Peterson's Four-Year Colleges

2005

THOMSON
PETERSON'S™

Australia • Canada • Mexico • Singapore • Spain • United Kingdom • United States

About Thomson Peterson's

Thomson Peterson's (www.petersons.com) is a leading provider of education information and advice, with books and online resources focusing on education search, test preparation, and financial aid. Its Web site offers searchable databases and interactive tools for contacting educational institutions, online practice tests and instruction, and planning tools for securing financial aid. Thomson Peterson's serves 110 million education consumers annually.

For more information, contact Thomson Peterson's, 2000 Lenox Drive, Lawrenceville, NJ 08648; 800-338-3282; or find us on the World Wide Web at www.petersons.com/about.

Previous editions published as *Peterson's Annual Guide to Undergraduate Study,* © 1970, 1971, 1972, 1973, 1974, 1975, 1976, 1977, 1978, 1979, 1980, 1981, 1982, and as *Peterson's Four-Year Colleges,* © 1983, 1984, 1985, 1986, 1987, 1988, 1989, 1990, 1991, 1992, 1993, 1994, 1995, 1996, 1997, 1998, 1999, 2000, 2001, 2002, 2003

Editor: Fern A. Oram; Production Editor: Linda Seghers; Copy Editors: Bret Bollmann, Jim Colbert, Michele N. Firestone, Michael Haines, Sally Ross, Jill C. Schwartz, Pam Sullivan, and Valerie Bolus Vaughan; Research Project Manager: Daniel Margolin; Research Associates: Mary Meyer-Penniston, Jared A. Stein, and Amy L. Weber; Programmer: Phyllis Johnson; Manufacturing Manager: Ray Golaszewski; Composition Manager: Linda M. Williams; Cover Design: Allison Sullivan; Client Relations Representatives: Mimi Kaufman, Lois Regina Milton, Mary Ann Murphy, Jim Swinarski, and Eric Wallace; CD Quality Assurance: Carol Aickley, Laura Laus, Jeff Pagano, and Josette Rossetti; Contributing Editors: Joe Krasowski, Charlotte Thomas, and Richard Woodland.

ISSN 1544-2330
ISBN 0-7689-1379-9

Printed in the United States of America

10 9 8 7 6 5 4 3 2 1 06 05 04

Thirty-fifth Edition

Contents

A Note from the Peterson's Editors

For more than thirty-five years, Peterson's has given students and parents the most comprehensive, up-to-date information on undergraduate institutions in the United States and Canada. *Peterson's Four-Year Colleges 2005* features advice and tips on the college search and selection process, such as how to consider the factors that truly make a difference during your college search, how to understand the application process, and how to file for financial aid. Peterson's researches the data published in *Peterson's Four-Year Colleges* each year. The information is furnished by the colleges and is accurate at the time of publishing.

Opportunities abound for students, and this guide can help you find what you want in a number of ways:

- For advice and guidance in the college search and selection process, just turn the page for our **SEARCH, FIND, SELECT** section. Providing a quick overview of the college application process, the "College Admissions Countdown Calendar" outlines pertinent month-by-month milestones. "Choosing Your Top Ten Colleges" gets you started on putting together the most important top ten list you have ever made. "Surviving Standardized Tests" describes the most frequently used tests and lists test dates for 2004–05. Of course, part of the college selection process involves visiting the schools themselves, and "The Whys and Whats of College Visits" is just the planner you need to make those trips well worth your while. Next, "Applying 101" provides advice on how best to approach the application phase of the process. If you can't make sense out of the early decision/early action conundrum, "The Early Decision Decision" helps to clear it up for you. "What International Students Need to Know About Admission to U.S. Colleges and Universities" has tips on college admissions for non–U.S. citizens and can also be useful to U.S. citizens. Finally, "Searching for Four-Year Colleges Online" outlines why you'll want to visit Petersons.com for even more college search and selection resources. Up next is the **MONEY, MONEY, MONEY** section, which provides all the essential information on how to meet your educational expenses, starting with the "Financial Aid Countdown Calendar" and followed by articles covering "What's Your BestCollegeDeal®?," "Who's Paying for This? Financial Aid Basics," and "Middle Income Families: Making the Financial Aid Process Work." And be sure to check out our **OPTIONS, OPTIONS, OPTIONS** section for some sneak peeks into specific institutions and programs that may be just right for you, including the latest on honors programs, public versus private colleges, women's colleges, and the military and higher education!
- Next, you'll want to read through "How to Use This Guide," which explains the information presented in the individual college profiles, how we collect our data, and how we determine eligibility for inclusion in this guide. Following that are the **PROFILES OF FOUR-YEAR COLLEGES.** Here you'll find our unparalleled and expanded college descriptions, arranged alphabetically by state. They provide a complete picture of need-to-know information about accredited four-year colleges—including admission rates, majors, current expenses, financial aid, student life, and campus safety. All the information you need to apply is placed together at the conclusion of each college profile. And if you still thirst for even more information, nearly 900 two-page narrative descriptions appear in the **IN-DEPTH DESCRIPTIONS OF FOUR-YEAR COLLEGES** section of the book. These descriptions are written by admissions deans and provide great detail about each college. They are edited to provide a consistent format across entries for your ease of comparison.
- If you already have specifics in mind, such as a particular institution or major, turn to the **INDEXES.** Here you can search for a school based on entrance difficulty, cost ranges, and majors. If you already have colleges in mind that pique your interest, you can use the "Alphabetical Listing of Colleges and Universities" to search for these schools. You'll also find a "Geographical Listing of In-Depth Descriptions." Page numbers referring to all information presented about a college are conveniently referenced.
- Finally, at the back of the book, you will find your bonus CD-ROM. This CD includes information on colleges and universities, standardized test preparation, financial aid, and Quick-Reference Charts. Within the Colleges and Universities Info tab, you'll find In-Depth Descriptions and access to colleges' Web sites and the ability to ask any question of the school via an "instant inquiry." The Test Prep tab and Financial Aid tab both feature access to Peterson's online tools: Peterson's Test Prep—SAT and ACT online courses—and BestCollegeDeals®. Refer to the color ad at the front of this book for the key activation code to get FREE 90-day BestCollegeDeals® access! You'll also find a FREE SAT practice test on the CD and, coming in the summer of 2004, you can go to www.petersons.com/testprep/satnew_cd for a FREE SAT

practice test for the new SAT! Be sure to check out the Quick-Reference Charts offered on the CD too—you'll find three At-a-Glance charts with colleges' general information, financial aid information, and admissions criteria!

Peterson's publishes a full line of resources to help you and your family with any information you need to guide you through the admissions process. Peterson's publications can be found at your local bookstore, library, and high school guidance office—or visit us on the Web at www.petersons.com.

Colleges will be pleased to know that Peterson's helped you in your selection. Admissions staff members are more than happy to answer questions, address specific problems, and help in any way they can. The editors at Peterson's wish you great success in your college search!

Search, Find, Select

College Admissions Countdown Calendar

This practical month-by-month calendar is designed to help you stay on top of the process of applying to college. For most students, the process begins in September of the junior year of high school and ends in June of the senior year. You may want to begin considering financial aid options, reviewing your academic schedule, and attending college fairs before your junior year.

JUNIOR YEAR

September

- ❒ Check with your counselor to make sure your course credits will meet college requirements.
- ❒ Be sure you are involved in one or two extracurricular activities.
- ❒ Begin building your personal list of colleges on the Undergraduate Channel of Petersons.com.

October

- ❒ Register for and take the PSAT.

November

- ❒ Strive to get the best grades you can. A serious effort will provide you with the most options during the application process.

December

- ❒ Get involved in a community service activity.
- ❒ Begin to read newspapers and a weekly news magazine.
- ❒ Buy **Peterson's Ultimate SAT Tool Kit, Peterson's Ultimate ACT Tool Kit,** or **Peterson's TOEFL Success** and begin to study for the tests.

January

- ❒ With your school counselor, decide when to take the ACT Assessment, SAT I, and SAT II Subject Tests (and which Subject Tests to take). If English is not your primary language and you are planning on attending a college in North America, decide when to take the TOEFL test.
- ❒ Keep your grades up!

February

- ❒ Plan a challenging schedule of classes for your senior year.
- ❒ Think about which teachers you will ask to write recommendations.
- ❒ Check www.nacac.com/fairs.html for schedules and locations of college fairs.

March

- ❒ Register for the tests you will take this spring (ACT Assessment, SAT I, SAT II, and the TOEFL test).
- ❒ Meet with your school counselor to discuss college choices.
- ❒ Review your transcript and test scores with your counselor to determine how competitive your range of choices should be.
- ❒ Visit Petersons.com to do college research.
- ❒ Develop a preliminary list of 15 to 20 colleges and universities and search for information on them.
- ❒ Start scheduling campus visits. When school is in session (but never during final exams) is the best time. Summers are OK, but will not show you what the college is really like. If possible, save your top college choices for the fall. Be aware, however, that fall is the busiest visit season, and you will need advance planning. Don't forget to write thank-you letters to your interviewers.

April

- ❒ Take any standardized tests for which you have registered.
- ❒ Create a list of your potential college choices and begin to record personal and academic information that can be later transferred to your college applications.

May

- ❒ Plan college visits and make appointments.
- ❒ Structure your summer plans to include advanced academic work, travel, volunteer work, or a job.
- ❒ Confirm your academic schedule for the fall.

Summer

- ❒ Write to any colleges on your list that do not accept the Common Application to request application forms.
- ❒ Begin working on your application essays.

SENIOR YEAR

September

- ❐ Register for the ACT Assessment, SAT I, SAT II, and TOEFL test, as necessary.
- ❐ Check with your school counselor for the fall visiting schedule of college reps.
- ❐ Ask appropriate teachers if they would write recommendations for you (don't forget to write thank-you letters when they accept).
- ❐ Meet with your counselor to compile your final list of colleges.

October

- ❐ Mail or send early applications electronically after carefully checking them to be sure they are completely filled out.
- ❐ Photocopy or print extra copies of your applications to use as a backup.
- ❐ Take the tests for which you have registered.
- ❐ Don't be late! Keep track of all deadlines for transcripts, recommendations, financial aid, etc.

November

- ❐ Be sure that you have requested your ACT Assessment and SAT scores be sent to your colleges of choice.
- ❐ Complete and submit all applications. Print or photocopy an extra copy for your records.

December

- ❐ Take any necessary ACT Assessment, SAT I, SAT II, or TOEFL tests.
- ❐ Meet with your counselor to verify that all is in order and that transcripts are out to colleges.

January

- ❐ Prepare the Free Application for Federal Student Aid (FAFSA), available at www.fafsa.ed.gov or through your school counseling office. An estimated income tax statement (which can be corrected later) can be used. The sooner you apply for financial aid, the better your chances.

February

- ❐ Send in your FAFSA via the Web or U.S. mail.
- ❐ Be sure your midyear report has gone out to the colleges to which you've applied.
- ❐ Let colleges know of any new honors or accomplishments that were not in your original application.

March

- ❐ Register for any Advanced Placement (AP) tests you might take.
- ❐ Be sure you have received a FAFSA acknowledgment.

April

- ❐ Review the acceptances and financial aid offers you receive.
- ❐ Go back to visit one or two of your top-choice colleges.
- ❐ Notify your college of choice that you have accepted its offer (and send in a deposit by May 1).
- ❐ Notify the colleges you have chosen not to attend of your decision.

May

- ❐ Take AP tests.

June

- ❐ Graduate! Congratulations and best of luck.

Choosing Your Top Ten Colleges

By using all the information in the various sections of this guide, you will find the colleges worthy of the most important top-ten list on the planet—yours.

The first thing you will need to do is decide what type of institution of higher learning you want to attend. Each of the thousands of four-year colleges and universities in the United States is as unique as the people applying to it. Although listening to the voices and media hype around you can make it sound as though there are only a few elite schools worth attending, this simply is not true. By considering some of the following criteria, you will soon find that the large pool of interesting colleges has been narrowed to a more reasonable number.

Size and Category. Schools come in all shapes and sizes, from tiny rural colleges of 400 students to massive state university systems serving 100,000 students or more. If you are coming from a small high school, a college with 3,500 students may seem large to you. If you are currently attending a high school with 3,000 students, selecting a college of a similar size may not feel like a new enough experience. Some students coming from very large impersonal high schools are looking for a place where they will be recognized from the beginning and offered a more personal approach. If you don't have a clue about what size might feel right to you, try visiting a couple of nearby colleges of varying sizes. You do not have to be seriously interested in them; just feel what impact the number of students on campus has on you.

Large Universities. Large universities offer a wide range of educational, athletic, and social experiences. Universities offer a full scope of undergraduate majors and award master's and doctoral degrees as well. Universities are usually composed of several smaller colleges. Depending on your interest in a major field or area of study, you would likely apply to a specific college within the university. Each college has the flexibility to set its own standards for admission, which may differ from the overall average of the university. For example, a student applying to a university's College of Arts and Sciences might need a minimum GPA of 3.2 and a minimum SAT I score of 1200. Another, applying to the College of Engineering, may find that a minimum GPA of 3.8 and SAT I score of 1280 are the standards. The colleges within a university system also set their own course requirements for earning a degree.

Universities may be public or private. Some large private universities, such as Harvard, Yale, Princeton, University of Pennsylvania, New York University, Northwestern, and Stanford, are well-known for their high entrance standards, the excellence of their education, and the success rates of their graduates. These institutions place a great deal of emphasis on research and compete aggressively for grants from the federal government to fund these projects. Large public universities, such as the State University of New York (SUNY) System, University of Michigan, University of Texas, University of Illinois, University of Washington, and University of North Carolina, also support excellent educational programs, compete for and win research funding, and have successful graduates. Public universities usually offer substantially lower tuition rates to in-state students, although their tuition rates for out-of-state residents are often comparable to those of private institutions.

At many large universities, sports play a major role on campus. Athletics can dominate the calendar and set the tone year-round at some schools. Alumni travel from far and wide to attend their alma mater's football or basketball games, and the campus, and frequently the entire town, grinds to a halt when there is a home game. Athletes are heroes and dominate campus social life.

What are some other features of life on a university campus? Every kind of club imaginable, from literature to bioengineering and chorus to politics, can be found on most college campuses. You will be able to play the intramural version of almost every sport in which the university fields interscholastic teams and join fraternities, sororities, and groups dedicated to social action. You can become a member of a band, an orchestra, or perhaps a chamber music group or work on the newspaper, the literary magazine, or the Web site. The list can go on and on. You may want to try out a new interest or two or pursue what you have always been interested in and make like-minded friends along the way.

Take a look at the size of the classrooms in the larger universities and envision yourself sitting in that atmosphere. Would this offer a learning environment that would benefit you?

Liberal Arts Colleges. If you have considered large universities and come to the conclusion that all that action could be a distraction, a small liberal arts college might be right for you. Ideally tucked away on a picture-perfect campus, a liberal arts college generally has fewer than 5,000 students. The mission of most liberal arts schools is learning for the sake of learning, with a strong emphasis on creating lifelong learners who will be able to apply their education to any number of careers. This contrasts with objectives of the profession-based preparation of specialized colleges.

Liberal arts colleges cannot offer the breadth of courses provided by the large universities. As a result, liberal arts colleges try to create a niche for themselves. For instance, a college may place its emphasis on its humanities departments, whose professors are all well-known published authors and international presenters in their areas of expertise. A college may highlight its science departments by providing state-of-the-art facilities where undergraduates conduct research side by side with top-notch professors and copublish their findings in the most prestigious scientific journals in the country. The personal approach is very important at liberal arts colleges. Whether in advisement, course selection, athletic programs tailored to students' interests, or dinner with the department head at her home, liberal arts colleges emphasize that they get to know their students.

If they are so perfect, why doesn't everyone choose a liberal arts college? Well, the small size limits options. Fewer people may mean less diversity. The fact that many of these colleges encourage a study-abroad option (a student elects to spend a semester or a year studying in another country) reduces the number of students on campus even further. Some liberal arts colleges have a certain reputation that does not appeal to some students. You should ask yourself questions about the campus life that most appeals to you. Will you fit in with the campus culture? Will the small size mean that you go through your social options quickly? Check out the activities listed on the Student Center bulletin board. Does the student body look diverse enough for you? Will what is happening keep you busy and interested? Do the students have input into decision making? Do they create the social climate of the school?

Small Universities. Smaller universities often combine stringent admissions policies, handpicked faculty members, and attractive scholarship packages. These institutions generally have undergraduate enrollments of about 4,000 students. Some are more famous for their graduate and professional schools, but have established strong undergraduate colleges. Smaller universities balance the great majors options of large universities with a smaller campus community. They offer choices but not to the same extent as large universities. On the other hand, by limiting admissions and enrollment, they manage to cultivate some of the characteristics of a liberal arts college. Like a liberal arts college, a small university may emphasize a particular program and go out of its way to draw strong candidates in a specific area, such as premed, to its campus. Universities such as the Johns Hopkins University, University of Notre Dame, Vanderbilt University, Washington University in St. Louis, and Wesleyan University in Connecticut are a few examples of this category.

Specialized Colleges. Another alternative to the liberal arts college or to the large university is the technical or otherwise specialized college. Their goal is to offer a specialized and saturated experience in a particular field of study. Such an institution might limit its course offerings to engineering and science, the performing or fine arts, or business. Schools such as the California Institute of Technology, Carnegie Mellon University, Massachusetts Institute of Technology, and Rensselaer Polytechnic Institute concentrate on attracting the finest math and science students in the country. At other schools, like Bentley College in Massachusetts or Bryant College in Rhode Island, students eat, sleep, and breathe business. These institutions are purists at heart and strong believers in the necessity of focused, specialized study to produce excellence in their graduates' achievements. If you are certain about your chosen path in life and want to immerse yourself in subjects such as math, music, or business to be best prepared for a particular kind of career, you will fit right in.

Religious Colleges. Many private colleges have religious origins, and many of these have become secular institutions with virtually no trace of their religious roots. Others remain dedicated to a religious way of education. What sets religious colleges apart is the way they combine faith, learning, and student life. Faculty members and administrators are hired with faith as a criterion as much as their academic credentials.

Single-Gender Colleges. There are strong arguments that being able to pursue one's education without the distraction, competition, and stress caused by the presence of the opposite sex helps a student evolve a stronger sense of her or his self-worth; achieve more academically; have a more fulfilling, less pressured social life; and achieve more later in life. For various historic, social, and psychological reasons, there are many more all-women than all-men colleges. A strict single-sex environment is rare. Even though the undergraduate day college adheres to an all-female or all-male admissions policy, coeducational evening classes or graduate programs and coordinate facilities and classes shared with nearby coed or opposite-sex institutions can result in a good number of students of the opposite sex being found on campus. Women's colleges, such as Scripps College, Smith College, Sweet Briar College, and Wellesley College, pride themselves on turning out leaders. If you want to concentrate on your studies and hone your leadership qualities, a single-gender school might be an option.

Location. Location and distance from home are two other important considerations. If you have always lived in the suburbs, choosing an urban campus can be an adventure, but after a week of the urban experience, will you long for a grassy campus and open space? On the other hand, if you choose a college in a rural area, will you run screaming into the Student Center some night looking for noise, lights, and people? The location—urban, rural, or suburban—can directly affect how easy or how difficult adjusting to college life will be for you.

Don't forget to factor in distance from home. Everyone going off to college wants to think he or she won't be homesick, but sometimes it's nice to get a home-cooked meal or to do the laundry in a place that does not require quarters. Even your kid sister may seem like less of a nuisance after a couple of months away.

Here are some questions you might ask yourself as you go through the selection process: In what part of the country do I want to be? How far away from home do I want to be? What is the cost of returning home? Do I need to be close to a city? How close? How large of a city? Would city life distract me? Would I concentrate better in a setting that is more rural or more suburban?

Entrance Difficulty. Many students will look at a college's entrance difficulty as an indicator of whether or not they will be admitted. For instance, if you have an excellent academic record, you might wish to primarily consider those colleges that are highly competitive. Although entrance difficulty does not translate directly to quality of education, it indicates which colleges are attracting large numbers of high-achieving students. A high-achieving student body usually translates into prestige for the college and its graduates. Prestige has some advantages but should definitely be viewed as a secondary factor that might tip the scales when all the other important factors are equal. Never base your decision on prestige alone!

The other principle to keep in mind when considering this factor is to not sell yourself short. If everything else tells you that a college might be right for you, but your numbers just miss that college's average range, apply there anyway. Your numbers—grades and test scores—are undeniably important in the admissions decision, but there are other considerations. First, lower grades in honors or AP courses will impress colleges more than top grades in regular-track courses because they demonstrate that you are the kind of student willing to accept challenges. Second, admissions directors are looking for different qualities in students that can be combined to create a multifaceted class. For example, if you did poorly in your freshman and sophomore years but made a great improvement in your grades in later years, this usually will impress a college. If you are likely to contribute to your class because of your special personal qualities, a strong sense of commitment and purpose, unusual and valuable experiences, or special interests and talents, these factors can outweigh numbers that are weaker than average. Nevertheless, be practical. Overreach yourself in a few applications, but put the bulk of your effort into gaining admission to colleges where you have a realistic chance for admission.

The Price of an Education. The price tag for higher education continues to rise, and it has become an increasingly important factor for people. While it is necessary to consider your family's resources when choosing a list of colleges to which you might apply, never eliminate a college solely because of cost. There are many ways to pay for college, including loans, and a college education will never depreciate in value, unlike other purchases. It is an investment in yourself and will pay back the expense many times over in your lifetime.

Surviving Standardized Tests

WHAT ARE STANDARDIZED TESTS?

Colleges and universities in the United States use tests to help evaluate applicants' readiness for admission or to place them in appropriate courses. The tests that are most frequently used by colleges are the ACT Assessment of American College Testing, Inc., and the College Board's SAT. In addition, the Educational Testing Service (ETS) offers the TOEFL test, which evaluates the English-language proficiency of nonnative speakers. The tests are offered at designated testing centers located at high schools and colleges throughout the United States and U.S. territories and at testing centers in various countries throughout the world. The ACT Assessment test and the SAT tests are each taken by more than a million students each year. The TOEFL test is taken by more than 700,000 students each year.

Upon request, special accommodations for students with documented visual, hearing, physical, or learning disabilities are available. Examples of special accommodations include tests in Braille or large print and such aids as a reader, recorder, magnifying glass, or sign language interpreter. Additional testing time may be allowed in some instances. Contact the appropriate testing program or your guidance counselor for details on how to request special accommodations.

College Board SAT Program

Currently, the SAT Program consists of the SAT I Reasoning Test and the SAT II Subject Tests. The SAT I is a 3-hour test made up of seven sections, primarily multiple-choice, that measures verbal and mathematical abilities. The three verbal sections test vocabulary, verbal reasoning, and critical reading skills. Emphasis is placed on reading passages, which are 400–850 words in length. Some reading passages are paired; the second opposes, supports, or in some way complements the point of view expressed in the first. The three mathematics sections test a student's ability to solve problems involving arithmetic, algebra, and geometry. They include questions that require students to produce their own responses, in addition to questions that students can choose from four or five answer choices. Calculators may be used on the SAT I mathematics sections. Beginning in the spring of 2005, the SAT will be a 3-hour and 35-minute test that focuses on college success skills of writing, critical reading, and mathematics. The new writing component will measure grammar and usage and include a short, student-written essay.

The SAT II Subject Tests are 1-hour tests, primarily multiple-choice, in specific subjects that measure students' knowledge of these subjects and their ability to apply that knowledge. Some colleges may require or recommend these tests for placement, or even admission. The Subject Tests measure a student's academic achievement in high school and may indicate readiness for certain college programs. Tests offered include Writing, Literature, U.S. History, World History, Mathematics Level IC, Mathematics Level IIC, Biology E/M (Ecological/Molecular), Chemistry, Physics, French, German, Modern Hebrew, Italian, Latin, and Spanish, as well as Foreign Language Tests with Listening in Chinese, French, German, Japanese, Korean, Spanish, and English Language Proficiency (ELPT). The Mathematics Level IC and IIC tests require the use of a scientific calculator.

SAT scores are automatically sent to each student who has taken the test. On average, they are mailed about three weeks after the test. Students may request that the scores be reported to their high schools or to the colleges to which they are applying.

ACT Assessment Program

The ACT Assessment Program is a comprehensive data collection, processing, and reporting service designed to assist in educational and career planning. The ACT Assessment instrument consists of four academic tests, taken under timed conditions, and a Student Profile Section and Interest Inventory, completed when students register for the ACT Assessment.

The academic tests cover four areas—English, mathematics, reading, and science reasoning. The ACT Assessment consists of 215 multiple-choice questions and takes approximately 3 hours and 30 minutes to complete with breaks (testing time is actually 2 hours and 55 minutes). They are designed to assess the student's educational development and readiness to handle college-level work. The minimum standard score is 1, the maximum is 36, and the national average is 21. Students should note that beginning in February 2005, an optional writing test will be offered.

The Student Profile Section requests information about each student's admission and enrollment plans, academic and out-of-class high school achievements and aspirations, and high school course work. The student is also asked to supply biographical data and self-reported high school grades in the four subject-matter areas covered by the academic tests.

The ACT Assessment has a number of career planning services, including the ACT Assessment Interest Inventory,

DON'T FORGET TO . . .

- Take the SAT or ACT Assessment before application deadlines.
- Note that test registration deadlines precede test dates by about six weeks.
- Register to take the TOEFL test if English is not your native language and you are planning on studying at a North American college.
- Practice your test-taking skills with **Peterson's Ultimate SAT Tool Kit, Peterson's Ultimate ACT Tool Kit,** and **Peterson's TOEFL Success** (all available with software).
- Contact the College Board or American College Testing, Inc., in advance if you need special accommodations when taking tests.

which is designed to measure six major dimensions of student interests–business contact, business operations, technical, science, arts, and social service. Results are used to compare the student's interests with those of college-bound students who later majored in each of a wide variety of areas. Inventory results are also used to help students compare their work-activity preferences with work activities that characterize twenty-three "job families."

Because the information resulting from the ACT Assessment Program is used in a variety of educational settings, American College Testing, Inc., prepares three reports for each student: the Student Report, the High School Report, and the College Report. The Student Report normally is sent to the student's high school, except after the June test date, when it is sent directly to the student's home address. The College Report is sent to the colleges the student designates.

Early in the school year, American College Testing, Inc., sends registration packets to high schools across the country that contain all the information a student needs to register for the ACT Assessment. High school guidance offices also receive a supply of *Preparing for the ACT Assessment*, a booklet that contains a complete practice test, an answer key, and general information about preparing for the test.

Test of English as a Foreign Language (TOEFL)

The TOEFL test is used by various organizations, such as colleges and universities, to determine English proficiency. The test is mainly offered in a computer-based format (TOEFL CBT), although the paper-based test is still offered in some areas. Eventually, the TOEFL will be completely computer-based.

The TOEFL tests students in the areas of listening, structure, reading comprehension, and writing. Score requirements are set by individual institutions. For more information on TOEFL, and to obtain a copy of the Information Bulletin, contact the Educational Testing Service.

Peterson's *TOEFL CBT Success* can help you prepare for the exam. The CD version of the book includes a TOEFL practice test and adaptive English skill building exercise. An online CBT test can also be taken for a small fee at petersons.com.

Contact your secondary school counselor for full information about the SAT and ACT Assessment programs and the TOEFL test.

2004–05 ACT ASSESSMENT AND SAT TEST DATES

ACT Assessment

September 25, 2004*
October 23, 2004
December 11, 2004
February 12, 2005**
April 9, 2005
June 11, 2005

All test dates fall on a Saturday. Tests are also given on the Sundays following the Saturday test dates for students who cannot take the test on Saturday because of religious reasons. The basic ACT Assessment registration fee for 2003–04 was $26 ($29 in Florida and $42 outside of the U.S.).

*The September test is available only in Arizona, California, Florida, Georgia, Illinois, Indiana, Maryland, Nevada, North Carolina, Pennsylvania, South Carolina, Texas, and Washington.

**The February test date is not available in New York.

SAT

October 9, 2004 (SAT I and SAT II)
November 6, 2004 (SAT I, SAT II, and Language Tests with Listening, including ELPT*)
December 4, 2004 (SAT I and SAT II)
January 22, 2005 (SAT I, SAT II, and ELPT)
March 12, 2005 (SAT I only)** NEW SAT
May 7, 2005 (SAT I and SAT II) NEW SAT
June 4, 2005 (SAT I and SAT II) NEW SAT

For the 2003–04 academic year, the basic fee for the SAT I Reasoning Test was $28.50, which included the $16 basic registration and reporting fee. The basic fee for the SAT II Subject Tests was $16 for the Writing Test, $13 for the Language Tests with Listening, and $8 each for all other Subject Tests. Students can take up to three SAT II Subject Tests on a single date, and a $16 basic registration and reporting fee should be added for each test date. Tests are also given on the Sundays following the Saturday test dates for students who cannot take the test on Saturday because of religious reasons. Fee waivers are available to juniors and seniors who cannot afford test fees.

*Language Tests with Listening (including the English Language Proficiency Test, or ELPT) are only offered on November 6; the ELPT is offered on November 6 and January 22 at some test centers. See the Registration Bulletin for details.

**The March 12 test date is only available in the U.S. and its territories.

The Whys and Whats of College Visits

Dawn B. Sova, Ph.D.

The campus visit should not be a passive activity for you and your parents, and you will have to take the initiative and use all of your senses to gather information beyond that provided in the official tour. You will see many important indicators during your visit that will tell you more about the true character of a college and its students than the tour guide will reveal. Know what to look for and how to assess the importance of such indicators.

WHAT SHOULD YOU ASK AND WHAT SHOULD YOU LOOK FOR?

Your first stop on a campus visit is the visitor center or admissions office, where you will probably have to wait to meet with a counselor. Colleges usually plan to greet visitors later than the appointed time in order to give them the opportunity to review some of the campus information that is liberally scattered throughout the visitor waiting room. Take advantage of the time to become even more familiar with the college by arriving 15 to 30 minutes before your appointment to observe the behavior of staff members and to browse through the yearbooks and student newspapers that will be available.

If you prepare in advance, you will have already reviewed the college catalog and map of the campus. These materials familiarize you with the academic offerings and the physical layout of the campus, but the true character of the college and its students emerges in other ways.

Begin your investigation with the visitor center staff members. As a student's first official contact with the college, they should make every effort to welcome prospective students and to project a friendly image.

- How do they treat you and other prospective students who are waiting? Are they friendly and willing to speak with you, or do they try their hardest to avoid eye contact and conversation?
- Are they friendly with each other and with students who enter the office, or are they curt and unwilling to help?
- Does the waiting room have a friendly feeling or is it cold and sterile?

If the visitor center staff members seem indifferent to *prospective* students, there is little reason to believe that they will be warm and welcoming to current students. View such behavior as a warning to watch very carefully the interaction of others with you during the tour. An indifferent or unfriendly reception in the admissions office may be simply the first of many signs that attending this college will not be a pleasant experience.

Look through several yearbooks and see the types of activities that are actually photographed, as opposed to the activities that colleges promise in their promotional literature. Some questions are impossible to answer if the college is very large, but for small and moderately sized colleges the yearbook is a good indicator of campus activity.

- Has the number of clubs and organizations increased or decreased in the past five years?
- Do the same students appear repeatedly in activities?
- Do sororities and fraternities dominate campus activities?
- Are participants limited to one sex or one ethnic group or are the participants diverse?
- Are all activities limited to the campus, or are students involved in activities in the community?

Use what you observe in the yearbooks as a means of forming a more complete understanding of the college, but don't base your entire impression on just one facet. If time permits, look through several copies of the school newspaper, which should reflect the major concerns and interests of the students. The paper is also a good way to learn about the campus social life.

- Does the paper contain a mix of national and local news?
- What products or services are advertised?
- How assertive are the editorials?
- With what topics are the columnists concerned?
- Are movies and concerts that meet your tastes advertised or reviewed?
- What types of ads appear in the classified section?

The newspaper should be a public forum for students, and, as such, should reflect the character of the campus and of the student body. A paper that deals only with seemingly safe and well-edited topics on the editorial page and in regular feature columns might indicate administrative censorship. A lack of ads for restaurants might indicate either a lack of good places to eat or that area restaurants do not welcome student business. A limited mention of movies, concerts, or other entertainment might reveal a severely limited campus social life. Even if ads and reviews are included, you can also learn a lot about how such activities reflect your tastes.

You will have only a limited amount of time to ask questions during your initial meeting with the admissions counselor, for very few schools include a formal interview in the initial campus visit or tour. Instead, this brief meeting is often just a nicety that allows the admissions office to begin a file for the student and to record some initial impressions. Save your questions for the tour guide and for campus members that you meet along the way.

HOW CAN YOU ASSESS THE TRUE CHARACTER OF A COLLEGE AND ITS STUDENTS?

Colleges do not train their tour guides to deceive prospective students, but they do caution guides to avoid unflattering topics and campus sites. Does this mean that you are condemned to see only a sugarcoated version of life on a particular college campus? Not at all, especially not if you are observant.

Most organized campus visits include such campus facilities as dormitories, dining halls, libraries, student activity and recreation centers, and the health and student services centers. Some may only be pointed out, while you will walk through others. Either way, you will find that many signs of the true character of the college emerge if you keep your eyes open.

Bulletin boards in dormitories and student centers contain a wealth of information about campus activities, student concerns, and campus groups. Read the posters, notices, and messages to learn what *really* interests students. Unlike ads in the school newspaper, posters put up by students advertise both on- and off-campus events, so they will give you an idea of what is also available in the surrounding community.

Review the notices, which may cover either campus-wide events or events that concern only small groups of students. The catalog may not mention a performance group, but an individual dormitory with its own small theater may offer regular productions. Poetry readings, jam sessions, writers' groups, and other activities may be announced and shows diversity of student interests.

Even the brief bulletin board messages offering objects for sale and noting objects that people want to purchase reveal a lot about a campus. Are most of the items computer related? Or do the messages specify compact discs, audio equipment, or musical instruments? Are offers to barter goods or services posted? Don't ignore the "ride wanted" messages. Students who want to share rides home during a break may specify widely diverse geographical locations. If so, then you know that the student body is not limited to only the immediate area or one locale. Other messages can also enhance your knowledge of the true character of the campus and its students.

As you walk through various buildings, examine their condition carefully.

- Is the paint peeling, and do the exteriors look worn?
- Are the exteriors and interiors of the building clean?
- Is the equipment in the classrooms up-to-date or outdated?

Pay particular attention to the dormitories, especially to factors that might affect your safety. Observe the appearance of the structure, and ask about the security measures in and around the dormitories.

- Are the dormitories noisy or quiet?
- Do they seem crowded?
- How good is the lighting around each dormitory?
- Are the dormitories spread throughout the campus or are they clustered in one main area?
- Who has access to the dormitories in addition to students?
- How secure are the means by which students enter and leave the dormitory?

While you are on the subject of dormitory safety, you should also ask about campus safety. Don't expect that the guide will rattle off a list of crimes that have been committed in the past year. To obtain that information, access the recent year of issues of *The Chronicle of Higher Education* and locate its yearly report on campus crime. Also ask the guide about safety measures that the campus police take and those that students have initiated.

- Can students request escorts to their residences late at night?
- Do campus shuttle buses run at frequent intervals all night?
- Are "blue-light" telephones liberally placed throughout the campus for students to use to call for help?
- Do the campus police patrol the campus regularly?

If the guide does not answer your questions satisfactorily, wait until after the tour to contact the campus police or traffic office for answers.

Campus tours usually just point out the health services center without taking the time to walk through. Even if you don't see the inside of the building, you should take a close look at the location of the health services center and ask the guide questions about services.

- How far is the health center from the dormitories?
- Is a doctor always on call?
- Does the campus transport sick students from their dormitories or must they walk?
- What are the operating hours of the health center?
- Does the health center refer students to a nearby hospital?

If the guide can't answer your questions, visit the health center later and ask someone there.

Most campus tours take pride in showing students their activities centers, which may contain snack bars, game rooms, workout facilities, and other means of entertainment. Should you scrutinize this building as carefully as the rest? Of course. Outdated and poorly maintained activity equipment contributes to your total impression of the college. You should also ask about the hours, availability, and cost (no, the activities are usually *not* free) of using the bowling alleys, pool tables, air hockey tables, and other items.

As you walk through campus with the tour, also look carefully at the appearance of the students who pass. The way in which both men and women groom themselves, the way they dress, and even their physical bearing communicate a lot more than any guidebook can. If everyone seems to conform to the same look, you might feel that you would be uncomfortable at the college, however nonconformist that look might be. On the other hand, you might not feel comfortable on a campus that stresses diversity of dress and behavior, and your observations now can save you discomfort later.

- Does every student seem to wear a sorority or fraternity t-shirt or jacket?
- Is everyone of your sex sporting the latest fad haircut?
- Do all of the men or the women seem to be wearing expensive name-brand clothes?
- Do most of the students seem to be working hard to look outrageous in regard to clothing, hair color, and body art?
- Would you feel uncomfortable in a room full of these students?

Is appearance important to you? If it is, then you should consider very seriously if you answer *yes* to any of the above questions. You don't have to be the same as everyone else on campus, but standing out too rigorously may make you unhappy.

As you observe the physical appearance of the students, also listen to their conversations as you pass them? What are they talking about? How are they speaking? Are their voices and accents all the same, or do you hear diversity in their speech? Are you offended by their language? Think how you will feel if surrounded by the same speech habits and patterns for four years.

WHERE SHOULD YOU VISIT ON YOUR OWN?

Your campus visit is not over when the tour ends because you will probably have many questions yet to be answered and many places to still be seen. Where you go depends upon the extent to which the organized tour covers the campus. Your tour should take you to view residential halls, health and student services centers, the gymnasium or field house, dining halls, the library, and recreational centers. If any of the facilities on this list have been omitted, visit them on your own and ask questions of the students and staff members you meet. In addition, you should step off campus and gain an impression of the surrounding community. You will probably become bored with life on campus and spend at least some time off campus. Make certain that you know what the surrounding area is like.

The campus tour leaves little time to ask impromptu questions of current students, but you can do so after the tour. Eat lunch in one of the dining halls. Most will allow visitors to pay cash to experience a typical student meal. Food may not be important to you now while you are living at home and can simply take anything you want from the refrigerator at any time, but it will be when you are away at college with only a meal ticket to feed you.

- How clean is the dining hall? Consider serving tables, floors, and seating.
- What is the quality of the food?
- How big are the portions?
- How much variety do students have at each meal?
- How healthy are the food choices?

While you are eating, try to strike up a conversation with students and tell them that you are considering attending their college. Their reactions and advice can be eye-opening. Ask them questions about the academic atmosphere and the professors.

- Are the classes large or small?
- Do the majority of the professors only lecture or are tutorials and seminars common?
- Is the emphasis of the faculty career-oriented or abstract?
- Are the teaching methods innovative and stimulating or boring and dull?
- Is the academic atmosphere pressured, lax, or somewhere in between?
- Which are the strong majors? The weak majors?
- Is the emphasis on grades or social life or a mix of both at the college?
- How hard do students have to work to receive high grades?

Current students can also give you the inside line on the true nature of the college social life. You may gain some idea through looking in the yearbook, in the newspaper, and on the bulletin boards, but students will reveal the true highs and lows of campus life. Ask them about drug use, partying, dating rituals, drinking, and anything else that may affect your life as a student.

- Which are the most popular club activities?
- What do students do on weekends? Do most go home?
- How frequently do concerts occur on campus? Which groups have recently performed?
- How can you become involved in specific activities (name them)?
- How strictly are campus rules enforced and how severe are penalties?
- What counseling services are available?
- Are academic tutoring services available?
- Do they feel that the faculty really cares about students, especially freshmen?

You will receive the most valuable information from current students, but you will only be able to speak with them after the tour is over. And you might have to risk rejection as you try to initiate conversations with students who might not want to reveal how they feel about the campus. Still, the value of this information is worth the chance.

If you have the time, you should also visit the library to see just how accessible research materials are and to observe the physical layout. The catalog usually specifies the days and hours of operation, as well as the number of volumes contained in the library and the number of periodicals to which it subscribes. A library also requires accessibility, good lighting, an adequate number of study carrels, and lounge areas for students. Many colleges have created 24-hour study lounges for students who find the residence halls too noisy for studying, although most colleges claim that they designate areas of the residences as "quiet study" areas. You may not be interested in any of this information, but when you are a student you will have to make frequent use of the campus library so you should know what is available. You should at least ask how extensive their holdings are in your proposed major area. If they have virtually nothing, you will have to spend a lot of time ordering items via interlibrary loan or making copies, which can become expensive. The ready answer of students that they will obtain their information from the Internet is unpleasantly countered by professors who demand journal articles with documentation.

Make a point of at least driving through the community surrounding the college, because you will be spending time there shopping, dining, working in a part-time job, or attending events. Even the largest and best-stocked campus will not meet all of your social and personal needs. If you can spare the time, stop in several stores to see if they welcome college students.

- Is the surrounding community suburban, urban, or rural?
- Does the community offer stores of interest, such as bookstores, craft shops, and boutiques?
- Do the businesses employ college students?
- Does the community have a movie or stage theater?
- Are there several types of interesting restaurants?
- Do there seem to be any clubs that court a college clientele?
- Is the center of activity easy to walk to, or do you need a car or other transportation?

You might feel that a day is not enough to answer all of your questions, but even answering some questions will provide you with a stronger basis for choosing a college. Many students visit a college campus several times before making their decision, as you also should. Keep in mind that for the rest of your life you will be associated with the college that you attend. You will spend four years of your life at this college. The effort of spending several days to obtain the information to make your decision is worthwhile.

Dawn B. Sova, Ph.D., is a former newspaper reporter and columnist, as well as the author of more than eight books and numerous magazine articles. She teaches creative and research writing, as well as scientific and technical writing, newswriting, and journalism.

Applying 101

The words "applying yourself" have several important meanings in the college application process. One meaning refers to the fact that you need to keep focused during this important time in your life, keep your priorities straight, and know the dates that your applications are due so you can apply on time. The phrase might also refer to the person who is really responsible for your application--you.

You are the only person who should compile your college application. You need to take ownership of this process. The intervention of others should be for advisement only. The guidance counselor is not responsible for completing your applications, and your parents shouldn't be typing them. College applications must be completed in addition to your normal workload at school, college visits, and SAT, ACT Assessment, or possibly, TOEFL testing.

THE APPLICATION

The application is your way of introducing yourself to a college admissions office. As with any introduction, you should try to make a good first impression. The first thing you should do in presenting your application is to find out what the college or university needs from you. Read the application carefully to find out the application fee and deadline, required standardized tests, number of essays, interview requirements, and anything else you can do or submit to help improve your chances for acceptance.

Completing college applications yourself helps you learn more about the schools to which you are applying. The information a college asks for in its application can tell you much about the school. State university applications often tell you how they are going to view their applicants. Usually, they select students based on GPAs and test scores. Colleges that request an interview, ask you to respond to a few open-ended questions, or require an essay are interested in a more personal approach to the application process and may be looking for different types of students than those sought by a state school.

In addition to submitting the actual application, there are several other items that are commonly required. You will be responsible for ensuring that your standardized test scores and your high school transcript arrive at the colleges to which you apply. Most colleges will ask that you submit teacher recommendations as well. Select teachers who know you and your abilities well and allow them plenty of time to complete the recommendations. When all portions of the application have been completed and sent in, whether electronically or by mail, make sure you follow up with the college to ensure their receipt.

FOLLOW THESE TIPS WHEN FILLING OUT YOUR APPLICATION

- **Follow the directions to the letter.** You don't want to be in a position to ask an admissions officer for exceptions due to your inattentiveness.
- **Make a photocopy** of the application and work through a rough draft before you actually fill out the application copy to be submitted.
- **Proofread all parts of your application,** including your essay. Again, the final product indicates to the admissions staff how meticulous and careful you are in your work.
- **Submit your application as early as possible,** provided all of the pieces are available. If there is a problem with your application, this will allow you to work through it with the admissions staff in plenty of time. If you wait until the last minute, it not only takes away that cushion but also reflects poorly on your sense of priorities.

THE APPLICATION ESSAY

Some colleges may request one essay or a combination of essays and short-answer topics to learn more about who you are and how well you can communicate your thoughts. Common essay topics cover such simple themes as writing about yourself and your experiences or why you want to attend that particular school. Other colleges will ask that you show your imaginative or creative side by writing about a favorite author, for instance, or commenting on a hypothetical situation. In such cases, they will be looking at your thought processes and your level of creativity.

Whereas the other portions of your application—your transcript, test scores, and involvement in extracurricular activities—are a reflection of what you've accomplished up to this point, your application essay is an opportunity to present yourself in the here and now. The essay shows your originality and verbal skills and is very important. Test scores and grades may represent your academic results, but your essay shows how you approach a topic or problem and express your opinion.

Admissions officers, particularly those at small or mid-size colleges, use the essay to determine how you, as a student, will fit into life at that college. The essay, therefore, is a critical component of the application process. Here are some tips for writing a winning essay:

- Colleges are looking for an honest representation of who you are and what you think. Make sure that the tone of the essay reflects enthusiasm, maturity, creativity, the ability to communicate, talent, and your leadership skills.

- Be sure you set aside enough time to write the essay, revise it, and revise it *again*. Running the "spell check" feature on your computer will only detect a fraction of the errors you probably made on your first pass at writing it. Take a break and then come back to it and reread it. You will probably notice other style, content, and grammar problems—and ways that you can improve the essay overall.
- Always answer the question that is being asked, making sure that you are specific, clear, and true to your personality.
- Enlist the help of reviewers who know you well—friends, parents, teachers—since they are likely to be the most honest and will keep you on track in the presentation of your true self.

THE PERSONAL INTERVIEW

Although it is relatively rare that a personal interview is required, many colleges recommend that you take this opportunity for a face-to-face discussion with a member of the admissions staff. Read through the application materials to determine whether or not a college places great emphasis on the interview. If they strongly recommend that you have one, it may work against you to forego it.

In contrast to a group interview and some alumni interviews, which are intended to provide information about a college, the personal interview is viewed both as an information session and as further evaluation of your skills and strengths. You will meet with a member of the admissions staff who will be assessing your personal qualities, high school preparation, and your capacity to contribute to undergraduate life at the institution. On average, these meetings last about 45 minutes—a relatively short amount of time in which to gather information and leave the desired impression—so here are some suggestions on how to make the most of it.

Scheduling Your Visit. Generally, students choose to visit campuses in the summer or fall of their senior year. Both times have their advantages. A summer visit, when the campus is not in session, generally allows for a less hectic visit and interview. Visiting in the fall, on the other hand, provides the opportunity to see what campus life is like in full swing. If you choose the fall, consider arranging an overnight trip so that you can stay in one of the college dormitories. At the very least, you should make your way around campus to take part in classes, athletic events, and social activities. Always make an appointment and avoid scheduling more than two college interviews on any given day. Multiple interviews in a single day hinder your chances of making a good impression, and your impressions of the colleges will blur into each other as you hurriedly make your way from place to place.

Preparation. Know the basics about the college before going for your interview. Read the college viewbook or catalog in addition to this guide. You will be better prepared to ask questions that are not answered in the literature and that will give you a better understanding of what the college has to offer. You should also spend some time thinking about your strengths and weaknesses and, in particular, what you are looking for in a college education. You will find that as you get a few interviews under your belt, they will get easier. You might consider starting with a college that is not a top contender on your list, where the stakes are not as high.

Asking Questions. Inevitably, your interviewer will ask you, "Do you have any questions?" Not having one may suggest that you're unprepared or, even worse, not interested. When you do ask questions, make sure that they are ones that matter to you and that have a bearing on your decision about whether or not to attend. The questions that you ask will give the interviewer some insight into your personality and priorities. Avoid asking questions that can be answered in the college literature—again, a sign of unpreparedness. Although the interviewer will undoubtedly pose questions to you, the interview should not be viewed merely as a question-and-answer session. If a conversation evolves out of a particular question, so much the better. Your interviewer can learn a great deal about you from how you sustain a conversation. Similarly, you will be able to learn a great deal about the college in a conversational format.

Separate the Interview from the Interviewer. Many students base their feelings about a college solely on their impressions of the interviewer. Try not to characterize a college based only on your personal reaction, however, since your impressions can be skewed by whether you and your interviewer hit it off. Pay lots of attention to everything else that you see, hear, and learn about a college. Once on campus, you may never see your interviewer again.

In the end, remember to relax and be yourself. Don't drink jitters-producing caffeinated beverages prior to the interview, and suppress nervous fidgets like leg-wagging, finger-drumming, or bracelet-jangling. Your interviewer will expect you to be somewhat nervous, which will relieve some of the pressure. Consider this an opportunity to put forth your best effort and to enhance everything that the college knows about you up to this point.

THE FINAL DECISION

Once you have received your acceptance letters, it is time to go back and look at the whole picture. Provided you received more than one acceptance, you are now in a position to compare your options. The best way to do this is to compare your original list of important college-ranking criteria with what you've discovered about each college along the way. In addition, you and your family will need to factor in the financial aid component. You will need to look beyond these cost issues and the quantifiable pros and cons of each college, however, and know that you have a good feeling about your final choice. Before sending off your acceptance letter, you need to feel confident that the college will feel like home for the next four years. Once the choice is made, the only hard part will be waiting for an entire summer before heading off to college!

The Early Decision Decision

Maybe a senior you knew last year didn't get into the college he wanted. He said it was because he didn't apply early decision. Maybe your friend's mom told your mom that unless students apply early decision, their chances of getting into top schools are slim to none, even though they have great grades and spectacular essays. Maybe you figure you'd better get in on the early decision action.

All of the above are true—well, sort of—because many students applying to college get the term "early decision" backwards. High school guidance and college counselors run into this kind of thinking all the time and suggest putting "decision" before "early"—as in making a wise decision about committing to a college before applying early. For some students, early decision is a great option. For others, early decision is loaded with pitfalls and dangers.

"When students come back in the fall of their senior year, I often hear 'I know I want to apply early. Can you help me choose the school?'" says Kathy Cleaver, Director of College Counseling at Durham Academy in Durham, North Carolina. She compares that to saying, "I know I want to get married, please help me pick the man." Continues Cleaver, "First you have to fall in love with the school and know it's your first choice and then join the circus for early decision." She's referring to the media hype flying around high school halls about early decision—it's easy to fall prey to the early decision madness. Hot competition to get into "top" schools creates early decision anxiety. Mickey Gilbert, Guidance Counselor at Passaic High School in Passaic, New Jersey, throws out some scary numbers that confirm that, yes, the competition for admittance to top schools is white-hot. There are about 30,000 high schools in the United States, and although the majority of high school seniors apply to institutions in their own states, there are still limited spaces in the "top" schools and the eight Ivy League schools. "No wonder kids think that early decision is the way to go," speculates Gilbert. Early decision panic sets in because students are convinced that if they get their applications in early, they have an edge. Sometimes early decision might make the difference, but there are many issues to consider before taking the early decision leap.

EARLY THIS, EARLY THAT

If you are paying attention to the buzz about early decision, do you really know what it means along with all the other early options, such as early action and early notification? And what about the variations of early decision? Each institution can have its own version of early decision, meaning that deadlines and criteria are different. There's the early decision that notifies students by December, there's the early decision round two, and then there is the early action/single choice.

Seeing the confusion, the National Association for College Admission Counseling (NACAC) developed a standard set of definitions. NACAC is an education association of secondary school counselors, college and university admissions and financial aid officers, counselors, and other individuals who work with students as they transition from high school to college. While each institution has its own variations of each early option, an understanding of the basic differences can help. The list below was adapted from the definitions found on the NACAC Web site.

Early Decision

- Early decision is the application process in which students make a commitment to a first-choice institution where, if admitted, they definitely will enroll. Should a student who applies for financial aid not be offered an award that makes attendance possible, the student may decline the offer of admission and be released from the early decision commitment.
- While pursuing admission under an early decision plan, students may apply to other institutions, but may have only one early decision application pending at any time.
- The institution must notify the applicant of the decision within a reasonable and clearly stated period of time after the early decision deadline. Usually, a nonrefundable deposit must be made well in advance of May 1.
- A student applying for financial aid must adhere to institutional early decision aid application deadlines.
- The institution will respond to an application for financial aid at or near the time of an offer of admission.
- The early decision application supercedes all other applications. Immediately upon acceptance of an offer of admission, a student must withdraw all other applications and make no subsequent applications.
- The application form will include a request for a parent and a counselor signature, in addition to the student's signature, indicating an understanding of the early decision commitment and agreement to abide by its terms.

Early Action

- Early action is the application process in which students make application to an institution of preference and receive a decision well in advance of the institution's regular response date. Students who are admitted under early action are not obligated to accept the institution's offer of admission or to submit a deposit until the regular reply date (not prior to May 1).
- A student may apply to other colleges without restriction.

- The institution must notify the applicant of the decision within a reasonable and clearly stated period of time after the early action deadline.
- A student applying for financial aid must adhere to institutional aid application deadlines. The student admitted under an early action plan may not be required to make a commitment prior to May 1, but may be encouraged to do so as soon as a final college choice is made. Colleges that solicit commitments to offers of early action admission and/or financial assistance prior to May 1 may do so provided those offers include a clear statement that written requests for extensions until May 1 will be granted, and that such requests will not jeopardize a student's status for admission or financial aid.

Regular Decision

- Regular decision is the application process in which a student submits an application to an institution by a specified date and receives a decision within a reasonable and clearly stated period of time, but not later than April 15.
- A student may apply to other colleges without restriction.
- The institution will state a deadline for completion of applications and will respond to completed applications by a specified date.
- A student applying for financial aid will adhere to institutional aid application deadlines.
- A student admitted under a regular decision plan may not be required to make a commitment prior to May 1, but may be encouraged to do so as soon as a final college choice is made. Colleges that solicit commitments to offers of admission and/or financial assistance prior to May 1 may do so provided those offers include a clear statement that written requests for extensions until May 1 will be granted, and that such requests will not jeopardize a student's status for admission or financial aid.

Rolling Admission

- Rolling admission is the application process in which an institution reviews applications as they are completed and renders admission decisions to students throughout the admission cycle.
- A student may apply to other colleges without restriction.
- The institution will respond to completed applications in a timely manner.
- A student applying for financial aid must adhere to institutional aid application deadlines.
- The student admitted under a rolling admission plan may not be required to make a commitment prior to May 1, but may be encouraged to do so as soon as a final college choice is made. Colleges that solicit commitments to offers of admission and/or financial assistance prior to May 1 may do so provided those offers include a clear statement that written requests for extensions until May 1 will be granted, and that such requests will not jeopardize a student's status for admission or financial aid.

PARENTS, SOME ADVICE FOR YOU

Though guidance counselors stress that high school students should make the final decision about which college to attend, they also say that parents are a very important part of the decision equation. Parents can help as organizers of all the information and provide the support needed to make a good choice. "Little things like setting up file folders and keeping track of deadlines can keep a student on track," advises Gibson.

Along with their children, parents also need to understand the basics of early option terminology as it applies to each institution being considered. Five different colleges might have five different early decision criteria. Read the fine print, and make note of deadlines.

What really will help—you, your child, and your wallet—is to understand the basics about financial aid. Says Leftwich, "Have an in-depth discussion with the financial aid officer so that you are aware of the ramifications, restrictions, and implications of the financial aid offer."

If possible, make an appointment to visit with a financial aid officer at the college while your child is visiting the campus. Bring your tax forms and discuss the prospects of financial aid. "Financial aid people are straight shooters. It's not in their best interest to tell you one thing to get your foot in the door and then turn around and pull the rug out from under you," says McClintick. "Parents might not like the answer they get from the financial aid officer, but they will get a candid assessment of their eligibility for financial aid."

Leftwich suggests having an honest discussion with your child early in the college selection process. Talk about what you can realistically afford, what colleges will appropriately challenge him or her, if location is a factor, and what kind of environment best suits your child. Whichever option your child uses to apply, you both will know the decision is an informed one.

Wait List

- Wait list is an admission decision option utilized by institutions to protect against shortfalls in enrollment. Wait lists are sometimes made necessary because of the uncertainty of the admission process, as students submit applications for admission to multiple institutions and may receive several offers of admission. By placing a student on the wait list, an institution does not initially offer or deny admission, but extends to a candidate the possibility of admission in the future before the institution's admission cycle is concluded.
- The institution will ensure that a wait list, if necessary, is of reasonable length and is maintained for a reasonable period of time, but never later than August 1.

- In the letter offering a wait list position, the institution should provide a past wait list history, which describes the number of students placed on the wait list(s), the number offered admission from the wait list, and the availability of financial aid. Students should be given an indication of when they can expect to be notified of final admission decision.
- An institution must resolve final status and notify wait list candidates as soon after May 1 as possible.
- The institution will not require students to submit deposits to remain on a wait list or pressure students for a commitment to enroll prior to sending an official offer of admission in writing.

There is one more option, called *early action/single choice* (EASC), that some highly selective schools such as Harvard, Yale, and Stanford have recently begun using. Early action/single choice is a nonbinding early admission option for freshman applicants that replaces early decision. With this change, students learn about their admission decision in December without being required to reply until May 1. This option allows students to apply to as many colleges as they want under a regular admission time frame. The difference is that the early action/single choice option does not allow a candidate to apply to other schools under any type of early action, early decision, or early notification program. Students are asked to sign a statement in their application agreeing to file only one early application.

Each of these options has variations, depending on the institution using them. Some schools have a November 1 deadline for early decision round one. Smaller schools have a deadline of November 15, while others have a December 1 deadline. Then there's an early decision round two. To make matters even more complicated, some schools with early decision say that students can't apply to other institutions if they've sent in an early decision application to their admissions office. Others say it's okay to apply to other schools at the same time you're applying early decision to them, but if they send you an acceptance, you must withdraw the other applications.

Just because two institutions have an application process called early decision or early action doesn't mean that their policies are identical. "There is no common terminology, even among the colleges that have early decision," says Christoph Guttentag, Director of Undergraduate Admissions at Duke University in Durham, North Carolina. He also points out that just when you think you've got the definitions figured out, institutions change them. "Colleges are always balancing the needs of their institution and the needs of students," he comments. Just last year, several well-known institutions were using early decision and then abruptly switched to early action.

EARLY DECISION: A MATCHMAKING TOOL OR A CLEVER STRATEGY?

Despite the differences in what actually constitutes early decision, it has become more of a strategy than a matchmaking tool, according to Bill McClintick, Director of College Counseling at Mercersburg Academy in Mercersburg, Pennsylvania. He also chairs the national steering committee on admissions standards for NACAC. The focus of early decision used to be on matching the student with the college and letting the admissions office know that that institution is where the student wants to be above all others. Today, early decision is misunderstood and misused. High school seniors think that they must use the early decision tactic to get an edge. The result, says McClintick is "at many of the top places, early decision applications have gone through the roof."

Though high school students may have exaggerated ideas of how much early decision can really help them, it is true that it does give a small segment of students at highly selective schools an advantage. Generally, the more selective the institution, the more small differences matter. "Even if it's a small increase, you need everything you can get," states John Latting, Director of Undergraduate Admissions at the Johns Hopkins University in Baltimore, Maryland.

"Remember," cautions McClintick, "we're only talking about a small slice of kids in the grand scheme of things." He mentions 5 percent of high school seniors nationally who aspire to the "top" institutions. State colleges and universities fill a much lower percentage of their freshman class with early decision applications. "I don't believe that more kids are chasing the same number of spots," says Jon Reider, Director of College Counseling at San Francisco University High School in San Francisco, California. "Students are applying to more and more schools, even with the early decision option on the side. This is inflating the selectivity of some colleges beyond what it used to be." In reality, 90 percent of students apply regular admission. Interest in early decision comes from a relatively small segment of the college applicant pool.

THE BENEFITS OF EARLY DECISION

There are clear benefits to students. Aside from the fact that early decision does play a role in acceptance rates for a relatively small percentage of students at a small number of schools, early decision is a good option. The caveat is that students must know, without a shred of doubt, that one institution, above all others, is the best match for their goals and their likes and dislikes, and that based on grades and test scores, they solidly match the institution's criteria for admission. The option to go early decision should be taken after extensive research, multiple visits to the campus, and talking to a lot of people. "Early decision is for those who can put their hearts and souls into one application," advises Cleaver.

There are other advantages. You have to make only one choice, and you will know by December if you've been accepted. You have to fill out only one application. You are not chewing your nails over your list of possibilities during the Christmas holiday. Instead, you know where you're going and can sit back and enjoy the rest of your senior year, while others in your class are madly filling out applications, writing essays, and agonizing over the thin envelopes that arrive in the mail. Says Guttentag, "The advantage of having that challenging process over with is not insignificant."

Early decision is helpful for admissions officers at selective colleges because it allows them to make decisions between well-qualified students and select those who really want to be at their institution. As Shawn Leftwich, Director of Admissions at Wheaton College in Illinois, points out, early decision is for the students who are strongly committed. "We like you. You like us. We know you're coming, and we can fill our freshman class." However, on the flip side, she adds that some students aren't so sure about which college they want to attend, and early decision only makes the process more stressful.

Before you decide early decision, consider early action. Many high school counselors lean toward early action, which is another good option. With early action you're able to apply later in the process. This means you will be able to take the SATs again. Your first-semester grades and AP classes taken in the first semester of your senior year can be used to evaluate your eligibility. You have September and October to visit several campuses while they are in session and plenty of time to do the research to put more than one school on your list.

THE PITFALLS OF EARLY DECISION

Though early decision has benefits, before you jump into it, look at the ramifications of that option. Advises Gilbert, "Early decision might give you an edge, but the tradeoff is not so great."

Perhaps the most compelling reason why students should seriously examine early decision before jumping at it is because they are bound by an agreement to attend that school if accepted. Students sign a pledge to attend that institution and are required to withdraw applications from all other schools. They also are obligated to accept the financial aid award that the institution gives them. An early decision is a binding decision. "Regardless," advises David Gibson, College Advisor at Baltimore City College High School in Baltimore, Maryland, "students don't learn about their financial aid awards until March or April, and if the award funding is not at all acceptable because the family's financial need was not met, they need to decline the offer and begin searching for a new college. March or April is not a good time to start applying to new colleges."

How binding is binding? Though no school can force a student to attend if they've signed an early action agreement, students who decide not to attend that school hurt others with that decision. High school counselors have to sign the binding agreement, along with parents, and must state that they will not send out transcripts to other institutions. Many institutions will not accept the application of a student who applied early decision elsewhere and backed out of the agreement. Admissions officers may find out in May that an early decision student is not coming, so they'll call the counselor and ask if the student applied to another school. If so, often a phone call to the other institution is made and acceptance denied. Sometimes the counselor loses a good reputation with that institution, putting applicants who follow in subsequent years at a disadvantage.

QUESTIONS TO ASK YOURSELF BEFORE APPLYING EARLY DECISION

What if you don't get accepted early decision—then what? Speaking from the experience of seeing students deal with early decision rejection letters, Reider says, "Some of your friends are getting acceptance letters, and you get one thin envelope and the pain of rejection. You've given the early decision institution your best shot and you lost." Cleaver has seen kids in her high school end up thinking they won't get in anywhere. "This is the first time they've faced a big rejection and news they don't want to hear," she says, noting that because of the timetable of early decision, letters often come right around exam time in December.

When students apply regular decision, meaning they wait until well into their senior year and apply to several different institutions, it's "all or some," quips Latting. "With early decision, it's all or nothing." Many application deadlines for regular decision are in January. If you get that rejection letter from the school you were counting on, that doesn't give you much time to apply to other schools, much less to visit them.

Are you ready to make such a drastic decision so early in your senior year? A lot can change in how you think about your future between the beginning of your senior year and graduation. With six or seven months behind you as a senior, you might be in a better position to compare colleges in April than you were back in September. Think about it—you're making the decision about where you want to spend the next four years of your life in early October of your senior year!

Have you given yourself enough time to pick one college above all others? If you want to apply early decision, you should start making plans to do so in your junior year. In order to apply early decision, you must have your ACTs or SATs taken, campus visits done, a final choice made, a dynamite essay written, a stellar application filled out, and teacher recommendation letters collected. That's a lot to cram into the end of your junior year and a few months into your senior year.

Have you given an admissions office enough information to make a decision about you? The more information the admissions office has about grades and classes you took and activities and leadership positions you held, the better they can decide if you're a good match for them. Do you really want decisions being made about you based on sophomore and junior grades and activities? What happens to that AP English class you finally felt ready to take the beginning of your senior year? What about that calculus class you finally kicked in the first semester of your senior year? Admissions won't be able to assess that on an early decision application.

After the consequences of signing a binding agreement, the financial aspect of early decision is the next biggest pitfall. "You can't compare financial aid offers," says Latting. "You have only one offer." Students won't know if they're eligible for Pell Grants or merit scholarships. Government FAFSA forms are not submitted until January, and students might not find out how much aid they can get until March or April, long after the early decision agreement was signed and sealed. "This means that if they are accepted, they are then obligated to a college that might not fund them to the level of their financial need," says Gibson. Students who apply early action or regular decision are in a better position to negotiate financial aid packages.

EARLY DECISION REJECTION

In case you haven't heard, fat is good, thin is bad. Thin envelopes from college admissions offices usually mean a single-page letter saying good luck, we wish you the best, but you're not going to be attending our school next fall. However stated, it's hard to be rejected, especially when you've applied early decision, which states to the college and to yourself that this is the college you've decided is the only one you really, really want to attend above all others.

But thin envelopes don't mean the end of the world. Cleaver advises to not let early decision get control of you. "There are too many choices of colleges for you not to get into college. You might not get into Princeton, but there are many other wonderful schools if you do the research to look for a good match. Early decision is a tool to use to apply, but it is not always the best tool."

Objecting to the term "perfect match," Reider asks, "Does it really matter what kind of car you drive? There are twenty different colleges that can get you where you want to go. You'll be successful in most places."

HOW TO DO EARLY DECISION THE RIGHT WAY

Taking the early decision option requires more than gathering information, filling out an application, writing an essay, and waiting for an envelope to come in the mail. If you're going to be serious about early decision, the time to start is in your junior year.

Research yourself and the institutions at the top of your list. Think through what you want out of college—not just in terms of a future career, but also factors such as location, size, distance from home, sports, and other activities. Think about who you want to be. "It has to be a love connection," says Cleaver. Tune out all the early decision talk and do your homework about each college. Then ask yourself if one stands out above all the others you've researched. Is this the one to which you can commit to a binding agreement? Are you in the competition to be admitted? Will you have the funds to attend this college?

"Admissions can tell if your application is from the heart," Cleaver cautions. Students ask her how to make their applications "look like they want to go there." She replies that what they put on an application and in an essay has to pour out of their hearts. Students who visit the campus and sit in on a class or a campus organization have the edge if something really clicked with them. They will write a convincing application. Perhaps they'll tell about how exciting the professor they heard was or how wonderful it is that the college has a chess club. Cleaver observes that kids usually write about an institution's sports team or about the ivy-covered walls of the campus on their application essay instead of writing about some interesting aspect of the university that spoke to them. This takes research, time, and reflection. "Don't make the mistake of chasing a name and not being a good consumer," cautions McClintick. Part of being a good consumer is to make sure you are a reasonably competitive applicant. This means looking at the school's admission criteria and statistics. What is the school's SAT range? What percentage of the freshman class is filled with early decision and early action students? If it's a high percentage, then you might want to reconsider where that school falls on your wish list. What is the persistence rate of students returning for their sophomore year? If more than 10 percent leave after their freshman year, that should tell you something about student satisfaction—and ultimately yours.

One of the most important ways to choose the right school is to visit the campus, perhaps multiple times and preferably with students on campus. "Campus visits are a critical time to talk with undergraduates and to find out what the academic, social, and physical climate is like," advises Guttentag. If you're staying in a dorm on Tuesday night during a visit, you can tell how serious kids are about their work. What kinds of conversations are they having? "Are these the kind of kids you want to spend four years of your life with?" asks McClintick.

After you've thoroughly investigated all the aspects of a college and decided it's at the absolute top of your list, after you are familiar with the early decision requirements at that institution, after you've determined that you have a good chance of getting into that institution, then early decision is for you. For those who are not so sure, fortunately, colleges and universities have plenty of other options for admission.

What International Students Need to Know About Admission to U.S. Colleges and Universities

Kitty M. Villa

Selecting an institution and securing admission require a significant investment of time and effort.

There are two principles to remember about admission to a university in the United States. First, applying is almost never a one-time request for admission but an ongoing process that may involve several exchanges of information between applicant and institution. "Admission process" or "application process" means that a "yes" or "no" is usually not immediate, and requests for additional information are to be expected. To successfully manage this process, you must be prepared to send additional information when requested and then wait for replies. You need a thoughtful balance of persistence to communicate regularly and effectively with your selected universities and patience to endure what can be a very long process.

The second principle involves a marketplace analogy. The most successful applicants are alert to opportunities to create a positive impression that sets them apart from other applicants. They are able to market themselves to their target institution. Institutions are also trying to attract the highest-quality student that they can. The admissions process presents you with the opportunity to analyze your strengths and weaknesses as a student and to look for ways to present yourself in the most marketable manner.

FIRST STEP—SELECTING INSTITUTIONS

With thousands of institutions of higher education in the U.S., how do you begin to narrow your choices down to the institutions that are best for you? There are many factors to consider, and you must ultimately decide which factors are most important to you.

Location

You may spend several years studying in the U.S. Do you prefer an urban or rural campus? Large or small metropolitan area? If you need to live on campus, will you be unhappy at a university where most students commute from off-campus housing? How do you feel about extremely hot summers or cold winters? Eliminating institutions that do not match your preferences in terms of location will narrow your choices.

Recommendations from Friends, Professors, or Others

There are valid academic reasons to consider the recommendations of people who know you well and have firsthand knowledge about particular institutions. Friends and contacts may be able to provide you with "inside information" about the campus or its academic programs to which published sources have no access. You should carefully balance anecdotal information with your own research and your own impressions. However, current and former students, professors, and others may provide excellent information during the application process.

Your Own Academic and Career Goals

Consideration of your academic goals is more complex than it may seem at first glance. All institutions do not offer the same academic programs. The application form usually provides a definitive listing of the academic programs offered by an institution. A course catalog describes the degree program and all the courses offered. In addition to printed sources, there is a tremendous amount of institutional information available through the Internet. Program descriptions, even course descriptions and course syllabi, are often available to peruse via computer.

You may be interested in the rankings of either the university or of a program of study. Keep in mind, however, that rankings usually assume that quality is quantifiable. Rankings are usually based on presumptions about how data relate to quality that are likely to be unproven. It is important to carefully consider the source and the criteria of any ranking information before believing and acting upon it.

Your Own Educational Background

You may be concerned about the interpretation of your educational credentials, since your country's degree nomenclature and the grading scale may differ from those in the U.S. Universities use reference books about the educational systems of other countries to help them understand specific educational credentials. Generally, these credentials are interpreted by each institution; there is not a single interpretation that applies to every institution. The lack of uniformity is good news for most students, since it means that students from a wide variety of educational backgrounds can find a U.S. university that is appropriate to their needs.

To choose an appropriate institution, you can and should do an informal self-evaluation of your educational background. This self-analysis involves three important questions:

How Many Years of Study Have You Completed?

Completion of secondary school with at least twelve total years of education usually qualifies students to apply for undergraduate (bachelor's) degree programs. Completion of a university degree program that involves at least sixteen years of total education qualifies one to apply for admission to graduate (master's) degree programs in the U.S.

Does the Education That You Have Completed in Your Country Provide Access to Further Study in the U.S.?

Consider the kind of institution where you completed your previous studies. If educational opportunities in your country are limited, it may be necessary to investigate many U.S. institutions and programs in order to find a match.

Are Your Previous Marks or Grades Excellent, Average, or Poor?

Your educational record influences your choice of U.S. institutions. If your grades are average or poor, it may be advisable to apply to several institutions with minimally difficult or noncompetitive entrance levels.

YOU are one of the best sources of information about the level and quality of your previous studies. Awareness of your educational assets and liabilities will serve you well throughout the application process.

SECOND STEP—PLANNING AND ASSEMBLING THE APPLICATION

Planning and assembling a university application can be compared to the construction of a building. First, you must start with a solid foundation, which is the application form itself. The application, often available online as well as in paper form, usually contains a wealth of useful information, such as deadlines, fees, and degree programs available at that institution. To build a solid application, it is best to begin well in advance of the application deadline.

How to Obtain the Application Form

Application forms and links to institutional Web sites may also be available at a U.S. educational advising center associated with the American Embassy or Consulate in your country. These centers are excellent resources for international students and provide information about standardized test administration, scholarships, and other matters to students who are interested in studying in the U.S. Your local U.S. Embassy or Consulate can guide you to the nearest educational advising center.

Completing the Application Form

Whether sent by mail or electronically, the application form must be neat and thoroughly filled out. Parts of the application may not seem to apply to you or your situation. Do your best to answer all the questions.

Remember that this is a process. You provide information, and your proposed university then requests clarification and further information. If you have questions, it is better to initiate the entire process by submitting the application form rather than asking questions before you apply. The university will be better able to respond to you after it has your application. Always complete as much as you can. Do not permit uncertainty about the completion of the application form to cause unnecessary delays.

What Are the Key Components of a Complete Application?

Institutional requirements vary, but the standard components of a complete application include:

- Transcript
- Required standardized examination scores
- Evidence of financial support
- Letters of recommendation
- Application fee

Transcript

A complete academic record or transcript includes all courses completed, grades earned, and degrees awarded. Most universities require an official transcript to be sent directly from the school or university. In many other countries, however, the practice is to issue official transcripts and degree certificates directly to the student. If you have only one official copy of your transcript, it may be a challenge to get additional certified copies that are acceptable to U.S. universities. Some institutions will issue additional official copies for application purposes.

If your institution does not provide this service, you may have to seek an alternate source of certification. As a last resort, you may send a photocopy of your official transcript, explain that you have only one original, and ask the university for advice on how to deal with this situation.

Required Standardized Examination Scores

Arranging to take standardized examinations and earning the required scores seem to cause the most anxiety for international students.

The university application form usually indicates which examinations are required. The standardized examination required most often for undergraduate admission is the Test of English as a Foreign Language (TOEFL). In most countries, TOEFL has changed from a paper-and-pencil test to a computer-based test. Institutions may also require the SAT I of undergraduate applicants. Some institutions also require the Test of Spoken English (TSE). These standardized examinations are administered by the Educational Testing Service (ETS). Please note: In September 2005, ETS will introduce a new TOEFL CBT, which will include a speaking section.

These examinations are offered in almost every country of the world. It is advisable to begin planning for standardized examinations at least six months prior to the application deadline of your desired institutions. Test centers fill up quickly, so it is important to register as soon as possible. Information about the examinations is available at U.S. educational advising centers associated with embassies or consulates.

FOR MORE INFORMATION

Questions about test formats, locations, dates, and registration may be addressed to:

TOEFL/TSE Services
P.O. Box 6151
Princeton, New Jersey 08541-6151
Web sites: http://www.ets.org
http://www.toefl.org
E-mail: toefl@ets.org
Telephone: 609-771-7100
Fax: 609-771-7500

Most universities require that the original test scores, not a student copy, be sent directly by the testing service. When you register for the test, be sure to indicate that the testing service should send the test scores directly to your proposed universities.

You should usually begin your application process before you receive your test scores. Delaying submission of your application until the test scores arrive may cause you to miss deadlines and negatively effect the outcome of your application. If you want to know your scores in order to assess your chances of admission to an institution with rigorous admission standards, you should take the tests early.

Many universities in the U.S. set minimum required scores on the TOEFL or on other standardized examinations. Test scores are an important factor, but most institutions also look at a number of other factors in their consideration of a candidate for admission.

Evidence of Financial Support

Evidence of financial support is required to issue immigration documents to admitted students. This is part of a complete application package but usually plays no role in determining admission. Most institutions make admissions decisions without regard to the source and amount of financial support.

Letters of Recommendation

Most institutions require one or more letters of recommendation. The best letters are written by former professors, employers, or others who can comment on your academic achievements or professional potential.

Some universities provide a special form for the letters of recommendation. If possible, use the forms provided. If you are applying to a large number of universities, however, or if your recommenders are not available to complete several forms, it may be necessary for you to duplicate a general recommendation letter.

Application Fee

Most universities also require an application fee, ranging from $25 to $100, which must be paid to initiate consideration of the application.

THIRD STEP—DISTINGUISH YOUR APPLICATION

To distinguish your application—to market yourself successfully—is ultimately the most important part of the application process. As you select your prospective universities, you begin to analyze your strengths and weaknesses as a prospective student. As you complete your application, you should strive to create a positive impression and set yourself apart from other applicants, to highlight your assets and bring these qualities to the attention of the appropriate university administrators and professors. Applying early is a very easy way to distinguish your application.

Deadline or Guideline?

The application deadline is the last date that an application for a given semester will be accepted. Often, the application will specify that all required documents and information be submitted before the deadline date. To meet the deadlines, start the application process early. This also gives you more time to take—and perhaps retake and improve—the required standardized tests.

Admissions deliberations may take several weeks or months. In the meantime, most institutions accept additional information, including improved test scores, after the posted deadline.

Even if your application is initially rejected, you may be able to provide additional information to change the decision. You can request reconsideration based on additional information, such as improved test scores, strong letters of recommendation, or information about your class rank. Applying early allows more time to improve your application. Also, some students may decide not to accept their offers of admission, leaving room for offers to students on a waiting list. Reconsideration of the admission decisions can occur well beyond the application deadline.

Think of the deadline as a guideline rather than an impermeable barrier. Many factors—the strength of the application, your research interests, the number of spaces available at the proposed institution—can override the enforcement of an application deadline. So, if you lack a test score or transcript by the official deadline, you may still be able to apply and be accepted.

Statement of Purpose

The statement of purpose is your first and perhaps best opportunity to present yourself as an excellent candidate for admission. Whether or not a personal history essay or statement of purpose is required, always include a carefully written statement of purpose with your applications. A compelling statement of purpose does not have to be lengthy, but it should include some basic components:

- Part One—Introduce yourself and describe your previous educational background. This is your opportunity to describe any facet of your educational experience that you wish to emphasize. Perhaps you attended a highly ranked secondary school or university in your home country. Mention the name and any noteworthy characteristics of the secondary school or university from which you graduated. Explain the grading scale used at your university. Do not forget to mention your rank in your graduating class and any honors you may have received. This is not the time to be modest.
- Part Two—Describe your current academic interests and goals. It is very important to describe in some detail your specific study or career interests. Think about how these will fit into those of the institution to which you are applying, and mention the reasons why you have selected that institution.
- Part Three—Describe your long-term goals. When you finish your program of study, what do you plan to do next? If you already have a job offer or a career plan, describe it. Give some thought to how you'll demonstrate that studying in the U.S. will ultimately benefit others.

Use Personal Contacts When Possible

Appropriate and judicious use of your own network of contacts can be very helpful. Friends, former professors, former students of your selected institutions, and others may be willing to advise you during the application process and provide you with introductions to key administrators or professors. If suggested, you may wish to contact certain professors or administrators by mail, telephone, or e-mail. A personal visit to discuss your interest in the institution may be appropriate. Whatever your choice of communication, try to make the encounter pleasant and personal. Your goal is to make a positive impression, not to rush the admission decision.

There is no single right way to be admitted to U.S. universities. The same characteristics that make the educational choice in the U.S. so difficult—the number of institutions and the variety of programs of study—are the same attributes that allow so many international students to find the institution that's right for them.

Kitty M. Villa is Assistant Director, International Office, at the University of Texas at Austin.

Searching for Four-Year Colleges Online

The Internet can be a great tool for gathering information about four-year colleges and universities. There are many worthwhile sites that are ready to help guide you through the various aspects of the selection process, including Peterson's Undergraduate Channel at www.petersons.com/ugchannel.

HOW PETERSON'S UNDERGRADUATE CHANNEL CAN HELP

Choosing a college involves a serious commitment of time and resources. Therefore, it is important to have the most up-to-date information about prospective schools at your fingertips. That is why Peterson's Undergraduate Channel is a great place to start your college search and selection process.

Find a College

Peterson's Undergraduate Channel is a comprehensive information resource that will help you make sense of the college admissions process. Peterson's Undergraduate Channel offers visitors enhanced search criteria and an easily navigable interface. The Channel is organized into various sections that make finding a program easy and fun. You can search for colleges based on name or location for starters, or do a detailed search on the following criteria:

- *Location*
- *Major*
- *Tuition*
- *Size*
- *Student/faculty ratio*
- *Average GPA*
- *Type of college*
- *Sports*
- *Religion*

Once you have found the school of your choice, simply click on it to get information about the institution, including majors, off-campus programs, costs, faculty, admission requirements, location, academic programs, academic facilities, athletics, student life, financial aid, student government, and application information and contacts.

E-mail the School

If, after looking at the information provided on Peterson's Undergraduate Channel, you still have questions, you can send an e-mail directly to the admissions department of the school. Just click on the "E-mail the School" button and send your message. In most instances, if you keep your questions short and to the point, you will receive an answer in no time at all.

School Web Site

For institutions that have provided information about their Web sites, simply click on the "School Web Site" button and you will be taken directly to that institution's Web page. Once you arrive at the school's Web site, look around and get a feel for the place. Often, schools offer virtual tours of the campus, complete with photos and commentary. If you have specific questions about the school, a visit to a school's Web site will often yield an answer.

Detailed Description

If the schools you are interested in have provided Peterson's with an **In-Depth Description,** you can do a keyword search on that description. Here, schools are given the opportunity to communicate unique features of their programs to prospective students.

Microsite

Several educational institutions provide students access to microsites, where more information about the types of resources and services offered can be found. In addition, students can take campus tours, apply for admissions, and explore academic majors.

Apply

The Apply link gives you the ability to directly apply to the school online.

Add to My List

The My List feature is designed to help you with your college planning. Here you can save the list of schools you're interested in, which you can then revisit at any time, access all the features of the site, and be reminded of important dates. You'll also be notified when new features are added to the site.

Get Recruited

Here's your chance to stop looking for colleges and let them find you with CollegesWantYou℠ (www.collegeswantyou.com), the new approach to the search and selection process. Unlike other college search and selection tools, CollegesWantYou℠ allows you to enter information on your preferences, test scores, and extracurricular activities into the online form, and before you know it, colleges that meet your specifications will be in touch with you. Registration is free, and all you need to do is complete a short profile indicating your preferences and then sit back and wait as colleges contact you directly!

Write Admissions Essays

This year, 500,000 college applicants will write 500,000 different admissions essays. Half will be rejected by their first-choice school, while only an 11 eleven percent will gain admission to the nation's most selective colleges. With acceptance rates at all-time lows, setting yourself apart requires more than just blockbuster SAT scores and impeccable transcripts-it requires the perfect application essay. Named "the world's premier application essay editing service" by the New York Times Learning Network and "one of the best essay services on the Internet" by the *Washington Post,* EssayEdge (www.essayedge.com) has helped more applicants write successful personal statements than any other company in the world. Learn more about EssayEdge and how it can give you an edge over hundreds of applicants with comparable academic credentials.

Practice for Your Test

At Peterson's, we understand that the college admissions process can be very stressful. With the stakes so high and the competition getting tighter every year, it's easy to feel like the process is out of your control. Fortunately, preparing for college admissions tests like the SAT, ACT, and PSAT helps you exert some control over the options you will have available to you. You can visit Peterson's Test Prep Channel (www.petersonstestprep.com) to learn more about how Peterson's can help you maximize your scores—and your options.

Use the Tools to Your Advantage

Choosing a college is an involved and complicated process. The tools available to you on www.petersons.com/ugchannel can help you to be more productive in this process. So, what are you waiting for? Fire up your computer; your future alma mater may be just a click away!

Money, Money, Money

Financial Aid Countdown Calendar

JUNIOR YEAR

Fall

Now is the time to get serious about the colleges in which you are interested. Meet with your guidance counselor to help you narrow down your choices. Hopefully by the spring, your list will have five to ten solid choices. College visits are always a great idea—remember this will be the place you spend the next four years, so start your campus visits soon!

- ❐ Register for the Preliminary SAT (PSAT).
- ❐ Check out local financial aid nights in the area. Be sure to attend these invaluable sessions, especially if this is the first time your family is sending someone off to college. Try to become familiar with common financial aid terms. Start reviewing some of the literature available and begin to familiarize yourself with the various programs. A good booklet is published by the U.S. Department of Education, "The Student Guide" and is available at any financial aid office or on the Web at http://studentaid.ed.gov/students/publications/student_guide.html#title.
- ❐ In October, take the PSAT and the National Merit Scholarship Qualifying Test.
- ❐ Do some Web browsing! There are many free scholarship search engines, such as Petersons.com. Also, head to the bookstore or library and pick up a copy of **Peterson's Scholarships, Grants & Prizes**. It features details on millions of dollars of aid from private sources.
- ❐ Ask your parents to contact their employers and church and fraternal organizations to learn about possible scholarship opportunities.
- ❐ Check with your high school guidance counselor for the qualifications and deadlines of local scholarship awards. Many guidance counselors report that there are few applicants for these awards.

Winter

- ❐ Keep checking for scholarships! Remember that this is the one area over which you have control. The harder you work, the better your chances for success!
- ❐ Register and study for the SAT (I and II). Most college-administered scholarship programs use the SATs in their selection process. Signing up for a prep course is usually money well spent (check out www.petersonstestprep.com). If you decide not to take a course, then your next best resource is the bookstore. The SAT is definitely not a test that you can cram for the night before. Invest in a comprehensive test-prep guide such as **Peterson's Ultimate SAT Tool Kit.** Using a study guide will help you get an idea of your math and verbal strengths and weaknesses. Set up a regular schedule to work on the areas that need improvement.

Spring

- ❐ Spring Break—a great time to visit colleges. Remember your top ten list? Time to start narrowing it down.
- ❐ Review the requirements for local scholarships. What can you do now and over the summer to improve your chances?
- ❐ Take the SATs. Good luck!
- ❐ Look for a summer job, especially one that ties in with your college plans. For example, if you want to major in premed, why not try to get a job at a hospital or with a laboratory?

Summer

- ❐ College visit time! Begin to ask yourself some questions: Is this where I see myself getting my undergraduate degree? Can I adjust to the seasons, the town surrounding the campus, the distance from home, the college size? Does this school feel right for me?

SENIOR YEAR

Fall

- ❒ How's the college list coming? Can you get your list down to five or six choices? Your guidance counselor can help with this process. Once you have your top choices, make a list of what each college requires for admission and financial aid. Be sure your list includes all deadlines.
- ❒ Do any of these colleges require the PROFILE financial aid application? Many private colleges use this form for institutional aid. You need to file this comprehensive form in late September or early October.
- ❒ Don't falter now in your scholarship search. Get the applications filed by the published deadlines.
- ❒ Register now if you are planning to retake the SAT.
- ❒ Attend a financial aid night presentation with your parents. Some of these sessions offer help in completing forms; others offer a broader view of the process. Contact the presenter (usually a local college professional) to be sure you are getting the information you need.

Winter

- ❒ Get the Free Application for Federal Student Aid (FAFSA). This is the key form for financial aid for every school across the country. Remember, watch your deadlines, but do not file until after January 1. Be sure to keep a copy of the form, whether you file electronically or with the paper application. Got some questions? Call the local financial aid office. Also, many states have special toll-free call-in programs in January and February, Financial Aid Awareness Month.
- ❒ As the letters of admission start to arrive, the financial aid award letters should be right behind them. Important question for parents: What is the bottom line? Remember, aid at a lower-cost state school will be less than a higher-cost private college. But what will *you* be required to pay? This can be confusing, so consider gift aid (scholarships and grants), student loans, and parent loans. The school with the lowest sticker price (tuition, fees, and room and board) might not be the best bargain when you factor in the overall financial aid package.

Spring

- ❒ Still not sure where to go? The financial aid package at your top choice just not enough? Call the financial aid office and the admissions office. Talk it over. While schools don't like to bargain, they are usually willing to take a second look. Is there something unusual about your family's financial situation that might impact your parents' ability to pay?
- ❒ By May 1, you must make your final decision. Notify your chosen college and find out what you need to do next. Tell the other colleges you are not accepting their offers of admission and financial aid.

Summer

- ❒ Time to crunch the numbers. Parents, get information from the college on the total charges for the coming fall term. Deduct the aid package and then plan for how the balance will be paid. Contact the college financial aid office for the best parental loan program. If you want to arrange for a payment plan, contact the Business Office for further information. Most schools have deferred payment plans available for a nominal fee.

Congratulations! Remember that you need to reapply for aid every year!

What's Your BestCollegeDeal®?

Today's students need all the help they can get in finding ways to pay for their college education. Skyrocketing tuition costs, state budget cuts, and diminished personal savings have combined to make college costs perhaps the number one concern for parents sending their children to college. College sticker shock is driving many families away from college. No wonder. The "purchasing power" of all aid programs from federal, state, and institutional sources has declined over the past two decades. State education budgets have been slashed. Tuition at a four-year public institution is increasing at an average annual rate of 14 percent; private tuition, by 6 percent. And it's not only lower-income families who are affected. Some fear they make too much money to qualify for financial aid. Regardless of their income, most families struggle to make sense of the college financing process and to decide which aid package is the right one for them.

Despite the seemingly dire situation, students and parents can and should continue to research as many sources as they can to find the money they need. With the right information, they can learn how to contain college costs, establish accurate savings targets, and find out what they should really expect to pay for a college education.

Peterson's knows that families need help that directly pertains to their personal financial situation-how to identify individual colleges' aid packages, analyze how much each college expects them to pay, and determine their own true college costs.

BestCollegeDeals®

The Internet's first online financial aid resource to provide truly personalized assistance, Peterson's BestCollegeDeals (www.BestCollegeDeals.com), allows participating families to assess the reality of their situation before they submit their paperwork to colleges for review. BestCollegeDeals has collected information on nearly 2,000 scholarships, grants, and other awards (both need- and non-need-based) that are generally not well publicized. No matter what their income, parents will discover what each college expects them to pay for freshman through senior years and find out the latest information on scholarships, tuition discounts, and other financial packages to help minimize out-of-pocket costs.

The architect of BestCollegeDeals, Carl Buck, has more than thirty years' experience as a financial aid expert. Currently Peterson's Vice President for Financial Aid Services, Carl was previously the Senior Vice President for the New Mexico Educational Assistance Foundation and the Director of Student Financial Services at a number of leading U.S. institutions, including Rice University; Rutgers, The State University of New Jersey; and the University of Utah.

Refer to the color ad at the front of this book for the key activation code to get FREE 90-day BestCollegeDeals® access!

WHAT'S IN IT FOR ME?

Through extensive secondary research, Peterson's has compiled the latest information on exceptional college deals-financial award packages, including the average grant award, offered by more than 1,800 accredited undergraduate institutions all over the country. Surprisingly, many institutions offer "free money" deals in the form of no-strings grants or scholarships, regardless of an applicant's income. In fact, there are nearly 2,000 of these "free money" deals in our database, which are available to students for performing community service, for being valedictorians, or for being the sibling of a current college student. All of the deals fall into one or more of the following categories:

- **First Generation** First generation deals are designed for students who are the first in their family to attend a postsecondary institution. Programs are generally structured to provide financial assistance to high school students who exhibit a high degree of motivation and academic potential.
- **Tuition** Tuition deals vary by school and include plans that provide discounts or tuition reciprocity, limit tuition increases, or pay for part or all of a student's tuition, room, board, and other expenses. Tuition deals may affect only a student's first year of college or be guaranteed for up to four years.
- **GPA/SAT/ACT** Restricted to students who have high grade point averages (GPA), usually 3.5 or above on a 4-point scale; a high class rank; and/or high SAT or ACT scores, as stipulated by the college or university. Other criteria may apply. Renewal of a GPA/SAT/ACT deal may be contingent upon a minimum cumulative GPA and/or full-time enrollment status.
- **National Merit** These deals primarily apply to National Merit Finalists who have formally listed specific institutions as their primary choice with the National Merit Scholarship Corporation.
- **Valedictorian** Many colleges offer scholarships to graduating high school seniors who rank first or second in

their class. Scholarships may cover tuition. Many of these awards are renewable for students who maintain a certain GPA while in college, usually a 3.0 or better.

- **Sibling** A number of schools offer tuition discounts or scholarships for students who have a sibling enrolled at the same college or university. In many instances, sibling deals are available only for the time that both siblings are enrolled. Other requirements, such as a minimum GPA, may apply. On average, the tuition discount is approximately 20 to 25 percent.
- **Minority** Students belonging to traditionally underrepresented ethnic minority groups may be eligible for annual awards at colleges and universities. As with other rewards, certain academic requirements may apply, including GPA, class rank, or SAT/ACT scores.
- **Community Service** A number of colleges and universities provide financial awards to students who are active in volunteer work or community service. In fact, community service deals are offered to incoming freshmen at more than 160 colleges and may be renewable from sophomore to senior years.
- **Exceptional Opportunity** This is a miscellaneous category that includes legacy discounts and more obscure deals, and these deals vary by university and are often very unique. For example, some schools offer incoming freshmen who are sons or daughters of alumni special tuition discounts or scholarships to offset college-related costs.

HOW DOES IT WORK?

The confusing methods many colleges use to assess a family's financial situation can make college financing a complex, frustrating experience. But it doesn't have to be. BestCollegeDeals helps you and your family better understand the financial aid process. And you'll discover quick and easy solutions to find the funding you need.

1. Calculate your estimated Expected Family Contribution (EFC), the amount of money you may be expected to pay toward your college education.
2. Choose location, enrollment size, and whether you're interested in a public, private, all-women's, or all-men's college or university.
3. Get a list of colleges and information about their financial aid offerings that match your preferences.
4. Discover great need- and merit-based financial aid deals that you can't find anywhere else!

TOP TEN REASONS TO MAKE BestCollegeDeals® WORK FOR YOU!

Every family's financial situation is different. Only BestCollegeDeals gives you the facts on how much colleges expect you to pay and provides you with information on scholarships, tuition discounts, and other financial aid packages that minimize your out-of-pocket costs.

10. Learn more about thousands of colleges.
9. Discover financial aid packages for years two to four, in addition to freshman year.
8. Get financial planning from a trusted source.
7. Compare, at a glance, financial packages of as many colleges as you choose.
6. Find a college that gives you the lowest debt burden upon graduation.
5. Estimate your Expected Family Contribution (what colleges expect you can pay).
4. Plan and save according to your income, your needs, and your budget.
3. Minimize your family's out-of-pocket college expenses.
2. Uncover hidden deals that can save you up to 100 percent on your college costs, such as free tuition or free room and board.
1. Fulfill your dreams at a college you never thought you could afford!

Who's Paying for This? Financial Aid Basics

A college education can be expensive—costing more than $100,000 for four years at some of the higher priced private colleges and universities. Even at the lower cost state colleges and universities, the cost of a four-year education can approach $50,000. Determining how you and your family will come up with the necessary funds to pay for your education requires planning, perseverance, and learning as much as you can about the options that are available to you.

Paying for college should not be looked on as a four-year financial commitment. For most families, paying the total cost of a student's college education out of current savings is usually not realistic. For families that have planned ahead and have financial savings established for higher education, the burden is a lot easier. But for most, meeting the cost of college requires the pooling of current income and assets and investing in longer-term loan options. These family resources, together with possible financial assistance from the state, federal, and institutional resources enable millions of students each year to attend the institution of their choice.

HOW NEED-BASED FINANCIAL AID IS AWARDED

When you apply for aid, your family's financial situation is analyzed using a government-approved formula called the Federal Methodology. This formula looks at five items:

1. Demographic information of the family.
2. Income of the parents.
3. Assets of the parents.
4. Income of the student.
5. Assets of the student.

This analysis determines the amount you and your family are expected to contribute toward your college expenses, called your Expected Family Contribution or EFC. If the EFC is equal to or more than the cost at a particular college, then you do not demonstrate financial need. However, even if you don't have financial need, you may still qualify for aid, as there are grants, scholarships, and loan programs that are not need-based.

If the cost of your education is greater than your EFC, then you do demonstrate financial need and qualify for assistance. The amount of your financial need that can be met varies from school to school. Some are able to meet your full need, while others can only cover a certain percentage of need. Here's the formula:

Cost of Attendance
− Expected Family Contribution
= Financial Need

The EFC remains constant, but your need will vary according to the costs of attendance at a particular college. In general, the higher the tuition and fees at a particular college, the higher the cost of attendance will be. Expenses for books and supplies, room and board, and other miscellaneous costs are included in the overall cost of attendance. It is important to remember that you do not have to be "needy" to qualify for financial aid. Many middle and upper-middle income families qualify for need-based financial aid.

SOURCES OF FINANCIAL AID

The largest single source of aid is the federal government, which awards almost $84 billion to more than 8.9 million students each year.

The next largest source of financial aid is found in the college and university community. Institutions award an estimated $20 billion to students each year. Most of this aid is awarded to students who have a demonstrated need based on the Federal Methodology. Some institutions use a different formula, the Institutional Methodology, to award their own funds in conjunction with other forms of aid. Institutional aid may be either need-based or non-need based. Aid that is not based on need is usually awarded for a student's academic performance (merit awards), specific talents or abilities, or to attract the type of students a college seeks to enroll.

Another source of financial aid is from state government, awarding more than $5.6 billion per year. All states offer grant and/or scholarship aid, most of which is need-based. However, more and more states are offering substantial merit-based aid programs. Most state programs award aid only to students attending college in their home state.

Other sources of financial aid include:

- Private agencies
- Foundations
- Corporations
- Clubs
- Fraternal and service organizations
- Civic associations

- Unions
- Religious groups that award grants, scholarships, and low-interest loans
- Employers that provide tuition reimbursement benefits for employees and their children

More information about these different sources of aid is available from high school guidance offices, public libraries, college financial aid offices, directly from the sponsoring organizations and on the Web at www.finaid.org.

APPLYING FOR FINANCIAL AID

Every student must complete the Free Application for Federal Student Aid (FAFSA) to be considered for financial aid. The FAFSA is available from your high school guidance office, many public libraries, colleges in your area, or directly from the U.S. Department of Education.

Students also can apply for federal student aid over the Internet using the interactive FAFSA on the Web. FAFSA on the Web can be accessed at http://www.fafsa.ed.gov. Both the student and at least one parent must apply for a federal pin number at http://www.pin.ed.gov. The pin number serves as your electronic signature when applying for aid on the Web.

To award their own funds, some colleges require an additional application, the Financial Aid PROFILE® form. The PROFILE asks supplemental questions that some colleges and awarding agencies feel provide a more accurate assessment of the family's ability to pay for college. It is up to the college to decide whether it will use only the FAFSA or both the FAFSA and the PROFILE. PROFILE applications are available from the high school guidance office and on the Web. Both the paper application and the Web site list those colleges and programs that require the PROFILE application.

If Every College You're Applying to for Fall 2005 Requires Just the FAFSA

. . . then it's pretty simple: Complete the FAFSA after January 1, 2005, being certain to send it in before any college-imposed deadlines. (You are not permitted to send in the 2005-06 FAFSA before January 1, 2005.) Most college FAFSA application deadlines are in February or early March. It is easier if you have all your financial records for the previous year available, but if that is not possible, you are strongly encouraged to use estimated figures.

After you send in your FAFSA, either with the paper application or electronically, you'll receive a Student Aid Report (SAR) that includes all of the information you reported and shows your EFC. If you provided an e-mail address, the SAR is sent to you electronically; otherwise, you will receive a paper copy in the mail. Be sure to review the SAR, checking to see if the information you reported is accurate. If you used estimated numbers to complete the FAFSA, you may have to resubmit the SAR with any corrections to the data. The college(s) you have designated on the FAFSA will receive the information you reported and will use that data to make their decision. In many instances, the colleges you've applied to will ask you to send copies of your and your parents' federal income tax returns for 2004, plus any other documents needed to verify the information you reported.

If a College Requires the PROFILE

Step 1: Register for the Financial Aid PROFILE in the fall of your senior year in high school.

Registering for the Financial Aid PROFILE begins the financial aid process. You can register by calling the College Scholarship Service at 1-800-778-6888 and providing basic demographic information, a list of colleges to which you are applying, and your credit card number to pay for the service. You can also apply for the PROFILE online at http://profileonline.collegeboard.com/index.jsp. Registration packets with a list of the colleges that require the PROFILE are available in most high school guidance offices. There is a fee for using the Financial Aid PROFILE application ($23 for the first college and $18 for each additional college). You must pay for the service by credit card when you register. If you do not have a credit card, you will be billed.

Step 2: Fill out your customized Financial Aid PROFILE.

A few weeks after you register, you'll receive in the mail a customized financial aid application that you can use to apply for institutional aid at the colleges you've designated, as well as from some private scholarship programs, like the National Merit Scholarship. (Note: If you've waited until winter and a college's financial aid application deadline is approaching, you can get overnight delivery by paying an extra fee.) The PROFILE contains all the questions necessary to calculate your "institutional" EFC, plus any additional questions that the colleges and organizations you've designated require you to answer. Your individualized packet will also contain a customized cover letter instructing you what to do and informing you about deadlines and requirements for the colleges and programs you designated when you registered for the PROFILE, codes that indicate which colleges wanted which additional questions, and supplemental forms (if any of the colleges to which you are applying require them—e.g. the Business/Farm Supplement for students whose parents own a business or farm or the Divorced/Separated Parents' Statement).

Make sure you submit your PROFILE by the earliest deadline listed. Two to four weeks after you do so, you will receive an acknowledgment and a report estimating your "institutional" EFC based on the data elements you provided on your PROFILE. Remember, this is a different formula from the federal system that uses the FAFSA.

FINANCIAL AID PROGRAMS

There are three types of financial aid:

1. Gift-aid—Scholarships and grants are funds that do not have to be repaid.
2. Loans—Loans must be repaid, usually after graduation; the amount you have to pay back is the total you've borrowed plus any accrued interest. This is considered a source of self-help aid.

3. Student employment—Student employment is a job arranged for you by the financial aid office. This is another source of self-help aid.

The federal government has two major grant programs—the Federal Pell Grant and the Federal Supplemental Educational Opportunity Grant. These grants are targeted to low-to-moderate income families with significant financial need. The federal government also sponsors a student employment program called Federal Work-Study, which offers jobs both on and off campus; and several loan programs, including those for students and for parents of undergraduate students.

There are two types of student loan programs, subsidized and unsubsidized. The Subsidized Stafford Loan and the Federal Perkins Loan are need-based, government-subsidized loans. Students who borrow through these programs do not have to pay interest on the loan until after they graduate or leave school. The Unsubsidized Stafford Loan and the Parent Loan Programs are not based on need, and borrowers are responsible for the interest while the student is in school. There are different methods on how these loans are administered. Once you choose your college, the financial aid office will guide you through this process.

After you've submitted your financial aid application and you've been accepted for admission, each college will send you a letter describing your financial aid award. Most award letters show estimated college costs, how much you and your family are expected to contribute, and the amount and types of aid you have been awarded. Most students are awarded aid from a combination of sources and programs. Hence, your award is often called a financial aid "package."

IF YOU DON'T QUALIFY FOR NEED-BASED AID

If you are not eligible for need-based aid, you can still find ways to lessen the burden on your parents.

Here are some suggestions:

- Search for merit scholarships. You can start at the initial stages of your application process. College merit awards are becoming increasingly important as more and more colleges award these grants to students they especially want to attract. As a result, applying to a college at which your qualifications put you at the top of the entering class may give you a larger merit award. Another source of aid to look for is private scholarships that are given for special skills and talents. Additional information can be found at petersons.com and at www.finaid.org.
- Seek employment during the summer and the academic year. The student employment office at your college can help you locate a school-year job. Many colleges and local businesses have vacancies remaining after they have hired students who are receiving Federal Work-Study financial aid.
- Borrow through the Unsubsidized Stafford Loan programs. These are open to all students. The terms and conditions are similar to the subsidized loans. The biggest difference is that the borrower is responsible for the interest while still in college, although most lenders permit students to delay paying the interest right away and add the accrued interest to the total amount owed. You must file the FAFSA to be considered.
- After you've secured what you can through scholarships, working, and borrowing, your parents will be expected to meet their share of the college bill (the Expected Family Contribution). Many colleges offer monthly payment plans that spread the cost over the academic year. If the monthly payments are too high, parents can borrow through the Federal Parent Loan for Undergraduate Students (PLUS program), through one of the many private education loan programs available, or through home equity loans and lines of credit. Families seeking assistance in financing college expenses should inquire at the financial aid office about what programs are available at the college. Some families seek the advice of professional financial advisers and tax consultants.

HOW IS YOUR FAMILY CONTRIBUTION CALCULATED?

The chart on the next page makes the following assumptions:

- two parent family where age of older parent is 45
- lower income families will file the 1040A or 1040EZ tax form
- student income is less than $2300
- there are no student assets
- there is only one family member in college

All figures are estimates and may vary when the complete FAFSA or PROFILE application is submitted.

Approximate Expected Family Contribution

		INCOME BEFORE TAXES								
ASSETS	**FAMILY SIZE**	**$20,000**	**30,000**	**40,000**	**50,000**	**60,000**	**70,000**	**80,000**	**90,000**	**100,000**
$ 20,000										
	3	$ 0	870	2,450	4,350	7,000	9,800	12,600	15,500	18,000
	4	0	80	1,670	3,350	5,600	8,300	11,000	14,000	17,100
	5	0	0	930	2,500	4,500	7,000	9,700	12,600	15,600
	6	0	0	100	1,700	3,350	5,500	8,100	11,000	14,000
$ 30,000										
	3	$ 0	870	2,450	4,350	7,000	9,800	12,600	15,500	18,000
	4	0	80	1,670	3,350	5,600	8,300	11,000	14,000	17,100
	5	0	0	930	2,500	4,500	7,000	9,700	12,600	15,600
	6	0	0	100	1,700	3,350	5,500	8,100	11,000	14,000
$ 40,000										
	3	$ 0	870	2,450	4,350	7,000	9,800	12,600	15,500	18,000
	4	0	80	1,670	3,350	5,600	8,300	11,000	14,000	17,100
	5	0	0	930	2,500	4,500	7,000	9,700	12,600	15,600
	6	0	0	100	1,700	3,350	5,500	8,100	11,000	14,000
$ 50,000										
	3	$ 0	870	2,450	4,350	7,500	10,300	13,000	16,000	19,000
	4	0	80	1,670	3,350	6,000	8,800	11,500	14,400	17,500
	5	0	0	930	2,500	4,700	7,400	10,100	13,000	16,100
	6	0	0	100	1,700	3,600	5,900	8,500	11,400	14,500
$ 60,000										
	3	$ 0	870	2,450	5,100	8,050	10,800	13,600	16,500	19,600
	4	0	80	1,670	3,950	6,550	9,300	12,200	15,000	18,100
	5	0	0	930	3,000	5,300	7,900	10,800	13,600	16,700
	6	0	0	100	2,150	4,000	6,300	9,100	12,000	15,000
$ 80,000										
	3	$ 0	870	2,450	6,000	9,200	12,000	14,800	17,600	20,700
	4	0	80	1,670	4,700	7,600	10,500	13,200	16,100	19,200
	5	0	0	930	3,700	6,100	9,000	11,800	14,700	17,800
	6	0	0	100	2,700	4,700	7,400	10,200	13,100	16,200
$ 100,000										
	3	$ 0	870	2,450	7,000	10,300	13,000	15,900	18,800	21,850
	4	0	80	1,670	5,600	8,700	11,500	14,300	17,200	20,300
	5	0	0	930	4,400	7,100	10,200	12,900	15,800	18,900
	6	0	0	100	3,300	5,500	8,500	11,300	14,200	17,300
$ 120,000										
	3	$ 0	870	2,450	8,100	11,400	14,200	17,000	19,900	23,000
	4	0	80	1,670	6,600	9,800	12,600	15,500	18,400	21,500
	5	0	0	930	5,300	8,200	11,300	14,100	17,000	20,000
	6	0	0	100	4,000	6,500	9,700	12,500	15,300	18,400
$ 140,000										
	3	$ 0	870	2,450	9,300	12,600	15,400	18,200	21,000	24,100
	4	0	80	1,670	7,600	11,000	13,900	16,700	19,500	22,600
	5	0	0	930	6,100	9,500	12,500	15,200	18,100	21,200
	6	0	0	100	4,700	7,600	10,800	13,600	16,500	19,600

Middle-Income Families: Making the Financial Aid Process Work

Richard Woodland

An August 2001 report from the U.S. Department of Education's National Center for Education Statistics took a close look at how middle-income families finance a college education. The report, Middle Income Undergraduates: Where They Enroll and How They Pay for Their Education, was one of the first detailed studies of these families. Even though 31 percent of middle-income families have the entire cost of attendance covered by financial aid, there is widespread angst among middle-income families that, while they earn too much to qualify for grant assistance, they are too financially strapped to pay the spiraling costs of higher education.

First, we have to agree on what constitutes a "middle-income" family. For the purposes of the federal study, middle income is defined as those families with incomes between $35,000 and $70,000. The good news is that 52 percent of these families received grants, while the balance received loans. Other sources of aid, including work-study, also helped close the gap.

So how do these families do it? Is there a magic key that will open the door to significant amounts of grants and scholarships?

The report found some interesting trends. One way families can make college more affordable is by choosing a less expensive college. In fact, in this income group, 29 percent choose to enroll in low- to moderate-cost schools. These include schools where the total cost is less than $8,500 per year. In this sector, we find the community colleges and lower-priced state colleges and universities. But almost half of these middle-income families choose schools in the upper-level tier, with costs ranging from $8,500 to $16,000. The remaining 23 percent enrolled at the highest-tier schools, with costs above $16,000. Clearly, while cost is a factor, middle-income families are not limiting their choices based on costs alone.

The report shows that families pay these higher costs with a combination of family assets, current income, and long-term borrowing. This is often referred to as the "past-present-future" model of financing. In fact, just by looking at the Expected Family Contributions, it is clear that there is a significant gap in what families need and what the financial aid process can provide. Families are closing this gap by making the financial sacrifices necessary to pay the price at higher-cost schools, especially if they think their child is academically strong. The report concludes that parents are more likely to pay for a higher-priced education if their child scores above 1200 on the SATs.

The best place for middle-income families to start is with the high school guidance office. This office has a lot of good information on financial aid and valuable leads on local scholarships. Most guidance officers report that there are far fewer applicants for these locally based scholarships than one would expect. So read the information they send home and check on the application process. A few of those $500–$1000 scholarships can add up!

Second, plan to attend a financial aid awareness program. If your school does not offer one, contact your local college financial aid office and see when and where they will be speaking. You can get a lot of "inside" information on how the financial aid process works.

Next, be sure to file the correct applications for aid. Remember, each school can have a different set of requirements. For example, many higher-cost private colleges will require the PROFILE application to be filed in September or October of your senior year. Other schools will have their own institutional aid application. All schools will require the Free Application for Federal Student Aid (FAFSA). Watch the deadlines! It is imperative that you meet the school's published application deadline. Generally, schools are not flexible about this, so be sure to double-check the due date of all applications.

Finally, become a smart educational consumer. Peterson's has a wide range of resources available to help you understand the process. Be sure to also check your local library, bookstore, and of course, the Internet. Two great Web sites to check are Petersons.com and www.finaid.org.

Once admitted to the various colleges and universities, you will receive an award notice outlining the aid you are eligible to receive. If you feel the offer is not sufficient, or if you have some unique financial circumstances, call the school's financial aid office to see if you can have your application reviewed again. The financial aid office is your best source for putting the pieces together and finding solutions for you.

The financial aid office will help you determine what the "net price" is. This is the actual out-of-pocket expenses that you will need to cover. Through a combination of student and parent loans, most families are able to meet these expenses not paid with other forms of financial aid and family resources.

Many students help meet their educational expenses by working while in school. While this works for many students, research shows that too many hours spent away from your studies will negatively impact on your academic success. Most experts feel that working 10 to 15 hours a week is optimal.

An overlooked source of aid is the recent tax credits given to middle-income families. Rather than extending eligibility for traditional sources of grant assistance to middle-income families, congress and the president have built into the federal tax system significant tax credits for middle-income families. While it may be seven or eight months before you see the tax credit, families in this income group can safely count on this benefit, usually about $1500 per student. This is real money in your pocket. You do not need to itemize your deductions to qualify for this tax credit.

Millions of middle-income families send their children to colleges and universities every year. Only 8 percent attend the lowest-priced schools. By using the concept of past-present-future financing, institutional assistance, meaningful targeted tax relief, and student earnings, you can afford even the highest-cost schools.

Richard Woodland is Director of Financial Aid at Rutgers University–Camden.

Options, Options, Options

Honors: An A+ Education

Dr. Joan Digby

WHO ARE HONORS STUDENTS?

If you are a strong student filled with ideas, longing for creative expression, and ready to take on career-shaping challenges, then an honors education is just for you. Honors programs and colleges offer some of the finest undergraduate degrees available in American colleges and do it with students in mind. The essence of honors is personal attention, top faculty members, enlightening seminars, illuminating study-travel experiences, research options, career-building internships-all designed to enhance a classic education and prepare you for life achievements. And here's an eye-opening bonus: honors programs and colleges may reward your past academic performance by giving you scholarships that will help you pay for your higher education.

Take your choice of institutions: community college, state or private four-year college, or large research university. There are honors opportunities in each. What they share in common is an unqualified commitment to academic excellence. Honors education teaches students to think and write clearly, to be excited by ideas, and to become independent, creative, self-confident learners. It prepares exceptional students for professional choices in every imaginable sphere of life: arts and sciences, engineering, business, health, education, medicine, theater, music, film, journalism, media, law, politics-invent your own professional goal, and honors will guide you to it! There are hundreds of honors programs and honors colleges around the country. Whichever one you choose, you can be sure to enjoy an extraordinarily fulfilling undergraduate education.

Who are you? Perhaps a high school junior making out your first college applications, a community college student seeking to transfer to a four-year college, or possibly a four-year college student doing better than you had expected. You might be an international student, a varsity athlete, captain of the debate team, or second violin in the campus orchestra. Whether you are the first person in your family to attend college or an adult with a grown family seeking a new career, honors might well be right for you. Honors programs admit students with every imaginable background and educational goal.

How does honors satisfy them and give them something special? Read what students in some of our member programs say. Although they refer to particular colleges, their experiences are typical of what students find exciting about honors education on hundreds of campuses around the country.

"Honors is not just a class or a degree but rather a family that you can count on. I was an out-of-state student, not knowing anyone, and honors helped me [make] the drastic change from high school student to college scholar. Through its educators as well as its students, honors has changed my life for the better."

Chris Whitford
Business major
University of Maine, Orono

"Having interested people who remember my name and monitor my progress made a big difference to me.... The crossover of disciplines is amazing. I use notes from philosophy class in botany and ecology. The text in ecology uses terms I studied in botany, and they all refer to Aristotle and algebra. Finishing this program has made it a part of me, and it will alter the outcome of my life."

Andre Chenault
Tulsa Community College

"Although the structure of my engineering courses makes involvement in the Honors Program difficult, my honors classes have been the perfect break from my major. Rather than sitting in yet another classroom with 20+ students being told how things are, through honors I get to sit in a classroom with 16 or fewer students and actually discuss the material. Discussion and paper assignments in my honors courses have kept me on my toes."

Colin Smith
Villanova University

"Through engaging discussions and readings in seminars like African Literature and Politics and Literature of the Apocalypse, Christ College has challenged me to examine my view of the world by introducing me to different ideas, cultures, beliefs, and lifestyles."

Gretchen Eelkema
Chemistry and French major
Valparaiso University, Christ College

"I went to an arts high school that allowed me to participate in . . music, theater, and the visual arts. . . I had trouble finding a college that would allow me to create a specialized major (and that would be within my budget!). I gave up and settled on Cal State Fullerton as a temporary solution . . . I was also accepted into their Honors Program and I soon discovered that it was the best thing I could have done. . . . To my surprise [my honors director] was an art professor and was excited to create a major specialized to my interests. Unexpectedly Cal State Fullerton became the perfect school for me, but it could not have come about without the special attention I received in the Honors Program."

Joy Shannon
College of the Arts, California State University, Fullerton

These portraits don't tell the whole story, but they should give you a sense of what it means to be part of an honors program or honors college. Outside of class, honors students often run track, run the student government, and write the college newspaper. They are everywhere on campus: in plays and concerts, in laboratories and libraries, in sororities and fraternities. Some are clear about their majors and professions; others need direction and advice. One of the great strengths of honors programs is that they are nurturing environments that encourage students to be well-rounded and help students make life choices.

WHAT IS AN HONORS PROGRAM?

An honors program is a sequence of courses designed specifically to encourage independent and creative learning. Whether you want to attend a large state university or a private one, a small or large four-year college, or your local community college, you can make the decision to join an honors program. For more than half a century, honors education, given definition by the National Collegiate Honors Council, has been an institution on American campuses. Although honors programs have many different designs, there are typical components. In two-year colleges, the programs often concentrate on special versions of general education courses and may have individual capstone projects that come out of the students' special interest. In four-year colleges and universities, honors programs are generally designed for students of almost every major in every college on campus. In some cases, they are given additional prominence as honors colleges. Whether a program or a college, honors is most often structured as a general education or core component followed by advanced courses (often called colloquia or seminars) and a thesis or creative project, which may or may not be in the departmental major. Almost always, honors curriculum is incorporated within whatever number of credits is required of every student for graduation. Honors very rarely requires students to take additional credits. Students who complete an honors program or honors college curriculum frequently receive transcript and diploma notations as well as certificates, medallions, or other citations at graduation ceremonies.

While researching honors programs and colleges, you will begin to see typical patterns of academic programming, and that is where you must choose the program or college best suited to your own needs. In every case, catering to the student as an individual plays a central role in honors course design. Most honors classes are small (under 20 students); most are discussion-oriented, giving students a chance to present their own interpretations of ideas and even teach a part of the course. Many classes are interdisciplinary, which means they are taught by faculty members from two or more departments, providing different perspectives on a subject. All honors classes help students develop and articulate their own perspectives by cultivating both verbal and written style. They help students mature intellectually, preparing them to engage in their own explorations and research. Some programs even extend the options for self-growth to study abroad and internships in science, government, the arts, or business related to the major. Other programs encourage or require community service as part of the honors experience. In every case, honors is an experiential education that deepens classroom learning and extends far beyond.

Despite their individual differences, all honors programs and honors colleges rely on faculty members who enjoy working with bright, independent students. The ideal honors faculty members are open-minded and encouraging master teachers. They want to see their students achieve at their highest capacity, and they are glad to spend time with students in discussions and laboratories, on field trips and at conferences, or online in e-mail. They often influence career decisions, provide inspiring models, and remain friends long after they have served as thesis advisers.

WHERE ARE HONORS PROGRAMS AND HONORS COLLEGES LOCATED?

Because honors programs and honors colleges include students from many different departments or colleges, they usually have their own offices and space on campus. Some have their own buildings. Most programs have honors centers or lounges where students gather together for informal conversations, luncheons, discussions, lectures, and special projects.

Many honors students have cultivated strong personal interests that have nothing to do with classes; they may be experts at using the Internet; they may be fine artists or poets, musicians or racing car enthusiasts. Some volunteer in hospitals or do landscape gardening to pay for college. Many work in retail stores and catering. Some inline skate and others collect antique watches. When they get together in honors lounges, there is always an interesting mixture of ideas.

In general, honors provides an environment in which students feel free to talk about their passionate interests and ideas, knowing they will find good listeners and sometimes arguers. There is no end to conversations among honors students. Like many students in honors, you may feel a great relief in finding a sympathetic group that respects your intelligence and creativity. In honors, you can be eccentric, you can be yourself! Some lifelong friendships, even marriages, are the result of social relationships developed in honors programs. Of course you will make other friends in classes, clubs, and elsewhere on campus, even through e-mail! But the honors program will build strong bonds too.

In the honors center, whether program or college, you will also find the honors director or dean. The honors director often serves as a personal adviser to all of the students in the program. Many programs also have peer counselors and mentors who are upperclass honors students and know the ropes from a student's perspective and experience. Some have specially assigned honors advisers who guide honors students through their degrees, assist in registration, and answer every imaginable question. The honors office area usually is a good place to meet people, ask questions, and solve problems.

ARE YOU READY FOR HONORS?

Admission to honors programs and honors colleges is generally based on a combination of several factors: high school or previous college grades, SAT or ACT Assessment scores, personal essay, and extra-curricular achievements. To stay in honors, students need to maintain a certain GPA (grade point average) and show progress toward the completion of the specific honors program or college requirements. Since you have probably exceeded admissions standards all along, maintaining your GPA will not be as big a problem as it sounds. Your faculty members and your honors director are there to help you succeed in the program. Most honors programs have very low attrition rates, because students enjoy classes and do well. You have every reason to believe that you can make the grade.

Of course, you must be careful about how you budget your time for studying. Honors encourages well-rounded, diversified students, and you should play a sport if you want to, work at the radio station, join the clubs that interest you, or pledge a sorority or fraternity. You might find a job in the food service or library that will help you pay for your car expenses, and that also is reasonable. But remember, each activity takes time, and you must strike a balance that will leave you enough time to do your homework, prepare for seminar discussions, do your research, and do well on exams. Choose the extracurricular activities and work opportunities on campus that attract you, but never let them overshadow your primary purpose-to be a student.

Sometimes even the very best students who apply for honors admissions are frightened by the thought of speaking in front of a group, giving seminar papers, or writing a thesis. But if you understand how the programs work, you will see that there is nothing about which to be frightened. The basis of honors is confidence in the student and building the student's self-confidence. Once you are admitted to an honors program, you have already demonstrated your academic achievement in high school or college classes. Once in an honors program, you will learn how to formulate and structure ideas so that you can apply critical judgment to sets of facts and opinions. In small seminar classes, you practice discussion and arguments, so by the time you come to the senior thesis or project, the method is second nature. For most honors students, the senior thesis, performance, or portfolio presentation is the project that gives them the greatest fulfillment and pride. In many honors programs and colleges, students present their work either to other students or to faculty members in their major departments. Students often present their work at regional and national honors conferences. Some students even publish their work jointly with their faculty mentors. These are great achievements, and they come naturally with the training. There is nothing to be afraid of. Just do it! Honors will make you ready for life.

Dr. Joan Digby is Director of the Honors Program at Long Island University, C.W. Post Campus.

THE APPLICATION PROCESS

READY, SET, GO!

The Standardized Tests

- The SAT I, the ACT Assessment®, or both tests are taken during your junior year of high school and, perhaps, again in your senior year if you are trying to improve your scores. If your native language is not English, you may also have to take the TOEFL.

The Application

- Find out what materials the college or university needs from you.
- Read the application carefully to find out the application fee and deadline, required standardized tests, number of essays, interview requirements, and anything else you can do or submit to help improve your chances for acceptance.
- Ensure that your standardized test scores and your high school transcript arrive at the colleges to which you have applied.
- Submit teacher recommendations, if required.
- Be sure you set aside enough time to write the application essay, revise it, and revise it again, as colleges are looking at your essay for an honest representation of who you are and what you think. Make sure that the tone of the essay reflects enthusiasm, maturity, creativity, the ability to communicate, talent, and your leadership skills. Finally, make sure that you have answered the question that is asked.
- Follow up with the college to ensure their receipt of your materials.

The Personal Interview

- Read through the application materials to determine whether or not a college places great emphasis on a personal interview and arrange one if it is strongly recommended. The personal interview is viewed both as an information session and as further evaluation of your skills and strengths. Be prepared, ask questions, and relax!

The Final Decision

- Compare your options, factor in the financial aid component, and feel confident in your choice! **CONGRATULATIONS!**

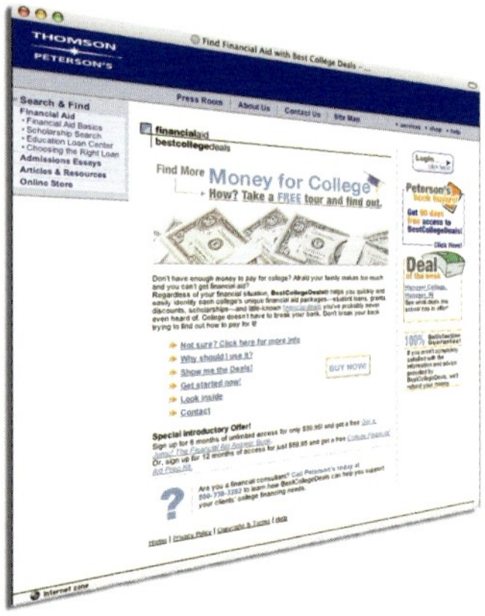

Public and Private Colleges and Universities—How to Choose

Debra Humphreys

As you survey the thousands of four-year colleges in the country and weigh the options before you, it is important to be aware of how colleges differ and what kind of educational experience each college offers you. In every state in the country, you will find both public and private colleges and universities. What are the differences between public and private colleges, and how should you approach the decision to attend one or the other? What are some common misconceptions regarding both public and private colleges that you should know about before you eliminate an entire category of institution from your list of prospective schools?

WHAT ARE THE BASIC CHARACTERISTICS OF PUBLIC AND PRIVATE INSTITUTIONS?

Over the course of the nation's history, what began as a small group of mostly church-affiliated colleges has grown in both size and complexity. Over the years, education in the United States became increasingly democratized, and more and more state-sponsored institutions and state systems of higher education emerged. These included small colleges, sometimes called "normal schools," designed to train school teachers for the expanding public school system; land-grant colleges and universities brought into existence with federal support in the mid-nineteenth century in order to prepare workers to expand the nation's agricultural and technological capacity; and large state systems that evolved in the twentieth century and now include two-year colleges, basic four-year institutions, and large research universities, all supported at least in part by state revenues.

Today, the United States boasts some 2,450 four-year colleges and universities, 622 of which are considered public institutions and 1,828 private. While there are some clear distinctions to be made, even some of the core characteristics of public and private colleges vary from state to state. In general, a public institution receives at least part of its operating budget from state tax revenues, operates with a mandate and mission from the state where it is located, and is accountable to the elected officials of that state. Most private colleges and universities are independent, not-for-profit institutions. They operate with revenues from tuition, income from endowments, private gifts and bequests, and federal, private, or corporate foundation grants. These institutions are primarily accountable to a board of trustees, usually made up of local or national business and community leaders and esteemed alumni.

There are also a small but growing number of for-profit colleges whose operating revenues include tuition dollars but also might include investor financing. Some of these colleges are owned and operated by publicly traded corporations. Most of the following generalizations about private institutions however refer to the more familiar not-for-profit independent college previously described.

While the distinction between public and private institutions might seem clear at first, these two kinds of colleges and universities actually share many characteristics. All accredited colleges and universities in the country—whether public or private, for profit or not—are entitled to receive public funds from the federal government in the form of direct grants and loans for eligible students, support for student work-study programs, and competitive grants to support research or campus programs. In exchange for this federal support, all schools undergo a peer-reviewed accreditation process by a regional accreditor authorized by the federal government's Department of Education.

Whether a college is public or private, you should know if it is accredited and therefore an institution whose students are eligible for all available federal financial aid. Accreditation status also provides you with assurance that the school operates in a fiscally responsible manner and that its academic programs have been deemed sound by an outside group of educators from its peer institutions.

HOW ARE PUBLIC AND PRIVATE COLLEGES AND UNIVERSITIES RUN?

In many ways, your experience as a student will not differ significantly based on what type of governance system a college or university uses. However, some knowledge of this might be useful in making choices among the various options. Private colleges and universities tend to have more independence and autonomy in how they are run, with boards of trustees that oversee financial and other broad matters of governance. Academic and student services leaders determine the nature of the academic program and life on campus at these schools. Public colleges and universities often have more complex governing structures with boards of regents or other types of oversight committees made up of politically appointed or elected officials exercising more or less oversight and intrusion into their day-to-day operations. New York, for instance, has a board of regents that oversees the system's sixty-four campuses and has become more actively involved in recent years in more than just fiscal matters. They have been actively involved in reviewing and revising curricular requirements that apply to institutions throughout the system. Other states have multiple public colleges, each with its own board overseeing each campus' operations with more or less intrusion into day-to-day operations.

Whether an institution is public or private, you will want to ask lots of questions about campus climate and academic programs in order to help you determine if a school is right for you. Being aware of some facts about public and private institutions will help you frame these questions to get truly useful answers.

ARE ALL PUBLIC COLLEGES AND UNIVERSITIES BIG AND IMPERSONAL?

Like private institutions, public colleges come in all shapes and sizes. Some are large institutions offering multiple degrees and majors to both undergraduate and graduate students alike. These institutions offer students many curricular options as well as access to leading scholars and an environment where cutting-edge academic research is conducted. While an institution of this size and scope might seem intimidating at first, remember that there are large institutions that do take very seriously their undergraduate programs. While you may receive less customized attention at a larger institution, many large public and private research universities now offer options such as smaller honors programs, academic learning communities with smaller cohorts of students, or theme residence halls that can minimize the potential that you will get lost in the crowd.

If you are considering a large research institution—whether it is public or private—you should ask questions about the undergraduate program. What is the student-faculty ratio for undergraduates? What is the average class size, especially for introductory first-year courses? How many courses are taught by graduate students, and what sort of teacher training do those students receive? Are there opportunities for undergraduate students to participate in research projects with university faculty members?

In addition to the large, public research universities, there are many other smaller, state-funded regional institutions that still offer a wide range of both liberal arts and sciences fields as well as professional fields of study. Many states also offer small, public liberal arts colleges that share many of the defining characteristics of traditional, private liberal arts colleges. In 1987, some of these institutions formed the Council of Public Liberal Arts Colleges (COPLAC). Now numbering twenty institutions, COPLAC schools pride themselves on providing students of high ability and from all backgrounds access to a quality liberal education. These colleges and universities have been nationally recognized as outstanding in many ways. They offer small classes, innovations in teaching, personal interactions with faculty members, opportunities for faculty-supervised research, and supportive atmospheres. Most of them are located on campuses in rural or small-town settings. In addition to offering rigorous and well-integrated undergraduate programs, these institutions often charge far less tuition than many private colleges do. More information can be found at http://www.coplac.org.

These public liberal arts colleges, along with more traditional private liberal arts institutions, do offer unique learning environments that research suggests often lead to higher levels of student achievement. Liberal arts colleges tend to offer a high degree of student-faculty interaction, high levels of student engagement with both in-class and out-of-class experiences, and lots of opportunities for collaborative and innovative learning practices. Businesses are also increasingly asking for exactly the set of skills and capacities that a liberal education provides, whether offered in a traditional liberal arts college setting or within a larger university that grants degrees in both liberal arts and other fields. Many public liberal arts and more comprehensive colleges and universities also now offer students a rigorous liberal education while integrating liberal learning into professional degree programs, for instance in health sciences, engineering, or education.

ARE PUBLIC COLLEGES CHEAPER THAN PRIVATE COLLEGES?

The cost of college is not easy to calculate and is not limited simply to the advertised price of tuition. It is absolutely not the case that attending a public college will always cost a student less money than attending a private institution. It is true that the basic tuition for in-state or out-of-state students attending public colleges is on average less expensive than the advertised tuition rate at private institutions. It is very important, however, to note that many private colleges and universities offer significant amounts of financial aid—often beyond the basic federal loans and grants available to all students wherever they might attend. Many, but not all, private colleges have large endowments that allow them to effectively discount the standard, published tuition rates for a great number of their students. The National Association of College and University Business Officers sampled a small group of private colleges and discovered that only 10 percent of entering students were paying the full, advertised tuition. Ninety percent of their students received price discounts in the form of scholarships or financial aid. In other words, don't write off a college simply because its tuition looks extremely high relative to other institutions.

Both private and public institutions, however, have been fiscally stressed in recent years because of declining values of stock portfolios in endowments or because of declining state revenues resulting from the deteriorating economy. It is safe to say that for many students in the coming years, it will become increasingly difficult to get large amounts of financial aid. Many institutions, however, remain committed to widening access to more students from less economically privileged backgrounds. In addition, students demonstrating high levels of academic achievement are being rewarded at both private and public institutions—both in terms of admission and financial aid.

It is important to look carefully at the tuition and the financial aid requirements and availability at each school you are considering, private or public. In-state and out-of-state tuitions and the difference between them varies substantially from state to state. Out-of-state tuition also varies from state to state but still tends to be lower than average private tuition levels. The differences between in-state and out-of-state tuition vary considerably.

Policies vary as well for determining state residency status. In many states, the policy for dependent students requires that their parents must have lived in the state for at least twelve months prior to attendance in order to qualify for in-state tuition. For independent students, the requirement of twelve months residence prior to enrollment applies to the student. Independent status must be verified and generally entails proof that a student receives no support from parents or other relatives living in or out of the state in question. Policies of this sort exist in many states, including those with large public systems such as California, Florida, Wisconsin, Ohio, and New York. As budgets have increasingly tightened, states like these and others have over the past several years made it increasingly difficult to establish in-state residence after matriculating at a school. Exceptions are sometimes made, however, for students from migrant, refugee, or military families.

IS IT EASIER TO GAIN ADMISSION TO A PUBLIC INSTITUTION ESPECIALLY AS A STATE RESIDENT?

Few public colleges and universities automatically admit students who graduate from a public high school in their state. Many, however, give preference in admissions and financial assistance to in-state residents. Moreover, some states, like Florida and California, have implemented policies that guarantee admission to at least one of the state's public institutions for all students graduating in a top percentage of their high school classes.

There are, indeed, more highly selective private than public institutions. Many public colleges and universities, however, do admit very few applicants. These highly selective institutions might draw their students from a national pool of applicants and can be among the most selective in the country. However, the ten national universities and liberal arts colleges with the lowest acceptance rates in the country are all private institutions.

While some public institutions offer virtually open admissions to state residents, it is important for all prospective students to realize that even an open-admission institution will require incoming students to meet certain academic standards before being admitted to credit-bearing courses. In most cases, public and private institutions give incoming students a series of placement exams that determines at what level the student can begin his or her course work. Depending on the results of these exams, a student may be required to take and pass one or more remedial courses before being admitted to courses that will actually count towards a degree.

Since each state's requirements are different and shift often, you should not assume that, regardless of your academic background, admission is automatic to your local state college. In the current climate—with costs rising and competition across systems tightening—admission rates are dropping at many public institutions.

IS THE CLIMATE ON A PUBLIC COLLEGE CAMPUS SIGNIFICANTLY DIFFERENT THAN ON A PRIVATE COLLEGE CAMPUS?

The social and academic climate at colleges and universities varies substantially and public institutions do not necessarily offer a distinctively different climate than private institutions do. As with the COPLAC schools mentioned earlier, you can find, at some public institutions, the small, residential environment traditionally associated with private liberal arts colleges.

You will also find the presence of fraternities and sororities at both public and private institutions. You should look carefully at whether a school in which you are interested has fraternities and sororities and how much influence the Greek system has on college life. At some institutions, fraternitics and sororities dominate the entire social life of the campus.

One campus environment that can only be found at a private institution is a highly religious environment. Many early colleges and universities were founded by churches or religious orders. Some of these institutions no longer retain a strong affiliation with one church or denomination. Others do retain a strong affiliation, and church traditions can heavily influence the climate of these institutions.

QUESTIONS TO ASK AS YOU EVALUATE PROSPECTIVE COLLEGES AND UNIVERSITIES

- Does the college offer a distinctive first-year experience?
- Does the college offer a small-size freshman seminar for all students?
- Are all students required to complete a senior project or assignment that allows them to integrate all that they have learned and demonstrate acquired skills and knowledge?
- Are students encouraged or required to complete internships and/or service learning courses?
- Are students encouraged to study abroad? Is support for study abroad provided to all students and are study abroad experiences integrated into a student's overall curricula?
- Does the college offer learning communities, especially in the student's early years?
- Are students required to complete rigorous writing courses not only in the freshman year but also across the curriculum in whatever major he or she chooses to pursue?
- Are there opportunities for students to pursue independent research or creative projects under the supervision of a senior faculty member?

Usually, these campuses will admit a student from any religious background, but they may require students to attend chapel services and/or take religion or theology courses to graduate. In addition, some college missions and curricula are influenced by their religious affiliations. For instance, many Catholic institutions have a strong commitment to community service and social justice. Students may find, at these institutions, curricula related to social justice issues and requirements that they complete a community-service learning activity or course to graduate. Institutions with a strong mission are also often able to develop more coherent, cohesive, and innovative curricula for their students.

Finally, other important climate factors to consider include whether a college or university is in an urban or rural setting; what the diversity of the student body is in terms of geographic, religious, or racial/ethnic background; if most students live on campus or commute from home; and finally if the college dominates the life of the community in which it is located. Each of these options has advantages and disadvantages you will want to weigh in making your decisions.

ARE PRIVATE COLLEGES MORE ACADEMICALLY RIGOROUS THAN PUBLIC COLLEGES?

Private colleges and universities are not necessarily more academically rigorous than public institutions. You will find rigorous, intellectually challenging, and innovative academic programs at both private and public institutions. There is also a common misconception that schools that are more highly selective have the most effective or engaging academic programs. Research suggests that there is no connection between the selectivity of an institution and the presence of effective or innovative teaching and learning practices. There is, however, preliminary research that suggests that the academic quality of one's peers does seem to have an impact on the grade point averages of fellow students.

Nothing could be more important in your decision-making process than evaluating the nature of academic programs at prospective colleges or universities. Across both public and private institutions, there have been exciting and important changes in how colleges and universities are organizing undergraduate curricula. Many promising programs have been proven to result in higher levels of student retention, graduation, satisfaction, and academic achievement.

Many colleges and universities also now participate in the National Survey of Student Engagement. This survey asks students in both their first and last years about a series of effective educational practices and the degree to which they are engaged in the academic life of their school. Issues that are examined in the survey include the level of academic challenge, active and collaborative learning opportunities, the nature of student-faculty interactions, the number of enriching educational experiences available, and the supportive nature of the campus environment. Ask if the school you are considering participates in this survey and if you can see the results from recent classes of students.

THE PRIVATE/PUBLIC CHOICE

While there are distinct differences between public and private colleges and universities you should not limit your choice—whatever your background—to only one type of institution. There are wonderful opportunities at many different kinds of schools. The availability of many kinds of financial aid may bring private institutions with high-tuition levels within reach for you, whatever your financial background. Whether a school is highly selective or has open admissions, you should also be able to find a college or university that will challenge you academically and provide you with a supportive environment in which to live, learn, and pursue a college degree of lasting value.

Debra Humphreys is Vice President for Communications and Public Affairs for the Association of American Colleges and Universities.

Why Not Women's Colleges?

Before we start talking about the many advantages that women's colleges offer, let's get some myths out of the way. It is almost certain that the minute you hear "women's colleges" in the same sentence with "choosing colleges" you immediately think: no boys, no fun, no way!

Maybe that is why some girls who visit Joan Jaffe's office at Mills College in San Francisco, California, rush in to tell her that they just saw some guys on the campus of this women's college. Jaffe, Associate Dean of Admissions, frequently gets this reaction from the young women who visit the campus. That's because many think that if they go to a women's college they are never going to see a guy within 2 miles of the campus gates, which, by the way, will clang shut behind them, leaving them secluded inside a heavily guarded male-free zone.

KISS MYTH NUMBER ONE GOOD-BYE

Forget iron gates. The first myth to get rid of is the one that assumes attending a women's college means kissing your social life good-bye. In fact, as Patricia Gibbs, Vice President of Enrollment Services and Student Affairs at Wesleyan College in Macon, Georgia, points out, "If you were a guy looking for a date, where would you go?" Not only that, the majority of women's colleges are near, if not next to, coed campuses. Most share activities with other colleges and universities, and many have reciprocal agreements so that guys can take classes at the women's college and vice versa.

When it comes to dating, women's colleges offer the best of both worlds. You can hang out with guys when you want to and then retreat to your own lovely environment (women's dorms usually are beautiful) and hang out with the girls. Julie Binder, who transferred from the University of Wisconsin to all-women's Barnard College in New York City, notes that there is open registration with Columbia University, which just happens to be right next door. "Campus life is shared. Sports are shared," she says.

As you dig deeper into this myth, you will find that attending a women's college is not about isolation, it's about options. You get to choose if you want to be in classes, clubs, and organizations only with women or to mingle with the men.

SCRATCH MYTH NUMBER TWO

On to myth number two. Women's colleges are just a bunch of catty, competitive females waiting for the right moment to scratch each other's eyes out. Scratch that myth, too. Instead, women's colleges cultivate an environment of sisterhood-women looking out for each other and helping each other. Most women's colleges encourage women in the upper-level classes to help their younger classmates. Talking to their "big sisters," newcomers find out what classes to take, which

THE RICH TRADITIONS IN WOMEN'S COLLEGES

Tradition plays an important part of the experience women have in women's colleges. They run the gamut from solemn ceremonies of passing along the bond of sisterhood to the fun of secret surprises. "Women's colleges have a strong sense of tradition," says Amy Shaver, Director of Enrollment Services at Stephens College in Columbia, Missouri. It's also a wonderful way to help women from all social, economic, religious, and ethnic backgrounds to share a common experience and pass it on to the next generation of students. "Traditions bond women over the generations," says Jennifer Rickard, Dean of Admissions and Financial Aid at Bryn Mawr College, who notes that it's not unusual at all to have students today singing songs and participating in ceremonies that the class of 1945 did and which will be the same when today's students have their twenty-year reunion.

Here's a sampling of the many traditions you'll find on women's college campuses:

Lantern Night At Bryn Mawr's Lantern Night, women gather around a fountain on campus. Each woman is given a lantern as a symbol for knowledge and learning. Each class has a color, and as the lanterns are passed from the sophomores to the first-year students, songs are sung in Greek that are the same as the ones sung 100 years ago around the same fountain.

Senior Paint Night Mills College seniors get the okay to paint the campus in their class color. Along with brushes and cans of paint, they are given a few guidelines as to what can and cannot be painted, but the rest is up to them.

The Crossing of the Bridge As women students come to Stephens to begin their college education, they cross over a bridge on campus in a ceremony symbolizing their entrance into the world of academia. At graduation, they cross over another bridge on campus and are welcomed into the alumnae society.

Candlelight Induction Ceremony Spelman students dressed in white dresses and black shoes light candles and hear the charge to be the best they can be. While the candles are still lit, they sing the Spelman hymn.

Midnight Breakfast At Barnard, the night before finals, the president of the College, deans, and professors make breakfast for the students.

professors are the best, and have sympathetic ears for the problems that most first-year college students face.

"The sense of community is very strong at women's colleges," observes Fran Samuels, Director of College Counseling at The Master's School in Dobbs Ferry, New York. "The myth is that a women's college will be cliquish. In truth, the women are supportive of each other." The strong bonds of sisterhood that naturally develop connect students to their college, its history, and its students, past, present, and future. Many women's colleges designate a rotating color for each incoming class. For example, if the freshman class you enter is dubbed the golden hearts, by the time you graduate, you are connected to all the golden hearts who graduated ahead of you and all the golden hearts who will graduate after you.

TOSS MYTH NUMBER THREE

Another myth that should be tossed out is that women's colleges don't prepare you for the "real world." Well, try saying that to the 12 women members of Congress who graduated from women's colleges. Or to the 15 women on *Business Week*'s list of the rising stars in corporate America. Although you are not in a totally coed situation, on the other hand you are in an environment in which you can gain skills to think critically and learn to meet challenges. Becky Marsh, Director of Communications at Whitfield School, in St. Louis, Missouri, points out that when you first ride a bike, training wheels allow you to learn how to balance. Once you are ready to race down the street, you take them off. Same with women's colleges. The focus is on your education and your strengths, and who you are. You graduate ready to take on the obstacles of the real world. "In high school, I had the feeling that boys were given more opportunities to share their knowledge. It was harder and more intimidating for me to share my opinions in a coed class," says Brittany Johnson, a first-year student at Spelman College in Atlanta, Georgia. "Now I feel like I can do anything."

Graduates of women's colleges feel empowered and willing to confront any limits to their abilities. While in college, they have many opportunities to assume leadership roles and see women in leadership positions as professors and deans. "They don't doubt whether they can do anything. Instead, they ask, 'Why can't I do it now?'" reports Amy Shaver, Director of Enrollment Services at Stephens College in Columbia, Missouri. Women can find their own voices and establish their own ways of approaching things that will ultimately make them successful in a male-dominated world. They learn from seeing other women students and professors engaged in the intellectual process.

THE ADVANTAGES

As more young women find out about the advantages that women's colleges offer them, they like what they see. Maybe that is why attendance at women's colleges is growing. Learning leadership skills tops the list of advantages. Says Shaver, "Women in a same-sex environment are more likely to take risks and speak up in class. They are more willing to stand up and voice an opinion." If you think about it, students get plenty of practice at a women's college because all the leadership roles go to women. From day one on a women's campus, you will see women leading the entire college or involved in interesting and significant research. You get more exposure to what leadership is and what to expect as a leader. "Leadership becomes ingrained," notes Jennifer Fondiller, Dean of Admissions at Barnard College in New York City.

You might not realize it, but women react differently in classrooms with all women. They tend to speak up with confidence and to test their ideas more readily when they are not competing with men. Researchers find that even as early as the fifth grade, girls are taught differently than boys. Teachers call on boys more frequently and don't ask girls the more thought-provoking questions or to critically analyze problems. In coed situations, the more aggressive and competitive guys take over, whereas in all-female classes, research indicates there is much more give-and-take and exchange of ideas.

Coming from a coed public school, Johnson realized that more attention was given to the guys in her classes, but at Spelman, she says, "Everyone is on the same path." Arlene Cash, Vice President for Enrollment Management at Spelman, notes that women don't have to vie for attention or retreat into the intellectual background in all-women classes. In a coed class, the environment becomes more adversarial. "Women feel they have to perform. In women's colleges they become more academically involved and interact with faculty members more frequently," says Debbie Greenberg, College Counselor at Whitfield School. Speaking of the rich interaction that occurs in her classes at Barnard, Binder says, "The diversity of experience around the discussion table is unparalleled."

YOU CAN SUCCEED

Shaver characterizes the environment in women's colleges as one in which there is no fear of failing when the social pressures and dynamics of men and women are removed from the classroom. Women's colleges give women the opportunity to explore different avenues without the fear of failing. "We challenge them to become what they want to become," says Gibbs from Wesleyan. "No one says, 'You can't do that because you are a woman.'" At the same time, you are interacting with other women who have the same goals as you, which reinforces who you are. "It is self-reaffirmation over and over again," says Spelman's Monica Rodgers, Associate Director of Admissions. Or, as Jennifer Rickard, Dean of Admissions and Financial Aid at Bryn Mawr College, in Bryn Mawr, Pennsylvania, points out, women are not just sitting in classes to do well on exams and get good grades. They also are figuring out what they want to do with their education. "There's less expectation to conform to an external measure," she says.

Many women's colleges foster self-government and give their students responsibilities they might not find in a coed institution. At Bryn Mawr, for instance, students pay a self-government association fee as part of their tuition. This is put into a fund that is controlled by a student government that takes ownership of how the students want to govern themselves. "This isn't student government making only recommendations to the administration as to how to allocate the budget to the different student groups vying for funds," notes Rickard. "You have students dealing with real-world management issues, such as resource allocation."

Since women's colleges are smaller than big coed universities, women receive all the benefits that students get from a small liberal arts college in addition to the advantages that only a women's college offers. A big plus is interaction with professors and staff, which is hard to achieve when you are one of 200 students in a lecture hall taught by a graduate student. Women's colleges tend to foster seminar-style classes taught by full professors, many of them women. "You have an expert teaching you," says Gibbs. Faculty members get to know their students and can challenge them intellectually on an individual basis. "Within two days, all my teachers knew my name," recalls Johnson, who says she was given each professor's e-mail address, home phone number, and all the contact information she needed and was encouraged to reach out to them.

Women are encouraged to achieve their intellectual goals. Professors often will point out specific programs that they know suits the student's interests. Add to this the opportunities to conduct research with a professor, and in many cases actually present research findings to a professional society, and you can see why women graduate with a terrific resume before they even start their careers. Rickard mentions the opportunity that Bryn Mawr students have to work on funded projects with professors during the summer and then present the results along with them at conferences. "It's a window into the academic world and the world of the intellectual," she notes. It's no surprise that women in women's colleges major in math and science at a higher national average than women in coed institutions.

Paid and unpaid internships, too, are more available for women at women's colleges, mainly because of the network of women graduates in business and industry who want to help their "sisters" at their alma maters. "I'm getting my professional edge as a 19-year-old," says Binder, who is interested in TV production and had a paid internship as a production assistant while a sophomore at Barnard. "You will have an amazing resume by the time you graduate," she says.

Peggy Hock, Ph.D., Director of College Counseling and Chair of the Counseling Department at Notre Dame High School in San Jose, California, points out that colleges naturally rely on their alumni to come forward with networking opportunities for students; however, the alumnae of women's colleges tend to be more loyal and willing to give of their time. This translates into many more opportunities for internships, mentoring, and job possibilities. At Barnard, for example, the career office has an alumna mentor network. Students can call, ask questions, and get advice about career choices. At alumnae events, current students mix with the graduates. Binder takes full advantage of the Web log of women who are working all over the world and willing to spend time online with Barnard students. She applied for a job at a

WHAT MADE YOU CHOOSE A WOMEN'S COLLEGE?

When she got to the point of choosing which college to attend, Wisambi Loundu had plenty of options. Coming from San Diego, the California universities were a logical choice. Women's colleges were not on her list. In fact, she hardly knew they existed. Her first thought when someone suggested a women's college to her was, "I'm not going to a school full of girls minus boys." Her second thought was just as negative. "If it's all girls, they will always be fighting." The third and fourth thought assumed that a women's college wouldn't prepare her for the real world, plus she would be isolated.

But then her math teacher's daughter told her about Bryn Mawr, and as Wisambi started exploring the possibility, the advantages of a women's college started lining up. However, it wasn't until she visited Bryn Mawr that she really began to see herself there. "I fell in love with the campus," says Wisambi. "It was like nothing I'd ever seen before." Her stay in the dorm added to her steadily growing thoughts that Bryn Mawr might be it. "The girls I stayed with in the dorm were so friendly. At first I was suspicious, but I saw it was not a front. Plus, there were girls from all over the world."

But Wisambi didn't make her final decision just yet. She decided to look at other schools, like Wellesley and the University of California schools, as well as Stanford. Meanwhile, her friend told her more about Bryn Mawr. "She said I'd make lasting friends and she talked about how the academics would train me for the outside world even if there were no men on campus. Bryn Mawr would build my identity as a woman.

She still wasn't convinced and made a second visit, along with visits to Wellesley and Stanford, which she says were nice, but too big. It would be too hard to make friends there, she thought. When the time came to make her final selection, she chose Bryn Mawr.

Now into the second semester of her first year, how does Wisambi feel about Bryn Mawr? The academics are more challenging than she anticipated but doable, and she is excited about the internships she will be able to access. She also finds that the staff and teachers at Bryn Mawr go out of their way to make her feel at home. "They match us up with a mentor and professor," she says.

How about dating? Since Bryn Mawr is part of a tri-college community, guys are around, though Wisambi says you have to make an effort to meet people on other campuses.

Talking to seniors who are getting ready to head out to the "real world," Wisambi can see that they are full of confidence and don't think for a minute that they won't do well. "And that's a positive," she says.

public relations firm in New York after contacting a fellow Barnard graduate working there. She met with her and subsequently got a letter of recommendation.

HOW TO CHOOSE

Choosing a women's college isn't any different from choosing a coed college. You should definitely visit the campus and don't be afraid to ask lots of questions—even the ones that might make you uncomfortable. Because women's colleges are similar to small coed liberal arts colleges, make sure that you don't compare a women's campus to a big university.

Janet Ashley, Interim Director for Admissions at Spelman College, advises high school women to ask what a women's college can give them academically. "Their choice depends on what their goals are," she says.

If you're worried about the dating scene, ask about the levels of interaction with guys and how close the relationships are with neighboring institutions.

"Look at the individuality of each women's college," suggests Rickard, "because each has its own personality." Look at the school before looking at the fact that it's a women's college, and on the flip side, don't rule out a school just because it is a women's college. "So many students make quick decisions about where to apply," warns Fondiller, noting that sometimes the decision hinges on what schools a friend is applying to rather than if that institution really fits the student. Many women's colleges specialize in certain fields like science, math, or theater.

FAMOUS FIRSTS FROM WOMEN'S COLLEGES

Quick, from where did the first woman to be named Secretary of State graduate? Or the woman scientist who identified Hong Kong flu? Or the first woman executive vice president of the American Stock Exchange? Here's a big clue. They were all graduates of women's colleges.

SENATORS

- Hillary Rodham Clinton (NY)—Wellesley College
- Blanche Lambert Lincoln (AR)—Randolph-Macon Woman's College
- Barbara Mikulski (MD)—Mount Saint Agnes College

REPRESENTATIVES

- Tammy Baldwin (WI)—Smith College
- Donna Christian-Christensen (VI)—St. Mary's College
- Rosa DeLauro (CT)—Marymount College
- Jane Harman (CA)—Smith College
- Eddie Bernice Johnson (TX)—Saint Mary's College
- Nancy L. Johnson (CT)—Radcliffe College
- Sue Kelly (NY)—Sarah Lawrence College
- Barbara Lee (CA)—Mills College
- Nita Lowey (NY)—Mount Holyoke College
- Betty McCollum (MN)—College of Saint Catherine
- Patsy Mink (HI)—University of Hawaii and Wilson College
- Anne Meagher Northup (KY)—Saint Mary's College
- Nancy Pelosi (CA), first woman elected as Democratic Whip in the House of Representatives (10/01), the highest post ever held by a woman in Congress—Trinity College

OTHER FAMOUS WOMEN FIRSTS

- Madeleine Albright, first woman to be named Secretary of State in the U.S., appointed in 1997—Wellesley
- Jane Amsterdam, first woman editor, the *New York Post*—Cedar Crest
- Emily Green Balch, first woman to receive the Nobel Peace Prize in 1946—Bryn Mawr
- Catherine Brewer Benson, first woman to receive a college bachelor's degree—Wesleyan
- Earla Biekert, first scientist to identify the Hong Kong flu virus—Wesleyan
- Cathleen Black, first woman leader of the American Newspaper Publishers Association—Trinity, Washington, D.C.
- Sarah Porter Boehmler, first woman executive vice president of American Stock Exchange—Sweet Briar
- Jane Matilda Bolin, first African-American woman judge in the U.S.—Wellesley
- Dorothy L. Brown, first African-American woman general surgeon in the South—Bennett
- Pearl S. Buck, first American woman to win the Nobel Prize in Literature—Randolph-Macon Woman's College
- Ila Burdett, Georgia's first female Rhodes Scholar—Agnes Scott
- Dorothy Vredenburgh Bush, first woman secretary of the Democratic National Party—Mississippi University for Women
- Hon. Audrey J. S. Carrion, first Hispanic woman judge Circuit Court for Baltimore City—College of Notre Dame of Maryland
- Barbara Cassani, first female and CEO of a commercial airline—Mount Holyoke
- Elaine L. Chao, U.S. Secretary of Labor, 2001; First Asian-American woman appointed to a President's cabinet in U.S. history—Mount Holyoke

Adapted from the Web site of the Women's College Coalition at http://www.womenscolleges.org.

The Military and Higher Education

The first part of this section offers an overview of the opportunities that exist today for students who wish to explore the possibility of financing their higher education by participating in ROTC or attending a service academy. This information is provided in order to help students and families make well-informed decisions about this important investment. The second part of this section presents, in the Army's own words and photos, a detailed description of one military financial aid option—the Army ROTC Program.

The Military as a Source of Financial Aid

One of the major problems facing families today is how to come up with the money to meet college expenses. Many people are unaware that the military is a source of financial aid. Its focus, however, is quite different from that of other sources: military financial aid programs do not consider need but are either a payment for training or a reward for service. This large source of money (about $1 billion each year) can prove quite helpful in assisting a wide range of students. The military financial aid programs are by far the largest source of college money that is not based on need.

HOW THE MILITARY PROVIDES FINANCIAL AID

One form of military financial aid is college money for officer candidates: tuition assistance and monthly pay in return for the student's promise to serve as an officer in the Army, Navy, Air Force, Marine Corps, Coast Guard, or Merchant Marine. Most of this money is awarded to high school seniors who go directly to college. The main benefits are reduced or free tuition and $100 to $150 per month if the student is enrolled in the Reserve Officers' Training Corps (ROTC) Scholarship Program or free tuition, room and board, and $500 per month if the student is enrolled at one of the service academies. ROTC units are located on college campuses and provide military training for a few hours a week. The five service academies (West Point, Annapolis, the Air Force Academy, the Coast Guard Academy, and the Merchant Marine Academy) are military establishments that combine education and training for the armed forces. For those already in college, financial aid is obtainable through ROTC scholarships for enrolled students or special commissioning programs.

By participating in ROTC, attending a service academy, or enrolling in a special program for military commissioning, a student not only can become an officer but also can become eligible for financial aid, thus turning the dream of an affordable college education into a reality. The military trains students to become officers and pays them to learn at the same time. (A detailed look at one such program, that of the Army ROTC, appears following this article.)

IS OFFICER TRAINING RIGHT FOR YOU?

Military scholarship programs exist largely to provide money to college students as they go through officer training, and, in return, the military receives from the students a commitment to serve in the armed forces. The military's goal is to produce, through this method of attracting outstanding young men and women, "entry-level" officers who are well educated both academically and in the workings of the military itself. Obviously, you would not be the ideal candidate for one of these programs if you had moral or religious reservations about serving your country as a military officer. You also should not apply if the program's main appeal for you is the money. The financial benefits may be very important, but their attraction should be balanced by genuine feelings on your part that you will seriously consider becoming an officer, you will undertake military training with a positive attitude, and you will be flexible and open-minded about your plans. Applicants are typically young men or women who are willing to serve at least four or five years as officers in exchange for four years of a good education at little or no cost.

First: Are You the Military Type?

At the outset, it is essential that you determine whether or not you are cut out to be in the military. Take a personal inventory: What are you like? How do you relate to others? What kind of organization do you want to be part of?

- Do you consider yourself intelligent, well-rounded, energetic, organized, and somewhat athletic? Are you a serious student with good grades in precollege courses and an aptitude for science and math?
- Are you outgoing? Does leadership appeal to you? Do you work well with others, both in groups and in one-on-one situations? Can you willingly take direction from others?
- Can you exist in a structured and disciplined environment? Do you have strong feelings of patriotism? Are you willing to defend your country in a time of war?
- If "yes" is your answer to most of these questions, you are the type of individual the military services are interested in. Even more important, you may be the type of person who can be comfortable with the military's lifestyle. Although there are many different types of military officers—from the quiet intellectual to the extroverted athlete—the average officer usually conforms to a set of general characteristics: a mixture of certain personal traits and a willingness to be part of and contribute to a large and very structured organization.

Second: What Kind of Military Training Might Be Appropriate for You?

If your personal inventory revealed you to be at least somewhat the "military type," your next step is to see which of the programs offered by the different services is best for you.

Now ask yourself which of the following most closely describes your feelings at present.

1. I have firsthand knowledge of military service. I can picture myself as an officer, perhaps even a career officer. I have experience with discipline, both in taking and in giving orders. I plan to major in science or engineering while I'm in college. Obtaining a top-quality education at very low cost is very important to me.
2. Service in the military is of interest to me. I don't have much direct experience, but I'm willing to learn more. I'm not sure whether I'm ready to immerse myself completely in a military environment as a college student. I've done well in math and science, but I may decide to major in another field. I can look forward to the prospect of four years of service as an officer before deciding whether to stay on. A tuition scholarship is appealing, and it would widen the range of colleges that are within my reach.
3. I don't have a negative attitude toward the military, but it's not something I know much about. I might be interested in giving it a look. Studying math and science may not be for me; my interests are probably in other areas. I'm concerned about paying for college, but my parents could help me for at least one or two years.
4. I don't think I'm the military type, but actually I haven't thought that much about it. I doubt if I would go for the discipline. Certainly, I wouldn't want to commit to anything until I've been in college for a few years and can see my choices more clearly. I might be able to see myself serving in the military—if I could get duty that matches my academic interests. I could use a scholarship, but I plan to seek financial aid through other sources.

When you've determined which of the foregoing paragraphs mostly closely describes your attitude toward military service, review the following items, the numbers of which generally relate to the numbers above.

1. Think seriously about competing for an appointment to a service academy. (You must be nominated by an official source, usually your congressional representative. Each member of Congress has a set number of nominees he or she can recommend for admission. Neither political influence nor a personal relationship with the member of Congress is necessary.)
2. Plan to enter the national ROTC four-year scholarship competition.
3. Join an ROTC unit in college and see what the military is like. Scholarship opportunities are available if you decide to stay on.
4. Don't get involved with a military program yet, but keep the service in mind for possible entrance after two years of college.
5. It should go without saying that it's best to avoid extreme discrepancies between the two lists. For example, if description number 4 applies, a military academy or even the four-year scholarship is probably not right for you. It would be far wiser to choose item three or four. Later on, after you are enrolled in college, you might find that certain aspects of the military complement your academic interests and that the military lifestyle is something you can adapt to. If, on the other hand, description number 1 suits you, it will be worth your while to pursue either the ROTC scholarship or service academy option when you graduate from high school. If you are this far along in your thinking about a possible future in the military, you can take advantage of both the financial benefits the services offer and the head start you will get toward a possible military career by trying for an officer training program.

Preparation While in High School

Enrolling in a precollege program while you're attending high school will improve your chances of winning a four-year ROTC scholarship or receiving an appointment to a service academy. For the most part, the services don't require that you take specific subjects (the exceptions are the Coast Guard Academy and the Merchant Marine Academy). Nonetheless, the Army, Navy, Air Force, and Marine Corps all stress the importance of a good high school curriculum. They suggest the following: 4 years of English, 4 years of math (through calculus), 2 years of a foreign language, 2 years of laboratory science, and 1 year of American history.

Being an active member of your school and community is also important, as is holding leadership positions in sports and/or other extracurricular activities. If your high school has a Junior ROTC unit, join the detachment; doing so could improve your chances of being selected for an ROTC scholarship or admitted to a service academy.

Standardized Tests

For entrance into the academies and most other colleges, be prepared to take the SAT I or ACT, used by college admission offices as one of the measures of a prospective college student's academic potential. For more details, see Surviving Standardized Tests.

Who Is a Successful Candidate?

A fictional though typical winner of a four-year ROTC scholarship or an appointment to a service academy exhibits certain kinds of characteristics. That person (whom we will call John Doe):

- Follows a curriculum that includes 4 years of English, 4 years of math, 3 or 4 years of a foreign language, 2 years of laboratory science, and 2 years of history—with some of the courses at the honors level. John maintains a B+ average and ranks in the top 15 percent of his class. On the SAT I, he received scores of 610 verbal and 640 math (based on original, rather than recentered, scores). (Had he taken the ACT, his composite score would have been 28.)
- Is a member of the National Honor Society. He holds an office in student government and is a candidate for Boys State. John has a leadership position on the student newspaper and is a member of both the debate panel and math club. He is active in varsity athletics and is cocaptain of the basketball team.
- Is one of the top all-around students in his class and makes a positive contribution to both his school and

community. He is described as intelligent, industrious, well-organized, self-confident, concerned, and emotionally mature.

- The services believe and expect that a person with John Doe's abilities and traits will do well in college—in both academic and military training—and will also have great potential to become a productive officer after graduation.

Facts About the Officer Training Programs

Officer Pay and Benefits. As a military officer, you will be paid the standard rate for all members of the armed forces of your rank and length of service. In addition to your salary, significant fringe benefits include free medical care and a generous retirement plan.

The Difference Between a Regular and a Reserve Officer. Officer training programs offer Regular and Reserve commissions. However, all initial commissions after September 30, 1996, have been Reserve only. You should be aware of the difference between the two designations.

When commissioned as a Regular officer, you are on a career path in the military. In the event that you choose not to serve at least twenty years, you must write a letter asking if you can resign your commission. Such requests are normally accepted once you have completed your minimum service obligation. If you plan to make the military your career, it is a definite advantage to be a Regular officer.

As a Reserve officer, you contract for a specific term, for example, four years of active duty in the case of an ROTC scholarship. Nearly all Air Force ROTC second lieutenants are in this category, along with about 85 percent of Army ROTC graduates. If you want to remain on active duty after your initial obligation, you must request to sign on for a second term.

There is another category of Reserve officer—those who are assigned to the Reserve Forces rather than to active duty. About 50 percent of the officers who are commissioned through the Army ROTC are given orders to the National Guard or Army Reserve. After attending the Basic Course for six months, these officers join the Reserve Forces to finish their obligated service as "weekend warriors." In this case, the time commitment is 7½ years in the Reserve, the first 5½ years involving drills one weekend per month and two weeks of active duty per year. During the last two years of obligated service, these officers are transferred to inactive Reserve status, in which drills are not required.

Women Officers. Virtually all of the officer training programs are open to women. With the exception of differences in height and weight standards and lower minimums on the physical fitness test, the eligibility rules, benefits, and obligations are the same for both genders. When it comes to duty assignments, however, there is a notable difference between men and women. Depending on the branch of the service, this law restricts the types of jobs women can choose. Other than the limits imposed by certain combat restrictions for women, the position of women within the military has improved considerably in the past ten years. There are variations among the services, but overall, women make up between 8 and 20 percent of the officers, and they are gradually but steadily moving into the higher-ranking positions.

Medical Requirements. Candidates for an ROTC scholarship must pass a medical examination. You need take only one physical, even if you apply for more than one type of scholarship. Medical standards vary considerably and can be quite complicated. Nevertheless, it is worth having an idea of the general medical requirements at the outset, particularly the eyesight and height and weight rules. Keep in mind, too, that medical standards change periodically, and some of them may be waived under certain conditions. (Service academy medical requirements for the Army and Navy/Marine Corps are the same as the ROTC requirements; the Air Force requirements are also the same except that flight training has its own height and vision standards; and the Coast Guard and Merchant Marine medical requirements are similar to Naval ROTC, except that eyesight standards for the Merchant Marine are more lenient.)

THE ROTC PROGRAMS

The predominant way for a college student to become a military officer is through the Reserve Officers' Training Corps program. ROTC is offered by the Army, Navy, and Air Force, while students taking the Marine Corps option participate in Naval ROTC. (The Coast Guard and Merchant Marine do not sponsor ROTC programs.)

Each service that has an ROTC program signs an agreement with a number of colleges to host a unit on their campuses. Each of these units has a commanding officer supervising a staff of active-duty officers and enlisted servicemembers who conduct the military training of cadets and midshipmen. This instruction includes regular class periods in which military science is taught as well as longer drill sessions in which students concentrate on developing leadership qualities through participation in military formations, physical fitness routines, and field exercises.

It is not necessary for you to attend a college that hosts a unit to participate in ROTC. You may attend any of the approved colleges that have a cross-enrollment contract and participate in ROTC at the host institution, provided you are accepted into the unit and you are able to arrange your schedule so that you have time to commute to the ROTC classes and drill sessions.

As a member of an ROTC unit, you are a part-time cadet or midshipman. You are required to wear a uniform and adhere to military discipline when you attend an ROTC class or drill, but not at other times. Since this involvement averages only about 4 hours per week, most of the time you will enjoy the same lifestyle as a typical college student. You must realize, however, that while you are an undergraduate, you are being trained to become an officer when you graduate. You therefore will have a number of obligations and responsibilities your classmates do not face. Nevertheless, the part-time nature of your military training is the major difference between participating in ROTC and enrolling at a service academy, where you are in a military environment 24 hours a day.

In each ROTC unit there are two types of student—scholarship and nonscholarship. Although the focus of this section is on military programs that provide tuition aid, it should be pointed out that you may join an ROTC unit after you get to college even if you don't receive a scholarship. You take the same ROTC courses as a scholarship student, and you may major in nearly any subject. You can drop out at any time prior to the start of your junior year. If you continue, you will be paid a monthly stipend for your last two years of college and be required to attend a summer training session between your junior and senior years. Upon graduation, you will be commissioned as a second lieutenant or ensign. For the Army, your minimum active-duty obligation is six months; four years if you are in the Air Force or Navy.

The major source of scholarships is the four-year tuition scholarship program. Four-year scholarships are awarded to high school seniors on the basis of a national competition. Each year, more than 4,000 winners are selected (roughly 2,000 Army, 1,300 Navy, and 1,300 Air Force) from about 25,000 applicants. Recipients of four-year Army, Air Force, and Naval ROTC scholarships may attend either a host college or approved cross-enrollment college. In return for an Army ROTC scholarship, you must serve eight years in the Active Army, Army Reserve, or Army National Guard or a combination thereof. For scholarships from other services, four years' active duty service is required. After you accept the scholarship, you have a one-year grace period before you incur a military obligation. Prior to beginning your sophomore year, you may simply withdraw from the program. If you drop out after that time, you may be permitted to leave without penalty, ordered to active duty as an enlisted servicemember, or required to repay the financial aid you have received. The military will choose one of these three options, depending on the circumstances of your withdrawal.

Should you decide to try for a four-year ROTC scholarship, it is important that you apply to a college to which you can bring an ROTC scholarship. Because there is always the possibility you may not be accepted at your first choice, it is a good idea to apply to more than one college with an ROTC affiliation. In the case of Army and Air Force ROTC scholarships, both of which may require you to major in a specified area, you also need to be admitted to the particular program for which the scholarship is offered. For example, if you win an Air Force ROTC scholarship designated for an engineering major, you must be accepted into the engineering program as well as to the college as a whole.

While the majority of new ROTC scholarships are four-year awards given to high school seniors, each service sets aside scholarships for students who are already enrolled in college and want to try for this kind of military financial aid for their last two or three years. These in-college scholarships are a rapidly growing area within the ROTC program, since the services are finding they can do a better job of selecting officer candidates after observing one or two years of college performance. Of further interest to applicants is the fact that for some of the services, the selection rate is quite a bit higher for the two- and three-year awards than it is for the four-year scholarship. For example, in a recent year, Air Force ROTC accepted 37 percent of its candidates for four-year awards and 63 percent of its candidates for two- and three-year awards. Most of these in-college scholarships are given to students who join an ROTC unit without a scholarship and then decide to try for a tuition grant. Since a cadet or midshipman takes the same ROTC courses whether on scholarship or not, it makes good sense for those who are not receiving aid to apply for an in-college award.

Even if you have not been a member of an ROTC unit during your first two years in college, it is possible to receive a two-year scholarship, provided you apply by the spring of your sophomore year. If you win a two-year scholarship, you will go to a military summer camp where you will receive training equivalent to the first two years of ROTC courses. You then join the ROTC unit for your junior and senior years. (There are also limited opportunities for non-ROTC members to try for a three-year in-college scholarship; interested students should check with an ROTC unit.)

If you receive a two- or three-year scholarship, your active-duty obligation is two to eight years. You will not have the one-year grace period four-year scholarship winners have in which to decide whether they want to remain in ROTC. You must make up your mind whether or not you want to stay when you attend your first military science class as a scholarship student.

You may be married and still receive an ROTC scholarship (you may not be married in the service academies). The benefits are the same regardless of whether you are married or single.

In summary, there are four ways to participate in ROTC: as a winner of a four-year scholarship (or, in some cases, a three-year award) for high school seniors; as a recipient of a two- or three-year scholarship for ROTC members who are not initially on scholarship; by receiving an in-college scholarship (usually for two years) designated for students who have not yet joined an ROTC unit; or as a nonscholarship student.

This section, adapted from *How the Military Will Help You Pay for College: The High School Student's Guide to ROTC, the Academies, and Special Programs,* second edition, by Don M. Betterton (Peterson's), has provided an overview of the options available if you choose to turn to the military as a source of financial aid. One such option, Army ROTC, is discussed in detail in the following pages.

The Army ROTC Program

Through Army ROTC, a student can become an officer while pursuing a regular college degree.

WHAT IS ROTC?

Army ROTC is a college program that enables students not only to graduate with a degree in their chosen college majors but also to receive officers' commissions in the U.S. Army, the Army National Guard, or the Army Reserve.

ROTC courses are like any other college elective. And most college students can try ROTC for a year without incurring any military service obligation.

ROTC cadets are eligible for numerous financial benefits, including scholarships worth up to $68,000.

ROTC graduates have the opportunity to serve full time as officers in the active Army or serve part time in the Army National Guard or Reserve while pursuing regular civilian careers or continuing their education.

Students at hundreds of colleges and universities nationwide have access to Army ROTC programs, and about 40,000 students participate each year.

WHAT ARE THE BENEFITS OF ARMY ROTC?

Army ROTC helps ensure a young person's success in college and in life. It builds confidence and teaches the planning and time-management skills needed to succeed in college and the leadership, management, and motivational skills critical to success in life. These skills are not just taught in class. ROTC cadets can practice them in special ROTC activities and summer training. ROTC classes last just a few hours a week and at most colleges fulfill elective requirements.

Army ROTC provides a competitive edge that will be of value in either a military or a civilian career. In fact, many civilian employers place a premium on the skills and experience gained through ROTC.

According to its headquarters at Fort Monroe, Virginia, Army ROTC describes the type of cadets it is seeking as, "scholars, athletes, and leaders." In other words, Army ROTC wants students who are:

- athletically inclined (even if they have not played team sports);
- attracted to physical challenge;
- at least a B student;
- have served in leadership positions in community or student organizations; and
- motivated by serving and doing for others.

Such young people, according to Army ROTC, are most likely to exhibit the personal and professional integrity and the ability to work as a team that are so critical to today's Army officer.

Army ROTC provides the leadership and management training that will help make students a success in college and in life.

WHAT TYPES OF FINANCIAL BENEFITS ARE AVAILABLE?

In the face of today's growing college costs, Army ROTC offers merit-based scholarships that can help pay tuition and on-campus educational expenses.

Juniors and seniors in ROTC, plus certain other ROTC cadets, receive allowances ranging from $2000 to $4000 each school year and are paid to attend a special summer leadership training course.

Students who enroll in Army ROTC at college and who also join the National Guard or Army Reserve are eligible for other financial benefits. For more information, students should contact the Professor of Military Science at the college they plan to attend.

WHAT IS THE COMMITMENT?

College freshmen can try Army ROTC without making any commitment to join the Army. That commitment does not usually come until the junior year.

When students graduate with officers' commissions, they serve in the active Army, the Army National Guard, the Army Reserve, or a combination for a total of eight years.

In the active Army, they serve full time as Army officers. In the Guard or Reserve, they serve part time, generally one weekend a month and two weeks during the summer, while pursuing their chosen civilian careers.

THE FOUR-YEAR PROGRAM

Army ROTC is traditionally a four-year college program consisting of a two-year Basic Course and a two-year Advanced Course.

The Basic Course is usually taken during a college student's freshman and sophomore years. The subjects taught cover such areas as management principles, military history and tactics, leadership development, communication skills, first aid, land navigation, and rappelling.

Most students incur no military obligation by participating in the Basic Course, and most necessary ROTC textbooks, materials, and uniforms are furnished without cost.

After completing the Basic Course, only students who have demonstrated leadership potential and who meet scholastic, physical, and moral standards are eligible to enroll in the Advanced Course.

The Advanced Course is normally taken during a college student's junior and senior years. Instruction includes further training in leadership, organization theory, management, military tactics, strategic thinking, and professional ethics.

ROTC cadets in the Advanced Course attend a paid leadership development course during the summer between their junior and senior years. This course further permits cadets to put into practice the principles and theories they have learned in the classroom. It also exposes them to Army life in a tactical and field environment.

All ROTC cadets in the Advanced Course receive an allowance of $3000 or $4000 each school year and are paid to attend the Summer Leadership Development course. They are also furnished, without cost, most necessary ROTC textbooks, materials, and uniforms.

Before entering the Advanced Course, ROTC cadets must sign contracts that certify an understanding of their future Army service obligation, which is for eight years. This obligation may be fulfilled through various combinations of full-time active duty and part-time reserve forces duty depend-

More than 20 percent of all current ROTC cadets are women.

ing upon a cadet's personal preference and the needs of the Army at the time of commissioning.

ROTC cadets selected for reserve forces duty actually serve on active duty for three to six months before they join a National Guard or Army Reserve unit. This is so that they can attend an Officer Basic Course to receive additional Army training. Reserve officers generally serve part time in the National Guard or Army Reserve while they pursue regular full-time civilian careers.

THE TWO-YEAR PROGRAM

Students can also be commissioned after only two years of ROTC instruction.

This program is open to students who did not take Army ROTC during their first two years of college. Two-year program cadets include community and junior college graduates who have transferred to a four-year institution, graduate students, high school students planning to attend a Military Junior College, veterans, and members of the National Guard or the Army Reserve.

Students can take advantage of the two-year program by successfully completing a paid Leaders Training course (usually attended between the sophomore and junior years of college) and entering the Advanced Course.

Veterans and members of the National Guard and Army Reserve do not have to attend the Leaders Training course since their prior military service serves as the prerequisite for entering the Advanced Course.

Students interested in the two-year ROTC program should contact the nearest on-campus Army ROTC office for information before the end of the sophomore year of college.

EXTRACURRICULAR ACTIVITIES

Like regular college students, ROTC cadets participate in a wide variety of social, educational, professional, and athletic activities. Most of these activities are sponsored by the colleges hosting Army ROTC, but some are sponsored by ROTC itself.

Ranger Challenge is sponsored by Army ROTC and includes competition in patrolling, marksmanship, rope-bridge building, and a 10-kilometer run. Each ROTC unit fields a Ranger Challenge team that competes against teams from ROTC units at other colleges and universities.

These and other challenging activities offer leadership opportunities that increase self-confidence.

THE SCHOLARSHIP PROGRAM

Army ROTC offers valuable four-year scholarships to students entering college as freshmen and two- or three-year scholarships to students with two or three years remaining toward their bachelor's degrees.

These scholarships may pay thousands of dollars toward college tuition and required educational fees. In addition, they provide a specified amount for textbooks, supplies, and equipment. Each scholarship recipient also receives a personal allowance of $2000 to $4000 for each school year the scholarship is in effect.

Army ROTC scholarships are merit scholarships awarded on a competitive basis. Selection is based on high school or college grades, SAT or ACT scores, personal recommendations, physical fitness, athletic and extracurricular activities, leadership potential, a personal interview, and other criteria as prescribed by regulation.

All ROTC units offer instruction in some type of adventure training, including rappelling, orienteering, mountaineering, or white-water rafting.

Many of these scholarships are specifically targeted to students pursuing degrees in engineering, nursing, the physical sciences, or other technical programs.

Army ROTC scholarship winners who fail to complete the ROTC program or do not accept commissions as Army officers will be required to pay back the amount of their scholarships or serve as enlisted soldiers in the Army. This provision is binding for three- and four-year scholarship winners when they enter the sophomore year and for two-year scholarship winners when they enter the junior year.

Completed applications for four-year Army ROTC scholarships must be postmarked by November 15 of a high school student's senior year. Applications for two- and three-year scholarships are usually due by March of a college student's freshman and sophomore years. Since special application forms and procedures are required, interested students should contact Army ROTC for information well before these deadlines.

ARMY NURSE CORPS

Army ROTC offers two-, three-, and four-year scholarships to qualified students who are seeking bachelor's degrees in nursing. Army ROTC nurse candidates join the Army Nurse Corps upon graduation from an accredited nursing program, successful completion of a state board examination, and commissioning as Army officers.

The management training provided through Army ROTC is just as important to a nursing career as it is to any other career, and nursing students enrolled in Army ROTC can receive special nursing leadership experiences.

Eligible students who desire to attend one of the historically black colleges or universities (HBCU) that host Army ROTC may apply for an ROTC four-year scholarship.

Students seeking a bachelor's degree in nursing are especially encouraged to enroll in Army ROTC.

In the summer between their junior and senior years, ROTC nursing cadets attend the ROTC Nurse Summer Training Program (NSTP). NSTP allows ROTC nurse cadets to develop both leadership and nursing skills. It introduces the cadets to the Army Medical Department and the roles and responsibilities of an Army Nurse Corps officer. NSTP cadets report to Army hospitals for clinical training under the supervision of Army Nurse Corps office "preceptors." These professionals work one-on-one with the cadets throughout the training, which concentrates on "hands-on" experiences in areas like medical-surgical wards and intensive care units.

The Army also provides Army nurses specialty training. Army nurses can apply for clinical specialty courses in such areas as obstetrics/gynecology, critical care, perioperative, and psychiatric health nursing. They can also become nurse anesthetists.

In addition to training, the Army offers nurses many unique benefits. Army nurses serve around the world, get thirty days paid vacation from the start of their career, and don't lose seniority when changing geographical areas or specialties.

OPPORTUNITIES FOR SCIENCE OR ENGINEERING STUDENTS

Army scientists designed America's first earth satellite, developed the first operational computer, and devised innovative production methods for transistors and titanium, among other scientific discoveries. All this was accomplished by giving priority to scientific knowledge and investing in students who put their scientific skills to work while serving the nation.

As Army officers, students have exciting opportunities to be a part of world-class science from the very beginning of their careers. The Army also provides many students fully funded graduate tuition programs for approved courses of study. No matter which scientific or technical course of college study students choose, the Army offers them a chance to gain technical skills and leadership experience sooner and in more fields than any other employer.

THE SIMULTANEOUS MEMBERSHIP PROGRAM

The Simultaneous Membership Program (SMP) allows students to attend college, participate in Army ROTC, serve part time in the Army National Guard or Army Reserve, and receive generous Army benefits.

SMP cadets receive their Guard or Reserve pay; G.I. Bill benefits, if eligible; and a monthly ROTC allowance. In many states, Guard and Reserve members are eligible for additional state benefits. In some states, this includes free tuition at state-supported colleges and universities.

OPPORTUNITIES FOR VETERANS

Veterans who attend college can enroll in Army ROTC and participate in the two-year program. Their prior military service could fulfill the requirements for the Basic Course, so they could start ROTC in the Advanced Course.

Army ROTC—Leadership Excellence Starts Here.

In addition to the Veterans Administration benefits to which they are already entitled, veterans in ROTC receive the annual ROTC allowance each school year and may apply for ROTC scholarships.

Soldiers who have two years of active duty may be eligible for an Army ROTC scholarship. These "Green-to-Gold" scholarships allow selected soldiers to be released from the Army in order to attend college. Interested soldiers should contact the nearest on-campus Army ROTC office or their installation Education Offices for details.

WHAT DOES BECOMING AN ARMY OFFICER MEAN?

Army officers are leaders, thinkers, doers, and decision makers, proudly serving their country in a role that is vital to the national defense. They are required to have traits such as courage, confidence, integrity, and self-discipline.

In the Army, ROTC graduates start out as Second Lieutenants. Most become eligible for promotion and new job assignments at regular intervals.

In addition to their pay, they qualify for excellent medical, educational, and retirement benefits as well as other entitlements.

In the active Army, ROTC graduates have the opportunity to serve on Army posts located across the nation as well as abroad. In the Army National Guard or Army Reserve, they are able to serve close to where they live and work.

ADDITIONAL INFORMATION

To get more information about Army ROTC and any of the specific programs described above, students should call 800-USA-ROTC (toll-free) or contact the Professor of Military Science at a college hosting Army ROTC. Students can also write: College Army ROTC, QUEST Center, Attn: Department PG99, P.O. Box 3279, Warminster, Pennsylvania 18974-9872. Information about Army ROTC is also available on the World Wide Web at www.armyrotc.com.

Army ROTC Colleges and Universities

Army ROTC is offered at the colleges and universities listed below. Students at other institutions can often take ROTC at a nearby college campus; note that affiliated schools may cross state boundaries. The four-digit code that follows each institution name should be used to identify the college when seeking further information.

ALABAMA

†• Alabama Agricultural and Mechanical University, Normal (1002)
■ Auburn University, Auburn (1009)
‡ Auburn University at Montgomery, Montgomery (8310)
‡ Jacksonville State University, Jacksonville (1020)
○ Marion Military Institute, Marion (1026)
■• Tuskegee University, Tuskegee (1050)
■ University of Alabama, Tuscaloosa (1051)
■ University of Alabama at Birmingham, Birmingham (1052)
‡ University of North Alabama, Florence (1016)
■ University of South Alabama, Mobile (1057)

ALASKA

† University of Alaska Fairbanks, Fairbanks (1063)

ARIZONA

■ Arizona State University, Tempe (1081)
■ Northern Arizona University, Flagstaff (1082)
■ University of Arizona, Tucson (1083)

ARKANSAS

■ Arkansas State University, State University (1090)
■ University of Arkansas, Fayetteville (1108)
‡• University of Arkansas at Pine Bluff, Pine Bluff (1086)
‡ University of Central Arkansas, Conway (1092)

CALIFORNIA

† California Polytechnic State University, San Luis Obispo (1143)
■ California State University, Fresno (1147)
California State University, Fullerton (1137)
† Claremont-McKenna College, Claremont (1168)
■ San Diego State University, San Diego (1151)
† Santa Clara University, Santa Clara (1326)
† University of California, Berkeley (1312)
† University of California, Davis (1313)
■ University of California, Los Angeles (1315)
† University of California, Santa Barbara (1320)
‡ University of San Francisco, San Francisco (1325)
■ University of Southern California, Los Angeles (1328)

COLORADO

† Colorado State University, Fort Collins (1350)
† University of Colorado at Boulder, Boulder (1370)
† University of Colorado at Colorado Springs, Colorado Springs (4509)

CONNECTICUT

■ University of Connecticut, Storrs (29013)

DELAWARE

■ University of Delaware, Newark (1431)

DISTRICT OF COLUMBIA

‡ Georgetown University, Washington (1445)
■• Howard University, Washington (1448)

FLORIDA

† Embry-Riddle Aeronautical University, Daytona (1479)
■• Florida Agricultural and Mechanical University, Tallahassee (1480)
Florida International University, Miami (9635)
† Florida Institute of Technology, Melbourne (1469)
Florida Southern College, Lakeland (1488)
‡ Florida State University, Tallahassee (1489)
■ University of Central Florida, Orlando (3954)
■ University of Florida, Gainesville (1535)
■ University of South Florida, Tampa (1537)
University of Tampa, Tampa (1538)
University of West Florida, Pensacola (3955)

GEORGIA

Augusta State University, Augusta (1552)
‡ Columbus State University, Columbus (1561)
†• Fort Valley State University, Fort Valley (1566)
† Georgia Institute of Technology, Atlanta (1569)
○ Georgia Military College, Milledgeville (1571)
■ Georgia Southern University, Statesboro (1572)
‡ Georgia State University, Atlanta (1574)
‡* North Georgia College, Dahlonega (1585)
† University of Georgia, Athens (1598)

GUAM

University of Guam, Mangilao (3935)

HAWAII

■ University of Hawaii, Honolulu (1610)

IDAHO

‡ Boise State University, Boise (1616)
† University of Idaho, Moscow (1626)

ILLINOIS

Eastern Illinois University, Charleston (1674)
Illinois State University, Normal (1692)
■ Northern Illinois University, DeKalb (1737)
† Southern Illinois University Carbondale, Carbondale (1758)
Southern Illinois University Edwardsville, Edwardsville (1759)
■ University of Illinois at Chicago, Chicago (1776)
‡ University of Illinois at Urbana-Champaign, Champaign (1775)
Western Illinois University, Macomb (1780)
Wheaton College, Wheaton (1781)

INDIANA

‡ Ball State University, Muncie (1786)
‡ Indiana University Bloomington, Bloomington (1809)
■ Indiana University-Purdue University Indianapolis, Indianapolis (1813)
■ Purdue University, West Lafayette (1825)
† Rose-Hulman Institute of Technology, Terre Haute (1830)
† University of Notre Dame, Notre Dame (1840)

IOWA

† Iowa State University of Science and Technology, Ames (1869)
■ University of Iowa, Iowa City (1892)
University of Northern Iowa, Cedar Falls (1890)

KANSAS

† Kansas State University, Manhattan (1928)
■ Pittsburg State University, Pittsburg (1926)
■ University of Kansas, Lawrence (1948)

KENTUCKY

‡ Eastern Kentucky University, Richmond (1963)

Morehead State University, Morehead (1976)
■ University of Kentucky, Lexington (1989)
■ University of Louisville, Louisville (1999)
■ Western Kentucky University, Bowling Green (2002)

LOUISIANA

‡• Grambling State University, Grambling (2006)
† Louisiana State University and Agricultural and Mechanical College, Baton Rouge (2010)
‡ Northwestern State University of Louisiana, Natchitoches (2021)
‡• Southern University and Agricultural and Mechanical College, Baton Rouge (9636)
† Tulane University, New Orleans (2029)

MAINE

■ University of Maine, Orono (2053)

MARYLAND

Bowie State College, Bowie (2062)
■ Johns Hopkins University, Baltimore (2077)
† Loyola College in Maryland, Baltimore (2078)
McDaniel College, Westminster (2109)
• Morgan State University, Baltimore (2083)
University of Maryland, College Park (2103)

MASSACHUSETTS

† Boston University, Boston (2130)
† Massachusetts Institute of Technology, Cambridge (2178)
■ Northeastern University, Boston (2199)
■ University of Massachusetts, Amherst (2221)
† Worcester Polytechnic Institute, Worcester (2233)

MICHIGAN

Central Michigan University, Mount Pleasant (2243)
‡ Eastern Michigan University, Ypsilanti (2259)
■ Michigan State University, East Lansing (2290)
† Michigan Technological University, Houghton (2292)
‡ Northern Michigan University, Marquette (2301)
■ University of Michigan, Ann Arbor (9092)
† Western Michigan University, Kalamazoo (2330)

MINNESOTA

■ Minnesota State University, Mankato, Mankato (2360)
St. John's University, Collegeville (2379)
■ University of Minnesota, Minneapolis (3969)

MISSISSIPPI

‡• Alcorn State University, Lorman (2396)
• Jackson State University, Jackson (2410)
† Mississippi State University, Mississippi State (2423)
† University of Mississippi, University (2440)
■ University of Southern Mississippi, Hattiesburg (2441)

MISSOURI

‡ Central Missouri State University, Warrensburg (2454)
• Lincoln University, Jefferson City (2479)
Missouri Western State College, St. Joseph (2490)
Southwest Missouri State University, Springfield (2503)
‡ Truman State University, Kirksville (2495)
■ University of Missouri-Columbia, Columbia (2516)
† University of Missouri-Rolla, Rolla (2517)
† Washington University in St. Louis, St. Louis (2520)
○ Wentworth Military Academy and Junior College, Lexington (2522)

MONTANA

■ Montana State University, Bozeman (2532)
University of Montana, Missoula (2536)

NEBRASKA

‡ Creighton University, Omaha (2542)
■ University of Nebraska, Lincoln (2565)

NEVADA

■ University of Nevada, Reno (2568)

NEW HAMPSHIRE

■ University of New Hampshire, Durham (2589)

NEW JERSEY

■ Princeton University, Princeton (2627)
† Rutgers, The State University of New Jersey, New Brunswick (6964)
‡ Seton Hall University, South Orange (2632)

NEW MEXICO

○ New Mexico Military Institute, Roswell (2656)
■ New Mexico State University, Las Cruces (2657)
University of New Mexico, Albuquerque (2663)

NEW YORK

Canisius College, Buffalo (2681)
† Clarkson University, Potsdam (2699)
† Cornell University, Ithaca (2711)
Fordham University, Bronx (2722)
† Hofstra University, Hempstead (2732)
‡ Niagara University, Niagara (2788)
† Rochester Institute of Technology, Rochester (2806)
St. Bonaventure University, St. Bonaventure (2817)
St. John's University, Jamaica (2823)
Siena College, Loudonville (2816)
State University of New York College at Brockport, Brockport (2841)
■ Syracuse University, Syracuse (2882)

NORTH CAROLINA

Appalachian State University, Boone (2906)
Campbell University, Buies Creek (2913)
■ Duke University, Durham (2920)
‡ East Carolina University, Greenville (2923)
Elizabeth City State University, Elizabeth City (2926)
■• North Carolina Agricultural and Technical State University, Greensboro (2905)
† North Carolina State University at Raleigh, Raleigh (2972)
• St. Augustine's College, Raleigh (2968)
■ University of North Carolina at Chapel Hill (2974)
■ University of North Carolina at Charlotte, Charlotte (2975)
Wake Forest University, Winston-Salem (2978)

NORTH DAKOTA

† North Dakota State University, Fargo (9265)
■ University of North Dakota, Grand Forks (3005)

OHIO

‡ Bowling Green State University, Bowling Green (3018)
‡ Capital University, Columbus (3023)
• Central State University, Wilberforce (3026)
John Carroll University, Cleveland (3050)
‡ Kent University, Kent (3051)
■ Ohio State University, Columbus (6883)
† Ohio University, Athens (3100)
■ University of Akron, Akron (3123)
■ University of Cincinnati, Cincinnati (3125)
† University of Dayton, Dayton (3127)
■ University of Toledo, Toledo (3131)
‡ Wright State University, Dayton (9168)
Xavier University, Cincinnati (3144)

OKLAHOMA

Cameron University, Lawton (3150)
† Oklahoma State University, Stillwater (3170)
‡ University of Central Oklahoma, Edmond (3152)
■ University of Oklahoma, Norman (3184)

OREGON

† Oregon State University, Corvallis (3210)
University of Oregon, Eugene (3223)
■ University of Portland, Portland (3224)

PENNSYLVANIA

† Bucknell University, Lewisburg (3238)
Dickinson College, Carlisle (3253)
† Drexel University, Philadelphia (3256)
Edinboro University of Pennsylvania, Edinboro (3321)
■ Gannon University, Erie (3266)
‡ Indiana University of Pennsylvania, Indiana (8810)
† Lehigh University, Bethlehem (3289)
Lock Haven University of Pennsylvania, Lock Haven (3323)
■ Pennsylvania State University, University Park Campus, University Park (6965)
Shippensburg University of Pennsylvania, Shippensburg (3326)
‡ Slippery Rock University of Pennsylvania, Slippery Rock (3327)
‡ Temple University, Pennsylvania (3371)
■ University of Pennsylvania, Philadelphia (3378)

■ University of Pittsburgh, Pittsburgh (3379)
‡ University of Scranton, Scranton (3384)
○ Valley Forge Military Academy and Junior College, Wayne (3386)
■ Widener University, Chester (3313)

PUERTO RICO

■ University of Puerto Rico, Mayaguez (3944)
University of Puerto Rico, Rio Piedras Campus, Rio Piedras (7108)

RHODE ISLAND

Providence College, Providence (3406)
■ University of Rhode Island, Kingston (3414)

SOUTH CAROLINA

†* The Citadel, Charleston (3423)
■ Clemson University, Clemson (3425)
Furman University, Greenville (3434)
Presbyterian College, Clinton (3445)
• South Carolina State University, Orangeburg (3446)
■ University of South Carolina, Columbia (3448)
Wofford College, Spartanburg (3457)

SOUTH DAKOTA

† South Dakota School of Mines and Technology, Rapid City (3470)
■ South Dakota State University, Brookings (3471)
University of South Dakota, Vermillion (10300)

TENNESSEE

‡ Austin Peay State University, Clarksville (3478)
‡ Carson-Newman College, Jefferson City (3481)
■ East Tennessee State University, Johnson City (3487)
‡ Middle Tennessee State University, Murfreesboro (3510)
■ Tennessee Technological University, Cookeville (3523)
■ The University of Memphis, Memphis (3509)
■ University of Tennessee, Knoxville, Knoxville (3530)
† University of Tennessee at Martin, Martin (3531)
■ Vanderbilt University, Nashville (3535)

TEXAS

■• Prairie View Agricultural and Mechanical University, Prairie View (3630)
† St. Mary's University of San Antonio, San Antonio (3623)
Sam Houston State University, Huntsville (3606)
Southwest Texas State University, Canyon (3615)
‡ Stephen F. Austin State University, Nacogdoches (3624)
Tarleton State University, Stephenville (3631)
† Texas Agricultural and Mechanical University, College Station (10366)
† Texas Agricultural and Mechanical University, Kingsville (3639)
‡ Texas Christian University, Fort Worth (3636)
■ Texas Tech University, Lubbock (3644)
† University of Houston, Houston (3652)
■ University of Texas at Arlington, Arlington (3656)
■ University of Texas at Austin, Austin (3658)
■ University of Texas at El Paso, El Paso (3661)
‡ University of Texas-Pan American, Edinburg (3599)
■ University of Texas at San Antonio, San Antonio (10115)

UTAH

■ Brigham Young University, Provo (3670)
■ University of Utah, Salt Lake City (3675)
‡ Weber State University, Ogden (3680)

VERMONT

■* Norwich University, Northfield (3692)
■ University of Vermont, Burlington (3696)

VIRGINIA

College of William and Mary, Williamsburg (3705)
George Mason University, Fairfax (3749)
‡• Hampton University, Hampton (3714)
‡ James Madison University, Harrisonburg (3721)
‡• Norfolk State University, Norfolk (3765)
■ Old Dominion University, Norfolk (3728)
University of Richmond, Richmond (3744)
■ University of Virginia, Charlottesville (6968)
†* Virginia Military Institute, Lexington (3753)
† Virginia Polytechnic Institute and State University, Blacksburg (3754)
• Virginia State University, Petersburg (3764)

WASHINGTON

Central Washington University, Ellensburg (3771)
■ Eastern Washington University, Cheney (3775)
■ Gonzaga University, Spokane (3778)
Pacific Lutheran University, Tacoma (3785)
■ Seattle University, Seattle (3790)
■ University of Washington, Seattle (3798)
■ Washington State University, Pullman (3800)

WEST VIRGINIA

‡ Marshall University, Huntington (3815)
• West Virginia State College, Institute (3826)
■ West Virginia University, Morgantown (3827)

WISCONSIN

■ Marquette University, Milwaukee (3863)
University of Wisconsin-LaCrosse, LaCrosse (3919)
■ University of Wisconsin-Madison, Madison (3895)
‡ University of Wisconsin-Oshkosh, Oshkosh (9630)
University of Wisconsin-Stevens Point, Stevens Point (3924)

WYOMING

■ University of Wyoming, Laramie (3932)

Becoming an Army officer is an exciting opportunity. And the best part is that, through Army ROTC, a student can become an officer while pursuing a regular college degree.

There are many ways to obtain a scholarship application or simply more information about Army ROTC:

1. Contact the Professor of Military Science at one of the colleges or universities listed on the previous pages.
2. Write to: College Army ROTC
   QUEST Center
   Attn: Department PG99
   P.O. Box 3279
   Warminster, PA 18974-9872
3. Call 800-USA-ROTC (toll-free).
4. Call the Army ROTC Advisor nearest you

New York/New England	978-796-2243/2547
Delaware Valley	609-562-3275
Mid-Atlantic	703-805-4040
Southeastern	910-396-8408
Florida/Georgia	912-692-8544
Midwest	847-266-3105
Bluegrass	502-624-4475
Ohio Valley	573-596-6680
Southern Central	256-955-7577
Northwest	253-967-6025
North Central	719-526-9261
Southwest	831-242-7726
Southwest Central	210-221-2055

5. Check out Army ROTC on the World Wide Web: http://www.armyrotc.com

How to Use This Guide

PROFILES OF FOUR-YEAR COLLEGES AND SPECIAL MESSAGES

The **Profiles of Four-Year Colleges** contain basic data in capsule form for quick review and comparison. The following outline of the profile format shows the section headings and the items that each section covers. Any item that does not apply to a particular college or for which no information was supplied is omitted from that college's profile. **Special Messages,** which appear in the profiles just below the bulleted highlights, have been written by those colleges that wished to supplement their profile data with additional information.

Bulleted Highlights

The bulleted highlights feature important information for quick reference and comparison. The number of *possible* bulleted highlights that an ideal profile would have if all questions were answered in a timely manner are represented below. However, not every institution provides all of the information necessary to fill out every bulleted line. In such instances, the line will not appear.

First bullet

Institutional control: Private institutions are designated as independent (nonprofit), proprietary (profit-making), or independent, with a specific religious denomination or affiliation. Nondenominational or interdenominational religious orientation is possible and would be indicated.

Public institutions are designated by the source of funding. Designations include federal, state, province, commonwealth (Puerto Rico), territory (U.S. territories), county, district (an educational administrative unit often having boundaries different from units of local government), city, state and local (local may refer to county, district, or city), or state-related (funded primarily by the state but administratively autonomous).

Religious affiliation is also noted here.

Institutional type: Each institution is classified as one of the following:

Primarily two-year college: Awards baccalaureate degrees, but the vast majority of students are enrolled in two-year programs.

Four-year college: Awards baccalaureate degrees; may also award associate degrees; does not award graduate (postbaccalaureate) degrees.

Five-year college: Awards a five-year baccalaureate in a professional field such as architecture or pharmacy; does not award graduate degrees.

Upper-level institution: Awards baccalaureate degrees, but entering students must have at least two years of previous college-level credit; may also offer graduate degrees.

Comprehensive institution: Awards baccalaureate degrees; may also award associate degrees; offers graduate degree programs, primarily at the master's, specialist's, or professional level, although one or two doctoral programs may be offered.

University: Offers four years of undergraduate work plus graduate degrees through the doctorate in more than two academic or professional fields.

Founding date: If the year an institution was chartered differs from the year when instruction actually began, the earlier date is given.

System or administrative affiliation: Any coordinate institutions or system affiliations are indicated. An institution that has separate colleges or campuses for men and women but shares facilities and courses is termed a coordinate institution. A formal administrative grouping of institutions, either private or public, of which the college is a part, or the name of a single institution with which the college is administratively affiliated, is a system.

Second bullet

Calendar: Most colleges indicate one of the following: *4-1-4, 4-4-1,* or a similar arrangement (two terms of equal length plus an abbreviated winter or spring term, with the numbers referring to months); *semesters; trimesters; quarters; 3-3* (three courses for each of three terms); *modular* (the academic year is divided into small blocks of time; courses of varying lengths are assembled according to individual programs); or *standard year* (for most Canadian institutions).

Third bullet

Degrees: This names the full range of levels of certificates, diplomas, and degrees, including prebaccalaureate, graduate, and professional, that are offered by this institution.

Associate degree: Normally requires at least two but fewer than four years of full-time college work or its equivalent.

Bachelor's degree (baccalaureate): Requires at least four years but not more than five years of full-time college-level work or its equivalent. This includes all bachelor's degrees in which the normal four years of work are completed in three years and bachelor's degrees conferred in a five-year cooperative (work-study plan) program. A cooperative plan provides for alternate class attendance and employment in business, industry, or government. This allows students to combine actual work experience with their college studies.

Master's degree: Requires the successful completion of a program of study of at least the full-time equivalent of one but not more than two years of work beyond the bachelor's degree.

Doctoral degree (doctorate): The highest degree in graduate study. The doctoral degree classification includes Doctor of Education, Doctor of Juridical Science, Doctor of Public Health, and the Doctor of Philosophy in any nonprofessional field.

First professional degree: The first postbaccalaureate degree in one of the following fields: chiropractic (DC, DCM), dentistry (DDS, DMD), medicine (MD), optometry (OD), osteopathic medicine (DO), rabbinical and Talmudic studies (MHL, Rav), pharmacy (BPharm, PharmD), podiatry (PodD, DP, DPM), veterinary medicine (DVM), law (JD), or divinity/ministry (BD, MDiv).

First professional certificate (postdegree): Requires completion of an organized program of study after completion of the first professional degree. Examples are refresher courses or additional units of study in a specialty or subspecialty.

Post-master's certificate: Requires completion of an organized program of study of 24 credit hours beyond the master's degree but does not meet the requirements of academic degrees at the doctoral level.

Fourth bullet

Setting: Schools are designated as *urban* (located within a major city), *suburban* (a residential area within commuting distance of a major city), *small-town* (a small but compactly settled area not within commuting distance of a major city), or *rural* (a remote and sparsely populated area). The phrase *easy access to* . . . indicates that the campus is within an hour's drive of the nearest major metropolitan area that has a population greater than 500,000.

Fifth bullet

Endowment: The total dollar value of donations to the institution or the multicampus educational system of which the institution is a part.

Sixth bullet

Student body: An institution is coed (coeducational—admits men and women), primarily (80 percent or more) women, primarily men, women only, or men only.

Undergraduate students: Represents the number of full-time and part-time students enrolled in undergraduate degree programs as of fall 2003. The percentage of full-time undergraduates and the percentages of men and women are given.

Seventh bullet

Entrance level: As reported by each school, classifications of levels of entrance difficulty are as follows: most difficult, very difficult, moderately difficult, minimally difficult, and noncompetitive.

Percent of applicants admitted: The percentage of applicants who were granted admission.

Special Messages

These messages have been written by those colleges that wished to supplement the profile data with additional, timely, important information.

Category Overviews

Undergraduates

For fall 2003, the number of full- and part-time undergraduate students is listed. This list provides the number of states and U.S. territories, including the District of Columbia and Puerto Rico (or, for Canadian institutions, provinces and territories), and other countries from which undergraduates come. Percentages are given of undergraduates who are from out of state; Native American, African American, and Asian American or Pacific Islander; international students; transfer students; and living on campus

Retention: The percentage of 2002 freshmen (or, for upper-level institutions, entering students) who returned for the fall 2003 term.

Freshmen

Admission: Figures are given for the number of students who applied for fall 2003 admission, the number of those who were admitted, and the number who enrolled. Freshman statistics include the average high school GPA; the percentage of freshmen who took the SAT I and received verbal and math scores above 500, above 600, and above 700; as well as the percentage of freshmen taking the ACT Assessment who received a composite score of 18 or higher.

Faculty

Total: The total number of faculty members; the percentage of full-time faculty members as of fall 2003; and the percentage of full-time faculty members who hold doctoral/first professional/terminal degrees.

Student-faculty ratio: The school's estimate of the ratio of matriculated undergraduate students to faculty members teaching undergraduate courses.

Majors

This section lists the major fields of study offered by the college.

Academic Programs

Details are given here on study options available at each college.

Accelerated degree program: Students may earn a bachelor's degree in three academic years.

Academic remediation for entering students: Instructional courses designed for students deficient in the general competencies necessary for a regular postsecondary curriculum and educational setting.

Adult/continuing education programs: Courses offered for nontraditional students who are currently working or are returning to formal education.

Advanced placement: Credit toward a degree awarded for acceptable scores on College Board Advanced Placement tests.

Cooperative (co-op) education programs: Formal arrangements with off-campus employers allowing students to combine work and study in order to gain degree-related experience, usually extending the time required to complete a degree.

Distance learning: For-credit courses that can be accessed off-campus via cable television, the Internet, satellite, videotape, correspondence course, or other media.

Double major: A program of study in which a student concurrently completes the requirements of two majors.

English as a second language (ESL): A course of study designed specifically for students whose native language is not English.

External degree programs: A program of study in which students earn credits toward a degree through a combination of independent study, college courses, proficiency examinations, and personal experience. External degree programs require minimal or no classroom attendance.

Freshmen honors college: A separate academic program for talented freshmen.

Honors programs: Any special program for very able students offering the opportunity for educational enrichment, independent study, acceleration, or some combination of these.

Independent study: Academic work, usually undertaken outside the regular classroom structure, chosen or designed by the student with departmental approval and instructor supervision.

Internships: Any short-term, supervised work experience usually related to a student's major field, for which the student earns academic credit. The work can be full- or part-time, on or off-campus, paid or unpaid.

Off-campus study: A formal arrangement with one or more domestic institutions under which students may take courses at the other institution(s) for credit.

Part-time degree program: Students may earn a degree through part-time enrollment in regular session (daytime) classes or evening, weekend, or summer classes.

Self-designed major: Program of study based on individual interests, designed by the student with the assistance of an adviser.

Services for LD students: Special help for learning-disabled students with resolvable difficulties, such as dyslexia.

Study abroad: An arrangement by which a student completes part of the academic program studying in another country. A college may operate a campus abroad or it may have a cooperative agreement with other U.S. institutions or institutions in other countries.

Summer session for credit: Summer courses through which students may make up degree work or accelerate their program.

Tutorials: Undergraduates can arrange for special in-depth academic assignments (not for remediation) working with faculty members one-on-one or in small groups.

ROTC: Army, Naval, or Air Force Reserve Officers' Training Corps programs offered either on campus or at a cooperating host institution [designated by (C)].

Unusual degree programs: Nontraditional programs such as a 3-2 degree program, in which 3 years of liberal arts study is followed by 2 years of study in a professional field at another institution (or in a professional division of the same institution), resulting in two bachelor's degrees or a bachelor's and a master's degree.

Library

This section lists the name of the main library; the number of other libraries on campus; numbers of books, microform titles, serials, commercial online services, and audiovisual materials.

Computers on Campus

This paragraph includes the number of on-campus computer terminals and PCs available for general student use and their locations; computer purchase or lease plans; PC requirements for entering students; and campuswide computer network, e-mail, and access to computer labs, the Internet, and software.

Student Life

Housing options: The institution's policy about whether students are permitted to live off-campus or are required to live on campus for a specified period; whether freshmen-only, coed, single-sex, cooperative, and disabled student housing options are available; whether campus housing is leased by the school and/or provided by a third party; whether freshman applicants are given priority for college housing. The phrase *college housing not available* indicates that no college-owned or -operated housing facilities are provided for undergraduates and that noncommuting students must arrange for their own accommodations.

Activities and organizations: Lists information on drama-theater groups, choral groups, marching bands, student-run campus newspapers, student-run radio stations, and social organizations (sororities, fraternities, eating clubs, etc.) and how many are represented on campus.

Campus security: Campus safety measures including 24-hour emergency response devices (telephones and alarms) and patrols by trained security personnel, student patrols, late-night transport-escort service, and controlled dormitory access (key, security card, etc.).

Student services: Information provided indicates services offered to students by the college, such as legal services, health clinics, personal-psychological counseling, and women's centers.

Athletics

Membership in one or more of the following athletic associations is indicated by initials.

NCAA: National Collegiate Athletic Association

NAIA: National Association of Intercollegiate Athletics

NCCAA: National Christian College Athletic Association

NSCAA: National Small College Athletic Association

NJCAA: National Junior College Athletic Association

CIS: Canadian Interuniversity Sports

The overall NCAA division in which all or most intercollegiate teams compete is designated by a roman numeral I, II, or III. All teams that do not compete in this division are listed as exceptions.

Sports offered by the college are divided into two groups: intercollegiate (**M** or **W** following the name of each sport indicates that it is offered for men or women) and intramural. An **s** in parentheses following an **M** or **W** for an intercollegiate sport indicates that athletic scholarships (or grants-in-aid) are offered for men or women in that sport, and a **c** indicates a club team as opposed to a varsity team.

Standardized Tests

The most commonly required standardized tests are the ACT Assessment, SAT I, and SAT II Subject Tests, including the SAT II: Writing Test. These and other standardized tests may be used for selective admission, as a basis for counseling or course placement, or for both purposes. This section notes if a test is used for admission or placement and whether it is required, required for some, or recommended.

In addition to the ACT Assessment and SAT I, the following standardized entrance and placement examinations are referred to by their initials:

ABLE: Adult Basic Learning Examination

ACT ASSET: ACT Assessment of Skills for Successful Entry and Transfer

ACT PEP: ACT Proficiency Examination Program

CAT: California Achievement Tests

CELT: Comprehensive English Language Test

CPAt: Career Programs Assessment

CPT: Computerized Placement Test

DAT: Differential Aptitude Test

LSAT: Law School Admission Test

MAPS: Multiple Assessment Program Service

MCAT: Medical College Admission Test

MMPI: Minnesota Multiphasic Personality Inventory

OAT: Optometry Admission Test

PAA: Prueba de Aptitude Académica (Spanish-language version of the SAT I)

PCAT: Pharmacy College Admission Test

PSAT: Preliminary SAT

SCAT: Scholastic College Aptitude Test

SRA: Scientific Research Association (administers verbal, arithmetical, and achievement tests)

TABE: Test of Adult Basic Education

TASP: Texas Academic Skills Program

TOEFL: Test of English as a Foreign Language (for international students whose native language is not English)

WPCT: Washington Pre-College Test

Costs

Costs are given for the 2004–05 academic year or for the 2003–04 academic year if 2004–05 figures were not yet available. Annual expenses may be expressed as a comprehensive fee (including full-time tuition, mandatory fees, and college room and board) or as separate figures for full-time tuition, fees, room and board, or room only. For public institutions where tuition differs according to residence, separate figures are given for area or state residents and for nonresidents. Part-time tuition is expressed in terms of a per-unit rate (per credit, per semester hour, etc.) as specified by the institution.

The tuition structure at some institutions is complex in that freshmen and sophomores may be charged a different rate from that for juniors and seniors, a professional or vocational division may have a different fee structure from the liberal arts division of the same institution, or part-time tuition may be prorated on a sliding scale according to the number of credit hours taken. Tuition and fees may vary according to academic program, campus/location, class time (day, evening, weekend), course/credit load, course level, degree level, reciprocity agreements, and student level. Room and board charges are reported as an average for one academic year and may vary according to the board plan selected, campus/location, type of housing facility, or student level. If no college-owned or -operated housing facilities are offered, the phrase *college housing not available* will appear in the Housing section of the Student Life paragraph.

Tuition payment plans that may be offered to undergraduates include tuition prepayment, installment payments, and deferred payment. A tuition prepayment plan gives a student the option of locking in the current tuition rate for the entire term of enrollment by paying the full amount in advance rather than year by year. Colleges that offer such a prepayment plan may also help the student to arrange financing.

The availability of full or partial undergraduate tuition waivers to minority students, children of alumni, employees or their children, adult students, and senior citizens may be listed.

Financial Aid

Financial aid information presented represents aid awarded to undergraduates for the 2003–04 academic year. Figures are given for the number of undergraduates who applied for aid, the number who were judged to have need, and the number who had their need met. The number of Federal Work-Study and/or part-time jobs and average earnings are listed, as well as the number of non-need-based awards that were made. Non-need-based awards are college-administered scholarships for which the college determines the recipient and amount of each award. These scholarships are awarded to full-time undergraduates on the basis of merit or personal attributes without regard to need, although they many certainly be given to students who also happen to need aid. The average percent of need met for those determined to have need, the average financial aid package awarded to undergraduates (the amount of scholarships, grants, work-study payments, or loans in the institutionally administered financial aid package divided by the number of students who received any financial aid-amounts used to pay the officially designated Expected Family Contribution (EFC), such as PLUS or other alternative loans, are excluded from the amounts reported), the average amount of need-based gift aid, and the average amount of non-need-based aid are given. Average indebtedness, which is the average per-borrower indebtedness of the last graduating undergraduate class from amounts borrowed at this institution through any loan programs, excluding parent loans, is listed last.

Applying

Application and admission options include the following:

Early admission: Highly qualified students may matriculate before graduating from high school.

Early action plan: An admission plan that allows students to apply and be notified of an admission decision well in advance of the regular notification dates. If accepted, the candidate is not committed to enroll; students may reply to the offer under the college's regular reply policy.

Early decision plan: A plan that permits students to apply and be notified of an admission decision (and financial aid offer, if applicable) well in advance of the regular notification date. Applicants agree to accept an offer of admission and to withdraw their applications from other colleges. Candidates who are not accepted under early decision are automatically considered with the regular applicant pool, without prejudice.

Deferred entrance: The practice of permitting accepted students to postpone enrollment, usually for a period of one academic term or year.

Application fee: The fee required with an application is noted. This is typically nonrefundable, although under certain specified conditions it may be waived or returned.

Requirements: Other application requirements are grouped into three categories: required for all, required for some, and recommended. They may include an essay, standardized test scores, a high school transcript, a minimum high school grade point average (expressed as a number on a scale of 0 to 4.0, where 4.0 equals A, 3.0 equals B, etc.), letters of recommendation, an interview on campus or with local alumni, and, for certain types of schools or programs, special requirements such as a musical audition or an art portfolio.

Application deadlines and notification dates: Admission application deadlines and dates for notification of acceptance or rejection are given either as specific dates or as *rolling* and *continuous*. Rolling means that applications are processed as they are received, and qualified students are accepted as long as there are openings. Continuous means that applicants are notified of acceptance or rejection as applications are processed up until the date indicated or the actual beginning of classes. The application deadline and the notification date for transfers are given if they differ from the dates for freshmen. Early decision and early action application deadlines and notification dates are also indicated when relevant.

Freshmen Application Contact

The name, title, and telephone number of the person to contact for application information are given at the end of the profile. The admission office address is listed. Toll-free telephone numbers may also be included. The admission office fax number and e-mail address, if available, are listed, provided the school wanted them printed for use by prospective students.

Additional Information

Each college that has an **In-Depth Description** in the guide will have a cross-reference appended to the profile, referring you directly to that **In-Depth Description.**

IN-DEPTH DESCRIPTIONS OF FOUR-YEAR COLLEGES

Nearly 1,000 two-page narrative descriptions provide an inside look at colleges and universities appearing in this section, shifting the focus to a variety of other factors, some of them intangible, that should also be considered. The descriptions presented in this section provide a wealth of statistics that are crucial components in the college decision-making equation—components such as tuition, financial aid, and major fields of study. Prepared exclusively by college officials, the descriptions are designed to help give students a better sense of the individuality of each institution, in terms that include campus environment, student activities, and lifestyle. Such quality-of-life intangibles can be the deciding factors in the college selection process. The absence from this section of any college or university does not constitute an editorial decision on the part of Peterson's. In essence, this section is an open forum for colleges and universities, on a voluntary basis, to communicate their particular message to prospective college students. The colleges included have paid a fee to Peterson's to provide this information. The descriptions are edited to provide a consistent format across entries for your ease of comparison and are presented alphabetically by the official name of the institution. You'll also find state-by-state listings of these descriptions in the **Geographical Listing of In-Depth Descriptions** index.

INDEXES

Entrance Difficulty

This index groups colleges by their own assessment of their entrance difficulty level. The colleges were asked to select the level that most closely corresponds to their entrance difficulty. Institutions for which high school class rank and/or standardized test scores do not apply as admission criteria were asked to select the level that best indicates their entrance difficulty as compared to other institutions.

Cost Ranges

Colleges are grouped into eleven price ranges, from under $2000 to $20,000 and over.

Majors

This index presents hundreds of undergraduate fields of study that are currently offered most widely, according to the colleges' responses on *Peterson's Annual Survey of Undergraduate Institutions.* The majors appear in alphabetical order, each followed by an alphabetical list of the schools that offer a bachelor's-level program in that field. Liberal Arts and Studies indicates a general program with no specified major.

The terms used for the majors are those of the U.S. Department of Education Classification of Instructional Programs (CIPs). Many institutions, however, use different terms. Readers should visit www.petersons.com in order to contact a college and ask for its catalog or refer to the In-Depth Description in this book for the school's exact terminology. In addition, although the term "major" is used in this guide, some colleges may use other terms, such as "concentration," "program of study," or "field."

CD

Finally, at the back of the book, you will find your bonus CD-ROM. This CD includes information on colleges and universities, standardized test preparation, financial aid, and Quick-Reference Charts. Within the Colleges and Universities Info tab, you'll find In-Depth Descriptions and access to colleges' Web sites and the ability to ask any question of the school via an "instant inquiry." The Test Prep tab and Financial Aid tab both feature access to Peterson's online tools: Peterson's Test Prep—SAT and ACT online courses—and BestCollegeDeals®. Refer to the color ad at the front of this book for the key activation code to get FREE 90-day BestCollegeDeals® access! You'll also find a FREE SAT practice test on the CD and, coming in the summer of 2004, you can go to www.petersons.com/testprep/satnew_cd for a FREE SAT practice test for the new SAT! Be sure to check out the Quick-Reference Charts offered on the CD too—you'll find three At-a-Glance charts with colleges' general information, financial aid information, and admissions criteria!

DATA COLLECTION PROCEDURES

The data contained in the **Four-Year College Profiles** and **Indexes** were researched between fall 2003 and spring 2004 through *Peterson's Annual Survey of Undergraduate Institutions.* Questionnaires were sent to the more than 2,000 colleges and universities that met the outlined inclusion criteria. All data included in this edition have been submitted by officials (usually admissions and financial aid officers, registrars, or institutional research personnel) at the colleges. In addition, many of the institutions that submitted data were contacted directly by the Peterson's research staff to verify unusual figures, resolve discrepancies, or obtain additional data. All usable information received in time for publication has been included. The omission of any particular item from the **Four-Year College Profiles** and **Indexes** listing signifies that the information is either not applicable to that institution or not available. Because of Peterson's comprehensive editorial review and because all material comes directly from college officials, we believe that the information presented in this guide is accurate. You should check with a specific college or university at the time of application to verify such figures as tuition and fees, which may have changed since the publication of this volume.

CRITERIA FOR INCLUSION IN THIS BOOK

The term "four-year college" is the commonly used designation for institutions that grant the baccalaureate degree. Four years is the expected amount of time required to earn this degree, although some bachelor's degree programs may be completed in three years, others require five years, and part-time programs may take considerably longer. Upper-level institutions offer only the junior and senior years and accept only students with two years of college-level credit. Therefore, "four-year college" is a conventional term that accurately describes most of the institutions included in this guide, but should not be taken literally in all cases.

To be included in this guide, an institution must have full accreditation or be a candidate for accreditation (preaccreditation) status by an institutional or specialized accrediting body recognized by the U.S. Department of Education or the Council for Higher Education Accreditation (CHEA). Institutional accrediting bodies, which review each institution as a whole, include the six regional associations of schools and colleges (Middle States, New England, North Central, Northwest, Southern, and Western), each of which is responsible for a specified portion of the United States and its territories. Other institutional accrediting bodies are national in scope and accredit specific kinds of institutions (e.g., Bible colleges, independent colleges, and rabbinical and Talmudic schools). Program registration by the New York State Board of Regents is considered to be the equivalent of institutional accreditation, since the board requires that all programs offered by an institution meet its standards before recognition is granted. A Canadian institution must be chartered and authorized to grant degrees by the provincial government, affiliated with a chartered institution, or accredited by a recognized U.S. accrediting body. This guide also includes institutions outside the United States that are accredited by these U.S. accrediting bodies. There are recognized specialized or professional accrediting bodies in more than forty different fields, each of which is authorized to accredit institutions or specific programs in its particular field. For specialized institutions that offer programs in one field only, we designate this to be the equivalent of institutional accreditation. A full explanation of the accrediting process and complete information on recognized, institutional (regional and national) and specialized accrediting bodies can be found online at www.chea.org or at www.ed.gov/admins/finaid/accred/index.html.

Profiles of Four-Year Colleges

U.S. AND U.S. TERRITORIES

ALABAMA

ALABAMA AGRICULTURAL AND MECHANICAL UNIVERSITY
Huntsville, Alabama

- **State-supported** university, founded 1875
- **Calendar** semesters
- **Degrees** bachelor's, master's, and doctoral
- **Suburban** 2001-acre campus
- **Endowment** $31.0 million
- **Coed,** 5,326 undergraduate students, 93% full-time, 53% women, 47% men
- **Minimally difficult** entrance level, 45% of applicants were admitted

AAMU is a dynamic and progressive multicultural institution with a strong commitment to academic excellence. Some 100 programs are offered through 6 schools. The School of Graduate Studies offers the MS, MBA, MSW, MEd, MURP, EdS, and PhD degrees. Serving more than 6,600 students, the research institution ably meets the challenges launched by the nation's 2nd-largest research park in Huntsville, Alabama, and the world beyond. Moreover, AAMU students placed on *USA Today*'s Academic Teams in 1997, 1998, 1999, 2000, and 2001. Scholarships are available in academics, athletics, music, and theater.

Undergraduates 4,946 full-time, 380 part-time. Students come from 48 states and territories, 54 other countries, 15% are from out of state, 93% African American, 0.2% Asian American or Pacific Islander, 0.4% Hispanic American, 0.2% Native American, 3% international, 4% transferred in, 45% live on campus. *Retention:* 74% of 2002 full-time freshmen returned.

Freshmen *Admission:* 8,295 applied, 3,697 admitted, 1,301 enrolled. *Average high school GPA:* 2.8. *Test scores:* ACT scores over 18: 44%; ACT scores over 24: 5%.

Faculty *Total:* 374, 79% full-time, 48% with terminal degrees. *Student/faculty ratio:* 16:1.

Majors Accounting; agricultural economics; animal sciences; biology/biological sciences; business administration and management; business/commerce; business/managerial economics; business statistics; chemistry; city/urban, community and regional planning; civil engineering; civil engineering technology; computer and information sciences; economics; electrical, electronics and communications engineering; elementary education; English; family and consumer economics related; finance; food science; kindergarten/preschool education; marketing/marketing management; mathematics; mechanical engineering; mechanical engineering/mechanical technology; music teacher education; physical education teaching and coaching; physics; political science and government; psychology; radio and television broadcasting technology; secondary education; social work; sociology; special education; special education (speech or language impaired).

Academic Programs *Special study options:* academic remediation for entering students, adult/continuing education programs, advanced placement credit, cooperative education, distance learning, double majors, honors programs, off-campus study, part-time degree program, services for LD students, summer session for credit. *ROTC:* Army (b).

Library J. F. Drake Learning Resources Center with 507,500 titles, 2,500 serial subscriptions, 33,000 audiovisual materials, an OPAC.

Computers on Campus 1000 computers available on campus for general student use. A campuswide network can be accessed from student residence rooms and from off campus. Internet access, at least one staffed computer lab available.

Student Life *Housing:* on-campus residence required through sophomore year. *Options:* men-only, women-only, disabled students. *Activities and organizations:* drama/theater group, student-run newspaper, radio and television station, choral group, marching band, University Voices Gospel Choir, University Choir and Band, Elementary/Early Childhood Club, National Alliance of Business Students, fraternities/sororities, national fraternities, national sororities. *Campus security:* 24-hour patrols, late-night transport/escort service, controlled dormitory access. *Student services:* health clinic, personal/psychological counseling.

Athletics Member NCAA. All Division I except football (Division I-AA). *Intercollegiate sports:* baseball M(s), basketball M(s)/W(s), cross-country running M(s)/W(s), golf M(s), soccer M(s), tennis M/W, track and field M(s)/W(s), volleyball W(s). *Intramural sports:* basketball M/W, cross-country running M/W, football M, golf M, soccer M, table tennis M/W, tennis M/W, track and field M/W, volleyball W.

Standardized Tests *Recommended:* ACT (for admission).

Costs (2004–05) *Tuition:* state resident $3352 full-time; nonresident $6184 full-time. Part-time tuition and fees vary according to course load and program. *Required fees:* $520 full-time. *Room and board:* $4500; room only: $2600. Room and board charges vary according to board plan and housing facility. *Payment plan:* installment. *Waivers:* employees or children of employees.

Financial Aid Of all full-time matriculated undergraduates who enrolled in 2002, 4,790 applied for aid, 4,613 were judged to have need, 2,601 had their need fully met. In 2002, 432 non-need-based awards were made. *Average percent of need met:* 61%. *Average financial aid package:* $7862. *Average need-based loan:* $5500. *Average need-based gift aid:* $2543. *Average non-need-based aid:* $5500. *Average indebtedness upon graduation:* $17,125.

Applying *Options:* common application, electronic application, deferred entrance. *Application fee:* $10. *Required:* high school transcript, minimum 2.0 GPA. *Recommended:* 1 letter of recommendation. *Application deadline:* 7/15 (freshmen), rolling (transfers). *Notification:* continuous (freshmen), continuous (transfers).

Admissions Contact Mr. Antonio Boyle, Director of Admissions, Alabama Agricultural and Mechanical University, PO Box 908, Normal, AL 35762. *Phone:* 256-372-5245. *Toll-free phone:* 800-553-0816. *Fax:* 256-851-9747. *E-mail:* aboyle@asnaam.aamu.edu.

ALABAMA STATE UNIVERSITY
Montgomery, Alabama

- **State-supported** comprehensive, founded 1867, part of Alabama Commission on Higher Education
- **Calendar** semesters
- **Degrees** associate, bachelor's, master's, and post-master's certificates
- **Urban** 172-acre campus
- **Endowment** $20.5 million
- **Coed,** 5,020 undergraduate students, 85% full-time, 59% women, 41% men
- **Minimally difficult** entrance level, 37% of applicants were admitted

Undergraduates 4,254 full-time, 766 part-time. Students come from 39 states and territories, 5 other countries, 35% are from out of state, 95% African American, 0.1% Asian American or Pacific Islander, 0.2% Hispanic American, 0.1% Native American, 0.3% international, 4% transferred in, 43% live on campus.

Freshmen *Admission:* 11,462 applied, 4,267 admitted, 1,249 enrolled. *Average high school GPA:* 2.68. *Test scores:* SAT verbal scores over 500: 13%; SAT math scores over 500: 9%; ACT scores over 18: 27%; SAT verbal scores over 600: 1%; SAT math scores over 600: 1%; ACT scores over 24: 2%.

Faculty *Total:* 408, 57% full-time, 45% with terminal degrees. *Student/faculty ratio:* 15:1.

Majors Accounting; administrative assistant and secretarial science; art; art teacher education; biology/biological sciences; business administration and management; business teacher education; chemistry; child development; clinical/medical laboratory technology; community organization and advocacy; computer science; criminal justice/law enforcement administration; dramatic/theatre arts; economics; education; elementary education; English; finance; French; health information/medical records administration; history; information science/studies; journalism; kindergarten/preschool education; liberal arts and sciences/liberal studies; marine biology and biological oceanography; marketing/marketing management; mass communication/media; mathematics; music; music teacher education; occupational therapy; parks, recreation and leisure; physical education teaching and coaching; political science and government; pre-medical studies; psychology; public relations/image management; radio and television; science teacher education; secondary education; social sciences; social work; sociology; Spanish; special education; speech and rhetoric; teacher assistant/aide.

Academic Programs *Special study options:* academic remediation for entering students, adult/continuing education programs, advanced placement credit, cooperative education, double majors, honors programs, internships, off-campus study, part-time degree program, study abroad, summer session for credit. *ROTC:* Army (c), Navy (b). *Unusual degree programs:* 3-2 engineering with Auburn University at Montgomery, Tuskegee University.

Library Levi Watkins Learning Center with 396,871 titles, 1,307 serial subscriptions, 42,319 audiovisual materials, an OPAC, a Web page.

Computers on Campus 380 computers available on campus for general student use. A campuswide network can be accessed from off campus that provide access to e-mail. Internet access, online (class) registration, at least one staffed computer lab available. Computer purchase or lease plan available.

Student Life *Housing options:* men-only, women-only. Campus housing is university owned. *Activities and organizations:* drama/theater group, student-run newspaper, choral group, marching band, Student Orientation Services Leaders, Voices of Praise Gospel Choir, Student Government Association, University bands, Commuter Student Association, national fraternities, national sororities. *Campus security:* 24-hour emergency response devices and patrols, late-night transport/escort service, self-defense education, well-lit campus. *Student services:* health clinic, personal/psychological counseling.

Athletics Member NCAA. All Division I except football (Division I-AA). *Intercollegiate sports:* baseball M(s), basketball M(s)/W(s), bowling W, cross-country running M(s)/W(s), golf M(s), softball W(s), tennis M(s)/W(s), track and field M(s)/W(s), volleyball W(s). *Intramural sports:* baseball M, basketball M/W, field hockey M, softball M/W, swimming M/W, tennis M/W, track and field M/W, volleyball M/W.

Standardized Tests *Recommended:* SAT I or ACT (for admission).

Costs (2003–04) *Tuition:* state resident $3600 full-time, $150 per credit part-time; nonresident $7200 full-time, $300 per credit part-time. Full-time tuition and fees vary according to student level. Part-time tuition and fees vary according to student level. *Room and board:* $3700; room only: $1980. *Payment plans:* installment, deferred payment. *Waivers:* employees or children of employees.

Financial Aid Of all full-time matriculated undergraduates who enrolled in 2002, 4,154 applied for aid, 3,823 were judged to have need, 463 had their need fully met. 678 Federal Work-Study jobs (averaging $2219). 65 state and other part-time jobs (averaging $1631). In 2002, 64 non-need-based awards were made. *Average percent of need met:* 61%. *Average financial aid package:* $7011. *Average need-based loan:* $3059. *Average need-based gift aid:* $3292. *Average non-need-based aid:* $4973. *Average indebtedness upon graduation:* $26,825.

Applying *Options:* common application, early admission, deferred entrance. *Required:* high school transcript, minimum 2.0 GPA. *Application deadlines:* 7/30 (freshmen), 7/30 (transfers). *Notification:* continuous (freshmen), continuous (transfers).

Admissions Contact Mrs. Danielle Kennedy-Lamar, Director of Admissions and Recruitment, Alabama State University, PO Box 271, Montgomery, AL 36101-0271. *Phone:* 334-229-4291. *Toll-free phone:* 800-253-5037. *Fax:* 334-229-4984. *E-mail:* dlamar@asunet.alasu.edu.

■ *See page 1138 for a narrative description.*

AMERICAN COLLEGE OF COMPUTER & INFORMATION SCIENCES

Birmingham, Alabama

- **Proprietary** comprehensive, founded 1988
- **Calendar** continuous
- **Degrees** bachelor's and master's (offers only distance learning degree programs)
- **Coed, primarily men,** 1,253 undergraduate students
- **Moderately difficult** entrance level

Undergraduates Students come from 120 other countries, 95% are from out of state.

Faculty *Total:* 43, 9% full-time, 56% with terminal degrees.

Majors Business administration and management; business/commerce; computer and information sciences; computer science; information science/studies; information technology; system administration.

Academic Programs *Special study options:* academic remediation for entering students, accelerated degree program, adult/continuing education programs, advanced placement credit, distance learning, external degree program, honors programs, part-time degree program.

Student Life *Housing:* college housing not available.

Athletics *Intramural sports:* rock climbing M/W.

Costs (2003–04) *Tuition:* $145 per credit hour part-time. No tuition increase for student's term of enrollment. *Payment plans:* tuition prepayment, installment, deferred payment.

Applying *Options:* common application, electronic application. *Application fee:* $40. *Required:* high school transcript. *Application deadline:* rolling (freshmen), rolling (transfers).

Admissions Contact Mr. David Lenhart, Admissions Coordinator, American College of Computer & Information Sciences, 2101 Magnolia Avenue, Birmingham, AL 35205. *Phone:* 205-323-6191. *Toll-free phone:* 800-767-2427. *Fax:* 205-328-2229. *E-mail:* admiss@accis.edu.

ANDREW JACKSON UNIVERSITY

Birmingham, Alabama

- **Private** comprehensive, founded 1994
- **Degrees** bachelor's and master's (offers primarily external degree programs)
- **Coed**
- **Noncompetitive** entrance level

Faculty *Student/faculty ratio:* 10:1.

Costs (2003–04) *Tuition:* $375 per course part-time. *Payment plans:* tuition prepayment, installment.

Applying *Application fee:* $75.

Admissions Contact Ms. Bell Woods, Director of Admissions, Andrew Jackson University, 10 Old Montgomery Highway, Birmingham, AL 35209. *Phone:* 205-871-9288. *Fax:* 800-321-9694. *E-mail:* info@aju.edu.

ATHENS STATE UNIVERSITY

Athens, Alabama

- **State-supported** upper-level, founded 1822, part of The Alabama College System
- **Calendar** semesters
- **Degree** certificates and bachelor's
- **Small-town** 45-acre campus
- **Coed,** 2,537 undergraduate students, 40% full-time, 68% women, 32% men
- **Noncompetitive** entrance level, 87% of applicants were admitted

Undergraduates 1,026 full-time, 1,511 part-time. Students come from 6 states and territories, 10% are from out of state, 11% African American, 0.5% Asian American or Pacific Islander, 0.6% Hispanic American, 3% Native American, 0.4% international, 23% transferred in.

Faculty *Total:* 194, 34% full-time, 26% with terminal degrees. *Student/faculty ratio:* 23:1.

Majors Accounting; art; behavioral sciences; biology/biological sciences; business administration and management; business, management, and marketing related; chemistry; computer science; criminal justice/law enforcement administration; elementary education; English; health science; history; humanities; human resources management; information science/studies; kindergarten/preschool education; mathematics; physical education teaching and coaching; physics; political science and government; psychology; religious studies; science teacher education; science technologies related; secondary education; sociology; special education; trade and industrial teacher education.

Academic Programs *Special study options:* adult/continuing education programs, advanced placement credit, cooperative education, distance learning, double majors, independent study, internships, off-campus study, part-time degree program, study abroad, summer session for credit.

Library Athens State University Library with 107,015 titles, 249 serial subscriptions, an OPAC, a Web page.

Computers on Campus 260 computers available on campus for general student use. A campuswide network can be accessed. Internet access, online (class) registration, at least one staffed computer lab available.

Student Life *Housing options:* coed. Campus housing is university owned. *Activities and organizations:* drama/theater group, student-run newspaper, national sororities. *Campus security:* 24-hour emergency response devices, controlled dormitory access. *Student services:* personal/psychological counseling.

Athletics Member NAIA. *Intercollegiate sports:* basketball M(s), softball W(s). *Intramural sports:* table tennis M/W, volleyball M/W.

Costs (2003–04) *Tuition:* state resident $3150 full-time, $105 per semester hour part-time; nonresident $6300 full-time, $210 per semester hour part-time. *Required fees:* $420 full-time, $14 per semester hour part-time. *Room only:* $900. *Waivers:* senior citizens and employees or children of employees.

Financial Aid Of all full-time matriculated undergraduates who enrolled in 2002, 2,092 applied for aid, 1,533 were judged to have need. 57 Federal Work-Study jobs (averaging $2587). *Average indebtedness upon graduation:* $9755.

Applying *Options:* deferred entrance. *Application fee:* $30. *Application deadline:* rolling (transfers). *Notification:* continuous (transfers).

Admissions Contact Ms. Necedah Henderson, Coordinator of Admissions, Athens State University, 300 North Beaty Street, Athens, AL 35611. *Phone:* 256-233-8217. *Toll-free phone:* 800-522-0272. *Fax:* 256-233-6565. *E-mail:* henden@athens.edu.

AUBURN UNIVERSITY

Auburn University, Alabama

- **State-supported** university, founded 1856
- **Calendar** semesters
- **Degrees** bachelor's, master's, doctoral, first professional, and post-master's certificates
- **Small-town** 1875-acre campus with easy access to Atlanta and Birmingham
- **Endowment** $251.8 million
- **Coed,** 19,251 undergraduate students, 91% full-time, 48% women, 52% men
- **Moderately difficult** entrance level, 78% of applicants were admitted

Auburn University (continued)

Undergraduates 17,584 full-time, 1,667 part-time. Students come from 54 states and territories, 65 other countries, 48% are from out of state, 7% African American, 1% Asian American or Pacific Islander, 1% Hispanic American, 0.5% Native American, 0.8% international, 7% transferred in, 15% live on campus. *Retention:* 84% of 2002 full-time freshmen returned.

Freshmen *Admission:* 12,439 applied, 9,653 admitted, 3,706 enrolled. *Average high school GPA:* 3.51. *Test scores:* SAT verbal scores over 500: 79%; SAT math scores over 500: 84%; ACT scores over 18: 98%; SAT verbal scores over 600: 27%; SAT math scores over 600: 37%; ACT scores over 24: 56%; SAT verbal scores over 700: 5%; SAT math scores over 700: 7%; ACT scores over 30: 10%.

Faculty *Total:* 1,314, 89% full-time, 88% with terminal degrees. *Student/faculty ratio:* 16:1.

Majors Accounting; adult and continuing education; aerospace, aeronautical and astronautical engineering; agricultural/biological engineering and bioengineering; agricultural economics; agricultural teacher education; agriculture; agronomy and crop science; airline pilot and flight crew; animal sciences; anthropology; apparel and textiles; applied mathematics; aquaculture; architectural engineering; architecture; art; audiology and speech-language pathology; aviation/airway management; biochemistry; biology/biological sciences; biomedical sciences; botany/plant biology; broadcast journalism; business administration and management; business/managerial economics; business teacher education; chemical engineering; chemistry; child development; civil engineering; clinical laboratory science/medical technology; clinical/medical laboratory technology; commercial and advertising art; communication and journalism related; computer and information sciences; computer engineering; computer engineering related; computer hardware engineering; computer software engineering; criminology; dairy science; dramatic/theatre arts; early childhood education; economics; electrical, electronics and communications engineering; elementary education; engineering; English; English as a second/foreign language (teaching); environmental design/architecture; environmental science; environmental studies; family and consumer sciences/human sciences; finance; fine/studio arts; food science; foods, nutrition, and wellness; foreign languages and literatures; forest sciences and biology; French; French language teacher education; geography; geological/geophysical engineering; geology/earth science; German; German language teacher education; health/health care administration; health teacher education; history; history teacher education; horticultural science; hospitality administration related; hotel/motel administration; housing and human environments; human development and family studies; human resources management; industrial design; industrial engineering; interior architecture; international business/trade/commerce; journalism; kindergarten/preschool education; landscape architecture; logistics and materials management; management information systems; marine biology and biological oceanography; marketing/marketing management; mass communication/media; materials engineering; mathematics; mechanical engineering; medical laboratory technology; medical microbiology and bacteriology; microbiology; molecular biology; music teacher education; nursing (registered nurse training); nutrition sciences; operations management; ornamental horticulture; parks, recreation and leisure; philosophy; physical education teaching and coaching; physics; physics teacher education; plant pathology/phytopathology; plant sciences; plant sciences related; political science and government; poultry science; pre-dentistry studies; pre-law studies; pre-medical studies; pre-pharmacy studies; pre-veterinary studies; psychology; public administration; public relations/image management; radio and television; science teacher education; secondary education; secondary school administration/principalship; social work; sociology; Spanish; Spanish language teacher education; special education; special education related; special education (vision impaired); speech and rhetoric; speech therapy; textile sciences and engineering; trade and industrial teacher education; wildlife and wildlands science and management; zoology/animal biology.

Academic Programs *Special study options:* accelerated degree program, adult/continuing education programs, advanced placement credit, cooperative education, distance learning, double majors, English as a second language, honors programs, independent study, internships, part-time degree program, services for LD students, study abroad, summer session for credit. *ROTC:* Army (b), Navy (b), Air Force (b).

Library R. B. Draughon Library plus 2 others with 2.6 million titles, 23,121 serial subscriptions, 219,454 audiovisual materials, an OPAC, a Web page.

Computers on Campus 600 computers available on campus for general student use. A campuswide network can be accessed from student residence rooms and from off campus. Online (class) registration, at least one staffed computer lab available.

Student Life *Housing options:* coed, men-only, women-only, disabled students. Campus housing is university owned. *Activities and organizations:* drama/theater group, student-run newspaper, radio and television station, choral group, marching band, Student Government Association, University Program Council, IMPACT-Volunteer opportunities, Panhellenic Council, Interfraternity Council, national fraternities, national sororities. *Campus security:* 24-hour emergency response devices and patrols, late-night transport/escort service, controlled dormitory access. *Student services:* health clinic, personal/psychological counseling.

Athletics Member NCAA. All Division I except football (Division I-A). *Intercollegiate sports:* baseball M(s), basketball M(s)/W(s), cross-country running M(s)/W(s), equestrian sports W(s), golf M(s)/W(s), gymnastics W(s), soccer W(s), softball W(s), swimming M(s)/W(s), tennis M(s)/W(s), track and field M(s)/W(s), volleyball W(s). *Intramural sports:* badminton M(c)/W(c), basketball M/W, bowling M/W, equestrian sports W, fencing M/W, football M/W, golf M/W, gymnastics M(c)/W(c), lacrosse M(c)/W(c), racquetball M/W, rugby M(c), sailing M/W, soccer M(c)/W(c), softball M/W, swimming M(c)/W(c), table tennis M/W, tennis M/W, track and field M/W, ultimate Frisbee M/W, volleyball M(c)/W(c), weight lifting M(c)/W(c), wrestling M(c).

Standardized Tests *Required:* SAT I or ACT (for admission).

Costs (2003–04) *Tuition:* state resident $4230 full-time, $175 per credit hour part-time; nonresident $12,690 full-time, $525 per credit hour part-time. Full-time tuition and fees vary according to program. Part-time tuition and fees vary according to program. *Required fees:* $196 full-time. *Room and board:* $5970; room only: $2500. Room and board charges vary according to housing facility. *Payment plan:* installment. *Waivers:* children of alumni and employees or children of employees.

Financial Aid Of all full-time matriculated undergraduates who enrolled in 2002, 8,026 applied for aid, 5,625 were judged to have need, 425 had their need fully met. 517 Federal Work-Study jobs (averaging $2611). In 2002, 787 non-need-based awards were made. *Average percent of need met:* 53%. *Average financial aid package:* $6551. *Average need-based loan:* $4044. *Average need-based gift aid:* $3094. *Average non-need-based aid:* $4166. *Average indebtedness upon graduation:* $18,535.

Applying *Options:* early admission, deferred entrance. *Application fee:* $25. *Required:* high school transcript, minimum 2.0 GPA. *Required for some:* minimum 3.0 GPA. *Application deadline:* 8/1 (freshmen), rolling (transfers). *Notification:* continuous (freshmen), continuous (transfers).

Admissions Contact Doyle Bickers, Director, Admissions and Records, Auburn University, 202 Mary Martin Hall, Auburn University, AL 36849-5145. *Phone:* 334-844-6444. *Toll-free phone:* 800-AUBURN9. *E-mail:* admissions@auburn.edu.

■ *See page 1196 for a narrative description.*

AUBURN UNIVERSITY MONTGOMERY

Montgomery, Alabama

- **State-supported** comprehensive, founded 1967, part of Auburn University
- **Calendar** semesters
- **Degrees** bachelor's, master's, doctoral, and post-master's certificates
- **Suburban** 500-acre campus
- **Endowment** $15.7 million
- **Coed,** 4,492 undergraduate students, 63% full-time, 64% women, 36% men
- **Moderately difficult** entrance level, 99% of applicants were admitted

Undergraduates 2,846 full-time, 1,646 part-time. Students come from 35 states and territories, 21 other countries, 3% are from out of state, 33% African American, 2% Asian American or Pacific Islander, 1% Hispanic American, 0.5% Native American, 0.9% international, 12% live on campus.

Freshmen *Admission:* 962 applied, 954 admitted, 906 enrolled. *Test scores:* ACT scores over 18: 72%; ACT scores over 24: 19%; ACT scores over 30: 1%.

Faculty *Total:* 311, 59% full-time. *Student/faculty ratio:* 17:1.

Majors Accounting; art; biology/biological sciences; business administration and management; business/commerce; business/managerial economics; communication/speech communication and rhetoric; criminal justice/safety; elementary education; English; finance; foreign languages and literatures; history; human resources management; liberal arts and sciences/liberal studies; management information systems; marketing/marketing management; mathematics; nursing (registered nurse training); physical sciences; political science and government; psychology; secondary education; sociology.

Academic Programs *Special study options:* academic remediation for entering students, accelerated degree program, adult/continuing education programs, advanced placement credit, cooperative education, distance learning, double majors, English as a second language, honors programs, independent study, internships, off-campus study, part-time degree program, services for LD students, student-designed majors, study abroad, summer session for credit. *ROTC:* Army (b), Air Force (c).

Library Auburn University Montgomery Library with 238,322 titles, 1,436 serial subscriptions, 24,743 audiovisual materials, an OPAC, a Web page.

Computers on Campus 285 computers available on campus for general student use. A campuswide network can be accessed from student residence rooms and from off campus. Internet access, online (class) registration, at least one staffed computer lab available.

Student Life *Housing options:* coed, disabled students. Campus housing is university owned and leased by the school. *Activities and organizations:* drama/theater group, student-run newspaper, choral group, Student Government Association, Baptist campus ministries, International Student Association, African-American Student Alliance, national fraternities, national sororities. *Campus security:* 24-hour emergency response devices and patrols, student patrols, late-night transport/escort service, controlled dormitory access. *Student services:* health clinic, personal/psychological counseling.

Athletics Member NAIA. *Intercollegiate sports:* baseball M(s), basketball M(s)/W(s), soccer M(s)/W(s), tennis M(s)/W(s). *Intramural sports:* basketball M/W, bowling M/W, football M/W, soccer M/W, softball M/W, tennis M/W, volleyball M/W.

Standardized Tests *Required:* SAT I or ACT (for admission).

Costs (2003–04) *Tuition:* state resident $3900 full-time, $130 per semester hour part-time; nonresident $11,700 full-time, $390 per semester hour part-time. Full-time tuition and fees vary according to course load. *Required fees:* $230 full-time, $5 per credit hour part-time, $40 per term part-time. *Room and board:* $4890; room only: $2400. *Payment plan:* deferred payment. *Waivers:* employees or children of employees.

Financial Aid Of all full-time matriculated undergraduates who enrolled in 2003, 55 Federal Work-Study jobs (averaging $4000). *Average financial aid package:* $5309.

Applying *Options:* electronic application, deferred entrance. *Application fee:* $25. *Required:* high school transcript. *Application deadline:* rolling (freshmen), rolling (transfers). *Notification:* continuous (freshmen), continuous (transfers).

Admissions Contact Ms. Valerie Samuel Crawford, Assistant Director, Enrollment Services, Auburn University Montgomery, PO Box 244023, Montgomery, AL 36124-4023. *Phone:* 334-244-3667. *Toll-free phone:* 800-227-2649. *Fax:* 334-244-3795. *E-mail:* auminfo@mail.aum.edu.

BIRMINGHAM-SOUTHERN COLLEGE

Birmingham, Alabama

- **Independent Methodist** comprehensive, founded 1856
- **Calendar** 4-1-4
- **Degrees** bachelor's and master's
- **Urban** 196-acre campus
- **Endowment** $131.9 million
- **Coed,** 1,303 undergraduate students, 98% full-time, 58% women, 42% men
- **Moderately difficult** entrance level, 89% of applicants were admitted

Birmingham–Southern is a nationally ranked institution noted for an outstanding record of job placement and graduate admission to medical, law, and professional schools. In addition, the Honors Program, service learning, leadership studies, and international programs are also excellent opportunities. *U.S. News & World Report, Money* magazine, and *National Review* have recognized Southern, which has one of the three Phi Beta Kappa chapters in Alabama.

Undergraduates 1,276 full-time, 27 part-time. Students come from 28 states and territories, 25% are from out of state, 6% African American, 2% Asian American or Pacific Islander, 0.9% Hispanic American, 0.3% Native American, 0.5% international, 3% transferred in, 85% live on campus. *Retention:* 82% of 2002 full-time freshmen returned.

Freshmen *Admission:* 1,080 applied, 956 admitted, 356 enrolled. *Average high school GPA:* 3.35. *Test scores:* SAT verbal scores over 500: 92%; SAT math scores over 500: 88%; ACT scores over 18: 100%; SAT verbal scores over 600: 59%; SAT math scores over 600: 52%; ACT scores over 24: 78%; SAT verbal scores over 700: 15%; SAT math scores over 700: 13%; ACT scores over 30: 28%.

Faculty *Total:* 121, 79% full-time, 82% with terminal degrees. *Student/faculty ratio:* 12:1.

Majors Accounting; art; art history, criticism and conservation; art teacher education; Asian studies; biology/biological sciences; business administration and management; chemistry; computer science; dance; dramatic/theatre arts; drawing; economics; education; elementary education; English; fine/studio arts; French; German; history; human resources management; interdisciplinary studies; international business/trade/commerce; kindergarten/preschool education; mathematics; music; music history, literature, and theory; music teacher education; painting; philosophy; physics; piano and organ; political science and government; pre-dentistry studies; pre-law studies; pre-medical studies; printmaking; psychology; religious studies; sculpture; secondary education; sociology; Spanish; voice and opera.

Academic Programs *Special study options:* adult/continuing education programs, advanced placement credit, double majors, honors programs, independent study, internships, off-campus study, part-time degree program, student-designed majors, study abroad, summer session for credit. *ROTC:* Army (c), Air Force (c). *Unusual degree programs:* 3-2 engineering with Auburn University, Columbia University, Washington University in St. Louis, University of Alabama at Birmingham; nursing with Vanderbilt University; environmental studies with Duke University.

Library Charles Andrew Rush Learning Center/N. E. Miles Library with 232,330 titles, 949 serial subscriptions, 31,471 audiovisual materials, an OPAC, a Web page.

Computers on Campus 156 computers available on campus for general student use. A campuswide network can be accessed from student residence rooms and from off campus. At least one staffed computer lab available.

Student Life *Housing:* on-campus residence required through senior year. *Options:* men-only, women-only, disabled students. Campus housing is university owned. *Activities and organizations:* drama/theater group, student-run newspaper, radio station, choral group, Southern Volunteer Services, Student Conservancy, Residence Hall Association, national fraternities, national sororities. *Campus security:* 24-hour emergency response devices and patrols, late-night transport/escort service, controlled dormitory access, vehicle safety inspection. *Student services:* health clinic, personal/psychological counseling.

Athletics Member NCAA. All Division I. *Intercollegiate sports:* baseball M(s), basketball M(s)/W(s), cross-country running M(s)/W(s), golf M(s)/W(s), riflery W(s), soccer M(s)/W(s), softball W(s), tennis M(s)/W(s), volleyball W(s). *Intramural sports:* basketball M/W, fencing M, football M/W, golf M/W, racquetball M, soccer M/W, softball M/W, tennis M/W, volleyball M/W.

Standardized Tests *Required:* SAT I or ACT (for admission).

Costs (2003–04) *Comprehensive fee:* $25,034 includes full-time tuition ($18,530), mandatory fees ($400), and room and board ($6104). *College room only:* $3444. *Payment plan:* installment. *Waivers:* employees or children of employees.

Financial Aid Of all full-time matriculated undergraduates who enrolled in 2003, 871 applied for aid, 520 were judged to have need, 177 had their need fully met. 142 Federal Work-Study jobs (averaging $1818). 157 state and other part-time jobs (averaging $1371). In 2003, 616 non-need-based awards were made. *Average percent of need met:* 82%. *Average financial aid package:* $16,015. *Average need-based loan:* $4560. *Average need-based gift aid:* $7342. *Average non-need-based aid:* $10,425. *Average indebtedness upon graduation:* $12,200. *Financial aid deadline:* 8/1.

Applying *Options:* common application, electronic application, early admission, early action, deferred entrance. *Application fee:* $25. *Required:* essay or personal statement, high school transcript, minimum 2.0 GPA, 1 letter of recommendation. *Required for some:* interview. *Recommended:* interview. *Application deadline:* rolling (freshmen), rolling (transfers). *Notification:* continuous (freshmen), 12/15 (early action), continuous (transfers).

Admissions Contact Ms. Sheryl E. Salmon, Associate Vice President for Admission, Birmingham-Southern College, Box 549008, Birmingham, AL 35254. *Phone:* 205-226-4696. *Toll-free phone:* 800-523-5793. *Fax:* 205-226-3074. *E-mail:* admissions@bsc.edu.

■ *See page 1264 for a narrative description.*

COLUMBIA SOUTHERN UNIVERSITY

Orange Beach, Alabama

- **Proprietary** comprehensive
- **Calendar** modular
- **Degrees** certificates, associate, bachelor's, and master's (offers only distance learning degree programs)
- **Coed,** 1,600 undergraduate students
- **Noncompetitive** entrance level

Undergraduates Students come from 54 states and territories, 42 other countries.

Faculty *Total:* 45, 2% full-time, 76% with terminal degrees.

Majors Business administration and management; computer management; criminal justice/safety; environmental studies; fire protection and safety technology; fire services administration; health/health care administration; human resources management and services related; international business/trade/commerce; management information systems and services related; marketing/marketing management; occupational safety and health technology; sport and fitness administration.

Academic Programs *Special study options:* academic remediation for entering students, adult/continuing education programs, distance learning, external degree program, part-time degree program.

Student Life *Housing:* college housing not available.

Costs (2003–04) *Tuition:* $3750 full-time, $125 per credit hour part-time. Full-time tuition and fees vary according to course load. Part-time tuition and fees vary according to course load. No tuition increase for student's term of enrollment. *Payment plans:* tuition prepayment, installment.

Columbia Southern University (continued)

Applying *Options:* common application, electronic application. *Application fee:* $25. *Required for some:* high school transcript. *Application deadline:* rolling (freshmen), rolling (transfers).

Admissions Contact Mr. Poche Waguespack, Dean of Students, Columbia Southern University, 24847 Commercial Avenue, Orange Beach, AL 36561. *Phone:* 251-981-3771 Ext. 110. *Toll-free phone:* 800-977-8449. *E-mail:* tommy@columbiasouthern.edu.

CONCORDIA COLLEGE
Selma, Alabama

- **Independent Lutheran** 4-year, founded 1922, part of Concordia University System
- **Calendar** semesters
- **Degrees** associate and bachelor's
- **Small-town** 22-acre campus with easy access to Birmingham
- **Endowment** $4.1 million
- **Coed,** 851 undergraduate students, 83% full-time, 78% women, 22% men
- **Noncompetitive** entrance level

Undergraduates 705 full-time, 146 part-time. Students come from 12 states and territories, 5 other countries, 0.1% are from out of state, 89% African American, 0.2% Asian American or Pacific Islander, 4% international, 8% transferred in, 21% live on campus. *Retention:* 95% of 2002 full-time freshmen returned.

Freshmen *Admission:* 179 enrolled. *Average high school GPA:* 2.50. *Test scores:* ACT scores over 18: 66%.

Faculty *Total:* 58, 29% full-time. *Student/faculty ratio:* 17:1.

Majors Business administration and management; early childhood education; elementary education; general studies.

Academic Programs *Special study options:* academic remediation for entering students, adult/continuing education programs, part-time degree program, services for LD students, summer session for credit.

Library Ellwinger-Hunt Learning Resource Center with 41,230 titles, 106 serial subscriptions.

Computers on Campus 40 computers available on campus for general student use. At least one staffed computer lab available.

Student Life *Housing options:* coed. Campus housing is university owned. Freshman campus housing is guaranteed. *Activities and organizations:* drama/theater group, student-run newspaper, choral group, Music Ensemble, Rotract Club, Phi Theta Kappa, Spiritual Life, Red Cross. *Campus security:* 24-hour patrols.

Athletics Member NSCAA. *Intercollegiate sports:* baseball M(s), basketball M(s)/W(s), cheerleading W(s), soccer M(s), softball W(s). *Intramural sports:* volleyball M/W.

Standardized Tests *Recommended:* ACT (for placement).

Costs (2003–04) *Comprehensive fee:* $9774 includes full-time tuition ($6000), mandatory fees ($174), and room and board ($3600). Full-time tuition and fees vary according to course load. Part-time tuition: $233 per credit hour. Part-time tuition and fees vary according to course load. *Required fees:* $87 per term part-time. *College room only:* $1600. Room and board charges vary according to housing facility. *Payment plan:* installment. *Waivers:* employees or children of employees.

Financial Aid Of all full-time matriculated undergraduates who enrolled in 2001, 800 applied for aid, 782 were judged to have need, 487 had their need fully met. 75 Federal Work-Study jobs, 25 state and other part-time jobs (averaging $2500). In 2001, 22 non-need-based awards were made. *Average percent of need met:* 92%. *Average financial aid package:* $4410. *Average need-based gift aid:* $1500. *Average non-need-based aid:* $500.

Applying *Options:* deferred entrance. *Application fee:* $10. *Required:* high school transcript, minimum 2.0 GPA. *Application deadlines:* 8/15 (freshmen), 8/15 (transfers). *Notification:* continuous (freshmen), continuous (transfers).

Admissions Contact Ms. Ruthie Orsborn, Director of Admissions, Concordia College, 1804 Green Street, PO Box 1329, Selma, AL 36701. *Phone:* 334-874-7143. *Fax:* 334-874-3728.

FAULKNER UNIVERSITY
Montgomery, Alabama

- **Independent** comprehensive, founded 1942, affiliated with Church of Christ
- **Calendar** semesters
- **Degrees** associate, bachelor's, master's, and first professional
- **Urban** 75-acre campus
- **Endowment** $9.7 million
- **Coed,** 2,303 undergraduate students, 72% full-time, 64% women, 36% men
- **Minimally difficult** entrance level, 55% of applicants were admitted

Undergraduates 1,659 full-time, 644 part-time. Students come from 25 states and territories, 3 other countries, 12% are from out of state, 73% transferred in, 59% live on campus. *Retention:* 55% of 2002 full-time freshmen returned.

Freshmen *Admission:* 575 applied, 316 admitted, 314 enrolled. *Test scores:* SAT verbal scores over 500: 64%; SAT math scores over 500: 56%; ACT scores over 18: 67%; SAT verbal scores over 600: 22%; SAT math scores over 600: 14%; ACT scores over 24: 28%; SAT verbal scores over 700: 2%; SAT math scores over 700: 2%; ACT scores over 30: 3%.

Faculty *Total:* 118, 53% full-time, 53% with terminal degrees. *Student/faculty ratio:* 22:1.

Majors Accounting; administrative assistant and secretarial science; athletic training; biblical studies; biology/biological sciences; biomedical technology; business administration and management; business teacher education; clinical laboratory science/medical technology; clinical/medical laboratory technology; computer management; computer typography and composition equipment operation; criminal justice/law enforcement administration; criminology; dietetics; divinity/ministry; dramatic/theatre arts; education; elementary education; emergency medical technology (EMT paramedic); engineering; English; health information/medical records administration; history; humanities; human resources management; industrial radiologic technology; information science/studies; kindergarten/preschool education; legal assistant/paralegal; liberal arts and sciences/liberal studies; marketing/marketing management; medical/clinical assistant; occupational therapy; pastoral studies/counseling; physical education teaching and coaching; physical sciences; physical therapy; political science and government; pre-engineering; pre-law studies; psychology; religious education; religious studies; respiratory care therapy; secondary education; social sciences; sport and fitness administration; theology.

Academic Programs *Special study options:* academic remediation for entering students, accelerated degree program, adult/continuing education programs, advanced placement credit, distance learning, double majors, freshman honors college, honors programs, independent study, internships, off-campus study, part-time degree program, services for LD students, summer session for credit. *ROTC:* Army (c), Air Force (c).

Library Gus Nichols Library plus 1 other with 118,039 titles, 1,183 serial subscriptions, 730 audiovisual materials, an OPAC, a Web page.

Computers on Campus 85 computers available on campus for general student use. A campuswide network can be accessed from student residence rooms and from off campus. Internet access, at least one staffed computer lab available.

Student Life *Housing:* on-campus residence required through junior year. *Options:* coed, men-only, women-only, disabled students. Campus housing is university owned. Freshman applicants given priority for college housing. *Activities and organizations:* drama/theater group, student-run newspaper, choral group, social clubs, student government, Senators, Christians In Action, acappella chorus. *Campus security:* 24-hour patrols, late-night transport/escort service. *Student services:* health clinic, personal/psychological counseling.

Athletics Member NAIA, NCCAA. *Intercollegiate sports:* baseball M(s), basketball M(s), cross-country running M/W, softball W(s), volleyball W(s). *Intramural sports:* basketball M/W, football M/W, softball M/W, volleyball M/W.

Standardized Tests *Required:* SAT I or ACT (for admission).

Costs (2004–05) *Comprehensive fee:* $15,200 includes full-time tuition ($10,200) and room and board ($5000). Part-time tuition: $340 per semester hour. *College room only:* $2400. Room and board charges vary according to board plan and housing facility. *Payment plan:* installment. *Waivers:* employees or children of employees.

Financial Aid Of all full-time matriculated undergraduates who enrolled in 2003, 1,452 applied for aid, 1,234 were judged to have need, 136 had their need fully met. 149 Federal Work-Study jobs (averaging $1430). 7 state and other part-time jobs (averaging $457). In 2003, 46 non-need-based awards were made. *Average percent of need met:* 62%. *Average financial aid package:* $7100. *Average need-based loan:* $4800. *Average need-based gift aid:* $2800. *Average non-need-based aid:* $1900. *Average indebtedness upon graduation:* $18,100.

Applying *Options:* common application, electronic application, early admission, deferred entrance. *Application fee:* $10. *Required:* high school transcript, minimum 2.0 GPA, 2 letters of recommendation. *Recommended:* essay or personal statement, interview. *Application deadline:* rolling (freshmen), rolling (transfers).

Admissions Contact Mr. Keith Mock, Director of Admissions, Faulkner University, 5345 Atlanta Highway, Montgomery, AL 36109. *Phone:* 334-386-7200. *Toll-free phone:* 800-879-9816. *Fax:* 334-386-7137. *E-mail:* admissions@faulkner.edu.

HERITAGE CHRISTIAN UNIVERSITY
Florence, Alabama

- **Independent** comprehensive, founded 1971, affiliated with Church of Christ
- **Calendar** semesters
- **Degrees** associate, bachelor's, and master's
- **Small-town** 43-acre campus
- **Endowment** $3.5 million
- **Coed, primarily men,** 127 undergraduate students, 40% full-time, 9% women, 91% men
- **Noncompetitive** entrance level

Undergraduates 51 full-time, 76 part-time. Students come from 18 states and territories, 10 other countries, 48% are from out of state, 12% African American, 3% Hispanic American, 12% international, 7% transferred in.

Freshmen *Admission:* 7 enrolled.

Faculty *Total:* 16, 81% full-time, 50% with terminal degrees. *Student/faculty ratio:* 9:1.

Majors Biblical studies.

Academic Programs *Special study options:* accelerated degree program, adult/continuing education programs, distance learning, external degree program, independent study, internships, part-time degree program, summer session for credit.

Library Overton Memorial Library plus 1 other with 51,000 titles, 309 serial subscriptions, 12,342 audiovisual materials, an OPAC.

Computers on Campus 12 computers available on campus for general student use. A campuswide network can be accessed. Internet access, at least one staffed computer lab available.

Student Life *Housing options:* Campus housing is university owned. *Activities and organizations:* Missions Club, preachers club, Student Government Association, Christian Ladies Organization. *Student services:* personal/psychological counseling.

Athletics *Intramural sports:* softball M/W.

Costs (2004–05) *Tuition:* $7420 full-time, $265 per hour part-time. *Required fees:* $480 full-time, $20 per hour part-time. *Room only:* $1500. *Payment plans:* installment, deferred payment. *Waivers:* employees or children of employees.

Financial Aid Of all full-time matriculated undergraduates who enrolled in 2002, 26 applied for aid, 26 were judged to have need, 18 had their need fully met. 10 Federal Work-Study jobs (averaging $1234). In 2002, 16 non-need-based awards were made. *Average percent of need met:* 69%. *Average financial aid package:* $3272. *Average need-based loan:* $4067. *Average need-based gift aid:* $2617. *Average indebtedness upon graduation:* $9908.

Applying *Options:* early admission, deferred entrance. *Application fee:* $25. *Required:* high school transcript, 3 letters of recommendation. *Recommended:* interview. *Application deadline:* rolling (freshmen), rolling (transfers). *Notification:* continuous until 7/1 (freshmen), continuous (transfers).

Admissions Contact Mr. Travis Harmon, Director of Admissions, Heritage Christian University, PO Box HCU, Florence, AL 35630-0050. *Phone:* 256-766-6610. *Toll-free phone:* 800-367-3565. *Fax:* 256-766-9289. *E-mail:* bcollins@hcu.edu.

HERZING COLLEGE
Birmingham, Alabama

- **Proprietary** primarily 2-year, founded 1965, part of Herzing Institutes, Inc.
- **Calendar** semesters
- **Degrees** diplomas, associate, and bachelor's
- **Urban** campus
- **Coed**
- **Minimally difficult** entrance level

Faculty *Student/faculty ratio:* 20:1.

Student Life *Campus security:* 24-hour emergency response devices, late-night transport/escort service, security guard.

Standardized Tests *Required:* (for admission).

Costs (2003–04) *Tuition:* $24,300 full-time, $270 per credit hour part-time. Full-time tuition and fees vary according to program.

Applying *Options:* early admission, deferred entrance.

Admissions Contact Ms. Tess Anderson, Admissions Coordinator, Herzing College, 280 West Valley Avenue, Birmingham, AL 35209. *Phone:* 205-916-2800. *Fax:* 205-916-2807.

HUNTINGDON COLLEGE
Montgomery, Alabama

- **Independent United Methodist** 4-year, founded 1854
- **Calendar** semesters
- **Degrees** associate and bachelor's
- **Suburban** 71-acre campus with easy access to Birmingham
- **Endowment** $32.9 million
- **Coed,** 660 undergraduate students, 96% full-time, 55% women, 45% men
- **Moderately difficult** entrance level, 59% of applicants were admitted

Undergraduates 631 full-time, 29 part-time. Students come from 19 states and territories, 20% are from out of state, 10% African American, 0.8% Asian American or Pacific Islander, 0.8% Hispanic American, 1% Native American, 3% international, 5% transferred in, 72% live on campus. *Retention:* 76% of 2002 full-time freshmen returned.

Freshmen *Admission:* 1,108 applied, 650 admitted, 201 enrolled. *Average high school GPA:* 3.26. *Test scores:* SAT verbal scores over 500: 91%; SAT math scores over 500: 76%; ACT scores over 18: 96%; SAT verbal scores over 600: 39%; SAT math scores over 600: 48%; ACT scores over 24: 50%; SAT verbal scores over 700: 4%; SAT math scores over 700: 7%; ACT scores over 30: 3%.

Faculty *Total:* 62, 53% full-time. *Student/faculty ratio:* 14:1.

Majors Accounting; American studies; applied art; art; art teacher education; athletic training; biology/biological sciences; business administration and management; business/managerial economics; cell biology and anatomical sciences related; chemistry; chemistry teacher education; computer and information sciences; computer graphics; computer science; counseling psychology; creative writing; dramatic/theatre arts; education; English; English/language arts teacher education; European studies; experimental psychology; history; history teacher education; interdisciplinary studies; international business/trade/commerce; international relations and affairs; kinesiology and exercise science; liberal arts and sciences/liberal studies; marketing/marketing management; mathematics; mathematics teacher education; multi-/interdisciplinary studies related; music; music teacher education; parks, recreation and leisure; physical education teaching and coaching; physical therapy; piano and organ; political science and government; public administration; religious education; religious studies; secondary education; Spanish; speech and rhetoric; sport and fitness administration; visual and performing arts related; voice and opera.

Academic Programs *Special study options:* accelerated degree program, adult/continuing education programs, advanced placement credit, cooperative education, double majors, honors programs, independent study, internships, off-campus study, part-time degree program, student-designed majors, study abroad, summer session for credit. *ROTC:* Army (c), Air Force (c). *Unusual degree programs:* 3-2 engineering with Auburn University, The University of Alabama at Birmingham.

Library Houghton Memorial Library with 97,436 titles, 443 serial subscriptions, 1,811 audiovisual materials, a Web page.

Computers on Campus 75 computers available on campus for general student use. A campuswide network can be accessed from student residence rooms and from off campus that provide access to personal computer given to each entering student. Internet access, at least one staffed computer lab available.

Student Life *Housing:* on-campus residence required through junior year. *Options:* coed, disabled students. Campus housing is university owned. Freshman campus housing is guaranteed. *Activities and organizations:* drama/theater group, student-run newspaper, choral group, Circle K, SGA, Civitan, International Student Association, BACCHUS, national fraternities, national sororities. *Campus security:* 24-hour emergency response devices and patrols, late-night transport/escort service, controlled dormitory access, electronic video surveillance. *Student services:* health clinic, personal/psychological counseling.

Athletics Member NCAA. All Division III except men's and women's cheerleading (Division II). *Intercollegiate sports:* baseball M, basketball M/W, cheerleading M(s)/W(s), crew M(c)/W(c), cross-country running M/W, football M, golf M, sailing M(c)/W(c), soccer M/W, softball W, tennis W, volleyball W. *Intramural sports:* basketball M/W, crew M/W, fencing M/W, football M/W, golf M/W, rock climbing M(c)/W(c), rugby M/W, soccer M/W, softball M/W, table tennis M/W, tennis M/W, ultimate Frisbee M(c)/W(c), volleyball M/W, weight lifting M/W.

Standardized Tests *Required:* SAT I or ACT (for admission).

Costs (2004–05) *Comprehensive fee:* $21,250 includes full-time tuition ($15,250) and room and board ($6000). Full-time tuition and fees vary according to class time, reciprocity agreements, and student level. Part-time tuition and fees vary according to class time. No tuition increase for student's term of enrollment. *Room and board:* Room and board charges vary according to housing facility. *Payment plan:* deferred payment. *Waivers:* employees or children of employees.

Financial Aid Of all full-time matriculated undergraduates who enrolled in 2002, 525 applied for aid, 421 were judged to have need, 218 had their need fully met. 126 Federal Work-Study jobs (averaging $796). In 2002, 119 non-need-based awards were made. *Average percent of need met:* 83%. *Average financial aid package:* $10,686. *Average need-based loan:* $3179. *Average need-based gift aid:* $6569. *Average non-need-based aid:* $5691. *Average indebtedness upon graduation:* $15,621.

Applying *Options:* common application, electronic application, early admission, deferred entrance. *Application fee:* $25. *Required:* high school transcript,

Huntingdon College (continued)
minimum 2.25 GPA. *Required for some:* essay or personal statement, 2 letters of recommendation, interview. *Recommended:* 3 letters of recommendation. *Application deadline:* rolling (freshmen), rolling (transfers).

Admissions Contact Ms. Christy C. Mehaffey, Director of Admissions, Huntingdon College, 1500 East Fairview Avenue, Montgomery, AL 36106. *Phone:* 334-833-4517. *Toll-free phone:* 800-763-0313. *Fax:* 334-833-4347. *E-mail:* admiss@huntingdon.edu.

■ *See page 1754 for a narrative description.*

ITT TECHNICAL INSTITUTE
Birmingham, Alabama

- **Proprietary** primarily 2-year, founded 1994, part of ITT Educational Services, Inc.
- **Calendar** quarters
- **Degrees** associate and bachelor's
- **Suburban** campus
- **Coed**
- **Minimally difficult** entrance level

Student Life *Campus security:* 24-hour emergency response devices.

Standardized Tests *Required:* Wonderlic aptitude test (for admission).

Costs (2003–04) *Tuition:* $347 per credit hour part-time.

Applying *Options:* deferred entrance. *Application fee:* $100. *Required:* high school transcript, interview. *Recommended:* letters of recommendation.

Admissions Contact Jesse L. Johnson, Director of Recruitment, ITT Technical Institute, 500 Riverhills Business Park, Birmingham, AL 35242. *Phone:* 205-991-5410. *Toll-free phone:* 800-488-7033. *Fax:* 205-991-5025.

JACKSONVILLE STATE UNIVERSITY
Jacksonville, Alabama

- **State-supported** comprehensive, founded 1883
- **Calendar** semesters
- **Degrees** bachelor's, master's, and post-master's certificates
- **Small-town** 459-acre campus with easy access to Birmingham
- **Endowment** $8.3 million
- **Coed,** 7,289 undergraduate students, 79% full-time, 58% women, 42% men
- **Minimally difficult** entrance level, 44% of applicants were admitted

Undergraduates 5,771 full-time, 1,518 part-time. Students come from 49 states and territories, 77 other countries, 15% are from out of state, 21% African American, 1% Asian American or Pacific Islander, 1% Hispanic American, 0.7% Native American, 1% international, 10% transferred in, 20% live on campus. *Retention:* 60% of 2002 full-time freshmen returned.

Freshmen *Admission:* 2,452 applied, 1,078 admitted, 1,078 enrolled. *Test scores:* SAT verbal scores over 500: 37%; SAT math scores over 500: 38%; ACT scores over 18: 70%; SAT verbal scores over 600: 8%; SAT math scores over 600: 9%; ACT scores over 24: 21%; SAT verbal scores over 700: 1%; ACT scores over 30: 3%.

Faculty *Total:* 433, 68% full-time. *Student/faculty ratio:* 21:1.

Majors Accounting; animal genetics; anthropology; Army R.O.T.C./military science; art; biology/biological sciences; business administration and management; chemistry; clothing/textiles; communication/speech communication and rhetoric; computer and information sciences; corrections; criminal justice/law enforcement administration; criminal justice/police science; dietetics; dramatic/theatre arts; ecology; economics; education; educational/instructional media design; educational psychology; electrical, electronic and communications engineering technology; elementary education; English; environmental biology; family and consumer sciences/home economics teacher education; family and consumer sciences/human sciences; finance; foods, nutrition, and wellness; forensic science and technology; French; geography; geology/earth science; German; health and physical education; health teacher education; history; industrial technology; kindergarten/preschool education; kinesiology and exercise science; marine biology and biological oceanography; marketing/marketing management; mathematics; middle school education; music; music teacher education; nursing (registered nurse training); occupational safety and health technology; parks, recreation and leisure; physical education teaching and coaching; physics; political science and government; psychology; secondary education; social work; sociology; Spanish; special education.

Academic Programs *Special study options:* academic remediation for entering students, accelerated degree program, adult/continuing education programs, advanced placement credit, cooperative education, distance learning, double majors, honors programs, independent study, internships, part-time degree program, services for LD students, summer session for credit. *ROTC:* Army (b).

Library Houston Cole Library with 420,583 titles, 4,791 serial subscriptions, 32,875 audiovisual materials, an OPAC, a Web page.

Computers on Campus 330 computers available on campus for general student use. A campuswide network can be accessed from student residence rooms and from off campus. At least one staffed computer lab available.

Student Life *Housing options:* coed, men-only, women-only, disabled students. Campus housing is university owned. *Activities and organizations:* drama/theater group, student-run newspaper, radio and television station, choral group, marching band, Student Government Association, archaeology club, Campus Fellowship clubs, computer science club, biology club, national fraternities, national sororities. *Campus security:* 24-hour emergency response devices and patrols, student patrols, late-night transport/escort service, night security officer in female residence halls. *Student services:* health clinic, personal/psychological counseling.

Athletics Member NCAA. All Division I except football (Division I-AA). *Intercollegiate sports:* baseball M(s), basketball M(s)/W(s), cross-country running M(s)/W(s), golf M(s)/W(s), riflery M(s)/W(s), softball W(s), tennis M(s)/W(s), volleyball W(s). *Intramural sports:* badminton M(c)/W(c), basketball M(c)/W(c), bowling M(c)/W(c), football M(c), golf M(c)/W(c), racquetball M(c)/W(c), soccer M(c)/W(c), softball M(c)/W(c), table tennis M(c)/W(c), tennis M(c)/W(c), volleyball M(c)/W(c).

Standardized Tests *Required:* SAT I or ACT (for admission).

Costs (2003–04) *Tuition:* state resident $3540 full-time, $148 per hour part-time; nonresident $7080 full-time, $296 per hour part-time. *Room and board:* $3288; room only: $1150. Room and board charges vary according to board plan and housing facility. *Waivers:* employees or children of employees.

Financial Aid Of all full-time matriculated undergraduates who enrolled in 2002, 304 Federal Work-Study jobs (averaging $2320). *Average indebtedness upon graduation:* $20,388.

Applying *Options:* early admission, deferred entrance. *Application fee:* $20. *Required:* high school transcript. *Application deadline:* rolling (freshmen), rolling (transfers). *Notification:* continuous (freshmen), continuous (transfers).

Admissions Contact Ms. Martha Mitchell, Director of Admission, Jacksonville State University, 700 Pelham Road North, Jacksonville, AL 36265. *Phone:* 256-782-5363. *Toll-free phone:* 800-231-5291. *Fax:* 256-782-5291. *E-mail:* info@jsucc.jsu.edu.

JUDSON COLLEGE
Marion, Alabama

- **Independent Baptist** 4-year, founded 1838
- **Calendar** semesters plus 2-month term
- **Degree** bachelor's
- **Rural** 80-acre campus with easy access to Birmingham
- **Endowment** $15.8 million
- **Women only,** 369 undergraduate students, 84% full-time
- **Moderately difficult** entrance level, 78% of applicants were admitted

Undergraduates 311 full-time, 58 part-time. Students come from 25 states and territories, 21% are from out of state, 15% African American, 2% Asian American or Pacific Islander, 1% Hispanic American, 0.8% Native American, 0.8% international, 8% transferred in, 63% live on campus. *Retention:* 65% of 2002 full-time freshmen returned.

Freshmen *Admission:* 81 enrolled. *Average high school GPA:* 3.11. *Test scores:* SAT verbal scores over 500: 80%; SAT math scores over 500: 80%; ACT scores over 18: 93%; SAT verbal scores over 600: 80%; SAT math scores over 600: 20%; ACT scores over 24: 34%; SAT verbal scores over 700: 60%; SAT math scores over 700: 20%; ACT scores over 30: 7%.

Faculty *Total:* 29, 97% full-time, 72% with terminal degrees. *Student/faculty ratio:* 13:1.

Majors Art; biology/biological sciences; business/commerce; chemistry; criminal justice/law enforcement administration; education; elementary education; English; English/language arts teacher education; history; interdisciplinary studies; mathematics; mathematics teacher education; middle school education; modern languages; multi-/interdisciplinary studies related; music; music teacher education; psychology; religious studies; Romance languages; science teacher education; secondary education; social science teacher education.

Academic Programs *Special study options:* academic remediation for entering students, accelerated degree program, adult/continuing education programs, advanced placement credit, distance learning, double majors, external degree program, honors programs, independent study, internships, off-campus study, part-time degree program, student-designed majors, study abroad, summer session for credit. *ROTC:* Army (c).

Library Bowling Library with 70,746 titles, 5,287 serial subscriptions, 7,359 audiovisual materials, an OPAC, a Web page.

Computers on Campus 40 computers available on campus for general student use. A campuswide network can be accessed. Internet access, at least one staffed computer lab available. Computer purchase or lease plan available.

Student Life *Housing:* on-campus residence required through senior year. *Options:* women-only. Campus housing is university owned. *Activities and organizations:* drama/theater group, student-run newspaper, choral group, marching band, Student Government Association, campus ministries, Choir, Ambassadors, Science Club. *Campus security:* 24-hour emergency response devices and patrols, late-night transport/escort service, controlled dormitory access. *Student services:* personal/psychological counseling.

Athletics Member NCCAA. *Intercollegiate sports:* basketball W(s), equestrian sports W, softball W(s), tennis W(s), volleyball W(s). *Intramural sports:* basketball W, field hockey W, softball W, tennis W, volleyball W.

Standardized Tests *Required:* SAT I or ACT (for admission).

Costs (2004–05) *Comprehensive fee:* $15,220 includes full-time tuition ($8900), mandatory fees ($470), and room and board ($5850). Full-time tuition and fees vary according to course load. Part-time tuition: $285 per semester hour. Part-time tuition and fees vary according to course load. *Payment plan:* installment. *Waivers:* employees or children of employees.

Financial Aid Of all full-time matriculated undergraduates who enrolled in 2003, 266 applied for aid, 206 were judged to have need, 54 had their need fully met. 62 Federal Work-Study jobs (averaging $1483). 76 state and other part-time jobs (averaging $1550). In 2003, 34 non-need-based awards were made. *Average percent of need met:* 82%. *Average financial aid package:* $11,500. *Average need-based loan:* $3462. *Average need-based gift aid:* $6884. *Average non-need-based aid:* $3395. *Average indebtedness upon graduation:* $15,339.

Applying *Options:* common application, electronic application, early admission. *Application fee:* $25. *Required:* high school transcript, minimum 2.0 GPA, 2 letters of recommendation, interview. *Recommended:* essay or personal statement. *Application deadline:* rolling (freshmen), rolling (transfers). *Notification:* continuous (freshmen), continuous (transfers).

Admissions Contact Mr. Michael Scotto, Director of Admissions, Judson College, PO Box 120, 302 Bibb Street, Marion, AL 36756. *Phone:* 334-683-5110 Ext. 110. *Toll-free phone:* 800-447-9472. *Fax:* 334-683-5158. *E-mail:* admissions@future.judson.edu.

MILES COLLEGE
Fairfield, Alabama

- **Independent Christian Methodist Episcopal** 4-year, founded 1905
- **Calendar** semesters
- **Degree** bachelor's
- **Small-town** 35-acre campus
- **Endowment** $10.7 million
- **Coed,** 1,660 undergraduate students, 93% full-time, 57% women, 43% men
- **Noncompetitive** entrance level, 58% of applicants were admitted

Undergraduates 1,550 full-time, 110 part-time. Students come from 22 states and territories, 98% African American, 0.1% international, 7% transferred in, 31% live on campus. *Retention:* 78% of 2002 full-time freshmen returned.

Freshmen *Admission:* 829 applied, 477 admitted, 352 enrolled. *Average high school GPA:* 2.34. *Test scores:* ACT scores over 18: 11%; ACT scores over 24: 1%.

Faculty *Total:* 134, 69% full-time, 31% with terminal degrees. *Student/faculty ratio:* 20:1.

Majors Accounting and business/management; African studies; behavioral sciences; biology/biological sciences; business administration and management; chemistry; communication and media related; computer and information sciences; criminal justice/law enforcement administration; early childhood education; education; elementary education; English; English/language arts teacher education; environmental science; history; mass communication/media; mathematics; mathematics teacher education; physics; political science and government; religious studies; secondary education; social sciences; social work.

Academic Programs *Special study options:* academic remediation for entering students, accelerated degree program, adult/continuing education programs, cooperative education, honors programs, internships, off-campus study, part-time degree program, services for LD students, summer session for credit. *ROTC:* Army (c), Air Force (c). *Unusual degree programs:* 3-2 engineering with Tuskegee University, University of Alabama at Birmingham, UAB Walker College, Tennessee State University; physics with Tuskegee University, Alabama Agricultural and Mechanical University.

Library C.A. Kirkeedoll Learning Resources Center with 180,000 titles, 250 serial subscriptions, an OPAC.

Computers on Campus 50 computers available on campus for general student use. Internet access, at least one staffed computer lab available.

Student Life *Housing options:* coed, men-only, women-only. Campus housing is university owned. *Activities and organizations:* drama/theater group, student-run newspaper, television station, choral group, marching band, Choir, Education Club, Student Government Association, Phi Beta Lambda Business Club, Communications Club, national fraternities, national sororities. *Campus security:* 24-hour emergency response devices and patrols. *Student services:* health clinic, personal/psychological counseling.

Athletics Member NCAA, NAIA. All NCAA Division III. *Intercollegiate sports:* baseball M(s), basketball M(s)/W(s), cheerleading W(s), cross-country running M(s), football M(s), softball W(s), track and field M(s). *Intramural sports:* basketball M/W, cross-country running M/W, tennis M/W, track and field M/W, volleyball W.

Standardized Tests *Recommended:* ACT (for admission), ACT ASSET.

Costs (2003–04) *Comprehensive fee:* $9808 includes full-time tuition ($5090), mandatory fees ($380), and room and board ($4338). Full-time tuition and fees vary according to course load, location, and program. Part-time tuition: $190 per credit. *Required fees:* $190 per term part-time. *College room only:* $2370. Room and board charges vary according to housing facility and location. *Payment plans:* installment, deferred payment. *Waivers:* employees or children of employees.

Financial Aid Of all full-time matriculated undergraduates who enrolled in 2002, 1,696 applied for aid, 1,673 were judged to have need, 1,254 had their need fully met. 355 Federal Work-Study jobs (averaging $804). In 2002, 23 non-need-based awards were made. *Average percent of need met:* 75%. *Average financial aid package:* $6702. *Average need-based loan:* $1382. *Average need-based gift aid:* $1939. *Average non-need-based aid:* $609. *Average indebtedness upon graduation:* $17,500.

Applying *Application fee:* $25. *Required for some:* high school transcript. *Application deadline:* 8/23 (freshmen), rolling (transfers). *Notification:* continuous (freshmen), continuous (transfers).

Admissions Contact Dr. Carolyn Ray, Director of Admissions and Recruitment, Miles College, 5500 Myron Massey Boulevard, Bell Building, Fairfield, AL 35064. *Phone:* 205-929-1657. *Toll-free phone:* 800-445-0708. *Fax:* 205-929-1627. *E-mail:* carolyn@miles.edu.

OAKWOOD COLLEGE
Huntsville, Alabama

- **Independent Seventh-day Adventist** 4-year, founded 1896
- **Calendar** semesters
- **Degrees** associate and bachelor's
- 1200-acre campus
- **Coed**
- **Minimally difficult** entrance level

Faculty *Student/faculty ratio:* 14:1.

Student Life *Campus security:* 24-hour patrols, student patrols, late-night transport/escort service.

Standardized Tests *Required:* SAT I or ACT (for admission).

Costs (2003–04) *Comprehensive fee:* $14,418 includes full-time tuition ($9420), mandatory fees ($378), and room and board ($4620). *College room only:* $2370.

Financial Aid Of all full-time matriculated undergraduates who enrolled in 2001, 1,422 applied for aid, 1,422 were judged to have need, 131 had their need fully met. *Average percent of need met:* 77. *Average financial aid package:* $6500. *Average need-based loan:* $4500. *Average need-based gift aid:* $2500. *Average non-need-based aid:* $2000. *Average indebtedness upon graduation:* $15,000.

Applying *Options:* common application, early action, deferred entrance. *Application fee:* $20. *Required:* high school transcript, letters of recommendation.

Admissions Contact Mr. Fred Pullins, Director of Enrollment Management, Oakwood College, 7000 Adventist Boulevard, NW, Huntsville, AL 35896. *Phone:* 256-726-7354. *Toll-free phone:* 800-358-3978. *Fax:* 256-726-7154. *E-mail:* admission@oakwood.edu.

REMINGTON COLLEGE–MOBILE CAMPUS
Mobile, Alabama

- **Proprietary** primarily 2-year, part of Education America
- **Calendar** quarters
- **Degrees** associate and bachelor's
- **Coed**
- **Noncompetitive** entrance level

Faculty *Student/faculty ratio:* 16:1.

Standardized Tests *Required:* Wonderlic aptitude test (for admission).

Costs (2003–04) *Tuition:* $27,840 full-time, $270 per credit hour part-time. Full-time tuition and fees vary according to class time, course level, course load,

Remington College–Mobile Campus (continued)
degree level, location, program, reciprocity agreements, and student level. No tuition increase for student's term of enrollment.

Financial Aid Of all full-time matriculated undergraduates who enrolled in 2001, 500 applied for aid, 500 were judged to have need. 22 Federal Work-Study jobs (averaging $1300). *Average percent of need met:* 45. *Average financial aid package:* $7043. *Average need-based loan:* $3000. *Average need-based gift aid:* $7043. *Average indebtedness upon graduation:* $14,000.

Applying *Application fee:* $50. *Required:* high school transcript, interview.

Admissions Contact Mr. Randall Olson, Director of Recruitment, Remington College–Mobile Campus, 828 Downtowner Loop West, Mobile, AL 36609. *Phone:* 251-343-8200 Ext. 221. *Toll-free phone:* 800-866-0850. *Fax:* 251-343-0577.

SAMFORD UNIVERSITY
Birmingham, Alabama

- **Independent Baptist** university, founded 1841
- **Calendar** 4-1-4
- **Degrees** certificates, associate, bachelor's, master's, doctoral, first professional, and post-master's certificates
- **Suburban** 180-acre campus
- **Endowment** $210.0 million
- **Coed,** 2,882 undergraduate students, 93% full-time, 64% women, 36% men
- **Moderately difficult** entrance level, 90% of applicants were admitted

A Samford education is carefully crafted to provide personal empowerment, academic and career competency, social and civic responsibility, and ethical and spiritual strength. It is built around broadening international awareness and the development of transferable skills, such as computer familiarity in every academic major, to keep Samford graduates on the leading edge in a constantly changing career environment.

Undergraduates 2,666 full-time, 216 part-time. Students come from 41 states and territories, 54% are from out of state, 6% African American, 0.3% Asian American or Pacific Islander, 0.6% Hispanic American, 0.5% Native American, 0.4% international, 3% transferred in, 65% live on campus. *Retention:* 89% of 2002 full-time freshmen returned.

Freshmen *Admission:* 2,074 applied, 1,859 admitted, 684 enrolled. *Average high school GPA:* 3.63. *Test scores:* SAT verbal scores over 500: 85%; SAT math scores over 500: 83%; ACT scores over 18: 99%; SAT verbal scores over 600: 35%; SAT math scores over 600: 38%; ACT scores over 24: 64%; SAT verbal scores over 700: 10%; SAT math scores over 700: 6%; ACT scores over 30: 12%.

Faculty *Total:* 419, 63% full-time, 65% with terminal degrees. *Student/faculty ratio:* 13:1.

Majors Accounting; art; Asian studies; athletic training; biochemistry; biology/biological sciences; biology teacher education; business administration and management; cartography; chemistry; classical, ancient Mediterranean and Near Eastern studies and archaeology; classics and languages, literatures and linguistics; commercial and advertising art; community organization and advocacy; computer science; counseling psychology; criminal justice/law enforcement administration; dramatic/theatre arts; engineering physics; engineering related; English; English/language arts teacher education; environmental science; environmental studies; foreign languages and literatures; French; general studies; geography; German; health and physical education; history; history teacher education; human development and family studies; human nutrition; human resources management; interior design; international business/trade/commerce; international relations and affairs; journalism; kinesiology and exercise science; Latin; Latin American studies; marine biology and biological oceanography; mathematics; music performance; music teacher education; music theory and composition; nursing (registered nurse training); philosophy; philosophy and religious studies related; physical education teaching and coaching; physics; piano and organ; political science and government; pre-medical studies; psychology; public administration; religious/sacred music; religious studies; science teacher education; science, technology and society; social sciences; social science teacher education; sociology; Spanish; speech and rhetoric; speech teacher education; visual and performing arts related; voice and opera.

Academic Programs *Special study options:* accelerated degree program, adult/continuing education programs, advanced placement credit, cooperative education, double majors, honors programs, internships, off-campus study, part-time degree program, services for LD students, study abroad, summer session for credit. *ROTC:* Army (c), Air Force (b). *Unusual degree programs:* 3-2 engineering with The University of Alabama at Birmingham, Auburn University, Washington University in St. Louis, Mercer University.

Library Samford University Library plus 3 others with 439,760 titles, 3,724 serial subscriptions, 14,362 audiovisual materials, an OPAC, a Web page.

Computers on Campus 350 computers available on campus for general student use. A campuswide network can be accessed from student residence rooms. Internet access, at least one staffed computer lab available. Computer purchase or lease plan available.

Student Life *Housing:* on-campus residence required through sophomore year. *Options:* men-only, women-only, disabled students. Campus housing is university owned. Freshman campus housing is guaranteed. *Activities and organizations:* drama/theater group, student-run newspaper, radio station, choral group, marching band, student ministries, student government, student bar, national fraternities, national sororities. *Campus security:* 24-hour emergency response devices and patrols, student patrols, late-night transport/escort service. *Student services:* health clinic, personal/psychological counseling.

Athletics Member NCAA. All Division I except football (Division I-AA). *Intercollegiate sports:* baseball M(s), basketball M(s)/W(s), cross-country running M(s)/W(s), golf M(s)/W(s), soccer M(c)/W(s), softball W(s), tennis M(s)/W(s), track and field M(s)/W(s), volleyball W(s). *Intramural sports:* basketball M/W, bowling M/W, cheerleading M/W, football M/W, golf M/W, racquetball M/W, rock climbing M/W, soccer M/W, softball M/W, table tennis M/W, tennis M/W, ultimate Frisbee M(c)/W(c), volleyball M/W.

Standardized Tests *Required:* SAT I or ACT (for admission).

Costs (2003–04) *Comprehensive fee:* $18,398 includes full-time tuition ($13,154) and room and board ($5244). Full-time tuition and fees vary according to course load. Part-time tuition: $437 per semester hour. Part-time tuition and fees vary according to course load. *College room only:* $2554. Room and board charges vary according to board plan and housing facility. *Waivers:* employees or children of employees.

Financial Aid Of all full-time matriculated undergraduates who enrolled in 2002, 1,458 applied for aid, 1,092 were judged to have need, 260 had their need fully met. 399 Federal Work-Study jobs (averaging $1508). 504 state and other part-time jobs (averaging $642). In 2002, 974 non-need-based awards were made. *Average percent of need met:* 72%. *Average financial aid package:* $9708. *Average need-based loan:* $3538. *Average need-based gift aid:* $5717. *Average non-need-based aid:* $5796. *Average indebtedness upon graduation:* $15,863.

Applying *Options:* early admission, deferred entrance. *Application fee:* $25. *Required:* essay or personal statement, high school transcript, 1 letter of recommendation, leadership resumé. *Recommended:* interview. *Application deadline:* 8/1 (transfers).

Admissions Contact Dr. Phil Kimrey, Dean of Admissions and Financial Aid, Samford University, 800 Lakeshore Drive, Samford Hall, Birmingham, AL 35229-0002. *Phone:* 205-726-3673. *Toll-free phone:* 800-888-7218. *Fax:* 205-726-2171. *E-mail:* admiss@samford.edu.

■ *See page 2342 for a narrative description.*

SOUTHEASTERN BIBLE COLLEGE
Birmingham, Alabama

- **Independent nondenominational** 4-year, founded 1935
- **Calendar** semesters
- **Degrees** diplomas, associate, and bachelor's
- **Suburban** 10-acre campus
- **Endowment** $1.4 million
- **Coed,** 228 undergraduate students, 83% full-time, 38% women, 62% men
- **Moderately difficult** entrance level, 63% of applicants were admitted

Undergraduates 190 full-time, 38 part-time. Students come from 15 states and territories, 1 other country, 30% are from out of state, 14% African American, 0.9% Asian American or Pacific Islander, 0.4% Hispanic American, 0.9% international, 20% transferred in, 41% live on campus. *Retention:* 62% of 2002 full-time freshmen returned.

Freshmen *Admission:* 279 applied, 176 admitted, 45 enrolled. *Average high school GPA:* 3.17. *Test scores:* SAT verbal scores over 500: 80%; SAT math scores over 500: 80%; ACT scores over 18: 85%; ACT scores over 24: 25%; ACT scores over 30: 2%.

Faculty *Total:* 22, 55% full-time, 55% with terminal degrees. *Student/faculty ratio:* 13:1.

Majors Biblical studies; education; music; pastoral studies/counseling; religious education; religious/sacred music; religious studies; theology.

Academic Programs *Special study options:* academic remediation for entering students, adult/continuing education programs, advanced placement credit, external degree program, internships, part-time degree program, summer session for credit.

Library Gannett-Estes Library with 38,510 titles, 114 serial subscriptions, 1,862 audiovisual materials, an OPAC.

Computers on Campus 10 computers available on campus for general student use. Internet access, at least one staffed computer lab available.

Student Life *Housing:* on-campus residence required for freshman year. *Options:* men-only, women-only. Campus housing is university owned. Freshman applicants given priority for college housing. *Activities and organizations:* choral group, Student Council, Student Missions Fellowship, chorale. *Campus security:* 24-hour emergency response devices, student patrols. *Student services:* health clinic, personal/psychological counseling.

Athletics *Intramural sports:* basketball M/W, soccer M/W, table tennis M/W, volleyball M/W.

Standardized Tests *Required:* SAT I or ACT (for admission).

Costs (2004–05) *Comprehensive fee:* $11,440 includes full-time tuition ($7500), mandatory fees ($200), and room and board ($3740). Full-time tuition and fees vary according to course load. Part-time tuition: $250 per semester hour. Part-time tuition and fees vary according to course load. *Required fees:* $50 per term part-time. *Payment plan:* installment. *Waivers:* employees or children of employees.

Financial Aid Of all full-time matriculated undergraduates who enrolled in 2003, 193 applied for aid, 163 were judged to have need. 10 Federal Work-Study jobs (averaging $1200). 10 state and other part-time jobs (averaging $2000). *Average percent of need met:* 70%. *Average financial aid package:* $6457. *Average need-based loan:* $4250. *Average need-based gift aid:* $4000. *Average indebtedness upon graduation:* $20,000.

Applying *Options:* common application, deferred entrance. *Application fee:* $20. *Required:* essay or personal statement, high school transcript, minimum 2.0 GPA, 3 letters of recommendation. *Required for some:* interview. *Application deadlines:* 8/1 (freshmen), 8/1 (transfers). *Notification:* 9/1 (freshmen), 9/1 (transfers).

Admissions Contact Mr. Adam McClendon, Admissions Director, Southeastern Bible College, 3001 Highway 280 East, Birmingham, AL 35243. *Phone:* 205-970-9209. *Toll-free phone:* 800-749-8878. *Fax:* 205-970-9207. *E-mail:* amcclendon@sebc.edu.

SOUTHERN CHRISTIAN UNIVERSITY
Montgomery, Alabama

- **Independent** comprehensive, founded 1967, affiliated with Church of Christ
- **Calendar** semesters
- **Degrees** bachelor's, master's, doctoral, and first professional
- **Urban** 9-acre campus
- **Endowment** $174,505
- **Coed,** 338 undergraduate students, 98% full-time, 47% women, 53% men
- **Minimally difficult** entrance level

Undergraduates 330 full-time, 8 part-time. Students come from 48 states and territories, 75% are from out of state, 24% African American, 0.9% Asian American or Pacific Islander, 2% Hispanic American, 0.6% Native American. *Retention:* 85% of 2002 full-time freshmen returned.

Faculty *Total:* 75, 81% full-time, 100% with terminal degrees. *Student/faculty ratio:* 10:1.

Majors Biblical studies; business/corporate communications; human resources management; liberal arts and sciences/liberal studies; marriage and family therapy/counseling; pastoral studies/counseling; public administration and social service professions related.

Academic Programs *Special study options:* accelerated degree program, adult/continuing education programs, advanced placement credit, distance learning, double majors, external degree program, internships, part-time degree program, summer session for credit.

Library Southern Christian University Library with 75,000 titles, 700 serial subscriptions, 800 audiovisual materials, an OPAC, a Web page.

Computers on Campus 5 computers available on campus for general student use. A campuswide network can be accessed from off campus. Internet access, online (class) registration, at least one staffed computer lab available.

Student Life *Housing:* college housing not available. *Student services:* personal/psychological counseling.

Costs (2003–04) *Tuition:* $8640 full-time. Part-time tuition and fees vary according to course load. *Required fees:* $800 full-time. *Payment plan:* tuition prepayment. *Waivers:* senior citizens and employees or children of employees.

Financial Aid Of all full-time matriculated undergraduates who enrolled in 2002, 300 applied for aid, 270 were judged to have need, 250 had their need fully met. In 2002, 20 non-need-based awards were made. *Average percent of need met:* 85%. *Average financial aid package:* $8500. *Average need-based loan:* $5500. *Average need-based gift aid:* $6500. *Average non-need-based aid:* $4000. *Average indebtedness upon graduation:* $18,000.

Applying *Options:* common application. *Application fee:* $50. *Required:* high school transcript, minimum 2.0 GPA. *Application deadline:* rolling (freshmen), rolling (transfers).

Admissions Contact Mr. Rick Johnson, Director of Enrollment Management, Southern Christian University, 1200 Taylor Road, Montgomery, AL 36117. *Phone:* 334-387-3877 Ext. 213. *Toll-free phone:* 800-351-4040 Ext. 213. *E-mail:* admissions@southernchristian.edu.

■ See page 2404 for a narrative description.

SOUTH UNIVERSITY
Montgomery, Alabama

- **Proprietary** 4-year, founded 1887
- **Calendar** quarters
- **Degrees** associate and bachelor's
- **Urban** 4-acre campus
- **Coed, primarily women,** 363 undergraduate students, 61% full-time, 81% women, 19% men
- **Minimally difficult** entrance level, 89% of applicants were admitted

Undergraduates 221 full-time, 142 part-time. Students come from 1 other state, 0.1% from out of state, 73% African American, 0.8% Asian American or Pacific Islander, 0.3% Hispanic American, 18% transferred in. *Retention:* 20% of 2002 full-time freshmen returned.

Freshmen *Admission:* 70 applied, 62 admitted, 62 enrolled. *Average high school GPA:* 2.5.

Faculty *Total:* 32, 38% full-time, 13% with terminal degrees. *Student/faculty ratio:* 15:1.

Majors Accounting; business administration and management; health science; information science/studies; legal assistant/paralegal; legal studies; medical/clinical assistant; physical therapist assistant.

Academic Programs *Special study options:* academic remediation for entering students, double majors, internships, part-time degree program, summer session for credit.

Library South College Library with 5,000 titles, 43 serial subscriptions.

Computers on Campus 37 computers available on campus for general student use. Internet access, at least one staffed computer lab available.

Student Life *Housing:* college housing not available. *Campus security:* 24-hour emergency response devices, evening security guard.

Standardized Tests *Required:* CPT (for admission). *Required for some:* SAT I or ACT (for admission).

Costs (2003–04) *Tuition:* $10,185 full-time, $2695 per term part-time. Full-time tuition and fees vary according to course load and program. Part-time tuition and fees vary according to course load and program. *Payment plans:* installment, deferred payment. *Waivers:* employees or children of employees.

Financial Aid Of all full-time matriculated undergraduates who enrolled in 2002, 221 applied for aid, 210 were judged to have need. 22 Federal Work-Study jobs (averaging $1474). *Average percent of need met:* 40%. *Average financial aid package:* $5600. *Average need-based loan:* $2625. *Average need-based gift aid:* $3000. *Average indebtedness upon graduation:* $9600.

Applying *Application fee:* $25. *Required:* high school transcript, interview. *Required for some:* 3 letters of recommendation. *Application deadline:* rolling (freshmen), rolling (transfers). *Notification:* continuous (freshmen), continuous (transfers).

Admissions Contact Ms. Anna Pearson, Director of Admissions, South University, 5355 Vaughn Road, Montgomery, AL 36116-1120. *Phone:* 334-395-8800. *Fax:* 334-395-8800. *E-mail:* mtgadmis@southuniversity.edu.

■ See page 2420 for a narrative description.

SPRING HILL COLLEGE
Mobile, Alabama

- **Independent Roman Catholic (Jesuit)** comprehensive, founded 1830
- **Calendar** semesters
- **Degrees** certificates, associate, bachelor's, master's, and postbachelor's certificates
- **Suburban** 450-acre campus
- **Endowment** $24.8 million
- **Coed,** 1,211 undergraduate students, 86% full-time, 62% women, 38% men
- **Moderately difficult** entrance level, 80% of applicants were admitted

Undergraduates 1,043 full-time, 168 part-time. Students come from 35 states and territories, 11 other countries, 49% are from out of state, 15% African American, 2% Asian American or Pacific Islander, 6% Hispanic American, 0.8% Native American, 2% international, 4% transferred in, 68% live on campus. *Retention:* 80% of 2002 full-time freshmen returned.

Freshmen *Admission:* 1,122 applied, 892 admitted, 309 enrolled. *Average high school GPA:* 3.38. *Test scores:* SAT verbal scores over 500: 73%; SAT math scores

Spring Hill College (continued)
over 500: 73%; ACT scores over 18: 96%; SAT verbal scores over 600: 40%; SAT math scores over 600: 29%; ACT scores over 24: 50%; SAT verbal scores over 700: 4%; SAT math scores over 700: 3%; ACT scores over 30: 6%.

Faculty *Total:* 138, 48% full-time, 63% with terminal degrees. *Student/faculty ratio:* 13:1.

Majors Accounting; arts management; art therapy; biochemistry; biology/biological sciences; business administration and management; chemistry; communication and journalism related; computer and information sciences; dramatic/theatre arts; early childhood education; education; elementary education; engineering related; English; English language and literature related; environmental science; finance; fine/studio arts; general studies; graphic design; history; humanities; international business/trade/commerce; international relations and affairs; journalism; marine biology and biological oceanography; marketing/marketing management; mathematics; multi-/interdisciplinary studies related; nursing (registered nurse training); philosophy; political science and government; pre-dentistry studies; pre-medical studies; pre-veterinary studies; psychology; radio and television; secondary education; Spanish; theology.

Academic Programs *Special study options:* academic remediation for entering students, accelerated degree program, adult/continuing education programs, advanced placement credit, distance learning, double majors, honors programs, independent study, internships, off-campus study, part-time degree program, services for LD students, student-designed majors, study abroad, summer session for credit. *ROTC:* Army (c), Air Force (c). *Unusual degree programs:* 3-2 engineering with Marquette University, University of Alabama at Birmingham, University of Florida, Auburn University, Texas A & M University; accounting.

Library Thomas Byrne Memorial Library with 180,098 titles, 573 serial subscriptions, 757 audiovisual materials, an OPAC, a Web page.

Computers on Campus 141 computers available on campus for general student use. A campuswide network can be accessed from student residence rooms and from off campus. Internet access, at least one staffed computer lab available.

Student Life *Housing:* on-campus residence required through junior year. *Options:* coed, men-only, women-only. Campus housing is university owned. Freshman campus housing is guaranteed. *Activities and organizations:* drama/theater group, student-run newspaper, choral group, Student Government Association, Multicultural Student Union, Circle K, Campus Programming Board, Habitat for Humanity, national fraternities, national sororities. *Campus security:* 24-hour emergency response devices and patrols, late-night transport/escort service, controlled dormitory access. *Student services:* health clinic, personal/psychological counseling.

Athletics Member NAIA. *Intercollegiate sports:* baseball M(s), basketball M(s)/W(s), cross-country running M(s)/W(s), golf M(s)/W(s), soccer M(s)/W(s), softball W(s), swimming M(s)/W(s), tennis M(s)/W(s), volleyball W(s). *Intramural sports:* basketball M/W, cheerleading M(c)/W(c), crew M(c)/W(c), football M/W, golf M/W, lacrosse M(c), racquetball M/W, rugby M(c), soccer M/W, softball M/W, swimming M/W, ultimate Frisbee M(c)/W(c), volleyball M/W.

Standardized Tests *Required:* SAT I or ACT (for admission).

Costs (2003–04) *Comprehensive fee:* $25,868 includes full-time tuition ($17,830), mandatory fees ($1170), and room and board ($6868). Part-time tuition: $668 per semester hour. *Required fees:* $38 per semester hour part-time. *College room only:* $3466. Room and board charges vary according to board plan and housing facility. *Payment plan:* installment. *Waivers:* employees or children of employees.

Financial Aid Of all full-time matriculated undergraduates who enrolled in 2003, 850 applied for aid, 725 were judged to have need, 113 had their need fully met. 201 Federal Work-Study jobs (averaging $1245). 93 state and other part-time jobs (averaging $844). In 2003, 119 non-need-based awards were made. *Average percent of need met:* 79%. *Average financial aid package:* $16,836. *Average need-based loan:* $3835. *Average need-based gift aid:* $12,057. *Average non-need-based aid:* $7936. *Average indebtedness upon graduation:* $13,421.

Applying *Options:* common application, electronic application, early admission, deferred entrance. *Application fee:* $25. *Required:* essay or personal statement, high school transcript, 1 letter of recommendation. *Recommended:* minimum 2.5 GPA, interview. *Application deadlines:* 7/1 (freshmen), 8/10 (transfers). *Notification:* continuous (freshmen), continuous (transfers).

Admissions Contact Ms. Florence W. Hines, Dean of Enrollment Management and Communications, Spring Hill College, 4000 Dauphin Street, Mobile, AL 36608-1791. *Phone:* 251-380-3030. *Toll-free phone:* 800-SHC-6704. *Fax:* 251-460-2186. *E-mail:* admit@shc.edu.

STILLMAN COLLEGE
Tuscaloosa, Alabama

Admissions Contact Mr. Mason Bonner, Director of Admissions, Stillman College, PO Box 1430, 3600 Stillman Boulevard, Tuscaloosa, AL 35403. *Phone:* 205-366-8817. *Toll-free phone:* 800-841-5722.

TALLADEGA COLLEGE
Talladega, Alabama

- **Independent** 4-year, founded 1867
- **Calendar** semesters
- **Degree** bachelor's
- **Small-town** 130-acre campus with easy access to Birmingham
- **Endowment** $4.1 million
- **Coed,** 468 undergraduate students, 88% full-time, 62% women, 38% men
- **Minimally difficult** entrance level, 42% of applicants were admitted

Undergraduates 412 full-time, 56 part-time. Students come from 24 states and territories, 2 other countries, 39% are from out of state, 96% African American, 0.6% Hispanic American, 3% international, 77% live on campus. *Retention:* 56% of 2002 full-time freshmen returned.

Freshmen *Admission:* 1,923 applied, 812 admitted, 182 enrolled. *Average high school GPA:* 2.60. *Test scores:* SAT math scores over 500: 50%; ACT scores over 18: 41%; ACT scores over 24: 9%.

Faculty *Total:* 44, 89% full-time, 48% with terminal degrees. *Student/faculty ratio:* 11:1.

Majors Accounting; African-American/Black studies; biology/biological sciences; biology teacher education; business administration and management; chemistry; chemistry teacher education; computer science; economics; education; English; English/language arts teacher education; finance; French; French language teacher education; history; history teacher education; marketing research; mathematics; mathematics teacher education; music; music teacher education; physics; pre-dentistry studies; pre-law studies; pre-medical studies; psychology; public administration; science teacher education; social work; sociology; Spanish; voice and opera.

Academic Programs *Special study options:* academic remediation for entering students, adult/continuing education programs, cooperative education, double majors, independent study, internships, off-campus study, part-time degree program. *ROTC:* Army (c). *Unusual degree programs:* 3-2 engineering with Tuskegee University, Georgia Institute of Technology, Florida Agricultural and Mechanical University; nursing with Jacksonville State University; veterinary medicine, allied health with Tuskegee University.

Library Savery Library with 41,112 titles, 10,110 serial subscriptions, 362 audiovisual materials, an OPAC.

Computers on Campus 105 computers available on campus for general student use. A campuswide network can be accessed from student residence rooms and from off campus. Internet access, at least one staffed computer lab available.

Student Life *Housing options:* men-only, women-only. Campus housing is university owned. Freshman campus housing is guaranteed. *Activities and organizations:* choral group, Student Government Association, Crimson Ambassadors, Greek letter organizations, academic major clubs, religious based organizations, national fraternities, national sororities. *Campus security:* 24-hour patrols, late-night transport/escort service, campus police. *Student services:* health clinic, personal/psychological counseling.

Athletics *Intramural sports:* baseball M, basketball M/W, football M, softball M/W, volleyball W.

Standardized Tests *Required:* SAT I or ACT (for admission).

Costs (2003–04) *One-time required fee:* $250. *Comprehensive fee:* $11,548 includes full-time tuition ($6720), mandatory fees ($408), and room and board ($4420). Full-time tuition and fees vary according to course load. Part-time tuition: $280 per credit hour. Part-time tuition and fees vary according to course load. *Required fees:* $204 per term part-time. *College room only:* $1760. *Payment plan:* deferred payment. *Waivers:* employees or children of employees.

Financial Aid Of all full-time matriculated undergraduates who enrolled in 2003, 407 applied for aid, 375 were judged to have need, 100 had their need fully met. 141 Federal Work-Study jobs (averaging $691). *Average percent of need met:* 90%. *Average financial aid package:* $5000. *Average need-based loan:* $5335. *Average need-based gift aid:* $3025. *Average non-need-based aid:* $5774. *Average indebtedness upon graduation:* $12,790. *Financial aid deadline:* 6/30.

Applying *Options:* common application, electronic application, early admission, deferred entrance. *Application fee:* $25. *Required:* essay or personal statement, high school transcript, minimum 2.0 GPA, 1 letter of recommendation. *Application deadline:* rolling (freshmen), rolling (transfers). *Notification:* continuous (transfers).

Admissions Contact Mr. Richard Blanks, Director of Admissions, Talladega College, 627 West Battle Street, Talladega, AL 35160. *Phone:* 256-761-6219. *Toll-free phone:* 800-762-2468 (in-state); 800-633-2440 (out-of-state). *Fax:* 205-362-0274. *E-mail:* rblanks@talladega.edu.

■ *See page 2482 for a narrative description.*

TROY STATE UNIVERSITY
Troy, Alabama

- **State-supported** comprehensive, founded 1887, part of Troy State University System
- **Calendar** semesters
- **Degrees** associate, bachelor's, master's, and post-master's certificates
- **Small-town** 577-acre campus
- **Endowment** $22.0 million
- **Coed,** 5,205 undergraduate students, 80% full-time, 59% women, 41% men
- **Moderately difficult** entrance level, 67% of applicants were admitted

Undergraduates 4,156 full-time, 1,049 part-time. Students come from 56 states and territories, 59 other countries, 13% are from out of state, 26% African American, 0.5% Asian American or Pacific Islander, 0.9% Hispanic American, 0.5% Native American, 6% international, 6% transferred in, 34% live on campus. *Retention:* 74% of 2002 full-time freshmen returned.

Freshmen *Admission:* 3,507 applied, 2,335 admitted, 1,007 enrolled. *Average high school GPA:* 3.21. *Test scores:* ACT scores over 18: 73%; ACT scores over 24: 24%; ACT scores over 30: 3%.

Faculty *Total:* 498, 48% full-time. *Student/faculty ratio:* 20:1.

Majors Accounting; art; art history, criticism and conservation; art teacher education; athletic training; biology/biological sciences; broadcast journalism; business administration and management; business/commerce; business teacher education; chemistry; computer and information sciences; corrections; dramatic/theatre arts; education; elementary education; English; environmental science; finance; fine/studio arts; health teacher education; history; journalism; kindergarten/preschool education; management information systems; marine biology and biological oceanography; marketing related; mathematics; music teacher education; nursing (registered nurse training); parks, recreation and leisure; physical education teaching and coaching; physical sciences; political science and government; pre-dentistry studies; pre-medical studies; pre-veterinary studies; psychology; science teacher education; secondary education; social sciences; social work; sociology; special education; speech and rhetoric.

Academic Programs *Special study options:* academic remediation for entering students, accelerated degree program, adult/continuing education programs, advanced placement credit, distance learning, double majors, English as a second language, honors programs, independent study, internships, part-time degree program, services for LD students, student-designed majors, summer session for credit. *ROTC:* Army (b), Air Force (b).

Library Wallace Library with 389,524 titles, 2,692 serial subscriptions, an OPAC, a Web page.

Computers on Campus 487 computers available on campus for general student use. A campuswide network can be accessed from student residence rooms and from off campus. Internet access, at least one staffed computer lab available.

Student Life *Housing:* on-campus residence required for freshman year. *Options:* coed, men-only, women-only. Campus housing is university owned. *Activities and organizations:* drama/theater group, student-run newspaper, television station, choral group, marching band, University band, University choir, yearbook, University Activities Council, national fraternities, national sororities. *Campus security:* 24-hour patrols, student patrols, late-night transport/escort service, controlled dormitory access. *Student services:* health clinic, personal/psychological counseling, women's center.

Athletics Member NCAA. All Division I. *Intercollegiate sports:* baseball M(s), basketball M(s)/W(s), cross-country running M(s)/W(s), football M(s), golf M(s)/W(s), soccer W(s), softball W(s), tennis M(s)/W(s), track and field M(s)/W(s), volleyball W(s). *Intramural sports:* basketball M/W, bowling M/W, cross-country running M, football M/W, golf M/W, soccer M, softball M/W, swimming M/W, tennis M/W, track and field M, volleyball M/W.

Standardized Tests *Required:* SAT I or ACT (for admission).

Costs (2003–04) *Tuition:* state resident $3530 full-time, $149 per credit hour part-time; nonresident $7060 full-time, $298 per credit hour part-time. *Required fees:* $312 full-time, $13 per credit hour part-time. *Room and board:* $4580; room only: $2240. Room and board charges vary according to board plan and housing facility. *Payment plan:* installment. *Waivers:* employees or children of employees.

Financial Aid Of all full-time matriculated undergraduates who enrolled in 2003, 3,939 applied for aid, 3,939 were judged to have need. *Average percent of need met:* 58%. *Average financial aid package:* $9000. *Average need-based loan:* $4000. *Average need-based gift aid:* $5000. *Average indebtedness upon graduation:* $17,125.

Applying *Options:* deferred entrance. *Application fee:* $20. *Required:* high school transcript. *Recommended:* interview. *Application deadline:* rolling (freshmen), rolling (transfers).

Admissions Contact Mr. Buddy Starling, Dean of Enrollment Management, Troy State University, Adams Administration Building, Room 134, Troy, AL 36082. *Phone:* 334-670-3243. *Toll-free phone:* 800-551-9716. *Fax:* 334-670-3733. *E-mail:* bstar@trojan.troyst.edu.

■ *See page 2532 for a narrative description.*

TROY STATE UNIVERSITY DOTHAN
Dothan, Alabama

- **State-supported** comprehensive, founded 1961, part of Troy State University System
- **Calendar** semesters
- **Degrees** associate, bachelor's, master's, and post-master's certificates
- **Small-town** 250-acre campus
- **Coed,** 1,581 undergraduate students, 50% full-time, 65% women, 35% men
- **Minimally difficult** entrance level, 70% of applicants were admitted

Undergraduates 792 full-time, 789 part-time. Students come from 7 states and territories, 7% are from out of state, 21% African American, 2% Asian American or Pacific Islander, 2% Hispanic American, 1% Native American, 25% transferred in. *Retention:* 67% of 2002 full-time freshmen returned.

Freshmen *Admission:* 139 applied, 97 admitted, 77 enrolled. *Average high school GPA:* 3.31. *Test scores:* ACT scores over 18: 100%; ACT scores over 24: 19%.

Faculty *Total:* 121, 49% full-time, 50% with terminal degrees. *Student/faculty ratio:* 15:1.

Majors Biology/biological sciences; business administration and management; business, management, and marketing related; computer and information sciences; criminal justice/safety; educational administration and supervision related; elementary education; English; history; human resources management; kindergarten/preschool education; liberal arts and sciences and humanities related; mathematics; physical sciences; psychology; science teacher education; secondary education; social and philosophical foundations of education; social sciences; sociology.

Academic Programs *Special study options:* academic remediation for entering students, advanced placement credit, cooperative education, distance learning, double majors, independent study, internships, part-time degree program, services for LD students, summer session for credit.

Library Troy State University Dotham Library with 101,136 titles, 455 serial subscriptions, 14,282 audiovisual materials, an OPAC, a Web page.

Computers on Campus 120 computers available on campus for general student use. A campuswide network can be accessed. Internet access, at least one staffed computer lab available.

Student Life *Housing:* college housing not available. *Activities and organizations:* Creative Writing Club, American Marketing Association, Alpha Upsilon Alpha, Gamma Beta Phi, Delta Mu Delta. *Campus security:* 24-hour patrols. *Student services:* personal/psychological counseling.

Standardized Tests *Required for some:* SAT I or ACT (for admission).

Costs (2003–04) *Tuition:* state resident $3530 full-time, $149 per credit hour part-time; nonresident $7060 full-time, $298 per credit hour part-time. *Required fees:* $312 full-time, $312 per year part-time. *Payment plans:* installment, deferred payment. *Waivers:* employees or children of employees.

Financial Aid Of all full-time matriculated undergraduates who enrolled in 2002, 682 applied for aid, 682 were judged to have need, 682 had their need fully met. 21 Federal Work-Study jobs (averaging $2140). *Average percent of need met:* 55%. *Average need-based loan:* $4281. *Average need-based gift aid:* $3174. *Average indebtedness upon graduation:* $6038.

Applying *Options:* common application, electronic application, deferred entrance. *Application fee:* $20. *Required:* high school transcript, minimum 2.0 GPA. *Recommended:* minimum 3.0 GPA. *Application deadline:* rolling (freshmen), rolling (transfers). *Notification:* continuous (freshmen), continuous (transfers).

Admissions Contact Mr. Andrew Rivers, Coordinator, Undergraduate Admissions, Troy State University Dothan, PO Box 8368, Dothan, AL 36303. *Phone:* 334-983-6556 Ext. 231. *Fax:* 334-983-6322. *E-mail:* rwillis@troyst.edu.

TROY STATE UNIVERSITY MONTGOMERY
Montgomery, Alabama

- **State-supported** comprehensive, founded 1965, part of Troy State University System
- **Calendar** semesters
- **Degrees** associate, bachelor's, master's, and post-master's certificates
- **Urban** 6-acre campus
- **Coed,** 3,182 undergraduate students, 34% full-time, 69% women, 31% men
- **Noncompetitive** entrance level, 99% of applicants were admitted

Troy State University Montgomery (continued)

Undergraduates 1,087 full-time, 2,095 part-time. 53% African American, 1% Asian American or Pacific Islander, 1% Hispanic American, 0.3% Native American.

Freshmen *Admission:* 553 applied, 550 admitted, 266 enrolled.

Faculty *Total:* 198, 18% full-time, 41% with terminal degrees.

Majors Accounting; business administration and management; business/commerce; computer and information sciences; English; finance; history; human resources management; liberal arts and sciences and humanities related; marketing research; mathematics; political science and government; psychology; social sciences.

Academic Programs *Special study options:* academic remediation for entering students, accelerated degree program, adult/continuing education programs, advanced placement credit, distance learning, double majors, external degree program, honors programs, independent study, part-time degree program, services for LD students, student-designed majors, summer session for credit. *ROTC:* Army (c), Air Force (c).

Library Rosa L. Parks Library and Museum with 26,041 titles, 476 serial subscriptions, 9,194 audiovisual materials, an OPAC, a Web page.

Computers on Campus 248 computers available on campus for general student use. A campuswide network can be accessed from off campus. Internet access, online (class) registration, at least one staffed computer lab available.

Student Life *Housing:* college housing not available. *Campus security:* 24-hour emergency response devices, late-night transport/escort service, evening patrols by security.

Standardized Tests *Required:* SAT I (for placement). *Recommended:* ACT (for placement).

Costs (2003–04) *Tuition:* state resident $3530 full-time, $149 per semester hour part-time; nonresident $7060 full-time, $298 per semester hour part-time. *Required fees:* $70 full-time, $35 per semester part-time. *Payment plan:* installment. *Waivers:* employees or children of employees.

Financial Aid Of all full-time matriculated undergraduates who enrolled in 2002, 685 applied for aid, 685 were judged to have need. *Average financial aid package:* $3512. *Average need-based loan:* $3706. *Average need-based gift aid:* $3235.

Applying *Options:* electronic application, early admission, deferred entrance. *Application fee:* $20. *Required:* high school transcript, minimum 2.0 GPA. *Application deadline:* rolling (freshmen), rolling (transfers).

Admissions Contact Mr. Larry Hawkins, Director of Enrollment Management, Troy State University Montgomery, PO Drawer 4419, Montgomery, AL 36103-4419. *Phone:* 334-241-9506. *Toll-free phone:* 800-355-TSUM. *E-mail:* admit@tsum.edu.

TUSKEGEE UNIVERSITY

Tuskegee, Alabama

- **Independent** comprehensive, founded 1881
- **Calendar** semesters
- **Degrees** bachelor's, master's, doctoral, and first professional
- **Small-town** 4390-acre campus
- **Coed,** 2,804 undergraduate students, 96% full-time, 63% women, 37% men
- **Moderately difficult** entrance level, 81% of applicants were admitted

Undergraduates 2,689 full-time, 115 part-time. Students come from 42 states and territories, 35 other countries, 57% are from out of state, 76% African American, 0.1% Asian American or Pacific Islander, 0.1% Hispanic American, 0.1% Native American, 0.8% international, 1% transferred in, 63% live on campus. *Retention:* 71% of 2002 full-time freshmen returned.

Freshmen *Admission:* 1,326 applied, 1,068 admitted, 518 enrolled. *Average high school GPA:* 3.20. *Test scores:* SAT verbal scores over 500: 22%; SAT math scores over 500: 29%; ACT scores over 18: 60%; SAT verbal scores over 600: 5%; SAT math scores over 600: 6%; ACT scores over 24: 10%; SAT verbal scores over 700: 1%; SAT math scores over 700: 3%; ACT scores over 30: 1%.

Faculty *Total:* 250, 87% full-time, 65% with terminal degrees. *Student/faculty ratio:* 12:1.

Majors Accounting; aerospace, aeronautical and astronautical engineering; agricultural business and management; agriculture; agronomy and crop science; animal sciences; architecture; biology/biological sciences; building/home/construction inspection; business administration and management; chemical engineering; chemistry; clinical laboratory science/medical technology; computer science; construction engineering technology; dietetics; economics; electrical, electronics and communications engineering; elementary education; engineering technology; English; environmental studies; finance; food science; foods, nutrition, and wellness; history; hospitality administration; hospitality and recreation marketing; management science; marketing/marketing management; mathematics; mechanical engineering; natural resources management and policy; nursing (registered nurse training); occupational therapy; physics; plant sciences; political science and government; poultry science; psychology; sales, distribution and marketing; social work; sociology.

Academic Programs *Special study options:* academic remediation for entering students, cooperative education, English as a second language, honors programs, internships, off-campus study, part-time degree program, summer session for credit. *ROTC:* Army (b), Air Force (b). *Unusual degree programs:* 3-2 forestry with Auburn University, Iowa State University of Science and Technology, University of Michigan, Idaho State University.

Library Hollis B. Frissell Library plus 3 others with 623,824 titles, 81,157 serial subscriptions, an OPAC.

Computers on Campus 1000 computers available on campus for general student use. A campuswide network can be accessed from student residence rooms and from off campus. Internet access, online (class) registration, at least one staffed computer lab available.

Student Life *Housing:* on-campus residence required through sophomore year. *Options:* Freshman applicants given priority for college housing. *Activities and organizations:* drama/theater group, student-run newspaper, choral group, marching band, national fraternities, national sororities. *Campus security:* 24-hour emergency response devices and patrols, late-night transport/escort service. *Student services:* health clinic, personal/psychological counseling.

Athletics Member NCAA. All Division II. *Intercollegiate sports:* baseball M(s), basketball M(s)/W(s), cross-country running M/W, football M(s), golf M(s), riflery M/W, soccer M, tennis M(s)/W(s), track and field M(s)/W(s), volleyball W(s). *Intramural sports:* badminton M/W, basketball M/W, football M, golf M, gymnastics M/W, riflery M/W, soccer M, swimming M/W, tennis M/W, track and field M/W, volleyball M/W.

Standardized Tests *Required:* SAT I or ACT (for admission).

Costs (2003–04) *Comprehensive fee:* $17,250 includes full-time tuition ($11,060), mandatory fees ($250), and room and board ($5940). Full-time tuition and fees vary according to course load and program. Part-time tuition: $450 per credit hour. Part-time tuition and fees vary according to course load and program. *Required fees:* $125 per term part-time. *Room and board:* Room and board charges vary according to housing facility. *Payment plan:* installment. *Waivers:* employees or children of employees.

Financial Aid Of all full-time matriculated undergraduates who enrolled in 2002, 2,519 applied for aid, 2,142 were judged to have need, 1,379 had their need fully met. 525 Federal Work-Study jobs (averaging $1879). 425 state and other part-time jobs (averaging $4739). *Average percent of need met:* 85%. *Average financial aid package:* $13,824. *Average need-based loan:* $6006. *Average need-based gift aid:* $8000. *Average non-need-based aid:* $6000. *Average indebtedness upon graduation:* $30,000.

Applying *Options:* electronic application, early admission. *Application fee:* $25. *Required:* high school transcript, minimum 2.0 GPA. *Application deadlines:* 4/15 (freshmen), 4/15 (transfers).

Admissions Contact Ms. Iolantha E. Spencer, Admissions, Tuskegee University, 102 Old Administration Building, Tuskegee, AL 36088. *Phone:* 334-727-8500. *Toll-free phone:* 800-622-6531.

THE UNIVERSITY OF ALABAMA

Tuscaloosa, Alabama

- **State-supported** university, founded 1831, part of The University of Alabama System
- **Calendar** semesters
- **Degrees** certificates, bachelor's, master's, doctoral, first professional, post-master's, and postbachelor's certificates
- **Suburban** 1000-acre campus with easy access to Birmingham
- **Endowment** $301.6 million
- **Coed,** 15,889 undergraduate students, 90% full-time, 54% women, 46% men
- **Moderately difficult** entrance level, 87% of applicants were admitted

Undergraduates 14,270 full-time, 1,619 part-time. Students come from 52 states and territories, 92 other countries, 20% are from out of state, 14% African American, 1% Asian American or Pacific Islander, 1% Hispanic American, 0.6% Native American, 1% international, 8% transferred in, 24% live on campus. *Retention:* 84% of 2002 full-time freshmen returned.

Freshmen *Admission:* 8,298 applied, 7,194 admitted, 3,077 enrolled. *Average high school GPA:* 3.33. *Test scores:* SAT verbal scores over 500: 78%; SAT math scores over 500: 76%; ACT scores over 18: 97%; SAT verbal scores over 600: 30%; SAT math scores over 600: 29%; ACT scores over 24: 46%; SAT verbal scores over 700: 8%; SAT math scores over 700: 6%; ACT scores over 30: 6%.

Faculty *Total:* 1,084, 83% full-time, 88% with terminal degrees. *Student/faculty ratio:* 19:1.

Majors Accounting; advertising; aerospace, aeronautical and astronautical engineering; American studies; anthropology; apparel and textiles; art history, criticism and conservation; athletic training; audiology and speech-language pathology; biological and physical sciences; biology/biological sciences; business administration and management; business/managerial economics; chemical engineering; chemistry; civil engineering; classics and languages, literatures and linguistics; computer and information sciences; consumer economics; criminal justice/safety; dance; dramatic/theatre arts; electrical, electronics and communications engineering; elementary education; English; family and consumer sciences/human sciences; family and consumer sciences/human sciences related; finance; fine/studio arts; foods, nutrition, and wellness; French; geography; geology/earth science; German; health professions related; history; hospital and health care facilities administration; hotel/motel administration; human development and family studies; industrial engineering; interdisciplinary studies; interior design; international relations and affairs; journalism; kindergarten/preschool education; Latin American studies; management information systems; management science; marine biology and biological oceanography; marketing/marketing management; mathematics; mechanical engineering; medical microbiology and bacteriology; metallurgical engineering; music; music teacher education; nursing (registered nurse training); philosophy; physical education teaching and coaching; physics; political science and government; psychology; public relations/image management; radio and television; religious studies; Russian; secondary education; social work; sociology; Spanish; special education; speech and rhetoric.

Academic Programs *Special study options:* academic remediation for entering students, accelerated degree program, adult/continuing education programs, advanced placement credit, cooperative education, distance learning, double majors, English as a second language, external degree program, freshman honors college, honors programs, independent study, internships, off-campus study, part-time degree program, services for LD students, student-designed majors, study abroad, summer session for credit. *ROTC:* Army (b), Air Force (b).

Library Amelia Gayle Gorgas Library plus 8 others with 2.3 million titles, 16,590 serial subscriptions, 495,484 audiovisual materials, an OPAC, a Web page.

Computers on Campus 2000 computers available on campus for general student use. A campuswide network can be accessed from student residence rooms and from off campus. Internet access, at least one staffed computer lab available.

Student Life *Housing:* on-campus residence required for freshman year. *Options:* coed, men-only, women-only, disabled students. Campus housing is university owned. Freshman applicants given priority for college housing. *Activities and organizations:* drama/theater group, student-run newspaper, radio and television station, choral group, marching band, Coordinating Council of Student Organizations, Residence Hall Association, International Student Association, Student Government Association, African-American Association, national fraternities, national sororities. *Campus security:* 24-hour emergency response devices and patrols, student patrols, late-night transport/escort service, controlled dormitory access, crime prevention programs, community police protection. *Student services:* health clinic, personal/psychological counseling, women's center, legal services.

Athletics Member NCAA. All Division I except football (Division I-A). *Intercollegiate sports:* baseball M(s), basketball M(s)/W(s), cross-country running M(s)/W(s), golf M(s)/W(s), gymnastics W(s), soccer W(s), softball W(s), swimming M(s)/W(s), tennis M(s)/W(s), track and field M(s)/W(s), volleyball W(s). *Intramural sports:* badminton M/W, basketball M/W, bowling M/W, cheerleading M/W, crew M(c)/W(c), football M/W, golf M/W, lacrosse M(c), racquetball M(c)/W(c), rugby M(c), soccer M/W, softball M/W, squash M/W, table tennis M/W, tennis M(c)/W(c), track and field M/W, ultimate Frisbee M(c)/W(c), volleyball M/W, water polo M(c)/W(c), wrestling M(c).

Standardized Tests *Required:* SAT I or ACT (for admission).

Costs (2003–04) *Tuition:* state resident $4134 full-time, $172 per credit hour part-time; nonresident $11,294 full-time, $471 per credit hour part-time. Full-time tuition and fees vary according to course load. Part-time tuition and fees vary according to course load. *Room and board:* $4906; room only: $2788. Room and board charges vary according to board plan and housing facility. *Payment plans:* installment, deferred payment. *Waivers:* employees or children of employees.

Financial Aid Of all full-time matriculated undergraduates who enrolled in 2002, 10,142 applied for aid, 5,394 were judged to have need, 1,029 had their need fully met. 700 Federal Work-Study jobs (averaging $3100). 1,500 state and other part-time jobs (averaging $4000). In 2002, 3843 non-need-based awards were made. *Average percent of need met:* 71%. *Average financial aid package:* $7549. *Average need-based loan:* $3931. *Average need-based gift aid:* $3355. *Average non-need-based aid:* $4126. *Average indebtedness upon graduation:* $19,319.

Applying *Options:* common application, electronic application, early admission, deferred entrance. *Application fee:* $25. *Required:* high school transcript, minimum 2.0 GPA. *Required for some:* interview. *Application deadline:* 8/1 (freshmen). *Notification:* 9/1 (freshmen), continuous (transfers).

Admissions Contact Ms. Mary K. Spiegel, Director of Admissions, The University of Alabama, Box 870132, 203 Student services Center, Tuscaloosa, AL 35487-0132. *Phone:* 205-348-5666. *Toll-free phone:* 800-933-BAMA. *Fax:* 205-348-9046. *E-mail:* admissions@ua.edu.

THE UNIVERSITY OF ALABAMA AT BIRMINGHAM

Birmingham, Alabama

- **State-supported** university, founded 1969, part of University of Alabama System
- **Calendar** semesters
- **Degrees** certificates, bachelor's, master's, doctoral, first professional, post-master's, and postbachelor's certificates
- **Urban** 265-acre campus
- **Endowment** $239.8 million
- **Coed,** 11,046 undergraduate students, 70% full-time, 60% women, 40% men
- **Moderately difficult** entrance level, 81% of applicants were admitted

Undergraduates 7,723 full-time, 3,323 part-time. Students come from 39 states and territories, 80 other countries, 6% are from out of state, 32% African American, 3% Asian American or Pacific Islander, 1% Hispanic American, 0.5% Native American, 4% international, 9% transferred in, 11% live on campus. *Retention:* 75% of 2002 full-time freshmen returned.

Freshmen *Admission:* 4,710 applied, 3,807 admitted, 1,708 enrolled. *Average high school GPA:* 3.18. *Test scores:* ACT scores over 18: 85%; ACT scores over 24: 30%; ACT scores over 30: 5%.

Faculty *Total:* 881, 89% full-time, 87% with terminal degrees. *Student/faculty ratio:* 18:1.

Majors Accounting; African-American/Black studies; anthropology; biological and physical sciences; biology/biological sciences; biomedical/medical engineering; business administration and management; business/managerial economics; chemistry; civil engineering; clinical laboratory science/medical technology; communication/speech communication and rhetoric; computer and information sciences; corrections and criminal justice related; cytotechnology; electrical, electronics and communications engineering; elementary education; English; finance; fine/studio arts; French; health information/medical records administration; health teacher education; history; kindergarten/preschool education; management information systems; marketing/marketing management; materials engineering; mathematics; mechanical engineering; medical radiologic technology; music; nuclear medical technology; nursing (registered nurse training); philosophy; physical education teaching and coaching; physician assistant; physics; political science and government; psychology; respiratory care therapy; secondary education; social sciences related; social work; sociology; Spanish; special education; visual and performing arts.

Academic Programs *Special study options:* academic remediation for entering students, adult/continuing education programs, advanced placement credit, cooperative education, double majors, honors programs, independent study, internships, off-campus study, part-time degree program, services for LD students, student-designed majors, study abroad, summer session for credit. *ROTC:* Army (b), Air Force (c). *Unusual degree programs:* 3-2 accounting.

Library Mervyn Sterne Library plus 1 other with 853,445 titles, 3,934 serial subscriptions, 78,017 audiovisual materials, an OPAC, a Web page.

Computers on Campus 400 computers available on campus for general student use. A campuswide network can be accessed from off campus. Internet access, online (class) registration, at least one staffed computer lab available.

Student Life *Housing options:* coed, women-only. Campus housing is university owned and is provided by a third party. *Activities and organizations:* drama/theater group, student-run newspaper, radio station, choral group, marching band, campus ministries, service-oriented groups, sports-affiliated groups, national fraternities, national sororities. *Campus security:* 24-hour emergency response devices and patrols, late-night transport/escort service, controlled dormitory access. *Student services:* health clinic, personal/psychological counseling, women's center.

Athletics Member NCAA. All Division I except football (Division I-A). *Intercollegiate sports:* baseball M(s), basketball M(s)/W(s), cross-country running W(s), golf M(s)/W(s), riflery M/W, soccer M(s)/W(s), softball W(s), swimming W(s), tennis M(s)/W(s), track and field W(s), volleyball W(s). *Intramural sports:* badminton M/W, baseball M, basketball M/W, bowling M/W, football M/W, golf M/W, racquetball M/W, soccer M/W, softball M/W, swimming M/W, table tennis M/W, tennis M/W, track and field M/W, ultimate Frisbee M/W, volleyball M/W, wrestling M.

Standardized Tests *Required:* SAT I or ACT (for admission).

Costs (2003–04) *Tuition:* state resident $3480 full-time, $116 per hour part-time; nonresident $8700 full-time, $290 per hour part-time. Full-time tuition and fees vary according to program. Part-time tuition and fees vary according to program. *Required fees:* $794 full-time. *Room only:* $2588. *Waivers:* employees or children of employees.

Financial Aid Of all full-time matriculated undergraduates who enrolled in 2003, 5,544 applied for aid, 4,101 were judged to have need, 527 had their need fully met. In 2003, 1654 non-need-based awards were made. *Average percent of*

The University of Alabama at Birmingham (continued)
need met: 43%. *Average financial aid package:* $8536. *Average need-based loan:* $4101. *Average need-based gift aid:* $3336. *Average non-need-based aid:* $5455. *Average indebtedness upon graduation:* $18,299.

Applying *Options:* early admission, deferred entrance. *Application fee:* $25. *Required:* high school transcript, minimum 2.0 GPA. *Application deadlines:* 7/1 (freshmen), 7/15 (transfers). *Notification:* continuous (freshmen), continuous (transfers).

Admissions Contact Ms. Chenise Ryan, Director of Undergraduate Admissions, The University of Alabama at Birmingham, Office of Undergraduate Admissions, HUC 260, 1530 3rd Avenue South, Birmingham, AL 35294-1150. *Phone:* 205-934-8221. *Toll-free phone:* 800-421-8743. *Fax:* 205-975-7114. *E-mail:* UndergradAdmit@uab.edu.

■ *See page 2564 for a narrative description.*

THE UNIVERSITY OF ALABAMA IN HUNTSVILLE
Huntsville, Alabama

- **State-supported** university, founded 1950, part of University of Alabama System
- **Calendar** semesters
- **Degrees** bachelor's, master's, doctoral, post-master's, and postbachelor's certificates
- **Suburban** 376-acre campus
- **Endowment** $18.9 million
- **Coed,** 5,481 undergraduate students, 71% full-time, 49% women, 51% men
- **Moderately difficult** entrance level, 88% of applicants were admitted

Undergraduates 3,873 full-time, 1,608 part-time. Students come from 45 states and territories, 55 other countries, 14% are from out of state, 14% African American, 4% Asian American or Pacific Islander, 2% Hispanic American, 2% Native American, 3% international, 12% transferred in, 17% live on campus. *Retention:* 76% of 2002 full-time freshmen returned.

Freshmen *Admission:* 1,785 applied, 1,563 admitted, 798 enrolled. *Average high school GPA:* 3.40. *Test scores:* SAT verbal scores over 500: 83%; SAT math scores over 500: 82%; ACT scores over 18: 100%; SAT verbal scores over 600: 38%; SAT math scores over 600: 37%; ACT scores over 24: 60%; SAT verbal scores over 700: 8%; SAT math scores over 700: 7%; ACT scores over 30: 9%.

Faculty *Total:* 447, 62% full-time, 71% with terminal degrees. *Student/faculty ratio:* 16:1.

Majors Accounting; art; biology/biological sciences; business administration and management; chemical engineering; chemistry; civil engineering; computer and information sciences; computer engineering; electrical, electronics and communications engineering; elementary education; engineering related; English; finance; foreign languages and literatures; history; industrial engineering; management information systems; marketing/marketing management; mathematics; mechanical engineering; music; nursing (registered nurse training); philosophy; physics; political science and government; psychology; sociology; speech and rhetoric.

Academic Programs *Special study options:* academic remediation for entering students, accelerated degree program, adult/continuing education programs, advanced placement credit, cooperative education, distance learning, double majors, English as a second language, honors programs, independent study, internships, off-campus study, part-time degree program, services for LD students, summer session for credit. *ROTC:* Army (c). *Unusual degree programs:* 3-2 engineering with Morris Brown College, Oakwood College, Moorehouse College, Clark Atlanta University, Fisk University.

Library University of Alabama in Huntsville Library with 277,878 titles, 1,120 serial subscriptions, 2,677 audiovisual materials, an OPAC, a Web page.

Computers on Campus 960 computers available on campus for general student use. A campuswide network can be accessed from student residence rooms and from off campus. Internet access, online (class) registration, at least one staffed computer lab available.

Student Life *Housing options:* coed. Campus housing is university owned. *Activities and organizations:* drama/theater group, student-run newspaper, choral group, Student Government Association, Association for Campus Entertainment, Circle K International, Anointed Voices, Institute of Electrical and Electronic Engineers, national fraternities, national sororities. *Campus security:* 24-hour emergency response devices and patrols, late-night transport/escort service, controlled dormitory access. *Student services:* health clinic, personal/psychological counseling.

Athletics Member NCAA. All Division II except ice hockey (Division I). *Intercollegiate sports:* baseball M(s), basketball M(s)/W(s), bowling M(c)/W(c), cross-country running M(s)/W(s), ice hockey M(s), soccer M(s)/W(s), softball W, tennis M(s)/W(s), track and field M/W, volleyball W(s). *Intramural sports:* badminton M/W, basketball M/W, crew M(c)/W(c), football M/W, soccer M/W, softball M/W, ultimate Frisbee M/W, volleyball M/W.

Standardized Tests *Required:* SAT I or ACT (for admission).

Costs (2003–04) *Tuition:* $926 per term part-time; state resident $4126 full-time, $926 per term part-time; nonresident $8702 full-time, $1945 per term part-time. Full-time tuition and fees vary according to course load. Part-time tuition and fees vary according to course load. *Room and board:* $5000; room only: $3400. Room and board charges vary according to board plan and housing facility. *Payment plan:* deferred payment. *Waivers:* employees or children of employees.

Financial Aid Of all full-time matriculated undergraduates who enrolled in 2003, 3,041 applied for aid, 1,682 were judged to have need, 266 had their need fully met. 142 Federal Work-Study jobs (averaging $1760). In 2003, 852 non-need-based awards were made. *Average percent of need met:* 53%. *Average financial aid package:* $5560. *Average need-based loan:* $3493. *Average need-based gift aid:* $3165. *Average non-need-based aid:* $2070. *Average indebtedness upon graduation:* $17,058. *Financial aid deadline:* 7/31.

Applying *Options:* common application, electronic application, early admission, deferred entrance. *Application fee:* $20. *Required:* high school transcript. *Application deadline:* 8/15 (freshmen). *Notification:* continuous (freshmen), continuous (transfers).

Admissions Contact Ms. Ginger Reed, Senior Associate Director of Admissions, The University of Alabama in Huntsville, 301 Sparkman Drive, Huntsville, AL 35899. *Phone:* 256-824-6070. *Toll-free phone:* 800-UAH-CALL. *Fax:* 256-824-6073. *E-mail:* admitme@email.uah.edu.

■ *See page 2566 for a narrative description.*

UNIVERSITY OF MOBILE
Mobile, Alabama

- **Independent Southern Baptist** comprehensive, founded 1961
- **Calendar** semesters
- **Degrees** associate, bachelor's, and master's
- **Suburban** 830-acre campus
- **Endowment** $9.0 million
- **Coed,** 1,663 undergraduate students, 74% full-time, 71% women, 29% men
- **Moderately difficult** entrance level, 67% of applicants were admitted

Undergraduates 1,238 full-time, 425 part-time. Students come from 21 states and territories, 19 other countries, 23% African American, 0.4% Asian American or Pacific Islander, 1% Hispanic American, 2% Native American, 2% international, 10% transferred in, 20% live on campus.

Freshmen *Admission:* 413 applied, 276 admitted, 212 enrolled. *Test scores:* ACT scores over 18: 79%; ACT scores over 24: 26%; ACT scores over 30: 5%.

Faculty *Total:* 153, 58% full-time, 41% with terminal degrees. *Student/faculty ratio:* 14:1.

Majors Accounting; art; athletic training; behavioral sciences; biblical studies; biological and physical sciences; biology/biological sciences; business administration and management; chemistry; computer science; dramatic/theatre arts; economics; elementary education; English; environmental studies; general studies; history; humanities; information science/studies; kindergarten/preschool education; mass communication/media; mathematics; music; nursing (registered nurse training); physical education teaching and coaching; political science and government; psychology; religious studies; secondary education; social sciences; sociology.

Academic Programs *Special study options:* academic remediation for entering students, accelerated degree program, adult/continuing education programs, advanced placement credit, double majors, English as a second language, honors programs, independent study, internships, part-time degree program, summer session for credit. *ROTC:* Army (c), Air Force (c). *Unusual degree programs:* 3-2 engineering with Auburn University and University of South Alabama; law with Tulane University.

Library J. L. Bedsole Library plus 2 others with 100,250 titles, 1,043 serial subscriptions, 2,222 audiovisual materials, an OPAC.

Computers on Campus 110 computers available on campus for general student use. A campuswide network can be accessed from off campus. Internet access, at least one staffed computer lab available.

Student Life *Housing:* on-campus residence required for freshman year. *Options:* men-only, women-only. Campus housing is university owned. Freshman campus housing is guaranteed. *Activities and organizations:* drama/theater group, student-run newspaper, choral group, Campus Activity Board, Baptist Campus Ministry, Student Government Association, Fellowship of Christian Athletes. *Campus security:* 24-hour emergency response devices and patrols. *Student services:* health clinic, personal/psychological counseling.

Athletics Member NAIA. *Intercollegiate sports:* baseball M(s), basketball M(s)/W(s), cross-country running M(s)/W(s), golf M(s)/W(s), soccer M(s)/W(s), softball W(s), tennis W(s), track and field M(s)/W(s). *Intramural sports:* badminton M/W, baseball M, basketball M/W, cross-country running M/W, football M/W, golf M/W, soccer M/W, softball M/W, swimming M/W, table tennis M/W, tennis M/W, track and field M/W, volleyball M/W, weight lifting M/W.

Standardized Tests *Required:* SAT I or ACT (for admission).

Costs (2003–04) *Comprehensive fee:* $14,960 includes full-time tuition ($9270), mandatory fees ($250), and room and board ($5440). Full-time tuition and fees vary according to course load. Part-time tuition: $309 per semester hour. Part-time tuition and fees vary according to course load. *Room and board:* Room and board charges vary according to board plan. *Payment plan:* installment. *Waivers:* employees or children of employees.

Financial Aid Of all full-time matriculated undergraduates who enrolled in 2002, 1,100 applied for aid, 798 were judged to have need. 88 Federal Work-Study jobs (averaging $1545). In 2002, 238 non-need-based awards were made. *Average percent of need met:* 56%. *Average financial aid package:* $7468. *Average need-based loan:* $4500. *Average need-based gift aid:* $3350. *Average indebtedness upon graduation:* $13,600.

Applying *Options:* common application, early admission, deferred entrance. *Application fee:* $30. *Required:* high school transcript, minimum 2.0 GPA. *Required for some:* interview. *Application deadline:* rolling (freshmen), rolling (transfers). *Notification:* continuous (freshmen), continuous (transfers).

Admissions Contact Mr. Brian Boyle, Director of Admissions, University of Mobile, PO Box 13220, Mobile, AL 36663-0220. *Phone:* 251-442-2287. *Toll-free phone:* 800-946-7267. *Fax:* 251-442-2498. *E-mail:* adminfo@umobile.edu.

UNIVERSITY OF MONTEVALLO

Montevallo, Alabama

- **State-supported** comprehensive, founded 1896
- **Calendar** semesters
- **Degrees** bachelor's, master's, and post-master's certificates
- **Small-town** 106-acre campus with easy access to Birmingham
- **Endowment** $2.0 million
- **Coed,** 2,644 undergraduate students, 89% full-time, 67% women, 33% men
- **Moderately difficult** entrance level, 79% of applicants were admitted

Undergraduates 2,361 full-time, 283 part-time. Students come from 18 states and territories, 22 other countries, 2% are from out of state, 12% African American, 0.8% Asian American or Pacific Islander, 1% Hispanic American, 0.6% Native American, 2% international, 11% transferred in, 37% live on campus. *Retention:* 76% of 2002 full-time freshmen returned.

Freshmen *Admission:* 1,334 applied, 1,050 admitted, 539 enrolled. *Average high school GPA:* 3.24. *Test scores:* ACT scores over 18: 94%; ACT scores over 24: 32%; ACT scores over 30: 3%.

Faculty *Total:* 188, 73% full-time, 64% with terminal degrees. *Student/faculty ratio:* 16:1.

Majors Accounting; art; art teacher education; audiology and speech-language pathology; biology/biological sciences; broadcast journalism; business administration and management; ceramic arts and ceramics; chemistry; commercial and advertising art; consumer merchandising/retailing management; dietetics; dramatic/theatre arts; drawing; elementary education; English; family and consumer economics related; family and consumer sciences/home economics teacher education; family and consumer sciences/human sciences; fashion merchandising; fine/studio arts; French; health and physical education; history; interior design; kindergarten/preschool education; management information systems; marketing/marketing management; mass communication/media; mathematics; music; music teacher education; photography; piano and organ; political science and government; pre-dentistry studies; pre-law studies; pre-medical studies; pre-veterinary studies; printmaking; psychology; radio and television; sculpture; social sciences; social work; sociology; Spanish; speech and rhetoric; voice and opera.

Academic Programs *Special study options:* academic remediation for entering students, accelerated degree program, advanced placement credit, double majors, honors programs, independent study, internships, part-time degree program, services for LD students, study abroad, summer session for credit. *ROTC:* Army (c), Air Force (c). *Unusual degree programs:* 3-2 engineering with Auburn University, University of Alabama at Birmingham.

Library Carmichael Library with 159,026 titles, 794 serial subscriptions, 3,185 audiovisual materials, an OPAC, a Web page.

Computers on Campus 250 computers available on campus for general student use. A campuswide network can be accessed from student residence rooms and from off campus. Internet access, online (class) registration, at least one staffed computer lab available.

Student Life *Housing:* on-campus residence required for freshman year. *Options:* coed, men-only, women-only. Campus housing is university owned. Freshman campus housing is guaranteed. *Activities and organizations:* drama/theater group, student-run newspaper, television station, choral group, Golden Key, Student Government Association, University Programming Council, campus ministries, African-American Association, national fraternities, national sororities. *Campus security:* 24-hour emergency response devices and patrols, late-night transport/escort service, controlled dormitory access. *Student services:* health clinic, personal/psychological counseling.

Athletics Member NCAA. All Division II. *Intercollegiate sports:* baseball M(s), basketball M(s)/W(s), golf M(s)/W(s), soccer M(s)/W(s), tennis W(s), volleyball W(s). *Intramural sports:* basketball M/W, bowling M, football M, golf M, tennis M/W, volleyball M/W.

Standardized Tests *Required:* SAT I or ACT (for admission). *Recommended:* ACT (for admission).

Costs (2003–04) *Tuition:* state resident $4500 full-time, $150 per credit hour part-time; nonresident $9000 full-time, $300 per credit hour part-time. Full-time tuition and fees vary according to course load. Part-time tuition and fees vary according to course load. *Required fees:* $284 full-time. *Room and board:* $3638; room only: $2318. Room and board charges vary according to board plan and housing facility. *Waivers:* employees or children of employees.

Financial Aid Of all full-time matriculated undergraduates who enrolled in 2003, 1,781 applied for aid, 1,327 were judged to have need, 450 had their need fully met. 136 Federal Work-Study jobs (averaging $1410). In 2003, 484 non-need-based awards were made. *Average percent of need met:* 77%. *Average financial aid package:* $6861. *Average need-based loan:* $2702. *Average need-based gift aid:* $5997. *Average non-need-based aid:* $3767. *Average indebtedness upon graduation:* $14,265.

Applying *Options:* common application, electronic application, early admission, deferred entrance. *Application fee:* $25. *Required:* high school transcript, minimum 2.0 GPA. *Recommended:* interview. *Application deadline:* 8/1 (freshmen), rolling (transfers).

Admissions Contact Mr. Lynn Gurganus, Director of Admissions, University of Montevallo, Station 6030, Montevallo, AL 35115-6030. *Phone:* 205-665-6030. *Toll-free phone:* 800-292-4349. *Fax:* 205-665-6032. *E-mail:* admissions@montevallo.edu.

■ See page 2658 for a narrative description.

UNIVERSITY OF NORTH ALABAMA

Florence, Alabama

- **State-supported** comprehensive, founded 1830, part of Alabama Commission on Higher Education
- **Calendar** semesters
- **Degrees** bachelor's, master's, and post-master's certificates
- **Urban** 125-acre campus
- **Endowment** $3.7 million
- **Coed,** 4,995 undergraduate students, 82% full-time, 58% women, 42% men
- **Minimally difficult** entrance level, 79% of applicants were admitted

Undergraduates 4,116 full-time, 879 part-time. Students come from 35 states and territories, 42 other countries, 23% are from out of state, 10% African American, 0.6% Asian American or Pacific Islander, 1% Hispanic American, 2% Native American, 5% international, 11% transferred in, 19% live on campus. *Retention:* 65% of 2002 full-time freshmen returned.

Freshmen *Admission:* 1,635 applied, 1,298 admitted, 803 enrolled. *Average high school GPA:* 2.97. *Test scores:* ACT scores over 18: 81%; ACT scores over 24: 29%; ACT scores over 30: 3%.

Faculty *Total:* 276, 72% full-time, 55% with terminal degrees. *Student/faculty ratio:* 22:1.

Majors Accounting; biological and biomedical sciences related; biology/biological sciences; business administration and management; business/managerial economics; chemistry; computer and information sciences; counseling psychology; criminal justice/law enforcement administration; education (multiple levels); elementary education; English; family and consumer sciences/human sciences; finance; fine arts related; fine/studio arts; foreign languages and literatures; general studies; geography; geology/earth science; history; kindergarten/preschool education; management information systems; marine biology and biological oceanography; marketing/marketing management; mathematics; music; nursing (registered nurse training); parks, recreation, and leisure related; physical sciences; physics; political science and government; psychology; secondary education; social work; sociology; special education; speech and rhetoric.

Academic Programs *Special study options:* academic remediation for entering students, accelerated degree program, adult/continuing education programs, advanced placement credit, cooperative education, distance learning, double majors, English as a second language, independent study, internships, part-time degree program, services for LD students, summer session for credit. *ROTC:* Army (b).

Library Collier Library with 358,393 titles, 3,126 serial subscriptions, 9,898 audiovisual materials, an OPAC, a Web page.

University of North Alabama (continued)

Computers on Campus 750 computers available on campus for general student use. A campuswide network can be accessed from student residence rooms and from off campus. Internet access, online (class) registration, at least one staffed computer lab available.

Student Life *Housing options:* coed, men-only, women-only. Campus housing is university owned. *Activities and organizations:* drama/theater group, student-run newspaper, radio station, choral group, marching band, Student Government Association, University Program Council, Baptist campus ministries, physical education majors club, Residence Hall Association, national fraternities, national sororities. *Campus security:* 24-hour emergency response devices and patrols, student patrols, late-night transport/escort service, controlled dormitory access. *Student services:* health clinic, personal/psychological counseling.

Athletics Member NCAA. All Division II. *Intercollegiate sports:* baseball M(s), basketball M(s)/W(s), cross-country running M(s)/W(s), football M(s), golf M(s), soccer W(s), softball W(s), tennis M(s)/W(s), volleyball W(s). *Intramural sports:* badminton M/W, baseball M, basketball M/W, bowling M/W, cross-country running M/W, football M/W, golf M, racquetball M/W, softball W, swimming M/W, table tennis M/W, tennis M/W, volleyball M/W, weight lifting M/W.

Standardized Tests *Required:* SAT I or ACT (for admission).

Costs (2003–04) *Tuition:* state resident $3048 full-time, $127 per credit hour part-time; nonresident $6096 full-time, $254 per credit hour part-time. Part-time tuition and fees vary according to course load. *Required fees:* $410 full-time, $18 per credit hour part-time. *Room and board:* $4272; room only: $1960. Room and board charges vary according to board plan and housing facility. *Payment plan:* installment. *Waivers:* senior citizens and employees or children of employees.

Financial Aid Of all full-time matriculated undergraduates who enrolled in 2001, 2,509 applied for aid, 2,009 were judged to have need, 818 had their need fully met. *Average percent of need met:* 41%. *Average financial aid package:* $4531. *Average need-based loan:* $4742. *Average need-based gift aid:* $2986. *Average indebtedness upon graduation:* $15,835.

Applying *Options:* electronic application, early admission, deferred entrance. *Application fee:* $25. *Required:* high school transcript. *Application deadline:* rolling (freshmen), rolling (transfers).

Admissions Contact Mrs. Kim O. Mauldin, Director of Admissions, University of North Alabama, Office of Admissions, Box 5011, Florence, AL 35632-0001. *Phone:* 256-765-4680. *Toll-free phone:* 800-TALKUNA. *Fax:* 256-765-4329. *E-mail:* admissions@una.edu.

UNIVERSITY OF SOUTH ALABAMA
Mobile, Alabama

- **State-supported** university, founded 1963
- **Calendar** semesters
- **Degrees** certificates, bachelor's, master's, doctoral, first professional, post-master's, and postbachelor's certificates
- **Suburban** 1225-acre campus
- **Endowment** $270.3 million
- **Coed,** 10,171 undergraduate students, 74% full-time, 59% women, 41% men
- **Moderately difficult** entrance level, 76% of applicants were admitted

Undergraduates 7,542 full-time, 2,629 part-time. Students come from 41 states and territories, 99 other countries, 22% are from out of state, 17% African American, 3% Asian American or Pacific Islander, 2% Hispanic American, 0.7% Native American, 4% international, 10% transferred in, 19% live on campus. *Retention:* 71% of 2002 full-time freshmen returned.

Freshmen *Admission:* 2,930 applied, 2,217 admitted, 1,376 enrolled. *Average high school GPA:* 3.21. *Test scores:* ACT scores over 18: 96%; ACT scores over 24: 37%; ACT scores over 30: 4%.

Faculty *Total:* 721, 66% full-time. *Student/faculty ratio:* 19:1.

Majors Accounting; anthropology; art; atmospheric sciences and meteorology; audiology and speech-language pathology; biology/biological sciences; biomedical sciences; business administration and management; business/commerce; chemical engineering; chemistry; civil engineering; clinical laboratory science/medical technology; communication/speech communication and rhetoric; computer and information sciences; computer engineering; criminal justice/law enforcement administration; dramatic/theatre arts; early childhood education; e-commerce; electrical, electronics and communications engineering; elementary education; English; finance; foreign languages and literatures; geography; geology/earth science; health/medical preparatory programs related; history; liberal arts and sciences and humanities related; marketing/marketing management; mathematics and statistics related; mechanical engineering; multi-/interdisciplinary studies related; music; nursing (registered nurse training); parks, recreation and leisure; philosophy; physical education teaching and coaching; physics; political science and government; psychology; radiologic technology/science; respiratory care therapy; secondary education; sociology; special education.

Academic Programs *Special study options:* academic remediation for entering students, accelerated degree program, adult/continuing education programs, advanced placement credit, cooperative education, distance learning, double majors, English as a second language, external degree program, freshman honors college, independent study, internships, part-time degree program, services for LD students, student-designed majors, study abroad, summer session for credit. *ROTC:* Army (b), Air Force (b).

Library University Library plus 1 other with 1.0 million titles, 5,215 serial subscriptions, an OPAC, a Web page.

Computers on Campus 500 computers available on campus for general student use. A campuswide network can be accessed from student residence rooms and from off campus. Internet access, online (class) registration, at least one staffed computer lab available.

Student Life *Housing options:* coed. Campus housing is university owned. *Activities and organizations:* drama/theater group, student-run newspaper, radio and television station, choral group, Student Government Association, Black Student Union, Non-Traditional Student Committee, national fraternities, national sororities. *Campus security:* 24-hour emergency response devices and patrols, late-night transport/escort service. *Student services:* health clinic, personal/psychological counseling, legal services.

Athletics Member NCAA. All Division I. *Intercollegiate sports:* baseball M(s), basketball M(s)/W(s), cross-country running M(s)/W(s), fencing M(c)/W(c), football M(c), golf M/W, soccer W(s), tennis M(s)/W(s), track and field M(s)/W(s), volleyball W(s). *Intramural sports:* badminton M/W, basketball M/W, bowling M/W, cheerleading M(c)/W(c), golf M/W, racquetball M/W, sailing M(c)/W(c), soccer M/W, softball M/W, table tennis M/W, tennis M/W, volleyball M/W, water polo M/W.

Standardized Tests *Required:* SAT I or ACT (for admission).

Costs (2003–04) *Tuition:* state resident $3390 full-time, $113 per semester hour part-time; nonresident $6780 full-time, $226 per semester hour part-time. *Required fees:* $380 full-time, $129 per term part-time. *Room and board:* $3990; room only: $2220. Room and board charges vary according to board plan, housing facility, and location. *Payment plan:* installment. *Waivers:* employees or children of employees.

Financial Aid Of all full-time matriculated undergraduates who enrolled in 2003, 3,786 applied for aid, 3,730 were judged to have need, 471 had their need fully met. In 2003, 890 non-need-based awards were made. *Average percent of need met:* 45%. *Average financial aid package:* $5702. *Average non-need-based aid:* $1978. *Average indebtedness upon graduation:* $9000.

Applying *Options:* early admission. *Application fee:* $25. *Required:* high school transcript. *Recommended:* minimum 2.0 GPA. *Application deadlines:* 7/15 (freshmen), 8/10 (transfers). *Notification:* continuous until 8/10 (freshmen), continuous until 8/10 (transfers).

Admissions Contact Ms. Melissa Jones, Director, University of South Alabama, 307 University Boulevard, Mobile, AL 36688-0002. *Phone:* 251-460-6141. *Toll-free phone:* 800-872-5247.

THE UNIVERSITY OF WEST ALABAMA
Livingston, Alabama

- **State-supported** comprehensive, founded 1835
- **Calendar** semesters
- **Degrees** associate, bachelor's, and master's
- **Small-town** 595-acre campus
- **Endowment** $425,431
- **Coed,** 1,692 undergraduate students, 90% full-time, 56% women, 44% men
- **Minimally difficult** entrance level, 78% of applicants were admitted

Undergraduates 1,525 full-time, 167 part-time. Students come from 22 states and territories, 9 other countries, 17% are from out of state, 41% African American, 0.5% Asian American or Pacific Islander, 0.4% Hispanic American, 0.2% Native American, 1% international, 12% transferred in, 35% live on campus. *Retention:* 80% of 2002 full-time freshmen returned.

Freshmen *Admission:* 730 applied, 572 admitted, 322 enrolled. *Test scores:* ACT scores over 18: 63%; ACT scores over 24: 13%; ACT scores over 30: 1%.

Faculty *Total:* 88, 94% full-time, 57% with terminal degrees. *Student/faculty ratio:* 23:1.

Majors Accounting; athletic training; biology/biological sciences; business administration and management; chemistry; early childhood education; elementary education; engineering technology; English; history; industrial technology; management information systems; marine biology and biological oceanography; mathematics; nursing (registered nurse training); physical education teaching and coaching; psychology; sociology; special education.

Academic Programs *Special study options:* academic remediation for entering students, accelerated degree program, advanced placement credit, double majors, honors programs, internships, off-campus study, part-time degree program, services for LD students, summer session for credit. *ROTC:* Army (c), Air Force (c). *Unusual degree programs:* 3-2 engineering with Auburn University; forestry with Auburn University.

Library Julia Tutwiler Library with 212,497 titles, 5,000 serial subscriptions, 3,008 audiovisual materials, an OPAC, a Web page.

Computers on Campus 400 computers available on campus for general student use. A campuswide network can be accessed from student residence rooms and from off campus. Internet access, at least one staffed computer lab available.

Student Life *Housing:* on-campus residence required through sophomore year. *Options:* coed, men-only, women-only. Campus housing is university owned. *Activities and organizations:* drama/theater group, student-run newspaper, choral group, Campus Outreach, national fraternities, national sororities. *Campus security:* 24-hour patrols. *Student services:* health clinic, personal/psychological counseling.

Athletics Member NCAA. All Division II. *Intercollegiate sports:* baseball M(s), basketball M(s)/W(s), cross-country running M(s)/W(s), football M(s), softball W(s), volleyball W(s). *Intramural sports:* basketball M/W, football M/W, golf M/W, softball M/W, table tennis M/W, tennis M/W, volleyball M/W.

Standardized Tests *Required:* SAT I or ACT (for admission).

Costs (2003–04) *Tuition:* state resident $3240 full-time, $136 per semester hour part-time; nonresident $6480 full-time, $272 per semester hour part-time. Part-time tuition and fees vary according to course level. *Required fees:* $470 full-time, $215 per semester part-time. *Room and board:* $2986; room only: $1460. Room and board charges vary according to board plan and housing facility. *Payment plan:* deferred payment. *Waivers:* employees or children of employees.

Financial Aid Of all full-time matriculated undergraduates who enrolled in 2002, 1,661 applied for aid, 1,259 were judged to have need. 176 Federal Work-Study jobs (averaging $1221). In 2002, 275 non-need-based awards were made. *Average financial aid package:* $8870. *Average need-based loan:* $4107. *Average need-based gift aid:* $3508. *Average non-need-based aid:* $2676. *Average indebtedness upon graduation:* $16,043.

Applying *Options:* common application, electronic application, early admission, deferred entrance. *Application fee:* $20. *Required:* high school transcript, minimum 2.0 GPA. *Application deadline:* rolling (freshmen), rolling (transfers). *Notification:* continuous (freshmen), continuous (transfers).

Admissions Contact Mr. Richard Hester, Vice President for Student Affairs, The University of West Alabama, Station 4, Livingston, AL 35470. *Phone:* 205-652-3400 Ext. 3578. *Toll-free phone:* 800-621-7742 (in-state); 800-621-8044 (out-of-state). *Fax:* 205-652-3522. *E-mail:* rhester@uwa.edu.

VIRGINIA COLLEGE AT BIRMINGHAM
Birmingham, Alabama

- **Proprietary** 4-year, founded 1989
- **Calendar** quarters
- **Degrees** diplomas, associate, and bachelor's
- **Urban** 1-acre campus
- **Coed,** 2,407 undergraduate students, 100% full-time, 66% women, 34% men
- **Moderately difficult** entrance level, 86% of applicants were admitted

Undergraduates 2,407 full-time. Students come from 7 states and territories, 0.1% are from out of state, 42% African American, 0.5% Asian American or Pacific Islander, 0.7% Hispanic American. *Retention:* 70% of 2002 full-time freshmen returned.

Freshmen *Admission:* 600 applied, 515 admitted, 515 enrolled. *Average high school GPA:* 2.5.

Faculty *Total:* 201, 69% full-time. *Student/faculty ratio:* 14:1.

Majors Accounting technology and bookkeeping; administrative assistant and secretarial science; baking and pastry arts; business administration and management; cooking and related culinary arts; culinary arts; diagnostic medical sonography and ultrasound technology; drafting and design technology; information technology; interior design; legal assistant/paralegal; massage therapy; medical/clinical assistant; medical insurance coding; medical insurance/medical billing; medical office assistant; medical office computer specialist; office management; surgical technology.

Library Elma Bell Library plus 2 others with 3,900 titles, 120 serial subscriptions, 40 audiovisual materials, an OPAC.

Computers on Campus 80 computers available on campus for general student use. A campuswide network can be accessed.

Student Life *Housing:* college housing not available. *Student services:* personal/psychological counseling.

Athletics *Intramural sports:* basketball M/W, softball M/W, volleyball M/W.

Standardized Tests *Required:* ACCUPLACER (for placement).

Costs (2003–04) *Tuition:* $8820 full-time, $245 per quarter hour part-time. Full-time tuition and fees vary according to program. Part-time tuition and fees vary according to program. No tuition increase for student's term of enrollment. *Payment plan:* installment. *Waivers:* employees or children of employees.

Financial Aid In 2002, 361 non-need-based awards were made. *Average financial aid package:* $7500.

Applying *Required:* high school transcript. *Application deadline:* rolling (freshmen). *Notification:* continuous (freshmen).

Admissions Contact Ms. Bibbie J. McLaughlin, Senior Vice President of Admissions, Virginia College at Birmingham, 65 Bagby Drive, PO Box 19249, Birmingham, AL 35209. *Phone:* 205-802-1200 Ext. 1207. *Fax:* 205-802-7045. *E-mail:* bibbie@vc.edu.

ALASKA

ALASKA BIBLE COLLEGE
Glennallen, Alaska

- **Independent nondenominational** 4-year, founded 1966
- **Calendar** semesters
- **Degrees** certificates, associate, and bachelor's
- **Rural** 80-acre campus
- **Endowment** $37,500
- **Coed,** 56 undergraduate students, 75% full-time, 39% women, 61% men
- **Minimally difficult** entrance level, 100% of applicants were admitted

Undergraduates 42 full-time, 14 part-time. Students come from 20 states and territories, 68% are from out of state, 2% Asian American or Pacific Islander, 4% Native American, 30% transferred in, 90% live on campus.

Freshmen *Admission:* 8 applied, 8 admitted, 7 enrolled.

Faculty *Total:* 5, 40% full-time, 20% with terminal degrees. *Student/faculty ratio:* 15:1.

Majors Biblical studies; English as a second/foreign language (teaching).

Academic Programs *Special study options:* academic remediation for entering students, advanced placement credit, double majors, internships, part-time degree program, student-designed majors.

Library Alaska Bible College Library Center with 27,911 titles, 130 serial subscriptions, 252 audiovisual materials.

Computers on Campus 10 computers available on campus for general student use. A campuswide network can be accessed. Internet access, at least one staffed computer lab available.

Student Life *Housing:* on-campus residence required through sophomore year. *Options:* men-only, women-only. Campus housing is university owned. Freshman campus housing is guaranteed. *Activities and organizations:* student-run radio station. *Campus security:* 24-hour emergency response devices. *Student services:* health clinic.

Athletics *Intramural sports:* basketball M(c)/W(c), volleyball M(c)/W(c).

Standardized Tests *Required:* SAT I or ACT (for admission).

Costs (2004–05) *Comprehensive fee:* $9800 includes full-time tuition ($5450) and room and board ($4350). Part-time tuition: $240 per credit. *Room and board:* Room and board charges vary according to board plan and housing facility. *Payment plan:* installment.

Financial Aid Of all full-time matriculated undergraduates who enrolled in 2003, 35 applied for aid, 30 were judged to have need. 16 state and other part-time jobs (averaging $1800). *Financial aid deadline:* 7/5.

Applying *Options:* deferred entrance. *Application fee:* $35. *Required:* essay or personal statement, high school transcript, minimum 2.0 GPA, 2 letters of recommendation, interview. *Application deadlines:* 7/1 (freshmen), 7/1 (transfers). *Notification:* 7/15 (freshmen), continuous until 7/15 (transfers).

Admissions Contact Ms. Jackie Colwell, Admissions Officer, Alaska Bible College, Box 289, 200 College Road, Glennallen, AK 99588-0289. *Phone:* 907-822-3201. *Toll-free phone:* 800-478-7884. *Fax:* 907-822-5027. *E-mail:* info@akbible.edu.

ALASKA PACIFIC UNIVERSITY
Anchorage, Alaska

- **Independent** comprehensive, founded 1959
- **Calendar** semesters
- **Degrees** certificates, associate, bachelor's, and master's
- **Suburban** 170-acre campus
- **Endowment** $31.9 million
- **Coed,** 478 undergraduate students, 59% full-time, 67% women, 33% men
- **Moderately difficult** entrance level, 91% of applicants were admitted

Undergraduates 284 full-time, 194 part-time. Students come from 34 states and territories, 26% are from out of state, 5% African American, 3% Asian

Alaska Pacific University (continued)
American or Pacific Islander, 4% Hispanic American, 16% Native American, 0.5% international, 15% transferred in, 22% live on campus. *Retention:* 79% of 2002 full-time freshmen returned.

Freshmen *Admission:* 117 applied, 107 admitted, 27 enrolled. *Average high school GPA:* 3.26. *Test scores:* SAT verbal scores over 500: 50%; SAT math scores over 500: 69%; ACT scores over 18: 80%; SAT verbal scores over 600: 30%; SAT math scores over 600: 15%; ACT scores over 24: 50%; SAT verbal scores over 700: 10%; ACT scores over 30: 10%.

Faculty *Total:* 85, 36% full-time, 35% with terminal degrees. *Student/faculty ratio:* 9:1.

Majors Accounting and business/management; business administration and management; elementary education; environmental science; human services; liberal arts and sciences/liberal studies; marine biology and biological oceanography; natural resources management and policy; parks, recreation and leisure; psychology.

Academic Programs *Special study options:* academic remediation for entering students, accelerated degree program, adult/continuing education programs, advanced placement credit, distance learning, double majors, independent study, internships, part-time degree program, services for LD students, student-designed majors, study abroad, summer session for credit.

Library Consortium Library with 676,745 titles, 3,842 serial subscriptions, an OPAC, a Web page.

Computers on Campus 40 computers available on campus for general student use. A campuswide network can be accessed from student residence rooms. Internet access, at least one staffed computer lab available.

Student Life *Housing:* on-campus residence required for freshman year. *Options:* coed. Freshman campus housing is guaranteed. *Activities and organizations:* drama/theater group, student-run newspaper, choral group, environmental club, Student Government Association, Psychology Club, Student Organization of Native Americans, Sife (Students for Free Enterprise). *Campus security:* 24-hour emergency response devices, controlled dormitory access. *Student services:* personal/psychological counseling.

Athletics *Intramural sports:* basketball M/W, skiing (cross-country) M/W, soccer M/W.

Standardized Tests *Required:* SAT I or ACT (for admission).

Costs (2003–04) *Comprehensive fee:* $21,828 includes full-time tuition ($16,218), mandatory fees ($110), and room and board ($5500). Full-time tuition and fees vary according to class time, location, and program. Part-time tuition: $675 per semester hour. Part-time tuition and fees vary according to class time, location, and program. No tuition increase for student's term of enrollment. *Required fees:* $55 per term part-time. *College room only:* $3000. Room and board charges vary according to board plan and housing facility. *Payment plan:* deferred payment. *Waivers:* adult students, senior citizens, and employees or children of employees.

Financial Aid Of all full-time matriculated undergraduates who enrolled in 2003, 163 applied for aid, 100 were judged to have need. 38 Federal Work-Study jobs (averaging $1444). In 2003, 41 non-need-based awards were made. *Average percent of need met:* 78%. *Average financial aid package:* $10,113. *Average need-based loan:* $4340. *Average need-based gift aid:* $4443. *Average non-need-based aid:* $6701. *Average indebtedness upon graduation:* $23,791.

Applying *Options:* electronic application, early decision, deferred entrance. *Application fee:* $25. *Required:* essay or personal statement, high school transcript, minimum 2.5 GPA, 2 letters of recommendation. *Required for some:* interview. *Application deadlines:* 2/1 (freshmen), 2/1 (transfers). *Early decision:* 1/1. *Notification:* 3/15 (freshmen), 1/15 (early decision), 3/15 (transfers).

Admissions Contact Mr. Michael Worner, Co-Director of Admissions, Alaska Pacific University, Anchorage, AK 99508. *Phone:* 907-564-8248. *Toll-free phone:* 800-252-7528. *Fax:* 907-564-8317. *E-mail:* admissions@alaskapacific.edu.

■ *See page 1140 for a narrative description.*

CHARTER COLLEGE
Anchorage, Alaska

Admissions Contact Ms. Lily Sirianni, Vice President, Charter College, 2221 East Northern Lights Boulevard, Suite 120, Anchorage, AK 99508-4157. *Phone:* 907-277-1000. *Toll-free phone:* 800-279-1008. *Fax:* 907-274-3342. *E-mail:* contact@chartercollege.org.

SHELDON JACKSON COLLEGE
Sitka, Alaska

- **Independent** 4-year, founded 1878, affiliated with Presbyterian Church (U.S.A.)
- **Calendar** semesters
- **Degrees** certificates, associate, and bachelor's
- **Small-town** 320-acre campus
- **Endowment** $1.4 million
- **Coed,** 221 undergraduate students, 56% full-time, 64% women, 36% men
- **Noncompetitive** entrance level, 66% of applicants were admitted

Undergraduates 123 full-time, 98 part-time. Students come from 25 states and territories, 51% are from out of state, 2% African American, 0.7% Asian American or Pacific Islander, 4% Hispanic American, 25% Native American, 16% transferred in, 80% live on campus. *Retention:* 60% of 2002 full-time freshmen returned.

Freshmen *Admission:* 242 applied, 160 admitted, 34 enrolled. *Average high school GPA:* 2.71.

Faculty *Total:* 38, 53% full-time, 34% with terminal degrees. *Student/faculty ratio:* 6:1.

Majors Business administration and management; education (specific levels and methods) related; elementary education; environmental science; general studies; human services; liberal arts and sciences/liberal studies; multi-/interdisciplinary studies related; parks, recreation and leisure; secondary education.

Academic Programs *Special study options:* academic remediation for entering students, advanced placement credit, double majors, independent study, internships, part-time degree program, services for LD students, student-designed majors.

Library Stratton Library with 46,000 titles, 150 serial subscriptions, an OPAC, a Web page.

Computers on Campus 50 computers available on campus for general student use. A campuswide network can be accessed from student residence rooms and from off campus. Internet access, at least one staffed computer lab available.

Student Life *Housing:* on-campus residence required through sophomore year. *Options:* coed, men-only, women-only. Campus housing is university owned. *Activities and organizations:* choral group, fly fishing, basketball, American Sign Language, American Fisheries Society, Student Ethnic Association. *Campus security:* 24-hour patrols, controlled dormitory access. *Student services:* personal/psychological counseling.

Athletics *Intramural sports:* basketball M(c)/W(c), racquetball M/W, rock climbing M/W, soccer M/W, swimming M/W, ultimate Frisbee M/W, volleyball M/W, weight lifting M/W.

Costs (2004–05) *Comprehensive fee:* $18,500 includes full-time tuition ($10,600), mandatory fees ($600), and room and board ($7300). Part-time tuition and fees vary according to course load and degree level. *College room only:* $3700. Room and board charges vary according to board plan and housing facility. *Payment plan:* installment. *Waivers:* children of alumni and employees or children of employees.

Financial Aid Of all full-time matriculated undergraduates who enrolled in 2003, 126 applied for aid, 123 were judged to have need, 87 had their need fully met. 52 Federal Work-Study jobs (averaging $2119). 32 state and other part-time jobs (averaging $1094). In 2003, 13 non-need-based awards were made. *Average percent of need met:* 71%. *Average financial aid package:* $11,974. *Average need-based loan:* $3198. *Average need-based gift aid:* $8713. *Average non-need-based aid:* $11,799. *Average indebtedness upon graduation:* $14,858. *Financial aid deadline:* 3/1.

Applying *Options:* common application, electronic application, deferred entrance. *Required:* high school transcript. *Recommended:* essay or personal statement, minimum 2.0 GPA. *Application deadline:* rolling (freshmen), rolling (transfers). *Notification:* continuous (freshmen), continuous (transfers).

Admissions Contact Mr. Michael Santarosa, Director of Admissions, Sheldon Jackson College, 801 Lincoln Street, Sitka, AK 99835. *Phone:* 907-747-5208. *Toll-free phone:* 800-478-4556. *Fax:* 907-747-6366. *E-mail:* admissions@sj-alaska.edu.

■ *See page 2374 for a narrative description.*

UNIVERSITY OF ALASKA ANCHORAGE
Anchorage, Alaska

- **State-supported** comprehensive, founded 1954, part of University of Alaska System
- **Calendar** semesters
- **Degrees** certificates, diplomas, associate, bachelor's, and master's
- **Urban** 428-acre campus
- **Endowment** $7.3 million
- **Coed**
- **Noncompetitive** entrance level

Faculty *Student/faculty ratio:* 18:1.

Student Life *Campus security:* 24-hour emergency response devices and patrols, student patrols, late-night transport/escort service, controlled dormitory access.

Athletics Member NCAA. All Division II.

Standardized Tests *Required:* SAT I or ACT (for admission).

Costs (2003–04) *Tuition:* state resident $2304 full-time; nonresident $6800 full-time. Part-time tuition and fees vary according to course level. *Required fees:* $352 full-time. *Room and board:* $6830; room only: $3730.

Financial Aid Of all full-time matriculated undergraduates who enrolled in 2003, 129 Federal Work-Study jobs (averaging $2557). *Average indebtedness upon graduation:* $15,621. *Financial aid deadline:* 8/1.

Applying *Options:* deferred entrance. *Application fee:* $40. *Required:* minimum 2.0 GPA. *Required for some:* high school transcript.

Admissions Contact Ms. Cecile Mitchell, Director of Enrollment Services, University of Alaska Anchorage, 3211 Providence Drive, Anchorage, AK 99508-8046. *Phone:* 907-786-1558. *Fax:* 907-786-4888. *E-mail:* enroll@uaa.alaska.edu.

■ *See page 2568 for a narrative description.*

UNIVERSITY OF ALASKA FAIRBANKS

Fairbanks, Alaska

- **State-supported** university, founded 1917, part of University of Alaska System
- **Calendar** semesters
- **Degrees** certificates, associate, bachelor's, master's, and doctoral
- **Small-town** 2250-acre campus
- **Coed,** 7,708 undergraduate students, 46% full-time, 59% women, 41% men
- **Minimally difficult** entrance level, 84% of applicants were admitted

UAF is America's premier institution of northern scholarship, discovery, and adventure. Located in Interior Alaska, a land of rivers, forests, mountains, wildlife, and the Northern Lights, the University is known for research in arctic phenomena, including global climate change. The 2,250-acre campus boasts state-of-the-art classrooms, laboratories, recreational facilities, and residence halls.

Undergraduates 3,537 full-time, 4,171 part-time. Students come from 58 states and territories, 27 other countries, 14% are from out of state, 4% African American, 3% Asian American or Pacific Islander, 2% Hispanic American, 18% Native American, 2% international, 7% transferred in, 28% live on campus. *Retention:* 70% of 2002 full-time freshmen returned.

Freshmen *Admission:* 1,895 applied, 1,587 admitted, 1,021 enrolled. *Average high school GPA:* 3.12. *Test scores:* SAT verbal scores over 500: 59%; SAT math scores over 500: 58%; ACT scores over 18: 72%; SAT verbal scores over 600: 24%; SAT math scores over 600: 22%; ACT scores over 24: 35%; SAT verbal scores over 700: 5%; SAT math scores over 700: 3%; ACT scores over 30: 5%.

Faculty *Total:* 311, 98% full-time. *Student/faculty ratio:* 19:1.

Majors Accounting; accounting technology and bookkeeping; administrative assistant and secretarial science; agricultural business technology; airframe mechanics and aircraft maintenance technology; American Indian/Native American studies; anthropology; applied mathematics; area studies related; art; aviation/airway management; biological and physical sciences; biology/biological sciences; business administration and management; chemistry; child care provision; civil engineering; communication/speech communication and rhetoric; community organization and advocacy; computer and information sciences; computer science; corrections and criminal justice related; culinary arts; dramatic/theatre arts; economics; education; electrical, electronics and communications engineering; elementary education; English; fire science; fishing and fisheries sciences and management; foreign languages and literatures; foreign languages related; geography; geological/geophysical engineering; geology/earth science; history; human resources management; industrial engineering; industrial technology; Japanese; journalism; kindergarten/preschool education; kinesiology and exercise science; legal assistant/paralegal; liberal arts and sciences/liberal studies; linguistics; mathematics; mechanical engineering; medical/clinical assistant; mental and social health services and allied professions related; mining and petroleum technologies related; multi-/interdisciplinary studies related; music; natural resources and conservation related; natural resources management and policy; office occupations and clerical services; petroleum engineering; philosophy; physical education teaching and coaching; physics; political science and government; psychology; public health; Russian studies; social work; sociology; speech and rhetoric; theatre design and technology; vehicle maintenance and repair technologies related; wildlife and wildlands science and management.

Academic Programs *Special study options:* academic remediation for entering students, accelerated degree program, advanced placement credit, cooperative education, distance learning, double majors, honors programs, independent study, internships, off-campus study, part-time degree program, services for LD students, student-designed majors, study abroad, summer session for credit. *ROTC:* Army (b).

Library Rasmuson Library plus 8 others with 608,575 titles, 2,754 serial subscriptions, 664,448 audiovisual materials, an OPAC, a Web page.

Computers on Campus 199 computers available on campus for general student use. A campuswide network can be accessed from student residence rooms and from off campus. Internet access, online (class) registration, at least one staffed computer lab available. Computer purchase or lease plan available.

Student Life *Housing options:* coed, disabled students. Campus housing is university owned. Freshman applicants given priority for college housing. *Activities and organizations:* drama/theater group, student-run newspaper, radio and television station, choral group, United Campus Ministry, Northern Star Chinese Student Association, Golden Key National Honor Society, UAF Good Time Swing Dance Club, University Women's Association, national fraternities, national sororities. *Campus security:* 24-hour emergency response devices and patrols, student patrols, late-night transport/escort service, controlled dormitory access, ID check at door of residence halls, crime prevention and safety workshops. *Student services:* health clinic, personal/psychological counseling, women's center, legal services.

Athletics Member NCAA. All Division II except ice hockey (Division I), men's and women's riflery (Division I). *Intercollegiate sports:* basketball M(s)/W(s), cross-country running M(s)/W(s), ice hockey M(s), riflery M(s)/W(s), skiing (cross-country) M(s)/W(s), volleyball W(s). *Intramural sports:* badminton M/W, basketball M/W, bowling M/W, cheerleading M(c)/W(c), cross-country running M/W, fencing M(c)/W(c), ice hockey M/W, racquetball M/W, riflery M/W, skiing (cross-country) M/W, skiing (downhill) M/W, soccer M/W, softball M/W, swimming M/W, table tennis M/W, tennis M/W, ultimate Frisbee M/W, volleyball M/W, water polo M/W, wrestling M/W.

Standardized Tests *Required:* SAT I or ACT (for admission), SAT I or ACT (for placement).

Costs (2004–05) *Tuition:* state resident $3165 full-time, $106 per credit part-time; nonresident $10,195 full-time, $337 per credit part-time. Full-time tuition and fees vary according to course level and course load. Part-time tuition and fees vary according to course level and course load. *Required fees:* $1000 full-time. *Room and board:* $5130; room only: $2690. Room and board charges vary according to board plan and housing facility. *Payment plan:* installment. *Waivers:* children of alumni, senior citizens, and employees or children of employees.

Financial Aid Of all full-time matriculated undergraduates who enrolled in 2003, 2,776 applied for aid, 1,464 were judged to have need, 479 had their need fully met. 94 Federal Work-Study jobs (averaging $4691). In 2003, 452 non-need-based awards were made. *Average percent of need met:* 71%. *Average financial aid package:* $9137. *Average need-based loan:* $6505. *Average need-based gift aid:* $4093. *Average non-need-based aid:* $2915. *Average indebtedness upon graduation:* $11,623.

Applying *Options:* electronic application, early admission, deferred entrance. *Application fee:* $35. *Required:* high school transcript, minimum 2.0 GPA. *Application deadlines:* 8/1 (freshmen), 8/1 (transfers). *Notification:* continuous (transfers).

Admissions Contact Ms. Nancy Dix, Director, Admissions, University of Alaska Fairbanks, PO Box 757480, Fairbanks, AK 99775-7480. *Phone:* 907-474-7500. *Toll-free phone:* 800-478-1823. *Fax:* 907-474-5379. *E-mail:* fyapply@uaf.edu.

■ *See page 2570 for a narrative description.*

UNIVERSITY OF ALASKA SOUTHEAST

Juneau, Alaska

- **State-supported** comprehensive, founded 1972, part of University of Alaska System
- **Calendar** semesters
- **Degrees** certificates, associate, bachelor's, and master's
- **Small-town** 198-acre campus
- **Coed,** 3,126 undergraduate students, 25% full-time, 62% women, 38% men
- **Noncompetitive** entrance level, 44% of applicants were admitted

Undergraduates 795 full-time, 2,331 part-time. Students come from 39 states and territories, 6 other countries, 15% are from out of state, 4% transferred in. *Retention:* 59% of 2002 full-time freshmen returned.

Freshmen *Admission:* 416 applied, 181 admitted, 145 enrolled. *Average high school GPA:* 3.10. *Test scores:* SAT verbal scores over 500: 60%; SAT math scores over 500: 56%; ACT scores over 18: 71%; SAT verbal scores over 600: 33%; SAT math scores over 600: 20%; ACT scores over 24: 47%; SAT verbal scores over 700: 11%; ACT scores over 30: 6%.

Faculty *Total:* 240, 40% full-time, 20% with terminal degrees. *Student/faculty ratio:* 12:1.

University of Alaska Southeast (continued)

Majors Accounting; administrative assistant and secretarial science; automobile/automotive mechanics technology; biology/biological sciences; business administration and management; construction engineering technology; education; elementary education; environmental studies; hospitality administration; kindergarten/preschool education; legal assistant/paralegal; liberal arts and sciences/liberal studies; marine biology and biological oceanography; marine technology; political science and government; tourism and travel services management.

Academic Programs *Special study options:* academic remediation for entering students, adult/continuing education programs, advanced placement credit, cooperative education, distance learning, independent study, internships, off-campus study, part-time degree program, services for LD students, student-designed majors, study abroad, summer session for credit.

Library Egan Memorial Library with 112,500 titles, 537 serial subscriptions, 2,763 audiovisual materials, an OPAC, a Web page.

Computers on Campus 75 computers available on campus for general student use. A campuswide network can be accessed from student residence rooms and from off campus. Internet access, at least one staffed computer lab available.

Student Life *Housing options:* coed, disabled students. *Activities and organizations:* drama/theater group, student-run newspaper, Native Student Club. *Campus security:* 24-hour emergency response devices and patrols, late-night transport/escort service, controlled dormitory access. *Student services:* health clinic, personal/psychological counseling.

Athletics *Intercollegiate sports:* riflery M(c)/W(c). *Intramural sports:* basketball M/W, racquetball M/W, riflery M/W, skiing (cross-country) M/W, skiing (downhill) M/W, softball M/W, tennis M/W, volleyball M/W.

Standardized Tests *Required:* SAT I or ACT (for admission).

Costs (2004–05) *Tuition:* state resident $3360 full-time, $112 per credit hour part-time; nonresident $10,290 full-time, $343 per credit hour part-time. *Required fees:* $423 full-time. *Room and board:* $5320; room only: $3350.

Financial Aid Of all full-time matriculated undergraduates who enrolled in 2003, 502 applied for aid, 315 were judged to have need, 69 had their need fully met. 27 Federal Work-Study jobs (averaging $3195). In 2003, 36 non-need-based awards were made. *Average percent of need met:* 64%. *Average financial aid package:* $6417. *Average need-based loan:* $3941. *Average need-based gift aid:* $3697. *Average non-need-based aid:* $2906. *Average indebtedness upon graduation:* $13,340.

Applying *Options:* early admission, deferred entrance. *Application fee:* $40. *Required:* high school transcript, minimum 2.0 GPA. *Required for some:* essay or personal statement. *Application deadline:* rolling (freshmen), rolling (transfers).

Admissions Contact Mr. Bill Stenberg, Director of Admissions, University of Alaska Southeast, 11120 Glacier Highway, Juneau, AK 99801-8625. *Phone:* 907-465-6239. *Toll-free phone:* 877-465-4827. *Fax:* 907-465-6365. *E-mail:* info.uas@uas.alaska.edu.

■ *See page 2572 for a narrative description.*

ARIZONA

American Indian College of the Assemblies of God, Inc.

Phoenix, Arizona

- **Independent** 4-year, founded 1957, affiliated with Assemblies of God
- **Calendar** semesters
- **Degrees** associate and bachelor's
- **Urban** 10-acre campus
- **Coed,** 73 undergraduate students, 82% full-time, 48% women, 52% men
- **Minimally difficult** entrance level, 44% of applicants were admitted

Undergraduates 60 full-time, 13 part-time. Students come from 10 states and territories, 29% are from out of state, 3% African American, 4% Asian American or Pacific Islander, 7% Hispanic American, 67% Native American, 1% international, 7% transferred in. *Retention:* 88% of 2002 full-time freshmen returned.

Freshmen *Admission:* 18 applied, 8 admitted, 8 enrolled. *Average high school GPA:* 2.61.

Faculty *Total:* 20, 25% full-time, 10% with terminal degrees. *Student/faculty ratio:* 8:1.

Majors Business administration and management; elementary education; pastoral studies/counseling.

Academic Programs *Special study options:* academic remediation for entering students, distance learning, double majors, independent study, internships.

Library Cummings Memorial Library with 19,899 titles, 120 serial subscriptions, an OPAC.

Computers on Campus 39 computers available on campus for general student use. A campuswide network can be accessed. Internet access, at least one staffed computer lab available.

Student Life *Housing:* on-campus residence required through senior year. *Activities and organizations:* drama/theater group, Missions Fellowship, Associated Student Body, yearbook. *Campus security:* student patrols. *Student services:* personal/psychological counseling.

Athletics *Intramural sports:* basketball M/W, bowling M/W, table tennis M/W, volleyball M/W.

Standardized Tests *Required:* SAT I or ACT (for admission).

Costs (2004–05) *Comprehensive fee:* $9275 includes full-time tuition ($4800), mandatory fees ($625), and room and board ($3850). Full-time tuition and fees vary according to course load. Part-time tuition: $160 per credit hour. Part-time tuition and fees vary according to course load.

Financial Aid In 2002, 7 non-need-based awards were made. *Average percent of need met:* 80%.

Applying *Required:* essay or personal statement, high school transcript, 1 letter of recommendation. *Application deadlines:* 8/15 (freshmen), 8/15 (transfers).

Admissions Contact Rev. Steve Clindaniel, Admissions Director, American Indian College of the Assemblies of God, Inc., 10020 North 15th Avenue, Phoenix, AZ 85021. *Phone:* 602-944-3335 Ext. 235. *Toll-free phone:* 800-933-3828. *Fax:* 602-943-8299. *E-mail:* aicadm@aicag.edu.

Argosy University/Phoenix

Phoenix, Arizona

- **Proprietary** upper-level, founded 1997, part of Argosy University
- **Calendar** semesters
- **Degrees** bachelor's, master's, and doctoral
- **Urban** 1-acre campus
- **Coed,** 14 undergraduate students, 100% full-time, 86% women, 14% men

Undergraduates 14 full-time. Students come from 50 states and territories, 5 other countries, 80% are from out of state.

Faculty *Total:* 26, 62% full-time, 100% with terminal degrees. *Student/faculty ratio:* 13:1.

Majors Psychology.

Student Life *Housing:* college housing not available. *Activities and organizations:* Diversity Club. *Campus security:* 24-hour emergency response devices.

Costs (2003–04) *Tuition:* $12,960 full-time, $360 per credit hour part-time. *Required fees:* $25 full-time.

Financial Aid Of all full-time matriculated undergraduates who enrolled in 2003, 6 applied for aid, 6 were judged to have need. *Average financial aid package:* $4213. *Average need-based loan:* $3208. *Average need-based gift aid:* $1342.

Admissions Contact Mr. Andy Hughes, Director of Admissions, Argosy University/Phoenix, 2301 West Dunlap Avenue, Suite 211, Phoenix, AZ 85021. *Phone:* 602-216-2600 Ext. 277. *Toll-free phone:* 866-216-2777. *Fax:* 602-216-2601. *E-mail:* ahughes@argosyu.edu.

Arizona State University

Tempe, Arizona

- **State-supported** university, founded 1885, part of Arizona State University
- **Calendar** semesters
- **Degrees** bachelor's, master's, doctoral, first professional, post-master's, and postbachelor's certificates
- **Suburban** 814-acre campus with easy access to Phoenix
- **Endowment** $221.2 million
- **Coed,** 38,627 undergraduate students, 80% full-time, 52% women, 48% men
- **Moderately difficult** entrance level, 88% of applicants were admitted

Undergraduates 30,935 full-time, 7,692 part-time. Students come from 53 states and territories, 108 other countries, 23% are from out of state, 4% African American, 5% Asian American or Pacific Islander, 12% Hispanic American, 2% Native American, 3% international, 10% transferred in, 18% live on campus. *Retention:* 77% of 2002 full-time freshmen returned.

Freshmen *Admission:* 19,785 applied, 17,490 admitted, 7,126 enrolled. *Average high school GPA:* 3.36. *Test scores:* SAT verbal scores over 500: 70%; SAT math scores over 500: 73%; ACT scores over 18: 92%; SAT verbal scores over 600: 26%; SAT math scores over 600: 32%; ACT scores over 24: 46%; SAT verbal scores over 700: 5%; SAT math scores over 700: 6%; ACT scores over 30: 7%.

Faculty *Total:* 1,844, 93% full-time, 82% with terminal degrees. *Student/faculty ratio:* 23:1.

Majors Accounting; aerospace, aeronautical and astronautical engineering; African-American/Black studies; American Indian/Native American studies;

anthropology; applied mathematics related; architecture; art; art history, criticism and conservation; biochemistry; biological and biomedical sciences related; biological specializations related; biology/biological sciences; biomedical/medical engineering; botany/plant biology; business administration and management; business, management, and marketing related; ceramic arts and ceramics; chemical engineering; chemistry; city/urban, community and regional planning; civil engineering; clinical laboratory science/medical technology; commercial and advertising art; communication disorders; communication/speech communication and rhetoric; computer engineering; computer science; conservation biology; construction engineering; criminal justice/safety; dance; dramatic/theatre arts; drawing; East Asian languages related; economics; electrical, electronics and communications engineering; elementary education; English; family resource management; finance; fine/studio arts; French; geography; geology/earth science; German; Hispanic-American, Puerto Rican, and Mexican-American/Chicano studies; history; humanities; industrial design; industrial engineering; interdisciplinary studies; interior architecture; Italian; journalism; kindergarten/preschool education; kinesiology and exercise science; landscape architecture; management information systems; marketing/marketing management; materials engineering; mathematics; mechanical engineering; medical microbiology and bacteriology; metal and jewelry arts; molecular biology; multi-/interdisciplinary studies related; music; music performance; music related; music theory and composition; music therapy; nursing (registered nurse training); parks, recreation and leisure; philosophy; photography; physics; political science and government; pre-law studies; printmaking; psychology; purchasing, procurement/acquisitions and contracts management; radio and television; real estate; religious studies; Russian; sculpture; secondary education; social work; sociology; Spanish; special education; women's studies.

Academic Programs *Special study options:* academic remediation for entering students, accelerated degree program, adult/continuing education programs, advanced placement credit, cooperative education, distance learning, double majors, honors programs, independent study, internships, off-campus study, part-time degree program, services for LD students, study abroad, summer session for credit. *ROTC:* Army (b), Air Force (b).

Library Hayden Library plus 4 others with 2.4 million titles, 28,159 serial subscriptions, 1.3 million audiovisual materials, an OPAC, a Web page.

Computers on Campus A campuswide network can be accessed from student residence rooms and from off campus. Internet access, online (class) registration, at least one staffed computer lab available. Computer purchase or lease plan available.

Student Life *Housing options:* coed, disabled students. Campus housing is university owned. *Activities and organizations:* drama/theater group, student-run newspaper, radio and television station, choral group, marching band, ski club, outing club, Students Against Discrimination (SAD), national fraternities, national sororities. *Campus security:* 24-hour emergency response devices and patrols, late-night transport/escort service. *Student services:* health clinic, personal/psychological counseling, women's center, legal services.

Athletics Member NCAA. All Division I except cheerleading (Division III), football (Division I-A). *Intercollegiate sports:* baseball M(s), basketball M(s)/W(s), cheerleading W, cross-country running M(s)/W(s), golf M(s)/W(s), gymnastics W(s), soccer W(s), softball W(s), swimming M(s)/W(s), tennis M(s)/W(s), track and field M(s)/W(s), volleyball W(s), water polo W, wrestling M(s). *Intramural sports:* badminton M(c)/W(c), basketball M/W, bowling M/W, crew M(c)/W(c), cross-country running M/W, equestrian sports M(c)/W(c), fencing M(c)/W(c), field hockey M(c), golf M/W, gymnastics M(c)/W(c), ice hockey M(c)/W(c), lacrosse M(c)/W(c), racquetball M/W, rugby M(c)/W(c), soccer M/W, softball M/W, swimming M/W, table tennis M/W, tennis M/W, track and field M/W, ultimate Frisbee M(c)/W(c), volleyball M/W, water polo W(c), weight lifting M/W, wrestling M.

Standardized Tests *Required:* SAT I or ACT (for admission).

Costs (2003–04) *Tuition:* state resident $3508 full-time, $183 per credit part-time; nonresident $12,028 full-time, $501 per credit part-time. Full-time tuition and fees vary according to program. Part-time tuition and fees vary according to program. *Required fees:* $87 full-time. *Room and board:* $6453; room only: $4101. Room and board charges vary according to board plan and housing facility. *Waivers:* employees or children of employees.

Financial Aid Of all full-time matriculated undergraduates who enrolled in 2002, 15,074 applied for aid, 11,283 were judged to have need, 1,092 had their need fully met. 670 Federal Work-Study jobs (averaging $2084). 4,203 state and other part-time jobs (averaging $3022). In 2002, 3219 non-need-based awards were made. *Average percent of need met:* 65%. *Average financial aid package:* $7225. *Average need-based loan:* $3898. *Average need-based gift aid:* $4175. *Average non-need-based aid:* $4043. *Average indebtedness upon graduation:* $17,780.

Applying *Options:* early action. *Required:* high school transcript, minimum 3.0 GPA. *Application deadline:* rolling (freshmen), rolling (transfers). *Notification:* continuous (freshmen), 12/1 (early action), continuous (transfers).

Admissions Contact Mr. Timothy J. Desch, Director of Undergraduate Admissions, Arizona State University, Box 870112, Tempe, AZ 85287-0112. *Phone:* 480-965-7788. *Fax:* 480-965-3610. *E-mail:* ugradinq@asu.edu.

ARIZONA STATE UNIVERSITY EAST
Mesa, Arizona

- **State-supported** comprehensive, founded 1995, part of Arizona State University
- **Calendar** semesters
- **Degrees** bachelor's and master's
- **Suburban** 600-acre campus with easy access to Phoenix
- **Endowment** $3.2 million
- **Coed,** 2,862 undergraduate students, 37% full-time, 48% women, 52% men
- **Moderately difficult** entrance level, 79% of applicants were admitted

Undergraduates 1,067 full-time, 1,795 part-time. Students come from 43 states and territories, 10% are from out of state, 2% African American, 4% Asian American or Pacific Islander, 10% Hispanic American, 2% Native American, 2% international, 13% transferred in, 7% live on campus.

Freshmen *Admission:* 484 applied, 380 admitted, 137 enrolled. *Average high school GPA:* 3.20. *Test scores:* SAT verbal scores over 500: 63%; SAT math scores over 500: 73%; ACT scores over 18: 93%; SAT verbal scores over 600: 20%; SAT math scores over 600: 29%; ACT scores over 24: 34%; SAT verbal scores over 700: 1%; ACT scores over 30: 2%.

Faculty *Total:* 99, 89% full-time, 100% with terminal degrees. *Student/faculty ratio:* 22:1.

Majors Aeronautical/aerospace engineering technology; agricultural business and management; biology/biological sciences; business/commerce; communication and journalism related; computer engineering technology; electrical, electronic and communications engineering technology; elementary education; foods, nutrition, and wellness; health and physical education related; health professions related; industrial technology; interdisciplinary studies; manufacturing technology; mechanical engineering/mechanical technology; multi-/interdisciplinary studies related; psychology related; science technologies related.

Academic Programs *Special study options:* accelerated degree program, advanced placement credit, distance learning, double majors, honors programs, independent study, internships, part-time degree program, services for LD students, student-designed majors, study abroad, summer session for credit. *ROTC:* Army (c), Air Force (c).

Library ASU East Library plus 1 other with 4.4 million titles, 206 serial subscriptions, 105 audiovisual materials, an OPAC, a Web page.

Computers on Campus 350 computers available on campus for general student use. A campuswide network can be accessed from off campus that provide access to specialized software applications. Internet access, online (class) registration, at least one staffed computer lab available. Computer purchase or lease plan available.

Student Life *Housing options:* coed, disabled students. Campus housing is university owned, leased by the school and is provided by a third party. Freshman applicants given priority for college housing. *Activities and organizations:* student-run newspaper, professional golf management club, Aero Management Tech—Student Advisory Committee, graphic information technology club, National Agri-Marketing Association, One Nation Club, national fraternities, national sororities. *Campus security:* 24-hour emergency response devices and patrols, late-night transport/escort service. *Student services:* health clinic, personal/psychological counseling.

Standardized Tests *Recommended:* SAT I or ACT (for admission).

Costs (2003–04) *Tuition:* state resident $3508 full-time, $183 per semester hour part-time; nonresident $12,028 full-time, $501 per semester hour part-time. Full-time tuition and fees vary according to degree level and location. Part-time tuition and fees vary according to course load, degree level, and location. *Required fees:* $36 full-time. *Room and board:* $4770; room only: $2610. Room and board charges vary according to board plan and housing facility. *Waivers:* employees or children of employees.

Financial Aid Of all full-time matriculated undergraduates who enrolled in 2002, 530 applied for aid, 380 were judged to have need, 13 had their need fully met. 23 Federal Work-Study jobs (averaging $2295). 140 state and other part-time jobs (averaging $3066). In 2002, 150 non-need-based awards were made. *Average percent of need met:* 62%. *Average financial aid package:* $6963. *Average need-based loan:* $4492. *Average need-based gift aid:* $3520. *Average non-need-based aid:* $5452.

Applying *Options:* common application, electronic application, early action. *Application fee:* $50. *Required:* high school transcript. *Required for some:* essay or personal statement, interview. *Recommended:* minimum 3.0 GPA. *Application deadline:* rolling (freshmen), rolling (transfers). *Notification:* 12/1 (early action).

Arizona State University East (continued)

Admissions Contact Stacie Dana, Student Recruitment/Retention Specialist, Arizona State University East, 7001 East Williams Field Road #350, Mesa, AZ 85212. *Phone:* 480-727-1165. *Fax:* 480-727-1008. *E-mail:* asueast@asu.edu.

ARIZONA STATE UNIVERSITY WEST

Phoenix, Arizona

- **State-supported** comprehensive, founded 1984, part of Arizona State University
- **Calendar** semesters
- **Degrees** bachelor's, master's, and postbachelor's certificates
- **Urban** 300-acre campus
- **Coed,** 5,751 undergraduate students, 67% full-time, 68% women, 32% men
- **Moderately difficult** entrance level, 62% of applicants were admitted

Undergraduates 3,853 full-time, 1,898 part-time. Students come from 29 states and territories, 23 other countries, 2% are from out of state, 5% African American, 4% Asian American or Pacific Islander, 18% Hispanic American, 2% Native American, 1% international, 21% transferred in, 2% live on campus. *Retention:* 75% of 2002 full-time freshmen returned.

Freshmen *Admission:* 961 applied, 600 admitted, 357 enrolled. *Average high school GPA:* 3.35. *Test scores:* SAT verbal scores over 500: 64%; SAT math scores over 500: 62%; ACT scores over 18: 85%; SAT verbal scores over 600: 25%; SAT math scores over 600: 18%; ACT scores over 24: 26%; SAT verbal scores over 700: 4%; SAT math scores over 700: 2%; ACT scores over 30: 2%.

Faculty *Total:* 335, 56% full-time, 64% with terminal degrees. *Student/faculty ratio:* 20:1.

Majors Accounting; American studies; biology/biological sciences; communication/speech communication and rhetoric; criminal justice/law enforcement administration; elementary education; English; history; interdisciplinary studies; international business/trade/commerce; multi-/interdisciplinary studies related; parks, recreation and leisure; political science and government; psychology; secondary education; social sciences; social work; sociology; Spanish; special education; visual and performing arts; women's studies.

Academic Programs *Special study options:* adult/continuing education programs, distance learning, double majors, honors programs, independent study, internships, part-time degree program, services for LD students, student-designed majors, summer session for credit.

Library ASU West Library with 334,625 titles, 3,318 serial subscriptions, 26,369 audiovisual materials, an OPAC, a Web page.

Computers on Campus 400 computers available on campus for general student use. A campuswide network can be accessed from off campus. Internet access, online (class) registration, at least one staffed computer lab available.

Student Life *Housing options:* coed, disabled students. Campus housing is provided by a third party. Freshman applicants given priority for college housing. *Activities and organizations:* student-run newspaper, justice studies club, American Marketing Association West, Beta Alpha Psi Accounting Honor Society, communication club, outdoor recreation club. *Campus security:* 24-hour emergency response devices and patrols, student patrols, late-night transport/escort service. *Student services:* health clinic, personal/psychological counseling, women's center.

Standardized Tests *Required:* SAT I or ACT (for admission).

Costs (2003–04) *Tuition:* state resident $3508 full-time, $183 per credit hour part-time; nonresident $12,028 full-time, $501 per credit hour part-time. Part-time tuition and fees vary according to course load. *Required fees:* $87 full-time, $19 per term part-time. *Room only:* $4101. *Payment plan:* installment. *Waivers:* employees or children of employees.

Financial Aid Of all full-time matriculated undergraduates who enrolled in 2002, 1,587 applied for aid, 1,346 were judged to have need, 1,346 had their need fully met. 87 Federal Work-Study jobs (averaging $2957). 207 state and other part-time jobs (averaging $2881). In 2002, 426 non-need-based awards were made. *Average percent of need met:* 100%. *Average financial aid package:* $6911. *Average need-based loan:* $4117. *Average need-based gift aid:* $3898. *Average non-need-based aid:* $3858.

Applying *Options:* common application, electronic application. *Required:* high school transcript. *Recommended:* minimum 3.0 GPA. *Application deadline:* rolling (freshmen), rolling (transfers). *Notification:* continuous (transfers).

Admissions Contact Ms. Deborah Moore, Program Coordinator, Arizona State University West, PO Box 37100, 4701 West Thunderbird Road, Phoenix, AZ 85069-7100. *Phone:* 602-543-8217. *Fax:* 602-543-8312.

THE ART CENTER DESIGN COLLEGE

Tucson, Arizona

Admissions Contact Ms. Colleen Gimbel-Froebe, Associate Director of Admissions and Placement, The Art Center Design College, 2525 North Country Club Road, Tucson, AZ 85716-2505. *Phone:* 520-325-0123. *Toll-free phone:* 800-825-8753. *Fax:* 520-325-5535.

THE ART INSTITUTE OF PHOENIX

Phoenix, Arizona

- **Proprietary** 4-year, founded 1995, part of The Art Institutes
- **Calendar** quarters
- **Degrees** diplomas, associate, and bachelor's
- **Suburban** 3-acre campus
- **Coed,** 1,216 undergraduate students, 86% full-time, 39% women, 61% men
- **Minimally difficult** entrance level

Undergraduates 1,045 full-time, 171 part-time. Students come from 32 states and territories, 40% are from out of state, 3% African American, 2% Asian American or Pacific Islander, 13% Hispanic American, 2% Native American, 0.1% international, 100% transferred in, 20% live on campus.

Freshmen *Admission:* 388 admitted, 388 enrolled. *Average high school GPA:* 2.75.

Faculty *Total:* 80, 39% full-time. *Student/faculty ratio:* 20:1.

Majors Advertising; animation, interactive technology, video graphics and special effects; apparel and accessories marketing; culinary arts; graphic design; interior design; web page, digital/multimedia and information resources design.

Academic Programs *Special study options:* academic remediation for entering students, advanced placement credit, cooperative education, distance learning, honors programs, independent study, internships, services for LD students.

Library Learning Resource Center with 11,000 titles, 120 serial subscriptions, 2,850 audiovisual materials.

Computers on Campus 120 computers available on campus for general student use. A campuswide network can be accessed. Internet access, at least one staffed computer lab available.

Student Life *Housing options:* men-only, women-only. Campus housing is provided by a third party. *Activities and organizations:* student-run newspaper, computer arts and animation club, Student Activities Council, Gay and Straight Student Alliance, American Institute of Graphic Arts, international student club. *Campus security:* 24-hour emergency response devices, late-night transport/escort service, security guard during open hours. *Student services:* personal/psychological counseling.

Standardized Tests *Recommended:* SAT I or ACT (for placement), ACT ASSET.

Costs (2004–05) *One-time required fee:* $100. *Tuition:* $16,320 full-time, $325 per credit part-time. No tuition increase for student's term of enrollment. *Payment plan:* installment. *Waivers:* employees or children of employees.

Applying *Options:* common application. *Application fee:* $50. *Required:* essay or personal statement, high school transcript, interview. *Recommended:* minimum 2.0 GPA. *Application deadline:* rolling (freshmen), rolling (transfers).

Admissions Contact Mr. Jerry Driskill, Director of Admissions, The Art Institute of Phoenix, 2233 West Dunlap Avenue, Phoenix, AZ 85021-2859. *Phone:* 602-678-4300 Ext. 102. *Toll-free phone:* 800-474-2479. *Fax:* 602-216-0439. *E-mail:* infoaipx@aii.edu.

■ *See page 1186 for a narrative description.*

CHAPARRAL COLLEGE

Tucson, Arizona

- **Proprietary** primarily 2-year, founded 1972
- **Calendar** 5 five-week modules
- **Degrees** certificates, diplomas, associate, and bachelor's (bachelor's degree in business administration only)
- **Suburban** campus with easy access to Phoenix
- **Coed,** 400 undergraduate students
- **Noncompetitive** entrance level

Undergraduates Students come from 1 other state, 3 other countries, 0.1% are from out of state.

Faculty *Total:* 38, 37% full-time, 58% with terminal degrees. *Student/faculty ratio:* 20:1.

Majors Accounting; administrative assistant and secretarial science; business administration and management; computer systems networking and telecommunications; criminal justice/safety.
Academic Programs *Special study options:* academic remediation for entering students, internships, summer session for credit.
Library 6,000 titles, 65 serial subscriptions, 500 audiovisual materials, a Web page.
Computers on Campus 150 computers available on campus for general student use. A campuswide network can be accessed. Internet access, at least one staffed computer lab available.
Student Life *Housing:* college housing not available. *Activities and organizations:* student-run newspaper. *Campus security:* 24-hour emergency response devices. *Student services:* personal/psychological counseling.
Standardized Tests *Required:* CPAt (for admission).
Applying *Options:* common application. *Application fee:* $35. *Required:* high school transcript, interview. *Required for some:* letters of recommendation, entrance test. *Application deadline:* rolling (freshmen), rolling (transfers).
Admissions Contact Chaparral College, 4585 East Speedway No. 204, Tucson, AZ 85712. *Phone:* 520-327-6866. *Fax:* 520-325-0108. *E-mail:* admissions@chap-col.edu.

College of the Humanities and Sciences
Tempe, Arizona

Admissions Contact 1105 East Broadway, Tempe, AZ 85282. *Toll-free phone:* 877-248-6724.

Collins College: A School of Design and Technology
Tempe, Arizona

- **Proprietary** 4-year, founded 1978, part of Career Education Corporation
- **Calendar** trimesters
- **Degrees** certificates, associate, and bachelor's
- **Urban** 3-acre campus with easy access to Phoenix
- **Coed**
- 65% of applicants were admitted

Standardized Tests *Recommended:* SAT I or ACT (for admission).
Costs (2003–04) *Tuition:* No tuition increase for student's term of enrollment. tuition varies by program. *Room and board:* Room and board charges vary according to housing facility and location.
Financial Aid Of all full-time matriculated undergraduates who enrolled in 2003, 2,736 applied for aid, 2,576 were judged to have need, 65 had their need fully met. 62 Federal Work-Study jobs (averaging $2400). In 2003, 27. *Average percent of need met:* 65. *Average financial aid package:* $11,500. *Average need-based loan:* $4880. *Average need-based gift aid:* $4000. *Average non-need-based aid:* $11,500. *Average indebtedness upon graduation:* $18,000.
Applying *Options:* common application, early admission, deferred entrance. *Required:* essay or personal statement, high school transcript, interview.
Admissions Contact Collins College: A School of Design and Technology, 1140 South Priest, Tempe, AZ 85281. *Phone:* 480-966-3000. *Toll-free phone:* 800-876-7070. *Fax:* 480-966-2599. *E-mail:* info@collinscollege.edu.

DeVry University
Mesa, Arizona

Admissions Contact 1201 South Alma School Road, Mesa, AZ 85210-2011.

DeVry University
Phoenix, Arizona

- **Proprietary** comprehensive, founded 1967, part of DeVry University
- **Calendar** semesters
- **Degrees** associate, bachelor's, master's, and postbachelor's certificates
- **Urban** 18-acre campus
- **Coed**
- **Minimally difficult** entrance level

Faculty *Student/faculty ratio:* 24:1.
Student Life *Campus security:* 24-hour emergency response devices, student patrols, late-night transport/escort service, trained security personnel on duty, lighted pathways/sidewalks.
Standardized Tests *Recommended:* SAT I, ACT or CPT.
Costs (2003–04) *Tuition:* $9990 full-time, $355 per credit hour part-time. Full-time tuition and fees vary according to course load. Part-time tuition and fees vary according to course load. *Required fees:* $165 full-time. *Payment plans:* installment, deferred payment.
Financial Aid Of all full-time matriculated undergraduates who enrolled in 2002, 1,911 applied for aid, 1,830 were judged to have need, 42 had their need fully met. In 2002, 97. *Average percent of need met:* 40. *Average financial aid package:* $9288. *Average need-based loan:* $6294. *Average need-based gift aid:* $4531. *Average non-need-based aid:* $10,981.
Applying *Options:* electronic application, deferred entrance. *Application fee:* $50. *Required:* high school transcript, interview.
Admissions Contact Mr. Jerry Driskill, Director of Admissions, DeVry University, 2149 West Dunlap Avenue, Phoenix, AZ 85021-2995. *Phone:* 602-870-9201. *Toll-free phone:* 800-528-0250. *Fax:* 602-331-1494. *E-mail:* admissions@phx.devry.edu.

Embry-Riddle Aeronautical University
Prescott, Arizona

- **Independent** comprehensive, founded 1978
- **Calendar** semesters
- **Degrees** bachelor's and master's
- **Small-town** 547-acre campus
- **Endowment** $35.9 million
- **Coed, primarily men,** 1,631 undergraduate students, 87% full-time, 16% women, 84% men
- **Moderately difficult** entrance level, 80% of applicants were admitted

Undergraduates 1,425 full-time, 206 part-time. Students come from 52 states and territories, 31 other countries, 77% are from out of state, 2% African American, 6% Asian American or Pacific Islander, 6% Hispanic American, 1% Native American, 2% international, 6% transferred in, 49% live on campus. *Retention:* 75% of 2002 full-time freshmen returned.
Freshmen *Admission:* 1,250 applied, 1,001 admitted, 304 enrolled. *Average high school GPA:* 3.00. *Test scores:* SAT verbal scores over 500: 70%; SAT math scores over 500: 80%; ACT scores over 18: 95%; SAT verbal scores over 600: 32%; SAT math scores over 600: 44%; ACT scores over 24: 57%; SAT verbal scores over 700: 4%; SAT math scores over 700: 7%; ACT scores over 30: 13%.
Faculty *Total:* 113, 79% full-time, 50% with terminal degrees. *Student/faculty ratio:* 15:1.
Majors Aeronautics/aviation/aerospace science and technology; aerospace, aeronautical and astronautical engineering; airline pilot and flight crew; computer engineering; computer software engineering; electrical, electronics and communications engineering; engineering; international relations and affairs; physics related; science, technology and society.
Academic Programs *Special study options:* academic remediation for entering students, adult/continuing education programs, advanced placement credit, cooperative education, distance learning, double majors, English as a second language, independent study, internships, part-time degree program, services for LD students, study abroad, summer session for credit. *ROTC:* Army (b), Air Force (b).
Library ERAU—Prescott Campus Library with 28,264 titles, 629 serial subscriptions, 2,518 audiovisual materials, an OPAC, a Web page.
Computers on Campus 200 computers available on campus for general student use. A campuswide network can be accessed from student residence rooms and from off campus. Internet access, online (class) registration, at least one staffed computer lab available.
Student Life *Housing:* on-campus residence required for freshman year. *Options:* coed, disabled students. Freshman campus housing is guaranteed. *Activities and organizations:* student-run newspaper, radio and television station, Hawaii club, Strike Eagles, Theta XI, American Institute of Aeronautics and Astronautics (AIAA), Arnold Air Society, national fraternities, national sororities. *Campus security:* 24-hour emergency response devices and patrols, student patrols, late-night transport/escort service. *Student services:* health clinic, personal/psychological counseling.
Athletics Member NAIA. *Intercollegiate sports:* volleyball W(s), wrestling M(s). *Intramural sports:* archery M/W, badminton M/W, basketball M/W, bowling M/W, cross-country running M/W, fencing M(c)/W(c), lacrosse M(c)/W(c), racquetball M/W, rugby M(c)/W(c), skiing (cross-country) M(c)/W(c), skiing (downhill) M(c)/W(c), soccer M(c)/W(c), softball M/W, swimming M/W, table tennis M/W, tennis M/W, track and field M/W, volleyball M/W, weight lifting M/W.
Standardized Tests *Required:* SAT I or ACT (for admission).
Costs (2004–05) *Comprehensive fee:* $28,386 includes full-time tuition ($21,530), mandatory fees ($650), and room and board ($6206). Full-time tuition and fees vary according to course load and program. Part-time tuition: $900 per credit hour. Part-time tuition and fees vary according to course load and program.

Embry-Riddle Aeronautical University (continued)

College room only: $3370. Room and board charges vary according to board plan, housing facility, and location. *Waivers:* employees or children of employees.

Financial Aid Of all full-time matriculated undergraduates who enrolled in 2003, 1,016 applied for aid, 913 were judged to have need. 47 Federal Work-Study jobs (averaging $1351). 572 state and other part-time jobs (averaging $1604). In 2003, 235 non-need-based awards were made. *Average financial aid package:* $12,420. *Average need-based loan:* $4810. *Average need-based gift aid:* $3899. *Average non-need-based aid:* $4649. *Average indebtedness upon graduation:* $33,433. *Financial aid deadline:* 6/30.

Applying *Options:* common application, electronic application, early admission, early decision, deferred entrance. *Application fee:* $30. *Required:* high school transcript, minimum 2.0 GPA. *Required for some:* minimum 3.0 GPA, medical examination for flight students. *Recommended:* essay or personal statement, letters of recommendation, interview. *Application deadlines:* 3/1 (freshmen), 7/1 (transfers). *Early decision:* 12/1. *Notification:* continuous (freshmen), 12/31 (early decision), continuous (transfers).

Admissions Contact Mr. Bill Thompson, Director of Admissions, Embry-Riddle Aeronautical University, 3700 Willow Creek Road, Prescott, AZ 86301-3720. *Phone:* 928-777-6692. *Toll-free phone:* 800-888-3728. *Fax:* 928-777-6606. *E-mail:* pradmit@erau.edu.

■ *See page 1586 for a narrative description.*

GRAND CANYON UNIVERSITY
Phoenix, Arizona

- **Independent Southern Baptist** comprehensive, founded 1949
- **Calendar** semesters
- **Degrees** certificates, diplomas, bachelor's, and master's
- **Suburban** 90-acre campus
- **Endowment** $5.4 million
- **Coed,** 1,609 undergraduate students, 82% full-time, 64% women, 36% men
- **Moderately difficult** entrance level, 69% of applicants were admitted

Grand Canyon University (GCU) is Arizona's only private, Christian, liberal arts university. For more than 50 years, GCU has provided a holistic approach to education, wherein the mind, body, and spirit are seen as essential components in the learning process. With approximately 4,000 students, GCU is committed to providing students with individual attention from faculty, staff, and administrators.

Undergraduates 1,327 full-time, 282 part-time. Students come from 40 states and territories, 14 other countries, 19% are from out of state, 3% African American, 2% Asian American or Pacific Islander, 7% Hispanic American, 1% Native American, 3% international, 19% transferred in, 30% live on campus. *Retention:* 76% of 2002 full-time freshmen returned.

Freshmen *Admission:* 823 applied, 567 admitted, 371 enrolled. *Average high school GPA:* 3.44. *Test scores:* ACT scores over 18: 82%; ACT scores over 24: 29%; ACT scores over 30: 7%.

Faculty *Total:* 274, 35% full-time, 22% with terminal degrees. *Student/faculty ratio:* 16:1.

Majors Accounting; art; art teacher education; athletic training; biblical studies; biology/biological sciences; business administration and management; business/managerial economics; business teacher education; chemistry; commercial and advertising art; criminal justice/law enforcement administration; divinity/ministry; dramatic/theatre arts; economics; elementary education; English; environmental biology; finance; fine/studio arts; history; human resources management; international business/trade/commerce; international relations and affairs; kinesiology and exercise science; liberal arts and sciences/liberal studies; literature; marketing/marketing management; mass communication/media; mathematics; music; music management and merchandising; music teacher education; nursing (registered nurse training); physical education teaching and coaching; physical sciences; piano and organ; political science and government; pre-dentistry studies; pre-law studies; pre-medical studies; pre-veterinary studies; psychology; religious/sacred music; religious studies; science teacher education; secondary education; social sciences; sociology; special education; speech and rhetoric; theology; voice and opera; wildlife biology; wind/percussion instruments.

Academic Programs *Special study options:* academic remediation for entering students, accelerated degree program, adult/continuing education programs, advanced placement credit, cooperative education, distance learning, double majors, English as a second language, freshman honors college, honors programs, independent study, internships, off-campus study, part-time degree program, study abroad, summer session for credit. *ROTC:* Army (b), Air Force (c). *Unusual degree programs:* 3-2 engineering with Arizona State University.

Library Fleming Library with 75,905 titles, 1,174 serial subscriptions, 404 audiovisual materials, an OPAC.

Computers on Campus 119 computers available on campus for general student use. Internet access, at least one staffed computer lab available.

Student Life *Housing:* on-campus residence required through sophomore year. *Options:* men-only, women-only. *Activities and organizations:* drama/theater group, student-run newspaper, choral group. *Campus security:* 24-hour emergency response devices and patrols, student patrols, late-night transport/escort service, controlled dormitory access. *Student services:* health clinic.

Athletics Member NCAA. All Division II. *Intercollegiate sports:* baseball M(s), basketball M(s)/W(s), golf M(s), soccer M(s)/W(s), tennis W(s), volleyball W(s). *Intramural sports:* basketball M/W, football M/W, softball M/W, volleyball M/W.

Standardized Tests *Required:* SAT I or ACT (for admission).

Costs (2003–04) *Comprehensive fee:* $21,630 includes full-time tuition ($14,500) and room and board ($7130). Full-time tuition and fees vary according to course load. Part-time tuition and fees vary according to course load. *Room and board:* Room and board charges vary according to board plan and housing facility. *Payment plan:* installment. *Waivers:* employees or children of employees.

Financial Aid Of all full-time matriculated undergraduates who enrolled in 2000, 993 applied for aid, 855 were judged to have need, 120 had their need fully met. In 2000, 241 non-need-based awards were made. *Average percent of need met:* 41%. *Average financial aid package:* $8405. *Average need-based gift aid:* $2918. *Average non-need-based aid:* $3958. *Average indebtedness upon graduation:* $46,640.

Applying *Application fee:* $50. *Required:* high school transcript, minimum 3.0 GPA. *Required for some:* essay or personal statement, 3 letters of recommendation, interview. *Application deadline:* rolling (freshmen), rolling (transfers). *Notification:* continuous until 9/1 (freshmen), continuous until 9/1 (transfers).

Admissions Contact Mrs. April Chapman, Director of Admissions, Grand Canyon University, 3300 West Camelback Road, PO Box 11097, Phoenix, AZ 86017-3030. *Phone:* 602-589-2855 Ext. 2811. *Toll-free phone:* 800-800-9776. *Fax:* 602-589-2580. *E-mail:* admissions@gcu.edu.

■ *See page 1684 for a narrative description.*

INTERNATIONAL BAPTIST COLLEGE
Tempe, Arizona

Admissions Contact Dr. Stanley Bushey, Administrative Services Director, International Baptist College, 2150 East Southern Avenue, Tempe, AZ 85282. *Phone:* 480-838-7070. *Toll-free phone:* 800-422-4858. *Fax:* 480-838-1533.

INTERNATIONAL IMPORT-EXPORT INSTITUTE
Phoenix, Arizona

Admissions Contact 2432 West Peoria Avenue, Suite 1026, Phoenix, AZ 85029. *Toll-free phone:* 800-474-8013.

INTERNATIONAL INSTITUTE OF THE AMERICAS
Phoenix, Arizona

- **Independent** primarily 2-year, founded 1979
- **Calendar** semesters
- **Degrees** certificates, diplomas, associate, and bachelor's
- **Coed**
- **Noncompetitive** entrance level

Faculty *Student/faculty ratio:* 17:1.

Student Life *Campus security:* 24-hour emergency response devices.

Costs (2003–04) *Tuition:* $8500 full-time, $283 per credit part-time. Full-time tuition and fees vary according to program. No tuition increase for student's term of enrollment. *Required fees:* $350 full-time.

Applying *Options:* electronic application, early admission, deferred entrance. *Required:* interview.

Admissions Contact International Institute of the Americas, 6049 North 43 Avenue, Phoenix, AZ 85019. *Phone:* 800-793-2428. *Toll-free phone:* 800-793-2428. *Fax:* 602-973-2572. *E-mail:* info@aibt.edu.

ITT TECHNICAL INSTITUTE
Phoenix, Arizona

- **Proprietary** primarily 2-year, founded 1972, part of ITT Educational Services, Inc.
- **Calendar** quarters
- **Degrees** associate and bachelor's
- **Urban** 2-acre campus
- **Coed**

■ **Minimally difficult** entrance level

Standardized Tests *Required:* Wonderlic aptitude test (for admission).
Costs (2003–04) *Tuition:* $347 per credit hour part-time.
Financial Aid Of all full-time matriculated undergraduates who enrolled in 2001, 10 Federal Work-Study jobs (averaging $4000).
Applying *Options:* deferred entrance. *Application fee:* $100. *Required:* high school transcript, interview. *Recommended:* letters of recommendation.
Admissions Contact Mr. Gene McWhorter, Director of Recruitment, ITT Technical Institute, 4837 East McDowell Road, Phoenix, AZ 85008. *Phone:* 602-252-2331. *Toll-free phone:* 800-879-4881. *Fax:* 602-267-8727.

ITT TECHNICAL INSTITUTE
Tucson, Arizona

■ **Proprietary** primarily 2-year, founded 1984, part of ITT Educational Services, Inc.
■ **Calendar** quarters
■ **Degrees** associate and bachelor's
■ **Urban** 3-acre campus
■ **Coed**
■ **Minimally difficult** entrance level

Standardized Tests *Required:* Wonderlic aptitude test (for admission).
Costs (2003–04) *Tuition:* $347 per credit hour part-time.
Applying *Options:* deferred entrance. *Application fee:* $100. *Required:* high school transcript, interview. *Recommended:* letters of recommendation.
Admissions Contact Ms. Linda Lemken, Director of Recruitment, ITT Technical Institute, 1455 West River Road, Tucson, AZ 85704. *Phone:* 520-408-7488. *Toll-free phone:* 800-870-9730. *Fax:* 520-292-9899.

METROPOLITAN COLLEGE OF COURT REPORTING
Phoenix, Arizona

Admissions Contact Ms. Shannon Buchanan, Admissions, Metropolitan College of Court Reporting, 4640 East Elwood Street, Suite 12, Phoenix, AZ 85040. *Phone:* 480-955-5900. *Fax:* 480-894-8999.

MIDWESTERN UNIVERSITY, GLENDALE CAMPUS
Glendale, Arizona

■ **Independent** upper-level, founded 1996
■ **Calendar** quarters
■ **Degrees** certificates, bachelor's, master's, doctoral, and postbachelor's certificates
■ **Coed**

Costs (2003–04) *Tuition:* $14,440 full-time. *Required fees:* $250 full-time.
Financial Aid Of all full-time matriculated undergraduates who enrolled in 2002, 110 applied for aid, 110 were judged to have need, 2 had their need fully met. 28 Federal Work-Study jobs (averaging $1519). *Average percent of need met:* 42. *Average financial aid package:* $30,333. *Average need-based loan:* $5458. *Average need-based gift aid:* $5310. *Financial aid deadline:* 4/15.
Admissions Contact Mr. James Walter, Director of Admissions, Midwestern University, Glendale Campus, 19555 North 59th Avenue, Glendale, AZ 85308. *Phone:* 623-572-3340. *Toll-free phone:* 888-247-9277 (in-state); 888-247-9271 (out-of-state). *Fax:* 623-572-3229. *E-mail:* admissionaz@arizona.midwestern.edu.

NORTHCENTRAL UNIVERSITY
Prescott, Arizona

■ **Proprietary** comprehensive
■ **Calendar** continuous
■ **Degrees** bachelor's, master's, and doctoral (distance learning only)
■ **Coed,** 132 undergraduate students, 44% women, 56% men
■ **Minimally difficult** entrance level

Undergraduates 132 part-time. Students come from 51 states and territories, 93% are from out of state, 14% African American, 3% Asian American or Pacific Islander, 5% Hispanic American, 2% Native American.
Freshmen *Admission:* 4 enrolled.
Faculty *Total:* 103, 9% full-time, 82% with terminal degrees. *Student/faculty ratio:* 1:1.
Majors Business administration and management; general studies; psychology.
Academic Programs *Special study options:* accelerated degree program, advanced placement credit, distance learning, external degree program, part-time degree program, summer session for credit.
Library Electronic Learning Resources Center with a Web page.
Student Life *Housing:* college housing not available.
Costs (2003–04) *Tuition:* $335 per credit part-time. *Payment plan:* installment. *Waivers:* employees or children of employees.
Applying *Options:* electronic application. *Application fee:* $100. *Required:* essay or personal statement, high school transcript. *Application deadline:* rolling (freshmen), rolling (transfers). *Notification:* continuous (freshmen), continuous (transfers).
Admissions Contact Ms. Poppy Keegan, Admissions Counselor, Northcentral University, 505 West Whipple Street, Prescott, AZ 86301. *Phone:* 888-327-2877 Ext. 8072. *Toll-free phone:* 888-327-2877. *Fax:* 928-541-7817. *E-mail:* info@ncu.edu.

NORTHERN ARIZONA UNIVERSITY
Flagstaff, Arizona

■ **State-supported** university, founded 1899, part of Arizona University System
■ **Calendar** semesters
■ **Degrees** certificates, bachelor's, master's, doctoral, first professional, post-master's, and postbachelor's certificates
■ **Small-town** 730-acre campus
■ **Endowment** $9.9 million
■ **Coed,** 13,015 undergraduate students, 85% full-time, 60% women, 40% men
■ **Moderately difficult** entrance level

Undergraduates 11,034 full-time, 1,981 part-time. Students come from 50 states and territories, 66 other countries, 15% are from out of state, 2% African American, 2% Asian American or Pacific Islander, 10% Hispanic American, 8% Native American, 2% international, 53% live on campus. *Retention:* 69% of 2002 full-time freshmen returned.
Freshmen *Average high school GPA:* 3.40. *Test scores:* SAT verbal scores over 500: 67%; SAT math scores over 500: 63%; ACT scores over 18: 87%; SAT verbal scores over 600: 23%; SAT math scores over 600: 22%; ACT scores over 24: 34%; SAT verbal scores over 700: 3%; SAT math scores over 700: 2%; ACT scores over 30: 3%.
Faculty *Total:* 1,142, 62% full-time, 61% with terminal degrees. *Student/faculty ratio:* 17:1.
Majors Accounting; advertising; American government and politics; American Indian/Native American studies; anthropology; art; art history, criticism and conservation; arts management; art teacher education; astronomy; biology/biological sciences; biology teacher education; botany/plant biology; business administration and management; business/commerce; business/managerial economics; cell biology and anatomical sciences related; chemistry; chemistry related; civil engineering; communication and journalism related; communication/speech communication and rhetoric; computer and information sciences; construction engineering technology; counselor education/school counseling and guidance; criminal justice/law enforcement administration; dental hygiene; drama and dance teacher education; dramatic/theatre arts; ecology; economics; education; educational leadership and administration; education (specific subject areas) related; electrical, electronics and communications engineering; elementary education; engineering; engineering physics; English; English as a second/foreign language (teaching); English/language arts teacher education; environmental/environmental health engineering; environmental studies; finance; forest sciences and biology; French; general studies; geochemistry; geography; geology/earth science; German; health teacher education; history; history teacher education; hotel/motel administration; humanities; interior design; international relations and affairs; journalism; kinesiology and exercise science; liberal arts and sciences and humanities related; liberal arts and sciences/liberal studies; management information systems; marine biology and biological oceanography; marketing/marketing management; mathematics; mathematics teacher education; mechanical engineering; medical microbiology and bacteriology; music; music performance; music teacher education; nursing (registered nurse training); parks, recreation and leisure; philosophy; photography; physical education teaching and coaching; physical sciences; physics; physics related; physics teacher education; political science and government; pre-law studies; pre-medical studies; pre-veterinary studies; psychology; public policy analysis; public relations/image management; radio and television; religious studies; science teacher education; science technologies related; social sciences; social science teacher education; social work; sociology; Spanish; Spanish language teacher education; special education; special education (speech or language impaired); speech and rhetoric; technology/industrial arts teacher education; wildlife and wildlands science and management; women's studies; zoology/animal biology.
Academic Programs *Special study options:* accelerated degree program, advanced placement credit, cooperative education, distance learning, double

Northern Arizona University (continued)

majors, English as a second language, freshman honors college, honors programs, independent study, internships, off-campus study, part-time degree program, services for LD students, study abroad, summer session for credit. *ROTC:* Army (b), Air Force (b).

Library Cline Library plus 1 other with 633,417 titles, 2,595 serial subscriptions, 31,746 audiovisual materials, an OPAC, a Web page.

Computers on Campus 903 computers available on campus for general student use. A campuswide network can be accessed from student residence rooms and from off campus that provide access to e-mail. Internet access, online (class) registration, at least one staffed computer lab available. Computer purchase or lease plan available.

Student Life *Housing options:* coed, men-only, women-only, disabled students. Campus housing is university owned and is provided by a third party. Freshman campus housing is guaranteed. *Activities and organizations:* drama/theater group, student-run newspaper, radio and television station, choral group, marching band, ASNAU, Black Student Union, New Student Organization, Cardinal Key, Blue Key, national fraternities, national sororities. *Campus security:* 24-hour emergency response devices and patrols, late-night transport/escort service, controlled dormitory access. *Student services:* health clinic, personal/psychological counseling, women's center, legal services.

Athletics Member NCAA. All Division I except football (Division I-AA). *Intercollegiate sports:* basketball M(s)/W(s), cross-country running M(s)/W(s), golf W(s), soccer W(s), swimming W(s), tennis M(s)/W(s), track and field M(s)/W(s), volleyball W(s). *Intramural sports:* archery M/W, badminton M/W, baseball M, basketball M/W, bowling M/W, cross-country running M/W, fencing M/W, football M/W, ice hockey M, lacrosse M/W, racquetball M/W, rugby M/W, skiing (cross-country) M/W, skiing (downhill) M/W, soccer M(c), softball M/W, swimming W, table tennis M/W, ultimate Frisbee M/W, volleyball M/W, water polo M/W, weight lifting M/W.

Standardized Tests *Required for some:* SAT I (for admission), ACT (for admission), SAT I or ACT (for admission).

Costs (2003–04) *Tuition:* state resident $3508 full-time, $183 per credit part-time; nonresident $12,028 full-time, $501 per credit part-time. Full-time tuition and fees vary according to program. Part-time tuition and fees vary according to course load and program. *Required fees:* $120 full-time, $22 per term part-time. *Room and board:* $5374; room only: $2708. Room and board charges vary according to board plan and housing facility. *Waivers:* employees or children of employees.

Financial Aid Of all full-time matriculated undergraduates who enrolled in 2003, 7,891 applied for aid, 6,063 were judged to have need, 2,187 had their need fully met. 624 Federal Work-Study jobs (averaging $1758). In 2003, 1344 non-need-based awards were made. *Average percent of need met:* 72%. *Average financial aid package:* $7898. *Average need-based loan:* $1909. *Average need-based gift aid:* $5157. *Average non-need-based aid:* $6039. *Average indebtedness upon graduation:* $16,310.

Applying *Options:* electronic application, deferred entrance. *Application fee:* $25. *Required:* high school transcript. *Required for some:* essay or personal statement, letters of recommendation, interview. *Recommended:* minimum 3.0 GPA. *Application deadline:* 8/1 (freshmen), rolling (transfers). *Notification:* continuous (freshmen), continuous (transfers).

Admissions Contact Janet Heinrichs, Assistant Director, Northern Arizona University, PO Box 4084, Flagstaff, AZ 86011. *Phone:* 928-523-6006. *Toll-free phone:* 888-MORE-NAU. *Fax:* 928-523-6023. *E-mail:* undergraduate.admissions@nau.edu.

■ See page 2100 for a narrative description.

PRESCOTT COLLEGE
Prescott, Arizona

- **Independent** comprehensive, founded 1966
- **Calendar** quarters (4-week blocks followed by 10-week terms for each quarter)
- **Degrees** certificates, bachelor's, and master's
- **Small-town** campus
- **Endowment** $150,000
- **Coed**
- **Moderately difficult** entrance level

Faculty *Student/faculty ratio:* 12:1.

Costs (2003–04) *Tuition:* $14,970 full-time, $453 per credit hour part-time. Full-time tuition and fees vary according to course load and program. Part-time tuition and fees vary according to course load and program. *Required fees:* $1652 full-time. Payment plan: installment. Waivers: employees or children of employees.

Financial Aid Of all full-time matriculated undergraduates who enrolled in 2002, 642 applied for aid, 590 were judged to have need. 165 Federal Work-Study jobs (averaging $1373). 64 state and other part-time jobs (averaging $1010). *Average percent of need met:* 67. *Average financial aid package:* $4560. *Average need-based loan:* $3790. *Average need-based gift aid:* $2725. *Average indebtedness upon graduation:* $14,255.

Applying *Options:* deferred entrance. *Application fee:* $25. *Required:* essay or personal statement, high school transcript, 2 letters of recommendation. *Required for some:* interview.

Admissions Contact Ms. Shari Sterling, Director of Admissions, Prescott College, 220 Grove Avenue, Prescott, AZ 86301. *Phone:* 928-778-2090 Ext. 2101. *Toll-free phone:* 877-350-2100. *Fax:* 928-776-5242. *E-mail:* admissions@prescott.edu.

■ See page 2194 for a narrative description.

REMINGTON COLLEGE–TEMPE CAMPUS
Tempe, Arizona

Admissions Contact Mr. Joe Drennen, Campus President, Remington College–Tempe Campus, 875 West Elliot Road, Suite 216, Tempe, AZ 85284. *Phone:* 480-834-1000. *Toll-free phone:* 800-395-4322.

SOUTHWESTERN COLLEGE
Phoenix, Arizona

- **Independent Conservative Baptist** 4-year, founded 1960
- **Calendar** 4-4-1
- **Degrees** associate and bachelor's
- **Urban** 19-acre campus
- **Coed,** 267 undergraduate students, 89% full-time, 52% women, 48% men
- **Minimally difficult** entrance level, 61% of applicants were admitted

Undergraduates 237 full-time, 30 part-time. Students come from 19 states and territories, 3 other countries, 16% are from out of state, 2% African American, 0.7% Asian American or Pacific Islander, 7% Hispanic American, 0.7% Native American, 1% international, 24% transferred in, 51% live on campus. *Retention:* 61% of 2002 full-time freshmen returned.

Freshmen *Admission:* 130 applied, 79 admitted, 29 enrolled. *Average high school GPA:* 3.30.

Faculty *Total:* 33, 27% full-time, 100% with terminal degrees. *Student/faculty ratio:* 17:1.

Majors Biblical studies; business administration and management; counseling psychology; elementary education; music teacher education; secondary education; youth ministry.

Academic Programs *Special study options:* academic remediation for entering students, accelerated degree program, adult/continuing education programs, advanced placement credit, internships, summer session for credit. *ROTC:* Air Force (c).

Library R. S. Beal Library with 32,000 titles, 293 serial subscriptions, 2,567 audiovisual materials.

Computers on Campus 27 computers available on campus for general student use. At least one staffed computer lab available.

Student Life *Housing:* on-campus residence required through sophomore year. *Options:* men-only, women-only, disabled students. Campus housing is university owned. Freshman campus housing is guaranteed. *Activities and organizations:* drama/theater group, student-run newspaper, choral group, Newspaper, Drama, Choral, Student Leadership Council. *Campus security:* controlled dormitory access.

Athletics Member NCCAA, NSCAA. *Intercollegiate sports:* basketball M/W, volleyball W. *Intramural sports:* basketball M/W, football M, softball M/W, table tennis M/W, ultimate Frisbee M/W, volleyball M/W.

Standardized Tests *Required:* SAT I and SAT II or ACT (for admission).

Costs (2004–05) *Comprehensive fee:* $15,240 includes full-time tuition ($10,600), mandatory fees ($440), and room and board ($4200). Full-time tuition and fees vary according to course load and program. Part-time tuition: $442 per credit hour. Part-time tuition and fees vary according to course load and program. *Required fees:* $220 per term part-time. *College room only:* $3200. Room and board charges vary according to housing facility. *Payment plan:* installment. *Waivers:* employees or children of employees.

Financial Aid Of all full-time matriculated undergraduates who enrolled in 2003, 147 applied for aid, 147 were judged to have need. 20 Federal Work-Study jobs (averaging $2000). In 2003, 99 non-need-based awards were made. *Average percent of need met:* 3%. *Average financial aid package:* $5500. *Average need-based loan:* $4500. *Average need-based gift aid:* $1400. *Average non-need-based aid:* $1100. *Average indebtedness upon graduation:* $17,125.

Applying *Options:* deferred entrance. *Application fee:* $25. *Required:* essay or personal statement, high school transcript, minimum 2.0 GPA, 1 letter of recommendation. *Application deadlines:* 8/1 (freshmen), 8/1 (transfers). *Notification:* continuous until 8/20 (freshmen), continuous (transfers).

Admissions Contact Lambur Cruz, Admissions/Financial Aid Counselor, Southwestern College, 2625 East Cactus Road, Administration Building, Phoenix, AZ 85015. *Phone:* 602-992-6101 Ext. 111. *Toll-free phone:* 800-247-2697. *Fax:* 602-404-2159. *E-mail:* admissions@swcaz.edu.

UNIVERSITY OF ADVANCING TECHNOLOGY
Tempe, Arizona

- **Proprietary** comprehensive, founded 1983
- **Calendar** semesters
- **Degrees** certificates, diplomas, associate, bachelor's, and master's
- **Urban** campus
- **Coed,** 744 undergraduate students, 100% full-time, 15% women, 85% men

Undergraduates 744 full-time. 4% African American, 4% Asian American or Pacific Islander, 8% Hispanic American, 2% Native American, 2% international.

Freshmen *Admission:* 459 admitted, 170 enrolled.

Faculty *Total:* 50, 82% full-time. *Student/faculty ratio:* 15:1.

Majors Cinematography and film/video production; commercial and advertising art; computer graphics; computer programming; computer systems analysis; data processing and data processing technology; design and visual communications.

Academic Programs *Special study options:* accelerated degree program, distance learning.

Library University of Advancing Computer Technology Library with a Web page.

Computers on Campus 190 computers available on campus for general student use. A campuswide network can be accessed from off campus. Internet access, online (class) registration, at least one staffed computer lab available.

Student Life *Housing:* college housing not available. *Options:* Campus housing is provided by a third party. *Activities and organizations:* student-run newspaper, television station, web club, gaming club, animation club, video club, student government. *Campus security:* 24-hour patrols. *Student services:* personal/psychological counseling.

Standardized Tests *Required:* SAT I or ACT (for admission). *Required for some:* Wonderlic aptitude test.

Costs (2003–04) *Comprehensive fee:* $21,400 includes full-time tuition ($13,600) and room and board ($7800). *College room only:* $4200.

Applying *Options:* early admission. *Required:* high school transcript, interview. *Required for some:* minimum 2.5 GPA. *Recommended:* essay or personal statement. *Application deadline:* rolling (freshmen).

Admissions Contact Mr. Dominic Pistillo, President, University of Advancing Technology, 2625 West Baseline Road, Tempe, AZ 85283-1042. *Phone:* 602-383-8228. *Toll-free phone:* 602-383-8228 (in-state); 800-658-5744 (out-of-state). *Fax:* 602-383-8222. *E-mail:* admissions@uact.edu.

■ *See page 2562 for a narrative description.*

THE UNIVERSITY OF ARIZONA
Tucson, Arizona

- **State-supported** university, founded 1885, part of Arizona Board of Regents
- **Calendar** semesters
- **Degrees** bachelor's, master's, doctoral, first professional, and postbachelor's certificates
- **Urban** 362-acre campus
- **Endowment** $297.7 million
- **Coed,** 28,482 undergraduate students, 85% full-time, 53% women, 47% men
- **Moderately difficult** entrance level, 85% of applicants were admitted

Undergraduates 24,217 full-time, 4,265 part-time. Students come from 56 states and territories, 135 other countries, 28% are from out of state, 3% African American, 6% Asian American or Pacific Islander, 15% Hispanic American, 2% Native American, 3% international, 20% live on campus. *Retention:* 77% of 2002 full-time freshmen returned.

Freshmen *Admission:* 20,924 applied, 17,796 admitted, 5,958 enrolled. *Average high school GPA:* 3.40. *Test scores:* SAT verbal scores over 500: 74%; SAT math scores over 500: 77%; ACT scores over 18: 91%; SAT verbal scores over 600: 31%; SAT math scores over 600: 36%; ACT scores over 24: 49%; SAT verbal scores over 700: 5%; SAT math scores over 700: 6%; ACT scores over 30: 7%.

Faculty *Total:* 1,362. *Student/faculty ratio:* 20:1.

Majors Accounting; aerospace, aeronautical and astronautical engineering; agricultural/biological engineering and bioengineering; agricultural economics; agricultural teacher education; agriculture; animal physiology; animal sciences; anthropology; architecture; art history, criticism and conservation; art teacher education; Asian studies (East); astronomy; atmospheric sciences and meteorology; biochemistry; biology/biological sciences; biology teacher education; business/commerce; business/managerial economics; cell biology and histology; chemical engineering; chemistry; chemistry teacher education; city/urban, community and regional planning; civil engineering; classics and languages, literatures and linguistics; clinical laboratory science/medical technology; communication disorders; communication/speech communication and rhetoric; computer and information sciences; computer engineering; consumer economics; creative writing; criminal justice/law enforcement administration; dance; drama and dance teacher education; dramatic/theatre arts; ecology; economics; education (specific subject areas) related; electrical, electronics and communications engineering; elementary education; engineering; engineering physics; engineering related; English; English/language arts teacher education; entrepreneurship; environmental studies; evolutionary biology; family and consumer sciences/home economics teacher education; finance; fine/studio arts; foreign language teacher education; French; French language teacher education; geography; geological/geophysical engineering; geology/earth science; German; German language teacher education; health/health care administration; health teacher education; Hispanic-American, Puerto Rican, and Mexican-American/Chicano studies; history; history teacher education; human development and family studies; humanities; human resources management; industrial engineering; Italian; Jewish/Judaic studies; journalism; kindergarten/preschool education; landscape architecture; Latin American studies; liberal arts and sciences/liberal studies; linguistics; management information systems; marketing/marketing management; materials science; mathematics; mathematics teacher education; mechanical engineering; medical microbiology and bacteriology; mining and mineral engineering; molecular biophysics; multi-/interdisciplinary studies related; music; music performance; music related; music teacher education; Near and Middle Eastern studies; nuclear engineering; nursing (registered nurse training); nutrition sciences; operations management; optical sciences; philosophy; physical education teaching and coaching; physics; physics teacher education; plant sciences; political science and government; pre-veterinary studies; psychology; public administration; radio and television; religious studies; Russian; science teacher education; science technologies related; secondary education; social science teacher education; social studies teacher education; sociology; soil science and agronomy; Spanish; Spanish language teacher education; special education; speech teacher education; systems engineering; theatre design and technology; visual and performing arts; water resources engineering; wildlife and wildlands science and management; women's studies.

Academic Programs *Special study options:* adult/continuing education programs, advanced placement credit, distance learning, double majors, English as a second language, freshman honors college, honors programs, independent study, internships, part-time degree program, services for LD students, study abroad, summer session for credit. *ROTC:* Army (b), Navy (b), Air Force (b). *Unusual degree programs:* 3-2 business administration with American Graduate School of International Management.

Library University of Arizona Main Library plus 5 others with 4.4 million titles, 23,790 serial subscriptions, 51,136 audiovisual materials, an OPAC, a Web page.

Computers on Campus 1950 computers available on campus for general student use. A campuswide network can be accessed from student residence rooms and from off campus. Internet access, at least one staffed computer lab available.

Student Life *Housing options:* coed, men-only, women-only. Campus housing is university owned and leased by the school. Freshman applicants given priority for college housing. *Activities and organizations:* drama/theater group, student-run newspaper, radio and television station, choral group, marching band, Student Government Association, national fraternities, national sororities. *Campus security:* 24-hour patrols, student patrols, late-night transport/escort service, emergency telephones. *Student services:* health clinic, personal/psychological counseling, women's center, legal services.

Athletics Member NCAA. All Division I except men's and women's cheerleading (Division III), football (Division I-A). *Intercollegiate sports:* baseball M(s), basketball M(s)/W(s), cheerleading M/W, cross-country running M(s)/W(s), golf M(s)/W(s), gymnastics W(s), ice hockey M(c), lacrosse M(c)/W(c), rugby M(c)/W(c), soccer M(c)/W(s), softball W(s), swimming M(s)/W(s), tennis M(s)/W(s), track and field M(s)/W(s), volleyball M(c)/W(s), wrestling M(c). *Intramural sports:* badminton M/W, basketball M/W, bowling M/W, cross-country running M/W, football M/W, golf M/W, racquetball M/W, soccer M/W, softball M/W, swimming M/W, table tennis M/W, tennis M/W, track and field M/W, ultimate Frisbee M(c)/W(c), volleyball M/W, water polo M/W, weight lifting M/W, wrestling M.

Standardized Tests *Required:* SAT I or ACT (for admission).

Costs (2003–04) *Tuition:* state resident $3508 full-time, $197 per unit part-time; nonresident $12,278 full-time, $526 per unit part-time. Full-time tuition and fees vary according to course load and program. Part-time tuition and fees vary according to course load. *Required fees:* $95 full-time. *Room and board:* $6810; room only: $3570. Room and board charges vary according to board plan and housing facility. *Waivers:* employees or children of employees.

The University of Arizona (continued)

Financial Aid Of all full-time matriculated undergraduates who enrolled in 2002, 19,264 applied for aid, 11,166 were judged to have need. *Average financial aid package:* $9993. *Average indebtedness upon graduation:* $16,881.

Applying *Options:* electronic application, early admission. *Required:* high school transcript. *Required for some:* minimum 3.0 GPA, letters of recommendation, interview. *Application deadlines:* 4/1 (freshmen), 6/1 (transfers). *Notification:* continuous until 8/1 (freshmen), 7/15 (transfers).

Admissions Contact Ms. Lori Goldman, Director of Admissions, The University of Arizona, PO Box 210011, Tucson, AZ 85721-0040. *Phone:* 520-621-3237. *Fax:* 520-621-9799. *E-mail:* appinfo@arizona.edu.

University of Phoenix Online Campus
Phoenix, Arizona

- **Proprietary** comprehensive, founded 1989
- **Calendar** continuous
- **Degrees** certificates, associate, bachelor's, master's, doctoral, post-master's, and postbachelor's certificates (courses conducted at 121 campuses and learning centers in 25 states)
- **Coed,** 27,799 undergraduate students, 100% full-time, 64% women, 36% men
- **Noncompetitive** entrance level

Undergraduates 27,799 full-time. 10% African American, 2% Asian American or Pacific Islander, 5% Hispanic American, 0.8% Native American, 9% international.

Freshmen *Admission:* 1,671 enrolled.

Faculty *Total:* 4,363, 0.2% full-time, 23% with terminal degrees. *Student/faculty ratio:* 12:1.

Majors Accounting; business administration and management; computer programming; corrections and criminal justice related; finance; general studies; health/health care administration; management science.

Academic Programs *Special study options:* accelerated degree program, adult/continuing education programs, advanced placement credit, distance learning, external degree program, independent study.

Library University Library with 27.1 million titles, 11,648 serial subscriptions, an OPAC, a Web page.

Computers on Campus A campuswide network can be accessed from off campus. At least one staffed computer lab available.

Student Life *Housing:* college housing not available.

Costs (2003–04) *Tuition:* $12,660 full-time, $422 per credit part-time. *Waivers:* employees or children of employees.

Financial Aid *Average financial aid package:* $1301.

Applying *Options:* deferred entrance. *Required:* 1 letter of recommendation, 2 years of work experience, 23 years of age. *Required for some:* high school transcript. *Application deadline:* rolling (freshmen), rolling (transfers).

Admissions Contact Ms. Beth Barilla, Director of Admissions, University of Phoenix Online Campus, 4615 East Elwood Street, Mail Stop AA-K101, Phoenix, AZ 85040-1958. *Phone:* 480-317-6000. *Toll-free phone:* 800-776-4867 (in-state); 800-228-7240 (out-of-state). *E-mail:* beth.barilla@apollogrp.edu.

University of Phoenix–Phoenix Campus
Phoenix, Arizona

- **Proprietary** comprehensive, founded 1976
- **Calendar** continuous
- **Degrees** certificates, associate, bachelor's, master's, doctoral, post-master's, and postbachelor's certificates (courses conducted at 121 campuses and learning centers in 25 states)
- **Urban** campus
- **Coed,** 3,071 undergraduate students, 100% full-time, 58% women, 42% men
- **Noncompetitive** entrance level

Undergraduates 3,071 full-time. 5% African American, 1% Asian American or Pacific Islander, 8% Hispanic American, 1% Native American, 5% international.

Freshmen *Admission:* 112 enrolled.

Faculty *Total:* 2,256, 2% full-time, 25% with terminal degrees. *Student/faculty ratio:* 9:1.

Majors Accounting; business administration and management; counseling psychology; criminal justice/law enforcement administration; entrepreneurship; finance; general studies; health/health care administration; information technology; management information systems; management science; marketing/marketing management; nursing science; public administration and social service professions related.

Academic Programs *Special study options:* accelerated degree program, adult/continuing education programs, advanced placement credit, distance learning, external degree program, independent study.

Library University Library with 27.1 million titles, 11,648 serial subscriptions, an OPAC, a Web page.

Computers on Campus A campuswide network can be accessed from off campus. Internet access, at least one staffed computer lab available.

Student Life *Housing:* college housing not available. *Campus security:* 24-hour patrols, late-night transport/escort service.

Costs (2003–04) *Tuition:* $8760 full-time, $292 per credit part-time. *Waivers:* employees or children of employees.

Financial Aid *Average financial aid package:* $1437.

Applying *Options:* deferred entrance. *Application fee:* $85. *Required:* 1 letter of recommendation, 2 years of work experience, 23 years of age. *Required for some:* high school transcript. *Application deadline:* rolling (freshmen), rolling (transfers).

Admissions Contact Ms. Beth Barilla, Director of Admissions, University of Phoenix–Phoenix Campus, 4615 East Elwood Street, Mail Stop AA-K101, Phoenix, AZ 85040-1958. *Phone:* 480-317-6000. *Toll-free phone:* 800-776-4867 (in-state); 800-228-7240 (out-of-state). *Fax:* 480-894-1758. *E-mail:* beth.barilla@phoenix.edu.

University of Phoenix–Southern Arizona Campus
Tucson, Arizona

- **Proprietary** comprehensive, founded 1979
- **Calendar** continuous
- **Degrees** certificates, associate, bachelor's, master's, doctoral, post-master's, and postbachelor's certificates (courses conducted at 121 campuses and learning centers in 25 states)
- **Urban** campus
- **Coed,** 1,107 undergraduate students, 100% full-time, 61% women, 39% men
- **Noncompetitive** entrance level

Undergraduates 1,107 full-time. 4% African American, 0.7% Asian American or Pacific Islander, 19% Hispanic American, 2% Native American, 16% international.

Freshmen *Admission:* 46 enrolled.

Faculty *Total:* 650, 1% full-time, 27% with terminal degrees. *Student/faculty ratio:* 8:1.

Majors Accounting; business administration and management; corrections and criminal justice related; finance; health/health care administration; information technology; management information systems; management science; marketing/marketing management; nursing (registered nurse training); nursing science; public administration and social service professions related.

Academic Programs *Special study options:* accelerated degree program, adult/continuing education programs, advanced placement credit, distance learning, external degree program, independent study.

Library University Library with 27.1 million titles, 11,648 serial subscriptions, an OPAC, a Web page.

Computers on Campus A campuswide network can be accessed from off campus. Internet access, at least one staffed computer lab available.

Student Life *Housing:* college housing not available.

Costs (2003–04) *Tuition:* $8490 full-time, $283 per credit part-time. *Waivers:* employees or children of employees.

Applying *Options:* deferred entrance. *Application fee:* $85. *Required:* 1 letter of recommendation, 2 years of work experience, 23 years of age. *Required for some:* high school transcript. *Application deadline:* rolling (freshmen), rolling (transfers).

Admissions Contact Ms. Beth Barilla, Director of Admissions, University of Phoenix–Southern Arizona Campus, 4615 East Elwood Street, Mail Stop AA-K101, Phoenix, AZ 85040-1958. *Phone:* 480-317-6000. *Toll-free phone:* 800-228-7240. *Fax:* 480-594-1756. *E-mail:* beth.barilla@phoenix.edu.

Western International University
Phoenix, Arizona

- **Proprietary** comprehensive, founded 1978
- **Calendar** continuous
- **Degrees** certificates, associate, bachelor's, and master's
- **Urban** 4-acre campus
- **Endowment** $20,000
- **Coed**
- **Moderately difficult** entrance level

Faculty *Student/faculty ratio:* 10:1.

Student Life *Campus security:* 24-hour emergency response devices and patrols, late-night transport/escort service.
Costs (2003–04) *Tuition:* $9180 full-time.
Applying *Options:* deferred entrance. *Application fee:* $85. *Required:* high school transcript, minimum 2.5 GPA, interview. *Required for some:* 3 letters of recommendation. *Recommended:* 3 letters of recommendation.
Admissions Contact Ms. Jo Arney, Director of Student services, Western International University, 9215 North Black Canyon Highway, Phoenix, AZ 85021. *Phone:* 602-943-2311 Ext. 139.

ARKANSAS

ARKANSAS BAPTIST COLLEGE
Little Rock, Arkansas

- **Independent Baptist** 4-year, founded 1884
- **Calendar** semesters
- **Degrees** certificates, associate, and bachelor's
- **Urban** campus
- **Endowment** $306,174
- **Coed,** 375 undergraduate students, 69% full-time, 56% women, 44% men
- **Minimally difficult** entrance level

Undergraduates 258 full-time, 117 part-time. 99% African American.
Freshmen *Admission:* 215 enrolled. *Average high school GPA:* 2.00.
Faculty *Total:* 31, 55% full-time, 23% with terminal degrees. *Student/faculty ratio:* 9:1.
Majors Adult and continuing education; business administration and management; computer science; elementary education; liberal arts and sciences/liberal studies; religious studies; secondary education; social work.
Academic Programs *Special study options:* academic remediation for entering students, accelerated degree program, adult/continuing education programs, part-time degree program, summer session for credit.
Computers on Campus 25 computers available on campus for general student use.
Student Life *Housing options:* Campus housing is university owned.
Athletics Member NAIA. *Intercollegiate sports:* basketball M/W, volleyball M/W.
Costs (2003–04) *Comprehensive fee:* $8288 includes full-time tuition ($3000), mandatory fees ($288), and room and board ($5000). Part-time tuition: $157 per hour. *Required fees:* $100 per term part-time.
Applying *Options:* deferred entrance. *Required:* high school transcript. *Application deadline:* rolling (freshmen).
Admissions Contact Mrs. Jamesetta Ballard, Director of Admissions and Enrollment, Arkansas Baptist College, 1600 Bishop Street, Little Rock, AR 72202. *Phone:* 501-374-7856.

ARKANSAS STATE UNIVERSITY
Jonesboro, Arkansas

- **State-supported** comprehensive, founded 1909, part of Arkansas State University System
- **Calendar** semesters
- **Degrees** certificates, associate, bachelor's, master's, doctoral, post-master's, and postbachelor's certificates
- **Small-town** 942-acre campus with easy access to Memphis
- **Endowment** $28.6 million
- **Coed,** 9,413 undergraduate students, 79% full-time, 59% women, 41% men
- **Moderately difficult** entrance level, 66% of applicants were admitted

Arkansas State University (ASU) is creating leaders. ASU is the only institution in Arkansas that offers a leadership minor in addition to a number leadership opportunities such as seminars, summer camps for high school students, and travel abroad. ASU is also the only university in Arkansas that offers the National Student Exchange Program.

Undergraduates 7,457 full-time, 1,956 part-time. Students come from 45 states and territories, 56 other countries, 10% are from out of state, 15% African American, 0.7% Asian American or Pacific Islander, 0.8% Hispanic American, 0.3% Native American, 1% international, 9% transferred in, 20% live on campus. *Retention:* 70% of 2002 full-time freshmen returned.
Freshmen *Admission:* 3,088 applied, 2,039 admitted, 1,525 enrolled. *Average high school GPA:* 3.2. *Test scores:* ACT scores over 18: 80%; ACT scores over 24: 35%; ACT scores over 30: 4%.
Faculty *Total:* 614, 73% full-time, 47% with terminal degrees. *Student/faculty ratio:* 19:1.
Majors Accounting; administrative assistant and secretarial science; agribusiness; agricultural teacher education; agriculture; animal sciences; art; art teacher education; athletic training; audiology and speech-language pathology; automobile/automotive mechanics technology; biology/biological sciences; biology teacher education; business administration and management; business/managerial economics; business teacher education; chemistry; chemistry teacher education; clinical laboratory science/medical technology; commercial and advertising art; computer and information sciences; criminal justice/law enforcement administration; criminal justice/police science; criminology; data processing and data processing technology; development economics and international development; dramatic/theatre arts; economics; education related; electrical, electronic and communications engineering technology; emergency medical technology (EMT paramedic); engineering; engineering technology; English; English/language arts teacher education; finance; forensic science and technology; French; French language teacher education; general studies; geography; health and physical education; health teacher education; history; international business/trade/commerce; journalism; kinesiology and exercise science; management information systems; marketing/marketing management; mathematics; mathematics teacher education; medical radiologic technology; middle school education; music; music performance; music teacher education; nursing (registered nurse training); philosophy; physical education teaching and coaching; physical therapist assistant; physics; physics teacher education; plant sciences; political science and government; psychology; radio and television; social science teacher education; social work; sociology; Spanish; Spanish language teacher education; special education; speech and rhetoric; sport and fitness administration; technology/industrial arts teacher education; tourism and travel services management; wildlife and wildlands science and management.
Academic Programs *Special study options:* academic remediation for entering students, accelerated degree program, advanced placement credit, cooperative education, distance learning, double majors, English as a second language, honors programs, independent study, internships, off-campus study, part-time degree program, services for LD students, study abroad, summer session for credit. *ROTC:* Army (b).
Library Dean B. Ellis Library with 567,535 titles, 1,760 serial subscriptions, 12,867 audiovisual materials, an OPAC, a Web page.
Computers on Campus 508 computers available on campus for general student use. A campuswide network can be accessed from student residence rooms and from off campus. Internet access, online (class) registration, at least one staffed computer lab available.
Student Life *Housing:* on-campus residence required for freshman year. *Options:* men-only, women-only. Campus housing is university owned. *Activities and organizations:* drama/theater group, student-run newspaper, radio and television station, choral group, marching band, Student Government Association, Greek organizations, intramurals, academic clubs, minority/international organizations, national fraternities, national sororities. *Campus security:* 24-hour emergency response devices and patrols. *Student services:* health clinic, personal/psychological counseling.
Athletics Member NCAA. All Division I except football (Division I-A). *Intercollegiate sports:* baseball M(s), basketball M(s)/W(s), bowling W(s), cross-country running M(s)/W(s), golf M(s)/W(s), soccer W(s), tennis W(s), track and field M(s)/W(s), volleyball W(s). *Intramural sports:* archery M/W, badminton M/W, basketball M/W, bowling M/W, football M/W, golf M/W, racquetball M/W, soccer M/W, softball M/W, table tennis M/W, tennis M/W, ultimate Frisbee M/W, volleyball M/W.
Standardized Tests *Required:* SAT I, ACT, ACT COMPASS, or ACT ASSET, ACT preferred (for admission).
Costs (2003–04) *Tuition:* state resident $3750 full-time, $125 per credit hour part-time; nonresident $9660 full-time, $322 per credit hour part-time. Full-time tuition and fees vary according to course load and location. Part-time tuition and fees vary according to course load and location. *Required fees:* $1060 full-time, $33 per credit hour part-time, $25 per term part-time. *Room and board:* $3640. Room and board charges vary according to board plan and housing facility. *Payment plan:* installment. *Waivers:* children of alumni, senior citizens, and employees or children of employees.
Financial Aid Of all full-time matriculated undergraduates who enrolled in 2002, 4,899 applied for aid, 4,646 were judged to have need, 1,791 had their need fully met. 353 Federal Work-Study jobs (averaging $1515). In 2002, 500 non-need-based awards were made. *Average percent of need met:* 55%. *Average financial aid package:* $3100. *Average need-based loan:* $2000. *Average need-based gift aid:* $2400. *Average non-need-based aid:* $2100. *Average indebtedness upon graduation:* $14,900. *Financial aid deadline:* 7/1.
Applying *Options:* common application, electronic application, early admission, deferred entrance. *Application fee:* $15. *Required:* high school transcript, minimum 2.0 GPA, proof of immunization, proof of enrollment in selective

Arkansas State University (continued)
service for men over 18. *Application deadline:* rolling (freshmen), rolling (transfers). *Notification:* continuous (freshmen), continuous (transfers).

Admissions Contact Ms. Paula James Lynn, Director of Admissions, Arkansas State University, PO Box 1630, State University, AR 72467. *Phone:* 870-972-3024. *Toll-free phone:* 800-382-3030. *Fax:* 870-910-8094. *E-mail:* admissions@astate.edu.

ARKANSAS TECH UNIVERSITY
Russellville, Arkansas

- **State-supported** comprehensive, founded 1909
- **Calendar** semesters
- **Degrees** certificates, associate, bachelor's, and master's
- **Small-town** 516-acre campus
- **Endowment** $8.6 million
- **Coed,** 5,889 undergraduate students, 87% full-time, 53% women, 47% men
- **Moderately difficult** entrance level, 56% of applicants were admitted

Undergraduates 5,126 full-time, 763 part-time. Students come from 35 states and territories, 32 other countries, 4% are from out of state, 4% African American, 0.9% Asian American or Pacific Islander, 2% Hispanic American, 1% Native American, 1% international, 5% transferred in, 29% live on campus. *Retention:* 66% of 2002 full-time freshmen returned.

Freshmen *Admission:* 2,990 applied, 1,683 admitted, 1,507 enrolled. *Average high school GPA:* 3.26. *Test scores:* SAT verbal scores over 500: 54%; SAT math scores over 500: 54%; ACT scores over 18: 83%; SAT verbal scores over 600: 27%; SAT math scores over 600: 18%; ACT scores over 24: 38%; SAT math scores over 700: 9%; ACT scores over 30: 2%.

Faculty *Total:* 351, 65% full-time. *Student/faculty ratio:* 19:1.

Majors Accounting; agribusiness; art; art teacher education; biology/biological sciences; biology teacher education; business administration and management; business teacher education; chemistry; chemistry teacher education; clinical laboratory science/medical technology; clinical/medical social work; computer and information sciences; computer systems analysis; creative writing; economics; education related; electrical, electronic and communications engineering technology; elementary education; engineering; engineering physics; English; English/language arts teacher education; foreign languages and literatures; foreign language teacher education; general studies; geology/earth science; health information/medical records administration; hospitality administration; humanities; industrial mechanics and maintenance technology; information science/studies; journalism; mathematics; mathematics teacher education; mechanical engineering; medical/clinical assistant; middle school education; music; music teacher education; nuclear engineering; nursing (registered nurse training); parks, recreation and leisure facilities management; physical education teaching and coaching; physical sciences; precision systems maintenance and repair technologies related; psychology; science teacher education; social studies teacher education; sociology; speech and rhetoric; speech teacher education; wildlife and wildlands science and management.

Academic Programs *Special study options:* academic remediation for entering students, adult/continuing education programs, advanced placement credit, distance learning, double majors, external degree program, honors programs, independent study, internships, off-campus study, part-time degree program, services for LD students, summer session for credit. *ROTC:* Army (c).

Library Ross Pendergraft Library and Technology Center with 239,398 titles, 1,136 serial subscriptions, 5,086 audiovisual materials, an OPAC, a Web page.

Computers on Campus 600 computers available on campus for general student use. A campuswide network can be accessed from student residence rooms and from off campus. Internet access, online (class) registration, at least one staffed computer lab available.

Student Life *Housing:* on-campus residence required through sophomore year. *Options:* coed, men-only, women-only, disabled students. Campus housing is university owned. Freshman campus housing is guaranteed. *Activities and organizations:* drama/theater group, student-run newspaper, radio and television station, choral group, marching band, Student Government Association, Student Activities Board, Wesley Foundation, Chi Alpha, Baptist Student Union, national fraternities, national sororities. *Campus security:* 24-hour patrols, late-night transport/escort service, controlled dormitory access. *Student services:* health clinic.

Athletics Member NCAA. All Division II. *Intercollegiate sports:* baseball M(s), basketball M(s)/W(s), cheerleading M/W, cross-country running W(s), football M(s), golf M(s), tennis W(s), volleyball W(s). *Intramural sports:* basketball M/W, football M, golf M/W, racquetball M/W, rock climbing M(c)/W(c), soccer M/W, softball M/W, swimming M/W, table tennis M/W, tennis M/W, ultimate Frisbee M/W, volleyball M/W.

Standardized Tests *Required:* SAT I or ACT (for admission). *Recommended:* ACT (for admission).

Costs (2003–04) *Tuition:* state resident $3540 full-time, $138 per hour part-time; nonresident $7080 full-time, $276 per hour part-time. Full-time tuition and fees vary according to course load. Part-time tuition and fees vary according to course load. *Required fees:* $280 full-time, $3 per hour part-time, $70 per term part-time. *Room and board:* $3725; room only: $2016. Room and board charges vary according to board plan and housing facility. *Payment plans:* installment, deferred payment. *Waivers:* senior citizens and employees or children of employees.

Financial Aid Of all full-time matriculated undergraduates who enrolled in 2002, 3,213 applied for aid, 2,802 were judged to have need, 615 had their need fully met. 252 Federal Work-Study jobs (averaging $999). 459 state and other part-time jobs (averaging $936). In 2002, 973 non-need-based awards were made. *Average percent of need met:* 48%. *Average financial aid package:* $4537. *Average need-based loan:* $2001. *Average need-based gift aid:* $2438. *Average non-need-based aid:* $4220. *Average indebtedness upon graduation:* $17,026.

Applying *Options:* electronic application, deferred entrance. *Required:* high school transcript, minimum 2.0 GPA. *Notification:* continuous (freshmen), continuous (transfers).

Admissions Contact Ms. Shauna Donnell, Director of Enrollment Management, Arkansas Tech University, L.L. "Doc" Bryan Student services Building, Suite 141, Russellville, AR 72801-2222. *Phone:* 479-968-0343. *Toll-free phone:* 800-582-6953. *Fax:* 479-964-0522. *E-mail:* tech.enroll@mail.atu.edu.

CENTRAL BAPTIST COLLEGE
Conway, Arkansas

- **Independent Baptist** 4-year, founded 1952
- **Calendar** semesters
- **Degrees** associate and bachelor's
- **Small-town** 11-acre campus
- **Endowment** $775,713
- **Coed,** 426 undergraduate students, 81% full-time, 43% women, 57% men
- **Minimally difficult** entrance level, 84% of applicants were admitted

Undergraduates 345 full-time, 81 part-time. Students come from 14 states and territories, 4 other countries, 1% are from out of state, 8% African American, 1% Asian American or Pacific Islander, 2% Hispanic American, 1% Native American, 1% international, 23% transferred in, 40% live on campus.

Freshmen *Admission:* 164 applied, 138 admitted, 104 enrolled. *Average high school GPA:* 3.08. *Test scores:* ACT scores over 18: 70%; ACT scores over 24: 17%.

Faculty *Total:* 50, 32% full-time, 24% with terminal degrees. *Student/faculty ratio:* 11:1.

Majors Biblical studies; business administration and management; counseling psychology; data processing and data processing technology; education; general studies; mathematics; music; music related; organizational behavior; religious education; religious/sacred music; theological and ministerial studies related; theology and religious vocations related.

Academic Programs *Special study options:* academic remediation for entering students, adult/continuing education programs, advanced placement credit, internships, part-time degree program, summer session for credit. *ROTC:* Army (c).

Library J. E. Cobb Library with 50,448 titles, 330 serial subscriptions, 3,413 audiovisual materials.

Computers on Campus 25 computers available on campus for general student use. A campuswide network can be accessed. Internet access, at least one staffed computer lab available.

Student Life *Housing:* on-campus residence required through senior year. *Activities and organizations:* drama/theater group, choral group. *Student services:* personal/psychological counseling.

Athletics Member NCCAA. *Intercollegiate sports:* baseball M/W, basketball M/W, volleyball W. *Intramural sports:* badminton M/W, basketball M, bowling M/W, cheerleading W, football M, golf M, softball M/W, table tennis M/W, tennis M/W, volleyball M/W.

Standardized Tests *Required:* ACT (for admission).

Costs (2003–04) *Comprehensive fee:* $11,656 includes full-time tuition ($6768), mandatory fees ($490), and room and board ($4398). *Room and board:* Room and board charges vary according to board plan. *Payment plans:* installment, deferred payment. *Waivers:* employees or children of employees.

Applying *Options:* common application, electronic application, early admission. *Application fee:* $25. *Required:* essay or personal statement, high school transcript, minimum 2.5 GPA, 2 letters of recommendation. *Application deadlines:* 8/15 (freshmen), 8/15 (transfers).

Admissions Contact Ms. Lindsay Watson, Admissions Counselor, Central Baptist College, 1501 College Avenue, Conway, AR 72034. *Phone:* 501-329-6872 Ext. 145. *Toll-free phone:* 800-205-6872. *Fax:* 501-329-2941. *E-mail:* ccalhoun@cbc.edu.

HARDING UNIVERSITY
Searcy, Arkansas

- **Independent** comprehensive, founded 1924, affiliated with Church of Christ
- **Calendar** semesters
- **Degrees** bachelor's and master's
- **Small-town** 200-acre campus with easy access to Little Rock
- **Endowment** $81.2 million
- **Coed,** 4,036 undergraduate students, 96% full-time, 55% women, 45% men
- **Moderately difficult** entrance level, 58% of applicants were admitted

Located in the beautiful foothills of the Ozark Mountains, Harding is one of America's more highly regarded private universities. At Harding, students build lifetime friendships and, upon graduation, are highly recruited. Harding's Christian environment and challenging academic program develop students who can compete and succeed.

Undergraduates 3,859 full-time, 177 part-time. Students come from 50 states and territories, 41 other countries, 71% are from out of state, 4% African American, 0.7% Asian American or Pacific Islander, 1% Hispanic American, 0.5% Native American, 4% international, 4% transferred in, 84% live on campus. *Retention:* 78% of 2002 full-time freshmen returned.

Freshmen *Admission:* 1,750 applied, 1,020 admitted, 971 enrolled. *Average high school GPA:* 3.34. *Test scores:* SAT verbal scores over 500: 75%; SAT math scores over 500: 65%; ACT scores over 18: 93%; SAT verbal scores over 600: 30%; SAT math scores over 600: 31%; ACT scores over 24: 47%; SAT verbal scores over 700: 6%; SAT math scores over 700: 6%; ACT scores over 30: 12%.

Faculty *Total:* 295, 69% full-time, 52% with terminal degrees. *Student/faculty ratio:* 19:1.

Majors Accounting; advertising; American studies; art teacher education; art therapy; athletic training; biochemistry; biology/biological sciences; biology teacher education; broadcast journalism; business administration and management; business/corporate communications; chemistry; Christian studies; clinical laboratory science/medical technology; communication and media related; communication disorders; communication/speech communication and rhetoric; computer and information sciences; computer engineering; computer science; corrections and criminal justice related; counselor education/school counseling and guidance; criminal justice/safety; design and applied arts related; dietetics; digital communication and media/multimedia; divinity/ministry; dramatic/theatre arts; early childhood education; economics; educational leadership and administration; education (multiple levels); elementary education; English; English/language arts teacher education; family and consumer sciences/home economics teacher education; family and consumer sciences/human sciences; fashion merchandising; fine/studio arts; French; general studies; graphic design; health/health care administration; health teacher education; history; human development and family studies related; humanities; human resources management; information technology; interior design; international business/trade/commerce; international/global studies; international relations and affairs; kindergarten/preschool education; kinesiology and exercise science; legal studies; marketing/marketing management; marriage and family therapy/counseling; mathematics; mathematics teacher education; middle school education; missionary studies and missiology; music; music teacher education; nursing (registered nurse training); painting; pastoral counseling and specialized ministries related; pastoral studies/counseling; physical education teaching and coaching; physics; political science and government; pre-dentistry studies; pre-medical studies; pre-veterinary studies; psychology; public administration; public relations/image management; reading teacher education; religious education; religious studies; sales, distribution and marketing; science teacher education; secondary education; social sciences; social studies teacher education; social work; Spanish; special education (early childhood); special education related; special education (specific learning disabilities); speech-language pathology; speech teacher education; sport and fitness administration; theology; youth ministry.

Academic Programs *Special study options:* academic remediation for entering students, accelerated degree program, adult/continuing education programs, advanced placement credit, cooperative education, double majors, English as a second language, freshman honors college, honors programs, internships, part-time degree program, services for LD students, student-designed majors, study abroad, summer session for credit. *ROTC:* Army (c). *Unusual degree programs:* 3-2 engineering with University of Arkansas, Georgia Institute of Technology, University of Missouri-Rolla, Louisiana Tech University, University of Southern California.

Library Brackett Library plus 1 other with 321,928 titles, 1,368 serial subscriptions, 7,481 audiovisual materials, an OPAC, a Web page.

Computers on Campus 192 computers available on campus for general student use. A campuswide network can be accessed from student residence rooms and from off campus. Internet access, online (class) registration, at least one staffed computer lab available.

Student Life *Housing:* on-campus residence required through senior year. *Options:* men-only, women-only. Campus housing is university owned. Freshman campus housing is guaranteed. *Activities and organizations:* drama/theater group, student-run newspaper, radio and television station, choral group, marching band, University Singers, RENEW (environmental group), JOY, concert choir, Omicron Delta Kappa. *Campus security:* 24-hour emergency response devices and patrols. *Student services:* health clinic, personal/psychological counseling.

Athletics Member NCAA. All Division II. *Intercollegiate sports:* baseball M(s), basketball M(s)/W(s), cheerleading M/W, cross-country running M(s)/W(s), football M(s), golf M, lacrosse M(c), soccer M/W(s), tennis M(s)/W(s), track and field M(s)/W(s), ultimate Frisbee M/W, volleyball W(s). *Intramural sports:* basketball M/W, bowling M/W, cross-country running M/W, football M/W, golf M/W, gymnastics W, racquetball M/W, rock climbing M(c)/W(c), soccer M/W, softball M/W, swimming M/W, table tennis M/W, tennis M/W, track and field M/W, ultimate Frisbee M/W, volleyball M/W, weight lifting M/W.

Standardized Tests *Required:* SAT I or ACT (for admission).

Costs (2003–04) *Comprehensive fee:* $14,890 includes full-time tuition ($9720), mandatory fees ($400), and room and board ($4770). Full-time tuition and fees vary according to course load. Part-time tuition: $324 per semester hour. Part-time tuition and fees vary according to course load. *Required fees:* $20 per semester hour part-time. *College room only:* $2240. Room and board charges vary according to board plan and housing facility. *Payment plans:* tuition prepayment, installment. *Waivers:* senior citizens and employees or children of employees.

Financial Aid Of all full-time matriculated undergraduates who enrolled in 2003, 3,642 applied for aid, 1,966 were judged to have need, 193 had their need fully met. 2,034 Federal Work-Study jobs (averaging $291). 1,629 state and other part-time jobs (averaging $512). In 2003, 1454 non-need-based awards were made. *Average percent of need met:* 64%. *Average financial aid package:* $8673. *Average need-based loan:* $4380. *Average need-based gift aid:* $5444. *Average non-need-based aid:* $7246. *Average indebtedness upon graduation:* $21,183.

Applying *Options:* common application, electronic application, early admission, deferred entrance. *Application fee:* $35. *Required:* high school transcript, 2 letters of recommendation, interview. *Application deadlines:* 7/1 (freshmen), 7/1 (transfers). *Notification:* continuous (freshmen), continuous (transfers).

Admissions Contact Mr. Glenn Dillard, Director of Enrollment Management, Harding University, Box 11255, Searcy, AR 72149-0001. *Phone:* 501-279-4407. *Toll-free phone:* 800-477-4407. *Fax:* 501-279-4865. *E-mail:* admissions@harding.edu.

■ *See page 1712 for a narrative description.*

HENDERSON STATE UNIVERSITY
Arkadelphia, Arkansas

- **State-supported** comprehensive, founded 1890
- **Calendar** semesters
- **Degrees** associate, bachelor's, and master's
- **Small-town** 139-acre campus with easy access to Little Rock
- **Coed,** 3,050 undergraduate students, 90% full-time, 57% women, 43% men
- **Moderately difficult** entrance level, 63% of applicants were admitted

Undergraduates 2,737 full-time, 313 part-time. Students come from 25 states and territories, 27 other countries, 10% are from out of state, 15% African American, 0.4% Asian American or Pacific Islander, 1% Hispanic American, 0.7% Native American, 3% international, 8% transferred in. *Retention:* 60% of 2002 full-time freshmen returned.

Freshmen *Admission:* 1,878 applied, 1,189 admitted, 412 enrolled. *Average high school GPA:* 3.29. *Test scores:* SAT verbal scores over 500: 56%; SAT math scores over 500: 64%; ACT scores over 18: 90%; SAT verbal scores over 600: 32%; SAT math scores over 600: 32%; ACT scores over 24: 39%; ACT scores over 30: 4%.

Faculty *Total:* 217, 72% full-time, 56% with terminal degrees. *Student/faculty ratio:* 13:1.

Majors Accounting; administrative assistant and secretarial science; airline pilot and flight crew; art; art teacher education; athletic training; biology/biological sciences; business/commerce; business teacher education; chemistry; child care and support services management; clinical laboratory science/medical technology; computer and information sciences; dramatic/theatre arts; education (specific subject areas) related; elementary education; English; family and consumer sciences/home economics teacher education; family and consumer sciences/human sciences; history; journalism; kindergarten/preschool education; management information systems; mathematics; middle school education; music; music performance; music teacher education; nursing (registered nurse training); painting; parks, recreation and leisure facilities management; physical education teaching and coaching; physics; political science and government; psychology; public administration; science teacher education; social work; sociology; Spanish; speech and rhetoric; speech teacher education; sport and fitness administration.

Henderson State University (continued)

Academic Programs *Special study options:* academic remediation for entering students, advanced placement credit, distance learning, honors programs, internships, off-campus study, part-time degree program, services for LD students, summer session for credit.

Library Huie Library with 262,572 titles, 1,516 serial subscriptions, 18,717 audiovisual materials, an OPAC, a Web page.

Computers on Campus 125 computers available on campus for general student use. A campuswide network can be accessed from student residence rooms and from off campus. At least one staffed computer lab available.

Student Life *Housing:* on-campus residence required for freshman year. *Options:* coed, men-only, women-only. Campus housing is university owned and is provided by a third party. Freshman applicants given priority for college housing. *Activities and organizations:* drama/theater group, student-run newspaper, radio and television station, choral group, marching band, Heart and Key, Student Government Association, Residence Hall Association, national fraternities, national sororities. *Campus security:* 24-hour emergency response devices and patrols, controlled dormitory access. *Student services:* health clinic, personal/psychological counseling.

Athletics Member NCAA. All Division II. *Intercollegiate sports:* baseball M(s), basketball M(s)/W(s), cross-country running W(s), football M(s), golf M, softball W(s), swimming M(s)/W(s), tennis M(s)/W(s), volleyball W(s). *Intramural sports:* basketball M/W, football M, golf M/W, soccer M, swimming M/W, tennis M/W, volleyball W.

Standardized Tests *Required:* SAT I or ACT (for admission). *Recommended:* ACT (for admission).

Costs (2003–04) *Tuition:* state resident $3380 full-time; nonresident $6760 full-time. Part-time tuition and fees vary according to course load. *Required fees:* $255 full-time. *Room and board:* $3984. Room and board charges vary according to board plan and housing facility. *Waivers:* children of alumni and employees or children of employees.

Financial Aid Of all full-time matriculated undergraduates who enrolled in 2000, 2,337 applied for aid, 1,423 were judged to have need, 408 had their need fully met. 107 state and other part-time jobs (averaging $1648). In 2000, 411 non-need-based awards were made. *Average percent of need met:* 72%. *Average financial aid package:* $5482. *Average need-based loan:* $3610. *Average need-based gift aid:* $4200. *Average non-need-based aid:* $5535. *Average indebtedness upon graduation:* $13,000.

Applying *Options:* electronic application, deferred entrance. *Required:* high school transcript. *Required for some:* essay or personal statement, 3 letters of recommendation. *Recommended:* minimum 2.5 GPA. *Application deadline:* 7/15 (freshmen), rolling (transfers). *Notification:* continuous (freshmen), continuous (transfers).

Admissions Contact Ms. Vikita Hardwrick, Director of University Relations/Admissions, Henderson State University, 1100 Henderson Street, PO Box 7560, Arkadelphia, AR 71999-0001. *Phone:* 870-230-5028. *Toll-free phone:* 800-228-7333. *Fax:* 870-230-5066. *E-mail:* hardwrv@hsu.edu.

HENDRIX COLLEGE
Conway, Arkansas

- **Independent United Methodist** comprehensive, founded 1876
- **Calendar** semesters
- **Degrees** bachelor's and master's
- **Suburban** 158-acre campus with easy access to Little Rock
- **Endowment** $115.0 million
- **Coed,** 1,050 undergraduate students, 98% full-time, 57% women, 43% men
- **Very difficult** entrance level, 86% of applicants were admitted

Undergraduates 1,031 full-time, 19 part-time. Students come from 36 states and territories, 12 other countries, 40% are from out of state, 4% African American, 2% Asian American or Pacific Islander, 3% Hispanic American, 1% Native American, 1% international, 2% transferred in, 80% live on campus. *Retention:* 85% of 2002 full-time freshmen returned.

Freshmen *Admission:* 891 applied, 770 admitted, 267 enrolled. *Average high school GPA:* 3.60. *Test scores:* SAT verbal scores over 500: 93%; SAT math scores over 500: 92%; ACT scores over 18: 100%; SAT verbal scores over 600: 67%; SAT math scores over 600: 61%; ACT scores over 24: 77%; SAT verbal scores over 700: 21%; SAT math scores over 700: 15%; ACT scores over 30: 27%.

Faculty *Total:* 100, 81% full-time, 87% with terminal degrees. *Student/faculty ratio:* 12:1.

Majors Accounting; anthropology; art; biology/biological sciences; business/managerial economics; chemistry; computer science; dramatic/theatre arts; economics; elementary education; English; French; German; history; interdisciplinary studies; international relations and affairs; mathematics; music; philosophy; physical education teaching and coaching; physics; political science and government; psychology; religious studies; sociology; Spanish.

Academic Programs *Special study options:* advanced placement credit, double majors, independent study, internships, off-campus study, student-designed majors, study abroad. *ROTC:* Army (c). *Unusual degree programs:* 3-2 engineering with Columbia University, Vanderbilt University, Washington University in St. Louis.

Library Olin C. and Marjorie H. Bailey Library with 211,374 titles, 819 serial subscriptions, 971 audiovisual materials, an OPAC, a Web page.

Computers on Campus 75 computers available on campus for general student use. A campuswide network can be accessed from student residence rooms and from off campus. At least one staffed computer lab available.

Student Life *Housing:* on-campus residence required through senior year. *Options:* coed, men-only, women-only. Campus housing is university owned. Freshman campus housing is guaranteed. *Activities and organizations:* drama/theater group, student-run newspaper, radio station, choral group, Volunteer Action Center, Student Government, Music Ensembles, Multicultural Development Committee, Social Committee. *Campus security:* 24-hour emergency response devices and patrols, late-night transport/escort service, controlled dormitory access. *Student services:* health clinic, personal/psychological counseling.

Athletics Member NCAA. All Division III. *Intercollegiate sports:* baseball M, basketball M/W, cheerleading M/W, cross-country running M/W, golf M/W, rugby M(c), soccer M/W, softball W, swimming M/W, tennis M/W, track and field M/W, volleyball W. *Intramural sports:* badminton M/W, basketball M/W, football M/W, racquetball M/W, soccer M/W, softball M/W, tennis M/W, ultimate Frisbee M/W, volleyball M/W.

Standardized Tests *Required:* SAT I or ACT (for admission).

Costs (2003–04) *Comprehensive fee:* $20,970 includes full-time tuition ($15,440), mandatory fees ($190), and room and board ($5340). Full-time tuition and fees vary according to course load. Part-time tuition: $488 per hour. Part-time tuition and fees vary according to course load. *College room only:* $2354. Room and board charges vary according to housing facility. *Payment plan:* installment. *Waivers:* employees or children of employees.

Financial Aid Of all full-time matriculated undergraduates who enrolled in 2003, 667 applied for aid, 548 were judged to have need, 187 had their need fully met. 275 Federal Work-Study jobs (averaging $1437). 151 state and other part-time jobs (averaging $1088). In 2003, 433 non-need-based awards were made. *Average percent of need met:* 86%. *Average financial aid package:* $13,995. *Average need-based loan:* $4103. *Average need-based gift aid:* $9949. *Average non-need-based aid:* $12,567. *Average indebtedness upon graduation:* $14,400.

Applying *Options:* common application, electronic application, deferred entrance. *Application fee:* $40. *Required:* essay or personal statement, high school transcript. *Required for some:* interview. *Recommended:* 1 letter of recommendation. *Application deadlines:* rolling (freshmen), 8/1 (transfers). *Notification:* continuous (freshmen), continuous (transfers).

Admissions Contact Ms. Karen R. Forest, Vice President for Enrollment, Hendrix College, 1600 Washington Avenue, Conway, AR 72032. *Phone:* 501-450-1362. *Toll-free phone:* 800-277-9017. *Fax:* 501-450-3843. *E-mail:* adm@hendrix.edu.

JOHN BROWN UNIVERSITY
Siloam Springs, Arkansas

- **Independent interdenominational** comprehensive, founded 1919
- **Calendar** semesters
- **Degrees** associate, bachelor's, and master's
- **Small-town** 200-acre campus
- **Endowment** $37.5 million
- **Coed,** 1,652 undergraduate students
- **Moderately difficult** entrance level, 82% of applicants were admitted

Undergraduates Students come from 44 states and territories, 37 other countries, 64% are from out of state, 2% African American, 1% Asian American or Pacific Islander, 2% Hispanic American, 2% Native American, 8% international, 69% live on campus. *Retention:* 83% of 2002 full-time freshmen returned.

Freshmen *Admission:* 620 applied, 511 admitted. *Average high school GPA:* 3.51. *Test scores:* SAT verbal scores over 500: 78%; SAT math scores over 500: 85%; ACT scores over 18: 84%; SAT verbal scores over 600: 37%; SAT math scores over 600: 35%; ACT scores over 24: 54%; SAT verbal scores over 700: 11%; SAT math scores over 700: 9%; ACT scores over 30: 12%.

Faculty *Total:* 122, 70% full-time. *Student/faculty ratio:* 16:1.

Majors Accounting; art; athletic training; biblical studies; biochemistry; biology/biological sciences; biology teacher education; broadcast journalism; business administration and management; business teacher education; chemistry; chemistry teacher education; clinical laboratory science/medical technology; commercial and advertising art; computer graphics; construction engineering; construction management; divinity/ministry; education; electrical, electronics and communications engineering; elementary education; engineering; engineering/industrial management; engineering technology; English; English as a second/foreign language (teaching); English/language arts teacher education; environmental science; environmental studies; health/health care administration; health teacher education; history; interdisciplinary studies; international business/trade/commerce; international relations and affairs; journalism; kindergarten/preschool education; kinesiology and exercise science; liberal arts and sciences/liberal studies; mass communication/media; mathematics; mechanical engineering; middle school education; missionary studies and missiology; music; music teacher education; parks, recreation and leisure facilities management; pastoral studies/counseling; physical education teaching and coaching; piano and organ; pre-law studies; pre-medical studies; pre-veterinary studies; psychology; public relations/image management; radio and television; religious education; religious studies; secondary education; social sciences; social studies teacher education; Spanish; special education; theology; voice and opera.

Academic Programs *Special study options:* academic remediation for entering students, adult/continuing education programs, advanced placement credit, double majors, English as a second language, external degree program, freshman honors college, honors programs, independent study, internships, services for LD students, study abroad. *ROTC:* Army (c), Air Force (c).

Library Arutunoff Learning Resource Center plus 4 others with 114,799 titles, 3,775 serial subscriptions, 10,697 audiovisual materials, an OPAC, a Web page.

Computers on Campus 93 computers available on campus for general student use. A campuswide network can be accessed from student residence rooms and from off campus. Internet access, at least one staffed computer lab available.

Student Life *Housing:* on-campus residence required through junior year. *Options:* coed, men-only, women-only. *Activities and organizations:* drama/theater group, student-run newspaper, radio and television station, choral group, Student Government Association, Student Ministries Organization, Student Missionary Fellowship, African Heritage Fellowship. *Campus security:* 24-hour emergency response devices and patrols, late-night transport/escort service. *Student services:* health clinic, personal/psychological counseling.

Athletics Member NAIA. *Intercollegiate sports:* basketball M(s)/W(s), soccer M(s)/W(s), swimming M(s)/W(s), tennis M(s)/W(s), volleyball W(s). *Intramural sports:* baseball M, basketball M/W, football M/W, racquetball M/W, rugby M, soccer M/W, softball M/W, tennis M/W, volleyball M/W.

Standardized Tests *Required:* SAT I or ACT (for admission).

Costs (2003–04) *Comprehensive fee:* $19,396 includes full-time tuition ($13,716), mandatory fees ($640), and room and board ($5040). Part-time tuition: $480 per credit hour. Part-time tuition and fees vary according to course load and program. *Room and board:* Room and board charges vary according to board plan and housing facility. *Waivers:* minority students, adult students, senior citizens, and employees or children of employees.

Financial Aid Of all full-time matriculated undergraduates who enrolled in 2003, 1,176 applied for aid, 1,035 were judged to have need, 104 had their need fully met. 278 Federal Work-Study jobs (averaging $1425). 241 state and other part-time jobs (averaging $1376). In 2003, 337 non-need-based awards were made. *Average percent of need met:* 65%. *Average financial aid package:* $11,400. *Average need-based loan:* $5935. *Average need-based gift aid:* $10,693. *Average non-need-based aid:* $3923. *Average indebtedness upon graduation:* $14,200.

Applying *Options:* common application, deferred entrance. *Application fee:* $25. *Required:* essay or personal statement, high school transcript, minimum 2.5 GPA, 2 letters of recommendation. *Recommended:* interview. *Application deadlines:* 3/1 (freshmen), 3/1 (transfers). *Notification:* 5/1 (freshmen), 5/1 (transfers).

Admissions Contact Mrs. Karen Elliott, Admissions Systems Manager, John Brown University, 200 West University Street, Siloam Springs, AR 72761-2121. *Phone:* 501-524-7454. *Toll-free phone:* 877-JBU-INFO. *Fax:* 501 524-4196. *E-mail:* jbuinfo@acc.jbu.edu.

LYON COLLEGE
Batesville, Arkansas

- **Independent Presbyterian** 4-year, founded 1872
- **Calendar** semesters
- **Degree** bachelor's
- **Small-town** 136-acre campus
- **Endowment** $38.1 million
- **Coed,** 490 undergraduate students, 92% full-time, 52% women, 48% men
- **Very difficult** entrance level, 72% of applicants were admitted

Lyon College is a private, residential, coeducational, undergraduate liberal arts college affiliated with the Presbyterian Church (U.S.A.) It is distinguished by its accomplished faculty, student-run honor system, innovative residential house system, and endowed international studies program. Lyon competes in the TranSouth Athletic Conference (NAIA). More information is available at the College Web site (http://www.lyon.edu).

Undergraduates 451 full-time, 39 part-time. Students come from 18 states and territories, 15 other countries, 14% are from out of state, 4% African American, 1% Asian American or Pacific Islander, 2% Hispanic American, 2% Native American, 4% international, 6% transferred in, 76% live on campus. *Retention:* 78% of 2002 full-time freshmen returned.

Freshmen *Admission:* 427 applied, 309 admitted, 120 enrolled. *Average high school GPA:* 3.46. *Test scores:* SAT verbal scores over 500: 81%; SAT math scores over 500: 74%; ACT scores over 18: 98%; SAT verbal scores over 600: 37%; SAT math scores over 600: 30%; ACT scores over 24: 59%; SAT verbal scores over 700: 11%; SAT math scores over 700: 8%; ACT scores over 30: 15%.

Faculty *Total:* 54, 81% full-time, 76% with terminal degrees. *Student/faculty ratio:* 10:1.

Majors Accounting; art; biology/biological sciences; business administration and management; chemistry; computer science; dramatic/theatre arts; economics; English; environmental studies; history; mathematics; music; philosophy and religious studies related; political science and government; psychology; Spanish.

Academic Programs *Special study options:* academic remediation for entering students, accelerated degree program, advanced placement credit, double majors, independent study, internships, part-time degree program, student-designed majors, study abroad, summer session for credit. *Unusual degree programs:* 3-2 engineering with University of Missouri-Rolla.

Library Mabee-Simpson Library with 172,738 titles, 854 serial subscriptions, 6,103 audiovisual materials, an OPAC, a Web page.

Computers on Campus 71 computers available on campus for general student use. A campuswide network can be accessed from student residence rooms and from off campus. Internet access, at least one staffed computer lab available.

Student Life *Housing:* on-campus residence required through senior year. *Options:* men-only, women-only. Campus housing is university owned. Freshman campus housing is guaranteed. *Activities and organizations:* drama/theater group, student-run newspaper, choral group, Baptist Christian Ministry, Phi Mu sorority, Student Activities Council, Alpha Xi Delta sorority, Pre-med club, national fraternities, national sororities. *Campus security:* 24-hour patrols, late-night transport/escort service. *Student services:* health clinic, personal/psychological counseling.

Athletics Member NAIA. *Intercollegiate sports:* baseball M(s), basketball M(s)/W(s), cross-country running M(s)/W(s), golf M(s)/W(s), soccer M(s)/W(s), tennis M(s)/W(s), volleyball W(s). *Intramural sports:* archery M/W, badminton M/W, basketball M/W, football M/W, softball M/W, table tennis M/W, tennis M/W, volleyball M/W.

Standardized Tests *Required:* SAT I or ACT (for admission).

Costs (2004–05) *One-time required fee:* $200. *Comprehensive fee:* $18,950 includes full-time tuition ($12,710), mandatory fees ($420), and room and board ($5820). Part-time tuition: $530 per credit hour. Part-time tuition and fees vary according to course load. *College room only:* $2390. *Payment plan:* installment. *Waivers:* employees or children of employees.

Financial Aid Of all full-time matriculated undergraduates who enrolled in 2003, 346 applied for aid, 300 were judged to have need, 95 had their need fully met. 113 Federal Work-Study jobs (averaging $1000). 40 state and other part-time jobs (averaging $1108). In 2003, 137 non-need-based awards were made. *Average percent of need met:* 83%. *Average financial aid package:* $13,491. *Average need-based loan:* $3868. *Average need-based gift aid:* $10,230. *Average non-need-based aid:* $10,132. *Average indebtedness upon graduation:* $15,383.

Applying *Options:* common application, electronic application, early admission, deferred entrance. *Application fee:* $25. *Required:* essay or personal statement, high school transcript. *Recommended:* minimum 2.5 GPA, 2 letters of recommendation. *Application deadline:* rolling (freshmen), rolling (transfers). *Notification:* continuous (freshmen), continuous (transfers).

Admissions Contact Mr. Denny Bardos, Vice President for Enrollment Services, Lyon College, PO Box 2317, Batesville, AR 72503-2317. *Phone:* 870-698-4250. *Toll-free phone:* 800-423-2542. *Fax:* 870-793-1791. *E-mail:* admissions@lyon.edu.

OUACHITA BAPTIST UNIVERSITY
Arkadelphia, Arkansas

- **Independent Baptist** 4-year, founded 1886
- **Calendar** semesters
- **Degrees** associate and bachelor's
- **Small-town** 84-acre campus with easy access to Little Rock
- **Endowment** $50.7 million
- **Coed,** 1,530 undergraduate students, 97% full-time, 54% women, 46% men
- **Moderately difficult** entrance level, 80% of applicants were admitted

Undergraduates 1,487 full-time, 43 part-time. Students come from 33 states and territories, 46% are from out of state, 6% African American, 0.3% Asian

Ouachita Baptist University (continued)
American or Pacific Islander, 0.9% Hispanic American, 0.3% Native American, 3% international, 4% transferred in, 86% live on campus. *Retention:* 79% of 2002 full-time freshmen returned.

Freshmen *Admission:* 879 applied, 704 admitted, 343 enrolled. *Average high school GPA:* 3.48. *Test scores:* SAT verbal scores over 500: 70%; SAT math scores over 500: 74%; ACT scores over 18: 93%; SAT verbal scores over 600: 32%; SAT math scores over 600: 29%; ACT scores over 24: 50%; SAT verbal scores over 700: 8%; SAT math scores over 700: 7%; ACT scores over 30: 6%.

Faculty *Total:* 153, 74% full-time, 63% with terminal degrees. *Student/faculty ratio:* 13:1.

Majors Accounting; art teacher education; athletic training; biblical studies; biology/biological sciences; business administration and management; business teacher education; chemistry; communication disorders sciences and services related; computer science; dietetics; dramatic/theatre arts; early childhood education; education; English; fine/studio arts; French; graphic design; health and physical education; history; mass communication/media; mathematics; middle school education; missionary studies and missiology; music; music history, literature, and theory; music performance; music teacher education; music theory and composition; pastoral counseling and specialized ministries related; pastoral studies/counseling; philosophy; physical education teaching and coaching; physics; piano and organ; political science and government; pre-dentistry studies; pre-medical studies; pre-nursing studies; pre-pharmacy studies; pre-veterinary studies; psychology; religious/sacred music; Russian; science teacher education; secondary education; social sciences; social studies teacher education; sociology; Spanish; speech and rhetoric; theology; voice and opera; youth ministry.

Academic Programs *Special study options:* academic remediation for entering students, accelerated degree program, advanced placement credit, cooperative education, double majors, English as a second language, honors programs, internships, off-campus study, part-time degree program, study abroad, summer session for credit. *ROTC:* Army (b).

Library Riley–Hickinbotham Library plus 1 other with 139,278 titles, 1,931 serial subscriptions, 8,306 audiovisual materials, an OPAC.

Computers on Campus 189 computers available on campus for general student use. A campuswide network can be accessed from student residence rooms and from off campus. Internet access, at least one staffed computer lab available.

Student Life *Housing:* on-campus residence required through senior year. *Options:* men-only, women-only. Campus housing is university owned and leased by the school. Freshman campus housing is guaranteed. *Activities and organizations:* drama/theater group, student-run newspaper, television station, choral group, marching band, Phi Beta Lambda, Campus Activities Board, Student Education Association, Student Foundation, international club. *Campus security:* 24-hour emergency response devices and patrols, controlled dormitory access. *Student services:* health clinic, personal/psychological counseling.

Athletics Member NCAA. All Division II. *Intercollegiate sports:* baseball M(s), basketball M(s)/W(s), cross-country running W(s), football M(s), golf M(s), soccer M/W, softball W(s), swimming M(s)/W(s), tennis M(s)/W(s), volleyball W(s). *Intramural sports:* basketball M/W, football M/W, soccer M, softball M/W, table tennis M/W, ultimate Frisbee M(c)/W(c).

Standardized Tests *Required:* SAT I or ACT (for admission).

Costs (2004–05) *Comprehensive fee:* $19,970 includes full-time tuition ($14,940), mandatory fees ($230), and room and board ($4800). Full-time tuition and fees vary according to course load. Part-time tuition: $400 per semester hour. Part-time tuition and fees vary according to course load. No tuition increase for student's term of enrollment. *Room and board:* Room and board charges vary according to housing facility. *Payment plans:* tuition prepayment, installment. *Waivers:* employees or children of employees.

Financial Aid Of all full-time matriculated undergraduates who enrolled in 2003, 969 applied for aid, 788 were judged to have need, 336 had their need fully met. 430 Federal Work-Study jobs (averaging $1367). 396 state and other part-time jobs (averaging $1538). In 2003, 686 non-need-based awards were made. *Average percent of need met:* 89%. *Average financial aid package:* $11,845. *Average need-based loan:* $3465. *Average need-based gift aid:* $4633. *Average non-need-based aid:* $5920. *Average indebtedness upon graduation:* $17,125. *Financial aid deadline:* 6/1.

Applying *Options:* early admission, deferred entrance. *Application fee:* $50. *Required:* high school transcript, minimum 2.75 GPA. *Recommended:* interview. *Application deadlines:* 8/15 (freshmen), 8/15 (transfers). *Notification:* continuous (freshmen), continuous (transfers).

Admissions Contact Mr. David Goodman, Director of Admissions Counseling, Ouachita Baptist University, OBU Box 3776, Arkadelphia, AR 71998-0001. *Phone:* 870-245-5110. *Toll-free phone:* 800-342-5628. *Fax:* 870-245-5500. *E-mail:* goodmand@obu.edu.

PHILANDER SMITH COLLEGE
Little Rock, Arkansas

Admissions Contact Mrs. Arnella Hayes, Admission Officer, Philander Smith College, 812 West 13th Street, Little Rock, AR 72202-3718. *Phone:* 501-370-5310. *Toll-free phone:* 800-446-6772. *Fax:* 501-370-5225. *E-mail:* admissions@philander.edu.

SOUTHERN ARKANSAS UNIVERSITY–MAGNOLIA
Magnolia, Arkansas

- **State-supported** comprehensive, founded 1909, part of Southern Arkansas University System
- **Calendar** semesters
- **Degrees** associate, bachelor's, and master's
- **Small-town** 781-acre campus
- **Endowment** $12.3 million
- **Coed,** 2,804 undergraduate students, 87% full-time, 56% women, 44% men
- **Moderately difficult** entrance level, 81% of applicants were admitted

Undergraduates 2,449 full-time, 355 part-time. Students come from 22 states and territories, 39 other countries, 19% are from out of state, 25% African American, 0.4% Asian American or Pacific Islander, 1% Hispanic American, 0.4% Native American, 5% international, 7% transferred in, 37% live on campus. *Retention:* 65% of 2002 full-time freshmen returned.

Freshmen *Admission:* 1,155 applied, 939 admitted, 565 enrolled. *Test scores:* ACT scores over 18: 77%; ACT scores over 24: 21%; ACT scores over 30: 1%.

Faculty *Total:* 199, 69% full-time, 44% with terminal degrees. *Student/faculty ratio:* 17:1.

Majors Accounting; administrative assistant and secretarial science; agricultural business and management; agricultural teacher education; agriculture; art; art teacher education; biological and physical sciences; biology/biological sciences; biology teacher education; broadcast journalism; business/commerce; business teacher education; chemistry; chemistry teacher education; clinical laboratory science/medical technology; community organization and advocacy; computer and information sciences; criminal justice/safety; dramatic/theatre arts; elementary education; engineering physics; English; English/language arts teacher education; general studies; history; industrial technology; journalism; kindergarten/preschool education; kinesiology and exercise science; mass communication/media; mathematics; mathematics teacher education; music teacher education; nursing (registered nurse training); physical education teaching and coaching; physics teacher education; political science and government; psychology; science teacher education; social studies teacher education; social work; sociology; Spanish; Spanish language teacher education.

Academic Programs *Special study options:* academic remediation for entering students, accelerated degree program, adult/continuing education programs, advanced placement credit, distance learning, double majors, independent study, internships, part-time degree program, services for LD students, study abroad, summer session for credit.

Library Magale Library with 197,635 titles, 1,235 serial subscriptions, 12,223 audiovisual materials, an OPAC, a Web page.

Computers on Campus 175 computers available on campus for general student use. A campuswide network can be accessed from off campus. Internet access, at least one staffed computer lab available.

Student Life *Housing:* on-campus residence required through sophomore year. *Options:* men-only, women-only. Campus housing is university owned. Freshman campus housing is guaranteed. *Activities and organizations:* drama/theater group, student-run newspaper, radio station, choral group, marching band, Student Government Association, IMPACT, national fraternities, national sororities. *Campus security:* 24-hour emergency response devices, student patrols, late-night transport/escort service, controlled dormitory access. *Student services:* health clinic, personal/psychological counseling.

Athletics Member NCAA. All Division II. *Intercollegiate sports:* baseball M(s), basketball M(s)/W(s), cross-country running M/W(s), football M(s), golf M, softball W(s), tennis W(s), track and field M/W, volleyball W(s). *Intramural sports:* badminton M/W, basketball M/W, football M, golf M, softball M/W, swimming M/W, table tennis M/W, tennis M/W, volleyball M/W.

Standardized Tests *Required:* ACT (for admission).

Costs (2003–04) *Tuition:* state resident $3250 full-time, $125 per credit hour part-time; nonresident $4940 full-time, $190 per credit hour part-time. Full-time tuition and fees vary according to course load. Part-time tuition and fees vary according to course load. *Required fees:* $246 full-time, $10 per credit hour part-time. *Room and board:* $3460. *Payment plans:* installment, deferred payment. *Waivers:* children of alumni, senior citizens, and employees or children of employees.

Financial Aid Of all full-time matriculated undergraduates who enrolled in 2003, 1,797 applied for aid, 1,584 were judged to have need, 1,530 had their need fully met. 1,034 Federal Work-Study jobs (averaging $2322). 328 state and other part-time jobs (averaging $2646). In 2003, 362 non-need-based awards were made. *Average percent of need met:* 100%. *Average financial aid package:* $6612. *Average need-based loan:* $3259. *Average need-based gift aid:* $3825. *Average non-need-based aid:* $3002. *Average indebtedness upon graduation:* $24,722.

Applying *Options:* early admission, deferred entrance. *Required:* high school transcript. *Required for some:* interview. *Application deadlines:* 8/27 (freshmen), 8/27 (transfers).

Admissions Contact Ms. Sarah Jennings, Dean of Enrollment Services, Southern Arkansas University–Magnolia, PO Box 9382, Magnolia, AR 71754-9382. *Phone:* 870-235-4040. *Toll-free phone:* 800-332-7286. *Fax:* 870-235-5005. *E-mail:* addanne@saumag.edu.

UNIVERSITY OF ARKANSAS

Fayetteville, Arkansas

- **State-supported** university, founded 1871, part of University of Arkansas System
- **Calendar** semesters
- **Degrees** bachelor's, master's, doctoral, first professional, post-master's, and postbachelor's certificates
- **Suburban** 357-acre campus
- **Endowment** $546.0 million
- **Coed,** 13,083 undergraduate students, 84% full-time, 49% women, 51% men
- **Moderately difficult** entrance level, 85% of applicants were admitted

The University of Arkansas's drive to emerge as one of the top 50 public research universities in America got a tremendous boost in April 2002, when the University received a $300-million gift from the Walton Family Charitable Support Foundation. The gift—the largest ever made to a public university—will be used to establish and endow an undergraduate honors college, providing full financial support to nearly 2,000 high-achieving students.

Undergraduates 11,037 full-time, 2,046 part-time. Students come from 50 states and territories, 107 other countries, 12% are from out of state, 6% African American, 3% Asian American or Pacific Islander, 2% Hispanic American, 2% Native American, 2% international, 9% transferred in, 23% live on campus. *Retention:* 83% of 2002 full-time freshmen returned.

Freshmen *Admission:* 5,491 applied, 4,661 admitted, 2,357 enrolled. *Average high school GPA:* 3.60. *Test scores:* SAT verbal scores over 500: 84%; SAT math scores over 500: 83%; ACT scores over 18: 99%; SAT verbal scores over 600: 45%; SAT math scores over 600: 49%; ACT scores over 24: 64%; SAT verbal scores over 700: 11%; SAT math scores over 700: 13%; ACT scores over 30: 19%.

Faculty *Total:* 839, 94% full-time, 87% with terminal degrees. *Student/faculty ratio:* 17:1.

Majors Accounting; adult and continuing education; agribusiness; agricultural/biological engineering and bioengineering; agricultural economics; agricultural production; agricultural teacher education; agronomy and crop science; American Sign Language related; American studies; animal sciences; anthropology; apparel and textiles; architecture; art; audiology and speech-language pathology; biology/biological sciences; botany/plant biology; business administration and management; business/commerce; business/managerial economics; cell biology and anatomical sciences related; chemical engineering; chemistry; civil engineering; classics and languages, literatures and linguistics; communication/speech communication and rhetoric; community health services counseling; comparative literature; computer and information sciences; computer engineering; computer systems analysis; counselor education/school counseling and guidance; creative writing; criminal justice/safety; curriculum and instruction; data processing and data processing technology; dramatic/theatre arts; economics; educational assessment, testing, and measurement; educational evaluation and research; educational/instructional media design; educational leadership and administration; educational statistics and research methods; electrical, electronics and communications engineering; elementary education; engineering; engineering related; English; entomology; environmental/environmental health engineering; environmental science; family and consumer sciences/home economics teacher education; family and consumer sciences/human sciences; finance; food science; foods, nutrition, and wellness; French; geography; geological and earth sciences/geosciences related; geology/earth science; German; gerontology; health and physical education; health professions related; higher education/higher education administration; history; horticultural science; housing and human environments; human development and family studies; industrial engineering; international business/trade/commerce; international relations and affairs; journalism; kinesiology and exercise science; landscape architecture; logistics and materials management; management science; marketing/marketing management; mathematics; mathematics teacher education; mechanical engineering; middle school education; multi-/interdisciplinary studies related; music performance; music teacher education; Near and Middle Eastern studies; nursing (registered nurse training); ornamental horticulture; parks, recreation and leisure; parks, recreation and leisure facilities management; philosophy; physical education teaching and coaching; physics; physics related; plant pathology/phytopathology; plant protection and integrated pest management; plant sciences; political science and government; poultry science; pre-medical studies; psychology; public administration; public policy analysis; secondary education; social work; sociology; Spanish; special education; special education related; statistics; technology/industrial arts teacher education; trade and industrial teacher education; transportation and highway engineering; vocational rehabilitation counseling.

Academic Programs *Special study options:* accelerated degree program, advanced placement credit, cooperative education, distance learning, double majors, English as a second language, freshman honors college, honors programs, independent study, internships, part-time degree program, services for LD students, study abroad, summer session for credit. *ROTC:* Army (b), Air Force (b). *Unusual degree programs:* 3-2 law.

Library David W. Mullins Library plus 5 others with 851,714 titles, 14,168 serial subscriptions, 22,006 audiovisual materials, an OPAC, a Web page.

Computers on Campus 1275 computers available on campus for general student use. A campuswide network can be accessed from student residence rooms and from off campus. Internet access, at least one staffed computer lab available.

Student Life *Housing:* on-campus residence required for freshman year. *Options:* coed, men-only, women-only. Campus housing is university owned. Freshman campus housing is guaranteed. *Activities and organizations:* drama/theater group, student-run newspaper, radio and television station, choral group, marching band, University programs, booster club, Associated Student Government, Black Students Association, Alpha Phi Omega, national fraternities, national sororities. *Campus security:* 24-hour emergency response devices and patrols, student patrols, late-night transport/escort service, controlled dormitory access, RAD (Rape Aggression Defense program). *Student services:* health clinic, personal/psychological counseling, women's center, legal services.

Athletics Member NCAA. All Division I except football (Division I-A). *Intercollegiate sports:* baseball M(s), basketball M(s)/W(s), cross-country running M(s)/W(s), golf M(s)/W(s), gymnastics W(s), soccer W(s), softball W(s), swimming W(s), tennis M(s)/W(s), track and field M(s)/W(s), volleyball W(s). *Intramural sports:* badminton M/W, basketball M/W, bowling M(c)/W(c), football M/W, golf M/W, racquetball M/W, rugby M(c)/W(c), soccer M/W, softball M/W, swimming M/W, table tennis M/W, tennis M/W, volleyball M(c)/W(c), water polo M/W.

Standardized Tests *Required:* SAT I or ACT (for admission).

Costs (2003–04) *Tuition:* state resident $3810 full-time, $127 per credit hour part-time; nonresident $10,560 full-time, $352 per credit hour part-time. *Required fees:* $958 full-time. *Room and board:* $5087; room only: $2812. Room and board charges vary according to board plan and housing facility. *Payment plan:* installment. *Waivers:* senior citizens and employees or children of employees.

Financial Aid Of all full-time matriculated undergraduates who enrolled in 2003, 6,019 applied for aid, 4,743 were judged to have need, 1,593 had their need fully met. 1,898 Federal Work-Study jobs (averaging $2000). In 2003, 2240 non-need-based awards were made. *Average percent of need met:* 74%. *Average financial aid package:* $8260. *Average need-based loan:* $4204. *Average need-based gift aid:* $3650. *Average non-need-based aid:* $5645. *Average indebtedness upon graduation:* $17,204.

Applying *Options:* common application, electronic application, early admission, early action, deferred entrance. *Application fee:* $30. *Required:* high school transcript. *Recommended:* minimum 3.0 GPA. *Application deadlines:* 8/15 (freshmen), 8/15 (transfers). *Notification:* 11/15 (freshmen), 12/15 (early action), continuous (transfers).

Admissions Contact Mr. Clark Adams, Assistant Director of Admissions, University of Arkansas, 200 Silas H. Hunt Hall, Fayetteville, AR 72701-1201. *Phone:* 479-575-7724. *Toll-free phone:* 800-377-5346 (in-state); 800-377-8632 (out-of-state). *Fax:* 479-575-7515. *E-mail:* uofa@uark.edu.

■ *See page 2574 for a narrative description.*

UNIVERSITY OF ARKANSAS AT FORT SMITH

Fort Smith, Arkansas

- **State and locally supported** 4-year, founded 1928, part of University of Arkansas System
- **Calendar** semesters
- **Degrees** certificates, associate, and bachelor's
- **Suburban** 120-acre campus
- **Endowment** $27.9 million
- **Coed,** 6,395 undergraduate students, 53% full-time, 59% women, 41% men
- **Noncompetitive** entrance level, 100% of applicants were admitted

University of Arkansas at Fort Smith (continued)

Undergraduates 3,389 full-time, 3,006 part-time. Students come from 32 states and territories, 10 other countries, 12% are from out of state, 4% African American, 4% Asian American or Pacific Islander, 2% Hispanic American, 4% Native American, 0.2% international, 5% transferred in. *Retention:* 58% of 2002 full-time freshmen returned.

Freshmen *Admission:* 2,295 applied, 2,295 admitted, 1,241 enrolled. *Average high school GPA:* 3.12. *Test scores:* ACT scores over 18: 78%; ACT scores over 24: 21%; ACT scores over 30: 1%.

Faculty *Total:* 332, 51% full-time. *Student/faculty ratio:* 19:1.

Majors Accounting; administrative assistant and secretarial science; biology teacher education; business administration and management; cartography; commercial and advertising art; computer and information sciences; computer and information sciences and support services related; criminal justice/law enforcement administration; dental hygiene; drafting; early childhood education; electrical/electronics equipment installation and repair; emergency medical technology (EMT paramedic); forensic science and technology; general studies; industrial technology; legal assistant/paralegal; liberal arts and sciences/liberal studies; mathematics teacher education; medical radiologic technology; middle school education; multi-/interdisciplinary studies related; music teacher education; nursing (registered nurse training); respiratory care therapy; surgical technology; visual and performing arts.

Academic Programs *Special study options:* academic remediation for entering students, accelerated degree program, adult/continuing education programs, advanced placement credit, cooperative education, distance learning, English as a second language, external degree program, honors programs, internships, off-campus study, part-time degree program, services for LD students, summer session for credit. *ROTC:* Air Force (c).

Library Boreham Library with 60,417 titles, 527 serial subscriptions, 3,037 audiovisual materials, an OPAC, a Web page.

Computers on Campus 1200 computers available on campus for general student use. A campuswide network can be accessed from off campus that provide access to online grade reports, online subscription databases. Internet access, online (class) registration, at least one staffed computer lab available.

Student Life *Housing:* college housing not available. *Options:* Campus housing is provided by a third party. *Activities and organizations:* choral group, Student Activities Council, Phi Beta Lambda, Alpha Lambda Delta, Colege Republicans, Baptist Collegiate Ministry. *Campus security:* 24-hour emergency response devices and patrols, late-night transport/escort service.

Athletics Member NJCAA. *Intercollegiate sports:* baseball M(s), basketball M(s)/W(s), cheerleading M/W, volleyball W(s). *Intramural sports:* basketball M/W.

Standardized Tests *Required for some:* ACT (for placement), ACT ASSET, ACT COMPASS. *Recommended:* ACT (for placement), ACT ASSET, ACT COMPASS.

Costs (2003–04) *Tuition:* area resident $1440 full-time; state resident $1740 full-time; nonresident $6360 full-time. Full-time tuition and fees vary according to course level. Part-time tuition and fees vary according to course level. *Required fees:* $480 full-time. *Payment plan:* installment. *Waivers:* employees or children of employees.

Financial Aid Of all full-time matriculated undergraduates who enrolled in 2001, 110 Federal Work-Study jobs (averaging $3000). 94 state and other part-time jobs (averaging $3000).

Applying *Options:* electronic application, early admission, deferred entrance. *Required:* high school transcript. *Application deadline:* rolling (freshmen), rolling (transfers).

Admissions Contact Ms. Michelle Cooper, Director of Enrollment Management and Communications, University of Arkansas at Fort Smith, 5210 Grand Avenue, PO Box 3649, Fort Smith, AR 72913-3649. *Phone:* 479-788-7127. *Toll-free phone:* 888-512-5466. *Fax:* 479-788-7016. *E-mail:* information@uafortsmith.edu.

University of Arkansas at Little Rock

Little Rock, Arkansas

- **State-supported** university, founded 1927, part of University of Arkansas System
- **Calendar** semesters
- **Degrees** certificates, associate, bachelor's, master's, doctoral, first professional, and post-master's certificates
- **Urban** 150-acre campus
- **Endowment** $7.6 million
- **Coed,** 9,330 undergraduate students, 61% full-time, 62% women, 38% men
- **Minimally difficult** entrance level, 99% of applicants were admitted

Undergraduates 5,733 full-time, 3,597 part-time. Students come from 45 states and territories, 43 other countries, 4% are from out of state, 32% African American, 2% Asian American or Pacific Islander, 2% Hispanic American, 0.6% Native American, 2% international, 8% transferred in, 3% live on campus. *Retention:* 64% of 2002 full-time freshmen returned.

Freshmen *Admission:* 2,531 applied, 2,514 admitted, 777 enrolled. *Test scores:* ACT scores over 18: 62%; ACT scores over 24: 18%; ACT scores over 30: 1%.

Faculty *Total:* 749, 57% full-time. *Student/faculty ratio:* 16:1.

Majors Accounting; advertising; anthropology; art; art history, criticism and conservation; audiology and speech-language pathology; biology/biological sciences; business administration and management; business/commerce; chemistry; computer engineering technology; computer programming; computer science; construction engineering technology; criminal justice/law enforcement administration; criminal justice/police science; dramatic/theatre arts; economics; education; electrical, electronic and communications engineering technology; elementary education; English; environmental health; finance; French; general studies; geology/earth science; health science; health teacher education; history; information science/studies; international business/trade/commerce; international relations and affairs; journalism; kindergarten/preschool education; landscape architecture; liberal arts and sciences/liberal studies; marketing/marketing management; mathematics; mechanical engineering/mechanical technology; music; nursing (registered nurse training); philosophy; physics; political science and government; psychology; radio and television; sign language interpretation and translation; social work; sociology; Spanish; special education (hearing impaired); speech and rhetoric; survey technology; technical and business writing.

Academic Programs *Special study options:* academic remediation for entering students, accelerated degree program, adult/continuing education programs, advanced placement credit, cooperative education, English as a second language, freshman honors college, honors programs, independent study, internships, off-campus study, part-time degree program, services for LD students, student-designed majors, study abroad, summer session for credit. *ROTC:* Army (b).

Library Ottenheimer Library plus 1 other with 3,998 serial subscriptions, an OPAC.

Computers on Campus 500 computers available on campus for general student use. A campuswide network can be accessed from off campus. Internet access, at least one staffed computer lab available.

Student Life *Housing options:* coed. *Activities and organizations:* student-run newspaper, choral group, national fraternities, national sororities. *Campus security:* 24-hour emergency response devices, student patrols, late-night transport/escort service. *Student services:* health clinic, personal/psychological counseling, women's center.

Athletics Member NCAA. All Division I. *Intercollegiate sports:* baseball M(s), basketball M(s), cross-country running M(s)/W(s), golf M(s)/W(s), soccer W(s), swimming W, tennis M(s)/W(s), track and field M/W(s), volleyball W(s). *Intramural sports:* archery M/W, badminton M/W, basketball M, bowling M/W, football M/W, golf M/W, swimming M/W, table tennis M/W, tennis M/W, volleyball M/W.

Standardized Tests *Required:* SAT I or ACT (for placement).

Costs (2003–04) *Tuition:* state resident $3780 full-time; nonresident $9720 full-time. *Required fees:* $818 full-time. *Room only:* $2700.

Financial Aid *Average financial aid package:* $7190.

Applying *Options:* early admission, deferred entrance. *Required:* high school transcript, minimum 2.5 GPA, proof of immunization. *Application deadline:* rolling (freshmen), rolling (transfers). *Notification:* continuous (freshmen), continuous (transfers).

Admissions Contact Mr. John Noah, Director of Admissions, University of Arkansas at Little Rock, 2801 South University Avenue, Little Rock, AR 72204-1099. *Phone:* 501-569-3127. *Toll-free phone:* 800-482-8892. *Fax:* 501-569-8915.

University of Arkansas at Monticello

Monticello, Arkansas

- **State-supported** comprehensive, founded 1909, part of University of Arkansas System
- **Calendar** semesters
- **Degrees** associate, bachelor's, master's, and postbachelor's certificates
- **Small-town** 400-acre campus
- **Coed,** 2,694 undergraduate students, 84% full-time, 60% women, 40% men
- **Noncompetitive** entrance level, 73% of applicants were admitted

Undergraduates 2,253 full-time, 441 part-time. Students come from 20 states and territories, 2 other countries, 9% are from out of state, 28% African American, 0.4% Asian American or Pacific Islander, 2% Hispanic American, 0.6% Native American, 0.4% international, 6% transferred in, 25% live on campus. *Retention:* 54% of 2002 full-time freshmen returned.

Freshmen *Admission:* 1,208 applied, 880 admitted, 751 enrolled.

Faculty *Total:* 247, 64% full-time, 34% with terminal degrees. *Student/faculty ratio:* 18:1.
Majors Accounting; agricultural production; agriculture; art; biology/biological sciences; business administration and management; business teacher education; chemistry; criminal justice/safety; education; elementary education; English; forestry; history; liberal arts and sciences/liberal studies; management information systems; mathematics; music; music teacher education; nursing (registered nurse training); physical education teaching and coaching; physical sciences; political science and government; pre-dentistry studies; pre-law studies; premedical studies; pre-veterinary studies; psychology; social work; special education; speech and rhetoric; wildlife and wildlands science and management; wood science and wood products/pulp and paper technology.
Academic Programs *Special study options:* academic remediation for entering students, accelerated degree program, advanced placement credit, freshman honors college, independent study, off-campus study, part-time degree program, summer session for credit.
Library 126,229 titles, 862 serial subscriptions.
Computers on Campus 140 computers available on campus for general student use. At least one staffed computer lab available.
Student Life *Housing options:* men-only, women-only. Campus housing is university owned. *Activities and organizations:* student-run newspaper, choral group, marching band, national fraternities, national sororities. *Campus security:* 24-hour emergency response devices and patrols. *Student services:* health clinic, personal/psychological counseling.
Athletics Member NCAA. All Division II. *Intercollegiate sports:* baseball M(s), basketball M(s)/W(s), cross-country running W, football M(s), golf M(s), softball W(s), tennis W. *Intramural sports:* baseball M, basketball M/W, cross-country running M/W, football M/W, golf M/W, racquetball M/W, soccer M/W, softball M/W, table tennis M/W, tennis M/W, track and field M/W, volleyball M/W.
Standardized Tests *Required:* SAT I or ACT (for placement). *Recommended:* ACT (for placement).
Costs (2003–04) *Tuition:* state resident $2700 full-time, $118 per hour part-time; nonresident $6120 full-time, $232 per hour part-time. *Required fees:* $685 full-time. *Room and board:* $3150. Room and board charges vary according to board plan and housing facility. *Waivers:* senior citizens and employees or children of employees.
Financial Aid Of all full-time matriculated undergraduates who enrolled in 2002, 190 Federal Work-Study jobs (averaging $991). 298 state and other part-time jobs (averaging $1020). *Average indebtedness upon graduation:* $13,599.
Applying *Options:* early admission, deferred entrance. *Required:* high school transcript, proof of immunization. *Application deadlines:* 8/1 (freshmen), 8/1 (transfers).
Admissions Contact Ms. Mary Whiting, Director of Admissions, University of Arkansas at Monticello, PO Box 3600, Monticello, AR 71656. *Phone:* 870-460-1026. *Toll-free phone:* 800-844-1826. *Fax:* 870-460-1321. *E-mail:* admissions@uamont.edu.

UNIVERSITY OF ARKANSAS AT PINE BLUFF
Pine Bluff, Arkansas

Admissions Contact Mrs. Erica W. Fulton, Director of Admissions and Academic Records, University of Arkansas at Pine Bluff, Mail Slot 4981, 1200 North University Drive, Pine Bluff, AR 71611. *Phone:* 870-575-8487. *Toll-free phone:* 800-264-6585. *Fax:* 870-543-8014. *E-mail:* fulton_e@uapb.edu.

UNIVERSITY OF ARKANSAS FOR MEDICAL SCIENCES
Little Rock, Arkansas

- **State-supported** upper-level, founded 1879, part of University of Arkansas System
- **Calendar** semesters
- **Degrees** certificates, associate, bachelor's, master's, doctoral, and first professional (bachelor's degree is upper-level)
- **Urban** 5-acre campus
- **Endowment** $22.1 million
- **Coed**

Student Life *Campus security:* 24-hour emergency response devices and patrols, late-night transport/escort service, controlled dormitory access.
Costs (2003–04) *Tuition:* $137 per semester hour part-time; state resident $3288 full-time, $331 per semester hour part-time; nonresident $7444 full-time. Full-time tuition and fees vary according to program. Part-time tuition and fees vary according to program. *Room only:* $1530.
Financial Aid Of all full-time matriculated undergraduates who enrolled in 2002, 576 applied for aid, 424 were judged to have need. 9 Federal Work-Study jobs (averaging $1201). *Average percent of need met:* 65. *Average financial aid package:* $3000. *Average need-based loan:* $4000. *Average need-based gift aid:* $500. *Average indebtedness upon graduation:* $7000.
Admissions Contact Ms. Mona Stiles, Admissions Officer, University of Arkansas for Medical Sciences, 4301 West Markham-Slot 601, Little Rock, AR 72205-7199. *Phone:* 501-686-5730.

UNIVERSITY OF CENTRAL ARKANSAS
Conway, Arkansas

- **State-supported** comprehensive, founded 1907
- **Calendar** semesters
- **Degrees** associate, bachelor's, master's, and doctoral
- **Small-town** 365-acre campus
- **Endowment** $9.2 million
- **Coed,** 8,580 undergraduate students, 94% full-time, 60% women, 40% men
- **Moderately difficult** entrance level, 70% of applicants were admitted

Undergraduates 8,055 full-time, 525 part-time. Students come from 39 states and territories, 58 other countries, 5% are from out of state, 17% African American, 1% Asian American or Pacific Islander, 1% Hispanic American, 0.9% Native American, 2% international, 7% transferred in, 39% live on campus. *Retention:* 70% of 2002 full-time freshmen returned.
Freshmen *Admission:* 5,655 applied, 3,979 admitted, 2,428 enrolled. *Average high school GPA:* 3.66. *Test scores:* ACT scores over 18: 87%; ACT scores over 24: 51%; ACT scores over 30: 7%.
Faculty *Total:* 542, 84% full-time. *Student/faculty ratio:* 18:1.
Majors Accounting; art; athletic training; audiology and speech-language pathology; biological and physical sciences; biology/biological sciences; business administration and management; business/commerce; business teacher education; chemistry; child care and support services management; clinical laboratory science/medical technology; computer and information sciences; economics; elementary and middle school administration/principalship; elementary education; English; English composition; English/language arts teacher education; environmental studies; family and consumer sciences/home economics teacher education; family and consumer sciences/human sciences; finance; French; general studies; geography; history; insurance; journalism; kinesiology and exercise science; management information systems; marketing/marketing management; mathematics; mathematics teacher education; medical radiologic technology; middle school education; music; music performance; nuclear medical technology; nursing (registered nurse training); occupational therapy; philosophy; physical education teaching and coaching; physical sciences; physical therapist assistant; physical therapy; physics; political science and government; psychology; public administration; reading teacher education; religious studies; science teacher education; social studies teacher education; sociology; Spanish; special education; speech and rhetoric.
Academic Programs *Special study options:* academic remediation for entering students, accelerated degree program, advanced placement credit, cooperative education, distance learning, double majors, English as a second language, freshman honors college, honors programs, independent study, internships, part-time degree program, study abroad, summer session for credit. *ROTC:* Army (b). *Unusual degree programs:* 3-2 engineering with Arkansas State University.
Library Torreyson Library with 587,714 titles, 1,824 serial subscriptions, an OPAC, a Web page.
Computers on Campus 1500 computers available on campus for general student use. A campuswide network can be accessed from student residence rooms and from off campus. Internet access, online (class) registration, at least one staffed computer lab available.
Student Life *Housing:* on-campus residence required for freshman year. *Options:* coed, men-only, women-only. Campus housing is university owned and leased by the school. Freshman campus housing is guaranteed. *Activities and organizations:* drama/theater group, student-run newspaper, radio and television station, choral group, marching band, Student Government Association, Royal Rooters, student orientation staff, Ambassadors, national fraternities, national sororities. *Campus security:* 24-hour emergency response devices and patrols, student patrols, late-night transport/escort service, controlled dormitory access, security personnel at entrances during evening hours. *Student services:* health clinic, personal/psychological counseling.
Athletics Member NCAA. All Division II. *Intercollegiate sports:* baseball M, basketball M(s)/W(s), cheerleading M(s)/W(s), cross-country running W, football M(s)/W, golf M/W, soccer M/W, softball W, tennis W, track and field W, volleyball W(s). *Intramural sports:* badminton M/W, basketball M/W, bowling M/W, cross-country running M/W, football M/W, racquetball M/W, rock climbing M(c)/W(c), soccer M(c)/W, softball M/W, swimming M/W, table tennis M/W, tennis M/W, track and field M/W, ultimate Frisbee M(c)/W(c), volleyball M/W.

University of Central Arkansas (continued)

Standardized Tests *Required:* SAT I or ACT (for admission).

Costs (2003–04) *Tuition:* state resident $3770 full-time, $170 per hour part-time; nonresident $7082 full-time, $308 per hour part-time. Part-time tuition and fees vary according to course load. *Required fees:* $735 full-time, $25 per hour part-time, $34 per hour part-time. *Room and board:* $3786; room only: $2112. Room and board charges vary according to board plan and housing facility. *Payment plan:* installment. *Waivers:* senior citizens and employees or children of employees.

Applying *Options:* electronic application, early admission, deferred entrance. *Required:* high school transcript. *Required for some:* minimum 2.75 GPA. *Application deadline:* rolling (freshmen), rolling (transfers). *Notification:* continuous (freshmen), continuous (transfers).

Admissions Contact Ms. Penny Hatfield, Director of Admissions, University of Central Arkansas, 201 Donaghey Avenue, Conway, AR 72035. *Phone:* 501-450-5145. *Toll-free phone:* 800-243-8245. *Fax:* 501-450-5228. *E-mail:* admissons@uca.edu.

UNIVERSITY OF PHOENIX–LITTLE ROCK CAMPUS

Little Rock, Arkansas

Admissions Contact 10800 Financial Center Parkway, Little Rock, AR 72211.

UNIVERSITY OF THE OZARKS

Clarksville, Arkansas

- **Independent Presbyterian** 4-year, founded 1834
- **Calendar** semesters
- **Degree** bachelor's
- **Small-town** 56-acre campus with easy access to Little Rock
- **Endowment** $56.1 million
- **Coed,** 734 undergraduate students, 94% full-time, 57% women, 43% men
- **Moderately difficult** entrance level, 84% of applicants were admitted

Undergraduates 690 full-time, 44 part-time. Students come from 22 states and territories, 20 other countries, 30% are from out of state, 3% African American, 1% Asian American or Pacific Islander, 3% Hispanic American, 4% Native American, 15% international, 4% transferred in, 64% live on campus. *Retention:* 67% of 2002 full-time freshmen returned.

Freshmen *Admission:* 654 applied, 548 admitted, 214 enrolled. *Average high school GPA:* 3.42. *Test scores:* SAT verbal scores over 500: 94%; SAT math scores over 500: 43%; ACT scores over 18: 93%; SAT verbal scores over 600: 17%; SAT math scores over 600: 10%; ACT scores over 24: 31%; SAT verbal scores over 700: 6%; SAT math scores over 700: 3%; ACT scores over 30: 5%.

Faculty *Total:* 66, 67% full-time, 58% with terminal degrees. *Student/faculty ratio:* 14:1.

Majors Accounting; art; art teacher education; biology/biological sciences; biology teacher education; business administration and management; business teacher education; chemistry; communication/speech communication and rhetoric; dramatic/theatre arts; education (multiple levels); English; English/language arts teacher education; environmental studies; general studies; history; marketing/marketing management; mathematics; mathematics teacher education; middle school education; music; philosophy and religious studies related; physical education teaching and coaching; political science and government; pre-dentistry studies; pre-medical studies; pre-veterinary studies; psychology; religious education; respiratory care therapy; science teacher education; secondary education; social sciences; social studies teacher education; sociology; special education.

Academic Programs *Special study options:* academic remediation for entering students, advanced placement credit, cooperative education, double majors, English as a second language, independent study, internships, off-campus study, part-time degree program, services for LD students, study abroad, summer session for credit. *Unusual degree programs:* 3-2 engineering with University of Arkansas; theology with University of Dubuque, marine biology with University of South Mississippi, respiratory therapy with Arkansas Valley Technical Institute.

Library Robson Library with 125,000 titles, 536 serial subscriptions, 4,000 audiovisual materials, an OPAC, a Web page.

Computers on Campus 145 computers available on campus for general student use. A campuswide network can be accessed from student residence rooms and from off campus. Internet access, at least one staffed computer lab available.

Student Life *Housing:* on-campus residence required through sophomore year. *Options:* coed, men-only, women-only. Campus housing is university owned. *Activities and organizations:* drama/theater group, student-run television station, choral group, Phi Beta Lambda, Planet Club, SGA, Student Foundation Board, Baptist Campus Ministries. *Campus security:* 24-hour emergency response devices, late-night transport/escort service. *Student services:* health clinic.

Athletics Member NCAA. All Division III. *Intercollegiate sports:* baseball M, basketball M/W, cheerleading M/W, cross-country running M/W, golf M, soccer M/W, softball W, tennis M/W. *Intramural sports:* badminton M/W, basketball M/W, bowling M/W, football M/W, racquetball M/W, soccer M, softball M/W, table tennis M/W, tennis M/W, ultimate Frisbee M/W, volleyball M/W, weight lifting M/W.

Standardized Tests *Required:* SAT I or ACT (for admission).

Costs (2003–04) *Comprehensive fee:* $16,460 includes full-time tuition ($11,520), mandatory fees ($360), and room and board ($4580). *Room and board:* Room and board charges vary according to board plan and housing facility. *Payment plan:* installment. *Waivers:* employees or children of employees.

Financial Aid Of all full-time matriculated undergraduates who enrolled in 2003, 608 applied for aid, 367 were judged to have need, 86 had their need fully met. 109 Federal Work-Study jobs (averaging $1391). 232 state and other part-time jobs (averaging $1625). In 2003, 259 non-need-based awards were made. *Average percent of need met:* 77%. *Average financial aid package:* $12,685. *Average need-based loan:* $3114. *Average need-based gift aid:* $9322. *Average non-need-based aid:* $11,784. *Average indebtedness upon graduation:* $13,900.

Applying *Options:* common application, electronic application, deferred entrance. *Application fee:* $10. *Required:* minimum 2.0 GPA. *Required for some:* essay or personal statement, high school transcript, letters of recommendation, interview. *Application deadlines:* rolling (freshmen), 8/15 (transfers). *Notification:* continuous (freshmen), continuous (transfers).

Admissions Contact Mr. James D. Decker, Director of Admissions, University of the Ozarks, 415 North College Avenue, Clarksville, AR 72830-2880. *Phone:* 479-979-1421. *Toll-free phone:* 800-264-8636. *Fax:* 479-979-1355. *E-mail:* admiss@ozarks.edu.

WILLIAMS BAPTIST COLLEGE

Walnut Ridge, Arkansas

- **Independent Southern Baptist** 4-year, founded 1941
- **Calendar** semesters
- **Degrees** associate and bachelor's
- **Rural** 180-acre campus
- **Endowment** $5.4 million
- **Coed,** 653 undergraduate students, 78% full-time, 56% women, 44% men
- **Minimally difficult** entrance level, 69% of applicants were admitted

Williams Baptist College is a 4-year liberal arts college in Walnut Ridge, Arkansas. Known for its caring, Christ-centered atmosphere, Williams makes the college experience a personal journey in higher learning. It features small classes and more than 25 academic programs. WBC's Eagles belong to the NAIA and field 8 varsity teams. Telephone: 800-722-4434 (toll-free); World Wide Web: http://www.wbcoll.edu.

Undergraduates 511 full-time, 142 part-time. Students come from 13 states and territories, 5 other countries, 20% are from out of state, 3% African American, 1% Asian American or Pacific Islander, 0.6% Hispanic American, 0.4% Native American, 0.4% international, 7% transferred in, 62% live on campus. *Retention:* 61% of 2002 full-time freshmen returned.

Freshmen *Admission:* 407 applied, 281 admitted, 121 enrolled. *Average high school GPA:* 3.20.

Faculty *Total:* 37, 73% full-time, 46% with terminal degrees. *Student/faculty ratio:* 13:1.

Majors Administrative assistant and secretarial science; art; art teacher education; biology/biological sciences; business administration and management; computer and information sciences; divinity/ministry; education; elementary education; English; fine/studio arts; history; kindergarten/preschool education; liberal arts and sciences/liberal studies; music; music teacher education; pastoral studies/counseling; physical education teaching and coaching; pre-dentistry studies; pre-law studies; pre-medical studies; psychology; religious education; religious/sacred music; religious studies; theology.

Academic Programs *Special study options:* academic remediation for entering students, adult/continuing education programs, advanced placement credit, double majors, honors programs, independent study, internships, off-campus study, part-time degree program, student-designed majors, study abroad, summer session for credit. *ROTC:* Army (c).

Library Felix Goodson Library with 57,321 titles, 284 serial subscriptions, an OPAC.

Computers on Campus 71 computers available on campus for general student use. A campuswide network can be accessed. Internet access, at least one staffed computer lab available.

Student Life *Housing:* on-campus residence required through senior year. *Options:* men-only, women-only. *Activities and organizations:* drama/theater group, choral group, campus ministries, Fellowship of Christian Athletes, international club, Alpha Psi Omega. *Campus security:* 24-hour emergency response devices, student patrols. *Student services:* personal/psychological counseling.

Athletics Member NAIA, NCCAA. *Intercollegiate sports:* baseball M(s), basketball M(s)/W(s), golf M(s), soccer M(s)/W(s), softball W(s), volleyball W(s). *Intramural sports:* basketball M/W, football M, golf M/W, racquetball M/W, softball M/W, table tennis M/W, tennis M/W, volleyball M/W.

Standardized Tests *Required:* SAT I or ACT (for admission).

Costs (2004–05) *Comprehensive fee:* $12,600 includes full-time tuition ($8000), mandatory fees ($600), and room and board ($4000). Part-time tuition and fees vary according to course load. *Room and board:* Room and board charges vary according to housing facility. *Payment plan:* installment. *Waivers:* senior citizens and employees or children of employees.

Financial Aid Of all full-time matriculated undergraduates who enrolled in 2002, 451 applied for aid, 336 were judged to have need. 197 Federal Work-Study jobs (averaging $1121). 51 state and other part-time jobs (averaging $851). In 2002, 76 non-need-based awards were made. *Average financial aid package:* $8886. *Average need-based loan:* $3121. *Average need-based gift aid:* $3015. *Average non-need-based aid:* $3066. *Average indebtedness upon graduation:* $12,752.

Applying *Options:* electronic application. *Application fee:* $20. *Required:* high school transcript, minimum 2.5 GPA. *Recommended:* essay or personal statement, interview. *Application deadline:* rolling (freshmen), rolling (transfers).

Admissions Contact Ms. Angela Flippo, Vice President for Enrollment, Williams Baptist College, PO Box 3665, Walnut Ridge, AR 72476. *Phone:* 870-759-4117. *Toll-free phone:* 800-722-4434. *Fax:* 870-886-3924. *E-mail:* admissions@wbcoll.edu.

CALIFORNIA

ACADEMY OF ART UNIVERSITY
San Francisco, California

- **Proprietary** comprehensive, founded 1929
- **Calendar** semesters
- **Degrees** certificates, diplomas, associate, bachelor's, and master's
- **Urban** 3-acre campus
- **Coed,** 5,693 undergraduate students, 64% full-time, 47% women, 53% men
- **Noncompetitive** entrance level

Undergraduates 3,630 full-time, 2,063 part-time. Students come from 53 states and territories, 52 other countries, 39% are from out of state, 12% transferred in, 10% live on campus. *Retention:* 58% of 2002 full-time freshmen returned.

Freshmen *Admission:* 1,814 applied, 1,397 enrolled. *Average high school GPA:* 2.60.

Faculty *Total:* 725, 17% full-time, 93% with terminal degrees. *Student/faculty ratio:* 15:1.

Majors Advertising; animation, interactive technology, video graphics and special effects; apparel and textiles; applied art; art; cinematography and film/video production; commercial and advertising art; computer graphics; digital communication and media/multimedia; drawing; fashion/apparel design; fashion merchandising; fiber, textile and weaving arts; film/cinema studies; fine/studio arts; graphic communications; graphic design; illustration; industrial design; interior design; metal and jewelry arts; painting; photography; printmaking; radio and television; sculpture; web/multimedia management and webmaster.

Academic Programs *Special study options:* academic remediation for entering students, adult/continuing education programs, English as a second language, independent study, internships, part-time degree program, summer session for credit.

Library Academy of Art College Library with 35,000 titles, 300 serial subscriptions, 115,000 audiovisual materials, an OPAC, a Web page.

Computers on Campus 600 computers available on campus for general student use. Internet access, online (class) registration, at least one staffed computer lab available. Computer purchase or lease plan available.

Student Life *Housing options:* coed. Campus housing is university owned and leased by the school. Freshman campus housing is guaranteed. *Activities and organizations:* Circle of Nations, advertising club, Western Art Directors Club, Pinoy and Pinay Artists Club, Taiwanese Student Association. *Campus security:* late-night transport/escort service, ID check at all buildings.

Athletics *Intramural sports:* soccer M/W.

Costs (2004–05) *Comprehensive fee:* $25,200 includes full-time tuition ($13,200) and room and board ($12,000). Full-time tuition and fees vary according to course load. Part-time tuition: $550 per unit. Part-time tuition and fees vary according to course load. *Required fees:* $30 per term part-time. *College room only:* $8400. Room and board charges vary according to housing facility. *Payment plan:* installment.

Financial Aid Of all full-time matriculated undergraduates who enrolled in 2002, 1,469 applied for aid, 1,203 were judged to have need, 31 had their need fully met. 82 Federal Work-Study jobs (averaging $2309). *Average percent of need met:* 39%. *Average financial aid package:* $6217. *Average need-based loan:* $3491. *Average need-based gift aid:* $5800. *Average indebtedness upon graduation:* $32,000.

Applying *Options:* common application, early admission, deferred entrance. *Application fee:* $100. *Required:* high school transcript. *Recommended:* minimum 2.0 GPA, interview, portfolio. *Application deadline:* rolling (freshmen), rolling (transfers).

Admissions Contact Admissions, Academy of Art University, 79 New Montgomery Street, San Francisco, CA 94105. *Phone:* 415-263-2219. *Toll-free phone:* 800-544-ARTS. *Fax:* 415-263-4130. *E-mail:* info@academyart.edu.

■ *See page 1128 for a narrative description.*

ALLIANT INTERNATIONAL UNIVERSITY
San Diego, California

- **Independent** university, founded 1952, part of Alliant International University
- **Calendar** semesters
- **Degrees** certificates, bachelor's, master's, doctoral, and postbachelor's certificates
- **Suburban** 60-acre campus
- **Endowment** $1.6 million
- **Coed,** 420 undergraduate students, 87% full-time, 55% women, 45% men
- **Moderately difficult** entrance level, 60% of applicants were admitted

Undergraduates 365 full-time, 55 part-time. Students come from 16 states and territories, 78 other countries, 16% are from out of state, 10% African American, 7% Asian American or Pacific Islander, 18% Hispanic American, 1% Native American, 32% international, 23% transferred in, 38% live on campus. *Retention:* 68% of 2002 full-time freshmen returned.

Freshmen *Admission:* 376 applied, 226 admitted, 71 enrolled. *Average high school GPA:* 2.91.

Faculty *Total:* 589, 27% full-time, 98% with terminal degrees. *Student/faculty ratio:* 15:1.

Majors Business administration and management; education related; hotel/motel administration; international business/trade/commerce; international relations and affairs; journalism; Latin American studies; management information systems; psychology; tourism and travel services management.

Academic Programs *Special study options:* academic remediation for entering students, adult/continuing education programs, advanced placement credit, English as a second language, honors programs, independent study, internships, part-time degree program, services for LD students, study abroad, summer session for credit. *ROTC:* Army (c).

Library Walter Library with 142,303 titles, 15,150 serial subscriptions, 1,658 audiovisual materials, an OPAC, a Web page.

Computers on Campus 80 computers available on campus for general student use. A campuswide network can be accessed from student residence rooms. Internet access, online (class) registration, at least one staffed computer lab available.

Student Life *Housing:* on-campus residence required for freshman year. *Options:* coed. Campus housing is university owned. *Activities and organizations:* student-run newspaper, Residence Hall Association, Latino Students Association, Finance Club, Student Government, Sigma Iota Epsilon. *Campus security:* 24-hour emergency response devices and patrols, student patrols, late-night transport/escort service. *Student services:* health clinic, personal/psychological counseling.

Athletics Member NAIA. *Intercollegiate sports:* cross-country running M(s)/W(s), soccer M(s)/W(s), tennis M(s)/W(s), track and field M(s)/W(s), volleyball W(s). *Intramural sports:* basketball M/W, cross-country running M/W, football M/W, soccer M/W, softball M/W, table tennis M/W, tennis M/W, volleyball M/W.

Costs (2004–05) *Comprehensive fee:* $26,790 includes full-time tuition ($18,990), mandatory fees ($370), and room and board ($7430). Full-time tuition and fees vary according to course load. Part-time tuition: $695 per unit. Part-time tuition and fees vary according to course load. *Room and board:* Room and board charges vary according to board plan and housing facility. *Payment plan:* installment. *Waivers:* children of alumni and employees or children of employees.

Financial Aid Of all full-time matriculated undergraduates who enrolled in 2002, 372 applied for aid, 342 were judged to have need, 51 had their need fully met. In 2002, 56 non-need-based awards were made. *Average percent of need met:*

Alliant International University (continued)
100%. *Average financial aid package:* $21,250. *Average need-based loan:* $4500. *Average non-need-based aid:* $2000. *Average indebtedness upon graduation:* $13,200.

Applying *Options:* common application, deferred entrance. *Application fee:* $40. *Required:* high school transcript, minimum 2.0 GPA. *Recommended:* minimum 3.0 GPA. *Application deadline:* rolling (freshmen). *Notification:* continuous (transfers).

Admissions Contact Mr. Hernan Bucheli, System Director of Enrollment Management, Alliant International University, 10455 Pomerado Road, San Diego, CA 92131-1799. *Phone:* 858-635-4777. *Toll-free phone:* 866-825-5426. *Fax:* 858-635-4739. *E-mail:* admissions@alliant.edu.

■ *See page 1154 for a narrative description.*

AMERICAN INTERCONTINENTAL UNIVERSITY
Los Angeles, California

- **Proprietary** comprehensive, founded 1982
- **Calendar** five 10-week terms
- **Degrees** associate, bachelor's, and master's
- **Urban** campus
- **Coed,** 1,304 undergraduate students, 63% full-time, 44% women, 56% men
- **Noncompetitive** entrance level, 38% of applicants were admitted

Undergraduates 827 full-time, 477 part-time. Students come from 50 states and territories, 21 other countries, 27% are from out of state, 3% African American, 2% Asian American or Pacific Islander, 3% Hispanic American, 0.7% Native American, 2% international, 10% live on campus. *Retention:* 63% of 2002 full-time freshmen returned.

Freshmen *Admission:* 720 applied, 270 admitted. *Average high school GPA:* 2.00.

Faculty *Total:* 133, 18% full-time, 29% with terminal degrees. *Student/faculty ratio:* 24:1.

Majors Business administration and management; cinematography and film/video production; commercial and advertising art; computer management; criminal justice/law enforcement administration; fashion/apparel design; fashion merchandising; interior design; management information systems; marketing/marketing management; photography.

Academic Programs *Special study options:* academic remediation for entering students, accelerated degree program, distance learning, double majors, internships, part-time degree program, study abroad, summer session for credit.

Library Library plus 1 other with 20,000 titles, 228 serial subscriptions.

Computers on Campus 40 computers available on campus for general student use. A campuswide network can be accessed from off campus. Internet access, at least one staffed computer lab available. Computer purchase or lease plan available.

Student Life *Housing options:* coed, men-only, women-only. Campus housing is provided by a third party. Freshman campus housing is guaranteed. *Activities and organizations:* drama/theater group, student-run newspaper. *Campus security:* 24-hour emergency response devices, late-night transport/escort service. *Student services:* personal/psychological counseling.

Applying *Options:* electronic application, early admission, deferred entrance. *Application fee:* $50. *Required:* essay or personal statement, high school transcript, interview. *Application deadline:* rolling (freshmen), rolling (transfers).

Admissions Contact Director of High School Admissions, American InterContinental University, 12655 West Jefferson Boulevard, Los Angeles, CA 90066. *Phone:* 310-302-2000 Ext. 2632. *Toll-free phone:* 800-333-2652. *Fax:* 310-302-2001.

ANTIOCH UNIVERSITY LOS ANGELES
Culver City, California

- **Independent** upper-level, founded 1972, part of Antioch University
- **Calendar** quarters
- **Degrees** bachelor's, master's, post-master's, and postbachelor's certificates
- **Urban** 1-acre campus with easy access to Los Angeles
- **Coed,** 188 undergraduate students, 43% full-time, 75% women, 25% men
- **Moderately difficult** entrance level, 88% of applicants were admitted

Undergraduates 81 full-time, 107 part-time. Students come from 1 other state, 0.1% are from out of state, 17% African American, 4% Asian American or Pacific Islander, 10% Hispanic American, 2% Native American, 100% transferred in.

Faculty *Total:* 172, 12% full-time, 52% with terminal degrees. *Student/faculty ratio:* 14:1.

Majors Liberal arts and sciences/liberal studies.

Academic Programs *Special study options:* academic remediation for entering students, accelerated degree program, adult/continuing education programs, advanced placement credit, cooperative education, distance learning, double majors, external degree program, independent study, internships, part-time degree program, services for LD students, student-designed majors, summer session for credit. *Unusual degree programs:* 3-2 education, management.

Library Ohiolink.

Computers on Campus 12 computers available on campus for general student use. A campuswide network can be accessed from off campus. Internet access, at least one staffed computer lab available.

Student Life *Housing:* college housing not available. *Campus security:* 24-hour emergency response devices, late-night transport/escort service. *Student services:* personal/psychological counseling.

Costs (2003–04) *Tuition:* $15,995 full-time, $405 per unit part-time. Full-time tuition and fees vary according to course load and program. Part-time tuition and fees vary according to course load and program. *Required fees:* $65 full-time. *Payment plan:* installment. *Waivers:* employees or children of employees.

Applying *Options:* deferred entrance. *Application fee:* $60. *Application deadline:* 8/1 (transfers). *Notification:* continuous until 10/1 (transfers).

Admissions Contact Ms. Kathie Rawding, Director of Admissions and Financial Aid, Antioch University Los Angeles, 400 Corporate Pointe, Culver City, CA 90230. *Phone:* 310-578-1080 Ext. 217. *Toll-free phone:* 800-7ANTIOCH. *Fax:* 310-822-4824. *E-mail:* admissions@antiochla.edu.

ANTIOCH UNIVERSITY SANTA BARBARA
Santa Barbara, California

- **Independent** upper-level, founded 1977, part of Antioch University
- **Calendar** quarters
- **Degrees** bachelor's and master's
- **Small-town** campus with easy access to Los Angeles
- **Coed,** 103 undergraduate students, 58% full-time, 75% women, 25% men
- **Minimally difficult** entrance level

Undergraduates 60 full-time, 43 part-time. 5% African American, 6% Asian American or Pacific Islander, 12% Hispanic American, 2% Native American, 2% international, 100% transferred in.

Faculty *Total:* 62, 19% full-time. *Student/faculty ratio:* 15:1.

Majors General studies.

Academic Programs *Special study options:* academic remediation for entering students, accelerated degree program, adult/continuing education programs, independent study, internships, part-time degree program, student-designed majors, summer session for credit.

Computers on Campus 14 computers available on campus for general student use. A campuswide network can be accessed from off campus. At least one staffed computer lab available.

Student Life *Housing:* college housing not available. *Campus security:* late-night transport/escort service.

Costs (2003–04) *Tuition:* $11,985 full-time, $395 per unit part-time. Full-time tuition and fees vary according to degree level. Part-time tuition and fees vary according to course load and degree level. *Required fees:* $48 full-time. *Payment plan:* installment. *Waivers:* employees or children of employees.

Financial Aid Of all full-time matriculated undergraduates who enrolled in 2003, 23 Federal Work-Study jobs (averaging $2120).

Applying *Options:* common application, deferred entrance. *Application fee:* $60. *Application deadline:* rolling (transfers).

Admissions Contact Mr. Richard Grisel, Director of Admissions, Antioch University Santa Barbara, 801 Garden Street, Santa Barbara, CA 93101-1580. *Phone:* 805-962-8179 Ext. 113. *Fax:* 805-962-4786. *E-mail:* admissions@antiochsb.edu.

ARGOSY UNIVERSITY/ORANGE COUNTY
Orange, California

- **Proprietary** upper-level
- **Calendar** semesters
- **Degrees** bachelor's, master's, and doctoral
- **Urban** campus with easy access to Los Angeles and San Diego
- **Coed,** 81 undergraduate students, 81% full-time, 59% women, 41% men
- **Moderately difficult** entrance level

Undergraduates 66 full-time, 15 part-time. 62% transferred in.

Faculty *Total:* 81, 14% full-time, 90% with terminal degrees. *Student/faculty ratio:* 22:1.

Academic Programs *Special study options:* academic remediation for entering students, distance learning, part-time degree program, services for LD students.
Library Carrie Lixey with 1,200 titles, 50 serial subscriptions, an OPAC.
Computers on Campus 12 computers available on campus for general student use. Internet access, online (class) registration, at least one staffed computer lab available.
Student Life *Housing:* college housing not available.
Costs (2003–04) *Tuition:* $360 per credit hour part-time. Full-time tuition and fees vary according to degree level and location. Part-time tuition and fees vary according to degree level and location. *Required fees:* $25 per year part-time. *Payment plan:* installment. *Waivers:* employees or children of employees.
Financial Aid Of all full-time matriculated undergraduates who enrolled in 2003, 28 applied for aid, 23 were judged to have need. 3 Federal Work-Study jobs (averaging $4660). *Average financial aid package:* $3586. *Average need-based loan:* $2185. *Average need-based gift aid:* $2349.
Applying *Options:* common application, electronic application, early admission, deferred entrance. *Application fee:* $50.
Admissions Contact Mark Betz, Director, Admissions, Argosy University/Orange County, 3745 West Chapman Avenue, Suite 100, Orange, CA 92868. *Phone:* 714-940-0025 Ext. 4815. *Toll-free phone:* 800-716-9598 Ext. 4819. *Fax:* 714-940-0767. *E-mail:* auocadmissions@argosyu.edu.

ARGOSY UNIVERSITY/SAN FRANCISCO BAY AREA

Point Richmond, California

- **Proprietary** upper-level, founded 1998
- **Calendar** semesters
- **Degrees** bachelor's, master's, and doctoral
- **Urban** campus with easy access to Oakland and San Francisco
- **Coed,** 45 undergraduate students, 100% full-time, 56% women, 44% men

Undergraduates 45 full-time. Students come from 1 other state, 2 other countries, 0.1% are from out of state, 27% African American, 9% Asian American or Pacific Islander, 20% Hispanic American, 4% international, 33% transferred in.
Faculty *Total:* 11, 9% full-time, 100% with terminal degrees. *Student/faculty ratio:* 10:1.
Student Life *Housing:* college housing not available.
Costs (2003–04) *Tuition:* $360 per credit hour part-time. Full-time tuition and fees vary according to course level and degree level. *Payment plans:* tuition prepayment, installment.
Financial Aid Of all full-time matriculated undergraduates who enrolled in 2003, 17 applied for aid, 16 were judged to have need. *Average financial aid package:* $2973. *Average need-based loan:* $2344. *Average need-based gift aid:* $1980.
Admissions Contact 999 Canal Boulevard, Suite A, Point Richmond, CA 94804. *Toll-free phone:* 866-215-2777 Ext. 205 (in-state); 866-215-2777 (out-of-state). *E-mail:* jstofan@argosyu.edu.

ART CENTER COLLEGE OF DESIGN

Pasadena, California

- **Independent** comprehensive, founded 1930
- **Calendar** trimesters
- **Degrees** bachelor's and master's
- **Suburban** 175-acre campus with easy access to Los Angeles
- **Endowment** $16.7 million
- **Coed,** 1,412 undergraduate students, 100% full-time, 42% women, 58% men
- **Very difficult** entrance level, 72% of applicants were admitted

Undergraduates 1,412 full-time. Students come from 36 states and territories, 32 other countries, 21% are from out of state, 2% African American, 31% Asian American or Pacific Islander, 11% Hispanic American, 0.7% Native American, 16% international, 2% transferred in. *Retention:* 94% of 2002 full-time freshmen returned.
Freshmen *Admission:* 949 applied, 687 admitted, 43 enrolled. *Average high school GPA:* 3.25.
Faculty *Total:* 407, 16% full-time. *Student/faculty ratio:* 12:1.
Majors Advertising; art; cinematography and film/video production; commercial and advertising art; commercial photography; design and applied arts related; environmental design/architecture; film/cinema studies; film/video and photographic arts related; fine arts related; fine/studio arts; graphic design; illustration; industrial design; interior design; intermedia/multimedia; painting; photography; visual and performing arts.
Academic Programs *Special study options:* accelerated degree program, adult/continuing education programs, advanced placement credit, independent study, internships, summer session for credit.
Library James LeMont Fogg Library with 77,000 titles, 400 serial subscriptions, 7,000 audiovisual materials, an OPAC.
Computers on Campus 225 computers available on campus for general student use. A campuswide network can be accessed from off campus. Internet access, at least one staffed computer lab available.
Student Life *Housing:* college housing not available. *Activities and organizations:* Contraste, Chroma, Women's Alliance, Korean Student Alliance, Industrial Design Society Student Chapter. *Campus security:* 24-hour emergency response devices and patrols. *Student services:* personal/psychological counseling.
Athletics *Intramural sports:* ultimate Frisbee M/W.
Standardized Tests *Required for some:* SAT I or ACT (for admission).
Costs (2004–05) *Tuition:* $23,450 full-time. *Payment plan:* installment. *Waivers:* employees or children of employees.
Financial Aid Of all full-time matriculated undergraduates who enrolled in 2003, 938 applied for aid, 891 were judged to have need. In 2003, 1 non-need-based awards were made. *Average percent of need met:* 60%. *Average financial aid package:* $21,214. *Average need-based loan:* $3964. *Average need-based gift aid:* $8195. *Average non-need-based aid:* $31,450. *Average indebtedness upon graduation:* $49,000.
Applying *Options:* deferred entrance. *Application fee:* $45. *Required:* essay or personal statement, high school transcript, portfolio. *Recommended:* minimum 3.0 GPA, interview. *Application deadline:* rolling (freshmen), rolling (transfers). *Notification:* continuous (freshmen).
Admissions Contact Ms. Kit Baron, Vice President of Admissions, Art Center College of Design, 1700 Lida Street, Pasadena, CA 91103-1999. *Phone:* 626-396-2373. *Fax:* 626-795-0578. *E-mail:* admissions@artcenter.edu.

THE ART INSTITUTE OF CALIFORNIA–LOS ANGELES

Santa Monica, California

Admissions Contact Director of Admissions, The Art Institute of California–Los Angeles, 2900 31st Street, Santa Monica, CA 90405-3035. *Phone:* 310-752-4700. *Toll-free phone:* 888-646-4610.

THE ART INSTITUTE OF CALIFORNIA–SAN DIEGO

San Diego, California

- **Proprietary** 4-year, founded 1981, part of The Art Institutes/Argosy
- **Calendar** quarters
- **Degrees** associate and bachelor's
- **Urban** campus
- **Coed,** 1,329 undergraduate students, 92% full-time, 42% women, 58% men
- **Minimally difficult** entrance level

Undergraduates 1,220 full-time, 109 part-time. Students come from 23 states and territories, 20% are from out of state, 4% African American, 13% Asian American or Pacific Islander, 21% Hispanic American, 1% Native American, 4% international. *Retention:* 85% of 2002 full-time freshmen returned.
Freshmen *Average high school GPA:* 2.53.
Faculty *Total:* 91. *Student/faculty ratio:* 22:1.
Majors Advertising; baking and pastry arts; commercial and advertising art; communication and journalism related; cooking and related culinary arts; culinary arts; design and applied arts related; digital communication and media/multimedia; graphic design; interior architecture; interior design; intermedia/multimedia; restaurant, culinary, and catering management; restaurant/food services management.
Academic Programs *Special study options:* cooperative education, double majors, internships, services for LD students, summer session for credit.
Library The Art Institute of California Library plus 1 other with 1,100 titles, 17 serial subscriptions, an OPAC.
Computers on Campus 150 computers available on campus for general student use. Internet access, at least one staffed computer lab available.
Student Life *Housing options:* Campus housing is leased by the school and is provided by a third party. Freshman applicants given priority for college housing. *Activities and organizations:* student-run newspaper, Advertising Club-AAF, Communicating Art Club, 3-D club, ASB, AIGA. *Campus security:* 24-hour emergency response devices.
Costs (2004–05) *Tuition:* $17,472 full-time, $364 per credit part-time. Full-time tuition and fees vary according to program. *Required fees:* $595 full-time. *Room only:* $8580. *Payment plans:* tuition prepayment, installment.

The Art Institute of California–San Diego (continued)

Applying *Options:* common application, electronic application, deferred entrance. *Application fee:* $50. *Required:* essay or personal statement, high school transcript, interview. *Application deadline:* rolling (freshmen), rolling (transfers). *Notification:* continuous (freshmen), continuous (transfers).

Admissions Contact Ms. Sandy Park, Director of Admissions, The Art Institute of California–San Diego, 7650 Mission Valley Road, San Diego, CA 92108. *Phone:* 858-598-1399 Ext. 1208. *Toll-free phone:* 800-591-2422 Ext. 3117. *Fax:* 619-291-3206. *E-mail:* info@aii.edu.

THE ART INSTITUTE OF CALIFORNIA–SAN FRANCISCO

San Francisco, California

- **Proprietary** 4-year, founded 1939, part of Education Management Corporation
- **Calendar** quarters
- **Degrees** associate and bachelor's
- **Urban** campus
- **Coed,** 918 undergraduate students
- **Moderately difficult** entrance level

Faculty *Total:* 66, 8% full-time. *Student/faculty ratio:* 16:1.

Majors Advertising; animation, interactive technology, video graphics and special effects; business, management, and marketing related; commercial and advertising art; computer graphics; computer programming (specific applications); fashion/apparel design; graphic design; interior design; web page, digital/multimedia and information resources design.

Academic Programs *Special study options:* accelerated degree program, distance learning, internships, part-time degree program, summer session for credit.

Computers on Campus At least one staffed computer lab available.

Student Life *Housing options:* Campus housing is leased by the school. *Activities and organizations:* student-run newspaper, Animation club, Game Art and Design Club, Fashion Salon, Society of Web Architects and Programmers, Student Federation. *Campus security:* 24-hour emergency response devices.

Costs (2003–04) *Tuition:* $17,472 full-time, $364 per credit hour part-time. *Required fees:* $150 full-time.

Applying *Options:* common application, deferred entrance. *Application fee:* $50. *Required:* essay or personal statement, high school transcript. *Recommended:* minimum 2.0 GPA, 2 letters of recommendation, interview. *Application deadline:* rolling (freshmen), rolling (transfers).

Admissions Contact Daniel Cardenas, Admissions Department, The Art Institute of California–San Francisco, 1170 Market Street, San Francisco, CA 94102-4908. *Phone:* 415-865-0198. *Toll-free phone:* 888-493-3261. *Fax:* 415-863-6344. *E-mail:* aisfadm@aii.edu.

AZUSA PACIFIC UNIVERSITY

Azusa, California

- **Independent nondenominational** comprehensive, founded 1899
- **Calendar** semesters
- **Degrees** bachelor's, master's, doctoral, and first professional
- **Small-town** 60-acre campus with easy access to Los Angeles
- **Endowment** $21.1 million
- **Coed,** 4,373 undergraduate students, 96% full-time, 64% women, 36% men
- **Moderately difficult** entrance level, 83% of applicants were admitted

At Azusa Pacific, a comprehensive Christian university, students are challenged academically, encouraged to participate in dynamic leadership experiences, and enabled to utilize the latest technology, gaining the skills needed to reach their goals. Located 26 miles northeast of Los Angeles, APU offers more than 40 undergraduate majors, 20 master's programs, 4 doctoral programs, and extensive credential and certificate programs.

Undergraduates 4,194 full-time, 179 part-time. Students come from 44 states and territories, 52 other countries, 19% are from out of state, 3% African American, 5% Asian American or Pacific Islander, 12% Hispanic American, 0.3% Native American, 2% international, 9% transferred in, 63% live on campus. *Retention:* 83% of 2002 full-time freshmen returned.

Freshmen *Admission:* 2,472 applied, 2,042 admitted, 912 enrolled. *Average high school GPA:* 3.62. *Test scores:* SAT verbal scores over 500: 67%; SAT math scores over 500: 68%; ACT scores over 18: 97%; SAT verbal scores over 600: 24%; SAT math scores over 600: 28%; ACT scores over 24: 44%; SAT verbal scores over 700: 3%; SAT math scores over 700: 3%; ACT scores over 30: 8%.

Faculty *Total:* 920, 29% full-time. *Student/faculty ratio:* 12:1.

Majors Accounting; applied art; art; athletic training; biblical studies; biochemistry; biology/biological sciences; business administration and management; chemistry; communication/speech communication and rhetoric; computer science; cultural studies; divinity/ministry; English; health science; history; international relations and affairs; liberal arts and sciences/liberal studies; management information systems; marketing/marketing management; mathematics; music; natural sciences; nursing (registered nurse training); philosophy; physical education teaching and coaching; physics; political science and government; pre-engineering; pre-law studies; psychology; religious studies; social sciences; social work; sociology; Spanish; theology; web page, digital/multimedia and information resources design.

Academic Programs *Special study options:* academic remediation for entering students, accelerated degree program, adult/continuing education programs, advanced placement credit, cooperative education, distance learning, double majors, English as a second language, freshman honors college, honors programs, internships, off-campus study, part-time degree program, services for LD students, study abroad, summer session for credit. *ROTC:* Army (c).

Library Marshburn Memorial Library plus 2 others with 176,679 titles, 14,000 serial subscriptions, 6,004 audiovisual materials, an OPAC, a Web page.

Computers on Campus 300 computers available on campus for general student use. A campuswide network can be accessed from off campus. Internet access, online (class) registration, at least one staffed computer lab available. Computer purchase or lease plan available.

Student Life *Housing options:* Campus housing is university owned and leased by the school. Freshman applicants given priority for college housing. *Activities and organizations:* drama/theater group, student-run newspaper, choral group, marching band, community service groups, choir, outreach ministries groups, Habitat for Humanity, Multi-Ethnic Student Alliance (MESA). *Campus security:* 24-hour emergency response devices and patrols, student patrols, late-night transport/escort service, controlled dormitory access. *Student services:* health clinic, personal/psychological counseling.

Athletics Member NAIA. *Intercollegiate sports:* baseball M(s), basketball M(s)/W(s), cross-country running M(s)/W(s), football M(s), golf M(s), soccer M(s)/W(s), softball W(s), tennis M(s), track and field M(s)/W(s), volleyball M/W(s). *Intramural sports:* basketball M/W, football M/W, golf M/W, skiing (downhill) M/W, soccer W, volleyball M/W.

Standardized Tests *Required:* SAT I or ACT (for admission).

Costs (2003–04) *Comprehensive fee:* $24,720 includes full-time tuition ($18,790), mandatory fees ($234), and room and board ($5696). Part-time tuition: $750 per credit hour. Part-time tuition and fees vary according to course load. *College room only:* $3150. Room and board charges vary according to board plan, housing facility, and student level. *Payment plan:* installment. *Waivers:* employees or children of employees.

Financial Aid Of all full-time matriculated undergraduates who enrolled in 2002, 2,709 applied for aid, 2,258 were judged to have need, 271 had their need fully met. 453 Federal Work-Study jobs (averaging $1500). In 2002, 1212 non-need-based awards were made. *Average percent of need met:* 72%. *Average financial aid package:* $12,616. *Average need-based loan:* $3984. *Average need-based gift aid:* $8335. *Average non-need-based aid:* $3485. *Average indebtedness upon graduation:* $24,000. *Financial aid deadline:* 7/1.

Applying *Options:* early admission, early action, deferred entrance. *Application fee:* $45. *Required:* essay or personal statement, high school transcript, minimum 2.5 GPA, 2 letters of recommendation. *Required for some:* interview. *Application deadlines:* 6/1 (freshmen), 6/1 (transfers). *Notification:* continuous (freshmen), 2/15 (early action), continuous (transfers).

Admissions Contact Mrs. Deana Porterfield, Dean of Enrollment, Azusa Pacific University, 901 East Alosta Avenue, PO Box 7000, Azusa, CA 91702-7000. *Phone:* 626-812-3016. *Toll-free phone:* 800-TALK-APU. *E-mail:* admissions@apu.edu.

■ *See page 1202 for a narrative description.*

BETHANY COLLEGE OF THE ASSEMBLIES OF GOD

Scotts Valley, California

- **Independent Assemblies of God** comprehensive, founded 1919
- **Calendar** semesters
- **Degrees** certificates, associate, bachelor's, and master's
- **Small-town** 40-acre campus with easy access to San Francisco and San Jose
- **Endowment** $500,000
- **Coed**
- **Minimally difficult** entrance level

Faculty *Student/faculty ratio:* 11:1.

Student Life *Campus security:* 24-hour emergency response devices, student patrols, controlled dormitory access.

Athletics Member NAIA.
Standardized Tests *Required:* SAT I or ACT (for admission).
Costs (2003–04) *Comprehensive fee:* $17,960 includes full-time tuition ($11,940), mandatory fees ($640), and room and board ($5380). Part-time tuition: $500 per unit. *Required fees:* $90 per term part-time. *College room only:* $2520.
Financial Aid Of all full-time matriculated undergraduates who enrolled in 2003, 370 applied for aid, 331 were judged to have need, 50 had their need fully met. 38 Federal Work-Study jobs (averaging $2011). In 2003, 15. *Average percent of need met:* 39. *Average financial aid package:* $10,250. *Average need-based loan:* $4570. *Average need-based gift aid:* $7423. *Average non-need-based aid:* $6000. *Average indebtedness upon graduation:* $21,000.
Applying *Options:* early admission, deferred entrance. *Application fee:* $35. *Required:* essay or personal statement, high school transcript, minimum 2.0 GPA, 2 letters of recommendation, Christian commitment.
Admissions Contact Ms. Pam Smallwood, Director of Admissions, Bethany College of the Assemblies of God, 800 Bethany Drive, Scotts Valley, CA 95066-2820. *Phone:* 831-438-3800 Ext. 1400. *Toll-free phone:* 800-843-9410. *Fax:* 831-438-4517. *E-mail:* info@bethany.edu.

BETHESDA CHRISTIAN UNIVERSITY
Anaheim, California

- **Independent** comprehensive, founded 1978, affiliated with Full Gospel World Mission
- **Calendar** semesters
- **Degrees** certificates, bachelor's, master's, and first professional
- **Suburban** campus with easy access to Los Angeles
- **Endowment** $7.0 million
- **Coed,** 164 undergraduate students, 79% full-time, 54% women, 46% men
- **Minimally difficult** entrance level

Undergraduates 129 full-time, 35 part-time. Students come from 3 states and territories, 3 other countries, 0.1% are from out of state, 30% Asian American or Pacific Islander, 70% international, 13% transferred in. *Retention:* 36% of 2002 full-time freshmen returned.
Freshmen *Admission:* 32 enrolled.
Faculty *Total:* 25, 24% full-time, 80% with terminal degrees. *Student/faculty ratio:* 15:1.
Majors Biblical studies; conducting; design and visual communications; divinity/ministry; early childhood education; missionary studies and missiology; music management and merchandising; music theory and composition; pastoral studies/counseling; piano and organ; religious education; religious/sacred music; violin, viola, guitar and other stringed instruments; voice and opera.
Academic Programs *Special study options:* accelerated degree program, adult/continuing education programs, double majors, English as a second language, independent study, internships, part-time degree program, study abroad, summer session for credit.
Library Library plus 1 other with 27,763 titles, 99 serial subscriptions, 3,042 audiovisual materials.
Computers on Campus 30 computers available on campus for general student use. Internet access, at least one staffed computer lab available.
Student Life *Housing:* college housing not available. *Activities and organizations:* Student Council, Ping Pong Team. *Campus security:* student patrols, late-night transport/escort service, 24-hour security monitor. *Student services:* personal/psychological counseling.
Athletics *Intramural sports:* ultimate Frisbee M/W.
Costs (2004–05) *Tuition:* $6000 full-time, $200 per credit part-time. *Required fees:* $120 full-time, $60 per term part-time. *Room only:* Room and board charges vary according to housing facility. *Payment plans:* installment, deferred payment.
Financial Aid Of all full-time matriculated undergraduates who enrolled in 2002, 52 applied for aid, 52 were judged to have need. *Average percent of need met:* 39%. *Average financial aid package:* $4557. *Average need-based loan:* $3253. *Average need-based gift aid:* $2617. *Average indebtedness upon graduation:* $5000.
Applying *Options:* common application, early admission. *Application fee:* $35. *Required:* essay or personal statement, high school transcript, minimum 2.0 GPA, 2 letters of recommendation, interview, 2 photographs. *Application deadline:* 8/11 (freshmen). *Notification:* continuous until 8/25 (freshmen).
Admissions Contact Mr. Samuel C. Jung, Director of Admission, Bethesda Christian University, 730 North Euclid Street, Anaheim, CA 92801. *Phone:* 714-517-1945. *Fax:* 714-517-1948. *E-mail:* admission@bcu.edu.

BIOLA UNIVERSITY
La Mirada, California

- **Independent interdenominational** university, founded 1908
- **Calendar** 4-1-4
- **Degrees** certificates, bachelor's, master's, doctoral, and first professional
- **Suburban** 95-acre campus with easy access to Los Angeles
- **Endowment** $16.7 million
- **Coed,** 3,232 undergraduate students, 90% full-time, 63% women, 37% men
- **Moderately difficult** entrance level, 78% of applicants were admitted

Undergraduates 2,904 full-time, 328 part-time. Students come from 47 states and territories, 40 other countries, 29% are from out of state, 4% African American, 7% Asian American or Pacific Islander, 9% Hispanic American, 0.3% Native American, 4% international, 6% transferred in, 69% live on campus. *Retention:* 84% of 2002 full-time freshmen returned.
Freshmen *Admission:* 1,901 applied, 1,483 admitted, 814 enrolled. *Average high school GPA:* 3.55. *Test scores:* SAT verbal scores over 500: 78%; SAT math scores over 500: 73%; ACT scores over 18: 96%; SAT verbal scores over 600: 37%; SAT math scores over 600: 32%; ACT scores over 24: 53%; SAT verbal scores over 700: 7%; SAT math scores over 700: 6%; ACT scores over 30: 7%.
Faculty *Total:* 404, 45% full-time, 62% with terminal degrees. *Student/faculty ratio:* 18:1.
Majors Adult and continuing education; anthropology; art; biblical studies; bilingual and multilingual education; biochemistry; biology/biological sciences; business administration and management; clinical psychology; commercial and advertising art; communication disorders; computer and information sciences; divinity/ministry; drawing; education; education (K-12); elementary education; English; fine/studio arts; history; humanities; kinesiology and exercise science; mathematics; missionary studies and missiology; music; nursing (registered nurse training); pastoral studies/counseling; philosophy; physical education teaching and coaching; physical sciences; pre-law studies; psychology; radio and television; religious education; religious studies; secondary education; social sciences; sociology; Spanish; theology.
Academic Programs *Special study options:* academic remediation for entering students, accelerated degree program, adult/continuing education programs, advanced placement credit, cooperative education, double majors, English as a second language, freshman honors college, honors programs, independent study, internships, off-campus study, part-time degree program, services for LD students, study abroad, summer session for credit. *ROTC:* Army (c), Air Force (c). *Unusual degree programs:* 3-2 engineering with University of Southern California; biblical and theological studies.
Library The Biola University Library with 270,456 titles, 13,123 serial subscriptions, 12,482 audiovisual materials, an OPAC, a Web page.
Computers on Campus 150 computers available on campus for general student use. A campuswide network can be accessed from student residence rooms and from off campus. Internet access, online (class) registration, at least one staffed computer lab available. Computer purchase or lease plan available.
Student Life *Housing:* on-campus residence required through sophomore year. *Options:* men-only, women-only. Campus housing is university owned and is provided by a third party. Freshman campus housing is guaranteed. *Activities and organizations:* drama/theater group, student-run newspaper, radio and television station, choral group, Korean Student Association, Brothers and Sisters in Christ, Accounting Society, Maharlika (Filipino Club), SOUL (Seeking Out Unity and Love). *Campus security:* 24-hour emergency response devices and patrols, student patrols, late-night transport/escort service, controlled dormitory access, access gates to roads through the middle of campus. *Student services:* health clinic, personal/psychological counseling, legal services.
Athletics Member NAIA. *Intercollegiate sports:* baseball M(s), basketball M(s)/W(s), cheerleading W(c), cross-country running M(s)/W(s), soccer M(s)/W(s), softball W(s), swimming M(s)/W(s), tennis W(s), track and field M(s)/W(s), volleyball W(s). *Intramural sports:* basketball M/W, football M/W, rock climbing M/W, softball M/W, ultimate Frisbee M/W, volleyball M/W, water polo M/W.
Standardized Tests *Required:* SAT I or ACT (for admission).
Costs (2003–04) *Comprehensive fee:* $25,531 includes full-time tuition ($19,564) and room and board ($5967). Full-time tuition and fees vary according to program. Part-time tuition and fees vary according to course load and program. *College room only:* $3207. Room and board charges vary according to board plan and housing facility. *Payment plan:* installment. *Waivers:* employees or children of employees.
Financial Aid Of all full-time matriculated undergraduates who enrolled in 2002, 1,770 applied for aid, 1,480 were judged to have need, 305 had their need

Biola University (continued)
fully met. 117 Federal Work-Study jobs (averaging $2564). In 2002, 302 non-need-based awards were made. *Average percent of need met:* 77%. *Average financial aid package:* $13,701. *Average need-based loan:* $3073. *Average need-based gift aid:* $8470. *Average non-need-based aid:* $7502. *Average indebtedness upon graduation:* $21,220.

Applying *Options:* common application, electronic application, early admission, early action, deferred entrance. *Application fee:* $45. *Required:* essay or personal statement, high school transcript, 2 letters of recommendation, interview. *Recommended:* minimum 3.0 GPA. *Application deadlines:* 3/1 (freshmen), 3/1 (transfers). *Notification:* 3/20 (freshmen), 12/20 (early action), 3/20 (transfers).

Admissions Contact Mr. Greg Vaughan, Director of Enrollment Management, Biola University, 13800 Biola Avenue, La Mirada, CA 90639. *Phone:* 562-903-4752. *Toll-free phone:* 800-652-4652. *Fax:* 562-903-4709. *E-mail:* admissions@biola.edu.

■ *See page 1262 for a narrative description.*

BROOKS INSTITUTE OF PHOTOGRAPHY
Santa Barbara, California

- **Proprietary** comprehensive, founded 1945
- **Calendar** trimesters
- **Degrees** diplomas, bachelor's, and master's
- **Suburban** 25-acre campus
- **Coed**
- **Moderately difficult** entrance level

Faculty *Student/faculty ratio:* 12:1.

Student Life *Campus security:* campus closed after 11:30 p.m.

Costs (2003–04) *Tuition:* $19,650 full-time. *Required fees:* $600 full-time.

Applying *Options:* deferred entrance. *Application fee:* $35. *Required:* essay or personal statement, high school transcript, minimum 3.0 GPA, 15 semester hours of college credit. *Recommended:* interview.

Admissions Contact Ms. Inge B. Kautzmann, Director of Admissions, Brooks Institute of Photography, 801 Alston Road, Santa Barbara, CA 93108. *Phone:* 805-966-3888 Ext. 4601. *Toll-free phone:* 888-304-3456. *Fax:* 805-564-1475. *E-mail:* admissions@brooks.edu.

CALIFORNIA BAPTIST UNIVERSITY
Riverside, California

- **Independent Southern Baptist** comprehensive, founded 1950
- **Calendar** 4-4-1-1
- **Degrees** bachelor's and master's
- **Suburban** 82-acre campus with easy access to Los Angeles
- **Endowment** $6.5 million
- **Coed,** 1,753 undergraduate students, 82% full-time, 66% women, 34% men
- **Minimally difficult** entrance level, 84% of applicants were admitted

Undergraduates 1,444 full-time, 309 part-time. Students come from 30 states and territories, 14 other countries, 8% are from out of state, 10% transferred in, 45% live on campus. *Retention:* 86% of 2002 full-time freshmen returned.

Freshmen *Admission:* 705 applied, 594 admitted, 221 enrolled. *Average high school GPA:* 3.20. *Test scores:* SAT verbal scores over 500: 53%; SAT math scores over 500: 56%; ACT scores over 18: 85%; SAT verbal scores over 600: 18%; SAT math scores over 600: 10%; ACT scores over 24: 18%; SAT verbal scores over 700: 1%; ACT scores over 30: 1%.

Faculty *Total:* 162, 51% full-time, 52% with terminal degrees. *Student/faculty ratio:* 16:1.

Majors Art; behavioral sciences; biblical studies; biology/biological sciences; business administration and management; Christian studies; communication and journalism related; communication/speech communication and rhetoric; computer/information technology services administration related; criminal justice/law enforcement administration; English; health and physical education related; history; information science/studies; kinesiology and exercise science; liberal arts and sciences/liberal studies; mathematics; music; music performance; music theory and composition; philosophy; political science and government; pre-theology/pre-ministerial studies; psychology; social sciences; sociology; theological and ministerial studies related; theology; visual and performing arts; youth ministry.

Academic Programs *Special study options:* accelerated degree program, adult/continuing education programs, advanced placement credit, double majors, independent study, internships, off-campus study, part-time degree program, study abroad, summer session for credit.

Library Annie Gabriel Library with 97,615 titles, 38 serial subscriptions, 4,271 audiovisual materials, an OPAC, a Web page.

Computers on Campus 130 computers available on campus for general student use. A campuswide network can be accessed from student residence rooms and from off campus that provide access to intranet. Internet access, at least one staffed computer lab available.

Student Life *Housing options:* men-only, women-only. Campus housing is university owned. Freshman applicants given priority for college housing. *Activities and organizations:* drama/theater group, student-run newspaper, choral group, Student Senate, Fellowship of Christian Athletes, Blue Crew, Christian student organizations, Community Life Committees. *Campus security:* 24-hour emergency response devices and patrols, student patrols, late-night transport/escort service, controlled dormitory access. *Student services:* health clinic, personal/psychological counseling.

Athletics Member NAIA. *Intercollegiate sports:* baseball M(s), basketball M(s)/W(s), cross-country running M(s)/W(s), soccer M(s)/W(s), softball W(s), swimming M(s)/W(s), volleyball M(s)/W(s), water polo M(s)/W(s). *Intramural sports:* basketball M/W, bowling M/W, football M/W, golf M, softball M/W, table tennis M/W, tennis M/W, volleyball M/W.

Standardized Tests *Required:* SAT I or ACT (for admission).

Costs (2004–05) *Comprehensive fee:* $22,250 includes full-time tuition ($14,950), mandatory fees ($990), and room and board ($6310). Full-time tuition and fees vary according to course load and program. Part-time tuition: $575 per semester hour. Part-time tuition and fees vary according to course load and program. *College room only:* $2640. Room and board charges vary according to board plan and housing facility. *Payment plans:* installment, deferred payment. *Waivers:* employees or children of employees.

Financial Aid Of all full-time matriculated undergraduates who enrolled in 2003, 1,269 applied for aid, 1,207 were judged to have need, 762 had their need fully met. 105 Federal Work-Study jobs (averaging $831). In 2003, 46 non-need-based awards were made. *Average percent of need met:* 78%. *Average financial aid package:* $10,700. *Average need-based loan:* $3750. *Average need-based gift aid:* $7250. *Average non-need-based aid:* $3650. *Average indebtedness upon graduation:* $18,800.

Applying *Options:* common application, early admission, early action, deferred entrance. *Application fee:* $45. *Required:* essay or personal statement, high school transcript, minimum 2.5 GPA, 2 letters of recommendation. *Recommended:* interview. *Application deadline:* rolling (freshmen). *Notification:* continuous until 9/6 (freshmen), 12/19 (early action), continuous (transfers).

Admissions Contact Mr. Allen Johnson, Director, Undergraduate Admissions, California Baptist University, 8432 Magnolia Avenue, Riverside, CA 92504-3297. *Phone:* 909-343-4212. *Toll-free phone:* 877-228-8866. *Fax:* 909-343-4525. *E-mail:* admissions@calbaptist.edu.

CALIFORNIA CHRISTIAN COLLEGE
Fresno, California

- **Independent religious** 4-year
- **Calendar** semesters
- **Degrees** associate and bachelor's
- **Urban** 5-acre campus with easy access to Fresno
- **Endowment** $60,000
- **Coed,** 52 undergraduate students, 87% full-time, 31% women, 69% men
- **Noncompetitive** entrance level, 100% of applicants were admitted

Undergraduates 45 full-time, 7 part-time. Students come from 4 states and territories, 2 other countries, 4% are from out of state, 15% African American, 13% Hispanic American, 2% Native American, 4% international, 17% transferred in, 21% live on campus. *Retention:* 22% of 2002 full-time freshmen returned.

Freshmen *Admission:* 5 applied, 5 admitted, 5 enrolled.

Faculty *Total:* 18, 39% full-time, 89% with terminal degrees. *Student/faculty ratio:* 8:1.

Majors Biblical studies; pre-theology/pre-ministerial studies.

Academic Programs *Special study options:* academic remediation for entering students, accelerated degree program, cooperative education, independent study, part-time degree program, summer session for credit.

Library Cortese Library with 13,154 titles, 7 serial subscriptions, 430 audiovisual materials.

Computers on Campus 6 computers available on campus for general student use. Internet access, at least one staffed computer lab available.

Student Life *Housing:* on-campus residence required through sophomore year. *Options:* coed. Campus housing is university owned. *Activities and organizations:* drama/theater group, student-run newspaper, choral group. *Student services:* personal/psychological counseling.

Athletics Member NCCAA. *Intercollegiate sports:* basketball M, volleyball W.

Standardized Tests *Required:* standardized Bible content tests (for placement). *Recommended:* SAT I or ACT (for admission).

Costs (2003–04) *Comprehensive fee:* $8900 includes full-time tuition ($5040), mandatory fees ($660), and room and board ($3200). Full-time tuition and fees vary according to course load. Part-time tuition: $210 per unit. Part-time tuition and fees vary according to course load. *Required fees:* $55 per term part-time. *Payment plan:* installment.

Financial Aid Of all full-time matriculated undergraduates who enrolled in 2003, 45 applied for aid, 40 were judged to have need, 2 had their need fully met. 8 Federal Work-Study jobs (averaging $963). *Average percent of need met:* 55%. *Average financial aid package:* $8730. *Average need-based loan:* $3491. *Average need-based gift aid:* $3794. *Average indebtedness upon graduation:* $17,750.

Applying *Application fee:* $40. *Required:* essay or personal statement, high school transcript, minimum 2.0 GPA, 3 letters of recommendation, statement of faith, moral/ethical statement. *Recommended:* interview. *Application deadline:* rolling (freshmen), rolling (transfers). *Notification:* continuous (freshmen), continuous (transfers).

Admissions Contact Mr. Brian Henderer, Director of Admissions, California Christian College, 4881 East University Avenue, Fresno, CA 93703. *Phone:* 559-251-4215 Ext. 5571. *Fax:* 559-251-4231. *E-mail:* cccfresno@aol.com.

CALIFORNIA COLLEGE FOR HEALTH SCIENCES

National City, California

- **Proprietary** comprehensive, founded 1978
- **Calendar** continuous
- **Degrees** certificates, diplomas, associate, bachelor's, and master's (offers primarily external degree programs)
- **Urban** 2-acre campus with easy access to San Diego
- **Coed**
- **Noncompetitive** entrance level

Costs (2003–04) *Tuition:* $13,975 full-time.

Financial Aid Of all full-time matriculated undergraduates who enrolled in 2001, 96 applied for aid, 96 were judged to have need. In 2001, 1. *Average percent of need met:* 60. *Average financial aid package:* $5082. *Average need-based loan:* $2366. *Average need-based gift aid:* $2057. *Average non-need-based aid:* $4000. *Average indebtedness upon graduation:* $14,125.

Applying *Options:* deferred entrance. *Application fee:* $50. *Required:* high school transcript. *Required for some:* employment in a health science field. *Recommended:* employment in a health science field.

Admissions Contact Ms. Loreli L. Relova, Student services Manager, California College for Health Sciences, 2423 Hoover Avenue, National City, CA 91950. *Phone:* 619-477-4800 Ext. 313. *Toll-free phone:* 800-221-7374. *Fax:* 619-477-4360. *E-mail:* admissions@cchs.edu.

CALIFORNIA COLLEGE OF THE ARTS

San Francisco, California

- **Independent** comprehensive, founded 1907
- **Calendar** semesters
- **Degrees** bachelor's and master's
- **Urban** 4-acre campus
- **Endowment** $18.2 million
- **Coed,** 1,303 undergraduate students, 89% full-time, 60% women, 40% men
- **Moderately difficult** entrance level, 79% of applicants were admitted

California College of the Arts (CCA) is the only regionally accredited school of art and design on the West Coast. The College is distinguished by the interdisciplinary nature and breadth of its programs in fine art, design, and architecture, which are taught by a faculty of practicing professionals. Current initiatives include new undergraduate majors in creative writing and visual studies.

Undergraduates 1,158 full-time, 145 part-time. Students come from 39 states and territories, 21 other countries, 27% are from out of state, 2% African American, 10% Asian American or Pacific Islander, 7% Hispanic American, 0.5% Native American, 6% international, 16% transferred in, 12% live on campus. *Retention:* 79% of 2002 full-time freshmen returned.

Freshmen *Admission:* 620 applied, 490 admitted, 164 enrolled. *Average high school GPA:* 3.17. *Test scores:* SAT verbal scores over 500: 75%; SAT math scores over 500: 63%; ACT scores over 18: 82%; SAT verbal scores over 600: 28%; SAT math scores over 600: 19%; ACT scores over 24: 55%; SAT verbal scores over 700: 3%; SAT math scores over 700: 3%; ACT scores over 30: 9%.

Faculty *Total:* 337, 10% full-time, 63% with terminal degrees. *Student/faculty ratio:* 9:1.

Majors Applied art; architecture; art; ceramic arts and ceramics; commercial and advertising art; drawing; fashion/apparel design; fiber, textile and weaving arts; film/cinema studies; fine/studio arts; industrial design; interior architecture; metal and jewelry arts; painting; photography; printmaking; sculpture.

Academic Programs *Special study options:* academic remediation for entering students, advanced placement credit, double majors, independent study, internships, off-campus study, services for LD students, student-designed majors, study abroad, summer session for credit.

Library Meyer Library plus 1 other with 39,000 titles, 340 serial subscriptions, 520 audiovisual materials, an OPAC, a Web page.

Computers on Campus 180 computers available on campus for general student use. A campuswide network can be accessed from student residence rooms and from off campus. Internet access, at least one staffed computer lab available.

Student Life *Housing options:* coed. Campus housing is university owned. *Activities and organizations:* student-run newspaper, American Institute of Architecture—student chapter, American Institute of Graphic Arts—student chapter, Women's Caucus for the Arts, international student club, Artists that are Queer. *Campus security:* 24-hour emergency response devices and patrols, late-night transport/escort service. *Student services:* personal/psychological counseling.

Standardized Tests *Recommended:* SAT I or ACT (for admission).

Costs (2003–04) *Comprehensive fee:* $31,280 includes full-time tuition ($22,970), mandatory fees ($280), and room and board ($8030). Full-time tuition and fees vary according to course load. Part-time tuition and fees vary according to course load. *College room only:* $5800. Room and board charges vary according to housing facility. *Payment plans:* installment, deferred payment. *Waivers:* employees or children of employees.

Financial Aid Of all full-time matriculated undergraduates who enrolled in 2003, 893 applied for aid, 834 were judged to have need, 34 had their need fully met. 56 state and other part-time jobs (averaging $2500). In 2003, 42 non-need-based awards were made. *Average percent of need met:* 57%. *Average financial aid package:* $18,896. *Average need-based loan:* $7050. *Average need-based gift aid:* $11,851. *Average non-need-based aid:* $5157. *Average indebtedness upon graduation:* $23,073.

Applying *Options:* common application, electronic application, deferred entrance. *Application fee:* $50. *Required:* essay or personal statement, high school transcript, minimum 2.0 GPA, 2 letters of recommendation, portfolio. *Required for some:* interview. *Application deadline:* 2/15 (freshmen), rolling (transfers). *Notification:* continuous (freshmen), continuous (transfers).

Admissions Contact Ms. Molly Ryan, Director of Admissions, California College of the Arts, 1111 Eighth Street at 16th and Wisconsin, San Francisco, CA 94107. *Phone:* 415-703-9523 Ext. 9532. *Toll-free phone:* 800-447-1ART. *Fax:* 415-703-9539. *E-mail:* enroll@ccac-art.edu.

■ *See page 1318 for a narrative description.*

CALIFORNIA INSTITUTE OF INTEGRAL STUDIES

San Francisco, California

Admissions Contact Mr. Henry B. Villareal, Dean of Enrollment Management, California Institute of Integral Studies, 1453 Mission Street, San Francisco, CA 94103. *Phone:* 415-575-6156. *Fax:* 415-575-1268. *E-mail:* info@ciis.edu.

CALIFORNIA INSTITUTE OF TECHNOLOGY

Pasadena, California

- **Independent** university, founded 1891
- **Calendar** 3 ten-week terms
- **Degrees** bachelor's, master's, and doctoral
- **Suburban** 124-acre campus with easy access to Los Angeles
- **Endowment** $1.2 billion
- **Coed,** 891 undergraduate students, 100% full-time, 33% women, 67% men
- **Most difficult** entrance level, 17% of applicants were admitted

Academics—with a focus on math, science, and engineering—in a research environment characterize Caltech. The core curriculum emphasizes the fundamentals of each of the sciences plus study in the humanities and social sciences. Caltech values and encourages study and research across disciplines. A renowned faculty and facilities, including the Jet Propulsion Laboratory, contribute to Caltech's reputation as one of the world's major research centers.

Undergraduates 891 full-time. Students come from 46 states and territories, 28 other countries, 59% are from out of state, 1% African American, 31% Asian American or Pacific Islander, 7% Hispanic American, 0.6% Native American, 8% international, 3% transferred in, 90% live on campus. *Retention:* 95% of 2002 full-time freshmen returned.

Freshmen *Admission:* 3,071 applied, 520 admitted, 191 enrolled. *Test scores:* SAT verbal scores over 500: 99%; SAT math scores over 500: 100%; SAT verbal scores over 600: 94%; SAT math scores over 600: 100%; SAT verbal scores over 700: 77%; SAT math scores over 700: 96%.

California Institute of Technology (continued)

Faculty *Total:* 324, 90% full-time, 94% with terminal degrees. *Student/faculty ratio:* 3:1.

Majors Aerospace, aeronautical and astronautical engineering; applied mathematics; astronomy; biochemistry; biology/biological sciences; business/managerial economics; chemical engineering; chemical physics; chemistry; civil engineering; computer engineering; computer science; economics; electrical, electronics and communications engineering; engineering; engineering physics; environmental/environmental health engineering; general studies; geochemistry; geology/earth science; geophysics and seismology; history; inorganic chemistry; literature; mathematics; mechanical engineering; organic chemistry; physical sciences; physics; planetary astronomy and science; science, technology and society; social sciences.

Academic Programs *Special study options:* double majors, English as a second language, independent study, internships, off-campus study, services for LD students, student-designed majors, study abroad. *ROTC:* Army (c), Air Force (c).

Library Millikan Library plus 10 others with 3.2 million titles, 3,500 serial subscriptions, an OPAC, a Web page.

Computers on Campus 600 computers available on campus for general student use. A campuswide network can be accessed from student residence rooms and from off campus. Internet access, at least one staffed computer lab available. Computer purchase or lease plan available.

Student Life *Housing:* on-campus residence required for freshman year. *Options:* coed. Campus housing is university owned. Freshman campus housing is guaranteed. *Activities and organizations:* drama/theater group, student-run newspaper, choral group, ASCIT, entrepreneur's club, instrumental music groups, glee club, Theater Arts. *Campus security:* 24-hour emergency response devices and patrols, late-night transport/escort service. *Student services:* health clinic, personal/psychological counseling, women's center.

Athletics Member NCAA. All Division III. *Intercollegiate sports:* baseball M, basketball M/W, cross-country running M/W, fencing M/W, golf M, ice hockey M(c), rugby M(c), soccer M/W(c), swimming M/W, tennis M/W, track and field M/W, volleyball M(c)/W, water polo M/W. *Intramural sports:* badminton M/W, baseball M, basketball M/W, cross-country running M/W, fencing M/W, football M/W, ice hockey M, racquetball M, soccer M/W, softball M/W, squash M/W, swimming M/W, table tennis M/W, tennis M/W, track and field M/W, ultimate Frisbee M/W, volleyball M/W, water polo M/W.

Standardized Tests *Required:* SAT I or ACT (for admission), SAT II: Writing Test (for admission), SAT II Subject Test in Math Level II C and either physics, chemistry, or biology (for admission).

Costs (2004–05) *Comprehensive fee:* $33,564 includes full-time tuition ($25,335), mandatory fees ($216), and room and board ($8013). *Payment plans:* installment, deferred payment. *Waivers:* employees or children of employees.

Financial Aid Of all full-time matriculated undergraduates who enrolled in 2003, 577 applied for aid, 527 were judged to have need, 527 had their need fully met. In 2003, 94 non-need-based awards were made. *Average percent of need met:* 100%. *Average financial aid package:* $26,230. *Average need-based loan:* $1212. *Average need-based gift aid:* $23,873. *Average non-need-based aid:* $24,729. *Average indebtedness upon graduation:* $7906.

Applying *Options:* electronic application, early admission, early action, deferred entrance. *Application fee:* $50. *Required:* essay or personal statement, high school transcript, 2 letters of recommendation. *Application deadlines:* 1/1 (freshmen), 3/1 (transfers). *Notification:* 4/1 (freshmen), 12/30 (early action), 6/1 (transfers).

Admissions Contact Mr. Daniel T. Langdale, Director of Admissions, California Institute of Technology, 1200 East California Boulevard, Pasadena, CA 91125-0001. *Phone:* 626-395-6341. *Fax:* 626-683-3026. *E-mail:* ugadmissions@caltech.edu.

■ *See page 1320 for a narrative description.*

California Institute of the Arts
Valencia, California

- **Independent** comprehensive, founded 1961
- **Calendar** semesters
- **Degrees** certificates, bachelor's, master's, and postbachelor's certificates
- **Suburban** 60-acre campus with easy access to Los Angeles
- **Endowment** $66.3 million
- **Coed,** 753 undergraduate students, 100% full-time, 43% women, 57% men
- **Very difficult** entrance level, 36% of applicants were admitted

Undergraduates 753 full-time. Students come from 51 states and territories, 40 other countries, 55% are from out of state, 7% African American, 11% Asian American or Pacific Islander, 10% Hispanic American, 1% Native American, 8% international, 7% transferred in, 40% live on campus. *Retention:* 76% of 2002 full-time freshmen returned.

Freshmen *Admission:* 2,838 applied, 1,033 admitted, 130 enrolled.

Faculty *Total:* 270, 50% full-time. *Student/faculty ratio:* 7:1.

Majors Acting; art; commercial and advertising art; computer graphics; dance; dramatic/theatre arts; dramatic/theatre arts and stagecraft related; film/cinema studies; film/video and photographic arts related; fine/studio arts; graphic design; jazz/jazz studies; music; music performance; music related; music theory and composition; photography; piano and organ; sculpture; theatre design and technology; theatre/theatre arts management; violin, viola, guitar and other stringed instruments; voice and opera.

Academic Programs *Special study options:* advanced placement credit, independent study, internships, services for LD students, student-designed majors, study abroad.

Library Main Library plus 1 other with 95,973 titles, 613 serial subscriptions, 20,611 audiovisual materials, an OPAC, a Web page.

Computers on Campus 87 computers available on campus for general student use. A campuswide network can be accessed from student residence rooms and from off campus. Internet access, at least one staffed computer lab available.

Student Life *Housing options:* coed, disabled students. Campus housing is university owned. Freshman applicants given priority for college housing. *Activities and organizations:* drama/theater group, student-run radio and television station, choral group. *Campus security:* 24-hour emergency response devices and patrols, late-night transport/escort service, controlled dormitory access. *Student services:* health clinic, personal/psychological counseling.

Costs (2003–04) *Comprehensive fee:* $31,805 includes full-time tuition ($23,920), mandatory fees ($765), and room and board ($7120). *College room only:* $3700. Room and board charges vary according to board plan, housing facility, and location. *Payment plan:* deferred payment. *Waivers:* employees or children of employees.

Financial Aid Of all full-time matriculated undergraduates who enrolled in 2003, 624 applied for aid, 544 were judged to have need, 41 had their need fully met. 198 Federal Work-Study jobs (averaging $1938). 15 state and other part-time jobs (averaging $1642). In 2003, 55 non-need-based awards were made. *Average percent of need met:* 78%. *Average financial aid package:* $20,922. *Average need-based loan:* $5499. *Average need-based gift aid:* $10,769. *Average non-need-based aid:* $5719. *Average indebtedness upon graduation:* $29,167.

Applying *Options:* deferred entrance. *Application fee:* $60. *Required:* essay or personal statement, high school transcript, 2 letters of recommendation, portfolio or audition. *Required for some:* interview. *Application deadline:* 1/5 (freshmen), rolling (transfers). *Notification:* continuous (freshmen).

Admissions Contact Ms. Carol Kim, Director of Enrollment Services, California Institute of the Arts, 24700 McBean Parkway, Valencia, CA 91355. *Phone:* 661-255-1050. *Toll-free phone:* 800-545-2787. *Fax:* 661-253-7710. *E-mail:* admiss@calarts.edu.

■ *See page 1322 for a narrative description.*

California Lutheran University
Thousand Oaks, California

- **Independent Lutheran** comprehensive, founded 1959
- **Calendar** semesters
- **Degrees** bachelor's, master's, doctoral, post-master's, and postbachelor's certificates
- **Suburban** 290-acre campus with easy access to Los Angeles
- **Endowment** $26.7 million
- **Coed,** 1,920 undergraduate students, 89% full-time, 56% women, 44% men
- **Moderately difficult** entrance level, 77% of applicants were admitted

California Lutheran University is a comprehensive, private university deeply rooted in the concept of freedom in matters of both faith and reason. A challenging interdisciplinary core curriculum supports 36 majors and 28 minors. Cal Lutheran is located in the southern California city of Thousand Oaks and on the Web at http://www.callutheran.edu.

Undergraduates 1,715 full-time, 205 part-time. Students come from 36 states and territories, 20 other countries, 21% are from out of state, 2% African American, 4% Asian American or Pacific Islander, 13% Hispanic American, 0.9% Native American, 2% international, 9% transferred in, 65% live on campus. *Retention:* 82% of 2002 full-time freshmen returned.

Freshmen *Admission:* 1,217 applied, 941 admitted, 336 enrolled. *Average high school GPA:* 3.50. *Test scores:* SAT verbal scores over 500: 77%; SAT math scores over 500: 77%; ACT scores over 18: 91%; SAT verbal scores over 600: 30%; SAT math scores over 600: 24%; ACT scores over 24: 50%; SAT verbal scores over 700: 3%; SAT math scores over 700: 2%; ACT scores over 30: 7%.

Faculty *Total:* 249, 49% full-time. *Student/faculty ratio:* 15:1.

Majors Accounting; art; art teacher education; athletic training; biochemistry; biology/biological sciences; biomedical/medical engineering; business administration and management; chemistry; computer and information sciences; computer science; criminal justice/law enforcement administration; digital communication and media/multimedia; dramatic/theatre arts; economics; English; French; French language teacher education; geology/earth science; German; German language teacher education; history; information science/studies; interdisciplinary studies; international relations and affairs; journalism; kinesiology and exercise science; liberal arts and sciences/liberal studies; marketing/marketing management; mass communication/media; mathematics; mathematics teacher education; molecular biology; multi-/interdisciplinary studies related; music; music teacher education; philosophy; physical education teaching and coaching; physics; political science and government; psychology; psychology teacher education; public relations, advertising, and applied communication related; public relations/image management; religious studies; science teacher education; social sciences; social science teacher education; sociology; Spanish; Spanish language teacher education.

Academic Programs *Special study options:* accelerated degree program, adult/continuing education programs, advanced placement credit, cooperative education, double majors, honors programs, independent study, internships, off-campus study, part-time degree program, student-designed majors, study abroad, summer session for credit. *ROTC:* Army (c), Air Force (c).

Library Pearson Library with 139,476 titles, 10,600 serial subscriptions, 1,457 audiovisual materials, an OPAC, a Web page.

Computers on Campus 262 computers available on campus for general student use. A campuswide network can be accessed from student residence rooms and from off campus. Internet access, at least one staffed computer lab available.

Student Life *Housing:* on-campus residence required through junior year. *Options:* coed, disabled students. Campus housing is university owned. Freshman campus housing is guaranteed. *Activities and organizations:* drama/theater group, student-run newspaper, radio and television station, choral group, student government, music and drama clubs, service organizations, campus ministry organizations, multicultural organizations. *Campus security:* 24-hour emergency response devices and patrols, late-night transport/escort service, controlled dormitory access, escort service; shuttle service. *Student services:* health clinic, personal/psychological counseling, women's center.

Athletics Member NCAA. All Division III. *Intercollegiate sports:* baseball M, basketball M/W, cheerleading M/W, cross-country running M/W, football M, golf M, soccer M/W, softball W, swimming M/W, tennis M/W, track and field M/W, volleyball W, water polo M/W. *Intramural sports:* basketball M/W, football M/W, rugby M(c), soccer M/W, softball M/W, tennis M/W, volleyball M(c)/W.

Standardized Tests *Required:* SAT I or ACT (for admission).

Costs (2003–04) *Comprehensive fee:* $27,600 includes full-time tuition ($20,200), mandatory fees ($200), and room and board ($7200). Part-time tuition: $665 per unit. *Required fees:* $200 per year part-time. *College room only:* $3550. Room and board charges vary according to board plan. *Payment plan:* installment. *Waivers:* employees or children of employees.

Financial Aid Of all full-time matriculated undergraduates who enrolled in 2002, 1,107 applied for aid, 913 were judged to have need, 252 had their need fully met. 374 Federal Work-Study jobs (averaging $1850). 26 state and other part-time jobs (averaging $3180). In 2002, 102 non-need-based awards were made. *Average percent of need met:* 86%. *Average financial aid package:* $16,800. *Average need-based loan:* $3360. *Average need-based gift aid:* $11,360. *Average non-need-based aid:* $2150. *Average indebtedness upon graduation:* $16,600.

Applying *Options:* common application, electronic application, early action, deferred entrance. *Application fee:* $45. *Required:* essay or personal statement, high school transcript, minimum 2.8 GPA, 1 letter of recommendation. *Recommended:* minimum 3.0 GPA, interview. *Application deadlines:* 6/1 (freshmen), 6/1 (transfers). *Notification:* continuous until 6/15 (freshmen), 12/1 (early action), continuous until 7/15 (transfers).

Admissions Contact Mr. Darryl Calkins, Dean of Undergraduate Enrollment, California Lutheran University, Office of Admission, #1350, Thousand Oaks, CA 91360. *Phone:* 805-493-3135. *Toll-free phone:* 877-258-3678. *Fax:* 805-493-3114. *E-mail:* cluadm@clunet.edu.

■ *See page 1324 for a narrative description.*

California Maritime Academy

Vallejo, California

- **State-supported** 4-year, founded 1929, part of California State University System
- **Calendar** semesters
- **Degree** bachelor's
- **Suburban** 64-acre campus with easy access to San Francisco
- **Coed, primarily men,** 670 undergraduate students, 100% full-time, 19% women, 81% men
- **Moderately difficult** entrance level, 61% of applicants were admitted

Undergraduates 670 full-time. Students come from 18 states and territories, 16 other countries, 14% are from out of state, 65% live on campus. *Retention:* 89% of 2002 full-time freshmen returned.

Freshmen *Admission:* 831 applied, 505 admitted. *Average high school GPA:* 3.40.

Faculty *Student/faculty ratio:* 17:1.

Majors Business administration and management; engineering technologies related; marine technology; mechanical engineering.

Academic Programs *Special study options:* academic remediation for entering students, advanced placement credit, distance learning, internships, summer session for credit.

Library Main Library plus 1 other with 28,377 titles, 273 serial subscriptions, 241 audiovisual materials, an OPAC, a Web page.

Computers on Campus 50 computers available on campus for general student use. A campuswide network can be accessed from student residence rooms and from off campus. Internet access, at least one staffed computer lab available.

Student Life *Housing:* on-campus residence required through junior year. *Options:* coed. *Activities and organizations:* student-run newspaper, sailing club, dive club, drill team. *Campus security:* 24-hour patrols, student patrols. *Student services:* health clinic, personal/psychological counseling.

Athletics Member NAIA. *Intercollegiate sports:* basketball M, crew M/W, golf M/W, rugby M, sailing M/W, soccer M/W, volleyball W, water polo M/W. *Intramural sports:* baseball M, basketball M/W, football M/W, golf M/W, racquetball M/W, rugby M, sailing M/W, softball M/W, tennis M/W, volleyball M/W.

Standardized Tests *Required:* SAT I or ACT (for admission).

Costs (2003–04) *Tuition:* state resident $0 full-time; nonresident $8460 full-time. Full-time tuition and fees vary according to program and student level. *Required fees:* $2396 full-time. *Room and board:* $6750; room only: $3130. Room and board charges vary according to board plan and housing facility. *Payment plan:* installment.

Financial Aid *Average percent of need met:* 50%. *Average financial aid package:* $15,329.

Applying *Options:* electronic application. *Application fee:* $55. *Required:* high school transcript, minimum 2.0 GPA, health form. *Application deadlines:* 4/1 (freshmen), 4/1 (transfers). *Notification:* continuous (freshmen), continuous (transfers).

Admissions Contact California Maritime Academy, PO Box 1392, Vallejo, CA 94590-0644. *Phone:* 707-654-1331. *Toll-free phone:* 800-561-1945. *Fax:* 707-654-1336. *E-mail:* admission@csum.edu.

■ *See page 1326 for a narrative description.*

California National University for Advanced Studies

Northridge, California

- **Proprietary** comprehensive, founded 1993
- **Calendar** trimesters
- **Degrees** certificates, bachelor's, master's, and postbachelor's certificates
- **Urban** campus
- **Coed**

Faculty *Student/faculty ratio:* 10:1.

Costs (2003–04) *Tuition:* $4230 full-time, $235 per semester hour part-time. Part-time tuition and fees vary according to degree level and program. *Required fees:* $175 full-time. *Payment plans:* installment, deferred payment.

Applying *Options:* common application, electronic application, deferred entrance. *Application fee:* $50. *Required:* essay or personal statement, high school transcript. *Required for some:* interview.

Admissions Contact Ms. Stephanie M. Smith, Registrar, California National University for Advanced Studies, California National University Admissions, 8550 Balboa Boulevard, Suite 210, Northridge, CA 91325. *Phone:* 818-830-2411. *Toll-free phone:* 800-744-2822 (in-state); 800-782-2422 (out-of-state). *Fax:* 818-830-2418. *E-mail:* cnuadms@mail.cnuas.edu.

California Polytechnic State University, San Luis Obispo

San Luis Obispo, California

- **State-supported** comprehensive, founded 1901, part of California State University System
- **Calendar** quarters
- **Degrees** bachelor's and master's
- **Small-town** 6000-acre campus

California Polytechnic State University, San Luis Obispo (continued)

- **Endowment** $2.7 million
- **Coed,** 17,257 undergraduate students, 95% full-time, 44% women, 56% men
- **Moderately difficult** entrance level, 38% of applicants were admitted

Undergraduates 16,425 full-time, 832 part-time. Students come from 48 states and territories, 41 other countries, 6% are from out of state, 1% African American, 11% Asian American or Pacific Islander, 10% Hispanic American, 0.8% Native American, 0.9% international, 5% transferred in, 17% live on campus. *Retention:* 89% of 2002 full-time freshmen returned.

Freshmen *Admission:* 20,827 applied, 7,989 admitted, 2,828 enrolled. *Average high school GPA:* 3.71. *Test scores:* SAT verbal scores over 500: 86%; SAT math scores over 500: 94%; ACT scores over 18: 98%; SAT verbal scores over 600: 36%; SAT math scores over 600: 62%; ACT scores over 24: 69%; SAT verbal scores over 700: 4%; SAT math scores over 700: 14%; ACT scores over 30: 9%.

Faculty *Total:* 1,268, 62% full-time, 49% with terminal degrees. *Student/faculty ratio:* 19:1.

Majors Aerospace, aeronautical and astronautical engineering; agricultural/biological engineering and bioengineering; agricultural business and management; agriculture; agronomy and crop science; animal sciences; applied art; architectural engineering; architecture; art; biochemistry; biology/biological sciences; business administration and management; chemistry; city/urban, community and regional planning; civil engineering; commercial and advertising art; computer engineering; computer science; dairy science; developmental and child psychology; economics; electrical, electronics and communications engineering; engineering science; English; environmental biology; environmental/environmental health engineering; farm and ranch management; food science; foods, nutrition, and wellness; forestry; graphic and printing equipment operation/production; history; horticultural science; human resources management; industrial engineering; industrial technology; journalism; kindergarten/preschool education; landscape architecture; liberal arts and sciences/liberal studies; management information systems; materials engineering; mathematics; mechanical engineering; mechanical engineering/mechanical technology; medical microbiology and bacteriology; music; ornamental horticulture; parks, recreation and leisure; philosophy; physical education teaching and coaching; physical sciences; physics; political science and government; pre-medical studies; psychology; social sciences; speech and rhetoric; statistics; trade and industrial teacher education.

Academic Programs *Special study options:* academic remediation for entering students, advanced placement credit, cooperative education, distance learning, double majors, English as a second language, external degree program, honors programs, independent study, internships, off-campus study, part-time degree program, services for LD students, study abroad, summer session for credit. *ROTC:* Army (b).

Library Kennedy Library with 763,651 titles, 5,529 serial subscriptions, 5,204 audiovisual materials, an OPAC, a Web page.

Computers on Campus 1880 computers available on campus for general student use. A campuswide network can be accessed from student residence rooms and from off campus. At least one staffed computer lab available.

Student Life *Housing options:* coed, men-only, women-only. *Activities and organizations:* drama/theater group, student-run newspaper, radio station, choral group, marching band, ski club, American Marketing Association, Rose Float Club, MECHA, Society of Women Engineers, national fraternities, national sororities. *Campus security:* 24-hour emergency response devices and patrols, student patrols, late-night transport/escort service, controlled dormitory access. *Student services:* health clinic, personal/psychological counseling, women's center, legal services.

Athletics Member NCAA. All Division I except football (Division I-AA). *Intercollegiate sports:* baseball M(s), basketball M(s)/W(s), cross-country running M(s)/W(s), equestrian sports M/W, golf M(s), gymnastics W(s), soccer M/W, softball W(s), swimming M/W, tennis M/W, track and field M(s)/W(s), volleyball W(s), wrestling M(s). *Intramural sports:* baseball M, basketball M, bowling M/W, crew M, fencing M/W, football M, golf M, gymnastics M, lacrosse M, racquetball M/W, rugby M, skiing (cross-country) M/W, skiing (downhill) M/W, soccer M/W, softball W, volleyball M/W, water polo M/W.

Standardized Tests *Required:* SAT I or ACT (for admission).

Costs (2004–05) *Tuition:* state resident $0 full-time; nonresident $6768 full-time, $188 per unit part-time. Full-time tuition and fees vary according to course load. Part-time tuition and fees vary according to course load. *Required fees:* $3459 full-time. *Room and board:* $7479; room only: $4221. Room and board charges vary according to board plan. *Payment plan:* installment. *Waivers:* senior citizens and employees or children of employees.

Financial Aid Of all full-time matriculated undergraduates who enrolled in 2001, 8,895 applied for aid, 5,870 were judged to have need, 516 had their need fully met. *Average percent of need met:* 76%. *Average financial aid package:* $6847. *Average need-based loan:* $3636. *Average need-based gift aid:* $1352. *Average indebtedness upon graduation:* $12,842.

Applying *Options:* electronic application, early admission, early decision. *Application fee:* $55. *Required:* high school transcript. *Application deadlines:* 11/30 (freshmen), 11/30 (transfers). *Early decision:* 10/31. *Notification:* 3/1 (freshmen), 12/15 (early decision), 3/1 (transfers).

Admissions Contact Mr. James Maraviglia, Director of Admissions and Evaluations, California Polytechnic State University, San Luis Obispo, San Luis Obispo, CA 93407. *Phone:* 805-756-2311. *Fax:* 805-756-5400. *E-mail:* admprosp@calpoly.edu.

CALIFORNIA STATE POLYTECHNIC UNIVERSITY, POMONA

Pomona, California

- **State-supported** comprehensive, founded 1938, part of California State University System
- **Calendar** quarters
- **Degrees** bachelor's and master's
- **Urban** 1400-acre campus with easy access to Los Angeles
- **Endowment** $17.2 million
- **Coed,** 17,650 undergraduate students, 83% full-time, 43% women, 57% men
- **Moderately difficult** entrance level, 30% of applicants were admitted

Undergraduates 14,611 full-time, 3,039 part-time. Students come from 52 states and territories, 116 other countries, 2% are from out of state, 3% African American, 33% Asian American or Pacific Islander, 24% Hispanic American, 0.5% Native American, 5% international, 7% transferred in, 9% live on campus. *Retention:* 82% of 2002 full-time freshmen returned.

Freshmen *Admission:* 11,040 applied, 3,345 admitted, 2,284 enrolled. *Average high school GPA:* 3.36. *Test scores:* SAT verbal scores over 500: 54%; SAT math scores over 500: 65%; ACT scores over 18: 76%; SAT verbal scores over 600: 12%; SAT math scores over 600: 26%; ACT scores over 24: 24%; SAT verbal scores over 700: 1%; SAT math scores over 700: 3%; ACT scores over 30: 2%.

Faculty *Total:* 1,224, 55% full-time, 40% with terminal degrees. *Student/faculty ratio:* 21:1.

Majors Accounting; aerospace, aeronautical and astronautical engineering; agricultural/biological engineering and bioengineering; agricultural business and management; agricultural teacher education; agriculture; agronomy and crop science; animal sciences; anthropology; applied mathematics; architecture; art; behavioral sciences; bilingual and multilingual education; biology/biological sciences; biology/biotechnology laboratory technician; botany/plant biology; business administration and management; chemical engineering; chemistry; city/urban, community and regional planning; civil engineering; commercial and advertising art; computer and information sciences; computer engineering; computer science; construction engineering technology; counselor education/school counseling and guidance; cultural studies; dietetics; dramatic/theatre arts; economics; electrical, electronic and communications engineering technology; electrical, electronics and communications engineering; engineering technologies related; engineering technology; English; ethnic, cultural minority, and gender studies related; family and consumer sciences/human sciences; farm and ranch management; finance; foods, nutrition, and wellness; geography; geology/earth science; history; horticultural science; hotel/motel administration; humanities; human resources management; industrial engineering; information science/studies; insurance; international business/trade/commerce; journalism; landscape architecture; liberal arts and sciences/liberal studies; marketing/marketing management; mass communication/media; materials engineering; mathematics; mechanical engineering; mechanical engineering/mechanical technology; medical microbiology and bacteriology; music; ornamental horticulture; petroleum engineering; philosophy; physical education teaching and coaching; physics; plant protection and integrated pest management; political science and government; pre-law studies; pre-medical studies; pre-veterinary studies; psychology; public administration; public relations/image management; radio, television, and digital communication related; real estate; social sciences; sociology; soil conservation; Spanish; statistics; survey technology; telecommunications; urban studies/affairs; zoology/animal biology.

Academic Programs *Special study options:* academic remediation for entering students, adult/continuing education programs, advanced placement credit, cooperative education, double majors, English as a second language, internships, off-campus study, part-time degree program, services for LD students, study abroad, summer session for credit. *ROTC:* Army (b), Air Force (c).

Library University Library with 465,018 titles, 6,017 serial subscriptions, 13,260 audiovisual materials, an OPAC, a Web page.

Computers on Campus 1864 computers available on campus for general student use. A campuswide network can be accessed from student residence rooms and from off campus. Internet access, at least one staffed computer lab available.

Student Life *Housing options:* coed, disabled students. Campus housing is university owned. Freshman applicants given priority for college housing. *Activi-*

ties and organizations: drama/theater group, student-run newspaper, choral group, Rose Float club, Ridge Runners Ski Club, Barkada (Asian club), American Marketing Association, Cal Poly Society of Accountants, national fraternities, national sororities. *Campus security:* 24-hour emergency response devices and patrols, student patrols, late-night transport/escort service, video camera surveillance. *Student services:* health clinic, personal/psychological counseling, women's center.

Athletics Member NCAA. All Division II. *Intercollegiate sports:* baseball M(s), basketball M(s)/W(s), cross-country running M(s)/W(s), soccer M(s)/W(s), tennis M(s)/W(s), track and field M(s)/W(s), volleyball W(s). *Intramural sports:* basketball M/W, bowling M/W, football M/W, softball M/W, tennis M/W, volleyball M/W.

Standardized Tests *Required:* SAT I or ACT (for admission).

Costs (2004–05) *Tuition:* area resident $0 full-time; state resident $0 full-time; nonresident $8460 full-time, $188 per unit part-time. *Required fees:* $2046 full-time, $682 per term part-time. *Room and board:* $6747. Room and board charges vary according to board plan and housing facility. *Payment plans:* installment, deferred payment.

Financial Aid Of all full-time matriculated undergraduates who enrolled in 2003, 8,796 applied for aid, 7,502 were judged to have need, 3,050 had their need fully met. 660 Federal Work-Study jobs (averaging $2800). In 2003, 105 non-need-based awards were made. *Average percent of need met:* 85%. *Average financial aid package:* $8258. *Average need-based loan:* $3751. *Average need-based gift aid:* $5277. *Average non-need-based aid:* $1798. *Average indebtedness upon graduation:* $11,258.

Applying *Options:* electronic application. *Application fee:* $55. *Required:* high school transcript, minimum 2.0 GPA. *Application deadlines:* 4/1 (freshmen), 5/1 (transfers). *Notification:* 11/1 (freshmen), 11/1 (transfers).

Admissions Contact Dr. George R. Bradshaw, Director, Admissions and Outreach, California State Polytechnic University, Pomona, Pomona, CA 91768. *Phone:* 909-869-3427. *Fax:* 909-869-4529. *E-mail:* cppadmit@csupomona.edu.

■ *See page 1328 for a narrative description.*

CALIFORNIA STATE UNIVERSITY, BAKERSFIELD

Bakersfield, California

- **State-supported** comprehensive, founded 1970, part of California State University System
- **Calendar** quarters
- **Degrees** bachelor's and master's
- **Urban** 575-acre campus
- **Coed**
- **Moderately difficult** entrance level

Student Life *Campus security:* 24-hour emergency response devices and patrols, late-night transport/escort service.

Athletics Member NCAA. All Division II except wrestling (Division I).

Standardized Tests *Required:* SAT I or ACT (for admission). *Recommended:* SAT II: Subject Tests (for admission).

Costs (2003–04) *Tuition:* state resident $0 full-time; nonresident $5640 full-time. *Required fees:* $2427 full-time. *Room and board:* Room and board charges vary according to board plan.

Financial Aid Of all full-time matriculated undergraduates who enrolled in 2002, 3,720 applied for aid, 3,244 were judged to have need, 388 had their need fully met. 194 Federal Work-Study jobs (averaging $1629). 29 state and other part-time jobs (averaging $2107). In 2002, 156. *Average percent of need met:* 81. *Average financial aid package:* $6150. *Average need-based loan:* $3489. *Average need-based gift aid:* $4372. *Average non-need-based aid:* $1895. *Average indebtedness upon graduation:* $3436.

Applying *Options:* electronic application, early admission, deferred entrance. *Application fee:* $55. *Required:* high school transcript.

Admissions Contact Dr. Homer S. Montalvo, Associate Dean of Admissions and Records, California State University, Bakersfield, 9001 Stockdale Highway, Balersfield, CA 93311-1099. *Phone:* 805-664-2160. *Toll-free phone:* 800-788-2782. *E-mail:* admissions@csub.edu.

CALIFORNIA STATE UNIVERSITY, CHICO

Chico, California

- **State-supported** comprehensive, founded 1887, part of California State University System
- **Calendar** semesters
- **Degrees** certificates, bachelor's, master's, post-master's, and postbachelor's certificates
- **Small-town** 119-acre campus
- **Endowment** $17.9 million
- **Coed,** 13,903 undergraduate students, 90% full-time, 54% women, 46% men
- **Moderately difficult** entrance level, 73% of applicants were admitted

Undergraduates 12,580 full-time, 1,323 part-time. Students come from 39 states and territories, 50 other countries, 1% are from out of state, 2% African American, 5% Asian American or Pacific Islander, 10% Hispanic American, 1% Native American, 2% international, 10% transferred in, 12% live on campus. *Retention:* 80% of 2002 full-time freshmen returned.

Freshmen *Admission:* 9,157 applied, 6,718 admitted, 2,001 enrolled. *Average high school GPA:* 3.27. *Test scores:* SAT verbal scores over 500: 60%; SAT math scores over 500: 65%; ACT scores over 18: 84%; SAT verbal scores over 600: 15%; SAT math scores over 600: 17%; ACT scores over 24: 28%; SAT verbal scores over 700: 1%; SAT math scores over 700: 1%; ACT scores over 30: 1%.

Faculty *Total:* 883, 60% full-time, 65% with terminal degrees. *Student/faculty ratio:* 20:1.

Majors Accounting; accounting and computer science; agricultural business and management; agricultural teacher education; agronomy and crop science; American studies; animal sciences; anthropology; applied mathematics; art; art history, criticism and conservation; art teacher education; Asian studies; biochemistry; biology/biological sciences; biology teacher education; business administration and management; business administration, management and operations related; chemistry; chemistry related; chemistry teacher education; city/urban, community and regional planning; civil engineering; clinical laboratory science/medical technology; communication disorders; computer and information sciences and support services related; computer engineering; computer graphics; computer science; construction engineering technology; criminal justice/safety; design and visual communications; desktop publishing and digital imaging design; dietetics; dramatic/theatre arts; dramatic/theatre arts and stagecraft related; early childhood education; ecology; economics; economics related; educational/instructional media design; electrical, electronics and communications engineering; engineering related; English; English/language arts teacher education; ethnic, cultural minority, and gender studies related; finance; fine/studio arts; French; French language teacher education; geography; geological and earth sciences/geosciences related; geology/earth science; German; German language teacher education; gerontology; graphic design; health and physical education; health services/allied health/health sciences; health teacher education; history; humanities; human resources management; hydrology and water resources science; information technology; interior design; international economics; international relations and affairs; Jewish/Judaic studies; journalism; kinesiology and exercise science; Latin American studies; legal assistant/paralegal; legal studies; liberal arts and sciences/liberal studies; linguistics; management information systems; management information systems and services related; marketing/marketing management; mathematics; mathematics teacher education; mechanical engineering; microbiology; multi-/interdisciplinary studies related; music; music performance; music related; music teacher education; music theory and composition; natural resources management and policy; nursing (registered nurse training); operations management; organizational communication; parks, recreation and leisure; parks, recreation and leisure facilities management; philosophy; physical education teaching and coaching; physics; physics related; piano and organ; political science and government; pre-dentistry studies; pre-medical studies; pre-veterinary studies; psychology; public administration; public relations/image management; radio and television; range science and management; religious studies; science teacher education; social sciences; social science teacher education; social work; sociology; Spanish; Spanish language teacher education; speech and rhetoric; statistics; therapeutic recreation; women's studies.

Academic Programs *Special study options:* academic remediation for entering students, adult/continuing education programs, advanced placement credit, cooperative education, distance learning, double majors, English as a second language, external degree program, honors programs, independent study, internships, off-campus study, part-time degree program, services for LD students, student-designed majors, study abroad, summer session for credit.

Library Meriam Library with 942,322 titles, 24,244 serial subscriptions, 23,608 audiovisual materials, an OPAC, a Web page.

Computers on Campus 840 computers available on campus for general student use. A campuswide network can be accessed from student residence rooms and from off campus that provide access to student account information, email, calendar, transcripts. Internet access, online (class) registration, at least one staffed computer lab available.

Student Life *Housing options:* coed, disabled students. Campus housing is university owned. Freshman applicants given priority for college housing. *Activities and organizations:* drama/theater group, student-run newspaper, radio station, choral group, Golden Key International Honor Society, Newman Catholic Campus Ministry, The Edge, national fraternities, national sororities. *Campus security:* 24-hour emergency response devices and patrols, student patrols, late-night transport/escort service, controlled dormitory access, crime prevention work-

California State University, Chico (continued)
shops, RAD self-defense program, Chico Safe Rides, blue light emergency phones. *Student services:* health clinic, personal/psychological counseling, women's center, legal services.

Athletics Member NCAA. All Division II. *Intercollegiate sports:* baseball M, basketball M/W, bowling M(c)/W(c), cross-country running M/W, golf M/W, lacrosse M(c)/W(c), rugby M(c)/W(c), soccer M/W, softball W, track and field M/W, ultimate Frisbee M(c)/W(c), volleyball M(c)/W, water polo M(c)/W(c). *Intramural sports:* basketball M/W, bowling M/W, fencing M(c)/W(c), football M/W, golf M/W, racquetball M/W, soccer M/W, softball M/W, swimming M/W, track and field M/W, ultimate Frisbee M/W, volleyball M/W, weight lifting M/W, wrestling M/W.

Standardized Tests *Required:* SAT I or ACT (for admission).

Costs (2003–04) *Tuition:* state resident $0 full-time; nonresident $10,506 full-time, $282 per unit part-time. Part-time tuition and fees vary according to course load. *Required fees:* $2796 full-time. *Room and board:* $7245; room only: $4910. Room and board charges vary according to board plan and housing facility. *Payment plans:* installment, deferred payment. *Waivers:* senior citizens and employees or children of employees.

Financial Aid Of all full-time matriculated undergraduates who enrolled in 2002, 355 Federal Work-Study jobs, 101 state and other part-time jobs (averaging $2071).

Applying *Options:* electronic application, deferred entrance. *Application fee:* $55. *Required:* high school transcript, GPA of 10th and 11th grade college prep courses only. *Application deadlines:* 11/30 (freshmen), 11/30 (transfers). *Notification:* 3/1 (freshmen), continuous (transfers).

Admissions Contact Dr. John F. Swiney, Director of Admissions, California State University, Chico, 400 West First Street, Chico, CA 95929-0722. *Phone:* 530-898-4879. *Toll-free phone:* 800-542-4426. *Fax:* 530-898-6456. *E-mail:* info@csuchico.edu.

California State University, Dominguez Hills

Carson, California

- **State-supported** comprehensive, founded 1960, part of California State University System
- **Calendar** semesters
- **Degrees** certificates, bachelor's, and master's
- **Urban** 350-acre campus with easy access to Los Angeles
- **Coed,** 8,134 undergraduate students, 62% full-time, 69% women, 31% men
- **Moderately difficult** entrance level, 47% of applicants were admitted

Undergraduates 5,008 full-time, 3,126 part-time. Students come from 29 states and territories, 42 other countries, 2% are from out of state, 28% African American, 9% Asian American or Pacific Islander, 34% Hispanic American, 0.5% Native American, 2% international, 16% transferred in. *Retention:* 62% of 2002 full-time freshmen returned.

Freshmen *Admission:* 1,937 applied, 920 admitted, 693 enrolled.

Faculty *Total:* 762, 42% full-time, 48% with terminal degrees.

Majors Accounting; African-American/Black studies; anthropology; applied art; art; art history, criticism and conservation; behavioral sciences; bilingual and multilingual education; biochemistry; biology/biological sciences; business administration and management; chemistry; child development; clinical laboratory science/medical technology; clinical/medical laboratory technology; commercial and advertising art; computer science; criminal justice/law enforcement administration; cytotechnology; dramatic/theatre arts; economics; English; finance; fine/studio arts; French; geography; geology/earth science; gerontology; health/health care administration; health science; Hispanic-American, Puerto Rican, and Mexican-American/Chicano studies; history; humanities; human resources management; human services; information science/studies; interdisciplinary studies; international business/trade/commerce; labor and industrial relations; liberal arts and sciences/liberal studies; linguistics; literature; management information systems; marketing/marketing management; mass communication/media; mathematics; medical/clinical assistant; medical microbiology and bacteriology; music; music teacher education; nuclear medical technology; nursing (registered nurse training); parks, recreation and leisure; philosophy; physical education teaching and coaching; physician assistant; physics; political science and government; pre-dentistry studies; pre-law studies; pre-medical studies; pre-veterinary studies; psychology; public administration; public health; public relations/image management; real estate; religious studies; sociology; Spanish.

Academic Programs *Special study options:* academic remediation for entering students, adult/continuing education programs, advanced placement credit, cooperative education, English as a second language, external degree program, honors programs, internships, off-campus study, part-time degree program, student-designed majors, study abroad, summer session for credit. *ROTC:* Army (c), Air Force (c).

Library Leo F. Cain Educational Resource Center with 440,181 titles, an OPAC, a Web page.

Computers on Campus 200 computers available on campus for general student use. At least one staffed computer lab available.

Student Life *Housing options:* coed. *Activities and organizations:* drama/theater group, student-run newspaper, television station, choral group, national fraternities, national sororities. *Campus security:* student patrols, late-night transport/escort service. *Student services:* health clinic, personal/psychological counseling, women's center, legal services.

Athletics Member NCAA. All Division II. *Intercollegiate sports:* badminton M(c)/W(c), basketball M(s)/W(s), soccer M(s)/W(s), volleyball W(s). *Intramural sports:* basketball M/W, soccer M/W, volleyball W.

Standardized Tests *Required for some:* SAT I or ACT (for admission).

Costs (2004–05) *Tuition:* state resident $0 full-time, $810 per unit part-time; nonresident $8460 full-time, $282 per unit part-time. Part-time tuition and fees vary according to course load. *Required fees:* $2478 full-time, $216 per term part-time. *Room only:* $5022. Room and board charges vary according to housing facility. *Payment plan:* installment. *Waivers:* employees or children of employees.

Financial Aid Of all full-time matriculated undergraduates who enrolled in 2002, 3,829 applied for aid, 3,785 were judged to have need, 1,969 had their need fully met. 241 Federal Work-Study jobs (averaging $2671). In 2002, 37 non-need-based awards were made. *Average percent of need met:* 60%. *Average financial aid package:* $7910. *Average need-based loan:* $4689. *Average need-based gift aid:* $4520. *Average non-need-based aid:* $3470. *Average indebtedness upon graduation:* $15,112. *Financial aid deadline:* 4/15.

Applying *Options:* electronic application, early admission. *Application fee:* $55. *Required:* high school transcript. *Application deadline:* rolling (freshmen), rolling (transfers). *Notification:* continuous (freshmen), continuous (transfers).

Admissions Contact Information Center, California State University, Dominguez Hills, 1000 East Victoria Street, Carson, CA 90747-0001. *Phone:* 310-243-3696.

■ *See page 1330 for a narrative description.*

California State University, Fresno

Fresno, California

- **State-supported** comprehensive, founded 1911, part of California State University System
- **Calendar** semesters
- **Degrees** certificates, bachelor's, master's, and doctoral
- **Urban** 1410-acre campus
- **Endowment** $58.5 million
- **Coed,** 18,574 undergraduate students, 77% full-time, 58% women, 42% men
- **Moderately difficult** entrance level, 70% of applicants were admitted

Undergraduates 14,294 full-time, 4,280 part-time. Students come from 50 states and territories, 74 other countries, 1% are from out of state, 5% African American, 12% Asian American or Pacific Islander, 26% Hispanic American, 0.9% Native American, 3% international, 11% transferred in, 5% live on campus. *Retention:* 64% of 2002 full-time freshmen returned.

Freshmen *Admission:* 10,374 applied, 7,247 admitted, 2,590 enrolled. *Average high school GPA:* 3.28. *Test scores:* SAT verbal scores over 500: 37%; SAT math scores over 500: 45%; ACT scores over 18: 60%; SAT verbal scores over 600: 9%; SAT math scores over 600: 11%; ACT scores over 24: 16%; SAT verbal scores over 700: 1%; SAT math scores over 700: 1%; ACT scores over 30: 1%.

Faculty *Total:* 1,234, 55% full-time. *Student/faculty ratio:* 18:1.

Majors Accounting; African-American/Black studies; agricultural business and management; agricultural teacher education; agronomy and crop science; animal physiology; animal sciences; anthropology; art; audiology and speech-language pathology; biological and physical sciences; biology/biological sciences; business administration and management; business teacher education; cell biology and histology; chemistry; child development; civil engineering; commercial and advertising art; communication disorders; computer engineering; computer science; construction engineering technology; criminology; dance; dietetics; dramatic/theatre arts; ecology; economics; electrical, electronics and communications engineering; elementary education; English; family and consumer economics related; finance; foods, nutrition, and wellness; French; geography; geology/earth science; health science; Hispanic-American, Puerto Rican, and Mexican-American/Chicano studies; history; human resources management; industrial arts; industrial engineering; industrial technology; interior design; international business/trade/commerce; journalism; liberal arts and sciences/liberal studies; linguistics; management information systems; marketing/marketing management; mass communication/media; mathematics; mechanical engineering; medical microbiology and bacteriology; molecular biology; music; music history, literature, and theory; music teacher education; natural sciences; nursing (registered nurse training); occupational health and industrial hygiene; occupational safety and health technology; ornamental horticulture; parks, recreation and leisure; philosophy; physical education teaching and coaching; physical therapy; physics; plant sciences; political science and government; pre-law studies; psychology; public administration; public relations/image management; radio and television; real estate; religious studies; social work; sociology; Spanish; speech and rhetoric; survey technology; trade and industrial teacher education; women's studies; zoology/animal biology.

Academic Programs *Special study options:* academic remediation for entering students, accelerated degree program, adult/continuing education programs, advanced placement credit, cooperative education, distance learning, double majors, English as a second language, freshman honors college, honors programs, independent study, internships, off-campus study, part-time degree program, services for LD students, student-designed majors, study abroad, summer session for credit. *ROTC:* Army (b), Air Force (b).

Library Henry Madden Library with 977,198 titles, 2,500 serial subscriptions, 71,482 audiovisual materials, an OPAC, a Web page.

Computers on Campus 853 computers available on campus for general student use. A campuswide network can be accessed from off campus that provide access to common applications. Internet access, at least one staffed computer lab available.

Student Life *Housing options:* coed. Campus housing is university owned. *Activities and organizations:* drama/theater group, student-run newspaper, radio station, choral group, marching band, national fraternities, national sororities. *Campus security:* 24-hour emergency response devices and patrols, late-night transport/escort service, controlled dormitory access. *Student services:* health clinic, personal/psychological counseling, women's center.

Athletics Member NCAA. All Division I except football (Division I-A). *Intercollegiate sports:* baseball M(s), basketball M(s)/W(s), cross-country running M(s)/W(s), equestrian sports W(s), golf M(s), soccer M(s)/W(s), softball W(s), swimming W(s), tennis M(s)/W(s), track and field M(s)/W(s), volleyball W(s), wrestling M(s). *Intramural sports:* archery M/W, badminton M/W, baseball M, basketball M/W, bowling M/W, cross-country running M/W, equestrian sports W, fencing M/W, golf M/W, gymnastics M/W, racquetball M/W, skiing (cross-country) M/W, softball W, swimming W, tennis M/W, ultimate Frisbee M/W, volleyball M/W, water polo M, wrestling M.

Standardized Tests *Required:* SAT I or ACT (for admission).

Costs (2004–05) *Tuition:* state resident $0 full-time; nonresident $10,874 full-time, $282 per unit part-time. *Required fees:* $2414 full-time, $778 per term part-time. *Room and board:* $7073. Room and board charges vary according to board plan.

Financial Aid Of all full-time matriculated undergraduates who enrolled in 2003, 11,413 applied for aid, 9,601 were judged to have need, 3,859 had their need fully met. 246 Federal Work-Study jobs (averaging $3352). In 2003, 272 non-need-based awards were made. *Average percent of need met:* 82%. *Average financial aid package:* $8026. *Average need-based loan:* $3702. *Average need-based gift aid:* $2903. *Average non-need-based aid:* $2436. *Average indebtedness upon graduation:* $15,000.

Applying *Options:* common application, electronic application. *Application fee:* $55. *Required:* high school transcript. *Application deadlines:* 7/28 (freshmen), 2/1 (transfers). *Notification:* 8/1 (freshmen).

Admissions Contact Ms. Vivian Franco, Director, California State University, Fresno, 5150 North Maple Avenue, M/S JA 57, Fresno, CA 93740-8026. *Phone:* 559-278-2261. *Fax:* 559-278-4812. *E-mail:* donna_mills@csufresno.edu.

CALIFORNIA STATE UNIVERSITY, FULLERTON

Fullerton, California

- **State-supported** comprehensive, founded 1957, part of California State University System
- **Calendar** semesters
- **Degrees** bachelor's and master's
- **Urban** 225-acre campus with easy access to Los Angeles
- **Coed,** 26,896 undergraduate students, 69% full-time, 60% women, 40% men
- **Moderately difficult** entrance level, 66% of applicants were admitted

Undergraduates 18,656 full-time, 8,240 part-time. Students come from 43 states and territories, 73 other countries, 1% are from out of state, 3% African American, 23% Asian American or Pacific Islander, 26% Hispanic American, 0.6% Native American, 4% international, 12% transferred in, 2% live on campus. *Retention:* 80% of 2002 full-time freshmen returned.

Freshmen *Admission:* 17,723 applied, 11,751 admitted, 3,271 enrolled. *Average high school GPA:* 3.21. *Test scores:* SAT verbal scores over 500: 41%; SAT math scores over 500: 51%; ACT scores over 18: 68%; SAT verbal scores over 600: 8%; SAT math scores over 600: 14%; ACT scores over 24: 17%; SAT math scores over 700: 1%; ACT scores over 30: 2%.

Faculty *Total:* 1,940, 41% full-time. *Student/faculty ratio:* 21:1.

Majors Accounting; advertising; African-American/Black studies; American studies; anthropology; applied mathematics; art; art history, criticism and conservation; art teacher education; Asian-American studies; audiology and speech-language pathology; biochemistry; biology/biological sciences; business administration and management; business/managerial economics; ceramic arts and ceramics; chemistry; civil engineering; clinical psychology; commercial and advertising art; communication disorders; communication/speech communication and rhetoric; comparative literature; computer science; criminal justice/law enforcement administration; cultural studies; dance; dramatic/theatre arts; drawing; early childhood education; economics; electrical, electronics and communications engineering; engineering; engineering science; English; entrepreneurship; finance; fine/studio arts; French; geography; geology/earth science; German; graphic design; health and physical education; health professions related; Hispanic-American, Puerto Rican, and Mexican-American/Chicano studies; history; illustration; information science/studies; Japanese; journalism; Latin American studies; liberal arts and sciences/liberal studies; linguistics; marketing/marketing management; mathematics; mechanical engineering; music; music history, literature, and theory; music performance; music teacher education; nursing (registered nurse training); nursing related; operations research; painting; philosophy; photography; physical education teaching and coaching; physics; piano and organ; political science and government; printmaking; psychology; public administration; public relations/image management; radio and television; religious studies; Russian studies; sculpture; sociology; Spanish; speech and rhetoric; statistics; taxation; violin, viola, guitar and other stringed instruments; voice and opera; wind/percussion instruments; women's studies.

Academic Programs *Special study options:* academic remediation for entering students, adult/continuing education programs, advanced placement credit, cooperative education, distance learning, double majors, English as a second language, honors programs, independent study, internships, off-campus study, part-time degree program, services for LD students, student-designed majors, study abroad, summer session for credit. *ROTC:* Army (b).

Library California State University, Fullerton Pollak Library with 743,945 titles, 7,454 serial subscriptions, 19,620 audiovisual materials, an OPAC.

Computers on Campus 1993 computers available on campus for general student use. A campuswide network can be accessed from student residence rooms and from off campus. Internet access, at least one staffed computer lab available.

Student Life *Housing options:* coed. Campus housing is university owned. *Activities and organizations:* drama/theater group, student-run newspaper, radio station, choral group, national fraternities, national sororities. *Campus security:* 24-hour emergency response devices and patrols, student patrols, late-night transport/escort service, controlled dormitory access. *Student services:* health clinic, personal/psychological counseling, women's center, legal services.

Athletics Member NCAA. All Division I. *Intercollegiate sports:* baseball M(s), basketball M(s)/W(s), bowling M(c)/W(c), cross-country running M(s)/W(s), fencing M(s)/W(s), gymnastics W(s), rugby M(c), soccer M(s)/W(s), softball W(s), tennis W(s), track and field M(s)/W(s), volleyball W(s), wrestling M(s). *Intramural sports:* archery M/W, badminton M/W, basketball M/W, bowling M/W, cross-country running M/W, fencing M/W, football M/W, gymnastics M/W, racquetball M/W, skiing (cross-country) M/W, skiing (downhill) M/W, soccer M/W, softball M/W, table tennis M/W, tennis M/W, volleyball M/W, wrestling M.

Standardized Tests *Required:* SAT I or ACT (for admission).

Costs (2003–04) *Tuition:* state resident $0 full-time; nonresident $8460 full-time, $282 per unit part-time. Full-time tuition and fees vary according to course load. Part-time tuition and fees vary according to course load. *Required fees:* $2516 full-time, $829 per term part-time. *Room only:* $4127. *Payment plan:* installment. *Waivers:* senior citizens and employees or children of employees.

Financial Aid Of all full-time matriculated undergraduates who enrolled in 2003, 10,411 applied for aid, 8,430 were judged to have need, 272 had their need fully met. 1,675 Federal Work-Study jobs (averaging $2952). In 2003, 1273 non-need-based awards were made. *Average percent of need met:* 67%. *Average financial aid package:* $6916. *Average need-based loan:* $3906. *Average need-based gift aid:* $6052. *Average non-need-based aid:* $4083. *Average indebtedness upon graduation:* $12,720.

Applying *Options:* electronic application. *Application fee:* $55. *Required:* high school transcript, minimum 2.0 GPA. *Application deadline:* 11/30 (freshmen), rolling (transfers). *Notification:* continuous (freshmen), continuous (transfers).

California State University, Fullerton (continued)

Admissions Contact Ms. Nancy J. Dority, Admissions Director, California State University, Fullerton, Office of Admissions and Records, PO Box 6900, 800 North State College Boulevard, Fullerton, CA 92834-6900. *Phone:* 714-278-2370.

CALIFORNIA STATE UNIVERSITY, HAYWARD
Hayward, California

- **State-supported** comprehensive, founded 1957, part of California State University System
- **Calendar** quarters
- **Degrees** certificates, bachelor's, master's, and postbachelor's certificates
- **Suburban** 343-acre campus with easy access to San Francisco
- **Endowment** $5.4 million
- **Coed,** 9,380 undergraduate students, 79% full-time, 63% women, 37% men
- **Moderately difficult** entrance level, 47% of applicants were admitted

California State University, Hayward, is the San Francisco Bay area's leading career development university. With 2 campuses in the scenic East Bay hills, CSUH is recognized for its professional focus, small classes, personalized instruction, and low fees, earning it a reputation as northern California's best value in public higher education.

Undergraduates 7,366 full-time, 2,014 part-time. Students come from 50 states and territories, 86 other countries, 10% African American, 27% Asian American or Pacific Islander, 12% Hispanic American, 0.6% Native American, 5% international, 14% transferred in, 4% live on campus. *Retention:* 82% of 2002 full-time freshmen returned.

Freshmen *Admission:* 4,665 applied, 2,177 admitted, 682 enrolled. *Average high school GPA:* 3.14. *Test scores:* SAT verbal scores over 500: 36%; SAT math scores over 500: 43%; ACT scores over 18: 52%; SAT verbal scores over 600: 8%; SAT math scores over 600: 9%; ACT scores over 24: 15%; SAT verbal scores over 700: 1%; SAT math scores over 700: 1%.

Faculty *Total:* 741, 45% full-time, 90% with terminal degrees. *Student/faculty ratio:* 21:1.

Majors Accounting; advertising; African-American/Black studies; American Indian/Native American studies; anthropology; applied mathematics; art history, criticism and conservation; arts management; Asian-American studies; athletic training; audiology and speech-language pathology; biochemistry; biology/biological sciences; biomedical technology; broadcast journalism; business administration and management; business/managerial economics; ceramic arts and ceramics; chemistry; child development; clinical/medical laboratory technology; commercial and advertising art; computer graphics; computer science; computer systems networking and telecommunications; corrections; creative writing; criminal justice/law enforcement administration; criminal justice/police science; cultural studies; dance; developmental and child psychology; dramatic/theatre arts; drawing; ecology; economics; English; environmental studies; finance; fine/studio arts; French; geography; geology/earth science; gerontology; health science; Hispanic-American, Puerto Rican, and Mexican-American/Chicano studies; history; human development and family studies; human ecology; human resources management; industrial and organizational psychology; industrial engineering; information science/studies; interdisciplinary studies; international relations and affairs; journalism; kinesiology and exercise science; Latin American studies; liberal arts and sciences/liberal studies; management information systems; marketing/marketing management; mass communication/media; mathematics; music; nursing (registered nurse training); painting; parks, recreation and leisure; philosophy; photography; physical education teaching and coaching; physical sciences; physics; political science and government; pre-dentistry studies; premedical studies; pre-veterinary studies; printmaking; psychology; public administration; public relations/image management; purchasing, procurement/acquisitions and contracts management; real estate; religious studies; sculpture; social work; sociology; Spanish; speech and rhetoric; statistics; telecommunications; therapeutic recreation.

Academic Programs *Special study options:* academic remediation for entering students, accelerated degree program, adult/continuing education programs, advanced placement credit, cooperative education, distance learning, double majors, English as a second language, honors programs, independent study, internships, off-campus study, part-time degree program, services for LD students, student-designed majors, study abroad, summer session for credit.

Library California State University, Hayward Library plus 1 other with 908,577 titles, 2,210 serial subscriptions, 28,416 audiovisual materials, an OPAC, a Web page.

Computers on Campus 700 computers available on campus for general student use. A campuswide network can be accessed from student residence rooms and from off campus. Internet access, online (class) registration, at least one staffed computer lab available.

Student Life *Housing options:* coed. *Activities and organizations:* drama/theater group, student-run newspaper, radio and television station, choral group, Vietnamese Student Association, Accounting Association, Philipino-American Students Association, Movimiento Estudiantil Chicano, Hayward Orientation Team, national fraternities, national sororities. *Campus security:* 24-hour emergency response devices and patrols, late-night transport/escort service. *Student services:* health clinic, personal/psychological counseling, legal services.

Athletics Member NCAA, NAIA. All NCAA Division III. *Intercollegiate sports:* baseball M, basketball M/W, cross-country running M/W, soccer M/W, softball W, swimming W, volleyball W, water polo W. *Intramural sports:* badminton M/W, basketball M/W, golf M/W, gymnastics M, racquetball M/W, soccer M/W, softball M/W, swimming M/W, tennis M/W, volleyball M/W, weight lifting M/W.

Standardized Tests *Required for some:* SAT I or ACT (for admission).

Costs (2004–05) *Tuition:* state resident $0 full-time; nonresident $8460 full-time, $188 per unit part-time. *Required fees:* $2418 full-time, $520 per term part-time. *Room only:* $3705.

Financial Aid Of all full-time matriculated undergraduates who enrolled in 2003, 3,347 applied for aid, 3,116 were judged to have need, 217 had their need fully met. *Average percent of need met:* 61%. *Average financial aid package:* $7251. *Average need-based loan:* $5309. *Average need-based gift aid:* $5588. *Average indebtedness upon graduation:* $12,584.

Applying *Options:* electronic application, deferred entrance. *Application fee:* $55. *Required:* high school transcript. *Application deadlines:* 9/7 (freshmen), 9/7 (transfers). *Notification:* continuous (freshmen), continuous (transfers).

Admissions Contact Ms. Susan Lakis, Associate Director of Admissions, California State University, Hayward, 25800 Carlos Bee Boulevard, Hayward, CA 94542-3035. *Phone:* 510-885-3248. *Fax:* 510-885-3816. *E-mail:* adminfo@csuhayward.edu.

CALIFORNIA STATE UNIVERSITY, LONG BEACH
Long Beach, California

- **State-supported** comprehensive, founded 1949, part of California State University System
- **Calendar** semesters
- **Degrees** bachelor's, master's, and postbachelor's certificates
- **Suburban** 320-acre campus with easy access to Los Angeles
- **Endowment** $52,656
- **Coed,** 28,067 undergraduate students, 77% full-time, 60% women, 40% men
- **Moderately difficult** entrance level, 49% of applicants were admitted

Undergraduates 21,678 full-time, 6,389 part-time. Students come from 45 states and territories, 89 other countries, 1% are from out of state, 6% African American, 21% Asian American or Pacific Islander, 24% Hispanic American, 0.6% Native American, 5% international, 11% transferred in, 7% live on campus. *Retention:* 87% of 2002 full-time freshmen returned.

Freshmen *Admission:* 27,869 applied, 13,751 admitted, 3,516 enrolled. *Average high school GPA:* 3.40. *Test scores:* SAT verbal scores over 500: 50%; SAT math scores over 500: 62%; ACT scores over 18: 78%; SAT verbal scores over 600: 13%; SAT math scores over 600: 20%; ACT scores over 24: 28%; SAT verbal scores over 700: 1%; SAT math scores over 700: 2%; ACT scores over 30: 3%.

Faculty *Total:* 2,080, 52% full-time, 55% with terminal degrees. *Student/faculty ratio:* 20:1.

Majors Accounting; acting; aerospace, aeronautical and astronautical engineering; African-American/Black studies; American studies; ancient/classical Greek; anthropology; apparel and textiles; applied mathematics; art; art history, criticism and conservation; art teacher education; Asian-American studies; Asian studies; athletic training; audiology and hearing sciences; audiology and speech-language pathology; biochemistry; biochemistry/biophysics and molecular biology; biology/biological sciences; biology teacher education; biomedical/medical engineering; botany/plant biology; broadcast journalism; business administration and management; business/managerial economics; cell biology and histology; ceramic arts and ceramics; chemical engineering; chemistry; child development; Chinese; cinematography and film/video production; civil engineering; classics and classical languages related; commercial and advertising art; communication disorders; comparative literature; computer engineering; computer engineering technology; computer science; construction engineering; construction engineering technology; construction management; creative writing; criminal justice/law enforcement administration; dance; dance related; dietetics; directing and theatrical production; dramatic/theatre arts; drawing; ecology; economics; electrical, electronic and communications engineering technology; electrical, electronics and communications engineering; engineering; engineering/industrial management; engineering related; engineering technology; English; English/language arts teacher education; environmental engineering technology; environmental science; family and consumer sciences/human sciences; family and consumer sciences/human sciences related; fashion merchandising; fiber, textile and weaving arts; film/cinema studies; finance; fine arts related; fine/studio arts; foods and nutrition related; French; geography; geology/earth science; German; graphic design; health and physical education related; health/health care administration; health science; Hispanic-American, Puerto Rican, and Mexican-American/Chicano studies; history; hotel/motel administration; human development and family studies; human resources management; illustration; industrial design; industrial engineering; industrial technology; interdisciplinary studies; interior design; international business/trade/commerce; international relations and affairs; Italian; Japanese; journalism; journalism related; kinesiology and exercise science; kinesiotherapy; liberal arts and sciences/liberal studies; literature; management information systems; manufacturing technology; marine biology and biological oceanography; marketing/marketing management; mass communication/media; materials engineering; mathematics; mathematics teacher education; mechanical engineering; mechanical engineering/mechanical technology; medical radiologic technology; metal and jewelry arts; microbiology; multi-/interdisciplinary studies related; music; music history, literature, and theory; music performance; music theory and composition; nursing (registered nurse training); ocean engineering; operations management; painting; parks, recreation and leisure; philosophy; photography; physical education teaching and coaching; physics; physiology; political science and government; printmaking; psychology; public health; public health education and promotion; public relations/image management; quality control technology; radio and television; religious studies; sculpture; social work; sociology; Spanish; speech and rhetoric; statistics; trade and industrial teacher education; voice and opera; women's studies; zoology/animal biology.

Academic Programs *Special study options:* academic remediation for entering students, accelerated degree program, adult/continuing education programs, advanced placement credit, distance learning, double majors, English as a second language, honors programs, independent study, internships, off-campus study, part-time degree program, services for LD students, student-designed majors, study abroad, summer session for credit. *ROTC:* Army (b).

Library University Library with 1.5 million titles, 3,965 serial subscriptions, 26,679 audiovisual materials, an OPAC, a Web page.

Computers on Campus 2000 computers available on campus for general student use. A campuswide network can be accessed from off campus. Internet access, at least one staffed computer lab available.

Student Life *Housing options:* coed. *Activities and organizations:* drama/theater group, student-run newspaper, radio and television station, choral group, national fraternities, national sororities. *Campus security:* 24-hour emergency response devices and patrols, student patrols, late-night transport/escort service. *Student services:* health clinic, personal/psychological counseling, women's center, legal services.

Athletics Member NCAA. All Division I. *Intercollegiate sports:* archery M(c)/W(c), badminton M(c)/W(c), basketball M(s)/W(s), bowling M(c)/W(c), crew M(c)/W(c), cross-country running M(s)/W(s), fencing M(c)/W(c), rugby M(c), sailing M(c)/W(c), skiing (downhill) M(c)/W(c), soccer M(c)/W(c), softball W(s), swimming M(s)/W(s), table tennis M(c), tennis W(s), track and field M(s)/W(s), volleyball M(s)/W(s), water polo M(s)/W(c). *Intramural sports:* basketball M/W, gymnastics M/W, racquetball M/W, softball W, swimming M/W, table tennis W(c), tennis W, track and field M(c)/W(c), volleyball M/W.

Standardized Tests *Required:* SAT I or ACT (for admission).

Costs (2004–05) *Tuition:* state resident $0 full-time; nonresident $8460 full-time, $282 per unit part-time. Full-time tuition and fees vary according to program. Part-time tuition and fees vary according to course load and program. *Required fees:* $2362 full-time, $752 per term part-time. *Room and board:* $5800. Room and board charges vary according to board plan. *Payment plan:* installment. *Waivers:* senior citizens and employees or children of employees.

Financial Aid Of all full-time matriculated undergraduates who enrolled in 2003, 12,525 applied for aid, 10,438 were judged to have need, 4,506 had their need fully met. 850 Federal Work-Study jobs (averaging $1882). In 2003, 644 non-need-based awards were made. *Average percent of need met:* 84%. *Average financial aid package:* $7635. *Average need-based loan:* $3270. *Average need-based gift aid:* $4100. *Average non-need-based aid:* $1737. *Average indebtedness upon graduation:* $6319.

Applying *Options:* electronic application. *Application fee:* $55. *Required:* high school transcript. *Required for some:* minimum 2.0 GPA, minimum GPA of 2.4 for nonresidents. *Application deadlines:* 11/30 (freshmen), 11/30 (transfers). *Notification:* continuous (freshmen), continuous (transfers).

Admissions Contact Mr. Thomas Enders, Director of Enrollment Services, California State University, Long Beach, Brotman Hall, 1250 Bellflower Boulevard, Long Beach, CA 90840. *Phone:* 562-985-4641.

CALIFORNIA STATE UNIVERSITY, LOS ANGELES

Los Angeles, California

- **State-supported** comprehensive, founded 1947, part of California State University System
- **Calendar** quarters
- **Degrees** bachelor's, master's, and doctoral
- **Urban** 173-acre campus
- **Coed,** 14,421 undergraduate students, 72% full-time, 62% women, 38% men
- **Moderately difficult** entrance level, 54% of applicants were admitted

Undergraduates 10,455 full-time, 3,966 part-time. 4% are from out of state, 8% African American, 19% Asian American or Pacific Islander, 48% Hispanic American, 0.4% Native American, 5% international. *Retention:* 75% of 2002 full-time freshmen returned.

Freshmen *Admission:* 12,198 applied, 6,642 admitted.

Faculty *Total:* 1,062, 58% full-time. *Student/faculty ratio:* 21:1.

Majors African-American/Black studies; anthropology; applied mathematics; art; biochemistry; biology/biological sciences; business administration and management; chemistry; Chinese; civil engineering; communication disorders; communication/speech communication and rhetoric; computer and information sciences; computer and information sciences and support services related; computer science; criminal justice/safety; dance; dietetics; dramatic/theatre arts; early childhood education; economics; electrical, electronics and communications engineering; engineering; English; fire services administration; foods, nutrition, and wellness; French; geography; geology/earth science; gerontology; graphic communications; health professions related; health science; Hispanic-American, Puerto Rican, and Mexican-American/Chicano studies; history; industrial technology; information technology; interdisciplinary studies; Japanese; kindergarten/preschool education; Latin American studies; liberal arts and sciences/liberal studies; manufacturing engineering; mathematics; mechanical engineering; microbiology; multi-/interdisciplinary studies related; music; music performance; natural sciences; nursing (registered nurse training); philosophy; physical education teaching and coaching; physics; political science and government; psychology; radio and television; rehabilitation therapy; social sciences; social work; sociology; Spanish; speech and rhetoric; technology/industrial arts teacher education; trade and industrial teacher education; vocational rehabilitation counseling.

Academic Programs *Special study options:* academic remediation for entering students, accelerated degree program, adult/continuing education programs, advanced placement credit, cooperative education, English as a second language, honors programs, internships, off-campus study, part-time degree program, services for LD students, student-designed majors, study abroad, summer session for credit. *ROTC:* Army (c), Air Force (c).

Library John F. Kennedy Memorial Library with 1.7 million titles, 2,724 serial subscriptions, 1,163 audiovisual materials, an OPAC, a Web page.

Computers on Campus 1500 computers available on campus for general student use. A campuswide network can be accessed from off campus. Internet access, at least one staffed computer lab available.

Student Life *Housing options:* coed. *Activities and organizations:* drama/theater group, student-run newspaper, choral group, Society of Hispanic, Engineering and Science Students, Institute of Electrical and Electronics Engineer, Sigma Delta PI, Asian Unified, Society of Automotive Engineers, national fraternities, national sororities. *Campus security:* 24-hour emergency response devices, student patrols, late-night transport/escort service. *Student services:* health clinic, personal/psychological counseling, women's center, legal services.

Athletics Member NCAA. All Division II. *Intercollegiate sports:* baseball M(s), basketball M(s)/W(s), cross-country running W(s), soccer M(s)/W(s), tennis W(s), track and field M(s)/W(s), volleyball W(s). *Intramural sports:* basketball M/W, bowling M/W, gymnastics M/W, racquetball M/W, skiing (cross-country) M/W, soccer M/W, softball M/W, swimming M/W, tennis M/W, track and field M/W, volleyball M/W, water polo M/W, wrestling M.

Standardized Tests *Required:* SAT I or ACT (for admission).

Costs (2003–04) *Tuition:* state resident $0 full-time; nonresident $9208 full-time, $188 per unit part-time. *Required fees:* $2440 full-time, $527 per term part-time. *Room only:* $3338.

Financial Aid Of all full-time matriculated undergraduates who enrolled in 2003, 7,685 applied for aid, 7,233 were judged to have need, 426 had their need fully met. 276 Federal Work-Study jobs (averaging $4402). *Average percent of need met:* 75%. *Average financial aid package:* $7416. *Average need-based loan:* $3592. *Average need-based gift aid:* $6523.

California State University, Los Angeles (continued)

Applying *Options:* common application, electronic application, early admission. *Application fee:* $55. *Required:* high school transcript. *Application deadlines:* 6/15 (freshmen), 6/15 (transfers).

Admissions Contact Mr. Vince Lopez, Assistant Director of Outreach and Recruitment, California State University, Los Angeles, 5151 State University Drive, Los Angeles, CA 90032-8530. *Phone:* 323-343-3839. *E-mail:* admission@calstatela.edu.

CALIFORNIA STATE UNIVERSITY, MONTEREY BAY

Seaside, California

Admissions Contact Ms. Valarie E. Brown, Director of Admissions and Records, California State University, Monterey Bay, 100 Campus Center, Building 47, Seaside, CA 93955. *Phone:* 831-582-4093. *Fax:* 831-582-3087. *E-mail:* moreinfo-prospective@csumb.edu.

CALIFORNIA STATE UNIVERSITY, NORTHRIDGE

Northridge, California

- **State-supported** comprehensive, founded 1958, part of California State University System
- **Calendar** semesters
- **Degrees** bachelor's and master's
- **Urban** 353-acre campus with easy access to Los Angeles
- **Endowment** $25.6 million
- **Coed**
- **Moderately difficult** entrance level

Student Life *Campus security:* 24-hour emergency response devices, late-night transport/escort service.

Athletics Member NCAA. All Division I except football (Division II).

Standardized Tests *Recommended:* SAT I or ACT (for admission).

Costs (2003–04) *Tuition:* state resident $0 full-time; nonresident $9024 full-time. *Required fees:* $2444 full-time. *Room and board:* $6400.

Financial Aid Of all full-time matriculated undergraduates who enrolled in 2003, 20,000 applied for aid, 16,900 were judged to have need, 5,000 had their need fully met. 859 Federal Work-Study jobs (averaging $1823). In 2003, 1200. *Average percent of need met:* 88. *Average financial aid package:* $12,046. *Average need-based loan:* $4000. *Average need-based gift aid:* $6046. *Average non-need-based aid:* $4300. *Average indebtedness upon graduation:* $5400.

Applying *Options:* electronic application, early admission, early action. *Application fee:* $55. *Required:* high school transcript.

Admissions Contact Ms. Mary Baxton, Associate Director of Admissions and Records, California State University, Northridge, 18111 Nordhoff Street, Northridge, CA 91330-8207. *Phone:* 818-677-3777. *Fax:* 818-677-3766. *E-mail:* admissions.records@csun.edu.

CALIFORNIA STATE UNIVERSITY, SACRAMENTO

Sacramento, California

- **State-supported** comprehensive, founded 1947, part of California State University System
- **Calendar** semesters
- **Degrees** bachelor's, master's, and doctoral
- **Urban** 300-acre campus
- **Coed,** 22,562 undergraduate students, 76% full-time, 58% women, 42% men
- **Moderately difficult** entrance level, 52% of applicants were admitted

Undergraduates 17,202 full-time, 5,360 part-time. Students come from 36 states and territories, 47 other countries, 1% are from out of state, 6% African American, 19% Asian American or Pacific Islander, 14% Hispanic American, 0.9% Native American, 2% international, 13% transferred in, 5% live on campus. *Retention:* 77% of 2002 full-time freshmen returned.

Freshmen *Admission:* 11,214 applied, 5,864 admitted, 2,446 enrolled. *Average high school GPA:* 3.20. *Test scores:* SAT verbal scores over 500: 40%; SAT math scores over 500: 49%; ACT scores over 18: 67%; SAT verbal scores over 600: 9%; SAT math scores over 600: 11%; ACT scores over 24: 16%; SAT verbal scores over 700: 1%; SAT math scores over 700: 1%.

Faculty *Total:* 1,587, 56% full-time, 56% with terminal degrees. *Student/faculty ratio:* 21:1.

Majors Accounting; accounting related; anthropology; apparel and textiles related; art; Asian studies; audiology and speech-language pathology; biology/biological sciences; biology/biotechnology laboratory technician; business administration and management; business, management, and marketing related; chemistry; chemistry related; civil engineering related; communication/speech communication and rhetoric; community health services counseling; computer and information sciences; computer engineering; conservation biology; construction engineering technology; criminal justice/law enforcement administration; cultural studies; dance; digital communication and media/multimedia; dramatic/theatre arts; economics; electrical, electronics and communications engineering; English; environmental studies; ethnic, cultural minority, and gender studies related; family and consumer economics related; finance; French; geography; geology/earth science; gerontology; graphic design; health and physical education; health and physical education related; health/health care administration; health professions related; health services/allied health/health sciences; history; humanities; human resources management; industrial and organizational psychology; insurance; interior design; international business/trade/commerce; journalism; kinesiology and exercise science; liberal arts and sciences/liberal studies; management information systems; marketing/marketing management; mass communication/media; mathematics; mechanical engineering; mechanical engineering/mechanical technology; molecular biology; music; music management and merchandising; music pedagogy; music related; music theory and composition; natural resources/conservation; nursing (registered nurse training); operations management; organizational communication; parks, recreation and leisure; parks, recreation and leisure facilities management; philosophy; philosophy and religious studies related; photography; physical sciences; physics; piano and organ; political science and government; psychology; real estate; social sciences; social work; sociology; Spanish; women's studies.

Academic Programs *Special study options:* academic remediation for entering students, accelerated degree program, advanced placement credit, cooperative education, distance learning, double majors, English as a second language, external degree program, independent study, internships, off-campus study, part-time degree program, services for LD students, student-designed majors, study abroad, summer session for credit. *ROTC:* Army (c), Air Force (b).

Library California State University, Sacramento Library with 967,418 titles, 4,071 serial subscriptions, 135,074 audiovisual materials, an OPAC, a Web page.

Computers on Campus 700 computers available on campus for general student use. A campuswide network can be accessed from student residence rooms and from off campus. Internet access, online (class) registration, at least one staffed computer lab available.

Student Life *Housing options:* coed. Campus housing is university owned. *Activities and organizations:* drama/theater group, student-run newspaper, radio station, choral group, marching band, ski club, American Marketing Association, Society for Advancement of Management, Accounting Society, Human Resources Management Association, national fraternities, national sororities. *Campus security:* 24-hour emergency response devices and patrols, student patrols, late-night transport/escort service, controlled dormitory access. *Student services:* health clinic, personal/psychological counseling, women's center, legal services.

Athletics Member NCAA. All Division I except football (Division I-AA). *Intercollegiate sports:* baseball M(s), basketball M(s)/W(s), bowling M(c)/W(c), cheerleading M/W, crew M(s)/W(s), cross-country running M(s)/W(s), golf M(s)/W, gymnastics W(s), ice hockey M(c), lacrosse M(c)/W(c), racquetball M(c)/W(c), rugby M(c), skiing (downhill) M(c)/W(c), soccer M(s)/W(s), softball W(s), tennis M(s)/W(s), track and field M(s)/W(s), volleyball M(c)/W(s). *Intramural sports:* badminton M/W, basketball M/W, bowling W, crew M/W, football M/W, golf M/W, ice hockey M, racquetball M/W, skiing (downhill) M/W, soccer M/W, softball M/W, table tennis M/W, tennis M/W, ultimate Frisbee M/W, volleyball M/W, water polo M/W, weight lifting M/W.

Standardized Tests *Required for some:* SAT I or ACT (for admission).

Costs (2003–04) *Tuition:* state resident $0 full-time; nonresident $8927 full-time, $282 per unit part-time. *Required fees:* $2513 full-time, $828 per term part-time. *Room and board:* $6523. Room and board charges vary according to board plan. *Payment plan:* installment. *Waivers:* senior citizens and employees or children of employees.

Financial Aid Of all full-time matriculated undergraduates who enrolled in 2002, 9,977 applied for aid, 8,419 were judged to have need, 652 had their need fully met. 652 Federal Work-Study jobs, 130 state and other part-time jobs. In 2002, 954 non-need-based awards were made. *Average percent of need met:* 70%. *Average financial aid package:* $7779. *Average need-based loan:* $3733. *Average need-based gift aid:* $1668. *Average non-need-based aid:* $5036. *Average indebtedness upon graduation:* $17,305.

Applying *Options:* electronic application, early action, deferred entrance. *Application fee:* $55. *Required:* high school transcript, minimum 2.0 GPA. *Application deadline:* 11/30 (freshmen). *Notification:* continuous until 11/1 (freshmen), 11/1 (early action), continuous until 11/1 (transfers).

Admissions Contact California State University, Sacramento, 6000 J Street, Lassen Hall, Sacramento, CA 95819-6048. *Phone:* 916-278-7362. *Fax:* 916-278-5603. *E-mail:* admissions@csus.edu.

CALIFORNIA STATE UNIVERSITY, SAN BERNARDINO

San Bernardino, California

- **State-supported** comprehensive, founded 1965, part of California State University System
- **Calendar** quarters
- **Degrees** bachelor's and master's
- **Suburban** 430-acre campus with easy access to Los Angeles
- **Coed,** 12,119 undergraduate students, 82% full-time, 65% women, 35% men
- **Moderately difficult** entrance level, 61% of applicants were admitted

Undergraduates 9,896 full-time, 2,223 part-time. 1% are from out of state, 12% African American, 7% Asian American or Pacific Islander, 31% Hispanic American, 0.8% Native American, 3% international, 14% transferred in, 7% live on campus. *Retention:* 81% of 2002 full-time freshmen returned.

Freshmen *Admission:* 6,463 applied, 3,948 admitted, 1,383 enrolled. *Average high school GPA:* 3.20. *Test scores:* SAT verbal scores over 500: 24%; SAT math scores over 500: 30%; ACT scores over 18: 59%; SAT verbal scores over 600: 4%; SAT math scores over 600: 6%; ACT scores over 24: 11%; ACT scores over 30: 1%.

Faculty *Total:* 981, 51% full-time. *Student/faculty ratio:* 21:1.

Majors Accounting; African-American/Black studies; American studies; anthropology; art; art history, criticism and conservation; biochemistry; biology/biological sciences; business administration and management; business/managerial economics; chemistry; commercial and advertising art; computer and information sciences; computer science; creative writing; criminal justice/law enforcement administration; developmental and child psychology; dietetics; dramatic/theatre arts; economics; English; environmental studies; finance; foods, nutrition, and wellness; French; geography; geology/earth science; health/health care administration; health science; health teacher education; Hispanic-American, Puerto Rican, and Mexican-American/Chicano studies; history; human development and family studies; humanities; human services; interdisciplinary studies; liberal arts and sciences/liberal studies; management information systems; marketing/marketing management; mass communication/media; mathematics; music; natural sciences; nursing (registered nurse training); philosophy; physical education teaching and coaching; physics; political science and government; psychology; public administration; social sciences; social work; sociology; Spanish; trade and industrial teacher education.

Academic Programs *Special study options:* academic remediation for entering students, adult/continuing education programs, advanced placement credit, cooperative education, distance learning, double majors, honors programs, independent study, internships, off-campus study, part-time degree program, services for LD students, student-designed majors, study abroad, summer session for credit. *ROTC:* Army (b), Air Force (b).

Library Pfau Library with 731,259 titles, 2,028 serial subscriptions, 15,252 audiovisual materials, an OPAC, a Web page.

Computers on Campus 1300 computers available on campus for general student use. A campuswide network can be accessed from student residence rooms and from off campus. Internet access, online (class) registration, at least one staffed computer lab available.

Student Life *Housing options:* coed, women-only. Campus housing is university owned. *Activities and organizations:* drama/theater group, student-run newspaper, radio station, choral group, national fraternities, national sororities. *Campus security:* 24-hour emergency response devices and patrols, student patrols, late-night transport/escort service, residence staff on call 24-hours. *Student services:* health clinic, personal/psychological counseling, women's center, legal services.

Athletics Member NCAA. All Division II. *Intercollegiate sports:* baseball M(s), basketball M(s)/W(s), golf M(s), soccer M(s)/W(s), softball W(s), swimming M(s)/W(s), volleyball W(s). *Intramural sports:* basketball M/W, field hockey M/W, football M/W, soccer M/W, softball M, volleyball M/W.

Standardized Tests *Required for some:* SAT I or ACT (for admission).

Costs (2003–04) *Tuition:* state resident $0 full-time; nonresident $6768 full-time, $188 per credit part-time. Part-time tuition and fees vary according to course load. *Required fees:* $1932 full-time, $404 per term part-time. *Room and board:* $5383; room only: $4205. Room and board charges vary according to board plan and housing facility. *Waivers:* employees or children of employees.

Applying *Options:* early admission. *Application fee:* $55. *Required:* high school transcript, minimum 2.0 GPA. *Application deadline:* rolling (freshmen), rolling (transfers). *Notification:* continuous (freshmen), continuous (transfers).

Admissions Contact Ms. Cynthia Shum, Admissions Counselor, California State University, San Bernardino, 5500 University Parkway, University Hall, Room 107, San Bernardino, CA 92407-2397. *Phone:* 909-880-5212. *Toll-free phone:* 909-880-5188. *Fax:* 909-880-7034. *E-mail:* moreinfo@mail.csusb.edu.

CALIFORNIA STATE UNIVERSITY, SAN MARCOS

San Marcos, California

- **State-supported** comprehensive, founded 1990, part of California State University System
- **Calendar** semesters
- **Degrees** bachelor's and master's
- **Suburban** 304-acre campus with easy access to San Diego
- **Endowment** $5.9 million
- **Coed,** 6,407 undergraduate students, 70% full-time, 60% women, 40% men
- **Moderately difficult** entrance level, 73% of applicants were admitted

Undergraduates 4,461 full-time, 1,946 part-time. 1% are from out of state, 3% African American, 10% Asian American or Pacific Islander, 19% Hispanic American, 0.8% Native American, 3% international, 16% transferred in, 2% live on campus. *Retention:* 71% of 2002 full-time freshmen returned.

Freshmen *Admission:* 4,317 applied, 3,166 admitted, 890 enrolled. *Average high school GPA:* 3.15. *Test scores:* SAT verbal scores over 500: 45%; SAT math scores over 500: 51%; SAT verbal scores over 600: 9%; SAT math scores over 600: 11%; SAT verbal scores over 700: 1%.

Faculty *Total:* 408, 49% full-time, 63% with terminal degrees. *Student/faculty ratio:* 19:1.

Majors Accounting; biochemistry; biology/biological sciences; business administration and management; cell biology and histology; chemistry; communication/speech communication and rhetoric; computer science; ecology; economics; English; history; liberal arts and sciences/liberal studies; mathematics; molecular biology; political science and government; psychology; science teacher education; social sciences; sociology; Spanish; visual and performing arts; women's studies.

Academic Programs *Special study options:* academic remediation for entering students, adult/continuing education programs, advanced placement credit, distance learning, double majors, English as a second language, independent study, internships, off-campus study, part-time degree program, services for LD students, student-designed majors, study abroad, summer session for credit. *ROTC:* Army (c), Navy (c), Air Force (c).

Library Library and Information Services with 179,439 titles, 2,984 serial subscriptions, 7,576 audiovisual materials, an OPAC, a Web page.

Computers on Campus 487 computers available on campus for general student use. A campuswide network can be accessed from student residence rooms and from off campus. Internet access, online (class) registration, at least one staffed computer lab available.

Student Life *Housing options:* men-only, women-only, disabled students. *Activities and organizations:* drama/theater group, student-run newspaper, choral group, accounting club, liberal studies club, MECHA, Sigma IOTA Epsilon, national fraternities, national sororities. *Campus security:* 24-hour patrols, student patrols, late-night transport/escort service. *Student services:* health clinic, personal/psychological counseling, women's center.

Athletics Member NAIA. *Intercollegiate sports:* cross-country running M/W, golf M(s)/W, track and field M/W. *Intramural sports:* basketball M/W, football M/W, soccer M/W, volleyball M/W.

Standardized Tests *Required:* SAT I or ACT (for admission).

Costs (2003–04) *Tuition:* state resident $0 full-time; nonresident $6768 full-time, $282 per credit hour part-time. Part-time tuition and fees vary according to course load. *Required fees:* $2414 full-time. *Room only:* $7470. Room and board charges vary according to housing facility. *Waivers:* senior citizens and employees or children of employees.

Financial Aid Of all full-time matriculated undergraduates who enrolled in 2002, 1,981 applied for aid, 1,637 were judged to have need. 193 Federal Work-Study jobs (averaging $2035). 18 state and other part-time jobs (averaging $821). *Average financial aid package:* $6068. *Average need-based loan:* $4067. *Average need-based gift aid:* $4496. *Average indebtedness upon graduation:* $12,762.

Applying *Options:* electronic application. *Application fee:* $55. *Required:* high school transcript, minimum 3.0 GPA. *Application deadlines:* 11/30 (freshmen), 11/30 (transfers). *Notification:* continuous (freshmen), continuous (transfers).

Admissions Contact Ms. Cherine Heckman, Director of Admissions, California State University, San Marcos, 333 South Twin Oaks Valley Road, San Marcos, CA 92096-0001. *Phone:* 760-750-4848. *Fax:* 760-750-3248. *E-mail:* apply@csusm.edu.

CALIFORNIA STATE UNIVERSITY, STANISLAUS

Turlock, California

- **State-supported** comprehensive, founded 1957, part of California State University System
- **Calendar** 4-1-4

California State University, Stanislaus (continued)
- **Degrees** bachelor's and master's
- **Small-town** 220-acre campus
- **Coed,** 6,154 undergraduate students, 68% full-time, 66% women, 34% men
- **Moderately difficult** entrance level, 64% of applicants were admitted

Undergraduates 4,177 full-time, 1,977 part-time. Students come from 25 states and territories, 71 other countries, 1% are from out of state, 3% African American, 10% Asian American or Pacific Islander, 25% Hispanic American, 1% Native American, 2% international, 14% transferred in, 6% live on campus. *Retention:* 82% of 2002 full-time freshmen returned.

Freshmen *Admission:* 2,687 applied, 1,733 admitted, 670 enrolled. *Average high school GPA:* 3.30. *Test scores:* SAT verbal scores over 500: 56%; SAT math scores over 500: 58%; ACT scores over 18: 65%; SAT verbal scores over 600: 10%; SAT math scores over 600: 12%; ACT scores over 24: 14%; SAT verbal scores over 700: 1%; SAT math scores over 700: 1%.

Faculty *Total:* 495, 57% full-time, 57% with terminal degrees.

Majors Agriculture; anthropology; art; biology/biological sciences; business administration and management; business, management, and marketing related; chemistry; cognitive psychology and psycholinguistics; communication/speech communication and rhetoric; computer and information sciences; criminal justice/law enforcement administration; dramatic/theatre arts; economics; English; fine/studio arts; French; geography; geology/earth science; history; information science/studies; liberal arts and sciences/liberal studies; mathematics; multi-/interdisciplinary studies related; music; music performance; nursing (registered nurse training); philosophy; physical education teaching and coaching; physical sciences; physics; political science and government; psychology; social sciences; sociology; Spanish.

Academic Programs *Special study options:* academic remediation for entering students, accelerated degree program, adult/continuing education programs, advanced placement credit, cooperative education, distance learning, double majors, English as a second language, external degree program, honors programs, independent study, internships, off-campus study, part-time degree program, services for LD students, student-designed majors, study abroad, summer session for credit.

Library Vasche Library with 347,674 titles, 1,924 serial subscriptions, 4,676 audiovisual materials, an OPAC, a Web page.

Computers on Campus 150 computers available on campus for general student use. A campuswide network can be accessed from student residence rooms and from off campus. Internet access, at least one staffed computer lab available.

Student Life *Housing options:* coed, disabled students. *Activities and organizations:* drama/theater group, student-run newspaper, radio station, choral group, marching band, Theta Chi fraternity, Phi Sigma Sigma sorority, Phi Delta Theta fraternity, Alpha XI Delta sorority, MECHA, national fraternities, national sororities. *Campus security:* 24-hour emergency response devices and patrols, student patrols, late-night transport/escort service, controlled dormitory access. *Student services:* health clinic, personal/psychological counseling, women's center.

Athletics Member NCAA. All Division II. *Intercollegiate sports:* baseball M, basketball M/W, cross-country running M/W, golf M, soccer M/W, softball W, track and field M/W, volleyball W.

Standardized Tests *Required:* SAT I or ACT (for admission).

Costs (2003–04) *Tuition:* state resident $0 full-time; nonresident $8460 full-time, $282 per unit part-time. *Required fees:* $2503 full-time, $691 per term part-time. *Room and board:* $7242; room only: $4322. Room and board charges vary according to board plan and housing facility. *Payment plans:* installment, deferred payment. *Waivers:* adult students, senior citizens, and employees or children of employees.

Financial Aid Of all full-time matriculated undergraduates who enrolled in 2003, 3,100 applied for aid, 2,726 were judged to have need, 220 had their need fully met. 168 Federal Work-Study jobs (averaging $2722). In 2003, 97 non-need-based awards were made. *Average percent of need met:* 59%. *Average financial aid package:* $7472. *Average need-based loan:* $3970. *Average need-based gift aid:* $5567. *Average non-need-based aid:* $1263. *Average indebtedness upon graduation:* $13,050.

Applying *Options:* electronic application, early decision, deferred entrance. *Application fee:* $55. *Required:* high school transcript. *Recommended:* minimum 3.0 GPA. *Application deadlines:* 5/1 (freshmen), 5/31 (transfers). *Early decision:* 11/30. *Notification:* 3/1 (early decision), 3/1 (transfers).

Admissions Contact California State University, Stanislaus, Enrollment Services, 801 West Monte Vista Avenue, Mary Stuart Rogers Gateway Center, Room 120, Turlock, CA 95382. *Phone:* 209-667-3070. *Toll-free phone:* 800-300-7420. *Fax:* 209-667-3788. *E-mail:* outreach_help_desk@stan.csustan.edu.

CHAPMAN UNIVERSITY
Orange, California

- **Independent** comprehensive, founded 1861, affiliated with Christian Church (Disciples of Christ)
- **Calendar** 4-1-4
- **Degrees** certificates, bachelor's, master's, first professional, and postbachelor's certificates
- **Suburban** 45-acre campus with easy access to Los Angeles
- **Endowment** $142.6 million
- **Coed,** 3,443 undergraduate students, 95% full-time, 57% women, 43% men
- **Moderately difficult** entrance level, 62% of applicants were admitted

Undergraduates 3,261 full-time, 182 part-time. Students come from 40 states and territories, 45 other countries, 26% are from out of state, 2% African American, 7% Asian American or Pacific Islander, 9% Hispanic American, 0.4% Native American, 3% international, 9% transferred in, 45% live on campus. *Retention:* 84% of 2002 full-time freshmen returned.

Freshmen *Admission:* 3,084 applied, 1,902 admitted, 850 enrolled. *Average high school GPA:* 3.56. *Test scores:* SAT verbal scores over 500: 94%; SAT math scores over 500: 95%; ACT scores over 18: 99%; SAT verbal scores over 600: 43%; SAT math scores over 600: 45%; ACT scores over 24: 61%; SAT verbal scores over 700: 7%; SAT math scores over 700: 5%; ACT scores over 30: 5%.

Faculty *Total:* 518, 45% full-time. *Student/faculty ratio:* 16:1.

Majors Accounting; advertising; American government and politics; American history; art; art history, criticism and conservation; athletic training; biology/biological sciences; biopsychology; broadcast journalism; business administration and management; business/managerial economics; chemistry; chemistry teacher education; cinematography and film/video production; communication/speech communication and rhetoric; computer and information sciences; computer science; creative writing; dance; dance related; dramatic/theatre arts; English; English/language arts teacher education; environmental science; European history; exercise physiology; film/cinema studies; fine/studio arts; French; graphic design; health and physical education; health science; history; international business/trade/commerce; legal studies; liberal arts and sciences/liberal studies; literature; mathematics; molecular biology; music; music performance; music teacher education; music theory and composition; music therapy; nutrition sciences; organizational behavior; peace studies and conflict resolution; philosophy; political science and government; psychology; religious studies; social work; sociology; Spanish; theatre design and technology; voice and opera; wind/percussion instruments.

Academic Programs *Special study options:* academic remediation for entering students, accelerated degree program, adult/continuing education programs, advanced placement credit, cooperative education, double majors, English as a second language, honors programs, independent study, internships, part-time degree program, services for LD students, study abroad, summer session for credit. *ROTC:* Army (c), Air Force (c). *Unusual degree programs:* 3-2 engineering with University of California, Irvine.

Library Thurmond Clarke Memorial Library plus 1 other with 188,682 titles, 1,777 serial subscriptions, 6,334 audiovisual materials, an OPAC, a Web page.

Computers on Campus 278 computers available on campus for general student use. A campuswide network can be accessed from off campus. Internet access, at least one staffed computer lab available. Computer purchase or lease plan available.

Student Life *Housing:* on-campus residence required for freshman year. *Options:* coed, women-only. Campus housing is university owned. Freshman campus housing is guaranteed. *Activities and organizations:* drama/theater group, student-run newspaper, radio station, choral group, Associated Students, Disciples on Campus, Gamma Beta Phi honor society, national fraternities, national sororities. *Campus security:* 24-hour emergency response devices and patrols, late-night transport/escort service, controlled dormitory access, full safety education program. *Student services:* health clinic, personal/psychological counseling.

Athletics Member NCAA. All Division III. *Intercollegiate sports:* baseball M, basketball M/W, cheerleading M/W, crew M(c)/W, cross-country running M/W, football M, golf M/W, lacrosse M(c), soccer M/W, softball W, swimming M(c)/W, tennis M/W, track and field W, ultimate Frisbee M(c)/W(c), volleyball W, water polo M/W. *Intramural sports:* basketball M/W, football M, soccer M/W, softball M/W, tennis M/W, ultimate Frisbee M/W, volleyball M/W.

Standardized Tests *Required:* SAT I or ACT (for admission). *Recommended:* SAT II: Subject Tests (for admission), SAT II: Subject Tests (for placement), SAT II: Writing Test (for placement).

Costs (2004–05) *Comprehensive fee:* $35,232 includes full-time tuition ($25,500), mandatory fees ($650), and room and board ($9082). Part-time tuition:

$795 per credit. Part-time tuition and fees vary according to course load. *Room and board:* Room and board charges vary according to board plan and housing facility. *Payment plans:* tuition prepayment, installment, deferred payment. *Waivers:* children of alumni and employees or children of employees.

Financial Aid Of all full-time matriculated undergraduates who enrolled in 2002, 2,725 applied for aid, 2,001 were judged to have need, 1,987 had their need fully met. 642 Federal Work-Study jobs (averaging $1695). In 2002, 667 non-need-based awards were made. *Average percent of need met:* 100%. *Average financial aid package:* $18,066. *Average need-based loan:* $4409. *Average need-based gift aid:* $14,642. *Average non-need-based aid:* $12,014. *Average indebtedness upon graduation:* $18,574.

Applying *Options:* common application, electronic application, early admission, early action. *Application fee:* $50. *Required:* essay or personal statement, high school transcript, minimum 2.75 GPA, 1 letter of recommendation. *Recommended:* minimum 3.5 GPA, interview. *Application deadlines:* 1/31 (freshmen), 3/15 (transfers). *Notification:* continuous (freshmen), 1/15 (early action), continuous (transfers).

Admissions Contact Mr. Michael O. Drummy, Associate Dean for Enrollment Services and Chief Admission Officer, Chapman University, One University Drive, Orange, CA 92866. *Phone:* 714-997-6711. *Toll-free phone:* 888-CUAPPLY. *Fax:* 714-997-6713. *E-mail:* admit@chapman.edu.

■ *See page 1388 for a narrative description.*

CHARLES R. DREW UNIVERSITY OF MEDICINE AND SCIENCE
Los Angeles, California

Admissions Contact Ms. Mala Sharma, Director of Enrollment Services, Charles R. Drew University of Medicine and Science, 1731 East 120th Street, Los Angeles, CA 90059. *Phone:* 323-563-4832.

CHRISTIAN HERITAGE COLLEGE
El Cajon, California

- **Independent nondenominational** 4-year, founded 1970
- **Calendar** semesters
- **Degrees** certificates, bachelor's, and postbachelor's certificates
- **Suburban** 55-acre campus with easy access to San Diego
- **Endowment** $262,641
- **Coed,** 524 undergraduate students, 89% full-time, 62% women, 38% men
- **Moderately difficult** entrance level, 71% of applicants were admitted

Undergraduates 467 full-time, 57 part-time. Students come from 25 states and territories, 6 other countries, 13% are from out of state, 7% African American, 4% Asian American or Pacific Islander, 10% Hispanic American, 0.5% Native American, 2% international, 18% transferred in, 44% live on campus. *Retention:* 54% of 2002 full-time freshmen returned.

Freshmen *Admission:* 208 applied, 147 admitted, 90 enrolled. *Average high school GPA:* 3.36. *Test scores:* SAT verbal scores over 500: 52%; SAT math scores over 500: 42%; ACT scores over 18: 79%; SAT verbal scores over 600: 7%; SAT math scores over 600: 17%; ACT scores over 24: 26%; SAT verbal scores over 700: 2%; ACT scores over 30: 5%.

Faculty *Total:* 71, 48% full-time, 24% with terminal degrees. *Student/faculty ratio:* 14:1.

Majors Adult and continuing education; athletic training; biblical studies; biology/biological sciences; business administration and management; communication/speech communication and rhetoric; counseling psychology; divinity/ministry; education; education (K-12); elementary education; English; history; human development and family studies; interdisciplinary studies; kinesiology and exercise science; liberal arts and sciences/liberal studies; mathematics; multi-/interdisciplinary studies related; music; music teacher education; pastoral studies/counseling; physical education teaching and coaching; psychology; religious/sacred music; secondary education; social sciences; theology; voice and opera.

Academic Programs *Special study options:* academic remediation for entering students, adult/continuing education programs, advanced placement credit, double majors, English as a second language, independent study, internships, part-time degree program, student-designed majors, study abroad, summer session for credit. *ROTC:* Army (c), Air Force (c).

Library Christian Heritage College Library with 71,000 titles, 6,250 serial subscriptions, 3,784 audiovisual materials, an OPAC.

Computers on Campus 50 computers available on campus for general student use. A campuswide network can be accessed from student residence rooms and from off campus. Internet access, at least one staffed computer lab available.

Student Life *Housing options:* men-only, women-only. Campus housing is leased by the school. *Activities and organizations:* drama/theater group, choral group, Senate, Missions Club, aviators club, Women of Influence, Hope Ministries. *Campus security:* 24-hour emergency response devices and patrols. *Student services:* health clinic, personal/psychological counseling.

Athletics Member NAIA, NCCAA. *Intercollegiate sports:* basketball M(s)/W(s), cross-country running M(s)/W(s), soccer M(s)/W(s), volleyball W(s). *Intramural sports:* basketball M/W, football M, soccer M/W, softball M/W, swimming M/W, tennis M/W, volleyball M/W.

Standardized Tests *Required:* SAT I or ACT (for admission).

Costs (2003–04) *Comprehensive fee:* $19,990 includes full-time tuition ($14,000) and room and board ($5990). Full-time tuition and fees vary according to class time, course load, and program. Part-time tuition: $470 per credit. Part-time tuition and fees vary according to class time, course load, and program. *Room and board:* Room and board charges vary according to housing facility. *Payment plan:* installment. *Waivers:* employees or children of employees.

Financial Aid Of all full-time matriculated undergraduates who enrolled in 2002, 478 applied for aid, 429 were judged to have need, 304 had their need fully met. 40 Federal Work-Study jobs (averaging $1569). 18 state and other part-time jobs (averaging $1324). In 2002, 129 non-need-based awards were made. *Average percent of need met:* 80%. *Average financial aid package:* $12,802. *Average need-based loan:* $3850. *Average need-based gift aid:* $7035. *Average non-need-based aid:* $3390. *Average indebtedness upon graduation:* $16,000.

Applying *Options:* electronic application, deferred entrance. *Application fee:* $25. *Required:* essay or personal statement, high school transcript, 2 letters of recommendation. *Recommended:* minimum 2.75 GPA, interview. *Application deadlines:* 9/1 (freshmen), 9/1 (transfers). *Notification:* continuous (freshmen), continuous (transfers).

Admissions Contact Ms. Misty Blount, Director of Admissions, Christian Heritage College, 2100 Greenfield Drive, El Cajon, CA 92019-1157. *Phone:* 619-588-7747. *Toll-free phone:* 800-676-2242. *Fax:* 619-440-0209. *E-mail:* chcadm@christianheritage.edu.

CLAREMONT MCKENNA COLLEGE
Claremont, California

- **Independent** 4-year, founded 1946, part of The Claremont Colleges Consortium
- **Calendar** semesters
- **Degree** bachelor's
- **Small-town** 50-acre campus with easy access to Los Angeles
- **Endowment** $286.0 million
- **Coed,** 1,050 undergraduate students, 100% full-time, 45% women, 55% men
- **Very difficult** entrance level, 29% of applicants were admitted

Claremont McKenna College (CMC) infuses a traditional liberal arts education with its own pragmatic sensibilities. CMC's focus on economics, government, and international relations allows it to fully prepare students for leadership in business, government, and other professions. CMC's enrollment of approximately 1,000 students ensures a personalized educational experience. However, with 4 other colleges—Harvey Mudd, Pitzer, Pomona, and Scripps—and 2 graduate schools right next door, CMC students also have access to the academic, intellectual, social, and athletic resources typical of a medium-sized university.

Undergraduates 1,050 full-time. Students come from 45 states and territories, 21 other countries, 51% are from out of state, 3% transferred in, 96% live on campus. *Retention:* 97% of 2002 full-time freshmen returned.

Freshmen *Admission:* 2,892 applied, 842 admitted, 284 enrolled. *Average high school GPA:* 3.91. *Test scores:* SAT verbal scores over 500: 100%; SAT math scores over 500: 100%; ACT scores over 18: 100%; SAT verbal scores over 600: 93%; SAT math scores over 600: 95%; ACT scores over 24: 98%; SAT verbal scores over 700: 46%; SAT math scores over 700: 51%; ACT scores over 30: 53%.

Faculty *Total:* 159, 89% full-time, 82% with terminal degrees. *Student/faculty ratio:* 7:1.

Majors Accounting; African-American/Black studies; American government and politics; American studies; anthropology; Arabic; archeology; area, ethnic, cultural, and gender studies related; area studies related; art; art history, criticism and conservation; Asian-American studies; Asian studies; biochemistry; biology/biological sciences; biophysics; chemistry; Chinese; Chinese studies; classics and languages, literatures and linguistics; computer and information sciences; computer science; dance; dramatic/theatre arts; East Asian languages related; economics; economics related; engineering; engineering/industrial management; engineering related; engineering science; English; environmental studies; ethnic, cultural minority, and gender studies related; European studies; European studies (Western); film/cinema studies; fine/studio arts; French; French studies; German; Germanic languages; German studies; Hispanic-American, Puerto Rican, and Mexican-American/Chicano studies; history; international business/trade/commerce; international economics; international relations and affairs; Italian;

Claremont McKenna College (continued)
Japanese; Japanese studies; Korean studies; Latin; Latin American studies; legal studies; literature; mathematics; modern Greek; modern languages; music; music related; Near and Middle Eastern studies; Pacific area/Pacific rim studies; philosophy; philosophy and religious studies related; philosophy related; physics; physiological psychology/psychobiology; political science and government; political science and government related; pre-dentistry studies; pre-law studies; premedical studies; psychology; religious studies; religious studies related; Russian; Russian studies; sociology; South Asian languages; Spanish; visual and performing arts; visual and performing arts related; women's studies.

Academic Programs *Special study options:* accelerated degree program, advanced placement credit, double majors, honors programs, independent study, internships, off-campus study, services for LD students, student-designed majors, study abroad. *ROTC:* Army (b), Air Force (c). *Unusual degree programs:* 3-2 business administration with Claremont Graduate School, University of Chicago; engineering with Stanford University, Harvey Mudd College, Columbia University, Washington University in St. Louis, University of California System schools, University of Southern California; education, management information systems, computer information systems with Claremont Graduate School, applied biology with Keck Graduate Institute.

Library Honnold Library plus 3 others with 2.0 million titles, 6,028 serial subscriptions, 606 audiovisual materials, an OPAC, a Web page.

Computers on Campus 120 computers available on campus for general student use. A campuswide network can be accessed from student residence rooms and from off campus. Internet access, at least one staffed computer lab available.

Student Life *Housing:* on-campus residence required for freshman year. *Options:* coed, disabled students. Campus housing is university owned. Freshman campus housing is guaranteed. *Activities and organizations:* drama/theater group, student-run newspaper, radio station, choral group, student government, Debate/ Forensics Club, newspaper, Volunteer Student Admission Committee, Civitas (community service club). *Campus security:* 24-hour emergency response devices and patrols, student patrols, late-night transport/escort service, controlled dormitory access. *Student services:* health clinic, personal/psychological counseling, women's center.

Athletics Member NCAA. All Division III. *Intercollegiate sports:* badminton M(c)/W(c), baseball M, basketball M/W, cheerleading M(c)/W(c), cross-country running M/W, football M, golf M, lacrosse M(c)/W, rugby M(c)/W(c), skiing (downhill) M(c)/W(c), soccer M/W, softball W, swimming M/W, tennis M/W, track and field M/W, volleyball M(c)/W, water polo M/W. *Intramural sports:* archery M/W, badminton M/W, basketball M/W, bowling M/W, crew M/W, equestrian sports M/W, fencing M/W, football M/W, golf W, racquetball M/W, sailing M/W, soccer M/W, softball M/W, squash M/W, swimming M/W, table tennis M/W, tennis M/W, ultimate Frisbee M/W, volleyball M/W, water polo M/W, weight lifting M/W.

Standardized Tests *Required:* SAT I or ACT (for admission). *Recommended:* SAT II: Subject Tests (for admission).

Costs (2003–04) *Comprehensive fee:* $36,880 includes full-time tuition ($27,500), mandatory fees ($200), and room and board ($9180). *College room only:* $4590. Room and board charges vary according to board plan and housing facility. *Payment plans:* tuition prepayment, installment. *Waivers:* employees or children of employees.

Financial Aid Of all full-time matriculated undergraduates who enrolled in 2002, 713 applied for aid, 635 were judged to have need, 635 had their need fully met. 358 Federal Work-Study jobs (averaging $1563). 195 state and other part-time jobs (averaging $1672). In 2002, 105 non-need-based awards were made. *Average percent of need met:* 100%. *Average financial aid package:* $23,920. *Average need-based loan:* $3614. *Average need-based gift aid:* $20,446. *Average non-need-based aid:* $5620. *Average indebtedness upon graduation:* $11,620. *Financial aid deadline:* 2/1.

Applying *Options:* common application, electronic application, early admission, early decision, deferred entrance. *Application fee:* $50. *Required:* essay or personal statement, high school transcript, minimum 3.0 GPA, 3 letters of recommendation. *Recommended:* interview. *Application deadlines:* 1/2 (freshmen), 4/1 (transfers). *Early decision:* 11/15 (for plan 1), 1/2 (for plan 2). *Notification:* 4/1 (freshmen), 12/15 (early decision plan 1), 2/15 (early decision plan 2), 5/15 (transfers).

Admissions Contact Mr. Richard C. Vos, Vice President/Dean of Admission and Financial Aid, Claremont McKenna College, 890 Columbia Avenue, Claremont, CA 91711. *Phone:* 909-621-8088. *Toll-free phone:* 909-621-8088. *Fax:* 909-621-8516. *E-mail:* admission@mckenna.edu.

■ *See page 1408 for a narrative description.*

CLEVELAND CHIROPRACTIC COLLEGE-LOS ANGELES CAMPUS

Los Angeles, California

- **Independent** upper-level, founded 1911
- **Calendar** trimesters
- **Degrees** associate, bachelor's, and first professional
- **Coed,** 113 undergraduate students, 65% full-time, 43% women, 57% men

Undergraduates 74 full-time, 39 part-time. 7% African American, 13% Asian American or Pacific Islander, 14% Hispanic American, 0.9% Native American, 4% international, 100% transferred in.

Majors Biology/biological sciences.

Student Life *Housing:* college housing not available.

Costs (2003–04) *Tuition:* $4752 full-time, $198 per credit part-time. *Required fees:* $200 full-time, $200 per year part-time.

Admissions Contact Ms. Melissa Denton, Director of MultiCampus Admissions, Cleveland Chiropractic College-Los Angeles Campus, 590 North Vermont Avenue, Los Angeles, CA 90004-2196. *Phone:* 323-906-2031. *Toll-free phone:* 800-446-CCLA. *Fax:* 323-906-2094. *E-mail:* la.admissions@cleveland.edu.

COGSWELL POLYTECHNICAL COLLEGE

Sunnyvale, California

- **Independent** 4-year, founded 1887, part of Foundation for Educational Achievement, San Diego
- **Calendar** trimesters
- **Degree** bachelor's
- **Suburban** 2-acre campus with easy access to San Francisco and San Jose
- **Endowment** $6.8 million
- **Coed, primarily men,** 376 undergraduate students, 46% full-time, 14% women, 86% men
- **Moderately difficult** entrance level, 90% of applicants were admitted

Cogswell College provides innovative and rigorous academic programs representing the contemporary fusion of art and engineering. Students learn the theory and gain practical skills to begin work immediately. Cogswell's historic legacy of academic excellence, personalized attention, small student-faculty ratios, and state-of-the-art technologies make a Cogswell education distinctive.

Undergraduates 172 full-time, 204 part-time. Students come from 20 states and territories, 5 other countries, 11% are from out of state, 4% African American, 14% Asian American or Pacific Islander, 7% Hispanic American, 0.5% Native American, 1% international, 18% transferred in, 9% live on campus. *Retention:* 87% of 2002 full-time freshmen returned.

Freshmen *Admission:* 30 applied, 27 admitted, 25 enrolled.

Faculty *Total:* 48, 29% full-time, 31% with terminal degrees. *Student/faculty ratio:* 15:1.

Majors Audio engineering; commercial and advertising art; computer graphics; electrical, electronic and communications engineering technology; electrical, electronics and communications engineering; engineering; fire science.

Academic Programs *Special study options:* adult/continuing education programs, advanced placement credit, distance learning, external degree program, internships, part-time degree program, summer session for credit.

Library Cogswell College Library with 11,257 titles, 102 serial subscriptions, 359 audiovisual materials, an OPAC.

Computers on Campus 125 computers available on campus for general student use. A campuswide network can be accessed from off campus. Internet access, at least one staffed computer lab available.

Student Life *Housing options:* men-only, women-only. Campus housing is provided by a third party. *Activities and organizations:* student-run newspaper, ASB. *Campus security:* 24-hour emergency response devices.

Standardized Tests *Recommended:* SAT I and SAT II or ACT (for admission).

Costs (2003–04) *Tuition:* $10,880 full-time, $470 per credit part-time. Full-time tuition and fees vary according to course load. Part-time tuition and fees vary according to course load. *Required fees:* $40 full-time, $10 per term part-time. *Room only:* $6300. *Payment plan:* deferred payment. *Waivers:* employees or children of employees.

Financial Aid Of all full-time matriculated undergraduates who enrolled in 2002, 180 applied for aid, 166 were judged to have need. 9 Federal Work-Study jobs (averaging $2556). *Average percent of need met:* 29%. *Average financial aid* *package:* $5960. *Average need-based loan:* $9216. *Average need-based gift aid:* $4764. *Average indebtedness upon graduation:* $31,689.

Applying *Options:* common application, deferred entrance. *Application fee:* $50. *Required:* essay or personal statement, high school transcript, minimum 2.5 GPA. *Required for some:* letters of recommendation, interview, portfolio. *Application deadlines:* 6/1 (freshmen), 6/1 (transfers). *Notification:* continuous (freshmen), continuous (transfers).

Admissions Contact Cogswell Polytechnical College, 1175 Bordeaux Drive, Sunnyvale, CA 94089. *Phone:* 408-541-0100 Ext. 107. *Toll-free phone:* 800-264-7955. *Fax:* 408-747-0764. *E-mail:* info@cogswell.edu.

■ *See page 1424 for a narrative description.*

THE COLBURN SCHOOL OF PERFORMING ARTS

Los Angeles, California

- **Independent** 4-year, founded 1980
- **Calendar** semesters
- **Degrees** certificates, diplomas, bachelor's, and postbachelor's certificates
- **Urban** campus with easy access to Los Angeles
- **Coed,** 7 undergraduate students, 100% full-time, 57% women, 43% men
- 90% of applicants were admitted

Undergraduates 7 full-time. Students come from 3 states and territories, 1 other country, 43% are from out of state, 29% Asian American or Pacific Islander, 14% international, 100% live on campus.

Freshmen *Admission:* 10 applied, 9 admitted, 7 enrolled.

Faculty *Total:* 9, 22% full-time, 22% with terminal degrees.

Majors Music performance; piano and organ; violin, viola, guitar and other stringed instruments.

Student Life *Housing:* college housing not available. *Options:* Campus housing is leased by the school and is provided by a third party. Freshman campus housing is guaranteed. *Campus security:* trained security personnel during open building hours. *Student services:* personal/psychological counseling.

Athletics *Intramural sports:* cheerleading M/W.

Standardized Tests *Recommended:* SAT I or ACT (for admission).

Costs (2004–05) *Comprehensive fee:* includes mandatory fees ($500).

Applying *Application fee:* $100. *Required:* essay or personal statement, high school transcript, 2 letters of recommendation, interview. *Application deadlines:* 1/2 (freshmen), 1/2 (transfers). *Notification:* 4/15 (freshmen), 4/15 (transfers).

Admissions Contact Ms. Kathleen Tesar, Director of Student Affairs/ Admissions, The Colburn School of Performing Arts, CA. *Phone:* 213-687-8500. *Fax:* 213-621-2110. *E-mail:* ktesar@colburnschool.edu.

COLEMAN COLLEGE

La Mesa, California

- **Independent** comprehensive, founded 1963
- **Calendar** quarters
- **Degrees** certificates, associate, bachelor's, and master's
- **Suburban** 3-acre campus with easy access to San Diego
- **Coed,** 704 undergraduate students, 100% full-time, 26% women, 74% men
- **Moderately difficult** entrance level

Undergraduates 704 full-time. Students come from 19 states and territories, 1% are from out of state, 8% African American, 11% Asian American or Pacific Islander, 14% Hispanic American, 1% international.

Freshmen *Admission:* 395 enrolled.

Faculty *Total:* 93, 67% full-time.

Majors Business administration, management and operations related; computer and information sciences; computer graphics; computer systems networking and telecommunications; system administration.

Academic Programs *Special study options:* accelerated degree program, part-time degree program, services for LD students, summer session for credit.

Library Coleman College LaMesa Library with 66,800 titles, 69 serial subscriptions.

Computers on Campus 420 computers available on campus for general student use. A campuswide network can be accessed. Internet access available.

Student Life *Housing:* college housing not available. *Campus security:* 24-hour emergency response devices and patrols, late-night transport/escort service. *Student services:* personal/psychological counseling.

Costs (2004–05) *Tuition:* $15,960 full-time, $220 per unit part-time. *Required fees:* $100 full-time.

Applying *Options:* common application, deferred entrance. *Application fee:* $100. *Required:* high school transcript, interview. *Application deadline:* 8/1 (freshmen), rolling (transfers). *Notification:* continuous (freshmen), continuous (transfers).

Admissions Contact Admissions Department, Coleman College, 7380 Parkway Drive, La Mesa, CA 91942-1500. *Phone:* 619-465-3990. *Fax:* 619-463-0162. *E-mail:* admissions@coleman.edu.

COLUMBIA COLLEGE HOLLYWOOD

Tarzana, California

- **Independent** 4-year, founded 1952
- **Calendar** quarters
- **Degrees** associate and bachelor's
- **Urban** 1-acre campus
- **Coed,** 150 undergraduate students, 100% full-time, 31% women, 69% men
- **Minimally difficult** entrance level, 77% of applicants were admitted

Undergraduates 150 full-time. Students come from 30 other countries, 50% are from out of state, 9% African American, 5% Asian American or Pacific Islander, 14% Hispanic American, 0.7% Native American, 10% international, 23% transferred in. *Retention:* 83% of 2002 full-time freshmen returned.

Freshmen *Admission:* 87 applied, 67 admitted, 60 enrolled. *Average high school GPA:* 3.3.

Faculty *Total:* 27. *Student/faculty ratio:* 5:1.

Majors Broadcast journalism; cinematography and film/video production; film/cinema studies; radio and television; telecommunications.

Academic Programs *Special study options:* accelerated degree program, adult/continuing education programs, part-time degree program, summer session for credit.

Library Joseph E. Blath Memorial Library with 5,500 titles, 23 serial subscriptions, 220 audiovisual materials, an OPAC.

Computers on Campus 12 computers available on campus for general student use. Internet access, at least one staffed computer lab available.

Student Life *Housing:* college housing not available. *Student services:* personal/psychological counseling.

Standardized Tests *Recommended:* SAT I (for admission).

Costs (2003–04) *Tuition:* $11,400 full-time, $4000 per term part-time. Full-time tuition and fees vary according to course level, course load, and program. *Required fees:* $225 full-time. *Payment plans:* installment, deferred payment.

Financial Aid Of all full-time matriculated undergraduates who enrolled in 2003, 103 applied for aid, 103 were judged to have need. 3 Federal Work-Study jobs (averaging $2023). *Average financial aid package:* $3827. *Average need-based gift aid:* $3745. *Average indebtedness upon graduation:* $35,125.

Applying *Options:* deferred entrance. *Application fee:* $50. *Required:* essay or personal statement, high school transcript, minimum 2.0 GPA, 2 letters of recommendation, interview. *Application deadline:* rolling (freshmen). *Notification:* continuous until 9/1 (freshmen), continuous (transfers).

Admissions Contact Mr. Adam McDaniel, Admissions and Marketing Coordinator, Columbia College Hollywood, 18618 Oxnard Street, Tarzana, CA 91356. *Phone:* 818-345-8414 Ext. 203. *Toll-free phone:* 800-785-0585 Ext. 105. *Fax:* 818-345-9053. *E-mail:* admissions@columbiacollege.edu.

■ *See page 1476 for a narrative description.*

CONCORDIA UNIVERSITY

Irvine, California

- **Independent** comprehensive, founded 1972, affiliated with Lutheran Church–Missouri Synod, part of The Ten-campus Concordia University System
- **Calendar** semesters
- **Degrees** associate, bachelor's, master's, and postbachelor's certificates (associate's degree is only offered for international students)
- **Suburban** 70-acre campus with easy access to Los Angeles
- **Endowment** $7.5 million
- **Coed,** 1,337 undergraduate students, 92% full-time, 65% women, 35% men
- **Moderately difficult** entrance level, 27% of applicants were admitted

Undergraduates 1,230 full-time, 107 part-time. Students come from 36 states and territories, 7 other countries, 15% are from out of state, 3% African American, 4% Asian American or Pacific Islander, 11% Hispanic American, 0.9% Native American, 2% international, 10% transferred in, 69% live on campus. *Retention:* 74% of 2002 full-time freshmen returned.

Freshmen *Admission:* 986 applied, 270 admitted, 261 enrolled. *Average high school GPA:* 3.60. *Test scores:* SAT verbal scores over 500: 66%; SAT math scores over 500: 68%; ACT scores over 18: 82%; SAT verbal scores over 600: 23%; SAT math scores over 600: 22%; ACT scores over 24: 35%; SAT verbal scores over 700: 3%; SAT math scores over 700: 3%; ACT scores over 30: 7%.

Faculty *Total:* 168, 44% full-time, 42% with terminal degrees. *Student/faculty ratio:* 15:1.

Concordia University (continued)

Majors Art; behavioral sciences; biology/biological sciences; business administration and management; chemistry; communication/speech communication and rhetoric; divinity/ministry; dramatic/theatre arts; English; history; humanities; information technology; kinesiology and exercise science; liberal arts and sciences/liberal studies; mathematics; music; psychology; religious education; social sciences related; theology.

Academic Programs *Special study options:* accelerated degree program, adult/continuing education programs, advanced placement credit, double majors, English as a second language, honors programs, independent study, internships, part-time degree program, student-designed majors, summer session for credit.

Library Concordia University Library with 94,250 titles, 377 serial subscriptions, 2,079 audiovisual materials, an OPAC, a Web page.

Computers on Campus 42 computers available on campus for general student use. A campuswide network can be accessed from student residence rooms and from off campus. Internet access, at least one staffed computer lab available.

Student Life *Housing:* on-campus residence required through junior year. *Options:* men-only, women-only. Campus housing is university owned. Freshman campus housing is guaranteed. *Activities and organizations:* drama/theater group, student-run newspaper, radio station, choral group, Student Senate, Spiritual Life Board, Student Activities Committee, intramurals, Outreach. *Campus security:* 24-hour patrols, student patrols, late-night transport/escort service, lighted walkways. *Student services:* health clinic, personal/psychological counseling.

Athletics Member NAIA. *Intercollegiate sports:* baseball M(s), basketball M(s)/W(s), cross-country running M(s)/W(s), soccer M(s)/W(s), softball W(s), volleyball W(s). *Intramural sports:* basketball M/W, bowling M/W, football M/W, rock climbing M/W, soccer M/W, softball M/W, table tennis M/W, track and field M/W, volleyball M/W.

Standardized Tests *Required:* SAT I or ACT (for admission).

Costs (2004–05) *Comprehensive fee:* $25,470 includes full-time tuition ($18,800) and room and board ($6670). Part-time tuition: $565 per unit. *College room only:* $4000. Room and board charges vary according to board plan. *Payment plan:* installment. *Waivers:* employees or children of employees.

Financial Aid Of all full-time matriculated undergraduates who enrolled in 2003, 1,101 applied for aid, 830 were judged to have need, 295 had their need fully met. 33 Federal Work-Study jobs (averaging $1910). 289 state and other part-time jobs (averaging $1782). In 2003, 179 non-need-based awards were made. *Average percent of need met:* 86%. *Average financial aid package:* $13,979. *Average need-based loan:* $3817. *Average need-based gift aid:* $7327. *Average non-need-based aid:* $5397. *Average indebtedness upon graduation:* $16,500. *Financial aid deadline:* 4/1.

Applying *Options:* common application, electronic application, deferred entrance. *Application fee:* $40. *Required:* high school transcript, 2 letters of recommendation. *Recommended:* minimum 2.8 GPA, interview. *Application deadline:* rolling (freshmen), rolling (transfers). *Notification:* continuous until 4/1 (freshmen), continuous until 4/1 (transfers).

Admissions Contact Ms. Lori McDonald, Executive Director of Enrollment Services, Concordia University, 1530 Concordia West, Irvine, CA 92612-3299. *Phone:* 949-854-8002 Ext. 1170. *Toll-free phone:* 800-229-1200. *Fax:* 949-854-6894. *E-mail:* admission@cui.edu.

DESIGN INSTITUTE OF SAN DIEGO
San Diego, California

- **Proprietary** 4-year, founded 1977
- **Calendar** semesters
- **Degree** bachelor's
- **Urban** campus
- **Coed,** 450 undergraduate students
- **Noncompetitive** entrance level

Undergraduates Students come from 10 states and territories, 15 other countries. *Retention:* 87% of 2002 full-time freshmen returned.

Freshmen *Average high school GPA:* 2.5.

Faculty *Total:* 50.

Majors Interior design.

Academic Programs *Special study options:* internships, part-time degree program, study abroad.

Library 5,000 titles, 90 serial subscriptions, an OPAC.

Computers on Campus 50 computers available on campus for general student use. At least one staffed computer lab available.

Student Life *Housing:* college housing not available. *Activities and organizations:* American Society of Interior Designers, International Interior Designers Association, Illuminating Electrical Society.

Costs (2004–05) *Tuition:* $11,800 full-time.

Applying *Application fee:* $25. *Required:* high school transcript, minimum 2.0 GPA. *Recommended:* interview. *Application deadline:* rolling (freshmen), rolling (transfers).

Admissions Contact Ms. Paula Parrish, Director of Admissions, Design Institute of San Diego, 8555 Commerce Avenue, San Diego, CA 92121. *Phone:* 858-566-1200. *Toll-free phone:* 800-619-4337. *Fax:* 858-566-2711. *E-mail:* admissions@disd.edu.

■ *See page 1532 for a narrative description.*

DEVRY UNIVERSITY
Elk Grove, California

Admissions Contact Sacramento Center, 2218 Kausen Drive, Elk Grove, CA 95758. *Toll-free phone:* 866-573-3879.

DEVRY UNIVERSITY
Fremont, California

- **Proprietary** comprehensive, founded 1998, part of DeVry University
- **Calendar** semesters
- **Degrees** associate, bachelor's, master's, and postbachelor's certificates
- **Suburban** 17-acre campus with easy access to San Francisco
- **Coed**
- **Minimally difficult** entrance level

Faculty *Student/faculty ratio:* 29:1.

Student Life *Campus security:* 24-hour emergency response devices and patrols, late-night transport/escort service, lighted pathways/sidewalks.

Standardized Tests *Recommended:* SAT I, ACT or CPT.

Costs (2003–04) *Tuition:* $11,100 full-time, $395 per credit hour part-time. Full-time tuition and fees vary according to course load. Part-time tuition and fees vary according to course load. *Required fees:* $165 full-time. *Payment plans:* installment, deferred payment.

Financial Aid Of all full-time matriculated undergraduates who enrolled in 2002, 1,580 applied for aid, 1,487 were judged to have need, 27 had their need fully met. In 2002, 125. *Average percent of need met:* 44. *Average financial aid package:* $10,351. *Average need-based loan:* $6394. *Average need-based gift aid:* $6863. *Average non-need-based aid:* $12,699.

Applying *Options:* electronic application, deferred entrance. *Application fee:* $50. *Required:* high school transcript, interview.

Admissions Contact Mr. Bruce Williams, New Student Coordinator, DeVry University, 6600 Dumbarton Circle, Fremont, CA 94555-3615. *Phone:* 510-574-1111. *Toll-free phone:* 888-201-9941. *Fax:* 510-742-0868.

DEVRY UNIVERSITY
Irvine, California

Admissions Contact 3333 Michelson Drive, Suite 420, Irvine, CA 92612-1682.

DEVRY UNIVERSITY
Long Beach, California

- **Proprietary** comprehensive, founded 1984, part of DeVry University
- **Calendar** semesters
- **Degrees** associate, bachelor's, master's, and postbachelor's certificates
- **Urban** 23-acre campus with easy access to Los Angeles
- **Coed**
- **Minimally difficult** entrance level

Student Life *Campus security:* 24-hour emergency response devices and patrols, late-night transport/escort service, motion detectors, closed hours.

Standardized Tests *Recommended:* SAT I, ACT or CPT.

Costs (2003–04) *Tuition:* $10,590 full-time, $370 per credit hour part-time. Full-time tuition and fees vary according to course load. Part-time tuition and fees vary according to course load. *Required fees:* $165 full-time. *Payment plans:* installment, deferred payment.

Financial Aid Of all full-time matriculated undergraduates who enrolled in 2003, 1,572 applied for aid, 1,498 were judged to have need, 46 had their need fully met. In 2003, 106. *Average percent of need met:* 43. *Average financial aid package:* $10,063. *Average need-based loan:* $5999. *Average need-based gift aid:* $5911. *Average non-need-based aid:* $13,231.

Applying *Options:* electronic application, deferred entrance. *Application fee:* $50. *Required:* high school transcript, interview.

Admissions Contact Ms. Lisa Flores, New Student Coordinator, DeVry University, 3880 Kilroy Airport Way, Long Beach, CA 90806-2449. *Phone:* 562-427-0861. *Toll-free phone:* 800-597-0444. *Fax:* 562-997-5371. *E-mail:* cblas@socal.devry.edu.

DeVry University
Pomona, California

- **Proprietary** comprehensive, founded 1983, part of DeVry University
- **Calendar** semesters
- **Degrees** associate, bachelor's, master's, and postbachelor's certificates
- **Urban** 15-acre campus with easy access to Los Angeles
- **Coed**
- **Minimally difficult** entrance level

Student Life *Campus security:* 24-hour emergency response devices, late-night transport/escort service.

Standardized Tests *Recommended:* SAT I, ACT or CPT.

Costs (2003–04) *Tuition:* $10,590 full-time, $370 per credit hour part-time. Full-time tuition and fees vary according to course load. Part-time tuition and fees vary according to course load. *Required fees:* $165 full-time. *Payment plans:* installment, deferred payment.

Financial Aid Of all full-time matriculated undergraduates who enrolled in 2002, 1,866 applied for aid, 1,791 were judged to have need, 54 had their need fully met. In 2002, 85. *Average percent of need met:* 43. *Average financial aid package:* $9829. *Average need-based loan:* $5977. *Average need-based gift aid:* $5797. *Average non-need-based aid:* $12,336.

Applying *Options:* electronic application, deferred entrance. *Application fee:* $50. *Required:* high school transcript, interview.

Admissions Contact Ms. Melanie Guerra, New Student Coordinator, DeVry University, 901 Corporate Center Drive, University Center, Pomona, CA 91768-2642. *Phone:* 909-622-8866. *Toll-free phone:* 800-882-7536. *Fax:* 909-868-4165.

DeVry University
San Diego, California

Admissions Contact 2655 Camino Del Rio North, Suite 201, San Diego, CA 92108-1633.

DeVry University
San Francisco, California

Admissions Contact 455 Market Street, Suite 1650, San Francisco, CA 94105-2472.

DeVry University
West Hills, California

- **Proprietary** comprehensive, founded 1999, part of DeVry University
- **Calendar** semesters
- **Degrees** associate, bachelor's, master's, and postbachelor's certificates
- **Suburban** 20-acre campus
- **Coed**
- **Minimally difficult** entrance level

Faculty *Student/faculty ratio:* 15:1.

Student Life *Campus security:* 24-hour emergency response devices, late-night transport/escort service, lighted pathways/sidewalks.

Standardized Tests *Recommended:* SAT I, ACT or CPT.

Costs (2003–04) *Tuition:* $10,590 full-time, $370 per credit hour part-time. Full-time tuition and fees vary according to course load. Part-time tuition and fees vary according to course load. *Required fees:* $165 full-time. *Payment plans:* installment, deferred payment.

Financial Aid Of all full-time matriculated undergraduates who enrolled in 2002, 759 applied for aid, 711 were judged to have need, 20 had their need fully met. In 2002, 57. *Average percent of need met:* 42. *Average financial aid package:* $9557. *Average need-based loan:* $5887. *Average need-based gift aid:* $6070. *Average non-need-based aid:* $11,795.

Applying *Options:* electronic application, deferred entrance. *Application fee:* $50. *Required:* high school transcript, interview.

Admissions Contact Ms. Denise Barba, Acting Director of Admissions, DeVry University, 22801 Roscoe Boulevard, West Hills, CA 91304-3200. *Phone:* 818-932-3001. *Toll-free phone:* 888-610-0800. *Fax:* 909-868-4165. *E-mail:* admissions@devry.edu.

Dominican School of Philosophy and Theology
Berkeley, California

- **Independent Roman Catholic** upper-level, founded 1932
- **Calendar** semesters
- **Degrees** bachelor's, master's, and first professional
- **Urban** campus with easy access to San Francisco
- **Endowment** $2.0 million
- **Coed**
- **Moderately difficult** entrance level

Faculty *Student/faculty ratio:* 5:1.

Student Life *Campus security:* late-night transport/escort service.

Costs (2003–04) *Tuition:* $9456 full-time, $394 per credit part-time. Full-time tuition and fees vary according to program. Part-time tuition and fees vary according to program. *Required fees:* $50 full-time, $50 per year part-time. *Room only:* $7081. Room and board charges vary according to housing facility.

Applying *Options:* electronic application, early admission, deferred entrance. *Application fee:* $30.

Admissions Contact Ms. Susan McGinnis Hardie, Director of Admissions, Dominican School of Philosophy and Theology, 2401 Ridge Road, Berkeley, CA 94709-1295. *Phone:* 510-883-2073. *Fax:* 510-849-1372. *E-mail:* admissions@dspt.edu.

Dominican University of California
San Rafael, California

- **Independent** comprehensive, founded 1890, affiliated with Roman Catholic Church
- **Calendar** semesters
- **Degrees** bachelor's, master's, and postbachelor's certificates
- **Suburban** 80-acre campus with easy access to San Francisco
- **Endowment** $9.8 million
- **Coed,** 1,124 undergraduate students, 76% full-time, 75% women, 25% men
- **Moderately difficult** entrance level, 55% of applicants were admitted

Undergraduates 855 full-time, 269 part-time. Students come from 19 states and territories, 21 other countries, 6% are from out of state, 9% African American, 13% Asian American or Pacific Islander, 13% Hispanic American, 1% Native American, 4% international, 14% transferred in, 42% live on campus. *Retention:* 70% of 2002 full-time freshmen returned.

Freshmen *Admission:* 1,792 applied, 980 admitted, 245 enrolled. *Average high school GPA:* 3.30. *Test scores:* SAT verbal scores over 500: 64%; SAT math scores over 500: 57%; SAT verbal scores over 600: 20%; SAT math scores over 600: 17%; SAT verbal scores over 700: 4%; SAT math scores over 700: 2%.

Faculty *Total:* 228, 30% full-time, 45% with terminal degrees. *Student/faculty ratio:* 10:1.

Majors Art; art history, criticism and conservation; biology/biological sciences; business administration and management; communication/speech communication and rhetoric; computer graphics; creative writing; e-commerce; education related; English; environmental studies; foreign languages and literatures; history; humanities; human resources management; international business/trade/commerce; international/global studies; liberal arts and sciences/liberal studies; music; music performance; nursing (registered nurse training); occupational therapy; political science and government; psychology; religious studies; visual and performing arts related.

Academic Programs *Special study options:* academic remediation for entering students, adult/continuing education programs, advanced placement credit, double majors, English as a second language, honors programs, independent study, internships, off-campus study, part-time degree program, services for LD students, student-designed majors, study abroad, summer session for credit.

Library Archbishop Alemany Library plus 1 other with 94,800 titles, 400 serial subscriptions, 775 audiovisual materials, an OPAC, a Web page.

Computers on Campus 52 computers available on campus for general student use. A campuswide network can be accessed from student residence rooms and from off campus. Internet access, at least one staffed computer lab available.

Student Life *Housing options:* coed. Campus housing is university owned. Freshman applicants given priority for college housing. *Activities and organizations:* drama/theater group, student-run newspaper, radio station, choral group, Students Promoting Dominican Islands, Perceptions, Science Club, Filipino Club, Scripture Union. *Campus security:* 24-hour emergency response devices and patrols, late-night transport/escort service, controlled dormitory access. *Student services:* health clinic, personal/psychological counseling.

Athletics Member NAIA. *Intercollegiate sports:* basketball M(s)/W(s), cheerleading W, soccer M(s)/W(s), softball W(s), tennis M(s)/W(s), volleyball W(s).

Dominican University of California (continued)

Standardized Tests *Required:* SAT I or ACT (for admission). *Recommended:* SAT II: Subject Tests (for admission).

Costs (2003–04) *Comprehensive fee:* $32,070 includes full-time tuition ($22,250), mandatory fees ($400), and room and board ($9420). Full-time tuition and fees vary according to class time, degree level, location, and program. Part-time tuition: $927 per unit. Part-time tuition and fees vary according to class time, degree level, location, and program. *Required fees:* $200 per term part-time. *Room and board:* Room and board charges vary according to board plan. *Payment plan:* installment. *Waivers:* senior citizens and employees or children of employees.

Financial Aid Of all full-time matriculated undergraduates who enrolled in 2003, 698 applied for aid, 622 were judged to have need, 144 had their need fully met. 335 Federal Work-Study jobs (averaging $2478). 53 state and other part-time jobs (averaging $4612). In 2003, 174 non-need-based awards were made. *Average percent of need met:* 23%. *Average financial aid package:* $19,762. *Average need-based loan:* $4159. *Average need-based gift aid:* $14,879. *Average non-need-based aid:* $9765. *Average indebtedness upon graduation:* $3160.

Applying *Options:* common application, electronic application, early admission, deferred entrance. *Application fee:* $40. *Required:* essay or personal statement, high school transcript, minimum 2.5 GPA, 1 letter of recommendation. *Required for some:* interview. *Application deadline:* 8/1 (freshmen), rolling (transfers). *Notification:* continuous until 9/1 (freshmen), continuous (transfers).

Admissions Contact Mr. Art Criss, Director of Undergraduate Admissions, Dominican University of California, 50 Acacia Avenue, San Rafael, CA 94901-2298. *Phone:* 415-257-1376. *Toll-free phone:* 888-323-6763. *Fax:* 415-385-3214. *E-mail:* enroll@dominican.edu.

■ *See page 1540 for a narrative description.*

D-Q University
Davis, California

Admissions Contact Ms. Irma Hernandez, Director of Admissions and Records, D-Q University, PO Box 409, Davis, CA 95617-0409. *Phone:* 530-758-0470 Ext. 1016. *Fax:* 530-758-4891.

Emmanuel Bible College
Pasadena, California

Admissions Contact Mr. Yeghia Babikian, President, Emmanuel Bible College, 1605 East Elizabeth Street, 1536 East Howard Street, Pasadena, CA 91104. *Phone:* 626-791-2575. *Fax:* 626-398-2424.

Fresno Pacific University
Fresno, California

- **Independent** comprehensive, founded 1944, affiliated with Mennonite Brethren Church
- **Calendar** semesters
- **Degrees** associate, bachelor's, and master's
- **Suburban** 42-acre campus
- **Endowment** $3.7 million
- **Coed,** 1,380 undergraduate students, 74% full-time, 61% women, 39% men
- **Moderately difficult** entrance level, 62% of applicants were admitted

Undergraduates 1,020 full-time, 360 part-time. Students come from 20 states and territories, 14 other countries, 3% are from out of state, 4% African American, 2% Asian American or Pacific Islander, 22% Hispanic American, 1% Native American, 3% international, 21% transferred in, 56% live on campus. *Retention:* 86% of 2002 full-time freshmen returned.

Freshmen *Admission:* 580 applied, 360 admitted, 191 enrolled. *Average high school GPA:* 3.71. *Test scores:* SAT verbal scores over 500: 57%; SAT math scores over 500: 50%; ACT scores over 18: 76%; SAT verbal scores over 600: 17%; SAT math scores over 600: 18%; ACT scores over 24: 18%; SAT verbal scores over 700: 2%; SAT math scores over 700: 2%.

Faculty *Total:* 92, 83% full-time. *Student/faculty ratio:* 16:1.

Majors Accounting; applied mathematics; athletic training; biblical studies; bilingual and multilingual education; biology/biological sciences; business administration and management; chemistry; computer and information sciences; developmental and child psychology; divinity/ministry; education; elementary education; English; finance; history; humanities; international business/trade/commerce; liberal arts and sciences/liberal studies; literature; marketing/marketing management; mass communication/media; mathematics; music; music teacher education; natural sciences; non-profit management; pastoral studies/counseling; physical education teaching and coaching; political science and government; pre-law studies; pre-medical studies; psychology; religious/sacred music; religious studies; science teacher education; secondary education; social sciences; social work; sociology; Spanish; sport and fitness administration.

Academic Programs *Special study options:* accelerated degree program, adult/continuing education programs, advanced placement credit, cooperative education, distance learning, double majors, English as a second language, independent study, internships, off-campus study, part-time degree program, services for LD students, student-designed majors, study abroad, summer session for credit.

Library Hiebert Library with 158,000 titles, 3,064 serial subscriptions, 9,400 audiovisual materials, an OPAC, a Web page.

Computers on Campus 68 computers available on campus for general student use. A campuswide network can be accessed from student residence rooms and from off campus.

Student Life *Housing:* on-campus residence required through sophomore year. *Options:* men-only, women-only. Campus housing is university owned. Freshman campus housing is guaranteed. *Activities and organizations:* drama/theater group, student-run newspaper, choral group, international club, Kid's Klub, Amigos Unidos, Slavic club, women's soccer club. *Campus security:* 24-hour emergency response devices and patrols, student patrols, late-night transport/escort service, controlled dormitory access, 24-hour monitored closed-circuit security cameras. *Student services:* health clinic, personal/psychological counseling.

Athletics Member NAIA. *Intercollegiate sports:* baseball M(c), basketball M(s)/W(s), cheerleading M(c)/W(c), cross-country running M(s)/W(s), soccer M(s)/W(s), track and field M(s)/W(s), volleyball M(c)/W(s). *Intramural sports:* basketball M/W, bowling M/W, football M/W, soccer M/W, volleyball M/W.

Standardized Tests *Required:* SAT I or ACT (for admission).

Costs (2003–04) *Comprehensive fee:* $22,462 includes full-time tuition ($17,370), mandatory fees ($222), and room and board ($4870). Full-time tuition and fees vary according to program. Part-time tuition: $615 per unit. Part-time tuition and fees vary according to program. *Required fees:* $72 per term part-time. *College room only:* $2130. Room and board charges vary according to board plan and housing facility. *Payment plan:* installment. *Waivers:* senior citizens and employees or children of employees.

Financial Aid Of all full-time matriculated undergraduates who enrolled in 2003, 854 applied for aid, 779 were judged to have need, 143 had their need fully met. 443 Federal Work-Study jobs (averaging $2728). In 2003, 59 non-need-based awards were made. *Average percent of need met:* 86%. *Average financial aid package:* $13,688. *Average need-based loan:* $3119. *Average need-based gift aid:* $8294. *Average non-need-based aid:* $2150. *Average indebtedness upon graduation:* $13,164.

Applying *Options:* electronic application, early admission, deferred entrance. *Application fee:* $40. *Required:* essay or personal statement, high school transcript, 1 letter of recommendation. *Recommended:* minimum 3.10 GPA. *Application deadline:* rolling (freshmen), rolling (transfers). *Notification:* continuous until 7/31 (freshmen), continuous until 7/31 (transfers).

Admissions Contact Ms. Suzana Dobric, Associate Director of Undergraduate Admissions, Fresno Pacific University, 1717 South Chestnut Avenue, Fresno, CA 93702-4709. *Phone:* 559-453-2233. *Toll-free phone:* 800-660-6089. *Fax:* 559-453-2007. *E-mail:* ugadmis@fresno.edu.

■ *See page 1656 for a narrative description.*

Golden Gate University
San Francisco, California

- **Independent** university, founded 1853
- **Calendar** trimesters
- **Degrees** certificates, associate, bachelor's, master's, doctoral, and first professional
- **Urban** campus
- **Endowment** $16.6 million
- **Coed,** 686 undergraduate students, 22% full-time, 53% women, 47% men
- **Moderately difficult** entrance level, 100% of applicants were admitted

Undergraduates 148 full-time, 538 part-time. Students come from 61 other countries, 5% are from out of state, 7% African American, 16% Asian American or Pacific Islander, 8% Hispanic American, 12% international, 18% transferred in. *Retention:* 80% of 2002 full-time freshmen returned.

Freshmen *Admission:* 2 applied, 2 admitted, 2 enrolled.

Faculty *Total:* 662, 5% full-time, 19% with terminal degrees. *Student/faculty ratio:* 14:1.

Majors Accounting; business administration and management; computer/information technology services administration related; finance; human resources management; information science/studies; international business/trade/commerce; marketing/marketing management; operations management; telecommunications.

Academic Programs *Special study options:* academic remediation for entering students, accelerated degree program, adult/continuing education programs, advanced placement credit, cooperative education, distance learning, English as a second language, internships, off-campus study, part-time degree program, summer session for credit.

Library Golden Gate University Library plus 1 other with 79,204 titles, 3,335 serial subscriptions, an OPAC.

Computers on Campus 52 computers available on campus for general student use. A campuswide network can be accessed. Internet access, at least one staffed computer lab available.

Student Life *Housing:* college housing not available. *Activities and organizations:* student-run newspaper, American Marketing Association, Korean Student Association, Japanese Student Association, Thai Student Association, computing society. *Campus security:* late-night transport/escort service. *Student services:* personal/psychological counseling.

Athletics *Intramural sports:* cross-country running M(c)/W(c), racquetball M(c)/W(c), tennis M(c)/W(c).

Costs (2003–04) *Tuition:* $9984 full-time, $1248 per course part-time. Full-time tuition and fees vary according to course load, degree level, and program. Part-time tuition and fees vary according to course load and program.

Financial Aid Of all full-time matriculated undergraduates who enrolled in 2003, 136 applied for aid, 98 were judged to have need, 26 had their need fully met. 2 Federal Work-Study jobs (averaging $5000). In 2003, 50 non-need-based awards were made. *Average percent of need met:* 27%. *Average financial aid package:* $2931. *Average need-based loan:* $2931. *Average need-based gift aid:* $1000. *Average non-need-based aid:* $2000. *Average indebtedness upon graduation:* $17,522.

Applying *Options:* common application, electronic application, deferred entrance. *Application fee:* $55. *Required:* high school transcript, minimum 2.0 GPA. *Required for some:* minimum 3.2 GPA, interview. *Recommended:* essay or personal statement, minimum 3.0 GPA. *Application deadlines:* 6/1 (freshmen), 6/1 (transfers). *Notification:* continuous (freshmen), continuous (transfers).

Admissions Contact Golden Gate University, 536 Mission Street, San Francisco, CA 94105-2968. *Phone:* 415-442-7800. *Toll-free phone:* 800-448-4968. *Fax:* 415-442-7807. *E-mail:* info@ggu.edu.

HARVEY MUDD COLLEGE
Claremont, California

- **Independent** 4-year, founded 1955, part of The Claremont Colleges Consortium
- **Calendar** semesters
- **Degrees** bachelor's and master's
- **Suburban** 33-acre campus with easy access to Los Angeles
- **Endowment** $163.2 million
- **Coed,** 704 undergraduate students, 99% full-time, 32% women, 68% men
- **Most difficult** entrance level, 40% of applicants were admitted

Undergraduates 700 full-time, 4 part-time. Students come from 47 states and territories, 14 other countries, 57% are from out of state, 0.4% African American, 18% Asian American or Pacific Islander, 5% Hispanic American, 0.4% Native American, 3% international, 0.9% transferred in, 96% live on campus. *Retention:* 95% of 2002 full-time freshmen returned.

Freshmen *Admission:* 1,773 applied, 709 admitted, 191 enrolled. *Average high school GPA:* 4.00. *Test scores:* SAT verbal scores over 500: 100%; SAT math scores over 500: 100%; SAT verbal scores over 600: 91%; SAT math scores over 600: 99%; SAT verbal scores over 700: 57%; SAT math scores over 700: 86%.

Faculty *Total:* 91, 91% full-time, 99% with terminal degrees. *Student/faculty ratio:* 9:1.

Majors Biology/biological sciences; chemistry; computer science; engineering; mathematics; physics.

Academic Programs *Special study options:* advanced placement credit, double majors, internships, off-campus study, services for LD students, student-designed majors, study abroad. *ROTC:* Army (c), Air Force (b). *Unusual degree programs:* 3-2 management/engineering with Claremont McKenna College.

Library Honnold Library plus 1 other with 1.4 million titles, 4,321 serial subscriptions, 606 audiovisual materials, an OPAC, a Web page.

Computers on Campus 360 computers available on campus for general student use. A campuswide network can be accessed from student residence rooms and from off campus. Internet access, at least one staffed computer lab available. Computer purchase or lease plan available.

Student Life *Housing:* on-campus residence required for freshman year. *Options:* coed. Campus housing is university owned. Freshman campus housing is guaranteed. *Activities and organizations:* drama/theater group, student-run newspaper, radio station, choral group, Delta "H" Outdoor Club, Etc. Players—Drama Club, club sports, Jazz Orchestra, Society of Women Engineers. *Campus security:* 24-hour emergency response devices and patrols, late-night transport/escort service. *Student services:* health clinic, personal/psychological counseling, women's center.

Athletics Member NCAA. All Division III. *Intercollegiate sports:* baseball M, basketball M/W, cross-country running M/W, football M, golf M, lacrosse W, soccer M/W, softball W, swimming M/W, tennis M/W, track and field M/W, volleyball W, water polo M/W. *Intramural sports:* badminton M(c), fencing M(c)/W(c), football M/W, ice hockey M(c), rugby M(c)/W(c), sailing M(c)/W(c), soccer M/W, swimming M/W, table tennis M(c)/W(c), tennis M/W, ultimate Frisbee M(c)/W(c), volleyball M/W, water polo M.

Standardized Tests *Required:* SAT I (for admission), SAT II: Writing Test (for admission), SAT II Subject Test in Math 2C, third SAT II Subject Test (Math 1C is not accepted) (for admission).

Costs (2004–05) *Comprehensive fee:* $38,080 includes full-time tuition ($28,012), mandatory fees ($648), and room and board ($9420). *College room only:* $4790. Room and board charges vary according to board plan. *Payment plan:* installment. *Waivers:* employees or children of employees.

Financial Aid Of all full-time matriculated undergraduates who enrolled in 2003, 456 applied for aid, 391 were judged to have need, 391 had their need fully met. 272 Federal Work-Study jobs (averaging $1886). 10 state and other part-time jobs (averaging $2115). In 2003, 174 non-need-based awards were made. *Average percent of need met:* 100%. *Average financial aid package:* $22,740. *Average need-based loan:* $4500. *Average need-based gift aid:* $18,438. *Average non-need-based aid:* $6563. *Average indebtedness upon graduation:* $21,881. *Financial aid deadline:* 2/1.

Applying *Options:* common application, electronic application, early decision, deferred entrance. *Application fee:* $50. *Required:* essay or personal statement, high school transcript, 3 letters of recommendation. *Recommended:* interview. *Application deadlines:* 1/15 (freshmen), 4/1 (transfers). *Early decision:* 11/15. *Notification:* 4/1 (freshmen), 12/15 (early decision), 5/1 (transfers).

Admissions Contact Mr. Deren Finks, Vice President and Dean of Admissions and Financial Aid, Harvey Mudd College, 301 East 12th Street, Claremont, CA 91711. *Phone:* 909-621-8011. *Fax:* 909-607-7046. *E-mail:* admission@hmc.edu.

■ *See page 1720 for a narrative description.*

HOLY NAMES COLLEGE
Oakland, California

- **Independent Roman Catholic** comprehensive, founded 1868
- **Calendar** semesters
- **Degrees** bachelor's, master's, and postbachelor's certificates
- **Urban** 60-acre campus with easy access to San Francisco
- **Endowment** $6.3 million
- **Coed, primarily women,** 593 undergraduate students, 66% full-time, 78% women, 22% men
- **Moderately difficult** entrance level, 62% of applicants were admitted

Undergraduates 391 full-time, 202 part-time. Students come from 15 states and territories, 11 other countries, 4% are from out of state, 32% African American, 6% Asian American or Pacific Islander, 16% Hispanic American, 1% Native American, 3% international, 18% transferred in, 27% live on campus. *Retention:* 62% of 2002 full-time freshmen returned.

Freshmen *Admission:* 211 applied, 131 admitted, 58 enrolled. *Average high school GPA:* 3.22. *Test scores:* SAT verbal scores over 500: 50%; SAT math scores over 500: 50%; ACT scores over 18: 50%; SAT verbal scores over 600: 8%; SAT math scores over 600: 8%.

Faculty *Total:* 127, 24% full-time, 55% with terminal degrees. *Student/faculty ratio:* 12:1.

Majors Biological and biomedical sciences related; biology/biological sciences; business administration and management; business/corporate communications; computer/information technology services administration related; computer software and media applications related; English; history; humanities; human resources management; human services; international relations and affairs; liberal arts and sciences/liberal studies; marketing/marketing management; music; music pedagogy; music performance; nursing (registered nurse training); nursing science; philosophy; philosophy and religious studies related; physiological psychology/psychobiology; psychology; religious studies; sociology; Spanish.

Academic Programs *Special study options:* academic remediation for entering students, accelerated degree program, adult/continuing education programs, advanced placement credit, distance learning, double majors, English as a second language, honors programs, independent study, internships, off-campus study, part-time degree program, services for LD students, student-designed majors, study abroad, summer session for credit. *ROTC:* Army (c), Air Force (c).

Library Cushing Library with 116,031 titles, 200 serial subscriptions, 4,378 audiovisual materials, a Web page.

Holy Names College (continued)

Computers on Campus 69 computers available on campus for general student use. A campuswide network can be accessed from student residence rooms and from off campus. Internet access, at least one staffed computer lab available.

Student Life *Housing options:* coed, women-only. Campus housing is university owned. Freshman campus housing is guaranteed. *Activities and organizations:* drama/theater group, choral group, drama club, Latinos Unidos, Black Student Union, biology club, hiking club. *Campus security:* 24-hour emergency response devices, late-night transport/escort service, controlled dormitory access, electronically operated main gate. *Student services:* personal/psychological counseling.

Athletics Member NAIA. *Intercollegiate sports:* basketball M(s)/W(s), cross-country running M(s)/W(s), golf M(s), soccer M(s)/W(s), volleyball W(s).

Standardized Tests *Required:* SAT I or ACT (for admission).

Costs (2004–05) *Comprehensive fee:* $28,780 includes full-time tuition ($20,770), mandatory fees ($210), and room and board ($7800). Full-time tuition and fees vary according to course load. Part-time tuition: $690 per unit. *Required fees:* $105 per term part-time. *College room only:* $4000. Room and board charges vary according to board plan. *Payment plan:* installment. *Waivers:* employees or children of employees.

Financial Aid Of all full-time matriculated undergraduates who enrolled in 2003, 283 applied for aid, 283 were judged to have need, 36 had their need fully met. 64 Federal Work-Study jobs (averaging $1795). In 2003, 2 non-need-based awards were made. *Average percent of need met:* 72%. *Average financial aid package:* $22,883. *Average need-based loan:* $4015. *Average need-based gift aid:* $9796. *Average non-need-based aid:* $3000. *Average indebtedness upon graduation:* $19,000.

Applying *Options:* common application, electronic application, deferred entrance. *Application fee:* $35. *Required:* essay or personal statement, high school transcript, 1 letter of recommendation. *Required for some:* interview. *Application deadlines:* 8/1 (freshmen), 8/1 (transfers). *Notification:* continuous (freshmen), continuous (transfers).

Admissions Contact Mr. Jeffrey D. Miller, Vice President for Enrollment Management, Holy Names College, 3200 Mountain Boulevard, Oakland, CA 94619. *Phone:* 510-436-1351. *Toll-free phone:* 800-430-1321. *Fax:* 510-436-1325. *E-mail:* admissions@admin.hnc.edu.

HOPE INTERNATIONAL UNIVERSITY

Fullerton, California

- **Independent** comprehensive, founded 1928, affiliated with Christian Churches and Churches of Christ
- **Calendar** 4-1-4
- **Degrees** certificates, associate, bachelor's, and master's
- **Suburban** 16-acre campus with easy access to Los Angeles
- **Endowment** $2.1 million
- **Coed**
- **Moderately difficult** entrance level

Faculty *Student/faculty ratio:* 15:1.

Student Life *Campus security:* 24-hour emergency response devices, student patrols.

Standardized Tests *Required:* SAT I or ACT (for admission).

Costs (2003–04) *Comprehensive fee:* $21,074 includes full-time tuition ($14,900), mandatory fees ($300), and room and board ($5874). *College room only:* $3098.

Financial Aid Of all full-time matriculated undergraduates who enrolled in 2003, 540 applied for aid, 488 were judged to have need, 73 had their need fully met. 62 Federal Work-Study jobs (averaging $2000). In 2003, 93. *Average percent of need met:* 60. *Average financial aid package:* $10,042. *Average need-based loan:* $3925. *Average need-based gift aid:* $7998. *Average non-need-based aid:* $10,583. *Average indebtedness upon graduation:* $18,045.

Applying *Options:* early admission, deferred entrance. *Application fee:* $20. *Required:* essay or personal statement, high school transcript, minimum 2.5 GPA, 2 letters of recommendation. *Required for some:* interview.

Admissions Contact Ms. Midge Madden, Office Manager, Hope International University, 2500 East Nutwood Avenue, Fullerton, CA 92831-3138. *Phone:* 714-879-3901 Ext. 2235. *Toll-free phone:* 800-762-1294. *Fax:* 714-526-0231. *E-mail:* mfmadden@hiu.edu.

HUMBOLDT STATE UNIVERSITY

Arcata, California

- **State-supported** comprehensive, founded 1913, part of California State University System
- **Calendar** semesters
- **Degrees** certificates, diplomas, bachelor's, and master's
- **Rural** 161-acre campus
- **Endowment** $10.2 million
- **Coed,** 6,682 undergraduate students, 89% full-time, 55% women, 45% men
- **Moderately difficult** entrance level, 67% of applicants were admitted

Undergraduates 5,947 full-time, 735 part-time. Students come from 50 states and territories, 24 other countries, 4% are from out of state, 12% transferred in, 18% live on campus. *Retention:* 72% of 2002 full-time freshmen returned.

Freshmen *Admission:* 5,521 applied, 3,677 admitted, 861 enrolled. *Average high school GPA:* 3.18. *Test scores:* SAT verbal scores over 500: 65%; SAT math scores over 500: 66%; ACT scores over 18: 79%; SAT verbal scores over 600: 26%; SAT math scores over 600: 21%; ACT scores over 24: 32%; SAT verbal scores over 700: 3%; SAT math scores over 700: 2%; ACT scores over 30: 3%.

Faculty *Total:* 489, 59% full-time, 56% with terminal degrees. *Student/faculty ratio:* 19:1.

Majors Accounting; American Indian/Native American studies; anthropology; applied mathematics; art; art history, criticism and conservation; art teacher education; biochemistry; biology/biological sciences; botany/plant biology; broadcast journalism; business administration and management; cell biology and histology; chemistry; child development; clinical laboratory science/medical technology; communication/speech communication and rhetoric; computer science; developmental and child psychology; dramatic/theatre arts; economics; education; elementary education; English; environmental biology; environmental/environmental health engineering; environmental studies; fine/studio arts; fish/game management; fishing and fisheries sciences and management; forestry; French; geography; geology/earth science; German; history; hydrology and water resources science; industrial arts; information science/studies; journalism; kindergarten/preschool education; kinesiology and exercise science; liberal arts and sciences/liberal studies; marine biology and biological oceanography; marketing/marketing management; mathematics; medical microbiology and bacteriology; molecular biology; music; music teacher education; natural resources/conservation; natural resources management and policy; natural sciences; nursing (registered nurse training); oceanography (chemical and physical); parks, recreation and leisure; parks, recreation and leisure facilities management; philosophy; physical education teaching and coaching; physical sciences; physics; political science and government; pre-dentistry studies; pre-law studies; pre-medical studies; pre-veterinary studies; psychology; range science and management; religious studies; secondary education; social sciences; social work; sociology; Spanish; speech and rhetoric; toxicology; wildlife and wildlands science and management; zoology/animal biology.

Academic Programs *Special study options:* academic remediation for entering students, adult/continuing education programs, advanced placement credit, cooperative education, distance learning, double majors, English as a second language, honors programs, independent study, internships, off-campus study, part-time degree program, services for LD students, student-designed majors, study abroad, summer session for credit.

Library 585,386 titles, 2,629 serial subscriptions, 4,947 audiovisual materials, an OPAC, a Web page.

Computers on Campus 778 computers available on campus for general student use. A campuswide network can be accessed from student residence rooms and from off campus. Internet access, online (class) registration, at least one staffed computer lab available.

Student Life *Housing options:* coed. Campus housing is university owned. *Activities and organizations:* drama/theater group, student-run newspaper, radio station, choral group, marching band, student radio station, Student Environmental Action Coalition, youth educational services, Ballet Folklorico, International Student Union, national fraternities, national sororities. *Campus security:* 24-hour emergency response devices and patrols, late-night transport/escort service, controlled dormitory access. *Student services:* health clinic, personal/psychological counseling, women's center, legal services.

Athletics Member NCAA. All Division II. *Intercollegiate sports:* basketball M(s)/W(s), crew M(c)/W, cross-country running M(s)/W(s), football M(s), lacrosse M(c)/W(c), rugby M(c)/W(c), soccer M(s)/W(s), softball W(s), track and field M(s)/W(s), volleyball M(c)/W(s). *Intramural sports:* baseball M(c), basketball M/W, fencing M(c)/W(c), racquetball M/W, soccer M/W, softball M/W, swimming M/W, ultimate Frisbee M(c)/W(c), volleyball M/W, water polo M/W.

Standardized Tests *Required for some:* SAT I or ACT (for admission).

Costs (2003–04) *Tuition:* state resident $0 full-time; nonresident $6768 full-time, $282 per unit part-time. *Required fees:* $2539 full-time. *Room and board:* $6861; room only: $3595. Room and board charges vary according to board plan and housing facility. *Payment plan:* installment. *Waivers:* senior citizens and employees or children of employees.

Financial Aid Of all full-time matriculated undergraduates who enrolled in 2003, 350 Federal Work-Study jobs (averaging $2000). *Average financial aid package:* $8050.

Applying *Options:* electronic application, deferred entrance. *Application fee:* $55. *Required:* high school transcript, minimum 2.0 GPA. *Application deadlines:* rolling (freshmen), 11/30 (transfers). *Notification:* continuous (freshmen), continuous (transfers).

Admissions Contact Ms. Rebecca Kalal, Assistant Director of Admissions, Humboldt State University, 1 Harpst Street, Arcata, CA 95521-8299. *Phone:* 707-826-4402. *Fax:* 707-826-6194. *E-mail:* hsuinfo@humboldt.edu.

HUMPHREYS COLLEGE
Stockton, California

Admissions Contact Ms. Wilma Okamoto Vaughn, Dean of Administration, Humphreys College, 6650 Inglewood Avenue, Stockton, CA 95207-3896. *Phone:* 209-478-0800. *Fax:* 209-478-8721.

INSTITUTE OF COMPUTER TECHNOLOGY
Los Angeles, California

- **Proprietary** 4-year, founded 1981
- **Calendar** quarters
- **Degrees** certificates, diplomas, associate, and bachelor's
- **Urban** campus
- **Coed**
- **Noncompetitive** entrance level

Faculty *Student/faculty ratio:* 21:1.

Student Life *Campus security:* 24-hour patrols.

Standardized Tests *Required:* CPAt (for admission).

Applying *Options:* common application. *Application fee:* $75. *Required:* high school transcript, interview.

Admissions Contact Mr. Randy Taylor, Director of Admissions, Institute of Computer Technology, 3200 Wilshire Boulevard 4th Floor, Los Angeles, CA 90010. *Phone:* 213-381-3333. *Toll-free phone:* 800-57 GO ICT. *Fax:* 213-383-9369.

INTERIOR DESIGNERS INSTITUTE
Newport Beach, California

Admissions Contact 1061 Camelback Road, Newport Beach, CA 92660. *Fax:* 949-759-0667. *E-mail:* contact@idi.edu.

INTERNATIONAL TECHNOLOGICAL UNIVERSITY
Santa Clara, California

- **Independent** upper-level
- **Calendar** trimesters
- **Degrees** certificates, bachelor's, master's, and postbachelor's certificates
- **Coed**

Faculty *Student/faculty ratio:* 6:1.

Costs (2003–04) *Tuition:* $8250 full-time, $275 per semester hour part-time. *Required fees:* $500 full-time, $75 per term part-time.

Applying *Options:* common application, electronic application.

Admissions Contact Chun Mou Peng, Director of Operations, International Technological University, 1650 Warbunton Avenue, Santa Clara, CA 95050. *Phone:* 408-556-9027. *E-mail:* chunmou@itu.edu.

ITT TECHNICAL INSTITUTE
Anaheim, California

- **Proprietary** primarily 2-year, founded 1982, part of ITT Educational Services, Inc.
- **Calendar** quarters
- **Degrees** associate and bachelor's
- **Suburban** 5-acre campus with easy access to Los Angeles
- **Coed**
- **Minimally difficult** entrance level

Standardized Tests *Required:* Wonderlic aptitude test (for admission).

Costs (2003–04) *Tuition:* $347 per credit hour part-time.

Financial Aid Of all full-time matriculated undergraduates who enrolled in 2001, 20 Federal Work-Study jobs (averaging $5000).

Applying *Options:* deferred entrance. *Application fee:* $100. *Required:* high school transcript, interview. *Recommended:* letters of recommendation.

Admissions Contact Mr. Albert A. Naranjo, Director of Recruitment, ITT Technical Institute, 525 North Muller Avenue, Anaheim, CA 92801. *Phone:* 714-535-3700. *Fax:* 714-535-1802.

ITT TECHNICAL INSTITUTE
Lathrop, California

- **Proprietary** primarily 2-year, part of ITT Educational Services
- **Calendar** quarters
- **Degrees** associate and bachelor's
- **Coed**
- **Minimally difficult** entrance level

Standardized Tests *Required:* Wonderlic aptitude test (for admission).

Costs (2003–04) *Tuition:* $347 per credit hour part-time.

Applying *Options:* deferred entrance. *Application fee:* $100. *Required:* high school transcript, interview. *Recommended:* letters of recommendation.

Admissions Contact Mr. Donald Fraser, Director of Recruitment, ITT Technical Institute, 16916 South Harlan Road, Lathrop, CA 95330. *Phone:* 209-858-0077. *Toll-free phone:* 800-346-1786. *Fax:* 209-858-0277.

ITT TECHNICAL INSTITUTE
Oxnard, California

- **Proprietary** primarily 2-year, founded 1993, part of ITT Educational Services, Inc.
- **Calendar** quarters
- **Degrees** associate and bachelor's
- **Urban** campus with easy access to Los Angeles
- **Coed**
- **Minimally difficult** entrance level

Student Life *Campus security:* 24-hour emergency response devices and patrols.

Standardized Tests *Required:* Wonderlic aptitude test (for admission).

Costs (2003–04) *Tuition:* $347 per credit hour part-time.

Applying *Options:* deferred entrance. *Application fee:* $100. *Required:* high school transcript, interview. *Recommended:* letters of recommendation.

Admissions Contact Mr. Dean K. Dunbar, Director of Recruitment, ITT Technical Institute, 2051 Solar Drive, Building B, Oxnard, CA 93036. *Phone:* 805-988-0143. *Toll-free phone:* 800-530-1582. *Fax:* 805-988-1813.

ITT TECHNICAL INSTITUTE
Rancho Cordova, California

- **Proprietary** primarily 2-year, founded 1954, part of ITT Educational Services, Inc.
- **Calendar** quarters
- **Degrees** associate and bachelor's
- **Urban** 5-acre campus
- **Coed**
- **Minimally difficult** entrance level

Standardized Tests *Required:* Wonderlic aptitude test (for admission).

Costs (2003–04) *Tuition:* $347 per credit hour part-time.

Applying *Options:* deferred entrance. *Application fee:* $100. *Required:* high school transcript, interview. *Recommended:* letters of recommendation.

Admissions Contact Mr. Robert Menszer, Director of Recruitment, ITT Technical Institute, 10863 Gold Center Drive, Rancho Cordova, CA 95670. *Phone:* 916-851-3900. *Toll-free phone:* 800-488-8466. *Fax:* 916-851-9225.

ITT TECHNICAL INSTITUTE
San Bernardino, California

- **Proprietary** primarily 2-year, founded 1987, part of ITT Educational Services, Inc.
- **Calendar** quarters
- **Degrees** associate and bachelor's
- **Urban** campus with easy access to Los Angeles
- **Coed**
- **Minimally difficult** entrance level

Standardized Tests *Required:* Wonderlic aptitude test (for admission).

Costs (2003–04) *Tuition:* $347 per credit hour part-time.

Applying *Options:* deferred entrance. *Application fee:* $100. *Required:* high school transcript, interview. *Recommended:* letters of recommendation.

ITT Technical Institute (continued)

Admissions Contact Ms. Maria Alamat, Director of Recruitment, ITT Technical Institute, 630 East Brier Drive, Suite 150, San Bernardino, CA 92408. *Phone:* 909-889-3800 Ext. 11. *Toll-free phone:* 800-888-3801. *Fax:* 909-888-6970.

ITT Technical Institute
San Diego, California

- **Proprietary** primarily 2-year, founded 1981, part of ITT Educational Services, Inc.
- **Calendar** quarters
- **Degrees** associate and bachelor's
- **Suburban** campus
- **Coed**
- **Minimally difficult** entrance level

Standardized Tests *Required:* Wonderlic aptitude test (for admission).

Costs (2003–04) *Tuition:* $347 per credit hour part-time.

Applying *Options:* deferred entrance. *Application fee:* $100. *Required:* high school transcript, interview. *Recommended:* letters of recommendation.

Admissions Contact Ms. Sheryl Schulgen, Director of Recruitment, ITT Technical Institute, 9680 Granite Ridge Drive, San Diego, CA 92123. *Phone:* 858-571-8500. *Toll-free phone:* 800-883-0380. *Fax:* 858-571-1277.

ITT Technical Institute
Sylmar, California

- **Proprietary** primarily 2-year, founded 1982, part of ITT Educational Services, Inc.
- **Calendar** quarters
- **Degrees** associate and bachelor's
- **Urban** campus with easy access to Los Angeles
- **Coed**
- **Minimally difficult** entrance level

Standardized Tests *Required:* Wonderlic aptitude test (for admission).

Costs (2003–04) *Tuition:* $347 per credit hour part-time.

Applying *Options:* deferred entrance. *Application fee:* $100. *Required:* high school transcript, interview. *Recommended:* letters of recommendation.

Admissions Contact Mr. Dominick Miciotta, Director of Recruitment, ITT Technical Institute, 12669 Encinitas Avenue, Sylmar, CA 91342. *Phone:* 818-364-5151. *Toll-free phone:* 800-363-2086. *Fax:* 818-364-5150.

ITT Technical Institute
Torrance, California

- **Proprietary** primarily 2-year, founded 1987, part of ITT Educational Services, Inc.
- **Calendar** quarters
- **Degrees** associate and bachelor's
- **Urban** campus with easy access to Los Angeles
- **Coed**
- **Minimally difficult** entrance level

Standardized Tests *Required:* Wonderlic aptitude test (for admission).

Costs (2003–04) *Tuition:* $347 per credit hour part-time.

Financial Aid Of all full-time matriculated undergraduates who enrolled in 2001, 6 Federal Work-Study jobs (averaging $4000).

Applying *Options:* deferred entrance. *Application fee:* $100. *Required:* high school transcript, interview. *Recommended:* letters of recommendation.

Admissions Contact Mr. Freddie Polk, Director of Recruitment, ITT Technical Institute, 20050 South Vermont Avenue, Torrance, CA 90502. *Phone:* 310-380-1555. *Fax:* 310-380-1557.

ITT Technical Institute
West Covina, California

- **Proprietary** primarily 2-year, founded 1982, part of ITT Educational Services, Inc.
- **Calendar** quarters
- **Degrees** associate and bachelor's
- **Suburban** 4-acre campus with easy access to Los Angeles
- **Coed**
- **Minimally difficult** entrance level

Standardized Tests *Required:* Wonderlic aptitude test (for admission).

Costs (2003–04) *Tuition:* $347 per credit hour part-time.

Financial Aid Of all full-time matriculated undergraduates who enrolled in 2001, 20 Federal Work-Study jobs (averaging $4500).

Applying *Options:* deferred entrance. *Application fee:* $100. *Required:* high school transcript, interview. *Recommended:* letters of recommendation.

Admissions Contact Mr. Michael Snyder, Director of Recruitment, ITT Technical Institute, 1530 West Cameron Avenue, West Covina, CA 91790. *Phone:* 626-960-8681. *Toll-free phone:* 800-414-6522. *Fax:* 626-337-5271.

John F. Kennedy University
Pleasant Hill, California

- **Independent** comprehensive, founded 1964
- **Calendar** quarters semesters for law school
- **Degrees** bachelor's, master's, doctoral, first professional, and postbachelor's certificates
- **Suburban** 5-acre campus with easy access to San Francisco
- **Coed,** 237 undergraduate students, 10% full-time, 77% women, 23% men
- **Noncompetitive** entrance level

Undergraduates 23 full-time, 214 part-time. 0.1% are from out of state, 9% African American, 8% Asian American or Pacific Islander, 5% Hispanic American, 1% Native American.

Faculty *Total:* 715, 5% full-time, 67% with terminal degrees. *Student/faculty ratio:* 12:1.

Majors Accounting; business administration and management; consumer merchandising/retailing management; humanities; liberal arts and sciences/liberal studies; psychology.

Academic Programs *Special study options:* adult/continuing education programs, advanced placement credit, independent study, off-campus study, part-time degree program, services for LD students, student-designed majors, summer session for credit.

Library Robert M. Fisher Library with 91,170 titles, 811 serial subscriptions, 1,854 audiovisual materials, an OPAC, a Web page.

Computers on Campus 50 computers available on campus for general student use. At least one staffed computer lab available.

Student Life *Housing:* college housing not available. *Activities and organizations:* student-run newspaper. *Campus security:* late-night transport/escort service. *Student services:* personal/psychological counseling.

Costs (2003–04) *Tuition:* $13,920 full-time, $290 per quarter hour part-time. Full-time tuition and fees vary according to course load and program. Part-time tuition and fees vary according to course load and program. *Required fees:* $27 full-time, $9 per term part-time. *Payment plan:* deferred payment. *Waivers:* employees or children of employees.

Financial Aid Of all full-time matriculated undergraduates who enrolled in 2002, 11 applied for aid, 11 were judged to have need, 11 had their need fully met. *Average percent of need met:* 60%. *Average financial aid package:* $7000. *Average need-based loan:* $6000. *Average need-based gift aid:* $1000. *Average indebtedness upon graduation:* $23,000.

Applying *Options:* common application, deferred entrance. *Application fee:* $50. *Application deadline:* rolling (transfers). *Notification:* continuous (transfers).

Admissions Contact Ms. Ellena Bloedorn, Director of Admissions and Records, John F. Kennedy University, 100 Ellinwood Way, Pleasant Hill, CA 94523-4817. *Phone:* 925-969-3330. *Toll-free phone:* 800-696-JFKU. *Fax:* 925-969-3328. *E-mail:* skierce@jfku.edu.

The King's College and Seminary
Van Nuys, California

Admissions Contact Ms. Marilyn J. Chappell, Director of Admissions, The King's College and Seminary, 14800 Sherman Way, Van Nuys, CA 91405-8040. *Phone:* 818-779-8040.

Laguna College of Art & Design
Laguna Beach, California

- **Independent** 4-year, founded 1962
- **Calendar** semesters
- **Degree** certificates and bachelor's
- **Small-town** 9-acre campus with easy access to Los Angeles
- **Endowment** $411,000
- **Coed,** 310 undergraduate students, 100% full-time, 47% women, 53% men

■ **Very difficult** entrance level, 88% of applicants were admitted

Laguna College of Art & Design (LCAD) hosts an annual open house to introduce prospective students and their families to the school. Individuals may schedule personal tours and portfolio reviews by contacting Anthony Padilla, Vice President of Enrollment, or Susan DeRosa, Assistant Dean of Admissions. Campus hours are Monday–Friday, 9 a.m. to 5 p.m.

Undergraduates 310 full-time. Students come from 32 states and territories, 42% are from out of state, 2% African American, 15% Asian American or Pacific Islander, 9% Hispanic American, 0.6% Native American, 6% international. *Retention:* 83% of 2002 full-time freshmen returned.

Freshmen *Admission:* 245 applied, 215 admitted, 70 enrolled. *Average high school GPA:* 3.45. *Test scores:* SAT verbal scores over 500: 88%; SAT math scores over 500: 80%; ACT scores over 18: 100%; SAT verbal scores over 600: 66%; SAT math scores over 600: 32%; ACT scores over 24: 80%; SAT verbal scores over 700: 16%; SAT math scores over 700: 10%; ACT scores over 30: 10%.

Faculty *Total:* 72, 14% full-time. *Student/faculty ratio:* 10:1.

Majors Art; commercial and advertising art; design and applied arts related; design and visual communications; drawing; fine/studio arts; graphic design; illustration; intermedia/multimedia; painting; printmaking; sculpture.

Academic Programs *Special study options:* academic remediation for entering students, adult/continuing education programs, advanced placement credit, English as a second language, independent study, internships, off-campus study, part-time degree program, summer session for credit.

Library Ruth Salyer Library plus 1 other with 16,000 titles, 100 serial subscriptions, 8 audiovisual materials, an OPAC.

Computers on Campus 85 computers available on campus for general student use. A campuswide network can be accessed from off campus. Internet access, at least one staffed computer lab available. Computer purchase or lease plan available.

Student Life *Housing:* college housing not available. *Activities and organizations:* student-run newspaper. *Campus security:* 24-hour emergency response devices. *Student services:* personal/psychological counseling.

Standardized Tests *Required:* SAT I or ACT (for admission).

Costs (2004–05) *Tuition:* $16,500 full-time, $688 per unit part-time. *Payment plan:* installment. *Waivers:* employees or children of employees.

Financial Aid Of all full-time matriculated undergraduates who enrolled in 2003, 302 applied for aid, 274 were judged to have need. 12 Federal Work-Study jobs (averaging $1500). In 2003, 31 non-need-based awards were made. *Average percent of need met:* 70%. *Average financial aid package:* $8000. *Average need-based loan:* $3500. *Average need-based gift aid:* $2000. *Average non-need-based aid:* $2000. *Average indebtedness upon graduation:* $35,125.

Applying *Options:* common application, electronic application, deferred entrance. *Application fee:* $45. *Required:* essay or personal statement, high school transcript, minimum 3.0 GPA, 1 letter of recommendation, interview, portfolio. *Recommended:* minimum 3.5 GPA. *Application deadlines:* 2/2 (freshmen), 3/2 (transfers). *Notification:* 5/1 (freshmen), 5/30 (transfers).

Admissions Contact Mr. Anthony Padilla, Vice President of Enrollment, Laguna College of Art & Design, 2222 Laguna Canyon Road, Laguna Beach, CA 92651-1136. *Phone:* 949-376-6000 Ext. 232. *Toll-free phone:* 800-255-0762. *Fax:* 949-376-6009. *E-mail:* admissions@lagunacollege.edu.

■ *See page 1836 for a narrative description.*

LA SIERRA UNIVERSITY
Riverside, California

■ **Independent Seventh-day Adventist** comprehensive, founded 1922
■ **Calendar** quarters
■ **Degrees** bachelor's, master's, doctoral, post-master's, and postbachelor's certificates
■ **Suburban** 630-acre campus with easy access to Los Angeles
■ **Endowment** $10.1 million
■ **Coed**
■ **Minimally difficult** entrance level

Faculty *Student/faculty ratio:* 16:1.

Student Life *Campus security:* 24-hour emergency response devices and patrols, student patrols, late-night transport/escort service.

Standardized Tests *Required:* SAT I or ACT (for placement). *Required for some:* SAT II: Writing Test (for placement).

Costs (2003–04) *Comprehensive fee:* $21,300 includes full-time tuition ($16,272), mandatory fees ($468), and room and board ($4560). *College room only:* $2700.

Applying *Application fee:* $30. *Required:* high school transcript, minimum 2.5 GPA, 2 letters of recommendation. *Required for some:* interview.

Admissions Contact Dr. Tom Smith, Director of Admissions, La Sierra University, 4700 Pierce Street, Riverside, CA 92515-8247. *Phone:* 909-785-2176. *Toll-free phone:* 800-874-5587. *Fax:* 909-785-2477. *E-mail:* ivy@lasierra.edu.

LIFE PACIFIC COLLEGE
San Dimas, California

■ **Independent** 4-year, founded 1923, affiliated with International Church of the Foursquare Gospel
■ **Calendar** semesters
■ **Degrees** associate and bachelor's
■ **Suburban** 9-acre campus with easy access to Los Angeles
■ **Endowment** $2.2 million
■ **Coed,** 446 undergraduate students, 80% full-time, 49% women, 51% men
■ **Moderately difficult** entrance level, 97% of applicants were admitted

Undergraduates 359 full-time, 87 part-time. Students come from 32 states and territories, 2 other countries, 41% are from out of state, 5% African American, 6% Asian American or Pacific Islander, 13% Hispanic American, 1% Native American, 0.4% international, 17% transferred in, 57% live on campus.

Freshmen *Admission:* 64 applied, 62 admitted, 51 enrolled. *Average high school GPA:* 3.14. *Test scores:* SAT verbal scores over 500: 50%; SAT math scores over 500: 24%; ACT scores over 18: 80%; SAT verbal scores over 600: 2%; SAT math scores over 600: 9%; ACT scores over 24: 40%; SAT math scores over 700: 3%.

Faculty *Total:* 36, 47% full-time, 28% with terminal degrees. *Student/faculty ratio:* 24:1.

Majors Biblical studies; pastoral studies/counseling; theology.

Academic Programs *Special study options:* adult/continuing education programs, advanced placement credit, cooperative education, distance learning, external degree program, independent study, internships, part-time degree program, services for LD students, summer session for credit.

Library LIFE Alumni Library with 38,084 titles, 244 serial subscriptions, 1,104 audiovisual materials, an OPAC.

Computers on Campus 35 computers available on campus for general student use. A campuswide network can be accessed from student residence rooms. Internet access, at least one staffed computer lab available.

Student Life *Housing:* on-campus residence required for freshman year. *Options:* men-only, women-only. Campus housing is university owned. Freshman campus housing is guaranteed. *Activities and organizations:* drama/theater group, student-run newspaper, choral group, tutoring, chorale. *Campus security:* 24-hour emergency response devices, student patrols, part-time security personnel. *Student services:* personal/psychological counseling.

Athletics Member NCCAA. *Intercollegiate sports:* basketball M/W, volleyball W. *Intramural sports:* cross-country running M/W, soccer M.

Standardized Tests *Required:* SAT I or ACT (for admission). *Recommended:* SAT II: Writing Test (for admission).

Costs (2003–04) *Comprehensive fee:* $11,300 includes full-time tuition ($7050), mandatory fees ($250), and room and board ($4000). Part-time tuition: $235 per credit hour. Part-time tuition and fees vary according to course load. *Payment plan:* installment. *Waivers:* children of alumni and employees or children of employees.

Financial Aid Of all full-time matriculated undergraduates who enrolled in 2002, 299 applied for aid, 266 were judged to have need, 13 had their need fully met. 23 Federal Work-Study jobs (averaging $1359). In 2002, 26 non-need-based awards were made. *Average percent of need met:* 53%. *Average financial aid package:* $5890. *Average need-based loan:* $3156. *Average need-based gift aid:* $3991. *Average non-need-based aid:* $1874. *Average indebtedness upon graduation:* $12,955.

Applying *Options:* common application, electronic application, deferred entrance. *Application fee:* $35. *Required:* essay or personal statement, high school transcript, minimum 2.0 GPA, 3 letters of recommendation, Christian testimony. *Application deadlines:* 7/1 (freshmen), 7/1 (transfers). *Notification:* continuous (freshmen), continuous (transfers).

Admissions Contact Mrs. Linda Hibdon, Admissions Director, Life Pacific College, 1100 Covina Boulevard, San Dimas, CA 91773-3298. *Phone:* 909-599-5433 Ext. 314. *Toll-free phone:* 877-886-5433. *Fax:* 909-706-3070. *E-mail:* adm@lifepacific.edu.

LINCOLN UNIVERSITY
Oakland, California

■ **Independent** comprehensive, founded 1919
■ **Calendar** semesters
■ **Degrees** certificates, bachelor's, and master's

Lincoln University (continued)
- **Urban** 2-acre campus
- **Coed**
- **Minimally difficult** entrance level

Faculty *Student/faculty ratio:* 14:1.
Student Life *Campus security:* 24-hour emergency response devices.
Standardized Tests *Required:* Michigan English Language Assessment Battery (for placement).
Costs (2003–04) *Tuition:* $6840 full-time. *Required fees:* $255 full-time.
Applying *Options:* deferred entrance. *Application fee:* $50. *Required:* high school transcript, minimum 2.0 GPA. *Required for some:* essay or personal statement, letters of recommendation, interview.
Admissions Contact Ms. Vivian Xu, Admissions Officer, Lincoln University, 401 15th Street, Oakland, CA 94612-2801. *Phone:* 415-221-1212 Ext. 115. *Fax:* 510-628-8012.

Loma Linda University
Loma Linda, California

- **Independent Seventh-day Adventist** upper-level, founded 1905
- **Calendar** quarters
- **Degrees** certificates, associate, bachelor's, master's, doctoral, first professional, and postbachelor's certificates (associate degree and nursing students may enter at the sophomore level)
- **Small-town** campus with easy access to Los Angeles
- **Endowment** $153.0 million
- **Coed,** 978 undergraduate students, 71% full-time, 75% women, 25% men
- 33% of applicants were admitted

Undergraduates 697 full-time, 281 part-time. Students come from 29 states and territories, 28 other countries, 23% are from out of state, 7% African American, 22% Asian American or Pacific Islander, 19% Hispanic American, 0.5% Native American, 6% international, 25% transferred in, 25% live on campus.
Faculty *Total:* 202, 72% full-time, 41% with terminal degrees. *Student/faculty ratio:* 5:1.
Majors Audiology and speech-language pathology; clinical laboratory science/medical technology; cytotechnology; dental hygiene; dietetics; emergency medical technology (EMT paramedic); health information/medical records administration; medical radiologic technology; nursing (registered nurse training); occupational therapist assistant; occupational therapy; physical therapist assistant; respiratory care therapy; surgical technology.
Academic Programs *Special study options:* distance learning, English as a second language, independent study, internships, off-campus study.
Library Del E. Webb Memorial Library with 322,657 titles, 1,394 serial subscriptions, an OPAC, a Web page.
Computers on Campus A campuswide network can be accessed from student residence rooms and from off campus that provide access to on-line courses. Internet access, online (class) registration, at least one staffed computer lab available.
Student Life *Housing:* on-campus residence required in senior year. *Options:* men-only, women-only. *Activities and organizations:* student-run newspaper, choral group, Students for International Mission Services, Students Computing Organization. *Campus security:* 24-hour emergency response devices and patrols, late-night transport/escort service. *Student services:* health clinic, personal/psychological counseling.
Athletics *Intramural sports:* basketball M/W, football M, racquetball M/W, soccer M/W, softball M/W, swimming M/W, tennis M/W, volleyball M/W.
Costs (2003–04) *Tuition:* $21,805 full-time. *Room only:* $2780.
Financial Aid Of all full-time matriculated undergraduates who enrolled in 2002, 542 applied for aid, 492 were judged to have need, 131 had their need fully met. 85 Federal Work-Study jobs (averaging $3029). In 2002, 54 non-need-based awards were made. *Average percent of need met:* 87%. *Average financial aid package:* $16,862. *Average need-based loan:* $4345. *Average need-based gift aid:* $3118. *Average non-need-based aid:* $12,582. *Average indebtedness upon graduation:* $28,245.
Applying *Options:* common application. *Application fee:* $60. *Application deadline:* 4/15 (freshmen).
Admissions Contact Admissions Office, Loma Linda University, Loma Linda, CA 92350. *Phone:* 909-558-1000.

Loyola Marymount University
Los Angeles, California

- **Independent Roman Catholic** comprehensive, founded 1911
- **Calendar** semesters
- **Degrees** bachelor's, master's, first professional, and postbachelor's certificates
- **Suburban** 128-acre campus
- **Endowment** $228.0 million
- **Coed,** 5,699 undergraduate students, 93% full-time, 60% women, 40% men
- **Very difficult** entrance level, 58% of applicants were admitted

Undergraduates 5,312 full-time, 387 part-time. Students come from 51 states and territories, 52 other countries, 23% are from out of state, 7% African American, 11% Asian American or Pacific Islander, 18% Hispanic American, 0.6% Native American, 2% international, 3% transferred in, 54% live on campus. *Retention:* 88% of 2002 full-time freshmen returned.
Freshmen *Admission:* 7,833 applied, 4,568 admitted, 1,335 enrolled. *Average high school GPA:* 3.37. *Test scores:* SAT verbal scores over 500: 87%; SAT math scores over 500: 88%; ACT scores over 18: 100%; SAT verbal scores over 600: 36%; SAT math scores over 600: 42%; ACT scores over 24: 72%; SAT verbal scores over 700: 4%; SAT math scores over 700: 6%; ACT scores over 30: 8%.
Faculty *Total:* 865, 48% full-time. *Student/faculty ratio:* 13:1.
Majors Accounting; African-American/Black studies; art history, criticism and conservation; Asian-American studies; biochemistry; biology/biological sciences; business administration and management; chemistry; cinematography and film/video production; civil engineering; classics and languages, literatures and linguistics; computer engineering; computer science; conducting; dance; dramatic/theatre arts; economics; electrical, electronics and communications engineering; engineering physics; English; European studies; fine/studio arts; French; Hispanic-American, Puerto Rican, and Mexican-American/Chicano studies; history; humanities; international economics; Latin; liberal arts and sciences/liberal studies; mass communication/media; mathematics; mechanical engineering; modern Greek; music; music history, literature, and theory; musicology and ethnomusicology; music theory and composition; natural sciences; philosophy; physics; playwriting and screenwriting; political science and government; psychology; sociology; Spanish; theology; urban studies/affairs; voice and opera.
Academic Programs *Special study options:* accelerated degree program, adult/continuing education programs, advanced placement credit, cooperative education, double majors, honors programs, independent study, internships, part-time degree program, services for LD students, student-designed majors, study abroad, summer session for credit. *ROTC:* Army (c), Air Force (b).
Library Charles von der Ahe Library plus 1 other with 484,273 titles, 36,650 serial subscriptions, 40,158 audiovisual materials, an OPAC, a Web page.
Computers on Campus 300 computers available on campus for general student use. A campuswide network can be accessed from student residence rooms and from off campus. Internet access, at least one staffed computer lab available. Computer purchase or lease plan available.
Student Life *Housing options:* coed, men-only, women-only. Campus housing is university owned. Freshman campus housing is guaranteed. *Activities and organizations:* drama/theater group, student-run newspaper, radio and television station, choral group, service clubs, Student Government and Activity Board, community service opportunities, student media opportunities, clubs and organizations, national fraternities, national sororities. *Campus security:* 24-hour emergency response devices and patrols, late-night transport/escort service, controlled dormitory access. *Student services:* health clinic, personal/psychological counseling.
Athletics Member NCAA. All Division I. *Intercollegiate sports:* baseball M(s), basketball M(s)/W(s), crew M/W(s), cross-country running M(s)/W(s), golf M(s), lacrosse M(c)/W(c), rugby M(c), soccer M(s)/W(s), softball W(s), swimming W(s), tennis M(s)/W(s), volleyball M(c)/W(s), water polo M(s)/W(s). *Intramural sports:* basketball M/W, football M/W, rock climbing M/W, soccer M/W, softball M/W, tennis M/W, volleyball M/W.
Standardized Tests *Required:* SAT I or ACT (for admission).
Costs (2003–04) *Comprehensive fee:* $32,194 includes full-time tuition ($23,504), mandatory fees ($430), and room and board ($8260). Part-time tuition: $979 per unit. Part-time tuition and fees vary according to course load. *College room only:* $6010. Room and board charges vary according to board plan and housing facility. *Payment plan:* installment. *Waivers:* employees or children of employees.
Financial Aid Of all full-time matriculated undergraduates who enrolled in 2003, 3,771 applied for aid, 2,952 were judged to have need, 899 had their need fully met. 1,600 Federal Work-Study jobs (averaging $2000). 579 state and other part-time jobs (averaging $2800). In 2003, 165 non-need-based awards were made. *Average percent of need met:* 78%. *Average financial aid package:* $18,095. *Average need-based loan:* $4807. *Average need-based gift aid:* $11,116. *Average non-need-based aid:* $6811. *Average indebtedness upon graduation:* $19,933.
Applying *Options:* electronic application, early admission, deferred entrance. *Application fee:* $50. *Required:* essay or personal statement, high school tran-

script, 1 letter of recommendation. *Recommended:* interview. *Application deadlines:* 2/1 (freshmen), 6/1 (transfers). *Notification:* continuous (freshmen), continuous (transfers).

Admissions Contact Mr. Matthew X. Fissinger, Director of Admissions, Loyola Marymount University, 1 LMU Drive Suite 100, Los Angeles, CA 90045-8350. *Phone:* 310-338-2750. *Toll-free phone:* 800-LMU-INFO. *E-mail:* admissions@lmu.edu.

■ *See page 1896 for a narrative description.*

THE MASTER'S COLLEGE AND SEMINARY

Santa Clarita, California

- **Independent nondenominational** comprehensive, founded 1927
- **Calendar** semesters
- **Degrees** certificates, bachelor's, master's, doctoral, first professional, and first professional certificates
- **Suburban** 110-acre campus with easy access to Los Angeles
- **Endowment** $3.8 million
- **Coed,** 1,132 undergraduate students, 86% full-time, 51% women, 49% men
- **Moderately difficult** entrance level, 54% of applicants were admitted

Undergraduates 971 full-time, 161 part-time. Students come from 42 states and territories, 24 other countries, 33% are from out of state, 3% African American, 3% Asian American or Pacific Islander, 6% Hispanic American, 0.6% Native American, 3% international, 11% transferred in, 75% live on campus. *Retention:* 83% of 2002 full-time freshmen returned.

Freshmen *Admission:* 412 applied, 221 admitted, 209 enrolled. *Average high school GPA:* 3.62. *Test scores:* SAT verbal scores over 500: 81%; SAT math scores over 500: 80%; ACT scores over 18: 97%; SAT verbal scores over 600: 40%; SAT math scores over 600: 32%; ACT scores over 24: 60%; SAT verbal scores over 700: 6%; SAT math scores over 700: 5%; ACT scores over 30: 12%.

Faculty *Total:* 140, 49% full-time, 51% with terminal degrees. *Student/faculty ratio:* 14:1.

Majors Accounting; actuarial science; American government and politics; ancient Near Eastern and biblical languages; applied mathematics; biblical studies; biological and physical sciences; biology/biological sciences; business administration and management; computer and information sciences; divinity/ministry; education; elementary education; English; environmental biology; family and consumer sciences/human sciences; finance; foods, nutrition, and wellness; health and physical education; history; liberal arts and sciences/liberal studies; management information systems; mass communication/media; mathematics; middle school education; music; music management and merchandising; music teacher education; natural sciences; pastoral studies/counseling; physical education teaching and coaching; physical sciences; piano and organ; political science and government; pre-law studies; pre-medical studies; public relations/image management; radio and television; religious education; religious/sacred music; religious studies; science teacher education; secondary education; speech and rhetoric; theology; voice and opera.

Academic Programs *Special study options:* academic remediation for entering students, accelerated degree program, adult/continuing education programs, advanced placement credit, cooperative education, double majors, external degree program, independent study, internships, part-time degree program, services for LD students, study abroad, summer session for credit.

Library Powell Library plus 1 other with 211,895 titles, 1,288 serial subscriptions, 7,001 audiovisual materials, an OPAC, a Web page.

Computers on Campus 57 computers available on campus for general student use. A campuswide network can be accessed from student residence rooms. Internet access, online (class) registration, at least one staffed computer lab available. Computer purchase or lease plan available.

Student Life *Housing:* on-campus residence required through sophomore year. *Options:* men-only, women-only. Campus housing is university owned and leased by the school. Freshman campus housing is guaranteed. *Activities and organizations:* choral group, college chorale, Summer Missions, intramurals, church ministries, drama club. *Campus security:* 24-hour patrols. *Student services:* health clinic, personal/psychological counseling.

Athletics Member NAIA, NCCAA. *Intercollegiate sports:* baseball M(s), basketball M(s)/W(s), cross-country running M(s)/W(s), golf M(s), soccer M(s)/W(s), softball W(s), volleyball W(s). *Intramural sports:* basketball M/W, football M/W, golf M/W, softball M/W, tennis M/W, volleyball M/W.

Standardized Tests *Required:* SAT I or ACT (for admission).

Costs (2003–04) *Comprehensive fee:* $23,250 includes full-time tuition ($17,000), mandatory fees ($200), and room and board ($6050). Full-time tuition and fees vary according to course load, degree level, and program. Part-time tuition: $710 per credit hour. Part-time tuition and fees vary according to course load, degree level, and program. *College room only:* $3370. Room and board charges vary according to board plan. *Payment plan:* installment. *Waivers:* employees or children of employees.

Financial Aid Of all full-time matriculated undergraduates who enrolled in 2003, 816 applied for aid, 738 were judged to have need, 163 had their need fully met. 45 Federal Work-Study jobs (averaging $2666). In 2003, 227 non-need-based awards were made. *Average percent of need met:* 74%. *Average financial aid package:* $14,157. *Average need-based loan:* $4119. *Average need-based gift aid:* $10,059. *Average non-need-based aid:* $8145. *Average indebtedness upon graduation:* $13,131.

Applying *Options:* electronic application, early admission, early action, deferred entrance. *Application fee:* $40. *Required:* essay or personal statement, high school transcript, minimum 2.50 GPA, 2 letters of recommendation, interview. *Application deadline:* 3/6 (transfers). *Notification:* 3/15 (freshmen), 12/22 (early action), continuous until 4/1 (transfers).

Admissions Contact Mr. Yaphet Peterson, Director of Enrollment, The Master's College and Seminary, Santa Clarita, CA 91321. *Phone:* 661-259-3540 Ext. 3365. *Toll-free phone:* 800-568-6248. *Fax:* 661-288-1037. *E-mail:* enrollment@masters.edu.

MENLO COLLEGE

Atherton, California

- **Independent** 4-year, founded 1927
- **Calendar** semesters
- **Degree** bachelor's
- **Small-town** 45-acre campus with easy access to San Francisco
- **Endowment** $7.4 million
- **Coed,** 660 undergraduate students, 91% full-time, 37% women, 63% men
- **Moderately difficult** entrance level, 56% of applicants were admitted

Undergraduates 599 full-time, 61 part-time. Students come from 24 states and territories, 34 other countries, 18% are from out of state, 7% African American, 15% Asian American or Pacific Islander, 13% Hispanic American, 0.5% Native American, 12% international, 16% transferred in, 66% live on campus. *Retention:* 48% of 2002 full-time freshmen returned.

Freshmen *Admission:* 1,061 applied, 598 admitted, 172 enrolled. *Average high school GPA:* 3.14. *Test scores:* SAT verbal scores over 500: 29%; SAT math scores over 500: 42%; ACT scores over 18: 62%; SAT verbal scores over 600: 3%; SAT math scores over 600: 9%; ACT scores over 24: 11%; SAT math scores over 700: 1%.

Faculty *Total:* 58, 43% full-time, 40% with terminal degrees. *Student/faculty ratio:* 17:1.

Majors Business administration and management; liberal arts and sciences/liberal studies; mass communication/media.

Academic Programs *Special study options:* academic remediation for entering students, accelerated degree program, adult/continuing education programs, advanced placement credit, double majors, honors programs, independent study, internships, part-time degree program, services for LD students, student-designed majors, study abroad, summer session for credit. *ROTC:* Army (c), Air Force (c).

Library Bowman Library with 55,000 titles, 172 serial subscriptions, 600 audiovisual materials, an OPAC, a Web page.

Computers on Campus 100 computers available on campus for general student use. A campuswide network can be accessed from student residence rooms. Internet access, online (class) registration, at least one staffed computer lab available.

Student Life *Housing:* on-campus residence required through sophomore year. *Options:* coed. Campus housing is university owned. Freshman campus housing is guaranteed. *Activities and organizations:* drama/theater group, student-run newspaper, radio and television station, international club, Residence Hall Association, French club, media network, Hawaiian club. *Campus security:* 24-hour emergency response devices and patrols. *Student services:* health clinic, personal/psychological counseling.

Athletics Member NCAA, NAIA. All NCAA Division III. *Intercollegiate sports:* baseball M, basketball M/W(c), cross-country running M/W, football M, golf M/W, soccer M/W, softball W, tennis M/W, track and field M/W, volleyball W. *Intramural sports:* basketball M, softball M/W.

Standardized Tests *Required:* SAT I or ACT (for admission).

Costs (2003–04) *Comprehensive fee:* $30,860 includes full-time tuition ($21,630), mandatory fees ($150), and room and board ($9080). Full-time tuition and fees vary according to program. Part-time tuition: $901 per unit. Part-time tuition and fees vary according to course load and program. *Required fees:* $50 per term part-time. *Room and board:* Room and board charges vary according to housing facility. *Payment plan:* installment. *Waivers:* employees or children of employees.

Financial Aid Of all full-time matriculated undergraduates who enrolled in 2003, 370 applied for aid, 348 were judged to have need, 52 had their need fully met. 239 Federal Work-Study jobs (averaging $1000). In 2003, 145 non-need-based awards were made. *Average percent of need met:* 73%. *Average financial*

Menlo College (continued)
aid package: $19,717. *Average need-based loan:* $4513. *Average need-based gift aid:* $15,312. *Average non-need-based aid:* $11,410. *Average indebtedness upon graduation:* $18,856.

Applying *Options:* common application, electronic application, early action, deferred entrance. *Application fee:* $40. *Required:* essay or personal statement, high school transcript, 1 letter of recommendation. *Recommended:* minimum 3.0 GPA, interview. *Application deadline:* rolling (freshmen), rolling (transfers). *Early decision:* 2/1. *Notification:* continuous (freshmen), continuous (out-of-state freshmen), 1/30 (early action), continuous (transfers).

Admissions Contact Dr. Greg Smith, Dean of Admission and Financial Aid, Menlo College, 1000 El Camino Real, Atherton, CA 94027. *Phone:* 650-543-3910. *Toll-free phone:* 800-556-3656. *Fax:* 650 617-2395. *E-mail:* admissions@menlo.edu.

■ *See page 1972 for a narrative description.*

MILLS COLLEGE
Oakland, California

- **Independent** comprehensive, founded 1852
- **Calendar** semesters
- **Degrees** certificates, bachelor's, master's, doctoral, and postbachelor's certificates
- **Urban** 135-acre campus with easy access to San Francisco
- **Endowment** $139.0 million
- **Women only,** 735 undergraduate students, 92% full-time
- **Moderately difficult** entrance level, 73% of applicants were admitted

Why Mills? Why a women's college? Because half of the College's professors are women, which is not the case at coeducational institutions, students have successful role models in every field. All of Mills' excellent undergraduate resources are committed to women. When women graduate from Mills, they know they can succeed. That confidence makes all the difference.

Undergraduates 676 full-time, 59 part-time. Students come from 35 states and territories, 6 other countries, 24% are from out of state, 11% African American, 8% Asian American or Pacific Islander, 10% Hispanic American, 0.7% Native American, 4% international, 16% transferred in, 52% live on campus. *Retention:* 72% of 2002 full-time freshmen returned.

Freshmen *Admission:* 115 enrolled. *Average high school GPA:* 3.54. *Test scores:* SAT verbal scores over 500: 80%; SAT math scores over 500: 74%; ACT scores over 18: 95%; SAT verbal scores over 600: 48%; SAT math scores over 600: 27%; ACT scores over 24: 63%; SAT verbal scores over 700: 12%; SAT math scores over 700: 5%; ACT scores over 30: 11%.

Faculty *Total:* 159, 60% full-time, 70% with terminal degrees. *Student/faculty ratio:* 10:1.

Majors American studies; anthropology; art; art history, criticism and conservation; biochemistry; biology/biological sciences; business/managerial economics; chemistry; comparative literature; computer science; creative writing; cultural studies; dance; developmental and child psychology; economics; engineering; English; environmental science; environmental studies; fine/studio arts; French; French studies; Hispanic-American, Puerto Rican, and Mexican-American/Chicano studies; history; interdisciplinary studies; intermedia/multimedia; international relations and affairs; liberal arts and sciences/liberal studies; mathematics; music; philosophy; physiological psychology/psychobiology; political science and government; psychology; public policy analysis; sociology; Spanish; women's studies.

Academic Programs *Special study options:* adult/continuing education programs, advanced placement credit, double majors, independent study, internships, off-campus study, part-time degree program, services for LD students, student-designed majors. *ROTC:* Army (c).

Library F. W. Olin Library plus 1 other with 189,814 titles, 2,029 serial subscriptions, 6,046 audiovisual materials, an OPAC, a Web page.

Computers on Campus 66 computers available on campus for general student use. A campuswide network can be accessed from student residence rooms and from off campus. At least one staffed computer lab available.

Student Life *Housing options:* women-only, cooperative. Campus housing is university owned. Freshman campus housing is guaranteed. *Activities and organizations:* drama/theater group, student-run newspaper, choral group, class organizations, MECHA, ASA (Asian Sisterhood Alliance), Mills Environmental Organization, BWC (Black Women's Collective). *Campus security:* 24-hour emergency response devices and patrols, late-night transport/escort service, controlled dormitory access. *Student services:* health clinic, personal/psychological counseling, women's center.

Athletics Member NCAA. All Division III. *Intercollegiate sports:* crew W, cross-country running W, soccer W, tennis W, volleyball W. *Intramural sports:* badminton W, basketball W, fencing W, soccer W, softball W, tennis W, volleyball W, weight lifting W.

Standardized Tests *Required:* SAT I or ACT (for admission). *Recommended:* SAT II: Subject Tests (for admission).

Costs (2003–04) *Comprehensive fee:* $33,371 includes full-time tuition ($23,000), mandatory fees ($1441), and room and board ($8930). Part-time tuition: $3835 per course. Part-time tuition and fees vary according to course load. *Room and board:* Room and board charges vary according to board plan and housing facility. *Payment plan:* installment. *Waivers:* employees or children of employees.

Financial Aid In 2002, 152 non-need-based awards were made. *Average percent of need met:* 86%. *Average financial aid package:* $20,357. *Average indebtedness upon graduation:* $17,163.

Applying *Options:* common application, early action, deferred entrance. *Application fee:* $40. *Required:* high school transcript, 3 letters of recommendation, essay or graded paper. *Recommended:* interview. *Application deadlines:* 3/1 (freshmen), 4/1 (transfers). *Notification:* 3/30 (freshmen), 12/30 (early action), 5/1 (transfers).

Admissions Contact Myrt Whitcomb, Dean of Admission, Mills College, 5000 MacArthur Boulevard, Oakland, CA 94613-1301. *Phone:* 510-430-2135. *Toll-free phone:* 800-87-MILLS. *Fax:* 510-430-3314. *E-mail:* admission@mills.edu.

■ *See page 1994 for a narrative description.*

MOUNT ST. MARY'S COLLEGE
Los Angeles, California

- **Independent Roman Catholic** comprehensive, founded 1925
- **Calendar** semesters
- **Degrees** certificates, associate, bachelor's, master's, and postbachelor's certificates
- **Suburban** 71-acre campus
- **Endowment** $44.0 million
- **Coed, primarily women,** 1,719 undergraduate students, 75% full-time, 95% women, 5% men
- **Moderately difficult** entrance level, 86% of applicants were admitted

Undergraduates 1,288 full-time, 431 part-time. Students come from 23 states and territories, 3% are from out of state, 12% African American, 16% Asian American or Pacific Islander, 46% Hispanic American, 0.2% Native American, 0.1% international, 6% transferred in. *Retention:* 79% of 2002 full-time freshmen returned.

Freshmen *Admission:* 544 applied, 469 admitted, 374 enrolled. *Average high school GPA:* 3.02. *Test scores:* SAT verbal scores over 500: 51%; SAT math scores over 500: 56%; SAT verbal scores over 600: 10%; SAT math scores over 600: 12%.

Faculty *Total:* 268, 27% full-time, 29% with terminal degrees. *Student/faculty ratio:* 17:1.

Majors Accounting; American studies; art; art teacher education; biochemistry; biology/biological sciences; business administration and management; business teacher education; chemistry; developmental and child psychology; education; elementary education; English; French; gerontology; health/health care administration; history; international business/trade/commerce; kindergarten/preschool education; liberal arts and sciences/liberal studies; marketing/marketing management; mathematics; music; music teacher education; nursing (registered nurse training); occupational therapist assistant; philosophy; physical therapist assistant; political science and government; pre-dentistry studies; pre-law studies; pre-medical studies; psychology; religious studies; secondary education; social sciences; sociology; Spanish; urban studies/affairs; voice and opera.

Academic Programs *Special study options:* academic remediation for entering students, accelerated degree program, adult/continuing education programs, advanced placement credit, double majors, English as a second language, freshman honors college, honors programs, independent study, internships, off-campus study, part-time degree program, services for LD students, student-designed majors, study abroad, summer session for credit.

Library Charles Williard Coe Memorial Library with 140,000 titles, 750 serial subscriptions, an OPAC, a Web page.

Computers on Campus 85 computers available on campus for general student use. A campuswide network can be accessed from student residence rooms and from off campus. At least one staffed computer lab available.

Student Life *Housing options:* Campus housing is university owned. Freshman applicants given priority for college housing. *Activities and organizations:* drama/theater group, student-run newspaper, choral group, Latinas Unidas, student government, Pi Theta Mu, Kappa Delta Chi, Student Ambassadors, national sororities. *Campus security:* 24-hour patrols, controlled dormitory access. *Student services:* health clinic, personal/psychological counseling, women's center.

Athletics *Intramural sports:* basketball W, cross-country running W, swimming W, tennis W, track and field W, volleyball W.

Standardized Tests *Required:* SAT I or ACT (for admission). *Recommended:* SAT I (for admission).

Costs (2003–04) *Comprehensive fee:* $28,980 includes full-time tuition ($19,722), mandatory fees ($1034), and room and board ($8224). Part-time tuition: $750 per unit. *Required fees:* $365 per term part-time.

Financial Aid Of all full-time matriculated undergraduates who enrolled in 2003, 1,099 applied for aid. *Financial aid deadline:* 5/15.

Applying *Options:* electronic application, early action, deferred entrance. *Application fee:* $40. *Required:* essay or personal statement, high school transcript, minimum 2.0 GPA, 1 letter of recommendation. *Recommended:* minimum 3.0 GPA, interview. *Application deadlines:* 2/15 (freshmen), 3/15 (transfers). *Notification:* continuous (freshmen), 1/1 (early action), continuous (transfers).

Admissions Contact Mr. Dean Kilgour, Director of Admissions, Mount St. Mary's College, 12001 Chalon Road, Los Angeles, CA 90049-1599. *Phone:* 310-954-4252. *Toll-free phone:* 800-999-9893. *E-mail:* admissions@msmc.la.edu.

MT. SIERRA COLLEGE
Monrovia, California

- **Proprietary** 4-year, founded 1990
- **Calendar** quarters
- **Degree** bachelor's
- **Suburban** 5-acre campus
- **Coed,** 1,100 undergraduate students, 99% full-time, 30% women, 70% men
- **Moderately difficult** entrance level, 73% of applicants were admitted

Undergraduates 1,085 full-time, 15 part-time. Students come from 7 states and territories, 5% are from out of state, 5% African American, 26% Asian American or Pacific Islander, 26% Hispanic American, 4% Native American, 5% transferred in. *Retention:* 70% of 2002 full-time freshmen returned.

Freshmen *Admission:* 380 applied, 279 admitted, 279 enrolled. *Average high school GPA:* 2.79.

Faculty *Total:* 50, 44% full-time, 14% with terminal degrees. *Student/faculty ratio:* 15:1.

Majors Business administration and management; business/commerce; commercial and advertising art; computer and information sciences; computer and information sciences and support services related; computer and information systems security; computer/information technology services administration related; computer programming; computer science; computer systems networking and telecommunications; design and applied arts related; e-commerce; graphic design; illustration; information science/studies; intermedia/multimedia; system administration; system, networking, and LAN/wan management; web/multimedia management and webmaster.

Academic Programs *Special study options:* accelerated degree program, adult/continuing education programs, distance learning, independent study, internships, summer session for credit.

Library Mt. Sierra College Learning Resource Center with 6,000 titles, 5,000 serial subscriptions, 100 audiovisual materials.

Computers on Campus 300 computers available on campus for general student use. A campuswide network can be accessed from off campus. Internet access, online (class) registration, at least one staffed computer lab available. Computer purchase or lease plan available.

Student Life *Housing:* college housing not available. *Campus security:* 24-hour emergency response devices, student patrols, late-night transport/escort service.

Costs (2004–05) *Tuition:* $16,200 full-time. *Payment plans:* installment, deferred payment. *Waivers:* employees or children of employees.

Financial Aid In 2002, 6 non-need-based awards were made. *Average percent of need met:* 85%. *Average indebtedness upon graduation:* $28,000.

Applying *Options:* electronic application. *Application fee:* $95. *Required:* essay or personal statement, high school transcript, interview. *Application deadline:* 10/8 (transfers). *Notification:* 10/1 (freshmen).

Admissions Contact Mr. Al Desrosiors, Director of Admissions, Mt. Sierra College, 101 East Huntington Drive, Monrovia, CA 91016. *Phone:* 626-873-2100 Ext. 213. *Toll-free phone:* 888-828-8800. *Fax:* 626-359-5528.

MUSICIANS INSTITUTE
Hollywood, California

- **Proprietary** 4-year, founded 1976
- **Calendar** quarters
- **Degrees** certificates, diplomas, associate, and bachelor's
- **Coed,** 650 undergraduate students
- **Minimally difficult** entrance level

Majors Music.

Computers on Campus At least one staffed computer lab available.

Student Life *Housing:* college housing not available.

Athletics *Intercollegiate sports:* cheerleading W(s). *Intramural sports:* rock climbing M/W.

Costs (2003–04) *Tuition:* $13,200 full-time, $220 per unit part-time. *Required fees:* $400 full-time, $100 per term part-time.

Financial Aid Of all full-time matriculated undergraduates who enrolled in 2002, 520 applied for aid, 465 were judged to have need. *Average percent of need met:* 40%. *Average financial aid package:* $6100. *Average need-based loan:* $3100. *Average indebtedness upon graduation:* $14,000.

Applying *Application fee:* $100. *Application deadline:* rolling (freshmen). *Notification:* continuous (freshmen).

Admissions Contact Mr. Steve Lunn, Admissions Representative, Musicians Institute, 1655 North McCadden Place, Hollywood, CA 90028. *Phone:* 323-462-1384 Ext. 156. *Toll-free phone:* 800-255-PLAY.

THE NATIONAL HISPANIC UNIVERSITY
San Jose, California

- **Independent** 4-year, founded 1981
- **Calendar** semesters
- **Degrees** certificates, associate, bachelor's, and postbachelor's certificates
- **Urban** 1-acre campus
- **Endowment** $1.0 million
- **Coed**
- **Minimally difficult** entrance level

Faculty *Student/faculty ratio:* 14:1.

Student Life *Campus security:* 24-hour emergency response devices and patrols.

Standardized Tests *Recommended:* SAT I and SAT II or ACT (for admission), SAT II: Writing Test (for admission).

Costs (2003–04) *Tuition:* $3360 full-time, $140 per credit hour part-time. *Required fees:* $200 full-time, $100 per term part-time.

Financial Aid Of all full-time matriculated undergraduates who enrolled in 2002, 120 applied for aid, 100 were judged to have need. 3 Federal Work-Study jobs (averaging $3000). In 2002, 40. *Average percent of need met:* 30. *Average need-based loan:* $3500. *Average need-based gift aid:* $2500. *Average non-need-based aid:* $3000.

Applying *Options:* common application, electronic application. *Application fee:* $50. *Required:* essay or personal statement, high school transcript, minimum 2.0 GPA, letters of recommendation, interview.

Admissions Contact Office of Admissions, The National Hispanic University, 14271 Story Road, San Jose, CA 95127-3823. *Phone:* 408-254-6900.

NATIONAL UNIVERSITY
La Jolla, California

- **Independent** comprehensive, founded 1971
- **Calendar** quarters
- **Degrees** certificates, diplomas, associate, bachelor's, master's, and postbachelor's certificates
- **Urban** campus
- **Endowment** $162.7 million
- **Coed,** 4,031 undergraduate students, 48% full-time, 57% women, 43% men
- **Noncompetitive** entrance level

Undergraduates 1,915 full-time, 2,116 part-time. Students come from 64 other countries, 0.1% are from out of state, 13% African American, 9% Asian American or Pacific Islander, 19% Hispanic American, 0.9% Native American, 1% international, 9% transferred in.

Freshmen *Admission:* 60 enrolled.

Faculty *Total:* 2,357, 8% full-time, 7% with terminal degrees. *Student/faculty ratio:* 17:1.

Majors Accounting; banking and financial support services; behavioral sciences; biological and biomedical sciences related; business administration and management; computer science; computer software engineering; construction engineering; criminal justice/law enforcement administration; drafting/design engineering technologies related; English; finance; geology/earth science; hospitality administration; human resources management; information science/studies; interdisciplinary studies; intermedia/multimedia; legal studies; liberal arts and sciences/liberal studies; marketing/marketing management; mathematics; nursing

National University (continued)
science; occupational safety and health technology; operations management; organizational behavior; psychology; sport and fitness administration.
Academic Programs *Special study options:* accelerated degree program, adult/continuing education programs, advanced placement credit, distance learning, double majors, English as a second language, independent study, internships, off-campus study, part-time degree program, services for LD students, summer session for credit. *ROTC:* Army (c), Air Force (c).
Library Central Library with 226,049 titles, 2,794 serial subscriptions, 5,539 audiovisual materials, an OPAC, a Web page.
Computers on Campus 2253 computers available on campus for general student use. A campuswide network can be accessed from off campus. Internet access, online (class) registration, at least one staffed computer lab available.
Student Life *Housing:* college housing not available. *Campus security:* 24-hour emergency response devices and patrols, late-night transport/escort service.
Costs (2003–04) *Tuition:* $8550 full-time, $950 per course part-time. *Waivers:* employees or children of employees.
Applying *Options:* deferred entrance. *Application fee:* $60. *Required:* high school transcript, interview. *Required for some:* essay or personal statement. *Application deadline:* rolling (freshmen), rolling (transfers). *Notification:* continuous (freshmen), continuous (transfers).
Admissions Contact Department of Admissions, National University, 11255 North Torrey Pines Road, La Jolla, CA 92037. *Phone:* 800-NAT-UNIV. *Toll-free phone:* 800-628-8648. *Fax:* 858-642-8710. *E-mail:* jwilson@nu.edu.

NEW COLLEGE OF CALIFORNIA
San Francisco, California

- **Independent** comprehensive, founded 1971
- **Calendar** semesters
- **Degrees** certificates, bachelor's, master's, and postbachelor's certificates
- **Urban** campus
- **Coed,** 618 undergraduate students, 99% full-time, 49% women, 51% men
- **Noncompetitive** entrance level

Undergraduates 611 full-time, 7 part-time. Students come from 5 other countries, 3% African American, 1% Asian American or Pacific Islander, 5% Hispanic American, 0.5% Native American, 0.5% international. *Retention:* 87% of 2002 full-time freshmen returned.
Freshmen *Admission:* 300 enrolled.
Faculty *Total:* 90, 44% full-time. *Student/faculty ratio:* 15:1.
Majors Creative writing; cultural studies; ecology; education; humanities; interdisciplinary studies; literature; psychology; social sciences.
Academic Programs *Special study options:* academic remediation for entering students, accelerated degree program, advanced placement credit, cooperative education, English as a second language, internships, part-time degree program, student-designed majors, study abroad.
Library New College Library with 24,000 titles, 50 serial subscriptions.
Computers on Campus 10 computers available on campus for general student use. At least one staffed computer lab available.
Student Life *Housing:* college housing not available. *Activities and organizations:* drama/theater group, student-run newspaper. *Campus security:* trained security personnel. *Student services:* personal/psychological counseling, legal services.
Costs (2004–05) *Tuition:* $12,023 full-time, $484 per unit part-time. *Required fees:* $200 full-time, $100 per term part-time.
Applying *Options:* deferred entrance. *Application fee:* $50. *Required:* essay or personal statement, high school transcript. *Required for some:* 2 letters of recommendation. *Recommended:* interview. *Application deadline:* rolling (freshmen), rolling (transfers). *Notification:* continuous (freshmen), continuous (transfers).
Admissions Contact Ms. Sarah Starpoli, Admissions Inquiry Office, New College of California, 777 Valencia Street, San Francisco, CA 94110. *Phone:* 415-437-3420. *Toll-free phone:* 888-437-3460. *Fax:* 415-865-2636. *E-mail:* admissions@newcollege.edu.

■ *See page 2068 for a narrative description.*

NEWSCHOOL OF ARCHITECTURE & DESIGN
San Diego, California

- **Proprietary** comprehensive, founded 1980
- **Calendar** quarters
- **Degrees** associate, bachelor's, master's, and first professional
- **Urban** 1-acre campus
- **Coed, primarily men**
- **Moderately difficult** entrance level

Faculty *Student/faculty ratio:* 15:1.
Student Life *Campus security:* 24-hour emergency response devices, controlled dormitory access.
Costs (2003–04) *Tuition:* $18,675 full-time. *Required fees:* $195 full-time.
Financial Aid Of all full-time matriculated undergraduates who enrolled in 2000, 71 applied for aid. 6 Federal Work-Study jobs (averaging $1544). In 2000, 6. *Average percent of need met:* 90. *Average financial aid package:* $9700. *Average non-need-based aid:* $5000. *Average indebtedness upon graduation:* $40,000.
Applying *Options:* early decision. *Required:* essay or personal statement, high school transcript, minimum 2.5 GPA, interview. *Required for some:* portfolio. *Recommended:* letters of recommendation.
Admissions Contact Ms. Lexi Rogers, Director of Admissions, Newschool of Architecture & Design, 1249 F Street, San Diego, CA 92101-6634. *Phone:* 619-235-4100 Ext. 106. *E-mail:* admissions@newschoolarch.edu.

NORTHWESTERN POLYTECHNIC UNIVERSITY
Fremont, California

- **Independent** comprehensive, founded 1984
- **Calendar** trimesters
- **Degrees** bachelor's, master's, and doctoral
- **Urban** 2-acre campus with easy access to San Francisco and San Jose
- **Coed,** 150 undergraduate students, 53% full-time, 35% women, 65% men
- 100% of applicants were admitted

Undergraduates 79 full-time, 71 part-time. Students come from 20 states and territories, 13 other countries, 5% are from out of state, 6% transferred in, 11% live on campus. *Retention:* 89% of 2002 full-time freshmen returned.
Freshmen *Admission:* 23 applied, 23 admitted, 15 enrolled. *Average high school GPA:* 2.70.
Faculty *Total:* 60, 15% full-time, 45% with terminal degrees. *Student/faculty ratio:* 10:1.
Majors Business administration and management; computer engineering; computer science; electrical, electronics and communications engineering.
Academic Programs *Special study options:* adult/continuing education programs, advanced placement credit, English as a second language, internships, part-time degree program, summer session for credit.
Library NPU Library plus 1 other with 12,000 titles, 200 serial subscriptions, 200 audiovisual materials.
Computers on Campus 200 computers available on campus for general student use. A campuswide network can be accessed from student residence rooms and from off campus that provide access to online learning resource services. Internet access, online (class) registration, at least one staffed computer lab available.
Student Life *Housing options:* coed, men-only, women-only. Campus housing is university owned. *Activities and organizations:* NPU Student Association, table tennis club, IEEE Student Chapter, softball club. *Campus security:* late-night transport/escort service.
Athletics *Intercollegiate sports:* table tennis M.
Costs (2004–05) *Tuition:* $6000 full-time, $250 per unit part-time. *Required fees:* $340 full-time, $170 per term part-time. *Room only:* $2800.
Applying *Options:* common application. *Application fee:* $50. *Required:* high school transcript, minimum 2.0 GPA. *Required for some:* essay or personal statement. *Recommended:* interview. *Application deadlines:* 8/12 (freshmen), 8/12 (transfers). *Notification:* continuous (freshmen), continuous (transfers).
Admissions Contact Ms. Alice Ye, Admission Officer, Northwestern Polytechnic University, 117 Fourier Avenue, Fremont, CA 94539. *Phone:* 510-657-0256. *Fax:* 510-657-8975. *E-mail:* admission@npu.edu.

NOTRE DAME DE NAMUR UNIVERSITY
Belmont, California

- **Independent Roman Catholic** comprehensive, founded 1851
- **Calendar** semesters
- **Degrees** bachelor's and master's
- **Suburban** 80-acre campus with easy access to San Francisco
- **Endowment** $5.9 million
- **Coed,** 988 undergraduate students, 65% full-time, 68% women, 32% men
- **Moderately difficult** entrance level, 89% of applicants were admitted

Undergraduates 645 full-time, 343 part-time. Students come from 24 states and territories, 17 other countries, 10% are from out of state, 7% African American, 14% Asian American or Pacific Islander, 18% Hispanic American, 1%

Native American, 4% international, 56% transferred in, 36% live on campus. *Retention:* 80% of 2002 full-time freshmen returned.

Freshmen *Admission:* 537 applied, 477 admitted, 191 enrolled. *Average high school GPA:* 3.00. *Test scores:* SAT verbal scores over 500: 44%; SAT math scores over 500: 53%; ACT scores over 18: 80%; SAT verbal scores over 600: 9%; SAT math scores over 600: 15%; ACT scores over 24: 19%; SAT verbal scores over 700: 2%; SAT math scores over 700: 1%; ACT scores over 30: 4%.

Faculty *Total:* 189, 30% full-time, 52% with terminal degrees. *Student/faculty ratio:* 13:1.

Majors Accounting; advertising; art; behavioral sciences; biochemistry; biology/biological sciences; business administration and management; business/managerial economics; commercial and advertising art; communication and journalism related; communication/speech communication and rhetoric; computer science; computer software engineering; dramatic/theatre arts; education; elementary education; English; finance; fine/studio arts; French; history; humanities; human services; international business/trade/commerce; liberal arts and sciences/liberal studies; marketing/marketing management; music; music performance; philosophy; piano and organ; political science and government; pre-dentistry studies; pre-law studies; pre-medical studies; psychology; religious studies; secondary education; social sciences; sociology; violin, viola, guitar and other stringed instruments; voice and opera.

Academic Programs *Special study options:* academic remediation for entering students, accelerated degree program, adult/continuing education programs, advanced placement credit, cooperative education, double majors, English as a second language, independent study, internships, off-campus study, part-time degree program, services for LD students, study abroad, summer session for credit. *ROTC:* Air Force (c). *Unusual degree programs:* 3-2 engineering with Boston University.

Library College of Notre Dame Library with 726 serial subscriptions, 8,314 audiovisual materials, an OPAC.

Computers on Campus 50 computers available on campus for general student use. A campuswide network can be accessed from off campus. Internet access, at least one staffed computer lab available.

Student Life *Housing options:* coed, men-only, women-only. *Activities and organizations:* drama/theater group, student-run newspaper, choral group, Associated Students of Notre Dame de Namur University, BizCom, social action club, Alianza Latina, Hawaiian club. *Campus security:* 24-hour emergency response devices and patrols, late-night transport/escort service, controlled dormitory access. *Student services:* health clinic, personal/psychological counseling.

Athletics Member NAIA. *Intercollegiate sports:* basketball M/W, soccer M/W, softball W, volleyball W.

Standardized Tests *Required:* SAT I or ACT (for admission).

Costs (2004–05) *Comprehensive fee:* $31,150 includes full-time tuition ($21,350), mandatory fees ($150), and room and board ($9650). Part-time tuition: $510 per unit. *Required fees:* $15 per term part-time. *Room and board:* Room and board charges vary according to board plan and housing facility. *Payment plan:* installment. *Waivers:* employees or children of employees.

Applying *Options:* early action, deferred entrance. *Application fee:* $40. *Required:* essay or personal statement, high school transcript, 1 letter of recommendation. *Required for some:* interview. *Application deadline:* rolling (freshmen), rolling (transfers). *Notification:* continuous (freshmen), continuous (transfers).

Admissions Contact Ms. Melissa Garcia, Assistant Director for Undergraduate Admission, Notre Dame de Namur University, 1500 Ralston Avenue, Belmont, CA 94002-1997. *Phone:* 650-508-3532. *Toll-free phone:* 800-263-0545. *Fax:* 650-508-3765. *E-mail:* admiss@ndnu.edu.

■ *See page 2114 for a narrative description.*

OCCIDENTAL COLLEGE
Los Angeles, California

- **Independent** comprehensive, founded 1887
- **Calendar** semesters
- **Degrees** bachelor's and master's
- **Urban** 120-acre campus
- **Endowment** $230.1 million
- **Coed,** 1,840 undergraduate students, 99% full-time, 58% women, 42% men
- **Very difficult** entrance level, 44% of applicants were admitted

Undergraduates 1,823 full-time, 17 part-time. Students come from 45 states and territories, 24 other countries, 32% are from out of state, 7% African American, 12% Asian American or Pacific Islander, 15% Hispanic American, 1% Native American, 4% international, 3% transferred in, 70% live on campus. *Retention:* 91% of 2002 full-time freshmen returned.

Freshmen *Admission:* 4,513 applied, 1,964 admitted, 441 enrolled. *Test scores:* SAT verbal scores over 500: 85%; SAT math scores over 500: 87%; SAT verbal scores over 600: 61%; SAT math scores over 600: 61%; SAT verbal scores over 700: 18%; SAT math scores over 700: 16%.

Faculty *Total:* 206, 66% full-time. *Student/faculty ratio:* 11:1.

Majors American studies; anthropology; art history, criticism and conservation; Asian studies; biochemistry; biology/biological sciences; business/managerial economics; chemistry; cognitive psychology and psycholinguistics; comparative literature; dramatic/theatre arts; economics; environmental studies; fine/studio arts; French; geology/earth science; geophysics and seismology; history; international relations and affairs; kinesiology and exercise science; mathematics; music; philosophy; physics; physiological psychology/psychobiology; political science and government; psychology; public policy analysis; religious studies; sociology; Spanish; women's studies.

Academic Programs *Special study options:* accelerated degree program, advanced placement credit, double majors, honors programs, independent study, internships, off-campus study, services for LD students, student-designed majors, study abroad, summer session for credit. *ROTC:* Army (c), Navy (c), Air Force (c). *Unusual degree programs:* 3-2 engineering with California Institute of Technology, Columbia University.

Library Mary Norton Clapp Library plus 2 others with 481,822 titles, 1,135 serial subscriptions, an OPAC, a Web page.

Computers on Campus 131 computers available on campus for general student use. A campuswide network can be accessed from student residence rooms and from off campus. Internet access, online (class) registration, at least one staffed computer lab available.

Student Life *Housing:* on-campus residence required for freshman year. *Options:* coed, women-only. Campus housing is university owned. Freshman campus housing is guaranteed. *Activities and organizations:* drama/theater group, student-run newspaper, radio station, choral group, Asian-Pacific Islander Alliance, community service, Inter-Faith Student Council, Black Student Alliance, MECHA/ALAS, national fraternities. *Campus security:* 24-hour emergency response devices and patrols, late-night transport/escort service, controlled dormitory access, lighted pathways and sidewalks; whistle alert program. *Student services:* health clinic, personal/psychological counseling, women's center, legal services.

Athletics Member NCAA. All Division III. *Intercollegiate sports:* baseball M, basketball M/W, cheerleading W(c), crew W(c), cross-country running M/W, football M, golf M/W, lacrosse M(c)/W(c), rugby M(c)/W(c), soccer M/W, softball W, swimming M/W, tennis M/W, track and field M/W, ultimate Frisbee M(c)/W(c), volleyball M(c)/W, water polo M/W. *Intramural sports:* basketball M/W, football M/W, soccer M(c), volleyball M/W.

Standardized Tests *Required:* SAT I or ACT (for admission). *Recommended:* SAT II: Subject Tests (for admission), SAT II: Writing Test (for admission).

Costs (2003–04) *Comprehensive fee:* $36,126 includes full-time tuition ($27,734), mandatory fees ($572), and room and board ($7820). Part-time tuition: $1156 per credit. *Required fees:* $179 per term part-time. *College room only:* $4300. Room and board charges vary according to board plan and housing facility. *Payment plan:* installment. *Waivers:* employees or children of employees.

Financial Aid Of all full-time matriculated undergraduates who enrolled in 2003, 1,090 applied for aid, 978 were judged to have need, 426 had their need fully met. 767 Federal Work-Study jobs (averaging $2175). 127 state and other part-time jobs (averaging $2005). In 2003, 311 non-need-based awards were made. *Average percent of need met:* 95%. *Average financial aid package:* $28,003. *Average need-based loan:* $5444. *Average need-based gift aid:* $21,725. *Average non-need-based aid:* $17,422. *Average indebtedness upon graduation:* $22,000.

Applying *Options:* common application, early admission, early decision, deferred entrance. *Application fee:* $50. *Required:* essay or personal statement, high school transcript, 2 letters of recommendation. *Recommended:* interview. *Application deadlines:* 1/10 (freshmen), 3/15 (transfers). *Early decision:* 11/15. *Notification:* 4/1 (freshmen), 12/15 (early decision), 5/1 (transfers).

Admissions Contact Mr. Vince Cuseo, Director of Admission, Occidental College, 1600 Campus Road M-18, Los Angeles, CA 90041. *Phone:* 323-259-2700. *Toll-free phone:* 800-825-5262. *Fax:* 323-341-4875. *E-mail:* admission@oxy.edu.

OTIS COLLEGE OF ART AND DESIGN
Los Angeles, California

- **Independent** comprehensive, founded 1918
- **Calendar** semesters
- **Degrees** bachelor's and master's
- **Urban** 5-acre campus
- **Coed,** 1,023 undergraduate students, 98% full-time, 65% women, 35% men
- **Moderately difficult** entrance level, 63% of applicants were admitted

Undergraduates 1,005 full-time, 18 part-time. 26% are from out of state, 2% African American, 30% Asian American or Pacific Islander, 12% Hispanic

Otis College of Art and Design (continued)
American, 0.6% Native American, 12% international, 17% transferred in. *Retention:* 69% of 2002 full-time freshmen returned.

Freshmen *Admission:* 629 applied, 395 admitted, 162 enrolled. *Average high school GPA:* 3.04. *Test scores:* SAT verbal scores over 500: 47%; SAT math scores over 500: 56%; ACT scores over 18: 83%; SAT verbal scores over 600: 19%; SAT math scores over 600: 16%; ACT scores over 24: 39%; SAT verbal scores over 700: 3%; SAT math scores over 700: 3%; ACT scores over 30: 4%.

Faculty *Total:* 214, 18% full-time, 41% with terminal degrees. *Student/faculty ratio:* 11:1.

Majors Applied art; art; commercial and advertising art; drawing; environmental design/architecture; fashion/apparel design; fine/studio arts; interior design; photography; sculpture.

Academic Programs *Special study options:* academic remediation for entering students, adult/continuing education programs, advanced placement credit, cooperative education, English as a second language, freshman honors college, honors programs, independent study, internships, off-campus study, study abroad, summer session for credit.

Library Milliard Sheets Library with 42,000 titles, 150 serial subscriptions, 2,500 audiovisual materials, an OPAC, a Web page.

Computers on Campus 220 computers available on campus for general student use. A campuswide network can be accessed. Internet access, at least one staffed computer lab available.

Student Life *Activities and organizations:* student-run newspaper, Student Government Association, international students organization, Otis Students in Service (OASIS), literary magazine (club), Campus Crusade. *Campus security:* 24-hour patrols. *Student services:* personal/psychological counseling.

Standardized Tests *Required:* SAT I or ACT (for admission).

Costs (2003–04) *Tuition:* $22,820 full-time, $761 per credit part-time. *Required fees:* $600 full-time. *Payment plan:* installment. *Waivers:* employees or children of employees.

Financial Aid Of all full-time matriculated undergraduates who enrolled in 2002, 740 applied for aid, 638 were judged to have need, 7 had their need fully met. In 2002, 102 non-need-based awards were made. *Average percent of need met:* 17%. *Average financial aid package:* $12,774. *Average need-based loan:* $3677. *Average need-based gift aid:* $8962. *Average non-need-based aid:* $3097. *Average indebtedness upon graduation:* $25,700.

Applying *Options:* early admission. *Application fee:* $50. *Required:* essay or personal statement, high school transcript, minimum 2.5 GPA, portfolio. *Recommended:* 1 letter of recommendation, interview. *Application deadline:* rolling (freshmen), rolling (transfers). *Notification:* continuous (freshmen), continuous (transfers).

Admissions Contact Mr. Marc D. Meredith, Dean of Admissions, Otis College of Art and Design, 9045 Lincoln Boulevard, Los Angeles, CA 90045-9785. *Phone:* 310-665-6820. *Toll-free phone:* 800-527-OTIS. *Fax:* 310-665-6821. *E-mail:* admissions@otis.edu.

■ *See page 2138 for a narrative description.*

PACIFIC OAKS COLLEGE
Pasadena, California

- **Independent** upper-level, founded 1945
- **Calendar** semesters summer sessions and 2 intensive sessions
- **Degrees** bachelor's, master's, post-master's, and postbachelor's certificates
- **Small-town** 2-acre campus with easy access to Los Angeles
- **Endowment** $7.0 million
- **Coed, primarily women,** 210 undergraduate students, 8% full-time, 92% women, 8% men

Undergraduates 17 full-time, 193 part-time. Students come from 34 states and territories, 19% are from out of state, 16% African American, 4% Asian American or Pacific Islander, 34% Hispanic American, 1% Native American, 18% transferred in.

Faculty *Total:* 68, 43% full-time. *Student/faculty ratio:* 9:1.

Majors Child development; elementary education; human development and family studies; human services; kindergarten/preschool education; special education.

Academic Programs *Special study options:* adult/continuing education programs, distance learning, independent study, internships, off-campus study, part-time degree program, summer session for credit.

Library Andrew Norman Library with 18,451 titles, 106 serial subscriptions, 161 audiovisual materials, an OPAC.

Computers on Campus 17 computers available on campus for general student use. A campuswide network can be accessed from off campus that provide access to on-line class listings. Internet access, at least one staffed computer lab available.

Student Life *Housing:* college housing not available. *Activities and organizations:* Latina/o Support Group, Student Empowerment Group, Teacher Education Student Association, Marriage, Family Therapy Student Association.

Costs (2004–05) *Tuition:* $18,900 full-time, $630 per unit part-time. Full-time tuition and fees vary according to program. Part-time tuition and fees vary according to program. *Required fees:* $60 full-time, $30 per term part-time. *Payment plan:* installment. *Waivers:* employees or children of employees.

Financial Aid Of all full-time matriculated undergraduates who enrolled in 2002, 34 applied for aid, 31 were judged to have need. 6 Federal Work-Study jobs (averaging $5000). *Average financial aid package:* $4750. *Average need-based loan:* $5500. *Average need-based gift aid:* $8000. *Average indebtedness upon graduation:* $40,000.

Applying *Options:* deferred entrance. *Application fee:* $55. *Application deadline:* 6/1 (transfers). *Notification:* continuous until 9/1 (transfers).

Admissions Contact Ms. Teresa Cook, Director of Admissions, Pacific Oaks College, 5 Westmoreland Place, Pasadena, CA 91103. *Phone:* 626-397-4945. *Toll-free phone:* 800-684-0900. *Fax:* 626-685-2531. *E-mail:* admissions@pacificoaks.edu.

PACIFIC STATES UNIVERSITY
Los Angeles, California

- **Independent** comprehensive, founded 1928
- **Calendar** quarters
- **Degrees** bachelor's and master's
- **Urban** 1-acre campus
- **Coed,** 38 undergraduate students, 100% full-time, 32% women, 68% men
- **Minimally difficult** entrance level, 93% of applicants were admitted

Undergraduates 38 full-time. 10% are from out of state, 100% Asian American or Pacific Islander. *Retention:* 75% of 2002 full-time freshmen returned.

Freshmen *Admission:* 86 applied, 80 admitted, 27 enrolled.

Faculty *Total:* 16, 25% full-time, 63% with terminal degrees. *Student/faculty ratio:* 20:1.

Majors Business administration and management; computer science; electrical, electronics and communications engineering.

Academic Programs *Special study options:* accelerated degree program, adult/continuing education programs, English as a second language, independent study, student-designed majors, study abroad, summer session for credit.

Library University Library plus 1 other with 15,000 titles, 108 serial subscriptions, an OPAC.

Computers on Campus 25 computers available on campus for general student use. At least one staffed computer lab available.

Student Life *Housing:* college housing not available. *Campus security:* patrols by trained security personnel during campus hours.

Costs (2003–04) *Tuition:* $8400 full-time. *Required fees:* $480 full-time.

Applying *Options:* common application, electronic application, early admission, deferred entrance. *Application fee:* $100. *Required:* essay or personal statement, high school transcript, minimum 2.5 GPA. *Application deadlines:* 9/21 (freshmen), 10/27 (transfers). *Notification:* continuous (freshmen).

Admissions Contact Ms. Marina Miller, Assistant Director of Admissions, Pacific States University, 1516 South Western Avenue, Los Angeles, CA 90006. *Phone:* 323-731-2383. *Toll-free phone:* 888-200-0383. *E-mail:* admission@psuca.edu.

PACIFIC UNION COLLEGE
Angwin, California

- **Independent Seventh-day Adventist** comprehensive, founded 1882
- **Calendar** quarters
- **Degrees** associate, bachelor's, and master's
- **Rural** 200-acre campus with easy access to San Francisco
- **Endowment** $13.1 million
- **Coed,** 1,494 undergraduate students, 99% full-time, 54% women, 46% men
- **Moderately difficult** entrance level, 35% of applicants were admitted

Undergraduates 1,484 full-time, 10 part-time. Students come from 18 states and territories, 20 other countries, 9% are from out of state, 4% African American, 20% Asian American or Pacific Islander, 12% Hispanic American, 0.2% Native American, 8% international, 6% transferred in, 70% live on campus.

Freshmen *Admission:* 1,688 applied, 589 admitted, 282 enrolled. *Average high school GPA:* 3.30. *Test scores:* SAT verbal scores over 500: 62%; SAT math scores over 500: 58%; ACT scores over 18: 79%; SAT verbal scores over 600: 24%; SAT math scores over 600: 24%; ACT scores over 24: 30%; SAT verbal scores over 700: 5%; SAT math scores over 700: 4%; ACT scores over 30: 3%.

Faculty *Total:* 104, 79% full-time, 55% with terminal degrees. *Student/faculty ratio:* 14:1.

Majors Accounting; advertising; applied mathematics; art; art history, criticism and conservation; artificial intelligence and robotics; astrophysics; audiology and speech-language pathology; behavioral sciences; biblical studies; biochemistry; biology/biological sciences; biophysics; business administration and management; business teacher education; chemistry; child care and support services management; child care provision; clinical laboratory science/medical technology; computer and information sciences; computer management; computer programming; computer science; data processing and data processing technology; dietitian assistant; divinity/ministry; drafting and design technology; education; education (K-12); electrical, electronic and communications engineering technology; elementary education; engineering; engineering related; engineering technology; English; finance; fine/studio arts; French; graphic and printing equipment operation/production; history; industrial arts; industrial technology; information science/studies; interdisciplinary studies; international business/trade/commerce; journalism; kindergarten/preschool education; kinesiology and exercise science; laser and optical technology; legal administrative assistant/secretary; liberal arts and sciences/liberal studies; management information systems; marketing/marketing management; mass communication/media; mathematics; medical administrative assistant and medical secretary; music; music teacher education; nursing (registered nurse training); parks, recreation and leisure; pastoral studies/counseling; photography; physical education teaching and coaching; physical sciences; physics; piano and organ; political science and government; pre-dentistry studies; pre-engineering; pre-law studies; pre-medical studies; pre-veterinary studies; psychology; public relations/image management; religious studies; social sciences; social work; sociology; Spanish; theology; transportation technology.

Academic Programs *Special study options:* academic remediation for entering students, accelerated degree program, adult/continuing education programs, advanced placement credit, cooperative education, distance learning, double majors, English as a second language, freshman honors college, honors programs, independent study, internships, off-campus study, part-time degree program, services for LD students, student-designed majors, study abroad, summer session for credit.

Library W. E. Nelson Memorial Library with 165,321 titles, 839 serial subscriptions, 55,502 audiovisual materials, an OPAC, a Web page.

Computers on Campus 134 computers available on campus for general student use. A campuswide network can be accessed from student residence rooms and from off campus. Internet access, at least one staffed computer lab available.

Student Life *Housing:* on-campus residence required through senior year. *Options:* men-only, women-only. Campus housing is university owned. *Activities and organizations:* drama/theater group, student-run newspaper, choral group, Student Association, business club, Asian Student Association, Korean Adventist Student Association, Black Student Forum. *Campus security:* 24-hour emergency response devices and patrols, late-night transport/escort service. *Student services:* health clinic, personal/psychological counseling.

Athletics Member NAIA. *Intercollegiate sports:* basketball M/W, cross-country running M/W, volleyball M/W. *Intramural sports:* baseball M/W, basketball M/W, cross-country running M/W, football M, golf M/W, gymnastics M/W, soccer M/W, softball M/W, tennis M/W, volleyball M/W.

Standardized Tests *Required:* SAT I and SAT II or ACT (for placement).

Costs (2003–04) *One-time required fee:* $30. *Comprehensive fee:* $22,257 includes full-time tuition ($17,235), mandatory fees ($120), and room and board ($4902). Part-time tuition: $492 per credit. No tuition increase for student's term of enrollment. *Required fees:* $40 per term part-time. *College room only:* $2952. *Payment plans:* installment, deferred payment. *Waivers:* senior citizens and employees or children of employees.

Financial Aid Of all full-time matriculated undergraduates who enrolled in 2003, 1,218 applied for aid, 1,051 were judged to have need, 160 had their need fully met. 101 Federal Work-Study jobs (averaging $895). In 2003, 30 non-need-based awards were made. *Average percent of need met:* 72%. *Average financial aid package:* $10,958. *Average need-based loan:* $4250. *Average need-based gift aid:* $6424. *Average non-need-based aid:* $7606. *Average indebtedness upon graduation:* $12,000.

Applying *Options:* electronic application, deferred entrance. *Application fee:* $30. *Required:* high school transcript, minimum 2.3 GPA, 3 letters of recommendation. *Application deadline:* rolling (freshmen), rolling (transfers).

Admissions Contact Mr. Sean Kootsey, Director of Enrollment Services, Pacific Union College, Enrollment Services, One Angwin Avenue, Angwin, CA 94508. *Phone:* 707-965-6425. *Toll-free phone:* 800-862-7080. *Fax:* 707-965-6432. *E-mail:* enroll@puc.edu.

PATTEN UNIVERSITY
Oakland, California

- **Independent interdenominational** comprehensive, founded 1944
- **Calendar** semesters
- **Degrees** certificates, associate, bachelor's, master's, and postbachelor's certificates
- **Urban** 5-acre campus with easy access to San Francisco
- **Endowment** $274,588
- **Coed**
- **Noncompetitive** entrance level

Faculty *Student/faculty ratio:* 14:1.

Student Life *Campus security:* 24-hour emergency response devices, student patrols, late-night transport/escort service.

Athletics Member NAIA, NCCAA.

Standardized Tests *Required:* SAT I or ACT (for admission).

Costs (2003–04) *Comprehensive fee:* $15,640 includes full-time tuition ($9840) and room and board ($5800).

Applying *Options:* early admission, deferred entrance. *Application fee:* $30. *Required:* essay or personal statement, high school transcript, minimum 2.5 GPA, 2 letters of recommendation. *Recommended:* interview.

Admissions Contact Ms. Inez Bailey, Director of Admissions, Patten University, 2433 Coolidge Avenue, Oakland, CA 94601. *Phone:* 510-261-8500 Ext. 765. *Fax:* 510-534-4344.

PEPPERDINE UNIVERSITY
Malibu, California

- **Independent** university, founded 1937, affiliated with Church of Christ
- **Calendar** semesters
- **Degrees** bachelor's, master's, doctoral, and first professional
- **Small-town** 830-acre campus with easy access to Los Angeles
- **Coed,** 3,098 undergraduate students, 83% full-time, 56% women, 44% men
- **Very difficult** entrance level, 23% of applicants were admitted

Undergraduates 2,575 full-time, 523 part-time. Students come from 51 states and territories, 70 other countries, 48% are from out of state, 7% African American, 10% Asian American or Pacific Islander, 10% Hispanic American, 2% Native American, 6% international, 2% transferred in, 48% live on campus. *Retention:* 88% of 2002 full-time freshmen returned.

Freshmen *Admission:* 6,719 applied, 1,555 admitted, 615 enrolled. *Average high school GPA:* 3.60. *Test scores:* SAT verbal scores over 500: 90%; SAT math scores over 500: 91%; ACT scores over 18: 99%; SAT verbal scores over 600: 48%; SAT math scores over 600: 59%; ACT scores over 24: 81%; SAT verbal scores over 700: 11%; SAT math scores over 700: 13%; ACT scores over 30: 21%.

Faculty *Total:* 332, 58% full-time. *Student/faculty ratio:* 12:1.

Majors Accounting; advertising; art; athletic training; biology/biological sciences; business administration and management; chemistry; communication/speech communication and rhetoric; computer science; dramatic/theatre arts; economics; education; elementary education; English; foods, nutrition, and wellness; French; German; history; humanities; interdisciplinary studies; international business/trade/commerce; international relations and affairs; journalism; liberal arts and sciences/liberal studies; mathematics; music; music teacher education; natural sciences; philosophy; physical education teaching and coaching; political science and government; pre-dentistry studies; pre-law studies; pre-medical studies; psychology; public relations/image management; religious education; religious studies; secondary education; sociology; Spanish; speech and rhetoric; telecommunications.

Academic Programs *Special study options:* accelerated degree program, advanced placement credit, double majors, honors programs, independent study, internships, part-time degree program, student-designed majors, study abroad, summer session for credit. *ROTC:* Army (c), Navy (c), Air Force (c). *Unusual degree programs:* 3-2 engineering with University of Southern California, Washington University in St. Louis, Boston University.

Library Payson Library plus 2 others with 315,078 titles, 3,182 serial subscriptions, 5,044 audiovisual materials, an OPAC, a Web page.

Computers on Campus 292 computers available on campus for general student use. A campuswide network can be accessed from student residence rooms. Internet access, online (class) registration, at least one staffed computer lab available. Computer purchase or lease plan available.

Student Life *Housing:* on-campus residence required through sophomore year. *Options:* men-only, women-only, disabled students. Campus housing is university owned. Freshman campus housing is guaranteed. *Activities and organizations:*

Pepperdine University (continued)
drama/theater group, student-run newspaper, radio and television station, choral group, Student Government Association, Black Student Union, international club, Alpha Chi Honor Society, Golden Key Honor Society, national fraternities, national sororities. *Campus security:* 24-hour emergency response devices and patrols, student patrols, late-night transport/escort service, front gate security, 24-hour security in residence halls, controlled access, crime prevention programs. *Student services:* health clinic, personal/psychological counseling.

Athletics Member NCAA. All Division I. *Intercollegiate sports:* baseball M(s), basketball M(s)/W(s), cheerleading M/W, crew M(c)/W(c), cross-country running M(s)/W(s), field hockey W(c), golf M(s)/W(s), lacrosse M(c), rugby M(c), sailing M(c)/W(c), soccer M(c)/W(s), swimming W(s), tennis M(s)/W(s), volleyball M(s)/W(s), water polo M(s)/W(c). *Intramural sports:* badminton M/W, basketball M/W, cross-country running M/W, football M/W, golf M/W, lacrosse M/W, soccer M/W, softball M/W, swimming M/W, tennis M/W, volleyball M/W.

Standardized Tests *Required:* SAT I or ACT (for admission).

Costs (2004–05) *Comprehensive fee:* $37,360 includes full-time tuition ($28,630), mandatory fees ($90), and room and board ($8640). Part-time tuition: $890 per unit. *Room and board:* Room and board charges vary according to board plan and housing facility. *Payment plans:* installment, deferred payment. *Waivers:* employees or children of employees.

Financial Aid Of all full-time matriculated undergraduates who enrolled in 2003, 1,634 applied for aid, 1,403 were judged to have need, 340 had their need fully met. 785 Federal Work-Study jobs (averaging $1809). 284 state and other part-time jobs (averaging $1999). In 2003, 243 non-need-based awards were made. *Average percent of need met:* 89%. *Average financial aid package:* $22,611. *Average need-based loan:* $5019. *Average need-based gift aid:* $16,191. *Average non-need-based aid:* $14,042. *Average indebtedness upon graduation:* $31,179.

Applying *Options:* common application, electronic application, early action. *Application fee:* $55. *Required:* essay or personal statement, high school transcript, 2 letters of recommendation. *Recommended:* interview. *Application deadlines:* 1/15 (freshmen), 1/15 (transfers). *Notification:* 4/1 (freshmen), 12/15 (early action), 4/1 (transfers).

Admissions Contact Mr. Paul A. Long, Dean of Admission and Enrollment Management, Pepperdine University, 24255 Pacific Coast Highway, Malibu, CA 90263-4392. *Phone:* 310-506-4392. *Fax:* 310-506-4861. *E-mail:* admission-seaver@pepperdine.edu.

■ *See page 2166 for a narrative description.*

PITZER COLLEGE
Claremont, California

- **Independent** 4-year, founded 1963, part of The Claremont Colleges Consortium
- **Calendar** semesters
- **Degree** bachelor's
- **Suburban** 35-acre campus with easy access to Los Angeles
- **Endowment** $43.4 million
- **Coed,** 942 undergraduate students, 95% full-time, 60% women, 40% men
- **Moderately difficult** entrance level, 50% of applicants were admitted

Undergraduates 892 full-time, 50 part-time. Students come from 44 states and territories, 11 other countries, 47% are from out of state, 5% African American, 10% Asian American or Pacific Islander, 13% Hispanic American, 1% Native American, 3% international, 2% transferred in, 71% live on campus. *Retention:* 84% of 2002 full-time freshmen returned.

Freshmen *Admission:* 2,425 applied, 1,215 admitted, 230 enrolled. *Average high school GPA:* 3.58. *Test scores:* SAT verbal scores over 500: 93%; SAT math scores over 500: 90%; ACT scores over 18: 98%; SAT verbal scores over 600: 61%; SAT math scores over 600: 60%; ACT scores over 24: 66%; SAT verbal scores over 700: 15%; SAT math scores over 700: 12%; ACT scores over 30: 14%.

Faculty *Total:* 91, 78% full-time, 93% with terminal degrees. *Student/faculty ratio:* 11:1.

Majors African-American/Black studies; American history; American studies; anthropology; art; art history, criticism and conservation; Asian-American studies; Asian studies; biochemistry; biology/biological sciences; chemistry; classics and languages, literatures and linguistics; creative writing; dance; dramatic/theatre arts; economics; engineering; English; environmental science; environmental studies; European history; European studies; film/cinema studies; fine/studio arts; French; German; Hispanic-American, Puerto Rican, and Mexican-American/Chicano studies; history; interdisciplinary studies; international relations and affairs; Latin American studies; linguistics; literature; mathematics; neuroscience; philosophy; physics; political science and government; pre-medical studies; psychology; religious studies; Romance languages; Russian; science, technology and society; sociology; Spanish; women's studies.

Academic Programs *Special study options:* adult/continuing education programs, advanced placement credit, cooperative education, double majors, English as a second language, honors programs, independent study, internships, off-campus study, part-time degree program, services for LD students, student-designed majors, study abroad. *Unusual degree programs:* 3-2 business administration with Claremont Graduate University; public administration, mathematics with Claremont Graduate University.

Library Honnold Library plus 3 others with 2.0 million titles, 6,000 serial subscriptions, 606 audiovisual materials, an OPAC, a Web page.

Computers on Campus 100 computers available on campus for general student use. A campuswide network can be accessed from student residence rooms and from off campus. Internet access, at least one staffed computer lab available.

Student Life *Housing:* on-campus residence required through junior year. *Options:* coed, women-only, cooperative, disabled students. Campus housing is university owned. Freshman campus housing is guaranteed. *Activities and organizations:* drama/theater group, student-run radio station, choral group, Student Senate, The Other Side, Without A Box, Residence Hall Association. *Campus security:* 24-hour emergency response devices and patrols, late-night transport/escort service, controlled dormitory access. *Student services:* health clinic, personal/psychological counseling, women's center.

Athletics Member NCAA. All Division III. *Intercollegiate sports:* baseball M, basketball M/W, cross-country running M/W, football M, golf M, soccer M/W, softball W, swimming M/W, tennis M/W, track and field M/W, volleyball W, water polo M/W, wrestling M. *Intramural sports:* badminton M/W, baseball M, basketball M/W, cheerleading W, fencing M(c)/W(c), football M, lacrosse M(c)/W(c), rugby M(c), sailing M(c)/W(c), skiing (downhill) M(c)/W(c), soccer M/W, softball W, tennis M/W, track and field M/W, ultimate Frisbee M/W, volleyball M(c)/W, water polo M(c)/W(c).

Standardized Tests *Required for some:* SAT I or ACT (for admission).

Costs (2003–04) *Comprehensive fee:* $37,590 includes full-time tuition ($26,640), mandatory fees ($3154), and room and board ($7796). Full-time tuition and fees vary according to course load. Part-time tuition: $3330 per course. Part-time tuition and fees vary according to course load. *College room only:* $4880. Room and board charges vary according to board plan. *Payment plans:* installment, deferred payment. *Waivers:* employees or children of employees.

Financial Aid Of all full-time matriculated undergraduates who enrolled in 2003, 397 applied for aid, 379 were judged to have need, 379 had their need fully met. 338 Federal Work-Study jobs (averaging $2562). In 2003, 33 non-need-based awards were made. *Average percent of need met:* 100%. *Average financial aid package:* $27,950. *Average need-based loan:* $4941. *Average need-based gift aid:* $21,101. *Average non-need-based aid:* $10,000. *Average indebtedness upon graduation:* $20,900. *Financial aid deadline:* 2/1.

Applying *Options:* common application, electronic application, early admission, early action, deferred entrance. *Application fee:* $50. *Required:* essay or personal statement, high school transcript, 3 letters of recommendation. *Recommended:* interview. *Application deadlines:* 1/15 (freshmen), 4/15 (transfers). *Notification:* 4/1 (freshmen), 1/1 (early action), 5/15 (transfers).

Admissions Contact Dr. Arnaldo Rodriguez, Vice President for Admission and Financial Aid, Pitzer College, 1050 North Mills Avenue, Claremont, CA 91711-6101. *Phone:* 909-621-8129. *Toll-free phone:* 800-748-9371. *Fax:* 909-621-8770. *E-mail:* admission@pitzer.edu.

■ *See page 2176 for a narrative description.*

PLATT COLLEGE SAN DIEGO
San Diego, California

- **Proprietary** primarily 2-year, founded 1879
- **Calendar** continuous
- **Degrees** certificates, diplomas, associate, and bachelor's
- **Suburban** campus with easy access to San Diego
- **Coed**

Faculty *Student/faculty ratio:* 20:1.

Student Life *Campus security:* 24-hour emergency response devices, video camera.

Costs (2003–04) *Tuition:* $13,952 full-time. Full-time tuition and fees vary according to program. *Required fees:* $75 full-time. *Payment plans:* tuition prepayment, installment.

Applying *Application fee:* $75. *Required:* high school transcript, interview.

Admissions Contact Carly Westerfield, Coordinator, Platt College San Diego, 6250 El Cajon Boulevard, San Diego, CA 92115-3919. *Phone:* 619-265-0107. *Toll-free phone:* 800-255-0613. *Fax:* 619-265-8655. *E-mail:* info@platt.edu.

Point Loma Nazarene University
San Diego, California

- **Independent Nazarene** comprehensive, founded 1902
- **Calendar** semesters
- **Degrees** bachelor's and master's
- **Suburban** 88-acre campus
- **Endowment** $22.6 million
- **Coed,** 2,375 undergraduate students, 95% full-time, 59% women, 41% men
- **Moderately difficult** entrance level, 64% of applicants were admitted

Undergraduates 2,249 full-time, 126 part-time. Students come from 42 states and territories, 17 other countries, 22% are from out of state, 2% African American, 5% Asian American or Pacific Islander, 8% Hispanic American, 0.6% Native American, 1% international, 7% transferred in, 65% live on campus. *Retention:* 82% of 2002 full-time freshmen returned.

Freshmen *Admission:* 1,672 applied, 1,076 admitted, 555 enrolled. *Average high school GPA:* 3.72. *Test scores:* SAT verbal scores over 500: 83%; SAT math scores over 500: 84%; ACT scores over 18: 95%; SAT verbal scores over 600: 35%; SAT math scores over 600: 39%; ACT scores over 24: 56%; SAT verbal scores over 700: 5%; SAT math scores over 700: 4%; ACT scores over 30: 9%.

Faculty *Total:* 272, 50% full-time, 42% with terminal degrees. *Student/faculty ratio:* 16:1.

Majors Accounting; art; athletic training; biochemistry; biology/biological sciences; broadcast journalism; business administration and management; business/corporate communications; chemistry; child development; communication and media related; communication/speech communication and rhetoric; computer science; development economics and international development; dramatic/theatre arts; engineering physics; English; family and consumer sciences/human sciences; family systems; foods, nutrition, and wellness; graphic communications; health and physical education; history; industrial and organizational psychology; journalism; kinesiology and exercise science; liberal arts and sciences/liberal studies; management information systems; mathematics; music; music performance; music teacher education; music theory and composition; nursing (registered nurse training); philosophy; philosophy and religious studies related; physics; political science and government; psychology; religious/sacred music; Romance languages; social sciences; social work; sociology; Spanish; theological and ministerial studies related.

Academic Programs *Special study options:* academic remediation for entering students, advanced placement credit, double majors, internships, off-campus study, part-time degree program, services for LD students, study abroad, summer session for credit. *ROTC:* Army (c), Navy (c), Air Force (c).

Library Ryan Library with 146,016 titles, 836 serial subscriptions, 18,685 audiovisual materials, an OPAC, a Web page.

Computers on Campus 125 computers available on campus for general student use. A campuswide network can be accessed from student residence rooms and from off campus. Internet access, online (class) registration, at least one staffed computer lab available. Computer purchase or lease plan available.

Student Life *Housing:* on-campus residence required through junior year. *Options:* men-only, women-only. Campus housing is university owned and leased by the school. Freshman campus housing is guaranteed. *Activities and organizations:* drama/theater group, student-run newspaper, radio station, choral group, Chi Delta Psi, Psi Omega Theta, SNAPL (nurses association), Chi Beta Sigma, national sororities. *Campus security:* 24-hour patrols, student patrols, late-night transport/escort service. *Student services:* health clinic, personal/psychological counseling, women's center.

Athletics Member NAIA. *Intercollegiate sports:* baseball M(s), basketball M(s)/W(s), cheerleading M(c)/W(c), cross-country running M(s)/W(s), golf M(s), soccer M(s), softball W(s), tennis M(s)/W(s), track and field M(s)/W(s), volleyball W(s). *Intramural sports:* badminton M/W, baseball M, basketball M/W, bowling M/W, cross-country running M/W, football M/W, golf M/W, racquetball M/W, rock climbing M(c)/W(c), sailing M/W, soccer M/W, softball M/W, swimming M/W, table tennis M/W, tennis M/W, track and field M/W, ultimate Frisbee M/W, volleyball M/W, water polo M/W, weight lifting M/W.

Standardized Tests *Required:* SAT I or ACT (for admission). *Recommended:* SAT I (for admission).

Costs (2003–04) *Comprehensive fee:* $24,880 includes full-time tuition ($18,000), mandatory fees ($500), and room and board ($6380). Full-time tuition and fees vary according to course load. Part-time tuition: $750 per unit. Part-time tuition and fees vary according to course load. *Required fees:* $20 per unit part-time. *Room and board:* Room and board charges vary according to board plan. *Payment plan:* installment. *Waivers:* senior citizens and employees or children of employees.

Financial Aid Of all full-time matriculated undergraduates who enrolled in 2002, 1,544 applied for aid, 1,265 were judged to have need, 290 had their need fully met. In 2002, 637 non-need-based awards were made. *Average percent of need met:* 70%. *Average financial aid package:* $12,676. *Average need-based loan:* $4432. *Average need-based gift aid:* $9560. *Average non-need-based aid:* $7777. *Average indebtedness upon graduation:* $11,029.

Applying *Options:* early action, deferred entrance. *Application fee:* $45. *Required:* essay or personal statement, high school transcript, minimum 2.8 GPA, 2 letters of recommendation. *Required for some:* interview. *Application deadline:* 3/1 (freshmen), rolling (transfers). *Notification:* continuous (freshmen), 1/15 (early action), continuous (transfers).

Admissions Contact Mr. Scott Shoemaker, Dean of Enrollment, Point Loma Nazarene University, 3900 Lomaland Drive, San Diego, CA 92106. *Phone:* 619-849-2273. *Toll-free phone:* 800-733-7770. *Fax:* 619-849-2601. *E-mail:* admissions@ptloma.edu.

■ *See page 2180 for a narrative description.*

Pomona College
Claremont, California

- **Independent** 4-year, founded 1887, part of The Claremont Colleges Consortium
- **Calendar** semesters
- **Degree** bachelor's
- **Suburban** 140-acre campus with easy access to Los Angeles
- **Endowment** $1.0 billion
- **Coed,** 1,555 undergraduate students, 100% full-time, 51% women, 49% men
- **Most difficult** entrance level, 21% of applicants were admitted

Pomona is one of the nation's premier liberal arts colleges. Its widely diverse, intellectually talented student body enjoys a broad range of resources and opportunities supported by one of the largest financial endowments of any college. Pomona is the founding member of the Claremont Colleges, offering the benefits of a university setting with the advantages of a small college.

Undergraduates 1,548 full-time, 7 part-time. Students come from 48 states and territories, 18 other countries, 65% are from out of state, 6% African American, 13% Asian American or Pacific Islander, 7% Hispanic American, 0.9% Native American, 2% international, 0.1% transferred in, 97% live on campus. *Retention:* 97% of 2002 full-time freshmen returned.

Freshmen *Admission:* 4,539 applied, 968 admitted, 399 enrolled. *Average high school GPA:* 3.90. *Test scores:* SAT verbal scores over 500: 100%; SAT math scores over 500: 100%; ACT scores over 18: 100%; SAT verbal scores over 600: 97%; SAT math scores over 600: 97%; ACT scores over 24: 95%; SAT verbal scores over 700: 74%; SAT math scores over 700: 70%; ACT scores over 30: 73%.

Faculty *Total:* 212, 75% full-time, 85% with terminal degrees. *Student/faculty ratio:* 8:1.

Majors African-American/Black studies; American studies; anthropology; art; art history, criticism and conservation; Asian studies; Asian studies (East); astronomy; biochemistry; biology/biological sciences; cell biology and histology; chemistry; Chinese; classics and languages, literatures and linguistics; computer science; dance; dramatic/theatre arts; ecology; economics; English; environmental studies; film/cinema studies; fine/studio arts; French; geochemistry; geology/earth science; German; Hispanic-American, Puerto Rican, and Mexican-American/Chicano studies; history; humanities; interdisciplinary studies; international relations and affairs; Japanese; liberal arts and sciences/liberal studies; linguistics; mathematics; medical microbiology and bacteriology; modern languages; molecular biology; music; neuroscience; philosophy; physics; political science and government; pre-medical studies; psychology; public policy analysis; religious studies; Romance languages; Russian; sociology; Spanish; women's studies.

Academic Programs *Special study options:* advanced placement credit, double majors, independent study, internships, off-campus study, student-designed majors, study abroad. *Unusual degree programs:* 3-2 engineering with California Institute of Technology, Washington University in St. Louis.

Library Honnold Library plus 3 others with 2.2 million titles, 5,968 serial subscriptions, 16,524 audiovisual materials, an OPAC, a Web page.

Computers on Campus 180 computers available on campus for general student use. A campuswide network can be accessed from student residence rooms and from off campus. Internet access, at least one staffed computer lab available. Computer purchase or lease plan available.

Student Life *Housing:* on-campus residence required for freshman year. *Options:* coed. Campus housing is university owned. Freshman campus housing is guaranteed. *Activities and organizations:* drama/theater group, student-run newspaper, radio station, choral group, student government, music/choral organizations, service organizations, intramural sports. *Campus security:* 24-hour emergency response devices and patrols, late-night transport/escort service, controlled dormitory access. *Student services:* health clinic, personal/psychological counseling, women's center.

Athletics Member NCAA. All Division III. *Intercollegiate sports:* baseball M, basketball M/W, cross-country running M/W, football M, golf M/W, soccer M/W,

Pomona College (continued)
softball W, swimming M/W, tennis M/W, track and field M/W, ultimate Frisbee M(c)/W(c), volleyball W, water polo M/W. *Intramural sports:* badminton M(c)/W(c), basketball M/W, cross-country running M/W, fencing M/W, field hockey W(c), football M, golf M/W, lacrosse M(c)/W(c), racquetball M/W, rugby M(c)/W(c), sailing M(c)/W(c), skiing (cross-country) M(c)/W(c), skiing (downhill) M(c)/W(c), soccer M/W, softball M/W, squash M/W, swimming M/W, tennis M/W, track and field M/W, ultimate Frisbee M, volleyball M/W, water polo M/W.

Standardized Tests *Required:* SAT I and SAT II or ACT (for admission), 3 SAT II Subject Tests (including SAT II: Writing Test) (for admission).

Costs (2003–04) *Comprehensive fee:* $37,130 includes full-time tuition ($26,890), mandatory fees ($260), and room and board ($9980). Part-time tuition: $4485 per course. *Room and board:* Room and board charges vary according to board plan. *Payment plan:* installment. *Waivers:* employees or children of employees.

Financial Aid Of all full-time matriculated undergraduates who enrolled in 2002, 920 applied for aid, 786 were judged to have need, 786 had their need fully met. 250 Federal Work-Study jobs (averaging $1650). 500 state and other part-time jobs (averaging $1650). In 2002, 88 non-need-based awards were made. *Average percent of need met:* 100%. *Average financial aid package:* $25,700. *Average need-based loan:* $3230. *Average need-based gift aid:* $20,860. *Average non-need-based aid:* $2428. *Average indebtedness upon graduation:* $15,600. *Financial aid deadline:* 2/1.

Applying *Options:* common application, electronic application, early admission, early decision, deferred entrance. *Application fee:* $60. *Required:* essay or personal statement, high school transcript, 2 letters of recommendation. *Recommended:* minimum 3.0 GPA, interview, portfolio or tapes for art and performing arts programs. *Application deadlines:* 1/2 (freshmen), 3/15 (transfers). *Early decision:* 11/15 (for plan 1), 12/28 (for plan 2). *Notification:* 4/10 (freshmen), 12/15 (early decision plan 1), 2/15 (early decision plan 2), 5/15 (transfers).

Admissions Contact Mr. Bruce Poch, Vice President and Dean of Admissions, Pomona College, 333 North College Way, Claremont, CA 91711. *Phone:* 909-621-8134. *Fax:* 909-621-8952. *E-mail:* admissions@pomona.edu.

■ *See page 2186 for a narrative description.*

REMINGTON COLLEGE–SAN DIEGO CAMPUS
San Diego, California

Admissions Contact Mr. Jose Cisneros, Campus President, Remington College–San Diego Campus, 123 Camino de la Reina, North Building, Suite 100, San Diego, CA 92108. *Phone:* 619-686-8600 Ext. 210. *Toll-free phone:* 800-214-7001.

SAINT MARY'S COLLEGE OF CALIFORNIA
Moraga, California

- **Independent Roman Catholic** comprehensive, founded 1863
- **Calendar** 4-1-4
- **Degrees** certificates, bachelor's, master's, and doctoral
- **Suburban** 420-acre campus with easy access to San Francisco
- **Endowment** $111.8 million
- **Coed,** 3,337 undergraduate students, 72% full-time, 60% women, 40% men
- **Moderately difficult** entrance level, 82% of applicants were admitted

Undergraduates 2,406 full-time, 931 part-time. Students come from 26 states and territories, 21 other countries, 17% are from out of state, 7% African American, 10% Asian American or Pacific Islander, 18% Hispanic American, 0.8% Native American, 3% international, 4% transferred in, 61% live on campus. *Retention:* 84% of 2002 full-time freshmen returned.

Freshmen *Admission:* 3,172 applied, 2,590 admitted, 562 enrolled. *Average high school GPA:* 3.33. *Test scores:* SAT verbal scores over 500: 75%; SAT math scores over 500: 76%; SAT verbal scores over 600: 22%; SAT math scores over 600: 27%; SAT verbal scores over 700: 3%; SAT math scores over 700: 2%.

Faculty *Total:* 524, 40% full-time. *Student/faculty ratio:* 12:1.

Majors Accounting; accounting related; American studies; anthropology; archeology; area, ethnic, cultural, and gender studies related; art; art history, criticism and conservation; biochemistry; biological and biomedical sciences related; biology/biological sciences; business administration and management; business/commerce; chemistry; chemistry related; communication and journalism related; communication/speech communication and rhetoric; dance; dramatic/theatre arts; economics; engineering; English; English language and literature related; European studies; finance and financial management services related; foreign languages related; French; German; health and physical education; health and physical education related; health professions related; historic preservation and conservation; history; industrial and organizational psychology; interdisciplinary studies; international business/trade/commerce; international relations and affairs; Italian; kinesiology and exercise science; Latin; Latin American studies; liberal arts and sciences and humanities related; liberal arts and sciences/liberal studies; literature; mathematics; mathematics and computer science; mathematics and statistics related; modern Greek; modern languages; multi-/interdisciplinary studies related; music; nursing (registered nurse training); philosophy; physics; physiological psychology/psychobiology; political science and government; political science and government related; psychology; psychology related; religious studies; social sciences; social sciences related; sociology; Spanish; sport and fitness administration; theatre literature, history and criticism; theology; visual and performing arts related; women's studies.

Academic Programs *Special study options:* adult/continuing education programs, advanced placement credit, double majors, external degree program, honors programs, independent study, internships, off-campus study, part-time degree program, student-designed majors, study abroad. *ROTC:* Army (c), Air Force (c). *Unusual degree programs:* 3-2 engineering with Washington University in St. Louis, University of Southern California, Boston University; nursing with Samuel Merritt College.

Library St. Albert Hall plus 1 other with 207,076 titles, 1,070 serial subscriptions, 6,296 audiovisual materials, an OPAC, a Web page.

Computers on Campus 250 computers available on campus for general student use. A campuswide network can be accessed from student residence rooms and from off campus. Internet access, online (class) registration, at least one staffed computer lab available.

Student Life *Housing options:* coed, women-only, disabled students. Campus housing is university owned. Freshman campus housing is guaranteed. *Activities and organizations:* drama/theater group, student-run newspaper, radio and television station, choral group, LASA-Latin American Student Association, Student Alumni Association, Black Student Union, Intervarsity Christian Fellowship, Asian Pacific America Student Association. *Campus security:* 24-hour emergency response devices and patrols, late-night transport/escort service. *Student services:* health clinic, personal/psychological counseling, women's center.

Athletics Member NCAA. All Division I except football (Division I-AA). *Intercollegiate sports:* baseball M(s), basketball M(s)/W(s), cheerleading M/W, crew M(c)/W, cross-country running M(s)/W(s), golf M(s), lacrosse M(c)/W, rugby M(c)/W(c), soccer M(s)/W(s), softball W(s), tennis M(s)/W(s), volleyball M(c)/W(s), water polo M(c)/W(c). *Intramural sports:* badminton M/W, basketball M/W, bowling M/W, crew M/W, cross-country running M/W, football M/W, golf M/W, lacrosse M/W, rugby M/W, skiing (cross-country) M/W, skiing (downhill) M/W, soccer M/W, softball M/W, table tennis M/W, tennis M/W, ultimate Frisbee M/W, volleyball M/W, water polo M/W.

Standardized Tests *Required:* SAT I or ACT (for admission).

Costs (2003–04) *Comprehensive fee:* $32,850 includes full-time tuition ($23,640), mandatory fees ($135), and room and board ($9075). Full-time tuition and fees vary according to program. Part-time tuition: $2750 per course. *College room only:* $5065. Room and board charges vary according to board plan and housing facility. *Payment plans:* tuition prepayment, installment. *Waivers:* employees or children of employees.

Financial Aid Of all full-time matriculated undergraduates who enrolled in 2003, 1,710 applied for aid, 1,554 were judged to have need, 454 had their need fully met. 385 Federal Work-Study jobs (averaging $1962). In 2003, 85 non-need-based awards were made. *Average percent of need met:* 76%. *Average financial aid package:* $20,460. *Average need-based loan:* $4303. *Average need-based gift aid:* $15,625. *Average non-need-based aid:* $7944. *Average indebtedness upon graduation:* $19,953. *Financial aid deadline:* 3/2.

Applying *Options:* common application, electronic application, early action, deferred entrance. *Application fee:* $45. *Required:* essay or personal statement, high school transcript, minimum 2.0 GPA, 1 letter of recommendation. *Required for some:* minimum 3.0 GPA, interview. *Recommended:* minimum 3.0 GPA. *Application deadlines:* 2/1 (freshmen), 7/1 (transfers). *Notification:* continuous until 3/15 (freshmen), 1/15 (early action), continuous (transfers).

Admissions Contact Ms. Dorothy Jones, Dean of Admissions, Saint Mary's College of California, PO Box 4800, Moraga, CA 94556-4800. *Phone:* 925-631-4224. *Toll-free phone:* 800-800-4SMC. *Fax:* 925-376-7193. *E-mail:* smcadmit@stmarys-ca.edu.

■ *See page 2314 for a narrative description.*

SAMUEL MERRITT COLLEGE
Oakland, California

- **Independent** comprehensive, founded 1909
- **Calendar** 4-1-4
- **Degrees** bachelor's, master's, doctoral, and first professional (bachelor's degree offered jointly with Saint Mary's College of California)
- **Urban** 1-acre campus with easy access to San Francisco
- **Endowment** $21.3 million

- **Coed, primarily women,** 285 undergraduate students, 87% full-time, 93% women, 7% men
- **Moderately difficult** entrance level, 63% of applicants were admitted

Undergraduates 249 full-time, 36 part-time. Students come from 1 other state, 0.1% are from out of state, 12% African American, 23% Asian American or Pacific Islander, 14% Hispanic American, 2% Native American, 18% transferred in, 11% live on campus. *Retention:* 92% of 2002 full-time freshmen returned.

Freshmen *Admission:* 86 applied, 54 admitted, 15 enrolled. *Average high school GPA:* 3.37. *Test scores:* SAT verbal scores over 500: 71%; SAT math scores over 500: 50%; ACT scores over 18: 100%; SAT verbal scores over 600: 21%; SAT math scores over 600: 14%; ACT scores over 24: 20%.

Faculty *Total:* 120, 48% full-time, 39% with terminal degrees. *Student/faculty ratio:* 11:1.

Majors Nursing (registered nurse training).

Academic Programs *Special study options:* academic remediation for entering students, advanced placement credit, distance learning, double majors, independent study, internships, off-campus study, services for LD students, study abroad, summer session for credit. *ROTC:* Army (c), Navy (c), Air Force (c).

Library John A. Graziano Memorial Library plus 1 other with 11,000 titles, 540 serial subscriptions, 900 audiovisual materials.

Computers on Campus 48 computers available on campus for general student use. A campuswide network can be accessed. Internet access, at least one staffed computer lab available.

Student Life *Housing options:* coed. Campus housing is university owned. *Activities and organizations:* student-run newspaper, Multicultural Group, California Nursing Students Association, Student Body Association. *Campus security:* 24-hour emergency response devices and patrols, late-night transport/escort service, controlled dormitory access, 24-hour controlled access. *Student services:* health clinic, personal/psychological counseling.

Standardized Tests *Required:* SAT I or ACT (for admission).

Costs (2003–04) *Comprehensive fee:* $30,669 includes full-time tuition ($21,790), mandatory fees ($50), and room and board ($8829). Part-time tuition: $911 per unit. *College room only:* $5661. *Payment plans:* installment, deferred payment.

Financial Aid Of all full-time matriculated undergraduates who enrolled in 2001, 244 applied for aid, 239 were judged to have need, 22 had their need fully met. 118 Federal Work-Study jobs (averaging $3300). 12 state and other part-time jobs (averaging $2678). *Average percent of need met:* 82%. *Average financial aid package:* $22,000. *Average need-based loan:* $4000. *Average need-based gift aid:* $4000. *Average indebtedness upon graduation:* $27,500.

Applying *Options:* common application, deferred entrance. *Application fee:* $35. *Required:* essay or personal statement, high school transcript, minimum 2.5 GPA, 1 letter of recommendation. *Required for some:* interview. *Application deadlines:* 3/1 (freshmen), 3/1 (transfers). *Notification:* continuous (freshmen), continuous (transfers).

Admissions Contact Ms. Anne Seed, Director of Admissions, Samuel Merritt College, 570 Hawthorne Avenue, Oakland, CA 94609. *Phone:* 510-869-6610. *Toll-free phone:* 800-607-MERRITT. *Fax:* 510-869-6525. *E-mail:* admission@samuelmerritt.edu.

SAN DIEGO STATE UNIVERSITY
San Diego, California

- **State-supported** university, founded 1897, part of California State University System
- **Calendar** semesters
- **Degrees** bachelor's, master's, doctoral, post-master's, and postbachelor's certificates
- **Urban** 300-acre campus
- **Endowment** $66.5 million
- **Coed,** 27,345 undergraduate students, 79% full-time, 58% women, 42% men
- **Moderately difficult** entrance level, 50% of applicants were admitted

Undergraduates 21,697 full-time, 5,648 part-time. Students come from 50 states and territories, 125 other countries, 7% are from out of state, 4% African American, 15% Asian American or Pacific Islander, 21% Hispanic American, 0.7% Native American, 3% international, 12% transferred in, 48% live on campus. *Retention:* 82% of 2002 full-time freshmen returned.

Freshmen *Admission:* 29,129 applied, 14,454 admitted, 3,730 enrolled. *Average high school GPA:* 3.52. *Test scores:* SAT verbal scores over 500: 67%; SAT math scores over 500: 75%; ACT scores over 18: 89%; SAT verbal scores over 600: 18%; SAT math scores over 600: 26%; ACT scores over 24: 39%; SAT verbal scores over 700: 1%; SAT math scores over 700: 2%; ACT scores over 30: 2%.

Faculty *Total:* 1,684, 60% full-time, 47% with terminal degrees. *Student/faculty ratio:* 19:1.

Majors Accounting; aerospace, aeronautical and astronautical engineering; African-American/Black studies; agricultural business and management; American studies; anthropology; applied mathematics; art; art history, criticism and conservation; art teacher education; Asian studies; astronomy; atomic/molecular physics; biology/biological sciences; biology teacher education; business administration and management; chemical engineering; chemistry; chemistry related; chemistry teacher education; child development; civil engineering; classics and languages, literatures and linguistics; communication and journalism related; communication disorders; comparative literature; computer and information sciences; computer engineering; computer teacher education; creative writing; criminal justice/law enforcement administration; dance; design and visual communications; drama and dance teacher education; dramatic/theatre arts; ecology; econometrics and quantitative economics; economics; education (specific subject areas) related; electrical, electronics and communications engineering; engineering; English; English/language arts teacher education; environmental studies; European studies; evolutionary biology; finance; finance and financial management services related; fine arts related; foods, nutrition, and wellness; foreign language teacher education; French; French language teacher education; geochemistry; geography; geological and earth sciences/geosciences related; geology/earth science; German; German language teacher education; gerontology; health professions related; Hispanic-American, Puerto Rican, and Mexican-American/Chicano studies; history; hospitality administration related; hotel/motel administration; humanities; industrial arts; information science/studies; interior design; international business/trade/commerce; international economics; international relations and affairs; Japanese; journalism; journalism related; Latin American studies; liberal arts and sciences/liberal studies; linguistics; marine biology and biological oceanography; marketing/marketing management; mass communication/media; mathematics; mathematics and computer science; mathematics teacher education; mechanical engineering; medical microbiology and bacteriology; multi-/interdisciplinary studies related; music; music related; nursing (registered nurse training); painting; paleontology; parks, recreation and leisure; philosophy; physical education teaching and coaching; physical sciences; physics; political science and government; pre-law studies; psychology; public administration; public relations/image management; radio and television; real estate; religious studies; Russian; Russian studies; sales and marketing/marketing and distribution teacher education; science teacher education; sculpture; social sciences; social sciences related; social science teacher education; social work; sociology; Spanish; Spanish language teacher education; speech and rhetoric; statistics; technical teacher education; theoretical and mathematical physics; tourism and travel services management; urban studies/affairs; women's studies; zoology/animal biology.

Academic Programs *Special study options:* academic remediation for entering students, advanced placement credit, distance learning, double majors, English as a second language, honors programs, independent study, internships, off-campus study, part-time degree program, services for LD students, student-designed majors, study abroad, summer session for credit. *ROTC:* Army (b), Navy (b), Air Force (b).

Library Malcolm A. Love Library with 1.3 million titles, 8,245 serial subscriptions, 12,616 audiovisual materials, an OPAC, a Web page.

Computers on Campus 400 computers available on campus for general student use. A campuswide network can be accessed from student residence rooms and from off campus. Internet access, online (class) registration, at least one staffed computer lab available.

Student Life *Housing options:* coed, disabled students. Campus housing is university owned. Freshman applicants given priority for college housing. *Activities and organizations:* drama/theater group, student-run newspaper, radio and television station, choral group, marching band, American Marketing Association, Associated Students, Student Accounting Society, Residence Hall Association, MECHA, national fraternities, national sororities. *Campus security:* 24-hour emergency response devices and patrols, student patrols, late-night transport/escort service. *Student services:* health clinic, personal/psychological counseling, women's center.

Athletics Member NCAA. All Division I except football (Division I-A). *Intercollegiate sports:* baseball M(s), basketball M(s)/W(s), cross-country running W(s), golf M(s)/W(s), soccer M(s)/W(s), softball W(s), swimming W(s), tennis M(s)/W(s), track and field W(s), volleyball M/W(s), water polo W(s). *Intramural sports:* badminton M(c)/W(c), basketball M/W, bowling M/W, crew M/W(c), football M/W, golf M/W, ice hockey M(c), lacrosse M(c), racquetball M/W, rugby M(c), sailing M(c)/W(c), skiing (downhill) M(c)/W(c), soccer M/W, softball M/W, table tennis M/W, tennis M/W, volleyball M/W.

Standardized Tests *Required:* SAT I or ACT (for admission).

Costs (2003–04) *Tuition:* state resident $0 full-time; nonresident $8460 full-time, $282 per unit part-time. *Required fees:* $2488 full-time, $815 per term part-time. *Room and board:* $8787; room only: $5096.

Financial Aid Of all full-time matriculated undergraduates who enrolled in 2003, 13,400 applied for aid, 10,000 were judged to have need, 2,500 had their

San Diego State University (continued)
need fully met. In 2003, 280 non-need-based awards were made. *Average percent of need met:* 86%. *Average financial aid package:* $8500. *Average need-based loan:* $2800. *Average need-based gift aid:* $4000. *Average non-need-based aid:* $1400. *Average indebtedness upon graduation:* $13,000.

Applying *Options:* electronic application. *Application fee:* $55. *Required:* high school transcript, minimum 2.0 GPA, 2.5 GPA for non-California residents. *Application deadlines:* 11/30 (freshmen), 11/30 (transfers). *Notification:* 3/1 (freshmen), 3/1 (transfers).

Admissions Contact Prospective Student Center, San Diego State University, 5500 Campanile Drive, San Diego, CA 92182-7455. *Phone:* 619-594-6886. *Fax:* 619-594-1250. *E-mail:* admissions@sdsu.edu.

SAN FRANCISCO ART INSTITUTE
San Francisco, California

- **Independent** comprehensive, founded 1871
- **Calendar** semesters
- **Degrees** certificates, bachelor's, master's, and postbachelor's certificates
- **Urban** 3-acre campus
- **Endowment** $8.3 million
- **Coed,** 407 undergraduate students, 84% full-time, 53% women, 47% men
- **Moderately difficult** entrance level, 83% of applicants were admitted

Small enough for students and faculty members to work closely together and develop important relationships, yet large enough so that students are exposed to a variety of work and artists, the San Francisco Art Institute provides an environment for focused art making that emphasizes vision, skill, intellectual development, hands-on experience, and engagement with the world.

Undergraduates 341 full-time, 66 part-time. Students come from 24 states and territories, 18 other countries, 33% are from out of state, 2% African American, 7% Asian American or Pacific Islander, 10% Hispanic American, 2% Native American, 6% international, 29% transferred in.

Freshmen *Admission:* 251 applied, 208 admitted, 39 enrolled.

Faculty *Total:* 115, 30% full-time. *Student/faculty ratio:* 6:1.

Majors Ceramic arts and ceramics; drawing; film/cinema studies; interdisciplinary studies; painting; photography; printmaking; sculpture; web page, digital/multimedia and information resources design.

Academic Programs *Special study options:* academic remediation for entering students, accelerated degree program, adult/continuing education programs, advanced placement credit, double majors, English as a second language, external degree program, independent study, internships, off-campus study, part-time degree program, services for LD students, study abroad, summer session for credit.

Library Anne Bremer Memorial Library with 35,500 titles, 210 serial subscriptions, 121,000 audiovisual materials.

Computers on Campus 39 computers available on campus for general student use. A campuswide network can be accessed. Internet access, at least one staffed computer lab available.

Student Life *Housing options:* Campus housing is provided by a third party. *Activities and organizations:* Student Senate. *Campus security:* 24-hour patrols, security cameras. *Student services:* personal/psychological counseling.

Standardized Tests *Required:* SAT I or ACT (for admission).

Costs (2004–05) *Comprehensive fee:* $33,690 includes full-time tuition ($24,240) and room and board ($9450). Part-time tuition: $1010 per unit. Part-time tuition and fees vary according to course load. *Payment plan:* installment. *Waivers:* employees or children of employees.

Financial Aid *Average percent of need met:* 75%.

Applying *Options:* deferred entrance. *Application fee:* $50. *Required:* essay or personal statement, high school transcript, portfolio. *Recommended:* interview. *Application deadline:* 8/27 (freshmen), rolling (transfers). *Notification:* continuous until 4/15 (freshmen), continuous (transfers).

Admissions Contact Mark Takiguchi, Director of Admissions, San Francisco Art Institute, 800 Chestnut Street, San Francisco, CA 94133. *Phone:* 415-749-4500. *Toll-free phone:* 800-345-SFAI. *E-mail:* admissions@sfai.edu.

■ *See page 2344 for a narrative description.*

SAN FRANCISCO CONSERVATORY OF MUSIC
San Francisco, California

- **Independent** comprehensive, founded 1917
- **Calendar** semesters
- **Degrees** diplomas, bachelor's, and master's
- **Urban** 2-acre campus
- **Endowment** $30.3 million
- **Coed**
- **Moderately difficult** entrance level

Faculty *Student/faculty ratio:* 6:1.

Student Life *Campus security:* late-night transport/escort service.

Standardized Tests *Required:* SAT I or ACT (for admission). *Recommended:* SAT I (for admission).

Costs (2003–04) *Tuition:* $23,500 full-time. *Required fees:* $280 full-time.

Financial Aid Of all full-time matriculated undergraduates who enrolled in 2003, 146 applied for aid, 135 were judged to have need, 88 had their need fully met. 34 Federal Work-Study jobs (averaging $2058). 33 state and other part-time jobs (averaging $2151). In 2003, 9. *Average percent of need met:* 85. *Average financial aid package:* $21,000. *Average need-based loan:* $4580. *Average need-based gift aid:* $15,433. *Average non-need-based aid:* $7500.

Applying *Options:* early admission. *Application fee:* $70. *Required:* high school transcript, 2 letters of recommendation, audition.

Admissions Contact Ms. Susan Dean, Director of Admissions, San Francisco Conservatory of Music, 1201 Ortega Street, San Francisco, CA 94122-4411. *Phone:* 415-759-3431. *Fax:* 415-759-3499. *E-mail:* admit@sfcm.edu.

SAN FRANCISCO STATE UNIVERSITY
San Francisco, California

- **State-supported** comprehensive, founded 1899, part of California State University System
- **Calendar** semesters
- **Degrees** certificates, bachelor's, master's, doctoral, and postbachelor's certificates
- **Urban** 90-acre campus
- **Endowment** $3.6 million
- **Coed,** 21,892 undergraduate students, 75% full-time, 59% women, 41% men
- **Moderately difficult** entrance level, 64% of applicants were admitted

Undergraduates 16,407 full-time, 5,485 part-time. Students come from 48 states and territories, 113 other countries, 1% are from out of state, 6% African American, 32% Asian American or Pacific Islander, 13% Hispanic American, 0.9% Native American, 6% international, 17% transferred in. *Retention:* 79% of 2002 full-time freshmen returned.

Freshmen *Admission:* 16,221 applied, 10,417 admitted, 2,499 enrolled. *Average high school GPA:* 3.18. *Test scores:* SAT verbal scores over 500: 50%; SAT math scores over 500: 55%; ACT scores over 18: 69%; SAT verbal scores over 600: 15%; SAT math scores over 600: 15%; ACT scores over 24: 20%; SAT verbal scores over 700: 1%; SAT math scores over 700: 1%; ACT scores over 30: 1%.

Faculty *Total:* 1,646, 54% full-time, 50% with terminal degrees. *Student/faculty ratio:* 18:1.

Majors Accounting; African-American/Black studies; American studies; animal physiology; anthropology; applied mathematics; art; astronomy; astrophysics; atmospheric sciences and meteorology; audiology and speech-language pathology; biochemistry; biological and physical sciences; biology/biological sciences; botany/plant biology; business administration and management; cell biology and histology; chemistry; Chinese; civil engineering; classics and languages, literatures and linguistics; clothing/textiles; comparative literature; computer science; consumer merchandising/retailing management; creative writing; criminal justice/law enforcement administration; dance; dietetics; dramatic/theatre arts; ecology; economics; electrical, electronics and communications engineering; English; family and consumer sciences/human sciences; film/cinema studies; finance; French; geography; geology/earth science; German; health science; health teacher education; Hispanic-American, Puerto Rican, and Mexican-American/Chicano studies; history; hospitality administration; humanities; industrial arts; industrial design; information science/studies; interior design; international business/trade/commerce; international relations and affairs; Italian; Japanese; journalism; labor and industrial relations; liberal arts and sciences/liberal studies; literature; marine biology and biological oceanography; marketing/marketing management; mathematics; mechanical engineering; medical microbiology and bacteriology; molecular biology; music; nursing (registered nurse training); parks, recreation and leisure; philosophy; physical education teaching and coaching; physical sciences; physics; political science and government; psychology; radio and television; real estate; religious studies; Russian; social sciences; social work; sociology; Spanish; special products marketing; speech and rhetoric; statistics; technical and business writing; trade and industrial teacher education; transportation technology; urban studies/affairs; women's studies; zoology/animal biology.

Academic Programs *Special study options:* academic remediation for entering students, accelerated degree program, adult/continuing education programs, advanced placement credit, cooperative education, distance learning, double majors, English as a second language, honors programs, independent study, internships, off-campus study, part-time degree program, services for LD students, student-designed majors, study abroad, summer session for credit.

Library J. Paul Leonard Library plus 2 others with 780,230 titles, 5,679 serial subscriptions, 72,245 audiovisual materials, an OPAC, a Web page.

Computers on Campus 1474 computers available on campus for general student use. A campuswide network can be accessed from student residence rooms and from off campus. At least one staffed computer lab available.

Student Life *Housing options:* coed, disabled students. *Activities and organizations:* drama/theater group, student-run newspaper, radio and television station, choral group, marching band, African Student Union, Asian Student Union, Laraza Student Organization, Filipino Collegial Endeavor, Sigma Sigma Sigma, national fraternities, national sororities. *Campus security:* 24-hour emergency response devices and patrols, student patrols, late-night transport/escort service, controlled dormitory access. *Student services:* health clinic, personal/psychological counseling, women's center, legal services.

Athletics Member NCAA. All Division II. *Intercollegiate sports:* baseball M(s)/W(s), basketball M(s)/W(s), cross-country running M(s)/W(s), soccer M(s)/W(s), softball W(s), swimming M(s)/W(s), track and field M(s)/W(s), volleyball W(s), wrestling M(s). *Intramural sports:* basketball M/W, swimming M/W, volleyball M/W, wrestling M.

Standardized Tests *Required for some:* SAT I or ACT (for admission).

Costs (2003–04) *Tuition:* state resident $0 full-time; nonresident $8460 full-time, $282 per unit part-time. *Required fees:* $2498 full-time. *Room and board:* $8090; room only: $5030. Room and board charges vary according to board plan and housing facility. *Payment plans:* installment, deferred payment. *Waivers:* employees or children of employees.

Financial Aid Of all full-time matriculated undergraduates who enrolled in 2002, 8,399 applied for aid, 7,616 were judged to have need, 1,071 had their need fully met. In 2002, 28 non-need-based awards were made. *Average percent of need met:* 69%. *Average financial aid package:* $8638. *Average need-based loan:* $4814. *Average need-based gift aid:* $5280. *Average non-need-based aid:* $1053. *Average indebtedness upon graduation:* $16,088.

Applying *Application fee:* $55. *Required:* high school transcript. *Application deadline:* rolling (freshmen). *Notification:* continuous (freshmen), continuous (transfers).

Admissions Contact Ms. Patricia Wade, Admissions Officer, San Francisco State University, 1600 Holloway Avenue, San Francisco, CA 94132. *Phone:* 415-338-2037. *Fax:* 415-338-7196. *E-mail:* ugadmit@sfsu.edu.

SAN JOSE STATE UNIVERSITY
San Jose, California

- **State-supported** comprehensive, founded 1857, part of California State University System
- **Calendar** semesters
- **Degrees** bachelor's and master's
- **Urban** 104-acre campus
- **Coed,** 21,396 undergraduate students, 72% full-time, 51% women, 49% men
- **Moderately difficult** entrance level, 52% of applicants were admitted

Undergraduates 15,431 full-time, 5,965 part-time. Students come from 38 states and territories, 83% are from out of state, 5% African American, 41% Asian American or Pacific Islander, 14% Hispanic American, 0.4% Native American, 0.1% international, 9% transferred in.

Freshmen *Admission:* 13,065 applied, 6,785 admitted, 1,978 enrolled. *Average high school GPA:* 3.14. *Test scores:* SAT verbal scores over 500: 42%; SAT math scores over 500: 56%; ACT scores over 18: 68%; SAT verbal scores over 600: 10%; SAT math scores over 600: 17%; ACT scores over 24: 20%; SAT math scores over 700: 2%; ACT scores over 30: 1%.

Faculty *Total:* 1,685, 46% full-time. *Student/faculty ratio:* 18:1.

Majors Accounting; accounting and computer science; advertising; aeronautics/aviation/aerospace science and technology; aerospace, aeronautical and astronautical engineering; African-American/Black studies; American studies; anthropology; applied mathematics; art; art history, criticism and conservation; atmospheric sciences and meteorology; behavioral sciences; biochemistry; biological specializations related; biology/biological sciences; business administration and management; business administration, management and operations related; chemical engineering; chemistry; Chinese; civil engineering; communication disorders; computer engineering; computer science; criminal justice/safety; dance; dietetics; dramatic/theatre arts; early childhood education; economics; electrical, electronics and communications engineering; engineering; English; environmental studies; finance; finance and financial management services related; fine/studio arts; food science; French; geography; geological and earth sciences/geosciences related; geology/earth science; German; graphic design; health and physical education; health/health care administration; health services/allied health/health sciences; history; hospitality administration; humanities; human resources management; industrial design; industrial engineering; information technology; interior design; international business/trade/commerce; Japanese; journalism; liberal arts and sciences/liberal studies; linguistics; marine biology and biological oceanography; marketing/marketing management; materials engineering; mathematics; mechanical engineering; molecular biology; multi-/interdisciplinary studies related; music; music performance; natural sciences; nursing (registered nurse training); occupational therapy; parks, recreation and leisure; philosophy; physics; physiology; political science and government; psychology; public relations/image management; quality control technology; radio and television; religious studies; social sciences; social work; sociology; Spanish; speech and rhetoric; visual and performing arts.

Academic Programs *Special study options:* academic remediation for entering students, accelerated degree program, adult/continuing education programs, advanced placement credit, cooperative education, distance learning, double majors, English as a second language, honors programs, independent study, internships, off-campus study, part-time degree program, services for LD students, student-designed majors, study abroad, summer session for credit. *ROTC:* Army (b), Air Force (b).

Library Robert D. Clark Library plus 1 other with 1.1 million titles, 2,504 serial subscriptions, 37,146 audiovisual materials, an OPAC, a Web page.

Computers on Campus A campuswide network can be accessed from student residence rooms and from off campus. Internet access, online (class) registration, at least one staffed computer lab available.

Student Life *Housing options:* coed. *Activities and organizations:* drama/theater group, student-run newspaper, radio station, choral group, marching band, national fraternities, national sororities. *Campus security:* 24-hour emergency response devices and patrols, student patrols, late-night transport/escort service. *Student services:* health clinic, personal/psychological counseling, women's center.

Athletics Member NCAA. All Division I except football (Division I-A). *Intercollegiate sports:* baseball M(s), basketball M(s)/W(s), bowling M(c)/W(c), cross-country running M(s)/W(s), golf M(s)/W(s), gymnastics W(s), sailing M(c)/W(c), soccer M(s)/W(s), softball W, swimming W(s), tennis W(s), volleyball W(s), water polo W(s). *Intramural sports:* badminton M/W, baseball M, basketball M/W, bowling M/W, cross-country running M(c)/W(c), fencing M(c)/W(c), field hockey W(c), football M, ice hockey M(c), lacrosse M(c), racquetball M/W, rugby M(c)/W(c), soccer M/W, softball M/W, table tennis M(c)/W(c), tennis M/W, track and field M(c)/W(c), volleyball M(c)/W, water polo M/W, wrestling M(c)/W(c).

Standardized Tests *Required for some:* SAT I or ACT (for admission).

Costs (2003–04) *Tuition:* state resident $0 full-time; nonresident $6768 full-time, $282 per unit part-time. Part-time tuition and fees vary according to course load. *Required fees:* $2562 full-time, $897 per term part-time. *Room and board:* $8465. Room and board charges vary according to board plan and housing facility. *Payment plan:* installment. *Waivers:* employees or children of employees.

Financial Aid Of all full-time matriculated undergraduates who enrolled in 2002, 8,365 applied for aid, 6,991 were judged to have need, 1,111 had their need fully met. 633 Federal Work-Study jobs (averaging $2751). In 2002, 172 non-need-based awards were made. *Average percent of need met:* 68%. *Average financial aid package:* $6439. *Average need-based loan:* $3429. *Average need-based gift aid:* $4994. *Average non-need-based aid:* $1799. *Average indebtedness upon graduation:* $9932.

Applying *Options:* common application, electronic application. *Application fee:* $55. *Required:* high school transcript. *Application deadline:* 11/30 (freshmen), rolling (transfers). *Notification:* continuous (freshmen), continuous (transfers).

Admissions Contact Mr. John Loera, Director of Admissions, San Jose State University, One Washington Square, San Jose, CA 95192-0001. *Phone:* 408-283-7500. *Fax:* 408-924-2050. *E-mail:* contact@sjsu.edu.

SANTA CLARA UNIVERSITY
Santa Clara, California

- **Independent Roman Catholic (Jesuit)** university, founded 1851
- **Calendar** quarters
- **Degrees** bachelor's, master's, doctoral, first professional, post-master's, postbachelor's, and first professional certificates
- **Suburban** 104-acre campus with easy access to San Francisco and San Jose
- **Endowment** $401.4 million
- **Coed,** 4,298 undergraduate students, 97% full-time, 55% women, 45% men
- **Moderately difficult** entrance level, 66% of applicants were admitted

Undergraduates 4,174 full-time, 124 part-time. Students come from 35 states and territories, 12 other countries, 34% are from out of state, 2% African American, 19% Asian American or Pacific Islander, 14% Hispanic American, 0.6% Native American, 3% international, 6% transferred in, 46% live on campus. *Retention:* 92% of 2002 full-time freshmen returned.

Freshmen *Admission:* 6,388 applied, 4,223 admitted, 897 enrolled. *Average high school GPA:* 3.53. *Test scores:* SAT verbal scores over 500: 87%; SAT math

Santa Clara University (continued)
scores over 500: 94%; ACT scores over 18: 99%; SAT verbal scores over 600: 43%; SAT math scores over 600: 58%; ACT scores over 24: 75%; SAT verbal scores over 700: 6%; SAT math scores over 700: 10%; ACT scores over 30: 13%.

Faculty *Total:* 695, 60% full-time, 77% with terminal degrees. *Student/faculty ratio:* 12:1.

Majors Accounting; ancient/classical Greek; anthropology; art; art history, criticism and conservation; biological and physical sciences; biology/biological sciences; business/managerial economics; chemistry; civil engineering; classics and languages, literatures and linguistics; communication/speech communication and rhetoric; computer engineering; computer science; dramatic/theatre arts; economics; electrical, electronics and communications engineering; engineering; engineering physics; English; environmental science; environmental studies; finance; French; history; interdisciplinary studies; Italian; Latin; liberal arts and sciences/liberal studies; management information systems; marketing/marketing management; mathematics; mechanical engineering; music; philosophy; physics; political science and government; psychology; religious studies; sociology; Spanish.

Academic Programs *Special study options:* advanced placement credit, cooperative education, double majors, honors programs, independent study, internships, student-designed majors, study abroad, summer session for credit. *ROTC:* Army (b), Air Force (c).

Library Orradre Library plus 1 other with 639,691 titles, 11,952 serial subscriptions, 12,622 audiovisual materials, an OPAC, a Web page.

Computers on Campus 682 computers available on campus for general student use. A campuswide network can be accessed from student residence rooms and from off campus. Internet access, online (class) registration, at least one staffed computer lab available. Computer purchase or lease plan available.

Student Life *Housing options:* coed. Campus housing is university owned and leased by the school. Freshman applicants given priority for college housing. *Activities and organizations:* drama/theater group, student-run newspaper, radio and television station, choral group, Community Action Program, Associated Students, Activities Programming Board, Multicultural Programming Board, Residence Hall Association. *Campus security:* 24-hour emergency response devices and patrols, late-night transport/escort service, controlled dormitory access. *Student services:* health clinic, personal/psychological counseling, legal services.

Athletics Member NCAA. All Division I. *Intercollegiate sports:* baseball M(s), basketball M(s)/W(s), crew M/W, cross-country running M(s)/W(s), golf M(s)/W(s), lacrosse M(c)/W(c), rugby M(c)/W(c), soccer M(s)/W(s), softball W(s), tennis M(s)/W(s), volleyball M(c)/W(s), water polo M(s). *Intramural sports:* basketball M/W, football M/W, soccer M/W, softball M/W, swimming M/W, table tennis M/W, tennis M/W, ultimate Frisbee M/W, volleyball M/W.

Standardized Tests *Required:* SAT I or ACT (for admission).

Costs (2003–04) *Comprehensive fee:* $34,701 includes full-time tuition ($25,365) and room and board ($9336). Part-time tuition and fees vary according to course load. *Room and board:* Room and board charges vary according to housing facility. *Payment plans:* tuition prepayment, installment, deferred payment. *Waivers:* employees or children of employees.

Financial Aid Of all full-time matriculated undergraduates who enrolled in 2003, 3,230 applied for aid, 2,423 were judged to have need, 1,429 had their need fully met. 487 Federal Work-Study jobs (averaging $2201). In 2003, 480 non-need-based awards were made. *Average percent of need met:* 78%. *Average financial aid package:* $18,400. *Average need-based loan:* $4766. *Average need-based gift aid:* $14,308. *Average non-need-based aid:* $5025. *Average indebtedness upon graduation:* $25,492.

Applying *Options:* common application, electronic application, early action, deferred entrance. *Application fee:* $55. *Required:* essay or personal statement, high school transcript, 1 letter of recommendation. *Recommended:* interview. *Application deadlines:* 1/15 (freshmen), 5/15 (transfers). *Notification:* continuous until 4/1 (freshmen), 12/31 (early action), continuous (transfers).

Admissions Contact Ms. Sandra Hayes, Dean of Undergraduate Admissions, Santa Clara University, 500 El Camino Real, Santa Clara, CA 95053. *Phone:* 408-554-4700. *Fax:* 408-554-5255. *E-mail:* ugadmissions@scu.edu.

■ *See page 2346 for a narrative description.*

SCRIPPS COLLEGE
Claremont, California

- **Independent** 4-year, founded 1926, part of The Claremont Colleges Consortium
- **Calendar** semesters
- **Degrees** bachelor's and postbachelor's certificates
- **Suburban** 30-acre campus with easy access to Los Angeles
- **Endowment** $162.6 million
- **Women only,** 819 undergraduate students, 99% full-time
- **Very difficult** entrance level, 54% of applicants were admitted

Undergraduates 809 full-time, 10 part-time. Students come from 45 states and territories, 56% are from out of state, 3% African American, 13% Asian American or Pacific Islander, 5% Hispanic American, 0.4% Native American, 2% international, 2% transferred in, 92% live on campus. *Retention:* 92% of 2002 full-time freshmen returned.

Freshmen *Admission:* 210 enrolled. *Average high school GPA:* 3.90. *Test scores:* SAT verbal scores over 500: 100%; SAT math scores over 500: 98%; ACT scores over 18: 100%; SAT verbal scores over 600: 87%; SAT math scores over 600: 82%; ACT scores over 24: 90%; SAT verbal scores over 700: 35%; SAT math scores over 700: 24%; ACT scores over 30: 39%.

Faculty *Total:* 89, 69% full-time, 88% with terminal degrees. *Student/faculty ratio:* 11:1.

Majors African-American/Black studies; American studies; anthropology; art; art history, criticism and conservation; Asian-American studies; Asian studies; Asian studies (East); biochemistry; biology/biological sciences; chemistry; Chinese; classics and languages, literatures and linguistics; computer science; dance; dramatic/theatre arts; economics; English; environmental science; environmental studies; European studies; film/video and photographic arts related; fine/studio arts; foreign languages and literatures; French; geology/earth science; German; Hispanic-American, Puerto Rican, and Mexican-American/Chicano studies; history; international relations and affairs; Italian; Japanese; Jewish/Judaic studies; Latin; Latin American studies; legal studies; linguistics; mathematics; modern languages; molecular biology; multi-/interdisciplinary studies related; music; neuroscience; organizational behavior; philosophy; physics; physiological psychology/psychobiology; political science and government; pre-medical studies; psychology; religious studies; Russian; science, technology and society; sociology; Spanish; visual and performing arts related; women's studies.

Academic Programs *Special study options:* accelerated degree program, advanced placement credit, double majors, honors programs, independent study, internships, off-campus study, part-time degree program, student-designed majors, study abroad. *ROTC:* Army (c), Air Force (c). *Unusual degree programs:* 3-2 business administration with Claremont Graduate University; engineering with Stanford University, University of Southern California, Harvey Mudd College, University of California, Berkeley, Washington University in St. Louis, Columbia University, Boston University; public policy, religion, government, international studies, economics, philosophy with Claremont Graduate University.

Library Honnold Library plus 4 others with 998,823 titles, 5,733 serial subscriptions, 4,361 audiovisual materials, an OPAC, a Web page.

Computers on Campus 72 computers available on campus for general student use. A campuswide network can be accessed from student residence rooms and from off campus. Internet access, at least one staffed computer lab available.

Student Life *Housing:* on-campus residence required for freshman year. *Options:* women-only, disabled students. Campus housing is university owned. Freshman campus housing is guaranteed. *Activities and organizations:* drama/theater group, student-run newspaper, radio station, choral group, College Council, Asian/Black/Latina clubs, National Organization for Women, Sexual Assault Task Force, Family. *Campus security:* 24-hour emergency response devices and patrols, late-night transport/escort service, controlled dormitory access. *Student services:* health clinic, personal/psychological counseling, women's center.

Athletics Member NCAA. All Division III. *Intercollegiate sports:* basketball W, cheerleading M/W, cross-country running W, fencing W(c), golf W, lacrosse W, rock climbing W(c), rugby W(c), skiing (downhill) W(c), soccer W, softball W, swimming W, tennis W, track and field W, volleyball W, water polo W. *Intramural sports:* basketball W, football W, soccer W, softball W, ultimate Frisbee W, volleyball W, water polo W.

Standardized Tests *Required:* SAT I or ACT (for admission).

Costs (2003–04) *Comprehensive fee:* $35,700 includes full-time tuition ($26,964), mandatory fees ($136), and room and board ($8600). Full-time tuition and fees vary according to program. Part-time tuition: $3371 per course. Part-time tuition and fees vary according to program. *College room only:* $4600. Room and board charges vary according to board plan. *Payment plan:* installment. *Waivers:* employees or children of employees.

Financial Aid Of all full-time matriculated undergraduates who enrolled in 2002, 479 applied for aid, 393 were judged to have need, 393 had their need fully met. 312 Federal Work-Study jobs (averaging $1610). In 2002, 67 non-need-based awards were made. *Average percent of need met:* 100%. *Average financial aid package:* $23,861. *Average need-based loan:* $3977. *Average need-based gift aid:* $18,691. *Average non-need-based aid:* $12,790. *Average indebtedness upon graduation:* $14,362.

Applying *Options:* common application, electronic application, early decision, deferred entrance. *Application fee:* $50. *Required:* essay or personal statement, high school transcript, 3 letters of recommendation, graded writing sample. *Recommended:* minimum 3.0 GPA, interview. *Application deadlines:* 2/1 (freshmen), 4/1 (transfers). *Early decision:* 11/1 (for plan 1), 1/1 (for plan 2). *Notification:* 4/1 (freshmen), 12/15 (early decision plan 1), 2/15 (early decision plan 2), 6/1 (transfers).

Admissions Contact Ms. Patricia F. Goldsmith, Dean of Admission and Financial Aid, Scripps College, 1030 Columbia Avenue, Claremont, CA 91711-3948. *Phone:* 909-621-8149. *Toll-free phone:* 800-770-1333. *Fax:* 909-607-7508. *E-mail:* admission@scrippscollege.edu.

■ *See page 2362 for a narrative description.*

SHASTA BIBLE COLLEGE
Redding, California

- **Independent nondenominational** comprehensive, founded 1971
- **Calendar** semesters
- **Degrees** certificates, diplomas, associate, bachelor's, and master's
- **Small-town** 25-acre campus
- **Endowment** $1.1 million
- **Coed,** 84 undergraduate students, 83% full-time, 36% women, 64% men
- **Noncompetitive** entrance level

Undergraduates 70 full-time, 14 part-time. Students come from 5 states and territories, 1 other country, 3% are from out of state, 1% African American, 1% Asian American or Pacific Islander, 1% Hispanic American, 4% international, 32% transferred in. *Retention:* 90% of 2002 full-time freshmen returned.

Freshmen *Admission:* 43 enrolled. *Average high school GPA:* 3.00.

Faculty *Total:* 28, 21% full-time, 82% with terminal degrees. *Student/faculty ratio:* 11:1.

Majors Biblical studies; education; educational leadership and administration.

Academic Programs *Special study options:* academic remediation for entering students, adult/continuing education programs, distance learning, double majors, independent study, part-time degree program.

Library The Library plus 1 other with 30,321 titles, 103 serial subscriptions.

Computers on Campus 6 computers available on campus for general student use.

Student Life *Housing options:* men-only, women-only. Campus housing is university owned. Freshman applicants given priority for college housing. *Activities and organizations:* student-run newspaper, choral group. *Campus security:* 24-hour emergency response devices. *Student services:* personal/psychological counseling, women's center.

Costs (2004–05) *Tuition:* $6000 full-time, $200 per unit part-time. *Required fees:* $300 full-time, $300 per year part-time. *Room only:* $1575. *Payment plan:* tuition prepayment. *Waivers:* senior citizens and employees or children of employees.

Financial Aid Of all full-time matriculated undergraduates who enrolled in 2003, 55 applied for aid, 42 were judged to have need. 7 Federal Work-Study jobs (averaging $1449). 14 state and other part-time jobs (averaging $1692). In 2003, 2 non-need-based awards were made. *Average percent of need met:* 59%. *Average financial aid package:* $4019. *Average non-need-based aid:* $3900.

Applying *Options:* common application. *Application fee:* $35. *Required:* essay or personal statement, high school transcript, 4 letters of recommendation.

Admissions Contact Mr. Mark A. Mueller, Registrar, Shasta Bible College, 2951 Goodwater Avenue, Redding, CA 96002. *Phone:* 530-221-4275 Ext. 206. *Toll-free phone:* 800-800-45BC (in-state); 800-800-6929 (out-of-state). *Fax:* 530-221-6929. *E-mail:* ggunn@shasta.edu.

SILICON VALLEY COLLEGE
Emeryville, California

- **Proprietary** primarily 2-year, founded 2001
- **Calendar** semesters
- **Degrees** certificates, diplomas, associate, and bachelor's
- **Coed**

Faculty *Student/faculty ratio:* 18:1.

Standardized Tests *Required:* ACT (for admission).

Applying *Options:* common application. *Application fee:* $125. *Required:* interview. *Required for some:* high school transcript.

Admissions Contact Ms. Marianne Dulay, Admissions Representative, Silicon Valley College, 1400 65th Street, Suite 200, Emeryville, CA 94608. *Phone:* 510-601-0133 Ext. 14. *Toll-free phone:* 800-750-5627. *E-mail:* mdulay@svcollege.com.

SILICON VALLEY COLLEGE
Fremont, California

- **Proprietary** primarily 2-year, founded 1989
- **Calendar** semesters
- **Degrees** certificates, diplomas, associate, and bachelor's
- **Coed**

Faculty *Student/faculty ratio:* 18:1.

Standardized Tests *Required:* ACT (for admission).

Costs (2003–04) *Tuition:* $9450 full-time. Full-time tuition and fees vary according to program. *Required fees:* $625 full-time.

Applying *Options:* common application. *Application fee:* $125. *Required:* interview. *Required for some:* high school transcript.

Admissions Contact Mr. Anton Croos, Admissions Director, Silicon Valley College, 41350 Christy Street, Fremont, CA 94538. *Phone:* 510-623-9966 Ext. 212. *Toll-free phone:* 800-750-5627. *Fax:* 510-623-9822. *E-mail:* acroos@svcollege.com.

SILICON VALLEY COLLEGE
San Jose, California

- **Proprietary** primarily 2-year, founded 1999
- **Calendar** semesters
- **Degrees** certificates, diplomas, associate, and bachelor's
- **Coed**

Faculty *Student/faculty ratio:* 20:1.

Standardized Tests *Required:* ACT (for admission).

Costs (2003–04) *Tuition:* $9450 full-time. Full-time tuition and fees vary according to program. *Required fees:* $625 full-time.

Applying *Options:* common application. *Application fee:* $125. *Required:* interview. *Required for some:* high school transcript.

Admissions Contact Ms. Patricia Fraser, Admissions Director, Silicon Valley College, 6201 San Ignacio Avenue, San Jose, CA 95119. *Phone:* 408-360-0840 Ext. 247. *Toll-free phone:* 800-750-5627. *E-mail:* pfraser@svcollege.com.

SILICON VALLEY COLLEGE
Walnut Creek, California

- **Proprietary** primarily 2-year, founded 1997
- **Calendar** continuous
- **Degrees** certificates, diplomas, associate, and bachelor's
- **Coed,** 472 undergraduate students, 100% full-time, 65% women, 35% men

Undergraduates 472 full-time. Students come from 4 states and territories, 0.1% are from out of state, 16% African American, 10% Asian American or Pacific Islander, 9% Hispanic American, 4% Native American, 0.4% international.

Faculty *Total:* 17, 71% full-time, 18% with terminal degrees.

Majors Animation, interactive technology, video graphics and special effects; architectural drafting and CAD/CADD; architectural technology; architecture; architecture related; CAD/CADD drafting/design technology; design and visual communications; desktop publishing and digital imaging design; drafting and design technology; graphic and printing equipment operation/production; graphic communications; health and medical administrative services related; information technology; mechanical drafting and CAD/CADD; medical administrative assistant and medical secretary; medical office assistant; pharmacology and toxicology; pharmacology and toxicology related; pharmacy technician; system administration; system, networking, and LAN/wan management.

Academic Programs *Special study options:* accelerated degree program, cooperative education.

Library Silicon Valley College plus 1 other with 1,000 titles, 50 audiovisual materials.

Computers on Campus Internet access, at least one staffed computer lab available.

Student Life *Housing:* college housing not available. *Campus security:* 24-hour emergency response devices.

Standardized Tests *Required:* CPAt (for admission).

Costs (2004–05) *Tuition:* $12,000 full-time. Full-time tuition and fees vary according to degree level. No tuition increase for student's term of enrollment. *Waivers:* employees or children of employees.

Applying *Application fee:* $125. *Required:* high school transcript, interview, entrance exam. *Required for some:* essay or personal statement. *Notification:* continuous (freshmen), continuous (transfers).

Admissions Contact Mr. Mark Millen, Admissions Director, Silicon Valley College, 2800 Mitchell Drive, Walnut Creek, CA 94598. *Phone:* 925-280-0235 Ext. 37. *Toll-free phone:* 800-750-5627. *E-mail:* mmillen@svcollege.com.

Silicon Valley University
San Jose, California

Admissions Contact 3590 North First Street, Suite 320, San Jose, CA 95134.

Simpson College and Graduate School
Redding, California

- **Independent** comprehensive, founded 1921, affiliated with The Christian and Missionary Alliance
- **Calendar** semesters
- **Degrees** certificates, associate, bachelor's, and master's
- **Suburban** 92-acre campus
- **Endowment** $3.4 million
- **Coed,** 964 undergraduate students, 97% full-time, 63% women, 37% men
- **Moderately difficult** entrance level, 95% of applicants were admitted

Undergraduates 935 full-time, 29 part-time. Students come from 24 states and territories, 14% are from out of state, 0.8% African American, 6% Asian American or Pacific Islander, 4% Hispanic American, 1% Native American, 0.5% international, 19% transferred in, 66% live on campus. *Retention:* 59% of 2002 full-time freshmen returned.

Freshmen *Admission:* 784 applied, 743 admitted, 154 enrolled. *Average high school GPA:* 3.28. *Test scores:* SAT verbal scores over 500: 57%; SAT math scores over 500: 44%; ACT scores over 18: 71%; SAT verbal scores over 600: 15%; SAT math scores over 600: 12%; ACT scores over 24: 26%; SAT verbal scores over 700: 2%; SAT math scores over 700: 1%; ACT scores over 30: 3%.

Faculty *Total:* 80, 53% full-time. *Student/faculty ratio:* 17:1.

Majors Biblical studies; business administration and management; communication/speech communication and rhetoric; elementary education; English; English/language arts teacher education; general studies; history; human resources management; liberal arts and sciences/liberal studies; management information systems; mathematics; missionary studies and missiology; music; music teacher education; organizational behavior; psychology; religious education; social science teacher education; theology and religious vocations related.

Academic Programs *Special study options:* accelerated degree program, adult/continuing education programs, advanced placement credit, distance learning, double majors, honors programs, independent study, internships, off-campus study, part-time degree program, services for LD students, student-designed majors, study abroad, summer session for credit.

Library Start-Kilgour Memorial Library with 62,237 titles, 327 serial subscriptions, 2,021 audiovisual materials, an OPAC, a Web page.

Computers on Campus 58 computers available on campus for general student use. A campuswide network can be accessed from student residence rooms and from off campus. Internet access, online (class) registration, at least one staffed computer lab available.

Student Life *Housing:* on-campus residence required through junior year. *Options:* men-only, women-only, disabled students. Campus housing is university owned. Freshman campus housing is guaranteed. *Activities and organizations:* drama/theater group, student-run newspaper, choral group, Summer Missions Trips, Worship Team (chapel), Student Senate, Spiritual Action Committee, Psychology Club. *Campus security:* 24-hour emergency response devices and patrols, student patrols, late-night transport/escort service, controlled dormitory access, emergency whistle program and monthly campus safety meetings. *Student services:* health clinic, personal/psychological counseling.

Athletics Member NAIA, NCCAA. *Intercollegiate sports:* baseball M, basketball M/W, soccer M/W, softball W, volleyball W. *Intramural sports:* baseball M(c), basketball M/W, cheerleading W(c), cross-country running M(c)/W(c), football M/W, golf M(c), soccer M, table tennis M/W, volleyball M(c)/W.

Standardized Tests *Required:* SAT I or ACT (for admission).

Costs (2003–04) *Comprehensive fee:* $20,500 includes full-time tuition ($14,760) and room and board ($5740). Part-time tuition: $620 per credit hour. *Room and board:* Room and board charges vary according to board plan. *Payment plans:* installment, deferred payment. *Waivers:* employees or children of employees.

Financial Aid Of all full-time matriculated undergraduates who enrolled in 2003, 894 applied for aid, 814 were judged to have need, 38 had their need fully met. In 2003, 36 non-need-based awards were made. *Average percent of need met:* 72%. *Average financial aid package:* $12,507. *Average need-based loan:* $5000. *Average need-based gift aid:* $7507. *Average non-need-based aid:* $3050. *Average indebtedness upon graduation:* $17,600.

Applying *Options:* electronic application, deferred entrance. *Application fee:* $20. *Required:* essay or personal statement, high school transcript, minimum 2.0 GPA, 2 letters of recommendation, Christian commitment. *Required for some:* interview. *Application deadline:* rolling (freshmen), rolling (transfers). *Notification:* continuous (freshmen), continuous (transfers).

Admissions Contact Mrs. Beth Spencer, Director of Enrollment Support, Simpson College and Graduate School, 2211 College View Drive, Redding, CA 96003. *Phone:* 530-226-4606 Ext. 2602. *Toll-free phone:* 800-598-2493. *Fax:* 530-226-4861. *E-mail:* admissions@simpsonca.edu.

Sonoma State University
Rohnert Park, California

- **State-supported** comprehensive, founded 1960, part of California State University System
- **Calendar** semesters
- **Degrees** bachelor's and master's
- **Small-town** 280-acre campus with easy access to San Francisco
- **Endowment** $18.7 million
- **Coed,** 6,996 undergraduate students, 86% full-time, 63% women, 37% men
- **Moderately difficult** entrance level, 84% of applicants were admitted

Undergraduates 6,019 full-time, 977 part-time. Students come from 39 states and territories, 36 other countries, 2% are from out of state, 2% African American, 5% Asian American or Pacific Islander, 11% Hispanic American, 1% Native American, 1% international, 12% transferred in, 34% live on campus. *Retention:* 77% of 2002 full-time freshmen returned.

Freshmen *Admission:* 6,366 applied, 5,361 admitted, 1,303 enrolled. *Average high school GPA:* 3.16. *Test scores:* SAT verbal scores over 500: 61%; SAT math scores over 500: 63%; ACT scores over 18: 86%; SAT verbal scores over 600: 17%; SAT math scores over 600: 16%; ACT scores over 24: 26%; SAT verbal scores over 700: 2%; SAT math scores over 700: 1%; ACT scores over 30: 2%.

Faculty *Total:* 590, 42% full-time, 61% with terminal degrees. *Student/faculty ratio:* 22:1.

Majors African-American/Black studies; American Indian/Native American studies; American studies; animal physiology; anthropology; applied mathematics; art; art history, criticism and conservation; biology/biological sciences; botany/plant biology; business administration and management; business/managerial economics; cell biology and histology; chemistry; clinical/medical laboratory technology; computer science; criminal justice/law enforcement administration; cultural studies; developmental and child psychology; dramatic/theatre arts; drawing; ecology; economics; English; environmental education; environmental studies; fine/studio arts; French; geography; geology/earth science; health science; Hispanic-American, Puerto Rican, and Mexican-American/Chicano studies; history; interdisciplinary studies; international relations and affairs; liberal arts and sciences/liberal studies; literature; marine biology and biological oceanography; mass communication/media; mathematics; medical microbiology and bacteriology; multi-/interdisciplinary studies related; music; music teacher education; nursing (registered nurse training); philosophy; physical education teaching and coaching; physics; political science and government; pre-dentistry studies; pre-law studies; pre-medical studies; pre-veterinary studies; printmaking; psychology; sculpture; sociology; Spanish; statistics; women's studies; zoology/animal biology.

Academic Programs *Special study options:* academic remediation for entering students, accelerated degree program, adult/continuing education programs, advanced placement credit, cooperative education, distance learning, double majors, English as a second language, honors programs, independent study, internships, off-campus study, part-time degree program, services for LD students, student-designed majors, study abroad, summer session for credit. *ROTC:* Army (c), Air Force (c).

Library Jean and Charles Schultz Information Center with 602,415 titles, 21,040 serial subscriptions, 27,799 audiovisual materials, an OPAC, a Web page.

Computers on Campus 300 computers available on campus for general student use. A campuswide network can be accessed from student residence rooms and from off campus. Internet access, at least one staffed computer lab available.

Student Life *Housing options:* coed, women-only. Freshman applicants given priority for college housing. *Activities and organizations:* drama/theater group, student-run newspaper, radio station, choral group, Accounting Forum, Sonoma Earth Action, Re-Entry Student Association, Lacrosse club, Intervarsity Christian Fellowship, national fraternities, national sororities. *Campus security:* 24-hour emergency response devices and patrols, student patrols, late-night transport/escort service. *Student services:* health clinic, personal/psychological counseling, women's center, legal services.

Athletics Member NCAA. All Division II. *Intercollegiate sports:* baseball M(s), basketball M(s)/W(s), cross-country running W(s), soccer M(s)/W(s), softball W(s), tennis M(s)/W(s), track and field W(s), volleyball W(s). *Intramural sports:* baseball M, basketball M/W, soccer M/W, softball M/W, track and field W, volleyball M/W.

Standardized Tests *Required:* SAT I or ACT (for admission).

Costs (2003–04) *Tuition:* state resident $0 full-time; nonresident $8460 full-time. Part-time tuition and fees vary according to course load. *Required fees:*

$3010 full-time. *Room and board:* $7411; room only: $4645. Room and board charges vary according to board plan and housing facility. *Payment plan:* deferred payment. *Waivers:* employees or children of employees.

Financial Aid Of all full-time matriculated undergraduates who enrolled in 2003, 3,386 applied for aid, 2,714 were judged to have need, 710 had their need fully met. 421 Federal Work-Study jobs (averaging $2822). 911 state and other part-time jobs (averaging $2488). In 2003, 100 non-need-based awards were made. *Average percent of need met:* 86%. *Average financial aid package:* $6838. *Average need-based loan:* $3937. *Average need-based gift aid:* $5005. *Average non-need-based aid:* $6182. *Average indebtedness upon graduation:* $7848.

Applying *Options:* electronic application, early admission. *Application fee:* $55. *Required:* high school transcript. *Application deadlines:* 12/31 (freshmen), 1/31 (transfers). *Notification:* continuous (freshmen), continuous (transfers).

Admissions Contact Mr. Gustavo Flores , Interim Director of Admissions, Sonoma State University, 1801 East Cotati Avenue, Rohnert Park, CA 94928. *Phone:* 707-664-2074. *Fax:* 707-664-2060. *E-mail:* csumentor@sonoma.edu.

SOUTHERN CALIFORNIA BIBLE COLLEGE & SEMINARY

El Cajon, California

Admissions Contact Donna Coombs, Director of Admissions, Southern California Bible College & Seminary, 2075 East Madison Avenue, El Cajon, CA 92019. *Phone:* 619-442-9841.

SOUTHERN CALIFORNIA INSTITUTE OF ARCHITECTURE

Los Angeles, California

- **Independent** comprehensive, founded 1972
- **Calendar** semesters
- **Degrees** bachelor's, master's, and first professional
- **Urban** campus
- **Coed,** 183 undergraduate students, 100% full-time, 27% women, 73% men
- **Moderately difficult** entrance level

Undergraduates 183 full-time. Students come from 35 states and territories, 17 other countries, 2% African American, 17% Asian American or Pacific Islander, 22% Hispanic American, 0.5% Native American, 12% international. *Retention:* 40% of 2002 full-time freshmen returned.

Freshmen *Admission:* 5 enrolled. *Average high school GPA:* 3.10. *Test scores:* SAT verbal scores over 500: 85%; SAT math scores over 500: 95%; ACT scores over 18: 100%; SAT verbal scores over 600: 35%; SAT math scores over 600: 50%.

Faculty *Total:* 80. *Student/faculty ratio:* 15:1.

Majors Architecture.

Academic Programs *Special study options:* academic remediation for entering students, advanced placement credit, cooperative education, English as a second language, internships, study abroad, summer session for credit.

Library Kappe Library with 10,000 titles, 70 serial subscriptions.

Computers on Campus 30 computers available on campus for general student use. A campuswide network can be accessed. Internet access, at least one staffed computer lab available.

Student Life *Housing:* college housing not available. *Activities and organizations:* student-run newspaper, Student Council, Academic Council. *Campus security:* 24-hour emergency response devices and patrols.

Standardized Tests *Required:* SAT I or ACT (for admission).

Costs (2004–05) *Tuition:* $18,376 full-time. *Required fees:* $70 full-time.

Financial Aid Of all full-time matriculated undergraduates who enrolled in 2003, 137 applied for aid, 134 were judged to have need. In 2003, 21 non-need-based awards were made. *Average percent of need met:* 25%. *Average financial aid package:* $9500. *Average need-based loan:* $5500. *Average need-based gift aid:* $4000. *Average non-need-based aid:* $16,000. *Average indebtedness upon graduation:* $33,000.

Applying *Options:* deferred entrance. *Application fee:* $60. *Required:* essay or personal statement, high school transcript, minimum 2.0 GPA, 3 letters of recommendation, portfolio. *Recommended:* interview. *Application deadline:* 2/1 (freshmen), rolling (transfers). *Notification:* continuous until 7/1 (freshmen), continuous until 7/1 (transfers).

Admissions Contact Ms. Wenona Colinco, Director of Admissions, Southern California Institute of Architecture, Freight Yard, 960 East 3rd Street, Los Angeles, CA 90013. *Phone:* 213-613-2200 Ext. 321. *Toll-free phone:* 800-774-7242. *Fax:* 213-613-2260. *E-mail:* admissions@sciarc.edu.

■ *See page 2402 for a narrative description.*

SOUTHERN CALIFORNIA INSTITUTE OF TECHNOLOGY

Anaheim, California

- **Proprietary** primarily 2-year
- **Degrees** associate, bachelor's, and master's
- 664 undergraduate students, 100% full-time

Faculty *Student/faculty ratio:* 24:1.

Financial Aid Of all full-time matriculated undergraduates who enrolled in 2001, 8 Federal Work-Study jobs (averaging $2800).

Admissions Contact Ms. Flor Rojas, Director of Admissions, Southern California Institute of Technology, 1900 West Crescent Avenue, Building B, Anaheim, CA 92801. *Phone:* 714-520-5552.

STANFORD UNIVERSITY

Stanford, California

- **Independent** university, founded 1891
- **Calendar** quarters
- **Degrees** bachelor's, master's, doctoral, and first professional
- **Suburban** 8180-acre campus with easy access to San Francisco
- **Endowment** $8.6 billion
- **Coed,** 7,054 undergraduate students, 91% full-time, 50% women, 50% men
- **Most difficult** entrance level, 13% of applicants were admitted

Undergraduates 6,442 full-time, 612 part-time. Students come from 52 states and territories, 62 other countries, 48% are from out of state, 10% African American, 25% Asian American or Pacific Islander, 12% Hispanic American, 2% Native American, 6% international, 1% transferred in, 94% live on campus. *Retention:* 98% of 2002 full-time freshmen returned.

Freshmen *Admission:* 18,628 applied, 2,343 admitted, 1,640 enrolled. *Average high school GPA:* 3.90. *Test scores:* SAT verbal scores over 500: 100%; SAT math scores over 500: 100%; ACT scores over 18: 100%; SAT verbal scores over 600: 91%; SAT math scores over 600: 95%; ACT scores over 24: 95%; SAT verbal scores over 700: 63%; SAT math scores over 700: 69%; ACT scores over 30: 66%.

Faculty *Total:* 1,749, 98% full-time, 99% with terminal degrees. *Student/faculty ratio:* 7:1.

Majors Aerospace, aeronautical and astronautical engineering; African studies; American Indian/Native American studies; American studies; anthropology; archeology; art; Asian studies; Asian studies (East); biology/biological sciences; chemical engineering; chemistry; Chinese; civil engineering; classics and languages, literatures and linguistics; communication/speech communication and rhetoric; comparative literature; computer science; dramatic/theatre arts; economics; electrical, electronics and communications engineering; engineering; English; environmental/environmental health engineering; environmental studies; French; geology/earth science; geophysics and seismology; German; Hispanic-American, Puerto Rican, and Mexican-American/Chicano studies; history; industrial engineering; interdisciplinary studies; international relations and affairs; Italian; Japanese; linguistics; materials engineering; materials science; mathematics; mathematics and computer science; mechanical engineering; music; petroleum engineering; philosophy; physics; political science and government; psychology; public policy analysis; religious studies; science, technology and society; Slavic languages; sociology; Spanish; systems science and theory; urban studies/affairs; women's studies.

Academic Programs *Special study options:* advanced placement credit, double majors, honors programs, independent study, internships, off-campus study, services for LD students, student-designed majors, study abroad, summer session for credit. *ROTC:* Army (c), Navy (c), Air Force (c).

Library Green Library plus 18 others with 8.0 million titles, 50,056 serial subscriptions, 1.3 million audiovisual materials, an OPAC, a Web page.

Computers on Campus 1000 computers available on campus for general student use. A campuswide network can be accessed from student residence rooms and from off campus. Internet access, online (class) registration, at least one staffed computer lab available.

Student Life *Housing:* on-campus residence required for freshman year. *Options:* coed, women-only, cooperative, disabled students. Campus housing is university owned. Freshman campus housing is guaranteed. *Activities and organizations:* drama/theater group, student-run newspaper, radio and television station, choral group, marching band, Ram's Head (theatre club), Axe Committee (athletic support), Business Association of Engineering Students, Asian American Student Association, Stanford Daily, national fraternities, national sororities. *Campus security:* 24-hour emergency response devices and patrols, late-night transport/escort service, controlled dormitory access. *Student services:* health clinic, personal/psychological counseling, women's center, legal services.

Athletics Member NCAA, NAIA. All NCAA Division I except football (Division I-A). *Intercollegiate sports:* baseball M(s), basketball M(s)/W(s), crew

Stanford University (continued)
M/W(s), cross-country running M(s)/W(s), equestrian sports M(c)/W(c), fencing M(s)/W(s), field hockey M(c)/W(s), golf M(s)/W(s), gymnastics M(s)/W(s), ice hockey M(c), lacrosse M(c)/W, racquetball M(c)/W(c), rugby M(c)/W(c), sailing M(c)/W, skiing (cross-country) M(c)/W(c), skiing (downhill) M(c)/W(c), soccer M(s)/W(s), softball W(s), squash M(c)/W(c), swimming M(s)/W(s), tennis M(s)/W(s), track and field M(s)/W(s), ultimate Frisbee M/W, volleyball M(s)/W(s), water polo M(s)/W(s), wrestling M(s). *Intramural sports:* archery M/W, badminton M/W, baseball M, basketball M/W, bowling M/W, cross-country running M/W, field hockey W, football M/W, golf M/W, gymnastics M/W, soccer M/W, softball M/W, swimming M/W, table tennis M/W, tennis M/W, track and field M/W, volleyball M/W, water polo M/W, wrestling M.

Standardized Tests *Required:* SAT I or ACT (for admission). *Recommended:* SAT II: Subject Tests (for admission), SAT II: Writing Test (for admission).

Costs (2004–05) *Comprehensive fee:* $39,347 includes full-time tuition ($29,847) and room and board ($9500). *College room only:* $5012. Room and board charges vary according to board plan.

Financial Aid Of all full-time matriculated undergraduates who enrolled in 2002, 3,657 applied for aid, 3,122 were judged to have need, 2,924 had their need fully met. 522 Federal Work-Study jobs (averaging $1834). 912 state and other part-time jobs (averaging $1611). In 2002, 661 non-need-based awards were made. *Average percent of need met:* 100%. *Average financial aid package:* $25,634. *Average need-based loan:* $2466. *Average need-based gift aid:* $22,356. *Average non-need-based aid:* $2760. *Average indebtedness upon graduation:* $16,045.

Applying *Options:* early action, deferred entrance. *Application fee:* $75. *Required:* essay or personal statement, high school transcript, 2 letters of recommendation. *Application deadlines:* 12/15 (freshmen), 3/15 (transfers). *Notification:* 4/1 (freshmen), 12/15 (early action), 5/25 (transfers).

Admissions Contact Ms. Robin G. Mamlet, Dean of Undergraduate Admissions and Financial Aid, Stanford University, Old Union 232, 520 Lasuen Mall, Stanford, CA 94305. *Phone:* 650-723-2091. *Fax:* 650-723-6050. *E-mail:* admission@stanford.edu.

■ *See page 2434 for a narrative description.*

THOMAS AQUINAS COLLEGE
Santa Paula, California

- **Independent Roman Catholic** 4-year, founded 1971
- **Calendar** semesters
- **Degree** bachelor's
- **Rural** 170-acre campus with easy access to Los Angeles
- **Endowment** $9.0 million
- **Coed,** 332 undergraduate students, 100% full-time, 54% women, 46% men
- **Very difficult** entrance level, 78% of applicants were admitted

Undergraduates 332 full-time. Students come from 42 states and territories, 7 other countries, 53% are from out of state, 0.3% African American, 4% Asian American or Pacific Islander, 5% Hispanic American, 0.9% Native American, 8% international, 99% live on campus. *Retention:* 86% of 2002 full-time freshmen returned.

Freshmen *Admission:* 184 applied, 144 admitted, 101 enrolled. *Average high school GPA:* 3.71. *Test scores:* SAT verbal scores over 500: 100%; SAT math scores over 500: 99%; ACT scores over 18: 100%; SAT verbal scores over 600: 88%; SAT math scores over 600: 61%; ACT scores over 24: 93%; SAT verbal scores over 700: 32%; SAT math scores over 700: 10%; ACT scores over 30: 41%.

Faculty *Total:* 33, 91% full-time, 73% with terminal degrees. *Student/faculty ratio:* 11:1.

Majors Interdisciplinary studies; liberal arts and sciences/liberal studies; multi-/interdisciplinary studies related; western civilization.

Library St. Bernardine Library with 51,000 titles, 80 serial subscriptions, 2,200 audiovisual materials.

Computers on Campus 15 computers available on campus for general student use. At least one staffed computer lab available.

Student Life *Housing:* on-campus residence required through senior year. *Options:* men-only, women-only. Campus housing is university owned. Freshman campus housing is guaranteed. *Activities and organizations:* drama/theater group, choral group, choir, drama club, Legion of Mary, language clubs, Pro-Life Ministry. *Campus security:* 24-hour emergency response devices, student patrols, daily security daytime patrol. *Student services:* health clinic, personal/psychological counseling.

Athletics *Intercollegiate sports:* cheerleading M/W. *Intramural sports:* basketball M/W, football M, soccer M/W, softball M/W, table tennis M/W, tennis M/W, ultimate Frisbee M/W, volleyball M/W.

Standardized Tests *Required:* SAT I or ACT (for admission).

Costs (2003–04) *Comprehensive fee:* $22,000 includes full-time tuition ($16,800) and room and board ($5200). *Payment plan:* installment.

Financial Aid Of all full-time matriculated undergraduates who enrolled in 2003, 248 applied for aid, 221 were judged to have need, 221 had their need fully met. 204 state and other part-time jobs (averaging $2868). In 2003, 5 non-need-based awards were made. *Average percent of need met:* 100%. *Average financial aid package:* $14,936. *Average need-based loan:* $3408. *Average need-based gift aid:* $10,124. *Average non-need-based aid:* $2960. *Average indebtedness upon graduation:* $13,250.

Applying *Options:* early admission, deferred entrance. *Required:* essay or personal statement, high school transcript, 3 letters of recommendation. *Required for some:* interview. *Recommended:* minimum 2.0 GPA. *Application deadline:* rolling (freshmen). *Notification:* continuous (freshmen).

Admissions Contact Mr. Thomas J. Susanka Jr., Director of Admissions, Thomas Aquinas College, 10000 North Ojai Road, Santa Paula, CA 93060-9980. *Phone:* 805-525-4417 Ext. 361. *Toll-free phone:* 800-634-9797. *Fax:* 805-525-9342. *E-mail:* admissions@thomasaquinas.edu.

TOURO UNIVERSITY INTERNATIONAL
Cypress, California

- **Independent** university
- **Calendar** four 12 week sessions per year
- **Degrees** certificates, bachelor's, master's, doctoral, and postbachelor's certificates (offers only online degree programs)
- **Coed,** 1,748 undergraduate students, 80% full-time, 33% women, 67% men
- **Minimally difficult** entrance level, 54% of applicants were admitted

Undergraduates 1,404 full-time, 344 part-time. Students come from 50 states and territories, 15 other countries, 90% are from out of state, 65% transferred in. *Retention:* 95% of 2002 full-time freshmen returned.

Freshmen *Admission:* 665 applied, 358 admitted, 112 enrolled. *Average high school GPA:* 3.10.

Faculty *Total:* 89, 69% full-time, 98% with terminal degrees. *Student/faculty ratio:* 18:1.

Majors Business/commerce; health/health care administration; health teacher education; hospitality administration; management information systems; public health.

Academic Programs *Special study options:* adult/continuing education programs, distance learning, off-campus study, part-time degree program, summer session for credit.

Library Touro Cyber Library with 18,352 titles, 12,000 serial subscriptions, an OPAC, a Web page.

Computers on Campus A campuswide network can be accessed from off campus. Internet access, online (class) registration available.

Student Life *Housing:* college housing not available.

Costs (2004–05) *Tuition:* $7200 full-time, $225 per credit part-time. *Payment plan:* deferred payment. *Waivers:* employees or children of employees.

Applying *Options:* common application, electronic application. *Application fee:* $75. *Required:* high school transcript, minimum 3.0 GPA. *Required for some:* essay or personal statement. *Recommended:* interview. *Application deadline:* rolling (freshmen). *Notification:* continuous (freshmen).

Admissions Contact Wei Ren, Registrar, Touro University International, 5336 Plaza Drive, 3rd Floor, Cypress, CA 90630. *Phone:* 714-816-0366. *Fax:* 714-827-7407. *E-mail:* registration@tourou.edu.

TRINITY LIFE BIBLE COLLEGE
Sacramento, California

Admissions Contact Ms. Kathy Clarke, Registrar, Trinity Life Bible College, 5225 Hillsdale Boulevard, Sacramento, CA 95842. *Phone:* 816-348-4689.

UNIVERSITY OF CALIFORNIA, BERKELEY
Berkeley, California

- **State-supported** university, founded 1868, part of University of California System
- **Calendar** semesters
- **Degrees** certificates, bachelor's, master's, doctoral, and first professional
- **Urban** 1232-acre campus with easy access to San Francisco
- **Endowment** $1.3 billion
- **Coed,** 23,206 undergraduate students, 95% full-time, 54% women, 46% men
- **Very difficult** entrance level, 24% of applicants were admitted

Undergraduates 21,942 full-time, 1,264 part-time. Students come from 53 states and territories, 100 other countries, 11% are from out of state, 4% African American, 41% Asian American or Pacific Islander, 11% Hispanic American, 0.6% Native American, 3% international, 7% transferred in, 35% live on campus. *Retention:* 95% of 2001 full-time freshmen returned.

Freshmen *Admission:* 36,976 applied, 8,832 admitted, 3,653 enrolled. *Average high school GPA:* 3.94. *Test scores:* SAT verbal scores over 500: 89%; SAT math scores over 500: 95%; SAT verbal scores over 600: 67%; SAT math scores over 600: 80%; SAT verbal scores over 700: 28%; SAT math scores over 700: 45%.

Faculty *Total:* 1,889, 78% full-time, 95% with terminal degrees. *Student/faculty ratio:* 16:1.

Majors African-American/Black studies; American Indian/Native American studies; American studies; ancient/classical Greek; anthropology; applied mathematics; architecture; art; art history, criticism and conservation; Asian-American studies; Asian studies; Asian studies (Southeast); astrophysics; biology/biological sciences; biomedical/medical engineering; botany/plant biology; business administration and management; cell and molecular biology; Celtic languages; chemical engineering; chemistry; chemistry related; Chinese; civil engineering; classical, ancient Mediterranean and Near Eastern studies and archaeology; classics and languages, literatures and linguistics; cognitive science; comparative literature; computer science; dance; dramatic/theatre arts; Dutch/Flemish; economics; electrical, electronics and communications engineering; engineering physics; engineering science; English; environmental/environmental health engineering; environmental science; environmental studies; ethnic, cultural minority, and gender studies related; film/cinema studies; foreign languages related; forestry; French; geography; geological/geophysical engineering; geology/earth science; German; Hispanic-American, Puerto Rican, and Mexican-American/Chicano studies; history; Italian; Japanese; landscape architecture; Latin; Latin American studies; legal studies; linguistics; manufacturing engineering; mass communication/media; materials science; mathematics; mechanical engineering; microbiology; multi-/interdisciplinary studies related; music; natural resources/conservation; natural resources management and policy; Near and Middle Eastern studies; nuclear engineering; nutrition sciences; operations research; peace studies and conflict resolution; philosophy; physical sciences; physics; political science and government; psychology; public health related; religious studies; Scandinavian languages; Slavic languages; social sciences related; social work; sociology; Spanish; speech and rhetoric; statistics; urban studies/affairs; women's studies.

Academic Programs *Special study options:* accelerated degree program, adult/continuing education programs, advanced placement credit, distance learning, double majors, English as a second language, honors programs, independent study, internships, off-campus study, services for LD students, student-designed majors, study abroad, summer session for credit. *ROTC:* Army (b), Navy (b), Air Force (b).

Library Doe Library plus 30 others with 13.9 million titles, 181,071 serial subscriptions, 100,560 audiovisual materials, an OPAC, a Web page.

Computers on Campus 600 computers available on campus for general student use. A campuswide network can be accessed from student residence rooms and from off campus. Internet access, online (class) registration, at least one staffed computer lab available. Computer purchase or lease plan available.

Student Life *Housing:* on-campus residence required for freshman year. *Options:* coed, men-only, women-only, cooperative, disabled students. Campus housing is university owned and is provided by a third party. Freshman campus housing is guaranteed. *Activities and organizations:* drama/theater group, student-run newspaper, radio and television station, choral group, marching band, national fraternities, national sororities. *Campus security:* 24-hour emergency response devices and patrols, late-night transport/escort service, controlled dormitory access, Office of Emergency Preparedness. *Student services:* health clinic, personal/psychological counseling, women's center, legal services.

Athletics Member NCAA. All Division I except football (Division I-A). *Intercollegiate sports:* baseball M(s), basketball M(s)/W(s), cheerleading M/W, crew M(s)/W(s), cross-country running M(s)/W(s), field hockey W(s), golf M(s)/W(s), gymnastics M(s)/W(s), lacrosse W(s), rugby M(s), soccer M(s)/W(s), softball W(s), swimming M(s)/W(s), tennis M(s)/W(s), track and field M(s)/W(s), volleyball W(s), water polo M(s)/W(s). *Intramural sports:* badminton M(c)/W(c), basketball M/W, crew M(c)/W(c), fencing M(c)/W(c), field hockey M(c), football M/W, gymnastics M(c)/W(c), ice hockey M(c)/W(c), lacrosse M(c), racquetball M(c)/W(c), rock climbing M(c)/W(c), rugby W(c), sailing M(c)/W(c), skiing (downhill) M(c)/W(c), soccer M/W(c), softball M/W, squash M(c)/W(c), tennis M(c)/W(c), ultimate Frisbee M(c)/W(c), volleyball M(c).

Standardized Tests *Required:* SAT I or ACT (for admission), SAT II: Subject Tests (for admission), SAT II: Writing Test (for admission).

Costs (2003–04) *Tuition:* state resident $0 full-time; nonresident $14,210 full-time. Full-time tuition and fees vary according to program. *Required fees:* $5250 full-time. *Room and board:* $11,212. Room and board charges vary according to board plan and housing facility. *Payment plan:* installment.

Financial Aid Of all full-time matriculated undergraduates who enrolled in 2003, 13,671 applied for aid, 11,061 were judged to have need, 5,533 had their need fully met. In 2003, 1335 non-need-based awards were made. *Average percent of need met:* 89%. *Average financial aid package:* $13,481. *Average need-based loan:* $4648. *Average need-based gift aid:* $9441. *Average non-need-based aid:* $3066. *Average indebtedness upon graduation:* $16,354. *Financial aid deadline:* 3/2.

Applying *Options:* electronic application. *Application fee:* $40. *Required:* essay or personal statement, high school transcript. *Application deadlines:* 11/30 (freshmen), 11/30 (transfers). *Notification:* 3/31 (freshmen), 4/30 (transfers).

Admissions Contact Pre-Admission Advising, Office of Undergraduate Admission and Relations With Schools, University of California, Berkeley, Berkeley, CA 94720. *Phone:* 510-642-3175. *Fax:* 510-642-7333. *E-mail:* ouars@uclink.berkeley.edu.

UNIVERSITY OF CALIFORNIA, DAVIS

Davis, California

- **State-supported** university, founded 1905, part of University of California System
- **Calendar** quarters
- **Degrees** bachelor's, master's, doctoral, first professional, and postbachelor's certificates
- **Suburban** 5993-acre campus with easy access to San Francisco
- **Endowment** $400.8 million
- **Coed,** 23,472 undergraduate students, 89% full-time, 56% women, 44% men
- **Very difficult** entrance level, 60% of applicants were admitted

Undergraduates 20,962 full-time, 2,510 part-time. Students come from 49 states and territories, 113 other countries, 4% are from out of state, 2% African American, 37% Asian American or Pacific Islander, 10% Hispanic American, 0.7% Native American, 2% international, 8% transferred in, 25% live on campus. *Retention:* 99% of 2002 full-time freshmen returned.

Freshmen *Admission:* 32,506 applied, 19,367 admitted, 4,786 enrolled. *Average high school GPA:* 3.72. *Test scores:* SAT verbal scores over 500: 80%; SAT math scores over 500: 92%; ACT scores over 18: 91%; SAT verbal scores over 600: 41%; SAT math scores over 600: 63%; ACT scores over 24: 57%; SAT verbal scores over 700: 8%; SAT math scores over 700: 16%; ACT scores over 30: 10%.

Faculty *Total:* 1,950, 83% full-time, 98% with terminal degrees. *Student/faculty ratio:* 20:1.

Majors Aerospace, aeronautical and astronautical engineering; African-American/Black studies; African studies; agricultural/biological engineering and bioengineering; agricultural business and management; agricultural economics; agricultural teacher education; American Indian/Native American studies; American studies; animal genetics; animal physiology; animal sciences; anthropology; apparel and textiles; art; art history, criticism and conservation; Asian studies (East); atmospheric sciences and meteorology; biochemistry; biology/biological sciences; biomedical/medical engineering; botany/plant biology; cell biology and histology; chemical engineering; chemistry; Chinese; civil engineering; comparative literature; computer engineering; design and visual communications; dramatic/theatre arts; economics; electrical, electronics and communications engineering; engineering; English; entomology; environmental biology; food science; foods, nutrition, and wellness; French; geology/earth science; German; Hispanic-American, Puerto Rican, and Mexican-American/Chicano studies; history; horticultural science; human development and family studies; international agriculture; international relations and affairs; Italian; Japanese; landscape architecture; linguistics; materials engineering; mathematics; mechanical engineering; medical microbiology and bacteriology; music; natural resources/conservation; philosophy; physical education teaching and coaching; physics; political science and government; poultry science; psychology; range science and management; religious studies; Russian; sociology; Spanish; speech and rhetoric; statistics; women's studies; zoology/animal biology.

Academic Programs *Special study options:* academic remediation for entering students, adult/continuing education programs, advanced placement credit, double majors, English as a second language, freshman honors college, honors programs, independent study, internships, part-time degree program, services for LD students, student-designed majors, study abroad, summer session for credit. *ROTC:* Army (b), Air Force (c).

Library Peter J. Shields Library plus 5 others with 2.9 million titles, 45,665 serial subscriptions, an OPAC, a Web page.

Computers on Campus 600 computers available on campus for general student use. A campuswide network can be accessed from student residence rooms and from off campus that provide access to software packages. Internet access, at least one staffed computer lab available.

Student Life *Housing options:* coed, men-only, women-only, cooperative. Campus housing is university owned, leased by the school and is provided by a

University of California, Davis (continued)

third party. Freshman campus housing is guaranteed. *Activities and organizations:* drama/theater group, student-run newspaper, radio station, choral group, marching band, Filipino Student Organization, Vietnamese Student Association, Jewish Student Union, Alpha Phi Omega, national fraternities, national sororities. *Campus security:* 24-hour emergency response devices and patrols, student patrols, late-night transport/escort service, controlled dormitory access, rape prevention programs. *Student services:* health clinic, personal/psychological counseling, women's center, legal services.

Athletics Member NCAA. All Division II except football (Division I-AA), gymnastics (Division I), wrestling (Division I). *Intercollegiate sports:* baseball M, basketball M/W, cross-country running M/W, golf M, gymnastics W, soccer M/W, softball W, swimming M/W, tennis M/W, track and field M/W, volleyball W, water polo M, wrestling M. *Intramural sports:* archery M(c)/W(c), badminton M(c)/W(c), basketball M/W, crew M(c)/W(c), equestrian sports M(c)/W(c), fencing M(c)/W(c), football M/W, golf M/W, gymnastics M(c), ice hockey M(c)/W, lacrosse M(c)/W(c), racquetball M(c)/W(c), riflery M(c)/W(c), rugby M(c), sailing M(c)/W(c), skiing (cross-country) M(c)/W(c), skiing (downhill) M(c)/W(c), soccer M/W, softball M/W, swimming W(c), table tennis M/W, tennis M/W, ultimate Frisbee M/W, volleyball M(c)/W, water polo W(c).

Standardized Tests *Required:* SAT I and SAT II or ACT (for admission), SAT II: Writing Test (for admission).

Costs (2003–04) *Tuition:* state resident $0 full-time; nonresident $14,210 full-time. *Required fees:* $5853 full-time. *Room and board:* $9143. Room and board charges vary according to board plan. *Payment plan:* installment.

Financial Aid Of all full-time matriculated undergraduates who enrolled in 2003, 12,506 applied for aid, 10,001 were judged to have need, 1,211 had their need fully met. In 2003, 1509 non-need-based awards were made. *Average percent of need met:* 76%. *Average financial aid package:* $9864. *Average need-based loan:* $4248. *Average need-based gift aid:* $6965. *Average non-need-based aid:* $2179.

Applying *Options:* electronic application. *Application fee:* $40. *Required:* essay or personal statement, high school transcript. *Application deadlines:* 11/30 (freshmen), 11/30 (transfers). *Notification:* continuous until 5/15 (freshmen), continuous until 5/1 (transfers).

Admissions Contact Dr. Gary Tudor, Director of Undergraduate Admissions, University of California, Davis, Undergraduate Admission and Outreach Services, 175 Mrak Hall, Davis, CA 95616. *Phone:* 530-752-2971. *Fax:* 530-752-1280. *E-mail:* thinkucd@ucdavis.edu.

University of California, Irvine

Irvine, California

- **State-supported** university, founded 1965, part of University of California System
- **Calendar** quarters
- **Degrees** bachelor's, master's, doctoral, first professional, and postbachelor's certificates
- **Suburban** 1477-acre campus with easy access to Los Angeles
- **Endowment** $128.3 million
- **Coed,** 19,967 undergraduate students, 96% full-time, 50% women, 50% men
- **Moderately difficult** entrance level, 54% of applicants were admitted

Undergraduates 19,201 full-time, 766 part-time. Students come from 45 states and territories, 38 other countries, 2% are from out of state, 2% African American, 50% Asian American or Pacific Islander, 11% Hispanic American, 0.4% Native American, 3% international, 9% transferred in, 30% live on campus.

Freshmen *Admission:* 34,417 applied, 18,517 admitted, 4,043 enrolled. *Average high school GPA:* 3.61. *Test scores:* SAT verbal scores over 500: 86%; SAT math scores over 500: 94%; SAT verbal scores over 600: 39%; SAT math scores over 600: 65%; SAT verbal scores over 700: 7%; SAT math scores over 700: 19%.

Faculty *Total:* 1,194, 71% full-time, 98% with terminal degrees. *Student/faculty ratio:* 18:1.

Majors Aerospace, aeronautical and astronautical engineering; African-American/Black studies; anthropology; area, ethnic, cultural, and gender studies related; art; art history, criticism and conservation; Asian-American studies; Asian studies (East); biology/biological sciences; biomedical/medical engineering; chemical engineering; chemistry; Chinese; civil engineering; classical, ancient Mediterranean and Near Eastern studies and archaeology; classics and languages, literatures and linguistics; comparative literature; computer and information sciences; computer and information sciences and support services related; computer engineering; computer science; criminology; cultural studies; dance; dramatic/theatre arts; ecology; economics; electrical, electronics and communications engineering; English; environmental design/architecture; environmental/environmental health engineering; European studies; film/cinema studies; fine/studio arts; French; geology/earth science; German; German studies; Hispanic-American, Puerto Rican, and Mexican-American/Chicano studies; history; human ecology; humanities; international/global studies; Japanese; journalism; linguistics; literature; materials engineering; mathematics; mechanical engineering; microbiology; molecular biochemistry; multi-/interdisciplinary studies related; music; music performance; neuroscience; philosophy; physics; political science and government; psychology; Russian; social psychology; social sciences; sociology; Spanish; women's studies.

Academic Programs *Special study options:* academic remediation for entering students, adult/continuing education programs, advanced placement credit, cooperative education, double majors, English as a second language, honors programs, independent study, internships, off-campus study, services for LD students, study abroad, summer session for credit. *ROTC:* Army (c), Air Force (c).

Library Main Library plus 1 other with 2.6 million titles, 28,416 serial subscriptions, 101,335 audiovisual materials, an OPAC, a Web page.

Computers on Campus 500 computers available on campus for general student use. A campuswide network can be accessed from student residence rooms and from off campus. Internet access, online (class) registration, at least one staffed computer lab available.

Student Life *Housing options:* coed, men-only, women-only, disabled students. Campus housing is university owned. Freshman campus housing is guaranteed. *Activities and organizations:* drama/theater group, student-run newspaper, radio station, choral group, ASUCI, Kababayan, national fraternities, national sororities. *Campus security:* 24-hour emergency response devices and patrols, late-night transport/escort service. *Student services:* health clinic, personal/psychological counseling, women's center, legal services.

Athletics Member NCAA. All Division I. *Intercollegiate sports:* baseball M, basketball M(s)/W(s), crew M/W, cross-country running M/W(s), golf M(s)/W, sailing M/W, soccer M/W, swimming M(s)/W(s), tennis M(s)/W(s), track and field M/W(s), volleyball M/W(s), water polo M(s)/W. *Intramural sports:* badminton M/W, baseball M, basketball M/W, bowling M(c)/W(c), crew W(c), cross-country running M/W, fencing M(c)/W(c), football M, golf M/W, ice hockey M(c)/W(c), lacrosse M(c)/W, racquetball M/W, rugby M(c), sailing M(c)/W(c), skiing (cross-country) M(c)/W(c), skiing (downhill) M(c)/W(c), soccer M/W, softball M/W, swimming M/W, table tennis M/W, tennis M/W, track and field M/W, ultimate Frisbee M(c)/W(c), volleyball M/W, water polo M/W, weight lifting M/W, wrestling M.

Standardized Tests *Required:* SAT I and SAT II or ACT (for admission), SAT II: Writing Test (for admission).

Costs (2003–04) *Tuition:* state resident $0 full-time; nonresident $14,210 full-time. *Required fees:* $6165 full-time. *Room and board:* $8055. Room and board charges vary according to board plan and housing facility. *Payment plan:* installment.

Financial Aid Of all full-time matriculated undergraduates who enrolled in 2003, 11,890 applied for aid, 9,545 were judged to have need, 1,901 had their need fully met. 3,755 Federal Work-Study jobs (averaging $1117). In 2003, 708 non-need-based awards were made. *Average percent of need met:* 80%. *Average financial aid package:* $10,882. *Average need-based loan:* $4626. *Average need-based gift aid:* $7606. *Average non-need-based aid:* $3535.

Applying *Options:* electronic application. *Application fee:* $40. *Required:* essay or personal statement, high school transcript, minimum 2.0 GPA. *Application deadlines:* 11/30 (freshmen), 11/30 (transfers). *Notification:* continuous until 3/1 (freshmen), continuous until 5/1 (transfers).

Admissions Contact Marguerit Bonous-Hammarth, Director of Admissions and Relations with Schools, University of California, Irvine, 204 Administration, Irvine, CA 92697-1075. *Phone:* 949-824-6703.

University of California, Los Angeles

Los Angeles, California

- **State-supported** university, founded 1919, part of University of California System
- **Calendar** quarters
- **Degrees** bachelor's, master's, doctoral, and first professional
- **Urban** 419-acre campus
- **Endowment** $1.2 billion
- **Coed,** 25,715 undergraduate students, 96% full-time, 56% women, 44% men
- **Very difficult** entrance level, 24% of applicants were admitted

Undergraduates 24,598 full-time, 1,117 part-time. Students come from 49 states and territories, 66 other countries, 4% are from out of state, 3% African American, 38% Asian American or Pacific Islander, 15% Hispanic American, 0.4% Native American, 3% international, 13% transferred in, 31% live on campus. *Retention:* 96% of 2002 full-time freshmen returned.

Freshmen *Admission:* 44,994 applied, 10,581 admitted, 4,268 enrolled. *Test scores:* SAT verbal scores over 500: 90%; SAT math scores over 500: 95%; ACT scores over 18: 98%; SAT verbal scores over 600: 64%; SAT math scores over

600: 76%; ACT scores over 24: 72%; SAT verbal scores over 700: 21%; SAT math scores over 700: 39%; ACT scores over 30: 24%.

Faculty *Total:* 2,462, 76% full-time, 98% with terminal degrees. *Student/faculty ratio:* 18:1.

Majors Aerospace, aeronautical and astronautical engineering; African-American/Black studies; African languages; African studies; agricultural/biological engineering and bioengineering; American Indian/Native American studies; American literature; American studies; ancient/classical Greek; anthropology; applied mathematics; Arabic; archeology; architecture; area studies related; art; art history, criticism and conservation; Asian-American studies; Asian studies; Asian studies (East); Asian studies (Southeast); astronomy; astrophysics; atmospheric sciences and meteorology; biochemistry; biology/biological sciences; biomathematics and bioinformatics related; biomedical/medical engineering; biophysics; biostatistics; biotechnology; botany/plant biology; business administration and management; business/managerial economics; cell and molecular biology; chemical engineering; chemistry; Chinese; city/urban, community and regional planning; civil engineering; classical, ancient Mediterranean and Near Eastern studies and archaeology; classics and classical languages related; classics and languages, literatures and linguistics; cognitive science; communication/speech communication and rhetoric; community health and preventive medicine; comparative literature; computational mathematics; computer engineering; computer science; dance; design and applied arts related; development economics and international development; dramatic/theatre arts; East Asian languages; ecology; economics; education; educational leadership and administration; electrical, electronics and communications engineering; engineering; English; English as a second/foreign language (teaching); English language and literature related; environmental health; environmental science; epidemiology; European studies; film/cinema studies; fine arts related; foreign languages related; French; geochemistry; geography; geography related; geological and earth sciences/geosciences related; geological/geophysical engineering; geology/earth science; geophysics and seismology; German; Germanic languages related; health services administration; Hebrew; Hispanic-American, Puerto Rican, and Mexican-American/Chicano studies; history; human/medical genetics; information science/studies; international economics; Islamic studies; Italian; Japanese; Jewish/Judaic studies; kinesiology and exercise science; Korean; Latin; Latin American studies; liberal arts and sciences and humanities related; liberal arts and sciences/liberal studies; library science related; linguistic and comparative language studies related; linguistics; manufacturing engineering; marine biology and biological oceanography; materials engineering; materials science; mathematics; mathematics related; mechanical engineering; medical microbiology and bacteriology; microbiological sciences and immunology related; Middle/ Near Eastern and Semitic languages related; modern Greek; molecular biochemistry; molecular biology; molecular pharmacology; molecular physiology; molecular toxicology; multi-/interdisciplinary studies related; music; music history, literature, and theory; musicology and ethnomusicology; Near and Middle Eastern studies; neurobiology and neurophysiology; neuroscience; nursing (registered nurse training); nursing related; pathology/experimental pathology; philosophy; physics; physiological psychology/psychobiology; physiology; plant sciences; political science and government; Portuguese; psychology; public administration; public health related; public policy analysis; religious studies; Russian; Russian studies; Scandinavian languages; Slavic languages; social work; sociology; Spanish; special education; statistics; visual and performing arts related; women's studies.

Academic Programs *Special study options:* academic remediation for entering students, adult/continuing education programs, advanced placement credit, distance learning, double majors, English as a second language, freshman honors college, honors programs, independent study, internships, off-campus study, services for LD students, student-designed majors, study abroad, summer session for credit. *ROTC:* Army (b), Navy (b), Air Force (b).

Library University Research Library plus 13 others with 7.6 million titles, 94,801 serial subscriptions, 4.6 million audiovisual materials, an OPAC, a Web page.

Computers on Campus A campuswide network can be accessed from student residence rooms and from off campus. Internet access, online (class) registration, at least one staffed computer lab available. Computer purchase or lease plan available.

Student Life *Housing options:* coed, cooperative. Campus housing is university owned. *Activities and organizations:* drama/theater group, student-run newspaper, radio station, choral group, marching band, Student Alumni Association, student government, Rally Committee, national fraternities, national sororities. *Campus security:* 24-hour emergency response devices, student patrols, late-night transport/escort service. *Student services:* health clinic, personal/psychological counseling, women's center, legal services.

Athletics Member NCAA. All Division I except football (Division I-A). *Intercollegiate sports:* baseball M(s), basketball M(s)/W(s), cross-country running M(s)/W(s), golf M(s)/W(s), gymnastics W(s), soccer M(s)/W(s), softball W(s), swimming W(s), tennis M(s)/W(s), track and field M(s)/W(s), volleyball M(s)/W(s), water polo M(s)/W(s). *Intramural sports:* archery W, badminton M/W, basketball M/W, bowling M/W, crew M/W, cross-country running M/W, fencing M/W, football M/W, golf M/W, gymnastics M/W, ice hockey M/W, lacrosse M/W, racquetball M/W, rugby M/W, sailing M/W, skiing (cross-country) M/W, skiing (downhill) M/W, soccer M/W, squash M/W, swimming M/W, tennis M/W, track and field M/W, volleyball M/W, water polo M/W, weight lifting M, wrestling M.

Standardized Tests *Required:* SAT I or ACT (for admission), SAT II: Subject Tests (for admission), SAT II: Writing Test (for admission), SAT II Subject Test in math, third SAT II Subject Test (for admission), SAT I or ACT (for placement), SAT II: Subject Tests (for placement).

Costs (2003–04) *Tuition:* state resident $0 full-time; nonresident $14,210 full-time. *Required fees:* $5820 full-time. *Room and board:* $10,452. Room and board charges vary according to board plan and housing facility.

Financial Aid Of all full-time matriculated undergraduates who enrolled in 2002, 15,137 applied for aid, 12,267 were judged to have need, 5,757 had their need fully met. 2,835 Federal Work-Study jobs (averaging $1809). 222 state and other part-time jobs (averaging $1369). In 2002, 1736 non-need-based awards were made. *Average percent of need met:* 82%. *Average financial aid package:* $10,634. *Average need-based loan:* $4708. *Average need-based gift aid:* $7641. *Average non-need-based aid:* $2244. *Average indebtedness upon graduation:* $12,775.

Applying *Options:* electronic application. *Application fee:* $40. *Required:* essay or personal statement, high school transcript. *Application deadlines:* 11/30 (freshmen), 11/30 (transfers). *Notification:* 3/30 (freshmen), 4/30 (transfers).

Admissions Contact Mr. Vu T. Tran, Director of Undergraduate Admissions, University of California, Los Angeles, 405 Hilgard Avenue, Box 951436, Los Angeles, CA 90095-1436. *Phone:* 310-825-3101. *E-mail:* ugadm@saonet.ucla.edu.

UNIVERSITY OF CALIFORNIA, RIVERSIDE

Riverside, California

- **State-supported** university, founded 1954, part of University of California System
- **Calendar** quarters
- **Degrees** bachelor's, master's, and doctoral
- **Urban** 1200-acre campus with easy access to Los Angeles
- **Endowment** $63.9 million
- **Coed,** 15,282 undergraduate students, 97% full-time, 54% women, 46% men
- **Very difficult** entrance level, 79% of applicants were admitted

Undergraduates 14,748 full-time, 534 part-time. Students come from 40 states and territories, 21 other countries, 1% are from out of state, 6% African American, 41% Asian American or Pacific Islander, 24% Hispanic American, 0.4% Native American, 2% international, 6% transferred in, 28% live on campus. *Retention:* 85% of 2002 full-time freshmen returned.

Freshmen *Admission:* 20,060 applied, 15,862 admitted, 3,889 enrolled. *Average high school GPA:* 3.42. *Test scores:* SAT verbal scores over 500: 55%; SAT math scores over 500: 72%; ACT scores over 18: 82%; SAT verbal scores over 600: 16%; SAT math scores over 600: 33%; ACT scores over 24: 25%; SAT verbal scores over 700: 2%; SAT math scores over 700: 6%; ACT scores over 30: 1%.

Faculty *Total:* 816, 81% full-time, 98% with terminal degrees. *Student/faculty ratio:* 19:1.

Majors African-American/Black studies; American Indian/Native American studies; anthropology; art history, criticism and conservation; Asian-American studies; Asian studies; biochemistry; biology/biological sciences; biomedical sciences; botany/plant biology; business administration and management; business/managerial economics; chemical engineering; chemistry; Chinese; classics and languages, literatures and linguistics; comparative literature; computer science; creative writing; cultural studies; dance; dramatic/theatre arts; economics; electrical, electronics and communications engineering; English; entomology; environmental/environmental health engineering; environmental studies; fine/studio arts; French; geology/earth science; geophysics and seismology; German; Hispanic-American, Puerto Rican, and Mexican-American/Chicano studies; history; human development and family studies; humanities; Latin American studies; liberal arts and sciences/liberal studies; linguistics; mathematics; mechanical engineering; music; neuroscience; philosophy; physical sciences; physics; physiological psychology/psychobiology; political science and government; pre-law studies; psychology; public administration; religious studies; Russian; Russian studies; social sciences; sociology; Spanish; statistics; women's studies.

Academic Programs *Special study options:* academic remediation for entering students, accelerated degree program, adult/continuing education programs, advanced placement credit, cooperative education, distance learning, double majors, English as a second language, freshman honors college, honors programs, independent study, internships, off-campus study, part-time degree program, services for LD students, student-designed majors, study abroad, summer session for credit. *ROTC:* Army (c), Air Force (c).

University of California, Riverside (continued)

Library Tomas Rivera Library plus 6 others with 2.1 million titles, 21,323 serial subscriptions, 141,663 audiovisual materials, an OPAC, a Web page.

Computers on Campus 600 computers available on campus for general student use. A campuswide network can be accessed from student residence rooms and from off campus. Internet access, online (class) registration, at least one staffed computer lab available.

Student Life *Housing options:* coed. Campus housing is university owned. Freshman applicants given priority for college housing. *Activities and organizations:* drama/theater group, student-run newspaper, radio station, choral group, Associated Students, UCR Ambassadors, Community Service/Human Corps Program, BEAR FACTS Student Orientation, national fraternities, national sororities. *Campus security:* 24-hour emergency response devices and patrols, student patrols, late-night transport/escort service, controlled dormitory access. *Student services:* health clinic, personal/psychological counseling, women's center, legal services.

Athletics Member NCAA. All Division I. *Intercollegiate sports:* baseball M(s), basketball M(s)/W(s), cross-country running M(s)/W(s), softball W(s), tennis M(s)/W(s), track and field M(s)/W(s), volleyball W(s). *Intramural sports:* badminton M(c)/W(c), basketball M/W, bowling M/W, cheerleading M(c)/W(c), field hockey M(c)/W(c), football M/W, golf M/W, racquetball M/W, skiing (cross-country) M(c)/W(c), skiing (downhill) M(c)/W(c), soccer M/W, softball M/W, tennis M/W, volleyball M/W.

Standardized Tests *Required:* SAT I or ACT (for admission), SAT II: Subject Tests (for admission), SAT II: Writing Test (for admission).

Costs (2003–04) *Tuition:* state resident $0 full-time; nonresident $13,731 full-time. *Required fees:* $5950 full-time. *Room and board:* $9350. Room and board charges vary according to board plan and housing facility. *Payment plan:* deferred payment.

Financial Aid Of all full-time matriculated undergraduates who enrolled in 2003, 10,951 applied for aid, 9,412 were judged to have need, 2,156 had their need fully met. 1,640 Federal Work-Study jobs (averaging $2557). In 2003, 1749 non-need-based awards were made. *Average percent of need met:* 79%. *Average financial aid package:* $10,439. *Average need-based loan:* $3793. *Average need-based gift aid:* $7500. *Average non-need-based aid:* $4744. *Average indebtedness upon graduation:* $13,382.

Applying *Options:* electronic application, early admission. *Application fee:* $40. *Required:* essay or personal statement, high school transcript, minimum 2.82 GPA. *Application deadlines:* 11/30 (freshmen), 11/30 (transfers). *Notification:* continuous (freshmen), continuous until 3/1 (transfers).

Admissions Contact LaRae Lundgren, Director of Undergraduate Admission, University of California, Riverside, 1138 Hinderaker Hall, 900 University Avenue, Riverside, CA 92521. *Phone:* 909-787-3411. *Fax:* 909-787-6344. *E-mail:* discover@pop.ucr.edu.

UNIVERSITY OF CALIFORNIA, SAN DIEGO
La Jolla, California

- **State-supported** university, founded 1959, part of University of California System
- **Calendar** quarters
- **Degrees** bachelor's, master's, doctoral, and first professional
- **Suburban** 1976-acre campus with easy access to San Diego
- **Endowment** $1.2 billion
- **Coed,** 19,872 undergraduate students, 100% full-time, 52% women, 48% men
- **Very difficult** entrance level, 42% of applicants were admitted

Undergraduates 19,872 full-time. 3% are from out of state, 1% African American, 37% Asian American or Pacific Islander, 10% Hispanic American, 0.4% Native American, 3% international, 8% transferred in, 33% live on campus. *Retention:* 93% of 2002 full-time freshmen returned.

Freshmen *Admission:* 43,438 applied, 18,118 admitted, 3,799 enrolled. *Average high school GPA:* 3.95. *Test scores:* SAT verbal scores over 500: 89%; SAT math scores over 500: 96%; ACT scores over 18: 97%; SAT verbal scores over 600: 56%; SAT math scores over 600: 77%; ACT scores over 24: 73%; SAT verbal scores over 700: 13%; SAT math scores over 700: 30%; ACT scores over 30: 18%.

Faculty *Total:* 1,092, 84% full-time, 98% with terminal degrees. *Student/faculty ratio:* 19:1.

Majors Aerospace, aeronautical and astronautical engineering; animal physiology; anthropology; applied mathematics; archeology; art; art history, criticism and conservation; atomic/molecular physics; biochemistry; biology/biological sciences; biomedical/medical engineering; biophysics; biotechnology; cell biology and histology; chemical engineering; chemistry; chemistry teacher education; Chinese; classics and languages, literatures and linguistics; cognitive psychology and psycholinguistics; computer engineering; computer science; creative writing; cultural studies; dance; dramatic/theatre arts; ecology; econometrics and quantitative economics; economics; electrical, electronics and communications engineering; engineering; engineering physics; engineering science; English; environmental studies; film/cinema studies; fine/studio arts; foreign languages and literatures; French; geology/earth science; German; history; human ecology; interdisciplinary studies; intermedia/multimedia; Italian; Japanese; Jewish/Judaic studies; Latin American studies; linguistics; literature; management science; mass communication/media; mathematics; mathematics teacher education; mechanical engineering; medical microbiology and bacteriology; medicinal and pharmaceutical chemistry; molecular biology; music; music history, literature, and theory; natural resources management and policy; philosophy; physics; physics teacher education; political science and government; psychology; religious studies; Russian; Russian studies; sociology; Spanish; structural engineering; systems engineering; urban studies/affairs; women's studies.

Academic Programs *Special study options:* accelerated degree program, advanced placement credit, cooperative education, double majors, English as a second language, freshman honors college, honors programs, independent study, internships, off-campus study, services for LD students, student-designed majors, study abroad, summer session for credit. *ROTC:* Army (c), Navy (c).

Library Geisel Library plus 7 others with 2.9 million titles, 19,517 serial subscriptions, 381,099 audiovisual materials, an OPAC, a Web page.

Computers on Campus 1020 computers available on campus for general student use. A campuswide network can be accessed from student residence rooms and from off campus that provide access to e-mail. Internet access, online (class) registration, at least one staffed computer lab available. Computer purchase or lease plan available.

Student Life *Housing options:* coed, disabled students. Campus housing is university owned. Freshman campus housing is guaranteed. *Activities and organizations:* drama/theater group, student-run newspaper, radio and television station, choral group, cultural organizations, IFC/Panhellenic, recreational clubs, service organizations, spiritual/religious organizations, national fraternities, national sororities. *Campus security:* 24-hour emergency response devices and patrols, student patrols, late-night transport/escort service, crime prevention programs. *Student services:* health clinic, personal/psychological counseling, women's center, legal services.

Athletics Member NCAA. All Division II. *Intercollegiate sports:* baseball M, basketball M/W, cheerleading M/W, crew M/W, cross-country running M/W, fencing M/W, golf M, soccer M/W, softball W, swimming M/W, tennis M/W, track and field M/W, volleyball M/W, water polo M/W. *Intramural sports:* archery M/W, badminton M(c)/W(c), basketball M/W, equestrian sports M(c)/W(c), fencing M(c)/W(c), football M(c)/W(c), golf M/W, gymnastics M/W, ice hockey M, lacrosse M(c)/W(c), racquetball M/W, rock climbing M/W, rugby M(c)/W(c), sailing M(c)/W(c), skiing (downhill) M(c)/W(c), soccer M/W, table tennis M/W, tennis M/W, track and field M/W, ultimate Frisbee M(c)/W(c), volleyball M/W, water polo M/W, wrestling M(c)/W(c).

Standardized Tests *Required:* SAT I or ACT (for admission), 3 SAT II Subject Tests (including SAT II: Writing Test) (for admission).

Costs (2003–04) *One-time required fee:* $597. *Tuition:* state resident $0 full-time; nonresident $13,730 full-time. Full-time tuition and fees vary according to location. *Required fees:* $5507 full-time. *Room and board:* $8620. Room and board charges vary according to board plan and location. *Payment plans:* installment, deferred payment.

Financial Aid Of all full-time matriculated undergraduates who enrolled in 2003, 11,839 applied for aid, 9,648 were judged to have need, 4,741 had their need fully met. 4,983 Federal Work-Study jobs (averaging $1894). In 2003, 640 non-need-based awards were made. *Average percent of need met:* 87%. *Average financial aid package:* $12,420. *Average need-based loan:* $4761. *Average need-based gift aid:* $8137. *Average non-need-based aid:* $5875. *Average indebtedness upon graduation:* $14,192.

Applying *Options:* electronic application. *Application fee:* $40. *Required:* essay or personal statement, high school transcript, minimum 2.8 GPA. *Required for some:* minimum 3.4 GPA. *Application deadlines:* 11/30 (freshmen), 11/30 (transfers). *Notification:* 3/31 (freshmen), 5/1 (transfers).

Admissions Contact Mr. Nathan Evans, Associate Director of Admissions and Relations with Schools, University of California, San Diego, 9500 Gilman Drive, 0021, La Jolla, CA 92093-0021. *Phone:* 858-534-4831. *E-mail:* admissionsinfo@ucsd.edu.

UNIVERSITY OF CALIFORNIA, SANTA BARBARA
Santa Barbara, California

- **State-supported** university, founded 1909, part of University of California System
- **Calendar** quarters plus 6-week summer term
- **Degrees** bachelor's, master's, doctoral, and first professional certificates
- **Suburban** 989-acre campus
- **Endowment** $44.2 million

- **Coed,** 17,844 undergraduate students, 96% full-time, 55% women, 45% men
- **Very difficult** entrance level, 50% of applicants were admitted

Undergraduates 17,199 full-time, 645 part-time. Students come from 51 states and territories, 110 other countries, 5% are from out of state, 3% African American, 15% Asian American or Pacific Islander, 16% Hispanic American, 0.7% Native American, 1% international, 8% transferred in, 21% live on campus. *Retention:* 91% of 2002 full-time freshmen returned.

Freshmen *Admission:* 37,599 applied, 18,780 admitted, 3,993 enrolled. *Average high school GPA:* 3.72. *Test scores:* SAT verbal scores over 500: 85%; SAT math scores over 500: 90%; ACT scores over 18: 98%; SAT verbal scores over 600: 45%; SAT math scores over 600: 57%; ACT scores over 24: 75%; SAT verbal scores over 700: 8%; SAT math scores over 700: 12%; ACT scores over 30: 14%.

Faculty *Total:* 1,036, 83% full-time. *Student/faculty ratio:* 19:1.

Majors African-American/Black studies; animal physiology; anthropology; aquatic biology/limnology; art history, criticism and conservation; Asian-American studies; Asian studies; biochemistry; biology/biological sciences; biopsychology; business/managerial economics; cell biology and histology; chemical engineering; chemistry; Chinese; classics and languages, literatures and linguistics; communication/speech communication and rhetoric; comparative literature; computer engineering; computer science; dance; dramatic/theatre arts; ecology; economics; electrical, electronic and communications engineering technology; electrical, electronics and communications engineering; English; environmental studies; film/cinema studies; fine/studio arts; French; geography; geology/earth science; geophysics and seismology; German; Hispanic-American, Puerto Rican, and Mexican-American/Chicano studies; history; interdisciplinary studies; Islamic studies; Italian; Japanese; Latin American studies; linguistics; marine biology and biological oceanography; mathematics; mechanical engineering; medical microbiology and bacteriology; medieval and Renaissance studies; molecular biology; multi-/interdisciplinary studies related; music; Near and Middle Eastern studies; pharmacology; philosophy; physics; political science and government; Portuguese; pre-law studies; psychology; public/applied history and archival administration; religious studies; Slavic languages; sociology; Spanish; statistics; women's studies; zoology/animal biology.

Academic Programs *Special study options:* accelerated degree program, advanced placement credit, cooperative education, distance learning, double majors, English as a second language, honors programs, independent study, internships, off-campus study, services for LD students, student-designed majors, study abroad, summer session for credit. *ROTC:* Army (b).

Library Davidson Library with 2.7 million titles, 18,898 serial subscriptions, 103,495 audiovisual materials, an OPAC, a Web page.

Computers on Campus 3000 computers available on campus for general student use. A campuswide network can be accessed from off campus. At least one staffed computer lab available.

Student Life *Housing options:* coed, cooperative. Campus housing is university owned and is provided by a third party. Freshman applicants given priority for college housing. *Activities and organizations:* drama/theater group, student-run newspaper, radio station, choral group, national fraternities, national sororities. *Campus security:* 24-hour emergency response devices, late-night transport/escort service. *Student services:* health clinic, personal/psychological counseling, women's center, legal services.

Athletics Member NCAA. All Division I. *Intercollegiate sports:* baseball M(s), basketball M(s)/W(s), bowling M(c)/W(c), crew M(c)/W(c), cross-country running M(s)/W(s), equestrian sports M(c)/W(c), fencing M(c)/W(c), field hockey W(c), golf M(s)/W(c), gymnastics M/W(s), lacrosse M(c)/W(c), rugby M(c), sailing M(c)/W(c), skiing (downhill) M(c)/W(c), soccer M(s)/W(s), softball W(s), swimming M(s)/W(s), tennis M(s)/W(s), track and field M(s)/W(s), ultimate Frisbee M(c)/W(c), volleyball M(s)/W(s), water polo M(s)/W(s). *Intramural sports:* badminton M/W, basketball M/W, bowling M/W, cheerleading M/W, crew M/W, cross-country running M/W, football M/W, golf M/W, gymnastics M/W, racquetball M/W, rock climbing M(c)/W(c), soccer M/W, softball M/W, squash M/W, tennis M/W, ultimate Frisbee M/W, volleyball M/W, water polo M/W.

Standardized Tests *Required:* SAT I or ACT (for admission), SAT II: Subject Tests (for admission), SAT II: Writing Test (for admission).

Costs (2003–04) *Tuition:* state resident $0 full-time; nonresident $13,731 full-time. *Required fees:* $5639 full-time. *Room and board:* $9236; room only: $6849. *Waivers:* employees or children of employees.

Financial Aid Of all full-time matriculated undergraduates who enrolled in 2003, 10,369 applied for aid, 8,063 were judged to have need, 2,402 had their need fully met. In 2003, 388 non-need-based awards were made. *Average percent of need met:* 79%. *Average financial aid package:* $11,068. *Average need-based loan:* $5407. *Average need-based gift aid:* $6960. *Average non-need-based aid:* $3913.

Applying *Options:* electronic application. *Application fee:* $40. *Required:* essay or personal statement, high school transcript. *Required for some:* interview. *Application deadlines:* 11/30 (freshmen), 11/30 (transfers). *Notification:* 3/15 (freshmen), 5/1 (transfers).

Admissions Contact Ms. Christine Van Gieson, Director of Admissions/Outreach Services, University of California, Santa Barbara, 1234 Cheadle Hall, Santa Barbara, CA 93106-2014. *Phone:* 805-893-2485. *Fax:* 805-893-2676. *E-mail:* appinfo@sa.ucsb.edu.

UNIVERSITY OF CALIFORNIA, SANTA CRUZ
Santa Cruz, California

- **State-supported** university, founded 1965, part of University of California System
- **Calendar** quarters
- **Degrees** certificates, bachelor's, master's, doctoral, and postbachelor's certificates
- **Small-town** 2000-acre campus with easy access to San Francisco and San Jose
- **Endowment** $85.3 million
- **Coed,** 13,660 undergraduate students, 95% full-time, 55% women, 45% men
- **Very difficult** entrance level, 80% of applicants were admitted

Undergraduates 13,002 full-time, 658 part-time. 5% are from out of state, 2% African American, 17% Asian American or Pacific Islander, 14% Hispanic American, 0.9% Native American, 0.9% international, 6% transferred in, 46% live on campus. *Retention:* 87% of 2002 full-time freshmen returned.

Freshmen *Admission:* 21,525 applied, 17,284 admitted, 3,434 enrolled. *Average high school GPA:* 3.48. *Test scores:* SAT verbal scores over 500: 79%; SAT math scores over 500: 84%; ACT scores over 18: 91%; SAT verbal scores over 600: 40%; SAT math scores over 600: 42%; ACT scores over 24: 53%; SAT verbal scores over 700: 8%; SAT math scores over 700: 6%; ACT scores over 30: 7%.

Faculty *Total:* 717, 72% full-time, 98% with terminal degrees. *Student/faculty ratio:* 19:1.

Majors American studies; ancient/classical Greek; anthropology; applied mathematics; art; art history, criticism and conservation; Asian studies; Asian studies (East); Asian studies (South); Asian studies (Southeast); astrophysics; biochemistry; biology/biological sciences; botany/plant biology; business/managerial economics; cell biology and histology; chemistry; Chinese; cinematography and film/video production; classics and languages, literatures and linguistics; cognitive psychology and psycholinguistics; comparative literature; computer engineering; computer science; creative writing; dance; developmental and child psychology; dramatic/theatre arts; drawing; ecology; economics; electrical, electronics and communications engineering; English language and literature related; environmental studies; European history; family and community services; film/cinema studies; foreign languages and literatures; French; geology/earth science; geophysics and seismology; German; Hispanic-American, Puerto Rican, and Mexican-American/Chicano studies; history; information science/studies; international economics; Italian; Italian studies; Japanese; Latin; Latin American studies; legal studies; linguistics; literature; marine biology and biological oceanography; mathematics; mathematics teacher education; molecular biology; music; peace studies and conflict resolution; philosophy; photography; physics; physiological psychology/psychobiology; plant sciences; political science and government; printmaking; psychology; religious studies; Russian studies; sculpture; social psychology; sociology; Spanish; theatre design and technology; women's studies.

Academic Programs *Special study options:* academic remediation for entering students, adult/continuing education programs, advanced placement credit, cooperative education, double majors, English as a second language, freshman honors college, honors programs, independent study, internships, off-campus study, part-time degree program, services for LD students, student-designed majors, study abroad, summer session for credit. *ROTC:* Army (c), Navy (c), Air Force (c). *Unusual degree programs:* 3-2 engineering with University of California, Berkeley.

Library McHenry Library plus 9 others with 1.5 million titles, 9,190 serial subscriptions, 43,785 audiovisual materials, an OPAC, a Web page.

Computers on Campus 200 computers available on campus for general student use. A campuswide network can be accessed from student residence rooms and from off campus. Internet access, at least one staffed computer lab available.

Student Life *Housing options:* coed, men-only, women-only. Campus housing is university owned. Freshman campus housing is guaranteed. *Activities and organizations:* drama/theater group, student-run newspaper, radio station, choral group, Asian Pacific Islander Student Alliance, African/Black Student Alliance, Movimiento Estudiantil Chicano de Aztlan, Students Alliance of North American Indians, Estudiantes Para Salud del Pueblo, national fraternities, national sororities. *Campus security:* 24-hour emergency response devices and patrols, late-night transport/escort service, controlled dormitory access, evening main gate security, campus police force and fire station. *Student services:* health clinic, personal/psychological counseling, women's center.

Athletics Member NCAA. All Division III. *Intercollegiate sports:* basketball M/W, cross-country running M(c)/W(c), equestrian sports M(c)/W(c), fencing

University of California, Santa Cruz (continued)

M(c)/W(c), lacrosse M(c)/W(c), rugby M(c)/W(c), sailing M(c)/W(c), soccer M, softball W(c), swimming M/W, tennis M/W, track and field M(c)/W(c), ultimate Frisbee M(c)/W(c), volleyball M/W, water polo M/W. *Intramural sports:* badminton M/W, basketball M/W, cross-country running M/W, fencing M/W, racquetball M/W, soccer M/W, softball M/W, tennis M/W, volleyball M/W.

Standardized Tests *Required:* SAT I and SAT II or ACT (for admission), SAT I or ACT composite score and three SAT II subject tests required including SAT II Writing, Math Level 1 or 2, and one test from each of the following areas: english literature, foreign language, science or social studies (for admission).

Costs (2003–04) *Tuition:* state resident $0 full-time; nonresident $18,109 full-time. *Required fees:* $4629 full-time. *Room and board:* $10,314. Room and board charges vary according to board plan and housing facility. *Payment plans:* installment, deferred payment. *Waivers:* employees or children of employees.

Financial Aid Of all full-time matriculated undergraduates who enrolled in 2002, 6,241 applied for aid, 5,119 were judged to have need, 1,043 had their need fully met. 2,568 Federal Work-Study jobs (averaging $2000). 2 state and other part-time jobs (averaging $1675). In 2002, 703 non-need-based awards were made. *Average percent of need met:* 90%. *Average financial aid package:* $11,124. *Average need-based loan:* $4264. *Average need-based gift aid:* $7568. *Average non-need-based aid:* $3305. *Average indebtedness upon graduation:* $13,282.

Applying *Options:* electronic application. *Application fee:* $40. *Required:* essay or personal statement, high school transcript. *Application deadlines:* 11/30 (freshmen), 11/30 (transfers). *Notification:* 3/1 (freshmen), 4/30 (transfers).

Admissions Contact Mr. Kevin M. Browne, Executive Director of Admissions and University Registrar, University of California, Santa Cruz, Admissions Office, Cook House, Santa Cruz, CA 95064. *Phone:* 831-459-5779. *Fax:* 831-459-4452. *E-mail:* admissions@ucsc.edu.

UNIVERSITY OF JUDAISM

Bel Air, California

- **Independent Jewish** comprehensive, founded 1947
- **Calendar** semesters
- **Degrees** bachelor's and master's
- **Suburban** 28-acre campus with easy access to Los Angeles
- **Coed,** 142 undergraduate students
- **Moderately difficult** entrance level, 79% of applicants were admitted

Undergraduates Students come from 22 states and territories, 4 other countries, 31% are from out of state, 4% African American, 11% Hispanic American, 6% international, 60% live on campus. *Retention:* 58% of 2002 full-time freshmen returned.

Freshmen *Admission:* 87 applied, 69 admitted. *Average high school GPA:* 3.40. *Test scores:* SAT verbal scores over 500: 62%; SAT math scores over 500: 62%; ACT scores over 18: 100%; SAT verbal scores over 600: 27%; SAT math scores over 600: 27%; ACT scores over 24: 25%; SAT verbal scores over 700: 5%; SAT math scores over 700: 5%.

Faculty *Total:* 91, 21% full-time, 42% with terminal degrees. *Student/faculty ratio:* 7:1.

Majors Business/managerial economics; interdisciplinary studies; Jewish/Judaic studies; liberal arts and sciences/liberal studies; literature; political science and government; pre-medical studies; psychology.

Academic Programs *Special study options:* academic remediation for entering students, accelerated degree program, adult/continuing education programs, advanced placement credit, honors programs, independent study, internships, off-campus study, part-time degree program, services for LD students, student-designed majors, study abroad. *Unusual degree programs:* 3-2 education.

Library Ostrow Library with 105,000 titles, 400 serial subscriptions, a Web page.

Computers on Campus 16 computers available on campus for general student use. At least one staffed computer lab available.

Student Life *Housing:* on-campus residence required through junior year. *Options:* coed. Campus housing is university owned. Freshman campus housing is guaranteed. *Activities and organizations:* drama/theater group, student-run newspaper, radio station, choral group, ASUJC, Graduate Student Association, Resident Life Council, College Urban Fellows, UJ Chorale. *Campus security:* 24-hour emergency response devices and patrols, controlled dormitory access. *Student services:* health clinic, personal/psychological counseling.

Athletics *Intramural sports:* basketball M/W, football M/W, softball M/W.

Standardized Tests *Required:* SAT I or ACT (for admission).

Costs (2004–05) *Comprehensive fee:* $27,830 includes full-time tuition ($17,500), mandatory fees ($750), and room and board ($9580). Part-time tuition: $730 per credit. *College room only:* $4970.

Financial Aid In 2002, 32 non-need-based awards were made. *Average percent of need met:* 100%. *Average financial aid package:* $19,214. *Average indebtedness upon graduation:* $17,000.

Applying *Options:* early admission, early decision, deferred entrance. *Application fee:* $35. *Required:* essay or personal statement, high school transcript, 2 letters of recommendation. *Required for some:* interview. *Recommended:* minimum 3.2 GPA, interview. *Application deadlines:* 1/31 (freshmen), 4/15 (transfers). *Early decision:* 11/15. *Notification:* continuous (freshmen), 12/15 (early decision), continuous (transfers).

Admissions Contact Ms. Shoshana Kapnek, Assistant Director of Undergraduate Admissions, University of Judaism, 15600 Mulholland Drive, Bel Air, CA 90077. *Phone:* 310-476-9777 Ext. 299. *Toll-free phone:* 888-853-6763. *Fax:* 310-471-3657. *E-mail:* admissions@uj.edu.

■ *See page 2622 for a narrative description.*

UNIVERSITY OF LA VERNE

La Verne, California

- **Independent** university, founded 1891
- **Calendar** 4-1-4
- **Degrees** certificates, associate, bachelor's, master's, doctoral, first professional, post-master's, and postbachelor's certificates (also offers continuing education program with significant enrollment not reflected in profile)
- **Suburban** 26-acre campus with easy access to Los Angeles
- **Endowment** $25.9 million
- **Coed,** 1,396 undergraduate students, 96% full-time, 63% women, 37% men
- **Moderately difficult** entrance level, 56% of applicants were admitted

The University of La Verne is an independent university located in southern California that emphasizes a liberal arts foundation in addition to career preparation. The 4-1-4 academic calendar and an enrollment of approximately 1,400 students translates into flexible scheduling, generous access to course work, and faculty focus on individual student success.

Undergraduates 1,343 full-time, 53 part-time. Students come from 13 states and territories, 9 other countries, 5% are from out of state, 10% African American, 6% Asian American or Pacific Islander, 36% Hispanic American, 0.6% Native American, 0.7% international, 8% transferred in, 37% live on campus. *Retention:* 88% of 2002 full-time freshmen returned.

Freshmen *Admission:* 1,432 applied, 805 admitted, 290 enrolled. *Average high school GPA:* 3.49. *Test scores:* SAT verbal scores over 500: 48%; SAT math scores over 500: 54%; ACT scores over 18: 81%; SAT verbal scores over 600: 6%; SAT math scores over 600: 9%; ACT scores over 24: 7%; SAT verbal scores over 700: 1%; SAT math scores over 700: 1%.

Faculty *Total:* 263, 40% full-time, 40% with terminal degrees. *Student/faculty ratio:* 9:1.

Majors Accounting; anthropology; art; art history, criticism and conservation; behavioral sciences; biology/biological sciences; broadcast journalism; business administration and management; business/managerial economics; chemistry; child development; communication/speech communication and rhetoric; comparative literature; computer science; criminology; dramatic/theatre arts; education; elementary education; English; environmental biology; French; German; health/health care administration; history; international business/trade/commerce; international relations and affairs; journalism; kindergarten/preschool education; legal assistant/paralegal; liberal arts and sciences/liberal studies; marketing/marketing management; mathematics; music; music teacher education; natural resources management and policy; natural sciences; organizational behavior; philosophy; physical education teaching and coaching; physics; political science and government; pre-dentistry studies; pre-law studies; pre-medical studies; pre-nursing studies; psychology; public administration; radio and television; religious studies; secondary education; social sciences; sociology; Spanish.

Academic Programs *Special study options:* academic remediation for entering students, accelerated degree program, adult/continuing education programs, advanced placement credit, distance learning, double majors, English as a second language, external degree program, freshman honors college, honors programs, independent study, internships, off-campus study, part-time degree program, services for LD students, student-designed majors, study abroad, summer session for credit.

Library Wilson Library with 215,000 titles, 4,500 serial subscriptions, an OPAC, a Web page.

Computers on Campus 150 computers available on campus for general student use. A campuswide network can be accessed from student residence rooms and from off campus that provide access to on-line grade information. Internet access, online (class) registration, at least one staffed computer lab available.

Student Life *Housing options:* coed, women-only. Campus housing is university owned and is provided by a third party. *Activities and organizations:* drama/theater group, student-run newspaper, radio and television station, choral group, Latino Student Forum, Inter-Fraternity/Sorority Council, African-American Student Association, Associated Students Federation, Alpha Kappa Psi, national fraternities, national sororities. *Campus security:* 24-hour emergency response devices and patrols, late-night transport/escort service, controlled dormitory access, whistle program. *Student services:* health clinic, personal/psychological counseling.

Athletics Member NCAA. All Division III. *Intercollegiate sports:* baseball M, basketball M/W, cross-country running M/W, football M, golf M, soccer M/W, softball W, swimming M/W, tennis M/W, track and field M/W, volleyball M/W, water polo M/W. *Intramural sports:* basketball M/W, cheerleading W, skiing (downhill) M/W, softball M/W, table tennis M/W, tennis M/W, volleyball M/W.

Standardized Tests *Required:* SAT I or ACT (for admission).

Costs (2004–05) *One-time required fee:* $110. *Comprehensive fee:* $30,010 includes full-time tuition ($21,500) and room and board ($8510). Full-time tuition and fees vary according to course load, degree level, location, and program. Part-time tuition and fees vary according to course load, degree level, location, and program. *College room only:* $4150. Room and board charges vary according to board plan, housing facility, and location. *Payment plans:* installment, deferred payment. *Waivers:* employees or children of employees.

Financial Aid Of all full-time matriculated undergraduates who enrolled in 2003, 1,173 applied for aid, 1,087 were judged to have need, 328 had their need fully met. 752 Federal Work-Study jobs (averaging $1997). In 2003, 148 non-need-based awards were made. *Average percent of need met:* 85%. *Average financial aid package:* $24,188. *Average need-based loan:* $5413. *Average need-based gift aid:* $10,027. *Average non-need-based aid:* $7144.

Applying *Options:* common application, electronic application, deferred entrance. *Application fee:* $50. *Required:* essay or personal statement, high school transcript, 2 letters of recommendation. *Recommended:* interview. *Application deadlines:* 2/1 (freshmen), 4/1 (transfers). *Notification:* continuous (freshmen), continuous (transfers).

Admissions Contact Ms. Ana Liza Zell, Director of Admissions, University of La Verne, 1950 Third Street, La Verne, CA 91750. *Phone:* 800-876-4858. *Toll-free phone:* 800-876-4858. *Fax:* 909-392-2714. *E-mail:* admissions@ulv.edu.

■ *See page 2624 for a narrative description.*

UNIVERSITY OF PHOENIX–NORTHERN CALIFORNIA CAMPUS

Pleasanton, California

- **Proprietary** comprehensive
- **Calendar** continuous
- **Degrees** certificates, associate, bachelor's, master's, doctoral, post-master's, and postbachelor's certificates (courses conducted at 121 campuses and learning centers in 25 states)
- **Urban** campus
- **Coed,** 3,731 undergraduate students, 100% full-time, 60% women, 40% men
- **Noncompetitive** entrance level

Undergraduates 3,731 full-time. 8% African American, 7% Asian American or Pacific Islander, 11% Hispanic American, 0.8% Native American, 12% international.

Freshmen *Admission:* 123 enrolled.

Faculty *Total:* 1,424, 0.3% full-time, 23% with terminal degrees. *Student/faculty ratio:* 8:1.

Majors Accounting; business administration and management; corrections and criminal justice related; health/health care administration; information technology; management information systems; management science; marketing/marketing management; nursing science; public administration and social service professions related.

Academic Programs *Special study options:* accelerated degree program, adult/continuing education programs, advanced placement credit, distance learning, external degree program, independent study.

Library University Library with 27.1 million titles, 11,648 serial subscriptions, an OPAC, a Web page.

Computers on Campus A campuswide network can be accessed from off campus. Internet access, at least one staffed computer lab available.

Student Life *Housing:* college housing not available.

Costs (2003–04) *Tuition:* $12,150 full-time, $405 per credit part-time. *Waivers:* employees or children of employees.

Financial Aid *Average financial aid package:* $1311.

Applying *Options:* deferred entrance. *Application fee:* $85. *Required:* 1 letter of recommendation, 2 years of work experience, 23 years of age. *Required for some:* high school transcript. *Application deadline:* rolling (freshmen), rolling (transfers).

Admissions Contact Ms. Beth Barilla, Director of Admissions, University of Phoenix–Northern California Campus, 4615 East Elwood Street, Mail Stop AA-K101, Phoenix, AZ 85040-1958. *Phone:* 480-317-6000. *Toll-free phone:* 877-4-STUDENT. *Fax:* 480-594-1758. *E-mail:* beth.barilla@phoenix.edu.

UNIVERSITY OF PHOENIX–SACRAMENTO CAMPUS

Sacramento, California

- **Proprietary** comprehensive, founded 1993
- **Calendar** continuous
- **Degrees** certificates, associate, bachelor's, master's, doctoral, post-master's, and postbachelor's certificates (courses conducted at 121 campuses and learning centers in 25 states)
- **Urban** campus
- **Coed,** 1,730 undergraduate students, 100% full-time, 62% women, 38% men
- **Noncompetitive** entrance level

Undergraduates 1,730 full-time. 8% African American, 5% Asian American or Pacific Islander, 6% Hispanic American, 0.9% Native American, 15% international.

Freshmen *Admission:* 45 enrolled.

Faculty *Total:* 608, 1% full-time, 18% with terminal degrees. *Student/faculty ratio:* 8:1.

Majors Accounting; business administration and management; corrections and criminal justice related; health/health care administration; human services; information technology; management information systems; management science; marketing/marketing management; nursing science; public administration and social service professions related.

Academic Programs *Special study options:* accelerated degree program, adult/continuing education programs, advanced placement credit, distance learning, external degree program, independent study.

Library University Library with 27.1 million titles, 11,648 serial subscriptions, an OPAC, a Web page.

Computers on Campus A campuswide network can be accessed from off campus. Internet access, at least one staffed computer lab available.

Student Life *Housing:* college housing not available.

Costs (2003–04) *Tuition:* $12,540 full-time, $418 per credit part-time. *Payment plan:* deferred payment. *Waivers:* employees or children of employees.

Financial Aid *Average financial aid package:* $1413.

Applying *Options:* deferred entrance. *Application fee:* $85. *Required:* 1 letter of recommendation, 2 years of work experience, 23 years of age. *Required for some:* high school transcript. *Application deadline:* rolling (freshmen), rolling (transfers).

Admissions Contact Ms. Beth Barilla, Director of Admissions, University of Phoenix–Sacramento Campus, 4615 East Elwood Street, Mail Stop AA-K101, Phoenix, AZ 85040-1958. *Phone:* 480-317-6000. *Toll-free phone:* 800-266-2107. *Fax:* 480-594-1758. *E-mail:* beth.barilla@phoenix.edu.

UNIVERSITY OF PHOENIX–SAN DIEGO CAMPUS

San Diego, California

- **Proprietary** comprehensive, founded 1988
- **Calendar** continuous
- **Degrees** certificates, associate, bachelor's, master's, doctoral, post-master's, and postbachelor's certificates (courses conducted at 121 campuses and learning centers in 25 states)
- **Urban** campus
- **Coed,** 1,829 undergraduate students, 100% full-time, 56% women, 44% men
- **Noncompetitive** entrance level

Undergraduates 1,829 full-time. 7% African American, 5% Asian American or Pacific Islander, 11% Hispanic American, 0.5% Native American, 11% international.

Freshmen *Admission:* 44 enrolled.

Faculty *Total:* 956, 0.8% full-time, 28% with terminal degrees. *Student/faculty ratio:* 9:1.

Majors Accounting; business administration and management; corrections and criminal justice related; health/health care administration; information technology; management information systems; marketing/marketing management; nursing science; public administration and social service professions related.

Academic Programs *Special study options:* accelerated degree program, adult/continuing education programs, advanced placement credit, distance learning, external degree program, independent study.

University of Phoenix–San Diego Campus (continued)
Library University Library with 27.1 million titles, 11,648 serial subscriptions, an OPAC, a Web page.
Computers on Campus A campuswide network can be accessed from off campus. Internet access, at least one staffed computer lab available.
Student Life *Housing:* college housing not available.
Costs (2003–04) *Tuition:* $11,760 full-time, $392 per credit part-time. *Waivers:* employees or children of employees.
Financial Aid *Average financial aid package:* $1229.
Applying *Options:* deferred entrance. *Application fee:* $85. *Required:* 1 letter of recommendation, 2 years of work experience, 23 years of age. *Required for some:* high school transcript. *Application deadline:* rolling (freshmen), rolling (transfers).
Admissions Contact Ms. Beth Barilla, Director of Admissions, University of Phoenix–San Diego Campus, 4615 East Elwood Street, Mail Stop AA-K101, Phoenix, AZ 85040-1958. *Phone:* 480-317-6000. *Toll-free phone:* 888-UOP-INFO. *Fax:* 480-594-1758. *E-mail:* beth.barilla@phoenix.edu.

UNIVERSITY OF PHOENIX–SOUTHERN CALIFORNIA CAMPUS
Fountain Valley, California

- **Proprietary** comprehensive, founded 1980
- **Calendar** continuous
- **Degrees** certificates, associate, bachelor's, master's, doctoral, post-master's, and postbachelor's certificates (courses conducted at 121 campuses and learning centers in 25 states)
- **Urban** campus
- **Coed,** 6,269 undergraduate students, 100% full-time, 59% women, 41% men
- **Noncompetitive** entrance level

Undergraduates 6,269 full-time. 11% African American, 5% Asian American or Pacific Islander, 16% Hispanic American, 0.6% Native American, 9% international.
Freshmen *Admission:* 205 enrolled.
Faculty *Total:* 2,890, 0.3% full-time, 28% with terminal degrees. *Student/faculty ratio:* 11:1.
Majors Accounting; business administration and management; corrections and criminal justice related; information technology; management information systems; marketing/marketing management; nursing science; public administration and social service professions related.
Academic Programs *Special study options:* accelerated degree program, adult/continuing education programs, advanced placement credit, distance learning, external degree program, independent study.
Library University Library with 27.1 million titles, 11,648 serial subscriptions, an OPAC, a Web page.
Computers on Campus A campuswide network can be accessed from off campus. Internet access, at least one staffed computer lab available.
Student Life *Housing:* college housing not available.
Costs (2003–04) *Tuition:* $12,660 full-time, $422 per credit part-time. *Waivers:* employees or children of employees.
Financial Aid *Average financial aid package:* $1346.
Applying *Options:* deferred entrance. *Application fee:* $85. *Required:* 1 letter of recommendation, 2 years of work experience, 23 years of age. *Required for some:* high school transcript. *Application deadline:* rolling (freshmen), rolling (transfers).
Admissions Contact Ms. Beth Barilla, Director of Admissions, University of Phoenix–Southern California Campus, 4615 East Elwood Street, Mail Stop AA-K101, Phoenix, AZ 85040-1958. *Phone:* 480-317-6000. *Toll-free phone:* 800-228-7240. *E-mail:* beth.barilla@phoenix.edu.

UNIVERSITY OF REDLANDS
Redlands, California

- **Independent** comprehensive, founded 1907
- **Calendar** 4-4-1
- **Degrees** bachelor's, master's, post-master's, and postbachelor's certificates
- **Small-town** 140-acre campus with easy access to Los Angeles
- **Endowment** $61.2 million
- **Coed,** 2,223 undergraduate students, 99% full-time, 59% women, 41% men
- **Moderately difficult** entrance level, 71% of applicants were admitted

Undergraduates 2,192 full-time, 31 part-time. Students come from 42 states and territories, 10 other countries, 27% are from out of state, 2% African American, 5% Asian American or Pacific Islander, 12% Hispanic American, 0.7% Native American, 0.9% international, 5% transferred in, 75% live on campus. *Retention:* 86% of 2002 full-time freshmen returned.
Freshmen *Admission:* 2,669 applied, 1,890 admitted, 574 enrolled. *Average high school GPA:* 3.52. *Test scores:* SAT verbal scores over 500: 89%; SAT math scores over 500: 89%; ACT scores over 18: 99%; SAT verbal scores over 600: 39%; SAT math scores over 600: 38%; ACT scores over 24: 56%; SAT verbal scores over 700: 5%; SAT math scores over 700: 6%; ACT scores over 30: 8%.
Faculty *Total:* 275, 57% full-time, 64% with terminal degrees. *Student/faculty ratio:* 12:1.
Majors Accounting; anthropology; art history, criticism and conservation; Asian studies; audiology and speech-language pathology; biology/biological sciences; business administration and management; business/commerce; chemistry; computer science; creative writing; economics; education; elementary education; English; environmental studies; fine/studio arts; French; German; history; interdisciplinary studies; international relations and affairs; liberal arts and sciences/liberal studies; literature; management information systems; mathematics; music; music history, literature, and theory; music performance; music teacher education; music theory and composition; philosophy; physics; piano and organ; political science and government; psychology; religious studies; secondary education; sociology; Spanish; speech therapy; voice and opera.
Academic Programs *Special study options:* academic remediation for entering students, adult/continuing education programs, advanced placement credit, double majors, freshman honors college, honors programs, independent study, internships, off-campus study, services for LD students, student-designed majors, study abroad.
Library Armacost Library with 251,053 titles, 7,786 serial subscriptions, 9,151 audiovisual materials, an OPAC, a Web page.
Computers on Campus 563 computers available on campus for general student use. A campuswide network can be accessed from student residence rooms and from off campus. Internet access, at least one staffed computer lab available.
Student Life *Housing:* on-campus residence required through senior year. *Options:* coed, men-only, women-only, cooperative, disabled students. Campus housing is university owned. Freshman campus housing is guaranteed. *Activities and organizations:* drama/theater group, student-run newspaper, choral group, Associated Students, service organizations, cultural organizations, social awareness groups. *Campus security:* 24-hour emergency response devices and patrols, student patrols, late-night transport/escort service, controlled dormitory access, safety whistles. *Student services:* health clinic, personal/psychological counseling, women's center.
Athletics Member NCAA. All Division III. *Intercollegiate sports:* baseball M, basketball M/W, cross-country running M/W, football M, golf M, lacrosse W, soccer M/W, softball W, swimming M/W, tennis M/W, track and field M/W, volleyball W, water polo M/W. *Intramural sports:* basketball M/W, football M/W, racquetball M/W, soccer M/W, softball M/W, table tennis M/W, ultimate Frisbee M/W, volleyball M/W, water polo M/W.
Standardized Tests *Required:* SAT I or ACT (for admission).
Costs (2003–04) *Comprehensive fee:* $32,574 includes full-time tuition ($23,796), mandatory fees ($300), and room and board ($8478). Part-time tuition: $744 per credit. Part-time tuition and fees vary according to course load. *Required fees:* $150 per term part-time. *Room and board:* Room and board charges vary according to board plan and housing facility. *Payment plan:* installment. *Waivers:* employees or children of employees.
Financial Aid Of all full-time matriculated undergraduates who enrolled in 2003, 1,834 applied for aid, 1,519 were judged to have need, 608 had their need fully met. 963 Federal Work-Study jobs (averaging $2023). 360 state and other part-time jobs (averaging $1991). In 2003, 141 non-need-based awards were made. *Average percent of need met:* 90%. *Average financial aid package:* $23,120. *Average need-based loan:* $4926. *Average need-based gift aid:* $13,162. *Average non-need-based aid:* $9525. *Average indebtedness upon graduation:* $22,358.
Applying *Options:* common application, electronic application, deferred entrance. *Application fee:* $40. *Required:* essay or personal statement, high school transcript, 2 letters of recommendation. *Recommended:* interview. *Application deadlines:* 12/15 (freshmen), 3/1 (transfers). *Notification:* continuous (freshmen), continuous (transfers).
Admissions Contact Mr. Paul Driscoll, Dean of Admissions, University of Redlands, PO Box 3080, Redlands, CA 92373-0999. *Phone:* 909-335-4074. *Toll-free phone:* 800-455-5064. *Fax:* 909-335-4089. *E-mail:* admissions@redlands.edu.

■ *See page 2690 for a narrative description.*

UNIVERSITY OF SAN DIEGO
San Diego, California

- **Independent Roman Catholic** university, founded 1949
- **Calendar** 4-1-4

- **Degrees** bachelor's, master's, doctoral, first professional, post-master's, postbachelor's, and first professional certificates
- **Urban** 180-acre campus
- **Endowment** $97.0 million
- **Coed,** 4,803 undergraduate students, 97% full-time, 62% women, 38% men
- **Very difficult** entrance level, 51% of applicants were admitted

The University of San Diego (USD) is located in a beautiful setting overlooking Mission Bay and the Pacific Ocean. USD is a Roman Catholic university that is committed to belief in the existence of God, the dignity of human beings, and service to the community.

Undergraduates 4,646 full-time, 157 part-time. Students come from 50 states and territories, 63 other countries, 38% are from out of state, 2% African American, 7% Asian American or Pacific Islander, 16% Hispanic American, 1% Native American, 2% international, 7% transferred in, 50% live on campus. *Retention:* 85% of 2002 full-time freshmen returned.

Freshmen *Admission:* 7,273 applied, 3,709 admitted, 1,064 enrolled. *Average high school GPA:* 3.80. *Test scores:* SAT verbal scores over 500: 85%; SAT math scores over 500: 90%; ACT scores over 18: 98%; SAT verbal scores over 600: 42%; SAT math scores over 600: 52%; ACT scores over 24: 70%; SAT verbal scores over 700: 3%; SAT math scores over 700: 9%; ACT scores over 30: 9%.

Faculty *Total:* 683, 51% full-time, 77% with terminal degrees. *Student/faculty ratio:* 14:1.

Majors Accounting; anthropology; art; biology/biological sciences; business administration and management; business/managerial economics; chemistry; computer science; economics; education; electrical, electronics and communications engineering; English; French; Hispanic-American, Puerto Rican, and Mexican-American/Chicano studies; history; humanities; industrial engineering; international relations and affairs; liberal arts and sciences/liberal studies; marine science/merchant marine officer; mass communication/media; mathematics; mechanical engineering; music; oceanography (chemical and physical); philosophy; physics; political science and government; pre-medical studies; psychology; religious studies; sociology; Spanish; urban studies/affairs.

Academic Programs *Special study options:* advanced placement credit, double majors, honors programs, independent study, internships, part-time degree program, services for LD students, study abroad, summer session for credit. *ROTC:* Army (c), Navy (b), Air Force (c).

Library Helen K. and James S. Copley Library plus 1 other with 500,000 titles, 4,986 serial subscriptions, 8,103 audiovisual materials, an OPAC.

Computers on Campus 260 computers available on campus for general student use. A campuswide network can be accessed from student residence rooms and from off campus. Internet access, online (class) registration, at least one staffed computer lab available.

Student Life *Housing:* on-campus residence required for freshman year. *Options:* coed, women-only, disabled students. Campus housing is university owned. Freshman campus housing is guaranteed. *Activities and organizations:* drama/theater group, student-run newspaper, television station, choral group, International Student Organization, Student Alumni Association, United Front/Multicultural Center, Associated Student Government, Panhellenic/interfraternity council, national fraternities, national sororities. *Campus security:* 24-hour emergency response devices and patrols, student patrols, late-night transport/escort service, controlled dormitory access. *Student services:* health clinic, personal/psychological counseling, women's center, legal services.

Athletics Member NCAA. All Division I. *Intercollegiate sports:* baseball M(s), basketball M(s)/W(s), crew M/W, cross-country running M(s)/W(s), equestrian sports W(c), football M, golf M(s), ice hockey M(c), lacrosse M(c)/W(c), rugby M(c), soccer M(s)/W(s), softball W, swimming W(s), tennis M(s)/W(s), volleyball M(c)/W(s). *Intramural sports:* basketball M/W, football M/W, golf M/W, sailing M(c)/W(c), skiing (downhill) M(c)/W(c), soccer M/W, softball M/W, tennis M/W, ultimate Frisbee M(c)/W(c), volleyball M/W, water polo M(c)/W(c), wrestling M(c).

Standardized Tests *Required:* SAT I or ACT (for admission), SAT I or ACT (for placement). *Recommended:* SAT II: Writing Test (for admission), SAT II: Writing Test (for placement).

Costs (2003–04) *Comprehensive fee:* $33,148 includes full-time tuition ($23,410), mandatory fees ($108), and room and board ($9630). Part-time tuition: $810 per unit. Part-time tuition and fees vary according to course load. *College room only:* $6970. Room and board charges vary according to board plan and housing facility. *Payment plan:* installment. *Waivers:* employees or children of employees.

Financial Aid Of all full-time matriculated undergraduates who enrolled in 2002, 3,420 applied for aid, 2,488 were judged to have need, 1,194 had their need fully met. 779 Federal Work-Study jobs (averaging $2432). 113 state and other part-time jobs (averaging $4899). In 2002, 679 non-need-based awards were made. *Average percent of need met:* 100%. *Average financial aid package:* $21,804. *Average need-based loan:* $4347. *Average need-based gift aid:* $16,473. *Average non-need-based aid:* $5241. *Average indebtedness upon graduation:* $25,631.

Applying *Options:* electronic application, early admission, early action. *Application fee:* $55. *Required:* essay or personal statement, high school transcript, 1 letter of recommendation. *Application deadlines:* 1/5 (freshmen), 3/1 (transfers). *Notification:* 4/15 (freshmen), 1/31 (early action), continuous until 6/1 (transfers).

Admissions Contact Mr. Stephen Pultz, Director of Admission, University of San Diego, 5998 Alcala Park, San Diego, CA 92110. *Phone:* 619-260-4506. *Toll-free phone:* 800-248-4873. *Fax:* 619-260-6836. *E-mail:* admissions@sandiego.edu.

■ *See page 2702 for a narrative description.*

UNIVERSITY OF SAN FRANCISCO

San Francisco, California

- **Independent Roman Catholic (Jesuit)** university, founded 1855
- **Calendar** 4-1-4
- **Degrees** certificates, bachelor's, master's, doctoral, first professional, and post-master's certificates
- **Urban** 55-acre campus with easy access to in San Francisco
- **Coed,** 4,718 undergraduate students, 95% full-time, 65% women, 35% men
- **Moderately difficult** entrance level, 82% of applicants were admitted

Undergraduates 4,493 full-time, 225 part-time. Students come from 51 states and territories, 70 other countries, 22% are from out of state, 4% African American, 26% Asian American or Pacific Islander, 13% Hispanic American, 0.5% Native American, 8% international, 7% transferred in, 48% live on campus. *Retention:* 84% of 2002 full-time freshmen returned.

Freshmen *Admission:* 4,634 applied, 3,798 admitted, 918 enrolled. *Average high school GPA:* 3.43. *Test scores:* SAT verbal scores over 500: 79%; SAT math scores over 500: 80%; ACT scores over 18: 95%; SAT verbal scores over 600: 31%; SAT math scores over 600: 31%; ACT scores over 24: 44%; SAT verbal scores over 700: 7%; SAT math scores over 700: 4%; ACT scores over 30: 9%.

Faculty *Total:* 767, 45% full-time. *Student/faculty ratio:* 14:1.

Majors Accounting; adult and continuing education; applied economics; architecture; art; art history, criticism and conservation; arts management; Asian studies; bilingual and multilingual education; biology/biological sciences; business administration and management; business/commerce; chemistry; city/urban, community and regional planning; communication/speech communication and rhetoric; computer and information sciences; computer science; drawing; economics; education; educational leadership and administration; elementary education; English; environmental science; environmental studies; finance; fine/studio arts; French; graphic design; health and physical education; history; hotel/motel administration; illustration; information science/studies; interdisciplinary studies; international business/trade/commerce; Japanese studies; Latin American studies; liberal arts and sciences/liberal studies; management information systems; marketing/marketing management; mass communication/media; mathematics; nursing administration; nursing (registered nurse training); organizational behavior; painting; philosophy; physical education teaching and coaching; physics; political science and government; pre-dentistry studies; pre-medical studies; pre-veterinary studies; printmaking; psychology; public administration; religious studies; restaurant/food services management; secondary education; sociology; Spanish; theology; visual and performing arts.

Academic Programs *Special study options:* academic remediation for entering students, adult/continuing education programs, advanced placement credit, cooperative education, distance learning, double majors, English as a second language, external degree program, honors programs, internships, off-campus study, part-time degree program, services for LD students, student-designed majors, study abroad, summer session for credit. *ROTC:* Army (b), Air Force (c). *Unusual degree programs:* 3-2 engineering with University of Southern California; physics.

Library Gleeson Library plus 2 others with 1.1 million titles, 5,560 serial subscriptions, 4,591 audiovisual materials, an OPAC, a Web page.

Computers on Campus 250 computers available on campus for general student use. A campuswide network can be accessed from student residence rooms and from off campus. Internet access, online (class) registration, at least one staffed computer lab available.

Student Life *Housing:* on-campus residence required through sophomore year. *Options:* coed, women-only. Campus housing is university owned and leased by the school. Freshman campus housing is guaranteed. *Activities and organizations:* drama/theater group, student-run newspaper, radio station, choral group, student leadership, student media, College Players, national fraternities, national sororities. *Campus security:* 24-hour emergency response devices and patrols, late-night transport/escort service, controlled dormitory access. *Student services:* health clinic, personal/psychological counseling.

University of San Francisco (continued)

Athletics Member NCAA. All Division I. *Intercollegiate sports:* baseball M(s), basketball M(s)/W(s), cross-country running M(s)/W(s), golf M(s)/W(s), riflery M(s)/W(s), soccer M(s)/W(s), softball M(c)/W(c), tennis M(s)/W(s), track and field W(s), volleyball M(c)/W(s). *Intramural sports:* basketball M/W, bowling M/W, fencing M(c)/W(c), football M/W, golf M(c)/W(c), ice hockey M(c)/W(c), lacrosse M(c), racquetball M/W, rugby M(c)/W(c), skiing (cross-country) M(c)/W(c), soccer M/W, softball M/W, swimming M/W, table tennis M/W, tennis M/W, volleyball M/W.

Standardized Tests *Required:* SAT I or ACT (for admission).

Costs (2004–05) *Comprehensive fee:* $34,700 includes full-time tuition ($24,800), mandatory fees ($120), and room and board ($9780). Full-time tuition and fees vary according to program. Part-time tuition: $886 per credit. *Required fees:* $120 per year part-time. *College room only:* $6180. Room and board charges vary according to board plan. *Payment plan:* installment. *Waivers:* employees or children of employees.

Financial Aid Of all full-time matriculated undergraduates who enrolled in 2003, 2,591 applied for aid, 2,375 were judged to have need, 294 had their need fully met. 713 Federal Work-Study jobs (averaging $3446). 394 state and other part-time jobs (averaging $3453). In 2003, 139 non-need-based awards were made. *Average percent of need met:* 72%. *Average financial aid package:* $19,440. *Average need-based loan:* $4989. *Average need-based gift aid:* $13,635. *Average non-need-based aid:* $13,247. *Average indebtedness upon graduation:* $22,075.

Applying *Options:* common application, electronic application, early action, deferred entrance. *Application fee:* $55. *Required:* essay or personal statement, high school transcript, minimum 2.8 GPA, 1 letter of recommendation. *Required for some:* interview. *Recommended:* minimum 3.0 GPA. *Application deadline:* 2/1 (freshmen), rolling (transfers). *Notification:* continuous until 8/15 (freshmen), 1/1 (early action), continuous until 8/15 (transfers).

Admissions Contact Mr. Tom Matos, Director, University of San Francisco, 2130 Fulton Street, San Francisco, CA 94117-1080. *Phone:* 415-422-6563. *Toll-free phone:* 800-CALL USF. *Fax:* 415-422-2217. *E-mail:* admissions@usfca.edu.

■ *See page 2704 for a narrative description.*

UNIVERSITY OF SOUTHERN CALIFORNIA

Los Angeles, California

- **Independent** university, founded 1880
- **Calendar** semesters
- **Degrees** bachelor's, master's, doctoral, first professional, post-master's, postbachelor's, and first professional certificates
- **Urban** 155-acre campus
- **Endowment** $2.1 billion
- **Coed,** 16,381 undergraduate students, 96% full-time, 50% women, 50% men
- **Most difficult** entrance level, 30% of applicants were admitted

Hailed for linking a powerful educational community with a diverse city and neighborhood, USC is the largest private university in the west. USC students benefit from a creative research and teaching menu. Majors and minors in demanding traditional liberal arts and science programs and 18 respected professional schools are offered. Living in Southern California gives students a comprehensive academic and hands-on experience.

Undergraduates 15,687 full-time, 694 part-time. Students come from 52 states and territories, 148 other countries, 33% are from out of state, 7% African American, 21% Asian American or Pacific Islander, 13% Hispanic American, 0.8% Native American, 8% international, 7% transferred in, 37% live on campus. *Retention:* 94% of 2001 full-time freshmen returned.

Freshmen *Admission:* 29,278 applied, 8,718 admitted, 2,976 enrolled. *Average high school GPA:* 3.99. *Test scores:* SAT verbal scores over 500: 99%; SAT math scores over 500: 100%; ACT scores over 18: 100%; SAT verbal scores over 600: 80%; SAT math scores over 600: 91%; ACT scores over 24: 97%; SAT verbal scores over 700: 28%; SAT math scores over 700: 42%; ACT scores over 30: 43%.

Faculty *Total:* 2,341, 62% full-time. *Student/faculty ratio:* 10:1.

Majors Accounting; acting; aerospace, aeronautical and astronautical engineering; African-American/Black studies; American literature; American studies; anthropology; anthropology related; architecture; art; art history, criticism and conservation; Asian-American studies; Asian studies (East); astronomy; biochemistry; biology/biological sciences; biomedical/medical engineering; biophysics; broadcast journalism; business administration and management; business administration, management and operations related; business, management, and marketing related; chemical engineering; chemistry; cinematography and film/video production; city/urban, community and regional planning; civil engineering; civil engineering related; classics and languages, literatures and linguistics; communication/speech communication and rhetoric; comparative literature; computer and information sciences; computer engineering; computer engineering related; computer science; construction engineering; creative writing; cultural studies; dental hygiene; directing and theatrical production; dramatic/theatre arts; East Asian languages; economics; education; electrical, electronics and communications engineering; engineering; English; English literature (British and Commonwealth); environmental/environmental health engineering; environmental studies; film/cinema studies; fine/studio arts; French; general studies; geography; geology/earth science; German; gerontology; health science; Hispanic-American, Puerto Rican, and Mexican-American/Chicano studies; history; interdisciplinary studies; international business/trade/commerce; international relations and affairs; Italian; jazz/jazz studies; Jewish/Judaic studies; journalism; kinesiology and exercise science; landscape architecture; linguistics; marine biology and biological oceanography; mass communication/media; materials science; mathematics; mechanical engineering; music; music management and merchandising; music performance; music related; music teacher education; music theory and composition; occupational therapy; petroleum engineering; philosophy; philosophy related; physical sciences; physics; physiological psychology/psychobiology; piano and organ; playwriting and screenwriting; political science and government; polymer/plastics engineering; Portuguese; psychology; public administration; public health education and promotion; public relations/image management; radio and television; religious studies; Russian; Slavic languages; sociology; Spanish; structural engineering; systems engineering; theatre design and technology; theatre/theatre arts management; urban studies/affairs; violin, viola, guitar and other stringed instruments; voice and opera; water resources engineering; wind/percussion instruments; women's studies.

Academic Programs *Special study options:* accelerated degree program, advanced placement credit, cooperative education, double majors, English as a second language, freshman honors college, honors programs, independent study, internships, off-campus study, part-time degree program, services for LD students, student-designed majors, study abroad, summer session for credit. *ROTC:* Army (b), Navy (b), Air Force (b). *Unusual degree programs:* 3-2 economics, mathematics, accounting.

Library Doheny Memorial Library plus 20 others with 3.5 million titles, 28,561 serial subscriptions, 3.2 million audiovisual materials, an OPAC, a Web page.

Computers on Campus 2500 computers available on campus for general student use. A campuswide network can be accessed from student residence rooms and from off campus that provide access to online degree progress, grades, financial aid summary. Internet access, online (class) registration, at least one staffed computer lab available. Computer purchase or lease plan available.

Student Life *Housing options:* coed, cooperative, disabled students. Campus housing is university owned. Freshman campus housing is guaranteed. *Activities and organizations:* drama/theater group, student-run newspaper, radio and television station, choral group, marching band, Troy Camp, USC Helenes, Program Board, Student Senate, Alpha Phi Omega, national fraternities, national sororities. *Campus security:* 24-hour emergency response devices and patrols, student patrols, late-night transport/escort service, controlled dormitory access. *Student services:* health clinic, personal/psychological counseling, women's center.

Athletics Member NCAA. All Division I except football (Division I-A). *Intercollegiate sports:* baseball M(s), basketball M(s)/W(s), crew W(s), cross-country running M(s)/W(s), golf M(s)/W(s), soccer W(s), swimming M(s)/W(s), tennis M(s)/W(s), track and field M(s)/W(s), volleyball M(s)/W(s), water polo M(s)/W(s). *Intramural sports:* archery M(c)/W(c), badminton M(c)/W(c), basketball M(c)/W(c), bowling M(c)/W(c), crew M(c), cross-country running M(c)/W(c), equestrian sports M(c)/W(c), fencing M(c)/W(c), football M/W, golf M(c)/W(c), ice hockey M(c)/W(c), lacrosse M(c)/W(c), racquetball M(c)/W(c), riflery M(c)/W(c), rugby M(c)/W(c), sailing M(c)/W(c), skiing (cross-country) M(c)/W(c), skiing (downhill) M(c)/W(c), soccer M(c)/W(c), softball W(c), swimming M(c)/W(c), tennis M(c)/W(c), volleyball M(c)/W(c), water polo M(c)/W(c), weight lifting M(c)/W(c), wrestling M(c)/W(c).

Standardized Tests *Required:* SAT I or ACT (for admission). *Required for some:* SAT II: Subject Tests (for admission).

Costs (2003–04) *Comprehensive fee:* $37,324 includes full-time tuition ($28,184), mandatory fees ($508), and room and board ($8632). Part-time tuition: $949 per credit hour. Part-time tuition and fees vary according to course load. *Required fees:* $508 per term part-time. *College room only:* $4750. Room and board charges vary according to board plan and housing facility. *Payment plans:* tuition prepayment, installment, deferred payment. *Waivers:* employees or children of employees.

Financial Aid Of all full-time matriculated undergraduates who enrolled in 2002, 9,326 applied for aid, 7,587 were judged to have need, 7,007 had their need fully met. 6,183 Federal Work-Study jobs (averaging $2218). In 2002, 2481 non-need-based awards were made. *Average percent of need met:* 100%. *Average financial aid package:* $25,521. *Average need-based loan:* $6078. *Average need-based gift aid:* $19,235. *Average non-need-based aid:* $12,288. *Average indebtedness upon graduation:* $19,176.

Applying *Options:* electronic application. *Application fee:* $65. *Required:* essay or personal statement, high school transcript. *Required for some:* letters of recommendation. *Recommended:* letters of recommendation, interview. *Application deadlines:* 1/10 (freshmen), 3/1 (transfers). *Notification:* 4/1 (freshmen), 5/1 (transfers).

Admissions Contact Ms. Laurel Baker-Tew, Director of Admission, University of Southern California, University Park Campus, Los Angeles, CA 90089. *Phone:* 213-740-1111. *Fax:* 213-740-6364. *E-mail:* admitusc@usc.edu.

■ *See page 2710 for a narrative description.*

UNIVERSITY OF THE PACIFIC
Stockton, California

- **Independent** university, founded 1851
- **Calendar** semesters
- **Degrees** bachelor's, master's, doctoral, and first professional
- **Suburban** 175-acre campus with easy access to Sacramento
- **Endowment** $136.7 million
- **Coed,** 3,357 undergraduate students, 96% full-time, 58% women, 42% men
- **Moderately difficult** entrance level, 70% of applicants were admitted

Comprehensive is the best word to describe the University of the Pacific. The integration of liberal arts and sciences with professional study provides undergraduate students with a wealth of academic opportunities in a personally supportive community. Located halfway between the San Francisco Bay and the Sierra Nevada mountains, Pacific offers its 3,100 undergraduate students a wide variety of educational, cultural, recreational, and social opportunities.

Undergraduates 3,239 full-time, 118 part-time. Students come from 41 states and territories, 16 other countries, 13% are from out of state, 3% African American, 27% Asian American or Pacific Islander, 11% Hispanic American, 0.7% Native American, 3% international, 7% transferred in, 55% live on campus. *Retention:* 85% of 2002 full-time freshmen returned.

Freshmen *Admission:* 4,501 applied, 3,173 admitted, 818 enrolled. *Average high school GPA:* 3.45. *Test scores:* SAT verbal scores over 500: 82%; SAT math scores over 500: 90%; ACT scores over 18: 98%; SAT verbal scores over 600: 35%; SAT math scores over 600: 50%; ACT scores over 24: 58%; SAT verbal scores over 700: 3%; SAT math scores over 700: 12%; ACT scores over 30: 5%.

Faculty *Total:* 627, 62% full-time, 87% with terminal degrees. *Student/faculty ratio:* 13:1.

Majors Art; art history, criticism and conservation; audiology and speech-language pathology; biochemistry; biology/biological sciences; biomedical/medical engineering; business administration and management; chemistry; chemistry related; civil engineering; classics and languages, literatures and linguistics; commercial and advertising art; communication/speech communication and rhetoric; computer engineering; computer science; dramatic/theatre arts; economics; education; electrical, electronics and communications engineering; engineering/industrial management; engineering physics; English; environmental studies; fine/studio arts; French; geology/earth science; German; history; information science/studies; interdisciplinary studies; international relations and affairs; Japanese; kinesiology and exercise science; mathematics; mechanical engineering; music; music history, literature, and theory; music management and merchandising; music teacher education; music theory and composition; music therapy; pharmacy; philosophy; physical sciences; physics; piano and organ; political science and government; psychology; religious studies; social sciences; sociology; Spanish; special education; voice and opera.

Academic Programs *Special study options:* academic remediation for entering students, accelerated degree program, adult/continuing education programs, advanced placement credit, cooperative education, double majors, English as a second language, honors programs, independent study, internships, part-time degree program, services for LD students, student-designed majors, study abroad, summer session for credit.

Library Holt Memorial Library plus 1 other with 268,365 titles, 1,361 serial subscriptions, 10,110 audiovisual materials, an OPAC, a Web page.

Computers on Campus 274 computers available on campus for general student use. A campuswide network can be accessed from student residence rooms and from off campus. Internet access, online (class) registration, at least one staffed computer lab available. Computer purchase or lease plan available.

Student Life *Housing:* on-campus residence required through sophomore year. *Options:* coed. Campus housing is university owned. *Activities and organizations:* drama/theater group, student-run newspaper, radio station, choral group, student government, cultural organizations, marketing club, Model United Nations, national fraternities, national sororities. *Campus security:* 24-hour emergency response devices and patrols, late-night transport/escort service, controlled dormitory access. *Student services:* health clinic, personal/psychological counseling, legal services.

Athletics Member NCAA. All Division I. *Intercollegiate sports:* baseball M(s), basketball M(s)/W(s), cross-country running W(s), field hockey W(s), golf M(s), soccer W(s), softball W(s), swimming M(s)/W(s), tennis M(s)/W(s), volleyball M(s)/W(s), water polo M(s)/W(s). *Intramural sports:* badminton M(c)/W(c), basketball M/W, bowling M/W, crew M(c)/W(c), equestrian sports M(c)/W(c), football M/W, golf M, lacrosse M(c)/W(c), rugby M(c), soccer M(c)/W(c), tennis M/W, volleyball M/W.

Standardized Tests *Required:* SAT I or ACT (for admission).

Costs (2003–04) *Comprehensive fee:* $31,090 includes full-time tuition ($23,180), mandatory fees ($420), and room and board ($7490). Part-time tuition and fees vary according to course load. *College room only:* $3736. Room and board charges vary according to board plan and housing facility. *Payment plan:* deferred payment. *Waivers:* employees or children of employees.

Financial Aid Of all full-time matriculated undergraduates who enrolled in 2003, 2,496 applied for aid, 2,219 were judged to have need, 784 had their need fully met. In 2003, 338 non-need-based awards were made. *Average financial aid package:* $22,096. *Average need-based loan:* $4721. *Average need-based gift aid:* $17,379. *Average non-need-based aid:* $7766.

Applying *Options:* common application, electronic application, early action. *Application fee:* $50. *Required:* essay or personal statement, high school transcript, minimum 2.5 GPA, 1 letter of recommendation. *Required for some:* audition for music program. *Recommended:* minimum 3.0 GPA, interview. *Application deadlines:* 1/15 (freshmen), 6/1 (transfers). *Notification:* continuous (freshmen), 1/15 (early action), continuous (transfers).

Admissions Contact Mr. Marc McGee, Director of Admissions, University of the Pacific, 3601 Pacific Avenue, Stockton, CA 95211. *Phone:* 209-946-2211. *Toll-free phone:* 800-959-2867. *Fax:* 209-946-2413. *E-mail:* admissions@pacific.edu.

■ *See page 2726 for a narrative description.*

UNIVERSITY OF THE WEST
Rosemead, California

- **Independent** comprehensive, founded 1991
- **Calendar** semesters
- **Degrees** certificates, bachelor's, master's, doctoral, first professional, and post-master's certificates
- **Coed**

Majors Asian history; Buddhist studies; business administration and management; Chinese studies; English; history; philosophy; psychology; religious studies related.

Student Life *Housing options:* Campus housing is university owned.

Costs (2004–05) *Comprehensive fee:* $11,750 includes full-time tuition ($6750), mandatory fees ($200), and room and board ($4800). Part-time tuition: $200 per unit.

Financial Aid Of all full-time matriculated undergraduates who enrolled in 2003, 30 applied for aid, 18 were judged to have need. 20 state and other part-time jobs.

Applying *Application fee:* $50. *Application deadlines:* 8/15 (freshmen), 7/31 (out-of-state freshmen).

Admissions Contact Ms. Grace Hsiao, Registrar and Admissions Officer, University of the West, 1409 North Walnut Grove Avenue, Rosemead, CA 91770. *Phone:* 626-571-8811 Ext. 120.

■ *See page 2732 for a narrative description.*

UNIVERSITY OF WEST LOS ANGELES
Inglewood, California

- **Independent** upper-level, founded 1966
- **Calendar** trimesters
- **Degrees** certificates, bachelor's, first professional, and postbachelor's certificates
- **Suburban** 2-acre campus with easy access to Los Angeles
- **Coed,** 71 undergraduate students, 30% full-time, 75% women, 25% men
- **Minimally difficult** entrance level

Undergraduates 21 full-time, 50 part-time. Students come from 1 other state, 0.1% are from out of state, 32% African American, 9% Asian American or Pacific Islander, 14% Hispanic American, 5% Native American, 10% transferred in.

Faculty *Total:* 21, 5% full-time, 95% with terminal degrees. *Student/faculty ratio:* 10:1.

Majors Legal administrative assistant/secretary; legal assistant/paralegal; legal studies; pre-law studies.

University of West Los Angeles (continued)

Academic Programs *Special study options:* academic remediation for entering students, adult/continuing education programs, independent study, internships, part-time degree program.

Library Kelton Library with 33,000 titles, 250 serial subscriptions.

Computers on Campus 20 computers available on campus for general student use. Internet access, at least one staffed computer lab available.

Student Life *Housing:* college housing not available. *Activities and organizations:* student-run newspaper, Black Law Students Association, American Trial Lawyers Association, Asian Pacific American Law Students Association, Toastmasters. *Campus security:* late-night transport/escort service.

Costs (2003–04) *Tuition:* $7650 full-time, $255 per unit part-time. *Required fees:* $360 full-time, $120 per term part-time. *Payment plan:* installment. *Waivers:* employees or children of employees.

Financial Aid Of all full-time matriculated undergraduates who enrolled in 2003, 83 applied for aid, 83 were judged to have need. In 2003, 1 non-need-based awards were made. *Average percent of need met:* 60%. *Average financial aid package:* $9797. *Average need-based loan:* $4162. *Average need-based gift aid:* $3950.

Applying *Options:* electronic application, deferred entrance. *Application fee:* $55. *Application deadline:* rolling (transfers).

Admissions Contact Ms. Yvonne Alwag, Admissions Counselor, University of West Los Angeles, School of Paralegal Studies, 1155 West Arbor Vitae Street, Inglewood, CA 90301-2902. *Phone:* 310-342-5287. *Fax:* 310-342-5296. *E-mail:* aalwag@uwla.edu.

■ *See page 2740 for a narrative description.*

VANGUARD UNIVERSITY OF SOUTHERN CALIFORNIA

Costa Mesa, California

- **Independent** comprehensive, founded 1920, affiliated with Assemblies of God
- **Calendar** semesters
- **Degrees** bachelor's and master's
- **Suburban** 38-acre campus with easy access to Los Angeles
- **Endowment** $2.1 million
- **Coed,** 1,340 undergraduate students, 98% full-time, 64% women, 36% men
- **Moderately difficult** entrance level, 80% of applicants were admitted

Founded in 1920, Vanguard University is a comprehensive Christian university of liberal arts and professional studies. Vanguard is committed to preparing students through an education marked by academic excellence and spiritual vitality for productive service in a variety of vocations and ministries that are matched to the marketplace of the 21st century.

Undergraduates 1,309 full-time, 31 part-time. Students come from 40 states and territories, 10 other countries, 21% are from out of state, 2% African American, 4% Asian American or Pacific Islander, 17% Hispanic American, 0.7% Native American, 1% international, 12% transferred in, 75% live on campus. *Retention:* 80% of 2002 full-time freshmen returned.

Freshmen *Admission:* 746 applied, 599 admitted, 347 enrolled. *Average high school GPA:* 3.39. *Test scores:* SAT verbal scores over 500: 57%; SAT math scores over 500: 53%; ACT scores over 18: 84%; SAT verbal scores over 600: 22%; SAT math scores over 600: 15%; ACT scores over 24: 35%; SAT verbal scores over 700: 2%; SAT math scores over 700: 1%; ACT scores over 30: 4%.

Faculty *Total:* 164, 46% full-time, 51% with terminal degrees. *Student/faculty ratio:* 16:1.

Majors Accounting; anthropology; athletic training; biblical studies; biological and physical sciences; biology/biological sciences; business administration and management; chemistry; cinematography and film/video production; communication/speech communication and rhetoric; dramatic/theatre arts; education; English; finance; health and physical education; history; interdisciplinary studies; international business/trade/commerce; kinesiology and exercise science; marketing/marketing management; mathematics; missionary studies and missiology; music; pastoral studies/counseling; physical education teaching and coaching; physical therapy; political science and government; pre-law studies; psychology; radio and television; religious education; religious studies; secondary education; sociology; Spanish; speech and rhetoric; youth ministry.

Academic Programs *Special study options:* accelerated degree program, adult/continuing education programs, advanced placement credit, double majors, external degree program, independent study, internships, off-campus study, part-time degree program, services for LD students, study abroad, summer session for credit. *ROTC:* Air Force (c).

Library O. Cope Budge Library with 144,952 titles, 1,066 serial subscriptions, 4,668 audiovisual materials, an OPAC, a Web page.

Computers on Campus 145 computers available on campus for general student use. A campuswide network can be accessed from student residence rooms and from off campus. Internet access, at least one staffed computer lab available. Computer purchase or lease plan available.

Student Life *Housing:* on-campus residence required through senior year. *Options:* men-only, women-only. Campus housing is university owned. Freshman applicants given priority for college housing. *Activities and organizations:* drama/theater group, student-run newspaper, choral group, student ministries, choral groups, orchestral bands. *Campus security:* 24-hour emergency response devices and patrols, late-night transport/escort service. *Student services:* personal/psychological counseling.

Athletics Member NAIA. *Intercollegiate sports:* baseball M(s), basketball M(s)/W(s), cross-country running M(s)/W(s), soccer M(s)/W(s), softball W(s), tennis M(s)/W(s), track and field M(s)/W(s), volleyball W(s). *Intramural sports:* basketball M/W, football M/W, soccer M/W, softball M/W, table tennis M/W, tennis M/W.

Standardized Tests *Required:* SAT I or ACT (for admission).

Costs (2003–04) *Comprehensive fee:* $21,868 includes full-time tuition ($15,928), mandatory fees ($430), and room and board ($5510). Part-time tuition: $664 per credit hour. *College room only:* $3060. Room and board charges vary according to board plan and housing facility. *Payment plan:* installment. *Waivers:* employees or children of employees.

Financial Aid Of all full-time matriculated undergraduates who enrolled in 2003, 1,264 applied for aid, 983 were judged to have need, 756 had their need fully met. 80 Federal Work-Study jobs (averaging $2000). In 2003, 284 non-need-based awards were made. *Average percent of need met:* 68%. *Average financial aid package:* $9700. *Average need-based loan:* $4281. *Average need-based gift aid:* $7400. *Average non-need-based aid:* $4051. *Average indebtedness upon graduation:* $17,500. *Financial aid deadline:* 3/2.

Applying *Options:* common application, electronic application, deferred entrance. *Application fee:* $45. *Required:* essay or personal statement, high school transcript, minimum 2.8 GPA, 1 letter of recommendation. *Required for some:* interview. *Application deadlines:* 12/1 (freshmen), 12/1 (transfers). *Notification:* continuous until 8/31 (freshmen), continuous until 8/31 (transfers).

Admissions Contact Ms. Jessica Mireles, Associate Vice President of Enrollment Management, Vanguard University of Southern California, 55 Fair Drive, Costa Mesa, CA 92626. *Phone:* 714-556-3610 Ext. 327. *Toll-free phone:* 800-722-6279. *Fax:* 714-966-5471. *E-mail:* admissions@vanguard.edu.

WESTMONT COLLEGE

Santa Barbara, California

- **Independent nondenominational** 4-year, founded 1937
- **Calendar** semesters
- **Degrees** bachelor's and postbachelor's certificates
- **Suburban** 133-acre campus with easy access to Los Angeles
- **Endowment** $17.2 million
- **Coed,** 1,343 undergraduate students, 100% full-time, 65% women, 35% men
- **Moderately difficult** entrance level, 85% of applicants were admitted

Undergraduates 1,337 full-time, 6 part-time. Students come from 41 states and territories, 34% are from out of state, 1% African American, 6% Asian American or Pacific Islander, 7% Hispanic American, 1% Native American, 0.8% international, 4% transferred in. *Retention:* 89% of 2002 full-time freshmen returned.

Freshmen *Admission:* 1,404 applied, 1,188 admitted, 355 enrolled. *Average high school GPA:* 3.65. *Test scores:* SAT verbal scores over 500: 92%; SAT math scores over 500: 94%; ACT scores over 18: 100%; SAT verbal scores over 600: 57%; SAT math scores over 600: 62%; ACT scores over 24: 78%; SAT verbal scores over 700: 12%; SAT math scores over 700: 21%; ACT scores over 30: 15%.

Faculty *Total:* 139, 60% full-time. *Student/faculty ratio:* 13:1.

Majors Anthropology; art; art teacher education; biology/biological sciences; business/commerce; business/managerial economics; chemistry; communication/speech communication and rhetoric; computer science; dance; dramatic/theatre arts; economics; education; elementary education; engineering physics; English; English/language arts teacher education; French; history; kinesiology and exercise science; liberal arts and sciences/liberal studies; mathematics; mathematics teacher education; modern languages; music; neuroscience; philosophy; physical education teaching and coaching; physics; political science and government; pre-dentistry studies; pre-law studies; pre-medical studies; pre-pharmacy studies; pre-theology/pre-ministerial studies; pre-veterinary studies; psychology; religious studies; secondary education; social sciences; social science teacher education; sociology; Spanish.

Academic Programs *Special study options:* accelerated degree program, advanced placement credit, cooperative education, double majors, honors programs, independent study, internships, off-campus study, services for LD students, student-designed majors, study abroad, summer session for credit. *ROTC:*

Army (c), Air Force (c). *Unusual degree programs:* 3-2 engineering with Washington University in St. Louis; Boston University; University of Southern California; University of California, Berkeley; Los Angeles; Santa Barbara; California Polytechnic State University; Stanford University.

Library Roger John Voskuyl Library with 165,512 titles, 3,211 serial subscriptions, 8,032 audiovisual materials, an OPAC.

Computers on Campus 100 computers available on campus for general student use. A campuswide network can be accessed from student residence rooms and from off campus. Internet access, at least one staffed computer lab available.

Student Life *Housing options:* coed, disabled students. Campus housing is university owned. Freshman campus housing is guaranteed. *Activities and organizations:* drama/theater group, student-run newspaper, radio station, choral group, Christian Concerns, student government, Leadership Development, music and theater ensembles, intramural athletics. *Campus security:* 24-hour emergency response devices and patrols, late-night transport/escort service, controlled dormitory access. *Student services:* health clinic, personal/psychological counseling, women's center.

Athletics Member NAIA. *Intercollegiate sports:* baseball M(s), basketball M(s)/W(s), cross-country running M(s)/W(s), lacrosse W(c), rugby M(c), soccer M(s)/W(s), tennis M(s)/W(s), track and field M(s)/W(s), volleyball M(c)/W(s). *Intramural sports:* badminton M/W, basketball M/W, bowling M/W, cheerleading M(c)/W(c), cross-country running M/W, football M/W, golf M/W, racquetball M/W, rock climbing M(c)/W(c), soccer M(c)/W, softball M/W, swimming M/W, table tennis M/W, tennis M/W, ultimate Frisbee M(c), volleyball M/W, water polo M/W.

Standardized Tests *Required:* SAT I or ACT (for admission). *Recommended:* SAT II: Writing Test (for admission).

Costs (2003–04) *Comprehensive fee:* $33,280 includes full-time tuition ($24,224), mandatory fees ($666), and room and board ($8390). *College room only:* $4888. Room and board charges vary according to board plan. *Payment plan:* installment. *Waivers:* employees or children of employees.

Financial Aid Of all full-time matriculated undergraduates who enrolled in 2003, 859 applied for aid, 752 were judged to have need, 61 had their need fully met. 186 Federal Work-Study jobs (averaging $1015). In 2003, 398 non-need-based awards were made. *Average percent of need met:* 68%. *Average financial aid package:* $16,571. *Average need-based loan:* $5317. *Average need-based gift aid:* $11,356. *Average non-need-based aid:* $8450. *Average indebtedness upon graduation:* $19,548.

Applying *Options:* common application, electronic application, early action. *Application fee:* $50. *Required:* essay or personal statement, high school transcript, 3 letters of recommendation. *Required for some:* interview. *Recommended:* minimum 3.0 GPA, interview. *Application deadlines:* 2/15 (freshmen), 3/15 (transfers). *Notification:* 4/1 (freshmen), 1/20 (early action), 4/1 (transfers).

Admissions Contact Mrs. Joyce Luy, Director of Admissions, Westmont College, 955 La Paz Road, Santa Barbara, CA 93108. *Phone:* 805-565-6200 Ext. 6005. *Toll-free phone:* 800-777-9011. *Fax:* 805-565-6234. *E-mail:* admissions@westmont.edu.

■ *See page 2828 for a narrative description.*

WESTWOOD COLLEGE OF AVIATION TECHNOLOGY–LOS ANGELES

Inglewood, California

- **Proprietary** primarily 2-year, founded 1942
- **Calendar** quarters
- **Degrees** associate and bachelor's
- **Urban** campus
- **Coed, primarily men**
- **Noncompetitive** entrance level

Applying *Application fee:* $75.

Admissions Contact Mr. Keith Watson, Director of Admissions, Westwood College of Aviation Technology–Los Angeles, 8911 Aviation Boulevard, Inglewood, CA 90301-2904. *Phone:* 310-337-4444. *Toll-free phone:* 800-597-8690. *Fax:* 310-337-1176. *E-mail:* info@westwood.edu.

WESTWOOD COLLEGE OF TECHNOLOGY–ANAHEIM

Anaheim, California

- **Proprietary** primarily 2-year
- **Degrees** associate and bachelor's
- **Coed**

Admissions Contact Mr. Dean Dunbar, Director of Admissions, Westwood College of Technology–Anaheim, 2461 West La Palma Avenue, Anaheim, CA 92801-2610. *Phone:* 714-226-9990. *Toll-free phone:* 877-650-6050. *Fax:* 714-826-7398. *E-mail:* info@westwood.edu.

WESTWOOD COLLEGE OF TECHNOLOGY–INLAND EMPIRE

Upland, California

- **Proprietary** primarily 2-year
- **Degrees** associate and bachelor's
- **Coed**

Admissions Contact Mr. Lyle Seavers, Director of Admissions, Westwood College of Technology–Inland Empire, 20 West 7th Street, Upland, CA 91786-7148. *Phone:* 909-931-7550. *Toll-free phone:* 866-288-9488. *Fax:* 909-931-9195. *E-mail:* info@westwood.edu.

WESTWOOD COLLEGE OF TECHNOLOGY–LONG BEACH

Long Beach, California

- **Proprietary** primarily 2-year, founded 2002, part of Alta Colleges
- **Calendar** continuous
- **Degrees** associate and bachelor's
- **Urban** 1-acre campus with easy access to Los Angeles
- **Coed,** 154 undergraduate students, 100% full-time, 31% women, 69% men
- 62% of applicants were admitted

Undergraduates 154 full-time. Students come from 4 states and territories, 2% are from out of state, 15% African American, 10% Asian American or Pacific Islander, 46% Hispanic American, 0.6% Native American.

Freshmen *Admission:* 45 applied, 28 admitted.

Faculty *Total:* 19, 11% full-time, 11% with terminal degrees. *Student/faculty ratio:* 15:1.

Majors CAD/CADD drafting/design technology; computer hardware engineering; design and visual communications; graphic design.

Student Life *Housing:* college housing not available. *Activities and organizations:* Westwood Expo, Mentorship Program, Director's Advisory Board. *Campus security:* 24-hour emergency response devices and patrols, late-night transport/escort service. *Student services:* personal/psychological counseling.

Athletics *Intramural sports:* basketball M/W, ultimate Frisbee M/W.

Standardized Tests *Required:* ACCUPLACER (for admission). *Recommended:* SAT I or ACT (for admission).

Costs (2004–05) *Tuition:* $18,645 full-time. Full-time tuition and fees vary according to course load and program. Part-time tuition and fees vary according to course load and program. *Required fees:* $2726 full-time. *Payment plans:* tuition prepayment, installment. *Waivers:* employees or children of employees.

Applying *Application fee:* $100. *Required:* high school transcript, interview. *Application deadline:* 10/4 (transfers). *Notification:* continuous (transfers).

Admissions Contact Mr. Craig McVey, Director of Admissions, Westwood College of Technology–Long Beach, 3901 Via Oro Avenue, Suite 103, Long Beach, CA 90810. *Phone:* 310-522-2088 Ext. 100. *Toll-free phone:* 888-403-3308. *Fax:* 310-522-2098. *E-mail:* cmcvey@westwood.edu.

WESTWOOD COLLEGE OF TECHNOLOGY–LOS ANGELES

Los Angeles, California

- **Proprietary** primarily 2-year
- **Degrees** associate and bachelor's
- **Coed**

Admissions Contact Mr. Ron Milman, Director of Admissions, Westwood College of Technology–Los Angeles, 3460 Wilshire Boulevard, Suite 700, Los Angeles, CA 90010-2210. *Phone:* 213-739-9999. *Toll-free phone:* 877-377-4600. *Fax:* 213-382-2468. *E-mail:* info@westwood.edu.

WHITTIER COLLEGE

Whittier, California

- **Independent** comprehensive, founded 1887
- **Calendar** 4-1-4

Whittier College (continued)

- **Degrees** bachelor's, master's, and first professional
- **Suburban** 95-acre campus with easy access to Los Angeles
- **Endowment** $55.0 million
- **Coed**
- **Moderately difficult** entrance level

Faculty *Student/faculty ratio:* 13:1.
Student Life *Campus security:* 24-hour emergency response devices and patrols, late-night transport/escort service, controlled dormitory access.
Athletics Member NCAA. All Division III.
Standardized Tests *Required:* SAT I or ACT (for admission). *Recommended:* SAT II: Subject Tests (for admission).
Costs (2003–04) *Comprehensive fee:* $31,080 includes full-time tuition ($23,192), mandatory fees ($300), and room and board ($7588). *College room only:* $4162.
Financial Aid Of all full-time matriculated undergraduates who enrolled in 2003, 1,161 applied for aid, 394 had their need fully met. In 2003, 244. *Average percent of need met:* 100. *Average financial aid package:* $25,619. *Average need-based gift aid:* $12,005. *Average non-need-based aid:* $11,212. *Average indebtedness upon graduation:* $22,104.
Applying *Options:* common application, electronic application, early action, deferred entrance. *Application fee:* $35. *Required:* essay or personal statement, high school transcript, minimum 2.0 GPA, 2 letters of recommendation. *Required for some:* minimum 3.5 GPA. *Recommended:* minimum 2.5 GPA, interview.
Admissions Contact Ms. Urmi Kar, Dean of Enrollment, Whittier College, PO Box 634, Whittier, CA 90608-0634. *Phone:* 562-907-4238. *Fax:* 562-907-4870. *E-mail:* admission@whittier.edu.

WILLIAM JESSUP UNIVERSITY
Rocklin, California

- **Independent nondenominational** 4-year, founded 1939
- **Calendar** quarters
- **Degrees** certificates, associate, and bachelor's
- **Suburban** 156-acre campus with easy access to Sacramento
- **Coed,** 328 undergraduate students
- **Noncompetitive** entrance level, 45% of applicants were admitted

Undergraduates Students come from 9 states and territories, 6% are from out of state, 8% African American, 16% Asian American or Pacific Islander, 12% Hispanic American, 1% Native American, 7% international, 25% live on campus. *Retention:* 66% of 2002 full-time freshmen returned.
Freshmen *Admission:* 187 applied, 85 admitted. *Average high school GPA:* 2.98. *Test scores:* SAT verbal scores over 500: 46%; SAT math scores over 500: 28%; ACT scores over 18: 56%; SAT verbal scores over 600: 9%; SAT math scores over 600: 5%.
Faculty *Total:* 35, 40% full-time. *Student/faculty ratio:* 9:1.
Majors Adult and continuing education; biblical studies; business administration, management and operations related; divinity/ministry; education; liberal arts and sciences/liberal studies; music; pastoral studies/counseling; religious studies; theology.
Academic Programs *Special study options:* academic remediation for entering students, accelerated degree program, advanced placement credit, cooperative education, double majors, internships, part-time degree program, summer session for credit.
Library San Jose Christian College Memorial Library with 31,689 titles, 157 serial subscriptions.
Computers on Campus 14 computers available on campus for general student use. A campuswide network can be accessed from off campus. Internet access, at least one staffed computer lab available.
Student Life *Housing:* on-campus residence required through sophomore year. *Options:* men-only, women-only. Campus housing is university owned. Freshman campus housing is guaranteed. *Activities and organizations:* drama/theater group, choral group, Missions Club, student leadership, drama team, music ensemble. *Campus security:* student patrols, late-night transport/escort service, day and evening patrols by trained security personnel. *Student services:* personal/psychological counseling.
Athletics *Intercollegiate sports:* basketball M/W, soccer M, volleyball W.
Standardized Tests *Required:* SAT I or ACT (for admission).
Costs (2003–04) *Comprehensive fee:* $17,721 includes full-time tuition ($11,664), mandatory fees ($582), and room and board ($5475). Full-time tuition and fees vary according to course load and program. Part-time tuition: $243 per quarter hour. Part-time tuition and fees vary according to course load and program. *Room and board:* Room and board charges vary according to board plan. *Payment plan:* deferred payment. *Waivers:* employees or children of employees.
Financial Aid Of all full-time matriculated undergraduates who enrolled in 2000, 226 applied for aid, 226 were judged to have need. 18 Federal Work-Study jobs (averaging $1792). *Average financial aid package:* $6244. *Average need-based loan:* $1737. *Average need-based gift aid:* $1514.
Applying *Options:* deferred entrance. *Application fee:* $35. *Required:* essay or personal statement, high school transcript, minimum 2.0 GPA, 1 letter of recommendation, letter of introduction, minimum SAT score of 830 or ACT score of 17. *Application deadlines:* 8/1 (freshmen), 8/1 (transfers). *Notification:* continuous (freshmen), continuous (transfers).
Admissions Contact Mr. Rob Jones, Director of Admissions, William Jessup University, 333 Sunset Boulevard, Rocklin, CA 95765. *Phone:* 408-278-4330. *Toll-free phone:* 800-355-7522. *Fax:* 916-624-1722. *E-mail:* admissions@jessup.edu.

■ *See page 2854 for a narrative description.*

WOODBURY UNIVERSITY
Burbank, California

- **Independent** comprehensive, founded 1884
- **Calendar** semesters
- **Degrees** bachelor's and master's
- **Suburban** 22-acre campus with easy access to Los Angeles
- **Endowment** $7.1 million
- **Coed**
- **Moderately difficult** entrance level

Faculty *Student/faculty ratio:* 18:1.
Student Life *Campus security:* 24-hour patrols, late-night transport/escort service, controlled dormitory access.
Standardized Tests *Required:* SAT I or ACT (for admission).
Costs (2003–04) *Comprehensive fee:* $27,493 includes full-time tuition ($20,070), mandatory fees ($240), and room and board ($7183). Full-time tuition and fees vary according to program. Part-time tuition and fees vary according to class time and program. *College room only:* $4298. Room and board charges vary according to board plan and housing facility. *Payment plans:* installment, deferred payment.
Financial Aid Of all full-time matriculated undergraduates who enrolled in 2003, 849 applied for aid, 597 were judged to have need, 30 had their need fully met. 100 Federal Work-Study jobs (averaging $1500). In 2003, 156. *Average percent of need met:* 61. *Average financial aid package:* $15,369. *Average need-based loan:* $4041. *Average need-based gift aid:* $11,938. *Average non-need-based aid:* $8481.
Applying *Options:* deferred entrance. *Application fee:* $30. *Required:* high school transcript, minimum 2.0 GPA. *Required for some:* portfolio. *Recommended:* essay or personal statement, minimum 3.0 GPA, 2 letters of recommendation, interview.
Admissions Contact Mr. Don St. Clair, Vice President of Enrollment Management and University Marketing, Woodbury University, 7500 Glenoaks Boulevard, Burbank, CA 91510-7846. *Phone:* 818-767-0888. *Toll-free phone:* 800-784-WOOD. *Fax:* 818-767-7520. *E-mail:* info@woodbury.edu.

■ *See page 2874 for a narrative description.*

YESHIVA OHR ELCHONON CHABAD/WEST COAST TALMUDICAL SEMINARY
Los Angeles, California

Admissions Contact Rabbi Ezra Binyomin Schochet, Dean, Yeshiva Ohr Elchonon Chabad/West Coast Talmudical Seminary, 7215 Waring Avenue, Los Angeles, CA 90046-7660. *Phone:* 213-937-3763.

COLORADO

ADAMS STATE COLLEGE
Alamosa, Colorado

- **State-supported** comprehensive, founded 1921, part of State Colleges in Colorado
- **Calendar** semesters
- **Degrees** associate, bachelor's, and master's
- **Small-town** 90-acre campus
- **Endowment** $7.5 million
- **Coed,** 2,423 undergraduate students, 67% full-time, 58% women, 42% men
- **Moderately difficult** entrance level, 75% of applicants were admitted

Undergraduates 1,612 full-time, 811 part-time. Students come from 46 states and territories, 5 other countries, 19% are from out of state, 5% African American, 0.8% Asian American or Pacific Islander, 26% Hispanic American, 1% Native American, 0.3% international, 6% transferred in, 45% live on campus. *Retention:* 54% of 2002 full-time freshmen returned.

Freshmen *Admission:* 1,903 applied, 1,418 admitted, 461 enrolled. *Average high school GPA:* 3.11. *Test scores:* SAT verbal scores over 500: 51%; SAT math scores over 500: 48%; ACT scores over 18: 70%; SAT verbal scores over 600: 11%; SAT math scores over 600: 15%; ACT scores over 24: 19%; SAT verbal scores over 700: 1%; ACT scores over 30: 1%.

Faculty *Total:* 198, 47% full-time, 41% with terminal degrees. *Student/faculty ratio:* 15:1.

Majors Art; biological and physical sciences; biology/biological sciences; business administration and management; chemistry; communication/speech communication and rhetoric; dramatic/theatre arts; elementary education; English; geology/earth science; history; kinesiology and exercise science; liberal arts and sciences/liberal studies; mathematics; music; music performance; political science and government; pre-dentistry studies; pre-engineering; pre-law studies; pre-medical studies; pre-nursing studies; pre-pharmacy studies; pre-veterinary studies; psychology; secondary education; social sciences; sociology; Spanish; speech and rhetoric.

Academic Programs *Special study options:* academic remediation for entering students, accelerated degree program, adult/continuing education programs, advanced placement credit, distance learning, double majors, independent study, internships, off-campus study, part-time degree program, services for LD students, student-designed majors, summer session for credit.

Library Nielsen Library with 472,594 titles, 1,646 serial subscriptions, 1,954 audiovisual materials, an OPAC, a Web page.

Computers on Campus 261 computers available on campus for general student use. A campuswide network can be accessed from student residence rooms and from off campus. Internet access, online (class) registration, at least one staffed computer lab available.

Student Life *Housing:* on-campus residence required through sophomore year. *Options:* coed, women-only. Freshman campus housing is guaranteed. *Activities and organizations:* drama/theater group, student-run newspaper, radio station, choral group, marching band, student government, Student Ambassadors, Program Council, Circle K, Tri Beta. *Campus security:* 24-hour emergency response devices and patrols, student patrols, late-night transport/escort service, controlled dormitory access. *Student services:* health clinic, personal/psychological counseling.

Athletics Member NCAA. All Division II. *Intercollegiate sports:* basketball M(s)/W(s), cross-country running M(s)/W(s), football M(s), golf M(s), softball W(s), track and field M(s)/W(s), volleyball W(s), wrestling M(s). *Intramural sports:* basketball M/W, football M/W, golf M/W, racquetball M/W, soccer M/W, softball M/W, swimming M/W, tennis M/W, volleyball M/W, water polo M/W.

Standardized Tests *Required:* SAT I or ACT (for admission).

Costs (2003–04) *Tuition:* state resident $1798 full-time; nonresident $7428 full-time. Full-time tuition and fees vary according to course load and reciprocity agreements. Part-time tuition and fees vary according to course load. *Required fees:* $694 full-time. *Room and board:* $5730; room only: $2880. Room and board charges vary according to board plan and housing facility. *Payment plans:* installment, deferred payment. *Waivers:* senior citizens and employees or children of employees.

Financial Aid Of all full-time matriculated undergraduates who enrolled in 2002, 1,422 applied for aid, 1,182 were judged to have need, 707 had their need fully met. In 2002, 417 non-need-based awards were made. *Average percent of need met:* 88%. *Average financial aid package:* $4586. *Average need-based loan:* $3568. *Average need-based gift aid:* $4127. *Average non-need-based aid:* $824. *Average indebtedness upon graduation:* $15,975.

Applying *Options:* common application, electronic application, early admission, deferred entrance. *Application fee:* $25. *Required:* high school transcript, minimum 2.0 GPA. *Required for some:* essay or personal statement, letters of recommendation, interview. *Application deadlines:* 8/1 (freshmen), 8/1 (transfers).

Admissions Contact Mr. Matt Gallegas, Director of Admissions, Adams State College, 208 Edgemont Boulevard, Alamosa, CO 81102. *Phone:* 719-587-7712. *Toll-free phone:* 800-824-6494. *Fax:* 719-587-7522. *E-mail:* ascadmit@adams.edu.

■ *See page 1130 for a narrative description.*

THE ART INSTITUTE OF COLORADO
Denver, Colorado

- **Proprietary** 4-year, founded 1952, part of Education Management Corporation
- **Calendar** quarters
- **Degrees** diplomas, associate, and bachelor's
- **Urban** campus
- **Coed,** 2,226 undergraduate students, 76% full-time, 46% women, 54% men
- **Minimally difficult** entrance level

Undergraduates 1,686 full-time, 540 part-time. Students come from 49 states and territories, 22 other countries, 50% are from out of state, 1% African American, 3% Asian American or Pacific Islander, 6% Hispanic American, 1% Native American, 0.5% transferred in, 9% live on campus. *Retention:* 65% of 2002 full-time freshmen returned.

Freshmen *Admission:* 748 applied, 674 enrolled.

Faculty *Total:* 135, 47% full-time, 13% with terminal degrees. *Student/faculty ratio:* 20:1.

Majors Advertising; art; cinematography and film/video production; commercial and advertising art; computer graphics; culinary arts; industrial design; interior design; intermedia/multimedia; photography.

Academic Programs *Special study options:* academic remediation for entering students, adult/continuing education programs, advanced placement credit, distance learning, external degree program, independent study, internships, part-time degree program, services for LD students, study abroad.

Library Colorado Institute of Art Learning Resource Center with 13,100 titles, 200 serial subscriptions, an OPAC.

Computers on Campus 400 computers available on campus for general student use. Internet access, at least one staffed computer lab available.

Student Life *Housing options:* coed. Campus housing is leased by the school. *Activities and organizations:* Culinary Student Forum, computer animation club, Student Chapter—American Society of Interior Designers. *Campus security:* 24-hour emergency response devices. *Student services:* personal/psychological counseling.

Costs (2003–04) *Comprehensive fee:* $24,512 includes full-time tuition ($18,752) and room and board ($5760). Full-time tuition and fees vary according to course load. Part-time tuition: $330 per credit. Part-time tuition and fees vary according to course load. No tuition increase for student's term of enrollment. *Payment plan:* installment. *Waivers:* employees or children of employees.

Financial Aid Of all full-time matriculated undergraduates who enrolled in 1999, 1,621 applied for aid, 1,621 were judged to have need. 34 state and other part-time jobs. *Average indebtedness upon graduation:* $30,000.

Applying *Options:* early admission, deferred entrance. *Application fee:* $50. *Required:* essay or personal statement, high school transcript, interview. *Application deadline:* rolling (freshmen), rolling (transfers).

Admissions Contact Ms. Barbara Browning, Vice President and Director of Admissions, The Art Institute of Colorado, 1200 Lincoln Street, Denver, CO 80203. *Phone:* 303-837-0825 Ext. 4729. *Toll-free phone:* 800-275-2420. *Fax:* 303-860-8520. *E-mail:* aicinfo@aii.edu.

ASPEN UNIVERSITY
Denver, Colorado

Admissions Contact Admissions, Aspen University, 501 South Cherry Street, Suite 350, Denver, CO 80246. *Phone:* 303-333-4224 Ext. 177. *Toll-free phone:* 800-441-4746 Ext. 177.

COLLEGEAMERICA–FORT COLLINS
Fort Collins, Colorado

- **Proprietary** 4-year, founded 1962
- **Calendar** continuous
- **Degrees** associate and bachelor's
- **Suburban** campus
- **Coed,** 232 undergraduate students
- **Noncompetitive** entrance level

Undergraduates Students come from 3 states and territories, 0.1% are from out of state.

Freshmen *Average high school GPA:* 2.69.

Faculty *Total:* 33, 33% full-time. *Student/faculty ratio:* 22:1.

Majors Accounting; administrative assistant and secretarial science; business administration and management; clinical/medical laboratory technology; communications systems installation and repair technology; computer and information sciences; computer graphics; computer installation and repair technology; computer programming; computer programming (specific applications); computer systems networking and telecommunications; medical/clinical assistant; web page, digital/multimedia and information resources design; word processing.

Academic Programs *Special study options:* independent study, internships.

Library Library with 12 serial subscriptions, 30 audiovisual materials.

CollegeAmerica–Fort Collins (continued)

Computers on Campus 86 computers available on campus for general student use. A campuswide network can be accessed. Internet access, at least one staffed computer lab available.

Student Life *Housing:* college housing not available.

Athletics *Intramural sports:* ultimate Frisbee M/W.

Costs (2004–05) *Comprehensive fee:* $14,325, $275 per credit part-time. Full-time tuition and fees vary according to program. No tuition increase for student's term of enrollment. Tuition includes books and fees. *Payment plans:* tuition prepayment, installment, deferred payment. *Waivers:* employees or children of employees.

Applying *Required:* essay or personal statement, high school transcript, interview. *Required for some:* letters of recommendation. *Recommended:* minimum 2.0 GPA. *Notification:* continuous (freshmen).

Admissions Contact Ms. Anna DiTorrice-Mull, Director of Admissions, CollegeAmerica–Fort Collins, 4601 South Mason Street, Fort Collins, CO 80525. *Phone:* 970-223-6060 Ext. 8002. *Toll-free phone:* 800-97-SKILLS. *Fax:* 970-225-6059. *E-mail:* anna@collegeamerica.edu.

COLORADO CHRISTIAN UNIVERSITY

Lakewood, Colorado

- **Independent interdenominational** comprehensive, founded 1914
- **Calendar** semesters
- **Degrees** associate, bachelor's, and master's
- **Suburban** 26-acre campus with easy access to Denver
- **Endowment** $8.4 million
- **Coed,** 1,462 undergraduate students, 78% full-time, 60% women, 40% men
- **Moderately difficult** entrance level, 76% of applicants were admitted

Undergraduates 1,135 full-time, 327 part-time. Students come from 45 states and territories, 9 other countries, 41% are from out of state, 4% African American, 1% Asian American or Pacific Islander, 5% Hispanic American, 1% Native American, 0.6% international, 4% transferred in, 65% live on campus. *Retention:* 58% of 2002 full-time freshmen returned.

Freshmen *Admission:* 920 applied, 702 admitted, 265 enrolled. *Average high school GPA:* 3.52. *Test scores:* SAT verbal scores over 500: 82%; SAT math scores over 500: 69%; ACT scores over 18: 97%; SAT verbal scores over 600: 35%; SAT math scores over 600: 29%; ACT scores over 24: 53%; SAT verbal scores over 700: 10%; SAT math scores over 700: 4%; ACT scores over 30: 5%.

Faculty *Total:* 334, 12% full-time, 33% with terminal degrees. *Student/faculty ratio:* 21:1.

Majors Accounting; art; biblical studies; biological and physical sciences; biology/biological sciences; business administration and management; communication/speech communication and rhetoric; computer and information sciences; dramatic/theatre arts; English; fine/studio arts; health and physical education; history; international/global studies; liberal arts and sciences/liberal studies; management information systems; management science; mathematics; music; music performance; music related; music teacher education; political science and government; psychology; social sciences; youth ministry.

Academic Programs *Special study options:* academic remediation for entering students, accelerated degree program, adult/continuing education programs, advanced placement credit, cooperative education, distance learning, double majors, honors programs, independent study, internships, off-campus study, part-time degree program, services for LD students, student-designed majors, study abroad, summer session for credit. *ROTC:* Army (c).

Library Clifton Fowler Library plus 1 other with 71,565 titles, 1,192 serial subscriptions, 4,200 audiovisual materials, an OPAC, a Web page.

Computers on Campus 141 computers available on campus for general student use. A campuswide network can be accessed from student residence rooms and from off campus. Internet access, online (class) registration, at least one staffed computer lab available.

Student Life *Housing:* on-campus residence required through sophomore year. *Options:* coed, men-only, women-only, disabled students. Campus housing is university owned and leased by the school. Freshman campus housing is guaranteed. *Activities and organizations:* drama/theater group, student-run newspaper, choral group, FAT Boys (inner city ministry to homeless), SALT (Snowboarding as a Living Testimony), Freedom, In His Service Honor Society, Trash Club. *Campus security:* 24-hour emergency response devices and patrols, student patrols. *Student services:* health clinic, personal/psychological counseling, women's center.

Athletics Member NCAA. All Division II. *Intercollegiate sports:* basketball M(s)/W(s), cross-country running M/W, golf M, soccer M(s)/W(s), tennis M/W, volleyball W(s). *Intramural sports:* badminton M/W, basketball M/W, football M/W, soccer M/W, softball M/W, table tennis M/W, tennis M/W, ultimate Frisbee M/W, volleyball M/W.

Standardized Tests *Required:* SAT I or ACT (for admission).

Costs (2004–05) *Comprehensive fee:* $21,182 includes full-time tuition ($15,040), mandatory fees ($100), and room and board ($6042). Full-time tuition and fees vary according to degree level, location, and program. Part-time tuition: $615 per semester hour. Part-time tuition and fees vary according to degree level, location, and program. *College room only:* $3452. Room and board charges vary according to board plan and housing facility. *Payment plan:* installment. *Waivers:* minority students and employees or children of employees.

Financial Aid Of all full-time matriculated undergraduates who enrolled in 2003, 802 applied for aid, 658 were judged to have need, 91 had their need fully met. 41 Federal Work-Study jobs (averaging $3503). In 2003, 284 non-need-based awards were made. *Average percent of need met:* 58%. *Average financial aid package:* $8771. *Average need-based loan:* $3907. *Average need-based gift aid:* $5856. *Average non-need-based aid:* $12,332. *Average indebtedness upon graduation:* $20,390.

Applying *Options:* common application, electronic application, deferred entrance. *Application fee:* $40. *Required:* essay or personal statement, high school transcript, 2 letters of recommendation. *Required for some:* minimum 2.8 GPA, 3 letters of recommendation, interview. *Application deadline:* 8/1 (freshmen). *Notification:* 11/1 (freshmen), continuous (transfers).

Admissions Contact Mr. Rodney Stanford, Director of Undergraduate Admission, Colorado Christian University, 180 South Garrison Street, Lakewood, CO 80226. *Phone:* 303-963-3203. *Toll-free phone:* 800-44-FAITH. *Fax:* 303-963-3201. *E-mail:* admission@ccu.edu.

■ *See page 1464 for a narrative description.*

THE COLORADO COLLEGE

Colorado Springs, Colorado

- **Independent** comprehensive, founded 1874
- **Calendar** modular
- **Degrees** bachelor's and master's (master's degree in education only)
- **Urban** 90-acre campus with easy access to Denver
- **Endowment** $343.0 million
- **Coed,** 1,941 undergraduate students, 99% full-time, 54% women, 46% men
- **Very difficult** entrance level, 56% of applicants were admitted

Founded in 1874, Colorado College is a private, 4-year, coeducational college. Its 90-acre campus is located in downtown Colorado Springs (metro population 508,870) on the front range of the Rocky Mountains, 70 miles south of Denver. It employs an innovative, one-course-at-a-time approach (the Block Plan) in structuring its traditional liberal arts and sciences curriculum.

Undergraduates 1,929 full-time, 12 part-time. Students come from 52 states and territories, 26 other countries, 70% are from out of state, 2% African American, 4% Asian American or Pacific Islander, 7% Hispanic American, 2% Native American, 2% international, 2% transferred in, 78% live on campus. *Retention:* 92% of 2002 full-time freshmen returned.

Freshmen *Admission:* 3,533 applied, 1,975 admitted, 524 enrolled. *Test scores:* SAT verbal scores over 500: 97%; SAT math scores over 500: 97%; ACT scores over 18: 99%; SAT verbal scores over 600: 70%; SAT math scores over 600: 70%; ACT scores over 24: 82%; SAT verbal scores over 700: 22%; SAT math scores over 700: 16%; ACT scores over 30: 23%.

Faculty *Total:* 211, 79% full-time. *Student/faculty ratio:* 9:1.

Majors Anthropology; art history, criticism and conservation; Asian studies; biochemistry; biology/biological sciences; chemistry; classics and languages, literatures and linguistics; comparative literature; creative writing; dance; dramatic/theatre arts; econometrics and quantitative economics; economics; economics related; English; environmental science; ethnic, cultural minority, and gender studies related; film/cinema studies; fine/studio arts; French; French studies; geology/earth science; German; Hispanic-American, Puerto Rican, and Mexican-American/Chicano studies; history; history related; international economics; Italian; liberal arts and sciences and humanities related; mathematics; mathematics and computer science; multi-/interdisciplinary studies related; music; neuroscience; philosophy; physics; political science and government; psychology; religious studies; Romance languages related; Russian; Russian studies; social sciences related; sociology; Spanish; women's studies.

Academic Programs *Special study options:* advanced placement credit, double majors, English as a second language, independent study, internships, off-campus study, services for LD students, student-designed majors, study abroad, summer session for credit. *ROTC:* Army (c). *Unusual degree programs:* 3-2 engineering with Rensselaer Polytechnic Institute, Washington University in St. Louis, University of Southern California, Columbia University.

Library Tutt Library plus 2 others with 535,657 titles, 1,313 serial subscriptions, 21,419 audiovisual materials, an OPAC, a Web page.

Computers on Campus 235 computers available on campus for general student use. A campuswide network can be accessed from student residence rooms

and from off campus. Internet access, online (class) registration, at least one staffed computer lab available. Computer purchase or lease plan available.

Student Life *Housing:* on-campus residence required through junior year. *Options:* coed, men-only, women-only. Campus housing is university owned. Freshman campus housing is guaranteed. *Activities and organizations:* drama/theater group, student-run newspaper, radio station, choral group, Community Service Center, student government, arts and crafts organizations, Outdoor Recreation Committee, theater workshop, national fraternities, national sororities. *Campus security:* 24-hour emergency response devices and patrols, late-night transport/escort service, controlled dormitory access, whistle program, student escort service. *Student services:* health clinic, personal/psychological counseling, women's center.

Athletics Member NCAA. All Division III except ice hockey (Division I), soccer (Division I). *Intercollegiate sports:* basketball M/W, cross-country running M/W, equestrian sports M(c)/W(c), field hockey M(c)/W(c), football M, ice hockey M(s)/W(c), lacrosse M/W, rugby M(c)/W(c), skiing (downhill) M(c)/W(c), soccer M/W(s), softball W, swimming M/W, tennis M/W, track and field M/W, ultimate Frisbee M(c)/W(c), volleyball M(c)/W, water polo M(c)/W(c). *Intramural sports:* basketball M/W, football M/W, ice hockey M/W, racquetball M/W, soccer M/W, softball M/W, ultimate Frisbee M/W, volleyball M/W.

Standardized Tests *Required:* SAT I or ACT (for admission).

Costs (2003–04) *Comprehensive fee:* $34,475 includes full-time tuition ($27,270), mandatory fees ($365), and room and board ($6840). Part-time tuition: $852 per credit hour. *College room only:* $3664. Room and board charges vary according to board plan. *Payment plan:* installment. *Waivers:* employees or children of employees.

Financial Aid Of all full-time matriculated undergraduates who enrolled in 2003, 965 applied for aid, 877 were judged to have need, 471 had their need fully met. 395 Federal Work-Study jobs (averaging $1730). 212 state and other part-time jobs (averaging $1740). In 2003, 267 non-need-based awards were made. *Average percent of need met:* 92%. *Average financial aid package:* $23,278. *Average need-based loan:* $3866. *Average need-based gift aid:* $19,275. *Average non-need-based aid:* $16,100. *Average indebtedness upon graduation:* $13,850.

Applying *Options:* common application, electronic application, early action, deferred entrance. *Application fee:* $50. *Required:* essay or personal statement, high school transcript, 3 letters of recommendation. *Recommended:* interview. *Application deadlines:* 1/15 (freshmen), 3/1 (transfers). *Notification:* 4/1 (freshmen), 1/1 (early action), 5/15 (transfers).

Admissions Contact Mr. Mark Hatch, Dean of Admission and Financial Aid, The Colorado College, 900 Block North Cascade, West, Colorado Springs, CO 80903-3294. *Phone:* 719-389-6344. *Toll-free phone:* 800-542-7214. *Fax:* 719-389-6816. *E-mail:* admission@coloradocollege.edu.

■ *See page 1466 for a narrative description.*

COLORADO SCHOOL OF MINES

Golden, Colorado

- **State-supported** university, founded 1874
- **Calendar** semesters
- **Degrees** bachelor's, master's, and doctoral
- **Small-town** 373-acre campus with easy access to Denver
- **Endowment** $133.5 million
- **Coed,** 2,664 undergraduate students, 97% full-time, 23% women, 77% men
- **Very difficult** entrance level, 79% of applicants were admitted

Undergraduates 2,582 full-time, 82 part-time. Students come from 51 states and territories, 62 other countries, 21% are from out of state, 1% African American, 5% Asian American or Pacific Islander, 7% Hispanic American, 0.9% Native American, 4% international, 3% transferred in, 25% live on campus. *Retention:* 88% of 2002 full-time freshmen returned.

Freshmen *Admission:* 3,049 applied, 2,422 admitted, 668 enrolled. *Average high school GPA:* 3.70. *Test scores:* SAT verbal scores over 500: 90%; SAT math scores over 500: 98%; ACT scores over 18: 100%; SAT verbal scores over 600: 52%; SAT math scores over 600: 79%; ACT scores over 24: 88%; SAT verbal scores over 700: 11%; SAT math scores over 700: 25%; ACT scores over 30: 26%.

Faculty *Total:* 282, 67% full-time, 78% with terminal degrees. *Student/faculty ratio:* 15:1.

Majors Chemical engineering; chemistry; civil engineering; computer science; economics; electrical, electronics and communications engineering; engineering; engineering physics; engineering science; environmental/environmental health engineering; geological/geophysical engineering; mathematics; mechanical engineering; metallurgical engineering; mining and mineral engineering; petroleum engineering.

Academic Programs *Special study options:* academic remediation for entering students, accelerated degree program, advanced placement credit, cooperative education, double majors, English as a second language, honors programs, independent study, internships, services for LD students, study abroad, summer session for credit. *ROTC:* Army (b).

Library Arthur Lakes Library with 150,000 titles, 4,883 serial subscriptions, 20 audiovisual materials, an OPAC, a Web page.

Computers on Campus 400 computers available on campus for general student use. A campuswide network can be accessed from student residence rooms and from off campus. Internet access, online (class) registration, at least one staffed computer lab available.

Student Life *Housing options:* coed. Campus housing is university owned. Freshman campus housing is guaranteed. *Activities and organizations:* drama/theater group, student-run newspaper, choral group, marching band, Residence Hall Association, Society of Women Engineers, American Institute of Chemical Engineers, national fraternities, national sororities. *Campus security:* 24-hour emergency response devices and patrols, late-night transport/escort service. *Student services:* health clinic, personal/psychological counseling.

Athletics Member NCAA. All Division II. *Intercollegiate sports:* baseball M(s), basketball M(s)/W(s), cross-country running M(s)/W(s), football M(s), golf M(s), skiing (downhill) M, soccer M, softball W(s), swimming M(s)/W(s), tennis M(s)/W(s), track and field M(s)/W(s), volleyball W(s), wrestling M(s). *Intramural sports:* badminton M/W, basketball M/W, cross-country running M/W, football M/W, racquetball M/W, soccer M/W, softball M/W, swimming M/W, tennis M/W, track and field M/W, ultimate Frisbee M(c)/W(c), volleyball M/W.

Standardized Tests *Required:* SAT I or ACT (for admission).

Costs (2004–05) *Tuition:* state resident $5700 full-time; nonresident $19,030 full-time. Part-time tuition and fees vary according to course load. *Required fees:* $733 full-time. *Room and board:* $6100; room only: $3200. Room and board charges vary according to board plan and housing facility. *Payment plan:* installment.

Financial Aid Of all full-time matriculated undergraduates who enrolled in 2003, 1,968 applied for aid, 1,838 were judged to have need, 1,470 had their need fully met. 273 Federal Work-Study jobs (averaging $850). 787 state and other part-time jobs (averaging $850). In 2003, 242 non-need-based awards were made. *Average percent of need met:* 90%. *Average financial aid package:* $13,100. *Average need-based loan:* $4000. *Average need-based gift aid:* $6900. *Average non-need-based aid:* $4910. *Average indebtedness upon graduation:* $17,500.

Applying *Options:* electronic application, deferred entrance. *Application fee:* $45. *Required:* high school transcript. *Required for some:* essay or personal statement, letters of recommendation, interview. *Recommended:* rank in upper one-third of high school class. *Application deadlines:* 6/1 (freshmen), 6/1 (transfers). *Notification:* continuous (freshmen), continuous (transfers).

Admissions Contact Ms. Tricia Douthit, Associate Director of Admissions, Colorado School of Mines, Student Center, 1600 Maple Street, Golden, CO 80401. *Phone:* 303-273-3224. *Toll-free phone:* 800-446-9488 Ext. 3220. *Fax:* 303-273-3509. *E-mail:* admit@mines.edu.

COLORADO STATE UNIVERSITY

Fort Collins, Colorado

- **State-supported** university, founded 1870, part of Colorado State University System
- **Calendar** semesters
- **Degrees** bachelor's, master's, doctoral, and first professional
- **Urban** 666-acre campus with easy access to Denver
- **Endowment** $135.8 million
- **Coed,** 21,689 undergraduate students, 88% full-time, 51% women, 49% men
- **Moderately difficult** entrance level, 79% of applicants were admitted

Undergraduates 19,078 full-time, 2,611 part-time. Students come from 50 other countries, 19% are from out of state, 2% African American, 3% Asian American or Pacific Islander, 6% Hispanic American, 1% Native American, 1% international, 7% transferred in, 24% live on campus. *Retention:* 82% of 2002 full-time freshmen returned.

Freshmen *Admission:* 12,027 applied, 9,520 admitted, 3,802 enrolled. *Average high school GPA:* 3.50. *Test scores:* SAT verbal scores over 500: 77%; SAT math scores over 500: 79%; ACT scores over 18: 99%; SAT verbal scores over 600: 27%; SAT math scores over 600: 33%; ACT scores over 24: 54%; SAT verbal scores over 700: 3%; SAT math scores over 700: 3%; ACT scores over 30: 7%.

Faculty *Total:* 901, 96% full-time, 99% with terminal degrees. *Student/faculty ratio:* 17:1.

Majors Accounting; agribusiness; agricultural and extension education; agricultural and horticultural plant breeding; agricultural economics; agricultural teacher education; agriculture; agronomy and crop science; American studies; animal sciences; anthropology; apparel and textiles; applied horticulture; applied mathematics; art; art history, criticism and conservation; art teacher education; Asian-American studies; Asian studies; athletic training; biochemistry; biology/

Colorado State University (continued)
biological sciences; biology teacher education; botany/plant biology; business administration and management; business teacher education; ceramic arts and ceramics; chemical engineering; chemistry; chemistry teacher education; civil engineering; commercial and advertising art; computer and information sciences; computer engineering; computer science; creative writing; criminal justice/safety; crop production; dance; dietetics; dramatic/theatre arts; drawing; economics; electrical, electronics and communications engineering; engineering physics; engineering science; English; English/language arts teacher education; entomology; environmental/environmental health engineering; environmental health; equestrian studies; family and consumer sciences/home economics teacher education; family and consumer sciences/human sciences; farm and ranch management; fiber, textile and weaving arts; finance; fine/studio arts; fishing and fisheries sciences and management; foods, nutrition, and wellness; foreign languages and literatures; forest sciences and biology; French; French language teacher education; geology/earth science; German; German language teacher education; history; horticultural science; hotel/motel administration; human development and family studies; humanities; information science/studies; interior design; journalism; kinesiology and exercise science; landscape architecture; landscaping and groundskeeping; Latin American studies; liberal arts and sciences/liberal studies; marketing/marketing management; mathematics; mathematics teacher education; mechanical engineering; medical microbiology and bacteriology; metal and jewelry arts; music; music performance; music teacher education; music therapy; natural resources management and policy; painting; parks, recreation and leisure facilities management; philosophy; photography; physical sciences; physics; physics teacher education; plant sciences; political science and government; pre-dentistry studies; pre-law studies; pre-medical studies; pre-veterinary studies; printmaking; psychology; public relations/image management; radio and television; range science and management; real estate; sales and marketing/marketing and distribution teacher education; science teacher education; sculpture; social sciences; social studies teacher education; social work; sociology; soil science and agronomy; Spanish; Spanish language teacher education; speech and rhetoric; turf and turfgrass management; wildlife and wildlands science and management; zoology/animal biology.

Academic Programs *Special study options:* accelerated degree program, adult/continuing education programs, advanced placement credit, cooperative education, distance learning, double majors, English as a second language, honors programs, independent study, internships, off-campus study, part-time degree program, services for LD students, student-designed majors, study abroad, summer session for credit. *ROTC:* Army (b), Air Force (b).

Library William E. Morgan Library plus 3 others with 1.9 million titles, 20,712 serial subscriptions, 31,850 audiovisual materials, an OPAC, a Web page.

Computers on Campus 2530 computers available on campus for general student use. A campuswide network can be accessed from student residence rooms and from off campus. Internet access, at least one staffed computer lab available.

Student Life *Housing:* on-campus residence required for freshman year. *Options:* coed. Campus housing is university owned. Freshman campus housing is guaranteed. *Activities and organizations:* drama/theater group, student-run newspaper, radio and television station, choral group, marching band, Club Sports Association, Associated Students (student government), Office of Community Services, Colorado Public Interest Research Group, national fraternities, national sororities. *Campus security:* 24-hour emergency response devices and patrols, student patrols, late-night transport/escort service, controlled dormitory access. *Student services:* health clinic, personal/psychological counseling, women's center, legal services.

Athletics Member NCAA. All Division I except football (Division I-A). *Intercollegiate sports:* basketball M(s)/W(s), cross-country running M(s)/W(s), golf M/W, softball W, swimming W(s), tennis W, track and field M(s)/W(s), volleyball W(s), water polo W(s). *Intramural sports:* badminton M(c)/W(c), baseball M(c)/W(c), basketball M/W, equestrian sports M/W, fencing M(c)/W(c), golf M/W, gymnastics M(c)/W(c), ice hockey M(c)/W(c), lacrosse M(c)/W(c), racquetball M(c)/W(c), riflery M(c)/W(c), rugby M(c)/W(c), skiing (downhill) M/W, soccer M/W, softball M/W, tennis M/W, ultimate Frisbee M/W, volleyball M/W, water polo M/W, weight lifting M/W, wrestling M.

Standardized Tests *Required:* SAT I or ACT (for admission).

Costs (2003–04) *Tuition:* state resident $2908 full-time, $162 per credit part-time; nonresident $13,380 full-time, $743 per credit part-time. *Required fees:* $836 full-time, $51 per credit part-time. *Room and board:* $6045. Room and board charges vary according to board plan and housing facility. *Payment plan:* installment. *Waivers:* employees or children of employees.

Financial Aid Of all full-time matriculated undergraduates who enrolled in 2002, 10,416 applied for aid, 7,254 were judged to have need, 3,521 had their need fully met. 691 Federal Work-Study jobs (averaging $1885). 1,245 state and other part-time jobs (averaging $1827). In 2002, 831 non-need-based awards were made. *Average percent of need met:* 82%. *Average financial aid package:* $7948. *Average need-based loan:* $5312. *Average need-based gift aid:* $4288. *Average non-need-based aid:* $1402. *Average indebtedness upon graduation:* $16,075.

Applying *Options:* electronic application, deferred entrance. *Application fee:* $50. *Required:* high school transcript. *Recommended:* essay or personal statement, letters of recommendation. *Application deadlines:* 7/1 (freshmen), 7/1 (transfers). *Notification:* continuous (freshmen), continuous (transfers).

Admissions Contact Ms. Mary Ontiveros, Director of Admissions, Colorado State University, Spruce Hall, Fort Collins, CO 80523-0015. *Phone:* 970-491-6909. *Fax:* 970-491-7799. *E-mail:* admissions@vines.colostate.edu.

■ *See page 1468 for a narrative description.*

COLORADO STATE UNIVERSITY-PUEBLO

Pueblo, Colorado

- **State-supported** comprehensive, founded 1933, part of Colorado State University System
- **Calendar** semesters
- **Degrees** bachelor's and master's
- **Suburban** 275-acre campus with easy access to Colorado Springs
- **Endowment** $3.5 million
- **Coed,** 6,078 undergraduate students, 55% full-time, 60% women, 40% men
- **Moderately difficult** entrance level, 95% of applicants were admitted

Undergraduates 3,320 full-time, 2,758 part-time. Students come from 44 states and territories, 37 other countries, 8% are from out of state, 4% African American, 2% Asian American or Pacific Islander, 29% Hispanic American, 2% Native American, 3% international, 6% transferred in, 18% live on campus. *Retention:* 64% of 2002 full-time freshmen returned.

Freshmen *Admission:* 1,665 applied, 1,587 admitted, 637 enrolled. *Average high school GPA:* 3.08. *Test scores:* SAT verbal scores over 500: 51%; SAT math scores over 500: 49%; ACT scores over 18: 63%; SAT verbal scores over 600: 7%; SAT math scores over 600: 11%; ACT scores over 24: 19%; SAT verbal scores over 700: 2%; ACT scores over 30: 2%.

Faculty *Total:* 293, 51% full-time, 43% with terminal degrees. *Student/faculty ratio:* 17:1.

Majors Accounting; advertising; applied art; art; art teacher education; athletic training; automobile/automotive mechanics technology; biology/biological sciences; biomedical technology; broadcast journalism; business administration and management; chemistry; cinematography and film/video production; civil engineering technology; clinical psychology; computer and information sciences; computer engineering technology; construction engineering technology; corrections; criminology; developmental and child psychology; education; elementary education; engineering technology; English; environmental biology; environmental health; experimental psychology; finance; history; industrial arts; industrial engineering; instrumentation technology; journalism; kinesiology and exercise science; marketing/marketing management; mass communication/media; mathematics; mathematics teacher education; mechanical engineering/mechanical technology; middle school education; music; music teacher education; nursing (registered nurse training); parks, recreation and leisure; physical education teaching and coaching; physics; political science and government; pre-dentistry studies; pre-law studies; pre-medical studies; pre-pharmacy studies; pre-veterinary studies; psychology; public relations/image management; radio and television; science teacher education; secondary education; social sciences; social studies teacher education; social work; sociology; Spanish; Spanish language teacher education; telecommunications.

Academic Programs *Special study options:* accelerated degree program, adult/continuing education programs, advanced placement credit, cooperative education, distance learning, double majors, English as a second language, external degree program, honors programs, independent study, internships, off-campus study, part-time degree program, services for LD students, study abroad, summer session for credit. *ROTC:* Army (c).

Library University of Southern Colorado Library with 270,761 titles, 1,327 serial subscriptions, 16,862 audiovisual materials, an OPAC, a Web page.

Computers on Campus 521 computers available on campus for general student use. A campuswide network can be accessed from student residence rooms and from off campus. Internet access, at least one staffed computer lab available.

Student Life *Housing:* on-campus residence required for freshman year. *Options:* coed. Campus housing is university owned and is provided by a third party. Freshman campus housing is guaranteed. *Activities and organizations:* student-run newspaper, radio and television station, choral group, Belmont Residence Hall Association, Associate Student Government, Hawaii club, Medical Science Society, Student Social Worker's Association, national fraternities, national sororities. *Campus security:* 24-hour emergency response devices and patrols, late-night transport/escort service, controlled dormitory access. *Student services:* health clinic, personal/psychological counseling.

Athletics Member NCAA. All Division II. *Intercollegiate sports:* baseball M, basketball M(s)/W(s), golf M(s), soccer M/W, softball W(s), tennis M(s)/W(s), volleyball W(s). *Intramural sports:* basketball M/W, cheerleading W, lacrosse M, racquetball M/W, rock climbing M/W, sailing M/W, skiing (cross-country) M/W, skiing (downhill) M/W, soccer M, softball M/W, tennis M/W, ultimate Frisbee M/W, volleyball M/W, weight lifting M/W.

Standardized Tests *Required:* SAT I or ACT (for admission).

Costs (2003–04) *Tuition:* state resident $2289 full-time, $104 per credit part-time; nonresident $12,279 full-time, $558 per credit part-time. Full-time tuition and fees vary according to reciprocity agreements. Part-time tuition and fees vary according to reciprocity agreements. *Required fees:* $641 full-time, $28 per credit part-time. *Room and board:* $5742; room only: $2794. Room and board charges vary according to board plan and housing facility. *Payment plans:* installment, deferred payment. *Waivers:* senior citizens and employees or children of employees.

Financial Aid Of all full-time matriculated undergraduates who enrolled in 2002, 2,396 applied for aid, 2,104 were judged to have need, 78 had their need fully met. In 2002, 501 non-need-based awards were made. *Average percent of need met:* 59%. *Average financial aid package:* $6560. *Average need-based loan:* $3234. *Average need-based gift aid:* $4209. *Average non-need-based aid:* $4414. *Average indebtedness upon graduation:* $5521.

Applying *Options:* common application, electronic application, deferred entrance. *Application fee:* $25. *Required:* high school transcript, minimum 2.0 GPA. *Required for some:* essay or personal statement, letters of recommendation. *Application deadlines:* 8/1 (freshmen), 8/1 (transfers). *Notification:* continuous until 8/1 (freshmen), continuous (transfers).

Admissions Contact Jennifer Jensen, Director of Admissions and Records (Interim), Colorado State University-Pueblo, 2200 Bonforte Boulevard, Pueblo, CO 81001. *Phone:* 719-549-2461. *Toll-free phone:* 877-872-9653. *Fax:* 719-549-2419. *E-mail:* info@uscolo.edu.

COLORADO TECHNICAL UNIVERSITY
Colorado Springs, Colorado

- **Proprietary** comprehensive, founded 1965, part of Whitman Education Group
- **Calendar** quarters
- **Degrees** certificates, associate, bachelor's, master's, doctoral, and postbachelor's certificates
- **Suburban** 14-acre campus with easy access to Denver
- **Coed**
- **Minimally difficult** entrance level

Faculty *Student/faculty ratio:* 20:1.

Student Life *Campus security:* 24-hour emergency response devices, late-night transport/escort service.

Standardized Tests *Required for some:* ACT COMPASS. *Recommended:* SAT I or ACT (for admission).

Costs (2003–04) *One-time required fee:* $100. *Tuition:* $9225 full-time, $205 per quarter hour part-time. Full-time tuition and fees vary according to course load. Part-time tuition and fees vary according to course load. *Required fees:* $213 full-time, $10 per credit part-time, $6 per term part-time.

Financial Aid Of all full-time matriculated undergraduates who enrolled in 2001, 35 Federal Work-Study jobs (averaging $4619).

Applying *Options:* electronic application, deferred entrance. *Application fee:* $50. *Required for some:* essay or personal statement. *Recommended:* high school transcript, minimum 3.0 GPA, interview.

Admissions Contact Mr. Ron Begora, Director of Admissions, Colorado Technical University, 4435 North Chestnut Street, Colorado Springs, CO 80907-3896. *Phone:* 719-598-0200. *Fax:* 719-598-3740. *E-mail:* rbegora@coloradotech.edu.

COLORADO TECHNICAL UNIVERSITY DENVER CAMPUS
Greenwood Village, Colorado

- **Proprietary** comprehensive, founded 1965, part of Whitman Education Group
- **Calendar** quarters
- **Degrees** certificates, associate, bachelor's, master's, and postbachelor's certificates
- **Urban** 1-acre campus with easy access to Denver
- **Coed**
- **Minimally difficult** entrance level

Faculty *Student/faculty ratio:* 14:1.

Student Life *Campus security:* 24-hour emergency response devices and patrols, late-night transport/escort service.

Standardized Tests *Required for some:* ACT COMPASS. *Recommended:* SAT I or ACT (for admission).

Costs (2003–04) *One-time required fee:* $100. *Tuition:* $9225 full-time, $205 per quarter hour part-time. Full-time tuition and fees vary according to course load. Part-time tuition and fees vary according to course load. *Required fees:* $213 full-time, $10 per credit part-time, $6 per term part-time.

Financial Aid Of all full-time matriculated undergraduates who enrolled in 2001, 2 Federal Work-Study jobs (averaging $3936).

Applying *Options:* electronic application, deferred entrance. *Application fee:* $50. *Required for some:* essay or personal statement. *Recommended:* high school transcript, minimum 3.0 GPA, interview.

Admissions Contact Ms. Suzanne Hyman, Director of Admissions, Colorado Technical University Denver Campus, 5775 DTC Boulevard, Suite 100, Greenwood Village, CO 80111. *Phone:* 303-694-6600. *Fax:* 303-694-6673. *E-mail:* ctudenver@coloradotech.edu.

DEVRY UNIVERSITY
Broomfield, Colorado

- **Proprietary** comprehensive, founded 2001, part of DeVry University
- **Calendar** semesters
- **Degrees** associate and bachelor's
- **Coed**
- **Minimally difficult** entrance level

Faculty *Student/faculty ratio:* 7:1.

Standardized Tests *Required:* (for admission). *Recommended:* SAT I or ACT (for admission).

Costs (2003–04) *Tuition:* $10,590 full-time, $370 per credit hour part-time. Full-time tuition and fees vary according to course load. Part-time tuition and fees vary according to course load. *Required fees:* $165 full-time. *Payment plans:* installment, deferred payment.

Financial Aid Of all full-time matriculated undergraduates who enrolled in 2001, 213 applied for aid, 193 were judged to have need, 1 had their need fully met. In 2001, 26. *Average percent of need met:* 37. *Average financial aid package:* $5040. *Average need-based loan:* $3430. *Average need-based gift aid:* $3420. *Average non-need-based aid:* $5663.

Applying *Options:* electronic application, deferred entrance. *Required:* high school transcript, interview, CPT.

Admissions Contact Mr. Rick Rodman, DeVry University, 12202 Airport Way, Suite 190, Broomfield, CO 80021-2588. *Phone:* 303-329-3340.

DEVRY UNIVERSITY
Colorado Springs, Colorado

- **Proprietary** comprehensive, founded 2001, part of DeVry University
- **Calendar** semesters
- **Degrees** associate, bachelor's, master's, and postbachelor's certificates
- **Urban** 9-acre campus
- **Coed**
- **Minimally difficult** entrance level

Student Life *Campus security:* 24-hour emergency response devices and patrols, late-night transport/escort service, safety pamphlets, lighted sidewalks/pathways.

Standardized Tests *Recommended:* SAT I, ACT or CPT.

Costs (2003–04) *Tuition:* $10,590 full-time, $370 per credit hour part-time. Full-time tuition and fees vary according to course load. Part-time tuition and fees vary according to course load. *Required fees:* $165 full-time. *Payment plans:* installment, deferred payment.

Financial Aid Of all full-time matriculated undergraduates who enrolled in 2003, 114 applied for aid, 109 were judged to have need. In 2003, 6. *Average percent of need met:* 36. *Average financial aid package:* $8534. *Average need-based loan:* $5145. *Average need-based gift aid:* $4919. *Average non-need-based aid:* $8253.

Applying *Options:* electronic application, deferred entrance. *Application fee:* $50. *Required:* high school transcript, interview.

Admissions Contact Mr. Rick Rodman, Director of Admissions, DeVry University, 225 South Union Boulevard, Colorado Springs, CO 80910-3124. *Phone:* 303-329-3340 Ext. 7221. *Fax:* 719-632-1909. *E-mail:* admitcs@cs.devry.edu.

DeVry University
Westminster, Colorado

Admissions Contact Pam Smith, DeVry University, 1870 West 122nd Avenue, Westminster, CO 80234-2010. *Phone:* 303-280-7585. *Toll-free phone:* 888-212-1857. *Fax:* 303-280-7606. *E-mail:* denver-admissions@den.devry.edu.

Fort Lewis College
Durango, Colorado

- **State-supported** 4-year, founded 1911
- **Calendar** modified trimesters
- **Degrees** associate and bachelor's
- **Small-town** 350-acre campus
- **Endowment** $6.5 million
- **Coed,** 4,182 undergraduate students, 92% full-time, 48% women, 52% men
- **Moderately difficult** entrance level, 78% of applicants were admitted

Undergraduates 3,828 full-time, 354 part-time. Students come from 49 states and territories, 15 other countries, 32% are from out of state, 0.9% African American, 0.8% Asian American or Pacific Islander, 5% Hispanic American, 17% Native American, 1% international, 8% transferred in, 34% live on campus. *Retention:* 56% of 2002 full-time freshmen returned.

Freshmen *Admission:* 3,146 applied, 2,440 admitted, 923 enrolled. *Average high school GPA:* 2.95. *Test scores:* SAT verbal scores over 500: 51%; SAT math scores over 500: 54%; ACT scores over 18: 80%; SAT verbal scores over 600: 15%; SAT math scores over 600: 11%; ACT scores over 24: 20%; SAT verbal scores over 700: 1%; ACT scores over 30: 2%.

Faculty *Total:* 243, 72% full-time, 58% with terminal degrees. *Student/faculty ratio:* 19:1.

Majors Accounting; agricultural business and management; anthropology; archeology; art; art teacher education; Asian studies; biochemistry; biology/biological sciences; business administration and management; cell biology and histology; chemistry; computer science; cultural studies; dramatic/theatre arts; economics; education; elementary education; engineering/industrial management; English; English language and literature related; environmental biology; European studies; finance; fine/studio arts; geology/earth science; history; humanities; information science/studies; international business/trade/commerce; kindergarten/preschool education; Latin American studies; liberal arts and sciences/liberal studies; literature; marketing/marketing management; mathematics; modern languages; molecular biology; music; music teacher education; philosophy; physical education teaching and coaching; physics; political science and government; pre-dentistry studies; pre-law studies; pre-medical studies; pre-veterinary studies; psychology; secondary education; sociology; Spanish; statistics; tourism and travel services management.

Academic Programs *Special study options:* academic remediation for entering students, accelerated degree program, adult/continuing education programs, advanced placement credit, cooperative education, distance learning, double majors, English as a second language, honors programs, independent study, internships, off-campus study, part-time degree program, services for LD students, student-designed majors, study abroad, summer session for credit. *Unusual degree programs:* 3-2 engineering with Colorado State University, Colorado School of Mines, University of New Mexico, University of Colorado at Boulder; forestry with Colorado State University, Northern Arizona University.

Library John F. Reed Library plus 1 other with 184,860 titles, 5,800 serial subscriptions, 4,334 audiovisual materials, an OPAC, a Web page.

Computers on Campus 517 computers available on campus for general student use. A campuswide network can be accessed from student residence rooms and from off campus. Internet access, online (class) registration, at least one staffed computer lab available. Computer purchase or lease plan available.

Student Life *Housing:* on-campus residence required for freshman year. *Options:* coed. Campus housing is university owned. Freshman applicants given priority for college housing. *Activities and organizations:* drama/theater group, student-run newspaper, radio station, choral group, marching band, business club, AISES (American Indian Science and Engineering Club), Circle K, cycling sport club, dance team. *Campus security:* 24-hour emergency response devices and patrols, late-night transport/escort service, controlled dormitory access. *Student services:* health clinic, personal/psychological counseling, legal services.

Athletics Member NCAA. All Division II. *Intercollegiate sports:* baseball M(c), basketball M(s)/W(s), cross-country running M(s)/W(s), football M(s), golf M(s), lacrosse M(c), rugby M(c)/W(c), skiing (cross-country) M(c)/W(c), skiing (downhill) M(c)/W(c), soccer M(s)/W(s), softball W(s), track and field M(c)/W(c), ultimate Frisbee M(c)/W(c), volleyball M(c)/W(s). *Intramural sports:* badminton M/W, basketball M/W, cross-country running M/W, football M/W, lacrosse M/W, racquetball M/W, soccer M/W, softball M/W, track and field M/W, ultimate Frisbee M/W, volleyball M/W, water polo M/W, wrestling M/W.

Standardized Tests *Required:* SAT I or ACT (for admission).

Costs (2003–04) *Tuition:* state resident $2020 full-time; nonresident $10,560 full-time. Full-time tuition and fees vary according to reciprocity agreements. Part-time tuition and fees vary according to course load and reciprocity agreements. *Required fees:* $768 full-time. *Room and board:* $5564; room only: $3014. Room and board charges vary according to board plan and housing facility. *Waivers:* minority students and employees or children of employees.

Financial Aid Of all full-time matriculated undergraduates who enrolled in 2002, 2,698 applied for aid, 2,207 were judged to have need, 444 had their need fully met. 196 Federal Work-Study jobs (averaging $1315). 186 state and other part-time jobs (averaging $1377). In 2002, 221 non-need-based awards were made. *Average percent of need met:* 76%. *Average financial aid package:* $7318. *Average need-based loan:* $3874. *Average need-based gift aid:* $3766. *Average non-need-based aid:* $1990. *Average indebtedness upon graduation:* $14,100.

Applying *Options:* electronic application. *Application fee:* $30. *Required:* high school transcript, minimum 2.0 GPA. *Recommended:* essay or personal statement, letters of recommendation, interview. *Application deadlines:* 8/1 (freshmen), 7/15 (transfers). *Notification:* continuous (freshmen), continuous (transfers).

Admissions Contact Ms. Gretchen Foster, Director of Admissions, Fort Lewis College, 1000 Rim Drive, Durango, CO 81301. *Phone:* 970-247-7184. *Fax:* 970-247-7179. *E-mail:* admission@fortlewis.edu.

ITT Technical Institute
Thornton, Colorado

- **Proprietary** primarily 2-year, founded 1984, part of ITT Educational Services, Inc.
- **Calendar** quarters
- **Degrees** associate and bachelor's
- **Suburban** 2-acre campus with easy access to Denver
- **Coed**
- **Minimally difficult** entrance level

Standardized Tests *Required:* Wonderlic aptitude test (for admission).

Costs (2003–04) *Tuition:* $347 per credit hour part-time.

Applying *Options:* deferred entrance. *Application fee:* $100. *Required:* high school transcript, interview. *Recommended:* letters of recommendation.

Admissions Contact Niki Donahue, Director of Recruitment, ITT Technical Institute, 500 East 84th Avenue, Suite B12, Thornton, CO 80229. *Phone:* 303-288-4488. *Toll-free phone:* 800-395-4488. *Fax:* 303-288-8166.

Johnson & Wales University
Denver, Colorado

- **Independent** 4-year, founded 1993
- **Calendar** modular
- **Degrees** associate and bachelor's
- **Small-town** campus
- **Endowment** $161.5 million
- **Coed,** 1,328 undergraduate students, 98% full-time, 46% women, 54% men
- **Minimally difficult** entrance level, 88% of applicants were admitted

Undergraduates 1,302 full-time, 26 part-time. Students come from 44 states and territories, 13 other countries, 42% are from out of state, 7% African American, 4% Asian American or Pacific Islander, 13% Hispanic American, 0.5% Native American, 1% international.

Freshmen *Admission:* 2,024 applied, 1,789 admitted. *Average high school GPA:* 2.99. *Test scores:* SAT verbal scores over 500: 45%; SAT math scores over 500: 48%; SAT verbal scores over 600: 14%; SAT math scores over 600: 14%; SAT verbal scores over 700: 1%; SAT math scores over 700: 2%.

Faculty *Total:* 70, 59% full-time.

Majors Business administration and management; culinary arts; marketing/marketing management.

Academic Programs *Special study options:* adult/continuing education programs, cooperative education, internships, part-time degree program, services for LD students, summer session for credit.

Library Johnson & Wales University Library plus 1 other with 14,000 titles, 150 serial subscriptions, 660 audiovisual materials, an OPAC, a Web page.

Computers on Campus 20 computers available on campus for general student use. A campuswide network can be accessed from student residence rooms and from off campus. Internet access, at least one staffed computer lab available.

Student Life *Housing:* on-campus residence required for freshman year. *Options:* coed. Campus housing is university owned. Freshman campus housing is guaranteed. *Campus security:* 24-hour emergency response devices and patrols, student patrols, late-night transport/escort service.

Athletics Member NAIA. *Intercollegiate sports:* baseball M, basketball M/W, cheerleading M/W, golf M, soccer M, tennis M/W. *Intramural sports:* basketball M/W, football M/W, volleyball M/W.

Standardized Tests *Required for some:* SAT I or ACT (for admission). *Recommended:* SAT I or ACT (for admission).

Costs (2004–05) *Comprehensive fee:* $28,107 includes full-time tuition ($19,182), mandatory fees ($810), and room and board ($8115). Full-time tuition and fees vary according to course load, location, and program. Part-time tuition: $355 per quarter hour. Part-time tuition and fees vary according to course load, location, and program. No tuition increase for student's term of enrollment. *Room and board:* Room and board charges vary according to housing facility and location. *Payment plans:* installment, deferred payment. *Waivers:* employees or children of employees.

Financial Aid Of all full-time matriculated undergraduates who enrolled in 2003, 1,089 applied for aid, 929 were judged to have need, 770 had their need fully met. In 2003, 87 non-need-based awards were made. *Average percent of need met:* 70%. *Average financial aid package:* $12,343. *Average need-based loan:* $5551. *Average need-based gift aid:* $4172. *Average non-need-based aid:* $4561. *Average indebtedness upon graduation:* $15,277.

Applying *Options:* common application, deferred entrance. *Required:* high school transcript. *Required for some:* minimum 3.0 GPA, interview. *Recommended:* minimum 2.0 GPA. *Application deadline:* rolling (freshmen), rolling (transfers). *Notification:* continuous (freshmen), continuous (transfers).

Admissions Contact Mr. Dave McKlveen, Director of Admissions, Johnson & Wales University, 7150 Montview Boulevard, Denver, CO 80220. *Phone:* 303-256-9300. *Toll-free phone:* 877-598-3368. *Fax:* 303-256-9333. *E-mail:* admissions@jwu.edu.

JONES INTERNATIONAL UNIVERSITY
Englewood, Colorado

- **Proprietary** comprehensive, founded 1995
- **Calendar** semesters
- **Degrees** certificates, bachelor's, and master's (offers only online degree programs)
- **Coed,** 312 undergraduate students, 48% women, 52% men
- **Noncompetitive** entrance level

Undergraduates 312 part-time. Students come from 45 states and territories, 90% are from out of state, 8% African American, 6% Asian American or Pacific Islander, 6% Hispanic American, 1% Native American. *Retention:* 99% of 2002 full-time freshmen returned.

Freshmen *Admission:* 24 applied.

Faculty *Total:* 93, 6% full-time, 67% with terminal degrees. *Student/faculty ratio:* 12:1.

Majors Business administration and management; business/corporate communications; educational assessment, evaluation, and research related; educational/instructional media design; educational leadership and administration; information technology; organizational communication; public relations, advertising, and applied communication related; secondary school administration/principalship.

Academic Programs *Special study options:* academic remediation for entering students, accelerated degree program, adult/continuing education programs, advanced placement credit, distance learning, double majors, external degree program, independent study, part-time degree program, student-designed majors, summer session for credit.

Library Jones e-global Library with a Web page.

Computers on Campus Online (class) registration available.

Applying *Options:* electronic application, deferred entrance. *Application fee:* $100. *Required:* essay or personal statement, high school transcript, minimum 2.5 GPA, 3 letters of recommendation. *Application deadline:* rolling (freshmen). *Notification:* continuous (freshmen).

Admissions Contact Ms. Candice Morrissey, Associate Director of Admissions, Jones International University, 9697 East Mineral Avenue, Englewood, CO 80112. *Phone:* 303-784-8247. *Toll-free phone:* 800-811-5663. *Fax:* 303-799-0966. *E-mail:* admissions@international.edu.

■ See page 1800 for a narrative description.

MESA STATE COLLEGE
Grand Junction, Colorado

- **State-supported** comprehensive, founded 1925, part of State Colleges in Colorado
- **Calendar** semesters
- **Degrees** certificates, associate, bachelor's, and master's
- **Small-town** 42-acre campus
- **Coed**
- **Minimally difficult** entrance level

Faculty *Student/faculty ratio:* 18:1.

Student Life *Campus security:* 24-hour emergency response devices and patrols, late-night transport/escort service, controlled dormitory access.

Athletics Member NCAA. All Division II.

Standardized Tests *Required:* SAT I or ACT (for admission).

Costs (2003–04) *Tuition:* state resident $1856 full-time; nonresident $7508 full-time. *Required fees:* $660 full-time. *Room and board:* $6266; room only: $3106.

Financial Aid Of all full-time matriculated undergraduates who enrolled in 2002, 3,385 applied for aid, 3,385 were judged to have need. 189 Federal Work-Study jobs (averaging $1428). 394 state and other part-time jobs (averaging $1669). *Average percent of need met:* 59. *Average financial aid package:* $6206. *Average need-based loan:* $3212. *Average need-based gift aid:* $2678. *Average indebtedness upon graduation:* $14,123.

Applying *Options:* common application, early admission, deferred entrance. *Application fee:* $30. *Required:* high school transcript, minimum 2.0 GPA. *Required for some:* 1 letter of recommendation, interview.

Admissions Contact Ms. Tyre Bush, Director of Admission, Mesa State College, 1100 North Avenue, Grand Junction, CO 81501. *Phone:* 970-248-1875. *Toll-free phone:* 800-982-MESA. *Fax:* 970-248-1973. *E-mail:* admissions@mesastate.edu.

METROPOLITAN STATE COLLEGE OF DENVER
Denver, Colorado

- **State-supported** 4-year, founded 1963
- **Calendar** semesters
- **Degree** certificates and bachelor's
- **Urban** 175-acre campus
- **Endowment** $2.3 million
- **Coed,** 20,261 undergraduate students, 58% full-time, 56% women, 44% men
- **Minimally difficult** entrance level, 79% of applicants were admitted

Undergraduates 11,772 full-time, 8,489 part-time. Students come from 40 states and territories, 58 other countries, 2% are from out of state, 6% African American, 4% Asian American or Pacific Islander, 13% Hispanic American, 1% Native American, 1% international, 13% transferred in. *Retention:* 62% of 2002 full-time freshmen returned.

Freshmen *Admission:* 4,550 applied, 3,575 admitted, 2,330 enrolled. *Average high school GPA:* 2.90. *Test scores:* SAT verbal scores over 500: 55%; SAT math scores over 500: 54%; ACT scores over 18: 76%; SAT verbal scores over 600: 13%; SAT math scores over 600: 12%; ACT scores over 24: 16%; SAT verbal scores over 700: 2%; SAT math scores over 700: 1%; ACT scores over 30: 1%.

Faculty *Total:* 1,000, 39% full-time, 35% with terminal degrees. *Student/faculty ratio:* 23:1.

Majors Accounting; African-American/Black studies; anthropology; art; atmospheric sciences and meteorology; aviation/airway management; behavioral sciences; biology/biological sciences; chemistry; civil engineering technology; computer and information sciences; computer science; criminal justice/law enforcement administration; economics; education (K-12); electrical, electronic and communications engineering technology; English; environmental studies; finance; foreign languages and literatures; health/health care administration; Hispanic-American, Puerto Rican, and Mexican-American/Chicano studies; history; hospitality administration; human services; industrial design; industrial technology; journalism; kinesiology and exercise science; land use planning and management; management science; marketing research; mathematics; mechanical engineering/mechanical technology; music performance; music teacher education; nursing (registered nurse training); parks, recreation and leisure; philosophy; physics; political science and government; psychology; public relations/image management; social work; sociology; Spanish; speech and rhetoric; survey technology; urban studies/affairs.

Academic Programs *Special study options:* accelerated degree program, adult/continuing education programs, advanced placement credit, cooperative education, distance learning, double majors, external degree program, honors programs, independent study, internships, off-campus study, part-time degree program, services for LD students, student-designed majors, study abroad, summer session for credit. *ROTC:* Air Force (c).

Library Auraria Library with 607,971 titles, 2,380 serial subscriptions, 16,309 audiovisual materials, an OPAC, a Web page.

Computers on Campus 800 computers available on campus for general student use. A campuswide network can be accessed from off campus. Internet access, online (class) registration, at least one staffed computer lab available.

Student Life *Activities and organizations:* drama/theater group, student-run newspaper, choral group, Political Science Association, Accounting Students

Metropolitan State College of Denver (continued)
Organization, Christian Students Organization, LGBTA, Golden Key National Honor Society. *Campus security:* 24-hour emergency response devices and patrols, late-night transport/escort service. *Student services:* health clinic, personal/psychological counseling, women's center, legal services.

Athletics Member NCAA. All Division II. *Intercollegiate sports:* baseball M(s), basketball M(s)/W(s), cheerleading M(s)/W(s), soccer M(s)/W(s), swimming M(s)/W(s), tennis M(s)/W(s), volleyball W(s). *Intramural sports:* badminton M(c)/W(c), baseball M/W, basketball M/W, football M/W, golf M/W, lacrosse M(c), racquetball M/W, rugby M(c), soccer M/W, softball M/W(c), swimming M/W, tennis M/W, ultimate Frisbee M(c)/W(c), volleyball M(c)/W(c), water polo M(c)/W(c).

Standardized Tests *Required for some:* SAT I or ACT (for admission).

Costs (2003–04) *One-time required fee:* $1025. *Tuition:* state resident $2130 full-time, $89 per credit part-time; nonresident $8737 full-time, $364 per credit part-time. Full-time tuition and fees vary according to course load and location. Part-time tuition and fees vary according to course load and location. *Required fees:* $538 full-time, $35 per credit part-time. *Payment plan:* deferred payment. *Waivers:* senior citizens.

Financial Aid Of all full-time matriculated undergraduates who enrolled in 2003, 6,194 applied for aid, 4,898 were judged to have need, 345 had their need fully met. 150 Federal Work-Study jobs (averaging $2909). 509 state and other part-time jobs (averaging $3362). In 2003, 684 non-need-based awards were made. *Average percent of need met:* 26%. *Average financial aid package:* $7481. *Average need-based loan:* $3814. *Average need-based gift aid:* $4549. *Average non-need-based aid:* $1836. *Average indebtedness upon graduation:* $9525.

Applying *Options:* common application, electronic application, deferred entrance. *Application fee:* $25. *Required:* high school transcript. *Required for some:* essay or personal statement, letters of recommendation. *Recommended:* minimum 2.0 GPA. *Application deadline:* 8/12 (freshmen), rolling (transfers). *Notification:* continuous (freshmen), continuous (transfers).

Admissions Contact Ms. Miriam Tapia, Associate Director, Metropolitan State College of Denver, PO Box 173362, Campus Box 16, Denver, CO 80217-3362. *Phone:* 303-556-2615. *Fax:* 303-556-6345.

NAROPA UNIVERSITY
Boulder, Colorado

- **Independent** comprehensive, founded 1974
- **Calendar** semesters
- **Degrees** bachelor's, master's, first professional, post-master's, and postbachelor's certificates
- **Urban** 12-acre campus with easy access to Denver
- **Endowment** $2.5 million
- **Coed,** 507 undergraduate students, 80% full-time, 61% women, 39% men
- **Moderately difficult** entrance level, 95% of applicants were admitted

Undergraduates 405 full-time, 102 part-time. Students come from 44 states and territories, 15 other countries, 73% are from out of state, 0.9% African American, 1% Asian American or Pacific Islander, 6% Hispanic American, 0.9% Native American, 4% international, 19% transferred in, 6% live on campus. *Retention:* 68% of 2002 full-time freshmen returned.

Freshmen *Admission:* 100 applied, 95 admitted, 39 enrolled. *Average high school GPA:* 2.82. *Test scores:* SAT verbal scores over 500: 83%; SAT math scores over 500: 67%; ACT scores over 18: 100%; SAT verbal scores over 600: 25%; SAT math scores over 600: 17%; SAT verbal scores over 700: 8%.

Faculty *Total:* 288, 16% full-time, 43% with terminal degrees. *Student/faculty ratio:* 12:1.

Majors American Indian/Native American studies; art; creative writing; dance; dramatic/theatre arts; ecology; English; environmental studies; fine/studio arts; health and physical education related; horticultural science; interdisciplinary studies; kindergarten/preschool education; literature; multi-/interdisciplinary studies related; music; psychology; religious studies; visual and performing arts.

Academic Programs *Special study options:* adult/continuing education programs, advanced placement credit, cooperative education, distance learning, double majors, independent study, internships, part-time degree program, services for LD students, student-designed majors, study abroad, summer session for credit.

Library Allen Ginsberg Library with 30,500 titles, 155 serial subscriptions, 12,000 audiovisual materials, an OPAC, a Web page.

Computers on Campus 48 computers available on campus for general student use. A campuswide network can be accessed. Internet access, online (class) registration, at least one staffed computer lab available.

Student Life *Housing options:* coed. Campus housing is university owned. Freshman applicants given priority for college housing. *Activities and organizations:* drama/theater group, student-run newspaper, choral group, Student Union of Naropa (SUN), GLBT Group, International Students' Group, Root Outdoor Organization, Greenworks Environmental Group. *Campus security:* late-night transport/escort service, controlled dormitory access, foot and vehicle patrol 4:30 pm–midnight. *Student services:* personal/psychological counseling.

Standardized Tests *Recommended:* SAT I or ACT (for admission).

Costs (2003–04) *Comprehensive fee:* $22,072 includes full-time tuition ($15,204), mandatory fees ($560), and room and board ($6308). Full-time tuition and fees vary according to course load. Part-time tuition: $543 per semester hour. Part-time tuition and fees vary according to course load. *Required fees:* $280 per term part-time. *College room only:* $4826. Room and board charges vary according to board plan. *Payment plan:* installment. *Waivers:* employees or children of employees.

Financial Aid Of all full-time matriculated undergraduates who enrolled in 2003, 298 applied for aid, 279 were judged to have need, 15 had their need fully met. 206 Federal Work-Study jobs (averaging $3778). 13 state and other part-time jobs (averaging $4973). *Average percent of need met:* 72%. *Average financial aid package:* $16,759. *Average need-based loan:* $7990. *Average need-based gift aid:* $8145. *Average indebtedness upon graduation:* $20,558.

Applying *Options:* electronic application, deferred entrance. *Application fee:* $35. *Required:* essay or personal statement, high school transcript, 2 letters of recommendation, interview. *Application deadline:* 1/15 (freshmen), rolling (transfers).

Admissions Contact Ms. Sally Forester, Admissions Counselor, Naropa University, 2130 Arapahoe Avenue, Boulder, CO 80302. *Phone:* 303-546-5285. *Toll-free phone:* 800-772-0410. *Fax:* 303-546-3583. *E-mail:* admissions@naropa.edu.

■ *See page 2056 for a narrative description.*

NATIONAL AMERICAN UNIVERSITY
Colorado Springs, Colorado

- **Proprietary** 4-year, founded 1941
- **Calendar** quarters
- **Degrees** certificates, diplomas, associate, bachelor's, and master's
- **Suburban** 1-acre campus with easy access to Denver
- **Coed,** 230 undergraduate students
- **Noncompetitive** entrance level

Undergraduates Students come from 25 states and territories, 16% African American, 6% Asian American or Pacific Islander, 18% Hispanic American. *Retention:* 73% of 2002 full-time freshmen returned.

Faculty *Total:* 37, 27% full-time. *Student/faculty ratio:* 15:1.

Majors Accounting; accounting and business/management; allied health and medical assisting services related; business administration and management; health/health care administration; hotel/motel administration; information science/studies; medical/clinical assistant; medical office management; tourism and travel services management.

Academic Programs *Special study options:* academic remediation for entering students, accelerated degree program, adult/continuing education programs, distance learning, English as a second language, external degree program, independent study, internships, off-campus study, part-time degree program, summer session for credit.

Library National American University Library with 15,000 titles, 100 serial subscriptions.

Computers on Campus 40 computers available on campus for general student use. A campuswide network can be accessed. At least one staffed computer lab available.

Student Life *Housing:* college housing not available. *Campus security:* late-night transport/escort service.

Costs (2004–05) *Tuition:* $10,575 full-time. *Required fees:* $200 full-time. *Payment plans:* installment, deferred payment. *Waivers:* employees or children of employees.

Applying *Options:* common application, deferred entrance. *Application fee:* $25. *Required:* high school transcript, interview. *Application deadline:* 9/1 (freshmen), rolling (transfers).

Admissions Contact National American University, 5125 North Academy Boulevard, Colorado Springs, CO 80918. *Phone:* 719-277-0588. *Fax:* 719-277-0589. *E-mail:* jwest@national.edu.

NATIONAL AMERICAN UNIVERSITY
Denver, Colorado

- **Proprietary** 4-year, founded 1974
- **Calendar** quarters
- **Degrees** certificates, diplomas, associate, bachelor's, and master's

- **Urban** campus
- **Coed**
- **Noncompetitive** entrance level

Undergraduates *Retention:* 60% of 2002 full-time freshmen returned.
Faculty *Total:* 35. *Student/faculty ratio:* 10:1.
Majors Accounting; business administration and management; computer and information sciences; computer and information sciences related; computer/information technology services administration related; computer programming; computer programming related; computer programming (specific applications); computer systems networking and telecommunications; data entry/microcomputer applications; health/health care administration; health services/allied health/health sciences; information science/studies; information technology; management information systems; medical/clinical assistant; medical/health management and clinical assistant; system administration; system, networking, and LAN/wan management; web page, digital/multimedia and information resources design.
Academic Programs *Special study options:* academic remediation for entering students, accelerated degree program, adult/continuing education programs, advanced placement credit, distance learning, double majors, English as a second language, independent study, internships, part-time degree program, summer session for credit.
Library NAU Library with 400 titles, 33 serial subscriptions.
Computers on Campus 47 computers available on campus for general student use. A campuswide network can be accessed from off campus. Internet access, at least one staffed computer lab available.
Student Life *Housing:* college housing not available.
Athletics *Intramural sports:* cheerleading W.
Standardized Tests *Recommended:* SAT I or ACT (for placement).
Costs (2004–05) *Tuition:* $8208 full-time. Full-time tuition and fees vary according to course load, location, and program. Part-time tuition and fees vary according to course load, location, and program. *Payment plan:* installment. *Waivers:* senior citizens and employees or children of employees.
Applying *Options:* common application, electronic application, early admission, deferred entrance. *Application fee:* $25. *Required:* high school transcript. *Application deadline:* rolling (freshmen), rolling (transfers).
Admissions Contact Ms. Karen Walker, Director of Admissions, National American University, 1325 South Colorado Blvd, Suite 100, Denver, CO 80222. *Phone:* 303-758-6700. *Fax:* 303-758-6810.

NAZARENE BIBLE COLLEGE
Colorado Springs, Colorado

- **Independent** 4-year, founded 1967, affiliated with Church of the Nazarene
- **Calendar** quarters
- **Degrees** diplomas, associate, and bachelor's
- **Urban** 64-acre campus with easy access to Denver
- **Endowment** $1.5 million
- **Coed**
- **Noncompetitive** entrance level

Faculty *Student/faculty ratio:* 15:1.
Student Life *Campus security:* student patrols.
Costs (2003–04) *Tuition:* $6624 full-time, $207 per semester hour part-time. *Required fees:* $300 full-time, $10 per term part-time.
Financial Aid Of all full-time matriculated undergraduates who enrolled in 2002, 208 applied for aid, 208 were judged to have need. 7 Federal Work-Study jobs (averaging $2800). *Average indebtedness upon graduation:* $19,045.
Applying *Options:* common application, electronic application, deferred entrance. *Application fee:* $20. *Required:* essay or personal statement, high school transcript, 2 letters of recommendation.
Admissions Contact Dr. David Phillips, Director of Admissions/Public Relations, Nazarene Bible College, 1111 Academy Park Loop, Colorado Springs, CO 80910-3704. *Phone:* 719-884-5031. *Toll-free phone:* 800-873-3873. *Fax:* 719-884-5199.

PLATT COLLEGE
Aurora, Colorado

Admissions Contact Admissions Office, Platt College, 3100 South Parker Road, Suite 200, Aurora, CO 80014-3141. *Phone:* 303-369-5151. *E-mail:* admissions@plattcolo.com.

REGIS UNIVERSITY
Denver, Colorado

- **Independent Roman Catholic (Jesuit)** comprehensive, founded 1877
- **Calendar** semesters
- **Degrees** bachelor's and master's
- **Suburban** 90-acre campus
- **Endowment** $24.2 million
- **Coed,** 1,268 undergraduate students, 30% full-time, 17% women, 13% men
- **Moderately difficult** entrance level, 83% of applicants were admitted

The Regis Guarantee ensures that entering freshmen will graduate in 4 years—or take the additional course work at no charge. The Learn and Earn Program offers every new freshman the opportunity to work on campus to gain valuable experience and money to help defray expenses. These programs, and its 126-year history of offering high-quality, value-oriented Jesuit education, make Regis a leader in the Rocky Mountain region.

Undergraduates 381 full-time. Students come from 40 states and territories, 11 other countries, 43% are from out of state, 29% transferred in. *Retention:* 79% of 2002 full-time freshmen returned.
Freshmen *Admission:* 1,528 applied, 1,268 admitted, 381 enrolled. *Average high school GPA:* 3.27. *Test scores:* SAT verbal scores over 500: 71%; SAT math scores over 500: 66%; ACT scores over 18: 97%; SAT verbal scores over 600: 23%; SAT math scores over 600: 21%; ACT scores over 24: 46%; SAT verbal scores over 700: 1%; SAT math scores over 700: 2%; ACT scores over 30: 7%.
Faculty *Total:* 1,225, 14% full-time. *Student/faculty ratio:* 14:1.
Majors Accounting; biochemistry; biology/biological sciences; business administration and management; chemistry; communication/speech communication and rhetoric; computer science; criminal justice/law enforcement administration; economics; education; elementary education; English; environmental studies; French; health information/medical records administration; history; human ecology; humanities; liberal arts and sciences/liberal studies; mathematics; neuroscience; nursing (registered nurse training); philosophy; political science and government; pre-dentistry studies; pre-law studies; pre-medical studies; preveterinary studies; psychology; religious studies; sociology; Spanish; visual and performing arts.
Academic Programs *Special study options:* academic remediation for entering students, accelerated degree program, adult/continuing education programs, advanced placement credit, cooperative education, double majors, external degree program, freshman honors college, honors programs, independent study, internships, off-campus study, part-time degree program, services for LD students, student-designed majors, study abroad, summer session for credit. *ROTC:* Army (c), Air Force (c). *Unusual degree programs:* 3-2 engineering with Washington University in St. Louis.
Library Dayton Memorial Library with 430,514 titles, 7,850 serial subscriptions, 104,887 audiovisual materials, an OPAC, a Web page.
Computers on Campus 300 computers available on campus for general student use. A campuswide network can be accessed from student residence rooms and from off campus. At least one staffed computer lab available.
Student Life *Housing:* on-campus residence required for freshman year. *Options:* coed. Campus housing is university owned. Freshman campus housing is guaranteed. *Activities and organizations:* drama/theater group, student-run newspaper, radio station, choral group, Programming Activities Council, hall governing boards, Student Executive Board, outdoor club, rugby club. *Campus security:* 24-hour emergency response devices and patrols, student patrols, late-night transport/escort service, controlled dormitory access. *Student services:* health clinic, personal/psychological counseling.
Athletics Member NCAA. All Division II. *Intercollegiate sports:* baseball M(s), basketball M(s)/W(s), golf M(s), lacrosse W(s), soccer M(s)/W(s), softball W(s), volleyball W(s). *Intramural sports:* basketball M/W, softball W, volleyball W.
Standardized Tests *Required:* SAT I or ACT (for admission). *Recommended:* SAT II: Subject Tests (for admission).
Costs (2003–04) *Comprehensive fee:* $28,500 includes full-time tuition ($20,700), mandatory fees ($200), and room and board ($7600). *College room only:* $4300.
Financial Aid Of all full-time matriculated undergraduates who enrolled in 2003, 869 applied for aid, 734 were judged to have need, 261 had their need fully met. 320 Federal Work-Study jobs (averaging $1175). 423 state and other part-time jobs (averaging $2510). In 2003, 436 non-need-based awards were made. *Average percent of need met:* 97%. *Average financial aid package:* $20,738. *Average need-based loan:* $5732. *Average need-based gift aid:* $10,698. *Average non-need-based aid:* $5876. *Average indebtedness upon graduation:* $22,000.
Applying *Options:* common application. *Application fee:* $40. *Required:* essay or personal statement, high school transcript, minimum 2.5 GPA, 1 letter of recommendation. *Required for some:* 2 letters of recommendation, interview. *Application deadlines:* rolling (freshmen), 8/1 (transfers). *Notification:* continuous (freshmen), continuous (transfers).

Regis University (continued)

Admissions Contact Mr. Vic Davolt, Director of Admissions, Regis University, 3333 Regis Boulevard, Denver, CO 80221-1099. *Phone:* 303-458-4905. *Toll-free phone:* 800-388-2366 Ext. 4900. *Fax:* 303-964-5534. *E-mail:* regisadm@regis.edu.

■ *See page 2222 for a narrative description.*

REMINGTON COLLEGE–COLORADO SPRINGS CAMPUS

Colorado Springs, Colorado

- **Proprietary** 4-year
- **Calendar** quarters
- **Degrees** associate and bachelor's
- **Urban** 3-acre campus
- **Coed,** 282 undergraduate students, 100% full-time, 51% women, 49% men
- **Noncompetitive** entrance level, 100% of applicants were admitted

Undergraduates 282 full-time. 16% African American, 4% Asian American or Pacific Islander, 17% Hispanic American, 1% Native American.

Freshmen *Admission:* 71 applied, 71 admitted, 71 enrolled.

Faculty *Total:* 30, 23% full-time, 10% with terminal degrees. *Student/faculty ratio:* 17:1.

Majors Computer systems networking and telecommunications; criminal justice/law enforcement administration; operations management.

Student Life *Housing:* college housing not available.

Costs (2004–05) *Tuition:* $15,240 full-time.

Admissions Contact Mr. Shibu Thomas, Campus Vice-President, Remington College–Colorado Springs Campus, 6050 Erin Park Drive, #250, Colorado Springs, CO 80918. *Phone:* 769-532-1234 Ext. 202.

REMINGTON COLLEGE–DENVER CAMPUS

Lakewood, Colorado

Admissions Contact Mr. Jim Ploskonka, Campus President, Remington College–Denver Campus, 11011 West 6th Avenue, Lakewood, CO 80215-0090. *Phone:* 303-445-0500. *Toll-free phone:* 800-999-5181.

REVANS UNIVERSITY–THE UNIVERSITY OF ACTION LEARNING

Boulder, Colorado

Admissions Contact Sally Brownell, Student Support Manager, Revans University–The University of Action Learning, 1650 38th Street, Suite 205W, Boulder, CO 80301. *Phone:* 303-442-6907.

ROCKY MOUNTAIN COLLEGE OF ART & DESIGN

Lakewood, Colorado

- **Proprietary** 4-year, founded 1963
- **Calendar** trimesters
- **Degree** bachelor's
- **Suburban** 23-acre campus
- **Coed,** 503 undergraduate students, 71% full-time, 55% women, 45% men
- **Moderately difficult** entrance level, 92% of applicants were admitted

Undergraduates 358 full-time, 145 part-time. Students come from 36 states and territories, 4 other countries, 24% are from out of state, 1% African American, 3% Asian American or Pacific Islander, 8% Hispanic American, 0.7% Native American, 1% international, 15% transferred in, 18% live on campus. *Retention:* 65% of 2002 full-time freshmen returned.

Freshmen *Admission:* 140 applied, 129 admitted, 54 enrolled. *Average high school GPA:* 2.9.

Faculty *Total:* 57, 32% full-time, 88% with terminal degrees. *Student/faculty ratio:* 12:1.

Majors Art teacher education; film/video and photographic arts related; graphic design; illustration; interior design; painting; sculpture.

Academic Programs *Special study options:* academic remediation for entering students, accelerated degree program, advanced placement credit, cooperative education, double majors, independent study, internships, part-time degree program, study abroad, summer session for credit.

Library Rocky Mountain College of Art and Design Library with 6,287 titles, 65 serial subscriptions.

Computers on Campus 47 computers available on campus for general student use. A campuswide network can be accessed. Internet access, at least one staffed computer lab available.

Student Life *Housing:* on-campus residence required for freshman year. *Options:* coed. Campus housing is leased by the school. Freshman applicants given priority for college housing. *Activities and organizations:* Artists Representative Team, The American Society of Interior Designers, The American Institute of Graphic Arts, Art Directors Club of Denver, International Animated Film Association. *Campus security:* 24-hour emergency response devices, late-night transport/escort service. *Student services:* personal/psychological counseling.

Costs (2003–04) *Tuition:* $14,184 full-time, $591 per credit part-time. *Required fees:* $90 full-time, $15 per term part-time. *Room only:* $3840. Room and board charges vary according to housing facility. *Payment plan:* installment. *Waivers:* employees or children of employees.

Financial Aid Of all full-time matriculated undergraduates who enrolled in 2001, 310 applied for aid, 227 were judged to have need. In 2001, 73 non-need-based awards were made. *Average percent of need met:* 55%. *Average financial aid package:* $3033. *Average need-based loan:* $2160. *Average need-based gift aid:* $1877. *Average non-need-based aid:* $1500.

Applying *Options:* common application, deferred entrance. *Application fee:* $50. *Required:* minimum 2.0 GPA, portfolio. *Application deadline:* rolling (freshmen), rolling (transfers).

Admissions Contact Ms. Sandy Sprock, Director of Admissions, Rocky Mountain College of Art & Design, 1600 Pierce Street, Lakewood, CO 80214. *Phone:* 303-753-6046. *Toll-free phone:* 800-888-ARTS. *Fax:* 303-759-4970. *E-mail:* admit@rmcad.edu.

TEIKYO LORETTO HEIGHTS UNIVERSITY

Denver, Colorado

Admissions Contact Teikyo Loretto Heights University, 3001 South Federal Boulevard, Denver, CO 80236-2711.

UNITED STATES AIR FORCE ACADEMY

Colorado Springs, Colorado

- **Federally supported** 4-year, founded 1954
- **Calendar** semesters
- **Degree** bachelor's
- **Suburban** 18,000-acre campus with easy access to Denver
- **Coed, primarily men,** 4,157 undergraduate students, 100% full-time, 17% women, 83% men
- **Most difficult** entrance level, 12% of applicants were admitted

Undergraduates 4,157 full-time. Students come from 54 states and territories, 21 other countries, 95% are from out of state, 5% African American, 5% Asian American or Pacific Islander, 6% Hispanic American, 1% Native American, 1% international, 100% live on campus. *Retention:* 82% of 2002 full-time freshmen returned.

Freshmen *Admission:* 10,780 applied, 1,291 admitted, 1,214 enrolled. *Average high school GPA:* 3.80. *Test scores:* SAT verbal scores over 500: 96%; SAT math scores over 500: 99%; SAT verbal scores over 600: 70%; SAT math scores over 600: 84%; SAT verbal scores over 700: 16%; SAT math scores over 700: 28%.

Faculty *Total:* 531, 100% full-time, 57% with terminal degrees. *Student/faculty ratio:* 8:1.

Majors Aerospace, aeronautical and astronautical engineering; area studies; atmospheric sciences and meteorology; behavioral sciences; biochemistry; biological and physical sciences; biology/biological sciences; business administration and management; chemistry; civil engineering; computer science; economics; electrical, electronics and communications engineering; engineering; engineering mechanics; engineering science; English; environmental/environmental health engineering; geography; history; humanities; interdisciplinary studies; legal studies; materials science; mathematics; mechanical engineering; military studies; operations research; physics; political science and government; social sciences.

Academic Programs *Special study options:* academic remediation for entering students, advanced placement credit, double majors, English as a second language, independent study, internships, off-campus study, student-designed majors, study abroad, summer session for credit.

Library United States Air Force Academy Library plus 2 others with 445,379 titles, 1,693 serial subscriptions, 4,458 audiovisual materials, an OPAC, a Web page.

Computers on Campus A campuswide network can be accessed from student residence rooms and from off campus. Computer purchase or lease plan available.

Student Life *Housing:* on-campus residence required through senior year. *Options:* coed. Campus housing is university owned. Freshman campus housing is guaranteed. *Activities and organizations:* drama/theater group, student-run newspaper, radio station, choral group, marching band, Cadet Ski Club, choir, scuba club, aviation club, Drum and Bugle Corps. *Campus security:* 24-hour emergency response devices and patrols, late-night transport/escort service, self-defense education, well-lit campus. *Student services:* health clinic, personal/psychological counseling, legal services.

Athletics Member NCAA. All Division I except football (Division I-A). *Intercollegiate sports:* baseball M, basketball M/W, cheerleading M/W, cross-country running M/W, fencing M/W, golf M, gymnastics M/W, ice hockey M, lacrosse M, riflery M/W, rugby W(c), skiing (cross-country) M(c)/W(c), skiing (downhill) M(c)/W(c), soccer M/W, softball W(c), swimming M/W, tennis M/W, track and field M/W, volleyball W, water polo M, weight lifting M(c)/W(c), wrestling M. *Intramural sports:* archery M(c)/W(c), basketball M/W, bowling M(c)/W(c), cross-country running M/W, racquetball M/W, rock climbing M/W, rugby M/W, soccer M/W, softball M/W, swimming M/W, tennis M/W, ultimate Frisbee M/W, volleyball M/W, water polo M/W, wrestling M.

Standardized Tests *Required:* SAT I or ACT (for admission). *Recommended:* SAT I or ACT (for placement).

Costs (2004–05) *Tuition:* Tuition, room and board, and medical and dental care are provided by the U.S. government. Each cadet receives a salary from which to pay for uniforms, supplies, and personal expenses. Entering freshmen are required to deposit $2500 to defray the initial cost of uniforms and equipment.

Applying *Required:* essay or personal statement, high school transcript, minimum 2.0 GPA, interview, authorized nomination. *Application deadlines:* 1/31 (freshmen), 1/31 (transfers). *Notification:* continuous until 5/15 (freshmen), continuous until 5/15 (transfers).

Admissions Contact Mr. Rolland Stoneman, Associate Director of Admissions/Selections, United States Air Force Academy, HQ USAFA/RR 2304 Cadet Drive, Suite 200, USAF Academy, CO 80840-5025. *Phone:* 719-333-2520. *Toll-free phone:* 800-443-9266. *Fax:* 719-333-3012. *E-mail:* rr_webmail@usafa.af.mil.

■ See page 2548 for a narrative description.

UNIVERSITY OF COLORADO AT BOULDER
Boulder, Colorado

- **State-supported** university, founded 1876, part of University of Colorado System
- **Calendar** semesters
- **Degrees** bachelor's, master's, doctoral, and first professional
- **Suburban** 600-acre campus with easy access to Denver
- **Endowment** $192.2 million
- **Coed,** 26,186 undergraduate students, 91% full-time, 47% women, 53% men
- **Moderately difficult** entrance level, 80% of applicants were admitted

Undergraduates 23,862 full-time, 2,324 part-time. Students come from 53 states and territories, 100 other countries, 33% are from out of state, 2% African American, 6% Asian American or Pacific Islander, 6% Hispanic American, 0.7% Native American, 1% international, 5% transferred in, 25% live on campus. *Retention:* 83% of 2002 full-time freshmen returned.

Freshmen *Admission:* 20,920 applied, 16,790 admitted, 5,630 enrolled. *Average high school GPA:* 3.52. *Test scores:* SAT verbal scores over 500: 89%; SAT math scores over 500: 91%; ACT scores over 18: 99%; SAT verbal scores over 600: 41%; SAT math scores over 600: 51%; ACT scores over 24: 69%; SAT verbal scores over 700: 6%; SAT math scores over 700: 9%; ACT scores over 30: 11%.

Faculty *Total:* 1,737, 68% full-time, 73% with terminal degrees. *Student/faculty ratio:* 17:1.

Majors Accounting; advertising; aerospace, aeronautical and astronautical engineering; anthropology; applied mathematics; architectural engineering; Asian studies; astronomy; biochemistry; broadcast journalism; business/commerce; cell and molecular biology; chemical engineering; chemistry; Chinese; civil engineering; classics and languages, literatures and linguistics; communication disorders; communication/speech communication and rhetoric; computer engineering; computer science; cultural studies; dance; dramatic/theatre arts; ecology, evolution, systematics and population biology related; economics; electrical, electronics and communications engineering; engineering physics; English; environmental design/architecture; environmental/environmental health engineering; environmental studies; film/cinema studies; finance; fine/studio arts; French; geography; geology/earth science; Germanic languages; history; humanities; international/global studies; Italian; Japanese; journalism; kinesiology and exercise science; linguistics; management information systems; marketing/marketing management; mathematics; mechanical engineering; multi-/interdisciplinary studies related; music; music performance; music teacher education; philosophy; physics; political science and government; psychology; religious studies; Russian studies; sociology; Spanish; women's studies.

Academic Programs *Special study options:* accelerated degree program, adult/continuing education programs, advanced placement credit, cooperative education, distance learning, double majors, English as a second language, freshman honors college, honors programs, independent study, internships, off-campus study, part-time degree program, services for LD students, student-designed majors, study abroad, summer session for credit. *ROTC:* Army (b), Navy (b), Air Force (b). *Unusual degree programs:* 3-2 nursing with University of Colorado Health Sciences Center; child health associate, dental hygiene, medical technology, pharmacy at University of Colorado Health Sciences Center.

Library Norlin Library plus 5 others with 2.2 million titles, 25,607 serial subscriptions, 63,314 audiovisual materials, an OPAC, a Web page.

Computers on Campus 1525 computers available on campus for general student use. A campuswide network can be accessed from student residence rooms and from off campus that provide access to standard and academic software, student government voting. Internet access, online (class) registration, at least one staffed computer lab available.

Student Life *Housing:* on-campus residence required for freshman year. *Options:* coed, disabled students. Campus housing is university owned and is provided by a third party. Freshman applicants given priority for college housing. *Activities and organizations:* drama/theater group, student-run newspaper, radio and television station, choral group, marching band, student government, ski and snowboard club, Environmental Center, AIESEC, Program Council, national fraternities, national sororities. *Campus security:* 24-hour emergency response devices and patrols, student patrols, late-night transport/escort service, University police department. *Student services:* health clinic, personal/psychological counseling, women's center, legal services.

Athletics Member NCAA. All Division I except football (Division I-A). *Intercollegiate sports:* baseball M(c), basketball M(s)/W(s), bowling M(c)/W(c), crew M(c)/W(c), cross-country running M(s)/W(s), equestrian sports M(c)/W(c), fencing M(c)/W(c), field hockey M(c)/W(c), golf M(s)/W(s), ice hockey M(c)/W(c), lacrosse M(c)/W(c), racquetball M(c)/W(c), rugby M(c)/W(c), skiing (cross-country) M(s)/W(s), skiing (downhill) M(s)/W(s), soccer M(c)/W(s), softball W(c), squash M(c)/W(c), swimming M(c)/W(c), tennis M(s)/W(s), track and field M(s)/W(s), ultimate Frisbee M(c)/W(c), volleyball M(c)/W(s), water polo M(c)/W(c), wrestling M(c). *Intramural sports:* badminton M/W, basketball M/W, cross-country running M(c)/W(c), football M/W(c), ice hockey M/W, racquetball M/W, skiing (cross-country) M(c)/W(c), skiing (downhill) M(c)/W(c), soccer M/W(c), softball M/W, squash M/W, table tennis M/W, tennis M/W, ultimate Frisbee M/W, volleyball M/W(c), water polo M/W.

Standardized Tests *Required:* SAT I or ACT (for admission).

Costs (2003–04) *Tuition:* state resident $3192 full-time; nonresident $19,508 full-time. Full-time tuition and fees vary according to program. Part-time tuition and fees vary according to course load and program. *Required fees:* $828 full-time. *Room and board:* $6754. Room and board charges vary according to board plan, housing facility, and location. *Payment plan:* deferred payment. *Waivers:* senior citizens.

Financial Aid Of all full-time matriculated undergraduates who enrolled in 2003, 13,680 applied for aid, 6,432 were judged to have need, 1,970 had their need fully met. 1,180 Federal Work-Study jobs (averaging $1665). 1,058 state and other part-time jobs (averaging $2106). In 2003, 4626 non-need-based awards were made. *Average percent of need met:* 73%. *Average financial aid package:* $9962. *Average need-based loan:* $4190. *Average need-based gift aid:* $4740. *Average non-need-based aid:* $5210. *Average indebtedness upon graduation:* $16,002.

Applying *Options:* electronic application, deferred entrance. *Application fee:* $50. *Required:* high school transcript, minimum 2.0 GPA. *Required for some:* audition for music program. *Recommended:* essay or personal statement, minimum 3.0 GPA, letters of recommendation. *Application deadlines:* 1/15 (freshmen), 4/1 (transfers). *Notification:* continuous (freshmen), continuous until 6/1 (transfers).

Admissions Contact Mr. Kevin MacLennan, Associate Director, University of Colorado at Boulder, 552 UCB, Boulder, CO 80309-0030. *Phone:* 303-492-1394. *Fax:* 303-492-7115.

■ See page 2588 for a narrative description.

UNIVERSITY OF COLORADO AT COLORADO SPRINGS
Colorado Springs, Colorado

- **State-supported** comprehensive, founded 1965
- **Calendar** semesters
- **Degrees** certificates, bachelor's, master's, and doctoral
- **Suburban** 400-acre campus with easy access to Denver
- **Endowment** $14.7 million
- **Coed,** 5,875 undergraduate students, 78% full-time, 62% women, 38% men
- **Moderately difficult** entrance level, 74% of applicants were admitted

University of Colorado at Colorado Springs (continued)

Undergraduates 4,569 full-time, 1,306 part-time. Students come from 44 states and territories, 26 other countries, 7% are from out of state, 4% African American, 5% Asian American or Pacific Islander, 8% Hispanic American, 1% Native American, 0.4% international, 10% live on campus. *Retention:* 63% of 2002 full-time freshmen returned.

Freshmen *Admission:* 2,551 applied, 1,886 admitted, 690 enrolled. *Average high school GPA:* 3.36. *Test scores:* SAT verbal scores over 500: 71%; SAT math scores over 500: 72%; ACT scores over 18: 92%; SAT verbal scores over 600: 24%; SAT math scores over 600: 31%; ACT scores over 24: 33%; SAT verbal scores over 700: 5%; SAT math scores over 700: 3%; ACT scores over 30: 3%.

Faculty *Total:* 423, 65% full-time, 73% with terminal degrees. *Student/faculty ratio:* 17:1.

Majors Accounting; anthropology; applied mathematics; art; biology/biological sciences; business administration and management; chemistry; communication/speech communication and rhetoric; computer and information sciences; computer engineering; computer science; ecology; economics; electrical, electronics and communications engineering; English; finance; fine/studio arts; geography; health science; history; marketing/marketing management; mathematics; mechanical engineering; nursing (registered nurse training); philosophy; physics; political science and government; pre-dentistry studies; pre-law studies; pre-medical studies; pre-veterinary studies; psychology; sociology; Spanish.

Academic Programs *Special study options:* accelerated degree program, advanced placement credit, cooperative education, distance learning, double majors, independent study, internships, part-time degree program, services for LD students, summer session for credit. *ROTC:* Army (b).

Library University of Colorado at Colorado Springs Kraemer Family Library with 391,638 titles, 2,201 serial subscriptions, 5,229 audiovisual materials, an OPAC, a Web page.

Computers on Campus 250 computers available on campus for general student use. A campuswide network can be accessed from student residence rooms and from off campus. At least one staffed computer lab available.

Student Life *Housing options:* coed, men-only, women-only. Campus housing is university owned. *Activities and organizations:* drama/theater group, student-run newspaper, choral group, business club, ski club, United Students of Color, psychology club. *Campus security:* 24-hour emergency response devices and patrols, student patrols, late-night transport/escort service, controlled dormitory access. *Student services:* health clinic, personal/psychological counseling, women's center.

Athletics Member NCAA. All Division II. *Intercollegiate sports:* baseball M(c), basketball M(s)/W(s), cross-country running M(s)/W(s), golf M(s), soccer M(s)/W(c), softball W(s), tennis M(s)/W(s), track and field M/W, volleyball M(c)/W(s). *Intramural sports:* badminton M/W, basketball M/W, bowling M/W, cross-country running M/W, fencing M(c)/W(c), ice hockey M(c), racquetball M/W, skiing (cross-country) M/W, skiing (downhill) M(c)/W(c), soccer M/W, softball M/W, table tennis M/W, tennis M/W, volleyball M/W, weight lifting M/W.

Standardized Tests *Required:* SAT I or ACT (for admission).

Costs (2003–04) *Tuition:* state resident $4378 full-time, $150 per credit hour part-time; nonresident $19,210 full-time, $768 per credit hour part-time. Full-time tuition and fees vary according to program and student level. Part-time tuition and fees vary according to program and student level. *Required fees:* $778 full-time, $389 per term part-time. *Room and board:* $6729. Room and board charges vary according to board plan and housing facility. *Payment plan:* deferred payment. *Waivers:* employees or children of employees.

Financial Aid Of all full-time matriculated undergraduates who enrolled in 2003, 3,488 applied for aid, 2,437 were judged to have need, 60 had their need fully met. 143 Federal Work-Study jobs (averaging $3763). 206 state and other part-time jobs (averaging $3940). In 2003, 414 non-need-based awards were made. *Average percent of need met:* 60%. *Average financial aid package:* $6859. *Average need-based loan:* $3642. *Average need-based gift aid:* $3873. *Average non-need-based aid:* $1774. *Average indebtedness upon graduation:* $16,724.

Applying *Options:* electronic application, deferred entrance. *Application fee:* $45. *Required:* high school transcript. *Application deadlines:* 7/1 (freshmen), 7/1 (transfers). *Notification:* continuous (freshmen), continuous (transfers).

Admissions Contact Mr. James Tidwell, Assistant Admissions Director, University of Colorado at Colorado Springs, PO Box 7150, Colorado Springs, CO 80918. *Phone:* 719-262-3383. *Toll-free phone:* 800-990-8227 Ext. 3383. *Fax:* 719-262-3116. *E-mail:* admrec@uccs.edu.

UNIVERSITY OF COLORADO AT DENVER

Denver, Colorado

- **State-supported** university, founded 1912, part of University of Colorado System
- **Calendar** semesters
- **Degrees** bachelor's, master's, and doctoral
- **Urban** 171-acre campus
- **Endowment** $10.0 million
- **Coed,** 8,903 undergraduate students, 54% full-time, 57% women, 43% men
- **Moderately difficult** entrance level, 70% of applicants were admitted

Undergraduates 4,823 full-time, 4,080 part-time. Students come from 51 states and territories, 117 other countries, 4% African American, 11% Asian American or Pacific Islander, 10% Hispanic American, 1% Native American, 7% international, 11% transferred in. *Retention:* 66% of 2002 full-time freshmen returned.

Freshmen *Admission:* 1,778 applied, 1,244 admitted, 645 enrolled. *Average high school GPA:* 3.30. *Test scores:* SAT verbal scores over 500: 62%; SAT math scores over 500: 63%; ACT scores over 18: 88%; SAT verbal scores over 600: 19%; SAT math scores over 600: 22%; ACT scores over 24: 34%; SAT verbal scores over 700: 2%; SAT math scores over 700: 1%; ACT scores over 30: 2%.

Faculty *Total:* 916, 50% full-time. *Student/faculty ratio:* 14:1.

Majors Anthropology; biology/biological sciences; business/commerce; chemistry; civil engineering; communication/speech communication and rhetoric; computer and information sciences; dramatic/theatre arts; economics; electrical, electronics and communications engineering; English; English composition; fine/studio arts; French; geography; history; mathematics; mechanical engineering; multi-/interdisciplinary studies related; music; philosophy; physics; political science and government; psychology; sociology; Spanish.

Academic Programs *Special study options:* accelerated degree program, adult/continuing education programs, advanced placement credit, cooperative education, distance learning, double majors, English as a second language, honors programs, independent study, internships, off-campus study, part-time degree program, services for LD students, student-designed majors, study abroad, summer session for credit. *ROTC:* Army (b), Air Force (c). *Unusual degree programs:* 3-2 liberal arts, public affairs.

Library Auraria Library with 588,582 titles, 4,364 serial subscriptions, 15,720 audiovisual materials, an OPAC, a Web page.

Computers on Campus 750 computers available on campus for general student use. A campuswide network can be accessed from student residence rooms and from off campus. Internet access, online (class) registration, at least one staffed computer lab available.

Student Life *Housing:* college housing not available. *Activities and organizations:* drama/theater group, student-run newspaper, television station, choral group, Gold Key National Honor Society, Meslim Student Association, Model United Nations (International Forum Club), Psi Chi Honor Society, Associated Engineering Students. *Campus security:* 24-hour emergency response devices and patrols, student patrols, late-night transport/escort service. *Student services:* health clinic, personal/psychological counseling, legal services.

Athletics *Intramural sports:* lacrosse M(c), rugby M(c), skiing (downhill) M(c)/W(c), water polo M(c)/W(c).

Standardized Tests *Required:* SAT I or ACT (for admission).

Costs (2003–04) *Tuition:* state resident $3028 full-time, $161 per semester hour part-time; nonresident $14,656 full-time, $880 per semester hour part-time. Full-time tuition and fees vary according to program and student level. Part-time tuition and fees vary according to program and student level. *Required fees:* $523 full-time, $249 per year part-time. *Payment plans:* installment, deferred payment. *Waivers:* employees or children of employees.

Financial Aid Of all full-time matriculated undergraduates who enrolled in 2002, 2,402 applied for aid, 1,943 were judged to have need, 246 had their need fully met. 157 Federal Work-Study jobs (averaging $4075). 256 state and other part-time jobs (averaging $3403). In 2002, 120 non-need-based awards were made. *Average percent of need met:* 69%. *Average financial aid package:* $6586. *Average need-based loan:* $3369. *Average need-based gift aid:* $4003. *Average non-need-based aid:* $1537. *Average indebtedness upon graduation:* $16,075.

Applying *Options:* electronic application, deferred entrance. *Application fee:* $40. *Required:* high school transcript, minimum 2.5 GPA. *Application deadlines:* 7/22 (freshmen), 7/22 (transfers). *Notification:* continuous (freshmen), continuous (transfers).

Admissions Contact Ms. Barbara Edwards, Director of Admissions, University of Colorado at Denver, PO Box 173364, Campus Box 167, Denver, CO 80217. *Phone:* 303-556-3287. *Fax:* 303-556-4838.

■ *See page 2590 for a narrative description.*

UNIVERSITY OF COLORADO HEALTH SCIENCES CENTER

Denver, Colorado

- **State-supported** upper-level, founded 1883, part of University of Colorado System

■ **Calendar** semesters or quarters depending on program
■ **Degrees** bachelor's, master's, doctoral, first professional, post-master's, and first professional certificates
■ **Urban** 40-acre campus
■ **Endowment** $454.0 million
■ **Coed,** 320 undergraduate students, 92% full-time, 92% women, 8% men
■ **Moderately difficult** entrance level

Undergraduates 294 full-time, 26 part-time. 3% are from out of state, 3% African American, 4% Asian American or Pacific Islander, 8% Hispanic American, 2% Native American, 49% transferred in.

Faculty *Total:* 2,573.

Majors Dental hygiene; nursing (registered nurse training).

Academic Programs *Special study options:* adult/continuing education programs, advanced placement credit, distance learning, internships, summer session for credit.

Library Denison Library plus 1 other with 250,000 titles, 1,650 serial subscriptions, an OPAC, a Web page.

Computers on Campus 55 computers available on campus for general student use. A campuswide network can be accessed from off campus. Internet access, online (class) registration, at least one staffed computer lab available.

Student Life *Housing:* college housing not available. *Campus security:* 24-hour patrols, late-night transport/escort service. *Student services:* health clinic, personal/psychological counseling.

Athletics *Intramural sports:* basketball M/W, football M/W, softball M/W, volleyball M/W.

Costs (2003–04) *Tuition:* state resident $5730 full-time; nonresident $20,010 full-time. *Required fees:* $380 full-time.

Financial Aid Of all full-time matriculated undergraduates who enrolled in 2003, 258 applied for aid, 219 were judged to have need. *Average financial aid package:* $12,452. *Average indebtedness upon graduation:* $18,997.

Applying *Options:* electronic application. *Application fee:* $40. *Application deadline:* 10/1 (transfers). *Notification:* continuous (transfers).

Admissions Contact Dr. Lynn Mason, Director of Admissions, University of Colorado Health Sciences Center, A-054, 4200 East 9th Avenue, Denver, CO 80262. *Phone:* 303-315-7676. *Fax:* 303-315-3358.

UNIVERSITY OF DENVER

Denver, Colorado

■ **Independent** university, founded 1864
■ **Calendar** quarters; semesters for law school
■ **Degrees** bachelor's, master's, doctoral, and first professional
■ **Suburban** 125-acre campus
■ **Endowment** $156.9 million
■ **Coed,** 4,456 undergraduate students, 89% full-time, 56% women, 44% men
■ **Moderately difficult** entrance level, 79% of applicants were admitted

Undergraduates 3,970 full-time, 486 part-time. Students come from 52 states and territories, 54 other countries, 50% are from out of state, 3% African American, 5% Asian American or Pacific Islander, 7% Hispanic American, 1% Native American, 4% international, 4% transferred in, 49% live on campus. *Retention:* 85% of 2002 full-time freshmen returned.

Freshmen *Admission:* 4,334 applied, 3,405 admitted, 1,031 enrolled. *Average high school GPA:* 3.49. *Test scores:* SAT verbal scores over 500: 79%; SAT math scores over 500: 82%; ACT scores over 18: 97%; SAT verbal scores over 600: 37%; SAT math scores over 600: 40%; ACT scores over 24: 63%; SAT verbal scores over 700: 6%; SAT math scores over 700: 6%; ACT scores over 30: 12%.

Faculty *Total:* 972, 45% full-time. *Student/faculty ratio:* 9:1.

Majors Accounting; animal sciences; anthropology; art; art history, criticism and conservation; art teacher education; Asian-American studies; biochemistry; biological and physical sciences; biology/biological sciences; biopsychology; business administration and management; business/commerce; business, management, and marketing related; business/managerial economics; chemistry; commercial and advertising art; communication/speech communication and rhetoric; computer and information sciences; computer engineering; computer systems analysis; construction management; creative writing; criminology; dramatic/theatre arts; economics; electrical, electronics and communications engineering; engineering; English; environmental studies; finance; fine/studio arts; French; geography; German; history; hospitality administration; hotel/motel administration; international business/trade/commerce; international relations and affairs; Italian; journalism; Latin American studies; management information systems; marketing/marketing management; mathematics; mechanical engineering; molecular biology; multi-/interdisciplinary studies related; music; musicology and ethnomusicology; music performance; operations research; philosophy; physics; political science and government; psychology; public administration; real estate; religious studies; Russian; social sciences; social sciences related; sociology; Spanish; statistics; women's studies.

Academic Programs *Special study options:* accelerated degree program, adult/continuing education programs, advanced placement credit, cooperative education, double majors, English as a second language, freshman honors college, honors programs, independent study, internships, part-time degree program, services for LD students, student-designed majors, study abroad, summer session for credit. *ROTC:* Army (c), Air Force (c).

Library Penrose Library with 1.2 million titles, 6,283 serial subscriptions, 6,293 audiovisual materials, an OPAC, a Web page.

Computers on Campus 130 computers available on campus for general student use. A campuswide network can be accessed from student residence rooms and from off campus that provide access to online grade reports. Internet access, online (class) registration, at least one staffed computer lab available.

Student Life *Housing:* on-campus residence required through sophomore year. *Options:* coed, men-only, women-only. Campus housing is university owned. Freshman campus housing is guaranteed. *Activities and organizations:* drama/theater group, student-run newspaper, choral group, student government, Club Sports Council, Programming Board, International Student Organization, Residence Hall Association, national fraternities, national sororities. *Campus security:* 24-hour emergency response devices and patrols, late-night transport/escort service, controlled dormitory access, 24-hour locked residence hall entrances. *Student services:* health clinic, personal/psychological counseling, women's center.

Athletics Member NCAA. All Division I. *Intercollegiate sports:* basketball M(s)/W(s), golf M(s)/W(s), gymnastics W(s), ice hockey M(s), lacrosse M(s)/W(s), skiing (cross-country) M(s)/W(s), skiing (downhill) M(s)/W(s), soccer M(s)/W(s), swimming M(s)/W(s), tennis M(s)/W(s), volleyball M(c)/W(s). *Intramural sports:* badminton M/W, baseball M(c)/W(c), basketball M/W, cross-country running M(c)/W(c), equestrian sports M(c)/W(c), football M/W, ice hockey M(c)/W(c), racquetball M/W, rock climbing M/W, rugby M(c)/W(c), skiing (downhill) M(c)/W(c), soccer M(c)/W(c), softball M/W, squash M/W, tennis M(c)/W(c), volleyball M(c)/W(c), water polo M(c)/W(c).

Standardized Tests *Required:* SAT I or ACT (for admission).

Costs (2004–05) *Comprehensive fee:* $34,973 includes full-time tuition ($25,956), mandatory fees ($654), and room and board ($8363). Part-time tuition: $721 per quarter hour. *College room only:* $5093.

Financial Aid Of all full-time matriculated undergraduates who enrolled in 2002, 2,876 applied for aid, 1,577 were judged to have need, 330 had their need fully met. 403 Federal Work-Study jobs (averaging $1718). 312 state and other part-time jobs (averaging $1819). In 2002, 906 non-need-based awards were made. *Average percent of need met:* 72%. *Average financial aid package:* $17,271. *Average need-based loan:* $4568. *Average need-based gift aid:* $12,743. *Average non-need-based aid:* $4839. *Average indebtedness upon graduation:* $23,138.

Applying *Options:* common application, electronic application, early admission, early action, deferred entrance. *Application fee:* $50. *Required:* essay or personal statement, high school transcript, 2 letters of recommendation. *Required for some:* minimum 2.0 GPA. *Recommended:* minimum 2.7 GPA, interview. *Application deadlines:* 1/15 (freshmen), 2/15 (transfers). *Notification:* 3/8 (freshmen), 1/5 (early action), 3/15 (transfers).

Admissions Contact Cezar Mesquita, Director of Admission Counselors, University of Denver, University Park, Denver, CO 80208. *Phone:* 303-871-3312. *Toll-free phone:* 800-525-9495. *Fax:* 303-871-3301. *E-mail:* admission@du.edu.

UNIVERSITY OF NORTHERN COLORADO

Greeley, Colorado

■ **State-supported** university, founded 1890
■ **Calendar** semesters
■ **Degrees** bachelor's, master's, and doctoral
■ **Suburban** 240-acre campus with easy access to Denver
■ **Coed,** 10,664 undergraduate students, 89% full-time, 62% women, 38% men
■ **Moderately difficult** entrance level, 71% of applicants were admitted

Undergraduates 9,488 full-time, 1,176 part-time. Students come from 48 states and territories, 10% are from out of state, 2% African American, 3% Asian American or Pacific Islander, 8% Hispanic American, 0.8% Native American, 0.4% international, 9% transferred in, 29% live on campus. *Retention:* 70% of 2002 full-time freshmen returned.

Freshmen *Admission:* 7,172 applied, 5,063 admitted, 2,140 enrolled. *Average high school GPA:* 3.32. *Test scores:* SAT verbal scores over 500: 62%; SAT math scores over 500: 63%; ACT scores over 18: 95%; SAT verbal scores over 600: 20%; SAT math scores over 600: 19%; ACT scores over 24: 35%; SAT verbal scores over 700: 2%; SAT math scores over 700: 1%; ACT scores over 30: 2%.

University of Northern Colorado (continued)

Faculty *Total:* 547, 76% full-time, 69% with terminal degrees. *Student/faculty ratio:* 21:1.

Majors Adult development and aging; African-American/Black studies; audiology and hearing sciences; biology/biological sciences; business administration and management; chemistry; clinical laboratory science/medical technology; communication/speech communication and rhetoric; criminal justice/safety; dietetics; dramatic/theatre arts; dramatic/theatre arts and stagecraft related; economics; English; fine/studio arts; foreign languages and literatures; French; geography; geology/earth science; German; Hispanic-American, Puerto Rican, and Mexican-American/Chicano studies; history; human services; interdisciplinary studies; journalism; kinesiology and exercise science; mathematics; multi-/interdisciplinary studies related; music; music teacher education; nursing (registered nurse training); parks, recreation and leisure facilities management; philosophy, physics; political science and government; psychology; public health education and promotion; social sciences; sociology; Spanish; special education; speech-language pathology; vocational rehabilitation counseling.

Academic Programs *Special study options:* academic remediation for entering students, adult/continuing education programs, advanced placement credit, cooperative education, distance learning, double majors, English as a second language, external degree program, honors programs, independent study, internships, off-campus study, part-time degree program, services for LD students, student-designed majors, study abroad, summer session for credit. *ROTC:* Army (b), Air Force (b).

Library James A. Michener Library plus 2 others with 1.0 million titles, 3,621 serial subscriptions, 44,843 audiovisual materials, an OPAC, a Web page.

Computers on Campus 1100 computers available on campus for general student use. A campuswide network can be accessed from student residence rooms and from off campus. Internet access, online (class) registration, at least one staffed computer lab available. Computer purchase or lease plan available.

Student Life *Housing:* on-campus residence required for freshman year. *Options:* coed, women-only, disabled students. Campus housing is university owned. Freshman campus housing is guaranteed. *Activities and organizations:* drama/theater group, student-run newspaper, radio station, choral group, marching band, national fraternities, national sororities. *Campus security:* 24-hour emergency response devices and patrols, student patrols, late-night transport/escort service, controlled dormitory access. *Student services:* health clinic, personal/psychological counseling, women's center, legal services.

Athletics Member NCAA. All Division II except golf (Division I). *Intercollegiate sports:* baseball M(s), basketball M(s)/W(s), cross-country running W(s), football M(s), golf M(s)/W(s), lacrosse M(c), rugby M(c)/W(c), soccer M(c)/W(s), softball W(s), swimming W(s), tennis M(s)/W(s), track and field M(s)/W(s), volleyball W(s), wrestling M(s). *Intramural sports:* basketball M/W, football M/W, soccer M/W, softball M/W, volleyball M/W, water polo M/W.

Standardized Tests *Required:* SAT I or ACT (for admission).

Costs (2003–04) *Tuition:* state resident $2520 full-time, $140 per credit hour part-time; nonresident $11,646 full-time, $647 per credit hour part-time. *Required fees:* $685 full-time, $35 per credit hour part-time. *Room and board:* $5782; room only: $2704. Room and board charges vary according to board plan and housing facility. *Waivers:* employees or children of employees.

Financial Aid Of all full-time matriculated undergraduates who enrolled in 2002, 7,158 applied for aid, 3,974 were judged to have need, 1,050 had their need fully met. 339 Federal Work-Study jobs (averaging $1476). 2,217 state and other part-time jobs (averaging $1662). In 2002, 1061 non-need-based awards were made. *Average percent of need met:* 86%. *Average financial aid package:* $7557. *Average need-based loan:* $3383. *Average need-based gift aid:* $3393. *Average non-need-based aid:* $2272.

Applying *Options:* electronic application, deferred entrance. *Application fee:* $30. *Required:* high school transcript, minimum 2.9 GPA. *Required for some:* interview. *Application deadline:* 8/1 (freshmen), rolling (transfers). *Notification:* continuous (transfers).

Admissions Contact Mr. Gary O. Gullickson, Director of Admissions, University of Northern Colorado, Campus Box 10, Carter Hall 3006, Greeley, CO 80639. *Phone:* 970-351-2881. *Toll-free phone:* 888-700-4UNC. *Fax:* 970-351-2984. *E-mail:* unc@mail.unco.edu.

UNIVERSITY OF PHOENIX–COLORADO CAMPUS

Lone Tree, Colorado

- **Proprietary** comprehensive
- **Calendar** continuous
- **Degrees** certificates, associate, bachelor's, master's, doctoral, post-master's, and postbachelor's certificates (courses conducted at 121 campuses and learning centers in 25 states)
- **Urban** campus
- **Coed,** 1,781 undergraduate students, 100% full-time, 53% women, 47% men
- **Noncompetitive** entrance level

Undergraduates 1,781 full-time. 5% African American, 2% Asian American or Pacific Islander, 7% Hispanic American, 1% Native American, 3% international.

Freshmen *Admission:* 88 enrolled.

Faculty *Total:* 827, 0.7% full-time, 29% with terminal degrees. *Student/faculty ratio:* 10:1.

Majors Accounting; business administration and management; criminal justice/law enforcement administration; information technology; management information systems; management science; nursing science; public administration and social service professions related.

Academic Programs *Special study options:* accelerated degree program, adult/continuing education programs, advanced placement credit, distance learning, external degree program, independent study.

Library University Library with 27.1 million titles, 1,648 serial subscriptions, an OPAC, a Web page.

Computers on Campus A campuswide network can be accessed from off campus. Internet access, at least one staffed computer lab available.

Student Life *Housing:* college housing not available.

Costs (2003–04) *Tuition:* $8610 full-time, $287 per credit part-time. *Waivers:* employees or children of employees.

Financial Aid *Average financial aid package:* $1400.

Applying *Options:* deferred entrance. *Application fee:* $100. *Required:* 1 letter of recommendation, 2 years of work experience, 23 years of age. *Required for some:* high school transcript. *Application deadline:* rolling (freshmen), rolling (transfers).

Admissions Contact Ms. Beth Barilla, Director of Admissions, University of Phoenix–Colorado Campus, 4615 East Elwood Street, Mail Stop AA-K101, Phoenix, AZ 85040-1958. *Phone:* 480-317-6000. *Toll-free phone:* 800-228-7240. *Fax:* 480-594-1758. *E-mail:* beth.barilla@phoenix.edu.

UNIVERSITY OF PHOENIX–SOUTHERN COLORADO CAMPUS

Colorado Springs, Colorado

- **Proprietary** comprehensive, founded 1999
- **Calendar** continuous
- **Degrees** certificates, associate, bachelor's, master's, doctoral, post-master's, and postbachelor's certificates (courses conducted at 121 campuses and learning centers in 25 states)
- **Urban** campus
- **Coed,** 461 undergraduate students, 100% full-time, 51% women, 49% men
- **Noncompetitive** entrance level

Undergraduates 461 full-time. 7% African American, 1% Asian American or Pacific Islander, 8% Hispanic American, 0.9% Native American, 16% international.

Freshmen *Admission:* 20 enrolled.

Faculty *Total:* 232, 1% full-time, 20% with terminal degrees. *Student/faculty ratio:* 7:1.

Majors Accounting; business administration and management; corrections and criminal justice related; information technology; management information systems; management science; marketing/marketing management; nursing science; public administration and social service professions related.

Academic Programs *Special study options:* accelerated degree program, adult/continuing education programs, advanced placement credit, distance learning, external degree program, independent study.

Library University Library with 27.1 million titles, 11,648 serial subscriptions, an OPAC, a Web page.

Computers on Campus A campuswide network can be accessed from off campus. Internet access, at least one staffed computer lab available.

Student Life *Housing:* college housing not available.

Costs (2003–04) *Tuition:* $8610 full-time, $287 per credit part-time. *Waivers:* employees or children of employees.

Financial Aid *Average financial aid package:* $1563.

Applying *Options:* deferred entrance. *Application fee:* $85. *Required:* 1 letter of recommendation, 2 years of work experience, 23 years of age. *Required for some:* high school transcript. *Application deadline:* rolling (freshmen), rolling (transfers).

Admissions Contact Ms. Beth Barilla, Director of Admissions, University of Phoenix–Southern Colorado Campus, 4615 East Elwood Street, Mail Stop AA-K101, Phoenix, AZ 85040-1958. *Phone:* 480-317-6000. *Toll-free phone:* 800-228-7240. *Fax:* 480-894-1758. *E-mail:* beth.barilla@phoenix.edu.

WESTERN STATE COLLEGE OF COLORADO
Gunnison, Colorado

- **State-supported** 4-year, founded 1901
- **Calendar** semesters
- **Degree** bachelor's
- **Small-town** 381-acre campus
- **Endowment** $7.2 million
- **Coed,** 2,385 undergraduate students, 91% full-time, 41% women, 59% men
- **Moderately difficult** entrance level, 79% of applicants were admitted

Western State College of Colorado is in the heart of the Colorado Rocky Mountains in Gunnison. Western offers award-winning bachelor's degree programs in 23 areas, including arts, business, recreation, kinesiology, natural sciences, education, and behavioral and social sciences. Western enrolls 2,400 students from all 50 states of the Union. For more information, students should call 800-876-5309 (toll-free) or visit http://www.western.edu.

Undergraduates 2,181 full-time, 204 part-time. Students come from 50 states and territories, 28% are from out of state, 1% African American, 0.9% Asian American or Pacific Islander, 6% Hispanic American, 1% Native American, 8% transferred in, 41% live on campus. *Retention:* 58% of 2002 full-time freshmen returned.

Freshmen *Admission:* 2,077 applied, 1,643 admitted, 634 enrolled. *Average high school GPA:* 2.93. *Test scores:* SAT verbal scores over 500: 51%; SAT math scores over 500: 49%; ACT scores over 18: 72%; SAT verbal scores over 600: 15%; SAT math scores over 600: 13%; ACT scores over 24: 11%; SAT verbal scores over 700: 2%; SAT math scores over 700: 1%; ACT scores over 30: 1%.

Faculty *Total:* 120, 83% full-time, 68% with terminal degrees. *Student/faculty ratio:* 21:1.

Majors Accounting; American studies; anthropology; art; art teacher education; athletic training; biology/biological sciences; business administration and management; chemistry; clinical psychology; commercial and advertising art; computer science; criminal justice/police science; dramatic/theatre arts; economics; education; elementary education; English; environmental studies; fine/studio arts; French; geology/earth science; history; human resources management; industrial arts; international business/trade/commerce; journalism; kinesiology and exercise science; management information systems; marketing/marketing management; mass communication/media; mathematics; molecular biology; music; music teacher education; parks, recreation and leisure; parks, recreation and leisure facilities management; physical education teaching and coaching; physics; political science and government; pre-dentistry studies; pre-law studies; pre-medical studies; pre-veterinary studies; psychology; public policy analysis; radio and television; science teacher education; secondary education; social sciences; sociology; Spanish; special education.

Academic Programs *Special study options:* accelerated degree program, adult/continuing education programs, advanced placement credit, cooperative education, double majors, honors programs, internships, off-campus study, part-time degree program, services for LD students, student-designed majors, study abroad, summer session for credit.

Library Savage Library with 158,698 titles, 719 serial subscriptions, 1,539 audiovisual materials, an OPAC, a Web page.

Computers on Campus 175 computers available on campus for general student use. A campuswide network can be accessed from student residence rooms and from off campus. Internet access, online (class) registration, at least one staffed computer lab available.

Student Life *Housing:* on-campus residence required for freshman year. *Options:* coed, men-only, women-only. Campus housing is university owned. Freshman applicants given priority for college housing. *Activities and organizations:* drama/theater group, student-run newspaper, radio and television station, choral group, Mountain Search and Rescue Team, student government association, rodeo club, wilderness pursuits, Peak Productions, national fraternities. *Campus security:* 24-hour emergency response devices and patrols, student patrols, late-night transport/escort service, controlled dormitory access. *Student services:* health clinic, personal/psychological counseling.

Athletics Member NCAA. All Division II. *Intercollegiate sports:* baseball M(c), basketball M(s)/W(s), cheerleading W(c), cross-country running M(s)/W(s), football M(s), ice hockey M(c), lacrosse M(c)/W(c), rugby M(c)/W(c), skiing (cross-country) M(s)/W(s), skiing (downhill) M(s)/W(s), soccer M(c)/W(c), track and field M(s)/W(s), volleyball M(c)/W(s), wrestling M(s)/W(c). *Intramural sports:* basketball M/W, football M/W, golf M/W, rock climbing M(c)/W(c), soccer M/W, softball M/W, tennis M/W, ultimate Frisbee M/W, volleyball M/W, wrestling M.

Standardized Tests *Required:* SAT I or ACT (for admission).

Costs (2003–04) *Tuition:* state resident $1783 full-time, $89 per credit hour part-time; nonresident $8965 full-time, $448 per credit hour part-time. Full-time tuition and fees vary according to course load. Part-time tuition and fees vary according to course load. *Required fees:* $781 full-time, $33 per credit hour part-time. *Room and board:* $5680; room only: $3524. Room and board charges vary according to board plan and housing facility. *Payment plans:* installment, deferred payment. *Waivers:* senior citizens and employees or children of employees.

Financial Aid Of all full-time matriculated undergraduates who enrolled in 2003, 1,368 applied for aid, 821 were judged to have need, 153 had their need fully met. 250 Federal Work-Study jobs (averaging $1500). 225 state and other part-time jobs (averaging $1500). In 2003, 387 non-need-based awards were made. *Average percent of need met:* 55%. *Average financial aid package:* $8800. *Average need-based loan:* $5000. *Average need-based gift aid:* $2500. *Average non-need-based aid:* $1000. *Average indebtedness upon graduation:* $13,700.

Applying *Options:* common application, deferred entrance. *Application fee:* $40. *Required:* high school transcript. *Required for some:* essay or personal statement, 2 letters of recommendation, interview. *Recommended:* minimum 2.5 GPA. *Application deadline:* 8/1 (freshmen). *Notification:* 11/1 (freshmen), continuous (transfers).

Admissions Contact Mr. Timothy L. Albers, Director of Admissions, Western State College of Colorado, Western State College of Colorado, 6 Admission Office, 600 North Adams, Gunnison, CO 81231. *Phone:* 970-943-2119. *Toll-free phone:* 800-876-5309. *Fax:* 970-943-2212. *E-mail:* discover@western.edu.

■ *See page 2818 for a narrative description.*

WESTWOOD COLLEGE OF TECHNOLOGY–DENVER NORTH
Denver, Colorado

- **Proprietary** primarily 2-year, founded 1953
- **Calendar** 5 terms
- **Degrees** diplomas, associate, and bachelor's
- **Suburban** 11-acre campus
- **Coed**
- **Moderately difficult** entrance level

Faculty *Student/faculty ratio:* 16:1.

Student Life *Campus security:* 24-hour emergency response devices.

Standardized Tests *Required for some:* Accuplacer. *Recommended:* SAT I and SAT II or ACT (for admission), SAT II: Writing Test (for admission).

Costs (2004–05) *Tuition:* $18,645 full-time, $2654 per term part-time. Full-time tuition and fees vary according to course load and program. Part-time tuition and fees vary according to course load and program. *Required fees:* $950 full-time, $404 per credit part-time.

Applying *Options:* deferred entrance. *Application fee:* $100. *Required:* high school transcript. *Recommended:* interview.

Admissions Contact Ms. Nicole Blaschko, New Student Coordinator, Westwood College of Technology–Denver North, 7350 North Broadway, Denver, CO 80221-3653. *Phone:* 303-650-5050 Ext. 329. *Toll-free phone:* 800-992-5050.

WESTWOOD COLLEGE OF TECHNOLOGY–DENVER SOUTH
Denver, Colorado

- **Proprietary** primarily 2-year
- **Degrees** associate and bachelor's
- **Coed**

Admissions Contact Mr. Ron DeJong, Director of Admissions, Westwood College of Technology–Denver South, 3150 South Sheridan Boulevard, Denver, CO 80227-5548. *Phone:* 303-934-2790. *Fax:* 303-934-2583. *E-mail:* info@westwood.edu.

YESHIVA TORAS CHAIM TALMUDICAL SEMINARY
Denver, Colorado

Admissions Contact Rabbi Israel Kagan, Dean, Yeshiva Toras Chaim Talmudical Seminary, 1400 Quitman Street, Denver, CO 80204-1415. *Phone:* 303-629-8200.

CONNECTICUT

ALBERTUS MAGNUS COLLEGE

New Haven, Connecticut

- **Independent Roman Catholic** comprehensive, founded 1925
- **Calendar** semesters
- **Degrees** associate, bachelor's, and master's
- **Suburban** 55-acre campus with easy access to New York City and Hartford
- **Endowment** $8.4 million
- **Coed,** 1,806 undergraduate students, 94% full-time, 69% women, 31% men
- **Moderately difficult** entrance level, 79% of applicants were admitted

For more than 75 years, the individual learning experience has been the focus of Albertus Magnus College's extraordinary educational program. This straight-arrow mission allows faculty members to develop the academic, personal, and professional strengths of each individual student. Students can visit the Web site (http://www.albertus.edu) or call (800-578-9160) for details.

Undergraduates 1,690 full-time, 116 part-time. Students come from 10 states and territories, 5 other countries, 4% are from out of state, 22% African American, 0.9% Asian American or Pacific Islander, 8% Hispanic American, 0.2% Native American, 0.3% international, 2% transferred in, 60% live on campus. *Retention:* 77% of 2002 full-time freshmen returned.

Freshmen *Admission:* 532 applied, 419 admitted, 229 enrolled. *Average high school GPA:* 2.63. *Test scores:* SAT math scores over 500: 29%; SAT math scores over 600: 8%; SAT math scores over 700: 1%.

Faculty *Student/faculty ratio:* 17:1.

Majors Accounting; accounting and finance; art; art history, criticism and conservation; art therapy; biology/biological sciences; business/managerial economics; chemistry; child development; classics and languages, literatures and linguistics; commercial and advertising art; criminal justice/law enforcement administration; curriculum and instruction; dramatic/theatre arts; economics; education; elementary education; English; finance; fine/studio arts; French; general studies; graphic design; health/health care administration; history; humanities; human resources management and services related; human services; information science/studies; interdisciplinary studies; international business/trade/commerce; international economics; Italian; liberal arts and sciences/liberal studies; management information systems; marketing/marketing management; mass communication/media; mathematics; mathematics teacher education; middle school education; philosophy; photography; political science and government; pre-dentistry studies; pre-law studies; pre-medical studies; pre-veterinary studies; psychology; religious studies; Romance languages; secondary education; social sciences; social work; sociology; Spanish; urban studies/affairs.

Academic Programs *Special study options:* academic remediation for entering students, accelerated degree program, adult/continuing education programs, advanced placement credit, distance learning, double majors, English as a second language, freshman honors college, honors programs, independent study, internships, part-time degree program, services for LD students, student-designed majors, summer session for credit.

Library Rosary Hall with 538 serial subscriptions, 817 audiovisual materials, an OPAC, a Web page.

Computers on Campus 130 computers available on campus for general student use. A campuswide network can be accessed from student residence rooms and from off campus. Internet access, at least one staffed computer lab available.

Student Life *Housing options:* coed, women-only. Campus housing is university owned. Freshman campus housing is guaranteed. *Activities and organizations:* drama/theater group, student-run newspaper, Student Government Association, College Drama, Minority Student Union. *Campus security:* 24-hour emergency response devices and patrols, late-night transport/escort service, controlled dormitory access. *Student services:* health clinic, personal/psychological counseling.

Athletics Member NCAA. All Division III. *Intercollegiate sports:* baseball M, basketball M/W, cross-country running M/W, soccer M/W, softball W, tennis M/W, volleyball W. *Intramural sports:* basketball M/W, racquetball M/W, soccer M/W, squash M/W, table tennis M/W.

Standardized Tests *Required:* SAT I or ACT (for admission). *Recommended:* SAT II: Subject Tests (for admission), SAT II: Writing Test (for admission).

Costs (2003–04) *Comprehensive fee:* $24,138 includes full-time tuition ($16,668), mandatory fees ($140), and room and board ($7330). Full-time tuition and fees vary according to class time and program. Part-time tuition and fees vary according to class time and program. *Payment plan:* installment. *Waivers:* senior citizens and employees or children of employees.

Financial Aid Of all full-time matriculated undergraduates who enrolled in 2003, 370 applied for aid, 370 were judged to have need, 260 had their need fully met. 83 Federal Work-Study jobs (averaging $1310). 46 state and other part-time jobs (averaging $2660). *Average percent of need met:* 87%. *Average financial aid package:* $8500. *Average need-based loan:* $4800. *Average need-based gift aid:* $7500. *Average non-need-based aid:* $7000. *Average indebtedness upon graduation:* $12,625.

Applying *Options:* deferred entrance. *Application fee:* $35. *Required:* high school transcript, 1 letter of recommendation. *Required for some:* minimum 2.5 GPA. *Recommended:* minimum 2.5 GPA, interview. *Application deadline:* 8/20 (freshmen), rolling (transfers). *Notification:* continuous (freshmen), continuous (transfers).

Admissions Contact Ms. Rebecca Kurber, Associate Dean of Admissions, Albertus Magnus College, 700 Prospect Street, New Haven, CT 06511-1189. *Phone:* 203-773-8501. *Toll-free phone:* 800-578-9160. *Fax:* 203-773-5248. *E-mail:* admissions@albertus.edu.

■ *See page 1142 for a narrative description.*

BETH BENJAMIN ACADEMY OF CONNECTICUT

Stamford, Connecticut

Admissions Contact Rabbi David Mayer, Director of Admissions, Beth Benjamin Academy of Connecticut, 132 Prospect Street, Stamford, CT 06901-1202. *Phone:* 203-325-4351.

CENTRAL CONNECTICUT STATE UNIVERSITY

New Britain, Connecticut

- **State-supported** comprehensive, founded 1849, part of Connecticut State University System
- **Calendar** semesters
- **Degrees** bachelor's, master's, doctoral, post-master's, and postbachelor's certificates
- **Suburban** 294-acre campus
- **Endowment** $15.1 million
- **Coed,** 9,401 undergraduate students, 72% full-time, 51% women, 49% men
- **Moderately difficult** entrance level, 55% of applicants were admitted

Undergraduates 6,780 full-time, 2,621 part-time. Students come from 26 states and territories, 50 other countries, 5% are from out of state, 8% African American, 3% Asian American or Pacific Islander, 6% Hispanic American, 0.4% Native American, 2% international, 10% transferred in, 24% live on campus. *Retention:* 72% of 2002 full-time freshmen returned.

Freshmen *Admission:* 5,503 applied, 3,024 admitted, 1,203 enrolled. *Test scores:* SAT verbal scores over 500: 62%; SAT math scores over 500: 59%; SAT verbal scores over 600: 13%; SAT math scores over 600: 12%; SAT verbal scores over 700: 1%; SAT math scores over 700: 1%.

Faculty *Total:* 856, 46% full-time, 37% with terminal degrees. *Student/faculty ratio:* 17:1.

Majors Accounting; anthropology; art; art teacher education; athletic training; biology/biological sciences; building/construction finishing, management, and inspection related; business administration and management; chemistry; civil engineering technology; communication/speech communication and rhetoric; computer and information sciences; criminology; design and visual communications; dramatic/theatre arts; early childhood education; economics; electrical, electronics and communications engineering; elementary education; engineering technology; English; finance; French; geography; geology/earth science; German; history; industrial production technologies related; interdisciplinary studies; international business/trade/commerce; Italian; management information systems; manufacturing technology; marketing/marketing management; mathematics; mechanical engineering/mechanical technology; multi-/interdisciplinary studies related; music; music teacher education; nursing (registered nurse training); philosophy; physical education teaching and coaching; physical sciences related; physics; plastics engineering technology; political science and government; psychology; social sciences; social work; sociology; Spanish; technology/industrial arts teacher education; tourism and travel services marketing.

Academic Programs *Special study options:* academic remediation for entering students, adult/continuing education programs, advanced placement credit, cooperative education, English as a second language, honors programs, internships, off-campus study, part-time degree program, services for LD students, student-designed majors, study abroad, summer session for credit. *ROTC:* Army (c), Air Force (c).

Library Burritt Library plus 1 other with 639,257 titles, 2,762 serial subscriptions, 5,669 audiovisual materials, an OPAC.

Computers on Campus 230 computers available on campus for general student use. A campuswide network can be accessed from student residence rooms and from off campus. Internet access, at least one staffed computer lab available.

Student Life *Housing options:* coed. *Activities and organizations:* drama/theater group, student-run newspaper, radio and television station, choral group,

Inter-Residence Council, student radio station, Program Council, outing club, NAACP, national fraternities, national sororities. *Campus security:* 24-hour emergency response devices and patrols, student patrols, late-night transport/escort service. *Student services:* health clinic, personal/psychological counseling, women's center.

Athletics Member NCAA. All Division I except football (Division I-AA). *Intercollegiate sports:* baseball M(s), basketball M(s)/W(s), cheerleading W(s), cross-country running M(s)/W(s), fencing M(c)/W(c), golf M(s)/W(s), lacrosse M(c)/W(s), soccer M(s)/W(s), softball W(s), swimming W(s), track and field M(s)/W(s), volleyball W(s). *Intramural sports:* badminton M/W, basketball M/W, equestrian sports M/W, field hockey W(c), football M, gymnastics W, rock climbing M/W, rugby M(c)/W(c), soccer M/W, softball M/W, volleyball M/W.

Standardized Tests *Required:* SAT I (for admission).

Costs (2003–04) *Tuition:* state resident $2648 full-time, $240 per credit part-time; nonresident $8570 full-time, $240 per credit part-time. Full-time tuition and fees vary according to class time, course level, and reciprocity agreements. Part-time tuition and fees vary according to class time and course level. *Required fees:* $2736 full-time, $50 per term part-time. *Room and board:* $6706; room only: $3826. Room and board charges vary according to board plan. *Payment plans:* installment, deferred payment. *Waivers:* senior citizens and employees or children of employees.

Financial Aid Of all full-time matriculated undergraduates who enrolled in 2003, 4,645 applied for aid, 3,514 were judged to have need, 374 had their need fully met. 289 Federal Work-Study jobs (averaging $1990). 110 state and other part-time jobs (averaging $544). In 2003, 30 non-need-based awards were made. *Average percent of need met:* 76%. *Average financial aid package:* $6704. *Average need-based loan:* $4358. *Average need-based gift aid:* $4523. *Average non-need-based aid:* $2408. *Average indebtedness upon graduation:* $10,471.

Applying *Options:* common application, electronic application. *Application fee:* $40. *Required:* high school transcript, minimum 2.0 GPA. *Required for some:* interview. *Recommended:* minimum 3.0 GPA, 1 letter of recommendation. *Application deadlines:* 6/1 (freshmen), 6/1 (transfers). *Notification:* continuous until 7/1 (freshmen), continuous until 7/1 (transfers).

Admissions Contact Ms. Myrna Garcia-Bowen, Director of Admissions, Central Connecticut State University, 1615 Stanley Street, New Britain, CT 06050. *Phone:* 860-832-2285. *Toll-free phone:* 800-755-2278. *Fax:* 860-832-2522. *E-mail:* admissions@ccsu.edu.

■ *See page 1376 for a narrative description.*

CHARTER OAK STATE COLLEGE
New Britain, Connecticut

- **State-supported** 4-year, founded 1973
- **Calendar** continuous
- **Degrees** associate and bachelor's (offers only external degree programs)
- **Small-town** campus
- **Endowment** $697,267
- **Coed,** 1,578 undergraduate students, 56% women, 44% men
- **Noncompetitive** entrance level

Undergraduates 1,578 part-time. Students come from 51 states and territories, 38% are from out of state, 10% African American, 2% Asian American or Pacific Islander, 4% Hispanic American, 2% Native American.

Faculty *Total:* 71, 77% with terminal degrees. *Student/faculty ratio:* 12:1.

Majors Liberal arts and sciences/liberal studies.

Academic Programs *Special study options:* accelerated degree program, adult/continuing education programs, advanced placement credit, distance learning, external degree program, independent study, part-time degree program, services for LD students, student-designed majors, summer session for credit.

Student Life *Housing:* college housing not available.

Costs (2003–04) *Tuition:* state resident $890 full-time, $140 per credit part-time; nonresident $1130 full-time, $195 per credit part-time. Part-time tuition and fees vary according to degree level. *Required fees:* $25 per term part-time. *Payment plan:* installment. *Waivers:* adult students.

Financial Aid Of all full-time matriculated undergraduates who enrolled in 2002, 355 applied for aid, 203 were judged to have need, 18 had their need fully met. *Average percent of need met:* 75%. *Average financial aid package:* $2983. *Average need-based loan:* $3600.

Applying *Options:* electronic application, deferred entrance. *Application fee:* $50. *Application deadline:* rolling (transfers). *Notification:* continuous (transfers).

Admissions Contact Ms. Lori Pendleton, Director of Admissions, Charter Oak State College, New Britain, CT 06053-2142. *Phone:* 860-832-3858. *Fax:* 860-832-3855. *E-mail:* info@charteroak.edu.

CONNECTICUT COLLEGE
New London, Connecticut

- **Independent** comprehensive, founded 1911
- **Calendar** semesters
- **Degrees** bachelor's and master's
- **Suburban** 702-acre campus
- **Endowment** $133.7 million
- **Coed,** 1,837 undergraduate students, 95% full-time, 59% women, 41% men
- **Very difficult** entrance level, 35% of applicants were admitted

Undergraduates 1,750 full-time, 87 part-time. Students come from 45 states and territories, 57 other countries, 84% are from out of state, 4% African American, 3% Asian American or Pacific Islander, 4% Hispanic American, 0.5% Native American, 9% international, 2% transferred in, 98% live on campus. *Retention:* 92% of 2002 full-time freshmen returned.

Freshmen *Admission:* 4,396 applied, 1,536 admitted, 511 enrolled. *Test scores:* SAT verbal scores over 500: 98%; SAT math scores over 500: 99%; SAT verbal scores over 600: 83%; SAT math scores over 600: 84%; SAT verbal scores over 700: 20%; SAT math scores over 700: 17%.

Faculty *Total:* 223, 68% full-time, 64% with terminal degrees. *Student/faculty ratio:* 10:1.

Majors African studies; American studies; anthropology; architecture; art; art history, criticism and conservation; Asian studies (East); astrophysics; biochemistry; biology/biological sciences; botany/plant biology; cell and molecular biology; cell biology and anatomical sciences related; chemistry; chemistry related; Chinese; classics and languages, literatures and linguistics; computer and information sciences; dance; dramatic/theatre arts; early childhood education; ecology; economics; education (multiple levels); elementary education; engineering physics; English; environmental studies; ethnic, cultural minority, and gender studies related; European studies (Central and Eastern); film/cinema studies; French; German; German studies; Hispanic-American, Puerto Rican, and Mexican-American/Chicano studies; history; human ecology; interdisciplinary studies; international relations and affairs; Italian; Italian studies; Japanese; kindergarten/preschool education; Latin American studies; mathematics; medieval and Renaissance studies; middle school education; museum studies; music; music pedagogy; music related; music teacher education; neurobiology and neurophysiology; neuroscience; philosophy; physics; physics teacher education; political science and government; psychology; religious studies; Russian; secondary education; Slavic studies; sociology; Spanish; urban studies/affairs; women's studies; zoology/animal biology.

Academic Programs *Special study options:* accelerated degree program, adult/continuing education programs, advanced placement credit, double majors, honors programs, independent study, internships, off-campus study, part-time degree program, student-designed majors, study abroad, summer session for credit. *Unusual degree programs:* 3-2 engineering with Washington University in St. Louis.

Library Charles Shain Library plus 1 other with 496,817 titles, 2,279 serial subscriptions, 155,884 audiovisual materials, an OPAC, a Web page.

Computers on Campus 461 computers available on campus for general student use. A campuswide network can be accessed from student residence rooms and from off campus. Internet access, at least one staffed computer lab available.

Student Life *Housing options:* coed, cooperative, disabled students. Campus housing is university owned. Freshman campus housing is guaranteed. *Activities and organizations:* drama/theater group, student-run newspaper, radio station, choral group, Student Government Association, Student Activity Council, unity clubs, sports clubs, student radio station. *Campus security:* 24-hour emergency response devices and patrols, late-night transport/escort service, controlled dormitory access. *Student services:* health clinic, personal/psychological counseling, women's center.

Athletics Member NCAA. All Division III. *Intercollegiate sports:* baseball M(c), basketball M/W, crew M/W, cross-country running M/W, equestrian sports M(c)/W(c), field hockey W, ice hockey M/W, lacrosse M/W, rugby W(c), sailing M/W, skiing (cross-country) M(c)/W(c), skiing (downhill) M(c)/W(c), soccer M/W, squash M/W, swimming M/W, tennis M/W, track and field M/W, ultimate Frisbee M(c)/W(c), volleyball M/W, water polo M/W. *Intramural sports:* basketball M/W, football M, golf M/W, ice hockey M/W, lacrosse M, soccer M/W, softball M/W, tennis M/W, volleyball M/W.

Standardized Tests *Required:* ACT or 3 SAT II Subject Tests (any 3) (for admission). *Recommended:* SAT I (for admission).

Costs (2004–05) *Comprehensive fee:* $37,900.

Financial Aid Of all full-time matriculated undergraduates who enrolled in 2003, 909 applied for aid, 789 were judged to have need, 789 had their need fully met. 637 Federal Work-Study jobs (averaging $1117). 12 state and other part-time jobs (averaging $1175). *Average percent of need met:* 100%. *Average financial*

Connecticut College (continued)
aid package: $24,120. *Average need-based loan:* $4181. *Average need-based gift aid:* $21,414. *Average indebtedness upon graduation:* $18,375. *Financial aid deadline:* 1/15.

Applying *Options:* common application, early decision, deferred entrance. *Application fee:* $55. *Required:* essay or personal statement, high school transcript, minimum 2.0 GPA, 2 letters of recommendation. *Recommended:* interview. *Application deadlines:* 1/1 (freshmen), 4/1 (transfers). *Early decision:* 11/15 (for plan 1), 1/1 (for plan 2). *Notification:* 4/1 (freshmen), 12/15 (early decision plan 1), 2/15 (early decision plan 2), 5/15 (transfers).

Admissions Contact Ms. Martha Merrill, Dean of Admissions and Financial Aid, Connecticut College, 270 Mohegan Avenue, New London, CT 06320-4196. *Phone:* 860-439-2200. *Fax:* 860-439-4301. *E-mail:* admission@conncoll.edu.

■ *See page 1490 for a narrative description.*

EASTERN CONNECTICUT STATE UNIVERSITY
Willimantic, Connecticut

- **State-supported** comprehensive, founded 1889, part of Connecticut State University System
- **Calendar** semesters
- **Degrees** associate, bachelor's, and master's
- **Small-town** 179-acre campus
- **Endowment** $60,000
- **Coed,** 4,716 undergraduate students, 77% full-time, 57% women, 43% men
- **Moderately difficult** entrance level, 58% of applicants were admitted

Undergraduates 3,619 full-time, 1,097 part-time. Students come from 19 states and territories, 26 other countries, 6% are from out of state, 6% African American, 1% Asian American or Pacific Islander, 4% Hispanic American, 0.9% Native American, 1% international, 9% transferred in. *Retention:* 75% of 2002 full-time freshmen returned.

Freshmen *Admission:* 3,116 applied, 1,822 admitted, 783 enrolled. *Test scores:* SAT verbal scores over 500: 59%; SAT math scores over 500: 61%; SAT verbal scores over 600: 11%; SAT math scores over 600: 13%; SAT verbal scores over 700: 1%; SAT math scores over 700: 1%.

Faculty *Total:* 361, 51% full-time, 59% with terminal degrees. *Student/faculty ratio:* 16:1.

Majors Accounting; art; biochemistry; biology/biological sciences; business administration and management; business/commerce; communication/speech communication and rhetoric; computer and information sciences; developmental and child psychology; early childhood education; economics; elementary education; English; environmental science; general studies; history; industrial and organizational psychology; kindergarten/preschool education; liberal arts and sciences/liberal studies; management information systems; mathematics; physical education teaching and coaching; political science and government; psychology; secondary education; social work; sociology; Spanish; sport and fitness administration; visual and performing arts.

Academic Programs *Special study options:* academic remediation for entering students, adult/continuing education programs, advanced placement credit, cooperative education, distance learning, double majors, freshman honors college, honors programs, independent study, internships, off-campus study, part-time degree program, services for LD students, student-designed majors, study abroad, summer session for credit. *ROTC:* Army (c), Air Force (c).

Library J. Eugene Smith Library with 234,319 titles, 2,068 serial subscriptions, 3,657 audiovisual materials, an OPAC, a Web page.

Computers on Campus 518 computers available on campus for general student use. A campuswide network can be accessed from student residence rooms and from off campus. Internet access, at least one staffed computer lab available.

Student Life *Housing options:* coed, women-only. Campus housing is university owned. Freshman campus housing is guaranteed. *Activities and organizations:* drama/theater group, student-run newspaper, radio and television station, choral group, M.A.L.E.S, Organization of Latin American Students, 180 Christian Fellowship, A.L.A.Y.A. *Campus security:* 24-hour emergency response devices and patrols, student patrols, late-night transport/escort service, controlled dormitory access. *Student services:* health clinic, personal/psychological counseling, women's center.

Athletics Member NCAA. All Division III. *Intercollegiate sports:* baseball M, basketball M/W, cheerleading W(c), cross-country running M/W, field hockey W, golf M(c), lacrosse M/W, soccer M/W, softball W, swimming W, track and field M/W, volleyball W. *Intramural sports:* badminton M/W, basketball M/W, bowling M(c)/W(c), cross-country running M/W, football M, gymnastics W, lacrosse W(c), racquetball M/W, rugby M, skiing (cross-country) M/W, skiing (downhill) M/W, soccer M/W, softball M/W, squash M/W, swimming M/W, tennis M/W, track and field M/W, ultimate Frisbee M/W, volleyball M/W, water polo M/W.

Standardized Tests *Required:* SAT I or ACT (for admission).

Costs (2004–05) *Tuition:* state resident $3010 full-time, $264 per credit part-time; nonresident $9744 full-time, $264 per credit part-time. Full-time tuition and fees vary according to degree level. Part-time tuition and fees vary according to course load, degree level, and reciprocity agreements. *Required fees:* $3112 full-time, $35 per term part-time. *Room and board:* $7266; room only: $3950. Room and board charges vary according to board plan and housing facility. *Payment plans:* installment, deferred payment. *Waivers:* senior citizens and employees or children of employees.

Financial Aid In 2002, 327 non-need-based awards were made. *Average percent of need met:* 80%.

Applying *Options:* common application, electronic application, early admission, deferred entrance. *Application fee:* $40. *Required:* high school transcript. *Required for some:* interview. *Recommended:* essay or personal statement, letters of recommendation, rank in upper 50% of high school class. *Application deadline:* 5/1 (freshmen). *Notification:* continuous (freshmen).

Admissions Contact Ms. Kimberly Crone, Director of Admissions and Enrollment Management, Eastern Connecticut State University, 83 Windham Street, Willimantic, CT 06336. *Phone:* 860-465-5286. *Toll-free phone:* 877-353-3278. *Fax:* 860-465-5544. *E-mail:* admissions@easternct.edu.

■ *See page 1554 for a narrative description.*

FAIRFIELD UNIVERSITY
Fairfield, Connecticut

- **Independent Roman Catholic (Jesuit)** comprehensive, founded 1942
- **Calendar** semesters
- **Degrees** bachelor's, master's, and post-master's certificates
- **Suburban** 200-acre campus with easy access to New York City
- **Endowment** $122.9 million
- **Coed,** 4,020 undergraduate students, 84% full-time, 58% women, 42% men
- **Moderately difficult** entrance level, 49% of applicants were admitted

Undergraduates 3,381 full-time, 639 part-time. Students come from 35 states and territories, 45 other countries, 76% are from out of state, 2% African American, 3% Asian American or Pacific Islander, 5% Hispanic American, 0.4% Native American, 1% international, 2% transferred in, 80% live on campus. *Retention:* 85% of 2002 full-time freshmen returned.

Freshmen *Admission:* 7,655 applied, 3,782 admitted, 789 enrolled. *Average high school GPA:* 3.39. *Test scores:* SAT verbal scores over 500: 94%; SAT math scores over 500: 96%; SAT verbal scores over 600: 46%; SAT math scores over 600: 57%; SAT verbal scores over 700: 5%; SAT math scores over 700: 7%.

Faculty *Total:* 426, 52% full-time, 73% with terminal degrees. *Student/faculty ratio:* 13:1.

Majors Accounting; American studies; art; biology/biological sciences; business administration and management; chemistry; clinical psychology; computer science; computer software engineering; economics; electrical, electronics and communications engineering; engineering related; English; finance; French; German; history; information science/studies; international relations and affairs; management information systems; marketing/marketing management; mass communication/media; mathematics; mechanical engineering; modern languages; music history, literature, and theory; nursing (registered nurse training); philosophy; physics; political science and government; psychology; religious studies; secondary education; sociology; Spanish.

Academic Programs *Special study options:* adult/continuing education programs, advanced placement credit, double majors, honors programs, independent study, internships, part-time degree program, services for LD students, student-designed majors, study abroad, summer session for credit. *Unusual degree programs:* 3-2 engineering with University of Connecticut, Rensselaer Polytechnic Institute, Columbia University, Stevens Institute of Technology.

Library Dimenna-Nyselius Library with 219,893 titles, 1,790 serial subscriptions, 9,924 audiovisual materials, an OPAC, a Web page.

Computers on Campus 150 computers available on campus for general student use. A campuswide network can be accessed from student residence rooms and from off campus. Internet access, online (class) registration, at least one staffed computer lab available. Computer purchase or lease plan available.

Student Life *Housing:* on-campus residence required through senior year. *Options:* coed, disabled students. Campus housing is university owned. Freshman campus housing is guaranteed. *Activities and organizations:* drama/theater group, student-run newspaper, radio and television station, choral group, student government, glee club, drama Club, multicultural organizations, Mission volunteers. *Campus security:* 24-hour emergency response devices and patrols, late-night transport/escort service, controlled dormitory access, bicycle patrols. *Student services:* health clinic, personal/psychological counseling, women's center.

Athletics Member NCAA. All Division I. *Intercollegiate sports:* baseball M(s), basketball M(s)/W(s), cheerleading M(c)/W(c), crew M(c)/W, cross-country running M/W, equestrian sports M(c)/W(c), field hockey W(s), golf M/W, lacrosse M(s)/W(s), rock climbing W(c), soccer M(s)/W(s), softball W(s), swimming M(s)/W(s), tennis M(s)/W(s), volleyball W(s). *Intramural sports:* basketball M/W, fencing M(c)/W(c), lacrosse M(c)/W(c), racquetball M/W, rugby M(c)/W(c), sailing M(c)/W(c), skiing (cross-country) M(c)/W(c), skiing (downhill) M/W, soccer M/W(c), softball W, table tennis M/W, tennis M/W, track and field M/W, ultimate Frisbee W, volleyball M/W.

Standardized Tests *Required:* SAT I or ACT (for admission).

Costs (2003–04) *One-time required fee:* $150. *Comprehensive fee:* $35,505 includes full-time tuition ($26,100), mandatory fees ($485), and room and board ($8920). Part-time tuition: $360 per credit. Part-time tuition and fees vary according to course load. *Required fees:* $60 per term part-time. *College room only:* $5270. Room and board charges vary according to board plan and housing facility. *Payment plan:* installment. *Waivers:* employees or children of employees.

Financial Aid Of all full-time matriculated undergraduates who enrolled in 2003, 2,220 applied for aid, 1,802 were judged to have need, 1,358 had their need fully met. 434 Federal Work-Study jobs (averaging $1472). In 2003, 254 non-need-based awards were made. *Average percent of need met:* 78%. *Average financial aid package:* $17,603. *Average need-based loan:* $4462. *Average need-based gift aid:* $10,642. *Average non-need-based aid:* $9483. *Average indebtedness upon graduation:* $25,194.

Applying *Options:* common application, early admission, early decision, deferred entrance. *Application fee:* $55. *Required:* essay or personal statement, high school transcript, minimum 3.0 GPA, 1 letter of recommendation, rank in upper 20% of high school class. *Recommended:* interview. *Application deadlines:* 1/15 (freshmen), 6/1 (transfers). *Early decision:* 11/15. *Notification:* 4/1 (freshmen), 12/15 (early decision), continuous (transfers).

Admissions Contact Ms. Marianne Gumpper, Interim Director of Admission, Fairfield University, 1073 North Benson Road, Fairfield, CT 06824-5195. *Phone:* 203-254-4100. *Fax:* 203-254-4199. *E-mail:* admis@mail.fairfield.edu.

■ *See page 1604 for a narrative description.*

HOLY APOSTLES COLLEGE AND SEMINARY
Cromwell, Connecticut

- **Independent Roman Catholic** comprehensive, founded 1956
- **Calendar** semesters
- **Degrees** certificates, associate, bachelor's, master's, first professional, and post-master's certificates
- **Suburban** 17-acre campus with easy access to Hartford, CT New Haven, CT
- **Coed**
- **Noncompetitive** entrance level

Faculty *Student/faculty ratio:* 10:1.

Student Life *Campus security:* 24-hour emergency response devices and patrols.

Costs (2003–04) *Comprehensive fee:* $15,380 includes full-time tuition ($8450), mandatory fees ($80), and room and board ($6850). Full-time tuition and fees vary according to program. Part-time tuition: $630 per course. Part-time tuition and fees vary according to program.

Applying *Options:* common application, deferred entrance. *Application fee:* $50. *Required:* high school transcript, interview. *Required for some:* letters of recommendation.

Admissions Contact Very Rev. Douglas Mosey CSB, Director of Admissions, Holy Apostles College and Seminary, 33 Prospect Hill Road, Cromwell, CT 06416-2005. *Phone:* 860-632-3010. *Toll-free phone:* 800-330-7272. *Fax:* 860-632-3075. *E-mail:* admissions@holyapostles.edu.

INTERNATIONAL COLLEGE OF HOSPITALITY MANAGEMENT, CÉSAR RITZ
Washington, Connecticut

- **Proprietary** primarily 2-year, founded 1992
- **Calendar** continuous
- **Degrees** certificates, associate, and bachelor's
- **Small-town** 27-acre campus with easy access to New York City
- **Coed**
- **Minimally difficult** entrance level

Faculty *Student/faculty ratio:* 6:1.

Student Life *Campus security:* 24-hour emergency response devices, student patrols, late-night transport/escort service, controlled dormitory access, weekend patrols by trained security personnel.

Standardized Tests *Recommended:* SAT I (for admission).

Applying *Options:* common application, electronic application, deferred entrance. *Application fee:* $25. *Required:* high school transcript, 2 letters of recommendation. *Required for some:* essay or personal statement, interview. *Recommended:* interview.

Admissions Contact Ms. Jacqueline Ocholla, Enrollment Coordinator, International College of Hospitality Management, *César Ritz*, 101 Wykeham Road, Washington, CT 06793-1310. *Phone:* 860-868-9555 Ext. 126. *Toll-free phone:* 800-955-0809. *Fax:* 860-868-2114. *E-mail:* admissions@ichm.cc.ct.us.

LYME ACADEMY COLLEGE OF FINE ARTS
Old Lyme, Connecticut

- **Independent** 4-year, founded 1976
- **Calendar** semesters
- **Degree** certificates and bachelor's
- **Small-town** 3-acre campus
- **Endowment** $2.4 million
- **Coed,** 160 undergraduate students, 44% full-time, 66% women, 34% men
- **Moderately difficult** entrance level, 47% of applicants were admitted

Undergraduates 71 full-time, 89 part-time. Students come from 18 states and territories, 20% are from out of state, 5% Hispanic American, 35% transferred in. *Retention:* 48% of 2002 full-time freshmen returned.

Freshmen *Admission:* 32 applied, 15 admitted, 14 enrolled. *Average high school GPA:* 3.0. *Test scores:* SAT verbal scores over 500: 83%; SAT math scores over 500: 50%; SAT verbal scores over 600: 33%; SAT math scores over 600: 25%.

Faculty *Total:* 22, 45% full-time, 45% with terminal degrees. *Student/faculty ratio:* 7:1.

Majors Drawing; painting; sculpture.

Academic Programs *Special study options:* off-campus study, part-time degree program, summer session for credit.

Library Krieble Library with 8,686 titles, 60 serial subscriptions, 14,232 audiovisual materials, an OPAC, a Web page.

Computers on Campus 6 computers available on campus for general student use. A campuswide network can be accessed. Internet access available.

Student Life *Housing:* college housing not available. *Activities and organizations:* student-run newspaper, Student Association. *Student services:* personal/psychological counseling.

Standardized Tests *Required:* SAT I or ACT (for admission).

Costs (2004–05) *Tuition:* $15,312 full-time, $638 per credit part-time. Part-time tuition and fees vary according to course level and student level. *Required fees:* $500 full-time. *Payment plan:* installment. *Waivers:* employees or children of employees.

Financial Aid In 2003, 3 non-need-based awards were made. *Average percent of need met:* 51%. *Average financial aid package:* $9356. *Average indebtedness upon graduation:* $7825. *Financial aid deadline:* 3/15.

Applying *Options:* electronic application, deferred entrance. *Application fee:* $35. *Required:* essay or personal statement, high school transcript, 2 letters of recommendation, portfolio. *Required for some:* interview. *Recommended:* minimum 2.0 GPA, interview. *Application deadline:* rolling (freshmen), rolling (transfers).

Admissions Contact Mr. John D. Werenko, Executive Director of Admission, Lyme Academy College of Fine Arts, 84 Lyme Street, Old Lyme, CT 06371. *Phone:* 860-434-5232 Ext. 119. *Fax:* 860-434-8725. *E-mail:* admissions@lymeacademy.edu.

MITCHELL COLLEGE
New London, Connecticut

- **Independent** 4-year, founded 1938
- **Calendar** semesters
- **Degrees** associate and bachelor's
- **Suburban** 67-acre campus with easy access to Hartford and Providence
- **Endowment** $6.0 million
- **Coed,** 555 undergraduate students, 80% full-time, 52% women, 48% men
- **Minimally difficult** entrance level, 58% of applicants were admitted

Undergraduates 442 full-time, 113 part-time. Students come from 22 states and territories, 5 other countries, 42% are from out of state, 12% African American, 0.4% Asian American or Pacific Islander, 3% Hispanic American, 5% Native American, 2% international, 7% transferred in, 80% live on campus.

Freshmen *Admission:* 1,158 applied, 675 admitted, 191 enrolled. *Average high school GPA:* 2.65. *Test scores:* SAT verbal scores over 500: 20%; SAT math scores over 500: 23%; ACT scores over 18: 57%; SAT verbal scores over 600: 2%; SAT math scores over 600: 2%; ACT scores over 24: 14%.

Mitchell College (continued)

Faculty *Total:* 66, 39% full-time, 41% with terminal degrees. *Student/faculty ratio:* 12:1.

Majors Accounting; athletic training; biological and physical sciences; business administration and management; child development; commercial and advertising art; criminal justice/law enforcement administration; developmental and child psychology; engineering; human development and family studies; human services; kindergarten/preschool education; liberal arts and sciences/liberal studies; marine biology and biological oceanography; parks, recreation and leisure; physical education teaching and coaching; physical sciences; psychology; sport and fitness administration; therapeutic recreation.

Academic Programs *Special study options:* adult/continuing education programs, advanced placement credit, cooperative education, double majors, English as a second language, internships, part-time degree program, services for LD students, summer session for credit.

Library Mitchell College Library plus 1 other with 80,000 titles, 120 serial subscriptions, 300 audiovisual materials, an OPAC, a Web page.

Computers on Campus 155 computers available on campus for general student use. A campuswide network can be accessed from student residence rooms and from off campus. Internet access, at least one staffed computer lab available. Computer purchase or lease plan available.

Student Life *Housing options:* coed, men-only, women-only. Campus housing is university owned. Freshman campus housing is guaranteed. *Activities and organizations:* drama/theater group, student-run newspaper, choral group, Multicultural Club, Business Club, student government, student newspaper, Outdoor Adventure Club. *Campus security:* 24-hour emergency response devices and patrols, student patrols, late-night transport/escort service, controlled dormitory access. *Student services:* health clinic, personal/psychological counseling.

Athletics Member NJCAA. *Intercollegiate sports:* baseball M(s), basketball M(s)/W(s), cross-country running M/W, golf M/W, lacrosse M(s), sailing M/W, soccer M(s)/W(s), softball W(s), tennis M/W, volleyball W(s). *Intramural sports:* badminton M/W, baseball M, basketball M/W, bowling M/W, cross-country running M/W, football M/W, golf M/W, ice hockey M, sailing M/W, soccer M/W, softball M/W, table tennis M/W, tennis M/W, volleyball M/W, weight lifting M/W.

Standardized Tests *Required:* SAT I or ACT (for admission).

Costs (2004–05) *Comprehensive fee:* $27,710 includes full-time tuition ($18,058), mandatory fees ($972), and room and board ($8680). Part-time tuition: $275 per credit hour. *Required fees:* $35 per term part-time. *College room only:* $4513. *Payment plan:* installment. *Waivers:* children of alumni and employees or children of employees.

Financial Aid Of all full-time matriculated undergraduates who enrolled in 2003, 475 applied for aid, 460 were judged to have need. 44 Federal Work-Study jobs (averaging $1000). In 2003, 108 non-need-based awards were made. *Average percent of need met:* 92%. *Average financial aid package:* $14,047. *Average need-based loan:* $3062. *Average need-based gift aid:* $10,645. *Average non-need-based aid:* $2447.

Applying *Options:* common application, electronic application, early admission, early decision, deferred entrance. *Application fee:* $30. *Required:* essay or personal statement, high school transcript, minimum 2.0 GPA, letters of recommendation. *Recommended:* interview. *Application deadline:* rolling (freshmen), rolling (transfers). *Early decision:* 11/15. *Notification:* continuous until 8/30 (freshmen), 12/15 (early decision), continuous until 8/30 (transfers).

Admissions Contact Ms. Kimberly Hodges, Associate Director of Enrollment Management and Marketing, Mitchell College, 437 Pequot Avenue, New London, CT 06320. *Phone:* 860-701-5038. *Toll-free phone:* 800-443-2811. *Fax:* 860-444-1209. *E-mail:* admissions@mitchell.edu.

■ See page 2008 for a narrative description.

PAIER COLLEGE OF ART, INC.
Hamden, Connecticut

- **Proprietary** 4-year, founded 1946
- **Calendar** semesters plus 1 summer session
- **Degrees** certificates, diplomas, associate, and bachelor's
- **Suburban** 3-acre campus with easy access to New York City
- **Coed,** 291 undergraduate students, 60% full-time, 59% women, 41% men
- **Minimally difficult** entrance level, 84% of applicants were admitted

Undergraduates 175 full-time, 116 part-time. Students come from 4 states and territories, 1 other country, 1% are from out of state, 7% transferred in. *Retention:* 78% of 2002 full-time freshmen returned.

Freshmen *Admission:* 93 applied, 78 admitted, 55 enrolled. *Test scores:* SAT verbal scores over 500: 42%; SAT math scores over 500: 27%; SAT verbal scores over 600: 20%; SAT math scores over 600: 5%; SAT verbal scores over 700: 4%; SAT math scores over 700: 1%.

Faculty *Total:* 38, 24% full-time, 13% with terminal degrees. *Student/faculty ratio:* 7:1.

Majors Art; commercial and advertising art; commercial photography; design and visual communications; fine/studio arts; interior design; painting; photography.

Academic Programs *Special study options:* academic remediation for entering students, advanced placement credit, independent study, part-time degree program, services for LD students, summer session for credit.

Library Adele K. Paier Memorial Library with 11,515 titles, 69 serial subscriptions, 66,136 audiovisual materials.

Computers on Campus 20 computers available on campus for general student use. At least one staffed computer lab available.

Student Life *Housing:* college housing not available. *Activities and organizations:* Student Council. *Campus security:* evening patrols by security. *Student services:* personal/psychological counseling.

Standardized Tests *Required:* SAT I or ACT (for admission).

Costs (2004–05) *Tuition:* $11,200 full-time. Full-time tuition and fees vary according to course load, degree level, and program. Part-time tuition and fees vary according to course load, degree level, and program. *Required fees:* $340 full-time. *Payment plan:* installment. *Waivers:* senior citizens and employees or children of employees.

Financial Aid Of all full-time matriculated undergraduates who enrolled in 1999, 102 applied for aid, 92 were judged to have need, 1 had their need fully met. *Average percent of need met:* 62%. *Average financial aid package:* $6717. *Average need-based loan:* $3446. *Average need-based gift aid:* $3460. *Average indebtedness upon graduation:* $13,536.

Applying *Options:* deferred entrance. *Application fee:* $25. *Required:* high school transcript, minimum 2.0 GPA, 2 letters of recommendation, interview, portfolio. *Recommended:* essay or personal statement. *Application deadline:* rolling (freshmen), rolling (transfers). *Notification:* continuous (freshmen), continuous (transfers).

Admissions Contact Ms. Lynn Pascale, Secretary to Admissions, Paier College of Art, Inc., 20 Gorham Avenue, Hamden, CT 06514-3902. *Phone:* 203-287-3031. *Fax:* 203-287-3021. *E-mail:* info@paierart.com.

■ See page 2148 for a narrative description.

QUINNIPIAC UNIVERSITY
Hamden, Connecticut

- **Independent** comprehensive, founded 1929
- **Calendar** semesters
- **Degrees** associate, bachelor's, master's, first professional, and postbachelor's certificates
- **Suburban** 400-acre campus with easy access to Hartford
- **Endowment** $123.3 million
- **Coed,** 5,470 undergraduate students, 93% full-time, 62% women, 38% men
- **Moderately difficult** entrance level, 62% of applicants were admitted

The $7-million Lender School of Business Center features local area network classrooms, satellite service, and the Ed McMahon Center for Mass Communications, one of the most advanced in higher education. The communications facilities include TV and radio studios, print journalism and desktop publishing laboratories, a news technology center, and audio and video equipment. The center establishes national recognition for the undergraduate and graduate communication and business programs.

Undergraduates 5,089 full-time, 381 part-time. Students come from 28 states and territories, 20 other countries, 72% are from out of state, 2% African American, 2% Asian American or Pacific Islander, 4% Hispanic American, 0.2% Native American, 1% international, 4% transferred in, 70% live on campus. *Retention:* 86% of 2002 full-time freshmen returned.

Freshmen *Admission:* 8,881 applied, 5,503 admitted, 1,318 enrolled. *Average high school GPA:* 3.30. *Test scores:* SAT verbal scores over 500: 76%; SAT math scores over 500: 84%; ACT scores over 18: 92%; SAT verbal scores over 600: 18%; SAT math scores over 600: 27%; ACT scores over 24: 53%; SAT verbal scores over 700: 1%; SAT math scores over 700: 2%; ACT scores over 30: 6%.

Faculty *Total:* 731, 37% full-time. *Student/faculty ratio:* 15:1.

Majors Accounting; actuarial science; advertising; applied mathematics; athletic training; biochemistry; biological and physical sciences; biology/biological sciences; broadcast journalism; business administration and management; business/managerial economics; chemistry; child development; cinematography and film/video production; communication and journalism related; computer science; criminal justice/safety; developmental and child psychology; economics; education; English; film/cinema studies; finance; gerontology; history; human resources management; human services; information science/studies; international business/trade/commerce; international relations and affairs; journalism; legal assistant/

paralegal; legal studies; liberal arts and sciences/liberal studies; literature; marketing/marketing management; mass communication/media; mathematics; medical laboratory technology; medical microbiology and bacteriology; nursing (registered nurse training); occupational therapy; physical therapy; physician assistant; physiological psychology/psychobiology; political science and government; pre-dentistry studies; pre-law studies; pre-medical studies; pre-veterinary studies; psychology; public relations/image management; radiologic technology/science; respiratory care therapy; sales, distribution and marketing; social sciences; sociology; Spanish; special products marketing; veterinary technology; web page, digital/multimedia and information resources design; zoology/animal biology.

Academic Programs *Special study options:* adult/continuing education programs, advanced placement credit, distance learning, double majors, honors programs, independent study, internships, part-time degree program, services for LD students, student-designed majors, study abroad, summer session for credit. *ROTC:* Army (c), Air Force (c).

Library Arnold Bernhard Library plus 1 other with 285,000 titles, 4,400 serial subscriptions, an OPAC, a Web page.

Computers on Campus 300 computers available on campus for general student use. A campuswide network can be accessed from student residence rooms and from off campus. Internet access, online (class) registration, at least one staffed computer lab available. Computer purchase or lease plan available.

Student Life *Housing options:* coed. Campus housing is university owned. Freshman campus housing is guaranteed. *Activities and organizations:* drama/theater group, student-run newspaper, radio and television station, choral group, student government, Social Programming Board, drama club, student newspaper, dance company, national fraternities, national sororities. *Campus security:* 24-hour emergency response devices and patrols, late-night transport/escort service, controlled dormitory access. *Student services:* health clinic, personal/psychological counseling, women's center.

Athletics Member NCAA. except baseball (Division I), men's and women's basketball (Division I), men's and women's cross-country running (Division I), field hockey (Division I), golf (Division I), men's and women's ice hockey (Division I), men's and women's lacrosse (Division I), men's and women's soccer (Division I), softball (Division I), men's and women's tennis (Division I), men's and women's track and field (Division I), volleyball (Division I) *Intercollegiate sports:* baseball M(s), basketball M(s)/W(s), cross-country running M(s)/W(s), field hockey W(s), golf M(s), ice hockey M(s)/W(s), lacrosse M(s)/W(s), soccer M(s)/W(s), softball W(s), tennis M(s)/W(s), track and field M(s)/W(s), volleyball W(s). *Intramural sports:* baseball M, basketball M/W, bowling M/W, field hockey M/W, soccer M/W, softball W, tennis M/W, volleyball M/W.

Standardized Tests *Required:* SAT I or ACT (for admission).

Costs (2004–05) *Comprehensive fee:* $32,400 includes full-time tuition ($21,540), mandatory fees ($960), and room and board ($9900). Part-time tuition: $530 per credit. Part-time tuition and fees vary according to course load. *Required fees:* $30 per credit part-time. *Room and board:* Room and board charges vary according to board plan and housing facility. *Payment plans:* installment, deferred payment. *Waivers:* employees or children of employees.

Financial Aid Of all full-time matriculated undergraduates who enrolled in 2003, 3,640 applied for aid, 3,034 were judged to have need, 377 had their need fully met. 1,490 Federal Work-Study jobs (averaging $1800). 39 state and other part-time jobs (averaging $1271). In 2003, 429 non-need-based awards were made. *Average percent of need met:* 67%. *Average financial aid package:* $13,160. *Average need-based loan:* $4264. *Average need-based gift aid:* $8534. *Average non-need-based aid:* $4928. *Average indebtedness upon graduation:* $20,510.

Applying *Options:* common application, electronic application, early admission, deferred entrance. *Application fee:* $45. *Required:* essay or personal statement, high school transcript, 1 letter of recommendation. *Required for some:* minimum 3.0 GPA. *Recommended:* minimum 2.5 GPA, interview. *Application deadlines:* 2/1 (freshmen), 6/1 (transfers). *Notification:* continuous until 3/1 (freshmen), continuous (transfers).

Admissions Contact Ms. Joan Isaac Mohr, Vice President and Dean of Admissions, Quinnipiac University, 275 Mount Carmel Avenue, Hamden, CT 06518-1940. *Phone:* 203-582-8600. *Toll-free phone:* 800-462-1944. *Fax:* 203-582-8906. *E-mail:* admissions@quinnipiac.edu.

■ *See page 2208 for a narrative description.*

SACRED HEART UNIVERSITY
Fairfield, Connecticut

- **Independent Roman Catholic** comprehensive, founded 1963
- **Calendar** semesters
- **Degrees** certificates, associate, bachelor's, master's, post-master's, and postbachelor's certificates (also offers part-time program with significant enrollment not reflected in profile)
- **Suburban** 56-acre campus with easy access to New York City
- **Endowment** $29.0 million
- **Coed,** 4,100 undergraduate students, 74% full-time, 61% women, 39% men
- **Moderately difficult** entrance level, 68% of applicants were admitted

Undergraduates 3,040 full-time, 1,060 part-time. Students come from 35 states and territories, 20 other countries, 50% are from out of state, 7% African American, 2% Asian American or Pacific Islander, 6% Hispanic American, 1% international, 4% transferred in, 66% live on campus. *Retention:* 81% of 2002 full-time freshmen returned.

Freshmen *Admission:* 4,701 applied, 3,219 admitted, 816 enrolled. *Average high school GPA:* 3.30. *Test scores:* SAT verbal scores over 500: 66%; SAT math scores over 500: 86%; ACT scores over 18: 92%; SAT verbal scores over 600: 12%; SAT math scores over 600: 35%; ACT scores over 24: 35%; SAT verbal scores over 700: 1%; SAT math scores over 700: 1%; ACT scores over 30: 3%.

Faculty *Total:* 457, 36% full-time, 49% with terminal degrees. *Student/faculty ratio:* 13:1.

Majors Accounting; art; athletic training; biochemistry; biological and physical sciences; biology/biological sciences; biology teacher education; business administration and management; business/managerial economics; Celtic languages; chemistry; chemistry teacher education; cinematography and film/video production; commercial and advertising art; computer and information sciences; computer science; criminal justice/law enforcement administration; data processing and data processing technology; dramatic/theatre arts; drawing; economics; education; elementary education; English; English/language arts teacher education; environmental biology; environmental science; European studies; film/cinema studies; finance; history; history teacher education; information technology; international business/trade/commerce; international relations and affairs; journalism; kindergarten/preschool education; kinesiology and exercise science; liberal arts and sciences/liberal studies; literature; marketing/marketing management; mass communication/media; mathematics; mathematics and computer science; mathematics teacher education; middle school education; modern languages; molecular biochemistry; music; nursing (registered nurse training); occupational therapy; philosophy; physical therapy; political science and government; pre-dentistry studies; pre-medical studies; pre-veterinary studies; psychology; radio and television; radio, television, and digital communication related; religious studies; science teacher education; secondary education; social science teacher education; social work; sociology; Spanish; sport and fitness administration.

Academic Programs *Special study options:* academic remediation for entering students, accelerated degree program, adult/continuing education programs, advanced placement credit, cooperative education, distance learning, double majors, English as a second language, honors programs, independent study, internships, off-campus study, part-time degree program, services for LD students, student-designed majors, study abroad, summer session for credit. *ROTC:* Army (b). *Unusual degree programs:* 3-2 physical therapy, occupational therapy.

Library Ryan-Matura Library with 98,000 titles, 4,100 serial subscriptions, 1,063 audiovisual materials, an OPAC, a Web page.

Computers on Campus 330 computers available on campus for general student use. A campuswide network can be accessed from student residence rooms and from off campus that provide access to Intranet. Internet access, at least one staffed computer lab available. Computer purchase or lease plan available.

Student Life *Housing options:* coed, disabled students. Campus housing is university owned and leased by the school. Freshman campus housing is guaranteed. *Activities and organizations:* drama/theater group, student-run newspaper, radio station, choral group, marching band, student government association, Greek Life, Marching/Pep Band, Campus Ministry, Multicultural/International Club. *Campus security:* 24-hour emergency response devices and patrols, late-night transport/escort service, controlled dormitory access, campus housing has sprinklers and fire alarms. *Student services:* health clinic, personal/psychological counseling, women's center.

Athletics Member NCAA. All Division I except football (Division I-AA). *Intercollegiate sports:* baseball M(s), basketball M(s)/W(s), bowling M/W(s), cheerleading W, crew W(s), cross-country running M(s)/W(s), equestrian sports W(s), fencing M/W(s), field hockey W(s), golf M(s)/W(s), ice hockey M(s)/W, lacrosse M(s)/W(s), soccer M(s)/W(s), softball W(s), swimming W(s), tennis M(s)/W(s), track and field M(s)/W(s), volleyball M(s)/W(s), wrestling M(s). *Intramural sports:* basketball M/W, bowling M/W, football M/W, golf M/W, gymnastics W, ice hockey M(c), rugby M(c)/W(c), skiing (downhill) M(c)/W(c), soccer M/W, softball M/W, table tennis M/W, tennis M/W, ultimate Frisbee M/W, volleyball M/W, weight lifting M/W.

Standardized Tests *Required:* SAT I or ACT (for admission).

Costs (2003–04) *Comprehensive fee:* $29,178 includes full-time tuition ($20,220), mandatory fees ($48), and room and board ($8910). Full-time tuition and fees vary according to program. Part-time tuition: $355. Part-time tuition and

Sacred Heart University (continued)
fees vary according to program. *College room only:* $6490. Room and board charges vary according to board plan. *Payment plan:* installment. *Waivers:* employees or children of employees.

Financial Aid Of all full-time matriculated undergraduates who enrolled in 2003, 2,515 applied for aid, 2,110 were judged to have need, 588 had their need fully met. 439 Federal Work-Study jobs (averaging $1320). 672 state and other part-time jobs (averaging $1109). In 2003, 455 non-need-based awards were made. *Average percent of need met:* 72%. *Average financial aid package:* $13,393. *Average need-based loan:* $5215. *Average need-based gift aid:* $8762. *Average non-need-based aid:* $9864. *Average indebtedness upon graduation:* $18,213.

Applying *Options:* common application, electronic application, early admission, early decision, deferred entrance. *Application fee:* $50. *Required:* essay or personal statement, high school transcript, minimum 3.0 GPA, 1 letter of recommendation. *Recommended:* minimum 3.2 GPA, interview. *Early decision:* 10/1 (for plan 1), 12/1 (for plan 2). *Notification:* continuous (freshmen), 10/15 (early decision plan 1), 12/15 (early decision plan 2), continuous (transfers).

Admissions Contact Ms. Karen N. Guastelle, Dean of Undergraduate Admissions, Sacred Heart University, 5151 Park Avenue, Fairfield, CT 06825-1000. *Phone:* 203-371-7880. *Fax:* 203-365-7607. *E-mail:* enroll@sacredheart.edu.

■ *See page 2270 for a narrative description.*

SAINT JOSEPH COLLEGE
West Hartford, Connecticut

- **Independent Roman Catholic** comprehensive, founded 1932
- **Calendar** semesters
- **Degrees** certificates, bachelor's, and master's
- **Suburban** 84-acre campus with easy access to Hartford
- **Endowment** $11.9 million
- **Women only,** 1,193 undergraduate students, 71% full-time
- **Moderately difficult** entrance level, 68% of applicants were admitted

Saint Joseph College provides outstanding academic, professional, and leadership opportunities for women. More than 25 majors are accompanied by internships locally or abroad. Success in every program springs from the liberal arts and sciences curriculum and active mentoring by faculty members, advisers, and alumnae. This mentoring guides students directly into postgraduate business, professional, and academic communities. Students serve on every College committee from strategic planning to Web site development, and, like the founding Sisters of Mercy, they perform community service around the world.

Undergraduates 847 full-time, 346 part-time. Students come from 10 states and territories, 1 other country, 20% are from out of state, 13% African American, 2% Asian American or Pacific Islander, 7% Hispanic American, 0.3% Native American, 0.1% international, 10% transferred in. *Retention:* 75% of 2002 full-time freshmen returned.

Freshmen *Admission:* 709 applied, 485 admitted, 215 enrolled. *Test scores:* SAT verbal scores over 500: 46%; SAT math scores over 500: 34%; SAT verbal scores over 600: 12%; SAT math scores over 600: 6%; SAT verbal scores over 700: 1%.

Faculty *Total:* 86, 91% full-time, 79% with terminal degrees. *Student/faculty ratio:* 12:1.

Majors American studies; art history, criticism and conservation; biochemistry; biology/biological sciences; business administration and management; chemistry; child development; dietetics; economics; education; elementary education; English; environmental studies; family and consumer economics related; family and consumer sciences/home economics teacher education; family and consumer sciences/human sciences; foods, nutrition, and wellness; history; kindergarten/preschool education; liberal arts and sciences/liberal studies; mathematics; natural sciences; nursing (registered nurse training); philosophy; political science and government; pre-law studies; pre-medical studies; psychology; religious studies; secondary education; social work; sociology; Spanish; special education.

Academic Programs *Special study options:* academic remediation for entering students, accelerated degree program, adult/continuing education programs, advanced placement credit, distance learning, double majors, English as a second language, honors programs, internships, off-campus study, part-time degree program, services for LD students, student-designed majors, study abroad, summer session for credit. *Unusual degree programs:* 3-2 psychology, counseling.

Library Pope Pius XII Library plus 1 other with 134,500 titles, 623 serial subscriptions, 3,000 audiovisual materials, an OPAC.

Computers on Campus 150 computers available on campus for general student use. A campuswide network can be accessed from student residence rooms and from off campus. Internet access, at least one staffed computer lab available.

Student Life *Housing options:* women-only. Campus housing is university owned. Freshman campus housing is guaranteed. *Activities and organizations:* drama/theater group, choral group, Student Government Association, Student Nurse Association, psychology club, SJC choir, business society. *Campus security:* 24-hour emergency response devices and patrols, late-night transport/escort service, controlled dormitory access. *Student services:* health clinic, personal/psychological counseling, legal services.

Athletics Member NCAA. All Division III. *Intercollegiate sports:* basketball W, cross-country running W, soccer W, softball W, swimming W, tennis W, volleyball W. *Intramural sports:* badminton W, basketball W, lacrosse W, soccer W, softball W, tennis W, volleyball W, water polo W.

Standardized Tests *Required:* SAT I or ACT (for admission).

Costs (2003–04) *Comprehensive fee:* $29,685 includes full-time tuition ($20,350), mandatory fees ($550), and room and board ($8785). Part-time tuition: $550 per credit. *Required fees:* $275 per semester hour part-time. *College room only:* $4140. Room and board charges vary according to board plan. *Payment plan:* installment. *Waivers:* employees or children of employees.

Financial Aid Of all full-time matriculated undergraduates who enrolled in 2003, 784 applied for aid, 739 were judged to have need, 160 had their need fully met. 175 Federal Work-Study jobs (averaging $1000). 125 state and other part-time jobs (averaging $1500). In 2003, 74 non-need-based awards were made. *Average percent of need met:* 72%. *Average financial aid package:* $16,273. *Average need-based loan:* $5756. *Average need-based gift aid:* $11,151. *Average non-need-based aid:* $12,346. *Average indebtedness upon graduation:* $17,649.

Applying *Options:* electronic application, early admission, early action, deferred entrance. *Application fee:* $35. *Required:* essay or personal statement, high school transcript, minimum 2.5 GPA, 1 letter of recommendation. *Recommended:* interview. *Application deadlines:* rolling (freshmen), 7/1 (transfers). *Notification:* continuous until 6/14 (freshmen), 12/15 (early action), continuous until 8/14 (transfers).

Admissions Contact Ms. Mary Yuskis, Director of Admissions, Saint Joseph College, 1678 Asylum Avenue, West Hartford, CT 06117. *Phone:* 860-231-5216. *Fax:* 860-233-5695. *E-mail:* admissions@mercy.sjc.edu.

■ *See page 2292 for a narrative description.*

SOUTHERN CONNECTICUT STATE UNIVERSITY
New Haven, Connecticut

- **State-supported** comprehensive, founded 1893, part of Connecticut State University System
- **Calendar** semesters
- **Degrees** bachelor's, master's, doctoral, and post-master's certificates
- **Urban** 168-acre campus with easy access to New York City
- **Endowment** $6.2 million
- **Coed,** 8,123 undergraduate students, 78% full-time, 60% women, 40% men
- **Moderately difficult** entrance level, 61% of applicants were admitted

Undergraduates 6,347 full-time, 1,776 part-time. Students come from 37 states and territories, 44 other countries, 6% are from out of state, 12% African American, 3% Asian American or Pacific Islander, 6% Hispanic American, 0.3% Native American, 2% international, 9% transferred in, 33% live on campus. *Retention:* 72% of 2002 full-time freshmen returned.

Freshmen *Admission:* 4,829 applied, 2,936 admitted, 1,337 enrolled. *Test scores:* SAT verbal scores over 500: 43%; SAT math scores over 500: 41%; SAT verbal scores over 600: 7%; SAT math scores over 600: 6%; SAT math scores over 700: 1%.

Faculty *Total:* 726, 55% full-time. *Student/faculty ratio:* 16:1.

Majors Accounting; art history, criticism and conservation; art teacher education; athletic training; biochemistry; biology/biological sciences; botany/plant biology; business administration and management; business/managerial economics; chemistry; commercial and advertising art; communication/speech communication and rhetoric; community organization and advocacy; computer science; creative writing; dramatic/theatre arts; economics; education; elementary education; English; finance; fine/studio arts; French; geography; geology/earth science; German; history; Italian; journalism; kindergarten/preschool education; liberal arts and sciences/liberal studies; library science; literature; management information systems and services related; marine biology and biological oceanography; mathematics; medical microbiology and bacteriology; music; nursing (registered nurse training); parks, recreation and leisure; philosophy; physical education teaching and coaching; physics; political science and government; pre-dentistry studies; pre-law studies; pre-medical studies; pre-veterinary studies; psychology; public health; science teacher education; secondary education; social sciences; social work; sociology; Spanish; special education; zoology/animal biology.

Academic Programs *Special study options:* academic remediation for entering students, accelerated degree program, adult/continuing education programs, advanced placement credit, cooperative education, distance learning, double

majors, freshman honors college, honors programs, independent study, internships, off-campus study, part-time degree program, services for LD students, student-designed majors, study abroad, summer session for credit. *ROTC:* Army (c), Air Force (c).

Library Hilton C. Buley Library with 495,660 titles, 3,549 serial subscriptions, an OPAC, a Web page.

Computers on Campus 300 computers available on campus for general student use. A campuswide network can be accessed from student residence rooms and from off campus. Internet access, online (class) registration, at least one staffed computer lab available. Computer purchase or lease plan available.

Student Life *Housing options:* coed. Campus housing is university owned. Freshman campus housing is guaranteed. *Activities and organizations:* drama/theater group, student-run newspaper, radio station, choral group, marching band, People to People, Pre-Law Society, Accounting Society, Crescent Players, Black Student Union, national fraternities, national sororities. *Campus security:* 24-hour emergency response devices and patrols, late-night transport/escort service, controlled dormitory access. *Student services:* health clinic, personal/psychological counseling, women's center.

Athletics Member NCAA. All Division II except gymnastics (Division I). *Intercollegiate sports:* baseball M, basketball M/W, cross-country running M/W, field hockey W, football M, golf M, gymnastics M/W, soccer M/W, softball W, swimming M/W, track and field M/W, volleyball W, wrestling M(s). *Intramural sports:* badminton M/W, basketball M/W, cross-country running M/W, football M, golf M/W, gymnastics M/W, ice hockey M(c), rugby M(c)/W(c), skiing (downhill) M/W, soccer M/W, softball W, volleyball M/W.

Standardized Tests *Required:* SAT I or ACT (for admission).

Costs (2004–05) *Tuition:* state resident $3010 full-time; nonresident $9744 full-time. *Required fees:* $2612 full-time. *Room and board:* $7019; room only: $3865. Room and board charges vary according to housing facility. *Payment plan:* installment. *Waivers:* senior citizens and employees or children of employees.

Financial Aid Of all full-time matriculated undergraduates who enrolled in 2003, 4,889 applied for aid, 1,747 were judged to have need, 969 had their need fully met. 91 Federal Work-Study jobs (averaging $2743). 15 state and other part-time jobs (averaging $3781). In 2003, 468 non-need-based awards were made. *Average percent of need met:* 84%. *Average financial aid package:* $5185. *Average need-based loan:* $3724. *Average non-need-based aid:* $3012.

Applying *Options:* common application, electronic application, deferred entrance. *Application fee:* $50. *Required:* essay or personal statement, high school transcript. *Recommended:* letters of recommendation. *Application deadlines:* 7/1 (freshmen), 8/1 (transfers). *Notification:* continuous (freshmen), continuous (transfers).

Admissions Contact Ms. Paula Kennedy, Associate Director of Admissions, Southern Connecticut State University, Admissions House, 131 Farnham Avenue, New Haven, CT 06515-1202. *Phone:* 203-392-5651. *Fax:* 203-392-5727.

■ *See page 2406 for a narrative description.*

TEIKYO POST UNIVERSITY
Waterbury, Connecticut

- **Independent** 4-year, founded 1890
- **Calendar** semesters (modular courses offered in the evening)
- **Degrees** certificates, associate, bachelor's, and postbachelor's certificates
- **Suburban** 70-acre campus with easy access to Hartford
- **Endowment** $1.3 million
- **Coed,** 1,325 undergraduate students, 54% full-time, 64% women, 36% men
- **Minimally difficult** entrance level, 66% of applicants were admitted

Western Connecticut's only 4-year, private, accredited, coeducational, international business and liberal arts university. This globally focused university is known for its comprehensive and affordable education, study-abroad programs, and ideal environment for learning and growth, where students experience large-university academics in a small, collegial atmosphere.

Undergraduates 719 full-time, 606 part-time. Students come from 12 states and territories, 13 other countries, 24% are from out of state, 18% African American, 2% Asian American or Pacific Islander, 10% Hispanic American, 0.7% Native American, 5% international, 2% transferred in, 52% live on campus. *Retention:* 75% of 2002 full-time freshmen returned.

Freshmen *Admission:* 1,111 applied, 733 admitted, 197 enrolled. *Average high school GPA:* 2.25. *Test scores:* SAT verbal scores over 500: 18%; SAT math scores over 500: 16%; SAT verbal scores over 600: 2%; SAT math scores over 600: 5%; SAT verbal scores over 700: 1%; SAT math scores over 700: 1%.

Faculty *Total:* 85, 33% full-time, 24% with terminal degrees. *Student/faculty ratio:* 12:1.

Majors Accounting; biology/biological sciences; business administration and management; business administration, management and operations related; child care and support services management; criminal justice/law enforcement administration; English; environmental science; environmental studies; equestrian studies; finance; history; human services; international business/trade/commerce; legal assistant/paralegal; liberal arts and sciences/liberal studies; management information systems; marketing/marketing management; psychology; sociology.

Academic Programs *Special study options:* academic remediation for entering students, accelerated degree program, adult/continuing education programs, advanced placement credit, cooperative education, distance learning, double majors, English as a second language, independent study, internships, part-time degree program, services for LD students, study abroad, summer session for credit.

Library Trauriq Library and Resource Center with 106,127 titles, 500 serial subscriptions, 600 audiovisual materials, an OPAC.

Computers on Campus 70 computers available on campus for general student use. A campuswide network can be accessed from student residence rooms and from off campus that provide access to software applications. Internet access, online (class) registration, at least one staffed computer lab available.

Student Life *Housing:* on-campus residence required for freshman year. *Options:* coed. Campus housing is university owned. Freshman campus housing is guaranteed. *Activities and organizations:* drama/theater group, student-run newspaper, choral group, Post Theatrical Players, Resident Hall Council, Student Government Association, Program Board. *Campus security:* 24-hour emergency response devices and patrols, late-night transport/escort service, controlled dormitory access. *Student services:* health clinic, personal/psychological counseling.

Athletics Member NCAA. All Division II. *Intercollegiate sports:* baseball M(s), basketball M(s)/W(s), cross-country running M(s)/W(s), equestrian sports M(s)/W(s), golf M(s), soccer M(s)/W(s), softball W(s), volleyball W(s). *Intramural sports:* cheerleading W(c), racquetball M(c)/W(c), soccer M/W.

Standardized Tests *Recommended:* SAT I or ACT (for admission).

Costs (2003–04) *Comprehensive fee:* $24,875 includes full-time tuition ($16,950), mandatory fees ($550), and room and board ($7375). Part-time tuition: $565 per credit. Part-time tuition and fees vary according to class time and course load. *Payment plan:* installment. *Waivers:* minority students, senior citizens, and employees or children of employees.

Financial Aid Of all full-time matriculated undergraduates who enrolled in 2002, 625 applied for aid, 625 were judged to have need. 234 Federal Work-Study jobs (averaging $729). 25 state and other part-time jobs (averaging $649). *Average percent of need met:* 75%. *Average financial aid package:* $8385. *Average need-based loan:* $5171. *Average need-based gift aid:* $4500. *Average non-need-based aid:* $5368. *Average indebtedness upon graduation:* $17,500.

Applying *Options:* common application, electronic application, deferred entrance. *Application fee:* $40. *Required:* high school transcript, 1 letter of recommendation. *Recommended:* essay or personal statement, interview. *Application deadline:* rolling (freshmen), rolling (transfers). *Notification:* continuous (freshmen), continuous (transfers).

Admissions Contact Mr. William Johnson, Senior Assistant Director of Admissions, Teikyo Post University, PO Box 2540, Waterbury, CT 06723. *Phone:* 203-596-4520. *Toll-free phone:* 800-345-2562. *Fax:* 203-756-5810. *E-mail:* tpuadmiss@teikyopost.edu.

■ *See page 2486 for a narrative description.*

TRINITY COLLEGE
Hartford, Connecticut

- **Independent** comprehensive, founded 1823
- **Calendar** semesters
- **Degrees** bachelor's and master's
- **Urban** 100-acre campus
- **Endowment** $340.0 million
- **Coed,** 2,188 undergraduate students, 91% full-time, 51% women, 49% men
- **Very difficult** entrance level, 36% of applicants were admitted

Undergraduates 2,001 full-time, 187 part-time. Students come from 44 states and territories, 28 other countries, 78% are from out of state, 5% African American, 6% Asian American or Pacific Islander, 5% Hispanic American, 0.2% Native American, 2% international, 0.4% transferred in, 96% live on campus. *Retention:* 91% of 2002 full-time freshmen returned.

Freshmen *Admission:* 5,510 applied, 1,993 admitted, 550 enrolled. *Test scores:* SAT verbal scores over 500: 97%; SAT math scores over 500: 98%; ACT scores over 18: 100%; SAT verbal scores over 600: 73%; SAT math scores over 600: 83%; ACT scores over 24: 87%; SAT verbal scores over 700: 26%; SAT math scores over 700: 30%; ACT scores over 30: 17%.

Faculty *Total:* 237, 79% full-time, 85% with terminal degrees. *Student/faculty ratio:* 10:1.

Majors American studies; anthropology; art; art history, criticism and conservation; biochemistry; biology/biological sciences; biomedical/medical engineer-

Trinity College (continued)
ing; chemistry; classics and languages, literatures and linguistics; comparative literature; computer engineering; computer science; creative writing; dance; dramatic/theatre arts; economics; education; electrical, electronics and communications engineering; engineering; English; environmental science; fine/studio arts; French; German; history; interdisciplinary studies; international relations and affairs; Italian; Jewish/Judaic studies; mathematics; mechanical engineering; modern languages; music; neuroscience; philosophy; physics; political science and government; psychology; public policy analysis; religious studies; Russian; sociology; Spanish; women's studies.

Academic Programs *Special study options:* accelerated degree program, adult/continuing education programs, advanced placement credit, double majors, honors programs, independent study, internships, off-campus study, student-designed majors, study abroad, summer session for credit. *ROTC:* Army (c).

Library Trinity College Library plus 2 others with 988,536 titles, 2,434 serial subscriptions, 226,532 audiovisual materials, an OPAC, a Web page.

Computers on Campus 315 computers available on campus for general student use. A campuswide network can be accessed from student residence rooms and from off campus that provide access to e-mail, web pages. Internet access, online (class) registration, at least one staffed computer lab available.

Student Life *Housing options:* coed, disabled students. Campus housing is university owned. Freshman campus housing is guaranteed. *Activities and organizations:* drama/theater group, student-run newspaper, radio and television station, choral group, Community Outreach, Habitat for Humanity, Activities Council, student government, Multi-Cultural Affairs Committee. *Campus security:* 24-hour emergency response devices and patrols, late-night transport/escort service, controlled dormitory access. *Student services:* health clinic, personal/psychological counseling, women's center.

Athletics Member NCAA. All Division III. *Intercollegiate sports:* baseball M, basketball M/W, crew M/W, cross-country running M/W, equestrian sports M(c)/W(c), fencing M(c)/W(c), field hockey W, football M, golf M, ice hockey M/W, lacrosse M/W, riflery M(c)/W(c), rugby M(c)/W(c), sailing M(c)/W(c), skiing (downhill) M(c)/W(c), soccer M/W, softball W, squash M/W, swimming M/W, tennis M/W, track and field M/W, ultimate Frisbee M(c)/W(c), volleyball M(c)/W, water polo M(c)/W(c), wrestling M. *Intramural sports:* basketball M/W, cheerleading M(c)/W(c), fencing M/W, field hockey W, football M, soccer M/W, softball M/W, squash M/W, swimming M/W, tennis M/W, track and field M/W, weight lifting M/W.

Standardized Tests *Required:* ACT or SAT I and SAT II Writing Test or SAT II Writing Test and two additional SAT II subject tests (for admission).

Costs (2003–04) *Comprehensive fee:* $38,040 includes full-time tuition ($28,740), mandatory fees ($1490), and room and board ($7810). Part-time tuition and fees vary according to program. *College room only:* $5020. Room and board charges vary according to board plan. *Payment plan:* installment. *Waivers:* adult students and employees or children of employees.

Financial Aid Of all full-time matriculated undergraduates who enrolled in 2002, 933 applied for aid, 852 were judged to have need, 852 had their need fully met. 635 Federal Work-Study jobs (averaging $1482). 7 state and other part-time jobs (averaging $1131). In 2002, 6 non-need-based awards were made. *Average percent of need met:* 100%. *Average financial aid package:* $22,161. *Average need-based loan:* $4206. *Average need-based gift aid:* $20,275. *Average non-need-based aid:* $16,557. *Average indebtedness upon graduation:* $15,850. *Financial aid deadline:* 3/1.

Applying *Options:* common application, electronic application, early admission, early decision, deferred entrance. *Application fee:* $50. *Required:* essay or personal statement, high school transcript, 3 letters of recommendation. *Recommended:* interview. *Application deadlines:* 1/15 (freshmen), 4/1 (transfers). *Early decision:* 11/15 (for plan 1), 1/15 (for plan 2). *Notification:* 4/1 (freshmen), 12/15 (early decision plan 1), 2/15 (early decision plan 2), 6/1 (transfers).

Admissions Contact Mr. Larry Dow, Dean of Admissions and Financial Aid, Trinity College, 300 Summit Street, Hartford, CT 06106-3100. *Phone:* 860-297-2180. *Fax:* 860-297-2287. *E-mail:* admissions.office@trincoll.edu.

■ *See page 2524 for a narrative description.*

UNITED STATES COAST GUARD ACADEMY
New London, Connecticut

- **Federally supported** 4-year, founded 1876
- **Calendar** semesters
- **Degree** bachelor's
- **Suburban** 110-acre campus with easy access to Providence and Hartford
- **Coed,** 1,016 undergraduate students, 100% full-time, 30% women, 70% men
- **Very difficult** entrance level, 7% of applicants were admitted

Undergraduates 1,016 full-time. Students come from 49 states and territories, 12 other countries, 93% are from out of state, 4% African American, 5% Asian American or Pacific Islander, 5% Hispanic American, 0.5% Native American, 1% international, 100% live on campus. *Retention:* 81% of 2002 full-time freshmen returned.

Freshmen *Admission:* 6,028 applied, 429 admitted, 309 enrolled. *Test scores:* SAT verbal scores over 500: 97%; SAT math scores over 500: 100%; ACT scores over 18: 100%; SAT verbal scores over 600: 64%; SAT math scores over 600: 83%; ACT scores over 24: 97%; SAT verbal scores over 700: 15%; SAT math scores over 700: 18%; ACT scores over 30: 21%.

Faculty *Student/faculty ratio:* 10:1.

Majors Civil engineering; electrical, electronics and communications engineering; management science; marine science/merchant marine officer; mechanical engineering; naval architecture and marine engineering; operations research; political science and government.

Academic Programs *Special study options:* cooperative education, double majors, honors programs, independent study, internships, off-campus study, summer session for credit.

Library Waesche Hall Library with an OPAC, a Web page.

Computers on Campus A campuswide network can be accessed from student residence rooms and from off campus that provide access to laptop for each student. Internet access, at least one staffed computer lab available. Computer purchase or lease plan available.

Student Life *Housing:* on-campus residence required through senior year. *Options:* coed. Campus housing is university owned. Freshman campus housing is guaranteed. *Activities and organizations:* drama/theater group, choral group, marching band. *Campus security:* 24-hour patrols, student patrols. *Student services:* health clinic, personal/psychological counseling, legal services.

Athletics Member NCAA. All Division III. *Intercollegiate sports:* baseball M, basketball M/W, bowling M(c)/W(c), crew M/W, cross-country running M/W, football M, golf M(c)/W(c), ice hockey M(c), lacrosse M(c)/W(c), riflery M/W, rugby M(c)/W(c), sailing M/W, soccer M/W, softball W, swimming M/W, tennis M/W(c), track and field M/W, volleyball W, water polo M(c), wrestling M. *Intramural sports:* basketball M/W, bowling M/W, cheerleading M/W, football M, golf M/W, racquetball M/W, rock climbing M(c)/W(c), sailing M/W, skiing (downhill) M(c)/W(c), soccer M/W, softball M/W, swimming M/W, table tennis M/W, track and field M/W, ultimate Frisbee M/W, volleyball M/W, water polo M, wrestling M.

Standardized Tests *Required:* SAT I or ACT (for admission).

Costs (2003–04) *Tuition:* Tuition, room and board, and medical and dental care are provided by the U.S. government. Each cadet receives a salary from which to pay for uniforms, supplies, and personal expenses. Entering freshmen are required to deposit $3000 to defray the initial cost of uniforms and equipment.

Applying *Options:* electronic application, early action. *Required:* essay or personal statement, high school transcript, 3 letters of recommendation, medical exam, physical fitness exam. *Recommended:* interview. *Application deadline:* 1/31 (freshmen). *Notification:* continuous (freshmen), 12/15 (early action).

Admissions Contact Capt. Susan D. Bibeau, Director of Admissions, United States Coast Guard Academy, 31 Mohegan Avenue, New London, CT 06320-4195. *Phone:* 860-444-8500. *Toll-free phone:* 800-883-8724. *Fax:* 860-701-6700. *E-mail:* admissions@cga.uscg.mil.

■ *See page 2550 for a narrative description.*

UNIVERSITY OF BRIDGEPORT
Bridgeport, Connecticut

- **Independent** comprehensive, founded 1927
- **Calendar** semesters
- **Degrees** certificates, associate, bachelor's, master's, doctoral, first professional, and post-master's certificates
- **Urban** 86-acre campus with easy access to New York City
- **Coed,** 1,261 undergraduate students, 80% full-time, 59% women, 41% men
- **Moderately difficult** entrance level, 84% of applicants were admitted

Undergraduates 1,003 full-time, 258 part-time. Students come from 37 states and territories, 52 other countries, 27% are from out of state, 31% African American, 5% Asian American or Pacific Islander, 13% Hispanic American, 0.3% Native American, 19% international, 11% transferred in, 46% live on campus. *Retention:* 68% of 2002 full-time freshmen returned.

Freshmen *Admission:* 1,796 applied, 1,514 admitted, 293 enrolled. *Average high school GPA:* 2.73. *Test scores:* SAT verbal scores over 500: 21%; SAT math scores over 500: 26%; ACT scores over 18: 75%; SAT verbal scores over 600: 6%; SAT math scores over 600: 6%; ACT scores over 24: 19%; SAT verbal scores over 700: 1%; SAT math scores over 700: 1%; ACT scores over 30: 4%.

Faculty *Total:* 341, 26% full-time. *Student/faculty ratio:* 12:1.

Majors Accounting; biology/biological sciences; business administration and management; clinical laboratory science/medical technology; computer engineering; computer science; dental hygiene; economics; English; fashion merchandising; finance; graphic design; humanities; human services; illustration; industrial design; information science/studies; interdisciplinary studies; interior architecture; interior design; international business/trade/commerce; international relations and affairs; journalism; liberal arts and sciences/liberal studies; marketing/marketing management; mass communication/media; mathematics; music; pre-dentistry studies; pre-law studies; pre-medical studies; pre-veterinary studies; psychology; religious studies; respiratory care therapy; social sciences.

Academic Programs *Special study options:* academic remediation for entering students, accelerated degree program, adult/continuing education programs, advanced placement credit, cooperative education, distance learning, double majors, English as a second language, honors programs, independent study, internships, off-campus study, part-time degree program, services for LD students, student-designed majors, summer session for credit. *ROTC:* Army (b).

Library Wahlstrom Library with 272,430 titles, 2,117 serial subscriptions, 5,485 audiovisual materials, an OPAC, a Web page.

Computers on Campus 500 computers available on campus for general student use. A campuswide network can be accessed from student residence rooms and from off campus. Internet access, at least one staffed computer lab available.

Student Life *Housing:* on-campus residence required through sophomore year. *Options:* coed. Campus housing is university owned. Freshman campus housing is guaranteed. *Activities and organizations:* student-run newspaper, radio station, choral group, Student Congress, international relations club, Black Students Alliance, scuba club, Japanese Student Association, national fraternities, national sororities. *Campus security:* 24-hour emergency response devices and patrols, student patrols, late-night transport/escort service. *Student services:* health clinic, personal/psychological counseling, women's center.

Athletics Member NCAA. All Division II. *Intercollegiate sports:* baseball M(s), basketball M(s)/W(s), cross-country running M/W, gymnastics W(s), soccer M(s)/W(s), softball W(s), swimming W(s), volleyball M/W(s). *Intramural sports:* basketball M/W, football M/W, golf M/W, racquetball M/W, soccer M/W, softball M/W, tennis M/W.

Standardized Tests *Required:* SAT I or ACT (for admission). *Required for some:* SAT II: Subject Tests (for admission).

Costs (2003–04) *Comprehensive fee:* $25,924 includes full-time tuition ($17,008), mandatory fees ($916), and room and board ($8000). Full-time tuition and fees vary according to program. Part-time tuition: $462 per credit. Part-time tuition and fees vary according to program. *Required fees:* $55 per term part-time. *Room and board:* Room and board charges vary according to board plan and student level. *Payment plans:* installment, deferred payment. *Waivers:* senior citizens and employees or children of employees.

Financial Aid *Average percent of need met:* 75%.

Applying *Options:* electronic application, early admission, early action, deferred entrance. *Application fee:* $25. *Required:* essay or personal statement, high school transcript, minimum 2.0 GPA. *Required for some:* interview, portfolio, audition. *Recommended:* 1 letter of recommendation, interview. *Application deadline:* rolling (freshmen), rolling (transfers). *Notification:* continuous until 8/1 (freshmen), 1/15 (early action).

Admissions Contact University of Bridgeport, 126 Park Avenue, Bridgeport, CT 06604. *Phone:* 203-576-4552. *Toll-free phone:* 800-EXCEL-UB (in-state); 800-243-9496 (out-of-state). *Fax:* 203-576-4941. *E-mail:* admit@bridgeport.edu.

UNIVERSITY OF CONNECTICUT

Storrs, Connecticut

- **State-supported** university, founded 1881
- **Calendar** semesters
- **Degrees** associate, bachelor's, master's, doctoral, first professional, post-master's, and postbachelor's certificates
- **Rural** 4104-acre campus
- **Endowment** $262.0 million
- **Coed,** 15,184 undergraduate students, 94% full-time, 52% women, 48% men
- **Moderately difficult** entrance level, 53% of applicants were admitted

Undergraduates 14,332 full-time, 852 part-time. Students come from 50 states and territories, 53 other countries, 24% are from out of state, 5% African American, 6% Asian American or Pacific Islander, 5% Hispanic American, 0.3% Native American, 1% international, 4% transferred in, 75% live on campus. *Retention:* 88% of 2002 full-time freshmen returned.

Freshmen *Admission:* 17,666 applied, 9,287 admitted, 3,208 enrolled. *Test scores:* SAT verbal scores over 500: 89%; SAT math scores over 500: 91%; SAT verbal scores over 600: 37%; SAT math scores over 600: 48%; SAT verbal scores over 700: 5%; SAT math scores over 700: 8%.

Faculty *Total:* 1,098, 77% full-time, 95% with terminal degrees. *Student/faculty ratio:* 17:1.

Majors Accounting; acting; actuarial science; agricultural economics; agricultural teacher education; agriculture; agronomy and crop science; allied health diagnostic, intervention, and treatment professions related; animal/livestock husbandry and production; animal physiology; animal sciences; anthropology; applied horticulture; applied mathematics; art history, criticism and conservation; biology/biological sciences; biomedical/medical engineering; biophysics; business/commerce; cell biology and anatomical sciences related; chemical engineering; chemistry; civil engineering; classics and languages, literatures and linguistics; clinical laboratory science/medical technology; communication/speech communication and rhetoric; computer engineering; computer science; cytotechnology; dietetics; dramatic/theatre arts; dramatic/theatre arts and stagecraft related; ecology; economics; electrical, electronics and communications engineering; elementary education; engineering physics; engineering related; English; environmental/environmental health engineering; environmental studies; European studies (Central and Eastern); finance; fine/studio arts; French; general studies; geography; geology/earth science; German; health/health care administration; history; horticultural science; human development and family studies; industrial engineering; insurance; Italian; journalism; landscape architecture; Latin American studies; linguistics; management information systems; management science; marine biology and biological oceanography; marketing/marketing management; materials engineering; mathematics; mechanical engineering; multi-/interdisciplinary studies related; music; music teacher education; natural resources/conservation; Near and Middle Eastern studies; nursing (registered nurse training); nutrition sciences; parks, recreation and leisure facilities management; pathology/experimental pathology; pharmacy; pharmacy, pharmaceutical sciences, and administration related; philosophy; physical education teaching and coaching; physical therapy; physics; political science and government; Portuguese; pre-pharmacy studies; psychology; real estate; Russian studies; sociology; Spanish; special education; statistics; theatre design and technology; theatre literature, history and criticism; urban studies/affairs; women's studies.

Academic Programs *Special study options:* academic remediation for entering students, accelerated degree program, adult/continuing education programs, advanced placement credit, cooperative education, distance learning, double majors, English as a second language, honors programs, independent study, internships, off-campus study, part-time degree program, services for LD students, student-designed majors, study abroad, summer session for credit. *ROTC:* Army (b), Air Force (b). *Unusual degree programs:* 3-2 education, pharmacy.

Library Homer Babbidge Library plus 3 others with 3.0 million titles, 17,378 serial subscriptions, 61,417 audiovisual materials, an OPAC, a Web page.

Computers on Campus 1318 computers available on campus for general student use. A campuswide network can be accessed from student residence rooms and from off campus that provide access to e-mail. Internet access, online (class) registration, at least one staffed computer lab available. Computer purchase or lease plan available.

Student Life *Housing options:* coed, men-only, women-only, disabled students. Campus housing is university owned and is provided by a third party. Freshman campus housing is guaranteed. *Activities and organizations:* drama/theater group, student-run newspaper, radio and television station, choral group, marching band, national fraternities, national sororities. *Campus security:* 24-hour emergency response devices, late-night transport/escort service. *Student services:* health clinic, personal/psychological counseling, women's center.

Athletics Member NCAA. All Division I except football (Division I-A). *Intercollegiate sports:* baseball M(s), basketball M(s)/W(s), crew W, cross-country running M(s)/W(s), field hockey W(s), golf M(s), ice hockey M(s)/W(s), lacrosse W, soccer M(s)/W(s), softball W(s), swimming M(s)/W(s), tennis M(s)/W(s), track and field M(s)/W(s), volleyball W(s). *Intramural sports:* badminton M/W, baseball M, basketball M/W, bowling M(c)/W(c), crew M(c), cross-country running M/W, equestrian sports M(c)/W(c), fencing M(c)/W(c), football M, gymnastics W(c), ice hockey M(c)/W(c), lacrosse M(c)/W(c), racquetball M/W, rugby M(c)/W(c), sailing M(c)/W(c), skiing (downhill) M(c)/W(c), soccer M/W, softball M/W, squash M/W, swimming M/W, table tennis M/W, tennis M/W, track and field M/W, volleyball M/W, water polo W, weight lifting M(c), wrestling M(c).

Standardized Tests *Required:* SAT I or ACT (for admission).

Costs (2004–05) *Tuition:* state resident $5720 full-time, $238 per credit part-time; nonresident $17,448 full-time, $727 per credit part-time. Part-time tuition and fees vary according to course load. *Required fees:* $1588 full-time, $809 per term part-time. *Room and board:* $7300; room only: $3872. Room and board charges vary according to board plan and housing facility. *Payment plans:* installment, deferred payment. *Waivers:* senior citizens and employees or children of employees.

Financial Aid Of all full-time matriculated undergraduates who enrolled in 2003, 9,671 applied for aid, 6,997 were judged to have need, 2,128 had their need fully met. 1,696 Federal Work-Study jobs (averaging $1522). 5,399 state and other part-time jobs (averaging $1818). In 2003, 1694 non-need-based awards were made. *Average percent of need met:* 75%. *Average financial aid package:* $8358. *Average need-based loan:* $3340. *Average need-based gift aid:* $5316. *Average non-need-based aid:* $5359. *Average indebtedness upon graduation:* $17,185.

University of Connecticut (continued)

Applying *Options:* common application, early admission, early action, deferred entrance. *Application fee:* $70. *Required:* essay or personal statement, high school transcript. *Recommended:* 1 letter of recommendation. *Application deadlines:* 2/1 (freshmen), 4/1 (transfers). *Notification:* 1/1 (early action), continuous until 7/1 (transfers).

Admissions Contact Mr. Brian Usher, Associate Director of Admissions, University of Connecticut, 2131 Hillside Road, Unit 3088, Storrs, CT 06269-3088. *Phone:* 860-486-3137. *Fax:* 860-486-1476. *E-mail:* beahusky@uconnvm.uconn.edu.

■ *See page 2592 for a narrative description.*

UNIVERSITY OF HARTFORD

West Hartford, Connecticut

- **Independent** comprehensive, founded 1877
- **Calendar** semesters
- **Degrees** certificates, diplomas, associate, bachelor's, master's, doctoral, post-master's, and postbachelor's certificates
- **Suburban** 320-acre campus with easy access to Hartford
- **Endowment** $73.1 million
- **Coed,** 5,612 undergraduate students, 81% full-time, 52% women, 48% men
- **Moderately difficult** entrance level, 64% of applicants were admitted

Undergraduates 4,533 full-time, 1,079 part-time. Students come from 47 states and territories, 46 other countries, 64% are from out of state, 10% African American, 2% Asian American or Pacific Islander, 4% Hispanic American, 0.3% Native American, 3% international, 5% transferred in, 66% live on campus. *Retention:* 71% of 2002 full-time freshmen returned.

Freshmen *Admission:* 12,009 applied, 7,658 admitted, 1,448 enrolled. *Test scores:* SAT verbal scores over 500: 67%; SAT math scores over 500: 71%; ACT scores over 18: 95%; SAT verbal scores over 600: 18%; SAT math scores over 600: 19%; ACT scores over 24: 41%; SAT verbal scores over 700: 1%; SAT math scores over 700: 2%; ACT scores over 30: 4%.

Faculty *Total:* 719, 44% full-time. *Student/faculty ratio:* 13:1.

Majors Accounting; architectural engineering technology; art history, criticism and conservation; audio engineering; biology/biological sciences; biomedical/medical engineering; business administration and management; business/managerial economics; ceramic arts and ceramics; chemistry; cinematography and film/video production; civil engineering; clinical laboratory science/medical technology; commercial and advertising art; communication/speech communication and rhetoric; community organization and advocacy; computer and information sciences; computer engineering; criminal justice/police science; dance; dramatic/theatre arts; drawing; early childhood education; economics; economics related; electrical and electronic engineering technologies related; electrical, electronic and communications engineering technology; electrical, electronics and communications engineering; elementary education; engineering; engineering technologies related; engineering technology; English; environmental/environmental health engineering; film/cinema studies; finance; fine arts related; foreign languages and literatures; general studies; health science; history; information science/studies; insurance; interdisciplinary studies; jazz/jazz studies; Jewish/Judaic studies; legal assistant/paralegal; legal studies; liberal arts and sciences and humanities related; liberal arts and sciences/liberal studies; management information systems; manufacturing engineering; mathematics; mathematics and statistics related; mechanical engineering; mechanical engineering technologies related; medical radiologic technology; multi-/interdisciplinary studies related; music; music history, literature, and theory; music management and merchandising; music performance; music related; music teacher education; music theory and composition; nursing (registered nurse training); occupational therapy; painting; philosophy; photography; physical therapy; physics; political science and government; pre-dentistry studies; pre-medical studies; pre-veterinary studies; psychology; respiratory care therapy; sculpture; secondary education; social sciences related; sociology; special education; technical and business writing; women's studies.

Academic Programs *Special study options:* academic remediation for entering students, adult/continuing education programs, advanced placement credit, cooperative education, distance learning, double majors, English as a second language, honors programs, independent study, internships, off-campus study, part-time degree program, services for LD students, student-designed majors, study abroad, summer session for credit. *ROTC:* Army (c), Air Force (c). *Unusual degree programs:* 3-2 engineering with Stonehill College.

Library Mortenson Library with 452,060 titles, 2,121 serial subscriptions, 30,811 audiovisual materials, an OPAC, a Web page.

Computers on Campus 380 computers available on campus for general student use. A campuswide network can be accessed from student residence rooms and from off campus that provide access to student web pages. Internet access, online (class) registration, at least one staffed computer lab available. Computer purchase or lease plan available.

Student Life *Housing options:* coed, women-only, disabled students. Campus housing is university owned and leased by the school. *Activities and organizations:* drama/theater group, student-run newspaper, radio and television station, choral group, Program Council, Brothers and Sisters United, Hillel, Student Government Association, Residence Hall Association, national fraternities, national sororities. *Campus security:* 24-hour emergency response devices and patrols, late-night transport/escort service, controlled dormitory access, bicycle patrols. *Student services:* health clinic, personal/psychological counseling, women's center, legal services.

Athletics Member NCAA. All Division I. *Intercollegiate sports:* badminton M(c)/W(c), baseball M(s), basketball M(s)/W(s), cross-country running M(s)/W(s), golf M(s)(c)/W(s)(c), lacrosse M(s), racquetball M(c)/W(c), rugby M(c)/W(c), soccer M(s)/W(s), softball W(s), squash M(c)/W(c), tennis M(s)/W(s), volleyball M(c)/W(s). *Intramural sports:* basketball M/W, racquetball M/W, soccer M/W, softball M/W, tennis M/W, ultimate Frisbee M/W, volleyball M/W, water polo M/W.

Standardized Tests *Required:* SAT I or ACT (for admission).

Costs (2003–04) *Comprehensive fee:* $31,080 includes full-time tuition ($21,330), mandatory fees ($1140), and room and board ($8610). Part-time tuition and fees vary according to course load. *College room only:* $5310. Room and board charges vary according to board plan and housing facility. *Payment plans:* tuition prepayment, installment. *Waivers:* senior citizens and employees or children of employees.

Financial Aid Of all full-time matriculated undergraduates who enrolled in 2002, 3,059 applied for aid, 2,747 were judged to have need, 2,066 had their need fully met. 455 Federal Work-Study jobs (averaging $1103). 93 state and other part-time jobs (averaging $8530). In 2002, 359 non-need-based awards were made. *Average percent of need met:* 73%. *Average financial aid package:* $18,271. *Average need-based loan:* $5344. *Average need-based gift aid:* $9800. *Average non-need-based aid:* $7642. *Average indebtedness upon graduation:* $23,938.

Applying *Options:* common application, electronic application, early admission, deferred entrance. *Application fee:* $35. *Required:* high school transcript. *Recommended:* essay or personal statement, 2 letters of recommendation, interview. *Application deadline:* rolling (freshmen), rolling (transfers). *Notification:* continuous (freshmen), continuous (transfers).

Admissions Contact Mr. Richard Zeiser, Dean of Admissions, University of Hartford, West Hartford, CT 06117. *Phone:* 860-768-4296. *Toll-free phone:* 800-947-4303. *Fax:* 860-768-4961. *E-mail:* admission@hartford.edu.

■ *See page 2612 for a narrative description.*

UNIVERSITY OF NEW HAVEN

West Haven, Connecticut

- **Independent** comprehensive, founded 1920
- **Calendar** 4-1-4
- **Degrees** certificates, associate, bachelor's, master's, and postbachelor's certificates
- **Suburban** 78-acre campus with easy access to Hartford, New Haven
- **Endowment** $6.0 million
- **Coed,** 2,627 undergraduate students, 76% full-time, 45% women, 55% men
- **Moderately difficult** entrance level, 67% of applicants were admitted

Undergraduates 2,000 full-time, 627 part-time. Students come from 30 states and territories, 58 other countries, 34% are from out of state, 11% African American, 2% Asian American or Pacific Islander, 6% Hispanic American, 0.5% Native American, 5% international, 6% transferred in, 62% live on campus. *Retention:* 78% of 2002 full-time freshmen returned.

Freshmen *Admission:* 3,025 applied, 2,039 admitted, 631 enrolled. *Average high school GPA:* 3.00. *Test scores:* SAT verbal scores over 500: 56%; SAT math scores over 500: 57%; SAT verbal scores over 600: 16%; SAT math scores over 600: 18%; SAT verbal scores over 700: 1%; SAT math scores over 700: 2%.

Faculty *Total:* 413, 43% full-time. *Student/faculty ratio:* 10:1.

Majors Accounting; aeronautical/aerospace engineering technology; art; aviation/airway management; biology/biotechnology laboratory technician; business administration and management; business/managerial economics; chemical engineering; chemistry; civil engineering; clinical laboratory science/medical technology; commercial and advertising art; computer and information sciences; corrections; criminalistics and criminal science; criminal justice/law enforcement administration; criminal justice/police science; criminal justice/safety; dental hygiene; dietetics; economics; electrical, electronics and communications engineering; engineering; English; environmental studies; finance; fire protection and safety technology; fire science; fire services administration; forensic science and technology; general studies; history; hospitality administration; hotel/motel administration; human resources management; industrial engineering; industrial technology; interior architecture; international business/trade/commerce; juvenile corrections; legal studies; liberal arts and sciences/liberal studies; marine biology and biological oceanography; marketing/marketing management; mathematics; mechanical engineering; mechanical engineering/mechanical technology; music; music management and merchandising; occupational safety and health technology; political science and government; psychology; security and loss prevention; sport and fitness administration; tourism and travel services management.

Academic Programs *Special study options:* academic remediation for entering students, accelerated degree program, adult/continuing education programs, advanced placement credit, cooperative education, double majors, English as a second language, honors programs, independent study, internships, part-time degree program, services for LD students, student-designed majors, summer session for credit. *ROTC:* Navy (c). *Unusual degree programs:* 3-2 environmental science.

Library Marvin K. Peterson Library with 165,044 titles, 1,294 serial subscriptions, 605 audiovisual materials, an OPAC, a Web page.

Computers on Campus 800 computers available on campus for general student use. A campuswide network can be accessed from student residence rooms and from off campus that provide access to e-mail. Internet access, at least one staffed computer lab available.

Student Life *Housing:* on-campus residence required through sophomore year. *Options:* coed. Campus housing is university owned. Freshman applicants given priority for college housing. *Activities and organizations:* drama/theater group, student-run newspaper, radio and television station, choral group, intramural athletics, WNHU (radio station), USGA (Undergraduate Student Government Association), American Criminal Justice Association, Black Student Union, national fraternities. *Campus security:* 24-hour emergency response devices and patrols, late-night transport/escort service, escort service, vehicle, bicycle and foot patrols, crime prevention programs. *Student services:* health clinic, personal/psychological counseling.

Athletics Member NCAA. All Division II. *Intercollegiate sports:* baseball M(s), basketball M(s)/W(s), cheerleading W, cross-country running M(s)/W(s), football M(s), golf M/W, lacrosse W(s), soccer M(s)/W(s), softball W(s), tennis W(s), track and field M(s)/W(s), volleyball M(s)/W(s). *Intramural sports:* basketball M/W, cross-country running M/W, football M, lacrosse M, racquetball M/W, soccer M/W, softball M/W, table tennis M/W, tennis M/W, volleyball M/W, weight lifting M/W.

Standardized Tests *Required:* SAT I or ACT (for admission). *Recommended:* SAT I (for admission).

Costs (2003–04) *Comprehensive fee:* $29,235 includes full-time tuition ($20,130), mandatory fees ($605), and room and board ($8500). Full-time tuition and fees vary according to course load and program. Part-time tuition: $671 per credit hour. Part-time tuition and fees vary according to class time, course load, location, and program. *College room only:* $5160. Room and board charges vary according to board plan and housing facility. *Payment plan:* installment. *Waivers:* employees or children of employees.

Financial Aid Of all full-time matriculated undergraduates who enrolled in 2002, 1,483 applied for aid, 1,317 were judged to have need, 419 had their need fully met. 123 Federal Work-Study jobs (averaging $1072). In 2002, 218 non-need-based awards were made. *Average percent of need met:* 76%. *Average financial aid package:* $14,583. *Average need-based loan:* $6120. *Average need-based gift aid:* $9373. *Average non-need-based aid:* $11,153. *Average indebtedness upon graduation:* $16,300.

Applying *Options:* common application, deferred entrance. *Application fee:* $50. *Required:* essay or personal statement, high school transcript. *Recommended:* minimum 2.75 GPA, interview. *Application deadline:* rolling (freshmen), rolling (transfers). *Notification:* continuous (freshmen), continuous (transfers).

Admissions Contact Ms. Jane C. Sangeloty, Director of Undergraduate Admissions, University of New Haven, Bayer Hall, 300 Orange Avenue, West Haven, CT 06516. *Phone:* 203-932-7319. *Toll-free phone:* 800-DIAL-UNH. *Fax:* 203-931-6093. *E-mail:* adminfo@newhaven.edu.

■ *See page 2670 for a narrative description.*

WESLEYAN UNIVERSITY
Middletown, Connecticut

- **Independent** university, founded 1831
- **Calendar** semesters
- **Degrees** bachelor's, master's, doctoral, and post-master's certificates
- **Small-town** 120-acre campus
- **Endowment** $472.3 million
- **Coed,** 2,730 undergraduate students, 99% full-time, 53% women, 47% men
- **Most difficult** entrance level, 27% of applicants were admitted

Undergraduates 2,704 full-time, 26 part-time. Students come from 50 states and territories, 47 other countries, 90% are from out of state, 8% African American, 8% Asian American or Pacific Islander, 6% Hispanic American, 0.3% Native American, 6% international, 2% transferred in, 94% live on campus. *Retention:* 95% of 2002 full-time freshmen returned.

Freshmen *Admission:* 6,955 applied, 1,854 admitted, 715 enrolled. *Test scores:* SAT verbal scores over 500: 99%; SAT math scores over 500: 100%; ACT scores over 18: 100%; SAT verbal scores over 600: 87%; SAT math scores over 600: 92%; ACT scores over 24: 97%; SAT verbal scores over 700: 51%; SAT math scores over 700: 44%; ACT scores over 30: 62%.

Faculty *Total:* 362, 91% full-time, 90% with terminal degrees. *Student/faculty ratio:* 9:1.

Majors African-American/Black studies; American studies; anthropology; art history, criticism and conservation; Asian studies (East); astronomy; biochemistry; biology/biological sciences; chemistry; classics and languages, literatures and linguistics; computer science; dance; dramatic/theatre arts; economics; English; environmental studies; European studies (Central and Eastern); film/cinema studies; fine/studio arts; French; geology/earth science; German; history; humanities; interdisciplinary studies; Italian; Latin American studies; liberal arts and sciences/liberal studies; mathematics; medieval and Renaissance studies; molecular biology; music; neuroscience; philosophy; physics; political science and government; psychology; religious studies; Romance languages; Russian; Russian studies; science, technology and society; social sciences; sociology; Spanish; women's studies.

Academic Programs *Special study options:* accelerated degree program, adult/continuing education programs, advanced placement credit, double majors, English as a second language, honors programs, independent study, internships, off-campus study, services for LD students, student-designed majors, study abroad, summer session for credit. *ROTC:* Air Force (c). *Unusual degree programs:* 3-2 engineering with Columbia University, California Institute of Technology.

Library Olin Memorial Library plus 3 others with 1.2 million titles, 4,281 serial subscriptions, 43,808 audiovisual materials, an OPAC, a Web page.

Computers on Campus 250 computers available on campus for general student use. A campuswide network can be accessed from student residence rooms and from off campus that provide access to electronic portfolio. Internet access, online (class) registration, at least one staffed computer lab available. Computer purchase or lease plan available.

Student Life *Housing:* on-campus residence required for freshman year. *Options:* coed. Campus housing is university owned and leased by the school. Freshman campus housing is guaranteed. *Activities and organizations:* drama/theater group, student-run newspaper, radio station, choral group, community service, Students of Color groups, theater (student and faculty productions), campus publications, intramurals, national fraternities, national sororities. *Campus security:* 24-hour emergency response devices and patrols, student patrols, late-night transport/escort service, controlled dormitory access. *Student services:* health clinic, personal/psychological counseling, women's center.

Athletics Member NCAA. All Division III. *Intercollegiate sports:* baseball M, basketball M/W, crew M/W, cross-country running M/W, equestrian sports M(c)/W(c), field hockey W, football M, golf M/W, ice hockey M/W, lacrosse M/W, rugby M(c)/W(c), sailing M(c)/W(c), skiing (downhill) M(c)/W(c), soccer M/W, softball W, squash M/W, swimming M/W, table tennis M(c)/W(c), tennis M/W, track and field M/W, ultimate Frisbee M(c)/W(c), volleyball M(c)/W, water polo M(c)/W(c), wrestling M. *Intramural sports:* badminton M/W, basketball M/W, bowling M/W, crew M/W, cross-country running M/W, ice hockey M/W, racquetball M/W, soccer M/W, softball M/W, squash M/W, table tennis M/W, tennis M/W, track and field M/W, ultimate Frisbee M/W, volleyball M/W.

Standardized Tests *Required:* SAT I and SAT II or ACT (for admission).

Costs (2003–04) *Comprehensive fee:* $38,224 includes full-time tuition ($29,784), mandatory fees ($214), and room and board ($8226). *College room only:* $5138. *Payment plan:* installment.

Financial Aid Of all full-time matriculated undergraduates who enrolled in 2002, 1,430 applied for aid, 1,304 were judged to have need, 1,304 had their need fully met. 1,121 Federal Work-Study jobs (averaging $1822). 92 state and other part-time jobs (averaging $1865). *Average percent of need met:* 100%. *Average financial aid package:* $24,553. *Average need-based loan:* $4760. *Average need-based gift aid:* $19,328. *Average indebtedness upon graduation:* $21,389. *Financial aid deadline:* 2/1.

Applying *Options:* common application, electronic application, early admission, early decision, deferred entrance. *Application fee:* $55. *Required:* essay or personal statement, high school transcript, 3 letters of recommendation. *Recommended:* interview. *Application deadlines:* 1/1 (freshmen), 3/15 (transfers). *Early decision:* 11/15 (for plan 1), 1/1 (for plan 2). *Notification:* 4/1 (freshmen), 12/15 (early decision plan 1), 2/15 (early decision plan 2), 5/15 (transfers).

Wesleyan University (continued)

Admissions Contact Ms. Nancy Hargrave Meislahn, Dean of Admission and Financial Aid, Wesleyan University, Stewart M Reid House, 70 Wyllys Avenue, Middletown, CT 06459-0265. *Phone:* 860-685-3000. *Fax:* 860-685-3001. *E-mail:* admissions@wesleyan.edu.

WESTERN CONNECTICUT STATE UNIVERSITY

Danbury, Connecticut

- **State-supported** comprehensive, founded 1903, part of Connecticut State University System
- **Calendar** semesters
- **Degrees** associate, bachelor's, and master's
- **Urban** 340-acre campus with easy access to New York City
- **Coed,** 5,236 undergraduate students, 73% full-time, 55% women, 45% men
- **Moderately difficult** entrance level, 55% of applicants were admitted

Undergraduates 3,814 full-time, 1,422 part-time. Students come from 25 states and territories, 19 other countries, 12% are from out of state, 6% African American, 3% Asian American or Pacific Islander, 6% Hispanic American, 0.3% Native American, 0.5% international, 6% transferred in, 33% live on campus. *Retention:* 71% of 2002 full-time freshmen returned.

Freshmen *Admission:* 3,626 applied, 2,008 admitted, 820 enrolled. *Test scores:* SAT verbal scores over 500: 47%; SAT math scores over 500: 43%; SAT verbal scores over 600: 8%; SAT math scores over 600: 10%; SAT verbal scores over 700: 1%; SAT math scores over 700: 1%.

Faculty *Total:* 443, 42% full-time. *Student/faculty ratio:* 17:1.

Majors Accounting; American studies; anthropology; art; atmospheric sciences and meteorology; biology/biological sciences; business administration and management; chemistry; clinical laboratory science/medical technology; commercial and advertising art; community health services counseling; computer science; criminal justice/police science; dramatic/theatre arts; economics; education; elementary education; English; environmental studies; finance; geology/earth science; health teacher education; history; liberal arts and sciences/liberal studies; management information systems; marketing/marketing management; mass communication/media; mathematics; music; music history, literature, and theory; music teacher education; nursing (registered nurse training); political science and government; pre-dentistry studies; pre-medical studies; psychology; secondary education; social sciences; social work; sociology; Spanish.

Academic Programs *Special study options:* academic remediation for entering students, accelerated degree program, adult/continuing education programs, advanced placement credit, cooperative education, distance learning, double majors, English as a second language, honors programs, independent study, internships, off-campus study, part-time degree program, services for LD students, student-designed majors, study abroad, summer session for credit. *ROTC:* Army (c), Air Force (c).

Library Ruth Haas Library plus 1 other with 182,915 titles, 1,273 serial subscriptions, 8,654 audiovisual materials, an OPAC, a Web page.

Computers on Campus 400 computers available on campus for general student use. A campuswide network can be accessed from student residence rooms and from off campus. Internet access, online (class) registration, at least one staffed computer lab available.

Student Life *Housing options:* coed, women-only. Campus housing is university owned. Freshman campus housing is guaranteed. *Activities and organizations:* drama/theater group, student-run newspaper, radio station, choral group, Justice and Law Club, Black Student Alliance, Student Government Association, Music Education National Conference, WXCI, national fraternities, national sororities. *Campus security:* 24-hour emergency response devices and patrols, student patrols, late-night transport/escort service, controlled dormitory access. *Student services:* health clinic, personal/psychological counseling.

Athletics Member NCAA. All Division III. *Intercollegiate sports:* baseball M, basketball M/W, football M, lacrosse W, soccer M/W, softball W, swimming W, tennis M/W, volleyball W. *Intramural sports:* basketball M/W, football M, ice hockey M(c), lacrosse M(c), rugby M(c), soccer M/W, softball M/W, ultimate Frisbee M/W, volleyball M/W.

Standardized Tests *Required:* SAT I or ACT (for admission).

Costs (2003–04) *Tuition:* state resident $2648 full-time, $250 per semester hour part-time; nonresident $9636 full-time, $250 per semester hour part-time. Full-time tuition and fees vary according to reciprocity agreements. *Required fees:* $2396 full-time, $55 per term part-time. *Room and board:* $6580; room only: $4240. Room and board charges vary according to housing facility. *Payment plan:* installment. *Waivers:* senior citizens and employees or children of employees.

Financial Aid Of all full-time matriculated undergraduates who enrolled in 2001, 2,211 applied for aid, 1,518 were judged to have need, 344 had their need fully met. 78 Federal Work-Study jobs (averaging $1180). 417 state and other part-time jobs (averaging $2273). In 2001, 141 non-need-based awards were made. *Average percent of need met:* 63%. *Average financial aid package:* $6314. *Average need-based loan:* $3480. *Average need-based gift aid:* $3348. *Average non-need-based aid:* $2056. *Financial aid deadline:* 4/15.

Applying *Options:* common application, electronic application, early admission, deferred entrance. *Application fee:* $40. *Required:* high school transcript. *Recommended:* essay or personal statement, letters of recommendation, interview. *Application deadlines:* 5/1 (freshmen), 7/1 (transfers). *Notification:* continuous (freshmen), continuous (transfers).

Admissions Contact Mr. William Hawkins, Enrollment Management Officer, Western Connecticut State University, 181 White Street, Danbury, CT 06810. *Phone:* 203-837-9000. *Toll-free phone:* 877-837-9278.

■ *See page 2810 for a narrative description.*

YALE UNIVERSITY

New Haven, Connecticut

- **Independent** university, founded 1701
- **Calendar** semesters
- **Degrees** bachelor's, master's, doctoral, first professional, and post-master's certificates
- **Urban** 200-acre campus with easy access to New York City
- **Endowment** $11.0 billion
- **Coed,** 5,354 undergraduate students, 99% full-time, 50% women, 50% men
- **Most difficult** entrance level, 11% of applicants were admitted

Undergraduates 5,292 full-time, 62 part-time. Students come from 50 states and territories, 70 other countries, 92% are from out of state, 8% African American, 13% Asian American or Pacific Islander, 6% Hispanic American, 0.6% Native American, 9% international, 0.4% transferred in, 83% live on campus. *Retention:* 98% of 2001 full-time freshmen returned.

Freshmen *Admission:* 17,735 applied, 2,014 admitted, 1,352 enrolled.

Faculty *Total:* 1,389, 72% full-time, 85% with terminal degrees. *Student/faculty ratio:* 7:1.

Majors African-American/Black studies; African studies; American studies; ancient/classical Greek; anthropology; applied mathematics; archeology; architecture; art; art history, criticism and conservation; Asian studies (East); astronomy; astrophysics; biology/biological sciences; biomedical/medical engineering; cell biology and anatomical sciences related; chemical engineering; chemistry; Chinese; classics and languages, literatures and linguistics; cognitive psychology and psycholinguistics; computer and information sciences; cultural studies; dramatic/theatre arts; ecology; economics; electrical, electronics and communications engineering; engineering physics; engineering science; English; environmental/environmental health engineering; environmental studies; ethnic, cultural minority, and gender studies related; evolutionary biology; film/cinema studies; foreign languages related; French; geological and earth sciences/geosciences related; German; history; humanities; Italian; Japanese; Jewish/Judaic studies; Latin; Latin American studies; linguistics; literature; mathematics; mathematics and computer science; mechanical engineering; molecular biology; multi-/interdisciplinary studies related; music; philosophy; physics; political science and government; Portuguese; psychology; religious studies; Russian; Russian studies; sociology; South Asian languages; Spanish; systems science and theory; women's studies.

Academic Programs *Special study options:* accelerated degree program, advanced placement credit, double majors, English as a second language, honors programs, independent study, part-time degree program, student-designed majors, study abroad, summer session for credit. *ROTC:* Army (c), Air Force (c).

Library Sterling Memorial Library plus 20 others with 10.8 million titles, 63,656 serial subscriptions, 2.9 million audiovisual materials, an OPAC, a Web page.

Computers on Campus 350 computers available on campus for general student use. A campuswide network can be accessed from student residence rooms and from off campus. At least one staffed computer lab available.

Student Life *Housing:* on-campus residence required through sophomore year. *Options:* coed. Campus housing is university owned. Freshman campus housing is guaranteed. *Activities and organizations:* drama/theater group, student-run newspaper, radio station, choral group, marching band, community service, intramural sports, theater productions, music groups, campus publications, national fraternities, national sororities. *Campus security:* 24-hour emergency response devices and patrols, late-night transport/escort service, controlled dormitory access. *Student services:* health clinic, personal/psychological counseling, women's center.

Athletics Member NCAA. All Division I except football (Division I-AA). *Intercollegiate sports:* baseball M, basketball M/W, cheerleading M(s)/W(s), crew M/W, cross-country running M/W, fencing M/W, field hockey W, golf M/W, gymnastics W, ice hockey M/W, lacrosse M/W, soccer M/W, softball W, squash M/W, swimming M/W, table tennis M(c), tennis M/W, track and field M/W, volleyball M(c)/W. *Intramural sports:* badminton M(c)/W(c), baseball M, basketball M/W, bowling M/W, crew M/W, cross-country running M/W, equestrian sports M(c)/W(c), field hockey W, football M/W, golf M/W, ice hockey M/W, racquetball M/W, riflery M(c)/W(c), rugby M(c)/W(c), sailing M(c)/W(c), skiing (cross-country) M(c)/W(c), skiing (downhill) M(c)/W(c), soccer M/W, softball M/W, squash M/W, swimming M/W, table tennis M/W, tennis M/W, ultimate Frisbee M/W, volleyball M/W, water polo M/W, wrestling M(c).

Standardized Tests *Required:* SAT I and SAT II or ACT (for admission).

Costs (2003–04) *Comprehensive fee:* $37,000 includes full-time tuition ($28,400) and room and board ($8600). *College room only:* $4700.

Financial Aid Of all full-time matriculated undergraduates who enrolled in 2003, 2,595 applied for aid, 2,096 were judged to have need, 2,096 had their need fully met. 1,202 Federal Work-Study jobs (averaging $1829). 334 state and other part-time jobs (averaging $2634). *Average percent of need met:* 100%. *Average financial aid package:* $26,978. *Average need-based loan:* $2591. *Average need-based gift aid:* $23,574. *Average indebtedness upon graduation:* $16,911.

Applying *Options:* electronic application, early admission, early decision, deferred entrance. *Application fee:* $65. *Required:* essay or personal statement, high school transcript, 3 letters of recommendation. *Recommended:* interview. *Application deadlines:* 12/31 (freshmen), 3/1 (transfers). *Early decision:* 11/1. *Notification:* 4/1 (freshmen), 12/15 (early decision), 6/4 (transfers).

Admissions Contact Admissions Director, Yale University, PO Box 208234, New Haven, CT 06520-8324. *Phone:* 203-432-9300. *Fax:* 203-432-9392. *E-mail:* undergraduate.admissions@yale.edu.

■ See page 2882 for a narrative description.

DELAWARE

DELAWARE STATE UNIVERSITY

Dover, Delaware

- **State-supported** comprehensive, founded 1891, part of Delaware Higher Education Commission
- **Calendar** semesters
- **Degrees** bachelor's, master's, and doctoral
- **Small-town** 400-acre campus
- **Endowment** $13.4 million
- **Coed,** 2,992 undergraduate students, 85% full-time, 58% women, 42% men
- **Moderately difficult** entrance level, 50% of applicants were admitted

Undergraduates 2,556 full-time, 436 part-time. Students come from 31 states and territories, 44% are from out of state, 80% African American, 1% Asian American or Pacific Islander, 2% Hispanic American, 0.3% Native American, 0.4% international, 6% transferred in, 46% live on campus. *Retention:* 68% of 2002 full-time freshmen returned.

Freshmen *Admission:* 3,204 applied, 1,601 admitted, 618 enrolled. *Average high school GPA:* 2.70. *Test scores:* SAT verbal scores over 500: 13%; SAT math scores over 500: 14%; SAT verbal scores over 600: 2%; SAT math scores over 600: 2%.

Faculty *Total:* 264, 70% full-time. *Student/faculty ratio:* 15:1.

Majors Accounting; agricultural and horticultural plant breeding; agricultural business and management; agriculture; agronomy and crop science; airline pilot and flight crew; animal sciences; art; arts management; art teacher education; aviation/airway management; banking and financial support services; biology/biological sciences; biology teacher education; biotechnology; broadcast journalism; business administration and management; business/managerial economics; business teacher education; chemistry; chemistry teacher education; civil engineering; clothing/textiles; community health liaison; computer and information sciences; computer science; criminal justice/law enforcement administration; dietetics; early childhood education; e-commerce; electrical, electronic and communications engineering technology; elementary education; engineering physics; English; English/language arts teacher education; environmental science; family and consumer sciences/human sciences; fashion merchandising; finance; fish/game management; foods, nutrition, and wellness; forestry; French; French language teacher education; history; hospitality administration; human resources management; information science/studies; journalism; kindergarten/preschool education; marketing/marketing management; mathematics; mathematics teacher education; mechanical engineering; mechanical engineering/mechanical technology; middle school education; music; musical instrument technology; music teacher education; nursing (registered nurse training); parks, recreation and leisure facilities management; physical education teaching and coaching; physics; physics teacher education; political science and government; poultry science; pre-engineering; pre-veterinary studies; psychology; public relations; radio and television; science teacher education; secondary education; social work; sociology; Spanish; Spanish language teacher education; special education; special education (early childhood); sport and fitness administration; systems engineering; tourism and travel services management; trade and industrial teacher education; voice and opera; wildlife and wildlands science and management.

Academic Programs *Special study options:* academic remediation for entering students, accelerated degree program, adult/continuing education programs, advanced placement credit, cooperative education, distance learning, double majors, English as a second language, honors programs, independent study, internships, off-campus study, part-time degree program, services for LD students, student-designed majors, summer session for credit. *ROTC:* Army (b), Air Force (b). *Unusual degree programs:* 3-2 engineering with University of Delaware.

Library William C. Jason Library with 204,127 titles, 3,094 serial subscriptions, 13,775 audiovisual materials, an OPAC.

Computers on Campus 641 computers available on campus for general student use. A campuswide network can be accessed from student residence rooms and from off campus that provide access to online grade access, e-mail. Internet access, online (class) registration, at least one staffed computer lab available.

Student Life *Activities and organizations:* drama/theater group, student-run newspaper, radio and television station, choral group, marching band, NAACP, Women's Senate, Men's Council, national fraternities, national sororities. *Campus security:* 24-hour emergency response devices and patrols, student patrols, late-night transport/escort service, controlled dormitory access. *Student services:* health clinic, personal/psychological counseling, women's center.

Athletics Member NCAA. All Division I except football (Division I-AA). *Intercollegiate sports:* baseball M, basketball M(s)/W(s), bowling W(s), cross-country running M(s)/W(s), softball W(s), tennis M(s)/W(s), track and field M(s)/W(s), volleyball W(s), wrestling M(s). *Intramural sports:* basketball M/W, bowling M/W, field hockey W, football M, racquetball M/W, swimming M/W, table tennis M/W, tennis M/W, volleyball M/W.

Standardized Tests *Required:* SAT I or ACT (for admission).

Costs (2003–04) *Tuition:* state resident $3996 full-time, $167 per credit hour part-time; nonresident $8976 full-time, $374 per credit hour part-time. *Required fees:* $300 full-time, $90 per term part-time. *Room and board:* $6344; room only: $4004.

Financial Aid Of all full-time matriculated undergraduates who enrolled in 2002, 2,335 applied for aid, 2,031 were judged to have need, 786 had their need fully met. In 2002, 528 non-need-based awards were made. *Average percent of need met:* 76%. *Average financial aid package:* $7691. *Average non-need-based aid:* $5306.

Applying *Options:* common application, electronic application, early admission. *Application fee:* $15. *Required:* high school transcript, minimum 2.0 GPA, 2 letters of recommendation. *Recommended:* interview. *Application deadlines:* 4/1 (freshmen), 4/1 (transfers).

Admissions Contact Mr. Jimmy Arrington, Assistant Vice President for Enrollment Management/Director of Admissions, Delaware State University, 1200 North Dupont Highway, Dover, DE 19901. *Phone:* 302-857-6344. *Toll-free phone:* 800-845-2544. *Fax:* 302-857-6352. *E-mail:* dadmiss@dsc.edu.

GOLDEY-BEACOM COLLEGE

Wilmington, Delaware

- **Independent** comprehensive, founded 1886
- **Calendar** semesters
- **Degrees** associate, bachelor's, and master's
- **Suburban** 27-acre campus with easy access to Philadelphia
- **Endowment** $1.7 million
- **Coed,** 1,049 undergraduate students, 98% full-time, 55% women, 45% men
- **Moderately difficult** entrance level, 78% of applicants were admitted

Goldey-Beacom is a small, private, nationally accredited college offering challenging undergraduate degrees in business as well as a master's in business administration. The College is known for dedicated faculty members, small class size, and individual attention and is recognized regionally as a leader in the business field. Apartment-style housing is available on the safe, suburban campus located 15 minutes from downtown Wilmington.

Undergraduates 1,028 full-time, 21 part-time. Students come from 15 states and territories, 50 other countries, 50% are from out of state, 24% African American, 10% Asian American or Pacific Islander, 5% Hispanic American, 16% live on campus. *Retention:* 82% of 2002 full-time freshmen returned.

Freshmen *Admission:* 408 applied, 319 admitted. *Average high school GPA:* 3.10. *Test scores:* SAT verbal scores over 500: 33%; SAT math scores over 500: 32%; SAT verbal scores over 600: 6%; SAT math scores over 600: 6%; SAT verbal scores over 700: 1%; SAT math scores over 700: 2%.

Faculty *Total:* 49, 51% full-time, 43% with terminal degrees. *Student/faculty ratio:* 28:1.

Goldey-Beacom College (continued)

Majors Accounting; business administration and management; finance; information science/studies; international business/trade/commerce; management information systems; marketing/marketing management.

Academic Programs *Special study options:* academic remediation for entering students, accelerated degree program, advanced placement credit, cooperative education, honors programs, internships, part-time degree program, study abroad, summer session for credit.

Library J. Wilbur Hirons Library with 29,700 titles, 817 serial subscriptions, a Web page.

Computers on Campus 136 computers available on campus for general student use. A campuswide network can be accessed from student residence rooms and from off campus. Internet access, at least one staffed computer lab available.

Student Life *Housing options:* coed. *Activities and organizations:* drama/theater group, student-run newspaper, choral group, Marketing/Management Association, Circle K International, Data Processing Management Association, GBC singers, national fraternities, national sororities. *Campus security:* 24-hour emergency response devices. *Student services:* health clinic.

Athletics Member NCAA. All Division II. *Intercollegiate sports:* basketball M(s)/W(s), field hockey W(c), soccer M(s)/W(s), softball W(s), volleyball W(s). *Intramural sports:* basketball M/W, football M, golf M/W, soccer M/W, softball M/W, tennis M/W, volleyball M/W.

Standardized Tests *Required:* SAT I (for admission). *Required for some:* DTLS, DTMS.

Costs (2003–04) *Tuition:* $11,025 full-time, $315 per credit hour part-time. *Required fees:* $324 full-time, $9 per credit hour part-time. *Room only:* $3937. *Payment plans:* installment, deferred payment. *Waivers:* employees or children of employees.

Applying *Options:* common application, electronic application, early admission, deferred entrance. *Application fee:* $30. *Required:* high school transcript, minimum 2.0 GPA. *Required for some:* 1 letter of recommendation, interview. *Application deadline:* rolling (freshmen), rolling (transfers). *Notification:* continuous until 8/15 (freshmen), continuous until 8/15 (transfers).

Admissions Contact Mr. Kevin M. McIntyre, Dean of Admissions, Goldey-Beacom College, 4701 Limestone Road, Wilmington, DE 19808-1999. *Phone:* 302-998-8814 Ext. 266. *Toll-free phone:* 800-833-4877. *Fax:* 302-996-5408. *E-mail:* mcintyrk@goldey.gbc.edu.

UNIVERSITY OF DELAWARE

Newark, Delaware

- **State-related** university, founded 1743
- **Calendar** 4-1-4
- **Degrees** associate, bachelor's, master's, and doctoral (enrollment data for undergraduate students does not include non-degree-seeking students)
- **Small-town** 1000-acre campus with easy access to Philadelphia and Baltimore
- **Endowment** $780.2 million
- **Coed,** 17,200 undergraduate students, 86% full-time, 58% women, 42% men
- **Moderately difficult** entrance level, 42% of applicants were admitted

Undergraduates 14,864 full-time, 2,336 part-time. Students come from 52 states and territories, 100 other countries, 58% are from out of state, 6% African American, 3% Asian American or Pacific Islander, 3% Hispanic American, 0.3% Native American, 1% international, 3% transferred in, 50% live on campus. *Retention:* 90% of 2002 full-time freshmen returned.

Freshmen *Admission:* 22,020 applied, 9,267 admitted, 3,384 enrolled. *Average high school GPA:* 3.5. *Test scores:* SAT verbal scores over 500: 88%; SAT math scores over 500: 91%; ACT scores over 18: 99%; SAT verbal scores over 600: 42%; SAT math scores over 600: 54%; ACT scores over 24: 71%; SAT verbal scores over 700: 6%; SAT math scores over 700: 9%; ACT scores over 30: 11%.

Faculty *Total:* 1,371, 81% full-time, 75% with terminal degrees. *Student/faculty ratio:* 13:1.

Majors Accounting; African-American/Black studies; agribusiness; agricultural/biological engineering and bioengineering; agricultural business and management; agricultural economics; agricultural teacher education; agriculture; agronomy and crop science; animal sciences; anthropology; applied art; art; art history, criticism and conservation; Asian studies (East); astronomy; astrophysics; athletic training; bilingual and multilingual education; biochemistry; biology/biological sciences; biology/biotechnology laboratory technician; biology teacher education; biotechnology; botany/plant biology; business administration and management; business/managerial economics; chemical engineering; chemistry; chemistry teacher education; child development; civil engineering; classics and languages, literatures and linguistics; clinical laboratory science/medical technology; commercial and advertising art; communication/speech communication and rhetoric; community organization and advocacy; comparative literature; computer and information sciences; computer engineering; computer science; consumer economics; criminal justice/law enforcement administration; developmental and child psychology; dietetics; ecology; economics; education; electrical, electronics and communications engineering; elementary education; engineering; English; English as a second/foreign language (teaching); English/language arts teacher education; entomology; environmental engineering technology; environmental/environmental health engineering; environmental studies; family and community services; family and consumer economics related; fashion/apparel design; fashion merchandising; film/cinema studies; finance; food science; foods, nutrition, and wellness; foreign languages and literatures; foreign language teacher education; French; geography; geology/earth science; geophysics and seismology; German; health and physical education; health teacher education; historic preservation and conservation; history; history teacher education; horticultural science; hospitality and recreation marketing; hotel/motel administration; human development and family studies; international relations and affairs; Italian; journalism; kindergarten/preschool education; kinesiology and exercise science; Latin; Latin American studies; liberal arts and sciences/liberal studies; linguistics; marketing/marketing management; mass communication/media; mathematics; mathematics teacher education; mechanical engineering; middle school education; music; music teacher education; music theory and composition; natural resources management and policy; neuroscience; nursing (registered nurse training); nursing science; nutrition sciences; operations management; ornamental horticulture; paleontology; parks, recreation and leisure facilities management; philosophy; physical education teaching and coaching; physics; physics teacher education; piano and organ; plant protection and integrated pest management; political science and government; pre-veterinary studies; psychology; public relations/image management; Russian; science teacher education; secondary education; sociology; soil conservation; soil science and agronomy; Spanish; special education; technical and business writing; theatre design and technology; voice and opera; wildlife and wildlands science and management; women's studies.

Academic Programs *Special study options:* academic remediation for entering students, accelerated degree program, adult/continuing education programs, advanced placement credit, cooperative education, distance learning, double majors, English as a second language, honors programs, independent study, internships, part-time degree program, services for LD students, student-designed majors, study abroad, summer session for credit. *ROTC:* Army (b), Air Force (b).

Library Hugh Morris Library plus 4 others with 2.5 million titles, 13,541 serial subscriptions, 16,315 audiovisual materials, an OPAC, a Web page.

Computers on Campus 900 computers available on campus for general student use. A campuswide network can be accessed from student residence rooms and from off campus. Internet access, online (class) registration, at least one staffed computer lab available.

Student Life *Housing:* on-campus residence required for freshman year. *Options:* coed, women-only, disabled students. Campus housing is university owned. Freshman campus housing is guaranteed. *Activities and organizations:* drama/theater group, student-run newspaper, radio and television station, choral group, marching band, Undergraduate Student Congress, Resident Student Association, Black Student Union, HOLA (Hispanic Student Association), national fraternities, national sororities. *Campus security:* 24-hour emergency response devices and patrols, student patrols, late-night transport/escort service, controlled dormitory access. *Student services:* health clinic, personal/psychological counseling, women's center.

Athletics Member NCAA. All Division I except football (Division I-AA). *Intercollegiate sports:* baseball M(s), basketball M(s)/W(s), bowling M(c)/W(c), cheerleading M(s)/W(s), crew M(c)/W(s), cross-country running M/W, equestrian sports M(c)/W(c), field hockey W(s), golf M, ice hockey M(c), lacrosse M(s)/W(s), rugby W(c), sailing M(c)/W(c), soccer M(s)/W(s), softball W(s), swimming M/W(s), tennis M/W, track and field M/W(s), volleyball W(s), wrestling M(c). *Intramural sports:* badminton M/W, basketball M/W, field hockey W(c), football M/W, golf M/W, lacrosse M(c)/W(c), racquetball M/W, soccer M/W(c), softball M/W, squash M/W, table tennis M/W, tennis M/W, ultimate Frisbee M/W, volleyball M(c)/W(c), water polo M/W.

Standardized Tests *Required:* SAT I or ACT (for admission). *Recommended:* SAT II: Subject Tests (for admission), SAT II: Writing Test (for admission).

Costs (2003–04) *Tuition:* state resident $5890 full-time, $246 per credit part-time; nonresident $15,420 full-time, $643 per credit part-time. *Required fees:* $608 full-time, $15 per term part-time. *Room and board:* $6118; room only: $3428. Room and board charges vary according to housing facility. *Payment plans:* tuition prepayment, installment. *Waivers:* senior citizens and employees or children of employees.

Financial Aid Of all full-time matriculated undergraduates who enrolled in 2003, 8,568 applied for aid, 5,773 were judged to have need, 2,672 had their need fully met. In 2003, 2989 non-need-based awards were made. *Average percent of need met:* 79%. *Average financial aid package:* $9750. *Average need-based loan:* $4600. *Average need-based gift aid:* $5600. *Average non-need-based aid:* $4070. *Average indebtedness upon graduation:* $13,806.

Applying *Options:* common application, electronic application, early decision, deferred entrance. *Application fee:* $60. *Required:* essay or personal statement, high school transcript, 1 letter of recommendation. *Application deadlines:* 2/15 (freshmen), 5/1 (transfers). *Early decision:* 11/15. *Notification:* 3/15 (freshmen), 12/15 (early decision), continuous (transfers).

Admissions Contact Mr. Lou Hirsh, Director of Admissions, University of Delaware, 116 Hullihen Hall, Newark, DE 19716. *Phone:* 302-831-8123. *Fax:* 302-831-6905. *E-mail:* admissions@udel.edu.

WESLEY COLLEGE

Dover, Delaware

- **Independent United Methodist** comprehensive, founded 1873
- **Calendar** semesters
- **Degrees** certificates, associate, bachelor's, master's, and postbachelor's certificates
- **Small-town** 40-acre campus
- **Endowment** $4.2 million
- **Coed,** 2,000 undergraduate students, 83% full-time, 55% women, 45% men
- **Moderately difficult** entrance level, 68% of applicants were admitted

Undergraduates 1,662 full-time, 338 part-time. Students come from 23 states and territories, 7 other countries, 64% are from out of state, 25% African American, 2% Asian American or Pacific Islander, 3% Hispanic American, 0.5% Native American, 0.9% international, 4% transferred in, 62% live on campus. *Retention:* 88% of 2002 full-time freshmen returned.

Freshmen *Admission:* 1,842 applied, 1,253 admitted, 429 enrolled. *Average high school GPA:* 2.92. *Test scores:* SAT verbal scores over 500: 42%; SAT math scores over 500: 49%; SAT verbal scores over 600: 8%; SAT math scores over 600: 8%; SAT verbal scores over 700: 1%; SAT math scores over 700: 1%.

Faculty *Total:* 101, 61% full-time, 63% with terminal degrees. *Student/faculty ratio:* 17:1.

Majors Accounting; American studies; biology/biological sciences; business administration and management; clinical laboratory science/medical technology; education; English; environmental studies; history; legal assistant/paralegal; liberal arts and sciences/liberal studies; marketing/marketing management; mass communication/media; nursing (registered nurse training); parks, recreation and leisure; physical education teaching and coaching; political science and government; psychology.

Academic Programs *Special study options:* academic remediation for entering students, accelerated degree program, adult/continuing education programs, advanced placement credit, double majors, English as a second language, external degree program, independent study, internships, part-time degree program, study abroad, summer session for credit. *ROTC:* Army (c).

Library Robert H. Parker Library with 95,719 titles, 232 serial subscriptions, 936 audiovisual materials, an OPAC, a Web page.

Computers on Campus 225 computers available on campus for general student use. A campuswide network can be accessed from student residence rooms. Internet access, at least one staffed computer lab available. Computer purchase or lease plan available.

Student Life *Housing:* on-campus residence required for freshman year. *Options:* coed, men-only, women-only. Campus housing is university owned. *Activities and organizations:* drama/theater group, student-run newspaper, choral group, Student Activity Board, Student Government Association, National Coeducation Community Service Organization, national fraternities, national sororities. *Campus security:* 24-hour patrols, controlled dormitory access. *Student services:* health clinic, personal/psychological counseling.

Athletics Member NCAA. All Division III. *Intercollegiate sports:* baseball M, basketball M/W, field hockey W, football M, golf M, lacrosse M/W, soccer M/W, softball W, tennis M/W. *Intramural sports:* basketball M/W, cross-country running M/W, football M/W, soccer M/W, track and field M/W, volleyball M/W.

Standardized Tests *Recommended:* SAT I (for admission).

Costs (2004–05) *Comprehensive fee:* $20,844 includes full-time tuition ($13,585), mandatory fees ($779), and room and board ($6480). Full-time tuition and fees vary according to class time. Part-time tuition: $529 per credit hour. *Required fees:* $10 per term part-time. *Room and board:* Room and board charges vary according to board plan. *Payment plan:* installment. *Waivers:* senior citizens and employees or children of employees.

Financial Aid Of all full-time matriculated undergraduates who enrolled in 2003, 1,479 applied for aid, 1,260 were judged to have need, 1,084 had their need fully met. 333 Federal Work-Study jobs (averaging $2250). In 2003, 232 non-need-based awards were made. *Average percent of need met:* 95%. *Average financial aid package:* $8200. *Average need-based loan:* $3400. *Average need-based gift aid:* $5700. *Average non-need-based aid:* $9150. *Average indebtedness upon graduation:* $17,125.

Applying *Options:* common application, electronic application, early admission, early decision, deferred entrance. *Application fee:* $20. *Required:* essay or personal statement, high school transcript, minimum 2.2 GPA, 1 letter of recommendation. *Recommended:* interview. *Application deadline:* rolling (freshmen), rolling (transfers). *Early decision:* 11/15. *Notification:* 12/1 (early decision).

Admissions Contact Mr. Art Jacobs, Director of Admissions, Wesley College, 120 North State Street, Dover, DE 19901-3875. *Phone:* 302-736-2400. *Toll-free phone:* 800-937-5398 Ext. 2400. *Fax:* 302-736-2301. *E-mail:* admissions@wesley.edu.

■ *See page 2804 for a narrative description.*

WILMINGTON COLLEGE

New Castle, Delaware

- **Independent** comprehensive, founded 1967
- **Calendar** semesters
- **Degrees** certificates, associate, bachelor's, master's, doctoral, post-master's, and postbachelor's certificates
- **Suburban** 17-acre campus with easy access to Philadelphia
- **Endowment** $10.1 million
- **Coed,** 4,110 undergraduate students, 46% full-time, 67% women, 33% men
- **Noncompetitive** entrance level

Wilmington College is a small career-oriented college that specializes in offering a personal learning atmosphere to every student. Wilmington College encourages applications from students who, in its judgment, show promise of academic achievement, regardless of past performance. Applications are reviewed and accepted on a continuous basis. Freshmen and transfer students are admitted to the fall, spring, and summer terms.

Undergraduates 1,896 full-time, 2,214 part-time. Students come from 14 states and territories, 14% are from out of state, 13% African American, 0.5% Asian American or Pacific Islander, 2% Hispanic American, 0.4% Native American, 7% transferred in. *Retention:* 63% of 2002 full-time freshmen returned.

Freshmen *Admission:* 494 enrolled.

Faculty *Total:* 473, 12% full-time. *Student/faculty ratio:* 20:1.

Majors Accounting; airframe mechanics and aircraft maintenance technology; aviation/airway management; avionics maintenance technology; behavioral sciences; business administration and management; communication and media related; criminal justice/law enforcement administration; design and visual communications; early childhood education; elementary education; finance; general studies; human resources management; information technology; kindergarten/preschool education; legal studies; marketing/marketing management; middle school education; nursing (registered nurse training); psychology; science teacher education; sport and fitness administration.

Academic Programs *Special study options:* academic remediation for entering students, accelerated degree program, adult/continuing education programs, cooperative education, distance learning, double majors, external degree program, independent study, internships, part-time degree program, summer session for credit. *ROTC:* Army (c), Air Force (c).

Library Robert C. and Dorothy M. Peoples Library plus 1 other with 111,000 titles, 500 serial subscriptions, 6,795 audiovisual materials, an OPAC, a Web page.

Computers on Campus 500 computers available on campus for general student use. Internet access, at least one staffed computer lab available.

Student Life *Housing:* college housing not available. *Campus security:* 24-hour emergency response devices and patrols, late-night transport/escort service.

Athletics Member NCAA. All Division II. *Intercollegiate sports:* baseball M(s), basketball M(s)/W(s), cross-country running M(s)/W(s), softball W(s), volleyball W(s).

Standardized Tests *Recommended:* SAT I or ACT (for placement).

Costs (2003–04) *Tuition:* $6930 full-time, $231 per credit part-time. Full-time tuition and fees vary according to course load, degree level, and location. Part-time tuition and fees vary according to course load, degree level, and location. *Required fees:* $50 full-time, $25 per term part-time. *Payment plan:* installment. *Waivers:* employees or children of employees.

Financial Aid Of all full-time matriculated undergraduates who enrolled in 2003, 958 applied for aid, 792 were judged to have need. 25 Federal Work-Study jobs (averaging $2000). In 2003, 125 non-need-based awards were made. *Average percent of need met:* 78%. *Average financial aid package:* $6960. *Average need-based loan:* $3654. *Average need-based gift aid:* $1290. *Average non-need-based aid:* $4750. *Average indebtedness upon graduation:* $15,400.

Applying *Options:* early admission, deferred entrance. *Application fee:* $25. *Required:* high school transcript. *Recommended:* letters of recommendation, interview. *Application deadline:* rolling (freshmen), rolling (transfers). *Notification:* continuous (freshmen), continuous (transfers).

Wilmington College (continued)

Admissions Contact Mr. Christopher Ferguson, Director of Admissions, Wilmington College, 320 DuPont Highway, New Castle, DE 19720-6491. *Phone:* 302-328-9407. *Toll-free phone:* 877-967-5464. *Fax:* 302-328-5902. *E-mail:* inquire@wilmcoll.edu.

■ See page 2864 for a narrative description.

DISTRICT OF COLUMBIA

AMERICAN UNIVERSITY
Washington, District of Columbia

- **Independent Methodist** university, founded 1893
- **Calendar** semesters
- **Degrees** certificates, associate, bachelor's, master's, doctoral, first professional, and postbachelor's certificates
- **Suburban** 84-acre campus
- **Endowment** $169.1 million
- **Coed,** 5,752 undergraduate students, 94% full-time, 62% women, 38% men
- **Very difficult** entrance level, 59% of applicants were admitted

American University (AU) attracts academically distinctive students who are committed to turning ideas into action and action into service—here and around the world. With more than 150 clubs, NCAA Division I league-winning teams, and on-campus concerts and speaker series, AU students can stay on campus or take advantage of all the options offered by the nation's capital. American's diverse campus community, location in Washington, D.C., Honors Program, more than 17 study-abroad options, and emphasis on internships and research prepare students to be major contributors in their fields.

Undergraduates 5,427 full-time, 325 part-time. Students come from 54 states and territories, 118 other countries, 95% are from out of state, 6% African American, 5% Asian American or Pacific Islander, 5% Hispanic American, 0.3% Native American, 7% international, 6% transferred in, 75% live on campus. *Retention:* 86% of 2002 full-time freshmen returned.

Freshmen *Admission:* 10,282 applied, 6,107 admitted, 1,238 enrolled. *Average high school GPA:* 3.42. *Test scores:* SAT verbal scores over 500: 95%; SAT math scores over 500: 95%; ACT scores over 18: 99%; SAT verbal scores over 600: 64%; SAT math scores over 600: 54%; ACT scores over 24: 85%; SAT verbal scores over 700: 17%; SAT math scores over 700: 10%; ACT scores over 30: 23%.

Faculty *Total:* 965, 51% full-time. *Student/faculty ratio:* 14:1.

Majors African studies; American studies; anthropology; applied mathematics; art; art history, criticism and conservation; Asian studies; audio engineering; biochemistry; biology/biological sciences; broadcast journalism; business administration and management; business/managerial economics; chemistry; cinematography and film/video production; commercial and advertising art; computer science; criminal justice/safety; development economics and international development; dramatic/theatre arts; economics; elementary education; entrepreneurship; environmental studies; European studies; finance; fine/studio arts; French; German; health science; history; human resources management; information science/studies; interdisciplinary studies; intermedia/multimedia; international business/trade/commerce; international economics; international finance; international marketing; international relations and affairs; Islamic studies; Jewish/Judaic studies; journalism; Latin American studies; legal studies; literature; management information systems; marine biology and biological oceanography; marketing/marketing management; mathematics; music; Near and Middle Eastern studies; peace studies and conflict resolution; philosophy; physics; political science and government; pre-dentistry studies; pre-law studies; pre-medical studies; pre-pharmacy studies; pre-veterinary studies; psychology; public relations/image management; Russian; Russian studies; secondary education; sociology; Spanish; sport and fitness administration; statistics; women's studies.

Academic Programs *Special study options:* accelerated degree program, advanced placement credit, cooperative education, double majors, honors programs, independent study, internships, off-campus study, part-time degree program, services for LD students, student-designed majors, study abroad, summer session for credit. *ROTC:* Army (c), Air Force (c). *Unusual degree programs:* 3-2 engineering with University of Maryland College Park.

Library American University Library plus 1 other with 763,000 titles, 3,100 serial subscriptions, 43,000 audiovisual materials, an OPAC, a Web page.

Computers on Campus 600 computers available on campus for general student use. A campuswide network can be accessed from student residence rooms and from off campus that provide access to online course support, wireless campus. Internet access, online (class) registration, at least one staffed computer lab available. Computer purchase or lease plan available.

Student Life *Housing options:* coed. Campus housing is university owned and leased by the school. Freshman campus housing is guaranteed. *Activities and organizations:* drama/theater group, student-run newspaper, radio and television station, choral group, Kennedy Political Union, Student Confederation, Freshman Service Experience, Student Union Board, DC Reads, national fraternities, national sororities. *Campus security:* 24-hour emergency response devices and patrols, late-night transport/escort service, controlled dormitory access. *Student services:* health clinic, personal/psychological counseling.

Athletics Member NCAA. All Division I. *Intercollegiate sports:* basketball M(s)/W(s), cross-country running M(s)/W(s), field hockey W(s), golf M(s), lacrosse W(s), soccer M(s)/W(s), swimming M/W, tennis M(s)/W(s), track and field M(s)/W(s), volleyball W(s), wrestling M(s). *Intramural sports:* basketball M/W, bowling M/W, cheerleading W, crew M(c)/W(c), fencing M(c)/W(c), golf M/W, ice hockey M(c)/W(c), lacrosse M(c)/W(c), rugby M(c)/W(c), soccer M/W, softball M/W, tennis M/W, ultimate Frisbee M(c)/W(c), volleyball M/W.

Standardized Tests *Required:* SAT I or ACT (for admission). *Required for some:* TOEFL for all whose first language is not English, regardless of citizenship. *Recommended:* SAT II: Subject Tests (for admission), SAT II: Writing Test (for admission).

Costs (2004–05) *Comprehensive fee:* $36,567 includes full-time tuition ($25,920), mandatory fees ($387), and room and board ($10,260). Part-time tuition: $864 per semester hour. *Required fees:* $130 per year part-time. *Room and board:* Room and board charges vary according to board plan and housing facility. *Payment plan:* installment. *Waivers:* employees or children of employees.

Financial Aid Of all full-time matriculated undergraduates who enrolled in 2002, 3,247 applied for aid, 2,557 were judged to have need, 1,271 had their need fully met. 2,098 Federal Work-Study jobs (averaging $2022). In 2002, 722 non-need-based awards were made. *Average percent of need met:* 79%. *Average financial aid package:* $24,370. *Average need-based loan:* $7454. *Average need-based gift aid:* $12,699. *Average non-need-based aid:* $12,410. *Average indebtedness upon graduation:* $18,716. *Financial aid deadline:* 3/1.

Applying *Options:* common application, electronic application, early admission, early decision, deferred entrance. *Application fee:* $45. *Required:* essay or personal statement, high school transcript, minimum 2.0 GPA, 2 letters of recommendation. *Recommended:* minimum 3.0 GPA, interview. *Application deadlines:* 2/1 (freshmen), 7/1 (transfers). *Early decision:* 11/15. *Notification:* 4/1 (freshmen), 12/31 (early decision), continuous (transfers).

Admissions Contact Dr. Sharon Alston, Director of Admissions, American University, 4400 Massachusetts Avenue, NW, Washington, DC 20016-8001. *Phone:* 202-885-6000. *Fax:* 202-885-1025. *E-mail:* afa@american.edu.

■ See page 1168 for a narrative description.

THE CATHOLIC UNIVERSITY OF AMERICA
Washington, District of Columbia

- **Independent** university, founded 1887, affiliated with Roman Catholic Church
- **Calendar** semesters
- **Degrees** bachelor's, master's, doctoral, first professional, and post-master's certificates
- **Urban** 144-acre campus
- **Endowment** $134.9 million
- **Coed,** 2,759 undergraduate students, 90% full-time, 56% women, 44% men
- **Moderately difficult** entrance level, 82% of applicants were admitted

Undergraduates 2,477 full-time, 282 part-time. Students come from 51 states and territories, 32 other countries, 96% are from out of state, 7% African American, 3% Asian American or Pacific Islander, 4% Hispanic American, 2% international, 6% transferred in, 66% live on campus. *Retention:* 85% of 2002 full-time freshmen returned.

Freshmen *Admission:* 2,748 applied, 2,251 admitted, 673 enrolled. *Average high school GPA:* 3.36. *Test scores:* SAT verbal scores over 500: 87%; SAT math scores over 500: 86%; ACT scores over 18: 96%; SAT verbal scores over 600: 46%; SAT math scores over 600: 44%; ACT scores over 24: 66%; SAT verbal scores over 700: 8%; SAT math scores over 700: 4%; ACT scores over 30: 10%.

Faculty *Total:* 676, 50% full-time. *Student/faculty ratio:* 8:1.

Majors Accounting; anthropology; architecture; art; art history, criticism and conservation; art teacher education; atomic/molecular physics; biochemistry; biology/biological sciences; biology teacher education; biomedical/medical engineering; business administration and management; business/commerce; chemistry; chemistry teacher education; civil engineering; classics and classical languages related; classics and languages, literatures and linguistics; clinical laboratory science/medical technology; communication/speech communication and rhetoric; computer engineering; computer science; drama and dance teacher education; dramatic/theatre arts; economics; education; educational psychology; electrical, electronics and communications engineering; elementary education; engineering; English; English/language arts teacher education; finance; fine arts related; fine/studio arts; foreign language teacher education; French; French language teacher education; general studies; German; German language teacher education; history; history teacher education; human resources management; interdisciplinary studies; international economics; international finance; international relations and affairs; kindergarten/preschool education; Latin; mathematics; mathematics teacher education; mechanical engineering; medieval and Renaissance studies; modern Greek; music; music history, literature, and theory; music performance; music teacher education; music theory and composition; nursing (registered nurse training); painting; philosophy; physics; piano and organ; political science and government; psychology; religious education; religious studies; Romance languages; sculpture; secondary education; social work; sociology; Spanish; Spanish language teacher education; voice and opera.

Academic Programs *Special study options:* accelerated degree program, adult/continuing education programs, advanced placement credit, double majors, English as a second language, freshman honors college, honors programs, independent study, internships, off-campus study, part-time degree program, services for LD students, study abroad, summer session for credit. *ROTC:* Army (c), Navy (c), Air Force (c).

Library Mullen Library plus 7 others with 1.0 million titles, 11,200 serial subscriptions, 38,200 audiovisual materials, an OPAC, a Web page.

Computers on Campus 450 computers available on campus for general student use. A campuswide network can be accessed from student residence rooms and from off campus. Internet access, online (class) registration, at least one staffed computer lab available. Computer purchase or lease plan available.

Student Life *Housing:* on-campus residence required through sophomore year. *Options:* coed, men-only, women-only. Campus housing is university owned. Freshman campus housing is guaranteed. *Activities and organizations:* drama/theater group, student-run newspaper, radio station, choral group, Knights of Columbus, Students for Life, College Republicans, Habitat for Humanity, College Democrats. *Campus security:* 24-hour emergency response devices and patrols, late-night transport/escort service, controlled dormitory access, controlled access of academic buildings. *Student services:* health clinic, personal/psychological counseling, women's center, legal services.

Athletics Member NCAA. All Division III. *Intercollegiate sports:* baseball M, basketball M/W, cross-country running M/W, field hockey W, football M, lacrosse M/W, soccer M/W, softball W, swimming M/W, tennis M/W, track and field M/W, volleyball W. *Intramural sports:* basketball M/W, crew M(c)/W(c), equestrian sports M(c)/W(c), football M/W, ice hockey M(c), racquetball M/W, rugby M(c), soccer M/W, softball M/W, tennis M/W, track and field M/W, volleyball M/W.

Standardized Tests *Required:* SAT I or ACT (for admission). *Recommended:* SAT II: Subject Tests (for admission), SAT II: Writing Test (for admission).

Costs (2004–05) *Comprehensive fee:* $34,248 includes full-time tuition ($23,600), mandatory fees ($1150), and room and board ($9498). Full-time tuition and fees vary according to program. Part-time tuition: $895 per credit. *Required fees:* $575 per term part-time. *College room only:* $5428. Room and board charges vary according to board plan and housing facility. *Payment plans:* installment, deferred payment. *Waivers:* employees or children of employees.

Financial Aid Of all full-time matriculated undergraduates who enrolled in 2003, 2,430 applied for aid, 2,161 were judged to have need, 387 had their need fully met. In 2003, 241 non-need-based awards were made. *Average percent of need met:* 57%. *Average financial aid package:* $14,945. *Average need-based loan:* $4648. *Average need-based gift aid:* $4478. *Average non-need-based aid:* $8533. *Financial aid deadline:* 2/1.

Applying *Options:* common application, electronic application, early admission, early decision, deferred entrance. *Application fee:* $55. *Required:* essay or personal statement, high school transcript, 1 letter of recommendation. *Recommended:* minimum 2.8 GPA. *Application deadlines:* 2/15 (freshmen), 8/1 (transfers). *Early decision:* 12/1. *Notification:* continuous until 3/20 (freshmen), 1/15 (early decision).

Admissions Contact Christine Mica, Director of Undergraduate Admission, The Catholic University of America, Cardinal Station, 620 Michigan Avenue, NE, Washington, DC 20064. *Phone:* 202-319-5305. *Toll-free phone:* 202-319-5305 (in-state); 800-673-2772 (out-of-state). *Fax:* 202-319-6533. *E-mail:* cua-admissions@cua.edu.

■ *See page 1368 for a narrative description.*

CORCORAN COLLEGE OF ART AND DESIGN
Washington, District of Columbia

- **Independent** 4-year, founded 1890
- **Calendar** semesters
- **Degrees** associate and bachelor's
- **Urban** 7-acre campus
- **Endowment** $29.5 million
- **Coed**
- **Moderately difficult** entrance level

Faculty *Student/faculty ratio:* 10:1.

Student Life *Campus security:* 24-hour patrols, ID check at all entrances.

Standardized Tests *Required:* SAT I or ACT (for admission).

Costs (2003–04) *Comprehensive fee:* $27,400 includes full-time tuition ($19,800), mandatory fees ($100), and room and board ($7500). *College room only:* $5700.

Financial Aid Of all full-time matriculated undergraduates who enrolled in 2003, 226 applied for aid, 226 were judged to have need. 51 Federal Work-Study jobs (averaging $439). In 2003, 67. *Average percent of need met:* 29. *Average financial aid package:* $8612. *Average need-based loan:* $4641. *Average need-based gift aid:* $5094. *Average non-need-based aid:* $3603. *Average indebtedness upon graduation:* $28,083.

Applying *Options:* early admission, deferred entrance. *Application fee:* $40. *Required:* high school transcript, minimum 2.5 GPA, portfolio. *Required for some:* essay or personal statement, 2 letters of recommendation, interview. *Recommended:* essay or personal statement, minimum 3.0 GPA, 2 letters of recommendation, interview.

Admissions Contact Ms. Anne E. Bowman, Director of Enrollment Management, Corcoran College of Art and Design, 500 17th Street, NW, Washington, DC 20006-4804. *Phone:* 202-639-1814. *Toll-free phone:* 888-CORCORAN. *Fax:* 202-639-1830. *E-mail:* admofc@corcoran.org.

GALLAUDET UNIVERSITY
Washington, District of Columbia

- **Independent** university, founded 1864
- **Calendar** semesters
- **Degrees** bachelor's, master's, and doctoral (all undergraduate programs open primarily to hearing-impaired)
- **Urban** 99-acre campus
- **Endowment** $126.6 million
- **Coed,** 1,168 undergraduate students, 96% full-time, 53% women, 47% men
- **Moderately difficult** entrance level, 71% of applicants were admitted

Undergraduates 1,120 full-time, 48 part-time. Students come from 56 states and territories, 27 other countries, 99% are from out of state, 11% African American, 5% Asian American or Pacific Islander, 7% Hispanic American, 1% Native American, 11% international, 4% transferred in, 62% live on campus. *Retention:* 65% of 2002 full-time freshmen returned.

Freshmen *Admission:* 603 applied, 426 admitted, 238 enrolled.

Faculty *Total:* 218, 100% full-time, 79% with terminal degrees. *Student/faculty ratio:* 7:1.

Majors Accounting; American government and politics; apparel and textiles; art; art history, criticism and conservation; art teacher education; biology/biological sciences; business administration and management; chemical engineering; chemistry; child development; civil engineering; commercial and advertising art; communication/speech communication and rhetoric; computer and information sciences; computer engineering; computer science; criminology; dramatic/theatre arts; economics; education; electrical, electronics and communications engineering; elementary education; engineering; engineering science; engineering technology; English; English composition; English/language arts teacher education; family systems; fine/studio arts; foods, nutrition, and wellness; French; history; information science/studies; international relations and affairs; kindergarten/preschool education; mass communication/media; mathematics; mechanical engineering; philosophy; photography; physical education teaching and coaching; physics; psychology; radio and television; secondary education; sign language interpretation and translation; social work; sociology; Spanish; therapeutic recreation.

Academic Programs *Special study options:* academic remediation for entering students, accelerated degree program, adult/continuing education programs, advanced placement credit, cooperative education, distance learning, double majors, English as a second language, honors programs, independent study, internships, off-campus study, part-time degree program, services for LD students, student-designed majors, study abroad, summer session for credit.

Library Merrill Learning Center with 159,142 titles, 1,649 serial subscriptions, 188,130 audiovisual materials, an OPAC, a Web page.

Computers on Campus 240 computers available on campus for general student use. A campuswide network can be accessed from student residence rooms and from off campus. Online (class) registration, at least one staffed computer lab available.

Student Life *Housing options:* coed. Campus housing is university owned. *Activities and organizations:* drama/theater group, student-run newspaper, Student Body Government, Delta Epsilon, Rainbow Society, Black Deaf Student Union, national fraternities, national sororities. *Campus security:* 24-hour emergency response devices and patrols, late-night transport/escort service, controlled dormitory access. *Student services:* health clinic, personal/psychological counseling.

Gallaudet University (continued)

Athletics Member NCAA. All Division III. *Intercollegiate sports:* baseball M, basketball M/W, cross-country running M/W, football M, soccer M/W, softball W, swimming M/W, tennis M/W, track and field M/W, volleyball W, wrestling M. *Intramural sports:* badminton M/W, basketball M/W, bowling M/W, cross-country running M/W, football M/W, golf M/W, gymnastics M(c)/W(c), racquetball M/W, soccer M, softball W.

Standardized Tests *Required:* SAT I or ACT (for admission).

Costs (2003–04) *Comprehensive fee:* $17,690 includes full-time tuition ($9000), mandatory fees ($660), and room and board ($8030). Part-time tuition: $450 per credit. *Room and board:* Room and board charges vary according to board plan. *Payment plan:* installment. *Waivers:* employees or children of employees.

Financial Aid Of all full-time matriculated undergraduates who enrolled in 2003, 952 applied for aid, 892 were judged to have need, 231 had their need fully met. 142 Federal Work-Study jobs (averaging $1559). In 2003, 49 non-need-based awards were made. *Average percent of need met:* 76%. *Average financial aid package:* $14,057. *Average need-based loan:* $3028. *Average need-based gift aid:* $12,342. *Average non-need-based aid:* $10,996. *Average indebtedness upon graduation:* $10,273.

Applying *Options:* early admission, deferred entrance. *Application fee:* $35. *Required:* essay or personal statement, high school transcript, 2 letters of recommendation, audiogram. *Required for some:* interview. *Application deadlines:* 8/1 (freshmen), 8/1 (transfers). *Notification:* continuous (freshmen), continuous (transfers).

Admissions Contact Ms. Deborah E. DeStefano, Director of Admissions, Gallaudet University, 800 Florida Avenue, NE, Washington, DC 20002-3625. *Phone:* 202-651-5750. *Toll-free phone:* 800-995-0550. *Fax:* 202-651-5774. *E-mail:* admissions@gallua.gallaudet.edu.

GEORGETOWN UNIVERSITY
Washington, District of Columbia

- **Independent Roman Catholic (Jesuit)** university, founded 1789
- **Calendar** semesters
- **Degrees** bachelor's, master's, doctoral, and first professional
- **Urban** 110-acre campus
- **Endowment** $610.3 million
- **Coed,** 6,550 undergraduate students, 97% full-time, 54% women, 46% men
- **Most difficult** entrance level, 23% of applicants were admitted

Undergraduates 6,326 full-time, 224 part-time. Students come from 50 states and territories, 92 other countries, 97% are from out of state, 7% African American, 10% Asian American or Pacific Islander, 5% Hispanic American, 0.1% Native American, 5% international, 4% transferred in, 80% live on campus. *Retention:* 95% of 2002 full-time freshmen returned.

Freshmen *Admission:* 15,420 applied, 3,505 admitted, 1,528 enrolled. *Average high school GPA:* 3.87. *Test scores:* SAT verbal scores over 500: 99%; SAT math scores over 500: 99%; ACT scores over 18: 99%; SAT verbal scores over 600: 88%; SAT math scores over 600: 91%; ACT scores over 24: 93%; SAT verbal scores over 700: 39%; SAT math scores over 700: 43%; ACT scores over 30: 54%.

Faculty *Total:* 1,036, 67% full-time, 81% with terminal degrees. *Student/faculty ratio:* 10:1.

Majors Accounting; American studies; Arabic; art; biochemistry; biology/biological sciences; business administration and management; chemistry; Chinese; classics and languages, literatures and linguistics; comparative literature; computer science; economics; English; finance; French; German; history; interdisciplinary studies; international business/trade/commerce; international economics; international relations and affairs; Italian; Japanese; liberal arts and sciences/liberal studies; linguistics; marketing/marketing management; mathematics; nursing (registered nurse training); philosophy; physics; political science and government; Portuguese; psychology; religious studies; Russian; science, technology and society; social sciences related; sociology; Spanish; women's studies.

Academic Programs *Special study options:* academic remediation for entering students, adult/continuing education programs, advanced placement credit, double majors, English as a second language, honors programs, independent study, internships, off-campus study, services for LD students, student-designed majors, study abroad, summer session for credit. *ROTC:* Army (b), Navy (c), Air Force (c). *Unusual degree programs:* 3-2 foreign service.

Library Lauinger Library plus 6 others with 2.2 million titles, 21,901 serial subscriptions, 15,730 audiovisual materials, an OPAC, a Web page.

Computers on Campus 360 computers available on campus for general student use. A campuswide network can be accessed from student residence rooms and from off campus that provide access to online grade reports. Internet access, online (class) registration, at least one staffed computer lab available.

Student Life *Housing:* on-campus residence required through sophomore year. *Options:* coed, disabled students. Campus housing is university owned. Freshman campus housing is guaranteed. *Activities and organizations:* drama/theater group, student-run newspaper, radio station, choral group, University Choir, Mask and Bauble, The Hoya (student newspaper), international relations club, The Voice (weekly news magazine). *Campus security:* 24-hour emergency response devices and patrols, late-night transport/escort service, controlled dormitory access, student guards at residence halls and academic facilities. *Student services:* health clinic, personal/psychological counseling.

Athletics Member NCAA. All Division I except football (Division I-AA). *Intercollegiate sports:* baseball M(s), basketball M(s)/W(s), crew M/W, cross-country running M(s)/W(s), field hockey W, golf M(s), ice hockey M(c), lacrosse M(s)/W(s), rugby M(c), sailing M/W, soccer M(s)/W(s), swimming M/W, tennis M/W(s), track and field M(s)/W(s), volleyball W(s). *Intramural sports:* basketball M/W, cross-country running M/W, football M/W, golf M/W, racquetball M/W, soccer M/W, softball M/W, squash M/W, table tennis M/W, tennis M/W, track and field M/W, ultimate Frisbee M, volleyball M/W.

Standardized Tests *Required:* SAT I or ACT (for admission). *Recommended:* SAT II: Subject Tests (for admission), SAT II: Writing Test (for admission).

Costs (2003–04) *Comprehensive fee:* $38,242 includes full-time tuition ($27,864), mandatory fees ($345), and room and board ($10,033). Part-time tuition: $1161 per credit hour. Part-time tuition and fees vary according to course load. *College room only:* $6653. Room and board charges vary according to board plan and housing facility. *Payment plans:* installment, deferred payment. *Waivers:* employees or children of employees.

Financial Aid Of all full-time matriculated undergraduates who enrolled in 2003, 2,775 applied for aid, 2,493 were judged to have need, 2,493 had their need fully met. 2,012 Federal Work-Study jobs (averaging $3200). In 2003, 5 non-need-based awards were made. *Average percent of need met:* 100%. *Average financial aid package:* $22,344. *Average need-based loan:* $3859. *Average need-based gift aid:* $15,663. *Average non-need-based aid:* $3500. *Average indebtedness upon graduation:* $21,500. *Financial aid deadline:* 2/1.

Applying *Options:* electronic application, early admission, early action, deferred entrance. *Application fee:* $60. *Required:* essay or personal statement, high school transcript, 2 letters of recommendation, interview. *Application deadlines:* 1/10 (freshmen), 3/1 (transfers). *Notification:* 4/1 (freshmen), 12/15 (early action), 6/1 (transfers).

Admissions Contact Mr. Charles A. Deacon, Dean of Undergraduate Admissions, Georgetown University, 37th and O Street, NW, Washington, DC 20057. *Phone:* 202-687-3600. *Fax:* 202-687-6660.

THE GEORGE WASHINGTON UNIVERSITY
Washington, District of Columbia

- **Independent** university, founded 1821
- **Calendar** semesters
- **Degrees** certificates, associate, bachelor's, master's, doctoral, first professional, post-master's, and postbachelor's certificates
- **Urban** 36-acre campus
- **Endowment** $621.1 million
- **Coed,** 10,436 undergraduate students, 89% full-time, 57% women, 43% men
- **Very difficult** entrance level, 39% of applicants were admitted

Undergraduates 9,280 full-time, 1,156 part-time. Students come from 55 states and territories, 101 other countries, 98% are from out of state, 5% African American, 9% Asian American or Pacific Islander, 5% Hispanic American, 0.2% Native American, 5% international, 4% transferred in, 62% live on campus. *Retention:* 93% of 2002 full-time freshmen returned.

Freshmen *Admission:* 18,442 applied, 7,103 admitted, 2,266 enrolled. *Test scores:* SAT verbal scores over 500: 97%; SAT math scores over 500: 98%; ACT scores over 18: 99%; SAT verbal scores over 600: 72%; SAT math scores over 600: 73%; ACT scores over 24: 88%; SAT verbal scores over 700: 20%; SAT math scores over 700: 18%; ACT scores over 30: 23%.

Faculty *Total:* 1,922, 42% full-time, 61% with terminal degrees. *Student/faculty ratio:* 14:1.

Majors Accounting; American studies; anthropology; applied mathematics; archeology; art; art history, criticism and conservation; Asian studies; Asian studies (East); audiology and speech-language pathology; biology/biological sciences; business administration and management; business/managerial economics; chemistry; Chinese; civil engineering; classics and languages, literatures and linguistics; clinical laboratory science/medical technology; clinical/medical laboratory technology; computer and information sciences; computer engineering; computer science; criminal justice/law enforcement administration; dance; dramatic/theatre arts; economics; electrical, electronics and communications engineering; emergency medical technology (EMT paramedic); engineering; English; environmental/environmental health engineering; environmental studies; European studies; finance; fine/studio arts; French; geography; geology/earth science; German; history; humanities; human resources management; human services; industrial radiologic technology; interdisciplinary studies; international business/trade/commerce; international relations and affairs; Jewish/Judaic studies; journalism; kinesiology and exercise science; Latin American studies; liberal arts and sciences/liberal studies; marketing/marketing management; mass communication/media; mathematics; mechanical engineering; medical laboratory technology; music; Near and Middle Eastern studies; nuclear medical technology; philosophy; physician assistant; physics; political science and government; pre-dentistry studies; pre-law studies; pre-medical studies; psychology; public policy analysis; radio and television; radiologic technology/science; religious studies; Russian; Russian studies; sociology; Spanish; speech and rhetoric; statistics; systems engineering.

Academic Programs *Special study options:* accelerated degree program, adult/continuing education programs, advanced placement credit, cooperative education, distance learning, double majors, English as a second language, honors programs, independent study, internships, off-campus study, part-time degree program, services for LD students, student-designed majors, study abroad, summer session for credit. *ROTC:* Army (c), Navy (b), Air Force (c). *Unusual degree programs:* 3-2 chemical toxicology, art therapy, economics, engineering economics, operations research.

Library Gelman Library plus 2 others with 2.0 million titles, 15,365 serial subscriptions, 171,397 audiovisual materials, an OPAC, a Web page.

Computers on Campus 550 computers available on campus for general student use. A campuswide network can be accessed from student residence rooms and from off campus. At least one staffed computer lab available.

Student Life *Housing options:* coed, women-only. Campus housing is university owned. Freshman campus housing is guaranteed. *Activities and organizations:* drama/theater group, student-run newspaper, radio and television station, choral group, marching band, Program Board, Student Association, Residence Hall Association, College Democrats, College Republicans, national fraternities, national sororities. *Campus security:* 24-hour emergency response devices and patrols, late-night transport/escort service, controlled dormitory access. *Student services:* health clinic, personal/psychological counseling, legal services.

Athletics Member NCAA. All Division I. *Intercollegiate sports:* baseball M(s), basketball M(s)/W(s), crew M(s)/W(s), cross-country running M(s)/W(s), golf M(s), gymnastics W(s), soccer M(s)/W(s), swimming M(s)/W(s), tennis M(s)/W(s), volleyball W(s), water polo M(s). *Intramural sports:* badminton M(c)/W(c), basketball M/W, bowling M(c)/W(c), equestrian sports M(c)/W(c), fencing M(c)/W(c), football M/W, lacrosse M(c), racquetball M/W, rugby M(c), sailing M(c)/W(c), soccer M/W, softball M/W, squash M(c)/W, swimming M/W, tennis M/W, volleyball M(c)/W, water polo M/W.

Standardized Tests *Required:* SAT I or ACT (for admission). *Required for some:* SAT II: Subject Tests (for admission). *Recommended:* SAT I (for admission), SAT II: Writing Test (for admission).

Costs (2004–05) *Comprehensive fee:* $41,030 includes full-time tuition ($30,790), mandatory fees ($30), and room and board ($10,210). Full-time tuition and fees vary according to student level. Part-time tuition: $964 per credit hour. *Required fees:* $1 per credit hour part-time. *College room only:* $7210. Room and board charges vary according to board plan and housing facility. *Payment plans:* installment, deferred payment. *Waivers:* employees or children of employees.

Financial Aid Of all full-time matriculated undergraduates who enrolled in 2002, 4,702 applied for aid, 3,456 were judged to have need, 2,729 had their need fully met. In 2002, 1927 non-need-based awards were made. *Average percent of need met:* 94%. *Average financial aid package:* $27,413. *Average need-based loan:* $6888. *Average need-based gift aid:* $15,891. *Average non-need-based aid:* $11,318. *Average indebtedness upon graduation:* $22,854.

Applying *Options:* common application, electronic application, early admission, early decision, deferred entrance. *Application fee:* $60. *Required:* essay or personal statement, high school transcript, 2 letters of recommendation. *Recommended:* interview. *Application deadline:* 1/15 (freshmen), rolling (transfers). *Early decision:* 12/1 (for plan 1), 1/15 (for plan 2). *Notification:* 12/15 (early decision plan 1), 2/1 (early decision plan 2), continuous (transfers).

Admissions Contact Dr. Kathryn M. Napper, Director of Admission, The George Washington University, 2121 I Street, NW, Suite 201, Washington, DC 20052. *Phone:* 202-994-6040. *Toll-free phone:* 800-447-3765. *Fax:* 202-944-0325. *E-mail:* gwadm@gwu.edu.

■ *See page 1668 for a narrative description.*

HOWARD UNIVERSITY
Washington, District of Columbia

- **Independent** university, founded 1867
- **Calendar** semesters
- **Degrees** certificates, bachelor's, master's, doctoral, first professional, post-master's, and first professional certificates
- **Urban** 256-acre campus
- **Endowment** $312.7 million
- **Coed,** 7,059 undergraduate students, 94% full-time, 67% women, 33% men
- **Moderately difficult** entrance level, 56% of applicants were admitted

Undergraduates 6,648 full-time, 411 part-time. Students come from 50 states and territories, 61 other countries, 86% are from out of state, 69% African American, 0.6% Asian American or Pacific Islander, 0.5% Hispanic American, 0.1% Native American, 10% international, 5% transferred in, 57% live on campus. *Retention:* 89% of 2002 full-time freshmen returned.

Freshmen *Admission:* 7,057 applied, 3,982 admitted, 1,455 enrolled. *Average high school GPA:* 3.2.

Faculty *Total:* 1,598, 70% full-time, 85% with terminal degrees. *Student/faculty ratio:* 8:1.

Majors Accounting; African-American/Black studies; anatomy; anthropology; applied art; architecture; art; art therapy; biology/biological sciences; broadcast journalism; business administration and management; ceramic arts and ceramics; chemical engineering; chemistry; civil engineering; classics and languages, literatures and linguistics; clinical laboratory science/medical technology; counselor education/school counseling and guidance; criminal justice/police science; dental hygiene; drama therapy; dramatic/theatre arts; economics; education; electrical, electronics and communications engineering; English; family and consumer economics related; fashion/apparel design; film/cinema studies; finance; foods, nutrition, and wellness; French; German; history; hotel/motel administration; industrial radiologic technology; information science/studies; insurance; interior design; international business/trade/commerce; international economics; journalism; kindergarten/preschool education; marketing/marketing management; mass communication/media; mathematics; mechanical engineering; music; nursing (registered nurse training); occupational therapy; pharmacy; philosophy; physical education teaching and coaching; physical therapy; physician assistant; physics; political science and government; psychology; radio and television; Russian; social work; sociology; Spanish; zoology/animal biology.

Academic Programs *Special study options:* academic remediation for entering students, accelerated degree program, adult/continuing education programs, advanced placement credit, cooperative education, double majors, freshman honors college, honors programs, independent study, internships, off-campus study, part-time degree program, services for LD students, student-designed majors, study abroad, summer session for credit. *ROTC:* Army (b), Air Force (b).

Library Founders Library plus 8 others with 2.5 million titles, 12,795 serial subscriptions, 40,872 audiovisual materials, an OPAC, a Web page.

Computers on Campus 5673 computers available on campus for general student use. A campuswide network can be accessed from student residence rooms and from off campus. Internet access, online (class) registration, at least one staffed computer lab available. Computer purchase or lease plan available.

Student Life *Housing:* on-campus residence required through sophomore year. *Options:* coed. Campus housing is university owned. Freshman applicants given priority for college housing. *Activities and organizations:* drama/theater group, student-run newspaper, radio and television station, choral group, marching band, Howard University Student Association, Undergraduate Student Assembly, Campus Pals, national fraternities, national sororities. *Campus security:* 24-hour emergency response devices and patrols, student patrols, late-night transport/escort service, controlled dormitory access, security lighting. *Student services:* health clinic, personal/psychological counseling.

Athletics Member NCAA. All Division I except football (Division I-AA). *Intercollegiate sports:* baseball M(s)/W(s), basketball M(s)/W(s), bowling W, cross-country running M(s)/W(s), lacrosse W, soccer M(s), swimming M(s)/W(s), tennis M(s)/W(s), track and field M(s)/W(s), volleyball W(s). *Intramural sports:* basketball M/W, bowling W, football M, soccer M/W, softball W, swimming M/W, table tennis M/W, tennis M/W, track and field M/W, volleyball M/W.

Standardized Tests *Required:* SAT I and SAT II or ACT (for admission), SAT II: Writing Test (for admission).

Costs (2003–04) *Comprehensive fee:* $16,505 includes full-time tuition ($10,130), mandatory fees ($805), and room and board ($5570). Part-time tuition: $422 per credit hour. *College room only:* $2182. Room and board charges vary according to board plan and housing facility. *Payment plan:* deferred payment. *Waivers:* employees or children of employees.

Financial Aid Of all full-time matriculated undergraduates who enrolled in 2002, 5,685 applied for aid, 4,624 were judged to have need, 1,122 had their need fully met. 356 Federal Work-Study jobs (averaging $3708). 239 state and other part-time jobs (averaging $3474). *Average percent of need met:* 55%. *Average financial aid package:* $17,111. *Average need-based loan:* $5015. *Average need-based gift aid:* $3473. *Average indebtedness upon graduation:* $17,548.

Applying *Options:* early admission, early action, deferred entrance. *Application fee:* $45. *Required:* high school transcript. *Required for some:* 2 letters of recommendation. *Application deadlines:* 2/15 (freshmen), 3/1 (transfers). *Notification:* continuous (freshmen), 12/24 (early action), continuous (transfers).

Howard University (continued)

Admissions Contact Ms. Ann-Marie Waterman, Interim Director of Admissions, Howard University, 2400 Sixth Street, NW, Washington, DC 20059-0002. *Phone:* 202-806-2700. *Toll-free phone:* 800-HOWARD-U. *Fax:* 202-806-4462. *E-mail:* admissions@howard.edu.

■ *See page 1750 for a narrative description.*

POTOMAC COLLEGE
Washington, District of Columbia

- **Proprietary** 4-year, founded 1991
- **Calendar** 6-week modules
- **Degree** bachelor's
- **Urban** campus
- **Coed**
- **Noncompetitive** entrance level

Faculty *Student/faculty ratio:* 11:1.

Student Life *Campus security:* 24-hour emergency response devices.

Costs (2003–04) *Tuition:* $13,380 full-time, $380 per credit hour part-time.

Applying *Required:* high school transcript, interview, 4 years post high school work experience; minimum employment of 20 hours per week.

Admissions Contact Ms. Florence Tate, President, Potomac College, 4000 Chesapeake Street, NW, Washington, DC 20016. *Phone:* 202-686-0876 Ext. 203. *Toll-free phone:* 888-686-0876. *Fax:* 202-686-0818. *E-mail:* cdresser@potomac.edu.

SOUTHEASTERN UNIVERSITY
Washington, District of Columbia

- **Independent** comprehensive, founded 1879
- **Calendar** quadmester (four 12-week semesters)
- **Degrees** certificates, associate, bachelor's, and master's
- **Urban** 1-acre campus
- **Endowment** $27,450
- **Coed**
- **Noncompetitive** entrance level

Faculty *Student/faculty ratio:* 15:1.

Student Life *Campus security:* late-night transport/escort service.

Costs (2003–04) *Tuition:* $8640 full-time, $240 per credit hour part-time. *Required fees:* $525 full-time.

Applying *Options:* deferred entrance. *Application fee:* $45. *Required:* high school transcript. *Recommended:* essay or personal statement, interview.

Admissions Contact Admissions Office, Southeastern University, 501 I Street, Washington, DC 20024. *Phone:* 202-265-5343 Ext. 211. *Fax:* 202-488-8162. *E-mail:* jackf@admin.seu.edu.

■ *See page 2400 for a narrative description.*

STRAYER UNIVERSITY
Washington, District of Columbia

- **Proprietary** comprehensive, founded 1892
- **Calendar** quarters
- **Degrees** certificates, diplomas, associate, bachelor's, master's, and postbachelor's certificates
- **Urban** campus
- **Coed,** 15,972 undergraduate students, 18% full-time, 59% women, 41% men
- **Noncompetitive** entrance level

Undergraduates 2,867 full-time, 13,105 part-time. 5% are from out of state.

Faculty *Total:* 881, 16% full-time. *Student/faculty ratio:* 20:1.

Majors Accounting; business administration and management; computer and information sciences and support services related; computer systems networking and telecommunications; economics; information science/studies; international business/trade/commerce; liberal arts and sciences/liberal studies; marketing/marketing management; purchasing, procurement/acquisitions and contracts management; web page, digital/multimedia and information resources design.

Academic Programs *Special study options:* academic remediation for entering students, accelerated degree program, adult/continuing education programs, advanced placement credit, cooperative education, distance learning, double majors, internships, off-campus study, part-time degree program, services for LD students, summer session for credit.

Library Wilkes Library plus 20 others with 34,000 titles, 600 serial subscriptions, 1,687 audiovisual materials, an OPAC, a Web page.

Computers on Campus 1500 computers available on campus for general student use. A campuswide network can be accessed. Internet access, online (class) registration, at least one staffed computer lab available.

Student Life *Housing:* college housing not available. *Activities and organizations:* honor society, international club, Association of Information Technology Professionals, business administration club, human resource management club. *Campus security:* patrols by trained personnel during operating hours.

Costs (2003–04) *Tuition:* $9841 full-time, $244 per quarter hour part-time. Full-time tuition and fees vary according to course load and degree level. Part-time tuition and fees vary according to course load and degree level. *Payment plan:* installment. *Waivers:* employees or children of employees.

Applying *Options:* electronic application, early admission, deferred entrance. *Application fee:* $35. *Required:* high school transcript. *Required for some:* 1 letter of recommendation. *Recommended:* essay or personal statement, 1 letter of recommendation, interview. *Application deadline:* rolling (freshmen), rolling (transfers). *Notification:* continuous (freshmen), continuous (transfers).

Admissions Contact Mr. Melvin Menns, Campus Manager, Strayer University, 1133 15th Street NW, Washington, DC 20005. *Phone:* 202-419-4190. *Toll-free phone:* 888-4-STRAYER. *Fax:* 202-419-1425. *E-mail:* mzm@strayer.edu.

TRINITY COLLEGE
Washington, District of Columbia

- **Independent Roman Catholic** comprehensive, founded 1897
- **Calendar** semesters
- **Degrees** bachelor's, master's, and postbachelor's certificates
- **Urban** 26-acre campus
- **Endowment** $10.0 million
- **Women only,** 1,011 undergraduate students, 55% full-time
- **Moderately difficult** entrance level, 78% of applicants were admitted

Undergraduates 561 full-time, 450 part-time. Students come from 17 states and territories, 50% are from out of state, 68% African American, 2% Asian American or Pacific Islander, 8% Hispanic American, 0.2% Native American, 4% international, 3% transferred in, 30% live on campus. *Retention:* 69% of 2002 full-time freshmen returned.

Freshmen *Admission:* 423 applied, 331 admitted, 162 enrolled. *Average high school GPA:* 2.80. *Test scores:* SAT verbal scores over 500: 22%; SAT math scores over 500: 19%; ACT scores over 18: 48%; SAT verbal scores over 600: 5%; SAT math scores over 600: 1%; ACT scores over 24: 4%.

Faculty *Total:* 164, 37% full-time. *Student/faculty ratio:* 9:1.

Majors Art history, criticism and conservation; biochemistry; biology/biological sciences; biomedical/medical engineering; business administration and management; chemistry; economics; education; elementary education; English; environmental studies; French; history; human development and family studies; interdisciplinary studies; international relations and affairs; kindergarten/preschool education; liberal arts and sciences/liberal studies; mass communication/media; mathematics; political science and government; pre-law studies; pre-medical studies; psychology; secondary education; Spanish; special education.

Academic Programs *Special study options:* academic remediation for entering students, accelerated degree program, adult/continuing education programs, advanced placement credit, cooperative education, double majors, English as a second language, external degree program, honors programs, independent study, internships, off-campus study, part-time degree program, services for LD students, student-designed majors, study abroad, summer session for credit. *ROTC:* Army (c). *Unusual degree programs:* 3-2 engineering with George Washington University; University of Maryland, College Park.

Library Sister Helen Sheehan Library plus 1 other with 207,000 titles, 498 serial subscriptions, 13,760 audiovisual materials, an OPAC, a Web page.

Computers on Campus 80 computers available on campus for general student use. A campuswide network can be accessed from student residence rooms and from off campus. Internet access, online (class) registration, at least one staffed computer lab available.

Student Life *Housing:* on-campus residence required through junior year. *Options:* women-only. *Activities and organizations:* drama/theater group, student-run newspaper, choral group, Campus Ministry, Athletic Association, international club, Black Student Alliance, Young Democrats/Republicans. *Campus security:* 24-hour emergency response devices and patrols, late-night transport/escort service, controlled dormitory access. *Student services:* health clinic, personal/psychological counseling.

Athletics Member NCAA. All Division III. *Intercollegiate sports:* basketball W(c), crew W, field hockey W, lacrosse W, soccer W, tennis W. *Intramural sports:* tennis W.

Standardized Tests *Recommended:* SAT I or ACT (for admission).

Costs (2004–05) *Comprehensive fee:* $24,150 includes full-time tuition ($16,700), mandatory fees ($160), and room and board ($7290). Part-time tuition:

$540 per credit hour. Part-time tuition and fees vary according to class time. *College room only:* $3190. Room and board charges vary according to board plan and housing facility. *Payment plans:* installment, deferred payment. *Waivers:* employees or children of employees.

Financial Aid Of all full-time matriculated undergraduates who enrolled in 2003, 488 applied for aid, 472 were judged to have need, 48 had their need fully met. 65 Federal Work-Study jobs (averaging $1500). In 2003, 31 non-need-based awards were made. *Average percent of need met:* 65%. *Average financial aid package:* $14,406. *Average need-based loan:* $4709. *Average need-based gift aid:* $10,606. *Average non-need-based aid:* $11,641. *Average indebtedness upon graduation:* $24,093.

Applying *Options:* common application, electronic application, early action, deferred entrance. *Application fee:* $35. *Required:* essay or personal statement, high school transcript, minimum 2.0 GPA, 1 letter of recommendation. *Recommended:* interview. *Application deadline:* 3/1 (freshmen). *Notification:* 1/1 (early action), continuous (transfers).

Admissions Contact Ms. Wendy Kares, Director of Admissions, Trinity College, 125 Michigan Avenue, NE, Washington, DC 20017-1094. *Phone:* 202-884-9400. *Toll-free phone:* 800-IWANTTC. *Fax:* 202-884-9403. *E-mail:* admissions@trinitydc.edu.

■ *See page 2526 for a narrative description.*

University of the District of Columbia
Washington, District of Columbia

- **District-supported** comprehensive, founded 1976
- **Calendar** semesters
- **Degrees** associate, bachelor's, and master's
- **Urban** 28-acre campus
- **Endowment** $16.5 million
- **Coed,** 5,006 undergraduate students, 37% full-time, 62% women, 38% men
- **Noncompetitive** entrance level, 91% of applicants were admitted

Undergraduates 1,862 full-time, 3,144 part-time. Students come from 54 states and territories, 125 other countries, 24% are from out of state, 72% African American, 2% Asian American or Pacific Islander, 5% Hispanic American, 0.2% Native American, 10% international, 12% transferred in. *Retention:* 60% of 2002 full-time freshmen returned.

Freshmen *Admission:* 2,002 applied, 1,825 admitted, 720 enrolled.

Faculty *Total:* 360, 72% full-time, 30% with terminal degrees. *Student/faculty ratio:* 13:1.

Majors Accounting; administrative assistant and secretarial science; advertising; aeronautics/aviation/aerospace science and technology; anthropology; architectural engineering technology; architecture; art; art teacher education; audiology and speech-language pathology; aviation/airway management; avionics maintenance technology; biology/biological sciences; biology/biotechnology laboratory technician; business administration and management; business teacher education; ceramic arts and ceramics; chemical engineering; chemistry; child development; city/urban, community and regional planning; civil engineering; civil engineering technology; clinical laboratory science/medical technology; clinical/medical laboratory technology; clothing/textiles; commercial and advertising art; computer engineering technology; computer science; construction management; corrections; criminal justice/law enforcement administration; criminal justice/police science; criminology; developmental and child psychology; dramatic/theatre arts; economics; electrical, electronic and communications engineering technology; electrical, electronics and communications engineering; electromechanical technology; elementary education; emergency medical technology (EMT paramedic); engineering technology; English; entrepreneurship; environmental engineering technology; environmental studies; family and consumer sciences/home economics teacher education; family and consumer sciences/human sciences; fashion merchandising; finance; fine/studio arts; fire science; food science; food services technology; forestry; French; funeral service and mortuary science; geography; graphic and printing equipment operation/production; graphic communications related; health teacher education; history; hospitality administration; hospitality administration related; human resources management and services related; hydrology and water resources science; industrial arts; industrial radiologic technology; information science/studies; kindergarten/preschool education; legal administrative assistant/secretary; library science; marine science/merchant marine officer; marketing/marketing management; mass communication/media; mathematics; mechanical engineering; mechanical engineering/mechanical technology; music; music teacher education; nursing (licensed practical/vocational nurse training); nursing (registered nurse training); nutrition sciences; ornamental horticulture; parks, recreation and leisure; philosophy; physical education teaching and coaching; physical sciences; physics; political science and government; psychology; public administration; purchasing, procurement/acquisitions and contracts management; respiratory care therapy; social work; sociology; Spanish; special education; trade and industrial teacher education; urban studies/affairs; water quality and wastewater treatment management and recycling technology.

Academic Programs *Special study options:* academic remediation for entering students, accelerated degree program, adult/continuing education programs, cooperative education, English as a second language, external degree program, honors programs, internships, off-campus study, part-time degree program, services for LD students, summer session for credit. *ROTC:* Army (c), Air Force (c).

Library Learning Resources Division Library plus 1 other with 544,412 titles, 594 serial subscriptions, 19,635 audiovisual materials, an OPAC, a Web page.

Computers on Campus 1500 computers available on campus for general student use. A campuswide network can be accessed. At least one staffed computer lab available.

Student Life *Housing:* college housing not available. *Activities and organizations:* drama/theater group, student-run newspaper, choral group, marching band, Caribbean Student Association, Theater Arts Ensemble, National Association for the Advancement of Colored People, national fraternities, national sororities. *Campus security:* 24-hour patrols. *Student services:* health clinic, personal/psychological counseling.

Athletics Member NCAA. All Division II. *Intercollegiate sports:* basketball M(s)/W(s), golf M(s), soccer M(s), tennis M(s)/W(s), track and field M(s)/W(s), volleyball W(s). *Intramural sports:* basketball M.

Standardized Tests *Recommended:* SAT I (for admission).

Costs (2004–05) *Tuition:* district resident $1800 full-time; nonresident $4440 full-time. Part-time tuition and fees vary according to course load. *Required fees:* $270 full-time. *Payment plans:* installment, deferred payment. *Waivers:* senior citizens and employees or children of employees.

Financial Aid Of all full-time matriculated undergraduates who enrolled in 2003, 2,465 applied for aid, 1,567 were judged to have need, 385 had their need fully met. 110 Federal Work-Study jobs (averaging $3000). In 2003, 66 non-need-based awards were made. *Average financial aid package:* $5927. *Average need-based loan:* $4447. *Average need-based gift aid:* $2822. *Average non-need-based aid:* $2147. *Average indebtedness upon graduation:* $16,270.

Applying *Options:* common application, deferred entrance. *Application fee:* $20. *Required:* high school transcript. *Required for some:* GED. *Application deadlines:* 8/1 (freshmen), 8/1 (transfers). *Notification:* continuous until 8/15 (freshmen), continuous until 8/15 (transfers).

Admissions Contact University of the District of Columbia, 4200 Connecticut Avenue NW, Building 39—A-Level, Washington, DC 20008. *Phone:* 202-274-6110. *Fax:* 202-274-5553.

■ *See page 2722 for a narrative description.*

FLORIDA

American College of Prehospital Medicine
Navarre, Florida

Admissions Contact Dr. Richard A. Clinchy, Chairman/CEO, American College of Prehospital Medicine, 7552 Navarre Parkway, Suite 1, Navarre, FL 32566-7312. *Phone:* 850-939-0840. *Toll-free phone:* 800-735-2276. *Fax:* 800-350-3870. *E-mail:* admit@acpm.edu.

American InterContinental University
Plantation, Florida

- **Proprietary** comprehensive
- **Calendar** five 10-week terms
- **Degrees** associate, bachelor's, and master's
- **Suburban** 3-acre campus
- **Coed**
- 100% of applicants were admitted

Faculty *Student/faculty ratio:* 24:1.

Applying *Options:* common application, electronic application. *Application fee:* $50.

Admissions Contact Ms. Lisa Bixler, Director of High School Admissions, American InterContinental University, American Inter Continental University, Admissions Office, 8151 West Peters Road, Plantation, FL 33324. *Phone:* 954-233-7421. *Toll-free phone:* 866-248-4723. *Fax:* 954-233-8127.

Argosy University/Sarasota
Sarasota, Florida

- **Proprietary** upper-level, founded 1974
- **Calendar** semesters

Argosy University/Sarasota (continued)
- **Degrees** bachelor's, master's, and doctoral
- **Coed,** 48 undergraduate students

Undergraduates 0.1% are from out of state, 17% African American, 4% Hispanic American.
Majors Business administration and management; business administration, management and operations related; business, management, and marketing related; e-commerce; management information systems and services related; psychology.
Student Life *Housing:* college housing not available.
Costs (2003–04) *Tuition:* $12,960 full-time, $360 per credit part-time. *Required fees:* $360 full-time, $10 per credit part-time. *Payment plan:* installment.
Financial Aid Of all full-time matriculated undergraduates who enrolled in 2003, 9 applied for aid, 6 were judged to have need. *Average financial aid package:* $6284. *Average need-based loan:* $3959. *Average need-based gift aid:* $2458.
Applying *Application fee:* $50. *Notification:* continuous (transfers).
Admissions Contact Ms. Linda Volz, Director of Admissions, Argosy University/Sarasota, 5250 17th Street, Sarasota, FL 34235. *Phone:* 800-331-5995 Ext. 222. *Toll-free phone:* 800-331-5995. *E-mail:* lvolz@argosyu.edu.

ARGOSY UNIVERSITY/TAMPA
Tampa, Florida

- **Proprietary** upper-level
- **Calendar** semesters
- **Degrees** bachelor's and master's
- **Urban** campus
- **Coed,** 49 undergraduate students, 53% full-time, 80% women, 20% men

Undergraduates 26 full-time, 23 part-time. 0.1% are from out of state, 20% African American, 4% Asian American or Pacific Islander, 6% Hispanic American.
Faculty *Total:* 9, 100% with terminal degrees. *Student/faculty ratio:* 9:1.
Majors Business administration and management; e-commerce; psychology.
Student Life *Activities and organizations:* Student Senate.
Costs (2003–04) *Tuition:* $360 per credit hour part-time. *Required fees:* $135 per year part-time. *Payment plan:* installment. *Waivers:* employees or children of employees.
Financial Aid Of all full-time matriculated undergraduates who enrolled in 2003, 25 applied for aid, 23 were judged to have need. *Average financial aid package:* $5298. *Average need-based loan:* $3602. *Average need-based gift aid:* $1844.
Applying *Application fee:* $50. *Notification:* continuous (transfers).
Admissions Contact Jean Graham, Director of Admissions, Argosy University/Tampa, 4401 North Himes Avenue Suite 150, Tampa, FL 33619. *Phone:* 813-393-5260. *Toll-free phone:* 800-850-6488 Ext. 5260 (in-state); 800-850-6488 (out-of-state). *Fax:* 813-246-4045. *E-mail:* jgraham@argosyu.edu.

THE ART INSTITUTE OF FORT LAUDERDALE
Fort Lauderdale, Florida

Admissions Contact Ms. Eileen L. Northrop, Vice President and Director of Admissions, The Art Institute of Fort Lauderdale, 1799 Southeast 17th Street Causeway, Fort Lauderdale, FL 33316-3000. *Phone:* 954-527-1799 Ext. 420. *Toll-free phone:* 800-275-7603. *Fax:* 954-728-8637.

AVE MARIA UNIVERSITY
Naples, Florida

- **Independent Roman Catholic** comprehensive, founded 2002
- **Calendar** semesters
- **Degrees** bachelor's and master's
- **Suburban** campus
- **Coed,** 109 undergraduate students, 92% full-time, 61% women, 39% men
- 44% of applicants were admitted

Undergraduates 100 full-time, 9 part-time. Students come from 32 states and territories, 80% are from out of state, 2% Asian American or Pacific Islander, 10% Hispanic American, 27% transferred in, 98% live on campus.
Freshmen *Admission:* 177 applied, 77 admitted, 51 enrolled. *Average high school GPA:* 3.35.
Faculty *Total:* 8, 88% full-time, 100% with terminal degrees. *Student/faculty ratio:* 12:1.
Majors American history; American literature; biology/biological sciences; classics and languages, literatures and linguistics; English; European history; Latin; mathematics; philosophy; pre-theology/pre-ministerial studies; theology.
Student Life *Housing:* on-campus residence required through senior year. *Options:* men-only, women-only. Campus housing is university owned. Freshman campus housing is guaranteed. *Activities and organizations:* student-run newspaper, choral group, Pro-Life Club, Student Government, Soccer Club, Hall Council, Ultimate Frisbee Club. *Campus security:* 24-hour patrols, controlled dormitory access.
Costs (2003–04) *Comprehensive fee:* $15,150 includes full-time tuition ($9650), mandatory fees ($500), and room and board ($5000). Part-time tuition: $300 per credit hour. *Required fees:* $40 per credit hour part-time. *Payment plan:* installment. *Waivers:* employees or children of employees.
Applying *Application fee:* $50. *Required:* essay or personal statement, high school transcript, minimum X GPA, letters of recommendation. *Recommended:* interview. *Notification:* continuous (freshmen), continuous (transfers).
Admissions Contact Mr. Richard Dittus, Director of Admissions, Ave Maria University, 1025 Commons Circle, Naples, FL 34119. *Phone:* 877-AVE-UNIV. *Toll-free phone:* 877-AVE-UNIV. *Fax:* 239-280-2559. *E-mail:* admissions@avemaria.edu.

THE BAPTIST COLLEGE OF FLORIDA
Graceville, Florida

- **Independent Southern Baptist** 4-year, founded 1943
- **Calendar** 4-4-2
- **Degrees** associate and bachelor's
- **Small-town** 165-acre campus
- **Endowment** $3.1 million
- **Coed,** 628 undergraduate students, 71% full-time, 33% women, 67% men
- **Noncompetitive** entrance level, 79% of applicants were admitted

Undergraduates 447 full-time, 181 part-time. Students come from 21 states and territories, 24% are from out of state, 7% African American, 1% Asian American or Pacific Islander, 4% Hispanic American, 0.5% Native American, 12% transferred in, 36% live on campus. *Retention:* 70% of 2002 full-time freshmen returned.
Freshmen *Admission:* 352 applied, 277 admitted, 60 enrolled. *Average high school GPA:* 3.01. *Test scores:* SAT verbal scores over 500: 71%; SAT math scores over 500: 50%; ACT scores over 18: 66%; SAT verbal scores over 600: 17%; SAT math scores over 600: 12%; ACT scores over 24: 22%; ACT scores over 30: 3%.
Faculty *Total:* 58, 38% full-time, 45% with terminal degrees. *Student/faculty ratio:* 15:1.
Majors Biblical studies; child care and support services management; education; elementary education; music teacher education; pastoral studies/counseling; religious education; religious/sacred music; theology.
Academic Programs *Special study options:* academic remediation for entering students, advanced placement credit, distance learning, double majors, independent study, internships, part-time degree program, services for LD students, summer session for credit.
Library Ida J. MacMillan Library with 68,419 titles, 484 serial subscriptions, 12,052 audiovisual materials, an OPAC, a Web page.
Computers on Campus 25 computers available on campus for general student use. A campuswide network can be accessed. Internet access, online (class) registration, at least one staffed computer lab available.
Student Life *Housing:* on-campus residence required through sophomore year. *Options:* men-only, women-only. Campus housing is university owned. Freshman applicants given priority for college housing. *Activities and organizations:* drama/theater group, choral group, Baptist Collegiate Ministry, student government, AACC. *Campus security:* student patrols, patrols by police officers 11 p.m. to 7 a.m. *Student services:* personal/psychological counseling.
Athletics *Intramural sports:* basketball M/W, football M/W, soccer M/W, softball M/W, table tennis M/W, tennis M/W, volleyball M/W.
Standardized Tests *Required:* SAT I or ACT (for admission).
Costs (2004–05) *Comprehensive fee:* $9794 includes full-time tuition ($5850), mandatory fees ($200), and room and board ($3744). Full-time tuition and fees vary according to course load. Part-time tuition: $200 per semester hour. Part-time tuition and fees vary according to course load. *Required fees:* $100 per term part-time. *Room and board:* Room and board charges vary according to board plan and housing facility. *Payment plan:* installment. *Waivers:* employees or children of employees.
Financial Aid Of all full-time matriculated undergraduates who enrolled in 2003, 506 applied for aid, 435 were judged to have need, 63 had their need fully met. 30 Federal Work-Study jobs (averaging $1025). In 2003, 53 non-need-based awards were made. *Average percent of need met:* 59%. *Average financial aid*

package: $3500. *Average need-based loan:* $2250. *Average non-need-based aid:* $600. *Average indebtedness upon graduation:* $12,824. *Financial aid deadline:* 4/15.

Applying *Options:* electronic application, deferred entrance. *Application fee:* $20. *Required:* essay or personal statement, high school transcript, 3 letters of recommendation. *Required for some:* interview. *Application deadline:* rolling (freshmen), rolling (transfers). *Notification:* continuous (freshmen), continuous (transfers).

Admissions Contact Mr. Christopher Bishop, Director of Admissions, The Baptist College of Florida, 5400 College Drive, Graceville, FL 32440-1898. *Phone:* 850-263-3261 Ext. 460. *Toll-free phone:* 800-328-2660 Ext. 460. *Fax:* 850-263-7506. *E-mail:* admissions@baptistcollege.edu.

BARRY UNIVERSITY

Miami Shores, Florida

- **Independent Roman Catholic** university, founded 1940
- **Calendar** semesters
- **Degrees** certificates, bachelor's, master's, doctoral, first professional, and postbachelor's certificates
- **Suburban** 122-acre campus with easy access to Miami
- **Endowment** $18.8 million
- **Coed,** 5,893 undergraduate students, 74% full-time, 67% women, 33% men
- **Moderately difficult** entrance level, 70% of applicants were admitted

Barry University represents a personalized educational experience that encourages students to think critically, expand their skills, and find answers. With more than 60 undergraduate programs and more than 50 graduate programs, Barry offers superb opportunities for study, community service, and professional growth. Barry University is a coeducational, Catholic university that is focused on quality academics, hands-on experience, and students' success.

Undergraduates 4,337 full-time, 1,556 part-time. Students come from 49 states and territories, 67 other countries, 12% are from out of state, 22% African American, 1% Asian American or Pacific Islander, 34% Hispanic American, 0.2% Native American, 5% international, 12% transferred in, 32% live on campus. *Retention:* 65% of 2002 full-time freshmen returned.

Freshmen *Admission:* 3,186 applied, 2,236 admitted, 518 enrolled. *Average high school GPA:* 3.03. *Test scores:* SAT verbal scores over 500: 43%; SAT math scores over 500: 36%; ACT scores over 18: 72%; SAT verbal scores over 600: 8%; SAT math scores over 600: 9%; ACT scores over 24: 19%; ACT scores over 30: 1%.

Faculty *Total:* 871, 39% full-time. *Student/faculty ratio:* 13:1.

Majors Accounting; acting; advertising; biology/biological sciences; broadcast journalism; business administration and management; chemistry; clinical laboratory science/medical technology; clinical/medical laboratory technology; communication/speech communication and rhetoric; computer science; criminology; cytotechnology; dramatic/theatre arts; ecology; economics; education; elementary education; engineering; English; English/language arts teacher education; finance; French; history; information science/studies; international business/trade/commerce; international relations and affairs; journalism; kindergarten/preschool education; kinesiology and exercise science; liberal arts and sciences/liberal studies; literature; management information systems; marine biology and biological oceanography; marketing/marketing management; mass communication/media; mathematics; nuclear medical technology; nursing (registered nurse training); philosophy; photography; physical education teaching and coaching; piano and organ; political science and government; pre-dentistry studies; pre-law studies; pre-medical studies; pre-pharmacy studies; pre-veterinary studies; psychology; public relations/image management; radio and television; sociology; Spanish; special education; sport and fitness administration; theology; voice and opera.

Academic Programs *Special study options:* academic remediation for entering students, accelerated degree program, adult/continuing education programs, advanced placement credit, distance learning, double majors, English as a second language, honors programs, independent study, internships, off-campus study, part-time degree program, services for LD students, study abroad, summer session for credit. *ROTC:* Air Force (c). *Unusual degree programs:* 3-2 engineering with University of Miami.

Library Monsignor William Barry Memorial Library plus 1 other with 233,938 titles, 2,880 serial subscriptions, 4,247 audiovisual materials, an OPAC, a Web page.

Computers on Campus 368 computers available on campus for general student use. A campuswide network can be accessed from student residence rooms and from off campus. Internet access, at least one staffed computer lab available. Computer purchase or lease plan available.

Student Life *Housing:* on-campus residence required for freshman year. *Options:* coed, men-only, women-only, disabled students. Campus housing is university owned. *Activities and organizations:* drama/theater group, student-run newspaper, radio and television station, choral group, Student Government Association, Campus Activities Board, Scuba Society, Caribbean Students Association, Jamaican Association, national fraternities, national sororities. *Campus security:* 24-hour emergency response devices and patrols, late-night transport/escort service. *Student services:* health clinic, personal/psychological counseling.

Athletics Member NCAA. All Division II. *Intercollegiate sports:* baseball M(s), basketball M(s)/W(s), crew W(s), golf M(s)/W(s), soccer M(s)/W(s), softball W(s), tennis M(s)/W(s), volleyball W(s). *Intramural sports:* basketball M/W, football M/W, golf M/W, soccer M/W, softball M/W, volleyball M/W.

Standardized Tests *Required:* SAT I or ACT (for admission).

Costs (2004–05) *Comprehensive fee:* $28,750 includes full-time tuition ($21,350) and room and board ($7400). Part-time tuition: $630 per credit.

Financial Aid Of all full-time matriculated undergraduates who enrolled in 2003, 3,499 applied for aid, 3,233 were judged to have need, 302 had their need fully met. 610 Federal Work-Study jobs (averaging $2582). In 2003, 386 non-need-based awards were made. *Average percent of need met:* 67%. *Average financial aid package:* $14,739. *Average need-based loan:* $4424. *Average need-based gift aid:* $6221. *Average non-need-based aid:* $5829. *Average indebtedness upon graduation:* $20,661.

Applying *Options:* common application, electronic application, early admission, deferred entrance. *Application fee:* $30. *Required:* high school transcript, minimum 2.0 GPA. *Required for some:* essay or personal statement. *Recommended:* interview. *Application deadline:* rolling (freshmen), rolling (transfers). *Notification:* continuous (freshmen), continuous (transfers).

Admissions Contact Ms. Tracey Lynn Dysart, Director of Admissions, Barry University, Kelly House, 11300 Northeast Second Avenue, Miami Shores, FL 33161. *Phone:* 305-899-3127. *Toll-free phone:* 800-695-2279. *Fax:* 305-899-2971. *E-mail:* admissions@mail.barry.edu.

■ *See page 1214 for a narrative description.*

BEACON COLLEGE

Leesburg, Florida

- **Independent** 4-year
- **Calendar** semesters
- **Degrees** associate and bachelor's
- **Small-town** 12-acre campus with easy access to Orlando
- **Coed,** 81 undergraduate students, 100% full-time, 41% women, 59% men
- 70% of applicants were admitted

Undergraduates 81 full-time. Students come from 27 states and territories, 80% are from out of state, 12% African American, 2% Asian American or Pacific Islander, 1% Hispanic American, 14% transferred in, 97% live on campus. *Retention:* 71% of 2002 full-time freshmen returned.

Freshmen *Admission:* 43 applied, 30 admitted, 30 enrolled.

Faculty *Total:* 15, 67% full-time, 47% with terminal degrees. *Student/faculty ratio:* 7:1.

Majors Human services; liberal arts and sciences and humanities related; liberal arts and sciences/liberal studies.

Student Life *Housing options:* men-only, women-only. Campus housing is university owned. Freshman campus housing is guaranteed. *Activities and organizations:* Student Government, Yearbook, Basketball, Book Club, Poets and Writers Association. *Student services:* personal/psychological counseling.

Costs (2003–04) *Comprehensive fee:* $25,900 includes full-time tuition ($19,700) and room and board ($6200). Part-time tuition: $610 per credit hour. *College room only:* $3600. *Payment plan:* installment.

Applying *Application fee:* $50. *Required:* essay or personal statement, high school transcript, 3 letters of recommendation, interview, Psycho-Educational Evaluation.

Admissions Contact Beacon College, 105 East Main Street, Leesburg, FL 34748. *Toll-free phone:* 852-787-7249 (in-state); 352-787-0721 (out-of-state). *Fax:* 352-787-0721. *E-mail:* admissions@beaconcollege.edu.

BETHUNE-COOKMAN COLLEGE

Daytona Beach, Florida

- **Independent Methodist** 4-year, founded 1904
- **Calendar** semesters
- **Degree** bachelor's
- **Urban** 60-acre campus with easy access to Orlando
- **Endowment** $21.7 million
- **Coed,** 2,794 undergraduate students, 94% full-time, 59% women, 41% men
- **Minimally difficult** entrance level, 67% of applicants were admitted

Bethune-Cookman College (continued)

Undergraduates 2,618 full-time, 176 part-time. Students come from 42 states and territories, 32 other countries, 29% are from out of state, 90% African American, 0.3% Asian American or Pacific Islander, 1% Hispanic American, 6% international, 4% transferred in, 59% live on campus. *Retention:* 80% of 2002 full-time freshmen returned.

Freshmen *Admission:* 4,024 applied, 2,681 admitted, 832 enrolled. *Average high school GPA:* 2.75. *Test scores:* SAT verbal scores over 500: 13%; SAT math scores over 500: 10%; ACT scores over 18: 21%; SAT verbal scores over 600: 1%; SAT math scores over 600: 1%; ACT scores over 24: 2%.

Faculty *Total:* 192, 73% full-time, 46% with terminal degrees. *Student/faculty ratio:* 17:1.

Majors Accounting; biology/biological sciences; biology teacher education; business administration and management; business teacher education; chemistry; chemistry teacher education; clinical laboratory science/medical technology; computer engineering; computer science; corrections and criminal justice related; elementary education; English; English/language arts teacher education; gerontology; history; hotel/motel administration; information science/studies; international business/trade/commerce; international relations and affairs; liberal arts and sciences/liberal studies; mass communication/media; mathematics; mathematics teacher education; music performance; music teacher education; nursing (registered nurse training); philosophy and religious studies related; physical education teaching and coaching; physics; physics teacher education; political science and government; psychology; social studies teacher education; sociology; special education (specific learning disabilities); speech and rhetoric.

Academic Programs *Special study options:* academic remediation for entering students, accelerated degree program, adult/continuing education programs, advanced placement credit, cooperative education, distance learning, double majors, honors programs, independent study, internships, part-time degree program, study abroad, summer session for credit. *ROTC:* Army (c), Air Force (c). *Unusual degree programs:* 3-2 engineering with Tuskegee University, University of Florida, Florida Atlantic University, Florida Agricultural and Mechanical University, University of Central Florida.

Library Carl S. Swisher Library plus 1 other with 166,772 titles, 770 serial subscriptions, 10,500 audiovisual materials, an OPAC, a Web page.

Computers on Campus 500 computers available on campus for general student use. A campuswide network can be accessed from student residence rooms and from off campus. Internet access, online (class) registration, at least one staffed computer lab available.

Student Life *Housing:* on-campus residence required for freshman year. *Options:* men-only, women-only. Campus housing is university owned. Freshman campus housing is guaranteed. *Activities and organizations:* drama/theater group, student-run newspaper, radio station, choral group, marching band, Greek organizations, concert chorale, marching band, Inspirational Gospel Choir, SGA, national fraternities, national sororities. *Campus security:* 24-hour emergency response devices and patrols, student patrols, late-night transport/escort service. *Student services:* health clinic, personal/psychological counseling.

Athletics Member NCAA. All Division I except football (Division I-AA). *Intercollegiate sports:* baseball M(s), basketball M(s)/W(s), bowling W(s), cross-country running M(s)/W(s), golf M(s)/W(s), softball W(s), tennis M(s)/W(s), track and field M(s)/W(s), volleyball W(s). *Intramural sports:* basketball M/W, football M, racquetball M/W, soccer M, table tennis M/W, volleyball M/W.

Standardized Tests *Required:* SAT I or ACT (for admission).

Costs (2003–04) *Comprehensive fee:* $16,480 includes full-time tuition ($10,106) and room and board ($6374). Part-time tuition: $421 per credit hour. *Waivers:* employees or children of employees.

Financial Aid Of all full-time matriculated undergraduates who enrolled in 2003, 2,597 applied for aid, 2,341 were judged to have need, 480 had their need fully met. 330 Federal Work-Study jobs (averaging $1660). 176 state and other part-time jobs (averaging $1660). In 2003, 71 non-need-based awards were made. *Average percent of need met:* 74%. *Average financial aid package:* $13,750. *Average need-based loan:* $3430. *Average need-based gift aid:* $6575. *Average non-need-based aid:* $7815. *Average indebtedness upon graduation:* $26,200.

Applying *Options:* early admission, deferred entrance. *Application fee:* $25. *Required:* high school transcript, minimum 2.25 GPA, medical history. *Required for some:* interview. *Application deadlines:* 6/30 (freshmen), 6/30 (transfers). *Notification:* continuous (freshmen), continuous (transfers).

Admissions Contact Mr. Les Ferrier, Director of Admissions, Bethune-Cookman College, 640 Dr. Mary McLeod Bethune Boulevard, Daytona Beach, FL 32114-3099. *Phone:* 386-481-2600. *Toll-free phone:* 800-448-0228. *Fax:* 386-481-2601. *E-mail:* admissions@cookman.edu.

■ *See page 1260 for a narrative description.*

CARLOS ALBIZU UNIVERSITY, MIAMI CAMPUS
Miami, Florida

- **Independent** comprehensive, founded 1980, part of Carlos Albizu University
- **Calendar** trimesters
- **Degrees** diplomas, bachelor's, master's, and doctoral
- **Urban** 2-acre campus
- **Coed, primarily women,** 357 undergraduate students, 40% full-time, 76% women, 24% men
- 64% of applicants were admitted

Undergraduates 143 full-time, 214 part-time. 0.1% are from out of state, 13% African American, 77% Hispanic American, 18% transferred in. *Retention:* 67% of 2002 full-time freshmen returned.

Freshmen *Admission:* 185 applied, 119 admitted, 64 enrolled. *Average high school GPA:* 2.00.

Faculty *Total:* 44, 9% full-time, 100% with terminal degrees. *Student/faculty ratio:* 13:1.

Majors Business administration and management; business administration, management and operations related; elementary education; psychology.

Academic Programs *Special study options:* academic remediation for entering students, accelerated degree program, adult/continuing education programs, advanced placement credit, cooperative education, English as a second language, external degree program, independent study, internships, part-time degree program, services for LD students, summer session for credit.

Library Albizu Library with 26,027 titles, 380 serial subscriptions, 1,081 audiovisual materials, an OPAC, a Web page.

Computers on Campus 65 computers available on campus for general student use. A campuswide network can be accessed. Internet access, at least one staffed computer lab available. Computer purchase or lease plan available.

Student Life *Housing:* college housing not available. *Activities and organizations:* student-run newspaper, Student Council, Psi Chi, Students for Cross Cultural Advancement, Black Student Association, P.R.I.D.E. Gay/Lesbian/Bisexual Student Association. *Campus security:* 24-hour emergency response devices and patrols, late-night transport/escort service.

Costs (2004–05) *Tuition:* $8250 full-time, $275 per credit part-time. Full-time tuition and fees vary according to course load and program. Part-time tuition and fees vary according to course load and program. *Required fees:* $669 full-time, $223 per term part-time. *Payment plan:* installment. *Waivers:* minority students and employees or children of employees.

Financial Aid Of all full-time matriculated undergraduates who enrolled in 2002, 121 applied for aid, 118 were judged to have need. 27 Federal Work-Study jobs (averaging $3059). *Average percent of need met:* 50%. *Average financial aid package:* $7925. *Average need-based loan:* $3549. *Average need-based gift aid:* $5300. *Average indebtedness upon graduation:* $23,000.

Applying *Options:* common application. *Application fee:* $25. *Required:* high school transcript, minimum 2.0 GPA. *Application deadline:* rolling (transfers).

Admissions Contact Ms. Miriam E. Matos, Admissions Officer, Carlos Albizu University, Miami Campus, 2173 Northwest 99th Avenue, Miami, FL 33172. *Phone:* 305-593-1223 Ext. 134. *Toll-free phone:* 800-672-3246. *Fax:* 305-593-1854. *E-mail:* jacevedo@albizu.edu.

CHIPOLA COLLEGE
Marianna, Florida

- **State-supported** primarily 2-year, founded 1947
- **Calendar** semesters
- **Degrees** certificates, associate, and bachelor's
- **Rural** 105-acre campus
- **Coed**
- **Noncompetitive** entrance level

Faculty *Student/faculty ratio:* 24:1.

Student Life *Campus security:* night security personnel.

Athletics Member NJCAA.

Standardized Tests *Required:* SAT I or ACT (for placement).

Costs (2003–04) *Tuition:* state resident $57 per semester hour part-time; nonresident $176 per semester hour part-time.

Applying *Options:* early admission. *Required:* high school transcript.

Admissions Contact Mrs. Annette Widner, Registrar and Admissions Director, Chipola College, Marianna, FL 32446. *Phone:* 850-526-2761 Ext. 2292. *Fax:* 850-718-2287.

CLEARWATER CHRISTIAN COLLEGE
Clearwater, Florida

- **Independent nondenominational** 4-year, founded 1966
- **Calendar** semesters
- **Degrees** associate and bachelor's
- **Suburban** 130-acre campus with easy access to Tampa–St. Petersburg
- **Endowment** $1.0 million
- **Coed,** 623 undergraduate students, 96% full-time, 52% women, 48% men
- **Minimally difficult** entrance level, 86% of applicants were admitted

Undergraduates 596 full-time, 27 part-time. Students come from 40 states and territories, 15 other countries, 0.1% are from out of state, 3% African American, 0.8% Asian American or Pacific Islander, 4% Hispanic American, 0.3% international, 15% transferred in, 70% live on campus. *Retention:* 59% of 2002 full-time freshmen returned.

Freshmen *Admission:* 526 applied, 453 admitted, 178 enrolled. *Average high school GPA:* 3.00. *Test scores:* SAT verbal scores over 500: 66%; SAT math scores over 500: 54%; ACT scores over 18: 82%; SAT verbal scores over 600: 27%; SAT math scores over 600: 15%; ACT scores over 24: 27%; SAT verbal scores over 700: 2%; SAT math scores over 700: 2%; ACT scores over 30: 3%.

Faculty *Total:* 53, 68% full-time. *Student/faculty ratio:* 15:1.

Majors Accounting; administrative assistant and secretarial science; banking and financial support services; biblical studies; biology/biological sciences; biology teacher education; business administration and management; business teacher education; communication/speech communication and rhetoric; education; education (K-12); elementary education; English; English/language arts teacher education; general studies; history; history teacher education; humanities; mathematics; mathematics teacher education; music; music teacher education; pastoral studies/counseling; physical education teaching and coaching; pre-law studies; pre-medical studies; psychology; religious/sacred music; science teacher education; secondary education; social studies teacher education; special education.

Academic Programs *Special study options:* academic remediation for entering students, advanced placement credit, double majors, internships, part-time degree program, services for LD students, summer session for credit. *ROTC:* Army (c), Air Force (c).

Library Easter Library with 106,000 titles, 700 serial subscriptions, an OPAC.

Computers on Campus 25 computers available on campus for general student use. A campuswide network can be accessed from student residence rooms and from off campus. Internet access, at least one staffed computer lab available.

Student Life *Housing:* on-campus residence required through senior year. *Options:* men-only, women-only. *Activities and organizations:* drama/theater group, student-run newspaper, choral group, drama club, Alpha Chi, College Republicans, science club, Student Missionary Fellowship. *Campus security:* 24-hour emergency response devices and patrols. *Student services:* personal/psychological counseling.

Athletics Member NCCAA. *Intercollegiate sports:* baseball M, basketball M/W, soccer M, softball W, volleyball W. *Intramural sports:* basketball M/W, tennis M/W, volleyball M/W.

Standardized Tests *Required:* SAT I or ACT (for admission).

Costs (2004–05) *Comprehensive fee:* $15,670 includes full-time tuition ($10,220), mandatory fees ($630), and room and board ($4820). Part-time tuition: $400 per credit hour. *Required fees:* $150 per semester hour part-time.

Financial Aid Of all full-time matriculated undergraduates who enrolled in 2003, 595 applied for aid, 595 were judged to have need, 17 had their need fully met. *Average percent of need met:* 61%. *Average financial aid package:* $6594. *Average need-based loan:* $3434. *Average need-based gift aid:* $3366. *Average indebtedness upon graduation:* $13,638.

Applying *Options:* early admission, deferred entrance. *Application fee:* $35. *Required:* essay or personal statement, high school transcript, minimum 2.0 GPA, 2 letters of recommendation, Christian testimony. *Recommended:* interview. *Application deadline:* rolling (freshmen), rolling (transfers). *Notification:* continuous (freshmen), continuous (transfers).

Admissions Contact Mr. Benjamin J. Puckett, Dean of Enrollment Services, Clearwater Christian College, 3400 Gulf-to-Bay Boulevard, Clearwater, FL 33759-4595. *Phone:* 727-726-1153. *Toll-free phone:* 800-348-4463. *Fax:* 813-726-8597. *E-mail:* admissions@clearwater.edu.

■ *See page 1414 for a narrative description.*

DEVRY UNIVERSITY
Miami, Florida

Admissions Contact 200 South Biscayne Boulevard, Suite 500, Miami, FL 33131-5351.

DEVRY UNIVERSITY
Miramar, Florida

- **Proprietary** comprehensive, founded 2002, part of DeVry University
- **Calendar** semesters
- **Degrees** associate, bachelor's, master's, and postbachelor's certificates
- **Coed**
- **Minimally difficult** entrance level

Standardized Tests *Recommended:* SAT I, ACT or CPT.

Costs (2003–04) *Tuition:* $10,590 full-time, $370 per credit hour part-time. *Required fees:* $165 full-time.

Financial Aid Of all full-time matriculated undergraduates who enrolled in 2003, 164 applied for aid, 161 were judged to have need, 2 had their need fully met. In 2003, 4. *Average percent of need met:* 41. *Average financial aid package:* $6248. *Average need-based loan:* $2778. *Average need-based gift aid:* $3847. *Average non-need-based aid:* $7853.

Applying *Application fee:* $50. *Required:* high school transcript, interview.

Admissions Contact Ms. Tammy Gardener, New Student Coordinator, DeVry University, 2300 Southwest 145th Avenue, Miramar, FL 33207-4150. *Phone:* 954-499-9707. *Toll-free phone:* 866-793-3879. *Fax:* 954-499-9723. *E-mail:* openhouse@mir.devry.edu.

DEVRY UNIVERSITY
Orlando, Florida

- **Proprietary** comprehensive, founded 2000, part of DeVry University
- **Calendar** semesters
- **Degrees** associate, bachelor's, master's, and postbachelor's certificates
- **Urban** 10-hectare campus
- **Coed**
- **Minimally difficult** entrance level

Student Life *Campus security:* 24-hour emergency response devices and patrols, late-night transport/escort service, lighted pathways/sidewalks.

Standardized Tests *Recommended:* SAT I, ACT or CPT.

Costs (2003–04) *Tuition:* $10,590 full-time, $370 per credit hour part-time. Full-time tuition and fees vary according to course load. Part-time tuition and fees vary according to course load. *Required fees:* $165 full-time. *Payment plans:* installment, deferred payment.

Financial Aid Of all full-time matriculated undergraduates who enrolled in 2002, 807 applied for aid, 784 were judged to have need, 2 had their need fully met. In 2002, 55. *Average percent of need met:* 37. *Average financial aid package:* $7922. *Average need-based loan:* $5178. *Average need-based gift aid:* $4030. *Average non-need-based aid:* $10,566.

Applying *Options:* electronic application, deferred entrance. *Application fee:* $50. *Required:* high school transcript, interview.

Admissions Contact Ms. Laura Dorsey, New Student Coordinator, DeVry University, 4000 Millenia Boulevard, Orlando, FL 32839-2426. *Phone:* 407-355-4833. *Toll-free phone:* 866-353-3879. *Fax:* 407-370-3198. *E-mail:* krochford@orl.devry.edu.

DEVRY UNIVERSITY
Tampa, Florida

Admissions Contact 3030 North Rocky Point Drive West, Suite 100, Tampa, FL 33607-5901.

ECKERD COLLEGE
St. Petersburg, Florida

- **Independent Presbyterian** 4-year, founded 1958
- **Calendar** 4-1-4
- **Degree** bachelor's
- **Suburban** 267-acre campus with easy access to Tampa
- **Endowment** $15.0 million
- **Coed,** 1,631 undergraduate students, 98% full-time, 55% women, 45% men
- **Moderately difficult** entrance level, 77% of applicants were admitted

Undergraduates 1,605 full-time, 26 part-time. Students come from 50 states and territories, 49 other countries, 69% are from out of state, 3% African American, 2% Asian American or Pacific Islander, 4% Hispanic American, 0.1% Native American, 8% international, 5% transferred in, 76% live on campus. *Retention:* 84% of 2002 full-time freshmen returned.

Freshmen *Admission:* 2,046 applied, 1,569 admitted, 433 enrolled. *Average high school GPA:* 3.30. *Test scores:* SAT verbal scores over 500: 79%; SAT math

Eckerd College (continued)
scores over 500: 77%; ACT scores over 18: 89%; SAT verbal scores over 600: 35%; SAT math scores over 600: 33%; ACT scores over 24: 51%; SAT verbal scores over 700: 7%; SAT math scores over 700: 4%; ACT scores over 30: 14%.

Faculty *Total:* 147, 69% full-time, 77% with terminal degrees. *Student/faculty ratio:* 13:1.

Majors American studies; anthropology; art; biology/biological sciences; business administration and management; chemistry; Chinese; clinical laboratory science/medical technology; communication/speech communication and rhetoric; comparative literature; computer science; creative writing; dramatic/theatre arts; East Asian languages; economics; English; environmental studies; foreign languages and literatures; French; German; history; human development and family studies; humanities; human resources management; interdisciplinary studies; international business/trade/commerce; international relations and affairs; literature; marine biology and biological oceanography; mathematics; modern languages; music; philosophy; physics; political science and government; psychology; religious studies; Russian; sociology; Spanish; women's studies.

Academic Programs *Special study options:* accelerated degree program, adult/continuing education programs, advanced placement credit, cooperative education, double majors, English as a second language, external degree program, honors programs, independent study, internships, off-campus study, part-time degree program, services for LD students, student-designed majors, study abroad, summer session for credit. *ROTC:* Army (c), Air Force (c). *Unusual degree programs:* 3-2 engineering with University of Miami, Columbia University, Washington University in St. Louis, Auburn University.

Library William Luther Cobb Library with 113,850 titles, 3,009 serial subscriptions, 1,941 audiovisual materials, an OPAC, a Web page.

Computers on Campus 144 computers available on campus for general student use. A campuswide network can be accessed from student residence rooms and from off campus. Internet access, at least one staffed computer lab available.

Student Life *Housing:* on-campus residence required for freshman year. *Options:* coed, men-only, women-only. Campus housing is university owned. Freshman campus housing is guaranteed. *Activities and organizations:* drama/theater group, student-run newspaper, radio and television station, choral group, Earth Society, Water Search and Rescue Team, Triton Tribune, College Choir, Organization of Students. *Campus security:* 24-hour emergency response devices and patrols, student patrols, late-night transport/escort service, controlled dormitory access. *Student services:* health clinic, personal/psychological counseling, women's center.

Athletics Member NCAA. All Division II. *Intercollegiate sports:* baseball M(s), basketball M(s)/W(s), cross-country running W(s), golf M(s), sailing M/W, soccer M(s)/W(s), softball W(s), swimming M(c)/W(c), tennis M(s)/W(s), volleyball M(c)/W(s). *Intramural sports:* basketball M/W, bowling M/W, cross-country running M/W, football M, golf M/W, sailing M/W, soccer M/W, softball M/W, swimming M/W, table tennis M/W, tennis M/W, volleyball M/W, weight lifting M/W.

Standardized Tests *Required:* SAT I or ACT (for admission). *Recommended:* SAT II: Subject Tests (for admission), SAT II: Writing Test (for admission).

Costs (2003–04) *Comprehensive fee:* $28,744 includes full-time tuition ($22,538), mandatory fees ($236), and room and board ($5970). *College room only:* $2812. Room and board charges vary according to board plan and housing facility. *Payment plan:* installment. *Waivers:* employees or children of employees.

Financial Aid Of all full-time matriculated undergraduates who enrolled in 2003, 1,012 applied for aid, 885 were judged to have need, 753 had their need fully met. 48 Federal Work-Study jobs (averaging $2000). 92 state and other part-time jobs (averaging $1370). *Average percent of need met:* 85%. *Average financial aid package:* $17,608. *Average indebtedness upon graduation:* $17,500.

Applying *Options:* common application, electronic application, early admission, deferred entrance. *Application fee:* $25. *Required:* essay or personal statement, high school transcript, 1 letter of recommendation. *Recommended:* minimum 3.0 GPA, interview. *Application deadline:* rolling (freshmen), rolling (transfers). *Notification:* continuous (freshmen), continuous (transfers).

Admissions Contact Dr. Richard R. Hallin, Dean of Admissions, Eckerd College, 4200 54th Avenue South, St. Petersburg, FL 33711. *Phone:* 727-864-8331. *Toll-free phone:* 800-456-9009. *Fax:* 727-866-2304. *E-mail:* admissions@eckerd.edu.

■ *See page 1568 for a narrative description.*

EDWARD WATERS COLLEGE
Jacksonville, Florida

Admissions Contact Ms. Sadie Milliner-Smith, Director of Admissions, Edward Waters College, 1658 Kings Road, Jacksonville, FL 32209-6199. *Phone:* 904-366-2715. *Toll-free phone:* 888-898-3191.

EMBRY-RIDDLE AERONAUTICAL UNIVERSITY
Daytona Beach, Florida

- **Independent** comprehensive, founded 1926
- **Calendar** semesters
- **Degrees** associate, bachelor's, and master's
- **Urban** 178-acre campus with easy access to Orlando
- **Endowment** $35.9 million
- **Coed, primarily men,** 4,518 undergraduate students, 92% full-time, 18% women, 82% men
- **Moderately difficult** entrance level, 82% of applicants were admitted

Embry-Riddle teaches science, theory, and business to meet all the demands of employers in the world of aviation and aerospace; the University's impact on the industry through its graduates is significant. Founded just 22 years after the Wright brothers first flew, Embry-Riddle students learn to solve problems in engineering, business, computer science, technology, maintenance, psychology, communication, and flight. Whatever field students choose, they learn from educators and practitioners who are on the leading edge.

Undergraduates 4,159 full-time, 359 part-time. Students come from 53 states and territories, 99 other countries, 71% are from out of state, 5% African American, 3% Asian American or Pacific Islander, 6% Hispanic American, 0.5% Native American, 9% international, 6% transferred in, 43% live on campus. *Retention:* 77% of 2002 full-time freshmen returned.

Freshmen *Admission:* 3,073 applied, 2,507 admitted, 1,017 enrolled. *Average high school GPA:* 3.00. *Test scores:* SAT verbal scores over 500: 73%; SAT math scores over 500: 82%; ACT scores over 18: 95%; SAT verbal scores over 600: 27%; SAT math scores over 600: 40%; ACT scores over 24: 56%; SAT verbal scores over 700: 3%; SAT math scores over 700: 5%; ACT scores over 30: 6%.

Faculty *Total:* 274, 76% full-time, 52% with terminal degrees. *Student/faculty ratio:* 19:1.

Majors Aeronautical/aerospace engineering technology; aeronautics/aviation/aerospace science and technology; aerospace, aeronautical and astronautical engineering; aircraft powerplant technology; airline pilot and flight crew; air traffic control; atmospheric sciences and meteorology; aviation/airway management; business administration, management and operations related; civil engineering related; communication/speech communication and rhetoric; computer engineering; computer software engineering; electrical and electronic engineering technologies related; engineering; engineering physics; engineering technologies related; environmental psychology; occupational safety and health technology.

Academic Programs *Special study options:* academic remediation for entering students, adult/continuing education programs, advanced placement credit, cooperative education, distance learning, double majors, English as a second language, independent study, internships, part-time degree program, services for LD students, study abroad, summer session for credit. *ROTC:* Army (b), Air Force (b).

Library Jack R. Hunt Memorial Library with 138,327 titles, 741 serial subscriptions, 7,030 audiovisual materials, an OPAC, a Web page.

Computers on Campus 817 computers available on campus for general student use. A campuswide network can be accessed from student residence rooms and from off campus. Internet access, online (class) registration, at least one staffed computer lab available.

Student Life *Housing:* on-campus residence required through sophomore year. *Options:* coed, disabled students. Campus housing is university owned. Freshman campus housing is guaranteed. *Activities and organizations:* drama/theater group, student-run newspaper, radio station, choral group, Eagle Wing, Future Professional Pilots Association, African Student Association, Caribbean Student Association, Sigma Gamma Tau, national fraternities, national sororities. *Campus security:* 24-hour emergency response devices and patrols, student patrols, late-night transport/escort service, controlled dormitory access. *Student services:* health clinic, personal/psychological counseling.

Athletics Member NAIA. *Intercollegiate sports:* baseball M(s), basketball M(s), cheerleading M(c)/W(c), cross-country running M/W, golf M(s), soccer M(s)/W(s), tennis M(s)/W, volleyball W(s). *Intramural sports:* badminton M/W, basketball M/W, bowling M(c)/W(c), crew M(c)/W(c), football M/W, golf M/W, ice hockey M(c), lacrosse M(c)/W(c), racquetball M/W, rugby M(c)/W(c), sailing M(c)/W(c), skiing (downhill) M/W, soccer M/W, softball M/W, swimming M/W, table tennis M/W, tennis M/W, volleyball M/W, water polo M/W, weight lifting M/W, wrestling M(c).

Standardized Tests *Required:* SAT I or ACT (for admission).

Costs (2004–05) *Comprehensive fee:* $28,820 includes full-time tuition ($21,530), mandatory fees ($660), and room and board ($6630). Full-time tuition and fees vary according to program. Part-time tuition: $900 per credit hour. Part-time tuition and fees vary according to program. *College room only:* $3600. Room and board charges vary according to board plan. *Payment plans:* installment, deferred payment. *Waivers:* employees or children of employees.

Financial Aid Of all full-time matriculated undergraduates who enrolled in 2003, 3,048 applied for aid, 2,735 were judged to have need. 281 Federal Work-Study jobs (averaging $980). 1,370 state and other part-time jobs (averaging $1938). In 2003, 574 non-need-based awards were made. *Average financial aid package:* $12,563. *Average need-based loan:* $5514. *Average need-based gift aid:* $3727. *Average non-need-based aid:* $3588. *Average indebtedness upon graduation:* $36,022. *Financial aid deadline:* 6/30.

Applying *Options:* common application, electronic application, early admission, early decision, deferred entrance. *Application fee:* $30. *Required:* high school transcript, minimum 2.0 GPA. *Required for some:* minimum 3.0 GPA, medical examination for flight students. *Recommended:* essay or personal statement, letters of recommendation, interview. *Application deadlines:* rolling (freshmen), 7/1 (transfers). *Early decision:* 12/1. *Notification:* continuous (freshmen), 12/31 (early decision), continuous (transfers).

Admissions Contact Mr. Michael Novak, Director of Admissions, Embry-Riddle Aeronautical University, 600 South Clyde Morris Boulevard, Daytona Beach, FL 32114-3900. *Phone:* 386-226-6112. *Toll-free phone:* 800-862-2416. *Fax:* 386-226-7070. *E-mail:* admit@erau.edu.

■ *See page 1588 for a narrative description.*

EMBRY-RIDDLE AERONAUTICAL UNIVERSITY, EXTENDED CAMPUS

Daytona Beach, Florida

- **Independent** comprehensive, founded 1970
- **Calendar** 5 9-week terms
- **Degrees** associate, bachelor's, and master's (programs offered at 100 military bases worldwide)
- **Endowment** $35.9 million
- **Coed, primarily men,** 7,671 undergraduate students, 2% full-time, 11% women, 89% men
- **Minimally difficult** entrance level

Undergraduates 176 full-time, 7,495 part-time. 8% African American, 3% Asian American or Pacific Islander, 7% Hispanic American, 1% Native American, 1% international.

Freshmen *Admission:* 213 enrolled.

Faculty *Total:* 3,499, 3% full-time, 20% with terminal degrees.

Majors Aeronautics/aviation/aerospace science and technology; aircraft powerplant technology; airline pilot and flight crew; aviation/airway management; business administration, management and operations related.

Academic Programs *Special study options:* adult/continuing education programs, advanced placement credit, cooperative education, external degree program, independent study, off-campus study, part-time degree program, services for LD students.

Library Jack R. Hunt Memorial Library with 138,237 titles, 741 serial subscriptions, 7,030 audiovisual materials, an OPAC, a Web page.

Student Life *Housing:* college housing not available.

Costs (2003–04) *Comprehensive fee:* $27,700 includes full-time tuition ($20,700), mandatory fees ($630), and room and board ($6370). Full-time tuition and fees vary according to location and program. Part-time tuition and fees vary according to location. *College room only:* $3440. *Waivers:* employees or children of employees.

Financial Aid Of all full-time matriculated undergraduates who enrolled in 2003, 38 applied for aid, 34 were judged to have need. *Average financial aid package:* $5206. *Average need-based loan:* $2201. *Average need-based gift aid:* $3156. *Average indebtedness upon graduation:* $7715. *Financial aid deadline:* 6/30.

Applying *Options:* deferred entrance. *Application fee:* $30. *Required for some:* essay or personal statement. *Application deadline:* rolling (freshmen), rolling (transfers). *Notification:* continuous (freshmen), continuous (transfers).

Admissions Contact Mrs. Pam Thomas, Director of Admissions, Records and Registration, Embry-Riddle Aeronautical University, Extended Campus, 600 South Clyde Morris Boulevard, Daytona Beach, FL 32114-3900. *Phone:* 386-226-7610. *Toll-free phone:* 800-522-6787. *Fax:* 386-226-6984. *E-mail:* ecinfo@erau.edu.

EVERGLADES UNIVERSITY

Boca Raton, Florida

- **Proprietary** comprehensive, founded 1989, part of Keiser College
- **Calendar** continuous
- **Degrees** bachelor's and master's
- **Urban** campus
- **Coed,** 300 undergraduate students
- **Noncompetitive** entrance level, 76% of applicants were admitted

Undergraduates 27% African American, 0.9% Asian American or Pacific Islander, 16% Hispanic American.

Freshmen *Admission:* 66 applied, 50 admitted.

Faculty *Total:* 29, 14% full-time. *Student/faculty ratio:* 35:1.

Majors Airline pilot and flight crew; aviation/airway management; business administration and management; information technology; management science.

Academic Programs *Special study options:* accelerated degree program, adult/continuing education programs, cooperative education, distance learning, external degree program, summer session for credit.

Computers on Campus 30 computers available on campus for general student use.

Student Life *Housing:* college housing not available.

Standardized Tests *Required for some:* SAT I (for admission), ACT (for admission), SAT I or ACT (for admission), Otis-Lennon School Ability Test.

Costs (2003–04) *Tuition:* $8928 full-time, $372 per credit hour part-time. *Required fees:* $800 full-time, $400 per term part-time.

Financial Aid Of all full-time matriculated undergraduates who enrolled in 2002, 408 applied for aid, 408 were judged to have need, 327 had their need fully met. 8 Federal Work-Study jobs (averaging $1481). *Average financial aid package:* $9728. *Average need-based loan:* $9728. *Average indebtedness upon graduation:* $35,125. *Financial aid deadline:* 6/1.

Applying *Options:* common application, electronic application. *Application fee:* $55. *Required:* high school transcript. *Notification:* continuous (freshmen), continuous (transfers).

Admissions Contact Ms. Andrea Lieberman, Everglades University, Everglades College, 1500 NW 49th Street, #600, Fort Lauderdale, FL 33309. *Phone:* 954-772-2655. *Toll-free phone:* 954-772-2655 (in-state); 888-772-6077 (out-of-state). *Fax:* 954-772-2695. *E-mail:* admissions@evergladecollege.edu.

EVERGLADES UNIVERSITY

Sarasota, Florida

Admissions Contact 6151 Lake Osprey Drive, Sarasota, FL 34240. *Toll-free phone:* 866-907-2262.

FLAGLER COLLEGE

St. Augustine, Florida

- **Independent** 4-year, founded 1968
- **Calendar** semesters
- **Degree** bachelor's
- **Small-town** 36-acre campus with easy access to Jacksonville
- **Endowment** $32.5 million
- **Coed,** 2,033 undergraduate students, 98% full-time, 61% women, 39% men
- **Moderately difficult** entrance level, 33% of applicants were admitted

Size, cost, location, and excellent academics are the characteristics most often cited by students in their decision to enroll at Flagler. Interested students are encouraged to visit historic St. Augustine and learn how Flagler offers high-quality education in a beautiful setting at a reasonable cost. The cost of tuition, room, and board for the 2003–04 year is just $11,860.

Undergraduates 1,986 full-time, 47 part-time. Students come from 49 states and territories, 28 other countries, 35% are from out of state, 1% African American, 0.8% Asian American or Pacific Islander, 3% Hispanic American, 0.2% Native American, 3% international, 6% transferred in, 36% live on campus. *Retention:* 71% of 2002 full-time freshmen returned.

Freshmen *Admission:* 1,897 applied, 628 admitted, 443 enrolled. *Average high school GPA:* 3.14. *Test scores:* SAT verbal scores over 500: 89%; SAT math scores over 500: 87%; ACT scores over 18: 100%; SAT verbal scores over 600: 34%; SAT math scores over 600: 28%; ACT scores over 24: 48%; SAT verbal scores over 700: 4%; SAT math scores over 700: 2%; ACT scores over 30: 2%.

Faculty *Total:* 155, 41% full-time, 41% with terminal degrees. *Student/faculty ratio:* 21:1.

Majors Accounting; art teacher education; business administration and management; communication/speech communication and rhetoric; dramatic/theatre arts; elementary education; English; fine/studio arts; graphic design; history; Latin American studies; liberal arts and sciences/liberal studies; philosophy; political science and government; psychology; public administration; religious studies; secondary education; social studies teacher education; sociology; Spanish; Spanish language teacher education; special education (emotionally disturbed); special education (hearing impaired); special education (mentally retarded); special education (multiply disabled); special education (specific learning disabilities); sport and fitness administration.

Flagler College (continued)

Academic Programs *Special study options:* academic remediation for entering students, advanced placement credit, distance learning, double majors, independent study, internships, off-campus study, services for LD students, study abroad, summer session for credit.

Library William L. Proctor Library with 80,473 titles, 572 serial subscriptions, 3,003 audiovisual materials, an OPAC, a Web page.

Computers on Campus 210 computers available on campus for general student use. A campuswide network can be accessed from off campus. Internet access, at least one staffed computer lab available.

Student Life *Housing:* on-campus residence required for freshman year. *Options:* men-only, women-only. Campus housing is university owned. Freshman campus housing is guaranteed. *Activities and organizations:* drama/theater group, student-run newspaper, radio station, choral group, Intervarsity, Student Government, Society for the Advancement of Management, Students in Free Enterprise, Deaf Awareness Club. *Campus security:* 24-hour emergency response devices and patrols, late-night transport/escort service, controlled dormitory access. *Student services:* health clinic, personal/psychological counseling.

Athletics Member NAIA. *Intercollegiate sports:* baseball M(s), basketball M(s)/W(s), cross-country running M(s)/W(s), golf M(s)/W, lacrosse M(c), soccer M(s)/W(s), tennis M(s)/W(s), volleyball M(c)/W(s). *Intramural sports:* badminton M/W, basketball M/W, bowling M/W, football M/W, soccer M/W, softball M/W, swimming M/W, table tennis M/W, tennis M/W, volleyball M/W, weight lifting M/W.

Standardized Tests *Required:* SAT I or ACT (for admission).

Costs (2004–05) *Comprehensive fee:* $12,750 includes full-time tuition ($8000) and room and board ($4750). Part-time tuition: $265 per credit hour. *Waivers:* employees or children of employees.

Financial Aid Of all full-time matriculated undergraduates who enrolled in 2002, 1,347 applied for aid, 830 were judged to have need, 254 had their need fully met. 232 Federal Work-Study jobs (averaging $540). 84 state and other part-time jobs (averaging $531). In 2002, 861 non-need-based awards were made. *Average percent of need met:* 74%. *Average financial aid package:* $7285. *Average need-based loan:* $3488. *Average need-based gift aid:* $2751. *Average non-need-based aid:* $4262. *Average indebtedness upon graduation:* $14,971.

Applying *Options:* electronic application, early admission, early decision, deferred entrance. *Application fee:* $30. *Required:* essay or personal statement, high school transcript, 1 letter of recommendation. *Recommended:* minimum 2.85 GPA, interview, rank in upper 50% of high school class. *Application deadlines:* 3/1 (freshmen), 3/1 (transfers). *Early decision:* 12/1 (for plan 1), 1/15 (for plan 2). *Notification:* 3/15 (freshmen), 12/15 (early decision plan 1), 2/1 (early decision plan 2), 3/15 (transfers).

Admissions Contact Mr. Marc G. Williar, Director of Admissions, Flagler College, PO Box 1027, St. Augustine, FL 32085-1027. *Phone:* 904-829-6481 Ext. 220. *Toll-free phone:* 800-304-4208. *E-mail:* admiss@flagler.edu.

■ *See page 1626 for a narrative description.*

Florida Agricultural and Mechanical University

Tallahassee, Florida

- **State-supported** university, founded 1887, part of State University System of Florida
- **Calendar** semesters
- **Degrees** associate, bachelor's, master's, doctoral, and first professional
- **Urban** 419-acre campus
- **Coed,** 11,164 undergraduate students, 89% full-time, 57% women, 43% men
- **Moderately difficult** entrance level, 71% of applicants were admitted

Undergraduates 9,971 full-time, 1,193 part-time. Students come from 47 states and territories, 73 other countries, 20% are from out of state, 3% transferred in. *Retention:* 80% of 2002 full-time freshmen returned.

Freshmen *Admission:* 5,467 applied, 3,875 admitted, 2,493 enrolled. *Average high school GPA:* 3.18. *Test scores:* SAT verbal scores over 500: 53%; SAT math scores over 500: 53%; ACT scores over 18: 83%; SAT verbal scores over 600: 11%; SAT math scores over 600: 13%; ACT scores over 24: 17%; SAT verbal scores over 700: 1%; SAT math scores over 700: 1%; ACT scores over 30: 1%.

Faculty *Total:* 592, 100% full-time, 89% with terminal degrees. *Student/faculty ratio:* 22:1.

Majors Accounting; accounting and business/management; actuarial science; administrative assistant and secretarial science; African-American/Black studies; agricultural business and management; agriculture; animal sciences; architectural engineering technology; architecture; art; art teacher education; biology/biological sciences; business administration and management; business teacher education; chemical engineering; chemistry; civil engineering; civil engineering technology; commercial and advertising art; computer and information sciences; computer engineering; construction engineering technology; criminal justice/law enforcement administration; dramatic/theatre arts; economics; education; electrical, electronic and communications engineering technology; electrical, electronics and communications engineering; elementary education; English; entomology; environmental science; finance; finance and financial management services related; French; geography; graphic and printing equipment operation/production; health and physical education; health/health care administration; health information/medical records administration; health teacher education; history; horticultural science; industrial arts; industrial engineering; information science/studies; jazz/jazz studies; journalism; kindergarten/preschool education; landscape architecture; liberal arts and sciences/liberal studies; management information systems; management information systems and services related; mass communication/media; mathematics; mechanical engineering; medical illustration and informatics related; molecular biology; music; music performance; music teacher education; nursing (registered nurse training); occupational therapy; ornamental horticulture; parks, recreation and leisure facilities management; pharmacy; philosophy; physical education teaching and coaching; physical therapy; physics; plant protection and integrated pest management; political science and government; pre-dentistry studies; psychology; public administration; public relations/image management; religious studies; respiratory care therapy; social sciences; social work; sociology; Spanish; trade and industrial teacher education.

Academic Programs *Special study options:* academic remediation for entering students, accelerated degree program, adult/continuing education programs, advanced placement credit, cooperative education, honors programs, internships, off-campus study, part-time degree program, services for LD students, summer session for credit. *ROTC:* Army (b), Navy (b), Air Force (c).

Library Coleman Memorial Library plus 5 others with 484,801 titles, 7,672 serial subscriptions, 73,957 audiovisual materials, an OPAC.

Computers on Campus A campuswide network can be accessed from student residence rooms and from off campus. Internet access, at least one staffed computer lab available.

Student Life *Housing:* on-campus residence required for freshman year. *Options:* men-only, women-only. *Activities and organizations:* drama/theater group, student-run newspaper, radio station, choral group, marching band, Gospel Choir, University Marching Band, Alpha Kappa Alpha, Alpha Phi Alpha, SBI, national fraternities, national sororities. *Campus security:* 24-hour emergency response devices and patrols, late-night transport/escort service. *Student services:* health clinic, personal/psychological counseling, women's center.

Athletics Member NCAA. All Division I except football (Division I-AA). *Intercollegiate sports:* baseball M, basketball M(s)/W(s), cross-country running M(s)/W(s), golf M(s)/W(s), softball W, swimming M(s)/W(s), tennis M(s)/W(s), track and field M(s)/W(s), volleyball W(s). *Intramural sports:* basketball M/W, cross-country running M, football M, soccer M/W, tennis M/W, volleyball M/W.

Standardized Tests *Required:* SAT I or ACT (for admission).

Costs (2003–04) *Tuition:* state resident $2703 full-time, $90 per credit hour part-time; nonresident $13,058 full-time, $435 per credit hour part-time. Full-time tuition and fees vary according to course load. Part-time tuition and fees vary according to course load. *Required fees:* $248 full-time. *Room and board:* $5238; room only: $3278. Room and board charges vary according to board plan and housing facility. *Payment plans:* tuition prepayment, deferred payment. *Waivers:* senior citizens and employees or children of employees.

Financial Aid Of all full-time matriculated undergraduates who enrolled in 2003, 9,005 applied for aid, 8,093 were judged to have need, 607 had their need fully met. 524 Federal Work-Study jobs (averaging $1227). In 2003, 397 non-need-based awards were made. *Average percent of need met:* 60%. *Average financial aid package:* $7926. *Average need-based loan:* $3356. *Average need-based gift aid:* $3047. *Average non-need-based aid:* $6572. *Average indebtedness upon graduation:* $30,454. *Financial aid deadline:* 6/30.

Applying *Options:* common application, electronic application, early admission, deferred entrance. *Application fee:* $20. *Required:* high school transcript, minimum 2.0 GPA. *Required for some:* essay or personal statement, letters of recommendation. *Recommended:* minimum 3.2 GPA. *Application deadlines:* 5/9 (freshmen), 5/1 (transfers). *Notification:* continuous until 8/1 (freshmen), continuous until 8/1 (transfers).

Admissions Contact Kimberly Davis, Director of Admissions, Florida Agricultural and Mechanical University, Office of Admissions, Tallahassee, FL 32307. *Phone:* 850-599-3866. *Fax:* 850-599-3069. *E-mail:* kimberly.davis@famu.edu.

■ *See page 1628 for a narrative description.*

Florida Atlantic University

Boca Raton, Florida

- **State-supported** university, founded 1961, part of State University System of Florida

- **Calendar** semesters
- **Degrees** certificates, associate, bachelor's, master's, doctoral, and post-master's certificates
- **Suburban** 850-acre campus with easy access to Miami
- **Endowment** $94.1 million
- **Coed,** 21,072 undergraduate students, 51% full-time, 61% women, 39% men
- **Moderately difficult** entrance level, 72% of applicants were admitted

Undergraduates 10,699 full-time, 10,373 part-time. Students come from 50 states and territories, 135 other countries, 6% are from out of state, 18% African American, 5% Asian American or Pacific Islander, 15% Hispanic American, 0.4% Native American, 5% international, 15% transferred in, 9% live on campus. *Retention:* 69% of 2002 full-time freshmen returned.

Freshmen *Admission:* 8,202 applied, 5,915 admitted, 2,440 enrolled. *Average high school GPA:* 3.40. *Test scores:* SAT verbal scores over 500: 57%; SAT math scores over 500: 59%; ACT scores over 18: 77%; SAT verbal scores over 600: 14%; SAT math scores over 600: 15%; ACT scores over 24: 18%; SAT verbal scores over 700: 2%; SAT math scores over 700: 1%; ACT scores over 30: 2%.

Faculty *Total:* 1,304, 56% full-time, 76% with terminal degrees. *Student/faculty ratio:* 18:1.

Majors Accounting; anthropology; architecture; art; biology/biological sciences; business administration and management; chemistry; city/urban, community and regional planning; civil engineering; clinical laboratory science/medical technology; computer and information sciences; computer engineering; criminal justice/safety; digital communication and media/multimedia; dramatic/theatre arts; economics; electrical, electronics and communications engineering; elementary education; English; English/language arts teacher education; finance; French; geography; geology/earth science; German; health/health care administration; health science; health services/allied health/health sciences; history; hospitality administration; human resources management; international business/trade/commerce; Jewish/Judaic studies; kinesiology and exercise science; liberal arts and sciences and humanities related; liberal arts and sciences/liberal studies; linguistics; management information systems; marketing/marketing management; mathematics; mathematics teacher education; mechanical engineering; music; music teacher education; nursing (registered nurse training); ocean engineering; philosophy; physics; physiological psychology/psychobiology; political science and government; psychology; public administration; real estate; science teacher education; social psychology; social sciences; social science teacher education; social work; sociology; Spanish; special education; speech and rhetoric.

Academic Programs *Special study options:* accelerated degree program, adult/continuing education programs, advanced placement credit, cooperative education, distance learning, double majors, English as a second language, freshman honors college, honors programs, independent study, internships, off-campus study, part-time degree program, services for LD students, study abroad, summer session for credit. *ROTC:* Army (c), Air Force (c).

Library S. E. Wimberly Library with 902,834 titles, 3,836 serial subscriptions, 11,107 audiovisual materials, an OPAC, a Web page.

Computers on Campus 822 computers available on campus for general student use. A campuswide network can be accessed from student residence rooms and from off campus. Internet access, online (class) registration, at least one staffed computer lab available.

Student Life *Housing:* on-campus residence required for freshman year. *Options:* coed, women-only. Campus housing is university owned. Freshman campus housing is guaranteed. *Activities and organizations:* drama/theater group, student-run newspaper, radio and television station, choral group, marching band, Latin American Student Organization, Alpha Tau Omega, Konbit Kreyol, Program Board, Owl Corral, national fraternities, national sororities. *Campus security:* 24-hour emergency response devices and patrols, student patrols, late-night transport/escort service, controlled dormitory access. *Student services:* health clinic, personal/psychological counseling, women's center, legal services.

Athletics Member NCAA. All Division I. *Intercollegiate sports:* baseball M(s), basketball M(s)/W(s), cheerleading W, cross-country running M(s)/W(s), football M(s), golf M(s)/W(s), soccer M(s)/W(s), softball W(s), swimming M(s)/W(s), tennis M(s)/W(s), track and field W(s), volleyball W(s). *Intramural sports:* basketball M/W, bowling M/W, cross-country running M/W, fencing M(c)/W(c), football M/W, golf M/W, ice hockey M(c)/W(c), rugby M(c)/W(c), soccer M/W, softball M/W, swimming M/W, table tennis M/W, tennis M/W, track and field M/W, volleyball M/W, weight lifting M/W.

Standardized Tests *Required:* SAT I or ACT (for admission).

Costs (2003–04) *Tuition:* state resident $2943 full-time, $98 per credit hour part-time; nonresident $13,955 full-time, $465 per credit hour part-time. Full-time tuition and fees vary according to course load. Part-time tuition and fees vary according to course load. *Room and board:* $5600. Room and board charges vary according to board plan and housing facility. *Payment plans:* installment, deferred payment. *Waivers:* senior citizens and employees or children of employees.

Financial Aid Of all full-time matriculated undergraduates who enrolled in 2001, 196 Federal Work-Study jobs (averaging $3062). *Average financial aid package:* $2100.

Applying *Options:* common application, electronic application, early admission, deferred entrance. *Application fee:* $20. *Required:* high school transcript, minimum 2.0 GPA. *Required for some:* 1 letter of recommendation. *Application deadlines:* 6/1 (freshmen), 6/1 (transfers). *Notification:* continuous (freshmen), continuous (transfers).

Admissions Contact Coordinator, Freshmen Recruitment, Florida Atlantic University, 777 Glades Road, PO Box 3091, Boca Raton, FL 33431-0991. *Phone:* 561-297-2458. *Toll-free phone:* 800-299-4FAU. *Fax:* 561-297-2758. *E-mail:* admisweb@fau.edu.

■ *See page 1630 for a narrative description.*

FLORIDA CHRISTIAN COLLEGE
Kissimmee, Florida

Admissions Contact Mr. Terry Davis, Admissions Director, Florida Christian College, 1011 Bill Beck Boulevard. *Phone:* 407-847-8966 Ext. 305.

FLORIDA COLLEGE
Temple Terrace, Florida

- **Independent** 4-year, founded 1944
- **Calendar** semesters
- **Degrees** associate and bachelor's
- **Small-town** 95-acre campus with easy access to Tampa
- **Endowment** $11.4 million
- **Coed,** 478 undergraduate students, 98% full-time, 48% women, 52% men
- **Moderately difficult** entrance level, 84% of applicants were admitted

Undergraduates 468 full-time, 10 part-time. Students come from 33 states and territories, 5 other countries, 68% are from out of state, 3% African American, 2% Hispanic American, 1% international, 4% transferred in, 85% live on campus. *Retention:* 73% of 2002 full-time freshmen returned.

Freshmen *Admission:* 326 applied, 274 admitted, 232 enrolled. *Test scores:* SAT verbal scores over 500: 62%; SAT math scores over 500: 57%; ACT scores over 18: 88%; SAT verbal scores over 600: 23%; SAT math scores over 600: 21%; ACT scores over 24: 40%; SAT verbal scores over 700: 5%; SAT math scores over 700: 4%; ACT scores over 30: 5%.

Faculty *Total:* 35, 83% full-time, 29% with terminal degrees. *Student/faculty ratio:* 15:1.

Majors Biblical studies; elementary education; liberal arts and sciences/liberal studies.

Academic Programs *Special study options:* academic remediation for entering students, advanced placement credit, independent study. *ROTC:* Army (c), Air Force (c).

Library Chatlos Library with 96,316 titles, 400 serial subscriptions, 5,920 audiovisual materials, an OPAC, a Web page.

Computers on Campus 76 computers available on campus for general student use. A campuswide network can be accessed from student residence rooms and from off campus. Internet access, at least one staffed computer lab available.

Student Life *Housing:* on-campus residence required through sophomore year. *Options:* men-only, women-only. Campus housing is university owned. Freshman campus housing is guaranteed. *Activities and organizations:* drama/theater group, choral group, Drama Workshop, concert band, chorus, SBGA, YWTO. *Campus security:* controlled dormitory access, evening patrols by trained security personnel. *Student services:* health clinic, personal/psychological counseling.

Athletics Member NJCAA. *Intercollegiate sports:* baseball M(s), basketball M(s), volleyball W(s). *Intramural sports:* basketball M/W, football M/W, soccer M/W, softball M/W, volleyball M/W.

Standardized Tests *Required:* SAT I or ACT (for admission).

Costs (2003–04) *Comprehensive fee:* $14,240 includes full-time tuition ($9100) and room and board ($5140). Part-time tuition: $370 per semester hour. *College room only:* $2400. Room and board charges vary according to board plan and housing facility. *Payment plan:* installment. *Waivers:* employees or children of employees.

Financial Aid Of all full-time matriculated undergraduates who enrolled in 2002, 202 applied for aid, 202 were judged to have need, 18 had their need fully met. In 2002, 80 non-need-based awards were made. *Average percent of need met:* 44%. *Average financial aid package:* $2888. *Average need-based loan:* $1798. *Average need-based gift aid:* $2777. *Average non-need-based aid:* $3159. *Average indebtedness upon graduation:* $6000. *Financial aid deadline:* 8/1.

Applying *Options:* electronic application. *Application fee:* $25. *Required:* high school transcript, minimum 2.0 GPA, letters of recommendation. *Required for*

Florida College (continued)
some: essay or personal statement. *Application deadlines:* 8/1 (freshmen), 8/1 (transfers). *Notification:* continuous (freshmen), continuous (transfers).

Admissions Contact Mrs. Mari Smith, Assistant Director of Admissions, Florida College, 119 North Glen Arven Avenue, Temple Terrace, FL 33617. *Phone:* 813-988-5131 Ext. 6716. *Toll-free phone:* 800-326-7655. *Fax:* 813-899-6772. *E-mail:* admissions@floridacollege.edu.

FLORIDA GULF COAST UNIVERSITY

Fort Myers, Florida

- **State-supported** comprehensive, founded 1991, part of State University System of Florida
- **Calendar** semesters
- **Degrees** certificates, associate, bachelor's, and master's
- **Suburban** 760-acre campus
- **Endowment** $18.4 million
- **Coed,** 4,836 undergraduate students, 70% full-time, 63% women, 37% men
- **Moderately difficult** entrance level, 72% of applicants were admitted

Undergraduates 3,388 full-time, 1,448 part-time. Students come from 34 states and territories, 3% are from out of state, 5% African American, 2% Asian American or Pacific Islander, 9% Hispanic American, 0.5% Native American, 0.8% international, 22% transferred in, 19% live on campus. *Retention:* 70% of 2002 full-time freshmen returned.

Freshmen *Admission:* 2,578 applied, 1,854 admitted, 880 enrolled. *Average high school GPA:* 3.44. *Test scores:* SAT verbal scores over 500: 60%; SAT math scores over 500: 60%; ACT scores over 18: 56%; SAT verbal scores over 600: 13%; SAT math scores over 600: 16%; ACT scores over 24: 22%; SAT verbal scores over 700: 1%; SAT math scores over 700: 1%; ACT scores over 30: 2%.

Faculty *Total:* 402, 48% full-time. *Student/faculty ratio:* 16:1.

Majors Accounting; biotechnology; business administration and management; computer and information sciences; criminal justice/safety; early childhood education; elementary education; finance; general studies; health services/allied health/health sciences; human services; kinesiology and exercise science; legal assistant/paralegal; liberal arts and sciences/liberal studies; management information systems; marketing/marketing management; mental health counseling; nursing (registered nurse training); occupational therapy; political science and government; resort management; special education.

Academic Programs *Special study options:* academic remediation for entering students, accelerated degree program, advanced placement credit, cooperative education, distance learning, double majors, honors programs, independent study, internships, off-campus study, part-time degree program, services for LD students, study abroad, summer session for credit.

Library Library Services with 282,357 titles, 1,429 serial subscriptions, 2,421 audiovisual materials, an OPAC, a Web page.

Computers on Campus 323 computers available on campus for general student use. A campuswide network can be accessed from student residence rooms and from off campus that provide access to online admissions and advising. Internet access, online (class) registration, at least one staffed computer lab available.

Student Life *Housing options:* coed. Campus housing is university owned. *Activities and organizations:* drama/theater group, student-run newspaper, Golden Key National Honor Society, student government, Student Nurses Association, Student Council for Exceptional Children, Physical Therapy Association, national fraternities, national sororities. *Campus security:* 24-hour emergency response devices and patrols, late-night transport/escort service. *Student services:* health clinic, personal/psychological counseling.

Athletics *Intercollegiate sports:* baseball M(s), basketball M(s)/W(s), cheerleading W, cross-country running M/W, golf M(s)/W(s), softball W(s), tennis M(s)/W(s), volleyball W(s). *Intramural sports:* basketball M/W, cross-country running M(c)/W(c), football M/W, soccer M/W, softball M/W, table tennis M/W, tennis M/W, volleyball M/W.

Standardized Tests *Required:* SAT I or ACT (for admission).

Costs (2003–04) *Tuition:* state resident $2850 full-time, $95 per credit part-time; nonresident $13,200 full-time, $440 per credit part-time. Full-time tuition and fees vary according to course load. Part-time tuition and fees vary according to course load. *Required fees:* $71 full-time, $36 per term part-time. *Room and board:* $8000; room only: $4220. Room and board charges vary according to board plan. *Waivers:* senior citizens and employees or children of employees.

Financial Aid Of all full-time matriculated undergraduates who enrolled in 2002, 2,062 applied for aid, 1,219 were judged to have need, 185 had their need fully met. 144 Federal Work-Study jobs (averaging $1608). In 2002, 683 non-need-based awards were made. *Average percent of need met:* 71%. *Average financial aid package:* $6313. *Average need-based loan:* $3641. *Average need-based gift aid:* $3599. *Average non-need-based aid:* $3198. *Average indebtedness upon graduation:* $14,094.

Applying *Options:* electronic application, early admission, deferred entrance. *Application fee:* $30. *Required:* high school transcript, minimum 2.0 GPA. *Required for some:* essay or personal statement, letters of recommendation, interview. *Application deadline:* 3/1 (freshmen), rolling (transfers). *Notification:* continuous (freshmen), continuous (transfers).

Admissions Contact Mr. Larry Stiles, Director of Admissions, Florida Gulf Coast University, 10501 FGCU Boulevard South, Fort Myers, FL 33965-6565. *Phone:* 239-590-7878. *Toll-free phone:* 800-590-7878 (in-state); 800-590-3428 (out-of-state). *Fax:* 239-590-7894. *E-mail:* oar@fgcu.edu.

FLORIDA HOSPITAL COLLEGE OF HEALTH SCIENCES

Orlando, Florida

- **Independent** primarily 2-year
- **Calendar** semesters
- **Degrees** certificates, associate, and bachelor's
- **Urban** 9-acre campus
- **Endowment** $906,128
- **Coed**
- **Minimally difficult** entrance level

Faculty *Student/faculty ratio:* 24:1.

Student Life *Campus security:* 24-hour emergency response devices and patrols, late-night transport/escort service, controlled dormitory access.

Standardized Tests *Required for some:* SAT I or ACT (for admission).

Costs (2004–05) *Tuition:* $5280 full-time, $220 per credit part-time. *Required fees:* $250 full-time, $125 per term part-time. *Room only:* $1680. Room and board charges vary according to housing facility.

Applying *Options:* common application, electronic application. *Application fee:* $20. *Required:* minimum 2.7 GPA. *Required for some:* essay or personal statement, high school transcript, 3 letters of recommendation.

Admissions Contact Ms. Fiona Ghosn, Director of Admissions, Florida Hospital College of Health Sciences, 800 Lake Estelle Drive, Orlando, FL 32803. *Phone:* 407-303-9798 Ext. 5548. *Toll-free phone:* 800-500-7747. *Fax:* 407-303-9408. *E-mail:* fiona.ghosn@fhchs.edu.

FLORIDA INSTITUTE OF TECHNOLOGY

Melbourne, Florida

- **Independent** university, founded 1958
- **Calendar** semesters
- **Degrees** bachelor's, master's, doctoral, and post-master's certificates
- **Small-town** 130-acre campus with easy access to Orlando
- **Endowment** $28.0 million
- **Coed,** 2,346 undergraduate students, 95% full-time, 30% women, 70% men
- **Moderately difficult** entrance level, 86% of applicants were admitted

Undergraduates 2,217 full-time, 129 part-time. Students come from 50 states and territories, 88 other countries, 46% are from out of state, 3% African American, 3% Asian American or Pacific Islander, 6% Hispanic American, 0.3% Native American, 20% international, 7% transferred in, 51% live on campus. *Retention:* 79% of 2002 full-time freshmen returned.

Freshmen *Admission:* 2,146 applied, 1,836 admitted, 551 enrolled. *Average high school GPA:* 3.54. *Test scores:* SAT verbal scores over 500: 77%; SAT math scores over 500: 90%; ACT scores over 18: 100%; SAT verbal scores over 600: 34%; SAT math scores over 600: 54%; ACT scores over 24: 63%; SAT verbal scores over 700: 4%; SAT math scores over 700: 10%; ACT scores over 30: 13%.

Faculty *Total:* 283, 77% full-time, 83% with terminal degrees. *Student/faculty ratio:* 12:1.

Majors Accounting; aeronautics/aviation/aerospace science and technology; aerospace, aeronautical and astronautical engineering; air transportation related; analytical chemistry; applied mathematics; aquatic biology/limnology; astrophysics; aviation/airway management; biochemistry; biological and physical sciences; biology/biological sciences; biology teacher education; biomedical sciences; business administration and management; business administration, management and operations related; chemical engineering; chemistry; chemistry related; chemistry teacher education; civil engineering; communication/speech communication and rhetoric; computer engineering; computer science; computer software engineering; computer teacher education; ecology; electrical, electronics and communications engineering; environmental science; forensic psychology; humanities; hydrology and water resources science; information science/studies; interdisciplinary studies; management information systems; marine biology and biological oceanography; mathematics teacher education; mechanical engineering; meteorology; molecular biology; multi-/interdisciplinary studies related; ocean engineering; oceanography (chemical and physical); physics; physics related; physics teacher education; psychology; science teacher education.

Academic Programs *Special study options:* academic remediation for entering students, accelerated degree program, adult/continuing education programs, advanced placement credit, cooperative education, double majors, English as a second language, internships, part-time degree program, services for LD students, study abroad, summer session for credit. *ROTC:* Army (b).

Library Evans Library with 146,419 titles, 6,079 serial subscriptions, 4,734 audiovisual materials, an OPAC, a Web page.

Computers on Campus 400 computers available on campus for general student use. A campuswide network can be accessed from student residence rooms and from off campus. Internet access, online (class) registration, at least one staffed computer lab available.

Student Life *Housing:* on-campus residence required for freshman year. *Options:* coed, men-only, women-only. Campus housing is university owned. Freshman campus housing is guaranteed. *Activities and organizations:* drama/theater group, student-run newspaper, radio and television station, choral group, marching band, Squamish, Luter-Fraternity Council, Muslim Student Association, Phi Eta Sigma, Chinese Student Scholars Association, national fraternities, national sororities. *Campus security:* 24-hour emergency response devices and patrols, late-night transport/escort service, self-defense education. *Student services:* health clinic, personal/psychological counseling, legal services.

Athletics Member NCAA. All Division II. *Intercollegiate sports:* baseball M(s), basketball M(s)/W(s), cheerleading M/W, crew M(s)/W(s), cross-country running M(s)/W(s), golf M(s)/W(s), soccer M(s)/W(s), softball W(s), tennis M(s)/W(s), volleyball W(s). *Intramural sports:* archery M(c)/W(c), badminton M/W, basketball M/W, bowling M(c)/W(c), fencing M(c)/W(c), football M/W, golf M/W, lacrosse M(c)/W(c), racquetball M/W, rugby M(c)/W(c), sailing M(c)/W(c), soccer M/W, softball M/W, table tennis M/W, tennis M/W, track and field M(c)/W(c), ultimate Frisbee M(c)/W(c), volleyball M/W, water polo M/W, weight lifting M/W, wrestling M.

Standardized Tests *Required:* SAT I or ACT (for admission).

Costs (2003–04) *Comprehensive fee:* $28,740 includes full-time tuition ($22,600) and room and board ($6140). Full-time tuition and fees vary according to course load and program. Part-time tuition: $695 per credit hour. Part-time tuition and fees vary according to course load and program. *College room only:* $3250. Room and board charges vary according to board plan and housing facility. *Payment plan:* installment. *Waivers:* senior citizens and employees or children of employees.

Financial Aid Of all full-time matriculated undergraduates who enrolled in 2003, 1,889 applied for aid, 1,349 were judged to have need, 323 had their need fully met. 532 Federal Work-Study jobs (averaging $1470). In 2003, 473 non-need-based awards were made. *Average percent of need met:* 83%. *Average financial aid package:* $20,497. *Average need-based loan:* $4868. *Average need-based gift aid:* $13,798. *Average non-need-based aid:* $7280. *Average indebtedness upon graduation:* $25,692.

Applying *Options:* common application, electronic application, early admission, deferred entrance. *Application fee:* $40. *Required:* high school transcript, minimum 2.5 GPA. *Required for some:* minimum 3.0 GPA. *Recommended:* essay or personal statement, minimum 2.8 GPA, interview. *Application deadline:* rolling (freshmen), rolling (transfers). *Notification:* continuous (freshmen), continuous (transfers).

Admissions Contact Ms. Judith Marino, Director of Undergraduate Admissions, Florida Institute of Technology, 150 West University Boulevard, Melbourne, FL 32901-6975. *Phone:* 321-674-8030. *Toll-free phone:* 800-888-4348. *Fax:* 321-723-9468. *E-mail:* admissions@fit.edu.

■ *See page 1632 for a narrative description.*

FLORIDA INTERNATIONAL UNIVERSITY
Miami, Florida

- **State-supported** university, founded 1965, part of State University System of Florida
- **Calendar** semesters
- **Degrees** bachelor's, master's, doctoral, and first professional
- **Urban** 573-acre campus
- **Endowment** $48.7 million
- **Coed,** 27,269 undergraduate students, 60% full-time, 57% women, 43% men
- **Moderately difficult** entrance level, 43% of applicants were admitted

Undergraduates 16,335 full-time, 10,934 part-time. Students come from 52 states and territories, 115 other countries, 6% are from out of state, 14% African American, 4% Asian American or Pacific Islander, 56% Hispanic American, 0.2% Native American, 6% international, 9% transferred in, 7% live on campus. *Retention:* 88% of 2002 full-time freshmen returned.

Freshmen *Admission:* 8,450 applied, 3,631 admitted, 3,071 enrolled. *Average high school GPA:* 3.59. *Test scores:* SAT verbal scores over 500: 92%; SAT math scores over 500: 94%; ACT scores over 18: 100%; SAT verbal scores over 600: 34%; SAT math scores over 600: 35%; ACT scores over 24: 75%; SAT verbal scores over 700: 4%; SAT math scores over 700: 4%; ACT scores over 30: 4%.

Faculty *Total:* 1,119, 67% full-time, 71% with terminal degrees. *Student/faculty ratio:* 17:1.

Majors Accounting; applied mathematics; architecture related; art history, criticism and conservation; art teacher education; Asian studies; biology/biological sciences; biomedical/medical engineering; broadcast journalism; business administration and management; chemical engineering; chemistry; civil engineering; communication/speech communication and rhetoric; computer and information sciences; computer engineering; computer science; construction engineering technology; criminal justice/safety; dance; dietetics; dramatic/theatre arts; economics; electrical, electronics and communications engineering; elementary education; English; English/language arts teacher education; environmental control technologies related; environmental design/architecture; environmental studies; family and consumer sciences/home economics teacher education; finance; fine/studio arts; foreign language teacher education; French; geography; geology/earth science; German; health/health care administration; health information/medical records administration; health science; health services/allied health/health sciences; health teacher education; history; hospitality administration; humanities; human resources management; information technology; insurance; interior design; international business/trade/commerce; international relations and affairs; Italian; kinesiology and exercise science; liberal arts and sciences/liberal studies; logistics and materials management; management information systems; marine biology and biological oceanography; marketing/marketing management; mathematics; mathematics teacher education; mechanical engineering; music; music teacher education; nursing (registered nurse training); occupational therapy; orthotics/prosthetics; parks, recreation and leisure facilities management; philosophy; physical education teaching and coaching; physics; political science and government; Portuguese; psychology; public administration; real estate; religious studies; science teacher education; social science teacher education; social work; sociology; Spanish; special education (emotionally disturbed); special education (mentally retarded); special education (specific learning disabilities); statistics; systems engineering; tourism and travel services management; trade and industrial teacher education; urban studies/affairs; women's studies.

Academic Programs *Special study options:* accelerated degree program, adult/continuing education programs, advanced placement credit, cooperative education, distance learning, double majors, English as a second language, freshman honors college, honors programs, independent study, internships, off-campus study, part-time degree program, services for LD students, study abroad, summer session for credit. *ROTC:* Army (b), Air Force (b).

Library University Park Library plus 2 others with 2.2 million titles, 14,978 serial subscriptions, 121,173 audiovisual materials, an OPAC, a Web page.

Computers on Campus 600 computers available on campus for general student use. A campuswide network can be accessed from student residence rooms and from off campus. Internet access, online (class) registration, at least one staffed computer lab available.

Student Life *Housing options:* coed. Campus housing is university owned. *Activities and organizations:* drama/theater group, student-run newspaper, radio station, choral group, marching band, Students for Community Service, Black Student Leadership Council, hospitality management student club, Hispanic Students Association, Haitian Students Organization, national fraternities, national sororities. *Campus security:* 24-hour emergency response devices and patrols, late-night transport/escort service, controlled dormitory access. *Student services:* health clinic, personal/psychological counseling, women's center, legal services.

Athletics Member NCAA. All Division I. *Intercollegiate sports:* baseball M(s), basketball M(s)/W(s), cross-country running M(s)/W(s), football M(s), golf W(s), soccer M(s)/W(s), softball W(s), tennis W(s), track and field M(s)/W(s), volleyball W(s). *Intramural sports:* basketball M/W, bowling M/W, cross-country running M/W, football M, golf M/W, lacrosse M, racquetball M/W, rugby M, sailing M/W, soccer M/W, softball M/W, swimming M/W, table tennis M/W, tennis M/W, volleyball M/W, weight lifting M/W.

Standardized Tests *Required:* SAT I or ACT (for admission).

Costs (2003–04) *Tuition:* state resident $2668 full-time, $89 per credit hour part-time; nonresident $13,696 full-time, $457 per credit hour part-time. Full-time tuition and fees vary according to course load. Part-time tuition and fees vary according to course load. *Required fees:* $221 full-time, $111 per term part-time. *Room and board:* $8822; room only: $5442. Room and board charges vary according to housing facility. *Payment plan:* tuition prepayment. *Waivers:* senior citizens and employees or children of employees.

Financial Aid Of all full-time matriculated undergraduates who enrolled in 2001, 8,112 applied for aid, 7,405 were judged to have need, 717 had their need fully met. 660 Federal Work-Study jobs (averaging $2558). In 2001, 2607

Florida International University (continued)
non-need-based awards were made. *Average percent of need met:* 56%. *Average financial aid package:* $6351. *Average need-based loan:* $4374. *Average need-based gift aid:* $2117. *Average non-need-based aid:* $1851. *Average indebtedness upon graduation:* $4547.

Applying *Options:* common application, electronic application, early admission, deferred entrance. *Application fee:* $25. *Required:* high school transcript, minimum 3.0 GPA. *Required for some:* 1 letter of recommendation. *Application deadline:* rolling (freshmen), rolling (transfers). *Notification:* continuous until 8/1 (freshmen), continuous until 8/1 (transfers).

Admissions Contact Ms. Carmen Brown, Director of Admissions, Florida International University, University Park, PC 140, 11200 SW 8 Street, PC140, Miami, FL 33199. *Phone:* 305-348-3675. *Fax:* 305-348-3648. *E-mail:* admiss@fiu.edu.

■ *See page 1634 for a narrative description.*

FLORIDA MEMORIAL COLLEGE
Miami-Dade, Florida

Admissions Contact Mrs. Peggy Murray Martin, Director of Admissions and International Student Advisor, Florida Memorial College, 15800 NW 42nd Avenue, Miami-Dade, FL 33054. *Phone:* 305-626-3147. *Toll-free phone:* 800-822-1362.

FLORIDA METROPOLITAN UNIVERSITY–BRANDON CAMPUS
Tampa, Florida

- **Proprietary** comprehensive, founded 1890, part of Corinthian Colleges, Inc.
- **Calendar** quarters
- **Degrees** associate, bachelor's, and master's
- **Urban** 5-acre campus
- **Coed,** 1,293 undergraduate students, 51% full-time, 73% women, 27% men
- **Minimally difficult** entrance level, 79% of applicants were admitted

Undergraduates 660 full-time, 633 part-time. Students come from 1 other state, 0.1% are from out of state, 27% African American, 0.9% Asian American or Pacific Islander, 15% Hispanic American, 0.1% international. *Retention:* 35% of 2002 full-time freshmen returned.

Freshmen *Admission:* 177 applied, 139 admitted, 52 enrolled.

Faculty *Total:* 68, 43% full-time. *Student/faculty ratio:* 19:1.

Majors Accounting; business administration and management; computer and information sciences; computer and information sciences and support services related; criminal justice/safety; legal assistant/paralegal; marketing/marketing management; medical/clinical assistant; pharmacy technician; surgical technology.

Academic Programs *Special study options:* academic remediation for entering students, accelerated degree program, adult/continuing education programs, cooperative education, double majors, external degree program, honors programs, internships, part-time degree program, services for LD students, summer session for credit.

Library Tampa College Library with 1,000 titles, 50 serial subscriptions, an OPAC, a Web page.

Computers on Campus 81 computers available on campus for general student use. A campuswide network can be accessed. Internet access, at least one staffed computer lab available.

Student Life *Housing:* college housing not available. *Activities and organizations:* student-run newspaper, Accounting Club, Medical Assistants Club, Paralegal Club. *Campus security:* 24-hour emergency response devices.

Standardized Tests *Required:* CPAt (for admission). *Recommended:* SAT I or ACT (for admission).

Costs (2003–04) *Tuition:* $8800 full-time, $235 per credit part-time. *Required fees:* $180 full-time, $45 per term part-time. *Payment plans:* installment, deferred payment.

Financial Aid Of all full-time matriculated undergraduates who enrolled in 2001, 1,000 applied for aid, 900 were judged to have need. 41 Federal Work-Study jobs (averaging $2500). In 2001, 200 non-need-based awards were made. *Average percent of need met:* 15%. *Average need-based loan:* $3500. *Average need-based gift aid:* $4000. *Average indebtedness upon graduation:* $15,000.

Applying *Options:* common application, early admission, deferred entrance. *Application fee:* $25. *Required:* high school transcript, interview, minimum CPAt score of 120. *Application deadline:* rolling (freshmen), rolling (transfers). *Notification:* continuous (freshmen), continuous (transfers).

Admissions Contact Mrs. Dee McKee, Director of Admissions, Florida Metropolitan University–Brandon Campus, Florida metropolitan University, 3924 Coconut Palm Drive, Tampa, FL 33619. *Phone:* 813-621-0041 Ext. 106. *Toll-free phone:* 877-338-0068. *Fax:* 813-623-5769. *E-mail:* dpearson@cci.edu.

FLORIDA METROPOLITAN UNIVERSITY–FORT LAUDERDALE CAMPUS
Pompano Beach, Florida

- **Proprietary** comprehensive, founded 1940, part of Corinthian Colleges, Inc.
- **Calendar** quarters
- **Degrees** associate, bachelor's, and master's
- **Urban** campus with easy access to Miami
- **Coed,** 1,522 undergraduate students, 62% full-time, 67% women, 33% men
- **Minimally difficult** entrance level

Undergraduates 941 full-time, 581 part-time. Students come from 25 states and territories, 8% African American, 0.1% Asian American or Pacific Islander, 2% Hispanic American, 0.1% international.

Freshmen *Admission:* 332 admitted.

Faculty *Total:* 70, 34% full-time. *Student/faculty ratio:* 17:1.

Majors Accounting; business administration and management; computer programming; criminal justice/police science; hotel/motel administration; international business/trade/commerce; legal assistant/paralegal; management information systems; marketing/marketing management.

Academic Programs *Special study options:* academic remediation for entering students, accelerated degree program, adult/continuing education programs, advanced placement credit, distance learning, English as a second language, internships, part-time degree program, summer session for credit.

Library Florida Metropolitan University Library plus 1 other with 14,500 titles, 61 serial subscriptions, an OPAC.

Computers on Campus 86 computers available on campus for general student use. Internet access, at least one staffed computer lab available. Computer purchase or lease plan available.

Student Life *Housing:* college housing not available. *Activities and organizations:* student-run newspaper, American Marketing Association, International Business Club. *Campus security:* late-night transport/escort service, building security. *Student services:* personal/psychological counseling.

Standardized Tests *Required:* CPAt (for admission). *Recommended:* SAT I or ACT (for admission).

Costs (2003–04) *Tuition:* $9000 full-time, $235 per quarter hour part-time. Full-time tuition and fees vary according to course load. *Required fees:* $150 full-time, $50 per term part-time. *Payment plan:* installment. *Waivers:* employees or children of employees.

Applying *Options:* common application, electronic application, deferred entrance. *Application fee:* $25. *Required:* essay or personal statement, high school transcript. *Required for some:* letters of recommendation. *Recommended:* interview. *Application deadline:* rolling (freshmen), rolling (transfers). *Notification:* continuous (freshmen), continuous (transfers).

Admissions Contact Ms. Fran Heaston, Director of Admissions, Florida Metropolitan University–Fort Lauderdale Campus, Fort Lauderdale, FL 33304. *Phone:* 954-783-7339. *Toll-free phone:* 800-468-0168. *Fax:* 954-568-2008.

FLORIDA METROPOLITAN UNIVERSITY–JACKSONVILLE CAMPUS
Jacksonville, Florida

- **Proprietary** comprehensive, founded 2000
- **Calendar** quarters
- **Degrees** diplomas, associate, bachelor's, and master's
- **Coed**
- **Minimally difficult** entrance level

Costs (2003–04) *Tuition:* $8460 full-time, $235 per quarter hour part-time. *Required fees:* $180 full-time, $60 per term part-time.

Admissions Contact Ms. Donna Wilhelm, Admissions Director, Florida Metropolitan University–Jacksonville Campus, 8226 Phillips Highway, Jacksonville, FL 32256. *Phone:* 904-731-4949. *Toll-free phone:* 888-741-4271.

FLORIDA METROPOLITAN UNIVERSITY–LAKELAND CAMPUS
Lakeland, Florida

- **Proprietary** comprehensive, founded 1890, part of Corinthian Colleges, Inc.
- **Calendar** quarters

- **Degrees** associate, bachelor's, and master's (bachelor's degree in business administration only)
- **Suburban** 3-acre campus with easy access to Orlando and Tampa–St. Petersburg
- **Coed,** 712 undergraduate students, 71% full-time, 77% women, 23% men
- **Minimally difficult** entrance level

Undergraduates 506 full-time, 206 part-time. Students come from 5 states and territories, 5 other countries, 5% are from out of state, 18% African American, 2% Asian American or Pacific Islander, 7% Hispanic American, 0.4% Native American, 1% international, 1% transferred in. *Retention:* 70% of 2002 full-time freshmen returned.
Freshmen *Admission:* 322 enrolled.
Faculty *Total:* 49, 20% full-time, 12% with terminal degrees. *Student/faculty ratio:* 15:1.
Majors Accounting; business administration and management; computer programming; computer science; criminal justice/safety; data processing and data processing technology; legal assistant/paralegal; marketing/marketing management.
Academic Programs *Special study options:* academic remediation for entering students, adult/continuing education programs, advanced placement credit, internships, part-time degree program, summer session for credit.
Library Tampa College Library with 5,000 titles, 30 serial subscriptions.
Computers on Campus 50 computers available on campus for general student use. At least one staffed computer lab available.
Student Life *Housing:* college housing not available. *Activities and organizations:* student-run newspaper, C. J. Association, Paralegal Society, Club Med, Phi Beta Lambda. *Campus security:* 24-hour patrols.
Standardized Tests *Required:* CPAt (for admission). *Recommended:* SAT I (for admission), ACT (for admission).
Costs (2003–04) *Tuition:* $8460 full-time, $235 per quarter hour part-time. *Required fees:* $180 full-time, $60 per term part-time.
Financial Aid Of all full-time matriculated undergraduates who enrolled in 2002, 679 applied for aid, 646 were judged to have need, 10 had their need fully met. 6 Federal Work-Study jobs (averaging $4863). *Average percent of need met:* 76%. *Average financial aid package:* $3510. *Average need-based loan:* $3875. *Average need-based gift aid:* $1000. *Average indebtedness upon graduation:* $29,852.
Applying *Options:* common application, early admission. *Application fee:* $25. *Required:* high school transcript, interview. *Recommended:* essay or personal statement, letters of recommendation.
Admissions Contact Ms. Diane Y. Walton, President, Florida Metropolitan University–Lakeland Campus, Suite 110, 995 East Memorial Boulevard, Lakeland, FL 33801. *Phone:* 863-686-1444. *Toll-free phone:* 877-225-0014. *Fax:* 863-686-1727. *E-mail:* astenbec@cci.edu.

FLORIDA METROPOLITAN UNIVERSITY–MELBOURNE CAMPUS
Melbourne, Florida

- **Proprietary** comprehensive, founded 1953, part of Corinthian Colleges, Inc.
- **Calendar** quarters
- **Degrees** associate, bachelor's, and master's
- **Small-town** 5-acre campus with easy access to Orlando
- **Coed**
- **Minimally difficult** entrance level

Faculty *Student/faculty ratio:* 18:1.
Student Life *Campus security:* 24-hour emergency response devices.
Standardized Tests *Required:* CPAt (for admission).
Costs (2003–04) *Tuition:* $8460 full-time, $235 per credit hour part-time. *Required fees:* $180 full-time.
Financial Aid *Average percent of need met:* 70.
Applying *Options:* common application, deferred entrance. *Application fee:* $25. *Required:* high school transcript, interview.
Admissions Contact Mr. Timothy Alexander, Director of Admissions, Florida Metropolitan University–Melbourne Campus, 2401 North Harbor City Boulevard, Melbourne, FL 32935-6657. *Phone:* 321-253-2929 Ext. 121.

FLORIDA METROPOLITAN UNIVERSITY–NORTH ORLANDO CAMPUS
Orlando, Florida

- **Proprietary** comprehensive, founded 1953, part of Corinthian Colleges, Inc.
- **Calendar** quarters
- **Degrees** associate, bachelor's, and master's
- **Urban** 1-acre campus
- **Coed**
- **Minimally difficult** entrance level

Faculty *Student/faculty ratio:* 15:1.
Student Life *Campus security:* door alarms.
Costs (2003–04) *Tuition:* $8460 full-time, $235 per quarter hour part-time. *Required fees:* $180 full-time, $60 per term part-time.
Financial Aid *Average financial aid package:* $8800.
Applying *Options:* common application, deferred entrance. *Required:* high school transcript.
Admissions Contact Ms. Charlene Donnelly, Director of Admissions, Florida Metropolitan University–North Orlando Campus, 5421 Diplomat Circle, Orlando, FL 32810-5674. *Phone:* 407-628-5870 Ext. 108. *Toll-free phone:* 800-628-5870.

FLORIDA METROPOLITAN UNIVERSITY–PINELLAS CAMPUS
Clearwater, Florida

- **Proprietary** comprehensive, founded 1890, part of Corinthian Colleges, Inc.
- **Calendar** quarters
- **Degrees** associate, bachelor's, and master's
- **Urban** 3-acre campus with easy access to Tampa–St. Petersburg
- **Coed**
- **Minimally difficult** entrance level

Faculty *Student/faculty ratio:* 24:1.
Student Life *Campus security:* 24-hour emergency response devices, late-night transport/escort service, evening patrols by security.
Standardized Tests *Required:* CPAt (for admission). *Recommended:* SAT I or ACT (for admission).
Costs (2003–04) *Tuition:* $8460 full-time, $235 per quarter hour part-time. *Required fees:* $180 full-time, $60 per term part-time.
Financial Aid Of all full-time matriculated undergraduates who enrolled in 2003, 864 applied for aid, 587 were judged to have need. *Average percent of need met:* 90. *Average financial aid package:* $7250. *Average need-based gift aid:* $2700. *Average indebtedness upon graduation:* $23,000.
Applying *Options:* common application, early admission, deferred entrance. *Application fee:* $25. *Required:* high school transcript, interview. *Recommended:* minimum 2.0 GPA.
Admissions Contact Mr. Wayne Childers, Director of Admissions, Florida Metropolitan University–Pinellas Campus, 2471 McMullen Booth Road, Suite 200, Clearwater, FL 33759. *Phone:* 727-725-2688 Ext. 702. *Toll-free phone:* 800-353-FMUS. *Fax:* 727-796-3722. *E-mail:* wchilder@cci.edu.

FLORIDA METROPOLITAN UNIVERSITY–SOUTH ORLANDO CAMPUS
Orlando, Florida

- **Proprietary** comprehensive
- **Calendar** quarters
- **Degrees** associate, bachelor's, and master's
- **Coed**
- **Minimally difficult** entrance level

Faculty *Student/faculty ratio:* 20:1.
Standardized Tests *Required:* (for admission).
Costs (2003–04) *Tuition:* $8460 full-time, $235 per quarter hour part-time. *Required fees:* $180 full-time, $60 per term part-time.
Financial Aid *Average percent of need met:* 90. *Average financial aid package:* $8000.
Applying *Application fee:* $50. *Required:* high school transcript, interview.
Admissions Contact Ms. Annette Cloin, Director of Admissions, Florida Metropolitan University–South Orlando Campus, 2411 Sand Lake Road, Orlando, FL 32809. *Phone:* 407-851-2525 Ext. 111. *Toll-free phone:* 407-851 Ext. 2525 (in-state); 866-508 Ext. 0007 (out-of-state). *Fax:* 407-851-1477.

FLORIDA METROPOLITAN UNIVERSITY–TAMPA CAMPUS
Tampa, Florida

- **Proprietary** comprehensive, founded 1890, part of Corinthian Colleges, Inc.
- **Calendar** quarters

Florida Metropolitan University–Tampa Campus (continued)
- **Degrees** associate, bachelor's, and master's
- **Urban** 4-acre campus
- **Coed,** 1,125 undergraduate students, 62% full-time, 61% women, 39% men
- **Minimally difficult** entrance level, 54% of applicants were admitted

Undergraduates 698 full-time, 427 part-time. Students come from 10 states and territories, 3% transferred in.

Freshmen *Admission:* 237 applied, 127 admitted, 127 enrolled.

Faculty *Total:* 93, 12% full-time, 14% with terminal degrees. *Student/faculty ratio:* 17:1.

Majors Accounting; business administration and management; commercial and advertising art; computer programming; computer science; criminal justice/law enforcement administration; data processing and data processing technology; legal assistant/paralegal; marketing/marketing management; medical/clinical assistant.

Academic Programs *Special study options:* accelerated degree program, adult/continuing education programs, advanced placement credit, cooperative education, distance learning, double majors, English as a second language, external degree program, independent study, internships, part-time degree program, student-designed majors, summer session for credit.

Library Tampa College Library with 4,000 titles, 125 serial subscriptions, 250 audiovisual materials, an OPAC, a Web page.

Computers on Campus 113 computers available on campus for general student use. Internet access, at least one staffed computer lab available.

Student Life *Housing:* college housing not available. *Activities and organizations:* Legal Network, Phi Beta Lambda, PC-MAC Users Group, international club, Art League. *Campus security:* 24-hour emergency response devices, evening and Saturday afternoon patrols by trained security personnel.

Standardized Tests *Required:* CPAt (for admission). *Required for some:* SAT I (for admission), ACT (for admission).

Costs (2003–04) *Tuition:* $8460 full-time, $245 per quarter hour part-time. Full-time tuition and fees vary according to program. Part-time tuition and fees vary according to program. *Required fees:* $180 full-time, $180 per term part-time. *Payment plan:* installment. *Waivers:* employees or children of employees.

Financial Aid Of all full-time matriculated undergraduates who enrolled in 2003, 1,309 applied for aid, 1,309 were judged to have need, 960 had their need fully met. 25 Federal Work-Study jobs (averaging $4000). *Average percent of need met:* 82%. *Average financial aid package:* $5000. *Average need-based loan:* $2625. *Average need-based gift aid:* $1500. *Average indebtedness upon graduation:* $12,000.

Applying *Options:* common application, deferred entrance. *Application fee:* $25. *Required:* high school transcript. *Application deadline:* rolling (freshmen), rolling (transfers). *Notification:* continuous (freshmen), continuous (transfers).

Admissions Contact Mr. Donnie Broughton, Director of Admissions, Florida Metropolitan University–Tampa Campus, 3319 West Hillsborough Avenue, Tampa, FL 33614. *Phone:* 813-879-6000 Ext. 129. *Fax:* 813-871-2483.

FLORIDA SOUTHERN COLLEGE
Lakeland, Florida

- **Independent** comprehensive, founded 1885, affiliated with United Methodist Church
- **Calendar** semesters
- **Degrees** bachelor's and master's
- **Suburban** 100-acre campus with easy access to Tampa and Orlando
- **Endowment** $61.6 million
- **Coed,** 1,841 undergraduate students, 96% full-time, 60% women, 40% men
- **Moderately difficult** entrance level, 75% of applicants were admitted

Undergraduates 1,767 full-time, 74 part-time. Students come from 42 states and territories, 44 other countries, 27% are from out of state, 6% African American, 0.8% Asian American or Pacific Islander, 6% Hispanic American, 0.4% Native American, 4% international, 8% transferred in, 64% live on campus. *Retention:* 68% of 2002 full-time freshmen returned.

Freshmen *Admission:* 1,735 applied, 1,295 admitted, 439 enrolled. *Average high school GPA:* 3.26. *Test scores:* SAT verbal scores over 500: 52%; SAT math scores over 500: 58%; ACT scores over 18: 86%; SAT verbal scores over 600: 16%; SAT math scores over 600: 15%; ACT scores over 24: 23%; SAT verbal scores over 700: 1%; SAT math scores over 700: 2%.

Faculty *Total:* 172, 62% full-time, 58% with terminal degrees. *Student/faculty ratio:* 14:1.

Majors Accounting; advertising; agricultural business and management; art; art teacher education; athletic training; biology/biological sciences; broadcast journalism; business administration and management; business/commerce; chemistry; commercial and advertising art; communication/speech communication and rhetoric; computer science; criminal justice/safety; dramatic/theatre arts; economics; education; elementary education; English; English composition; environmental studies; finance; fine/studio arts; history; horticultural science; hotel/motel administration; humanities; human resources management; international business/trade/commerce; journalism; kindergarten/preschool education; management information systems; marketing/marketing management; mathematics; music; music management and merchandising; music teacher education; natural sciences; nursing (registered nurse training); operations management; ornamental horticulture; physical education teaching and coaching; political science and government; pre-dentistry studies; pre-medical studies; pre-veterinary studies; psychology; public relations/image management; religious education; religious/sacred music; religious studies; secondary education; social sciences; sociology; Spanish; special education (specific learning disabilities).

Academic Programs *Special study options:* academic remediation for entering students, adult/continuing education programs, advanced placement credit, double majors, honors programs, independent study, internships, off-campus study, part-time degree program, study abroad, summer session for credit. *ROTC:* Army (b). *Unusual degree programs:* 3-2 engineering with Washington University in St. Louis, University of Miami; forestry with Duke University.

Library E. T. Roux Library with 172,803 titles, 939 serial subscriptions, 11,490 audiovisual materials, an OPAC, a Web page.

Computers on Campus 250 computers available on campus for general student use. A campuswide network can be accessed from student residence rooms and from off campus that provide access to campus portal. Internet access, online (class) registration, at least one staffed computer lab available. Computer purchase or lease plan available.

Student Life *Housing:* on-campus residence required through junior year. *Options:* men-only, women-only. Campus housing is university owned. Freshman campus housing is guaranteed. *Activities and organizations:* drama/theater group, student-run newspaper, choral group, Fellowship of Christian Athletes, Student Government Association, Student Union Board, Shades of Color, International Student Association, national fraternities, national sororities. *Campus security:* 24-hour emergency response devices and patrols, student patrols, late-night transport/escort service, controlled dormitory access. *Student services:* health clinic, personal/psychological counseling.

Athletics Member NCAA. All Division II. *Intercollegiate sports:* baseball M(s), basketball M(s)/W(s), cheerleading W, cross-country running M(s)/W(s), golf M(s)/W(s), soccer M(s)/W(s), softball W(s), swimming M/W, tennis M(s)/W(s), volleyball M(c)/W(s). *Intramural sports:* basketball M/W, cheerleading W(c), football M/W, soccer W, softball M/W, tennis M/W, volleyball M/W.

Standardized Tests *Required:* SAT I or ACT (for admission).

Costs (2003–04) *Comprehensive fee:* $23,542 includes full-time tuition ($17,142), mandatory fees ($350), and room and board ($6050). Full-time tuition and fees vary according to student level. Part-time tuition: $430 per credit hour. *Required fees:* $350 per year part-time. *College room only:* $3350. Room and board charges vary according to board plan and housing facility. *Payment plan:* installment. *Waivers:* children of alumni and employees or children of employees.

Financial Aid Of all full-time matriculated undergraduates who enrolled in 2003, 1,527 applied for aid, 1,322 were judged to have need, 417 had their need fully met. 352 Federal Work-Study jobs (averaging $1367). 73 state and other part-time jobs (averaging $1639). In 2003, 201 non-need-based awards were made. *Average percent of need met:* 65%. *Average financial aid package:* $15,001. *Average need-based loan:* $4937. *Average need-based gift aid:* $10,988. *Average non-need-based aid:* $10,453. *Average indebtedness upon graduation:* $13,703. *Financial aid deadline:* 8/1.

Applying *Options:* common application, electronic application, early admission, deferred entrance. *Application fee:* $30. *Required:* essay or personal statement, high school transcript, minimum 2.0 GPA, 3 letters of recommendation. *Recommended:* minimum 3.0 GPA, interview. *Application deadline:* rolling (transfers). *Notification:* continuous (freshmen), continuous (transfers).

Admissions Contact Mr. Barry Conners, Director of Admissions, Florida Southern College, 111 Lake Hollingsworth Drive, Lakeland, FL 33801-5698. *Phone:* 863-680-3909. *Toll-free phone:* 800-274-4131. *Fax:* 863-680-4120. *E-mail:* fscadm@flsouthern.edu.

■ *See page 1636 for a narrative description.*

FLORIDA STATE UNIVERSITY
Tallahassee, Florida

- **State-supported** university, founded 1851, part of State University System of Florida
- **Calendar** semesters
- **Degrees** certificates, associate, bachelor's, master's, doctoral, first professional, post-master's, and postbachelor's certificates
- **Suburban** 448-acre campus
- **Endowment** $323.6 million

■ **Coed,** 29,630 undergraduate students, 88% full-time, 57% women, 43% men
■ **Very difficult** entrance level, 42% of applicants were admitted

Undergraduates 25,959 full-time, 3,671 part-time. Students come from 51 states and territories, 120 other countries, 13% are from out of state, 12% African American, 3% Asian American or Pacific Islander, 10% Hispanic American, 0.4% Native American, 0.6% international, 6% transferred in, 16% live on campus. *Retention:* 85% of 2002 full-time freshmen returned.

Freshmen *Admission:* 31,264 applied, 13,037 admitted, 6,081 enrolled. *Average high school GPA:* 3.8. *Test scores:* SAT verbal scores over 500: 87%; SAT math scores over 500: 91%; ACT scores over 18: 99%; SAT verbal scores over 600: 40%; SAT math scores over 600: 43%; ACT scores over 24: 59%; SAT verbal scores over 700: 5%; SAT math scores over 700: 5%; ACT scores over 30: 4%.

Faculty *Total:* 1,403, 77% full-time, 92% with terminal degrees. *Student/faculty ratio:* 23:1.

Majors Accounting; acting; actuarial science; advertising; African-American/Black studies; American studies; anthropology; apparel and textile marketing management; apparel and textiles; applied economics; applied mathematics; art; art history, criticism and conservation; art teacher education; Asian studies; athletic training; atmospheric sciences and meteorology; audiology and speech-language pathology; bilingual and multilingual education; bilingual, multilingual, and multicultural education related; biochemistry; biology/biological sciences; biomathematics and bioinformatics related; biomedical/medical engineering; business administration and management; business/commerce; Caribbean studies; cell and molecular biology; chemical engineering; chemistry; chemistry related; child development; cinematography and film/video production; civil engineering; classics and languages, literatures and linguistics; commercial and advertising art; communication and media related; communication/speech communication and rhetoric; community health services counseling; computer and information sciences; computer engineering; computer programming; computer science; computer software and media applications related; computer software engineering; creative writing; criminal justice/safety; criminology; dance; dietetics; dramatic/theatre arts; early childhood education; ecology; economics; electrical, electronics and communications engineering; elementary education; English; English/language arts teacher education; entrepreneurial and small business related; environmental biology; environmental/environmental health engineering; environmental studies; European studies (Central and Eastern); evolutionary biology; family and consumer economics related; family and consumer sciences/home economics teacher education; family and consumer sciences/human sciences; fashion/apparel design; fashion merchandising; film/cinema studies; finance; fine/studio arts; foods, nutrition, and wellness; foreign language teacher education; French; geography; geology/earth science; German; gerontology; graphic design; health teacher education; history; hospitality administration; hospitality administration related; housing and human environments; human development and family studies; humanities; human resources management; industrial engineering; information science/studies; insurance; interior design; international business/trade/commerce; international relations and affairs; Italian; jazz/jazz studies; kindergarten/preschool education; kinesiology and exercise science; Latin; Latin American studies; liberal arts and sciences/liberal studies; literature; management information systems; marine biology and biological oceanography; marketing/marketing management; mass communication/media; materials engineering; mathematics; mathematics teacher education; mechanical engineering; meteorology; middle school education; modern Greek; multicultural education; music; music history, literature, and theory; music pedagogy; music performance; music teacher education; music theory and composition; music therapy; neurobiology and neurophysiology; nursing (registered nurse training); nutrition sciences; parks, recreation and leisure facilities management; philosophy; physical education teaching and coaching; physical sciences; physical sciences related; physics; piano and organ; plant physiology; political science and government; pre-dentistry studies; pre-law studies; pre-medical studies; pre-pharmacy studies; pre-theology/pre-ministerial studies; pre-veterinary studies; psychology; public relations/image management; radio and television; radio, television, and digital communication related; real estate; religious studies; Russian; Russian studies; sales, distribution and marketing; science teacher education; secondary education; social sciences; social science teacher education; social work; sociology; Spanish; special education (emotionally disturbed); special education (mentally retarded); special education (specific learning disabilities); special education (vision impaired); sport and fitness administration; statistics; technical and business writing; textile science; theatre design and technology; violin, viola, guitar and other stringed instruments; vocational rehabilitation counseling; voice and opera; wind/percussion instruments; women's studies; zoology/animal biology.

Academic Programs *Special study options:* accelerated degree program, adult/continuing education programs, advanced placement credit, cooperative education, distance learning, double majors, English as a second language, honors programs, independent study, internships, off-campus study, part-time degree program, services for LD students, study abroad, summer session for credit. *ROTC:* Army (b), Navy (c), Air Force (b). *Unusual degree programs:* 3-2 emotional disturbances/learning disabilities.

Library Robert Manning Strozier Library plus 6 others with 2.5 million titles, 19,309 serial subscriptions, 43,275 audiovisual materials, an OPAC, a Web page.

Computers on Campus 2707 computers available on campus for general student use. A campuswide network can be accessed from student residence rooms and from off campus that provide access to course home pages, course search, online fee payment. Internet access, online (class) registration, at least one staffed computer lab available. Computer purchase or lease plan available.

Student Life *Housing options:* coed, women-only, cooperative, disabled students. Campus housing is university owned. Freshman applicants given priority for college housing. *Activities and organizations:* drama/theater group, student-run newspaper, radio and television station, choral group, marching band, student government, honors program, Gold Key, Marching Chiefs, intramural sports, national fraternities, national sororities. *Campus security:* 24-hour emergency response devices and patrols, late-night transport/escort service, controlled dormitory access. *Student services:* health clinic, personal/psychological counseling, women's center, legal services.

Athletics Member NCAA. All Division I except football (Division I-A). *Intercollegiate sports:* baseball M(s), basketball M(s)/W(s), bowling M(c)/W(c), cheerleading M/W, cross-country running M(s)/W(s), golf M(s)/W(s), rugby M(c)/W(c), soccer M(c)/W(s), softball W(s), swimming M(s)/W(s), table tennis M(c)/W(c), tennis M(s)/W(s), track and field M(s)/W(s), volleyball M(c)/W(s), wrestling M(c)/W(c). *Intramural sports:* badminton M(c)/W(c), basketball M/W, bowling M/W, crew M(c)/W(c), equestrian sports M(c)/W(c), fencing M(c)/W(c), football M/W, golf M/W, ice hockey M(c)/W(c), lacrosse M(c)/W(c), racquetball M/W, sailing M(c)/W(c), soccer M/W, softball M/W, squash M(c)/W(c), swimming M/W, table tennis M/W, tennis M/W, track and field M/W, ultimate Frisbee M(c)/W(c), volleyball M/W, water polo M(c)/W(c), weight lifting M/W, wrestling M/W.

Standardized Tests *Required:* SAT I or ACT (for admission).

Costs (2003–04) *Tuition:* state resident $2860 full-time, $95 per credit hour part-time; nonresident $13,888 full-time, $463 per credit hour part-time. Full-time tuition and fees vary according to location. Part-time tuition and fees vary according to location. *Room and board:* $6168; room only: $3280. Room and board charges vary according to board plan and housing facility. *Payment plans:* tuition prepayment, installment. *Waivers:* senior citizens and employees or children of employees.

Financial Aid Of all full-time matriculated undergraduates who enrolled in 2003, 14,983 applied for aid, 10,732 were judged to have need, 3,012 had their need fully met. 871 Federal Work-Study jobs (averaging $1787). In 2003, 2713 non-need-based awards were made. *Average percent of need met:* 81%. *Average financial aid package:* $5512. *Average need-based loan:* $3719. *Average need-based gift aid:* $3812. *Average non-need-based aid:* $2454. *Average indebtedness upon graduation:* $17,112.

Applying *Options:* common application, electronic application, early admission. *Application fee:* $30. *Required:* high school transcript. *Required for some:* audition. *Recommended:* essay or personal statement, minimum 3.0 GPA. *Application deadlines:* 3/1 (freshmen), 7/1 (transfers). *Notification:* continuous until 3/15 (freshmen), continuous until 7/15 (transfers).

Admissions Contact Office of Admissions, Florida State University, A2500 University Center, Tallahassee, FL 32306-2400. *Phone:* 850-644-6200. *Fax:* 850-644-0197. *E-mail:* admissions@admin.fsu.edu.

■ *See page 1638 for a narrative description.*

HOBE SOUND BIBLE COLLEGE
Hobe Sound, Florida

Admissions Contact Mrs. Ann French, Director of Admissions, Hobe Sound Bible College, PO Box 1065, Hobe Sound, FL 33475-1065. *Phone:* 561-546-5534 Ext. 415. *Toll-free phone:* 800-881-5534. *Fax:* 561-545-1422. *E-mail:* hsbcuwin@aol.com.

INTERNATIONAL ACADEMY OF DESIGN & TECHNOLOGY
Tampa, Florida

■ **Proprietary** 4-year, founded 1984, part of Career Education Corporation
■ **Calendar** quarters
■ **Degrees** associate and bachelor's
■ **Urban** 1-acre campus
■ **Coed,** 2,043 undergraduate students
■ **Noncompetitive** entrance level, 62% of applicants were admitted

International Academy of Design & Technology (continued)

Undergraduates Students come from 27 states and territories, 9 other countries, 22% are from out of state, 13% African American, 3% Asian American or Pacific Islander, 17% Hispanic American, 1% Native American, 3% international. *Retention:* 62% of 2002 full-time freshmen returned.

Freshmen *Admission:* 667 applied, 416 admitted.

Faculty *Total:* 151, 13% full-time, 12% with terminal degrees. *Student/faculty ratio:* 14:1.

Majors Commercial and advertising art; computer graphics; design and visual communications; fashion/apparel design; interior design; intermedia/multimedia.

Academic Programs *Special study options:* academic remediation for entering students, accelerated degree program, adult/continuing education programs, advanced placement credit, distance learning, internships, study abroad, summer session for credit.

Library International Academy Library with 6,321 titles, 236 serial subscriptions, 421 audiovisual materials, an OPAC.

Computers on Campus 310 computers available on campus for general student use. A campuswide network can be accessed. Internet access, at least one staffed computer lab available.

Student Life *Housing:* college housing not available. *Activities and organizations:* Student Chapter ASID, Dean's Team, Fashion Design International, computer animation club, marketing club. *Campus security:* 24-hour emergency response devices, late night patrols by trained security personnel.

Costs (2004–05) *Tuition:* $16,320 full-time, $340 per credit part-time. *Required fees:* $300 full-time, $100 per term part-time. *Payment plans:* installment, deferred payment. *Waivers:* employees or children of employees.

Financial Aid *Average percent of need met:* 48%.

Applying *Options:* common application, electronic application, early admission, deferred entrance. *Application fee:* $100. *Required:* essay or personal statement, interview. *Recommended:* minimum 2.0 GPA. *Application deadline:* rolling (freshmen), rolling (transfers).

Admissions Contact Mr. Harold Saulsby, Vice President of Admissions and Marketing, International Academy of Design & Technology, 5225 Memorial Highway, Tampa, FL 33634-7350. *Phone:* 813-880-8019. *Toll-free phone:* 800-ACADEMY. *Fax:* 813-881-0008. *E-mail:* leads@academy.edu.

INTERNATIONAL COLLEGE
Naples, Florida

- **Independent** comprehensive, founded 1990
- **Calendar** trimesters
- **Degrees** associate, bachelor's, and master's
- **Suburban** campus with easy access to Miami
- **Coed,** 1,333 undergraduate students, 74% full-time, 63% women, 37% men
- **Minimally difficult** entrance level

Undergraduates 985 full-time, 348 part-time. 0.1% are from out of state, 13% African American, 1% Asian American or Pacific Islander, 14% Hispanic American, 0.5% Native American, 23% transferred in.

Freshmen *Admission:* 138 enrolled.

Faculty *Total:* 107, 50% full-time, 48% with terminal degrees. *Student/faculty ratio:* 16:1.

Majors Accounting; business administration and management; business administration, management and operations related; computer/information technology services administration related; criminal justice/safety; health/health care administration; health information/medical records technology; health/medical preparatory programs related; information technology; legal assistant/paralegal; legal professions and studies related; medical/clinical assistant; multi-/interdisciplinary studies related.

Academic Programs *Special study options:* academic remediation for entering students, accelerated degree program, adult/continuing education programs, advanced placement credit, cooperative education, distance learning, double majors, English as a second language, external degree program, internships, part-time degree program, services for LD students, summer session for credit.

Library Information Resource Center plus 1 other with 25,751 titles, 227 serial subscriptions, 249 audiovisual materials, an OPAC, a Web page.

Computers on Campus 300 computers available on campus for general student use. A campuswide network can be accessed. Internet access, at least one staffed computer lab available.

Student Life *Housing:* college housing not available. *Activities and organizations:* Ambassadors, Paralegal club, Institute of Managerial Accountants, running club, Entrepreneurial Club. *Campus security:* late-night transport/escort service, building security. *Student services:* personal/psychological counseling.

Athletics *Intramural sports:* cheerleading M/W.

Standardized Tests *Required:* CPAt (for admission). *Recommended:* SAT I (for admission), ACT (for admission).

Costs (2003–04) *Tuition:* $8160 full-time, $340 per credit part-time. *Required fees:* $380 full-time, $190 per term part-time. *Payment plan:* installment. *Waivers:* employees or children of employees.

Financial Aid Of all full-time matriculated undergraduates who enrolled in 2003, 821 applied for aid, 745 were judged to have need, 358 had their need fully met. 28 Federal Work-Study jobs. In 2003, 16 non-need-based awards were made. *Average percent of need met:* 65%. *Average financial aid package:* $4500. *Average need-based loan:* $2600. *Average need-based gift aid:* $2340. *Average non-need-based aid:* $1000. *Average indebtedness upon graduation:* $17,500.

Applying *Options:* common application, electronic application, deferred entrance. *Application fee:* $20. *Required:* essay or personal statement, high school transcript, interview. *Required for some:* 2 letters of recommendation. *Application deadline:* rolling (freshmen), rolling (transfers). *Notification:* continuous (freshmen), continuous (transfers).

Admissions Contact Ms. Rita Lampus, Director of Admissions, International College, 2655 Northbrooke Drive, Naples, FL 34119. *Phone:* 239-513-1122 Ext. 104. *Toll-free phone:* 800-466-8017. *E-mail:* admit@internationalcollege.edu.

ITT TECHNICAL INSTITUTE
Fort Lauderdale, Florida

- **Proprietary** primarily 2-year, founded 1991, part of ITT Educational Services, Inc.
- **Calendar** quarters
- **Degrees** associate and bachelor's
- **Suburban** campus with easy access to Miami
- **Coed**
- **Minimally difficult** entrance level

Standardized Tests *Required:* Wonderlic aptitude test (for admission).

Costs (2003–04) *Tuition:* $347 per credit hour part-time.

Applying *Options:* deferred entrance. *Application fee:* $100. *Required:* high school transcript, interview. *Recommended:* letters of recommendation.

Admissions Contact Mr. Bob Bixler, Director of Recruitment, ITT Technical Institute, 3401 South University Drive, Fort Lauderdale, FL 33328. *Phone:* 954-476-9300. *Toll-free phone:* 800-488-7797. *Fax:* 954-476-6889.

ITT TECHNICAL INSTITUTE
Jacksonville, Florida

- **Proprietary** primarily 2-year, founded 1991, part of ITT Educational Services, Inc.
- **Calendar** quarters
- **Degrees** associate and bachelor's
- **Urban** 1-acre campus
- **Coed**
- **Minimally difficult** entrance level

Standardized Tests *Required:* Wonderlic aptitude test (for admission).

Costs (2003–04) *Tuition:* $347 per credit hour part-time.

Financial Aid Of all full-time matriculated undergraduates who enrolled in 2001, 5 Federal Work-Study jobs.

Applying *Options:* deferred entrance. *Application fee:* $100. *Required:* high school transcript, interview. *Recommended:* letters of recommendation.

Admissions Contact Mr. Jorge Torres, Director of Recruitment, ITT Technical Institute, 6600-10 Youngerman Circle, Jacksonville, FL 32244. *Phone:* 904-573-9100. *Toll-free phone:* 800-318-1264. *Fax:* 904-573-0512.

ITT TECHNICAL INSTITUTE
Maitland, Florida

- **Proprietary** primarily 2-year, founded 1989, part of ITT Educational Services, Inc.
- **Calendar** quarters
- **Degrees** associate and bachelor's
- **Suburban** 1-acre campus with easy access to Orlando
- **Coed**
- **Minimally difficult** entrance level

Standardized Tests *Required:* Wonderlic aptitude test (for admission).

Costs (2003–04) *Tuition:* $347 per credit hour part-time.

Applying *Options:* deferred entrance. *Application fee:* $100. *Required:* high school transcript, interview. *Recommended:* letters of recommendation.

Admissions Contact Mr. Larry Johnson, Director of Recruitment, ITT Technical Institute, 2600 Lake Lucien Drive, Suite 140, Maitland, FL 32751. *Phone:* 407-660-2900. *Fax:* 407-660-2566.

ITT TECHNICAL INSTITUTE
Miami, Florida

- **Proprietary** primarily 2-year, founded 1996, part of ITT Educational Services, Inc.
- **Calendar** quarters
- **Degrees** associate and bachelor's
- **Coed**
- **Minimally difficult** entrance level

Standardized Tests *Required:* Wonderlic aptitude test (for admission).
Costs (2003–04) *Tuition:* $347 per credit hour part-time.
Applying *Options:* deferred entrance. *Application fee:* $100. *Required:* high school transcript, interview. *Recommended:* letters of recommendation.
Admissions Contact Mrs. Rosa Sacarello Daratany, Director of Recruitment, ITT Technical Institute, 7955 NW 12th Street, Suite 119, Miami, FL 33126. *Phone:* 305-477-3080. *Fax:* 305-477-7561.

ITT TECHNICAL INSTITUTE
Tampa, Florida

- **Proprietary** primarily 2-year, founded 1981, part of ITT Educational Services, Inc.
- **Calendar** quarters
- **Degrees** associate and bachelor's
- **Suburban** campus with easy access to St. Petersburg
- **Coed**
- **Minimally difficult** entrance level

Standardized Tests *Required:* Wonderlic aptitude test (for admission).
Costs (2003–04) *Tuition:* $347 per credit hour part-time.
Applying *Options:* deferred entrance. *Application fee:* $100. *Required:* high school transcript, interview. *Recommended:* letters of recommendation.
Admissions Contact Mr. Joseph E. Rostkowski, Director of Recruitment, ITT Technical Institute, 4809 Memorial Highway, Tampa, FL 33634. *Phone:* 813-885-2244. *Toll-free phone:* 800-825-2831. *Fax:* 813-888-8451.

JACKSONVILLE UNIVERSITY
Jacksonville, Florida

- **Independent** comprehensive, founded 1934
- **Calendar** semesters
- **Degrees** bachelor's, master's, and first professional certificates
- **Suburban** 260-acre campus
- **Endowment** $24.0 million
- **Coed,** 2,214 undergraduate students, 86% full-time, 50% women, 50% men
- **Moderately difficult** entrance level, 70% of applicants were admitted

Undergraduates 1,900 full-time, 314 part-time. Students come from 46 states and territories, 61 other countries, 37% are from out of state, 15% African American, 3% Asian American or Pacific Islander, 5% Hispanic American, 0.7% Native American, 3% international, 10% transferred in, 59% live on campus. *Retention:* 69% of 2002 full-time freshmen returned.
Freshmen *Admission:* 1,684 applied, 1,179 admitted, 451 enrolled. *Average high school GPA:* 3.17. *Test scores:* SAT verbal scores over 500: 62%; SAT math scores over 500: 65%; ACT scores over 18: 90%; SAT verbal scores over 600: 18%; SAT math scores over 600: 24%; ACT scores over 24: 37%; SAT verbal scores over 700: 2%; SAT math scores over 700: 3%; ACT scores over 30: 5%.
Faculty *Total:* 264, 47% full-time, 51% with terminal degrees. *Student/faculty ratio:* 13:1.
Majors Accounting; airline pilot and flight crew; art; art history, criticism and conservation; aviation/airway management; biology/biological sciences; business administration and management; business/commerce; chemistry; communication/speech communication and rhetoric; computer and information sciences; dance; design and visual communications; drama and dance teacher education; dramatic/theatre arts; economics; electrical, electronics and communications engineering; elementary education; engineering physics; English; environmental studies; finance; fine/studio arts; French; geography; history; humanities; interdisciplinary studies; international business/trade/commerce; international relations and affairs; kinesiology and exercise science; liberal arts and sciences/liberal studies; management information systems; marine science/merchant marine officer; marketing/marketing management; mathematics; mechanical engineering; music; music management and merchandising; music performance; music teacher education; music theory and composition; nursing (registered nurse training); philosophy; physical education teaching and coaching; physics; political science and government; predentistry studies; pre-law studies; pre-medical studies; pre-veterinary studies; psychology; secondary education; sociology; Spanish; special education; visual and performing arts; voice and opera.
Academic Programs *Special study options:* academic remediation for entering students, accelerated degree program, adult/continuing education programs, advanced placement credit, cooperative education, distance learning, double majors, honors programs, independent study, internships, off-campus study, part-time degree program, services for LD students, student-designed majors, study abroad, summer session for credit. *ROTC:* Navy (b). *Unusual degree programs:* 3-2 engineering with University of Florida, Georgia Institute of Technology, Columbia University, University of Miami, Stevens Institute of Technology, Washington University in St. Louis, Mercer University.
Library Carl S. Swisher Library with 374,016 titles, 686 serial subscriptions, 32,887 audiovisual materials, a Web page.
Computers on Campus 450 computers available on campus for general student use. A campuswide network can be accessed from student residence rooms and from off campus. Internet access, online (class) registration, at least one staffed computer lab available.
Student Life *Housing:* on-campus residence required through junior year. *Options:* coed, men-only, women-only, disabled students. Campus housing is university owned. Freshman campus housing is guaranteed. *Activities and organizations:* drama/theater group, student-run newspaper, radio and television station, choral group, Student Government Association, Baptist Campus Ministry, national fraternities, national sororities. *Campus security:* 24-hour emergency response devices and patrols, student patrols, late-night transport/escort service, controlled dormitory access, code lock doors in residence halls, trained security patrols during evening hours. *Student services:* health clinic, personal/psychological counseling.
Athletics Member NCAA. All Division I except football (Division I-AA). *Intercollegiate sports:* baseball M(s), basketball M(s)/W(s), crew M(s)/W(s), cross-country running M/W(s), golf M(s)/W(s), soccer M(s)/W(s), softball W(s), tennis M(s)/W(s), track and field W(s), volleyball W(s). *Intramural sports:* basketball M/W, bowling M/W, cross-country running M/W, football M/W, golf M/W, racquetball M/W, soccer M, softball M/W, swimming M/W, table tennis M/W, tennis M/W, track and field M, volleyball M/W.
Standardized Tests *Required:* SAT I or ACT (for admission).
Costs (2003–04) *Comprehensive fee:* $24,040 includes full-time tuition ($17,700), mandatory fees ($240), and room and board ($6100). Part-time tuition: $590 per hour. Part-time tuition and fees vary according to course load. *College room only:* $2800. Room and board charges vary according to board plan and housing facility. *Payment plan:* installment. *Waivers:* employees or children of employees.
Financial Aid Of all full-time matriculated undergraduates who enrolled in 2003, 1,249 applied for aid, 1,104 were judged to have need, 423 had their need fully met. 200 Federal Work-Study jobs (averaging $2000). In 2003, 469 non-need-based awards were made. *Average percent of need met:* 82%. *Average financial aid package:* $15,853. *Average need-based loan:* $4014. *Average need-based gift aid:* $12,438. *Average non-need-based aid:* $5234.
Applying *Options:* common application, electronic application, early admission, deferred entrance. *Application fee:* $30. *Required:* essay or personal statement, high school transcript, minimum 2.0 GPA. *Recommended:* letters of recommendation, interview. *Application deadline:* rolling (freshmen), rolling (transfers).
Admissions Contact Mr. John P. Grundig, Director of Admissions, Jacksonville University, 2800 University Boulevard North, Office of Admissions, Jacksonville, FL 32211. *Phone:* 904-256-7000. *Toll-free phone:* 800-225-2027. *Fax:* 904-256-7012. *E-mail:* admissions@ju.edu.

■ *See page 1780 for a narrative description.*

JOHNSON & WALES UNIVERSITY
North Miami, Florida

- **Independent** 4-year, founded 1992
- **Calendar** quarters
- **Degrees** associate and bachelor's
- **Suburban** 8-acre campus with easy access to Miami
- **Endowment** $161.5 million
- **Coed,** 2,379 undergraduate students, 96% full-time, 55% women, 45% men
- **Minimally difficult** entrance level, 87% of applicants were admitted

Undergraduates 2,287 full-time, 92 part-time. Students come from 39 states and territories, 51 other countries, 35% African American, 2% Asian American or Pacific Islander, 23% Hispanic American, 0.3% Native American, 7% international.
Freshmen *Admission:* 4,954 applied, 4,296 admitted. *Average high school GPA:* 2.80. *Test scores:* SAT verbal scores over 500: 31%; SAT math scores over 500: 31%; SAT verbal scores over 600: 7%; SAT math scores over 600: 8%; SAT verbal scores over 700: 1%.
Faculty *Total:* 80, 74% full-time.

Johnson & Wales University (continued)

Majors Accounting; advertising; criminal justice/law enforcement administration; culinary arts; fashion merchandising; hospitality administration; hotel/motel administration; international business/trade/commerce; marketing/marketing management; special products marketing; tourism and travel services management.

Academic Programs *Special study options:* academic remediation for entering students, accelerated degree program, advanced placement credit, cooperative education, English as a second language, honors programs, independent study, internships, part-time degree program, services for LD students, study abroad, summer session for credit.

Library Florida Campus Library with 11,875 titles, 243 serial subscriptions, 1,822 audiovisual materials, an OPAC.

Computers on Campus 141 computers available on campus for general student use. A campuswide network can be accessed from off campus. Internet access, at least one staffed computer lab available.

Student Life *Housing:* on-campus residence required for freshman year. *Options:* coed. Campus housing is university owned and leased by the school. Freshman campus housing is guaranteed. *Activities and organizations:* Vocational Industrial Clubs of America, American Culinary Federation, Collegiate Ambassador Team, New Frontiers, Tasters of the Vine, national fraternities, national sororities. *Campus security:* 24-hour emergency response devices and patrols, video camera surveillance throughout campus. *Student services:* personal/psychological counseling.

Athletics Member NAIA. *Intramural sports:* basketball M/W, football M, golf M/W, soccer M/W, softball M/W, table tennis M/W, tennis M/W, volleyball M/W.

Standardized Tests *Required for some:* SAT I or ACT (for admission). *Recommended:* SAT I or ACT (for admission).

Costs (2004–05) *Tuition:* $19,182 full-time, $6395 per term part-time. Full-time tuition and fees vary according to course load, location, and program. Part-time tuition and fees vary according to course load, location, and program. No tuition increase for student's term of enrollment. *Required fees:* $810 full-time. *Room only:* $7185. Room and board charges vary according to board plan and housing facility. *Payment plan:* installment. *Waivers:* employees or children of employees.

Financial Aid Of all full-time matriculated undergraduates who enrolled in 2003, 2,036 applied for aid, 1,891 were judged to have need, 1,566 had their need fully met. In 2003, 55 non-need-based awards were made. *Average percent of need met:* 66%. *Average financial aid package:* $13,053. *Average need-based loan:* $5858. *Average need-based gift aid:* $4926. *Average non-need-based aid:* $4539. *Average indebtedness upon graduation:* $21,958.

Applying *Options:* common application, early admission, deferred entrance. *Required:* high school transcript. *Required for some:* essay or personal statement, letters of recommendation, interview. *Recommended:* minimum 2.0 GPA. *Application deadline:* rolling (freshmen), rolling (transfers). *Notification:* continuous (freshmen), continuous (transfers).

Admissions Contact Mr. Jeff Greenip, Director of Admissions, Johnson & Wales University, 1701 Northeast 127th Street, North Miami, FL 33181. *Phone:* 305-892-7002. *Toll-free phone:* 800-232-2433. *Fax:* 305-892-7020. *E-mail:* admissions@jwu.edu.

JONES COLLEGE
Jacksonville, Florida

- **Independent** 4-year, founded 1918
- **Calendar** trimesters
- **Degrees** associate and bachelor's
- **Urban** 5-acre campus
- **Coed,** 641 undergraduate students, 32% full-time, 79% women, 21% men
- **Noncompetitive** entrance level, 72% of applicants were admitted

Undergraduates 205 full-time, 436 part-time. Students come from 3 states and territories, 57% African American, 3% Asian American or Pacific Islander, 2% Hispanic American, 0.2% Native American, 0.5% international. *Retention:* 68% of 2002 full-time freshmen returned.

Freshmen *Admission:* 290 applied, 209 admitted, 51 enrolled.

Faculty *Total:* 57, 12% full-time, 79% with terminal degrees. *Student/faculty ratio:* 14:1.

Majors Accounting; administrative assistant and secretarial science; business administration and management; information science/studies; interdisciplinary studies; legal assistant/paralegal; medical/clinical assistant.

Academic Programs *Special study options:* academic remediation for entering students, accelerated degree program, adult/continuing education programs, advanced placement credit, cooperative education, distance learning, double majors, internships, part-time degree program, student-designed majors, summer session for credit.

Library James V. Forrestal Library plus 2 others with 34,000 titles, 161 serial subscriptions, a Web page.

Computers on Campus 80 computers available on campus for general student use. A campuswide network can be accessed. Internet access, at least one staffed computer lab available.

Student Life *Housing:* college housing not available. *Activities and organizations:* PBL, national fraternities. *Campus security:* late-night transport/escort service. *Student services:* personal/psychological counseling.

Costs (2004–05) *Tuition:* $6000 full-time, $250 per credit hour part-time. *Required fees:* $90 full-time, $45 per term part-time.

Applying *Options:* early admission, deferred entrance. *Required:* high school transcript, interview. *Application deadline:* rolling (freshmen). *Notification:* continuous (transfers).

Admissions Contact Mr. Barry Durden, Director of Admissions, Jones College, 5355 Arlington Expressway, Jacksonville, FL 32211. *Phone:* 904-743-1122 Ext. 115. *Fax:* 904-743-4446. *E-mail:* bdurden@jones.edu.

JONES COLLEGE
Miami, Florida

- **Independent** 4-year, founded 1987
- **Calendar** trimesters
- **Degrees** associate and bachelor's
- **Suburban** campus
- **Coed,** 837 undergraduate students, 75% women, 25% men

Undergraduates 837 part-time. 49% African American, 1% Asian American or Pacific Islander, 16% Hispanic American, 0.5% Native American, 0.8% international.

Freshmen *Admission:* 145 admitted.

Faculty *Total:* 246, 74% full-time, 80% with terminal degrees.

Majors Business administration and management; clinical/medical laboratory assistant; computer and information sciences; health services/allied health/health sciences; interdisciplinary studies; legal assistant/paralegal.

Costs (2004–05) *Tuition:* $6000 full-time, $250 per credit part-time. *Required fees:* $90 full-time, $45 per term part-time.

Admissions Contact Ms. LeAnne Osburne, Director of Admissions, Jones College, 11430 North Kendall Drive, Suite 200, Miami, FL 33176. *Phone:* 904-743-1122 Ext. 135.

KEISER COLLEGE
Fort Lauderdale, Florida

Admissions Contact Mr. Brian Woods, Vice President of Enrollment Management, Keiser College, 1500 Northwest 49th Street, Fort Lauderdale, FL 33309. *Phone:* 954-776-4476. *Toll-free phone:* 800-749-4456. *Fax:* 954-351-4030. *E-mail:* admissions@keisercollege.edu.

LYNN UNIVERSITY
Boca Raton, Florida

- **Independent** comprehensive, founded 1962
- **Calendar** semesters plus 3 summer sessions
- **Degrees** certificates, bachelor's, master's, and doctoral
- **Suburban** 123-acre campus with easy access to Fort Lauderdale
- **Endowment** $5.0 million
- **Coed,** 1,620 undergraduate students, 94% full-time, 48% women, 52% men
- **Minimally difficult** entrance level, 77% of applicants were admitted

The University, ideally located between Palm Beach and Fort Lauderdale, enrolls approximately 2,100 students. The faculty-student ratio of 1:16 provides an academic environment in which the well-being and development of the individual are assured. The University currently hosts students from 46 states and 93 nations, creating a community in which each student is provided with a rich multicultural experience and global awareness.

Undergraduates 1,525 full-time, 95 part-time. Students come from 44 states and territories, 89 other countries, 45% are from out of state, 9% transferred in, 45% live on campus. *Retention:* 82% of 2002 full-time freshmen returned.

Freshmen *Admission:* 2,607 applied, 2,017 admitted, 501 enrolled. *Average high school GPA:* 2.55. *Test scores:* SAT verbal scores over 500: 25%; SAT math scores over 500: 26%; ACT scores over 18: 57%; SAT verbal scores over 600: 3%; SAT math scores over 600: 5%; ACT scores over 24: 8%.

Faculty *Total:* 247, 28% full-time, 39% with terminal degrees. *Student/faculty ratio:* 14:1.

Majors Accounting; adult and continuing education; airline pilot and flight crew; aviation/airway management; business administration and management; commercial and advertising art; drafting and design technology; education; elementary education; English; environmental studies; fashion/apparel design; fashion merchandising; funeral service and mortuary science; gerontology; health/health care administration; history; hotel/motel administration; humanities; international business/trade/commerce; kindergarten/preschool education; liberal arts and sciences/liberal studies; marketing/marketing management; mass communication/media; middle school education; music; natural sciences; nursing (registered nurse training); parks, recreation and leisure facilities management; physical therapy; political science and government; pre-law studies; pre-medical studies; psychology; secondary education; social sciences; special products marketing; sport and fitness administration; tourism and travel services management.

Academic Programs *Special study options:* academic remediation for entering students, adult/continuing education programs, advanced placement credit, cooperative education, distance learning, double majors, English as a second language, freshman honors college, honors programs, internships, part-time degree program, services for LD students, study abroad, summer session for credit. *ROTC:* Air Force (c).

Library Eugene M. and Christine E. Lynn Library with 235,000 titles, 10,450 serial subscriptions, 2,000 audiovisual materials, an OPAC.

Computers on Campus 150 computers available on campus for general student use. A campuswide network can be accessed from student residence rooms and from off campus. Internet access, online (class) registration, at least one staffed computer lab available.

Student Life *Housing:* on-campus residence required through sophomore year. *Options:* coed, women-only, disabled students. Campus housing is university owned. Freshman campus housing is guaranteed. *Activities and organizations:* drama/theater group, student-run newspaper, radio station, choral group, Knights of the Round Table, intramural groups, student newspaper, Residence Hall Council, Activities Board, national fraternities, national sororities. *Campus security:* 24-hour patrols, late-night transport/escort service, video monitor at residence entrances. *Student services:* health clinic, personal/psychological counseling.

Athletics Member NCAA. All Division II. *Intercollegiate sports:* baseball M(s), basketball M(s)/W(s), cross-country running M/W, golf M(s)/W(s), soccer M(s)/W(s), softball W, tennis M(s)/W(s), volleyball W. *Intramural sports:* baseball M, basketball M/W, bowling M/W, cheerleading M/W, crew M, cross-country running M/W, equestrian sports M/W, football M/W, golf M/W, ice hockey M/W, lacrosse M/W, rugby M, soccer M/W, softball M/W, swimming M/W, table tennis M/W, tennis M/W, ultimate Frisbee M/W, volleyball M/W, water polo M/W, weight lifting M/W.

Standardized Tests *Required:* SAT I or ACT (for admission).

Costs (2003–04) *Comprehensive fee:* $30,750 includes full-time tuition ($22,000), mandatory fees ($750), and room and board ($8000). Part-time tuition: $660 per credit. Part-time tuition and fees vary according to class time. *Required fees:* $300 per year part-time. *Room and board:* Room and board charges vary according to housing facility. *Payment plans:* installment, deferred payment. *Waivers:* employees or children of employees.

Financial Aid Of all full-time matriculated undergraduates who enrolled in 2003, 686 applied for aid, 590 were judged to have need, 188 had their need fully met. 171 Federal Work-Study jobs (averaging $1263). 34 state and other part-time jobs (averaging $4732). In 2003, 490 non-need-based awards were made. *Average percent of need met:* 74%. *Average financial aid package:* $19,285. *Average need-based loan:* $9208. *Average need-based gift aid:* $11,449. *Average non-need-based aid:* $11,083. *Average indebtedness upon graduation:* $15,154.

Applying *Options:* common application, electronic application, early admission, deferred entrance. *Application fee:* $35. *Required:* essay or personal statement, high school transcript, minimum 2.5 GPA, 1 letter of recommendation. *Recommended:* essay or personal statement, minimum 3.0 GPA, interview. *Application deadline:* rolling (freshmen), rolling (out-of-state freshmen), rolling (transfers). *Notification:* continuous (freshmen), continuous (out-of-state freshmen), continuous (transfers).

Admissions Contact Ms. Melanie Glines, Director of Admissions, Lynn University, 3601 North Military Trail, Boca Raton, FL 33431-5598. *Phone:* 561-237-7900. *Toll-free phone:* 800-888-LYNN Ext. 1 (in-state); 800-544-8035 (out-of-state). *Fax:* 561-237-7100. *E-mail:* admission@lynn.edu.

■ *See page 1908 for a narrative description.*

MIAMI DADE COLLEGE

Miami, Florida

- **State and locally supported** primarily 2-year, founded 1960, part of Florida Community College System
- **Calendar** 16-16-6-6
- **Degrees** certificates, associate, and bachelor's
- **Urban** campus
- **Endowment** $106.5 million
- **Coed,** 58,490 undergraduate students, 36% full-time, 62% women, 38% men
- **Noncompetitive** entrance level, 100% of applicants were admitted

Undergraduates 21,009 full-time, 37,481 part-time. Students come from 37 states and territories, 155 other countries, 1% are from out of state, 22% African American, 1% Asian American or Pacific Islander, 65% Hispanic American, 0.1% Native American, 3% international, 2% transferred in.

Freshmen *Admission:* 16,216 applied, 16,216 admitted, 8,623 enrolled. *Test scores:* SAT verbal scores over 500: 18%; SAT math scores over 500: 16%; ACT scores over 18: 36%; SAT verbal scores over 600: 2%; SAT math scores over 600: 2%; ACT scores over 24: 2%.

Faculty *Total:* 2,081, 34% full-time, 15% with terminal degrees. *Student/faculty ratio:* 29:1.

Majors Accounting technology and bookkeeping; administrative assistant and secretarial science; aeronautics/aviation/aerospace science and technology; agriculture; airline pilot and flight crew; air traffic control; American studies; anthropology; architectural drafting and CAD/CADD; architectural engineering technology; art; art teacher education; Asian studies; aviation/airway management; behavioral sciences; biology/biological sciences; biology teacher education; biomedical technology; business administration and management; chemistry; chemistry teacher education; child development; cinematography and film/video production; civil engineering technology; clinical/medical laboratory technology; commercial and advertising art; computer engineering technology; computer graphics; computer programming; computer science; computer software technology; computer technology/computer systems technology; construction engineering technology; court reporting; criminal justice/law enforcement administration; criminal justice/police science; dance; data processing and data processing technology; dental hygiene; diagnostic medical sonography and ultrasound technology; dietetics; dietetic technician; drafting and design technology; dramatic/theatre arts; economics; education; education (specific subject areas) related; electrical and electronic engineering technologies related; electrical, electronic and communications engineering technology; elementary education; emergency medical technology (EMT paramedic); engineering; engineering related; engineering technology; English; environmental engineering technology; finance; fire science; food science; forestry; French; funeral service and mortuary science; general studies; geology/earth science; German; health information/medical records administration; heating, air conditioning and refrigeration technology; heating, air conditioning, ventilation and refrigeration maintenance technology; histologic technician; history; horticultural science; hospitality administration; humanities; human services; industrial technology; information science/studies; interior design; international relations and affairs; Italian; journalism; kindergarten/preschool education; landscaping and groundskeeping; Latin American studies; legal administrative assistant/secretary; legal assistant/paralegal; literature; management information systems; marketing/marketing management; mass communication/media; mathematics; mathematics teacher education; medical/clinical assistant; middle school education; music; music performance; music teacher education; natural sciences; non-profit management; nuclear medical technology; nursing midwifery; nursing (registered nurse training); ophthalmic technology; ornamental horticulture; parks, recreation and leisure; philosophy; photographic and film/video technology; photography; physical education teaching and coaching; physical sciences; physical therapist assistant; physical therapy; physics; physics teacher education; plant nursery management; political science and government; Portuguese; pre-dentistry studies; pre-engineering; pre-medical studies; pre-nursing studies; pre-pharmacy studies; pre-veterinary studies; psychology; public administration; radio and television; radio and television broadcasting technology; radiologic technology/science; recording arts technology; respiratory care therapy; respiratory therapy technician; science teacher education; sign language interpretation and translation; social sciences; social work; sociology; Spanish; special education; substance abuse/addiction counseling; teacher assistant/aide; telecommunications technology; tourism and travel services management; veterinary sciences.

Academic Programs *Special study options:* academic remediation for entering students, adult/continuing education programs, advanced placement credit, cooperative education, distance learning, English as a second language, honors programs, independent study, internships, part-time degree program, services for LD students, study abroad, summer session for credit. *ROTC:* Army (c), Air Force (c).

Library Main Library plus 8 others with 347,302 titles, 3,586 serial subscriptions, 17,186 audiovisual materials, an OPAC, a Web page.

Computers on Campus 6136 computers available on campus for general student use. A campuswide network can be accessed from off campus. Internet access, online (class) registration, at least one staffed computer lab available.

Student Life *Housing:* college housing not available. *Activities and organizations:* drama/theater group, student-run newspaper, radio station, choral group, Welcome Back, Hispanic Heritage Month, Black History Month, Renaissance

Miami Dade College (continued)
Dinner (3 nights), Paella Festival. *Campus security:* 24-hour patrols. *Student services:* personal/psychological counseling, women's center.

Athletics Member NJCAA. *Intercollegiate sports:* baseball M(s), basketball M(s)/W(s), softball W(s), volleyball W(s). *Intramural sports:* basketball M/W, racquetball M/W, soccer M/W, softball M/W, swimming M/W, tennis M/W, track and field M/W, volleyball M/W, weight lifting M/W.

Standardized Tests *Required:* (for placement). *Recommended:* SAT I and SAT II or ACT (for placement), SAT II: Subject Tests (for placement), SAT II: Writing Test (for placement).

Costs (2003–04) *Tuition:* state resident $1419 full-time, $47 per credit part-time; nonresident $5286 full-time, $176 per credit part-time. Full-time tuition and fees vary according to degree level. Part-time tuition and fees vary according to degree level. *Required fees:* $276 full-time, $9 per credit part-time. *Waivers:* employees or children of employees.

Financial Aid Of all full-time matriculated undergraduates who enrolled in 2001, 800 Federal Work-Study jobs (averaging $5000). 125 state and other part-time jobs (averaging $5000).

Applying *Options:* electronic application, early admission. *Application fee:* $20. *Required:* high school transcript. *Application deadline:* rolling (freshmen). *Notification:* continuous (freshmen), continuous (transfers).

Admissions Contact Mr. Steven Kelly, College Registrar, Miami Dade College, 11011 SW 104th Street, Miami, FL 33176. *Phone:* 305-237-0633. *Fax:* 305-237-2964. *E-mail:* jstewart@mdcc.edu.

MIAMI INTERNATIONAL UNIVERSITY OF ART & DESIGN

Miami, Florida

- **Proprietary** comprehensive, founded 1965
- **Calendar** quarters
- **Degrees** associate, bachelor's, and master's
- **Urban** 4-acre campus
- **Coed,** 1,150 undergraduate students, 100% full-time, 60% women, 40% men
- **Moderately difficult** entrance level, 55% of applicants were admitted

Undergraduates 1,150 full-time. Students come from 45 states and territories, 50 other countries, 40% live on campus.

Freshmen *Admission:* 603 applied, 330 admitted, 330 enrolled. *Average high school GPA:* 2.70.

Faculty *Total:* 91, 48% full-time. *Student/faculty ratio:* 18:1.

Majors Art; cinematography and film/video production; commercial and advertising art; computer graphics; fashion/apparel design; fashion merchandising; interior design; visual and performing arts.

Academic Programs *Special study options:* academic remediation for entering students, English as a second language, internships, services for LD students, summer session for credit.

Library Daniel Stack Memorial Library plus 2 others with 14,022 titles, 87 serial subscriptions.

Computers on Campus 144 computers available on campus for general student use. Internet access, at least one staffed computer lab available.

Student Life *Housing options:* coed. *Activities and organizations:* student-run newspaper, Caribbean Students Association, student government, DECA. *Campus security:* 24-hour emergency response devices, student patrols, late-night transport/escort service, controlled dormitory access, security service. *Student services:* personal/psychological counseling.

Standardized Tests *Recommended:* SAT I and SAT II or ACT (for admission), SAT II: Writing Test (for admission).

Costs (2004–05) *Tuition:* $17,520 full-time. *Required fees:* $50 full-time. *Room only:* $4600.

Applying *Options:* common application, deferred entrance. *Application fee:* $50. *Required:* high school transcript, minimum 2.0 GPA, interview, 2 photographs, art portfolio. *Recommended:* essay or personal statement, 2 letters of recommendation. *Application deadline:* rolling (freshmen), rolling (transfers). *Notification:* continuous (freshmen), continuous (transfers).

Admissions Contact Ms. Elsia Suarez, Director of Admissions, Miami International University of Art & Design, 1501 Biscayne Boulevard, Suite 100, Miami, FL 33132-1418. *Phone:* 305-428-5600. *Toll-free phone:* 800-225-9023.

NEW COLLEGE OF FLORIDA

Sarasota, Florida

- **State-supported** 4-year, founded 1960, part of State University System of Florida
- **Calendar** 4-1-4
- **Degree** bachelor's
- **Suburban** 144-acre campus with easy access to Tampa–St. Petersburg
- **Endowment** $30.8 million
- **Coed,** 671 undergraduate students, 100% full-time, 61% women, 39% men
- **Very difficult** entrance level, 61% of applicants were admitted

New College offers serious students the opportunity to pursue rigorous academic study in an environment designed to promote depth in thinking, free exchange of ideas, and highly individualized interaction with faculty members. Study is focused in the liberal arts and sciences and is highly accelerated and independent.

Undergraduates 671 full-time. Students come from 40 states and territories, 12 other countries, 23% are from out of state, 2% African American, 3% Asian American or Pacific Islander, 7% Hispanic American, 0.3% Native American, 2% international, 6% transferred in, 70% live on campus. *Retention:* 75% of 2002 full-time freshmen returned.

Freshmen *Admission:* 565 applied, 343 admitted, 157 enrolled. *Average high school GPA:* 3.82. *Test scores:* SAT verbal scores over 500: 99%; SAT math scores over 500: 97%; ACT scores over 18: 100%; SAT verbal scores over 600: 92%; SAT math scores over 600: 73%; ACT scores over 24: 94%; SAT verbal scores over 700: 42%; SAT math scores over 700: 15%; ACT scores over 30: 28%.

Faculty *Total:* 72, 86% full-time, 94% with terminal degrees. *Student/faculty ratio:* 11:1.

Majors Anthropology; art history, criticism and conservation; biology/biological sciences; chemistry; classics and classical languages related; comparative literature; economics; English; environmental studies; fine/studio arts; foreign languages and literatures; French; French studies; general studies; German; Germanic languages; history; humanities; international/global studies; liberal arts and sciences/liberal studies; literature; marine biology and biological oceanography; mathematics; medieval and Renaissance studies; music; music history, literature, and theory; natural sciences; neurobiology and neurophysiology; philosophy; physics; political science and government; psychology; public policy analysis; religious studies; Russian; social sciences; sociology; Spanish; urban studies/affairs.

Academic Programs *Special study options:* accelerated degree program, double majors, honors programs, independent study, internships, off-campus study, services for LD students, student-designed majors, study abroad.

Library Jane Bancroft Cook Library with 256,581 titles, 1,925 serial subscriptions, 4,246 audiovisual materials, an OPAC, a Web page.

Computers on Campus 41 computers available on campus for general student use. A campuswide network can be accessed from student residence rooms and from off campus. Internet access, at least one staffed computer lab available. Computer purchase or lease plan available.

Student Life *Housing:* on-campus residence required through sophomore year. *Options:* coed, disabled students. Campus housing is university owned. Freshman campus housing is guaranteed. *Activities and organizations:* drama/theater group, student-run newspaper, radio station, choral group, Nice Random Acts of Kindness, Interfaith groups, New College Student Alliance, Feminist Majority Leadership Alliance, Sailing Club. *Campus security:* 24-hour emergency response devices and patrols, late-night transport/escort service. *Student services:* health clinic, personal/psychological counseling, women's center.

Standardized Tests *Required:* SAT I or ACT (for admission).

Costs (2003–04) *Tuition:* state resident $3240 full-time; nonresident $16,473 full-time. *Room and board:* $5658; room only: $3533. Room and board charges vary according to board plan and housing facility. *Payment plans:* tuition prepayment, installment, deferred payment.

Financial Aid Of all full-time matriculated undergraduates who enrolled in 2003, 373 applied for aid, 278 were judged to have need, 52 had their need fully met. 29 state and other part-time jobs (averaging $2241). In 2003, 309 non-need-based awards were made. *Average percent of need met:* 79%. *Average financial aid package:* $8886. *Average need-based loan:* $3600. *Average need-based gift aid:* $6542. *Average non-need-based aid:* $3247. *Average indebtedness upon graduation:* $9612.

Applying *Options:* common application, electronic application, early admission, deferred entrance. *Application fee:* $30. *Required:* essay or personal statement, high school transcript, 2 letters of recommendation. *Required for some:* interview. *Recommended:* minimum 3.0 GPA, interview, analytical paper. *Notification:* continuous until 5/1 (freshmen), continuous until 5/1 (transfers).

Admissions Contact Ms. Kathleen M. Killian, Interim Dean of Admissions and Financial Aid, New College of Florida, 5700 North Tamiami Trail, Sarasota, FL 34243-2197. *Phone:* 941-359-4269. *Fax:* 941-359-4435. *E-mail:* admissions@ncf.edu.

■ *See page 2070 for a narrative description.*

NEW WORLD SCHOOL OF THE ARTS
Miami, Florida

- **State-supported** 4-year, founded 1984
- **Calendar** semesters
- **Degrees** diplomas, associate, and bachelor's
- **Urban** 5-acre campus
- **Endowment** $3.2 million
- **Coed,** 359 undergraduate students, 100% full-time, 52% women, 48% men
- **Noncompetitive** entrance level, 61% of applicants were admitted

Undergraduates 359 full-time. Students come from 12 states and territories, 25% are from out of state, 11% African American, 4% Asian American or Pacific Islander, 51% Hispanic American, 6% transferred in. *Retention:* 80% of 2002 full-time freshmen returned.

Freshmen *Admission:* 287 applied, 176 admitted, 113 enrolled. *Average high school GPA:* 2.80.

Faculty *Total:* 96, 21% full-time. *Student/faculty ratio:* 8:1.

Majors Acting; applied art; dance; dance related; drawing; graphic design; intermedia/multimedia; music performance; music theory and composition; painting; photography; piano and organ; printmaking; sculpture; violin, viola, guitar and other stringed instruments; voice and opera; wind/percussion instruments.

Academic Programs *Special study options:* academic remediation for entering students, advanced placement credit, cooperative education, distance learning, English as a second language, freshman honors college, honors programs, internships, services for LD students, summer session for credit.

Library Miami-Dade Community College library (Wolfson Campus) plus 1 other with an OPAC, a Web page.

Computers on Campus 100 computers available on campus for general student use. A campuswide network can be accessed from student residence rooms and from off campus. Internet access, online (class) registration, at least one staffed computer lab available.

Student Life *Housing:* college housing not available. *Activities and organizations:* drama/theater group, student-run newspaper, student government. *Campus security:* 24-hour patrols. *Student services:* personal/psychological counseling.

Standardized Tests *Recommended:* SAT I or ACT (for placement).

Costs (2003–04) *Tuition:* state resident $2034 full-time, $57 per credit part-time; nonresident $7110 full-time, $198 per credit part-time. Full-time tuition and fees vary according to degree level. Part-time tuition and fees vary according to degree level.

Applying *Required:* essay or personal statement, high school transcript, 2 letters of recommendation, interview, audition. *Application deadline:* rolling (freshmen). *Notification:* continuous until 8/1 (freshmen), continuous until 8/1 (transfers).

Admissions Contact Ms. Pamela Neumann, Recruitment and Admissions Coordinator, New World School of the Arts, 300 NE Second Avenue, Miami, FL 33132. *Phone:* 305-237-7007. *Fax:* 305-237-3794. *E-mail:* nwsaadm@mdc.edu.

NORTHWOOD UNIVERSITY, FLORIDA CAMPUS
West Palm Beach, Florida

- **Independent** 4-year, founded 1982
- **Calendar** quarters
- **Degrees** associate and bachelor's
- **Suburban** 90-acre campus with easy access to Miami
- **Endowment** $54.4 million
- **Coed,** 959 undergraduate students, 81% full-time, 46% women, 54% men
- **Moderately difficult** entrance level, 61% of applicants were admitted

Undergraduates 772 full-time, 187 part-time. Students come from 35 states and territories, 47 other countries, 39% are from out of state, 9% African American, 0.9% Asian American or Pacific Islander, 9% Hispanic American, 0.1% Native American, 23% international, 14% transferred in, 42% live on campus. *Retention:* 60% of 2002 full-time freshmen returned.

Freshmen *Admission:* 878 applied, 532 admitted, 156 enrolled. *Average high school GPA:* 2.92. *Test scores:* SAT verbal scores over 500: 33%; SAT math scores over 500: 45%; ACT scores over 18: 72%; SAT verbal scores over 600: 3%; SAT math scores over 600: 13%; ACT scores over 24: 16%.

Faculty *Total:* 54, 26% full-time, 24% with terminal degrees. *Student/faculty ratio:* 25:1.

Majors Accounting; advertising; banking and financial support services; business administration and management; computer and information sciences; computer management; hotel/motel administration; international business/trade/commerce; management information systems; marketing/marketing management; vehicle and vehicle parts and accessories marketing.

Academic Programs *Special study options:* academic remediation for entering students, accelerated degree program, adult/continuing education programs, advanced placement credit, cooperative education, distance learning, double majors, English as a second language, external degree program, honors programs, independent study, internships, part-time degree program, study abroad, summer session for credit.

Library Peter C. Cook Library with 20,295 titles, 144 serial subscriptions, 504 audiovisual materials, an OPAC.

Computers on Campus 68 computers available on campus for general student use. A campuswide network can be accessed from student residence rooms and from off campus. Internet access, at least one staffed computer lab available.

Student Life *Housing:* on-campus residence required through sophomore year. *Options:* men-only, women-only. Campus housing is university owned. Freshman campus housing is guaranteed. *Activities and organizations:* Student Government Association, International Club, Auto Show. *Campus security:* 24-hour emergency response devices and patrols, student patrols. *Student services:* health clinic, personal/psychological counseling.

Athletics Member NAIA. *Intercollegiate sports:* baseball M(s), cheerleading M(s)/W(s), golf M(s)/W(s), soccer M(s)/W(s), softball W(s), tennis M(s)/W(s), volleyball W(s). *Intramural sports:* basketball M/W, bowling M/W, racquetball M/W, tennis M/W, ultimate Frisbee M/W.

Standardized Tests *Required:* SAT I or ACT (for admission).

Costs (2003–04) *Comprehensive fee:* $20,835 includes full-time tuition ($13,485), mandatory fees ($510), and room and board ($6840). Part-time tuition: $281 per credit. *College room only:* $3420. Room and board charges vary according to board plan and location. *Payment plan:* installment. *Waivers:* children of alumni and employees or children of employees.

Financial Aid Of all full-time matriculated undergraduates who enrolled in 2003, 350 applied for aid, 310 were judged to have need, 39 had their need fully met. 75 Federal Work-Study jobs (averaging $2063). In 2003, 130 non-need-based awards were made. *Average percent of need met:* 70%. *Average financial aid package:* $12,505. *Average need-based loan:* $3561. *Average need-based gift aid:* $9561. *Average non-need-based aid:* $4006. *Average indebtedness upon graduation:* $13,495.

Applying *Options:* common application, electronic application, early admission, deferred entrance. *Application fee:* $25. *Required:* essay or personal statement, high school transcript. *Recommended:* minimum 2.0 GPA, 1 letter of recommendation, interview. *Application deadline:* rolling (freshmen), rolling (transfers). *Notification:* continuous (freshmen), continuous (transfers).

Admissions Contact Mr. John M. Letvinchuck, Director of Admissions, Northwood University, Florida Campus, 2600 North Military Trail, West Palm Beach, FL 33409-2911. *Phone:* 561-478-5500. *Toll-free phone:* 800-458-8325. *Fax:* 561-640-3328. *E-mail:* fladmit@northwood.edu.

■ *See page 2106 for a narrative description.*

NOVA SOUTHEASTERN UNIVERSITY
Fort Lauderdale, Florida

- **Independent** university, founded 1964
- **Calendar** trimesters
- **Degrees** associate, bachelor's, master's, doctoral, first professional, post-master's, and first professional certificates
- **Suburban** 300-acre campus
- **Coed,** 5,223 undergraduate students, 60% full-time, 75% women, 25% men
- **Moderately difficult** entrance level, 64% of applicants were admitted

Nova Southeastern's Alvin Sherman Library, Research, and Information Technology Center accommodates 1,000 user seats equipped with Internet access, 700 workstations, the 500-seat Rose and Alfred Miniaci Performing Arts Center, and twenty electronic classrooms. The Library, with the capacity to house 1.4 million volumes of reference materials, is the largest in Florida.

Undergraduates 3,131 full-time, 2,092 part-time. Students come from 37 other countries, 27% African American, 3% Asian American or Pacific Islander, 24% Hispanic American, 0.4% Native American, 8% international, 10% live on campus. *Retention:* 75% of 2002 full-time freshmen returned.

Freshmen *Admission:* 1,550 applied, 993 admitted, 393 enrolled. *Average high school GPA:* 3.48. *Test scores:* SAT verbal scores over 500: 43%; SAT math scores over 500: 54%; ACT scores over 18: 83%; SAT verbal scores over 600: 9%; SAT math scores over 600: 17%; ACT scores over 24: 27%; SAT verbal scores over 700: 1%; SAT math scores over 700: 3%; ACT scores over 30: 2%.

Faculty *Total:* 1,509, 35% full-time. *Student/faculty ratio:* 14:1.

Majors Accounting; athletic training; biology/biological sciences; business administration and management; computer and information sciences; computer science; elementary education; English; environmental science; environmental studies; finance; health services/allied health/health sciences; history; humanities; interdisciplinary studies; kindergarten/preschool education; legal assistant/paralegal; liberal arts and sciences/liberal studies; management science; marine

Nova Southeastern University (continued)

biology and biological oceanography; multi-/interdisciplinary studies related; nursing (registered nurse training); physician assistant; pre-dentistry studies; pre-law studies; pre-medical studies; psychology; special education; sport and fitness administration.

Academic Programs *Special study options:* academic remediation for entering students, accelerated degree program, adult/continuing education programs, advanced placement credit, cooperative education, distance learning, internships, part-time degree program, study abroad, summer session for credit. *Unusual degree programs:* 3-2 marine biology, occupational therapy.

Library Library, Research, and Information Technology Center plus 4 others with 395,927 titles, 12,750 serial subscriptions, 12,421 audiovisual materials, an OPAC, a Web page.

Computers on Campus 2000 computers available on campus for general student use. A campuswide network can be accessed from student residence rooms and from off campus. Internet access, online (class) registration, at least one staffed computer lab available.

Student Life *Housing:* on-campus residence required through sophomore year. *Options:* coed, disabled students. Campus housing is university owned. Freshman campus housing is guaranteed. *Activities and organizations:* drama/theater group, student-run newspaper, radio station, Pre-Pharmacy Society, Pre-Med Society, Beta Theta Pi, Delta Phi Epsilon, Nova International Muslim Association, national fraternities, national sororities. *Campus security:* 24-hour emergency response devices and patrols, late-night transport/escort service, controlled dormitory access, shuttle bus service. *Student services:* health clinic, personal/psychological counseling, women's center.

Athletics Member NAIA. *Intercollegiate sports:* baseball M(s), basketball M(s)/W(s), cheerleading W(s), cross-country running W(s), golf M(s)/W(s), soccer M(s)/W(s), softball W(s), volleyball W(s). *Intramural sports:* basketball M, cross-country running M/W, football M, golf M, soccer M/W, softball W, tennis M/W, volleyball W.

Standardized Tests *Required:* SAT I or ACT (for admission).

Costs (2003–04) *Comprehensive fee:* $23,346 includes full-time tuition ($15,000), mandatory fees ($220), and room and board ($8126). Full-time tuition and fees vary according to class time and program. Part-time tuition: $500 per credit hour. Part-time tuition and fees vary according to class time, course load, and program. *College room only:* $5662. Room and board charges vary according to board plan and housing facility. *Payment plans:* installment, deferred payment. *Waivers:* employees or children of employees.

Financial Aid Of all full-time matriculated undergraduates who enrolled in 2003, 3,108 applied for aid, 85 had their need fully met. 776 Federal Work-Study jobs (averaging $6370). 269 state and other part-time jobs (averaging $4020). In 2003, 503 non-need-based awards were made. *Average percent of need met:* 50%. *Average financial aid package:* $14,294. *Average need-based loan:* $5535. *Average need-based gift aid:* $7356. *Average non-need-based aid:* $4956. *Average indebtedness upon graduation:* $21,607.

Applying *Options:* common application, electronic application, early admission, deferred entrance. *Application fee:* $50. *Required:* high school transcript. *Recommended:* minimum 2.5 GPA, letters of recommendation, interview. *Application deadline:* rolling (freshmen), rolling (transfers). *Notification:* continuous (freshmen), continuous (transfers).

Admissions Contact Ms. Maria Dillard, Director of Enrollment Management, Nova Southeastern University, Enrollment Processing Services, 3301 College Avenue, PO Box 299000, Ft. Lauderdale, FL 33329-9905. *Phone:* 954-262-8000. *Toll-free phone:* 800-541-NOVA. *Fax:* 954-262-3811. *E-mail:* nsuinfo@nova.edu.

■ *See page 2116 for a narrative description.*

PALM BEACH ATLANTIC UNIVERSITY
West Palm Beach, Florida

- **Independent nondenominational** comprehensive, founded 1968
- **Calendar** semesters
- **Degrees** associate, bachelor's, master's, and first professional
- **Urban** 25-acre campus with easy access to Miami
- **Endowment** $50.1 million
- **Coed,** 2,420 undergraduate students, 92% full-time, 65% women, 35% men
- **Moderately difficult** entrance level, 87% of applicants were admitted

Palm Beach Atlantic University is a comprehensive, Christian university offering bachelor's, master's, and doctoral degrees to 3,000 students. Located on a 25-acre campus in downtown West Palm Beach, Florida, and facing the Intracoastal Waterway, the University features excellent facilities, including Oceanview, the new 188-bed freshman men's residence hall.

Undergraduates 2,216 full-time, 204 part-time. Students come from 47 states and territories, 25 other countries, 23% are from out of state, 15% African American, 2% Asian American or Pacific Islander, 8% Hispanic American, 0.5% Native American, 4% international, 9% transferred in, 55% live on campus. *Retention:* 73% of 2002 full-time freshmen returned.

Freshmen *Admission:* 970 applied, 846 admitted, 443 enrolled. *Average high school GPA:* 3.40. *Test scores:* SAT verbal scores over 500: 76%; SAT math scores over 500: 70%; ACT scores over 18: 95%; SAT verbal scores over 600: 24%; SAT math scores over 600: 21%; ACT scores over 24: 43%; SAT verbal scores over 700: 3%; SAT math scores over 700: 1%; ACT scores over 30: 1%.

Faculty *Total:* 223, 54% full-time. *Student/faculty ratio:* 16:1.

Majors Accounting and finance; acting; art teacher education; biblical studies; biology/biological sciences; broadcast journalism; business administration and management; business administration, management and operations related; communication/speech communication and rhetoric; computer and information sciences; dance; dramatic/theatre arts; education; elementary education; engineering; English; entrepreneurship; fine/studio arts; general studies; graphic design; history; human resources management; international business/trade/commerce; journalism; marketing/marketing management; mathematics; music; music performance; music teacher education; music theory and composition; nursing (registered nurse training); organizational communication; philosophy; physical education teaching and coaching; piano and organ; playwriting and screenwriting; political science and government; pre-law studies; psychology; radio and television; religious/sacred music; religious studies; secondary education; theological and ministerial studies related; voice and opera; wind/percussion instruments.

Academic Programs *Special study options:* academic remediation for entering students, accelerated degree program, adult/continuing education programs, advanced placement credit, cooperative education, double majors, English as a second language, freshman honors college, honors programs, independent study, internships, part-time degree program, study abroad, summer session for credit.

Library E. C. Blomeyer Library with 99,763 titles, 1,061 serial subscriptions, 4,156 audiovisual materials, an OPAC, a Web page.

Computers on Campus A campuswide network can be accessed from student residence rooms and from off campus. Internet access, online (class) registration, at least one staffed computer lab available.

Student Life *Housing:* on-campus residence required through sophomore year. *Options:* men-only, women-only. Campus housing is university owned. Freshman applicants given priority for college housing. *Activities and organizations:* drama/theater group, student-run newspaper, radio and television station, choral group. *Campus security:* 24-hour emergency response devices and patrols, late-night transport/escort service, controlled dormitory access. *Student services:* health clinic, personal/psychological counseling.

Athletics Member NCAA. All Division III. *Intercollegiate sports:* baseball M, basketball M/W, cheerleading M/W, cross-country running M/W, golf M/W, soccer M/W, softball W, tennis M/W, volleyball M/W. *Intramural sports:* basketball M/W, bowling M/W, football M/W, golf M/W, racquetball M/W, soccer M/W, softball M/W, table tennis M/W, ultimate Frisbee M/W, volleyball M/W.

Standardized Tests *Required:* SAT I or ACT (for admission).

Costs (2003–04) *Comprehensive fee:* $20,690 includes full-time tuition ($14,690), mandatory fees ($200), and room and board ($5800). Full-time tuition and fees vary according to course load, degree level, program, and reciprocity agreements. Part-time tuition: $360 per credit hour. Part-time tuition and fees vary according to course load, degree level, program, and reciprocity agreements. *Required fees:* $80 per term part-time. *College room only:* $3150. Room and board charges vary according to board plan and housing facility. *Payment plan:* installment. *Waivers:* employees or children of employees.

Financial Aid Of all full-time matriculated undergraduates who enrolled in 2003, 1,827 applied for aid, 1,577 were judged to have need, 249 had their need fully met. 215 Federal Work-Study jobs (averaging $1673). In 2003, 636 non-need-based awards were made. *Average percent of need met:* 63%. *Average financial aid package:* $10,659. *Average need-based loan:* $3256. *Average need-based gift aid:* $2059. *Average non-need-based aid:* $1684. *Average indebtedness upon graduation:* $14,181.

Applying *Options:* common application, electronic application, early admission, deferred entrance. *Application fee:* $25. *Required:* high school transcript, minimum 2.0 GPA, 2 letters of recommendation. *Recommended:* minimum 3.0 GPA, interview, class rank. *Application deadline:* rolling (freshmen). *Notification:* continuous (freshmen).

Admissions Contact Mr. Buck James, Vice President of Enrollment Services, Palm Beach Atlantic University, PO Box 24708, West Palm Beach, FL 33416-4708. *Phone:* 561-803-2100. *Toll-free phone:* 800-238-3998. *Fax:* 561-803-2115. *E-mail:* admit@pba.edu.

■ See page 2152 for a narrative description.

REMINGTON COLLEGE–JACKSONVILLE CAMPUS
Jacksonville, Florida

Admissions Contact Mr. Tony Galang, Campus President, Remington College–Jacksonville Campus, 7011 A.C. Skinner Parkway, Jacksonville, FL 32256. *Phone:* 904-296-3435 Ext. 218.

REMINGTON COLLEGE–TAMPA CAMPUS
Tampa, Florida

- **Proprietary** primarily 2-year, founded 1948
- **Calendar** quarters
- **Degrees** diplomas, associate, and bachelor's
- **Urban** 10-acre campus
- **Coed**
- **Noncompetitive** entrance level

Student Life *Campus security:* late-night transport/escort service.
Standardized Tests *Required:* Wonderlic aptitude test (for admission).
Costs (2003–04) *Tuition:* $281 per credit hour part-time.
Financial Aid Of all full-time matriculated undergraduates who enrolled in 2001, 12 Federal Work-Study jobs (averaging $8000).
Applying *Options:* common application, deferred entrance. *Application fee:* $50. *Required:* high school transcript, interview.
Admissions Contact Ms. Kathy Miller, Director of Admissions, Remington College–Tampa Campus, 2410 East Busch Boulevard, Tampa, FL 33612. *Phone:* 813-935-5700 Ext. 211. *Toll-free phone:* 800-992-4850.

RINGLING SCHOOL OF ART AND DESIGN
Sarasota, Florida

- **Independent** 4-year, founded 1931
- **Calendar** semesters
- **Degree** bachelor's
- **Small-town** 37-acre campus with easy access to Tampa–St. Petersburg
- **Endowment** $8.0 million
- **Coed,** 989 undergraduate students, 97% full-time, 47% women, 53% men
- **Moderately difficult** entrance level, 67% of applicants were admitted

Undergraduates 962 full-time, 27 part-time. Students come from 44 states and territories, 34 other countries, 46% are from out of state, 3% African American, 4% Asian American or Pacific Islander, 8% Hispanic American, 1% Native American, 6% international, 12% transferred in, 48% live on campus. *Retention:* 78% of 2002 full-time freshmen returned.
Freshmen *Admission:* 1,030 applied, 686 admitted, 174 enrolled. *Average high school GPA:* 3.54. *Test scores:* SAT verbal scores over 500: 63%; SAT math scores over 500: 58%; ACT scores over 18: 100%; SAT verbal scores over 600: 18%; SAT math scores over 600: 11%; SAT verbal scores over 700: 7%.
Faculty *Total:* 118, 53% full-time, 62% with terminal degrees. *Student/faculty ratio:* 12:1.
Majors Design and applied arts related; fine/studio arts; graphic design; illustration; interior design; photography.
Academic Programs *Special study options:* academic remediation for entering students, advanced placement credit, independent study, internships, off-campus study, part-time degree program, services for LD students, study abroad.
Library Verman Kimbrough Memorial Library with 42,436 titles, 320 serial subscriptions, 113,143 audiovisual materials, an OPAC, a Web page.
Computers on Campus 500 computers available on campus for general student use. A campuswide network can be accessed from student residence rooms and from off campus. Internet access, at least one staffed computer lab available.
Student Life *Housing options:* coed, men-only, women-only, disabled students. Campus housing is university owned. Freshman applicants given priority for college housing. *Activities and organizations:* drama/theater group, FEWS, Nontraditional Student Group, Phi Delta Theta, Sigma Sigma Sigma, Ringling Ambassadors, national fraternities, national sororities. *Campus security:* 24-hour emergency response devices and patrols, late-night transport/escort service, controlled dormitory access, lighted campus. *Student services:* personal/psychological counseling.
Athletics *Intramural sports:* basketball M/W, soccer M/W, softball M/W.
Standardized Tests *Recommended:* SAT I and SAT II or ACT (for placement).
Costs (2003–04) *One-time required fee:* $165. *Comprehensive fee:* $27,530 includes full-time tuition ($18,860), mandatory fees ($200), and room and board ($8470). Full-time tuition and fees vary according to course load, program, and student level. Part-time tuition: $900 per credit hour. Part-time tuition and fees vary according to course load, program, and student level. *College room only:* $4545. Room and board charges vary according to board plan and housing facility. *Payment plan:* installment. *Waivers:* employees or children of employees.
Financial Aid Of all full-time matriculated undergraduates who enrolled in 2003, 694 applied for aid, 615 were judged to have need, 44 had their need fully met. 100 Federal Work-Study jobs (averaging $2034). In 2003, 100 non-need-based awards were made. *Average percent of need met:* 25%. *Average financial aid package:* $10,100. *Average need-based loan:* $5680. *Average need-based gift aid:* $5581. *Average non-need-based aid:* $13,094. *Average indebtedness upon graduation:* $31,276.
Applying *Options:* electronic application, deferred entrance. *Application fee:* $35. *Required:* essay or personal statement, high school transcript, minimum 2.0 GPA, 2 letters of recommendation, portfolio, resume. *Recommended:* interview. *Application deadline:* rolling (freshmen), rolling (transfers). *Notification:* continuous (freshmen).
Admissions Contact Amy Fischer, Associate Dean of Admissions, Ringling School of Art and Design, 2700 North Tamiami Trail, Sarasota, FL 34234-5895. *Phone:* 941-351-5100 Ext. 5034. *Toll-free phone:* 800-255-7695. *Fax:* 937-359-7517. *E-mail:* admissions@ringling.edu.

ROLLINS COLLEGE
Winter Park, Florida

- **Independent** comprehensive, founded 1885
- **Calendar** semesters
- **Degrees** bachelor's and master's
- **Suburban** 70-acre campus with easy access to Orlando
- **Endowment** $143.3 million
- **Coed,** 1,733 undergraduate students, 100% full-time, 61% women, 39% men
- **Very difficult** entrance level, 66% of applicants were admitted

Undergraduates 1,733 full-time. Students come from 46 states and territories, 51 other countries, 57% are from out of state, 4% African American, 3% Asian American or Pacific Islander, 7% Hispanic American, 0.6% Native American, 4% international, 4% transferred in, 62% live on campus. *Retention:* 83% of 2002 full-time freshmen returned.
Freshmen *Admission:* 2,271 applied, 1,510 admitted, 497 enrolled. *Average high school GPA:* 3.40. *Test scores:* SAT verbal scores over 500: 89%; SAT math scores over 500: 90%; ACT scores over 18: 98%; SAT verbal scores over 600: 39%; SAT math scores over 600: 42%; ACT scores over 24: 58%; SAT verbal scores over 700: 6%; SAT math scores over 700: 6%; ACT scores over 30: 8%.
Faculty *Total:* 179. *Student/faculty ratio:* 11:1.
Majors Anthropology; art history, criticism and conservation; biochemistry; biology/biological sciences; chemistry; classics and languages, literatures and linguistics; computer science; dramatic/theatre arts; economics; education; English; environmental studies; European studies; fine/studio arts; French; history; interdisciplinary studies; international business/trade/commerce; international relations and affairs; Latin American studies; mathematics; music; philosophy; physics; political science and government; pre-dentistry studies; pre-law studies; pre-medical studies; psychology; religious studies; sociology; Spanish.
Academic Programs *Special study options:* academic remediation for entering students, accelerated degree program, adult/continuing education programs, advanced placement credit, double majors, honors programs, independent study, internships, off-campus study, part-time degree program, services for LD students, student-designed majors, study abroad. *Unusual degree programs:* 3-2 engineering with Washington University in St. Louis, Columbia University, Georgia Institute of Technology, Case Western Reserve University, Auburn University; forestry with Duke University; nursing with Emory University; medical technology, environmental management with Duke University.
Library Olin Library with 237,333 titles, 2,259 serial subscriptions, 4,853 audiovisual materials, an OPAC, a Web page.
Computers on Campus 200 computers available on campus for general student use. A campuswide network can be accessed from student residence rooms and from off campus. Internet access, at least one staffed computer lab available.
Student Life *Housing options:* coed, disabled students. Campus housing is university owned. Freshman campus housing is guaranteed. *Activities and organizations:* drama/theater group, student-run newspaper, radio and television station, choral group, national fraternities, national sororities. *Campus security:* 24-hour emergency response devices and patrols, late-night transport/escort service, controlled dormitory access. *Student services:* health clinic, personal/psychological counseling.

Rollins College (continued)

Athletics Member NCAA. All Division II. *Intercollegiate sports:* baseball M(s), basketball M(s)/W(s), cheerleading M/W, crew M/W, cross-country running M/W, golf M(s)/W(s), sailing M(c)/W(c), soccer M(s)/W(s), softball W(s), swimming M/W, tennis M(s)/W(s), volleyball W(s). *Intramural sports:* basketball M/W, bowling M/W, football M/W, soccer M/W, softball M, table tennis M/W, tennis M/W, volleyball M/W.

Standardized Tests *Required:* SAT I or ACT (for admission).

Costs (2003–04) *Comprehensive fee:* $34,300 includes full-time tuition ($25,500), mandatory fees ($750), and room and board ($8050). *College room only:* $4650. *Payment plans:* tuition prepayment, installment. *Waivers:* employees or children of employees.

Financial Aid Of all full-time matriculated undergraduates who enrolled in 2003, 828 applied for aid, 739 were judged to have need, 445 had their need fully met. In 2003, 228 non-need-based awards were made. *Average percent of need met:* 92%. *Average financial aid package:* $26,005. *Average need-based loan:* $3923. *Average need-based gift aid:* $20,887. *Average non-need-based aid:* $7982. *Average indebtedness upon graduation:* $14,049. *Financial aid deadline:* 3/1.

Applying *Options:* common application, electronic application, early admission, early decision, deferred entrance. *Application fee:* $40. *Required:* essay or personal statement, high school transcript, 1 letter of recommendation. *Recommended:* interview. *Application deadlines:* 2/15 (freshmen), 4/15 (transfers). *Early decision:* 11/15 (for plan 1), 1/15 (for plan 2). *Notification:* 4/1 (freshmen), 12/15 (early decision plan 1), 2/1 (early decision plan 2), continuous (transfers).

Admissions Contact Mr. David Erdmann, Dean of Admission and Enrollment, Rollins College, 1000 Holt Avenue, Box 2720, Winter Park, FL 32789-4499. *Phone:* 407-646-2161. *Fax:* 407-646-1502. *E-mail:* admission@rollins.edu.

■ *See page 2256 for a narrative description.*

ST. JOHN VIANNEY COLLEGE SEMINARY

Miami, Florida

Admissions Contact Br. Edward Van Merrienboer, Academic Dean, St. John Vianney College Seminary, 2900 Southwest 87th Avenue, Miami, FL 33165-3244. *Phone:* 305-223-4561 Ext. 13. *E-mail:* academic@sjvcs.edu.

SAINT LEO UNIVERSITY

Saint Leo, Florida

- **Independent Roman Catholic** comprehensive, founded 1889
- **Calendar** semesters
- **Degrees** associate, bachelor's, and master's
- **Rural** 186-acre campus with easy access to Tampa and Orlando
- **Endowment** $6.6 million
- **Coed,** 1,083 undergraduate students, 95% full-time, 55% women, 45% men
- **Moderately difficult** entrance level, 59% of applicants were admitted

Undergraduates 1,032 full-time, 51 part-time. Students come from 33 states and territories, 35 other countries, 28% are from out of state, 8% African American, 1% Asian American or Pacific Islander, 7% Hispanic American, 0.6% Native American, 5% international, 8% transferred in, 69% live on campus. *Retention:* 67% of 2002 full-time freshmen returned.

Freshmen *Admission:* 1,933 applied, 1,145 admitted, 376 enrolled. *Average high school GPA:* 3.1. *Test scores:* SAT verbal scores over 500: 46%; SAT math scores over 500: 46%; ACT scores over 18: 82%; SAT verbal scores over 600: 8%; SAT math scores over 600: 7%; ACT scores over 24: 22%; SAT verbal scores over 700: 1%; SAT math scores over 700: 1%; ACT scores over 30: 3%.

Faculty *Total:* 108, 56% full-time, 58% with terminal degrees. *Student/faculty ratio:* 14:1.

Majors Accounting; biology/biological sciences; business administration and management; clinical laboratory science/medical technology; community organization and advocacy; creative writing; criminal justice/safety; elementary education; English; English language and literature related; environmental studies; health/health care administration; history; hospital and health care facilities administration; hospitality administration; hospitality administration related; human resources management; human services; international business/trade/commerce; international relations and affairs; liberal arts and sciences/liberal studies; literature; management information systems; marketing/marketing management; operations management; political science and government; psychology; social work; sociology; sport and fitness administration; theology.

Academic Programs *Special study options:* academic remediation for entering students, adult/continuing education programs, advanced placement credit, distance learning, double majors, English as a second language, honors programs, independent study, internships, part-time degree program, services for LD students, study abroad, summer session for credit. *ROTC:* Army (b), Air Force (c).

Library Cannon Memorial Library with 141,521 titles, 700 serial subscriptions, 6,437 audiovisual materials, an OPAC, a Web page.

Computers on Campus 750 computers available on campus for general student use. A campuswide network can be accessed from student residence rooms and from off campus. Internet access, online (class) registration, at least one staffed computer lab available.

Student Life *Housing:* on-campus residence required through junior year. *Options:* coed, men-only, women-only, disabled students. Campus housing is university owned. Freshman applicants given priority for college housing. *Activities and organizations:* drama/theater group, student-run newspaper, television station, choral group, Student Government Union, Circle K, Samaritans, American Marketing Association, Campus Activities Board, national fraternities, national sororities. *Campus security:* 24-hour emergency response devices and patrols, late-night transport/escort service, controlled dormitory access. *Student services:* health clinic, personal/psychological counseling.

Athletics Member NCAA. All Division II. *Intercollegiate sports:* baseball M(s), basketball M(s)/W(s), cross-country running M/W, golf M(s)/W, soccer M(s)/W(s), softball W(s), tennis M(s)/W(s), volleyball W(s). *Intramural sports:* basketball M/W, cheerleading M/W, football M/W, racquetball M/W, rock climbing M/W, sailing M/W, soccer M/W, softball M/W, table tennis M/W, tennis M/W, volleyball M/W.

Standardized Tests *Required:* SAT I or ACT (for admission).

Costs (2003–04) *Comprehensive fee:* $20,600 includes full-time tuition ($13,150), mandatory fees ($420), and room and board ($7030). Full-time tuition and fees vary according to location. Part-time tuition: $361 per credit hour. Part-time tuition and fees vary according to location. *College room only:* $3700. Room and board charges vary according to board plan and housing facility. *Payment plan:* installment. *Waivers:* children of alumni.

Financial Aid Of all full-time matriculated undergraduates who enrolled in 2002, 802 applied for aid, 659 were judged to have need, 191 had their need fully met. In 2002, 183 non-need-based awards were made. *Average percent of need met:* 88%. *Average financial aid package:* $17,695. *Average need-based loan:* $3691. *Average need-based gift aid:* $12,077. *Average non-need-based aid:* $5760. *Average indebtedness upon graduation:* $12,000.

Applying *Options:* common application, electronic application, early admission, deferred entrance. *Application fee:* $35. *Required:* essay or personal statement, high school transcript, minimum 2.3 GPA, 1 letter of recommendation. *Required for some:* interview. *Recommended:* minimum 3.0 GPA, interview. *Application deadlines:* 8/15 (freshmen), 8/1 (transfers). *Notification:* continuous (freshmen), continuous (transfers).

Admissions Contact Mr. Gary Bracken, Vice President for Enrollment, Saint Leo University, MC 2008, PO Box 6665, Saint Leo, FL 33574-6665. *Phone:* 352-588-8283. *Toll-free phone:* 800-334-5532. *Fax:* 352-588-8257. *E-mail:* admission@saintleo.edu.

■ *See page 2304 for a narrative description.*

ST. PETERSBURG COLLEGE

St. Petersburg, Florida

- **State and locally supported** primarily 2-year, founded 1927
- **Calendar** semesters
- **Degrees** certificates, diplomas, associate, and bachelor's
- **Suburban** campus
- **Endowment** $12.0 million
- **Coed**
- **Noncompetitive** entrance level

Student Life *Campus security:* late-night transport/escort service.

Athletics Member NJCAA.

Standardized Tests *Required for some:* SAT I and SAT II or ACT (for placement), SAT II: Writing Test (for placement), CPT.

Costs (2003–04) *Tuition:* state resident $1493 full-time, $50 per credit part-time; nonresident $5975 full-time, $199 per credit part-time. Full-time tuition and fees vary according to degree level and program. Part-time tuition and fees vary according to degree level and program. *Required fees:* $254 full-time, $8 per credit part-time.

Financial Aid Of all full-time matriculated undergraduates who enrolled in 2001, 350 Federal Work-Study jobs (averaging $2500).

Applying *Options:* common application, electronic application, early admission, deferred entrance. *Application fee:* $35. *Required:* high school transcript.

Admissions Contact St. Petersburg College, PO Box 13489, St. Petersburg, FL 33733-3489. *Phone:* 727-712-5892. *Fax:* 727-712-5872. *E-mail:* information@spcollege.edu.

St. Petersburg Theological Seminary

St. Petersburg, Florida

Admissions Contact Jane Cargile, Director of Admissions, St. Petersburg Theological Seminary, 10830 Navajo Drive, St. Petersburg, FL 33708. *Phone:* 727-399-0276.

St. Thomas University

Miami Gardens, Florida

- **Independent Roman Catholic** comprehensive, founded 1961
- **Calendar** semesters
- **Degrees** bachelor's, master's, first professional, post-master's, and postbachelor's certificates
- **Suburban** 140-acre campus
- **Endowment** $9.1 million
- **Coed,** 1,171 undergraduate students, 93% full-time, 61% women, 39% men
- **Moderately difficult** entrance level, 43% of applicants were admitted

Undergraduates 1,089 full-time, 82 part-time. Students come from 25 states and territories, 58 other countries, 6% are from out of state, 26% African American, 0.5% Asian American or Pacific Islander, 47% Hispanic American, 0.1% Native American, 13% international, 16% transferred in, 10% live on campus. *Retention:* 68% of 2002 full-time freshmen returned.

Freshmen *Admission:* 818 applied, 349 admitted, 209 enrolled. *Average high school GPA:* 2.94. *Test scores:* SAT verbal scores over 500: 22%; SAT math scores over 500: 25%; ACT scores over 18: 52%; SAT verbal scores over 600: 2%; SAT math scores over 600: 6%; ACT scores over 24: 12%; SAT verbal scores over 700: 1%; ACT scores over 30: 9%.

Faculty *Total:* 214, 39% full-time. *Student/faculty ratio:* 15:1.

Majors Accounting; biology/biological sciences; business administration and management; chemistry; computer science; criminal justice/law enforcement administration; elementary education; English; finance; history; hotel/motel administration; information science/studies; international business/trade/commerce; liberal arts and sciences/liberal studies; marketing/marketing management; mass communication/media; pastoral studies/counseling; political science and government; pre-dentistry studies; pre-law studies; pre-medical studies; psychology; public administration; religious studies; secondary education; sociology; sport and fitness administration; tourism and travel services management.

Academic Programs *Special study options:* academic remediation for entering students, adult/continuing education programs, advanced placement credit, distance learning, double majors, freshman honors college, honors programs, independent study, part-time degree program, services for LD students, summer session for credit. *ROTC:* Army (c), Air Force (c).

Library St. Thomas University Library plus 1 other with 154,017 titles, 898 serial subscriptions, 7,894 audiovisual materials, a Web page.

Computers on Campus 60 computers available on campus for general student use. A campuswide network can be accessed. At least one staffed computer lab available.

Student Life *Housing options:* men-only, women-only. *Activities and organizations:* student-run newspaper, television station, choral group, International Student Organization, pre-med club, Hispanic Heritage Club, Inter-Dorm Council, communicators club. *Campus security:* 24-hour emergency response devices and patrols, late-night transport/escort service, controlled dormitory access. *Student services:* health clinic, personal/psychological counseling.

Athletics Member NAIA. *Intercollegiate sports:* baseball M(s), cross-country running M(s)/W(s), golf M(s)/W(s), soccer M(s)/W(s), softball W(s), tennis M(s)/W(s), volleyball W(s). *Intramural sports:* baseball M, basketball M/W, cross-country running M/W, football M, golf M, soccer M/W, softball M/W, table tennis M/W, tennis M/W, volleyball M/W, water polo M/W, weight lifting M/W.

Standardized Tests *Required:* SAT I and SAT II or ACT (for admission).

Costs (2003–04) *Comprehensive fee:* $26,400 includes full-time tuition ($16,200) and room and board ($10,200). *Room and board:* Room and board charges vary according to housing facility. *Payment plan:* installment. *Waivers:* minority students, children of alumni, and employees or children of employees.

Financial Aid Of all full-time matriculated undergraduates who enrolled in 2002, 1,307 applied for aid, 1,307 were judged to have need. 227 Federal Work-Study jobs (averaging $2325). 47 state and other part-time jobs (averaging $3277). In 2002, 224 non-need-based awards were made. *Average non-need-based aid:* $4000. *Average indebtedness upon graduation:* $17,000.

Applying *Options:* common application, electronic application, early admission, deferred entrance. *Application fee:* $40. *Required:* high school transcript, minimum 2.0 GPA. *Recommended:* essay or personal statement, 1 letter of recommendation, interview. *Application deadline:* rolling (freshmen), rolling (transfers). *Notification:* continuous (freshmen), continuous (transfers).

Admissions Contact Mr. Andre Lightbourne, Associate Director of Admissions, St. Thomas University, 1540 Northwest 32nd Avenue, Miami, FL 33054-6459. *Phone:* 305-628-6546. *Toll-free phone:* 800-367-9010. *Fax:* 305-628-6591. *E-mail:* signup@stu.edu.

■ *See page 2330 for a narrative description.*

Schiller International University

Dunedin, Florida

- **Independent** comprehensive, founded 1991, part of Schiller International University
- **Calendar** semesters
- **Degrees** certificates, diplomas, associate, bachelor's, and master's
- **Suburban** campus with easy access to Tampa
- **Coed,** 108 undergraduate students, 95% full-time, 40% women, 60% men
- **Noncompetitive** entrance level

Schiller International University (SIU) is an independent American university with campuses in England, France, Germany, Spain, Switzerland, and the United States. In addition, students can transfer without loss of credit. English is the language of instruction at all campuses. SIU offers undergraduate and graduate students an American education in an international setting.

Undergraduates 103 full-time, 5 part-time. Students come from 60 other countries. *Retention:* 22% of 2002 full-time freshmen returned.

Freshmen *Admission:* 20 enrolled.

Faculty *Total:* 34, 12% full-time.

Majors Hotel/motel administration; interdisciplinary studies; international business/trade/commerce; international relations and affairs; liberal arts and sciences/liberal studies; marketing/marketing management; tourism and travel services management.

Academic Programs *Special study options:* accelerated degree program, adult/continuing education programs, advanced placement credit, English as a second language, internships, part-time degree program, student-designed majors, study abroad, summer session for credit.

Library SIU Library with 1,918 titles, 30 serial subscriptions.

Computers on Campus 17 computers available on campus for general student use. Internet access, at least one staffed computer lab available.

Student Life *Housing options:* coed. Campus housing is university owned. *Activities and organizations:* student-run newspaper, student government, student newspaper, yearbook staff, Model United Nations. *Campus security:* night patrols. *Student services:* personal/psychological counseling.

Athletics *Intramural sports:* basketball M/W, sailing M/W, soccer M/W, softball M/W, swimming M/W, volleyball M/W.

Costs (2003–04) *Comprehensive fee:* $21,540 includes full-time tuition ($14,400), mandatory fees ($640), and room and board ($6500). Part-time tuition: $417 per credit. *Required fees:* $150 per term part-time.

Applying *Options:* common application, deferred entrance. *Application fee:* $35. *Required:* essay or personal statement, high school transcript. *Recommended:* minimum 2.0 GPA. *Application deadline:* rolling (freshmen), rolling (transfers).

Admissions Contact Ms. Kamala Dontamsetti, Associate Director of Admissions, Schiller International University, 453 Edgewater Drive, Dunedin, FL 34698-7532. *Phone:* 727-736-5082 Ext. 240. *Toll-free phone:* 800-336-4133. *Fax:* 727-734-0359. *E-mail:* admissions@schiller.edu.

■ *See page 2354 for a narrative description.*

Southeastern College of the Assemblies of God

Lakeland, Florida

- **Independent** 4-year, founded 1935, affiliated with Assemblies of God
- **Calendar** semesters
- **Degree** diplomas and bachelor's
- **Suburban** 62-acre campus with easy access to Tampa and Orlando
- **Endowment** $1.2 million
- **Coed,** 1,675 undergraduate students, 92% full-time, 53% women, 47% men
- **Minimally difficult** entrance level, 85% of applicants were admitted

Undergraduates 1,535 full-time, 140 part-time. Students come from 46 states and territories, 53% are from out of state, 6% African American, 1% Asian American or Pacific Islander, 9% Hispanic American, 0.5% Native American, 0.8% international, 60% live on campus. *Retention:* 70% of 2002 full-time freshmen returned.

Freshmen *Admission:* 589 applied, 503 admitted, 360 enrolled.

Southeastern College of the Assemblies of God (continued)

Faculty *Total:* 97, 47% full-time, 41% with terminal degrees. *Student/faculty ratio:* 25:1.

Majors Accounting; biblical studies; biology/biological sciences; business, management, and marketing related; communication/speech communication and rhetoric; dramatic/theatre arts; elementary education; English; English/language arts teacher education; interdisciplinary studies; marketing/marketing management; mathematics teacher education; missionary studies and missiology; music performance; music teacher education; pastoral studies/counseling; pre-medical studies; psychology; religious/sacred music; science teacher education; social studies teacher education; social work; theological and ministerial studies related.

Academic Programs *Special study options:* advanced placement credit, internships, part-time degree program, summer session for credit. *ROTC:* Army (c), Air Force (c).

Library Steelman Library plus 3 others with 96,000 titles, 490 serial subscriptions, an OPAC.

Computers on Campus 26 computers available on campus for general student use. A campuswide network can be accessed from student residence rooms and from off campus that provide access to network programs. Internet access, at least one staffed computer lab available.

Student Life *Housing:* on-campus residence required through senior year. *Options:* men-only, women-only. *Activities and organizations:* drama/theater group, student-run newspaper, radio and television station, choral group, Spanish club, travel music groups, Impact (cross-cultural awareness), Psyche, Student Broadcast Organization. *Campus security:* 24-hour emergency response devices and patrols, late-night transport/escort service. *Student services:* health clinic, personal/psychological counseling.

Athletics Member NCCAA. *Intercollegiate sports:* baseball M, basketball M/W, golf M, soccer M, tennis W, volleyball W. *Intramural sports:* basketball M, bowling M/W, football M, soccer M/W, softball M/W, tennis M/W, volleyball M/W, weight lifting M/W.

Standardized Tests *Required:* SAT I or ACT (for placement).

Costs (2003–04) *Comprehensive fee:* $14,449 includes full-time tuition ($9000), mandatory fees ($120), and room and board ($5329). Part-time tuition: $375 per credit. Part-time tuition and fees vary according to course load, program, and reciprocity agreements. *Room and board:* Room and board charges vary according to board plan and housing facility. *Payment plan:* installment. *Waivers:* employees or children of employees.

Financial Aid Of all full-time matriculated undergraduates who enrolled in 2003, 1,328 applied for aid, 1,129 were judged to have need, 121 had their need fully met. 106 Federal Work-Study jobs (averaging $1164). In 2003, 347 non-need-based awards were made. *Average percent of need met:* 59%. *Average financial aid package:* $6922. *Average need-based loan:* $3205. *Average need-based gift aid:* $4628. *Average non-need-based aid:* $7890. *Average indebtedness upon graduation:* $16,580.

Applying *Options:* electronic application, early admission, deferred entrance. *Application fee:* $40. *Required:* high school transcript, 2 letters of recommendation. *Required for some:* essay or personal statement, interview. *Application deadlines:* 8/1 (freshmen), 8/1 (transfers). *Notification:* continuous until 8/1 (freshmen), continuous until 8/1 (transfers).

Admissions Contact Mr. Omar Rashed, Director of Admission, Southeastern College of the Assemblies of God, 1000 Longfellow Boulevard, Lakeland, FL 33801. *Phone:* 863-667-5000. *Toll-free phone:* 800-500-8760. *Fax:* 863-667-5200. *E-mail:* admission@secollege.edu.

SOUTH UNIVERSITY
West Palm Beach, Florida

- **Proprietary** 2-year, founded 1899
- **Calendar** quarters
- **Degrees** associate, bachelor's
- **Suburban** campus
- **Coed,** 450 undergraduate students

Faculty *Total:* 60. *Student/faculty ratio:* 8:1.

Majors Accounting; administrative assistant and secretarial science; business administration and management; health services/allied health/health sciences; information science/studies; infomation technology; legal administrative assistant/secretary; legal assistant/paralegal; legal studies; medical/clinical assistant; nursing (registered nurse training); physical therapist assistant; pre-nursing studies.

Costs (2003–04) *Tuition:* $10,185 full-time.

Applying *Application fee:* $25. *Required:* high school transcript. *Application deadline:* rolling.

Admissions Contact Mr. Peter Grosfeld, Director of Admissions, South University, 1760 North Congress Avenue, West Palm Beach, FL 33409-5178. *Phone:* 561-697-9200. *Toll-free phone:* 866-629-2902 (in-state); 866-629-9200 (out-of-state). *Fax:* 561-697-9944. *E-mail:* wpbadmiss@southuniversity.edu.

■ **See page 2422 for a narrative description.**

SPURGEON BAPTIST BIBLE COLLEGE
Mulberry, Florida

Admissions Contact Ms. Linda Stutzman, Director of Admissions and Student Development, Spurgeon Baptist Bible College, 4440 Spurgeon Drive, Mulberry, FL 33860-9531. *Phone:* 863-425-3429.

STETSON UNIVERSITY
DeLand, Florida

- **Independent** comprehensive, founded 1883
- **Calendar** semesters
- **Degrees** bachelor's, master's, first professional, post-master's, and first professional certificates
- **Small-town** 170-acre campus with easy access to Orlando
- **Endowment** $103.3 million
- **Coed,** 2,161 undergraduate students, 96% full-time, 57% women, 43% men
- **Moderately difficult** entrance level, 76% of applicants were admitted

Stetson University is nationally known for its superior programs and course offerings, many of which are found at few other schools. Great professors committed to teaching and helping students set career goals are the heart of the University. Maintaining a more than century-old commitment to values and social responsibility, Stetson is also committed to making top-quality private education affordable to a diverse group of qualified students. Four colleges and schools on four beautiful Florida campuses offer the best of two worlds: the rich variety of a university program coupled with the close student-faculty interaction found at small colleges.

Undergraduates 2,070 full-time, 91 part-time. Students come from 40 states and territories, 35 other countries, 20% are from out of state, 4% African American, 2% Asian American or Pacific Islander, 5% Hispanic American, 0.4% Native American, 3% international, 6% transferred in, 65% live on campus. *Retention:* 81% of 2002 full-time freshmen returned.

Freshmen *Admission:* 1,992 applied, 1,510 admitted, 529 enrolled. *Average high school GPA:* 3.54. *Test scores:* SAT verbal scores over 500: 86%; SAT math scores over 500: 82%; ACT scores over 18: 99%; SAT verbal scores over 600: 36%; SAT math scores over 600: 33%; ACT scores over 24: 56%; SAT verbal scores over 700: 7%; SAT math scores over 700: 4%; ACT scores over 30: 7%.

Faculty *Total:* 251, 74% full-time. *Student/faculty ratio:* 11:1.

Majors Accounting; American studies; aquatic biology/limnology; art; biochemistry; biology/biological sciences; business administration and management; business/managerial economics; chemistry; clinical laboratory science/medical technology; communication/speech communication and rhetoric; computer science; dramatic/theatre arts; e-commerce; economics; education; elementary education; English; environmental studies; finance; French; geography; German; health services/allied health/health sciences; history; humanities; international business/trade/commerce; international relations and affairs; kinesiology and exercise science; Latin American studies; management science; marketing/marketing management; mathematics; molecular biology; music; music performance; music teacher education; music theory and composition; philosophy; physics; piano and organ; political science and government; pre-dentistry studies; pre-law studies; pre-medical studies; pre-veterinary studies; psychology; religious studies; Russian studies; secondary education; social sciences; social science teacher education; sociology; Spanish; sport and fitness administration; violin, viola, guitar and other stringed instruments; visual and performing arts related; voice and opera; web page, digital/multimedia and information resources design.

Academic Programs *Special study options:* accelerated degree program, adult/continuing education programs, advanced placement credit, double majors, honors programs, independent study, internships, off-campus study, part-time degree program, student-designed majors, study abroad, summer session for credit. *ROTC:* Army (c). *Unusual degree programs:* 3-2 engineering with University of Florida, University of Miami; forestry with Duke University.

Library DuPont-Ball Library plus 2 others with 377,319 titles, 10,079 serial subscriptions, 18,769 audiovisual materials, an OPAC, a Web page.

Computers on Campus 320 computers available on campus for general student use. A campuswide network can be accessed from student residence rooms and from off campus. Internet access, at least one staffed computer lab available.

Student Life *Housing:* on-campus residence required through junior year. *Options:* coed, men-only, women-only. Campus housing is university owned. Freshman campus housing is guaranteed. *Activities and organizations:* drama/theater group, student-run newspaper, radio station, choral group, Into the Streets,

Multi-Cultural Student Council, Black Student Association, Best Buddies, Habitat For Humanity, national fraternities, national sororities. *Campus security:* 24-hour emergency response devices and patrols, late-night transport/escort service. *Student services:* health clinic, personal/psychological counseling, women's center.

Athletics Member NCAA. All Division I. *Intercollegiate sports:* baseball M(s), basketball M(s)/W(s), crew M/W, cross-country running M(s)/W(s), golf M(s)/W(s), soccer M(s)/W(s), softball W(s), tennis M(s)/W(s), volleyball W(s). *Intramural sports:* basketball M/W, bowling M/W, football M/W, sailing M(c)/W(c), soccer M/W, softball M/W, swimming M(c)/W(c), table tennis M/W, tennis M/W, ultimate Frisbee M/W, volleyball M/W, water polo M/W.

Standardized Tests *Required:* SAT I or ACT (for admission).

Costs (2003–04) *One-time required fee:* $260. *Comprehensive fee:* $29,235 includes full-time tuition ($21,300), mandatory fees ($1080), and room and board ($6855). Part-time tuition: $685 per credit hour. Part-time tuition and fees vary according to course load. *College room only:* $3845. Room and board charges vary according to board plan and housing facility. *Payment plan:* installment. *Waivers:* employees or children of employees.

Financial Aid Of all full-time matriculated undergraduates who enrolled in 2003, 1,372 applied for aid, 1,188 were judged to have need, 308 had their need fully met. 568 Federal Work-Study jobs (averaging $2325). 133 state and other part-time jobs (averaging $2011). In 2003, 659 non-need-based awards were made. *Average percent of need met:* 82%. *Average financial aid package:* $19,406. *Average need-based loan:* $5002. *Average need-based gift aid:* $14,369. *Average non-need-based aid:* $11,283. *Average indebtedness upon graduation:* $20,000.

Applying *Options:* common application, electronic application, early admission, early decision. *Application fee:* $40. *Required:* essay or personal statement, high school transcript, letters of recommendation. *Recommended:* interview. *Application deadline:* 3/1 (freshmen), rolling (transfers). *Early decision:* 11/1. *Notification:* 11/15 (early decision), continuous (transfers).

Admissions Contact Ms. Deborah Thompson, Vice President for Admissions, Stetson University, Unit 8378, Griffith Hall, DeLand, FL 32723. *Phone:* 386-822-7100. *Toll-free phone:* 800-688-0101. *Fax:* 386-822-8832. *E-mail:* admissions@stetson.edu.

■ *See page 2462 for a narrative description.*

TALMUDIC COLLEGE OF FLORIDA
Miami Beach, Florida

- **Independent Jewish** comprehensive, founded 1974
- **Calendar** semesters
- **Degrees** bachelor's, master's, and doctoral
- **Urban** campus with easy access to Miami
- **Men only,** 30 undergraduate students, 100% full-time
- **Moderately difficult** entrance level, 70% of applicants were admitted

Undergraduates 30 full-time. Students come from 8 states and territories, 7 other countries, 90% are from out of state, 67% transferred in, 90% live on campus. *Retention:* 50% of 2002 full-time freshmen returned.

Freshmen *Admission:* 5 enrolled. *Average high school GPA:* 3.50.

Faculty *Total:* 6, 100% full-time, 100% with terminal degrees. *Student/faculty ratio:* 5:1.

Majors Biblical studies; Jewish/Judaic studies; rabbinical studies; religious education; talmudic studies.

Academic Programs *Special study options:* academic remediation for entering students, adult/continuing education programs, English as a second language, honors programs, independent study, part-time degree program, study abroad, summer session for credit.

Library Beis Medrash plus 1 other with 23,000 titles, a Web page.

Computers on Campus 14 computers available on campus for general student use. A campuswide network can be accessed. Internet access, at least one staffed computer lab available.

Student Life *Housing:* on-campus residence required through senior year. *Options:* men-only. Campus housing is university owned. Freshman campus housing is guaranteed. *Student services:* personal/psychological counseling.

Athletics *Intramural sports:* basketball M, football M, golf M, soccer M, swimming M, tennis M, weight lifting M.

Costs (2004–05) *Comprehensive fee:* $12,500 includes full-time tuition ($7500) and room and board ($5000). No tuition increase for student's term of enrollment. *College room only:* $2500. *Payment plans:* installment, deferred payment.

Financial Aid Of all full-time matriculated undergraduates who enrolled in 2002, 55 applied for aid, 49 were judged to have need, 6 had their need fully met. 12 Federal Work-Study jobs (averaging $2200). In 2002, 9 non-need-based awards were made. *Average percent of need met:* 57%. *Average financial aid package:* $7125. *Average need-based loan:* $2780. *Average non-need-based aid:* $4600. *Average indebtedness upon graduation:* $6300.

Applying *Options:* common application, early admission, deferred entrance. *Application fee:* $250. *Required:* interview, placement exam. *Required for some:* high school transcript. *Recommended:* essay or personal statement, 2 letters of recommendation. *Application deadline:* rolling (freshmen). *Notification:* continuous (transfers).

Admissions Contact Rabbi Ira Hill, Admissions Director, Talmudic College of Florida, 1910 Alton Road, Miami Beach, FL 33139. *Phone:* 305-534-7050 Ext. 11. *Toll-free phone:* 888-825-6834. *Fax:* 305-534-8444. *E-mail:* ryhill@talmudicu.edu.

TRINITY BAPTIST COLLEGE
Jacksonville, Florida

- **Independent Baptist** comprehensive, founded 1974
- **Calendar** semesters
- **Degrees** diplomas, associate, bachelor's, and master's
- **Urban** 148-acre campus
- **Coed,** 383 undergraduate students, 88% full-time, 48% women, 52% men
- **Moderately difficult** entrance level, 74% of applicants were admitted

Undergraduates 336 full-time, 47 part-time. Students come from 28 states and territories, 4 other countries, 42% are from out of state, 6% African American, 1% Asian American or Pacific Islander, 3% Hispanic American, 1% international, 7% transferred in, 55% live on campus. *Retention:* 66% of 2002 full-time freshmen returned.

Freshmen *Admission:* 171 applied, 126 admitted, 100 enrolled.

Faculty *Total:* 51, 25% full-time, 29% with terminal degrees. *Student/faculty ratio:* 14:1.

Majors Administrative assistant and secretarial science; biblical studies; elementary education; missionary studies and missiology; pastoral studies/counseling; secondary education.

Academic Programs *Special study options:* academic remediation for entering students, accelerated degree program, adult/continuing education programs, advanced placement credit, independent study, internships, part-time degree program, services for LD students, summer session for credit.

Library Travis Hudson Library with 33,000 titles, 210 serial subscriptions.

Computers on Campus 35 computers available on campus for general student use. A campuswide network can be accessed from student residence rooms. Internet access, at least one staffed computer lab available.

Student Life *Housing:* on-campus residence required through senior year. *Options:* men-only, women-only. Campus housing is university owned. Freshman campus housing is guaranteed. *Activities and organizations:* drama/theater group, choral group. *Campus security:* 24-hour emergency response devices, student patrols, controlled dormitory access, evening security. *Student services:* health clinic, personal/psychological counseling.

Athletics Member NCCAA. *Intercollegiate sports:* basketball M, volleyball W. *Intramural sports:* baseball M, basketball M/W, football M, softball M/W, table tennis M/W, volleyball M/W.

Standardized Tests *Required:* SAT I or ACT (for admission).

Costs (2004–05) *Comprehensive fee:* $8800 includes full-time tuition ($4520), mandatory fees ($550), and room and board ($3730). Part-time tuition: $185 per semester hour. *College room only:* $1930. Room and board charges vary according to board plan. *Payment plan:* installment. *Waivers:* employees or children of employees.

Financial Aid Of all full-time matriculated undergraduates who enrolled in 2001, 264 applied for aid, 168 were judged to have need, 37 had their need fully met. In 2001, 10 non-need-based awards were made. *Average percent of need met:* 55%. *Average financial aid package:* $4458. *Average need-based loan:* $2912. *Average need-based gift aid:* $2791. *Average non-need-based aid:* $1279. *Average indebtedness upon graduation:* $6425. *Financial aid deadline:* 4/15.

Applying *Options:* common application. *Application fee:* $30. *Required:* essay or personal statement, high school transcript, minimum 2.0 GPA, 3 letters of recommendation. *Application deadline:* rolling (freshmen), rolling (transfers). *Notification:* continuous until 8/15 (freshmen), continuous until 8/15 (transfers).

Admissions Contact Mr. Larry Appleby, Administrative Dean, Trinity Baptist College, 800 Hammond Boulevard, Jacksonville, FL 32221. *Phone:* 904-596-2538. *Toll-free phone:* 800-786-2206. *Fax:* 904-596-2531. *E-mail:* trinity@tbc.edu.

TRINITY COLLEGE OF FLORIDA
New Port Richey, Florida

- **Independent nondenominational** 4-year, founded 1932
- **Calendar** semesters

Trinity College of Florida (continued)

- **Degrees** certificates, associate, and bachelor's
- **Small-town** 40-acre campus with easy access to Tampa
- **Endowment** $1.3 million
- **Coed,** 207 undergraduate students, 54% full-time, 46% women, 54% men
- **Minimally difficult** entrance level, 52% of applicants were admitted

Undergraduates 112 full-time, 95 part-time. Students come from 15 states and territories, 6 other countries, 9% are from out of state, 3% African American, 2% Hispanic American, 4% international, 20% transferred in, 28% live on campus. *Retention:* 60% of 2002 full-time freshmen returned.

Freshmen *Admission:* 103 applied, 54 admitted, 30 enrolled. *Average high school GPA:* 3.00. *Test scores:* SAT verbal scores over 500: 75%; SAT math scores over 500: 40%; ACT scores over 18: 66%; SAT verbal scores over 600: 20%; SAT math scores over 600: 20%; ACT scores over 24: 12%; SAT verbal scores over 700: 5%; SAT math scores over 700: 5%.

Faculty *Total:* 21, 29% full-time, 33% with terminal degrees. *Student/faculty ratio:* 15:1.

Majors Biblical studies; business/commerce; counseling psychology; elementary education; missionary studies and missiology; pastoral studies/counseling; theological and ministerial studies related; youth ministry.

Academic Programs *Special study options:* academic remediation for entering students, adult/continuing education programs, advanced placement credit, double majors, external degree program, independent study, internships, part-time degree program, services for LD students, summer session for credit.

Library Raymond H. Center, M.D. Library with 40,523 titles, 275 serial subscriptions, 2,300 audiovisual materials.

Computers on Campus 16 computers available on campus for general student use. Internet access, at least one staffed computer lab available.

Student Life *Housing:* on-campus residence required for freshman year. *Options:* men-only, women-only. Campus housing is university owned and leased by the school. Freshman campus housing is guaranteed. *Activities and organizations:* drama/theater group, choral group, Great Commission Missionary Fellowship, Men's Basketball/Soccer Leagues, music club, Bible and Theology Club, Student Government. *Campus security:* controlled dormitory access, on-campus security personnel. *Student services:* personal/psychological counseling.

Athletics Member NCCAA. *Intramural sports:* basketball M(c), soccer M(c), table tennis M/W, volleyball M/W.

Standardized Tests *Required:* SAT I or ACT (for admission).

Costs (2003–04) *Comprehensive fee:* $10,766 includes full-time tuition ($6900), mandatory fees ($356), and room and board ($3510). Part-time tuition: $288 per credit hour. Part-time tuition and fees vary according to course load. *Required fees:* $178 per term part-time. *Payment plan:* deferred payment. *Waivers:* children of alumni, senior citizens, and employees or children of employees.

Financial Aid Of all full-time matriculated undergraduates who enrolled in 2002, 28 Federal Work-Study jobs (averaging $2232). In 2002, 129 non-need-based awards were made.

Applying *Options:* common application, electronic application, early admission, deferred entrance. *Application fee:* $25. *Required:* essay or personal statement, high school transcript, 3 letters of recommendation, interview. *Recommended:* minimum 2.75 GPA. *Application deadlines:* 7/15 (freshmen), 7/1 (out-of-state freshmen), 7/1 (transfers). *Notification:* continuous until 7/31 (freshmen), continuous until 7/15 (out-of-state freshmen), continuous (transfers).

Admissions Contact Mr. Kevin Bonsignore, Assistant Director, Enrollment, Trinity College of Florida, 2430 Welbilt Boulevard, New Port Richey, FL 34655. *Phone:* 727-376-6911 Ext. 1108. *Toll-free phone:* 888-776-4999. *Fax:* 727-376-0781. *E-mail:* admissions@trinitycollege.edu.

UNIVERSIDAD FLET
Miami, Florida

Admissions Contact 14540 SW 136th Street, Suite 200, Miami, FL 33186. *Toll-free phone:* 800-487-0340.

UNIVERSITY OF CENTRAL FLORIDA
Orlando, Florida

- **State-supported** university, founded 1963, part of State University System of Florida
- **Calendar** semesters
- **Degrees** certificates, associate, bachelor's, master's, doctoral, and postbachelor's certificates
- **Suburban** 1415-acre campus
- **Endowment** $53.8 million
- **Coed,** 34,170 undergraduate students, 75% full-time, 55% women, 45% men
- **Moderately difficult** entrance level, 60% of applicants were admitted

Undergraduates 25,757 full-time, 8,413 part-time. Students come from 52 states and territories, 131 other countries, 3% are from out of state, 8% African American, 5% Asian American or Pacific Islander, 12% Hispanic American, 0.6% Native American, 1% international, 10% transferred in, 20% live on campus. *Retention:* 83% of 2002 full-time freshmen returned.

Freshmen *Admission:* 20,533 applied, 12,289 admitted, 5,965 enrolled. *Average high school GPA:* 3.80. *Test scores:* SAT verbal scores over 500: 84%; SAT math scores over 500: 87%; ACT scores over 18: 100%; SAT verbal scores over 600: 32%; SAT math scores over 600: 38%; ACT scores over 24: 62%; SAT verbal scores over 700: 4%; SAT math scores over 700: 5%; ACT scores over 30: 5%.

Faculty *Total:* 1,628, 71% full-time, 64% with terminal degrees. *Student/faculty ratio:* 25:1.

Majors Accounting; actuarial science; advertising; aerospace, aeronautical and astronautical engineering; anthropology; art; art teacher education; audiology and speech-language pathology; biology/biological sciences; business administration and management; business/commerce; business/managerial economics; business teacher education; chemistry; cinematography and film/video production; civil engineering; clinical laboratory science/medical technology; computer and information sciences; computer engineering; computer technology/computer systems technology; criminal justice/safety; dramatic/theatre arts; early childhood education; economics; electrical, electronic and communications engineering technology; electrical, electronics and communications engineering; elementary education; engineering technology; English; English/language arts teacher education; environmental/environmental health engineering; finance; fine/studio arts; foreign languages and literatures; foreign language teacher education; forensic science and technology; French; health/health care administration; health information/medical records administration; health science; health services/allied health/health sciences; history; hospitality administration; humanities; industrial engineering; information technology; intermedia/multimedia; journalism; legal assistant/paralegal; liberal arts and sciences/liberal studies; management information systems; marketing/marketing management; mass communication/media; mathematics; mathematics teacher education; mechanical engineering; mechanical engineering technologies related; medical microbiology and bacteriology; medical radiologic technology; music performance; music teacher education; nursing (registered nurse training); philosophy; photography; physical education teaching and coaching; physics; political science and government; psychology; public administration; radio and television; respiratory care therapy; science teacher education; social sciences; social science teacher education; social work; sociology; Spanish; special education; speech and rhetoric; statistics; trade and industrial teacher education.

Academic Programs *Special study options:* accelerated degree program, adult/continuing education programs, advanced placement credit, cooperative education, distance learning, double majors, English as a second language, external degree program, freshman honors college, honors programs, independent study, internships, off-campus study, part-time degree program, services for LD students, student-designed majors, study abroad, summer session for credit. *ROTC:* Army (b), Air Force (b). *Unusual degree programs:* 3-2 history.

Library University Library with 1.2 million titles, 9,866 serial subscriptions, 35,233 audiovisual materials, an OPAC, a Web page.

Computers on Campus 2420 computers available on campus for general student use. A campuswide network can be accessed from student residence rooms and from off campus. Internet access, online (class) registration, at least one staffed computer lab available. Computer purchase or lease plan available.

Student Life *Housing options:* coed, men-only, women-only. Campus housing is university owned and is provided by a third party. Freshman applicants given priority for college housing. *Activities and organizations:* drama/theater group, student-run newspaper, radio station, choral group, marching band, student government, Hispanic American Student Association, Volunteer UCF, Pre-Professional Medical Society and Student Nurses Association, African-American Student Union, national fraternities, national sororities. *Campus security:* 24-hour emergency response devices and patrols, late-night transport/escort service, controlled dormitory access. *Student services:* health clinic, personal/psychological counseling, women's center, legal services.

Athletics Member NCAA. All Division I except football (Division I-A). *Intercollegiate sports:* baseball M(s), basketball M(s)/W(s), cheerleading M(s)/W(s), crew W, cross-country running M(s)/W(s), golf M(s)/W(s), soccer M(s)/W(s), tennis M(s)/W(s), track and field W(s), volleyball W(s). *Intramural sports:* baseball M(c), basketball M/W, bowling M(c)/W(c), crew M(c), fencing M(c)/W(c), golf M/W, ice hockey M(c)/W(c), lacrosse M(c)/W(c), racquetball M/W, rock climbing M(c)/W(c), rugby M(c)/W(c), sailing M(c)/W(c), soccer M(c)/W(c), softball M/W, table tennis M(c)/W(c), tennis M(c)/W(c), ultimate Frisbee M(c)/W(c), volleyball M(c)/W(c), water polo M(c)/W(c), weight lifting M/W, wrestling M.

Standardized Tests *Required:* SAT I or ACT (for admission).

Costs (2003–04) *Tuition:* state resident $2833 full-time, $94 per credit part-time; nonresident $13,861 full-time, $462 per credit part-time. Full-time tuition and fees vary according to course load. Part-time tuition and fees vary according to course load. *Required fees:* $180 full-time, $6 per credit part-time. *Room and board:* $7026; room only: $4200. Room and board charges vary according to board plan and housing facility. *Payment plans:* tuition prepayment, deferred payment. *Waivers:* senior citizens and employees or children of employees.

Financial Aid Of all full-time matriculated undergraduates who enrolled in 2003, 14,103 applied for aid, 13,612 were judged to have need, 6,899 had their need fully met. In 2003, 1441 non-need-based awards were made. *Average percent of need met:* 71%. *Average financial aid package:* $5397. *Average need-based loan:* $3982. *Average need-based gift aid:* $3709. *Average non-need-based aid:* $1728. *Average indebtedness upon graduation:* $12,780. *Financial aid deadline:* 6/30.

Applying *Options:* common application, electronic application, early admission. *Application fee:* $30. *Required:* high school transcript, minimum 2.0 GPA. *Recommended:* essay or personal statement. *Application deadlines:* 5/1 (freshmen), 5/1 (transfers). *Notification:* continuous until 8/1 (freshmen), continuous until 8/1 (transfers).

Admissions Contact Undergraduate Admissions Office, University of Central Florida, PO Box 160111, Orlando, FL 32816. *Phone:* 407-823-3000. *Fax:* 407-823-5625. *E-mail:* admission@mail.ucf.edu.

■ *See page 2580 for a narrative description.*

UNIVERSITY OF FLORIDA
Gainesville, Florida

- **State-supported** university, founded 1853, part of State University System of Florida
- **Calendar** semesters
- **Degrees** bachelor's, master's, doctoral, and first professional
- **Suburban** 2000-acre campus with easy access to Jacksonville
- **Coed,** 33,982 undergraduate students, 92% full-time, 53% women, 47% men
- **Very difficult** entrance level, 52% of applicants were admitted

Undergraduates 31,217 full-time, 2,765 part-time. Students come from 52 states and territories, 114 other countries, 4% are from out of state, 9% African American, 7% Asian American or Pacific Islander, 12% Hispanic American, 0.5% Native American, 0.9% international, 6% transferred in, 21% live on campus. *Retention:* 93% of 2002 full-time freshmen returned.

Freshmen *Admission:* 22,973 applied, 12,029 admitted, 6,596 enrolled. *Average high school GPA:* 3.8. *Test scores:* SAT verbal scores over 500: 92%; SAT math scores over 500: 95%; ACT scores over 18: 98%; SAT verbal scores over 600: 59%; SAT math scores over 600: 69%; ACT scores over 24: 80%; SAT verbal scores over 700: 14%; SAT math scores over 700: 19%; ACT scores over 30: 21%.

Faculty *Total:* 1,720, 98% full-time, 92% with terminal degrees. *Student/faculty ratio:* 22:1.

Majors Accounting; advertising; aerospace, aeronautical and astronautical engineering; agricultural and food products processing; agricultural/biological engineering and bioengineering; agricultural economics; agricultural teacher education; agronomy and crop science; American studies; animal sciences; anthropology; architecture; art history, criticism and conservation; art teacher education; Asian studies; astronomy; audiology and speech-language pathology; botany/plant biology; business administration and management; chemical engineering; chemistry; civil engineering; classics and languages, literatures and linguistics; community health services counseling; computer and information sciences; computer engineering; construction engineering technology; criminology; dairy science; dance; dramatic/theatre arts; East Asian languages related; economics; electrical, electronics and communications engineering; elementary education; engineering science; English; entomology; environmental/environmental health engineering; environmental science; family and community services; finance; fine/studio arts; fire science; food science; forestry; French; geography; geology/earth science; German; graphic design; health services/allied health/health sciences; health teacher education; history; horticultural science; industrial engineering; insurance; interior design; intermedia/multimedia; Jewish/Judaic studies; journalism; kinesiology and exercise science; landscape architecture; linguistics; management science; marketing/marketing management; materials engineering; mathematics; mechanical engineering; medical microbiology and bacteriology; middle school education; multi-/interdisciplinary studies related; music; music teacher education; nuclear engineering; nursing (registered nurse training); parks, recreation and leisure facilities management; philosophy; physics; plant pathology/phytopathology; plant sciences; political science and government; Portuguese; poultry science; psychology; public relations/image management; radio and television; real estate; religious studies; Russian; sociology; soil science and agronomy; Spanish; special education; statistics; survey technology; systems engineering; zoology/animal biology.

Academic Programs *Special study options:* accelerated degree program, adult/continuing education programs, advanced placement credit, cooperative education, distance learning, double majors, English as a second language, external degree program, honors programs, independent study, internships, off-campus study, part-time degree program, services for LD students, student-designed majors, study abroad, summer session for credit. *ROTC:* Army (b), Navy (b), Air Force (b). *Unusual degree programs:* 3-2 mathematics.

Library George A. Smathers Library plus 8 others with 5.0 million titles, 28,103 serial subscriptions, 36,078 audiovisual materials, an OPAC, a Web page.

Computers on Campus 472 computers available on campus for general student use. A campuswide network can be accessed from student residence rooms and from off campus. Internet access, online (class) registration, at least one staffed computer lab available. Computer purchase or lease plan available.

Student Life *Housing options:* coed, women-only, cooperative, disabled students. Campus housing is university owned. Freshman applicants given priority for college housing. *Activities and organizations:* drama/theater group, student-run newspaper, radio and television station, choral group, marching band, Blue Key, student government, Black Student Union, Hispanic Student Association, Reitz Union Program Council, national fraternities, national sororities. *Campus security:* 24-hour emergency response devices and patrols, student patrols, late-night transport/escort service, controlled dormitory access, crime and rape prevention programs. *Student services:* health clinic, personal/psychological counseling, women's center, legal services.

Athletics Member NCAA. All Division I except football (Division I-A). *Intercollegiate sports:* baseball M(s), basketball M(s)/W(s), cheerleading M/W, cross-country running M(s)/W(s), golf M(s)/W(s), gymnastics W(s), soccer W(s), softball W(s), swimming M(s)/W(s), tennis M(s)/W(s), track and field M(s)/W(s), volleyball W(s). *Intramural sports:* archery M/W, badminton M(c)/W(c), baseball M, basketball M/W, bowling M/W, crew M(c)/W(c), cross-country running M/W, equestrian sports M(c)/W(c), fencing M(c)/W(c), field hockey M/W, football M, golf M/W, gymnastics W, ice hockey M(c), lacrosse M(c)/W(c), racquetball M(c)/W(c), rugby M(c)/W(c), sailing M(c)/W(c), soccer M(c)/W, softball W, swimming M/W, table tennis M(c)/W(c), tennis M/W, track and field M/W, ultimate Frisbee W(c), volleyball M(c)/W, water polo M(c)/W(c), weight lifting M, wrestling M(c).

Standardized Tests *Required:* SAT I or ACT (for admission).

Costs (2003–04) *Tuition:* state resident $2780 full-time, $93 per semester hour part-time; nonresident $13,808 full-time, $460 per semester hour part-time. *Room and board:* $5800; room only: $3580. Room and board charges vary according to board plan and housing facility. *Payment plan:* tuition prepayment. *Waivers:* senior citizens and employees or children of employees.

Financial Aid Of all full-time matriculated undergraduates who enrolled in 2002, 16,288 applied for aid, 12,876 were judged to have need, 4,088 had their need fully met. 1,477 Federal Work-Study jobs (averaging $1378). 4,209 state and other part-time jobs (averaging $1659). In 2002, 14195 non-need-based awards were made. *Average percent of need met:* 85%. *Average financial aid package:* $9380. *Average need-based loan:* $3633. *Average need-based gift aid:* $4577. *Average non-need-based aid:* $3662. *Average indebtedness upon graduation:* $13,744.

Applying *Options:* common application, electronic application, early admission, early decision. *Application fee:* $30. *Required:* high school transcript. *Application deadline:* 1/12 (freshmen). *Early decision:* 10/1. *Notification:* continuous (freshmen), 12/1 (early decision).

Admissions Contact Office of Admissions, University of Florida, 201 Criser Hall, PO Box 114000, Gainesville, FL 32611-4000. *Phone:* 352-392-1365. *E-mail:* freshmen@ufl.edu.

UNIVERSITY OF MIAMI
Coral Gables, Florida

- **Independent** university, founded 1925
- **Calendar** semesters
- **Degrees** certificates, bachelor's, master's, doctoral, first professional, post-master's, and postbachelor's certificates
- **Suburban** 260-acre campus with easy access to Miami
- **Endowment** $413.8 million
- **Coed,** 9,996 undergraduate students, 92% full-time, 58% women, 42% men
- **Very difficult** entrance level, 44% of applicants were admitted

Undergraduates 9,184 full-time, 812 part-time. Students come from 53 states and territories, 99 other countries, 45% are from out of state, 10% African American, 6% Asian American or Pacific Islander, 24% Hispanic American, 0.3% Native American, 7% international, 6% transferred in, 40% live on campus. *Retention:* 87% of 2002 full-time freshmen returned.

Freshmen *Admission:* 16,851 applied, 7,490 admitted, 2,078 enrolled. *Test scores:* SAT verbal scores over 500: 93%; SAT math scores over 500: 95%; ACT

University of Miami (continued)
scores over 18: 100%; SAT verbal scores over 600: 54%; SAT math scores over 600: 64%; ACT scores over 24: 91%; SAT verbal scores over 700: 13%; SAT math scores over 700: 18%; ACT scores over 30: 28%.

Faculty *Total:* 1,194, 71% full-time, 77% with terminal degrees. *Student/faculty ratio:* 13:1.

Majors Accounting; advertising; aerospace, aeronautical and astronautical engineering; African-American/Black studies; American studies; anthropology; architectural engineering; architecture; art; art history, criticism and conservation; athletic training; atmospheric sciences and meteorology; biochemistry; biology/biological sciences; biomedical/medical engineering; biophysics; broadcast journalism; business administration and management; business administration, management and operations related; business/managerial economics; ceramic arts and ceramics; chemistry; chemistry related; cinematography and film/video production; civil engineering; commercial and advertising art; communication and journalism related; communication/speech communication and rhetoric; computer and information sciences; computer engineering; computer science; computer systems analysis; conducting; creative writing; criminology; dance; dramatic/theatre arts; education; electrical, electronics and communications engineering; elementary education; engineering science; English; English literature (British and Commonwealth); entrepreneurial and small business related; entrepreneurship; environmental/environmental health engineering; environmental studies; family and community services; film/cinema studies; finance; fine/studio arts; French; general studies; geography; geological and earth sciences/geosciences related; geology/earth science; German; health and medical administrative services related; health/medical preparatory programs related; health professions related; history; human resources management; industrial engineering; information science/studies; international business/trade/commerce; international relations and affairs; Italian; Jewish/Judaic studies; journalism; kinesiology and exercise science; Latin American studies; liberal arts and sciences/liberal studies; marine biology and biological oceanography; marketing/marketing management; mass communication/media; mathematics; mathematics and statistics related; mechanical engineering; medical microbiology and bacteriology; music; music management and merchandising; musicology and ethnomusicology; music performance; music related; music teacher education; music theory and composition; music therapy; natural resources and conservation related; natural resources management and policy; neurobiology and neurophysiology; neuroscience; nursing (registered nurse training); oceanography (chemical and physical); painting; philosophy; photography; physics; physics related; physiological psychology/psychobiology; piano and organ; political science and government; pre-pharmacy studies; printmaking; psychology; public relations/image management; radio and television; religious studies; sculpture; secondary education; sociology; Spanish; special education; visual and performing arts; voice and opera; wildlife and wildlands science and management; women's studies.

Academic Programs *Special study options:* academic remediation for entering students, accelerated degree program, adult/continuing education programs, advanced placement credit, distance learning, double majors, English as a second language, honors programs, independent study, internships, part-time degree program, services for LD students, student-designed majors, study abroad, summer session for credit. *ROTC:* Army (c), Air Force (b). *Unusual degree programs:* 3-2 physical therapy, biomedical engineering, marine geology.

Library Otto G. Richter Library plus 7 others with 1.4 million titles, 16,305 serial subscriptions, 109,900 audiovisual materials, an OPAC, a Web page.

Computers on Campus 1800 computers available on campus for general student use. A campuswide network can be accessed from student residence rooms and from off campus that provide access to online student account and grade information. Internet access, online (class) registration, at least one staffed computer lab available. Computer purchase or lease plan available.

Student Life *Housing:* on-campus residence required for freshman year. *Options:* coed, disabled students. Campus housing is university owned. Freshman campus housing is guaranteed. *Activities and organizations:* drama/theater group, student-run newspaper, radio and television station, choral group, marching band, student government, international student organizations, sports and recreation clubs, Association of Commuter Students, United Black Students, national fraternities, national sororities. *Campus security:* 24-hour emergency response devices and patrols, student patrols, late-night transport/escort service, controlled dormitory access, crime prevention and safety workshops, residential college crime watch. *Student services:* health clinic, personal/psychological counseling, women's center.

Athletics Member NCAA. All Division I except football (Division I-A). *Intercollegiate sports:* badminton M(c)/W(c), baseball M(s), basketball M(s)/W(s), cheerleading M/W, crew W(s), cross-country running M(s)/W(s), golf W(s), racquetball M(c)/W(c), soccer W(s), softball W(c), squash M(c)/W(c), swimming W(s), tennis M(s)/W(s), track and field M(s)/W(s), volleyball M(c)/W(s), water polo M(c)/W(c). *Intramural sports:* badminton M, basketball M/W, bowling M(c)/W(c), crew M(c)/W(c), equestrian sports M(c)/W(c), fencing M(c)/W(c), football M/W, golf M(c)/W(c), lacrosse M(c)/W(c), racquetball M/W, rock climbing M(c)/W(c), rugby M(c)/W(c), sailing M(c)/W(c), soccer M(c)/W(c), softball M/W, squash M/W, swimming M(c)/W(c), table tennis M(c)/W(c), tennis M(c)/W(c), ultimate Frisbee M(c)/W(c), volleyball M/W, water polo M/W.

Standardized Tests *Required:* SAT I or ACT (for admission). *Required for some:* SAT II: Subject Tests (for admission).

Costs (2003–04) *Comprehensive fee:* $35,045 includes full-time tuition ($26,280), mandatory fees ($442), and room and board ($8323). Full-time tuition and fees vary according to course load, degree level, location, and program. Part-time tuition and fees vary according to course load, degree level, location, and program. *College room only:* $4858. Room and board charges vary according to board plan and housing facility. *Payment plans:* tuition prepayment, installment. *Waivers:* employees or children of employees.

Financial Aid Of all full-time matriculated undergraduates who enrolled in 2003, 5,612 applied for aid, 4,978 were judged to have need, 1,247 had their need fully met. 3,198 Federal Work-Study jobs (averaging $2358). 220 state and other part-time jobs (averaging $4358). In 2003, 1873 non-need-based awards were made. *Average percent of need met:* 82%. *Average financial aid package:* $22,940. *Average need-based loan:* $5113. *Average need-based gift aid:* $16,363. *Average non-need-based aid:* $12,776. *Average indebtedness upon graduation:* $29,046.

Applying *Options:* common application, electronic application, early admission, early decision, early action, deferred entrance. *Application fee:* $55. *Required:* essay or personal statement, high school transcript, 1 letter of recommendation, counselor evaluation form. *Required for some:* interview. *Recommended:* minimum 3.0 GPA. *Application deadlines:* 2/1 (freshmen), 3/1 (transfers). *Early decision:* 11/1. *Notification:* 4/15 (freshmen), 12/15 (early decision), 1/15 (early action), 4/15 (transfers).

Admissions Contact Mr. Edward M. Gillis, Associate Dean of Enrollment and Director of Admission, University of Miami, PO Box 248025, Ashe Building Room 132, 1252 Memorial Drive, Coral Gables, FL 33146-4616. *Phone:* 305-284-4323. *Fax:* 305-284-2507. *E-mail:* admission@miami.edu.

UNIVERSITY OF NORTH FLORIDA
Jacksonville, Florida

- **State-supported** comprehensive, founded 1965, part of State University System of Florida
- **Calendar** semesters
- **Degrees** associate, bachelor's, master's, doctoral, post-master's, and postbachelor's certificates (doctoral degree in education only)
- **Urban** 1300-acre campus
- **Endowment** $43.8 million
- **Coed,** 11,970 undergraduate students, 69% full-time, 58% women, 42% men
- **Very difficult** entrance level, 66% of applicants were admitted

Undergraduates 8,247 full-time, 3,723 part-time. Students come from 48 states and territories, 56 other countries, 5% are from out of state, 9% African American, 5% Asian American or Pacific Islander, 5% Hispanic American, 0.4% Native American, 0.7% international, 8% transferred in, 18% live on campus. *Retention:* 76% of 2002 full-time freshmen returned.

Freshmen *Admission:* 7,887 applied, 5,224 admitted, 1,998 enrolled. *Average high school GPA:* 3.51. *Test scores:* SAT verbal scores over 500: 79%; SAT math scores over 500: 78%; ACT scores over 18: 98%; SAT verbal scores over 600: 28%; SAT math scores over 600: 29%; ACT scores over 24: 20%; SAT verbal scores over 700: 4%; SAT math scores over 700: 3%.

Faculty *Total:* 646, 64% full-time, 59% with terminal degrees. *Student/faculty ratio:* 22:1.

Majors Accounting; anthropology; art; art teacher education; banking and financial support services; biological and physical sciences; biology/biological sciences; business administration and management; business/managerial economics; chemistry; civil engineering; communication/speech communication and rhetoric; computer and information sciences; construction engineering technology; criminal justice/safety; economics; electrical, electronics and communications engineering; elementary education; English; finance; fine/studio arts; general studies; health services/allied health/health sciences; history; international business/trade/commerce; international relations and affairs; jazz/jazz studies; liberal arts and sciences/liberal studies; marketing/marketing management; mathematics; mathematics teacher education; mechanical engineering; middle school education; music; music performance; music teacher education; nursing (registered nurse training); philosophy; physical education teaching and coaching; physics; political science and government; psychology; science teacher education; secondary education; sociology; Spanish; special education; statistics; trade and industrial teacher education; transportation management.

Academic Programs *Special study options:* accelerated degree program, adult/continuing education programs, advanced placement credit, cooperative education, distance learning, double majors, freshman honors college, honors programs, independent study, internships, off-campus study, part-time degree program, services for LD students, study abroad, summer session for credit. *ROTC:* Navy (c).

Library Thomas G. Carpenter Library with 746,604 titles, 3,466 serial subscriptions, 67,208 audiovisual materials, an OPAC, a Web page.

Computers on Campus 750 computers available on campus for general student use. A campuswide network can be accessed from student residence rooms and from off campus that provide access to applications software. Internet access, online (class) registration, at least one staffed computer lab available.

Student Life *Housing options:* coed, disabled students. Campus housing is university owned. Freshman applicants given priority for college housing. *Activities and organizations:* drama/theater group, student-run newspaper, radio and television station, choral group, International Student Association, Filipino Student Association, Student Physical Therapy Association, National Education Association, Student Government Association, national fraternities, national sororities. *Campus security:* 24-hour emergency response devices and patrols, student patrols, late-night transport/escort service, controlled dormitory access, electronic parking lot security. *Student services:* health clinic, personal/psychological counseling, women's center.

Athletics Member NCAA. All Division II except golf (Division I), swimming (Division I). *Intercollegiate sports:* baseball M(s), basketball M(s)/W(s), cheerleading M/W, cross-country running M(s)/W(s), golf M(s), soccer M(s)/W(s), softball W(s), swimming W(s), tennis M(s)/W(s), track and field M(s)/W(s), volleyball W(s). *Intramural sports:* badminton M/W, basketball M/W, bowling M/W, fencing M(c)/W(c), football M/W, golf M/W, lacrosse M(c)/W(c), racquetball M(c)/W(c), rugby M, sailing M/W, soccer M/W, softball M/W, squash M/W, swimming M/W, table tennis M/W, tennis M/W, track and field M/W, ultimate Frisbee M(c)/W(c), volleyball M(c)/W(c), water polo M/W, weight lifting M/W, wrestling M/W.

Standardized Tests *Required:* SAT I or ACT (for admission).

Costs (2003–04) *Tuition:* state resident $2913 full-time, $97 per semester hour part-time; nonresident $13,268 full-time, $442 per semester hour part-time. *Room and board:* $5856; room only: $3574. Room and board charges vary according to housing facility. *Payment plan:* deferred payment. *Waivers:* senior citizens and employees or children of employees.

Financial Aid Of all full-time matriculated undergraduates who enrolled in 2003, 6,408 applied for aid, 5,273 were judged to have need, 1,229 had their need fully met. 85 Federal Work-Study jobs (averaging $3012). In 2003, 980 non-need-based awards were made. *Average percent of need met:* 73%. *Average financial aid package:* $2237. *Average need-based loan:* $3634. *Average need-based gift aid:* $1908. *Average non-need-based aid:* $3168. *Average indebtedness upon graduation:* $12,346.

Applying *Options:* common application, electronic application, early admission, early action, deferred entrance. *Application fee:* $20. *Required:* essay or personal statement, high school transcript, minimum 2.0 GPA. *Required for some:* essay or personal statement, letters of recommendation. *Recommended:* minimum 3.0 GPA. *Application deadlines:* 7/2 (freshmen), 7/2 (transfers). *Notification:* continuous (freshmen), 12/2 (early action), continuous (transfers).

Admissions Contact Mr. John Yancey, Director of Admissions, University of North Florida, 4567 St. Johns Bluff Road South, Jacksonville, FL 32224. *Phone:* 904-620-2624. *Fax:* 904-620-2014. *E-mail:* admissions@unf.edu.

UNIVERSITY OF PHOENIX–FORT LAUDERDALE CAMPUS
Fort Lauderdale, Florida

- **Proprietary** comprehensive
- **Calendar** continuous
- **Degrees** certificates, associate, bachelor's, master's, doctoral, post-master's, and postbachelor's certificates (courses conducted at 121 campuses and learning centers in 25 states)
- **Urban** campus
- **Coed,** 1,460 undergraduate students
- **Noncompetitive** entrance level

Undergraduates 25% African American, 0.9% Asian American or Pacific Islander, 20% Hispanic American, 0.3% Native American, 14% international.

Faculty *Total:* 171, 2% full-time, 36% with terminal degrees. *Student/faculty ratio:* 10:1.

Majors Accounting; business administration and management; computer and information sciences; entrepreneurship; management information systems; management science; marketing/marketing management; nursing science.

Academic Programs *Special study options:* accelerated degree program, adult/continuing education programs, advanced placement credit, distance learning, external degree program, independent study.

Library University Library with 27.1 million titles, 11,648 serial subscriptions, an OPAC, a Web page.

Computers on Campus A campuswide network can be accessed from off campus. Internet access, at least one staffed computer lab available.

Student Life *Housing:* college housing not available.

Costs (2003–04) *Tuition:* $8850 full-time, $295 per credit part-time. *Waivers:* employees or children of employees.

Financial Aid *Average financial aid package:* $1418.

Applying *Options:* deferred entrance. *Application fee:* $100. *Required:* 1 letter of recommendation, 2 years of work experience, 23 years of age. *Required for some:* high school transcript. *Application deadline:* rolling (freshmen), rolling (transfers).

Admissions Contact Ms. Beth Barilla, Director of Admissions, University of Phoenix–Fort Lauderdale Campus, 4615 East Elwood Street, Mail Stop AA-K101, Phoenix, AZ 85040-1958. *Phone:* 480-317-6000. *Toll-free phone:* 800-228-7240. *Fax:* 480-594-1758. *E-mail:* beth.barilla@phoenix.edu.

UNIVERSITY OF PHOENIX–JACKSONVILLE CAMPUS
Jacksonville, Florida

- **Proprietary** comprehensive, founded 1976
- **Calendar** continuous
- **Degrees** certificates, associate, bachelor's, master's, doctoral, post-master's, and postbachelor's certificates (courses conducted at 121 campuses and learning centers in 25 states)
- **Urban** campus
- **Coed,** 1,186 undergraduate students, 100% full-time, 58% women, 42% men
- **Noncompetitive** entrance level

Undergraduates 1,186 full-time. 16% African American, 2% Asian American or Pacific Islander, 4% Hispanic American, 0.6% Native American, 7% international.

Freshmen *Admission:* 73 enrolled.

Faculty *Total:* 184, 3% full-time, 33% with terminal degrees. *Student/faculty ratio:* 9:1.

Majors Accounting; business administration and management; e-commerce; entrepreneurship; health/health care administration; information science/studies; management information systems; management science; marketing/marketing management; nursing science.

Academic Programs *Special study options:* accelerated degree program, adult/continuing education programs, advanced placement credit, distance learning, external degree program, independent study.

Library University Library with 27.1 million titles, 11,648 serial subscriptions, an OPAC, a Web page.

Computers on Campus A campuswide network can be accessed from off campus. Internet access, at least one staffed computer lab available.

Student Life *Housing:* college housing not available.

Costs (2003–04) *Tuition:* $8850 full-time, $295 per credit part-time. *Waivers:* employees or children of employees.

Financial Aid *Average financial aid package:* $1351.

Applying *Options:* deferred entrance. *Application fee:* $100. *Required:* 1 letter of recommendation, 2 years of work experience, 23 years of age. *Required for some:* high school transcript. *Application deadline:* rolling (freshmen), rolling (transfers).

Admissions Contact Ms. Beth Barilla, Director of Admissions, University of Phoenix–Jacksonville Campus, 4615 East Elwood Street, Mail Stop AA-K101, Phoenix, AZ 85040-1958. *Phone:* 480-317-6000. *Toll-free phone:* 800-228-7240. *Fax:* 480-594-1758. *E-mail:* beth.barilla@phoenix.edu.

UNIVERSITY OF PHOENIX–ORLANDO CAMPUS
Maitland, Florida

- **Proprietary** comprehensive, founded 1996
- **Calendar** continuous
- **Degrees** certificates, associate, bachelor's, master's, doctoral, post-master's, and postbachelor's certificates (courses conducted at 121 campuses and learning centers in 25 states)
- **Urban** campus
- **Coed,** 833 undergraduate students, 100% full-time, 66% women, 34% men
- **Noncompetitive** entrance level

Undergraduates 833 full-time. 13% African American, 1% Asian American or Pacific Islander, 10% Hispanic American, 0.4% Native American, 30% international.

University of Phoenix–Orlando Campus (continued)

Freshmen *Admission:* 63 enrolled.

Faculty *Total:* 243, 1% full-time, 31% with terminal degrees. *Student/faculty ratio:* 10:1.

Majors Accounting; business administration and management; computer and information sciences; corrections and criminal justice related; management information systems; management science; marketing/marketing management; nursing science; public administration and social service professions related.

Academic Programs *Special study options:* accelerated degree program, adult/continuing education programs, advanced placement credit, distance learning, external degree program, independent study.

Library University Library with 27.1 million titles, 11,648 serial subscriptions, an OPAC, a Web page.

Computers on Campus A campuswide network can be accessed from off campus. Internet access, at least one staffed computer lab available.

Student Life *Housing:* college housing not available.

Costs (2003–04) *Tuition:* $8850 full-time, $295 per credit part-time. *Waivers:* employees or children of employees.

Financial Aid *Average financial aid package:* $1353.

Applying *Options:* deferred entrance. *Application fee:* $85. *Required:* minimum 1 GPA, 2 years of work experience, 23 years of age. *Required for some:* high school transcript. *Application deadline:* rolling (freshmen), rolling (transfers).

Admissions Contact Ms. Beth Barilla, Director of Admissions, University of Phoenix–Orlando Campus, 4615 East Elwood Street, Mail Stop AA-K101, Phoenix, AZ 85040-1958. *Phone:* 480-317-6000. *Toll-free phone:* 800-228-7240. *Fax:* 480-594-1758. *E-mail:* beth.barilla@phoenix.edu.

UNIVERSITY OF PHOENIX–TAMPA CAMPUS

Tampa, Florida

- **Proprietary** comprehensive
- **Calendar** continuous
- **Degrees** associate, bachelor's, master's, doctoral, post-master's, and postbachelor's certificates (courses conducted at 121 campuses and learning centers in 25 states)
- **Coed,** 870 undergraduate students, 100% full-time, 62% women, 38% men
- **Noncompetitive** entrance level

Undergraduates 870 full-time. 17% African American, 1% Asian American or Pacific Islander, 9% Hispanic American, 0.7% Native American, 6% international.

Freshmen *Admission:* 59 enrolled.

Faculty *Total:* 209, 3% full-time, 25% with terminal degrees. *Student/faculty ratio:* 9:1.

Majors Accounting; business administration and management; computer and information sciences; corrections and criminal justice related; health/health care administration; management information systems; management science; marketing/marketing management; nursing (registered nurse training); public administration and social service professions related.

Academic Programs *Special study options:* accelerated degree program, adult/continuing education programs, advanced placement credit, distance learning, external degree program, independent study.

Library University Library with 27.1 million titles, 11,648 serial subscriptions, an OPAC, a Web page.

Computers on Campus A campuswide network can be accessed from off campus. Internet access, at least one staffed computer lab available.

Student Life *Housing:* college housing not available.

Costs (2003–04) *Tuition:* $8850 full-time, $295 per credit part-time. *Waivers:* employees or children of employees.

Financial Aid *Average financial aid package:* $1271.

Applying *Options:* deferred entrance. *Application fee:* $85. *Required:* 2 years of work experience, 23 years of age. *Required for some:* high school transcript. *Application deadline:* rolling (freshmen), rolling (transfers).

Admissions Contact Ms. Beth Barilla, Director of Admissions, University of Phoenix–Tampa Campus, 4615 East Elwood Street, Mail Stop AA-K101, Phoenix, AZ 85040-1958. *Phone:* 480-317-6000. *Toll-free phone:* 800-228-7240. *Fax:* 480-594-1758. *E-mail:* beth.barilla@phoenix.edu.

UNIVERSITY OF SOUTH FLORIDA

Tampa, Florida

- **State-supported** university, founded 1956, part of State University System of Florida
- **Calendar** semesters
- **Degrees** associate, bachelor's, master's, doctoral, first professional, and postbachelor's certificates
- **Urban** 1913-acre campus
- **Coed,** 32,127 undergraduate students, 67% full-time, 59% women, 41% men
- **Moderately difficult** entrance level, 62% of applicants were admitted

Undergraduates 21,604 full-time, 10,523 part-time. Students come from 52 states and territories, 120 other countries, 5% are from out of state, 13% African American, 6% Asian American or Pacific Islander, 11% Hispanic American, 0.5% Native American, 1% international, 13% transferred in, 13% live on campus. *Retention:* 81% of 2002 full-time freshmen returned.

Freshmen *Admission:* 15,491 applied, 9,567 admitted, 5,051 enrolled. *Average high school GPA:* 3.6. *Test scores:* SAT verbal scores over 500: 71%; SAT math scores over 500: 75%; ACT scores over 18: 94%; SAT verbal scores over 600: 22%; SAT math scores over 600: 26%; ACT scores over 24: 36%; SAT verbal scores over 700: 2%; SAT math scores over 700: 3%; ACT scores over 30: 4%.

Faculty *Total:* 2,295, 72% full-time, 81% with terminal degrees. *Student/faculty ratio:* 16:1.

Majors Accounting; African-American/Black studies; American studies; anthropology; art; art teacher education; athletic training; audiology and speech-language pathology; biological and physical sciences; biology/biological sciences; business administration and management; business/commerce; business/managerial economics; business teacher education; chemical engineering; chemistry; civil engineering; classics and languages, literatures and linguistics; clinical laboratory science/medical technology; communication/speech communication and rhetoric; computer and information sciences; computer engineering; computer/information technology services administration related; criminal justice/safety; dance; drama and dance teacher education; dramatic/theatre arts; economics; education; electrical, electronics and communications engineering; elementary education; engineering; English; English/language arts teacher education; environmental studies; finance; foreign language teacher education; French; general studies; geography; geology/earth science; German; gerontology; history; hospitality administration; humanities; industrial engineering; information science/studies; international business/trade/commerce; international relations and affairs; Italian; kindergarten/preschool education; liberal arts and sciences/liberal studies; management information systems; management science; marketing/marketing management; mathematics; mathematics teacher education; mechanical engineering; medical microbiology and bacteriology; modern languages; music performance; music teacher education; nursing (registered nurse training); philosophy; physical education teaching and coaching; physics; political science and government; psychology; religious studies; Russian; science teacher education; social sciences; social science teacher education; social work; sociology; Spanish; special education; special education (emotionally disturbed); special education (mentally retarded); special education (specific learning disabilities); speech and rhetoric; trade and industrial teacher education; women's studies.

Academic Programs *Special study options:* academic remediation for entering students, accelerated degree program, adult/continuing education programs, advanced placement credit, cooperative education, distance learning, double majors, external degree program, freshman honors college, honors programs, independent study, internships, off-campus study, part-time degree program, services for LD students, student-designed majors, study abroad, summer session for credit. *ROTC:* Army (b), Navy (b), Air Force (b).

Library Tampa Campus Library plus 2 others with 1.7 million titles, 15,263 serial subscriptions, 154,199 audiovisual materials, an OPAC, a Web page.

Computers on Campus 593 computers available on campus for general student use. A campuswide network can be accessed from student residence rooms and from off campus. Internet access, online (class) registration, at least one staffed computer lab available.

Student Life *Housing options:* coed, men-only, women-only, cooperative, disabled students. Campus housing is university owned. *Activities and organizations:* drama/theater group, student-run newspaper, radio and television station, choral group, marching band, student government, Campus Activities Board, USF Ambassadors, student admissions representatives, national fraternities, national sororities. *Campus security:* 24-hour emergency response devices and patrols, student patrols, late-night transport/escort service, controlled dormitory access, residence hall lobby personnel 8 p.m. to 6 a.m. *Student services:* health clinic, personal/psychological counseling, women's center, legal services.

Athletics Member NCAA. All Division I. *Intercollegiate sports:* baseball M(s), basketball M(s)/W(s), cross-country running M(s)/W(s), football M(s), golf M(s)/W(s), soccer M(s)/W(s), softball W(s), tennis M(s)/W(s), track and field M(s)/W(s), volleyball W(s). *Intramural sports:* badminton M/W, basketball M/W, bowling M/W, cross-country running M/W, football M, golf M/W, racquetball M/W, soccer M/W, softball M/W, swimming M/W, tennis M/W, track and field M/W, volleyball M/W, wrestling M.

Standardized Tests *Required:* SAT I or ACT (for admission).

Costs (2003–04) *Tuition:* state resident $2909 full-time, $97 per credit hour part-time; nonresident $13,937 full-time, $465 per credit hour part-time. Full-time tuition and fees vary according to course level, course load, and location. Part-time tuition and fees vary according to course level, course load, and location. *Required fees:* $74 full-time. *Room and board:* $6508; room only: $3408. Room and board charges vary according to board plan, housing facility, and location. *Payment plans:* tuition prepayment, installment. *Waivers:* senior citizens.

Financial Aid Of all full-time matriculated undergraduates who enrolled in 2003, 13,070 applied for aid, 10,922 were judged to have need, 2,821 had their need fully met. 811 Federal Work-Study jobs (averaging $3600). In 2003, 1432 non-need-based awards were made. *Average percent of need met:* 81%. *Average financial aid package:* $8799. *Average need-based loan:* $4015. *Average need-based gift aid:* $3681. *Average non-need-based aid:* $1707. *Average indebtedness upon graduation:* $16,969.

Applying *Options:* common application, electronic application, early admission. *Application fee:* $30. *Required:* high school transcript, minimum 2.0 GPA. *Required for some:* letters of recommendation. *Application deadlines:* 5/1 (freshmen), 5/1 (transfers). *Notification:* continuous (freshmen), continuous (transfers).

Admissions Contact Mr. Dewey Holleman, Director of Admissions, University of South Florida, 4202 East Fowler Avenue, SVC 1036, Tampa, FL 33620-9951. *Phone:* 813-974-3350. *Toll-free phone:* 877-USF-BULLS. *Fax:* 813-974-9689. *E-mail:* bullseye@admin.usf.edu.

■ *See page 2714 for a narrative description.*

THE UNIVERSITY OF TAMPA

Tampa, Florida

- **Independent** comprehensive, founded 1931
- **Calendar** semesters
- **Degrees** certificates, associate, bachelor's, and master's
- **Urban** 90-acre campus
- **Endowment** $18.6 million
- **Coed,** 4,125 undergraduate students, 88% full-time, 63% women, 37% men
- **Moderately difficult** entrance level, 61% of applicants were admitted

Undergraduates 3,627 full-time, 498 part-time. Students come from 50 states and territories, 100 other countries, 54% are from out of state, 7% African American, 2% Asian American or Pacific Islander, 9% Hispanic American, 0.6% Native American, 5% international, 6% transferred in, 62% live on campus. *Retention:* 73% of 2002 full-time freshmen returned.

Freshmen *Admission:* 5,269 applied, 3,202 admitted, 1,079 enrolled. *Average high school GPA:* 3.22. *Test scores:* SAT verbal scores over 500: 69%; SAT math scores over 500: 71%; ACT scores over 18: 96%; SAT verbal scores over 600: 20%; SAT math scores over 600: 20%; ACT scores over 24: 41%; SAT verbal scores over 700: 1%; SAT math scores over 700: 2%; ACT scores over 30: 3%.

Faculty *Total:* 364, 52% full-time, 63% with terminal degrees. *Student/faculty ratio:* 17:1.

Majors Accounting; art; biochemistry; biology/biological sciences; business administration and management; chemistry; computer graphics; computer programming; creative writing; criminology; dramatic/theatre arts; economics; education (K-12); elementary education; English; environmental biology; environmental studies; finance; geography; history; information science/studies; international business/trade/commerce; international relations and affairs; kinesiology and exercise science; liberal arts and sciences/liberal studies; marine science/merchant marine officer; marketing/marketing management; mass communication/media; mathematics; music; nursing (registered nurse training); philosophy; physical education teaching and coaching; political science and government; pre-dentistry studies; pre-law studies; pre-medical studies; pre-veterinary studies; psychology; secondary education; social sciences; sociology; Spanish; urban studies/affairs; visual and performing arts.

Academic Programs *Special study options:* academic remediation for entering students, adult/continuing education programs, advanced placement credit, cooperative education, double majors, English as a second language, honors programs, independent study, internships, off-campus study, part-time degree program, services for LD students, student-designed majors, study abroad, summer session for credit. *ROTC:* Army (b), Air Force (c).

Library Macdonald Library with 252,147 titles, 10,854 serial subscriptions, 4,181 audiovisual materials, an OPAC, a Web page.

Computers on Campus 454 computers available on campus for general student use. A campuswide network can be accessed from student residence rooms and from off campus. Internet access, online (class) registration, at least one staffed computer lab available. Computer purchase or lease plan available.

Student Life *Housing options:* coed, women-only. Campus housing is university owned. Freshman applicants given priority for college housing. *Activities and organizations:* drama/theater group, student-run newspaper, radio and television station, choral group, Greek Life, PEACE, Kappa Delta Pi, Student Productions, Minaret, national fraternities, national sororities. *Campus security:* 24-hour emergency response devices and patrols, late-night transport/escort service, controlled dormitory access. *Student services:* health clinic, personal/psychological counseling.

Athletics Member NCAA. All Division II. *Intercollegiate sports:* baseball M(s), basketball M(s)/W(s), crew M/W(s), cross-country running M(s)/W(s), golf M(s), soccer M(s)/W(s), softball W(s), swimming M/W, tennis W(s), volleyball W(s). *Intramural sports:* baseball M/W, basketball M/W, bowling M/W, crew M, equestrian sports W, field hockey W, football M, golf M/W, soccer M/W, softball M/W, swimming M/W, tennis W, volleyball M/W.

Standardized Tests *Required:* SAT I or ACT (for admission).

Costs (2003–04) *Comprehensive fee:* $23,982 includes full-time tuition ($16,670), mandatory fees ($902), and room and board ($6410). Part-time tuition: $356 per hour. Part-time tuition and fees vary according to class time. *Required fees:* $35 per term part-time. *College room only:* $3430. Room and board charges vary according to board plan and housing facility. *Payment plan:* installment. *Waivers:* employees or children of employees.

Financial Aid Of all full-time matriculated undergraduates who enrolled in 2003, 2,545 applied for aid, 2,155 were judged to have need, 516 had their need fully met. In 2003, 389 non-need-based awards were made. *Average percent of need met:* 84%. *Average financial aid package:* $14,162. *Average need-based loan:* $3533. *Average need-based gift aid:* $6704. *Average non-need-based aid:* $6520. *Average indebtedness upon graduation:* $22,791.

Applying *Options:* common application, electronic application, early admission, deferred entrance. *Application fee:* $35. *Required:* essay or personal statement, high school transcript, minimum 2.0 GPA, 1 letter of recommendation. *Recommended:* interview. *Application deadline:* rolling (freshmen), rolling (transfers). *Notification:* continuous (transfers).

Admissions Contact Ms. Barbara P. Strickler, Vice President for Enrollment, The University of Tampa, 401 West Kennedy Boulevard, Tampa, FL 33606-1480. *Phone:* 813-253-6211. *Toll-free phone:* 888-646-2438 (in-state); 888-MINARET (out-of-state). *Fax:* 813-258-7398. *E-mail:* admissions@ut.edu.

■ *See page 2716 for a narrative description.*

UNIVERSITY OF WEST FLORIDA

Pensacola, Florida

- **State-supported** comprehensive, founded 1963, part of State University System of Florida
- **Calendar** semesters
- **Degrees** associate, bachelor's, master's, and doctoral
- **Suburban** 1600-acre campus
- **Endowment** $44.0 million
- **Coed,** 7,911 undergraduate students, 71% full-time, 59% women, 41% men
- **Moderately difficult** entrance level, 66% of applicants were admitted

The University of West Florida (UWF)—near historic Pensacola and the world-famous beaches of the Gulf of Mexico—offers an inviting, environmentally friendly setting for study. Small classes, opportunities for individually tailored educational experiences, and scholarships for academic performance help make UWF an extraordinary value in higher education.

Undergraduates 5,599 full-time, 2,312 part-time. Students come from 49 states and territories, 85 other countries, 13% are from out of state, 10% African American, 5% Asian American or Pacific Islander, 4% Hispanic American, 1% Native American, 1% international, 16% transferred in, 16% live on campus. *Retention:* 72% of 2002 full-time freshmen returned.

Freshmen *Admission:* 3,011 applied, 1,996 admitted, 940 enrolled. *Average high school GPA:* 3.43. *Test scores:* SAT verbal scores over 500: 77%; SAT math scores over 500: 79%; ACT scores over 18: 100%; SAT verbal scores over 600: 28%; SAT math scores over 600: 26%; ACT scores over 24: 50%; SAT verbal scores over 700: 3%; SAT math scores over 700: 2%; ACT scores over 30: 6%.

Faculty *Total:* 479, 52% full-time. *Student/faculty ratio:* 22:1.

Majors Accounting; anthropology; art; art history, criticism and conservation; art teacher education; biological and physical sciences; biology/biological sciences; business administration and management; business/managerial economics; chemistry; clinical laboratory science/medical technology; communication/speech communication and rhetoric; community health services counseling; computer and information sciences; computer engineering; criminal justice/safety; dramatic/theatre arts; early childhood education; electrical, electronics and communications engineering; elementary education; engineering technology; English; English/language arts teacher education; environmental studies; finance; fine/studio arts; foreign language teacher education; health and physical education; history; hospitality administration; humanities; international relations and affairs; legal assistant/paralegal; management information systems; marine biology and biological oceanography; marketing/marketing management; mathematics; mathematics teacher education; middle school education; music performance; music teacher education; nursing (registered nurse training); philosophy; physics;

University of West Florida (continued)
political science and government; psychology; religious studies; science teacher education; social sciences; social sciences related; social science teacher education; social work; sociology; special education; special education (mentally retarded); trade and industrial teacher education.

Academic Programs *Special study options:* advanced placement credit, cooperative education, distance learning, English as a second language, honors programs, independent study, internships, off-campus study, part-time degree program, services for LD students, study abroad, summer session for credit. *ROTC:* Army (b), Air Force (b).

Library Pace Library with 414,418 titles, 3,236 serial subscriptions, 4,303 audiovisual materials, an OPAC, a Web page.

Computers on Campus 900 computers available on campus for general student use. A campuswide network can be accessed from student residence rooms and from off campus. Internet access, online (class) registration, at least one staffed computer lab available.

Student Life *Housing options:* coed. Campus housing is university owned. *Activities and organizations:* drama/theater group, student-run newspaper, choral group, Marketing Association, Student Council for Exceptional Children, Intervarsity Christian Fellowship, Baptist Student Ministry, Golden Key Honor Society, national fraternities, national sororities. *Campus security:* 24-hour emergency response devices and patrols, student patrols, late-night transport/escort service, controlled dormitory access. *Student services:* health clinic, personal/psychological counseling.

Athletics Member NCAA. All Division II. *Intercollegiate sports:* baseball M(s), basketball M(s)/W(s), cross-country running M(s)/W(s), golf M(s), soccer M(s)/W(s), softball W(s), tennis M(s)/W(s), volleyball W. *Intramural sports:* basketball M/W, bowling M/W, fencing M/W, football M/W, sailing M/W, soccer M/W, swimming M/W, tennis M/W, volleyball M/W.

Standardized Tests *Required:* SAT I or ACT (for admission).

Costs (2003–04) *Tuition:* state resident $1902 full-time, $63 per semester hour part-time; nonresident $12,930 full-time, $431 per semester hour part-time. Full-time tuition and fees vary according to location. Part-time tuition and fees vary according to location. *Required fees:* $953 full-time, $32 per semester hour part-time. *Room and board:* $6000. Room and board charges vary according to housing facility. *Payment plan:* tuition prepayment. *Waivers:* senior citizens and employees or children of employees.

Financial Aid Of all full-time matriculated undergraduates who enrolled in 2002, 178 Federal Work-Study jobs (averaging $2350). 1,545 state and other part-time jobs.

Applying *Options:* electronic application, early admission, deferred entrance. *Application fee:* $20. *Required:* high school transcript, minimum 2.0 GPA. *Application deadlines:* 6/30 (freshmen), 6/30 (transfers). *Notification:* continuous (freshmen), continuous (transfers).

Admissions Contact Mr. Richard M. Hulett, Director of Admissions, University of West Florida, Admissions, 11000 University Parkway, Pensacola, FL 32514. *Phone:* 850-474-2230. *Toll-free phone:* 800-263-1074. *E-mail:* admissions@uwf.edu.

■ *See page 2738 for a narrative description.*

WARNER SOUTHERN COLLEGE
Lake Wales, Florida

- **Independent** comprehensive, founded 1968, affiliated with Church of God
- **Calendar** semesters
- **Degrees** certificates, associate, bachelor's, and master's
- **Rural** 320-acre campus with easy access to Tampa and Orlando
- **Endowment** $6.1 million
- **Coed,** 1,144 undergraduate students, 86% full-time, 57% women, 43% men
- **Minimally difficult** entrance level, 70% of applicants were admitted

Undergraduates 982 full-time, 162 part-time. Students come from 27 states and territories, 17 other countries, 12% are from out of state, 17% African American, 0.5% Asian American or Pacific Islander, 8% Hispanic American, 0.6% Native American, 3% international, 11% transferred in, 20% live on campus. *Retention:* 60% of 2002 full-time freshmen returned.

Freshmen *Admission:* 279 applied, 194 admitted, 120 enrolled. *Average high school GPA:* 3.27. *Test scores:* SAT verbal scores over 500: 32%; SAT math scores over 500: 31%; ACT scores over 18: 60%; SAT verbal scores over 600: 4%; SAT math scores over 600: 4%; ACT scores over 24: 18%; SAT verbal scores over 700: 2%; SAT math scores over 700: 2%; ACT scores over 30: 2%.

Faculty *Total:* 120, 43% full-time, 41% with terminal degrees. *Student/faculty ratio:* 19:1.

Majors Accounting; biblical studies; biology/biological sciences; business administration and management; business teacher education; communication/speech communication and rhetoric; computer and information sciences; elementary education; English; English/language arts teacher education; finance; general studies; history; kinesiology and exercise science; marketing/marketing management; music teacher education; physical education teaching and coaching; pre-law studies; psychology; religious/sacred music; science teacher education; social sciences; social science teacher education; social work; special education; sport and fitness administration; theology.

Academic Programs *Special study options:* academic remediation for entering students, accelerated degree program, adult/continuing education programs, advanced placement credit, distance learning, double majors, independent study, internships, part-time degree program, summer session for credit.

Library Pontious Learning Resource Center plus 1 other with 56,419 titles, 224 serial subscriptions, 14,935 audiovisual materials, an OPAC, a Web page.

Computers on Campus 75 computers available on campus for general student use. A campuswide network can be accessed. Internet access, at least one staffed computer lab available.

Student Life *Housing:* on-campus residence required through junior year. *Options:* men-only, women-only. Campus housing is university owned. Freshman campus housing is guaranteed. *Activities and organizations:* choral group, Concert Choir, Fellowship of Christian Athletes, Young Americans, Student Government Association. *Campus security:* 24-hour emergency response devices and patrols, late-night transport/escort service, controlled dormitory access. *Student services:* health clinic, personal/psychological counseling.

Athletics Member NAIA. *Intercollegiate sports:* baseball M(s), basketball M(s)/W(s), cheerleading M(s)/W(s), cross-country running M(s)/W(s), golf M(s)/W(s), soccer M(s)/W(s), softball W(s), track and field M(s)/W(s), volleyball W(s).

Standardized Tests *Required:* SAT I or ACT (for admission).

Costs (2003–04) *Comprehensive fee:* $16,651 includes full-time tuition ($11,290), mandatory fees ($90), and room and board ($5271). Part-time tuition: $380 per hour. *Required fees:* $45 per term part-time. *College room only:* $2640. Room and board charges vary according to board plan. *Payment plans:* installment, deferred payment. *Waivers:* employees or children of employees.

Financial Aid Of all full-time matriculated undergraduates who enrolled in 2001, 891 applied for aid, 578 were judged to have need. 147 Federal Work-Study jobs (averaging $2000). In 2001, 313 non-need-based awards were made. *Average financial aid package:* $10,091. *Average need-based loan:* $3178. *Average need-based gift aid:* $3325. *Average non-need-based aid:* $5031. *Average indebtedness upon graduation:* $6046. *Financial aid deadline:* 10/1.

Applying *Options:* common application, deferred entrance. *Application fee:* $20. *Required:* high school transcript, minimum 2.25 GPA, 1 letter of recommendation. *Required for some:* interview. *Recommended:* essay or personal statement. *Application deadline:* rolling (freshmen), rolling (transfers). *Notification:* continuous (freshmen), continuous (transfers).

Admissions Contact Mr. Jason Roe, Director of Admissions, Warner Southern College, Warner Southern Center, 13895 US 27, Lake Wales, FL 33859. *Phone:* 863-638-7212 Ext. 7213. *Toll-free phone:* 800-949-7248. *Fax:* 863-638-1472. *E-mail:* admissions@warner.edu.

WEBBER INTERNATIONAL UNIVERSITY
Babson Park, Florida

- **Independent** comprehensive, founded 1927
- **Calendar** semesters
- **Degrees** associate, bachelor's, and master's
- **Small-town** 110-acre campus with easy access to Orlando
- **Endowment** $4.6 million
- **Coed,** 588 undergraduate students, 90% full-time, 40% women, 60% men
- **Moderately difficult** entrance level, 50% of applicants were admitted

Webber International University celebrated its 75th anniversary with a name change that reflects the mission of the institution. The University attracts more than 140 international students from every continent except Antarctica. Worldwide business is the focus of the curriculum and successful employment is a key goal. Students are encouraged to follow careers as executives in established companies, leaders in their home countries, and groundbreaking entrepreneurs in the world of business.

Undergraduates 530 full-time, 58 part-time. Students come from 19 states and territories, 30 other countries, 5% are from out of state, 21% African American, 1% Asian American or Pacific Islander, 6% Hispanic American, 0.2% Native American, 14% international, 12% transferred in, 38% live on campus. *Retention:* 59% of 2002 full-time freshmen returned.

Freshmen *Admission:* 418 applied, 209 admitted, 121 enrolled. *Average high school GPA:* 2.94. *Test scores:* SAT verbal scores over 500: 18%; SAT math scores over 500: 22%; ACT scores over 18: 43%; SAT math scores over 600: 3%; ACT scores over 24: 5%.

Faculty *Total:* 40, 43% full-time, 38% with terminal degrees. *Student/faculty ratio:* 22:1.

Majors Accounting; business administration and management; business/commerce; computer and information sciences; finance; hotel/motel administration; international business/trade/commerce; marketing/marketing management; pre-law studies; sport and fitness administration; tourism and travel services management.

Academic Programs *Special study options:* academic remediation for entering students, accelerated degree program, adult/continuing education programs, advanced placement credit, cooperative education, double majors, internships, part-time degree program, services for LD students, study abroad, summer session for credit.

Library Grace and Roger Babson Library plus 1 other with 25,000 titles, 89 serial subscriptions, 210 audiovisual materials.

Computers on Campus 100 computers available on campus for general student use. A campuswide network can be accessed. Internet access, at least one staffed computer lab available.

Student Life *Housing:* on-campus residence required for freshman year. *Options:* men-only, women-only. Campus housing is university owned. Freshman campus housing is guaranteed. *Activities and organizations:* student-run newspaper, Fellowship of Christian Athletes, PBL, student government, Society of Hosteleurs, Webber Ambassadors. *Campus security:* 24-hour emergency response devices and patrols, late-night transport/escort service, controlled dormitory access. *Student services:* health clinic, personal/psychological counseling.

Athletics Member NAIA. *Intercollegiate sports:* baseball M(s), basketball M(s)/W(s), cross-country running M(s)/W(s), football M(s), golf M(s)/W(s), soccer M(s)/W(s), softball W(s), tennis M(s)/W(s), track and field M(s)/W(s). *Intramural sports:* basketball M/W, cheerleading M/W, football M/W, soccer M/W, softball W, table tennis M/W, tennis M/W, volleyball M/W.

Standardized Tests *Required:* SAT I or ACT (for admission). *Required for some:* SAT I and SAT II or ACT (for admission).

Costs (2004–05) *Comprehensive fee:* $17,440 includes full-time tuition ($12,400), mandatory fees ($530), and room and board ($4510). Full-time tuition and fees vary according to class time. Part-time tuition: $170 per credit hour. *Room and board:* Room and board charges vary according to board plan. *Payment plan:* installment. *Waivers:* children of alumni, adult students, senior citizens, and employees or children of employees.

Financial Aid Of all full-time matriculated undergraduates who enrolled in 2003, 349 applied for aid, 323 were judged to have need, 43 had their need fully met. 51 Federal Work-Study jobs (averaging $700). 60 state and other part-time jobs (averaging $615). In 2003, 36 non-need-based awards were made. *Average percent of need met:* 72%. *Average financial aid package:* $11,999. *Average need-based loan:* $4549. *Average need-based gift aid:* $8273. *Average non-need-based aid:* $3540. *Average indebtedness upon graduation:* $11,200. *Financial aid deadline:* 8/1.

Applying *Options:* early action. *Application fee:* $35. *Required:* high school transcript, minimum 2.0 GPA, letters of recommendation. *Required for some:* interview. *Recommended:* essay or personal statement. *Application deadlines:* 8/1 (freshmen), 8/1 (transfers).

Admissions Contact Ms. Jacquie Guiley, Director of Admission, Webber International University, 1201 Scenic Highway, North, Babson Park, FL 33827. *Phone:* 863-638-2910. *Toll-free phone:* 800-741-1844. *Fax:* 863-638-1591. *E-mail:* admissions@webber.edu.

■ *See page 2792 for a narrative description.*

WEBSTER COLLEGE
Holiday, Florida

- **Proprietary** primarily 2-year
- **Degrees** diplomas, associate, and bachelor's
- 209 undergraduate students
- 100% of applicants were admitted

Faculty *Student/faculty ratio:* 12:1.

Standardized Tests *Required:* Wonderlic aptitude test (for admission).

Financial Aid Of all full-time matriculated undergraduates who enrolled in 2001, 6 Federal Work-Study jobs.

Applying *Required:* high school transcript, minimum 2.0 GPA, interview. *Required for some:* essay or personal statement.

Admissions Contact Ms. Claire L. Walker, Senior Admissions Representative, Webster College, 2127 Grand Boulevard, Holiday, FL 34690. *Phone:* 727-942-0069. *Toll-free phone:* 888-729-7247. *Fax:* 813-938-5709.

YESHIVA GEDOLAH RABBINICAL COLLEGE
Miami Beach, Florida

Admissions Contact 1140 Alton Road, Miami Beach, FL 33139.

GEORGIA

AGNES SCOTT COLLEGE
Decatur, Georgia

- **Independent** comprehensive, founded 1889, affiliated with Presbyterian Church (U.S.A.)
- **Calendar** semesters
- **Degrees** bachelor's, master's, and postbachelor's certificates
- **Urban** 100-acre campus with easy access to Atlanta
- **Endowment** $281.4 million
- **Women only,** 898 undergraduate students, 95% full-time
- **Very difficult** entrance level, 66% of applicants were admitted

Undergraduates 852 full-time, 46 part-time. Students come from 41 states and territories, 29 other countries, 50% are from out of state, 19% African American, 4% Asian American or Pacific Islander, 3% Hispanic American, 8% international, 2% transferred in, 82% live on campus. *Retention:* 84% of 2002 full-time freshmen returned.

Freshmen *Admission:* 213 enrolled. *Average high school GPA:* 3.64. *Test scores:* SAT verbal scores over 500: 91%; SAT math scores over 500: 83%; ACT scores over 18: 100%; SAT verbal scores over 600: 62%; SAT math scores over 600: 43%; ACT scores over 24: 76%; SAT verbal scores over 700: 16%; SAT math scores over 700: 4%; ACT scores over 30: 25%.

Faculty *Total:* 111, 69% full-time, 84% with terminal degrees. *Student/faculty ratio:* 10:1.

Majors Anthropology; art; astrophysics; biochemistry; biology/biological sciences; chemistry; classics and languages, literatures and linguistics; creative writing; dramatic/theatre arts; economics; English; French; German; history; interdisciplinary studies; international relations and affairs; literature; mathematics; music; philosophy; physics; political science and government; psychology; religious studies; sociology; Spanish; women's studies.

Academic Programs *Special study options:* accelerated degree program, adult/continuing education programs, advanced placement credit, double majors, independent study, internships, off-campus study, part-time degree program, services for LD students, student-designed majors, study abroad, summer session for credit. *ROTC:* Navy (c), Air Force (c). *Unusual degree programs:* 3-2 engineering with Georgia Institute of Technology; art and architecture with Washington University in St. Louis.

Library McCain Library with 171,891 titles, 1,118 serial subscriptions, 17,828 audiovisual materials, an OPAC, a Web page.

Computers on Campus 372 computers available on campus for general student use. A campuswide network can be accessed from student residence rooms and from off campus. Internet access, at least one staffed computer lab available.

Student Life *Housing:* on-campus residence required through senior year. *Options:* women-only. Campus housing is university owned. Freshman campus housing is guaranteed. *Activities and organizations:* drama/theater group, student-run newspaper, choral group, marching band, Student Government Association, Blackfriars, Joyful Noise, Witkaze (African-American Student organization), Volunteer Board. *Campus security:* 24-hour emergency response devices and patrols, late-night transport/escort service, security systems in apartments, public safety facility, surveillance equipment. *Student services:* health clinic, personal/psychological counseling.

Athletics Member NCAA. All Division III. *Intercollegiate sports:* basketball W, cross-country running W, soccer W, softball W, swimming W, tennis W, volleyball W. *Intramural sports:* basketball W, field hockey W, football W, golf W, rock climbing W, soccer W, softball W, swimming W, tennis W, track and field W, ultimate Frisbee W, volleyball W.

Standardized Tests *Required:* SAT I or ACT (for admission). *Required for some:* SAT II: Subject Tests (for admission).

Costs (2003–04) *Comprehensive fee:* $28,230 includes full-time tuition ($20,310), mandatory fees ($160), and room and board ($7760). Part-time tuition: $845 per credit hour. Part-time tuition and fees vary according to course load. *Required fees:* $160 per year part-time. *Room and board:* Room and board charges vary according to board plan and housing facility. *Payment plan:* installment. *Waivers:* employees or children of employees.

Financial Aid Of all full-time matriculated undergraduates who enrolled in 2003, 632 applied for aid, 530 were judged to have need, 402 had their need fully met. 382 Federal Work-Study jobs (averaging $1909). 154 state and other part-time jobs (averaging $1783). In 2003, 218 non-need-based awards were made. *Average percent of need met:* 97%. *Average financial aid package:* $21,263. *Average need-based loan:* $3923. *Average need-based gift aid:* $15,042. *Average non-need-based aid:* $10,451. *Average indebtedness upon graduation:* $20,321. *Financial aid deadline:* 5/1.

Applying *Options:* common application, electronic application, early admission, early decision, deferred entrance. *Application fee:* $35. *Required:* essay or

Agnes Scott College (continued)
personal statement, high school transcript, 2 letters of recommendation. *Recommended:* minimum 3.0 GPA, interview. *Application deadlines:* 3/1 (freshmen), 3/1 (transfers). *Early decision:* 11/15. *Notification:* continuous until 5/1 (freshmen), 12/15 (early decision), continuous (transfers).

Admissions Contact Ms. Stephanie Balmer, Dean of Admission, Agnes Scott College, 141 East College Avenue, Decatur, GA 30030-3797. *Phone:* 404-471-6285. *Toll-free phone:* 800-868-8602. *Fax:* 404-471-6414. *E-mail:* admission@agnesscott.edu.

■ *See page 1136 for a narrative description.*

ALBANY STATE UNIVERSITY
Albany, Georgia

- **State-supported** comprehensive, founded 1903, part of University System of Georgia
- **Calendar** semesters
- **Degrees** bachelor's, master's, and postbachelor's certificates
- **Urban** 144-acre campus
- **Endowment** $2.0 million
- **Coed,** 3,169 undergraduate students, 83% full-time, 66% women, 34% men
- **Minimally difficult** entrance level, 24% of applicants were admitted

Undergraduates 2,625 full-time, 544 part-time. 91% African American, 0.2% Asian American or Pacific Islander, 0.6% Hispanic American, 0.1% Native American, 3% international, 35% live on campus. *Retention:* 82% of 2002 full-time freshmen returned.

Freshmen *Admission:* 2,751 applied, 652 admitted, 466 enrolled. *Average high school GPA:* 2.93. *Test scores:* SAT verbal scores over 500: 18%; SAT math scores over 500: 18%; ACT scores over 18: 38%; SAT verbal scores over 600: 2%; SAT math scores over 600: 1%.

Faculty *Total:* 220, 66% full-time, 59% with terminal degrees. *Student/faculty ratio:* 16:1.

Majors Accounting; administrative assistant and secretarial science; art; biology/biological sciences; business administration and management; business teacher education; chemistry; computer and information sciences; criminal justice/safety; education related; English; French; health professions related; history; kindergarten/preschool education; marketing/marketing management; mathematics; middle school education; music; nursing (registered nurse training); physical education teaching and coaching; political science and government; psychology; science teacher education; social work; sociology; Spanish; special education; speech and rhetoric.

Academic Programs *Special study options:* academic remediation for entering students, adult/continuing education programs, advanced placement credit, cooperative education, distance learning, double majors, honors programs, independent study, internships, off-campus study, part-time degree program, services for LD students, study abroad, summer session for credit. *ROTC:* Army (b). *Unusual degree programs:* 3-2 engineering with Georgia Institute of Technology.

Library James Pendergrast Memorial Library with 338,744 titles, 1,066 serial subscriptions, 3,301 audiovisual materials, an OPAC, a Web page.

Computers on Campus 1000 computers available on campus for general student use. A campuswide network can be accessed from student residence rooms and from off campus that provide access to email. Internet access, at least one staffed computer lab available.

Student Life *Housing options:* coed, men-only, women-only. *Activities and organizations:* drama/theater group, student-run newspaper, choral group, marching band, Gospel Choir, Religious Life Organization, Business Professionals of America, Concert Chorale, NAACP ASU Chapter, national fraternities, national sororities. *Campus security:* 24-hour emergency response devices and patrols, late-night transport/escort service, controlled dormitory access. *Student services:* health clinic, personal/psychological counseling, women's center.

Athletics Member NCAA. All Division II. *Intercollegiate sports:* baseball M(s), basketball M(s)/W(s), cross-country running M(s)/W(s), football M(s), softball W(s), tennis M(s), track and field M(s)/W(s), volleyball W(s). *Intramural sports:* basketball M/W, softball M, swimming M/W.

Standardized Tests *Required:* SAT I or ACT (for admission).

Costs (2003–04) *Tuition:* state resident $2212 full-time, $93 per credit hour part-time; nonresident $8848 full-time, $369 per credit hour part-time. *Required fees:* $562 full-time, $281 per term part-time. *Room and board:* $3760; room only: $1770.

Financial Aid Of all full-time matriculated undergraduates who enrolled in 2003, 2,524 applied for aid, 2,182 were judged to have need, 615 had their need fully met. 440 Federal Work-Study jobs (averaging $1050). 178 state and other part-time jobs (averaging $1655). In 2003, 164 non-need-based awards were made. *Average percent of need met:* 68%. *Average financial aid package:* $7057.

Applying *Options:* early admission, deferred entrance. *Application fee:* $20. *Required:* high school transcript, minimum 2.0 GPA. *Required for some:* interview. *Application deadlines:* 7/1 (freshmen), 7/1 (transfers).

Admissions Contact Mrs. Patricia Price, Assistant Director of Recruitment and Admissions, Albany State University, 504 College Drive, Albany, GA 31705. *Phone:* 229-430-4645. *Toll-free phone:* 800-822-RAMS. *Fax:* 229-430-3936. *E-mail:* fsuttles@asurams.edu.

AMERICAN INTERCONTINENTAL UNIVERSITY
Atlanta, Georgia

- **Proprietary** 4-year, founded 1977
- **Calendar** five 10-week terms
- **Degrees** associate, bachelor's, and master's
- **Urban** 3-acre campus
- **Coed,** 1,274 undergraduate students, 55% full-time, 67% women, 33% men
- **Noncompetitive** entrance level

Undergraduates 699 full-time, 575 part-time. Students come from 31 states and territories, 39 other countries, 39% are from out of state, 16% African American, 0.5% Asian American or Pacific Islander, 0.9% Hispanic American, 0.2% Native American, 1% international, 54% transferred in, 14% live on campus. *Retention:* 44% of 2002 full-time freshmen returned.

Freshmen *Admission:* 544 enrolled.

Faculty *Total:* 115, 18% full-time, 91% with terminal degrees. *Student/faculty ratio:* 11:1.

Majors Cinematography and film/video production; design and visual communications; fashion/apparel design; fashion merchandising; interior design; international business/trade/commerce; marketing/marketing management.

Academic Programs *Special study options:* academic remediation for entering students, accelerated degree program, adult/continuing education programs, cooperative education, double majors, English as a second language, external degree program, independent study, internships, part-time degree program, study abroad, summer session for credit.

Library American Intercontinental University Library-Backhead Campus with 21,691 titles, 244 serial subscriptions, 1,212 audiovisual materials, an OPAC.

Computers on Campus 86 computers available on campus for general student use. A campuswide network can be accessed from off campus. Internet access, at least one staffed computer lab available.

Student Life *Activities and organizations:* student-run newspaper, Student Government Association, Positive Image (Black History), International Student Association, Ministries in Action, Fashion Association. *Campus security:* 24-hour patrols. *Student services:* personal/psychological counseling.

Standardized Tests *Recommended:* SAT I or ACT (for admission), SAT II: Subject Tests (for admission).

Costs (2003–04) *Tuition:* $14,805 full-time, $414 per credit part-time. *Room only:* $4500.

Financial Aid *Average financial aid package:* $6850.

Applying *Options:* early admission, deferred entrance. *Application fee:* $50. *Recommended:* essay or personal statement, high school transcript, minimum 2.0 GPA, 2 letters of recommendation, interview. *Application deadline:* 10/15 (freshmen), rolling (transfers). *Notification:* continuous (freshmen), continuous (transfers).

Admissions Contact Ms. Knitra Watson, Vice President of Admissions and Marketing, American InterContinental University, 3330 Peachtree Road, NE, Atlanta, GA 30326-1016. *Phone:* 404-965-5772. *Toll-free phone:* 888-999-4248. *Fax:* 404-965-5701. *E-mail:* acatl@ix.netcom.com.

■ *See page 1164 for a narrative description.*

AMERICAN INTERCONTINENTAL UNIVERSITY
Atlanta, Georgia

Admissions Contact Mr. Jeff Bostick, Director of Admissions, American InterContinental University, 6600 Peachtree-Dunwoody Road, 500 Embassy Row, Atlanta, GA 30328. *Phone:* 404-965-8050. *Toll-free phone:* 800-255-6839. *E-mail:* info@aiuniv.edu.

ARGOSY UNIVERSITY/ATLANTA
Atlanta, Georgia

- **Proprietary** upper-level, founded 1990
- **Calendar** semesters
- **Degrees** bachelor's, master's, doctoral, and post-master's certificates
- **Suburban** campus

■ **Coed,** 13 undergraduate students, 31% full-time, 85% women, 15% men
■ 72% of applicants were admitted

Undergraduates 4 full-time, 9 part-time. Students come from 1 other state, 38% African American, 308% transferred in.

Faculty *Total:* 13, 8% full-time, 92% with terminal degrees. *Student/faculty ratio:* 40:1.

Student Life *Housing:* college housing not available. *Activities and organizations:* student-run newspaper, SGA, Student Senate.

Costs (2003–04) *Tuition:* $4320 full-time, $360 per credit hour part-time. Full-time tuition and fees vary according to course load. Part-time tuition and fees vary according to course load. No tuition increase for student's term of enrollment. *Required fees:* $11 full-time, $11 per year part-time. *Payment plan:* installment. *Waivers:* employees or children of employees.

Financial Aid Of all full-time matriculated undergraduates who enrolled in 2003, 13 applied for aid, 13 were judged to have need. 1 Federal Work-Study job (averaging $441). *Average financial aid package:* $4789. *Average need-based loan:* $5708. *Average need-based gift aid:* $2352.

Applying *Application fee:* $50. *Notification:* continuous (transfers).

Admissions Contact Mr. Andrew Horn, Director of Admissions, Argosy University/Atlanta, 990 Hammond Drive, 11th Floor, Atlanta, GA 30328-5505. *Phone:* 770-671-1200 Ext. 1014. *Toll-free phone:* 888-671-4777.

ARMSTRONG ATLANTIC STATE UNIVERSITY
Savannah, Georgia

■ **State-supported** comprehensive, founded 1935, part of University System of Georgia
■ **Calendar** semesters
■ **Degrees** associate, bachelor's, and master's
■ **Suburban** 250-acre campus
■ **Endowment** $4.0 million
■ **Coed,** 5,743 undergraduate students, 60% full-time, 68% women, 32% men
■ **Minimally difficult** entrance level, 65% of applicants were admitted

Undergraduates 3,446 full-time, 2,297 part-time. Students come from 46 states and territories, 71 other countries, 11% are from out of state, 23% African American, 3% Asian American or Pacific Islander, 3% Hispanic American, 0.5% Native American, 2% international, 10% transferred in, 10% live on campus. *Retention:* 68% of 2002 full-time freshmen returned.

Freshmen *Admission:* 1,685 applied, 1,099 admitted, 847 enrolled. *Average high school GPA:* 3.05. *Test scores:* SAT verbal scores over 500: 60%; SAT math scores over 500: 49%; ACT scores over 18: 81%; SAT verbal scores over 600: 16%; SAT math scores over 600: 12%; ACT scores over 24: 15%; SAT verbal scores over 700: 1%; SAT math scores over 700: 1%; ACT scores over 30: 1%.

Faculty *Total:* 408, 57% full-time. *Student/faculty ratio:* 16:1.

Majors Art; art teacher education; biology/biological sciences; business teacher education; chemistry; clinical laboratory science/medical technology; computer science; criminal justice/police science; dental hygiene; dramatic/theatre arts; economics; English; health professions related; health science; health teacher education; history; information science/studies; information technology; kindergarten/preschool education; liberal arts and sciences/liberal studies; mathematics; middle school education; music; music teacher education; nursing (registered nurse training); physical education teaching and coaching; physical therapy; physics; political science and government; psychology; respiratory care therapy; Spanish; special education; visual and performing arts.

Academic Programs *Special study options:* academic remediation for entering students, adult/continuing education programs, advanced placement credit, cooperative education, distance learning, double majors, honors programs, independent study, internships, off-campus study, part-time degree program, services for LD students, study abroad, summer session for credit. *ROTC:* Army (b), Navy (c). *Unusual degree programs:* 3-2 engineering with Georgia Institute of Technology.

Library Lane Library with 223,412 titles, 1,166 serial subscriptions, 15,618 audiovisual materials, an OPAC, a Web page.

Computers on Campus 160 computers available on campus for general student use. A campuswide network can be accessed from student residence rooms and from off campus. Internet access, online (class) registration, at least one staffed computer lab available.

Student Life *Housing options:* coed. Campus housing is provided by a third party. *Activities and organizations:* drama/theater group, student-run newspaper, choral group, Wesley Fellowship, Hispanic Student Society, Ebony Coalition, American Chemical Society, Phi Alpha Theta, national fraternities, national sororities. *Campus security:* 24-hour emergency response devices and patrols, student patrols, late-night transport/escort service. *Student services:* health clinic, personal/psychological counseling.

Athletics Member NCAA. All Division II. *Intercollegiate sports:* baseball M(s), basketball M(s)/W(s), golf M(s), softball W(s), tennis M(s)/W(s), volleyball W(s). *Intramural sports:* badminton M/W, basketball M/W, bowling M/W, cheerleading M/W, football M/W, golf M/W, soccer M/W, softball M/W, table tennis M/W, tennis M/W, volleyball M/W, water polo M/W.

Standardized Tests *Required:* SAT I or ACT (for admission). *Required for some:* SAT II: Subject Tests (for admission).

Costs (2003–04) *Tuition:* state resident $2212 full-time, $93 per hour part-time; nonresident $8848 full-time, $369 per hour part-time. Full-time tuition and fees vary according to program. Part-time tuition and fees vary according to course load and program. *Required fees:* $390 full-time. *Room only:* $4500. *Waivers:* senior citizens and employees or children of employees.

Financial Aid Of all full-time matriculated undergraduates who enrolled in 2002, 2,660 applied for aid, 2,395 were judged to have need, 2,155 had their need fully met. 103 Federal Work-Study jobs (averaging $4000). In 2002, 763 non-need-based awards were made. *Average percent of need met:* 90%. *Average financial aid package:* $6625. *Average need-based loan:* $5000. *Average need-based gift aid:* $1500. *Average non-need-based aid:* $1000. *Average indebtedness upon graduation:* $11,000.

Applying *Options:* early admission, deferred entrance. *Application fee:* $20. *Required:* high school transcript, proof of immunization. *Application deadlines:* 7/1 (freshmen), 7/1 (transfers). *Notification:* continuous (freshmen), continuous (transfers).

Admissions Contact Ms. Melanie Mirande, Assistant Director of Recruitment, Armstrong Atlantic State University, Savannah, GA 31419. *Phone:* 912-925-5275. *Toll-free phone:* 800-633-2349. *Fax:* 912-921-5462.

THE ART INSTITUTE OF ATLANTA
Atlanta, Georgia

■ **Proprietary** 4-year, founded 1949, part of The Art Institutes
■ **Calendar** quarters
■ **Degrees** associate and bachelor's
■ **Suburban** 7-acre campus
■ **Coed,** 2,699 undergraduate students, 87% full-time, 47% women, 53% men
■ **Minimally difficult** entrance level

Undergraduates 2,338 full-time, 361 part-time. Students come from 44 states and territories, 38 other countries, 27% are from out of state, 34% African American, 3% Asian American or Pacific Islander, 4% Hispanic American, 0.4% Native American, 3% international, 13% live on campus.

Freshmen *Admission:* 370 enrolled.

Faculty *Total:* 169, 54% full-time, 49% with terminal degrees. *Student/faculty ratio:* 21:1.

Majors Advertising; animation, interactive technology, video graphics and special effects; cinematography and film/video production; commercial and advertising art; commercial photography; culinary arts; interior design; intermedia/multimedia; restaurant, culinary, and catering management; web page, digital/multimedia and information resources design.

Academic Programs *Special study options:* academic remediation for entering students, adult/continuing education programs, advanced placement credit, distance learning, independent study, internships, part-time degree program, services for LD students, study abroad, summer session for credit.

Library Library with 35,872 titles, 157 serial subscriptions, 2,548 audiovisual materials, an OPAC.

Computers on Campus 282 computers available on campus for general student use. A campuswide network can be accessed. Internet access, at least one staffed computer lab available.

Student Life *Housing options:* coed, disabled students. Campus housing is leased by the school. Freshman campus housing is guaranteed. *Activities and organizations:* student-run newspaper, AIGA (American Institute of Graphic Artists, student chapter), ASID (American Society of Interior Designers, student chapter), SGA—Student Government Association, Housing Council, Haven. *Campus security:* 24-hour emergency response devices and patrols, late-night transport/escort service, controlled dormitory access. *Student services:* personal/psychological counseling.

Athletics *Intramural sports:* football M/W.

Costs (2003–04) *One-time required fee:* $655. *Tuition:* $16,560 full-time, $345 per credit part-time. No tuition increase for student's term of enrollment. *Required fees:* $345 per credit part-time. *Room only:* $6645. Room and board charges vary according to housing facility. *Payment plans:* installment, deferred payment. *Waivers:* employees or children of employees.

Financial Aid Of all full-time matriculated undergraduates who enrolled in 2003, 2,233 applied for aid, 2,048 were judged to have need. *Average percent of need met:* 65%. *Average financial aid package:* $10,854. *Average need-based loan:* $3500. *Average need-based gift aid:* $2551.

The Art Institute of Atlanta (continued)

Applying *Options:* electronic application, early admission, deferred entrance. *Application fee:* $50. *Required:* essay or personal statement, minimum 2.0 GPA, interview. *Required for some:* high school transcript. *Notification:* continuous (freshmen), continuous (transfers).

Admissions Contact Donna Scott, Director of Admissions, The Art Institute of Atlanta, 6600 Peachtree Dunwoody Road, 100 Embassy Row, Atlanta, GA 30328. *Phone:* 770-394-8300. *Toll-free phone:* 800-275-4242. *Fax:* 770-394-0008. *E-mail:* aiaadm@aii.edu.

ATLANTA CHRISTIAN COLLEGE
East Point, Georgia

- **Independent Christian** 4-year, founded 1937
- **Calendar** semesters
- **Degrees** associate and bachelor's
- **Suburban** 52-acre campus with easy access to Atlanta
- **Endowment** $30.0 million
- **Coed,** 394 undergraduate students, 81% full-time, 48% women, 52% men
- **Moderately difficult** entrance level, 36% of applicants were admitted

Undergraduates 319 full-time, 75 part-time. Students come from 13 states and territories, 12% are from out of state, 19% African American, 2% Asian American or Pacific Islander, 0.8% Hispanic American, 47% live on campus.

Freshmen *Admission:* 737 applied, 265 admitted. *Average high school GPA:* 2.80.

Faculty *Student/faculty ratio:* 16:1.

Majors Biblical studies; business administration and management; business/commerce; counseling psychology; humanities; kindergarten/preschool education; music; pre-theology/pre-ministerial studies; theology.

Academic Programs *Special study options:* academic remediation for entering students, advanced placement credit, double majors, independent study, internships, part-time degree program, services for LD students, summer session for credit.

Library Atlanta Christian College Library with 50,000 titles, 187 serial subscriptions, an OPAC.

Computers on Campus 30 computers available on campus for general student use. A campuswide network can be accessed from student residence rooms and from off campus. Internet access, online (class) registration, at least one staffed computer lab available.

Student Life *Housing:* on-campus residence required for freshman year. *Options:* men-only, women-only. Campus housing is university owned. Freshman campus housing is guaranteed. *Activities and organizations:* drama/theater group, student-run radio station, choral group. *Campus security:* controlled dormitory access, 12-hour patrols by security personnel. *Student services:* health clinic, personal/psychological counseling.

Athletics Member NAIA, NCCAA. *Intercollegiate sports:* baseball M, basketball M/W, golf M, soccer M/W, softball W, volleyball W. *Intramural sports:* basketball M/W, golf M(c), table tennis M/W, tennis M/W, ultimate Frisbee M/W, volleyball M/W.

Standardized Tests *Required:* SAT I or ACT (for admission).

Costs (2003–04) *Comprehensive fee:* $14,950 includes full-time tuition ($10,250), mandatory fees ($550), and room and board ($4150). Full-time tuition and fees vary according to course load and student level. Part-time tuition and fees vary according to course load and student level. *Room and board:* Room and board charges vary according to board plan. *Payment plan:* installment. *Waivers:* senior citizens and employees or children of employees.

Applying *Options:* electronic application, early admission, early decision, deferred entrance. *Application fee:* $25. *Required:* high school transcript, minimum 2.0 GPA, 2 letters of recommendation, medical history. *Application deadlines:* 8/1 (freshmen), 8/1 (transfers). *Early decision:* 11/15.

Admissions Contact Mr. Keith Wagner, Director of Admissions, Atlanta Christian College, 2605 Ben Hill Road, East Point, GA 30344-1999. *Phone:* 404-761-8861. *Toll-free phone:* 800-776-1ACC. *Fax:* 404-669-2024. *E-mail:* admissions@acc.edu.

ATLANTA COLLEGE OF ART
Atlanta, Georgia

- **Independent** 4-year, founded 1928
- **Calendar** semesters
- **Degree** bachelor's
- **Urban** 2-acre campus
- **Endowment** $3.6 million
- **Coed,** 322 undergraduate students, 94% full-time, 49% women, 51% men
- **Moderately difficult** entrance level, 64% of applicants were admitted

Atlanta College of Art, founded in 1905, is the oldest private college of art and design in the Southeast and, as a founding division of the Woodruff Arts Center, is the only school in the nation to share its campus with three internationally recognized cultural institutions: the High Museum of Art, Alliance Theater Company, and Atlanta Symphony Orchestra.

Undergraduates 303 full-time, 19 part-time. Students come from 30 states and territories, 17 other countries, 50% are from out of state, 23% African American, 3% Asian American or Pacific Islander, 3% Hispanic American, 0.3% Native American, 6% international, 30% live on campus. *Retention:* 71% of 2002 full-time freshmen returned.

Freshmen *Admission:* 221 applied, 142 admitted. *Average high school GPA:* 2.97. *Test scores:* SAT verbal scores over 500: 48%; SAT math scores over 500: 42%; ACT scores over 18: 90%; SAT verbal scores over 600: 21%; SAT math scores over 600: 15%; ACT scores over 24: 37%; ACT scores over 30: 11%.

Faculty *Total:* 60, 40% full-time. *Student/faculty ratio:* 8:1.

Majors Cinematography and film/video production; commercial and advertising art; computer graphics; design and visual communications; drawing; fine/studio arts; illustration; painting; photography; printmaking; sculpture; web page, digital/multimedia and information resources design.

Academic Programs *Special study options:* academic remediation for entering students, advanced placement credit, independent study, internships, off-campus study, part-time degree program, services for LD students, student-designed majors, study abroad, summer session for credit.

Library Atlanta College of Art Library with 30,000 titles, 200 serial subscriptions, 98,000 audiovisual materials.

Computers on Campus 80 computers available on campus for general student use. A campuswide network can be accessed. Internet access, at least one staffed computer lab available.

Student Life *Housing options:* coed. Campus housing is university owned. Freshman applicants given priority for college housing. *Activities and organizations:* Cipher of Peace, outing club, performance art club, student activities club, graphic design club. *Campus security:* 24-hour patrols, late-night transport/escort service, security cameras. *Student services:* health clinic, personal/psychological counseling.

Standardized Tests *Required:* SAT I or ACT (for admission).

Costs (2004–05) *Tuition:* $16,900 full-time, $705 per semester hour part-time. Full-time tuition and fees vary according to course load. Part-time tuition and fees vary according to course load. *Required fees:* $600 full-time, $80 per year part-time. *Room only:* $5100. *Payment plan:* installment. *Waivers:* employees or children of employees.

Financial Aid Of all full-time matriculated undergraduates who enrolled in 2003, 229 applied for aid, 212 were judged to have need, 25 had their need fully met. 65 Federal Work-Study jobs (averaging $1898). 40 state and other part-time jobs (averaging $1898). In 2003, 16 non-need-based awards were made. *Average percent of need met:* 63%. *Average financial aid package:* $11,738. *Average need-based loan:* $3925. *Average need-based gift aid:* $8086. *Average non-need-based aid:* $13,799. *Average indebtedness upon graduation:* $22,830.

Applying *Options:* electronic application, deferred entrance. *Application fee:* $30. *Required:* essay or personal statement, high school transcript, minimum 2.0 GPA, portfolio. *Required for some:* letters of recommendation. *Recommended:* letters of recommendation, interview. *Application deadline:* rolling (freshmen), rolling (transfers). *Notification:* continuous (freshmen), continuous (transfers).

Admissions Contact Ms. Lucy Leusch, Vice President of Enrollment Management, Atlanta College of Art, 1280 Peachtree Street, NE, Atlanta, GA 30309. *Phone:* 404-733-5101. *Toll-free phone:* 800-832-2104. *Fax:* 404-733-5107. *E-mail:* acainfo@woodruffcenter.org.

■ *See page 1194 for a narrative description.*

AUGUSTA STATE UNIVERSITY
Augusta, Georgia

- **State-supported** comprehensive, founded 1925, part of University System of Georgia
- **Calendar** semesters
- **Degrees** certificates, associate, bachelor's, master's, and post-master's certificates
- **Urban** 72-acre campus
- **Endowment** $298,174
- **Coed,** 5,257 undergraduate students, 67% full-time, 64% women, 36% men
- **Minimally difficult** entrance level, 65% of applicants were admitted

Undergraduates 3,501 full-time, 1,756 part-time. Students come from 47 states and territories, 56 other countries, 11% are from out of state, 26% African

American, 3% Asian American or Pacific Islander, 3% Hispanic American, 0.4% Native American, 1% international, 8% transferred in. *Retention:* 66% of 2002 full-time freshmen returned.

Freshmen *Admission:* 1,714 applied, 1,106 admitted, 917 enrolled. *Average high school GPA:* 2.80. *Test scores:* SAT verbal scores over 500: 46%; SAT math scores over 500: 45%; SAT verbal scores over 600: 11%; SAT math scores over 600: 9%; SAT math scores over 700: 1%.

Faculty *Total:* 312, 63% full-time, 57% with terminal degrees. *Student/faculty ratio:* 19:1.

Majors Accounting; biology/biological sciences; business administration and management; chemistry; clinical laboratory science/medical technology; communication/speech communication and rhetoric; computer and information sciences; criminal justice/safety; elementary education; English; finance; French; history; intermedia/multimedia; kindergarten/preschool education; liberal arts and sciences/liberal studies; marketing/marketing management; mathematics; middle school education; music; music performance; music teacher education; nursing (registered nurse training); physical education teaching and coaching; physical sciences; physics; political science and government; psychology; sociology; Spanish; special education; special education (mentally retarded).

Academic Programs *Special study options:* academic remediation for entering students, adult/continuing education programs, advanced placement credit, cooperative education, double majors, English as a second language, honors programs, independent study, internships, off-campus study, part-time degree program, services for LD students, study abroad, summer session for credit. *ROTC:* Army (b).

Library Reese Library plus 1 other with 430,938 titles, 1,276 serial subscriptions, 5,807 audiovisual materials, an OPAC, a Web page.

Computers on Campus 325 computers available on campus for general student use. A campuswide network can be accessed from off campus. Internet access, online (class) registration, at least one staffed computer lab available.

Student Life *Activities and organizations:* drama/theater group, student-run newspaper, choral group, Jazz Ensemble, Baptist Student Union, ASU Orchestra, Student Art Association, Black Student Union, national fraternities, national sororities. *Campus security:* 24-hour patrols, late-night transport/escort service. *Student services:* personal/psychological counseling.

Athletics Member NCAA, NAIA. All NCAA Division II. *Intercollegiate sports:* baseball M, basketball M(s)/W(s), cross-country running M(s)/W(s), softball W, tennis M(s)/W(s), volleyball W(s). *Intramural sports:* softball W, volleyball M/W, weight lifting M/W.

Standardized Tests *Required:* SAT I or ACT (for admission).

Costs (2003–04) *Tuition:* state resident $2212 full-time; nonresident $8846 full-time. *Required fees:* $380 full-time. *Waivers:* senior citizens and employees or children of employees.

Financial Aid Of all full-time matriculated undergraduates who enrolled in 2002, 1,745 applied for aid, 1,359 were judged to have need, 90 had their need fully met. 100 Federal Work-Study jobs (averaging $2783). 200 state and other part-time jobs (averaging $1713). In 2002, 198 non-need-based awards were made. *Average percent of need met:* 70%. *Average financial aid package:* $7284. *Average need-based loan:* $3231. *Average need-based gift aid:* $4799. *Average non-need-based aid:* $1824. *Average indebtedness upon graduation:* $15,685. *Financial aid deadline:* 5/1.

Applying *Options:* common application, early admission, deferred entrance. *Application fee:* $20. *Required:* high school transcript, minimum 2.0 GPA. *Application deadline:* 7/21 (freshmen), rolling (transfers). *Notification:* continuous (freshmen), continuous (transfers).

Admissions Contact Latoya Ward, Contact Coordinator, Augusta State University, 2500 Walton Way, Augusta, GA 30904-2200. *Phone:* 706-737-1632. *Toll-free phone:* 800-341-4373. *Fax:* 706-667-4355. *E-mail:* admissions@ac.edu.

BEACON COLLEGE AND GRADUATE SCHOOL
Columbus, Georgia

- **Independent religious** comprehensive, founded 1993
- **Calendar** semesters
- **Degrees** certificates, associate, bachelor's, master's, and doctoral
- **Urban** 12-acre campus
- **Coed,** 107 undergraduate students
- 88% of applicants were admitted

Undergraduates Students come from 4 states and territories, 2 other countries, 27% are from out of state, 43% African American, 5% Hispanic American, 2% international. *Retention:* 95% of 2002 full-time freshmen returned.

Freshmen *Admission:* 49 applied, 43 admitted. *Average high school GPA:* 2.90.

Faculty *Student/faculty ratio:* 5:1.

Majors Biblical studies; business administration and management; psychology.

Academic Programs *Special study options:* academic remediation for entering students, accelerated degree program, adult/continuing education programs, advanced placement credit, distance learning, double majors, external degree program, independent study, off-campus study, part-time degree program, summer session for credit.

Library Beacon College Library plus 1 other with 25,000 titles, 67 serial subscriptions, a Web page.

Computers on Campus 30 computers available on campus for general student use. A campuswide network can be accessed. Internet access, at least one staffed computer lab available.

Student Life *Housing:* college housing not available. *Activities and organizations:* student-run newspaper, Student Government Association, practical ministry. *Student services:* personal/psychological counseling.

Standardized Tests *Required for some:* ACT COMPASS. *Recommended:* SAT I or ACT (for admission).

Costs (2003–04) *Tuition:* $3150 full-time, $150 per semester hour part-time. *Required fees:* $170 full-time, $85 per term part-time. *Payment plan:* installment. *Waivers:* employees or children of employees.

Financial Aid Of all full-time matriculated undergraduates who enrolled in 2002, 55 applied for aid, 55 were judged to have need, 55 had their need fully met. *Average percent of need met:* 100%. *Average financial aid package:* $6500. *Average need-based gift aid:* $6500. *Average indebtedness upon graduation:* $5194.

Applying *Options:* common application, early admission. *Application fee:* $25. *Required:* high school transcript, minimum 2.0 GPA, 3 letters of recommendation, interview. *Application deadline:* rolling (freshmen), rolling (transfers).

Admissions Contact Dr. Robert Thomas, Dean of Student services, Beacon College and Graduate School, 6003 Veterans Parkway, Columbus, GA 31909. *Phone:* 706-323-5364 Ext. 259. *Fax:* 706-323-5891. *E-mail:* beacon@beacon.edu.

BERRY COLLEGE
Mount Berry, Georgia

- **Independent interdenominational** comprehensive, founded 1902
- **Calendar** semesters
- **Degrees** bachelor's, master's, and post-master's certificates
- **Suburban** 28,000-acre campus with easy access to Atlanta
- **Endowment** $575.9 million
- **Coed,** 1,895 undergraduate students, 98% full-time, 63% women, 37% men
- **Moderately difficult** entrance level, 83% of applicants were admitted

Undergraduates 1,855 full-time, 40 part-time. Students come from 34 states and territories, 22 other countries, 20% are from out of state, 3% African American, 1% Asian American or Pacific Islander, 0.8% Hispanic American, 0.1% Native American, 2% international, 4% transferred in, 69% live on campus. *Retention:* 76% of 2002 full-time freshmen returned.

Freshmen *Admission:* 1,846 applied, 1,531 admitted, 505 enrolled. *Average high school GPA:* 3.64. *Test scores:* SAT verbal scores over 500: 89%; SAT math scores over 500: 85%; ACT scores over 18: 98%; SAT verbal scores over 600: 49%; SAT math scores over 600: 39%; ACT scores over 24: 64%; SAT verbal scores over 700: 8%; SAT math scores over 700: 6%; ACT scores over 30: 12%.

Faculty *Total:* 175, 85% full-time, 80% with terminal degrees. *Student/faculty ratio:* 12:1.

Majors Accounting; animal sciences; anthropology; art; biochemistry; biology/biological sciences; business administration and management; chemistry; communication and journalism related; computer science; early childhood education; economics; engineering technology; English; environmental science; finance; French; German; history; international relations and affairs; marketing/marketing management; mathematics; middle school education; multi-/interdisciplinary studies related; music; music management and merchandising; music teacher education; nursing (registered nurse training); philosophy and religious studies related; physical education teaching and coaching; physics; political science and government; psychology; social sciences; sociology; Spanish.

Academic Programs *Special study options:* accelerated degree program, adult/continuing education programs, advanced placement credit, cooperative education, double majors, honors programs, independent study, internships, part-time degree program, student-designed majors, study abroad, summer session for credit. *Unusual degree programs:* 3-2 engineering with Georgia Institute of Technology, Mercer University; nursing with Emory University.

Library Memorial Library plus 1 other with 291,337 titles, 1,400 serial subscriptions, an OPAC, a Web page.

Computers on Campus 100 computers available on campus for general student use. A campuswide network can be accessed from student residence rooms. Internet access, at least one staffed computer lab available.

Student Life *Housing:* on-campus residence required through sophomore year. *Options:* coed, men-only, women-only. Campus housing is university owned.

Berry College (continued)
Freshman applicants given priority for college housing. *Activities and organizations:* drama/theater group, student-run newspaper, television station, choral group, Student Government Association, Baptist Student Union, equestrian, Campus Outreach, Viking crew team. *Campus security:* 24-hour emergency response devices and patrols, controlled dormitory access, lighted pathways. *Student services:* health clinic, personal/psychological counseling.

Athletics Member NAIA. *Intercollegiate sports:* baseball M(s), basketball M(s)/W(s), cheerleading M/W, crew M(c)/W(c), cross-country running M(s)/W(s), equestrian sports M(c)/W(c), golf M(s)/W(s), lacrosse M(c)/W(c), soccer M(s)/W(s), tennis M(s)/W(s), track and field M(s)/W(s), volleyball W. *Intramural sports:* badminton M/W, basketball M/W, bowling M/W, football M/W, golf M/W, racquetball M/W, soccer M/W, softball M/W, table tennis M/W, tennis M/W, track and field M/W, ultimate Frisbee M/W, volleyball M/W, water polo M/W.

Standardized Tests *Required:* SAT I or ACT (for admission).

Costs (2003–04) *Comprehensive fee:* $21,410 includes full-time tuition ($15,220) and room and board ($6190). Part-time tuition: $506 per credit hour. *College room only:* $3470. Room and board charges vary according to board plan and housing facility. *Payment plan:* installment. *Waivers:* senior citizens and employees or children of employees.

Financial Aid Of all full-time matriculated undergraduates who enrolled in 2003, 1,916 applied for aid, 1,085 were judged to have need, 259 had their need fully met. In 2003, 779 non-need-based awards were made. *Average percent of need met:* 86%. *Average financial aid package:* $13,396. *Average need-based loan:* $3271. *Average need-based gift aid:* $10,046. *Average non-need-based aid:* $11,228. *Average indebtedness upon graduation:* $12,000.

Applying *Options:* common application, electronic application, early admission, deferred entrance. *Application fee:* $25. *Required:* high school transcript. *Application deadlines:* 7/23 (freshmen), 7/23 (transfers). *Notification:* continuous (freshmen), continuous (transfers).

Admissions Contact Mr. Garreth M. Johnson, Dean of Admissions, Berry College, PO Box 490159, 2277 Martha Berry Highway, NW, Mount Berry, GA 30149-0159. *Phone:* 706-236-2215. *Toll-free phone:* 800-237-7942. *Fax:* 706-290-2178. *E-mail:* admissions@berry.edu.

BEULAH HEIGHTS BIBLE COLLEGE
Atlanta, Georgia

- **Independent Pentecostal** 4-year, founded 1918
- **Calendar** semesters
- **Degrees** certificates, associate, and bachelor's
- **Urban** 10-acre campus
- **Endowment** $19,881
- **Coed**
- **Noncompetitive** entrance level

Faculty *Student/faculty ratio:* 17:1.

Student Life *Campus security:* 24-hour emergency response devices, student patrols.

Standardized Tests *Recommended:* SAT I or ACT (for admission), SAT II: Writing Test (for admission).

Costs (2003–04) *Tuition:* $4080 full-time, $170 per credit hour part-time. Full-time tuition and fees vary according to course load. *Required fees:* $150 full-time, $150 per term part-time. *Room only:* $4400. *Payment plans:* installment, deferred payment.

Financial Aid Of all full-time matriculated undergraduates who enrolled in 2003, 166 applied for aid, 166 were judged to have need. 10 Federal Work-Study jobs (averaging $4134). *Average percent of need met:* 80. *Average financial aid package:* $3126. *Average need-based loan:* $1920. *Average need-based gift aid:* $1864. *Average indebtedness upon graduation:* $23,000.

Applying *Options:* common application, early admission. *Application fee:* $20. *Required:* high school transcript, minimum 2.0 GPA, 2 letters of recommendation. *Recommended:* interview.

Admissions Contact Mr. John Dreher, Associate Director of Admissions, Beulah Heights Bible College, 892 Berne Street, SE, PO Box 18145, Atlanta, GA 30316. *Phone:* 404-627-2681 Ext. 114. *Toll-free phone:* 888-777-BHBC. *Fax:* 404-627-0702. *E-mail:* admissions@beulah.org.

BRENAU UNIVERSITY
Gainesville, Georgia

- **Independent** comprehensive, founded 1878
- **Calendar** semesters
- **Degrees** bachelor's and master's (also offers coed evening and weekend programs with significant enrollment not reflected in profile)
- **Small-town** 57-acre campus with easy access to Atlanta
- **Endowment** $47.6 million
- **Women only,** 586 undergraduate students, 92% full-time
- **Moderately difficult** entrance level, 74% of applicants were admitted

Undergraduates 538 full-time, 48 part-time. Students come from 22 states and territories, 22 other countries, 12% are from out of state, 14% African American, 2% Asian American or Pacific Islander, 3% Hispanic American, 0.5% Native American, 3% international, 17% transferred in, 56% live on campus. *Retention:* 73% of 2002 full-time freshmen returned.

Freshmen *Admission:* 333 applied, 247 admitted, 121 enrolled. *Test scores:* SAT verbal scores over 500: 51%; SAT math scores over 500: 43%; ACT scores over 18: 75%; SAT verbal scores over 600: 17%; SAT math scores over 600: 9%; ACT scores over 24: 32%; SAT verbal scores over 700: 2%; ACT scores over 30: 2%.

Faculty *Total:* 105, 75% full-time, 65% with terminal degrees. *Student/faculty ratio:* 6:1.

Majors Accounting; arts management; art teacher education; biology/biological sciences; business administration and management; business/corporate communications; commercial and advertising art; dance; drama and dance teacher education; dramatic/theatre arts; education; English; environmental studies; fashion merchandising; fine/studio arts; general studies; history; interior design; international relations and affairs; kindergarten/preschool education; legal professions and studies related; marketing/marketing management; mass communication/media; middle school education; music; music related; music teacher education; nursing (registered nurse training); occupational therapy; piano and organ; political science and government; pre-law studies; psychology; special education; voice and opera.

Academic Programs *Special study options:* academic remediation for entering students, advanced placement credit, cooperative education, distance learning, double majors, honors programs, independent study, internships, part-time degree program, services for LD students, study abroad, summer session for credit.

Library Trustee Library with 61,059 titles, 205 serial subscriptions, 2,104 audiovisual materials, an OPAC, a Web page.

Computers on Campus 198 computers available on campus for general student use. A campuswide network can be accessed from student residence rooms and from off campus. Internet access, online (class) registration, at least one staffed computer lab available.

Student Life *Housing:* on-campus residence required through junior year. *Options:* women-only. Campus housing is university owned. Freshman campus housing is guaranteed. *Activities and organizations:* drama/theater group, student-run newspaper, radio and television station, choral group, Student Government/Campus Activities Board, Silhouettes (diversity awareness), Recreation Association, DIVAS Peer Education, international club, national sororities. *Campus security:* 24-hour emergency response devices and patrols, late-night transport/escort service. *Student services:* health clinic, personal/psychological counseling.

Athletics Member NAIA. *Intercollegiate sports:* cross-country running W(s), soccer W(s), tennis W(s), volleyball W(s).

Standardized Tests *Required:* SAT I or ACT (for admission).

Costs (2004–05) *Comprehensive fee:* $22,670. Part-time tuition: $487 per semester hour. *Room and board:* Room and board charges vary according to board plan and housing facility. *Payment plan:* installment. *Waivers:* employees or children of employees.

Financial Aid Of all full-time matriculated undergraduates who enrolled in 2003, 419 applied for aid, 371 were judged to have need, 114 had their need fully met. 109 Federal Work-Study jobs (averaging $1750). 11 state and other part-time jobs (averaging $1785). In 2003, 104 non-need-based awards were made. *Average percent of need met:* 82%. *Average financial aid package:* $14,512. *Average need-based loan:* $3648. *Average need-based gift aid:* $11,856. *Average non-need-based aid:* $7965. *Average indebtedness upon graduation:* $15,409.

Applying *Options:* electronic application, early admission, deferred entrance. *Application fee:* $35. *Required:* essay or personal statement, high school transcript, minimum 2.5 GPA, minimum SAT I score of 900 or ACT score of 19. *Required for some:* interview. *Recommended:* letters of recommendation. *Application deadline:* rolling (freshmen), rolling (transfers). *Notification:* continuous (freshmen), continuous (transfers).

Admissions Contact Ms. Christina Cochran, Coordinator of Women's College Admission, Brenau University, Admissions, 1 Centennial Circle, Gainesville, GA 30501. *Phone:* 770-718-5320 Ext. 5320. *Toll-free phone:* 800-252-5119. *Fax:* 770-538-4306. *E-mail:* wcadmissions@lib.brenau.edu.

■ *See page 1286 for a narrative description.*

BREWTON-PARKER COLLEGE
Mt. Vernon, Georgia

- **Independent Southern Baptist** 4-year, founded 1904
- **Calendar** semesters

■ **Degrees** associate and bachelor's
■ **Rural** 280-acre campus
■ **Endowment** $12.0 million
■ **Coed,** 1,109 undergraduate students, 79% full-time, 65% women, 35% men
■ **Minimally difficult** entrance level, 96% of applicants were admitted

Undergraduates 877 full-time, 232 part-time. Students come from 19 states and territories, 15 other countries, 6% are from out of state, 19% African American, 0.5% Asian American or Pacific Islander, 1% Hispanic American, 0.4% Native American, 2% international, 8% transferred in, 32% live on campus. *Retention:* 56% of 2002 full-time freshmen returned.

Freshmen *Admission:* 522 applied, 500 admitted, 282 enrolled. *Test scores:* SAT verbal scores over 500: 41%; SAT math scores over 500: 33%; ACT scores over 18: 53%; SAT verbal scores over 600: 11%; SAT math scores over 600: 7%; ACT scores over 24: 2%; SAT verbal scores over 700: 2%.

Faculty *Total:* 155, 35% full-time, 33% with terminal degrees. *Student/faculty ratio:* 10:1.

Majors Accounting; biology/biological sciences; biology teacher education; business administration and management; communication/speech communication and rhetoric; computer and information sciences; early childhood education; education; English; English/language arts teacher education; general studies; health and physical education related; history; history teacher education; information science/studies; mathematics; mathematics teacher education; middle school education; music; music performance; music teacher education; physical education teaching and coaching; political science and government; pre-law studies; psychology; religious studies; science teacher education; secondary education; social sciences; sociology; theology.

Academic Programs *Special study options:* academic remediation for entering students, adult/continuing education programs, advanced placement credit, cooperative education, honors programs, internships, part-time degree program, services for LD students, summer session for credit.

Library Fountain-New Library with 70,352 titles, 350 serial subscriptions, 5,567 audiovisual materials, an OPAC, a Web page.

Computers on Campus 87 computers available on campus for general student use. A campuswide network can be accessed from student residence rooms. Internet access, online (class) registration, at least one staffed computer lab available.

Student Life *Housing:* on-campus residence required through sophomore year. *Options:* men-only, women-only. Campus housing is university owned. Freshman campus housing is guaranteed. *Activities and organizations:* drama/theater group, student-run newspaper, choral group, Council of Intramural Activities, Student Activities Council, Rotaract, Circle K, Baptist Student Union. *Campus security:* 24-hour emergency response devices and patrols, controlled dormitory access. *Student services:* health clinic, personal/psychological counseling.

Athletics Member NAIA. *Intercollegiate sports:* baseball M(s), basketball M(s)/W(s), cheerleading M(s)/W(s), soccer M(s)/W(s), softball W(s), volleyball W(s). *Intramural sports:* basketball M/W, football M/W, softball M/W, table tennis M/W, tennis M/W, ultimate Frisbee M/W, volleyball M/W.

Standardized Tests *Required:* SAT I or ACT (for admission).

Costs (2004–05) *Comprehensive fee:* $15,520 includes full-time tuition ($10,720), mandatory fees ($350), and room and board ($4450). Part-time tuition: $335 per credit hour. *College room only:* $2150. Room and board charges vary according to board plan and housing facility. *Payment plan:* installment. *Waivers:* senior citizens and employees or children of employees.

Financial Aid Of all full-time matriculated undergraduates who enrolled in 2002, 825 applied for aid, 749 were judged to have need, 89 had their need fully met. 242 Federal Work-Study jobs (averaging $800). 26 state and other part-time jobs (averaging $1386). In 2002, 106 non-need-based awards were made. *Average percent of need met:* 61%. *Average financial aid package:* $8431. *Average need-based loan:* $3020. *Average need-based gift aid:* $6036. *Average non-need-based aid:* $5630. *Average indebtedness upon graduation:* $16,340.

Applying *Options:* common application, early admission. *Application fee:* $25. *Required:* high school transcript, minimum 2.0 GPA. *Recommended:* interview. *Application deadline:* rolling (freshmen), rolling (transfers). *Notification:* continuous (freshmen), continuous (transfers).

Admissions Contact Mr. Brad Kissell, Dean of Enrollment Management, Brewton-Parker College, Highway 280, Mt. Vernon, GA 30445-0197. *Phone:* 912-583-3268 Ext. 268. *Toll-free phone:* 800-342-1087. *Fax:* 912-583-4498. *E-mail:* admissions@pbc.edu.

CARVER BIBLE COLLEGE
Atlanta, Georgia

■ **Independent nondenominational** 4-year, founded 1943
■ **Calendar** semesters
■ **Degree** certificates and bachelor's
■ **Coed**
■ **Noncompetitive** entrance level

Faculty *Student/faculty ratio:* 10:1.

Athletics Member NCCAA.

Costs (2003–04) *Required fees:* $160 full-time. *Room and board:* $2400.

Applying *Options:* common application. *Required:* essay or personal statement, high school transcript, minimum 2.0 GPA, 4 letters of recommendation. *Required for some:* interview.

Admissions Contact Ms. Patsy S. Singh, Director of Admissions, Carver Bible College, 437 Nelson Street, Atlanta, GA 30313. *Phone:* 404-527-4520.

CLARK ATLANTA UNIVERSITY
Atlanta, Georgia

■ **Independent United Methodist** university, founded 1865
■ **Calendar** semesters
■ **Degrees** bachelor's, master's, doctoral, post-master's, and postbachelor's certificates
■ **Urban** 113-acre campus with easy access to Atlanta
■ **Endowment** $31.4 million
■ **Coed,** 3,920 undergraduate students, 97% full-time, 71% women, 29% men
■ **Moderately difficult** entrance level, 53% of applicants were admitted

Undergraduates 3,793 full-time, 127 part-time. Students come from 43 states and territories, 60% are from out of state, 94% African American, 0.1% Asian American or Pacific Islander, 0.2% Hispanic American, 0.1% Native American, 10% transferred in, 37% live on campus. *Retention:* 72% of 2002 full-time freshmen returned.

Freshmen *Admission:* 6,939 applied, 3,664 admitted, 953 enrolled. *Average high school GPA:* 3.06. *Test scores:* SAT verbal scores over 500: 61%; SAT math scores over 500: 54%; ACT scores over 18: 31%; SAT verbal scores over 600: 42%; SAT math scores over 600: 41%; ACT scores over 24: 7%; SAT math scores over 700: 1%; ACT scores over 30: 1%.

Faculty *Total:* 291, 100% full-time, 80% with terminal degrees. *Student/faculty ratio:* 16:1.

Majors Accounting; art; art teacher education; biology/biological sciences; business administration and management; business teacher education; chemistry; computer and information sciences; computer science; criminal justice/law enforcement administration; developmental and child psychology; dramatic/theatre arts; early childhood education; economics; education; elementary education; engineering; English; fashion/apparel design; French; health information/medical records administration; health teacher education; history; history teacher education; information science/studies; interdisciplinary studies; kindergarten/preschool education; marketing related; mass communication/media; mathematics; medical illustration; middle school education; music; music teacher education; philosophy; physical education teaching and coaching; physics; political science and government; psychology; religious studies; science teacher education; secondary education; social sciences; social work; sociology; Spanish; speech and rhetoric.

Academic Programs *Special study options:* academic remediation for entering students, accelerated degree program, adult/continuing education programs, advanced placement credit, cooperative education, distance learning, English as a second language, freshman honors college, honors programs, internships, off-campus study, part-time degree program, services for LD students, study abroad, summer session for credit. *ROTC:* Army (b), Air Force (b). *Unusual degree programs:* 3-2 engineering with Georgia Institute of Technology, Boston University, North Carolina Agricultural and Technical State University.

Library Robert W. Woodruff Library with 836,593 serial subscriptions, 10,555 audiovisual materials, an OPAC, a Web page.

Computers on Campus 300 computers available on campus for general student use. A campuswide network can be accessed from off campus. Internet access, online (class) registration, at least one staffed computer lab available.

Student Life *Housing options:* coed, men-only, women-only. Campus housing is university owned and is provided by a third party. Freshman applicants given priority for college housing. *Activities and organizations:* drama/theater group, student-run newspaper, radio and television station, choral group, marching band, Spirit Boosters, Pre alumni Council, Campus Activities Board (CAB), Orientation Guides, National Association for the Advancement of Colored People (NAACP), national fraternities, national sororities. *Campus security:* 24-hour emergency response devices and patrols, late-night transport/escort service, controlled dormitory access. *Student services:* health clinic, personal/psychological counseling.

Athletics Member NCAA. All Division II. *Intercollegiate sports:* basketball M(s)/W(s), cheerleading W(s), cross-country running M(s)/W(s), football M(s), golf M(s), softball W, tennis M(s)/W(s), track and field M(s)/W, volleyball W. *Intramural sports:* basketball M/W, football M/W, swimming M/W, tennis M/W, track and field M/W, volleyball M/W.

Clark Atlanta University (continued)

Standardized Tests *Required:* SAT I or ACT (for admission).

Costs (2003–04) *Comprehensive fee:* $19,300 includes full-time tuition ($12,312), mandatory fees ($550), and room and board ($6438). Part-time tuition: $513 per credit. *Required fees:* $550 per year part-time. *College room only:* $3778. Room and board charges vary according to board plan and housing facility. *Payment plan:* deferred payment. *Waivers:* employees or children of employees.

Financial Aid Of all full-time matriculated undergraduates who enrolled in 2002, 3,537 applied for aid, 3,386 were judged to have need, 1,103 had their need fully met. 297 Federal Work-Study jobs (averaging $1931). *Average percent of need met:* 5%. *Average financial aid package:* $3197. *Average need-based loan:* $2813. *Average need-based gift aid:* $2501. *Average indebtedness upon graduation:* $17,751.

Applying *Options:* common application, early admission, deferred entrance. *Application fee:* $35. *Required:* essay or personal statement, high school transcript, minimum 2.0 GPA, 2 letters of recommendation. *Recommended:* minimum 2.5 GPA, interview. *Application deadlines:* 7/1 (freshmen), 7/1 (transfers). *Notification:* continuous (freshmen), continuous (transfers).

Admissions Contact Office of Admissions, Clark Atlanta University, 223 James P. Brawley Drive, SW, 101 Trevor Arnett Hall, Atlanta, GA 30314. *Phone:* 404-880-8784 Ext. 6650. *Toll-free phone:* 800-688-3228. *Fax:* 404-880-6174.

■ *See page 1410 for a narrative description.*

CLAYTON COLLEGE & STATE UNIVERSITY

Morrow, Georgia

- **State-supported** 4-year, founded 1969, part of University System of Georgia
- **Calendar** semesters
- **Degrees** certificates, associate, and bachelor's
- **Suburban** 163-acre campus with easy access to Atlanta
- **Coed,** 5,661 undergraduate students, 47% full-time, 69% women, 31% men
- **Minimally difficult** entrance level

Undergraduates 2,656 full-time, 3,005 part-time. Students come from 45 states and territories, 25 other countries, 5% are from out of state, 47% African American, 4% Asian American or Pacific Islander, 3% Hispanic American, 0.5% Native American, 4% international, 11% transferred in. *Retention:* 61% of 2002 full-time freshmen returned.

Freshmen *Admission:* 617 enrolled.

Faculty *Total:* 364, 43% full-time. *Student/faculty ratio:* 16:1.

Majors Accounting; administrative assistant and secretarial science; agricultural business and management; agricultural mechanization; agriculture; airframe mechanics and aircraft maintenance technology; apparel and accessories marketing; architectural engineering technology; art; artificial intelligence and robotics; art teacher education; aviation/airway management; avionics maintenance technology; biological and physical sciences; biology/biological sciences; business administration and management; business teacher education; chemistry; clinical laboratory science/medical technology; clinical/medical laboratory technology; communication and media related; computer engineering technology; computer/information technology services administration related; computer science; criminal justice/law enforcement administration; data processing and data processing technology; dental hygiene; drafting and design technology; dramatic/theatre arts; economics; education; electrical, electronic and communications engineering technology; electromechanical technology; elementary education; emergency medical technology (EMT paramedic); engineering; engineering technology; English; family and consumer sciences/human sciences; fashion merchandising; finance; forestry; French; geology/earth science; health/health care administration; health information/medical records administration; health teacher education; history; human services; information science/studies; instrumentation technology; journalism; kindergarten/preschool education; legal administrative assistant/secretary; legal assistant/paralegal; legal studies; management information systems; marketing/marketing management; marketing related; mass communication/media; mathematics; mechanical design technology; medical/clinical assistant; medical illustration; merchandising; merchandising, sales, and marketing operations related (general); merchandising, sales, and marketing operations related (specialized); middle school education; multi-/interdisciplinary studies related; music; music performance; music theory and composition; nursing (registered nurse training); occupational therapy; parks, recreation and leisure; pharmacy; philosophy; physical education teaching and coaching; physical therapy; physics; political science and government; pre-engineering; psychology; psychology related; public/applied history and archival administration; radiologic technology/science; social sciences; sociology; Spanish; speech and rhetoric; telecommunications; urban studies/affairs; veterinary sciences.

Academic Programs *Special study options:* academic remediation for entering students, adult/continuing education programs, advanced placement credit, cooperative education, distance learning, double majors, freshman honors college, honors programs, independent study, internships, off-campus study, part-time degree program, services for LD students, student-designed majors, study abroad, summer session for credit. *ROTC:* Army (c).

Library Clayton College and State University Library plus 1 other with 77,043 titles, 4,250 serial subscriptions, 5,636 audiovisual materials, an OPAC, a Web page.

Computers on Campus 110 computers available on campus for general student use. A campuswide network can be accessed from off campus. Internet access, online (class) registration, at least one staffed computer lab available.

Student Life *Housing:* college housing not available. *Activities and organizations:* drama/theater group, student-run newspaper, choral group, accounting club, international awareness club, Black Cultural Awareness Association, Student Government Association, music club, national fraternities, national sororities. *Campus security:* 24-hour emergency response devices and patrols, late-night transport/escort service, lighted pathways. *Student services:* health clinic, personal/psychological counseling.

Athletics Member NCAA. All Division II. *Intercollegiate sports:* basketball M(s)/W(s), cheerleading W(s)(c), cross-country running M(s)/W(s), golf M(s), soccer M(s)/W(s), tennis W(s), track and field M(s)/W(s). *Intramural sports:* bowling M/W, softball M/W, table tennis M/W, volleyball M/W.

Standardized Tests *Required:* SAT I or ACT (for admission). *Required for some:* SAT II: Subject Tests (for admission).

Costs (2003–04) *Tuition:* state resident $2244 full-time, $109 per credit hour part-time; nonresident $8848 full-time, $369 per credit hour part-time. Part-time tuition and fees vary according to program. *Required fees:* $458 full-time, $229 per term part-time. *Waivers:* senior citizens and employees or children of employees.

Financial Aid Of all full-time matriculated undergraduates who enrolled in 2003, 1,901 applied for aid, 1,458 were judged to have need, 433 had their need fully met. 59 Federal Work-Study jobs. In 2003, 266 non-need-based awards were made.

Applying *Options:* early admission, deferred entrance. *Application fee:* $5. *Required:* high school transcript, proof of immunization. *Application deadline:* 7/17 (freshmen). *Notification:* continuous (freshmen), continuous (transfers).

Admissions Contact Ms. Carol S. Montgomery, Admissions, Clayton College & State University, 5900 North Lee Street, Morrow, GA 30260-0285. *Phone:* 770-961-3500. *Fax:* 770-961-3752. *E-mail:* csc-info@ce.clayton.peachnet.edu.

COLUMBUS STATE UNIVERSITY

Columbus, Georgia

- **State-supported** comprehensive, founded 1958, part of University System of Georgia
- **Calendar** semesters
- **Degrees** certificates, associate, bachelor's, master's, and post-master's certificates
- **Suburban** 132-acre campus with easy access to Atlanta
- **Coed,** 5,994 undergraduate students, 66% full-time, 62% women, 38% men
- **Minimally difficult** entrance level, 70% of applicants were admitted

Undergraduates 3,981 full-time, 2,013 part-time. Students come from 35 states and territories, 40 other countries, 13% are from out of state, 30% African American, 2% Asian American or Pacific Islander, 3% Hispanic American, 0.4% Native American, 1% international, 8% transferred in, 14% live on campus. *Retention:* 71% of 2002 full-time freshmen returned.

Freshmen *Admission:* 2,637 applied, 1,859 admitted, 1,157 enrolled. *Average high school GPA:* 3.01. *Test scores:* SAT verbal scores over 500: 42%; SAT math scores over 500: 38%; ACT scores over 18: 70%; SAT verbal scores over 600: 10%; SAT math scores over 600: 8%; ACT scores over 24: 13%; SAT verbal scores over 700: 1%; ACT scores over 30: 1%.

Faculty *Total:* 373, 53% full-time, 50% with terminal degrees. *Student/faculty ratio:* 18:1.

Majors Accounting; applied mathematics; art; art teacher education; athletic training; biology/biological sciences; biology teacher education; business administration and management; business/commerce; business/managerial economics; chemistry; chemistry teacher education; computer management; computer science; creative writing; criminal justice/law enforcement administration; drama and dance teacher education; dramatic/theatre arts; early childhood education; education (K-12); engineering; English; English/language arts teacher education; finance; forest engineering; forestry; French language teacher education; geology/earth science; health science; health services/allied health/health sciences; health teacher education; history; history teacher education; information science/studies; kinesiology and exercise science; liberal arts and sciences/liberal studies; literature; marketing/marketing management; mass communication/media; mathematics; mathematics teacher education; medical radiologic technology; middle school education; music; music pedagogy; music teacher education; nursing (registered nurse training); physical education teaching and coaching; piano and organ;

political science and government; pre-dentistry studies; pre-engineering; pre-law studies; pre-medical studies; pre-pharmacy studies; pre-veterinary studies; psychology; public relations/image management; science teacher education; secondary education; social science teacher education; sociology; Spanish language teacher education; special education; speech/theater education; violin, viola, guitar and other stringed instruments; voice and opera; wind/percussion instruments.

Academic Programs *Special study options:* academic remediation for entering students, adult/continuing education programs, advanced placement credit, cooperative education, distance learning, freshman honors college, honors programs, independent study, internships, part-time degree program, services for LD students, study abroad, summer session for credit. *ROTC:* Army (b).

Library Simon Schwob Memorial Library with 250,000 titles, 1,400 serial subscriptions, 2,500 audiovisual materials, an OPAC, a Web page.

Computers on Campus 300 computers available on campus for general student use. A campuswide network can be accessed from student residence rooms and from off campus. Internet access, online (class) registration, at least one staffed computer lab available.

Student Life *Housing options:* coed, disabled students. *Activities and organizations:* drama/theater group, student-run newspaper, choral group, Student Government Association, Student Programming Council, Greek life, Baptist Student Union, national fraternities, national sororities. *Campus security:* 24-hour emergency response devices and patrols, late-night transport/escort service. *Student services:* health clinic, personal/psychological counseling.

Athletics Member NCAA. All Division II. *Intercollegiate sports:* baseball M(s), basketball M(s)/W(s), cross-country running M(s)/W(s), golf M(s), soccer W(s), softball W(s), tennis M(s)/W(s). *Intramural sports:* badminton M/W, basketball M/W, bowling M/W, cross-country running M/W, football M/W, golf M/W, racquetball M/W, skiing (downhill) M/W, soccer M/W, softball M/W, table tennis M/W, tennis M/W, volleyball M/W.

Standardized Tests *Required:* SAT I or ACT (for admission). *Required for some:* SAT II: Subject Tests (for admission).

Costs (2003–04) *Tuition:* state resident $2212 full-time, $93 per semester hour part-time; nonresident $8848 full-time, $369 per semester hour part-time. *Required fees:* $464 full-time, $168 per semester hour part-time. *Room and board:* $5270; room only: $2900. Room and board charges vary according to board plan and location. *Waivers:* senior citizens and employees or children of employees.

Financial Aid Of all full-time matriculated undergraduates who enrolled in 2003, 2,816 applied for aid, 1,574 were judged to have need, 1,317 had their need fully met. 56 Federal Work-Study jobs (averaging $2302). In 2003, 718 non-need-based awards were made. *Average percent of need met:* 69%. *Average financial aid package:* $3995. *Average need-based loan:* $3481. *Average need-based gift aid:* $3284. *Average non-need-based aid:* $1764. *Average indebtedness upon graduation:* $14,237.

Applying *Options:* common application, electronic application, early admission, deferred entrance. *Application fee:* $25. *Required:* high school transcript, minimum 2.5 GPA, proof of immunization. *Application deadlines:* 7/28 (freshmen), 7/28 (transfers).

Admissions Contact Ms. Susan Lovell, Associate Director of Admissions, Columbus State University, 4225 University Avenue, Columbus, GA 31907-5645. *Phone:* 706-568-2035 Ext. 1681. *Toll-free phone:* 866-264-2035. *Fax:* 706-568-5272.

COVENANT COLLEGE
Lookout Mountain, Georgia

- **Independent** comprehensive, founded 1955, affiliated with Presbyterian Church in America
- **Calendar** semesters
- **Degrees** diplomas, associate, bachelor's, and master's (master's degree in education only)
- **Suburban** 250-acre campus
- **Endowment** $14.0 million
- **Coed,** 1,198 undergraduate students, 98% full-time, 59% women, 41% men
- **Moderately difficult** entrance level, 61% of applicants were admitted

Undergraduates 1,171 full-time, 27 part-time. Students come from 49 states and territories, 7 other countries, 76% are from out of state, 6% African American, 3% Asian American or Pacific Islander, 2% Hispanic American, 0.6% Native American, 1% international, 3% transferred in, 88% live on campus. *Retention:* 79% of 2002 full-time freshmen returned.

Freshmen *Admission:* 715 applied, 433 admitted, 243 enrolled. *Average high school GPA:* 3.60. *Test scores:* SAT verbal scores over 500: 86%; SAT math scores over 500: 81%; ACT scores over 18: 99%; SAT verbal scores over 600: 58%; SAT math scores over 600: 49%; ACT scores over 24: 64%; SAT verbal scores over 700: 16%; SAT math scores over 700: 10%; ACT scores over 30: 17%.

Faculty *Total:* 61, 87% full-time, 79% with terminal degrees. *Student/faculty ratio:* 15:1.

Majors Art; biblical studies; biology/biological sciences; business administration and management; chemistry; computer science; economics; elementary education; English; foreign languages and literatures; health science; history; interdisciplinary studies; mathematics; middle school education; music; natural sciences; nursing (registered nurse training); philosophy; physics; pre-engineering; pre-law studies; pre-medical studies; pre-nursing studies; psychology; sociology.

Academic Programs *Special study options:* academic remediation for entering students, adult/continuing education programs, advanced placement credit, double majors, independent study, internships, off-campus study, part-time degree program, student-designed majors, summer session for credit. *Unusual degree programs:* 3-2 nursing with Vanderbilt University.

Library Kresge Memorial Library with 85,000 titles, 475 serial subscriptions, 4,300 audiovisual materials, an OPAC, a Web page.

Computers on Campus 135 computers available on campus for general student use. A campuswide network can be accessed from off campus. Internet access, at least one staffed computer lab available.

Student Life *Housing:* on-campus residence required through junior year. *Options:* men-only, women-only. Campus housing is university owned. Freshman campus housing is guaranteed. *Activities and organizations:* drama/theater group, student-run newspaper, choral group, psychology club, interpretive dance group, drama club, backpacking club, various ministries. *Campus security:* night security guards. *Student services:* health clinic, personal/psychological counseling, women's center.

Athletics Member NAIA. *Intercollegiate sports:* basketball M(s)/W(s), cross-country running M(s)/W(s), soccer M(s)/W(s), volleyball W(s). *Intramural sports:* basketball M/W, football M, golf M, soccer M/W, tennis M/W, volleyball M/W.

Standardized Tests *Required:* SAT I or ACT (for admission). *Recommended:* ACT (for admission).

Costs (2003–04) *Comprehensive fee:* $23,830 includes full-time tuition ($17,750), mandatory fees ($480), and room and board ($5600). Full-time tuition and fees vary according to course load. Part-time tuition and fees vary according to course load. *Room and board:* Room and board charges vary according to board plan and housing facility. *Payment plan:* installment. *Waivers:* senior citizens and employees or children of employees.

Financial Aid Of all full-time matriculated undergraduates who enrolled in 2002, 819 applied for aid, 588 were judged to have need, 170 had their need fully met. 313 Federal Work-Study jobs (averaging $1931). 69 state and other part-time jobs (averaging $1681). In 2002, 175 non-need-based awards were made. *Average percent of need met:* 84%. *Average financial aid package:* $15,903. *Average need-based loan:* $4280. *Average need-based gift aid:* $11,658. *Average non-need-based aid:* $4748. *Average indebtedness upon graduation:* $13,565.

Applying *Options:* early admission, deferred entrance. *Application fee:* $25. *Required:* essay or personal statement, high school transcript, minimum 2.5 GPA, 2 letters of recommendation, interview. *Application deadline:* rolling (freshmen), rolling (transfers). *Notification:* continuous (freshmen).

Admissions Contact Mrs. Elysa Lochstampfor, Admissions Administrative Assistant, Covenant College, 14049 Scenic Highway, Lookout Mountain, GA 30750. *Phone:* 706-419-1149. *Toll-free phone:* 888-451-2683. *Fax:* 706-419-2255. *E-mail:* admissions@covenant.edu.

DALTON STATE COLLEGE
Dalton, Georgia

- **State-supported** 4-year, founded 1963, part of University System of Georgia
- **Calendar** semesters
- **Degrees** certificates, associate, and bachelor's
- **Small-town** 141-acre campus
- **Endowment** $9.6 million
- **Coed,** 4,201 undergraduate students, 43% full-time, 64% women, 36% men
- **Noncompetitive** entrance level, 62% of applicants were admitted

Undergraduates 1,792 full-time, 2,409 part-time. Students come from 4 states and territories, 0.9% are from out of state.

Freshmen *Admission:* 2,178 applied, 1,347 admitted, 554 enrolled. *Average high school GPA:* 3.00. *Test scores:* SAT verbal scores over 500: 42%; SAT math scores over 500: 36%; ACT scores over 18: 73%; SAT verbal scores over 600: 11%; SAT math scores over 600: 7%; ACT scores over 24: 14%; SAT verbal scores over 700: 1%; SAT math scores over 700: 1%; ACT scores over 30: 1%.

Faculty *Total:* 153, 73% full-time. *Student/faculty ratio:* 27:1.

Majors Agriculture; biological and physical sciences; biology/biological sciences; business administration and management; business/commerce; chemistry; clinical laboratory science/medical technology; clinical/medical laboratory technology; computer and information sciences; computer engineering technology; computer/information technology services administration related; computer instal-

Dalton State College (continued)

lation and repair technology; computer science; computer technology/computer systems technology; criminal justice/law enforcement administration; criminal justice/police science; criminology; dental hygiene; drafting and design technology; economics; education; electrical, electronic and communications engineering technology; elementary education; English; family and consumer economics related; foreign languages and literatures; forestry; general studies; geography; geology/earth science; health information/medical records administration; history; industrial arts; industrial electronics technology; industrial mechanics and maintenance technology; industrial technology; information science/studies; journalism; machine shop technology; management information systems; marketing/marketing management; mathematics; medical office management; medical transcription; middle school education; nuclear medical technology; nursing (registered nurse training); occupational therapy; office management; operations management; philosophy; physical therapy; physician assistant; physics; political science and government; pre-pharmacy studies; psychology; radiologic technology/science; respiratory care therapy; sales, distribution and marketing; secondary education; social work; sociology; speech and rhetoric.

Academic Programs *Special study options:* academic remediation for entering students, adult/continuing education programs, advanced placement credit, distance learning, English as a second language, internships, off-campus study, part-time degree program, services for LD students, study abroad, summer session for credit.

Library Derrell C. Roberts Library with 710 serial subscriptions, 6,064 audiovisual materials, an OPAC, a Web page.

Computers on Campus 559 computers available on campus for general student use. A campuswide network can be accessed. Internet access, at least one staffed computer lab available.

Student Life *Housing:* college housing not available. *Activities and organizations:* student-run newspaper, Baptist Student Union, Social Work Club, International Students Association, Medical Laboratory Technicians, Phi Theta Kappa. *Campus security:* 24-hour emergency response devices and patrols.

Athletics *Intercollegiate sports:* basketball M(c)/W(c), golf W(c), softball M(c)/W(c), table tennis M(c)/W(c), tennis M(c)/W(c), volleyball M(c)/W(c). *Intramural sports:* badminton M/W, basketball M/W, football M/W, softball M/W, table tennis M/W, tennis M/W, volleyball M/W.

Standardized Tests *Required for some:* SAT I or ACT (for admission), SAT II: Subject Tests (for admission).

Costs (2004–05) *Tuition:* state resident $1522 full-time; nonresident $5716 full-time. Full-time tuition and fees vary according to program. *Waivers:* senior citizens.

Financial Aid Of all full-time matriculated undergraduates who enrolled in 2003, 91 Federal Work-Study jobs (averaging $1433). 98 state and other part-time jobs (averaging $3665). *Average indebtedness upon graduation:* $4049.

Applying *Options:* common application, early admission. *Application fee:* $20. *Required:* high school transcript. *Application deadline:* rolling (freshmen), rolling (transfers). *Notification:* continuous (freshmen), continuous (transfers).

Admissions Contact Dr. Angela Harris, Assistant Director of Admissions, Dalton State College, 213 North College Drive, Dalton, GA 30720-3797. *Phone:* 706-272-4476. *Toll-free phone:* 800-829-4436. *Fax:* 706-272-2530. *E-mail:* aharris@em.daltonstate.edu.

DEVRY UNIVERSITY
Alpharetta, Georgia

- **Proprietary** comprehensive, founded 1997, part of DeVry University
- **Calendar** semesters
- **Degrees** associate, bachelor's, master's, and postbachelor's certificates
- **Suburban** 9-acre campus with easy access to Atlanta
- **Coed**
- **Minimally difficult** entrance level

Student Life *Campus security:* 24-hour emergency response devices, late-night transport/escort service, lighted pathways, video recorder (CCTV).

Standardized Tests *Recommended:* SAT I, ACT, or CPT.

Costs (2003–04) *Tuition:* $9990 full-time, $355 per credit hour part-time. Full-time tuition and fees vary according to course load. Part-time tuition and fees vary according to course load. *Required fees:* $165 full-time. *Payment plans:* installment, deferred payment.

Financial Aid Of all full-time matriculated undergraduates who enrolled in 2002, 1,047 applied for aid, 957 were judged to have need, 41 had their need fully met. In 2002, 133. *Average percent of need met:* 46. *Average financial aid package:* $8858. *Average need-based loan:* $5520. *Average need-based gift aid:* $3799. *Average non-need-based aid:* $8453.

Applying *Options:* electronic application, deferred entrance. *Application fee:* $50. *Required:* high school transcript, interview.

Admissions Contact Ms. Kristi Franklin, New Student Coordinator, DeVry University, 2555 Northwinds Parkway, Alpharetta, GA 30004-2232. *Phone:* 770-521-4900. *Toll-free phone:* 800-221-4771. *Fax:* 770-664-8824. *E-mail:* admissions@devry.edu.

DEVRY UNIVERSITY
Atlanta, Georgia

Admissions Contact Fifteen Piedmont Center, Plaza Level 100, Atlanta, GA 30305-1543.

DEVRY UNIVERSITY
Decatur, Georgia

- **Proprietary** comprehensive, founded 1969, part of DeVry University
- **Calendar** semesters
- **Degrees** associate, bachelor's, master's, and postbachelor's certificates
- **Suburban** 21-acre campus with easy access to Atlanta
- **Coed**
- **Minimally difficult** entrance level

Student Life *Campus security:* 24-hour emergency response devices and patrols, late-night transport/escort service, lighted pathways/sidewalks.

Standardized Tests *Recommended:* SAT I, ACT or CPT.

Costs (2003–04) *Tuition:* $9990 full-time, $355 per credit hour part-time. Full-time tuition and fees vary according to course load. Part-time tuition and fees vary according to course load. *Required fees:* $165 full-time. *Payment plans:* installment, deferred payment.

Financial Aid Of all full-time matriculated undergraduates who enrolled in 2002, 2,255 applied for aid, 2,195 were judged to have need, 49 had their need fully met. In 2002, 137. *Average percent of need met:* 47. *Average financial aid package:* $9862. *Average need-based loan:* $5600. *Average need-based gift aid:* $4432. *Average non-need-based aid:* $8842.

Applying *Options:* electronic application, deferred entrance. *Application fee:* $50. *Required:* high school transcript, interview.

Admissions Contact Ms. Karen Krumenaker, New Student Coordinator, DeVry University, 250 North Arcadia Avenue, Decatur, GA 30030-2198. *Phone:* 404-292-2645. *Toll-free phone:* 800-221-4771. *Fax:* 404-292-7011. *E-mail:* dsilva@admin.atl.devry.edu.

DEVRY UNIVERSITY
Duluth, Georgia

Admissions Contact 3505 Koger Boulevard, Suite 170, Duluth, GA 30096-7671.

EMMANUEL COLLEGE
Franklin Springs, Georgia

- **Independent** 4-year, founded 1919, affiliated with Pentecostal Holiness Church
- **Calendar** semesters
- **Degrees** associate and bachelor's
- **Rural** 90-acre campus with easy access to Atlanta
- **Endowment** $3.8 million
- **Coed,** 742 undergraduate students, 86% full-time, 57% women, 43% men
- **Minimally difficult** entrance level, 49% of applicants were admitted

Undergraduates 637 full-time, 105 part-time. Students come from 25 states and territories, 4 other countries, 23% are from out of state, 16% African American, 2% Asian American or Pacific Islander, 1% Hispanic American, 0.4% Native American, 0.8% international, 8% transferred in, 41% live on campus. *Retention:* 62% of 2002 full-time freshmen returned.

Freshmen *Admission:* 672 applied, 331 admitted, 192 enrolled.

Faculty *Total:* 63, 76% full-time, 52% with terminal degrees. *Student/faculty ratio:* 14:1.

Majors American history; biblical studies; biology/biological sciences; business administration and management; business teacher education; computer and information sciences; computer teacher education; elementary education; English; English/language arts teacher education; European history; health/medical preparatory programs related; kinesiology and exercise science; liberal arts and sciences/liberal studies; mass communication/media; mathematics; mathematics teacher education; middle school education; music; music teacher education; office management; organizational communication; pastoral studies/counseling;

pre-law studies; pre-pharmacy studies; psychology; religious/sacred music; social science teacher education; sport and fitness administration; youth ministry.

Academic Programs *Special study options:* academic remediation for entering students, advanced placement credit, distance learning, independent study, internships, part-time degree program, summer session for credit.

Library Shaw–Leslie Library with 75,780 titles, 143 serial subscriptions, 3,117 audiovisual materials, an OPAC, a Web page.

Computers on Campus 50 computers available on campus for general student use. A campuswide network can be accessed from student residence rooms and from off campus. Internet access, at least one staffed computer lab available.

Student Life *Housing:* on-campus residence required through sophomore year. *Options:* men-only, women-only. Campus housing is university owned. Freshman campus housing is guaranteed. *Activities and organizations:* drama/theater group, student-run newspaper, choral group, SIFE, FCA, SOS, BSU, International Students Club. *Campus security:* 24-hour patrols, controlled dormitory access. *Student services:* health clinic, personal/psychological counseling.

Athletics Member NAIA, NCCAA. *Intercollegiate sports:* baseball M(s), basketball M(s)/W(s), soccer M(s)/W(s), softball W(s), tennis M(s)/W(s). *Intramural sports:* basketball M/W, football M/W, golf M/W, soccer M/W, tennis M/W, track and field M/W, volleyball M/W, weight lifting M/W.

Standardized Tests *Required:* SAT I or ACT (for admission).

Costs (2003–04) *Comprehensive fee:* $13,140 includes full-time tuition ($8734), mandatory fees ($270), and room and board ($4136). Part-time tuition: $306 per semester hour. *Required fees:* $75 per term part-time. *College room only:* $1950. Room and board charges vary according to board plan. *Payment plan:* installment. *Waivers:* adult students, senior citizens, and employees or children of employees.

Financial Aid Of all full-time matriculated undergraduates who enrolled in 2001, 636 applied for aid, 493 were judged to have need, 136 had their need fully met. 209 Federal Work-Study jobs (averaging $2474). 105 state and other part-time jobs (averaging $1408). In 2001, 133 non-need-based awards were made. *Average percent of need met:* 53%. *Average financial aid package:* $8948. *Average need-based loan:* $3319. *Average need-based gift aid:* $3080. *Average non-need-based aid:* $3368. *Average indebtedness upon graduation:* $16,575.

Applying *Options:* early admission, deferred entrance. *Application fee:* $25. *Required:* high school transcript. *Application deadlines:* 8/1 (freshmen), 8/1 (transfers). *Notification:* 8/1 (freshmen), continuous until 8/1 (transfers).

Admissions Contact Mrs. Angie Thompson, Associate Director of Admissions, Emmanuel College, PO Box 129, 181 Spring Street, Franklin Springs, GA 30639-0129. *Phone:* 706-245-7226 Ext. 2872. *Toll-free phone:* 800-860-8800. *Fax:* 706-245-4424. *E-mail:* admissions@eclions.net.

EMORY UNIVERSITY
Atlanta, Georgia

- **Independent Methodist** university, founded 1836
- **Calendar** semesters
- **Degrees** associate, bachelor's, master's, doctoral, and first professional (enrollment figures include Emory University, Oxford College; application data for main campus only)
- **Suburban** 631-acre campus
- **Endowment** $3.8 billion
- **Coed,** 6,297 undergraduate students, 98% full-time, 56% women, 44% men
- **Most difficult** entrance level, 42% of applicants were admitted

For information on Emory University's Oxford campus, students should refer to *Peterson's Guide to Colleges in the South*. Oxford provides an intimate living-learning environment for students who want to begin their Emory education in a personalized setting with leadership opportunities. After completing the Oxford program, students automatically continue to Emory in Atlanta for their junior and senior years. See Oxford's Web site at http://www.emory.edu/OXFORD for additional information.

Undergraduates 6,193 full-time, 104 part-time. Students come from 52 states and territories, 64 other countries, 80% are from out of state, 9% African American, 16% Asian American or Pacific Islander, 3% Hispanic American, 0.2% Native American, 4% international, 2% transferred in, 70% live on campus. *Retention:* 94% of 2002 full-time freshmen returned.

Freshmen *Admission:* 10,372 applied, 4,357 admitted, 1,606 enrolled. *Average high school GPA:* 3.80. *Test scores:* SAT verbal scores over 500: 100%; SAT math scores over 500: 100%; ACT scores over 18: 100%; SAT verbal scores over 600: 90%; SAT math scores over 600: 95%; ACT scores over 24: 100%; SAT verbal scores over 700: 40%; SAT math scores over 700: 51%; ACT scores over 30: 54%.

Faculty *Total:* 2,938, 86% full-time, 99% with terminal degrees. *Student/faculty ratio:* 7:1.

Majors Accounting; African-American/Black studies; African studies; anthropology; art history, criticism and conservation; Asian studies; biology/biological sciences; biomedical sciences; business administration and management; business/managerial economics; chemistry; Chinese; classics and languages, literatures and linguistics; comparative literature; computer science; creative writing; dance; dramatic/theatre arts; economics; education; elementary education; English; European studies (Central and Eastern); film/cinema studies; finance; French; German; history; human ecology; international relations and affairs; Italian; Japanese; Jewish/Judaic studies; Latin; Latin American studies; liberal arts and sciences/liberal studies; literature; marketing/marketing management; mathematics; medieval and Renaissance studies; modern Greek; music; neuroscience; nursing (registered nurse training); philosophy; physics; political science and government; psychology; religious studies; Russian; secondary education; sociology; Spanish; women's studies.

Academic Programs *Special study options:* accelerated degree program, advanced placement credit, double majors, honors programs, internships, off-campus study, services for LD students, study abroad, summer session for credit. *ROTC:* Air Force (c). *Unusual degree programs:* 3-2 engineering with Georgia Institute of Technology.

Library Robert W. Woodruff Library plus 7 others with 2.5 million titles, 24,687 serial subscriptions, an OPAC, a Web page.

Computers on Campus 600 computers available on campus for general student use. A campuswide network can be accessed from student residence rooms and from off campus. Internet access, online (class) registration, at least one staffed computer lab available.

Student Life *Housing:* on-campus residence required through sophomore year. *Options:* coed, women-only, disabled students. Campus housing is university owned. Freshman campus housing is guaranteed. *Activities and organizations:* drama/theater group, student-run newspaper, radio and television station, choral group, Volunteer Emory, music/theater, student government, Outdoor Emory, national fraternities, national sororities. *Campus security:* 24-hour emergency response devices and patrols, student patrols, late-night transport/escort service. *Student services:* health clinic, personal/psychological counseling, women's center, legal services.

Athletics Member NCAA. All Division III. *Intercollegiate sports:* badminton M(c)/W(c), baseball M, basketball M/W, bowling M(c)/W(c), crew M(c)/W(c), cross-country running M/W, equestrian sports M(c)/W(c), fencing M(c)/W(c), field hockey W(c), golf M, gymnastics M(c)/W(c), ice hockey M(c), lacrosse M(c)/W(c), racquetball M(c)/W(c), rugby M(c), sailing M(c)/W(c), soccer M/W, softball W, swimming M/W, table tennis M(c)/W(c), tennis M/W, track and field M/W, ultimate Frisbee M(c)/W(c), volleyball M(c)/W, water polo M(c)/W(c), wrestling M(c). *Intramural sports:* badminton M/W, baseball M, basketball M/W, bowling M/W, cheerleading M/W, crew M/W, cross-country running M/W, fencing M/W, field hockey W, football M/W, golf M/W, ice hockey M, lacrosse M, racquetball M/W, rock climbing M/W, rugby M, sailing M/W, soccer M/W, softball M/W, swimming M/W, tennis M/W, track and field M/W, volleyball M/W, water polo M/W, weight lifting M/W, wrestling M.

Standardized Tests *Required:* SAT I or ACT (for admission). *Recommended:* SAT II: Subject Tests (for admission).

Costs (2003–04) *Comprehensive fee:* $36,872 includes full-time tuition ($27,600), mandatory fees ($352), and room and board ($8920). *College room only:* $5612. Room and board charges vary according to board plan, housing facility, and student level. *Payment plans:* tuition prepayment, installment. *Waivers:* employees or children of employees.

Financial Aid Of all full-time matriculated undergraduates who enrolled in 2003, 2,805 applied for aid, 2,337 were judged to have need, 2,337 had their need fully met. 1,896 Federal Work-Study jobs (averaging $1890). 86 state and other part-time jobs (averaging $4932). In 2003, 389 non-need-based awards were made. *Average percent of need met:* 100%. *Average financial aid package:* $25,238. *Average need-based loan:* $4715. *Average need-based gift aid:* $18,962. *Average non-need-based aid:* $16,422. *Average indebtedness upon graduation:* $18,803. *Financial aid deadline:* 4/1.

Applying *Options:* common application, electronic application, early admission, early decision, deferred entrance. *Application fee:* $40. *Required:* essay or personal statement, high school transcript, 1 letter of recommendation. *Recommended:* minimum 3.0 GPA. *Application deadlines:* 1/15 (freshmen), 6/1 (transfers). *Early decision:* 11/1 (for plan 1), 1/1 (for plan 2). *Notification:* 4/1 (freshmen), 12/15 (early decision plan 1), 2/1 (early decision plan 2), continuous (transfers).

Admissions Contact Mr. Daniel C. Walls, Dean of Admission, Emory University, 200 Boisfeuillet Jones Center, Atlanta, GA 30322-1100. *Phone:* 404-727-6036. *Toll-free phone:* 800-727-6036. *E-mail:* admiss@unix.cc.emory.edu.

■ *See page 1596 for a narrative description.*

FORT VALLEY STATE UNIVERSITY
Fort Valley, Georgia

- **State-supported** comprehensive, founded 1895, part of University System of Georgia

Fort Valley State University (continued)

- **Calendar** semesters
- **Degrees** associate, bachelor's, master's, doctoral, and first professional
- **Small-town** 1365-acre campus
- **Endowment** $1.0 million
- **Coed,** 2,291 undergraduate students, 86% full-time, 56% women, 44% men
- **Moderately difficult** entrance level, 48% of applicants were admitted

Undergraduates 1,979 full-time, 312 part-time. Students come from 28 states and territories, 21 other countries, 6% are from out of state, 95% African American, 0.4% Asian American or Pacific Islander, 0.3% Hispanic American, 1% international, 0.6% transferred in, 59% live on campus. *Retention:* 72% of 2002 full-time freshmen returned.

Freshmen *Admission:* 2,484 applied, 1,194 admitted, 511 enrolled. *Average high school GPA:* 2.67.

Faculty *Total:* 114, 93% full-time, 54% with terminal degrees. *Student/faculty ratio:* 22:1.

Majors Accounting; administrative assistant and secretarial science; agricultural/biological engineering and bioengineering; agricultural economics; agronomy and crop science; animal sciences; biology/biological sciences; botany/plant biology; business administration and management; chemistry; computer science; criminal justice/law enforcement administration; developmental and child psychology; economics; electrical, electronic and communications engineering technology; family and consumer sciences/home economics teacher education; foods, nutrition, and wellness; French; health teacher education; kindergarten/preschool education; marketing/marketing management; mass communication/media; mathematics; ornamental horticulture; physical education teaching and coaching; political science and government; pre-engineering; psychology; social sciences; social work; sociology; veterinary sciences; veterinary technology; zoology/animal biology.

Academic Programs *Special study options:* academic remediation for entering students, adult/continuing education programs, advanced placement credit, cooperative education, distance learning, double majors, freshman honors college, honors programs, internships, off-campus study, part-time degree program, services for LD students, study abroad, summer session for credit. *ROTC:* Army (b). *Unusual degree programs:* 3-2 engineering with University of Nevada, Las Vegas; math, geological science with University of Oklahoma.

Library Henry A. Hunt Memorial Library plus 2 others with 186,365 titles, 1,213 serial subscriptions, an OPAC.

Computers on Campus 633 computers available on campus for general student use. A campuswide network can be accessed from off campus that provide access to on-line grade reports. At least one staffed computer lab available.

Student Life *Housing options:* coed, men-only, women-only. *Activities and organizations:* drama/theater group, student-run newspaper, radio and television station, choral group, marching band, Drama Group, Christian Student Organization, Habitat for Humanity, debate club, national fraternities, national sororities. *Campus security:* 24-hour emergency response devices and patrols, student patrols, late-night transport/escort service. *Student services:* health clinic, personal/psychological counseling.

Athletics Member NCAA. All Division II. *Intercollegiate sports:* basketball M(s)/W(s), cheerleading M/W, football M(s), golf M(s), tennis M(s)/W(s), track and field M(s)/W(s), volleyball W(s). *Intramural sports:* rock climbing M(c)/W(c), ultimate Frisbee M(c)/W(c).

Standardized Tests *Required:* SAT I or ACT (for admission).

Costs (2003–04) *Tuition:* state resident $2212 full-time; nonresident $8848 full-time. Full-time tuition and fees vary according to course load. Part-time tuition and fees vary according to course load. *Required fees:* $570 full-time. *Room and board:* $4178. Room and board charges vary according to board plan. *Waivers:* senior citizens and employees or children of employees.

Financial Aid *Average percent of need met:* 89%. *Average financial aid package:* $7200.

Applying *Options:* common application, electronic application, early admission, deferred entrance. *Application fee:* $20. *Required:* high school transcript. *Application deadlines:* 8/1 (freshmen), 8/1 (transfers). *Notification:* continuous until 8/10 (freshmen), continuous until 8/10 (transfers).

Admissions Contact Mrs. Debra McGhee, Dean of Admissions and Enrollment Management, Fort Valley State University, 1005 State University Drive, Fort Valley, GA 31030. *Phone:* 478-825-6307. *Toll-free phone:* 800-248-7343. *Fax:* 478-825-6169. *E-mail:* admissap@fvsu.edu.

■ *See page 1642 for a narrative description.*

Georgia College & State University
Milledgeville, Georgia

- **State-supported** comprehensive, founded 1889, part of University System of Georgia
- **Calendar** semesters
- **Degrees** bachelor's, master's, and post-master's certificates
- **Small-town** 590-acre campus
- **Endowment** $1.5 million
- **Coed,** 4,662 undergraduate students, 86% full-time, 60% women, 40% men
- **Moderately difficult** entrance level, 62% of applicants were admitted

Undergraduates 4,002 full-time, 660 part-time. Students come from 25 states and territories, 47 other countries, 2% are from out of state, 10% African American, 1% Asian American or Pacific Islander, 0.9% Hispanic American, 0.2% Native American, 2% international, 8% transferred in, 30% live on campus. *Retention:* 75% of 2002 full-time freshmen returned.

Freshmen *Admission:* 2,547 applied, 1,590 admitted, 1,031 enrolled. *Average high school GPA:* 3.17. *Test scores:* SAT verbal scores over 500: 79%; SAT math scores over 500: 76%; ACT scores over 18: 99%; SAT verbal scores over 600: 21%; SAT math scores over 600: 19%; ACT scores over 24: 29%; SAT verbal scores over 700: 2%; SAT math scores over 700: 1%; ACT scores over 30: 1%.

Faculty *Total:* 420, 64% full-time. *Student/faculty ratio:* 15:1.

Majors Accounting; art; arts management; biology/biological sciences; business administration and management; business/commerce; business/managerial economics; chemistry; computer and information sciences; creative writing; criminal justice/law enforcement administration; dramatic/theatre arts; early childhood education; English; environmental science; French; health teacher education; history; international business/trade/commerce; journalism; logistics and materials management; management sciences and quantitative methods related; marketing/marketing management; mathematics; middle school education; music; music teacher education; music therapy; nursing (registered nurse training); office management; parks, recreation and leisure; physical education teaching and coaching; political science and government; psychology; sociology; Spanish; special education; speech and rhetoric.

Academic Programs *Special study options:* academic remediation for entering students, accelerated degree program, advanced placement credit, distance learning, double majors, English as a second language, freshman honors college, honors programs, independent study, internships, part-time degree program, services for LD students, student-designed majors, study abroad, summer session for credit. *ROTC:* Army (c). *Unusual degree programs:* 3-2 engineering with Georgia Institute of Technology.

Library Ina Dillard Russell Library with 156,738 titles, 1,080 serial subscriptions, 4,586 audiovisual materials, an OPAC, a Web page.

Computers on Campus 425 computers available on campus for general student use. A campuswide network can be accessed from student residence rooms and from off campus. Internet access, online (class) registration, at least one staffed computer lab available.

Student Life *Housing options:* coed, men-only, women-only. Campus housing is university owned. Freshman applicants given priority for college housing. *Activities and organizations:* drama/theater group, student-run newspaper, radio and television station, choral group, Baptist Student Union, national fraternities, national sororities. *Campus security:* 24-hour emergency response devices and patrols, student patrols, late-night transport/escort service, controlled dormitory access. *Student services:* health clinic, personal/psychological counseling.

Athletics Member NCAA. All Division II. *Intercollegiate sports:* baseball M(s), basketball M(s)/W(s), cross-country running M(s)/W(s), fencing M(c)/W(c), golf M(s), softball W(s), tennis M(s)/W(s). *Intramural sports:* basketball M/W, bowling M/W, football M/W, golf M, racquetball M/W, rugby M(c), soccer M/W, softball M/W, swimming M/W, tennis M/W, ultimate Frisbee M/W, volleyball M/W.

Standardized Tests *Required:* SAT I or ACT (for admission).

Costs (2003–04) *Tuition:* state resident $3002 full-time; nonresident $12,008 full-time. Part-time tuition and fees vary according to course load. *Required fees:* $594 full-time. *Room and board:* $6282. Room and board charges vary according to board plan and housing facility. *Waivers:* employees or children of employees.

Financial Aid Of all full-time matriculated undergraduates who enrolled in 2002, 3,384 applied for aid, 777 were judged to have need. In 2002, 123 non-need-based awards were made. *Average indebtedness upon graduation:* $10,759.

Applying *Options:* electronic application, early admission, deferred entrance. *Application fee:* $25. *Required:* essay or personal statement, high school transcript, minimum 2.22 GPA, proof of immunization, essay. *Recommended:* interview. *Application deadlines:* 7/15 (freshmen), 7/15 (transfers). *Notification:* continuous (freshmen), continuous (transfers).

Admissions Contact Ms. Maryllis Wolfgang, Director of Admissions, Georgia College & State University, CPO Box 023, Milledgeville, GA 31061. *Phone:* 478-445-2774. *Toll-free phone:* 800-342-0471. *Fax:* 478-445-1914. *E-mail:* info@gcsu.edu.

GEORGIA INSTITUTE OF TECHNOLOGY
Atlanta, Georgia

- **State-supported** university, founded 1885, part of University System of Georgia
- **Calendar** semesters
- **Degrees** bachelor's, master's, and doctoral
- **Urban** 400-acre campus
- **Endowment** $1.0 billion
- **Coed,** 11,257 undergraduate students, 92% full-time, 28% women, 72% men
- **Very difficult** entrance level, 63% of applicants were admitted

Undergraduates 10,367 full-time, 890 part-time. Students come from 52 states and territories, 90 other countries, 35% are from out of state, 7% African American, 15% Asian American or Pacific Islander, 3% Hispanic American, 0.2% Native American, 5% international, 4% transferred in, 50% live on campus. *Retention:* 90% of 2002 full-time freshmen returned.

Freshmen *Admission:* 8,573 applied, 5,386 admitted, 2,235 enrolled. *Average high school GPA:* 3.74. *Test scores:* SAT verbal scores over 500: 99%; SAT math scores over 500: 100%; SAT verbal scores over 600: 77%; SAT math scores over 600: 95%; SAT verbal scores over 700: 23%; SAT math scores over 700: 50%.

Faculty *Total:* 818, 99% full-time, 95% with terminal degrees. *Student/faculty ratio:* 13:1.

Majors Aerospace, aeronautical and astronautical engineering; applied mathematics related; architecture; architecture related; atmospheric sciences and meteorology; biology/biological sciences; biomedical/medical engineering; business administration and management; business/managerial economics; chemical engineering; chemistry; chemistry related; civil engineering; computer and information sciences; computer engineering; electrical, electronics and communications engineering; geological and earth sciences/geosciences related; history and philosophy of science and technology; industrial and organizational psychology; industrial design; industrial engineering; international economics; international relations and affairs; management science; materials engineering; mathematics; mechanical engineering; metallurgical engineering; modern languages; multi-/interdisciplinary studies related; nuclear engineering; operations management; physics; polymer chemistry; public policy analysis; science, technology and society; textile sciences and engineering.

Academic Programs *Special study options:* academic remediation for entering students, accelerated degree program, advanced placement credit, cooperative education, distance learning, double majors, English as a second language, honors programs, independent study, internships, off-campus study, part-time degree program, services for LD students, student-designed majors, study abroad, summer session for credit. *ROTC:* Army (b), Navy (b), Air Force (b).

Library Library and Information Center with 2.3 million titles, 21,248 serial subscriptions, 84,941 audiovisual materials, an OPAC, a Web page.

Computers on Campus 180 computers available on campus for general student use. A campuswide network can be accessed from student residence rooms and from off campus. Internet access, online (class) registration, at least one staffed computer lab available.

Student Life *Housing:* on-campus residence required for freshman year. *Options:* coed, men-only, women-only, disabled students. Campus housing is university owned. Freshman campus housing is guaranteed. *Activities and organizations:* drama/theater group, student-run newspaper, radio station, choral group, marching band, Christian Campus Fellowship, IEEE, Mechanical Engineering Graduate Student Association, Gamma Beta Phi Society, national fraternities, national sororities. *Campus security:* 24-hour emergency response devices and patrols, student patrols, late-night transport/escort service, controlled dormitory access, self defense education, lighted pathways and walks, video cameras. *Student services:* health clinic, personal/psychological counseling, women's center, legal services.

Athletics Member NCAA. All Division I except football (Division I-A). *Intercollegiate sports:* baseball M(s), basketball M(s)/W(s), cross-country running M(s)/W(s), equestrian sports M(c)/W(c), golf M(s), ice hockey M(c), lacrosse M(c)/W(c), rugby M(c), softball W(s), swimming M(s)/W(s), tennis M(s)/W(s), track and field M(s)/W(s), volleyball W(s), wrestling M(c). *Intramural sports:* badminton M/W, baseball M(c), basketball M/W, bowling M(c)/W(c), crew M(c)/W(c), equestrian sports M/W, fencing M(c)/W(c), football M, golf M(c)/W(c), gymnastics M(c)/W(c), ice hockey M(c)/W(c), lacrosse M(c)/W(c), racquetball M(c)/W(c), sailing M(c)/W(c), skiing (cross-country) M(c)/W(c), skiing (downhill) M(c)/W(c), soccer M(c)/W(c), softball W, squash M/W, swimming M/W, table tennis M(c)/W(c), tennis M(c)/W(c), track and field M/W, ultimate Frisbee M/W, volleyball M(c)/W(c), water polo M(c)/W(c), weight lifting M(c)/W(c).

Standardized Tests *Required:* SAT I or ACT (for admission). *Required for some:* SAT II: Subject Tests (for admission). *Recommended:* SAT I (for admission).

Costs (2003–04) *Tuition:* state resident $3208 full-time; nonresident $15,134 full-time. Part-time tuition and fees vary according to course load. *Required fees:* $868 full-time. *Room and board:* $6264; room only: $3624. Room and board charges vary according to board plan and housing facility.

Financial Aid Of all full-time matriculated undergraduates who enrolled in 2003, 5,988 applied for aid, 3,432 were judged to have need, 1,464 had their need fully met. 250 Federal Work-Study jobs (averaging $2310). In 2003, 798 non-need-based awards were made. *Average percent of need met:* 64%. *Average financial aid package:* $7444. *Average need-based loan:* $3679. *Average need-based gift aid:* $3499. *Average non-need-based aid:* $3201. *Average indebtedness upon graduation:* $16,972.

Applying *Options:* electronic application, early admission. *Application fee:* $50. *Required:* essay or personal statement, high school transcript. *Application deadlines:* 1/15 (freshmen), 5/1 (transfers). *Notification:* 3/15 (freshmen), continuous (transfers).

Admissions Contact Ms. Ingrid Hayes, Director of Admissions (Undergraduate), Georgia Institute of Technology, 225 North Avenue, NW, Atlanta, GA 30332-0320. *Phone:* 404-894-4154. *Fax:* 404-894-9511. *E-mail:* admission@gatech.edu.

GEORGIA SOUTHERN UNIVERSITY
Statesboro, Georgia

- **State-supported** comprehensive, founded 1906, part of University System of Georgia
- **Calendar** semesters
- **Degrees** bachelor's, master's, doctoral, and post-master's certificates
- **Small-town** 634-acre campus
- **Endowment** $18.9 million
- **Coed,** 13,696 undergraduate students, 89% full-time, 50% women, 50% men
- **Moderately difficult** entrance level, 54% of applicants were admitted

Undergraduates 12,247 full-time, 1,449 part-time. Students come from 46 states and territories, 67 other countries, 4% are from out of state, 25% African American, 1% Asian American or Pacific Islander, 1% Hispanic American, 0.2% Native American, 1% international, 6% transferred in, 25% live on campus. *Retention:* 76% of 2002 full-time freshmen returned.

Freshmen *Admission:* 7,921 applied, 4,277 admitted, 2,764 enrolled. *Average high school GPA:* 3.07. *Test scores:* SAT verbal scores over 500: 66%; SAT math scores over 500: 65%; ACT scores over 18: 92%; SAT verbal scores over 600: 14%; SAT math scores over 600: 16%; ACT scores over 24: 21%; SAT verbal scores over 700: 1%; SAT math scores over 700: 1%; ACT scores over 30: 1%.

Faculty *Total:* 702, 89% full-time, 74% with terminal degrees. *Student/faculty ratio:* 19:1.

Majors Accounting; anthropology; apparel and textiles; art; art teacher education; athletic training; biology/biological sciences; biology teacher education; business administration and management; business/managerial economics; business teacher education; chemistry; chemistry teacher education; civil engineering technology; clinical laboratory science/medical technology; communication/speech communication and rhetoric; computer and information sciences; construction engineering technology; criminal justice/safety; development economics and international development; dramatic/theatre arts; economics; education; electrical, electronic and communications engineering technology; English; English/language arts teacher education; family and consumer sciences/home economics teacher education; finance; foods, nutrition, and wellness; French; French language teacher education; general studies; geography; geology/earth science; German; German language teacher education; graphic and printing equipment operation/production; health and physical education; history; history teacher education; hotel/motel administration; human development and family studies; industrial production technologies related; industrial technology; interior design; international business/trade/commerce; international relations and affairs; journalism; kindergarten/preschool education; kinesiology and exercise science; logistics and materials management; management information systems; marketing/marketing management; mathematics; mathematics teacher education; mechanical engineering/mechanical technology; middle school education; music; music performance; music teacher education; music theory and composition; nursing (registered nurse training); parks, recreation and leisure; philosophy; physical education teaching and coaching; physics; physics teacher education; political science and government; psychology; public health education and promotion; public relations/image management; radio and television; sociology; Spanish; Spanish language teacher education; special education; speech and rhetoric; sport and fitness administration; technology/industrial arts teacher education.

Academic Programs *Special study options:* academic remediation for entering students, accelerated degree program, adult/continuing education programs, advanced placement credit, cooperative education, distance learning, double majors, English as a second language, honors programs, independent study, internships, off-campus study, part-time degree program, services for LD stu-

Georgia Southern University (continued)
dents, study abroad, summer session for credit. *ROTC:* Army (b). *Unusual degree programs:* 3-2 physics with Georgia Institute of Technology.

Library Henderson Library with 532,722 titles, 3,470 serial subscriptions, 29,552 audiovisual materials, an OPAC, a Web page.

Computers on Campus 1425 computers available on campus for general student use. A campuswide network can be accessed from student residence rooms and from off campus. Internet access, online (class) registration, at least one staffed computer lab available.

Student Life *Housing options:* coed, men-only, women-only, disabled students. Campus housing is university owned. *Activities and organizations:* drama/theater group, student-run newspaper, radio station, choral group, marching band, Panhellenic and Interfraternity Council, Residence Hall Association, Campus Religious Ministries, Multicultural Student Center, Eagle Entertainment, national fraternities, national sororities. *Campus security:* 24-hour emergency response devices and patrols, student patrols, late-night transport/escort service, residence hall security, locked residence hall entrances. *Student services:* health clinic, personal/psychological counseling.

Athletics Member NCAA. All Division I except football (Division I-AA). *Intercollegiate sports:* baseball M(s), basketball M(s)/W(s), bowling M(c)/W(c), cheerleading M/W, cross-country running W(s), equestrian sports M(c)/W(c), fencing M(c)/W(c), golf M(s), lacrosse M(c), rugby M(c)/W(c), soccer M(s)/W(s), softball W(s), swimming W(s), tennis M(s)/W(s), track and field W(s), ultimate Frisbee M(c)/W(c), volleyball W(s), wrestling M(c)/W(c). *Intramural sports:* baseball M(c), basketball M/W, bowling M/W, football M/W, golf M/W, soccer M/W, softball M/W, tennis M/W, track and field M(c)/W(c), volleyball M/W.

Standardized Tests *Required:* SAT I or ACT (for admission). *Required for some:* SAT II: Writing Test (for admission).

Costs (2003–04) *Tuition:* state resident $2212 full-time, $93 per semester hour part-time; nonresident $8848 full-time, $369 per semester hour part-time. Full-time tuition and fees vary according to location. Part-time tuition and fees vary according to course load and location. *Required fees:* $700 full-time, $350 per term part-time. *Room and board:* $5628; room only: $3428. Room and board charges vary according to board plan and housing facility. *Waivers:* senior citizens and employees or children of employees.

Financial Aid Of all full-time matriculated undergraduates who enrolled in 2002, 10,287 applied for aid, 5,783 were judged to have need, 1,281 had their need fully met. 349 Federal Work-Study jobs (averaging $1336). In 2002, 350 non-need-based awards were made. *Average percent of need met:* 74%. *Average financial aid package:* $6469. *Average need-based loan:* $3655. *Average need-based gift aid:* $4085. *Average non-need-based aid:* $1283. *Average indebtedness upon graduation:* $17,557.

Applying *Options:* common application, electronic application, early admission, deferred entrance. *Application fee:* $20. *Required:* high school transcript, minimum 2.0 GPA, proof of immunization. *Application deadlines:* 8/1 (freshmen), 7/1 (transfers). *Notification:* continuous (freshmen), continuous (transfers).

Admissions Contact Dr. Teresa Thompson, Associate Vice President of Admissions, Georgia Southern University, GSU PO Box 8024, Building #805, Forest Drive, Statesboro, GA 30460. *Phone:* 912-681-5391. *Fax:* 912-486-7240. *E-mail:* admissions@georgiasouthern.edu.

GEORGIA SOUTHWESTERN STATE UNIVERSITY
Americus, Georgia

- **State-supported** comprehensive, founded 1906, part of University System of Georgia
- **Calendar** semesters
- **Degrees** associate, bachelor's, master's, and post-master's certificates
- **Small-town** 255-acre campus
- **Endowment** $24.4 million
- **Coed,** 2,094 undergraduate students, 72% full-time, 66% women, 34% men
- **Moderately difficult** entrance level, 74% of applicants were admitted

Undergraduates 1,510 full-time, 584 part-time. Students come from 15 states and territories, 37 other countries, 2% are from out of state, 31% African American, 0.5% Asian American or Pacific Islander, 0.8% Hispanic American, 0.5% Native American, 4% international, 12% transferred in, 38% live on campus. *Retention:* 66% of 2002 full-time freshmen returned.

Freshmen *Admission:* 1,128 applied, 833 admitted, 386 enrolled. *Average high school GPA:* 3.20. *Test scores:* SAT verbal scores over 500: 47%; SAT math scores over 500: 39%; ACT scores over 18: 81%; SAT verbal scores over 600: 8%; SAT math scores over 600: 7%; ACT scores over 24: 11%; SAT verbal scores over 700: 1%.

Faculty *Total:* 141, 77% full-time, 64% with terminal degrees. *Student/faculty ratio:* 16:1.

Majors Accounting; accounting technology and bookkeeping; administrative assistant and secretarial science; aircraft powerplant technology; airframe mechanics and aircraft maintenance technology; applied horticulture; art; autobody/collision and repair technology; automobile/automotive mechanics technology; avionics maintenance technology; biology/biological sciences; business administration and management; chemistry; clinical laboratory science/medical technology; computer and information sciences; computer engineering technology; computer programming (specific applications); computer science; criminal justice/safety; diesel mechanics technology; drafting and design technology; dramatic/theatre arts; education; electrical/electronics equipment installation and repair; electrician; electromechanical and instrumentation and maintenance technologies related; elementary education; English; geology/earth science; heating, air conditioning, ventilation and refrigeration maintenance technology; heavy equipment maintenance technology; history; human resources management; machine shop technology; machine tool technology; management information systems; marketing/marketing management; mathematics; medical/clinical assistant; middle school education; music; nursing (licensed practical/vocational nurse training); nursing (registered nurse training); office management; office occupations and clerical services; parks, recreation and leisure facilities management; physical education teaching and coaching; physical sciences; political science and government; pre-dentistry studies; pre-medical studies; pre-veterinary studies; psychology; social sciences; sociology; special education; welding technology.

Academic Programs *Special study options:* academic remediation for entering students, adult/continuing education programs, advanced placement credit, cooperative education, distance learning, double majors, English as a second language, freshman honors college, honors programs, internships, off-campus study, part-time degree program, services for LD students, study abroad, summer session for credit. *Unusual degree programs:* 3-2 business administration with Georgia Institute of Technology; engineering with Georgia Institute of Technology; math, physics with Georgia Institute of Technology.

Library James Earl Carter Library with 190,000 titles, 59 serial subscriptions, 1,849 audiovisual materials, an OPAC, a Web page.

Computers on Campus 336 computers available on campus for general student use. A campuswide network can be accessed from off campus. Internet access, online (class) registration, at least one staffed computer lab available.

Student Life *Housing:* on-campus residence required through sophomore year. *Options:* coed, men-only, women-only. Campus housing is university owned. Freshman campus housing is guaranteed. *Activities and organizations:* drama/theater group, student-run newspaper, television station, choral group, Greek organizations, religious clubs and organizations, SABU (Black Student Organization), biology club, Gamma Beta Phi, national fraternities, national sororities. *Campus security:* 24-hour emergency response devices and patrols, late-night transport/escort service, controlled dormitory access. *Student services:* health clinic, personal/psychological counseling, women's center.

Athletics Member NAIA. *Intercollegiate sports:* baseball M(s), basketball M(s)/W(s), softball W(s), tennis M(s)/W(s), volleyball W(s). *Intramural sports:* baseball M/W, basketball M/W, football M/W, golf M/W, soccer M, softball M/W, swimming M/W, tennis M/W, track and field M/W, volleyball M/W.

Standardized Tests *Required:* SAT I or ACT (for admission).

Costs (2003–04) *Tuition:* state resident $2212 full-time, $93 per semester hour part-time; nonresident $8848 full-time, $369 per semester hour part-time. Part-time tuition and fees vary according to course load. *Required fees:* $570 full-time, $293 per term part-time. *Room and board:* $4204; room only: $2160. Room and board charges vary according to board plan and housing facility. *Waivers:* senior citizens.

Financial Aid Of all full-time matriculated undergraduates who enrolled in 2002, 1,110 applied for aid, 915 were judged to have need, 62 had their need fully met. 96 Federal Work-Study jobs (averaging $1470). In 2002, 271 non-need-based awards were made. *Average percent of need met:* 58%. *Average financial aid package:* $6002. *Average need-based loan:* $3111. *Average need-based gift aid:* $3029. *Average non-need-based aid:* $3091.

Applying *Options:* common application, electronic application, early admission, early decision. *Application fee:* $20. *Required:* high school transcript, minimum 2.0 GPA, proof of immunization. *Recommended:* interview. *Application deadline:* rolling (freshmen), rolling (transfers). *Early decision:* 12/15. *Notification:* continuous until 8/1 (freshmen), 1/15 (early decision), continuous until 8/1 (transfers).

Admissions Contact Mrs. Gaye S. Hayes, Interim Director of Admissions, Georgia Southwestern State University, 800 Wheatley Street. *Phone:* 229-928-1273. *Toll-free phone:* 800-338-0082. *Fax:* 229-931-2983. *E-mail:* gswapps@canes.gsw.edu.

GEORGIA STATE UNIVERSITY
Atlanta, Georgia

- **State-supported** university, founded 1913, part of University System of Georgia
- **Calendar** semesters
- **Degrees** certificates, bachelor's, master's, doctoral, first professional, post-master's, postbachelor's, and first professional certificates
- **Urban** 44-acre campus
- **Endowment** $50.1 million
- **Coed,** 20,177 undergraduate students, 67% full-time, 61% women, 39% men
- **Moderately difficult** entrance level, 56% of applicants were admitted

Undergraduates 13,511 full-time, 6,666 part-time. Students come from 49 states and territories, 149 other countries, 3% are from out of state, 35% African American, 10% Asian American or Pacific Islander, 3% Hispanic American, 0.3% Native American, 3% international, 11% transferred in, 10% live on campus. *Retention:* 81% of 2002 full-time freshmen returned.

Freshmen *Admission:* 8,177 applied, 4,563 admitted, 2,008 enrolled. *Average high school GPA:* 3.34. *Test scores:* SAT verbal scores over 500: 75%; SAT math scores over 500: 75%; ACT scores over 18: 92%; SAT verbal scores over 600: 26%; SAT math scores over 600: 27%; ACT scores over 24: 33%; SAT verbal scores over 700: 3%; SAT math scores over 700: 4%; ACT scores over 30: 1%.

Faculty *Total:* 1,363, 73% full-time. *Student/faculty ratio:* 18:1.

Majors Accounting; actuarial science; African-American/Black studies; anthropology; art; art teacher education; biology/biological sciences; business administration and management; business/managerial economics; chemistry; classics and languages, literatures and linguistics; computer and information sciences; criminal justice/safety; dramatic/theatre arts; early childhood education; economics; elementary education; English; film/cinema studies; finance; fine/studio arts; foods, nutrition, and wellness; French; geography; geology/earth science; German; history; human resources development; insurance; journalism; marketing/marketing management; mathematics; middle school education; multi-/interdisciplinary studies related; music management and merchandising; music performance; nursing (registered nurse training); parks, recreation and leisure facilities management; philosophy; physical education teaching and coaching; physics; political science and government; psychology; real estate; religious studies; respiratory care therapy; social work; sociology; Spanish; speech and rhetoric; urban studies/affairs; women's studies.

Academic Programs *Special study options:* academic remediation for entering students, accelerated degree program, adult/continuing education programs, cooperative education, distance learning, double majors, English as a second language, honors programs, independent study, internships, off-campus study, part-time degree program, services for LD students, student-designed majors, study abroad, summer session for credit.

Library Pullen Library plus 1 other with 1.3 million titles, 8,929 serial subscriptions, 18,396 audiovisual materials, an OPAC, a Web page.

Computers on Campus 500 computers available on campus for general student use. A campuswide network can be accessed from student residence rooms and from off campus. At least one staffed computer lab available.

Student Life *Housing options:* coed. Campus housing is leased by the school. Freshman applicants given priority for college housing. *Activities and organizations:* drama/theater group, student-run newspaper, radio and television station, choral group, Spotlight Programs Board, Sports Club Council, Student Government Association, Cinefest Movie Theatre, WRAS (radio station), national fraternities, national sororities. *Campus security:* 24-hour emergency response devices and patrols, late-night transport/escort service, controlled dormitory access. *Student services:* health clinic, personal/psychological counseling, legal services.

Athletics Member NCAA. All Division I. *Intercollegiate sports:* badminton M/W, baseball M(s), basketball M(s)/W(s), bowling M/W, crew M/W, cross-country running M(s)/W(s), fencing M/W, golf M(s)/W(s), ice hockey M, sailing M/W, soccer M(s)/W(s), softball W(s), swimming W, table tennis M/W, tennis M(s)/W(s), track and field M(s)/W(s), volleyball W(s). *Intramural sports:* archery M/W, badminton M/W, basketball M/W, bowling M/W, crew M(c)/W(c), cross-country running M/W, equestrian sports M/W, fencing M(c)/W(c), field hockey M/W, football M/W, racquetball M/W, rock climbing M/W, sailing M(c)/W(c), skiing (cross-country) M/W, skiing (downhill) M/W, soccer M/W(c), softball M/W, swimming M/W, table tennis M/W, tennis M/W, track and field M/W, volleyball M/W, weight lifting M/W, wrestling M/W.

Standardized Tests *Required:* SAT I or ACT (for admission). *Required for some:* SAT II: Subject Tests (for admission).

Costs (2004–05) *Tuition:* state resident $3529 full-time; nonresident $14,115 full-time. Full-time tuition and fees vary according to course load, degree level, and program. Part-time tuition and fees vary according to course load, degree level, and program. *Required fees:* $783 full-time. *Room and board:* $7118; room only: $5130. Room and board charges vary according to housing facility. *Waivers:* employees or children of employees.

Financial Aid Of all full-time matriculated undergraduates who enrolled in 2002, 11,504 applied for aid, 6,661 were judged to have need, 2,907 had their need fully met. 344 Federal Work-Study jobs (averaging $2160). In 2002, 1819 non-need-based awards were made. *Average percent of need met:* 20%. *Average financial aid package:* $6062. *Average need-based loan:* $3585. *Average need-based gift aid:* $4757. *Average non-need-based aid:* $3722. *Average indebtedness upon graduation:* $11,723.

Applying *Options:* deferred entrance. *Application fee:* $50. *Required:* high school transcript. *Required for some:* interview. *Recommended:* essay or personal statement. *Application deadlines:* 3/1 (freshmen), 6/1 (transfers). *Notification:* continuous (transfers).

Admissions Contact Ms. Diane Weber, Dean of Admissions and Acting Dean for Enrollment Services, Georgia State University, PO Box 4009, Atlanta, GA 30302-4009. *Phone:* 404-651-2365. *Fax:* 404-651-4811.

HERZING COLLEGE
Atlanta, Georgia

Admissions Contact Stacy Johnston, Director of Admissions, Herzing College, 3355 Lenox Road, Suite 100, Atlanta, GA 30326. *Phone:* 404-816-4533. *Toll-free phone:* 800-573-4533. *Fax:* 404-816-5576. *E-mail:* leec@atl.herzing.edu.

ITT TECHNICAL INSTITUTE
Duluth, Georgia

- **Proprietary** primarily 2-year, founded 2003, part of ITT Educational Services, Inc.
- **Calendar** quarters
- **Degrees** associate and bachelor's
- **Coed**
- **Minimally difficult** entrance level

Standardized Tests *Required:* (for admission).

Costs (2003–04) *Tuition:* $347 per credit hour part-time.

Applying *Options:* deferred entrance. *Application fee:* $100. *Required:* high school transcript, interview. *Recommended:* letters of recommendation.

Admissions Contact Mr. Chip Hinton, Director of Recruitment, ITT Technical Institute, 10700 Abbotts Bridge Road, Suite 190, Duluth, GA 30097. *Phone:* 678-957-8510.

KENNESAW STATE UNIVERSITY
Kennesaw, Georgia

- **State-supported** comprehensive, founded 1963, part of University System of Georgia
- **Calendar** semesters
- **Degrees** bachelor's and master's
- **Suburban** 185-acre campus with easy access to Atlanta
- **Coed,** 15,581 undergraduate students, 64% full-time, 62% women, 38% men
- **Moderately difficult** entrance level, 70% of applicants were admitted

Undergraduates 10,045 full-time, 5,536 part-time. Students come from 37 states and territories, 129 other countries, 4% are from out of state, 10% African American, 3% Asian American or Pacific Islander, 3% Hispanic American, 0.3% Native American, 3% international, 10% transferred in. *Retention:* 73% of 2002 full-time freshmen returned.

Freshmen *Admission:* 5,738 applied, 4,035 admitted, 2,345 enrolled. *Average high school GPA:* 3.05. *Test scores:* SAT verbal scores over 500: 65%; SAT math scores over 500: 60%; ACT scores over 18: 95%; SAT verbal scores over 600: 17%; SAT math scores over 600: 14%; ACT scores over 24: 22%; SAT verbal scores over 700: 1%; SAT math scores over 700: 1%; ACT scores over 30: 2%.

Faculty *Total:* 805, 58% full-time, 52% with terminal degrees. *Student/faculty ratio:* 22:1.

Majors Accounting; art; art teacher education; biochemistry; biology/biological sciences; biology teacher education; biotechnology research; business administration and management; business/managerial economics; cartography; chemistry; chemistry teacher education; communication/speech communication and rhetoric; computer and information sciences; computer science; criminal justice/safety; dramatic/theatre arts; early childhood education; economics; elementary education; English; English/language arts teacher education; finance; fine/studio arts; French; French language teacher education; history; information science/studies; international relations and affairs; kinesiology and exercise science;

Kennesaw State University (continued)
marketing/marketing management; mathematics; mathematics teacher education; middle school education; music; music teacher education; nursing (registered nurse training); operations management; physical education teaching and coaching; political science and government; psychology; social science teacher education; social work; sociology; Spanish; Spanish language teacher education; sport and fitness administration; voice and opera.

Academic Programs *Special study options:* academic remediation for entering students, adult/continuing education programs, advanced placement credit, cooperative education, freshman honors college, honors programs, internships, off-campus study, part-time degree program, services for LD students, study abroad, summer session for credit. *ROTC:* Army (b), Air Force (b).

Library Horace W. Sturgis Library with 608,342 titles, 4,580 serial subscriptions, 10,500 audiovisual materials, an OPAC, a Web page.

Computers on Campus 542 computers available on campus for general student use. A campuswide network can be accessed from off campus. Internet access, online (class) registration, at least one staffed computer lab available.

Student Life *Housing options:* Campus housing is provided by a third party. Freshman applicants given priority for college housing. *Activities and organizations:* drama/theater group, student-run newspaper, choral group, Golden Key National Honor Society, Student Government Association, Campus Activities Board, African-American Student Alliance, International Student Association, national fraternities, national sororities. *Campus security:* 24-hour emergency response devices and patrols, student patrols, late-night transport/escort service. *Student services:* health clinic, personal/psychological counseling.

Athletics Member NCAA. All Division II. *Intercollegiate sports:* baseball M(s), basketball M(s)/W(s), cheerleading W, cross-country running M(s)/W(s), golf M(s), softball W(s), tennis W(s). *Intramural sports:* basketball M/W, bowling M/W, football M/W, soccer M/W, softball M/W, swimming M/W, tennis M/W, volleyball M/W, weight lifting M/W.

Standardized Tests *Required:* SAT I or ACT (for admission). *Required for some:* SAT II: Subject Tests (for admission).

Costs (2003–04) *Tuition:* state resident $2778 full-time, $93 per credit hour part-time; nonresident $9414 full-time, $369 per credit hour part-time. *Required fees:* $566 full-time, $213 per term part-time. *Room only:* $3897. Room and board charges vary according to housing facility. *Payment plan:* deferred payment.

Financial Aid Of all full-time matriculated undergraduates who enrolled in 2003, 7,715 applied for aid, 3,577 were judged to have need, 653 had their need fully met. In 2003, 654 non-need-based awards were made. *Average percent of need met:* 20%. *Average financial aid package:* $3907. *Average need-based loan:* $1625. *Average need-based gift aid:* $1324. *Average non-need-based aid:* $770. *Average indebtedness upon graduation:* $14,331.

Applying *Options:* electronic application, deferred entrance. *Application fee:* $40. *Required:* high school transcript, minimum 2.5 GPA, proof of immunization. *Application deadlines:* 5/30 (freshmen), 7/18 (transfers). *Notification:* continuous (freshmen), continuous (transfers).

Admissions Contact Mr. Joe F. Head, Director of Admissions and Dean of Enrollment Services, Kennesaw State University, 1000 Chastain Road, Campus Box 0115, Kennesaw, GA 30144. *Phone:* 770-423-6300. *Fax:* 770-423-6541. *E-mail:* ksuadmit@kennesaw.edu.

LAGRANGE COLLEGE
LaGrange, Georgia

- **Independent United Methodist** comprehensive, founded 1831
- **Calendar** quarters
- **Degrees** associate, bachelor's, and master's
- **Small-town** 120-acre campus with easy access to Atlanta
- **Endowment** $64.4 million
- **Coed,** 971 undergraduate students, 88% full-time, 62% women, 38% men
- **Moderately difficult** entrance level, 90% of applicants were admitted

Undergraduates 850 full-time, 121 part-time. Students come from 17 states and territories, 24 other countries, 12% are from out of state, 15% African American, 0.9% Asian American or Pacific Islander, 1% Hispanic American, 0.5% Native American, 7% transferred in, 52% live on campus. *Retention:* 76% of 2002 full-time freshmen returned.

Freshmen *Admission:* 563 applied, 506 admitted, 195 enrolled. *Average high school GPA:* 3.12. *Test scores:* SAT verbal scores over 500: 62%; SAT math scores over 500: 54%; ACT scores over 18: 84%; SAT verbal scores over 600: 20%; SAT math scores over 600: 16%; ACT scores over 24: 31%; SAT verbal scores over 700: 1%.

Faculty *Total:* 103, 64% full-time, 65% with terminal degrees. *Student/faculty ratio:* 11:1.

Majors Accounting; biochemistry; biology/biological sciences; business administration and management; business/commerce; business/managerial economics; chemistry; computer and information sciences; computer science; dramatic/theatre arts; early childhood education; economics; education; elementary education; English; history; human services; liberal arts and sciences/liberal studies; mathematics; middle school education; music; nursing (registered nurse training); organizational behavior; political science and government; pre-dentistry studies; pre-engineering; pre-law studies; pre-medical studies; pre-veterinary studies; psychology; religious education; religious studies; social work; Spanish; visual and performing arts.

Academic Programs *Special study options:* adult/continuing education programs, advanced placement credit, double majors, independent study, internships, part-time degree program, study abroad, summer session for credit. *Unusual degree programs:* 3-2 engineering with Georgia Institute of Technology, Auburn University.

Library William and Evelyn Banks Library with 108,389 titles, 512 serial subscriptions, 3,451 audiovisual materials, an OPAC, a Web page.

Computers on Campus 175 computers available on campus for general student use. A campuswide network can be accessed from student residence rooms and from off campus. Internet access, online (class) registration, at least one staffed computer lab available.

Student Life *Housing:* on-campus residence required through senior year. *Options:* coed, men-only, women-only. Campus housing is university owned. Freshman campus housing is guaranteed. *Activities and organizations:* drama/theater group, student-run newspaper, choral group, Student Government Association, Greek system, drama/theater groups, Habitat for Humanity, BSU/Wesley Fellowship, national fraternities, national sororities. *Campus security:* 24-hour patrols, controlled dormitory access. *Student services:* health clinic, personal/psychological counseling.

Athletics Member NCAA. All Division III. *Intercollegiate sports:* baseball M, basketball M/W, cross-country running M/W, golf M, soccer M/W, softball W, swimming M/W, tennis M/W, volleyball W. *Intramural sports:* badminton M/W, basketball M/W, football M, soccer M/W, softball M/W, swimming M/W, tennis M/W, volleyball M/W.

Standardized Tests *Required:* SAT I or ACT (for admission).

Costs (2003–04) *Comprehensive fee:* $20,500 includes full-time tuition ($14,482) and room and board ($6018). Full-time tuition and fees vary according to location. Part-time tuition: $597 per hour. Part-time tuition and fees vary according to location. *Payment plan:* installment. *Waivers:* employees or children of employees.

Financial Aid Of all full-time matriculated undergraduates who enrolled in 2002, 787 applied for aid, 546 were judged to have need, 125 had their need fully met. 99 Federal Work-Study jobs (averaging $856). 282 state and other part-time jobs (averaging $935). *Average percent of need met:* 75%. *Average financial aid package:* $11,309. *Average need-based loan:* $3378. *Average need-based gift aid:* $8888. *Average non-need-based aid:* $3658. *Average indebtedness upon graduation:* $18,600. *Financial aid deadline:* 3/1.

Applying *Options:* common application, electronic application, early admission, deferred entrance. *Application fee:* $20. *Required:* essay or personal statement, high school transcript, minimum 2.0 GPA. *Required for some:* 1 letter of recommendation, interview. *Application deadlines:* 8/30 (freshmen), 8/15 (transfers). *Notification:* continuous (freshmen), continuous (transfers).

Admissions Contact Mr. Andy Geeter, Director of Admission, LaGrange College, 601 Broad Street, LaGrange, GA 30240-2999. *Phone:* 706-880-8253. *Toll-free phone:* 800-593-2885. *Fax:* 706-880-8010. *E-mail:* lgcadmis@langrange.edu.

■ *See page 1834 for a narrative description.*

LIFE UNIVERSITY
Marietta, Georgia

- **Independent** comprehensive, founded 1974
- **Calendar** quarters
- **Degrees** associate, bachelor's, master's, and first professional
- **Suburban** 96-acre campus
- **Endowment** $29.0 million
- **Coed,** 410 undergraduate students, 80% full-time, 53% women, 47% men
- **Noncompetitive** entrance level, 48% of applicants were admitted

Undergraduates 330 full-time, 80 part-time. Students come from 19 states and territories, 42 other countries, 60% are from out of state, 17% African American, 2% Asian American or Pacific Islander, 2% Hispanic American, 0.5% Native American, 9% international.

Freshmen *Admission:* 246 applied, 118 admitted, 33 enrolled. *Average high school GPA:* 2.60. *Test scores:* SAT verbal scores over 500: 29%; SAT math scores over 500: 18%; ACT scores over 18: 33%; SAT math scores over 600: 6%; SAT math scores over 700: 6%.

Faculty *Total:* 30, 63% full-time, 80% with terminal degrees. *Student/faculty ratio:* 15:1.
Majors Biology/biological sciences; business administration and management; computer management.
Academic Programs *Special study options:* academic remediation for entering students, accelerated degree program, advanced placement credit, cooperative education, double majors, English as a second language, independent study, internships, off-campus study, part-time degree program, services for LD students, summer session for credit.
Library Nell K. Williams Learning Resource Center with 53,619 titles, 3,000 serial subscriptions, 9,601 audiovisual materials, an OPAC, a Web page.
Computers on Campus 35 computers available on campus for general student use. A campuswide network can be accessed from student residence rooms and from off campus. Internet access, at least one staffed computer lab available.
Student Life *Housing options:* Campus housing is university owned.
Athletics *Intramural sports:* basketball M/W, football M, rugby M, softball M/W, volleyball M/W.
Standardized Tests *Required:* SAT I or ACT (for admission).
Costs (2003–04) *Tuition:* state resident $5040 full-time, $140 per hour part-time; nonresident $5040 full-time, $140 per hour part-time. *Required fees:* $104 per term part-time.
Financial Aid Of all full-time matriculated undergraduates who enrolled in 2003, 346 applied for aid, 333 were judged to have need, 67 had their need fully met. 114 Federal Work-Study jobs (averaging $1400). In 2003, 12 non-need-based awards were made. *Average percent of need met:* 22%. *Average financial aid package:* $7600. *Average need-based loan:* $5100. *Average need-based gift aid:* $3400. *Average non-need-based aid:* $3800. *Average indebtedness upon graduation:* $12,450.
Applying *Options:* common application. *Application fee:* $50. *Required:* high school transcript, minimum 2.0 GPA. *Notification:* continuous (freshmen), continuous (transfers).
Admissions Contact Dr. Gary Craft, Office of Admissions, Life University, 1269 Barclay Circle, Marietta, GA 30060. *Phone:* 770-426-2884. *Toll-free phone:* 800-543-3202. *E-mail:* admissions@life.edu.

LUTHER RICE BIBLE COLLEGE AND SEMINARY
Lithonia, Georgia

- **Independent Baptist** comprehensive, founded 1962
- **Calendar** semesters
- **Degrees** bachelor's, master's, and doctoral
- **Urban** 5-acre campus with easy access to Atlanta
- **Endowment** $121,000
- **Coed**
- **Noncompetitive** entrance level

Student Life *Campus security:* 24-hour emergency response devices, late-night transport/escort service.
Standardized Tests *Required:* Bible examination (for admission).
Costs (2003–04) *Tuition:* $3480 full-time, $435 per course part-time. *Required fees:* $100 full-time, $50 per term part-time.
Financial Aid Of all full-time matriculated undergraduates who enrolled in 2003, 5 applied for aid, 5 were judged to have need, 5 had their need fully met. 2 Federal Work-Study jobs. *Average percent of need met:* 100. *Average financial aid package:* $7220. *Average need-based loan:* $2895. *Average need-based gift aid:* $5345.
Applying *Options:* common application, electronic application, early admission. *Application fee:* $50. *Required:* high school transcript, letters of recommendation.
Admissions Contact Mr. Russ Sorrow, Director of Admissions and Records, Luther Rice Bible College and Seminary, 3038 Evans Mill Road, Lithonia, GA 30038-2454. *Phone:* 770-484-1204 Ext. 231. *Toll-free phone:* 800-442-1577. *E-mail:* lrs@lrs.edu.

MACON STATE COLLEGE
Macon, Georgia

- **State-supported** 4-year, founded 1968, part of University System of Georgia
- **Calendar** semesters
- **Degrees** certificates, associate, and bachelor's
- **Urban** 167-acre campus
- **Endowment** $8.0 million
- **Coed,** 5,400 undergraduate students, 40% full-time, 67% women, 33% men
- **Minimally difficult** entrance level

Undergraduates 2,173 full-time, 3,227 part-time. 36% African American, 2% Asian American or Pacific Islander, 2% Hispanic American, 0.2% Native American, 0.3% international. *Retention:* 60% of 2002 full-time freshmen returned.
Freshmen *Admission:* 1,147 admitted. *Average high school GPA:* 2.88.
Faculty *Total:* 262, 56% full-time, 34% with terminal degrees. *Student/faculty ratio:* 21:1.
Majors Accounting; administrative assistant and secretarial science; agriculture; art; biology/biological sciences; business administration and management; business/commerce; business teacher education; chemistry; civil engineering; clinical/medical laboratory technology; communication and media related; computer programming; computer programming (specific applications); computer science; corrections; criminal justice/law enforcement administration; criminal justice/police science; data processing and data processing technology; dramatic/theatre arts; economics; education; electrical, electronics and communications engineering; elementary education; engineering; engineering technology; English; environmental studies; food science; general studies; health/health care administration; health information/medical records administration; health information/medical records technology; health science; history; humanities; information science/studies; journalism; liberal arts and sciences/liberal studies; marketing related; mass communication/media; mathematics; mechanical engineering; modern languages; music; nursing (registered nurse training); physical education teaching and coaching; physical therapy; physics; political science and government; postal management; pre-engineering; pre-pharmacy studies; psychology; public administration; respiratory care therapy; sociology; speech and rhetoric.
Academic Programs *Special study options:* academic remediation for entering students, adult/continuing education programs, advanced placement credit, cooperative education, distance learning, honors programs, internships, part-time degree program, services for LD students, study abroad, summer session for credit.
Library Macon State College Library with 80,000 titles, 513 serial subscriptions, an OPAC, a Web page.
Computers on Campus 95 computers available on campus for general student use. A campuswide network can be accessed from off campus. At least one staffed computer lab available.
Student Life *Housing:* college housing not available. *Activities and organizations:* drama/theater group, student-run newspaper, choral group, student government, Macon College Association of Nursing Students, Macon State College Association for Respiratory Education (MSCARE), Phi Beta Lambda, Baptist Student Union. *Campus security:* 24-hour emergency response devices and patrols, late-night transport/escort service. *Student services:* personal/psychological counseling.
Athletics *Intramural sports:* basketball M(c)/W(c), football M(c)/W(c), golf M(c)/W(c), softball M(c)/W(c), tennis M(c)/W(c), volleyball M(c)/W(c).
Standardized Tests *Required:* SAT I or ACT (for admission). *Required for some:* SAT II: Subject Tests (for admission).
Costs (2003–04) *Tuition:* state resident $1606 full-time; nonresident $5592 full-time. Full-time tuition and fees vary according to course level, degree level, and student level. Part-time tuition and fees vary according to course level, course load, degree level, and student level. *Required fees:* $158 full-time. *Waivers:* senior citizens.
Financial Aid Of all full-time matriculated undergraduates who enrolled in 2003, 2,613 applied for aid, 1,698 were judged to have need. 110 Federal Work-Study jobs (averaging $1574). *Average percent of need met:* 60%. *Average financial aid package:* $6580. *Average need-based loan:* $3500. *Average need-based gift aid:* $3000. *Average indebtedness upon graduation:* $16,519.
Applying *Options:* common application, electronic application, early admission. *Application fee:* $20. *Required:* high school transcript, minimum 1.8 GPA. *Application deadline:* rolling (freshmen), rolling (transfers). *Notification:* continuous (freshmen), continuous (transfers).
Admissions Contact Mr. Wesley Rauls, Admissions Representative, Macon State College, Macon, GA 31206. *Phone:* 478-471-2800 Ext. 2056. *Toll-free phone:* 800-272-7619. *Fax:* 478-471-5343.

MEDICAL COLLEGE OF GEORGIA
Augusta, Georgia

- **State-supported** upper-level, founded 1828, part of University System of Georgia
- **Calendar** semesters
- **Degrees** certificates, bachelor's, master's, doctoral, first professional, and postbachelor's certificates
- **Urban** 100-acre campus
- **Coed,** 773 undergraduate students, 87% full-time, 87% women, 13% men
- **Moderately difficult** entrance level

Undergraduates 676 full-time, 97 part-time. Students come from 18 states and territories, 11% are from out of state, 14% African American, 3% Asian American

Medical College of Georgia (continued)
or Pacific Islander, 1% Hispanic American, 0.3% Native American, 0.4% international, 52% transferred in, 13% live on campus.

Faculty *Total:* 741, 84% full-time, 88% with terminal degrees.

Majors Clinical laboratory science/medical technology; dental hygiene; diagnostic medical sonography and ultrasound technology; health information/medical records administration; nuclear medical technology; nursing (registered nurse training); occupational therapy; physician assistant; radiologic technology/science; respiratory care therapy.

Academic Programs *Special study options:* distance learning, off-campus study, summer session for credit.

Library Robert B. Greenblatt MD Library with 164,154 titles, 2,458 serial subscriptions, 3,410 audiovisual materials, an OPAC, a Web page.

Computers on Campus 322 computers available on campus for general student use. A campuswide network can be accessed. At least one staffed computer lab available.

Student Life *Housing options:* coed. Campus housing is university owned. *Activities and organizations:* student-run newspaper, choral group, Student Government Association, Baptist Student Union, international club, Campus Outreach, Medical Student Auxiliary. *Campus security:* 24-hour emergency response devices and patrols, late-night transport/escort service. *Student services:* health clinic, personal/psychological counseling.

Athletics *Intramural sports:* basketball M/W, cheerleading M(c)/W(c), football M/W, golf M, racquetball M, soccer M/W, softball M/W, table tennis M/W, volleyball M/W.

Costs (2003–04) *Tuition:* state resident $3208 full-time, $134 per hour part-time; nonresident $12,832 full-time, $535 per hour part-time. Full-time tuition and fees vary according to location. Part-time tuition and fees vary according to course load and location. *Required fees:* $586 full-time, $293 per term part-time. *Room only:* $2835. Room and board charges vary according to housing facility.

Financial Aid Of all full-time matriculated undergraduates who enrolled in 2003, 447 applied for aid, 397 were judged to have need, 48 had their need fully met. 134 Federal Work-Study jobs (averaging $2142). In 2003, 138 non-need-based awards were made. *Average percent of need met:* 55%. *Average financial aid package:* $8830. *Average need-based loan:* $5992. *Average need-based gift aid:* $4415. *Average non-need-based aid:* $5888. *Average indebtedness upon graduation:* $14,802.

Admissions Contact Ms. Carol S. Nobles, Director of Student Recruitment and Admissions, Medical College of Georgia, AA-170 Administration-Kelly Building, Augusta, GA 30912. *Phone:* 706-721-2725. *Toll-free phone:* 800-519-3388. *Fax:* 706-721-7279. *E-mail:* underadm@mail.mcg.edu.

MERCER UNIVERSITY
Macon, Georgia

- **Independent Baptist** comprehensive, founded 1833
- **Calendar** semesters
- **Degrees** bachelor's, master's, doctoral, first professional, post-master's, postbachelor's, and first professional certificates
- **Suburban** 150-acre campus with easy access to Atlanta
- **Endowment** $156.0 million
- **Coed,** 4,580 undergraduate students, 84% full-time, 67% women, 33% men
- **Moderately difficult** entrance level, 79% of applicants were admitted

Undergraduates 3,826 full-time, 754 part-time. Students come from 30 states and territories, 35 other countries, 20% are from out of state, 28% African American, 3% Asian American or Pacific Islander, 1% Hispanic American, 0.2% Native American, 3% international, 2% transferred in, 61% live on campus. *Retention:* 79% of 2002 full-time freshmen returned.

Freshmen *Admission:* 3,034 applied, 2,403 admitted, 696 enrolled. *Average high school GPA:* 3.60. *Test scores:* SAT verbal scores over 500: 89%; SAT math scores over 500: 89%; ACT scores over 18: 98%; SAT verbal scores over 600: 42%; SAT math scores over 600: 50%; ACT scores over 24: 64%; SAT verbal scores over 700: 8%; SAT math scores over 700: 11%; ACT scores over 30: 16%.

Faculty *Total:* 547, 60% full-time, 65% with terminal degrees. *Student/faculty ratio:* 14:1.

Majors African-American/Black studies; art; biochemistry; biology/biological sciences; business administration, management and operations related; business/commerce; chemistry; Christian studies; classics and languages, literatures and linguistics; communication and journalism related; community organization and advocacy; computer science; criminal justice/safety; dramatic/theatre arts; economics; education related; elementary education; engineering; English; environmental science; environmental studies; French; German; health/medical preparatory programs related; history; human services; information science/studies; international relations and affairs; journalism; Latin; liberal arts and sciences/liberal studies; mass communication/media; mathematics; middle school education; multi-/interdisciplinary studies related; music; music performance; music related; music teacher education; nursing (registered nurse training); philosophy; physics; political science and government; pre-dentistry studies; pre-medical studies; psychology; regional studies; sociology; Spanish.

Academic Programs *Special study options:* accelerated degree program, adult/continuing education programs, advanced placement credit, cooperative education, double majors, English as a second language, honors programs, independent study, internships, off-campus study, part-time degree program, services for LD students, student-designed majors, study abroad, summer session for credit. *ROTC:* Army (b).

Library Jack Tarver Library plus 3 others with 391,800 titles, 5,729 serial subscriptions, 59,733 audiovisual materials, an OPAC, a Web page.

Computers on Campus 140 computers available on campus for general student use. A campuswide network can be accessed from student residence rooms and from off campus. Internet access, at least one staffed computer lab available.

Student Life *Housing:* on-campus residence required through sophomore year. *Options:* coed, men-only, women-only, disabled students. Campus housing is university owned. Freshman campus housing is guaranteed. *Activities and organizations:* drama/theater group, student-run newspaper, choral group, AGAPE, Baptist Student Union, Student Government Association, Reformed University Worship, Organization of Black Students, national fraternities, national sororities. *Campus security:* 24-hour emergency response devices and patrols, student patrols, late-night transport/escort service, controlled dormitory access, patrols by police officers. *Student services:* health clinic, personal/psychological counseling.

Athletics Member NCAA. All Division I. *Intercollegiate sports:* baseball M(s), basketball M(s)/W(s), cross-country running M(s)/W(s), golf M(s)/W(s), riflery M(s)/W(s), soccer M(s)/W(s), softball W(s), tennis M(s)/W(s), volleyball W(s). *Intramural sports:* basketball M/W, bowling M/W, football M/W, golf M/W, racquetball M/W, soccer M/W, softball M/W, tennis M/W, ultimate Frisbee M/W, volleyball M/W, water polo M/W.

Standardized Tests *Required:* SAT I or ACT (for admission).

Costs (2003–04) *Comprehensive fee:* $27,516 includes full-time tuition ($20,796) and room and board ($6720). Full-time tuition and fees vary according to class time, course load, and location. Part-time tuition: $693 per credit hour. Part-time tuition and fees vary according to class time, course load, and location. *College room only:* $3240. Room and board charges vary according to board plan, housing facility, and location. *Payment plan:* installment. *Waivers:* employees or children of employees.

Financial Aid Of all full-time matriculated undergraduates who enrolled in 2003, 1,860 applied for aid, 1,546 were judged to have need, 807 had their need fully met. 471 Federal Work-Study jobs (averaging $1856). In 2003, 428 non-need-based awards were made. *Average percent of need met:* 89%. *Average financial aid package:* $21,250. *Average need-based loan:* $6486. *Average need-based gift aid:* $12,688. *Average non-need-based aid:* $14,016. *Average indebtedness upon graduation:* $15,549.

Applying *Options:* common application, electronic application, early admission, early decision, deferred entrance. *Application fee:* $50. *Required:* high school transcript, minimum 3.0 GPA. *Required for some:* 2 letters of recommendation, interview. *Recommended:* interview, counselor's evaluation. *Application deadline:* 6/1 (freshmen), rolling (transfers). *Early decision:* 12/1. *Notification:* continuous (freshmen), 12/15 (early decision), continuous (transfers).

Admissions Contact Mercer University, 1400 Coleman Avenue, Macon, GA 31207-0003. *Phone:* 478-301-2650. *Toll-free phone:* 800-840-8577. *Fax:* 478-301-2828. *E-mail:* admissions@mercer.edu.

■ *See page 1974 for a narrative description.*

MOREHOUSE COLLEGE
Atlanta, Georgia

- **Independent** 4-year, founded 1867
- **Calendar** semesters
- **Degree** bachelor's
- **Urban** 61-acre campus
- **Endowment** $88.8 million
- **Men only,** 2,859 undergraduate students, 95% full-time
- **Moderately difficult** entrance level, 72% of applicants were admitted

Undergraduates 2,716 full-time, 143 part-time. Students come from 45 states and territories, 18 other countries, 73% are from out of state, 93% African American, 0.3% Hispanic American, 0.1% Native American, 4% international, 3% transferred in, 56% live on campus. *Retention:* 85% of 2002 full-time freshmen returned.

Freshmen *Admission:* 766 enrolled. *Average high school GPA:* 3.14. *Test scores:* SAT verbal scores over 500: 63%; SAT math scores over 500: 66%; ACT scores over 18: 84%; SAT verbal scores over 600: 18%; SAT math scores over

600: 24%; ACT scores over 24: 28%; SAT verbal scores over 700: 2%; SAT math scores over 700: 2%; ACT scores over 30: 2%.

Faculty *Total:* 205, 77% full-time, 62% with terminal degrees. *Student/faculty ratio:* 15:1.

Majors Accounting; adult and continuing education; African-American/Black studies; art; biology/biological sciences; business administration and management; chemistry; computer and information sciences; dramatic/theatre arts; economics; elementary education; engineering; English; finance; French; German; history; interdisciplinary studies; international relations and affairs; marketing/marketing management; mathematics; middle school education; music; philosophy; physical education teaching and coaching; physics; political science and government; psychology; religious studies; secondary education; sociology; Spanish; urban studies/affairs.

Academic Programs *Special study options:* academic remediation for entering students, advanced placement credit, cooperative education, double majors, honors programs, internships, off-campus study, part-time degree program, services for LD students, study abroad, summer session for credit. *ROTC:* Army (b), Navy (b), Air Force (c). *Unusual degree programs:* 3-2 engineering with Georgia Institute of Technology, Boston University, Auburn University, Rensselaer Polytechnic University, Rochester Institute of Technology.

Library Woodruff Library plus 1 other with 560,000 titles, 1,000 serial subscriptions, an OPAC.

Computers on Campus 490 computers available on campus for general student use. A campuswide network can be accessed from student residence rooms and from off campus. Internet access, online (class) registration, at least one staffed computer lab available.

Student Life *Housing options:* men-only. Campus housing is university owned. Freshman campus housing is guaranteed. *Activities and organizations:* drama/theater group, student-run newspaper, choral group, marching band, glee club, political science club, STRIPES, national fraternities. *Campus security:* 24-hour emergency response devices and patrols, late-night transport/escort service. *Student services:* health clinic, personal/psychological counseling.

Athletics Member NCAA. All Division II. *Intercollegiate sports:* basketball M(s), cross-country running M(s), football M(s), tennis M(s), track and field M(s). *Intramural sports:* baseball M, basketball M, bowling M, football M, table tennis M, tennis M.

Standardized Tests *Required:* SAT I or ACT (for admission).

Costs (2003–04) *Comprehensive fee:* $22,728 includes full-time tuition ($11,786), mandatory fees ($2524), and room and board ($8418). Part-time tuition: $495 per semester hour. No tuition increase for student's term of enrollment. *College room only:* $4814. *Waivers:* employees or children of employees.

Financial Aid Of all full-time matriculated undergraduates who enrolled in 2002, 2,310 applied for aid, 2,296 were judged to have need, 33 had their need fully met. *Average percent of need met:* 27%. *Average financial aid package:* $10,986. *Average need-based loan:* $3854. *Average need-based gift aid:* $3534. *Average non-need-based aid:* $10,495. *Average indebtedness upon graduation:* $18,000.

Applying *Options:* common application, electronic application, early admission, early decision, deferred entrance. *Application fee:* $45. *Required:* essay or personal statement, high school transcript, minimum 2.8 GPA, letters of recommendation. *Recommended:* minimum 3.0 GPA, interview. *Application deadlines:* 2/15 (freshmen), 2/15 (transfers). *Early decision:* 10/15. *Notification:* continuous until 4/1 (freshmen), 12/15 (early decision), 4/1 (transfers).

Admissions Contact Mr. Terrance Dixon, Associate Dean for Admissions and Recruitment, Morehouse College, 830 Westview Drive, SW, Atlanta, GA 30314. *Phone:* 404-215-2632. *Toll-free phone:* 800-851-1254. *Fax:* 404-524-5635. *E-mail:* admissions@morehouse.edu.

NORTH GEORGIA COLLEGE & STATE UNIVERSITY

Dahlonega, Georgia

- **State-supported** comprehensive, founded 1873, part of University System of Georgia
- **Calendar** semesters
- **Degrees** certificates, associate, bachelor's, master's, post-master's, and postbachelor's certificates
- **Small-town** 140-acre campus with easy access to Atlanta
- **Coed,** 3,946 undergraduate students, 80% full-time, 62% women, 38% men
- **Moderately difficult** entrance level, 63% of applicants were admitted

Part of the University System of Georgia, NGCSU enrolls 4,600 undergraduate and graduate students and, as the Military College of Georgia, has a cadet corps of 620 men and women. Located 90 minutes from Atlanta, NGCSU offers 50 academic programs in liberal arts and preprofessional disciplines and is one of the safest campuses in America.

Undergraduates 3,145 full-time, 801 part-time. Students come from 40 states and territories, 46 other countries, 5% are from out of state, 2% African American, 1% Asian American or Pacific Islander, 2% Hispanic American, 0.6% Native American, 2% international, 10% transferred in, 31% live on campus. *Retention:* 75% of 2002 full-time freshmen returned.

Freshmen *Admission:* 1,797 applied, 1,133 admitted, 728 enrolled. *Average high school GPA:* 3.23. *Test scores:* SAT verbal scores over 500: 71%; SAT math scores over 500: 68%; ACT scores over 18: 90%; SAT verbal scores over 600: 17%; SAT math scores over 600: 18%; ACT scores over 24: 25%; SAT verbal scores over 700: 1%; SAT math scores over 700: 1%; ACT scores over 30: 2%.

Faculty *Total:* 287, 55% full-time, 22% with terminal degrees. *Student/faculty ratio:* 18:1.

Majors Accounting; art; art teacher education; biology/biological sciences; business administration and management; business/managerial economics; chemistry; computer and information sciences; computer science; crafts, folk art and artisanry; criminal justice/law enforcement administration; criminal justice/safety; drawing; education; educational leadership and administration; elementary education; English; English/language arts teacher education; family practice nursing/nurse practitioner; finance; French; history; information science/studies; kindergarten/preschool education; marketing/marketing management; mathematics; mathematics teacher education; middle school education; music; music teacher education; nursing (registered nurse training); physical education teaching and coaching; physics; political science and government; pre-dentistry studies; pre-medical studies; pre-veterinary studies; psychology; public administration; purchasing, procurement/acquisitions and contracts management; reading teacher education; science teacher education; secondary education; social sciences; social science teacher education; sociology; Spanish; special education.

Academic Programs *Special study options:* academic remediation for entering students, advanced placement credit, cooperative education, distance learning, double majors, freshman honors college, honors programs, internships, part-time degree program, services for LD students, study abroad, summer session for credit. *ROTC:* Army (b). *Unusual degree programs:* 3-2 engineering with Georgia Institute of Technology, Clemson University; industrial management, computer science with Georgia Institute of Technology.

Library Stewart Library with 143,613 titles, 2,554 serial subscriptions, 3,215 audiovisual materials, an OPAC, a Web page.

Computers on Campus 125 computers available on campus for general student use. A campuswide network can be accessed from student residence rooms and from off campus. Internet access, online (class) registration, at least one staffed computer lab available.

Student Life *Housing:* on-campus residence required through sophomore year. *Options:* men-only, women-only. Campus housing is university owned. *Activities and organizations:* drama/theater group, student-run newspaper, choral group, marching band, Student Government Association, Greek organizations, College Union Board, Resident Student Affairs Board, Baptist Student Union, national fraternities, national sororities. *Campus security:* 24-hour emergency response devices and patrols, late-night transport/escort service, controlled dormitory access. *Student services:* health clinic, personal/psychological counseling.

Athletics Member NAIA. *Intercollegiate sports:* baseball M, basketball M(s)/W(s), cheerleading W, cross-country running M(c)/W(c), riflery M(s)/W(s), soccer M(c)/W(c), softball W, tennis M(s)/W(s), track and field M/W. *Intramural sports:* basketball M/W, football M(c)/W(c), golf M(c)/W(c), softball M(c), volleyball M(c)/W(c).

Standardized Tests *Required:* SAT I or ACT (for admission).

Costs (2003–04) *Tuition:* state resident $2212 full-time, $93 per semester hour part-time; nonresident $8848 full-time, $369 per semester hour part-time. Part-time tuition and fees vary according to course load. *Required fees:* $612 full-time. *Room and board:* $4160; room only: $2080. Room and board charges vary according to board plan and housing facility. *Waivers:* senior citizens and employees or children of employees.

Financial Aid Of all full-time matriculated undergraduates who enrolled in 2002, 2,947 applied for aid, 962 were judged to have need, 351 had their need fully met. In 2002, 1154 non-need-based awards were made. *Average percent of need met:* 40%. *Average financial aid package:* $5973. *Average need-based loan:* $3037. *Average need-based gift aid:* $2639. *Average non-need-based aid:* $2831.

Applying *Options:* electronic application, early admission, deferred entrance. *Application fee:* $25. *Required:* high school transcript, minimum 2.0 GPA, proof of immunization. *Application deadline:* 7/1 (freshmen), rolling (transfers). *Notification:* continuous (freshmen), continuous (transfers).

Admissions Contact Robert J. LaVerriere, Director of Admissions and Recruitment, North Georgia College & State University, Admissions Center, 32 College Circle, Dahlonega, GA 30597. *Phone:* 706-864-1800. *Toll-free phone:* 800-498-9581. *Fax:* 706-864-1478. *E-mail:* admissions@ngcsu.edu.

Oglethorpe University
Atlanta, Georgia

- **Independent** comprehensive, founded 1835
- **Calendar** semesters
- **Degrees** bachelor's and master's
- **Suburban** 118-acre campus
- **Endowment** $17.5 million
- **Coed,** 945 undergraduate students, 83% full-time, 65% women, 35% men
- **Very difficult** entrance level, 66% of applicants were admitted

Undergraduates 784 full-time, 161 part-time. Students come from 36 states and territories, 21 other countries, 37% are from out of state, 20% African American, 3% Asian American or Pacific Islander, 3% Hispanic American, 0.1% Native American, 3% international, 7% transferred in, 70% live on campus. *Retention:* 87% of 2002 full-time freshmen returned.

Freshmen *Admission:* 746 applied, 492 admitted, 167 enrolled. *Average high school GPA:* 3.67. *Test scores:* SAT verbal scores over 500: 88%; SAT math scores over 500: 79%; ACT scores over 18: 97%; SAT verbal scores over 600: 54%; SAT math scores over 600: 40%; ACT scores over 24: 66%; SAT verbal scores over 700: 14%; SAT math scores over 700: 6%; ACT scores over 30: 13%.

Faculty *Total:* 80, 69% full-time, 88% with terminal degrees. *Student/faculty ratio:* 11:1.

Majors Accounting; American studies; art; biology/biological sciences; business administration and management; business/managerial economics; chemistry; computer science; economics; education; elementary education; English; history; interdisciplinary studies; international relations and affairs; kindergarten/preschool education; mass communication/media; mathematics; middle school education; philosophy; physics; political science and government; pre-dentistry studies; pre-law studies; pre-medical studies; pre-veterinary studies; psychology; secondary education; social work; sociology; urban studies/affairs.

Academic Programs *Special study options:* accelerated degree program, adult/continuing education programs, advanced placement credit, cooperative education, double majors, honors programs, independent study, internships, off-campus study, part-time degree program, services for LD students, student-designed majors, study abroad, summer session for credit. *Unusual degree programs:* 3-2 engineering with Auburn University, Georgia Institute of Technology, University of Florida, University of Southern California; art with Atlanta College of Art.

Library Philip Weltner Library with 150,000 titles, 710 serial subscriptions, an OPAC, a Web page.

Computers on Campus 60 computers available on campus for general student use. A campuswide network can be accessed from student residence rooms and from off campus. At least one staffed computer lab available.

Student Life *Housing options:* coed, men-only, women-only. *Activities and organizations:* drama/theater group, student-run newspaper, radio station, choral group, Alpha Phi Omega, Christian Fellowship, international club, Playmakers, national fraternities, national sororities. *Campus security:* 24-hour emergency response devices and patrols, student patrols, late-night transport/escort service, controlled dormitory access. *Student services:* health clinic, personal/psychological counseling.

Athletics Member NCAA. All Division III. *Intercollegiate sports:* baseball M, basketball M/W, cross-country running M/W, golf M/W, soccer M/W, tennis M/W, track and field M/W, volleyball W. *Intramural sports:* badminton M/W, basketball M/W, football M/W, softball M/W, table tennis M/W, ultimate Frisbee M/W, volleyball M/W.

Standardized Tests *Required:* SAT I or ACT (for admission).

Costs (2003–04) *Comprehensive fee:* $26,920 includes full-time tuition ($19,920), mandatory fees ($450), and room and board ($6550). Part-time tuition: $830 per credit hour. Part-time tuition and fees vary according to class time. *Room and board:* Room and board charges vary according to board plan and housing facility. *Payment plans:* tuition prepayment, installment. *Waivers:* employees or children of employees.

Financial Aid Of all full-time matriculated undergraduates who enrolled in 2003, 525 applied for aid, 444 were judged to have need, 141 had their need fully met. In 2003, 264 non-need-based awards were made. *Average percent of need met:* 86%. *Average financial aid package:* $20,779. *Average need-based loan:* $2288. *Average need-based gift aid:* $12,198. *Average non-need-based aid:* $10,542. *Average indebtedness upon graduation:* $16,273. *Financial aid deadline:* 9/1.

Applying *Options:* common application, electronic application, early action, deferred entrance. *Application fee:* $30. *Required:* essay or personal statement, high school transcript, 1 letter of recommendation. *Required for some:* interview. *Recommended:* minimum 2.5 GPA, interview. *Application deadline:* rolling (freshmen), rolling (transfers). *Notification:* continuous (freshmen), 12/20 (early action), continuous (transfers).

Admissions Contact Mr. David Rhodes, Vice President for Enrollment Management, Oglethorpe University, 4484 Peachtree Road, NE, Atlanta, GA 30319. *Phone:* 404-364-8307. *Toll-free phone:* 800-428-4484. *Fax:* 404-364-8491. *E-mail:* admission@oglethorpe.edu.

■ *See page 2122 for a narrative description.*

Paine College
Augusta, Georgia

- **Independent Methodist** 4-year, founded 1882
- **Calendar** semesters
- **Degree** bachelor's
- **Urban** 55-acre campus with easy access to Atlanta
- **Endowment** $10.7 million
- **Coed,** 972 undergraduate students, 88% full-time, 70% women, 30% men
- **Minimally difficult** entrance level, 7% of applicants were admitted

Undergraduates 858 full-time, 114 part-time. Students come from 30 states and territories, 3 other countries, 17% are from out of state, 98% African American, 0.1% Asian American or Pacific Islander, 0.5% Hispanic American, 0.5% international, 4% transferred in, 58% live on campus. *Retention:* 62% of 2002 full-time freshmen returned.

Freshmen *Admission:* 3,837 applied, 287 admitted, 264 enrolled. *Average high school GPA:* 2.83. *Test scores:* SAT verbal scores over 500: 9%; SAT math scores over 500: 13%; ACT scores over 18: 21%; SAT verbal scores over 600: 1%; SAT math scores over 600: 1%; ACT scores over 24: 3%.

Faculty *Total:* 104, 79% full-time, 44% with terminal degrees. *Student/faculty ratio:* 11:1.

Majors Accounting and business/management; biology/biological sciences; biology teacher education; broadcast journalism; business administration and management; chemistry; counseling psychology; criminology; dramatic/theatre arts; elementary education; English; English/language arts teacher education; environmental science; experimental psychology; history; history teacher education; international business/trade/commerce; journalism; management information systems; mathematics; mathematics and computer science; mathematics teacher education; middle school education; philosophy; psychology; public relations, advertising, and applied communication related; religious studies; social psychology; sociology.

Academic Programs *Special study options:* academic remediation for entering students, accelerated degree program, advanced placement credit, cooperative education, honors programs, independent study, internships, off-campus study, part-time degree program, study abroad, summer session for credit. *ROTC:* Army (c). *Unusual degree programs:* 3-2 engineering with Tennessee State University, Tuskegee University.

Library Collins–Callaway Library with 88,809 titles, 5,447 serial subscriptions, 1,655 audiovisual materials.

Computers on Campus 100 computers available on campus for general student use. A campuswide network can be accessed from student residence rooms and from off campus. Internet access, at least one staffed computer lab available.

Student Life *Housing options:* men-only, women-only. Campus housing is university owned. Freshman applicants given priority for college housing. *Activities and organizations:* drama/theater group, student-run newspaper, choral group, marching band, national fraternities, national sororities. *Campus security:* 24-hour emergency response devices and patrols, late-night transport/escort service. *Student services:* health clinic, personal/psychological counseling.

Athletics Member NCAA. All Division II. *Intercollegiate sports:* baseball M(s), basketball M(s)/W(s), cross-country running M(s)/W(s), softball W(s), track and field M(s)/W(s), volleyball W(s). *Intramural sports:* baseball M, basketball M/W, cheerleading M/W, football M, softball M/W, table tennis M/W, tennis M/W, track and field M/W, volleyball M/W, weight lifting M/W.

Standardized Tests *Required:* SAT I or ACT (for admission).

Costs (2003–04) *Comprehensive fee:* $13,022 includes full-time tuition ($8448), mandatory fees ($634), and room and board ($3940). Full-time tuition and fees vary according to course load and reciprocity agreements. Part-time tuition: $352 per credit hour. Part-time tuition and fees vary according to course load, location, and reciprocity agreements. *Required fees:* $317 per term part-time. *Room and board:* Room and board charges vary according to housing facility. *Payment plan:* installment. *Waivers:* children of alumni and employees or children of employees.

Financial Aid *Average financial aid package:* $185. *Average indebtedness upon graduation:* $2304.

Applying *Options:* early admission, deferred entrance. *Application fee:* $20. *Required:* essay or personal statement, high school transcript, minimum 2.0 GPA, 3 letters of recommendation, medical history. *Application deadlines:* 8/1 (freshmen), 8/1 (transfers). *Notification:* continuous (freshmen), continuous (transfers).

Admissions Contact Mr. Joseph Tinsley, Director of Admissions, Paine College, 1235 15th Street, Augusta, GA 30901-3182. *Phone:* 706-821-8320. *Toll-free phone:* 800-476-7703. *Fax:* 706-821-8691. *E-mail:* tinsleyj@mail.paine.edu.

■ See page 2150 for a narrative description.

PIEDMONT COLLEGE
Demorest, Georgia

- **Independent** comprehensive, founded 1897, affiliated with United Church of Christ
- **Calendar** semesters
- **Degrees** bachelor's, master's, and post-master's certificates
- **Rural** 115-acre campus with easy access to Atlanta
- **Endowment** $42.8 million
- **Coed,** 1,010 undergraduate students, 85% full-time, 63% women, 37% men
- **Moderately difficult** entrance level, 54% of applicants were admitted

Undergraduates 858 full-time, 152 part-time. Students come from 15 states and territories, 24 other countries, 4% are from out of state, 7% African American, 0.4% Asian American or Pacific Islander, 1% Hispanic American, 0.2% Native American, 0.9% international, 16% transferred in, 16% live on campus. *Retention:* 73% of 2002 full-time freshmen returned.

Freshmen *Admission:* 542 applied, 291 admitted, 142 enrolled. *Average high school GPA:* 3.03. *Test scores:* SAT verbal scores over 500: 54%; SAT math scores over 500: 54%; ACT scores over 18: 80%; SAT verbal scores over 600: 20%; SAT math scores over 600: 17%; ACT scores over 24: 20%; SAT verbal scores over 700: 1%; SAT math scores over 700: 1%; ACT scores over 30: 2%.

Faculty *Total:* 195, 48% full-time, 83% with terminal degrees. *Student/faculty ratio:* 15:1.

Majors Biology/biological sciences; business administration and management; chemistry; computer science; criminal justice/law enforcement administration; dramatic/theatre arts; elementary and middle school administration/principalship; English; environmental science; environmental studies; fine/studio arts; history; interdisciplinary studies; kindergarten/preschool education; mass communication/media; mathematics; mathematics and computer science; middle school education; music; music performance; nursing (registered nurse training); philosophy; political science and government; psychology; religious studies; social sciences; sociology; Spanish; special education.

Academic Programs *Special study options:* academic remediation for entering students, accelerated degree program, adult/continuing education programs, advanced placement credit, cooperative education, distance learning, double majors, honors programs, independent study, internships, off-campus study, part-time degree program, services for LD students, student-designed majors, study abroad, summer session for credit.

Library Arrendale Library with 116,750 titles, 366 serial subscriptions, 725 audiovisual materials, an OPAC, a Web page.

Computers on Campus 100 computers available on campus for general student use. A campuswide network can be accessed from student residence rooms and from off campus that provide access to e-mail. Internet access, at least one staffed computer lab available.

Student Life *Housing:* on-campus residence required through junior year. *Options:* coed, men-only, women-only, disabled students. Campus housing is university owned. Freshman campus housing is guaranteed. *Activities and organizations:* drama/theater group, student-run newspaper, radio and television station, choral group, student government, Student Georgia Association of Educators, Students In Free Enterprise, psychology club, alternatives. *Campus security:* 24-hour emergency response devices and patrols, late-night transport/escort service. *Student services:* personal/psychological counseling.

Athletics Member NCAA, NCCAA. All NCAA Division III. *Intercollegiate sports:* baseball M, basketball M/W, cross-country running M/W, golf M/W, soccer M/W, softball W, volleyball W. *Intramural sports:* rock climbing M/W, ultimate Frisbee M/W.

Standardized Tests *Required:* SAT I or ACT (for admission).

Costs (2004–05) *Comprehensive fee:* $18,200 includes full-time tuition ($13,500) and room and board ($4700). Full-time tuition and fees vary according to course load and program. Part-time tuition: $563 per hour. Part-time tuition and fees vary according to course load and program. *College room only:* $2450. Room and board charges vary according to board plan and housing facility. *Payment plan:* installment. *Waivers:* employees or children of employees.

Financial Aid Of all full-time matriculated undergraduates who enrolled in 2003, 841 applied for aid, 740 were judged to have need, 326 had their need fully met. 120 Federal Work-Study jobs (averaging $1696). 85 state and other part-time jobs (averaging $2839). In 2003, 87 non-need-based awards were made. *Average percent of need met:* 74%. *Average financial aid package:* $8642. *Average need-based loan:* $5744. *Average need-based gift aid:* $3049. *Average non-need-based aid:* $2542. *Average indebtedness upon graduation:* $13,702.

Applying *Options:* common application, electronic application, early admission, deferred entrance. *Required:* high school transcript, minimum 2.0 GPA. *Required for some:* interview. *Recommended:* essay or personal statement. *Application deadline:* rolling (freshmen), rolling (transfers).

Admissions Contact Mr. Jem Clement, Dean of Students, Piedmont College, PO Box 10, 165 Central Avenue, Demorest, GA 30535. *Phone:* 706-776-0103 Ext. 1188. *Toll-free phone:* 800-277-7020. *Fax:* 706-776-6635. *E-mail:* jclement@piedmont.edu.

REINHARDT COLLEGE
Waleska, Georgia

- **Independent** 4-year, founded 1883, affiliated with United Methodist Church
- **Calendar** semesters
- **Degrees** associate and bachelor's
- **Rural** 600-acre campus with easy access to Atlanta
- **Endowment** $38.0 million
- **Coed,** 1,308 undergraduate students, 89% full-time, 59% women, 41% men
- **Moderately difficult** entrance level, 70% of applicants were admitted

Undergraduates 1,166 full-time, 142 part-time. Students come from 15 states and territories, 5 other countries, 3% are from out of state, 8% African American, 1% Asian American or Pacific Islander, 2% Hispanic American, 0.3% Native American, 0.8% international, 1% transferred in, 39% live on campus. *Retention:* 61% of 2002 full-time freshmen returned.

Freshmen *Admission:* 773 applied, 542 admitted, 258 enrolled. *Average high school GPA:* 3.03. *Test scores:* ACT scores over 18: 60%; ACT scores over 24: 11%.

Faculty *Total:* 115, 44% full-time. *Student/faculty ratio:* 15:1.

Majors Accounting; art; biblical studies; biology/biological sciences; business administration and management; business/commerce; education; English; entrepreneurship; health and physical education related; history; information science/studies; kindergarten/preschool education; liberal arts and sciences/liberal studies; mass communication/media; middle school education; music; nursing (registered nurse training); physical education teaching and coaching; psychology; sociology; sport and fitness administration.

Academic Programs *Special study options:* academic remediation for entering students, adult/continuing education programs, advanced placement credit, cooperative education, double majors, external degree program, honors programs, independent study, internships, part-time degree program, services for LD students, study abroad, summer session for credit.

Library Hill Freeman Library with 46,750 titles, 329 serial subscriptions, 17,300 audiovisual materials, an OPAC, a Web page.

Computers on Campus 164 computers available on campus for general student use. A campuswide network can be accessed from student residence rooms and from off campus. Internet access, at least one staffed computer lab available.

Student Life *Housing:* on-campus residence required through sophomore year. *Options:* men-only, women-only. Campus housing is university owned. Freshman campus housing is guaranteed. *Activities and organizations:* student-run newspaper, television station, choral group, Real Deal, International & Historical Film Society, Student Government Association, SOAR-Student Orientation Leaders, communication club. *Campus security:* 24-hour patrols, student patrols, late-night transport/escort service. *Student services:* health clinic, personal/psychological counseling.

Athletics Member NAIA. *Intercollegiate sports:* baseball M, basketball M(s)/W(s), cross-country running M/W, golf M(s), soccer M(s)/W(s), softball W, tennis M(s)/W(s). *Intramural sports:* basketball M/W, football M/W, soccer M/W, softball M/W, volleyball M/W.

Standardized Tests *Required:* SAT I or ACT (for admission).

Costs (2004–05) *Comprehensive fee:* $17,962 includes full-time tuition ($12,000), mandatory fees ($200), and room and board ($5762). Full-time tuition and fees vary according to course load and location. Part-time tuition: $400 per credit hour. Part-time tuition and fees vary according to course load and location. *Room and board:* Room and board charges vary according to board plan and housing facility. *Payment plan:* installment. *Waivers:* employees or children of employees.

Financial Aid Of all full-time matriculated undergraduates who enrolled in 2002, 68 Federal Work-Study jobs (averaging $1400). 156 state and other part-time jobs (averaging $870). *Average financial aid package:* $6500.

Applying *Options:* common application, electronic application, early admission, deferred entrance. *Application fee:* $25. *Required:* high school transcript, minimum 2.0 GPA. *Recommended:* essay or personal statement, interview. *Application deadline:* rolling (freshmen), rolling (transfers). *Notification:* continuous (freshmen), continuous (transfers).

Reinhardt College (continued)

Admissions Contact Ms. Julie T. Cook, Director of Admissions, Reinhardt College, 7300 Reinhardt College Circle, Waleska, GA 30183-0128. *Phone:* 770-720-5526. *Toll-free phone:* 87-REINHARDT. *Fax:* 770-720-5602. *E-mail:* admissions@mail.reinhardt.edu.

SAVANNAH COLLEGE OF ART AND DESIGN

Savannah, Georgia

- **Independent** comprehensive, founded 1978
- **Calendar** quarters
- **Degrees** bachelor's and master's
- **Urban** campus
- **Coed,** 5,318 undergraduate students, 91% full-time, 49% women, 51% men
- **Moderately difficult** entrance level, 75% of applicants were admitted

The College is situated in Savannah's renowned historic district, a creative environment conducive to study, research, and artistic expression. The College exists to prepare talented students for careers, offering a well-rounded curriculum that emphasizes individual attention. The student body represents all 50 states and more than 75 countries.

Undergraduates 4,822 full-time, 496 part-time. Students come from 54 states and territories, 78 other countries, 78% are from out of state, 5% African American, 2% Asian American or Pacific Islander, 3% Hispanic American, 0.3% Native American, 5% international, 8% transferred in, 36% live on campus. *Retention:* 81% of 2002 full-time freshmen returned.

Freshmen *Admission:* 3,515 applied, 2,648 admitted, 1,041 enrolled. *Test scores:* SAT verbal scores over 500: 72%; SAT math scores over 500: 65%; ACT scores over 18: 92%; SAT verbal scores over 600: 29%; SAT math scores over 600: 25%; ACT scores over 24: 43%; SAT verbal scores over 700: 4%; SAT math scores over 700: 3%; ACT scores over 30: 4%.

Faculty *Total:* 331, 89% full-time, 80% with terminal degrees. *Student/faculty ratio:* 18:1.

Majors Animation, interactive technology, video graphics and special effects; applied art; architectural history and criticism; architecture; art history, criticism and conservation; cinematography and film/video production; computer graphics; design and applied arts related; design and visual communications; digital communication and media/multimedia; dramatic/theatre arts; fashion/apparel design; fiber, textile and weaving arts; graphic design; historic preservation and conservation; illustration; industrial design; interior design; metal and jewelry arts; painting; photography; recording arts technology.

Academic Programs *Special study options:* advanced placement credit, double majors, English as a second language, independent study, internships, off-campus study, part-time degree program, services for LD students, study abroad, summer session for credit.

Library Jen Library plus 1 other with 85,000 titles, 917 serial subscriptions, 3,976 audiovisual materials, an OPAC, a Web page.

Computers on Campus 2220 computers available on campus for general student use. A campuswide network can be accessed from student residence rooms and from off campus. Internet access, online (class) registration, at least one staffed computer lab available. Computer purchase or lease plan available.

Student Life *Housing options:* coed, women-only, disabled students. Campus housing is university owned. Freshman applicants given priority for college housing. *Activities and organizations:* drama/theater group, student-run newspaper, radio station, choral group, United Student Forum, Inter-Club Council, American Institute of Architecture Students, Intercultural Council, American Society of Interior Designers. *Campus security:* 24-hour emergency response devices and patrols, late-night transport/escort service, video camera surveillance. *Student services:* health clinic, personal/psychological counseling.

Athletics Member NCAA, NAIA. All NCAA Division III. *Intercollegiate sports:* baseball M, basketball M/W, cheerleading W, crew M/W, cross-country running M/W, equestrian sports M/W, fencing M(c)/W(c), golf M/W, sailing M(c)/W(c), soccer M/W, softball W, swimming M/W, tennis M/W, volleyball W. *Intramural sports:* basketball M/W, bowling M/W, equestrian sports M(c)/W(c), football M, lacrosse M(c), rock climbing M/W, softball M/W, volleyball M/W.

Standardized Tests *Required:* SAT I or ACT (for admission).

Costs (2004–05) *One-time required fee:* $500. *Comprehensive fee:* $28,580 includes full-time tuition ($20,250) and room and board ($8330). Part-time tuition: $2250 per course. *College room only:* $5300. Room and board charges vary according to board plan and housing facility. *Payment plan:* installment. *Waivers:* employees or children of employees.

Financial Aid Of all full-time matriculated undergraduates who enrolled in 2003, 2,940 applied for aid, 2,373 were judged to have need, 936 had their need fully met. 151 Federal Work-Study jobs (averaging $1905). 198 state and other part-time jobs (averaging $2574). In 2003, 1260 non-need-based awards were made. *Average percent of need met:* 24%. *Average financial aid package:* $8727. *Average need-based loan:* $4056. *Average need-based gift aid:* $3307. *Average non-need-based aid:* $3618. *Average indebtedness upon graduation:* $18,000.

Applying *Options:* electronic application, early admission. *Application fee:* $50. *Required:* high school transcript, 3 letters of recommendation. *Recommended:* interview. *Application deadline:* rolling (freshmen), rolling (transfers). *Notification:* continuous (freshmen), continuous (transfers).

Admissions Contact Ms. Eve Seibert, Director of Recruitment, Savannah College of Art and Design, 342 Bull Street, PO Box 3146, Savannah, GA 31402-3146. *Phone:* 912-525-5100. *Toll-free phone:* 800-869-7223. *Fax:* 912-525-5983. *E-mail:* admission@scad.edu.

■ See page 2350 for a narrative description.

SAVANNAH STATE UNIVERSITY

Savannah, Georgia

- **State-supported** comprehensive, founded 1890, part of University System of Georgia
- **Calendar** semesters
- **Degrees** bachelor's and master's
- **Suburban** 165-acre campus
- **Endowment** $72,919
- **Coed**
- **Minimally difficult** entrance level

Faculty *Student/faculty ratio:* 15:1.

Student Life *Campus security:* 24-hour patrols.

Athletics Member NCAA. All Division II.

Standardized Tests *Required:* SAT I or ACT (for admission). *Required for some:* SAT II: Subject Tests (for admission). *Recommended:* SAT I (for admission).

Costs (2003–04) *Tuition:* state resident $2830 full-time; nonresident $9466 full-time. *Room and board:* $4498. Room and board charges vary according to student level.

Financial Aid *Average percent of need met:* 75. *Average financial aid package:* $3200. *Average indebtedness upon graduation:* $11,000.

Applying *Options:* common application, electronic application, early admission, deferred entrance. *Application fee:* $20. *Required:* high school transcript, minimum 2.0 GPA.

Admissions Contact Mrs. Gwendolyn J. Moore, Associate Director of Admissions, Savannah State University, PO Box 20209, Savannah, GA 31404. *Phone:* 912-356-2181. *Toll-free phone:* 800-788-0478. *Fax:* 912-356-2256.

■ See page 2352 for a narrative description.

SHORTER COLLEGE

Rome, Georgia

- **Independent Baptist** comprehensive, founded 1873
- **Calendar** semesters
- **Degrees** associate, bachelor's, and master's
- **Small-town** 155-acre campus with easy access to Atlanta
- **Endowment** $23.3 million
- **Coed,** 884 undergraduate students, 95% full-time, 61% women, 39% men
- **Moderately difficult** entrance level, 83% of applicants were admitted

Undergraduates 841 full-time, 43 part-time. Students come from 21 states and territories, 20 other countries, 9% are from out of state, 6% African American, 0.9% Asian American or Pacific Islander, 2% Hispanic American, 0.3% Native American, 5% international, 8% transferred in, 75% live on campus. *Retention:* 74% of 2002 full-time freshmen returned.

Freshmen *Admission:* 555 applied, 460 admitted, 185 enrolled. *Average high school GPA:* 3.34. *Test scores:* SAT verbal scores over 500: 64%; SAT math scores over 500: 64%; ACT scores over 18: 85%; SAT verbal scores over 600: 22%; SAT math scores over 600: 20%; ACT scores over 24: 34%; SAT verbal scores over 700: 4%; SAT math scores over 700: 1%; ACT scores over 30: 3%.

Faculty *Total:* 115, 54% full-time, 45% with terminal degrees. *Student/faculty ratio:* 11:1.

Majors Accounting; art; art teacher education; biology/biological sciences; business administration and management; business/managerial economics; chemistry; computer and information sciences; divinity/ministry; dramatic/theatre arts; economics; elementary education; English; environmental studies; fine/studio arts; French; general studies; history; liberal arts and sciences/liberal studies; mathematics; mathematics teacher education; middle school education; music; music teacher education; natural sciences; organizational communication; parks, recreation and leisure; piano and organ; pre-theology/pre-ministerial studies;

psychology; public relations, advertising, and applied communication related; religious/sacred music; religious studies; social sciences; sociology; Spanish; therapeutic recreation; voice and opera.

Academic Programs *Special study options:* academic remediation for entering students, adult/continuing education programs, advanced placement credit, double majors, honors programs, independent study, internships, off-campus study, part-time degree program, services for LD students, student-designed majors, study abroad, summer session for credit.

Library Livingston Library with 100,366 titles, 596 serial subscriptions, 11,226 audiovisual materials, an OPAC, a Web page.

Computers on Campus 100 computers available on campus for general student use. A campuswide network can be accessed from student residence rooms that provide access to e-mail. Internet access, at least one staffed computer lab available.

Student Life *Housing:* on-campus residence required through senior year. *Options:* men-only, women-only, disabled students. Campus housing is university owned. Freshman applicants given priority for college housing. *Activities and organizations:* drama/theater group, student-run newspaper, radio and television station, choral group, marching band, Baptist Student Union, Student Government Association, Fellowship of Christian Athletes, Shorter Players, Habitat for Humanity. *Campus security:* 24-hour emergency response devices and patrols. *Student services:* health clinic, personal/psychological counseling.

Athletics Member NAIA. *Intercollegiate sports:* baseball M(s), basketball M(s)/W(s), cheerleading M/W, cross-country running M(s)/W(s), golf M(s)/W(s), soccer M(s)/W(s), tennis M(s)/W(s), track and field M(s)/W(s), volleyball M(s)/W(s). *Intramural sports:* basketball M/W, bowling M/W, soccer M/W, table tennis M/W, tennis M/W, ultimate Frisbee M/W, volleyball M/W.

Standardized Tests *Required:* SAT I or ACT (for admission).

Costs (2003–04) *Comprehensive fee:* $17,370 includes full-time tuition ($11,440), mandatory fees ($265), and room and board ($5665). Full-time tuition and fees vary according to course load. Part-time tuition: $260. *College room only:* $3165. Room and board charges vary according to board plan and housing facility. *Payment plan:* installment. *Waivers:* senior citizens and employees or children of employees.

Financial Aid Of all full-time matriculated undergraduates who enrolled in 2002, 651 applied for aid, 542 were judged to have need, 143 had their need fully met. 91 Federal Work-Study jobs (averaging $1286). 99 state and other part-time jobs (averaging $702). In 2002, 285 non-need-based awards were made. *Average percent of need met:* 68%. *Average financial aid package:* $10,018. *Average need-based loan:* $3529. *Average need-based gift aid:* $7379. *Average non-need-based aid:* $9042. *Average indebtedness upon graduation:* $16,718.

Applying *Options:* early admission, deferred entrance. *Application fee:* $25. *Required:* essay or personal statement, high school transcript. *Required for some:* interview, audition for music and theater programs. *Recommended:* minimum 2.0 GPA, 1 letter of recommendation, interview. *Application deadlines:* 8/20 (freshmen), 8/25 (transfers). *Notification:* continuous (freshmen), continuous (transfers).

Admissions Contact Mr. John Head, Vice President for Enrollment Management, Shorter College, 315 Shorter Avenue, Rome, GA 30165. *Phone:* 706-233-7342. *Toll-free phone:* 800-868-6980. *Fax:* 706-236-7224. *E-mail:* admissions@shorter.edu.

■ *See page 2382 for a narrative description.*

SOUTHERN POLYTECHNIC STATE UNIVERSITY
Marietta, Georgia

- **State-supported** comprehensive, founded 1948, part of University System of Georgia
- **Calendar** semesters
- **Degrees** certificates, associate, bachelor's, master's, and postbachelor's certificates
- **Suburban** 200-acre campus with easy access to Atlanta
- **Coed,** 3,185 undergraduate students, 63% full-time, 18% women, 82% men
- **Moderately difficult** entrance level, 85% of applicants were admitted

Undergraduates 1,997 full-time, 1,188 part-time. Students come from 40 states and territories, 6% are from out of state, 22% African American, 6% Asian American or Pacific Islander, 3% Hispanic American, 0.2% Native American, 6% international, 12% transferred in, 12% live on campus. *Retention:* 67% of 2002 full-time freshmen returned.

Freshmen *Admission:* 779 applied, 666 admitted, 472 enrolled. *Average high school GPA:* 3.17. *Test scores:* SAT verbal scores over 500: 75%; SAT math scores over 500: 88%; ACT scores over 18: 96%; SAT verbal scores over 600: 22%; SAT math scores over 600: 35%; ACT scores over 24: 26%; SAT verbal scores over 700: 2%; SAT math scores over 700: 2%.

Faculty *Total:* 228, 57% full-time. *Student/faculty ratio:* 17:1.

Majors Architectural engineering technology; architecture; biology/biological sciences; civil engineering technology; computer and information sciences; computer and information sciences and support services related; computer engineering technology; construction engineering technology; electrical and electronic engineering technologies related; electrical, electronic and communications engineering technology; entrepreneurship; industrial production technologies related; industrial technology; information science/studies; international relations and affairs; liberal arts and sciences/liberal studies; mathematics; mechanical engineering/mechanical technology; organizational behavior; physics; survey technology; technical and business writing; telecommunications.

Academic Programs *Special study options:* adult/continuing education programs, advanced placement credit, cooperative education, distance learning, double majors, independent study, internships, part-time degree program, services for LD students, study abroad, summer session for credit. *ROTC:* Army (c), Navy (c), Air Force (c).

Library Lawrence V. Johnson Library with 117,963 titles, 1,320 serial subscriptions, 60 audiovisual materials, an OPAC.

Computers on Campus 1500 computers available on campus for general student use. A campuswide network can be accessed from student residence rooms and from off campus. Internet access, online (class) registration, at least one staffed computer lab available.

Student Life *Housing options:* coed. Campus housing is university owned and is provided by a third party. *Activities and organizations:* student-run newspaper, radio station, International Student Association, Campus Activities Board, National Society of Black Engineers, Aerial Robotics Team, Intergreek Council, national fraternities, national sororities. *Campus security:* 24-hour emergency response devices and patrols, late-night transport/escort service, controlled dormitory access. *Student services:* health clinic, personal/psychological counseling.

Athletics Member NAIA. *Intercollegiate sports:* baseball M(s), basketball M(s)/W(s), tennis M(s). *Intramural sports:* badminton M/W, basketball M/W, football M/W, golf M/W, racquetball M/W, soccer M/W, softball M/W, table tennis M/W, tennis M/W, ultimate Frisbee M/W, volleyball M/W.

Standardized Tests *Required:* SAT I or ACT (for admission). *Required for some:* SAT II: Subject Tests (for admission).

Costs (2003–04) *Tuition:* state resident $2312 full-time; nonresident $9248 full-time. *Required fees:* $442 full-time. *Room and board:* $4866; room only: $2660. Room and board charges vary according to board plan. *Waivers:* senior citizens and employees or children of employees.

Financial Aid Of all full-time matriculated undergraduates who enrolled in 2002, 1,685 applied for aid, 775 were judged to have need, 214 had their need fully met. In 2002, 303 non-need-based awards were made. *Average percent of need met:* 78%. *Average financial aid package:* $4463. *Average need-based loan:* $2780. *Average need-based gift aid:* $2800. *Average non-need-based aid:* $4525. *Average indebtedness upon graduation:* $15,351.

Applying *Options:* early admission. *Application fee:* $20. *Required:* high school transcript, minimum 2.0 GPA, proof of immunization. *Application deadlines:* 8/1 (freshmen), 8/1 (transfers). *Notification:* continuous (freshmen), continuous (transfers).

Admissions Contact Ms. Virginia A. Head, Director of Admissions, Southern Polytechnic State University, 1100 South Marietta Parkway, Marietta, GA 30060-2896. *Phone:* 770-528-7281. *Toll-free phone:* 800-635-3204. *Fax:* 770-528-7292. *E-mail:* admissions@spsu.edu.

SOUTH UNIVERSITY
Savannah, Georgia

- **Proprietary** comprehensive, founded 1899
- **Calendar** quarters
- **Degrees** associate, bachelor's, master's, and doctoral
- **Urban** 9-acre campus
- **Coed,** 506 undergraduate students
- **Minimally difficult** entrance level

Undergraduates Students come from 20 states and territories, 3 other countries, 12% are from out of state, 33% African American, 1% Asian American or Pacific Islander, 3% Hispanic American.

Freshmen *Admission:* 39 admitted. *Test scores:* SAT verbal scores over 500: 36%; SAT math scores over 500: 32%; ACT scores over 18: 56%; ACT scores over 24: 12%.

Faculty *Total:* 87.

Majors Accounting; business administration and management; information science/studies; information technology; legal assistant/paralegal; legal studies; medical/clinical assistant; physical therapist assistant; physician assistant.

Academic Programs *Special study options:* academic remediation for entering students, accelerated degree program, adult/continuing education programs, double majors, internships, part-time degree program, summer session for credit.

South University (continued)

Library South College Library with 11,181 titles, 3,065 serial subscriptions, 3,268 audiovisual materials.

Computers on Campus 83 computers available on campus for general student use. A campuswide network can be accessed from off campus. Internet access, online (class) registration, at least one staffed computer lab available.

Student Life *Housing:* college housing not available. *Activities and organizations:* Medical Assisting Club, Paralegal Club, Student Advisory Committee. *Campus security:* late-night transport/escort service. *Student services:* personal/psychological counseling.

Standardized Tests *Required:* SAT I, ACT, or CPT (for admission).

Costs (2003–04) *Tuition:* $10,185 full-time. *Waivers:* employees or children of employees.

Financial Aid Of all full-time matriculated undergraduates who enrolled in 2002, 382 applied for aid, 279 were judged to have need. *Average percent of need met:* 85%.

Applying *Options:* deferred entrance. *Application fee:* $25. *Required:* high school transcript, interview. *Required for some:* essay or personal statement, 3 letters of recommendation. *Application deadline:* rolling (freshmen), rolling (transfers). *Notification:* continuous (freshmen), continuous (transfers).

Admissions Contact Mr. Robin Manning, Director of Admissions, South University, 709 Mall Boulevard, Savannah, GA 31406. *Phone:* 912-201-8014. *Toll-free phone:* 866-629-2901. *Fax:* 912-201-8070. *E-mail:* cshall@southuniversity.edu.

■ See page 2424 for a narrative description.

SPELMAN COLLEGE
Atlanta, Georgia

- **Independent** 4-year, founded 1881
- **Calendar** semesters
- **Degree** bachelor's
- **Urban** 32-acre campus
- **Endowment** $219.4 million
- **Women only,** 2,063 undergraduate students, 96% full-time
- **Very difficult** entrance level, 39% of applicants were admitted

Spelman College is a historically black, privately endowed, 4-year liberal arts college for women. Founded in 1881 as the Atlanta Baptist Female Seminary, Spelman today is one of America's top liberal arts colleges, providing academic excellence for women as well as an environment that encourages leadership development and community service experience. Spelman's commitment to excellence is demonstrated by its dedicated, accessible faculty and low student-faculty ratio as well as by the outstanding success of students and alumnae.

Undergraduates 1,980 full-time, 83 part-time. Students come from 42 states and territories, 18 other countries, 70% are from out of state, 95% African American, 0.1% Hispanic American, 2% international, 1% transferred in, 53% live on campus. *Retention:* 91% of 2002 full-time freshmen returned.

Freshmen *Admission:* 493 enrolled. *Average high school GPA:* 3.40. *Test scores:* SAT verbal scores over 500: 77%; SAT math scores over 500: 72%; ACT scores over 18: 97%; SAT verbal scores over 600: 20%; SAT math scores over 600: 17%; ACT scores over 24: 32%; SAT verbal scores over 700: 3%; SAT math scores over 700: 1%.

Faculty *Total:* 227, 70% full-time, 72% with terminal degrees. *Student/faculty ratio:* 11:1.

Majors Anthropology; art; biochemistry; biology/biological sciences; chemistry; computer science; developmental and child psychology; dramatic/theatre arts; economics; engineering; English; environmental studies; French; history; mathematics; music; natural sciences; philosophy; physics; political science and government; psychology; religious studies; sociology; Spanish; women's studies.

Academic Programs *Special study options:* academic remediation for entering students, adult/continuing education programs, advanced placement credit, double majors, honors programs, independent study, internships, off-campus study, part-time degree program, services for LD students, student-designed majors, study abroad. *ROTC:* Army (c), Air Force (c). *Unusual degree programs:* 3-2 engineering with North Carolina Agricultural and Technical State University, Rensselaer Polytechnic Institute, Georgia Institute of Technology, Boston University, The University of Alabama in Huntsville, Auburn University.

Library Robert Woodruff Library with 727,767 titles, 1,549 serial subscriptions, 10,656 audiovisual materials, an OPAC, a Web page.

Computers on Campus 105 computers available on campus for general student use. A campuswide network can be accessed from off campus. Internet access, online (class) registration, at least one staffed computer lab available.

Student Life *Housing options:* women-only. Campus housing is university owned and leased by the school. Freshman applicants given priority for college housing. *Activities and organizations:* drama/theater group, student-run newspaper, choral group, Student Government Association, Spotlight (newspaper), Health Careers Club, NAACP (campus organization), SHAPE (health organization), national sororities. *Campus security:* 24-hour emergency response devices and patrols, late-night transport/escort service, controlled dormitory access. *Student services:* health clinic, personal/psychological counseling, women's center.

Athletics Member NCAA. *Intercollegiate sports:* basketball W, cross-country running W, golf W, soccer W, tennis W, track and field W, volleyball W. *Intramural sports:* softball W, swimming W.

Standardized Tests *Required:* SAT I or ACT (for admission).

Costs (2003–04) *Comprehensive fee:* $21,750 includes full-time tuition ($11,950), mandatory fees ($2175), and room and board ($7625). Part-time tuition: $500 per hour. Part-time tuition and fees vary according to course load. *Payment plan:* deferred payment. *Waivers:* employees or children of employees.

Financial Aid *Average financial aid package:* $3250. *Average indebtedness upon graduation:* $13,600.

Applying *Options:* common application, electronic application, early admission, early action, deferred entrance. *Application fee:* $35. *Required:* essay or personal statement, high school transcript, minimum 2.0 GPA, 2 letters of recommendation. *Required for some:* interview. *Application deadlines:* 2/1 (freshmen), 2/1 (transfers). *Notification:* 4/1 (freshmen), 4/1 (transfers).

Admissions Contact Ms. Arlene Cash, Vice President for Admissions and Orientation, Spelman College, 350 Spelman Lane, SW, Atlanta, GA 30314-4399. *Phone:* 404-681-3643. *Toll-free phone:* 800-982-2411. *Fax:* 404-270-5201. *E-mail:* admiss@spelman.edu.

■ See page 2430 for a narrative description.

STATE UNIVERSITY OF WEST GEORGIA
Carrollton, Georgia

- **State-supported** comprehensive, founded 1933, part of University System of Georgia
- **Calendar** semesters
- **Degrees** bachelor's, master's, doctoral, and post-master's certificates
- **Small-town** 394-acre campus with easy access to Atlanta
- **Endowment** $9.5 million
- **Coed,** 8,045 undergraduate students, 84% full-time, 60% women, 40% men
- **Minimally difficult** entrance level, 62% of applicants were admitted

Undergraduates 6,741 full-time, 1,304 part-time. Students come from 42 states and territories, 34 other countries, 4% are from out of state, 22% African American, 1% Asian American or Pacific Islander, 1% Hispanic American, 0.2% Native American, 0.8% international, 8% transferred in, 29% live on campus. *Retention:* 69% of 2002 full-time freshmen returned.

Freshmen *Admission:* 4,848 applied, 3,026 admitted, 1,788 enrolled. *Average high school GPA:* 2.98. *Test scores:* SAT verbal scores over 500: 54%; SAT math scores over 500: 51%; ACT scores over 18: 88%; SAT verbal scores over 600: 12%; SAT math scores over 600: 11%; ACT scores over 24: 17%; SAT verbal scores over 700: 2%; SAT math scores over 700: 1%; ACT scores over 30: 1%.

Faculty *Total:* 477, 78% full-time, 72% with terminal degrees. *Student/faculty ratio:* 20:1.

Majors Accounting; anthropology; art; biology/biological sciences; biology teacher education; business administration and management; business/managerial economics; business teacher education; chemistry; chemistry teacher education; computer and information sciences; criminal justice/safety; dramatic/theatre arts; economics; economics related; elementary education; English; environmental studies; finance; French; geography; geological and earth sciences/geosciences related; geology/earth science; German; history; international economics; international relations and affairs; journalism; management information systems; marketing/marketing management; mathematics; microbiological sciences and immunology related; middle school education; music performance; music teacher education; music theory and composition; nursing (registered nurse training); office management; parks, recreation and leisure facilities management; philosophy; physical education teaching and coaching; physics; physics teacher education; political science and government; pre-law studies; pre-medical studies; pre-veterinary studies; psychology; real estate; secondary education; sociology; Spanish; special education (mentally retarded); speech-language pathology.

Academic Programs *Special study options:* academic remediation for entering students, accelerated degree program, adult/continuing education programs, advanced placement credit, cooperative education, distance learning, double majors, external degree program, honors programs, independent study, internships, off-campus study, part-time degree program, services for LD students, study abroad, summer session for credit. *ROTC:* Army (b). *Unusual degree programs:* 3-2 engineering with Georgia Institute of Technology, Auburn University.

Library Irvine Sullivan Ingram Library with 378,656 titles, 1,342 serial subscriptions, 9,494 audiovisual materials, an OPAC, a Web page.

Computers on Campus 745 computers available on campus for general student use. A campuswide network can be accessed from student residence rooms and from off campus. Internet access, online (class) registration, at least one staffed computer lab available.

Student Life *Housing:* on-campus residence required for freshman year. *Options:* coed, men-only, women-only. Campus housing is university owned. Freshman campus housing is guaranteed. *Activities and organizations:* drama/theater group, student-run newspaper, radio and television station, choral group, marching band, Black Student Alliance, Student Activities Council, Baptist Student Union, Campus Outreach, United Voices Gospel Choir, national fraternities, national sororities. *Campus security:* 24-hour emergency response devices and patrols, late-night transport/escort service, controlled dormitory access. *Student services:* health clinic, personal/psychological counseling.

Athletics Member NCAA. All Division II. *Intercollegiate sports:* baseball M(s), basketball M(s)/W(s), cheerleading M(s)/W(s), cross-country running M(s)/W(s), football M(s), softball W(s), volleyball W(s). *Intramural sports:* badminton M/W, basketball M/W, football M/W, golf M/W, racquetball M/W, soccer M/W, softball M/W, swimming M/W, table tennis M/W, tennis M/W, track and field M/W, ultimate Frisbee M/W, volleyball M/W, water polo M/W, weight lifting M/W.

Standardized Tests *Required:* SAT I or ACT (for admission).

Costs (2003–04) *Tuition:* state resident $2212 full-time, $93 per semester hour part-time; nonresident $8848 full-time, $369 per semester hour part-time. Part-time tuition and fees vary according to course load. *Required fees:* $562 full-time, $15 per semester hour part-time, $100 per term part-time. *Room and board:* $4406; room only: $2420. Room and board charges vary according to board plan and housing facility. *Waivers:* minority students, adult students, senior citizens, and employees or children of employees.

Financial Aid Of all full-time matriculated undergraduates who enrolled in 2003, 4,758 applied for aid, 3,544 were judged to have need, 796 had their need fully met. 538 Federal Work-Study jobs (averaging $2400). In 2003, 145 non-need-based awards were made. *Average percent of need met:* 69%. *Average financial aid package:* $7337. *Average need-based loan:* $2715. *Average need-based gift aid:* $4344. *Average non-need-based aid:* $1833. *Average indebtedness upon graduation:* $18,230.

Applying *Options:* common application, electronic application, early admission, deferred entrance. *Application fee:* $20. *Required:* high school transcript, proof of immunization. *Required for some:* 2 letters of recommendation, interview. *Application deadlines:* 7/1 (freshmen), 6/1 (transfers). *Notification:* continuous until 8/1 (freshmen), continuous (transfers).

Admissions Contact Dr. Robert Johnson, Director of Admissions, State University of West Georgia, 1600 Maple Street, Carrollton, GA 30118. *Phone:* 770-836-6416. *Toll-free phone:* 770-836-6416. *Fax:* 770-836-4659. *E-mail:* admiss@westga.edu.

■ *See page 2456 for a narrative description.*

THOMAS UNIVERSITY
Thomasville, Georgia

- **Independent** comprehensive, founded 1950
- **Calendar** semesters
- **Degrees** associate, bachelor's, master's, and postbachelor's certificates
- **Small-town** 24-acre campus
- **Endowment** $2.1 million
- **Coed,** 674 undergraduate students, 74% full-time, 69% women, 31% men
- **Noncompetitive** entrance level

Undergraduates 502 full-time, 172 part-time. Students come from 6 states and territories, 11 other countries, 6% are from out of state, 33% African American, 0.9% Asian American or Pacific Islander, 1% Hispanic American, 0.3% Native American, 7% international, 12% transferred in, 9% live on campus. *Retention:* 59% of 2002 full-time freshmen returned.

Freshmen *Admission:* 62 applied, 68 enrolled.

Faculty *Total:* 69, 64% full-time, 57% with terminal degrees. *Student/faculty ratio:* 10:1.

Majors Accounting; biology/biological sciences; business administration and management; business/commerce; communication/speech communication and rhetoric; criminal justice/law enforcement administration; criminology; early childhood education; English; humanities; kindergarten/preschool education; liberal arts and sciences/liberal studies; mathematics; middle school education; nursing (registered nurse training); parks, recreation and leisure facilities management; political science and government; psychology; rehabilitation therapy; secondary education; social sciences; social work; sociology.

Academic Programs *Special study options:* academic remediation for entering students, accelerated degree program, adult/continuing education programs, advanced placement credit, cooperative education, distance learning, double majors, independent study, internships, part-time degree program, services for LD students, study abroad, summer session for credit.

Library Thomas University Library with 50,442 titles, 418 serial subscriptions, an OPAC.

Computers on Campus 50 computers available on campus for general student use. A campuswide network can be accessed. At least one staffed computer lab available.

Student Life *Housing options:* coed. Campus housing is university owned. Freshman applicants given priority for college housing. *Activities and organizations:* student-run newspaper, choral group, Nursing Club, Psychology Club, Baptist Student Union. *Campus security:* late-night transport/escort service, evening security guards. *Student services:* personal/psychological counseling.

Athletics Member NAIA. *Intercollegiate sports:* baseball M(s), golf M(s), soccer M(s)/W(s), softball W(s), tennis W(s). *Intramural sports:* football M/W, table tennis M/W, tennis M/W, volleyball M/W.

Standardized Tests *Required:* MAPS (for placement). *Recommended:* SAT I or ACT (for placement).

Costs (2003–04) *Tuition:* $8550 full-time, $285 per semester hour part-time. *Required fees:* $470 full-time, $117 per term part-time. *Room only:* $2400. *Waivers:* senior citizens and employees or children of employees.

Financial Aid Of all full-time matriculated undergraduates who enrolled in 2002, 634 applied for aid, 634 were judged to have need, 279 had their need fully met. 16 Federal Work-Study jobs (averaging $3723). *Average percent of need met:* 48%. *Average financial aid package:* $5119. *Average need-based loan:* $3475. *Average need-based gift aid:* $2652. *Average indebtedness upon graduation:* $11,451.

Applying *Options:* electronic application, early admission, deferred entrance. *Application fee:* $25. *Required:* high school transcript, minimum 2.0 GPA. *Application deadline:* rolling (freshmen), rolling (transfers).

Admissions Contact Ms. Darla M. Glass, Director of Student Affairs, Thomas University, 1501 Millpond Road, Thomasville, GA 31792. *Phone:* 229-226-1621 Ext. 122. *Toll-free phone:* 800-538-9784. *Fax:* 229-227-1653.

TOCCOA FALLS COLLEGE
Toccoa Falls, Georgia

- **Independent interdenominational** 4-year, founded 1907
- **Calendar** semesters
- **Degrees** diplomas, associate, and bachelor's
- **Small-town** 500-acre campus
- **Endowment** $2.0 million
- **Coed,** 847 undergraduate students, 91% full-time, 58% women, 42% men
- **Moderately difficult** entrance level, 75% of applicants were admitted

Undergraduates 774 full-time, 73 part-time. Students come from 38 states and territories, 12 other countries, 37% are from out of state, 2% African American, 5% Asian American or Pacific Islander, 2% Hispanic American, 3% international, 7% transferred in, 63% live on campus. *Retention:* 77% of 2002 full-time freshmen returned.

Freshmen *Admission:* 430 applied, 324 admitted, 171 enrolled. *Average high school GPA:* 3.40. *Test scores:* SAT verbal scores over 500: 71%; SAT math scores over 500: 56%; ACT scores over 18: 85%; SAT verbal scores over 600: 24%; SAT math scores over 600: 13%; ACT scores over 24: 32%; SAT verbal scores over 700: 4%; SAT math scores over 700: 2%; ACT scores over 30: 4%.

Faculty *Total:* 68, 66% full-time, 47% with terminal degrees. *Student/faculty ratio:* 15:1.

Majors Biblical studies; business administration and management; counseling psychology; early childhood education; English; English/language arts teacher education; general studies; history teacher education; mass communication/media; middle school education; missionary studies and missiology; music; music performance; music teacher education; organizational communication; philosophy; religious education; religious/sacred music; youth ministry.

Academic Programs *Special study options:* academic remediation for entering students, accelerated degree program, advanced placement credit, double majors, independent study, internships, services for LD students, summer session for credit.

Library Seby Jones Library with 125,667 titles, 280 serial subscriptions, 5,161 audiovisual materials, a Web page.

Computers on Campus 50 computers available on campus for general student use. A campuswide network can be accessed from student residence rooms and from off campus. Internet access, at least one staffed computer lab available.

Student Life *Housing:* on-campus residence required through junior year. *Options:* men-only, women-only. Campus housing is university owned. Freshman campus housing is guaranteed. *Activities and organizations:* drama/theater group, student-run newspaper, radio station, choral group, Outdoor Club, Hmong Stu-

Toccoa Falls College (continued)
dent Fellowship, Impact, Student Missionary Fellowship, Fellowship of Christian Athletes. *Campus security:* student patrols. *Student services:* health clinic, personal/psychological counseling.

Athletics Member NCCAA. *Intercollegiate sports:* baseball M, basketball M/W, soccer M/W, volleyball W. *Intramural sports:* basketball M/W, golf M/W, soccer M/W.

Standardized Tests *Required:* SAT I or ACT (for admission).

Costs (2004–05) *One-time required fee:* $450. *Comprehensive fee:* $15,900 includes full-time tuition ($11,450) and room and board ($4450). Full-time tuition and fees vary according to course load. Part-time tuition: $477 per credit hour. Part-time tuition and fees vary according to course load. *Room and board:* Room and board charges vary according to board plan and housing facility. *Waivers:* employees or children of employees.

Financial Aid Of all full-time matriculated undergraduates who enrolled in 2003, 679 applied for aid, 621 were judged to have need, 89 had their need fully met. 326 Federal Work-Study jobs (averaging $1911). 89 state and other part-time jobs (averaging $2094). In 2003, 126 non-need-based awards were made. *Average percent of need met:* 46%. *Average financial aid package:* $10,132. *Average need-based loan:* $3773. *Average need-based gift aid:* $3960. *Average non-need-based aid:* $4720. *Average indebtedness upon graduation:* $16,152.

Applying *Options:* common application, electronic application, early admission, deferred entrance. *Application fee:* $20. *Required:* essay or personal statement, high school transcript, minimum 2.0 GPA, 1 letter of recommendation. *Required for some:* interview. *Application deadline:* rolling (freshmen), rolling (transfers). *Notification:* continuous (freshmen), continuous (transfers).

Admissions Contact Mr. Tristam Aldridge, Director of Admissions, Toccoa Falls College, Office of Admissions, PO Box 800899, Toccoa Falls, GA 30598-1000. *Phone:* 706-886-6831 Ext. 5380. *Fax:* 706-282-6012. *E-mail:* admissions@tfc.edu.

■ *See page 2512 for a narrative description.*

TRUETT-MCCONNELL COLLEGE
Cleveland, Georgia

- **Independent Baptist** primarily 2-year, founded 1946
- **Calendar** semesters
- **Degrees** certificates, associate, and bachelor's
- **Rural** 310-acre campus with easy access to Atlanta
- **Endowment** $6.7 million
- **Coed**
- **Minimally difficult** entrance level

Faculty *Student/faculty ratio:* 11:1.

Student Life *Campus security:* 24-hour weekday patrols, 10-hour weekend patrols by trained security personnel.

Athletics Member NJCAA.

Standardized Tests *Required:* SAT I or ACT (for admission).

Costs (2003–04) *Comprehensive fee:* $14,028 includes full-time tuition ($9828) and room and board ($4200). Part-time tuition: $330 per credit hour. *College room only:* $2000.

Applying *Options:* early admission, deferred entrance. *Required:* high school transcript, minimum 2.0 GPA, minimum SAT score of 720 or ACT score of 15. *Required for some:* interview.

Admissions Contact Mr. Alan Coker, Dean for Admissions, Truett-McConnell College, 100 Alumni Drive, Cleveland, GA 30528-9799. *Phone:* 706-865-2134 Ext. 129. *Toll-free phone:* 800-226-8621. *Fax:* 706-865-7615. *E-mail:* admissions@truett.edu.

UNIVERSITY OF GEORGIA
Athens, Georgia

- **State-supported** university, founded 1785, part of University System of Georgia
- **Calendar** semesters
- **Degrees** associate, bachelor's, master's, doctoral, and first professional
- **Suburban** 1289-acre campus with easy access to Atlanta
- **Endowment** $414.4 million
- **Coed,** 25,415 undergraduate students, 90% full-time, 57% women, 43% men
- **Moderately difficult** entrance level, 75% of applicants were admitted

Undergraduates 22,971 full-time, 2,444 part-time. Students come from 54 states and territories, 105 other countries, 11% are from out of state, 5% African American, 4% Asian American or Pacific Islander, 2% Hispanic American, 0.1% Native American, 0.7% international, 5% transferred in, 27% live on campus. *Retention:* 93% of 2002 full-time freshmen returned.

Freshmen *Admission:* 11,813 applied, 8,885 admitted, 5,177 enrolled. *Average high school GPA:* 3.61. *Test scores:* SAT verbal scores over 500: 93%; SAT math scores over 500: 94%; ACT scores over 18: 99%; SAT verbal scores over 600: 52%; SAT math scores over 600: 56%; ACT scores over 24: 70%; SAT verbal scores over 700: 10%; SAT math scores over 700: 10%; ACT scores over 30: 11%.

Faculty *Total:* 2,024, 83% full-time, 88% with terminal degrees. *Student/faculty ratio:* 14:1.

Majors Accounting; advertising; African-American/Black studies; agricultural/biological engineering and bioengineering; agricultural business and management; agricultural economics; agricultural teacher education; agronomy and crop science; ancient/classical Greek; animal genetics; animal sciences; anthropology; apparel and textiles; applied horticulture; art; art history, criticism and conservation; art teacher education; astronomy; biochemistry; biological and physical sciences; biology/biological sciences; biotechnology; botany/plant biology; broadcast journalism; business administration and management; business/commerce; business/managerial economics; business teacher education; cell biology and histology; chemistry; classics and languages, literatures and linguistics; cognitive psychology and psycholinguistics; communication disorders; comparative literature; computer and information sciences; consumer economics; criminal justice/safety; dairy science; dietetics; drama and dance teacher education; dramatic/theatre arts; ecology; economics; educational psychology; English; English/language arts teacher education; entomology; environmental health; family and consumer sciences/home economics teacher education; fashion merchandising; film/cinema studies; finance; fine/studio arts; fishing and fisheries sciences and management; food science; foods, nutrition, and wellness; foreign languages and literatures; foreign language teacher education; forestry; forest sciences and biology; French; geography; geology/earth science; German; health teacher education; history; housing and human environments; human development and family studies; insurance; international business/trade/commerce; Italian; Japanese; journalism; kindergarten/preschool education; landscape architecture; landscaping and groundskeeping; Latin; liberal arts and sciences/liberal studies; linguistics; management information systems; marketing/marketing management; mass communication/media; mathematics; mathematics teacher education; medical microbiology and bacteriology; middle school education; music; music performance; music teacher education; music theory and composition; music therapy; pharmacy; philosophy; physical education teaching and coaching; plant protection and integrated pest management; political science and government; poultry science; psychology; public relations/image management; radio and television broadcasting technology; reading teacher education; real estate; religious studies; Russian; sales and marketing/marketing and distribution teacher education; science teacher education; Slavic languages; social science teacher education; social work; sociology; Spanish; special education; speech and rhetoric; sport and fitness administration; statistics; technology/industrial arts teacher education; turf and turfgrass management; wildlife and wildlands science and management; women's studies.

Academic Programs *Special study options:* academic remediation for entering students, accelerated degree program, adult/continuing education programs, advanced placement credit, cooperative education, distance learning, double majors, English as a second language, honors programs, independent study, internships, off-campus study, part-time degree program, services for LD students, student-designed majors, study abroad, summer session for credit. *ROTC:* Army (b), Air Force (b). *Unusual degree programs:* 3-2 engineering with Georgia Institute of Technology.

Library Ilah Dunlap Little Memorial Library plus 2 others with 3.8 million titles, 46,431 serial subscriptions, 108,612 audiovisual materials, an OPAC, a Web page.

Computers on Campus 2500 computers available on campus for general student use. A campuswide network can be accessed from student residence rooms and from off campus that provide access to e-mail, web pages. Internet access, online (class) registration, at least one staffed computer lab available.

Student Life *Housing options:* coed, men-only, women-only, disabled students. Campus housing is university owned. Freshman campus housing is guaranteed. *Activities and organizations:* drama/theater group, student-run newspaper, radio and television station, choral group, marching band, intramurals, recreational sports program, Communiversity, University Union, Red Coat Band, national fraternities, national sororities. *Campus security:* 24-hour emergency response devices and patrols, late-night transport/escort service, controlled dormitory access. *Student services:* health clinic, personal/psychological counseling, legal services.

Athletics Member NCAA. All Division I except football (Division I-A). *Intercollegiate sports:* baseball M(s), basketball M(s)/W(s), cheerleading M/W, cross-country running M(s)/W(s), equestrian sports M(s)/W(s), golf M(s)/W(s), gymnastics W(s), soccer M(c)/W(s), swimming M(s)/W(s), tennis M(s)/W(s), track and field M(s)/W(s), volleyball M(c)/W(s). *Intramural sports:* badminton M(c)/W(c), basketball M/W, bowling M/W, crew M(c), cross-country running M/W, equestrian sports M(c)/W(c), fencing M(c), football M/W, golf M/W, ice hockey M(c), lacrosse M(c)/W(c), racquetball M/W, rugby M(c), soccer M/W, softball M/W, swimming M/W, tennis M/W, track and field M/W, volleyball M/W, weight lifting M/W, wrestling M(c).

Standardized Tests *Required:* SAT I or ACT (for admission). *Required for some:* SAT I and SAT II or ACT (for admission), SAT II: Writing Test (for admission).

Costs (2003–04) *Tuition:* state resident $3208 full-time, $134 per credit part-time; nonresident $13,984 full-time, $583 per credit part-time. Full-time tuition and fees vary according to course load, location, program, and reciprocity agreements. Part-time tuition and fees vary according to course load, location, program, and reciprocity agreements. *Required fees:* $870 full-time, $435 per term part-time. *Room and board:* $5756; room only: $3182. Room and board charges vary according to board plan and housing facility. *Waivers:* senior citizens and employees or children of employees.

Financial Aid Of all full-time matriculated undergraduates who enrolled in 2003, 10,729 applied for aid, 6,308 were judged to have need, 2,008 had their need fully met. 488 Federal Work-Study jobs (averaging $2534). In 2003, 1201 non-need-based awards were made. *Average percent of need met:* 73%. *Average financial aid package:* $7323. *Average need-based loan:* $3771. *Average need-based gift aid:* $5664. *Average non-need-based aid:* $1927. *Average indebtedness upon graduation:* $13,193.

Applying *Options:* electronic application, early admission, early action, deferred entrance. *Application fee:* $50. *Required:* high school transcript. *Recommended:* essay or personal statement, minimum 2.0 GPA. *Application deadlines:* 2/1 (freshmen), 4/1 (transfers). *Notification:* 4/1 (freshmen), 12/15 (early action), continuous (transfers).

Admissions Contact Mr. J. Robert Spatig, Associate Director of Admissions, University of Georgia, Athens, GA 30602. *Phone:* 706-542-3000. *Fax:* 706-542-1466. *E-mail:* undergrad@admissions.uga.edu.

■ *See page 2606 for a narrative description.*

UNIVERSITY OF PHOENIX–ATLANTA CAMPUS
Atlanta, Georgia

- **Proprietary** comprehensive
- **Calendar** continuous
- **Degrees** certificates, associate, bachelor's, master's, doctoral, post-master's, and postbachelor's certificates (courses conducted at 121 campuses and learning centers in 25 states)
- **Urban** campus
- **Coed,** 702 undergraduate students, 100% full-time, 62% women, 38% men
- **Noncompetitive** entrance level

Undergraduates 702 full-time. 42% African American, 0.7% Asian American or Pacific Islander, 2% Hispanic American, 0.7% Native American, 10% international.

Freshmen *Admission:* 33 enrolled.

Faculty *Total:* 41, 10% full-time, 32% with terminal degrees. *Student/faculty ratio:* 9:1.

Majors Accounting; business administration and management; computer and information sciences; computer programming; computer systems networking and telecommunications; data modeling/warehousing and database administration; entrepreneurship; management information systems; management science; marketing/marketing management; nursing science; web/multimedia management and webmaster.

Academic Programs *Special study options:* accelerated degree program, adult/continuing education programs, advanced placement credit, distance learning, external degree program, independent study.

Library University Library with 27.1 million titles, 11,648 serial subscriptions, an OPAC, a Web page.

Computers on Campus A campuswide network can be accessed from off campus. Internet access, at least one staffed computer lab available.

Student Life *Housing:* college housing not available.

Costs (2003–04) *Tuition:* $9420 full-time, $314 per credit part-time. *Waivers:* employees or children of employees.

Financial Aid *Average financial aid package:* $1740.

Applying *Options:* deferred entrance. *Application fee:* $100. *Required:* 1 letter of recommendation, 2 years of work experience, 23 years of age. *Required for some:* high school transcript. *Application deadline:* rolling (freshmen), rolling (transfers).

Admissions Contact Ms. Beth Barilla, Director of Admissions, University of Phoenix–Atlanta Campus, 4615 East Elwood Street, Mail Stop AA-K101, Phoenix, AZ 85040-1958. *Phone:* 480-317-6000. *Toll-free phone:* 800-228-7240. *Fax:* 480-594-1758. *E-mail:* beth.barilla@phoenix.edu.

UNIVERSITY OF PHOENIX–COLUMBUS GEORGIA CAMPUS
Columbus, Georgia

Admissions Contact 18 Ninth Street, Columbus, GA 31901.

VALDOSTA STATE UNIVERSITY
Valdosta, Georgia

- **State-supported** university, founded 1906, part of University System of Georgia
- **Calendar** semesters
- **Degrees** associate, bachelor's, master's, doctoral, and post-master's certificates
- **Small-town** 200-acre campus with easy access to Jacksonville
- **Endowment** $5.8 million
- **Coed,** 8,801 undergraduate students, 80% full-time, 60% women, 40% men
- **Moderately difficult** entrance level, 68% of applicants were admitted

Undergraduates 7,024 full-time, 1,777 part-time. Students come from 46 states and territories, 69 other countries, 7% are from out of state, 22% African American, 1% Asian American or Pacific Islander, 1% Hispanic American, 0.3% Native American, 1% international, 8% transferred in, 15% live on campus. *Retention:* 74% of 2002 full-time freshmen returned.

Freshmen *Admission:* 5,400 applied, 3,694 admitted, 2,001 enrolled. *Average high school GPA:* 3.05. *Test scores:* SAT verbal scores over 500: 54%; SAT math scores over 500: 52%; ACT scores over 18: 91%; SAT verbal scores over 600: 10%; SAT math scores over 600: 11%; ACT scores over 24: 16%; SAT verbal scores over 700: 1%; SAT math scores over 700: 1%; ACT scores over 30: 1%.

Faculty *Total:* 557, 76% full-time, 63% with terminal degrees. *Student/faculty ratio:* 20:1.

Majors Accounting; accounting technology and bookkeeping; administrative assistant and secretarial science; air traffic control; applied horticulture; applied mathematics; art; art teacher education; astronomy; autobody/collision and repair technology; automobile/automotive mechanics technology; biology/biological sciences; building/property maintenance and management; business administration and management; business/commerce; business/managerial economics; business teacher education; cabinetmaking and millwork; carpentry; chemistry; chemistry teacher education; communication/speech communication and rhetoric; computer and information sciences; computer systems analysis; cosmetology; criminal justice/safety; dental assisting; dental hygiene; diesel mechanics technology; early childhood education; economics; electrical/electronics equipment installation and repair; electrician; elementary education; emergency medical technology (EMT paramedic); engineering technology; English; English/language arts teacher education; finance; foreign language teacher education; French; general studies; health and physical education; heating, air conditioning, ventilation and refrigeration maintenance technology; heavy equipment maintenance technology; history; industrial mechanics and maintenance technology; information science/studies; interior design; kinesiology and exercise science; legal assistant/paralegal; liberal arts and sciences/liberal studies; machine shop technology; marketing/marketing management; masonry; mathematics; mathematics teacher education; medical/clinical assistant; medical radiologic technology; middle school education; music; music performance; music teacher education; natural resources/conservation; nuclear medical technology; nursing (registered nurse training); office occupations and clerical services; pharmacy technician; philosophy; physical education teaching and coaching; physics; plumbing technology; political science and government; precision production trades; psychology; school psychology; science teacher education; secondary education; social studies teacher education; sociology; Spanish; special education; special education (mentally retarded); speech-language pathology; surgical technology; trade and industrial teacher education; visual and performing arts; welding technology.

Academic Programs *Special study options:* academic remediation for entering students, accelerated degree program, adult/continuing education programs, advanced placement credit, cooperative education, distance learning, English as a second language, freshman honors college, honors programs, internships, off-campus study, part-time degree program, services for LD students, study abroad, summer session for credit. *ROTC:* Air Force (b). *Unusual degree programs:* 3-2 engineering with Georgia Institute of Technology.

Library Odom Library plus 2 others with 290,295 titles, 3,097 serial subscriptions, 19,400 audiovisual materials, an OPAC.

Computers on Campus 2400 computers available on campus for general student use. A campuswide network can be accessed from student residence rooms and from off campus. Internet access, online (class) registration, at least one staffed computer lab available.

Student Life *Housing:* on-campus residence required for freshman year. *Options:* coed, men-only, women-only, disabled students. Campus housing is

Valdosta State University (continued)
university owned. *Activities and organizations:* drama/theater group, student-run newspaper, radio and television station, choral group, marching band, Blazing Brigade (marching band), Student Government Association, Greek organizations, intramural athletics, Baptist Student Union, national fraternities, national sororities. *Campus security:* 24-hour emergency response devices and patrols, student patrols, late-night transport/escort service, controlled dormitory access, bicycle patrols, security cameras. *Student services:* health clinic, personal/psychological counseling.

Athletics Member NCAA. All Division II. *Intercollegiate sports:* baseball M(s), basketball M(s)/W(s), cross-country running M(s)/W(s), football M(s), golf M(s), softball W(s), tennis M(s)/W(s), volleyball W(s). *Intramural sports:* badminton M/W, basketball M/W, bowling M/W, cross-country running M/W, field hockey M/W, football M/W, golf M/W, soccer M/W, softball M/W, swimming M/W, table tennis M/W, tennis M/W, ultimate Frisbee M/W, volleyball M/W, weight lifting M/W.

Standardized Tests *Required:* SAT I or ACT (for admission).

Costs (2003–04) *Tuition:* state resident $2212 full-time, $93 per semester hour part-time; nonresident $8848 full-time, $369 per semester hour part-time. Part-time tuition and fees vary according to course load. *Required fees:* $648 full-time. *Room and board:* $5002; room only: $2556. Room and board charges vary according to board plan. *Waivers:* senior citizens and employees or children of employees.

Financial Aid Of all full-time matriculated undergraduates who enrolled in 2003, 6,146 applied for aid, 3,583 were judged to have need, 1,130 had their need fully met. 185 Federal Work-Study jobs (averaging $2443). In 2003, 945 non-need-based awards were made. *Average percent of need met:* 70%. *Average financial aid package:* $6484. *Average need-based loan:* $3174. *Average need-based gift aid:* $3026. *Average non-need-based aid:* $6182. *Average indebtedness upon graduation:* $22,361.

Applying *Options:* electronic application, early admission, deferred entrance. *Application fee:* $20. *Required:* high school transcript, minimum 2.0 GPA, proof of immunization. *Application deadlines:* 7/1 (freshmen), 8/1 (transfers). *Notification:* continuous (freshmen), continuous (transfers).

Admissions Contact Mr. Walter Peacock, Director of Admissions, Valdosta State University, Valdosta, GA 31698. *Phone:* 229-333-5791. *Toll-free phone:* 800-618-1878 Ext. 1. *Fax:* 229-333-5482. *E-mail:* admissions@valdosta.edu.

WESLEYAN COLLEGE
Macon, Georgia

- **Independent United Methodist** comprehensive, founded 1836
- **Calendar** semesters
- **Degrees** bachelor's and master's
- **Suburban** 200-acre campus with easy access to Atlanta
- **Endowment** $31.3 million
- **Women only,** 661 undergraduate students, 79% full-time
- **Moderately difficult** entrance level, 77% of applicants were admitted

Undergraduates 525 full-time, 136 part-time. Students come from 27 states and territories, 31 other countries, 21% are from out of state, 29% African American, 2% Asian American or Pacific Islander, 2% Hispanic American, 19% international, 5% transferred in, 70% live on campus. *Retention:* 78% of 2002 full-time freshmen returned.

Freshmen *Admission:* 92 enrolled. *Average high school GPA:* 3.60. *Test scores:* SAT verbal scores over 500: 73%; SAT math scores over 500: 62%; ACT scores over 18: 88%; SAT verbal scores over 600: 33%; SAT math scores over 600: 24%; ACT scores over 24: 38%; SAT verbal scores over 700: 5%; SAT math scores over 700: 6%.

Faculty *Total:* 72, 65% full-time, 69% with terminal degrees. *Student/faculty ratio:* 11:1.

Majors Advertising; American studies; art history, criticism and conservation; biology/biological sciences; business administration and management; chemistry; communication/speech communication and rhetoric; computer and information sciences; early childhood education; economics; education; English; fine/studio arts; French; history; humanities; interdisciplinary studies; international business/trade/commerce; international relations and affairs; mathematics; middle school education; music; philosophy; physical sciences; physics; political science and government; psychology; religious studies; social sciences; Spanish.

Academic Programs *Special study options:* adult/continuing education programs, advanced placement credit, cooperative education, double majors, honors programs, independent study, internships, off-campus study, part-time degree program, student-designed majors, study abroad, summer session for credit. *Unusual degree programs:* 3-2 engineering with Georgia Institute of Technology, Mercer University, Auburn University.

Library Lucy Lester Willet Memorial Library with 140,923 titles, 506 serial subscriptions, 4,259 audiovisual materials, an OPAC, a Web page.

Computers on Campus 100 computers available on campus for general student use. A campuswide network can be accessed from student residence rooms and from off campus. Internet access, online (class) registration, at least one staffed computer lab available.

Student Life *Housing:* on-campus residence required through senior year. *Options:* women-only. Campus housing is university owned. Freshman campus housing is guaranteed. *Activities and organizations:* drama/theater group, student-run newspaper, choral group, Student Recreation Council, Campus Activities Board, Student Government Association, Council on Religious Concerns, Christian Fellowship. *Campus security:* 24-hour emergency response devices and patrols, late-night transport/escort service, controlled dormitory access. *Student services:* health clinic, personal/psychological counseling, women's center.

Athletics Member NCAA. All Division III. *Intercollegiate sports:* basketball W, equestrian sports W, soccer W, softball W, tennis W, volleyball W. *Intramural sports:* basketball W, cheerleading M/W, rock climbing M/W, soccer W, softball W, ultimate Frisbee M(c)/W(c), volleyball W.

Standardized Tests *Required:* SAT I or ACT (for admission).

Costs (2003–04) *Comprehensive fee:* $17,870 includes full-time tuition ($9570), mandatory fees ($850), and room and board ($7450). Full-time tuition and fees vary according to class time and course load. Part-time tuition: $360 per semester hour. Part-time tuition and fees vary according to class time, course load, and program. *Room and board:* Room and board charges vary according to board plan and housing facility. *Waivers:* senior citizens and employees or children of employees.

Financial Aid Of all full-time matriculated undergraduates who enrolled in 2003, 406 applied for aid, 319 were judged to have need, 78 had their need fully met. 97 Federal Work-Study jobs (averaging $1200). 147 state and other part-time jobs (averaging $1200). *Average percent of need met:* 81%. *Average financial aid package:* $10,811. *Average need-based loan:* $3731. *Average need-based gift aid:* $7441. *Average non-need-based aid:* $12,223. *Average indebtedness upon graduation:* $20,627.

Applying *Options:* common application, early admission, early decision, early action, deferred entrance. *Application fee:* $30. *Required:* essay or personal statement, high school transcript, 1 letter of recommendation. *Recommended:* 2 letters of recommendation, interview. *Application deadline:* 3/1 (freshmen), rolling (transfers). *Early decision:* 11/15 (for plan 1), 1/15 (for plan 2). *Notification:* 4/1 (freshmen), 12/15 (early decision plan 1), 2/15 (early decision plan 2), 3/1 (early action), continuous until 8/1 (transfers).

Admissions Contact Ms. Rachel Powell, Director of Recruitment, Wesleyan College, 4760 Forsyth Road, Macon, GA 31210-4462. *Phone:* 478-757-5206. *Toll-free phone:* 800-447-6610. *Fax:* 478-757-4030. *E-mail:* admissions@wesleyancollege.edu.

■ *See page 2802 for a narrative description.*

HAWAII

ARGOSY UNIVERSITY/HONOLULU
Honolulu, Hawaii

Admissions Contact 400 ASB Tower, 1001 Bishop Street, Honolulu, HI 96813. *Toll-free phone:* 888-323-2777.

BRIGHAM YOUNG UNIVERSITY–HAWAII
Laie, Hawaii

- **Independent Latter-day Saints** 4-year, founded 1955
- **Calendar** 4-4-2-2
- **Degrees** associate, bachelor's, and postbachelor's certificates
- **Small-town** 60-acre campus with easy access to Honolulu
- **Endowment** $43.2 million
- **Coed,** 2,703 undergraduate students, 90% full-time, 54% women, 46% men
- **Moderately difficult** entrance level, 29% of applicants were admitted

Undergraduates 2,431 full-time, 272 part-time. Students come from 44 states and territories, 68 other countries, 37% are from out of state, 0.1% African American, 18% Asian American or Pacific Islander, 1% Hispanic American, 0.5% Native American, 47% international, 8% transferred in, 52% live on campus. *Retention:* 60% of 2002 full-time freshmen returned.

Freshmen *Admission:* 2,989 applied, 860 admitted, 262 enrolled. *Average high school GPA:* 3.20. *Test scores:* ACT scores over 18: 82%; ACT scores over 24: 28%; ACT scores over 30: 2%.

Faculty *Total:* 208, 59% full-time, 37% with terminal degrees. *Student/faculty ratio:* 16:1.

Majors Accounting; anthropology; area, ethnic, cultural, and gender studies related; art; art teacher education; biochemistry; biology/biological sciences; biology teacher education; business administration and management; business teacher education; chemistry; chemistry teacher education; communication and journalism related; communication/speech communication and rhetoric; computer programming; computer science; cultural studies; dramatic/theatre arts; education; elementary education; English; English as a second/foreign language (teaching); English/language arts teacher education; health and physical education; history; hotel/motel administration; humanities; information science/studies; interdisciplinary studies; international business/trade/commerce; kinesiology and exercise science; mathematics; mathematics teacher education; multi-/interdisciplinary studies related; music; music performance; music teacher education; Pacific area/Pacific rim studies; physical education teaching and coaching; physical sciences; physics teacher education; piano and organ; political science and government; psychology; science teacher education; secondary education; social science teacher education; social work; special education; tourism and travel services management; voice and opera.

Academic Programs *Special study options:* academic remediation for entering students, accelerated degree program, adult/continuing education programs, advanced placement credit, cooperative education, double majors, English as a second language, freshman honors college, honors programs, internships, off-campus study, part-time degree program, services for LD students, summer session for credit. *ROTC:* Army (c), Navy (c), Air Force (c).

Library Joseph F. Smith Library with 321,400 titles, 11,325 serial subscriptions, 7,000 audiovisual materials, an OPAC, a Web page.

Computers on Campus 465 computers available on campus for general student use. A campuswide network can be accessed from student residence rooms. Internet access, online (class) registration, at least one staffed computer lab available.

Student Life *Housing:* on-campus residence required for freshman year. *Options:* men-only, women-only. Campus housing is university owned. Freshman applicants given priority for college housing. *Activities and organizations:* drama/theater group, student-run newspaper, choral group, Tonga club, Samoa club, Hawaiian club, Hong Kong club, Japanese club. *Campus security:* 24-hour patrols, late-night transport/escort service. *Student services:* health clinic, personal/psychological counseling.

Athletics Member NCAA. All Division II. *Intercollegiate sports:* basketball M(s), cross-country running M(s)/W(s), softball W(s), tennis M(s)/W(s), volleyball W(s), water polo M(s). *Intramural sports:* badminton M(c)/W(c), basketball M/W, bowling M/W, cross-country running M/W, golf M/W, gymnastics M/W, racquetball M/W, rugby M/W, soccer M(c)/W(c), softball M/W, swimming M/W, table tennis M/W, tennis M/W, volleyball M/W, water polo M, weight lifting M/W, wrestling M/W.

Standardized Tests *Required:* SAT I or ACT (for admission). *Recommended:* ACT (for admission).

Costs (2003–04) *Comprehensive fee:* $7240 includes full-time tuition ($2580) and room and board ($4660). Full-time tuition and fees vary according to program. Part-time tuition: $175 per credit. Part-time tuition and fees vary according to program. *College room only:* $2000. Room and board charges vary according to board plan and housing facility. *Payment plan:* installment. *Waivers:* employees or children of employees.

Financial Aid Of all full-time matriculated undergraduates who enrolled in 2002, 2,000 applied for aid, 1,800 were judged to have need, 1,300 had their need fully met. 600 state and other part-time jobs (averaging $3500). In 2002, 600 non-need-based awards were made. *Average percent of need met:* 80%. *Average financial aid package:* $2850. *Average need-based loan:* $1410. *Average need-based gift aid:* $3000. *Average non-need-based aid:* $1245. *Average indebtedness upon graduation:* $8400.

Applying *Options:* common application, electronic application, early admission, deferred entrance. *Application fee:* $25. *Required:* essay or personal statement, high school transcript, minimum 3.0 GPA, resume of activities, ecclesiastical endorsement. *Required for some:* letters of recommendation. *Application deadlines:* 2/15 (freshmen), 3/15 (transfers). *Notification:* continuous (freshmen), continuous (transfers).

Admissions Contact Mr. Jeffrey N. Bunker, Dean for Admissions and Records, Brigham Young University–Hawaii, 55-220 Kulanui Street, BYUH 1973, Laie, Oahu, HI 96762. *Phone:* 808-293-3731. *Fax:* 808-293-3741. *E-mail:* admissions@byuh.edu.

CHAMINADE UNIVERSITY OF HONOLULU
Honolulu, Hawaii

- **Independent Roman Catholic** comprehensive, founded 1955
- **Calendar** semesters
- **Degrees** associate, bachelor's, master's, and postbachelor's certificates
- **Urban** 62-acre campus
- **Endowment** $3.7 million
- **Coed,** 1,063 undergraduate students, 97% full-time, 68% women, 32% men
- **Moderately difficult** entrance level, 96% of applicants were admitted

Undergraduates 1,026 full-time, 37 part-time. Students come from 41 states and territories, 11 other countries, 43% are from out of state, 5% African American, 63% Asian American or Pacific Islander, 5% Hispanic American, 1% Native American, 3% international, 11% transferred in. *Retention:* 55% of 2002 full-time freshmen returned.

Freshmen *Admission:* 830 applied, 799 admitted, 254 enrolled. *Average high school GPA:* 3.06. *Test scores:* SAT verbal scores over 500: 38%; SAT math scores over 500: 44%; ACT scores over 18: 88%; SAT verbal scores over 600: 9%; SAT math scores over 600: 11%; ACT scores over 24: 27%; SAT math scores over 700: 1%.

Faculty *Total:* 182, 42% full-time, 40% with terminal degrees. *Student/faculty ratio:* 14:1.

Majors Accounting; behavioral sciences; biology/biological sciences; business administration and management; computer and information sciences; criminology; early childhood education; elementary education; English; environmental studies; forensic science and technology; general studies; history; humanities; interior design; international relations and affairs; marketing/marketing management; mass communication/media; philosophy; political science and government; psychology; religious studies; social sciences.

Academic Programs *Special study options:* academic remediation for entering students, accelerated degree program, adult/continuing education programs, advanced placement credit, distance learning, double majors, independent study, internships, off-campus study, part-time degree program, student-designed majors, summer session for credit. *ROTC:* Army (c), Air Force (c). *Unusual degree programs:* 3-2 engineering with University of Dayton, St. Mary's University of San Antonio; mathematics with St. Mary's University of San Antonio.

Library Sullivan Library with 78,000 titles, 6,730 serial subscriptions, 566 audiovisual materials, an OPAC, a Web page.

Computers on Campus 90 computers available on campus for general student use. A campuswide network can be accessed from student residence rooms and from off campus. Internet access, at least one staffed computer lab available.

Student Life *Housing options:* coed, women-only. Campus housing is university owned and leased by the school. *Activities and organizations:* drama/theater group, student-run newspaper, choral group, Lumana O Samoa-(Samoan Club), Kaimi Lalakea-(Hawaiian Club), Rotaract Club, Residence Hall Association, Chaminade Student Government Association. *Campus security:* 24-hour emergency response devices and patrols, late-night transport/escort service, controlled dormitory access. *Student services:* personal/psychological counseling.

Athletics Member NCAA. All Division II. *Intercollegiate sports:* basketball M(s), cross-country running M(s)/W(s), softball W(s), tennis M(s)/W(s), volleyball W(s), water polo M(s).

Standardized Tests *Required:* SAT I or ACT (for admission).

Costs (2003–04) *Comprehensive fee:* $21,430 includes full-time tuition ($13,380), mandatory fees ($120), and room and board ($7930). *College room only:* $4150. *Payment plan:* installment. *Waivers:* employees or children of employees.

Financial Aid Of all full-time matriculated undergraduates who enrolled in 2003, 817 applied for aid, 735 were judged to have need, 132 had their need fully met. 115 Federal Work-Study jobs (averaging $1500). In 2003, 81 non-need-based awards were made. *Average percent of need met:* 66%. *Average financial aid package:* $12,201. *Average need-based loan:* $3771. *Average need-based gift aid:* $9004. *Average non-need-based aid:* $4693. *Average indebtedness upon graduation:* $21,105.

Applying *Options:* common application, electronic application, deferred entrance. *Application fee:* $50. *Required:* high school transcript. *Required for some:* interview. *Recommended:* minimum 2.0 GPA. *Application deadline:* rolling (freshmen), rolling (transfers). *Notification:* continuous (freshmen), continuous (transfers).

Admissions Contact Ao' Lani Lorenzo, Admissions Counselor, Chaminade University of Honolulu, 3140 Waialae Avenue, Honolulu, HI 96816-1578. *Phone:* 808-735-4735. *Toll-free phone:* 800-735-3733. *Fax:* 808-739-4647. *E-mail:* admissions@chaminade.edu.

■ *See page 1384 for a narrative description.*

HAWAI'I PACIFIC UNIVERSITY
Honolulu, Hawaii

- **Independent** comprehensive, founded 1965
- **Calendar** 4-1-4
- **Degrees** certificates, associate, bachelor's, master's, post-master's, and postbachelor's certificates
- **Urban** 140-acre campus

Hawai'i Pacific University (continued)
- **Endowment** $56.0 million
- **Coed,** 6,735 undergraduate students, 60% full-time, 56% women, 44% men
- **Moderately difficult** entrance level, 81% of applicants were admitted

Strategically situated at the crossroads of East and West, Hawai'i Pacific University is the ideal location for anyone interested in living and learning in an international setting. Over 8,000 students from all 50 states and more than 100 countries make HPU one of the most diverse universities in the United States.

Undergraduates 4,052 full-time, 2,683 part-time. Students come from 52 states and territories, 85 other countries, 27% are from out of state, 8% African American, 31% Asian American or Pacific Islander, 7% Hispanic American, 1% Native American, 15% international, 8% transferred in, 10% live on campus. *Retention:* 65% of 2002 full-time freshmen returned.

Freshmen *Admission:* 2,710 applied, 2,194 admitted, 590 enrolled. *Average high school GPA:* 3.24. *Test scores:* SAT verbal scores over 500: 58%; SAT math scores over 500: 55%; ACT scores over 18: 77%; SAT verbal scores over 600: 14%; SAT math scores over 600: 18%; ACT scores over 24: 45%; SAT verbal scores over 700: 1%; SAT math scores over 700: 2%; ACT scores over 30: 11%.

Faculty *Total:* 582, 39% full-time, 48% with terminal degrees. *Student/faculty ratio:* 18:1.

Majors Accounting; advertising; anthropology; applied mathematics; area studies; area studies related; behavioral sciences; biology/biological sciences; business administration and management; business/corporate communications; business/managerial economics; communication and journalism related; communication/speech communication and rhetoric; computer and information sciences; computer science; criminal justice/law enforcement administration; data processing and data processing technology; economics; engineering related; English; English as a second/foreign language (teaching); entrepreneurship; environmental science; environmental studies; finance; history; history related; human development and family studies; humanities; human resources management; human services; information science/studies; interdisciplinary studies; international business/trade/commerce; international relations and affairs; journalism; liberal arts and sciences/liberal studies; literature; management information systems; marine biology and biological oceanography; marketing/marketing management; mass communication/media; military studies; multi-/interdisciplinary studies related; nursing (registered nurse training); oceanography (chemical and physical); political science and government; pre-medical studies; psychology; public administration; public relations/image management; social sciences; social work; sociology; tourism and travel services management.

Academic Programs *Special study options:* academic remediation for entering students, accelerated degree program, adult/continuing education programs, advanced placement credit, cooperative education, distance learning, double majors, English as a second language, freshman honors college, honors programs, independent study, internships, part-time degree program, services for LD students, student-designed majors, study abroad, summer session for credit. *ROTC:* Army (c), Air Force (c). *Unusual degree programs:* 3-2 engineering with Washington University in St. Louis, University of Southern California.

Library Meader Library plus 2 others with 160,000 titles, 12,000 serial subscriptions, 8,695 audiovisual materials, an OPAC, a Web page.

Computers on Campus 500 computers available on campus for general student use. A campuswide network can be accessed from student residence rooms and from off campus. Internet access, online (class) registration, at least one staffed computer lab available. Computer purchase or lease plan available.

Student Life *Housing options:* coed. Campus housing is university owned and is provided by a third party. Freshman applicants given priority for college housing. *Activities and organizations:* drama/theater group, student-run newspaper, choral group, Association of Students of HPU, Swedish Student Association, President's Hosts, Akamai Advertising, Christian Fellowship. *Campus security:* 24-hour emergency response devices and patrols, student patrols, late-night transport/escort service, controlled dormitory access. *Student services:* health clinic, personal/psychological counseling.

Athletics Member NCAA. All Division II. *Intercollegiate sports:* baseball M(s), basketball M(s), cheerleading M(s)/W(s), cross-country running M(s)/W(s), golf M(s)/W(s), soccer M(s)(c)/W(s)(c), softball W(s), tennis M(s)/W(s), volleyball W(s). *Intramural sports:* soccer M/W, volleyball M/W.

Standardized Tests *Required:* SAT I or ACT (for admission).

Costs (2003–04) *Comprehensive fee:* $19,138 includes full-time tuition ($10,368) and room and board ($8770). Full-time tuition and fees vary according to program and student level. Part-time tuition: $200 per credit. Part-time tuition and fees vary according to course load. *Room and board:* Room and board charges vary according to housing facility. *Payment plan:* installment. *Waivers:* employees or children of employees.

Financial Aid Of all full-time matriculated undergraduates who enrolled in 2002, 2,456 applied for aid, 1,525 were judged to have need, 355 had their need fully met. 152 Federal Work-Study jobs (averaging $1950). In 2002, 706 non-need-based awards were made. *Average percent of need met:* 77%. *Average financial aid package:* $10,392. *Average need-based loan:* $4611. *Average need-based gift aid:* $3866. *Average non-need-based aid:* $4074. *Average indebtedness upon graduation:* $17,759.

Applying *Options:* common application, electronic application, early admission, deferred entrance. *Application fee:* $50. *Required:* high school transcript, minimum 2.5 GPA. *Required for some:* interview. *Recommended:* essay or personal statement, 2 letters of recommendation. *Application deadline:* rolling (freshmen), rolling (transfers). *Notification:* continuous (transfers).

Admissions Contact Mr. Scott Stensrud, Associate Vice President Enrollment Management, Hawai'i Pacific University, 1164 Bishop Street, Honolulu, HI 96813-2785. *Phone:* 808-544-0238. *Toll-free phone:* 866-225-5478. *Fax:* 808-544-1136. *E-mail:* admissions@hpu.edu.

■ *See page 1724 for a narrative description.*

International College and Graduate School
Honolulu, Hawaii

- **Independent interdenominational** upper-level, founded 1967
- **Calendar** semesters
- **Degrees** certificates, bachelor's, master's, and first professional
- **Urban** campus
- **Coed,** 26 undergraduate students, 46% full-time, 19% women, 81% men

Undergraduates 12 full-time, 14 part-time. Students come from 1 other state, 4 other countries, 0.1% are from out of state, 4% African American, 31% Asian American or Pacific Islander, 4% Hispanic American, 42% international.

Faculty *Total:* 39, 8% full-time. *Student/faculty ratio:* 12:1.

Majors Theology.

Academic Programs *Special study options:* adult/continuing education programs, advanced placement credit, independent study, internships, part-time degree program, study abroad, summer session for credit.

Library J. W. Cook Memorial Library with 20,000 titles, 65 serial subscriptions, 703 audiovisual materials.

Computers on Campus 6 computers available on campus for general student use. A campuswide network can be accessed from off campus.

Student Life *Housing:* college housing not available.

Financial Aid Of all full-time matriculated undergraduates who enrolled in 2003, 18 applied for aid, 18 were judged to have need, 18 had their need fully met. *Average percent of need met:* 100%. *Average financial aid package:* $3500. *Average need-based gift aid:* $3500. *Financial aid deadline:* 6/1.

Applying *Options:* deferred entrance. *Application fee:* $50. *Application deadline:* rolling (transfers). *Notification:* continuous (transfers).

Admissions Contact Mr. Jon Rawlings, Director of Admissions, International College and Graduate School, 20 Dowsett Avenue, Honolulu, HI 96817. *Phone:* 808-595-4247 Ext. 108. *Fax:* 808-595-4779. *E-mail:* icgs@hawaii.rr.com.

Remington College–Honolulu Campus
Honolulu, Hawaii

Admissions Contact Mr. Kenneth G. Heinemann, Campus President, Remington College–Honolulu Campus, 1111 Bishop Street, Suite 400, Honolulu, HI 96813. *Phone:* 808-942-1000.

University of Hawaii at Hilo
Hilo, Hawaii

- **State-supported** comprehensive, founded 1970, part of University of Hawaii System
- **Calendar** semesters
- **Degrees** certificates, bachelor's, and master's
- **Small-town** 115-acre campus
- **Endowment** $1.5 million
- **Coed,** 3,214 undergraduate students
- **Moderately difficult** entrance level, 134% of applicants were admitted

Undergraduates Students come from 48 states and territories, 40 other countries, 21% are from out of state, 1% African American, 36% Asian American or Pacific Islander, 2% Hispanic American, 0.6% Native American, 10% international, 29% live on campus. *Retention:* 58% of 2002 full-time freshmen returned.

Freshmen *Admission:* 1,470 applied, 1,967 admitted. *Average high school GPA:* 3.20. *Test scores:* SAT verbal scores over 500: 47%; SAT math scores over

500: 56%; SAT verbal scores over 600: 12%; SAT math scores over 600: 15%; SAT verbal scores over 700: 2%; SAT math scores over 700: 2%.

Faculty *Total:* 243, 70% full-time, 58% with terminal degrees. *Student/faculty ratio:* 14:1.

Majors Agricultural business and management; agriculture; animal sciences; anthropology; art; biology/biological sciences; business administration and management; chemistry; computer science; economics; elementary education; English; geography; geology/earth science; history; horticultural science; interdisciplinary studies; Japanese; linguistics; mathematics; music; natural sciences; nursing (registered nurse training); philosophy; physics; political science and government; psychology; secondary education; sociology.

Academic Programs *Special study options:* advanced placement credit, distance learning, double majors, English as a second language, honors programs, independent study, internships, off-campus study, part-time degree program, services for LD students, student-designed majors, study abroad, summer session for credit.

Library Edwin H. Mookini Library with 250,000 titles, 2,500 serial subscriptions, an OPAC, a Web page.

Computers on Campus 600 computers available on campus for general student use. A campuswide network can be accessed from student residence rooms and from off campus. Internet access, online (class) registration, at least one staffed computer lab available.

Student Life *Housing options:* coed. Campus housing is university owned. *Activities and organizations:* drama/theater group, student-run newspaper, choral group, International Student Association, Hawaiian Leadership and Development, Delta Sigma Pi Business Fraternity, University canoe club, Samoan club. *Campus security:* 24-hour emergency response devices and patrols, controlled dormitory access. *Student services:* health clinic, personal/psychological counseling, women's center.

Athletics Member NCAA. All Division II except baseball (Division I). *Intercollegiate sports:* baseball M(s), basketball M(s), cross-country running M(s)/W(s), golf M(s), softball W(s), tennis M(s)/W(s), volleyball W(s). *Intramural sports:* archery M/W, badminton M/W, basketball M/W, bowling M/W, golf M/W, soccer M/W, softball M/W, table tennis M/W, tennis M/W, volleyball M/W, weight lifting M/W.

Standardized Tests *Required:* SAT I or ACT (for admission).

Costs (2004–05) *Tuition:* state resident $2424 full-time, $101 per credit hour part-time; nonresident $7992 full-time, $333 per credit hour part-time. Full-time tuition and fees vary according to course level and student level. Part-time tuition and fees vary according to course level and student level. *Required fees:* $114 full-time, $32 per term part-time. *Room and board:* $5081; room only: $2360. Room and board charges vary according to board plan and housing facility.

Financial Aid Of all full-time matriculated undergraduates who enrolled in 2000, 1,631 applied for aid, 974 were judged to have need, 310 had their need fully met. 135 Federal Work-Study jobs (averaging $2941). 319 state and other part-time jobs (averaging $2647). In 2000, 112 non-need-based awards were made. *Average percent of need met:* 76%. *Average financial aid package:* $6372. *Average need-based loan:* $3227. *Average need-based gift aid:* $3675. *Average non-need-based aid:* $915. *Average indebtedness upon graduation:* $10,698.

Applying *Options:* common application, electronic application, deferred entrance. *Application fee:* $40. *Required:* high school transcript. *Required for some:* letters of recommendation. *Recommended:* minimum 3.0 GPA. *Application deadlines:* 7/1 (freshmen), 7/1 (transfers). *Notification:* 7/31 (freshmen), 7/31 (transfers).

Admissions Contact Mr. James Cromwell, UH Student services Specialist III/Director of Admissions, University of Hawaii at Hilo, 200 West Kawili Street, Hilo, HI 96720-4091. *Phone:* 808-974-7414. *Toll-free phone:* 808-974-7414 (in-state); 800-897-4456 (out-of-state). *E-mail:* uhhao@hawaii.edu.

■ *See page 2614 for a narrative description.*

UNIVERSITY OF HAWAII AT MANOA

Honolulu, Hawaii

- **State-supported** university, founded 1907
- **Calendar** semesters
- **Degrees** bachelor's, master's, doctoral, first professional, and postbachelor's certificates
- **Urban** 300-acre campus
- **Endowment** $180.7 million
- **Coed,** 13,755 undergraduate students, 81% full-time, 56% women, 44% men
- **Moderately difficult** entrance level, 59% of applicants were admitted

Undergraduates 11,078 full-time, 2,677 part-time. Students come from 83 other countries, 16% are from out of state, 0.9% African American, 56% Asian American or Pacific Islander, 2% Hispanic American, 0.3% Native American, 5% international, 12% transferred in, 13% live on campus. *Retention:* 77% of 2002 full-time freshmen returned.

Freshmen *Admission:* 6,028 applied, 3,566 admitted, 1,996 enrolled. *Average high school GPA:* 3.37. *Test scores:* SAT verbal scores over 500: 65%; SAT math scores over 500: 82%; ACT scores over 18: 96%; SAT verbal scores over 600: 19%; SAT math scores over 600: 34%; ACT scores over 24: 36%; SAT verbal scores over 700: 2%; SAT math scores over 700: 5%; ACT scores over 30: 4%.

Faculty *Total:* 1,215, 93% full-time, 81% with terminal degrees. *Student/faculty ratio:* 13:1.

Majors Accounting; agricultural/biological engineering and bioengineering; agricultural economics; agricultural production; agricultural teacher education; American studies; ancient/classical Greek; anthropology; apparel and textiles; applied horticulture; architecture; art; art teacher education; Asian studies; atmospheric sciences and meteorology; audiology and speech-language pathology; biology/biological sciences; botany/plant biology; business administration and management; business administration, management and operations related; business/commerce; business/managerial economics; business teacher education; chemistry; Chinese; civil engineering; clinical laboratory science/medical technology; communication/speech communication and rhetoric; computer and information sciences; counselor education/school counseling and guidance; dance; dental hygiene; dramatic/theatre arts; East Asian languages related; economics; education; education (specific subject areas) related; electrical, electronics and communications engineering; elementary education; engineering; English; English as a second/foreign language (teaching); English/language arts teacher education; entomology; environmental design/architecture; ethnic, cultural minority, and gender studies related; family and consumer economics related; family and consumer sciences/home economics teacher education; family and consumer sciences/human sciences; Filipino/Tagalog; finance; foreign languages related; foreign language teacher education; French; geography; geological and earth sciences/geosciences related; geology/earth science; German; health and physical education; health teacher education; hospitality administration related; human development and family studies; human resources management; interior architecture; international business/trade/commerce; Japanese; journalism; kinesiology and exercise science; landscape architecture; Latin; liberal arts and sciences/liberal studies; management information systems; marketing/marketing management; mathematics; mathematics teacher education; mechanical engineering; multi-/interdisciplinary studies related; music performance; music teacher education; nursing (registered nurse training); parks, recreation and leisure; philosophy; physical education teaching and coaching; physics; political science and government; psychology; real estate; religious studies; Russian; sales and marketing/marketing and distribution teacher education; science teacher education; secondary education; social science teacher education; social studies teacher education; social work; sociology; Spanish; special education; speech and rhetoric; technology/industrial arts teacher education; trade and industrial teacher education; zoology/animal biology.

Academic Programs *Special study options:* accelerated degree program, adult/continuing education programs, advanced placement credit, cooperative education, distance learning, double majors, English as a second language, honors programs, independent study, internships, off-campus study, part-time degree program, services for LD students, student-designed majors, study abroad, summer session for credit. *ROTC:* Army (b), Air Force (b).

Library Hamilton Library plus 6 others with 3.2 million titles, 27,328 serial subscriptions, 53,383 audiovisual materials, an OPAC, a Web page.

Computers on Campus 1000 computers available on campus for general student use. A campuswide network can be accessed from student residence rooms and from off campus that provide access to telephone registration. Internet access, at least one staffed computer lab available.

Student Life *Housing options:* coed, men-only, women-only, disabled students. Campus housing is university owned. *Activities and organizations:* drama/theater group, student-run newspaper, radio station, choral group, marching band, Associated Students of University of Hawaii, Campus Center Board, Broadcast Communication Authority, Board of Publications, Student Activities and Program Fee Board, national fraternities, national sororities. *Campus security:* 24-hour emergency response devices and patrols, student patrols, late-night transport/escort service, controlled dormitory access. *Student services:* health clinic, personal/psychological counseling, women's center.

Athletics Member NCAA. All Division I except football (Division I-A). *Intercollegiate sports:* baseball M(s), basketball M(s)/W(s), cross-country running W(s), golf M(s)/W(s), rugby M(c), sailing M/W, soccer W(s), softball W(s), swimming M(s)/W(s), tennis M(s)/W(s), track and field W(s), volleyball M(s)/W(s), water polo W(s). *Intramural sports:* badminton M/W, basketball M/W, cross-country running M/W, golf M/W, soccer M/W, softball M/W, table tennis M/W, tennis M/W, track and field M/W, volleyball M/W, weight lifting M/W.

Standardized Tests *Required:* SAT I or ACT (for admission).

Costs (2003–04) *Tuition:* $138 per credit part-time; state resident $3408 full-time, $138 per credit part-time; nonresident $9888 full-time, $408 per credit part-time. Full-time tuition and fees vary according to class time, course load, and program. Part-time tuition and fees vary according to class time, course load, and

University of Hawaii at Manoa (continued)
program. *Required fees:* $153 full-time, $69 per credit part-time. *Room and board:* $5675; room only: $3314. Room and board charges vary according to board plan and housing facility. *Waivers:* minority students and employees or children of employees.

Financial Aid Of all full-time matriculated undergraduates who enrolled in 2002, 5,295 applied for aid, 3,668 were judged to have need, 1,187 had their need fully met. 344 Federal Work-Study jobs (averaging $1630). In 2002, 399 non-need-based awards were made. *Average percent of need met:* 75%. *Average financial aid package:* $6092. *Average need-based loan:* $2432. *Average need-based gift aid:* $3203. *Average non-need-based aid:* $5700. *Average indebtedness upon graduation:* $13,707.

Applying *Application fee:* $40. *Required:* high school transcript, minimum 2.8 GPA, minimum SAT I score of 510 for verbal and math sections. *Application deadlines:* 5/1 (freshmen), 5/1 (transfers). *Notification:* continuous (freshmen), continuous (transfers).

Admissions Contact Ms. Janice Heu, Interim Director of Admissions and Records, University of Hawaii at Manoa, 2600 Campus Road, Room 001, Honolulu, HI 96822. *Phone:* 808-956-8975. *Toll-free phone:* 800-823-9771. *Fax:* 808-956-4148. *E-mail:* ar-info@hawaii.edu.

UNIVERSITY OF HAWAII–WEST OAHU
Pearl City, Hawaii

- **State-supported** upper-level, founded 1976, part of University of Hawaii System
- **Calendar** semesters
- **Degree** certificates and bachelor's
- **Small-town** campus with easy access to Honolulu
- **Coed**
- **Moderately difficult** entrance level

Faculty *Student/faculty ratio:* 13:1.

Student Life *Campus security:* 24-hour emergency response devices and patrols, late-night transport/escort service.

Costs (2003–04) *Tuition:* state resident $2112 full-time, $88 per credit part-time; nonresident $7248 full-time, $302 per credit part-time. *Required fees:* $10 full-time, $5 per term part-time.

Financial Aid Of all full-time matriculated undergraduates who enrolled in 2002, 138 applied for aid, 138 were judged to have need. 7 Federal Work-Study jobs (averaging $862). *Average financial aid package:* $4636. *Average need-based loan:* $3358. *Average need-based gift aid:* $3518.

Applying *Application fee:* $25.

Admissions Contact Jean M. Osumi, Dean of Student services, University of Hawaii–West Oahu, 96-043 Ala Ike, Pearl City, HI 96782. *Phone:* 808-453-4700. *Fax:* 805-453-6076. *E-mail:* jeano@uhwo.hawaii.edu.

UNIVERSITY OF PHOENIX–HAWAII CAMPUS
Honolulu, Hawaii

- **Proprietary** comprehensive
- **Calendar** continuous
- **Degrees** certificates, associate, bachelor's, master's, doctoral, post-master's, and postbachelor's certificates (courses conducted at 121 campuses and learning centers in 25 states)
- **Urban** campus
- **Coed,** 816 undergraduate students, 100% full-time, 63% women, 37% men
- **Noncompetitive** entrance level

Undergraduates 816 full-time. 4% African American, 35% Asian American or Pacific Islander, 4% Hispanic American, 1% Native American, 7% international, 5% transferred in.

Freshmen *Admission:* 22 enrolled.

Faculty *Total:* 292, 2% full-time, 26% with terminal degrees. *Student/faculty ratio:* 10:1.

Majors Accounting; e-commerce; finance; general studies; health/health care administration; information technology; management information systems; management science; marketing/marketing management; nursing (registered nurse training); nursing science; public administration and social service professions related.

Academic Programs *Special study options:* accelerated degree program, adult/continuing education programs, advanced placement credit, distance learning, external degree program, independent study.

Library University Library with 27.1 million titles, 11,648 serial subscriptions, an OPAC, a Web page.

Computers on Campus A campuswide network can be accessed from off campus. Internet access, at least one staffed computer lab available.

Student Life *Housing:* college housing not available.

Costs (2003–04) *Tuition:* $11,070 full-time, $369 per credit part-time. *Waivers:* employees or children of employees.

Financial Aid *Average financial aid package:* $1402.

Applying *Options:* deferred entrance. *Application fee:* $100. *Required:* 1 letter of recommendation, 2 years of work experience, 23 years of age. *Required for some:* high school transcript. *Application deadline:* rolling (freshmen), rolling (transfers).

Admissions Contact Ms. Beth Barilla, Director of Admissions, University of Phoenix–Hawaii Campus, 4615 East Elwood Street, Mail Stop AA-K101, Phoenix, AZ 85040-1958. *Phone:* 480-317-6300. *Toll-free phone:* 800-228-7240. *Fax:* 480-594-1758. *E-mail:* beth.barilla@phoenix.edu.

IDAHO

ALBERTSON COLLEGE OF IDAHO
Caldwell, Idaho

- **Independent** comprehensive, founded 1891
- **Calendar** semesters plus 6-week Winter term
- **Degrees** bachelor's and master's
- **Suburban** 50-acre campus
- **Endowment** $47.1 million
- **Coed,** 821 undergraduate students, 96% full-time, 54% women, 46% men
- **Moderately difficult** entrance level, 79% of applicants were admitted

Undergraduates 790 full-time, 31 part-time. Students come from 21 states and territories, 25% are from out of state, 0.2% African American, 3% Asian American or Pacific Islander, 3% Hispanic American, 0.6% Native American, 1% international, 5% transferred in, 56% live on campus. *Retention:* 73% of 2002 full-time freshmen returned.

Freshmen *Admission:* 643 applied, 507 admitted, 182 enrolled. *Average high school GPA:* 3.50. *Test scores:* SAT verbal scores over 500: 82%; SAT math scores over 500: 80%; ACT scores over 18: 96%; SAT verbal scores over 600: 33%; SAT math scores over 600: 39%; ACT scores over 24: 60%; SAT verbal scores over 700: 6%; SAT math scores over 700: 4%; ACT scores over 30: 7%.

Faculty *Total:* 69, 83% full-time, 88% with terminal degrees. *Student/faculty ratio:* 13:1.

Majors Accounting; anthropology; art; biology/biological sciences; business administration and management; chemistry; computer science; creative writing; dramatic/theatre arts; economics; English; history; international business/trade/commerce; international economics; kinesiology and exercise science; mathematics; music; philosophy; physical education teaching and coaching; physics; political science and government; pre-medical studies; psychology; religious studies; sociology; Spanish; sport and fitness administration.

Academic Programs *Special study options:* advanced placement credit, double majors, English as a second language, honors programs, independent study, internships, off-campus study, part-time degree program, services for LD students, student-designed majors, study abroad. *Unusual degree programs:* 3-2 engineering with University of Idaho, Columbia University, Washington University in St. Louis.

Library Terteling Library with 183,308 titles, 703 serial subscriptions, an OPAC, a Web page.

Computers on Campus 240 computers available on campus for general student use. A campuswide network can be accessed from student residence rooms and from off campus that provide access to online course syllabi, course assignments, course discussion. Internet access, at least one staffed computer lab available.

Student Life *Housing:* on-campus residence required through sophomore year. *Options:* coed, women-only. Campus housing is university owned. Freshman campus housing is guaranteed. *Activities and organizations:* drama/theater group, student-run newspaper, choral group, Scarlet Masque Drama Group, Latino American Students, International Studies Association, national fraternities, national sororities. *Campus security:* 24-hour emergency response devices and patrols, student patrols, late-night transport/escort service, controlled dormitory access. *Student services:* health clinic, personal/psychological counseling.

Athletics Member NAIA. *Intercollegiate sports:* baseball M(s), basketball M(s)/W(s), golf M(s)/W(s), skiing (cross-country) M/W, skiing (downhill) M(s)/W(s), soccer M(s)/W(s), softball W(s), tennis M(s)/W(s), volleyball W(s). *Intramural sports:* badminton M/W, basketball M/W, football M/W, soccer M/W, softball M/W, swimming M/W, table tennis M/W, tennis M/W, volleyball M/W.

Standardized Tests *Required:* SAT I or ACT (for admission).

Costs (2003–04) *Comprehensive fee:* $19,450 includes full-time tuition ($13,900), mandatory fees ($500), and room and board ($5050). Part-time tuition: $580 per credit. Part-time tuition and fees vary according to course load. No tuition increase for student's term of enrollment. *Required fees:* $600 per term part-time. *College room only:* $2450. Room and board charges vary according to board plan and housing facility. *Waivers:* children of alumni, adult students, senior citizens, and employees or children of employees.

Financial Aid Of all full-time matriculated undergraduates who enrolled in 2003, 813 applied for aid, 558 were judged to have need, 377 had their need fully met. 199 Federal Work-Study jobs (averaging $947). 166 state and other part-time jobs (averaging $812). In 2003, 174 non-need-based awards were made. *Average percent of need met:* 83%. *Average financial aid package:* $14,738. *Average need-based loan:* $5224. *Average need-based gift aid:* $4499. *Average non-need-based aid:* $7585. *Average indebtedness upon graduation:* $17,181.

Applying *Options:* common application, electronic application, early admission, early action, deferred entrance. *Application fee:* $50. *Required:* essay or personal statement, high school transcript, 1 letter of recommendation. *Recommended:* interview. *Application deadlines:* 6/1 (freshmen), 8/1 (transfers). *Notification:* 12/15 (early action), continuous (transfers).

Admissions Contact Ms. Brandie Holly, Associate Dean of Admission, Albertson College of Idaho, 2112 Cleveland Boulevard, Caldwell, ID 83605-4494. *Phone:* 208-459-5305. *Toll-free phone:* 800-224-3246. *Fax:* 208-459-5757. *E-mail:* admission@albertson.edu.

BOISE BIBLE COLLEGE
Boise, Idaho

- **Independent nondenominational** 4-year, founded 1945
- **Calendar** semesters
- **Degrees** certificates, associate, and bachelor's
- **Suburban** 17-acre campus
- **Endowment** $507,870
- **Coed**
- **Minimally difficult** entrance level

Faculty *Student/faculty ratio:* 13:1.

Student Life *Campus security:* patrols by police officers.

Costs (2003–04) *Comprehensive fee:* $10,288 includes full-time tuition ($6000), mandatory fees ($88), and room and board ($4200).

Financial Aid Of all full-time matriculated undergraduates who enrolled in 2003, 84 applied for aid, 80 were judged to have need, 20 had their need fully met. 7 Federal Work-Study jobs (averaging $1464). In 2003, 2. *Average percent of need met:* 48. *Average financial aid package:* $4380. *Average need-based loan:* $2539. *Average need-based gift aid:* $3660. *Average non-need-based aid:* $3500. *Average indebtedness upon graduation:* $8648.

Applying *Options:* deferred entrance. *Application fee:* $25. *Required:* essay or personal statement, high school transcript, minimum 2.0 GPA, 3 letters of recommendation. *Recommended:* interview.

Admissions Contact Mr. Ross Knudsen, Director of Admissions, Boise Bible College, 8695 Marigold Street, Boise, ID 83704. *Phone:* 208-376-7731. *Toll-free phone:* 800-893-7755. *Fax:* 208-376-7743. *E-mail:* boibible@micron.net.

BOISE STATE UNIVERSITY
Boise, Idaho

- **State-supported** comprehensive, founded 1932, part of Idaho System of Higher Education
- **Calendar** semesters
- **Degrees** certificates, diplomas, associate, bachelor's, master's, and doctoral
- **Urban** 130-acre campus
- **Endowment** $42.1 million
- **Coed,** 16,551 undergraduate students, 63% full-time, 54% women, 46% men
- **Minimally difficult** entrance level, 92% of applicants were admitted

Undergraduates 10,455 full-time, 6,096 part-time. Students come from 43 states and territories, 47 other countries, 7% are from out of state, 1% African American, 3% Asian American or Pacific Islander, 6% Hispanic American, 1% Native American, 1% international, 6% transferred in, 8% live on campus. *Retention:* 60% of 2002 full-time freshmen returned.

Freshmen *Admission:* 3,900 applied, 3,602 admitted, 2,137 enrolled. *Average high school GPA:* 3.20. *Test scores:* SAT verbal scores over 500: 50%; SAT math scores over 500: 51%; ACT scores over 18: 74%; SAT verbal scores over 600: 15%; SAT math scores over 600: 16%; ACT scores over 24: 32%; SAT verbal scores over 700: 2%; SAT math scores over 700: 1%; ACT scores over 30: 2%.

Faculty *Total:* 1,015, 61% full-time, 68% with terminal degrees. *Student/faculty ratio:* 21:1.

Majors Accounting; advertising; anthropology; art; art history, criticism and conservation; art teacher education; athletic training; automobile/automotive mechanics technology; bilingual and multilingual education; biology/biological sciences; business administration and management; business machine repair; business/managerial economics; business teacher education; chemistry; child development; civil engineering; clinical laboratory science/medical technology; commercial and advertising art; computer and information sciences; computer science; computer systems networking and telecommunications; construction management; criminal justice/law enforcement administration; culinary arts; cultural studies; drafting and design technology; dramatic/theatre arts; drawing; economics; education; electrical and electronic engineering technologies related; electrical, electronic and communications engineering technology; electrical, electronics and communications engineering; elementary education; English; environmental health; environmental studies; finance; French; geology/earth science; geophysics and seismology; German; health information/medical records administration; health science; heating, air conditioning, ventilation and refrigeration maintenance technology; history; horticultural science; human resources management; industrial radiologic technology; industrial technology; information science/studies; interdisciplinary studies; international business/trade/commerce; kindergarten/preschool education; kinesiology and exercise science; legal assistant/paralegal; liberal arts and sciences/liberal studies; literature; machine tool technology; marketing/marketing management; mass communication/media; mathematics; mechanical engineering/mechanical technology; medical administrative assistant and medical secretary; music; music management and merchandising; music teacher education; nursing (registered nurse training); operations management; perfusion technology; philosophy; physical education teaching and coaching; physician assistant; physics; political science and government; pre-dentistry studies; pre-engineering; pre-medical studies; pre-veterinary studies; psychology; public administration; public health; radiologic technology/science; reading teacher education; respiratory care therapy; science teacher education; secondary education; social sciences; social work; sociology; Spanish; special education; surgical technology; teacher assistant/aide; technical and business writing; welding technology.

Academic Programs *Special study options:* academic remediation for entering students, adult/continuing education programs, advanced placement credit, cooperative education, distance learning, double majors, English as a second language, freshman honors college, honors programs, independent study, internships, off-campus study, part-time degree program, services for LD students, student-designed majors, study abroad, summer session for credit. *ROTC:* Army (b).

Library Albertsons Library with 505,618 titles, 4,797 serial subscriptions, an OPAC, a Web page.

Computers on Campus 900 computers available on campus for general student use. A campuswide network can be accessed from student residence rooms and from off campus. Internet access, online (class) registration, at least one staffed computer lab available.

Student Life *Housing options:* coed. Campus housing is university owned. *Activities and organizations:* drama/theater group, student-run newspaper, choral group, marching band, Latter-Day Saints Student Association, Residence Hall Association, Organization of Student Social Workers, Marching Band Association, Teacher Education Association, national fraternities, national sororities. *Campus security:* 24-hour emergency response devices and patrols. *Student services:* health clinic, personal/psychological counseling, women's center, legal services.

Athletics Member NCAA. All Division I except football (Division I-A). *Intercollegiate sports:* basketball M(s)/W(s), cross-country running M(s)/W(s), golf M(s)/W(s), gymnastics W(s), soccer W, tennis M(s)/W(s), track and field M(s)/W(s), volleyball W(s), wrestling M(s). *Intramural sports:* basketball M/W, bowling M/W, lacrosse W(c), racquetball M/W, skiing (downhill) M(c)/W(c), soccer M/W, softball M/W, tennis M/W, volleyball M/W, weight lifting M/W.

Standardized Tests *Required for some:* SAT I or ACT (for admission).

Costs (2003–04) *Tuition:* state resident $3251 full-time, $162 per credit part-time; nonresident $9971 full-time, $162 per credit part-time. Part-time tuition and fees vary according to course load. *Room and board:* $4426. Room and board charges vary according to board plan and housing facility. *Payment plan:* deferred payment. *Waivers:* senior citizens and employees or children of employees.

Financial Aid Of all full-time matriculated undergraduates who enrolled in 2003, 7,249 applied for aid, 6,566 were judged to have need, 951 had their need fully met. In 2003, 1229 non-need-based awards were made. *Average percent of need met:* 75%. *Average financial aid package:* $6978. *Average need-based loan:* $3540. *Average need-based gift aid:* $3072. *Average non-need-based aid:* $1306. *Financial aid deadline:* 6/1.

Applying *Options:* electronic application. *Application fee:* $30. *Required for some:* high school transcript, minimum 2.0 GPA. *Application deadlines:* 7/14 (freshmen), 7/14 (transfers). *Notification:* continuous (freshmen), continuous (transfers).

Boise State University (continued)

Admissions Contact Ms. Barbara Fortin, Dean of Admissions, Boise State University, Enrollment Services, 1910 University Drive, Boise, ID 83725. *Phone:* 208-426-1177. *Toll-free phone:* 800-632-6586 (in-state); 800-824-7017 (out-of-state). *E-mail:* bsuinfo@boisestate.edu.

Idaho State University
Pocatello, Idaho

- **State-supported** university, founded 1901
- **Calendar** semesters
- **Degrees** certificates, diplomas, associate, bachelor's, master's, doctoral, first professional, post-master's, postbachelor's, and first professional certificates
- **Small-town** 972-acre campus
- **Endowment** $22.5 million
- **Coed,** 11,451 undergraduate students, 69% full-time, 55% women, 45% men
- **Minimally difficult** entrance level, 74% of applicants were admitted

Undergraduates 7,952 full-time, 3,499 part-time. Students come from 46 states and territories, 62 other countries, 5% are from out of state, 0.5% African American, 1% Asian American or Pacific Islander, 3% Hispanic American, 1% Native American, 1% international, 11% transferred in, 6% live on campus. *Retention:* 58% of 2002 full-time freshmen returned.

Freshmen *Admission:* 3,573 applied, 2,644 admitted, 1,971 enrolled. *Average high school GPA:* 3.31. *Test scores:* SAT verbal scores over 500: 63%; SAT math scores over 500: 57%; ACT scores over 18: 79%; SAT verbal scores over 600: 21%; SAT math scores over 600: 27%; ACT scores over 24: 25%; SAT verbal scores over 700: 4%; SAT math scores over 700: 2%; ACT scores over 30: 1%.

Faculty *Total:* 615, 89% full-time, 54% with terminal degrees. *Student/faculty ratio:* 17:1.

Majors Accounting; administrative assistant and secretarial science; aircraft powerplant technology; American Native/Native American languages; American Sign Language (ASL); American studies; anthropology; art; audiology and speech-language pathology; autobody/collision and repair technology; automobile/automotive mechanics technology; biochemistry; biology/biological sciences; botany/plant biology; business administration and management; business/commerce; business machine repair; carpentry; chemistry; child care and support services management; civil engineering; civil engineering technology; clinical laboratory science/medical technology; communication/speech communication and rhetoric; communications systems installation and repair technology; computer and information sciences; computer programming (specific applications); criminal justice/police science; criminal justice/safety; culinary arts; dental hygiene; dental laboratory technology; diesel mechanics technology; dietetics; drafting and design technology; drafting/design engineering technologies related; dramatic/theatre arts; ecology; economics; electrical, electronic and communications engineering technology; electrical, electronics and communications engineering; electrical/electronics equipment installation and repair; electromechanical technology; elementary education; emergency medical technology (EMT paramedic); engineering; engineering related; English; family and consumer sciences/human sciences; farm and ranch management; finance; fire science; foods, nutrition, and wellness; French; general studies; geology/earth science; German; graphic and printing equipment operation/production; health/health care administration; health information/medical records technology; health services/allied health/health sciences; health teacher education; history; human resources management; information science/studies; instrumentation technology; laser and optical technology; Latin; machine tool technology; marketing/marketing management; mass communication/media; mathematics; mechanical engineering; mechanics and repair; medical/clinical assistant; medical microbiology and bacteriology; medical radiologic technology; microbiology; multi-/interdisciplinary studies related; music; music performance; music teacher education; nursing (registered nurse training); occupational therapist assistant; pharmacy technician; philosophy; physical education teaching and coaching; physical therapist assistant; physics; political science and government; psychology; Russian; secondary education; sign language interpretation and translation; social work; sociology; Spanish; special education; survey technology; welding technology; zoology/animal biology.

Academic Programs *Special study options:* academic remediation for entering students, adult/continuing education programs, advanced placement credit, distance learning, double majors, English as a second language, external degree program, honors programs, independent study, internships, off-campus study, part-time degree program, services for LD students, student-designed majors, study abroad, summer session for credit. *ROTC:* Army (c).

Library Eli M. Oboler Library with 682,954 titles, 3,800 serial subscriptions, 701 audiovisual materials, an OPAC, a Web page.

Computers on Campus 562 computers available on campus for general student use. A campuswide network can be accessed from student residence rooms and from off campus. Internet access, online (class) registration, at least one staffed computer lab available.

Student Life *Housing options:* coed, men-only, women-only, disabled students. Campus housing is university owned. Freshman campus housing is guaranteed. *Activities and organizations:* drama/theater group, student-run newspaper, radio station, choral group, International Students Association, Vocational Industrial Clubs of America, Latter Day Saints Student Association, Student American Dental Hygienists Association, Academy of Students of Pharmacy, national fraternities, national sororities. *Campus security:* 24-hour emergency response devices and patrols, student patrols, late-night transport/escort service, controlled dormitory access. *Student services:* health clinic, personal/psychological counseling, women's center, legal services.

Athletics Member NCAA. All Division I except football (Division I-AA). *Intercollegiate sports:* basketball M(s)/W(s), cross-country running M(s)/W(s), golf M(s)/W(s), skiing (downhill) M/W, tennis M(s)/W(s), track and field M(s)/W(s), volleyball W(s). *Intramural sports:* basketball M/W, bowling M/W, cross-country running M/W, field hockey M/W, football M, racquetball M/W, riflery M/W, rugby M, skiing (cross-country) M/W, skiing (downhill) M/W, soccer M/W, softball M/W, table tennis M/W, tennis M/W, track and field M/W, volleyball M/W, water polo M/W.

Standardized Tests *Required:* SAT I or ACT (for admission).

Costs (2003–04) *Tuition:* state resident $0 full-time, $172 per credit hour part-time; nonresident $6600 full-time, $267 per credit hour part-time. Full-time tuition and fees vary according to reciprocity agreements. Part-time tuition and fees vary according to reciprocity agreements. *Required fees:* $3448 full-time. *Room and board:* $4680; room only: $1980. Room and board charges vary according to board plan and housing facility. *Payment plan:* deferred payment. *Waivers:* senior citizens and employees or children of employees.

Financial Aid Of all full-time matriculated undergraduates who enrolled in 2003, 920 Federal Work-Study jobs (averaging $1159). 2,700 state and other part-time jobs (averaging $1666). *Average indebtedness upon graduation:* $19,039.

Applying *Options:* common application, electronic application, early admission, deferred entrance. *Application fee:* $35. *Required:* high school transcript, minimum 2.0 GPA. *Application deadlines:* 8/1 (freshmen), 8/1 (transfers). *Notification:* continuous (transfers).

Admissions Contact Mr. Nathan Peterson, Associate Director of Recruitment, Idaho State University, Campus Box 8270, Pocatello, ID 83209. *Phone:* 208-282-3277. *Fax:* 208-282-4231. *E-mail:* info@isu.edu.

ITT Technical Institute
Boise, Idaho

- **Proprietary** primarily 2-year, founded 1906, part of ITT Educational Services, Inc.
- **Calendar** quarters
- **Degrees** associate and bachelor's
- **Urban** 1-acre campus
- **Coed**
- **Minimally difficult** entrance level

Standardized Tests *Required:* Wonderlic aptitude test (for admission).

Costs (2003–04) *Tuition:* $347 per credit hour part-time.

Financial Aid Of all full-time matriculated undergraduates who enrolled in 2001, 9 Federal Work-Study jobs (averaging $5500).

Applying *Options:* deferred entrance. *Application fee:* $100. *Required:* high school transcript, interview. *Recommended:* letters of recommendation.

Admissions Contact Terry G. Lowder, Director of Recruitment, ITT Technical Institute, 12302 West Explorer Drive, Boise, ID 83713. *Phone:* 208-322-8844. *Toll-free phone:* 800-666-4888. *Fax:* 208-322-0173.

Lewis-Clark State College
Lewiston, Idaho

- **State-supported** 4-year, founded 1893
- **Calendar** semesters
- **Degrees** certificates, associate, and bachelor's
- **Small-town** 44-acre campus
- **Coed,** 3,471 undergraduate students, 65% full-time, 61% women, 39% men
- **Minimally difficult** entrance level, 64% of applicants were admitted

Undergraduates 2,255 full-time, 1,216 part-time. Students come from 20 states and territories, 30 other countries, 13% are from out of state, 0.4% African American, 0.9% Asian American or Pacific Islander, 4% Hispanic American, 5% Native American, 3% international, 11% transferred in, 10% live on campus. *Retention:* 52% of 2002 full-time freshmen returned.

Freshmen *Admission:* 1,246 applied, 796 admitted, 514 enrolled. *Average high school GPA:* 3.11. *Test scores:* SAT verbal scores over 500: 44%; SAT math scores over 500: 50%; ACT scores over 18: 68%; SAT verbal scores over 600: 11%; SAT math scores over 600: 15%; ACT scores over 24: 19%; SAT verbal scores over 700: 2%; SAT math scores over 700: 3%; ACT scores over 30: 1%.

Faculty *Total:* 186, 73% full-time, 49% with terminal degrees. *Student/faculty ratio:* 17:1.

Majors Accounting technology and bookkeeping; administrative assistant and secretarial science; autobody/collision and repair technology; automobile/automotive mechanics technology; behavioral sciences; biology/biological sciences; business administration and management; chemistry; child development; communication/speech communication and rhetoric; computer and information sciences; computer science; corrections; creative writing; diesel mechanics technology; drafting and design technology; electrical/electronics equipment installation and repair; elementary education; English; English/language arts teacher education; fire science; graphic and printing equipment operation/production; heating, air conditioning, ventilation and refrigeration maintenance technology; hospitality administration; industrial electronics technology; interdisciplinary studies; kinesiology and exercise science; legal administrative assistant/secretary; legal assistant/paralegal; liberal arts and sciences/liberal studies; manufacturing technology; mathematics; mathematics teacher education; mechanics and repair; medical/health management and clinical assistant; medical office assistant; multi-/interdisciplinary studies related; natural sciences; nursing (licensed practical/vocational nurse training); nursing (registered nurse training); physical education teaching and coaching; psychology; radiologic technology/science; science teacher education; small business administration; social sciences; social science teacher education; social work; web/multimedia management and webmaster; welding technology.

Academic Programs *Special study options:* academic remediation for entering students, accelerated degree program, adult/continuing education programs, advanced placement credit, cooperative education, distance learning, double majors, English as a second language, external degree program, independent study, internships, off-campus study, part-time degree program, services for LD students, student-designed majors, study abroad, summer session for credit. *ROTC:* Army (b), Navy (c), Air Force (b). *Unusual degree programs:* 3-2 engineering with Boise State University.

Library Lewis-Clark State College Library with 139,499 titles, 1,612 serial subscriptions, 6,957 audiovisual materials, an OPAC, a Web page.

Computers on Campus 88 computers available on campus for general student use. A campuswide network can be accessed from student residence rooms and from off campus. Internet access, online (class) registration, at least one staffed computer lab available.

Student Life *Housing options:* coed, cooperative. Campus housing is university owned. *Activities and organizations:* drama/theater group, student-run newspaper, radio and television station, choral group, Business Students Organization, Ambassadors Club, international club, honors society, Explorers. *Campus security:* 24-hour emergency response devices and patrols, student patrols, late-night transport/escort service. *Student services:* health clinic, personal/psychological counseling.

Athletics Member NAIA. *Intercollegiate sports:* baseball M(s), basketball M(s)/W(s), cross-country running M(s)/W(s), golf M(s)/W(s), tennis M(s)/W(s), volleyball W(s). *Intramural sports:* badminton M/W, baseball M/W, basketball M/W, bowling M/W, field hockey M/W, football M/W, golf M/W, lacrosse M/W, rock climbing M/W, rugby M/W, skiing (downhill) M/W, soccer M/W, softball M/W, table tennis M/W, tennis M/W, track and field M/W, volleyball M/W, weight lifting M/W.

Standardized Tests *Required for some:* SAT I or ACT (for admission), ACT COMPASS.

Costs (2003–04) *Tuition:* state resident $0 full-time; nonresident $5998 full-time. Full-time tuition and fees vary according to course load and reciprocity agreements. *Required fees:* $3126 full-time, $153 per credit part-time. *Room and board:* $4336; room only: $1880. Room and board charges vary according to board plan and housing facility. *Payment plan:* deferred payment. *Waivers:* senior citizens and employees or children of employees.

Financial Aid Of all full-time matriculated undergraduates who enrolled in 2002, 1,551 applied for aid, 1,376 were judged to have need, 200 had their need fully met. 109 Federal Work-Study jobs (averaging $1190). 79 state and other part-time jobs (averaging $1241). In 2002, 140 non-need-based awards were made. *Average percent of need met:* 15%. *Average financial aid package:* $5239. *Average need-based loan:* $3365. *Average need-based gift aid:* $2890. *Average non-need-based aid:* $2982.

Applying *Options:* electronic application, deferred entrance. *Application fee:* $35. *Required:* high school transcript, minimum 2.0 GPA. *Required for some:* interview. *Application deadline:* rolling (freshmen), rolling (transfers). *Notification:* continuous (freshmen), continuous (transfers).

Admissions Contact Ms. Tracy Waffle, Admissions Supervisor, Lewis-Clark State College, 500 8th Avenue, Lewiston, ID 83501. *Phone:* 208-792-2210. *Toll-free phone:* 800-933-LCSC Ext. 2210. *Fax:* 208-792-2876. *E-mail:* admissions@lcsc.edu.

NEW SAINT ANDREWS COLLEGE

Moscow, Idaho

Admissions Contact PO Box 9025, Moscow, ID 83843.

NORTHWEST NAZARENE UNIVERSITY

Nampa, Idaho

- **Independent comprehensive, founded 1913, affiliated with Church of the Nazarene**
- **Calendar quarters**
- **Degrees bachelor's and master's**
- **Small-town 85-acre campus**
- **Endowment $12.8 million**
- **Coed, 1,156 undergraduate students, 94% full-time, 56% women, 44% men**
- **Moderately difficult entrance level, 70% of applicants were admitted**

A Christian university located in southern Idaho, NNU is consistently ranked by *U.S. News & World Report* as a top university and best value choice in the West. New facilities, nearby outdoor recreational areas, and opportunities for international study and service make NNU a place to challenge a student's mind and spirit.

Undergraduates 1,090 full-time, 66 part-time. Students come from 22 states and territories, 56% are from out of state, 0.6% African American, 1% Asian American or Pacific Islander, 1% Hispanic American, 0.3% Native American, 0.4% international, 6% transferred in, 68% live on campus. *Retention:* 70% of 2002 full-time freshmen returned.

Freshmen *Admission:* 814 applied, 571 admitted, 283 enrolled. *Average high school GPA:* 3.44. *Test scores:* ACT scores over 18: 86%; ACT scores over 24: 38%; ACT scores over 30: 3%.

Faculty *Total:* 98, 98% full-time, 62% with terminal degrees. *Student/faculty ratio:* 13:1.

Majors Accounting; ancient Near Eastern and biblical languages; art; art teacher education; athletic training; biochemistry; biology/biological sciences; biology teacher education; business administration and management; ceramic arts and ceramics; chemistry; chemistry teacher education; commercial and advertising art; communication/speech communication and rhetoric; computer science; divinity/ministry; elementary education; engineering physics; English; English/language arts teacher education; finance; forensic science and technology; graphic design; health and physical education; history; history teacher education; international business/trade/commerce; international relations and affairs; kinesiology and exercise science; liberal arts and sciences/liberal studies; marketing/marketing management; mass communication/media; mathematics; mathematics teacher education; missionary studies and missiology; music; music performance; music teacher education; music theory and composition; nursing (registered nurse training); painting; parks, recreation and leisure; pastoral studies/counseling; philosophy; physical education teaching and coaching; physical therapy; physics; political science and government; pre-law studies; pre-medical studies; psychology; public relations/image management; radio and television broadcasting technology; religious education; religious/sacred music; religious studies; sculpture; secondary education; social sciences; social science teacher education; social work; Spanish; Spanish language teacher education; theology.

Academic Programs *Special study options:* academic remediation for entering students, accelerated degree program, advanced placement credit, cooperative education, freshman honors college, honors programs, independent study, internships, off-campus study, part-time degree program, services for LD students, student-designed majors, study abroad, summer session for credit. *ROTC:* Army (b). *Unusual degree programs:* 3-2 engineering with University of Idaho, Boise State University, Walla Walla College.

Library John E. Riley Library with 100,966 titles, 821 serial subscriptions, an OPAC, a Web page.

Computers on Campus 400 computers available on campus for general student use. A campuswide network can be accessed from student residence rooms and from off campus that provide access to various software packages. Internet access, at least one staffed computer lab available.

Student Life *Housing:* on-campus residence required through sophomore year. *Options:* coed, men-only, women-only. Campus housing is university owned. Freshman campus housing is guaranteed. *Activities and organizations:* drama/theater group, student-run newspaper, choral group, student government, Are You Serving Him (RUSH), ministry clubs, service clubs, science clubs. *Campus security:* 24-hour patrols, student patrols, late-night transport/escort service, controlled dormitory access, residence hall check-in system, on-campus police hub. *Student services:* health clinic, personal/psychological counseling.

Athletics Member NCAA. All Division II. *Intercollegiate sports:* baseball M(s), basketball M(s)/W(s), cross-country running M(s)/W(s), golf M(s), soccer W(s),

Northwest Nazarene University (continued)
softball W(s), track and field M(s)/W(s), volleyball M(c)/W(s). *Intramural sports:* basketball M/W, cheerleading M/W, cross-country running M/W, fencing M/W, football M/W, golf M, softball M/W, table tennis M/W, tennis M/W, ultimate Frisbee M/W, volleyball M/W.

Standardized Tests *Required:* ACT (for admission).

Costs (2004–05) *Comprehensive fee:* $21,200 includes full-time tuition ($15,980), mandatory fees ($590), and room and board ($4630). Part-time tuition: $693 per credit. Part-time tuition and fees vary according to course load. *Required fees:* $70 per term part-time. *Room and board:* Room and board charges vary according to board plan and student level. *Payment plans:* tuition prepayment, installment. *Waivers:* employees or children of employees.

Financial Aid Of all full-time matriculated undergraduates who enrolled in 2003, 804 applied for aid, 695 were judged to have need, 161 had their need fully met. 337 Federal Work-Study jobs (averaging $1406). In 2003, 108 non-need-based awards were made. *Average percent of need met:* 76%. *Average financial aid package:* $12,598. *Average need-based loan:* $4711. *Average need-based gift aid:* $2887. *Average non-need-based aid:* $8153. *Average indebtedness upon graduation:* $21,073.

Applying *Options:* electronic application, early admission, early action, deferred entrance. *Application fee:* $25. *Required:* essay or personal statement, high school transcript, minimum 2.5 GPA, 2 letters of recommendation. *Required for some:* interview. *Application deadlines:* 8/8 (freshmen), 8/8 (transfers). *Notification:* continuous (freshmen), 1/15 (early action), continuous (transfers).

Admissions Contact Ms. Dianna Gibney, Director of Admissions, Northwest Nazarene University, 623 Holly Street, Admissions Welcome Center, Nampa, ID 83686. *Phone:* 208-467-8000. *Toll-free phone:* 877-NNU-4YOU. *Fax:* 208-467-8645. *E-mail:* admissions@nnu.edu.

UNIVERSITY OF IDAHO

Moscow, Idaho

- **State-supported** university, founded 1889
- **Calendar** semesters
- **Degrees** certificates, bachelor's, master's, doctoral, first professional, and post-master's certificates
- **Small-town** 1450-acre campus
- **Endowment** $143.5 million
- **Coed,** 9,607 undergraduate students, 87% full-time, 45% women, 55% men
- **Moderately difficult** entrance level, 81% of applicants were admitted

Undergraduates 8,403 full-time, 1,204 part-time. Students come from 25 other countries, 22% are from out of state, 0.9% African American, 2% Asian American or Pacific Islander, 4% Hispanic American, 1% Native American, 2% international, 8% transferred in, 55% live on campus. *Retention:* 82% of 2002 full-time freshmen returned.

Freshmen *Admission:* 3,973 applied, 3,202 admitted, 1,650 enrolled. *Average high school GPA:* 3.40. *Test scores:* SAT verbal scores over 500: 72%; SAT math scores over 500: 75%; ACT scores over 18: 92%; SAT verbal scores over 600: 30%; SAT math scores over 600: 34%; ACT scores over 24: 46%; SAT verbal scores over 700: 5%; SAT math scores over 700: 5%; ACT scores over 30: 8%.

Faculty *Total:* 585, 93% full-time, 79% with terminal degrees. *Student/faculty ratio:* 20:1.

Majors Accounting; administrative assistant and secretarial science; agricultural/biological engineering and bioengineering; agricultural business and management; agricultural economics; agricultural mechanization; agricultural teacher education; agriculture; American studies; animal sciences; anthropology; apparel and textiles; applied mathematics; architecture; art; art teacher education; athletic training; biology/biological sciences; biomedical/medical engineering; botany/plant biology; business teacher education; cartography; chemical engineering; chemistry; child development; civil engineering; classics and languages, literatures and linguistics; clinical laboratory science/medical technology; communication/speech communication and rhetoric; computer engineering; computer science; criminal justice/safety; dance; dramatic/theatre arts; economics; electrical, electronics and communications engineering; elementary education; engineering; English; entomology; environmental studies; family and consumer sciences/home economics teacher education; finance; fine/studio arts; fish/game management; food science; foods, nutrition, and wellness; foreign languages and literatures; forestry; French; general studies; geography; geological/geophysical engineering; geology/earth science; German; history; horticultural science; human resources management; industrial engineering; industrial technology; interior architecture; interior design; international relations and affairs; journalism; landscape architecture; Latin; Latin American studies; liberal arts and sciences/liberal studies; management information systems; marketing/marketing management; mathematics; mechanical engineering; medical microbiology and bacteriology; metallurgical engineering; military technologies; mining and mineral engineering; molecular biology; multi-/interdisciplinary studies related; music history, literature, and theory; music management and merchandising; music performance; music teacher education; music theory and composition; natural resources management and policy; operations management; parks, recreation and leisure; philosophy; photography; physical education teaching and coaching; physics; plant sciences; political science and government; pre-medical studies; psychology; public relations/image management; radio and television; range science and management; secondary education; sociology; soil science and agronomy; Spanish; special education; technical teacher education; technology/industrial arts teacher education; trade and industrial teacher education; voice and opera; wildlife and wildlands science and management; wood science and wood products/pulp and paper technology; zoology/animal biology.

Academic Programs *Special study options:* academic remediation for entering students, accelerated degree program, adult/continuing education programs, advanced placement credit, cooperative education, distance learning, double majors, honors programs, independent study, internships, off-campus study, part-time degree program, services for LD students, student-designed majors, study abroad, summer session for credit. *ROTC:* Army (b), Navy (b), Air Force (c).

Library University of Idaho Library plus 1 other with 1.4 million titles, 14,230 serial subscriptions, 8,717 audiovisual materials, an OPAC, a Web page.

Computers on Campus 670 computers available on campus for general student use. A campuswide network can be accessed from student residence rooms and from off campus that provide access to student evaluations of teaching. Internet access, online (class) registration, at least one staffed computer lab available. Computer purchase or lease plan available.

Student Life *Housing options:* coed, men-only, women-only, cooperative, disabled students. Campus housing is university owned. Freshman campus housing is guaranteed. *Activities and organizations:* drama/theater group, student-run newspaper, radio and television station, choral group, marching band, Alpha Phi Omega, Campus Crusade for Christ, Student International Association, OELA, Students of Human Resource Management, national fraternities, national sororities. *Campus security:* late-night transport/escort service, controlled dormitory access. *Student services:* health clinic, personal/psychological counseling, women's center, legal services.

Athletics Member NCAA. All Division I except football (Division I-A). *Intercollegiate sports:* baseball M(c), basketball M(s)/W(s), cross-country running M(s)/W(s), golf M(s)/W(s), ice hockey M(c), riflery M(c)/W(c), rugby M(c)/W(c), skiing (cross-country) M(c)/W(c), skiing (downhill) M(c)/W(c), soccer M(c)/W(s), tennis M(s)/W(s), track and field M(s)/W(s), volleyball W(s). *Intramural sports:* baseball M, basketball M/W, equestrian sports M/W, fencing M, football M/W, golf M/W, ice hockey M, racquetball M/W, riflery M/W, rugby M/W, skiing (cross-country) M/W, skiing (downhill) M/W, soccer M/W, softball M/W, squash M/W, swimming M/W, table tennis M/W, tennis M/W, track and field M/W, volleyball W, water polo M, weight lifting M/W, wrestling M.

Standardized Tests *Required:* SAT I or ACT (for admission). *Recommended:* SAT I (for admission).

Costs (2003–04) *Tuition:* state resident $0 full-time; nonresident $7392 full-time, $167 per credit part-time. Full-time tuition and fees vary according to degree level and program. Part-time tuition and fees vary according to course load, degree level, and program. *Required fees:* $3348 full-time. *Room and board:* $4868. Room and board charges vary according to board plan and housing facility. *Payment plan:* deferred payment. *Waivers:* minority students, children of alumni, senior citizens, and employees or children of employees.

Financial Aid Of all full-time matriculated undergraduates who enrolled in 2002, 6,076 applied for aid, 4,875 were judged to have need, 1,503 had their need fully met. 498 Federal Work-Study jobs (averaging $1483). 231 state and other part-time jobs (averaging $1757). In 2002, 2306 non-need-based awards were made. *Average percent of need met:* 79%. *Average financial aid package:* $8951. *Average need-based loan:* $5660. *Average need-based gift aid:* $3945. *Average non-need-based aid:* $3413. *Average indebtedness upon graduation:* $19,299.

Applying *Options:* common application, electronic application, deferred entrance. *Application fee:* $40. *Required:* high school transcript, minimum 2.2 GPA. *Required for some:* essay or personal statement. *Application deadline:* 8/1 (freshmen), rolling (transfers). *Notification:* continuous (freshmen), continuous (transfers).

Admissions Contact Mr. Dan Davenport, Director of Admissions, University of Idaho, PO Box 444264, Moscow, ID 83844-4264. *Phone:* 208-885-6326. *Toll-free phone:* 888-884-3246. *Fax:* 208-885-9119. *E-mail:* admappl@uidaho.edu.

■ *See page 2618 for a narrative description.*

UNIVERSITY OF PHOENIX–IDAHO CAMPUS

Meridian, Idaho

- **Proprietary** comprehensive
- **Calendar** continuous

■ **Degrees** certificates, associate, bachelor's, master's, doctoral, post-master's, and postbachelor's certificates (courses conducted at 121 campuses and learning centers in 25 states)
■ **Urban** campus
■ **Coed,** 376 undergraduate students
■ **Noncompetitive** entrance level

Undergraduates 0.8% African American, 2% Asian American or Pacific Islander, 0.8% Hispanic American, 0.5% Native American, 52% international.
Faculty *Total:* 26, 4% full-time, 27% with terminal degrees. *Student/faculty ratio:* 7:1.
Majors Accounting; business administration, management and operations related; computer and information sciences; e-commerce; health/health care administration; marketing/marketing management.
Academic Programs *Special study options:* accelerated degree program, adult/continuing education programs, advanced placement credit, distance learning, external degree program, independent study.
Library University Library with 27.1 million titles, 11,648 serial subscriptions, an OPAC, a Web page.
Computers on Campus A campuswide network can be accessed from off campus. Internet access, at least one staffed computer lab available. Computer purchase or lease plan available.
Student Life *Housing:* college housing not available.
Costs (2003–04) *Tuition:* $9000 full-time, $300 per credit part-time. *Waivers:* employees or children of employees.
Financial Aid *Average financial aid package:* $1162.
Applying *Options:* deferred entrance. *Application fee:* $100. *Required:* 1 letter of recommendation, 2 years of work experience, 23 years of age. *Notification:* continuous (freshmen), continuous (transfers).
Admissions Contact Ms. Beth Barilla, Director of Admissions, University of Phoenix–Idaho Campus, 4615 East Elwood Street, Mail Stop AA-K101, Phoenix, AZ 85040-1958. *Phone:* 480-317-6000. *Toll-free phone:* 800-228-7240. *Fax:* 480-574-1758. *E-mail:* beth.barilla@phoenix.edu.

ILLINOIS

AMERICAN ACADEMY OF ART
Chicago, Illinois

■ **Proprietary** comprehensive, founded 1923
■ **Calendar** trimesters
■ **Degrees** bachelor's and master's
■ **Urban** campus
■ **Coed,** 360 undergraduate students, 76% full-time, 34% women, 66% men
■ **Moderately difficult** entrance level, 100% of applicants were admitted

Undergraduates 272 full-time, 88 part-time. Students come from 8 states and territories, 2% are from out of state, 9% African American, 3% Asian American or Pacific Islander, 24% Hispanic American, 0.6% international, 7% transferred in. *Retention:* 82% of 2002 full-time freshmen returned.
Freshmen *Admission:* 87 applied, 87 admitted, 87 enrolled.
Faculty *Total:* 30, 87% full-time, 73% with terminal degrees. *Student/faculty ratio:* 15:1.
Majors Advertising; applied art; art; commercial and advertising art; computer graphics; design and visual communications; drawing; fine/studio arts; painting; visual and performing arts.
Academic Programs *Special study options:* academic remediation for entering students, accelerated degree program, adult/continuing education programs, independent study, internships, part-time degree program, study abroad, summer session for credit.
Library Irving Shapiro Library with 1,730 titles, 62 serial subscriptions, 101 audiovisual materials.
Computers on Campus 2 computers available on campus for general student use.
Student Life *Housing:* college housing not available. *Campus security:* 24-hour emergency response devices.
Costs (2003–04) *Tuition:* $17,780 full-time. Full-time tuition and fees vary according to course load. Part-time tuition and fees vary according to course load. *Payment plan:* installment. *Waivers:* employees or children of employees.
Financial Aid *Average percent of need met:* 70%.
Applying *Options:* electronic application. *Application fee:* $25. *Required:* high school transcript, 2 letters of recommendation, interview, portfolio review. *Application deadline:* rolling (freshmen), rolling (transfers).
Admissions Contact Mr. Stuart Rosenbloom, Director of Admissions, American Academy of Art, 332 South Michigan Avenue, Suite 300, Chicago, IL 60604-4302. *Phone:* 312-461-0600 Ext. 143. *E-mail:* stuartrnet@comcast.net.

■ *See page 1162 for a narrative description.*

AMERICAN INTERCONTINENTAL UNIVERSITY ONLINE
Hoffman Estates, Illinois

■ **Proprietary** comprehensive, founded 1970, part of American InterContinental University
■ **Calendar** quarters
■ **Degrees** associate, bachelor's, and master's (only offers online degree programs)
■ **Suburban** 1-acre campus
■ **Coed**

Majors Accounting and finance; business administration, management and operations related; computer programming; corrections and criminal justice related; data processing and data processing technology; design and visual communications; health/health care administration; human resources management; information technology; marketing/marketing management; system, networking, and LAN/wan management.
Applying *Application fee:* $50. *Required:* interview, documentation of high school graduation or its equivalency. *Recommended:* essay or personal statement. *Application deadline:* rolling (freshmen), rolling (transfers). *Notification:* continuous (freshmen), continuous (transfers).
Admissions Contact Mr. Steve Fireng, Senior Vice President of Admissions and Marketing, American InterContinental University Online, 5550 Prairie Stone Parkway, Suite 400, Hoffman Estates, IL 60192. *Phone:* 877-701-3800. *Toll-free phone:* 877-701-3800. *E-mail:* info@aiu-online.com.

ARGOSY UNIVERSITY/CHICAGO
Chicago, Illinois

■ **Proprietary** upper-level, founded 1976
■ **Calendar** semesters
■ **Degrees** bachelor's, master's, and doctoral
■ **Urban** campus
■ **Coed,** 23 undergraduate students, 48% full-time, 87% women, 13% men
■ 65% of applicants were admitted

Undergraduates 11 full-time, 12 part-time. 39% African American, 4% Asian American or Pacific Islander.
Faculty *Total:* 4.
Majors Business administration and management; psychology.
Student Life *Housing:* college housing not available. *Activities and organizations:* student-run newspaper. *Campus security:* 24-hour patrols.
Costs (2003–04) *Tuition:* $12,000 full-time, $360 per credit part-time. *Required fees:* $120 full-time, $80 per year part-time. *Payment plan:* installment. *Waivers:* employees or children of employees.
Financial Aid Of all full-time matriculated undergraduates who enrolled in 2003, 7 applied for aid, 6 were judged to have need. 1 Federal Work-Study job (averaging $1363). *Average financial aid package:* $7745. *Average need-based loan:* $3021. *Average need-based gift aid:* $3607.
Applying *Application fee:* $50. *Notification:* continuous (transfers).
Admissions Contact Ms. Ashley Delaney, Director of Admissions, Argosy University/Chicago, Admissions Department, 20 South Clark Street Third Floor, Chicago, IL 60603. *Phone:* 800-626-4123 Ext. 3906. *Toll-free phone:* 800-626-4123. *Fax:* 312-357-2736. *E-mail:* chicagoadmissions@argosyu.edu.

ARGOSY UNIVERSITY/CHICAGO NORTHWEST
Rolling Meadows, Illinois

■ **Proprietary** upper-level, founded 1979
■ **Calendar** semesters
■ **Degrees** bachelor's, master's, doctoral, and post-master's certificates
■ **Suburban** campus with easy access to Chicago
■ **Coed**

Majors Business/commerce; psychology.
Student Life *Housing:* college housing not available.
Athletics *Intramural sports:* cheerleading M/W.

Argosy University/Chicago Northwest (continued)

Costs (2003–04) *Tuition:* $360 per credit hour part-time. *Required fees:* $40 per term part-time.

Financial Aid Of all full-time matriculated undergraduates who enrolled in 2003, 8 applied for aid, 7 were judged to have need. *Average financial aid package:* $6617. *Average need-based loan:* $3572. *Average need-based gift aid:* $3531.

Applying *Application fee:* $50. *Notification:* continuous (transfers).

Admissions Contact Mr. Jamal Scott, Director of Admissions, Argosy University/Chicago Northwest, 1000 North Plaza Drive, Suite 100, Schaumburg, IL 60173. *Phone:* 847-290-7400. *Toll-free phone:* 866-290-2777. *Fax:* 312-201-1907. *E-mail:* jscott@argosyu.edu.

AUGUSTANA COLLEGE
Rock Island, Illinois

- **Independent** 4-year, founded 1860, affiliated with Evangelical Lutheran Church in America
- **Calendar** quarters
- **Degree** bachelor's
- **Suburban** 115-acre campus
- **Endowment** $73.6 million
- **Coed,** 2,309 undergraduate students, 99% full-time, 58% women, 42% men
- **Moderately difficult** entrance level, 68% of applicants were admitted

Undergraduates 2,277 full-time, 32 part-time. Students come from 26 states and territories, 19 other countries, 13% are from out of state, 2% African American, 2% Asian American or Pacific Islander, 3% Hispanic American, 0.3% Native American, 0.9% international, 3% transferred in, 72% live on campus. *Retention:* 85% of 2002 full-time freshmen returned.

Freshmen *Admission:* 3,021 applied, 2,060 admitted, 614 enrolled. *Average high school GPA:* 3.53. *Test scores:* ACT scores over 18: 100%; ACT scores over 24: 72%; ACT scores over 30: 17%.

Faculty *Total:* 223, 65% full-time, 68% with terminal degrees. *Student/faculty ratio:* 12:1.

Majors Accounting; anthropology; art; art history, criticism and conservation; art teacher education; Asian studies; biology/biological sciences; business administration and management; chemistry; Chinese; classics and languages, literatures and linguistics; computer science; creative writing; dramatic/theatre arts; economics; education; elementary education; engineering physics; engineering related; English; environmental studies; finance; fine/studio arts; French; geography; geology/earth science; German; history; Japanese; jazz/jazz studies; Latin; liberal arts and sciences/liberal studies; literature; marketing/marketing management; mass communication/media; mathematics; mathematics and computer science; music; music performance; music teacher education; occupational therapy; philosophy; physical education teaching and coaching; physics; piano and organ; political science and government; pre-dentistry studies; pre-law studies; premedical studies; pre-veterinary studies; psychology; public administration; religious/sacred music; religious studies; Scandinavian languages; science teacher education; secondary education; sociology; Spanish; speech and rhetoric; speech-language pathology; speech therapy; Swedish; violin, viola, guitar and other stringed instruments; voice and opera; wind/percussion instruments; women's studies.

Academic Programs *Special study options:* accelerated degree program, advanced placement credit, double majors, honors programs, independent study, internships, part-time degree program, services for LD students, study abroad, summer session for credit. *Unusual degree programs:* 3-2 engineering with Washington University in St. Louis, University of Illinois, Iowa State University of Science and Technology, Purdue University; forestry with Duke University; occupational therapy with Washington University in St. Louis, landscape architecture with University of Illinois, environmental studies with Duke University.

Library Augustana College Library plus 3 others with 190,641 titles, 1,705 serial subscriptions, 2,019 audiovisual materials, an OPAC, a Web page.

Computers on Campus 600 computers available on campus for general student use. A campuswide network can be accessed from student residence rooms and from off campus. Internet access, at least one staffed computer lab available.

Student Life *Housing:* on-campus residence required through junior year. *Options:* coed, men-only, women-only. Campus housing is university owned. Freshman campus housing is guaranteed. *Activities and organizations:* drama/theater group, student-run newspaper, radio station, choral group, College Union Board of Managers, Student Government Association, Literacy Council, student radio station. *Campus security:* 24-hour emergency response devices and patrols, late-night transport/escort service, controlled dormitory access. *Student services:* health clinic, personal/psychological counseling, women's center.

Athletics Member NCAA. All Division III. *Intercollegiate sports:* baseball M, basketball M/W, cross-country running M/W, football M, golf M/W, lacrosse M(c), soccer M/W, softball W, swimming M/W, tennis M/W, track and field M/W, ultimate Frisbee M(c)/W(c), volleyball M(c)/W, wrestling M. *Intramural sports:* badminton M/W, basketball M/W, bowling M/W, crew M, cross-country running M/W, football M/W, golf M/W, racquetball M/W, rugby M, skiing (cross-country) M/W, skiing (downhill) M/W, soccer M/W, softball M/W, swimming M/W, table tennis M/W, tennis M/W, track and field M/W, ultimate Frisbee M/W, volleyball M/W, wrestling M.

Standardized Tests *Required:* SAT I or ACT (for admission).

Costs (2003–04) *Comprehensive fee:* $26,610 includes full-time tuition ($20,397), mandatory fees ($432), and room and board ($5781). Full-time tuition and fees vary according to course load. Part-time tuition: $855 per credit hour. *College room only:* $2928. Room and board charges vary according to housing facility. *Payment plans:* tuition prepayment, installment. *Waivers:* employees or children of employees.

Financial Aid Of all full-time matriculated undergraduates who enrolled in 2003, 1,819 applied for aid, 1,526 were judged to have need, 755 had their need fully met. 1,007 Federal Work-Study jobs (averaging $1303). In 2003, 278 non-need-based awards were made. *Average percent of need met:* 86%. *Average financial aid package:* $15,207. *Average need-based loan:* $4409. *Average need-based gift aid:* $10,723. *Average non-need-based aid:* $6976. *Average indebtedness upon graduation:* $17,076.

Applying *Options:* common application, deferred entrance. *Application fee:* $25. *Required:* high school transcript. *Required for some:* essay or personal statement, 2 letters of recommendation, interview. *Application deadline:* rolling (freshmen), rolling (transfers). *Notification:* continuous (freshmen), continuous (transfers).

Admissions Contact Mr. Martin Sauer, Director of Admissions, Augustana College, 639 38th Street, Rock Island, IL 61201-2296. *Phone:* 309-794-7341. *Toll-free phone:* 800-798-8100. *Fax:* 309-794-7422. *E-mail:* admissions@augustana.edu.

AURORA UNIVERSITY
Aurora, Illinois

- **Independent** comprehensive, founded 1893
- **Calendar** trimesters
- **Degrees** bachelor's, master's, doctoral, and post-master's certificates
- **Suburban** 26-acre campus with easy access to Chicago
- **Coed,** 1,646 undergraduate students, 87% full-time, 64% women, 36% men
- **Moderately difficult** entrance level, 56% of applicants were admitted

Aurora University combines a residential and commuter population. The curriculum emphasizes human services offered through the College of Education and George Williams College (social work, nursing, human services), as well as traditional majors offered through the College of Arts, Sciences, and Business. The YMCA Senior Director Certificate Program is a supplemental major offered in cooperation with the YMCA of the USA.

Undergraduates 1,440 full-time, 206 part-time. Students come from 14 states and territories, 5% are from out of state, 16% African American, 2% Asian American or Pacific Islander, 12% Hispanic American, 0.3% Native American, 0.1% international, 20% transferred in, 33% live on campus. *Retention:* 71% of 2002 full-time freshmen returned.

Freshmen *Admission:* 1,485 applied, 834 admitted, 333 enrolled. *Average high school GPA:* 3.19. *Test scores:* SAT verbal scores over 500: 38%; SAT math scores over 500: 57%; ACT scores over 18: 93%; ACT scores over 24: 26%; ACT scores over 30: 2%.

Faculty *Total:* 216, 45% full-time, 54% with terminal degrees. *Student/faculty ratio:* 19:1.

Majors Accounting; biology/biological sciences; business/commerce; business/managerial economics; chemistry; clinical laboratory science/medical technology; communication/speech communication and rhetoric; computer and information sciences; computer systems networking and telecommunications; criminal justice/law enforcement administration; criminal justice/safety; economics; elementary education; engineering physics; English; English composition; environmental studies; finance; health/medical preparatory programs related; history; humanities; management information systems; marketing/marketing management; mathematics; nursing (registered nurse training); operations management; philosophy; physical education teaching and coaching; political science and government; psychology; social work; sociology.

Academic Programs *Special study options:* academic remediation for entering students, adult/continuing education programs, advanced placement credit, distance learning, double majors, independent study, internships, off-campus study, part-time degree program, services for LD students, student-designed majors, study abroad, summer session for credit. *ROTC:* Army (c).

Library Charles B. Phillips Library plus 1 other with 115,642 titles, 749 serial subscriptions, 6,015 audiovisual materials, an OPAC, a Web page.

Computers on Campus 90 computers available on campus for general student use. A campuswide network can be accessed from student residence rooms and from off campus. Internet access, at least one staffed computer lab available.

Student Life *Housing options:* coed. Campus housing is university owned and leased by the school. *Activities and organizations:* drama/theater group, choral group, Black Student Association, Aurora University Student Association, Student Nursing Association, Social Work Association, national fraternities, national sororities. *Campus security:* 24-hour patrols, late-night transport/escort service, controlled dormitory access. *Student services:* health clinic, personal/psychological counseling.

Athletics Member NCAA. All Division III. *Intercollegiate sports:* baseball M, basketball M/W, football M, golf M, soccer M/W, softball W, tennis M/W, volleyball W. *Intramural sports:* basketball M/W, football M/W, soccer M/W, softball M/W, volleyball M/W.

Standardized Tests *Recommended:* SAT I or ACT (for admission).

Costs (2004–05) *Comprehensive fee:* $21,364 includes full-time tuition ($14,750) and room and board ($6614). Full-time tuition and fees vary according to course load, location, and program. Part-time tuition: $507 per semester hour. Part-time tuition and fees vary according to location and program. *College room only:* $2968. Room and board charges vary according to board plan and housing facility. *Payment plans:* installment, deferred payment. *Waivers:* senior citizens and employees or children of employees.

Financial Aid Of all full-time matriculated undergraduates who enrolled in 2003, 1,417 applied for aid, 1,135 were judged to have need, 393 had their need fully met. 478 Federal Work-Study jobs (averaging $1535). In 2003, 253 non-need-based awards were made. *Average percent of need met:* 82%. *Average financial aid package:* $15,470. *Average need-based loan:* $3663. *Average need-based gift aid:* $5496. *Average non-need-based aid:* $7653. *Average indebtedness upon graduation:* $15,983.

Applying *Options:* common application, electronic application, early admission, deferred entrance. *Application fee:* $25. *Required:* high school transcript, minimum 2.0 GPA. *Required for some:* essay or personal statement, 2 letters of recommendation, interview. *Recommended:* essay or personal statement, interview. *Application deadline:* rolling (freshmen), rolling (transfers). *Notification:* continuous (freshmen), continuous (transfers).

Admissions Contact Mr. James Lancaster, Freshman Recruitment Coordinator, Aurora University, 347 South Gladstone Avenue, Aurora, IL 60506-4892. *Phone:* 630-844-5533. *Toll-free phone:* 800-742-5281. *Fax:* 630-844-5535. *E-mail:* admission@aurora.edu.

■ *See page 1198 for a narrative description.*

Benedictine University
Lisle, Illinois

- **Independent Roman Catholic** comprehensive, founded 1887
- **Calendar** semesters
- **Degrees** associate, bachelor's, master's, and doctoral
- **Suburban** 108-acre campus with easy access to Chicago
- **Endowment** $7.5 million
- **Coed,** 2,114 undergraduate students, 70% full-time, 63% women, 37% men
- **Moderately difficult** entrance level

Undergraduates 1,472 full-time, 642 part-time. Students come from 25 states and territories, 8 other countries, 4% are from out of state, 10% African American, 13% Asian American or Pacific Islander, 8% Hispanic American, 2% international, 12% transferred in, 23% live on campus. *Retention:* 77% of 2002 full-time freshmen returned.

Freshmen *Admission:* 303 enrolled. *Average high school GPA:* 3.40. *Test scores:* ACT scores over 18: 93%; ACT scores over 24: 47%; ACT scores over 30: 6%.

Faculty *Total:* 313, 30% full-time. *Student/faculty ratio:* 13:1.

Majors Accounting; arts management; biochemistry; biology/biological sciences; business administration and management; business/commerce; business, management, and marketing related; business/managerial economics; chemistry; clinical laboratory science/medical technology; communication/speech communication and rhetoric; computer science; economics; education; elementary education; engineering science; English; environmental studies; finance; fine/studio arts; health/health care administration; health science; history; information science/studies; international business/trade/commerce; international relations and affairs; marketing/marketing management; mathematics; molecular biology; music; music teacher education; nuclear medical technology; nursing science; nutrition sciences; organizational behavior; philosophy; physics; political science and government; pre-dentistry studies; pre-law studies; pre-medical studies; pre-veterinary studies; psychology; publishing; science teacher education; secondary education; social sciences; sociology; Spanish; special education.

Academic Programs *Special study options:* academic remediation for entering students, accelerated degree program, adult/continuing education programs, advanced placement credit, distance learning, double majors, English as a second language, honors programs, independent study, internships, off-campus study, part-time degree program, services for LD students, study abroad, summer session for credit. *ROTC:* Army (c). *Unusual degree programs:* 3-2 engineering with University of Illinois at Urbana–Champaign, Illinois Institute of Technology, Purdue University; nursing with Rush University.

Library Benedictine Library with 166,341 titles, 8,900 serial subscriptions, 9,349 audiovisual materials, an OPAC, a Web page.

Computers on Campus 102 computers available on campus for general student use. A campuswide network can be accessed from student residence rooms and from off campus. At least one staffed computer lab available.

Student Life *Housing options:* coed, men-only, women-only. Freshman campus housing is guaranteed. *Activities and organizations:* drama/theater group, student-run newspaper, television station, choral group, Student Government Association, campus ministry, choir/gospel choir. *Campus security:* 24-hour emergency response devices and patrols, late-night transport/escort service, controlled dormitory access. *Student services:* health clinic, personal/psychological counseling.

Athletics Member NCAA. All Division III. *Intercollegiate sports:* baseball M, basketball M/W, cross-country running M/W, football M, golf M, soccer M/W, softball W, swimming M/W, tennis W, track and field M/W, volleyball W. *Intramural sports:* badminton M/W, baseball M, basketball M/W, bowling M/W, football M/W, racquetball M/W, soccer M/W, softball M/W, swimming M/W, table tennis M/W, tennis M/W, volleyball M/W, water polo M/W, weight lifting M/W.

Standardized Tests *Required:* ACT (for admission).

Costs (2004–05) *Comprehensive fee:* $23,840 includes full-time tuition ($16,960), mandatory fees ($510), and room and board ($6370). Full-time tuition and fees vary according to class time and degree level. Part-time tuition: $570 per credit hour. Part-time tuition and fees vary according to class time and degree level. *Required fees:* $15 per credit hour part-time. *Room and board:* Room and board charges vary according to board plan and housing facility. *Payment plan:* installment. *Waivers:* children of alumni and employees or children of employees.

Financial Aid Of all full-time matriculated undergraduates who enrolled in 2003, 1,029 applied for aid, 872 were judged to have need, 147 had their need fully met. 59 Federal Work-Study jobs (averaging $1500). In 2003, 576 non-need-based awards were made. *Average percent of need met:* 68%. *Average financial aid package:* $11,489. *Average need-based loan:* $3692. *Average need-based gift aid:* $5273. *Average non-need-based aid:* $6632. *Average indebtedness upon graduation:* $6727. *Financial aid deadline:* 4/15.

Applying *Options:* deferred entrance. *Application fee:* $40. *Required:* essay or personal statement, high school transcript, letters of recommendation. *Required for some:* interview. *Recommended:* rank in top 50% of high school class, ACT score of 21. *Application deadline:* rolling (freshmen), rolling (transfers). *Notification:* continuous (freshmen), continuous (transfers).

Admissions Contact Ms. Kari Gibbons, Dean of Undergraduate Admissions, Benedictine University, 5700 College Road, Lisle, IL 60532-0900. *Phone:* 630-829-6306. *Toll-free phone:* 888-829-6363. *Fax:* 630-960-1126. *E-mail:* admissions@ben.edu.

■ *See page 1236 for a narrative description.*

Blackburn College
Carlinville, Illinois

- **Independent Presbyterian** 4-year, founded 1837
- **Calendar** semesters
- **Degree** bachelor's
- **Small-town** 80-acre campus with easy access to St. Louis
- **Endowment** $10.4 million
- **Coed,** 615 undergraduate students, 97% full-time, 58% women, 42% men
- **Moderately difficult** entrance level, 56% of applicants were admitted

Undergraduates 599 full-time, 16 part-time. Students come from 12 states and territories, 8 other countries, 6% African American, 0.9% Asian American or Pacific Islander, 0.9% Hispanic American, 0.3% Native American, 3% international. *Retention:* 65% of 2002 full-time freshmen returned.

Freshmen *Admission:* 792 applied, 442 admitted, 176 enrolled. *Average high school GPA:* 3.22. *Test scores:* ACT scores over 18: 80%; ACT scores over 24: 20%; ACT scores over 30: 1%.

Faculty *Total:* 51, 69% full-time, 53% with terminal degrees. *Student/faculty ratio:* 16:1.

Majors Accounting; art; art history, criticism and conservation; biology/biological sciences; business administration and management; chemistry; clinical laboratory science/medical technology; clinical psychology; communication/speech communication and rhetoric; computer science; criminal justice/law

Blackburn College (continued)
enforcement administration; elementary education; English; environmental science; experimental psychology; history; interdisciplinary studies; liberal arts and sciences/liberal studies; literature; marketing/marketing management; mathematics; molecular biology; music; physical education teaching and coaching; political science and government; pre-dentistry studies; pre-law studies; pre-medical studies; pre-veterinary studies; psychology; public administration; secondary education; Spanish; speech and rhetoric.

Academic Programs *Special study options:* advanced placement credit, cooperative education, double majors, honors programs, independent study, internships, off-campus study, part-time degree program, student-designed majors, study abroad. *Unusual degree programs:* 3-2 engineering with Washington University in St. Louis; nursing with St. John's College.

Library Lumpkin Library with 87,175 titles, 17,000 serial subscriptions, 1,940 audiovisual materials.

Computers on Campus 25 computers available on campus for general student use. A campuswide network can be accessed from student residence rooms. Internet access, at least one staffed computer lab available.

Student Life *Housing:* on-campus residence required through junior year. *Options:* coed, men-only, women-only. Campus housing is university owned. Freshman campus housing is guaranteed. *Activities and organizations:* drama/theater group, student-run newspaper, choral group, Cultural Expressions, Residence Hall Association, New Student Orientation Committee, choral groups, student government. *Campus security:* student patrols, late-night transport/escort service. *Student services:* personal/psychological counseling.

Athletics Member NCAA. All Division III. *Intercollegiate sports:* baseball M, basketball M/W, cheerleading M/W, cross-country running M/W, football M, golf M/W, soccer M/W, softball W, tennis W, volleyball W. *Intramural sports:* badminton M/W, basketball M/W, racquetball M/W, soccer M/W, tennis W, volleyball M/W.

Standardized Tests *Required:* SAT I or ACT (for admission).

Costs (2004–05) *Comprehensive fee:* $15,940 includes full-time tuition ($12,360) and room and board ($3580). Full-time tuition and fees vary according to program. Part-time tuition: $487 per semester hour. *College room only:* $1680. *Payment plan:* installment. *Waivers:* employees or children of employees.

Financial Aid *Average percent of need met:* 85%.

Applying *Options:* electronic application, deferred entrance. *Required:* essay or personal statement, high school transcript, minimum 2.0 GPA. *Required for some:* 1 letter of recommendation, interview. *Application deadline:* rolling (freshmen), rolling (transfers). *Notification:* continuous (transfers).

Admissions Contact Mr. John Malin, Dean of Enrollment Management, Blackburn College, 700 College Avenue, Carlinville, IL 62626-1498. *Phone:* 217-854-3231 Ext. 4252. *Toll-free phone:* 800-233-3550. *Fax:* 217-854-3713. *E-mail:* admit@mail.blackburn.edu.

BLESSING-RIEMAN COLLEGE OF NURSING
Quincy, Illinois

- **Independent** 4-year, founded 1985
- **Calendar** semesters
- **Degree** bachelor's
- **Small-town** 1-acre campus
- **Endowment** $7.0 million
- **Coed, primarily women,** 178 undergraduate students, 86% full-time, 96% women, 4% men
- **Moderately difficult** entrance level, 70% of applicants were admitted

Undergraduates 153 full-time, 25 part-time. Students come from 8 states and territories, 35% are from out of state, 3% African American, 1% Asian American or Pacific Islander, 1% Hispanic American, 0.6% Native American, 11% transferred in, 82% live on campus. *Retention:* 87% of 2002 full-time freshmen returned.

Freshmen *Admission:* 148 applied, 103 admitted, 26 enrolled. *Average high school GPA:* 3.60. *Test scores:* ACT scores over 18: 100%; ACT scores over 24: 25%.

Faculty *Total:* 13, 100% full-time, 31% with terminal degrees. *Student/faculty ratio:* 12:1.

Majors Nursing (registered nurse training).

Academic Programs *Special study options:* academic remediation for entering students, adult/continuing education programs, advanced placement credit, distance learning, double majors, honors programs, internships, part-time degree program, summer session for credit.

Library Blessing Health Professions Library plus 1 other with 4,275 titles, 123 serial subscriptions, 570 audiovisual materials, an OPAC, a Web page.

Computers on Campus 21 computers available on campus for general student use. A campuswide network can be accessed. Internet access, at least one staffed computer lab available.

Student Life *Housing:* on-campus residence required through sophomore year. *Options:* coed. Campus housing is university owned. Freshman campus housing is guaranteed. *Activities and organizations:* drama/theater group, student-run newspaper, radio station, choral group, Student Nurses Organization, national fraternities, national sororities. *Campus security:* 24-hour patrols, late-night transport/escort service, controlled dormitory access. *Student services:* health clinic, personal/psychological counseling.

Athletics *Intercollegiate sports:* baseball M(s)/W(s), basketball M(s)/W(s), football M(s), soccer M(s)/W(s), volleyball M(s)/W(s). *Intramural sports:* baseball M/W, basketball M/W, football M, soccer M/W, volleyball M/W.

Standardized Tests *Required:* SAT I or ACT (for admission).

Costs (2003–04) *Comprehensive fee:* $18,200 includes full-time tuition ($12,400), mandatory fees ($350), and room and board ($5450). Full-time tuition and fees vary according to course load, location, and student level. Part-time tuition: $325 per credit. Part-time tuition and fees vary according to course load, location, and student level. *Room and board:* Room and board charges vary according to location. *Waivers:* employees or children of employees.

Financial Aid Of all full-time matriculated undergraduates who enrolled in 2002, 74 applied for aid, 74 were judged to have need. *Average percent of need met:* 75%. *Average indebtedness upon graduation:* $11,000.

Applying *Options:* electronic application, deferred entrance. *Required:* high school transcript, minimum 3.0 GPA. *Recommended:* essay or personal statement, interview. *Application deadline:* rolling (freshmen), rolling (transfers).

Admissions Contact Ms. Heather Mutter, Admissions Counselor, Blessing-Rieman College of Nursing, PO Box 7005, Quincy, IL 62305-7005. *Phone:* 800-897-9140 Ext. 6961. *Toll-free phone:* 800-877-9140 Ext. 6964. *Fax:* 217-223-4661. *E-mail:* admissions@brcn.edu.

BRADLEY UNIVERSITY
Peoria, Illinois

- **Independent** comprehensive, founded 1897
- **Calendar** semesters
- **Degrees** bachelor's and master's
- **Urban** 75-acre campus with easy access to Chicago and St. Louis
- **Endowment** $144.3 million
- **Coed,** 5,305 undergraduate students, 93% full-time, 54% women, 46% men
- **Moderately difficult** entrance level, 69% of applicants were admitted

Undergraduates 4,927 full-time, 378 part-time. Students come from 42 states and territories, 55 other countries, 14% are from out of state, 6% African American, 3% Asian American or Pacific Islander, 2% Hispanic American, 0.4% Native American, 1% international, 7% transferred in, 42% live on campus. *Retention:* 89% of 2002 full-time freshmen returned.

Freshmen *Admission:* 5,207 applied, 3,570 admitted, 1,105 enrolled. *Test scores:* SAT verbal scores over 500: 81%; SAT math scores over 500: 82%; ACT scores over 18: 99%; SAT verbal scores over 600: 40%; SAT math scores over 600: 46%; ACT scores over 24: 68%; SAT verbal scores over 700: 4%; SAT math scores over 700: 8%; ACT scores over 30: 12%.

Faculty *Total:* 528, 63% full-time, 52% with terminal degrees. *Student/faculty ratio:* 15:1.

Majors Accounting; actuarial science; advertising; art; art history, criticism and conservation; biochemistry; biology/biological sciences; broadcast journalism; business administration and management; business/managerial economics; chemistry; civil engineering; civil engineering related; clinical laboratory science/medical technology; communication and journalism related; communication/speech communication and rhetoric; computer and information sciences; construction engineering; criminal justice/law enforcement administration; dramatic/theatre arts; ecology; economics; education (specific subject areas) related; electrical, electronic and communications engineering technology; electrical, electronics and communications engineering; elementary education; engineering physics; English; environmental/environmental health engineering; family resource management; finance; fine/studio arts; French; geology/earth science; German; health professions related; health science; history; industrial engineering; industrial technology; information science/studies; insurance; international business/trade/commerce; international relations and affairs; journalism; kindergarten/preschool education; liberal arts and sciences/liberal studies; management information systems; marketing/marketing management; mathematics; mathematics and statistics related; mechanical engineering; molecular biology; music; music management and merchandising; music performance; music teacher education; music theory and composition; nursing (registered nurse training); philosophy; physical therapy; physics; political science and government; psychology; public relations/image management; radio and television; religious studies; social work;

sociology; Spanish; special education (emotionally disturbed); special education (mentally retarded); special education (specific learning disabilities); speech and rhetoric.

Academic Programs *Special study options:* academic remediation for entering students, accelerated degree program, adult/continuing education programs, advanced placement credit, cooperative education, distance learning, double majors, honors programs, independent study, internships, off-campus study, part-time degree program, student-designed majors, study abroad, summer session for credit. *ROTC:* Army (b).

Library Cullom-Davis Library with 424,753 titles, 1,996 serial subscriptions, 9,574 audiovisual materials, an OPAC, a Web page.

Computers on Campus 2000 computers available on campus for general student use. A campuswide network can be accessed from student residence rooms and from off campus. Internet access, online (class) registration, at least one staffed computer lab available.

Student Life *Housing:* on-campus residence required through sophomore year. *Options:* coed. Campus housing is university owned and is provided by a third party. Freshman campus housing is guaranteed. *Activities and organizations:* drama/theater group, student-run newspaper, radio and television station, choral group, Alpha Phi Omega, Student Activities Council, Student Action for Environment, investment club, Student Senate, national fraternities, national sororities. *Campus security:* 24-hour emergency response devices and patrols, late-night transport/escort service, controlled dormitory access, bicycle patrol. *Student services:* health clinic, personal/psychological counseling.

Athletics Member NCAA. All Division I. *Intercollegiate sports:* baseball M(s), basketball M(s)/W(s), cheerleading M/W, cross-country running M(s)/W(s), fencing M(c)/W(c), golf M(s)/W(s), ice hockey M(c), soccer M(s)/W(c), softball W(s), table tennis M(c)/W(c), tennis M(s)/W(s), track and field W(s), volleyball W(s). *Intramural sports:* badminton M/W, basketball M/W, bowling M/W, football M/W, golf M/W, lacrosse M(c), racquetball M/W, soccer M/W, softball M/W, swimming M/W, table tennis M/W, tennis M/W, ultimate Frisbee M(c)/W(c), volleyball M/W, water polo M/W, wrestling M.

Standardized Tests *Required:* SAT I or ACT (for admission).

Costs (2003–04) *Comprehensive fee:* $22,910 includes full-time tuition ($16,800), mandatory fees ($130), and room and board ($5980). Full-time tuition and fees vary according to program. Part-time tuition: $460 per credit. Part-time tuition and fees vary according to course load. *College room only:* $3400. Room and board charges vary according to board plan. *Payment plans:* installment, deferred payment. *Waivers:* senior citizens and employees or children of employees.

Financial Aid Of all full-time matriculated undergraduates who enrolled in 2003, 4,349 applied for aid, 3,758 were judged to have need, 2,220 had their need fully met. In 2003, 1056 non-need-based awards were made. *Average percent of need met:* 83%. *Average financial aid package:* $12,636. *Average need-based loan:* $4955. *Average need-based gift aid:* $8755. *Average non-need-based aid:* $8980. *Average indebtedness upon graduation:* $15,944.

Applying *Options:* common application, electronic application, early admission, deferred entrance. *Application fee:* $35. *Required:* essay or personal statement, high school transcript. *Recommended:* minimum 3.0 GPA, letters of recommendation, interview. *Application deadline:* rolling (freshmen). *Notification:* continuous (freshmen), continuous (transfers).

Admissions Contact Mr. Thomas Richmond, Director of Admissions, Bradley University, 1501 West Bradley Avenue, 100 Swords Hall, Peoria, IL 61625-0002. *Phone:* 309-677-1000. *Toll-free phone:* 800-447-6460. *E-mail:* admissions@bradley.edu.

■ *See page 1282 for a narrative description.*

CHICAGO STATE UNIVERSITY

Chicago, Illinois

- **State-supported** comprehensive, founded 1867
- **Calendar** semesters
- **Degrees** bachelor's and master's
- **Urban** 161-acre campus
- **Coed,** 4,904 undergraduate students, 65% full-time, 73% women, 27% men
- **Moderately difficult** entrance level, 42% of applicants were admitted

Undergraduates 3,203 full-time, 1,701 part-time. Students come from 12 states and territories, 8 other countries, 1% are from out of state, 86% African American, 0.5% Asian American or Pacific Islander, 6% Hispanic American, 0.1% Native American, 0.1% international, 12% transferred in. *Retention:* 62% of 2002 full-time freshmen returned.

Freshmen *Admission:* 2,425 applied, 1,019 admitted, 542 enrolled. *Average high school GPA:* 2.69. *Test scores:* ACT scores over 18: 51%; ACT scores over 24: 4%.

Faculty *Total:* 364, 87% full-time, 59% with terminal degrees. *Student/faculty ratio:* 12:1.

Majors Accounting; African studies; anthropology; applied art; art history, criticism and conservation; art teacher education; bilingual and multilingual education; biology/biological sciences; broadcast journalism; business administration and management; business teacher education; ceramic arts and ceramics; chemistry; commercial and advertising art; computer science; consumer merchandising/retailing management; corrections; creative writing; criminal justice/law enforcement administration; criminal justice/police science; data processing and data processing technology; drawing; economics; education; elementary education; English; finance; fine/studio arts; geography; health information/medical records administration; health teacher education; history; hotel/motel administration; industrial arts; information science/studies; jazz/jazz studies; kindergarten/preschool education; literature; management information systems; marketing/marketing management; mathematics; modern languages; music; music teacher education; nursing (registered nurse training); occupational therapy; parks, recreation and leisure; physical education teaching and coaching; political science and government; pre-dentistry studies; pre-law studies; pre-medical studies; pre-veterinary studies; psychology; radio and television; reading teacher education; science teacher education; secondary education; sociology; Spanish; special education; technical and business writing; wind/percussion instruments.

Academic Programs *Special study options:* academic remediation for entering students, accelerated degree program, adult/continuing education programs, advanced placement credit, cooperative education, distance learning, double majors, English as a second language, external degree program, honors programs, internships, part-time degree program, services for LD students, student-designed majors, study abroad, summer session for credit. *ROTC:* Army (b), Navy (c), Air Force (c).

Library Paul and Emily Douglas Library with 320,000 titles, 1,539 serial subscriptions.

Computers on Campus 40 computers available on campus for general student use. At least one staffed computer lab available.

Student Life *Housing options:* coed. Campus housing is university owned. *Activities and organizations:* drama/theater group, student-run newspaper, radio station, choral group, math/computer science club, geographic society club, gospel choir, movie club, national fraternities, national sororities. *Campus security:* 24-hour emergency response devices and patrols, student patrols, controlled dormitory access. *Student services:* health clinic, personal/psychological counseling, women's center.

Athletics Member NCAA, NAIA. All NCAA Division I. *Intercollegiate sports:* baseball M, basketball M(s)/W(s), cross-country running M(s)/W(s), golf M/W, tennis M/W, track and field M(s)/W(s), volleyball W(s).

Standardized Tests *Required:* SAT I or ACT (for admission).

Costs (2004–05) *Tuition:* state resident $4830 full-time, $161 per credit hour part-time; nonresident $9660 full-time, $322 per credit hour part-time. *Required fees:* $1313 full-time, $210 per term part-time. *Room and board:* $6032.

Applying *Application fee:* $20. *Required:* high school transcript. *Application deadlines:* 7/15 (freshmen), 7/15 (transfers). *Notification:* continuous (freshmen), continuous (transfers).

Admissions Contact Ms. Addie Epps, Director of Admissions, Chicago State University, 95th Street at King Drive, ADM 200, Chicago, IL 60628. *Phone:* 773-995-2513. *E-mail:* ug-admissions@csu.edu.

CHRISTIAN LIFE COLLEGE

Mount Prospect, Illinois

- **Independent religious** 4-year
- **Degrees** diplomas, associate, and bachelor's
- **Coed**
- 57% of applicants were admitted

Faculty *Student/faculty ratio:* 10:1.

Costs (2003–04) *Tuition:* $6000 full-time, $250 per credit hour part-time. *Required fees:* $700 full-time. *Room only:* $3500.

Financial Aid Of all full-time matriculated undergraduates who enrolled in 2002, 33 applied for aid, 28 were judged to have need. 4 Federal Work-Study jobs (averaging $1646). In 2002, 6. *Average percent of need met:* 75. *Average financial aid package:* $4464. *Average need-based loan:* $2393. *Average need-based gift aid:* $3160. *Average non-need-based aid:* $871.

Admissions Contact Mr. Jim Spenner, Director of Admissions, Christian Life College, 400 East Gregory Street, Mount Prospect, IL 60056. *Phone:* 847-259-1840 Ext. 17.

COLUMBIA COLLEGE CHICAGO
Chicago, Illinois

- **Independent** comprehensive, founded 1890
- **Calendar** semesters
- **Degrees** bachelor's, master's, and postbachelor's certificates
- **Urban** campus
- **Endowment** $69.7 million
- **Coed,** 9,265 undergraduate students, 84% full-time, 52% women, 48% men
- **Noncompetitive** entrance level, 90% of applicants were admitted

Undergraduates 7,792 full-time, 1,473 part-time. Students come from 50 states and territories, 73 other countries, 15% are from out of state, 16% African American, 4% Asian American or Pacific Islander, 11% Hispanic American, 0.6% Native American, 2% international, 14% transferred in.

Freshmen *Admission:* 3,293 applied, 2,964 admitted, 1,557 enrolled. *Test scores:* ACT scores over 18: 63%; ACT scores over 24: 22%; ACT scores over 30: 2%.

Faculty *Total:* 1,662, 18% full-time. *Student/faculty ratio:* 11:1.

Majors Acting; advertising; area, ethnic, cultural, and gender studies related; art; arts management; broadcast journalism; business administration and management; cinematography and film/video production; commercial and advertising art; computer and information sciences and support services related; creative writing; dance; dance therapy; dramatic/theatre arts; early childhood education; education (specific levels and methods) related; education (specific subject areas) related; fashion/apparel design; film/cinema studies; fine/studio arts; industrial design; interdisciplinary studies; interior design; intermedia/multimedia; journalism; kindergarten/preschool education; liberal arts and sciences/liberal studies; marketing/marketing management; multi-/interdisciplinary studies related; music; music management and merchandising; music performance; photography; playwriting and screenwriting; public relations/image management; radio and television; recording arts technology; sign language interpretation and translation; theatre design and technology; web page, digital/multimedia and information resources design.

Academic Programs *Special study options:* academic remediation for entering students, advanced placement credit, English as a second language, independent study, internships, off-campus study, part-time degree program, services for LD students, student-designed majors, study abroad, summer session for credit.

Library Columbia College Library with 219,952 titles, 1,150 serial subscriptions, an OPAC, a Web page.

Computers on Campus 730 computers available on campus for general student use. A campuswide network can be accessed. Internet access, at least one staffed computer lab available.

Student Life *Housing:* on-campus residence required for freshman year. *Options:* coed. Campus housing is university owned and leased by the school. Freshman applicants given priority for college housing. *Activities and organizations:* drama/theater group, student-run newspaper, radio and television station, choral group, Columbia Urban Music Association, International Student Organization, Acianza Latina, marketing club. *Campus security:* 24-hour emergency response devices and patrols, late-night transport/escort service, controlled dormitory access, escort upon request. *Student services:* health clinic, personal/psychological counseling.

Athletics *Intramural sports:* basketball M/W, soccer M/W, volleyball M/W.

Standardized Tests *Recommended:* SAT I or ACT (for admission).

Costs (2004–05) *Comprehensive fee:* $24,144 includes full-time tuition ($14,880), mandatory fees ($390), and room and board ($8874). Part-time tuition: $575 per semester hour. *Required fees:* $85 per term part-time. *College room only:* $7155. Room and board charges vary according to housing facility. *Payment plan:* installment. *Waivers:* employees or children of employees.

Applying *Options:* deferred entrance. *Application fee:* $35. *Required:* essay or personal statement, high school transcript, letters of recommendation. *Recommended:* minimum 2.0 GPA, interview. *Application deadline:* 7/1 (freshmen). *Notification:* continuous (transfers).

Admissions Contact Mr. Murphy Monroe, Director of Admissions and Recruitment, Columbia College Chicago, 600 South Michigan Avenue, Chicago, IL 60605-1996. *Phone:* 312-663-1600 Ext. 7133. *Toll-free phone:* 312-663-1600 Ext. 7130. *Fax:* 312-344-8024. *E-mail:* admissions@colum.edu.

■ *See page 1474 for a narrative description.*

CONCORDIA UNIVERSITY
River Forest, Illinois

- **Independent** comprehensive, founded 1864, affiliated with Lutheran Church–Missouri Synod, part of Concordia University System
- **Calendar** semesters
- **Degrees** bachelor's, master's, doctoral, post-master's, and postbachelor's certificates
- **Suburban** 40-acre campus with easy access to Chicago
- **Endowment** $12.1 million
- **Coed,** 1,203 undergraduate students, 83% full-time, 63% women, 37% men
- **Moderately difficult** entrance level, 21% of applicants were admitted

Undergraduates 997 full-time, 206 part-time. Students come from 26 states and territories, 35% are from out of state, 6% African American, 2% Asian American or Pacific Islander, 5% Hispanic American, 0.1% Native American, 0.4% international, 8% transferred in, 50% live on campus. *Retention:* 72% of 2002 full-time freshmen returned.

Freshmen *Admission:* 1,094 applied, 228 admitted, 227 enrolled. *Average high school GPA:* 3.17. *Test scores:* ACT scores over 18: 84%; ACT scores over 24: 39%; ACT scores over 30: 7%.

Faculty *Total:* 66. *Student/faculty ratio:* 11:1.

Majors Accounting; ancient Near Eastern and biblical languages; art; art teacher education; biological and physical sciences; biology/biological sciences; biology teacher education; business administration and management; chemistry; commercial and advertising art; communication/speech communication and rhetoric; computer science; computer teacher education; dramatic/theatre arts; education; elementary education; English; English/language arts teacher education; environmental studies; geography; history; history teacher education; information science/studies; kindergarten/preschool education; kinesiology and exercise science; legal studies; mathematics; mathematics teacher education; music; music teacher education; natural sciences; nursing (registered nurse training); pastoral studies/counseling; philosophy; physical education teaching and coaching; physical sciences; piano and organ; political science and government; pre-dentistry studies; pre-law studies; pre-medical studies; pre-theology/pre-ministerial studies; psychology; religious education; religious/sacred music; science teacher education; secondary education; social science teacher education; social work; sociology; speech teacher education; theology; voice and opera; wind/percussion instruments.

Academic Programs *Special study options:* academic remediation for entering students, accelerated degree program, adult/continuing education programs, advanced placement credit, distance learning, double majors, honors programs, independent study, internships, off-campus study, part-time degree program, services for LD students, study abroad, summer session for credit.

Library Klinck Memorial Library plus 10 others with 171,510 titles, 256 serial subscriptions, 6,010 audiovisual materials, an OPAC, a Web page.

Computers on Campus 70 computers available on campus for general student use. A campuswide network can be accessed from student residence rooms and from off campus. Internet access, at least one staffed computer lab available.

Student Life *Housing options:* coed, women-only. Campus housing is university owned. *Activities and organizations:* drama/theater group, student-run newspaper, choral group, Concordia Youth Ministries, Kappelle Choir, Wind Symphony, student government, intramural sports. *Campus security:* 24-hour emergency response devices and patrols, student patrols, late-night transport/escort service, emergency call boxes. *Student services:* personal/psychological counseling, legal services.

Athletics Member NCAA. All Division III. *Intercollegiate sports:* baseball M, basketball M/W, cheerleading M/W, cross-country running M/W, football M, golf M, soccer M/W, softball W, tennis M/W, track and field M/W, volleyball W. *Intramural sports:* badminton M/W, basketball M/W, bowling M/W, football W, swimming M/W, table tennis M/W, tennis M/W, volleyball M/W.

Standardized Tests *Required:* SAT I or ACT (for admission).

Costs (2003–04) *Comprehensive fee:* $23,600 includes full-time tuition ($17,900), mandatory fees ($300), and room and board ($5400). Full-time tuition and fees vary according to program. Part-time tuition: $530 per semester hour. Part-time tuition and fees vary according to program. No tuition increase for student's term of enrollment. *Required fees:* $10 per semester hour part-time. *Payment plan:* installment. *Waivers:* minority students, children of alumni, senior citizens, and employees or children of employees.

Financial Aid Of all full-time matriculated undergraduates who enrolled in 2003, 960 applied for aid, 818 were judged to have need, 354 had their need fully met. 350 Federal Work-Study jobs (averaging $356). In 2003, 185 non-need-based awards were made. *Average percent of need met:* 45%. *Average financial aid package:* $11,333. *Average need-based loan:* $3670. *Average need-based gift aid:* $5179. *Average non-need-based aid:* $6928. *Average indebtedness upon graduation:* $15,700.

Applying *Options:* electronic application, deferred entrance. *Application fee:* $100. *Required:* high school transcript, minimum 2.0 GPA, 1 letter of recommendation, minimum ACT score of 20 or SAT I score of 930. *Required for some:* essay or personal statement, interview. *Application deadline:* rolling (freshmen), rolling (transfers).

Admissions Contact Dr. Evelyn Burdick, Vice President for Enrollment Services, Concordia University, 7400 Augusta Street, River Forest, IL 60305. *Phone:* 708-209-3100. *Toll-free phone:* 800-285-2668. *Fax:* 708-209-3473. *E-mail:* crfadmis@curf.edu.

DEPAUL UNIVERSITY
Chicago, Illinois

- **Independent Roman Catholic** university, founded 1898
- **Calendar** quarters; semesters for law school
- **Degrees** certificates, bachelor's, master's, doctoral, first professional, post-master's, and postbachelor's certificates
- **Urban** 36-acre campus
- **Coed,** 14,585 undergraduate students, 74% full-time, 58% women, 42% men
- **Moderately difficult** entrance level, 73% of applicants were admitted

Undergraduates 10,847 full-time, 3,738 part-time. Students come from 50 states and territories, 74 other countries, 13% are from out of state, 11% African American, 9% Asian American or Pacific Islander, 13% Hispanic American, 0.3% Native American, 2% international, 9% transferred in, 20% live on campus. *Retention:* 83% of 2002 full-time freshmen returned.

Freshmen *Admission:* 9,463 applied, 6,903 admitted, 2,261 enrolled. *Average high school GPA:* 3.30. *Test scores:* SAT verbal scores over 500: 78%; SAT math scores over 500: 75%; SAT verbal scores over 600: 34%; SAT math scores over 600: 28%; SAT verbal scores over 700: 5%; SAT math scores over 700: 4%.

Faculty *Total:* 1,516, 53% full-time. *Student/faculty ratio:* 17:1.

Majors Accounting; acting; adult and continuing education; advertising; African-American/Black studies; African studies; American studies; anthropology; applied art; applied mathematics; art; art history, criticism and conservation; arts management; Asian studies (East); biochemistry; biology/biological sciences; business administration and management; business administration, management and operations related; business/commerce; business/managerial economics; chemistry; city/urban, community and regional planning; clinical laboratory science/medical technology; clinical/medical laboratory technology; commercial and advertising art; communication/speech communication and rhetoric; comparative literature; computer and information sciences; computer and information sciences related; computer graphics; computer programming; computer programming (specific applications); computer science; computer systems networking and telecommunications; counselor education/school counseling and guidance; creative writing; dramatic/theatre arts; dramatic/theatre arts and stagecraft related; drawing; economics; education; elementary education; English; environmental studies; finance; fine/studio arts; French; general studies; geography; German; health teacher education; history; human resources management; information science/studies; interdisciplinary studies; international business/trade/commerce; international relations and affairs; Italian; Japanese; jazz/jazz studies; Jewish/Judaic studies; kindergarten/preschool education; Latin American studies; literature; management information systems; marketing/marketing management; mass communication/media; mathematics; modern languages; music; music management and merchandising; music performance; music teacher education; music theory and composition; nursing (registered nurse training); operations research; philosophy; physical education teaching and coaching; physics; piano and organ; playwriting and screenwriting; political science and government; pre-law studies; psychology; public policy analysis; religious studies; sculpture; secondary education; social sciences; sociology; Spanish; statistics; theatre design and technology; theatre literature, history and criticism; urban studies/affairs; violin, viola, guitar and other stringed instruments; voice and opera; web page, digital/multimedia and information resources design; wind/percussion instruments; women's studies.

Academic Programs *Special study options:* academic remediation for entering students, accelerated degree program, adult/continuing education programs, advanced placement credit, cooperative education, distance learning, double majors, English as a second language, freshman honors college, honors programs, independent study, internships, part-time degree program, services for LD students, study abroad, summer session for credit. *ROTC:* Army (b). *Unusual degree programs:* 3-2 engineering with University of Illinois at Urbana-Champaign, University of Illinois at Chicago, University of Detroit Mercy, University of Southern California, Northwestern University, Iowa State University, Ohio State University.

Library John T. Richardson Library plus 2 others with 1.4 million titles, 14,585 serial subscriptions, 96,669 audiovisual materials, a Web page.

Computers on Campus 850 computers available on campus for general student use. A campuswide network can be accessed from student residence rooms and from off campus. Internet access, online (class) registration, at least one staffed computer lab available.

Student Life *Housing options:* coed. Campus housing is university owned and leased by the school. Freshman applicants given priority for college housing. *Activities and organizations:* drama/theater group, student-run newspaper, choral group, Student Ambassadors, DePaul Activities Board, DePaul Community Service Association, national fraternities, national sororities. *Campus security:* 24-hour emergency response devices and patrols, late-night transport/escort service, controlled dormitory access, security lighting, prevention/awareness programs, on-campus police officers, video cameras, smoke detectors in residence halls. *Student services:* health clinic, personal/psychological counseling, women's center, legal services.

Athletics Member NCAA. All Division I. *Intercollegiate sports:* basketball M(s)/W(s), cheerleading M/W, cross-country running M(s)/W(s), golf M(s)/W, soccer M(s)/W(s), softball W(s), tennis M(s)/W(s), track and field M(s)/W(s), volleyball W(s). *Intramural sports:* badminton M/W, baseball M, basketball M/W, crew M/W, cross-country running M/W, football M/W, golf M, ice hockey M/W, racquetball M/W, rugby M/W, skiing (downhill) M/W, soccer M/W, softball W, swimming M/W, table tennis M/W, tennis M/W, track and field M/W, ultimate Frisbee M/W, volleyball W, weight lifting M/W, wrestling M.

Standardized Tests *Required:* SAT I or ACT (for admission).

Costs (2003–04) *One-time required fee:* $140. *Comprehensive fee:* $27,580 includes full-time tuition ($18,750), mandatory fees ($40), and room and board ($8790). Full-time tuition and fees vary according to program. Part-time tuition: $348 per quarter hour. Part-time tuition and fees vary according to program. *College room only:* $5970. Room and board charges vary according to board plan and housing facility. *Payment plans:* installment, deferred payment. *Waivers:* employees or children of employees.

Financial Aid Of all full-time matriculated undergraduates who enrolled in 2002, 7,497 applied for aid, 6,700 were judged to have need, 1,066 had their need fully met. 815 Federal Work-Study jobs (averaging $1650). In 2002, 210 non-need-based awards were made. *Average percent of need met:* 74%. *Average financial aid package:* $14,106. *Average need-based loan:* $4277. *Average need-based gift aid:* $9161. *Average non-need-based aid:* $6485. *Average indebtedness upon graduation:* $16,500. *Financial aid deadline:* 4/1.

Applying *Options:* common application, electronic application, early admission, early action, deferred entrance. *Application fee:* $40. *Required:* high school transcript, minimum 2.0 GPA, 1 letter of recommendation. *Required for some:* minimum 3.0 GPA, interview, audition. *Recommended:* minimum 3.0 GPA. *Application deadline:* rolling (freshmen), rolling (transfers). *Notification:* 1/15 (early action).

Admissions Contact Carlene Klaas, Undergraduate Admissions, DePaul University, 1 East Jackson Boulevard, Suite 9100, Chicago, IL 60604. *Phone:* 312-362-8300. *E-mail:* admitdpu@depaul.edu.

■ *See page 1528 for a narrative description.*

DEVRY UNIVERSITY
Addison, Illinois

- **Proprietary** 4-year, founded 1982, part of DeVry University
- **Calendar** semesters
- **Degrees** associate, bachelor's, and postbachelor's certificates
- **Suburban** 14-acre campus with easy access to Chicago
- **Coed**
- **Minimally difficult** entrance level

Student Life *Campus security:* 24-hour emergency response devices, lighted pathways/sidewalks.

Standardized Tests *Recommended:* SAT I, ACT or CPT.

Costs (2003–04) *Tuition:* $10,100 full-time, $360 per credit hour part-time. Full-time tuition and fees vary according to course load. Part-time tuition and fees vary according to course load. *Required fees:* $165 full-time. *Payment plans:* installment, deferred payment.

Financial Aid Of all full-time matriculated undergraduates who enrolled in 2002, 1,955 applied for aid, 1,769 were judged to have need, 78 had their need fully met. In 2002, 308. *Average percent of need met:* 52. *Average financial aid package:* $8431. *Average need-based loan:* $3451. *Average need-based gift aid:* $5239. *Average non-need-based aid:* $7973.

Applying *Options:* electronic application, deferred entrance. *Application fee:* $50. *Required:* high school transcript, interview.

Admissions Contact Ms. Jane Miritello, Assistant New Student Coordinator, DeVry University, 1221 North Swift Road, Addison, IL 60101-6106. *Phone:* 708-342-3300. *Toll-free phone:* 800-346-5420. *Fax:* 630-953-1236. *E-mail:* mbutler@dpg.devry.edu.

DEVRY UNIVERSITY
Chicago, Illinois

- **Proprietary** comprehensive, founded 1931, part of DeVry University
- **Calendar** semesters
- **Degrees** associate, bachelor's, and postbachelor's certificates

DeVry University (continued)
- **Urban** 17-acre campus
- **Coed**
- **Minimally difficult** entrance level

Student Life *Campus security:* 24-hour emergency response devices and patrols, late-night transport/escort service, lighted pathways/sidewalks.

Standardized Tests *Recommended:* SAT I, ACT or CPT.

Costs (2003–04) *Tuition:* $10,100 full-time, $360 per credit hour part-time. Full-time tuition and fees vary according to course load. Part-time tuition and fees vary according to course load. *Required fees:* $165 full-time. *Payment plans:* installment, deferred payment.

Financial Aid Of all full-time matriculated undergraduates who enrolled in 2002, 1,927 applied for aid, 1,886 were judged to have need, 27 had their need fully met. In 2002, 71. *Average percent of need met:* 53. *Average financial aid package:* $11,079. *Average need-based loan:* $5487. *Average need-based gift aid:* $6731. *Average non-need-based aid:* $8082.

Applying *Options:* electronic application, deferred entrance. *Application fee:* $50. *Required:* high school transcript, interview.

Admissions Contact Ms. Christine Hierl, Director of Admissions, DeVry University, 3300 North Campbell Avenue, Chicago, IL 60618-5994. *Phone:* 773-929-6550. *Toll-free phone:* 800-383-3879. *Fax:* 773-697-2710. *E-mail:* admissions2@devry.edu.

DeVry University
Elgin, Illinois

Admissions Contact 385 Airport Road, Elgin, IL 60123-9341.

DeVry University
Gurnee, Illinois

Admissions Contact 1075 Tri-State Parkway, Suite 800, Gurnee, IL 60031-9126. *Toll-free phone:* 866-563-3879.

DeVry University
Naperville, Illinois

Admissions Contact 2056 Westings Avenue, Suite 40, Naperville, IL 60563-2361.

DeVry University
Oakbrook Terrace, Illinois

Admissions Contact One Tower Lane, Oakbrook Terrace, IL 60181.

DeVry University
Tinley Park, Illinois

- **Proprietary** comprehensive, founded 2000, part of DeVry University
- **Calendar** semesters
- **Degrees** associate, bachelor's, master's, and postbachelor's certificates
- **Suburban** 12-acre campus
- **Coed**
- **Minimally difficult** entrance level

Faculty *Student/faculty ratio:* 27:1.

Student Life *Campus security:* 24-hour emergency response devices, late-night transport/escort service, lighted pathways/sidewalks, security patrols.

Standardized Tests *Recommended:* SAT I, ACT or CPT.

Costs (2003–04) *Tuition:* $10,100 full-time, $360 per credit hour part-time. Full-time tuition and fees vary according to course load. Part-time tuition and fees vary according to course load. *Required fees:* $165 full-time. *Payment plans:* installment, deferred payment.

Financial Aid Of all full-time matriculated undergraduates who enrolled in 2002, 1,574 applied for aid, 1,023 were judged to have need, 3 had their need fully met. In 2002, 94. *Average percent of need met:* 52. *Average financial aid package:* $9695. *Average need-based loan:* $5510. *Average need-based gift aid:* $6226. *Average non-need-based aid:* $9996.

Applying *Options:* electronic application, deferred entrance. *Application fee:* $50. *Required:* high school transcript, interview.

Admissions Contact Ms. Kerrie Flynn, Assistant New Student Coordinator, DeVry University, 18624 West Creek Drive, Tinley Park, IL 60477-6243. *Phone:* 708-342-3300. *Toll-free phone:* 877-305-8184. *Fax:* 708-342-3505. *E-mail:* imccauley@tp.devry.edu.

Dominican University
River Forest, Illinois

- **Independent Roman Catholic** comprehensive, founded 1901
- **Calendar** semesters
- **Degrees** certificates, bachelor's, master's, and post-master's certificates
- **Suburban** 30-acre campus with easy access to Chicago
- **Endowment** $14.5 million
- **Coed,** 1,211 undergraduate students, 83% full-time, 69% women, 31% men
- **Moderately difficult** entrance level, 82% of applicants were admitted

Undergraduates 1,010 full-time, 201 part-time. Students come from 21 states and territories, 18 other countries, 11% are from out of state, 5% African American, 2% Asian American or Pacific Islander, 16% Hispanic American, 2% international, 35% live on campus. *Retention:* 81% of 2002 full-time freshmen returned.

Freshmen *Admission:* 665 applied, 548 admitted, 241 enrolled. *Average high school GPA:* 3.48. *Test scores:* ACT scores over 18: 94%; ACT scores over 24: 39%; ACT scores over 30: 6%.

Faculty *Total:* 251, 39% full-time, 66% with terminal degrees. *Student/faculty ratio:* 12:1.

Majors Accounting; American studies; art; art history, criticism and conservation; biochemistry; biology/biological sciences; business administration and management; chemistry; clinical laboratory science/medical technology; commercial and advertising art; computer engineering; computer graphics; computer science; criminology; dietetics; dramatic/theatre arts; economics; education (K-12); electrical, electronics and communications engineering; elementary education; English; environmental studies; fashion/apparel design; fashion merchandising; fine/studio arts; food science; foodservice systems administration; foods, nutrition, and wellness; French; gerontology; history; information science/studies; international business/trade/commerce; Italian; mass communication/media; mathematics; philosophy; photography; political science and government; pre-dentistry studies; pre-law studies; pre-medical studies; pre-veterinary studies; psychology; religious studies; social sciences; sociology; Spanish; special products marketing.

Academic Programs *Special study options:* accelerated degree program, adult/continuing education programs, advanced placement credit, distance learning, double majors, English as a second language, honors programs, independent study, internships, off-campus study, part-time degree program, services for LD students, student-designed majors, study abroad, summer session for credit. *Unusual degree programs:* 3-2 engineering with with Illinois Institute of Technology; occupational therapy with Rush University.

Library Rebecca Crown Library with 280,475 titles, 4,422 serial subscriptions, 7,000 audiovisual materials, an OPAC, a Web page.

Computers on Campus 212 computers available on campus for general student use. A campuswide network can be accessed from student residence rooms and from off campus that provide access to email. Internet access, online (class) registration, at least one staffed computer lab available.

Student Life *Housing options:* coed, men-only, women-only. Campus housing is university owned. Freshman applicants given priority for college housing. *Activities and organizations:* drama/theater group, student-run newspaper, choral group, student government, Torch, Center Stage, Resident Student Association, international club. *Campus security:* 24-hour emergency response devices and patrols, student patrols, late-night transport/escort service, controlled dormitory access, door alarms. *Student services:* health clinic, personal/psychological counseling.

Athletics Member NCAA. All Division III. *Intercollegiate sports:* baseball M, basketball M/W, cheerleading M/W, cross-country running M/W, soccer M/W, softball W, tennis M/W, volleyball W. *Intramural sports:* basketball M/W, bowling M/W, football M/W, racquetball M/W, soccer M/W, softball W, tennis M/W, volleyball W.

Standardized Tests *Required:* SAT I or ACT (for admission).

Costs (2004–05) *One-time required fee:* $100. *Comprehensive fee:* $24,890 includes full-time tuition ($18,900), mandatory fees ($100), and room and board ($5890). Part-time tuition: $630 per semester hour. Part-time tuition and fees vary according to location and program. *Required fees:* $10 per course part-time. *Room and board:* Room and board charges vary according to board plan and housing facility. *Payment plans:* tuition prepayment, installment. *Waivers:* children of alumni and employees or children of employees.

Financial Aid Of all full-time matriculated undergraduates who enrolled in 2002, 781 applied for aid, 683 were judged to have need, 175 had their need fully

met. 152 Federal Work-Study jobs (averaging $1919). 150 state and other part-time jobs (averaging $1566). In 2002, 105 non-need-based awards were made. *Average percent of need met:* 81%. *Average financial aid package:* $11,710. *Average need-based loan:* $3303. *Average need-based gift aid:* $8709. *Average non-need-based aid:* $9635. *Average indebtedness upon graduation:* $15,138.

Applying *Options:* common application, deferred entrance. *Application fee:* $20. *Required:* essay or personal statement, high school transcript, minimum 2.75 GPA. *Required for some:* 2 letters of recommendation, interview. *Recommended:* letters of recommendation, interview. *Application deadline:* rolling (freshmen), rolling (transfers). *Notification:* continuous (freshmen), continuous (transfers).

Admissions Contact Mr. Glenn Hamilton, Director of Freshman Admission, Dominican University, 7900 West Division Street, River Forest, IL 60305. *Phone:* 708-524-6800. *Toll-free phone:* 800-828-8475. *Fax:* 708-366-5360. *E-mail:* domadmis@dom.edu.

■ *See page 1538 for a narrative description.*

EASTERN ILLINOIS UNIVERSITY

Charleston, Illinois

- **State-supported** comprehensive, founded 1895
- **Calendar** semesters
- **Degrees** bachelor's, master's, post-master's, and postbachelor's certificates
- **Small-town** 320-acre campus
- **Endowment** $23.7 million
- **Coed,** 9,845 undergraduate students, 90% full-time, 58% women, 42% men
- **Moderately difficult** entrance level, 78% of applicants were admitted

Undergraduates 8,890 full-time, 955 part-time. Students come from 38 states and territories, 36 other countries, 3% are from out of state, 7% African American, 0.8% Asian American or Pacific Islander, 2% Hispanic American, 0.2% Native American, 0.7% international, 11% transferred in.

Freshmen *Admission:* 8,103 applied, 6,313 admitted, 1,918 enrolled. *Test scores:* ACT scores over 18: 94%; ACT scores over 24: 28%; ACT scores over 30: 1%.

Faculty *Total:* 682, 87% full-time, 71% with terminal degrees. *Student/faculty ratio:* 16:1.

Majors Accounting; African-American/Black studies; art; biology/biological sciences; business administration and management; chemistry; clinical laboratory science/medical technology; communication disorders; computer and information sciences related; computer/information technology services administration related; dramatic/theatre arts; economics; elementary education; engineering related; English; family and consumer sciences/human sciences; finance; foreign languages and literatures; geography; geology/earth science; health teacher education; history; industrial technology; journalism; kindergarten/preschool education; liberal arts and sciences/liberal studies; management information systems; management science; marketing/marketing management; mathematics; mathematics and computer science; middle school education; multi-/interdisciplinary studies related; music; parks, recreation and leisure facilities management; philosophy; physical education teaching and coaching; physics; political science and government; psychology; social science teacher education; sociology; special education; speech and rhetoric; technical teacher education.

Academic Programs *Special study options:* academic remediation for entering students, adult/continuing education programs, advanced placement credit, double majors, English as a second language, external degree program, honors programs, independent study, internships, part-time degree program, services for LD students, study abroad, summer session for credit. *ROTC:* Army (b). *Unusual degree programs:* 3-2 engineering with University of Illinois.

Library Booth Library with 955,245 titles, 3,510 serial subscriptions, 33,460 audiovisual materials, an OPAC, a Web page.

Computers on Campus 1336 computers available on campus for general student use. A campuswide network can be accessed from student residence rooms and from off campus. Internet access, online (class) registration, at least one staffed computer lab available. Computer purchase or lease plan available.

Student Life *Housing:* on-campus residence required for freshman year. *Options:* coed, men-only, women-only. Campus housing is university owned. Freshman campus housing is guaranteed. *Activities and organizations:* drama/theater group, student-run newspaper, radio and television station, choral group, marching band, Greek organizations, Black Student Union, national fraternities, national sororities. *Campus security:* 24-hour emergency response devices and patrols, student patrols. *Student services:* health clinic, personal/psychological counseling, women's center, legal services.

Athletics Member NCAA. All Division I except football (Division I-AA). *Intercollegiate sports:* baseball M(s), basketball M(s)/W(s), cross-country running M(s)/W(s), golf M(s)/W(s), rugby W(s), soccer M(s)/W(s), softball W(s), swimming M(s)/W(s), tennis M(s)/W(s), track and field M(s)/W(s), volleyball W(s), wrestling M(s). *Intramural sports:* baseball M, basketball M/W, bowling M/W, cross-country running M/W, football M, lacrosse M(c), racquetball M/W, rugby M, soccer M/W, softball M/W, swimming M/W, table tennis M/W, tennis M/W, track and field M/W, volleyball M/W, weight lifting M/W, wrestling M.

Standardized Tests *Required:* SAT I or ACT (for admission).

Costs (2003–04) *Tuition:* $119 per credit hour part-time; state resident $3563 full-time, $119 per credit hour part-time; nonresident $10,688 full-time, $356 per credit hour part-time. Full-time tuition and fees vary according to course load. Part-time tuition and fees vary according to course load. *Required fees:* $1419 full-time, $51 per credit hour part-time. *Room and board:* $6210. Room and board charges vary according to board plan. *Payment plan:* installment. *Waivers:* employees or children of employees.

Financial Aid Of all full-time matriculated undergraduates who enrolled in 2003, 6,235 applied for aid, 4,618 were judged to have need, 3,322 had their need fully met. 639 Federal Work-Study jobs (averaging $1310). In 2003, 295 non-need-based awards were made. *Average percent of need met:* 19%. *Average financial aid package:* $8766. *Average need-based loan:* $3181. *Average need-based gift aid:* $2587. *Average non-need-based aid:* $5729. *Average indebtedness upon graduation:* $13,997.

Applying *Application fee:* $30. *Required:* high school transcript, audition for music program. *Required for some:* essay or personal statement, 3 letters of recommendation. *Application deadline:* rolling (freshmen), rolling (transfers). *Notification:* continuous (freshmen), continuous (transfers).

Admissions Contact Mr. Dale W. Wolf, Director of Admissions, Eastern Illinois University, 600 Lincoln Avenue, Charleston, IL 61920-3099. *Phone:* 217-581-2223. *Toll-free phone:* 800-252-5711. *Fax:* 217-581-7060. *E-mail:* admissns@eiu.edu.

EAST-WEST UNIVERSITY

Chicago, Illinois

- **Independent** 4-year, founded 1978
- **Calendar** quarters
- **Degrees** associate and bachelor's
- **Urban** campus
- **Endowment** $15.0 million
- **Coed**
- **Minimally difficult** entrance level

Faculty *Student/faculty ratio:* 20:1.

Standardized Tests *Recommended:* ACT (for placement).

Costs (2003–04) *Tuition:* $9900 full-time, $3300 per term part-time. Full-time tuition and fees vary according to course level. *Required fees:* $495 full-time, $465 per term part-time.

Financial Aid Of all full-time matriculated undergraduates who enrolled in 2001, 1,339 applied for aid, 1,339 were judged to have need. 37 Federal Work-Study jobs (averaging $2308). *Average percent of need met:* 90. *Average financial aid package:* $8720. *Average indebtedness upon graduation:* $2625.

Applying *Options:* common application, electronic application. *Application fee:* $30. *Required:* essay or personal statement, high school transcript, interview. *Required for some:* 1 letter of recommendation.

Admissions Contact Mr. William Link, Director of Admissions, East-West University, 819 South Wabash Avenue, Chicago, IL 60605-2103. *Phone:* 312-939-0111 Ext. 1830. *Fax:* 312-939-0083. *E-mail:* seeyou@eastwest.edu.

ELMHURST COLLEGE

Elmhurst, Illinois

- **Independent** comprehensive, founded 1871, affiliated with United Church of Christ
- **Calendar** 4-1-4
- **Degrees** bachelor's and master's
- **Suburban** 38-acre campus with easy access to Chicago
- **Endowment** $59.9 million
- **Coed,** 2,396 undergraduate students, 86% full-time, 66% women, 34% men
- **Moderately difficult** entrance level, 73% of applicants were admitted

Undergraduates 2,068 full-time, 328 part-time. Students come from 26 states and territories, 21 other countries, 8% are from out of state, 6% African American, 3% Asian American or Pacific Islander, 6% Hispanic American, 0.2% Native American, 1% international, 11% transferred in, 40% live on campus. *Retention:* 83% of 2002 full-time freshmen returned.

Freshmen *Admission:* 1,511 applied, 1,100 admitted, 366 enrolled. *Average high school GPA:* 3.36. *Test scores:* ACT scores over 18: 89%; ACT scores over 24: 46%; ACT scores over 30: 6%.

Elmhurst College (continued)

Faculty *Total:* 278, 40% full-time, 44% with terminal degrees. *Student/faculty ratio:* 13:1.

Majors Accounting; actuarial science; American studies; art; art teacher education; audiology and speech-language pathology; biology/biological sciences; biology teacher education; business administration and management; chemistry; chemistry teacher education; clinical laboratory science/medical technology; communication/speech communication and rhetoric; computer science; cytotechnology; dramatic/theatre arts; economics; education; elementary education; English; English/language arts teacher education; environmental studies; finance; French; French language teacher education; geography; German; German language teacher education; health and physical education; history; history teacher education; interdisciplinary studies; international business/trade/commerce; kindergarten/preschool education; kinesiology and exercise science; logistics and materials management; management information systems; marketing/marketing management; mathematics; mathematics teacher education; music; music management and merchandising; music teacher education; nursing (registered nurse training); nutrition sciences; occupational therapy; philosophy; physical education teaching and coaching; physical therapy; physician assistant; physics; physics teacher education; political science and government; pre-dentistry studies; pre-law studies; pre-medical studies; pre-pharmacy studies; pre-veterinary studies; psychology; secondary education; sociology; Spanish; Spanish language teacher education; special education; sport and fitness administration; theology; urban studies/affairs.

Academic Programs *Special study options:* academic remediation for entering students, accelerated degree program, adult/continuing education programs, advanced placement credit, cooperative education, double majors, honors programs, independent study, internships, off-campus study, part-time degree program, services for LD students, study abroad, summer session for credit. *ROTC:* Army (c), Air Force (c). *Unusual degree programs:* 3-2 engineering with Illinois Institute of Technology, Northwestern University, Washington University in St. Louis, University of Illinois at Chicago, University of Southern California.

Library Buehler Library with 222,441 titles, 2,010 serial subscriptions, 7,537 audiovisual materials, an OPAC, a Web page.

Computers on Campus 345 computers available on campus for general student use. A campuswide network can be accessed from student residence rooms and from off campus. Internet access, online (class) registration, at least one staffed computer lab available.

Student Life *Housing options:* coed. Campus housing is university owned and is provided by a third party. Freshman applicants given priority for college housing. *Activities and organizations:* drama/theater group, student-run newspaper, radio station, choral group, Programming Board and Student Government, theater and music groups, Black Student Union, residence life groups, Hablamos, national fraternities, national sororities. *Campus security:* 24-hour emergency response devices and patrols, late-night transport/escort service, controlled dormitory access. *Student services:* health clinic, personal/psychological counseling.

Athletics Member NCAA. All Division III. *Intercollegiate sports:* baseball M, basketball M/W, cross-country running M/W, football M, golf M/W, soccer W, softball W, tennis M/W, track and field M/W, volleyball W, wrestling M. *Intramural sports:* basketball M/W, football M, golf M/W, racquetball M/W, soccer M, softball M/W, volleyball M/W.

Standardized Tests *Required:* SAT I or ACT (for admission).

Costs (2003–04) *Comprehensive fee:* $24,630 includes full-time tuition ($18,600) and room and board ($6030). Part-time tuition: $529 per credit hour. *College room only:* $3460. Room and board charges vary according to board plan and housing facility. *Payment plan:* installment. *Waivers:* senior citizens and employees or children of employees.

Financial Aid Of all full-time matriculated undergraduates who enrolled in 2003, 1,600 applied for aid, 1,453 were judged to have need, 1,178 had their need fully met. 345 Federal Work-Study jobs (averaging $1250). 225 state and other part-time jobs (averaging $1285). In 2003, 303 non-need-based awards were made. *Average percent of need met:* 95%. *Average financial aid package:* $15,400. *Average need-based loan:* $4538. *Average need-based gift aid:* $11,297. *Average non-need-based aid:* $8871. *Average indebtedness upon graduation:* $15,225.

Applying *Options:* electronic application, deferred entrance. *Application fee:* $25. *Required:* high school transcript. *Required for some:* essay or personal statement, letters of recommendation, interview. *Recommended:* essay or personal statement, interview. *Application deadline:* 7/15 (freshmen). *Notification:* continuous (freshmen), continuous (transfers).

Admissions Contact Mr. Andrew B. Sison, Director of Admission, Elmhurst College, 190 Prospect Avenue, Elmhurst, IL 60126. *Phone:* 630-617-3400 Ext. 3068. *Toll-free phone:* 800-697-1871. *Fax:* 630-617-5501. *E-mail:* admit@elmhurst.edu.

■ *See page 1578 for a narrative description.*

EUREKA COLLEGE
Eureka, Illinois

- **Independent** 4-year, founded 1855, affiliated with Christian Church (Disciples of Christ)
- **Calendar** 4 8-week terms
- **Degree** bachelor's
- **Small-town** 112-acre campus
- **Endowment** $10.7 million
- **Coed,** 516 undergraduate students, 98% full-time, 56% women, 44% men
- **Moderately difficult** entrance level, 75% of applicants were admitted

Undergraduates 505 full-time, 11 part-time. Students come from 15 states and territories, 2 other countries, 9% African American, 0.8% Asian American or Pacific Islander, 1% Hispanic American, 1% international, 8% transferred in, 84% live on campus. *Retention:* 67% of 2002 full-time freshmen returned.

Freshmen *Admission:* 635 applied, 474 admitted, 138 enrolled. *Average high school GPA:* 3.10. *Test scores:* ACT scores over 18: 88%; ACT scores over 24: 48%; ACT scores over 30: 19%.

Faculty *Total:* 69, 61% full-time, 55% with terminal degrees. *Student/faculty ratio:* 13:1.

Majors Accounting; art; athletic training; biological and physical sciences; biology/biological sciences; business administration and management; chemistry; clinical laboratory science/medical technology; computer science; dramatic/theatre arts; economics; education; educational leadership and administration; elementary education; English; finance; history; kinesiology and exercise science; liberal arts and sciences/liberal studies; literature; management information systems; mass communication/media; mathematics; music; music teacher education; natural sciences; nursing (registered nurse training); philosophy; physical education teaching and coaching; physical sciences; political science and government; pre-dentistry studies; pre-law studies; pre-medical studies; pre-veterinary studies; psychology; religious studies; science teacher education; secondary education; social sciences; sociology; voice and opera.

Academic Programs *Special study options:* advanced placement credit, cooperative education, double majors, English as a second language, honors programs, independent study, internships, part-time degree program, student-designed majors, study abroad, summer session for credit. *Unusual degree programs:* 3-2 engineering with Washington University in St. Louis; nursing with Mennonite College of Nursing; occupational therapy with Washington University in St. Louis.

Library Melick Library with 75,000 titles, 330 serial subscriptions, 500 audiovisual materials, an OPAC.

Computers on Campus 95 computers available on campus for general student use. A campuswide network can be accessed from student residence rooms and from off campus. Internet access, at least one staffed computer lab available.

Student Life *Housing:* on-campus residence required through senior year. *Options:* coed. Campus housing is university owned. Freshman campus housing is guaranteed. *Activities and organizations:* drama/theater group, student-run newspaper, choral group, College Choral, theater, Campus Activities Board, intercollegiate athletics, national fraternities, national sororities. *Campus security:* 24-hour emergency response devices, late night patrols. *Student services:* health clinic, personal/psychological counseling.

Athletics Member NCAA. All Division III. *Intercollegiate sports:* baseball M, basketball M/W, football M, golf M/W, softball W, swimming M/W, tennis M/W, track and field M/W, volleyball W. *Intramural sports:* basketball M/W, football M, golf M/W, soccer M/W, softball W, swimming M/W, tennis M/W, track and field M/W, volleyball M/W.

Standardized Tests *Required:* SAT I or ACT (for admission).

Costs (2004–05) *Comprehensive fee:* $19,280 includes full-time tuition ($13,000), mandatory fees ($400), and room and board ($5880). Part-time tuition: $375 per semester hour. *College room only:* $2820. Room and board charges vary according to housing facility. *Payment plan:* installment. *Waivers:* children of alumni, senior citizens, and employees or children of employees.

Financial Aid Of all full-time matriculated undergraduates who enrolled in 2003, 481 applied for aid, 479 were judged to have need, 415 had their need fully met. 109 Federal Work-Study jobs (averaging $743). 67 state and other part-time jobs (averaging $1231). In 2003, 10 non-need-based awards were made. *Average percent of need met:* 86%. *Average financial aid package:* $12,677. *Average need-based loan:* $3621. *Average need-based gift aid:* $7954. *Average non-need-based aid:* $5610. *Average indebtedness upon graduation:* $12,968.

Applying *Options:* electronic application, deferred entrance. *Required:* high school transcript, minimum 2.0 GPA, 1 letter of recommendation. *Required for some:* essay or personal statement, 3 letters of recommendation. *Recommended:* interview. *Application deadlines:* 8/15 (freshmen), 8/15 (transfers). *Notification:* continuous (freshmen), continuous (transfers).

Admissions Contact Dr. Brian Sajko, Dean of Admissions and Financial Aid, Eureka College, 300 East College Avenue, Eureka, IL 61530-0128. *Phone:* 309-467-6350. *Toll-free phone:* 888-4-EUREKA. *Fax:* 309-467-6576. *E-mail:* admissions@eureka.edu.

■ *See page 1600 for a narrative description.*

GOVERNORS STATE UNIVERSITY
University Park, Illinois

- **State-supported** upper-level, founded 1969
- **Calendar** trimesters
- **Degrees** bachelor's and master's
- **Suburban** 750-acre campus with easy access to Chicago
- **Coed,** 2,618 undergraduate students, 33% full-time, 71% women, 29% men
- **Moderately difficult** entrance level

Undergraduates 856 full-time, 1,762 part-time. Students come from 8 states and territories, 22 other countries, 3% are from out of state, 32% African American, 2% Asian American or Pacific Islander, 6% Hispanic American, 0.3% Native American, 2% international.

Faculty *Total:* 204, 86% full-time, 71% with terminal degrees. *Student/faculty ratio:* 17:1.

Majors Accounting; art; art history, criticism and conservation; audiology and speech-language pathology; biology/biological sciences; business administration and management; chemistry; communication/speech communication and rhetoric; computer science; consumer merchandising/retailing management; criminal justice/law enforcement administration; drawing; early childhood education; elementary education; English; finance; fine/studio arts; health/health care administration; human resources management; kindergarten/preschool education; labor and industrial relations; liberal arts and sciences/liberal studies; management information systems; marketing/marketing management; mass communication/media; mental health/rehabilitation; middle school education; nursing (registered nurse training); photography; psychology; public administration; science teacher education; social sciences; social work; speech and rhetoric.

Academic Programs *Special study options:* academic remediation for entering students, adult/continuing education programs, advanced placement credit, distance learning, external degree program, honors programs, independent study, internships, off-campus study, part-time degree program, services for LD students, student-designed majors, study abroad, summer session for credit. *ROTC:* Army (c), Air Force (c).

Library University Library with 252,000 titles, 2,200 serial subscriptions, 2,700 audiovisual materials, an OPAC, a Web page.

Computers on Campus 165 computers available on campus for general student use. A campuswide network can be accessed from off campus. At least one staffed computer lab available.

Student Life *Housing:* college housing not available. *Activities and organizations:* student-run newspaper, choral group, Future Teachers of America, American College of Health Executives, Circle K, counseling club, African-American Student Association. *Campus security:* 24-hour emergency response devices and patrols, late-night transport/escort service. *Student services:* personal/psychological counseling.

Athletics *Intramural sports:* badminton M/W, basketball M/W, racquetball M/W, skiing (cross-country) M/W, softball M/W, table tennis M/W, volleyball M/W.

Costs (2003–04) *Tuition:* state resident $2832 full-time, $118 per credit part-time; nonresident $8496 full-time, $354 per credit part-time. Full-time tuition and fees vary according to location. Part-time tuition and fees vary according to course load and location. *Required fees:* $360 full-time, $225 per term part-time. *Payment plans:* installment, deferred payment. *Waivers:* senior citizens and employees or children of employees.

Applying *Options:* electronic application, deferred entrance. *Application deadlines:* rolling (freshmen), 7/15 (transfers).

Admissions Contact Mr. Larry Polselli, Executive Director of Enrollment Services, Governors State University, One University Parkway, University Park, IL 60466. *Phone:* 708-534-3148. *Fax:* 708-534-1640. *E-mail:* gsunow@govst.edu.

GREENVILLE COLLEGE
Greenville, Illinois

- **Independent Free Methodist** comprehensive, founded 1892
- **Calendar** 4-1-4
- **Degrees** bachelor's and master's
- **Small-town** 12-acre campus with easy access to St. Louis
- **Endowment** $7.7 million
- **Coed,** 1,188 undergraduate students, 95% full-time, 52% women, 48% men
- **Moderately difficult** entrance level, 95% of applicants were admitted

Undergraduates 1,128 full-time, 60 part-time. Students come from 40 states and territories, 14 other countries, 30% are from out of state, 8% African American, 1% Asian American or Pacific Islander, 2% Hispanic American, 1% Native American, 1% international, 14% transferred in, 62% live on campus. *Retention:* 72% of 2002 full-time freshmen returned.

Freshmen *Admission:* 697 applied, 665 admitted, 263 enrolled. *Average high school GPA:* 3.19. *Test scores:* SAT verbal scores over 500: 70%; SAT math scores over 500: 67%; ACT scores over 18: 85%; SAT verbal scores over 600: 27%; SAT math scores over 600: 22%; ACT scores over 24: 42%; SAT verbal scores over 700: 3%; ACT scores over 30: 7%.

Faculty *Total:* 133, 45% full-time, 42% with terminal degrees. *Student/faculty ratio:* 14:1.

Majors Accounting; art; art teacher education; audiovisual communications technologies related; biology/biological sciences; biology teacher education; business administration and management; chemistry; chemistry teacher education; communication and media related; computer and information sciences and support services related; computer science; criminal justice/law enforcement administration; dramatic/theatre arts; early childhood education; elementary education; English; English/language arts teacher education; environmental biology; foreign languages and literatures; French; kinesiology and exercise science; liberal arts and sciences/liberal studies; management information systems; management information systems and services related; marketing/marketing management; mass communication/media; mathematics; mathematics teacher education; modern languages; multi-/interdisciplinary studies related; music; music related; music teacher education; organizational behavior; parks, recreation and leisure; pastoral counseling and specialized ministries related; pastoral studies/counseling; philosophy; philosophy and religious studies related; physical education teaching and coaching; physics; physics teacher education; psychology; public relations/image management; religious/sacred music; religious studies; social sciences related; social studies teacher education; social work; sociology; Spanish; Spanish language teacher education; special education; speech and rhetoric; sport and fitness administration; web/multimedia management and webmaster; youth ministry.

Academic Programs *Special study options:* academic remediation for entering students, accelerated degree program, adult/continuing education programs, advanced placement credit, cooperative education, double majors, honors programs, independent study, internships, off-campus study, part-time degree program, student-designed majors, study abroad, summer session for credit. *Unusual degree programs:* 3-2 engineering with University of Illinois at Urbana–Champaign; Washington University in St. Louis.

Library Ruby E. Dare Library with 126,210 titles, 490 serial subscriptions, 4,377 audiovisual materials, an OPAC, a Web page.

Computers on Campus 65 computers available on campus for general student use. A campuswide network can be accessed from student residence rooms and from off campus that provide access to intranet. Internet access, at least one staffed computer lab available.

Student Life *Housing:* on-campus residence required through senior year. *Options:* men-only, women-only. Campus housing is university owned and leased by the school. Freshman campus housing is guaranteed. *Activities and organizations:* drama/theater group, student-run newspaper, radio station, choral group, Campus Activity Board, Intramurals, Greenville Student Outreach, Habitat for Humanity, Student Senate. *Campus security:* 24-hour emergency response devices, student patrols, late-night transport/escort service, controlled dormitory access. *Student services:* personal/psychological counseling.

Athletics Member NCAA, NCCAA. All NCAA Division III. *Intercollegiate sports:* baseball M, basketball M/W, cross-country running M/W, football M, soccer M/W, softball W, tennis M/W, track and field M/W, volleyball W. *Intramural sports:* badminton M/W, basketball M/W, cheerleading W, football M/W, soccer M/W, softball M/W, table tennis M/W, tennis M/W, track and field M/W, volleyball W.

Standardized Tests *Required:* SAT I or ACT (for admission).

Costs (2003–04) *Comprehensive fee:* $21,342 includes full-time tuition ($15,666), mandatory fees ($110), and room and board ($5566). Part-time tuition: $330 per credit hour. Part-time tuition and fees vary according to course load. *College room only:* $2634. Room and board charges vary according to housing facility. *Waivers:* senior citizens and employees or children of employees.

Financial Aid Of all full-time matriculated undergraduates who enrolled in 2002, 863 applied for aid, 787 were judged to have need, 141 had their need fully met. 248 Federal Work-Study jobs (averaging $796). 45 state and other part-time jobs (averaging $1250). In 2002, 147 non-need-based awards were made. *Average percent of need met:* 80%. *Average financial aid package:* $12,660. *Average need-based loan:* $4069. *Average need-based gift aid:* $8924. *Average non-need-based aid:* $6947. *Average indebtedness upon graduation:* $17,560.

Greenville College (continued)

Applying *Options:* electronic application, early admission, deferred entrance. *Application fee:* $25. *Required:* essay or personal statement, high school transcript, minimum 2.5 GPA, 2 letters of recommendation, agreement to code of conduct. *Required for some:* interview. *Application deadlines:* 8/1 (freshmen), 8/1 (transfers). *Notification:* continuous (freshmen), continuous (transfers).

Admissions Contact Dr. R. Pepper Dill, Vice President for Enrollment Management, Greenville College, 315 East College Avenue, Greenville, IL 62246. *Phone:* 618-664-7100. *Toll-free phone:* 800-345-4440. *Fax:* 618-664-9841. *E-mail:* admissions@greenville.edu.

HARRINGTON COLLEGE OF DESIGN
Chicago, Illinois

- **Proprietary** 4-year, founded 1931, part of Career Education Corporation
- **Calendar** semesters
- **Degrees** certificates, diplomas, associate, and bachelor's
- **Urban** campus
- **Coed, primarily women,** 1,364 undergraduate students, 47% full-time, 90% women, 10% men
- **Noncompetitive** entrance level, 73% of applicants were admitted

Undergraduates 646 full-time, 718 part-time. Students come from 14 states and territories, 9% are from out of state, 10% African American, 4% Asian American or Pacific Islander, 8% Hispanic American, 0.3% Native American, 18% transferred in, 6% live on campus. *Retention:* 43% of 2002 full-time freshmen returned.

Freshmen *Admission:* 411 applied, 302 admitted, 203 enrolled.

Faculty *Total:* 123, 8% full-time, 36% with terminal degrees. *Student/faculty ratio:* 11:1.

Majors Commercial photography; interior design.

Academic Programs *Special study options:* adult/continuing education programs, internships, off-campus study, part-time degree program, study abroad.

Library Harrington Institute Design Library with 22,000 titles, 90 serial subscriptions, 26,000 audiovisual materials, an OPAC.

Computers on Campus 25 computers available on campus for general student use. Internet access, at least one staffed computer lab available.

Student Life *Housing options:* coed. Campus housing is provided by a third party. Freshman applicants given priority for college housing. *Activities and organizations:* American Society of Interior Designers, International Interior Design Association, Green Design Club, Student Government. *Campus security:* 24-hour patrols.

Costs (2004–05) *Tuition:* $12,600 full-time, $500 per credit part-time. Full-time tuition and fees vary according to course load. Part-time tuition and fees vary according to course load. *Required fees:* $200 full-time. *Room only:* $4800. Room and board charges vary according to housing facility. *Payment plan:* installment. *Waivers:* employees or children of employees.

Financial Aid *Average percent of need met:* 30%. *Average financial aid package:* $3500.

Applying *Options:* deferred entrance. *Application fee:* $60. *Required:* high school transcript, interview. *Recommended:* essay or personal statement, 1 letter of recommendation. *Application deadline:* rolling (freshmen). *Notification:* continuous (freshmen), continuous (transfers).

Admissions Contact Melissa Laurentius, Director of Admissions, Harrington College of Design, 200 West Madison, Chicago, IL 60606. *Phone:* 877-939-4975 Ext. 1167. *Toll-free phone:* 877-939-4975. *Fax:* 312-939-8032. *E-mail:* barrington@interiordesign.edu.

■ *See page 1714 for a narrative description.*

HEBREW THEOLOGICAL COLLEGE
Skokie, Illinois

Admissions Contact Rabbi Berish Cardash, Hebrew Theological College, 7135 North Carpenter Road, Skokie, IL 60077-3263. *Phone:* 847-982-2500.

ILLINOIS COLLEGE
Jacksonville, Illinois

- **Independent interdenominational** 4-year, founded 1829
- **Calendar** semesters
- **Degree** bachelor's
- **Small-town** 62-acre campus with easy access to St. Louis
- **Endowment** $112.0 million
- **Coed,** 1,016 undergraduate students, 98% full-time, 56% women, 44% men
- **Moderately difficult** entrance level, 72% of applicants were admitted

Undergraduates 999 full-time, 17 part-time. Students come from 15 states and territories, 7 other countries, 3% are from out of state, 2% African American, 0.4% Asian American or Pacific Islander, 2% Hispanic American, 0.2% Native American, 0.9% international, 4% transferred in, 75% live on campus. *Retention:* 75% of 2002 full-time freshmen returned.

Freshmen *Admission:* 1,005 applied, 723 admitted, 318 enrolled. *Average high school GPA:* 3.31. *Test scores:* SAT verbal scores over 500: 86%; SAT math scores over 500: 90%; ACT scores over 18: 99%; SAT verbal scores over 600: 48%; SAT math scores over 600: 52%; ACT scores over 24: 49%; SAT verbal scores over 700: 10%; SAT math scores over 700: 14%; ACT scores over 30: 5%.

Faculty *Total:* 93, 66% full-time, 62% with terminal degrees. *Student/faculty ratio:* 14:1.

Majors Accounting; art; biology/biological sciences; business administration and management; business/managerial economics; chemistry; clinical laboratory science/medical technology; computer science; cytotechnology; dramatic/theatre arts; early childhood education; economics; education; education (K-12); elementary education; English; environmental studies; finance; French; German; history; information science/studies; interdisciplinary studies; international relations and affairs; liberal arts and sciences/liberal studies; management information systems; mass communication/media; mathematics; music; occupational therapy; philosophy; physical education teaching and coaching; physics; political science and government; pre-dentistry studies; pre-law studies; pre-medical studies; pre-veterinary studies; psychology; religious studies; secondary education; sociology; Spanish; speech and rhetoric.

Academic Programs *Special study options:* accelerated degree program, advanced placement credit, double majors, independent study, internships, study abroad, summer session for credit. *Unusual degree programs:* 3-2 engineering with University of Illinois at Urbana-Champaign, Washington University in St. Louis; nursing with Mennonite College of Nursing; occupational therapy with Washington University in St. Louis.

Library Schewe Library plus 1 other with 143,500 titles, 620 serial subscriptions, an OPAC, a Web page.

Computers on Campus 97 computers available on campus for general student use. A campuswide network can be accessed from student residence rooms and from off campus. Internet access, at least one staffed computer lab available.

Student Life *Housing:* on-campus residence required through sophomore year. *Options:* coed, men-only, women-only. Campus housing is university owned. Freshman campus housing is guaranteed. *Activities and organizations:* drama/theater group, student-run newspaper, television station, choral group, Student Activity Board, Forum, Homecoming Committee, literary societies, B.A.S.I.C. (Brothers and Sisters in Christ). *Campus security:* 24-hour emergency response devices and patrols, late-night transport/escort service, controlled dormitory access. *Student services:* health clinic, personal/psychological counseling.

Athletics Member NCAA. All Division III. *Intercollegiate sports:* baseball M, cheerleading W, cross-country running M/W, football M, golf M/W, soccer M/W, softball W, tennis M/W, track and field M/W, volleyball W, wrestling M. *Intramural sports:* badminton M/W, basketball M/W, fencing M/W, football M, racquetball M/W, softball M/W, swimming M/W, volleyball M/W, weight lifting M/W.

Standardized Tests *Required:* SAT I or ACT (for admission).

Costs (2003–04) *Comprehensive fee:* $19,100 includes full-time tuition ($13,300) and room and board ($5800). Part-time tuition: $555 per credit hour. *Payment plans:* installment, deferred payment. *Waivers:* employees or children of employees.

Financial Aid Of all full-time matriculated undergraduates who enrolled in 2003, 906 applied for aid, 778 were judged to have need, 242 had their need fully met. 499 Federal Work-Study jobs (averaging $1165). 443 state and other part-time jobs (averaging $1077). In 2003, 153 non-need-based awards were made. *Average percent of need met:* 69%. *Average financial aid package:* $13,273. *Average need-based loan:* $4044. *Average need-based gift aid:* $6106. *Average non-need-based aid:* $5074. *Average indebtedness upon graduation:* $16,320.

Applying *Options:* common application, electronic application. *Application fee:* $25. *Required:* high school transcript, 1 letter of recommendation. *Required for some:* essay or personal statement. *Recommended:* essay or personal statement, minimum 2.5 GPA, interview. *Application deadlines:* 7/1 (freshmen), 7/1 (transfers). *Notification:* continuous until 8/15 (freshmen), continuous until 8/15 (transfers).

Admissions Contact Mr. Rick Bystry, Associate Director of Admission, Illinois College, 1101 West College, Jacksonville, IL 62650. *Phone:* 217-245-3030. *Toll-free phone:* 866-464-5265. *Fax:* 217-245-3034. *E-mail:* admissions@ic.edu.

THE ILLINOIS INSTITUTE OF ART
Chicago, Illinois

- **Proprietary** 4-year, founded 1916, part of The Art Institutes
- **Calendar** quarters
- **Degrees** associate and bachelor's
- **Urban** 2-acre campus
- **Coed,** 1,950 undergraduate students
- **Minimally difficult** entrance level, 93% of applicants were admitted

Undergraduates Students come from 42 states and territories, 26 other countries, 30% are from out of state. *Retention:* 70% of 2002 full-time freshmen returned.
Freshmen *Admission:* 535 applied, 495 admitted. *Average high school GPA:* 2.50.
Faculty *Total:* 110. *Student/faculty ratio:* 20:1.
Majors Commercial and advertising art; computer graphics; fashion/apparel design; fashion merchandising; interior design.
Academic Programs *Special study options:* academic remediation for entering students, accelerated degree program, adult/continuing education programs, advanced placement credit, cooperative education, independent study, internships, off-campus study, part-time degree program, services for LD students, summer session for credit.
Library The Illinois Institute of Art Library plus 1 other with 11,324 titles, 264 serial subscriptions, 502 audiovisual materials, an OPAC, a Web page.
Computers on Campus 150 computers available on campus for general student use. Internet access, at least one staffed computer lab available.
Student Life *Housing options:* Campus housing is provided by a third party. *Activities and organizations:* student-run newspaper, Student Activities Committee, American Society of Interior Designers Club, commercial art club, Student Ambassador Program, Fashion Focus. *Campus security:* 24-hour emergency response devices and patrols. *Student services:* personal/psychological counseling.
Standardized Tests *Recommended:* SAT I or ACT (for placement).
Costs (2004–05) *Tuition:* $16,848 full-time, $351 per credit part-time. *Required fees:* $100 full-time.
Applying *Options:* common application, electronic application, early admission, deferred entrance. *Application fee:* $50. *Required:* essay or personal statement, high school transcript, interview. *Required for some:* letters of recommendation, portfolio. *Recommended:* minimum 2.0 GPA. *Application deadline:* rolling (freshmen), rolling (transfers).
Admissions Contact Ms. Janis Anton, Vice President/Director of Admissions, The Illinois Institute of Art, 350 North Orleans Street, Chicago, IL 60654-1510. *Phone:* 312-280-3500 Ext. 132. *Toll-free phone:* 800-351-3450. *Fax:* 312-280-8562. *E-mail:* janton@aii.edu.

■ *See page 1758 for a narrative description.*

THE ILLINOIS INSTITUTE OF ART-SCHAUMBURG
Schaumburg, Illinois

- **Proprietary** 4-year, part of The Arts Institutes International
- **Calendar** quarters
- **Degree** certificates and bachelor's
- **Suburban** campus
- **Coed,** 1,107 undergraduate students, 73% full-time, 45% women, 55% men
- **Minimally difficult** entrance level, 75% of applicants were admitted

Undergraduates 808 full-time, 299 part-time. Students come from 10 states and territories, 8 other countries, 10% are from out of state, 2% African American, 7% Asian American or Pacific Islander, 10% Hispanic American, 0.5% Native American, 1% international, 7% transferred in. *Retention:* 8% of 2002 full-time freshmen returned.
Freshmen *Admission:* 750 applied, 565 admitted, 270 enrolled. *Average high school GPA:* 2.70. *Test scores:* ACT scores over 18: 78%; ACT scores over 24: 20%.
Faculty *Total:* 55, 49% full-time, 18% with terminal degrees. *Student/faculty ratio:* 16:1.
Majors Advertising; animation, interactive technology, video graphics and special effects; design and visual communications; digital communication and media/multimedia; interior design; web page, digital/multimedia and information resources design.
Academic Programs *Special study options:* accelerated degree program, advanced placement credit, double majors, independent study, internships, off-campus study, services for LD students, student-designed majors, summer session for credit.
Library Resource Center.
Computers on Campus 260 computers available on campus for general student use. Internet access, at least one staffed computer lab available.
Student Life *Housing options:* Campus housing is leased by the school. *Activities and organizations:* student-run newspaper, animation club, ASID, newspaper, music club, A.I.G.A. (graphic design). *Campus security:* 24-hour emergency response devices and patrols, student patrols. *Student services:* personal/psychological counseling.
Standardized Tests *Recommended:* SAT I and SAT II or ACT (for admission).
Costs (2004–05) *Tuition:* $16,200 full-time, $360 per credit hour part-time. No tuition increase for student's term of enrollment. *Payment plan:* installment.
Financial Aid *Average percent of need met:* 61%. *Average financial aid package:* $10,122. *Average indebtedness upon graduation:* $21,550.
Applying *Options:* common application, electronic application. *Application fee:* $50. *Required:* essay or personal statement, high school transcript, minimum 2.0 GPA. *Required for some:* letters of recommendation, interview. *Application deadline:* rolling (freshmen), rolling (transfers).
Admissions Contact Mr. Sam Hinojosa, Director of Admissions, The Illinois Institute of Art-Schaumburg, 1000 Plaza Drive, Schaumburg, IL 60173. *Phone:* 847-619-3450 Ext. 4506. *Toll-free phone:* 800-314-3450. *Fax:* 847-619-3064.

ILLINOIS INSTITUTE OF TECHNOLOGY
Chicago, Illinois

- **Independent** university, founded 1890
- **Calendar** semesters
- **Degrees** certificates, bachelor's, master's, doctoral, first professional, and postbachelor's certificates
- **Urban** 120-acre campus
- **Endowment** $179.0 million
- **Coed,** 1,941 undergraduate students, 86% full-time, 25% women, 75% men
- **Very difficult** entrance level, 59% of applicants were admitted

IIT is a private, PhD-granting university located in Chicago providing small class sizes, hands-on projects, undergraduate research, co-op and internship opportunities, and a distinguished faculty. Areas of study include architecture, engineering, sciences, psychology, business administration, premed, prelaw, and prepharmacy. IIT offers substantial need-based and merit scholarships.

Undergraduates 1,670 full-time, 271 part-time. Students come from 50 states and territories, 58 other countries, 37% are from out of state, 5% African American, 15% Asian American or Pacific Islander, 7% Hispanic American, 0.4% Native American, 17% international, 6% transferred in, 58% live on campus. *Retention:* 81% of 2002 full-time freshmen returned.
Freshmen *Admission:* 2,538 applied, 1,502 admitted, 398 enrolled. *Average high school GPA:* 3.6. *Test scores:* SAT verbal scores over 500: 92%; SAT math scores over 500: 99%; ACT scores over 18: 100%; SAT verbal scores over 600: 63%; SAT math scores over 600: 84%; ACT scores over 24: 94%; SAT verbal scores over 700: 18%; SAT math scores over 700: 41%; ACT scores over 30: 35%.
Faculty *Total:* 524, 58% full-time. *Student/faculty ratio:* 12:1.
Majors Aerospace, aeronautical and astronautical engineering; applied mathematics; architectural engineering; architecture; biochemistry/biophysics and molecular biology; biology/biological sciences; biomedical/medical engineering; biophysics; business/commerce; chemical engineering; chemistry; civil engineering; communication and journalism related; computer engineering; computer science; design and visual communications; electrical, electronics and communications engineering; engineering/industrial management; environmental/environmental health engineering; industrial technology; information science/studies; information technology; manufacturing technology; materials engineering; mechanical engineering; metallurgical engineering; multi-/interdisciplinary studies related; physics; political science and government; psychology; technical and business writing.
Academic Programs *Special study options:* accelerated degree program, advanced placement credit, cooperative education, distance learning, double majors, independent study, internships, part-time degree program, services for LD students, study abroad, summer session for credit. *ROTC:* Army (b), Navy (b), Air Force (b).
Library Paul V. Galvin Library plus 5 others with 854,771 titles, 773 serial subscriptions, 52,368 audiovisual materials, an OPAC, a Web page.
Computers on Campus 650 computers available on campus for general student use. A campuswide network can be accessed from student residence rooms and from off campus. Internet access, online (class) registration, at least one staffed computer lab available. Computer purchase or lease plan available.
Student Life *Housing:* on-campus residence required for freshman year. *Options:* coed, men-only, women-only. Campus housing is university owned and is provided by a third party. Freshman campus housing is guaranteed. *Activities*

Illinois Institute of Technology (continued)

and organizations: drama/theater group, student-run newspaper, radio station, choral group, Union Board, Student Government Association, Residence Hall Association, Techmate Commuters, International Student Organization, national fraternities, national sororities. *Campus security:* 24-hour emergency response devices and patrols, late-night transport/escort service, controlled dormitory access. *Student services:* health clinic, personal/psychological counseling, women's center.

Athletics Member NAIA. *Intercollegiate sports:* baseball M(s), basketball M(s)/W(s), cross-country running M(s)/W(s), soccer M(s)/W(s), swimming M(s)/W(s), volleyball W(s). *Intramural sports:* basketball M/W, football M, racquetball M/W, rock climbing M/W, soccer M/W, softball M/W, swimming M/W, tennis M/W, ultimate Frisbee M/W, volleyball M/W.

Standardized Tests *Required:* SAT I or ACT (for admission). *Recommended:* SAT II: Subject Tests (for admission).

Costs (2004–05) *Comprehensive fee:* $28,288 includes full-time tuition ($20,764), mandatory fees ($578), and room and board ($6946). Part-time tuition: $647 per credit hour. *Room and board:* Room and board charges vary according to board plan. *Payment plan:* installment. *Waivers:* employees or children of employees.

Financial Aid Of all full-time matriculated undergraduates who enrolled in 2002, 952 applied for aid, 880 were judged to have need, 276 had their need fully met. 233 Federal Work-Study jobs (averaging $1686). In 2002, 620 non-need-based awards were made. *Average percent of need met:* 88%. *Average financial aid package:* $19,588. *Average need-based loan:* $5250. *Average need-based gift aid:* $13,613. *Average non-need-based aid:* $10,106. *Average indebtedness upon graduation:* $17,264.

Applying *Options:* common application, electronic application, deferred entrance. *Application fee:* $30. *Required:* essay or personal statement, high school transcript, minimum 3.0 GPA, 1 letter of recommendation, SAT score over 1150; ACT score over 24. *Required for some:* interview. *Application deadline:* rolling (freshmen), rolling (transfers). *Notification:* continuous (freshmen), continuous (transfers).

Admissions Contact Mr. Brent Benner, Director of Undergraduate Admission, Illinois Institute of Technology, 10 West 33rd Street PH101, Chicago, IL 60616-3793. *Phone:* 312-567-3025. *Toll-free phone:* 800-448-2329. *Fax:* 312-567-6939. *E-mail:* admission@iit.edu.

■ *See page 1760 for a narrative description.*

ILLINOIS STATE UNIVERSITY

Normal, Illinois

- **State-supported** university, founded 1857
- **Calendar** semesters
- **Degrees** bachelor's, master's, doctoral, post-master's, and postbachelor's certificates
- **Urban** 850-acre campus
- **Endowment** $32.7 million
- **Coed,** 18,097 undergraduate students, 93% full-time, 58% women, 42% men
- **Moderately difficult** entrance level, 75% of applicants were admitted

Undergraduates 16,811 full-time, 1,286 part-time. Students come from 48 states and territories, 55 other countries, 2% are from out of state, 6% African American, 2% Asian American or Pacific Islander, 3% Hispanic American, 0.3% Native American, 0.8% international, 10% transferred in, 40% live on campus. *Retention:* 83% of 2002 full-time freshmen returned.

Freshmen *Admission:* 10,075 applied, 7,570 admitted, 3,097 enrolled. *Test scores:* ACT scores over 18: 97%; ACT scores over 24: 48%; ACT scores over 30: 4%.

Faculty *Total:* 1,084, 78% full-time, 72% with terminal degrees. *Student/faculty ratio:* 19:1.

Majors Accounting; accounting and business/management; agribusiness; agriculture; anthropology; art; athletic training; audiology and speech-language pathology; biochemistry; biology/biological sciences; business administration and management; business teacher education; chemistry; clinical laboratory science/medical technology; computer science; computer systems networking and telecommunications; criminal justice/safety; dramatic/theatre arts; economics; elementary education; English; environmental health; family and consumer sciences/human sciences; finance; fine/studio arts; French; geography; geology/earth science; German; health information/medical records administration; health teacher education; history; industrial technology; information technology; insurance; international business/trade/commerce; kindergarten/preschool education; liberal arts and sciences/liberal studies; marketing/marketing management; mass communication/media; mathematics; middle school education; music; music performance; music teacher education; nursing (registered nurse training); occupational health and industrial hygiene; parks, recreation and leisure facilities management; philosophy; physical education teaching and coaching; physics; political science and government; psychology; public relations/image management; social studies teacher education; social work; sociology; Spanish; special education; speech and rhetoric; technology/industrial arts teacher education; visual and performing arts related.

Academic Programs *Special study options:* academic remediation for entering students, accelerated degree program, adult/continuing education programs, advanced placement credit, cooperative education, distance learning, double majors, English as a second language, honors programs, independent study, internships, off-campus study, part-time degree program, services for LD students, student-designed majors, study abroad, summer session for credit. *ROTC:* Army (b). *Unusual degree programs:* 3-2 engineering with University of Illinois.

Library Milner Library with 1.5 million titles, 4,873 serial subscriptions, an OPAC, a Web page.

Computers on Campus 2100 computers available on campus for general student use. A campuswide network can be accessed from student residence rooms and from off campus. Internet access, at least one staffed computer lab available.

Student Life *Housing:* on-campus residence required through sophomore year. *Options:* coed, women-only, disabled students. Campus housing is university owned. Freshman campus housing is guaranteed. *Activities and organizations:* drama/theater group, student-run newspaper, radio and television station, choral group, marching band, national fraternities, national sororities. *Campus security:* 24-hour emergency response devices and patrols, late-night transport/escort service, controlled dormitory access. *Student services:* health clinic, personal/psychological counseling, women's center, legal services.

Athletics Member NCAA. All Division I except football (Division I-AA). *Intercollegiate sports:* baseball M(s), basketball M(s)/W(s), cross-country running M(s)/W(s), golf M(s)/W(s), gymnastics W(s), soccer W(s), softball W(s), swimming W(s), tennis M(s)/W(s), track and field M(s)/W(s), volleyball W(s). *Intramural sports:* badminton M/W, baseball M, basketball M/W, bowling M(c)/W(c), field hockey M/W, football M, golf M/W, gymnastics M(c), ice hockey M(c), lacrosse M(c), racquetball M/W, rugby M(c)/W(c), soccer M/W, softball M/W, tennis M/W, ultimate Frisbee M/W, volleyball M(c)/W.

Standardized Tests *Required:* SAT I or ACT (for admission). *Recommended:* ACT (for admission).

Costs (2003–04) *Tuition:* state resident $4123 full-time, $137 per credit hour part-time; nonresident $8593 full-time, $286 per credit hour part-time. Full-time tuition and fees vary according to course load. Part-time tuition and fees vary according to course load. No tuition increase for student's term of enrollment. *Required fees:* $1407 full-time, $41 per credit hour part-time, $609 per term part-time. *Room and board:* $5414; room only: $2682. Room and board charges vary according to board plan. *Payment plan:* installment. *Waivers:* minority students, senior citizens, and employees or children of employees.

Financial Aid Of all full-time matriculated undergraduates who enrolled in 2003, 11,868 applied for aid, 7,782 were judged to have need, 4,122 had their need fully met. 848 Federal Work-Study jobs (averaging $1921). 16 state and other part-time jobs (averaging $3414). In 2003, 413 non-need-based awards were made. *Average percent of need met:* 82%. *Average financial aid package:* $7801. *Average need-based loan:* $4176. *Average need-based gift aid:* $5853. *Average non-need-based aid:* $3465. *Average indebtedness upon graduation:* $13,780.

Applying *Options:* electronic application. *Application fee:* $30. *Required:* essay or personal statement, high school transcript. *Application deadline:* 3/1 (freshmen), rolling (transfers). *Notification:* continuous (freshmen), continuous (transfers).

Admissions Contact Molly Arnold, Acting Director of Admissions, Illinois State University, Campus Box 2200, Normal, IL 61790-2200. *Phone:* 309-438-2181. *Toll-free phone:* 800-366-2478. *Fax:* 309-438-3932. *E-mail:* ugradadm@ilstu.edu.

ILLINOIS WESLEYAN UNIVERSITY

Bloomington, Illinois

- **Independent** 4-year, founded 1850
- **Calendar** 4-4-1
- **Degree** bachelor's
- **Suburban** 79-acre campus
- **Endowment** $141.7 million
- **Coed,** 2,106 undergraduate students, 100% full-time, 57% women, 43% men
- **Very difficult** entrance level, 43% of applicants were admitted

Undergraduates 2,098 full-time, 8 part-time. Students come from 36 states and territories, 20 other countries, 13% are from out of state, 3% African American, 2% Asian American or Pacific Islander, 2% Hispanic American, 0.1% Native American, 2% international, 0.2% transferred in, 83% live on campus. *Retention:* 93% of 2002 full-time freshmen returned.

Freshmen *Admission:* 3,331 applied, 1,431 admitted, 578 enrolled. *Test scores:* SAT verbal scores over 500: 98%; SAT math scores over 500: 99%; ACT scores over 18: 100%; SAT verbal scores over 600: 68%; SAT math scores over 600: 76%; ACT scores over 24: 95%; SAT verbal scores over 700: 23%; SAT math scores over 700: 23%; ACT scores over 30: 37%.

Faculty *Total:* 208, 76% full-time, 82% with terminal degrees. *Student/faculty ratio:* 12:1.

Majors Accounting; American studies; anthropology; area studies related; art; arts management; Asian studies; biology/biological sciences; biology teacher education; business administration and management; chemistry; chemistry teacher education; classics and languages, literatures and linguistics; computer science; dramatic/theatre arts; economics; education; elementary education; English; English/language arts teacher education; environmental studies; European studies (Western); French; French language teacher education; German; history; history teacher education; insurance; interdisciplinary studies; international business/trade/commerce; international/global studies; Latin American studies; mathematics; mathematics teacher education; music; music teacher education; nursing (registered nurse training); philosophy; physics; physics teacher education; piano and organ; political science and government; psychology; religious studies; science teacher education; secondary education; sociology; Spanish; Spanish language teacher education; violin, viola, guitar and other stringed instruments; visual and performing arts related; voice and opera; wind/percussion instruments; women's studies.

Academic Programs *Special study options:* advanced placement credit, cooperative education, double majors, honors programs, independent study, internships, off-campus study, student-designed majors, study abroad, summer session for credit. *ROTC:* Army (c). *Unusual degree programs:* 3-2 engineering with Case Western Reserve University, Northwestern University, Washington University in St. Louis, Dartmouth College; forestry with Duke University; occupational therapy.

Library Sheean Library with 307,861 titles, 14,264 serial subscriptions, 13,833 audiovisual materials, an OPAC, a Web page.

Computers on Campus 490 computers available on campus for general student use. A campuswide network can be accessed from student residence rooms and from off campus. Internet access, online (class) registration, at least one staffed computer lab available.

Student Life *Housing:* on-campus residence required through sophomore year. *Options:* coed. Campus housing is university owned. Freshman campus housing is guaranteed. *Activities and organizations:* drama/theater group, student-run newspaper, radio and television station, choral group, Alpha Phi Omega, Christian Fellowship, Students for a Just Society, Black Student Union, Habitat for Humanity, national fraternities, national sororities. *Campus security:* 24-hour emergency response devices and patrols, late-night transport/escort service, Emergency Response Team. *Student services:* health clinic, personal/psychological counseling.

Athletics Member NCAA. All Division III. *Intercollegiate sports:* baseball M, basketball M/W, cheerleading M(c)/W(c), cross-country running M/W, football M, golf M/W, lacrosse M(c), soccer M/W, softball W, swimming M/W, tennis M/W, track and field M/W, volleyball M(c)/W, water polo M(c). *Intramural sports:* badminton M/W, basketball M/W, golf M/W, racquetball M/W, soccer M/W, softball M/W, swimming M/W, table tennis M/W, tennis M/W, ultimate Frisbee M(c)/W(c), volleyball W.

Standardized Tests *Required:* SAT I or ACT (for admission).

Costs (2004–05) *Comprehensive fee:* $32,270 includes full-time tuition ($25,980), mandatory fees ($150), and room and board ($6140). Part-time tuition: $3250 per course. *College room only:* $3680. Room and board charges vary according to board plan and housing facility. *Payment plan:* installment. *Waivers:* employees or children of employees.

Financial Aid Of all full-time matriculated undergraduates who enrolled in 2003, 1,457 applied for aid, 1,250 were judged to have need, 297 had their need fully met. 228 Federal Work-Study jobs (averaging $2028). 582 state and other part-time jobs (averaging $1984). In 2003, 616 non-need-based awards were made. *Average percent of need met:* 85%. *Average financial aid package:* $17,044. *Average need-based loan:* $4478. *Average need-based gift aid:* $11,863. *Average indebtedness upon graduation:* $20,803. *Financial aid deadline:* 3/1.

Applying *Options:* common application, electronic application, early admission, deferred entrance. *Required:* essay or personal statement, high school transcript, minimum 2.0 GPA. *Recommended:* minimum 3.0 GPA, 3 letters of recommendation, interview. *Application deadline:* 2/15 (freshmen). *Notification:* 4/15 (freshmen), continuous (transfers).

Admissions Contact Mr. Jerry Pope, Dean of Admissions, Illinois Wesleyan University, PO Box 2900, Bloomington, IL 61702-2900. *Phone:* 309-556-3031. *Toll-free phone:* 800-332-2498. *Fax:* 309-556-3820. *E-mail:* iwuadmit@titan.iwu.edu.

INTERNATIONAL ACADEMY OF DESIGN & TECHNOLOGY
Chicago, Illinois

- **Proprietary** 4-year, founded 1977, part of Career Education Corporation
- **Calendar** quarters
- **Degrees** certificates, associate, and bachelor's
- **Urban** 1-acre campus
- **Coed,** 2,769 undergraduate students, 93% full-time, 66% women, 34% men
- **Minimally difficult** entrance level, 54% of applicants were admitted

Undergraduates 2,565 full-time, 204 part-time. Students come from 28 states and territories, 23 other countries, 6% are from out of state, 39% African American, 4% Asian American or Pacific Islander, 20% Hispanic American, 0.5% Native American, 0.8% international, 6% transferred in. *Retention:* 74% of 2002 full-time freshmen returned.

Freshmen *Admission:* 1,405 applied, 758 admitted, 755 enrolled. *Average high school GPA:* 2.25.

Faculty *Total:* 183, 11% full-time, 3% with terminal degrees. *Student/faculty ratio:* 14:1.

Majors Commercial and advertising art; computer and information sciences and support services related; computer graphics; design and visual communications; fashion/apparel design; fashion merchandising; information technology; interior design; intermedia/multimedia.

Academic Programs *Special study options:* academic remediation for entering students, adult/continuing education programs, advanced placement credit, independent study, internships, part-time degree program, study abroad, summer session for credit.

Library International Academy of Design and Technology Library with 5,000 titles, 90 serial subscriptions, 500 audiovisual materials, an OPAC, a Web page.

Computers on Campus 300 computers available on campus for general student use. A campuswide network can be accessed. Internet access, at least one staffed computer lab available.

Student Life *Housing:* college housing not available. *Options:* Campus housing is provided by a third party. *Activities and organizations:* student-run newspaper, ASID/IDSA (Interior Design Student Organization), Byte-Me Club/AIGA (American Institute of Graphic Artists), International club, Fashion Council, Adult Student Support Group. *Campus security:* 24-hour emergency response devices, building security during hours of operation. *Student services:* personal/psychological counseling.

Standardized Tests *Recommended:* SAT I and SAT II or ACT (for placement), SAT II: Writing Test (for placement).

Costs (2004–05) *Tuition:* $18,400 full-time, $1200 per course part-time. Full-time tuition and fees vary according to course load and program. Part-time tuition and fees vary according to program. *Required fees:* $300 full-time. *Payment plans:* tuition prepayment, installment, deferred payment. *Waivers:* employees or children of employees.

Financial Aid Of all full-time matriculated undergraduates who enrolled in 2002, 30 Federal Work-Study jobs.

Applying *Options:* common application, early admission. *Application fee:* $50. *Required:* high school transcript, interview. *Required for some:* GED. *Recommended:* essay or personal statement, minimum 2.0 GPA. *Application deadline:* rolling (freshmen), rolling (transfers).

Admissions Contact Ms. Laura Wincup, Associate Director of Student Management, International Academy of Design & Technology, One North State Street, Suite 400, Chicago, IL 60602. *Phone:* 312-980-9200. *Toll-free phone:* 877-ACADEMY. *Fax:* 312-541-3929. *E-mail:* academy@iadtchicago.com.

■ See page 1768 for a narrative description.

ITT TECHNICAL INSTITUTE
Mount Prospect, Illinois

- **Proprietary** primarily 2-year, founded 1986, part of ITT Educational Services, Inc.
- **Calendar** quarters
- **Degrees** associate and bachelor's
- **Suburban** 1-acre campus with easy access to Chicago
- **Coed**
- **Minimally difficult** entrance level

Standardized Tests *Required:* Wonderlic aptitude test (for admission).

Costs (2003–04) *Tuition:* $347 per credit hour part-time.

ITT Technical Institute (continued)

Applying *Options:* deferred entrance. *Application fee:* $100. *Required:* high school transcript, interview. *Recommended:* letters of recommendation.

Admissions Contact Mr. Ernest Lloyd, Director of Recruitment, ITT Technical Institute, 1401 Feehanville Drive, Mount Prospect, IL 60056. *Phone:* 847-375-8800. *Fax:* 847-375-9022.

JUDSON COLLEGE

Elgin, Illinois

- **Independent Baptist** 4-year, founded 1963
- **Calendar** semesters
- **Degrees** bachelor's and master's
- **Suburban** 80-acre campus with easy access to Chicago
- **Endowment** $5.4 million
- **Coed,** 1,123 undergraduate students, 79% full-time, 57% women, 43% men
- **Moderately difficult** entrance level, 79% of applicants were admitted

Undergraduates 892 full-time, 231 part-time. Students come from 21 states and territories, 18 other countries, 35% are from out of state, 5% African American, 1% Asian American or Pacific Islander, 5% Hispanic American, 0.4% Native American, 4% international, 8% transferred in, 62% live on campus. *Retention:* 65% of 2002 full-time freshmen returned.

Freshmen *Admission:* 532 applied, 420 admitted, 132 enrolled. *Average high school GPA:* 3.00. *Test scores:* SAT verbal scores over 500: 60%; SAT math scores over 500: 63%; ACT scores over 18: 96%; SAT verbal scores over 600: 20%; SAT math scores over 600: 33%; ACT scores over 24: 40%; SAT math scores over 700: 3%; ACT scores over 30: 5%.

Faculty *Total:* 114, 47% full-time, 47% with terminal degrees. *Student/faculty ratio:* 16:1.

Majors Accounting; anthropology; architecture; art; biblical studies; biological and physical sciences; biology/biological sciences; business administration and management; chemistry; commercial and advertising art; computer graphics; computer science; criminal justice/safety; dramatic/theatre arts; drawing; education; elementary education; English; fine/studio arts; history; human resources management; human services; information science/studies; international business/trade/commerce; journalism; kindergarten/preschool education; linguistics; literature; management information systems; mass communication/media; mathematics; music; music teacher education; nursing (registered nurse training); philosophy; physical education teaching and coaching; physical sciences; pre-law studies; pre-medical studies; psychology; religious studies; science teacher education; secondary education; social sciences; sociology; speech and rhetoric; sport and fitness administration; voice and opera.

Academic Programs *Special study options:* academic remediation for entering students, accelerated degree program, adult/continuing education programs, advanced placement credit, distance learning, double majors, honors programs, independent study, internships, off-campus study, part-time degree program, student-designed majors, study abroad.

Library Benjamin P. Browne Library plus 2 others with 104,331 titles, 450 serial subscriptions, 12,500 audiovisual materials, an OPAC, a Web page.

Computers on Campus 90 computers available on campus for general student use. A campuswide network can be accessed from student residence rooms. Internet access, at least one staffed computer lab available.

Student Life *Housing:* on-campus residence required through junior year. *Options:* coed, men-only, women-only. *Activities and organizations:* drama/theater group, student-run newspaper, choral group, Judson Choir, Nowhere Near Broadway, philosophy and religion club, Phi Beta Lambda. *Campus security:* 24-hour emergency response devices and patrols, controlled dormitory access. *Student services:* health clinic, personal/psychological counseling.

Athletics Member NAIA, NCCAA. *Intercollegiate sports:* baseball M(s), basketball M(s)/W(s), cross-country running M(s)/W(s), soccer M(s)/W(s), softball W(s), tennis M(s)/W(s), volleyball W(s). *Intramural sports:* badminton M/W, basketball M/W, football M, golf M, racquetball M/W, soccer M/W, softball W, tennis M/W, ultimate Frisbee M(c)/W(c), volleyball M/W.

Standardized Tests *Required:* SAT I or ACT (for admission).

Costs (2003–04) *Comprehensive fee:* $22,050 includes full-time tuition ($15,800), mandatory fees ($250), and room and board ($6000). Part-time tuition: $515 per term. Part-time tuition and fees vary according to course load. *Required fees:* $56 per term part-time. *Room and board:* Room and board charges vary according to board plan. *Payment plan:* installment. *Waivers:* senior citizens and employees or children of employees.

Financial Aid *Average indebtedness upon graduation:* $12,386.

Applying *Options:* early admission. *Application fee:* $30. *Required:* essay or personal statement, high school transcript, minimum 2.0 GPA. *Required for some:* 2 letters of recommendation, interview. *Application deadline:* rolling (freshmen), rolling (transfers). *Notification:* 7/1 (freshmen), continuous (transfers).

Admissions Contact Mr. Billy Dean, Director of Admissions, Judson College, 1151 North State Street, Elgin, IL 60123-1498. *Phone:* 847-695-2500 Ext. 2322. *Toll-free phone:* 800-839-5376. *Fax:* 847-695-0216. *E-mail:* admission@judsoncollege.edu.

KENDALL COLLEGE

Chicago, Illinois

- **Independent United Methodist** 4-year, founded 1934
- **Calendar** quarters
- **Degrees** certificates, associate, and bachelor's
- **Urban** 1-acre campus
- **Endowment** $3.0 million
- **Coed,** 628 undergraduate students, 72% full-time, 54% women, 46% men
- **Minimally difficult** entrance level, 79% of applicants were admitted

Undergraduates 454 full-time, 174 part-time. Students come from 20 states and territories, 19 other countries, 38% are from out of state, 14% African American, 5% Asian American or Pacific Islander, 6% Hispanic American, 0.6% Native American, 5% international, 19% transferred in, 33% live on campus.

Freshmen *Admission:* 629 applied, 496 admitted, 70 enrolled. *Average high school GPA:* 2.50. *Test scores:* ACT scores over 18: 78%; ACT scores over 24: 11%.

Faculty *Total:* 74, 41% with terminal degrees. *Student/faculty ratio:* 9:1.

Majors Baking and pastry arts; business administration and management; cooking and related culinary arts; culinary arts; early childhood education; education; educational administration and supervision related; educational leadership and administration; education related; education (specific levels and methods) related; elementary education; entrepreneurial and small business related; entrepreneurship; hospitality administration; hospitality administration related; hospitality and recreation marketing; hotel/motel administration; human services; institutional food workers; kindergarten/preschool education; marketing/marketing management; restaurant, culinary, and catering management; restaurant/food services management; small business administration.

Academic Programs *Special study options:* academic remediation for entering students, accelerated degree program, adult/continuing education programs, advanced placement credit, cooperative education, English as a second language, independent study, internships, part-time degree program, student-designed majors, study abroad, summer session for credit.

Library Kendall Library plus 1 other with 37,000 titles, 215 serial subscriptions, 150 audiovisual materials.

Computers on Campus 48 computers available on campus for general student use. A campuswide network can be accessed from student residence rooms and from off campus. Internet access, at least one staffed computer lab available.

Student Life *Housing options:* coed. Campus housing is university owned. *Activities and organizations:* student-run newspaper, culinary competition group, student culinary board, ECHO (early childhood organization), Volunteer Club, student government. *Campus security:* student patrols, late night security in dorms. *Student services:* personal/psychological counseling.

Standardized Tests *Required:* SAT I or ACT (for admission).

Costs (2003–04) *Comprehensive fee:* $21,578 includes full-time tuition ($14,445), mandatory fees ($305), and room and board ($6828). Full-time tuition and fees vary according to program. Part-time tuition: $436 per quarter hour. Part-time tuition and fees vary according to program. *Required fees:* $127 per term part-time. *Room and board:* Room and board charges vary according to housing facility. *Payment plan:* installment. *Waivers:* employees or children of employees.

Financial Aid Of all full-time matriculated undergraduates who enrolled in 2003, 360 were judged to have need. 50 Federal Work-Study jobs (averaging $1162). *Average percent of need met:* 26%. *Average indebtedness upon graduation:* $14,125.

Applying *Options:* common application, deferred entrance. *Application fee:* $30. *Required:* essay or personal statement, high school transcript, minimum ACT score of 18. *Required for some:* letters of recommendation, interview. *Recommended:* minimum 2.0 GPA, interview. *Application deadline:* rolling (freshmen), rolling (transfers). *Notification:* continuous (freshmen), continuous (transfers).

Admissions Contact Carl Goodmonson, Director of Admissions, Kendall College, 900 North Branch Street, Chicago, IL 60622. *Phone:* 847-866-1300 Ext. 1307. *Toll-free phone:* 877-588-8860. *Fax:* 847-448-2120. *E-mail:* admissions@kendall.edu.

■ *See page 1810 for a narrative description.*

Knox College
Galesburg, Illinois

- **Independent** 4-year, founded 1837
- **Calendar** three courses for each of three terms
- **Degree** bachelor's
- **Small-town** 82-acre campus with easy access to Peoria
- **Endowment** $44.2 million
- **Coed,** 1,127 undergraduate students, 98% full-time, 53% women, 47% men
- **Very difficult** entrance level, 73% of applicants were admitted

Undergraduates 1,105 full-time, 22 part-time. Students come from 46 states and territories, 50 other countries, 44% are from out of state, 4% African American, 5% Asian American or Pacific Islander, 4% Hispanic American, 0.5% Native American, 9% international, 5% transferred in, 95% live on campus. *Retention:* 87% of 2002 full-time freshmen returned.

Freshmen *Admission:* 1,538 applied, 1,129 admitted, 268 enrolled. *Test scores:* SAT verbal scores over 500: 88%; SAT math scores over 500: 87%; ACT scores over 18: 99%; SAT verbal scores over 600: 59%; SAT math scores over 600: 56%; ACT scores over 24: 82%; SAT verbal scores over 700: 23%; SAT math scores over 700: 9%; ACT scores over 30: 25%.

Faculty *Total:* 116, 79% full-time, 84% with terminal degrees. *Student/faculty ratio:* 12:1.

Majors African-American/Black studies; agriculture; American studies; anthropology; art; art history, criticism and conservation; biochemistry; biology/biological sciences; chemistry; classics and languages, literatures and linguistics; computer and information sciences; creative writing; dramatic/theatre arts; economics; education; English; environmental studies; foreign languages and literatures; French; German; history; international relations and affairs; mathematics; multi-/interdisciplinary studies related; music; philosophy; physics; political science and government; psychology; Russian; Russian studies; sociology; Spanish; women's studies.

Academic Programs *Special study options:* academic remediation for entering students, advanced placement credit, double majors, English as a second language, honors programs, independent study, internships, off-campus study, part-time degree program, services for LD students, student-designed majors, study abroad. *Unusual degree programs:* 3-2 engineering with Columbia University, Washington University in St. Louis, Rensselaer Polytechnic Institute, University of Illinois at Urbana-Champaign; forestry with Duke University; social work with University of Chicago; nursing, occupational therapy, medical technology with Columbia University, Rush University; Optometry with Illinois College of Optometry.

Library Seymour Library plus 2 others with 185,923 titles, 1,037 serial subscriptions, 6,336 audiovisual materials, an OPAC, a Web page.

Computers on Campus 171 computers available on campus for general student use. A campuswide network can be accessed from student residence rooms and from off campus that provide access to software applications. Internet access, at least one staffed computer lab available.

Student Life *Housing:* on-campus residence required through senior year. *Options:* coed, men-only, women-only. Campus housing is university owned. Freshman campus housing is guaranteed. *Activities and organizations:* drama/theater group, student-run newspaper, radio station, choral group, International Club, Allied Blacks for Liberty and Equality, Sexual Equality Awareness Coalition, Union Board, campus radio station, national fraternities, national sororities. *Campus security:* 24-hour emergency response devices and patrols, late-night transport/escort service. *Student services:* personal/psychological counseling.

Athletics Member NCAA. except baseball (Division III), men's and women's basketball (Division III), men's and women's cross-country running (Division III), football (Division III), men's and women's golf (Division III), men's and women's soccer (Division III), softball (Division III), men's and women's swimming (Division III), men's and women's tennis (Division III), men's and women's track and field (Division III), volleyball (Division III), wrestling (Division III) *Intercollegiate sports:* baseball M, basketball M/W, cross-country running M/W, football M, golf M/W, soccer M/W, softball W, swimming M/W, tennis M/W, track and field M/W, volleyball W, wrestling M. *Intramural sports:* baseball M, basketball M/W, cross-country running M/W, fencing M/W, lacrosse M/W, soccer M/W, softball M/W, swimming M/W, tennis M/W, track and field M/W, ultimate Frisbee M/W, volleyball M/W, water polo M/W, weight lifting M/W.

Standardized Tests *Required:* SAT I or ACT (for admission).

Costs (2004–05) *Comprehensive fee:* $31,338 includes full-time tuition ($24,960), mandatory fees ($276), and room and board ($6102). *College room only:* $2703. Room and board charges vary according to board plan. *Payment plan:* installment. *Waivers:* employees or children of employees.

Financial Aid Of all full-time matriculated undergraduates who enrolled in 2003, 909 applied for aid, 803 were judged to have need, 429 had their need fully met. 607 Federal Work-Study jobs (averaging $1378). 113 state and other part-time jobs (averaging $1441). In 2003, 235 non-need-based awards were made. *Average percent of need met:* 97%. *Average financial aid package:* $20,770. *Average need-based loan:* $5266. *Average need-based gift aid:* $15,483. *Average non-need-based aid:* $10,280. *Average indebtedness upon graduation:* $18,221.

Applying *Options:* common application, electronic application, early admission, early action, deferred entrance. *Application fee:* $35. *Required:* essay or personal statement, high school transcript, 2 letters of recommendation. *Recommended:* interview. *Application deadlines:* 2/1 (freshmen), 4/1 (transfers). *Notification:* 3/31 (freshmen), 12/31 (early action), 4/30 (transfers).

Admissions Contact Mr. Paul Steenis, Director of Admissions, Knox College, Box K-148, Galesburg, IL 61401. *Phone:* 309-341-7100. *Toll-free phone:* 800-678-KNOX. *Fax:* 309-341-7070. *E-mail:* admission@knox.edu.

■ *See page 1826 for a narrative description.*

Lake Forest College
Lake Forest, Illinois

- **Independent** comprehensive, founded 1857
- **Calendar** semesters
- **Degrees** bachelor's and master's
- **Suburban** 110-acre campus with easy access to Chicago
- **Endowment** $55.9 million
- **Coed,** 1,336 undergraduate students, 98% full-time, 57% women, 43% men
- **Very difficult** entrance level, 68% of applicants were admitted

Undergraduates 1,314 full-time, 22 part-time. Students come from 47 states and territories, 50 other countries, 52% are from out of state, 5% African American, 4% Asian American or Pacific Islander, 4% Hispanic American, 0.2% Native American, 10% international, 5% transferred in, 82% live on campus. *Retention:* 81% of 2002 full-time freshmen returned.

Freshmen *Admission:* 1,835 applied, 1,240 admitted, 347 enrolled. *Average high school GPA:* 3.40. *Test scores:* SAT verbal scores over 500: 82%; SAT math scores over 500: 85%; ACT scores over 18: 97%; SAT verbal scores over 600: 44%; SAT math scores over 600: 44%; ACT scores over 24: 68%; SAT verbal scores over 700: 8%; SAT math scores over 700: 8%; ACT scores over 30: 16%.

Faculty *Total:* 151, 58% full-time, 74% with terminal degrees. *Student/faculty ratio:* 12:1.

Majors American studies; anthropology; art history, criticism and conservation; Asian studies; biology/biological sciences; business/managerial economics; chemistry; communication/speech communication and rhetoric; computer science; economics; education; elementary education; English; environmental studies; finance; fine/studio arts; French; history; international relations and affairs; Latin American studies; mathematics; music; philosophy; physics; political science and government; pre-dentistry studies; pre-law studies; pre-medical studies; pre-veterinary studies; psychology; secondary education; sociology; Spanish.

Academic Programs *Special study options:* accelerated degree program, adult/continuing education programs, advanced placement credit, double majors, freshman honors college, honors programs, independent study, internships, off-campus study, part-time degree program, services for LD students, student-designed majors, study abroad, summer session for credit. *Unusual degree programs:* 3-2 engineering with Washington University in St. Louis.

Library Donnelley Library plus 1 other with 268,760 titles, 886 serial subscriptions, 12,125 audiovisual materials, an OPAC, a Web page.

Computers on Campus 120 computers available on campus for general student use. A campuswide network can be accessed from student residence rooms and from off campus that provide access to file storage. Internet access, at least one staffed computer lab available. Computer purchase or lease plan available.

Student Life *Housing:* on-campus residence required for freshman year. *Options:* coed, women-only. Campus housing is university owned. Freshman campus housing is guaranteed. *Activities and organizations:* drama/theater group, student-run newspaper, radio station, choral group, Garrick Players Drama Group, League for Environmental Awareness and Protection, International Student Organization, Ambassadors Host Organization, national fraternities. *Campus security:* 24-hour emergency response devices and patrols, student patrols, late-night transport/escort service. *Student services:* health clinic, personal/psychological counseling, women's center.

Athletics Member NCAA. All Division III. *Intercollegiate sports:* baseball M(c), basketball M/W, cross-country running M/W, fencing M(c)/W(c), football M, ice hockey M/W, lacrosse M(c)/W(c), rugby M(c), soccer M/W, softball W, swimming M/W, tennis M/W, ultimate Frisbee M(c)/W(c), volleyball M(c)/W, water polo M. *Intramural sports:* basketball M/W, football M, golf M/W, ice hockey M/W, racquetball M/W, sailing M/W, soccer M/W, squash M/W, tennis M/W, volleyball M/W.

Standardized Tests *Required:* SAT I or ACT (for admission).

Lake Forest College (continued)

Costs (2003–04) *One-time required fee:* $200. *Comprehensive fee:* $30,170 includes full-time tuition ($24,096), mandatory fees ($310), and room and board ($5764). Part-time tuition: $3012 per course. *Required fees:* $155 per term part-time. *College room only:* $3164. Room and board charges vary according to housing facility. *Payment plan:* installment. *Waivers:* employees or children of employees.

Financial Aid Of all full-time matriculated undergraduates who enrolled in 2003, 1,165 applied for aid, 1,006 were judged to have need, 1,006 had their need fully met. 460 Federal Work-Study jobs (averaging $1732). In 2003, 158 non-need-based awards were made. *Average percent of need met:* 100%. *Average financial aid package:* $19,466. *Average need-based loan:* $3315. *Average need-based gift aid:* $16,147. *Average non-need-based aid:* $10,606. *Average indebtedness upon graduation:* $17,285.

Applying *Options:* common application, electronic application, early admission, early decision, early action, deferred entrance. *Application fee:* $40. *Required:* essay or personal statement, high school transcript, 2 letters of recommendation, graded paper. *Recommended:* interview. *Application deadline:* 3/1 (freshmen), rolling (transfers). *Early decision:* 1/1. *Notification:* 3/23 (freshmen), 1/21 (early decision), 12/20 (early action), continuous (transfers).

Admissions Contact Mr. William G. Motzer Jr., Director of Admissions, Lake Forest College, 555 North Sheridan Road, Lake Forest, IL 60045-2399. *Phone:* 847-735-5000. *Toll-free phone:* 800-828-4751. *Fax:* 847-735-6271. *E-mail:* admissions@lakeforest.edu.

■ *See page 1840 for a narrative description.*

LAKEVIEW COLLEGE OF NURSING
Danville, Illinois

- **Independent** upper-level, founded 1987, part of Danville Area Community College
- **Calendar** semesters
- **Degree** bachelor's
- **Small-town** 1-acre campus
- **Endowment** $6.2 million
- **Coed**
- **Moderately difficult** entrance level

Faculty *Student/faculty ratio:* 8:1.

Student Life *Campus security:* 24-hour emergency response devices.

Costs (2003–04) *Tuition:* $8250 full-time, $275 per credit hour part-time. *Required fees:* $1050 full-time, $35 per credit hour part-time.

Financial Aid *Average percent of need met:* 58. *Average financial aid package:* $3200.

Applying *Options:* common application, deferred entrance. *Application fee:* $50.

Admissions Contact Kelly M. Holden MS Ed, Registrar, Lakeview College of Nursing, 903 North Logan Avenue, Danville, IL 61832. *Phone:* 217-443-5238 Ext. 5385. *Toll-free phone:* 217-443-5238 Ext. 5454 (in-state); 217-443-5238 (out-of-state). *Fax:* 217-442-2279. *E-mail:* kholden@lakeviewcol.edu.

LEWIS UNIVERSITY
Romeoville, Illinois

- **Independent** comprehensive, founded 1932, affiliated with Roman Catholic Church
- **Calendar** semesters
- **Degrees** certificates, associate, bachelor's, master's, and postbachelor's certificates
- **Small-town** 375-acre campus with easy access to Chicago
- **Endowment** $17.6 million
- **Coed,** 3,214 undergraduate students, 70% full-time, 59% women, 41% men
- **Moderately difficult** entrance level, 66% of applicants were admitted

Lewis University offers bachelor's degrees in more than 60 majors as well as graduate programs in business administration, counseling psychology, criminal/social justice, education, nursing, organizational leadership, public safety administration, and school counseling and guidance. A Catholic university, sponsored by the De La Salle Christian Brothers, Lewis is located in Romeoville, Illinois, just 30 minutes from Chicago on the interstate highways. Lewis has a widely recognized aviation program and an airport adjacent to the main campus.

Undergraduates 2,250 full-time, 964 part-time. Students come from 24 states and territories, 31 other countries, 4% are from out of state, 14% African American, 2% Asian American or Pacific Islander, 7% Hispanic American, 0.2% Native American, 4% international, 10% transferred in, 27% live on campus. *Retention:* 79% of 2002 full-time freshmen returned.

Freshmen *Admission:* 1,595 applied, 1,056 admitted, 458 enrolled. *Average high school GPA:* 3.02. *Test scores:* SAT verbal scores over 500: 75%; SAT math scores over 500: 75%; ACT scores over 18: 94%; SAT verbal scores over 600: 25%; SAT math scores over 600: 25%; ACT scores over 24: 29%.

Faculty *Total:* 157, 92% full-time, 61% with terminal degrees. *Student/faculty ratio:* 13:1.

Majors Accounting; airframe mechanics and aircraft maintenance technology; airline pilot and flight crew; American studies; area studies related; art; art teacher education; aviation/airway management; avionics maintenance technology; biochemistry; biology/biological sciences; broadcast journalism; business administration and management; business/managerial economics; chemistry; clinical laboratory science/medical technology; commercial and advertising art; computer science; criminal justice/law enforcement administration; dramatic/theatre arts; drawing; economics; education; education (K-12); elementary education; English; environmental studies; finance; fine/studio arts; health/health care administration; history; human resources management; journalism; liberal arts and sciences/liberal studies; management information systems; management information systems and services related; marketing/marketing management; mass communication/media; mathematics; music; music management and merchandising; nursing (registered nurse training); painting; philosophy; physical education teaching and coaching; physics; political science and government; pre-dentistry studies; pre-law studies; pre-medical studies; pre-veterinary studies; psychology; public administration; public relations/image management; radio and television broadcasting technology; religious studies; secondary education; security and protective services related; social work; sociology; special education; speech and rhetoric; speech/theater education.

Academic Programs *Special study options:* academic remediation for entering students, accelerated degree program, adult/continuing education programs, advanced placement credit, distance learning, double majors, English as a second language, honors programs, independent study, internships, part-time degree program, student-designed majors, study abroad, summer session for credit. *ROTC:* Army (c), Air Force (c).

Library Lewis University Library with 149,870 titles, 1,990 serial subscriptions, 2,281 audiovisual materials, an OPAC, a Web page.

Computers on Campus 310 computers available on campus for general student use. A campuswide network can be accessed from student residence rooms and from off campus that provide access to e-mail. Internet access, online (class) registration, at least one staffed computer lab available.

Student Life *Housing options:* coed, disabled students. Campus housing is university owned. Freshman campus housing is guaranteed. *Activities and organizations:* drama/theater group, student-run newspaper, radio and television station, choral group, Phi Kappa Theta, Scholars Academy, Black Student Union, Fellowship of Justice, Latin American Student Organization, national fraternities, national sororities. *Campus security:* 24-hour emergency response devices and patrols, student patrols, late-night transport/escort service, controlled dormitory access. *Student services:* health clinic, personal/psychological counseling.

Athletics Member NCAA. All Division II. *Intercollegiate sports:* baseball M(s), basketball M(s)/W(s), cheerleading M/W, cross-country running M(s)/W(s), golf M(s)/W(s), soccer M(s)/W(s), softball W(s), swimming M(s)/W(s), tennis M(s)/W(s), track and field M(s)/W(s), volleyball M(s)/W(s). *Intramural sports:* basketball M/W, bowling M/W, cheerleading M/W, cross-country running M/W, football M/W, golf M/W, racquetball M/W, soccer M/W, softball W, swimming M/W, tennis M/W, track and field M/W, volleyball M/W.

Standardized Tests *Required:* SAT I or ACT (for admission).

Costs (2004–05) *Comprehensive fee:* $24,106 includes full-time tuition ($16,906) and room and board ($7200). Full-time tuition and fees vary according to course load and program. Part-time tuition: $546 per credit. Part-time tuition and fees vary according to course load and program. *College room only:* $4850. Room and board charges vary according to board plan and housing facility. *Payment plan:* installment. *Waivers:* children of alumni and employees or children of employees.

Financial Aid Of all full-time matriculated undergraduates who enrolled in 2003, 2,007 applied for aid, 1,588 were judged to have need, 608 had their need fully met. 361 Federal Work-Study jobs (averaging $2800). 170 state and other part-time jobs (averaging $2800). In 2003, 218 non-need-based awards were made. *Average percent of need met:* 78%. *Average financial aid package:* $13,302. *Average need-based loan:* $3941. *Average need-based gift aid:* $5814. *Average non-need-based aid:* $4800. *Average indebtedness upon graduation:* $19,246.

Applying *Options:* common application, electronic application, deferred entrance. *Application fee:* $35. *Required:* high school transcript, minimum 2.0 GPA. *Required for some:* interview. *Application deadline:* 8/1 (freshmen), rolling (transfers).

Admissions Contact Mr. Ryan Cockerill, Admission Counselor, Lewis University, Box 297, One University Parkway, Romeoville, IL 60446. *Phone:* 815-838-0500 Ext. 5237. *Toll-free phone:* 800-897-9000. *Fax:* 815-836-5002. *E-mail:* admissions@lewisu.edu.

■ *See page 1866 for a narrative description.*

LEXINGTON COLLEGE
Chicago, Illinois

- **Independent** 4-year, founded 1977
- **Calendar** semesters
- **Degrees** associate and bachelor's
- **Urban** campus
- **Endowment** $29,600
- **Women only,** 41 undergraduate students, 98% full-time
- **Noncompetitive** entrance level, 53% of applicants were admitted

Undergraduates 40 full-time, 1 part-time. Students come from 5 states and territories, 2 other countries, 12% are from out of state, 34% African American, 5% Asian American or Pacific Islander, 20% Hispanic American, 5% international, 2% transferred in.

Freshmen *Admission:* 14 enrolled. *Average high school GPA:* 2.60. *Test scores:* ACT scores over 18: 30%; ACT scores over 24: 8%.

Faculty *Total:* 17, 24% full-time, 100% with terminal degrees. *Student/faculty ratio:* 2:1.

Majors Cooking and related culinary arts; culinary arts; culinary arts related; food preparation; food service and dining room management; hospitality administration; hospitality administration related; hotel/motel administration; institutional food workers; personal and culinary services related; restaurant, culinary, and catering management; restaurant/food services management.

Academic Programs *Special study options:* academic remediation for entering students, adult/continuing education programs, cooperative education, internships, part-time degree program.

Library Lexington College Library with 2,000 titles, 40 serial subscriptions, an OPAC.

Computers on Campus 25 computers available on campus for general student use. A campuswide network can be accessed. Internet access, at least one staffed computer lab available.

Student Life *Housing:* college housing not available. *Campus security:* 24-hour emergency response devices and patrols, patrols by municipal security personnel.

Standardized Tests *Required:* SAT I or ACT (for admission).

Costs (2003–04) *Tuition:* $12,600 full-time, $450 per credit hour part-time. *Required fees:* $750 full-time. *Payment plan:* installment. *Waivers:* employees or children of employees.

Financial Aid Of all full-time matriculated undergraduates who enrolled in 2003, 44 applied for aid, 41 were judged to have need. 5 Federal Work-Study jobs. In 2003, 3 non-need-based awards were made. *Average percent of need met:* 83%. *Average financial aid package:* $10,000. *Average need-based loan:* $2300. *Average need-based gift aid:* $7600. *Average non-need-based aid:* $333. *Average indebtedness upon graduation:* $3500. *Financial aid deadline:* 10/1.

Applying *Application fee:* $30. *Required:* essay or personal statement, high school transcript, minimum 2.0 GPA. *Required for some:* 2 letters of recommendation. *Recommended:* interview. *Application deadline:* rolling (freshmen). *Notification:* continuous (transfers).

Admissions Contact Ms. Giselle Castillo, Director of Admissions, Lexington College, 310 South Peoria Street, Chicago, IL 60607-3534. *Phone:* 312-226-6294 Ext. 225. *Fax:* 312-226-6405. *E-mail:* adm@lexingtoncollege.edu.

LINCOLN CHRISTIAN COLLEGE
Lincoln, Illinois

- **Independent** 4-year, founded 1944, affiliated with Christian Churches and Churches of Christ
- **Calendar** semesters
- **Degrees** certificates, associate, and bachelor's
- **Small-town** 227-acre campus
- **Coed**
- **Moderately difficult** entrance level

Faculty *Student/faculty ratio:* 16:1.

Student Life *Campus security:* 24-hour emergency response devices, student patrols.

Athletics Member NCCAA.

Standardized Tests *Required:* SAT I or ACT (for admission).

Costs (2003–04) *Comprehensive fee:* $13,558 includes full-time tuition ($7890), mandatory fees ($1200), and room and board ($4468). Part-time tuition: $263 per semester hour. Part-time tuition and fees vary according to course load and program. *Required fees:* $40 per semester hour part-time. *Payment plans:* installment, deferred payment.

Financial Aid Of all full-time matriculated undergraduates who enrolled in 2002, 554 applied for aid. 86 Federal Work-Study jobs (averaging $956). In 2002, 30. *Average percent of need met:* 80. *Average financial aid package:* $8000. *Average indebtedness upon graduation:* $13,529.

Applying *Options:* deferred entrance. *Application fee:* $20. *Required:* essay or personal statement, high school transcript, 3 letters of recommendation. *Required for some:* interview.

Admissions Contact Mrs. Mary K. Davis, Assistant Director of Admissions, Lincoln Christian College, 100 Campus View Drive, Lincoln, IL 62656. *Phone:* 217-732-3168 Ext. 2251. *Toll-free phone:* 888-522-5228. *Fax:* 217-732-4199. *E-mail:* coladmis@lccs.edu.

LINCOLN COLLEGE
Normal, Illinois

- **Independent** primarily 2-year, founded 1865
- **Calendar** semesters
- **Degrees** certificates, associate, and bachelor's
- **Suburban** 10-acre campus
- **Endowment** $14.0 million
- **Coed**
- **Minimally difficult** entrance level

Faculty *Student/faculty ratio:* 14:1.

Student Life *Campus security:* 24-hour emergency response devices and patrols, student patrols, late-night transport/escort service, controlled dormitory access.

Athletics Member NJCAA.

Standardized Tests *Required for some:* SAT I or ACT (for admission).

Costs (2003–04) *Comprehensive fee:* $18,470 includes full-time tuition ($12,400), mandatory fees ($570), and room and board ($5500). Full-time tuition and fees vary according to program. Part-time tuition: $413 per credit hour. Part-time tuition and fees vary according to course load. No tuition increase for student's term of enrollment. *Required fees:* $25 per term part-time. *College room only:* $3700. Room and board charges vary according to board plan.

Applying *Options:* common application, electronic application, deferred entrance. *Application fee:* $25. *Required:* high school transcript, interview. *Required for some:* 2 letters of recommendation.

Admissions Contact Mr. Joe Hendrix, Director of Admissions, Lincoln College, 715 West Raab Road, Normal, IL 61761. *Phone:* 800-569-0558. *Toll-free phone:* 800-569-0558. *Fax:* 309-454-5652. *E-mail:* admissions@lincoln.mclean.il.us.

LOYOLA UNIVERSITY CHICAGO
Chicago, Illinois

- **Independent Roman Catholic (Jesuit)** university, founded 1870
- **Calendar** semesters
- **Degrees** certificates, bachelor's, master's, doctoral, first professional, post-master's, and postbachelor's certificates (also offers adult part-time program with significant enrollment not reflected in profile)
- **Urban** 105-acre campus
- **Endowment** $197.7 million
- **Coed,** 7,916 undergraduate students, 83% full-time, 66% women, 34% men
- **Moderately difficult** entrance level, 82% of applicants were admitted

Undergraduates 6,592 full-time, 1,324 part-time. Students come from 50 states and territories, 60 other countries, 34% are from out of state, 8% African American, 11% Asian American or Pacific Islander, 11% Hispanic American, 0.2% Native American, 2% international, 7% transferred in, 29% live on campus. *Retention:* 84% of 2002 full-time freshmen returned.

Freshmen *Admission:* 11,009 applied, 9,078 admitted, 1,915 enrolled. *Average high school GPA:* 3.53. *Test scores:* SAT verbal scores over 500: 86%; SAT math scores over 500: 80%; ACT scores over 18: 97%; SAT verbal scores over 600: 44%; SAT math scores over 600: 40%; ACT scores over 24: 63%; SAT verbal scores over 700: 8%; SAT math scores over 700: 5%; ACT scores over 30: 10%.

Faculty *Total:* 975, 54% full-time. *Student/faculty ratio:* 13:1.

Majors Accounting; ancient/classical Greek; anthropology; art; art history, criticism and conservation; biochemistry; biology/biological sciences; business administration and management; business/managerial economics; ceramic arts and ceramics; chemistry; classics and languages, literatures and linguistics; communication and journalism related; communication/speech communication

Loyola University Chicago (continued)
and rhetoric; computer science; criminal justice/safety; dramatic/theatre arts; economics; elementary education; English; environmental studies; finance; fine arts related; foods, nutrition, and wellness; French; German; history; humanities; human resources management; information science/studies; international relations and affairs; Italian; journalism; kindergarten/preschool education; Latin; management information systems; marketing/marketing management; mathematics; mathematics and computer science; metal and jewelry arts; music; natural sciences; nursing (registered nurse training); operations management; philosophy; photography; physics; political science and government; pre-dentistry studies; pre-law studies; pre-medical studies; pre-theology/pre-ministerial studies; pre-veterinary studies; psychology; psychology related; social psychology; social work; sociology; Spanish; special education; statistics; theology.

Academic Programs *Special study options:* academic remediation for entering students, accelerated degree program, adult/continuing education programs, advanced placement credit, double majors, English as a second language, honors programs, internships, off-campus study, part-time degree program, services for LD students, study abroad, summer session for credit. *ROTC:* Army (c), Navy (c). *Unusual degree programs:* 3-2 engineering with University of Illinois at Urbana-Champaign, Washington University in St. Louis.

Library Cudahy Library plus 4 others with 1.1 million titles, 68,886 serial subscriptions, 35,090 audiovisual materials, an OPAC, a Web page.

Computers on Campus 318 computers available on campus for general student use. A campuswide network can be accessed from student residence rooms and from off campus. Internet access, at least one staffed computer lab available.

Student Life *Housing options:* coed, women-only. Campus housing is university owned. Freshman campus housing is guaranteed. *Activities and organizations:* drama/theater group, student-run newspaper, radio station, choral group, Campus Life Union Board, Activities Programming Board, student government, national fraternities, national sororities. *Campus security:* 24-hour emergency response devices and patrols, late-night transport/escort service, controlled dormitory access. *Student services:* health clinic, personal/psychological counseling, women's center.

Athletics Member NCAA. All Division I. *Intercollegiate sports:* basketball M(s)/W(s), cross-country running M(s)/W(s), golf M(s)/W(s), soccer M(s)/W(s), softball W(s), track and field M(s)/W(s), volleyball M(s)/W(s). *Intramural sports:* badminton M/W, baseball M(c), basketball M/W, football M, racquetball M/W, rugby M(c), sailing M/W, soccer M/W, softball M/W, table tennis M/W, tennis M/W, volleyball M/W.

Standardized Tests *Required:* SAT I or ACT (for admission).

Costs (2004–05) *Comprehensive fee:* $31,164 includes full-time tuition ($21,780), mandatory fees ($560), and room and board ($8824). Part-time tuition: $429 per semester hour. Part-time tuition and fees vary according to course load. *Required fees:* $75 per term part-time. *College room only:* $5974. Room and board charges vary according to board plan and housing facility. *Payment plan:* installment. *Waivers:* employees or children of employees.

Financial Aid Of all full-time matriculated undergraduates who enrolled in 2003, 5,903 applied for aid, 4,677 were judged to have need, 777 had their need fully met. In 2003, 1022 non-need-based awards were made. *Average percent of need met:* 78%. *Average financial aid package:* $20,488. *Average need-based loan:* $4457. *Average need-based gift aid:* $17,942. *Average non-need-based aid:* $8557. *Average indebtedness upon graduation:* $16,168.

Applying *Options:* common application, electronic application, deferred entrance. *Application fee:* $25. *Required:* essay or personal statement, high school transcript. *Recommended:* interview. *Application deadlines:* 4/1 (freshmen), 8/1 (transfers). *Notification:* continuous (freshmen), continuous (transfers).

Admissions Contact Ms. April Hansen, Director of Admissions, Loyola University Chicago, 820 North Michigan Avenue, Suite 613, Chicago, IL 60611-9810. *Phone:* 773-508-3080. *Toll-free phone:* 800-262-2373. *Fax:* 312-915-7216. *E-mail:* admission@luc.edu.

■ *See page 1898 for a narrative description.*

MACMURRAY COLLEGE
Jacksonville, Illinois

- **Independent United Methodist** 4-year, founded 1846
- **Calendar** 4-1-4
- **Degrees** associate and bachelor's
- **Small-town** 60-acre campus
- **Endowment** $11.2 million
- **Coed,** 673 undergraduate students, 91% full-time, 59% women, 41% men
- **Moderately difficult** entrance level, 64% of applicants were admitted

Undergraduates 615 full-time, 58 part-time. Students come from 21 states and territories, 7 other countries, 15% are from out of state, 11% African American, 0.3% Asian American or Pacific Islander, 4% Hispanic American, 0.3% Native American, 1% international, 13% transferred in, 55% live on campus. *Retention:* 66% of 2002 full-time freshmen returned.

Freshmen *Admission:* 1,082 applied, 690 admitted, 162 enrolled. *Average high school GPA:* 3.14. *Test scores:* SAT verbal scores over 500: 31%; SAT math scores over 500: 31%; ACT scores over 18: 78%; SAT verbal scores over 600: 15%; SAT math scores over 600: 8%; ACT scores over 24: 25%; ACT scores over 30: 4%.

Faculty *Total:* 70, 57% full-time, 41% with terminal degrees. *Student/faculty ratio:* 12:1.

Majors Accounting; art; art history, criticism and conservation; biology/biological sciences; business administration and management; chemistry; criminal justice/law enforcement administration; criminal justice/police science; dramatic/theatre arts; elementary education; English; finance; fine/studio arts; history; information science/studies; liberal arts and sciences/liberal studies; management information systems; marketing/marketing management; mathematics; music; music teacher education; nursing (registered nurse training); philosophy; physical education teaching and coaching; physics; political science and government; pre-dentistry studies; pre-law studies; pre-medical studies; pre-veterinary studies; psychology; religious studies; secondary education; sign language interpretation and translation; social work; Spanish; special education; special education (hearing impaired); sport and fitness administration.

Academic Programs *Special study options:* academic remediation for entering students, advanced placement credit, double majors, honors programs, independent study, internships, off-campus study, part-time degree program, services for LD students, summer session for credit. *Unusual degree programs:* 3-2 engineering with Washington University in St. Louis, Columbia University, University of Missouri-Rolla.

Library Henry Pfeiffer Library with 935,000 titles, 235 serial subscriptions, 936 audiovisual materials, an OPAC, a Web page.

Computers on Campus 100 computers available on campus for general student use. A campuswide network can be accessed from student residence rooms that provide access to various software packages. Internet access, at least one staffed computer lab available.

Student Life *Housing:* on-campus residence required through sophomore year. *Options:* coed, women-only. Campus housing is university owned. Freshman campus housing is guaranteed. *Activities and organizations:* drama/theater group, student-run newspaper, choral group, Campus Activity Board, MacMurray Student Association, Sigma Tau Gamma, Alpha Phi Omega, Circle K, national fraternities. *Campus security:* 24-hour emergency response devices, student patrols, late-night transport/escort service, controlled dormitory access. *Student services:* health clinic, personal/psychological counseling.

Athletics Member NCAA. All Division III. *Intercollegiate sports:* baseball M, basketball M/W, cheerleading M/W, cross-country running M/W, football M, golf M/W, soccer M/W, softball W, swimming M/W, tennis M/W, volleyball W, wrestling M. *Intramural sports:* badminton M/W, basketball M/W, football M/W, soccer M/W, softball M/W, table tennis M/W, tennis M/W, volleyball M/W.

Standardized Tests *Required:* SAT I or ACT (for admission).

Costs (2004–05) *Comprehensive fee:* $20,270 includes full-time tuition ($14,500), mandatory fees ($150), and room and board ($5620). Part-time tuition: $235 per credit hour. *College room only:* $2850. Room and board charges vary according to board plan and housing facility. *Payment plan:* installment. *Waivers:* minority students, children of alumni, senior citizens, and employees or children of employees.

Financial Aid Of all full-time matriculated undergraduates who enrolled in 2003, 609 applied for aid, 570 were judged to have need, 191 had their need fully met. 48 Federal Work-Study jobs (averaging $1333). 86 state and other part-time jobs (averaging $1139). In 2003, 39 non-need-based awards were made. *Average percent of need met:* 93%. *Average financial aid package:* $16,659. *Average need-based loan:* $3858. *Average need-based gift aid:* $11,651. *Average non-need-based aid:* $5200. *Average indebtedness upon graduation:* $17,477.

Applying *Options:* common application, electronic application, early admission. *Required:* high school transcript. *Required for some:* essay or personal statement, minimum 2.5 GPA, letters of recommendation, interview. *Application deadline:* rolling (freshmen), rolling (transfers). *Notification:* continuous (freshmen), continuous (transfers).

Admissions Contact Ms. Rhonda Cors, vice President for Enrollment, MacMurray College, 447 East College Avenue, Jacksonville, IL 62650. *Phone:* 217-479-7056. *Toll-free phone:* 800-252-7485. *Fax:* 217-291-0702. *E-mail:* admiss@mac.edu.

MCKENDREE COLLEGE
Lebanon, Illinois

- **Independent** 4-year, founded 1828, affiliated with United Methodist Church
- **Calendar** semesters
- **Degrees** bachelor's and master's

- **Small-town** 80-acre campus with easy access to St. Louis
- **Endowment** $15.9 million
- **Coed,** 2,115 undergraduate students, 74% full-time, 61% women, 39% men
- **Moderately difficult** entrance level, 73% of applicants were admitted

Undergraduates 1,561 full-time, 554 part-time. Students come from 23 states and territories, 15 other countries, 31% are from out of state, 10% African American, 1% Asian American or Pacific Islander, 1% Hispanic American, 0.2% Native American, 1% international, 13% transferred in, 50% live on campus. *Retention:* 79% of 2002 full-time freshmen returned.

Freshmen *Admission:* 1,182 applied, 865 admitted, 310 enrolled. *Average high school GPA:* 3.70. *Test scores:* ACT scores over 18: 97%; ACT scores over 24: 56%; ACT scores over 30: 7%.

Faculty *Total:* 204, 34% full-time, 38% with terminal degrees. *Student/faculty ratio:* 12:1.

Majors Accounting; art; art teacher education; athletic training; biology/biological sciences; biology teacher education; business administration and management; business teacher education; chemistry; clinical laboratory science/medical technology; computer science; criminal justice/law enforcement administration; economics; education (K-12); elementary education; English; English/language arts teacher education; finance; history; history teacher education; information science/studies; international relations and affairs; marketing/marketing management; mass communication/media; mathematics; mathematics teacher education; middle school education; music; music teacher education; nursing (registered nurse training); occupational therapy; organizational communication; philosophy; physical education teaching and coaching; political science and government; pre-dentistry studies; pre-law studies; pre-medical studies; pre-veterinary studies; psychology; public relations/image management; religious studies; sales, distribution and marketing; secondary education; social sciences; social science teacher education; social work; sociology; speech and rhetoric; speech/theater education.

Academic Programs *Special study options:* academic remediation for entering students, accelerated degree program, advanced placement credit, double majors, honors programs, independent study, internships, off-campus study, part-time degree program, services for LD students, student-designed majors, study abroad, summer session for credit. *ROTC:* Army (c), Air Force (c). *Unusual degree programs:* 3-2 occupational therapy with Washington University in St. Louis.

Library Holman Library with 105,000 titles, 450 serial subscriptions, 9,500 audiovisual materials, an OPAC, a Web page.

Computers on Campus 140 computers available on campus for general student use. A campuswide network can be accessed from student residence rooms and from off campus. Internet access, at least one staffed computer lab available.

Student Life *Housing:* on-campus residence required for freshman year. *Options:* coed, women-only. Campus housing is university owned and leased by the school. Freshman campus housing is guaranteed. *Activities and organizations:* drama/theater group, student-run newspaper, choral group, marching band, Model United Nations, Campus Christian Fellowship, Team Bogey, Student Government Association, Students Against Social Injustice, national fraternities. *Campus security:* 24-hour emergency response devices and patrols, student patrols, late-night transport/escort service, controlled dormitory access. *Student services:* health clinic, personal/psychological counseling.

Athletics Member NAIA. *Intercollegiate sports:* baseball M(s), basketball M(s)/W(s), bowling M(s)/W(s), cheerleading M(s)/W(s), cross-country running M(s)/W(s), football M(s), golf M(s)/W(s), ice hockey M, soccer M(s)/W(s), softball W(s), tennis M(s)/W(s), track and field M(s)/W(s), volleyball W(s), wrestling M(s). *Intramural sports:* basketball M/W, football M/W, softball M/W, table tennis M/W, ultimate Frisbee M/W, volleyball M/W.

Standardized Tests *Required:* SAT I or ACT (for admission).

Costs (2003–04) *One-time required fee:* $50. *Comprehensive fee:* $21,120 includes full-time tuition ($15,200) and room and board ($5920). Full-time tuition and fees vary according to class time, course load, and location. Part-time tuition: $510 per credit. Part-time tuition and fees vary according to class time, course load, and location. *Room and board:* Room and board charges vary according to board plan and housing facility. *Payment plan:* installment. *Waivers:* employees or children of employees.

Financial Aid Of all full-time matriculated undergraduates who enrolled in 2003, 1,138 applied for aid, 1,011 were judged to have need, 269 had their need fully met. 420 Federal Work-Study jobs (averaging $1250). In 2003, 232 non-need-based awards were made. *Average percent of need met:* 79%. *Average financial aid package:* $12,400. *Average need-based loan:* $3211. *Average need-based gift aid:* $9763. *Average non-need-based aid:* $8371. *Average indebtedness upon graduation:* $14,592.

Applying *Options:* common application, electronic application, deferred entrance. *Application fee:* $40. *Required:* essay or personal statement, high school transcript, minimum 2.5 GPA, 1 letter of recommendation, top half of class, ACT of 20 or greater. *Required for some:* essay or personal statement, interview. *Application deadline:* rolling (freshmen), rolling (transfers). *Notification:* continuous (freshmen), continuous (transfers).

Admissions Contact Mr. Mark Campbell, Vice President for Admissions and Financial Aid, McKendree College, 701 College Road, Lebanon, IL 62254. *Phone:* 800-232-7228 Ext. 6835. *Toll-free phone:* 800-232-7228 Ext. 6831. *Fax:* 618-537-6496. *E-mail:* inquiry@mckendree.edu.

MIDSTATE COLLEGE
Peoria, Illinois

- **Proprietary** primarily 2-year, founded 1888
- **Calendar** quarters
- **Degrees** diplomas, associate, and bachelor's
- **Urban** 1-acre campus
- **Coed, primarily women**
- **Moderately difficult** entrance level

Faculty *Student/faculty ratio:* 13:1.

Student Life *Campus security:* late-night transport/escort service.

Standardized Tests *Required:* Wonderlic aptitude test (for admission).

Costs (2003–04) *Tuition:* $11,600 full-time, $775 per course part-time.

Financial Aid Of all full-time matriculated undergraduates who enrolled in 2001, 20 Federal Work-Study jobs (averaging $618).

Applying *Options:* common application, early admission, deferred entrance. *Application fee:* $25. *Required:* high school transcript. *Recommended:* interview.

Admissions Contact Ms. Jessica Auer, Director of Admissions, Midstate College, 411 West Northmoor Road, Peoria, IL 61614. *Phone:* 309-692-4092. *Fax:* 309-692-3893.

MILLIKIN UNIVERSITY
Decatur, Illinois

- **Independent** comprehensive, founded 1901, affiliated with Presbyterian Church (U.S.A.)
- **Calendar** semesters
- **Degrees** bachelor's and master's
- **Suburban** 70-acre campus
- **Endowment** $52.8 million
- **Coed,** 2,602 undergraduate students, 97% full-time, 56% women, 44% men
- **Moderately difficult** entrance level, 74% of applicants were admitted

Undergraduates 2,512 full-time, 90 part-time. Students come from 33 states and territories, 15% are from out of state, 8% African American, 1% Asian American or Pacific Islander, 3% Hispanic American, 0.3% Native American, 0.3% international, 5% transferred in, 70% live on campus. *Retention:* 85% of 2002 full-time freshmen returned.

Freshmen *Admission:* 2,823 applied, 2,097 admitted, 598 enrolled. *Test scores:* SAT verbal scores over 500: 67%; SAT math scores over 500: 66%; ACT scores over 18: 94%; SAT verbal scores over 600: 32%; SAT math scores over 600: 28%; ACT scores over 24: 46%; SAT verbal scores over 700: 6%; SAT math scores over 700: 2%; ACT scores over 30: 6%.

Majors Accounting; American studies; arts management; art teacher education; art therapy; athletic training; biology/biological sciences; business administration and management; chemistry; commercial and advertising art; communication/speech communication and rhetoric; computer and information sciences; creative writing; dramatic/theatre arts; elementary education; English; experimental psychology; finance; fine/studio arts; foreign languages and literatures; French; German; history; human resources management; human services; interdisciplinary studies; international business/trade/commerce; international relations and affairs; management information systems; marketing/marketing management; mathematics; music; music management and merchandising; music performance; music teacher education; nursing (registered nurse training); philosophy; physical education teaching and coaching; physics; political science and government; pre-dentistry studies; pre-law studies; pre-medical studies; pre-veterinary studies; psychology; religious/sacred music; social science teacher education; sociology; Spanish; sport and fitness administration; voice and opera.

Academic Programs *Special study options:* advanced placement credit, double majors, honors programs, independent study, internships, off-campus study, part-time degree program, services for LD students, student-designed majors, study abroad, summer session for credit. *Unusual degree programs:* 3-2 engineering with Washington University in St. Louis; physical therapy, occupational therapy, medical technology, pharmacy with Midwestern University.

Library Staley Library with 199,660 titles, 927 serial subscriptions, 9,017 audiovisual materials, an OPAC, a Web page.

Millikin University (continued)

Computers on Campus 189 computers available on campus for general student use. A campuswide network can be accessed from student residence rooms that provide access to e-mail. Internet access, online (class) registration, at least one staffed computer lab available. Computer purchase or lease plan available.

Student Life *Housing:* on-campus residence required through junior year. *Options:* coed, men-only, women-only, disabled students. Campus housing is university owned, leased by the school and is provided by a third party. Freshman campus housing is guaranteed. *Activities and organizations:* drama/theater group, student-run newspaper, radio station, choral group, University Center Board, Millikin Marketing Association, Panhellenic Council, Interfraternity Council, Residence Hall Association, national fraternities, national sororities. *Campus security:* 24-hour emergency response devices and patrols, late-night transport/escort service, controlled dormitory access. *Student services:* health clinic, personal/psychological counseling.

Athletics Member NCAA. All Division III. *Intercollegiate sports:* baseball M, basketball M/W, cross-country running M/W, football M, golf M/W, soccer M/W, softball W, swimming M/W, tennis M/W, track and field M/W, volleyball W, wrestling M. *Intramural sports:* basketball M/W, bowling M/W, softball M/W, table tennis M/W, tennis M/W, ultimate Frisbee M(c)/W(c), volleyball M/W.

Standardized Tests *Required:* SAT I or ACT (for admission).

Costs (2003–04) *Comprehensive fee:* $25,357 includes full-time tuition ($18,834), mandatory fees ($400), and room and board ($6123). Full-time tuition and fees vary according to course load. Part-time tuition: $554 per credit. *College room only:* $3315. Room and board charges vary according to board plan and housing facility. *Payment plan:* installment. *Waivers:* employees or children of employees.

Financial Aid Of all full-time matriculated undergraduates who enrolled in 2002, 2,208 applied for aid, 1,722 were judged to have need, 1,221 had their need fully met. In 2002, 655 non-need-based awards were made. *Average percent of need met:* 88%. *Average financial aid package:* $16,233. *Average need-based loan:* $3748. *Average need-based gift aid:* $9951. *Average non-need-based aid:* $6535. *Average indebtedness upon graduation:* $17,100. *Financial aid deadline:* 6/1.

Applying *Options:* common application, electronic application, deferred entrance. *Required:* high school transcript, minimum 2.0 GPA, 2 letters of recommendation. *Required for some:* audition for school of music; portfolio review for art program. *Recommended:* interview. *Application deadline:* rolling (freshmen). *Notification:* continuous (freshmen), continuous (transfers).

Admissions Contact Mr. Lin Stoner, Dean of Admission, Millikin University, 1184 West Main Street, Decatur, IL 62522-2084. *Phone:* 217-424-6210. *Toll-free phone:* 800-373-7733. *Fax:* 217-425-4669. *E-mail:* admis@millikin.edu.

MONMOUTH COLLEGE
Monmouth, Illinois

- **Independent** 4-year, founded 1853, affiliated with Presbyterian Church
- **Calendar** semesters
- **Degree** bachelor's
- **Small-town** 80-acre campus with easy access to Peoria
- **Endowment** $48.0 million
- **Coed,** 1,162 undergraduate students, 99% full-time, 52% women, 48% men
- **Moderately difficult** entrance level, 76% of applicants were admitted

Undergraduates 1,155 full-time, 7 part-time. Students come from 20 states and territories, 15 other countries, 7% are from out of state, 3% African American, 0.9% Asian American or Pacific Islander, 2% Hispanic American, 0.2% Native American, 2% international, 7% transferred in, 94% live on campus. *Retention:* 80% of 2002 full-time freshmen returned.

Freshmen *Admission:* 1,480 applied, 1,128 admitted, 357 enrolled. *Average high school GPA:* 3.31. *Test scores:* SAT verbal scores over 500: 72%; SAT math scores over 500: 14%; ACT scores over 18: 96%; SAT verbal scores over 600: 43%; ACT scores over 24: 38%; SAT verbal scores over 700: 14%; ACT scores over 30: 3%.

Faculty *Total:* 111, 62% full-time, 61% with terminal degrees. *Student/faculty ratio:* 14:1.

Majors Accounting; art; biochemistry; biochemistry/biophysics and molecular biology; biological and biomedical sciences related; biology/biological sciences; business administration and management; chemistry; classics and languages, literatures and linguistics; computer science; dramatic/theatre arts; economics; education; elementary education; English; environmental science; French; history; humanities; Latin; liberal arts and sciences/liberal studies; mathematics; modern Greek; modern languages; music; natural sciences; philosophy; physical education teaching and coaching; physics; political science and government; political science and government related; psychology; public relations/image management; religious studies; secondary education; sociology; Spanish; speech and rhetoric.

Academic Programs *Special study options:* advanced placement credit, double majors, honors programs, independent study, internships, off-campus study, part-time degree program, student-designed majors, study abroad. *ROTC:* Army (c). *Unusual degree programs:* 3-2 engineering with Case Western Reserve University, Washington University in St. Louis; nursing with Rush University.

Library Hewes Library with 176,470 titles, 514 serial subscriptions, 3,975 audiovisual materials, an OPAC, a Web page.

Computers on Campus 300 computers available on campus for general student use. A campuswide network can be accessed from student residence rooms and from off campus. Internet access, online (class) registration, at least one staffed computer lab available.

Student Life *Housing:* on-campus residence required through senior year. *Options:* coed, men-only, women-only, disabled students. Campus housing is university owned. *Activities and organizations:* drama/theater group, student-run newspaper, radio and television station, choral group, Student Service Organization, Student Association, M-Club, Greek life, Crimson Masque, national fraternities, national sororities. *Campus security:* 24-hour emergency response devices, late-night transport/escort service, night security. *Student services:* personal/psychological counseling.

Athletics Member NCAA. All Division III. *Intercollegiate sports:* baseball M, basketball M/W, cheerleading M/W, cross-country running M/W, football M, golf M/W, soccer M/W, softball W, swimming M/W, tennis M/W, track and field M/W, volleyball W. *Intramural sports:* archery M/W, badminton M/W, basketball M/W, bowling M/W, football M/W, golf M/W, rock climbing M/W, soccer M/W, softball M/W, table tennis M/W, track and field M/W, ultimate Frisbee M/W, volleyball M/W.

Standardized Tests *Required:* SAT I or ACT (for admission).

Costs (2004–05) *Comprehensive fee:* $24,800 includes full-time tuition ($19,350) and room and board ($5450). Part-time tuition: $810 per semester hour. *Room and board:* Room and board charges vary according to board plan and housing facility. *Payment plan:* installment. *Waivers:* employees or children of employees.

Financial Aid Of all full-time matriculated undergraduates who enrolled in 2003, 1,003 applied for aid, 864 were judged to have need, 353 had their need fully met. In 2003, 139 non-need-based awards were made. *Average percent of need met:* 97%. *Average financial aid package:* $15,432. *Average need-based loan:* $3998. *Average need-based gift aid:* $12,028. *Average non-need-based aid:* $9352. *Average indebtedness upon graduation:* $18,286.

Applying *Options:* common application, electronic application, deferred entrance. *Required:* high school transcript. *Required for some:* essay or personal statement, 2 letters of recommendation. *Recommended:* interview. *Application deadline:* rolling (freshmen), rolling (transfers). *Notification:* continuous (freshmen), continuous (transfers).

Admissions Contact Ms. Christine Johnston, Director of New Student Recruitment, Monmouth College, 700 East Broadway, Monmouth, IL 61462-1998. *Phone:* 309-457-2140. *Toll-free phone:* 800-747-2687. *Fax:* 309-457-2141. *E-mail:* admit@monm.edu.

MOODY BIBLE INSTITUTE
Chicago, Illinois

- **Independent nondenominational** comprehensive, founded 1886
- **Calendar** semesters
- **Degrees** bachelor's, master's, and first professional
- **Urban** 25-acre campus
- **Coed,** 1,431 undergraduate students, 99% full-time, 42% women, 58% men
- **Moderately difficult** entrance level, 50% of applicants were admitted

Undergraduates 1,423 full-time, 8 part-time. Students come from 48 states and territories, 41 other countries, 69% are from out of state, 2% African American, 3% Asian American or Pacific Islander, 5% Hispanic American, 0.3% Native American, 7% international, 90% live on campus. *Retention:* 84% of 2002 full-time freshmen returned.

Freshmen *Admission:* 1,330 applied, 671 admitted. *Average high school GPA:* 3.46. *Test scores:* ACT scores over 18: 97%; ACT scores over 24: 61%; ACT scores over 30: 8%.

Faculty *Total:* 100, 84% full-time, 73% with terminal degrees. *Student/faculty ratio:* 20:1.

Majors Avionics maintenance technology; biblical studies; communication/speech communication and rhetoric; English as a second/foreign language (teaching); linguistics; missionary studies and missiology; pre-theology/pre-ministerial studies; religious education; religious/sacred music.

Academic Programs *Special study options:* adult/continuing education programs, advanced placement credit, distance learning, double majors, English as a second language, external degree program, independent study, internships, off-campus study, part-time degree program, study abroad, summer session for credit.

Library Henry Crowell Learning Center plus 1 other with 135,000 titles, 987 serial subscriptions.

Computers on Campus 26 computers available on campus for general student use. A campuswide network can be accessed from student residence rooms and from off campus. Internet access, at least one staffed computer lab available.

Student Life *Housing:* on-campus residence required through senior year. *Options:* men-only, women-only. Campus housing is university owned. *Activities and organizations:* drama/theater group, student-run newspaper, radio station, choral group, Student Missionary Fellowship, Big Brother/Big Sister, music groups, Drama Group. *Campus security:* 24-hour emergency response devices and patrols, student patrols, late-night transport/escort service, controlled dormitory access. *Student services:* health clinic, personal/psychological counseling.

Athletics Member NCCAA. *Intercollegiate sports:* basketball M/W, soccer M, volleyball M/W. *Intramural sports:* basketball M/W, cross-country running M/W, football M/W, golf M/W, soccer W, volleyball M/W, water polo M/W.

Standardized Tests *Required:* SAT I and SAT II or ACT (for admission).

Costs (2003–04) *Comprehensive fee:* includes mandatory fees ($1401) and room and board ($6340). All students are awarded full-tuition scholarships. *College room only:* $3620.

Financial Aid Of all full-time matriculated undergraduates who enrolled in 2003, 300 applied for aid, 300 were judged to have need. *Average percent of need met:* 25%. *Average need-based loan:* $4000. *Average need-based gift aid:* $750. *Average indebtedness upon graduation:* $3000.

Applying *Options:* early admission, early decision. *Application fee:* $35. *Required:* essay or personal statement, high school transcript, minimum 2.3 GPA, 4 letters of recommendation, Christian testimony. *Required for some:* interview. *Application deadlines:* 3/1 (freshmen), 3/1 (transfers). *Early decision:* 12/1. *Notification:* continuous until 8/1 (freshmen), 1/15 (early decision), continuous until 8/1 (transfers).

Admissions Contact Mrs. Marthe Campa, Application Coordinator, Moody Bible Institute, 820 North LaSalle Boulevard, Chicago, IL 60610. *Phone:* 312-329-4266. *Toll-free phone:* 800-967-4MBI. *Fax:* 312-329-8987. *E-mail:* admissions@moody.edu.

NAES College
Chicago, Illinois

Admissions Contact Ms. Christine Redcloud, Registrar, NAES College, 2838 West Peterson Avenue, Chicago, IL 60659-3813. *Phone:* 773-761-5000. *Fax:* 773-761-3808.

National-Louis University
Chicago, Illinois

- **Independent** university, founded 1886
- **Calendar** quarters
- **Degrees** bachelor's, master's, doctoral, post-master's, and postbachelor's certificates
- **Urban** 12-acre campus
- **Endowment** $15.3 million
- **Coed,** 2,534 undergraduate students, 76% full-time, 73% women, 27% men
- **Minimally difficult** entrance level

Undergraduates 1,919 full-time, 615 part-time. Students come from 18 states and territories, 1% are from out of state, 15% African American, 1% Asian American or Pacific Islander, 5% Hispanic American, 0.1% Native American, 0.1% international, 22% transferred in, 5% live on campus. *Retention:* 100% of 2002 full-time freshmen returned.

Freshmen *Admission:* 67 enrolled.

Faculty *Total:* 284, 100% full-time, 17% with terminal degrees. *Student/faculty ratio:* 16:1.

Majors Accounting; anthropology; art; behavioral sciences; biological and physical sciences; biology/biological sciences; business administration and management; clinical laboratory science/medical technology; computer management; dramatic/theatre arts; elementary education; English; gerontology; health/health care administration; human development and family studies; human services; industrial radiologic technology; information science/studies; international business/trade/commerce; kindergarten/preschool education; liberal arts and sciences/liberal studies; mathematics; psychology; respiratory care therapy; social sciences; substance abuse/addiction counseling.

Academic Programs *Special study options:* academic remediation for entering students, accelerated degree program, adult/continuing education programs, advanced placement credit, English as a second language, external degree program, honors programs, independent study, internships, part-time degree program, services for LD students, summer session for credit.

Library NLU Library plus 5 others with 5,043 audiovisual materials, an OPAC.

Computers on Campus A campuswide network can be accessed from off campus. Internet access, at least one staffed computer lab available.

Student Life *Housing options:* coed. Campus housing is university owned. *Activities and organizations:* drama/theater group, choral group, Student Council, Nosotros Unidos, Accounting club, African-American club. *Campus security:* 24-hour emergency response devices and patrols. *Student services:* health clinic, personal/psychological counseling.

Standardized Tests *Required for some:* SAT I or ACT (for admission).

Costs (2003–04) *Comprehensive fee:* $23,049 includes full-time tuition ($16,200), mandatory fees ($936), and room and board ($5913). Part-time tuition: $360 per quarter hour. *Room and board:* Room and board charges vary according to board plan. *Waivers:* employees or children of employees.

Financial Aid *Average indebtedness upon graduation:* $8840.

Applying *Options:* deferred entrance. *Application fee:* $25. *Required:* high school transcript, minimum 2.0 GPA. *Required for some:* 2 letters of recommendation. *Recommended:* interview. *Application deadline:* rolling (freshmen), rolling (transfers). *Notification:* continuous (freshmen), continuous (transfers).

Admissions Contact Ms. Pat Petillo, Director of Admissions, National-Louis University, 122 South Michigan Avenue, Chicago, IL 60603. *Phone:* 888-NLU-TODAY. *Toll-free phon*[illegible]88-NLU-TODAY (in-state); 800-443-5522 (out-of-state).

North Central College
Naperville, Illinois

- **Independent United Methodist** comprehensive, founded 1861
- **Calendar** trimesters
- **Degrees** bachelor's and master's
- **Suburban** 56-acre campus with easy access to Chicago
- **Endowment** $49.2 million
- **Coed,** 2,086 undergraduate students, 86% full-time, 59% women, 41% men
- **Moderately difficult** entrance level, 71% of applicants were admitted

Undergraduates 1,801 full-time, 285 part-time. Students come from 26 states and territories, 18 other countries, 9% are from out of state, 5% African American, 3% Asian American or Pacific Islander, 4% Hispanic American, 0.1% Native American, 1% international, 9% transferred in, 58% live on campus. *Retention:* 76% of 2002 full-time freshmen returned.

Freshmen *Admission:* 1,654 applied, 1,171 admitted, 408 enrolled. *Average high school GPA:* 3.53. *Test scores:* SAT verbal scores over 500: 84%; SAT math scores over 500: 84%; ACT scores over 18: 99%; SAT verbal scores over 600: 45%; SAT math scores over 600: 47%; ACT scores over 24: 59%; SAT verbal scores over 700: 12%; SAT math scores over 700: 12%; ACT scores over 30: 9%.

Faculty *Total:* 217, 58% full-time, 60% with terminal degrees. *Student/faculty ratio:* 14:1.

Majors Accounting; actuarial science; American history; applied mathematics; art; art teacher education; athletic training; biochemistry; biology/biological sciences; broadcast journalism; business administration and management; chemistry; computer science; dramatic/theatre arts; economics; education; elementary education; English; finance; French; German; history; humanities; international business/trade/commerce; Japanese; jazz/jazz studies; liberal arts and sciences/liberal studies; literature; management information systems; marketing/marketing management; mass communication/media; mathematics; music; natural sciences; philosophy; physical education teaching and coaching; physics; political science and government; pre-dentistry studies; pre-law studies; pre-medical studies; pre-veterinary studies; psychology; religious studies; science teacher education; secondary education; social sciences; sociology; Spanish; speech and rhetoric.

Academic Programs *Special study options:* academic remediation for entering students, accelerated degree program, adult/continuing education programs, advanced placement credit, cooperative education, double majors, English as a second language, honors programs, independent study, internships, off-campus study, part-time degree program, services for LD students, student-designed majors, study abroad, summer session for credit. *ROTC:* Army (c), Air Force (c). *Unusual degree programs:* 3-2 engineering with Washington University in St. Louis; University of Illinois at Urbana-Champaign; Marquette University; University of Minnesota, Twin Cities Campus; medical technology with Rush University.

Library Oesterle Library with 145,707 titles, 707 serial subscriptions, 3,367 audiovisual materials, an OPAC, a Web page.

Computers on Campus 200 computers available on campus for general student use. A campuswide network can be accessed from student residence rooms and from off campus that provide access to software packages. Internet access, online (class) registration, at least one staffed computer lab available. Computer purchase or lease plan available.

North Central College (continued)

Student Life *Housing options:* coed, men-only, women-only. Campus housing is university owned. Freshman applicants given priority for college housing. *Activities and organizations:* drama/theater group, student-run newspaper, radio station, choral group, College Union Activities Board, student radio station, Cards in Action (service group), Black Student Organization, Residence Hall Association. *Campus security:* 24-hour emergency response devices and patrols, late-night transport/escort service. *Student services:* health clinic, personal/psychological counseling.

Athletics Member NCAA. All Division III. *Intercollegiate sports:* baseball M, basketball M/W, cheerleading W, cross-country running M/W, football M, golf M/W, soccer M/W, softball W, swimming M/W, tennis M/W, track and field M/W, volleyball W, wrestling M. *Intramural sports:* badminton M/W, basketball M/W, bowling M/W, cross-country running M/W, football M/W, golf M/W, racquetball M/W, skiing (cross-country) M/W, skiing (downhill) M/W, soccer M/W, softball M/W, swimming M/W, table tennis M/W, tennis M/W, track and field M/W, volleyball M/W.

Standardized Tests *Required:* SAT I or ACT (for admission). *Recommended:* ACT (for admission).

Costs (2003–04) *Comprehensive fee:* $25,656 includes full-time tuition ($19,041), mandatory fees ($240), and room and board ($6375). Part-time tuition: $485 per semester hour. *Required fees:* $60 per year part-time. *Room and board:* Room and board charges vary according to housing facility. *Payment plan:* installment. *Waivers:* senior citizens and employees or children of employees.

Financial Aid Of all full-time matriculated undergraduates who enrolled in 2003, 1,389 applied for aid, 1,197 were judged to have need, 496 had their need fully met. 399 Federal Work-Study jobs (averaging $376). 811 state and other part-time jobs (averaging $2669). In 2003, 347 non-need-based awards were made. *Average percent of need met:* 87%. *Average financial aid package:* $18,212. *Average need-based loan:* $5239. *Average need-based gift aid:* $11,475. *Average non-need-based aid:* $7673. *Average indebtedness upon graduation:* $13,726.

Applying *Options:* common application, early admission, deferred entrance. *Application fee:* $25. *Required:* high school transcript, minimum 2.0 GPA. *Required for some:* interview. *Recommended:* essay or personal statement, 1 letter of recommendation. *Application deadline:* rolling (freshmen), rolling (transfers). *Notification:* continuous (freshmen), continuous (transfers).

Admissions Contact Mr. Michael Brown, Director of Freshman Admission, North Central College, 30 North Brainard Street, PO Box 3063, Naperville, IL 60566-7063. *Phone:* 630-637-5800. *Toll-free phone:* 800-411-1861. *Fax:* 630-637-5819. *E-mail:* ncadm@noctrl.edu.

■ *See page 2096 for a narrative description.*

NORTHEASTERN ILLINOIS UNIVERSITY
Chicago, Illinois

- **State-supported** comprehensive, founded 1961
- **Calendar** semesters
- **Degrees** bachelor's and master's
- **Urban** 67-acre campus
- **Endowment** $1.4 million
- **Coed,** 8,985 undergraduate students, 57% full-time, 63% women, 37% men
- **Minimally difficult** entrance level, 71% of applicants were admitted

Undergraduates 5,077 full-time, 3,908 part-time. Students come from 18 states and territories, 45 other countries, 1% are from out of state, 12% African American, 11% Asian American or Pacific Islander, 29% Hispanic American, 0.2% Native American, 3% international, 12% transferred in. *Retention:* 69% of 2002 full-time freshmen returned.

Freshmen *Admission:* 2,695 applied, 1,905 admitted, 1,120 enrolled. *Average high school GPA:* 2.80. *Test scores:* ACT scores over 18: 53%; ACT scores over 24: 8%; ACT scores over 30: 1%.

Faculty *Total:* 627, 63% full-time, 53% with terminal degrees. *Student/faculty ratio:* 18:1.

Majors Accounting; anthropology; art; bilingual and multilingual education; biology/biological sciences; business administration and management; business/commerce; chemistry; community health services counseling; computer and information sciences; computer science; criminal justice/safety; early childhood education; economics; elementary education; English; environmental studies; finance; French; geography; geology/earth science; history; human resources management; kindergarten/preschool education; liberal arts and sciences/liberal studies; linguistics; marketing/marketing management; mathematics; music; philosophy; physical education teaching and coaching; physics; political science and government; psychology; public administration and social service professions related; social work; sociology; Spanish; special education; speech and rhetoric; urban studies/affairs; women's studies.

Academic Programs *Special study options:* academic remediation for entering students, adult/continuing education programs, advanced placement credit, cooperative education, distance learning, double majors, English as a second language, external degree program, honors programs, independent study, internships, off-campus study, part-time degree program, services for LD students, study abroad, summer session for credit. *ROTC:* Army (c), Air Force (c).

Library Ronald Williams Library with 441,911 titles, 3,421 serial subscriptions, 6,034 audiovisual materials, an OPAC, a Web page.

Computers on Campus 360 computers available on campus for general student use. A campuswide network can be accessed from off campus that provide access to productivity software. Internet access, online (class) registration, at least one staffed computer lab available.

Student Life *Housing:* college housing not available. *Activities and organizations:* drama/theater group, student-run newspaper, radio station, student government, Chimexla, WZRD radio club, business and management club, Black Heritage Gospel Choir, national sororities. *Campus security:* 24-hour emergency response devices and patrols, late-night transport/escort service. *Student services:* health clinic, personal/psychological counseling, women's center.

Athletics *Intramural sports:* badminton M/W, baseball M, basketball M/W, cross-country running M/W, ice hockey M(c), racquetball M/W, soccer M/W, softball M/W, swimming M/W, table tennis M/W, tennis M/W, volleyball M/W, water polo M/W, weight lifting M/W.

Standardized Tests *Required:* ACT (for admission).

Costs (2004–05) *Tuition:* state resident $3720 full-time, $124 per credit hour part-time; nonresident $7440 full-time, $248 per credit hour part-time. Full-time tuition and fees vary according to student level. *Required fees:* $515 full-time.

Financial Aid Of all full-time matriculated undergraduates who enrolled in 2003, 3,442 applied for aid, 2,615 were judged to have need, 439 had their need fully met. 230 Federal Work-Study jobs (averaging $1899). 512 state and other part-time jobs (averaging $1792). In 2003, 134 non-need-based awards were made. *Average percent of need met:* 67%. *Average financial aid package:* $5591. *Average need-based loan:* $2171. *Average need-based gift aid:* $4922. *Average non-need-based aid:* $1415. *Average indebtedness upon graduation:* $10,125.

Applying *Options:* deferred entrance. *Application fee:* $25. *Required:* high school transcript. *Application deadlines:* 7/1 (freshmen), 7/1 (transfers). *Notification:* continuous (transfers).

Admissions Contact Ms. Kay D. Gulli, Administrative Assistant, Northeastern Illinois University, 5500 North St. Louis Avenue, Chicago, IL 60625. *Phone:* 773-442-4000. *Fax:* 773-794-6243. *E-mail:* admrec@neiu.edu.

NORTHERN ILLINOIS UNIVERSITY
De Kalb, Illinois

- **State-supported** university, founded 1895
- **Calendar** semesters
- **Degrees** bachelor's, master's, doctoral, and first professional
- **Small-town** 589-acre campus with easy access to Chicago
- **Endowment** $744,941
- **Coed,** 18,275 undergraduate students, 90% full-time, 53% women, 47% men
- **Moderately difficult** entrance level, 62% of applicants were admitted

Undergraduates 16,398 full-time, 1,877 part-time. Students come from 50 states and territories, 105 other countries, 3% are from out of state, 13% African American, 6% Asian American or Pacific Islander, 6% Hispanic American, 0.2% Native American, 1% international, 12% transferred in, 36% live on campus. *Retention:* 76% of 2002 full-time freshmen returned.

Freshmen *Admission:* 16,128 applied, 10,028 admitted, 3,253 enrolled. *Test scores:* ACT scores over 18: 88%; ACT scores over 24: 34%; ACT scores over 30: 3%.

Faculty *Total:* 1,146, 79% full-time. *Student/faculty ratio:* 17:1.

Majors Accounting; anthropology; apparel and textiles; applied mathematics; art; art history, criticism and conservation; art teacher education; atmospheric sciences and meteorology; biology/biological sciences; business administration and management; business/commerce; chemistry; clinical laboratory science/medical technology; communication disorders; communication/speech communication and rhetoric; computational mathematics; computer science; dramatic/theatre arts; economics; education; electrical, electronics and communications engineering; elementary education; engineering technology; English; family and consumer sciences/home economics teacher education; finance; fine/studio arts; foods, nutrition, and wellness; French; geography; geology/earth science; German; health science; health teacher education; history; human development and family studies; industrial engineering; industrial technology; journalism; kindergarten/preschool education; liberal arts and sciences/liberal studies; management information systems; marketing/marketing management; mathematical statistics and probability; mathematics; mechanical engineering; music; music teacher education; nursing (registered nurse training); operations management; philosophy;

physical education teaching and coaching; physical therapy; physics; political science and government; psychology; public health/community nursing; Russian; sociology; Spanish; special education.

Academic Programs *Special study options:* accelerated degree program, adult/continuing education programs, advanced placement credit, cooperative education, double majors, honors programs, independent study, internships, off-campus study, part-time degree program, services for LD students, student-designed majors, study abroad, summer session for credit. *ROTC:* Army (b), Air Force (c). *Unusual degree programs:* 3-2 engineering with University of Illinois.

Library Founders Memorial Library plus 8 others with 1.7 million titles, 17,000 serial subscriptions, 50,182 audiovisual materials, an OPAC, a Web page.

Computers on Campus 1200 computers available on campus for general student use. A campuswide network can be accessed from student residence rooms and from off campus. At least one staffed computer lab available.

Student Life *Housing:* on-campus residence required for freshman year. *Options:* coed. Campus housing is university owned. Freshman applicants given priority for college housing. *Activities and organizations:* drama/theater group, student-run newspaper, radio station, choral group, marching band, American Marketing Association, Delta Sigma Pi, Pi Sigma Epsilon, Black Choir, Student Volunteer Choir, national fraternities, national sororities. *Campus security:* 24-hour emergency response devices and patrols, student patrols, late-night transport/escort service, controlled dormitory access. *Student services:* health clinic, personal/psychological counseling, women's center, legal services.

Athletics Member NCAA. All Division I except football (Division I-A). *Intercollegiate sports:* baseball M(s), basketball M(s)/W(s), cross-country running W, golf M(s)/W(s), gymnastics W(s), soccer M(s)/W(s), softball W(s), swimming M(s)/W(s), tennis M(s)/W(s), volleyball W(s), wrestling M(s). *Intramural sports:* archery M(c)/W(c), badminton M/W, basketball M/W, bowling M(c)/W(c), cross-country running W, football M/W, golf M/W, ice hockey M(c)/W(c), lacrosse M(c)/W(c), racquetball M/W, rugby M(c)/W(c), skiing (downhill) M(c)/W(c), soccer M/W, softball M/W, table tennis M/W, tennis M/W, track and field M(c)/W(c), volleyball M/W, water polo M(c)/W(c), weight lifting M(c)/W(c).

Standardized Tests *Required:* SAT I or ACT (for admission).

Costs (2003–04) *Tuition:* state resident $3903 full-time; nonresident $7815 full-time. Full-time tuition and fees vary according to course load. Part-time tuition and fees vary according to course load. *Required fees:* $1261 full-time. *Room and board:* $5360. Room and board charges vary according to board plan and housing facility. *Payment plan:* installment. *Waivers:* minority students and employees or children of employees.

Financial Aid Of all full-time matriculated undergraduates who enrolled in 2002, 11,236 applied for aid, 7,570 were judged to have need, 4,635 had their need fully met. In 2002, 1143 non-need-based awards were made. *Average percent of need met:* 82%. *Average financial aid package:* $8948. *Average need-based loan:* $3478. *Average need-based gift aid:* $5839. *Average non-need-based aid:* $3200.

Applying *Options:* electronic application. *Required:* high school transcript, high school rank. *Application deadlines:* 8/1 (freshmen), 8/1 (transfers). *Notification:* continuous (freshmen), continuous (transfers).

Admissions Contact Dr. Robert Burk, Director of Admissions, Northern Illinois University, De Kalb, IL 60115-2854. *Phone:* 815-753-0446. *Toll-free phone:* 800-892-3050. *E-mail:* admission-info@niu.edu.

NORTH PARK UNIVERSITY
Chicago, Illinois

- **Independent** comprehensive, founded 1891, affiliated with Evangelical Covenant Church
- **Calendar** semesters
- **Degrees** bachelor's, master's, doctoral, and first professional
- **Urban** 30-acre campus
- **Endowment** $36.4 million
- **Coed,** 1,573 undergraduate students, 80% full-time, 62% women, 38% men
- **Moderately difficult** entrance level, 74% of applicants were admitted

North Park blends two traditions—faith and freedom—and two rich environments—the small, residential University and the vibrant city of Chicago. North Park offers broad exposure to the liberal arts and specific education in a profession. Faculty members are superbly credentialed and devoted to teaching. North Park's Chicago location means unparalleled educational, cultural, recreational, spiritual, and artistic opportunities. Several hundred internships are available in every imaginable vocation. North Park's Outreach Ministries program has served as a national prototype for urban collegiate service opportunities. An outstanding honors program includes generous scholarships, special courses, study abroad, and opportunities for mentoring by and research with faculty.

Undergraduates 1,252 full-time, 321 part-time. Students come from 38 states and territories, 32 other countries, 39% are from out of state, 12% African American, 5% Asian American or Pacific Islander, 10% Hispanic American, 0.4% Native American, 5% international, 12% transferred in. *Retention:* 70% of 2002 full-time freshmen returned.

Freshmen *Admission:* 1,068 applied, 791 admitted, 320 enrolled. *Test scores:* SAT verbal scores over 500: 82%; SAT math scores over 500: 80%; ACT scores over 18: 89%; SAT verbal scores over 600: 46%; SAT math scores over 600: 38%; ACT scores over 24: 42%; SAT verbal scores over 700: 11%; SAT math scores over 700: 9%; ACT scores over 30: 9%.

Faculty *Total:* 121, 73% full-time, 64% with terminal degrees. *Student/faculty ratio:* 16:1.

Majors Accounting; anthropology; art; art teacher education; athletic training; biblical studies; biological and physical sciences; biology/biological sciences; business administration and management; chemistry; clinical laboratory science/medical technology; community organization and advocacy; divinity/ministry; dramatic/theatre arts; economics; education; elementary education; English; finance; fine/studio arts; French; history; international business/trade/commerce; international relations and affairs; kindergarten/preschool education; kinesiology and exercise science; literature; marketing/marketing management; mass communication/media; mathematics; modern languages; music; music management and merchandising; music teacher education; natural sciences; nursing (registered nurse training); philosophy; physical education teaching and coaching; physics; political science and government; pre-dentistry studies; pre-law studies; pre-medical studies; pre-veterinary studies; psychology; religious/sacred music; religious studies; Scandinavian languages; secondary education; social sciences; sociology; Spanish; speech and rhetoric; theology; urban studies/affairs; voice and opera.

Academic Programs *Special study options:* academic remediation for entering students, accelerated degree program, adult/continuing education programs, advanced placement credit, English as a second language, freshman honors college, honors programs, internships, off-campus study, part-time degree program, student-designed majors, study abroad, summer session for credit. *Unusual degree programs:* 3-2 engineering with University of Illinois at Urbana–Champaign, Case Western Reserve University, Washington University in St. Louis, University of Minnesota, Twin Cities Campus; physical therapy.

Library Consolidated Library plus 4 others with 260,685 titles, 1,178 serial subscriptions, an OPAC, a Web page.

Computers on Campus 105 computers available on campus for general student use. A campuswide network can be accessed from student residence rooms and from off campus. At least one staffed computer lab available.

Student Life *Housing:* on-campus residence required through junior year. *Options:* men-only, women-only. *Activities and organizations:* drama/theater group, student-run newspaper, choral group, Student Association, Urban Outreach, College Life, College Music. *Campus security:* 24-hour emergency response devices and patrols, late-night transport/escort service. *Student services:* health clinic, personal/psychological counseling.

Athletics Member NCAA. All Division III. *Intercollegiate sports:* baseball M, basketball M/W, cross-country running M/W, football M, golf M, soccer M/W, softball W, tennis W, track and field M/W, volleyball M/W. *Intramural sports:* basketball M/W, football M/W, golf M/W, volleyball M/W.

Standardized Tests *Required:* SAT I or ACT (for admission).

Costs (2004–05) *Comprehensive fee:* $26,860 includes full-time tuition ($20,350) and room and board ($6510). Full-time tuition and fees vary according to program. Part-time tuition and fees vary according to program. *Room and board:* Room and board charges vary according to board plan, housing facility, and student level. *Payment plan:* installment. *Waivers:* adult students and employees or children of employees.

Financial Aid *Average indebtedness upon graduation:* $15,814.

Applying *Options:* early admission. *Application fee:* $20. *Required:* essay or personal statement, high school transcript, minimum 2.0 GPA, 2 letters of recommendation. *Required for some:* interview. *Recommended:* minimum 3.0 GPA. *Application deadline:* rolling (freshmen), rolling (transfers). *Notification:* continuous (freshmen), continuous (transfers).

Admissions Contact Office of Admissions, North Park University, 3225 West Foster Avenue, Chicago, IL 60625-4895. *Phone:* 773-244-5500. *Toll-free phone:* 800-888-NPC8. *Fax:* 773-583-0858. *E-mail:* afao@northpark.edu.

■ *See page 2104 for a narrative description.*

NORTHWESTERN UNIVERSITY
Evanston, Illinois

- **Independent** university, founded 1851
- **Calendar** quarters
- **Degrees** certificates, bachelor's, master's, doctoral, first professional, and post-master's certificates
- **Suburban** 250-acre campus with easy access to Chicago
- **Endowment** $3.1 billion

Northwestern University (continued)

- **Coed,** 8,001 undergraduate students, 97% full-time, 53% women, 47% men
- **Most difficult** entrance level, 33% of applicants were admitted

Undergraduates 7,797 full-time, 204 part-time. Students come from 51 states and territories, 51 other countries, 75% are from out of state, 5% African American, 17% Asian American or Pacific Islander, 5% Hispanic American, 0.2% Native American, 5% international, 2% transferred in, 65% live on campus. *Retention:* 97% of 2002 full-time freshmen returned.

Freshmen *Admission:* 14,137 applied, 4,702 admitted, 1,941 enrolled. *Test scores:* SAT verbal scores over 500: 98%; SAT math scores over 500: 99%; ACT scores over 18: 99%; SAT verbal scores over 600: 90%; SAT math scores over 600: 93%; ACT scores over 24: 95%; SAT verbal scores over 700: 50%; SAT math scores over 700: 56%; ACT scores over 30: 70%.

Faculty *Total:* 1,078, 83% full-time, 100% with terminal degrees. *Student/faculty ratio:* 7:1.

Majors African-American/Black studies; African studies; American studies; anthropology; applied mathematics; area studies related; art; art history, criticism and conservation; Asian studies; astronomy; audiology and hearing sciences; audiology and speech-language pathology; biochemistry; biological and physical sciences; biology/biological sciences; biomedical/medical engineering; Caribbean studies; cell biology and histology; chemical engineering; chemistry; civil engineering; classics and languages, literatures and linguistics; cognitive psychology and psycholinguistics; communication and media related; communication disorders; communication/speech communication and rhetoric; community organization and advocacy; community psychology; comparative literature; computer and information sciences; computer engineering; computer science; counseling psychology; dance; dramatic/theatre arts; East Asian languages related; ecology; economics; education; electrical, electronics and communications engineering; engineering; engineering related; engineering science; English; environmental/environmental health engineering; environmental science; environmental studies; film/cinema studies; French; general studies; geography; geology/earth science; German; history; humanities; industrial engineering; information science/studies; interdisciplinary studies; international relations and affairs; Italian; jazz/jazz studies; journalism; legal studies; liberal arts and sciences/liberal studies; linguistics; manufacturing engineering; materials engineering; materials science; mathematics; mathematics teacher education; mechanical engineering; molecular biology; multi-/interdisciplinary studies related; music; music history, literature, and theory; musicology and ethnomusicology; music performance; music related; music teacher education; music theory and composition; neuroscience; organizational behavior; philosophy; physics; piano and organ; political science and government; pre-medical studies; psychology; public policy analysis; radio and television; religious studies; science, technology and society; secondary education; Slavic languages; Slavic studies; social and philosophical foundations of education; social sciences related; sociology; South Asian languages; Spanish; special education (specific learning disabilities); speech and rhetoric; speech-language pathology; speech therapy; statistics; theatre literature, history and criticism; urban studies/affairs; violin, viola, guitar and other stringed instruments; visual and performing arts; voice and opera; wind/percussion instruments; women's studies.

Academic Programs *Special study options:* accelerated degree program, adult/continuing education programs, advanced placement credit, cooperative education, double majors, honors programs, independent study, internships, part-time degree program, services for LD students, student-designed majors, study abroad, summer session for credit. *ROTC:* Army (c), Navy (b), Air Force (c).

Library University Library plus 6 others with 4.2 million titles, 39,423 serial subscriptions, 72,837 audiovisual materials, an OPAC, a Web page.

Computers on Campus 608 computers available on campus for general student use. A campuswide network can be accessed from student residence rooms and from off campus. Internet access, online (class) registration, at least one staffed computer lab available. Computer purchase or lease plan available.

Student Life *Housing options:* coed, men-only, women-only. Campus housing is university owned. Freshman campus housing is guaranteed. *Activities and organizations:* drama/theater group, student-run newspaper, radio and television station, choral group, marching band, Associated Student Government, Asian Christian Ministry, Activities and Organization Board, Dance Marathon, Arts Alliance, national fraternities, national sororities. *Campus security:* 24-hour emergency response devices and patrols, late-night transport/escort service, controlled dormitory access. *Student services:* health clinic, personal/psychological counseling, women's center.

Athletics Member NCAA. All Division I except football (Division I-A). *Intercollegiate sports:* baseball M(s), basketball M(s)/W(s), cheerleading M/W, cross-country running W(s), fencing W(s), field hockey W(s), golf M(s)/W(s), lacrosse W(s), soccer M(s)/W(s), softball W(s), swimming M(s)/W(s), tennis M(s)/W(s), volleyball W(s), wrestling M(s). *Intramural sports:* baseball M(c), basketball M(c)/W(c), crew M(c)/W(c), cross-country running M(c)/W(c), equestrian sports M(c)/W(c), fencing M(c), football M/W, ice hockey M(c)/W(c), lacrosse M(c)/W(c), rugby M(c)/W(c), sailing M(c)/W(c), skiing (downhill) M(c)/W(c), soccer M(c)/W(c), softball M/W, squash M(c)/W(c), swimming M(c)/W(c), table tennis M/W, tennis M/W, ultimate Frisbee M(c)/W(c), volleyball M(c)/W(c), water polo M(c)/W(c).

Standardized Tests *Required:* SAT I or ACT (for admission). *Required for some:* SAT II: Subject Tests (for admission), SAT II: Writing Test (for admission). *Recommended:* SAT II: Subject Tests (for admission), SAT II: Writing Test (for admission).

Costs (2004–05) *Comprehensive fee:* $39,478 includes full-time tuition ($29,940), mandatory fees ($145), and room and board ($9393). Part-time tuition: $3552 per course. *College room only:* $5398. Room and board charges vary according to board plan and housing facility. *Payment plan:* installment. *Waivers:* employees or children of employees.

Financial Aid Of all full-time matriculated undergraduates who enrolled in 2003, 3,890 applied for aid, 3,423 were judged to have need, 3,423 had their need fully met. 1,690 Federal Work-Study jobs (averaging $1715). 1,162 state and other part-time jobs (averaging $2500). In 2003, 29 non-need-based awards were made. *Average percent of need met:* 100%. *Average financial aid package:* $24,508. *Average need-based loan:* $3876. *Average need-based gift aid:* $18,857. *Average non-need-based aid:* $4793. *Average indebtedness upon graduation:* $15,136.

Applying *Options:* electronic application, early admission, early decision, deferred entrance. *Application fee:* $65. *Required:* essay or personal statement, high school transcript, 1 letter of recommendation. *Required for some:* audition for music program. *Application deadlines:* 1/1 (freshmen), 6/1 (transfers). *Early decision:* 11/1. *Notification:* 4/15 (freshmen), 12/15 (early decision), continuous until 7/1 (transfers).

Admissions Contact Ms. Carol Lunkenheimer, Dean of Undergraduate Admission, Northwestern University, PO Box 3060, Evanston, IL 60204-3060. *Phone:* 847-491-7271. *E-mail:* ug-admission@northwestern.edu.

Olivet Nazarene University

Bourbonnais, Illinois

- **Independent** comprehensive, founded 1907, affiliated with Church of the Nazarene
- **Calendar** semesters
- **Degrees** associate, bachelor's, and master's
- **Small-town** 200-acre campus with easy access to Chicago
- **Endowment** $12.9 million
- **Coed,** 2,427 undergraduate students, 87% full-time, 59% women, 41% men
- **Minimally difficult** entrance level, 78% of applicants were admitted

Undergraduates 2,122 full-time, 305 part-time. Students come from 41 states and territories, 15 other countries, 51% are from out of state, 8% African American, 1% Asian American or Pacific Islander, 3% Hispanic American, 0.2% Native American, 1% international, 8% transferred in, 79% live on campus. *Retention:* 74% of 2002 full-time freshmen returned.

Freshmen *Admission:* 1,902 applied, 1,493 admitted, 594 enrolled. *Test scores:* ACT scores over 18: 86%; ACT scores over 24: 43%; ACT scores over 30: 9%.

Faculty *Total:* 123, 70% full-time. *Student/faculty ratio:* 21:1.

Majors Accounting; art; art teacher education; athletic training; biblical studies; biochemistry; biological and physical sciences; biology/biological sciences; broadcast journalism; business administration and management; business/managerial economics; chemistry; child development; clinical laboratory science/medical technology; clothing/textiles; commercial and advertising art; computer science; criminal justice/law enforcement administration; developmental and child psychology; dietetics; economics; education; elementary education; engineering; English; environmental studies; family and community services; family and consumer sciences/home economics teacher education; family and consumer sciences/human sciences; fashion merchandising; film/cinema studies; finance; food science; geology/earth science; history; human resources management; information science/studies; interdisciplinary studies; journalism; kindergarten/preschool education; kinesiology and exercise science; liberal arts and sciences/liberal studies; literature; marketing/marketing management; mass communication/media; mathematics; modern languages; music; music teacher education; natural sciences; nursing (registered nurse training); pastoral studies/counseling; philosophy; physical education teaching and coaching; physical sciences; piano and organ; pre-dentistry studies; pre-law studies; pre-medical studies; pre-veterinary studies; psychology; radio and television; religious education; religious/sacred music; religious studies; Romance languages; science teacher education; secondary education; social sciences; Spanish; speech and rhetoric; sport and fitness administration; theology; violin, viola, guitar and other stringed instruments; voice and opera; wind/percussion instruments; zoology/animal biology.

Academic Programs *Special study options:* academic remediation for entering students, adult/continuing education programs, advanced placement credit, double majors, independent study, internships, part-time degree program, study abroad, summer session for credit. *ROTC:* Army (b).

Library Benner Library with 160,039 titles, 925 serial subscriptions, 6,818 audiovisual materials, an OPAC, a Web page.

Computers on Campus 339 computers available on campus for general student use. A campuswide network can be accessed from student residence rooms and from off campus. Internet access, online (class) registration, at least one staffed computer lab available. Computer purchase or lease plan available.

Student Life *Housing:* on-campus residence required through senior year. *Options:* men-only, women-only. Campus housing is university owned. Freshman campus housing is guaranteed. *Activities and organizations:* drama/theater group, student-run newspaper, radio station, choral group, Fellowship of Christian Athletes, C.A.U.S.E. College and University Serving and Enabling, Diakonia, Student Education Association, Women's Residence Association. *Campus security:* 24-hour patrols, late-night transport/escort service. *Student services:* health clinic, personal/psychological counseling.

Athletics Member NAIA, NCCAA. *Intercollegiate sports:* baseball M(s), basketball M(s)/W(s), cheerleading M(s)/W(s), cross-country running M(s)/W(s), football M(s), golf M(s), soccer M(s)/W(s), softball W(s), tennis M(s)/W(s), track and field M(s)/W(s), volleyball W(s). *Intramural sports:* baseball M, basketball M/W, football M/W, golf M/W, racquetball M/W, soccer M/W, softball M/W, table tennis M/W, tennis M/W, track and field M/W, volleyball M/W.

Standardized Tests *Required:* ACT (for admission).

Costs (2004–05) *Comprehensive fee:* $21,540 includes full-time tuition ($14,900), mandatory fees ($840), and room and board ($5800). Full-time tuition and fees vary according to course load. Part-time tuition: $621 per hour. Part-time tuition and fees vary according to course load. *Required fees:* $10 per term part-time. *College room only:* $2900. Room and board charges vary according to board plan. *Payment plan:* installment. *Waivers:* employees or children of employees.

Financial Aid Of all full-time matriculated undergraduates who enrolled in 2003, 1,667 applied for aid, 1,469 were judged to have need, 625 had their need fully met. 297 Federal Work-Study jobs (averaging $918). 625 state and other part-time jobs (averaging $829). In 2003, 525 non-need-based awards were made. *Average percent of need met:* 76%. *Average financial aid package:* $11,634. *Average need-based loan:* $4203. *Average need-based gift aid:* $4915. *Average non-need-based aid:* $6647. *Average indebtedness upon graduation:* $17,103.

Applying *Options:* electronic application, deferred entrance. *Required:* high school transcript, minimum 2.0 GPA, 2 letters of recommendation. *Recommended:* essay or personal statement, interview. *Application deadline:* rolling (freshmen), rolling (transfers). *Notification:* continuous (freshmen), continuous (transfers).

Admissions Contact Ms. Mary Cary, Applicant Coordinator, Olivet Nazarene University, One University Avenue, Bourbonnais, IL 60914. *Phone:* 800-648-1463 Ext. 5200. *Toll-free phone:* 800-648-1463. *Fax:* 815-935-4998. *E-mail:* admissions@olivet.edu.

■ *See page 2134 for a narrative description.*

PRINCIPIA COLLEGE
Elsah, Illinois

- **Independent Christian Science** 4-year, founded 1910
- **Calendar** quarters
- **Degree** bachelor's
- **Rural** 2600-acre campus with easy access to St. Louis
- **Endowment** $398.3 million
- **Coed,** 552 undergraduate students, 99% full-time, 55% women, 45% men
- **Moderately difficult** entrance level, 85% of applicants were admitted

Undergraduates 545 full-time, 7 part-time. Students come from 37 states and territories, 28 other countries, 91% are from out of state, 0.2% African American, 0.7% Asian American or Pacific Islander, 1% Hispanic American, 0.2% Native American, 12% international, 3% transferred in, 100% live on campus. *Retention:* 92% of 2002 full-time freshmen returned.

Freshmen *Admission:* 247 applied, 211 admitted, 147 enrolled. *Average high school GPA:* 3.32. *Test scores:* SAT verbal scores over 500: 80%; SAT math scores over 500: 86%; ACT scores over 18: 100%; SAT verbal scores over 600: 49%; SAT math scores over 600: 44%; ACT scores over 24: 63%; SAT verbal scores over 700: 13%; SAT math scores over 700: 14%; ACT scores over 30: 12%.

Faculty *Total:* 66, 73% full-time, 70% with terminal degrees. *Student/faculty ratio:* 9:1.

Majors Anthropology; art history, criticism and conservation; biology/biological sciences; business administration and management; chemistry; computer and information sciences; dramatic/theatre arts; economics; elementary education; engineering related; English; environmental studies; fine/studio arts; foreign languages and literatures; French; German; history; humanities; mass communication/media; mathematics; music; philosophy; physics; political science and government; religious studies; sociology; Spanish; sport and fitness administration.

Academic Programs *Special study options:* accelerated degree program, advanced placement credit, double majors, English as a second language, honors programs, independent study, internships, student-designed majors, study abroad. *Unusual degree programs:* 3-2 engineering with Washington University in St. Louis, Southern Illinois University at Edwardsville, University of Southern California.

Library Marshall Brooks Library plus 1 other with 208,197 titles, 10,547 serial subscriptions, 7,273 audiovisual materials, an OPAC, a Web page.

Computers on Campus 180 computers available on campus for general student use. A campuswide network can be accessed from student residence rooms and from off campus. Internet access, at least one staffed computer lab available.

Student Life *Housing:* on-campus residence required through senior year. *Options:* men-only, women-only. Campus housing is university owned. Freshman campus housing is guaranteed. *Activities and organizations:* drama/theater group, student-run newspaper, radio and television station, choral group, Christian Science Organization, student newspaper, International Students Association, student radio station, student government. *Campus security:* 24-hour patrols. *Student services:* health clinic.

Athletics Member NCAA. All Division III. *Intercollegiate sports:* baseball M, basketball M/W, cross-country running M/W, football M, golf M, soccer M/W, swimming M/W, tennis M/W, track and field M/W, volleyball W. *Intramural sports:* basketball M/W, rugby M(c), soccer M/W, softball M/W.

Standardized Tests *Required:* SAT I or ACT (for admission).

Costs (2004–05) *Comprehensive fee:* $26,286 includes full-time tuition ($19,185), mandatory fees ($270), and room and board ($6831). Part-time tuition: $426 per quarter hour. *College room only:* $3315. *Payment plan:* installment. *Waivers:* employees or children of employees.

Financial Aid Of all full-time matriculated undergraduates who enrolled in 2002, 441 applied for aid, 316 were judged to have need, 300 had their need fully met. 181 state and other part-time jobs (averaging $1154). In 2002, 93 non-need-based awards were made. *Average percent of need met:* 95%. *Average financial aid package:* $16,787. *Average need-based loan:* $3335. *Average need-based gift aid:* $10,739. *Average non-need-based aid:* $13,092. *Average indebtedness upon graduation:* $11,314. *Financial aid deadline:* 3/1.

Applying *Options:* deferred entrance. *Application fee:* $40. *Required:* essay or personal statement, high school transcript, minimum 2.0 GPA, 4 letters of recommendation, Christian Science commitment. *Required for some:* interview. *Recommended:* interview. *Application deadlines:* 3/1 (freshmen), 3/1 (transfers). *Notification:* continuous (freshmen), continuous (transfers).

Admissions Contact Mrs. Martha Green Quirk, Dean of Admissions, Principia College, One Maybeck Place, Elsah, IL 62028. *Phone:* 618-374-5180. *Toll-free phone:* 800-277-4648 Ext. 2802. *Fax:* 618-374-4000. *E-mail:* collegeadmissions@prin.edu.

QUINCY UNIVERSITY
Quincy, Illinois

- **Independent Roman Catholic** comprehensive, founded 1860
- **Calendar** semesters
- **Degrees** associate, bachelor's, and master's
- **Small-town** 75-acre campus
- **Coed,** 1,130 undergraduate students, 86% full-time, 55% women, 45% men
- **Moderately difficult** entrance level, 94% of applicants were admitted

Undergraduates 970 full-time, 160 part-time. Students come from 22 states and territories, 5 other countries, 26% are from out of state, 6% African American, 0.2% Asian American or Pacific Islander, 3% Hispanic American, 0.3% Native American, 0.7% international, 11% transferred in, 77% live on campus. *Retention:* 71% of 2002 full-time freshmen returned.

Freshmen *Admission:* 1,056 applied, 988 admitted, 222 enrolled. *Average high school GPA:* 3.1. *Test scores:* SAT verbal scores over 500: 53%; SAT math scores over 500: 53%; ACT scores over 18: 87%; SAT verbal scores over 600: 13%; SAT math scores over 600: 20%; ACT scores over 24: 27%; ACT scores over 30: 1%.

Faculty *Total:* 115, 42% full-time, 50% with terminal degrees. *Student/faculty ratio:* 15:1.

Majors Accounting; airline pilot and flight crew; arts management; aviation/airway management; biology/biological sciences; business administration and management; chemistry; clinical laboratory science/medical technology; communication/speech communication and rhetoric; computer and information sciences; computer science; criminal justice/safety; elementary education; English; finance; graphic design; history; humanities; information science/studies; journalism; marketing/marketing management; music; music teacher education; nursing (registered nurse training); philosophy; physical education teaching and coaching; political science and government; pre-dentistry studies; pre-medical studies;

Quincy University (continued)
pre-veterinary studies; psychology; public administration and social service professions related; public relations/image management; radio and television; social work; special education; sport and fitness administration; theological and ministerial studies related; theology; visual and performing arts.

Academic Programs *Special study options:* academic remediation for entering students, accelerated degree program, adult/continuing education programs, advanced placement credit, distance learning, double majors, English as a second language, honors programs, independent study, internships, part-time degree program, student-designed majors, study abroad, summer session for credit. *Unusual degree programs:* 3-2 engineering with Washington University in St. Louis.

Library Brenner Library with 239,368 titles, 814 serial subscriptions, 5,640 audiovisual materials, an OPAC, a Web page.

Computers on Campus 200 computers available on campus for general student use. A campuswide network can be accessed from student residence rooms and from off campus. Internet access, online (class) registration, at least one staffed computer lab available.

Student Life *Housing:* on-campus residence required through sophomore year. *Options:* coed, men-only, women-only. Campus housing is university owned. Freshman campus housing is guaranteed. *Activities and organizations:* drama/theater group, student-run newspaper, radio station, choral group, Student Senate, campus ministry, Student Programming Board, BACCHUS, Students in Free Enterprise, national fraternities, national sororities. *Campus security:* 24-hour emergency response devices and patrols, student patrols, late-night transport/escort service, controlled dormitory access. *Student services:* health clinic, personal/psychological counseling.

Athletics Member NCAA. All Division II. *Intercollegiate sports:* baseball M(s), basketball M(s)/W(s), golf M(s)/W(s), soccer M(s)/W(s), softball W(s), tennis M(s)/W(s), volleyball M(s)/W(s). *Intramural sports:* badminton M/W, baseball M, basketball M/W, bowling M/W, football M/W, golf M, soccer M/W, softball M/W, tennis M/W, volleyball M/W.

Standardized Tests *Required:* SAT I or ACT (for admission).

Costs (2003–04) *Comprehensive fee:* $23,585 includes full-time tuition ($16,400), mandatory fees ($450), and room and board ($6735). Part-time tuition: $460 per credit hour. No tuition increase for student's term of enrollment. *College room only:* $3265. Room and board charges vary according to board plan and housing facility. *Payment plan:* installment. *Waivers:* senior citizens and employees or children of employees.

Financial Aid Of all full-time matriculated undergraduates who enrolled in 2003, 821 applied for aid, 707 were judged to have need, 187 had their need fully met. 569 Federal Work-Study jobs (averaging $1500). 35 state and other part-time jobs (averaging $3000). In 2003, 202 non-need-based awards were made. *Average percent of need met:* 85%. *Average financial aid package:* $14,835. *Average need-based loan:* $4373. *Average need-based gift aid:* $9365. *Average non-need-based aid:* $3867. *Average indebtedness upon graduation:* $16,134.

Applying *Options:* common application, electronic application, early admission, deferred entrance. *Application fee:* $25. *Required:* high school transcript. *Recommended:* minimum 2.0 GPA, interview. *Application deadline:* rolling (freshmen), rolling (transfers). *Notification:* continuous (freshmen), continuous (transfers).

Admissions Contact Mr. Kevin A. Brown, Director of Admissions, Quincy University, 1800 College Avenue, Quincy, IL 62301-2699. *Phone:* 217-222-8020 Ext. 5215. *Toll-free phone:* 800-688-4295. *E-mail:* admissions@quincy.edu.

■ *See page 2206 for a narrative description.*

ROBERT MORRIS COLLEGE
Chicago, Illinois

- **Independent** 4-year, founded 1913
- **Calendar** 5 ten-week academic sessions per year
- **Degrees** certificates, diplomas, associate, and bachelor's
- **Urban** campus
- **Endowment** $23.8 million
- **Coed,** 5,139 undergraduate students, 91% full-time, 68% women, 32% men
- **Minimally difficult** entrance level, 76% of applicants were admitted

Undergraduates 4,688 full-time, 451 part-time. Students come from 17 other countries, 1% are from out of state, 41% African American, 3% Asian American or Pacific Islander, 23% Hispanic American, 0.3% Native American, 0.6% international, 19% transferred in. *Retention:* 63% of 2002 full-time freshmen returned.

Freshmen *Admission:* 3,043 applied, 2,310 admitted, 1,011 enrolled. *Average high school GPA:* 2.59.

Faculty *Total:* 365, 34% full-time, 24% with terminal degrees. *Student/faculty ratio:* 21:1.

Majors Accounting technology and bookkeeping; administrative assistant and secretarial science; business administration and management; commercial and advertising art; computer programming (specific applications); computer systems networking and telecommunications; culinary arts; design and applied arts related; executive assistant/executive secretary; health and physical education; information technology; interior design; intermedia/multimedia; legal administrative assistant/secretary; legal assistant/paralegal; management information systems; medical/clinical assistant; tourism and travel services management; web page, digital/multimedia and information resources design.

Academic Programs *Special study options:* academic remediation for entering students, accelerated degree program, adult/continuing education programs, advanced placement credit, cooperative education, distance learning, honors programs, internships, part-time degree program, study abroad, summer session for credit.

Library Thomas Jefferson Library plus 4 others with 101,130 titles, 709 serial subscriptions, 9,800 audiovisual materials, an OPAC, a Web page.

Computers on Campus 1884 computers available on campus for general student use. A campuswide network can be accessed. Internet access, at least one staffed computer lab available.

Student Life *Housing:* college housing not available. *Activities and organizations:* drama/theater group, student-run newspaper, choral group, Fitness in Transition, Sigma Beta Delta (honor society), Eagle (newspaper), National Phlebotomy, Association for Medical Assistants. *Campus security:* 24-hour emergency response devices and patrols. *Student services:* personal/psychological counseling.

Athletics Member NAIA. *Intercollegiate sports:* baseball M(s), basketball M(s)/W(s), cross-country running M(s)/W(s), golf M(s)/W(s), ice hockey M(s)/W(s), soccer M(s)/W(s), softball W(s), tennis W(s), volleyball W(s). *Intramural sports:* basketball M(c)/W(c), ice hockey M(c)/W(c), soccer M(c)/W(c).

Costs (2004–05) *Tuition:* $14,250 full-time, $1580 per course part-time. *Payment plan:* installment. *Waivers:* employees or children of employees.

Financial Aid Of all full-time matriculated undergraduates who enrolled in 2003, 4,473 applied for aid, 4,351 were judged to have need, 161 had their need fully met. 290 Federal Work-Study jobs (averaging $635). In 2003, 121 non-need-based awards were made. *Average percent of need met:* 54%. *Average financial aid package:* $10,605. *Average need-based loan:* $3340. *Average need-based gift aid:* $8069. *Average non-need-based aid:* $7631. *Average indebtedness upon graduation:* $12,857.

Applying *Options:* common application, electronic application, deferred entrance. *Application fee:* $20. *Required:* high school transcript, minimum 2.0 GPA, interview. *Application deadline:* rolling (freshmen), rolling (transfers). *Notification:* continuous (freshmen), continuous (transfers).

Admissions Contact Admissions Information Office, Robert Morris College, 401 South State Street, Chicago, IL 60605. *Phone:* 312-935-6835. *Toll-free phone:* 800-225-1520. *Fax:* 312-935-6819. *E-mail:* enroll@robertmorris.edu.

■ *See page 2242 for a narrative description.*

ROCKFORD COLLEGE
Rockford, Illinois

- **Independent** comprehensive, founded 1847
- **Calendar** semesters
- **Degrees** bachelor's and master's
- **Suburban** 130-acre campus with easy access to Chicago
- **Endowment** $13.6 million
- **Coed,** 976 undergraduate students, 79% full-time, 63% women, 38% men
- **Moderately difficult** entrance level, 59% of applicants were admitted

Undergraduates 774 full-time, 202 part-time. Students come from 8 states and territories, 10 other countries, 4% are from out of state, 14% transferred in, 36% live on campus. *Retention:* 55% of 2002 full-time freshmen returned.

Freshmen *Admission:* 654 applied, 384 admitted, 131 enrolled. *Average high school GPA:* 3.03. *Test scores:* SAT verbal scores over 500: 60%; SAT math scores over 500: 63%; ACT scores over 18: 80%; SAT verbal scores over 600: 28%; SAT math scores over 600: 23%; ACT scores over 24: 33%; SAT verbal scores over 700: 14%; SAT math scores over 700: 5%; ACT scores over 30: 5%.

Faculty *Total:* 162, 46% full-time, 43% with terminal degrees. *Student/faculty ratio:* 10:1.

Majors Accounting; anthropology; art; art history, criticism and conservation; art teacher education; biochemistry; biological and physical sciences; biology/biological sciences; business administration and management; business/managerial economics; chemistry; classics and languages, literatures and linguistics; computer science; criminal justice/law enforcement administration; developmental and child psychology; dramatic/theatre arts; economics; education; elementary education; English; finance; fine/studio arts; French; German; history; humanities; international economics; international relations and affairs; Latin; literature;

management information systems; marketing/marketing management; mathematics; modern Greek; music history, literature, and theory; nursing (registered nurse training); philosophy; physical education teaching and coaching; political science and government; pre-dentistry studies; pre-law studies; pre-medical studies; pre-veterinary studies; psychology; science teacher education; social sciences; social work; sociology; Spanish; urban studies/affairs.

Academic Programs *Special study options:* academic remediation for entering students, adult/continuing education programs, advanced placement credit, double majors, English as a second language, honors programs, internships, off-campus study, part-time degree program, student-designed majors, study abroad, summer session for credit. *ROTC:* Army (c). *Unusual degree programs:* 3-2 engineering with Washington University in St. Louis, University of Southern California, University of Illinois.

Library Howard Colman Library with 140,000 titles, 831 serial subscriptions, 9,723 audiovisual materials, an OPAC.

Computers on Campus 65 computers available on campus for general student use. A campuswide network can be accessed from student residence rooms. Internet access, at least one staffed computer lab available.

Student Life *Housing:* on-campus residence required through senior year. *Options:* coed, men-only, women-only. Campus housing is university owned. *Activities and organizations:* drama/theater group, student-run newspaper, radio station, choral group, student government, intercultural club, 4Ts (Tomorrow's Teachers Together Today), Psychology Society, Nursing Student Organization. *Campus security:* 24-hour emergency response devices and patrols, late-night transport/escort service, controlled dormitory access. *Student services:* health clinic, personal/psychological counseling.

Athletics Member NCAA. All Division III. *Intercollegiate sports:* baseball M, basketball M/W, football M, golf M, soccer M/W, softball W, tennis M/W, volleyball M(c)/W. *Intramural sports:* archery M/W, badminton M/W, basketball M/W, bowling M/W, football M/W, table tennis M/W, tennis M/W, volleyball M/W.

Standardized Tests *Required:* SAT I or ACT (for admission).

Costs (2004–05) *Tuition:* $21,200 full-time, $560 per credit hour part-time. *Room only:* Room and board charges vary according to board plan and housing facility. *Waivers:* employees or children of employees.

Financial Aid Of all full-time matriculated undergraduates who enrolled in 2001, 677 applied for aid, 677 were judged to have need, 677 had their need fully met. In 2001, 17 non-need-based awards were made. *Average percent of need met:* 99%. *Average indebtedness upon graduation:* $16,000.

Applying *Options:* common application, electronic application, early admission, deferred entrance. *Application fee:* $35. *Required:* high school transcript. *Required for some:* essay or personal statement, minimum 2.5 GPA, 2 letters of recommendation. *Recommended:* minimum 2.5 GPA, interview, campus visit. *Application deadline:* rolling (freshmen), rolling (transfers).

Admissions Contact Mr. William Laffey, Director of Admission, Rockford College, Nelson Hall, Rockford, IL 61108-2393. *Phone:* 815-226-4050 Ext. 3330. *Toll-free phone:* 800-892-2984. *Fax:* 815-226-2822. *E-mail:* admission@rockford.edu.

■ *See page 2250 for a narrative description.*

ROOSEVELT UNIVERSITY
Chicago, Illinois

- **Independent** comprehensive, founded 1945
- **Calendar** semesters
- **Degrees** bachelor's, master's, doctoral, and postbachelor's certificates
- **Urban** campus
- **Coed,** 4,290 undergraduate students, 43% full-time, 67% women, 33% men
- **Moderately difficult** entrance level, 51% of applicants were admitted

Inaugurated in 1998, Roosevelt Scholars is a distinctive honors program open to students who demonstrate outstanding scholarship along with leadership in school/community activities. In addition to enriched academic experiences and scholarship support that averages $6000 annually, students are mentored by Chicago's political, business, and social leaders and participate in internship and research opportunities in their areas of interest.

Undergraduates 1,855 full-time, 2,435 part-time. Students come from 24 states and territories, 70 other countries, 4% are from out of state, 26% African American, 5% Asian American or Pacific Islander, 10% Hispanic American, 0.4% Native American, 3% international, 15% transferred in, 5% live on campus. *Retention:* 68% of 2002 full-time freshmen returned.

Freshmen *Admission:* 1,433 applied, 735 admitted, 277 enrolled. *Average high school GPA:* 3.18. *Test scores:* SAT verbal scores over 500: 68%; SAT math scores over 500: 57%; ACT scores over 18: 84%; SAT verbal scores over 600: 33%; SAT math scores over 600: 23%; ACT scores over 24: 39%; SAT verbal scores over 700: 5%; SAT math scores over 700: 2%; ACT scores over 30: 5%.

Faculty *Total:* 662, 32% full-time. *Student/faculty ratio:* 11:1.

Majors Accounting; actuarial science; African-American/Black studies; American studies; art; art history, criticism and conservation; biology/biological sciences; biotechnology; business administration and management; business/commerce; business/managerial economics; business operations support and secretarial services related; chemistry; clinical laboratory science/medical technology; clinical/medical laboratory science and allied professions related; communication/speech communication and rhetoric; community organization and advocacy; comparative literature; computer science; computer systems networking and telecommunications; criminal justice/safety; cytotechnology; dramatic/theatre arts; economics; education; education related; electrical, electronic and communications engineering technology; elementary education; English; environmental science; environmental studies; finance; foreign languages and literatures; French; geography; gerontology; health/health care administration; health/medical preparatory programs related; health science; history; hospitality administration; human resources management; human services; industrial engineering; insurance; international business/trade/commerce; international relations and affairs; jazz/jazz studies; journalism; journalism related; kindergarten/preschool education; labor and industrial relations; legal assistant/paralegal; legal studies; liberal arts and sciences/liberal studies; literature; management science; marketing/marketing management; mathematics; medical laboratory technology; medical radiologic technology; music; music history, literature, and theory; music pedagogy; music performance; music related; music teacher education; music theory and composition; nuclear medical technology; parks, recreation, and leisure related; philosophy; piano and organ; political science and government; pre-dentistry studies; pre-law studies; pre-medical studies; pre-pharmacy studies; psychology; public administration; public administration and social service professions related; public relations/image management; radio and television; secondary education; social sciences; social sciences related; sociology; Spanish; special education; statistics; telecommunications; urban studies/affairs; violin, viola, guitar and other stringed instruments; voice and opera; wind/percussion instruments; women's studies.

Academic Programs *Special study options:* academic remediation for entering students, accelerated degree program, adult/continuing education programs, advanced placement credit, distance learning, double majors, English as a second language, external degree program, honors programs, independent study, internships, off-campus study, part-time degree program, services for LD students, student-designed majors, summer session for credit.

Library Murray-Green Library plus 4 others with 233,016 titles, 1,195 serial subscriptions, 9,897 audiovisual materials, an OPAC, a Web page.

Computers on Campus 646 computers available on campus for general student use. A campuswide network can be accessed from off campus. Internet access, online (class) registration, at least one staffed computer lab available. Computer purchase or lease plan available.

Student Life *Housing options:* coed. Campus housing is university owned. *Activities and organizations:* drama/theater group, student-run newspaper, radio station, choral group, International Student Union, RU 10%, Associacion de Latinos Unidos, Black Support Union, Residence Hall Council. *Campus security:* 24-hour emergency response devices and patrols, controlled dormitory access. *Student services:* personal/psychological counseling.

Standardized Tests *Required:* SAT I or ACT (for admission).

Costs (2003–04) *Comprehensive fee:* $22,580 includes full-time tuition ($15,180), mandatory fees ($250), and room and board ($7150). Full-time tuition and fees vary according to program. Part-time tuition and fees vary according to program. *College room only:* $5300. *Payment plans:* installment, deferred payment. *Waivers:* employees or children of employees.

Financial Aid Of all full-time matriculated undergraduates who enrolled in 2002, 1,517 applied for aid, 1,233 were judged to have need, 97 had their need fully met. In 2002, 585 non-need-based awards were made. *Average percent of need met:* 75%. *Average financial aid package:* $11,395. *Average need-based gift aid:* $6180. *Average non-need-based aid:* $5481.

Applying *Options:* common application, electronic application, deferred entrance. *Application fee:* $25. *Required:* essay or personal statement, high school transcript, minimum 2.0 GPA, audition for music and theater programs. *Required for some:* letters of recommendation, interview. *Application deadlines:* 8/15 (freshmen), 9/1 (transfers). *Notification:* continuous (freshmen), continuous (transfers).

Admissions Contact Roosevelt University, 430 South Michigan Avenue, Room 576, Chicago, IL 60605-1394. *Phone:* 847-619-8620. *Toll-free phone:* 877-APPLYRU. *Fax:* 312-341-3523. *E-mail:* applyru@roosevelt.edu.

■ *See page 2258 for a narrative description.*

RUSH UNIVERSITY
Chicago, Illinois

- **Independent** upper-level, founded 1969
- **Calendar** quarters

Rush University (continued)

- **Degrees** bachelor's, master's, doctoral, first professional, and post-master's certificates
- **Urban** 35-acre campus
- **Endowment** $340.2 million
- **Coed,** 186 undergraduate students, 93% full-time, 88% women, 12% men
- **Moderately difficult** entrance level, 55% of applicants were admitted

Undergraduates 173 full-time, 13 part-time. Students come from 13 states and territories, 4 other countries, 12% are from out of state, 11% African American, 13% Asian American or Pacific Islander, 6% Hispanic American, 0.5% international, 47% transferred in, 27% live on campus.

Faculty *Total:* 796, 100% full-time. *Student/faculty ratio:* 8:1.

Majors Clinical laboratory science/medical technology; nursing (registered nurse training); perfusion technology.

Academic Programs *Special study options:* accelerated degree program, distance learning, part-time degree program. *Unusual degree programs:* 3-2 occupational therapy.

Library Library of Rush University with 120,042 titles, 1,100 serial subscriptions, 4,750 audiovisual materials, an OPAC, a Web page.

Computers on Campus 150 computers available on campus for general student use. A campuswide network can be accessed from student residence rooms and from off campus. Internet access, at least one staffed computer lab available. Computer purchase or lease plan available.

Student Life *Housing options:* coed. Campus housing is university owned. *Campus security:* 24-hour emergency response devices and patrols, late-night transport/escort service, controlled dormitory access. *Student services:* health clinic, personal/psychological counseling.

Athletics *Intramural sports:* ultimate Frisbee M/W.

Costs (2003–04) *Tuition:* $15,600 full-time, $450 per quarter hour part-time. Full-time tuition and fees vary according to program. Part-time tuition and fees vary according to program. *Room only:* $11,970. Room and board charges vary according to housing facility. *Payment plans:* installment, deferred payment. *Waivers:* employees or children of employees.

Financial Aid Of all full-time matriculated undergraduates who enrolled in 2003, 152 applied for aid, 145 were judged to have need, 80 had their need fully met. 10 Federal Work-Study jobs (averaging $950). 50 state and other part-time jobs (averaging $4500). In 2003, 28 non-need-based awards were made. *Average percent of need met:* 100%. *Average financial aid package:* $18,000. *Average need-based loan:* $5000. *Average need-based gift aid:* $9000. *Average non-need-based aid:* $3000. *Average indebtedness upon graduation:* $20,000. *Financial aid deadline:* 5/1.

Applying *Options:* common application, electronic application. *Application fee:* $40. *Application deadline:* rolling (transfers). *Notification:* continuous (transfers).

Admissions Contact Ms. Hicela Castruita Woods, Director of College Admission Services, Rush University, 600 South Paulina—Suite 440, College Admissions Services, Chicago, IL 60612-3878. *Phone:* 312-942-7100. *Fax:* 312-942-2219. *E-mail:* rush_admissions@rush.edu.

SAINT ANTHONY COLLEGE OF NURSING
Rockford, Illinois

- **Independent Roman Catholic** upper-level, founded 1915
- **Calendar** semesters
- **Degree** bachelor's
- **Urban** 17-acre campus with easy access to Chicago
- **Coed, primarily women,** 95 undergraduate students, 88% full-time, 91% women, 9% men
- **Moderately difficult** entrance level

Undergraduates 84 full-time, 11 part-time. Students come from 2 states and territories, 3% are from out of state, 4% African American, 2% Asian American or Pacific Islander, 4% Hispanic American, 1% international, 34% transferred in.

Faculty *Total:* 12, 92% full-time, 17% with terminal degrees. *Student/faculty ratio:* 8:1.

Majors Nursing (registered nurse training).

Academic Programs *Special study options:* accelerated degree program, advanced placement credit, independent study, internships, off-campus study, part-time degree program, services for LD students, summer session for credit.

Library Sister Mary Linus Learning Resource Center plus 1 other with 1,394 titles, 3,136 serial subscriptions, 163 audiovisual materials, an OPAC, a Web page.

Computers on Campus 10 computers available on campus for general student use. A campuswide network can be accessed from off campus. Internet access, at least one staffed computer lab available.

Student Life *Housing:* college housing not available. *Activities and organizations:* Student Organization. *Campus security:* 24-hour emergency response devices and patrols, late-night transport/escort service. *Student services:* health clinic, personal/psychological counseling, legal services.

Costs (2004–05) *One-time required fee:* $90. *Tuition:* $14,700 full-time, $460 per credit part-time. Full-time tuition and fees vary according to course load. Part-time tuition and fees vary according to course load. *Required fees:* $112 full-time, $55 per term part-time. *Payment plans:* installment, deferred payment. *Waivers:* employees or children of employees.

Financial Aid Of all full-time matriculated undergraduates who enrolled in 2002, 81 applied for aid, 81 were judged to have need. *Average percent of need met:* 50%. *Average financial aid package:* $13,145. *Average need-based loan:* $7002. *Average need-based gift aid:* $4382. *Average indebtedness upon graduation:* $19,000.

Applying *Options:* electronic application, deferred entrance. *Application fee:* $50. *Application deadline:* rolling (transfers). *Notification:* continuous (transfers).

Admissions Contact Ms. Nancy Sanders, Assistant Dean for Admissions and Student Affairs, Saint Anthony College of Nursing, 5658 East State Street, Rockford, IL 61108-2468. *Phone:* 815-395-5100. *Fax:* 815-395-2275. *E-mail:* cheryldelgado@sacn.edu.

ST. AUGUSTINE COLLEGE
Chicago, Illinois

- **Independent** 4-year, founded 1980
- **Calendar** semesters
- **Degrees** certificates, associate, and bachelor's (bilingual Spanish/English degree programs)
- **Urban** 4-acre campus
- **Endowment** $400,000
- **Coed,** 1,710 undergraduate students, 83% full-time, 78% women, 22% men
- **Noncompetitive** entrance level

Undergraduates 1,416 full-time, 294 part-time. Students come from 3 states and territories, 1% are from out of state, 7% African American, 5% Asian American or Pacific Islander, 86% Hispanic American, 1% international, 3% transferred in. *Retention:* 69% of 2002 full-time freshmen returned.

Freshmen *Admission:* 673 enrolled. *Average high school GPA:* 2.80.

Faculty *Total:* 159, 18% full-time. *Student/faculty ratio:* 10:1.

Majors Accounting technology and bookkeeping; administrative assistant and secretarial science; business administration and management; business administration, management and operations related; child care and support services management; computer and information sciences; culinary arts; early childhood education; general studies; liberal arts and sciences/liberal studies; management information systems; mental health/rehabilitation; respiratory care therapy; social work; special education; substance abuse/addiction counseling.

Academic Programs *Special study options:* academic remediation for entering students, cooperative education, English as a second language, independent study, internships, part-time degree program, summer session for credit.

Library 15,500 titles.

Computers on Campus A campuswide network can be accessed. Internet access, at least one staffed computer lab available.

Student Life *Housing:* college housing not available. *Activities and organizations:* student-run newspaper, choral group, ENLACE. *Campus security:* 24-hour patrols, late-night transport/escort service. *Student services:* personal/psychological counseling.

Athletics *Intercollegiate sports:* cheerleading M(s)/W(s).

Standardized Tests *Required:* Ability-To-Benefit Admissions Test (for admission).

Costs (2003–04) *Tuition:* $7128 full-time, $297 per credit part-time. *Payment plan:* installment. *Waivers:* employees or children of employees.

Financial Aid Of all full-time matriculated undergraduates who enrolled in 2002, 3,226 applied for aid, 2,966 were judged to have need. 59 Federal Work-Study jobs. In 2002, 22 non-need-based awards were made. *Average non-need-based aid:* $1639.

Applying *Options:* deferred entrance. *Application deadline:* rolling (freshmen), rolling (transfers).

Admissions Contact Ms. Gloria Quiroz, Director of Recruitment, St. Augustine College, 1345 West Argyle Street, Chicago, IL 60604-3501. *Phone:* 773-878-3256. *E-mail:* info@staugustinecollege.edu.

SAINT FRANCIS MEDICAL CENTER COLLEGE OF NURSING
Peoria, Illinois

- **Independent Roman Catholic** upper-level, founded 1986
- **Calendar** semesters
- **Degrees** bachelor's and master's
- **Urban** campus
- **Coed, primarily women,** 183 undergraduate students, 86% full-time, 91% women, 9% men
- **Moderately difficult** entrance level, 100% of applicants were admitted

Undergraduates 157 full-time, 26 part-time. Students come from 2 states and territories, 2% African American, 0.5% Asian American or Pacific Islander, 1% Hispanic American, 28% live on campus.

Faculty *Total:* 19, 100% full-time. *Student/faculty ratio:* 8:1.

Majors Nursing (registered nurse training).

Academic Programs *Special study options:* advanced placement credit, distance learning, independent study, part-time degree program, summer session for credit.

Library 6,215 titles, 125 serial subscriptions.

Computers on Campus 6 computers available on campus for general student use. Internet access, at least one staffed computer lab available.

Student Life *Housing options:* coed. Campus housing is university owned. *Activities and organizations:* choral group, Student Senate, SNAI. *Campus security:* 24-hour emergency response devices, controlled dormitory access. *Student services:* health clinic, personal/psychological counseling.

Costs (2003–04) *Tuition:* $10,088 full-time, $402 per semester hour part-time. Full-time tuition and fees vary according to course load. Part-time tuition and fees vary according to course load. *Required fees:* $200 full-time. *Room only:* $1680. *Payment plans:* installment, deferred payment. *Waivers:* employees or children of employees.

Financial Aid Of all full-time matriculated undergraduates who enrolled in 2003, 151 applied for aid, 106 were judged to have need, 32 had their need fully met. In 2003, 41 non-need-based awards were made. *Average percent of need met:* 88%. *Average financial aid package:* $9398. *Average need-based loan:* $6700. *Average need-based gift aid:* $7722. *Average non-need-based aid:* $5220. *Average indebtedness upon graduation:* $10,620.

Applying *Options:* common application, deferred entrance. *Application fee:* $50. *Application deadline:* rolling (transfers). *Notification:* continuous (transfers).

Admissions Contact Mrs. Janice Farquharson, Director of Admissions and Registrar, Saint Francis Medical Center College of Nursing, 511 Greenleaf Street, Peoria, IL 61603-3783. *Phone:* 309-624-8980. *Fax:* 309-624-8973. *E-mail:* janice.farquharson@osfhealthcare.org.

ST. JOHN'S COLLEGE
Springfield, Illinois

- **Independent Roman Catholic** upper-level, founded 1886
- **Calendar** semesters
- **Degree** bachelor's
- **Urban** campus
- **Endowment** $739,410
- **Coed, primarily women,** 64 undergraduate students, 92% full-time, 95% women, 5% men
- **Moderately difficult** entrance level, 100% of applicants were admitted

Undergraduates 59 full-time, 5 part-time. Students come from 2 states and territories, 1 other country, 2% are from out of state, 2% international, 50% transferred in.

Faculty *Total:* 15, 93% full-time, 7% with terminal degrees. *Student/faculty ratio:* 4:1.

Majors Nursing (registered nurse training).

Academic Programs *Special study options:* part-time degree program.

Library St. John's Health Science Library with 7,715 titles, 349 serial subscriptions, 735 audiovisual materials, an OPAC.

Computers on Campus 10 computers available on campus for general student use. A campuswide network can be accessed. Internet access, at least one staffed computer lab available.

Student Life *Housing:* college housing not available. *Activities and organizations:* NSNA, class/student government. *Campus security:* 24-hour emergency response devices and patrols, late-night transport/escort service. *Student services:* health clinic, personal/psychological counseling.

Costs (2003–04) *Tuition:* $9220 full-time. Full-time tuition and fees vary according to course load. Part-time tuition and fees vary according to course load. *Required fees:* $338 full-time. *Payment plan:* installment.

Financial Aid Of all full-time matriculated undergraduates who enrolled in 2002, 56 applied for aid, 52 were judged to have need, 13 had their need fully met. 3 Federal Work-Study jobs (averaging $2953). *Average percent of need met:* 80%. *Average financial aid package:* $8943. *Average need-based loan:* $4438. *Average need-based gift aid:* $8500. *Average indebtedness upon graduation:* $7850.

Applying *Options:* early action. *Application fee:* $25. *Notification:* continuous (transfers).

Admissions Contact Ms. Beth Beasley, Student Development Officer, St. John's College, 421 North Ninth Street, Springfield, IL 62702-5317. *Phone:* 217-525-5628 Ext. 45468. *Fax:* 217-757-6870. *E-mail:* college@st-johns.org.

SAINT XAVIER UNIVERSITY
Chicago, Illinois

- **Independent Roman Catholic** comprehensive, founded 1847
- **Calendar** semesters
- **Degrees** certificates, bachelor's, master's, post-master's, and postbachelor's certificates
- **Urban** 70-acre campus
- **Endowment** $6.5 million
- **Coed,** 3,062 undergraduate students, 76% full-time, 71% women, 29% men
- **Moderately difficult** entrance level, 68% of applicants were admitted

Undergraduates 2,331 full-time, 731 part-time. Students come from 21 states and territories, 4 other countries, 4% are from out of state, 18% African American, 2% Asian American or Pacific Islander, 11% Hispanic American, 0.3% Native American, 0.3% international, 15% transferred in, 19% live on campus. *Retention:* 80% of 2002 full-time freshmen returned.

Freshmen *Admission:* 1,701 applied, 1,159 admitted, 384 enrolled. *Average high school GPA:* 3.17. *Test scores:* ACT scores over 18: 94%; ACT scores over 24: 22%; ACT scores over 30: 1%.

Faculty *Total:* 339, 47% full-time, 51% with terminal degrees. *Student/faculty ratio:* 15:1.

Majors Accounting; art; art teacher education; biological and physical sciences; biology/biological sciences; biology teacher education; botany/plant biology; business/commerce; chemistry; communication/speech communication and rhetoric; computer and information sciences; computer science; counseling psychology; criminal justice/safety; elementary education; English; English/language arts teacher education; history; history teacher education; industrial and organizational psychology; international business/trade/commerce; international relations and affairs; kindergarten/preschool education; liberal arts and sciences/liberal studies; mathematics; mathematics teacher education; music; music performance; music teacher education; nursing (registered nurse training); philosophy; political science and government; psychology; religious studies; social sciences; sociology; Spanish; Spanish language teacher education; speech-language pathology.

Academic Programs *Special study options:* academic remediation for entering students, accelerated degree program, adult/continuing education programs, advanced placement credit, cooperative education, double majors, English as a second language, honors programs, independent study, internships, part-time degree program, services for LD students, student-designed majors, study abroad, summer session for credit. *ROTC:* Air Force (c).

Library Byrne Memorial Library with 170,753 titles, 717 serial subscriptions, 3,112 audiovisual materials, an OPAC, a Web page.

Computers on Campus 306 computers available on campus for general student use. A campuswide network can be accessed from student residence rooms and from off campus. Internet access, at least one staffed computer lab available.

Student Life *Housing options:* coed. Campus housing is university owned. *Activities and organizations:* drama/theater group, student-run newspaper, radio station, choral group, marching band, Student Activities Board, Black Student Union, UNIDOS (Hispanic Organization), Student Nurses Association, Business Students Association. *Campus security:* 24-hour emergency response devices and patrols, late-night transport/escort service. *Student services:* health clinic, personal/psychological counseling, women's center.

Athletics Member NAIA. *Intercollegiate sports:* baseball M(s), basketball M(s), cross-country running W(s), football M(s), golf M(s), soccer M(s)/W(s), softball W(s), volleyball W(s). *Intramural sports:* basketball M, bowling M/W, volleyball M/W, weight lifting M.

Standardized Tests *Required:* SAT I or ACT (for admission).

Saint Xavier University (continued)

Costs (2003–04) *Comprehensive fee:* $23,144 includes full-time tuition ($16,500), mandatory fees ($180), and room and board ($6464). Full-time tuition and fees vary according to course load. Part-time tuition: $550 per credit hour. Part-time tuition and fees vary according to course load. *College room only:* $3688. Room and board charges vary according to board plan. *Payment plan:* installment. *Waivers:* senior citizens and employees or children of employees.

Financial Aid Of all full-time matriculated undergraduates who enrolled in 2003, 2,152 applied for aid, 1,932 were judged to have need, 400 had their need fully met. 1,253 Federal Work-Study jobs (averaging $2143). 40 state and other part-time jobs (averaging $5377). In 2003, 327 non-need-based awards were made. *Average percent of need met:* 82%. *Average financial aid package:* $14,282. *Average need-based loan:* $3932. *Average need-based gift aid:* $8775. *Average non-need-based aid:* $3683. *Average indebtedness upon graduation:* $19,374.

Applying *Options:* common application, electronic application, deferred entrance. *Application fee:* $25. *Required:* high school transcript. *Required for some:* interview. *Recommended:* essay or personal statement, minimum 2.5 GPA, interview. *Application deadline:* rolling (freshmen), rolling (transfers). *Notification:* continuous (freshmen), continuous (transfers).

Admissions Contact Elizabeth A. Gierach, Director of Enrollment Services, Saint Xavier University, 3700 West 103rd Street, Chicago, IL 60655-3105. *Phone:* 773-298-3063. *Toll-free phone:* 800-462-9288. *Fax:* 773-298-3076. *E-mail:* admissions@sxu.edu.

■ *See page 2334 for a narrative description.*

SCHOOL OF THE ART INSTITUTE OF CHICAGO

Chicago, Illinois

- **Independent** comprehensive, founded 1866
- **Calendar** semesters
- **Degrees** certificates, bachelor's, and master's
- **Urban** 1-acre campus
- **Endowment** $225.0 million
- **Coed,** 2,159 undergraduate students, 82% full-time, 66% women, 34% men
- **Moderately difficult** entrance level, 83% of applicants were admitted

Undergraduates 1,773 full-time, 386 part-time. Students come from 50 states and territories, 23 other countries, 78% are from out of state, 3% African American, 10% Asian American or Pacific Islander, 7% Hispanic American, 0.8% Native American, 15% international, 11% transferred in, 35% live on campus. *Retention:* 79% of 2002 full-time freshmen returned.

Freshmen *Admission:* 1,215 applied, 1,006 admitted, 345 enrolled.

Faculty *Total:* 468, 26% full-time. *Student/faculty ratio:* 13:1.

Majors Animation, interactive technology, video graphics and special effects; architecture related; art; art history, criticism and conservation; art teacher education; ceramic arts and ceramics; cinematography and film/video production; commercial and advertising art; computer graphics; crafts, folk art and artisanry; design and applied arts related; design and visual communications; digital communication and media/multimedia; drawing; fashion/apparel design; fiber, textile and weaving arts; film/cinema studies; film/video and photographic arts related; fine arts related; fine/studio arts; graphic communications; graphic design; illustration; interior architecture; interior design; intermedia/multimedia; metal and jewelry arts; music related; painting; photography; printmaking; sculpture; visual and performing arts; visual and performing arts related; web page, digital/multimedia and information resources design.

Academic Programs *Special study options:* academic remediation for entering students, advanced placement credit, cooperative education, double majors, English as a second language, independent study, internships, off-campus study, part-time degree program, services for LD students, student-designed majors, study abroad, summer session for credit.

Library Flaxman Memorial Library plus 1 other with 72,490 titles, 334 serial subscriptions, 4,067 audiovisual materials, an OPAC, a Web page.

Computers on Campus 360 computers available on campus for general student use. A campuswide network can be accessed from student residence rooms and from off campus. Internet access, at least one staffed computer lab available. Computer purchase or lease plan available.

Student Life *Housing options:* coed. Campus housing is university owned. *Activities and organizations:* drama/theater group, student-run newspaper, radio and television station, Student Government/Student Union Galleries, N.I.A. (black student union), L.A.S.O. (Latin Art Student organization), Soccer Group/Kickball League, Student Diversity Council. *Campus security:* 24-hour emergency response devices and patrols, late-night transport/escort service, controlled dormitory access. *Student services:* health clinic, personal/psychological counseling.

Standardized Tests *Required:* SAT I or ACT (for admission).

Costs (2003–04) *Tuition:* $24,000 full-time, $800 per credit hour part-time. *Room only:* $7300. *Waivers:* employees or children of employees.

Financial Aid In 2002, 101 non-need-based awards were made.

Applying *Options:* deferred entrance. *Application fee:* $65. *Required:* essay or personal statement, high school transcript, 1 letter of recommendation, portfolio. *Recommended:* interview. *Application deadlines:* 9/1 (freshmen), 9/1 (transfers). *Notification:* continuous (freshmen), continuous (transfers).

Admissions Contact Ms. Kendra E. Dane, Executive Director of Admissions and Marketing, School of the Art Institute of Chicago, 37 South Wabash, Chicago, IL 60603. *Phone:* 312-899-5219. *Toll-free phone:* 800-232-SAIC. *E-mail:* admiss@artic.edu.

■ *See page 2356 for a narrative description.*

SHIMER COLLEGE

Waukegan, Illinois

- **Independent** 4-year, founded 1853
- **Calendar** semesters
- **Degrees** bachelor's and postbachelor's certificates
- **Suburban** 3-acre campus with easy access to Chicago and Milwaukee
- **Coed,** 126 undergraduate students, 90% full-time, 33% women, 67% men
- **Moderately difficult** entrance level, 88% of applicants were admitted

Undergraduates 114 full-time, 12 part-time. Students come from 20 states and territories, 4 other countries, 42% are from out of state, 12% African American, 0.8% Asian American or Pacific Islander, 4% international, 12% transferred in, 50% live on campus. *Retention:* 66% of 2002 full-time freshmen returned.

Freshmen *Admission:* 59 applied, 52 admitted, 26 enrolled. *Average high school GPA:* 2.6. *Test scores:* SAT verbal scores over 500: 100%; SAT math scores over 500: 60%; ACT scores over 18: 85%; SAT verbal scores over 600: 100%; SAT math scores over 600: 20%; ACT scores over 24: 62%; ACT scores over 30: 15%.

Faculty *Total:* 15, 87% full-time, 93% with terminal degrees. *Student/faculty ratio:* 8:1.

Majors General studies; humanities; liberal arts and sciences and humanities related; liberal arts and sciences/liberal studies; literature; natural sciences; social sciences.

Academic Programs *Special study options:* adult/continuing education programs, cooperative education, distance learning, double majors, independent study, internships, off-campus study, part-time degree program, student-designed majors, study abroad, summer session for credit.

Library 200,000 titles, 200 serial subscriptions.

Computers on Campus 9 computers available on campus for general student use. A campuswide network can be accessed from student residence rooms and from off campus. Internet access, at least one staffed computer lab available.

Student Life *Housing options:* coed. Campus housing is university owned and leased by the school. Freshman campus housing is guaranteed. *Activities and organizations:* drama/theater group, student-run newspaper, choral group, student government, Drama Group, Quality of Life Committee. *Campus security:* 24-hour emergency response devices, late-night transport/escort service. *Student services:* personal/psychological counseling.

Athletics *Intramural sports:* basketball M/W, football M/W, volleyball M/W.

Standardized Tests *Required for some:* SAT I or ACT (for admission). *Recommended:* SAT I or ACT (for admission).

Costs (2003–04) *Comprehensive fee:* $19,530 includes full-time tuition ($16,100), mandatory fees ($650), and room and board ($2780). Full-time tuition and fees vary according to class time and course load. Part-time tuition: $575 per credit hour. Part-time tuition and fees vary according to class time and course load. *Required fees:* $250 per term part-time. *Room and board:* Room and board charges vary according to housing facility. *Payment plan:* installment. *Waivers:* adult students, senior citizens, and employees or children of employees.

Financial Aid Of all full-time matriculated undergraduates who enrolled in 2003, 122 applied for aid, 112 were judged to have need. 57 Federal Work-Study jobs (averaging $1500). 8 state and other part-time jobs (averaging $1500). In 2003, 4 non-need-based awards were made. *Average percent of need met:* 75%. *Average financial aid package:* $14,000. *Average need-based loan:* $4200. *Average need-based gift aid:* $4000. *Average non-need-based aid:* $16,500.

Applying *Options:* common application, electronic application, early admission, deferred entrance. *Application fee:* $25. *Required:* essay or personal statement, high school transcript, 1 letter of recommendation, interview. *Application deadlines:* 8/30 (freshmen), 8/30 (transfers). *Notification:* continuous (freshmen), continuous (transfers).

Admissions Contact Mr. Bill Paterson, Associate Director of Admissions, Shimer College, PO Box 500, Waukegan, IL 60079. *Phone:* 847-249-7175. *Toll-free phone:* 800-215-7173. *Fax:* 847-249-8798. *E-mail:* admissions@shimer.edu.

SOUTHERN ILLINOIS UNIVERSITY CARBONDALE
Carbondale, Illinois

- **State-supported** university, founded 1869, part of Southern Illinois University
- **Calendar** semesters plus 8-week summer session
- **Degrees** associate, bachelor's, master's, doctoral, first professional, postbachelor's, and first professional certificates
- **Rural** 1133-acre campus with easy access to St. Louis
- **Endowment** $45.3 million
- **Coed,** 16,366 undergraduate students, 90% full-time, 44% women, 56% men
- **Moderately difficult** entrance level, 77% of applicants were admitted

Undergraduates 14,675 full-time, 1,691 part-time. Students come from 50 states and territories, 110 other countries, 12% are from out of state, 13% African American, 1% Asian American or Pacific Islander, 3% Hispanic American, 0.3% Native American, 3% international, 12% transferred in, 27% live on campus. *Retention:* 68% of 2002 full-time freshmen returned.

Freshmen *Admission:* 8,627 applied, 6,665 admitted, 2,624 enrolled. *Test scores:* SAT verbal scores over 500: 58%; SAT math scores over 500: 60%; ACT scores over 18: 89%; SAT verbal scores over 600: 24%; SAT math scores over 600: 28%; ACT scores over 24: 30%; SAT verbal scores over 700: 4%; SAT math scores over 700: 7%; ACT scores over 30: 4%.

Faculty *Total:* 1,116, 81% full-time, 78% with terminal degrees. *Student/faculty ratio:* 18:1.

Majors Accounting; agricultural economics; agriculture; airline pilot and flight crew; animal sciences; anthropology; apparel and textiles; architecture; art; automotive engineering technology; aviation/airway management; avionics maintenance technology; biology/biological sciences; botany/plant biology; business administration and management; business/managerial economics; chemistry; cinematography and film/video production; civil engineering; classics and languages, literatures and linguistics; communication disorders; computer engineering; computer science; construction engineering technology; criminal justice/law enforcement administration; dental hygiene; dental laboratory technology; design and visual communications; dramatic/theatre arts; economics; electrical and electronic engineering technologies related; electrical, electronics and communications engineering; elementary education; engineering technology; English; finance; fine/studio arts; fire services administration; foods, nutrition, and wellness; foreign languages related; forestry; French; funeral service and mortuary science; geography; geology/earth science; German; health teacher education; history; industrial technology; information science/studies; interior design; journalism; legal assistant/paralegal; liberal arts and sciences/liberal studies; linguistics; management science; marketing/marketing management; mathematics; mechanical engineering; medical radiologic technology; microbiology; mining and mineral engineering; multi-/interdisciplinary studies related; music; parks, recreation and leisure; philosophy; physical education teaching and coaching; physical therapist assistant; physician assistant; physics; physiology; plant sciences; political science and government; psychology; radio and television; rehabilitation and therapeutic professions related; respiratory care therapy; social sciences; social work; sociology; Spanish; special education; speech and rhetoric; trade and industrial teacher education; zoology/animal biology.

Academic Programs *Special study options:* academic remediation for entering students, accelerated degree program, adult/continuing education programs, advanced placement credit, cooperative education, distance learning, double majors, English as a second language, honors programs, independent study, internships, off-campus study, part-time degree program, services for LD students, study abroad, summer session for credit. *ROTC:* Army (b), Air Force (b).

Library Morris Library plus 1 other with 4.2 million titles, 18,271 serial subscriptions, 371,180 audiovisual materials, an OPAC, a Web page.

Computers on Campus 1681 computers available on campus for general student use. A campuswide network can be accessed from student residence rooms and from off campus. Internet access, at least one staffed computer lab available. Computer purchase or lease plan available.

Student Life *Housing:* on-campus residence required for freshman year. *Options:* coed, men-only, women-only, disabled students. Campus housing is university owned. Freshman campus housing is guaranteed. *Activities and organizations:* drama/theater group, student-run newspaper, radio and television station, choral group, marching band, Undergraduate Student Government, International Student Council, Black Togetherness Organization, Black Affairs Council, Hispanic Council, national fraternities, national sororities. *Campus security:* 24-hour emergency response devices and patrols, student patrols, late-night transport/escort service, well-lit pathways, night safety vans, student transit system. *Student services:* health clinic, personal/psychological counseling, women's center, legal services.

Athletics Member NCAA. All Division I except football (Division I-AA). *Intercollegiate sports:* baseball M(s), basketball M(s)/W(s), cross-country running M(s)/W(s), golf M(s)/W(s), softball W(s), swimming M(s)/W(s), tennis M(s)/W(s), track and field M(s)/W(s), volleyball W(s). *Intramural sports:* archery M(c)/W(c), badminton M(c)/W(c), baseball M(c), basketball M/W, bowling M(c), cross-country running M/W, equestrian sports M(c)/W(c), fencing M(c)/W(c), football M/W, golf M/W, lacrosse M(c), racquetball M(c)/W(c), riflery M(c)/W(c), rock climbing M(c)/W(c), rugby M(c)/W(c), sailing M(c)/W(c), soccer M(c)/W(c), softball M/W, squash M(c)/W, table tennis M(c)/W, tennis M/W, track and field M(c)/W(c), ultimate Frisbee M(c)/W(c), volleyball M(c)/W(c), water polo M(c)/W, weight lifting M(c)/W(c), wrestling M(c).

Standardized Tests *Required:* SAT I or ACT (for admission).

Costs (2003–04) *Tuition:* state resident $4245 full-time, $142 per semester hour part-time; nonresident $8490 full-time, $283 per semester hour part-time. Full-time tuition and fees vary according to course load. Part-time tuition and fees vary according to course load. *Required fees:* $1276 full-time. *Room and board:* $4903; room only: $2492. Room and board charges vary according to board plan and housing facility. *Payment plan:* installment. *Waivers:* senior citizens and employees or children of employees.

Financial Aid Of all full-time matriculated undergraduates who enrolled in 2002, 10,444 applied for aid, 8,348 were judged to have need, 6,699 had their need fully met. 1,840 Federal Work-Study jobs (averaging $1142). 4,529 state and other part-time jobs (averaging $1611). In 2002, 1457 non-need-based awards were made. *Average percent of need met:* 94%. *Average financial aid package:* $7969. *Average need-based loan:* $3293. *Average need-based gift aid:* $4550. *Average non-need-based aid:* $2631. *Average indebtedness upon graduation:* $12,413.

Applying *Options:* electronic application, deferred entrance. *Application fee:* $30. *Required:* high school transcript. *Application deadline:* rolling (freshmen), rolling (transfers). *Notification:* continuous (freshmen), continuous (transfers).

Admissions Contact Dr. Anne DeLuca, Assistant Vice Chancellor, Student Affairs and Enrollment Management and Director of Admissions, Southern Illinois University Carbondale, Mail Code 4710, Carbondale, IL 62901-4710. *Phone:* 618-453-2908. *Fax:* 618-453-3250. *E-mail:* joinsiuc@siu.edu.

■ *See page 2408 for a narrative description.*

SOUTHERN ILLINOIS UNIVERSITY EDWARDSVILLE
Edwardsville, Illinois

- **State-supported** comprehensive, founded 1957, part of Southern Illinois University
- **Calendar** semesters
- **Degrees** bachelor's, master's, first professional, post-master's, postbachelor's, and first professional certificates
- **Suburban** 2660-acre campus with easy access to St. Louis
- **Endowment** $8.6 million
- **Coed,** 10,563 undergraduate students, 84% full-time, 55% women, 45% men
- **Moderately difficult** entrance level, 81% of applicants were admitted

Undergraduates 8,844 full-time, 1,719 part-time. Students come from 47 states and territories, 53 other countries, 10% are from out of state, 11% African American, 2% Asian American or Pacific Islander, 2% Hispanic American, 0.3% Native American, 1% international, 12% transferred in, 27% live on campus. *Retention:* 75% of 2002 full-time freshmen returned.

Freshmen *Admission:* 4,383 applied, 3,542 admitted, 1,743 enrolled. *Test scores:* ACT scores over 18: 89%; ACT scores over 24: 33%; ACT scores over 30: 3%.

Faculty *Total:* 763, 68% full-time. *Student/faculty ratio:* 17:1.

Majors Accounting; anthropology; art; audiology and speech-language pathology; biology/biological sciences; business administration and management; business/managerial economics; chemistry; civil engineering; computer engineering; computer science; construction engineering technology; criminal justice/safety; dramatic/theatre arts; early childhood education; economics; electrical, electronics and communications engineering; elementary education; English; fine/studio arts; foreign languages and literatures; geography; health and physical education; health teacher education; history; industrial engineering; liberal arts and sciences/liberal studies; management information systems; manufacturing engineering; mass communication/media; mathematics; mechanical engineering; music; nursing (registered nurse training); philosophy; physics; political science and government; psychology; science teacher education; social work; sociology; special education; speech and rhetoric.

Academic Programs *Special study options:* academic remediation for entering students, accelerated degree program, adult/continuing education programs, advanced placement credit, cooperative education, distance learning, double majors, English as a second language, honors programs, independent study,

Southern Illinois University Edwardsville (continued)
internships, off-campus study, part-time degree program, services for LD students, student-designed majors, study abroad, summer session for credit. *ROTC:* Army (b), Air Force (b).

Library Lovejoy Library with 783,050 titles, 14,807 serial subscriptions, 29,183 audiovisual materials, an OPAC, a Web page.

Computers on Campus 600 computers available on campus for general student use. A campuswide network can be accessed from student residence rooms and from off campus. Internet access, at least one staffed computer lab available. Computer purchase or lease plan available.

Student Life *Housing options:* coed, disabled students. Campus housing is university owned. *Activities and organizations:* drama/theater group, student-run newspaper, radio station, choral group, student government, Greek Council, campus newspaper, University Center Board, International Student Council, national fraternities, national sororities. *Campus security:* 24-hour emergency response devices and patrols, student patrols, late-night transport/escort service, controlled dormitory access, 24-hour ID check at residence hall entrances, emergency call boxes located throughout campus. *Student services:* health clinic, personal/psychological counseling, legal services.

Athletics Member NCAA. All Division II. *Intercollegiate sports:* baseball M(s), basketball M(s)/W(s), cross-country running M(s)/W(s), golf W(s), soccer M(s)/W(s), softball W(s), tennis M(s)/W(s), track and field M(s)/W(s), volleyball W(s), wrestling M(s). *Intramural sports:* badminton M/W, basketball M/W, bowling M/W, football M/W, golf M/W, racquetball M/W, soccer M/W, softball M/W, table tennis M/W, tennis M/W, ultimate Frisbee M/W, volleyball M/W, weight lifting M/W.

Standardized Tests *Required:* SAT I or ACT (for admission).

Costs (2003–04) *Tuition:* state resident $3360 full-time, $112 per semester hour part-time; nonresident $6720 full-time, $224 per semester hour part-time. Full-time tuition and fees vary according to course load. Part-time tuition and fees vary according to course load. *Required fees:* $823 full-time, $234 per term part-time. *Room and board:* $5364; room only: $3077. Room and board charges vary according to board plan and housing facility. *Payment plan:* installment. *Waivers:* employees or children of employees.

Financial Aid Of all full-time matriculated undergraduates who enrolled in 2003, 5,908 applied for aid, 4,591 were judged to have need, 852 had their need fully met. 662 Federal Work-Study jobs (averaging $1095). 1,185 state and other part-time jobs (averaging $4486). In 2003, 818 non-need-based awards were made. *Average percent of need met:* 77%. *Average financial aid package:* $7890. *Average need-based loan:* $3236. *Average need-based gift aid:* $5184. *Average non-need-based aid:* $3389. *Average indebtedness upon graduation:* $14,755.

Applying *Options:* electronic application, early admission, deferred entrance. *Application fee:* $30. *Required:* high school transcript. *Application deadlines:* 5/31 (freshmen), 7/31 (transfers). *Notification:* continuous until 8/7 (freshmen), continuous until 8/7 (transfers).

Admissions Contact Mr. Boyd Bradshaw, Assistant Vice Chancellor for Enrollment Management, Southern Illinois University Edwardsville, Campus Box 1600, Edwardsville, IL 62026-1600. *Phone:* 618-650-2298. *Toll-free phone:* 800-447-SIUE. *Fax:* 618-650-5013. *E-mail:* admis@siue.edu.

TELSHE YESHIVA–CHICAGO

Chicago, Illinois

Admissions Contact Rosh Hayeshiva, Telshe Yeshiva–Chicago, 3535 West Foster Avenue, Chicago, IL 60625-5598. *Phone:* 773-463-7738.

TRINITY CHRISTIAN COLLEGE

Palos Heights, Illinois

- **Independent Christian Reformed** 4-year, founded 1959
- **Calendar** semesters plus 2 week interim term
- **Degree** bachelor's
- **Suburban** 53-acre campus with easy access to Chicago
- **Endowment** $4.0 million
- **Coed,** 1,263 undergraduate students, 82% full-time, 63% women, 37% men
- **Moderately difficult** entrance level, 93% of applicants were admitted

Undergraduates 1,032 full-time, 231 part-time. Students come from 37 states and territories, 10 other countries, 42% are from out of state, 5% African American, 2% Asian American or Pacific Islander, 4% Hispanic American, 0.2% Native American, 2% international, 6% transferred in, 67% live on campus. *Retention:* 79% of 2002 full-time freshmen returned.

Freshmen *Admission:* 589 applied, 548 admitted, 255 enrolled. *Average high school GPA:* 3.26. *Test scores:* SAT verbal scores over 500: 71%; SAT math scores over 500: 66%; ACT scores over 18: 85%; SAT verbal scores over 600: 21%; SAT math scores over 600: 24%; ACT scores over 24: 51%; SAT math scores over 700: 3%; ACT scores over 30: 9%.

Faculty *Total:* 124, 52% full-time, 46% with terminal degrees. *Student/faculty ratio:* 12:1.

Majors Accounting; art; art teacher education; biology/biological sciences; biology teacher education; business administration and management; business administration, management and operations related; business/commerce; business teacher education; ceramic arts and ceramics; chemistry; chemistry teacher education; commercial and advertising art; communication/speech communication and rhetoric; computer science; drawing; education; elementary education; English; English/language arts teacher education; financial planning and services; history; history teacher education; human resources management; information science/studies; management information systems; marketing/marketing management; mathematics; mathematics teacher education; middle school education; music; music performance; music teacher education; nursing (registered nurse training); painting; philosophy; photography; physical education teaching and coaching; piano and organ; pre-dentistry studies; pre-medical studies; pre-theology/pre-ministerial studies; pre-veterinary studies; printmaking; psychology; public relations/image management; religious education; religious studies; sales, distribution and marketing; science teacher education; sculpture; secondary education; social work; sociology; Spanish; special education; special education (emotionally disturbed); special education (mentally retarded); special education (specific learning disabilities); theology; voice and opera.

Academic Programs *Special study options:* academic remediation for entering students, adult/continuing education programs, advanced placement credit, cooperative education, double majors, honors programs, independent study, internships, off-campus study, part-time degree program, services for LD students, study abroad.

Library Jenny Huizenga Memorial Library with 77,833 titles, 441 serial subscriptions, 762 audiovisual materials, an OPAC, a Web page.

Computers on Campus 115 computers available on campus for general student use. A campuswide network can be accessed from student residence rooms and from off campus. Internet access, at least one staffed computer lab available.

Student Life *Housing:* on-campus residence required through senior year. *Options:* coed. Campus housing is university owned. Freshman campus housing is guaranteed. *Activities and organizations:* drama/theater group, student-run newspaper, choral group, Student Association, student ministries, student-run campus newspaper, Pro-Life Task Force, PACE (prison tutoring program). *Campus security:* 24-hour emergency response devices, student patrols, late-night transport/escort service. *Student services:* personal/psychological counseling.

Athletics Member NAIA, NCCAA. *Intercollegiate sports:* baseball M(s), basketball M(s)/W(s), cross-country running M(s)/W(s), soccer M(s)/W(s), softball W(s), track and field M(s)/W(s), volleyball M(s)/W(s). *Intramural sports:* badminton M/W, basketball M/W, racquetball M/W, soccer M/W, table tennis M/W, tennis M/W, track and field M/W, volleyball M/W.

Standardized Tests *Required:* SAT I or ACT (for admission).

Costs (2003–04) *Comprehensive fee:* $21,490 includes full-time tuition ($15,490) and room and board ($6000). Part-time tuition: $520 per semester hour. Part-time tuition and fees vary according to course load. *College room only:* $3100. Room and board charges vary according to board plan. *Payment plan:* installment. *Waivers:* senior citizens and employees or children of employees.

Financial Aid Of all full-time matriculated undergraduates who enrolled in 2001, 659 applied for aid, 582 were judged to have need, 126 had their need fully met. In 2001, 120 non-need-based awards were made. *Average percent of need met:* 67%. *Average financial aid package:* $9875. *Average need-based loan:* $3920. *Average need-based gift aid:* $2572. *Average non-need-based aid:* $1908. *Average indebtedness upon graduation:* $15,728.

Applying *Options:* deferred entrance. *Application fee:* $20. *Required:* essay or personal statement, high school transcript, minimum 2.0 GPA, interview. *Required for some:* 1 letter of recommendation. *Application deadline:* rolling (freshmen). *Notification:* continuous (freshmen), continuous (transfers).

Admissions Contact Mr. Josh Lenarz, Director of Admissions, Trinity Christian College, 6601 West College Drive, Palos Heights, IL 60463. *Phone:* 708-239-4708. *Toll-free phone:* 800-748-0085. *Fax:* 708-239-4826. *E-mail:* admissions@trnty.edu.

■ See page 2522 for a narrative description.

TRINITY COLLEGE OF NURSING AND HEALTH SCIENCES

Rock Island, Illinois

- **Independent** 4-year, founded 1994
- **Calendar** semesters
- **Degrees** certificates, diplomas, associate, and bachelor's (general education requirements are taken off campus, usually at Black Hawk College, Eastern Iowa Community College District and Western Illinois University)
- **Urban** 2-acre campus

- **Endowment** $1.0 million
- **Coed,** 165 undergraduate students, 66% full-time, 79% women, 21% men
- **Most difficult** entrance level, 43% of applicants were admitted

Undergraduates 109 full-time, 56 part-time. Students come from 2 states and territories, 28% are from out of state, 0.6% African American, 0.6% Asian American or Pacific Islander, 4% Hispanic American, 30% transferred in.

Freshmen *Admission:* 115 applied, 50 admitted, 5 enrolled. *Average high school GPA:* 2.50. *Test scores:* ACT scores over 18: 90%.

Faculty *Total:* 14, 86% full-time. *Student/faculty ratio:* 10:1.

Majors Emergency care attendant (EMT ambulance); medical radiologic technology; nursing (registered nurse training); nursing science; surgical technology.

Academic Programs *Special study options:* academic remediation for entering students, adult/continuing education programs, distance learning, honors programs, independent study, off-campus study, part-time degree program, services for LD students, summer session for credit.

Library Trinity Medical Center Library with a Web page.

Computers on Campus A campuswide network can be accessed. At least one staffed computer lab available.

Student Life *Housing:* college housing not available. *Activities and organizations:* Student Nurses Association, student government, BSN Honor Society, Phi Theta Kappa, Alpha Beta Gamma—Radiology Honor Society. *Campus security:* 24-hour emergency response devices, controlled dormitory access. *Student services:* personal/psychological counseling.

Standardized Tests *Required:* SAT I or ACT (for admission).

Costs (2003–04) *Tuition:* $8780 full-time. Full-time tuition and fees vary according to degree level. Part-time tuition and fees vary according to degree level. *Required fees:* $320 full-time. *Payment plan:* deferred payment.

Financial Aid Of all full-time matriculated undergraduates who enrolled in 2001, 87 applied for aid, 40 were judged to have need, 2 had their need fully met. 5 Federal Work-Study jobs (averaging $1500). In 2001, 29 non-need-based awards were made. *Average non-need-based aid:* $750. *Average indebtedness upon graduation:* $5000.

Applying *Options:* common application. *Application fee:* $50. *Required:* high school transcript, minimum 2.75 GPA, minimum ACT score of 21. *Application deadlines:* 6/1 (freshmen), 6/1 (transfers).

Admissions Contact Ms. Barbara Kimpe, Admissions Representative, Trinity College of Nursing and Health Sciences, 2122 25th Avenue, Rock Island, IL 61201. *Phone:* 309-779-7812. *Fax:* 309-779-7748. *E-mail:* con@trinityqc.com.

TRINITY INTERNATIONAL UNIVERSITY

Deerfield, Illinois

- **Independent** university, founded 1897, affiliated with Evangelical Free Church of America
- **Calendar** semesters
- **Degrees** bachelor's, master's, doctoral, first professional, and postbachelor's certificates
- **Suburban** 108-acre campus with easy access to Chicago
- **Endowment** $7.5 million
- **Coed,** 1,428 undergraduate students, 91% full-time, 59% women, 41% men
- **Moderately difficult** entrance level, 87% of applicants were admitted

Undergraduates 1,304 full-time, 124 part-time. Students come from 33 states and territories, 6 other countries, 52% are from out of state, 2% African American, 1% Asian American or Pacific Islander, 1% Hispanic American, 0.4% international, 4% transferred in, 80% live on campus. *Retention:* 85% of 2002 full-time freshmen returned.

Freshmen *Admission:* 498 applied, 431 admitted, 431 enrolled. *Average high school GPA:* 3.28. *Test scores:* SAT verbal scores over 500: 85%; SAT math scores over 500: 76%; ACT scores over 18: 95%; SAT verbal scores over 600: 39%; SAT math scores over 600: 44%; ACT scores over 24: 42%; SAT verbal scores over 700: 10%; SAT math scores over 700: 10%; ACT scores over 30: 7%.

Faculty *Total:* 155, 28% full-time, 32% with terminal degrees. *Student/faculty ratio:* 17:1.

Majors Accounting; athletic training; biblical studies; biology/biological sciences; business administration and management; chemistry; communication and media related; computer science; education; education (K-12); elementary education; English; history; humanities; human resources development; human resources management; international business/trade/commerce; liberal arts and sciences/liberal studies; management science; marketing/marketing management; mathematics; music; music history, literature, and theory; music pedagogy; music related; music teacher education; music theory and composition; non-profit management; pastoral counseling and specialized ministries related; philosophy; physical education teaching and coaching; pre-medical studies; pre-nursing studies; pre-theology/pre-ministerial studies; psychology; religious/sacred music; secondary education; social sciences; youth ministry.

Academic Programs *Special study options:* academic remediation for entering students, adult/continuing education programs, advanced placement credit, double majors, honors programs, independent study, internships, off-campus study, part-time degree program, study abroad.

Library Rolfing Memorial Library with 155,811 titles, 1,332 serial subscriptions, 4,332 audiovisual materials, an OPAC, a Web page.

Computers on Campus 80 computers available on campus for general student use. A campuswide network can be accessed from student residence rooms and from off campus. Internet access, online (class) registration, at least one staffed computer lab available.

Student Life *Housing:* on-campus residence required through junior year. *Options:* men-only, women-only. Campus housing is university owned. Freshman campus housing is guaranteed. *Activities and organizations:* drama/theater group, student-run newspaper, choral group, Student Senate, College Union, Trinity Summer Mission, student newspaper, yearbook. *Campus security:* 24-hour patrols, controlled dormitory access. *Student services:* health clinic, personal/psychological counseling.

Athletics Member NAIA, NCCAA. *Intercollegiate sports:* baseball M(s), basketball M(s)/W(s), football M(s), soccer M(s)/W(s), softball W(s), track and field M/W, volleyball W(s). *Intramural sports:* baseball M, basketball M/W, football M, racquetball M/W, soccer M/W, volleyball W.

Standardized Tests *Required:* SAT I or ACT (for admission).

Costs (2003–04) *Comprehensive fee:* $22,980 includes full-time tuition ($16,900), mandatory fees ($250), and room and board ($5830). Full-time tuition and fees vary according to location. Part-time tuition: $705 per hour. Part-time tuition and fees vary according to location. *Required fees:* $125 per term part-time. *College room only:* $3060. Room and board charges vary according to board plan. *Payment plan:* installment. *Waivers:* employees or children of employees.

Financial Aid Of all full-time matriculated undergraduates who enrolled in 2003, 991 applied for aid, 884 were judged to have need, 35 had their need fully met. 400 Federal Work-Study jobs (averaging $1900). In 2003, 54 non-need-based awards were made. *Average percent of need met:* 27%. *Average financial aid package:* $12,980. *Average need-based loan:* $4252. *Average need-based gift aid:* $7313. *Average non-need-based aid:* $1624. *Average indebtedness upon graduation:* $15,809.

Applying *Options:* electronic application, early admission, deferred entrance. *Application fee:* $25. *Required:* essay or personal statement, high school transcript, minimum 2.5 GPA, 1 letter of recommendation. *Required for some:* interview. *Recommended:* minimum 3.0 GPA. *Application deadline:* rolling (freshmen), rolling (transfers). *Notification:* continuous until 9/1 (freshmen).

Admissions Contact Mr. Matt Yoder, Director of Undergraduate Admissions, Trinity International University, 2065 Half Day Road, Deerfield, IL 60015-1284. *Phone:* 847-317-7000. *Toll-free phone:* 800-822-3225. *Fax:* 847-317-8097. *E-mail:* tcdadm@tiu.edu.

UNIVERSITY OF CHICAGO

Chicago, Illinois

- **Independent** university, founded 1891
- **Calendar** quarters
- **Degrees** bachelor's, master's, doctoral, and first professional
- **Urban** 211-acre campus
- **Coed,** 4,355 undergraduate students, 98% full-time, 51% women, 49% men
- **Most difficult** entrance level, 40% of applicants were admitted

The Undergraduate College of the University of Chicago is at the heart of one of the world's great intellectual communities and centers of learning, where 73 Nobel laureates have researched, studied, or taught. The College offers 50 concentrations of study and the first established and most extensive general education curriculum.

Undergraduates 4,261 full-time, 94 part-time. Students come from 52 states and territories, 59 other countries, 78% are from out of state, 4% African American, 15% Asian American or Pacific Islander, 8% Hispanic American, 0.3% Native American, 8% international, 1% transferred in.

Freshmen *Admission:* 9,100 applied, 3,605 admitted, 1,155 enrolled. *Test scores:* SAT verbal scores over 500: 100%; SAT math scores over 500: 99%; ACT scores over 18: 99%; SAT verbal scores over 600: 90%; SAT math scores over 600: 91%; ACT scores over 24: 94%; SAT verbal scores over 700: 57%; SAT math scores over 700: 53%; ACT scores over 30: 55%.

Faculty *Total:* 1,934, 87% full-time. *Student/faculty ratio:* 4:1.

Majors African-American/Black studies; African studies; American Sign Language related; American studies; ancient/classical Greek; ancient Near Eastern and biblical languages; anthropology; applied mathematics; Arabic; area, ethnic, cultural, and gender studies related; art; art history, criticism and conservation; Asian studies; Asian studies (East); Asian studies (South); Asian studies (South-

University of Chicago (continued)
east); behavioral sciences; Bengali; biochemistry; biology/biological sciences; chemistry; Chinese; classics and languages, literatures and linguistics; comparative literature; computer science; creative writing; economics; English; English language and literature related; environmental studies; European studies (Central and Eastern); film/cinema studies; fine/studio arts; French; geography; geophysics and seismology; German; Hindi; history; human development and family studies; humanities; interdisciplinary studies; international/global studies; Italian; Japanese; Jewish/Judaic studies; Latin; Latin American studies; liberal arts and sciences/liberal studies; linguistics; mathematics; medieval and Renaissance studies; modern languages; music; music history, literature, and theory; Near and Middle Eastern studies; philosophy; physics; political science and government; psychology; public policy analysis; religious studies; Romance languages; Russian; Russian studies; Sanskrit and classical Indian languages; Slavic languages; social sciences; sociology; South Asian languages; Spanish; statistics; Tamil; Tibetan; Turkish; Urdu.

Academic Programs *Special study options:* accelerated degree program, adult/continuing education programs, advanced placement credit, double majors, independent study, internships, off-campus study, student-designed majors, study abroad, summer session for credit. *ROTC:* Army (c), Air Force (c). *Unusual degree programs:* 3-2 law, public policy, teacher education.

Library Joseph Regenstein Library plus 8 others with 5.8 million titles, 47,000 serial subscriptions, an OPAC, a Web page.

Computers on Campus 1000 computers available on campus for general student use. A campuswide network can be accessed from student residence rooms and from off campus. At least one staffed computer lab available.

Student Life *Housing:* on-campus residence required for freshman year. *Options:* coed, cooperative, disabled students. Freshman campus housing is guaranteed. *Activities and organizations:* drama/theater group, student-run newspaper, radio station, choral group, Model United Nations, University Theater, documentary films club, Major Activities Board, student radio station, national fraternities, national sororities. *Campus security:* 24-hour emergency response devices and patrols, student patrols, late-night transport/escort service, controlled dormitory access. *Student services:* health clinic, personal/psychological counseling, women's center.

Athletics Member NCAA. All Division III. *Intercollegiate sports:* baseball M, basketball M/W, cross-country running M/W, football M, soccer M/W, softball W, swimming M/W, tennis M/W, track and field M/W, volleyball W, wrestling M. *Intramural sports:* archery M/W, badminton M/W, basketball M/W, crew M(c)/W(c), cross-country running M/W, fencing M(c)/W(c), football M/W, gymnastics M(c)/W(c), ice hockey M(c), lacrosse M(c)/W(c), racquetball M/W, rugby M(c)/W(c), sailing M(c)/W(c), softball M/W, squash M(c)/W(c), swimming M/W, table tennis M/W, tennis M/W, track and field M/W, volleyball M(c).

Standardized Tests *Required:* SAT I or ACT (for admission).

Costs (2003–04) *Comprehensive fee:* $38,553 includes full-time tuition ($28,689), mandatory fees ($549), and room and board ($9315). Full-time tuition and fees vary according to course load. Part-time tuition and fees vary according to course load. *Room and board:* Room and board charges vary according to board plan. *Payment plans:* tuition prepayment, installment. *Waivers:* employees or children of employees.

Applying *Options:* electronic application, early admission, early action, deferred entrance. *Application fee:* $60. *Required:* essay or personal statement, high school transcript, 3 letters of recommendation. *Recommended:* interview. *Application deadlines:* 1/1 (freshmen), 4/11 (transfers). *Notification:* 4/1 (freshmen), 12/15 (early action), 5/15 (transfers).

Admissions Contact Mr. Theodore O'Neill, Dean of Admissions, University of Chicago, 1116 East 59th Street, Chicago, IL 60637-1513. *Phone:* 773-702-8650. *Fax:* 773-702-4199.

■ *See page 2584 for a narrative description.*

UNIVERSITY OF ILLINOIS AT CHICAGO

Chicago, Illinois

- **State-supported** university, founded 1946, part of University of Illinois System
- **Calendar** semesters
- **Degrees** bachelor's, master's, doctoral, first professional, and first professional certificates
- **Urban** 240-acre campus
- **Endowment** $109.4 million
- **Coed,** 16,012 undergraduate students, 89% full-time, 55% women, 45% men
- **Moderately difficult** entrance level, 61% of applicants were admitted

Undergraduates 14,276 full-time, 1,736 part-time. Students come from 52 states and territories, 48 other countries, 3% are from out of state, 9% African American, 25% Asian American or Pacific Islander, 16% Hispanic American, 0.2% Native American, 1% international, 8% transferred in, 11% live on campus. *Retention:* 78% of 2002 full-time freshmen returned.

Freshmen *Admission:* 12,250 applied, 7,425 admitted, 2,942 enrolled. *Test scores:* ACT scores over 18: 97%; ACT scores over 24: 45%; ACT scores over 30: 6%.

Faculty *Total:* 1,456, 82% full-time, 80% with terminal degrees. *Student/faculty ratio:* 16:1.

Majors Accounting; African-American/Black studies; anthropology; architecture; art history, criticism and conservation; art teacher education; biochemistry; biology/biological sciences; biology teacher education; biomedical/medical engineering; business administration and management; chemical engineering; chemistry; chemistry teacher education; cinematography and film/video production; civil engineering; classics and languages, literatures and linguistics; clinical laboratory science/medical technology; commercial and advertising art; computer and information sciences; computer engineering; criminal justice/safety; dietetics; dramatic/theatre arts; economics; electrical, electronics and communications engineering; elementary education; engineering/industrial management; engineering physics; English; English/language arts teacher education; entrepreneurship; finance; fine/studio arts; foreign language teacher education; French; French language teacher education; geology/earth science; German; German language teacher education; graphic design; health information/medical records administration; history; history teacher education; industrial design; industrial engineering; Italian; kinesiology and exercise science; Latin American studies; management information systems; marketing/marketing management; mathematics; mathematics and computer science; mathematics teacher education; mechanical engineering; music; nursing (registered nurse training); philosophy; photography; physics; physics teacher education; Polish; political science and government; pre-dentistry studies; pre-law studies; psychology; Russian; science teacher education; secondary education; Slavic languages; social science teacher education; social work; sociology; Spanish; Spanish language teacher education; speech and rhetoric; statistics.

Academic Programs *Special study options:* academic remediation for entering students, accelerated degree program, advanced placement credit, cooperative education, distance learning, double majors, English as a second language, honors programs, independent study, internships, off-campus study, part-time degree program, services for LD students, student-designed majors, study abroad, summer session for credit. *ROTC:* Army (b), Navy (c), Air Force (c).

Library Richard J. Daley Library plus 7 others with 2.2 million titles, 21,571 serial subscriptions, 28,436 audiovisual materials, an OPAC, a Web page.

Computers on Campus 1100 computers available on campus for general student use. A campuswide network can be accessed from student residence rooms and from off campus. At least one staffed computer lab available.

Student Life *Housing options:* coed. Campus housing is university owned. *Activities and organizations:* drama/theater group, student-run newspaper, radio station, choral group, Golden Key National Honor Society, Chinese Students and Scholars Friendship Association, Muslim Student Association, MBA Association, Alternative Spring Break, national fraternities, national sororities. *Campus security:* 24-hour emergency response devices and patrols, student patrols, late-night transport/escort service, controlled dormitory access, housing ID stickers, guest escort policy, 24-hour closed circuit videos for exits and entrances, security screen for first floor. *Student services:* health clinic, personal/psychological counseling, women's center, legal services.

Athletics Member NCAA. All Division I. *Intercollegiate sports:* baseball M(s), basketball M(s)/W(s), cross-country running M(s)/W(s), gymnastics M(s)/W(s), soccer M(s), softball W(s), swimming M(s)/W(s), tennis M(s)/W(s), track and field M(s)/W(s), ultimate Frisbee M(c)/W(c), volleyball W(s). *Intramural sports:* badminton M/W, basketball M/W, bowling M/W, cross-country running M/W, fencing M(c)/W(c), field hockey M/W, football M/W, golf M/W, lacrosse M(c)/W(c), racquetball M/W, rugby M(c)/W(c), soccer M/W, softball M/W, squash M/W, table tennis M/W, tennis M/W, volleyball M(c)/W, water polo M(c)/W(c), wrestling M.

Standardized Tests *Required:* SAT I or ACT (for admission).

Costs (2004–05) *Tuition:* state resident $5682 full-time; nonresident $16,930 full-time. Full-time tuition and fees vary according to course load and program. Part-time tuition and fees vary according to course load and program. No tuition increase for student's term of enrollment. *Required fees:* $2178 full-time. *Room and board:* $6884. Room and board charges vary according to board plan and housing facility. *Waivers:* senior citizens and employees or children of employees.

Financial Aid Of all full-time matriculated undergraduates who enrolled in 2003, 10,080 applied for aid, 7,841 were judged to have need, 4,064 had their need fully met. 657 Federal Work-Study jobs (averaging $1100). 2,635 state and other part-time jobs (averaging $2600). In 2003, 1013 non-need-based awards were made. *Average percent of need met:* 90%. *Average financial aid package:* $11,600. *Average need-based loan:* $3819. *Average need-based gift aid:* $7032. *Average non-need-based aid:* $3009. *Average indebtedness upon graduation:* $17,000.

Applying *Options:* electronic application. *Application fee:* $40. *Required:* high school transcript. *Required for some:* essay or personal statement, interview. *Application deadlines:* 1/15 (freshmen), 3/1 (transfers). *Notification:* continuous (freshmen), continuous (transfers).

Admissions Contact Mr. Thomas E. Glenn, Executive Director of Admissions, University of Illinois at Chicago, Box 5220, Chicago, IL 60680-5220. *Phone:* 312-996-4350. *Fax:* 312-413-7628. *E-mail:* uic.admit@uic.edu.

UNIVERSITY OF ILLINOIS AT SPRINGFIELD

Springfield, Illinois

- **State-supported** upper-level, founded 1969, part of University of Illinois
- **Calendar** semesters
- **Degrees** certificates, bachelor's, master's, and doctoral
- **Suburban** 746-acre campus
- **Endowment** $4.5 million
- **Coed,** 2,569 undergraduate students, 58% full-time, 61% women, 39% men
- **Minimally difficult** entrance level, 52% of applicants were admitted

Undergraduates 1,497 full-time, 1,072 part-time. Students come from 26 states and territories, 2% are from out of state, 8% African American, 2% Asian American or Pacific Islander, 2% Hispanic American, 0.3% Native American, 0.7% international, 24% transferred in, 12% live on campus.

Faculty *Total:* 300, 57% full-time. *Student/faculty ratio:* 15:1.

Majors Accounting; anthropology; art; biology/biological sciences; business administration and management; chemistry; child development; computer science; criminal justice/law enforcement administration; economics; elementary education; English; family and consumer sciences/home economics teacher education; health/health care administration; history; interdisciplinary studies; legal studies; liberal arts and sciences/liberal studies; mass communication/media; mathematics; medical laboratory technology; nursing (registered nurse training); political science and government; psychology; secondary education; social work; sociology.

Academic Programs *Special study options:* academic remediation for entering students, adult/continuing education programs, cooperative education, external degree program, internships, off-campus study, part-time degree program, student-designed majors, summer session for credit.

Library Brookens Library with 521,389 titles, 2,014 serial subscriptions, 40,171 audiovisual materials, an OPAC, a Web page.

Computers on Campus 160 computers available on campus for general student use. A campuswide network can be accessed from student residence rooms and from off campus. Internet access, at least one staffed computer lab available.

Student Life *Housing options:* coed. Campus housing is university owned. *Activities and organizations:* student-run newspaper, radio and television station, USAS—United Students Against Sweatshops, OLAS—Organization of Latin American Students, Culturazzi, Christian Student Fellowship, Blue Crew. *Campus security:* 24-hour patrols, late-night transport/escort service. *Student services:* health clinic, personal/psychological counseling, women's center.

Athletics Member NAIA. *Intercollegiate sports:* basketball M(s)/W(s), soccer M(s), softball W(s), tennis M(s)/W(s), volleyball W(s). *Intramural sports:* basketball M/W, bowling M/W, cross-country running M/W, fencing M/W, football M/W, golf M/W, soccer W, softball M, table tennis M/W, tennis M/W, volleyball M/W.

Costs (2003–04) *Tuition:* state resident $3450 full-time, $115 per credit part-time; nonresident $10,350 full-time, $345 per credit part-time. *Required fees:* $860 full-time, $430 per term part-time. *Room and board:* $7000. Room and board charges vary according to housing facility. *Payment plan:* installment. *Waivers:* senior citizens and employees or children of employees.

Financial Aid Of all full-time matriculated undergraduates who enrolled in 2003, 1,087 applied for aid, 870 were judged to have need, 340 had their need fully met. 55 Federal Work-Study jobs (averaging $2345). 294 state and other part-time jobs (averaging $1701). In 2003, 199 non-need-based awards were made. *Average percent of need met:* 83%. *Average financial aid package:* $7226. *Average need-based loan:* $3805. *Average need-based gift aid:* $4759. *Average non-need-based aid:* $2915. *Average indebtedness upon graduation:* $10,407. *Financial aid deadline:* 11/15.

Applying *Options:* deferred entrance. *Application fee:* $40. *Application deadline:* rolling (freshmen), rolling (transfers). *Notification:* continuous (transfers).

Admissions Contact Office of Enrollment Services, University of Illinois at Springfield, Building SAB. *Phone:* 217-206-6626. *Toll-free phone:* 888-977-4847. *Fax:* 217-206-6620.

UNIVERSITY OF ILLINOIS AT URBANA–CHAMPAIGN

Champaign, Illinois

- **State-supported** university, founded 1867, part of University of Illinois System
- **Calendar** semesters
- **Degrees** certificates, bachelor's, master's, doctoral, first professional, and post-master's certificates
- **Small-town** 1470-acre campus
- **Endowment** $619.2 million
- **Coed,** 29,226 undergraduate students, 96% full-time, 47% women, 53% men
- **Very difficult** entrance level, 63% of applicants were admitted

Undergraduates 28,095 full-time, 1,131 part-time. Students come from 52 states and territories, 70 other countries, 12% are from out of state, 8% African American, 13% Asian American or Pacific Islander, 6% Hispanic American, 0.3% Native American, 3% international, 4% transferred in, 30% live on campus. *Retention:* 93% of 2002 full-time freshmen returned.

Freshmen *Admission:* 22,269 applied, 13,939 admitted, 6,811 enrolled. *Test scores:* SAT verbal scores over 500: 91%; SAT math scores over 500: 97%; ACT scores over 18: 99%; SAT verbal scores over 600: 58%; SAT math scores over 600: 79%; ACT scores over 24: 86%; SAT verbal scores over 700: 14%; SAT math scores over 700: 37%; ACT scores over 30: 34%.

Faculty *Total:* 2,537, 86% full-time, 87% with terminal degrees. *Student/faculty ratio:* 12:1.

Majors Accounting; actuarial science; advertising; aerospace, aeronautical and astronautical engineering; agribusiness; agricultural/biological engineering and bioengineering; agricultural communication/journalism; agricultural economics; agricultural mechanization; agriculture; agronomy and crop science; animal sciences; anthropology; architecture related; area studies related; art history, criticism and conservation; art teacher education; Asian studies (East); astronomy; audiology and speech-language pathology; biochemistry; biological and biomedical sciences related; biology/biological sciences; biomedical/medical engineering; biophysics; botany/plant biology; broadcast journalism; business/commerce; business teacher education; cell and molecular biology; cell biology and histology; chemical engineering; chemistry; city/urban, community and regional planning; civil engineering; classics and languages, literatures and linguistics; communication and journalism related; community health and preventive medicine; comparative literature; computer engineering; computer science; computer teacher education; crafts, folk art and artisanry; dance; dramatic/theatre arts; ecology; economics; economics related; electrical, electronics and communications engineering; elementary education; engineering; engineering mechanics; engineering physics; English; English composition; English/language arts teacher education; entomology; environmental science; fashion merchandising; finance; food science; foreign language teacher education; forestry; French; French language teacher education; geography; geology/earth science; German; German language teacher education; graphic design; history; horticultural science; human development and family studies; humanities; industrial and organizational psychology; industrial design; industrial engineering; Italian; journalism; kindergarten/preschool education; kinesiology and exercise science; landscape architecture; Latin American studies; Latin teacher education; liberal arts and sciences/liberal studies; linguistics; marketing related; mass communication/media; materials science; mathematics; mathematics and computer science; mechanical engineering; microbiology; music; music history, literature, and theory; music performance; music teacher education; music theory and composition; nuclear engineering; ornamental horticulture; painting; parks, recreation and leisure; philosophy; photography; physics; physiology; political science and government; Portuguese; pre-veterinary studies; psychology; public health related; religious studies; restaurant, culinary, and catering management; Russian; Russian studies; sales, distribution and marketing; sculpture; social studies teacher education; sociology; Spanish; Spanish language teacher education; special education; speech and rhetoric; statistics; voice and opera.

Academic Programs *Special study options:* accelerated degree program, advanced placement credit, cooperative education, distance learning, double majors, honors programs, internships, off-campus study, services for LD students, student-designed majors, study abroad, summer session for credit. *ROTC:* Army (b), Air Force (b). *Unusual degree programs:* 3-2 accounting.

Library University Library plus 42 others with 9.9 million titles, 90,707 serial subscriptions, 1.0 million audiovisual materials, an OPAC, a Web page.

Computers on Campus 3500 computers available on campus for general student use. A campuswide network can be accessed from student residence rooms and from off campus. Internet access, online (class) registration, at least one staffed computer lab available. Computer purchase or lease plan available.

Student Life *Housing:* on-campus residence required for freshman year. *Options:* coed, men-only, women-only, cooperative, disabled students. Campus housing is university owned and is provided by a third party. Freshman campus

University of Illinois at Urbana–Champaign (continued)
housing is guaranteed. *Activities and organizations:* drama/theater group, student-run newspaper, radio and television station, choral group, marching band, Volunteer Illini Project, Alpha Phi Omega, Indian Student Organization, Panhellenic Interfraternity Council, Residence Hall Association, national fraternities, national sororities. *Campus security:* 24-hour emergency response devices and patrols, student patrols, late-night transport/escort service, controlled dormitory access, safety training classes, ID cards with safety numbers. *Student services:* health clinic, personal/psychological counseling, women's center, legal services.

Athletics Member NCAA. All Division I except football (Division I-A). *Intercollegiate sports:* baseball M(s), basketball M(s)/W(s), cheerleading M/W, cross-country running M(s)/W(s), golf M(s)/W(s), gymnastics M(s)/W(s), soccer W(s), swimming W(s), tennis M(s)/W(s), track and field M(s)/W(s), volleyball W(s), wrestling M(s). *Intramural sports:* archery M/W, badminton M/W, basketball M/W, bowling M/W, cross-country running M/W, equestrian sports M(c)/W(c), fencing M(c)/W(c), field hockey W(c), football M/W, golf M/W, gymnastics M(c)/W(c), ice hockey M/W, lacrosse M(c)/W(c), racquetball M/W, riflery M(c)/W(c), rugby M(c)/W(c), sailing M(c)/W(c), skiing (cross-country) M(c)/W(c), skiing (downhill) M(c)/W(c), soccer M/W, softball M/W, squash M(c)/W(c), swimming M/W, table tennis M/W, tennis M/W, volleyball M/W, water polo M/W, weight lifting M(c)/W(c), wrestling M/W.

Standardized Tests *Required:* SAT I or ACT (for admission).

Costs (2004–05) *Tuition:* state resident $7922 full-time; nonresident $19,404 full-time. Full-time tuition and fees vary according to course load, program, and student level. No tuition increase for student's term of enrollment. *Required fees:* $1462 full-time. *Room and board:* $6848; room only: $2831. Room and board charges vary according to board plan and housing facility. *Payment plan:* installment. *Waivers:* senior citizens and employees or children of employees.

Financial Aid Of all full-time matriculated undergraduates who enrolled in 2003, 16,277 applied for aid, 11,726 were judged to have need, 6,039 had their need fully met. 1,655 Federal Work-Study jobs (averaging $1500). In 2003, 3460 non-need-based awards were made. *Average percent of need met:* 90%. *Average financial aid package:* $8521. *Average need-based loan:* $3748. *Average need-based gift aid:* $6195. *Average non-need-based aid:* $3172. *Average indebtedness upon graduation:* $15,100.

Applying *Options:* deferred entrance. *Application fee:* $40. *Required:* essay or personal statement, high school transcript. *Required for some:* audition, statement of professional interest. *Application deadlines:* 1/1 (freshmen), 3/15 (transfers). *Notification:* continuous (freshmen), continuous (transfers).

Admissions Contact Mr. Abel Montoya, Acting Associate Director, University of Illinois at Urbana–Champaign, 901 West Illinois, Urbana, IL 61801. *Phone:* 217-333-0302. *E-mail:* admissions@oar.uiuc.edu.

University of Phoenix–Chicago Campus
Schaumburg, Illinois

- **Proprietary** comprehensive, founded 2002
- **Calendar** continuous
- **Degrees** certificates, associate, bachelor's, master's, doctoral, post-master's, and postbachelor's certificates (courses conducted at 121 campuses and learning centers in 25 states)
- **Coed,** 453 undergraduate students, 100% full-time, 51% women, 49% men
- **Noncompetitive** entrance level

Undergraduates 453 full-time. 15% African American, 5% Asian American or Pacific Islander, 9% Hispanic American, 7% international.

Freshmen *Admission:* 35 enrolled.

Faculty *Total:* 36, 8% full-time, 25% with terminal degrees.

Majors Accounting; business administration and management; management information systems; management science; marketing/marketing management.

Academic Programs *Special study options:* accelerated degree program, adult/continuing education programs, advanced placement credit, distance learning, external degree program, independent study.

Library University Library with 27.1 million titles, 11,648 serial subscriptions, an OPAC, a Web page.

Computers on Campus A campuswide network can be accessed from off campus. At least one staffed computer lab available.

Student Life *Housing:* college housing not available.

Costs (2003–04) *Tuition:* $9900 full-time, $330 per credit part-time. *Waivers:* employees or children of employees.

Financial Aid *Average financial aid package:* $1171.

Applying *Options:* deferred entrance. *Application fee:* $100. *Required:* 1 letter of recommendation, 2 years of work experience, 23 years of age. *Required for some:* high school transcript. *Application deadline:* rolling (freshmen), rolling (transfers).

Admissions Contact Ms. Beth Barilla, Director of Admissions, University of Phoenix–Chicago Campus, 4615 East Elwood Street, Mail Stop AA-K101, Phoenix, AZ 85040-1958. *Phone:* 480-317-6000. *Toll-free phone:* 800-228-7240. *Fax:* 480-594-1758. *E-mail:* beth.barilla@phoenix.edu.

University of St. Francis
Joliet, Illinois

- **Independent Roman Catholic** comprehensive, founded 1920
- **Calendar** semesters
- **Degrees** certificates, bachelor's, master's, and postbachelor's certificates
- **Suburban** 17-acre campus with easy access to Chicago
- **Endowment** $10.3 million
- **Coed,** 1,143 undergraduate students, 92% full-time, 67% women, 33% men
- **Moderately difficult** entrance level, 58% of applicants were admitted

Founded in 1920, the University of St. Francis, in Joliet, Illinois, offers a rich tradition of excellence in higher education. With more than 60 areas of academic study, the University's academic quality is matched only by its commitment to technology and innovation in course delivery, as well as a long-standing belief in providing the best service and personal attention to University of St. Francis students.

Undergraduates 1,054 full-time, 89 part-time. Students come from 8 states and territories, 2 other countries, 2% are from out of state, 7% African American, 2% Asian American or Pacific Islander, 8% Hispanic American, 0.3% Native American, 0.2% international, 18% transferred in, 25% live on campus. *Retention:* 72% of 2002 full-time freshmen returned.

Freshmen *Admission:* 768 applied, 443 admitted, 189 enrolled. *Average high school GPA:* 3.33. *Test scores:* ACT scores over 18: 80%; ACT scores over 24: 22%.

Faculty *Total:* 189, 36% full-time, 38% with terminal degrees. *Student/faculty ratio:* 14:1.

Majors Accounting; biology/biological sciences; business administration and management; clinical laboratory science/medical technology; computer science; computer systems networking and telecommunications; elementary education; English; English/language arts teacher education; environmental science; finance; history; information technology; journalism; liberal arts and sciences/liberal studies; marketing/marketing management; mass communication/media; mathematics; mathematics teacher education; medical radiologic technology; nuclear medical technology; nursing (registered nurse training); parks, recreation and leisure facilities management; political science and government; pre-dentistry studies; pre-medical studies; pre-veterinary studies; psychology; radiologic technology/science; science teacher education; social studies teacher education; social work; special education; theology; visual and performing arts; web/multimedia management and webmaster.

Academic Programs *Special study options:* academic remediation for entering students, accelerated degree program, adult/continuing education programs, advanced placement credit, distance learning, double majors, external degree program, independent study, internships, off-campus study, part-time degree program, student-designed majors, study abroad, summer session for credit. *Unusual degree programs:* 3-2 computer science engineering with Illinois Institute of Technology.

Library University of St. Francis Library with 105,121 titles, 953 serial subscriptions, 8,601 audiovisual materials, an OPAC, a Web page.

Computers on Campus 147 computers available on campus for general student use. A campuswide network can be accessed from student residence rooms. Internet access, online (class) registration, at least one staffed computer lab available.

Student Life *Housing options:* coed. Campus housing is university owned and leased by the school. Freshman campus housing is guaranteed. *Activities and organizations:* drama/theater group, student-run newspaper, radio and television station, choral group, Ethnic Affairs Council, Student Activities Board, Student Government Association, Sometimes Thespians, Student Business Association. *Campus security:* 24-hour emergency response devices and patrols, late-night transport/escort service, controlled dormitory access, First Response trained security personnel. *Student services:* health clinic, personal/psychological counseling.

Athletics Member NAIA. *Intercollegiate sports:* baseball M(s), basketball M(s)/W(s), cheerleading W(s), cross-country running W(s), football M(s), golf M(s)/W(s), soccer M(s)/W(s), softball W(s), tennis M(s)/W(s), track and field W(s), volleyball W(s). *Intramural sports:* basketball M/W, bowling M/W, golf M/W, racquetball M/W, skiing (downhill) M/W, table tennis M/W, tennis M/W, volleyball M/W.

Standardized Tests *Required:* SAT I or ACT (for admission).

Costs (2003–04) *Comprehensive fee:* $22,870 includes full-time tuition ($16,480), mandatory fees ($360), and room and board ($6030). Part-time tuition:

$480 per semester hour. Part-time tuition and fees vary according to course load. *Required fees:* $15 per semester part-time. *College room only:* $2930. *Payment plan:* installment. *Waivers:* children of alumni and employees or children of employees.

Financial Aid Of all full-time matriculated undergraduates who enrolled in 2003, 1,029 applied for aid, 732 were judged to have need, 587 had their need fully met. 218 Federal Work-Study jobs (averaging $1780). 246 state and other part-time jobs (averaging $1417). In 2003, 239 non-need-based awards were made. *Average percent of need met:* 81%. *Average financial aid package:* $13,695. *Average need-based loan:* $4109. *Average need-based gift aid:* $8401. *Average non-need-based aid:* $4806. *Average indebtedness upon graduation:* $16,359.

Applying *Options:* electronic application, deferred entrance. *Application fee:* $20. *Required:* high school transcript, minimum 2.0 GPA. *Required for some:* essay or personal statement, 2 letters of recommendation, interview. *Application deadline:* 9/1 (freshmen). *Notification:* continuous (freshmen), continuous (transfers).

Admissions Contact Ms. Jean Norris, Vice President, Admissions and Enrollment Services, University of St. Francis, 500 North Wilcox Street, Joliet, IL 60435-6188. *Phone:* 815-740-3366. *Toll-free phone:* 800-735-3500. *Fax:* 815-740-5032. *E-mail:* admissions@stfrancis.edu.

■ *See page 2698 for a narrative description.*

VanderCook College of Music

Chicago, Illinois

- **Independent** comprehensive, founded 1909
- **Calendar** semesters
- **Degrees** bachelor's and master's
- **Urban** 1-acre campus
- **Endowment** $432,276
- **Coed**
- **Moderately difficult** entrance level

Faculty *Student/faculty ratio:* 8:1.

Student Life *Campus security:* 24-hour emergency response devices and patrols, late-night transport/escort service, controlled dormitory access.

Standardized Tests *Required:* SAT I or ACT (for admission).

Costs (2004–05) *Comprehensive fee:* $22,660 includes full-time tuition ($15,130), mandatory fees ($630), and room and board ($6900). Part-time tuition: $635 per semester hour. Part-time tuition and fees vary according to course load. *Required fees:* $315 per term part-time. *Room and board:* Room and board charges vary according to board plan and housing facility.

Financial Aid *Average financial aid package:* $7983. *Average indebtedness upon graduation:* $18,500. *Financial aid deadline:* 6/7.

Applying *Options:* deferred entrance. *Application fee:* $35. *Required:* essay or personal statement, high school transcript, 3 letters of recommendation, interview, audition. *Required for some:* minimum 3.0 GPA. *Recommended:* minimum 3.0 GPA.

Admissions Contact Ms. Tamara V. Trutwin, Student Recruiter, VanderCook College of Music, 3140 South Federal Street, Chicago, IL 60616. *Phone:* 800-448-2655 Ext. 241. *Toll-free phone:* 800-448-2655 Ext. 230. *Fax:* 312-225-5211. *E-mail:* admissions@vandercook.edu.

■ *See page 2754 for a narrative description.*

Western Illinois University

Macomb, Illinois

- **State-supported** comprehensive, founded 1899
- **Calendar** semesters
- **Degrees** bachelor's, master's, post-master's, and postbachelor's certificates
- **Small-town** 1050-acre campus
- **Endowment** $17.6 million
- **Coed,** 11,027 undergraduate students, 89% full-time, 49% women, 51% men
- **Moderately difficult** entrance level, 66% of applicants were admitted

Western Illinois University guarantees a fixed rate of tuition, fees, room, and board for all new undergraduate students. The program establishes and freezes a per-semester-hour cost for students for 4 years as long as they maintain continuous enrollment at Western. All new undergraduate students entering the University are automatically included.

Undergraduates 9,790 full-time, 1,237 part-time. Students come from 33 states and territories, 44 other countries, 6% are from out of state, 7% African American, 1% Asian American or Pacific Islander, 3% Hispanic American, 0.2% Native American, 1% international, 12% transferred in, 51% live on campus. *Retention:* 76% of 2002 full-time freshmen returned.

Freshmen *Admission:* 7,612 applied, 5,032 admitted, 1,961 enrolled. *Test scores:* ACT scores over 18: 90%; ACT scores over 24: 25%; ACT scores over 30: 2%.

Faculty *Total:* 685, 91% full-time, 66% with terminal degrees. *Student/faculty ratio:* 17:1.

Majors Accounting; African-American/Black studies; agriculture; art; bilingual and multilingual education; biology/biological sciences; business administration and management; business/managerial economics; chemistry; clinical laboratory science/medical technology; communication disorders; communication/speech communication and rhetoric; computer and information sciences; criminal justice/law enforcement administration; dramatic/theatre arts; economics; educational/instructional media design; elementary education; English; family and consumer sciences/human sciences; finance; fine/studio arts; French; geography; geology/earth science; graphic and printing equipment operation/production; health/health care administration; health teacher education; history; human resources management; industrial technology; journalism; liberal arts and sciences/liberal studies; management information systems; manufacturing technology; marketing/marketing management; mathematics; meteorology; music; music related; parks, recreation and leisure facilities management; philosophy; physical education teaching and coaching; physics; political science and government; psychology; radio and television; social work; sociology; Spanish; special education; trade and industrial teacher education; women's studies.

Academic Programs *Special study options:* academic remediation for entering students, adult/continuing education programs, advanced placement credit, distance learning, double majors, English as a second language, external degree program, freshman honors college, honors programs, independent study, internships, off-campus study, part-time degree program, services for LD students, student-designed majors, study abroad, summer session for credit. *ROTC:* Army (b). *Unusual degree programs:* 3-2 engineering with University of Illinois at Urbana–Champaign, Case Western Reserve University.

Library Leslie Malpass Library plus 4 others with 998,041 titles, 3,200 serial subscriptions, 3,445 audiovisual materials, an OPAC, a Web page.

Computers on Campus 1000 computers available on campus for general student use. A campuswide network can be accessed from student residence rooms and from off campus that provide access to course registration. Internet access, online (class) registration, at least one staffed computer lab available.

Student Life *Housing:* on-campus residence required through sophomore year. *Options:* coed, men-only, women-only. Campus housing is university owned. Freshman campus housing is guaranteed. *Activities and organizations:* drama/theater group, student-run newspaper, radio and television station, choral group, marching band, Student Government Association, Black Student Association, University Union Board, International Friendship Club, Bureau of Cultural Affairs, national fraternities, national sororities. *Campus security:* 24-hour emergency response devices and patrols, student patrols, late-night transport/escort service, controlled dormitory access. *Student services:* health clinic, personal/psychological counseling, women's center, legal services.

Athletics Member NCAA. All Division I except football (Division I-AA). *Intercollegiate sports:* baseball M(s), basketball M(s)/W(s), cross-country running M(s)/W(s), golf M(s)/W, soccer M(s)/W(s), softball W(s), swimming M(s)/W(s), tennis M(s)/W(s), track and field M(s)/W(s), volleyball W(s). *Intramural sports:* badminton M/W, basketball M/W, bowling M/W, cheerleading M/W, cross-country running M/W, football M/W, golf M/W, lacrosse M, racquetball M/W, rugby M/W, soccer M/W, softball M/W, swimming M/W, table tennis M/W, tennis M/W, volleyball M/W, water polo M/W.

Standardized Tests *Required:* SAT I or ACT (for admission).

Costs (2003–04) *Tuition:* state resident $3915 full-time, $131 per credit hour part-time; nonresident $7830 full-time, $261 per credit hour part-time. Full-time tuition and fees vary according to location. Part-time tuition and fees vary according to location. No tuition increase for student's term of enrollment. *Required fees:* $1487 full-time, $36 per credit hour part-time. *Room and board:* $5366; room only: $3122. *Waivers:* senior citizens and employees or children of employees.

Financial Aid Of all full-time matriculated undergraduates who enrolled in 2003, 6,905 applied for aid, 5,495 were judged to have need, 1,972 had their need fully met. 305 Federal Work-Study jobs (averaging $1540). 1,763 state and other part-time jobs (averaging $806). In 2003, 555 non-need-based awards were made. *Average percent of need met:* 68%. *Average financial aid package:* $7428. *Average need-based loan:* $3411. *Average need-based gift aid:* $4794. *Average non-need-based aid:* $1862. *Average indebtedness upon graduation:* $13,800.

Applying *Options:* electronic application, deferred entrance. *Application fee:* $30. *Required:* high school transcript. *Application deadline:* 8/1 (freshmen), rolling (transfers). *Notification:* continuous until 8/3 (freshmen), continuous (transfers).

Western Illinois University (continued)

Admissions Contact Ms. Karen Helmers, Director of Admissions, Western Illinois University, 1 University Circle, 115 Sherman Hall, Macomb, IL 61455-1390. *Phone:* 309-298-3157. *Toll-free phone:* 877-742-5948. *Fax:* 309-298-3111. *E-mail:* kl-helmers@wiu.edu.

■ *See page 2812 for a narrative description.*

WEST SUBURBAN COLLEGE OF NURSING

Oak Park, Illinois

- **Independent** upper-level, founded 1982
- **Calendar** semesters
- **Degree** bachelor's
- **Suburban** 10-acre campus with easy access to Chicago
- **Coed, primarily women**
- **Moderately difficult** entrance level

Faculty *Student/faculty ratio:* 14:1.

Student Life *Campus security:* 24-hour emergency response devices and patrols, late-night transport/escort service, controlled dormitory access.

Costs (2003–04) *Tuition:* $17,745 full-time, $600 per semester hour part-time. *Required fees:* $250 full-time, $125 per term part-time.

Applying *Options:* deferred entrance.

Admissions Contact Ms. Cindy Valdez, Director of Admission and Records/Registrar, West Suburban College of Nursing, 3 Erie Court, Oak Park, IL 60302. *Phone:* 708-763-6530. *Fax:* 708-763-1531.

WESTWOOD COLLEGE OF TECHNOLOGY-CHICAGO DU PAGE

Woodridge, Illinois

- **Proprietary** primarily 2-year
- **Degrees** associate and bachelor's
- **Coed**

Admissions Contact Mr. Scott Kawall, Director of Admissions, Westwood College of Technology-Chicago Du Page, 7155 James Avenue, Woodridge, IL 60517-2321. *Phone:* 630-434-8244. *Toll-free phone:* 888-721-7646. *Fax:* 630-434-8255. *E-mail:* info@westwood.edu.

WESTWOOD COLLEGE OF TECHNOLOGY–CHICAGO RIVER OAKS

Calumet City, Illinois

- **Proprietary** primarily 2-year
- **Degrees** associate and bachelor's
- **Coed**

Admissions Contact Mr. Barry McDonald, Director of Admissions, Westwood College of Technology–Chicago River Oaks, 80 River Oaks Drive, Suite D-49, Calumet City, IL 60409-5820. *Phone:* 708-832-1988. *Toll-free phone:* 888-549-6873. *Fax:* 708-832-9617. *E-mail:* info@westwood.edu.

WHEATON COLLEGE

Wheaton, Illinois

- **Independent nondenominational** comprehensive, founded 1860
- **Calendar** semesters
- **Degrees** bachelor's, master's, doctoral, and postbachelor's certificates
- **Suburban** 80-acre campus with easy access to Chicago
- **Endowment** $233.0 million
- **Coed,** 2,430 undergraduate students, 97% full-time, 51% women, 49% men
- **Very difficult** entrance level, 53% of applicants were admitted

Undergraduates 2,349 full-time, 81 part-time. Students come from 51 states and territories, 16 other countries, 69% are from out of state, 2% African American, 7% Asian American or Pacific Islander, 2% Hispanic American, 0.3% Native American, 1% international, 4% transferred in, 89% live on campus. *Retention:* 93% of 2002 full-time freshmen returned.

Freshmen *Admission:* 2,170 applied, 1,146 admitted, 576 enrolled. *Average high school GPA:* 3.71. *Test scores:* SAT verbal scores over 500: 100%; SAT math scores over 500: 98%; ACT scores over 18: 100%; SAT verbal scores over 600: 85%; SAT math scores over 600: 82%; ACT scores over 24: 92%; SAT verbal scores over 700: 37%; SAT math scores over 700: 29%; ACT scores over 30: 45%.

Faculty *Total:* 279, 68% full-time, 74% with terminal degrees. *Student/faculty ratio:* 11:1.

Majors Anthropology; archeology; art; biblical studies; biology/biological sciences; business/managerial economics; chemistry; communication/speech communication and rhetoric; computer science; economics; elementary education; engineering related; English; environmental studies; French; geology/earth science; German; health/medical preparatory programs related; history; international relations and affairs; kinesiology and exercise science; mathematics; multi-/interdisciplinary studies related; music; music history, literature, and theory; music management and merchandising; music performance; music related; music teacher education; music theory and composition; philosophy; physics; political science and government; psychology; religious education; religious studies; science teacher education; social studies teacher education; sociology; Spanish.

Academic Programs *Special study options:* advanced placement credit, double majors, independent study, internships, off-campus study, services for LD students, student-designed majors, study abroad, summer session for credit. *ROTC:* Army (b), Air Force (c). *Unusual degree programs:* 3-2 engineering with University of Illinois, Case Western Reserve University, Washington University in St. Louis, Illinois Institute of Technology; nursing with Rush University, Emory University, Goshen College, University of Rochester.

Library Buswell Memorial Library plus 1 other with 429,892 titles, 2,751 serial subscriptions, 38,591 audiovisual materials, an OPAC, a Web page.

Computers on Campus 238 computers available on campus for general student use. A campuswide network can be accessed from student residence rooms and from off campus. Internet access, online (class) registration, at least one staffed computer lab available.

Student Life *Housing:* on-campus residence required through senior year. *Options:* men-only, women-only, cooperative. Campus housing is university owned. Freshman campus housing is guaranteed. *Activities and organizations:* drama/theater group, student-run newspaper, radio and television station, choral group, intramurals, Discipleship small groups, Christian Service Council, Orientation Committee, Resident Assistant Staff. *Campus security:* 24-hour emergency response devices and patrols, student patrols, late-night transport/escort service, controlled dormitory access. *Student services:* health clinic, personal/psychological counseling.

Athletics Member NCAA. All Division III. *Intercollegiate sports:* baseball M, basketball M/W, crew M(c)/W(c), cross-country running M/W, field hockey W(c), football M, golf M/W, ice hockey M(c), lacrosse M(c)/W(c), soccer M/W, softball W, swimming M/W, tennis M/W, track and field M/W, volleyball M(c)/W, water polo W, wrestling M. *Intramural sports:* badminton M/W, basketball M/W, football M/W, golf M/W, soccer M/W, softball M/W, table tennis M/W, tennis M/W, volleyball M/W, weight lifting M/W.

Standardized Tests *Required:* SAT I or ACT (for admission). *Recommended:* SAT II: Writing Test (for admission), SAT II Subject Test in French, German, Latin, Spanish or Hebrew.

Costs (2004–05) *Comprehensive fee:* $26,466 includes full-time tuition ($20,000) and room and board ($6466). Part-time tuition and fees vary according to course load. *College room only:* $3784. Room and board charges vary according to board plan and housing facility. *Payment plans:* installment, deferred payment. *Waivers:* employees or children of employees.

Financial Aid Of all full-time matriculated undergraduates who enrolled in 2003, 1,717 applied for aid, 1,200 were judged to have need, 191 had their need fully met. 335 Federal Work-Study jobs (averaging $1327). In 2003, 429 non-need-based awards were made. *Average percent of need met:* 86%. *Average financial aid package:* $16,040. *Average need-based loan:* $5227. *Average need-based gift aid:* $10,582. *Average non-need-based aid:* $3702. *Average indebtedness upon graduation:* $16,476.

Applying *Options:* early action, deferred entrance. *Application fee:* $50. *Required:* essay or personal statement, high school transcript, 2 letters of recommendation. *Recommended:* interview. *Application deadlines:* 1/15 (freshmen), 3/1 (transfers). *Notification:* 4/10 (freshmen), 12/31 (early action), 4/10 (transfers).

Admissions Contact Ms. Shawn Leftwich, Director of Admissions, Wheaton College, 501 College Avenue, Wheaton, IL 60187. *Phone:* 630-752-5011. *Toll-free phone:* 800-222-2419. *Fax:* 630-752-5285. *E-mail:* admissions@wheaton.edu.

■ *See page 2834 for a narrative description.*

INDIANA

ANDERSON UNIVERSITY

Anderson, Indiana

- **Independent** comprehensive, founded 1917, affiliated with Church of God
- **Calendar** semesters
- **Degrees** associate, bachelor's, master's, doctoral, and first professional

- **Suburban** 100-acre campus with easy access to Indianapolis
- **Endowment** $7.1 million
- **Coed**
- **Moderately difficult** entrance level

Faculty *Student/faculty ratio:* 13:1.
Student Life *Campus security:* 24-hour emergency response devices and patrols, student patrols, late-night transport/escort service, 24-hour crime line.
Athletics Member NCAA. All Division III.
Standardized Tests *Required:* SAT I or ACT (for admission).
Costs (2003–04) *Comprehensive fee:* $22,610 includes full-time tuition ($17,050) and room and board ($5560). Part-time tuition and fees vary according to course load. *College room only:* $3330. Room and board charges vary according to board plan.
Financial Aid Of all full-time matriculated undergraduates who enrolled in 2003, 1,662 applied for aid, 1,491 were judged to have need, 332 had their need fully met. 1,092 Federal Work-Study jobs (averaging $2076). In 2003, 408. *Average percent of need met:* 96. *Average financial aid package:* $16,684. *Average need-based loan:* $4959. *Average need-based gift aid:* $10,784. *Average non-need-based aid:* $7516. *Average indebtedness upon graduation:* $14,500.
Applying *Options:* deferred entrance. *Application fee:* $20. *Required:* high school transcript, minimum 2.0 GPA, 2 letters of recommendation, lifestyle statement. *Required for some:* interview. *Recommended:* essay or personal statement.
Admissions Contact Mr. Jim King, Director of Admissions, Anderson University, 1100 East 5th Street, Anderson, IN 46012-3495. *Phone:* 765-641-4080. *Toll-free phone:* 800-421-3014 (in-state); 800-428-6414 (out-of-state). *Fax:* 765-641-3851. *E-mail:* info@anderson.edu.

BALL STATE UNIVERSITY
Muncie, Indiana

- **State-supported** university, founded 1918
- **Calendar** semesters
- **Degrees** associate, bachelor's, master's, doctoral, post-master's, and postbachelor's certificates
- **Suburban** 955-acre campus with easy access to Indianapolis
- **Coed,** 17,641 undergraduate students, 93% full-time, 53% women, 47% men
- **Moderately difficult** entrance level, 76% of applicants were admitted

Undergraduates 16,319 full-time, 1,322 part-time. Students come from 49 states and territories, 9% are from out of state, 6% African American, 0.6% Asian American or Pacific Islander, 1% Hispanic American, 0.3% Native American, 0.1% international, 5% transferred in, 41% live on campus. *Retention:* 80% of 2002 full-time freshmen returned.
Freshmen *Admission:* 10,695 applied, 8,117 admitted, 3,987 enrolled. *Test scores:* SAT verbal scores over 500: 59%; SAT math scores over 500: 60%; ACT scores over 18: 89%; SAT verbal scores over 600: 18%; SAT math scores over 600: 18%; ACT scores over 24: 36%; SAT verbal scores over 700: 2%; SAT math scores over 700: 2%; ACT scores over 30: 3%.
Faculty *Total:* 1,162, 77% full-time, 64% with terminal degrees. *Student/faculty ratio:* 17:1.
Majors Accounting; actuarial science; administrative assistant and secretarial science; advertising; animal genetics; anthropology; architecture; art; art teacher education; athletic training; audiology and speech-language pathology; biology/biological sciences; botany/plant biology; business administration and management; business/managerial economics; business teacher education; cartography; cell biology and histology; ceramic arts and ceramics; chemical engineering; chemistry; city/urban, community and regional planning; classics and languages, literatures and linguistics; clinical laboratory science/medical technology; commercial and advertising art; computer science; criminal justice/law enforcement administration; criminology; dance; dietetics; dramatic/theatre arts; drawing; ecology; economics; education; educational/instructional media design; elementary education; emergency medical technology (EMT paramedic); English; environmental design/architecture; environmental studies; family and consumer economics related; family and consumer sciences/home economics teacher education; family and consumer sciences/human sciences; fashion merchandising; finance; fine/studio arts; French; geography; geology/earth science; German; graphic and printing equipment operation/production; health science; health teacher education; history; human resources management; industrial arts; industrial radiologic technology; industrial technology; information science/studies; insurance; Japanese; journalism; kindergarten/preschool education; kinesiology and exercise science; landscape architecture; Latin; Latin American studies; legal administrative assistant/secretary; legal assistant/paralegal; liberal arts and sciences/liberal studies; management information systems; marine biology and biological oceanography; marketing/marketing management; mathematics; medical microbiology and bacteriology; modern Greek; modern languages; molecular biology; music; musical instrument fabrication and repair; music teacher education; natural resources management and policy; nuclear medical technology; nursing (registered nurse training); occupational safety and health technology; parks, recreation and leisure facilities management; philosophy; photography; physical education teaching and coaching; physics; piano and organ; plastics engineering technology; political science and government; polymer/plastics engineering; pre-dentistry studies; pre-law studies; pre-medical studies; printmaking; psychology; public relations/image management; real estate; religious studies; respiratory care therapy; science teacher education; sculpture; secondary education; social sciences; social work; sociology; soil conservation; Spanish; special education; special products marketing; speech and rhetoric; sport and fitness administration; telecommunications; tourism and travel services management; trade and industrial teacher education; violin, viola, guitar and other stringed instruments; voice and opera; wildlife biology; wind/percussion instruments; zoology/animal biology.
Academic Programs *Special study options:* academic remediation for entering students, adult/continuing education programs, advanced placement credit, cooperative education, distance learning, double majors, English as a second language, freshman honors college, honors programs, independent study, internships, part-time degree program, study abroad, summer session for credit. *ROTC:* Army (b). *Unusual degree programs:* 3-2 engineering with Purdue University, Tri-State University.
Library Bracken Library plus 3 others with 1.1 million titles, 2,937 serial subscriptions, 506,303 audiovisual materials, an OPAC, a Web page.
Computers on Campus 1500 computers available on campus for general student use. A campuswide network can be accessed from student residence rooms and from off campus. At least one staffed computer lab available.
Student Life *Housing:* on-campus residence required for freshman year. *Options:* coed, men-only, women-only, cooperative, disabled students. *Activities and organizations:* drama/theater group, student-run newspaper, radio and television station, choral group, marching band, Student Association, Excellence in Leadership, fraternities/sororities, Black Student Association, student voluntary services, national fraternities, national sororities. *Campus security:* 24-hour emergency response devices and patrols, late-night transport/escort service, controlled dormitory access. *Student services:* health clinic, personal/psychological counseling, women's center, legal services.
Athletics Member NCAA. All Division I except football (Division I-A). *Intercollegiate sports:* baseball M(s), basketball M(s)/W(s), cross-country running M(s)/W(s), equestrian sports M(c)/W(c), field hockey W(s), golf M(s), gymnastics W(s), ice hockey M(c), rugby M(c)/W(c), sailing M(c)/W(c), soccer M(c)/W, softball W(s), swimming M(s)/W(s), tennis M(s)/W(s), track and field M(s)/W(s), volleyball M(s)/W(s), water polo M(c), wrestling M(c). *Intramural sports:* archery M/W, badminton M(c)/W(c), basketball M/W, bowling M(c)/W(c), cross-country running M/W, fencing M(c)/W(c), football M, golf M, lacrosse M(c), racquetball M/W, soccer M, softball M/W, squash M/W, swimming M/W, table tennis M(c)/W(c), tennis M/W, track and field M/W, volleyball M/W, weight lifting M(c)/W(c).
Standardized Tests *Required for some:* SAT I or ACT (for admission).
Costs (2003–04) *Tuition:* state resident $5532 full-time; nonresident $13,950 full-time. Part-time tuition and fees vary according to course load. *Required fees:* $398 full-time. *Room and board:* $5880. Room and board charges vary according to board plan and housing facility. *Payment plan:* installment. *Waivers:* employees or children of employees.
Financial Aid Of all full-time matriculated undergraduates who enrolled in 2003, 12,027 applied for aid, 9,025 were judged to have need, 3,078 had their need fully met. 1,091 Federal Work-Study jobs (averaging $2395). 5,702 state and other part-time jobs (averaging $1099). In 2003, 1223 non-need-based awards were made. *Average percent of need met:* 69%. *Average financial aid package:* $6836. *Average need-based loan:* $3318. *Average need-based gift aid:* $4442. *Average non-need-based aid:* $2840. *Average indebtedness upon graduation:* $17,053.
Applying *Options:* common application, deferred entrance. *Application fee:* $25. *Required:* high school transcript. *Required for some:* essay or personal statement, letters of recommendation, interview. *Application deadline:* 5/1 (freshmen), rolling (transfers). *Notification:* continuous (freshmen), continuous (transfers).
Admissions Contact Dr. Lawrence Waters, Dean of Admissions and Financial Aid, Ball State University, 2000 University Avenue, Muncie, IN 47306. *Phone:* 765-285-8300. *Toll-free phone:* 800-482-4BSU. *Fax:* 765-285-1632. *E-mail:* askus@bsu.edu.

■ *See page 1208 for a narrative description.*

BETHEL COLLEGE
Mishawaka, Indiana

- **Independent** comprehensive, founded 1947, affiliated with Missionary Church

Bethel College (continued)
- **Calendar** semesters
- **Degrees** associate, bachelor's, and master's
- **Suburban** 70-acre campus
- **Endowment** $4.2 million
- **Coed,** 1,740 undergraduate students, 74% full-time, 63% women, 37% men
- **Minimally difficult** entrance level, 65% of applicants were admitted

Undergraduates 1,289 full-time, 451 part-time. Students come from 32 states and territories, 13 other countries, 33% are from out of state, 8% African American, 1% Asian American or Pacific Islander, 2% Hispanic American, 0.6% Native American, 2% international, 8% transferred in, 49% live on campus. *Retention:* 87% of 2002 full-time freshmen returned.

Freshmen *Admission:* 684 applied, 445 admitted, 306 enrolled. *Average high school GPA:* 3.30. *Test scores:* SAT verbal scores over 500: 64%; SAT math scores over 500: 66%; ACT scores over 18: 88%; SAT verbal scores over 600: 22%; SAT math scores over 600: 25%; ACT scores over 24: 40%; SAT verbal scores over 700: 2%; SAT math scores over 700: 2%; ACT scores over 30: 9%.

Faculty *Total:* 149, 40% full-time, 34% with terminal degrees. *Student/faculty ratio:* 14:1.

Majors Accounting; aerospace, aeronautical and astronautical engineering; agriculture and agriculture operations related; American Sign Language (ASL); ancient Near Eastern and biblical languages; art; biblical studies; biology/biological sciences; business administration and management; business teacher education; chemical engineering; chemistry; Christian studies; civil engineering; communication/speech communication and rhetoric; computer and information sciences; computer engineering; computer science; creative writing; criminal justice/safety; design and visual communications; divinity/ministry; dramatic/theatre arts; early childhood education; education; electrical, electronics and communications engineering; elementary education; engineering; English; English/language arts teacher education; environmental biology; health and physical education; history; human services; industrial engineering; interior design; international business/trade/commerce; journalism; kindergarten/preschool education; kinesiology and exercise science; liberal arts and sciences/liberal studies; mathematics; mathematics and computer science; mathematics teacher education; mechanical engineering; middle school education; missionary studies and missiology; music; music performance; music teacher education; nursing (registered nurse training); pastoral studies/counseling; philosophy; photography; physical education teaching and coaching; physics; piano and organ; pre-dentistry studies; pre-law studies; pre-medical studies; pre-veterinary studies; psychology; religious/sacred music; science teacher education; secondary education; sign language interpretation and translation; social sciences; social studies teacher education; sociology; sport and fitness administration; voice and opera; youth ministry.

Academic Programs *Special study options:* academic remediation for entering students, accelerated degree program, adult/continuing education programs, advanced placement credit, double majors, honors programs, independent study, internships, off-campus study, part-time degree program, study abroad, summer session for credit. *ROTC:* Army (c), Air Force (c). *Unusual degree programs:* 3-2 engineering with University of Notre Dame, Tri-State University.

Library Otis and Elizabeth Bowen Library with 106,584 titles, 450 serial subscriptions, 3,926 audiovisual materials, an OPAC, a Web page.

Computers on Campus 110 computers available on campus for general student use. A campuswide network can be accessed from student residence rooms and from off campus. Internet access, at least one staffed computer lab available.

Student Life *Housing:* on-campus residence required through sophomore year. *Options:* men-only, women-only. Campus housing is university owned. *Activities and organizations:* drama/theater group, student-run newspaper, radio station, choral group, "Task Force" Mission Teams, Student Council, Center for Community Service, Fellowship of Christian Athletes. *Campus security:* 24-hour emergency response devices and patrols, student patrols, late-night transport/escort service, controlled dormitory access. *Student services:* health clinic, personal/psychological counseling.

Athletics Member NAIA, NCCAA. *Intercollegiate sports:* baseball M(s), basketball M(s)/W(s), cheerleading M(s)/W(s), cross-country running M(s)/W(s), golf M(s)/W(s), soccer M(s)/W(s), softball W(s), tennis M(s)/W(s), track and field M(s)/W(s), volleyball W(s), wrestling M(s). *Intramural sports:* badminton M/W, basketball M/W, bowling M/W, football M/W, racquetball M/W, soccer M/W, softball M/W, table tennis M/W, tennis M/W, track and field M/W, volleyball M/W, weight lifting M/W.

Standardized Tests *Required:* SAT I or ACT (for admission).

Costs (2003–04) *Comprehensive fee:* $19,210 includes full-time tuition ($14,390), mandatory fees ($140), and room and board ($4680). Part-time tuition: $270 per hour. Part-time tuition and fees vary according to course load. *Room and board:* Room and board charges vary according to board plan and housing facility. *Payment plan:* installment. *Waivers:* employees or children of employees.

Financial Aid Of all full-time matriculated undergraduates who enrolled in 2003, 1,466 applied for aid, 1,193 were judged to have need, 650 had their need fully met. In 2003, 109 non-need-based awards were made. *Average percent of need met:* 90%. *Average financial aid package:* $12,313. *Average need-based loan:* $4133. *Average need-based gift aid:* $3310. *Average non-need-based aid:* $8925. *Average indebtedness upon graduation:* $16,509.

Applying *Options:* common application, electronic application, early admission, deferred entrance. *Application fee:* $25. *Required:* essay or personal statement, high school transcript, minimum 2.0 GPA, 1 letter of recommendation. *Recommended:* minimum 2.5 GPA, interview. *Application deadlines:* 8/6 (freshmen), 8/6 (transfers). *Notification:* continuous (freshmen), continuous (transfers).

Admissions Contact Mr. Randy Beachy, Assistant Vice President of Enrollment/Marketing, Bethel College, 1001 West McKinley Avenue, Mishawaka, IN 46545-5591. *Phone:* 574-257-3319. *Toll-free phone:* 800-422-4101. *Fax:* 574-257-3335. *E-mail:* admissions@bethelcollege.edu.

BUTLER UNIVERSITY
Indianapolis, Indiana

- **Independent** comprehensive, founded 1855
- **Calendar** semesters
- **Degrees** associate, bachelor's, master's, first professional, and postbachelor's certificates
- **Urban** 290-acre campus
- **Endowment** $100.9 million
- **Coed,** 3,657 undergraduate students, 98% full-time, 63% women, 37% men
- **Moderately difficult** entrance level, 77% of applicants were admitted

Butler offers a dual PharmD/MBA program. The dual program allows pharmacy students to develop management skills and entrepreneurial capabilities. Students take courses in both the College of Pharmacy and Health Sciences and the College of Business Administration. Upon completion of the program, students attain both a PharmD and MBA degree.

Undergraduates 3,580 full-time, 77 part-time. Students come from 42 states and territories, 51 other countries, 40% are from out of state, 4% African American, 2% Asian American or Pacific Islander, 2% Hispanic American, 0.2% Native American, 2% international, 4% transferred in, 63% live on campus. *Retention:* 88% of 2002 full-time freshmen returned.

Freshmen *Admission:* 4,329 applied, 3,350 admitted, 976 enrolled. *Average high school GPA:* 3.60. *Test scores:* SAT verbal scores over 500: 88%; SAT math scores over 500: 88%; ACT scores over 18: 100%; SAT verbal scores over 600: 45%; SAT math scores over 600: 52%; ACT scores over 24: 79%; SAT verbal scores over 700: 8%; SAT math scores over 700: 9%; ACT scores over 30: 18%.

Faculty *Total:* 425, 63% full-time, 60% with terminal degrees. *Student/faculty ratio:* 13:1.

Majors Accounting; actuarial science; anthropology; arts management; audiology and speech-language pathology; biology/biological sciences; business administration and management; business/managerial economics; chemistry; computer science; criminal justice/safety; dance; dramatic/theatre arts; economics; elementary education; English; finance; French; German; history; information science/studies; international business/trade/commerce; international relations and affairs; journalism; Latin; liberal arts and sciences/liberal studies; marketing/marketing management; mathematics; medicinal and pharmaceutical chemistry; modern Greek; music; music history, literature, and theory; music management and merchandising; music teacher education; pharmacy; philosophy; physician assistant; physics; piano and organ; political science and government; psychology; public relations/image management; religious studies; science, technology and society; secondary education; sociology; Spanish; speech and rhetoric; telecommunications; violin, viola, guitar and other stringed instruments; voice and opera; wind/percussion instruments.

Academic Programs *Special study options:* adult/continuing education programs, advanced placement credit, cooperative education, double majors, English as a second language, honors programs, independent study, internships, off-campus study, part-time degree program, student-designed majors, study abroad, summer session for credit. *ROTC:* Army (c), Air Force (c). *Unusual degree programs:* 3-2 engineering with Indiana University-Purdue University Indianapolis; forestry with Duke University.

Library Irwin Library System plus 1 other with 308,689 titles, 2,000 serial subscriptions, 13,091 audiovisual materials, an OPAC, a Web page.

Computers on Campus 250 computers available on campus for general student use. A campuswide network can be accessed from student residence rooms and from off campus that provide access to e-mail. Internet access, at least one staffed computer lab available.

Student Life *Housing:* on-campus residence required for freshman year. *Options:* coed, women-only. Campus housing is university owned. Freshman campus housing is guaranteed. *Activities and organizations:* drama/theater group, student-run newspaper, radio and television station, choral group, marching band, University YMCA, Student Government Association, Academic Service Honoraries, Alpha Phi Omega, Mortar Board, national fraternities, national sororities. *Campus security:* 24-hour emergency response devices and patrols, late-night transport/escort service, controlled dormitory access. *Student services:* health clinic, personal/psychological counseling.

Athletics Member NCAA. All Division I except football (Division III). *Intercollegiate sports:* baseball M(s), basketball M(s)/W(s), crew M(c)/W(c), cross-country running M(s)/W(s), football M, golf M(s)/W(s), ice hockey M(c), lacrosse M(s), rugby M(c), soccer M(s)/W(s), softball W(s), swimming M/W, tennis M(s)/W(s), track and field M/W, volleyball W(s). *Intramural sports:* badminton M/W, baseball M, basketball M/W, bowling M/W, football M, soccer M/W, softball M/W, swimming M/W, table tennis M/W, tennis M/W, track and field M/W, volleyball M/W, weight lifting M/W.

Standardized Tests *Required:* SAT I or ACT (for admission). *Recommended:* SAT II: Subject Tests (for admission).

Costs (2003–04) *Comprehensive fee:* $28,250 includes full-time tuition ($20,990), mandatory fees ($220), and room and board ($7040). Full-time tuition and fees vary according to program. Part-time tuition: $880 per credit. Part-time tuition and fees vary according to program. *College room only:* $3240. Room and board charges vary according to housing facility. *Payment plans:* tuition prepayment, installment. *Waivers:* employees or children of employees.

Financial Aid Of all full-time matriculated undergraduates who enrolled in 2003, 3,475 applied for aid, 2,295 were judged to have need, 486 had their need fully met. In 2003, 936 non-need-based awards were made. *Average financial aid package:* $16,400. *Average need-based loan:* $5000. *Average need-based gift aid:* $12,000. *Average non-need-based aid:* $7990.

Applying *Options:* common application, electronic application, early action, deferred entrance. *Application fee:* $35. *Required:* essay or personal statement, high school transcript. *Required for some:* interview, audition. *Application deadlines:* 8/15 (freshmen), 8/15 (transfers). *Notification:* continuous (freshmen), 1/15 (early action), continuous (transfers).

Admissions Contact Mr. William Preble, Dean of Admissions, Butler University, 4600 Sunset Avenue, Indianapolis, IN 46208-3485. *Phone:* 317-940-8100 Ext. 8124. *Toll-free phone:* 888-940-8100. *Fax:* 317-940-8150. *E-mail:* admission@butler.edu.

■ *See page 1312 for a narrative description.*

CALUMET COLLEGE OF SAINT JOSEPH
Whiting, Indiana

- **Independent Roman Catholic** comprehensive, founded 1951
- **Calendar** semesters
- **Degrees** certificates, associate, bachelor's, and master's
- **Urban** 25-acre campus with easy access to Chicago
- **Endowment** $2.9 million
- **Coed,** 1,214 undergraduate students, 37% full-time, 59% women, 41% men
- **Minimally difficult** entrance level, 73% of applicants were admitted

Undergraduates 446 full-time, 768 part-time. Students come from 4 states and territories, 29% are from out of state, 32% African American, 0.1% Asian American or Pacific Islander, 19% Hispanic American, 0.4% Native American, 16% transferred in. *Retention:* 69% of 2002 full-time freshmen returned.

Freshmen *Admission:* 160 applied, 117 admitted, 108 enrolled. *Average high school GPA:* 2.55. *Test scores:* SAT verbal scores over 500: 17%; SAT math scores over 500: 21%; ACT scores over 18: 55%; SAT verbal scores over 600: 4%; SAT math scores over 600: 4%; ACT scores over 24: 5%.

Faculty *Total:* 123, 24% full-time, 33% with terminal degrees. *Student/faculty ratio:* 14:1.

Majors Accounting; art teacher education; business administration and management; business teacher education; communication and media related; communication/speech communication and rhetoric; computer science; computer typography and composition equipment operation; criminal justice/law enforcement administration; elementary education; English; English/language arts teacher education; general studies; health/health care administration; human services; information science/studies; intermedia/multimedia; legal assistant/paralegal; liberal arts and sciences/liberal studies; political science and government; pre-law studies; psychology; religious studies; science teacher education; secondary education; social studies teacher education; substance abuse/addiction counseling; theology.

Academic Programs *Special study options:* academic remediation for entering students, accelerated degree program, adult/continuing education programs, advanced placement credit, cooperative education, double majors, external degree program, independent study, internships, part-time degree program, student-designed majors, summer session for credit.

Library Mary Gorman Specker Memorial Library with 93,055 titles, 354 serial subscriptions, 6,412 audiovisual materials, an OPAC, a Web page.

Computers on Campus 80 computers available on campus for general student use. Internet access, at least one staffed computer lab available.

Student Life *Housing:* college housing not available. *Activities and organizations:* drama/theater group, student-run newspaper, choral group, student government, Los Amigos Hispanic Club, Criminal Justice Club, Drama Club, Black Student Union. *Campus security:* late-night transport/escort service, night security. *Student services:* personal/psychological counseling.

Athletics Member NAIA. *Intercollegiate sports:* baseball M, basketball M/W, cheerleading W, soccer M/W, softball W, volleyball M/W. *Intramural sports:* ultimate Frisbee M(c)/W(c).

Standardized Tests *Required for some:* ACT COMPASS. *Recommended:* SAT I or ACT (for admission).

Costs (2003–04) *Tuition:* $9000 full-time, $300 per credit hour part-time. *Payment plan:* installment. *Waivers:* children of alumni, senior citizens, and employees or children of employees.

Financial Aid Of all full-time matriculated undergraduates who enrolled in 2003, 27 Federal Work-Study jobs (averaging $2708). 8 state and other part-time jobs (averaging $2250). *Average indebtedness upon graduation:* $21,000.

Applying *Options:* common application, electronic application, deferred entrance. *Required:* high school transcript. *Required for some:* essay or personal statement. *Recommended:* minimum 2.0 GPA, interview. *Application deadline:* rolling (freshmen), rolling (transfers). *Notification:* continuous (transfers).

Admissions Contact Mr. Chuck Walz, Director of Admissions, Calumet College of Saint Joseph, 2400 New York Avenue, Whiting, IN 46394. *Phone:* 219-473-4215 Ext. 379. *Toll-free phone:* 877-700-9100. *Fax:* 219-473-4259. *E-mail:* admissions@ccsj.edu.

CROSSROADS BIBLE COLLEGE
Indianapolis, Indiana

- **Independent Baptist** 4-year, founded 1980
- **Calendar** semesters
- **Degrees** certificates, associate, and bachelor's
- **Urban** 6-acre campus
- **Coed,** 203 undergraduate students, 32% full-time, 39% women, 61% men
- **Noncompetitive** entrance level, 84% of applicants were admitted

Undergraduates 65 full-time, 138 part-time. 46% African American, 3% Hispanic American, 0.5% Native American. *Retention:* 66% of 2002 full-time freshmen returned.

Freshmen *Admission:* 37 applied, 31 admitted, 31 enrolled. *Average high school GPA:* 2.65. *Test scores:* SAT verbal scores over 500: 70%; SAT math scores over 500: 70%; ACT scores over 18: 100%; SAT verbal scores over 600: 10%; SAT math scores over 600: 10%; ACT scores over 24: 20%.

Faculty *Total:* 25, 20% full-time, 80% with terminal degrees. *Student/faculty ratio:* 22:1.

Majors Biblical studies; elementary education; missionary studies and missiology; pastoral counseling and specialized ministries related; pre-theology/pre-ministerial studies; religious education; urban studies/affairs; youth ministry.

Student Life *Housing options:* Campus housing is leased by the school.

Costs (2004–05) *Tuition:* $6600 full-time, $200 per credit hour part-time. *Required fees:* $140 full-time, $140 per term part-time. *Room only:* $3000.

Financial Aid Of all full-time matriculated undergraduates who enrolled in 2001, 119 applied for aid, 44 were judged to have need, 7 had their need fully met. 3 Federal Work-Study jobs, 3 state and other part-time jobs. *Average percent of need met:* 60%. *Average financial aid package:* $1100. *Average need-based gift aid:* $600.

Applying *Application fee:* $10. *Application deadline:* 8/8 (freshmen).

Admissions Contact Ms. Bethanie Holdcroft, Director of Admissions, Crossroads Bible College, 601 North Shortridge Road, Indianapolis, IN 46219. *Phone:* 317-352-8736 Ext. 230. *Toll-free phone:* 800-273-2224.

DEPAUW UNIVERSITY
Greencastle, Indiana

- **Independent** 4-year, founded 1837, affiliated with United Methodist Church
- **Calendar** 4-1-4
- **Degree** bachelor's
- **Small-town** 655-acre campus with easy access to Indianapolis
- **Endowment** $373.7 million
- **Coed,** 2,365 undergraduate students, 98% full-time, 55% women, 45% men
- **Moderately difficult** entrance level, 63% of applicants were admitted

Undergraduates 2,326 full-time, 39 part-time. Students come from 41 states and territories, 19 other countries, 49% are from out of state, 6% African

DePauw University (continued)
American, 2% Asian American or Pacific Islander, 3% Hispanic American, 0.3% Native American, 2% international, 0.3% transferred in, 94% live on campus. *Retention:* 93% of 2002 full-time freshmen returned.

Freshmen *Admission:* 3,651 applied, 2,296 admitted, 581 enrolled. *Average high school GPA:* 3.66. *Test scores:* SAT verbal scores over 500: 95%; SAT math scores over 500: 96%; ACT scores over 18: 99%; SAT verbal scores over 600: 54%; SAT math scores over 600: 63%; ACT scores over 24: 84%; SAT verbal scores over 700: 13%; SAT math scores over 700: 12%; ACT scores over 30: 24%.

Faculty *Total:* 249, 84% full-time, 88% with terminal degrees. *Student/faculty ratio:* 10:1.

Majors African-American/Black studies; ancient/classical Greek; anthropology; art history, criticism and conservation; Asian studies (East); athletic training; biochemistry; biology/biological sciences; chemistry; classics and languages, literatures and linguistics; computer science; dramatic/theatre arts; economics; elementary education; English; English composition; environmental studies; fine/studio arts; French; geology/earth science; German; history; interdisciplinary studies; kinesiology and exercise science; Latin; mass communication/media; mathematics; multi-/interdisciplinary studies related; music; music management and merchandising; music performance; music teacher education; music theory and composition; peace studies and conflict resolution; philosophy; physical education teaching and coaching; physics; political science and government; psychology; religious studies; Romance languages; Russian studies; sociology; Spanish; women's studies.

Academic Programs *Special study options:* advanced placement credit, double majors, honors programs, independent study, internships, off-campus study, part-time degree program, student-designed majors, study abroad. *ROTC:* Army (c), Air Force (c). *Unusual degree programs:* 3-2 engineering with Columbia University, Washington University in St. Louis, Case Western Reserve University.

Library Roy O. West Library plus 3 others with 545,736 titles, 2,134 serial subscriptions, 12,126 audiovisual materials, an OPAC, a Web page.

Computers on Campus 158 computers available on campus for general student use. A campuswide network can be accessed from student residence rooms and from off campus. Internet access, online (class) registration, at least one staffed computer lab available. Computer purchase or lease plan available.

Student Life *Housing:* on-campus residence required through senior year. *Options:* coed, men-only, women-only. Campus housing is university owned. Freshman campus housing is guaranteed. *Activities and organizations:* drama/theater group, student-run newspaper, radio and television station, choral group, Community Service Program, Union Board, Student Congress, Resident Students Association, Independent Council, national fraternities, national sororities. *Campus security:* 24-hour emergency response devices and patrols, student patrols, late-night transport/escort service, controlled dormitory access. *Student services:* health clinic, personal/psychological counseling.

Athletics Member NCAA. All Division III. *Intercollegiate sports:* baseball M, basketball M/W, cheerleading M(c)/W(c), crew M(c)/W(c), cross-country running M/W, field hockey W, football M, golf M/W, rugby M(c), soccer M/W, softball W, swimming M/W, tennis M/W, track and field M/W, volleyball W. *Intramural sports:* badminton M/W, basketball M/W, bowling M/W, football M/W, golf M, racquetball M/W, rock climbing M(c)/W(c), soccer M/W, softball M/W, table tennis M/W, tennis M/W, ultimate Frisbee M/W, volleyball M/W.

Standardized Tests *Required:* SAT I or ACT (for admission).

Costs (2003–04) *Comprehensive fee:* $31,500 includes full-time tuition ($24,000), mandatory fees ($450), and room and board ($7050). Part-time tuition: $764 per semester hour. *College room only:* $3650. *Payment plans:* tuition prepayment, installment, deferred payment. *Waivers:* employees or children of employees.

Financial Aid Of all full-time matriculated undergraduates who enrolled in 2003, 1,655 applied for aid, 1,355 were judged to have need, 1,284 had their need fully met. 703 Federal Work-Study jobs (averaging $1579). 26 state and other part-time jobs (averaging $480). *Average percent of need met:* 99%. *Average financial aid package:* $20,208. *Average need-based loan:* $4241. *Average need-based gift aid:* $16,693. *Average non-need-based aid:* $12,135. *Average indebtedness upon graduation:* $15,635. *Financial aid deadline:* 2/15.

Applying *Options:* common application, electronic application, early admission, early decision, early action, deferred entrance. *Required:* essay or personal statement, high school transcript, 1 letter of recommendation. *Recommended:* minimum 3.25 GPA, interview. *Application deadlines:* 2/1 (freshmen), 3/1 (transfers). *Early decision:* 11/1. *Notification:* 4/1 (freshmen), 1/1 (early decision), 2/15 (early action), 4/1 (transfers).

Admissions Contact Director of Admission, DePauw University, 101 East Seminary Street, Greencastle, IN 46135-0037. *Phone:* 765-658-4006. *Toll-free phone:* 800-447-2495. *Fax:* 765-658-4007. *E-mail:* admission@depauw.edu.

■ *See page 1530 for a narrative description.*

DeVry University
Indianapolis, Indiana

Admissions Contact 9100 Keystone Crossing, Suite 350, Indianapolis, IN 46240-2158. *E-mail:* ahein@keller.edu.

DeVry University
Merrillville, Indiana

Admissions Contact Twin Towers, 1000 East 80th Place, Suite 222 Mall, Merrillville, IN 46410-5673.

Earlham College
Richmond, Indiana

- **Independent** comprehensive, founded 1847, affiliated with Society of Friends
- **Calendar** semesters
- **Degrees** bachelor's, master's, and first professional
- **Small-town** 800-acre campus with easy access to Cincinnati, Indianapolis, and Dayton
- **Endowment** $311.9 million
- **Coed,** 1,170 undergraduate students, 97% full-time, 56% women, 44% men
- **Moderately difficult** entrance level, 77% of applicants were admitted

Undergraduates 1,135 full-time, 35 part-time. Students come from 46 states and territories, 34 other countries, 74% are from out of state, 6% African American, 2% Asian American or Pacific Islander, 2% Hispanic American, 0.2% Native American, 4% international, 2% transferred in, 82% live on campus. *Retention:* 84% of 2002 full-time freshmen returned.

Freshmen *Admission:* 1,410 applied, 1,088 admitted, 348 enrolled. *Average high school GPA:* 3.45. *Test scores:* SAT verbal scores over 500: 90%; SAT math scores over 500: 89%; ACT scores over 18: 97%; SAT verbal scores over 600: 63%; SAT math scores over 600: 45%; ACT scores over 24: 67%; SAT verbal scores over 700: 25%; SAT math scores over 700: 14%; ACT scores over 30: 26%.

Faculty *Total:* 111, 86% full-time, 77% with terminal degrees. *Student/faculty ratio:* 11:1.

Majors African-American/Black studies; art; biology/biological sciences; business administration and management; chemistry; classics and languages, literatures and linguistics; computer science; dramatic/theatre arts; economics; education; English; environmental studies; French; geology/earth science; German; history; interdisciplinary studies; international relations and affairs; Japanese studies; Latin American studies; mathematics; music; peace studies and conflict resolution; philosophy; physics; political science and government; pre-law studies; pre-medical studies; psychology; religious studies; sociology; Spanish; women's studies.

Academic Programs *Special study options:* accelerated degree program, advanced placement credit, double majors, independent study, internships, off-campus study, services for LD students, student-designed majors, study abroad. *Unusual degree programs:* 3-2 business administration with Washington University in St. Louis; engineering with Columbia University, University of Michigan, Rensselaer Polytechnic Institute; forestry with Duke University; nursing with Case Western Reserve University, Washington University in St. Louis, Emory University, Columbia University; architecture with Washington University in St. Louis.

Library Lilly Library plus 1 other with 392,100 titles, 1,660 serial subscriptions, 53,000 audiovisual materials, an OPAC, a Web page.

Computers on Campus 154 computers available on campus for general student use. A campuswide network can be accessed from student residence rooms. Internet access, online (class) registration, at least one staffed computer lab available. Computer purchase or lease plan available.

Student Life *Housing:* on-campus residence required through senior year. *Options:* coed, men-only, women-only, cooperative. Campus housing is university owned. Freshman campus housing is guaranteed. *Activities and organizations:* drama/theater group, student-run newspaper, radio station, choral group, Gospel Revelations Chorus, Dance Alloy, club sports, student government, Black Leadership Action Coalition. *Campus security:* 24-hour emergency response devices and patrols, student patrols, late-night transport/escort service, controlled dormitory access. *Student services:* health clinic, personal/psychological counseling, women's center.

Athletics Member NCAA. All Division III. *Intercollegiate sports:* baseball M, basketball M/W, cross-country running M/W, equestrian sports M(c)/W(c), field hockey W, football M, lacrosse M(c)/W(c), rugby M(c), soccer M/W, tennis M/W, track and field M/W, ultimate Frisbee M(c)/W(c), volleyball M(c)/W. *Intramural sports:* basketball M/W, football M/W, racquetball M/W, soccer M/W, softball M/W, tennis M/W, volleyball M/W.

Standardized Tests *Required:* SAT I or ACT (for admission). *Recommended:* SAT I (for admission).

Costs (2003–04) *Comprehensive fee:* $29,976 includes full-time tuition ($23,920), mandatory fees ($640), and room and board ($5416). Part-time tuition: $797 per credit hour. *College room only:* $2650. Room and board charges vary according to board plan. *Payment plans:* tuition prepayment, installment, deferred payment. *Waivers:* employees or children of employees.

Financial Aid Of all full-time matriculated undergraduates who enrolled in 2003, 830 applied for aid, 739 were judged to have need, 160 had their need fully met. In 2003, 182 non-need-based awards were made. *Average percent of need met:* 95%. *Average financial aid package:* $21,215. *Average need-based loan:* $4300. *Average need-based gift aid:* $12,829. *Average non-need-based aid:* $6153. *Average indebtedness upon graduation:* $15,088.

Applying *Options:* common application, electronic application, early admission, early decision, early action, deferred entrance. *Application fee:* $30. *Required:* essay or personal statement, high school transcript, minimum 3.0 GPA, 2 letters of recommendation. *Recommended:* interview. *Application deadlines:* 2/15 (freshmen), 4/1 (transfers). *Early decision:* 12/1. *Notification:* 3/15 (freshmen), 12/15 (early decision), 2/1 (early action), 3/15 (transfers).

Admissions Contact Mr. Jeff Rickey, Dean of Admissions and Financial Aid, Earlham College, 801 National Road West, Richmond, IN 47374. *Phone:* 765-983-1600. *Toll-free phone:* 800-327-5426. *Fax:* 765-983-1560. *E-mail:* admission@earlham.edu.

■ *See page 1552 for a narrative description.*

FRANKLIN COLLEGE
Franklin, Indiana

- **Independent** 4-year, founded 1834, affiliated with American Baptist Churches in the U.S.A.
- **Calendar** 4-1-4
- **Degree** bachelor's
- **Small-town** 74-acre campus with easy access to Indianapolis
- **Endowment** $65.5 million
- **Coed,** 1,038 undergraduate students, 95% full-time, 56% women, 44% men
- **Moderately difficult** entrance level, 86% of applicants were admitted

A Franklin College education combines traditional liberal arts learning with career-oriented preparation in order to create a solid foundation for lifelong leadership skills and professional success. The College's nationally recognized Leadership and Professional Development Programs are distinguishing features of the Franklin curriculum and serve as proof of their commitment to developing students' broad-based communication, professional, and problem-solving skills. Students are offered a wide variety of diverse opportunities for creative learning and benefit from the small class sizes and personalized relationships with the faculty.

Undergraduates 983 full-time, 55 part-time. Students come from 19 states and territories, 7 other countries, 6% are from out of state, 4% African American, 0.1% Asian American or Pacific Islander, 1% Hispanic American, 0.2% Native American, 0.9% international, 2% transferred in, 74% live on campus. *Retention:* 70% of 2002 full-time freshmen returned.

Freshmen *Admission:* 681 applied, 587 admitted, 277 enrolled. *Average high school GPA:* 3.24. *Test scores:* SAT verbal scores over 500: 53%; SAT math scores over 500: 57%; ACT scores over 18: 82%; SAT verbal scores over 600: 14%; SAT math scores over 600: 12%; ACT scores over 24: 28%; SAT verbal scores over 700: 2%; SAT math scores over 700: 2%; ACT scores over 30: 4%.

Faculty *Total:* 111, 53% full-time, 62% with terminal degrees. *Student/faculty ratio:* 13:1.

Majors Accounting; American studies; athletic training; biology/biological sciences; biology teacher education; business/commerce; Canadian studies; chemistry; chemistry teacher education; computer and information sciences; computer science; dramatic/theatre arts; economics; elementary education; English; English/language arts teacher education; French; French language teacher education; history; journalism; mathematics; mathematics teacher education; parks, recreation, and leisure related; philosophy; physical education teaching and coaching; political science and government; psychology; religious studies; social studies teacher education; sociology; Spanish; Spanish language teacher education.

Academic Programs *Special study options:* academic remediation for entering students, advanced placement credit, double majors, independent study, internships, off-campus study, part-time degree program, services for LD students, study abroad, summer session for credit. *ROTC:* Army (c). *Unusual degree programs:* 3-2 engineering with Washington University in St. Louis; forestry with Duke University; nursing with Rush University; public health with University of South Florida.

Library Hamilton Library plus 1 other with 122,605 titles, 484 serial subscriptions, 7,388 audiovisual materials, an OPAC, a Web page.

Computers on Campus 150 computers available on campus for general student use. A campuswide network can be accessed from student residence rooms and from off campus. Internet access, online (class) registration, at least one staffed computer lab available.

Student Life *Housing:* on-campus residence required through junior year. *Options:* coed. Campus housing is university owned. Freshman campus housing is guaranteed. *Activities and organizations:* drama/theater group, student-run newspaper, radio and television station, choral group, FLOW, FC Volunteers, Student Entertainment Board, Student Congress, national fraternities, national sororities. *Campus security:* 24-hour emergency response devices and patrols, late-night transport/escort service. *Student services:* health clinic, personal/psychological counseling.

Athletics Member NCAA. All Division III. *Intercollegiate sports:* baseball M, basketball M/W, cross-country running M/W, football M, golf M/W, soccer M/W, softball W, tennis M/W, track and field M/W, volleyball W. *Intramural sports:* basketball M/W, softball M/W, volleyball M/W.

Standardized Tests *Required:* SAT I or ACT (for admission).

Costs (2003–04) *Comprehensive fee:* $22,195 includes full-time tuition ($16,750), mandatory fees ($175), and room and board ($5270). Part-time tuition and fees vary according to course load. *College room only:* $3080. Room and board charges vary according to board plan and housing facility. *Payment plan:* installment. *Waivers:* senior citizens and employees or children of employees.

Financial Aid Of all full-time matriculated undergraduates who enrolled in 2002, 903 applied for aid, 783 were judged to have need, 160 had their need fully met. 219 Federal Work-Study jobs (averaging $605). 129 state and other part-time jobs (averaging $368). In 2002, 183 non-need-based awards were made. *Average percent of need met:* 88%. *Average financial aid package:* $12,519. *Average need-based loan:* $3561. *Average need-based gift aid:* $9760. *Average non-need-based aid:* $9479. *Average indebtedness upon graduation:* $18,054. *Financial aid deadline:* 3/1.

Applying *Options:* common application, electronic application, deferred entrance. *Application fee:* $30. *Required:* essay or personal statement, high school transcript, 1 letter of recommendation, TOEFL for international students. *Recommended:* interview. *Application deadline:* 5/1 (freshmen). *Notification:* 10/1 (freshmen), continuous (transfers).

Admissions Contact Ms. Kathryn D. Coffman, Director of Admissions, Franklin College, 501 East Monroe Street, Franklin, IN 46131-2598. *Phone:* 317-738-8062. *Toll-free phone:* 800-852-0232. *Fax:* 317-738-8274. *E-mail:* admissions@franklincollege.edu.

■ *See page 1650 for a narrative description.*

GOSHEN COLLEGE
Goshen, Indiana

- **Independent Mennonite** 4-year, founded 1894
- **Calendar** semesters
- **Degree** bachelor's
- **Small-town** 135-acre campus
- **Endowment** $88.8 million
- **Coed,** 920 undergraduate students, 86% full-time, 62% women, 38% men
- **Moderately difficult** entrance level, 61% of applicants were admitted

Undergraduates 787 full-time, 133 part-time. Students come from 36 states and territories, 30 other countries, 43% are from out of state, 3% African American, 1% Asian American or Pacific Islander, 4% Hispanic American, 0.2% Native American, 9% international, 8% transferred in, 64% live on campus. *Retention:* 77% of 2002 full-time freshmen returned.

Freshmen *Admission:* 608 applied, 371 admitted, 182 enrolled. *Average high school GPA:* 3.25. *Test scores:* SAT verbal scores over 500: 78%; SAT math scores over 500: 83%; ACT scores over 18: 98%; SAT verbal scores over 600: 49%; SAT math scores over 600: 44%; ACT scores over 24: 64%; SAT verbal scores over 700: 18%; SAT math scores over 700: 10%; ACT scores over 30: 23%.

Faculty *Total:* 124, 56% full-time, 49% with terminal degrees. *Student/faculty ratio:* 10:1.

Majors Accounting; art; art teacher education; art therapy; biblical studies; bilingual and multilingual education; biology/biological sciences; broadcast journalism; business administration and management; business teacher education; chemistry; child development; computer science; dramatic/theatre arts; economics; education; elementary education; English; English as a second/foreign language (teaching); environmental studies; family and community services; German; Hispanic-American, Puerto Rican, and Mexican-American/Chicano studies; history; information science/studies; journalism; kindergarten/preschool education; liberal arts and sciences/liberal studies; mass communication/media; mathematics; music; music teacher education; natural sciences; nursing (registered nurse training); peace studies and conflict resolution; physical education teaching and coaching; physical sciences; physics; political science and govern-

Goshen College (continued)
ment; pre-dentistry studies; pre-law studies; pre-medical studies; pre-veterinary studies; psychology; religious studies; science teacher education; secondary education; sign language interpretation and translation; social work; sociology; Spanish.

Academic Programs *Special study options:* academic remediation for entering students, accelerated degree program, adult/continuing education programs, advanced placement credit, cooperative education, distance learning, double majors, English as a second language, freshman honors college, honors programs, independent study, internships, off-campus study, part-time degree program, services for LD students, student-designed majors, study abroad, summer session for credit. *Unusual degree programs:* 3-2 engineering with Case Western Reserve University, Washington University in St. Louis, Pennsylvania State University—University Park Campus, University of Illinois.

Library Harold and Wilma Good Library plus 2 others with 127,028 titles, 750 serial subscriptions, 3,250 audiovisual materials, an OPAC, a Web page.

Computers on Campus 160 computers available on campus for general student use. A campuswide network can be accessed from student residence rooms and from off campus that provide access to online services. Internet access, at least one staffed computer lab available.

Student Life *Housing:* on-campus residence required through junior year. *Options:* coed, women-only. Campus housing is university owned. Freshman campus housing is guaranteed. *Activities and organizations:* drama/theater group, student-run newspaper, radio and television station, choral group, business club, Black Student Union, Non-Traditional Student Network, Goshen Student Women's Organization, international student club. *Campus security:* 24-hour emergency response devices and patrols, late-night transport/escort service. *Student services:* health clinic, personal/psychological counseling, women's center.

Athletics Member NAIA. *Intercollegiate sports:* baseball M(s), basketball M(s)/W(s), cross-country running M(s)/W(s), golf M(s), soccer M(s)/W(s), softball W(s), tennis M(s)/W(s), track and field M(s)/W(s), volleyball W(s). *Intramural sports:* badminton M/W, basketball M/W, cross-country running M/W, racquetball M/W, skiing (cross-country) M/W, soccer M/W, softball W, swimming M/W, table tennis M/W, tennis M/W, volleyball M/W, weight lifting M/W.

Standardized Tests *Required:* SAT I or ACT (for admission).

Costs (2003–04) *Comprehensive fee:* $22,450 includes full-time tuition ($16,320), mandatory fees ($330), and room and board ($5800). Part-time tuition: $640 per credit hour. Part-time tuition and fees vary according to course load. *College room only:* $3000. Room and board charges vary according to board plan and student level. *Payment plan:* installment. *Waivers:* employees or children of employees.

Financial Aid Of all full-time matriculated undergraduates who enrolled in 2003, 732 applied for aid, 518 were judged to have need, 180 had their need fully met. 633 Federal Work-Study jobs (averaging $629). 20 state and other part-time jobs (averaging $865). In 2003, 44 non-need-based awards were made. *Average percent of need met:* 88%. *Average financial aid package:* $1562. *Average need-based loan:* $5189. *Average need-based gift aid:* $10,034. *Average non-need-based aid:* $7486. *Average indebtedness upon graduation:* $16,319.

Applying *Options:* common application, electronic application, early admission, early action, deferred entrance. *Application fee:* $25. *Required:* essay or personal statement, high school transcript, minimum 2.5 GPA, 2 letters of recommendation, rank in upper 50% of high school class, minimum SAT score of 1000, ACT score of 22. *Recommended:* interview. *Application deadlines:* 8/15 (freshmen), 8/15 (transfers). *Notification:* continuous (freshmen), 1/1 (early action), continuous (transfers).

Admissions Contact Ms. Karen Lowe Raftus, Director of Admission, Goshen College, 1700 South Main Street, Goshen, IN 46526-4794. *Phone:* 574-535-7535. *Toll-free phone:* 800-348-7422. *Fax:* 574-535-7609. *E-mail:* admissions@goshen.edu.

■ *See page 1676 for a narrative description.*

GRACE COLLEGE
Winona Lake, Indiana

- **Independent** comprehensive, founded 1948, affiliated with Fellowship of Grace Brethren Churches
- **Calendar** semesters
- **Degrees** associate, bachelor's, and master's
- **Small-town** 160-acre campus
- **Endowment** $5.2 million
- **Coed,** 1,086 undergraduate students, 88% full-time, 50% women, 50% men
- **Moderately difficult** entrance level, 71% of applicants were admitted

Grace College is a 4-year Christian liberal arts college that applies biblical values in strengthening character, sharpening competence, and preparing for service. Grace offers a variety of academic majors and programs, coupled with many ministry and service opportunities, to equip students to make an impact in whatever career they choose.

Undergraduates 955 full-time, 131 part-time. Students come from 35 states and territories, 8 other countries, 38% are from out of state, 6% African American, 0.2% Asian American or Pacific Islander, 1% Hispanic American, 0.3% Native American, 1% international, 4% transferred in, 68% live on campus. *Retention:* 72% of 2002 full-time freshmen returned.

Freshmen *Admission:* 768 applied, 549 admitted, 181 enrolled. *Average high school GPA:* 3.46. *Test scores:* SAT verbal scores over 500: 67%; SAT math scores over 500: 67%; ACT scores over 18: 92%; SAT verbal scores over 600: 27%; SAT math scores over 600: 19%; ACT scores over 24: 49%; SAT verbal scores over 700: 3%; SAT math scores over 700: 3%; ACT scores over 30: 7%.

Faculty *Total:* 91, 45% full time, 44% with terminal degrees. *Student/faculty ratio:* 17:1.

Majors Accounting; administrative assistant and secretarial science; art; art teacher education; biblical studies; biology/biological sciences; business administration and management; business/commerce; commercial and advertising art; counseling psychology; criminal justice/law enforcement administration; divinity/ministry; drawing; elementary education; English; English/language arts teacher education; French; French language teacher education; German; German language teacher education; international business/trade/commerce; journalism; journalism related; management information systems; mass communication/media; mathematics; mathematics teacher education; music teacher education; painting; pastoral studies/counseling; physical education teaching and coaching; piano and organ; psychology; science teacher education; social work; sociology; Spanish; Spanish language teacher education; special education.

Academic Programs *Special study options:* academic remediation for entering students, accelerated degree program, adult/continuing education programs, advanced placement credit, distance learning, double majors, independent study, internships, off-campus study, part-time degree program, services for LD students, study abroad, summer session for credit.

Library Morgan Library with 142,865 titles, 12,500 serial subscriptions, 3,583 audiovisual materials, an OPAC, a Web page.

Computers on Campus 85 computers available on campus for general student use. A campuswide network can be accessed from student residence rooms and from off campus. Internet access, at least one staffed computer lab available.

Student Life *Housing:* on-campus residence required through senior year. *Options:* men-only, women-only. Campus housing is university owned. Freshman campus housing is guaranteed. *Activities and organizations:* drama/theater group, student-run newspaper, choral group, Grace Ministries in Action, Student Activities Board, Funfest, women's ministries, Breakout. *Campus security:* student patrols, late-night transport/escort service, controlled dormitory access, evening patrols by trained security personnel. *Student services:* health clinic, personal/psychological counseling.

Athletics Member NAIA, NCCAA. *Intercollegiate sports:* baseball M(s), basketball M(s)/W(s), cheerleading M(s)/W(s), cross-country running M(s)/W(s), golf M(s), soccer M(s)/W(s), softball W(s), tennis M(s)/W(s), track and field M(s)/W(s), volleyball W(s). *Intramural sports:* basketball M/W, football M, soccer M/W, softball M/W, table tennis M/W, tennis M/W, volleyball M/W.

Standardized Tests *Required:* SAT I or ACT (for admission).

Costs (2003–04) *Comprehensive fee:* $19,825 includes full-time tuition ($13,690), mandatory fees ($380), and room and board ($5755). Part-time tuition: $255 per credit. Part-time tuition and fees vary according to course load. *Required fees:* $230 per year part-time. *College room only:* $2865. Room and board charges vary according to board plan and housing facility. *Payment plan:* installment. *Waivers:* employees or children of employees.

Financial Aid Of all full-time matriculated undergraduates who enrolled in 2003, 695 applied for aid, 649 were judged to have need, 158 had their need fully met. In 2003, 120 non-need-based awards were made. *Average percent of need met:* 85%. *Average financial aid package:* $12,437. *Average need-based loan:* $5597. *Average need-based gift aid:* $7559. *Average non-need-based aid:* $9058. *Average indebtedness upon graduation:* $19,709.

Applying *Options:* electronic application, early admission, deferred entrance. *Application fee:* $20. *Required:* high school transcript, minimum 2.3 GPA, 2 letters of recommendation, personal statement of faith. *Required for some:* interview. *Application deadlines:* 8/1 (freshmen), 8/1 (transfers). *Notification:* continuous until 8/15 (freshmen), continuous until 8/15 (transfers).

Admissions Contact Ms. Lisa Middleton, Assistant Director of Admissions/Registrar, Grace College, 200 Seminary Drive, Winona Lake, IN 46590-1294. *Phone:* 574-372-5100 Ext. 6412. *Toll-free phone:* 800-54-GRACE Ext. 6412 (in-state); 800-54 GRACE Ext. 6412 (out-of-state). *Fax:* 574-372-5114. *E-mail:* enroll@grace.edu.

■ *See page 1680 for a narrative description.*

HANOVER COLLEGE
Hanover, Indiana

- **Independent Presbyterian** 4-year, founded 1827
- **Calendar** 4-4-1
- **Degree** bachelor's
- **Rural** 630-acre campus with easy access to Louisville
- **Endowment** $102.0 million
- **Coed,** 997 undergraduate students, 99% full-time, 54% women, 46% men
- **Moderately difficult** entrance level, 79% of applicants were admitted

Hanover College, the oldest private college in Indiana, offers a classic liberal arts education. Nestled among 650 acres overlooking the Ohio River, Hanover is home to 1,000 students from 36 states and 18 countries who want a challenging college experience. Hanover has been consistently ranked as one of the best buys among private liberal arts colleges in the nation.

Undergraduates 988 full-time, 9 part-time. Students come from 35 states and territories, 15 other countries, 29% are from out of state, 2% African American, 3% Asian American or Pacific Islander, 2% Hispanic American, 0.2% Native American, 4% international, 1% transferred in, 93% live on campus. *Retention:* 75% of 2002 full-time freshmen returned.

Freshmen *Admission:* 1,364 applied, 1,073 admitted, 292 enrolled. *Test scores:* SAT verbal scores over 500: 79%; SAT math scores over 500: 87%; ACT scores over 18: 99%; SAT verbal scores over 600: 39%; SAT math scores over 600: 43%; ACT scores over 24: 64%; SAT verbal scores over 700: 6%; SAT math scores over 700: 8%; ACT scores over 30: 8%.

Faculty *Total:* 91, 93% full-time, 96% with terminal degrees. *Student/faculty ratio:* 10:1.

Majors Anthropology; art; art history, criticism and conservation; biology/biological sciences; business administration and management; chemistry; classics and languages, literatures and linguistics; computer science; dramatic/theatre arts; economics; English; French; geology/earth science; German; history; international/global studies; Latin American studies; mass communication/media; mathematics; medieval and Renaissance studies; music; philosophy; physical education teaching and coaching; physics; political science and government; psychology; sociology; Spanish; theology.

Academic Programs *Special study options:* accelerated degree program, advanced placement credit, double majors, independent study, internships, off-campus study, study abroad.

Library Duggan Library with 224,478 titles, 1,035 serial subscriptions, 5,080 audiovisual materials, an OPAC, a Web page.

Computers on Campus 90 computers available on campus for general student use. A campuswide network can be accessed from student residence rooms and from off campus. Internet access, at least one staffed computer lab available.

Student Life *Housing:* on-campus residence required through senior year. *Options:* coed, men-only, women-only. Campus housing is university owned and leased by the school. Freshman campus housing is guaranteed. *Activities and organizations:* drama/theater group, student-run newspaper, television station, choral group, Christian Life, Baptist Collegiate Ministries, Student Programming Board, Link, American Chemical Society, national fraternities, national sororities. *Campus security:* 24-hour emergency response devices and patrols, late-night transport/escort service, controlled dormitory access. *Student services:* health clinic, personal/psychological counseling.

Athletics Member NCAA. All Division III. *Intercollegiate sports:* baseball M, basketball M/W, cross-country running M/W, field hockey W, football M, golf M/W, soccer M/W, softball W, tennis M/W, track and field M/W, volleyball W. *Intramural sports:* basketball M/W, football M/W, soccer M/W, volleyball M/W.

Standardized Tests *Required:* SAT I or ACT (for admission).

Costs (2003–04) *Comprehensive fee:* $20,600 includes full-time tuition ($14,300), mandatory fees ($400), and room and board ($5900). Full-time tuition and fees vary according to reciprocity agreements. Part-time tuition and fees vary according to course load and reciprocity agreements. *College room only:* $2800. Room and board charges vary according to housing facility. *Payment plan:* installment. *Waivers:* senior citizens and employees or children of employees.

Financial Aid Of all full-time matriculated undergraduates who enrolled in 2003, 956 applied for aid, 847 were judged to have need, 336 had their need fully met. In 2003, 136 non-need-based awards were made. *Average percent of need met:* 73%. *Average financial aid package:* $14,788. *Average need-based loan:* $3038. *Average need-based gift aid:* $12,594. *Average non-need-based aid:* $15,625. *Average indebtedness upon graduation:* $11,583.

Applying *Options:* common application, electronic application, early admission, early action, deferred entrance. *Application fee:* $30. *Required:* essay or personal statement, high school transcript, 1 letter of recommendation. *Recommended:* interview. *Application deadline:* 3/1 (freshmen), rolling (transfers). *Notification:* continuous (freshmen), 12/20 (early action), continuous (transfers).

Admissions Contact Mr. Kenneth Moyer, Dean of Admission, Hanover College, PO Box 108, Hanover, IN 47243-0108. *Phone:* 812-866-7021. *Toll-free phone:* 800-213-2178. *Fax:* 812-866-7098. *E-mail:* admission@hanover.edu.

■ *See page 1710 for a narrative description.*

HUNTINGTON COLLEGE
Huntington, Indiana

- **Independent** comprehensive, founded 1897, affiliated with Church of the United Brethren in Christ
- **Calendar** 4-1-4
- **Degrees** diplomas, associate, bachelor's, master's, and postbachelor's certificates
- **Small-town** 200-acre campus with easy access to Fort Wayne
- **Endowment** $14.8 million
- **Coed,** 923 undergraduate students, 92% full-time, 57% women, 43% men
- **Moderately difficult** entrance level, 92% of applicants were admitted

Huntington College is ranked as a top 10 Midwest Comprehensive College by *U.S. News & World Report.* Since 1897, Huntington has been educating men and women to impact the world for Christ. Huntington offers more than 60 areas of study, including nationally recognized programs in youth ministry and theater. Prospective students can find out more about Huntingdon's programs and build their own personalized brochure at http://www.huntingdon.edu/brochure.

Undergraduates 848 full-time, 75 part-time. Students come from 27 states and territories, 15 other countries, 40% are from out of state, 1% African American, 0.7% Asian American or Pacific Islander, 0.7% Hispanic American, 0.1% Native American, 3% international, 3% transferred in, 68% live on campus. *Retention:* 77% of 2002 full-time freshmen returned.

Freshmen *Admission:* 620 applied, 570 admitted, 192 enrolled. *Average high school GPA:* 3.45. *Test scores:* SAT verbal scores over 500: 78%; SAT math scores over 500: 79%; ACT scores over 18: 92%; SAT verbal scores over 600: 33%; SAT math scores over 600: 33%; ACT scores over 24: 48%; SAT verbal scores over 700: 8%; SAT math scores over 700: 6%; ACT scores over 30: 9%.

Faculty *Total:* 97, 57% full-time, 53% with terminal degrees. *Student/faculty ratio:* 18:1.

Majors Accounting; art; art teacher education; biblical studies; biological and physical sciences; biology/biological sciences; broadcast journalism; business administration and management; business/managerial economics; business teacher education; chemistry; commercial and advertising art; communication/speech communication and rhetoric; computer science; digital communication and media/multimedia; divinity/ministry; dramatic/theatre arts; economics; education; elementary education; English; history; journalism; kinesiology and exercise science; mass communication/media; mathematics; music; music teacher education; natural resources management and policy; parks, recreation and leisure; philosophy; physical education teaching and coaching; piano and organ; pre-dentistry studies; pre-law studies; pre-medical studies; pre-veterinary studies; psychology; public relations/image management; religious studies; science teacher education; secondary education; sociology; special education; theology; voice and opera.

Academic Programs *Special study options:* academic remediation for entering students, accelerated degree program, adult/continuing education programs, advanced placement credit, distance learning, double majors, English as a second language, independent study, internships, off-campus study, part-time degree program, study abroad, summer session for credit.

Library RichLyn Library with 91,709 titles, 553 serial subscriptions, 4,323 audiovisual materials, a Web page.

Computers on Campus 190 computers available on campus for general student use. A campuswide network can be accessed from student residence rooms and from off campus. Internet access, at least one staffed computer lab available.

Student Life *Housing:* on-campus residence required through junior year. *Options:* men-only, women-only. Campus housing is university owned. Freshman campus housing is guaranteed. *Activities and organizations:* drama/theater group, student-run newspaper, radio and television station, choral group, Joe Mertz Volunteer Center, Student Senate, Ministry groups, student publications, Chapel Worship Team. *Campus security:* 24-hour emergency response devices, late-night transport/escort service, night patrols by trained security personnel. *Student services:* health clinic, personal/psychological counseling.

Athletics Member NAIA. *Intercollegiate sports:* baseball M(s), basketball M(s)/W(s), cheerleading M/W, cross-country running M(s)/W(s), golf M(s), soccer M(s)/W(s), softball W(s), tennis M(s)/W(s), track and field M(s)/W(s), volleyball W(s). *Intramural sports:* basketball M, football M, racquetball M/W, rock climbing M/W, softball M/W, ultimate Frisbee M/W, volleyball M/W.

Standardized Tests *Required:* SAT I or ACT (for admission).

Costs (2003–04) *Comprehensive fee:* $23,590 includes full-time tuition ($17,280), mandatory fees ($420), and room and board ($5890). Part-time tuition:

Huntington College (continued)
$500 per semester hour. Part-time tuition and fees vary according to course load. No tuition increase for student's term of enrollment. *Room and board:* Room and board charges vary according to board plan. *Payment plan:* installment. *Waivers:* minority students, children of alumni, adult students, senior citizens, and employees or children of employees.

Financial Aid Of all full-time matriculated undergraduates who enrolled in 2003, 678 applied for aid, 600 were judged to have need, 71 had their need fully met. 166 Federal Work-Study jobs (averaging $1812). In 2003, 60 non-need-based awards were made. *Average percent of need met:* 69%. *Average financial aid package:* $13,794. *Average need-based loan:* $4164. *Average need-based gift aid:* $8574. *Average non-need-based aid:* $5282. *Average indebtedness upon graduation:* $16,952.

Applying *Options:* electronic application, deferred entrance. *Application fee:* $20. *Required:* essay or personal statement, high school transcript, minimum 2.3 GPA. *Recommended:* interview. *Application deadline:* 8/15 (freshmen), rolling (transfers). *Notification:* continuous (freshmen), continuous (transfers).

Admissions Contact Mr. Jeff Berggren, Dean of Enrollment, Huntington College, 2303 College Avenue, Huntington, IN 46750-1299. *Phone:* 260-356-6000 Ext. 4016. *Toll-free phone:* 800-642-6493. *Fax:* 260-356-9448. *E-mail:* admissions@huntington.edu.

INDIANA INSTITUTE OF TECHNOLOGY

Fort Wayne, Indiana

- **Independent** comprehensive, founded 1930
- **Calendar** semesters
- **Degrees** associate, bachelor's, and master's
- **Urban** 25-acre campus
- **Endowment** $17.0 million
- **Coed,** 2,971 undergraduate students, 52% full-time, 56% women, 44% men
- **Moderately difficult** entrance level, 92% of applicants were admitted

Undergraduates 1,545 full-time, 1,426 part-time. 35% are from out of state, 18% African American, 0.5% Asian American or Pacific Islander, 2% Hispanic American, 0.5% Native American, 0.8% international, 44% live on campus. *Retention:* 56% of 2002 full-time freshmen returned.

Freshmen *Admission:* 1,989 applied, 1,826 admitted, 749 enrolled. *Average high school GPA:* 2.93. *Test scores:* SAT verbal scores over 500: 55%; SAT math scores over 500: 46%; ACT scores over 18: 74%; SAT verbal scores over 600: 22%; SAT math scores over 600: 12%; ACT scores over 24: 19%; SAT verbal scores over 700: 2%; ACT scores over 30: 2%.

Faculty *Total:* 272, 15% full-time, 9% with terminal degrees. *Student/faculty ratio:* 17:1.

Majors Accounting; business administration and management; computer engineering; computer science; electrical, electronics and communications engineering; human resources management; human services; information science/studies; information technology; marketing/marketing management; mechanical engineering; parks, recreation and leisure facilities management; psychology; therapeutic recreation.

Academic Programs *Special study options:* academic remediation for entering students, accelerated degree program, adult/continuing education programs, advanced placement credit, distance learning, double majors, English as a second language, external degree program, independent study, internships, part-time degree program, services for LD students, student-designed majors, summer session for credit.

Library McMillen Library with 35,200 titles, 158 serial subscriptions, 92 audiovisual materials, an OPAC.

Computers on Campus 79 computers available on campus for general student use. A campuswide network can be accessed from student residence rooms and from off campus. At least one staffed computer lab available.

Student Life *Housing:* on-campus residence required through sophomore year. *Options:* coed. Campus housing is university owned. *Activities and organizations:* student-run newspaper, choral group, national fraternities, national sororities. *Campus security:* 24-hour emergency response devices and patrols, controlled dormitory access. *Student services:* personal/psychological counseling.

Athletics Member NAIA. *Intercollegiate sports:* baseball M(s), basketball M(s)/W(s), cheerleading M(s)/W(s), soccer M(s)/W(s), softball W(s). *Intramural sports:* basketball M/W, bowling M/W, football M/W, golf M/W, softball M/W, volleyball M/W.

Standardized Tests *Required:* SAT I or ACT (for admission).

Costs (2004–05) *Comprehensive fee:* $22,952 includes full-time tuition ($16,680) and room and board ($6272). Full-time tuition and fees vary according to class time, course load, and program. Part-time tuition: $556 per credit hour. Part-time tuition and fees vary according to class time, course load, and program. *College room only:* $3136. Room and board charges vary according to housing facility and student level. *Payment plan:* installment. *Waivers:* employees or children of employees.

Financial Aid *Average financial aid package:* $9125. *Average indebtedness upon graduation:* $16,500.

Applying *Options:* electronic application, early admission, deferred entrance. *Application fee:* $50. *Required:* high school transcript. *Recommended:* minimum 3.0 GPA, interview, 2 references. *Notification:* continuous until 10/15 (freshmen), continuous until 2/1 (transfers).

Admissions Contact Ms. Allison Carnahan, Director of Admissions, Indiana Institute of Technology, 1600 East Washington Boulevard, Fort Wayne, IN 46803. *Phone:* 260-422-5561 Ext. 2206. *Toll-free phone:* 800-937-2448 (in-state); 888-666-TECH (out-of-state). *Fax:* 260-422-7696. *E-mail:* admissions@indtech.edu.

INDIANA STATE UNIVERSITY

Terre Haute, Indiana

- **State-supported** university, founded 1865
- **Calendar** semesters
- **Degrees** associate, bachelor's, master's, doctoral, post-master's, and postbachelor's certificates
- **Small-town** 91-acre campus with easy access to Indianapolis
- **Endowment** $36.1 million
- **Coed,** 9,615 undergraduate students, 88% full-time, 52% women, 48% men
- **Moderately difficult** entrance level, 86% of applicants were admitted

Undergraduates 8,417 full-time, 1,198 part-time. Students come from 41 states and territories, 41 other countries, 8% are from out of state, 11% African American, 0.6% Asian American or Pacific Islander, 1% Hispanic American, 0.3% Native American, 2% international, 7% transferred in, 45% live on campus. *Retention:* 70% of 2002 full-time freshmen returned.

Freshmen *Admission:* 5,568 applied, 4,800 admitted, 2,016 enrolled. *Average high school GPA:* 2.91. *Test scores:* SAT verbal scores over 500: 39%; SAT math scores over 500: 39%; ACT scores over 18: 68%; SAT verbal scores over 600: 7%; SAT math scores over 600: 6%; ACT scores over 24: 17%; ACT scores over 30: 1%.

Faculty *Total:* 715, 78% full-time. *Student/faculty ratio:* 16:1.

Majors Accounting; administrative assistant and secretarial science; aeronautics/aviation/aerospace science and technology; African-American/Black studies; airline pilot and flight crew; anthropology; apparel and textiles; architectural drafting and CAD/CADD; architectural engineering technology; art; art teacher education; athletic training; audiology and speech-language pathology; automotive engineering technology; aviation/airway management; biology/biological sciences; business administration and management; business teacher education; chemistry; clinical laboratory science/medical technology; communication and journalism related; communication/speech communication and rhetoric; community health services counseling; computer and information sciences; computer and information sciences related; computer engineering technology; criminology; dramatic/theatre arts; early childhood education; economics; educational/instructional media design; electrical, electronic and communications engineering technology; elementary education; English; environmental health; family and consumer sciences/human sciences; finance; fine arts related; foods, nutrition, and wellness; foreign languages and literatures; French; general studies; geography; geology/earth science; German; graphic and printing equipment operation/production; health teacher education; history; human development and family studies; humanities; human resources management; industrial production technologies related; industrial technology; insurance; interior architecture; journalism; liberal arts and sciences/liberal studies; management information systems; management sciences and quantitative methods related; marketing/marketing management; mathematics; mechanical engineering technologies related; music; music related; nursing (registered nurse training); occupational safety and health technology; office management; operations management; parks, recreation and leisure facilities management; philosophy; physical education teaching and coaching; physics; political science and government; psychology; radio and television; robotics technology; science teacher education; social studies teacher education; social work; sociology; Spanish; special education; speech-language pathology; trade and industrial teacher education.

Academic Programs *Special study options:* academic remediation for entering students, accelerated degree program, adult/continuing education programs, advanced placement credit, cooperative education, distance learning, double majors, English as a second language, honors programs, independent study, internships, off-campus study, part-time degree program, services for LD students, study abroad, summer session for credit. *ROTC:* Army (b), Air Force (b).

Library Cunningham Memorial Library plus 2 others with 2.5 million titles, 2,827 serial subscriptions, an OPAC, a Web page.

Computers on Campus 500 computers available on campus for general student use. A campuswide network can be accessed from student residence rooms and from off campus. Internet access, at least one staffed computer lab available.

Student Life *Housing:* on-campus residence required for freshman year. *Options:* coed, men-only, women-only. Campus housing is university owned. Freshman campus housing is guaranteed. *Activities and organizations:* drama/theater group, student-run newspaper, radio station, choral group, marching band, Union Boards, Student Government Association, Black Student Union, Student Alumni Association, Panhellenic, National Panhellenic, and Interfraternity Council, national fraternities, national sororities. *Campus security:* 24-hour emergency response devices and patrols, student patrols, late-night transport/escort service. *Student services:* health clinic, personal/psychological counseling, women's center, legal services.

Athletics Member NCAA. All Division I except football (Division I-AA). *Intercollegiate sports:* baseball M(s), basketball M(s)/W(s), bowling M(c)/W(c), cross-country running M(s)/W(s), soccer M(c)/W(c), softball W(s), swimming M(c)/W(c), tennis M(s)/W(s), track and field M(s)/W(s), volleyball M(c)/W(s). *Intramural sports:* badminton M/W, basketball M/W, bowling M/W, cross-country running M/W, golf M/W, racquetball M/W, soccer M/W, softball M/W, swimming M/W, table tennis M/W, tennis M/W, track and field M/W, volleyball M(c)/W, weight lifting M/W.

Standardized Tests *Required:* SAT I or ACT (for admission).

Costs (2003–04) *Tuition:* state resident $5322 full-time, $192 per credit part-time; nonresident $11,790 full-time, $416 per credit part-time. *Required fees:* $100 full-time, $50 per term part-time. *Room and board:* $5297; room only: $2790. Room and board charges vary according to board plan, housing facility, and student level. *Payment plans:* installment, deferred payment. *Waivers:* employees or children of employees.

Financial Aid Of all full-time matriculated undergraduates who enrolled in 2003, 6,224 applied for aid, 4,935 were judged to have need, 376 had their need fully met. 175 Federal Work-Study jobs (averaging $2075). In 2003, 630 non-need-based awards were made. *Average percent of need met:* 43%. *Average financial aid package:* $5836. *Average need-based loan:* $3398. *Average need-based gift aid:* $4313. *Average non-need-based aid:* $2887. *Average indebtedness upon graduation:* $16,242.

Applying *Options:* electronic application, deferred entrance. *Application fee:* $25. *Required:* high school transcript, minimum 2.0 GPA. *Required for some:* letters of recommendation, interview. *Application deadline:* 8/1 (freshmen). *Notification:* continuous (freshmen), continuous (transfers).

Admissions Contact Mr. Ronald Brown, Director of Admissions, Indiana State University, Tirey Hall 134, 210 North 7th Street, Terre Haute, IN 47809. *Phone:* 812-237-2121. *Toll-free phone:* 800-742-0891. *Fax:* 812-237-8023. *E-mail:* admissions@indstate.edu.

■ *See page 1764 for a narrative description.*

INDIANA UNIVERSITY BLOOMINGTON
Bloomington, Indiana

- **State-supported** university, founded 1820, part of Indiana University System
- **Calendar** semesters plus 2 summer sessions
- **Degrees** certificates, diplomas, associate, bachelor's, master's, doctoral, first professional, post-master's, and postbachelor's certificates
- **Small-town** 1931-acre campus with easy access to Indianapolis
- **Endowment** $613.7 million
- **Coed,** 30,319 undergraduate students, 94% full-time, 52% women, 48% men
- **Moderately difficult** entrance level, 81% of applicants were admitted

Undergraduates 28,559 full-time, 1,760 part-time. Students come from 56 states and territories, 135 other countries, 30% are from out of state, 4% African American, 3% Asian American or Pacific Islander, 2% Hispanic American, 0.2% Native American, 4% international, 3% transferred in, 36% live on campus. *Retention:* 88% of 2002 full-time freshmen returned.

Freshmen *Admission:* 22,178 applied, 17,992 admitted, 6,784 enrolled. *Test scores:* SAT verbal scores over 500: 73%; SAT math scores over 500: 76%; ACT scores over 18: 97%; SAT verbal scores over 600: 28%; SAT math scores over 600: 35%; ACT scores over 24: 61%; SAT verbal scores over 700: 4%; SAT math scores over 700: 6%; ACT scores over 30: 10%.

Faculty *Total:* 2,071, 85% full-time, 65% with terminal degrees. *Student/faculty ratio:* 19:1.

Majors Accounting; African-American/Black studies; African studies; ancient/classical Greek; anthropology; apparel and textiles; applied art; art; art history, criticism and conservation; art teacher education; Asian studies; Asian studies (East); astronomy; astrophysics; athletic training; audiology and hearing sciences; audiology and speech-language pathology; bilingual and multilingual education; biochemistry; biology/biological sciences; biology teacher education; broadcast journalism; business administration and management; business/commerce; business/managerial economics; ceramic arts and ceramics; chemistry; chemistry teacher education; child development; Chinese; city/urban, community and regional planning; classics and languages, literatures and linguistics; clothing/textiles; cognitive psychology and psycholinguistics; commercial and advertising art; communication/speech communication and rhetoric; comparative literature; computer and information sciences; consumer merchandising/retailing management; criminal justice/safety; dance; dietetics; dramatic/theatre arts; drawing; economics; education; elementary education; English; English/language arts teacher education; environmental studies; European studies (Central and Eastern); family and consumer economics related; fashion/apparel design; fashion merchandising; finance; fine/studio arts; folklore; foods, nutrition, and wellness; forensic science and technology; French; French language teacher education; general studies; geography; geology/earth science; German; German language teacher education; history; human development and family studies; interior design; Italian; Japanese; jazz/jazz studies; Jewish/Judaic studies; journalism; kindergarten/preschool education; labor and industrial relations; laser and optical technology; Latin; Latin American studies; linguistics; literature; management information systems; marketing/marketing management; mass communication/media; mathematics; mathematics teacher education; medical microbiology and bacteriology; metal and jewelry arts; music; musical instrument fabrication and repair; music history, literature, and theory; music teacher education; Near and Middle Eastern studies; occupational safety and health technology; ophthalmic laboratory technology; ophthalmic/optometric services; optometric technician; parks, recreation and leisure; parks, recreation and leisure facilities management; philosophy; photography; physical education teaching and coaching; physics; physics teacher education; piano and organ; political science and government; Portuguese; pre-dentistry studies; pre-law studies; pre-medical studies; psychology; public administration; public health; public policy analysis; radio and television; real estate; religious studies; Russian; Russian studies; science teacher education; sculpture; secondary education; Slavic languages; social studies teacher education; social work; sociology; Spanish; Spanish language teacher education; special education; speech and rhetoric; speech teacher education; speech therapy; sport and fitness administration; systems science and theory; telecommunications; theatre design and technology; therapeutic recreation; urban studies/affairs; voice and opera; wind/percussion instruments; women's studies.

Academic Programs *Special study options:* academic remediation for entering students, accelerated degree program, adult/continuing education programs, advanced placement credit, cooperative education, distance learning, double majors, English as a second language, external degree program, freshman honors college, honors programs, independent study, internships, off-campus study, part-time degree program, services for LD students, student-designed majors, study abroad, summer session for credit. *ROTC:* Army (b), Air Force (b). *Unusual degree programs:* 3-2 accounting.

Library Indiana University Library plus 32 others with 6.5 million titles, 60,019 serial subscriptions, 252,801 audiovisual materials, an OPAC, a Web page.

Computers on Campus 1500 computers available on campus for general student use. A campuswide network can be accessed from student residence rooms and from off campus that provide access to various software packages. Internet access, at least one staffed computer lab available.

Student Life *Housing options:* coed, men-only, women-only, cooperative, disabled students. Campus housing is university owned. *Activities and organizations:* drama/theater group, student-run newspaper, radio and television station, choral group, marching band, Union Board, Student Association, Student Foundation, Habitat for Humanity, Student Athletic Board, national fraternities, national sororities. *Campus security:* 24-hour emergency response devices and patrols, late-night transport/escort service, safety seminars, lighted pathways, escort service, shuttle bus service, emergency telephones. *Student services:* health clinic, personal/psychological counseling, women's center, legal services.

Athletics Member NCAA. All Division I except football (Division I-A). *Intercollegiate sports:* baseball M(s), basketball M(s)/W(s), crew W(s), cross-country running M(s)/W(s), field hockey W, golf M(s)/W(s), soccer M(s)/W(s), softball W(s), swimming M(s)/W(s), tennis M(s)/W(s), track and field M(s)/W(s), volleyball W(s), water polo W(s), wrestling M(s). *Intramural sports:* archery M/W, badminton M(c)/W(c), baseball M/W, basketball M/W, bowling M(c)/W(c), crew M(c)/W(c), cross-country running M/W, equestrian sports M(c)/W(c), fencing M(c)/W(c), field hockey W(c), golf M/W, gymnastics M/W, ice hockey M/W, lacrosse M(c)/W(c), racquetball M(c)/W(c), riflery M(c)/W(c), rugby M(c)/W(c), sailing M(c)/W(c), skiing (downhill) M(c)/W(c), soccer M/W(c), softball M/W, squash M/W, swimming M/W, table tennis M/W, tennis M(c)/W, track and field M/W, volleyball M/W, water polo M(c)/W, weight lifting M(c)/W(c), wrestling M(c).

Standardized Tests *Required:* SAT I or ACT (for admission). *Recommended:* SAT II: Subject Tests (for admission).

Costs (2003–04) *Tuition:* state resident $5756 full-time, $148 per credit hour part-time; nonresident $16,791 full-time, $494 per credit hour part-time. Part-time tuition and fees vary according to course load. *Required fees:* $761 full-time. *Room and board:* $5872; room only: $3482. Room and board charges vary

Indiana University Bloomington (continued)
according to board plan and housing facility. *Payment plan:* deferred payment. *Waivers:* employees or children of employees.

Financial Aid Of all full-time matriculated undergraduates who enrolled in 2003, 18,916 applied for aid, 10,973 were judged to have need, 983 had their need fully met. 2,177 Federal Work-Study jobs (averaging $1919). In 2003, 5097 non-need-based awards were made. *Average percent of need met:* 63%. *Average financial aid package:* $7425. *Average need-based loan:* $3854. *Average need-based gift aid:* $4877. *Average non-need-based aid:* $3592. *Average indebtedness upon graduation:* $18,423.

Applying *Options:* electronic application, deferred entrance. *Application fee:* $45. *Required:* high school transcript. *Recommended:* interview. *Application deadline:* 4/1 (freshmen), rolling (transfers). *Notification:* continuous (freshmen), continuous (transfers).

Admissions Contact Mr. Don Hossler, Vice Chancellor for Enrollment Services, Indiana University Bloomington, 300 North Jordan Avenue, Bloomington, IN 47405-1106. *Phone:* 812-855-0661. *Fax:* 812-855-5102. *E-mail:* iuadmit@indiana.edu.

INDIANA UNIVERSITY EAST
Richmond, Indiana

- **State-supported** 4-year, founded 1971, part of Indiana University System
- **Calendar** semesters
- **Degrees** associate, bachelor's, and postbachelor's certificates
- **Small-town** 194-acre campus with easy access to Indianapolis
- **Endowment** $6.3 million
- **Coed,** 2,505 undergraduate students, 51% full-time, 70% women, 30% men
- **Moderately difficult** entrance level, 79% of applicants were admitted

Undergraduates 1,285 full-time, 1,220 part-time. Students come from 7 states and territories, 10% are from out of state, 5% African American, 0.4% Asian American or Pacific Islander, 0.9% Hispanic American, 0.5% Native American, 0.4% international, 4% transferred in. *Retention:* 61% of 2002 full-time freshmen returned.

Freshmen *Admission:* 599 applied, 474 admitted, 474 enrolled. *Test scores:* SAT verbal scores over 500: 30%; SAT math scores over 500: 24%; ACT scores over 18: 65%; SAT verbal scores over 600: 8%; SAT math scores over 600: 2%; ACT scores over 24: 14%; SAT verbal scores over 700: 1%; SAT math scores over 700: 1%; ACT scores over 30: 2%.

Faculty *Total:* 204, 38% full-time, 20% with terminal degrees. *Student/faculty ratio:* 14:1.

Majors Biological and physical sciences; biology/biological sciences; business/commerce; clinical laboratory science/medical technology; communication/speech communication and rhetoric; computer programming; criminal justice/safety; education; elementary education; English; general studies; geology/earth science; history; human services; mathematics; nursing (registered nurse training); psychology; secondary education; social work; sociology; visual and performing arts.

Academic Programs *Special study options:* academic remediation for entering students, adult/continuing education programs, advanced placement credit, cooperative education, distance learning, double majors, external degree program, independent study, internships, off-campus study, part-time degree program, services for LD students, summer session for credit.

Library Library and Media Services plus 1 other with 67,036 titles, 435 serial subscriptions, 2,222 audiovisual materials.

Computers on Campus 110 computers available on campus for general student use. A campuswide network can be accessed from off campus. Internet access, at least one staffed computer lab available.

Student Life *Housing:* college housing not available. *Activities and organizations:* drama/theater group, student-run newspaper, television station, Student Government Association, Phi Beta Lambda, Multicultural Awareness Association, psychology club, sociology club. *Campus security:* 24-hour emergency response devices, late-night transport/escort service, safety awareness, lighted pathways, 14-hour foot and vehicle patrol. *Student services:* personal/psychological counseling.

Athletics *Intramural sports:* basketball M(c)/W(c), softball M/W, volleyball M/W.

Standardized Tests *Recommended:* SAT I or ACT (for admission).

Costs (2003–04) *Tuition:* state resident $4118 full-time, $137 per credit hour part-time; nonresident $10,068 full-time, $336 per credit hour part-time. Full-time tuition and fees vary according to course load. Part-time tuition and fees vary according to course load. *Required fees:* $315 full-time. *Payment plan:* deferred payment. *Waivers:* employees or children of employees.

Financial Aid Of all full-time matriculated undergraduates who enrolled in 2003, 1,079 applied for aid, 910 were judged to have need, 46 had their need fully met. 54 Federal Work-Study jobs (averaging $3854). In 2003, 46 non-need-based awards were made. *Average percent of need met:* 54%. *Average financial aid package:* $5838. *Average need-based loan:* $2880. *Average need-based gift aid:* $4474. *Average non-need-based aid:* $600. *Average indebtedness upon graduation:* $17,547.

Applying *Options:* early admission, deferred entrance. *Application fee:* $25. *Required:* high school transcript. *Recommended:* minimum 2.0 GPA. *Application deadline:* rolling (transfers). *Notification:* continuous (freshmen).

Admissions Contact Ms. Susanna Tanner, Admissions Counselor, Indiana University East, 2325 Chester Boulevard, WZ 116, Richmond, IN 47374-1289. *Phone:* 765-973-8415. *Toll-free phone:* 800-959-EAST. *Fax:* 765-973-8288. *E-mail:* eaadmit@indiana.edu.

INDIANA UNIVERSITY KOKOMO
Kokomo, Indiana

- **State-supported** comprehensive, founded 1945, part of Indiana University System
- **Calendar** semesters
- **Degrees** certificates, associate, bachelor's, master's, and postbachelor's certificates
- **Small-town** 51-acre campus with easy access to Indianapolis
- **Endowment** $2.5 million
- **Coed,** 2,730 undergraduate students, 52% full-time, 71% women, 29% men
- **Minimally difficult** entrance level, 86% of applicants were admitted

Undergraduates 1,424 full-time, 1,306 part-time. Students come from 3 states and territories, 1% are from out of state, 4% African American, 0.7% Asian American or Pacific Islander, 2% Hispanic American, 0.4% Native American, 0.5% international, 7% transferred in. *Retention:* 60% of 2002 full-time freshmen returned.

Freshmen *Admission:* 837 applied, 723 admitted, 557 enrolled. *Test scores:* SAT verbal scores over 500: 37%; SAT math scores over 500: 34%; ACT scores over 18: 67%; SAT verbal scores over 600: 5%; SAT math scores over 600: 6%; ACT scores over 24: 10%.

Faculty *Total:* 177, 50% full-time, 37% with terminal degrees. *Student/faculty ratio:* 17:1.

Majors Behavioral sciences; biological and physical sciences; biology/biological sciences; business/commerce; clinical laboratory science/medical technology; communication/speech communication and rhetoric; criminal justice/safety; data processing and data processing technology; elementary education; English; general studies; humanities; labor and industrial relations; mathematics; nursing (registered nurse training); psychology; sociology.

Academic Programs *Special study options:* academic remediation for entering students, adult/continuing education programs, advanced placement credit, distance learning, external degree program, freshman honors college, honors programs, independent study, internships, part-time degree program, services for LD students, study abroad, summer session for credit. *ROTC:* Army (c).

Library Main Library plus 1 other with 132,424 titles, 1,513 serial subscriptions, 1,466 audiovisual materials.

Computers on Campus 120 computers available on campus for general student use. Internet access, at least one staffed computer lab available.

Student Life *Housing:* college housing not available. *Activities and organizations:* drama/theater group, student-run newspaper, choral group. *Campus security:* 24-hour patrols, late-night transport/escort service, campus police, lighted pathways. *Student services:* personal/psychological counseling.

Athletics *Intramural sports:* basketball M, soccer M/W, softball M/W, volleyball M/W.

Standardized Tests *Required:* SAT I or ACT (for admission).

Costs (2003–04) *Tuition:* state resident $4118 full-time, $137 per credit hour part-time; nonresident $10,068 full-time, $336 per credit hour part-time. *Required fees:* $345 full-time. *Waivers:* employees or children of employees.

Financial Aid Of all full-time matriculated undergraduates who enrolled in 2003, 869 applied for aid, 603 were judged to have need, 94 had their need fully met. 37 Federal Work-Study jobs (averaging $1738). In 2003, 70 non-need-based awards were made. *Average percent of need met:* 70%. *Average financial aid package:* $5654. *Average need-based loan:* $2833. *Average need-based gift aid:* $4283. *Average non-need-based aid:* $1137. *Average indebtedness upon graduation:* $11,681.

Applying *Options:* early admission, deferred entrance. *Application fee:* $30. *Required:* high school transcript. *Application deadline:* 8/3 (freshmen). *Notification:* continuous (freshmen), continuous (transfers).

Admissions Contact Ms. Patty Young, Admissions Director, Indiana University Kokomo, PO Box 9003, Kelley Student Center 230A, Kokomo, IN 46904-9003. *Phone:* 765-455-9217. *Toll-free phone:* 888-875-4485. *Fax:* 765-455-9537. *E-mail:* iuadmis@iuk.edu.

INDIANA UNIVERSITY NORTHWEST

Gary, Indiana

- **State-supported** comprehensive, founded 1959, part of Indiana University System
- **Calendar** semesters
- **Degrees** certificates, associate, bachelor's, master's, and postbachelor's certificates
- **Urban** 38-acre campus with easy access to Chicago
- **Endowment** $4.7 million
- **Coed,** 4,476 undergraduate students, 54% full-time, 69% women, 31% men
- **Minimally difficult** entrance level, 67% of applicants were admitted

Undergraduates 2,437 full-time, 2,039 part-time. Students come from 6 states and territories, 1% are from out of state, 21% African American, 1% Asian American or Pacific Islander, 11% Hispanic American, 0.5% Native American, 0.4% international, 6% transferred in. *Retention:* 62% of 2002 full-time freshmen returned.

Freshmen *Admission:* 1,803 applied, 1,212 admitted, 860 enrolled. *Test scores:* SAT verbal scores over 500: 34%; SAT math scores over 500: 29%; ACT scores over 18: 64%; SAT verbal scores over 600: 10%; SAT math scores over 600: 7%; ACT scores over 24: 17%; SAT math scores over 700: 1%; ACT scores over 30: 2%.

Faculty *Total:* 380, 49% full-time, 30% with terminal degrees. *Student/faculty ratio:* 13:1.

Majors Accounting; actuarial science; African-American/Black studies; art; biology/biological sciences; biology teacher education; business administration and management; chemistry; chemistry teacher education; clinical/medical laboratory technology; criminal justice/law enforcement administration; data processing and data processing technology; dental hygiene; dramatic/theatre arts; economics; education; elementary education; English; English/language arts teacher education; French; French language teacher education; general studies; geology/earth science; health/health care administration; health information/medical records administration; history; labor and industrial relations; mass communication/media; mathematics; mathematics teacher education; medical radiologic technology; nursing (registered nurse training); philosophy; political science and government; psychology; public administration; public relations/image management; radiologic technology/science; respiratory care therapy; secondary education; social studies teacher education; sociology; Spanish; Spanish language teacher education.

Academic Programs *Special study options:* academic remediation for entering students, accelerated degree program, adult/continuing education programs, advanced placement credit, cooperative education, distance learning, double majors, external degree program, honors programs, independent study, internships, off-campus study, part-time degree program, services for LD students, student-designed majors, study abroad, summer session for credit. *ROTC:* Army (b).

Library IUN Library with 251,508 titles, 1,541 serial subscriptions, 331 audiovisual materials, an OPAC, a Web page.

Computers on Campus 250 computers available on campus for general student use. A campuswide network can be accessed from off campus. Internet access, online (class) registration, at least one staffed computer lab available.

Student Life *Housing:* college housing not available. *Activities and organizations:* drama/theater group, student-run newspaper, choral group, Student Government Association, Student Guides Organization, Nursing Association, Dental Association, international affairs club, national fraternities, national sororities. *Campus security:* 24-hour emergency response devices and patrols, late-night transport/escort service, lighted pathways. *Student services:* personal/psychological counseling.

Athletics Member NAIA. *Intercollegiate sports:* baseball M, basketball M, golf M/W, softball W, volleyball W. *Intramural sports:* basketball M(c), bowling M(c)/W(c), fencing M(c)/W(c), soccer M(c), softball M(c)/W(c), table tennis M(c)/W(c), tennis M(c)/W(c), volleyball M(c)/W(c).

Standardized Tests *Required:* SAT I or ACT (for admission).

Costs (2003–04) *Tuition:* state resident $4118 full-time, $121 per credit hour part-time; nonresident $10,068 full-time, $319 per credit hour part-time. Full-time tuition and fees vary according to course level. Part-time tuition and fees vary according to course level. *Required fees:* $420 full-time. *Payment plans:* installment, deferred payment. *Waivers:* senior citizens and employees or children of employees.

Financial Aid Of all full-time matriculated undergraduates who enrolled in 2003, 1,610 applied for aid, 992 were judged to have need, 117 had their need fully met. 353 Federal Work-Study jobs (averaging $2550). In 2003, 147 non-need-based awards were made. *Average percent of need met:* 65%. *Average financial aid package:* $6261. *Average need-based loan:* $2842. *Average need-based gift aid:* $4516. *Average non-need-based aid:* $1428. *Average indebtedness upon graduation:* $14,444.

Applying *Options:* early admission, deferred entrance. *Application fee:* $25. *Required:* high school transcript, minimum 2.0 GPA. *Application deadline:* 8/1 (freshmen), rolling (transfers). *Notification:* continuous (freshmen), continuous (transfers).

Admissions Contact Dr. Linda B. Templeton, Director of Admissions, Indiana University Northwest, Hawthorne 100, 3400 Broadway, Gary, IN 46408-1197. *Phone:* 219-980-6767. *Toll-free phone:* 800-968-7486. *Fax:* 219-981-4219. *E-mail:* admit@iun.edu.

INDIANA UNIVERSITY–PURDUE UNIVERSITY FORT WAYNE

Fort Wayne, Indiana

- **State-supported** comprehensive, founded 1917, part of Indiana University System and Purdue University System
- **Calendar** semesters
- **Degrees** certificates, associate, bachelor's, master's, and postbachelor's certificates
- **Urban** 565-acre campus
- **Endowment** $15.4 million
- **Coed,** 11,068 undergraduate students, 57% full-time, 58% women, 42% men
- **Minimally difficult** entrance level, 97% of applicants were admitted

Undergraduates 6,324 full-time, 4,744 part-time. Students come from 41 states and territories, 72 other countries, 6% are from out of state, 5% African American, 2% Asian American or Pacific Islander, 2% Hispanic American, 0.4% Native American, 1% international, 8% transferred in. *Retention:* 62% of 2002 full-time freshmen returned.

Freshmen *Admission:* 2,486 applied, 2,402 admitted, 1,643 enrolled. *Average high school GPA:* 2.93. *Test scores:* SAT verbal scores over 500: 40%; SAT math scores over 500: 42%; ACT scores over 18: 74%; SAT verbal scores over 600: 9%; SAT math scores over 600: 10%; ACT scores over 24: 21%; SAT verbal scores over 700: 1%; SAT math scores over 700: 1%; ACT scores over 30: 1%.

Faculty *Total:* 690, 49% full-time, 51% with terminal degrees. *Student/faculty ratio:* 17:1.

Majors Accounting; anthropology; architectural engineering technology; art teacher education; audiology and hearing sciences; biology/biological sciences; biology teacher education; business administration and management; business/managerial economics; chemical technology; chemistry; chemistry teacher education; civil engineering technology; clinical laboratory science/medical technology; commercial and advertising art; communication and media related; community health services counseling; computational mathematics; computer engineering; computer engineering technology; computer science; computer software and media applications related; construction engineering technology; crafts, folk art and artisanry; creative writing; criminal justice/safety; dental hygiene; dental laboratory technology; drama and dance teacher education; dramatic/theatre arts; drawing; early childhood education; economics; education; electrical, electronic and communications engineering technology; electrical, electronics and communications engineering; elementary education; English; English/language arts teacher education; English literature (British and Commonwealth); finance; fine/studio arts; French; French language teacher education; general studies; geology/earth science; German; German language teacher education; graphic design; health services administration; history; hospitality administration; human services; industrial technology; interior design; labor studies; legal studies; marketing/marketing management; mathematics; mathematics teacher education; mechanical engineering; mechanical engineering/mechanical technology; music; music teacher education; music therapy; nursing (registered nurse training); operations management; organizational communication; painting; philosophy; photography; physics; physics teacher education; piano and organ; political science and government; pre-dentistry studies; pre-medical studies; printmaking; psychology; public administration; public administration and social service professions related; public policy analysis; radiologic technology/science; science teacher education; sculpture; secondary education; social studies teacher education; sociology; Spanish; Spanish language teacher education; speech teacher education; statistics; substance abuse/addiction counseling; therapeutic recreation; voice and opera; women's studies; youth services.

Academic Programs *Special study options:* academic remediation for entering students, accelerated degree program, adult/continuing education programs, advanced placement credit, cooperative education, distance learning, double majors, English as a second language, honors programs, independent study, internships, off-campus study, part-time degree program, services for LD students, student-designed majors, study abroad, summer session for credit.

Library Helmke Library with 479,992 titles, 10,964 serial subscriptions, 1,000 audiovisual materials, an OPAC, a Web page.

Computers on Campus 285 computers available on campus for general student use. A campuswide network can be accessed from off campus that provide

Indiana University–Purdue University Fort Wayne (continued)
access to students academic records. Internet access, online (class) registration, at least one staffed computer lab available.

Student Life *Housing:* college housing not available. *Activities and organizations:* drama/theater group, student-run newspaper, television station, choral group, Campus Ministry, Hispanos Unidos, Sigma Phi Epsilon, Psi Chi, United Sexualities, national fraternities, national sororities. *Campus security:* 24-hour emergency response devices and patrols, late-night transport/escort service. *Student services:* health clinic, personal/psychological counseling, women's center.

Athletics Member NCAA. All Division I. *Intercollegiate sports:* baseball M(s), basketball M(s)/W(s), cross-country running M(s)/W(s), soccer M(s)/W(s), softball W(s), tennis M(s)/W(s), track and field W(s), volleyball M(s)/W(s). *Intramural sports:* badminton M/W, basketball M/W, football M, golf M/W, racquetball M/W, softball M/W, table tennis M/W, tennis M/W, volleyball M/W.

Standardized Tests *Required:* SAT I or ACT (for admission).

Costs (2003–04) *Tuition:* state resident $4535 full-time, $170 per semester hour part-time; nonresident $10,983 full-time, $385 per semester hour part-time. Full-time tuition and fees vary according to course load and student level. Part-time tuition and fees vary according to course load and student level. *Required fees:* $573 full-time, $19 per semester hour part-time. *Payment plans:* installment, deferred payment. *Waivers:* employees or children of employees.

Financial Aid Of all full-time matriculated undergraduates who enrolled in 2002, 4,335 applied for aid, 3,164 were judged to have need, 427 had their need fully met. 181 Federal Work-Study jobs (averaging $1291). In 2002, 939 non-need-based awards were made. *Average percent of need met:* 85%. *Average financial aid package:* $5101. *Average need-based loan:* $2771. *Average need-based gift aid:* $3523. *Average non-need-based aid:* $1030. *Average indebtedness upon graduation:* $15,481.

Applying *Options:* electronic application, early admission, deferred entrance. *Application fee:* $30. *Required:* high school transcript. *Recommended:* rank in upper 50% of high school class. *Application deadline:* 8/1 (freshmen). *Notification:* continuous (freshmen), continuous (transfers).

Admissions Contact Ms. Carol Isaacs, Director of Admissions, Indiana University–Purdue University Fort Wayne, 2101 East Coliseum Boulevard, Fort Wayne, IN 46805-1499. *Phone:* 260-481-6812. *Toll-free phone:* 800-324-4739. *Fax:* 260-481-6880. *E-mail:* ipfwadms@ipfw.edu.

INDIANA UNIVERSITY–PURDUE UNIVERSITY INDIANAPOLIS

Indianapolis, Indiana

- **State-supported** university, founded 1969, part of Indiana University System
- **Calendar** semesters
- **Degrees** certificates, associate, bachelor's, master's, doctoral, first professional, and postbachelor's certificates
- **Urban** 511-acre campus
- **Endowment** $305.1 million
- **Coed,** 21,388 undergraduate students, 63% full-time, 59% women, 41% men
- **Moderately difficult** entrance level, 77% of applicants were admitted

Undergraduates 13,371 full-time, 8,017 part-time. Students come from 40 states and territories, 2% are from out of state, 10% African American, 2% Asian American or Pacific Islander, 2% Hispanic American, 0.4% Native American, 2% international, 7% transferred in. *Retention:* 67% of 2002 full-time freshmen returned.

Freshmen *Admission:* 5,698 applied, 4,373 admitted, 2,826 enrolled. *Test scores:* SAT verbal scores over 500: 48%; SAT math scores over 500: 47%; ACT scores over 18: 79%; SAT verbal scores over 600: 10%; SAT math scores over 600: 13%; ACT scores over 24: 20%; SAT verbal scores over 700: 1%; SAT math scores over 700: 1%; ACT scores over 30: 1%.

Faculty *Total:* 2,919, 68% full-time, 65% with terminal degrees. *Student/faculty ratio:* 17:1.

Majors Anthropology; architectural drafting and CAD/CADD; architectural engineering technology; art history, criticism and conservation; art teacher education; biology/biological sciences; biomedical/medical engineering; biomedical technology; business/commerce; chemistry; civil engineering technology; clinical laboratory science/medical technology; communication/speech communication and rhetoric; computer and information sciences; computer engineering; criminal justice/safety; cytotechnology; dental hygiene; economics; education; electrical, electronic and communications engineering technology; electrical, electronics and communications engineering; elementary education; emergency medical technology (EMT paramedic); engineering; English; English/language arts teacher education; fine/studio arts; French; French language teacher education; general studies; geography; geology/earth science; German; German language teacher education; health/health care administration; health information/medical records administration; health teacher education; history; hospitality administration related; hotel/motel administration; interior design; journalism; kindergarten/preschool education; labor and industrial relations; mathematics; mechanical drafting and CAD/CADD; mechanical engineering; mechanical engineering/mechanical technology; medical radiologic technology; nuclear medical technology; nursing (registered nurse training); occupational therapy; operations management; philosophy; physical education teaching and coaching; physical therapy; physics; political science and government; pre-dentistry studies; pre-law studies; pre-medical studies; pre-veterinary studies; psychology; public administration; public health; religious studies; respiratory care therapy; robotics technology; secondary education; sign language interpretation and translation; social studies teacher education; social work; sociology; Spanish; Spanish language teacher education; speech teacher education.

Academic Programs *Special study options:* academic remediation for entering students, adult/continuing education programs, advanced placement credit, cooperative education, distance learning, double majors, English as a second language, external degree program, honors programs, independent study, internships, off-campus study, part-time degree program, services for LD students, study abroad, summer session for credit. *ROTC:* Army (b), Navy (c), Air Force (c).

Library University Library plus 5 others with 1.5 million titles, 14,673 serial subscriptions, 1,663 audiovisual materials, an OPAC, a Web page.

Computers on Campus 500 computers available on campus for general student use. A campuswide network can be accessed from off campus. Internet access, at least one staffed computer lab available.

Student Life *Housing options:* coed. Campus housing is university owned. *Activities and organizations:* drama/theater group, student-run newspaper, choral group, Undergraduate Student Assembly, Black Student Union, Student Activities Programming Board, national fraternities, national sororities. *Campus security:* 24-hour emergency response devices and patrols, late-night transport/escort service, controlled dormitory access, lighted pathways, self-defense education. *Student services:* health clinic, personal/psychological counseling, women's center.

Athletics Member NCAA. All Division I. *Intercollegiate sports:* basketball M(s)/W(s), cross-country running M(s)/W(s), golf M(s)/W, soccer M(s)/W(s), softball W(s), swimming M(s)/W(s), tennis M(s)/W(s), volleyball W(s). *Intramural sports:* badminton M/W, baseball M, basketball M/W, cross-country running M/W, football M, golf M/W, racquetball M/W, soccer M/W, softball M/W, swimming M/W, table tennis M/W, tennis M/W, track and field M/W, volleyball M/W, water polo M/W.

Standardized Tests *Required:* SAT I or ACT (for admission).

Costs (2003–04) *Tuition:* state resident $5151 full-time, $172 per credit hour part-time; nonresident $14,334 full-time, $478 per credit hour part-time. Full-time tuition and fees vary according to course load. Part-time tuition and fees vary according to course load. *Required fees:* $552 full-time. *Room only:* $2554. Room and board charges vary according to board plan and housing facility. *Payment plans:* installment, deferred payment. *Waivers:* employees or children of employees.

Financial Aid Of all full-time matriculated undergraduates who enrolled in 2003, 8,909 applied for aid, 7,509 were judged to have need, 319 had their need fully met. 167 Federal Work-Study jobs (averaging $3440). In 2003, 965 non-need-based awards were made. *Average percent of need met:* 50%. *Average financial aid package:* $6534. *Average need-based loan:* $3643. *Average need-based gift aid:* $4732. *Average non-need-based aid:* $2490. *Average indebtedness upon graduation:* $19,660.

Applying *Options:* electronic application, early admission, deferred entrance. *Application fee:* $45. *Required:* high school transcript. *Required for some:* interview. *Recommended:* portfolio for art program. *Application deadline:* rolling (freshmen), rolling (transfers). *Notification:* continuous (freshmen), continuous (transfers).

Admissions Contact Michael Donahue, Director of Admissions, Indiana University–Purdue University Indianapolis, 425 North University Boulevard, Cavanaugh Hall Room 129, Indianapolis, IN 46202-5143. *Phone:* 317-274-4591. *Fax:* 317-278-1862. *E-mail:* apply@iupui.edu.

INDIANA UNIVERSITY SOUTH BEND

South Bend, Indiana

- **State-supported** comprehensive, founded 1922, part of Indiana University System
- **Calendar** semesters
- **Degrees** certificates, diplomas, associate, bachelor's, master's, and postbachelor's certificates
- **Suburban** 73-acre campus with easy access to Chicago
- **Endowment** $4.7 million
- **Coed,** 6,093 undergraduate students, 56% full-time, 63% women, 37% men
- **Moderately difficult** entrance level, 83% of applicants were admitted

Undergraduates 3,434 full-time, 2,659 part-time. Students come from 13 states and territories, 2% are from out of state, 6% African American, 1% Asian American or Pacific Islander, 3% Hispanic American, 0.5% Native American, 3% international, 7% transferred in. *Retention:* 70% of 2002 full-time freshmen returned.

Freshmen *Admission:* 1,553 applied, 1,292 admitted, 895 enrolled. *Test scores:* SAT verbal scores over 500: 43%; SAT math scores over 500: 41%; ACT scores over 18: 74%; SAT verbal scores over 600: 10%; SAT math scores over 600: 7%; ACT scores over 24: 24%; SAT verbal scores over 700: 1%; SAT math scores over 700: 1%; ACT scores over 30: 2%.

Faculty *Total:* 541, 49% full-time, 36% with terminal degrees. *Student/faculty ratio:* 14:1.

Majors Applied mathematics; art; biology/biological sciences; biology teacher education; business/commerce; chemistry; chemistry teacher education; computer science; criminal justice/law enforcement administration; dental hygiene; dramatic/theatre arts; economics; education; elementary education; English; English/language arts teacher education; film/cinema studies; finance; fine/studio arts; French; French language teacher education; general studies; German; German language teacher education; health/health care administration; history; jazz/jazz studies; kindergarten/preschool education; labor and industrial relations; legal assistant/paralegal; marketing/marketing management; mass communication/media; mathematics; mathematics teacher education; medical radiologic technology; music performance; music teacher education; nursing (registered nurse training); philosophy; physics; physics teacher education; political science and government; psychology; public administration; science teacher education; secondary education; social studies teacher education; sociology; Spanish; Spanish language teacher education; special education; speech and rhetoric; women's studies.

Academic Programs *Special study options:* accelerated degree program, adult/continuing education programs, distance learning, double majors, English as a second language, external degree program, honors programs, internships, off-campus study, part-time degree program, study abroad, summer session for credit. *ROTC:* Army (c), Navy (c), Air Force (c).

Library Franklin D. Schurz Library plus 1 other with 300,202 titles, 1,937 serial subscriptions, 13,001 audiovisual materials.

Computers on Campus 200 computers available on campus for general student use. Internet access, at least one staffed computer lab available.

Student Life *Housing:* college housing not available. *Activities and organizations:* drama/theater group, student-run newspaper, choral group, national fraternities. *Campus security:* 24-hour emergency response devices and patrols, late-night transport/escort service, safety seminars, lighted pathways. *Student services:* personal/psychological counseling, women's center.

Athletics Member NAIA. *Intercollegiate sports:* basketball M(s)/W(s). *Intramural sports:* badminton M/W, baseball M, basketball M/W, cheerleading W, cross-country running M/W, golf M/W, racquetball M/W, soccer M/W, volleyball M/W.

Standardized Tests *Required:* SAT I or ACT (for admission).

Costs (2003–04) *Tuition:* state resident $4181 full-time, $123 per credit hour part-time; nonresident $10,773 full-time, $342 per credit hour part-time. Full-time tuition and fees vary according to course load. Part-time tuition and fees vary according to course load. *Required fees:* $390 full-time. *Payment plans:* installment, deferred payment. *Waivers:* employees or children of employees.

Financial Aid Of all full-time matriculated undergraduates who enrolled in 2003, 2,423 applied for aid, 1,767 were judged to have need, 121 had their need fully met. 73 Federal Work-Study jobs (averaging $2290). In 2003, 55 non-need-based awards were made. *Average percent of need met:* 58%. *Average financial aid package:* $5320. *Average need-based loan:* $3407. *Average need-based gift aid:* $3372. *Average non-need-based aid:* $2309. *Average indebtedness upon graduation:* $16,334.

Applying *Options:* deferred entrance. *Application fee:* $40. *Required:* high school transcript, minimum 2.0 GPA. *Application deadlines:* 7/1 (freshmen), 6/1 (transfers). *Notification:* continuous (freshmen), continuous (transfers).

Admissions Contact Jeff Johnston, Director of Recruitment/Admissions, Indiana University South Bend, 1700 Mishawaka Avenue, Administration Building, Room 169, PO Box 7111, South Bend, IN 46634-7111. *Phone:* 574-237-4480. *Toll-free phone:* 877-GO-2-IUSB. *Fax:* 574-237-4834. *E-mail:* admissio@iusb.edu.

INDIANA UNIVERSITY SOUTHEAST

New Albany, Indiana

- **State-supported** comprehensive, founded 1941, part of Indiana University System
- **Calendar** semesters
- **Degrees** certificates, associate, bachelor's, master's, and postbachelor's certificates
- **Suburban** 177-acre campus with easy access to Louisville
- **Endowment** $5.9 million
- **Coed,** 5,581 undergraduate students, 56% full-time, 62% women, 38% men
- **Minimally difficult** entrance level, 85% of applicants were admitted

Undergraduates 3,145 full-time, 2,436 part-time. Students come from 3 states and territories, 19% are from out of state, 3% African American, 0.8% Asian American or Pacific Islander, 0.7% Hispanic American, 0.2% Native American, 0.6% international, 6% transferred in. *Retention:* 67% of 2002 full-time freshmen returned.

Freshmen *Admission:* 1,268 applied, 1,083 admitted, 824 enrolled. *Test scores:* SAT verbal scores over 500: 38%; SAT math scores over 500: 37%; ACT scores over 18: 72%; SAT verbal scores over 600: 7%; SAT math scores over 600: 6%; ACT scores over 24: 12%; SAT verbal scores over 700: 1%; ACT scores over 30: 1%.

Faculty *Total:* 446, 44% full-time, 39% with terminal degrees. *Student/faculty ratio:* 15:1.

Majors Art; biology/biological sciences; biology teacher education; business/commerce; business/managerial economics; chemistry; clinical laboratory science/medical technology; communication/speech communication and rhetoric; computer science; cytotechnology; economics; education; elementary education; English; English/language arts teacher education; fine/studio arts; French; general studies; geography; German; history; journalism; labor and industrial relations; mathematics; mathematics teacher education; music; nursing (registered nurse training); parks, recreation and leisure facilities management; philosophy; political science and government; psychology; science teacher education; secondary education; social studies teacher education; sociology; Spanish; special education.

Academic Programs *Special study options:* academic remediation for entering students, accelerated degree program, adult/continuing education programs, advanced placement credit, double majors, external degree program, independent study, internships, off-campus study, part-time degree program, services for LD students, study abroad, summer session for credit. *ROTC:* Army (c), Air Force (c).

Library Main Library plus 1 other with 215,429 titles, 962 serial subscriptions, 9,360 audiovisual materials.

Computers on Campus 200 computers available on campus for general student use. A campuswide network can be accessed from off campus. Internet access available.

Student Life *Housing:* college housing not available. *Activities and organizations:* drama/theater group, student-run newspaper, choral group, national fraternities, national sororities. *Campus security:* 24-hour emergency response devices and patrols, self-defense education, lighted pathways, police department on campus. *Student services:* personal/psychological counseling.

Athletics Member NAIA. *Intercollegiate sports:* baseball M, basketball M(s)/W(s), tennis M/W, volleyball W(s). *Intramural sports:* basketball M/W, bowling M/W, cross-country running M/W, softball M/W, tennis M/W, volleyball W.

Standardized Tests *Required:* SAT I or ACT (for admission).

Costs (2003–04) *Tuition:* state resident $4118 full-time, $137 per credit hour part-time; nonresident $10,068 full-time, $356 per credit hour part-time. Full-time tuition and fees vary according to course load. Part-time tuition and fees vary according to course load. *Required fees:* $386 full-time. *Waivers:* employees or children of employees.

Financial Aid Of all full-time matriculated undergraduates who enrolled in 2003, 2,120 applied for aid, 1,407 were judged to have need, 129 had their need fully met. 171 Federal Work-Study jobs (averaging $1918). In 2003, 156 non-need-based awards were made. *Average percent of need met:* 62%. *Average financial aid package:* $5556. *Average need-based loan:* $3209. *Average need-based gift aid:* $4192. *Average non-need-based aid:* $1702. *Average indebtedness upon graduation:* $12,973.

Applying *Options:* early admission, deferred entrance. *Application fee:* $30. *Required:* high school transcript. *Required for some:* interview. *Application deadlines:* 7/15 (freshmen), 7/1 (transfers). *Notification:* continuous (freshmen), continuous (transfers).

Admissions Contact Mr. David B. Campbell, Director of Admissions, Indiana University Southeast, University Center Building, Room 100, 4201 Grant Line Road, New Albany, IN 47150. *Phone:* 812-941-2212. *Toll-free phone:* 800-852-8835. *Fax:* 812-941-2595. *E-mail:* admissions@ius.edu.

INDIANA WESLEYAN UNIVERSITY

Marion, Indiana

- **Independent Wesleyan** comprehensive, founded 1920
- **Calendar** 4-4-1
- **Degrees** associate, bachelor's, and master's (also offers adult program with significant enrollment not reflected in profile)
- **Small-town** 132-acre campus with easy access to Indianapolis
- **Endowment** $15.6 million

Indiana Wesleyan University (continued)
- **Coed**
- **Moderately difficult** entrance level

Faculty *Student/faculty ratio:* 17:1.
Student Life *Campus security:* 24-hour emergency response devices and patrols, late-night transport/escort service, controlled dormitory access.
Athletics Member NAIA, NCCAA.
Standardized Tests *Required:* SAT I or ACT (for admission).
Costs (2003–04) *Comprehensive fee:* $19,900 includes full-time tuition ($14,420) and room and board ($5480). Part-time tuition: $482 per credit hour. Part-time tuition and fees vary according to course load. *College room only:* $2550. Room and board charges vary according to board plan.
Applying *Options:* electronic application, deferred entrance. *Application fee:* $25. *Required:* essay or personal statement, high school transcript, minimum 2.0 GPA, 1 letter of recommendation. *Required for some:* interview.
Admissions Contact Ms. Gaytha Holloway, Director of Admissions, Indiana Wesleyan University, 4201 South Washington Street, Marion, IN 46953. *Phone:* 765-677-2138. *Toll-free phone:* 800-332-6901. *Fax:* 765-677-2333. *E-mail:* admissions@indwes.edu.

INTERNATIONAL BUSINESS COLLEGE
Fort Wayne, Indiana

- **Proprietary** primarily 2-year, founded 1889, part of Bradford Schools, Inc.
- **Calendar** semesters
- **Degrees** diplomas, associate, and bachelor's
- **Suburban** 2-acre campus
- **Coed, primarily women**
- **Minimally difficult** entrance level

Faculty *Student/faculty ratio:* 24:1.
Student Life *Campus security:* controlled dormitory access.
Costs (2003–04) *Tuition:* $10,100 full-time. *Room only:* $4600.
Applying *Options:* deferred entrance. *Application fee:* $50. *Required:* high school transcript.
Admissions Contact Mr. Steve Kinzer, School Director, International Business College, 5699 Coventry Lane, Fort Wayne, IN 46804. *Phone:* 219-459-4513. *Toll-free phone:* 800-589-6363. *Fax:* 219-436-1896.

ITT TECHNICAL INSTITUTE
Fort Wayne, Indiana

- **Proprietary** primarily 2-year, founded 1967, part of ITT Educational Services, Inc.
- **Calendar** quarters
- **Degrees** associate and bachelor's
- **Coed**
- **Minimally difficult** entrance level

Standardized Tests *Required:* Wonderlic aptitude test (for admission).
Costs (2003–04) *Tuition:* $347 per credit hour part-time.
Applying *Options:* deferred entrance. *Application fee:* $100. *Required:* high school transcript, interview. *Recommended:* letters of recommendation.
Admissions Contact Mr. Michael D. Frantom, ITT Technical Institute, 4919 Coldwater Road, Fort Wayne, IN 46825. *Phone:* 260-484-4107. *Toll-free phone:* 800-866-4488. *Fax:* 260-484-0860.

ITT TECHNICAL INSTITUTE
Indianapolis, Indiana

- **Proprietary** founded 1966, part of ITT Educational Services, Inc.
- **Calendar** quarters
- **Degrees** diplomas, associate, and bachelor's
- **Suburban** 10-acre campus
- **Coed**
- **Minimally difficult** entrance level

Standardized Tests *Required:* Wonderlic aptitude test (for admission).
Costs (2003–04) *Tuition:* $330—$347 per credit hour.
Applying *Options:* deferred entrance. *Application fee:* $100. *Required:* high school transcript, interview. *Recommended:* letters of recommendation.
Admissions Contact Ms. Martha Watson, ITT Technical Institute, 9511 Angola Court, Indianapolis, IN 46268. *Phone:* 317-875-8640. *Toll-free phone:* 800-937-4488. *Fax:* 317-875-8641.

ITT TECHNICAL INSTITUTE
Newburgh, Indiana

- **Proprietary** primarily 2-year, founded 1966, part of ITT Educational Services, Inc.
- **Calendar** quarters
- **Degrees** associate and bachelor's
- **Coed**
- **Minimally difficult** entrance level

Standardized Tests *Required:* Wonderlic aptitude test (for admission).
Costs (2003–04) *Tuition:* $347 per credit hour part-time.
Applying *Options:* deferred entrance. *Application fee:* $100. *Required:* high school transcript, interview. *Recommended:* letters of recommendation.
Admissions Contact Mr. Jim Smolinski, Director of Recruitment, ITT Technical Institute, 10999 Stahl Road, Newburgh, IN 47630. *Phone:* 812-858-1600. *Toll-free phone:* 800-832-4488. *Fax:* 812-858-0646.

MANCHESTER COLLEGE
North Manchester, Indiana

- **Independent** comprehensive, founded 1889, affiliated with Church of the Brethren
- **Calendar** 4-1-4
- **Degrees** associate, bachelor's, and master's
- **Small-town** 125-acre campus
- **Endowment** $25.2 million
- **Coed,** 1,153 undergraduate students, 96% full-time, 55% women, 45% men
- **Moderately difficult** entrance level, 79% of applicants were admitted

Undergraduates 1,107 full-time, 46 part-time. Students come from 23 states and territories, 29 other countries, 10% are from out of state, 3% African American, 0.6% Asian American or Pacific Islander, 2% Hispanic American, 0.7% Native American, 7% international, 2% transferred in, 77% live on campus. *Retention:* 74% of 2002 full-time freshmen returned.
Freshmen *Admission:* 1,085 applied, 854 admitted, 335 enrolled. *Test scores:* SAT verbal scores over 500: 56%; SAT math scores over 500: 51%; ACT scores over 18: 84%; SAT verbal scores over 600: 18%; SAT math scores over 600: 14%; ACT scores over 24: 39%; SAT verbal scores over 700: 2%; SAT math scores over 700: 1%; ACT scores over 30: 4%.
Faculty *Total:* 92, 74% full-time, 72% with terminal degrees. *Student/faculty ratio:* 14:1.
Majors Accounting; art; art teacher education; athletic training; biology/biological sciences; broadcast journalism; business administration and management; business/commerce; chemistry; clinical laboratory science/medical technology; computer science; creative writing; criminal justice/safety; dramatic/theatre arts; ecology; economics; education; elementary education; engineering science; English; environmental studies; finance; fine/studio arts; French; German; gerontology; health science; health teacher education; history; interdisciplinary studies; journalism; kindergarten/preschool education; kinesiology and exercise science; literature; marketing/marketing management; mass communication/media; mathematics; music; music teacher education; non-profit management; peace studies and conflict resolution; philosophy; physical education teaching and coaching; physics; political science and government; pre-dentistry studies; pre-law studies; pre-medical studies; pre-theology/pre-ministerial studies; pre-veterinary studies; psychology; religious studies; science teacher education; secondary education; social work; sociology; Spanish; special education; speech and rhetoric.
Academic Programs *Special study options:* adult/continuing education programs, advanced placement credit, double majors, honors programs, independent study, internships, off-campus study, part-time degree program, services for LD students, student-designed majors, study abroad, summer session for credit. *Unusual degree programs:* 3-2 engineering with Washington University in St. Louis; nursing with Goshen College; physical therapy, occupational therapy.
Library Funderburg Library with 172,822 titles, 733 serial subscriptions, 5,188 audiovisual materials, an OPAC, a Web page.
Computers on Campus 168 computers available on campus for general student use. A campuswide network can be accessed from student residence rooms and from off campus. Internet access, at least one staffed computer lab available. Computer purchase or lease plan available.
Student Life *Housing:* on-campus residence required through junior year. *Options:* coed, women-only, disabled students. Campus housing is university owned. Freshman campus housing is guaranteed. *Activities and organizations:* drama/theater group, student-run newspaper, radio station, choral group, volunteer services, Campus Ministry Board, accounting club, Manchester Admissions Recruiting Corps, Student Alumni Council. *Campus security:* 24-hour emergency

response devices and patrols, student patrols, late-night transport/escort service, alarm system, locked residence hall entrances. *Student services:* health clinic, personal/psychological counseling.

Athletics Member NCAA. All Division III. *Intercollegiate sports:* baseball M, basketball M/W, cheerleading M/W, cross-country running M/W, football M, golf M/W, soccer M/W, softball W, tennis M/W, track and field M/W, volleyball W, wrestling M. *Intramural sports:* badminton M/W, basketball M/W, bowling M/W, football M/W, racquetball M/W, soccer M/W, table tennis M/W, tennis M/W, track and field M/W, ultimate Frisbee M/W, volleyball M/W.

Standardized Tests *Required:* SAT I or ACT (for admission).

Costs (2004–05) *Comprehensive fee:* $24,710 includes full-time tuition ($17,950), mandatory fees ($110), and room and board ($6650). Part-time tuition: $600 per credit hour. *College room only:* $4150. Room and board charges vary according to board plan and housing facility. *Payment plan:* installment. *Waivers:* employees or children of employees.

Financial Aid Of all full-time matriculated undergraduates who enrolled in 2003, 950 applied for aid, 845 were judged to have need, 338 had their need fully met. In 2003, 120 non-need-based awards were made. *Average percent of need met:* 92%. *Average financial aid package:* $16,033. *Average need-based loan:* $3422. *Average need-based gift aid:* $12,666. *Average non-need-based aid:* $5424. *Average indebtedness upon graduation:* $12,084.

Applying *Options:* common application, electronic application, deferred entrance. *Application fee:* $20. *Required:* high school transcript, 1 letter of recommendation, rank in upper 50% of high school class. *Required for some:* essay or personal statement, minimum 3.0 GPA, interview. *Recommended:* minimum 2.3 GPA, interview. *Application deadline:* rolling (freshmen), rolling (transfers). *Notification:* continuous (freshmen), continuous (transfers).

Admissions Contact Ms. Jolane Rohr, Director of Admissions, Manchester College, 604 East College Avenue, North Manchester, IN 46962. *Phone:* 260-982-5055. *Toll-free phone:* 800-852-3648. *Fax:* 260-982-5239. *E-mail:* admitinfo@manchester.edu.

■ *See page 1914 for a narrative description.*

MARIAN COLLEGE
Indianapolis, Indiana

- **Independent Roman Catholic** comprehensive, founded 1851
- **Calendar** semesters
- **Degrees** associate, bachelor's, and master's
- **Urban** 114-acre campus
- **Endowment** $6.2 million
- **Coed,** 1,547 undergraduate students, 67% full-time, 74% women, 26% men
- **Moderately difficult** entrance level, 75% of applicants were admitted

Undergraduates 1,039 full-time, 508 part-time. Students come from 23 states and territories, 16 other countries, 10% are from out of state, 17% African American, 0.8% Asian American or Pacific Islander, 2% Hispanic American, 0.4% Native American, 2% international, 7% transferred in, 40% live on campus. *Retention:* 69% of 2002 full-time freshmen returned.

Freshmen *Admission:* 859 applied, 640 admitted, 471 enrolled. *Average high school GPA:* 3.10. *Test scores:* SAT verbal scores over 500: 49%; SAT math scores over 500: 46%; ACT scores over 18: 90%; SAT verbal scores over 600: 12%; SAT math scores over 600: 7%; ACT scores over 24: 26%.

Faculty *Total:* 132, 49% full-time. *Student/faculty ratio:* 12:1.

Majors Accounting; art; art history, criticism and conservation; art teacher education; biology/biological sciences; business administration and management; chemistry; education; elementary education; English; finance; fine/studio arts; French; history; interior design; kindergarten/preschool education; liberal arts and sciences/liberal studies; mass communication/media; mathematics; music; music teacher education; nursing (registered nurse training); philosophy; physical education teaching and coaching; pre-dentistry studies; pre-engineering; pre-law studies; pre-medical studies; pre-veterinary studies; psychology; religious education; secondary education; sociology; Spanish; special education; theology.

Academic Programs *Special study options:* academic remediation for entering students, accelerated degree program, adult/continuing education programs, advanced placement credit, cooperative education, double majors, honors programs, independent study, internships, off-campus study, part-time degree program, services for LD students, study abroad, summer session for credit. *ROTC:* Army (c). *Unusual degree programs:* 3-2 engineering with University of Detroit Mercy.

Library Mother Theresa Hackelmeier Memorial Library with 132,000 titles, 300 serial subscriptions, 100 audiovisual materials, an OPAC, a Web page.

Computers on Campus 130 computers available on campus for general student use. A campuswide network can be accessed from student residence rooms. Internet access, at least one staffed computer lab available.

Student Life *Housing:* on-campus residence required through senior year. *Options:* coed, men-only, women-only, disabled students. Campus housing is university owned. Freshman campus housing is guaranteed. *Activities and organizations:* drama/theater group, student-run newspaper, choral group, Fellowship of Christian Athletics, Marian College Student Association, Residence Hall Council, business club, Booster Club. *Campus security:* 24-hour patrols, late-night transport/escort service. *Student services:* health clinic, personal/psychological counseling.

Athletics Member NAIA. *Intercollegiate sports:* baseball M(s), basketball M(s)/W(s), cheerleading M(s)/W(s), cross-country running M(s)/W(s), golf M(s)/W(s), soccer M(s)/W(s), softball W(s), tennis M(s)/W(s), track and field M(s)/W(s), volleyball W(s). *Intramural sports:* basketball M/W, football M/W, racquetball M/W, table tennis M/W, tennis M/W, volleyball M/W.

Standardized Tests *Required:* SAT I or ACT (for admission).

Costs (2003–04) *Comprehensive fee:* $23,260 includes full-time tuition ($16,800), mandatory fees ($660), and room and board ($5800). Part-time tuition: $735 per credit. Part-time tuition and fees vary according to class time and course load. *Room and board:* Room and board charges vary according to board plan and housing facility. *Payment plans:* installment, deferred payment. *Waivers:* children of alumni, senior citizens, and employees or children of employees.

Financial Aid Of all full-time matriculated undergraduates who enrolled in 2003, 904 applied for aid, 836 were judged to have need, 277 had their need fully met. 200 Federal Work-Study jobs (averaging $1500). In 2003, 57 non-need-based awards were made. *Average percent of need met:* 78%. *Average financial aid package:* $13,717. *Average need-based loan:* $3019. *Average need-based gift aid:* $7633. *Average non-need-based aid:* $9301. *Average indebtedness upon graduation:* $14,815.

Applying *Options:* common application, electronic application, early admission, deferred entrance. *Application fee:* $20. *Required:* high school transcript, minimum 2.00 GPA. *Required for some:* essay or personal statement, letters of recommendation, interview. *Application deadlines:* 8/15 (freshmen), 8/1 (transfers). *Notification:* continuous until 8/24 (freshmen), continuous until 8/24 (transfers).

Admissions Contact Mrs. Karen Full, Director of Admission, Marian College, 3200 Cold Spring Road, Indianapolis, IN 46222-1997. *Phone:* 317-955-6300. *Toll-free phone:* 800-772-7264.

■ *See page 1924 for a narrative description.*

MARTIN UNIVERSITY
Indianapolis, Indiana

- **Independent** comprehensive, founded 1977
- **Calendar** semesters
- **Degrees** bachelor's and master's
- **Urban** 5-acre campus
- **Coed,** 465 undergraduate students, 47% full-time, 76% women, 24% men
- **Noncompetitive** entrance level

Undergraduates 219 full-time, 246 part-time. Students come from 1 other state, 6 other countries, 0.1% are from out of state, 92% African American, 0.2% Hispanic American, 0.2% Native American, 1% international. *Retention:* 90% of 2002 full-time freshmen returned.

Freshmen *Admission:* 156 admitted, 49 enrolled.

Faculty *Total:* 38, 84% full-time. *Student/faculty ratio:* 20:1.

Majors Accounting; adult and continuing education; African-American/Black studies; biology/biological sciences; business administration and management; chemistry; communication/speech communication and rhetoric; computer engineering technology; counselor education/school counseling and guidance; criminal justice/law enforcement administration; education; elementary education; English; fine/studio arts; history; humanities; human resources management; insurance; kindergarten/preschool education; marketing/marketing management; mathematics; music; political science and government; psychology; religious studies; secondary education; sociology; substance abuse/addiction counseling.

Academic Programs *Special study options:* academic remediation for entering students, accelerated degree program, adult/continuing education programs, advanced placement credit, double majors, honors programs, independent study, internships, off-campus study, part-time degree program, student-designed majors, summer session for credit.

Computers on Campus 20 computers available on campus for general student use. At least one staffed computer lab available.

Student Life *Housing:* college housing not available. *Activities and organizations:* drama/theater group, choral group. *Campus security:* building security, security personnel from 7 a.m. to 9:30 p.m. *Student services:* health clinic, personal/psychological counseling.

Standardized Tests *Required for some:* Wonderlic aptitude test, Wide Range Achievement Test.

Martin University (continued)

Costs (2003–04) *Tuition:* $10,200 full-time, $340 per credit part-time. *Required fees:* $120 full-time.

Financial Aid Of all full-time matriculated undergraduates who enrolled in 2003, 214 applied for aid, 206 were judged to have need, 3 had their need fully met. 9 Federal Work-Study jobs (averaging $2445). *Average percent of need met:* 69%. *Average financial aid package:* $8779. *Average need-based loan:* $3192. *Average need-based gift aid:* $6705. *Average indebtedness upon graduation:* $27,193.

Applying *Options:* early admission, deferred entrance. *Application fee:* $25. *Required:* essay or personal statement, high school transcript, interview, writing sample. *Application deadline:* rolling (freshmen), rolling (transfers). *Notification:* continuous (freshmen), continuous (transfers).

Admissions Contact Ms. Brenda Shaheed, Director of Enrollment Management, Martin University, PO Box 18567, 2171 Avondale Place, Indianapolis, IN 46218-3867. *Phone:* 317-543-3237. *Fax:* 317-543-4790.

MID-AMERICA COLLEGE OF FUNERAL SERVICE
Jeffersonville, Indiana

- **Independent** primarily 2-year, founded 1905
- **Calendar** quarters
- **Degrees** associate and bachelor's
- **Small-town** 3-acre campus with easy access to Louisville
- **Coed, primarily men**
- **Minimally difficult** entrance level

Faculty *Student/faculty ratio:* 13:1.

Applying *Options:* deferred entrance. *Application fee:* $25. *Required:* high school transcript.

Admissions Contact Mr. Richard Nelson, Dean of Students, Mid-America College of Funeral Service, 3111 Hamburg Pike, Jeffersonville, IN 47130-9630. *Phone:* 812-288-8878. *Toll-free phone:* 800-221-6158. *E-mail:* macfs@mindspring.com.

OAKLAND CITY UNIVERSITY
Oakland City, Indiana

- **Independent General Baptist** comprehensive, founded 1885
- **Calendar** semesters
- **Degrees** certificates, diplomas, associate, bachelor's, master's, doctoral, and first professional
- **Rural** 20-acre campus
- **Endowment** $2.5 million
- **Coed,** 1,486 undergraduate students, 82% full-time, 53% women, 47% men
- **Minimally difficult** entrance level, 99% of applicants were admitted

Undergraduates 1,212 full-time, 274 part-time. Students come from 5 states and territories, 23% are from out of state, 12% African American, 0.5% Asian American or Pacific Islander, 1% Hispanic American, 0.8% Native American, 0.1% international, 9% transferred in, 49% live on campus. *Retention:* 91% of 2002 full-time freshmen returned.

Freshmen *Admission:* 339 applied, 334 admitted, 319 enrolled. *Average high school GPA:* 3.10. *Test scores:* SAT verbal scores over 500: 29%; SAT math scores over 500: 36%; ACT scores over 18: 79%; SAT math scores over 600: 10%; ACT scores over 24: 24%.

Faculty *Total:* 168, 26% full-time, 20% with terminal degrees. *Student/faculty ratio:* 17:1.

Majors Accounting; administrative assistant and secretarial science; applied art; applied horticulture; applied mathematics; art; art teacher education; automobile/automotive mechanics technology; biblical studies; biological and physical sciences; biology/biological sciences; biology teacher education; business administration and management; business administration, management and operations related; business teacher education; chemistry; computer engineering technology; computer graphics; computer management; computer programming; computer science; criminal justice/law enforcement administration; culinary arts; divinity/ministry; early childhood education; education; elementary education; English; English/language arts teacher education; general studies; heating, air conditioning, ventilation and refrigeration maintenance technology; humanities; human resources management; industrial design; information science/studies; interdisciplinary studies; liberal arts and sciences/liberal studies; management science; mathematics; mathematics teacher education; middle school education; music; music performance; music teacher education; organizational behavior; physical education teaching and coaching; pre-law studies; pre-medical studies; preveterinary studies; religious education; religious studies; science teacher education; secondary education; social sciences; social science teacher education; social studies teacher education; special education (mentally retarded); theology; welding technology.

Academic Programs *Special study options:* academic remediation for entering students, accelerated degree program, adult/continuing education programs, advanced placement credit, external degree program, part-time degree program, services for LD students, summer session for credit.

Library Founders Memorial Library with 75,000 titles, 350 serial subscriptions, an OPAC.

Computers on Campus 92 computers available on campus for general student use. Internet access, at least one staffed computer lab available.

Student Life *Housing:* on-campus residence required for freshman year. *Options:* Campus housing is university owned. *Activities and organizations:* drama/theater group, student-run newspaper, choral group, Student Government Association, Good News Players, Art Guild. *Campus security:* 24-hour patrols, student patrols. *Student services:* personal/psychological counseling.

Athletics Member NAIA, NCCAA, NSCAA. *Intercollegiate sports:* baseball M(s), basketball M(s)/W(s), cross-country running M(s)/W(s), golf M/W, soccer M/W, softball W(s), volleyball W(s). *Intramural sports:* archery M/W, badminton M/W, basketball M/W, bowling M/W, golf M/W, soccer M/W, softball M/W, table tennis M/W, tennis M/W, volleyball M/W.

Standardized Tests *Required:* SAT I or ACT (for admission).

Costs (2004–05) *Comprehensive fee:* $17,720 includes full-time tuition ($12,600), mandatory fees ($320), and room and board ($4800). Full-time tuition and fees vary according to location and program. Part-time tuition: $420 per hour. Part-time tuition and fees vary according to location and program. *College room only:* $1550. Room and board charges vary according to housing facility. *Payment plans:* installment, deferred payment. *Waivers:* minority students, senior citizens, and employees or children of employees.

Financial Aid Of all full-time matriculated undergraduates who enrolled in 2002, 150 Federal Work-Study jobs (averaging $1600). 4 state and other part-time jobs (averaging $1500). *Average percent of need met:* 90%.

Applying *Options:* common application, early admission, deferred entrance. *Application fee:* $35. *Required:* essay or personal statement, high school transcript, minimum 2.0 GPA, 1 letter of recommendation. *Recommended:* interview. *Application deadline:* rolling (freshmen). *Notification:* continuous (freshmen), continuous (transfers).

Admissions Contact Mr. Buddy Harris, Director of Admissions, Oakland City University, 143 North Lucretia Street, Oakland City, IN 47660-1099. *Phone:* 812-749-1222. *Toll-free phone:* 800-737-5125.

PURDUE UNIVERSITY
West Lafayette, Indiana

- **State-supported** university, founded 1869, part of Purdue University System
- **Calendar** semesters
- **Degrees** certificates, associate, bachelor's, master's, doctoral, and first professional
- **Suburban** 1579-acre campus with easy access to Indianapolis
- **Endowment** $1.1 billion
- **Coed,** 30,851 undergraduate students, 94% full-time, 41% women, 59% men
- **Moderately difficult** entrance level, 79% of applicants were admitted

Undergraduates 29,051 full-time, 1,800 part-time. Students come from 51 states and territories, 96 other countries, 25% are from out of state, 3% African American, 5% Asian American or Pacific Islander, 2% Hispanic American, 0.4% Native American, 6% international, 3% transferred in, 39% live on campus. *Retention:* 89% of 2002 full-time freshmen returned.

Freshmen *Admission:* 22,977 applied, 18,076 admitted, 6,371 enrolled. *Test scores:* SAT verbal scores over 500: 78%; SAT math scores over 500: 83%; ACT scores over 18: 99%; SAT verbal scores over 600: 31%; SAT math scores over 600: 42%; ACT scores over 24: 68%; SAT verbal scores over 700: 5%; SAT math scores over 700: 10%; ACT scores over 30: 15%.

Faculty *Total:* 1,977, 97% full-time, 98% with terminal degrees. *Student/faculty ratio:* 16:1.

Majors Accounting; aeronautical/aerospace engineering technology; aeronautics/aviation/aerospace science and technology; aerospace, aeronautical and astronautical engineering; African-American/Black studies; agricultural/biological engineering and bioengineering; agricultural economics; agricultural mechanization; agricultural teacher education; agriculture; agronomy and crop science; animal sciences; apparel and textiles; architectural engineering technology; art; audiology and speech-language pathology; biochemistry; biological and physical sciences; biology/biological sciences; botany/plant biology; business administration and management; chemical engineering; chemistry; civil engineering; clinical laboratory science/medical technology; communication/speech communication and rhetoric; computer and information sciences; computer and information sciences and support services related; computer engineering; construction engineering; design and visual communications; dramatic/theatre arts; early childhood education; economics; education; electrical, electronic and communications engineering technology; electrical, electronics and communications engineering; elementary education; engineering related; English; entomology; family and consumer sciences/human sciences; food science; foods, nutrition, and wellness; foreign languages and literatures; forestry; geology/earth science; health professions related; history; horticultural science; hospitality administration related; hotel/motel administration; human development and family studies; humanities; industrial engineering; interdisciplinary studies; kindergarten/preschool education; landscape architecture; management information systems and services related; materials engineering; mathematics; mechanical drafting and CAD/CADD; mechanical engineering; mechanical engineering technologies related; multi-/interdisciplinary studies related; natural resources/conservation; nuclear engineering; nursing (registered nurse training); operations management; pharmacy; philosophy; physical education teaching and coaching; physics; political science and government; psychology; robotics technology; social sciences; sociology; statistics; survey technology; technology/industrial arts teacher education; trade and industrial teacher education; veterinary/animal health technology; wildlife and wildlands science and management.

Academic Programs *Special study options:* adult/continuing education programs, advanced placement credit, cooperative education, distance learning, double majors, freshman honors college, honors programs, independent study, internships, part-time degree program, services for LD students, study abroad, summer session for credit. *ROTC:* Army (b), Navy (b), Air Force (b).

Library Hicks Undergraduate Library plus 14 others with 1.2 million titles, 18,374 serial subscriptions, 12,733 audiovisual materials, an OPAC, a Web page.

Computers on Campus 2100 computers available on campus for general student use. A campuswide network can be accessed from student residence rooms and from off campus. Internet access, at least one staffed computer lab available.

Student Life *Housing options:* coed, men-only, women-only, cooperative, disabled students. Campus housing is university owned. Freshman applicants given priority for college housing. *Activities and organizations:* drama/theater group, student-run newspaper, radio and television station, choral group, marching band, student government, Alpha Phi Omega, Society of Women Engineers, ballroom dancing, Golden Key National Honor Society, national fraternities, national sororities. *Campus security:* 24-hour emergency response devices and patrols, student patrols, late-night transport/escort service, controlled dormitory access. *Student services:* health clinic, personal/psychological counseling, women's center.

Athletics Member NCAA. All Division I except football (Division I-A). *Intercollegiate sports:* archery M(c)/W(c), badminton M(c)/W(c), baseball M(s), basketball M(s)/W(s), crew M(c)/W(c), cross-country running M(s)/W(s), equestrian sports M(c)/W(c), fencing M(c)/W(c), golf M(s)/W(s), gymnastics M(c)/W(c), ice hockey M(c), lacrosse M(c)/W(c), racquetball M(c)/W(c), riflery M(c)/W(c), rugby M(c)/W(c), sailing M(c)/W(c), skiing (downhill) M(c)/W(c), soccer M(c)/W(s), softball W(s), squash M(c)/W(c), swimming M(s)/W(s), table tennis M(c)/W(c), tennis M(s)/W(s), track and field M(s)/W(s), volleyball M(c)/W(s), water polo M(c)/W(c), weight lifting M(c)/W(c), wrestling M(s). *Intramural sports:* archery M/W, badminton M/W, basketball M/W, bowling M/W, cross-country running M/W, football M, golf M/W, racquetball M/W, riflery M/W, soccer M/W, softball M/W, squash M, swimming M/W, table tennis M/W, tennis M/W, track and field M/W, volleyball M/W, water polo M/W.

Standardized Tests *Required:* SAT I or ACT (for admission).

Costs (2003–04) *Tuition:* state resident $5860 full-time, $210 per credit part-time; nonresident $17,480 full-time, $600 per credit part-time. Full-time tuition and fees vary according to course load and program. Part-time tuition and fees vary according to course load. *Room and board:* $6700. Room and board charges vary according to board plan and housing facility. *Payment plan:* installment. *Waivers:* senior citizens and employees or children of employees.

Financial Aid Of all full-time matriculated undergraduates who enrolled in 2003, 17,394 applied for aid, 12,276 were judged to have need, 4,500 had their need fully met. 1,147 Federal Work-Study jobs (averaging $1825). In 2003, 3661 non-need-based awards were made. *Average percent of need met:* 90%. *Average financial aid package:* $8796. *Average need-based loan:* $3946. *Average need-based gift aid:* $6879. *Average non-need-based aid:* $10,502. *Average indebtedness upon graduation:* $16,641.

Applying *Options:* electronic application, early admission, deferred entrance. *Application fee:* $30. *Required:* high school transcript. *Application deadline:* 3/1 (freshmen), rolling (transfers). *Notification:* continuous (freshmen).

Admissions Contact Director of Admissions, Purdue University, 1080 Schleman Hall, West Lafayette, IN 47907-1080. *Phone:* 765-494-1776. *Fax:* 765-494-0544. *E-mail:* admissions@purdue.edu.

PURDUE UNIVERSITY CALUMET
Hammond, Indiana

- **State-supported** comprehensive, founded 1951, part of Purdue University System
- **Calendar** semesters
- **Degrees** certificates, associate, bachelor's, master's, and postbachelor's certificates
- **Urban** 167-acre campus with easy access to Chicago
- **Coed**
- **Minimally difficult** entrance level

Faculty *Student/faculty ratio:* 21:1.

Student Life *Campus security:* 24-hour emergency response devices and patrols, student patrols, late-night transport/escort service.

Athletics Member NAIA.

Standardized Tests *Required for some:* SAT I or ACT (for admission).

Costs (2003–04) *Tuition:* state resident $4099 full-time, $146 per credit hour part-time; nonresident $9570 full-time, $342 per credit hour part-time. Full-time tuition and fees vary according to program. Part-time tuition and fees vary according to course load and program. *Required fees:* $316 full-time, $12 per credit hour part-time.

Financial Aid Of all full-time matriculated undergraduates who enrolled in 2003, 2,904 applied for aid, 2,265 were judged to have need, 117 had their need fully met. 113 Federal Work-Study jobs (averaging $2800). 2 state and other part-time jobs (averaging $1500). In 2003, 30. *Average percent of need met:* 74. *Average financial aid package:* $5324. *Average need-based loan:* $2879. *Average need-based gift aid:* $4106. *Average non-need-based aid:* $2261. *Average indebtedness upon graduation:* $13,905.

Applying *Options:* common application, early admission. *Required:* high school transcript.

Admissions Contact Mr. Paul McGuinness, Director of Admissions, Purdue University Calumet, 173rd and Woodmar Avenue, Hammond, IN 46323-2094. *Phone:* 219-989-2213. *Toll-free phone:* 800-447-8738. *E-mail:* adms@calumet.purdue.edu.

PURDUE UNIVERSITY NORTH CENTRAL
Westville, Indiana

- **State-supported** comprehensive, founded 1967, part of Purdue University System
- **Calendar** semesters
- **Degrees** certificates, associate, bachelor's, and master's
- **Rural** 305-acre campus with easy access to Chicago
- **Endowment** $600,852
- **Coed,** 3,443 undergraduate students, 59% full-time, 60% women, 40% men
- **Minimally difficult** entrance level, 83% of applicants were admitted

Undergraduates 2,031 full-time, 1,412 part-time. Students come from 5 states and territories, 1% are from out of state, 4% African American, 1% Asian American or Pacific Islander, 4% Hispanic American, 0.9% Native American, 0.2% international, 4% transferred in. *Retention:* 54% of 2002 full-time freshmen returned.

Freshmen *Admission:* 973 applied, 812 admitted, 617 enrolled. *Average high school GPA:* 2.80. *Test scores:* SAT verbal scores over 500: 38%; SAT math scores over 500: 37%; ACT scores over 18: 75%; SAT verbal scores over 600: 7%; SAT math scores over 600: 7%; ACT scores over 24: 12%; SAT math scores over 700: 1%.

Faculty *Total:* 244, 34% full-time, 27% with terminal degrees. *Student/faculty ratio:* 18:1.

Majors Accounting; architectural engineering technology; biology/biological sciences; business administration and management; civil engineering technology; computer engineering technology; computer programming; construction engineering technology; electrical, electronic and communications engineering technology; elementary education; English; industrial technology; information science/studies; liberal arts and sciences/liberal studies; marketing/marketing management; mechanical engineering/mechanical technology; nursing (registered nurse training); pre-engineering; sales, distribution and marketing.

Academic Programs *Special study options:* academic remediation for entering students, adult/continuing education programs, advanced placement credit, cooperative education, distance learning, double majors, honors programs, internships, part-time degree program, services for LD students, student-designed majors, study abroad, summer session for credit.

Library Purdue University North Central Library with 87,675 titles, 403 serial subscriptions, 602 audiovisual materials, an OPAC, a Web page.

Computers on Campus 450 computers available on campus for general student use. A campuswide network can be accessed from off campus. Internet

Purdue University North Central (continued)

access, online (class) registration, at least one staffed computer lab available. Computer purchase or lease plan available.

Student Life *Housing:* college housing not available. *Activities and organizations:* drama/theater group, student-run newspaper, Student Cultural Society, Student Education Association, construction club. *Campus security:* 24-hour emergency response devices, late-night transport/escort service. *Student services:* personal/psychological counseling.

Athletics Member NAIA. *Intercollegiate sports:* cheerleading M/W, softball W(c). *Intramural sports:* basketball M/W, cheerleading M/W, softball W.

Standardized Tests *Required for some:* SAT I or ACT (for admission). *Recommended:* SAT I (for admission), ACT (for admission).

Costs (2003–04) *Tuition:* state resident $4344 full-time, $145 per credit hour part-time; nonresident $10,503 full-time, $350 per credit hour part-time. Full-time tuition and fees vary according to course load, location, and program. Part-time tuition and fees vary according to course load, location, and program. *Required fees:* $368 full-time, $12 per credit hour part-time. *Payment plan:* installment.

Financial Aid Of all full-time matriculated undergraduates who enrolled in 2002, 1,444 applied for aid, 1,171 were judged to have need, 272 had their need fully met. 60 Federal Work-Study jobs (averaging $1600). In 2002, 33 non-need-based awards were made. *Average percent of need met:* 80%. *Average financial aid package:* $4893. *Average need-based loan:* $2909. *Average need-based gift aid:* $4236. *Average non-need-based aid:* $1361. *Average indebtedness upon graduation:* $8270.

Applying *Options:* early admission. *Required:* high school transcript. *Required for some:* essay or personal statement, minimum 2.0 GPA, interview. *Application deadlines:* 8/6 (freshmen), 8/1 (transfers). *Notification:* continuous (freshmen), continuous until 8/6 (transfers).

Admissions Contact Ms. Cathy Buckman, Director of Admissions, Purdue University North Central, 1401 South U.S. Highway 421, Westville, IN 46391. *Phone:* 219-785-5458. *Toll-free phone:* 800-872-1231. *E-mail:* cbuckman@purduenc.edu.

ROSE-HULMAN INSTITUTE OF TECHNOLOGY

Terre Haute, Indiana

- **Independent** comprehensive, founded 1874
- **Calendar** quarters
- **Degrees** bachelor's and master's
- **Suburban** 200-acre campus with easy access to Indianapolis
- **Endowment** $160.8 million
- **Coed, primarily men,** 1,721 undergraduate students, 99% full-time, 18% women, 82% men
- **Very difficult** entrance level, 71% of applicants were admitted

Undergraduates 1,709 full-time, 12 part-time. Students come from 49 states and territories, 9 other countries, 52% are from out of state, 2% African American, 3% Asian American or Pacific Islander, 1% Hispanic American, 0.1% Native American, 0.9% international, 1% transferred in, 51% live on campus. *Retention:* 91% of 2002 full-time freshmen returned.

Freshmen *Admission:* 3,188 applied, 2,261 admitted, 490 enrolled. *Test scores:* SAT verbal scores over 500: 99%; SAT math scores over 500: 100%; ACT scores over 18: 100%; SAT verbal scores over 600: 64%; SAT math scores over 600: 90%; ACT scores over 24: 94%; SAT verbal scores over 700: 22%; SAT math scores over 700: 47%; ACT scores over 30: 49%.

Faculty *Total:* 145, 96% full-time, 95% with terminal degrees. *Student/faculty ratio:* 13:1.

Majors Biology/biological sciences; biomedical/medical engineering; chemical engineering; chemistry; civil engineering; computer engineering; computer science; computer software engineering; economics; electrical, electronics and communications engineering; engineering physics; engineering related; mathematics; mechanical engineering; physics.

Academic Programs *Special study options:* accelerated degree program, adult/continuing education programs, advanced placement credit, cooperative education, double majors, honors programs, independent study, off-campus study, services for LD students, study abroad, summer session for credit. *ROTC:* Army (b), Air Force (b).

Library Logan Library with 77,348 titles, 280 serial subscriptions, 493 audiovisual materials, an OPAC, a Web page.

Computers on Campus 150 computers available on campus for general student use. A campuswide network can be accessed from student residence rooms and from off campus. Internet access, online (class) registration, at least one staffed computer lab available. Computer purchase or lease plan available.

Student Life *Housing:* on-campus residence required for freshman year. *Options:* coed, men-only, women-only. Campus housing is university owned. Freshman campus housing is guaranteed. *Activities and organizations:* drama/theater group, student-run newspaper, radio station, choral group, intramurals, band, drama club, student government, national fraternities, national sororities. *Campus security:* 24-hour emergency response devices and patrols, late-night transport/escort service, controlled dormitory access. *Student services:* health clinic, personal/psychological counseling.

Athletics Member NCAA. All Division III. *Intercollegiate sports:* baseball M, basketball M/W, cheerleading M/W, cross-country running M/W, football M, golf M/W, riflery M/W, soccer M/W, softball W, swimming M/W, tennis M/W, track and field M/W, volleyball W, wrestling M. *Intramural sports:* basketball M/W, bowling M(c)/W(c), cross-country running M/W, fencing M(c)/W(c), football M/W, golf M/W, lacrosse M(c)/W(c), racquetball M/W, riflery M(c)/W(c), soccer M/W, softball M/W, tennis M/W, ultimate Frisbee M(c)/W(c), volleyball M/W.

Standardized Tests *Required:* SAT I or ACT (for admission).

Costs (2003–04) *One-time required fee:* $3125. *Comprehensive fee:* $31,425 includes full-time tuition ($24,255), mandatory fees ($450), and room and board ($6720). Full-time tuition and fees vary according to course load and student level. Part-time tuition: $696 per credit. Part-time tuition and fees vary according to course load. *College room only:* $3840. Room and board charges vary according to board plan. *Payment plans:* tuition prepayment, installment. *Waivers:* employees or children of employees.

Financial Aid Of all full-time matriculated undergraduates who enrolled in 2003, 1,435 applied for aid, 1,229 were judged to have need, 126 had their need fully met. 543 Federal Work-Study jobs (averaging $1598). 485 state and other part-time jobs (averaging $1552). In 2003, 395 non-need-based awards were made. *Average percent of need met:* 83%. *Average financial aid package:* $15,261. *Average need-based loan:* $5341. *Average need-based gift aid:* $5746. *Average non-need-based aid:* $5557. *Average indebtedness upon graduation:* $27,000.

Applying *Options:* common application, electronic application, deferred entrance. *Application fee:* $40. *Required:* high school transcript, 1 letter of recommendation. *Recommended:* essay or personal statement, interview. *Application deadline:* 3/1 (freshmen). *Notification:* continuous (freshmen), continuous (transfers).

Admissions Contact Mr. Charles G. Howard, Dean of Admissions/Vice President, Rose-Hulman Institute of Technology, 5500 Wabash Avenue, CM 1, Terre Haute, IN 47803-3920. *Phone:* 812-877-8213. *Toll-free phone:* 800-248-7448. *Fax:* 812-877-8941. *E-mail:* admis.ofc@rose-hulman.edu.

SAINT JOSEPH'S COLLEGE

Rensselaer, Indiana

- **Independent Roman Catholic** comprehensive, founded 1889
- **Calendar** semesters
- **Degrees** certificates, diplomas, associate, bachelor's, and master's
- **Small-town** 180-acre campus with easy access to Chicago
- **Endowment** $8.0 million
- **Coed,** 998 undergraduate students, 84% full-time, 58% women, 42% men
- **Moderately difficult** entrance level, 76% of applicants were admitted

Undergraduates 842 full-time, 156 part-time. Students come from 20 states and territories, 3 other countries, 29% are from out of state, 5% African American, 0.4% Asian American or Pacific Islander, 5% Hispanic American, 0.4% Native American, 0.3% international, 3% transferred in, 70% live on campus. *Retention:* 69% of 2002 full-time freshmen returned.

Freshmen *Admission:* 1,169 applied, 885 admitted, 259 enrolled. *Average high school GPA:* 2.84. *Test scores:* SAT verbal scores over 500: 52%; SAT math scores over 500: 46%; ACT scores over 18: 83%; SAT verbal scores over 600: 9%; SAT math scores over 600: 15%; ACT scores over 24: 32%; SAT verbal scores over 700: 2%; SAT math scores over 700: 2%; ACT scores over 30: 3%.

Faculty *Total:* 85, 64% full-time, 72% with terminal degrees. *Student/faculty ratio:* 14:1.

Majors Accounting; art teacher education; biochemistry; biology/biological sciences; business/commerce; chemistry; clinical laboratory science/medical technology; communication/speech communication and rhetoric; computer and information sciences; creative writing; criminal justice/safety; economics; elementary education; English; environmental science; fine/studio arts; history; international relations and affairs; management information systems; mass communication/media; mathematics; mathematics and computer science; music history, literature, and theory; music management and merchandising; nursing (registered nurse training); pastoral studies/counseling; philosophy; philosophy and religious studies related; physical education teaching and coaching; political science and government; psychology; religious/sacred music; secondary education; social work; sociology.

Academic Programs *Special study options:* academic remediation for entering students, accelerated degree program, advanced placement credit, double majors, honors programs, independent study, internships, part-time degree program, services for LD students, student-designed majors, study abroad, summer session for credit.

Library Robinson Memorial Library with 157,481 titles, 498 serial subscriptions, 22,416 audiovisual materials, an OPAC, a Web page.

Computers on Campus 69 computers available on campus for general student use. A campuswide network can be accessed from student residence rooms. Internet access, at least one staffed computer lab available.

Student Life *Housing:* on-campus residence required through senior year. *Options:* coed, men-only, women-only, disabled students. Campus housing is university owned. Freshman campus housing is guaranteed. *Activities and organizations:* drama/theater group, student-run newspaper, radio and television station, choral group, marching band, Student Association, Student Senate, Student Union, Campus Ministry, Business Club. *Campus security:* 24-hour emergency response devices and patrols, student patrols, late-night transport/escort service. *Student services:* health clinic, personal/psychological counseling.

Athletics Member NCAA. All Division II. *Intercollegiate sports:* baseball M(s), basketball M(s)/W(s), cheerleading M/W, cross-country running M(s)/W(s), football M(s), golf M(s)/W(s), soccer M(s)/W(s), softball W(s), tennis M(s)/W(s), track and field M(s)/W(s), volleyball W(s). *Intramural sports:* basketball M/W, softball M/W, volleyball M/W.

Standardized Tests *Required:* SAT I or ACT (for admission).

Costs (2004–05) *Comprehensive fee:* $25,460 includes full-time tuition ($19,000), mandatory fees ($160), and room and board ($6300). Part-time tuition: $640 per credit. *Room and board:* Room and board charges vary according to housing facility. *Waivers:* minority students, children of alumni, and employees or children of employees.

Financial Aid Of all full-time matriculated undergraduates who enrolled in 2002, 766 applied for aid, 651 were judged to have need, 293 had their need fully met. 144 Federal Work-Study jobs (averaging $761). In 2002, 65 non-need-based awards were made. *Average percent of need met:* 85%. *Average financial aid package:* $13,000. *Average need-based loan:* $4000. *Average need-based gift aid:* $10,500. *Average non-need-based aid:* $6000. *Average indebtedness upon graduation:* $18,566.

Applying *Options:* electronic application, early admission, early decision, deferred entrance. *Application fee:* $25. *Required:* high school transcript, minimum 2.0 GPA. *Required for some:* interview. *Recommended:* essay or personal statement, letters of recommendation. *Application deadline:* rolling (freshmen), rolling (transfers). *Early decision:* 10/1. *Notification:* continuous (freshmen), 10/15 (early decision), continuous (transfers).

Admissions Contact Mr. Jeremy Spencer, Director of Admissions, Saint Joseph's College, PO Box 815, Rensselaer, IN 47978-0850. *Phone:* 219-866-6170. *Toll-free phone:* 800-447-8781. *Fax:* 219-866-6122. *E-mail:* admissions@saintjoe.edu.

■ *See page 2294 for a narrative description.*

SAINT MARY-OF-THE-WOODS COLLEGE

Saint Mary-of-the-Woods, Indiana

- **Independent Roman Catholic** comprehensive, founded 1840
- **Calendar** semesters
- **Degrees** certificates, associate, bachelor's, master's, post-master's, and postbachelor's certificates (also offers external degree program with significant enrollment reflected in profile)
- **Rural** 67-acre campus with easy access to Indianapolis
- **Endowment** $9.5 million
- **Women only,** 1,565 undergraduate students, 30% full-time
- **Moderately difficult** entrance level, 78% of applicants were admitted

Undergraduates 462 full-time, 1,103 part-time. Students come from 26 states and territories, 5 other countries, 30% are from out of state, 4% African American, 0.9% Asian American or Pacific Islander, 2% Hispanic American, 0.9% Native American, 0.2% international, 10% transferred in, 67% live on campus. *Retention:* 68% of 2002 full-time freshmen returned.

Freshmen *Admission:* 553 applied, 430 admitted, 282 enrolled. *Average high school GPA:* 3.20. *Test scores:* SAT verbal scores over 500: 50%; SAT math scores over 500: 49%; ACT scores over 18: 91%; SAT verbal scores over 600: 13%; SAT math scores over 600: 15%; ACT scores over 24: 34%; SAT verbal scores over 700: 2%; SAT math scores over 700: 2%; ACT scores over 30: 6%.

Faculty *Total:* 67, 97% full-time, 64% with terminal degrees. *Student/faculty ratio:* 12:1.

Majors Accounting; accounting related; adult development and aging; animal/livestock husbandry and production; art; art teacher education; biological and physical sciences; biology/biological sciences; business administration and management; business administration, management and operations related; child care and support services management; child care provision; clinical laboratory science/medical technology; communications technologies and support services related; communications technology; computer and information sciences; cultural studies; design and visual communications; dramatic/theatre arts; education; education (K-12); elementary education; English; English language and literature related; equestrian studies; fine/studio arts; French; gerontology; history; humanities; human resources management; human services; information science/studies; journalism; kindergarten/preschool education; legal assistant/paralegal; liberal arts and sciences/liberal studies; marketing/marketing management; mass communication/media; mathematics; music; music performance; music teacher education; music therapy; non-profit management; pastoral studies/counseling; photography; pre-dentistry studies; pre-law studies; pre-medical studies; pre-pharmacy studies; pre-veterinary studies; professional studies; psychology; public relations/image management; religious studies; secondary education; social sciences; Spanish; special education; theology.

Academic Programs *Special study options:* academic remediation for entering students, accelerated degree program, adult/continuing education programs, advanced placement credit, distance learning, double majors, external degree program, independent study, internships, off-campus study, part-time degree program, student-designed majors, study abroad, summer session for credit. *ROTC:* Army (c), Air Force (c).

Library College Library with 152,162 titles, 301 serial subscriptions, 522 audiovisual materials, an OPAC.

Computers on Campus 65 computers available on campus for general student use. A campuswide network can be accessed from student residence rooms and from off campus. Internet access, at least one staffed computer lab available.

Student Life *Housing:* on-campus residence required through senior year. *Options:* women-only. Campus housing is university owned. Freshman campus housing is guaranteed. *Activities and organizations:* drama/theater group, student-run newspaper, choral group, Student Senate, In-Law, student newspaper, chorale, Diversity "Worldwide Woodsies". *Campus security:* 24-hour patrols. *Student services:* health clinic, personal/psychological counseling.

Athletics *Intercollegiate sports:* basketball W(s), equestrian sports W(s), soccer W(s), softball W(s). *Intramural sports:* soccer W, softball W.

Standardized Tests *Required for some:* SAT I or ACT (for admission).

Costs (2003–04) *Comprehensive fee:* $23,280 includes full-time tuition ($16,530), mandatory fees ($500), and room and board ($6250). Part-time tuition: $319 per hour. Part-time tuition and fees vary according to course load and program. *Required fees:* $25 per term part-time. *College room only:* $2440. *Payment plan:* installment. *Waivers:* minority students, children of alumni, and employees or children of employees.

Applying *Options:* common application, electronic application, early admission, deferred entrance. *Application fee:* $30. *Required:* minimum 2.0 GPA, 1 letter of recommendation. *Required for some:* essay or personal statement, high school transcript, interview. *Application deadlines:* 8/15 (freshmen), 8/15 (transfers). *Notification:* continuous until 8/20 (freshmen), continuous until 8/20 (transfers).

Admissions Contact Director, Saint Mary-of-the-Woods College, Guerin Hall, Saint Mary-of-the-Woods, IN 47876. *Phone:* 812-535-5106. *Toll-free phone:* 800-926-SMWC. *Fax:* 812-535-4900. *E-mail:* smwcadms@smwc.edu.

SAINT MARY'S COLLEGE

Notre Dame, Indiana

- **Independent Roman Catholic** 4-year, founded 1844
- **Calendar** semesters
- **Degree** bachelor's
- **Suburban** 275-acre campus
- **Endowment** $79.6 million
- **Women only,** 1,475 undergraduate students, 98% full-time
- **Moderately difficult** entrance level, 82% of applicants were admitted

Undergraduates 1,440 full-time, 35 part-time. Students come from 47 states and territories, 12 other countries, 73% are from out of state, 1% African American, 2% Asian American or Pacific Islander, 5% Hispanic American, 0.3% Native American, 1% international, 2% transferred in, 83% live on campus. *Retention:* 85% of 2002 full-time freshmen returned.

Freshmen *Admission:* 402 enrolled. *Average high school GPA:* 3.65. *Test scores:* SAT verbal scores over 500: 78%; SAT math scores over 500: 81%; ACT scores over 18: 98%; SAT verbal scores over 600: 32%; SAT math scores over 600: 31%; ACT scores over 24: 60%; SAT verbal scores over 700: 4%; SAT math scores over 700: 3%; ACT scores over 30: 5%.

Faculty *Total:* 186, 61% full-time. *Student/faculty ratio:* 11:1.

Majors Applied mathematics related; art; art teacher education; biology/biological sciences; business administration and management; business teacher education; chemistry; clinical laboratory science/medical technology; communication/speech communication and rhetoric; creative writing; cytotechnology; dramatic/theatre arts; economics; education; elementary education; English literature (British and Commonwealth); finance; French; history; humanities; interdisciplinary studies; international business/trade/commerce; management information

Saint Mary's College (continued)

systems; marketing/marketing management; mathematics; mathematics and computer science; music; music teacher education; nursing (registered nurse training); philosophy; political science and government; psychology; religious studies; social work; sociology; Spanish.

Academic Programs *Special study options:* academic remediation for entering students, accelerated degree program, advanced placement credit, cooperative education, double majors, independent study, internships, off-campus study, part-time degree program, services for LD students, student-designed majors, study abroad, summer session for credit. *ROTC:* Army (c), Navy (c), Air Force (c). *Unusual degree programs:* 3-2 engineering with University of Notre Dame.

Library Cushwa-Leighton Library with 210,812 titles, 776 serial subscriptions, 2,471 audiovisual materials, an OPAC, a Web page.

Computers on Campus 198 computers available on campus for general student use. A campuswide network can be accessed from student residence rooms and from off campus. Internet access, online (class) registration, at least one staffed computer lab available.

Student Life *Housing options:* women-only. Campus housing is university owned. Freshman campus housing is guaranteed. *Activities and organizations:* drama/theater group, student-run newspaper, radio station, choral group, marching band, Circle K, Toastmasters, Volunteers in Support of Admissions (VISA), Student Government Association, academic clubs. *Campus security:* 24-hour emergency response devices and patrols, late-night transport/escort service, controlled dormitory access. *Student services:* health clinic, personal/psychological counseling, women's center.

Athletics Member NCAA. All Division III. *Intercollegiate sports:* basketball W, crew W(c), cross-country running W(c), equestrian sports W(c), field hockey W(c), gymnastics W(c), sailing W(c), skiing (downhill) W(c), soccer W, softball W, swimming W, tennis W, ultimate Frisbee W(c), volleyball W, water polo W(c). *Intramural sports:* cheerleading W, golf W, lacrosse W, skiing (cross-country) W.

Standardized Tests *Required:* SAT I or ACT (for admission).

Costs (2003–04) *Comprehensive fee:* $29,263 includes full-time tuition ($21,624), mandatory fees ($350), and room and board ($7289). Full-time tuition and fees vary according to location. Part-time tuition: $855 per semester hour. *Room and board:* Room and board charges vary according to housing facility. *Payment plan:* installment. *Waivers:* senior citizens and employees or children of employees.

Financial Aid Of all full-time matriculated undergraduates who enrolled in 2003, 1,084 applied for aid, 1,017 were judged to have need, 269 had their need fully met. 273 Federal Work-Study jobs (averaging $1201). 455 state and other part-time jobs (averaging $1446). In 2003, 323 non-need-based awards were made. *Average percent of need met:* 79%. *Average financial aid package:* $17,358. *Average need-based loan:* $2773. *Average need-based gift aid:* $8283. *Average non-need-based aid:* $6721. *Average indebtedness upon graduation:* $20,356.

Applying *Options:* electronic application, early admission, early decision, deferred entrance. *Application fee:* $30. *Required:* essay or personal statement, high school transcript, 1 letter of recommendation. *Recommended:* interview. *Application deadline:* 3/1 (freshmen), rolling (transfers). *Early decision:* 11/15. *Notification:* continuous (freshmen), 12/15 (early decision), continuous (transfers).

Admissions Contact Ms. Mary Pat Nolan, Director of Admission, Saint Mary's College, Notre Dame, IN 46556. *Phone:* 574-284-4587. *Toll-free phone:* 800-551-7621. *E-mail:* admission@saintmarys.edu.

■ *See page 2312 for a narrative description.*

TAYLOR UNIVERSITY

Upland, Indiana

- **Independent interdenominational** comprehensive, founded 1846
- **Calendar** 4-1-4
- **Degrees** certificates, associate, bachelor's, and master's
- **Rural** 250-acre campus with easy access to Indianapolis
- **Endowment** $28.8 million
- **Coed,** 1,834 undergraduate students, 98% full-time, 53% women, 47% men
- **Very difficult** entrance level, 84% of applicants were admitted

Since 1846, the mark of a Taylor education has been to enlighten the mind and ignite the soul. Within the context of our vibrant covenant-based community, students and faculty pursue learning through a relentless commitment to scholarship, research, and service.

Undergraduates 1,789 full-time, 45 part-time. Students come from 47 states and territories, 67% are from out of state, 1% African American, 2% Asian American or Pacific Islander, 1% Hispanic American, 0.4% Native American, 0.9% international, 2% transferred in, 85% live on campus. *Retention:* 87% of 2002 full-time freshmen returned.

Freshmen *Admission:* 1,312 applied, 1,100 admitted, 470 enrolled. *Average high school GPA:* 3.57. *Test scores:* SAT verbal scores over 500: 89%; SAT math scores over 500: 84%; ACT scores over 18: 85%; SAT verbal scores over 600: 53%; SAT math scores over 600: 44%; ACT scores over 24: 31%; SAT verbal scores over 700: 10%; SAT math scores over 700: 10%; ACT scores over 30: 2%.

Faculty *Total:* 162, 73% full-time, 60% with terminal degrees. *Student/faculty ratio:* 14:1.

Majors Accounting; ancient Near Eastern and biblical languages; art; art teacher education; athletic training; biblical studies; biology/biological sciences; biology teacher education; business administration and management; chemistry; clinical laboratory science/medical technology; commercial and advertising art; communication/speech communication and rhetoric; computer engineering; computer graphics; computer programming; computer science; creative writing; dramatic/theatre arts; economics; education; elementary education; engineering physics; English; environmental biology; environmental studies; finance; French; history; history teacher education; human resources management; information science/studies; international business/trade/commerce; international economics; international relations and affairs; kindergarten/preschool education; literature; management information systems; marketing/marketing management; mass communication/media; mathematics; middle school education; music; music management and merchandising; music performance; music teacher education; natural sciences; parks, recreation and leisure; philosophy; physical education teaching and coaching; physics; piano and organ; political science and government; pre-dentistry studies; pre-law studies; pre-medical studies; pre-veterinary studies; psychology; religious education; religious/sacred music; religious studies; science teacher education; secondary education; social sciences; social science teacher education; social work; sociology; Spanish; Spanish language teacher education; speech teacher education; sport and fitness administration; theology; voice and opera.

Academic Programs *Special study options:* academic remediation for entering students, advanced placement credit, cooperative education, distance learning, double majors, honors programs, independent study, internships, off-campus study, part-time degree program, services for LD students, student-designed majors, study abroad, summer session for credit. *Unusual degree programs:* 3-2 engineering with Washington University in St. Louis; medical technology.

Library Zondervan Library with 193,343 titles, 902 serial subscriptions, 6,653 audiovisual materials, an OPAC, a Web page.

Computers on Campus 228 computers available on campus for general student use. A campuswide network can be accessed from student residence rooms and from off campus. Internet access, online (class) registration, at least one staffed computer lab available.

Student Life *Housing:* on-campus residence required through junior year. *Options:* men-only, women-only. Campus housing is university owned and is provided by a third party. Freshman campus housing is guaranteed. *Activities and organizations:* drama/theater group, student-run newspaper, radio and television station, choral group, Student Activities Council, World Outreach, Youth Conference, Inter-Class Council, Senate. *Campus security:* 24-hour patrols, student patrols, late-night transport/escort service. *Student services:* health clinic, personal/psychological counseling.

Athletics Member NAIA, NCCAA. *Intercollegiate sports:* baseball M(s), basketball M(s)/W(s), cross-country running M(s)/W(s), equestrian sports M(c)/W(c), football M(s), golf M(s), lacrosse M(c)/W(c), soccer M(s)/W(s), softball W(s), tennis M(s)/W(s), track and field M(s)/W(s), volleyball M(c)/W(s). *Intramural sports:* badminton M/W, basketball M/W, football M/W, racquetball M/W, soccer M/W, softball M/W, table tennis M/W, tennis M/W, volleyball W.

Standardized Tests *Required:* SAT I or ACT (for admission).

Costs (2003–04) *Comprehensive fee:* $23,820 includes full-time tuition ($18,306), mandatory fees ($222), and room and board ($5292). Part-time tuition: $655 per credit. *Required fees:* $30 per term part-time. *College room only:* $2572. Room and board charges vary according to housing facility. *Payment plan:* installment. *Waivers:* senior citizens and employees or children of employees.

Financial Aid Of all full-time matriculated undergraduates who enrolled in 2003, 1,206 applied for aid, 1,009 were judged to have need, 229 had their need fully met. 810 Federal Work-Study jobs (averaging $610). In 2003, 448 non-need-based awards were made. *Average percent of need met:* 81%. *Average financial aid package:* $13,351. *Average need-based loan:* $4174. *Average need-based gift aid:* $9618. *Average non-need-based aid:* $3137. *Average indebtedness upon graduation:* $15,467. *Financial aid deadline:* 3/10.

Applying *Options:* electronic application, early action, deferred entrance. *Application fee:* $25. *Required:* essay or personal statement, high school transcript, 2 letters of recommendation, interview. *Recommended:* minimum 2.8 GPA. *Appli-*

cation deadline: 1/15 (freshmen), rolling (transfers). *Notification:* 2/5 (freshmen), 12/20 (early action), continuous (transfers).

Admissions Contact Mr. Stephen R. Mortland, Director of Admissions, Taylor University, 236 West Reade Avenue, Upland, IN 46989-1001. *Phone:* 765-998-5134. *Toll-free phone:* 800-882-3456. *Fax:* 765-998-4925. *E-mail:* admissions_u@tayloru.edu.

■ See page 2484 for a narrative description.

TAYLOR UNIVERSITY, FORT WAYNE CAMPUS
Fort Wayne, Indiana

- **Independent interdenominational** comprehensive, founded 1992, part of Taylor University
- **Calendar** 4-1-4
- **Degrees** associate, bachelor's, master's, and postbachelor's certificates
- **Suburban** 32-acre campus
- **Endowment** $6.4 million
- **Coed,** 637 undergraduate students, 63% full-time, 62% women, 38% men
- **Moderately difficult** entrance level, 83% of applicants were admitted

Undergraduates 401 full-time, 236 part-time. Students come from 24 states and territories, 3 other countries, 23% are from out of state, 5% African American, 0.8% Asian American or Pacific Islander, 2% Hispanic American, 0.2% Native American, 0.8% international, 5% transferred in, 46% live on campus. *Retention:* 64% of 2002 full-time freshmen returned.

Freshmen *Admission:* 313 applied, 260 admitted, 119 enrolled. *Average high school GPA:* 3.13. *Test scores:* SAT verbal scores over 500: 58%; SAT math scores over 500: 52%; ACT scores over 18: 89%; SAT verbal scores over 600: 19%; SAT math scores over 600: 15%; ACT scores over 24: 39%; SAT verbal scores over 700: 6%; SAT math scores over 700: 1%; ACT scores over 30: 3%.

Faculty *Total:* 52, 50% full-time, 46% with terminal degrees. *Student/faculty ratio:* 14:1.

Majors Biblical studies; business administration and management; communication and journalism related; computer and information sciences; criminal justice/law enforcement administration; criminal justice/safety; elementary education; English; interdisciplinary studies; international business/trade/commerce; liberal arts and sciences/liberal studies; music; pastoral studies/counseling; prelaw studies; psychology; public relations/image management; religious education; social work; urban studies/affairs; youth ministry.

Academic Programs *Special study options:* academic remediation for entering students, accelerated degree program, advanced placement credit, cooperative education, distance learning, double majors, independent study, internships, off-campus study, part-time degree program, services for LD students, student-designed majors, study abroad, summer session for credit.

Library S. A. Lehman Memorial Library with 78,662 titles, 670 serial subscriptions, 4,699 audiovisual materials, an OPAC, a Web page.

Computers on Campus 40 computers available on campus for general student use. A campuswide network can be accessed from off campus. Internet access, at least one staffed computer lab available.

Student Life *Housing:* on-campus residence required through junior year. *Options:* men-only, women-only. Campus housing is university owned. Freshman applicants given priority for college housing. *Activities and organizations:* drama/theater group, student-run newspaper, choral group, Taylor Student Organization, Youth Conference Committee, Multicultrual Activities Council, World Outreach, Student Activities Council. *Campus security:* student patrols, late-night transport/escort service, controlled dormitory access, 12-hour night patrols by trained personnel. *Student services:* health clinic, personal/psychological counseling.

Athletics Member NCCAA. *Intercollegiate sports:* basketball M/W, cheerleading M/W, soccer M, softball W(c), volleyball W. *Intramural sports:* badminton M/W, baseball M(c), basketball M/W, football M/W, soccer M/W, table tennis M/W, tennis M/W, volleyball M/W, weight lifting M/W.

Standardized Tests *Required:* SAT I or ACT (for admission).

Costs (2003–04) *Comprehensive fee:* $20,584 includes full-time tuition ($15,790), mandatory fees ($114), and room and board ($4680). Part-time tuition: $180 per hour. Part-time tuition and fees vary according to course load. *Required fees:* $25 per hour part-time. *College room only:* $2040. Room and board charges vary according to board plan. *Payment plan:* installment. *Waivers:* children of alumni, senior citizens, and employees or children of employees.

Financial Aid Of all full-time matriculated undergraduates who enrolled in 2002, 367 applied for aid, 344 were judged to have need, 61 had their need fully met. 118 Federal Work-Study jobs (averaging $1009). In 2002, 37 non-need-based awards were made. *Average percent of need met:* 87%. *Average financial aid package:* $15,298. *Average need-based loan:* $3426. *Average need-based gift aid:* $11,712. *Average non-need-based aid:* $2488. *Average indebtedness upon graduation:* $14,567.

Applying *Options:* electronic application, deferred entrance. *Application fee:* $20. *Required:* essay or personal statement, high school transcript, minimum 2.0 GPA, 2 letters of recommendation. *Recommended:* minimum 3.0 GPA, interview. *Application deadline:* rolling (freshmen), rolling (transfers).

Admissions Contact Mr. Leo Gonot, Associate Vice President for Enrollment Management, Taylor University, Fort Wayne Campus, 1025 West Rudisill Boulevard, Fort Wayne, IN 46807-2197. *Phone:* 219-744-8689. *Toll-free phone:* 800-233-3922. *Fax:* 260-744-8660. *E-mail:* admissions_f@tayloru.edu.

TRI-STATE UNIVERSITY
Angola, Indiana

- **Independent** comprehensive, founded 1884
- **Calendar** semesters
- **Degrees** associate, bachelor's, and master's
- **Small-town** 400-acre campus
- **Endowment** $19.3 million
- **Coed,** 1,186 undergraduate students, 87% full-time, 36% women, 64% men
- **Moderately difficult** entrance level, 72% of applicants were admitted

Within six months of graduation, 90% of Tri-State University's graduates in engineering, technology, business, education, mathematics, computer science, science, criminal justice, psychology, sport management, golf management, and communications have accepted full-time positions in their major areas, with average salaries at or above national averages for their disciplines.

Undergraduates 1,033 full-time, 153 part-time. Students come from 23 states and territories, 15 other countries, 40% are from out of state, 2% African American, 0.7% Asian American or Pacific Islander, 1% Hispanic American, 0.3% Native American, 2% international, 6% transferred in, 48% live on campus. *Retention:* 68% of 2002 full-time freshmen returned.

Freshmen *Admission:* 1,852 applied, 1,330 admitted, 335 enrolled. *Average high school GPA:* 3.33. *Test scores:* SAT verbal scores over 500: 62%; SAT math scores over 500: 76%; ACT scores over 18: 93%; SAT verbal scores over 600: 19%; SAT math scores over 600: 38%; ACT scores over 24: 48%; SAT verbal scores over 700: 1%; SAT math scores over 700: 6%; ACT scores over 30: 6%.

Faculty *Total:* 98, 69% full-time, 46% with terminal degrees. *Student/faculty ratio:* 15:1.

Majors Accounting; biological and physical sciences; biology/biological sciences; business administration and management; chemical engineering; chemistry; civil engineering; communication/speech communication and rhetoric; computer and information sciences; computer engineering; computer science; criminal justice/law enforcement administration; drafting and design technology; education; electrical, electronics and communications engineering; elementary education; engineering/industrial management; engineering technology; English; English/language arts teacher education; environmental studies; forensic science and technology; industrial technology; liberal arts and sciences/liberal studies; management information systems; marketing/marketing management; mathematics; mathematics teacher education; mechanical engineering; operations management; parks, recreation and leisure facilities management; physical education teaching and coaching; physical sciences; pre-law studies; pre-medical studies; pre-veterinary studies; psychology; science teacher education; secondary education; social sciences; social studies teacher education; sport and fitness administration.

Academic Programs *Special study options:* academic remediation for entering students, adult/continuing education programs, advanced placement credit, cooperative education, distance learning, double majors, internships, part-time degree program, study abroad, summer session for credit.

Library Perry Ford Library with 82,474 titles, 336 serial subscriptions, 625 audiovisual materials, an OPAC, a Web page.

Computers on Campus 150 computers available on campus for general student use. A campuswide network can be accessed from student residence rooms and from off campus. Internet access, at least one staffed computer lab available.

Student Life *Housing:* on-campus residence required through sophomore year. *Options:* coed. Campus housing is university owned. Freshman campus housing is guaranteed. *Activities and organizations:* drama/theater group, student-run newspaper, radio station, choral group, Circle K, drama club, International Student Association, student newspaper, student radio station, national fraternities. *Campus security:* 24-hour emergency response devices and patrols, late-night transport/escort service. *Student services:* personal/psychological counseling.

Athletics Member NAIA. *Intercollegiate sports:* baseball M, basketball M/W, cross-country running M/W, football M, golf M/W, soccer M/W, softball W, tennis M/W, track and field M/W, volleyball W. *Intramural sports:* badminton M/W, basketball M/W, football M, golf M/W, racquetball M/W, softball M/W, table tennis M/W, volleyball M/W.

Standardized Tests *Required:* SAT I or ACT (for admission).

Tri-State University (continued)

Costs (2003–04) *Comprehensive fee:* $23,600 includes full-time tuition ($18,000) and room and board ($5600). Part-time tuition: $562 per semester hour. *Payment plan:* installment. *Waivers:* employees or children of employees.

Financial Aid Of all full-time matriculated undergraduates who enrolled in 2003, 1,034 applied for aid, 1,025 were judged to have need, 804 had their need fully met. 431 Federal Work-Study jobs (averaging $662). *Average percent of need met:* 75%. *Average financial aid package:* $12,100. *Average need-based loan:* $3578. *Average need-based gift aid:* $3362. *Average non-need-based aid:* $2514. *Average indebtedness upon graduation:* $16,510. *Financial aid deadline:* 3/10.

Applying *Options:* common application, electronic application. *Application fee:* $20. *Required:* high school transcript, minimum 2.0 GPA. *Recommended:* letters of recommendation, interview. *Application deadlines:* 6/1 (freshmen), 8/1 (transfers). *Notification:* continuous until 8/15 (freshmen), continuous until 8/15 (transfers).

Admissions Contact Ms. Sara Yarian, Admissions Officer, Tri-State University, 1 University Avenue, Angola, IN 46703. *Phone:* 260-665-4365. *Toll-free phone:* 800-347-4TSU. *Fax:* 260-665-4578. *E-mail:* admit@tristate.edu.

■ *See page 2530 for a narrative description.*

UNIVERSITY OF EVANSVILLE
Evansville, Indiana

- **Independent** comprehensive, founded 1854, affiliated with United Methodist Church
- **Calendar** semesters
- **Degrees** associate, bachelor's, and master's
- **Suburban** 75-acre campus
- **Endowment** $59.7 million
- **Coed,** 2,566 undergraduate students, 89% full-time, 62% women, 38% men
- **Moderately difficult** entrance level, 86% of applicants were admitted

For 10 consecutive years, the University of Evansville has been ranked by *U.S. News & World Report* as one of the top 10 outstanding Midwest regional universities and as one of the best values in the Midwest. The University of Evansville is a comprehensive university offering Division I sports.

Undergraduates 2,275 full-time, 291 part-time. Students come from 44 states and territories, 38 other countries, 34% are from out of state, 2% African American, 0.9% Asian American or Pacific Islander, 0.9% Hispanic American, 0.3% Native American, 6% international, 3% transferred in, 70% live on campus. *Retention:* 80% of 2002 full-time freshmen returned.

Freshmen *Admission:* 2,292 applied, 1,972 admitted, 663 enrolled. *Average high school GPA:* 3.54. *Test scores:* SAT verbal scores over 500: 79%; SAT math scores over 500: 81%; ACT scores over 18: 95%; SAT verbal scores over 600: 41%; SAT math scores over 600: 39%; ACT scores over 24: 55%; SAT verbal scores over 700: 9%; SAT math scores over 700: 7%; ACT scores over 30: 9%.

Faculty *Total:* 232, 72% full-time. *Student/faculty ratio:* 13:1.

Majors Accounting; anthropology; archeology; art; art history, criticism and conservation; arts management; art teacher education; athletic training; biblical studies; biochemistry; biology/biological sciences; business administration and management; business/managerial economics; ceramic arts and ceramics; chemistry; civil engineering; classics and languages, literatures and linguistics; clinical laboratory science/medical technology; commercial and advertising art; computer engineering; computer science; creative writing; criminal justice/law enforcement administration; dramatic/theatre arts; drawing; economics; electrical, electronics and communications engineering; elementary education; engineering/industrial management; English; environmental studies; finance; French; German; gerontology; health/health care administration; history; international business/trade/commerce; international relations and affairs; kinesiology and exercise science; legal studies; liberal arts and sciences/liberal studies; literature; marketing/marketing management; mass communication/media; mathematics; mechanical engineering; music; music management and merchandising; music teacher education; music therapy; nursing (registered nurse training); philosophy; physical education teaching and coaching; physical therapist assistant; physical therapy; physics; physiological psychology/psychobiology; political science and government; pre-dentistry studies; pre-law studies; pre-medical studies; pre-veterinary studies; psychology; religious studies; science teacher education; sculpture; secondary education; sociology; Spanish; special education.

Academic Programs *Special study options:* accelerated degree program, adult/continuing education programs, advanced placement credit, cooperative education, distance learning, double majors, English as a second language, external degree program, freshman honors college, honors programs, independent study, internships, part-time degree program, services for LD students, student-designed majors, study abroad, summer session for credit.

Library Bower Suhrheinrich Library plus 1 other with 275,980 titles, 1,320 serial subscriptions, 10,094 audiovisual materials, an OPAC, a Web page.

Computers on Campus 375 computers available on campus for general student use. A campuswide network can be accessed from student residence rooms and from off campus. Internet access, online (class) registration, at least one staffed computer lab available. Computer purchase or lease plan available.

Student Life *Housing:* on-campus residence required for freshman year. *Options:* coed. Campus housing is university owned. Freshman campus housing is guaranteed. *Activities and organizations:* drama/theater group, student-run newspaper, radio station, choral group, Kappa Chi, Admission Ambassadors, Student Activities Board, Phi Eta Sigma, Mortar Board, national fraternities, national sororities. *Campus security:* 24-hour emergency response devices and patrols, late-night transport/escort service, controlled dormitory access. *Student services:* health clinic, personal/psychological counseling.

Athletics Member NCAA. All Division I. *Intercollegiate sports:* baseball M(s), basketball M(s)/W(s), cross-country running M(s)/W(s), golf M(s), soccer M(s)/W, softball W, swimming M(s)/W(s), tennis M(s)/W(s), volleyball W(s). *Intramural sports:* badminton W, basketball M/W, bowling M/W, cheerleading M/W, cross-country running M/W, golf M/W, soccer M/W, swimming M/W, table tennis M/W, tennis M/W, track and field M/W, volleyball M/W, wrestling M.

Standardized Tests *Required:* SAT I or ACT (for admission).

Costs (2003–04) *Comprehensive fee:* $24,740 includes full-time tuition ($18,900), mandatory fees ($330), and room and board ($5510). Part-time tuition: $525 per hour. Part-time tuition and fees vary according to course load. *Required fees:* $30 per term part-time. *College room only:* $2600. Room and board charges vary according to board plan and housing facility. *Payment plan:* installment. *Waivers:* minority students, children of alumni, senior citizens, and employees or children of employees.

Financial Aid Of all full-time matriculated undergraduates who enrolled in 2003, 2,183 applied for aid, 1,583 were judged to have need, 504 had their need fully met. 397 Federal Work-Study jobs (averaging $1284). 62 state and other part-time jobs (averaging $1248). In 2003, 473 non-need-based awards were made. *Average percent of need met:* 91%. *Average financial aid package:* $17,375. *Average need-based loan:* $4283. *Average need-based gift aid:* $12,915. *Average non-need-based aid:* $7764. *Average indebtedness upon graduation:* $21,141.

Applying *Options:* common application, electronic application, early admission, early action, deferred entrance. *Application fee:* $35. *Required:* essay or personal statement, high school transcript, minimum 2.0 GPA, 1 letter of recommendation. *Required for some:* interview. *Recommended:* minimum 3.0 GPA, interview. *Application deadlines:* rolling (freshmen), 7/1 (transfers). *Notification:* continuous until 3/1 (freshmen), 12/15 (early action), continuous (transfers).

Admissions Contact Dr. Tom Bear, Dean of Admission, University of Evansville, 1800 Lincoln Avenue, Evansville, IN 47722-0002. *Phone:* 812-479-2468. *Toll-free phone:* 800-423-8633. *Fax:* 812-474-4076. *E-mail:* admission@evansville.edu.

■ *See page 2602 for a narrative description.*

UNIVERSITY OF INDIANAPOLIS
Indianapolis, Indiana

- **Independent** comprehensive, founded 1902, affiliated with United Methodist Church
- **Calendar** 4-4-1
- **Degrees** associate, bachelor's, master's, and doctoral
- **Suburban** 60-acre campus
- **Endowment** $53.0 million
- **Coed,** 3,007 undergraduate students, 70% full-time, 66% women, 34% men
- **Moderately difficult** entrance level, 74% of applicants were admitted

Undergraduates 2,092 full-time, 915 part-time. Students come from 31 states and territories, 55 other countries, 8% are from out of state, 9% African American, 1% Asian American or Pacific Islander, 1% Hispanic American, 0.3% Native American, 4% international, 4% transferred in, 31% live on campus. *Retention:* 80% of 2002 full-time freshmen returned.

Freshmen *Admission:* 2,828 applied, 2,103 admitted, 661 enrolled. *Average high school GPA:* 3.05. *Test scores:* SAT verbal scores over 500: 52%; SAT math scores over 500: 60%; ACT scores over 18: 86%; SAT verbal scores over 600: 12%; SAT math scores over 600: 16%; ACT scores over 24: 27%; SAT verbal scores over 700: 2%; SAT math scores over 700: 1%; ACT scores over 30: 2%.

Faculty *Total:* 358, 45% full-time, 59% with terminal degrees. *Student/faculty ratio:* 14:1.

Majors Accounting; anatomy; anthropology; archeology; art; art history, criticism and conservation; art teacher education; art therapy; athletic training; banking and financial support services; biology/biological sciences; business administration and management; business/managerial economics; business teacher education; chemistry; clinical laboratory science/medical technology; commercial and advertising art; communication/speech communication and rhetoric; computer programming; computer science; corrections; criminal justice/law enforcement administration; dramatic/theatre arts; education; electrical, electronics and communications engineering; elementary education; English; English/language arts teacher education; environmental studies; fine/studio arts; French; French language teacher education; geology/earth science; German; history; human resources management; information science/studies; international business/trade/commerce; international relations and affairs; legal assistant/paralegal; liberal arts and sciences/liberal studies; marketing/marketing management; mathematics; mathematics teacher education; music; music performance; music teacher education; nursing (registered nurse training); operations management; philosophy; physical education teaching and coaching; physical therapist assistant; physics; political science and government; pre-dentistry studies; pre-law studies; pre-medical studies; pre-theology/pre-ministerial studies; pre-veterinary studies; psychology; religious studies; science teacher education; secondary education; social studies teacher education; social work; sociology; Spanish; Spanish language teacher education; speech teacher education.

Academic Programs *Special study options:* academic remediation for entering students, accelerated degree program, adult/continuing education programs, advanced placement credit, cooperative education, distance learning, double majors, English as a second language, honors programs, independent study, internships, off-campus study, part-time degree program, services for LD students, student-designed majors, study abroad, summer session for credit. *ROTC:* Army (c). *Unusual degree programs:* 3-2 engineering with Indiana University & Purdue University Indianapolis; physical therapy, occupational therapy.

Library Krannert Memorial Library with 173,363 titles, 1,015 serial subscriptions, 5,324 audiovisual materials, an OPAC, a Web page.

Computers on Campus 218 computers available on campus for general student use. A campuswide network can be accessed from student residence rooms and from off campus. Internet access, at least one staffed computer lab available.

Student Life *Housing options:* coed, women-only. Campus housing is university owned. *Activities and organizations:* drama/theater group, student-run newspaper, radio station, choral group, Fellowship of Christian Athletes, Intercultural Association, Circle K, Indianapolis Student Government, Residence Hall Association. *Campus security:* 24-hour emergency response devices and patrols, student patrols, late-night transport/escort service, emergency call boxes. *Student services:* health clinic, personal/psychological counseling.

Athletics Member NCAA. All Division II. *Intercollegiate sports:* baseball M(s), basketball M(s)/W(s), cross-country running M(s)/W(s), football M(s), golf M(s)/W(s), soccer M(s)/W(s), softball W(s), swimming M(s)/W(s), tennis M(s)/W(s), track and field M(s)/W(s), volleyball W(s), wrestling M(s). *Intramural sports:* badminton M/W, basketball M/W, cheerleading M/W, football M/W, racquetball M/W, softball M/W, table tennis M/W, tennis M/W, volleyball M/W.

Standardized Tests *Required:* SAT I or ACT (for admission).

Costs (2004–05) *Comprehensive fee:* $23,350 includes full-time tuition ($17,200) and room and board ($6150). Full-time tuition and fees vary according to program. Part-time tuition and fees vary according to class time. *Room and board:* Room and board charges vary according to board plan and housing facility. *Payment plan:* deferred payment. *Waivers:* senior citizens and employees or children of employees.

Financial Aid Of all full-time matriculated undergraduates who enrolled in 2002, 1,227 applied for aid, 1,086 were judged to have need, 368 had their need fully met. 344 Federal Work-Study jobs (averaging $776). In 2002, 210 non-need-based awards were made. *Average percent of need met:* 85%. *Average financial aid package:* $14,721. *Average need-based loan:* $4315. *Average need-based gift aid:* $8455. *Average non-need-based aid:* $7622. *Average indebtedness upon graduation:* $18,968.

Applying *Options:* electronic application, deferred entrance. *Application fee:* $20. *Required:* high school transcript, minimum 2.0 GPA. *Required for some:* interview. *Application deadline:* rolling (freshmen), rolling (transfers). *Notification:* continuous (freshmen), continuous (transfers).

Admissions Contact Mr. Ronald W. Wilks, Director of Admissions, University of Indianapolis, 1400 East Hanna Avenue, Indianapolis, IN 46227-3697. *Phone:* 317-788-3216. *Toll-free phone:* 800-232-8634 Ext. 3216. *Fax:* 317-778-3300. *E-mail:* admissions@uindy.edu.

■ *See page 2620 for a narrative description.*

UNIVERSITY OF NOTRE DAME

Notre Dame, Indiana

- **Independent Roman Catholic** university, founded 1842
- **Calendar** semesters
- **Degrees** bachelor's, master's, doctoral, and first professional
- **Suburban** 1250-acre campus
- **Endowment** $2.6 billion
- **Coed,** 8,311 undergraduate students, 100% full-time, 47% women, 53% men
- **Most difficult** entrance level, 29% of applicants were admitted

Undergraduates 8,293 full-time, 18 part-time. Students come from 54 states and territories, 65 other countries, 87% are from out of state, 4% African American, 5% Asian American or Pacific Islander, 8% Hispanic American, 0.6% Native American, 4% international, 2% transferred in, 75% live on campus.

Freshmen *Admission:* 12,095 applied, 3,524 admitted, 1,996 enrolled. *Test scores:* SAT verbal scores over 500: 97%; SAT math scores over 500: 99%; ACT scores over 18: 100%; SAT verbal scores over 600: 84%; SAT math scores over 600: 90%; ACT scores over 24: 97%; SAT verbal scores over 700: 39%; SAT math scores over 700: 51%; ACT scores over 30: 78%.

Majors Accounting; aerospace, aeronautical and astronautical engineering; American studies; ancient/classical Greek; anthropology; Arabic; architecture; art history, criticism and conservation; biochemistry; biology/biological sciences; business administration, management and operations related; business/commerce; chemical engineering; chemistry; chemistry related; Chinese; civil engineering; classics and languages, literatures and linguistics; computer and information sciences; computer and information sciences and support services related; computer engineering; design and visual communications; dramatic/theatre arts; economics; electrical, electronics and communications engineering; English; environmental/environmental health engineering; finance; fine/studio arts; French; geology/earth science; German; history; Italian; Japanese; Latin; liberal arts and sciences/liberal studies; management information systems; marketing/marketing management; mathematics; mechanical engineering; medieval and Renaissance studies; music; philosophy; philosophy and religious studies related; physics; physics related; political science and government; pre-medical studies; psychology; Russian; science teacher education; sociology; Spanish; theology.

Academic Programs *Special study options:* accelerated degree program, advanced placement credit, cooperative education, distance learning, double majors, honors programs, independent study, internships, off-campus study, services for LD students, student-designed majors, study abroad, summer session for credit. *ROTC:* Army (b), Navy (b), Air Force (b). *Unusual degree programs:* 3-2 business administration.

Library University Libraries of Notre Dame plus 9 others with 2.7 million titles, 19,232 serial subscriptions, 23,497 audiovisual materials, an OPAC, a Web page.

Computers on Campus 880 computers available on campus for general student use. A campuswide network can be accessed from student residence rooms and from off campus. Internet access, online (class) registration, at least one staffed computer lab available. Computer purchase or lease plan available.

Student Life *Housing:* on-campus residence required for freshman year. *Options:* men-only, women-only. Campus housing is university owned. Freshman campus housing is guaranteed. *Activities and organizations:* drama/theater group, student-run newspaper, radio station, choral group, marching band, marching band, Circle K, finance club, Notre Dame/St. Mary's Right to Life. *Campus security:* 24-hour emergency response devices and patrols, student patrols, late-night transport/escort service, controlled dormitory access, crime prevention and personal safety workshops, full time trained police investigators, sprinkler fire suppression in all residence hal. *Student services:* health clinic, personal/psychological counseling, women's center, legal services.

Athletics Member NCAA. All Division I except football (Division I-A). *Intercollegiate sports:* baseball M(s), basketball M(s)/W(s), crew W(s), cross-country running M(s)/W(s), fencing M(s)/W(s), golf M(s)/W(s), ice hockey M(s), lacrosse M(s)/W(s), soccer M(s)/W(s), softball W(s), swimming M(s)/W(s), tennis M(s)/W(s), track and field M(s)/W(s), volleyball W(s). *Intramural sports:* badminton M/W, baseball M, basketball M/W, bowling M(c)/W(c), crew M(c), cross-country running M/W, equestrian sports M(c)/W(c), field hockey M(c)/W(c), football M/W, golf M/W, gymnastics M(c)/W(c), ice hockey M/W, lacrosse M/W, racquetball M/W, sailing M(c)/W(c), skiing (cross-country) M(c)/W(c), skiing (downhill) M(c)/W(c), soccer M/W, softball M/W, squash M/W, table tennis M/W, tennis M/W, ultimate Frisbee M(c)/W(c), volleyball M(c)/W(c), water polo M(c)/W(c).

Standardized Tests *Required:* SAT I or ACT (for admission).

Costs (2003–04) *Comprehensive fee:* $34,542 includes full-time tuition ($27,170), mandatory fees ($442), and room and board ($6930). Part-time tuition: $1132 per credit. *Room and board:* Room and board charges vary according to board plan and housing facility. *Payment plan:* installment. *Waivers:* employees or children of employees.

Financial Aid Of all full-time matriculated undergraduates who enrolled in 2003, 4,674 applied for aid, 3,947 were judged to have need, 3,933 had their need fully met. 1,742 Federal Work-Study jobs (averaging $1738). 3,086 state and other part-time jobs (averaging $2256). In 2003, 211 non-need-based awards were made. *Average percent of need met:* 100%. *Average financial aid package:* $23,412. *Average need-based loan:* $5101. *Average need-based gift aid:* $17,160. *Average non-need-based aid:* $7963. *Average indebtedness upon graduation:* $25,653. *Financial aid deadline:* 2/15.

University of Notre Dame (continued)

Applying *Options:* electronic application, early action, deferred entrance. *Application fee:* $50. *Required:* essay or personal statement, high school transcript, 1 letter of recommendation. *Application deadlines:* 1/9 (freshmen), 4/15 (transfers). *Notification:* 4/1 (freshmen), 12/15 (early action), 7/15 (transfers).

Admissions Contact Mr. Daniel J. Saracino, Assistant Provost for Admissions, University of Notre Dame, 220 Main Building, Notre Dame, IN 46556-5612. *Phone:* 574-631-7505. *Fax:* 574-631-8865. *E-mail:* admissio.1@nd.edu.

UNIVERSITY OF PHOENIX–INDIANAPOLIS CAMPUS

Indianapolis, Indiana

Admissions Contact 7999 Knue Road Drive, Suite 150, Indianapolis, IN 46250.

UNIVERSITY OF SAINT FRANCIS

Fort Wayne, Indiana

- **Independent Roman Catholic** comprehensive, founded 1890
- **Calendar** semesters
- **Degrees** certificates, associate, bachelor's, master's, and postbachelor's certificates
- **Suburban** 73-acre campus
- **Endowment** $2.4 million
- **Coed,** 1,608 undergraduate students, 76% full-time, 71% women, 29% men
- **Moderately difficult** entrance level, 73% of applicants were admitted

Undergraduates 1,229 full-time, 379 part-time. Students come from 8 states and territories, 9% are from out of state, 6% African American, 0.4% Asian American or Pacific Islander, 2% Hispanic American, 0.4% Native American, 0.2% international, 12% transferred in, 25% live on campus. *Retention:* 67% of 2002 full-time freshmen returned.

Freshmen *Admission:* 931 applied, 684 admitted, 348 enrolled. *Average high school GPA:* 3.09. *Test scores:* SAT verbal scores over 500: 38%; SAT math scores over 500: 44%; ACT scores over 18: 78%; SAT verbal scores over 600: 9%; SAT math scores over 600: 7%; ACT scores over 24: 15%.

Faculty *Total:* 211, 44% full-time, 26% with terminal degrees. *Student/faculty ratio:* 11:1.

Majors Accounting; art; art teacher education; biological and physical sciences; biology/biological sciences; biology teacher education; business administration and management; business teacher education; chemistry; chemistry teacher education; clinical laboratory science/medical technology; commercial and advertising art; communication/speech communication and rhetoric; design and applied arts related; economics; education; elementary education; emergency medical technology (EMT paramedic); English; English/language arts teacher education; environmental studies; finance; fine arts related; health professions related; health science; health teacher education; history; human resources management; human services; international business/trade/commerce; liberal arts and sciences/liberal studies; marketing/marketing management; mass communication/media; medical radiologic technology; nursing (registered nurse training); nursing related; occupational therapist assistant; physical therapist assistant; physician assistant; pre-dentistry studies; pre-law studies; pre-medical studies; pre-pharmacy studies; pre-veterinary studies; psychology; public administration and social service professions related; religious studies; science teacher education; secondary education; social studies teacher education; social work; special education; surgical technology; theological and ministerial studies related.

Academic Programs *Special study options:* academic remediation for entering students, adult/continuing education programs, advanced placement credit, cooperative education, distance learning, double majors, freshman honors college, honors programs, independent study, internships, part-time degree program, services for LD students, study abroad, summer session for credit.

Library University Library plus 1 other with 47,877 titles, 449 serial subscriptions, an OPAC, a Web page.

Computers on Campus 135 computers available on campus for general student use. A campuswide network can be accessed. Internet access, online (class) registration, at least one staffed computer lab available.

Student Life *Housing:* on-campus residence required through sophomore year. *Options:* coed. Campus housing is university owned. *Activities and organizations:* drama/theater group, student-run newspaper, Student Activities Council, art club, Student Government Organization, Student Nursing Association, Residence Hall Council. *Campus security:* 24-hour emergency response devices and patrols, late-night transport/escort service, controlled dormitory access. *Student services:* personal/psychological counseling.

Athletics Member NAIA. *Intercollegiate sports:* baseball M(s), basketball M(s)/W(s), cheerleading M(s)/W(s), cross-country running M(s)/W(s), football M(s), golf M(s), soccer M(s)/W(s), softball W(s), tennis W(s), track and field M(s)/W(s), volleyball W(s). *Intramural sports:* basketball M/W, soccer M/W, volleyball M/W.

Standardized Tests *Recommended:* SAT I or ACT (for admission).

Costs (2003–04) *Comprehensive fee:* $20,964 includes full-time tuition ($14,900), mandatory fees ($614), and room and board ($5450). Full-time tuition and fees vary according to course load. Part-time tuition: $470 per semester hour. Part-time tuition and fees vary according to course load. *Room and board:* Room and board charges vary according to housing facility. *Payment plans:* installment, deferred payment. *Waivers:* children of alumni, senior citizens, and employees or children of employees.

Financial Aid Of all full-time matriculated undergraduates who enrolled in 2003, 1,151 applied for aid, 1,012 were judged to have need, 316 had their need fully met. 827 Federal Work-Study jobs (averaging $1531). In 2003, 143 non-need-based awards were made. *Average percent of need met:* 79%. *Average financial aid package:* $12,668. *Average need-based loan:* $3101. *Average need-based gift aid:* $9101. *Average non-need-based aid:* $8913. *Average indebtedness upon graduation:* $13,046. *Financial aid deadline:* 6/30.

Applying *Options:* electronic application, deferred entrance. *Application fee:* $20. *Required:* high school transcript, minimum 2.0 GPA. *Required for some:* letters of recommendation, interview. *Recommended:* essay or personal statement. *Application deadline:* rolling (freshmen), rolling (transfers). *Notification:* continuous until 8/15 (freshmen), continuous until 8/15 (transfers).

Admissions Contact Mr. Ron Schumacher, Vice President for Enrollment Management, University of Saint Francis, 2701 Spring Street, Fort Wayne, IN 46808. *Phone:* 260-434-3279. *Toll-free phone:* 800-729-4732. *E-mail:* admiss@sfc.edu.

UNIVERSITY OF SOUTHERN INDIANA

Evansville, Indiana

- **State-supported** comprehensive, founded 1965, part of Indiana Commission for Higher Education
- **Calendar** semesters
- **Degrees** certificates, associate, bachelor's, master's, and postbachelor's certificates
- **Suburban** 330-acre campus
- **Coed,** 9,154 undergraduate students, 80% full-time, 60% women, 40% men
- **Noncompetitive** entrance level, 93% of applicants were admitted

Undergraduates 7,292 full-time, 1,862 part-time. Students come from 28 states and territories, 34 other countries, 10% are from out of state, 4% African American, 0.6% Asian American or Pacific Islander, 0.6% Hispanic American, 0.3% Native American, 0.6% international, 7% transferred in, 32% live on campus. *Retention:* 62% of 2002 full-time freshmen returned.

Freshmen *Admission:* 4,368 applied, 4,048 admitted, 2,079 enrolled. *Average high school GPA:* 2.90. *Test scores:* SAT verbal scores over 500: 40%; SAT math scores over 500: 37%; ACT scores over 18: 74%; SAT verbal scores over 600: 10%; SAT math scores over 600: 8%; ACT scores over 24: 19%; SAT verbal scores over 700: 1%; ACT scores over 30: 1%.

Faculty *Total:* 573, 52% full-time, 40% with terminal degrees. *Student/faculty ratio:* 18:1.

Majors Accounting; advertising; art; biological and physical sciences; biology/biological sciences; biophysics; business administration and management; business/commerce; business, management, and marketing related; business teacher education; chemistry; communication/speech communication and rhetoric; computer and information sciences; data processing and data processing technology; dental assisting; dental hygiene; dramatic/theatre arts; e-commerce; economics; education; elementary education; engineering; engineering technologies related; English; entrepreneurship; finance; French; geology/earth science; German; health professions related; history; international relations and affairs; journalism; kinesiology and exercise science; liberal arts and sciences/liberal studies; management information systems and services related; marketing/marketing management; mathematics; medical radiologic technology; nursing (registered nurse training); occupational therapist assistant; occupational therapy; office management; philosophy; physical education teaching and coaching; political science and government; psychology; public relations/image management; radio and television; respiratory care therapy; social sciences; social work; sociology; Spanish; special education related.

Academic Programs *Special study options:* academic remediation for entering students, adult/continuing education programs, advanced placement credit, cooperative education, distance learning, double majors, English as a second language, honors programs, independent study, internships, part-time degree program, services for LD students, study abroad, summer session for credit. *ROTC:* Army (b).

Library David L. Rice Library plus 1 other with 234,406 titles, 3,035 serial subscriptions, 7,924 audiovisual materials, an OPAC, a Web page.

Computers on Campus 778 computers available on campus for general student use. A campuswide network can be accessed from student residence rooms and from off campus. Internet access, online (class) registration, at least one staffed computer lab available.

Student Life *Housing options:* coed. Campus housing is university owned. *Activities and organizations:* drama/theater group, student-run newspaper, radio station, choral group, student government, national fraternities, national sororities. *Campus security:* 24-hour emergency response devices and patrols, student patrols, late-night transport/escort service, controlled dormitory access. *Student services:* health clinic, personal/psychological counseling.

Athletics Member NCAA. All Division II. *Intercollegiate sports:* baseball M(s), basketball M(s)/W(s), cheerleading M/W, cross-country running M(s)/W(s), golf M(s)/W(s), ice hockey M(c), rugby M(c), soccer M(s)/W(s), softball W(s), tennis M(s)/W(s), ultimate Frisbee M(c)/W(c), volleyball W(s). *Intramural sports:* badminton M/W, basketball M/W, bowling M/W, cross-country running M/W, football M/W, golf M/W, rock climbing M/W, skiing (downhill) M/W, soccer M, softball M/W, table tennis M/W, tennis M/W, volleyball M/W.

Standardized Tests *Required:* SAT I or ACT (for admission).

Costs (2003–04) *Tuition:* state resident $3825 full-time, $128 per semester hour part-time; nonresident $9128 full-time, $304 per semester hour part-time. Full-time tuition and fees vary according to course load and reciprocity agreements. Part-time tuition and fees vary according to course load and reciprocity agreements. *Required fees:* $60 full-time, $23 per term part-time. *Room and board:* $5140; room only: $2740. Room and board charges vary according to board plan and housing facility. *Payment plan:* installment. *Waivers:* senior citizens and employees or children of employees.

Financial Aid Of all full-time matriculated undergraduates who enrolled in 2003, 5,738 applied for aid, 4,405 were judged to have need, 611 had their need fully met. 178 Federal Work-Study jobs (averaging $1638). In 2003, 503 non-need-based awards were made. *Average percent of need met:* 59%. *Average financial aid package:* $5134. *Average need-based loan:* $3102. *Average need-based gift aid:* $4060. *Average non-need-based aid:* $2068. *Average indebtedness upon graduation:* $13,487. *Financial aid deadline:* 3/1.

Applying *Options:* common application, electronic application. *Application fee:* $25. *Required:* high school transcript. *Required for some:* interview. *Recommended:* essay or personal statement, minimum 2.0 GPA. *Application deadline:* 8/15 (freshmen). *Notification:* continuous until 8/27 (freshmen), continuous (transfers).

Admissions Contact Mr. Eric Otto, Director of Admission, University of Southern Indiana, 8600 University Boulevard, Evansville, IN 47712-3590. *Phone:* 812-464-1765. *Toll-free phone:* 800-467-1965. *Fax:* 812-465-7154. *E-mail:* enroll@usi.edu.

VALPARAISO UNIVERSITY
Valparaiso, Indiana

- **Independent** comprehensive, founded 1859, affiliated with Lutheran Church
- **Calendar** semesters
- **Degrees** certificates, associate, bachelor's, master's, first professional, post-master's, and postbachelor's certificates
- **Small-town** 310-acre campus with easy access to Chicago
- **Endowment** $115.3 million
- **Coed,** 3,026 undergraduate students, 94% full-time, 53% women, 47% men
- **Moderately difficult** entrance level, 82% of applicants were admitted

Undergraduates 2,848 full-time, 178 part-time. Students come from 47 states and territories, 41 other countries, 67% are from out of state, 3% African American, 2% Asian American or Pacific Islander, 3% Hispanic American, 0.2% Native American, 2% international, 3% transferred in, 64% live on campus. *Retention:* 86% of 2002 full-time freshmen returned.

Freshmen *Admission:* 3,576 applied, 2,929 admitted, 795 enrolled. *Test scores:* SAT verbal scores over 500: 84%; SAT math scores over 500: 83%; ACT scores over 18: 99%; SAT verbal scores over 600: 41%; SAT math scores over 600: 45%; ACT scores over 24: 71%; SAT verbal scores over 700: 10%; SAT math scores over 700: 12%; ACT scores over 30: 18%.

Faculty *Total:* 344, 67% full-time, 75% with terminal degrees. *Student/faculty ratio:* 13:1.

Majors Accounting; actuarial science; American studies; art; art history, criticism and conservation; art teacher education; Asian studies (East); astronomy; athletic training; atmospheric sciences and meteorology; biochemistry; biological and physical sciences; biology/biological sciences; biology teacher education; chemistry; chemistry teacher education; civil engineering; classics and languages, literatures and linguistics; communication and journalism related; communication/speech communication and rhetoric; computer engineering; computer science; criminology; drama and dance teacher education; dramatic/theatre arts; economics; economics related; electrical, electronics and communications engineering; elementary education; English; English/language arts teacher education; environmental science; finance; fine/studio arts; foreign language teacher education; French; French language teacher education; geography; geography teacher education; geology/earth science; German; German language teacher education; health and physical education; history; history teacher education; humanities; international business/trade/commerce; international economics; international relations and affairs; journalism; kinesiology and exercise science; management science; management sciences and quantitative methods related; marketing/marketing management; mass communication/media; mathematics; mathematics teacher education; mechanical engineering; middle school education; multi-/interdisciplinary studies related; music; music management and merchandising; music performance; music teacher education; music theory and composition; nursing (registered nurse training); organizational communication; philosophy; physical education teaching and coaching; physics; physics teacher education; piano and organ; political science and government; psychology; psychology teacher education; public relations/image management; radio and television; religious/sacred music; science teacher education; secondary education; social sciences; social science teacher education; social work; sociology; Spanish; Spanish language teacher education; sport and fitness administration; theology; voice and opera.

Academic Programs *Special study options:* accelerated degree program, adult/continuing education programs, advanced placement credit, cooperative education, distance learning, double majors, English as a second language, freshman honors college, honors programs, independent study, internships, off-campus study, part-time degree program, student-designed majors, study abroad, summer session for credit. *ROTC:* Air Force (b).

Library Moellering Library plus 1 other with 521,907 titles, 5,282 serial subscriptions, 13,413 audiovisual materials, an OPAC, a Web page.

Computers on Campus 585 computers available on campus for general student use. A campuswide network can be accessed from student residence rooms and from off campus. Internet access, at least one staffed computer lab available.

Student Life *Housing:* on-campus residence required through junior year. *Options:* coed, women-only. Campus housing is university owned. Freshman campus housing is guaranteed. *Activities and organizations:* drama/theater group, student-run newspaper, radio station, choral group, Union Board, student government, student volunteer organization, chapel programs, national fraternities. *Campus security:* 24-hour emergency response devices and patrols, late-night transport/escort service, controlled dormitory access. *Student services:* health clinic, personal/psychological counseling, legal services.

Athletics Member NCAA. All Division I. *Intercollegiate sports:* baseball M(s), basketball M(s)/W(s), cheerleading M(c)/W(c), cross-country running M(s)/W(s), football M, soccer M(s)/W(s), softball W(s), swimming M(s)/W(s), tennis M(s)/W(s), volleyball W(s). *Intramural sports:* badminton M/W, baseball M, basketball M/W, bowling M/W, football M/W, golf M/W, ice hockey M, racquetball M/W, soccer M/W, softball M/W, swimming M/W, table tennis M/W, tennis M/W, track and field M/W, ultimate Frisbee M/W, volleyball M/W, water polo M.

Standardized Tests *Required:* SAT I or ACT (for admission).

Costs (2003–04) *Comprehensive fee:* $26,112 includes full-time tuition ($20,000), mandatory fees ($632), and room and board ($5480). Part-time tuition: $860 per credit hour. Part-time tuition and fees vary according to course load. *Required fees:* $50 per term part-time. *College room only:* $3480. Room and board charges vary according to housing facility and student level. *Payment plans:* installment, deferred payment. *Waivers:* employees or children of employees.

Financial Aid Of all full-time matriculated undergraduates who enrolled in 2003, 2,265 applied for aid, 1,933 were judged to have need, 995 had their need fully met. 390 Federal Work-Study jobs (averaging $872). 730 state and other part-time jobs (averaging $1027). In 2003, 692 non-need-based awards were made. *Average percent of need met:* 92%. *Average financial aid package:* $17,404. *Average need-based loan:* $5345. *Average need-based gift aid:* $17,310. *Average non-need-based aid:* $7593. *Average indebtedness upon graduation:* $20,270.

Applying *Options:* common application, electronic application, early action, deferred entrance. *Application fee:* $30. *Required:* essay or personal statement, high school transcript. *Required for some:* interview. *Recommended:* 2 letters of recommendation. *Application deadline:* 8/15 (freshmen). *Notification:* 12/1 (early action), continuous (transfers).

Admissions Contact Ms. Joyce Lantz, Director of Admissions, Valparaiso University, Kretzmann Hall, 1700 Chapel Drive, Valparaiso, IN 46383-6493. *Phone:* 219-464-5011. *Toll-free phone:* 888-GO-VALPO. *Fax:* 219-464-6898. *E-mail:* undergrad.admissions@valpo.edu.

■ *See page 2750 for a narrative description.*

Wabash College
Crawfordsville, Indiana

- **Independent** 4-year, founded 1832
- **Calendar** semesters
- **Degree** bachelor's
- **Small-town** 50-acre campus with easy access to Indianapolis
- **Endowment** $266.6 million
- **Men only,** 863 undergraduate students, 100% full-time
- **Moderately difficult** entrance level, 50% of applicants were admitted

Undergraduates 859 full-time, 4 part-time. Students come from 34 states and territories, 14 other countries, 27% are from out of state, 8% African American, 3% Asian American or Pacific Islander, 5% Hispanic American, 0.2% Native American, 4% international, 0.8% transferred in, 99% live on campus. *Retention:* 87% of 2002 full-time freshmen returned.

Freshmen *Admission:* 239 enrolled. *Average high school GPA:* 3.61. *Test scores:* SAT verbal scores over 500: 83%; SAT math scores over 500: 88%; SAT verbal scores over 600: 39%; SAT math scores over 600: 56%; SAT verbal scores over 700: 9%; SAT math scores over 700: 14%.

Faculty *Total:* 88, 98% full-time, 92% with terminal degrees. *Student/faculty ratio:* 10:1.

Majors Art; biology/biological sciences; chemistry; classics and languages, literatures and linguistics; dramatic/theatre arts; economics; English; French; German; history; Latin; mathematics; modern Greek; music; philosophy; physics; political science and government; pre-law studies; pre-medical studies; pre-veterinary studies; psychology; religious studies; Spanish; speech and rhetoric.

Academic Programs *Special study options:* accelerated degree program, advanced placement credit, cooperative education, double majors, independent study, internships, off-campus study, services for LD students, study abroad. *ROTC:* Army (c). *Unusual degree programs:* 3-2 engineering with Columbia University, Washington University in St. Louis.

Library Lilly Library with 420,906 titles, 1,634 serial subscriptions, 10,557 audiovisual materials, an OPAC, a Web page.

Computers on Campus 160 computers available on campus for general student use. A campuswide network can be accessed from student residence rooms and from off campus. Internet access, at least one staffed computer lab available. Computer purchase or lease plan available.

Student Life *Housing:* on-campus residence required through sophomore year. *Options:* men-only. Campus housing is university owned and is provided by a third party. Freshman campus housing is guaranteed. *Activities and organizations:* drama/theater group, student-run newspaper, radio station, choral group, Sphinx Club, Alpha Phi Omega, The Bachelor, Malcolm X Institute, Christian Fellowship, national fraternities. *Campus security:* 24-hour emergency response devices and patrols, late-night transport/escort service. *Student services:* health clinic, personal/psychological counseling.

Athletics Member NCAA. All Division III. *Intercollegiate sports:* baseball M, basketball M, crew M(c), cross-country running M, football M, golf M, lacrosse M(c), rugby M(c), sailing M(c), soccer M, swimming M, tennis M, track and field M, water polo M(c), wrestling M. *Intramural sports:* badminton M, basketball M, bowling M, cheerleading M/W, cross-country running M, football M, golf M, racquetball M, soccer M, softball M, swimming M, table tennis M, tennis M, track and field M, ultimate Frisbee M/W, volleyball M, weight lifting M, wrestling M.

Standardized Tests *Required:* SAT I or ACT (for admission).

Costs (2004–05) *Comprehensive fee:* $29,328 includes full-time tuition ($21,870), mandatory fees ($405), and room and board ($7053). Part-time tuition: $3472 per course. Part-time tuition and fees vary according to course load. *College room only:* $2609. Room and board charges vary according to board plan and housing facility. *Payment plans:* tuition prepayment, installment. *Waivers:* employees or children of employees.

Financial Aid Of all full-time matriculated undergraduates who enrolled in 2003, 680 applied for aid, 605 were judged to have need, 605 had their need fully met. 654 state and other part-time jobs (averaging $2230). In 2003, 215 non-need-based awards were made. *Average percent of need met:* 100%. *Average financial aid package:* $19,944. *Average need-based loan:* $2564. *Average need-based gift aid:* $14,921. *Average non-need-based aid:* $11,261. *Average indebtedness upon graduation:* $17,818. *Financial aid deadline:* 3/1.

Applying *Options:* common application, electronic application, early admission, early decision, early action, deferred entrance. *Application fee:* $30. *Required:* essay or personal statement, high school transcript, minimum 2.0 GPA, 1 letter of recommendation. *Recommended:* minimum 3.0 GPA, interview. *Application deadlines:* 3/15 (freshmen), 3/15 (transfers). *Early decision:* 11/15. *Notification:* continuous until 4/1 (freshmen), 12/15 (early decision), 1/15 (early action), continuous until 4/1 (transfers).

Admissions Contact Mr. Steve Klein, Director of Admissions, Wabash College, PO Box 362, Crawfordsville, IN 47933-0352. *Phone:* 765-361-6225. *Toll-free phone:* 800-345-5385. *Fax:* 765-361-6437. *E-mail:* admissions@wabash.edu.

■ *See page 2774 for a narrative description.*

IOWA

Allen College
Waterloo, Iowa

- **Independent** comprehensive, founded 1989
- **Calendar** semesters
- **Degrees** associate, bachelor's, and master's (liberal arts and general education courses are taken at either University of North Iowa or Wartburg College)
- **Suburban** 20-acre campus
- **Endowment** $949,250
- **Coed, primarily women,** 276 undergraduate students, 84% full-time, 93% women, 7% men
- **Moderately difficult** entrance level, 67% of applicants were admitted

Undergraduates 233 full-time, 43 part-time. Students come from 1 other state, 1% are from out of state, 1% African American, 1% Asian American or Pacific Islander, 1% Hispanic American, 0.4% Native American, 24% transferred in, 14% live on campus. *Retention:* 77% of 2002 full-time freshmen returned.

Freshmen *Admission:* 67 applied, 45 admitted, 33 enrolled. *Average high school GPA:* 3.45. *Test scores:* ACT scores over 18: 92%; ACT scores over 24: 22%.

Faculty *Total:* 24, 67% full-time, 8% with terminal degrees. *Student/faculty ratio:* 19:1.

Majors Nursing (registered nurse training); radiologic technology/science.

Academic Programs *Special study options:* advanced placement credit, distance learning, independent study, internships, off-campus study, part-time degree program. *ROTC:* Army (c).

Library Barrett Library with 2,797 titles, 184 serial subscriptions, 421 audiovisual materials, a Web page.

Computers on Campus 27 computers available on campus for general student use. Internet access, at least one staffed computer lab available.

Student Life *Housing options:* coed, men-only, women-only. Campus housing is provided by a third party. *Activities and organizations:* student-run newspaper, Allen Student Nurses' Association, Nurses' Christian Fellowship, Allen Student Organization. *Campus security:* 24-hour patrols. *Student services:* health clinic, personal/psychological counseling, women's center.

Standardized Tests *Required:* SAT I and SAT II or ACT (for admission).

Costs (2003–04) *One-time required fee:* $300. *Comprehensive fee:* $15,468 includes full-time tuition ($9324), mandatory fees ($1214), and room and board ($4930). Full-time tuition and fees vary according to course load, location, program, and student level. Part-time tuition: $356 per credit hour. Part-time tuition and fees vary according to program. *Required fees:* $25 per credit hour part-time, $185 per term part-time. *College room only:* $2465. Room and board charges vary according to board plan and housing facility. *Payment plan:* installment.

Financial Aid Of all full-time matriculated undergraduates who enrolled in 2003, 214 applied for aid, 173 were judged to have need, 24 had their need fully met. 17 Federal Work-Study jobs (averaging $2000). In 2003, 29 non-need-based awards were made. *Average percent of need met:* 65%. *Average financial aid package:* $7580. *Average need-based loan:* $3491. *Average need-based gift aid:* $4528. *Average non-need-based aid:* $1153. *Average indebtedness upon graduation:* $16,494.

Applying *Options:* electronic application. *Application fee:* $50. *Required:* essay or personal statement, high school transcript, 1 letter of recommendation. *Required for some:* interview. *Recommended:* minimum 2.3 GPA. *Application deadlines:* 8/1 (freshmen), 8/1 (transfers). *Notification:* continuous until 8/20 (freshmen), continuous until 8/20 (transfers).

Admissions Contact Ms. Lois Hagedorn, Student services Assistant, Allen College, Barrett Forum, 1825 Logan Avenue, Waterloo, IA 50703. *Phone:* 319-226-2000. *Fax:* 319-226-2051. *E-mail:* hagedole@ihs.org.

Briar Cliff University
Sioux City, Iowa

- **Independent Roman Catholic** comprehensive, founded 1930
- **Calendar** (3 10-week terms plus 2 5-week summer sessions)
- **Degrees** associate, bachelor's, and master's

■ **Suburban** 70-acre campus
■ **Endowment** $7.0 million
■ **Coed,** 1,063 undergraduate students, 83% full-time, 60% women, 40% men
■ **Moderately difficult** entrance level, 80% of applicants were admitted

At Briar Cliff University, learning is about a high-quality education. It's about a values-based Franciscan experience that changes a student's life. It's about getting involved and making a difference . . . exploring new ideas and discovering different perspectives. It's about a student's classroom learning connecting with life's work and becoming the person he or she wants to be. It all happens at this Catholic Franciscan learning place.

Undergraduates 884 full-time, 179 part-time. Students come from 25 states and territories, 1 other country, 32% are from out of state, 2% African American, 1% Asian American or Pacific Islander, 4% Hispanic American, 2% Native American, 0.1% international, 11% transferred in, 42% live on campus. *Retention:* 73% of 2002 full-time freshmen returned.

Freshmen *Admission:* 1,297 applied, 1,040 admitted, 258 enrolled. *Average high school GPA:* 3.20. *Test scores:* SAT verbal scores over 500: 50%; SAT math scores over 500: 50%; ACT scores over 18: 91%; SAT verbal scores over 600: 50%; SAT math scores over 600: 50%; ACT scores over 24: 22%; ACT scores over 30: 2%.

Faculty *Total:* 53, 89% full-time, 57% with terminal degrees. *Student/faculty ratio:* 12:1.

Majors Accounting; art; art teacher education; biology/biological sciences; business administration and management; chemistry; clinical laboratory science/medical technology; commercial and advertising art; computer and information systems security; computer science; creative writing; criminal justice/law enforcement administration; dramatic/theatre arts; education; education (K-12); elementary education; engineering; English; environmental studies; health and physical education related; health teacher education; history; human resources management; industrial radiologic technology; interdisciplinary studies; liberal arts and sciences/liberal studies; management information systems; mass communication/media; mathematics; music; nursing (registered nurse training); pharmacy; philosophy; physical education teaching and coaching; physical therapy; political science and government; pre-dentistry studies; pre-engineering; pre-law studies; pre-medical studies; pre-pharmacy studies; pre-veterinary studies; professional studies; psychology; secondary education; social work; sociology; Spanish; speech/theater education; theology.

Academic Programs *Special study options:* academic remediation for entering students, accelerated degree program, adult/continuing education programs, advanced placement credit, distance learning, double majors, English as a second language, independent study, internships, off-campus study, part-time degree program, services for LD students, student-designed majors, summer session for credit.

Library Mueller Library with 83,737 titles, 6,366 serial subscriptions, 9,791 audiovisual materials, an OPAC, a Web page.

Computers on Campus 114 computers available on campus for general student use. A campuswide network can be accessed from student residence rooms and from off campus. Internet access, at least one staffed computer lab available.

Student Life *Housing:* on-campus residence required through junior year. *Options:* coed. Campus housing is university owned. Freshman campus housing is guaranteed. *Activities and organizations:* drama/theater group, student-run newspaper, radio station, choral group, Student Government Association, ethnic relations club, Residence Hall Association, Vision: Campus Programming Board, peer advising leaders. *Campus security:* 24-hour emergency response devices and patrols, student patrols, late-night transport/escort service, controlled dormitory access. *Student services:* health clinic, personal/psychological counseling.

Athletics Member NAIA. *Intercollegiate sports:* baseball M(s), basketball M(s)/W(s), cross-country running M(s)/W(s), football M(s), golf M(s)/W(s), soccer M(s)/W(s), softball W(s), track and field M(s)/W(s), volleyball W(s), wrestling M(s). *Intramural sports:* basketball M/W, bowling M/W, cross-country running M/W, football M, golf M/W, racquetball M/W, skiing (cross-country) M/W, soccer M/W, softball W, table tennis M/W, tennis M/W, volleyball M/W, weight lifting M/W.

Standardized Tests *Required:* SAT I or ACT (for admission).

Costs (2003–04) *Comprehensive fee:* $21,660 includes full-time tuition ($15,960), mandatory fees ($390), and room and board ($5310). Part-time tuition: $532 per hour. Part-time tuition and fees vary according to class time and course load. *Required fees:* $13 per credit hour part-time. *College room only:* $2655. Room and board charges vary according to board plan and housing facility. *Payment plan:* deferred payment. *Waivers:* adult students, senior citizens, and employees or children of employees.

Financial Aid Of all full-time matriculated undergraduates who enrolled in 2002, 688 applied for aid, 527 were judged to have need, 511 had their need fully met. In 2002, 678 non-need-based awards were made. *Average percent of need met:* 91%. *Average financial aid package:* $15,950. *Average need-based loan:* $4775. *Average need-based gift aid:* $4625. *Average non-need-based aid:* $2675. *Average indebtedness upon graduation:* $18,900. *Financial aid deadline:* 3/15.

Applying *Options:* common application, electronic application, early admission, deferred entrance. *Application fee:* $20. *Required:* high school transcript, minimum 2.0 GPA, minimum ACT score of 18. *Required for some:* 3 letters of recommendation, interview. *Recommended:* essay or personal statement. *Application deadline:* rolling (freshmen), rolling (transfers). *Notification:* continuous (transfers).

Admissions Contact Ms. Tammy Namminga, Applications Specialist, Briar Cliff University, 3303 Rebecca Street, Sioux City, IA 51104. *Phone:* 712-279-5200 Ext. 5460. *Toll-free phone:* 800-662-3303 Ext. 5200. *Fax:* 712-279-1632. *E-mail:* admissions@briarcliff.edu.

BUENA VISTA UNIVERSITY
Storm Lake, Iowa

■ **Independent** comprehensive, founded 1891, affiliated with Presbyterian Church (U.S.A.)
■ **Calendar** 4-1-4
■ **Degrees** bachelor's and master's
■ **Small-town** 60-acre campus
■ **Endowment** $91.2 million
■ **Coed,** 1,288 undergraduate students, 98% full-time, 53% women, 47% men
■ **Moderately difficult** entrance level, 84% of applicants were admitted

Undergraduates 1,257 full-time, 31 part-time. Students come from 17 states and territories, 4 other countries, 18% are from out of state, 1% African American, 1% Asian American or Pacific Islander, 2% Hispanic American, 0.4% Native American, 0.3% international, 5% transferred in, 87% live on campus. *Retention:* 75% of 2002 full-time freshmen returned.

Freshmen *Admission:* 1,333 applied, 1,125 admitted, 378 enrolled. *Average high school GPA:* 3.34. *Test scores:* ACT scores over 18: 92%; ACT scores over 24: 37%; ACT scores over 30: 3%.

Faculty *Total:* 114, 71% full-time, 55% with terminal degrees. *Student/faculty ratio:* 15:1.

Majors Accounting; art; arts management; art teacher education; athletic training; banking and financial support services; biological and physical sciences; biology/biological sciences; biology teacher education; business/managerial economics; business teacher education; chemistry; chemistry teacher education; commercial and advertising art; communication/speech communication and rhetoric; computer science; computer teacher education; criminal justice/safety; elementary education; English; English/language arts teacher education; entrepreneurship; history; history teacher education; international business/trade/commerce; management information systems; management information systems and services related; marketing/marketing management; mass communication/media; mathematics; mathematics teacher education; modern languages; multi-/interdisciplinary studies related; music performance; music teacher education; organizational communication; philosophy and religious studies related; physical education teaching and coaching; physics; physics teacher education; political science and government; political science and government related; psychology; psychology related; public administration; public relations, advertising, and applied communication related; science teacher education; secondary education; social sciences; social science teacher education; social work; sociology; Spanish; Spanish language teacher education; special education; speech teacher education; sport and fitness administration; theatre literature, history and criticism.

Academic Programs *Special study options:* academic remediation for entering students, adult/continuing education programs, advanced placement credit, distance learning, double majors, English as a second language, freshman honors college, honors programs, independent study, internships, off-campus study, part-time degree program, services for LD students, student-designed majors, study abroad, summer session for credit. *Unusual degree programs:* 3-2 engineering with Washington University in St. Louis.

Library BVU Library with 153,084 titles, 698 serial subscriptions, 4,158 audiovisual materials, an OPAC, a Web page.

Computers on Campus 400 computers available on campus for general student use. A campuswide network can be accessed from student residence rooms and from off campus. Internet access, online (class) registration, at least one staffed computer lab available.

Student Life *Housing:* on-campus residence required through senior year. *Options:* coed. Campus housing is university owned. *Activities and organizations:* drama/theater group, student-run newspaper, radio and television station, choral group, Student Activities Board, student orientation staff, Esprit De Corps, Student Senate, Marketing Association. *Campus security:* 24-hour emergency response devices, late-night transport/escort service, controlled dormitory access, night security patrols. *Student services:* health clinic, personal/psychological counseling.

Buena Vista University (continued)

Athletics Member NCAA. All Division III. *Intercollegiate sports:* baseball M, basketball M/W, cross-country running M/W, football M, golf M/W, soccer M/W, softball W, swimming M/W, tennis M/W, track and field M/W, volleyball W, wrestling M. *Intramural sports:* baseball M, basketball M/W, football M/W, racquetball M/W, softball M/W, swimming M/W, tennis M/W, volleyball M/W, weight lifting M/W.

Standardized Tests *Required:* SAT I or ACT (for admission).

Costs (2003–04) *Comprehensive fee:* $25,406 includes full-time tuition ($19,862) and room and board ($5544). Part-time tuition: $668 per semester hour.

Financial Aid Of all full-time matriculated undergraduates who enrolled in 2003, 1,211 applied for aid, 1,153 were judged to have need, 296 had their need fully met. 621 Federal Work-Study jobs (averaging $1104). 158 state and other part-time jobs (averaging $1046). In 2003, 36 non need-based awards were made. *Average percent of need met:* 95%. *Average financial aid package:* $19,049. *Average need-based loan:* $4614. *Average need-based gift aid:* $12,115. *Average non-need-based aid:* $13,033. *Average indebtedness upon graduation:* $22,566.

Applying *Options:* common application, electronic application, early admission, deferred entrance. *Required:* high school transcript, letters of recommendation. *Required for some:* essay or personal statement, interview. *Recommended:* minimum 3.0 GPA. *Notification:* continuous (freshmen), continuous (transfers).

Admissions Contact Ms. Louise Cummings-Simmons, Director of Admissions, Buena Vista University, 610 West Fourth Street, Storm Lake, IA 50588. *Phone:* 712-749-2235. *Toll-free phone:* 800-383-9600. *E-mail:* admissions@bvu.edu.

CENTRAL COLLEGE
Pella, Iowa

- **Independent** 4-year, founded 1853, affiliated with Reformed Church in America
- **Calendar** semesters
- **Degree** bachelor's
- **Small-town** 133-acre campus with easy access to Des Moines
- **Endowment** $49.1 million
- **Coed,** 1,698 undergraduate students, 97% full-time, 57% women, 43% men
- **Moderately difficult** entrance level, 83% of applicants were admitted

Undergraduates 1,652 full-time, 46 part-time. Students come from 33 states and territories, 13 other countries, 19% are from out of state, 0.9% African American, 1% Asian American or Pacific Islander, 2% Hispanic American, 0.3% Native American, 1% international, 4% transferred in, 86% live on campus. *Retention:* 84% of 2002 full-time freshmen returned.

Freshmen *Admission:* 1,865 applied, 1,549 admitted, 417 enrolled. *Average high school GPA:* 3.43. *Test scores:* ACT scores over 18: 97%; ACT scores over 24: 49%; ACT scores over 30: 5%.

Faculty *Total:* 153, 63% full-time, 65% with terminal degrees. *Student/faculty ratio:* 14:1.

Majors Accounting; art; biology/biological sciences; business administration and management; chemistry; communication/speech communication and rhetoric; computer science; dramatic/theatre arts; economics; elementary education; English; environmental studies; European studies (Western); French; general studies; German; history; information science/studies; interdisciplinary studies; international business/trade/commerce; kinesiology and exercise science; Latin American studies; linguistics; mathematics; mathematics and computer science; music; music teacher education; philosophy; physics; political science and government; psychology; religious studies; secondary education; social sciences; sociology; Spanish.

Academic Programs *Special study options:* academic remediation for entering students, double majors, honors programs, independent study, internships, off-campus study, part-time degree program, services for LD students, student-designed majors, study abroad, summer session for credit. *Unusual degree programs:* 3-2 engineering with Washington University in St. Louis, Iowa State University of Science and Technology, The University of Iowa.

Library Geisler Library plus 3 others with 220,526 titles, 1,161 serial subscriptions, 13,160 audiovisual materials, an OPAC, a Web page.

Computers on Campus 256 computers available on campus for general student use. A campuswide network can be accessed from student residence rooms and from off campus that provide access to student academic records and data. Internet access, at least one staffed computer lab available. Computer purchase or lease plan available.

Student Life *Housing:* on-campus residence required through senior year. *Options:* coed, men-only, women-only. Campus housing is university owned. Freshman campus housing is guaranteed. *Activities and organizations:* drama/theater group, student-run newspaper, radio station, choral group, Students Concerned About the Environment, Intervarsity, FCA, Coalition for Multicultural Campus, Student Senate, national fraternities, national sororities. *Campus security:* 24-hour emergency response devices, student patrols, late-night transport/escort service, controlled dormitory access. *Student services:* health clinic, personal/psychological counseling.

Athletics Member NCAA. All Division III. *Intercollegiate sports:* baseball M, basketball M/W, cheerleading W(c), cross-country running M/W, football M, golf M/W, soccer M/W, softball W, tennis M/W, track and field M/W, ultimate Frisbee M(c)/W(c), volleyball W, wrestling M. *Intramural sports:* basketball M/W, football M, racquetball M/W, rock climbing M(c)/W(c), rugby M, soccer M/W, softball M/W, volleyball M/W.

Standardized Tests *Required:* SAT I or ACT (for admission).

Costs (2003–04) *Comprehensive fee:* $23,898 includes full-time tuition ($17,609), mandatory fees ($144), and room and board ($6145). Part-time tuition: $611 per credit hour. Part-time tuition and fees vary according to course load. *College room only:* $3132. Room and board charges vary according to board plan. *Payment plan:* installment. *Waivers:* employees or children of employees.

Financial Aid Of all full-time matriculated undergraduates who enrolled in 2003, 1,409 applied for aid, 1,284 were judged to have need, 206 had their need fully met. 903 Federal Work-Study jobs (averaging $1104). 505 state and other part-time jobs (averaging $1117). In 2003, 278 non-need-based awards were made. *Average percent of need met:* 82%. *Average financial aid package:* $16,020. *Average need-based loan:* $4493. *Average need-based gift aid:* $11,650. *Average non-need-based aid:* $8710. *Average indebtedness upon graduation:* $25,846.

Applying *Options:* common application, electronic application, deferred entrance. *Application fee:* $25. *Required:* high school transcript. *Required for some:* essay or personal statement, 3 letters of recommendation, interview. *Recommended:* minimum 2.0 GPA, interview. *Application deadline:* rolling (freshmen), rolling (transfers). *Notification:* continuous (transfers).

Admissions Contact Mr. John Olsen, Vice President for Admission and Student Enrollment Services, Central College, 812 University Street, Pella, IA 50219-1999. *Phone:* 641-628-7600. *Toll-free phone:* 800-458-5503. *Fax:* 641-628-5316. *E-mail:* admissions@central.edu.

CLARKE COLLEGE
Dubuque, Iowa

- **Independent Roman Catholic** comprehensive, founded 1843
- **Calendar** semesters
- **Degrees** associate, bachelor's, and master's
- **Urban** 55-acre campus
- **Endowment** $11.2 million
- **Coed,** 1,005 undergraduate students, 80% full-time, 70% women, 30% men
- **Moderately difficult** entrance level, 56% of applicants were admitted

Undergraduates 799 full-time, 206 part-time. Students come from 10 states and territories, 10 other countries, 38% are from out of state, 2% African American, 0.3% Asian American or Pacific Islander, 2% Hispanic American, 0.4% Native American, 2% international, 7% transferred in, 65% live on campus. *Retention:* 78% of 2002 full-time freshmen returned.

Freshmen *Admission:* 704 applied, 391 admitted, 171 enrolled. *Average high school GPA:* 3.37. *Test scores:* ACT scores over 18: 93%; ACT scores over 24: 29%; ACT scores over 30: 4%.

Faculty *Total:* 92, 89% full-time, 63% with terminal degrees. *Student/faculty ratio:* 12:1.

Majors Accounting; advertising; art; art history, criticism and conservation; art teacher education; athletic training; biology/biological sciences; business administration and management; chemistry; computer science; dramatic/theatre arts; economics; education; elementary education; English; fine/studio arts; French; history; information science/studies; international business/trade/commerce; kindergarten/preschool education; liberal arts and sciences/liberal studies; management information systems; marketing/marketing management; mass communication/media; mathematics; middle school education; music; music teacher education; nursing science; philosophy; physical education teaching and coaching; physical therapy; psychology; public relations/image management; religious studies; secondary education; social work; sociology; Spanish; special education; voice and opera.

Academic Programs *Special study options:* adult/continuing education programs, advanced placement credit, cooperative education, distance learning, double majors, English as a second language, honors programs, independent study, internships, off-campus study, part-time degree program, student-designed majors, study abroad, summer session for credit.

Library Nicholas J. Schrupp Library with 127,089 titles, 897 serial subscriptions, 1,504 audiovisual materials, an OPAC, a Web page.

Computers on Campus 237 computers available on campus for general student use. A campuswide network can be accessed from student residence rooms and from off campus. Internet access, at least one staffed computer lab available.

Student Life *Housing:* on-campus residence required through junior year. *Options:* coed, men-only, women-only. Campus housing is university owned. Freshman campus housing is guaranteed. *Activities and organizations:* drama/theater group, student-run newspaper, radio station, choral group, Admissions Student Team, Student Multicultural Organization, concert choir, campus ministry, student government. *Campus security:* 24-hour emergency response devices and patrols, late-night transport/escort service, controlled dormitory access. *Student services:* health clinic, personal/psychological counseling.

Athletics Member NCAA. All Division III. *Intercollegiate sports:* baseball M, basketball M/W, cross-country running M/W, golf M/W, soccer M/W, softball W, tennis M/W, volleyball M/W. *Intramural sports:* badminton M/W, basketball M/W, bowling M/W, football M/W, golf M/W, racquetball M/W, skiing (cross-country) M/W, skiing (downhill) M/W, softball M/W, swimming M/W, table tennis M/W, tennis M/W, track and field M/W, volleyball M/W, water polo M/W, weight lifting M/W.

Standardized Tests *Required:* SAT I or ACT (for admission).

Costs (2003–04) *Comprehensive fee:* $23,165 includes full-time tuition ($16,580), mandatory fees ($510), and room and board ($6075). Full-time tuition and fees vary according to class time. Part-time tuition: $422 per credit. Part-time tuition and fees vary according to class time. *College room only:* $2970. Room and board charges vary according to board plan and housing facility. *Payment plans:* installment, deferred payment. *Waivers:* children of alumni, adult students, senior citizens, and employees or children of employees.

Financial Aid Of all full-time matriculated undergraduates who enrolled in 2003, 711 applied for aid, 651 were judged to have need, 154 had their need fully met. 263 Federal Work-Study jobs (averaging $1398). 170 state and other part-time jobs (averaging $1415). In 2003, 110 non-need-based awards were made. *Average percent of need met:* 100%. *Average financial aid package:* $14,654. *Average need-based loan:* $4039. *Average need-based gift aid:* $10,751. *Average non-need-based aid:* $9948. *Average indebtedness upon graduation:* $17,399.

Applying *Options:* common application, electronic application, deferred entrance. *Application fee:* $25. *Required:* high school transcript, minimum 2.0 GPA, rank in upper 50% of high school class, minimum ACT score of 21 or SAT score of 1000. *Required for some:* interview. *Application deadline:* rolling (freshmen), rolling (transfers). *Notification:* continuous until 7/15 (freshmen), continuous until 8/15 (transfers).

Admissions Contact Mr. Omar G. Correa, Executive Director of Admissions and Financial Aid, Clarke College, 1550 Clarke Drive, Dubuque, IA 52001-3198. *Phone:* 563-588-6316. *Toll-free phone:* 800-383-2345. *Fax:* 319-588-6789. *E-mail:* admissions@clarke.edu.

COE COLLEGE
Cedar Rapids, Iowa

- **Independent** comprehensive, founded 1851, affiliated with Presbyterian Church
- **Calendar** 4-4-1
- **Degrees** bachelor's and master's
- **Urban** 53-acre campus
- **Endowment** $56.1 million
- **Coed,** 1,290 undergraduate students, 91% full-time, 56% women, 44% men
- **Moderately difficult** entrance level, 71% of applicants were admitted

Listed among the top 100 liberal arts colleges in America, Coe College is a private, coeducational liberal arts college located in Cedar Rapids, Iowa. Coe offers 41 majors, 65 student clubs, and NCAA Division III Iowa Conference competition in 11 men's and 10 women's sports. Ninety-eight percent of Coe graduates are in jobs or graduate school within 6 months of graduation.

Undergraduates 1,177 full-time, 113 part-time. Students come from 34 states and territories, 16 other countries, 30% are from out of state, 2% African American, 0.8% Asian American or Pacific Islander, 0.2% Native American, 3% international, 4% transferred in, 85% live on campus. *Retention:* 81% of 2002 full-time freshmen returned.

Freshmen *Admission:* 1,336 applied, 943 admitted, 322 enrolled. *Average high school GPA:* 3.58. *Test scores:* SAT verbal scores over 500: 81%; SAT math scores over 500: 78%; ACT scores over 18: 100%; SAT verbal scores over 600: 42%; SAT math scores over 600: 42%; ACT scores over 24: 51%; SAT verbal scores over 700: 3%; SAT math scores over 700: 9%; ACT scores over 30: 8%.

Faculty *Total:* 127, 58% full-time, 76% with terminal degrees. *Student/faculty ratio:* 12:1.

Majors Accounting; acting; African-American/Black studies; American studies; architecture; area, ethnic, cultural, and gender studies related; art; art teacher education; Asian studies; athletic training; biochemistry; biological and physical sciences; biology/biological sciences; business administration and management; ceramic arts and ceramics; chemistry; classics and languages, literatures and linguistics; computer science; creative writing; directing and theatrical production; dramatic/theatre arts; economics; education; elementary education; English; environmental studies; fine/studio arts; French; French studies; German; German studies; health and physical education related; history; interdisciplinary studies; liberal arts and sciences/liberal studies; literature; mathematics; molecular biology; music; music performance; music teacher education; music theory and composition; nursing (registered nurse training); painting; philosophy; photography; physical education teaching and coaching; physical sciences; physics; political science and government; pre-dentistry studies; pre-law studies; pre-medical studies; pre-veterinary studies; psychology; public relations/image management; religious studies; science teacher education; secondary education; sociology; Spanish; Spanish and Iberian studies; speech and rhetoric; theatre design and technology.

Academic Programs *Special study options:* accelerated degree program, adult/continuing education programs, advanced placement credit, double majors, English as a second language, honors programs, independent study, internships, off-campus study, part-time degree program, services for LD students, student-designed majors, study abroad, summer session for credit. *ROTC:* Army (c), Air Force (c). *Unusual degree programs:* 3-2 social service administration with University of Chicago.

Library Stewart Memorial Library plus 1 other with 213,270 titles, 750 serial subscriptions, 8,653 audiovisual materials, an OPAC, a Web page.

Computers on Campus 260 computers available on campus for general student use. A campuswide network can be accessed from student residence rooms and from off campus. Internet access, at least one staffed computer lab available.

Student Life *Housing:* on-campus residence required through senior year. *Options:* coed, men-only, women-only. Campus housing is university owned. Freshman campus housing is guaranteed. *Activities and organizations:* drama/theater group, student-run newspaper, radio station, choral group, Student Activities Committee, international club, Student Alumni Association, C-Club, Coe Alliance, national fraternities, national sororities. *Campus security:* 24-hour emergency response devices and patrols, late-night transport/escort service, controlled dormitory access. *Student services:* health clinic, personal/psychological counseling.

Athletics Member NCAA. All Division III. *Intercollegiate sports:* baseball M, basketball M/W, cheerleading W, cross-country running M/W, football M, golf M/W, soccer M/W, softball W, swimming M/W, tennis M/W, track and field M/W, volleyball W, wrestling M. *Intramural sports:* basketball M/W, football M/W, racquetball M/W, rugby M(c)/W(c), soccer M/W, softball M/W, squash M/W, table tennis M/W, tennis M/W, ultimate Frisbee M(c)/W(c), volleyball M/W.

Standardized Tests *Required:* SAT I or ACT (for admission).

Costs (2003–04) *Comprehensive fee:* $27,385 includes full-time tuition ($21,280), mandatory fees ($325), and room and board ($5780). Part-time tuition: $1040 per course. *College room only:* $2720. Room and board charges vary according to board plan and housing facility. *Payment plan:* installment. *Waivers:* children of alumni, adult students, senior citizens, and employees or children of employees.

Financial Aid Of all full-time matriculated undergraduates who enrolled in 2003, 1,007 applied for aid, 932 were judged to have need, 399 had their need fully met. In 2003, 212 non-need-based awards were made. *Average percent of need met:* 88%. *Average financial aid package:* $18,882. *Average need-based loan:* $5412. *Average need-based gift aid:* $13,274. *Average non-need-based aid:* $10,264. *Average indebtedness upon graduation:* $22,157.

Applying *Options:* common application, electronic application, early admission, early action, deferred entrance. *Required:* essay or personal statement, high school transcript, 1 letter of recommendation. *Recommended:* minimum 3.0 GPA, interview. *Application deadline:* 3/1 (freshmen), rolling (transfers). *Notification:* 3/15 (freshmen), 1/20 (early action), continuous (transfers).

Admissions Contact Mr. John Sullivan, Executive Director of Admission and Financial Aid, Coe College, 1220 1st Avenue, NE, Cedar Rapids, IA 52402-5070. *Phone:* 319-399-8500. *Toll-free phone:* 877-225-5263. *Fax:* 319-399-8816. *E-mail:* admission@coe.edu.

■ *See page 1422 for a narrative description.*

CORNELL COLLEGE
Mount Vernon, Iowa

- **Independent Methodist** 4-year, founded 1853
- **Calendar** 9 3½-week terms
- **Degree** bachelor's
- **Small-town** 129-acre campus
- **Endowment** $55.7 million
- **Coed,** 1,117 undergraduate students, 99% full-time, 59% women, 41% men
- **Moderately difficult** entrance level, 69% of applicants were admitted

Undergraduates 1,105 full-time, 12 part-time. Students come from 42 states and territories, 14 other countries, 69% are from out of state, 2% African

Cornell College (continued)
American, 0.8% Asian American or Pacific Islander, 3% Hispanic American, 0.6% Native American, 1% international, 3% transferred in, 92% live on campus. *Retention:* 81% of 2002 full-time freshmen returned.

Freshmen *Admission:* 1,555 applied, 1,067 admitted, 367 enrolled. *Average high school GPA:* 3.54. *Test scores:* SAT verbal scores over 500: 94%; SAT math scores over 500: 91%; ACT scores over 18: 97%; SAT verbal scores over 600: 59%; SAT math scores over 600: 54%; ACT scores over 24: 68%; SAT verbal scores over 700: 17%; SAT math scores over 700: 16%; ACT scores over 30: 25%.

Faculty *Total:* 101, 84% full-time, 82% with terminal degrees. *Student/faculty ratio:* 12:1.

Majors Architecture; art; art history, criticism and conservation; biochemistry; biology/biological sciences; chemistry; classics and languages, literatures and linguistics; computer science; cultural studies; dramatic/theatre arts; economics; elementary education; English; environmental studies; ethnic, cultural minority, and gender studies related; French; geology/earth science; German; health and physical education related; history; interdisciplinary studies; international business/trade/commerce; international relations and affairs; Latin; Latin American studies; liberal arts and sciences/liberal studies; mathematics; medieval and Renaissance studies; modern Greek; modern languages; multi-/interdisciplinary studies related; music; music teacher education; philosophy; physical education teaching and coaching; physics; political science and government; psychology; religious studies; Russian; secondary education; sociology; Spanish; speech and rhetoric; women's studies.

Academic Programs *Special study options:* adult/continuing education programs, advanced placement credit, double majors, English as a second language, independent study, internships, off-campus study, student-designed majors, study abroad. *Unusual degree programs:* 3-2 engineering with Washington University in St. Louis; forestry with Duke University; environmental management with Duke University, architecture with Washington University in St. Louis.

Library Cole Library with 197,780 titles, 1,236 serial subscriptions, 4,471 audiovisual materials, an OPAC, a Web page.

Computers on Campus 100 computers available on campus for general student use. A campuswide network can be accessed from student residence rooms and from off campus. Internet access, at least one staffed computer lab available.

Student Life *Housing:* on-campus residence required through senior year. *Options:* coed, men-only, women-only. Campus housing is university owned. Freshman campus housing is guaranteed. *Activities and organizations:* drama/theater group, student-run newspaper, radio station, choral group, social groups, Student-initiated Living-learning Community, Lunch Buddies/Youth Mentoring, chess and games club, PAAC (Performing Arts and Activities Council). *Campus security:* 24-hour emergency response devices and patrols. *Student services:* health clinic, personal/psychological counseling, women's center.

Athletics Member NCAA. All Division III. *Intercollegiate sports:* baseball M, basketball M/W, cross-country running M/W, football M, golf M/W, soccer M/W, softball W, tennis M/W, track and field M/W, volleyball M(c)/W, wrestling M. *Intramural sports:* badminton M/W, basketball M/W, bowling M/W, cheerleading M/W, cross-country running M/W, fencing M/W, football M, golf M/W, racquetball M/W, soccer M/W, softball M/W, table tennis M/W, tennis M/W, track and field M/W, ultimate Frisbee M/W, volleyball M/W, weight lifting M/W, wrestling M/W.

Standardized Tests *Required:* SAT I or ACT (for admission).

Costs (2003–04) *Comprehensive fee:* $27,825 includes full-time tuition ($21,630), mandatory fees ($160), and room and board ($6035). Full-time tuition and fees vary according to reciprocity agreements. Part-time tuition and fees vary according to course load. *College room only:* $2825. Room and board charges vary according to board plan. *Payment plan:* installment. *Waivers:* adult students, senior citizens, and employees or children of employees.

Financial Aid Of all full-time matriculated undergraduates who enrolled in 2003, 957 applied for aid, 854 were judged to have need, 482 had their need fully met. 554 Federal Work-Study jobs (averaging $1045). 182 state and other part-time jobs (averaging $1000). In 2003, 249 non-need-based awards were made. *Average percent of need met:* 98%. *Average financial aid package:* $19,455. *Average need-based loan:* $4210. *Average need-based gift aid:* $15,585. *Average non-need-based aid:* $11,210. *Average indebtedness upon graduation:* $17,850. *Financial aid deadline:* 3/1.

Applying *Options:* common application, electronic application, deferred entrance. *Application fee:* $25. *Required:* essay or personal statement, high school transcript, 1 letter of recommendation. *Recommended:* minimum 2.80 GPA, interview. *Application deadlines:* 2/1 (freshmen), 2/1 (transfers). *Notification:* continuous (freshmen), continuous (transfers).

Admissions Contact Mr. Jonathan Stroud, Dean of Admissions and Financial Assistance, Cornell College, 600 First Street West, Mount Vernon, IA 52314-1098. *Phone:* 319-895-4477. *Toll-free phone:* 800-747-1112. *Fax:* 319-895-4451. *E-mail:* admissions@cornellcollege.edu.

■ See page 1494 for a narrative description.

DIVINE WORD COLLEGE
Epworth, Iowa

Admissions Contact Vice President of Recruitment/Director of Admissions, Divine Word College, 102 Jacoby Drive SW, Epworth, IA 52045-0380. *Phone:* 563-876-3332. *Toll-free phone:* 800-553-3321. *Fax:* 319-876-3407.

DORDT COLLEGE
Sioux Center, Iowa

- **Independent Christian Reformed** comprehensive, founded 1955
- **Calendar** semesters
- **Degrees** associate, bachelor's, and master's
- **Small-town** 100-acre campus
- **Endowment** $22.0 million
- **Coed,** 1,287 undergraduate students, 96% full-time, 54% women, 46% men
- **Moderately difficult** entrance level, 92% of applicants were admitted

Undergraduates 1,233 full-time, 54 part-time. Students come from 32 states and territories, 12 other countries, 58% are from out of state, 0.6% African American, 1% Asian American or Pacific Islander, 0.4% Hispanic American, 13% international, 3% transferred in, 90% live on campus. *Retention:* 83% of 2002 full-time freshmen returned.

Freshmen *Admission:* 780 applied, 717 admitted, 351 enrolled. *Average high school GPA:* 3.40. *Test scores:* SAT verbal scores over 500: 95%; SAT math scores over 500: 95%; ACT scores over 18: 96%; SAT verbal scores over 600: 57%; SAT math scores over 600: 58%; ACT scores over 24: 57%; SAT verbal scores over 700: 24%; SAT math scores over 700: 25%; ACT scores over 30: 10%.

Faculty *Total:* 116, 69% full-time, 53% with terminal degrees. *Student/faculty ratio:* 15:1.

Majors Accounting; administrative assistant and secretarial science; agricultural business and management; agricultural teacher education; agriculture; animal/livestock husbandry and production; animal sciences; art; biology/biological sciences; biology teacher education; business administration and management; business teacher education; chemistry; chemistry teacher education; clinical laboratory science/medical technology; commercial and advertising art; computer engineering; computer/information technology services administration related; computer programming; computer science; computer teacher education; criminal justice/law enforcement administration; data processing and data processing technology; drama and dance teacher education; dramatic/theatre arts; education; education (K-12); electrical, electronics and communications engineering; elementary education; engineering; engineering mechanics; engineering technology; English; environmental studies; general studies; German; graphic design; health and physical education; history; history teacher education; journalism; kinesiology and exercise science; legal administrative assistant/secretary; management information systems; mass communication/media; mathematics; mechanical engineering; missionary studies and missiology; music; music performance; music teacher education; natural sciences; nursing (registered nurse training); parks, recreation and leisure; pastoral studies/counseling; philosophy; physical education teaching and coaching; physics; piano and organ; political science and government; pre-dentistry studies; pre-law studies; pre-medical studies; pre-nursing studies; pre-pharmacy studies; pre-veterinary studies; psychology; reading teacher education; religious studies; science teacher education; secondary education; social sciences; social science teacher education; social studies teacher education; social work; sociology; Spanish; Spanish language teacher education; speech teacher education; system administration; teacher assistant/aide; theology; voice and opera; youth ministry.

Academic Programs *Special study options:* academic remediation for entering students, advanced placement credit, distance learning, double majors, English as a second language, independent study, internships, off-campus study, part-time degree program, services for LD students, student-designed majors, study abroad.

Library Dordt College Library plus 1 other with 160,000 titles, 6,597 serial subscriptions, 1,989 audiovisual materials, an OPAC, a Web page.

Computers on Campus 250 computers available on campus for general student use. A campuswide network can be accessed from student residence rooms and from off campus. Internet access, online (class) registration, at least one staffed computer lab available.

Student Life *Housing:* on-campus residence required through senior year. *Options:* men-only, women-only, disabled students. Campus housing is university owned. Freshman campus housing is guaranteed. *Activities and organizations:* drama/theater group, student-run newspaper, radio station, choral group, PLIA, Future Teachers, Ag Club, lacrosse club, Defenders of Life. *Campus security:* 24-hour emergency response devices, student patrols, late-night transport/escort service, controlled dormitory access. *Student services:* health clinic, personal/psychological counseling.

Athletics Member NAIA. *Intercollegiate sports:* baseball M(s), basketball M(s)/W(s), cross-country running M(s)/W(s), golf M(s), ice hockey M(s), lacrosse

M, soccer M(s)/W(s), softball W(s), tennis M(s)/W(s), track and field M(s)/W(s), volleyball W(s). *Intramural sports:* basketball M/W, bowling M/W, field hockey M/W, gymnastics M/W, ice hockey M, lacrosse M, racquetball M/W, skiing (cross-country) M/W, soccer M/W, softball M/W, swimming M/W, table tennis M/W, tennis M/W, track and field M/W, volleyball M/W, weight lifting M/W.

Standardized Tests *Required:* SAT I or ACT (for admission).

Costs (2003–04) *Comprehensive fee:* $20,170 includes full-time tuition ($15,550), mandatory fees ($220), and room and board ($4400). Part-time tuition: $650 per credit hour. *Required fees:* $110 per term part-time. *College room only:* $2310. Room and board charges vary according to board plan and housing facility. *Payment plan:* installment. *Waivers:* children of alumni, senior citizens, and employees or children of employees.

Financial Aid Of all full-time matriculated undergraduates who enrolled in 2003, 1,063 applied for aid, 968 were judged to have need, 95 had their need fully met. 601 Federal Work-Study jobs (averaging $1300). 458 state and other part-time jobs (averaging $1300). In 2003, 170 non-need-based awards were made. *Average percent of need met:* 85%. *Average financial aid package:* $14,665. *Average need-based loan:* $4354. *Average need-based gift aid:* $7820. *Average non-need-based aid:* $7331. *Average indebtedness upon graduation:* $15,434.

Applying *Options:* electronic application, deferred entrance. *Application fee:* $25. *Required:* high school transcript, minimum 2.25 GPA, minimum ACT composite score of 19 or combined SAT I score of 920. *Required for some:* essay or personal statement, interview. *Application deadline:* 8/1 (transfers). *Notification:* continuous until 8/1 (freshmen), continuous until 9/1 (transfers).

Admissions Contact Mr. Quentin Van Essen, Executive Director of Admissions, Dordt College, 498 4th Avenue, NE, Sioux Center, IA 51250-1697. *Phone:* 712-722-6080. *Toll-free phone:* 800-343-6738. *Fax:* 712-722-1967. *E-mail:* admissions@dordt.edu.

DRAKE UNIVERSITY
Des Moines, Iowa

- **Independent** university, founded 1881
- **Calendar** semesters
- **Degrees** bachelor's, master's, doctoral, first professional, and post-master's certificates
- **Suburban** 120-acre campus
- **Endowment** $100.2 million
- **Coed,** 3,434 undergraduate students, 92% full-time, 59% women, 41% men
- **Moderately difficult** entrance level, 83% of applicants were admitted

Undergraduates 3,160 full-time, 274 part-time. Students come from 40 states and territories, 53 other countries, 61% are from out of state, 5% transferred in, 57% live on campus. *Retention:* 83% of 2002 full-time freshmen returned.

Freshmen *Admission:* 3,174 applied, 2,647 admitted, 815 enrolled. *Average high school GPA:* 3.60. *Test scores:* SAT verbal scores over 500: 87%; SAT math scores over 500: 87%; ACT scores over 18: 99%; SAT verbal scores over 600: 46%; SAT math scores over 600: 52%; ACT scores over 24: 73%; SAT verbal scores over 700: 7%; SAT math scores over 700: 12%; ACT scores over 30: 16%.

Faculty *Total:* 362, 65% full-time. *Student/faculty ratio:* 18:1.

Majors Accounting; accounting and finance; acting; actuarial science; advertising; anthropology; Army R.O.T.C./military science; art; art history, criticism and conservation; astronomy; biology/biological sciences; broadcast journalism; business administration and management; business/commerce; business teacher education; chemistry; commercial and advertising art; computer science; directing and theatrical production; dramatic/theatre arts; dramatic/theatre arts and stagecraft related; drawing; economics; elementary education; English; environmental science; environmental studies; finance; fine/studio arts; graphic design; history; human resources management and services related; information science/studies; international business/trade/commerce; international relations and affairs; jazz/jazz studies; journalism; marketing/marketing management; mass communication/media; mathematics; music; music management and merchandising; music performance; music teacher education; painting; pharmacy; pharmacy administration/pharmaceutics; philosophy; physics; piano and organ; political science and government; pre-dentistry studies; pre-law studies; pre-medical studies; pre-veterinary studies; printmaking; psychology; public relations/image management; radio and television; radio, television, and digital communication related; religious/sacred music; religious studies; science teacher education; sculpture; secondary education; sociology; speech and rhetoric; voice and opera.

Academic Programs *Special study options:* accelerated degree program, advanced placement credit, cooperative education, distance learning, double majors, English as a second language, honors programs, independent study, internships, off-campus study, part-time degree program, services for LD students, student-designed majors, study abroad, summer session for credit. *ROTC:* Army (b), Air Force (c). *Unusual degree programs:* 3-2 engineering with Washington University in St. Louis, Cornell University; journalism and law, arts and sciences and law, accounting.

Library Cowles Library plus 1 other with 472,110 titles, 2,000 serial subscriptions, 858 audiovisual materials, an OPAC, a Web page.

Computers on Campus 360 computers available on campus for general student use. A campuswide network can be accessed from student residence rooms and from off campus. Internet access, at least one staffed computer lab available.

Student Life *Housing:* on-campus residence required through sophomore year. *Options:* coed. Campus housing is university owned. Freshman campus housing is guaranteed. *Activities and organizations:* drama/theater group, student-run newspaper, radio and television station, choral group, marching band, Student Activities Board, international student organizations, Coalition of Black Students, Alpha Phi Omega Service Organization, Residence Hall Association, national fraternities, national sororities. *Campus security:* 24-hour emergency response devices and patrols, late-night transport/escort service, 24-hour desk attendants in residence halls. *Student services:* health clinic, personal/psychological counseling, women's center, legal services.

Athletics Member NCAA. All Division I except football (Division I-AA). *Intercollegiate sports:* basketball M(s)/W(s), cheerleading M(s)/W(s), crew W, cross-country running M(s)/W(s), golf M(s), soccer M(s)/W(s), softball W(s), tennis M(s)/W(s), track and field M(s)/W(s), volleyball W(s). *Intramural sports:* badminton M/W, basketball M/W, football M/W, golf M/W, racquetball M/W, soccer M/W, softball M/W, swimming M/W, table tennis M/W, tennis M/W, volleyball M/W.

Standardized Tests *Required:* SAT I or ACT (for admission). *Required for some:* PCAT for pharmacy transfers.

Costs (2003–04) *Comprehensive fee:* $25,120 includes full-time tuition ($19,100), mandatory fees ($320), and room and board ($5700). Full-time tuition and fees vary according to course load and student level. Part-time tuition: $387 per hour. Part-time tuition and fees vary according to class time. *Required fees:* $7 per hour part-time. *College room only:* $2760. Room and board charges vary according to board plan. *Payment plan:* installment. *Waivers:* children of alumni, senior citizens, and employees or children of employees.

Financial Aid Of all full-time matriculated undergraduates who enrolled in 2002, 2,409 applied for aid, 2,044 were judged to have need, 561 had their need fully met. 922 Federal Work-Study jobs (averaging $1532). 38 state and other part-time jobs (averaging $5921). In 2002, 1056 non-need-based awards were made. *Average percent of need met:* 98%. *Average financial aid package:* $16,354. *Average need-based loan:* $5606. *Average need-based gift aid:* $11,441. *Average non-need-based aid:* $8936. *Average indebtedness upon graduation:* $22,115.

Applying *Options:* common application, electronic application, early admission, deferred entrance. *Application fee:* $25. *Required:* high school transcript. *Recommended:* essay or personal statement, interview. *Application deadline:* 3/1 (freshmen), rolling (transfers). *Notification:* continuous (freshmen), continuous until 8/1 (transfers).

Admissions Contact Mr. Thomas F. Willoughby, Vice President for Admission and Financial Aid, Drake University, 2507 University Avenue, Des Moines, IA 50311. *Phone:* 515-271-3181. *Toll-free phone:* 800-44DRAKE Ext. 3181. *Fax:* 515-271-2831. *E-mail:* admission@drake.edu.

■ *See page 1542 for a narrative description.*

EMMAUS BIBLE COLLEGE
Dubuque, Iowa

- **Independent nondenominational** 4-year, founded 1941
- **Calendar** semesters
- **Degrees** certificates, associate, and bachelor's
- **Small-town** 22-acre campus
- **Endowment** $1.2 million
- **Coed**
- **Noncompetitive** entrance level

Faculty *Student/faculty ratio:* 12:1.

Student Life *Campus security:* 24-hour emergency response devices, student patrols, controlled dormitory access.

Athletics Member NCCAA.

Standardized Tests *Required:* SAT I or ACT (for placement).

Costs (2003–04) *Comprehensive fee:* $10,611 includes full-time tuition ($6900), mandatory fees ($231), and room and board ($3480). Part-time tuition and fees vary according to course load.

Financial Aid Of all full-time matriculated undergraduates who enrolled in 2002, 219 applied for aid, 195 were judged to have need. *Average percent of need*

Emmaus Bible College (continued)
met: 68. *Average financial aid package:* $4000. *Average need-based loan:* $3750. *Average need-based gift aid:* $500. *Average indebtedness upon graduation:* $17,850. *Financial aid deadline:* 6/10.

Applying *Options:* deferred entrance. *Application fee:* $25. *Required:* essay or personal statement, high school transcript, 3 letters of recommendation.

Admissions Contact Mr. Steve Schimpf, Enrollment Services Manager, Emmaus Bible College, 2570 Asbury Road, Dubuque, IA 52001. *Phone:* 563-588-8000 Ext. 1310. *Toll-free phone:* 800-397-2425. *Fax:* 563-557-0573. *E-mail:* admissions@emmaus.edu.

FAITH BAPTIST BIBLE COLLEGE AND THEOLOGICAL SEMINARY

Ankeny, Iowa

- **Independent** comprehensive, founded 1921, affiliated with General Association of Regular Baptist Churches
- **Calendar** semesters
- **Degrees** certificates, associate, bachelor's, master's, and first professional
- **Small-town** 52-acre campus
- **Endowment** $3.0 million
- **Coed,** 392 undergraduate students, 92% full-time, 54% women, 46% men
- **Minimally difficult** entrance level, 50% of applicants were admitted

Undergraduates 362 full-time, 30 part-time. Students come from 29 states and territories, 51% are from out of state, 0.8% African American, 0.8% Asian American or Pacific Islander, 0.8% Hispanic American, 0.3% Native American, 0.3% international, 5% transferred in, 81% live on campus. *Retention:* 74% of 2002 full-time freshmen returned.

Freshmen *Admission:* 226 applied, 113 admitted, 113 enrolled. *Average high school GPA:* 3.24. *Test scores:* SAT verbal scores over 500: 20%; SAT math scores over 500: 30%; ACT scores over 18: 79%; SAT verbal scores over 600: 10%; SAT math scores over 600: 10%; ACT scores over 24: 30%; ACT scores over 30: 5%.

Faculty *Total:* 30, 57% full-time, 47% with terminal degrees. *Student/faculty ratio:* 18:1.

Majors Administrative assistant and secretarial science; biblical studies; divinity/ministry; elementary education; English/language arts teacher education; missionary studies and missiology; music teacher education; pastoral studies/counseling; religious education; religious/sacred music.

Academic Programs *Special study options:* academic remediation for entering students, adult/continuing education programs, advanced placement credit, double majors, independent study, internships, part-time degree program, summer session for credit.

Library Patten Hall with 63,123 titles, 492 serial subscriptions, 6,629 audiovisual materials, an OPAC, a Web page.

Computers on Campus 50 computers available on campus for general student use. A campuswide network can be accessed from student residence rooms. Internet access, at least one staffed computer lab available. Computer purchase or lease plan available.

Student Life *Housing:* on-campus residence required through senior year. *Options:* men-only, women-only. Campus housing is university owned. Freshman campus housing is guaranteed. *Activities and organizations:* drama/theater group, choral group, Student Association, Student Missions Fellowship. *Campus security:* 24-hour emergency response devices and patrols, late-night transport/escort service. *Student services:* personal/psychological counseling.

Athletics Member NCCAA. *Intercollegiate sports:* basketball M/W, cheerleading W, soccer M/W, volleyball W. *Intramural sports:* basketball M/W, cheerleading W(c), football M.

Standardized Tests *Required:* SAT I or ACT (for admission).

Costs (2003–04) *Comprehensive fee:* $14,424 includes full-time tuition ($10,042), mandatory fees ($376), and room and board ($4006). Full-time tuition and fees vary according to course load. Part-time tuition: $365 per semester hour. *Required fees:* $188 per term part-time. *College room only:* $1866. *Waivers:* employees or children of employees.

Financial Aid Of all full-time matriculated undergraduates who enrolled in 2002, 324 applied for aid, 303 were judged to have need. In 2002, 22 non-need-based awards were made. *Average percent of need met:* 29%. *Average financial aid package:* $6417. *Average need-based loan:* $3315. *Average need-based gift aid:* $2873. *Average non-need-based aid:* $2041. *Average indebtedness upon graduation:* $10,623.

Applying *Options:* early admission, deferred entrance. *Application fee:* $25. *Required:* 2 letters of recommendation. *Required for some:* interview. *Application deadline:* 5/1 (freshmen). *Notification:* continuous (transfers).

Admissions Contact Faith Baptist Bible College and Theological Seminary, 1900 NW 4th Street, Ankeny, IA 50021. *Phone:* 515-964-0601 Ext. 238. *Toll-free phone:* 888-FAITH 4U. *Fax:* 515-964-1638. *E-mail:* admissions@faith.edu.

THE FRANCISCAN UNIVERSITY

Clinton, Iowa

- **Independent Roman Catholic** 4-year, founded 1918
- **Calendar** semesters
- **Degrees** bachelor's and master's
- **Small-town** 24-acre campus with easy access to Chicago
- **Endowment** $1.2 million
- **Coed,** 426 undergraduate students, 88% full-time, 56% women, 44% men
- **Minimally difficult** entrance level, 82% of applicants were admitted

The Franciscan University holds an annual academic scholarship competition in February. Students with a GPA of at least 3.0 are invited to attend. At stake are renewable major scholarships in many academic areas: accounting, athletic administration, biology, business administration, information systems, criminal justice, cytotechnology, education (elementary and secondary), environmental studies, health-care management, literature, marketing communications, mathematics, music, pre-medical studies, pre-physical therapy, prelaw, psychology, religious studies, social science, and visual arts.

Undergraduates 373 full-time, 53 part-time. Students come from 11 states and territories, 10 other countries, 40% are from out of state, 6% African American, 0.7% Asian American or Pacific Islander, 3% Hispanic American, 0.2% Native American, 3% international, 28% transferred in, 36% live on campus. *Retention:* 69% of 2002 full-time freshmen returned.

Freshmen *Admission:* 208 applied, 171 admitted, 54 enrolled. *Average high school GPA:* 2.84. *Test scores:* ACT scores over 18: 72%; ACT scores over 24: 13%.

Faculty *Total:* 52, 52% full-time, 33% with terminal degrees. *Student/faculty ratio:* 12:1.

Majors Accounting; athletic training; biology/biological sciences; business administration and management; business teacher education; communication and journalism related; computer and information sciences; criminal justice/safety; cytotechnology; education; elementary education; English; general studies; health/health care administration; history related; humanities; human services; journalism; kindergarten/preschool education; liberal arts and sciences/liberal studies; middle school education; multi-/interdisciplinary studies related; music; music teacher education; pre-law studies; pre-medical studies; psychology; religious studies; science teacher education; secondary education; social sciences; visual and performing arts.

Academic Programs *Special study options:* academic remediation for entering students, advanced placement credit, distance learning, double majors, English as a second language, external degree program, freshman honors college, honors programs, independent study, internships, part-time degree program, student-designed majors, study abroad, summer session for credit.

Library Mount St. Clare Library with 80,759 titles, 1,442 serial subscriptions, 363 audiovisual materials, an OPAC, a Web page.

Computers on Campus 109 computers available on campus for general student use. Internet access, at least one staffed computer lab available.

Student Life *Housing:* on-campus residence required through junior year. *Options:* coed, women-only. Campus housing is university owned. Freshman campus housing is guaranteed. *Activities and organizations:* drama/theater group, student-run newspaper, choral group, Student Senate, Student Ambassadors, Hall Council, Black Student Union, Student Iowa State Education Association. *Campus security:* 24-hour emergency response devices and patrols, student patrols, late-night transport/escort service, controlled dormitory access, self-defense education, lighted pathways. *Student services:* health clinic, personal/psychological counseling.

Athletics Member NAIA. *Intercollegiate sports:* baseball M(s), basketball M(s)/W(s), cross-country running M(s)/W(s), golf M(s), soccer M(s)/W(s), softball W(s), track and field M(s)/W(s), volleyball W(s). *Intramural sports:* football M/W, golf M, skiing (downhill) M/W, track and field M/W, volleyball M/W.

Standardized Tests *Required:* SAT I or ACT (for admission).

Costs (2003–04) *Comprehensive fee:* $19,430 includes full-time tuition ($13,920), mandatory fees ($260), and room and board ($5250). *College room only:* $2500. Room and board charges vary according to board plan and housing facility. *Payment plans:* tuition prepayment, installment, deferred payment. *Waivers:* children of alumni, senior citizens, and employees or children of employees.

Financial Aid Of all full-time matriculated undergraduates who enrolled in 2003, 347 applied for aid, 320 were judged to have need, 85 had their need fully met. In 2003, 36 non-need-based awards were made. *Average percent of need met:* 79%. *Average financial aid package:* $11,041. *Average need-based loan:* $3935. *Average need-based gift aid:* $7707. *Average non-need-based aid:* $8632. *Average indebtedness upon graduation:* $15,868. *Financial aid deadline:* 8/1.

Applying *Options:* common application, electronic application, early admission, deferred entrance. *Application fee:* $20. *Required:* high school transcript. *Required for some:* letters of recommendation, interview. *Recommended:* minimum 2.0 GPA, interview. *Application deadline:* 8/15 (freshmen), rolling (transfers). *Notification:* continuous (freshmen), continuous (transfers).

Admissions Contact Ms. Waunita M. Sullivan, Director of Enrollment, The Franciscan University, 400 North Bluff Boulevard, PO Box 2967, Clinton, IA 52733-2967. *Phone:* 563-242-4023 Ext. 3401. *Toll-free phone:* 800-242-4153. *Fax:* 563-243-6102. *E-mail:* admissns@tfu.edu.

GRACELAND UNIVERSITY
Lamoni, Iowa

- **Independent Community of Christ** comprehensive, founded 1895
- **Calendar** 4-1-4
- **Degrees** bachelor's, master's, and post-master's certificates
- **Small-town** 169-acre campus with easy access to Des Moines
- **Endowment** $55.2 million
- **Coed,** 2,033 undergraduate students, 66% full-time, 66% women, 34% men
- **Moderately difficult** entrance level, 58% of applicants were admitted

Undergraduates 1,343 full-time, 690 part-time. Students come from 49 states and territories, 37 other countries, 60% are from out of state, 3% African American, 2% Asian American or Pacific Islander, 2% Hispanic American, 0.6% Native American, 7% international, 6% transferred in, 64% live on campus. *Retention:* 70% of 2002 full-time freshmen returned.

Freshmen *Admission:* 1,016 applied, 585 admitted, 254 enrolled. *Average high school GPA:* 3.23. *Test scores:* SAT verbal scores over 500: 41%; SAT math scores over 500: 56%; ACT scores over 18: 80%; SAT verbal scores over 600: 11%; SAT math scores over 600: 16%; ACT scores over 24: 28%; SAT verbal scores over 700: 2%; SAT math scores over 700: 2%; ACT scores over 30: 3%.

Faculty *Total:* 118, 80% full-time, 46% with terminal degrees. *Student/faculty ratio:* 14:1.

Majors Accounting; art; art teacher education; athletic training; biology/biological sciences; business administration and management; chemistry; clinical laboratory science/medical technology; commercial and advertising art; computer science; criminal justice/law enforcement administration; dramatic/theatre arts; economics; education; education (K-12); elementary education; English; English composition; fine/studio arts; foreign languages and literatures; German; health science; health teacher education; history; human services; international business/trade/commerce; international relations and affairs; liberal arts and sciences/liberal studies; literature; management information systems; mathematics; music; music teacher education; nursing (registered nurse training); parks, recreation and leisure; philosophy and religious studies related; physical education teaching and coaching; physical sciences; pre-dentistry studies; pre-law studies; pre-medical studies; psychology; publishing; religious studies; science teacher education; secondary education; social sciences; social work; sociology; Spanish; speech and rhetoric; speech/theater education; sport and fitness administration; substance abuse/addiction counseling.

Academic Programs *Special study options:* academic remediation for entering students, accelerated degree program, adult/continuing education programs, advanced placement credit, cooperative education, distance learning, double majors, English as a second language, external degree program, honors programs, independent study, internships, off-campus study, part-time degree program, services for LD students, student-designed majors, study abroad, summer session for credit.

Library Frederick Madison Smith Library with 143,523 titles, 5,545 serial subscriptions, 3,500 audiovisual materials, an OPAC, a Web page.

Computers on Campus 106 computers available on campus for general student use. A campuswide network can be accessed from student residence rooms and from off campus. Internet access, at least one staffed computer lab available.

Student Life *Housing:* on-campus residence required through sophomore year. *Options:* men-only, women-only. Campus housing is university owned. Freshman campus housing is guaranteed. *Activities and organizations:* drama/theater group, student-run newspaper, choral group, student political organizations, Black Student Union (BSU), Habitat for Humanity, international club, Students in Free Enterprise (SIFE). *Campus security:* 24-hour emergency response devices and patrols, late-night transport/escort service, controlled dormitory access. *Student services:* health clinic, personal/psychological counseling.

Athletics Member NAIA. *Intercollegiate sports:* baseball M(s), basketball M(s)/W(s), cross-country running M(s)/W(s), football M(s), golf M(s)/W(s), soccer M(s)/W(s), softball W(s), tennis M(s)/W(s), track and field M(s)/W(s), volleyball M(s)/W(s). *Intramural sports:* badminton M/W, baseball M/W, basketball M/W, cheerleading W, cross-country running M/W, football M/W, golf M/W, racquetball M/W, soccer M/W, softball M/W, swimming M/W, table tennis M/W, tennis M/W, track and field M/W, volleyball M/W, weight lifting M/W, wrestling M.

Standardized Tests *Required:* SAT I or ACT (for admission).

Costs (2003–04) *Comprehensive fee:* $19,550 includes full-time tuition ($14,650), mandatory fees ($150), and room and board ($4750). Full-time tuition and fees vary according to course load. Part-time tuition: $460 per semester hour. Part-time tuition and fees vary according to location. *College room only:* $1770. Room and board charges vary according to board plan, housing facility, and location. *Payment plan:* installment. *Waivers:* senior citizens and employees or children of employees.

Financial Aid Of all full-time matriculated undergraduates who enrolled in 2003, 1,078 applied for aid, 922 were judged to have need, 282 had their need fully met. 400 Federal Work-Study jobs (averaging $1544). 297 state and other part-time jobs (averaging $1228). In 2003, 262 non-need-based awards were made. *Average percent of need met:* 85%. *Average financial aid package:* $14,192. *Average need-based loan:* $5172. *Average need-based gift aid:* $9610. *Average non-need-based aid:* $8506. *Average indebtedness upon graduation:* $19,772.

Applying *Options:* common application, electronic application, early admission, deferred entrance. *Application fee:* $50. *Required:* high school transcript, minimum 2.5 GPA. *Required for some:* essay or personal statement, 2 letters of recommendation, interview. *Recommended:* minimum SAT score of 960 or ACT score of 21. *Application deadline:* rolling (freshmen), rolling (transfers). *Notification:* continuous (freshmen), continuous (transfers).

Admissions Contact Mr. Brian Shantz, Dean of Admissions, Graceland University, 1 University Place, Lamoni, IA 50140. *Phone:* 641-784-5110. *Toll-free phone:* 866-GRACELAND. *Fax:* 641-784-5480. *E-mail:* admissions@graceland.edu.

■ *See page 1682 for a narrative description.*

GRAND VIEW COLLEGE
Des Moines, Iowa

- **Independent** 4-year, founded 1896, affiliated with Evangelical Lutheran Church in America
- **Calendar** semesters
- **Degrees** certificates, associate, bachelor's, and postbachelor's certificates
- **Urban** 25-acre campus
- **Endowment** $7.3 million
- **Coed,** 1,630 undergraduate students, 73% full-time, 70% women, 30% men
- **Minimally difficult** entrance level, 95% of applicants were admitted

Undergraduates 1,182 full-time, 448 part-time. Students come from 27 states and territories, 13 other countries, 8% are from out of state, 3% African American, 2% Asian American or Pacific Islander, 1% Hispanic American, 0.4% Native American, 1% international, 21% transferred in, 23% live on campus. *Retention:* 75% of 2002 full-time freshmen returned.

Freshmen *Admission:* 438 applied, 414 admitted, 167 enrolled. *Average high school GPA:* 3.10. *Test scores:* SAT verbal scores over 500: 67%; SAT math scores over 500: 67%; ACT scores over 18: 78%; SAT verbal scores over 600: 34%; SAT math scores over 600: 34%; ACT scores over 24: 25%; ACT scores over 30: 1%.

Faculty *Total:* 163, 47% full-time, 37% with terminal degrees. *Student/faculty ratio:* 13:1.

Majors Accounting; applied mathematics; art; biology/biological sciences; business administration and management; computer science; criminal justice/law enforcement administration; dramatic/theatre arts; elementary education; English; fine/studio arts; graphic communications; graphic design; history; human services; information science/studies; journalism; liberal arts and sciences/liberal studies; management information systems; mass communication/media; music; nursing (registered nurse training); physical sciences; political science and government; pre-law studies; psychology; radio and television; religious studies; sociology.

Academic Programs *Special study options:* academic remediation for entering students, accelerated degree program, adult/continuing education programs, advanced placement credit, cooperative education, distance learning, double majors, freshman honors college, honors programs, independent study, internships, off-campus study, part-time degree program, services for LD students, student-designed majors, study abroad, summer session for credit. *ROTC:* Army (c), Air Force (c). *Unusual degree programs:* 3-2 engineering with Iowa State University; hospital administration with The University of Iowa.

Library Grand View College Library with 103,468 titles, 3,412 serial subscriptions, 6,360 audiovisual materials, an OPAC, a Web page.

Computers on Campus 277 computers available on campus for general student use. A campuswide network can be accessed from student residence rooms and from off campus. Internet access, at least one staffed computer lab available.

Student Life *Housing:* on-campus residence required through sophomore year. *Options:* coed, men-only, women-only. Campus housing is university owned. Freshman campus housing is guaranteed. *Activities and organizations:* drama/

Grand View College (continued)
theater group, student-run newspaper, radio and television station, choral group, Nursing Student Association (NSA), art club, science club, education club, business club. *Campus security:* 24-hour emergency response devices, night security patrols. *Student services:* health clinic, personal/psychological counseling.

Athletics Member NAIA. *Intercollegiate sports:* baseball M(s), basketball M(s)/W(s), cross-country running M(s)/W(s), golf M(s)/W(s), soccer M(s)/W(s), softball W(s), volleyball W(s). *Intramural sports:* basketball M/W, cheerleading W, football M/W, rock climbing M/W, soccer M/W, table tennis M/W, ultimate Frisbee M/W, volleyball M/W.

Standardized Tests *Required:* SAT I or ACT (for admission).

Costs (2003–04) *Comprehensive fee:* $19,972 includes full-time tuition ($14,460), mandatory fees ($280), and room and board ($5232). Part-time tuition: $410 per credit hour. Part-time tuition and fees vary according to class time. *Room and board:* Room and board charges vary according to board plan and housing facility. *Payment plan:* installment. *Waivers:* senior citizens and employees or children of employees.

Financial Aid Of all full-time matriculated undergraduates who enrolled in 2003, 1,118 applied for aid, 1,103 were judged to have need, 180 had their need fully met. *Average percent of need met:* 76%. *Average financial aid package:* $11,670. *Average need-based loan:* $3954. *Average need-based gift aid:* $7855. *Average non-need-based aid:* $8654. *Average indebtedness upon graduation:* $18,938.

Applying *Options:* common application, electronic application. *Required:* high school transcript. *Recommended:* minimum 2.0 GPA. *Application deadlines:* 8/15 (freshmen), 8/15 (transfers). *Notification:* 9/15 (freshmen), continuous until 9/15 (transfers).

Admissions Contact Ms. Diane Johnson Schaefer, Director of Admissions, Grand View College, 1200 Grandview Avenue, Des Moines, IA 50316-1599. *Phone:* 515-263-2810. *Toll-free phone:* 800-444-6083. *Fax:* 515-263-2974. *E-mail:* admiss@gvc.edu.

■ *See page 1688 for a narrative description.*

GRINNELL COLLEGE

Grinnell, Iowa

- **Independent** 4-year, founded 1846
- **Calendar** semesters
- **Degree** bachelor's
- **Small-town** 120-acre campus
- **Endowment** $1.1 billion
- **Coed,** 1,524 undergraduate students, 97% full-time, 55% women, 45% men
- **Very difficult** entrance level, 63% of applicants were admitted

For the past 15 years, Grinnell College has been named one of the 15 best liberal arts colleges by *U.S. News & World Report* and was ranked 12th in 2002. Grinnell has an open curriculum, with no general education, core, or distribution requirements. The College has a $1-billion endowment and awarded more than $15 million in grants and scholarships last year.

Undergraduates 1,485 full-time, 39 part-time. Students come from 52 states and territories, 52 other countries, 87% are from out of state, 4% African American, 5% Asian American or Pacific Islander, 4% Hispanic American, 0.9% Native American, 10% international, 0.9% transferred in, 85% live on campus. *Retention:* 92% of 2002 full-time freshmen returned.

Freshmen *Admission:* 2,284 applied, 1,443 admitted, 404 enrolled. *Test scores:* SAT verbal scores over 500: 95%; SAT math scores over 500: 97%; ACT scores over 18: 100%; SAT verbal scores over 600: 82%; SAT math scores over 600: 85%; ACT scores over 24: 93%; SAT verbal scores over 700: 42%; SAT math scores over 700: 43%; ACT scores over 30: 62%.

Faculty *Total:* 142, 98% full-time, 98% with terminal degrees. *Student/faculty ratio:* 10:1.

Majors African-American/Black studies; American studies; anthropology; archeology; art; Asian studies (East); biochemistry; biological and physical sciences; biology/biological sciences; chemistry; Chinese; classics and languages, literatures and linguistics; computer science; dramatic/theatre arts; economics; education; elementary education; English; environmental biology; environmental studies; European studies (Central and Eastern); European studies (Western); French; German; history; interdisciplinary studies; international/global studies; Latin American studies; linguistics; mathematics; music; philosophy; physics; political science and government; pre-medical studies; psychology; religious studies; Russian; science, technology and society; secondary education; sociology; Spanish; women's studies.

Academic Programs *Special study options:* accelerated degree program, advanced placement credit, double majors, independent study, internships, off-campus study, services for LD students, student-designed majors, study abroad. *Unusual degree programs:* 3-2 engineering with Columbia University, California Institute of Technology, Rensselaer Polytechnic Institute, Washington University in St. Louis; architecture with Washington University in St. Louis, law at Columbia University.

Library Burling Library plus 2 others with 1.0 million titles, 3,470 serial subscriptions, 28,368 audiovisual materials, an OPAC, a Web page.

Computers on Campus 208 computers available on campus for general student use. A campuswide network can be accessed from student residence rooms and from off campus that provide access to e-mail. Internet access, at least one staffed computer lab available.

Student Life *Housing:* on-campus residence required through sophomore year. *Options:* coed, cooperative. Campus housing is university owned. Freshman campus housing is guaranteed. *Activities and organizations:* drama/theater group, student-run newspaper, radio station, choral group, Dagorhir, International Student Organization, Alternative Happy Hour, Campus Democrats, Davi's Buddies. *Campus security:* 24-hour emergency response devices and patrols, student patrols, late-night transport/escort service, controlled dormitory access. *Student services:* health clinic, personal/psychological counseling.

Athletics Member NCAA. All Division III. *Intercollegiate sports:* baseball M, basketball M/W, cross-country running M/W, football M, golf M/W, soccer M/W, softball W, swimming M/W, tennis M/W, track and field M/W, volleyball W. *Intramural sports:* badminton M/W, basketball M/W, cheerleading W, fencing M(c)/W(c), field hockey M/W, lacrosse M(c)/W(c), rugby M(c)/W(c), soccer M/W, softball M/W, tennis M/W, ultimate Frisbee M/W, volleyball M(c)/W(c), water polo M/W.

Standardized Tests *Required:* SAT I or ACT (for admission).

Costs (2003–04) *Comprehensive fee:* $31,060 includes full-time tuition ($23,898), mandatory fees ($592), and room and board ($6570). Part-time tuition: $747 per credit hour. No tuition increase for student's term of enrollment. *College room only:* $3080. Room and board charges vary according to board plan and housing facility. *Payment plans:* tuition prepayment, installment. *Waivers:* employees or children of employees.

Financial Aid Of all full-time matriculated undergraduates who enrolled in 2003, 898 applied for aid, 878 were judged to have need, 878 had their need fully met. 469 Federal Work-Study jobs (averaging $1630). 273 state and other part-time jobs (averaging $1400). In 2003, 408 non-need-based awards were made. *Average percent of need met:* 100%. *Average financial aid package:* $20,298. *Average need-based loan:* $4884. *Average need-based gift aid:* $15,616. *Average non-need-based aid:* $8890. *Average indebtedness upon graduation:* $16,818. *Financial aid deadline:* 2/1.

Applying *Options:* common application, electronic application, early admission, early decision, deferred entrance. *Application fee:* $30. *Required:* essay or personal statement, high school transcript, 3 letters of recommendation. *Recommended:* interview. *Application deadlines:* 1/20 (freshmen), 5/1 (transfers). *Early decision:* 11/20. *Notification:* 4/1 (freshmen), 12/20 (early decision), 5/15 (transfers).

Admissions Contact Mr. James Sumner, Dean for Admission and Financial Aid, Grinnell College, 1103 Park Street, Grinnell, IA 50112. *Phone:* 641-269-3600. *Toll-free phone:* 800-247-0113. *Fax:* 641-269-4800. *E-mail:* askgrin@grinnell.edu.

■ *See page 1692 for a narrative description.*

HAMILTON COLLEGE

Cedar Rapids, Iowa

- **Proprietary** primarily 2-year, founded 1900
- **Calendar** quarters
- **Degrees** certificates, diplomas, associate, and bachelor's (branch locations in Des Moines, Mason City, and Cedar Falls with significant enrollment reflected in profile)
- **Suburban** 4-acre campus
- **Coed**
- **Moderately difficult** entrance level

Faculty *Student/faculty ratio:* 25:1.

Student Life *Campus security:* 24-hour emergency response devices.

Standardized Tests *Required:* CPAt (for admission).

Costs (2003–04) *Tuition:* $14,160 full-time. *Payment plans:* tuition prepayment, installment.

Financial Aid Of all full-time matriculated undergraduates who enrolled in 2001, 10 Federal Work-Study jobs (averaging $889). 3 state and other part-time jobs (averaging $1885).

Applying *Options:* common application, early admission, deferred entrance. *Application fee:* $25. *Required:* high school transcript, minimum 2.0 GPA, interview.

Admissions Contact Mr. Brad Knudson, Director of Admissions, Hamilton College, 1924 D Street SW, Cedar Rapids, IA 52404. *Phone:* 319-363-0481. *Toll-free phone:* 800-728-0481. *Fax:* 319-363-3812.

HAMILTON TECHNICAL COLLEGE

Davenport, Iowa

- **Proprietary** 4-year, founded 1969
- **Calendar** continuous
- **Degrees** diplomas, associate, and bachelor's
- **Urban** campus
- **Coed,** 420 undergraduate students
- **Noncompetitive** entrance level

Freshmen *Admission:* 393 admitted.
Faculty *Total:* 18. *Student/faculty ratio:* 20:1.
Majors Drafting and design technology; electrical, electronic and communications engineering technology.
Academic Programs *Special study options:* accelerated degree program.
Library Hamilton Technical College Library with 4,500 titles, 30 serial subscriptions.
Computers on Campus 110 computers available on campus for general student use. Internet access, at least one staffed computer lab available.
Student Life *Housing:* college housing not available. *Campus security:* 24-hour emergency response devices.
Athletics *Intramural sports:* ultimate Frisbee M/W.
Costs (2003–04) *Tuition:* $6600 full-time, $220 per credit part-time. No tuition increase for student's term of enrollment.
Applying *Options:* common application, deferred entrance. *Application fee:* $25. *Required:* high school transcript, interview. *Application deadline:* rolling (freshmen), rolling (transfers).
Admissions Contact Mr. Chad Nelson, Admissions, Hamilton Technical College, 1011 East 53rd Street, Davenport, IA 52807. *Phone:* 563-386-3570. *Fax:* 563-386-6756.

IOWA STATE UNIVERSITY OF SCIENCE AND TECHNOLOGY

Ames, Iowa

- **State-supported** university, founded 1858
- **Calendar** semesters
- **Degrees** bachelor's, master's, doctoral, first professional, and post-master's certificates
- **Suburban** 1788-acre campus
- **Endowment** $335.9 million
- **Coed,** 22,230 undergraduate students, 93% full-time, 44% women, 56% men
- **Moderately difficult** entrance level, 90% of applicants were admitted

Undergraduates 20,682 full-time, 1,548 part-time. Students come from 54 states and territories, 113 other countries, 19% are from out of state, 3% African American, 3% Asian American or Pacific Islander, 2% Hispanic American, 0.3% Native American, 4% international, 6% transferred in, 32% live on campus. *Retention:* 84% of 2002 full-time freshmen returned.
Freshmen *Admission:* 9,035 applied, 8,116 admitted, 3,897 enrolled. *Average high school GPA:* 3.49. *Test scores:* SAT verbal scores over 500: 82%; SAT math scores over 500: 89%; ACT scores over 18: 97%; SAT verbal scores over 600: 48%; SAT math scores over 600: 61%; ACT scores over 24: 59%; SAT verbal scores over 700: 14%; SAT math scores over 700: 20%; ACT scores over 30: 12%.
Faculty *Total:* 1,659, 85% full-time, 87% with terminal degrees. *Student/faculty ratio:* 16:1.
Majors Accounting; advertising; aerospace, aeronautical and astronautical engineering; agricultural/biological engineering and bioengineering; agricultural business and management; agricultural mechanization; agricultural teacher education; agriculture; agronomy and crop science; animal sciences; anthropology; apparel and textiles; applied horticulture; architecture; art; atmospheric sciences and meteorology; biochemistry; biology/biological sciences; biophysics; botany/plant biology; business administration and management; business, management, and marketing related; chemical engineering; chemistry; city/urban, community and regional planning; civil engineering; commercial and advertising art; computer and information sciences; computer engineering; dairy science; design and visual communications; dietetics; dramatic/theatre arts; early childhood education; ecology; economics; education; electrical, electronics and communications engineering; elementary education; engineering; engineering related; engineering science; English; entomology; entrepreneurship; environmental studies; family and community services; family and consumer economics related; family and consumer sciences/home economics teacher education; family and consumer sciences/human sciences; family resource management; farm and ranch management; fashion/apparel design; finance; fish/game management; food services technology; foods, nutrition, and wellness; forestry; French; genetics; geology/earth science; German; graphic design; health and physical education; health teacher education; history; horticultural science; hotel/motel administration; housing and human environments; industrial engineering; interdisciplinary studies; interior design; international agriculture; international business/trade/commerce; international relations and affairs; journalism; landscape architecture; liberal arts and sciences/liberal studies; linguistics; logistics and materials management; management information systems; marketing/marketing management; mass communication/media; materials engineering; mathematics; mechanical engineering; medical illustration; microbiology; multi-/interdisciplinary studies related; music; music teacher education; natural resources management and policy; operations management; ornamental horticulture; philosophy; physics; plant protection and integrated pest management; political science and government; pre-dentistry studies; pre-law studies; pre-medical studies; pre-veterinary studies; psychology; public administration; religious studies; Russian studies; secondary education; sociology; Spanish; special products marketing; speech and rhetoric; statistics; technical and business writing; trade and industrial teacher education; visual and performing arts; women's studies; zoology/animal biology.
Academic Programs *Special study options:* academic remediation for entering students, accelerated degree program, adult/continuing education programs, advanced placement credit, cooperative education, distance learning, double majors, English as a second language, external degree program, freshman honors college, honors programs, independent study, internships, off-campus study, part-time degree program, services for LD students, student-designed majors, study abroad, summer session for credit. *ROTC:* Army (b), Navy (b), Air Force (b). *Unusual degree programs:* 3-2 engineering with William Penn College.
Library University Library plus 1 other with 2.3 million titles, 29,681 serial subscriptions, 58,055 audiovisual materials, an OPAC, a Web page.
Computers on Campus 2700 computers available on campus for general student use. A campuswide network can be accessed from student residence rooms and from off campus that provide access to e-mail, network services. Internet access, online (class) registration, at least one staffed computer lab available. Computer purchase or lease plan available.
Student Life *Housing options:* coed, men-only, women-only, disabled students. Campus housing is university owned. Freshman applicants given priority for college housing. *Activities and organizations:* drama/theater group, student-run newspaper, radio and television station, choral group, marching band, student government, Student Alumni Association, Residence Hall Associations, national fraternities, national sororities. *Campus security:* 24-hour emergency response devices and patrols, student patrols, late-night transport/escort service, controlled dormitory access, crime prevention programs, threat assessment team, motor vehicle help van. *Student services:* health clinic, personal/psychological counseling, women's center, legal services.
Athletics Member NCAA. All Division I except football (Division I-A). *Intercollegiate sports:* basketball M(s)/W(s), cross-country running M(s)/W(s), golf M(s)/W(s), gymnastics W(s), soccer W(s), softball W(s), swimming M(s)/W(s), tennis W(s), track and field M(s)/W(s), volleyball W(s), wrestling M(s). *Intramural sports:* archery M(c)/W(c), badminton M(c)/W(c), basketball M/W, bowling M(c)/W(c), cross-country running M/W, equestrian sports M(c)/W(c), fencing M(c)/W(c), football M/W, golf M/W, ice hockey M(c)/W(c), lacrosse M(c)/W(c), racquetball M(c)/W(c), riflery M(c)/W(c), rugby M(c)/W(c), sailing M(c)/W(c), skiing (cross-country) M(c)/W(c), skiing (downhill) M(c)/W(c), soccer M(c)/W(c), softball M/W, squash M/W, swimming M/W, table tennis M(c)/W(c), tennis M/W, volleyball M(c)/W(c), water polo M(c)/W(c), weight lifting M(c)/W(c), wrestling M/W.
Standardized Tests *Required:* SAT I or ACT (for admission).
Costs (2004–05) *Tuition:* state resident $4702 full-time, $196 per semester hour part-time; nonresident $14,404 full-time, $601 per semester hour part-time. Full-time tuition and fees vary according to class time, degree level, and program. Part-time tuition and fees vary according to class time, course load, degree level, and program. *Required fees:* $724 full-time. *Room and board:* $6121; room only: $3350. Room and board charges vary according to board plan and housing facility. *Payment plans:* installment, deferred payment.
Financial Aid Of all full-time matriculated undergraduates who enrolled in 2003, 13,749 applied for aid, 9,352 were judged to have need, 6,103 had their need fully met. 1,620 Federal Work-Study jobs (averaging $1828). In 2003, 3410 non-need-based awards were made. *Average percent of need met:* 73%. *Average financial aid package:* $7395. *Average need-based loan:* $4204. *Average need-based gift aid:* $3159. *Average non-need-based aid:* $3140. *Average indebtedness upon graduation:* $17,065.

Iowa State University of Science and Technology (continued)

Applying *Options:* common application, electronic application, deferred entrance. *Application fee:* $30. *Required:* high school transcript, rank in upper 50% of high school class. *Application deadlines:* 8/1 (freshmen), 8/1 (transfers). *Notification:* continuous (transfers).

Admissions Contact Mr. Phil Caffrey, Associate Director for Freshman Admissions, Iowa State University of Science and Technology, 100 Alumni Hall, Ames, IA 50011-2010. *Phone:* 515-294-5836. *Toll-free phone:* 800-262-3810. *Fax:* 515-294-2592. *E-mail:* admissions@iastate.edu.

■ *See page 1776 for a narrative description.*

IOWA WESLEYAN COLLEGE
Mount Pleasant, Iowa

- **Independent United Methodist** 4-year, founded 1842
- **Calendar** semesters
- **Degree** bachelor's
- **Small-town** 60-acre campus
- **Endowment** $5.9 million
- **Coed,** 753 undergraduate students, 71% full-time, 60% women, 40% men
- **Moderately difficult** entrance level, 53% of applicants were admitted

Undergraduates 531 full-time, 222 part-time. Students come from 22 states and territories, 7 other countries, 17% are from out of state, 9% African American, 1% Asian American or Pacific Islander, 4% Hispanic American, 0.1% Native American, 3% international, 10% transferred in, 57% live on campus. *Retention:* 55% of 2002 full-time freshmen returned.

Freshmen *Admission:* 680 applied, 358 admitted, 118 enrolled. *Average high school GPA:* 2.72. *Test scores:* ACT scores over 18: 59%; ACT scores over 24: 11%; ACT scores over 30: 2%.

Faculty *Total:* 63, 67% full-time, 33% with terminal degrees. *Student/faculty ratio:* 14:1.

Majors Accounting; adult and continuing education; art; art teacher education; biological and physical sciences; biology/biological sciences; business administration and management; chemistry; computer programming; computer science; criminal justice/law enforcement administration; education; elementary education; English; environmental biology; environmental health; fine/studio arts; history; information science/studies; kindergarten/preschool education; kinesiology and exercise science; liberal arts and sciences/liberal studies; mass communication/media; mathematics; music; music teacher education; natural sciences; nursing (registered nurse training); physical education teaching and coaching; pre-dentistry studies; pre-law studies; pre-medical studies; pre-pharmacy studies; pre-veterinary studies; psychology; secondary education; sport and fitness administration.

Academic Programs *Special study options:* academic remediation for entering students, adult/continuing education programs, advanced placement credit, distance learning, double majors, English as a second language, independent study, internships, off-campus study, part-time degree program, services for LD students, student-designed majors, study abroad, summer session for credit. *Unusual degree programs:* 3-2 forestry with Iowa State University of Science and Technology, Duke University.

Library Chadwick Library plus 1 other with 107,227 titles, 431 serial subscriptions, 6,553 audiovisual materials, an OPAC, a Web page.

Computers on Campus 72 computers available on campus for general student use. Internet access, at least one staffed computer lab available.

Student Life *Housing:* on-campus residence required through junior year. *Options:* men-only, women-only. Campus housing is university owned. Freshman campus housing is guaranteed. *Activities and organizations:* student-run newspaper, radio station, choral group, commuter club, Student Senate, international club, behavioral science club, Blue Key, national fraternities, national sororities. *Campus security:* 24-hour patrols, late-night transport/escort service, controlled dormitory access. *Student services:* health clinic, personal/psychological counseling.

Athletics Member NAIA. *Intercollegiate sports:* baseball M(s), basketball M(s)/W(s), cheerleading W, football M(s), soccer M(s)/W(s), softball W(s), track and field M(s)/W(s), volleyball W(s). *Intramural sports:* badminton M/W, basketball M/W, bowling M/W, football M/W, soccer M/W, softball M/W, swimming M/W, table tennis M/W, tennis M/W, track and field M/W, volleyball M/W, water polo M/W, weight lifting M/W.

Standardized Tests *Required:* SAT I or ACT (for admission).

Costs (2004–05) *Comprehensive fee:* $20,990 includes full-time tuition ($16,070) and room and board ($4920). Part-time tuition: $375 per credit hour. Part-time tuition and fees vary according to class time. *College room only:* $2050. Room and board charges vary according to board plan and housing facility. *Payment plans:* installment, deferred payment. *Waivers:* employees or children of employees.

Financial Aid Of all full-time matriculated undergraduates who enrolled in 2002, 460 applied for aid, 432 were judged to have need, 33 had their need fully met. 30 state and other part-time jobs (averaging $1000). In 2002, 26 non-need-based awards were made. *Average percent of need met:* 85%. *Average financial aid package:* $10,775. *Average need-based loan:* $2746. *Average need-based gift aid:* $6200. *Average non-need-based aid:* $3021. *Average indebtedness upon graduation:* $14,428.

Applying *Options:* common application, electronic application, early admission, deferred entrance. *Required:* high school transcript, minimum 2.0 GPA. *Required for some:* essay or personal statement, letters of recommendation. *Recommended:* interview. *Application deadlines:* 8/15 (freshmen), 8/15 (transfers). *Notification:* continuous (transfers).

Admissions Contact Mr. Cary A. Owens, Dean of Enrollment Management, Iowa Wesleyan College, 601 North Main Street, Mount Pleasant, IA 52641-1398. *Phone:* 319-385-6230. *Toll-free phone:* 800-582-2383. *Fax:* 319-385-6296. *E-mail:* admitrwl@iwc.edu.

KAPLAN COLLEGE
Davenport, Iowa

- **Proprietary** primarily 2-year, founded 1937, part of Kaplan Higher Education
- **Calendar** quarters
- **Degrees** certificates, diplomas, associate, and bachelor's
- **Suburban** campus
- **Coed,** 9,194 undergraduate students, 18% full-time, 72% women, 28% men
- **Minimally difficult** entrance level, 94% of applicants were admitted

Undergraduates 1,648 full-time, 7,546 part-time. Students come from 2 states and territories, 91% are from out of state, 1% African American, 0.1% Asian American or Pacific Islander, 0.4% Hispanic American, 0.1% Native American, 16% transferred in.

Freshmen *Admission:* 5,017 applied, 4,695 admitted, 4,635 enrolled.

Faculty *Total:* 411, 14% full-time, 23% with terminal degrees. *Student/faculty ratio:* 11:1.

Majors Accounting; business administration and management; business/commerce; court reporting; criminal justice/safety; information technology; legal assistant/paralegal; management information systems; medical/clinical assistant; medical transcription; multi-/interdisciplinary studies related; tourism and travel services management; web page, digital/multimedia and information resources design.

Academic Programs *Special study options:* academic remediation for entering students, adult/continuing education programs, cooperative education, distance learning, double majors, independent study, internships, part-time degree program, summer session for credit.

Library Academic Resource Center with 7,000 titles, 120 serial subscriptions, 504 audiovisual materials, an OPAC.

Computers on Campus 120 computers available on campus for general student use. A campuswide network can be accessed. Internet access, at least one staffed computer lab available.

Student Life *Housing:* college housing not available. *Activities and organizations:* academic department clubs. *Student services:* personal/psychological counseling.

Costs (2003–04) *Tuition:* $10,620 full-time, $236 per credit part-time. *Waivers:* employees or children of employees.

Applying *Options:* early admission, deferred entrance. *Application fee:* $25. *Required:* high school transcript, interview. *Application deadline:* rolling (freshmen), rolling (transfers).

Admissions Contact Mr. Robert Hoffmann, Director of Admissions, Kaplan College, 1801 East Kimberly Road, Suite 1, Davenport, IA 52807. *Phone:* 563-441-2496. *Toll-free phone:* 800-747-1035. *Fax:* 563-355-1320. *E-mail:* infoke@kaplancollege.edu.

LORAS COLLEGE
Dubuque, Iowa

- **Independent Roman Catholic** comprehensive, founded 1839
- **Calendar** semesters
- **Degrees** associate, bachelor's, and master's
- **Suburban** 60-acre campus
- **Endowment** $23.0 million
- **Coed,** 1,613 undergraduate students, 96% full-time, 51% women, 49% men
- **Moderately difficult** entrance level, 96% of applicants were admitted

Undergraduates 1,553 full-time, 60 part-time. Students come from 22 states and territories, 10 other countries, 46% are from out of state, 1% African American, 0.6% Asian American or Pacific Islander, 1% Hispanic American,

0.1% Native American, 1% international, 6% transferred in, 63% live on campus. *Retention:* 74% of 2002 full-time freshmen returned.

Freshmen *Admission:* 1,453 applied, 1,388 admitted, 414 enrolled. *Average high school GPA:* 3.21. *Test scores:* SAT verbal scores over 500: 76%; SAT math scores over 500: 81%; ACT scores over 18: 94%; SAT verbal scores over 600: 14%; SAT math scores over 600: 19%; ACT scores over 24: 38%; SAT verbal scores over 700: 10%; SAT math scores over 700: 5%; ACT scores over 30: 3%.

Faculty *Total:* 173, 68% full-time, 64% with terminal degrees. *Student/faculty ratio:* 12:1.

Majors Accounting; art teacher education; athletic training; biochemistry; biology/biological sciences; business administration and management; business/commerce; chemistry; clinical laboratory science/medical technology; computer science; creative writing; criminal justice/safety; early childhood education; economics; education; elementary education; engineering physics; engineering related; English; finance; fine/studio arts; French; health and physical education; history; human resources management; international business/trade/commerce; international relations and affairs; journalism; kindergarten/preschool education; kinesiology and exercise science; liberal arts and sciences/liberal studies; management information systems; marketing/marketing management; mass communication/media; mathematics; music; nuclear medical technology; philosophy; physical education teaching and coaching; physical sciences; physics; political science and government; pre-theology/pre-ministerial studies; psychology; public relations/image management; religious studies; secondary education; social work; sociology; Spanish; special education (emotionally disturbed); special education (mentally retarded); sport and fitness administration; visual and performing arts.

Academic Programs *Special study options:* academic remediation for entering students, adult/continuing education programs, advanced placement credit, cooperative education, double majors, English as a second language, honors programs, independent study, internships, off-campus study, part-time degree program, services for LD students, student-designed majors, study abroad, summer session for credit. *Unusual degree programs:* 3-2 engineering with Iowa State University of Science and Technology, University of Illinois, University of Notre Dame, University of Iowa; nursing with University of Iowa.

Library Academic Resource Center with 290,517 titles, 912 serial subscriptions, 1,676 audiovisual materials, an OPAC, a Web page.

Computers on Campus 105 computers available on campus for general student use. A campuswide network can be accessed from student residence rooms and from off campus. Internet access, at least one staffed computer lab available. Computer purchase or lease plan available.

Student Life *Housing:* on-campus residence required through junior year. *Options:* coed. Campus housing is university owned. Freshman campus housing is guaranteed. *Activities and organizations:* drama/theater group, student-run newspaper, radio and television station, choral group, Student Senate, campus ministry, College Activities Board, residence hall councils, national sororities. *Campus security:* 24-hour emergency response devices and patrols, late-night transport/escort service, controlled dormitory access. *Student services:* health clinic, personal/psychological counseling.

Athletics Member NCAA. All Division III. *Intercollegiate sports:* baseball M, basketball M/W, cross-country running M/W, football M, golf M/W, ice hockey M(c), rugby M(c), skiing (downhill) M(c), soccer M/W, softball W, swimming M/W, tennis M/W, track and field M/W, volleyball M(c)/W, wrestling M. *Intramural sports:* badminton M/W, baseball M, basketball M/W, cross-country running M/W, football M/W, golf M/W, ice hockey M, racquetball M/W, rugby M, skiing (cross-country) M/W, skiing (downhill) M/W, soccer M/W, softball M/W, swimming M/W, table tennis M/W, tennis M/W, track and field M/W, volleyball M/W, water polo M/W, weight lifting M/W, wrestling M.

Standardized Tests *Required:* SAT I or ACT (for admission).

Costs (2003–04) *Comprehensive fee:* $24,233 includes full-time tuition ($17,370), mandatory fees ($968), and room and board ($5895). Full-time tuition and fees vary according to course load and degree level. Part-time tuition: $385 per credit. *College room only:* $2900. Room and board charges vary according to board plan and housing facility. *Payment plan:* installment. *Waivers:* senior citizens and employees or children of employees.

Financial Aid Of all full-time matriculated undergraduates who enrolled in 2003, 1,320 applied for aid, 1,188 were judged to have need, 389 had their need fully met. 280 Federal Work-Study jobs (averaging $942). 254 state and other part-time jobs (averaging $2581). In 2003, 173 non-need-based awards were made. *Average percent of need met:* 92%. *Average financial aid package:* $16,479. *Average need-based loan:* $5329. *Average need-based gift aid:* $6449. *Average non-need-based aid:* $6330. *Average indebtedness upon graduation:* $18,325.

Applying *Options:* electronic application, deferred entrance. *Application fee:* $25. *Required:* high school transcript, minimum 2.5 GPA. *Required for some:* interview. *Recommended:* essay or personal statement, 1 letter of recommendation. *Application deadline:* rolling (freshmen), rolling (transfers). *Notification:* continuous (freshmen), continuous (transfers).

Admissions Contact Mr. Tim Hauber, Director of Admissions, Loras College, 1450 Alta Vista, Dubuque, IA 52004-0178. *Phone:* 563-588-7829. *Toll-free phone:* 800-245-6727. *Fax:* 563-588-7119. *E-mail:* adms@loras.edu.

■ *See page 1888 for a narrative description.*

LUTHER COLLEGE

Decorah, Iowa

- **Independent** 4-year, founded 1861, affiliated with Evangelical Lutheran Church in America
- **Calendar** 4-1-4
- **Degree** bachelor's
- **Small-town** 800-acre campus
- **Endowment** $60.2 million
- **Coed,** 2,565 undergraduate students, 98% full-time, 60% women, 40% men
- **Moderately difficult** entrance level, 77% of applicants were admitted

Undergraduates 2,503 full-time, 62 part-time. Students come from 35 states and territories, 32 other countries, 64% are from out of state, 0.5% African American, 1% Asian American or Pacific Islander, 1% Hispanic American, 0.2% Native American, 4% international, 2% transferred in, 83% live on campus. *Retention:* 85% of 2002 full-time freshmen returned.

Freshmen *Admission:* 1,998 applied, 1,537 admitted, 668 enrolled. *Average high school GPA:* 3.60. *Test scores:* SAT verbal scores over 500: 86%; SAT math scores over 500: 88%; ACT scores over 18: 98%; SAT verbal scores over 600: 44%; SAT math scores over 600: 54%; ACT scores over 24: 66%; SAT verbal scores over 700: 12%; SAT math scores over 700: 10%; ACT scores over 30: 12%.

Faculty *Total:* 235, 75% full-time, 68% with terminal degrees. *Student/faculty ratio:* 13:1.

Majors Accounting; African-American/Black studies; ancient/classical Greek; ancient Near Eastern and biblical languages; anthropology; art; arts management; biology/biological sciences; business administration and management; chemistry; classics and languages, literatures and linguistics; communication and journalism related; computer management; computer science; dance; economics; elementary education; English; French; German; health and physical education; health teacher education; history; interdisciplinary studies; international relations and affairs; Latin; management information systems; mathematics; music; nursing (registered nurse training); philosophy; physical education teaching and coaching; physics; physiological psychology/psychobiology; political science and government; psychology; religious studies; Scandinavian studies; social work; sociology; Spanish; sport and fitness administration; statistics; theatre/theatre arts management.

Academic Programs *Special study options:* academic remediation for entering students, advanced placement credit, double majors, honors programs, independent study, internships, off-campus study, part-time degree program, student-designed majors, study abroad, summer session for credit. *Unusual degree programs:* 3-2 engineering with Washington University in St. Louis; University of Minnesota, Twin Cities Campus; environmental management, resource management with Duke University.

Library Preus Library with 336,605 titles, 1,600 serial subscriptions, 7,000 audiovisual materials, an OPAC, a Web page.

Computers on Campus 526 computers available on campus for general student use. A campuswide network can be accessed from student residence rooms and from off campus. Internet access, online (class) registration, at least one staffed computer lab available.

Student Life *Housing:* on-campus residence required through senior year. *Options:* coed. Campus housing is university owned. Freshman campus housing is guaranteed. *Activities and organizations:* drama/theater group, student-run newspaper, radio station, choral group, Alpha Phi Omega—National Coed Service Fraternity, Student Activities Council, intramural clubs and organizations, Campus Ministry, national fraternities. *Campus security:* 24-hour emergency response devices and patrols, late-night transport/escort service, controlled dormitory access. *Student services:* health clinic, personal/psychological counseling.

Athletics Member NCAA. All Division III except men's and women's cheerleading (Division I). *Intercollegiate sports:* baseball M, basketball M/W, cheerleading M/W, cross-country running M/W, football M, golf M/W, soccer M/W, softball W, swimming M/W, tennis M/W, track and field M/W, volleyball W, wrestling M. *Intramural sports:* archery M/W, badminton M/W, basketball M/W, bowling M/W, football M/W, golf M/W, racquetball M/W, rock climbing M/W, rugby M(c)/W(c), skiing (downhill) M(c)/W(c), soccer M/W, softball M/W, table tennis M/W, tennis M/W, track and field M/W, ultimate Frisbee M/W, volleyball M(c)/W, water polo M/W.

Standardized Tests *Required:* SAT I or ACT (for admission).

Costs (2004–05) *Comprehensive fee:* $27,240 includes full-time tuition ($23,070) and room and board ($4170). Full-time tuition and fees vary according to course load. Part-time tuition: $824 per semester hour. Part-time tuition and

Luther College (continued)

fees vary according to course load. *College room only:* $2040. Room and board charges vary according to housing facility. *Payment plan:* installment. *Waivers:* employees or children of employees.

Financial Aid Of all full-time matriculated undergraduates who enrolled in 2002, 2,066 applied for aid, 1,798 were judged to have need, 571 had their need fully met. 950 Federal Work-Study jobs (averaging $1040). 1,000 state and other part-time jobs (averaging $976). In 2002, 220 non-need-based awards were made. *Average percent of need met:* 86%. *Average financial aid package:* $16,612. *Average need-based loan:* $4615. *Average need-based gift aid:* $11,104. *Average non-need-based aid:* $6423. *Average indebtedness upon graduation:* $17,312.

Applying *Options:* common application, electronic application, early admission, deferred entrance. *Application fee:* $25. *Required:* essay or personal statement, high school transcript, 1 letter of recommendation. *Recommended:* interview. *Notification:* continuous (freshmen), continuous (transfers).

Admissions Contact Mr. Jon Lund, Vice President for Enrollment and Marketing, Luther College, 700 College Drive, Decorah, IA 52101. *Phone:* 563-387-1287. *Toll-free phone:* 800-458-8437. *Fax:* 563-387-2159. *E-mail:* admissions@luther.edu.

■ See page 1902 for a narrative description.

MAHARISHI UNIVERSITY OF MANAGEMENT
Fairfield, Iowa

- **Independent** university, founded 1971
- **Calendar** semesters
- **Degrees** certificates, bachelor's, master's, doctoral, and postbachelor's certificates
- **Small-town** 272-acre campus
- **Endowment** $9.3 million
- **Coed,** 251 undergraduate students, 95% full-time, 47% women, 53% men
- **Moderately difficult** entrance level, 69% of applicants were admitted

Undergraduates 239 full-time, 12 part-time. Students come from 32 states and territories, 22 other countries, 48% are from out of state, 2% African American, 4% Asian American or Pacific Islander, 2% Hispanic American, 0.4% Native American, 30% international, 24% transferred in, 73% live on campus. *Retention:* 74% of 2002 full-time freshmen returned.

Freshmen *Admission:* 91 applied, 63 admitted, 59 enrolled. *Average high school GPA:* 3.38. *Test scores:* SAT verbal scores over 500: 88%; SAT math scores over 500: 86%; ACT scores over 18: 97%; SAT verbal scores over 600: 48%; SAT math scores over 600: 43%; ACT scores over 24: 59%; SAT verbal scores over 700: 11%; SAT math scores over 700: 6%; ACT scores over 30: 12%.

Faculty *Total:* 59, 76% full-time, 59% with terminal degrees. *Student/faculty ratio:* 14:1.

Majors Ayurvedic medicine; business administration and management; cinematography and film/video production; computer science; elementary education; English; environmental studies; fine/studio arts; mathematics; secondary education.

Academic Programs *Special study options:* academic remediation for entering students, adult/continuing education programs, advanced placement credit, cooperative education, distance learning, double majors, English as a second language, honors programs, independent study, internships, services for LD students, student-designed majors, study abroad.

Library Maharishi University of Management Library plus 1 other with 113,580 titles, 868 serial subscriptions, 21,850 audiovisual materials, an OPAC, a Web page.

Computers on Campus 120 computers available on campus for general student use. A campuswide network can be accessed from student residence rooms and from off campus. Internet access, at least one staffed computer lab available.

Student Life *Housing:* on-campus residence required through senior year. *Options:* men-only, women-only, disabled students. Campus housing is university owned. Freshman campus housing is guaranteed. *Activities and organizations:* drama/theater group, student-run newspaper, radio station, choral group, Student Senate, Soccer Club, Global Student Council, Fencing Club, Knitting Club. *Campus security:* 24-hour emergency response devices and patrols, late-night transport/escort service, controlled dormitory access. *Student services:* health clinic, personal/psychological counseling, legal services.

Athletics *Intercollegiate sports:* golf M/W, soccer M(c)/W(c). *Intramural sports:* archery M/W, badminton M/W, basketball M/W, fencing M/W, rock climbing M/W, sailing M/W, soccer M/W, table tennis M/W, tennis M/W, ultimate Frisbee M/W, weight lifting M/W.

Standardized Tests *Required:* SAT I or ACT (for admission).

Costs (2004–05) *One-time required fee:* $2500. *Comprehensive fee:* $30,430 includes full-time tuition ($24,000), mandatory fees ($430), and room and board ($6000). Part-time tuition: $550 per unit. Part-time tuition and fees vary according to course load. *College room only:* $2800. *Payment plan:* installment. *Waivers:* employees or children of employees.

Financial Aid Of all full-time matriculated undergraduates who enrolled in 2003, 192 applied for aid, 187 were judged to have need, 76 had their need fully met. 89 Federal Work-Study jobs (averaging $1589). 22 state and other part-time jobs (averaging $2753). In 2003, 18 non-need-based awards were made. *Average percent of need met:* 92%. *Average financial aid package:* $22,649. *Average need-based loan:* $8061. *Average need-based gift aid:* $17,720. *Average non-need-based aid:* $5950. *Average indebtedness upon graduation:* $18,996.

Applying *Options:* common application, electronic application, early admission, deferred entrance. *Application fee:* $25. *Required:* essay or personal statement, high school transcript, minimum 2.5 GPA, 2 letters of recommendation, minimum SAT score of 950 or ACT score of 19. *Recommended:* interview. *Application deadlines:* 8/1 (freshmen), 8/1 (transfers). *Notification:* continuous until 8/15 (freshmen), continuous (transfers).

Admissions Contact Mrs. Lois Neate, Associate Director of Admissions, Maharishi University of Management, Office of Admissions, Fairfield, IA 52557. *Phone:* 641-472-1110. *Toll-free phone:* 800-369-6480. *Fax:* 641-472-1179. *E-mail:* admissions@mum.edu.

MERCY COLLEGE OF HEALTH SCIENCES
Des Moines, Iowa

Admissions Contact Ms. Sandi Nagel, Admissions Representative, Mercy College of Health Sciences, IA. *Phone:* 515-643-6605. *Toll-free phone:* 800-637-2994.

MORNINGSIDE COLLEGE
Sioux City, Iowa

- **Independent** comprehensive, founded 1894, affiliated with United Methodist Church
- **Calendar** semesters
- **Degrees** bachelor's and master's
- **Suburban** 41-acre campus
- **Endowment** $25.3 million
- **Coed,** 942 undergraduate students, 92% full-time, 57% women, 43% men
- **Moderately difficult** entrance level, 74% of applicants were admitted

The Morningside College experience cultivates a passion for lifelong learning and a dedication to ethical leadership and civic responsibility. Students develop various dimensions of themselves through the liberal arts core curriculum, a complete range of majors, internships, independent study, and career and graduate school advising services. Typical merit scholarship candidates are students who make a difference in a variety of areas, both in and out of the classroom; those who have an alumni connection; or students with a tie to the United Methodist Church. Within 6 months of graduation, more than 95% are employed or admitted to graduate school.

Undergraduates 871 full-time, 71 part-time. Students come from 23 states and territories, 8 other countries, 29% are from out of state, 3% African American, 0.7% Asian American or Pacific Islander, 3% Hispanic American, 0.3% Native American, 2% international, 9% transferred in, 70% live on campus. *Retention:* 64% of 2002 full-time freshmen returned.

Freshmen *Admission:* 1,130 applied, 839 admitted, 273 enrolled. *Average high school GPA:* 3.27. *Test scores:* ACT scores over 18: 87%; ACT scores over 24: 35%; ACT scores over 30: 2%.

Faculty *Total:* 111, 57% full-time, 48% with terminal degrees. *Student/faculty ratio:* 14:1.

Majors Accounting; art; art teacher education; biology/biological sciences; biopsychology; business administration and management; business/corporate communications; business teacher education; chemistry; clinical laboratory science/medical technology; commercial and advertising art; computer science; counseling psychology; dramatic/theatre arts; education; elementary education; engineering physics; English; fine/studio arts; history; interdisciplinary studies; literature; management information systems; marketing/marketing management; mass communication/media; mathematics; music; music teacher education; nursing (registered nurse training); philosophy; photography; physics; political science and government; pre-dentistry studies; pre-law studies; pre-medical studies; pre-veterinary studies; psychology; religious studies; science teacher education; secondary education; Spanish; special education.

Academic Programs *Special study options:* academic remediation for entering students, adult/continuing education programs, advanced placement credit, double majors, English as a second language, honors programs, independent study, internships, off-campus study, part-time degree program, services for LD students, student-designed majors, study abroad, summer session for credit.

Library Hickman-Johnson-Furrow Library with 114,250 titles, 571 serial subscriptions, 5,372 audiovisual materials, an OPAC, a Web page.

Computers on Campus 800 computers available on campus for general student use. A campuswide network can be accessed from student residence rooms and from off campus. Internet access, at least one staffed computer lab available. Computer purchase or lease plan available.

Student Life *Housing:* on-campus residence required through junior year. *Options:* coed. Campus housing is university owned. Freshman campus housing is guaranteed. *Activities and organizations:* drama/theater group, student-run newspaper, radio and television station, choral group, Student Government/Activities Council, Student Ambassadors, fraternities and sororities, Homecoming Committee, New Student Orientation, national fraternities, national sororities. *Campus security:* 24-hour emergency response devices, student patrols, late-night transport/escort service, controlled dormitory access, 18-hour patrols by trained security personnel. *Student services:* health clinic, personal/psychological counseling, women's center.

Athletics Member NAIA. *Intercollegiate sports:* baseball M(s), basketball M(s)/W(s), cross-country running M(s)/W(s), football M(s), golf M(s)/W(s), soccer M(s)/W(s), softball W(s), swimming M(s)/W(s), tennis M(s)/W(s), track and field M(s)/W(s), volleyball W(s). *Intramural sports:* basketball M/W, bowling M/W, ultimate Frisbee M/W, volleyball M/W.

Standardized Tests *Required:* SAT I or ACT (for admission).

Costs (2003–04) *Comprehensive fee:* $21,610 includes full-time tuition ($15,450), mandatory fees ($900), and room and board ($5260). Part-time tuition: $500 per semester hour. *College room only:* $2750. Room and board charges vary according to board plan. *Payment plan:* installment. *Waivers:* children of alumni, senior citizens, and employees or children of employees.

Financial Aid Of all full-time matriculated undergraduates who enrolled in 2003, 835 applied for aid, 777 were judged to have need, 457 had their need fully met. 318 Federal Work-Study jobs (averaging $1096). 125 state and other part-time jobs (averaging $1406). In 2003, 94 non-need-based awards were made. *Average percent of need met:* 81%. *Average financial aid package:* $15,716. *Average need-based loan:* $3815. *Average need-based gift aid:* $5645. *Average non-need-based aid:* $5794. *Average indebtedness upon graduation:* $19,025.

Applying *Options:* electronic application, deferred entrance. *Application fee:* $25. *Required:* high school transcript, minimum SAT score of 930 or ACT score of 20 and rank in top 50% of high school class or achieved GPA of 2.5 or better. *Required for some:* 2 letters of recommendation. *Recommended:* interview. *Application deadline:* rolling (freshmen), rolling (transfers). *Notification:* continuous (freshmen), continuous (transfers).

Admissions Contact Mr. Joel Weyand, Director of Admissions, Morningside College, 1501 Morningside Avenue, Sioux City, IA 51106. *Phone:* 712-274-5111. *Toll-free phone:* 800-831-0806 Ext. 5111. *Fax:* 712-274-5101. *E-mail:* mscadm@morningside.edu.

■ *See page 2032 for a narrative description.*

MOUNT MERCY COLLEGE

Cedar Rapids, Iowa

- **Independent Roman Catholic** 4-year, founded 1928
- **Calendar** 4-1-4
- **Degree** bachelor's
- **Suburban** 40-acre campus
- **Endowment** $12.6 million
- **Coed**, 1,473 undergraduate students, 66% full-time, 70% women, 30% men
- **Moderately difficult** entrance level, 84% of applicants were admitted

Undergraduates 975 full-time, 498 part-time. Students come from 23 states and territories, 13% are from out of state, 2% African American, 1% Asian American or Pacific Islander, 1% Hispanic American, 0.3% Native American, 0.1% international, 14% transferred in, 28% live on campus. *Retention:* 77% of 2002 full-time freshmen returned.

Freshmen *Admission:* 488 applied, 408 admitted, 196 enrolled. *Average high school GPA:* 3.43. *Test scores:* ACT scores over 18: 98%; ACT scores over 24: 33%; ACT scores over 30: 3%.

Faculty *Total:* 135, 53% full-time, 43% with terminal degrees. *Student/faculty ratio:* 13:1.

Majors Accounting; art; art teacher education; biology/biological sciences; business administration and management; clinical laboratory science/medical technology; communication/speech communication and rhetoric; computer and information sciences; computer science; criminal justice/law enforcement administration; dramatic/theatre arts; education; elementary education; English; history; international relations and affairs; liberal arts and sciences/liberal studies; marketing/marketing management; mathematics; middle school education; music; music teacher education; nursing (registered nurse training); political science and government; pre-dentistry studies; pre-law studies; pre-medical studies; pre-veterinary studies; psychology; religious studies; science teacher education; secondary education; social work; sociology; speech and rhetoric; urban studies/affairs; voice and opera.

Academic Programs *Special study options:* academic remediation for entering students, accelerated degree program, adult/continuing education programs, advanced placement credit, double majors, freshman honors college, honors programs, independent study, internships, off-campus study, part-time degree program, services for LD students, student-designed majors, summer session for credit.

Library Busse Center with 118,000 titles, 1,000 serial subscriptions, 5,000 audiovisual materials, an OPAC, a Web page.

Computers on Campus 115 computers available on campus for general student use. A campuswide network can be accessed from student residence rooms and from off campus. Internet access, at least one staffed computer lab available.

Student Life *Housing options:* coed. Campus housing is university owned. Freshman campus housing is guaranteed. *Activities and organizations:* drama/theater group, student-run newspaper, choral group, Student Government Association, Students in Free Enterprise, Tomorrow's Nurses Today, Student-Iowa State Education Association. *Campus security:* 24-hour emergency response devices and patrols, student patrols, late-night transport/escort service, controlled dormitory access. *Student services:* health clinic, personal/psychological counseling, legal services.

Athletics Member NAIA. *Intercollegiate sports:* baseball M, basketball M/W, cheerleading W, cross-country running M/W, golf M/W, soccer M/W, softball W, track and field M/W, volleyball W. *Intramural sports:* baseball M, basketball M/W, football M/W, racquetball M/W, tennis M/W, volleyball M/W, weight lifting M/W.

Standardized Tests *Required:* SAT I or ACT (for admission).

Costs (2003–04) *Comprehensive fee:* $21,400 includes full-time tuition ($16,070) and room and board ($5330). Full-time tuition and fees vary according to course load. Part-time tuition: $445 per credit hour. Part-time tuition and fees vary according to course load. *College room only:* $2164. Room and board charges vary according to board plan. *Payment plan:* installment. *Waivers:* employees or children of employees.

Financial Aid Of all full-time matriculated undergraduates who enrolled in 2003, 862 applied for aid, 808 were judged to have need, 267 had their need fully met. 313 Federal Work-Study jobs (averaging $1482). 103 state and other part-time jobs (averaging $1545). In 2003, 93 non-need-based awards were made. *Average percent of need met:* 81%. *Average financial aid package:* $13,649. *Average need-based loan:* $4878. *Average need-based gift aid:* $8788. *Average non-need-based aid:* $9624. *Average indebtedness upon graduation:* $19,656.

Applying *Options:* electronic application, early admission, deferred entrance. *Application fee:* $20. *Required:* high school transcript, minimum 2.5 GPA, 1 letter of recommendation. *Required for some:* interview. *Recommended:* essay or personal statement, minimum 3.0 GPA. *Application deadlines:* 8/30 (freshmen), 8/30 (transfers). *Notification:* continuous (freshmen), continuous (transfers).

Admissions Contact Ms. Margaret M. Jackson, Dean of Admission, Mount Mercy College, 1330 Elmhurst Drive, NE, Cedar Rapids, IA 52402. *Phone:* 319-368-6460. *Toll-free phone:* 800-248-4504. *Fax:* 319-363-5270. *E-mail:* admission@mmc.mtmercy.edu.

■ *See page 2046 for a narrative description.*

NORTHWESTERN COLLEGE

Orange City, Iowa

- **Independent** 4-year, founded 1882, affiliated with Reformed Church in America
- **Calendar** semesters
- **Degrees** associate and bachelor's
- **Rural** 45-acre campus
- **Endowment** $32.0 million
- **Coed**, 1,285 undergraduate students, 95% full-time, 61% women, 39% men
- **Moderately difficult** entrance level, 83% of applicants were admitted

Ranked in the top tier of comprehensive Midwestern colleges by *U.S. News and World Report*, Northwestern College combines academic rigor with a Christian perspective and numerous opportunities for service and extracurricular preparation. A growing campus with state-of-the-art facilities has enabled Northwestern to accommodate record-setting enrollments for 4 consecutive years.

Undergraduates 1,227 full-time, 58 part-time. Students come from 29 states and territories, 12 other countries, 41% are from out of state, 0.5% African American, 0.9% Asian American or Pacific Islander, 1% Hispanic American, 3% international, 3% transferred in, 89% live on campus. *Retention:* 78% of 2002 full-time freshmen returned.

Northwestern College (continued)

Freshmen *Admission:* 1,311 applied, 1,090 admitted, 311 enrolled. *Average high school GPA:* 3.49. *Test scores:* ACT scores over 18: 96%; ACT scores over 24: 55%; ACT scores over 30: 8%.

Faculty *Total:* 121, 64% full-time, 52% with terminal degrees. *Student/faculty ratio:* 14:1.

Majors Accounting; actuarial science; administrative assistant and secretarial science; agribusiness; art; art teacher education; biology/biological sciences; biology teacher education; business administration and management; business teacher education; chemistry; clinical laboratory science/medical technology; computer science; dramatic/theatre arts; economics; education (K-12); elementary education; English; environmental science; history; humanities; kinesiology and exercise science; mass communication/media; mathematics; music; music teacher education; philosophy; physical education teaching and coaching; political science and government; psychology; religious education; religious studies; secondary education; social work; sociology; Spanish; speech and rhetoric; speech/theater education.

Academic Programs *Special study options:* academic remediation for entering students, accelerated degree program, advanced placement credit, cooperative education, double majors, English as a second language, freshman honors college, honors programs, independent study, internships, off-campus study, part-time degree program, student-designed majors, study abroad, summer session for credit. *Unusual degree programs:* 3-2 engineering with Washington University in St. Louis; nursing with Trinity Christian College, Briar Cliff College.

Library Ramaker Library plus 1 other with 125,000 titles, 615 serial subscriptions, 5,000 audiovisual materials, an OPAC.

Computers on Campus 250 computers available on campus for general student use. A campuswide network can be accessed from student residence rooms and from off campus. Internet access, online (class) registration, at least one staffed computer lab available.

Student Life *Housing:* on-campus residence required through senior year. *Options:* men-only, women-only, disabled students. Campus housing is university owned. *Activities and organizations:* drama/theater group, student-run newspaper, television station, choral group, Phi Beta Lambda, Student Ministries Board, Student Iowa State Education Association, Fellowship of Christian Athletes, international club. *Campus security:* 24-hour emergency response devices, controlled dormitory access. *Student services:* health clinic, personal/psychological counseling.

Athletics Member NAIA. *Intercollegiate sports:* baseball M(s), basketball M(s)/W(s), cross-country running M(s)/W(s), football M(s), golf M(s)/W(s), soccer M(s)/W(s), softball W(s), tennis M(s)/W(s), track and field M(s)/W(s), volleyball W(s), wrestling M(s). *Intramural sports:* badminton M/W, basketball M/W, bowling M/W, cheerleading M/W, cross-country running M/W, football M/W, golf M/W, lacrosse M/W, racquetball M/W, softball M, table tennis M/W, tennis M/W, ultimate Frisbee M(c)/W(c), volleyball M/W.

Standardized Tests *Required:* SAT I or ACT (for admission).

Costs (2003–04) *Comprehensive fee:* $19,640 includes full-time tuition ($15,290) and room and board ($4350). Part-time tuition: $320 per credit. Part-time tuition and fees vary according to course load. *College room only:* $1850. Room and board charges vary according to housing facility. *Payment plan:* installment. *Waivers:* employees or children of employees.

Financial Aid Of all full-time matriculated undergraduates who enrolled in 2002, 1,167 applied for aid, 1,049 were judged to have need, 547 had their need fully met. 389 Federal Work-Study jobs (averaging $950). 414 state and other part-time jobs (averaging $950). In 2002, 100 non-need-based awards were made. *Average percent of need met:* 88%. *Average financial aid package:* $13,738. *Average need-based loan:* $5192. *Average need-based gift aid:* $4635. *Average non-need-based aid:* $2086. *Average indebtedness upon graduation:* $18,267.

Applying *Options:* common application, electronic application, deferred entrance. *Application fee:* $25. *Required:* essay or personal statement, high school transcript, minimum 2.0 GPA, 1 letter of recommendation. *Recommended:* minimum 2.5 GPA, interview. *Application deadline:* rolling (freshmen), rolling (transfers). *Notification:* continuous until 8/30 (freshmen), continuous until 8/30 (transfers).

Admissions Contact Mr. Ronald K. DeJong, Director of Admissions, Northwestern College, 101 College Lane, Orange City, IA 51041-1996. *Phone:* 712-737-7130. *Toll-free phone:* 800-747-4757. *Fax:* 712-707-7164. *E-mail:* markb@nwciowa.edu.

PALMER COLLEGE OF CHIROPRACTIC

Davenport, Iowa

- **Independent** comprehensive, founded 1897, part of Palmer Chiropractic University System
- **Calendar** trimesters
- **Degrees** certificates, associate, incidental bachelor's, master's, and first professional
- **Urban** campus
- **Coed,** 97 undergraduate students, 86% full-time, 58% women, 42% men
- **Moderately difficult** entrance level

Undergraduates 83 full-time, 14 part-time. 5% African American, 5% Asian American or Pacific Islander, 1% Hispanic American.

Freshmen *Admission:* 33 enrolled. *Average high school GPA:* 2.8.

Faculty *Total:* 112, 100% full-time. *Student/faculty ratio:* 17:1.

Majors Biological and physical sciences; medical/clinical assistant.

Academic Programs *Special study options:* academic remediation for entering students, internships, services for LD students, summer session for credit.

Library D. D. Palmer Health Sciences Library with 51,445 titles, 894 serial subscriptions, 22,869 audiovisual materials, an OPAC.

Computers on Campus 75 computers available on campus for general student use. A campuswide network can be accessed from off campus. Internet access, at least one staffed computer lab available.

Student Life *Housing:* college housing not available. *Activities and organizations:* student-run newspaper, Gonstead Club, intramural sports, campus guides, Student International Chiropractic Association, Palmer Student Alumni Foundation. *Campus security:* 24-hour emergency response devices and patrols, late-night transport/escort service. *Student services:* health clinic, personal/psychological counseling.

Athletics *Intramural sports:* baseball M(c), basketball M(c)/W(c), golf M, ice hockey M(c), rugby M/W, soccer M, softball M/W, table tennis M/W, tennis M/W, volleyball M/W.

Costs (2003–04) *Tuition:* $5325 full-time, $126 per credit part-time. *Required fees:* $200 per term part-time. *Payment plan:* deferred payment. *Waivers:* employees or children of employees.

Financial Aid Of all full-time matriculated undergraduates who enrolled in 2003, 4 Federal Work-Study jobs (averaging $2200). *Average indebtedness upon graduation:* $14,013.

Applying *Options:* common application, electronic application, deferred entrance. *Application fee:* $50. *Required:* high school transcript, minimum 2.0 GPA, minimum 2.0 in math, science, and English courses. *Required for some:* essay or personal statement, interview. *Application deadline:* rolling (freshmen). *Notification:* continuous (freshmen).

Admissions Contact Ms. Lisa Walden, Interim Director of Admissions, Palmer College of Chiropractic, 1000 Brady Street, Davenport, IA 52803-5287. *Phone:* 563-884-5656. *Toll-free phone:* 800-722-3648. *Fax:* 563-884-5414. *E-mail:* pcadmit@palmer.edu.

ST. AMBROSE UNIVERSITY

Davenport, Iowa

- **Independent Roman Catholic** comprehensive, founded 1882
- **Calendar** 4-1-4
- **Degrees** certificates, bachelor's, master's, doctoral, post-master's, and postbachelor's certificates
- **Urban** 11-acre campus
- **Endowment** $30.6 million
- **Coed,** 2,483 undergraduate students, 80% full-time, 59% women, 41% men
- **Moderately difficult** entrance level, 87% of applicants were admitted

Undergraduates 1,983 full-time, 500 part-time. Students come from 23 states and territories, 15 other countries, 38% are from out of state, 11% transferred in, 45% live on campus. *Retention:* 75% of 2002 full-time freshmen returned.

Freshmen *Admission:* 1,112 applied, 971 admitted, 436 enrolled. *Average high school GPA:* 3.13. *Test scores:* ACT scores over 18: 89%; ACT scores over 24: 36%; ACT scores over 30: 4%.

Faculty *Total:* 293, 55% full-time, 42% with terminal degrees. *Student/faculty ratio:* 15:1.

Majors Accounting; advertising; art; art teacher education; biology/biological sciences; biology teacher education; business administration and management; business/commerce; business teacher education; chemistry; chemistry teacher education; computer science; computer systems analysis; computer systems networking and telecommunications; criminal justice/safety; design and visual communications; dramatic/theatre arts; early childhood education; economics; education; education (K-12); elementary education; engineering physics; English; English/language arts teacher education; finance; fine/studio arts; forensic psychology; French; French language teacher education; German; German language teacher education; graphic design; health and physical education; health teacher education; history; history teacher education; industrial engineering; information science/studies; international business/trade/commerce; journalism; management science; marketing/marketing management; mass communication/media; mathematics; mathematics teacher education; multi-/interdisciplinary studies related; music; music teacher education; nursing (registered nurse training); organizational behavior; philosophy; physical education teaching and coaching; physics; physics teacher education; political science and government; psychology; psychology teacher education; public administration; public relations/image management; radio and television; science teacher education; secondary education; security and protective services related; social science teacher education; sociology; Spanish; Spanish language teacher education; speech teacher education; speech/theater education; sport and fitness administration; theology.

Academic Programs *Special study options:* academic remediation for entering students, accelerated degree program, adult/continuing education programs, advanced placement credit, cooperative education, distance learning, double majors, external degree program, independent study, internships, off-campus study, part-time degree program, services for LD students, student-designed majors, study abroad, summer session for credit. *Unusual degree programs:* 3-2 physical therapy, occupational therapy, special education.

Library O'Keefe Library plus 1 other with 135,920 titles, 735 serial subscriptions, 2,930 audiovisual materials, an OPAC, a Web page.

Computers on Campus 190 computers available on campus for general student use. A campuswide network can be accessed from student residence rooms and from off campus that provide access to on-line course syllabi, class listings,grades. Internet access, online (class) registration, at least one staffed computer lab available. Computer purchase or lease plan available.

Student Life *Housing:* on-campus residence required through sophomore year. *Options:* coed, men-only, women-only, disabled students. Campus housing is university owned. Freshman campus housing is guaranteed. *Activities and organizations:* drama/theater group, student-run newspaper, radio and television station, choral group, Student Government Association, Student Alumni Association, Social Action Group, College Activities Board, Ambrosian's for Peace and Justice. *Campus security:* 24-hour emergency response devices and patrols, late-night transport/escort service, controlled dormitory access, police officer on campus 10 p.m. to 6 a.m. *Student services:* health clinic, personal/psychological counseling, women's center.

Athletics Member NAIA. *Intercollegiate sports:* baseball M(s), basketball M(s)/W(s), cross-country running M(s)/W(s), football M(s), golf M(s)/W(s), soccer M(s)/W(s), softball W(s), tennis M(s)/W(s), track and field M(s)/W(s), volleyball M(s)/W(s). *Intramural sports:* badminton M/W, baseball M/W, basketball M/W, bowling M/W, football M/W, golf M/W, racquetball M/W, skiing (downhill) M/W, soccer M/W, softball M/W, table tennis M/W, tennis M/W, volleyball M/W.

Standardized Tests *Required:* SAT I or ACT (for admission). *Recommended:* ACT (for admission).

Costs (2004–05) *One-time required fee:* $100. *Comprehensive fee:* $24,200 includes full-time tuition ($17,565) and room and board ($6635). Full-time tuition and fees vary according to course load and location. Part-time tuition: $547 per semester hour. Part-time tuition and fees vary according to course load and location. *College room only:* $3380. Room and board charges vary according to board plan and housing facility. *Payment plan:* installment. *Waivers:* minority students, children of alumni, senior citizens, and employees or children of employees.

Financial Aid Of all full-time matriculated undergraduates who enrolled in 2003, 1,865 applied for aid, 1,496 were judged to have need, 312 had their need fully met. 576 Federal Work-Study jobs (averaging $1269). 116 state and other part-time jobs (averaging $1441). In 2003, 369 non-need-based awards were made. *Average percent of need met:* 43%. *Average financial aid package:* $12,467. *Average need-based loan:* $4316. *Average need-based gift aid:* $4788. *Average non-need-based aid:* $5297. *Average indebtedness upon graduation:* $16,732.

Applying *Options:* common application, electronic application, deferred entrance. *Application fee:* $25. *Required:* high school transcript, minimum 2.5 GPA, minimum ACT score of 20 or rank in top 50% of high school class. *Required for some:* letters of recommendation, interview. *Recommended:* interview. *Application deadline:* rolling (freshmen), rolling (transfers). *Notification:* 10/1 (freshmen), continuous (transfers).

Admissions Contact Ms. Meg Halligan, Director of Admissions, St. Ambrose University, 518 West Locust Street, Davenport, IA 52803-2898. *Phone:* 563-333-6300 Ext. 6311. *Toll-free phone:* 800-383-2627. *Fax:* 563-333-6297. *E-mail:* halliganmegf@sau.edu.

■ *See page 2272 for a narrative description.*

SIMPSON COLLEGE
Indianola, Iowa

- **Independent United Methodist** 4-year, founded 1860
- **Calendar** 4-4-1
- **Degrees** diplomas, bachelor's, and postbachelor's certificates
- **Small-town** 74-acre campus
- **Endowment** $57.3 million
- **Coed,** 1,937 undergraduate students, 74% full-time, 59% women, 41% men
- **Moderately difficult** entrance level, 86% of applicants were admitted

Simpson is more than a beautiful campus. The College has an outstanding faculty and renowned curricula, including more than 40 majors, minors, and preprofessional programs. A 4-4-1 calendar provides students with many learning opportunities, including internships, career observations, and study programs both abroad and in the United States. The campus is located just 12 miles from Des Moines, Iowa's capital. Simpson's ideal location allows students the opportunity to enjoy both a large metropolitan area and small-town charm.

Undergraduates 1,436 full-time, 501 part-time. Students come from 27 states and territories, 20 other countries, 12% are from out of state, 0.9% African American, 1% Asian American or Pacific Islander, 1% Hispanic American, 0.2% Native American, 2% international, 4% transferred in, 82% live on campus. *Retention:* 81% of 2002 full-time freshmen returned.

Freshmen *Admission:* 1,271 applied, 1,097 admitted, 413 enrolled. *Test scores:* ACT scores over 18: 98%; ACT scores over 24: 55%; ACT scores over 30: 6%.

Faculty *Total:* 140, 60% full-time. *Student/faculty ratio:* 14:1.

Majors Accounting; advertising; art; art teacher education; athletic training; biochemistry; biological and physical sciences; biology/biological sciences; business administration and management; business/corporate communications; chemistry; clinical laboratory science/medical technology; commercial and advertising art; computer management; computer science; criminal justice/law enforcement administration; dramatic/theatre arts; economics; education; elementary education; English; environmental biology; French; German; history; information science/studies; international business/trade/commerce; international relations and affairs; kindergarten/preschool education; mass communication/media; mathematics; music; music performance; music teacher education; philosophy; physical education teaching and coaching; physical therapy; political science and government; pre-dentistry studies; pre-law studies; pre-medical studies; preveterinary studies; psychology; religious studies; secondary education; social sciences; sociology; Spanish; speech and rhetoric; sport and fitness administration.

Academic Programs *Special study options:* academic remediation for entering students, accelerated degree program, adult/continuing education programs, advanced placement credit, cooperative education, double majors, freshman honors college, honors programs, independent study, internships, off-campus study, part-time degree program, services for LD students, student-designed majors, study abroad, summer session for credit. *Unusual degree programs:* 3-2 engineering with Washington University in St. Louis.

Library Dunn Library plus 1 other with 151,359 titles, 599 serial subscriptions, 5,357 audiovisual materials, an OPAC, a Web page.

Computers on Campus 274 computers available on campus for general student use. A campuswide network can be accessed from student residence rooms and from off campus. Internet access, at least one staffed computer lab available.

Student Life *Housing:* on-campus residence required through junior year. *Options:* coed, men-only, women-only. Campus housing is university owned. Freshman campus housing is guaranteed. *Activities and organizations:* drama/theater group, student-run newspaper, radio station, choral group, intramurals, Religious Life Council, Campus Activities Board, student government, national fraternities, national sororities. *Campus security:* 24-hour emergency response devices and patrols, student patrols, late-night transport/escort service, controlled dormitory access. *Student services:* health clinic, personal/psychological counseling.

Athletics Member NCAA. All Division III. *Intercollegiate sports:* baseball M, basketball M/W, cheerleading M/W, cross-country running M/W, football M, golf M/W, rugby M(c)/W(c), soccer M/W, softball W, swimming M(c)/W, tennis M/W, track and field M/W, volleyball W, wrestling M. *Intramural sports:* badminton M/W, basketball M/W, bowling M/W, football M/W, racquetball M/W, soccer M/W, softball M/W, swimming M/W, ultimate Frisbee M/W, volleyball M/W, water polo M/W.

Standardized Tests *Required:* SAT I or ACT (for admission).

Costs (2003–04) *Comprehensive fee:* $24,159 includes full-time tuition ($17,908), mandatory fees ($189), and room and board ($6062). Part-time tuition and fees vary according to class time and course load. *College room only:* $3170. Room and board charges vary according to board plan and housing facility. *Payment plan:* installment. *Waivers:* employees or children of employees.

Financial Aid Of all full-time matriculated undergraduates who enrolled in 2003, 1,422 applied for aid, 1,261 were judged to have need, 315 had their need fully met. 484 Federal Work-Study jobs (averaging $612). 575 state and other part-time jobs (averaging $813). In 2003, 160 non-need-based awards were made. *Average percent of need met:* 87%. *Average financial aid package:* $17,124. *Average need-based loan:* $3757. *Average need-based gift aid:* $11,381. *Average non-need-based aid:* $7800. *Average indebtedness upon graduation:* $21,581.

Simpson College (continued)

Applying *Options:* electronic application, early admission, deferred entrance. *Required:* high school transcript, 1 letter of recommendation. *Recommended:* rank in upper 50% of high school class. *Application deadlines:* 8/15 (freshmen), 8/15 (transfers). *Notification:* continuous (freshmen), continuous (transfers).

Admissions Contact Ms. Deborah Tierney, Vice President for Enrollment, Simpson College, 701 North C Street, Indianola, IA 50125. *Phone:* 515-961-1624. *Toll-free phone:* 800-362-2454. *Fax:* 515-961-1870. *E-mail:* admiss@simpson.edu.

■ *See page 2392 for a narrative description.*

UNIVERSITY OF DUBUQUE

Dubuque, Iowa

- **Independent Presbyterian** comprehensive, founded 1852
- **Calendar** semesters
- **Degrees** associate, bachelor's, master's, doctoral, and first professional
- **Suburban** 56-acre campus
- **Coed,** 990 undergraduate students, 95% full-time, 35% women, 65% men
- **Moderately difficult** entrance level, 82% of applicants were admitted

Undergraduates 936 full-time, 54 part-time. Students come from 37 states and territories, 2 other countries, 46% are from out of state, 10% African American, 0.9% Asian American or Pacific Islander, 3% Hispanic American, 2% Native American, 1% international, 10% transferred in, 52% live on campus. *Retention:* 70% of 2002 full-time freshmen returned.

Freshmen *Admission:* 746 applied, 609 admitted, 313 enrolled. *Average high school GPA:* 3.00. *Test scores:* SAT verbal scores over 500: 38%; SAT math scores over 500: 44%; ACT scores over 18: 82%; SAT verbal scores over 600: 10%; SAT math scores over 600: 15%; ACT scores over 24: 19%; SAT verbal scores over 700: 1%; ACT scores over 30: 1%.

Faculty *Total:* 148, 41% full-time, 46% with terminal degrees. *Student/faculty ratio:* 14:1.

Majors Accounting; airline pilot and flight crew; animation, interactive technology, video graphics and special effects; aviation/airway management; biological and physical sciences; biology/biological sciences; biology teacher education; business administration and management; computer and information sciences; computer graphics; computer science; criminal justice/law enforcement administration; elementary education; English; English/language arts teacher education; environmental biology; environmental science; environmental studies; mass communication/media; nursing (registered nurse training); parks, recreation and leisure; philosophy; physical education teaching and coaching; professional studies; psychology; religious studies; secondary education; sociology; speech and rhetoric; theology; web/multimedia management and webmaster; web page, digital/multimedia and information resources design.

Academic Programs *Special study options:* academic remediation for entering students, accelerated degree program, adult/continuing education programs, advanced placement credit, distance learning, double majors, English as a second language, independent study, internships, off-campus study, part-time degree program, services for LD students, student-designed majors, study abroad, summer session for credit. *ROTC:* Army (b). *Unusual degree programs:* 3-2 communications.

Library Charles C. Myer's Library with 166,331 titles, 565 serial subscriptions, 525 audiovisual materials, an OPAC, a Web page.

Computers on Campus 220 computers available on campus for general student use. A campuswide network can be accessed from student residence rooms and from off campus that provide access to intranet. Internet access, at least one staffed computer lab available.

Student Life *Housing:* on-campus residence required through sophomore year. *Options:* coed, men-only, women-only. Campus housing is university owned. Freshman campus housing is guaranteed. *Activities and organizations:* drama/theater group, student-run newspaper, choral group, Alpha Phi Omega, Students in Free Enterprise, Student Activities Board, Student Government Association, Web of Life (environmental science). *Campus security:* 24-hour patrols, late-night transport/escort service, controlled dormitory access. *Student services:* health clinic, personal/psychological counseling.

Athletics Member NCAA. All Division III. *Intercollegiate sports:* baseball M, basketball M/W, cross-country running M/W, football M, golf M/W, soccer M/W, softball W, tennis M/W, track and field M/W, volleyball W, wrestling M. *Intramural sports:* archery M/W, badminton M/W, baseball M, basketball M/W, bowling M/W, cheerleading M/W, football M, golf M/W, racquetball M/W, soccer M/W, softball M/W, table tennis M/W, tennis M/W, track and field M/W, ultimate Frisbee M/W, volleyball M/W, wrestling M.

Standardized Tests *Required:* SAT I or ACT (for admission).

Costs (2004–05) *Comprehensive fee:* $21,680 includes full-time tuition ($16,100), mandatory fees ($160), and room and board ($5420). Part-time tuition: $360 per credit. *College room only:* $2610. Room and board charges vary according to board plan and housing facility. *Payment plans:* installment, deferred payment. *Waivers:* children of alumni and employees or children of employees.

Financial Aid Of all full-time matriculated undergraduates who enrolled in 2003, 958 applied for aid, 900 were judged to have need, 357 had their need fully met. 175 Federal Work-Study jobs (averaging $1500). 150 state and other part-time jobs (averaging $1500). In 2003, 70 non-need-based awards were made. *Average percent of need met:* 83%. *Average financial aid package:* $15,986. *Average need-based loan:* $8042. *Average need-based gift aid:* $8515. *Average non-need-based aid:* $15,657. *Average indebtedness upon graduation:* $26,000.

Applying *Options:* common application, electronic application. *Application fee:* $25. *Required:* essay or personal statement, high school transcript, minimum 2.0 GPA, 2 letters of recommendation. *Recommended:* interview. *Application deadline:* rolling (freshmen), rolling (transfers). *Notification:* continuous (freshmen), continuous (transfers).

Admissions Contact Mr. Jesse James, Director of Admissions, University of Dubuque, 2000 University Avenue, Dubuque, IA 52001-5099. *Phone:* 563-589-3214. *Toll-free phone:* 800-722-5583. *Fax:* 563-589-3690. *E-mail:* admssns@dbq.edu.

■ *See page 2600 for a narrative description.*

THE UNIVERSITY OF IOWA

Iowa City, Iowa

- **State-supported** university, founded 1847
- **Calendar** semesters
- **Degrees** bachelor's, master's, doctoral, and first professional
- **Small-town** 1900-acre campus
- **Endowment** $697.7 million
- **Coed,** 20,233 undergraduate students, 88% full-time, 54% women, 46% men
- **Moderately difficult** entrance level, 82% of applicants were admitted

Undergraduates 17,774 full-time, 2,459 part-time. Students come from 52 states and territories, 65 other countries, 33% are from out of state, 2% African American, 3% Asian American or Pacific Islander, 2% Hispanic American, 0.4% Native American, 1% international, 6% transferred in, 27% live on campus. *Retention:* 81% of 2002 full-time freshmen returned.

Freshmen *Admission:* 13,337 applied, 10,979 admitted, 4,083 enrolled. *Average high school GPA:* 3.54. *Test scores:* SAT verbal scores over 500: 84%; SAT math scores over 500: 88%; ACT scores over 18: 98%; SAT verbal scores over 600: 47%; SAT math scores over 600: 53%; ACT scores over 24: 64%; SAT verbal scores over 700: 11%; SAT math scores over 700: 14%; ACT scores over 30: 10%.

Faculty *Total:* 1,705, 95% full-time, 96% with terminal degrees. *Student/faculty ratio:* 15:1.

Majors Accounting; actuarial science; African-American/Black studies; African studies; Air Force R.O.T.C./air science; American Indian/Native American studies; American Sign Language related; American studies; ancient/classical Greek; ancient studies; anthropology; applied mathematics related; Army R.O.T.C./military science; art; art history, criticism and conservation; arts management; art teacher education; Asian studies; astronomy; athletic training; audiology and hearing sciences; audiology and speech-language pathology; biochemistry; biology/biological sciences; biology teacher education; biomedical/medical engineering; business administration and management; business/managerial economics; ceramic arts and ceramics; chemical engineering; chemistry; chemistry teacher education; Chinese; cinematography and film/video production; civil engineering; classics and languages, literatures and linguistics; clinical laboratory science/medical technology; communication/speech communication and rhetoric; comparative literature; computer and information sciences; computer science; dance; drama and dance teacher education; dramatic/theatre arts; drawing; economics; electrical, electronics and communications engineering; elementary education; engineering; English; English as a second/foreign language (teaching); English language and literature related; entrepreneurship; environmental science; environmental studies; film/cinema studies; film/video and photographic arts related; finance; fine/studio arts; French; French language teacher education; geography; geography teacher education; geology/earth science; German; German language teacher education; history; history teacher education; human resources management; industrial engineering; interdisciplinary studies; international/global studies; Italian; Japanese; jazz/jazz studies; journalism; kinesiology and exercise science; labor and industrial relations; Latin; Latin American studies; Latin teacher education; liberal arts and sciences/liberal studies; linguistics; literature; management information systems; management science; management sciences and quantitative methods related; marketing/marketing management; marketing related; mass communication/media; mathematics; mathematics teacher education; mechanical engineering; medieval and Renaissance studies; metal and jewelry arts; microbiology; modern Greek; museum studies; music; music management and merchandising; music teacher education; music theory and composition;

music therapy; nuclear medical technology; nursing (registered nurse training); painting; parks, recreation and leisure; pharmacy; philosophy; photography; physics; physics teacher education; piano and organ; political science and government; Portuguese; pre-dentistry studies; pre-law studies; pre-medical studies; pre-pharmacy studies; pre-veterinary studies; printmaking; psychology; radiologic technology/science; religious studies; Russian; Russian studies; science teacher education; sculpture; secondary education; social studies teacher education; social work; sociology; Spanish; Spanish language teacher education; speech and rhetoric; speech teacher education; sport and fitness administration; statistics; theatre/theatre arts management; therapeutic recreation; violin, viola, guitar and other stringed instruments; voice and opera; wind/percussion instruments; women's studies.

Academic Programs *Special study options:* academic remediation for entering students, accelerated degree program, adult/continuing education programs, advanced placement credit, cooperative education, distance learning, double majors, English as a second language, external degree program, honors programs, independent study, internships, off-campus study, part-time degree program, services for LD students, student-designed majors, study abroad, summer session for credit. *ROTC:* Army (b), Air Force (b).

Library Main Library plus 12 others with 4.0 million titles, 44,644 serial subscriptions, 267,192 audiovisual materials, an OPAC, a Web page.

Computers on Campus 1200 computers available on campus for general student use. A campuswide network can be accessed from student residence rooms and from off campus that provide access to online degree process, grades, financial aid summary, bills. Internet access, online (class) registration, at least one staffed computer lab available. Computer purchase or lease plan available.

Student Life *Housing options:* coed. Campus housing is university owned. Freshman applicants given priority for college housing. *Activities and organizations:* drama/theater group, student-run newspaper, radio station, choral group, marching band, Association of Students of Engineering, Association of Residence Halls, Newman Center, Friendship Association of Chinese Scholars, May Co., national fraternities, national sororities. *Campus security:* 24-hour emergency response devices and patrols, late-night transport/escort service, controlled dormitory access. *Student services:* health clinic, personal/psychological counseling, women's center, legal services.

Athletics Member NCAA. All Division I except football (Division I-A). *Intercollegiate sports:* baseball M(s), basketball M(s)/W(s), cheerleading M(s)/W(s), crew M(c)/W(s), cross-country running M(s)/W(s), field hockey W(s), golf M(s)/W(s), gymnastics M(s)/W(s), ice hockey M(c), lacrosse M(c)/W(c), rugby M(c)/W(c), sailing M(c)/W(c), soccer M(c)/W(s), softball W(s), swimming M(s)/W(s), table tennis M(c)/W(c), tennis M(s)/W(s), track and field M(s)/W(s), ultimate Frisbee M(c)/W(c), volleyball M(c)/W(s), wrestling M(s). *Intramural sports:* badminton M/W, basketball M/W, bowling M/W, fencing M(c)/W(c), football M/W, golf M/W, racquetball M/W, rock climbing M/W, rugby M(c)/W(c), sailing M(c)/W(c), skiing (cross-country) M(c)/W(c), skiing (downhill) M(c)/W(c), soccer M/W, softball M/W, tennis M/W, track and field M/W, ultimate Frisbee M/W, volleyball M/W, water polo M(c)/W(c), wrestling M.

Standardized Tests *Required:* SAT I or ACT (for admission).

Costs (2004–05) *Tuition:* state resident $4702 full-time, $196 per semester hour part-time; nonresident $15,354 full-time, $640 per semester hour part-time. Full-time tuition and fees vary according to course load and program. Part-time tuition and fees vary according to course load and program. *Required fees:* $694 full-time, $347 per term part-time. *Room and board:* $6350. Room and board charges vary according to board plan and housing facility. *Payment plan:* installment.

Financial Aid Of all full-time matriculated undergraduates who enrolled in 2003, 12,455 applied for aid, 9,243 were judged to have need, 6,557 had their need fully met. 1,200 Federal Work-Study jobs (averaging $2500). In 2003, 3866 non-need-based awards were made. *Average percent of need met:* 88%. *Average financial aid package:* $7386. *Average need-based loan:* $3861. *Average need-based gift aid:* $4497. *Average non-need-based aid:* $4192. *Average indebtedness upon graduation:* $16,750.

Applying *Options:* electronic application, early admission, deferred entrance. *Application fee:* $30. *Required:* high school transcript, rank in top 50% for residents, rank in top 30% for nonresidents. *Application deadlines:* 4/1 (freshmen), 4/1 (transfers). *Notification:* continuous (freshmen), continuous (transfers).

Admissions Contact Mr. Michael Barron, Director of Admissions, The University of Iowa, 107 Calvin Hall, Iowa City, IA 52242. *Phone:* 319-335-3847. *Toll-free phone:* 800-553-4692. *Fax:* 319-335-1535. *E-mail:* admissions@uiowa.edu.

UNIVERSITY OF NORTHERN IOWA

Cedar Falls, Iowa

- **State-supported** comprehensive, founded 1876, part of Board of Regents, State of Iowa
- **Calendar** semesters
- **Degrees** bachelor's, master's, and doctoral
- **Small-town** 916-acre campus
- **Endowment** $41.0 million
- **Coed,** 11,910 undergraduate students, 88% full-time, 58% women, 42% men
- **Moderately difficult** entrance level, 80% of applicants were admitted

Undergraduates 10,484 full-time, 1,426 part-time. Students come from 44 states and territories, 66 other countries, 4% are from out of state, 3% African American, 1% Asian American or Pacific Islander, 2% Hispanic American, 0.2% Native American, 2% international, 9% transferred in, 34% live on campus. *Retention:* 81% of 2002 full-time freshmen returned.

Freshmen *Admission:* 4,375 applied, 3,509 admitted, 1,785 enrolled. *Test scores:* SAT verbal scores over 500: 60%; SAT math scores over 500: 60%; ACT scores over 18: 95%; SAT verbal scores over 600: 31%; SAT math scores over 600: 39%; ACT scores over 24: 41%; SAT verbal scores over 700: 7%; SAT math scores over 700: 6%; ACT scores over 30: 4%.

Faculty *Total:* 799, 84% full-time, 74% with terminal degrees. *Student/faculty ratio:* 16:1.

Majors Accounting; acting; actuarial science; American studies; anthropology; apparel and textiles; applied economics; applied mathematics; art; art history, criticism and conservation; art teacher education; Asian studies; athletic training; biochemistry; biological and physical sciences; biology/biological sciences; biotechnology; broadcast journalism; business administration and management; business teacher education; chemistry; chemistry related; communication/speech communication and rhetoric; community health services counseling; computer and information sciences related; computer science; construction management; criminology; digital communication and media/multimedia; dramatic/theatre arts; driver and safety teacher education; ecology; econometrics and quantitative economics; economics; electromechanical technology; elementary education; engineering physics; English; English as a second/foreign language (teaching); environmental science; European studies; family and community services; family and consumer economics related; finance; fine/studio arts; foods, nutrition, and wellness; foreign languages and literatures; foreign languages related; foreign language teacher education; French; geography; geological and earth sciences/geosciences related; geology/earth science; German; gerontology; graphic communications; health and physical education; health professions related; health teacher education; history; housing and human environments; humanities; industrial technology; interior design; kindergarten/preschool education; Latin American studies; liberal arts and sciences/liberal studies; management information systems; manufacturing technology; marketing/marketing management; mathematics; mathematics teacher education; microbiology; middle school education; music; music performance; music teacher education; music theory and composition; organizational communication; parks, recreation and leisure; philosophy; physical education teaching and coaching; physics; physics related; political science and government; political science and government related; psychology; public administration; public relations/image management; radio and television; reading teacher education; real estate; religious studies; Russian; Russian studies; science teacher education; social science teacher education; social studies teacher education; social work; sociology; Spanish; special education; special education (early childhood); special education (mentally retarded); special education (multiply disabled); speech and rhetoric; speech-language pathology; speech teacher education; technology/industrial arts teacher education; theatre design and technology; theatre literature, history and criticism.

Academic Programs *Special study options:* academic remediation for entering students, accelerated degree program, adult/continuing education programs, advanced placement credit, cooperative education, distance learning, double majors, English as a second language, honors programs, independent study, internships, off-campus study, part-time degree program, services for LD students, student-designed majors, study abroad, summer session for credit. *ROTC:* Army (b). *Unusual degree programs:* 3-2 nursing with University of Iowa.

Library Rod Library with 760,595 titles, 7,226 serial subscriptions, 22,883 audiovisual materials, an OPAC, a Web page.

Computers on Campus 1284 computers available on campus for general student use. A campuswide network can be accessed from student residence rooms and from off campus that provide access to course registration, student account and grade information. Internet access, online (class) registration, at least one staffed computer lab available. Computer purchase or lease plan available.

Student Life *Housing options:* coed, men-only, women-only. Campus housing is university owned. *Activities and organizations:* drama/theater group, student-run newspaper, radio station, choral group, marching band, American Marketing Association, Public Relations Student Society, Iowa State Education Association, United Students of Iowa, Golden Key, national fraternities, national sororities. *Campus security:* 24-hour emergency response devices and patrols, student patrols, late-night transport/escort service, controlled dormitory access. *Student services:* health clinic, personal/psychological counseling.

University of Northern Iowa (continued)

Athletics Member NCAA. All Division I except football (Division I-AA). *Intercollegiate sports:* baseball M(s), basketball M(s)/W(s), cross-country running M(s)/W(s), golf M(s)/W(s), soccer W(s), softball W(s), swimming W(s), tennis M/W(s), track and field M(s)/W(s), volleyball W(s), wrestling M(s). *Intramural sports:* badminton M/W, basketball M/W, bowling M(c)/W(c), cheerleading M/W, crew M(c)/W(c), football M/W, golf M/W, ice hockey M(c), racquetball M(c)/W(c), rugby M(c)/W(c), skiing (cross-country) M(c)/W(c), skiing (downhill) M(c)/W(c), soccer M(c)/W(c), softball M/W, swimming W, table tennis M/W, tennis M/W, track and field M/W, volleyball M(c)/W(c), weight lifting M/W, wrestling M.

Standardized Tests *Required:* SAT I or ACT (for admission).

Costs (2003–04) *Tuition:* state resident $4342 full-time, $181 per hour part-time; nonresident $11,300 full-time, $471 per hour part-time. Full-time tuition and fees vary according to course load. Part-time tuition and fees vary according to course load. *Required fees:* $574 full-time. *Room and board:* $4918; room only: $2272. Room and board charges vary according to board plan and housing facility. *Payment plan:* installment.

Financial Aid Of all full-time matriculated undergraduates who enrolled in 2003, 8,217 applied for aid, 6,524 were judged to have need, 1,522 had their need fully met. 724 Federal Work-Study jobs (averaging $1997). 87 state and other part-time jobs (averaging $1944). In 2003, 745 non-need-based awards were made. *Average percent of need met:* 71%. *Average financial aid package:* $6705. *Average need-based loan:* $3976. *Average need-based gift aid:* $3122. *Average non-need-based aid:* $2655. *Average indebtedness upon graduation:* $16,716.

Applying *Options:* electronic application, deferred entrance. *Application fee:* $30. *Required:* high school transcript, rank in upper 50% of high school class. *Required for some:* interview. *Application deadlines:* 8/15 (freshmen), 8/15 (transfers). *Notification:* continuous (freshmen), continuous (transfers).

Admissions Contact Mr. Clark Elmer, Director of Enrollment Management and Admissions, University of Northern Iowa, 120 Gilchrist Hall, Cedar Falls, IA 50614-0018. *Phone:* 319-273-2281. *Toll-free phone:* 800-772-2037. *Fax:* 319-273-2885. *E-mail:* admissions@uni.edu.

UPPER IOWA UNIVERSITY
Fayette, Iowa

- **Independent** comprehensive, founded 1857
- **Calendar** 4 8-week terms
- **Degrees** associate, bachelor's, and master's (also offers continuing education program with significant enrollment not reflected in profile)
- **Rural** 80-acre campus
- **Coed,** 683 undergraduate students, 92% full-time, 40% women, 60% men
- **Moderately difficult** entrance level, 56% of applicants were admitted

Undergraduates 627 full-time, 56 part-time. Students come from 25 states and territories, 7 other countries, 42% are from out of state, 15% African American, 5% Asian American or Pacific Islander, 5% Hispanic American, 0.1% Native American, 2% international, 14% transferred in, 70% live on campus. *Retention:* 65% of 2002 full-time freshmen returned.

Freshmen *Admission:* 853 applied, 479 admitted, 146 enrolled. *Average high school GPA:* 2.96. *Test scores:* ACT scores over 18: 73%; ACT scores over 24: 25%.

Faculty *Total:* 65, 88% full-time, 62% with terminal degrees. *Student/faculty ratio:* 14:1.

Majors Accounting; agricultural business and management; art; arts management; art teacher education; athletic training; biological and physical sciences; biology/biological sciences; business administration and management; business teacher education; chemistry; commercial and advertising art; criminology; education; elementary education; English; environmental science; health/health care administration; human services; kinesiology and exercise science; liberal arts and sciences/liberal studies; management information systems; marketing/marketing management; mass communication/media; mathematics; natural resources/conservation; parks, recreation and leisure; physical education teaching and coaching; pre-dentistry studies; pre-medical studies; pre-veterinary studies; psychology; public administration; reading teacher education; science teacher education; social sciences; social science teacher education; sociology; trade and industrial teacher education.

Academic Programs *Special study options:* academic remediation for entering students, accelerated degree program, adult/continuing education programs, advanced placement credit, distance learning, double majors, external degree program, independent study, internships, part-time degree program, student-designed majors, study abroad, summer session for credit.

Library Henderson Wilder Library with 64,043 titles, 3,241 serial subscriptions, 4,031 audiovisual materials, an OPAC, a Web page.

Computers on Campus 75 computers available on campus for general student use. A campuswide network can be accessed. Internet access, at least one staffed computer lab available.

Student Life *Housing:* on-campus residence required through sophomore year. *Options:* coed, men-only, women-only. Campus housing is university owned. Freshman campus housing is guaranteed. *Activities and organizations:* drama/theater group, student-run newspaper, choral group, outdoor pursuits, Sigma Delta Phi, Alpha Nu Omega, psychology club, Campus Events Council. *Campus security:* late-night transport/escort service, controlled dormitory access. *Student services:* health clinic, personal/psychological counseling.

Athletics Member NCAA. All Division II except softball (Division III), men's and women's track and field (Division III). *Intercollegiate sports:* baseball M, basketball M/W, cheerleading M/W, football M, golf M/W, soccer M/W, softball W, tennis M/W, track and field M/W, volleyball M/W, wrestling M. *Intramural sports:* badminton M/W, basketball M/W, football M, golf M/W, rock climbing M/W, skiing (cross-country) M/W, softball M/W, table tennis M/W, tennis M/W.

Standardized Tests *Required:* SAT I or ACT (for admission).

Costs (2004–05) *Comprehensive fee:* $21,828 includes full-time tuition ($16,556) and room and board ($5272). Full-time tuition and fees vary according to course load. Part-time tuition: $550 per credit hour. *College room only:* $2188. Room and board charges vary according to board plan and housing facility. *Payment plan:* installment. *Waivers:* employees or children of employees.

Financial Aid *Average financial aid package:* $6000. *Average indebtedness upon graduation:* $17,125.

Applying *Options:* common application, early admission, deferred entrance. *Application fee:* $15. *Required:* high school transcript, minimum 2.0 GPA. *Required for some:* essay or personal statement, letters of recommendation, interview. *Application deadline:* rolling (freshmen), rolling (transfers).

Admissions Contact Ms. Linda Hoopes, Director of Admissions, Upper Iowa University, Box 1859, 605 Washington Street, Fayette, IA 52142-1857. *Phone:* 563-425-5281 Ext. 5279. *Toll-free phone:* 800-553-4150 Ext. 2. *Fax:* 563-425-5323. *E-mail:* admission@uiu.edu.

VENNARD COLLEGE
University Park, Iowa

- **Independent interdenominational** 4-year, founded 1996
- **Calendar** semesters
- **Degrees** certificates, associate, and bachelor's
- **Small-town** 70-acre campus with easy access to Des Moines
- **Endowment** $465,154
- **Coed,** 109 undergraduate students, 81% full-time, 43% women, 57% men
- 47% of applicants were admitted

Undergraduates 88 full-time, 21 part-time. Students come from 22 states and territories, 2 other countries, 66% are from out of state, 3% African American, 2% Asian American or Pacific Islander, 2% Hispanic American, 4% international, 7% transferred in, 76% live on campus. *Retention:* 66% of 2002 full-time freshmen returned.

Freshmen *Admission:* 51 applied, 24 admitted, 20 enrolled. *Average high school GPA:* 3.01. *Test scores:* SAT verbal scores over 500: 33%; SAT math scores over 500: 33%; ACT scores over 18: 65%; ACT scores over 24: 10%.

Faculty *Total:* 12, 42% full-time, 25% with terminal degrees. *Student/faculty ratio:* 12:1.

Majors Biblical studies; business administration and management; Christian studies; communications technology; computer/information technology services administration related; elementary education; general studies; missionary studies and missiology; multi-/interdisciplinary studies related; pastoral counseling and specialized ministries related; pastoral studies/counseling; psychology; religious education; religious/sacred music; religious studies; secondary education; theology; youth ministry.

Academic Programs *Special study options:* academic remediation for entering students, advanced placement credit, cooperative education, distance learning, double majors, external degree program, independent study, internships, off-campus study, part-time degree program, services for LD students, student-designed majors, summer session for credit.

Library Jessop-Bruner Library with 17,950 titles, 538,323 serial subscriptions, an OPAC, a Web page.

Computers on Campus 17 computers available on campus for general student use. Internet access, at least one staffed computer lab available.

Student Life *Housing:* on-campus residence required through sophomore year. *Options:* men-only, women-only. Campus housing is university owned. Freshman campus housing is guaranteed. *Campus security:* student patrols.

Athletics Member NCCAA. *Intercollegiate sports:* basketball M/W, soccer M, volleyball W. *Intramural sports:* golf M, soccer M/W, volleyball M/W.

Standardized Tests *Required for some:* SAT I or ACT (for admission), SAT I and SAT II or ACT (for admission).

Costs (2003–04) *Tuition:* Full-time tuition and fees vary according to course load. Part-time tuition and fees vary according to course load. Full-time (12+hours) tuition is $255 per credit hour. *Required fees:* $860 full-time. *Room and board:* $4300. *Payment plan:* installment. *Waivers:* employees or children of employees.

Financial Aid In 2002, 4 non-need-based awards were made. *Average percent of need met:* 60%. *Average financial aid package:* $7000. *Average indebtedness upon graduation:* $12,000.

Applying *Options:* common application, electronic application, early admission. *Application fee:* $20. *Required:* essay or personal statement, high school transcript, minimum 2.2 GPA, 3 letters of recommendation. *Notification:* continuous (transfers).

Admissions Contact Ms. Robyn Chrisman, Director of Admissions, Vennard College, PO Box 29, University Park, IA 52595. *Phone:* 641-673-8391 Ext. 116. *Toll-free phone:* 800-686-8391. *Fax:* 641-673-8365.

WALDORF COLLEGE

Forest City, Iowa

- **Independent Lutheran** 4-year, founded 1903
- **Calendar** semesters
- **Degree** bachelor's
- **Small-town** 29-acre campus
- **Coed,** 592 undergraduate students, 83% full-time, 50% women, 50% men
- **Moderately difficult** entrance level, 72% of applicants were admitted

Undergraduates 493 full-time, 99 part-time. Students come from 20 states and territories, 13 other countries, 33% are from out of state, 4% African American, 1% Asian American or Pacific Islander, 0.3% Hispanic American, 5% international, 8% transferred in, 93% live on campus. *Retention:* 75% of 2002 full-time freshmen returned.

Freshmen *Admission:* 585 applied, 424 admitted, 295 enrolled. *Average high school GPA:* 3.01. *Test scores:* ACT scores over 18: 75%; ACT scores over 24: 18%.

Faculty *Total:* 53, 68% full-time, 30% with terminal degrees. *Student/faculty ratio:* 13:1.

Majors Art teacher education; broadcast journalism; business administration and management; chemical engineering; cinematography and film/video production; creative writing; drama and dance teacher education; dramatic/theatre arts; early childhood education; education; education (multiple levels); elementary education; English; English/language arts teacher education; finance; health science; health teacher education; history; humanities; information science/studies; journalism; kindergarten/preschool education; marketing/marketing management; mass communication/media; middle school education; music management and merchandising; music performance; music teacher education; physical education teaching and coaching; psychology; social studies teacher education.

Academic Programs *Special study options:* academic remediation for entering students, accelerated degree program, adult/continuing education programs, advanced placement credit, cooperative education, double majors, English as a second language, freshman honors college, honors programs, internships, part-time degree program, services for LD students, study abroad, summer session for credit.

Library Voss Memorial Library with 33,422 titles, 55,989 serial subscriptions, 274 audiovisual materials, an OPAC.

Computers on Campus A campuswide network can be accessed from student residence rooms and from off campus that provide access to all students receive laptops. Internet access, at least one staffed computer lab available.

Student Life *Housing:* on-campus residence required through sophomore year. *Options:* coed, men-only, women-only. Campus housing is university owned. Freshman campus housing is guaranteed. *Activities and organizations:* drama/theater group, student-run newspaper, radio and television station, choral group, student government, FCA, drama club, intramurals, Amnesty International. *Campus security:* late-night transport/escort service, evening and night patrols by trained security personnel. *Student services:* health clinic, personal/psychological counseling.

Athletics Member NAIA. *Intercollegiate sports:* baseball M(s), basketball M(s)/W(s), football M(s), golf M(s)/W(s), soccer M(s)/W(s), softball W(s), volleyball W(s), wrestling M(s). *Intramural sports:* basketball M/W, football M, racquetball M/W, skiing (cross-country) M/W, skiing (downhill) M/W, soccer M/W, softball M/W, tennis M/W, volleyball M/W.

Standardized Tests *Required:* SAT I or ACT (for admission).

Costs (2003–04) *Comprehensive fee:* $17,862 includes full-time tuition ($13,000), mandatory fees ($662), and room and board ($4200). Full-time tuition and fees vary according to class time and course load. Part-time tuition: $180 per credit. *Required fees:* $35 per semester hour part-time. *College room only:* $2100. Room and board charges vary according to board plan and housing facility. *Payment plans:* installment, deferred payment. *Waivers:* employees or children of employees.

Financial Aid Of all full-time matriculated undergraduates who enrolled in 2003, 381 applied for aid, 368 were judged to have need, 70 had their need fully met. 296 Federal Work-Study jobs (averaging $1527). 97 state and other part-time jobs (averaging $906). In 2003, 66 non-need-based awards were made. *Average percent of need met:* 85%. *Average financial aid package:* $15,752. *Average need-based loan:* $4677. *Average need-based gift aid:* $11,062. *Average non-need-based aid:* $8717. *Average indebtedness upon graduation:* $10,500.

Applying *Options:* common application, electronic application, early admission. *Required:* high school transcript, 1 letter of recommendation. *Required for some:* interview. *Recommended:* minimum 2.0 GPA. *Application deadline:* rolling (freshmen), rolling (transfers). *Notification:* continuous (freshmen), continuous (transfers).

Admissions Contact Mr. Steve Hall, Assistant Dean of Admission, Waldorf College, 106 South 6th Street, Forest City, IA 50436. *Phone:* 641-585-8119. *Toll-free phone:* 800-292-1903. *Fax:* 641-585-8125. *E-mail:* admissions@waldorf.edu.

WARTBURG COLLEGE

Waverly, Iowa

- **Independent Lutheran** 4-year, founded 1852
- **Calendar** 4-4-1
- **Degree** bachelor's
- **Small-town** 118-acre campus
- **Endowment** $34.6 million
- **Coed,** 1,775 undergraduate students, 96% full-time, 55% women, 45% men
- **Moderately difficult** entrance level, 83% of applicants were admitted

Wartburg's integrated approach to education combines the liberal arts with an emphasis on leadership education, global and multicultural studies, and hands-on learning. Cultural immersion programs offer academic credit and give students the opportunity to live and work for one month, one term, or the entire year in settings throughout the United States and around the world.

Undergraduates 1,705 full-time, 70 part-time. Students come from 23 states and territories, 32 other countries, 19% are from out of state, 4% African American, 1% Asian American or Pacific Islander, 0.7% Hispanic American, 0.1% Native American, 4% international, 3% transferred in, 76% live on campus. *Retention:* 77% of 2002 full-time freshmen returned.

Freshmen *Admission:* 1,841 applied, 1,531 admitted, 504 enrolled. *Average high school GPA:* 3.46. *Test scores:* SAT verbal scores over 500: 71%; SAT math scores over 500: 70%; ACT scores over 18: 95%; SAT verbal scores over 600: 38%; SAT math scores over 600: 53%; ACT scores over 24: 50%; SAT verbal scores over 700: 5%; SAT math scores over 700: 5%; ACT scores over 30: 8%.

Faculty *Total:* 162, 64% full-time, 60% with terminal degrees. *Student/faculty ratio:* 14:1.

Majors Accounting; art; arts management; art teacher education; biochemistry; biology/biological sciences; broadcast journalism; business administration and management; chemistry; clinical laboratory science/medical technology; commercial and advertising art; computer science; economics; elementary education; engineering; English; English composition; finance; French; German; history; history teacher education; information science/studies; international business/trade/commerce; international relations and affairs; journalism; kindergarten/preschool education; marketing/marketing management; mass communication/media; mathematics; mathematics teacher education; music; music performance; music teacher education; music theory and composition; music therapy; occupational therapy; philosophy; physical education teaching and coaching; physics; political science and government; psychology; public relations/image management; religious/sacred music; religious studies; secondary education; social science teacher education; social work; sociology; Spanish; speech/theater education; sport and fitness administration.

Academic Programs *Special study options:* academic remediation for entering students, accelerated degree program, advanced placement credit, double majors, independent study, internships, off-campus study, part-time degree program, student-designed majors, study abroad, summer session for credit. *Unusual degree programs:* 3-2 engineering with Iowa State University of Science and Technology, University of Iowa, University of Illinois at Urbana-Champaign, Washington University in St. Louis; occupational therapy with Washington University in St. Louis.

Library Vogel Library with 171,852 titles, 826 serial subscriptions, 3,754 audiovisual materials, an OPAC, a Web page.

Computers on Campus 250 computers available on campus for general student use. A campuswide network can be accessed from student residence rooms and from off campus. Internet access, at least one staffed computer lab available.

Wartburg College (continued)

Student Life *Housing:* on-campus residence required through senior year. *Options:* coed, men-only, women-only, disabled students. Campus housing is university owned. Freshman campus housing is guaranteed. *Activities and organizations:* drama/theater group, student-run newspaper, radio and television station, choral group, Entertainment To Knight, choir, Student Senate, campus ministry, band. *Campus security:* 24-hour emergency response devices and patrols, late-night transport/escort service, controlled dormitory access. *Student services:* health clinic, personal/psychological counseling.

Athletics Member NCAA. All Division III. *Intercollegiate sports:* baseball M, basketball M/W, cheerleading W, cross-country running M/W, football M, golf M/W, soccer M/W, softball W, tennis M/W, track and field M/W, volleyball W, wrestling M. *Intramural sports:* badminton M/W, basketball M/W, golf M/W, racquetball M/W, rugby W, softball M/W, tennis M/W, ultimate Frisbee M/W, volleyball M/W

Standardized Tests *Required:* SAT I or ACT (for admission).

Costs (2003–04) *Comprehensive fee:* $23,730 includes full-time tuition ($18,150), mandatory fees ($400), and room and board ($5180). Part-time tuition: $670 per credit. Part-time tuition and fees vary according to class time and course load. *Required fees:* $15 per term part-time. *College room only:* $2530. Room and board charges vary according to board plan and housing facility. *Payment plan:* installment. *Waivers:* senior citizens and employees or children of employees.

Financial Aid Of all full-time matriculated undergraduates who enrolled in 2003, 1,577 applied for aid, 1,406 were judged to have need, 959 had their need fully met. 466 Federal Work-Study jobs (averaging $1490). 594 state and other part-time jobs (averaging $1661). In 2003, 337 non-need-based awards were made. *Average percent of need met:* 95%. *Average financial aid package:* $17,031. *Average need-based loan:* $6460. *Average need-based gift aid:* $11,123. *Average non-need-based aid:* $19,090. *Average indebtedness upon graduation:* $22,809.

Applying *Options:* common application, electronic application, deferred entrance. *Application fee:* $20. *Required:* high school transcript, minimum 2.0 GPA. *Required for some:* interview. *Recommended:* letters of recommendation, secondary school report. *Notification:* continuous (freshmen), continuous (transfers).

Admissions Contact Mr. Doug Bowman, Dean of Admissions/Financial Aid, Wartburg College, 100 Wartburg Boulevard, PO Box 1003, Waverly, IA 50677-0903. *Phone:* 319-352-8264. *Toll-free phone:* 800-772-2085. *Fax:* 319-352-8579. *E-mail:* admissions@wartburg.edu.

■ *See page 2784 for a narrative description.*

WILLIAM PENN UNIVERSITY
Oskaloosa, Iowa

- **Independent** 4-year, founded 1873, affiliated with Society of Friends
- **Calendar** semesters
- **Degrees** associate and bachelor's
- **Rural** 60-acre campus with easy access to Des Moines
- **Endowment** $4.2 million
- **Coed,** 1,499 undergraduate students, 94% full-time, 48% women, 52% men
- **Moderately difficult** entrance level, 65% of applicants were admitted

Undergraduates 1,411 full-time, 88 part-time. Students come from 42 states and territories, 12 other countries, 28% are from out of state, 8% African American, 0.5% Asian American or Pacific Islander, 3% Hispanic American, 0.3% Native American, 1% international, 8% transferred in, 40% live on campus. *Retention:* 55% of 2002 full-time freshmen returned.

Freshmen *Admission:* 717 applied, 465 admitted, 230 enrolled. *Average high school GPA:* 2.78. *Test scores:* ACT scores over 18: 75%; ACT scores over 24: 13%.

Faculty *Total:* 52, 67% full-time, 37% with terminal degrees. *Student/faculty ratio:* 14:1.

Majors Accounting; biology/biological sciences; business administration and management; business teacher education; communication/speech communication and rhetoric; computer science; criminology; driver and safety teacher education; education; elementary education; engineering technology; English as a second/foreign language (teaching); English/language arts teacher education; environmental biology; health and physical education; health teacher education; history; human services; industrial arts; industrial technology; journalism; mass communication/media; mathematics teacher education; mechanical engineering; parks, recreation and leisure; physical education teaching and coaching; political science and government; pre-dentistry studies; pre-law studies; pre-medical studies; psychology; public relations/image management; reading teacher education; science teacher education; secondary education; social science teacher education; sociology; special education; sport and fitness administration.

Academic Programs *Special study options:* academic remediation for entering students, adult/continuing education programs, advanced placement credit, cooperative education, double majors, English as a second language, independent study, internships, part-time degree program, services for LD students, student-designed majors, study abroad, summer session for credit. *Unusual degree programs:* 3-2 engineering with Washington University in St. Louis, Iowa State University of Science and Technology.

Library Wilcox Library with 72,907 titles, 354 serial subscriptions, 738 audiovisual materials, an OPAC, a Web page.

Computers on Campus 85 computers available on campus for general student use. A campuswide network can be accessed from student residence rooms and from off campus. Internet access, at least one staffed computer lab available. Computer purchase or lease plan available.

Student Life *Housing:* on-campus residence required through junior year. *Options:* coed, men-only, women-only. Campus housing is university owned. Freshman campus housing is guaranteed. *Activities and organizations:* drama/theater group, student-run newspaper, radio station, choral group, Fellowship of Christian Athletes, Greek Life, Literacy Tutoring Project, student government. *Campus security:* 24-hour emergency response devices and patrols, controlled dormitory access. *Student services:* health clinic, personal/psychological counseling.

Athletics Member NAIA. *Intercollegiate sports:* baseball M(s), basketball M(s)/W(s), cheerleading M(s)/W(s), cross-country running M(s)/W(s), football M(s), golf M(s), soccer M(s)/W(s), softball W(s), track and field M(s)/W(s), volleyball W(s), wrestling M(s). *Intramural sports:* basketball M/W, bowling M/W, football M, golf M, table tennis M/W, volleyball M/W, weight lifting M/W.

Standardized Tests *Required:* SAT I or ACT (for admission).

Costs (2004–05) *Comprehensive fee:* $19,350 includes full-time tuition ($14,234), mandatory fees ($370), and room and board ($4746). Part-time tuition and fees vary according to course load. *College room only:* $1852. Room and board charges vary according to board plan and housing facility. *Payment plan:* installment. *Waivers:* senior citizens and employees or children of employees.

Financial Aid Of all full-time matriculated undergraduates who enrolled in 2002, 310 Federal Work-Study jobs (averaging $1091). *Average indebtedness upon graduation:* $22,800.

Applying *Options:* electronic application, deferred entrance. *Application fee:* $20. *Required:* high school transcript, minimum 2.0 GPA. *Required for some:* essay or personal statement, letters of recommendation, interview. *Notification:* continuous (freshmen), continuous (transfers).

Admissions Contact Mrs. Mary Boyd, Director of Admissions, William Penn University, 201 Trueblood Avenue, Oskaloosa, IA 52577-1799. *Phone:* 641-673-1012. *Toll-free phone:* 800-779-7366. *Fax:* 641-673-2113. *E-mail:* admissions@wmpenn.edu.

■ *See page 2860 for a narrative description.*

KANSAS

BAKER UNIVERSITY
Baldwin City, Kansas

- **Independent United Methodist** comprehensive, founded 1858
- **Calendar** 4-1-4, semesters for nursing program
- **Degrees** bachelor's and master's
- **Small-town** 26-acre campus with easy access to Kansas City
- **Endowment** $27.8 million
- **Coed,** 1,015 undergraduate students, 95% full-time, 57% women, 43% men
- **Moderately difficult** entrance level, 82% of applicants were admitted

Undergraduates 960 full-time, 55 part-time. Students come from 21 states and territories, 7 other countries, 27% are from out of state, 5% African American, 0.7% Asian American or Pacific Islander, 2% Hispanic American, 1% Native American, 0.7% international, 4% transferred in, 90% live on campus. *Retention:* 74% of 2002 full-time freshmen returned.

Freshmen *Admission:* 945 applied, 771 admitted, 226 enrolled. *Average high school GPA:* 3.45. *Test scores:* SAT verbal scores over 500: 61%; SAT math scores over 500: 67%; ACT scores over 18: 96%; SAT verbal scores over 600: 19%; SAT math scores over 600: 20%; ACT scores over 24: 48%; SAT verbal scores over 700: 2%; ACT scores over 30: 8%.

Faculty *Total:* 101, 62% full-time, 51% with terminal degrees. *Student/faculty ratio:* 12:1.

Majors Accounting; art history, criticism and conservation; art teacher education; biology/biological sciences; business administration and management; chemistry; computer science; dramatic/theatre arts; economics; elementary education; engineering; English; fine/studio arts; French; German; history; information science/studies; international business/trade/commerce; mass communication/media; mathematics; molecular biochemistry; music; music teacher education; nursing (registered nurse training); philosophy; physical education teaching and coaching; physics; political science and government; psychology; religious studies; sociology; Spanish; speech and rhetoric; web/multimedia management and webmaster; wildlife biology.

Academic Programs *Special study options:* advanced placement credit, double majors, honors programs, independent study, internships, services for LD students, student-designed majors, study abroad, summer session for credit. *ROTC:* Army (c), Air Force (c). *Unusual degree programs:* 3-2 engineering with Washington University in St. Louis, University of Kansas; forestry with Duke University.

Library Collins Library with 84,114 titles, 507 serial subscriptions, 1,139 audiovisual materials, an OPAC, a Web page.

Computers on Campus 129 computers available on campus for general student use. A campuswide network can be accessed from student residence rooms. Internet access, at least one staffed computer lab available.

Student Life *Housing:* on-campus residence required through senior year. *Options:* coed, men-only, women-only, disabled students. Campus housing is university owned. Freshman campus housing is guaranteed. *Activities and organizations:* drama/theater group, student-run newspaper, radio station, choral group, Delta Sigma Pi, Earth We Are, Mungano, Fellowship of Christian Athletes, national fraternities, national sororities. *Campus security:* 24-hour emergency response devices and patrols, student patrols, controlled dormitory access. *Student services:* health clinic, personal/psychological counseling.

Athletics Member NAIA. *Intercollegiate sports:* baseball M(s), basketball M(s)/W(s), cheerleading M(s)/W(s), cross-country running M(s)/W(s), football M(s), golf M(s)/W(s), soccer M(s)/W(s), softball W(s), tennis M(s)/W(s), track and field M(s)/W(s), volleyball W(s). *Intramural sports:* basketball M/W, football M, softball M/W, volleyball M/W.

Standardized Tests *Required:* SAT I or ACT (for admission).

Costs (2003–04) *One-time required fee:* $80. *Comprehensive fee:* $19,860 includes full-time tuition ($14,210), mandatory fees ($350), and room and board ($5300). Full-time tuition and fees vary according to location and program. Part-time tuition: $455 per credit hour. Part-time tuition and fees vary according to course load. *Required fees:* $15 per credit hour part-time. *College room only:* $2400. Room and board charges vary according to board plan and housing facility. *Payment plan:* installment. *Waivers:* senior citizens and employees or children of employees.

Financial Aid Of all full-time matriculated undergraduates who enrolled in 2002, 926 applied for aid, 695 were judged to have need. 176 Federal Work-Study jobs (averaging $1050). 248 state and other part-time jobs (averaging $1053). In 2002, 231 non-need-based awards were made. *Average financial aid package:* $10,900. *Average need-based loan:* $5360. *Average need-based gift aid:* $4033. *Average non-need-based aid:* $5156. *Average indebtedness upon graduation:* $17,682.

Applying *Options:* electronic application, deferred entrance. *Application fee:* $20. *Required:* high school transcript, 1 letter of recommendation. *Required for some:* essay or personal statement, interview. *Recommended:* minimum 3.0 GPA, minimum ACT score of 21. *Application deadline:* rolling (freshmen), rolling (transfers).

Admissions Contact Ms. Annette Galluzzi, Vice President for Marketing, Baker University, PO Box 65, Baldwin City, KS 66006-0065. *Phone:* 785-594-6451 Ext. 344. *Toll-free phone:* 800-873-4282. *Fax:* 785-594-8372. *E-mail:* admission@bakeru.edu.

■ *See page 1206 for a narrative description.*

Barclay College
Haviland, Kansas

- **Independent** 4-year, founded 1917, affiliated with Society of Friends
- **Calendar** semesters
- **Degrees** certificates, associate, and bachelor's
- **Rural** 13-acre campus
- **Endowment** $835,322
- **Coed,** 185 undergraduate students, 92% full-time, 50% women, 50% men
- **Minimally difficult** entrance level, 66% of applicants were admitted

Barclay College is a coed, 4-year, interdenominational, accredited college located in Haviland, Kansas. Founded in 1917 by the Evangelical Friends, Barclay offers bachelor's degrees in Bible/theology, business administration, Christian school elementary education, church music, pastoral ministries, psychology/family counseling, and youth ministries, along with associate degrees. Tuition, room and board, and fees total $11,200.

Undergraduates 171 full-time, 14 part-time. Students come from 21 states and territories, 1 other country, 44% are from out of state, 5% African American, 2% Asian American or Pacific Islander, 2% Hispanic American, 2% Native American, 1% international, 10% transferred in. *Retention:* 60% of 2002 full-time freshmen returned.

Freshmen *Admission:* 137 applied, 90 admitted, 29 enrolled. *Test scores:* SAT verbal scores over 500: 25%; SAT math scores over 500: 25%; ACT scores over 18: 75%; SAT math scores over 600: 25%; ACT scores over 24: 25%.

Faculty *Total:* 38, 21% full-time, 8% with terminal degrees. *Student/faculty ratio:* 7:1.

Majors Biblical studies; business administration and management; divinity/ministry; elementary education; pastoral studies/counseling; psychology; religious education; religious/sacred music.

Academic Programs *Special study options:* academic remediation for entering students, accelerated degree program, adult/continuing education programs, advanced placement credit, distance learning, double majors, external degree program, independent study, internships, part-time degree program, student-designed majors.

Library Worden Memorial Library with 60,397 titles, 6,959 serial subscriptions, 2,291 audiovisual materials, an OPAC.

Computers on Campus 20 computers available on campus for general student use. A campuswide network can be accessed from off campus that provide access to on-line library catalog. Internet access, at least one staffed computer lab available. Computer purchase or lease plan available.

Student Life *Housing:* on-campus residence required through senior year. *Options:* men-only, women-only. Campus housing is university owned. Freshman campus housing is guaranteed. *Activities and organizations:* drama/theater group, choral group, pep club, drama club, missions club. *Campus security:* student patrols. *Student services:* personal/psychological counseling.

Athletics Member NSCAA. *Intercollegiate sports:* baseball M, basketball M/W, cheerleading M/W, soccer M, tennis M/W, volleyball W. *Intramural sports:* baseball M/W, basketball M/W, volleyball M/W.

Standardized Tests *Required:* SAT I or ACT (for admission).

Costs (2004–05) *Comprehensive fee:* $14,650 includes full-time tuition ($9250), mandatory fees ($700), and room and board ($4700). Part-time tuition and fees vary according to course load. *College room only:* $1850. Room and board charges vary according to board plan. *Payment plan:* installment. *Waivers:* employees or children of employees.

Financial Aid Of all full-time matriculated undergraduates who enrolled in 2003, 163 applied for aid, 163 were judged to have need, 145 had their need fully met. 33 Federal Work-Study jobs (averaging $1200). 67 state and other part-time jobs (averaging $600). In 2003, 4 non-need-based awards were made. *Average percent of need met:* 85%. *Average financial aid package:* $6700. *Average need-based loan:* $3750. *Average need-based gift aid:* $1500. *Average non-need-based aid:* $1500. *Average indebtedness upon graduation:* $10,000.

Applying *Options:* early admission, deferred entrance. *Application fee:* $15. *Required:* essay or personal statement, high school transcript, minimum 2.3 GPA, 2 letters of recommendation. *Application deadlines:* 9/1 (freshmen), 9/1 (transfers).

Admissions Contact Ryan Haase, Director of Admissions, Barclay College, 607 North Kingman, Haviland, KS 67059. *Phone:* 620-862-5252 Ext. 41. *Toll-free phone:* 800-862-0226. *Fax:* 620-862-5242. *E-mail:* admissions@barclaycollege.edu.

Benedictine College
Atchison, Kansas

- **Independent Roman Catholic** comprehensive, founded 1859
- **Calendar** semesters
- **Degrees** associate, bachelor's, and master's
- **Small-town** 225-acre campus with easy access to Kansas City
- **Endowment** $8.9 million
- **Coed,** 1,271 undergraduate students, 77% full-time, 52% women, 48% men
- **Moderately difficult** entrance level, 96% of applicants were admitted

Benedictine College, in Atchison, Kansas, enjoys more than 145 years of Catholic Benedictine commitment to learning, ethics, and spirituality. Its combination of tradition, experience, and dedication gives students a uniquely creative, collaborative, and challenging learning experience enabling them to succeed in every aspect of their lives.

Undergraduates 977 full-time, 294 part-time. Students come from 38 states and territories, 18 other countries, 53% are from out of state, 4% African American, 1% Asian American or Pacific Islander, 8% Hispanic American, 0.5% Native American, 3% international, 5% transferred in, 74% live on campus. *Retention:* 84% of 2002 full-time freshmen returned.

Freshmen *Admission:* 580 applied, 556 admitted, 253 enrolled. *Average high school GPA:* 3.23. *Test scores:* SAT verbal scores over 500: 68%; SAT math scores over 500: 64%; ACT scores over 18: 92%; SAT verbal scores over 600: 16%; SAT math scores over 600: 19%; ACT scores over 24: 37%; SAT verbal scores over 700: 3%; SAT math scores over 700: 3%; ACT scores over 30: 4%.

Benedictine College (continued)

Faculty *Total:* 96, 56% full-time, 51% with terminal degrees. *Student/faculty ratio:* 16:1.

Majors Accounting; arts management; astronomy; athletic training; biochemistry; biology/biological sciences; business administration and management; chemistry; computer science; dramatic/theatre arts; economics; elementary education; English; French; history; liberal arts and sciences/liberal studies; mass communication/media; mathematics; music; music teacher education; natural sciences; philosophy; physical education teaching and coaching; physics; political science and government; psychology; religious studies; secondary education; social sciences; sociology; Spanish; special education; youth ministry.

Academic Programs *Special study options:* academic remediation for entering students, advanced placement credit, cooperative education, English as a second language, independent study, internships, off-campus study, part-time degree program, student-designed majors, study abroad, summer session for credit. *ROTC:* Army (b). *Unusual degree programs:* 3-2 engineering with Kansas State University, University of Missouri–Columbia, South Dakota School of Mines and Technology; occupational therapy with Washington University in St. Louis.

Library Benedictine College Library with 366,212 titles, 501 serial subscriptions, 831 audiovisual materials, an OPAC, a Web page.

Computers on Campus 80 computers available on campus for general student use. A campuswide network can be accessed from student residence rooms and from off campus. Internet access, at least one staffed computer lab available.

Student Life *Housing:* on-campus residence required through senior year. *Options:* coed, men-only, women-only. Campus housing is university owned. Freshman campus housing is guaranteed. *Activities and organizations:* drama/theater group, student-run newspaper, choral group, student government, Students in Free Enterprise, Knights of Columbus, Concert Chorale/Chamber Singers, Campus Activities Board. *Campus security:* 24-hour emergency response devices and patrols, late-night transport/escort service. *Student services:* health clinic, personal/psychological counseling.

Athletics Member NAIA. *Intercollegiate sports:* baseball M(s), basketball M(s)/W(s), cheerleading M(s)/W(s), cross-country running M(s)/W(s), football M(s), golf M(s)/W(s), soccer M(s)/W(s), softball W(s), tennis M(s)/W(s), track and field M(s)/W(s), volleyball W(s). *Intramural sports:* basketball M/W, football M/W, racquetball M/W, soccer M/W, softball M/W, table tennis M/W, ultimate Frisbee M(c)/W(c), volleyball M/W.

Standardized Tests *Required:* SAT I or ACT (for admission).

Costs (2003–04) *Comprehensive fee:* $20,533 includes full-time tuition ($14,083), mandatory fees ($530), and room and board ($5920). Full-time tuition and fees vary according to course load and degree level. Part-time tuition: $300 per credit hour. Part-time tuition and fees vary according to course load and degree level. *College room only:* $2560. Room and board charges vary according to board plan and housing facility. *Payment plan:* installment. *Waivers:* senior citizens and employees or children of employees.

Financial Aid Of all full-time matriculated undergraduates who enrolled in 2003, 955 applied for aid, 680 were judged to have need, 98 had their need fully met. 422 Federal Work-Study jobs (averaging $1064). 145 state and other part-time jobs (averaging $1535). In 2003, 56 non-need-based awards were made. *Average percent of need met:* 74%. *Average financial aid package:* $12,667. *Average need-based loan:* $4618. *Average need-based gift aid:* $7843. *Average non-need-based aid:* $5297. *Average indebtedness upon graduation:* $20,684.

Applying *Options:* common application, electronic application, deferred entrance. *Application fee:* $25. *Required:* high school transcript, minimum 2.0 GPA. *Required for some:* interview. *Notification:* continuous (freshmen), continuous (transfers).

Admissions Contact Ms. Kelly Vowels, Dean of Enrollment Management, Benedictine College, 1020 North 2nd Street, Atchison, KS 66002. *Phone:* 913-367-5340 Ext. 2476. *Toll-free phone:* 800-467-5340. *Fax:* 913-367-5462. *E-mail:* bcadmiss@benedictine.edu.

■ *See page 1234 for a narrative description.*

BETHANY COLLEGE
Lindsborg, Kansas

- **Independent Lutheran** 4-year, founded 1881
- **Calendar** 4-1-4
- **Degree** bachelor's
- **Small-town** 80-acre campus
- **Endowment** $19.5 million
- **Coed,** 631 undergraduate students, 92% full-time, 44% women, 56% men
- **Moderately difficult** entrance level, 71% of applicants were admitted

Undergraduates 579 full-time, 52 part-time. Students come from 27 states and territories, 10 other countries, 41% are from out of state, 8% African American, 2% Asian American or Pacific Islander, 4% Hispanic American, 2% Native American, 2% international, 7% transferred in, 72% live on campus. *Retention:* 66% of 2002 full-time freshmen returned.

Freshmen *Admission:* 775 applied, 548 admitted, 172 enrolled. *Average high school GPA:* 3.30. *Test scores:* SAT verbal scores over 500: 30%; SAT math scores over 500: 50%; ACT scores over 18: 85%; SAT verbal scores over 600: 1%; SAT math scores over 600: 7%; ACT scores over 24: 26%; ACT scores over 30: 3%.

Faculty *Total:* 69, 59% full-time, 38% with terminal degrees. *Student/faculty ratio:* 13:1.

Majors Accounting; art; art teacher education; athletic training; biology/biological sciences; biology teacher education; business administration and management; business/managerial economics; business teacher education; ceramic arts and ceramics; chemistry; chemistry teacher education; Christian studies; communication/speech communication and rhetoric; criminal justice/safety; drawing; education; elementary education; English; English/language arts teacher education; financial planning and services; history; international business/trade/commerce; legal professions and studies related; mathematics; mathematics teacher education; music; music teacher education; painting; parks, recreation and leisure; philosophy; physical education teaching and coaching; political science and government; psychology; religious studies; sculpture; social studies teacher education; social work; sociology.

Academic Programs *Special study options:* accelerated degree program, advanced placement credit, double majors, independent study, internships, off-campus study, services for LD students, student-designed majors, summer session for credit. *Unusual degree programs:* 3-2 engineering with Wichita State University.

Library Wallerstedt Library plus 1 other with 609 serial subscriptions, 3,518 audiovisual materials.

Computers on Campus 50 computers available on campus for general student use. A campuswide network can be accessed from student residence rooms and from off campus. Internet access, online (class) registration, at least one staffed computer lab available.

Student Life *Housing:* on-campus residence required through junior year. *Options:* coed, women-only. Campus housing is university owned. Freshman campus housing is guaranteed. *Activities and organizations:* drama/theater group, student-run newspaper, choral group, Business Club, Bethany Student Education Association, Multicultural Student Association, Bethany Youth Ministry Team, Bio Chem Club. *Campus security:* 24-hour emergency response devices, student patrols, late-night transport/escort service, controlled dormitory access, night patrols by security personnel. *Student services:* health clinic, personal/psychological counseling.

Athletics Member NAIA. *Intercollegiate sports:* baseball M(s), basketball M(s)/W(s), cross-country running M(s)/W(s), football M(s), golf M(s), soccer M(s)/W(s), softball W(s), tennis M(s)/W(s), track and field M(s)/W(s), volleyball W(s). *Intramural sports:* archery M/W, badminton M/W, basketball M/W, bowling M/W, cross-country running M/W, field hockey M/W, football M/W, golf M/W, racquetball M/W, soccer M/W, softball M/W, table tennis M/W, tennis M/W, track and field M/W, volleyball M/W, weight lifting M/W.

Standardized Tests *Required:* SAT I or ACT (for admission).

Costs (2004–05) *Comprehensive fee:* $19,950 includes full-time tuition ($14,800) and room and board ($5150). Full-time tuition and fees vary according to location. Part-time tuition: $265 per credit hour. Part-time tuition and fees vary according to course load. *College room only:* $2800. Room and board charges vary according to board plan and housing facility. *Payment plan:* installment. *Waivers:* employees or children of employees.

Financial Aid Of all full-time matriculated undergraduates who enrolled in 2003, 551 applied for aid, 476 were judged to have need, 173 had their need fully met. 211 Federal Work-Study jobs (averaging $650). 154 state and other part-time jobs (averaging $650). In 2003, 32 non-need-based awards were made. *Average percent of need met:* 93%. *Average financial aid package:* $15,310. *Average need-based loan:* $5012. *Average need-based gift aid:* $4881. *Average non-need-based aid:* $4086. *Average indebtedness upon graduation:* $15,167.

Applying *Options:* deferred entrance. *Application fee:* $20. *Required:* high school transcript, minimum 2.5 GPA. *Required for some:* essay or personal statement, letters of recommendation, interview. *Application deadline:* 7/1 (freshmen), rolling (transfers). *Notification:* continuous (freshmen), continuous (transfers).

Admissions Contact Thandabantu Maceo, Enrollment Management, Bethany College, 421 North First Street, Lindsborg, KS 67456. *Phone:* 785-227-3311 Ext.

8274. *Toll-free phone:* 800-826-2281 (in-state); 800-826-8993 (out-of-state). *Fax:* 785-227-2004. *E-mail:* admissions@bethanylb.edu.

■ *See page 1252 for a narrative description.*

BETHEL COLLEGE

North Newton, Kansas

- **Independent** 4-year, founded 1887, affiliated with Mennonite Church USA
- **Calendar** 4-1-4
- **Degree** bachelor's
- **Small-town** 60-acre campus with easy access to Wichita
- **Endowment** $15.2 million
- **Coed,** 470 undergraduate students, 93% full-time, 53% women, 47% men
- **Moderately difficult** entrance level, 72% of applicants were admitted

Undergraduates 435 full-time, 35 part-time. Students come from 26 states and territories, 15 other countries, 29% are from out of state, 6% African American, 2% Asian American or Pacific Islander, 5% Hispanic American, 0.2% Native American, 4% international, 13% transferred in, 68% live on campus. *Retention:* 76% of 2002 full-time freshmen returned.

Freshmen *Admission:* 527 applied, 378 admitted, 98 enrolled. *Average high school GPA:* 3.50. *Test scores:* SAT verbal scores over 500: 56%; SAT math scores over 500: 67%; ACT scores over 18: 94%; SAT verbal scores over 600: 22%; SAT math scores over 600: 22%; ACT scores over 24: 53%; SAT math scores over 700: 22%; ACT scores over 30: 11%.

Faculty *Total:* 53, 85% full-time, 58% with terminal degrees. *Student/faculty ratio:* 9:1.

Majors Athletic training; biology/biological sciences; business/commerce; chemistry; computer science; criminology; dramatic/theatre arts; elementary education; English; fine/studio arts; Germanic languages; health and physical education; history; management information systems; mass communication/media; mathematics; music related; natural sciences; nursing (registered nurse training); peace studies and conflict resolution; physics; psychology; religious studies; social sciences related; social work; Spanish; system administration; visual and performing arts; youth ministry.

Academic Programs *Special study options:* academic remediation for entering students, advanced placement credit, cooperative education, double majors, independent study, internships, off-campus study, part-time degree program, services for LD students, study abroad, summer session for credit. *Unusual degree programs:* 3-2 engineering with Kansas State University, University of Kansas, Wichita State University.

Library Mantz Library plus 1 other with 99,287 titles, 560 serial subscriptions, 161,396 audiovisual materials, an OPAC, a Web page.

Computers on Campus 38 computers available on campus for general student use. A campuswide network can be accessed from student residence rooms and from off campus. Internet access, at least one staffed computer lab available.

Student Life *Housing:* on-campus residence required through senior year. *Options:* coed, disabled students. Campus housing is university owned. Freshman campus housing is guaranteed. *Activities and organizations:* drama/theater group, student-run newspaper, radio station, choral group, Bethel College Service Corps, The Collegian (newspaper), Student Alumni Association, Student Senate, Student Activities Board. *Campus security:* 24-hour emergency response devices, student patrols, community police patrols. *Student services:* health clinic, personal/psychological counseling.

Athletics Member NCAA. All Division II. *Intercollegiate sports:* basketball M(s)/W(s), cross-country running M(s)/W(s), football M(s), golf M(s)/W(s), soccer M(s)/W(s), tennis M(s)/W(s), track and field M(s)/W(s), volleyball W(s). *Intramural sports:* badminton M/W, baseball M, basketball M/W, bowling M/W, cross-country running M/W, golf M/W, soccer M/W, softball M/W, table tennis M/W, tennis M/W, ultimate Frisbee M/W, volleyball M/W.

Standardized Tests *Required:* SAT I or ACT (for admission).

Costs (2003–04) *Comprehensive fee:* $19,800 includes full-time tuition ($13,900) and room and board ($5900). Full-time tuition and fees vary according to course load. Part-time tuition: $495 per credit hour. Part-time tuition and fees vary according to course load. *Room and board:* Room and board charges vary according to board plan and housing facility. *Payment plans:* installment, deferred payment. *Waivers:* children of alumni, senior citizens, and employees or children of employees.

Financial Aid Of all full-time matriculated undergraduates who enrolled in 2002, 384 applied for aid, 379 were judged to have need, 125 had their need fully met. 235 Federal Work-Study jobs (averaging $1566). 9 state and other part-time jobs (averaging $1250). In 2002, 46 non-need-based awards were made. *Average percent of need met:* 86%. *Average financial aid package:* $14,161. *Average need-based loan:* $4931. *Average need-based gift aid:* $4017. *Average non-need-based aid:* $5714. *Average indebtedness upon graduation:* $15,927.

Applying *Options:* deferred entrance. *Application fee:* $20. *Required:* high school transcript, minimum 2.5 GPA. *Required for some:* essay or personal statement, 2 letters of recommendation. *Recommended:* interview. *Application deadlines:* 8/1 (freshmen), 8/1 (transfers). *Notification:* continuous (freshmen), continuous (transfers).

Admissions Contact Mr. Allan Bartel, Director of Admissions and Enrollment, Bethel College, 300 East 27th Street, North Newton, KS 67117-0531. *Phone:* 316-284-5230. *Toll-free phone:* 800-522-1887 Ext. 230. *Fax:* 316-284-5870. *E-mail:* admissions@bethelks.edu.

■ *See page 1256 for a narrative description.*

CENTRAL CHRISTIAN COLLEGE OF KANSAS

McPherson, Kansas

- **Independent Free Methodist** 4-year, founded 1884
- **Calendar** 4-1-4
- **Degrees** associate and bachelor's
- **Small-town** 16-acre campus
- **Endowment** $5.4 million
- **Coed,** 320 undergraduate students, 94% full-time, 52% women, 48% men
- **Moderately difficult** entrance level, 98% of applicants were admitted

Undergraduates 300 full-time, 20 part-time. Students come from 28 states and territories, 3 other countries, 62% are from out of state, 10% African American, 6% Hispanic American, 2% Native American, 3% international, 81% live on campus. *Retention:* 65% of 2002 full-time freshmen returned.

Freshmen *Admission:* 363 applied, 354 admitted. *Average high school GPA:* 3.26. *Test scores:* ACT scores over 18: 66%; ACT scores over 24: 20%; ACT scores over 30: 2%.

Faculty *Total:* 24, 67% full-time, 13% with terminal degrees. *Student/faculty ratio:* 14:1.

Majors Accounting; accounting and business/management; accounting and finance; acting; agricultural business and management; airline pilot and flight crew; American history; architectural engineering technology; architecture; art; art teacher education; athletic training; behavioral sciences; biblical studies; biological and physical sciences; biology/biological sciences; biology teacher education; business administration and management; business automation/technology/data entry; business/commerce; business/corporate communications; business/managerial economics; business teacher education; chemistry; chemistry teacher education; communication/speech communication and rhetoric; computer and information sciences; computer science; computer teacher education; conducting; counseling psychology; counselor education/school counseling and guidance; criminal justice/law enforcement administration; criminal justice/safety; developmental and child psychology; divinity/ministry; drafting and design technology; drama and dance teacher education; dramatic/theatre arts; drawing; economics; education; elementary education; engineering; English; English composition; English/language arts teacher education; environmental science; environmental studies; family and community services; finance; general studies; health and physical education; health services/allied health/health sciences; health teacher education; history; history teacher education; humanities; human resources management; journalism; kindergarten/preschool education; legal studies; liberal arts and sciences and humanities related; liberal arts and sciences/liberal studies; marketing/marketing management; marriage and family therapy/counseling; mass communication/media; mathematics; mathematics teacher education; middle school education; missionary studies and missiology; music; music history, literature, and theory; music management and merchandising; music performance; music teacher education; music theory and composition; natural sciences; nursing assistant/aide and patient care assistant; nursing (licensed practical/vocational nurse training); nursing (registered nurse training); painting; parks, recreation and leisure; pastoral studies/counseling; photography; physical education teaching and coaching; physical sciences; physical therapist assistant; physical therapy; physician assistant; piano and organ; pre-dentistry studies; pre-law studies; pre-medical studies; pre-nursing studies; pre-pharmacy studies; pre-theology/pre-ministerial studies; pre-veterinary studies; psychology; psychology teacher education; religious studies; sales and marketing/marketing and distribution teacher education; science teacher education; secondary education; small business administration; social psychology; social sciences; social science teacher education; social studies teacher education; social work; sociology; Spanish; Spanish language teacher education; speech teacher education; sport and fitness administration; theology; voice and opera; western civilization; wildlife biology; youth ministry; zoology/animal biology.

Academic Programs *Special study options:* academic remediation for entering students, adult/continuing education programs, advanced placement credit, cooperative education, double majors, independent study, internships, off-campus study, part-time degree program, services for LD students, student-designed majors, study abroad.

Central Christian College of Kansas (continued)

Library Briner Library with 26,700 titles, 95 serial subscriptions, 988 audiovisual materials, an OPAC, a Web page.

Computers on Campus 35 computers available on campus for general student use. A campuswide network can be accessed. Internet access, at least one staffed computer lab available.

Student Life *Housing:* on-campus residence required through junior year. *Options:* men-only, women-only. Campus housing is university owned. Freshman campus housing is guaranteed. *Activities and organizations:* drama/theater group, student-run newspaper, choral group, C.O.L.O.R.S. (Cross Over Lines of Racial Stereotype), performing arts club, Student Activities Committee, Fellowship of Christian Athletes, Phi Beta Lambda Business Club. *Campus security:* controlled dormitory access. *Student services:* health clinic, personal/psychological counseling.

Athletics Member NAIA, NCCAA. *Intercollegiate sports:* baseball M(s), basketball M(s)/W(s), cheerleading M(s)/W(s), cross-country running M(s)/W(s), golf M(s)/W(s), soccer M(s)/W(s), softball W(s), tennis M(s)/W(s), volleyball W(s). *Intramural sports:* basketball M/W, football M, soccer M/W, table tennis M/W, track and field M/W, volleyball M/W.

Standardized Tests *Required:* SAT I or ACT (for admission).

Costs (2004–05) *Comprehensive fee:* $17,225 includes full-time tuition ($12,625), mandatory fees ($500), and room and board ($4100). Full-time tuition and fees vary according to course load. Part-time tuition: $350 per credit hour. Part-time tuition and fees vary according to course load. *College room only:* $1900. Room and board charges vary according to board plan and gender. *Payment plan:* installment. *Waivers:* employees or children of employees.

Financial Aid Of all full-time matriculated undergraduates who enrolled in 2003, 269 applied for aid, 254 were judged to have need. In 2003, 30 non-need-based awards were made. *Average percent of need met:* 73%. *Average financial aid package:* $10,313. *Average need-based loan:* $4694. *Average need-based gift aid:* $3440. *Average non-need-based aid:* $4041. *Average indebtedness upon graduation:* $20,000.

Applying *Options:* electronic application, deferred entrance. *Application fee:* $20. *Required:* high school transcript, minimum 2.5 GPA, 2 letters of recommendation. *Recommended:* essay or personal statement, interview. *Application deadline:* rolling (freshmen), rolling (transfers). *Notification:* continuous (freshmen), continuous (transfers).

Admissions Contact Dr. David Ferrell, Dean of Admissions, Central Christian College of Kansas, PO Box 1403, McPherson, KS 67460. *Phone:* 620-241-0723 Ext. 380. *Toll-free phone:* 800-835-0078 Ext. 337. *Fax:* 620-241-6032. *E-mail:* admissions@centralchristian.edu.

EMPORIA STATE UNIVERSITY

Emporia, Kansas

- **State-supported** comprehensive, founded 1863, part of Kansas Board of Regents
- **Calendar** semesters
- **Degrees** certificates, bachelor's, master's, doctoral, post-master's, and postbachelor's certificates
- **Small-town** 207-acre campus with easy access to Wichita
- **Endowment** $39.2 million
- **Coed,** 4,434 undergraduate students, 87% full-time, 61% women, 39% men
- **Noncompetitive** entrance level, 74% of applicants were admitted

Undergraduates 3,852 full-time, 582 part-time. Students come from 41 states and territories, 49 other countries, 4% are from out of state, 4% African American, 0.9% Asian American or Pacific Islander, 4% Hispanic American, 0.7% Native American, 2% international, 10% transferred in, 25% live on campus. *Retention:* 67% of 2002 full-time freshmen returned.

Freshmen *Admission:* 1,477 applied, 1,090 admitted, 817 enrolled. *Test scores:* ACT scores over 18: 84%; ACT scores over 24: 33%; ACT scores over 30: 3%.

Faculty *Total:* 273, 91% full-time, 77% with terminal degrees. *Student/faculty ratio:* 19:1.

Majors Accounting; art; athletic training; biology/biological sciences; business administration and management; chemistry; communication/speech communication and rhetoric; computer and information sciences; dramatic/theatre arts; economics; elementary education; English; foreign languages and literatures; general studies; geology/earth science; history; information science/studies; marketing/marketing management; mathematics; multi-/interdisciplinary studies related; music; music teacher education; nursing (registered nurse training); parks, recreation and leisure; physical sciences; physics; political science and government; psychology; secondary education; social sciences; social science teacher education; sociology; vocational rehabilitation counseling.

Academic Programs *Special study options:* academic remediation for entering students, accelerated degree program, adult/continuing education programs, advanced placement credit, distance learning, double majors, English as a second language, honors programs, independent study, internships, off-campus study, part-time degree program, services for LD students, study abroad, summer session for credit. *Unusual degree programs:* 3-2 engineering with Kansas State University, University of Kansas, Wichita State University.

Library William Allen White Library with 558,565 titles, 1,416 serial subscriptions, 7,649 audiovisual materials, an OPAC, a Web page.

Computers on Campus 410 computers available on campus for general student use. A campuswide network can be accessed from student residence rooms and from off campus that provide access to various software packages. Internet access, online (class) registration, at least one staffed computer lab available.

Student Life *Housing:* on-campus residence required for freshman year. *Options:* coed, men-only, women-only, disabled students. Campus housing is university owned. Freshman campus housing is guaranteed. *Activities and organizations:* drama/theater group, student-run newspaper, choral group, marching band, Union Activities Council, Associated Student Government, Panhellenic Association, Interfraternity Council, Black Student Union, national fraternities, national sororities. *Campus security:* 24-hour emergency response devices and patrols, student patrols, late-night transport/escort service, controlled dormitory access, 24-hour residence hall monitoring, safety and self-awareness programs. *Student services:* health clinic, personal/psychological counseling, women's center, legal services.

Athletics Member NCAA. All Division II. *Intercollegiate sports:* baseball M(s), basketball M(s)/W(s), cheerleading M(s)/W(s), cross-country running M(s)/W(s), football M(s), soccer W(s), softball W(s), tennis M(s)/W(s), track and field M(s)/W(s), volleyball W(s). *Intramural sports:* badminton M/W, basketball M/W, bowling M(c)/W(c), fencing M(c)/W(c), football M/W, racquetball M/W, rugby M(c), soccer M(c)/W(c), softball M/W, swimming M/W, table tennis M/W, tennis M/W, volleyball M/W.

Standardized Tests *Required:* SAT I or ACT (for admission).

Costs (2003–04) *Tuition:* state resident $2200 full-time, $73 per credit hour part-time; nonresident $8338 full-time, $278 per credit hour part-time. *Required fees:* $576 full-time, $35 per credit hour part-time. *Room and board:* $4222; room only: $2104. Room and board charges vary according to board plan and housing facility. *Payment plans:* installment, deferred payment. *Waivers:* senior citizens and employees or children of employees.

Financial Aid Of all full-time matriculated undergraduates who enrolled in 2002, 3,056 applied for aid, 2,267 were judged to have need, 790 had their need fully met. 270 Federal Work-Study jobs (averaging $1158). 37 state and other part-time jobs (averaging $695). In 2002, 419 non-need-based awards were made. *Average percent of need met:* 80%. *Average financial aid package:* $4937. *Average need-based loan:* $2452. *Average need-based gift aid:* $1628. *Average non-need-based aid:* $822. *Average indebtedness upon graduation:* $13,036.

Applying *Options:* electronic application, early admission, deferred entrance. *Application fee:* $30. *Required:* high school transcript. *Recommended:* minimum 2.0 GPA. *Application deadline:* rolling (freshmen), rolling (transfers). *Notification:* continuous (transfers).

Admissions Contact Ms. Laura Eddy, Director of Admissions (Interim), Emporia State University, 1200 Commercial Street, Campus Box 4034, Plumb Hall Room 106, Emporia, KS 66801-5087. *Phone:* 620-341-5465. *Toll-free phone:* 877-GOTOESU (in-state); 877-468-6378 (out-of-state). *Fax:* 620-341-5599. *E-mail:* go2esu@emporia.edu.

FORT HAYS STATE UNIVERSITY

Hays, Kansas

- **State-supported** comprehensive, founded 1902, part of Kansas Board of Regents
- **Calendar** semesters
- **Degrees** certificates, associate, bachelor's, master's, and post-master's certificates
- **Small-town** 200-acre campus
- **Endowment** $27.6 million
- **Coed,** 5,920 undergraduate students, 70% full-time, 54% women, 46% men
- **Noncompetitive** entrance level, 94% of applicants were admitted

Undergraduates 4,126 full-time, 1,794 part-time. Students come from 48 states and territories, 15 other countries, 10% are from out of state, 1% African American, 0.6% Asian American or Pacific Islander, 3% Hispanic American, 0.5% Native American, 16% international, 21% transferred in, 20% live on campus. *Retention:* 72% of 2002 full-time freshmen returned.

Freshmen *Admission:* 1,938 applied, 1,813 admitted, 904 enrolled. *Average high school GPA:* 3.31. *Test scores:* ACT scores over 18: 87%; ACT scores over 24: 31%; ACT scores over 30: 3%.

Faculty *Total:* 291, 87% full-time, 66% with terminal degrees. *Student/faculty ratio:* 17:1.

Majors Accounting; administrative assistant and secretarial science; agricultural business and management; agriculture; agronomy and crop science; animal sciences; art; art teacher education; audiology and speech-language pathology; biological and physical sciences; biology/biological sciences; business administration and management; business/managerial economics; business teacher education; chemistry; clinical laboratory science/medical technology; commercial and advertising art; criminal justice/safety; economics; elementary education; English; finance; French; geology/earth science; German; history; industrial arts; industrial radiologic technology; information science/studies; journalism; kindergarten/preschool education; liberal arts and sciences/liberal studies; marketing/marketing management; mass communication/media; mathematics; music; music teacher education; natural resources management and policy; nursing (registered nurse training); philosophy; physical education teaching and coaching; physical sciences; physics; political science and government; pre-law studies; psychology; public relations/image management; radio and television; range science and management; school psychology; science teacher education; social work; sociology; Spanish; wildlife and wildlands science and management.

Academic Programs *Special study options:* academic remediation for entering students, adult/continuing education programs, advanced placement credit, distance learning, double majors, English as a second language, external degree program, internships, off-campus study, part-time degree program, services for LD students, student-designed majors, study abroad, summer session for credit. *Unusual degree programs:* 3-2 engineering with Kansas State University, University of Kansas.

Library Forsyth Library with 624,637 titles, 1,689 serial subscriptions, an OPAC, a Web page.

Computers on Campus 813 computers available on campus for general student use. A campuswide network can be accessed from student residence rooms and from off campus. Internet access, at least one staffed computer lab available. Computer purchase or lease plan available.

Student Life *Housing:* on-campus residence required for freshman year. *Options:* coed, men-only, women-only. Campus housing is university owned. Freshman campus housing is guaranteed. *Activities and organizations:* drama/theater group, student-run newspaper, radio and television station, choral group, marching band, Student Government Association, University Activities Board, Residence Hall Association, International Student Union, Block and Bridle, national fraternities, national sororities. *Campus security:* 24-hour emergency response devices and patrols, late-night transport/escort service, controlled dormitory access. *Student services:* health clinic, personal/psychological counseling, women's center.

Athletics Member NCAA. All Division II. *Intercollegiate sports:* baseball M(s), basketball M(s)/W(s), cross-country running M(s)/W(s), football M(s), golf M(s), softball W, tennis W(s), track and field M(s)/W(s), volleyball W(s), wrestling M(s). *Intramural sports:* archery M/W, badminton M/W, basketball M/W, bowling M/W, cross-country running M/W, fencing M, field hockey M/W, football M/W, golf M/W, racquetball M/W, rugby M/W, soccer M/W, softball M/W, swimming M/W, table tennis M/W, tennis M/W, track and field M/W, volleyball M/W, water polo M/W, weight lifting M/W, wrestling M.

Standardized Tests *Required:* SAT I or ACT (for admission).

Costs (2003–04) *Tuition:* state resident $2032 full-time, $85 per credit hour part-time; nonresident $8165 full-time, $272 per credit hour part-time. Full-time tuition and fees vary according to course load, location, and reciprocity agreements. Part-time tuition and fees vary according to course load and location. *Required fees:* $507 full-time. *Room and board:* $4843; room only: $2146. Room and board charges vary according to board plan, housing facility, and student level. *Payment plan:* installment. *Waivers:* senior citizens.

Financial Aid Of all full-time matriculated undergraduates who enrolled in 2002, 2,902 applied for aid, 2,368 were judged to have need, 653 had their need fully met. 400 Federal Work-Study jobs. In 2002, 1049 non-need-based awards were made. *Average percent of need met:* 72%. *Average financial aid package:* $5542. *Average need-based loan:* $3160. *Average need-based gift aid:* $3015. *Average non-need-based aid:* $2749. *Average indebtedness upon graduation:* $15,061.

Applying *Options:* common application, electronic application. *Application fee:* $30. *Required:* high school transcript. *Application deadline:* rolling (freshmen), rolling (transfers). *Notification:* continuous (freshmen), continuous (transfers).

Admissions Contact Ms. Christy Befort, Senior Administrative Assistant, Office of Admissions, Fort Hays State University, 600 Park Street, Hays, KS 67601-4099. *Phone:* 785-628-5830. *Toll-free phone:* 800-628-FHSU. *Fax:* 800-432-0248. *E-mail:* tigers@fhsu.edu.

FRIENDS UNIVERSITY
Wichita, Kansas

Admissions Contact Mr. Tony Myers, Director of Admissions, Friends University, 2100 West University Street, Wichita, KS 67213. *Phone:* 316-295-5100. *Toll-free phone:* 800-577-2233. *Fax:* 316-262-5027. *E-mail:* tmyers@friends.edu.

HASKELL INDIAN NATIONS UNIVERSITY
Lawrence, Kansas

- **Federally supported** 4-year, founded 1884
- **Calendar** semesters
- **Degrees** associate and bachelor's
- **Suburban** 320-acre campus
- **Coed,** 1,028 undergraduate students, 90% full-time, 47% women, 53% men
- **Minimally difficult** entrance level

Undergraduates 922 full-time, 106 part-time. Students come from 37 states and territories, 100% Native American, 9% transferred in.

Freshmen *Admission:* 350 enrolled.

Faculty *Total:* 48, 100% full-time. *Student/faculty ratio:* 15:1.

Majors American Indian/Native American studies; American literature; business administration and management; computer and information sciences; creative writing; elementary education; entrepreneurial and small business related; environmental science; film/video and photographic arts related; health and physical education; liberal arts and sciences/liberal studies; natural sciences; social work; theatre/theatre arts management.

Academic Programs *Special study options:* academic remediation for entering students, advanced placement credit, distance learning, independent study, internships, off-campus study, part-time degree program, services for LD students, student-designed majors, summer session for credit. *ROTC:* Air Force (c).

Library 50,000 titles, 400 serial subscriptions, an OPAC.

Computers on Campus 35 computers available on campus for general student use. At least one staffed computer lab available.

Student Life *Housing options:* coed, men-only, women-only. Campus housing is university owned. Freshman applicants given priority for college housing. *Activities and organizations:* drama/theater group, student-run newspaper, Phi Beta Lambda, Aises, H-Club, Navajo club, Unity. *Campus security:* night patrol only. *Student services:* health clinic, personal/psychological counseling.

Athletics Member NCAA. *Intercollegiate sports:* basketball M/W, cheerleading M/W, cross-country running M/W, football M, golf M, softball W, track and field M/W, volleyball W. *Intramural sports:* racquetball M/W.

Standardized Tests *Required:* ACT (for admission).

Costs (2003–04) *Tuition:* state resident $0 full-time; nonresident $0 full-time. *Required fees:* $210 full-time, $105 per term part-time. *Room and board:* $70.

Applying *Options:* common application, electronic application. *Application fee:* $10. *Required:* high school transcript, minimum 2.0 GPA. *Required for some:* 2 letters of recommendation. *Application deadlines:* 7/30 (freshmen), 7/30 (transfers). *Notification:* continuous (freshmen), continuous (transfers).

Admissions Contact Ms. Patty Grant, Recruitment Officer, Haskell Indian Nations University, 155 Indian Avenue, #5031, Lawrence, KS 66046. *Phone:* 785-749-8437 Ext. 437. *Fax:* 785-749-8429.

KANSAS STATE UNIVERSITY
Manhattan, Kansas

- **State-supported** university, founded 1863, part of Kansas Board of Regents
- **Calendar** semesters
- **Degrees** associate, bachelor's, master's, doctoral, and first professional
- **Suburban** 668-acre campus with easy access to Kansas City
- **Endowment** $155.2 million
- **Coed,** 19,083 undergraduate students, 85% full-time, 48% women, 52% men
- **Noncompetitive** entrance level, 60% of applicants were admitted

Undergraduates 16,285 full-time, 2,798 part-time. Students come from 50 states and territories, 100 other countries, 10% are from out of state, 3% African American, 1% Asian American or Pacific Islander, 2% Hispanic American, 0.5% Native American, 1% international, 9% transferred in, 33% live on campus. *Retention:* 79% of 2002 full-time freshmen returned.

Kansas State University (continued)

Freshmen *Admission:* 7,952 applied, 4,736 admitted, 3,439 enrolled. *Average high school GPA:* 3.47. *Test scores:* ACT scores over 18: 93%; ACT scores over 24: 49%; ACT scores over 30: 8%.

Faculty *Total:* 976, 87% full-time, 83% with terminal degrees. *Student/faculty ratio:* 12:1.

Majors Accounting; aeronautics/aviation/aerospace science and technology; agricultural and food products processing; agricultural/biological engineering and bioengineering; agricultural business and management; agricultural economics; agricultural mechanization; agronomy and crop science; aircraft powerplant technology; airframe mechanics and aircraft maintenance technology; airline pilot and flight crew; animal sciences; anthropology; apparel and textiles; architectural engineering; architecture; art; athletic training; biochemistry; biology/biological sciences; business administration and management; chemical engineering; chemistry; child development; civil engineering; civil engineering technology; clinical laboratory science/medical technology; communication disorders; communication/speech communication and rhetoric; computer and information sciences; computer engineering; computer engineering technology; computer programming; computer systems analysis; dietetics; dramatic/theatre arts; economics; electrical, electronic and communications engineering technology; electrical, electronics and communications engineering; elementary education; English; environmental engineering technology; finance; food science; foods, nutrition, and wellness; foreign languages and literatures; geography; geology/earth science; health science; history; horticultural science; hotel/motel administration; human development and family studies; human ecology; humanities; industrial engineering; industrial technology; information science/studies; interdisciplinary studies; interior architecture; interior design; journalism; kinesiology and exercise science; landscape architecture; marketing/marketing management; mathematics; mechanical engineering; mechanical engineering/mechanical technology; music; music teacher education; nuclear engineering; parks, recreation and leisure facilities management; philosophy; physical sciences; physics; political science and government; pre-dentistry studies; pre-medical studies; pre-veterinary studies; psychology; secondary education; social sciences; social work; sociology; statistics; survey technology; wildlife biology; women's studies.

Academic Programs *Special study options:* academic remediation for entering students, accelerated degree program, adult/continuing education programs, advanced placement credit, cooperative education, distance learning, double majors, English as a second language, freshman honors college, honors programs, independent study, internships, off-campus study, part-time degree program, services for LD students, study abroad, summer session for credit. *ROTC:* Army (b), Air Force (b). *Unusual degree programs:* 3-2 agriculture.

Library Hale Library plus 3 others with 1.6 million titles, 1,365 serial subscriptions, 5,056 audiovisual materials, an OPAC, a Web page.

Computers on Campus 556 computers available on campus for general student use. A campuswide network can be accessed from student residence rooms and from off campus. Internet access, online (class) registration, at least one staffed computer lab available.

Student Life *Housing options:* coed, men-only, women-only, cooperative. Campus housing is university owned. *Activities and organizations:* drama/theater group, student-run newspaper, radio station, choral group, marching band, athletic department groups, marching band, Union Governing Board, theater productions, debate team, national fraternities, national sororities. *Campus security:* 24-hour emergency response devices and patrols, late-night transport/escort service, controlled dormitory access. *Student services:* health clinic, personal/psychological counseling, women's center, legal services.

Athletics Member NCAA. All Division I except football (Division I-A). *Intercollegiate sports:* baseball M(s), basketball M(s)/W(s), crew W(s), cross-country running M(s)/W(s), golf M(s)/W(s), tennis W(s), track and field M(s)/W(s), volleyball W(s). *Intramural sports:* badminton M/W, basketball M/W, bowling M/W, crew M/W, cross-country running M/W, football M/W, golf M/W, ice hockey M, lacrosse M, racquetball M/W, rugby M/W, soccer M/W, softball M/W, table tennis M/W, tennis M/W, track and field M/W, volleyball M/W, water polo M/W, weight lifting M/W, wrestling M.

Standardized Tests *Required:* SAT I or ACT (for admission). *Recommended:* ACT (for admission).

Costs (2003–04) *Tuition:* state resident $3510 full-time, $117 per credit hour part-time; nonresident $11,400 full-time, $380 per credit hour part-time. *Required fees:* $549 full-time, $19 per credit hour part-time, $66 per term part-time. *Room and board:* $5080. Room and board charges vary according to board plan. *Payment plans:* installment, deferred payment. *Waivers:* employees or children of employees.

Financial Aid Of all full-time matriculated undergraduates who enrolled in 2002, 12,155 applied for aid, 9,067 were judged to have need, 1,813 had their need fully met. In 2002, 873 non-need-based awards were made. *Average percent of need met:* 80%. *Average financial aid package:* $5512. *Average need-based loan:* $2916. *Average need-based gift aid:* $1372. *Average non-need-based aid:* $1538. *Average indebtedness upon graduation:* $17,000.

Applying *Options:* common application, electronic application. *Application fee:* $30. *Required:* high school transcript, minimum 2.0 GPA. *Application deadline:* rolling (freshmen), rolling (transfers). *Notification:* continuous (freshmen), continuous (transfers).

Admissions Contact Ms. Christy Crenshaw, Associate Director of Admissions, Kansas State University, 119 Anderson Hall, Manhattan, KS 66506. *Phone:* 785-532-6250. *Toll-free phone:* 800-432-8270. *Fax:* 785-532-6393. *E-mail:* kstate@ksu.edu.

■ *See page 1804 for a narrative description.*

KANSAS WESLEYAN UNIVERSITY
Salina, Kansas

- **Independent United Methodist** comprehensive, founded 1886
- **Calendar** 2 semesters with a summer term
- **Degrees** associate, bachelor's, and master's
- **Urban** 28-acre campus
- **Endowment** $13.5 million
- **Coed,** 768 undergraduate students, 78% full-time, 59% women, 41% men
- **Moderately difficult** entrance level, 53% of applicants were admitted

Undergraduates 597 full-time, 171 part-time. Students come from 24 states and territories, 4 other countries, 39% are from out of state, 6% African American, 2% Asian American or Pacific Islander, 5% Hispanic American, 1% Native American, 0.4% international, 17% transferred in, 65% live on campus. *Retention:* 74% of 2002 full-time freshmen returned.

Freshmen *Admission:* 1,097 applied, 577 admitted, 147 enrolled. *Average high school GPA:* 3.36. *Test scores:* ACT scores over 18: 92%; ACT scores over 24: 26%; ACT scores over 30: 2%.

Faculty *Total:* 59, 71% full-time, 54% with terminal degrees. *Student/faculty ratio:* 18:1.

Majors Accounting; art; arts management; art teacher education; biology/biological sciences; business administration and management; chemistry; computer science; criminal justice/law enforcement administration; dramatic/theatre arts; education; elementary education; engineering; English; health teacher education; history; information science/studies; kindergarten/preschool education; liberal arts and sciences/liberal studies; literature; mass communication/media; mathematics; mental health/rehabilitation; nursing (registered nurse training); physical education teaching and coaching; physics; pre-dentistry studies; pre-law studies; pre-medical studies; pre-veterinary studies; psychology; religious education; religious studies; social sciences; sociology; Spanish; special education; speech and rhetoric; substance abuse/addiction counseling.

Academic Programs *Special study options:* academic remediation for entering students, adult/continuing education programs, advanced placement credit, distance learning, double majors, English as a second language, external degree program, independent study, internships, off-campus study, part-time degree program, student-designed majors, study abroad, summer session for credit. *Unusual degree programs:* 3-2 engineering with Columbia University, Washington University in St. Louis; agriculture with Kansas State University.

Library Memorial Library with 370 serial subscriptions, 1,055 audiovisual materials, an OPAC, a Web page.

Computers on Campus 72 computers available on campus for general student use. A campuswide network can be accessed from student residence rooms and from off campus. Internet access, at least one staffed computer lab available.

Student Life *Housing:* on-campus residence required through sophomore year. *Options:* men-only, women-only. Campus housing is university owned. Freshman campus housing is guaranteed. *Activities and organizations:* drama/theater group, student-run newspaper, choral group, Fellowship of Christian Athletes, student government, Wesleyan Chorale, Multicultural Student Association, business club. *Campus security:* 24-hour emergency response devices, student patrols, late-night transport/escort service, controlled dormitory access, evening patrols by security. *Student services:* personal/psychological counseling.

Athletics Member NAIA, NSCAA. *Intercollegiate sports:* baseball M(s), basketball M(s)/W(s), cheerleading M(s)/W(s), cross-country running M(s)/W(s), football M(s), golf M(s)/W(s), soccer M(s)/W(s), softball W(s), tennis M(s)/W(s), track and field M(s)/W(s), volleyball W(s). *Intramural sports:* basketball M/W, bowling M/W, fencing M/W, football W, golf M/W, racquetball M/W, softball M/W, table tennis M/W, volleyball M/W, weight lifting M/W.

Standardized Tests *Required:* SAT I or ACT (for admission). *Recommended:* SAT I (for admission), ACT (for admission).

Costs (2004–05) *Comprehensive fee:* $20,400 includes full-time tuition ($15,000) and room and board ($5400). Part-time tuition: $200 per credit hour. Part-time tuition and fees vary according to course load. *College room only:*

$2400. *Payment plan:* installment. *Waivers:* children of alumni, senior citizens, and employees or children of employees.

Financial Aid Of all full-time matriculated undergraduates who enrolled in 2001, 497 applied for aid, 452 were judged to have need, 429 had their need fully met. 100 Federal Work-Study jobs (averaging $790). 62 state and other part-time jobs (averaging $790). In 2001, 45 non-need-based awards were made. *Average percent of need met:* 95%. *Average financial aid package:* $15,495. *Average need-based loan:* $3739. *Average need-based gift aid:* $4346. *Average non-need-based aid:* $6553.

Applying *Options:* common application, electronic application, deferred entrance. *Application fee:* $20. *Required:* high school transcript, minimum 2.5 GPA, minimum ACT composite score of 18. *Application deadline:* rolling (freshmen), rolling (transfers). *Notification:* continuous (freshmen), continuous (transfers).

Admissions Contact Ms. Tina Thayer, Director of Admissions, Kansas Wesleyan University, 100 East Claflin Avenue, Salina, KS 67401-6196. *Phone:* 785-829-5541 Ext. 1283. *Toll-free phone:* 800-874-1154 Ext. 1285. *Fax:* 785-827-0927. *E-mail:* admissions@kwu.edu.

MANHATTAN CHRISTIAN COLLEGE

Manhattan, Kansas

- **Independent** 4-year, founded 1927, affiliated with Christian Churches and Churches of Christ
- **Calendar** semesters
- **Degrees** certificates, diplomas, associate, and bachelor's
- **Small-town** 10-acre campus
- **Endowment** $939,895
- **Coed,** 336 undergraduate students, 73% full-time, 49% women, 51% men
- **Minimally difficult** entrance level, 84% of applicants were admitted

Undergraduates 246 full-time, 90 part-time. Students come from 13 states and territories, 2 other countries, 28% are from out of state, 3% African American, 0.3% Asian American or Pacific Islander, 1% Hispanic American, 0.6% international, 8% transferred in, 65% live on campus. *Retention:* 60% of 2002 full-time freshmen returned.

Freshmen *Admission:* 118 applied, 99 admitted, 76 enrolled. *Average high school GPA:* 3.34. *Test scores:* SAT verbal scores over 500: 55%; SAT math scores over 500: 55%; ACT scores over 18: 82%; SAT verbal scores over 600: 22%; SAT math scores over 600: 22%; ACT scores over 24: 36%; ACT scores over 30: 8%.

Faculty *Total:* 31, 32% full-time, 26% with terminal degrees. *Student/faculty ratio:* 17:1.

Majors Biblical studies; business administration and management; divinity/ministry; missionary studies and missiology; pastoral studies/counseling; religious education; religious/sacred music; religious studies; theology.

Academic Programs *Special study options:* academic remediation for entering students, adult/continuing education programs, advanced placement credit, distance learning, double majors, independent study, internships, off-campus study, summer session for credit. *ROTC:* Army (c), Air Force (c). *Unusual degree programs:* 3-2 business administration with Kansas State University; engineering with Kansas State University; nursing with Wichita State University, Washburn University, Kansas Wesleyan University; social work with Kansas State University; education with Kansas State University.

Library Manhattan Christian College Library with 2,500 titles, 45 serial subscriptions, an OPAC, a Web page.

Computers on Campus 12 computers available on campus for general student use. A campuswide network can be accessed from student residence rooms. Internet access, at least one staffed computer lab available.

Student Life *Housing:* on-campus residence required through sophomore year. *Options:* men-only, women-only. Campus housing is university owned. Freshman campus housing is guaranteed. *Activities and organizations:* drama/theater group, student-run newspaper, choral group, Student Council, Unspoken Message (drama and dance team), praise bands, Drama Team, Prison Ministry. *Student services:* personal/psychological counseling.

Athletics Member NCCAA. *Intercollegiate sports:* basketball M/W, soccer M/W, tennis M/W, volleyball W. *Intramural sports:* softball M/W.

Standardized Tests *Required:* SAT I or ACT (for admission).

Costs (2003–04) *Comprehensive fee:* $13,356 includes full-time tuition ($8332), mandatory fees ($30), and room and board ($4994). Part-time tuition: $347 per hour. Part-time tuition and fees vary according to course load. *Room and board:* Room and board charges vary according to board plan. *Payment plan:* deferred payment. *Waivers:* senior citizens and employees or children of employees.

Financial Aid Of all full-time matriculated undergraduates who enrolled in 2002, 272 applied for aid, 243 were judged to have need, 36 had their need fully met. 66 Federal Work-Study jobs (averaging $1134). In 2002, 68 non-need-based awards were made. *Average percent of need met:* 67%. *Average financial aid package:* $7420. *Average need-based loan:* $3396. *Average need-based gift aid:* $5030. *Average non-need-based aid:* $2980. *Average indebtedness upon graduation:* $13,139.

Applying *Application fee:* $25. *Required:* essay or personal statement, high school transcript, minimum 2.0 GPA, 3 letters of recommendation. *Required for some:* interview. *Application deadlines:* 8/1 (freshmen), 8/1 (transfers). *Notification:* continuous (freshmen), continuous (transfers).

Admissions Contact Mr. Scott Jenkins, Director of Admissions, Manhattan Christian College, 1415 Anderson Avenue, Manhattan, KS 66502-4081. *Phone:* 785-539-3571 Ext. 323. *Toll-free phone:* 877-246-4622. *Fax:* 785-776-9251. *E-mail:* admit@mccks.edu.

MCPHERSON COLLEGE

McPherson, Kansas

- **Independent** 4-year, founded 1887, affiliated with Church of the Brethren
- **Calendar** 4-1-4
- **Degrees** associate and bachelor's
- **Small-town** 26-acre campus
- **Endowment** $31.4 million
- **Coed,** 436 undergraduate students, 89% full-time, 39% women, 61% men
- **Moderately difficult** entrance level, 73% of applicants were admitted

Undergraduates 386 full-time, 50 part-time. Students come from 30 states and territories, 9% African American, 0.5% Asian American or Pacific Islander, 7% Hispanic American, 0.2% Native American, 1% international, 14% transferred in, 70% live on campus. *Retention:* 83% of 2002 full-time freshmen returned.

Freshmen *Admission:* 532 applied, 390 admitted, 133 enrolled. *Average high school GPA:* 2.98. *Test scores:* SAT verbal scores over 500: 56%; SAT math scores over 500: 52%; ACT scores over 18: 92%; SAT verbal scores over 600: 9%; SAT math scores over 600: 22%; ACT scores over 24: 23%.

Faculty *Total:* 54, 74% full-time, 52% with terminal degrees. *Student/faculty ratio:* 10:1.

Majors Accounting; agricultural business and management; agricultural economics; art; art teacher education; automobile/automotive mechanics technology; behavioral sciences; biology/biological sciences; business administration and management; business teacher education; chemistry; computer programming; computer science; dramatic/theatre arts; education; education (K-12); elementary education; English; environmental studies; finance; history; industrial arts; interdisciplinary studies; international business/trade/commerce; kindergarten/preschool education; mathematics; music; music teacher education; philosophy; physical education teaching and coaching; physical sciences; pre-dentistry studies; pre-engineering; pre-law studies; pre-medical studies; pre-pharmacy studies; pre-veterinary studies; psychology; religious studies; secondary education; social sciences; sociology; Spanish; special education; speech/theater education.

Academic Programs *Special study options:* academic remediation for entering students, adult/continuing education programs, advanced placement credit, double majors, independent study, internships, off-campus study, part-time degree program, services for LD students, student-designed majors, study abroad, summer session for credit.

Library Miller Library with 89,946 titles, 345 serial subscriptions, 4,465 audiovisual materials, an OPAC, a Web page.

Computers on Campus 60 computers available on campus for general student use. A campuswide network can be accessed from student residence rooms and from off campus. Internet access, at least one staffed computer lab available.

Student Life *Housing:* on-campus residence required through senior year. *Options:* coed, men-only, disabled students. *Activities and organizations:* drama/theater group, student-run newspaper, choral group, Today's Educators, Spectator (newspaper), drama productions, athletics, choir. *Campus security:* student patrols, controlled dormitory access. *Student services:* health clinic, personal/psychological counseling.

Athletics Member NAIA. *Intercollegiate sports:* basketball M/W, cross-country running M/W, football M, softball W, track and field M/W, volleyball W. *Intramural sports:* basketball M/W, football M/W, racquetball M/W, soccer M/W, softball M/W, table tennis M/W, volleyball M/W.

Standardized Tests *Required:* SAT I or ACT (for admission). *Recommended:* ACT (for admission).

Costs (2004–05) *Comprehensive fee:* $20,265 includes full-time tuition ($14,385), mandatory fees ($260), and room and board ($5620). Part-time tuition: $450 per credit hour. Part-time tuition and fees vary according to course load. *College room only:* $2345. Room and board charges vary according to board plan. *Payment plan:* installment. *Waivers:* senior citizens and employees or children of employees.

Financial Aid Of all full-time matriculated undergraduates who enrolled in 2003, 352 applied for aid, 321 were judged to have need, 90 had their need fully met. 183 Federal Work-Study jobs (averaging $1562). In 2003, 51 non-need-

McPherson College (continued)

based awards were made. *Average percent of need met:* 92%. *Average financial aid package:* $16,475. *Average need-based loan:* $5690. *Average need-based gift aid:* $5258. *Average non-need-based aid:* $7524. *Average indebtedness upon graduation:* $14,450.

Applying *Options:* electronic application, deferred entrance. *Application fee:* $25. *Required:* high school transcript, minimum 2.0 GPA. *Application deadline:* rolling (freshmen), rolling (transfers). *Notification:* continuous (freshmen), continuous (transfers).

Admissions Contact Mr. Fred Schmidt, Dean of Enrollment, McPherson College, 1600 East Euclid, McPherson, KS 67460. *Phone:* 620-241-0731 Ext. 1270. *Toll-free phone:* 800-365-7402. *Fax:* 620-241-8443. *E-mail:* admiss@mcpherson.edu.

MIDAMERICA NAZARENE UNIVERSITY
Olathe, Kansas

- **Independent** comprehensive, founded 1966, affiliated with Church of the Nazarene
- **Calendar** semesters
- **Degrees** associate, bachelor's, and master's
- **Suburban** 105-acre campus with easy access to Kansas City
- **Endowment** $16.6 million
- **Coed,** 1,438 undergraduate students, 89% full-time, 54% women, 46% men
- **Minimally difficult** entrance level, 41% of applicants were admitted

MidAmerica is a comprehensive, Christian liberal arts university committed to transforming students for a life of service to God, their country, and their world. The University offers undergraduate and graduate degrees with 42 majors in such areas as business, education, nursing, psychology, and criminal justice. The University is located just 20 miles from Kansas City.

Undergraduates 1,278 full-time, 160 part-time. Students come from 40 states and territories, 11 other countries, 39% are from out of state, 7% African American, 1% Asian American or Pacific Islander, 2% Hispanic American, 1% Native American, 2% international, 8% transferred in, 62% live on campus. *Retention:* 75% of 2002 full-time freshmen returned.

Freshmen *Admission:* 629 applied, 260 admitted, 260 enrolled. *Average high school GPA:* 3.36. *Test scores:* SAT verbal scores over 500: 56%; SAT math scores over 500: 52%; ACT scores over 18: 84%; SAT verbal scores over 600: 22%; SAT math scores over 600: 22%; ACT scores over 24: 41%; SAT verbal scores over 700: 3%; SAT math scores over 700: 3%; ACT scores over 30: 5%.

Faculty *Total:* 163, 47% full-time, 25% with terminal degrees. *Student/faculty ratio:* 19:1.

Majors Accounting; agricultural business and management; athletic training; biology/biological sciences; business administration and management; business teacher education; chemistry; computer science; criminal justice/law enforcement administration; divinity/ministry; elementary education; English; English/language arts teacher education; graphic design; history; human resources management; international agriculture; kinesiology and exercise science; liberal arts and sciences/liberal studies; mass communication/media; mathematics; mathematics teacher education; middle school education; missionary studies and missiology; music; music teacher education; nursing (registered nurse training); physical education teaching and coaching; physics; psychology; public relations/image management; religious education; religious/sacred music; religious studies; secondary education; social studies teacher education; sociology; Spanish; Spanish language teacher education; sport and fitness administration; voice and opera.

Academic Programs *Special study options:* academic remediation for entering students, accelerated degree program, adult/continuing education programs, advanced placement credit, double majors, independent study, internships, off-campus study, part-time degree program, services for LD students, study abroad, summer session for credit. *ROTC:* Army (c), Air Force (c).

Library Mabee Library with 428,450 titles, 1,225 serial subscriptions, 7,391 audiovisual materials, an OPAC, a Web page.

Computers on Campus 85 computers available on campus for general student use. A campuswide network can be accessed from student residence rooms and from off campus. Internet access, at least one staffed computer lab available.

Student Life *Housing:* on-campus residence required through senior year. *Options:* men-only, women-only. Campus housing is university owned. Freshman campus housing is guaranteed. *Activities and organizations:* drama/theater group, student-run newspaper, radio and television station, choral group, Associated Student Government, Residence Hall Government, ministry groups, intramurals, Gospel Station. *Campus security:* 24-hour emergency response devices and patrols, student patrols, late-night transport/escort service, controlled dormitory access. *Student services:* health clinic, personal/psychological counseling.

Athletics Member NAIA, NCCAA. *Intercollegiate sports:* baseball M(s), basketball M(s)/W(s), cheerleading M(s)/W(s), cross-country running M(s)/W(s), football M(s), soccer M(s)/W(s), softball W(s), track and field M(s)/W(s), volleyball W(s). *Intramural sports:* basketball M/W, football M/W, softball M/W, table tennis M/W, tennis M/W, volleyball M/W.

Standardized Tests *Required:* SAT I or ACT (for admission).

Costs (2003–04) *Comprehensive fee:* $18,738 includes full-time tuition ($11,910), mandatory fees ($1000), and room and board ($5828). Full-time tuition and fees vary according to course load. Part-time tuition: $397 per semester hour. Part-time tuition and fees vary according to course load. *Required fees:* $500 per term part-time. *Room and board:* Room and board charges vary according to board plan and housing facility. *Waivers:* senior citizens and employees or children of employees.

Financial Aid Of all full-time matriculated undergraduates who enrolled in 2003, 1,048 applied for aid, 946 were judged to have need, 83 had their need fully met. 93 Federal Work-Study jobs (averaging $1764). In 2003, 177 non-need-based awards were made. *Average percent of need met:* 66%. *Average financial aid package:* $11,189. *Average need-based loan:* $5038. *Average need-based gift aid:* $6434. *Average non-need-based aid:* $3506. *Average indebtedness upon graduation:* $24,812.

Applying *Options:* early admission, deferred entrance. *Application fee:* $15. *Required:* high school transcript, minimum 2.0 GPA, 1 letter of recommendation. *Application deadlines:* 8/1 (freshmen), 8/1 (transfers). *Notification:* continuous (freshmen), continuous (transfers).

Admissions Contact Mr. Mike Redwine, Vice President for Enrollment Development, MidAmerica Nazarene University, 2030 East College Way, Olathe, KS 66062-1899. *Phone:* 913-791-3380 Ext. 481. *Toll-free phone:* 800-800-8887. *Fax:* 913-791-3481. *E-mail:* admissions@mnu.edu.

NEWMAN UNIVERSITY
Wichita, Kansas

- **Independent Roman Catholic** comprehensive, founded 1933
- **Calendar** semesters
- **Degrees** certificates, associate, bachelor's, and master's
- **Urban** 61-acre campus
- **Coed,** 1,757 undergraduate students, 62% full-time, 64% women, 36% men
- **Minimally difficult** entrance level

Undergraduates 1,086 full-time, 671 part-time. Students come from 34 states and territories, 11% are from out of state, 9% African American, 3% Asian American or Pacific Islander, 8% Hispanic American, 1% Native American, 14% live on campus. *Retention:* 64% of 2002 full-time freshmen returned.

Freshmen *Admission:* 188 admitted. *Average high school GPA:* 3.28. *Test scores:* SAT verbal scores over 500: 67%; SAT math scores over 500: 73%; ACT scores over 18: 87%; SAT verbal scores over 600: 11%; SAT math scores over 600: 12%; ACT scores over 24: 42%; SAT math scores over 700: 6%; ACT scores over 30: 3%.

Faculty *Total:* 192, 35% full-time. *Student/faculty ratio:* 14:1.

Majors Accounting; art; biology/biological sciences; business administration and management; chemistry; counseling psychology; criminal justice/law enforcement administration; education; elementary education; English; health science; history; information science/studies; liberal arts and sciences/liberal studies; management information systems; marketing/marketing management; mass communication/media; mathematics; mental health/rehabilitation; nursing (registered nurse training); occupational therapy; pastoral studies/counseling; pre-dentistry studies; pre-engineering; pre-law studies; pre-medical studies; pre-veterinary studies; psychology; radiologic technology/science; respiratory care therapy; secondary education; sociology; substance abuse/addiction counseling; theology.

Academic Programs *Special study options:* academic remediation for entering students, accelerated degree program, adult/continuing education programs, advanced placement credit, cooperative education, distance learning, double majors, external degree program, independent study, internships, off-campus study, part-time degree program, services for LD students, study abroad, summer session for credit. *Unusual degree programs:* 3-2 physical therapy with Washington University in St. Louis.

Library Ryan Library with 107,911 titles, 478 serial subscriptions, 2,042 audiovisual materials, an OPAC, a Web page.

Computers on Campus 90 computers available on campus for general student use. A campuswide network can be accessed from student residence rooms and from off campus. Internet access, at least one staffed computer lab available. Computer purchase or lease plan available.

Student Life *Housing:* on-campus residence required through sophomore year. *Options:* coed, women-only. Campus housing is university owned. Freshman campus housing is guaranteed. *Activities and organizations:* drama/theater group, student-run newspaper, choral group, Student Activities Board, chorale, international club, chemistry/pre-med club, Newman Occupational Therapy Student

Association. *Campus security:* 24-hour patrols, late-night transport/escort service. *Student services:* personal/psychological counseling.

Athletics Member NAIA. *Intercollegiate sports:* baseball M(s), basketball M(s)/W(s), bowling M(s)/W(s), cheerleading M(s)/W(s), cross-country running M(s)/W(s), golf M(s)/W(s), soccer M(s)/W(s), softball W(s), tennis M(s)/W(s), volleyball M(s)/W(s). *Intramural sports:* baseball M, basketball M/W, bowling M/W, cross-country running M/W, football M/W, golf M/W, soccer M/W, softball M/W, table tennis M/W, volleyball M/W, weight lifting M/W.

Standardized Tests *Required:* SAT I or ACT (for admission).

Costs (2003–04) *Comprehensive fee:* $18,168 includes full-time tuition ($13,198), mandatory fees ($150), and room and board ($4820). Full-time tuition and fees vary according to location. Part-time tuition: $365 per credit hour. Part-time tuition and fees vary according to location. *Required fees:* $5 per credit hour part-time. *Room and board:* Room and board charges vary according to housing facility. *Payment plan:* installment. *Waivers:* employees or children of employees.

Financial Aid Of all full-time matriculated undergraduates who enrolled in 2002, 1,025 applied for aid, 773 were judged to have need, 94 had their need fully met. 77 Federal Work-Study jobs (averaging $760). 97 state and other part-time jobs (averaging $963). In 2002, 52 non-need-based awards were made. *Average percent of need met:* 60%. *Average financial aid package:* $9191. *Average need-based loan:* $3919. *Average need-based gift aid:* $3551. *Average non-need-based aid:* $3056. *Average indebtedness upon graduation:* $16,699.

Applying *Options:* electronic application, early admission, deferred entrance. *Application fee:* $20. *Required:* high school transcript, minimum 2.0 GPA. *Recommended:* interview. *Application deadline:* rolling (freshmen), rolling (transfers). *Notification:* continuous (freshmen), continuous (transfers).

Admissions Contact Mrs. Marla Sexson, Dean of Admissions, Newman University, 3100 McCormick Avenue, Wichita, KS 67213. *Phone:* 316-942-4291 Ext. 2144. *Toll-free phone:* 877-NEWMANU Ext. 2144. *Fax:* 316-942-4483. *E-mail:* admissions@newmanu.edu.

OTTAWA UNIVERSITY

Ottawa, Kansas

- **Independent American Baptist Churches in the USA** comprehensive, founded 1865
- **Calendar** semesters
- **Degrees** bachelor's (also offers master's, adult, international and on-line education programs with significant enrollment not reflected in profile)
- **Small-town** 60-acre campus with easy access to Kansas City
- **Endowment** $12.7 million
- **Coed,** 530 undergraduate students, 89% full-time, 45% women, 55% men
- **Moderately difficult** entrance level, 44% of applicants were admitted

Undergraduates 471 full-time, 59 part-time. Students come from 25 states and territories, 4 other countries, 33% are from out of state, 11% African American, 2% Asian American or Pacific Islander, 4% Hispanic American, 2% Native American, 7% international, 14% transferred in, 52% live on campus. *Retention:* 64% of 2002 full-time freshmen returned.

Freshmen *Admission:* 561 applied, 245 admitted, 116 enrolled. *Average high school GPA:* 3.15. *Test scores:* ACT scores over 18: 78%; ACT scores over 24: 26%; ACT scores over 30: 1%.

Faculty *Total:* 37, 51% full-time, 27% with terminal degrees. *Student/faculty ratio:* 19:1.

Majors Art; art teacher education; biology/biological sciences; business administration and management; dramatic/theatre arts; elementary education; English; history; human services; information science/studies; mass communication/media; mathematics; music; music teacher education; physical education teaching and coaching; political science and government; psychology; religious studies; sociology.

Academic Programs *Special study options:* advanced placement credit, double majors, English as a second language, independent study, internships, part-time degree program, student-designed majors, summer session for credit. *Unusual degree programs:* 3-2 engineering with Kansas State University.

Library Myers Library with 80,500 titles, 310 serial subscriptions.

Computers on Campus 71 computers available on campus for general student use. A campuswide network can be accessed from student residence rooms and from off campus. Internet access, online (class) registration, at least one staffed computer lab available.

Student Life *Housing:* on-campus residence required through junior year. *Options:* men-only, women-only. Campus housing is university owned. Freshman campus housing is guaranteed. *Activities and organizations:* drama/theater group, student-run newspaper, radio station, choral group, Christian Faith In Action, Student Activities Force, education club, Whole Earth club, Fellowship of Christian Athletes. *Campus security:* 24-hour emergency response devices and patrols, locked residence hall entrances. *Student services:* health clinic, personal/psychological counseling.

Athletics Member NAIA. *Intercollegiate sports:* baseball M(s), basketball M(s)/W(s), cheerleading M(s)/W(s), cross-country running M(s)/W(s), football M(s), golf M(s), soccer M(s)/W(s), softball W(s), track and field M(s)/W(s), volleyball W(s). *Intramural sports:* badminton M/W, basketball M/W, bowling M/W, golf M/W, racquetball M/W, tennis M/W, volleyball M/W, weight lifting M/W.

Standardized Tests *Required:* SAT I or ACT (for admission).

Costs (2004–05) *Comprehensive fee:* $19,600 includes full-time tuition ($13,850), mandatory fees ($300), and room and board ($5450). Full-time tuition and fees vary according to course load. Part-time tuition and fees vary according to course load. *College room only:* $2400. Room and board charges vary according to board plan and housing facility. *Waivers:* senior citizens and employees or children of employees.

Applying *Options:* electronic application. *Application fee:* $15. *Required:* high school transcript, minimum 2.5 GPA. *Required for some:* essay or personal statement. *Recommended:* 2 letters of recommendation, interview. *Application deadline:* rolling (freshmen), rolling (transfers). *Notification:* continuous (freshmen), continuous (transfers).

Admissions Contact Ms. Ina Agnew, Dean of Student Affairs, Ottawa University, 1001 South Cedar #17, Ottawa, KS 66067-3399. *Phone:* 785-242-5200 Ext. 5561. *Toll-free phone:* 800-755-5200. *Fax:* 785-242-7429. *E-mail:* admiss@ottawa.edu.

PITTSBURG STATE UNIVERSITY

Pittsburg, Kansas

- **State-supported** comprehensive, founded 1903, part of Kansas Board of Regents
- **Calendar** semesters
- **Degrees** certificates, associate, bachelor's, and master's
- **Small-town** 233-acre campus
- **Endowment** $34.4 million
- **Coed,** 5,531 undergraduate students, 91% full-time, 50% women, 50% men
- **Noncompetitive** entrance level, 54% of applicants were admitted

Undergraduates 5,054 full-time, 477 part-time. Students come from 50 states and territories, 47 other countries, 19% are from out of state, 2% African American, 0.5% Asian American or Pacific Islander, 1% Hispanic American, 2% Native American, 4% international, 14% live on campus. *Retention:* 75% of 2002 full-time freshmen returned.

Freshmen *Admission:* 1,690 applied, 908 admitted. *Average high school GPA:* 3.30. *Test scores:* ACT scores over 18: 83%; ACT scores over 24: 29%; ACT scores over 30: 3%.

Faculty *Total:* 288. *Student/faculty ratio:* 18:1.

Majors Accounting; adult and continuing education; advertising; art; art teacher education; automobile/automotive mechanics technology; automotive engineering technology; biology/biological sciences; biology teacher education; broadcast journalism; business administration and management; business/managerial economics; cell and molecular biology; chemistry; chemistry teacher education; child development; clinical laboratory science/medical technology; commercial and advertising art; communication and journalism related; computer and information sciences; computer and information sciences related; computer engineering technology; computer graphics; computer programming; computer science; construction engineering technology; construction management; counselor education/school counseling and guidance; criminal justice/law enforcement administration; criminal justice/safety; economics; education; education related; electrical and electronic engineering technologies related; electrical, electronic and communications engineering technology; elementary education; engineering technology; English; English/language arts teacher education; environmental biology; environmental studies; family and consumer sciences/home economics teacher education; family and consumer sciences/human sciences; fashion merchandising; finance; fine/studio arts; fish/game management; French; general studies; geography; graphic and printing equipment operation/production; health and physical education; health teacher education; heavy equipment maintenance technology; history; history teacher education; industrial arts; industrial design; industrial technology; information science/studies; interior design; journalism; kindergarten/preschool education; marketing/marketing management; mass communication/media; mathematics; mathematics teacher education; mechanical design technology; mechanical engineering/mechanical technology; mental health/rehabilitation; music; music performance; music teacher education; nursing (registered nurse training); physical education teaching and coaching; physical sciences; physical therapy; physics; physics teacher education; piano and organ; plant molecular biology; plant physiology; plastics engineering technology; political science and government; pre-dentistry studies; pre-law studies; pre-medical studies; pre-

Pittsburg State University (continued)
veterinary studies; psychology; psychology teacher education; public relations, advertising, and applied communication related; public relations/image management; radio and television; science teacher education; secondary education; social sciences; social studies teacher education; social work; sociology; Spanish; technical and business writing; technology/industrial arts teacher education; therapeutic recreation; trade and industrial teacher education; violin, viola, guitar and other stringed instruments; voice and opera; wildlife and wildlands science and management; wind/percussion instruments; wood science and wood products/pulp and paper technology.

Academic Programs *Special study options:* academic remediation for entering students, adult/continuing education programs, advanced placement credit, cooperative education, double majors, English as a second language, external degree program, freshman honors college, honors programs, independent study, internships, off-campus study, part-time degree program, services for LD students, student-designed majors, study abroad, summer session for credit. *ROTC:* Army (b). *Unusual degree programs:* 3-2 engineering with Kansas State University, University of Kansas.

Library Leonard H. Axe Library plus 2 others with 290,798 titles, 1,368 serial subscriptions, an OPAC, a Web page.

Computers on Campus 213 computers available on campus for general student use. A campuswide network can be accessed from student residence rooms and from off campus. Internet access, online (class) registration, at least one staffed computer lab available.

Student Life *Housing:* on-campus residence required for freshman year. *Options:* coed. Campus housing is university owned. *Activities and organizations:* drama/theater group, student-run newspaper, radio and television station, choral group, marching band, Student Government Association, student yearbook, student newspaper, national fraternities, national sororities. *Campus security:* 24-hour emergency response devices and patrols, student patrols, controlled dormitory access. *Student services:* health clinic, personal/psychological counseling, legal services.

Athletics Member NCAA. All Division II. *Intercollegiate sports:* baseball M(s), basketball M(s)/W(s), cross-country running M(s)/W(s), football M(s), golf M(s), softball W(s), track and field M(s)/W(s), volleyball W(s). *Intramural sports:* basketball M/W, football M/W, racquetball M/W, rugby M(c), soccer M(c), softball M/W, table tennis M/W, tennis M/W, ultimate Frisbee M/W, volleyball M/W.

Standardized Tests *Required:* ACT (for admission).

Costs (2003–04) *Tuition:* state resident $2962 full-time, $105 per credit hour part-time; nonresident $8784 full-time, $299 per credit hour part-time. *Room and board:* $4166. Room and board charges vary according to board plan. *Payment plan:* installment. *Waivers:* employees or children of employees.

Financial Aid Of all full-time matriculated undergraduates who enrolled in 2003, 3,378 applied for aid, 2,821 were judged to have need, 429 had their need fully met. 324 Federal Work-Study jobs (averaging $1330). 1,250 state and other part-time jobs (averaging $1770). In 2003, 411 non-need-based awards were made. *Average percent of need met:* 88%. *Average financial aid package:* $6666. *Average need-based loan:* $3679. *Average need-based gift aid:* $3219. *Average non-need-based aid:* $1793. *Average indebtedness upon graduation:* $9792.

Applying *Options:* common application, electronic application, early admission, deferred entrance. *Application fee:* $30. *Required:* high school transcript. *Required for some:* minimum 2.0 GPA. *Application deadline:* rolling (freshmen), rolling (transfers).

Admissions Contact Ms. Ange Peterson, Director of Admission and Retention, Pittsburg State University, Pittsburg, KS 66762. *Phone:* 620-235-4251. *Toll-free phone:* 800-854-7488 Ext. 1. *Fax:* 316-235-6003. *E-mail:* psuadmit@pittstate.edu.

SOUTHWESTERN COLLEGE
Winfield, Kansas

- **Independent United Methodist** comprehensive, founded 1885
- **Calendar** semesters
- **Degrees** bachelor's and master's
- **Small-town** 70-acre campus with easy access to Wichita
- **Endowment** $15.3 million
- **Coed,** 1,218 undergraduate students, 63% full-time, 47% women, 53% men
- **Moderately difficult** entrance level, 71% of applicants were admitted

Undergraduates 765 full-time, 453 part-time. Students come from 23 states and territories, 7 other countries, 20% are from out of state, 8% African American, 1% Asian American or Pacific Islander, 4% Hispanic American, 2% Native American, 2% international, 7% transferred in, 63% live on campus. *Retention:* 71% of 2002 full-time freshmen returned.

Freshmen *Admission:* 540 applied, 385 admitted, 177 enrolled. *Average high school GPA:* 3.39. *Test scores:* SAT verbal scores over 500: 36%; SAT math scores over 500: 46%; ACT scores over 18: 91%; SAT verbal scores over 600: 9%; SAT math scores over 600: 12%; ACT scores over 24: 38%; SAT verbal scores over 700: 2%; SAT math scores over 700: 2%; ACT scores over 30: 3%.

Faculty *Total:* 173, 29% full-time, 16% with terminal degrees. *Student/faculty ratio:* 10:1.

Majors Athletic training; biochemistry; biology/biological sciences; business administration and management; business/corporate communications; chemistry; communication and media related; computer programming; computer science; computer technology/computer systems technology; criminal justice/law enforcement administration; early childhood education; elementary education; engineering physics; English; general studies; health and physical education; history; human resources management; industrial production technologies related; liberal arts and sciences and humanities related; liberal arts and sciences/liberal studies; management information systems; management science; manufacturing technology; marine biology and biological oceanography; mathematics; music; music teacher education; nursing (registered nurse training); pastoral studies/counseling; philosophy and religious studies related; physics; psychology; purchasing, procurement/acquisitions and contracts management; securities services administration; sport and fitness administration.

Academic Programs *Special study options:* academic remediation for entering students, adult/continuing education programs, advanced placement credit, double majors, external degree program, honors programs, independent study, internships, off-campus study, part-time degree program, student-designed majors, study abroad, summer session for credit. *Unusual degree programs:* 3-2 engineering with Washington University in St. Louis.

Library Memorial Library plus 1 other with 77,000 titles, 320 serial subscriptions, 320 audiovisual materials, an OPAC, a Web page.

Computers on Campus 55 computers available on campus for general student use. A campuswide network can be accessed from student residence rooms and from off campus that provide access to laptops, wireless campus. Internet access, at least one staffed computer lab available.

Student Life *Housing:* on-campus residence required for freshman year. *Options:* coed, men-only, women-only. Campus housing is university owned. Freshman campus housing is guaranteed. *Activities and organizations:* drama/theater group, student-run newspaper, radio and television station, choral group, Student Activities Association, student government, Fellowship of Christian Athletes, Campus Council on Ministries, International Club, national fraternities. *Campus security:* 24-hour emergency response devices, late-night transport/escort service. *Student services:* health clinic, personal/psychological counseling.

Athletics Member NAIA. *Intercollegiate sports:* basketball M(s)/W(s), cheerleading M(s)/W(s), cross-country running M(s)/W(s), football M(s), golf M(s)/W(s), soccer M(s)/W(s), softball W(s), tennis M(s)/W(s), track and field M(s)/W(s), volleyball W(s). *Intramural sports:* baseball M/W, basketball M/W, bowling M/W, softball M/W, ultimate Frisbee M/W.

Standardized Tests *Required:* SAT I or ACT (for admission).

Costs (2004–05) *Comprehensive fee:* $20,447 includes full-time tuition ($15,349) and room and board ($5098). Full-time tuition and fees vary according to degree level and location. Part-time tuition: $638 per semester hour. Part-time tuition and fees vary according to degree level and location. *College room only:* $2288. Room and board charges vary according to board plan, housing facility, and location. *Payment plan:* installment.

Financial Aid Of all full-time matriculated undergraduates who enrolled in 2001, 539 applied for aid, 479 were judged to have need, 207 had their need fully met. In 2001, 99 non-need-based awards were made. *Average percent of need met:* 88%. *Average financial aid package:* $12,576. *Average need-based loan:* $5203. *Average need-based gift aid:* $7931. *Average non-need-based aid:* $4400. *Average indebtedness upon graduation:* $15,206. *Financial aid deadline:* 8/1.

Applying *Options:* common application, electronic application, deferred entrance. *Application fee:* $20. *Required:* essay or personal statement, high school transcript, minimum 2.25 GPA. *Required for some:* interview. *Application deadlines:* 3/1 (freshmen), 8/15 (transfers). *Notification:* continuous (freshmen), continuous (transfers).

Admissions Contact Mr. Todd Moore, Director of Admission, Southwestern College, 100 College Street, Winfield, KS 67156. *Phone:* 620-229-6236. *Toll-free phone:* 800-846-1543. *Fax:* 620-229-6344. *E-mail:* scadmit@sckans.edu.

STERLING COLLEGE
Sterling, Kansas

- **Independent Presbyterian** 4-year, founded 1887
- **Calendar** 4-1-4
- **Degree** bachelor's
- **Rural** 46-acre campus
- **Endowment** $5.5 million
- **Coed,** 495 undergraduate students, 87% full-time, 51% women, 49% men
- **Moderately difficult** entrance level, 57% of applicants were admitted

Undergraduates 433 full-time, 62 part-time. Students come from 28 states and territories, 14 other countries, 42% are from out of state, 8% African American, 0.4% Asian American or Pacific Islander, 4% Hispanic American, 1% Native American, 3% international, 11% transferred in, 80% live on campus. *Retention:* 46% of 2002 full-time freshmen returned.

Freshmen *Admission:* 465 applied, 263 admitted, 126 enrolled. *Average high school GPA:* 3.29. *Test scores:* SAT verbal scores over 500: 24%; SAT math scores over 500: 19%; ACT scores over 18: 86%; SAT math scores over 600: 5%; ACT scores over 24: 38%; ACT scores over 30: 5%.

Faculty *Total:* 64, 61% full-time, 39% with terminal degrees. *Student/faculty ratio:* 12:1.

Majors Art; athletic training; behavioral sciences; biology/biological sciences; business administration and management; communication and journalism related; computer and information sciences; dramatic/theatre arts; elementary education; English; health and physical education; history; interdisciplinary studies; mathematics; music; music teacher education; philosophy and religious studies related; physical education teaching and coaching; religious education.

Academic Programs *Special study options:* advanced placement credit, double majors, honors programs, independent study, internships, off-campus study, services for LD students, student-designed majors, study abroad.

Library Mabee Library with 76,637 titles, 350 serial subscriptions, 2,159 audiovisual materials, an OPAC, a Web page.

Computers on Campus 93 computers available on campus for general student use. A campuswide network can be accessed from student residence rooms. Internet access, at least one staffed computer lab available.

Student Life *Housing:* on-campus residence required through senior year. *Options:* men-only, women-only. Campus housing is university owned. Freshman campus housing is guaranteed. *Activities and organizations:* drama/theater group, student-run newspaper, choral group, Fellowship of Christian Athletes, Student Activities Council, My Brother's Keeper, Habitat for Humanity, youth ministries. *Campus security:* controlled dormitory access, late night security patrol. *Student services:* personal/psychological counseling.

Athletics Member NAIA. *Intercollegiate sports:* baseball M(s), basketball M(s)/W(s), cross-country running M(s)/W(s), football M(s), soccer M(s)/W(s), softball W(s), track and field M(s)/W(s), volleyball W(s). *Intramural sports:* basketball M/W, golf M/W, softball M/W, table tennis M/W, volleyball M/W.

Standardized Tests *Required:* SAT I or ACT (for admission).

Costs (2003–04) *Comprehensive fee:* $19,033 includes full-time tuition ($13,150), mandatory fees ($370), and room and board ($5513). Part-time tuition and fees vary according to course load. *College room only:* $2170. Room and board charges vary according to board plan and housing facility. *Payment plan:* installment. *Waivers:* senior citizens and employees or children of employees.

Financial Aid Of all full-time matriculated undergraduates who enrolled in 2002, 430 applied for aid, 332 were judged to have need, 143 had their need fully met. 169 Federal Work-Study jobs (averaging $501). 196 state and other part-time jobs (averaging $808). In 2002, 92 non-need-based awards were made. *Average percent of need met:* 94%. *Average financial aid package:* $13,719. *Average need-based loan:* $4288. *Average need-based gift aid:* $7204. *Average non-need-based aid:* $6844. *Average indebtedness upon graduation:* $9647.

Applying *Options:* common application, electronic application, early action, deferred entrance. *Application fee:* $25. *Required:* high school transcript, minimum 2.2 GPA. *Required for some:* 2 letters of recommendation, audition required for fine arts majors. *Recommended:* essay or personal statement, interview. *Application deadline:* 7/1 (freshmen), rolling (transfers). *Notification:* continuous (freshmen), 12/1 (early action), continuous (transfers).

Admissions Contact Mr. Dennis Dutton, Vice President for Enrollment Services, Sterling College, PO Box 98, Administration Building, 125 West Cooper, Sterling, KS 67579-0098. *Phone:* 620-278-4364 Ext. 364. *Toll-free phone:* 800-346-1017. *Fax:* 620-278-4416. *E-mail:* admissions@sterling.edu.

TABOR COLLEGE
Hillsboro, Kansas

- **Independent Mennonite Brethren** comprehensive, founded 1908
- **Calendar** 4-1-4
- **Degrees** associate, bachelor's, and master's
- **Small-town** 26-acre campus with easy access to Wichita
- **Endowment** $3.5 million
- **Coed,** 522 undergraduate students, 79% full-time, 48% women, 52% men
- **Moderately difficult** entrance level, 40% of applicants were admitted

Undergraduates 411 full-time, 111 part-time. Students come from 27 states and territories, 4 other countries, 30% are from out of state, 4% African American, 1% Asian American or Pacific Islander, 3% Hispanic American, 1% Native American, 1% international, 5% transferred in, 81% live on campus. *Retention:* 69% of 2002 full-time freshmen returned.

Freshmen *Admission:* 382 applied, 153 admitted, 86 enrolled. *Average high school GPA:* 3.51. *Test scores:* ACT scores over 18: 98%; ACT scores over 24: 42%; ACT scores over 30: 12%.

Faculty *Total:* 43, 74% full-time, 44% with terminal degrees. *Student/faculty ratio:* 10:1.

Majors Accounting; actuarial science; administrative assistant and secretarial science; adult and continuing education; agricultural business and management; art teacher education; athletic training; biblical studies; biological and physical sciences; biology/biological sciences; business administration and management; business teacher education; chemistry; clinical laboratory science/medical technology; communication/speech communication and rhetoric; computer science; divinity/ministry; education; education (K-12); elementary education; English; environmental biology; health teacher education; history; humanities; interdisciplinary studies; international relations and affairs; journalism; kindergarten/preschool education; legal administrative assistant/secretary; marketing/marketing management; mass communication/media; mathematics; medical administrative assistant and medical secretary; music; music management and merchandising; music teacher education; natural sciences; pastoral studies/counseling; philosophy; physical education teaching and coaching; piano and organ; pre-dentistry studies; pre-medical studies; psychology; public relations/image management; religious studies; science teacher education; secondary education; social sciences; sociology; special education; voice and opera.

Academic Programs *Special study options:* academic remediation for entering students, accelerated degree program, adult/continuing education programs, advanced placement credit, cooperative education, distance learning, double majors, honors programs, independent study, internships, off-campus study, part-time degree program, services for LD students, student-designed majors, study abroad, summer session for credit.

Library Tabor College Library with 80,754 titles, 265 serial subscriptions, 945 audiovisual materials, an OPAC, a Web page.

Computers on Campus 57 computers available on campus for general student use. A campuswide network can be accessed from student residence rooms and from off campus. Internet access, at least one staffed computer lab available.

Student Life *Housing:* on-campus residence required through senior year. *Options:* men-only, women-only, disabled students. Campus housing is university owned. Freshman campus housing is guaranteed. *Activities and organizations:* drama/theater group, student-run newspaper, choral group, Student Activities Board, Student Senate, Campus Ministries Council, Fellowship of Christian Athletes, Share, Prayer, and Dare. *Campus security:* student patrols. *Student services:* personal/psychological counseling.

Athletics Member NAIA. *Intercollegiate sports:* baseball M(s), basketball M(s)/W(s), cheerleading M/W(s), cross-country running M(s)/W(s), football M(s), golf M(s)/W(s), rugby M(c), soccer M(s)/W(s), softball W(s), tennis M(s)/W(s), track and field M(s)/W(s), volleyball W(s). *Intramural sports:* basketball M/W, football M/W, golf M/W, racquetball M/W, soccer M/W, table tennis M/W, tennis M/W, track and field M/W, volleyball M/W, weight lifting M/W.

Standardized Tests *Required:* SAT I or ACT (for admission).

Costs (2003–04) *Comprehensive fee:* $19,500 includes full-time tuition ($13,990), mandatory fees ($360), and room and board ($5150). Full-time tuition and fees vary according to course load. Part-time tuition and fees vary according to course load. *College room only:* $2000. Room and board charges vary according to board plan, housing facility, and location. *Payment plan:* installment. *Waivers:* employees or children of employees.

Financial Aid Of all full-time matriculated undergraduates who enrolled in 2002, 391 applied for aid, 363 were judged to have need, 104 had their need fully met. 128 Federal Work-Study jobs (averaging $675). 275 state and other part-time jobs (averaging $527). In 2002, 87 non-need-based awards were made. *Average percent of need met:* 87%. *Average financial aid package:* $13,837. *Average need-based loan:* $5842. *Average need-based gift aid:* $3608. *Average non-need-based aid:* $4488. *Average indebtedness upon graduation:* $21,695. *Financial aid deadline:* 8/15.

Applying *Options:* common application, electronic application, deferred entrance. *Application fee:* $20. *Required:* essay or personal statement, high school transcript, minimum 2.0 GPA, 2 letters of recommendation, ACT-18. *Recommended:* minimum 3.0 GPA, interview. *Application deadlines:* 8/1 (freshmen), 8/1 (transfers). *Notification:* continuous (freshmen), continuous (transfers).

Admissions Contact Mr. Rusty Allen, Director of Admissions, Tabor College, 400 South Jefferson, Hillsboro, KS 67063. *Phone:* 620-947-3121 Ext. 1727. *Toll-free phone:* 800-822-6799. *Fax:* 620-947-2607. *E-mail:* admissions@tabor.edu.

UNIVERSITY OF KANSAS
Lawrence, Kansas

- **State-supported** university, founded 1866
- **Calendar** semesters

University of Kansas (continued)

- **Degrees** bachelor's, master's, doctoral, first professional, and post-master's certificates (University of Kansas is a single institution with academic programs and facilities at two primary locations: Lawrence and Kansas City. Undergraduate, graduate, and professional education are the principal missions of the Lawrence campus, with medicine and related professional education the focus of the Kansas City campus)
- **Suburban** 1100-acre campus with easy access to Kansas City
- **Endowment** $1.0 billion
- **Coed,** 20,866 undergraduate students, 88% full-time, 52% women, 48% men
- **Moderately difficult** entrance level, 67% of applicants were admitted

Undergraduates 18,272 full-time, 2,594 part-time. Students come from 53 states and territories, 111 other countries, 24% are from out of state, 3% African American, 4% Asian American or Pacific Islander, 3% Hispanic American, 1% Native American, 3% international, 7% transferred in, 22% live on campus. *Retention:* 82% of 2002 full-time freshmen returned.

Freshmen *Admission:* 9,573 applied, 6,458 admitted, 4,066 enrolled. *Average high school GPA:* 3.43. *Test scores:* ACT scores over 18: 96%; ACT scores over 24: 54%; ACT scores over 30: 10%.

Faculty *Total:* 1,332, 90% full-time, 86% with terminal degrees. *Student/faculty ratio:* 19:1.

Majors Accounting; advertising; aerospace, aeronautical and astronautical engineering; African-American/Black studies; African studies; American studies; ancient studies; anthropology; architectural engineering; architectural history and criticism; architecture; art history, criticism and conservation; art teacher education; astronomy; athletic training; atmospheric sciences and meteorology; behavioral sciences; biochemistry/biophysics and molecular biology; biological and biomedical sciences related; biology/biological sciences; broadcast journalism; business/commerce; ceramic arts and ceramics; chemical engineering; chemistry; civil engineering; classics and languages, literatures and linguistics; clinical laboratory science/medical technology; cognitive psychology and psycholinguistics; communication disorders; community health services counseling; computer and information sciences; computer engineering; cytotechnology; dance; design and visual communications; dramatic/theatre arts; East Asian languages; economics; electrical, electronics and communications engineering; elementary education; engineering physics; English; environmental studies; European studies; fiber, textile and weaving arts; fine/studio arts; French; geography; geology/earth science; Germanic languages; graphic design; health and physical education; health information/medical records administration; history; humanities; illustration; industrial design; interior design; international relations and affairs; journalism; Latin American studies; liberal arts and sciences/liberal studies; linguistics; mathematics; mechanical engineering; metal and jewelry arts; microbiology; middle school education; molecular biology; music; music history, literature, and theory; music teacher education; music theory and composition; music therapy; nursing (registered nurse training); nursing science; occupational therapy; painting; petroleum engineering; pharmacy; philosophy; physical education teaching and coaching; physics; piano and organ; political science and government; printmaking; psychology; radio and television; religious studies; respiratory care therapy; Russian studies; sculpture; secondary education; Slavic languages; social work; sociology; Spanish; speech and rhetoric; theatre design and technology; violin, viola, guitar and other stringed instruments; voice and opera; wind/percussion instruments; women's studies.

Academic Programs *Special study options:* academic remediation for entering students, accelerated degree program, adult/continuing education programs, advanced placement credit, cooperative education, distance learning, double majors, English as a second language, honors programs, independent study, internships, part-time degree program, services for LD students, study abroad, summer session for credit. *ROTC:* Army (b), Navy (b), Air Force (b).

Library Watson Library plus 11 others with 4.6 million titles, 33,874 serial subscriptions, 51,153 audiovisual materials, an OPAC, a Web page.

Computers on Campus 1100 computers available on campus for general student use. A campuswide network can be accessed from student residence rooms and from off campus. Internet access, online (class) registration, at least one staffed computer lab available.

Student Life *Housing options:* coed, women-only, cooperative. Campus housing is university owned. *Activities and organizations:* drama/theater group, student-run newspaper, radio and television station, choral group, marching band, Center for Community Outreach, Graduate and Professional Association, St. Lawrence Catholic Campus Center, Panhellenic, International Student Association, national fraternities, national sororities. *Campus security:* 24-hour emergency response devices and patrols, late-night transport/escort service, controlled dormitory access, University police department; security guards are included. *Student services:* health clinic, personal/psychological counseling, women's center, legal services.

Athletics Member NCAA. All Division I except football (Division I-A). *Intercollegiate sports:* baseball M(s), basketball M(s)/W(s), crew M(c)/W(s), cross-country running M(s)/W(s), fencing M(c)/W(c), golf M(s)/W(s), rugby M(c)/W(c), soccer W(s), softball W(s), swimming W(s), tennis W(s), track and field M(s)/W(s), volleyball W(s). *Intramural sports:* basketball M/W, bowling M/W, cheerleading M/W, crew M(c)/W(c), football M/W, golf M/W, gymnastics M(c)/W(c), ice hockey M(c)/W(c), lacrosse M(c)/W(c), racquetball M/W, rock climbing M(c)/W(c), sailing M(c)/W(c), soccer M(c)/W(c), softball M/W, table tennis M/W, tennis M/W, ultimate Frisbee M(c)/W(c), volleyball M(c)/W(c), water polo M(c)/W(c), wrestling M(c).

Standardized Tests *Required:* SAT I or ACT (for admission).

Costs (2003–04) *Tuition:* state resident $3527 full-time, $118 per credit hour part-time; nonresident $11,003 full-time, $367 per credit hour part-time. Full-time tuition and fees vary according to program and reciprocity agreements. Part-time tuition and fees vary according to program and reciprocity agreements. *Required fees:* $574 full-time, $48 per credit hour part-time. *Room and board:* $4822; room only: $2498. Room and board charges vary according to board plan and housing facility. *Waivers:* employees or children of employees.

Financial Aid Of all full-time matriculated undergraduates who enrolled in 2002, 8,631 applied for aid, 6,166 were judged to have need, 1,530 had their need fully met. 658 Federal Work-Study jobs (averaging $1690). 104 state and other part-time jobs (averaging $3703). In 2002, 2178 non-need-based awards were made. *Average percent of need met:* 74%. *Average financial aid package:* $6445. *Average need-based loan:* $3592. *Average need-based gift aid:* $2976. *Average non-need-based aid:* $3764. *Average indebtedness upon graduation:* $18,271.

Applying *Options:* electronic application, deferred entrance. *Application fee:* $30. *Required:* high school transcript, minimum 2.0 GPA, Kansas Board of Regents admissions criteria with GPA of 2.0/2.5; top third of high school class; minimum ACT score of 24 or minimum SAT score of 1090. *Required for some:* minimum 2.5 GPA. *Application deadlines:* 4/1 (freshmen), 5/1 (transfers). *Notification:* continuous (freshmen), continuous (transfers).

Admissions Contact Ms. Lisa Pinamonti, Director of Admissions and Scholarships, University of Kansas, KU Visitor Center, 1502 Iowa Street, Lawrence, KS 66045-7576. *Phone:* 785-864-3911. *Toll-free phone:* 888-686-7323. *Fax:* 785-864-5006. *E-mail:* adm@ku.edu.

UNIVERSITY OF PHOENIX–WICHITA CAMPUS
Wichita, Kansas

Admissions Contact 3020 North Cypress Drive, Suite 150, Wichita, KS 67226.

UNIVERSITY OF SAINT MARY
Leavenworth, Kansas

- **Independent Roman Catholic** comprehensive, founded 1923
- **Calendar** semesters
- **Degrees** associate, bachelor's, and master's
- **Small-town** 240-acre campus with easy access to Kansas City
- **Endowment** $7.8 million
- **Coed,** 580 undergraduate students, 67% full-time, 54% women, 46% men
- **Moderately difficult** entrance level, 47% of applicants were admitted

Undergraduates 389 full-time, 191 part-time. Students come from 24 states and territories, 4 other countries, 30% are from out of state, 12% African American, 2% Asian American or Pacific Islander, 7% Hispanic American, 0.2% Native American, 0.9% international, 3% transferred in. *Retention:* 70% of 2002 full-time freshmen returned.

Freshmen *Admission:* 541 applied, 252 admitted, 91 enrolled. *Test scores:* ACT scores over 18: 90%; ACT scores over 24: 24%; ACT scores over 30: 1%.

Faculty *Total:* 94, 44% full-time, 35% with terminal degrees. *Student/faculty ratio:* 12:1.

Majors Accounting; art; biology/biological sciences; business administration and management; chemistry; child development; community organization and advocacy; community psychology; computer and information sciences; curriculum and instruction; dramatic/theatre arts; education; elementary education; English; history; information science/studies; interdisciplinary studies; liberal arts and sciences/liberal studies; mass communication/media; mathematics; multi-/interdisciplinary studies related; pastoral studies/counseling; political science and government; psychology; sociology; sport and fitness administration; theology; visual and performing arts.

Academic Programs *Special study options:* adult/continuing education programs, advanced placement credit, cooperative education, distance learning, double majors, honors programs, independent study, internships, off-campus study, part-time degree program, student-designed majors, study abroad, summer session for credit. *ROTC:* Army (c).

Library De Paul Library with 117,070 titles, 223 serial subscriptions, 1,907 audiovisual materials, an OPAC, a Web page.

Computers on Campus 95 computers available on campus for general student use. A campuswide network can be accessed from student residence rooms. Internet access, online (class) registration, at least one staffed computer lab available.

Student Life *Housing:* on-campus residence required through senior year. *Options:* coed. Campus housing is university owned. Freshman campus housing is guaranteed. *Activities and organizations:* drama/theater group, student-run newspaper, choral group, Student Government Association, BACCHUS, Theatrical Union, Campus Ministry, Amnesty International. *Campus security:* late-night transport/escort service, controlled dormitory access. *Student services:* health clinic, personal/psychological counseling.

Athletics Member NAIA. *Intercollegiate sports:* baseball M(s), basketball M(s)/W(s), football M(s), soccer M(s)/W(s), softball W(s), volleyball W(s). *Intramural sports:* badminton M/W, basketball M/W, bowling M/W, cross-country running M/W, football M/W, racquetball M/W, soccer M/W, softball M/W, swimming M/W, table tennis M/W, tennis M/W, ultimate Frisbee M/W, volleyball M/W, weight lifting M/W.

Standardized Tests *Required:* SAT I or ACT (for admission).

Costs (2003–04) *Comprehensive fee:* $19,028 includes full-time tuition ($13,574), mandatory fees ($160), and room and board ($5294). Part-time tuition: $254 per credit. Part-time tuition and fees vary according to course load. *Required fees:* $55 per term part-time. *College room only:* $2300. Room and board charges vary according to student level. *Payment plan:* installment. *Waivers:* minority students, adult students, senior citizens, and employees or children of employees.

Financial Aid *Average percent of need met:* 82%.

Applying *Options:* common application, electronic application. *Application fee:* $25. *Required:* high school transcript, minimum 2.5 GPA, 1 letter of recommendation. *Recommended:* interview. *Application deadline:* rolling (freshmen), rolling (transfers). *Notification:* continuous (freshmen), continuous (transfers).

Admissions Contact Ms. Judy Wiedower, Director of Admissions and Financial Aid, University of Saint Mary, 4100 South Fourth Street, Leavenworth, KS 66048. *Phone:* 913-682-5151 Ext. 6118. *Toll-free phone:* 800-752-7043. *Fax:* 913-758-6140. *E-mail:* admiss@stmary.edu.

WASHBURN UNIVERSITY
Topeka, Kansas

- **City-supported** comprehensive, founded 1865
- **Calendar** semesters
- **Degrees** associate, bachelor's, master's, and first professional
- **Urban** 160-acre campus with easy access to Kansas City
- **Endowment** $108.0 million
- **Coed,** 6,045 undergraduate students, 65% full-time, 63% women, 37% men
- **Noncompetitive** entrance level, 100% of applicants were admitted

Undergraduates 3,934 full-time, 2,111 part-time. Students come from 49 states and territories, 45 other countries, 4% are from out of state, 6% African American, 2% Asian American or Pacific Islander, 4% Hispanic American, 2% Native American, 13% live on campus. *Retention:* 75% of 2002 full-time freshmen returned.

Freshmen *Admission:* 1,705 applied, 1,705 admitted. *Average high school GPA:* 3.30. *Test scores:* ACT scores over 18: 85%; ACT scores over 24: 34%; ACT scores over 30: 4%.

Faculty *Total:* 497, 51% full-time. *Student/faculty ratio:* 15:1.

Majors Accounting; actuarial science; administrative assistant and secretarial science; anthropology; art; art history, criticism and conservation; art teacher education; biological and physical sciences; biology/biological sciences; business administration and management; chemistry; child development; clinical laboratory science/medical technology; communication/speech communication and rhetoric; corrections; criminal justice/law enforcement administration; criminal justice/police science; dramatic/theatre arts; economics; education; electrical, electronic and communications engineering technology; elementary education; English; finance; fine/studio arts; French; German; health information/medical records administration; health services administration; health teacher education; history; hospitality administration; humanities; industrial radiologic technology; information science/studies; journalism; kindergarten/preschool education; legal administrative assistant/secretary; legal assistant/paralegal; liberal arts and sciences/liberal studies; marketing/marketing management; mass communication/media; mathematics; medical administrative assistant and medical secretary; mental health/rehabilitation; music; music teacher education; nursing (registered nurse training); occupational safety and health technology; philosophy; physical education teaching and coaching; physical therapy; physics; piano and organ; political science and government; postal management; pre-engineering; pre-law studies; pre-medical studies; psychology; public administration; radio and television; radiologic technology/science; religious studies; respiratory care therapy; social work; sociology; Spanish; speech and rhetoric; violin, viola, guitar and other stringed instruments; voice and opera.

Academic Programs *Special study options:* academic remediation for entering students, adult/continuing education programs, advanced placement credit, cooperative education, distance learning, double majors, English as a second language, honors programs, independent study, internships, off-campus study, part-time degree program, services for LD students, student-designed majors, study abroad, summer session for credit. *ROTC:* Army (b), Air Force (c). *Unusual degree programs:* 3-2 engineering with University of Kansas, Kansas State University.

Library Mabee Library plus 2 others with 1.5 million titles, 14,000 serial subscriptions, an OPAC, a Web page.

Computers on Campus 200 computers available on campus for general student use. A campuswide network can be accessed from off campus. Internet access, online (class) registration, at least one staffed computer lab available.

Student Life *Housing options:* coed. Campus housing is university owned. *Activities and organizations:* drama/theater group, student-run newspaper, television station, choral group, marching band, Washburn Student Association, Campus Activities Board, Student Alumni Association, Learning in the Community, Washburn Education Association, national fraternities, national sororities. *Campus security:* 24-hour emergency response devices and patrols, late-night transport/escort service. *Student services:* health clinic, personal/psychological counseling, legal services.

Athletics Member NCAA. All Division II. *Intercollegiate sports:* baseball M(s), basketball M(s)/W(s), cheerleading M/W, crew M(c)/W(c), football M(s), golf M(s), soccer W, softball W(s), tennis M(s)/W(s), volleyball W(s), wrestling M(c). *Intramural sports:* archery M, basketball M/W, bowling M/W, crew M/W, football M, golf M, racquetball M/W, swimming M/W, tennis M/W, volleyball M/W, wrestling M.

Standardized Tests *Required:* ACT (for admission).

Costs (2004–05) *Room and board:* $4860.

Financial Aid Of all full-time matriculated undergraduates who enrolled in 2002, 2,549 applied for aid, 1,562 were judged to have need, 402 had their need fully met. 138 Federal Work-Study jobs (averaging $2682). 9 state and other part-time jobs (averaging $5364). In 2002, 1477 non-need-based awards were made. *Average percent of need met:* 48%. *Average financial aid package:* $4300. *Average need-based loan:* $3400. *Average need-based gift aid:* $2300. *Average non-need-based aid:* $1642. *Average indebtedness upon graduation:* $12,000.

Applying *Options:* electronic application, early admission. *Application fee:* $20. *Required:* high school transcript. *Application deadlines:* rolling (freshmen), 8/1 (transfers). *Notification:* continuous (freshmen), continuous (transfers).

Admissions Contact Kirk R. Haskins, Director of Admission, Washburn University, 1700 SW College Avenue, Topeka, KS 66621. *Phone:* 785-231-1010 Ext. 1293. *Toll-free phone:* 800-332-0291. *Fax:* 785-231-1089. *E-mail:* zzhansen@acc.washburn.edu.

WICHITA STATE UNIVERSITY
Wichita, Kansas

- **State-supported** university, founded 1895, part of Kansas Board of Regents
- **Calendar** semesters
- **Degrees** certificates, associate, bachelor's, master's, doctoral, post-master's, and postbachelor's certificates
- **Urban** 335-acre campus
- **Endowment** $125,100
- **Coed,** 11,692 undergraduate students, 63% full-time, 56% women, 44% men
- **Noncompetitive** entrance level, 63% of applicants were admitted

Undergraduates 7,377 full-time, 4,315 part-time. Students come from 45 states and territories, 83 other countries, 3% are from out of state, 6% African American, 7% Asian American or Pacific Islander, 5% Hispanic American, 1% Native American, 5% international, 11% transferred in, 6% live on campus. *Retention:* 71% of 2002 full-time freshmen returned.

Freshmen *Admission:* 3,037 applied, 1,917 admitted, 1,211 enrolled. *Average high school GPA:* 3.30. *Test scores:* ACT scores over 18: 85%; ACT scores over 24: 37%; ACT scores over 30: 4%.

Faculty *Total:* 540, 86% full-time, 72% with terminal degrees. *Student/faculty ratio:* 18:1.

Majors Accounting; aerospace, aeronautical and astronautical engineering; anthropology; art; art history, criticism and conservation; art teacher education; audiology and speech-language pathology; biology/biological sciences; business administration and management; chemistry; clinical laboratory science/medical technology; commercial and advertising art; communication/speech communication and rhetoric; computer and information sciences; computer engineering; criminal justice/safety; dental hygiene; dramatic/theatre arts; economics; electrical, electronic and communications engineering technology; electrical, electronics and communications engineering; elementary education; English; finance; French; geology/earth science; gerontology; health/health care administration; history; humanities; human resources management; industrial engineering; inter-

Wichita State University (continued)
national business/trade/commerce; Latin; legal assistant/paralegal; liberal arts and sciences/liberal studies; management information systems; marketing/marketing management; mathematics; mechanical engineering; music; music teacher education; nursing science; occupational therapist assistant; philosophy; physical education teaching and coaching; physical therapist assistant; physician assistant; physics; political science and government; psychology; sales, distribution and marketing; science teacher education; secondary education; social work; sociology; Spanish; visual and performing arts; women's studies.

Academic Programs *Special study options:* academic remediation for entering students, accelerated degree program, advanced placement credit, cooperative education, distance learning, double majors, English as a second language, freshman honors college, honors programs, independent study, internships, off-campus study, part-time degree program, services for LD students, student-designed majors, study abroad, summer session for credit. *Unusual degree programs:* 3-2 accounting.

Library Ablah Library plus 2 others with 1.6 million titles, 15,169 serial subscriptions, 47,558 audiovisual materials, an OPAC, a Web page.

Computers on Campus 1500 computers available on campus for general student use. A campuswide network can be accessed from student residence rooms and from off campus that provide access to online grades, e-mail. Internet access, online (class) registration, at least one staffed computer lab available.

Student Life *Housing:* on-campus residence required for freshman year. *Options:* coed. Campus housing is university owned. *Activities and organizations:* drama/theater group, student-run newspaper, radio and television station, choral group, Association of Malaysian Students, Organization of Pakistani Students, psychology club, nursing students, Institute of Aeronautics, national fraternities, national sororities. *Campus security:* 24-hour emergency response devices and patrols, student patrols, late-night transport/escort service, controlled dormitory access, bicycle patrols by campus security. *Student services:* health clinic, personal/psychological counseling, women's center, legal services.

Athletics Member NCAA. All Division I. *Intercollegiate sports:* baseball M(s), basketball M(s)/W(s), bowling M(c)/W(c), cheerleading M/W, crew M(c)/W(c), cross-country running M(s)/W(s), golf M(s)/W(s), ice hockey M(c)/W(c), racquetball M(c)/W(c), rugby M(c), soccer M(c)/W(c), softball W(s), swimming M(c)/W(c), tennis M(s)/W(s), track and field M(s)/W(s), volleyball M(c)/W(s), wrestling M(c). *Intramural sports:* badminton M/W, basketball M/W, bowling M/W, football M/W, golf M/W, racquetball M/W, soccer M/W, softball M/W, swimming M/W, table tennis M/W, tennis M/W, ultimate Frisbee M/W, volleyball M/W, weight lifting M/W.

Standardized Tests *Required for some:* ACT (for admission).

Costs (2003–04) *Tuition:* state resident $2866 full-time, $96 per credit hour part-time; nonresident $10,320 full-time, $344 per credit hour part-time. Full-time tuition and fees vary according to course load. *Required fees:* $640 full-time, $20 per credit hour part-time, $17 per term part-time. *Room and board:* $4620. Room and board charges vary according to board plan and housing facility. *Payment plan:* installment. *Waivers:* senior citizens and employees or children of employees.

Financial Aid Of all full-time matriculated undergraduates who enrolled in 2002, 5,706 applied for aid, 5,112 were judged to have need, 557 had their need fully met. 195 Federal Work-Study jobs (averaging $2576). In 2002, 919 non-need-based awards were made. *Average percent of need met:* 50%. *Average financial aid package:* $5344. *Average need-based loan:* $3567. *Average need-based gift aid:* $3243. *Average non-need-based aid:* $1408. *Average indebtedness upon graduation:* $17,342.

Applying *Options:* electronic application, deferred entrance. *Application fee:* $30. *Required:* high school transcript. *Required for some:* minimum 2.0 GPA. *Application deadline:* rolling (freshmen), rolling (transfers). *Notification:* continuous (freshmen), continuous (transfers).

Admissions Contact Ms. Gina Crabtree, Director of Admissions, Wichita State University, 1845 North Fairmount, Wichita, KS 67260-0124. *Phone:* 316-978-3085. *Toll-free phone:* 800-362-2594. *Fax:* 316-978-3174. *E-mail:* admissions@wichita.edu.

KENTUCKY

ALICE LLOYD COLLEGE
Pippa Passes, Kentucky

- **Independent** 4-year, founded 1923
- **Calendar** semesters
- **Degree** bachelor's
- **Rural** 175-acre campus
- **Endowment** $16.1 million
- **Coed,** 617 undergraduate students, 96% full-time, 54% women, 46% men
- **Moderately difficult** entrance level, 58% of applicants were admitted

Undergraduates 595 full-time, 22 part-time. Students come from 6 states and territories, 4 other countries, 19% are from out of state, 1% African American, 0.5% Asian American or Pacific Islander, 0.6% Hispanic American, 0.3% Native American, 0.5% international, 4% transferred in, 76% live on campus. *Retention:* 62% of 2002 full-time freshmen returned.

Freshmen *Admission:* 870 applied, 503 admitted, 204 enrolled. *Average high school GPA:* 3.33. *Test scores:* SAT verbal scores over 500: 60%; SAT math scores over 500: 30%; ACT scores over 18: 83%; SAT verbal scores over 600: 40%; SAT math scores over 600: 10%; ACT scores over 24: 14%; ACT scores over 30: 4%.

Faculty *Total:* 36, 75% full-time, 50% with terminal degrees. *Student/faculty ratio:* 18:1.

Majors Biological and physical sciences; biology/biological sciences; business administration and management; elementary education; English; history; interdisciplinary studies; physical education teaching and coaching; pre-dentistry studies; pre-law studies; pre-medical studies; pre-veterinary studies; science teacher education; secondary education.

Academic Programs *Special study options:* academic remediation for entering students, advanced placement credit, double majors, independent study, part-time degree program.

Library McGaw Library and Learning Center with 74,216 titles, 118 serial subscriptions, 1,225 audiovisual materials, an OPAC, a Web page.

Computers on Campus 85 computers available on campus for general student use. A campuswide network can be accessed from student residence rooms. Internet access, at least one staffed computer lab available.

Student Life *Housing:* on-campus residence required through senior year. *Options:* Campus housing is university owned. *Activities and organizations:* drama/theater group, student-run newspaper, radio station, choral group, choral group, Phi Beta Lambda, All Scholastic Society, math/science club, Allied Health Sciences Club. *Campus security:* 24-hour patrols, late-night transport/escort service. *Student services:* health clinic, personal/psychological counseling.

Athletics Member NAIA. *Intercollegiate sports:* baseball M(s), basketball M(s)/W(s), golf M, softball W. *Intramural sports:* badminton M/W, basketball M/W, bowling M/W, cross-country running M/W, football M, racquetball M/W, soccer M/W, softball M/W, swimming M/W, table tennis M/W, tennis M/W, volleyball M/W, weight lifting M/W.

Standardized Tests *Required:* SAT I or ACT (for admission).

Costs (2004–05) *Comprehensive fee:* includes mandatory fees ($1040) and room and board ($3600). Part-time tuition: $212 per credit hour. Full-time students in the 108-county service area are granted guaranteed tuiton. *College room only:* $1650.

Financial Aid Of all full-time matriculated undergraduates who enrolled in 2003, 595 applied for aid, 476 were judged to have need, 65 had their need fully met. 438 Federal Work-Study jobs (averaging $1751). 157 state and other part-time jobs (averaging $1910). In 2003, 175 non-need-based awards were made. *Average percent of need met:* 70%. *Average financial aid package:* $8305. *Average need-based loan:* $747. *Average need-based gift aid:* $6629. *Average non-need-based aid:* $6360. *Average indebtedness upon graduation:* $5694.

Applying *Options:* deferred entrance. *Required:* high school transcript, minimum 2.25 GPA. *Required for some:* essay or personal statement, 1 letter of recommendation, interview. *Application deadline:* 7/1 (freshmen), rolling (transfers). *Notification:* continuous until 8/1 (freshmen), 12/1 (transfers).

Admissions Contact Mr. Sean Damron, Director of Admissions, Alice Lloyd College, 100 Purpose Road, Pippa Passes, KY 41844. *Phone:* 606-368-2101 Ext. 6134. *Fax:* 606-368-6215. *E-mail:* admissions@alc.edu.

ASBURY COLLEGE
Wilmore, Kentucky

- **Independent nondenominational** comprehensive, founded 1890
- **Calendar** semesters
- **Degrees** bachelor's and master's
- **Small-town** 400-acre campus with easy access to Lexington
- **Endowment** $23.9 million
- **Coed,** 1,191 undergraduate students, 96% full-time, 58% women, 42% men
- **Moderately difficult** entrance level, 73% of applicants were admitted

Undergraduates 1,141 full-time, 50 part-time. Students come from 43 states and territories, 10 other countries, 70% are from out of state, 0.9% African American, 0.9% Asian American or Pacific Islander, 1% Hispanic American, 0.3% Native American, 1% international, 5% transferred in, 90% live on campus. *Retention:* 83% of 2002 full-time freshmen returned.

Freshmen *Admission:* 820 applied, 598 admitted, 258 enrolled. *Average high school GPA:* 3.55. *Test scores:* SAT verbal scores over 500: 86%; SAT math scores over 500: 71%; ACT scores over 18: 96%; SAT verbal scores over 600: 47%; SAT math scores over 600: 37%; ACT scores over 24: 55%; SAT verbal scores over 700: 14%; SAT math scores over 700: 6%; ACT scores over 30: 11%.

Faculty *Total:* 143, 63% full-time, 57% with terminal degrees. *Student/faculty ratio:* 11:1.

Majors Accounting; ancient/classical Greek; applied mathematics; art teacher education; biblical studies; biochemistry; biology/biological sciences; business/commerce; chemistry; classics and languages, literatures and linguistics; elementary education; English; fine/studio arts; French; health and physical education; health/medical preparatory programs related; history; journalism; Latin; mathematics; middle school education; missionary studies and missiology; music; music teacher education; parks, recreation and leisure facilities management; philosophy; physical education teaching and coaching; physical sciences; psychology; radio and television broadcasting technology; religious education; social sciences; social work; sociology; Spanish; speech and rhetoric; sport and fitness administration.

Academic Programs *Special study options:* academic remediation for entering students, advanced placement credit, double majors, independent study, internships, part-time degree program, study abroad, summer session for credit. *ROTC:* Army (c), Air Force (c). *Unusual degree programs:* 3-2 engineering with University of Kentucky; nursing with University of Kentucky; computer science with University of Kentucky.

Library Kinlaw Library with 155,320 titles, 14,550 serial subscriptions, 8,974 audiovisual materials, an OPAC, a Web page.

Computers on Campus 183 computers available on campus for general student use. A campuswide network can be accessed from student residence rooms and from off campus. Internet access, at least one staffed computer lab available. Computer purchase or lease plan available.

Student Life *Housing:* on-campus residence required through senior year. *Options:* men-only, women-only, disabled students. Campus housing is university owned. Freshman campus housing is guaranteed. *Activities and organizations:* drama/theater group, student-run newspaper, radio and television station, choral group, Fellowship of Christian Athletes, Impact (community service), Christian Service Association, ministry teams, Student-Faculty Council. *Campus security:* 24-hour emergency response devices, late-night transport/escort service, controlled dormitory access, late night security personnel. *Student services:* health clinic, personal/psychological counseling.

Athletics Member NAIA, NCCAA. *Intercollegiate sports:* basketball M/W, cross-country running M/W, soccer M/W, softball W, swimming M/W, tennis M/W, track and field M/W, volleyball W. *Intramural sports:* badminton M/W, basketball M/W, football M/W, golf M/W, racquetball M/W, soccer M/W, softball M/W, swimming M/W, tennis M/W, ultimate Frisbee M/W, volleyball M/W.

Standardized Tests *Required:* SAT I or ACT (for admission).

Costs (2004–05) *Comprehensive fee:* $22,306 includes full-time tuition ($17,660), mandatory fees ($148), and room and board ($4498). Full-time tuition and fees vary according to course load. Part-time tuition: $679 per semester hour. Part-time tuition and fees vary according to course load. *College room only:* $2560. Room and board charges vary according to board plan, housing facility, and location. *Payment plans:* installment, deferred payment. *Waivers:* senior citizens and employees or children of employees.

Financial Aid Of all full-time matriculated undergraduates who enrolled in 2003, 936 applied for aid, 792 were judged to have need, 175 had their need fully met. 527 Federal Work-Study jobs (averaging $1300). In 2003, 111 non-need-based awards were made. *Average percent of need met:* 78%. *Average financial aid package:* $12,170. *Average need-based loan:* $3991. *Average need-based gift aid:* $7041. *Average non-need-based aid:* $6648. *Average indebtedness upon graduation:* $18,885. *Financial aid deadline:* 7/30.

Applying *Options:* early admission, early action, deferred entrance. *Application fee:* $30. *Required:* essay or personal statement, high school transcript, minimum 2.5 GPA, 3 letters of recommendation. *Required for some:* interview. *Application deadline:* rolling (freshmen), rolling (transfers). *Notification:* continuous (freshmen), continuous (transfers).

Admissions Contact Mr. Stan F. Wiggam, Dean of Admissions, Asbury College, 1 Macklem Drive, Wilmore, KY 40390. *Phone:* 859-858-3511 Ext. 2142. *Toll-free phone:* 800-888-1818. *Fax:* 859-858-3921. *E-mail:* admissions@asbury.edu.

■ See page 1188 for a narrative description.

BELLARMINE UNIVERSITY
Louisville, Kentucky

- **Independent Roman Catholic** comprehensive, founded 1950
- **Calendar** semesters
- **Degrees** certificates, bachelor's, master's, doctoral, post-master's, and postbachelor's certificates
- **Suburban** 120-acre campus
- **Endowment** $19.4 million
- **Coed,** 2,561 undergraduate students, 62% full-time, 60% women, 40% men
- **Moderately difficult** entrance level, 82% of applicants were admitted

Undergraduates 1,586 full-time, 975 part-time. Students come from 39 states and territories, 31% are from out of state, 4% African American, 2% Asian American or Pacific Islander, 0.8% Hispanic American, 0.3% Native American, 0.3% international, 4% transferred in, 37% live on campus. *Retention:* 78% of 2002 full-time freshmen returned.

Freshmen *Admission:* 1,485 applied, 1,212 admitted, 453 enrolled. *Average high school GPA:* 3.53. *Test scores:* SAT verbal scores over 500: 79%; SAT math scores over 500: 74%; ACT scores over 18: 99%; SAT verbal scores over 600: 33%; SAT math scores over 600: 28%; ACT scores over 24: 53%; SAT verbal scores over 700: 2%; SAT math scores over 700: 4%; ACT scores over 30: 6%.

Faculty *Total:* 251, 46% full-time. *Student/faculty ratio:* 13:1.

Majors Accounting; actuarial science; art; arts management; biology/biological sciences; business administration and management; business/managerial economics; cardiopulmonary technology; chemistry; clinical laboratory science/medical technology; clinical/medical laboratory science and allied professions related; communication/speech communication and rhetoric; community organization and advocacy; computer and information sciences; computer engineering; computer science; criminal justice/safety; cytotechnology; economics; education; elementary education; English; French; German; health services/allied health/health sciences; history; human resources management; international business/trade/commerce; international relations and affairs; liberal arts and sciences/liberal studies; mathematics; middle school education; music; musical instrument fabrication and repair; music management and merchandising; nursing (registered nurse training); painting; pastoral studies/counseling; philosophy; political science and government; pre-dentistry studies; pre-law studies; pre-medical studies; pre-pharmacy studies; pre-veterinary studies; psychology; respiratory care therapy; sculpture; secondary education; sociology; Spanish; special education; theology; voice and opera.

Academic Programs *Special study options:* accelerated degree program, adult/continuing education programs, advanced placement credit, double majors, honors programs, independent study, internships, off-campus study, part-time degree program, services for LD students, student-designed majors, study abroad, summer session for credit. *ROTC:* Army (c), Air Force (c).

Library W.L. Lyons Brown Library with 97,737 titles, 401 serial subscriptions, 3,853 audiovisual materials, an OPAC, a Web page.

Computers on Campus 160 computers available on campus for general student use. A campuswide network can be accessed from student residence rooms. Internet access, at least one staffed computer lab available.

Student Life *Housing:* on-campus residence required through junior year. *Options:* coed, men-only, women-only, disabled students. Campus housing is university owned. Freshman campus housing is guaranteed. *Activities and organizations:* drama/theater group, student-run newspaper, choral group, student government, Delta Sigma Pi, Fellowship of Christian Athletes, campus ministry, Bellarmine Activities Council, national fraternities, national sororities. *Campus security:* 24-hour emergency response devices and patrols, student patrols, late-night transport/escort service, controlled dormitory access, 24-hour locked residence hall entrances, security cameras. *Student services:* health clinic, personal/psychological counseling.

Athletics Member NCAA. All Division II except lacrosse (Division I). *Intercollegiate sports:* baseball M(s), basketball M(s)/W(s), cross-country running M(s)/W(s), field hockey W(s), golf M(s)/W(s), lacrosse M(s), soccer M(s)/W(s), softball W(s), tennis M(s)/W(s), track and field M(s)/W(s), volleyball W(s). *Intramural sports:* basketball M/W, football M/W, golf M/W, soccer M/W, table tennis M/W, tennis M/W, volleyball M/W, weight lifting M/W.

Standardized Tests *Required:* SAT I or ACT (for admission).

Costs (2004–05) *Comprehensive fee:* $25,730 includes full-time tuition ($19,250), mandatory fees ($700), and room and board ($5780). Full-time tuition and fees vary according to degree level and program. Part-time tuition: $450 per credit. Part-time tuition and fees vary according to course load, degree level, and program. *Required fees:* $25 per course part-time. *College room only:* $3290. Room and board charges vary according to board plan and housing facility. *Payment plans:* installment, deferred payment. *Waivers:* minority students, children of alumni, adult students, senior citizens, and employees or children of employees.

Financial Aid In 2002, 390 non-need-based awards were made. *Average percent of need met:* 89%. *Average financial aid package:* $13,762. *Average indebtedness upon graduation:* $15,900.

Applying *Options:* common application, electronic application, early admission, early action, deferred entrance. *Application fee:* $25. *Required:* essay or personal statement, high school transcript, minimum 2.0 GPA, letters of recommendation. *Recommended:* interview. *Application deadlines:* 2/1 (freshmen), 8/15 (transfers). *Notification:* 12/1 (early action), continuous (transfers).

Bellarmine University (continued)

Admissions Contact Mr. Timothy A. Sturgeon, Dean of Admission, Bellarmine University, 2001 Newburg Road, Louisville, KY 40205-0671. *Phone:* 502-452-8131. *Toll-free phone:* 800-274-4723 Ext. 8131. *Fax:* 502-452-8002. *E-mail:* admissions@bellarmine.edu.

BEREA COLLEGE
Berea, Kentucky

- **Independent** 4-year, founded 1855
- **Calendar** 4-1-4
- **Degree** bachelor's
- **Small-town** 140-acre campus
- **Endowment** $695.8 million
- **Coed,** 1,560 undergraduate students, 97% full-time, 60% women, 40% men
- **Very difficult** entrance level, 25% of applicants were admitted

Berea College is a small, residential, nonsectarian Christian college recognized for its distinctive academic and work programs and for its special interest in Appalachia. Financial need is an absolute prerequisite for admission. Every accepted student is awarded a full tuition scholarship that is currently worth $19,900 per year. All students participate in a work program on campus for 10–15 hours per week.

Undergraduates 1,515 full-time, 45 part-time. Students come from 44 states and territories, 65 other countries, 59% are from out of state, 17% African American, 1% Asian American or Pacific Islander, 1% Hispanic American, 0.7% Native American, 7% international, 1% transferred in, 81% live on campus. *Retention:* 80% of 2002 full-time freshmen returned.

Freshmen *Admission:* 2,119 applied, 530 admitted, 396 enrolled. *Average high school GPA:* 3.37. *Test scores:* SAT verbal scores over 500: 71%; SAT math scores over 500: 72%; ACT scores over 18: 94%; SAT verbal scores over 600: 30%; SAT math scores over 600: 25%; ACT scores over 24: 40%; SAT verbal scores over 700: 6%; SAT math scores over 700: 1%; ACT scores over 30: 4%.

Faculty *Total:* 161, 81% full-time. *Student/faculty ratio:* 11:1.

Majors Agricultural business and management; agriculture; art; art history, criticism and conservation; art teacher education; biology/biological sciences; biology teacher education; business administration and management; chemistry; child development; classics and languages, literatures and linguistics; developmental and child psychology; dietetics; dramatic/theatre arts; economics; education; elementary education; English; English/language arts teacher education; family and consumer economics related; family and consumer sciences/home economics teacher education; fine/studio arts; foreign language teacher education; French; French language teacher education; German; German language teacher education; history; industrial arts; industrial technology; kindergarten/preschool education; mass communication/media; mathematics; mathematics teacher education; middle school education; music; music teacher education; nursing (registered nurse training); philosophy; physical education teaching and coaching; physics; political science and government; pre-dentistry studies; premedical studies; pre-veterinary studies; psychology; religious studies; secondary education; sociology; Spanish; Spanish language teacher education; women's studies.

Academic Programs *Special study options:* academic remediation for entering students, advanced placement credit, double majors, honors programs, independent study, internships, off-campus study, services for LD students, student-designed majors, study abroad, summer session for credit. *Unusual degree programs:* 3-2 engineering with Washington University in St. Louis, University of Kentucky.

Library Hutchins Library plus 2 others with 330,401 titles, 1,069 serial subscriptions, 10,178 audiovisual materials, an OPAC, a Web page.

Computers on Campus 260 computers available on campus for general student use. A campuswide network can be accessed from student residence rooms and from off campus. Internet access, online (class) registration, at least one staffed computer lab available.

Student Life *Housing:* on-campus residence required through senior year. *Options:* men-only, women-only. Campus housing is university owned. Freshman campus housing is guaranteed. *Activities and organizations:* drama/theater group, student-run newspaper, choral group, Campus Activities Board, Cosmopolitan club, Students for Appalachia, flag football and basketball intramurals, Baptist Student Union. *Campus security:* 24-hour emergency response devices and patrols, late-night transport/escort service, controlled dormitory access, crime prevention programs. *Student services:* health clinic, personal/psychological counseling, women's center.

Athletics Member NAIA. *Intercollegiate sports:* baseball M, basketball M/W, cheerleading M(c)/W(c), cross-country running M/W, golf M, rock climbing W(c), soccer M/W, softball W, swimming M/W, tennis M/W, track and field M/W, volleyball W. *Intramural sports:* basketball M/W, football M/W, racquetball M/W, soccer M/W, softball M/W, ultimate Frisbee M/W, volleyball M/W.

Standardized Tests *Required:* SAT I or ACT (for admission).

Costs (2003–04) *Comprehensive fee:* includes mandatory fees ($507) and room and board ($4523). Financial aid is provided to all students for tuition costs. *College room only:* $2415. *Payment plan:* deferred payment.

Financial Aid Of all full-time matriculated undergraduates who enrolled in 2003, 1,510 applied for aid, 1,510 were judged to have need, 239 had their need fully met. *Average percent of need met:* 82%. *Average financial aid package:* $24,668. *Average need-based loan:* $1509. *Average need-based gift aid:* $23,110. *Average indebtedness upon graduation:* $6275. *Financial aid deadline:* 8/1.

Applying *Required:* essay or personal statement, high school transcript, interview, financial aid application. *Recommended:* 2 letters of recommendation. *Application deadline:* rolling (freshmen), rolling (transfers). *Notification:* 4/20 (freshmen), continuous (transfers).

Admissions Contact Mr. Jamie Ealy, Director of Admissions, Berea College, CPO 2220, Berea, KY 40404. *Phone:* 859-985-3500. *Toll-free phone:* 800-326-5948. *Fax:* 859-985-3512. *E-mail:* admissions@berea.edu.

■ *See page 1242 for a narrative description.*

BRESCIA UNIVERSITY
Owensboro, Kentucky

- **Independent Roman Catholic** comprehensive, founded 1950
- **Calendar** semesters
- **Degrees** certificates, associate, bachelor's, and master's
- **Urban** 9-acre campus
- **Endowment** $9.0 million
- **Coed**
- **Moderately difficult** entrance level, 80% of applicants were admitted

Undergraduates Students come from 18 states and territories, 19 other countries, 16% are from out of state, 4% African American, 0.5% Asian American or Pacific Islander, 0.8% Hispanic American, 0.3% Native American, 5% international, 34% live on campus. *Retention:* 67% of 2002 full-time freshmen returned.

Freshmen *Admission:* 264 applied, 210 admitted. *Average high school GPA:* 3.24.

Faculty *Total:* 72. *Student/faculty ratio:* 14:1.

Majors Accounting; applied mathematics; art; art teacher education; art therapy; audiology and speech-language pathology; biological and physical sciences; biology/biological sciences; business/commerce; chemistry; clinical laboratory science/medical technology; commercial and advertising art; education; elementary education; engineering; English; finance; history; human resources management; liberal arts and sciences/liberal studies; marketing/marketing management; mathematics and computer science; middle school education; pre-engineering; psychology; religious studies; secondary education; social sciences; social studies teacher education; social work; Spanish; special education; theological and ministerial studies related.

Academic Programs *Special study options:* academic remediation for entering students, adult/continuing education programs, advanced placement credit, double majors, English as a second language, honors programs, independent study, internships, off-campus study, part-time degree program, services for LD students, student-designed majors, study abroad, summer session for credit.

Library Brescia University Library with 2,466 serial subscriptions, 6,717 audiovisual materials, an OPAC, a Web page.

Computers on Campus 41 computers available on campus for general student use. A campuswide network can be accessed from student residence rooms and from off campus. Internet access, at least one staffed computer lab available.

Student Life *Housing:* on-campus residence required for freshman year. *Options:* coed, men-only, women-only. *Activities and organizations:* drama/theater group, student-run newspaper, choral group, Student Government Association, Ichabod Society, National Student Speech-Language-Hearing Association, social work club, Spanish club. *Campus security:* late-night transport/escort service, controlled dormitory access. *Student services:* personal/psychological counseling, women's center.

Athletics Member NAIA. *Intercollegiate sports:* baseball M(s), basketball M(s)/W(s), golf M(s)/W(s), soccer M(s)/W(s), softball W(s), tennis W(s), volleyball W(s). *Intramural sports:* badminton M/W, basketball M/W, bowling M/W, racquetball M/W, table tennis M/W, volleyball M/W.

Standardized Tests *Required:* SAT I or ACT (for admission).

Costs (2003–04) *Comprehensive fee:* $15,620 includes full-time tuition ($10,600), mandatory fees ($220), and room and board ($4800). Part-time tuition and fees vary according to course load. *College room only:* $3600. Room and board charges vary according to board plan and housing facility. *Payment plan:* deferred payment. *Waivers:* children of alumni, senior citizens, and employees or children of employees.

Financial Aid Of all full-time matriculated undergraduates who enrolled in 2002, 869 applied for aid, 767 were judged to have need, 129 had their need fully

met. In 2002, 126 non-need-based awards were made. *Average percent of need met:* 53%. *Average financial aid package:* $6494. *Average need-based loan:* $3070. *Average need-based gift aid:* $5219. *Average non-need-based aid:* $8770.

Applying *Options:* common application, electronic application, deferred entrance. *Application fee:* $25. *Required:* essay or personal statement, high school transcript, minimum 2.5 GPA. *Required for some:* 1 letter of recommendation, interview. *Application deadline:* rolling (freshmen), rolling (transfers). *Notification:* continuous (freshmen), continuous (transfers).

Admissions Contact Sr. Mary Austin Blank, Director of Admissions, Brescia University, 717 Frederica Street, Owensboro, KY 42301. *Phone:* 270-686-4241 Ext. 241. *Toll-free phone:* 877-273-7242. *Fax:* 270-686-4201. *E-mail:* admissions@brescia.edu.

■ *See page 1288 for a narrative description.*

CAMPBELLSVILLE UNIVERSITY
Campbellsville, Kentucky

- **Independent** comprehensive, founded 1906, affiliated with Kentucky Baptist Convention
- **Calendar** semesters
- **Degrees** certificates, associate, bachelor's, master's, and postbachelor's certificates
- **Small-town** 80-acre campus
- **Endowment** $5.2 million
- **Coed,** 1,721 undergraduate students, 68% full-time, 56% women, 44% men
- **Moderately difficult** entrance level, 80% of applicants were admitted

Undergraduates 1,175 full-time, 546 part-time. Students come from 24 states and territories, 18 other countries, 7% are from out of state, 6% African American, 0.5% Asian American or Pacific Islander, 0.6% Hispanic American, 0.2% Native American, 4% international, 6% transferred in, 53% live on campus. *Retention:* 66% of 2002 full-time freshmen returned.

Freshmen *Admission:* 1,053 applied, 839 admitted, 365 enrolled. *Average high school GPA:* 3.18. *Test scores:* SAT verbal scores over 500: 51%; SAT math scores over 500: 48%; ACT scores over 18: 75%; SAT verbal scores over 600: 16%; SAT math scores over 600: 12%; ACT scores over 24: 27%; SAT math scores over 700: 3%; ACT scores over 30: 4%.

Faculty *Total:* 183, 40% full-time, 26% with terminal degrees. *Student/faculty ratio:* 18:1.

Majors Accounting; administrative assistant and secretarial science; art; art teacher education; athletic training; biblical studies; biology/biological sciences; biology teacher education; business administration and management; business/managerial economics; business teacher education; chemistry; chemistry teacher education; clinical laboratory science/medical technology; criminal justice/law enforcement administration; data processing and data processing technology; divinity/ministry; economics; elementary education; English; English/language arts teacher education; health teacher education; history; history teacher education; information science/studies; journalism; marketing/marketing management; mass communication/media; mathematics; mathematics teacher education; music; music teacher education; parks, recreation and leisure; pastoral studies/counseling; physical education teaching and coaching; piano and organ; political science and government; pre-dentistry studies; pre-law studies; pre-medical studies; pre-veterinary studies; psychology; psychology teacher education; religious education; religious/sacred music; religious studies; science teacher education; secondary education; social sciences; social science teacher education; social studies teacher education; social work; sociology; voice and opera.

Academic Programs *Special study options:* academic remediation for entering students, accelerated degree program, adult/continuing education programs, advanced placement credit, distance learning, double majors, English as a second language, honors programs, independent study, internships, off-campus study, part-time degree program, study abroad, summer session for credit. *Unusual degree programs:* 3-2 engineering with University of Kentucky; nursing with Eastern Kentucky University.

Library Montgomery Library plus 2 others with 162,492 titles, 15,993 audiovisual materials, a Web page.

Computers on Campus 125 computers available on campus for general student use. Internet access, at least one staffed computer lab available.

Student Life *Housing:* on-campus residence required through sophomore year. *Options:* men-only, women-only. Campus housing is university owned. Freshman campus housing is guaranteed. *Activities and organizations:* drama/theater group, student-run newspaper, radio and television station, choral group, marching band, Student Government Association, Baptist Student Union, Phi Beta Lambda, African-American Leadership League, Fellowship of Christian Athletics. *Campus security:* 24-hour emergency response devices and patrols, student patrols, late-night transport/escort service, controlled dormitory access. *Student services:* health clinic, personal/psychological counseling.

Athletics Member NAIA. *Intercollegiate sports:* baseball M(s), basketball M(s)/W(s), cheerleading M(s)/W(s), cross-country running M(s)/W(s), football M(s), golf M(s)/W(s), soccer M(s)/W(s), softball W(s), tennis M(s)/W(s), track and field M(s)/W(s), volleyball W(s). *Intramural sports:* basketball M/W, football M/W, racquetball M/W, soccer M/W, swimming M/W, table tennis M/W, tennis M/W, volleyball M/W, weight lifting M/W.

Standardized Tests *Required:* SAT I or ACT (for admission).

Costs (2003–04) *Comprehensive fee:* $17,800 includes full-time tuition ($12,504), mandatory fees ($320), and room and board ($4976). Part-time tuition: $521 per credit. *Required fees:* $50 per term part-time. *College room only:* $2290. *Payment plan:* installment. *Waivers:* senior citizens and employees or children of employees.

Financial Aid Of all full-time matriculated undergraduates who enrolled in 2003, 1,142 applied for aid, 1,066 were judged to have need, 172 had their need fully met. 308 Federal Work-Study jobs (averaging $1600). 70 state and other part-time jobs (averaging $1800). In 2003, 71 non-need-based awards were made. *Average percent of need met:* 74%. *Average financial aid package:* $12,431. *Average need-based loan:* $3483. *Average need-based gift aid:* $9191. *Average non-need-based aid:* $9428. *Average indebtedness upon graduation:* $5300.

Applying *Options:* common application, electronic application, deferred entrance. *Application fee:* $20. *Required:* high school transcript, minimum 2.0 GPA. *Recommended:* essay or personal statement, minimum 3.0 GPA, letters of recommendation, interview. *Application deadline:* rolling (freshmen), rolling (transfers). *Notification:* continuous (freshmen), continuous (transfers).

Admissions Contact Mr. David Walters, Vice President for Admissions and Student services, Campbellsville University, 1 University Drive, Campbellsville, KY 42718-2799. *Phone:* 270-789-5220 Ext. 5007. *Toll-free phone:* 800-264-6014. *Fax:* 270-789-5071. *E-mail:* admissions@campbellsville.edu.

CENTRE COLLEGE
Danville, Kentucky

- **Independent** 4-year, founded 1819, affiliated with Presbyterian Church (U.S.A.)
- **Calendar** 4-1-4
- **Degree** bachelor's
- **Small-town** 100-acre campus
- **Endowment** $126.7 million
- **Coed,** 1,062 undergraduate students, 100% full-time, 52% women, 48% men
- **Very difficult** entrance level, 75% of applicants were admitted

Undergraduates 1,058 full-time, 4 part-time. Students come from 33 states and territories, 10 other countries, 30% are from out of state, 2% African American, 3% Asian American or Pacific Islander, 0.3% Hispanic American, 0.2% Native American, 1% international, 1% transferred in, 90% live on campus. *Retention:* 90% of 2002 full-time freshmen returned.

Freshmen *Admission:* 1,409 applied, 1,063 admitted, 272 enrolled. *Average high school GPA:* 3.70. *Test scores:* SAT verbal scores over 500: 97%; SAT math scores over 500: 91%; ACT scores over 18: 100%; SAT verbal scores over 600: 62%; SAT math scores over 600: 56%; ACT scores over 24: 85%; SAT verbal scores over 700: 20%; SAT math scores over 700: 12%; ACT scores over 30: 24%.

Faculty *Total:* 100, 90% full-time, 94% with terminal degrees. *Student/faculty ratio:* 11:1.

Majors Anthropology; art; art history, criticism and conservation; biochemistry; biology/biological sciences; chemistry; classics and languages, literatures and linguistics; computer science; dramatic/theatre arts; economics; elementary education; English; French; German; history; international relations and affairs; mathematics; molecular biology; music; philosophy; physics; physiological psychology/psychobiology; political science and government; psychology; religious studies; secondary education; sociology; Spanish.

Academic Programs *Special study options:* advanced placement credit, double majors, independent study, internships, off-campus study, part-time degree program, services for LD students, student-designed majors, study abroad. *ROTC:* Army (c), Air Force (c). *Unusual degree programs:* 3-2 engineering with Washington University in St. Louis, Columbia University, Vanderbilt University, University of Kentucky.

Library Doherty Library plus 1 other with 217,751 titles, 750 serial subscriptions, an OPAC, a Web page.

Computers on Campus 150 computers available on campus for general student use. A campuswide network can be accessed from student residence rooms and from off campus. Internet access, at least one staffed computer lab available.

Student Life *Housing:* on-campus residence required through sophomore year. *Options:* coed, men-only, women-only. Campus housing is university owned. Freshman campus housing is guaranteed. *Activities and organizations:* drama/theater group, student-run newspaper, choral group, CARE (Centre Action Reaches Everyone), Christian Fellowship, College Democrats and Republicans,

Centre College (continued)
Student Congress, outdoors club, national fraternities, national sororities. *Campus security:* 24-hour emergency response devices and patrols, late-night transport/escort service, controlled dormitory access. *Student services:* health clinic, personal/psychological counseling.

Athletics Member NCAA. All Division III. *Intercollegiate sports:* baseball M, basketball M/W, cheerleading W, cross-country running M/W, field hockey W, football M, golf M/W, soccer M/W, softball W, swimming M/W, tennis M/W, track and field M/W, volleyball W. *Intramural sports:* badminton M/W, basketball M/W, bowling M/W, equestrian sports M/W, football M/W, golf M/W, racquetball M/W, rock climbing M/W, soccer M/W, softball M/W, swimming M/W, table tennis M/W, tennis M/W, track and field M/W, ultimate Frisbee M/W, volleyball M/W, weight lifting M/W, wrestling M.

Standardized Tests *Required:* SAT I or ACT (for admission).

Costs (2003–04) *Comprehensive fee.* $27,300 includes full-time tuition ($20,400) and room and board ($6900). Part-time tuition: $650 per credit hour. Part-time tuition and fees vary according to course load. *College room only:* $3500. Room and board charges vary according to board plan. *Payment plan:* installment. *Waivers:* children of alumni and employees or children of employees.

Financial Aid Of all full-time matriculated undergraduates who enrolled in 2003, 779 applied for aid, 677 were judged to have need, 270 had their need fully met. 311 Federal Work-Study jobs (averaging $1342). 22 state and other part-time jobs (averaging $1920). In 2003, 316 non-need-based awards were made. *Average percent of need met:* 90%. *Average financial aid package:* $17,012. *Average need-based loan:* $3875. *Average need-based gift aid:* $14,139. *Average non-need-based aid:* $8013. *Average indebtedness upon graduation:* $14,200. *Financial aid deadline:* 3/1.

Applying *Options:* common application, electronic application, early admission, early action, deferred entrance. *Application fee:* $40. *Required:* essay or personal statement, high school transcript, 1 letter of recommendation. *Recommended:* interview. *Application deadlines:* 2/1 (freshmen), 6/1 (transfers). *Notification:* 3/1 (freshmen), 1/15 (early action), continuous until 7/1 (transfers).

Admissions Contact Mr. J. Carey Thompson, Dean of Admission and Financial Aid, Centre College, 600 West Walnut Street, Danville, KY 40422-1394. *Phone:* 859-238-5350. *Toll-free phone:* 800-423-6236. *Fax:* 859-238-5373. *E-mail:* admission@centre.edu.

CLEAR CREEK BAPTIST BIBLE COLLEGE
Pineville, Kentucky

- **Independent Southern Baptist** 4-year, founded 1926
- **Calendar** semesters
- **Degrees** certificates, diplomas, associate, and bachelor's
- **Rural** 700-acre campus
- **Coed, primarily men,** 212 undergraduate students, 73% full-time, 22% women, 78% men
- **Noncompetitive** entrance level

Undergraduates 154 full-time, 58 part-time. *Retention:* 82% of 2002 full-time freshmen returned.

Freshmen *Admission:* 22 admitted.

Faculty *Total:* 16, 50% full-time.

Majors Biblical studies; divinity/ministry.

Academic Programs *Special study options:* off-campus study, part-time degree program, summer session for credit.

Library Carolyn Boatman Brooks Memorial Library with 38,000 titles, 300 serial subscriptions, an OPAC.

Computers on Campus 15 computers available on campus for general student use. A campuswide network can be accessed. Internet access, at least one staffed computer lab available.

Student Life *Housing options:* coed. *Activities and organizations:* choral group. *Campus security:* 24-hour emergency response devices, student patrols. *Student services:* health clinic, personal/psychological counseling.

Athletics *Intramural sports:* basketball M/W, table tennis M/W, tennis M/W, volleyball M/W.

Costs (2004–05) *Comprehensive fee:* $7710 includes full-time tuition ($4110), mandatory fees ($290), and room and board ($3310). Part-time tuition: $186 per semester hour. *Required fees:* $145 per term part-time. *College room only:* $1870.

Financial Aid Of all full-time matriculated undergraduates who enrolled in 2002, 155 applied for aid, 127 were judged to have need. 24 Federal Work-Study jobs (averaging $1595). In 2002, 33 non-need-based awards were made. *Average percent of need met:* 53%. *Average financial aid package:* $6836. *Average non-need-based aid:* $887.

Applying *Options:* common application, electronic application, deferred entrance. *Application fee:* $40. *Required:* essay or personal statement, 4 letters of recommendation. *Recommended:* high school transcript, interview. *Application deadlines:* 7/15 (freshmen), 7/15 (transfers). *Notification:* continuous (freshmen), continuous (transfers).

Admissions Contact Mr. Billy Howell, Director of Admissions, Clear Creek Baptist Bible College, 300 Clear Creek Road, Pineville, KY 40977-9754. *Phone:* 606-337-3196 Ext. 103. *Fax:* 606-337-2372. *E-mail:* ccbbc@ccbbc.edu.

CUMBERLAND COLLEGE
Williamsburg, Kentucky

- **Independent Kentucky Baptist** comprehensive, founded 1889
- **Calendar** semesters
- **Degrees** associate, bachelor's, and master's
- **Rural** 50-acre campus with easy access to Knoxville
- **Endowment** $49.7 million
- **Coed,** 1,604 undergraduate students, 84% full-time, 53% women, 47% men
- **Moderately difficult** entrance level, 72% of applicants were admitted

Cumberland College is a 4-year, private, liberal arts college situated in the foothills of the Kentucky mountains. Founded in 1889, the College strives to provide a high-quality education at a reasonable cost while maintaining a strong commitment to the Christian values established by its founders.

Undergraduates 1,353 full-time, 251 part-time. Students come from 36 states and territories, 21 other countries, 39% are from out of state, 7% African American, 0.4% Asian American or Pacific Islander, 1% Hispanic American, 0.2% Native American, 2% international, 5% transferred in, 53% live on campus. *Retention:* 60% of 2002 full-time freshmen returned.

Freshmen *Admission:* 1,105 applied, 791 admitted, 414 enrolled. *Average high school GPA:* 3.37. *Test scores:* SAT verbal scores over 500: 54%; SAT math scores over 500: 47%; ACT scores over 18: 85%; SAT verbal scores over 600: 14%; SAT math scores over 600: 13%; ACT scores over 24: 24%; SAT verbal scores over 700: 1%; SAT math scores over 700: 2%; ACT scores over 30: 3%.

Faculty *Total:* 96, 93% full-time, 64% with terminal degrees. *Student/faculty ratio:* 16:1.

Majors Accounting; art teacher education; biology/biological sciences; business/commerce; business teacher education; chemistry; clinical laboratory science/medical technology; communication/speech communication and rhetoric; community health services counseling; computer and information sciences; dramatic/theatre arts; elementary education; English; executive assistant/executive secretary; fine/studio arts; general studies; health and physical education; health teacher education; history; mathematics; middle school education; music; music teacher education; organizational behavior; philosophy and religious studies related; physical education teaching and coaching; physics; political science and government; psychology; religious education; social studies teacher education; social work; special education; speech and rhetoric.

Academic Programs *Special study options:* academic remediation for entering students, accelerated degree program, adult/continuing education programs, advanced placement credit, cooperative education, distance learning, double majors, freshman honors college, honors programs, independent study, internships, part-time degree program, student-designed majors, study abroad, summer session for credit. *ROTC:* Army (b).

Library Norma Perkins Hagan Memorial Library with 191,701 titles, 3,655 serial subscriptions, 7,043 audiovisual materials, an OPAC, a Web page.

Computers on Campus 300 computers available on campus for general student use. A campuswide network can be accessed from student residence rooms and from off campus. Internet access, online (class) registration, at least one staffed computer lab available.

Student Life *Housing:* on-campus residence required through junior year. *Options:* men-only, women-only. Campus housing is university owned. Freshman campus housing is guaranteed. *Activities and organizations:* drama/theater group, student-run newspaper, television station, choral group, marching band, Baptist Student Union, Student Government Association, Campus Activity Board, Mountain Outreach, Fellowship of Christian Athletes. *Campus security:* 24-hour emergency response devices, student patrols, late-night transport/escort service, patrols by trained security personnel 11pm–7am. *Student services:* health clinic, personal/psychological counseling.

Athletics Member NAIA. *Intercollegiate sports:* baseball M(s), basketball M(s)/W(s), cheerleading M(s)/W(s), cross-country running M(s)/W(s), football M(s), golf M(s)/W(s), soccer M(s)/W(s), softball W(s), swimming M(s)/W(s), tennis M(s)/W(s), track and field M(s)/W(s), volleyball W(s), wrestling M(s)/W(s). *Intramural sports:* basketball M/W, football M/W, soccer M/W, softball M/W, table tennis M/W, tennis M/W, volleyball M/W.

Standardized Tests *Required:* SAT I or ACT (for admission).

Costs (2004–05) *Comprehensive fee:* $16,984 includes full-time tuition ($11,498), mandatory fees ($360), and room and board ($5126). Part-time tuition and fees vary according to course load. *Payment plan:* installment. *Waivers:* employees or children of employees.

Financial Aid Of all full-time matriculated undergraduates who enrolled in 2003, 1,202 applied for aid, 1,108 were judged to have need, 454 had their need fully met. 438 Federal Work-Study jobs (averaging $1622). 131 state and other part-time jobs (averaging $1586). In 2003, 142 non-need-based awards were made. *Average percent of need met:* 90%. *Average financial aid package:* $12,416. *Average need-based loan:* $3541. *Average need-based gift aid:* $4921. *Average non-need-based aid:* $5810. *Average indebtedness upon graduation:* $12,503.

Applying *Options:* common application. *Application fee:* $30. *Required:* essay or personal statement, high school transcript, minimum 2.0 GPA, 1 letter of recommendation. *Recommended:* interview. *Application deadline:* rolling (freshmen). *Notification:* continuous (freshmen), continuous (transfers).

Admissions Contact Mrs. Erica Harris, Director of Admissions, Cumberland College, 6178 College Station Drive, Williamsburg, KY 40769. *Phone:* 606-539-4241. *Toll-free phone:* 800-343-1609. *Fax:* 606-539-4303. *E-mail:* admiss@cumberlandcollege.edu.

■ *See page 1506 for a narrative description.*

EASTERN KENTUCKY UNIVERSITY

Richmond, Kentucky

- **State-supported** comprehensive, founded 1906, part of Kentucky Council on Post Secondary Education
- **Calendar** semesters
- **Degrees** certificates, associate, bachelor's, master's, post-master's, and postbachelor's certificates
- **Small-town** 500-acre campus with easy access to Lexington
- **Coed,** 13,567 undergraduate students, 77% full-time, 61% women, 39% men
- **Noncompetitive** entrance level, 76% of applicants were admitted

Undergraduates 10,449 full-time, 3,118 part-time. Students come from 51 states and territories, 56 other countries, 5% are from out of state, 4% African American, 1% Asian American or Pacific Islander, 0.7% Hispanic American, 0.4% Native American, 0.6% international, 7% transferred in, 33% live on campus. *Retention:* 65% of 2002 full-time freshmen returned.

Freshmen *Admission:* 5,513 applied, 4,211 admitted, 2,561 enrolled. *Average high school GPA:* 3.13. *Test scores:* SAT verbal scores over 500: 47%; SAT math scores over 500: 44%; ACT scores over 18: 76%; SAT verbal scores over 600: 15%; SAT math scores over 600: 12%; ACT scores over 24: 19%; SAT verbal scores over 700: 1%; SAT math scores over 700: 1%; ACT scores over 30: 1%.

Faculty *Total:* 987, 55% full-time. *Student/faculty ratio:* 17:1.

Majors Accounting; administrative assistant and secretarial science; agricultural business and management; agricultural production; agriculture; agriculture and agriculture operations related; airline pilot and flight crew; anthropology; applied mathematics; architectural engineering technology; art; art teacher education; audiology and speech-language pathology; biology/biological sciences; broadcast journalism; business administration and management; business/commerce; business/managerial economics; business teacher education; chemistry; child care/guidance; child care provision; child development; clinical laboratory science/medical technology; clinical/medical laboratory technology; commercial and advertising art; community health liaison; community health services counseling; computer and information sciences; computer engineering technology; computer maintenance technology; computer science; computer technology/computer systems technology; construction engineering technology; consumer merchandising/retailing management; corrections; criminal justice/law enforcement administration; criminal justice/police science; dietetics; dietician assistant; drafting; drafting and design technology; dramatic/theatre arts; ecology; economics; education; education (specific subject areas) related; electrical, electronic and communications engineering technology; elementary education; emergency medical technology (EMT paramedic); engineering related; English; environmental engineering technology; environmental health; environmental studies; family and community services; family and consumer sciences/home economics teacher education; family and consumer sciences/human sciences; farm and ranch management; fashion merchandising; finance; fine/studio arts; fire protection and safety technology; foods, nutrition, and wellness; forensic science and technology; French; general studies; geography; geology/earth science; graphic/printing equipment; health/health care administration; health information/medical records administration; health information/medical records technology; health teacher education; history; home furnishings; home furnishings and equipment installation; horticultural science; housing and human environments; human development and family studies; industrial arts; industrial technology; information science/studies; insurance; interior design; journalism; kindergarten/preschool education; landscape architecture; legal assistant/paralegal; management information systems; marketing/marketing management; mass communication/media; mathematics; medical/clinical assistant; medical microbiology and bacteriology; medical office management; middle school education; music; music teacher education; natural sciences; nursing (registered nurse training); nursing related; occupational therapy; office management; parks, recreation and leisure facilities management; philosophy; physical education teaching and coaching; physical sciences; physics; political science and government; pre-engineering; psychology; public relations, advertising, and applied communication related; public relations/image management; quality control technology; radio and television; real estate; science teacher education; secondary education; security and loss prevention; sign language interpretation and translation; social work; sociology; Spanish; special education; special education (hearing impaired); special education (speech or language impaired); speech and rhetoric; speech therapy; statistics; technical teacher education; technology/industrial arts teacher education; trade and industrial teacher education; transportation technology; wildlife and wildlands science and management.

Academic Programs *Special study options:* academic remediation for entering students, accelerated degree program, adult/continuing education programs, advanced placement credit, cooperative education, distance learning, double majors, English as a second language, external degree program, honors programs, independent study, internships, part-time degree program, services for LD students, student-designed majors, summer session for credit. *ROTC:* Army (b), Air Force (c). *Unusual degree programs:* 3-2 engineering with Georgia Institute of Technology, University of Kentucky, Auburn University.

Library John Grant Crabbe Library plus 2 others with 768,300 titles, 3,128 serial subscriptions, 13,580 audiovisual materials, an OPAC, a Web page.

Computers on Campus 1200 computers available on campus for general student use. A campuswide network can be accessed from student residence rooms and from off campus. Internet access, online (class) registration, at least one staffed computer lab available. Computer purchase or lease plan available.

Student Life *Housing:* on-campus residence required through senior year. *Options:* coed, men-only, women-only. Campus housing is university owned. Freshman campus housing is guaranteed. *Activities and organizations:* drama/theater group, student-run newspaper, radio station, choral group, marching band, fraternities, sororities, Honor Society, Regular Society, national fraternities, national sororities. *Campus security:* 24-hour emergency response devices and patrols, student patrols, late-night transport/escort service. *Student services:* health clinic, personal/psychological counseling.

Athletics Member NCAA. All Division I. *Intercollegiate sports:* baseball M(s), basketball M(s)/W(s), cheerleading M/W, cross-country running M(s)/W(s), football M(s), golf M(s)/W(s), softball W(s), tennis M(s)/W(s), track and field M(s)/W(s), volleyball W(s). *Intramural sports:* badminton M/W, basketball M/W, fencing M(c)/W(c), football M/W, golf M/W, ice hockey M(c), racquetball M/W, rugby M(c)/W(c), soccer M(c)/W(c), softball M/W, tennis M/W, track and field M/W, ultimate Frisbee M/W, volleyball M/W, weight lifting M/W.

Standardized Tests *Required:* ACT (for admission).

Costs (2004–05) *Tuition:* state resident $3298 full-time; nonresident $8990 full-time. Part-time tuition and fees vary according to course load. *Room and board:* $5450; room only: $2730. Room and board charges vary according to board plan and housing facility. *Payment plan:* deferred payment. *Waivers:* senior citizens and employees or children of employees.

Financial Aid Of all full-time matriculated undergraduates who enrolled in 2003, 7,248 applied for aid, 5,725 were judged to have need, 1,613 had their need fully met. 1,573 Federal Work-Study jobs (averaging $1712). 1,288 state and other part-time jobs (averaging $1749). In 2003, 2618 non-need-based awards were made. *Average percent of need met:* 87%. *Average financial aid package:* $6183. *Average need-based loan:* $2547. *Average need-based gift aid:* $3877. *Average non-need-based aid:* $1835. *Average indebtedness upon graduation:* $15,508.

Applying *Options:* deferred entrance. *Application fee:* $25. *Required:* high school transcript, minimum 2.0 GPA. *Application deadline:* 8/15 (freshmen), rolling (transfers). *Notification:* continuous (freshmen), continuous (transfers).

Admissions Contact Stephen A. Byrn, Director of Admissions, Eastern Kentucky University, SSB CPO 54, 521 Lancaster Avenue, Richmond, KY 40475-3102. *Phone:* 859-622-2106. *Toll-free phone:* 800-465-9191. *Fax:* 859-622-8024. *E-mail:* admissions@eku.edu.

GEORGETOWN COLLEGE

Georgetown, Kentucky

- **Independent** comprehensive, founded 1829, affiliated with Baptist Church
- **Calendar** semesters
- **Degrees** bachelor's, master's, and post-master's certificates
- **Suburban** 110-acre campus with easy access to Cincinnati
- **Endowment** $28.3 million

Georgetown College (continued)

■ **Coed,** 1,321 undergraduate students, 94% full-time, 57% women, 43% men
■ **Moderately difficult** entrance level, 80% of applicants were admitted

Undergraduates 1,243 full-time, 78 part-time. Students come from 24 states and territories, 12 other countries, 18% are from out of state, 4% African American, 0.5% Asian American or Pacific Islander, 0.5% Hispanic American, 0.1% Native American, 1% international, 3% transferred in, 86% live on campus. *Retention:* 71% of 2002 full-time freshmen returned.

Freshmen *Admission:* 1,065 applied, 849 admitted, 368 enrolled. *Average high school GPA:* 3.52. *Test scores:* SAT verbal scores over 500: 60%; SAT math scores over 500: 59%; ACT scores over 18: 97%; SAT verbal scores over 600: 20%; SAT math scores over 600: 17%; ACT scores over 24: 50%; SAT verbal scores over 700: 8%; SAT math scores over 700: 2%; ACT scores over 30: 9%.

Faculty *Total:* 144, 65% full-time, 64% with terminal degrees. *Student/faculty ratio:* 12:1.

Majors Accounting; American studies; art; biology/biological sciences; business administration and management; chemistry; computer and information sciences; computer science; dramatic/theatre arts; ecology; economics; education; elementary education; English; environmental studies; European studies; finance; fine/studio arts; French; German; history; information science/studies; international business/trade/commerce; kindergarten/preschool education; management information systems; marketing/marketing management; mass communication/media; mathematics; middle school education; multi-/interdisciplinary studies related; music; music teacher education; parks, recreation and leisure; philosophy; physics; piano and organ; political science and government; pre-dentistry studies; pre-law studies; pre-medical studies; psychology; religious studies; secondary education; sociology; Spanish; speech and rhetoric; voice and opera.

Academic Programs *Special study options:* advanced placement credit, cooperative education, double majors, honors programs, independent study, internships, off-campus study, part-time degree program, student-designed majors, study abroad, summer session for credit. *ROTC:* Army (c), Air Force (c). *Unusual degree programs:* 3-2 engineering with University of Kentucky, Washington University in St. Louis; nursing with University of Kentucky.

Library Anna Ashcraft Ensor Learning Resource Center plus 1 other with 152,531 titles, 733 serial subscriptions, 4,064 audiovisual materials, an OPAC, a Web page.

Computers on Campus 175 computers available on campus for general student use. A campuswide network can be accessed from student residence rooms and from off campus. Internet access, at least one staffed computer lab available.

Student Life *Housing:* on-campus residence required through senior year. *Options:* men-only, women-only. Campus housing is university owned. Freshman campus housing is guaranteed. *Activities and organizations:* drama/theater group, student-run newspaper, radio station, choral group, Campus Ministries, Association of Georgetown Students, Harper-Gatton Leadership Center, President's Ambassadors, Phi Beta Lambda, national fraternities, national sororities. *Campus security:* 24-hour patrols, late-night transport/escort service. *Student services:* health clinic, personal/psychological counseling.

Athletics Member NAIA. *Intercollegiate sports:* baseball M(s), basketball M(s)/W(s), cheerleading W(s), cross-country running M(s)/W(s), football M(s), golf M(s)/W(s), soccer M(s)/W(s), softball W(s), tennis M(s)/W(s), track and field M(s)/W(s), volleyball W(s). *Intramural sports:* basketball M/W, football M/W, golf M/W, racquetball M/W, soccer M/W, softball M/W, table tennis M/W, tennis M/W, ultimate Frisbee M/W, volleyball M/W.

Standardized Tests *Required:* SAT I or ACT (for admission). *Recommended:* ACT (for admission).

Costs (2003–04) *Comprehensive fee:* $21,560 includes full-time tuition ($15,690), mandatory fees ($680), and room and board ($5190). Part-time tuition: $620 per hour. *College room only:* $2500. Room and board charges vary according to board plan and housing facility. *Payment plans:* installment, deferred payment. *Waivers:* employees or children of employees.

Financial Aid Of all full-time matriculated undergraduates who enrolled in 2003, 993 applied for aid, 869 were judged to have need, 415 had their need fully met. 409 Federal Work-Study jobs (averaging $1094). In 2003, 314 non-need-based awards were made. *Average percent of need met:* 90%. *Average financial aid package:* $14,574. *Average need-based loan:* $3638. *Average need-based gift aid:* $6850. *Average non-need-based aid:* $7258. *Average indebtedness upon graduation:* $15,481.

Applying *Options:* electronic application, deferred entrance. *Application fee:* $30. *Required:* essay or personal statement, high school transcript, minimum 2.5 GPA. *Required for some:* letters of recommendation, interview. *Application deadline:* 7/1 (freshmen), rolling (transfers). *Notification:* continuous (freshmen), continuous (transfers).

Admissions Contact Mr. Johnnie Johnson, Director of Admissions, Georgetown College, 400 East College Street, Georgetown, KY 40324. *Phone:* 502-863-8009. *Toll-free phone:* 800-788-9985. *Fax:* 502-868-7733. *E-mail:* admissions@georgetowncollege.edu.

■ *See page 1666 for a narrative description.*

ITT Technical Institute
Louisville, Kentucky

■ **Proprietary** primarily 2-year, founded 1993, part of ITT Educational Services, Inc.
■ **Calendar** quarters
■ **Degrees** associate and bachelor's
■ **Suburban** campus
■ **Coed**
■ **Minimally difficult** entrance level

Standardized Tests *Required:* Wonderlic aptitude test (for admission).

Costs (2003–04) *Tuition:* $347 per credit hour part-time.

Applying *Options:* deferred entrance. *Application fee:* $100. *Required:* high school transcript, interview. *Recommended:* letters of recommendation.

Admissions Contact Mr. Chuck Taylor, Director of Recruitment, ITT Technical Institute, 10509 Timberwood Circle, Louisville, KY 40223. *Phone:* 502-327-7424. *Fax:* 502-327-7624.

Kentucky Christian College
Grayson, Kentucky

■ **Independent** comprehensive, founded 1919, affiliated with Christian Churches and Churches of Christ
■ **Calendar** semesters
■ **Degrees** associate, bachelor's, and master's
■ **Rural** 124-acre campus
■ **Endowment** $3.4 million
■ **Coed,** 544 undergraduate students, 97% full-time, 57% women, 43% men
■ **Moderately difficult** entrance level, 76% of applicants were admitted

Undergraduates 530 full-time, 14 part-time. Students come from 26 states and territories, 7 other countries, 67% are from out of state, 0.6% African American, 0.7% Asian American or Pacific Islander, 0.4% Hispanic American, 0.6% Native American, 2% international, 8% transferred in, 88% live on campus. *Retention:* 70% of 2002 full-time freshmen returned.

Freshmen *Admission:* 285 applied, 216 admitted, 127 enrolled. *Average high school GPA:* 3.17. *Test scores:* SAT verbal scores over 500: 44%; SAT math scores over 500: 55%; ACT scores over 18: 79%; SAT verbal scores over 600: 6%; SAT math scores over 600: 17%; ACT scores over 24: 29%; SAT math scores over 700: 6%; ACT scores over 30: 2%.

Faculty *Total:* 58, 72% full-time, 52% with terminal degrees. *Student/faculty ratio:* 16:1.

Majors Administrative assistant and secretarial science; business administration and management; elementary education; history; interdisciplinary studies; middle school education; music; music teacher education; nursing (registered nurse training); pastoral studies/counseling; psychology; religious education; social work.

Academic Programs *Special study options:* academic remediation for entering students, accelerated degree program, advanced placement credit, cooperative education, double majors, independent study, internships, off-campus study, part-time degree program, services for LD students, summer session for credit.

Library Young Library with 103,323 titles, 395 serial subscriptions, 1,755 audiovisual materials, an OPAC, a Web page.

Computers on Campus 50 computers available on campus for general student use. A campuswide network can be accessed from student residence rooms and from off campus. Internet access, at least one staffed computer lab available.

Student Life *Housing:* on-campus residence required through senior year. *Options:* men-only, women-only. Campus housing is university owned. *Activities and organizations:* drama/theater group, student-run newspaper, choral group, Rotaract, SIFE, Matheteuo, Pi Chi Delta, Laos Alpha. *Campus security:* 24-hour emergency response devices, late-night transport/escort service, controlled dormitory access, patrols by trained security personel (6pm-6am). *Student services:* health clinic, personal/psychological counseling.

Athletics Member NCCAA. *Intercollegiate sports:* basketball M/W, cross-country running M/W, soccer M/W, volleyball W. *Intramural sports:* basketball M/W, cheerleading M/W, football M/W, racquetball M/W, softball M/W, table tennis M/W, volleyball M/W.

Standardized Tests *Required:* SAT I and SAT II or ACT (for admission).

Costs (2004–05) *Comprehensive fee:* $14,995 includes full-time tuition ($10,560), mandatory fees ($80), and room and board ($4355). Full-time tuition and fees vary according to course load. Part-time tuition: $330 per credit hour. Part-time tuition and fees vary according to course load. *Room and board:* Room and board charges vary according to board plan and housing facility. *Payment plan:* installment. *Waivers:* minority students and employees or children of employees.

Financial Aid Of all full-time matriculated undergraduates who enrolled in 2003, 474 applied for aid, 416 were judged to have need, 76 had their need fully met. 241 Federal Work-Study jobs (averaging $1772). 43 state and other part-time jobs (averaging $2155). In 2003, 112 non-need-based awards were made. *Average percent of need met:* 79%. *Average financial aid package:* $6856. *Average need-based loan:* $3790. *Average need-based gift aid:* $4207. *Average non-need-based aid:* $3999. *Average indebtedness upon graduation:* $25,587.

Applying *Options:* common application, electronic application, early action, deferred entrance. *Application fee:* $25. *Required:* essay or personal statement, high school transcript, 3 letters of recommendation. *Required for some:* interview. *Recommended:* minimum 2.0 GPA. *Application deadline:* rolling (freshmen), rolling (transfers). *Notification:* continuous (freshmen), continuous (transfers).

Admissions Contact Ms. Sandra Deakins, Director of Admissions, Kentucky Christian College, 100 Academic Parkway, Box 2021, Grayson, KY 41143-2205. *Phone:* 606-474-3266. *Toll-free phone:* 800-522-3181. *Fax:* 606-474-3155. *E-mail:* sdeakins@email.kcc.edu.

KENTUCKY MOUNTAIN BIBLE COLLEGE

Vancleve, Kentucky

- **Independent interdenominational** 4-year, founded 1931
- **Calendar** semesters
- **Degrees** associate and bachelor's
- **Rural** 35-acre campus
- **Endowment** $350,000
- **Coed,** 82 undergraduate students
- **Moderately difficult** entrance level

Undergraduates Students come from 17 states and territories, 71% are from out of state, 1% African American, 12% international, 93% live on campus. *Retention:* 64% of 2002 full-time freshmen returned.

Freshmen *Admission:* 25 admitted. *Average high school GPA:* 3.33.

Faculty *Total:* 14, 64% full-time, 14% with terminal degrees. *Student/faculty ratio:* 6:1.

Majors Mass communication/media; missionary studies and missiology; pre-theology/pre-ministerial studies; religious education; religious studies.

Academic Programs *Special study options:* academic remediation for entering students, adult/continuing education programs, internships, part-time degree program.

Library Gibson Library with 23,520 titles, 175 serial subscriptions, 1,263 audiovisual materials, an OPAC.

Computers on Campus 12 computers available on campus for general student use. Internet access, at least one staffed computer lab available.

Student Life *Housing:* on-campus residence required through senior year. *Options:* men-only, women-only. Campus housing is university owned. Freshman campus housing is guaranteed. *Activities and organizations:* choral group, Drama Team, choral groups, Student Council, band, Student Involvement (missionary group). *Campus security:* student patrols. *Student services:* personal/psychological counseling.

Standardized Tests *Required:* ACT (for admission).

Costs (2003–04) *Comprehensive fee:* $7930 includes full-time tuition ($4500), mandatory fees ($430), and room and board ($3000). Full-time tuition and fees vary according to course load. Part-time tuition: $150 per credit hour. Part-time tuition and fees vary according to course load. *Required fees:* $30 per term part-time. *College room only:* $950. Room and board charges vary according to housing facility. *Payment plan:* installment. *Waivers:* employees or children of employees.

Financial Aid Of all full-time matriculated undergraduates who enrolled in 2003, 55 applied for aid, 55 were judged to have need. 40 Federal Work-Study jobs (averaging $480). In 2003, 2 non-need-based awards were made. *Average percent of need met:* 30%. *Average financial aid package:* $2000. *Average need-based loan:* $2600. *Average need-based gift aid:* $1500. *Average non-need-based aid:* $3800. *Average indebtedness upon graduation:* $2000.

Applying *Options:* deferred entrance. *Application fee:* $25. *Required:* essay or personal statement, high school transcript, minimum 2.0 GPA, letters of recommendation. *Recommended:* interview. *Application deadline:* rolling (freshmen), rolling (transfers). *Notification:* continuous (freshmen), continuous (transfers).

Admissions Contact Mr. Dana Beland, Director of Recruiting, Kentucky Mountain Bible College, PO Box 10, 855 Route 41, Vancleve, KY 41385. *Phone:* 606-693-5000 Ext. 130. *Toll-free phone:* 800-879-KMBC Ext. 130 (in-state); 800-879-KMBC Ext. 136 (out-of-state). *Fax:* 606-693-4884. *E-mail:* jnelson@kmbc.edu.

KENTUCKY STATE UNIVERSITY

Frankfort, Kentucky

- **State-related** comprehensive, founded 1886
- **Calendar** semesters
- **Degrees** associate, bachelor's, and master's
- **Small-town** 485-acre campus with easy access to Louisville
- **Coed,** 2,166 undergraduate students, 77% full-time, 59% women, 41% men
- **Minimally difficult** entrance level, 52% of applicants were admitted

Undergraduates 1,659 full-time, 507 part-time. Students come from 35 states and territories, 27 other countries, 34% are from out of state, 67% African American, 0.8% Asian American or Pacific Islander, 0.8% Hispanic American, 0.1% Native American, 0.2% international, 1% transferred in, 36% live on campus. *Retention:* 67% of 2002 full-time freshmen returned.

Freshmen *Admission:* 2,200 applied, 1,147 admitted, 333 enrolled. *Average high school GPA:* 2.7. *Test scores:* SAT verbal scores over 500: 14%; SAT math scores over 500: 15%; ACT scores over 18: 15%; SAT verbal scores over 600: 2%; SAT math scores over 600: 5%; ACT scores over 24: 2%; ACT scores over 30: 1%.

Faculty *Total:* 155, 95% full-time. *Student/faculty ratio:* 15:1.

Majors Apparel and textiles; applied mathematics; art teacher education; biology/biological sciences; business administration and management; chemistry; clinical laboratory science/medical technology; computer and information sciences; criminal justice/safety; drafting and design technology; electrical, electronic and communications engineering technology; elementary education; English; executive assistant/executive secretary; fine/studio arts; health and physical education; history; human development and family studies; liberal arts and sciences/liberal studies; mathematics; music performance; music teacher education; nursing (registered nurse training); physical education teaching and coaching; political science and government; psychology; public administration; secondary education; social studies teacher education; social work; sociology.

Academic Programs *Special study options:* academic remediation for entering students, accelerated degree program, adult/continuing education programs, advanced placement credit, cooperative education, English as a second language, honors programs, independent study, internships, off-campus study, part-time degree program, services for LD students, student-designed majors, study abroad, summer session for credit. *ROTC:* Air Force (c). *Unusual degree programs:* 3-2 engineering with University of Kentucky, University of Maryland College Park.

Library Blazer Library with 296,631 titles, 1,097 serial subscriptions, 3,025 audiovisual materials, an OPAC.

Computers on Campus 230 computers available on campus for general student use. A campuswide network can be accessed from off campus that provide access to e-mail. Internet access, at least one staffed computer lab available.

Student Life *Housing:* on-campus residence required through sophomore year. *Options:* men-only, women-only. Campus housing is university owned. *Activities and organizations:* drama/theater group, student-run newspaper, choral group, marching band, Baptist Student Union, student government, national fraternities, national sororities. *Campus security:* 24-hour patrols, controlled dormitory access. *Student services:* health clinic, personal/psychological counseling.

Athletics Member NCAA. All Division II. *Intercollegiate sports:* baseball M, basketball M(s)/W(s), cross-country running M(s)/W(s), football M(s), golf M(s), softball W, tennis M(s)/W(s), track and field M(s)/W(s), volleyball W(s). *Intramural sports:* archery M/W, basketball M/W, bowling M/W, football M/W, soccer M/W, swimming M/W, tennis M/W, track and field M/W, volleyball M/W.

Standardized Tests *Required:* SAT I or ACT (for admission). *Recommended:* ACT (for admission).

Costs (2003–04) *Tuition:* state resident $2828 full-time, $118 per credit part-time; nonresident $8472 full-time, $172 per credit part-time. *Required fees:* $542 full-time, $18 per credit part-time, $43 per term part-time. *Room and board:* $5394; room only: $2366. *Payment plans:* installment, deferred payment. *Waivers:* senior citizens and employees or children of employees.

Financial Aid Of all full-time matriculated undergraduates who enrolled in 2003, 1,679 applied for aid, 1,595 were judged to have need, 338 had their need fully met. 500 Federal Work-Study jobs. In 2003, 381 non-need-based awards were made. *Average percent of need met:* 85%. *Average financial aid package:* $11,500. *Average non-need-based aid:* $4000. *Average indebtedness upon graduation:* $30,000. *Financial aid deadline:* 5/31.

Applying *Options:* early admission. *Application fee:* $17. *Required:* high school transcript. *Required for some:* essay or personal statement, minimum 3.0 GPA, 2 letters of recommendation, interview. *Recommended:* minimum 2.0 GPA. *Application deadline:* rolling (freshmen), rolling (transfers).

Admissions Contact Mr. James Burrell, Director of Admission, Kentucky State University, 400 East Main Street, Frankfort, KY 40601-9957. *Phone:*

Kentucky State University (continued)
502-597-6322. *Toll-free phone:* 800-633-9415 (in-state); 800-325-1716 (out-of-state). *Fax:* 502-597-5814. *E-mail:* jburrell@gwmail.kysu.edu.

■ *See page 1814 for a narrative description.*

KENTUCKY WESLEYAN COLLEGE
Owensboro, Kentucky

- **Independent Methodist** 4-year, founded 1858
- **Calendar** semesters
- **Degree** bachelor's
- **Suburban** 52-acre campus
- **Endowment** $22.4 million
- **Coed,** 614 undergraduate students, 93% full-time, 51% women, 49% men
- **Moderately difficult** entrance level, 75% of applicants were admitted

Undergraduates 571 full-time, 43 part-time. Students come from 13 states and territories, 22% are from out of state, 7% African American, 0.5% Asian American or Pacific Islander, 0.8% Hispanic American, 0.8% international, 9% transferred in, 43% live on campus. *Retention:* 60% of 2002 full-time freshmen returned.

Freshmen *Admission:* 813 applied, 611 admitted, 165 enrolled. *Average high school GPA:* 3.34. *Test scores:* SAT verbal scores over 500: 49%; SAT math scores over 500: 42%; ACT scores over 18: 89%; SAT verbal scores over 600: 6%; SAT math scores over 600: 11%; ACT scores over 24: 25%; ACT scores over 30: 1%.

Faculty *Total:* 72, 47% full-time, 51% with terminal degrees. *Student/faculty ratio:* 12:1.

Majors Accounting; art teacher education; biology/biological sciences; biology teacher education; business administration and management; chemistry; chemistry teacher education; clinical laboratory science/medical technology; communication/speech communication and rhetoric; computer and information sciences; computer science; criminal justice/safety; elementary education; engineering related; English; English/language arts teacher education; environmental studies; fine arts related; history; human services; interdisciplinary studies; journalism; mathematics; mathematics teacher education; middle school education; multi-/interdisciplinary studies related; philosophy; physical education teaching and coaching; physics; political science and government; pre-dentistry studies; pre-law studies; pre-medical studies; pre-veterinary studies; psychology; public administration and social service professions related; secondary education; social studies teacher education; sociology; Spanish; Spanish language teacher education; sport and fitness administration.

Academic Programs *Special study options:* academic remediation for entering students, advanced placement credit, distance learning, double majors, independent study, internships, off-campus study, part-time degree program, student-designed majors, study abroad, summer session for credit. *Unusual degree programs:* 3-2 engineering with Auburn University, University of Kentucky.

Library Library Learning Center with a Web page.

Computers on Campus A campuswide network can be accessed from student residence rooms. At least one staffed computer lab available.

Student Life *Housing:* on-campus residence required through junior year. *Options:* coed, men-only, women-only. Campus housing is university owned. Freshman campus housing is guaranteed. *Activities and organizations:* drama/theater group, student-run newspaper, radio station, choral group, marching band, Student Government Association, Student Activities Programming Board, Leadership KWC, Pre-Professional Society, Wesley club, national fraternities, national sororities. *Campus security:* late-night transport/escort service, 12-hour patrols by trained security personnel. *Student services:* health clinic, personal/psychological counseling.

Athletics Member NCAA. All Division II. *Intercollegiate sports:* baseball M(s), basketball M(s)/W(s), cheerleading M/W, football M(s), golf M(s)/W(s), soccer M(s)/W(s), softball W(s), tennis W, volleyball W(s). *Intramural sports:* basketball M/W, racquetball M/W, soccer M/W, softball M, table tennis M/W, volleyball M/W.

Standardized Tests *Required:* SAT I or ACT (for admission).

Costs (2004–05) *Comprehensive fee:* $17,960 includes full-time tuition ($12,160), mandatory fees ($350), and room and board ($5450). Full-time tuition and fees vary according to course load. Part-time tuition: $375 per credit hour. Part-time tuition and fees vary according to course load. *Required fees:* $25 per term part-time. *College room only:* $2500. *Payment plans:* installment, deferred payment. *Waivers:* children of alumni, senior citizens, and employees or children of employees.

Financial Aid Of all full-time matriculated undergraduates who enrolled in 2003, 570 applied for aid, 500 were judged to have need, 133 had their need fully met. 180 Federal Work-Study jobs (averaging $1000). In 2003, 70 non-need-based awards were made. *Average percent of need met:* 75%. *Average financial aid package:* $11,416. *Average need-based loan:* $2949. *Average need-based gift aid:* $9177. *Average non-need-based aid:* $8739. *Average indebtedness upon graduation:* $18,606.

Applying *Options:* common application, electronic application, early admission, deferred entrance. *Application fee:* $20. *Required:* high school transcript. *Required for some:* letters of recommendation. *Application deadlines:* 9/1 (freshmen), 9/1 (transfers). *Notification:* continuous (freshmen), continuous (transfers).

Admissions Contact Mr. Ken Rasp, Dean of Admission and Financial Aid, Kentucky Wesleyan College, 3000 Frederica Street, PO Box 1039, Owensboro, KY 42302-1039. *Phone:* 270-852-3120. *Toll-free phone:* 800-999-0592 (in-state); 800-990-0592 (out-of-state). *Fax:* 270-852-3133. *E-mail:* admitme@kwc.edu.

■ *See page 1816 for a narrative description.*

LINDSEY WILSON COLLEGE
Columbia, Kentucky

- **Independent United Methodist** comprehensive, founded 1903
- **Calendar** semesters
- **Degrees** associate, bachelor's, and master's
- **Rural** 45-acre campus
- **Endowment** $12.0 million
- **Coed,** 1,536 undergraduate students, 88% full-time, 65% women, 35% men
- **Minimally difficult** entrance level, 73% of applicants were admitted

Undergraduates 1,356 full-time, 180 part-time. Students come from 23 states and territories, 32 other countries, 8% are from out of state, 6% African American, 1% Asian American or Pacific Islander, 1% Hispanic American, 0.2% Native American, 5% international, 10% transferred in, 47% live on campus. *Retention:* 48% of 2002 full-time freshmen returned.

Freshmen *Admission:* 1,270 applied, 932 admitted, 434 enrolled. *Average high school GPA:* 3.04. *Test scores:* ACT scores over 18: 64%; ACT scores over 24: 18%; ACT scores over 30: 1%.

Faculty *Total:* 123, 50% full-time, 37% with terminal degrees. *Student/faculty ratio:* 19:1.

Majors Accounting; American studies; art; art teacher education; biology/biological sciences; biology teacher education; business administration and management; chemistry; computer and information sciences related; computer programming; criminal justice/law enforcement administration; early childhood education; education; elementary education; English; health services/allied health/health sciences; history; humanities; human services; journalism; management information systems; mass communication/media; mathematics; mathematics teacher education; middle school education; physical education teaching and coaching; pre-dentistry studies; pre-law studies; pre-medical studies; pre-pharmacy studies; pre-veterinary studies; psychology; religious studies related; secondary education; social sciences; social science teacher education.

Academic Programs *Special study options:* academic remediation for entering students, accelerated degree program, adult/continuing education programs, advanced placement credit, cooperative education, double majors, English as a second language, external degree program, independent study, internships, off-campus study, part-time degree program, services for LD students, student-designed majors, study abroad, summer session for credit. *ROTC:* Army (c).

Library Katie Murrell Library with 80,000 titles, 1,500 serial subscriptions.

Computers on Campus 80 computers available on campus for general student use. A campuswide network can be accessed from student residence rooms and from off campus. Internet access, online (class) registration, at least one staffed computer lab available.

Student Life *Housing:* on-campus residence required through senior year. *Options:* men-only, women-only, disabled students. Campus housing is university owned. Freshman campus housing is guaranteed. *Activities and organizations:* drama/theater group, student-run newspaper, choral group. *Campus security:* 24-hour emergency response devices and patrols. *Student services:* health clinic, personal/psychological counseling.

Athletics Member NAIA. *Intercollegiate sports:* baseball M(s), basketball M(s)/W(s), bowling M(s)/W(s), cheerleading M(s)/W(s), cross-country running M(s)/W(s), golf M(s)/W(s), soccer M(s)/W(s), softball W(s), tennis M(s)/W(s), track and field M(s)/W(s), volleyball W(s). *Intramural sports:* basketball M, football M/W, softball M/W, table tennis M/W, tennis M/W, volleyball M/W, weight lifting M/W.

Standardized Tests *Required for some:* SAT I or ACT (for admission).

Costs (2003–04) *Comprehensive fee:* $18,086 includes full-time tuition ($12,456), mandatory fees ($146), and room and board ($5484). Part-time tuition: $519 per credit hour. *College room only:* $2024. *Payment plan:* installment. *Waivers:* employees or children of employees.

Applying *Options:* common application, electronic application. *Required:* high school transcript. *Recommended:* interview. *Application deadline:* rolling (freshmen), rolling (transfers). *Notification:* continuous (freshmen), continuous (transfers).

Admissions Contact Mr. David Alls, Director of Admissions, Lindsey Wilson College, 210 Lindsey Wilson Street, Columbia, KY 42728-1298. *Phone:* 270-384-8100 Ext. 8007. *Toll-free phone:* 800-264-0138. *Fax:* 270-384-8200. *E-mail:* allsd@lindsey.edu.

MID-CONTINENT COLLEGE
Mayfield, Kentucky

- **Independent Southern Baptist** 4-year, founded 1949
- **Calendar** semesters
- **Degree** certificates and bachelor's
- **Small-town** 60-acre campus
- **Endowment** $2.1 million
- **Coed,** 683 undergraduate students, 88% full-time, 48% women, 52% men
- **Minimally difficult** entrance level, 88% of applicants were admitted

Undergraduates 603 full-time, 80 part-time. Students come from 17 states and territories, 10 other countries, 24% are from out of state, 9% African American, 1% Hispanic American, 0.1% Native American, 4% international, 6% transferred in, 33% live on campus. *Retention:* 58% of 2002 full-time freshmen returned.

Freshmen *Admission:* 99 applied, 87 admitted, 75 enrolled. *Average high school GPA:* 2.96. *Test scores:* SAT verbal scores over 500: 50%; SAT math scores over 500: 50%; ACT scores over 18: 59%; ACT scores over 24: 9%; ACT scores over 30: 2%.

Faculty *Total:* 43, 47% full-time, 35% with terminal degrees. *Student/faculty ratio:* 15:1.

Majors Ancient Near Eastern and biblical languages; biblical studies; business administration and management; counseling psychology; elementary education; English; general studies; missionary studies and missiology; multi-/interdisciplinary studies related; organizational behavior; psychology; religious education; social sciences.

Academic Programs *Special study options:* academic remediation for entering students, accelerated degree program, advanced placement credit, double majors, English as a second language, independent study, part-time degree program, study abroad, summer session for credit.

Library Anne P. Markham Library with 33,255 titles, 148 serial subscriptions, 1,970 audiovisual materials, an OPAC.

Computers on Campus 24 computers available on campus for general student use. A campuswide network can be accessed from student residence rooms and from off campus. Internet access, at least one staffed computer lab available.

Student Life *Housing:* on-campus residence required through sophomore year. *Options:* men-only, women-only. Campus housing is university owned. *Activities and organizations:* student-run newspaper, SGA, Baptist Student Union, Psych Club, International Club, Ministry Association. *Campus security:* student patrols. *Student services:* personal/psychological counseling.

Athletics Member NAIA, NCCAA. *Intercollegiate sports:* baseball M(s), cross-country running M(s)/W(s), soccer M(s), softball W(s), volleyball W(s). *Intramural sports:* badminton M/W, basketball M/W, bowling M/W, field hockey M/W, lacrosse M/W, soccer M/W, table tennis M/W, ultimate Frisbee M/W, weight lifting M/W.

Standardized Tests *Required:* SAT I or ACT (for admission).

Costs (2003–04) *Comprehensive fee:* $14,480 includes full-time tuition ($7830), mandatory fees ($1250), and room and board ($5400). Full-time tuition and fees vary according to course load and program. Part-time tuition: $261 per credit hour. Part-time tuition and fees vary according to course load and program. *Required fees:* $303 per term part-time. *Room and board:* Room and board charges vary according to board plan and housing facility. *Waivers:* employees or children of employees.

Financial Aid Of all full-time matriculated undergraduates who enrolled in 2003, 532 applied for aid, 461 were judged to have need, 87 had their need fully met. 40 Federal Work-Study jobs (averaging $1650). In 2003, 108 non-need-based awards were made. *Average percent of need met:* 63%. *Average financial aid package:* $6199. *Average need-based loan:* $2577. *Average need-based gift aid:* $4620. *Average non-need-based aid:* $5445. *Average indebtedness upon graduation:* $9272.

Applying *Options:* common application, early admission. *Application fee:* $20. *Required:* essay or personal statement, high school transcript, minimum 2.0 GPA, 2 letters of recommendation. *Required for some:* interview. *Application deadline:* rolling (freshmen), rolling (transfers). *Notification:* continuous (freshmen), continuous (transfers).

Admissions Contact Mrs. Darla Zakowicz, Vice President for Student Development, Mid-Continent College, 99 Powell Road East, Mayfield, KY 42068. *Phone:* 270-247-8521 Ext. 311. *E-mail:* admissions@midcontinent.edu.

MIDWAY COLLEGE
Midway, Kentucky

- **Independent** 4-year, founded 1847, affiliated with Christian Church (Disciples of Christ)
- **Calendar** semesters
- **Degrees** associate and bachelor's
- **Small-town** 105-acre campus with easy access to Louisville and Lexington
- **Endowment** $9.8 million
- **Women only,** 1,154 undergraduate students, 62% full-time
- **Minimally difficult** entrance level, 74% of applicants were admitted

Undergraduates 721 full-time, 433 part-time. Students come from 30 states and territories, 8 other countries, 9% are from out of state, 5% African American, 0.2% Asian American or Pacific Islander, 0.3% Hispanic American, 0.5% Native American, 0.8% international, 15% transferred in, 14% live on campus. *Retention:* 57% of 2002 full-time freshmen returned.

Freshmen *Admission:* 342 applied, 252 admitted, 121 enrolled. *Average high school GPA:* 3.00. *Test scores:* SAT verbal scores over 500: 70%; SAT math scores over 500: 55%; ACT scores over 18: 77%; SAT verbal scores over 600: 10%; SAT math scores over 600: 20%; ACT scores over 24: 9%; SAT verbal scores over 700: 5%; SAT math scores over 700: 5%.

Faculty *Total:* 131, 32% full-time, 26% with terminal degrees. *Student/faculty ratio:* 12:1.

Majors Biology/biological sciences; business administration and management; chemistry; computer and information sciences; data processing and data processing technology; education; elementary education; English; environmental biology; equestrian studies; farm and ranch management; health/health care administration; liberal arts and sciences/liberal studies; mathematics; middle school education; nursing (registered nurse training); psychology; secondary education.

Academic Programs *Special study options:* academic remediation for entering students, adult/continuing education programs, advanced placement credit, distance learning, honors programs, independent study, internships, off-campus study, part-time degree program, services for LD students, study abroad, summer session for credit. *ROTC:* Army (c).

Library Little Memorial Library with 96,236 titles, 250 serial subscriptions, 9,213 audiovisual materials, an OPAC, a Web page.

Computers on Campus 60 computers available on campus for general student use. A campuswide network can be accessed from student residence rooms and from off campus. Internet access, at least one staffed computer lab available.

Student Life *Housing:* on-campus residence required through sophomore year. *Options:* women-only. Freshman campus housing is guaranteed. *Activities and organizations:* student-run newspaper, choral group, student government, Midway Chorale, Midway Association of Nursing Students, Council on Religious Activities, Midway Horse Women's Association. *Campus security:* 24-hour emergency response devices and patrols, late-night transport/escort service. *Student services:* health clinic, personal/psychological counseling, women's center.

Athletics Member NAIA. *Intercollegiate sports:* basketball W(s), equestrian sports W(s), soccer W(s), softball W(s), tennis W(s), volleyball W(s). *Intramural sports:* basketball W, equestrian sports W, softball W, tennis W, volleyball W.

Standardized Tests *Required:* SAT I or ACT (for admission).

Costs (2003–04) *Comprehensive fee:* $17,650 includes full-time tuition ($11,700), mandatory fees ($150), and room and board ($5800). Full-time tuition and fees vary according to program. Part-time tuition: $390 per semester hour. Part-time tuition and fees vary according to class time and course load. *College room only:* $2800. Room and board charges vary according to board plan and housing facility. *Payment plan:* deferred payment. *Waivers:* senior citizens and employees or children of employees.

Financial Aid Of all full-time matriculated undergraduates who enrolled in 2003, 619 applied for aid, 533 were judged to have need, 178 had their need fully met. 112 Federal Work-Study jobs (averaging $1523). 16 state and other part-time jobs (averaging $2306). In 2003, 27 non-need-based awards were made. *Average percent of need met:* 84%. *Average financial aid package:* $9028. *Average need-based loan:* $3298. *Average need-based gift aid:* $6626. *Average non-need-based aid:* $2974. *Average indebtedness upon graduation:* $12,910.

Applying *Options:* common application, electronic application, early admission, deferred entrance. *Application fee:* $25. *Required:* high school transcript. *Required for some:* essay or personal statement, letters of recommendation, interview. *Recommended:* minimum 2.2 GPA. *Application deadline:* rolling (freshmen), rolling (transfers). *Notification:* continuous (freshmen), continuous (transfers).

Midway College (continued)

Admissions Contact Mr. Jim Wombles, Vice President of Admissions, Midway College, 512 East Stephens Street, Pinkerton Building, Midway, KY 40347-1120. *Phone:* 859-846-5799. *Toll-free phone:* 800-755-0031. *Fax:* 859-846-5823. *E-mail:* admissions@midway.edu.

■ *See page 1988 for a narrative description.*

MOREHEAD STATE UNIVERSITY

Morehead, Kentucky

- **State-supported** comprehensive, founded 1922
- **Calendar** semesters
- **Degrees** associate, bachelor's, master's, and post-master's certificates
- **Small-town** 1016-acre campus
- **Endowment** $16.8 million
- **Coed,** 7,921 undergraduate students, 84% full-time, 60% women, 40% men
- **Minimally difficult** entrance level, 71% of applicants were admitted

Undergraduates 6,627 full-time, 1,294 part-time. Students come from 38 states and territories, 22 other countries, 17% are from out of state; 4% African American, 0.2% Asian American or Pacific Islander, 0.6% Hispanic American, 0.3% Native American, 0.7% international, 5% transferred in, 38% live on campus. *Retention:* 66% of 2002 full-time freshmen returned.

Freshmen *Admission:* 5,183 applied, 3,686 admitted, 1,520 enrolled. *Average high school GPA:* 3.11. *Test scores:* ACT scores over 18: 70%; ACT scores over 24: 17%; ACT scores over 30: 1%.

Faculty *Total:* 475, 76% full-time. *Student/faculty ratio:* 19:1.

Majors Accounting; agribusiness; agriculture; biology/biological sciences; business administration and management; business/managerial economics; business teacher education; chemistry; clinical laboratory science/medical technology; communication/speech communication and rhetoric; computer and information sciences; dramatic/theatre arts; ecology; elementary education; English; family and consumer sciences/human sciences related; finance; fine/studio arts; French; general studies; geography; geology/earth science; health teacher education; history; industrial technology; kindergarten/preschool education; kinesiology and exercise science; legal assistant/paralegal; management information systems; manufacturing technology; marketing/marketing management; mathematics; medical radiologic technology; middle school education; music; nursing (registered nurse training); philosophy; physical education teaching and coaching; physics; political science and government; psychology; real estate; respiratory care therapy; social sciences; social work; sociology; Spanish; special education; speech and rhetoric; sport and fitness administration; veterinary/animal health technology.

Academic Programs *Special study options:* academic remediation for entering students, accelerated degree program, adult/continuing education programs, advanced placement credit, cooperative education, distance learning, double majors, honors programs, independent study, internships, off-campus study, part-time degree program, services for LD students, student-designed majors, study abroad, summer session for credit. *ROTC:* Army (b).

Library Camden Carroll Library with 333,518 titles, 2,627 serial subscriptions, 1,808 audiovisual materials, an OPAC, a Web page.

Computers on Campus 1000 computers available on campus for general student use. A campuswide network can be accessed from student residence rooms and from off campus. Internet access, online (class) registration, at least one staffed computer lab available.

Student Life *Housing:* on-campus residence required through sophomore year. *Options:* coed, men-only, women-only, disabled students. Campus housing is university owned. Freshman applicants given priority for college housing. *Activities and organizations:* drama/theater group, student-run newspaper, radio and television station, choral group, marching band, national fraternities, national sororities. *Campus security:* 24-hour emergency response devices and patrols, late-night transport/escort service, controlled dormitory access. *Student services:* health clinic, personal/psychological counseling.

Athletics Member NCAA. All Division I except football (Division I-AA). *Intercollegiate sports:* baseball M(s), basketball M(s)/W(s), bowling M(c)/W(c), cross-country running M(s)/W(s), equestrian sports M(c)/W(c), golf M(s), riflery M(s)/W(s), soccer W, softball W(s), tennis M(s)/W(s), track and field M(s)/W(s), volleyball W(s). *Intramural sports:* archery M/W, badminton M/W, basketball M/W, bowling M/W, football M/W, golf M/W, racquetball M/W, soccer M(c)/W(c), softball M/W, swimming M/W, table tennis M/W, tennis M/W, track and field M/W, volleyball M/W.

Standardized Tests *Required:* SAT I or ACT (for admission). *Recommended:* ACT (for admission).

Costs (2003–04) *Tuition:* state resident $3364 full-time; nonresident $8948 full-time. *Room and board:* $4100. Room and board charges vary according to board plan and housing facility. *Payment plans:* installment, deferred payment. *Waivers:* children of alumni, senior citizens, and employees or children of employees.

Financial Aid Of all full-time matriculated undergraduates who enrolled in 2003, 5,347 applied for aid, 4,404 were judged to have need, 2,030 had their need fully met. 573 Federal Work-Study jobs (averaging $1680). 526 state and other part-time jobs (averaging $1111). In 2003, 1229 non-need-based awards were made. *Average percent of need met:* 90%. *Average financial aid package:* $6799. *Average need-based loan:* $2762. *Average need-based gift aid:* $4085. *Average non-need-based aid:* $2589. *Average indebtedness upon graduation:* $14,191.

Applying *Options:* electronic application, early admission, deferred entrance. *Required:* high school transcript. *Required for some:* letters of recommendation. *Application deadline:* rolling (freshmen), rolling (transfers). *Notification:* continuous (freshmen), continuous (transfers).

Admissions Contact Mr. Joel Pace, Director of Admissions, Morehead State University, Howell McDowell 301, Morehead, KY 40351. *Phone:* 606-783-2000. *Toll-free phone:* 800-585-6781. *Fax:* 606-783-5038. *E-mail:* admissions@morehead-st.edu.

MURRAY STATE UNIVERSITY

Murray, Kentucky

- **State-supported** comprehensive, founded 1922, part of Kentucky Council on Post Secondary Education
- **Calendar** semesters
- **Degrees** associate, bachelor's, master's, post-master's, and postbachelor's certificates
- **Small-town** 238-acre campus
- **Endowment** $38.0 million
- **Coed,** 8,378 undergraduate students, 82% full-time, 59% women, 41% men
- **Moderately difficult** entrance level, 63% of applicants were admitted

Undergraduates 6,901 full-time, 1,477 part-time. Students come from 43 states and territories, 59 other countries, 29% are from out of state, 6% African American, 0.8% Asian American or Pacific Islander, 0.8% Hispanic American, 0.5% Native American, 2% international, 7% transferred in, 40% live on campus. *Retention:* 74% of 2002 full-time freshmen returned.

Freshmen *Admission:* 2,972 applied, 1,873 admitted, 1,511 enrolled. *Average high school GPA:* 3.5. *Test scores:* ACT scores over 18: 96%; ACT scores over 24: 39%; ACT scores over 30: 3%.

Faculty *Total:* 540, 73% full-time, 64% with terminal degrees. *Student/faculty ratio:* 16:1.

Majors Accounting; administrative assistant and secretarial science; agricultural business and management; agricultural teacher education; agriculture; apparel and textiles; art teacher education; audiology and speech-language pathology; biology/biological sciences; biology teacher education; business administration and management; business/commerce; business teacher education; chemical engineering; chemical technology; chemistry; chemistry teacher education; child care provision; civil engineering technology; clinical laboratory science/medical technology; computer and information sciences; computer engineering technology; criminal justice/safety; drafting and design technology; dramatic/theatre arts; early childhood education; economics; electrical, electronic and communications engineering technology; electromechanical technology; elementary education; engineering physics; engineering technology; English; English as a second/foreign language (teaching); English/language arts teacher education; environmental engineering technology; equestrian studies; executive assistant/executive secretary; family and consumer economics related; family and consumer sciences/home economics teacher education; finance; fine/studio arts; fishing and fisheries sciences and management; foodservice systems administration; foods, nutrition, and wellness; foreign language teacher education; French; French language teacher education; general studies; geography; geology/earth science; German; German language teacher education; graphic and printing equipment operation/production; health teacher education; history; history teacher education; horticultural science; human development and family studies; industrial technology; information science/studies; international business/trade/commerce; international relations and affairs; journalism; kinesiology and exercise science; liberal arts and sciences/liberal studies; library science; management information systems; manufacturing technology; marketing/marketing management; mass communication/media; mathematics; mathematics teacher education; mechanical drafting and CAD/CADD; mechanical engineering; mechanical engineering/mechanical technology; middle school education; music; music teacher education; nursing (registered nurse training); occupational safety and health technology; office management; parks, recreation and leisure facilities management; perioperative/operating room and surgical nursing; philosophy; physical education teaching and coaching; physics; physics teacher education; political science and government; psychology; public administration; public relations, advertising, and applied communication related; public relations/image management; radio and television; reading teacher education; science teacher education; secondary education; social science teacher education; social studies teacher education; social work; sociology; Spanish; Spanish language teacher education; special education; speech and rhetoric; speech teacher education; speech therapy; technical and business writing; technology/industrial arts teacher education; telecommunications; trade and industrial teacher education; veterinary/animal health technology; water quality and wastewater treatment management and recycling technology; wildlife and wildlands science and management.

Academic Programs *Special study options:* academic remediation for entering students, accelerated degree program, adult/continuing education programs, advanced placement credit, cooperative education, distance learning, double majors, English as a second language, external degree program, freshman honors college, honors programs, independent study, internships, off-campus study, part-time degree program, services for LD students, study abroad, summer session for credit. *ROTC:* Army (c). *Unusual degree programs:* 3-2 engineering with University of Louisville, University of Kentucky; social work with University of Louisville.

Library Harry Lee Waterfield Library plus 1 other with 470,000 titles, 3,000 serial subscriptions, an OPAC, a Web page.

Computers on Campus 1500 computers available on campus for general student use. A campuswide network can be accessed from student residence rooms and from off campus. Internet access, at least one staffed computer lab available.

Student Life *Housing:* on-campus residence required through sophomore year. *Options:* coed, women-only. Campus housing is university owned. Freshman campus housing is guaranteed. *Activities and organizations:* drama/theater group, student-run newspaper, radio and television station, choral group, marching band, student government, Baptist Student Union, Phi Mu Alpha, Residential Colleges, Interfraternity and Panhellenic Councils, national fraternities, national sororities. *Campus security:* 24-hour emergency response devices and patrols, student patrols, late-night transport/escort service, controlled dormitory access. *Student services:* health clinic, personal/psychological counseling, women's center, legal services.

Athletics Member NCAA. All Division I except football (Division I-AA). *Intercollegiate sports:* baseball M(s), basketball M(s)/W(s), bowling M/W, cheerleading M(s)/W(s), crew M(s)/W(s), cross-country running M(s)/W(s), equestrian sports M/W, golf M(s)/W(s), riflery M(s)/W(s), soccer W(s), tennis M(s)/W(s), track and field M(s)/W(s), volleyball W(s). *Intramural sports:* archery M/W, badminton M/W, basketball M/W, bowling M/W, crew M/W, cross-country running M/W, equestrian sports M/W, fencing M/W, football M, golf M/W, gymnastics W, racquetball M/W, riflery M/W, rock climbing M/W, rugby M/W, sailing M/W, soccer M/W, softball M/W, swimming M/W, tennis M/W, track and field M/W, ultimate Frisbee M/W, volleyball M/W, weight lifting M/W.

Standardized Tests *Required:* ACT (for admission).

Costs (2003–04) *Tuition:* state resident $2944 full-time, $123 per hour part-time; nonresident $5000 full-time, $211 per hour part-time. Full-time tuition and fees vary according to reciprocity agreements. Part-time tuition and fees vary according to reciprocity agreements. $5000 full-time and $200 per hour part-time regional out of state tuition for Illinois, Indiana, Tennessee, and Missouri students. *Required fees:* $492 full-time, $20 per hour part-time. *Room and board:* $4380; room only: $2174. Room and board charges vary according to board plan. *Payment plan:* installment. *Waivers:* children of alumni, senior citizens, and employees or children of employees.

Financial Aid Of all full-time matriculated undergraduates who enrolled in 2003, 5,870 applied for aid, 3,266 were judged to have need, 2,939 had their need fully met. 470 Federal Work-Study jobs (averaging $1234). 1,910 state and other part-time jobs (averaging $1623). In 2003, 2236 non-need-based awards were made. *Average percent of need met:* 89%. *Average financial aid package:* $4610. *Average need-based loan:* $1950. *Average need-based gift aid:* $2180. *Average non-need-based aid:* $2550. *Average indebtedness upon graduation:* $14,034.

Applying *Options:* electronic application, early admission, deferred entrance. *Application fee:* $25. *Required:* high school transcript, minimum 3.0 GPA, rank in top 50% of graduating class. *Required for some:* letters of recommendation. *Recommended:* interview. *Application deadlines:* rolling (freshmen), 8/1 (out-of-state freshmen), rolling (transfers). *Notification:* continuous (freshmen), continuous (transfers).

Admissions Contact Mrs. Stacy Bell, Admission Clerk, Murray State University, PO Box 9, Murray, KY 42071-0009. *Phone:* 270-762-3035. *Toll-free phone:* 800-272-4678. *Fax:* 270-762-3050. *E-mail:* admissions@murraystate.edu.

NORTHERN KENTUCKY UNIVERSITY

Highland Heights, Kentucky

- **State-supported** comprehensive, founded 1968
- **Calendar** semesters
- **Degrees** certificates, associate, bachelor's, master's, and first professional
- **Suburban** 320-acre campus with easy access to Cincinnati
- **Endowment** $1.5 million
- **Coed**
- **Noncompetitive** entrance level

Faculty *Student/faculty ratio:* 18:1.

Student Life *Campus security:* 24-hour emergency response devices and patrols, late-night transport/escort service, controlled dormitory access.

Athletics Member NCAA. All Division II.

Standardized Tests *Required:* SAT I or ACT (for admission). *Recommended:* ACT (for admission).

Costs (2003–04) *Tuition:* state resident $3744 full-time, $156 per credit hour part-time; nonresident $7992 full-time, $333 per credit hour part-time. Full-time tuition and fees vary according to location and reciprocity agreements. Part-time tuition and fees vary according to location. *Room and board:* $5066; room only: $3026. Room and board charges vary according to board plan, housing facility, and location.

Financial Aid Of all full-time matriculated undergraduates who enrolled in 2002, 6,788 applied for aid, 5,362 were judged to have need. 244 Federal Work-Study jobs (averaging $1867). 1,227 state and other part-time jobs (averaging $1394). In 2002, 910. *Average percent of need met:* 85. *Average financial aid package:* $7378. *Average need-based loan:* $5306. *Average need-based gift aid:* $3744. *Average non-need-based aid:* $2872. *Average indebtedness upon graduation:* $20,787.

Applying *Options:* electronic application, early admission, early action, deferred entrance. *Application fee:* $25. *Required:* high school transcript.

Admissions Contact Mr. Dave Merriss, Associate Director of Admissions, Northern Kentucky University, Administrative Center 400, Highland Heights, KY 41099-7010. *Phone:* 606-572-5220 Ext. 5154. *Toll-free phone:* 800-637-9948. *Fax:* 859-572-5566. *E-mail:* admitnku@nku.edu.

■ *See page 2102 for a narrative description.*

PIKEVILLE COLLEGE

Pikeville, Kentucky

- **Independent** comprehensive, founded 1889, affiliated with Presbyterian Church (U.S.A.)
- **Calendar** semesters
- **Degrees** associate, bachelor's, first professional, and postbachelor's certificates
- **Small-town** 25-acre campus
- **Endowment** $15.4 million
- **Coed,** 762 undergraduate students, 94% full-time, 57% women, 43% men
- **Noncompetitive** entrance level, 100% of applicants were admitted

Undergraduates 720 full-time, 42 part-time. Students come from 28 states and territories, 18% are from out of state, 8% African American, 0.1% Asian American or Pacific Islander, 0.9% Hispanic American, 0.1% Native American, 7% transferred in, 44% live on campus. *Retention:* 54% of 2002 full-time freshmen returned.

Freshmen *Admission:* 615 applied, 615 admitted, 149 enrolled. *Average high school GPA:* 3.21. *Test scores:* ACT scores over 18: 64%; ACT scores over 24: 20%; ACT scores over 30: 1%.

Faculty *Total:* 72, 85% full-time, 44% with terminal degrees. *Student/faculty ratio:* 12:1.

Majors Art; biology/biological sciences; biology teacher education; business administration and management; chemistry; chemistry teacher education; communication/speech communication and rhetoric; community psychology; computer and information sciences; criminal justice/safety; education (K-12); elementary education; English; English/language arts teacher education; history; mathematics; mathematics teacher education; middle school education; nursing (registered nurse training); psychology; religious studies; social sciences; social studies teacher education; sociology.

Academic Programs *Special study options:* academic remediation for entering students, advanced placement credit, double majors, independent study, internships, off-campus study, part-time degree program, services for LD students, study abroad, summer session for credit.

Library Allara Library plus 1 other with 61,071 titles, 8,302 serial subscriptions, 1,598 audiovisual materials, an OPAC, a Web page.

Computers on Campus 170 computers available on campus for general student use. A campuswide network can be accessed from student residence rooms and from off campus. Internet access, at least one staffed computer lab available.

Student Life *Housing options:* coed, men-only, women-only. Campus housing is university owned and leased by the school. Freshman applicants given priority for college housing. *Activities and organizations:* drama/theater group, student-run newspaper, choral group, Pre-Professional, Phi Beta Lambda, Rotaract, Psychology Round Table, nursing club. *Campus security:* 24-hour patrols, controlled dormitory access. *Student services:* personal/psychological counseling.

Athletics Member NAIA. *Intercollegiate sports:* baseball M(s), basketball M(s)/W(s), bowling M(s)/W(s), cheerleading M/W, cross-country running M(s)/

Pikeville College (continued)
W(s), football M(s), golf M(s)/W(s), softball W(s), tennis M(s)/W(s), volleyball W(s). *Intramural sports:* badminton M/W, basketball M/W, bowling M/W, football M/W, softball M/W, table tennis M/W, tennis M/W, volleyball M/W.

Standardized Tests *Required:* SAT I or ACT (for placement).

Costs (2003–04) *Comprehensive fee:* $14,900 includes full-time tuition ($9900) and room and board ($5000). Part-time tuition: $412 per credit hour. *College room only:* $2500. *Payment plan:* installment. *Waivers:* senior citizens and employees or children of employees.

Financial Aid Of all full-time matriculated undergraduates who enrolled in 2003, 664 applied for aid, 551 were judged to have need, 284 had their need fully met. 198 Federal Work-Study jobs (averaging $1629). In 2003, 41 non-need-based awards were made. *Average percent of need met:* 84%. *Average financial aid package:* $11,622. *Average need-based loan:* $3660. *Average need-based gift aid:* $5545. *Average non-need-based aid:* $5591. *Average indebtedness upon graduation:* $12,070.

Applying *Options:* electronic application, early admission, deferred entrance. *Required:* high school transcript. *Application deadlines:* 8/20 (freshmen), 8/20 (transfers). *Notification:* continuous (freshmen), continuous (transfers).

Admissions Contact Ms. Missy McCoy, Director of Admissions, Pikeville College, 147 Sycamore Street, Pikeville, KY 41501. *Phone:* 606-218-5251. *Toll-free phone:* 866-232-7700. *Fax:* 606-218-5255. *E-mail:* wewantyou@pc.edu.

SOUTHERN BAPTIST THEOLOGICAL SEMINARY
Louisville, Kentucky

Admissions Contact Mr. Scott Davis, Director of Admissions, Southern Baptist Theological Seminary, 2825 Lexington Road, Louisville, KY 40280-0004. *Phone:* 502-897-4011 Ext. 4617.

SPALDING UNIVERSITY
Louisville, Kentucky

- **Independent** comprehensive, founded 1814, affiliated with Roman Catholic Church
- **Calendar** semesters
- **Degrees** certificates, associate, bachelor's, master's, and doctoral
- **Urban** 5-acre campus
- **Endowment** $4.9 million
- **Coed**
- **Moderately difficult** entrance level

Faculty *Student/faculty ratio:* 12:1.

Student Life *Campus security:* 24-hour emergency response devices and patrols, late-night transport/escort service.

Athletics Member NAIA.

Standardized Tests *Required:* SAT I or ACT (for admission).

Costs (2003–04) *Comprehensive fee:* $19,324 includes full-time tuition ($13,750), mandatory fees ($240), and room and board ($5334). Full-time tuition and fees vary according to course load and program. Part-time tuition: $420 per hour. *Required fees:* $8 per hour part-time. *College room only:* $2569. Room and board charges vary according to board plan.

Financial Aid Of all full-time matriculated undergraduates who enrolled in 2002, 36 Federal Work-Study jobs (averaging $1073). 77 state and other part-time jobs (averaging $1268). *Average percent of need met:* 75. *Average financial aid package:* $11,500.

Applying *Options:* common application, electronic application, early admission, deferred entrance. *Application fee:* $20. *Required:* high school transcript, minimum 2.0 GPA. *Recommended:* minimum 3.0 GPA, interview.

Admissions Contact Ms. Kathleen C. Hodapp, Director of Admission, Spalding University, Louisville, KY 40203. *Phone:* 502-585-7111 Ext. 2226. *Toll-free phone:* 800-896-8941 Ext. 2111. *Fax:* 502-992-2148. *E-mail:* admissions@spalding.edu.

SULLIVAN UNIVERSITY
Louisville, Kentucky

- **Proprietary** comprehensive, founded 1864
- **Calendar** quarters
- **Degrees** certificates, diplomas, associate, bachelor's, and master's
- **Suburban** 10-acre campus
- **Coed,** 4,639 undergraduate students
- **Minimally difficult** entrance level

Undergraduates Students come from 22 states and territories, 11 other countries, 13% are from out of state, 18% African American, 2% Hispanic American, 0.4% Native American, 0.6% international, 9% live on campus. *Retention:* 60% of 2002 full-time freshmen returned.

Faculty *Total:* 136, 49% full-time, 12% with terminal degrees. *Student/faculty ratio:* 20:1.

Majors Accounting; administrative assistant and secretarial science; business administration and management; computer science; consumer merchandising/retailing management; culinary arts; hotel/motel administration; legal administrative assistant/secretary; legal assistant/paralegal; marketing/marketing management; medical administrative assistant and medical secretary; tourism and travel services management.

Academic Programs *Special study options:* academic remediation for entering students, accelerated degree program, adult/continuing education programs, advanced placement credit, cooperative education, distance learning, double majors, independent study, part-time degree program, summer session for credit. *ROTC:* Army (c).

Library McWhorter Library with 22,500 titles, 222 serial subscriptions, an OPAC, a Web page.

Computers on Campus 125 computers available on campus for general student use. A campuswide network can be accessed from student residence rooms and from off campus. Internet access, at least one staffed computer lab available.

Student Life *Housing options:* coed. Campus housing is leased by the school. Freshman campus housing is guaranteed. *Activities and organizations:* student government, travel club, Sullivan Student Paralegal Association, American Marketing Association, Society of Hosteurs. *Campus security:* 24-hour patrols.

Athletics *Intramural sports:* basketball M/W, bowling M/W, football M/W, softball M/W, volleyball M/W.

Standardized Tests *Required:* ACT or CPAt (for admission). *Recommended:* ACT (for admission).

Costs (2004–05) *Tuition:* $12,240 full-time, $204 per credit part-time. Full-time tuition and fees vary according to program. Part-time tuition and fees vary according to program. No tuition increase for student's term of enrollment. *Required fees:* $415 full-time, $25 per course part-time. *Room only:* $3690. *Payment plan:* installment. *Waivers:* employees or children of employees.

Financial Aid Of all full-time matriculated undergraduates who enrolled in 2002, 6,028 applied for aid, 5,247 were judged to have need. 31 Federal Work-Study jobs (averaging $2065). In 2002, 374 non-need-based awards were made. *Average non-need-based aid:* $2000. *Average indebtedness upon graduation:* $15,000.

Applying *Application fee:* $90. *Required:* high school transcript, interview. *Application deadline:* rolling (freshmen), rolling (transfers). *Notification:* continuous (freshmen), continuous (transfers).

Admissions Contact Mr. Greg Cawthon, Director of Admissions, Sullivan University, 3101 Bardstown Road, Louisville, KY 40205. *Phone:* 502-456-6505 Ext. 370. *Toll-free phone:* 800-844-1354. *Fax:* 502-456-0040. *E-mail:* admissions@sullivan.edu.

■ *See page 2472 for a narrative description.*

THOMAS MORE COLLEGE
Crestview Hills, Kentucky

- **Independent Roman Catholic** comprehensive, founded 1921
- **Calendar** semesters
- **Degrees** certificates, associate, bachelor's, and master's
- **Suburban** 100-acre campus with easy access to Cincinnati
- **Endowment** $8.8 million
- **Coed,** 1,390 undergraduate students, 75% full-time, 51% women, 49% men
- **Moderately difficult** entrance level, 61% of applicants were admitted

Thomas More College is dedicated to the individual learning experience, offering majors and preprofessional programs. The College provides an outstanding liberal arts education that is carefully combined with practical professional training through cooperative education. The Thomas More experience is an education for all seasons of life.

Undergraduates 1,049 full-time, 341 part-time. Students come from 16 states and territories, 10 other countries, 34% are from out of state, 5% African American, 1% Asian American or Pacific Islander, 0.4% Hispanic American, 0.2% Native American, 1% international, 20% live on campus. *Retention:* 62% of 2002 full-time freshmen returned.

Freshmen *Admission:* 1,363 applied, 835 admitted. *Average high school GPA:* 3.20. *Test scores:* SAT verbal scores over 500: 63%; SAT math scores over 500: 58%; ACT scores over 18: 87%; SAT verbal scores over 600: 21%; SAT math scores over 600: 27%; ACT scores over 24: 26%; SAT math scores over 700: 3%; ACT scores over 30: 3%.

Faculty *Total:* 123, 58% full-time. *Student/faculty ratio:* 15:1.

Majors Accounting; art history, criticism and conservation; art teacher education; biology/biological sciences; business/commerce; business teacher education; chemistry; clinical laboratory science/medical technology; communication/speech communication and rhetoric; computer and information sciences; criminal justice/law enforcement administration; data processing and data processing technology; dramatic/theatre arts; economics; education (specific subject areas) related; elementary education; English; fine/studio arts; gerontology; history; international relations and affairs; kinesiology and exercise science; liberal arts and sciences/liberal studies; mathematics; middle school education; music; nursing (registered nurse training); nursing related; philosophy; physics; political science and government; pre-law studies; psychology; religious studies; social studies teacher education; sociology; Spanish; speech and rhetoric; visual and performing arts.

Academic Programs *Special study options:* academic remediation for entering students, accelerated degree program, adult/continuing education programs, advanced placement credit, cooperative education, double majors, external degree program, honors programs, independent study, internships, off-campus study, part-time degree program, services for LD students, student-designed majors, study abroad, summer session for credit. *ROTC:* Army (c), Air Force (c). *Unusual degree programs:* 3-2 engineering with University of Dayton, University of Kentucky, University of Detroit Mercy, University of Cincinnati, University of Notre Dame, University of Louisville.

Library Thomas More Library with 127,429 titles, 609 serial subscriptions, 2,178 audiovisual materials, a Web page.

Computers on Campus 100 computers available on campus for general student use. A campuswide network can be accessed from student residence rooms and from off campus. Internet access, at least one staffed computer lab available.

Student Life *Housing options:* coed, men-only, women-only. Campus housing is university owned. *Activities and organizations:* drama/theater group, Student Government Association, orientation team, ACT More Program Board, outdoors club, business society. *Campus security:* 24-hour patrols, late-night transport/escort service, controlled dormitory access. *Student services:* health clinic, personal/psychological counseling.

Athletics Member NCAA. All Division III. *Intercollegiate sports:* baseball M, basketball M/W, football M, golf M/W, soccer M/W, softball W, tennis M/W, volleyball W. *Intramural sports:* basketball M/W, cheerleading W, football M/W, golf M/W, racquetball M/W, softball M/W, volleyball M/W.

Standardized Tests *Required:* SAT I or ACT (for admission).

Costs (2003–04) *Comprehensive fee:* $21,400 includes full-time tuition ($15,550), mandatory fees ($450), and room and board ($5400). Part-time tuition: $395 per credit hour. Part-time tuition and fees vary according to course load and program. *Required fees:* $20 per credit hour part-time, $10 per term part-time. *College room only:* $2600. Room and board charges vary according to board plan and housing facility. *Payment plans:* installment, deferred payment. *Waivers:* children of alumni and employees or children of employees.

Financial Aid Of all full-time matriculated undergraduates who enrolled in 2002, 799 applied for aid, 788 were judged to have need, 782 had their need fully met. 81 Federal Work-Study jobs (averaging $2100). 134 state and other part-time jobs (averaging $2100). *Average percent of need met:* 91%. *Average financial aid package:* $12,484. *Average need-based loan:* $2665. *Average need-based gift aid:* $4534. *Average non-need-based aid:* $4035. *Average indebtedness upon graduation:* $21,980.

Applying *Options:* common application, electronic application, deferred entrance. *Application fee:* $25. *Required:* high school transcript, minimum 2.0 GPA, rank in top 50%, admissions committee may consider those not meeting criteria. *Required for some:* essay or personal statement, 2 letters of recommendation. *Recommended:* interview. *Application deadlines:* 8/15 (freshmen), 8/15 (transfers). *Notification:* continuous (freshmen), continuous (transfers).

Admissions Contact Mr. James E. Harter, Vice President for Enrollment Management and Marketing, Thomas More College, 333 Thomas More Parkway, Crestview Hills, KY 41017-3495. *Phone:* 859-344-3332. *Toll-free phone:* 800-825-4557. *Fax:* 859-344-3444. *E-mail:* admissions@thomasmore.edu.

■ *See page 2508 for a narrative description.*

TRANSYLVANIA UNIVERSITY
Lexington, Kentucky

- **Independent** 4-year, founded 1780, affiliated with Christian Church (Disciples of Christ)
- **Calendar** 4-4-1
- **Degree** bachelor's
- **Urban** 35-acre campus with easy access to Cincinnati and Louisville
- **Endowment** $109.0 million
- **Coed,** 1,134 undergraduate students, 99% full-time, 57% women, 43% men
- **Very difficult** entrance level, 88% of applicants were admitted

Undergraduates 1,123 full-time, 11 part-time. Students come from 32 states and territories, 3 other countries, 20% are from out of state, 3% African American, 2% Asian American or Pacific Islander, 1% Hispanic American, 0.4% Native American, 0.3% international, 1% transferred in, 80% live on campus. *Retention:* 84% of 2002 full-time freshmen returned.

Freshmen *Admission:* 1,098 applied, 965 admitted, 300 enrolled. *Average high school GPA:* 3.50. *Test scores:* SAT verbal scores over 500: 86%; SAT math scores over 500: 84%; ACT scores over 18: 100%; SAT verbal scores over 600: 49%; SAT math scores over 600: 51%; ACT scores over 24: 74%; SAT verbal scores over 700: 15%; SAT math scores over 700: 10%; ACT scores over 30: 18%.

Faculty *Total:* 91, 87% full-time, 80% with terminal degrees. *Student/faculty ratio:* 13:1.

Majors Accounting; anthropology; art; art teacher education; biology/biological sciences; business administration and management; chemistry; computer science; dramatic/theatre arts; economics; elementary education; English; fine/studio arts; French; history; kinesiology and exercise science; mathematics; middle school education; music performance; music teacher education; philosophy; physical education teaching and coaching; physics; political science and government; psychology; religious studies; social sciences related; sociology; Spanish.

Academic Programs *Special study options:* advanced placement credit, double majors, independent study, internships, off-campus study, part-time degree program, student-designed majors, study abroad, summer session for credit. *ROTC:* Army (c), Air Force (c). *Unusual degree programs:* 3-2 engineering with Washington University in St. Louis, University of Kentucky, Vanderbilt University.

Library Transylvania Library with 93,019 titles, 500 serial subscriptions, 1,860 audiovisual materials, an OPAC, a Web page.

Computers on Campus 250 computers available on campus for general student use. A campuswide network can be accessed from student residence rooms and from off campus. Internet access, at least one staffed computer lab available.

Student Life *Housing:* on-campus residence required through junior year. *Options:* coed, men-only, women-only. Campus housing is university owned. Freshman campus housing is guaranteed. *Activities and organizations:* drama/theater group, student-run newspaper, radio station, choral group, Student Alumni Association, Student Government Association, Student Activities Board, Crimson Crew, Alternative Spring Break, national fraternities, national sororities. *Campus security:* 24-hour emergency response devices and patrols, late-night transport/escort service. *Student services:* health clinic, personal/psychological counseling.

Athletics Member NCAA. All Division III. *Intercollegiate sports:* baseball M, basketball M/W, cross-country running M/W, field hockey W, golf M/W, soccer M/W, softball W, swimming M/W, tennis M/W, volleyball W. *Intramural sports:* badminton M/W, basketball M/W, bowling M/W, cheerleading W, cross-country running M/W, football M/W, golf M/W, racquetball M/W, soccer M/W, softball M/W, swimming M/W, table tennis M/W, tennis M/W, ultimate Frisbee M/W, volleyball M/W.

Standardized Tests *Required:* SAT I or ACT (for admission).

Costs (2003–04) *Comprehensive fee:* $23,780 includes full-time tuition ($17,010), mandatory fees ($650), and room and board ($6120). Part-time tuition: $1890 per course. *Required fees:* $70 per course part-time. *College room only:* $3420. Room and board charges vary according to board plan and location. *Payment plans:* tuition prepayment, installment, deferred payment. *Waivers:* employees or children of employees.

Financial Aid Of all full-time matriculated undergraduates who enrolled in 2003, 791 applied for aid, 683 were judged to have need, 209 had their need fully met. 366 Federal Work-Study jobs (averaging $1088). 151 state and other part-time jobs (averaging $1875). In 2003, 419 non-need-based awards were made. *Average percent of need met:* 87%. *Average financial aid package:* $15,115. *Average need-based loan:* $3790. *Average need-based gift aid:* $11,343. *Average non-need-based aid:* $9575. *Average indebtedness upon graduation:* $16,005.

Applying *Options:* common application, electronic application, early admission, early action, deferred entrance. *Application fee:* $30. *Required:* essay or personal statement, high school transcript, minimum 2.75 GPA, 2 letters of recommendation. *Required for some:* interview. *Recommended:* interview. *Application deadline:* 2/1 (freshmen), rolling (transfers). *Notification:* 3/1 (freshmen), 12/24 (early action).

Admissions Contact Ms. Sarah Coen, Director of Admissions, Transylvania University, 300 North Broadway, Lexington, KY 40508-1797. *Phone:* 859-233-8242. *Toll-free phone:* 800-872-6798. *Fax:* 859-233-8797. *E-mail:* admissions@transy.edu.

■ *See page 2516 for a narrative description.*

UNION COLLEGE
Barbourville, Kentucky

- **Independent United Methodist** comprehensive, founded 1879
- **Calendar** semesters
- **Degrees** bachelor's and master's
- **Small-town** 110-acre campus
- **Endowment** $12.9 million
- **Coed,** 589 undergraduate students, 94% full-time, 51% women, 49% men
- **Moderately difficult** entrance level, 73% of applicants were admitted

Undergraduates 552 full-time, 37 part-time. Students come from 21 states and territories, 3 other countries, 22% are from out of state, 10% African American, 0.5% Asian American or Pacific Islander, 2% Hispanic American, 1% Native American, 1% international, 12% transferred in, 46% live on campus. *Retention:* 68% of 2002 full-time freshmen returned.

Freshmen *Admission:* 579 applied, 422 admitted, 130 enrolled. *Average high school GPA:* 2.87. *Test scores:* ACT scores over 18: 62%; ACT scores over 24: 11%; ACT scores over 30: 1%.

Faculty *Total:* 76, 59% full-time, 47% with terminal degrees. *Student/faculty ratio:* 12:1.

Majors Accounting; biology/biological sciences; business administration and management; business teacher education; chemistry; communication/speech communication and rhetoric; criminal justice/law enforcement administration; education; elementary education; health teacher education; history; mathematics; middle school education; parks, recreation and leisure facilities management; physical education teaching and coaching; psychology; religious studies; secondary education; social sciences; special education; sport and fitness administration.

Academic Programs *Special study options:* accelerated degree program, advanced placement credit, cooperative education, double majors, internships, off-campus study, part-time degree program, student-designed majors, study abroad, summer session for credit. *Unusual degree programs:* 3-2 engineering with University of Kentucky.

Library Weeks-Townsend Memorial Library plus 1 other with 130,667 titles, 2,469 serial subscriptions, 5,164 audiovisual materials, an OPAC, a Web page.

Computers on Campus 70 computers available on campus for general student use. A campuswide network can be accessed from student residence rooms and from off campus. Internet access, online (class) registration, at least one staffed computer lab available.

Student Life *Housing:* on-campus residence required through sophomore year. *Options:* coed, men-only, women-only. Campus housing is university owned. Freshman campus housing is guaranteed. *Activities and organizations:* drama/theater group, student-run newspaper, choral group, Fellowship of Christian Athletes, Baptist Student Union, Thespian Society, Newman Club, Psychology Club. *Campus security:* 24-hour emergency response devices and patrols, late-night transport/escort service, controlled dormitory access. *Student services:* health clinic, personal/psychological counseling.

Athletics Member NAIA. *Intercollegiate sports:* baseball M(s), basketball M(s)/W(s), cheerleading M(s)/W(s), football M(s), golf M(s)/W(s), soccer M(s)/W(s), softball W(s), volleyball W(s). *Intramural sports:* basketball M/W, football M, softball M/W, table tennis M/W, tennis M/W, volleyball M/W, weight lifting M/W.

Standardized Tests *Required:* SAT I or ACT (for admission).

Costs (2003–04) *Comprehensive fee:* $17,600 includes full-time tuition ($13,150), mandatory fees ($50), and room and board ($4400). Part-time tuition: $230 per hour. *College room only:* $1600. Room and board charges vary according to board plan and housing facility. *Payment plan:* installment. *Waivers:* minority students, children of alumni, senior citizens, and employees or children of employees.

Financial Aid Of all full-time matriculated undergraduates who enrolled in 2003, 548 applied for aid, 521 were judged to have need, 140 had their need fully met. 189 Federal Work-Study jobs (averaging $1000). In 2003, 12 non-need-based awards were made. *Average percent of need met:* 77%. *Average financial aid package:* $12,420. *Average need-based loan:* $4470. *Average need-based gift aid:* $7979. *Average non-need-based aid:* $9128. *Average indebtedness upon graduation:* $11,253.

Applying *Options:* common application, electronic application, early admission, deferred entrance. *Application fee:* $20. *Required:* high school transcript, minimum 2.0 GPA. *Required for some:* essay or personal statement, letters of recommendation. *Recommended:* interview. *Application deadlines:* 8/1 (freshmen), 8/31 (transfers). *Notification:* continuous (freshmen), continuous until 9/1 (transfers).

Admissions Contact Mr. Andre Washington, Dean of Admission and Financial Aid, Union College, 310 College Street, Barbourville, KY 40906. *Phone:* 606-546-1220. *Toll-free phone:* 800-489-8646. *Fax:* 606-546-1667. *E-mail:* enroll@unionky.edu.

■ *See page 2540 for a narrative description.*

UNIVERSITY OF KENTUCKY
Lexington, Kentucky

- **State-supported** university, founded 1865
- **Calendar** semesters
- **Degrees** bachelor's, master's, doctoral, first professional, and post-master's certificates
- **Urban** 685-acre campus with easy access to Cincinnati and Louisville
- **Endowment** $420.8 million
- **Coed,** 18,108 undergraduate students, 90% full-time, 52% women, 48% men
- **Moderately difficult** entrance level, 81% of applicants were admitted

Undergraduates 16,274 full-time, 1,834 part-time. Students come from 53 states and territories, 123 other countries, 14% are from out of state, 5% African American, 2% Asian American or Pacific Islander, 1% Hispanic American, 0.1% Native American, 1% international, 7% transferred in, 31% live on campus. *Retention:* 77% of 2002 full-time freshmen returned.

Freshmen *Admission:* 9,418 applied, 7,603 admitted, 3,688 enrolled. *Average high school GPA:* 3.56. *Test scores:* SAT verbal scores over 500: 80%; SAT math scores over 500: 80%; ACT scores over 18: 99%; SAT verbal scores over 600: 34%; SAT math scores over 600: 39%; ACT scores over 24: 54%; SAT verbal scores over 700: 6%; SAT math scores over 700: 7%; ACT scores over 30: 9%.

Faculty *Total:* 1,725, 70% full-time. *Student/faculty ratio:* 16:1.

Majors Accounting; advertising; agricultural/biological engineering and bioengineering; agricultural economics; agriculture and agriculture operations related; agronomy and crop science; animal sciences; anthropology; apparel and textiles; architecture; art history, criticism and conservation; arts management; art teacher education; audiology and speech-language pathology; biology/biological sciences; business/commerce; business/managerial economics; cell biology and anatomical sciences related; chemical engineering; chemistry; civil engineering; classics and languages, literatures and linguistics; clinical laboratory science/medical technology; communication/speech communication and rhetoric; computer and information sciences; dramatic/theatre arts; economics; education (specific subject areas) related; electrical, electronics and communications engineering; elementary education; English; family and consumer sciences/human sciences; finance; fine/studio arts; food science; foods, nutrition, and wellness; forest sciences and biology; French; geography; geology/earth science; German; health/health care administration; health teacher education; history; hospitality administration; interdisciplinary studies; interior design; journalism; kindergarten/preschool education; landscape architecture; Latin American studies; linguistics; management science; marketing/marketing management; materials engineering; mathematics; mechanical engineering; middle school education; mining and mineral engineering; multi-/interdisciplinary studies related; music history, literature, and theory; music performance; music teacher education; natural resources/conservation; nursing (registered nurse training); nursing related; philosophy; physical education teaching and coaching; physical therapy; physics; political science and government; psychology; radio and television; Russian; science teacher education; social sciences; social work; sociology; Spanish; special education.

Academic Programs *Special study options:* academic remediation for entering students, accelerated degree program, adult/continuing education programs, advanced placement credit, cooperative education, distance learning, double majors, English as a second language, honors programs, independent study, internships, off-campus study, part-time degree program, services for LD students, student-designed majors, study abroad, summer session for credit. *ROTC:* Army (b), Air Force (b).

Library William T. Young Library plus 15 others with 2.9 million titles, 29,850 serial subscriptions, 78,136 audiovisual materials, an OPAC, a Web page.

Computers on Campus 1400 computers available on campus for general student use. A campuswide network can be accessed from student residence rooms and from off campus that provide access to various software packages. Internet access, online (class) registration, at least one staffed computer lab available.

Student Life *Housing options:* coed, men-only, women-only, disabled students. Campus housing is university owned and leased by the school. *Activities and organizations:* drama/theater group, student-run newspaper, radio station, choral group, marching band, Student Activities Board, Student Government Association, Campus Progressive Coalition, ski and snowboard club, Society of Women

Engineers, national fraternities, national sororities. *Campus security:* 24-hour emergency response devices and patrols, late-night transport/escort service, controlled dormitory access. *Student services:* health clinic, personal/psychological counseling, women's center, legal services.

Athletics Member NCAA. All Division I except football (Division I-A). *Intercollegiate sports:* baseball M(s), basketball M(s)/W(s), cross-country running M(s)/W(s), golf M(s)/W(s), gymnastics W(s), riflery M(s)/W(s), soccer M(s)/W(s), softball W(s), swimming M(s)/W(s), tennis M(s)/W(s), track and field M(s)/W(s), volleyball W(s). *Intramural sports:* archery M/W, badminton M/W, basketball M/W, fencing M/W, football M/W, golf M/W, ice hockey M, lacrosse M, rugby M, soccer M/W, softball M/W, swimming M/W, table tennis M/W, tennis M/W, track and field M/W, ultimate Frisbee M(c)/W(c), volleyball M/W.

Standardized Tests *Required:* SAT I or ACT (for admission).

Costs (2003–04) *Tuition:* state resident $4002 full-time, $167 per credit hour part-time; nonresident $10,682 full-time, $446 per credit hour part-time. Full-time tuition and fees vary according to degree level, program, and reciprocity agreements. Part-time tuition and fees vary according to degree level, program, and reciprocity agreements. *Required fees:* $545 full-time, $14 per credit hour part-time. *Room and board:* $4285; room only: $2785. Room and board charges vary according to board plan and housing facility. *Payment plan:* installment.

Financial Aid Of all full-time matriculated undergraduates who enrolled in 2003, 8,533 applied for aid, 6,244 were judged to have need, 2,145 had their need fully met. In 2003, 640 non-need-based awards were made. *Average percent of need met:* 79%. *Average financial aid package:* $7421. *Average need-based loan:* $3632. *Average need-based gift aid:* $4533. *Average non-need-based aid:* $3728. *Average indebtedness upon graduation:* $16,584.

Applying *Options:* electronic application, early admission. *Application fee:* $30. *Required:* high school transcript, minimum 2.0 GPA. *Application deadlines:* 2/15 (freshmen), 8/1 (transfers). *Notification:* continuous (freshmen), continuous (transfers).

Admissions Contact Ms. Michelle Nordin, Associate Director of Admissions, University of Kentucky, 100 W.D. Funkhouser Building, Lexington, KY 40506-0054. *Phone:* 859-257-2000. *Toll-free phone:* 800-432-0967. *E-mail:* admissio@uky.edu.

University of Louisville
Louisville, Kentucky

- **State-supported** university, founded 1798
- **Calendar** semesters
- **Degrees** certificates, diplomas, associate, bachelor's, master's, doctoral, first professional, post-master's, and postbachelor's certificates
- **Urban** 169-acre campus
- **Endowment** $475.2 million
- **Coed,** 14,724 undergraduate students, 73% full-time, 53% women, 47% men
- **Moderately difficult** entrance level, 79% of applicants were admitted

Undergraduates 10,676 full-time, 4,048 part-time. Students come from 51 states and territories, 63 other countries, 10% are from out of state, 14% African American, 3% Asian American or Pacific Islander, 1% Hispanic American, 0.2% Native American, 1% international, 0.8% transferred in, 17% live on campus. *Retention:* 77% of 2002 full-time freshmen returned.

Freshmen *Admission:* 5,284 applied, 4,189 admitted, 2,251 enrolled. *Average high school GPA:* 3.41. *Test scores:* ACT scores over 18: 98%; ACT scores over 24: 45%; ACT scores over 30: 7%.

Faculty *Total:* 1,253, 62% full-time, 58% with terminal degrees. *Student/faculty ratio:* 19:1.

Majors Accounting; African-American/Black studies; anthropology; art history, criticism and conservation; biology/biological sciences; business administration and management; business administration, management and operations related; business/managerial economics; chemical engineering; chemistry; civil engineering; communication/speech communication and rhetoric; computer engineering; criminal justice/law enforcement administration; dental hygiene; dramatic/theatre arts; economics; electrical, electronics and communications engineering; elementary education; engineering; English; finance; fine/studio arts; French; geography; health and physical education; health/medical preparatory programs related; history; industrial engineering; legal assistant/paralegal; liberal arts and sciences and humanities related; liberal arts and sciences/liberal studies; management information systems; marketing/marketing management; mathematics; mechanical engineering; music; music teacher education; music therapy; nursing (registered nurse training); philosophy; physics; political science and government; psychology; sign language interpretation and translation; sociology; Spanish; sport and fitness administration; trade and industrial teacher education; women's studies.

Academic Programs *Special study options:* academic remediation for entering students, accelerated degree program, adult/continuing education programs, advanced placement credit, cooperative education, distance learning, double majors, English as a second language, external degree program, honors programs, independent study, internships, off-campus study, part-time degree program, services for LD students, student-designed majors, study abroad, summer session for credit. *ROTC:* Army (b), Air Force (b).

Library William F. Ekstrom Library plus 5 others with 1.8 million titles, 16,078 serial subscriptions, 33,109 audiovisual materials, an OPAC, a Web page.

Computers on Campus 265 computers available on campus for general student use. A campuswide network can be accessed from student residence rooms and from off campus. Internet access, online (class) registration, at least one staffed computer lab available. Computer purchase or lease plan available.

Student Life *Housing options:* coed, disabled students. Campus housing is university owned and is provided by a third party. Freshman applicants given priority for college housing. *Activities and organizations:* drama/theater group, student-run newspaper, radio station, choral group, marching band, Spirit Club—"L" Raisers, Baptist Student Union, Golden Key, Sigma Chi, Phi Eta Sigma, national fraternities, national sororities. *Campus security:* 24-hour emergency response devices and patrols, late-night transport/escort service, controlled dormitory access. *Student services:* health clinic, personal/psychological counseling, women's center, legal services.

Athletics Member NCAA. All Division I except football (Division I-A). *Intercollegiate sports:* baseball M(s), basketball M(s)/W(s), cheerleading M(s)/W(s), crew W(s), cross-country running M(s)/W(s), field hockey W(s), golf M(s)/W(s), soccer M(s)/W(s), softball W(s), swimming M(s)/W(s), tennis M(s)/W(s), track and field M(s)/W(s), volleyball W(s). *Intramural sports:* badminton M/W, basketball M/W, bowling M/W, cross-country running M/W, fencing M/W, football M/W, golf M/W, ice hockey M, racquetball M/W, soccer M/W, softball M/W, swimming M/W, table tennis M/W, tennis M/W, track and field M/W, ultimate Frisbee M/W, volleyball M/W.

Standardized Tests *Required:* SAT I or ACT (for admission).

Costs (2003–04) *Tuition:* state resident $4344 full-time, $181 per hour part-time; nonresident $11,856 full-time, $494 per hour part-time. Part-time tuition and fees vary according to course load. *Room and board:* $4312; room only: $2772. Room and board charges vary according to board plan and housing facility. *Payment plan:* installment. *Waivers:* senior citizens and employees or children of employees.

Financial Aid Of all full-time matriculated undergraduates who enrolled in 2003, 6,244 applied for aid, 5,584 were judged to have need, 592 had their need fully met. In 2003, 1564 non-need-based awards were made. *Average percent of need met:* 53%. *Average financial aid package:* $7510. *Average need-based loan:* $3801. *Average need-based gift aid:* $4827. *Average non-need-based aid:* $4304. *Average indebtedness upon graduation:* $14,498.

Applying *Options:* electronic application, early admission, deferred entrance. *Application fee:* $30. *Required:* high school transcript, minimum 2.50 GPA. *Application deadline:* rolling (freshmen). *Notification:* continuous (freshmen), continuous (transfers).

Admissions Contact Ms. Jenny Sawyer, Executive Director for Admissions, University of Louisville, 2211 South Brook, Louisville, KY 40292. *Phone:* 502-852-6531. *Toll-free phone:* 502-852-6531 (in-state); 800-334-8635 (out-of-state). *Fax:* 502-852-4776. *E-mail:* admitme@gwise.louisville.edu.

Western Kentucky University
Bowling Green, Kentucky

- **State-supported** comprehensive, founded 1906
- **Calendar** semesters
- **Degrees** certificates, associate, bachelor's, master's, and first professional certificates
- **Suburban** 223-acre campus with easy access to Nashville
- **Endowment** $56.4 million
- **Coed,** 15,787 undergraduate students, 82% full-time, 59% women, 41% men
- **Moderately difficult** entrance level, 93% of applicants were admitted

Undergraduates 12,931 full-time, 2,856 part-time. Students come from 46 states and territories, 46 other countries, 18% are from out of state, 8% African American, 0.9% Asian American or Pacific Islander, 0.9% Hispanic American, 0.3% Native American, 1% international, 5% transferred in, 31% live on campus. *Retention:* 75% of 2002 full-time freshmen returned.

Freshmen *Admission:* 6,373 applied, 5,927 admitted, 3,076 enrolled. *Average high school GPA:* 3.15. *Test scores:* SAT verbal scores over 500: 52%; SAT math scores over 500: 56%; ACT scores over 18: 77%; SAT verbal scores over 600: 14%; SAT math scores over 600: 12%; ACT scores over 24: 24%; SAT verbal scores over 700: 2%; SAT math scores over 700: 2%; ACT scores over 30: 2%.

Faculty *Total:* 1,159, 56% full-time, 46% with terminal degrees. *Student/faculty ratio:* 20:1.

Majors Accounting; advertising; agricultural production; agriculture; anthropology; apparel and textiles; architectural drafting and CAD/CADD; art teacher

Western Kentucky University (continued)
education; biochemistry; biology/biological sciences; business administration and management; business/managerial economics; business teacher education; chemistry; civil engineering; clinical laboratory science/medical technology; commercial and advertising art; communication and journalism related; communication/speech communication and rhetoric; community health services counseling; computer and information sciences; data processing and data processing technology; dental hygiene; dramatic/theatre arts; economics; electrical, electronics and communications engineering; elementary education; emergency medical technology (EMT paramedic); engineering technologies related; English; English language and literature related; environmental engineering technology; executive assistant/executive secretary; family and consumer sciences/home economics teacher education; finance; fine/studio arts; foods, nutrition, and wellness; French; general studies; geography; geology/earth science; German; health/health care administration; health information/medical records technology; history; hotel/motel administration; housing and human environments; industrial production technologies related; industrial technology; journalism; kindergarten/preschool education; legal assistant/paralegal; management information systems; marketing/marketing management; mathematics; mechanical engineering; middle school education; multi-/interdisciplinary studies related; music; music related; music teacher education; nursing (registered nurse training); nursing related; parks, recreation and leisure facilities management; philosophy; physical education teaching and coaching; physical science technologies related; physics; political science and government; psychology; public relations/image management; radio and television; religious studies; respiratory care therapy; science teacher education; social sciences; social work; sociology; Spanish; special education; special education (speech or language impaired); speech and rhetoric; technical teacher education; trade and industrial teacher education; visual and performing arts.

Academic Programs *Special study options:* academic remediation for entering students, accelerated degree program, adult/continuing education programs, advanced placement credit, cooperative education, distance learning, double majors, English as a second language, honors programs, internships, part-time degree program, services for LD students, student-designed majors, study abroad, summer session for credit. *ROTC:* Army (b), Air Force (c).

Library Helm-Cravens Library plus 3 others with 570,299 titles, 4,564 serial subscriptions, 93,298 audiovisual materials, an OPAC, a Web page.

Computers on Campus 1200 computers available on campus for general student use. A campuswide network can be accessed from student residence rooms and from off campus that provide access to on-line grade reports. Internet access, online (class) registration, at least one staffed computer lab available.

Student Life *Housing:* on-campus residence required for freshman year. *Options:* coed, men-only, women-only, disabled students. Campus housing is university owned. Freshman applicants given priority for college housing. *Activities and organizations:* drama/theater group, student-run newspaper, radio and television station, choral group, marching band, Student Government Association, Campus Activities Board, Campus Crusade for Christ, campus ministries, Residence Hall Association, national fraternities, national sororities. *Campus security:* 24-hour emergency response devices and patrols, student patrols, late-night transport/escort service, controlled dormitory access. *Student services:* health clinic, personal/psychological counseling, women's center.

Athletics Member NCAA. All Division I except football (Division I-AA). *Intercollegiate sports:* baseball M(s), basketball M(s)/W(s), cheerleading M/W, cross-country running M(s)/W(s), golf M(s)/W(s), riflery M(c)/W(c), soccer M(s), softball W(s), swimming M(s)/W(s), tennis M(s)/W(s), track and field M(s)/W(s), volleyball W(s). *Intramural sports:* archery M/W, badminton M/W, basketball M/W, bowling M/W, equestrian sports M/W, fencing M(c)/W(c), golf M/W, lacrosse M(c)/W(c), racquetball M/W, rugby M(c)/W(c), soccer M/W, softball M/W(c), swimming M(c)/W(c), table tennis M/W, volleyball M(c)/W(c), water polo M/W, wrestling M.

Standardized Tests *Required:* SAT I or ACT (for admission).

Costs (2004–05) *Tuition:* state resident $169 per hour part-time; nonresident $371 per hour part-time. Full-time tuition and fees vary according to location and reciprocity agreements. Part-time tuition and fees vary according to location and reciprocity agreements. *Room and board:* Room and board charges vary according to board plan and housing facility. *Payment plan:* installment. *Waivers:* senior citizens and employees or children of employees.

Financial Aid Of all full-time matriculated undergraduates who enrolled in 2002, 8,559 applied for aid, 6,282 were judged to have need, 2,367 had their need fully met. 655 Federal Work-Study jobs (averaging $1371). 1,413 state and other part-time jobs (averaging $1677). In 2002, 3081 non-need-based awards were made. *Average percent of need met:* 39%. *Average financial aid package:* $5895. *Average need-based loan:* $2921. *Average need-based gift aid:* $3478. *Average non-need-based aid:* $1668. *Average indebtedness upon graduation:* $13,401.

Applying *Application fee:* $30. *Required:* high school transcript, minimum 2.5 GPA. *Application deadlines:* 8/1 (freshmen), 6/1 (out-of-state freshmen), 8/1 (transfers). *Notification:* continuous (freshmen), continuous (out-of-state freshmen), continuous (transfers).

Admissions Contact Dr. Dean R. Kahler, Director of Admissions and Academic Services, Western Kentucky University, Potter Hall 117, 1 Big Red Way, Bowling Green, KY 42101-3576. *Phone:* 270-745-2551. *Toll-free phone:* 800-495-8463. *Fax:* 270-745-6133. *E-mail:* admission@wku.edu.

LOUISIANA

CENTENARY COLLEGE OF LOUISIANA
Shreveport, Louisiana

- **Independent United Methodist** comprehensive, founded 1825
- **Calendar** 4-4-1
- **Degrees** bachelor's and master's
- **Suburban** 65-acre campus
- **Endowment** $98.1 million
- **Coed,** 845 undergraduate students, 97% full-time, 59% women, 41% men
- **Moderately difficult** entrance level, 74% of applicants were admitted

Undergraduates 817 full-time, 28 part-time. Students come from 36 states and territories, 14 other countries, 39% are from out of state, 7% African American, 2% Asian American or Pacific Islander, 2% Hispanic American, 1% Native American, 3% international, 3% transferred in. *Retention:* 80% of 2002 full-time freshmen returned.

Freshmen *Admission:* 802 applied, 594 admitted, 197 enrolled. *Average high school GPA:* 3.24. *Test scores:* SAT verbal scores over 500: 84%; SAT math scores over 500: 80%; ACT scores over 18: 99%; SAT verbal scores over 600: 46%; SAT math scores over 600: 41%; ACT scores over 24: 71%; SAT verbal scores over 700: 6%; SAT math scores over 700: 5%; ACT scores over 30: 14%.

Faculty *Total:* 117, 63% full-time, 71% with terminal degrees. *Student/faculty ratio:* 12:1.

Majors Accounting; art; art teacher education; audiology and speech-language pathology; biochemistry; biology/biological sciences; biology teacher education; biophysics; business administration and management; business/managerial economics; business teacher education; chemistry; chemistry teacher education; communication and journalism related; communication and media related; dance; drama and dance teacher education; dramatic/theatre arts; economics; education (K-12); education related; elementary education; English; English/language arts teacher education; environmental studies; film/cinema studies; finance; fine/studio arts; foreign languages and literatures; French; French language teacher education; geology/earth science; German; German language teacher education; health science; health teacher education; history; interdisciplinary studies; kinesiology and exercise science; Latin; Latin teacher education; liberal arts and sciences/liberal studies; mathematics; mathematics teacher education; museum studies; music; music performance; music teacher education; music theory and composition; neuroscience; occupational therapy; philosophy; physical education teaching and coaching; physical therapy; physics; physics teacher education; piano and organ; political science and government; pre-dentistry studies; pre-law studies; pre-medical studies; pre-veterinary studies; psychology; religious/sacred music; religious studies; science teacher education; secondary education; social studies teacher education; sociology; Spanish; Spanish language teacher education; visual and performing arts; voice and opera.

Academic Programs *Special study options:* adult/continuing education programs, advanced placement credit, double majors, honors programs, independent study, internships, off-campus study, part-time degree program, student-designed majors, study abroad, summer session for credit. *ROTC:* Army (c). *Unusual degree programs:* 3-2 engineering with Columbia University, Tulane University, Case Western Reserve University, Texas A&M University, Louisiana Tech University, Southern Methodist University, University of Arkansas, Washington University in St. Louis; forestry with Duke University; computer science with Southern Methodist University, communication disorders with Louisiana State University Medical Center School of Medicine in Shreveport.

Library Magale Library plus 1 other with 325,671 titles, 59,899 serial subscriptions, 5,945 audiovisual materials, an OPAC, a Web page.

Computers on Campus 250 computers available on campus for general student use. A campuswide network can be accessed from student residence rooms and from off campus. Internet access, online (class) registration, at least one staffed computer lab available.

Student Life *Housing:* on-campus residence required through senior year. *Options:* coed, men-only, women-only. Campus housing is university owned. Freshman campus housing is guaranteed. *Activities and organizations:* drama/theater group, student-run newspaper, radio station, choral group, intramural sports, Student Activities Board, crew, Church Career/Campus Ministries, student media, national fraternities, national sororities. *Campus security:* 24-hour emergency response devices and patrols, late-night transport/escort service, controlled dormitory access. *Student services:* health clinic, personal/psychological counseling.

Athletics Member NCAA. All Division I. *Intercollegiate sports:* baseball M(s), basketball M(s)/W(s), crew M(c)/W(c), cross-country running M(s)/W(s), golf M(s)/W(s), gymnastics W(s), riflery M(s)/W(s), sailing M(c)/W(c), soccer M(s)/W(s), softball W(s), tennis M(s)/W(s), volleyball W(s). *Intramural sports:* basketball M/W, cheerleading W, football M/W, golf M, soccer M/W, softball M/W, table tennis M/W, tennis M/W, ultimate Frisbee M/W, volleyball M/W.

Standardized Tests *Required:* SAT I or ACT (for admission). *Required for some:* SAT II: Subject Tests (for admission).

Costs (2003–04) *Comprehensive fee:* $23,100 includes full-time tuition ($16,750), mandatory fees ($500), and room and board ($5850). Full-time tuition and fees vary according to course load. Part-time tuition: $560 per semester hour. *Required fees:* $50 per term part-time. *College room only:* $2900. Room and board charges vary according to board plan and housing facility. *Payment plans:* installment, deferred payment. *Waivers:* employees or children of employees.

Financial Aid Of all full-time matriculated undergraduates who enrolled in 2003, 800 applied for aid, 543 were judged to have need, 205 had their need fully met. 175 Federal Work-Study jobs (averaging $1575). 64 state and other part-time jobs (averaging $1017). In 2003, 185 non-need-based awards were made. *Average percent of need met:* 78%. *Average financial aid package:* $13,207. *Average need-based loan:* $3687. *Average need-based gift aid:* $10,913. *Average non-need-based aid:* $9575. *Average indebtedness upon graduation:* $15,659.

Applying *Options:* common application, early admission, early decision, early action, deferred entrance. *Required:* essay or personal statement, high school transcript, minimum 2.0 GPA, 1 letter of recommendation. *Recommended:* interview, class rank. *Application deadlines:* 2/15 (freshmen), 8/15 (transfers). *Early decision:* 12/15. *Notification:* 1/1 (early decision), 1/1 (early action), continuous (transfers).

Admissions Contact Mr. Tim Crowley, Director of Admissions, Centenary College of Louisiana, Office of Admissions, Centenary College of Louisiana, 2911 Centenary Boulevard, PO box 41188, Shreveport, LA 71134-1188. *Phone:* 318-869-5134. *Toll-free phone:* 800-234-4448. *Fax:* 318-869-5005. *E-mail:* egregory@centenary.edu.

DILLARD UNIVERSITY
New Orleans, Louisiana

- **Independent interdenominational** 4-year, founded 1869
- **Calendar** semesters
- **Degree** bachelor's
- **Urban** 55-acre campus
- **Endowment** $44.6 million
- **Coed,** 2,312 undergraduate students, 90% full-time, 78% women, 22% men
- **Moderately difficult** entrance level, 64% of applicants were admitted

Undergraduates 2,074 full-time, 238 part-time. Students come from 32 states and territories, 54% are from out of state, 99% African American, 0.1% Asian American or Pacific Islander, 0.3% Hispanic American, 0.1% international, 3% transferred in, 30% live on campus. *Retention:* 78% of 2002 full-time freshmen returned.

Freshmen *Admission:* 3,372 applied, 2,155 admitted, 609 enrolled. *Average high school GPA:* 3.20. *Test scores:* SAT verbal scores over 500: 30%; SAT math scores over 500: 30%; ACT scores over 18: 68%; SAT verbal scores over 600: 10%; SAT math scores over 600: 6%; ACT scores over 24: 8%; SAT verbal scores over 700: 2%; SAT math scores over 700: 1%.

Faculty *Total:* 182, 72% full-time, 53% with terminal degrees. *Student/faculty ratio:* 15:1.

Majors Accounting; art; art teacher education; biology/biological sciences; biology teacher education; business administration and management; chemistry; computer science; dramatic/theatre arts; economics; education; elementary education; English; English composition; French; German; health/health care administration; health teacher education; history; information science/studies; international business/trade/commerce; Japanese; kindergarten/preschool education; mass communication/media; mathematics; modern languages; music; music performance; music teacher education; music therapy; nursing (registered nurse training); physical education teaching and coaching; physics; piano and organ; political science and government; pre-dentistry studies; pre-law studies; premedical studies; pre-veterinary studies; psychology; public health; public health education and promotion; religious studies; science teacher education; secondary education; social work; sociology; Spanish; special education; speech and rhetoric; urban studies/affairs.

Academic Programs *Special study options:* academic remediation for entering students, advanced placement credit, cooperative education, double majors, honors programs, internships, part-time degree program, services for LD students, study abroad, summer session for credit. *ROTC:* Army (c), Air Force (c). *Unusual degree programs:* 3-2 engineering with Auburn University, Columbia University, Georgia Institute of Technology; urban studies with Columbia University, allied health with Howard University, Tuskegee University.

Library Will W. Alexander Library with 116,700 titles, 7,789 serial subscriptions, 369 audiovisual materials, an OPAC, a Web page.

Computers on Campus 195 computers available on campus for general student use. A campuswide network can be accessed from student residence rooms and from off campus. Internet access, at least one staffed computer lab available. Computer purchase or lease plan available.

Student Life *Housing options:* men-only, women-only. Campus housing is university owned, leased by the school and is provided by a third party. Freshman campus housing is guaranteed. *Activities and organizations:* drama/theater group, student-run newspaper, radio station, choral group, SGA (Student Government Association), National Panhellenic Council, Pre-Alumni Council, SOUL-Students' Outreach of the Urban League, Students' Arts and Activities Committee, national fraternities, national sororities. *Campus security:* 24-hour patrols. *Student services:* health clinic, personal/psychological counseling.

Athletics Member NAIA. *Intercollegiate sports:* basketball M(s)/W(s), cross-country running M(s)/W(s), tennis M(s)/W(s), volleyball W(s). *Intramural sports:* basketball M/W, football M/W, softball M/W, tennis M/W, volleyball M/W, weight lifting M.

Standardized Tests *Required:* SAT I or ACT (for admission). *Recommended:* SAT II: Subject Tests (for admission).

Costs (2003–04) *Comprehensive fee:* $17,305 includes full-time tuition ($10,600), mandatory fees ($265), and room and board ($6440). Full-time tuition and fees vary according to class time and course load. Part-time tuition: $442 per credit hour. Part-time tuition and fees vary according to class time. *Required fees:* $165 per term part-time. *Room and board:* Room and board charges vary according to board plan and housing facility. *Payment plans:* installment, deferred payment. *Waivers:* adult students and employees or children of employees.

Financial Aid Of all full-time matriculated undergraduates who enrolled in 2003, 2,156 applied for aid, 1,998 were judged to have need, 1,998 had their need fully met. 203 Federal Work-Study jobs (averaging $1912). 31 state and other part-time jobs (averaging $2839). In 2003, 143 non-need-based awards were made. *Average percent of need met:* 85%. *Average financial aid package:* $13,443. *Average need-based loan:* $3337. *Average need-based gift aid:* $3603. *Average non-need-based aid:* $3924. *Average indebtedness upon graduation:* $25,247.

Applying *Options:* common application, electronic application. *Application fee:* $20. *Required:* essay or personal statement, high school transcript, minimum 2.2 GPA, 2 letters of recommendation. *Recommended:* interview. *Application deadlines:* 7/1 (freshmen), 7/1 (transfers). *Notification:* continuous until 8/1 (freshmen), continuous (transfers).

Admissions Contact Ms. Linda Nash, Director of Admissions, Dillard University, 2601 Gentilly Boulevard, New Orleans, LA 70122. *Phone:* 504-816-4670 Ext.4673. *Toll-free phone:* 800-216-6637. *Fax:* 504-816-4895. *E-mail:* admissions@dillard.edu.

GRAMBLING STATE UNIVERSITY
Grambling, Louisiana

- **State-supported** university, founded 1901, part of University of Louisiana System Board of Supervisors
- **Calendar** semesters
- **Degrees** certificates, associate, bachelor's, master's, and doctoral
- **Small-town** 380-acre campus
- **Endowment** $1.9 million
- **Coed,** 4,175 undergraduate students
- **Noncompetitive** entrance level, 62% of applicants were admitted

Undergraduates Students come from 39 states and territories, 17 other countries, 40% are from out of state, 95% African American, 0.1% Asian American or Pacific Islander, 0.3% Hispanic American, 0.2% Native American, 1% international.

Freshmen *Admission:* 2,923 applied, 1,811 admitted. *Average high school GPA:* 2.65. *Test scores:* ACT scores over 18: 48%.

Faculty *Total:* 268, 91% full-time. *Student/faculty ratio:* 17:1.

Majors Accounting; architectural engineering technology; art; art teacher education; biology/biological sciences; business administration and management; business/managerial economics; business teacher education; chemistry; child development; computer science; criminal justice/law enforcement administration; criminal justice/police science; drafting and design technology; dramatic/theatre arts; electrical, electronic and communications engineering technology; elementary education; English; English/language arts teacher education; family and

Grambling State University (continued)
consumer sciences/home economics teacher education; French; French language teacher education; history; hotel/motel administration; industrial technology; information science/studies; institutional food workers; kindergarten/preschool education; legal assistant/paralegal; marketing/marketing management; mass communication/media; mathematics; music performance; music teacher education; nursing (registered nurse training); physical education teaching and coaching; physics; political science and government; pre-law studies; psychology; public administration; science teacher education; secondary education; social science teacher education; social work; sociology; Spanish; special education; speech-language pathology; speech/theater education; technology/industrial arts teacher education.

Academic Programs *Special study options:* academic remediation for entering students, adult/continuing education programs, advanced placement credit, cooperative education, distance learning, honors programs, internships, off-campus study, part-time degree program, study abroad, summer session for credit. *ROTC:* Army (b), Air Force (b).

Library A. C. Lewis Memorial Library with 208,935 titles, 1,253 serial subscriptions, 5,661 audiovisual materials, an OPAC, a Web page.

Computers on Campus 250 computers available on campus for general student use. A campuswide network can be accessed from student residence rooms and from off campus. Internet access, at least one staffed computer lab available. Computer purchase or lease plan available.

Student Life *Housing:* on-campus residence required for freshman year. *Options:* men-only, women-only. Campus housing is university owned. *Activities and organizations:* drama/theater group, student-run newspaper, radio station, choral group, marching band, national fraternities, national sororities. *Campus security:* 24-hour patrols, student patrols, controlled dormitory access. *Student services:* health clinic, personal/psychological counseling.

Athletics Member NCAA. All Division I except football (Division I-AA). *Intercollegiate sports:* baseball M(s), basketball M(s)/W(s), bowling W(s), cross-country running M/W, golf M(s)/W(s), tennis M(s)/W(s), track and field M(s)/W(s), volleyball W(s). *Intramural sports:* bowling W, gymnastics M/W, softball M/W, swimming M/W, table tennis M/W, tennis M, track and field M/W, volleyball M/W, weight lifting M/W.

Standardized Tests *Required:* SAT I or ACT (for admission).

Costs (2003–04) *Tuition:* state resident $3182 full-time, $1591 per term part-time; nonresident $8532 full-time, $4261 per term part-time. *Required fees:* $8447 full-time, $1487 per term part-time, $3939 per term part-time. *Room and board:* $3356; room only: $3356. *Waivers:* children of alumni, senior citizens, and employees or children of employees.

Financial Aid Of all full-time matriculated undergraduates who enrolled in 2003, 3,679 applied for aid, 3,336 were judged to have need, 413 had their need fully met. 621 Federal Work-Study jobs (averaging $1030). 229 state and other part-time jobs (averaging $1996). In 2003, 257 non-need-based awards were made. *Average percent of need met:* 80%. *Average financial aid package:* $6800. *Average need-based loan:* $3875. *Average need-based gift aid:* $4000. *Average non-need-based aid:* $2826. *Average indebtedness upon graduation:* $30,000. *Financial aid deadline:* 6/1.

Applying *Options:* common application, early admission, early decision, deferred entrance. *Application fee:* $20. *Required:* high school transcript. *Application deadlines:* 7/15 (freshmen), 7/15 (transfers). *Early decision:* 4/15. *Notification:* continuous until 8/1 (freshmen), 4/20 (early decision), continuous until 8/1 (transfers).

Admissions Contact Ms. Norma Taylor, Director of Admissions, Grambling State University, PO Drawer 1165, 100 Main Street, Grambling, LA 71245. *Phone:* 318-274-6183. *E-mail:* bingamann@medgar.gram.edu.

GRANTHAM UNIVERSITY
Slidell, Louisiana

- **Proprietary** comprehensive, founded 1951
- **Calendar** continuous
- **Degrees** associate, bachelor's, and master's (offers only external degree programs)
- **Small-town** campus
- **Coed, primarily men,** 4,500 undergraduate students
- **Noncompetitive** entrance level

Undergraduates Students come from 52 states and territories, 25 other countries. *Retention:* 70% of 2002 full-time freshmen returned.

Majors Business administration and management; computer engineering technology; computer science; computer software engineering; electrical, electronic and communications engineering technology; engineering/industrial management; information science/studies.

Academic Programs *Special study options:* accelerated degree program, adult/continuing education programs, advanced placement credit, cooperative education, distance learning, external degree program, honors programs, independent study, part-time degree program.

Computers on Campus Internet access, online (class) registration available.

Student Life *Housing:* college housing not available.

Costs (2003–04) *Tuition:* $3489 full-time, $3489 per term part-time. No tuition increase for student's term of enrollment. *Required fees:* $335 per credit hour part-time. *Payment plans:* tuition prepayment, installment.

Applying *Application deadline:* rolling (freshmen), rolling (transfers). *Notification:* continuous (freshmen), continuous (transfers).

Admissions Contact Mr. Bill Wells, Admissions Office, Grantham University, 34641 Grantham College Road, Slidell, LA 70460-6815. *Phone:* 985-649-4191 Ext. 237. *Toll-free phone:* 800-955-2527. *Fax:* 985-649-4183. *E-mail:* admissions@grantham.edu.

HERZING COLLEGE
Kenner, Louisiana

Admissions Contact Genny Bordelon, Director of Admissions, Herzing College, 2400 Veterans Boulevard, Kenner, LA 70062. *Phone:* 504-733-0074.

ITT TECHNICAL INSTITUTE
St. Rose, Louisiana

- **Proprietary** primarily 2-year, part of ITT Educational Services, Inc.
- **Calendar** quarters
- **Degrees** associate and bachelor's
- **Coed**
- **Minimally difficult** entrance level

Standardized Tests *Required:* Wonderlic aptitude test (for admission).

Costs (2003–04) *Tuition:* $347 per credit hour part-time.

Applying *Options:* deferred entrance. *Application fee:* $100. *Required:* high school transcript, interview. *Recommended:* letters of recommendation.

Admissions Contact Mr. Richard Beard, Director of Recruitment, ITT Technical Institute, 140 James Drive East, Saint Rose, LA 70087. *Phone:* 504-463-0338. *Toll-free phone:* 866-463-0338. *Fax:* 504-463-0979.

LOUISIANA COLLEGE
Pineville, Louisiana

- **Independent Southern Baptist** 4-year, founded 1906
- **Calendar** semesters
- **Degree** bachelor's
- **Small-town** 81-acre campus
- **Endowment** $24.0 million
- **Coed,** 1,135 undergraduate students, 86% full-time, 57% women, 43% men
- **Moderately difficult** entrance level, 85% of applicants were admitted

Undergraduates 976 full-time, 159 part-time. Students come from 16 states and territories, 9% are from out of state, 7% African American, 1% Asian American or Pacific Islander, 2% Hispanic American, 0.2% Native American, 0.8% international, 5% transferred in, 50% live on campus. *Retention:* 59% of 2002 full-time freshmen returned.

Freshmen *Admission:* 727 applied, 618 admitted, 266 enrolled. *Average high school GPA:* 3.48. *Test scores:* SAT verbal scores over 500: 44%; SAT math scores over 500: 47%; ACT scores over 18: 95%; SAT verbal scores over 600: 9%; SAT math scores over 600: 25%; ACT scores over 24: 42%; SAT math scores over 700: 3%; ACT scores over 30: 7%.

Faculty *Total:* 100, 68% full-time, 43% with terminal degrees. *Student/faculty ratio:* 13:1.

Majors Accounting; adult and continuing education; advertising; art; art teacher education; athletic training; biology/biological sciences; broadcast journalism; business administration and management; business teacher education; chemistry; clinical laboratory science/medical technology; commercial and advertising art; criminal justice/law enforcement administration; criminal justice/police science; dramatic/theatre arts; economics; elementary education; English; family and consumer economics related; finance; fine/studio arts; French; health teacher education; history; interdisciplinary studies; journalism; kindergarten/preschool education; kinesiology and exercise science; liberal arts and sciences/liberal studies; marketing/marketing management; mass communication/media; mathematics; modern languages; music; music teacher education; nursing (registered nurse training); philosophy; physical education teaching and coaching; physics; piano and organ; pre-law studies; psychology; public administration; religious education; religious/sacred music; religious studies; science teacher education; secondary education; social work; sociology; Spanish; special education; speech and rhetoric; theology; voice and opera.

Academic Programs *Special study options:* academic remediation for entering students, accelerated degree program, adult/continuing education programs, advanced placement credit, double majors, honors programs, independent study, internships, part-time degree program, services for LD students, student-designed majors, study abroad, summer session for credit. *ROTC:* Army (b).

Library Richard W. Morton Memorial Library with 134,454 titles, 432 serial subscriptions, 3,000 audiovisual materials, an OPAC, a Web page.

Computers on Campus 242 computers available on campus for general student use. A campuswide network can be accessed from off campus. Internet access, at least one staffed computer lab available.

Student Life *Housing:* on-campus residence required through senior year. *Options:* men-only, women-only. Campus housing is university owned. Freshman campus housing is guaranteed. *Activities and organizations:* drama/theater group, student-run newspaper, choral group, Baptist Student Union, Delta Xi Omega, Student Government Association, Union Board, Lambda Chi Beta. *Campus security:* 24-hour patrols, student patrols, late-night transport/escort service, controlled dormitory access. *Student services:* health clinic, personal/psychological counseling.

Athletics Member NCAA, NCCAA. All NCAA Division III. *Intercollegiate sports:* baseball M, basketball M/W, cheerleading M/W, cross-country running M/W, football M, golf M/W, sailing M/W, soccer M/W, softball M/W, swimming M/W, tennis W. *Intramural sports:* badminton M/W, basketball M/W, bowling M/W, football M/W, golf M/W, softball M/W, swimming M/W, table tennis M/W, tennis M/W, ultimate Frisbee M/W, volleyball M/W, weight lifting M/W.

Standardized Tests *Required:* SAT I or ACT (for admission).

Costs (2003–04) *Comprehensive fee:* $13,260 includes full-time tuition ($8850), mandatory fees ($800), and room and board ($3610). Part-time tuition: $295 per hour. No tuition increase for student's term of enrollment. *College room only:* $1550. Room and board charges vary according to board plan and housing facility. *Payment plan:* installment. *Waivers:* senior citizens and employees or children of employees.

Financial Aid Of all full-time matriculated undergraduates who enrolled in 2003, 750 applied for aid, 576 were judged to have need, 182 had their need fully met. In 2003, 336 non-need-based awards were made. *Average percent of need met:* 79%. *Average financial aid package:* $10,014. *Average need-based loan:* $3942. *Average need-based gift aid:* $3251. *Average non-need-based aid:* $4063. *Average indebtedness upon graduation:* $5742.

Applying *Options:* electronic application, early admission. *Application fee:* $25. *Required:* high school transcript, letters of recommendation. *Required for some:* minimum 2.0 GPA, 3 letters of recommendation, class rank. *Recommended:* interview. *Application deadlines:* 8/15 (freshmen), 8/1 (transfers). *Notification:* continuous (freshmen), continuous (transfers).

Admissions Contact Mrs. Mary Wagner, Director of Enrollment Management and Institutional Research, Louisiana College, 1140 College Drive, Box 560, Pineville, LA 71359. *Phone:* 318-487-7259 Ext. 7301. *Toll-free phone:* 800-487-1906. *Fax:* 318-487-7550. *E-mail:* admissions@lacollege.edu.

LOUISIANA STATE UNIVERSITY AND AGRICULTURAL AND MECHANICAL COLLEGE

Baton Rouge, Louisiana

- **State-supported** university, founded 1860, part of Louisiana State University System
- **Calendar** semesters
- **Degrees** bachelor's, master's, doctoral, first professional, and post-master's certificates
- **Urban** 2000-acre campus with easy access to New Orleans
- **Endowment** $226.2 million
- **Coed,** 26,156 undergraduate students, 91% full-time, 53% women, 47% men
- **Moderately difficult** entrance level, 81% of applicants were admitted

Undergraduates 23,706 full-time, 2,450 part-time. Students come from 49 states and territories, 93 other countries, 10% are from out of state, 9% African American, 3% Asian American or Pacific Islander, 2% Hispanic American, 0.3% Native American, 2% international, 3% transferred in, 24% live on campus. *Retention:* 84% of 2002 full-time freshmen returned.

Freshmen *Admission:* 10,147 applied, 8,171 admitted, 5,428 enrolled. *Average high school GPA:* 3.49. *Test scores:* ACT scores over 18: 99%; ACT scores over 24: 54%; ACT scores over 30: 7%.

Faculty *Total:* 1,548, 84% full-time, 77% with terminal degrees. *Student/faculty ratio:* 21:1.

Majors Accounting; agricultural business and management; animal sciences; anthropology; architecture; audiology and speech-language pathology; biochemistry; biology/biological sciences; biomedical/medical engineering; biotechnology; business administration and management; business/managerial economics; chemical engineering; chemistry; civil engineering; computer engineering; computer science; construction management; dramatic/theatre arts; early childhood education; economics; education (specific subject areas) related; electrical, electronics and communications engineering; elementary education; English; environmental/environmental health engineering; environmental science; family and consumer sciences/human sciences; fashion merchandising; finance; fine/studio arts; food science; forest/forest resources management; French; general studies; geography; geology/earth science; German; history; industrial engineering; interior architecture; international business/trade/commerce; international/global studies; landscape architecture; Latin; liberal arts and sciences/liberal studies; management science; marketing/marketing management; mass communication/media; mathematics; mechanical engineering; microbiology; music; music performance; music teacher education; nutrition sciences; petroleum engineering; philosophy; physical education teaching and coaching; physics; plant sciences; political science and government; psychology; Russian studies; secondary education; sociology; Spanish; speech and rhetoric; wildlife and wildlands science and management; women's studies.

Academic Programs *Special study options:* accelerated degree program, adult/continuing education programs, advanced placement credit, cooperative education, distance learning, double majors, English as a second language, freshman honors college, honors programs, independent study, internships, off-campus study, part-time degree program, services for LD students, student-designed majors, study abroad, summer session for credit. *ROTC:* Army (b), Navy (c), Air Force (b).

Library Troy H. Middleton Library plus 7 others with 1.4 million titles, 24,304 serial subscriptions, 24,788 audiovisual materials, an OPAC, a Web page.

Computers on Campus 7000 computers available on campus for general student use. A campuswide network can be accessed from student residence rooms and from off campus that provide access to e-mail, wireless, grades, payroll, storage. Internet access, online (class) registration, at least one staffed computer lab available.

Student Life *Housing options:* coed, men-only, women-only, disabled students. Campus housing is university owned. *Activities and organizations:* drama/theater group, student-run newspaper, radio and television station, choral group, marching band, intramural athletics, student political organizations, Greek organizations, student professional organizations, religious organizations, national fraternities, national sororities. *Campus security:* 24-hour emergency response devices and patrols, late-night transport/escort service, controlled dormitory access, self-defense education, crime prevention programs. *Student services:* health clinic, personal/psychological counseling, women's center, legal services.

Athletics Member NCAA. All Division I except football (Division I-A). *Intercollegiate sports:* baseball M(s), basketball M(s)/W(s), cheerleading M/W, cross-country running M(s)/W(s), golf M(s)/W(s), gymnastics W(s), soccer W(s), softball W(s), swimming M(s)/W(s), tennis M(s)/W(s), track and field M(s)/W(s), volleyball W(s). *Intramural sports:* badminton M/W, basketball M/W, equestrian sports W(c), fencing M(c)/W(c), football M/W, golf M/W, lacrosse M(c), racquetball M/W, rugby M(c)/W(c), sailing M(c)/W(c), soccer M(c)/W(c), softball M/W, squash M, table tennis M/W, tennis M/W, track and field M/W, ultimate Frisbee M(c)/W(c), volleyball M(c)/W(c), weight lifting M(c)/W(c).

Standardized Tests *Required:* SAT I or ACT (for admission). *Required for some:* SAT I and SAT II or ACT (for admission).

Costs (2003–04) *Tuition:* state resident $2739 full-time; nonresident $8039 full-time. Part-time tuition and fees vary according to course load. *Required fees:* $1171 full-time. *Room and board:* $5216; room only: $3150. Room and board charges vary according to board plan and housing facility. *Payment plan:* deferred payment. *Waivers:* children of alumni and employees or children of employees.

Financial Aid Of all full-time matriculated undergraduates who enrolled in 2002, 17,422 applied for aid, 10,819 were judged to have need, 2,406 had their need fully met. 1,119 Federal Work-Study jobs (averaging $1308). 6,196 state and other part-time jobs (averaging $2072). In 2002, 8506 non-need-based awards were made. *Average percent of need met:* 68%. *Average financial aid package:* $6223. *Average need-based loan:* $3859. *Average need-based gift aid:* $4190. *Average non-need-based aid:* $3657. *Average indebtedness upon graduation:* $17,572.

Applying *Options:* early admission. *Application fee:* $40. *Required:* high school transcript, minimum 2.8 GPA, minimum ACT score of 20 or SAT I score of 940. *Required for some:* essay or personal statement, 3 letters of recommendation, interview. *Application deadlines:* 4/15 (freshmen), 4/15 (transfers). *Notification:* continuous (freshmen), continuous (transfers).

Admissions Contact Mr. Cleve Brooks, Director of Admissions, Louisiana State University and Agricultural and Mechanical College, 110 Thomas Boyd Hall, Baton Rouge, LA 70803. *Phone:* 225-578-1175. *Fax:* 225-578-4433. *E-mail:* admissions@lsu.edu.

■ *See page 1890 for a narrative description.*

LOUISIANA STATE UNIVERSITY AT ALEXANDRIA
Alexandria, Louisiana

- **State-supported** primarily 2-year, founded 1960, part of Louisiana State University System
- **Calendar** semesters
- **Degrees** certificates, associate, and bachelor's
- **Rural** 3114-acre campus
- **Endowment** $508,942
- **Coed**
- **Noncompetitive** entrance level

Faculty *Student/faculty ratio:* 21:1.

Student Life *Campus security:* 24-hour patrols.

Standardized Tests *Recommended:* ACT (for placement).

Costs (2003–04) *Tuition:* area resident $2205 full-time; nonresident $3967 full-time. *Required fees:* $150 full-time.

Financial Aid Of all full-time matriculated undergraduates who enrolled in 2001, 53 Federal Work-Study jobs (averaging $1226). 76 state and other part-time jobs (averaging $1261).

Applying *Options:* early admission. *Application fee:* $20. *Required:* high school transcript. *Required for some:* essay or personal statement, 3 letters of recommendation, interview.

Admissions Contact Ms. Shelly Kieffer, Recruiter/Admissions Counselor, Louisiana State University at Alexandria, 8100 Highway 71 South, Alexandria, LA 71302-9121. *Phone:* 318-473-6508. *Toll-free phone:* 888-473-6417. *Fax:* 318-473-6418. *E-mail:* skieffer@lsua.edu.

LOUISIANA STATE UNIVERSITY HEALTH SCIENCES CENTER
New Orleans, Louisiana

- **State-supported** university, founded 1931, part of Louisiana State University System
- **Calendar** semesters
- **Degrees** associate, bachelor's, master's, doctoral, and first professional
- **Urban** 80-acre campus with easy access to New Orleans
- **Endowment** $41.2 million
- **Coed,** 718 undergraduate students, 92% full-time, 84% women, 16% men

Undergraduates 660 full-time, 58 part-time. Students come from 3 states and territories, 1% are from out of state.

Faculty *Total:* 1,242.

Majors Cardiovascular technology; clinical laboratory science/medical technology; cytotechnology; dental assisting; dental hygiene; dental laboratory technology; electroneurodiagnostic/electroencephalographic technology; nursing (registered nurse training); ophthalmic technology; respiratory care therapy.

Academic Programs *Special study options:* academic remediation for entering students, advanced placement credit, independent study, internships, services for LD students, summer session for credit.

Library John P. Ische Library plus 2 others with 389,486 titles, 3,500 serial subscriptions, 9,454 audiovisual materials, an OPAC, a Web page.

Computers on Campus 100 computers available on campus for general student use. A campuswide network can be accessed from student residence rooms and from off campus. At least one staffed computer lab available.

Student Life *Housing options:* coed. Campus housing is university owned. *Activities and organizations:* choral group. *Campus security:* 24-hour emergency response devices and patrols, late-night transport/escort service, controlled dormitory access. *Student services:* health clinic, personal/psychological counseling.

Athletics *Intramural sports:* baseball M, football M, golf M, soccer M, softball M, volleyball M/W.

Costs (2003–04) *Tuition:* state resident $3214 full-time; nonresident $5714 full-time. Full-time tuition and fees vary according to program. Part-time tuition and fees vary according to program. *Room only:* $2012. Room and board charges vary according to housing facility. *Payment plan:* installment.

Applying *Application fee:* $50. *Application deadline:* 3/1 (transfers).

Admissions Contact Mr. W. Bryant Faust IV, Registrar, Louisiana State University Health Sciences Center, 433 Bolivar Street, New Orleans, LA 70112-2223. *Phone:* 504-568-4829.

LOUISIANA STATE UNIVERSITY IN SHREVEPORT
Shreveport, Louisiana

- **State-supported** comprehensive, founded 1965, part of Louisiana State University System
- **Calendar** semesters plus 8-week and two 4-week summer terms
- **Degrees** bachelor's, master's, and post-master's certificates
- **Urban** 200-acre campus
- **Endowment** $5.7 million
- **Coed,** 3,655 undergraduate students, 70% full-time, 62% women, 38% men
- **Noncompetitive** entrance level, 68% of applicants were admitted

Undergraduates 2,562 full-time, 1,093 part-time. Students come from 29 states and territories, 6 other countries, 4% are from out of state, 22% African American, 2% Asian American or Pacific Islander, 2% Hispanic American, 0.8% Native American, 0.5% international, 13% transferred in, 5% live on campus. *Retention:* 53% of 2002 full-time freshmen returned.

Freshmen *Admission:* 848 applied, 579 admitted, 579 enrolled. *Average high school GPA:* 3.06. *Test scores:* ACT scores over 18: 77%; ACT scores over 24: 20%; ACT scores over 30: 2%.

Faculty *Total:* 254, 61% full-time, 53% with terminal degrees. *Student/faculty ratio:* 16:1.

Majors Accounting; art; art teacher education; audiology and speech-language pathology; biological and biomedical sciences related; biological and physical sciences; biology/biological sciences; biology teacher education; business administration and management; business/managerial economics; chemistry; chemistry teacher education; computer science; criminal justice/safety; elementary education; English; English/language arts teacher education; environmental studies; finance; French; French language teacher education; general studies; geography; history; information science/studies; marketing/marketing management; mass communication/media; mathematics; mathematics teacher education; physical education teaching and coaching; physics; physics teacher education; political science and government; psychology; public health education and promotion; social studies teacher education; sociology; Spanish; special education; speech and rhetoric.

Academic Programs *Special study options:* academic remediation for entering students, accelerated degree program, adult/continuing education programs, advanced placement credit, cooperative education, distance learning, double majors, honors programs, independent study, internships, off-campus study, part-time degree program, services for LD students, student-designed majors, summer session for credit. *ROTC:* Army (b).

Library Noel Memorial Library with 279,821 titles, 1,190 serial subscriptions, 1,914 audiovisual materials, an OPAC, a Web page.

Computers on Campus A campuswide network can be accessed from off campus. Internet access, at least one staffed computer lab available. Computer purchase or lease plan available.

Student Life *Housing options:* coed, men-only, women-only. Campus housing is university owned. *Activities and organizations:* student-run newspaper, choral group, American Humanics, The Louisiana Association of Educators, Catholic Student Union, biology/health club, psychology club, national fraternities, national sororities. *Campus security:* 24-hour patrols, student patrols, controlled dormitory access. *Student services:* personal/psychological counseling.

Athletics Member NAIA. *Intercollegiate sports:* baseball M(s), basketball M/W. *Intramural sports:* archery M, basketball M/W, football M/W, lacrosse M, racquetball M/W, softball M/W, table tennis M/W, volleyball M/W.

Standardized Tests *Recommended:* ACT (for admission), SAT I or ACT (for admission), SAT II: Subject Tests (for admission).

Costs (2003–04) *Tuition:* state resident $2194 full-time, $94 per credit part-time; nonresident $6524 full-time, $269 per credit part-time. *Required fees:* $690 full-time. *Room only:* $2196. *Payment plan:* installment. *Waivers:* senior citizens and employees or children of employees.

Applying *Options:* early admission, deferred entrance. *Application fee:* $10. *Required:* high school transcript, minimum 2.0 GPA. *Required for some:* minimum ACT score of 17 for nonresidents. *Application deadlines:* 8/1 (freshmen), 8/1 (transfers). *Notification:* continuous (freshmen).

Admissions Contact Louisiana State University in Shreveport, One University Place, Shreveport, LA 71115-2399. *Phone:* 318-797-5061. *Toll-free phone:* 800-229-5957. *Fax:* 318-797-5286. *E-mail:* admissions@pilot.lsus.edu.

LOUISIANA TECH UNIVERSITY
Ruston, Louisiana

- **State-supported** university, founded 1894, part of University of Louisiana System
- **Calendar** quarters
- **Degrees** associate, bachelor's, master's, doctoral, and first professional certificates
- **Small-town** 247-acre campus
- **Endowment** $39.1 million
- **Coed,** 9,739 undergraduate students, 82% full-time, 48% women, 52% men
- **Moderately difficult** entrance level, 92% of applicants were admitted

Louisiana Tech University is known for high graduation rates, entrance exam scores, and overall academic quality. Quarter terms provide flexible scheduling. The family atmosphere enhances creativity and opportunity for participation in the many student organizations.

Undergraduates 7,942 full-time, 1,797 part-time. Students come from 48 states and territories, 70 other countries, 12% are from out of state, 15% African American, 0.8% Asian American or Pacific Islander, 1% Hispanic American, 0.7% Native American, 2% international, 5% transferred in, 30% live on campus. *Retention:* 74% of 2002 full-time freshmen returned.

Freshmen *Admission:* 3,768 applied, 3,454 admitted, 2,107 enrolled. *Average high school GPA:* 3.30. *Test scores:* ACT scores over 18: 89%; ACT scores over 24: 34%; ACT scores over 30: 4%.

Faculty *Total:* 496, 80% full-time, 67% with terminal degrees. *Student/faculty ratio:* 23:1.

Majors Accounting; aeronautics/aviation/aerospace science and technology; agricultural business and management; agricultural teacher education; animal sciences; architecture; art; art teacher education; audiology and speech-language pathology; aviation/airway management; biology/biological sciences; biology teacher education; biomedical/medical engineering; business administration and management; business/managerial economics; business teacher education; chemical engineering; chemistry; chemistry teacher education; child development; civil engineering; clinical laboratory science/medical technology; commercial and advertising art; computer science; construction engineering technology; consumer economics; dietetics; early childhood education; education (specific subject areas) related; electrical, electronic and communications engineering technology; electrical, electronics and communications engineering; elementary education; English; English/language arts teacher education; environmental studies; family and consumer sciences/home economics teacher education; finance; forestry; French; French language teacher education; general studies; geography; geology/earth science; health and physical education; health information/medical records administration; health information/medical records technology; history; human resources management; industrial engineering; interior architecture; journalism; kindergarten/preschool education; management information systems; management science; marketing/marketing management; mathematics; mathematics teacher education; mechanical engineering; middle school education; music; music performance; music teacher education; natural resources/conservation; nursing (registered nurse training); operations management; photography; physical education teaching and coaching; physics; physics teacher education; plant sciences; political science and government; psychology; social studies teacher education; sociology; Spanish; special education; special education (speech or language impaired); speech and rhetoric; speech teacher education.

Academic Programs *Special study options:* academic remediation for entering students, adult/continuing education programs, advanced placement credit, cooperative education, distance learning, double majors, English as a second language, honors programs, independent study, internships, off-campus study, part-time degree program, study abroad, summer session for credit. *ROTC:* Army (c), Navy (b).

Library Prescott Memorial Library with 3,319 titles, 2,469 serial subscriptions, 14,532 audiovisual materials, an OPAC, a Web page.

Computers on Campus 1800 computers available on campus for general student use. A campuswide network can be accessed from student residence rooms and from off campus. At least one staffed computer lab available.

Student Life *Housing:* on-campus residence required through sophomore year. *Options:* men-only, women-only, disabled students. *Activities and organizations:* drama/theater group, student-run newspaper, radio station, choral group, marching band, Student Government Association, Association of Women's Studies, Union Board, national fraternities, national sororities. *Campus security:* 24-hour emergency response devices and patrols, student patrols, late-night transport/escort service, controlled dormitory access. *Student services:* health clinic, personal/psychological counseling, legal services.

Athletics Member NCAA. All Division I except football (Division I-A). *Intercollegiate sports:* baseball M(s), basketball M(s)/W(s), cross-country running M(s)/W(s), golf M(s), softball W(s), tennis W(s), track and field M(s)/W(s), volleyball W(s), weight lifting M/W. *Intramural sports:* basketball M/W, bowling M/W, cross-country running M/W, football M/W, golf M, racquetball M/W, soccer M, softball M/W, tennis M/W, track and field M/W, volleyball M/W.

Standardized Tests *Required:* SAT I or ACT (for admission). *Recommended:* ACT (for admission).

Costs (2003–04) *Tuition:* state resident $3270 full-time; nonresident $7065 full-time. *Room and board:* $3885; room only: $2025.

Financial Aid Of all full-time matriculated undergraduates who enrolled in 2003, 6,292 applied for aid, 4,142 were judged to have need, 586 had their need fully met. 400 Federal Work-Study jobs (averaging $2675). 1,200 state and other part-time jobs (averaging $1780). In 2003, 2109 non-need-based awards were made. *Average percent of need met:* 64%. *Average financial aid package:* $5980. *Average need-based loan:* $2852. *Average need-based gift aid:* $4404. *Average non-need-based aid:* $5160. *Average indebtedness upon graduation:* $16,938.

Applying *Options:* early admission. *Application fee:* $20. *Required:* high school transcript, minimum 2.2 GPA. *Application deadline:* 7/31 (freshmen), rolling (transfers). *Notification:* continuous (freshmen), continuous (transfers).

Admissions Contact Mrs. Jan B. Albritton, Director of Admissions, Louisiana Tech University, PO Box 3178, Ruston, LA 71272. *Phone:* 318-257-3036. *Toll-free phone:* 800-528-3241. *Fax:* 318-257-2499. *E-mail:* bulldog@latech.edu.

■ *See page 1892 for a narrative description.*

LOYOLA UNIVERSITY NEW ORLEANS
New Orleans, Louisiana

- **Independent Roman Catholic (Jesuit)** comprehensive, founded 1912
- **Calendar** semesters
- **Degrees** bachelor's, master's, first professional, and postbachelor's certificates
- **Urban** 26-acre campus
- **Endowment** $275.6 million
- **Coed,** 3,747 undergraduate students, 88% full-time, 62% women, 38% men
- **Moderately difficult** entrance level, 69% of applicants were admitted

Holding fast to its core Jesuit values, Loyola University New Orleans strives to instill in its students a sense of social responsibility, a respect for the dignity of their fellow man, and the ability to discern truth in the midst of ambiguity. A unique combination of high-quality faculty members and academic programs and facilities, an ideal size that fosters a positive learning environment and individual student attention, and the centuries-old Jesuit tradition of educating the whole person distinguishes Loyola from other institutions.

Undergraduates 3,303 full-time, 444 part-time. Students come from 52 states and territories, 55 other countries, 55% are from out of state, 9% African American, 5% Asian American or Pacific Islander, 11% Hispanic American, 0.5% Native American, 3% international, 4% transferred in, 40% live on campus. *Retention:* 82% of 2002 full-time freshmen returned.

Freshmen *Admission:* 3,609 applied, 2,485 admitted, 864 enrolled. *Average high school GPA:* 3.72. *Test scores:* SAT verbal scores over 500: 97%; SAT math scores over 500: 97%; ACT scores over 18: 100%; SAT verbal scores over 600: 67%; SAT math scores over 600: 59%; ACT scores over 24: 84%; SAT verbal scores over 700: 11%; SAT math scores over 700: 7%; ACT scores over 30: 11%.

Faculty *Total:* 469, 62% full-time, 73% with terminal degrees. *Student/faculty ratio:* 13:1.

Majors Accounting; art; behavioral sciences; biology/biological sciences; business administration and management; business/managerial economics; chemistry; classics and languages, literatures and linguistics; commercial and advertising art; communication/speech communication and rhetoric; computer and information sciences; creative writing; criminal justice/safety; dramatic/theatre arts; economics; education; elementary education; English; finance; forensic science and technology; French; general studies; German; history; humanities; information science/studies; international business/trade/commerce; jazz/jazz studies; marketing/marketing management; mathematics; music; music management and merchandising; music performance; music teacher education; music theory and composition; nursing (registered nurse training); philosophy; physics; piano and organ; political science and government; psychology; religious education; religious/sacred music; religious studies; Russian; social sciences; sociology; Spanish; visual and performing arts.

Academic Programs *Special study options:* academic remediation for entering students, accelerated degree program, adult/continuing education programs, advanced placement credit, distance learning, double majors, English as a second language, honors programs, independent study, internships, off-campus study, part-time degree program, services for LD students, student-designed majors, study abroad, summer session for credit. *ROTC:* Army (c), Navy (c), Air Force (c). *Unusual degree programs:* 3-2 engineering with Tulane University.

Library University Library plus 1 other with 401,548 titles, 4,948 serial subscriptions, 15,484 audiovisual materials, an OPAC, a Web page.

Computers on Campus 458 computers available on campus for general student use. A campuswide network can be accessed from student residence rooms and from off campus. Internet access, online (class) registration, at least one staffed computer lab available. Computer purchase or lease plan available.

Student Life *Housing:* on-campus residence required for freshman year. *Options:* coed, women-only, disabled students. Freshman campus housing is guaranteed. *Activities and organizations:* drama/theater group, student-run newspaper, radio and television station, choral group, University Programming Board, Community Action Program, Black Student Union, Student Government Association, national fraternities, national sororities. *Campus security:* 24-hour emergency response devices and patrols, late-night transport/escort service, controlled dormitory access, self-defense education, bicycle patrols, closed circuit TV

Loyola University New Orleans (continued)

monitors, door alarms, crime prevention programs. *Student services:* health clinic, personal/psychological counseling, women's center.

Athletics Member NAIA. *Intercollegiate sports:* baseball M, basketball M/W, bowling M(c)/W(c), cheerleading M(c)/W(c), crew M(c)/W(c), cross-country running M/W, golf M(c)/W(c), rugby M(c), soccer M(c)/W, swimming M(c)/W(c), tennis M(c)/W(c), track and field M/W, ultimate Frisbee M(c)/W(c), wrestling M(c). *Intramural sports:* basketball M/W, racquetball M/W, soccer M/W, softball M/W, swimming M/W, tennis M/W, volleyball M/W, water polo M/W, weight lifting M/W.

Standardized Tests *Required:* SAT I or ACT (for admission). *Required for some:* PAA.

Costs (2004–05) *Comprehensive fee:* $31,612 includes full-time tuition ($22,812), mandatory fees ($806), and room and board ($7994). Full-time tuition and fees vary according to student level. Part-time tuition: $663 per credit hour. *Required fees:* $335 per year part-time. *College room only:* $4924. Room and board charges vary according to board plan and housing facility. *Payment plan:* installment. *Waivers:* senior citizens and employees or children of employees.

Financial Aid Of all full-time matriculated undergraduates who enrolled in 2003, 2,228 applied for aid, 1,783 were judged to have need, 801 had their need fully met. 764 Federal Work-Study jobs (averaging $1858). In 2003, 1049 non-need-based awards were made. *Average percent of need met:* 82%. *Average financial aid package:* $16,895. *Average need-based loan:* $3878. *Average need-based gift aid:* $11,964. *Average non-need-based aid:* $8868. *Average indebtedness upon graduation:* $18,125.

Applying *Options:* common application, electronic application, early admission, deferred entrance. *Application fee:* $20. *Required:* essay or personal statement, high school transcript, 1 letter of recommendation. *Required for some:* interview. *Recommended:* interview. *Application deadline:* 1/15 (freshmen), rolling (transfers). *Notification:* continuous (freshmen).

Admissions Contact Ms. Deborah C. Stieffel, Dean of Admission and Enrollment Management, Loyola University New Orleans, 6363 Saint Charles Avenue, Box 18, New Orleans, LA 70118-6195. *Phone:* 504-865-3240. *Toll-free phone:* 800-4-LOYOLA. *Fax:* 504-865-3383. *E-mail:* admit@loyno.edu.

■ *See page 1900 for a narrative description.*

McNEESE STATE UNIVERSITY
Lake Charles, Louisiana

- **State-supported** comprehensive, founded 1939, part of University of Louisiana System
- **Calendar** semesters
- **Degrees** associate, bachelor's, master's, post-master's, and postbachelor's certificates
- **Suburban** 580-acre campus
- **Endowment** $31.2 million
- **Coed,** 7,330 undergraduate students, 82% full-time, 58% women, 42% men
- **Moderately difficult** entrance level, 88% of applicants were admitted

Undergraduates 6,023 full-time, 1,307 part-time. Students come from 33 states and territories, 37 other countries, 6% are from out of state, 20% African American, 0.7% Asian American or Pacific Islander, 1% Hispanic American, 0.8% Native American, 1% international, 5% transferred in, 12% live on campus. *Retention:* 68% of 2002 full-time freshmen returned.

Freshmen *Admission:* 2,183 applied, 1,927 admitted, 1,563 enrolled. *Average high school GPA:* 3.07. *Test scores:* ACT scores over 18: 77%; ACT scores over 24: 18%; ACT scores over 30: 1%.

Faculty *Total:* 393, 74% full-time, 57% with terminal degrees. *Student/faculty ratio:* 22:1.

Majors Accounting; agricultural teacher education; agriculture; applied art; art; art teacher education; biology/biological sciences; biology teacher education; business administration and management; business teacher education; ceramic arts and ceramics; chemistry; chemistry teacher education; clinical laboratory science/medical technology; computer typography and composition equipment operation; criminal justice/safety; dramatic/theatre arts; drawing; early childhood education; education; educational leadership and administration; education related; electrical, electronic and communications engineering technology; elementary education; engineering; engineering technologies related; engineering technology; English; English/language arts teacher education; environmental science; family and consumer sciences/home economics teacher education; family and consumer sciences/human sciences; finance; foods, nutrition, and wellness; foreign language teacher education; French; general studies; geology/earth science; history; information technology; instrumentation technology; kindergarten/preschool education; kinesiology and exercise science; legal assistant/paralegal; liberal arts and sciences/liberal studies; marketing/marketing management; mass communication/media; mathematics; mathematics teacher education; medical radiologic technology; music; music performance; music teacher education; nursing (registered nurse training); petroleum technology; photography; physical education teaching and coaching; physics; political science and government; printmaking; psychology; secondary education; social studies teacher education; sociology; Spanish; special education; speech and rhetoric; speech teacher education; wildlife and wildlands science and management.

Academic Programs *Special study options:* academic remediation for entering students, accelerated degree program, adult/continuing education programs, advanced placement credit, cooperative education, distance learning, double majors, English as a second language, freshman honors college, honors programs, independent study, internships, off-campus study, part-time degree program, services for LD students, study abroad, summer session for credit.

Library Frazer Memorial Library plus 2 others with 351,708 titles, 1,679 serial subscriptions, 3,635 audiovisual materials, an OPAC, a Web page.

Computers on Campus 700 computers available on campus for general student use. A campuswide network can be accessed from student residence rooms and from off campus. Internet access, online (class) registration, at least one staffed computer lab available.

Student Life *Housing:* on-campus residence required for freshman year. *Options:* coed, men-only, women-only. Campus housing is university owned and is provided by a third party. *Activities and organizations:* drama/theater group, student-run newspaper, choral group, marching band, Student Government Association, International Students Association, Resident Student Association, national fraternities, national sororities. *Campus security:* 24-hour emergency response devices and patrols, late-night transport/escort service, controlled dormitory access. *Student services:* health clinic, personal/psychological counseling, women's center.

Athletics Member NCAA. All Division I except football (Division I-AA). *Intercollegiate sports:* baseball M(s), basketball M(s)/W(s), cross-country running M(s)/W(s), golf M(s)/W(s), riflery M/W, soccer W(s), softball W(s), tennis W(s), track and field M(s)/W(s), volleyball W(s), weight lifting M(c)/W(c). *Intramural sports:* badminton M/W, baseball M, basketball M/W, football M/W, golf M/W, racquetball M/W, soccer M/W, softball W, swimming M/W, table tennis M/W, tennis M/W, volleyball M/W, water polo M/W, weight lifting M/W.

Standardized Tests *Required:* SAT I or ACT (for admission).

Costs (2003–04) *Tuition:* state resident $2050 full-time, $519 per term part-time; nonresident $8116 full-time, $519 per term part-time. Full-time tuition and fees vary according to course load. Part-time tuition and fees vary according to course load. *Required fees:* $722 full-time, $249 per term part-time. *Room and board:* $3788. Room and board charges vary according to board plan and housing facility. *Payment plans:* installment, deferred payment. *Waivers:* senior citizens and employees or children of employees.

Financial Aid In 2002, 2610 non-need-based awards were made. *Average percent of need met:* 58%.

Applying *Options:* electronic application, early admission. *Application fee:* $20. *Required:* high school transcript. *Application deadline:* rolling (freshmen), rolling (transfers). *Notification:* continuous (freshmen), continuous (transfers).

Admissions Contact Ms. Tammie Pettis, Director of Admissions, McNeese State University, Box 92495, Kaufman Hall, 4100 Ryan Street, Lake Charles, LA 70609. *Phone:* 337-475-5148. *Toll-free phone:* 800-622-3352. *Fax:* 337-475-5189. *E-mail:* info@mail.mcneese.edu.

■ *See page 1968 for a narrative description.*

NEW ORLEANS BAPTIST THEOLOGICAL SEMINARY
New Orleans, Louisiana

Admissions Contact Dr. Paul E. Gregoire Jr., Registrar/Director of Admissions, New Orleans Baptist Theological Seminary, 3939 Gentilly Boulevard, New Orleans, LA 70126-4858. *Phone:* 504-282-4455 Ext. 3337. *Toll-free phone:* 800-662-8701.

NICHOLLS STATE UNIVERSITY
Thibodaux, Louisiana

- **State-supported** comprehensive, founded 1948, part of University of Louisiana System
- **Calendar** semesters
- **Degrees** certificates, associate, bachelor's, master's, and post-master's certificates
- **Small-town** 210-acre campus with easy access to New Orleans
- **Endowment** $3.1 million
- **Coed,** 6,517 undergraduate students, 81% full-time, 62% women, 38% men
- **Noncompetitive** entrance level, 99% of applicants were admitted

Undergraduates 5,304 full-time, 1,213 part-time. Students come from 30 states and territories, 29 other countries, 3% are from out of state, 17% African American, 0.7% Asian American or Pacific Islander, 1% Hispanic American, 2% Native American, 0.7% international, 5% transferred in, 15% live on campus. *Retention:* 64% of 2002 full-time freshmen returned.

Freshmen *Admission:* 2,472 applied, 2,447 admitted, 1,456 enrolled. *Average high school GPA:* 2.97. *Test scores:* SAT verbal scores over 500: 36%; SAT math scores over 500: 44%; ACT scores over 18: 68%; SAT verbal scores over 600: 12%; SAT math scores over 600: 3%; ACT scores over 24: 14%; ACT scores over 30: 1%.

Faculty *Total:* 285, 99% full-time, 56% with terminal degrees. *Student/faculty ratio:* 22:1.

Majors Accounting; agricultural business and management; art; art teacher education; audiology and speech-language pathology; biology/biological sciences; business administration and management; business/commerce; business teacher education; chemical technology; chemistry; child care and support services management; computer science; criminal justice/police science; culinary arts; dietetics; early childhood education; education; elementary education; emergency medical technology (EMT paramedic); English; environmental biology; family and consumer sciences/human sciences; finance; French; general studies; health services/allied health/health sciences; health teacher education; history; institutional food workers; kindergarten/preschool education; legal assistant/paralegal; management information systems; marine biology and biological oceanography; marketing/marketing management; mass communication/media; mathematics; mechanical engineering/mechanical technology; middle school education; music; music teacher education; nursing (registered nurse training); petroleum technology; physical education teaching and coaching; political science and government; pre-dentistry studies; pre-medical studies; psychology; respiratory care therapy; science teacher education; secondary education; sociology; special education; survey technology.

Academic Programs *Special study options:* academic remediation for entering students, accelerated degree program, adult/continuing education programs, advanced placement credit, cooperative education, distance learning, double majors, English as a second language, honors programs, independent study, internships, off-campus study, part-time degree program, services for LD students, study abroad, summer session for credit.

Library Allen J. Ellender Memorial Library with 303,962 titles, 1,341 serial subscriptions, 3,374 audiovisual materials, an OPAC, a Web page.

Computers on Campus 250 computers available on campus for general student use. A campuswide network can be accessed from student residence rooms and from off campus. Internet access, at least one staffed computer lab available.

Student Life *Housing options:* coed, men-only, women-only, disabled students. Campus housing is university owned. *Activities and organizations:* drama/theater group, student-run newspaper, radio and television station, choral group, marching band, Student Government Association, Student Programming Association, Residence Hall Association, Food Advisory Association, Intra-Fraternity Council, national fraternities, national sororities. *Campus security:* 24-hour emergency response devices and patrols, student patrols, late-night transport/escort service. *Student services:* health clinic, personal/psychological counseling, women's center, legal services.

Athletics Member NCAA. All Division I except football (Division I-AA). *Intercollegiate sports:* baseball M(s), basketball M(s)/W(s), cross-country running M(s)/W(s), golf M(s), soccer M/W(s), softball W(s), tennis W(s), track and field M(s)/W(s), volleyball W(s). *Intramural sports:* badminton M/W, baseball M, basketball M/W, bowling M/W, cheerleading M/W, cross-country running M/W, football M/W, golf M/W, racquetball M/W, soccer M/W, softball M/W, swimming M/W, table tennis M/W, tennis M/W, track and field M/W, volleyball M/W, weight lifting M/W.

Standardized Tests *Recommended:* ACT (for admission).

Costs (2003–04) *Tuition:* state resident $2115 full-time; nonresident $7563 full-time. Part-time tuition and fees vary according to course load. *Required fees:* $878 full-time. *Room and board:* $3402; room only: $1750. *Payment plan:* deferred payment. *Waivers:* employees or children of employees.

Financial Aid Of all full-time matriculated undergraduates who enrolled in 2002, 4,155 applied for aid, 2,579 were judged to have need, 1,629 had their need fully met. 250 Federal Work-Study jobs (averaging $972). 676 state and other part-time jobs (averaging $1546). In 2002, 90 non-need-based awards were made. *Average percent of need met:* 88%. *Average financial aid package:* $4935. *Average need-based loan:* $2675. *Average need-based gift aid:* $2863. *Average non-need-based aid:* $2425.

Applying *Options:* electronic application, early admission, deferred entrance. *Application fee:* $20. *Required:* high school transcript. *Application deadline:* 7/21 (freshmen), rolling (transfers). *Notification:* continuous until 8/28 (freshmen), continuous until 8/28 (transfers).

Admissions Contact Mrs. Becky L. Durocher, Director of Admissions, Nicholls State University, PO Box 2004-NSU, Thibodaux, LA 70310. *Phone:* 985-448-4507. *Toll-free phone:* 877-NICHOLLS. *Fax:* 985-448-4929. *E-mail:* nicholls@nicholls.edu.

NORTHWESTERN STATE UNIVERSITY OF LOUISIANA

Natchitoches, Louisiana

- **State-supported** comprehensive, founded 1884, part of University of Louisiana System
- **Calendar** semesters
- **Degrees** certificates, associate, bachelor's, master's, doctoral, and post-master's certificates
- **Small-town** 916-acre campus
- **Endowment** $3.0 million
- **Coed,** 9,351 undergraduate students, 75% full-time, 66% women, 34% men
- **Noncompetitive** entrance level, 98% of applicants were admitted

Undergraduates 6,968 full-time, 2,383 part-time. Students come from 43 states and territories, 24 other countries, 6% are from out of state, 30% African American, 0.9% Asian American or Pacific Islander, 2% Hispanic American, 2% Native American, 0.4% international, 5% transferred in, 24% live on campus. *Retention:* 65% of 2002 full-time freshmen returned.

Freshmen *Admission:* 4,389 applied, 4,313 admitted, 2,173 enrolled. *Average high school GPA:* 3.00. *Test scores:* SAT verbal scores over 500: 57%; SAT math scores over 500: 48%; ACT scores over 18: 67%; SAT verbal scores over 600: 19%; SAT math scores over 600: 21%; ACT scores over 24: 15%; SAT verbal scores over 700: 2%; SAT math scores over 700: 1%; ACT scores over 30: 1%.

Faculty *Total:* 511, 58% full-time. *Student/faculty ratio:* 23:1.

Majors Accounting; administrative assistant and secretarial science; anthropology; art; biology/biological sciences; business administration and management; chemistry; clinical laboratory science/medical technology; criminal justice/police science; criminal justice/safety; dramatic/theatre arts; early childhood education; electrical, electronic and communications engineering technology; elementary education; English; family and consumer sciences/human sciences; general studies; history; hospitality administration; industrial technology; information science/studies; journalism; liberal arts and sciences/liberal studies; mathematics; medical radiologic technology; middle school education; music performance; music teacher education; nursing (registered nurse training); physical education teaching and coaching; physics; political science and government; psychology; secondary education; social sciences; social work; sociology; special education; veterinary/animal health technology.

Academic Programs *Special study options:* academic remediation for entering students, accelerated degree program, adult/continuing education programs, advanced placement credit, distance learning, double majors, freshman honors college, honors programs, internships, off-campus study, part-time degree program, student-designed majors, study abroad, summer session for credit. *ROTC:* Army (b).

Library Eugene P. Watson Memorial Library with 330,145 titles, 1,749 serial subscriptions, 5,282 audiovisual materials, an OPAC.

Computers on Campus 748 computers available on campus for general student use. A campuswide network can be accessed from student residence rooms and from off campus. Internet access, online (class) registration, at least one staffed computer lab available.

Student Life *Housing options:* coed, men-only, women-only. Campus housing is university owned. *Activities and organizations:* drama/theater group, student-run newspaper, radio and television station, choral group, marching band, Sigma Sigma Sigma Sorority, Phi Mu Sorority, Baptist Collegiate Ministry, Catholic Student Organization, Sigma Nu Fraternity, national fraternities, national sororities. *Campus security:* 24-hour emergency response devices and patrols, late-night transport/escort service, controlled dormitory access. *Student services:* health clinic, personal/psychological counseling.

Athletics Member NCAA. All Division I except football (Division I-AA). *Intercollegiate sports:* baseball M(s), basketball M(s)/W(s), cross-country running M(s)/W(s), soccer W(s), softball W(s), tennis W(s), track and field M(s)/W(s), volleyball W(s). *Intramural sports:* basketball M/W, bowling M/W, cheerleading M(c)/W(c), crew M(c)/W, football M/W, racquetball M/W, riflery M/W, soccer M/W, softball M/W, tennis M/W, track and field M/W, volleyball M/W.

Standardized Tests *Required:* SAT I or ACT (for admission).

Costs (2004–05) *Tuition:* state resident $3006 full-time, $833 per term part-time; nonresident $9084 full-time, $833 per term part-time. Full-time tuition and fees vary according to course load. Part-time tuition and fees vary according to course load. *Required fees:* $99 per term part-time. *Room and board:* $3326;

Northwestern State University of Louisiana (continued)
room only: $1850. Room and board charges vary according to board plan, housing facility, and location. *Payment plan:* installment.

Financial Aid Of all full-time matriculated undergraduates who enrolled in 2002, 5,328 applied for aid, 3,841 were judged to have need, 1,356 had their need fully met. 490 Federal Work-Study jobs (averaging $948). 238 state and other part-time jobs (averaging $1054). In 2002, 1609 non-need-based awards were made. *Average percent of need met:* 95%. *Average financial aid package:* $3350. *Average need-based loan:* $1562. *Average need-based gift aid:* $2119. *Average non-need-based aid:* $1736. *Average indebtedness upon graduation:* $22,000.

Applying *Options:* early admission. *Application fee:* $20. *Required:* high school transcript. *Notification:* continuous (freshmen), continuous (transfers).

Admissions Contact Ms. Jana Lucky, Director of Recruiting and Admissions, Northwestern State University of Louisiana, Roy Hall, Room 209, Natchitoches, LA 71497. *Phone:* 318-357-4503. *Toll-free phone:* 800-426 3754 (in-state); 800-327-1903 (out-of-state). *Fax:* 318-357-4257. *E-mail:* admissions@nsula.edu.

OUR LADY OF HOLY CROSS COLLEGE

New Orleans, Louisiana

- **Independent Roman Catholic** comprehensive, founded 1916
- **Calendar** semesters plus summer sessions
- **Degrees** associate, bachelor's, master's, and postbachelor's certificates
- **Suburban** 40-acre campus with easy access to New Orleans
- **Endowment** $7.0 million
- **Coed,** 1,296 undergraduate students, 63% full-time, 77% women, 23% men
- **Minimally difficult** entrance level, 97% of applicants were admitted

Our Lady of Holy Cross College, a Catholic, coeducational liberal arts college, was founded in 1916. With a low student-faculty ratio, Our Lady of Holy Cross College provides high-quality education at reasonable tuition rates. Associate, baccalaureate, and master's programs are offered, and financial aid is available.

Undergraduates 810 full-time, 486 part-time. Students come from 4 states and territories, 3 other countries, 4% are from out of state, 16% African American, 2% Asian American or Pacific Islander, 5% Hispanic American, 0.5% Native American, 0.5% international, 11% transferred in. *Retention:* 64% of 2002 full-time freshmen returned.

Freshmen *Admission:* 320 applied, 309 admitted, 157 enrolled. *Average high school GPA:* 2.8. *Test scores:* ACT scores over 18: 71%; ACT scores over 24: 4%.

Faculty *Total:* 123, 32% full-time, 43% with terminal degrees. *Student/faculty ratio:* 22:1.

Majors Accounting; behavioral sciences; biology/biological sciences; business administration and management; business teacher education; clinical laboratory science/medical technology; counselor education/school counseling and guidance; education; education (K-12); elementary education; English; general studies; health science; history; mathematics; nursing (registered nurse training); reading teacher education; respiratory care therapy; sales, distribution and marketing; science teacher education; secondary education; social sciences; teacher assistant/aide; tourism and travel services management; tourism promotion.

Academic Programs *Special study options:* academic remediation for entering students, adult/continuing education programs, advanced placement credit, cooperative education, distance learning, double majors, independent study, internships, off-campus study, part-time degree program, services for LD students, study abroad, summer session for credit. *ROTC:* Army (c), Air Force (c). *Unusual degree programs:* 3-2 social work with Tulane University.

Library Blaine Kern Library with 83,631 titles, 1,002 serial subscriptions, 11,949 audiovisual materials, an OPAC, a Web page.

Computers on Campus 68 computers available on campus for general student use. A campuswide network can be accessed. Internet access, at least one staffed computer lab available.

Student Life *Housing:* college housing not available. *Activities and organizations:* drama/theater group, student-run newspaper, Innovators, student government, Association of Student Nurses, Delta Sigma Pi, Louisiana Association of Educators/Student Programs. *Campus security:* 24-hour patrols. *Student services:* personal/psychological counseling.

Athletics *Intramural sports:* baseball M, football M, golf M, volleyball M/W.

Standardized Tests *Required:* SAT I or ACT (for placement). *Recommended:* ACT (for placement).

Costs (2003–04) *Tuition:* $5400 full-time, $225 per semester hour part-time. *Required fees:* $490 full-time. *Payment plan:* installment. *Waivers:* employees or children of employees.

Financial Aid Of all full-time matriculated undergraduates who enrolled in 2003, 1,063 applied for aid, 918 were judged to have need, 38 had their need fully met. 45 Federal Work-Study jobs (averaging $2698). In 2003, 183 non-need-based awards were made. *Average percent of need met:* 35%. *Average financial aid package:* $4128. *Average need-based loan:* $2865. *Average need-based gift aid:* $3301. *Average non-need-based aid:* $4664. *Average indebtedness upon graduation:* $22,000.

Applying *Options:* common application, electronic application, deferred entrance. *Application fee:* $15. *Required:* high school transcript. *Recommended:* minimum 2.0 GPA. *Application deadline:* 7/20 (freshmen), rolling (transfers). *Notification:* continuous (freshmen), continuous (transfers).

Admissions Contact Ms. Kristine Hatfield Kopecky, Vice President for Student Affairs and Admissions, Our Lady of Holy Cross College, 4123 Woodland Drive, New Orleans, LA 70131-7399. *Phone:* 504-394-7744 Ext. 185. *Toll-free phone:* 800-259-7744 Ext. 175. *Fax:* 504-391-2421.

OUR LADY OF THE LAKE COLLEGE

Baton Rouge, Louisiana

- **Independent Roman Catholic** 4-year, founded 1990
- **Calendar** semesters
- **Degrees** certificates, associate, and bachelor's
- **Suburban** 5-acre campus with easy access to New Orleans
- **Coed, primarily women,** 1,807 undergraduate students
- **Noncompetitive** entrance level, 91% of applicants were admitted

Undergraduates Students come from 3 states and territories, 1% are from out of state, 18% African American, 2% Asian American or Pacific Islander, 2% Hispanic American, 0.7% Native American. *Retention:* 55% of 2002 full-time freshmen returned.

Freshmen *Admission:* 241 applied, 219 admitted. *Average high school GPA:* 3.0. *Test scores:* ACT scores over 18: 83%; ACT scores over 24: 7%.

Faculty *Total:* 134, 49% full-time, 64% with terminal degrees. *Student/faculty ratio:* 12:1.

Majors Biological and biomedical sciences related; biology/biological sciences; biomedical sciences; clinical laboratory science/medical technology; clinical/medical laboratory technology; emergency medical technology (EMT paramedic); forensic science and technology; general studies; health/health care administration; humanities; industrial radiologic technology; nursing (registered nurse training); physical therapist assistant; surgical technology.

Academic Programs *Special study options:* academic remediation for entering students, adult/continuing education programs, advanced placement credit, external degree program, off-campus study, part-time degree program, services for LD students, summer session for credit. *ROTC:* Army (c), Air Force (c).

Library Learning Resource Center plus 1 other with 12,409 titles, 328 serial subscriptions, an OPAC.

Computers on Campus 100 computers available on campus for general student use. A campuswide network can be accessed. Internet access, at least one staffed computer lab available.

Student Life *Housing:* college housing not available. *Activities and organizations:* student-run newspaper, Student Government Association, Cultural Arts Association, Christian Fellowship Association, Mathematics/Science Association. *Campus security:* 24-hour patrols. *Student services:* health clinic, personal/psychological counseling.

Standardized Tests *Required:* ACT (for admission), ACT ASSET (for admission).

Costs (2004–05) *Tuition:* $6450 full-time, $215 per credit hour part-time. *Required fees:* $360 full-time, $75 per term part-time. *Payment plans:* installment, deferred payment. *Waivers:* employees or children of employees.

Financial Aid Of all full-time matriculated undergraduates who enrolled in 2002, 25 Federal Work-Study jobs (averaging $3500). *Average indebtedness upon graduation:* $30,000.

Applying *Options:* common application. *Application fee:* $35. *Required:* high school transcript, minimum 2.0 GPA. *Application deadline:* rolling (freshmen), rolling (transfers). *Notification:* 8/1 (freshmen).

Admissions Contact Mr. Mark Wetmore, Director of Admissions, Our Lady of the Lake College, 7434 Perkins Road, Baton Rouge, LA 70808. *Phone:* 225-768-1718. *Toll-free phone:* 877-242-3509. *E-mail:* admission@ololcollege.edu.

SAINT JOSEPH SEMINARY COLLEGE

Saint Benedict, Louisiana

- **Independent Roman Catholic** 4-year, founded 1891
- **Calendar** semesters
- **Degrees** bachelor's (Religious Studies Institute is co-ed)
- **Rural** 1300-acre campus with easy access to New Orleans
- **Endowment** $127,793
- **Men only,** 167 undergraduate students, 46% full-time

■ **Minimally difficult** entrance level

Undergraduates 77 full-time, 90 part-time. Students come from 8 states and territories, 42% are from out of state, 3% African American, 6% Asian American or Pacific Islander, 21% Hispanic American, 15% transferred in, 100% live on campus. *Retention:* 91% of 2002 full-time freshmen returned.

Freshmen *Admission:* 10 enrolled. *Average high school GPA:* 3.32. *Test scores:* ACT scores over 18: 55%; ACT scores over 24: 22%.

Faculty *Total:* 36, 39% full-time, 36% with terminal degrees. *Student/faculty ratio:* 3:1.

Majors Liberal arts and sciences/liberal studies.

Academic Programs *Special study options:* academic remediation for entering students, adult/continuing education programs, advanced placement credit, English as a second language.

Library Pere Rouquette Library plus 1 other with 70,000 titles, 137 serial subscriptions, 1,500 audiovisual materials, an OPAC, a Web page.

Computers on Campus 15 computers available on campus for general student use. Internet access, at least one staffed computer lab available.

Student Life *Housing:* on-campus residence required through senior year. *Options:* men-only. Campus housing is university owned. Freshman campus housing is guaranteed. *Activities and organizations:* drama/theater group, student-run newspaper, choral group, student government. *Campus security:* 24-hour emergency response devices, controlled dormitory access, entrance gate. *Student services:* health clinic, personal/psychological counseling.

Athletics *Intramural sports:* baseball M, basketball M, football M, golf M, racquetball M, soccer M, softball M, squash M, swimming M, table tennis M, tennis M, volleyball M, water polo M, weight lifting M.

Standardized Tests *Required:* ACT (for admission).

Costs (2003–04) *One-time required fee:* $85. *Comprehensive fee:* $14,760 includes full-time tuition ($8150), mandatory fees ($460), and room and board ($6150).

Financial Aid Of all full-time matriculated undergraduates who enrolled in 2001, 33 applied for aid, 19 were judged to have need, 19 had their need fully met. 15 Federal Work-Study jobs (averaging $1000). 8 state and other part-time jobs (averaging $700). In 2001, 13 non-need-based awards were made. *Average percent of need met:* 100%. *Average financial aid package:* $12,386. *Average need-based loan:* $1614. *Average need-based gift aid:* $9530. *Average non-need-based aid:* $2285. *Average indebtedness upon graduation:* $12,400.

Applying *Options:* early admission, deferred entrance. *Application fee:* $10. *Required:* high school transcript, minimum 2.0 GPA, letters of recommendation, interview. *Application deadline:* rolling (freshmen), rolling (transfers). *Notification:* continuous (freshmen), continuous (transfers).

Admissions Contact Br. Bernard Boudreaux OSB, Academic Assistant, Saint Joseph Seminary College, 75376 River Road, St. Benedict, LA 70457. *Phone:* 985-867-2248. *E-mail:* asec@sjasc.edu.

SOUTHEASTERN LOUISIANA UNIVERSITY
Hammond, Louisiana

■ **State-supported** comprehensive, founded 1925, part of University of Louisiana System
■ **Calendar** semesters
■ **Degrees** associate, bachelor's, and master's
■ **Small-town** 375-acre campus with easy access to New Orleans
■ **Endowment** $21.0 million
■ **Coed,** 13,629 undergraduate students, 84% full-time, 62% women, 38% men
■ 96% of applicants were admitted

Undergraduates 11,420 full-time, 2,209 part-time. Students come from 42 states and territories, 41 other countries, 2% are from out of state, 15% African American, 0.5% Asian American or Pacific Islander, 1% Hispanic American, 0.4% Native American, 0.7% international, 6% transferred in, 12% live on campus. *Retention:* 67% of 2002 full-time freshmen returned.

Freshmen *Admission:* 3,488 applied, 3,341 admitted, 2,681 enrolled. *Test scores:* ACT scores over 18: 75%; ACT scores over 24: 13%; ACT scores over 30: 1%.

Faculty *Total:* 715, 70% full-time, 47% with terminal degrees. *Student/faculty ratio:* 27:1.

Majors Accounting; administrative assistant and secretarial science; art; arts management; art teacher education; athletic training; biology/biological sciences; business administration and management; chemistry; communication/speech communication and rhetoric; computer science; criminal justice/police science; criminal justice/safety; elementary education; English; English/language arts teacher education; family and consumer sciences/human sciences; finance; French; French language teacher education; general studies; history; horticultural science; industrial technology; liberal arts and sciences/liberal studies; marketing/marketing management; mathematics; mathematics teacher education; music performance; music teacher education; nursing (registered nurse training); physical education teaching and coaching; physics; political science and government; psychology; public health education and promotion; science teacher education; social studies teacher education; social work; sociology; Spanish; Spanish language teacher education; special education; special education (speech or language impaired); speech teacher education.

Academic Programs *Special study options:* academic remediation for entering students, adult/continuing education programs, advanced placement credit, distance learning, double majors, honors programs, independent study, internships, off-campus study, part-time degree program, services for LD students, study abroad, summer session for credit. *ROTC:* Army (c).

Library Sims Memorial Library with 572,563 titles, 2,387 serial subscriptions, 48,752 audiovisual materials, an OPAC, a Web page.

Computers on Campus 819 computers available on campus for general student use. A campuswide network can be accessed from student residence rooms and from off campus that provide access to campus webmail. Internet access, online (class) registration, at least one staffed computer lab available.

Student Life *Housing:* on-campus residence required through sophomore year. *Options:* coed, men-only, women-only. Campus housing is university owned and leased by the school. Freshman applicants given priority for college housing. *Activities and organizations:* drama/theater group, student-run newspaper, radio station, choral group, Gamma Beta Phi, Alpha Omicron Pi, Management Honor Society, Baptist Collegiate Ministries, Black Student Union Caucus, national fraternities, national sororities. *Campus security:* 24-hour emergency response devices and patrols, late-night transport/escort service, controlled dormitory access, video cameras, motorist assistance. *Student services:* health clinic, personal/psychological counseling, legal services.

Athletics Member NCAA. All Division I. *Intercollegiate sports:* baseball M(s), basketball M(s)/W(s), cheerleading M/W, cross-country running M(s)/W(s), golf M(s), soccer W(s), softball W(s), tennis M(s)/W(s), track and field M(s)/W(s), volleyball W(s). *Intramural sports:* badminton M/W, basketball M/W, football M/W, racquetball M/W, rugby M(c), soccer M/W, softball M/W, tennis M/W, volleyball M/W, weight lifting M/W.

Standardized Tests *Required:* SAT I or ACT (for admission). *Recommended:* ACT (for admission).

Costs (2003–04) *Tuition:* state resident $2951 full-time, $123 per credit hour part-time; nonresident $8279 full-time, $345 per credit hour part-time. Full-time tuition and fees vary according to course load. Part-time tuition and fees vary according to course load. *Room and board:* $3840; room only: $1900. Room and board charges vary according to board plan and housing facility. *Payment plans:* installment, deferred payment. *Waivers:* senior citizens and employees or children of employees.

Financial Aid Of all full-time matriculated undergraduates who enrolled in 2002, 8,727 applied for aid, 7,888 were judged to have need. 716 Federal Work-Study jobs (averaging $1279). 1,378 state and other part-time jobs (averaging $1229). In 2002, 3605 non-need-based awards were made. *Average financial aid package:* $6033. *Average need-based loan:* $3132. *Average need-based gift aid:* $3011. *Average non-need-based aid:* $2307. *Average indebtedness upon graduation:* $12,527.

Applying *Options:* electronic application, early admission, deferred entrance. *Application fee:* $20. *Required:* high school transcript, proof of immunization. *Required for some:* minimum 2.0 GPA. *Application deadline:* 7/15 (freshmen), rolling (transfers). *Notification:* continuous (freshmen), continuous (transfers).

Admissions Contact Ms. Pat Duplessis, University Admissions Analyst, Southeastern Louisiana University, SLU 10752, North Campus-Basic Studies, Hammond, LA 70402. *Phone:* 985-549-2066. *Toll-free phone:* 800-222-7358. *Fax:* 985-549-5632. *E-mail:* admissions@selu.edu.

SOUTHERN UNIVERSITY AND AGRICULTURAL AND MECHANICAL COLLEGE
Baton Rouge, Louisiana

■ **State-supported** comprehensive, founded 1880, part of Southern University System
■ **Calendar** semesters
■ **Degrees** associate, bachelor's, master's, and doctoral
■ **Suburban** 964-acre campus
■ **Endowment** $3.9 million
■ **Coed,** 7,571 undergraduate students, 92% full-time, 60% women, 40% men
■ **Moderately difficult** entrance level, 57% of applicants were admitted

Undergraduates 6,988 full-time, 583 part-time. Students come from 40 states and territories, 25 other countries, 16% are from out of state, 97% African

Southern University and Agricultural and Mechanical College (continued)
American, 0.4% Asian American or Pacific Islander, 0.1% Hispanic American, 0.8% international, 3% transferred in, 37% live on campus. *Retention:* 72% of 2002 full-time freshmen returned.

Freshmen *Admission:* 4,217 applied, 2,389 admitted, 1,298 enrolled. *Average high school GPA:* 2.83. *Test scores:* SAT verbal scores over 500: 20%; SAT math scores over 500: 20%; ACT scores over 18: 46%; SAT verbal scores over 600: 5%; SAT math scores over 600: 5%; ACT scores over 24: 3%.

Faculty *Total:* 551, 79% full-time, 60% with terminal degrees. *Student/faculty ratio:* 17:1.

Majors Accounting; agricultural economics; animal sciences; animal sciences related; architecture; art; audiology and speech-language pathology; biology/biological sciences; business administration and management; business/managerial economics; chemistry; civil engineering; computer science; criminal justice/police science; criminal justice/safety; dramatic/theatre arts; electrical, electronic and communications engineering technology; electrical, electronics and communications engineering; elementary education; English; finance; French; history; human development and family studies; jazz/jazz studies; kindergarten/preschool education; marketing/marketing management; mass communication/media; mathematics; mechanical engineering; music performance; music teacher education; nursing (registered nurse training); physics; political science and government; psychology; rehabilitation and therapeutic professions related; rehabilitation therapy; secondary education; social work; sociology; Spanish; special education; speech and rhetoric; therapeutic recreation; urban forestry.

Academic Programs *Special study options:* academic remediation for entering students, adult/continuing education programs, advanced placement credit, cooperative education, distance learning, honors programs, internships, off-campus study, part-time degree program, services for LD students, study abroad, summer session for credit. *ROTC:* Army (b), Navy (b), Air Force (c).

Library John B. Cade Library plus 2 others with 807,825 titles, 1,931 serial subscriptions, 42,217 audiovisual materials, an OPAC, a Web page.

Computers on Campus 1300 computers available on campus for general student use. A campuswide network can be accessed from student residence rooms and from off campus. Internet access, online (class) registration, at least one staffed computer lab available.

Student Life *Housing options:* men-only, women-only. Campus housing is university owned. *Activities and organizations:* drama/theater group, student-run newspaper, choral group, marching band, Student Government Association, Pan Hellenic Council, Association for Women Students (AWS), Men's Federation, Honor's Association, national fraternities, national sororities. *Campus security:* 24-hour emergency response devices and patrols, late-night transport/escort service, controlled dormitory access. *Student services:* health clinic, personal/psychological counseling, women's center, legal services.

Athletics Member NCAA. All Division I except men's and women's cheerleading (Division III), football (Division I-AA). *Intercollegiate sports:* baseball M, basketball M(s)/W(s), bowling W(s), cheerleading M/W, cross-country running M(s), golf M(s)/W(s), softball W(s), tennis M(s)/W(s), track and field M(s)/W(s), volleyball W(s). *Intramural sports:* archery M/W, basketball M/W, football M/W, track and field M/W, volleyball M/W, weight lifting M/W.

Standardized Tests *Required:* SAT I or ACT (for admission).

Costs (2003–04) *Tuition:* state resident $3066 full-time; nonresident $8858 full-time. Part-time tuition and fees vary according to course load and location. *Room and board:* $4306. Room and board charges vary according to board plan and housing facility. *Waivers:* children of alumni, senior citizens, and employees or children of employees.

Financial Aid Of all full-time matriculated undergraduates who enrolled in 2002, 6,419 applied for aid, 5,787 were judged to have need, 476 had their need fully met. 900 Federal Work-Study jobs (averaging $1800). 300 state and other part-time jobs (averaging $2500). In 2002, 224 non-need-based awards were made. *Average percent of need met:* 67%. *Average financial aid package:* $7310. *Average need-based loan:* $4600. *Average need-based gift aid:* $3800. *Average non-need-based aid:* $4600. *Average indebtedness upon graduation:* $17,000.

Applying *Options:* common application, early admission. *Application fee:* $5. *Required:* high school transcript, minimum 2.2 GPA. *Application deadlines:* 7/1 (freshmen), 7/1 (transfers). *Notification:* continuous (freshmen), continuous (transfers).

Admissions Contact Ms. Velva Thomas, Director of Admissions, Southern University and Agricultural and Mechanical College, PO Box 9901, Baton Rouge, LA 70813. *Phone:* 225-771-2430. *Toll-free phone:* 800-256-1531. *Fax:* 225-771-2500. *E-mail:* admit@subr.edu.

SOUTHERN UNIVERSITY AT NEW ORLEANS

New Orleans, Louisiana

Admissions Contact Registrar/Director of Admissions, Southern University at New Orleans, 6400 Press Drive, New Orleans, LA 70126-1009. *Phone:* 504-286-5314.

TULANE UNIVERSITY

New Orleans, Louisiana

- **Independent** university, founded 1834
- **Calendar** semesters plus 3 summer sessions
- **Degrees** associate, bachelor's, master's, doctoral, first professional, and postbachelor's certificates
- **Urban** 110-acre campus
- **Endowment** $606.5 million
- **Coed,** 7,862 undergraduate students, 76% full-time, 53% women, 47% men
- **Very difficult** entrance level, 56% of applicants were admitted

Undergraduates 5,989 full-time, 1,873 part-time. 8% African American, 4% Asian American or Pacific Islander, 4% Hispanic American, 0.5% Native American, 3% international, 2% transferred in, 42% live on campus. *Retention:* 86% of 2002 full-time freshmen returned.

Freshmen *Admission:* 13,931 applied, 7,801 admitted, 1,678 enrolled. *Test scores:* SAT verbal scores over 500: 97%; SAT math scores over 500: 98%; SAT verbal scores over 600: 84%; SAT math scores over 600: 79%; SAT verbal scores over 700: 32%; SAT math scores over 700: 25%.

Faculty *Total:* 1,095, 96% full-time, 99% with terminal degrees. *Student/faculty ratio:* 10:1.

Majors Accounting; African studies; American studies; anatomy; anthropology; architecture; art; art history, criticism and conservation; Asian studies; biochemistry; biology/biological sciences; biomedical/medical engineering; biostatistics; business administration and management; business/commerce; cell biology and anatomical sciences related; cell biology and histology; chemical engineering; chemistry; civil engineering; classics and classical languages related; classics and languages, literatures and linguistics; cognitive psychology and psycholinguistics; communication and journalism related; communication/speech communication and rhetoric; computer and information sciences; computer engineering; computer science; corrections; criminal justice/safety; dramatic/theatre arts; ecology; economics; electrical, electronics and communications engineering; engineering science; English; environmental biology; environmental/environmental health engineering; environmental studies; evolutionary biology; finance; fine/studio arts; foreign languages and literatures; French; geology/earth science; German; Hispanic-American, Puerto Rican, and Mexican-American/Chicano studies; history; information science/studies; international relations and affairs; Italian; Jewish/Judaic studies; kinesiology and exercise science; Latin; Latin American studies; legal assistant/paralegal; legal professions and studies related; liberal arts and sciences and humanities related; liberal arts and sciences/liberal studies; linguistics; marketing/marketing management; mass communication/media; mathematics; mathematics and statistics related; mechanical engineering; medieval and Renaissance studies; modern Greek; molecular biology; multi-/interdisciplinary studies related; music; neuroscience; nutrition sciences; philosophy; physics; political science and government; Portuguese; psychology; religious studies; Russian; Russian studies; sociology; Spanish; sport and fitness administration; statistics; women's studies.

Academic Programs *Special study options:* accelerated degree program, adult/continuing education programs, advanced placement credit, cooperative education, double majors, English as a second language, freshman honors college, honors programs, independent study, internships, off-campus study, part-time degree program, services for LD students, student-designed majors, study abroad, summer session for credit. *ROTC:* Army (b), Navy (b), Air Force (b). *Unusual degree programs:* 3-2 public health, tropical medicine.

Library Howard Tilton Memorial Library plus 8 others with 2.3 million titles, 15,308 serial subscriptions, 92,904 audiovisual materials, an OPAC, a Web page.

Computers on Campus 900 computers available on campus for general student use. A campuswide network can be accessed from student residence rooms and from off campus that provide access to wireless access to the Internet. Internet access, online (class) registration, at least one staffed computer lab available. Computer purchase or lease plan available.

Student Life *Housing:* on-campus residence required for freshman year. *Options:* coed, women-only. Campus housing is university owned. Freshman campus housing is guaranteed. *Activities and organizations:* drama/theater group, student-run newspaper, radio and television station, choral group, marching band, Community Action Council, Campus Programming, African-American Congress, club sports, Tsunami, national fraternities, national sororities. *Campus security:* 24-hour emergency response devices and patrols, student patrols, late-night transport/escort service, controlled dormitory access, on and off-campus shuttle service, crime prevention programs, lighted pathways. *Student services:* health clinic, personal/psychological counseling, women's center, legal services.

Athletics Member NCAA. All Division I except football (Division I-A). *Intercollegiate sports:* baseball M(s), basketball M(s)/W(s), crew M(c)/W(c), cross-country running M(s)/W(s), golf M(s)/W(s), gymnastics M(c)/W(c), ice hockey M(c)/W(c), lacrosse M(c)/W(c), rugby M(c), sailing M(c)/W(c), soccer M(c)/W(s), swimming M(c)/W(s), tennis M(s)/W(s), track and field M(c)/W(s), volleyball M(c)/W(s), water polo M(c)/W(c). *Intramural sports:* baseball M(c), cheerleading M(c)/W(c), crew M(c)/W(c), cross-country running M(c), fencing M(c)/W(c), field hockey M(c)/W(c), gymnastics M(c)/W(c), ice hockey M(c), lacrosse M(c)/W(c), racquetball M(c)/W(c), rock climbing M(c)/W(c), rugby M(c), sailing M(c)/W(c), soccer M(c)/W(c), swimming M(c)/W(c), tennis M(c)/W(c), track and field M(c)/W, ultimate Frisbee M(c)/W(c), volleyball M(c)/W(c), water polo M(c)/W(c).

Standardized Tests *Required:* SAT I or ACT (for admission). *Required for some:* SAT II: Subject Tests (for admission). *Recommended:* SAT II: Subject Tests (for admission).

Costs (2003–04) *Comprehensive fee:* $39,761 includes full-time tuition ($29,810), mandatory fees ($2310), and room and board ($7641). Part-time tuition: $1213 per credit hour. *Required fees:* $800 per term part-time. *College room only:* $4541. Room and board charges vary according to board plan and housing facility. *Payment plan:* installment. *Waivers:* employees or children of employees.

Financial Aid Of all full-time matriculated undergraduates who enrolled in 1999, 3,137 applied for aid, 2,528 were judged to have need, 1,736 had their need fully met. In 1999, 1303 non-need-based awards were made. *Average percent of need met:* 94%. *Average financial aid package:* $22,948. *Average need-based loan:* $5217. *Average need-based gift aid:* $16,286. *Average non-need-based aid:* $13,797. *Average indebtedness upon graduation:* $20,040. *Financial aid deadline:* 2/1.

Applying *Options:* common application, electronic application, early admission, early decision, early action, deferred entrance. *Application fee:* $55. *Required:* essay or personal statement, high school transcript, 1 letter of recommendation. *Application deadlines:* 1/15 (freshmen), 6/1 (transfers). *Early decision:* 11/1. *Notification:* continuous until 4/15 (freshmen), 12/15 (early decision), 12/15 (early action), continuous (transfers).

Admissions Contact Mr. Richard Whiteside, Vice President of Enrollment Management, Tulane University, Office of Admissions, 210 Gibson Hall, New Orleans, LA 70118. *Phone:* 504-865-5731. *Toll-free phone:* 800-873-9283. *Fax:* 504-862-8715. *E-mail:* undergrad.admission@tulane.edu.

■ *See page 2536 for a narrative description.*

UNIVERSITY OF LOUISIANA AT LAFAYETTE

Lafayette, Louisiana

- **State-supported** university, founded 1898, part of University of Louisiana System
- **Calendar** semesters
- **Degrees** bachelor's, master's, doctoral, and post-master's certificates
- **Urban** 1375-acre campus
- **Endowment** $72.6 million
- **Coed,** 14,585 undergraduate students, 82% full-time, 57% women, 43% men
- **Moderately difficult** entrance level, 88% of applicants were admitted

Undergraduates 12,025 full-time, 2,560 part-time. Students come from 48 states and territories, 82 other countries, 3% are from out of state, 19% African American, 2% Asian American or Pacific Islander, 1% Hispanic American, 0.5% Native American, 2% international, 5% transferred in, 12% live on campus. *Retention:* 71% of 2002 full-time freshmen returned.

Freshmen *Admission:* 4,431 applied, 3,888 admitted, 2,683 enrolled. *Average high school GPA:* 3.08. *Test scores:* ACT scores over 18: 83%; ACT scores over 24: 22%; ACT scores over 30: 2%.

Faculty *Total:* 698, 78% full-time, 66% with terminal degrees. *Student/faculty ratio:* 23:1.

Majors Accounting; agribusiness; agriculture; animal sciences; anthropology; apparel and textiles related; architecture; architecture related; art; athletic training; audiology and speech-language pathology; biological specializations related; biology/biological sciences; biology teacher education; business administration and management; business/commerce; business/managerial economics; chemical engineering; chemistry; chemistry teacher education; civil engineering; communication/speech communication and rhetoric; computer and information sciences; computer engineering; computer science; computer systems analysis; criminal justice/safety; dental hygiene; dietetics; dramatic/theatre arts; education; education (specific subject areas) related; electrical, electronics and communications engineering; elementary education; engineering; English; fashion/apparel design; fashion merchandising; finance; French; French language teacher education; general studies; geology/earth science; German language teacher education; health information/medical records administration; health professions related; history; horticultural science; hospitality administration related; human development and family studies related; industrial design; industrial technology; insurance; interior architecture; jazz/jazz studies; marketing/marketing management; mass communication/media; mathematics; mechanical engineering; medical microbiology and bacteriology; modern languages; music; music pedagogy; music performance; music related; music teacher education; music theory and composition; natural resources and conservation related; natural resources/conservation; nursing (registered nurse training); petroleum engineering; philosophy; physical education teaching and coaching; physics; physics teacher education; plant sciences; political science and government; pre-law studies; psychology; public relations/image management; science teacher education; secondary education; social studies teacher education; sociology; Spanish; Spanish language teacher education; special education; speech teacher education; visual and performing arts.

Academic Programs *Special study options:* academic remediation for entering students, adult/continuing education programs, advanced placement credit, cooperative education, double majors, honors programs, independent study, internships, part-time degree program, services for LD students, study abroad, summer session for credit. *ROTC:* Army (b).

Library Edith Garland Dupre Library with 925,339 titles, 5,174 serial subscriptions, 8,930 audiovisual materials, an OPAC, a Web page.

Computers on Campus 548 computers available on campus for general student use. A campuswide network can be accessed from off campus. Internet access, online (class) registration, at least one staffed computer lab available.

Student Life *Housing:* on-campus residence required for freshman year. *Options:* men-only, women-only. Campus housing is university owned. Freshman campus housing is guaranteed. *Activities and organizations:* drama/theater group, student-run newspaper, radio station, choral group, marching band, Student Government Association, Resident Hall Association, Newman Club, Union Program Council, Chi Alpha, national fraternities, national sororities. *Campus security:* 24-hour emergency response devices and patrols, late-night transport/escort service. *Student services:* health clinic, personal/psychological counseling, women's center, legal services.

Athletics Member NCAA. All Division I except football (Division I-A). *Intercollegiate sports:* baseball M(s), basketball M(s)/W(s), cross-country running M(s)/W(s), golf M(s), soccer W, softball W(s), tennis M(s)/W(s), track and field M(s)/W(s), volleyball W(s). *Intramural sports:* badminton M(c)/W(c), baseball M, basketball M/W, bowling M(c)/W(c), cross-country running M/W, football M/W, golf M/W, racquetball M/W, rugby M(c)/W(c), sailing M(c)/W(c), soccer M(c)/W(c), softball M/W, swimming M/W, table tennis M/W, tennis M/W, track and field M/W, volleyball M/W, water polo M/W, weight lifting M/W.

Standardized Tests *Required:* SAT I or ACT (for admission).

Costs (2003–04) *Tuition:* state resident $2700 full-time; nonresident $8960 full-time. Part-time tuition and fees vary according to course load. *Room and board:* $3126. Room and board charges vary according to board plan and housing facility. *Payment plan:* deferred payment. *Waivers:* children of alumni, senior citizens, and employees or children of employees.

Financial Aid Of all full-time matriculated undergraduates who enrolled in 2003, 10,589 applied for aid, 7,903 were judged to have need, 5,927 had their need fully met. 775 Federal Work-Study jobs (averaging $1338). 507 state and other part-time jobs (averaging $569). *Average percent of need met:* 88%. *Average financial aid package:* $4500. *Average need-based loan:* $4200. *Average need-based gift aid:* $2200. *Average non-need-based aid:* $2631.

Applying *Options:* early admission, deferred entrance. *Application fee:* $20. *Required:* high school transcript, minimum 2.0 GPA. *Application deadline:* rolling (freshmen), rolling (transfers).

Admissions Contact Mr. Dan Rosenfield, Dean of Enrollment Management, University of Louisiana at Lafayette, PO Drawer 41210, Lafayette, LA 70504. *Phone:* 337-482-6553. *Toll-free phone:* 800-752-6553. *Fax:* 337-482-6195. *E-mail:* dan@louisiana.edu.

■ *See page 2626 for a narrative description.*

UNIVERSITY OF LOUISIANA AT MONROE

Monroe, Louisiana

Admissions Contact Ms. Carlette Browder, Associate Registrar, University of Louisiana at Monroe, Monroe, LA 71209-1115. *Phone:* 318-342-5252. *Toll-free phone:* 800-372-5127. *Fax:* 318-342-5274. *E-mail:* rebrowder@ulm.edu.

UNIVERSITY OF NEW ORLEANS

New Orleans, Louisiana

- **State-supported** university, founded 1958, part of Louisiana State University System
- **Calendar** semesters
- **Degrees** bachelor's, master's, doctoral, and postbachelor's certificates
- **Urban** 345-acre campus
- **Endowment** $12.5 million
- **Coed,** 13,338 undergraduate students, 72% full-time, 56% women, 44% men
- **Moderately difficult** entrance level, 70% of applicants were admitted

Undergraduates 9,598 full-time, 3,740 part-time. Students come from 50 states and territories, 69 other countries, 4% are from out of state, 24% African American, 6% Asian American or Pacific Islander, 7% Hispanic American, 0.4% Native American, 3% international, 9% transferred in, 9% live on campus. *Retention:* 67% of 2002 full-time freshmen returned.

Freshmen *Admission:* 5,467 applied, 3,810 admitted, 2,284 enrolled. *Test scores:* SAT verbal scores over 500: 65%; SAT math scores over 500: 58%; ACT scores over 18: 81%; SAT verbal scores over 600: 30%; SAT math scores over 600: 24%; ACT scores over 24: 22%; SAT verbal scores over 700: 6%; SAT math scores over 700: 5%; ACT scores over 30: 2%.

Faculty *Total:* 598, 82% full-time, 65% with terminal degrees. *Student/faculty ratio:* 26:1.

Majors Accounting; anthropology; art history, criticism and conservation; biology/biological sciences; business administration and management; business/managerial economics; chemistry; civil engineering; clinical laboratory science/medical technology; communication/speech communication and rhetoric; computer science; early childhood education; economics; electrical, electronics and communications engineering; elementary education; engineering science; English; English/language arts teacher education; environmental studies; finance; fine/studio arts; foreign language teacher education; French; general studies; geography; geology/earth science; geophysics and seismology; history; hospitality administration; international/global studies; management information systems; marketing/marketing management; mathematics; mathematics teacher education; mechanical engineering; middle school education; music; music teacher education; naval architecture and marine engineering; philosophy; physical education teaching and coaching; physics; political science and government; psychology; science teacher education; social studies teacher education; sociology; Spanish; urban studies/affairs; women's studies.

Academic Programs *Special study options:* academic remediation for entering students, adult/continuing education programs, advanced placement credit, cooperative education, distance learning, double majors, English as a second language, honors programs, independent study, internships, off-campus study, part-time degree program, services for LD students, student-designed majors, study abroad, summer session for credit. *ROTC:* Army (c), Navy (c), Air Force (c). *Unusual degree programs:* 3-2 engineering with Xavier University of Louisiana, Southern University at New Orleans, Loyola University, New Orleans.

Library Earl K. Long Library with 896,000 titles, 4,950 serial subscriptions, 125,600 audiovisual materials, an OPAC, a Web page.

Computers on Campus 1084 computers available on campus for general student use. A campuswide network can be accessed from student residence rooms and from off campus. Internet access, at least one staffed computer lab available.

Student Life *Housing options:* coed. Campus housing is university owned. *Activities and organizations:* drama/theater group, student-run newspaper, choral group, Student Government Association, Student Government Activities Council, Circle K International, International Student Organization, Progressive Black Student Union, national fraternities, national sororities. *Campus security:* 24-hour emergency response devices and patrols, late-night transport/escort service, controlled dormitory access. *Student services:* health clinic, personal/psychological counseling, women's center, legal services.

Athletics Member NCAA. All Division I. *Intercollegiate sports:* baseball M(s), basketball M(s)/W(s), cross-country running M(s)/W(s), golf M(s)/W(s), tennis M(s)/W(s), track and field M(s)/W(s), volleyball W(s). *Intramural sports:* basketball M/W, bowling M/W, cheerleading M/W, football M/W, racquetball M/W, soccer M/W, softball M/W, table tennis M/W, tennis M/W, volleyball M/W.

Standardized Tests *Required:* SAT I or ACT (for admission).

Costs (2004–05) *Tuition:* state resident $3084 full-time, $488 per course part-time; nonresident $10,128 full-time, $1826 per course part-time. Part-time tuition and fees vary according to course load. *Required fees:* $150 full-time, $5 per semester hour part-time, $10 per term part-time. *Room only:* $4122. Room and board charges vary according to board plan and housing facility. *Payment plan:* deferred payment. *Waivers:* senior citizens and employees or children of employees.

Financial Aid Of all full-time matriculated undergraduates who enrolled in 2003, 5,283 applied for aid, 5,260 were judged to have need, 154 had their need fully met. 283 Federal Work-Study jobs (averaging $1556). 1,352 state and other part-time jobs (averaging $1616). In 2003, 208 non-need-based awards were made. *Average percent of need met:* 70%. *Average financial aid package:* $3269. *Average need-based loan:* $3455. *Average need-based gift aid:* $3132. *Average non-need-based aid:* $1319. *Average indebtedness upon graduation:* $22,000.

Applying *Options:* common application, electronic application, early admission, deferred entrance. *Application fee:* $20. *Required:* high school transcript. *Required for some:* essay or personal statement, minimum 2.0 GPA, 3 letters of recommendation, interview, 2.0 high school GPA on high school core program. *Application deadlines:* rolling (freshmen), 8/28 (transfers). *Notification:* continuous (freshmen), continuous (transfers).

Admissions Contact Ms. Roslyn S. Sheley, Director of Admissions, University of New Orleans, Lake Front, New Orleans, LA 70148. *Phone:* 504-280-7013. *Toll-free phone:* 800-256-5866. *Fax:* 504-280-5522. *E-mail:* admissions@uno.edu.

■ *See page 2672 for a narrative description.*

UNIVERSITY OF PHOENIX–LOUISIANA CAMPUS

Metairie, Louisiana

- **Proprietary** comprehensive, founded 1976
- **Calendar** continuous
- **Degrees** certificates, associate, bachelor's, master's, doctoral, post-master's, and postbachelor's certificates (courses conducted at 121 campuses and learning centers in 25 states)
- **Urban** campus
- **Coed,** 1,408 undergraduate students
- **Noncompetitive** entrance level

Undergraduates 33% African American, 0.8% Asian American or Pacific Islander, 2% Hispanic American, 0.3% Native American, 13% international.

Faculty *Total:* 239, 1% full-time, 27% with terminal degrees. *Student/faculty ratio:* 10:1.

Majors Accounting; business administration and management; computer and information sciences; entrepreneurship; general studies; nursing science; public administration and social service professions related.

Academic Programs *Special study options:* accelerated degree program, adult/continuing education programs, advanced placement credit, distance learning, external degree program, independent study.

Library University Library with 27.1 million titles, 11,648 serial subscriptions, an OPAC, a Web page.

Computers on Campus A campuswide network can be accessed from off campus. Internet access, at least one staffed computer lab available.

Student Life *Housing:* college housing not available.

Costs (2003–04) *Tuition:* $8160 full-time, $272 per credit part-time. *Waivers:* employees or children of employees.

Financial Aid *Average financial aid package:* $1439.

Applying *Options:* deferred entrance. *Application fee:* $100. *Required:* 1 letter of recommendation, 2 years of work experience, 23 years of age. *Required for some:* high school transcript. *Application deadline:* rolling (freshmen), rolling (transfers).

Admissions Contact Ms. Beth Barilla, Director of Admissions, University of Phoenix–Louisiana Campus, 4615 East Elwood Street, Mail Stop AA-K101, Phoenix, AZ 85040-1958. *Phone:* 480-317-6000. *Toll-free phone:* 800-228-7240. *Fax:* 480-594-1758. *E-mail:* beth.barilla@phoenix.edu.

XAVIER UNIVERSITY OF LOUISIANA

New Orleans, Louisiana

- **Independent Roman Catholic** comprehensive, founded 1925
- **Calendar** semesters
- **Degrees** bachelor's, master's, and first professional
- **Urban** 23-acre campus with easy access to New Orleans
- **Endowment** $39.8 million
- **Coed,** 3,145 undergraduate students, 95% full-time, 75% women, 25% men
- **Moderately difficult** entrance level, 84% of applicants were admitted

Undergraduates 3,000 full-time, 145 part-time. Students come from 41 states and territories, 9 other countries, 49% are from out of state, 85% African American, 4% Asian American or Pacific Islander, 0.4% Hispanic American, 0.1% Native American, 2% international, 5% transferred in, 27% live on campus. *Retention:* 73% of 2002 full-time freshmen returned.

Freshmen *Admission:* 4,172 applied, 3,508 admitted, 913 enrolled. *Average high school GPA:* 3.05. *Test scores:* SAT verbal scores over 500: 54%; SAT math scores over 500: 52%; ACT scores over 18: 80%; SAT verbal scores over 600: 12%; SAT math scores over 600: 12%; ACT scores over 24: 21%; SAT math scores over 700: 1%.

Faculty *Total:* 284, 83% full-time, 80% with terminal degrees. *Student/faculty ratio:* 15:1.

Majors Accounting; art; art teacher education; biochemistry; biology/biological sciences; biology teacher education; business administration and management; chemistry; chemistry teacher education; computer and information sciences; computer engineering; computer science; early childhood education; education; elementary education; English; environmental studies; French; French language teacher education; health teacher education; history; history teacher education; marketing/marketing management; mass communication/media; mathematics; medical microbiology and bacteriology; middle school education; music; music performance; music teacher education; philosophy; physical education teaching and coaching; physics; piano and organ; political science and government; pre-dentistry studies; pre-law studies; pre-medical studies; pre-veterinary studies; psychology; science teacher education; secondary education; social studies teacher education; sociology; Spanish; Spanish language teacher education; special education; special education related; speech-language pathology; speech therapy; statistics; theology; violin, viola, guitar and other stringed instruments; wind/percussion instruments.

Academic Programs *Special study options:* academic remediation for entering students, accelerated degree program, adult/continuing education programs, advanced placement credit, cooperative education, double majors, freshman honors college, honors programs, internships, off-campus study, part-time degree program, services for LD students, study abroad, summer session for credit. *ROTC:* Army (c), Navy (c), Air Force (c). *Unusual degree programs:* 3-2 business administration with Tulane University; engineering with Tulane University, University of Maryland, University of New Orleans, Georgia Institute of Technology, University of Wisconsin-Madison, Morgan State University, Southern University and Agricultural and Mechanical College; biostatistics with Louisiana State University Medical Center.

Library Xavier Library plus 1 other with 157,436 titles, 1,868 serial subscriptions, 5,093 audiovisual materials.

Computers on Campus 250 computers available on campus for general student use. A campuswide network can be accessed from student residence rooms and from off campus. At least one staffed computer lab available.

Student Life *Housing options:* coed, men-only, women-only. Campus housing is university owned and leased by the school. *Activities and organizations:* student-run newspaper, television station, choral group, Mobilization at Xavier, AWARE, NAACP, California club, Beta Beta Beta, national fraternities, national sororities. *Campus security:* 24-hour emergency response devices and patrols, student patrols, bicycle patrols. *Student services:* health clinic, personal/psychological counseling.

Athletics Member NAIA. *Intercollegiate sports:* basketball M(s)/W(s), cross-country running M/W, tennis M(s)/W(s). *Intramural sports:* badminton M/W, basketball M/W, football M/W, golf M/W, softball M/W, swimming M/W, table tennis M/W, tennis M/W, track and field M/W, volleyball M/W.

Standardized Tests *Required:* SAT I or ACT (for admission).

Costs (2003–04) *Comprehensive fee:* $17,600 includes full-time tuition ($10,500), mandatory fees ($900), and room and board ($6200). Part-time tuition: $435 per credit hour. *Room and board:* Room and board charges vary according to location. *Payment plan:* installment. *Waivers:* employees or children of employees.

Financial Aid Of all full-time matriculated undergraduates who enrolled in 2003, 2,980 applied for aid, 2,655 were judged to have need, 10 had their need fully met. In 2003, 100 non-need-based awards were made. *Average percent of need met:* 74%. *Average financial aid package:* $4695. *Average need-based loan:* $4400. *Average need-based gift aid:* $3886. *Average non-need-based aid:* $3046. *Average indebtedness upon graduation:* $15,292.

Applying *Options:* common application, early action. *Application fee:* $25. *Required:* high school transcript, minimum 2.0 GPA, 1 letter of recommendation. *Required for some:* interview. *Application deadlines:* 3/1 (freshmen), 6/1 (transfers). *Notification:* 4/15 (freshmen), 2/1 (early action), 7/1 (transfers).

Admissions Contact Mr. Winston Brown, Dean of Admissions, Xavier University of Louisiana, One Drexel Drive, New Orleans, LA 70125. *Phone:* 504-520-7388. *Toll-free phone:* 877-XAVIERU. *Fax:* 504-520-7941. *E-mail:* apply@xula.edu.

MAINE

BATES COLLEGE
Lewiston, Maine

- **Independent** 4-year, founded 1855
- **Calendar** 4-4-1
- **Degree** bachelor's
- **Small-town** 109-acre campus
- **Endowment** $158.6 million
- **Coed,** 1,746 undergraduate students, 100% full-time, 52% women, 48% men
- **Most difficult** entrance level, 31% of applicants were admitted

Undergraduates 1,746 full-time. Students come from 44 states and territories, 68 other countries, 88% are from out of state, 2% African American, 3% Asian American or Pacific Islander, 2% Hispanic American, 0.3% Native American, 6% international, 1% transferred in, 90% live on campus. *Retention:* 93% of 2002 full-time freshmen returned.

Freshmen *Admission:* 4,089 applied, 1,254 admitted, 487 enrolled. *Test scores:* SAT verbal scores over 500: 99%; SAT math scores over 500: 100%; SAT verbal scores over 600: 92%; SAT math scores over 600: 93%; SAT verbal scores over 700: 29%; SAT math scores over 700: 34%.

Faculty *Total:* 183, 89% full-time, 95% with terminal degrees. *Student/faculty ratio:* 10:1.

Majors African-American/Black studies; American studies; anthropology; art; Asian studies (East); biochemistry; biology/biological sciences; chemistry; Chinese; classical, ancient Mediterranean and Near Eastern studies and archaeology; dramatic/theatre arts; economics; engineering; English; environmental studies; French; geology/earth science; German; history; Japanese; mathematics; multi-/interdisciplinary studies related; music; neuroscience; philosophy; physics; political science and government; psychology; religious studies; Russian; sociology; Spanish; speech and rhetoric; women's studies.

Academic Programs *Special study options:* accelerated degree program, advanced placement credit, double majors, honors programs, independent study, internships, off-campus study, services for LD students, student-designed majors, study abroad. *Unusual degree programs:* 3-2 engineering with Columbia University, Rensselaer Polytechnic Institute, Case Western Reserve University, Washington University in St. Louis, Dartmouth College.

Library Ladd Library with 568,750 titles, 2,311 serial subscriptions, 29,196 audiovisual materials, an OPAC, a Web page.

Computers on Campus 1150 computers available on campus for general student use. A campuswide network can be accessed from student residence rooms and from off campus that provide access to course web pages, course evaluation, financial records. Internet access, online (class) registration, at least one staffed computer lab available. Computer purchase or lease plan available.

Student Life *Housing:* on-campus residence required for freshman year. *Options:* coed, men-only, women-only. Campus housing is university owned. Freshman campus housing is guaranteed. *Activities and organizations:* drama/theater group, student-run newspaper, radio and television station, choral group, Representative Assembly, international club, outing club (outdoor recreation), student radio station, The Student (newspaper). *Campus security:* 24-hour emergency response devices and patrols, student patrols, late-night transport/escort service, controlled dormitory access. *Student services:* health clinic, personal/psychological counseling, women's center.

Athletics Member NCAA. All Division III. *Intercollegiate sports:* badminton M(c)/W(c), baseball M, basketball M/W, crew M/W, cross-country running M/W, equestrian sports M(c)/W(c), fencing M(c)/W(c), field hockey W, football M, golf M/W, ice hockey M(c)/W(c), lacrosse M/W, rugby M(c)/W(c), sailing M(c)/W(c), skiing (cross-country) M/W, skiing (downhill) M/W, soccer M/W, softball W, squash M/W, swimming M/W, tennis M/W, track and field M/W, ultimate Frisbee M(c)/W(c), volleyball M(c)/W, water polo M(c)/W(c). *Intramural sports:* badminton M/W, basketball M/W, golf M/W, ice hockey M/W, racquetball M/W, rugby M/W, sailing M/W, soccer M/W, softball M/W, squash M/W, swimming M/W, table tennis M/W, tennis M/W, ultimate Frisbee M/W, volleyball M/W, water polo M/W.

Costs (2004–05) *Comprehensive fee:* $37,500.

Financial Aid Of all full-time matriculated undergraduates who enrolled in 2003, 846 applied for aid, 748 were judged to have need, 661 had their need fully met. 519 Federal Work-Study jobs (averaging $1704). 73 state and other part-time jobs (averaging $1720). *Average percent of need met:* 100%. *Average financial aid package:* $24,457. *Average need-based loan:* $3335. *Average need-based gift aid:* $21,234. *Average indebtedness upon graduation:* $14,401. *Financial aid deadline:* 2/1.

Applying *Options:* common application, electronic application, early admission, early decision, deferred entrance. *Application fee:* $60. *Required:* essay or personal statement, high school transcript, 3 letters of recommendation. *Recommended:* interview. *Application deadlines:* 1/15 (freshmen), 3/1 (transfers). *Early decision:* 11/15 (for plan 1), 1/1 (for plan 2). *Notification:* 4/1 (freshmen), 12/20 (early decision plan 1), 2/15 (early decision plan 2), 4/1 (transfers).

Admissions Contact Mr. Wylie L. Mitchell, Dean of Admissions, Bates College, 23 Campus Avenue, Lewiston, ME 04240-6028. *Phone:* 207-786-6000. *Fax:* 207-786-6025. *E-mail:* admissions@bates.edu.

BOWDOIN COLLEGE
Brunswick, Maine

- **Independent** 4-year, founded 1794
- **Calendar** semesters
- **Degree** bachelor's
- **Small-town** 200-acre campus with easy access to Portland
- **Endowment** $452.4 million
- **Coed,** 1,647 undergraduate students, 100% full-time, 49% women, 51% men
- **Most difficult** entrance level, 24% of applicants were admitted

Undergraduates 1,640 full-time, 7 part-time. Students come from 50 states and territories, 29 other countries, 87% are from out of state, 5% African American, 10% Asian American or Pacific Islander, 5% Hispanic American, 0.8% Native American, 3% international, 0.5% transferred in, 92% live on campus. *Retention:* 93% of 2002 full-time freshmen returned.

Freshmen *Admission:* 4,719 applied, 1,154 admitted, 465 enrolled. *Test scores:* SAT verbal scores over 500: 99%; SAT math scores over 500: 99%; SAT verbal scores over 600: 92%; SAT math scores over 600: 91%; SAT verbal scores over 700: 47%; SAT math scores over 700: 40%.

Faculty *Total:* 179, 86% full-time, 92% with terminal degrees. *Student/faculty ratio:* 10:1.

Majors African-American/Black studies; African studies; anthropology; archeology; art; art history, criticism and conservation; Asian studies; biochemistry; biology/biological sciences; chemical physics; chemistry; classics and languages, literatures and linguistics; computer science; dramatic/theatre arts and stagecraft related; economics; English; environmental studies; European studies (Central and Eastern); fine/studio arts; French; geochemistry; geology/earth science; geophysics and seismology; German; history; interdisciplinary studies; Latin American studies; mathematics; mathematics and computer science; mathematics related; music; neuroscience; philosophy; physics; political science and government; pre-medical studies; psychology; religious studies; Romance languages; Russian; sociology; Spanish; women's studies.

Academic Programs *Special study options:* accelerated degree program, advanced placement credit, double majors, independent study, off-campus study, services for LD students, student-designed majors, study abroad. *Unusual degree programs:* 3-2 engineering with California Institute of Technology, Columbia University; law with Columbia University.

Library Hawthorne-Longfellow Library plus 6 others with 948,879 titles, 1,983 serial subscriptions, 20,214 audiovisual materials, an OPAC, a Web page.

Computers on Campus 310 computers available on campus for general student use. A campuswide network can be accessed from student residence rooms and from off campus. Internet access, at least one staffed computer lab available. Computer purchase or lease plan available.

Student Life *Housing:* on-campus residence required through sophomore year. *Options:* coed, disabled students. Campus housing is university owned. Freshman campus housing is guaranteed. *Activities and organizations:* drama/theater group, student-run newspaper, radio and television station, choral group, outing club, men's and women's rugby, volunteer programs, ballroom dance club, Campus Activities Board. *Campus security:* 24-hour emergency response devices and patrols, student patrols, late-night transport/escort service, controlled dormitory access, self-defense education, whistle program. *Student services:* health clinic, personal/psychological counseling, women's center.

Athletics Member NCAA. All Division III except men's and women's skiing (cross-country) (Division I). *Intercollegiate sports:* baseball M, basketball M/W, crew M(c)/W(c), cross-country running M/W, field hockey W, football M, golf M/W, ice hockey M/W, lacrosse M/W, rugby M(c)/W(c), sailing M/W, skiing (cross-country) M/W, soccer M/W, softball W, squash M/W, swimming M/W, tennis M/W, track and field M/W, ultimate Frisbee M(c)/W(c), volleyball W, water polo M(c)/W(c). *Intramural sports:* basketball M/W, cross-country running M/W, equestrian sports M(c)/W(c), field hockey M/W, football M, ice hockey M(c)/W(c), rock climbing M(c)/W(c), sailing M/W, skiing (cross-country) M(c)/W(c), skiing (downhill) M(c)/W(c), soccer M/W, softball M/W, squash M/W, tennis M/W, volleyball M(c)/W(c), water polo M/W.

Costs (2003–04) *Comprehensive fee:* $37,790 includes full-time tuition ($29,470), mandatory fees ($650), and room and board ($7670). *College room only:* $3450. Room and board charges vary according to board plan. *Payment plans:* installment, deferred payment. *Waivers:* employees or children of employees.

Financial Aid Of all full-time matriculated undergraduates who enrolled in 2003, 880 applied for aid, 736 were judged to have need, 736 had their need fully met. 385 Federal Work-Study jobs (averaging $1400). 192 state and other part-time jobs (averaging $1285). In 2003, 20 non-need-based awards were made. *Average percent of need met:* 100%. *Average financial aid package:* $26,003. *Average need-based loan:* $3544. *Average need-based gift aid:* $22,086. *Average non-need-based aid:* $1000. *Average indebtedness upon graduation:* $14,830. *Financial aid deadline:* 2/15.

Applying *Options:* common application, electronic application, early decision, deferred entrance. *Application fee:* $60. *Required:* essay or personal statement, high school transcript, 3 letters of recommendation. *Recommended:* interview. *Application deadlines:* 1/1 (freshmen), 3/1 (transfers). *Early decision:* 11/15 (for plan 1), 1/1 (for plan 2). *Notification:* 4/5 (freshmen), 12/31 (early decision plan 1), 2/15 (early decision plan 2), 4/1 (transfers).

Admissions Contact Mr. Scott Steinberg, Director of Admissions Operations, Bowdoin College, 5000 College Station, Brunswick, ME 04011-8441. *Phone:* 207-725-3197. *Fax:* 207-725-3101. *E-mail:* admissions@bowdoin.edu.

■ *See page 1276 for a narrative description.*

COLBY COLLEGE
Waterville, Maine

- **Independent** 4-year, founded 1813
- **Calendar** 4-1-4
- **Degree** bachelor's
- **Small-town** 714-acre campus
- **Endowment** $321.6 million
- **Coed,** 1,768 undergraduate students, 100% full-time, 54% women, 46% men
- **Most difficult** entrance level, 34% of applicants were admitted

Undergraduates 1,768 full-time. Students come from 48 states and territories, 69 other countries, 87% are from out of state, 2% African American, 5% Asian American or Pacific Islander, 3% Hispanic American, 0.3% Native American, 7% international, 0.4% transferred in, 94% live on campus. *Retention:* 93% of 2002 full-time freshmen returned.

Freshmen *Admission:* 4,126 applied, 1,388 admitted, 474 enrolled. *Test scores:* SAT verbal scores over 500: 98%; SAT math scores over 500: 99%; ACT scores over 18: 100%; SAT verbal scores over 600: 88%; SAT math scores over 600: 89%; ACT scores over 24: 96%; SAT verbal scores over 700: 34%; SAT math scores over 700: 37%; ACT scores over 30: 36%.

Faculty *Total:* 202, 78% full-time, 91% with terminal degrees. *Student/faculty ratio:* 10:1.

Majors African-American/Black studies; American studies; anthropology; area studies related; art; art history, criticism and conservation; Asian studies (East); biochemistry; biology/biological sciences; cell biology and histology; chemistry; classics and languages, literatures and linguistics; computer science; creative writing; dramatic/theatre arts; economics; English; environmental science; environmental studies; fine/studio arts; foreign languages related; French; geology/earth science; German; history; international relations and affairs; Latin American studies; mathematics; molecular biology; multi-/interdisciplinary studies related; music; neuroscience; philosophy; physics; political science and government; psychology; religious studies; Russian studies; science, technology and society; sociology; Spanish; women's studies.

Academic Programs *Special study options:* advanced placement credit, double majors, honors programs, independent study, internships, off-campus study, part-time degree program, services for LD students, student-designed majors, study abroad. *ROTC:* Army (c). *Unusual degree programs:* 3-2 engineering with Dartmouth College.

Library Miller Library plus 2 others with 350,000 titles, 1,850 serial subscriptions, 20,645 audiovisual materials, an OPAC, a Web page.

Computers on Campus 300 computers available on campus for general student use. A campuswide network can be accessed from student residence rooms and from off campus. Internet access, online (class) registration, at least one staffed computer lab available.

Student Life *Housing:* on-campus residence required through senior year. *Options:* coed. Campus housing is university owned. Freshman campus housing is guaranteed. *Activities and organizations:* drama/theater group, student-run newspaper, radio station, choral group, outing club, volunteer center, WMHB-FM (College Radio Station), student government, Powder and Wig (theater). *Campus security:* 24-hour emergency response devices and patrols, late-night transport/escort service, controlled dormitory access, campus lighting, student emergency response team, self-defense class, property id program, party monitors. *Student services:* health clinic, personal/psychological counseling, women's center.

Athletics Member NCAA. All Division III except men's and women's skiing (cross-country) (Division I), men's and women's skiing (downhill) (Division I). *Intercollegiate sports:* badminton M(c)/W(c), baseball M, basketball M/W, cheerleading M/W, crew M/W, cross-country running M/W, equestrian sports M(c)/W(c), fencing M(c)/W(c), field hockey W, football M, golf M/W, ice hockey M/W, lacrosse M/W, rugby M(c)/W(c), sailing M(c)/W(c), skiing (cross-country) M/W, skiing (downhill) M/W, soccer M/W, softball W, squash M/W, swimming M/W, tennis M/W, track and field M/W, ultimate Frisbee M(c)/W(c), volleyball M(c)/W, water polo M(c)/W(c). *Intramural sports:* basketball M/W, football M/W, rock climbing M/W, soccer M/W, softball M/W.

Standardized Tests *Required:* SAT I or ACT (for admission).

Costs (2004–05) *Comprehensive fee:* $37,570.

Financial Aid Of all full-time matriculated undergraduates who enrolled in 2003, 807 applied for aid, 705 were judged to have need, 705 had their need fully met. 463 Federal Work-Study jobs (averaging $1483). 54 state and other part-time jobs (averaging $1492). *Average percent of need met:* 100%. *Average financial aid package:* $24,111. *Average need-based loan:* $2991. *Average need-based gift aid:* $22,766. *Average indebtedness upon graduation:* $17,809. *Financial aid deadline:* 2/1.

Applying *Options:* common application, electronic application, early admission, early decision, deferred entrance. *Application fee:* $55. *Required:* essay or personal statement, high school transcript, 2 letters of recommendation. *Recommended:* interview. *Application deadlines:* 1/1 (freshmen), 3/1 (transfers). *Early decision:* 11/15 (for plan 1), 1/1 (for plan 2). *Notification:* 4/1 (freshmen), 12/15 (early decision plan 1), 2/1 (early decision plan 2), 5/15 (transfers).

Admissions Contact Mr. Steve Thomas, Director of Admissions, Colby College, Office of Admissions and Financial Aid, 4800 Mayflower Hill, Waterville, ME 04901-8848. *Phone:* 207-872-3471. *Toll-free phone:* 800-723-3032. *Fax:* 207-872-3474. *E-mail:* admissions@colby.edu.

■ See page 1426 for a narrative description.

COLLEGE OF THE ATLANTIC
Bar Harbor, Maine

- **Independent** comprehensive, founded 1969
- **Calendar** 3 10-week terms
- **Degrees** bachelor's and master's
- **Small-town** 35-acre campus
- **Endowment** $8.6 million
- **Coed,** 250 undergraduate students, 92% full-time, 54% women, 46% men
- **Very difficult** entrance level, 69% of applicants were admitted

Undergraduates 229 full-time, 21 part-time. Students come from 37 states and territories, 32 other countries, 63% are from out of state, 0.8% African American, 0.8% Asian American or Pacific Islander, 0.8% Hispanic American, 17% international, 8% transferred in, 40% live on campus. *Retention:* 91% of 2002 full-time freshmen returned.

Freshmen *Admission:* 270 applied, 186 admitted, 67 enrolled. *Average high school GPA:* 3.4. *Test scores:* SAT verbal scores over 500: 95%; SAT math scores over 500: 85%; ACT scores over 18: 100%; SAT verbal scores over 600: 64%; SAT math scores over 600: 48%; ACT scores over 24: 100%; SAT verbal scores over 700: 13%; ACT scores over 30: 25%.

Faculty *Total:* 28, 64% full-time. *Student/faculty ratio:* 10:1.

Majors Art; biological and physical sciences; biology/biological sciences; botany/plant biology; ceramic arts and ceramics; computer graphics; drawing; ecology; economics; education; elementary education; English; environmental biology; environmental design/architecture; environmental education; environmental studies; evolutionary biology; human ecology; interdisciplinary studies; landscape architecture; legal studies; liberal arts and sciences/liberal studies; literature; marine biology and biological oceanography; maritime science; middle school education; museum studies; music; natural sciences; philosophy; preveterinary studies; psychology; public policy analysis; science teacher education; secondary education; wildlife biology; zoology/animal biology.

Academic Programs *Special study options:* academic remediation for entering students, accelerated degree program, advanced placement credit, cooperative education, independent study, internships, off-campus study, part-time degree program, services for LD students, student-designed majors, study abroad.

Library Thorndike Library with 37,049 titles, 469 serial subscriptions, 2,162 audiovisual materials, an OPAC, a Web page.

Computers on Campus 48 computers available on campus for general student use. A campuswide network can be accessed from student residence rooms and from off campus. Internet access, at least one staffed computer lab available. Computer purchase or lease plan available.

Student Life *Housing options:* coed. Campus housing is university owned. Freshman campus housing is guaranteed. *Activities and organizations:* drama/theater group, student-run newspaper, choral group, outing club, Environmental Awareness Club, Students for a Free Tibet, All-Campus Meeting, choral group. *Campus security:* 24-hour emergency response devices and patrols, late-night transport/escort service. *Student services:* health clinic, personal/psychological counseling, women's center.

Athletics *Intercollegiate sports:* soccer M(c)/W(c). *Intramural sports:* basketball M, bowling M/W, sailing M/W, skiing (cross-country) M/W, volleyball M/W, water polo M/W.

Standardized Tests *Recommended:* SAT I and SAT II or ACT (for admission).

Costs (2003–04) *Comprehensive fee:* $30,504 includes full-time tuition ($23,601), mandatory fees ($360), and room and board ($6543). Part-time tuition: $7867 per term. *Required fees:* $120 per term part-time. *College room only:* $4116. Room and board charges vary according to board plan. *Payment plan:* installment. *Waivers:* adult students, senior citizens, and employees or children of employees.

Financial Aid Of all full-time matriculated undergraduates who enrolled in 2003, 240 applied for aid, 235 were judged to have need, 175 had their need fully met. 147 Federal Work-Study jobs (averaging $2094). 49 state and other part-time jobs (averaging $1200). In 2003, 4 non-need-based awards were made. *Average percent of need met:* 85%. *Average financial aid package:* $21,823. *Average need-based loan:* $4077. *Average need-based gift aid:* $18,900. *Average non-need-based aid:* $2250. *Average indebtedness upon graduation:* $13,882.

Applying *Options:* common application, electronic application, early admission, early decision, deferred entrance. *Application fee:* $45. *Required:* essay or personal statement, high school transcript, 3 letters of recommendation. *Required for some:* interview. *Recommended:* minimum 3.0 GPA, interview. *Application deadlines:* 2/15 (freshmen), 4/1 (transfers). *Early decision:* 12/1 (for plan 1), 1/10 (for plan 2). *Notification:* 4/1 (freshmen), 12/15 (early decision plan 1), 1/25 (early decision plan 2), 4/25 (transfers).

Admissions Contact Ms. Sarah G. Baker, Director of Admission, College of the Atlantic, 105 Eden Street, Bar Harbor, ME 04609-1198. *Phone:* 207-288-5015 Ext. 233. *Toll-free phone:* 800-528-0025. *Fax:* 207-288-4126. *E-mail:* inquiry@ecology.coa.edu.

■ See page 1460 for a narrative description.

HUSSON COLLEGE
Bangor, Maine

- **Independent** comprehensive, founded 1898
- **Calendar** semesters
- **Degrees** associate, bachelor's, master's, post-master's, and postbachelor's certificates
- **Suburban** 170-acre campus
- **Endowment** $3.0 million
- **Coed,** 1,767 undergraduate students, 64% full-time, 60% women, 40% men
- **Moderately difficult** entrance level, 97% of applicants were admitted

Undergraduates 1,133 full-time, 634 part-time. Students come from 35 states and territories, 12 other countries, 15% are from out of state, 2% African American, 1% Asian American or Pacific Islander, 0.5% Hispanic American, 0.3% Native American, 3% international, 6% transferred in, 51% live on campus. *Retention:* 66% of 2002 full-time freshmen returned.

Freshmen *Admission:* 656 applied, 639 admitted, 305 enrolled. *Average high school GPA:* 3.12. *Test scores:* SAT verbal scores over 500: 32%; SAT math scores over 500: 34%; ACT scores over 18: 75%; SAT verbal scores over 600: 4%; SAT math scores over 600: 7%; ACT scores over 24: 42%; SAT math scores over 700: 1%; ACT scores over 30: 25%.

Faculty *Total:* 110, 45% full-time, 52% with terminal degrees. *Student/faculty ratio:* 19:1.

Majors Accounting; accounting and computer science; banking and financial support services; biology/biological sciences; biology teacher education; business administration and management; clinical psychology; computer programming; computer programming (specific applications); criminal justice/police science; criminal justice/safety; criminology; elementary education; finance; hospitality administration; information science/studies; international business/trade/commerce; legal assistant/paralegal; liberal arts and sciences/liberal studies; management information systems; marketing/marketing management; nursing (registered nurse training); occupational therapy; physical education teaching and coaching; physical therapy; sales, distribution and marketing; small business administration; sport and fitness administration.

Academic Programs *Special study options:* academic remediation for entering students, adult/continuing education programs, advanced placement credit, cooperative education, distance learning, double majors, English as a second language, independent study, internships, part-time degree program, services for LD students, student-designed majors, summer session for credit. *ROTC:* Army (c), Navy (c).

Library Husson College Library with 36,294 titles, 500 serial subscriptions, 220 audiovisual materials, an OPAC, a Web page.

Computers on Campus 110 computers available on campus for general student use. A campuswide network can be accessed from student residence rooms. Internet access, at least one staffed computer lab available.

Student Life *Housing:* on-campus residence required through senior year. *Options:* coed. Campus housing is university owned. Freshman campus housing is guaranteed. *Activities and organizations:* drama/theater group, student-run newspaper, radio station, student government, Organization of Student Nurses, Organization of Physical Therapy Students, Accounting Society, Phi Beta Lambda, national fraternities. *Campus security:* 24-hour emergency response devices and patrols. *Student services:* health clinic, personal/psychological counseling.

Husson College (continued)

Athletics Member NCAA. All Division III. *Intercollegiate sports:* baseball M, basketball M/W, cross-country running M/W, field hockey W, football M, golf M/W, soccer M/W, softball W, volleyball W. *Intramural sports:* baseball M, basketball M/W, cheerleading M/W, football M, ice hockey M/W, lacrosse M, soccer M/W, softball M/W, swimming M/W, tennis M/W, volleyball M/W, water polo M/W, wrestling M.

Standardized Tests *Required:* SAT I or ACT (for admission).

Costs (2003–04) *Comprehensive fee:* $16,380 includes full-time tuition ($10,470), mandatory fees ($230), and room and board ($5680). Full-time tuition and fees vary according to class time. Part-time tuition: $349 per credit hour. Part-time tuition and fees vary according to class time and course load. *Payment plans:* tuition prepayment, installment. *Waivers:* senior citizens and employees or children of employees.

Financial Aid Of all full-time matriculated undergraduates who enrolled in 2003, 1,362 applied for aid, 1,140 were judged to have need, 273 had their need fully met. 412 Federal Work-Study jobs (averaging $1256). In 2003, 298 non-need-based awards were made. *Average percent of need met:* 75%. *Average financial aid package:* $8287. *Average need-based loan:* $3143. *Average need-based gift aid:* $5799. *Average non-need-based aid:* $5291. *Average indebtedness upon graduation:* $17,125.

Applying *Options:* common application, electronic application, early admission, early action, deferred entrance. *Application fee:* $25. *Required:* essay or personal statement, high school transcript, 1 letter of recommendation. *Recommended:* interview. *Application deadlines:* 9/1 (freshmen), 9/1 (transfers). *Notification:* continuous (freshmen), 1/2 (early action), continuous until 9/1 (transfers).

Admissions Contact Mrs. Jane Goodwin, Director of Admissions, Husson College, One College Circle, Bangor, ME 04401-2999. *Phone:* 207-941-7100. *Toll-free phone:* 800-4-HUSSON. *Fax:* 207-941-7935. *E-mail:* admit@husson.edu.

■ *See page 1756 for a narrative description.*

MAINE COLLEGE OF ART
Portland, Maine

- **Independent** comprehensive, founded 1882
- **Calendar** semesters
- **Degrees** bachelor's and master's
- **Urban** campus with easy access to Boston
- **Endowment** $2.6 million
- **Coed,** 384 undergraduate students, 89% full-time, 63% women, 37% men
- **Moderately difficult** entrance level, 87% of applicants were admitted

Undergraduates 342 full-time, 42 part-time. Students come from 29 states and territories, 6 other countries, 35% are from out of state, 0.3% African American, 1% Asian American or Pacific Islander, 2% Hispanic American, 0.5% Native American, 0.8% international, 12% transferred in, 25% live on campus. *Retention:* 69% of 2002 full-time freshmen returned.

Freshmen *Admission:* 368 applied, 319 admitted, 94 enrolled. *Average high school GPA:* 3.16. *Test scores:* SAT verbal scores over 500: 71%; SAT math scores over 500: 51%; ACT scores over 18: 67%; SAT verbal scores over 600: 26%; SAT math scores over 600: 15%; ACT scores over 24: 17%; SAT verbal scores over 700: 4%; SAT math scores over 700: 1%.

Faculty *Total:* 57, 40% full-time, 77% with terminal degrees. *Student/faculty ratio:* 10:1.

Majors Ceramic arts and ceramics; graphic design; intermedia/multimedia; metal and jewelry arts; painting; photography; printmaking; sculpture; visual and performing arts related.

Academic Programs *Special study options:* adult/continuing education programs, cooperative education, double majors, independent study, internships, off-campus study, part-time degree program, services for LD students, student-designed majors, study abroad.

Library Joanne Waxman Library at the Maine College of Art with 20,797 titles, 100 serial subscriptions, 182 audiovisual materials, an OPAC, a Web page.

Computers on Campus 52 computers available on campus for general student use. A campuswide network can be accessed. Internet access, at least one staffed computer lab available.

Student Life *Housing options:* coed. Campus housing is university owned and is provided by a third party. Freshman applicants given priority for college housing. *Activities and organizations:* student-run newspaper, Student Representative Association, outdoor group, The Canvas—student newspaper, ski and snowboard club, movie club. *Campus security:* 24-hour emergency response devices and patrols, controlled dormitory access. *Student services:* health clinic, personal/psychological counseling.

Standardized Tests *Required:* SAT I or ACT (for admission).

Costs (2003–04) *Comprehensive fee:* $29,590 includes full-time tuition ($20,614), mandatory fees ($518), and room and board ($8458). Full-time tuition and fees vary according to course load. Part-time tuition: $859 per credit hour. Part-time tuition and fees vary according to course load. *College room only:* $5508. Room and board charges vary according to board plan and housing facility. *Payment plan:* installment. *Waivers:* employees or children of employees.

Financial Aid Of all full-time matriculated undergraduates who enrolled in 2003, 357 applied for aid, 325 were judged to have need, 38 had their need fully met. 75 Federal Work-Study jobs (averaging $1773). In 2003, 78 non-need-based awards were made. *Average percent of need met:* 58%. *Average financial aid package:* $12,591. *Average need-based loan:* $3935. *Average need-based gift aid:* $8691. *Average non-need-based aid:* $8422. *Average indebtedness upon graduation:* $21,429.

Applying *Options:* common application, electronic application, early admission, deferred entrance. *Application fee:* $40. *Required:* essay or personal statement, high school transcript, 2 letters of recommendation, portfolio. *Recommended:* minimum 2.0 GPA, interview. *Application deadline:* rolling (freshmen), rolling (transfers). *Notification:* continuous until 8/31 (freshmen), continuous until 8/31 (transfers).

Admissions Contact Ms. Kathryn Quin-Easter, Admissions Coordinator, Maine College of Art, 97 Spring Street, Portland, ME 04101-3987. *Phone:* 207-775-5157 Ext. 226. *Toll-free phone:* 800-639-4808. *Fax:* 207-772-5069. *E-mail:* admissions@meca.edu.

■ *See page 1910 for a narrative description.*

MAINE MARITIME ACADEMY
Castine, Maine

- **State-supported** comprehensive, founded 1941
- **Calendar** semesters
- **Degrees** associate, bachelor's, and master's
- **Small-town** 35-acre campus
- **Endowment** $16.0 million
- **Coed, primarily men,** 846 undergraduate students, 88% full-time, 16% women, 84% men
- **Moderately difficult** entrance level, 68% of applicants were admitted

Maine Maritime, a public college of 750 students, is a world leader in maritime engineering, transportation, and sciences featuring a safe, beautiful coastal campus, numerous labs/vessels, an active waterfront, ten majors, hands-on application of classroom instruction, required co-ops/cruises with worldwide travel, intercollegiate athletics, Navy ROTC, outstanding job placement, and great starting salaries. Web site: http://www.mainemaritime.edu.

Undergraduates 747 full-time, 99 part-time. Students come from 37 states and territories, 8 other countries, 48% are from out of state, 0.3% African American, 0.3% Asian American or Pacific Islander, 0.7% Hispanic American, 0.7% Native American, 4% international, 0.4% transferred in, 80% live on campus. *Retention:* 80% of 2002 full-time freshmen returned.

Freshmen *Admission:* 659 applied, 449 admitted, 241 enrolled. *Average high school GPA:* 2.8.

Faculty *Total:* 74, 78% full-time, 51% with terminal degrees. *Student/faculty ratio:* 12:1.

Majors Business administration and management; engineering; engineering technology; international business/trade/commerce; logistics and materials management; marine biology and biological oceanography; marine science/merchant marine officer; maritime science; naval architecture and marine engineering; oceanography (chemical and physical); systems engineering; transportation technology.

Academic Programs *Special study options:* academic remediation for entering students, adult/continuing education programs, advanced placement credit, distance learning, internships. *ROTC:* Navy (b).

Library Nutting Memorial Library with 68,200 titles, 453 serial subscriptions, an OPAC, a Web page.

Computers on Campus 40 computers available on campus for general student use. A campuswide network can be accessed from student residence rooms. Internet access, online (class) registration, at least one staffed computer lab available.

Student Life *Housing:* on-campus residence required through junior year. *Options:* coed. Campus housing is university owned. Freshman campus housing is guaranteed. *Activities and organizations:* drama/theater group, choral group, Alpha Phi Omega, yacht club, outing club, Social Council, drill team. *Campus security:* 24-hour patrols, student patrols. *Student services:* health clinic, personal/psychological counseling, women's center.

Athletics Member NCAA. All Division III. *Intercollegiate sports:* basketball M/W, cross-country running M/W, football M, lacrosse M, sailing M/W, soccer M/W, softball W, volleyball W. *Intramural sports:* basketball M/W, golf M/W, ice hockey M, racquetball M/W, riflery M/W, rugby M, sailing M/W, skiing (downhill) M/W, softball M/W, squash M/W, swimming M/W, tennis M/W, volleyball M, weight lifting M/W.

Standardized Tests *Required:* SAT I or ACT (for admission).

Costs (2003–04) *Tuition:* state resident $5700 full-time, $190 per credit part-time; nonresident $10,750 full-time, $355 per credit part-time. *Required fees:* $860 full-time. *Room and board:* $5820; room only: $2020. *Payment plan:* installment.

Financial Aid Of all full-time matriculated undergraduates who enrolled in 2002, 534 applied for aid, 451 were judged to have need, 78 had their need fully met. 171 Federal Work-Study jobs (averaging $969). In 2002, 81 non-need-based awards were made. *Average percent of need met:* 77%. *Average financial aid package:* $8257. *Average need-based loan:* $4473. *Average need-based gift aid:* $4535. *Average non-need-based aid:* $7613. *Average indebtedness upon graduation:* $24,856.

Applying *Options:* electronic application, early admission, early decision, deferred entrance. *Application fee:* $15. *Required:* high school transcript, 1 letter of recommendation, physical examination. *Recommended:* interview. *Application deadlines:* 7/1 (freshmen), 7/1 (transfers). *Early decision:* 12/20. *Notification:* 1/1 (early decision).

Admissions Contact Mr. Jeffrey C. Wright, Director of Admissions, Maine Maritime Academy, Castine, ME 04420. *Phone:* 207-326-2215. *Toll-free phone:* 800-464-6565 (in-state); 800-227-8465 (out-of-state). *Fax:* 207-326-2515. *E-mail:* admissions@mma.edu.

NEW ENGLAND SCHOOL OF COMMUNICATIONS

Bangor, Maine

- **Independent** 4-year, founded 1981
- **Calendar** semesters
- **Degrees** certificates, associate, and bachelor's
- **Small-town** 200-acre campus
- **Coed,** 222 undergraduate students, 98% full-time, 27% women, 73% men
- **Minimally difficult** entrance level, 32% of applicants were admitted

Undergraduates 218 full-time, 4 part-time. Students come from 9 states and territories, 16% are from out of state, 1% African American, 1% Hispanic American, 0.5% Native American, 6% transferred in, 54% live on campus.

Freshmen *Admission:* 362 applied, 115 admitted, 94 enrolled. *Average high school GPA:* 2.70.

Faculty *Total:* 32, 22% full-time, 75% with terminal degrees. *Student/faculty ratio:* 18:1.

Majors Advertising; animation, interactive technology, video graphics and special effects; audio engineering; broadcast journalism; cinematography and film/video production; communication and journalism related; communications technologies and support services related; computer graphics; computer software and media applications related; film/video and photographic arts related; graphic communications; intermedia/multimedia; marketing/marketing management; photographic and film/video technology; public relations/image management; radio and television; radio and television broadcasting technology; recording arts technology; web/multimedia management and webmaster; web page, digital/multimedia and information resources design.

Academic Programs *Special study options:* adult/continuing education programs, advanced placement credit, double majors, English as a second language, independent study, internships, part-time degree program, services for LD students, student-designed majors, summer session for credit.

Library Husson College Library plus 1 other with a Web page.

Computers on Campus 150 computers available on campus for general student use. A campuswide network can be accessed from student residence rooms and from off campus. Internet access, at least one staffed computer lab available. Computer purchase or lease plan available.

Student Life *Housing options:* coed. Campus housing is university owned. Freshman applicants given priority for college housing. *Activities and organizations:* drama/theater group, student-run newspaper, radio and television station, choral group, marching band, drama, Greek organizations, newspaper, student government, radio station, national fraternities, national sororities. *Campus security:* 24-hour emergency response devices and patrols, late-night transport/escort service. *Student services:* health clinic, personal/psychological counseling.

Athletics *Intramural sports:* basketball M/W, lacrosse M/W, soccer M/W, softball M/W, swimming M/W, table tennis M/W, tennis M/W, volleyball M/W.

Standardized Tests *Required:* Wonderlic aptitude test (for admission). *Recommended:* SAT I or ACT (for admission).

Costs (2004–05) *Comprehensive fee:* $15,245 includes full-time tuition ($8290), mandatory fees ($1105), and room and board ($5850). Part-time tuition: $275 per credit. Part-time tuition and fees vary according to course load. *Payment plan:* installment. *Waivers:* employees or children of employees.

Financial Aid Of all full-time matriculated undergraduates who enrolled in 2003, 148 applied for aid, 148 were judged to have need, 72 had their need fully met. 2 state and other part-time jobs (averaging $1000). *Average percent of need met:* 92%. *Average financial aid package:* $6320. *Average need-based loan:* $3100. *Average need-based gift aid:* $6000. *Average indebtedness upon graduation:* $12,000.

Applying *Options:* electronic application, early admission, deferred entrance. *Application fee:* $15. *Required:* essay or personal statement, high school transcript, 2 letters of recommendation, interview, Wonderlic Scholastic Test. *Application deadline:* rolling (freshmen), rolling (transfers). *Notification:* continuous (freshmen), continuous (transfers).

Admissions Contact Ms. Louise G. Grant, Director of Admissions, New England School of Communications, 1 College Circle, Bangor, ME 04401. *Phone:* 207-941-7176 Ext. 1093. *Toll-free phone:* 888-877-1876. *Fax:* 207-947-3987. *E-mail:* info@nescom.edu.

SAINT JOSEPH'S COLLEGE OF MAINE

Standish, Maine

- **Independent** comprehensive, founded 1912, affiliated with Roman Catholic Church
- **Calendar** semesters
- **Degrees** associate, bachelor's, and master's (profile does not include enrollment in distance learning master's program)
- **Small-town** 330-acre campus
- **Endowment** $3.3 million
- **Coed,** 953 undergraduate students, 97% full-time, 66% women, 34% men
- **Moderately difficult** entrance level, 79% of applicants were admitted

Saint Joseph's College of Maine offers academic excellence in a magnificent setting. Founded in 1912 and sponsored by the Sisters of Mercy, the College's mission focuses on the intellectual, spiritual, and social growth of its students within a values-centered environment. A new four-story academic center with sweeping views of Sebago Lake opens in fall 2004.

Undergraduates 929 full-time, 24 part-time. Students come from 16 states and territories, 3 other countries, 35% are from out of state, 4% transferred in, 85% live on campus. *Retention:* 78% of 2002 full-time freshmen returned.

Freshmen *Admission:* 962 applied, 763 admitted, 247 enrolled. *Average high school GPA:* 3.10. *Test scores:* SAT verbal scores over 500: 51%; SAT math scores over 500: 47%; SAT verbal scores over 600: 13%; SAT math scores over 600: 11%; SAT verbal scores over 700: 1%.

Faculty *Total:* 115, 56% full-time, 83% with terminal degrees. *Student/faculty ratio:* 13:1.

Majors Accounting; adult and continuing education administration; advertising; American history; banking and financial support services; biology/biological sciences; biology teacher education; business administration and management; chemistry; chemistry teacher education; clinical/medical laboratory assistant; computer and information sciences; criminal justice/safety; digital communication and media/multimedia; education; elementary education; English; English/language arts teacher education; environmental science; environmental studies; finance; forest harvesting production technology; general studies; health and medical administrative services related; health/health care administration; health services/allied health/health sciences; history; history teacher education; human development and family studies related; international business/trade/commerce; journalism; kinesiology and exercise science; liberal arts and sciences/liberal studies; marine biology and biological oceanography; marketing/marketing management; mathematics; mathematics teacher education; medical radiologic technology; nursing (registered nurse training); philosophy; physical education teaching and coaching; psychology; public relations/image management; radiologic technology/science; religious studies; respiratory therapy technician; science teacher education; social studies teacher education; social work; sociology; sport and fitness administration; theology.

Academic Programs *Special study options:* adult/continuing education programs, advanced placement credit, cooperative education, distance learning, double majors, external degree program, freshman honors college, honors programs, independent study, internships, off-campus study, part-time degree program, services for LD students, study abroad, summer session for credit. *ROTC:* Army (c). *Unusual degree programs:* 3-2 pharmacy, Massachusetts College of Pharmacy.

Library Wellehan Library with 95,650 titles, 392 serial subscriptions, 1,200 audiovisual materials, an OPAC, a Web page.

Computers on Campus 71 computers available on campus for general student use. A campuswide network can be accessed from student residence rooms and from off campus. Internet access, at least one staffed computer lab available. Computer purchase or lease plan available.

Student Life *Housing options:* coed, men-only, women-only. Campus housing is university owned. Freshman campus housing is guaranteed. *Activities and*

Saint Joseph's College of Maine (continued)

organizations: drama/theater group, student-run newspaper, radio station, choral group, campus ministry, Superkids, Student Government Association and Senate, business club, Inter-Hall Council. *Campus security:* 24-hour emergency response devices and patrols, late-night transport/escort service, controlled dormitory access. *Student services:* health clinic, personal/psychological counseling.

Athletics Member NCAA. All Division III. *Intercollegiate sports:* baseball M, basketball M/W, cheerleading M(c)/W(c), cross-country running M/W, field hockey W, golf M, ice hockey M(c)/W(c), soccer M/W, softball W, volleyball W. *Intramural sports:* basketball M/W, lacrosse M(c)/W(c), rock climbing M/W, skiing (cross-country) M/W, skiing (downhill) M/W, soccer M/W, softball M/W, swimming M/W, volleyball M/W, weight lifting M/W.

Standardized Tests *Required:* SAT I or ACT (for admission).

Costs (2003–04) *Comprehensive fee:* $25,600 includes full-time tuition ($17,430), mandatory fees ($640), and room and board ($7530). Full-time tuition and fees vary according to program. Part-time tuition: $295 per credit hour. Part-time tuition and fees vary according to program. *Required fees:* $490 per year part-time. *Payment plan:* installment. *Waivers:* employees or children of employees.

Financial Aid Of all full-time matriculated undergraduates who enrolled in 2003, 859 applied for aid, 789 were judged to have need, 243 had their need fully met. 339 Federal Work-Study jobs (averaging $1133). In 2003, 134 non-need-based awards were made. *Average percent of need met:* 80%. *Average financial aid package:* $15,022. *Average need-based loan:* $5584. *Average need-based gift aid:* $9531. *Average non-need-based aid:* $10,430. *Average indebtedness upon graduation:* $23,350.

Applying *Options:* common application, electronic application, early action, deferred entrance. *Application fee:* $35. *Required:* essay or personal statement, high school transcript, minimum 2.0 GPA, 1 letter of recommendation. *Recommended:* interview. *Application deadline:* rolling (freshmen), rolling (transfers). *Notification:* continuous until 12/15 (freshmen), 12/15 (early action), continuous (transfers).

Admissions Contact Dr. Alexander Popovics, Vice President for Enrollment and Dean of Admission and Financial Aid, Saint Joseph's College of Maine, 278 Whites Bridge Road, Standish, ME 04084-5263. *Phone:* 207-893-7746 Ext. 7741. *Toll-free phone:* 800-338-7057. *Fax:* 207-893-7862. *E-mail:* admission@sjcme.edu.

■ *See page 2298 for a narrative description.*

THOMAS COLLEGE

Waterville, Maine

- **Independent** comprehensive, founded 1894
- **Calendar** semesters
- **Degrees** associate, bachelor's, and master's
- **Small-town** 70-acre campus
- **Endowment** $1.2 million
- **Coed,** 695 undergraduate students, 78% full-time, 53% women, 47% men
- **Minimally difficult** entrance level, 73% of applicants were admitted

Undergraduates 542 full-time, 153 part-time. Students come from 13 states and territories, 2 other countries, 9% are from out of state, 0.9% African American, 0.7% Asian American or Pacific Islander, 0.5% Hispanic American, 0.5% Native American, 0.2% international, 4% transferred in, 60% live on campus. *Retention:* 66% of 2002 full-time freshmen returned.

Freshmen *Admission:* 588 applied, 428 admitted, 179 enrolled. *Average high school GPA:* 2.72. *Test scores:* SAT verbal scores over 500: 23%; SAT math scores over 500: 31%; ACT scores over 18: 33%; SAT verbal scores over 600: 2%; SAT math scores over 600: 6%.

Faculty *Total:* 86, 27% full-time, 31% with terminal degrees. *Student/faculty ratio:* 14:1.

Majors Accounting; administrative assistant and secretarial science; business administration and management; business teacher education; computer and information sciences; computer management; computer programming; computer science; consumer merchandising/retailing management; criminal justice/law enforcement administration; education (K-12); elementary education; fashion merchandising; finance; hotel/motel administration; human resources management; international business/trade/commerce; legal administrative assistant/secretary; legal assistant/paralegal; management information systems; marketing/marketing management; mathematics teacher education; medical administrative assistant and medical secretary; professional studies; psychology; sales, distribution and marketing; sport and fitness administration.

Academic Programs *Special study options:* academic remediation for entering students, adult/continuing education programs, advanced placement credit, cooperative education, internships, off-campus study, part-time degree program, study abroad, summer session for credit.

Library Marriner Library with 20,000 titles, 1,000 serial subscriptions, 300 audiovisual materials, an OPAC, a Web page.

Computers on Campus 90 computers available on campus for general student use. A campuswide network can be accessed from student residence rooms and from off campus. Internet access, online (class) registration, at least one staffed computer lab available.

Student Life *Housing:* on-campus residence required through senior year. *Options:* coed. Campus housing is university owned and leased by the school. Freshman campus housing is guaranteed. *Activities and organizations:* drama/theater group, student-run newspaper, Phi Beta Lambda, students club, GLOBE, Campus Activity Board, peer advisors, national fraternities, national sororities. *Campus security:* 24-hour emergency response devices and patrols, student patrols. *Student services:* health clinic, personal/psychological counseling.

Athletics Member NCAA, NAIA. All NCAA Division III. *Intercollegiate sports:* baseball M, basketball M/W, field hockey W, golf M, soccer M/W, softball W, volleyball W. *Intramural sports:* baseball M, basketball M/W, bowling M/W, football M, ice hockey M(c), lacrosse M(c), skiing (cross-country) M/W, skiing (downhill) M/W, soccer M/W, softball M/W, tennis M/W, volleyball M/W, weight lifting M/W.

Standardized Tests *Required:* SAT I or ACT (for admission).

Costs (2004–05) *Comprehensive fee:* $22,630 includes full-time tuition ($15,520), mandatory fees ($350), and room and board ($6760). *Payment plan:* deferred payment. *Waivers:* employees or children of employees.

Financial Aid Of all full-time matriculated undergraduates who enrolled in 2003, 508 applied for aid, 471 were judged to have need, 12 had their need fully met. 108 Federal Work-Study jobs (averaging $1700). In 2003, 37 non-need-based awards were made. *Average percent of need met:* 85%. *Average financial aid package:* $11,366. *Average need-based loan:* $5447. *Average need-based gift aid:* $5919. *Average non-need-based aid:* $9128. *Average indebtedness upon graduation:* $19,125.

Applying *Options:* electronic application, early action, deferred entrance. *Application fee:* $40. *Required:* essay or personal statement, high school transcript, 1 letter of recommendation. *Recommended:* minimum 2.0 GPA, interview, rank in upper 50% of high school class. *Application deadline:* rolling (freshmen), rolling (transfers). *Notification:* continuous (freshmen), 12/31 (early action), continuous (transfers).

Admissions Contact Mr. Robert Callahan, Vice President, Enrollment Management, Thomas College, 180 West River Road, Waterville, ME 04901. *Phone:* 207-859-1101. *Toll-free phone:* 800-339-7001. *Fax:* 207-859-1114. *E-mail:* admiss@thomas.edu.

UNITY COLLEGE

Unity, Maine

- **Independent** 4-year, founded 1965
- **Calendar** semesters
- **Degrees** associate and bachelor's
- **Rural** 265-acre campus
- **Endowment** $2.4 million
- **Coed,** 488 undergraduate students, 97% full-time, 34% women, 66% men
- **Moderately difficult** entrance level, 89% of applicants were admitted

Unity College offers a unique combination of liberal arts and professional preparation in environmental fields. The emphasis on fieldwork enables students to take classroom theory and find practical applications to tackle environmental issues. That combination of rigorous academics and hands-on experience ensures that Unity graduates will become the leaders in environmental stewardship.

Undergraduates 474 full-time, 14 part-time. Students come from 21 states and territories, 2 other countries, 62% are from out of state, 0.4% African American, 0.4% international, 10% transferred in, 72% live on campus. *Retention:* 98% of 2002 full-time freshmen returned.

Freshmen *Admission:* 451 applied, 403 admitted, 180 enrolled. *Average high school GPA:* 3.01. *Test scores:* SAT verbal scores over 500: 50%; SAT math scores over 500: 50%; SAT verbal scores over 600: 16%; SAT math scores over 600: 14%; SAT verbal scores over 700: 1%; SAT math scores over 700: 1%.

Faculty *Total:* 44, 77% full-time, 75% with terminal degrees. *Student/faculty ratio:* 12:1.

Majors Ecology; environmental biology; environmental education; environmental engineering technology; environmental studies; fishing and fisheries sciences and management; forestry; interdisciplinary studies; marine biology and biological oceanography; natural resources/conservation; natural resources management; natural resources management and policy; parks, recreation and leisure facilities management; wildlife biology.

Academic Programs *Special study options:* academic remediation for entering students, accelerated degree program, advanced placement credit, cooperative education, English as a second language, honors programs, independent study, internships, off-campus study, part-time degree program, services for LD students, student-designed majors, summer session for credit. *ROTC:* Army (c).

Library Dorothy Webb Quimby Library with 46,000 titles, 650 serial subscriptions, a Web page.

Computers on Campus 42 computers available on campus for general student use. A campuswide network can be accessed from student residence rooms and from off campus. At least one staffed computer lab available.

Student Life *Housing:* on-campus residence required through sophomore year. *Options:* coed. *Activities and organizations:* drama/theater group, student-run newspaper. *Campus security:* 24-hour patrols. *Student services:* health clinic, personal/psychological counseling.

Athletics Member NSCAA. *Intercollegiate sports:* basketball M(s), cross-country running M(s)/W(s), soccer M(s), volleyball W(s). *Intramural sports:* badminton M/W, baseball M, basketball M/W, cross-country running M/W, football M/W, golf M/W, ice hockey M/W, lacrosse M/W, skiing (cross-country) M/W, skiing (downhill) M/W, soccer W, softball M/W, table tennis M/W, tennis M/W, volleyball M/W, weight lifting M/W.

Standardized Tests *Recommended:* SAT I or ACT (for placement).

Costs (2004–05) *Comprehensive fee:* $23,045 includes full-time tuition ($15,790), mandatory fees ($735), and room and board ($6520). Part-time tuition and fees vary according to course load. *Payment plan:* installment. *Waivers:* employees or children of employees.

Financial Aid Of all full-time matriculated undergraduates who enrolled in 2003, 431 applied for aid, 381 were judged to have need, 110 had their need fully met. 289 Federal Work-Study jobs (averaging $1942). 12 state and other part-time jobs (averaging $1106). In 2003, 76 non-need-based awards were made. *Average percent of need met:* 79%. *Average financial aid package:* $12,407. *Average need-based loan:* $4903. *Average need-based gift aid:* $6931. *Average non-need-based aid:* $9034.

Applying *Options:* common application, electronic application, early admission, early action, deferred entrance. *Application fee:* $25. *Required:* essay or personal statement, high school transcript, 2 letters of recommendation. *Required for some:* interview. *Recommended:* minimum 2.0 GPA, interview. *Application deadline:* rolling (freshmen), rolling (transfers). *Notification:* 2/1 (early action).

Admissions Contact Ms. Kay Fiedler, Director of Admissions, Unity College, PO Box 532, Unity, ME 04988-0532. *Phone:* 207-948-3131. *Fax:* 207-948-6277.

UNIVERSITY OF MAINE

Orono, Maine

- **State-supported** university, founded 1865, part of University of Maine System
- **Calendar** semesters
- **Degrees** bachelor's, master's, doctoral, post-master's, and postbachelor's certificates
- **Small-town** 3300-acre campus
- **Endowment** $125.3 million
- **Coed,** 8,972 undergraduate students, 82% full-time, 52% women, 48% men
- **Moderately difficult** entrance level, 76% of applicants were admitted

Undergraduates 7,334 full-time, 1,638 part-time. Students come from 40 states and territories, 47 other countries, 15% are from out of state, 0.8% African American, 1% Asian American or Pacific Islander, 0.8% Hispanic American, 2% Native American, 2% international, 6% transferred in, 57% live on campus. *Retention:* 78% of 2002 full-time freshmen returned.

Freshmen *Admission:* 5,540 applied, 4,204 admitted, 1,662 enrolled. *Average high school GPA:* 3.25. *Test scores:* SAT verbal scores over 500: 69%; SAT math scores over 500: 72%; ACT scores over 18: 91%; SAT verbal scores over 600: 24%; SAT math scores over 600: 28%; ACT scores over 24: 52%; SAT verbal scores over 700: 3%; SAT math scores over 700: 4%; ACT scores over 30: 9%.

Faculty *Total:* 726, 70% full-time, 70% with terminal degrees. *Student/faculty ratio:* 15:1.

Majors Agricultural/biological engineering and bioengineering; agricultural economics; animal sciences; anthropology; art; art history, criticism and conservation; art teacher education; biochemistry; biology/biological sciences; botany/plant biology; business administration and management; chemical engineering; chemistry; child development; civil engineering; classics and languages, literatures and linguistics; clinical laboratory science/medical technology; communication disorders; communication/speech communication and rhetoric; computer engineering; computer science; construction engineering technology; drafting and design technology; dramatic/theatre arts; economics; education; educational/instructional media design; education (K-12); electrical, electronic and communications engineering technology; electrical, electronics and communications engineering; elementary education; engineering physics; engineering technology; English; fine/studio arts; food science; foods, nutrition, and wellness; forest engineering; forestry; French; geology/earth science; German; health teacher education; history; human development and family studies; international relations and affairs; journalism; kindergarten/preschool education; landscaping and groundskeeping; Latin; marine biology and biological oceanography; mass communication/media; mathematics; mechanical engineering; mechanical engineering/mechanical technology; medical microbiology and bacteriology; modern languages; molecular biology; music; music teacher education; natural resources management and policy; nursing (registered nurse training); parks, recreation and leisure facilities management; philosophy; physical education teaching and coaching; physics; political science and government; pre-medical studies; pre-veterinary studies; psychology; public administration; Romance languages; secondary education; social work; sociology; soil science and agronomy; Spanish; speech/theater education; surveying engineering; survey technology; systems engineering; wildlife and wildlands science and management; women's studies; wood science and wood products/pulp and paper technology; zoology/animal biology.

Academic Programs *Special study options:* adult/continuing education programs, advanced placement credit, cooperative education, distance learning, double majors, English as a second language, external degree program, freshman honors college, honors programs, independent study, internships, off-campus study, part-time degree program, services for LD students, student-designed majors, study abroad, summer session for credit. *ROTC:* Army (b), Navy (b).

Library Fogler Library plus 2 others with 851,736 titles, 16,667 serial subscriptions, 25,137 audiovisual materials, an OPAC, a Web page.

Computers on Campus 520 computers available on campus for general student use. A campuswide network can be accessed from student residence rooms and from off campus that provide access to on-line grade information, e-mail. Internet access, online (class) registration, at least one staffed computer lab available. Computer purchase or lease plan available.

Student Life *Housing:* on-campus residence required for freshman year. *Options:* coed, disabled students. Campus housing is university owned. Freshman campus housing is guaranteed. *Activities and organizations:* drama/theater group, student-run newspaper, radio station, choral group, marching band, Volunteers in Community Efforts/VOICE, Circle K, Campus Crusade for Christ, outing club, Wilde Stein, national fraternities, national sororities. *Campus security:* 24-hour emergency response devices and patrols, late-night transport/escort service, controlled dormitory access. *Student services:* health clinic, personal/psychological counseling, women's center, legal services.

Athletics Member NCAA. All Division I except football (Division I-A). *Intercollegiate sports:* baseball M(s), basketball M(s)/W(s), cross-country running M(s)/W(s), field hockey W(s), ice hockey M(s)/W(s), soccer M(s)/W(s), softball W(s), swimming M/W(s), track and field M(s)/W(s), volleyball W(s). *Intramural sports:* badminton M/W, basketball M/W, cross-country running M/W, fencing M(c)/W(c), field hockey M/W, golf M/W, lacrosse M(c)/W(c), racquetball M/W, rock climbing M(c)/W(c), rugby M(c)/W(c), skiing (cross-country) M/W, skiing (downhill) M(c)/W(c), soccer M/W, softball M/W, swimming M/W, table tennis M/W, tennis M/W, track and field M/W, ultimate Frisbee M(c)/W(c), volleyball M/W, water polo M/W, weight lifting M(c)/W(c), wrestling M(c).

Standardized Tests *Required:* SAT I or ACT (for admission).

Costs (2003–04) *Tuition:* state resident $4710 full-time, $157 per credit hour part-time; nonresident $13,410 full-time, $447 per credit hour part-time. Full-time tuition and fees vary according to course load and reciprocity agreements. Part-time tuition and fees vary according to course load and reciprocity agreements. *Required fees:* $1204 full-time. *Room and board:* $6166; room only: $3182. Room and board charges vary according to board plan and housing facility. *Payment plan:* installment. *Waivers:* employees or children of employees.

Financial Aid Of all full-time matriculated undergraduates who enrolled in 2003, 5,884 applied for aid, 4,861 were judged to have need, 1,246 had their need fully met. 1,408 Federal Work-Study jobs (averaging $1973). In 2003, 1257 non-need-based awards were made. *Average percent of need met:* 86%. *Average financial aid package:* $8853. *Average need-based loan:* $4220. *Average need-based gift aid:* $4931. *Average non-need-based aid:* $5096. *Average indebtedness upon graduation:* $18,922.

Applying *Options:* common application, electronic application, early admission, deferred entrance. *Application fee:* $40. *Required:* essay or personal statement, high school transcript, 1 letter of recommendation. *Application deadline:* rolling (freshmen), rolling (transfers). *Notification:* continuous until 12/15 (freshmen), continuous until 12/15 (transfers).

Admissions Contact Mr. Jonathan H. Henry, Director, University of Maine, 5713 Chadbourne Hall, Orono, ME 04469-5713. *Phone:* 207-581-1561. *Toll-free phone:* 877-486-2364. *Fax:* 207-581-1213. *E-mail:* um-admit@maine.edu.

■ *See page 2628 for a narrative description.*

THE UNIVERSITY OF MAINE AT AUGUSTA
Augusta, Maine

- **State-supported** 4-year, founded 1965, part of University of Maine System
- **Calendar** semesters
- **Degrees** certificates, associate, bachelor's, and postbachelor's certificates (also offers some graduate courses and continuing education programs with significant enrollment not reflected in profile)
- **Small-town** 159-acre campus
- **Endowment** $1.1 million
- **Coed,** 5,942 undergraduate students, 28% full-time, 75% women, 25% men
- **Noncompetitive** entrance level

Undergraduates 1,691 full-time, 4,251 part-time. Students come from 16 states and territories, 3% are from out of state, 0.6% African American, 0.3% Asian American or Pacific Islander, 0.5% Hispanic American, 3% Native American, 0.1% international, 9% transferred in.

Freshmen *Admission:* 660 enrolled. *Average high school GPA:* 3.1.

Faculty *Total:* 305, 30% full-time, 12% with terminal degrees. *Student/faculty ratio:* 22:1.

Majors Accounting; applied horticulture; architectural technology; biology/biological sciences; business administration and management; clinical/medical laboratory assistant; computer and information sciences; criminal justice/law enforcement administration; criminal justice/safety; dental assisting; dental hygiene; English language and literature related; financial planning and services; fine/studio arts; general studies; human services; liberal arts and sciences/liberal studies; library assistant; library science; mental and social health services and allied professions related; music; nursing (registered nurse training); photography; public administration; social sciences; veterinary/animal health technology.

Academic Programs *Special study options:* academic remediation for entering students, adult/continuing education programs, advanced placement credit, cooperative education, double majors, honors programs, independent study, internships, off-campus study, part-time degree program, services for LD students, student-designed majors, study abroad, summer session for credit.

Library The Bennett D. Katz Library with 44,000 titles, 560 serial subscriptions, an OPAC.

Computers on Campus 142 computers available on campus for general student use. A campuswide network can be accessed from off campus. At least one staffed computer lab available.

Student Life *Housing:* college housing not available. *Activities and organizations:* Honors Program Student Association, Arts and Architecture Students of UMA, Student Nurse Association, Student-American Dental Hygiene Association, International Student Club. *Campus security:* late-night transport/escort service. *Student services:* personal/psychological counseling.

Athletics Member NSCAA. *Intercollegiate sports:* basketball M(s)/W(s), soccer M(c)/W(s). *Intramural sports:* golf M/W, racquetball M/W, skiing (cross-country) M/W, skiing (downhill) M/W, softball M/W, tennis M/W, volleyball M/W.

Costs (2003–04) *Tuition:* area resident $5535 full-time; state resident $3690 full-time, $123 per credit part-time; nonresident $8940 full-time, $298 per credit part-time. Full-time tuition and fees vary according to reciprocity agreements. Part-time tuition and fees vary according to reciprocity agreements. *Required fees:* $705 full-time, $24 per credit part-time. *Payment plan:* installment. *Waivers:* senior citizens and employees or children of employees.

Financial Aid Of all full-time matriculated undergraduates who enrolled in 2003, 1,448 applied for aid, 199 had their need fully met. 223 Federal Work-Study jobs (averaging $1625). In 2003, 87 non-need-based awards were made. *Average percent of need met:* 67%. *Average financial aid package:* $6778. *Average need-based loan:* $3409. *Average need-based gift aid:* $4788. *Average non-need-based aid:* $3856. *Average indebtedness upon graduation:* $11,993.

Applying *Options:* common application, electronic application, early admission, deferred entrance. *Application fee:* $25. *Required:* high school transcript. *Required for some:* letters of recommendation, interview, music audition. *Recommended:* essay or personal statement. *Application deadline:* 6/15 (freshmen), rolling (transfers). *Notification:* 9/1 (freshmen), continuous (transfers).

Admissions Contact Ms. Sheri Cranston-Fraser, Interim Director of Admissions, The University of Maine at Augusta, 46 University Drive, Robinson Hall, Augusta, ME 04330. *Phone:* 207-621-3390. *Toll-free phone:* 877-862-1234 Ext. 3185. *Fax:* 207-621-3116. *E-mail:* umaar@maine.edu.

UNIVERSITY OF MAINE AT FARMINGTON
Farmington, Maine

- **State-supported** 4-year, founded 1863, part of University of Maine System
- **Calendar** semesters plus May term and 2 5-week summer terms
- **Degree** certificates and bachelor's
- **Small-town** 50-acre campus
- **Endowment** $6.2 million
- **Coed,** 2,420 undergraduate students, 87% full-time, 67% women, 33% men
- **Moderately difficult** entrance level, 72% of applicants were admitted

Undergraduates 2,100 full-time, 320 part-time. Students come from 23 states and territories, 23% are from out of state, 0.3% African American, 0.7% Asian American or Pacific Islander, 0.6% Hispanic American, 1% Native American, 0.5% international, 6% transferred in, 44% live on campus. *Retention:* 70% of 2002 full-time freshmen returned.

Freshmen *Admission:* 1,521 applied, 1,095 admitted, 523 enrolled. *Test scores:* SAT verbal scores over 500: 64%; SAT math scores over 500: 62%; SAT verbal scores over 600: 22%; SAT math scores over 600: 16%; SAT verbal scores over 700: 2%; SAT math scores over 700: 2%.

Faculty *Total:* 157, 76% full-time, 68% with terminal degrees. *Student/faculty ratio:* 16:1.

Majors Anthropology; art; biology/biological sciences; biology teacher education; business/managerial economics; computer science; creative writing; dramatic/theatre arts; elementary education; English; English/language arts teacher education; environmental studies; general studies; geography; geology/earth science; health occupations teacher education; health teacher education; history; interdisciplinary studies; international relations and affairs; kindergarten/preschool education; liberal arts and sciences/liberal studies; mathematics; mathematics teacher education; mental health/rehabilitation; music; philosophy; political science and government; psychology; rehabilitation therapy; religious studies; science teacher education; secondary education; social science teacher education; sociology; special education; special education (emotionally disturbed); special education (mentally retarded); special education (specific learning disabilities); women's studies.

Academic Programs *Special study options:* academic remediation for entering students, accelerated degree program, advanced placement credit, distance learning, double majors, honors programs, independent study, internships, off-campus study, part-time degree program, services for LD students, student-designed majors, study abroad, summer session for credit.

Library Mantor Library with 104,313 titles, 2,399 serial subscriptions, 8,572 audiovisual materials, an OPAC, a Web page.

Computers on Campus 175 computers available on campus for general student use. A campuswide network can be accessed from student residence rooms and from off campus. Internet access, at least one staffed computer lab available.

Student Life *Housing options:* coed, women-only. Campus housing is university owned and is provided by a third party. Freshman campus housing is guaranteed. *Activities and organizations:* drama/theater group, student-run newspaper, radio station, choral group, Program Board, Intramural Board, Campus Residence Council, campus radio station, Commuter Council. *Campus security:* 24-hour emergency response devices and patrols, late-night transport/escort service, controlled dormitory access, safety whistles. *Student services:* health clinic, personal/psychological counseling.

Athletics Member NCAA, NAIA. All NCAA Division III. *Intercollegiate sports:* baseball M, basketball M/W, cross-country running M/W, field hockey W, golf M/W, ice hockey M(c), lacrosse M(c), soccer M/W, softball W, volleyball W. *Intramural sports:* basketball M/W, cheerleading M/W, football M/W, ice hockey M(c)/W(c), rugby M(c)/W(c), skiing (cross-country) M(c)/W(c), skiing (downhill) M(c)/W(c), soccer M/W, softball M/W, ultimate Frisbee M/W, volleyball M/W.

Standardized Tests *Recommended:* SAT I or ACT (for placement).

Costs (2003–04) *Tuition:* state resident $4290 full-time, $143 per credit hour part-time; nonresident $10,470 full-time, $349 per credit hour part-time. Full-time tuition and fees vary according to course load, reciprocity agreements, and student level. Part-time tuition and fees vary according to course load, reciprocity agreements, and student level. *Required fees:* $582 full-time. *Room and board:* $5318; room only: $2848. Room and board charges vary according to board plan and housing facility. *Payment plan:* installment. *Waivers:* minority students, senior citizens, and employees or children of employees.

Financial Aid Of all full-time matriculated undergraduates who enrolled in 2002, 1,593 applied for aid, 1,284 were judged to have need, 345 had their need fully met. 453 Federal Work-Study jobs (averaging $1117). 550 state and other part-time jobs (averaging $1585). In 2002, 50 non-need-based awards were made. *Average percent of need met:* 76%. *Average financial aid package:* $8056. *Average need-based loan:* $3361. *Average need-based gift aid:* $3833. *Average non-need-based aid:* $1952. *Average indebtedness upon graduation:* $15,754.

Applying *Options:* electronic application, early admission, early action, deferred entrance. *Application fee:* $40. *Required:* essay or personal statement, high school transcript, minimum 2.0 GPA, 1 letter of recommendation. *Recommended:* interview. *Application deadline:* rolling (freshmen). *Notification:* continuous (freshmen), 1/8 (early action), continuous (transfers).

Admissions Contact Mr. James G. Collins, Associate Director of Admissions, University of Maine at Farmington, 246 Main Street, Farmington, ME 04938-1994. *Phone:* 207-778-7050. *Fax:* 207-778-8182. *E-mail:* umfadmit@maine.edu.

■ *See page 2630 for a narrative description.*

UNIVERSITY OF MAINE AT FORT KENT
Fort Kent, Maine

- **State-supported** 4-year, founded 1878, part of University of Maine System
- **Calendar** semesters
- **Degrees** associate and bachelor's
- **Rural** 52-acre campus
- **Endowment** $1.3 million
- **Coed,** 924 undergraduate students, 72% full-time, 65% women, 35% men
- **Moderately difficult** entrance level, 91% of applicants were admitted

Undergraduates 668 full-time, 256 part-time. Students come from 15 states and territories, 16 other countries, 4% are from out of state, 2% African American, 0.2% Asian American or Pacific Islander, 0.4% Hispanic American, 2% Native American, 28% international, 30% live on campus. *Retention:* 59% of 2002 full-time freshmen returned.

Freshmen *Admission:* 292 applied, 267 admitted. *Average high school GPA:* 2.43. *Test scores:* SAT verbal scores over 500: 24%; SAT math scores over 500: 34%; SAT verbal scores over 600: 8%; SAT math scores over 600: 14%; SAT math scores over 700: 2%.

Faculty *Total:* 67, 52% full-time, 40% with terminal degrees. *Student/faculty ratio:* 15:1.

Majors Behavioral sciences; bilingual and multilingual education; biology/biological sciences; business administration and management; business teacher education; computer science; criminal justice/law enforcement administration; education; education (K-12); elementary education; English; English/language arts teacher education; environmental studies; forestry; forestry technology; French; French language teacher education; general studies; human services; liberal arts and sciences/liberal studies; mathematics teacher education; nursing (registered nurse training); public administration; social sciences; social science teacher education.

Academic Programs *Special study options:* advanced placement credit, distance learning, double majors, English as a second language, external degree program, honors programs, independent study, internships, part-time degree program, services for LD students, student-designed majors, summer session for credit.

Library Waneta Blake Library plus 1 other with 69,189 titles, 377 serial subscriptions, 4,116 audiovisual materials, an OPAC, a Web page.

Computers on Campus 100 computers available on campus for general student use. A campuswide network can be accessed from student residence rooms and from off campus that provide access to e-mail. Internet access, online (class) registration, at least one staffed computer lab available.

Student Life *Housing options:* coed. Campus housing is university owned. *Activities and organizations:* drama/theater group, choral group, Performing Arts Club, Student Teachers Educational Professional Society, Student Nurses Organization, Diversity Club, Dorm Council, national fraternities, national sororities. *Campus security:* controlled dormitory access, 8-hour night patrols by security personnel 11pm-7am. *Student services:* health clinic, personal/psychological counseling.

Athletics Member NAIA. *Intercollegiate sports:* basketball M/W, cheerleading W, cross-country running M/W, golf M/W, skiing (cross-country) M/W, skiing (downhill) M/W, soccer M/W. *Intramural sports:* baseball M, basketball M/W, cross-country running M/W, golf M/W, ice hockey M, racquetball M/W, skiing (cross-country) M/W, skiing (downhill) M/W, soccer M/W, softball M/W, table tennis M/W, tennis M/W, volleyball M/W, weight lifting M/W.

Standardized Tests *Required for some:* SAT I (for admission), SAT I and SAT II or ACT (for admission). *Recommended:* SAT I and SAT II or ACT (for admission).

Costs (2004–05) *Tuition:* state resident $3960 full-time, $132 per credit hour part-time; nonresident $9600 full-time, $320 per credit hour part-time. Full-time tuition and fees vary according to course load. Part-time tuition and fees vary according to course load. *Required fees:* $554 full-time, $17 per credit hour part-time. *Room and board:* $5564; room only: $3026. *Payment plan:* installment. *Waivers:* employees or children of employees.

Financial Aid Of all full-time matriculated undergraduates who enrolled in 2003, 553 applied for aid, 458 were judged to have need, 97 had their need fully met. 209 Federal Work-Study jobs (averaging $1012). 41 state and other part-time jobs (averaging $943). In 2003, 36 non-need-based awards were made. *Average percent of need met:* 83%. *Average financial aid package:* $4995. *Average need-based loan:* $3639. *Average need-based gift aid:* $3704. *Average non-need-based aid:* $3600. *Average indebtedness upon graduation:* $10,483.

Applying *Options:* common application, electronic application, early admission, deferred entrance. *Application fee:* $25. *Required:* essay or personal statement, high school transcript. *Required for some:* interview. *Recommended:* letters of recommendation. *Application deadline:* rolling (freshmen), rolling (transfers). *Notification:* continuous (freshmen), continuous (transfers).

Admissions Contact Mr. Melik Peter Khoury, Director of Admissions, University of Maine at Fort Kent, 23 University Drive, Fort Kent, ME 04743. *Phone:* 207-834-7600 Ext. 608. *Toll-free phone:* 888-TRY-UMFK. *Fax:* 207-834-7609. *E-mail:* umfkadm@maine.maine.edu.

■ *See page 2632 for a narrative description.*

UNIVERSITY OF MAINE AT MACHIAS
Machias, Maine

- **State-supported** 4-year, founded 1909, part of University of Maine System
- **Calendar** semesters
- **Degree** bachelor's
- **Rural** 42-acre campus
- **Endowment** $721,736
- **Coed,** 1,313 undergraduate students, 44% full-time, 72% women, 28% men
- **Moderately difficult** entrance level, 82% of applicants were admitted

Undergraduates 577 full-time, 736 part-time. Students come from 26 states and territories, 16 other countries, 24% are from out of state, 1% African American, 0.8% Asian American or Pacific Islander, 1% Hispanic American, 4% Native American, 7% international, 4% transferred in, 42% live on campus. *Retention:* 73% of 2002 full-time freshmen returned.

Freshmen *Admission:* 510 applied, 416 admitted, 160 enrolled. *Test scores:* SAT verbal scores over 500: 35%; SAT math scores over 500: 34%; SAT verbal scores over 600: 10%; SAT math scores over 600: 5%; SAT verbal scores over 700: 1%.

Faculty *Total:* 83, 37% full-time, 48% with terminal degrees. *Student/faculty ratio:* 17:1.

Majors Accounting; administrative assistant and secretarial science; art; behavioral sciences; biology/biological sciences; biology teacher education; business administration and management; business teacher education; conservation biology; creative writing; dramatic/theatre arts; ecology; education; elementary education; English; English/language arts teacher education; environmental education; environmental studies; general studies; history; history teacher education; hotel/motel administration; human services; marine biology and biological oceanography; marketing/marketing management; mathematics teacher education; music; parks, recreation and leisure; parks, recreation and leisure facilities management; pre-medical studies; psychology; public administration; science teacher education; social science teacher education; tourism and travel services management; visual and performing arts.

Academic Programs *Special study options:* academic remediation for entering students, adult/continuing education programs, advanced placement credit, cooperative education, distance learning, double majors, English as a second language, external degree program, honors programs, independent study, internships, off-campus study, part-time degree program, services for LD students, student-designed majors, study abroad, summer session for credit.

Library Merrill Library plus 1 other with 82,664 titles, 316 serial subscriptions, 3,647 audiovisual materials, an OPAC, a Web page.

Computers on Campus 185 computers available on campus for general student use. A campuswide network can be accessed from student residence rooms and from off campus. Internet access, online (class) registration, at least one staffed computer lab available.

Student Life *Housing options:* coed. Campus housing is university owned. *Activities and organizations:* drama/theater group, student-run radio station, choral group, Student Senate, 100% Society, International Club, MRPASS, Softball Club, national fraternities, national sororities. *Campus security:* 24-hour emergency response devices, late-night transport/escort service, controlled dormitory access, night security guard until 3:00 a.m., day security 8-5 p.m. *Student services:* health clinic, personal/psychological counseling.

Athletics Member NAIA. *Intercollegiate sports:* basketball M/W, cross-country running M/W, lacrosse M(c)/W(c), soccer M/W, volleyball W. *Intramural sports:* basketball M/W, cheerleading W, fencing M/W, football M/W, soccer M/W, softball W, water polo M/W.

Standardized Tests *Required:* SAT I or ACT (for admission).

Costs (2003–04) *Tuition:* state resident $3636 full-time, $121 per credit hour part-time; nonresident $9630 full-time, $321 per credit hour part-time. *Required fees:* $485 full-time, $16 per credit hour part-time, $20 per term part-time. *Room and board:* $5150; room only: $2592. *Payment plans:* installment, deferred payment. *Waivers:* minority students, senior citizens, and employees or children of employees.

University of Maine at Machias (continued)

Financial Aid Of all full-time matriculated undergraduates who enrolled in 2002, 512 applied for aid, 419 were judged to have need, 108 had their need fully met. 140 Federal Work-Study jobs (averaging $1621). 83 state and other part-time jobs (averaging $1660). In 2002, 44 non-need-based awards were made. *Average percent of need met:* 83%. *Average financial aid package:* $8182. *Average need-based loan:* $3356. *Average need-based gift aid:* $4847. *Average non-need-based aid:* $5051. *Average indebtedness upon graduation:* $14,873.

Applying *Options:* common application, electronic application, early admission, early action, deferred entrance. *Application fee:* $25. *Required:* essay or personal statement, high school transcript, 1 letter of recommendation. *Required for some:* minimum 2.0 GPA, interview. *Recommended:* minimum 2.5 GPA, 2 letters of recommendation, interview. *Application deadlines:* 8/15 (freshmen), 8/15 (transfers). *Notification:* continuous (freshmen), 1/15 (early action), continuous (transfers).

Admissions Contact Director of Admissions, University of Maine at Machias, 9 O'Brien Avenue, Machias, ME 04654. *Phone:* 207-255-1318. *Toll-free phone:* 888-GOTOUMM. *Fax:* 207-255-1363. *E-mail:* ummadmissions@maine.edu.

■ See page 2634 for a narrative description.

UNIVERSITY OF MAINE AT PRESQUE ISLE
Presque Isle, Maine

- **State-supported** 4-year, founded 1903, part of University of Maine System
- **Calendar** semesters
- **Degrees** certificates, associate, and bachelor's
- **Small-town** 150-acre campus
- **Endowment** $775,287
- **Coed,** 1,546 undergraduate students, 70% full-time, 67% women, 33% men
- **Minimally difficult** entrance level, 87% of applicants were admitted

Undergraduates 1,079 full-time, 467 part-time. Students come from 20 states and territories, 6 other countries, 2% are from out of state, 0.5% African American, 0.7% Asian American or Pacific Islander, 0.9% Hispanic American, 3% Native American, 12% international, 14% transferred in, 28% live on campus. *Retention:* 67% of 2002 full-time freshmen returned.

Freshmen *Admission:* 520 applied, 454 admitted, 222 enrolled. *Average high school GPA:* 3.0. *Test scores:* SAT verbal scores over 500: 32%; SAT math scores over 500: 30%; SAT verbal scores over 600: 7%; SAT math scores over 600: 6%; SAT math scores over 700: 1%.

Faculty *Total:* 123, 49% full-time, 54% with terminal degrees. *Student/faculty ratio:* 14:1.

Majors Accounting; applied art; art; art teacher education; athletic training; behavioral sciences; biology/biological sciences; business administration and management; clinical/medical laboratory technology; creative writing; criminal justice/law enforcement administration; education; elementary education; English; environmental studies; fine/studio arts; foods, nutrition, and wellness; forest/forest resources management; geology/earth science; health teacher education; international relations and affairs; liberal arts and sciences/liberal studies; parks, recreation and leisure; physical education teaching and coaching; political science and government; science teacher education; secondary education; social work; sociology.

Academic Programs *Special study options:* academic remediation for entering students, accelerated degree program, adult/continuing education programs, advanced placement credit, distance learning, double majors, honors programs, independent study, internships, off-campus study, part-time degree program, services for LD students, student-designed majors, study abroad, summer session for credit.

Library UMPI Library with 455,372 titles, 2,500 serial subscriptions, 1,281 audiovisual materials, an OPAC, a Web page.

Computers on Campus 82 computers available on campus for general student use. A campuswide network can be accessed from student residence rooms and from off campus that provide access to e-mail. Internet access, at least one staffed computer lab available.

Student Life *Housing options:* coed. Campus housing is university owned and leased by the school. *Activities and organizations:* drama/theater group, student-run newspaper, radio station, choral group, Student Senate, OAPI-Outdoor Adventure Program International, Student Activities Board, Student Organization of Social Work, Campus Crusade for Christ, national fraternities, national sororities. *Campus security:* student patrols, late-night transport/escort service, crime prevention programs, lighted pathways. *Student services:* health clinic, personal/psychological counseling.

Athletics Member NAIA. *Intercollegiate sports:* baseball M, basketball M/W, cross-country running M/W, golf M, soccer M/W, softball W, volleyball W. *Intramural sports:* archery M/W, badminton M/W, basketball M/W, bowling M/W, cross-country running M/W, football M/W, ice hockey M/W, skiing (cross-country) M/W, skiing (downhill) M/W, soccer M/W, softball M/W, table tennis M/W, tennis M/W, track and field M/W, volleyball M/W, weight lifting M/W.

Standardized Tests *Recommended:* SAT I or ACT (for admission).

Costs (2003–04) *Tuition:* state resident $3690 full-time, $123 per credit hour part-time; nonresident $9240 full-time, $308 per credit hour part-time. Full-time tuition and fees vary according to course load and reciprocity agreements. Part-time tuition and fees vary according to course load and reciprocity agreements. *Required fees:* $500 full-time, $18 per credit hour part-time. *Room and board:* $4965; room only: $2835. Room and board charges vary according to board plan. *Payment plans:* installment, deferred payment. *Waivers:* minority students, senior citizens, and employees or children of employees.

Financial Aid Of all full-time matriculated undergraduates who enrolled in 2003, 773 applied for aid, 695 were judged to have need, 249 had their need fully met. 283 Federal Work-Study jobs (averaging $1318). In 2003, 70 non-need-based awards were made. *Average percent of need met:* 87%. *Average financial aid package:* $6853. *Average need-based loan:* $2820. *Average need-based gift aid:* $4501. *Average non-need-based aid:* $4219. *Average indebtedness upon graduation:* $11,128.

Applying *Options:* common application, electronic application, early admission, early action, deferred entrance. *Application fee:* $25. *Required:* essay or personal statement, high school transcript, minimum 2.0 GPA. *Required for some:* 1 letter of recommendation, interview. *Application deadline:* rolling (freshmen). *Notification:* continuous (freshmen), continuous (transfers).

Admissions Contact Mr. Brian Manter, Director of Admissions, University of Maine at Presque Isle, 181 Main Street, Presque Isle, ME 04769. *Phone:* 207-768-9536. *Fax:* 207-768-9777. *E-mail:* adventure@umpi.maine.edu.

UNIVERSITY OF NEW ENGLAND
Biddeford, Maine

- **Independent** comprehensive, founded 1831
- **Calendar** semesters
- **Degrees** associate, bachelor's, master's, first professional, post-master's, and postbachelor's certificates
- **Small-town** 410-acre campus
- **Endowment** $18.6 million
- **Coed**
- **Moderately difficult** entrance level

Faculty *Student/faculty ratio:* 9:1.

Student Life *Campus security:* 24-hour emergency response devices and patrols, late-night transport/escort service, controlled dormitory access.

Athletics Member NCAA. All Division III.

Standardized Tests *Required:* SAT I or ACT (for admission). *Required for some:* SAT II: Subject Tests (for admission).

Costs (2003–04) *Comprehensive fee:* $27,200 includes full-time tuition ($18,990), mandatory fees ($650), and room and board ($7560). Part-time tuition: $680 per credit.

Financial Aid Of all full-time matriculated undergraduates who enrolled in 2003, 1,105 applied for aid, 1,038 were judged to have need, 89 had their need fully met. 463 Federal Work-Study jobs (averaging $1200). In 2003, 142. *Average percent of need met:* 77. *Average financial aid package:* $17,240. *Average need-based loan:* $9248. *Average need-based gift aid:* $8249. *Average non-need-based aid:* $6264. *Average indebtedness upon graduation:* $28,421.

Applying *Options:* common application, electronic application, early admission, early decision, deferred entrance. *Application fee:* $40. *Required:* high school transcript. *Required for some:* interview. *Recommended:* interview.

Admissions Contact Mr. Robert Pecchia, Associate Dean of Admissions, University of New England, Hills Beach Road, Biddeford, ME 04005-9526. *Phone:* 207-283-0170 Ext. 2297. *Toll-free phone:* 800-477-4UNE. *Fax:* 207-294-5900. *E-mail:* admissions@une.edu.

■ See page 2666 for a narrative description.

UNIVERSITY OF SOUTHERN MAINE
Portland, Maine

- **State-supported** comprehensive, founded 1878, part of University of Maine System
- **Calendar** semesters
- **Degrees** associate, bachelor's, master's, doctoral, first professional, and post-master's certificates
- **Suburban** 144-acre campus
- **Endowment** $13.1 million
- **Coed,** 8,613 undergraduate students, 54% full-time, 61% women, 39% men

■ **Moderately difficult** entrance level, 72% of applicants were admitted

Combining a small-school atmosphere with the choices of a larger university, USM is just 2 hours from Boston, with access to the ocean, lakes, and ski resorts. Features include dedicated faculty members, small class sizes, a diverse student body, internships and cooperative education, a new field house and ice arena, and a dual residential campus (urban and rural). USM provides students with real value: a high-quality education at an affordable cost.

Undergraduates 4,668 full-time, 3,945 part-time. Students come from 31 states and territories, 11% are from out of state, 1% African American, 2% Asian American or Pacific Islander, 0.7% Hispanic American, 1% Native American, 9% transferred in, 40% live on campus. *Retention:* 68% of 2002 full-time freshmen returned.

Freshmen *Admission:* 3,585 applied, 2,588 admitted, 934 enrolled. *Average high school GPA:* 3.09. *Test scores:* SAT verbal scores over 500: 62%; SAT math scores over 500: 58%; ACT scores over 18: 88%; SAT verbal scores over 600: 18%; SAT math scores over 600: 12%; ACT scores over 24: 31%; SAT verbal scores over 700: 1%; SAT math scores over 700: 1%.

Faculty *Total:* 611, 62% full-time, 50% with terminal degrees. *Student/faculty ratio:* 13:1.

Majors Accounting; anthropology; art; art teacher education; athletic training; biology/biological sciences; biotechnology; business administration and management; chemistry; classics and languages, literatures and linguistics; communication/speech communication and rhetoric; computer science; criminology; dramatic/theatre arts; economics; electrical, electronics and communications engineering; English; environmental health; environmental studies; French; geography; geology/earth science; health science; Hispanic-American, Puerto Rican, and Mexican-American/Chicano studies; history; industrial arts; international relations and affairs; linguistics; mass communication/media; mathematics; modern languages; music; music performance; music teacher education; nursing (registered nurse training); philosophy; physics; political science and government; psychology; Russian studies; social sciences; social work; sociology; therapeutic recreation; trade and industrial teacher education; women's studies.

Academic Programs *Special study options:* academic remediation for entering students, adult/continuing education programs, advanced placement credit, cooperative education, distance learning, double majors, English as a second language, external degree program, honors programs, independent study, internships, off-campus study, part-time degree program, services for LD students, student-designed majors, study abroad, summer session for credit. *ROTC:* Army (c), Air Force (c). *Unusual degree programs:* 3-2 education.

Library University of Southern Maine Library plus 4 others with 431,978 titles, 3,339 serial subscriptions, 2,556 audiovisual materials, an OPAC, a Web page.

Computers on Campus 532 computers available on campus for general student use. A campuswide network can be accessed from student residence rooms and from off campus. Internet access, online (class) registration, at least one staffed computer lab available. Computer purchase or lease plan available.

Student Life *Housing options:* coed. Campus housing is university owned. Freshman applicants given priority for college housing. *Activities and organizations:* drama/theater group, student-run newspaper, radio and television station, choral group, outing and ski clubs, fraternities and sororities, Gorham Events Board, Commuter Student Group, Circle K, national fraternities, national sororities. *Campus security:* 24-hour emergency response devices and patrols, student patrols, late-night transport/escort service, controlled dormitory access, security lighting, preventive programs within residence halls. *Student services:* health clinic, personal/psychological counseling, women's center, legal services.

Athletics Member NCAA. All Division III. *Intercollegiate sports:* baseball M, basketball M/W, cheerleading M/W, cross-country running M/W, field hockey W, golf M/W, ice hockey M/W, lacrosse M/W, sailing M/W, soccer M/W, softball W, tennis M/W, track and field M/W, volleyball W, wrestling M. *Intramural sports:* basketball M/W, cheerleading W, football M/W, ice hockey M/W, lacrosse M(c)/W(c), racquetball M/W, rugby M(c)/W(c), skiing (downhill) M(c)/W(c), soccer M/W, softball M/W, squash M/W, table tennis M/W, tennis M/W, ultimate Frisbee M/W, volleyball M/W, weight lifting M/W.

Standardized Tests *Required:* SAT I or ACT (for admission).

Costs (2003–04) *One-time required fee:* $15. *Tuition:* state resident $4320 full-time; nonresident $12,000 full-time. Full-time tuition and fees vary according to course load, degree level, and reciprocity agreements. Part-time tuition and fees vary according to course load, degree level, and reciprocity agreements. *Required fees:* $878 full-time. *Room and board:* $6014; room only: $3224. Room and board charges vary according to board plan, housing facility, and location. *Payment plan:* installment. *Waivers:* minority students, senior citizens, and employees or children of employees.

Financial Aid Of all full-time matriculated undergraduates who enrolled in 2003, 3,937 applied for aid, 3,419 were judged to have need, 804 had their need fully met. In 2003, 386 non-need-based awards were made. *Average percent of need met:* 81%. *Average financial aid package:* $8937. *Average need-based loan:* $4382. *Average need-based gift aid:* $3833. *Average non-need-based aid:* $4266. *Average indebtedness upon graduation:* $21,720.

Applying *Options:* common application, electronic application, early admission, deferred entrance. *Application fee:* $40. *Required:* essay or personal statement, high school transcript. *Required for some:* interview, auditions for music majors. *Recommended:* minimum 2.8 GPA, 1 letter of recommendation, interview. *Application deadlines:* 2/15 (freshmen), 2/15 (transfers). *Notification:* continuous (freshmen), continuous (transfers).

Admissions Contact Mr. Jon Barker, Associate Director, University of Southern Maine, 37 College Avenue, Gorham, ME 04038. *Phone:* 207-780-5724. *Toll-free phone:* 800-800-4USM Ext. 5670. *Fax:* 207-780-5640. *E-mail:* usmadm@usm.maine.edu.

■ *See page 2712 for a narrative description.*

MARYLAND

BALTIMORE HEBREW UNIVERSITY
Baltimore, Maryland

■ **Independent** comprehensive, founded 1919
■ **Calendar** semesters
■ **Degrees** associate, bachelor's, master's, and doctoral
■ **Urban** 2-acre campus
■ **Coed**
■ **Moderately difficult** entrance level

Faculty *Student/faculty ratio:* 4:1.

Student Life *Campus security:* 24-hour patrols, guards on duty during class hours, patrols by security, well-lit parking lots.

Costs (2003–04) *Tuition:* $8800 full-time, $1100 per course part-time. *Required fees:* $30 full-time.

Financial Aid Of all full-time matriculated undergraduates who enrolled in 2001, 54 applied for aid, 54 were judged to have need, 54 had their need fully met. *Average percent of need met:* 100. *Average financial aid package:* $8000.

Applying *Options:* common application, early admission, deferred entrance. *Application fee:* $20. *Required:* essay or personal statement, high school transcript, interview. *Required for some:* 3 letters of recommendation.

Admissions Contact Ms. Essie Keyser, Director of Admissions, Baltimore Hebrew University, 5800 Park Heights Avenue, Baltimore, MD 21209. *Phone:* 410-578-6967. *Toll-free phone:* 888-248-7420. *Fax:* 410-578-6940. *E-mail:* bhu@bhu.edu.

BALTIMORE INTERNATIONAL COLLEGE
Baltimore, Maryland

■ **Independent** primarily 2-year, founded 1972
■ **Calendar** semesters
■ **Degrees** certificates, associate, and bachelor's
■ **Urban** 6-acre campus with easy access to Washington, DC
■ **Endowment** $94,812
■ **Coed,** 571 undergraduate students, 93% full-time, 52% women, 48% men
■ **Minimally difficult** entrance level, 28% of applicants were admitted

Undergraduates 531 full-time, 40 part-time. Students come from 17 states and territories, 4 other countries, 47% African American, 4% Asian American or Pacific Islander, 2% Hispanic American, 0.4% Native American, 0.9% international, 5% transferred in, 24% live on campus. *Retention:* 50% of 2002 full-time freshmen returned.

Freshmen *Admission:* 825 applied, 233 admitted, 144 enrolled.

Faculty *Total:* 32, 41% full-time, 75% with terminal degrees. *Student/faculty ratio:* 9:1.

Majors Business administration and management; culinary arts; hospitality administration; hotel/motel administration.

Academic Programs *Special study options:* academic remediation for entering students, accelerated degree program, adult/continuing education programs, advanced placement credit, cooperative education, double majors, honors programs, internships, off-campus study, study abroad.

Library George A. Piendak Library with 13,000 titles, 200 serial subscriptions, 1,000 audiovisual materials.

Computers on Campus 35 computers available on campus for general student use. A campuswide network can be accessed from off campus. Internet access, at least one staffed computer lab available.

Student Life *Housing:* on-campus residence required for freshman year. *Options:* coed. Campus housing is university owned. Freshman campus housing

Baltimore International College (continued)

is guaranteed. *Activities and organizations:* student-run newspaper, American Culinary Federation, Beta Iota Kappa. *Campus security:* late-night transport/escort service, controlled dormitory access. *Student services:* health clinic, personal/psychological counseling.

Standardized Tests *Required for some:* SAT I or ACT (for admission).

Costs (2004–05) *Comprehensive fee:* $20,057 includes full-time tuition ($14,049), mandatory fees ($102), and room and board ($5906). *Room and board:* Room and board charges vary according to housing facility. *Payment plans:* tuition prepayment, installment. *Waivers:* employees or children of employees.

Applying *Options:* common application, electronic application, deferred entrance. *Application fee:* $35. *Required:* high school transcript. *Required for some:* essay or personal statement. *Recommended:* interview. *Application deadline:* rolling (freshmen), rolling (transfers). *Notification:* continuous until 8/15 (freshmen), continuous until 8/15 (transfers).

Admissions Contact Ms. Lori Makowski, Director of Admissions, Baltimore International College, Commerce Exchange, 17 Commerce Street, Baltimore, MD 21202-3230. *Phone:* 410-752-4710 Ext. 124. *Toll-free phone:* 800-624-9926 Ext. 120. *Fax:* 410-752-3730. *E-mail:* admissions@bic.edu.

■ *See page 1210 for a narrative description.*

BOWIE STATE UNIVERSITY
Bowie, Maryland

- **State-supported** comprehensive, founded 1865, part of University System of Maryland
- **Calendar** semesters
- **Degrees** certificates, bachelor's, master's, doctoral, and postbachelor's certificates
- **Small-town** 312-acre campus with easy access to Baltimore and Washington, DC
- **Endowment** $2.3 million
- **Coed,** 3,988 undergraduate students, 78% full-time, 63% women, 37% men
- **Minimally difficult** entrance level, 48% of applicants were admitted

Undergraduates 3,122 full-time, 866 part-time. Students come from 33 states and territories, 47 other countries, 8% are from out of state, 90% African American, 1% Asian American or Pacific Islander, 1% Hispanic American, 0.3% Native American, 1% international, 12% transferred in, 24% live on campus. *Retention:* 70% of 2002 full-time freshmen returned.

Freshmen *Admission:* 3,537 applied, 1,704 admitted, 771 enrolled. *Average high school GPA:* 2.73. *Test scores:* SAT verbal scores over 500: 19%; SAT math scores over 500: 18%; SAT verbal scores over 600: 2%; SAT math scores over 600: 3%.

Faculty *Total:* 306, 53% full-time, 43% with terminal degrees. *Student/faculty ratio:* 20:1.

Majors Accounting; applied mathematics; art; biology/biological sciences; broadcast journalism; business administration and management; computer and information sciences; computer graphics; creative writing; criminal justice/law enforcement administration; economics; education; elementary education; English; history; kindergarten/preschool education; marketing/marketing management; mass communication/media; mathematics; mathematics teacher education; nursing (registered nurse training); political science and government; psychology; public relations/image management; science teacher education; secondary education; social work; sociology; special education.

Academic Programs *Special study options:* academic remediation for entering students, adult/continuing education programs, advanced placement credit, cooperative education, distance learning, double majors, external degree program, honors programs, independent study, internships, off-campus study, part-time degree program, services for LD students, study abroad, summer session for credit. *ROTC:* Army (b). *Unusual degree programs:* 3-2 engineering with George Washington University, University of Maryland College Park, Howard University.

Library Thurgood Marshall Library with 409,036 titles, 1,319 serial subscriptions, 4,475 audiovisual materials, an OPAC, a Web page.

Computers on Campus 3144 computers available on campus for general student use. A campuswide network can be accessed from student residence rooms and from off campus. Internet access, online (class) registration, at least one staffed computer lab available.

Student Life *Housing options:* coed, men-only, women-only. Campus housing is university owned. *Activities and organizations:* drama/theater group, student-run newspaper, radio and television station, choral group, marching band, Orientation, NSAP Student Leadership Institute, Football games, Basketball games, Honda Campus All-Star Challenge, national fraternities, national sororities. *Campus security:* 24-hour emergency response devices and patrols, student patrols, late-night transport/escort service, controlled dormitory access. *Student services:* health clinic, personal/psychological counseling.

Athletics Member NCAA. All Division II. *Intercollegiate sports:* basketball M(s)/W(s), bowling W, cross-country running M(s)/W(s), football M(s), softball W(s), tennis W(s), track and field M(s)/W(s), volleyball W(s).

Standardized Tests *Required:* SAT I or ACT (for admission).

Costs (2003–04) *Tuition:* state resident $3551 full-time, $162 per credit part-time; nonresident $10,894 full-time, $475 per credit part-time. Part-time tuition and fees vary according to course load. *Required fees:* $1171 full-time, $186 per term part-time. *Room and board:* $6020; room only: $4337. Room and board charges vary according to board plan and housing facility. *Payment plans:* installment, deferred payment. *Waivers:* senior citizens and employees or children of employees.

Financial Aid Of all full-time matriculated undergraduates who enrolled in 2003, 2,642 applied for aid, 2,023 were judged to have need, 223 had their need fully met. 161 Federal Work-Study jobs (averaging $1370). In 2003, 353 non-need-based awards were made. *Average percent of need met:* 60%. *Average financial aid package:* $7377. *Average need-based loan:* $3728. *Average need-based gift aid:* $4312. *Average non-need-based aid:* $4361. *Average indebtedness upon graduation:* $10,842.

Applying *Options:* electronic application. *Application fee:* $40. *Required:* high school transcript, minimum 2.0 GPA. *Required for some:* letters of recommendation. *Recommended:* letters of recommendation. *Application deadlines:* 4/1 (freshmen), 4/1 (transfers). *Notification:* continuous (freshmen), continuous (transfers).

Admissions Contact Shingiral Chanaiwa, Coordinator of Undergraduate Enrollment, Bowie State University, 14000 Jericho Park Road, Henry Building, Bowie, MD 20715-9465. *Phone:* 301-860-3425. *Toll-free phone:* 877-772-6943. *Fax:* 301-860-3438. *E-mail:* dkiah@bowiestate.edu.

■ *See page 1278 for a narrative description.*

CAPITOL COLLEGE
Laurel, Maryland

- **Independent** comprehensive, founded 1964
- **Calendar** semesters
- **Degrees** certificates, associate, bachelor's, master's, and postbachelor's certificates
- **Suburban** 52-acre campus with easy access to Baltimore and Washington, DC
- **Endowment** $3.0 million
- **Coed,** 630 undergraduate students, 51% full-time, 23% women, 77% men
- **Minimally difficult** entrance level, 90% of applicants were admitted

Capitol College specializes in focused quality degree programs that include both in-depth theory and extensive hands-on experience. A new computer science program offers students a broad range of theoretical and practical knowledge. Courses include programming with the latest computer languages, techniques, networks, and security.

Undergraduates 319 full-time, 311 part-time. Students come from 15 states and territories, 21 other countries, 14% are from out of state, 37% African American, 7% Asian American or Pacific Islander, 2% Hispanic American, 0.4% Native American, 4% international, 5% transferred in, 17% live on campus.

Freshmen *Admission:* 213 applied, 191 admitted, 61 enrolled. *Average high school GPA:* 3.13. *Test scores:* SAT verbal scores over 500: 33%; SAT math scores over 500: 56%; SAT verbal scores over 600: 2%; SAT math scores over 600: 13%; SAT verbal scores over 700: 1%; SAT math scores over 700: 1%.

Faculty *Total:* 54, 28% full-time, 24% with terminal degrees. *Student/faculty ratio:* 12:1.

Majors Computer engineering; computer engineering technology; electrical, electronic and communications engineering technology; electrical, electronics and communications engineering; laser and optical technology; management information systems; telecommunications.

Academic Programs *Special study options:* academic remediation for entering students, accelerated degree program, adult/continuing education programs, advanced placement credit, cooperative education, English as a second language, part-time degree program, summer session for credit. *ROTC:* Army (c).

Library Puente Library with 10,000 titles, 100 serial subscriptions, 117 audiovisual materials, an OPAC.

Computers on Campus 42 computers available on campus for general student use. A campuswide network can be accessed from off campus. Internet access, at least one staffed computer lab available.

Student Life *Housing options:* coed. Campus housing is university owned. Freshman campus housing is guaranteed. *Activities and organizations:* student-run newspaper, IEEE, NSDE, SWE. *Campus security:* night security patrols. *Student services:* personal/psychological counseling.

Athletics *Intramural sports:* basketball M, bowling M/W, football M, soccer M, table tennis M/W, volleyball M/W.

Standardized Tests *Required:* SAT I or ACT (for admission).
Costs (2004–05) *Tuition:* $16,854 full-time, $538 per credit part-time. *Required fees:* $600 full-time, $10 per credit part-time. *Room only:* $3850. Room and board charges vary according to housing facility. *Payment plans:* installment, deferred payment. *Waivers:* employees or children of employees.
Financial Aid Of all full-time matriculated undergraduates who enrolled in 2002, 127 applied for aid, 121 were judged to have need, 19 had their need fully met. 35 Federal Work-Study jobs (averaging $2000). 30 state and other part-time jobs (averaging $3800). In 2002, 9 non-need-based awards were made. *Average percent of need met:* 42%. *Average financial aid package:* $7893. *Average need-based loan:* $3937. *Average need-based gift aid:* $5689. *Average non-need-based aid:* $7728. *Average indebtedness upon graduation:* $26,542.
Applying *Options:* electronic application, deferred entrance. *Application fee:* $25. *Required:* high school transcript. *Required for some:* essay or personal statement, 2 letters of recommendation, interview. *Recommended:* minimum 2.2 GPA, interview. *Application deadline:* rolling (freshmen), rolling (transfers).
Admissions Contact Mr. Darnell Edwards, Director of Admissions, Capitol College, 11301 Springfield Road, Laurel, MD 20708. *Phone:* 301-953-3200 Ext. 3032. *Toll-free phone:* 800-950-1992. *E-mail:* admissions@capitol-college.edu.

■ *See page 1344 for a narrative description.*

COLLEGE OF NOTRE DAME OF MARYLAND
Baltimore, Maryland

- **Independent Roman Catholic** comprehensive, founded 1873
- **Calendar** 4-1-4
- **Degrees** bachelor's, master's, and postbachelor's certificates
- **Suburban** 58-acre campus
- **Women only,** 1,582 undergraduate students, 39% full-time
- **Moderately difficult** entrance level, 73% of applicants were admitted

The College of Notre Dame of Maryland is a Catholic, liberal arts college committed to educating women as leaders. Located in Baltimore, undergraduate and graduate programs challenge students to strive for intellectual and professional excellence, to build inclusive communities, to engage in service to others, and to promote social responsibility.

Undergraduates 622 full-time, 960 part-time. Students come from 26 states and territories, 15 other countries, 8% are from out of state, 26% African American, 3% Asian American or Pacific Islander, 2% Hispanic American, 0.8% Native American, 1% international, 4% transferred in, 57% live on campus. *Retention:* 86% of 2002 full-time freshmen returned.
Freshmen *Admission:* 397 applied, 288 admitted, 170 enrolled. *Average high school GPA:* 3.30. *Test scores:* SAT verbal scores over 500: 58%; SAT math scores over 500: 54%; SAT verbal scores over 600: 18%; SAT math scores over 600: 15%; SAT verbal scores over 700: 4%; SAT math scores over 700: 1%.
Faculty *Total:* 86, 94% full-time, 81% with terminal degrees. *Student/faculty ratio:* 13:1.
Majors Art; biology/biological sciences; business administration and management; chemistry; classics and languages, literatures and linguistics; computer science; economics; education; elementary education; engineering science; English; history; human services; information science/studies; interdisciplinary studies; international business/trade/commerce; international relations and affairs; kindergarten/preschool education; liberal arts and sciences/liberal studies; mass communication/media; mathematics; modern languages; music; nursing (registered nurse training); physics; physiological psychology/psychobiology; political science and government; pre-law studies; pre-medical studies; pre-veterinary studies; psychology; religious studies; special education.
Academic Programs *Special study options:* accelerated degree program, adult/continuing education programs, advanced placement credit, double majors, English as a second language, honors programs, independent study, internships, off-campus study, part-time degree program, services for LD students, student-designed majors, study abroad, summer session for credit. *ROTC:* Army (c). *Unusual degree programs:* 3-2 engineering with University of Maryland College Park, Johns Hopkins University; nursing with Johns Hopkins University; radiological science with Johns Hopkins University.
Library Loyola/Notre Dame Library with 400,000 titles, 1,800 serial subscriptions, 27,000 audiovisual materials, an OPAC, a Web page.
Computers on Campus 80 computers available on campus for general student use. A campuswide network can be accessed from student residence rooms and from off campus that provide access to online classroom assignments and information. Internet access, at least one staffed computer lab available. Computer purchase or lease plan available.
Student Life *Housing:* on-campus residence required through sophomore year. *Options:* women-only. Campus housing is university owned. Freshman campus housing is guaranteed. *Activities and organizations:* drama/theater group, student-run newspaper, radio and television station, choral group, Black Student Association, Kymry, Commuter Association, Community Service Organization, campus ministry. *Campus security:* 24-hour emergency response devices and patrols, late-night transport/escort service, controlled dormitory access, emergency call boxes. *Student services:* health clinic, personal/psychological counseling, women's center.
Athletics Member NCAA. All Division III. *Intercollegiate sports:* basketball W, field hockey W, lacrosse W, soccer W, swimming W, tennis W, volleyball W. *Intramural sports:* cross-country running W, softball W.
Standardized Tests *Required:* SAT I or ACT (for admission).
Costs (2004–05) *Comprehensive fee:* $28,100 includes full-time tuition ($19,900), mandatory fees ($400), and room and board ($7800). Part-time tuition: $325 per credit. *Required fees:* $40 per term part-time.
Financial Aid Of all full-time matriculated undergraduates who enrolled in 2003, 539 applied for aid, 488 were judged to have need, 264 had their need fully met. 168 Federal Work-Study jobs (averaging $1368). In 2003, 98 non-need-based awards were made. *Average percent of need met:* 100%. *Average financial aid package:* $19,127. *Average need-based loan:* $4749. *Average need-based gift aid:* $14,417. *Average non-need-based aid:* $9640. *Average indebtedness upon graduation:* $17,178.
Applying *Options:* common application, electronic application, early admission, early action, deferred entrance. *Application fee:* $25. *Required:* essay or personal statement, high school transcript, minimum 2.0 GPA, 2 letters of recommendation. *Recommended:* minimum 3.0 GPA, interview, resume. *Application deadlines:* 2/15 (freshmen), 2/15 (transfers). *Notification:* continuous until 6/30 (freshmen), 1/1 (early action), continuous until 6/30 (transfers).
Admissions Contact Ms. Sharon Bogdan, Associate Vice President for Enrollment Management, College of Notre Dame of Maryland, 4701 North Charles Street, Baltimore, MD 21210. *Phone:* 410-532-5330. *Toll-free phone:* 800-435-0200 (in-state); 800-435-0300 (out-of-state). *Fax:* 410-532-6287. *E-mail:* admiss@ndm.edu.

■ *See page 1446 for a narrative description.*

COLUMBIA UNION COLLEGE
Takoma Park, Maryland

- **Independent Seventh-day Adventist** comprehensive, founded 1904
- **Calendar** semesters
- **Degrees** associate, bachelor's, and master's
- **Suburban** 19-acre campus with easy access to Washington, DC
- **Endowment** $3.3 million
- **Coed,** 1,159 undergraduate students, 66% full-time, 64% women, 36% men
- **Minimally difficult** entrance level, 54% of applicants were admitted

Undergraduates 762 full-time, 397 part-time. Students come from 39 states and territories, 42% are from out of state, 52% African American, 7% Asian American or Pacific Islander, 10% Hispanic American, 0.4% Native American, 0.9% international, 6% transferred in, 47% live on campus. *Retention:* 64% of 2002 full-time freshmen returned.
Freshmen *Admission:* 851 applied, 460 admitted, 187 enrolled. *Average high school GPA:* 2.99. *Test scores:* SAT verbal scores over 500: 29%; SAT math scores over 500: 25%; ACT scores over 18: 50%; SAT verbal scores over 600: 10%; SAT math scores over 600: 4%; ACT scores over 24: 14%; SAT verbal scores over 700: 1%; SAT math scores over 700: 1%.
Faculty *Total:* 56, 95% full-time, 43% with terminal degrees. *Student/faculty ratio:* 13:1.
Majors Accounting; biochemistry; biology/biological sciences; broadcast journalism; business administration and management; chemistry; computer science; counseling psychology; early childhood education; elementary education; engineering; English; English/language arts teacher education; general studies; health and physical education; health/health care administration; history; information science/studies; journalism; liberal arts and sciences/liberal studies; mass communication/media; mathematics; mathematics teacher education; music; music performance; music teacher education; nursing (registered nurse training); political science and government; pre-dentistry studies; pre-law studies; pre-medical studies; pre-veterinary studies; psychology; religious education; respiratory care therapy; theology.
Academic Programs *Special study options:* academic remediation for entering students, accelerated degree program, adult/continuing education programs, advanced placement credit, cooperative education, distance learning, double majors, English as a second language, external degree program, independent study, internships, off-campus study, part-time degree program, student-designed majors, study abroad, summer session for credit. *Unusual degree programs:* 3-2 engineering with University of Maryland College Park.
Library Theofield G. Weis Library with 131,617 titles, 5,358 serial subscriptions, 7,500 audiovisual materials, an OPAC, a Web page.

Columbia Union College (continued)

Computers on Campus 50 computers available on campus for general student use. A campuswide network can be accessed from student residence rooms and from off campus. Internet access, at least one staffed computer lab available.

Student Life *Housing options:* men-only, women-only. Campus housing is university owned. Freshman campus housing is guaranteed. *Activities and organizations:* drama/theater group, student-run newspaper, radio station, choral group, Student Association. *Campus security:* 24-hour emergency response devices, student patrols, late-night transport/escort service. *Student services:* health clinic, personal/psychological counseling.

Athletics Member NCAA. All Division II. *Intercollegiate sports:* baseball M, basketball M(s)/W(s), cross-country running M(s)/W(s), soccer M(s)/W(s), softball W(s), track and field M(s)/W(s). *Intramural sports:* basketball M/W, cross-country running M/W, football M, golf M, gymnastics M/W, racquetball M/W, soccer M/W, track and field M/W.

Standardized Tests *Required:* SAT I or ACT (for admission).

Costs (2003–04) *Comprehensive fee:* $20,543 includes full-time tuition ($14,698), mandatory fees ($550), and room and board ($5295). Part-time tuition: $612 per semester hour. Part-time tuition and fees vary according to class time. *Required fees:* $275 per term part-time. *Payment plan:* installment. *Waivers:* senior citizens and employees or children of employees.

Financial Aid *Average indebtedness upon graduation:* $16,225.

Applying *Options:* electronic application, early admission, deferred entrance. *Application fee:* $25. *Required:* high school transcript, minimum 2.50 GPA, 2 letters of recommendation. *Required for some:* essay or personal statement, interview. *Application deadline:* 8/1 (freshmen), rolling (transfers). *Notification:* continuous (freshmen), continuous (transfers).

Admissions Contact Mr. Emil John, Director of Admissions, Columbia Union College, 7600 Flower Avenue, Takoma Park, MD 20412. *Phone:* 301-891-4502. *Toll-free phone:* 800-835-4212. *Fax:* 301-891-4230. *E-mail:* enroll@cuc.edu.

■ *See page 1478 for a narrative description.*

COPPIN STATE UNIVERSITY
Baltimore, Maryland

Admissions Contact Ms. Michelle Gross, Director of Admissions, Coppin State University, 2500 W North Avenue, Baltimore, MD 21216. *Phone:* 410-951-3600. *Toll-free phone:* 800-635-3674. *E-mail:* mgross@coppin.edu.

DEVRY UNIVERSITY
Bethesda, Maryland

Admissions Contact 4550 Montgomery Avenue, Suite 100 N, Bethesda, MD 20814-3304.

FROSTBURG STATE UNIVERSITY
Frostburg, Maryland

- **State-supported** comprehensive, founded 1898, part of University System of Maryland
- **Calendar** semesters
- **Degrees** certificates, bachelor's, master's, post-master's, and postbachelor's certificates
- **Small-town** 260-acre campus with easy access to Baltimore and Washington, DC
- **Endowment** $6.4 million
- **Coed,** 4,588 undergraduate students, 93% full-time, 51% women, 49% men
- **Moderately difficult** entrance level, 79% of applicants were admitted

Undergraduates 4,264 full-time, 324 part-time. Students come from 23 states and territories, 20 other countries, 12% are from out of state, 12% African American, 2% Asian American or Pacific Islander, 2% Hispanic American, 0.6% Native American, 0.6% international, 8% transferred in, 34% live on campus. *Retention:* 70% of 2002 full-time freshmen returned.

Freshmen *Admission:* 3,905 applied, 3,068 admitted, 990 enrolled. *Average high school GPA:* 3.07. *Test scores:* SAT verbal scores over 500: 55%; SAT math scores over 500: 58%; ACT scores over 18: 63%; SAT verbal scores over 600: 13%; SAT math scores over 600: 15%; ACT scores over 24: 10%; SAT verbal scores over 700: 1%; SAT math scores over 700: 1%.

Faculty *Total:* 339, 71% full-time, 56% with terminal degrees. *Student/faculty ratio:* 18:1.

Majors Accounting; actuarial science; biological specializations related; biology/biological sciences; business administration and management; business teacher education; chemistry; city/urban, community and regional planning; communication/speech communication and rhetoric; computer and information sciences; criminal justice/law enforcement administration; criminal justice/police science; dance; dramatic/theatre arts; economics; electrical, electronics and communications engineering; elementary education; English; environmental studies; foreign languages and literatures; geography; history; information science/studies; international relations and affairs; kindergarten/preschool education; kinesiology and exercise science; liberal arts and sciences/liberal studies; mass communication/media; mathematics; mechanical engineering; multi-/interdisciplinary studies related; music; natural resources/conservation; parks, recreation and leisure; philosophy; physical education teaching and coaching; physical sciences related; physics; political science and government; psychology; secondary education; social sciences; social work; sociology; speech and rhetoric; sport and fitness administration; visual and performing arts; wildlife and wildlands science and management.

Academic Programs *Special study options:* adult/continuing education programs, advanced placement credit, distance learning, double majors, freshman honors college, honors programs, independent study, internships, off-campus study, part-time degree program, services for LD students, study abroad, summer session for credit. *Unusual degree programs:* 3-2 engineering with University of Maryland, College Park.

Library Lewis J. Ort Library with 261,712 titles, 2,430 serial subscriptions, 32,224 audiovisual materials, an OPAC, a Web page.

Computers on Campus 577 computers available on campus for general student use. A campuswide network can be accessed from student residence rooms and from off campus. Internet access, online (class) registration, at least one staffed computer lab available.

Student Life *Housing options:* coed, men-only, women-only. Campus housing is university owned. *Activities and organizations:* drama/theater group, student-run newspaper, radio and television station, choral group, marching band, Student Government Association, Black Student Association, Campus Activities Board, Residence Hall Association, national fraternities, national sororities. *Campus security:* 24-hour emergency response devices and patrols, student patrols, late-night transport/escort service, controlled dormitory access, bicycle patrols. *Student services:* health clinic, personal/psychological counseling, women's center.

Athletics Member NCAA. All Division III. *Intercollegiate sports:* baseball M, basketball M/W, cross-country running M/W, field hockey W, football M, lacrosse W, soccer M/W, softball W, swimming M/W, tennis M/W, track and field M/W, volleyball W. *Intramural sports:* badminton M/W, basketball M/W, field hockey M/W, football M/W, golf M/W, lacrosse M(c)/W, racquetball M/W, rugby M(c), soccer M/W, softball M/W, squash M/W, table tennis M/W, tennis M/W, volleyball M(c)/W, water polo M/W, weight lifting M/W, wrestling M.

Standardized Tests *Required:* SAT I or ACT (for admission).

Costs (2004–05) *Tuition:* state resident $4720 full-time, $196 per credit hour part-time; nonresident $12,264 full-time, $346 per credit hour part-time. Full-time tuition and fees vary according to course load and program. Part-time tuition and fees vary according to course load and program. *Required fees:* $1110 full-time, $45 per credit hour part-time, $9 per term part-time. *Room and board:* $5772; room only: $2954. Room and board charges vary according to board plan and housing facility. *Payment plans:* installment, deferred payment. *Waivers:* senior citizens and employees or children of employees.

Financial Aid Of all full-time matriculated undergraduates who enrolled in 2003, 3,035 applied for aid, 2,130 were judged to have need, 732 had their need fully met. 196 Federal Work-Study jobs (averaging $958). 535 state and other part-time jobs (averaging $360). In 2003, 452 non-need-based awards were made. *Average percent of need met:* 77%. *Average financial aid package:* $6589. *Average need-based loan:* $3335. *Average need-based gift aid:* $4217. *Average non-need-based aid:* $3563. *Average indebtedness upon graduation:* $15,174.

Applying *Options:* electronic application, early admission. *Application fee:* $30. *Required:* high school transcript, minimum 2.0 GPA. *Required for some:* essay or personal statement. *Recommended:* letters of recommendation, interview. *Application deadline:* rolling (freshmen), rolling (transfers).

Admissions Contact Ms. Trish Gregory, Associate Director for Admissions, Frostburg State University, 101 Braddock Road, Frostburg, MD 21532-1099. *Phone:* 301-687-4201. *Fax:* 301-687-7074. *E-mail:* fsuadmissions@frostburg.edu.

■ *See page 1658 for a narrative description.*

GEORGE MEANY CENTER FOR LABOR STUDIES-THE NATIONAL LABOR COLLEGE
Silver Spring, Maryland

Admissions Contact Carrie Spruill, Acting Chief Financial Aid Officer/Student services, George Meany Center for Labor Studies-The National Labor College, 10000 New Hampshire Avenue, Silver Spring, MD 20903. *Phone:* 301-431-5404. *Toll-free phone:* 800-GMC-4CDP.

GOUCHER COLLEGE
Baltimore, Maryland

- **Independent** comprehensive, founded 1885
- **Calendar** semesters
- **Degrees** bachelor's, master's, and postbachelor's certificates
- **Suburban** 287-acre campus
- **Endowment** $136.6 million
- **Coed,** 1,310 undergraduate students, 97% full-time, 68% women, 32% men
- **Moderately difficult** entrance level, 65% of applicants were admitted

Undergraduates 1,268 full-time, 42 part-time. 63% are from out of state, 6% African American, 3% Asian American or Pacific Islander, 3% Hispanic American, 0.2% Native American, 0.9% international, 3% transferred in, 71% live on campus. *Retention:* 80% of 2002 full-time freshmen returned.

Freshmen *Admission:* 2,751 applied, 1,779 admitted, 342 enrolled. *Average high school GPA:* 3.23. *Test scores:* SAT verbal scores over 500: 96%; SAT math scores over 500: 91%; ACT scores over 18: 100%; SAT verbal scores over 600: 61%; SAT math scores over 600: 51%; ACT scores over 24: 81%; SAT verbal scores over 700: 14%; SAT math scores over 700: 8%; ACT scores over 30: 22%.

Faculty *Total:* 98. *Student/faculty ratio:* 10:1.

Majors American studies; art; biology/biological sciences; chemistry; computer science; dance; dramatic/theatre arts; economics; education; elementary education; English; French; historic preservation and conservation; history; interdisciplinary studies; international relations and affairs; management science; mass communication/media; mathematics; music; philosophy; physics; political science and government; psychology; religious studies; Russian; sociology; Spanish; special education; women's studies.

Academic Programs *Special study options:* adult/continuing education programs, advanced placement credit, distance learning, double majors, honors programs, independent study, internships, off-campus study, part-time degree program, services for LD students, student-designed majors, study abroad. *Unusual degree programs:* 3-2 engineering with Johns Hopkins University.

Library Julia Rogers Library with 303,364 titles, 1,098 serial subscriptions, 5,691 audiovisual materials, an OPAC, a Web page.

Computers on Campus 150 computers available on campus for general student use. A campuswide network can be accessed from student residence rooms and from off campus. Internet access, at least one staffed computer lab available.

Student Life *Housing:* on-campus residence required through sophomore year. *Options:* coed, women-only. Campus housing is university owned. Freshman campus housing is guaranteed. *Activities and organizations:* drama/theater group, student-run newspaper, radio and television station, choral group, CAUSE (Community Auxiliary for Service), Umoja: The African Alliance, Quindecim (newspaper), BGlad, Hillel. *Campus security:* 24-hour emergency response devices and patrols, late-night transport/escort service, controlled dormitory access. *Student services:* health clinic, personal/psychological counseling, women's center.

Athletics Member NCAA. All Division III. *Intercollegiate sports:* basketball M/W, cross-country running M/W, equestrian sports M/W, field hockey W, lacrosse M/W, soccer M/W, swimming M/W, tennis M/W, volleyball W. *Intramural sports:* equestrian sports M(c)/W(c), fencing M(c)/W(c), football M/W, golf M/W, racquetball M/W, soccer M/W, softball M/W(c), squash M/W, tennis M/W, volleyball M/W.

Standardized Tests *Required:* SAT I or ACT (for admission). *Recommended:* SAT II: Subject Tests (for admission), SAT II: Writing Test (for admission).

Costs (2003–04) *Comprehensive fee:* $32,800 includes full-time tuition ($24,150), mandatory fees ($300), and room and board ($8350). Part-time tuition: $865 per credit hour. *College room only:* $2675. Room and board charges vary according to board plan. *Payment plan:* installment. *Waivers:* employees or children of employees.

Financial Aid Of all full-time matriculated undergraduates who enrolled in 2002, 844 applied for aid, 726 were judged to have need, 207 had their need fully met. 208 Federal Work-Study jobs (averaging $486). 550 state and other part-time jobs (averaging $934). In 2002, 94 non-need-based awards were made. *Average percent of need met:* 72%. *Average financial aid package:* $18,813. *Average need-based loan:* $4068. *Average non-need-based aid:* $9363. *Average indebtedness upon graduation:* $16,062.

Applying *Options:* common application, electronic application, early admission, early action, deferred entrance. *Application fee:* $40. *Required:* essay or personal statement, high school transcript, minimum 2.0 GPA, 3 letters of recommendation. *Recommended:* minimum 3.0 GPA, interview. *Application deadlines:* 2/1 (freshmen), 4/1 (transfers). *Notification:* 4/1 (freshmen), 1/15 (early action), 4/15 (transfers).

Admissions Contact Mr. Carlton E. Surbeck III, Director of Admissions, Goucher College, 1021 Dulaney Valley Road, Baltimore, MD 21204-2794. *Phone:* 410-337-6100. *Toll-free phone:* 800-468-2437. *Fax:* 410-337-6354. *E-mail:* admission@goucher.edu.

■ *See page 1678 for a narrative description.*

GRIGGS UNIVERSITY
Silver Spring, Maryland

- **Independent Seventh-day Adventist** 4-year, founded 1990, part of Seventh-day Adventist Parochial School System
- **Calendar** continuous
- **Degrees** associate and bachelor's (offers only external degree programs)
- **Suburban** campus with easy access to Washington D.C.
- **Coed,** 358 undergraduate students
- **Minimally difficult** entrance level

Faculty *Total:* 39, 56% with terminal degrees.

Majors Business administration and management; religious education; religious studies; theology.

Academic Programs *Special study options:* accelerated degree program, adult/continuing education programs, advanced placement credit, distance learning, double majors, external degree program, independent study, part-time degree program, summer session for credit.

Student Life *Housing:* college housing not available.

Costs (2004–05) *Tuition:* $6900 full-time, $230 per semester hour part-time. Full-time tuition and fees vary according to course load. Part-time tuition and fees vary according to course load. *Required fees:* $70 full-time, $70 per year part-time. *Payment plan:* installment. *Waivers:* senior citizens and employees or children of employees.

Applying *Options:* common application, early admission, deferred entrance. *Application fee:* $50. *Required:* essay or personal statement, high school transcript, minimum 2.0 GPA. *Application deadline:* rolling (freshmen), rolling (transfers).

Admissions Contact Ms. Eva Michel, Enrollment Officer, Griggs University, PO Box 4437, Silver Spring, MD 20914-4437. *Phone:* 301-680-6593. *Toll-free phone:* 800-782-4769. *Fax:* 301-680-6577. *E-mail:* emichel@hsi.edu.

HOOD COLLEGE
Frederick, Maryland

- **Independent** comprehensive, founded 1893
- **Calendar** semesters
- **Degrees** bachelor's, master's, and postbachelor's certificates (also offers adult program with significant enrollment not reflected in profile)
- **Suburban** 50-acre campus with easy access to Baltimore and Washington, DC
- **Endowment** $50.6 million
- **Coed,** 864 undergraduate students, 80% full-time, 85% women, 15% men
- **Moderately difficult** entrance level, 55% of applicants were admitted

Undergraduates 687 full-time, 177 part-time. Students come from 27 states and territories, 22 other countries, 21% are from out of state, 13% African American, 2% Asian American or Pacific Islander, 2% Hispanic American, 0.2% Native American, 6% international, 13% transferred in, 54% live on campus. *Retention:* 75% of 2002 full-time freshmen returned.

Freshmen *Admission:* 1,001 applied, 546 admitted, 181 enrolled. *Average high school GPA:* 3.50. *Test scores:* SAT verbal scores over 500: 71%; SAT math scores over 500: 71%; ACT scores over 18: 89%; SAT verbal scores over 600: 31%; SAT math scores over 600: 26%; ACT scores over 24: 31%; SAT verbal scores over 700: 5%; SAT math scores over 700: 2%; ACT scores over 30: 5%.

Faculty *Total:* 175, 43% full-time, 63% with terminal degrees. *Student/faculty ratio:* 10:1.

Majors Art; biochemistry; biology/biological sciences; business administration and management; chemistry; communication and media related; computer and information sciences; economics; engineering; English; environmental studies; French; German; history; kindergarten/preschool education; Latin American studies; legal studies; mathematics; multi-/interdisciplinary studies related; music; philosophy; political science and government; psychology; religious studies; Romance languages related; social work; sociology; Spanish; special education.

Academic Programs *Special study options:* academic remediation for entering students, accelerated degree program, adult/continuing education programs, advanced placement credit, distance learning, double majors, English as a second

Hood College (continued)
language, honors programs, independent study, internships, off-campus study, part-time degree program, services for LD students, student-designed majors, study abroad, summer session for credit. *ROTC:* Army (c). *Unusual degree programs:* 3-2 engineering with George Washington University; computer science, biomedical science.

Library Beneficial-Hodson Library and Information Technology Center with 182,786 titles, 1,057 serial subscriptions, 3,864 audiovisual materials, an OPAC, a Web page.

Computers on Campus 277 computers available on campus for general student use. A campuswide network can be accessed from student residence rooms and from off campus. Internet access, at least one staffed computer lab available.

Student Life *Housing:* on-campus residence required through sophomore year. *Options:* coed, women-only, disabled students. Campus housing is university owned. Freshman campus housing is guaranteed. *Activities and organizations:* drama/theater group, student-run newspaper, choral group, education club, Black Student Union, Campus Activities Board, international club, Hood Today (newspaper). *Campus security:* 24-hour emergency response devices and patrols, late-night transport/escort service, controlled dormitory access, residence hall security. *Student services:* health clinic, personal/psychological counseling, women's center.

Athletics Member NCAA. All Division III. *Intercollegiate sports:* basketball M/W, cheerleading M/W, cross-country running M(c)/W(c), equestrian sports W(c), field hockey W, golf M(c)/W(c), lacrosse W, soccer W, softball W, swimming M/W, tennis M/W, volleyball W.

Standardized Tests *Required:* SAT I or ACT (for admission). *Recommended:* SAT II: Subject Tests (for admission).

Costs (2003–04) *Comprehensive fee:* $27,795 includes full-time tuition ($19,940), mandatory fees ($335), and room and board ($7520). Part-time tuition: $575 per credit. Part-time tuition and fees vary according to course load. *Required fees:* $105 per term part-time. *College room only:* $3920. Room and board charges vary according to board plan. *Payment plans:* tuition prepayment, installment, deferred payment. *Waivers:* children of alumni and employees or children of employees.

Financial Aid Of all full-time matriculated undergraduates who enrolled in 2003, 589 applied for aid, 519 were judged to have need, 220 had their need fully met. 135 Federal Work-Study jobs (averaging $1636). 100 state and other part-time jobs (averaging $1627). In 2003, 147 non-need-based awards were made. *Average percent of need met:* 90%. *Average financial aid package:* $17,518. *Average need-based loan:* $4731. *Average need-based gift aid:* $13,899. *Average non-need-based aid:* $14,337. *Average indebtedness upon graduation:* $17,392.

Applying *Options:* common application, electronic application, early admission, early action, deferred entrance. *Application fee:* $35. *Required:* essay or personal statement, high school transcript, 1 letter of recommendation. *Recommended:* interview. *Application deadline:* 2/1 (freshmen). *Notification:* 3/15 (freshmen), 1/2 (early action), continuous (transfers).

Admissions Contact Dr. Susan Hallenbeck, Dean of Admissions, Hood College, 401 Rosemont Avenue, Frederick, MD 21701. *Phone:* 301-696-3400. *Toll-free phone:* 800-922-1599. *Fax:* 301-696-3819. *E-mail:* admissions@hood.edu.

THE JOHNS HOPKINS UNIVERSITY

Baltimore, Maryland

- **Independent** university, founded 1876
- **Calendar** 4-1-4
- **Degrees** certificates, diplomas, bachelor's, master's, doctoral, first professional, post-master's, and postbachelor's certificates
- **Urban** 140-acre campus with easy access to Washington, DC
- **Endowment** $1.7 billion
- **Coed,** 4,177 undergraduate students, 99% full-time, 43% women, 57% men
- **Most difficult** entrance level, 30% of applicants were admitted

Since its founding in 1876 as America's first great research university, Johns Hopkins University has been attracting brilliant thinkers. Johns Hopkins puts the power of education directly into the hands of students through opportunities to engage with professors and peers in the areas of humanities, social and behavioral sciences, engineering, and natural sciences. This, combined with a small undergraduate enrollment, affords unparalleled exposure to creative investigation and discovery beginning in the freshman year.

Undergraduates 4,136 full-time, 41 part-time. Students come from 51 states and territories, 50 other countries, 80% are from out of state, 5% African American, 21% Asian American or Pacific Islander, 4% Hispanic American, 0.3% Native American, 6% international, 0.5% transferred in, 50% live on campus. *Retention:* 95% of 2002 full-time freshmen returned.

Freshmen *Admission:* 10,022 applied, 3,052 admitted, 1,048 enrolled. *Average high school GPA:* 3.66. *Test scores:* SAT verbal scores over 500: 99%; SAT math scores over 500: 100%; ACT scores over 18: 100%; SAT verbal scores over 600: 88%; SAT math scores over 600: 94%; ACT scores over 24: 98%; SAT verbal scores over 700: 38%; SAT math scores over 700: 59%; ACT scores over 30: 59%.

Faculty *Total:* 478, 95% full-time.

Majors American studies; anthropology; applied mathematics; art history, criticism and conservation; Asian studies (East); behavioral sciences; biological and physical sciences; biology/biological sciences; biomedical/medical engineering; biophysics; business/commerce; chemical engineering; chemistry; civil engineering; classics and languages, literatures and linguistics; cognitive psychology and psycholinguistics; computer and information sciences; computer engineering; creative writing; economics; electrical, electronics and communications engineering; electroneurodiagnostic/electroencephalographic technology; engineering; engineering mechanics; English; environmental/environmental health engineering; environmental studies; film/cinema studies; French; geography; geology/earth science; German; history; history and philosophy of science and technology; industrial engineering; interdisciplinary studies; international relations and affairs; Italian; Latin American studies; liberal arts and sciences and humanities related; liberal arts and sciences/liberal studies; literature; materials engineering; materials science; mathematics; mechanical engineering; music; music performance; music teacher education; music theory and composition; natural sciences; Near and Middle Eastern studies; neuroscience; nursing (registered nurse training); philosophy; physics; physiological psychology/psychobiology; political science and government; psychology; public administration; public health; social sciences; sociology; Spanish.

Academic Programs *Special study options:* accelerated degree program, adult/continuing education programs, advanced placement credit, double majors, English as a second language, honors programs, independent study, internships, off-campus study, part-time degree program, services for LD students, student-designed majors, study abroad, summer session for credit. *ROTC:* Army (b), Air Force (c). *Unusual degree programs:* 3-2 international studies with Johns Hopkins University, School of Advanced International Studies (Washington, DC); education.

Library Milton S. Eisenhower Library plus 6 others with 3.5 million titles, 30,023 serial subscriptions, 299,605 audiovisual materials, an OPAC, a Web page.

Computers on Campus 460 computers available on campus for general student use. A campuswide network can be accessed from student residence rooms and from off campus. Internet access, online (class) registration, at least one staffed computer lab available.

Student Life *Housing:* on-campus residence required through sophomore year. *Options:* coed, men-only, women-only, disabled students. Campus housing is university owned. Freshman campus housing is guaranteed. *Activities and organizations:* drama/theater group, student-run newspaper, radio station, choral group, The Outdoors Club, The Hopkins Organization for Programs, The Barn Stormers (theater group), Inter-Asian Council, Olé (Latino Student organization), national fraternities, national sororities. *Campus security:* 24-hour emergency response devices and patrols, student patrols, late-night transport/escort service, controlled dormitory access. *Student services:* health clinic, personal/psychological counseling.

Athletics Member NCAA. All Division III except men's and women's lacrosse (Division I). *Intercollegiate sports:* baseball M, basketball M/W, cheerleading M/W, crew M/W, cross-country running M/W, fencing M/W, field hockey W, football M, golf M(c)/W(c), ice hockey M(c), lacrosse M(s)/W(s), rugby M(c)/W(c), soccer M/W, softball W(c), swimming M/W, table tennis M(c)/W(c), tennis M/W, track and field M/W, volleyball W, water polo M, wrestling M. *Intramural sports:* basketball M/W, football M/W, lacrosse M/W, soccer M/W, tennis M(c)/W(c), ultimate Frisbee M(c)/W(c), volleyball M/W.

Standardized Tests *Required:* SAT I and SAT II or ACT (for admission), SAT II: Writing Test (for admission).

Costs (2003–04) *Comprehensive fee:* $38,372 includes full-time tuition ($28,730), mandatory fees ($500), and room and board ($9142). *Room and board:* Room and board charges vary according to board plan and housing facility. *Payment plan:* installment. *Waivers:* employees or children of employees.

Financial Aid Of all full-time matriculated undergraduates who enrolled in 2002, 2,192 applied for aid, 1,671 were judged to have need, 1,507 had their need fully met. 1,381 Federal Work-Study jobs (averaging $1878). In 2002, 231 non-need-based awards were made. *Average percent of need met:* 95%. *Average financial aid package:* $25,210. *Average need-based loan:* $3815. *Average need-based gift aid:* $20,046. *Average non-need-based aid:* $14,982. *Average indebtedness upon graduation:* $13,600. *Financial aid deadline:* 2/15.

Applying *Options:* common application, electronic application, early admission, early decision, deferred entrance. *Application fee:* $60. *Required:* essay or personal statement, high school transcript, 1 letter of recommendation. *Recom-*

mended: interview. *Application deadlines:* 1/1 (freshmen), 3/15 (transfers). *Early decision:* 11/15. *Notification:* 4/1 (freshmen), 12/15 (early decision), 4/15 (transfers).

Admissions Contact Mr. John Latting, Director of Undergraduate Admissions, The Johns Hopkins University, 140 Garland Hall, 3400 North Charles Street, Baltimore, MD 21218-2699. *Phone:* 410-516-8341. *Fax:* 410-516-6025. *E-mail:* gotojhu@jhu.edu.

■ **See pages 1790 and 1792 for narrative descriptions.**

LOYOLA COLLEGE IN MARYLAND

Baltimore, Maryland

- **Independent Roman Catholic (Jesuit)** comprehensive, founded 1852
- **Calendar** semesters
- **Degrees** bachelor's, master's, doctoral, and post-master's certificates
- **Urban** 89-acre campus with easy access to Washington, DC
- **Endowment** $118.9 million
- **Coed,** 3,413 undergraduate students, 98% full-time, 58% women, 42% men
- **Moderately difficult** entrance level, 71% of applicants were admitted

Undergraduates 3,350 full-time, 63 part-time. Students come from 38 states and territories, 19 other countries, 80% are from out of state, 5% African American, 2% Asian American or Pacific Islander, 2% Hispanic American, 0.1% Native American, 0.6% international, 1% transferred in, 79% live on campus. *Retention:* 92% of 2002 full-time freshmen returned.

Freshmen *Admission:* 6,611 applied, 4,675 admitted, 916 enrolled. *Average high school GPA:* 3.41. *Test scores:* SAT verbal scores over 500: 96%; SAT math scores over 500: 97%; SAT verbal scores over 600: 52%; SAT math scores over 600: 62%; SAT verbal scores over 700: 11%; SAT math scores over 700: 10%.

Faculty *Total:* 514, 55% full-time. *Student/faculty ratio:* 13:1.

Majors Accounting; applied mathematics; art; biology/biological sciences; business/commerce; chemistry; classics and languages, literatures and linguistics; communication/speech communication and rhetoric; computer and information sciences; creative writing; economics; education; electrical, electronics and communications engineering; elementary education; engineering; English; finance; French; German; history; interdisciplinary studies; international business/trade/commerce; mathematics; philosophy; physics; political science and government; psychology; religious studies; sociology; Spanish; special education; speech-language pathology.

Academic Programs *Special study options:* accelerated degree program, advanced placement credit, double majors, honors programs, independent study, internships, off-campus study, part-time degree program, services for LD students, study abroad, summer session for credit. *ROTC:* Army (b), Air Force (c).

Library Loyola/Notre Dame Library with 293,639 titles, 2,126 serial subscriptions, 28,878 audiovisual materials, an OPAC, a Web page.

Computers on Campus 292 computers available on campus for general student use. A campuswide network can be accessed from student residence rooms and from off campus. Internet access, at least one staffed computer lab available.

Student Life *Housing:* on-campus residence required for freshman year. *Options:* coed. Campus housing is university owned. Freshman applicants given priority for college housing. *Activities and organizations:* drama/theater group, student-run newspaper, choral group. *Campus security:* 24-hour emergency response devices and patrols, late-night transport/escort service, controlled dormitory access. *Student services:* health clinic, personal/psychological counseling.

Athletics Member NCAA. All Division I except men's and women's cheerleading (Division III). *Intercollegiate sports:* basketball M/W, cheerleading M/W, crew M/W, cross-country running M/W, golf M, lacrosse M/W, soccer M/W, swimming M/W, tennis M/W, volleyball W. *Intramural sports:* ultimate Frisbee M(c)/W(c).

Standardized Tests *Required:* SAT I (for admission).

Costs (2003–04) *Comprehensive fee:* $35,240 includes full-time tuition ($26,010), mandatory fees ($600), and room and board ($8630). Full-time tuition and fees vary according to student level. Part-time tuition: $441 per credit. *Required fees:* $25 per term part-time. *College room only:* $6630. Room and board charges vary according to board plan. *Waivers:* employees or children of employees.

Financial Aid Of all full-time matriculated undergraduates who enrolled in 2003, 1,968 applied for aid, 1,611 were judged to have need, 1,514 had their need fully met. 376 Federal Work-Study jobs (averaging $1870). 66 state and other part-time jobs (averaging $9025). In 2003, 493 non-need-based awards were made. *Average percent of need met:* 98%. *Average financial aid package:* $17,370. *Average need-based loan:* $5370. *Average need-based gift aid:* $10,050. *Average non-need-based aid:* $9767. *Average indebtedness upon graduation:* $15,870. *Financial aid deadline:* 2/15.

Applying *Options:* common application, early admission, deferred entrance. *Application fee:* $30. *Required:* essay or personal statement, high school transcript. *Recommended:* interview. *Application deadlines:* 1/15 (freshmen), 7/15 (transfers). *Notification:* 4/15 (freshmen).

Admissions Contact Mr. David Dukor-Jackson, Director of Undergraduate Admissions, Loyola College in Maryland, 4501 North Charles Street, Baltimore, MD 21210. *Phone:* 410-617-2015. *Toll-free phone:* 800-221-9107 Ext. 2252. *Fax:* 410-617-2176.

■ *See page 1894 for a narrative description.*

MAPLE SPRINGS BAPTIST BIBLE COLLEGE AND SEMINARY

Capitol Heights, Maryland

Admissions Contact Ms. Mazie Murphy, Assistant Director of Admissions and Records, Maple Springs Baptist Bible College and Seminary, 4130 Belt Road, Capitol Heights, MD 20743. *Phone:* 301-736-3631. *Fax:* 301-735-6507.

MARYLAND INSTITUTE COLLEGE OF ART

Baltimore, Maryland

- **Independent** comprehensive, founded 1826
- **Calendar** semesters
- **Degrees** bachelor's, master's, and postbachelor's certificates
- **Urban** 12-acre campus with easy access to Washington, DC
- **Endowment** $33.3 million
- **Coed,** 1,290 undergraduate students, 99% full-time, 62% women, 38% men
- **Very difficult** entrance level, 50% of applicants were admitted

Undergraduates 1,273 full-time, 17 part-time. Students come from 44 states and territories, 52 other countries, 76% are from out of state, 4% African American, 8% Asian American or Pacific Islander, 5% Hispanic American, 0.5% Native American, 5% international, 5% transferred in, 88% live on campus. *Retention:* 85% of 2002 full-time freshmen returned.

Freshmen *Admission:* 1,944 applied, 971 admitted, 385 enrolled. *Average high school GPA:* 3.49. *Test scores:* SAT verbal scores over 500: 87%; SAT math scores over 500: 80%; SAT verbal scores over 600: 51%; SAT math scores over 600: 35%; SAT verbal scores over 700: 10%; SAT math scores over 700: 4%.

Faculty *Total:* 217, 54% full-time, 77% with terminal degrees. *Student/faculty ratio:* 10:1.

Majors Art; art teacher education; ceramic arts and ceramics; drawing; fiber, textile and weaving arts; film/video and photographic arts related; fine/studio arts; graphic design; illustration; interior design; intermedia/multimedia; painting; photography; printmaking; sculpture; visual and performing arts.

Academic Programs *Special study options:* academic remediation for entering students, accelerated degree program, adult/continuing education programs, advanced placement credit, distance learning, double majors, independent study, internships, off-campus study, services for LD students, student-designed majors, study abroad, summer session for credit. *ROTC:* Army (c).

Library Decker Library plus 1 other with 53,000 titles, 305 serial subscriptions, 4,600 audiovisual materials, an OPAC, a Web page.

Computers on Campus 250 computers available on campus for general student use. A campuswide network can be accessed from student residence rooms and from off campus that provide access to e-mail. Internet access, at least one staffed computer lab available.

Student Life *Housing options:* coed, disabled students. Campus housing is university owned. Freshman applicants given priority for college housing. *Activities and organizations:* drama/theater group, choral group, a Cappela, soccer teams, Black Student Union, Channel Organix, knitting club. *Campus security:* 24-hour emergency response devices and patrols, student patrols, late-night transport/escort service, controlled dormitory access, self-defense education, 24-hour building security, safety awareness programs, campus patrols by city police. *Student services:* health clinic, personal/psychological counseling.

Athletics *Intramural sports:* soccer M(c)/W(c).

Standardized Tests *Required:* SAT I or ACT (for admission).

Costs (2003–04) *Comprehensive fee:* $30,890 includes full-time tuition ($22,980), mandatory fees ($730), and room and board ($7180). Part-time tuition: $960 per credit. *Required fees:* $220 per term part-time. *College room only:* $5000. Room and board charges vary according to board plan and housing facility. *Payment plan:* installment. *Waivers:* employees or children of employees.

Financial Aid *Average indebtedness upon graduation:* $17,472.

Applying *Options:* electronic application, early admission, early decision, deferred entrance. *Application fee:* $50. *Required:* essay or personal statement, high school transcript, art portfolio. *Recommended:* 3 letters of recommendation, interview. *Application deadlines:* 1/15 (freshmen), 3/15 (transfers). *Early decision:* 11/15. *Notification:* 3/15 (freshmen), 12/15 (early decision), 4/15 (transfers).

Maryland Institute College of Art (continued)

Admissions Contact Mr. Hans Ever, Director of Undergraduate Admission, Maryland Institute College of Art, 1300 Mount Royal Avenue, Baltimore, MD 21217-4191. *Phone:* 410-225-2222. *Fax:* 410-225-2337. *E-mail:* admissions@mica.edu.

■ *See page 1940 for a narrative description.*

McDANIEL COLLEGE
Westminster, Maryland

- **Independent** comprehensive, founded 1867
- **Calendar** 4-1-4
- **Degrees** bachelor's and master's
- **Suburban** 160-acre campus with easy access to Baltimore and Washington, DC
- **Endowment** $56.4 million
- **Coed,** 1,744 undergraduate students, 97% full-time, 57% women, 43% men
- **Moderately difficult** entrance level, 83% of applicants were admitted

Undergraduates 1,684 full-time, 60 part-time. Students come from 30 states and territories, 12 other countries, 26% are from out of state, 9% African American, 1% Asian American or Pacific Islander, 1% Hispanic American, 0.6% Native American, 2% international, 4% transferred in, 77% live on campus. *Retention:* 83% of 2002 full-time freshmen returned.

Freshmen *Admission:* 2,008 applied, 1,676 admitted, 451 enrolled. *Average high school GPA:* 3.40. *Test scores:* SAT verbal scores over 500: 74%; SAT math scores over 500: 78%; SAT verbal scores over 600: 28%; SAT math scores over 600: 28%; SAT verbal scores over 700: 5%; SAT math scores over 700: 3%.

Faculty *Total:* 180, 52% full-time, 61% with terminal degrees. *Student/faculty ratio:* 13:1.

Majors Art; art history, criticism and conservation; biochemistry; biology/biological sciences; business administration and management; chemistry; communication/speech communication and rhetoric; computer and information sciences; dramatic/theatre arts; economics; English; French; German; history; kinesiology and exercise science; mathematics; multi-/interdisciplinary studies related; music; philosophy; physics; political science and government; psychology; religious studies; social work; sociology; Spanish.

Academic Programs *Special study options:* academic remediation for entering students, adult/continuing education programs, advanced placement credit, double majors, honors programs, independent study, internships, off-campus study, part-time degree program, services for LD students, student-designed majors, study abroad, summer session for credit. *ROTC:* Army (b). *Unusual degree programs:* 3-2 engineering with University of Maryland College Park, Washington University in St. Louis; forestry with Duke University.

Library Hoover Library with 629,965 titles, 3,500 serial subscriptions, 11,125 audiovisual materials, an OPAC, a Web page.

Computers on Campus 171 computers available on campus for general student use. A campuswide network can be accessed from student residence rooms and from off campus. Internet access, at least one staffed computer lab available.

Student Life *Housing:* on-campus residence required through junior year. *Options:* coed, men-only, women-only, disabled students. Campus housing is university owned. Freshman campus housing is guaranteed. *Activities and organizations:* drama/theater group, student-run newspaper, radio and television station, choral group, national fraternities, national sororities. *Campus security:* 24-hour emergency response devices and patrols, late-night transport/escort service, controlled dormitory access. *Student services:* health clinic, personal/psychological counseling.

Athletics Member NCAA. All Division III. *Intercollegiate sports:* baseball M, basketball M/W, cross-country running M/W, field hockey W, football M, golf M/W, lacrosse M/W, soccer M/W, softball W, swimming M/W, tennis M/W, track and field M/W, volleyball W, wrestling M. *Intramural sports:* badminton M/W, basketball M/W, cheerleading M(c)/W(c), football M, golf M/W, racquetball M/W, soccer M/W, softball M/W, swimming M/W, tennis M/W, ultimate Frisbee M(c)/W(c), volleyball M/W, weight lifting M/W.

Standardized Tests *Required:* SAT I or ACT (for admission). *Recommended:* SAT II: Subject Tests (for admission).

Costs (2003–04) *Comprehensive fee:* $28,440 includes full-time tuition ($22,860), mandatory fees ($300), and room and board ($5280). Part-time tuition: $714 per credit. *Required fees:* $150 per term part-time. *College room only:* $2690. Room and board charges vary according to board plan and housing facility. *Payment plans:* tuition prepayment, installment. *Waivers:* employees or children of employees.

Financial Aid Of all full-time matriculated undergraduates who enrolled in 2003, 1,222 applied for aid, 1,047 were judged to have need, 313 had their need fully met. 195 Federal Work-Study jobs (averaging $783). 102 state and other part-time jobs (averaging $1189). In 2003, 418 non-need-based awards were made. *Average percent of need met:* 92%. *Average financial aid package:* $18,978. *Average need-based loan:* $4505. *Average need-based gift aid:* $7823. *Average non-need-based aid:* $7876. *Average indebtedness upon graduation:* $17,784.

Applying *Options:* common application, electronic application, early admission, early action, deferred entrance. *Application fee:* $40. *Required:* essay or personal statement, high school transcript, minimum 2.5 GPA. *Required for some:* interview. *Recommended:* letters of recommendation, interview. *Application deadlines:* 2/1 (freshmen), 6/1 (transfers). *Notification:* 4/1 (freshmen), 12/15 (early action), 7/15 (transfers).

Admissions Contact Ms. M. Martha O'Connell, Dean of Admissions, McDaniel College, 2 College Hill, Westminster, MD 21157-4390. *Phone:* 410-857-2230. *Toll-free phone:* 800-638-5005. *Fax:* 410-857-2757. *E-mail:* admissions@mcdaniel.edu.

■ *See page 1962 for a narrative description.*

MORGAN STATE UNIVERSITY
Baltimore, Maryland

- **State-supported** university, founded 1867
- **Calendar** semesters
- **Degrees** bachelor's, master's, and doctoral
- **Urban** 143-acre campus with easy access to Washington, DC
- **Coed,** 6,005 undergraduate students, 89% full-time, 58% women, 42% men
- **Moderately difficult** entrance level, 34% of applicants were admitted

Undergraduates 5,328 full-time, 677 part-time. Students come from 47 states and territories, 30 other countries, 91% African American, 0.5% Asian American or Pacific Islander, 0.5% Hispanic American, 0.2% Native American, 4% international, 5% transferred in, 30% live on campus. *Retention:* 71% of 2002 full-time freshmen returned.

Freshmen *Admission:* 11,387 applied, 3,900 admitted, 1,285 enrolled. *Average high school GPA:* 3.00. *Test scores:* SAT verbal scores over 500: 24%; SAT math scores over 500: 25%; ACT scores over 18: 21%; SAT verbal scores over 600: 3%; SAT math scores over 600: 3%; ACT scores over 24: 9%.

Faculty *Total:* 458, 79% full-time, 63% with terminal degrees. *Student/faculty ratio:* 15:1.

Majors Accounting; African-American/Black studies; African studies; art; art history, criticism and conservation; behavioral sciences; biology/biological sciences; business administration and management; business/managerial economics; business teacher education; chemistry; civil engineering; clinical laboratory science/medical technology; clinical/medical laboratory technology; computer science; dietetics; dramatic/theatre arts; economics; education; electrical, electronics and communications engineering; elementary education; engineering; engineering physics; English; family and consumer sciences/human sciences; finance; foods, nutrition, and wellness; health teacher education; history; hospitality administration; hotel/motel administration; human ecology; industrial engineering; information science/studies; management information systems; marketing/marketing management; mass communication/media; mathematics; mental health/rehabilitation; music; parks, recreation and leisure; philosophy; physical education teaching and coaching; physics; political science and government; pre-dentistry studies; pre-law studies; pre-medical studies; psychology; religious studies; secondary education; social work; sociology; speech and rhetoric; sport and fitness administration; telecommunications.

Academic Programs *Special study options:* academic remediation for entering students, accelerated degree program, adult/continuing education programs, advanced placement credit, cooperative education, honors programs, independent study, internships, off-campus study, part-time degree program, services for LD students, summer session for credit. *ROTC:* Army (b).

Library Morris Soper Library with 333,101 titles, 2,526 serial subscriptions, an OPAC.

Computers on Campus 65 computers available on campus for general student use. A campuswide network can be accessed from student residence rooms and from off campus that provide access to engineering lab supercomputer. Internet access, online (class) registration, at least one staffed computer lab available.

Student Life *Housing options:* coed. *Activities and organizations:* drama/theater group, student-run newspaper, radio station, choral group, marching band, Student Government Association, choir, band, national fraternities, national sororities. *Campus security:* 24-hour emergency response devices and patrols, late-night transport/escort service, controlled dormitory access. *Student services:* health clinic, personal/psychological counseling.

Athletics Member NCAA. All Division I except football (Division I-AA). *Intercollegiate sports:* basketball M(s)/W(s), bowling W, cross-country running M(s)/W(s), softball W, tennis M(s)/W(s), track and field M(s)/W(s), volleyball W. *Intramural sports:* badminton M/W, basketball M/W, bowling M/W, cross-country running M/W, field hockey M/W, football M, golf M/W, gymnastics

M/W, racquetball M/W, soccer M/W, softball M/W, swimming M/W, table tennis M/W, tennis M/W, track and field M/W, volleyball M/W, weight lifting M/W.
Standardized Tests *Required:* SAT I or ACT (for admission).
Costs (2004–05) *Tuition:* state resident $5718 full-time, $223 per credit part-time; nonresident $12,958 full-time, $480 per credit part-time. *Room and board:* $6780; room only: $4303. Room and board charges vary according to board plan and housing facility. *Payment plans:* installment, deferred payment. *Waivers:* senior citizens and employees or children of employees.
Financial Aid *Average percent of need met:* 97%.
Applying *Options:* common application, electronic application, early admission, deferred entrance. *Application fee:* $25. *Required:* high school transcript, minimum 2.0 GPA. *Required for some:* 2 letters of recommendation, interview. *Recommended:* essay or personal statement. *Application deadline:* rolling (freshmen), rolling (transfers). *Notification:* continuous (freshmen), continuous (transfers).
Admissions Contact Mr. Edwin T. Johnson, Director of Admissions and Recruitment, Morgan State University, 1700 East Cold Spring Lane, Baltimore, MD 21251. *Phone:* 443-885-3000. *Toll-free phone:* 800-332-6674.

■ *See page 2030 for a narrative description.*

Mount Saint Mary's College and Seminary
Emmitsburg, Maryland

■ **Independent Roman Catholic** comprehensive, founded 1808
■ **Calendar** semesters
■ **Degrees** bachelor's, master's, first professional, and postbachelor's certificates
■ **Rural** 1400-acre campus with easy access to Baltimore and Washington, DC
■ **Endowment** $27.2 million
■ **Coed,** 1,593 undergraduate students, 86% full-time, 57% women, 43% men
■ **Moderately difficult** entrance level, 90% of applicants were admitted

The Mount has expanded the concentrations in the business administration major to include sports management as well as finance, international business, management, and marketing. The sports management concentration includes courses in sport history, marketing, economics, and a required internship in the field. More than one half of Mount students enhance their majors with internships and study abroad programs. The Mount is proud to award academic scholarships ranging from $5000 to more than $21,000 per year for qualified students.

Undergraduates 1,371 full-time, 222 part-time. Students come from 24 states and territories, 5 other countries, 44% are from out of state, 5% African American, 2% Asian American or Pacific Islander, 3% Hispanic American, 0.3% Native American, 0.6% international, 2% transferred in, 83% live on campus. *Retention:* 78% of 2002 full-time freshmen returned.
Freshmen *Admission:* 1,803 applied, 1,624 admitted, 396 enrolled. *Average high school GPA:* 3.12. *Test scores:* SAT verbal scores over 500: 71%; SAT math scores over 500: 70%; SAT verbal scores over 600: 27%; SAT math scores over 600: 26%; SAT verbal scores over 700: 4%; SAT math scores over 700: 3%.
Faculty *Total:* 149, 62% full-time, 60% with terminal degrees. *Student/faculty ratio:* 13:1.
Majors Accounting; art; biochemistry; biology/biological sciences; business/commerce; chemistry; communication/speech communication and rhetoric; computer and information sciences; criminal justice/safety; economics; elementary education; English; French; German; history; information resources management; international relations and affairs; mathematics; multi-/interdisciplinary studies related; philosophy; political science and government; psychology; secondary education; social sciences; sociology; Spanish; theology.
Academic Programs *Special study options:* academic remediation for entering students, accelerated degree program, adult/continuing education programs, advanced placement credit, double majors, honors programs, independent study, internships, off-campus study, part-time degree program, services for LD students, student-designed majors, study abroad, summer session for credit. *ROTC:* Army (c). *Unusual degree programs:* 3-2 nursing with Johns Hopkins University.
Library Phillips Library with 211,158 titles, 905 serial subscriptions, 4,825 audiovisual materials, an OPAC, a Web page.
Computers on Campus 135 computers available on campus for general student use. A campuswide network can be accessed from student residence rooms and from off campus. Internet access, online (class) registration, at least one staffed computer lab available. Computer purchase or lease plan available.
Student Life *Housing:* on-campus residence required for freshman year. *Options:* coed, disabled students. Campus housing is university owned. Freshman campus housing is guaranteed. *Activities and organizations:* drama/theater group, student-run newspaper, radio and television station, choral group, campus ministry, rugby team club, ice hockey club, Circle K, International Affairs Organization. *Campus security:* 24-hour emergency response devices and patrols, late-night transport/escort service, controlled dormitory access. *Student services:* health clinic, personal/psychological counseling.
Athletics Member NCAA. All Division I. *Intercollegiate sports:* baseball M(s), basketball M(s)/W(s), cross-country running M(s)/W(s), equestrian sports M(c)/W(c), golf M(s)/W(s), ice hockey M(c), lacrosse M(s)/W(s), rugby M(c)/W(c), soccer M(s)/W(s), softball W(s), tennis M(s)/W(s), track and field M(s)/W(s). *Intramural sports:* basketball M/W, cheerleading W, field hockey W, football M, racquetball M/W, skiing (downhill) M/W, soccer M/W, softball M/W, swimming M/W, tennis M/W, volleyball M/W.
Standardized Tests *Required:* SAT I or ACT (for admission).
Costs (2003–04) *Comprehensive fee:* $28,400 includes full-time tuition ($20,800), mandatory fees ($200), and room and board ($7400). Part-time tuition: $694 per credit. *Required fees:* $5 per credit part-time. *College room only:* $3600. Room and board charges vary according to board plan. *Payment plan:* installment. *Waivers:* employees or children of employees.
Financial Aid Of all full-time matriculated undergraduates who enrolled in 2003, 1,020 applied for aid, 847 were judged to have need, 242 had their need fully met. 210 Federal Work-Study jobs (averaging $1305). 171 state and other part-time jobs (averaging $1400). In 2003, 462 non-need-based awards were made. *Average percent of need met:* 79%. *Average financial aid package:* $15,125. *Average need-based loan:* $4147. *Average need-based gift aid:* $11,425. *Average non-need-based aid:* $13,127. *Average indebtedness upon graduation:* $15,940. *Financial aid deadline:* 2/15.
Applying *Options:* electronic application, early action, deferred entrance. *Application fee:* $35. *Required:* high school transcript, minimum 2.0 GPA, 1 letter of recommendation. *Recommended:* essay or personal statement, minimum 3.0 GPA, interview. *Application deadlines:* rolling (freshmen), 6/1 (transfers). *Notification:* continuous (freshmen), 12/15 (early action), continuous (transfers).
Admissions Contact Mr. Stephen Neitz, Executive Director of Admissions and Financial Aid, Mount Saint Mary's College and Seminary, 16300 Old Emmitsburg Road, Emmitsburg, MD 21727. *Phone:* 301-447-5214. *Toll-free phone:* 800-448-4347. *Fax:* 301-447-5860. *E-mail:* admissions@msmary.edu.

■ *See page 2050 for a narrative description.*

Ner Israel Rabbinical College
Baltimore, Maryland

■ **Independent Jewish** comprehensive, founded 1933
■ **Calendar** semesters
■ **Degrees** bachelor's, master's, doctoral, and first professional
■ **Suburban** 54-acre campus
■ **Men only**
■ **Moderately difficult** entrance level

Costs (2003–04) *Comprehensive fee:* $13,750 includes full-time tuition ($6750) and room and board ($7000). *College room only:* $3500.
Applying *Options:* early admission, deferred entrance. *Required:* letters of recommendation. *Recommended:* interview.
Admissions Contact Rabbi Berel Weisbord, Dean of Admissions, Ner Israel Rabbinical College, Baltimore, MD. *Phone:* 410-484-7200.

Peabody Conservatory of Music of The Johns Hopkins University
Baltimore, Maryland

■ **Independent** comprehensive, founded 1857
■ **Calendar** semesters
■ **Degrees** certificates, diplomas, bachelor's, master's, doctoral, and postbachelor's certificates
■ **Urban** 1-acre campus with easy access to Washington, DC
■ **Endowment** $62.8 million
■ **Coed,** 302 undergraduate students, 97% full-time, 47% women, 53% men
■ **Very difficult** entrance level, 49% of applicants were admitted

Undergraduates 292 full-time, 10 part-time. Students come from 38 states and territories, 9 other countries, 67% are from out of state, 4% African American, 13% Asian American or Pacific Islander, 2% Hispanic American, 13% international, 6% transferred in. *Retention:* 78% of 2002 full-time freshmen returned.
Freshmen *Admission:* 567 applied, 275 admitted, 77 enrolled. *Test scores:* SAT verbal scores over 500: 89%; SAT math scores over 500: 88%; SAT verbal scores over 600: 59%; SAT math scores over 600: 52%; SAT verbal scores over 700: 22%; SAT math scores over 700: 22%.
Faculty *Total:* 162, 24% with terminal degrees. *Student/faculty ratio:* 4:1.

Peabody Conservatory of Music of The Johns Hopkins University (continued)

Majors Audio engineering; jazz/jazz studies; music; music teacher education; piano and organ; violin, viola, guitar and other stringed instruments; voice and opera; wind/percussion instruments.

Academic Programs *Special study options:* academic remediation for entering students, accelerated degree program, advanced placement credit, double majors, English as a second language, honors programs, independent study, internships, off-campus study, services for LD students.

Library Arthur Friedheim Library with 82,816 titles, 261 serial subscriptions, 22,269 audiovisual materials, an OPAC, a Web page.

Computers on Campus 40 computers available on campus for general student use. A campuswide network can be accessed from student residence rooms and from off campus that provide access to word processing, music processing. Internet access, at least one staffed computer lab available.

Student Life *Housing:* on-campus residence required through sophomore year. *Options:* coed, women-only. Campus housing is university owned. Freshman campus housing is guaranteed. *Activities and organizations:* choral group. *Campus security:* 24-hour emergency response devices and patrols, late-night transport/escort service, controlled dormitory access. *Student services:* health clinic, personal/psychological counseling.

Athletics *Intramural sports:* ultimate Frisbee M/W.

Standardized Tests *Required for some:* SAT I or ACT (for admission).

Costs (2003–04) *Comprehensive fee:* $35,100 includes full-time tuition ($25,850), mandatory fees ($300), and room and board ($8950). Part-time tuition: $750 per semester hour. *Room and board:* Room and board charges vary according to board plan. *Payment plan:* installment.

Financial Aid Of all full-time matriculated undergraduates who enrolled in 2002, 207 applied for aid, 183 were judged to have need, 5 had their need fully met. 116 Federal Work-Study jobs (averaging $1834). 121 state and other part-time jobs (averaging $1150). In 2002, 15 non-need-based awards were made. *Average percent of need met:* 85%. *Average financial aid package:* $15,856. *Average need-based loan:* $5326. *Average need-based gift aid:* $6949. *Average non-need-based aid:* $5400. *Average indebtedness upon graduation:* $25,640.

Applying *Application fee:* $55. *Required:* essay or personal statement, high school transcript, 3 letters of recommendation, interview, audition. *Application deadlines:* 12/15 (freshmen), 12/15 (transfers). *Notification:* 4/1 (freshmen), 4/1 (transfers).

Admissions Contact Mr. David Lane, Director of Admissions, Peabody Conservatory of Music of The Johns Hopkins University, Peabody Conservatory Admissions Office, One East Mount Vernon Place, Baltimore, MD 21202-2397. *Phone:* 410-659-8110. *Toll-free phone:* 800-368-2521.

ST. JOHN'S COLLEGE
Annapolis, Maryland

- **Independent** comprehensive, founded 1784
- **Calendar** semesters
- **Degrees** bachelor's and master's
- **Small-town** 36-acre campus with easy access to Baltimore and Washington, DC
- **Endowment** $51.4 million
- **Coed,** 472 undergraduate students, 100% full-time, 46% women, 54% men
- **Moderately difficult** entrance level, 73% of applicants were admitted

Undergraduates 470 full-time, 2 part-time. Students come from 47 states and territories, 6 other countries, 86% are from out of state, 0.6% African American, 1% Asian American or Pacific Islander, 3% Hispanic American, 0.6% Native American, 1% international, 75% live on campus. *Retention:* 83% of 2002 full-time freshmen returned.

Freshmen *Admission:* 531 applied, 389 admitted, 138 enrolled. *Test scores:* SAT verbal scores over 500: 99%; SAT math scores over 500: 98%; SAT verbal scores over 600: 92%; SAT math scores over 600: 75%; SAT verbal scores over 700: 51%; SAT math scores over 700: 25%.

Faculty *Total:* 80, 91% full-time, 68% with terminal degrees. *Student/faculty ratio:* 8:1.

Majors Interdisciplinary studies; liberal arts and sciences/liberal studies; western civilization.

Academic Programs *Special study options:* internships, off-campus study.

Library Greenfield Library plus 1 other with 93,668 titles, 114 serial subscriptions, 1,965 audiovisual materials, an OPAC, a Web page.

Computers on Campus 16 computers available on campus for general student use. A campuswide network can be accessed from student residence rooms and from off campus. Internet access, at least one staffed computer lab available.

Student Life *Housing:* on-campus residence required for freshman year. *Options:* coed. Campus housing is university owned. Freshman campus housing is guaranteed. *Activities and organizations:* drama/theater group, student-run newspaper, choral group, marching band, King William Players, Project Politae, Political Forum, Student Committee on Instruction, rowing club. *Campus security:* 24-hour emergency response devices and patrols, late-night transport/escort service, controlled dormitory access. *Student services:* health clinic, personal/psychological counseling.

Athletics *Intercollegiate sports:* cheerleading M(c)/W(c), crew M(c)/W(c), fencing M(c)/W(c), ultimate Frisbee M(c)/W(c). *Intramural sports:* badminton M/W, basketball M/W, fencing M/W, football M, racquetball M/W, sailing M/W, soccer M/W, softball M/W, squash M/W, table tennis M/W, tennis M/W, track and field M/W, ultimate Frisbee M/W, volleyball M/W, weight lifting M/W.

Standardized Tests *Required for some:* SAT I or ACT (for admission). *Recommended:* SAT I or ACT (for admission).

Costs (2004–05) *Comprehensive fee:* $38,160 includes full-time tuition ($30,350), mandatory fees ($200), and room and board ($7610). *Room and board:* Room and board charges vary according to board plan. *Payment plans:* tuition prepayment, installment. *Waivers:* employees or children of employees.

Financial Aid Of all full-time matriculated undergraduates who enrolled in 2003, 265 applied for aid, 260 were judged to have need, 250 had their need fully met. 136 Federal Work-Study jobs (averaging $2460). 20 state and other part-time jobs (averaging $2460). *Average percent of need met:* 90%. *Average financial aid package:* $22,262. *Average need-based loan:* $4860. *Average need-based gift aid:* $17,385. *Average indebtedness upon graduation:* $18,125.

Applying *Options:* common application, early admission, deferred entrance. *Required:* essay or personal statement, high school transcript, 2 letters of recommendation. *Recommended:* interview. *Application deadline:* rolling (freshmen), rolling (transfers). *Notification:* continuous (freshmen), continuous (transfers).

Admissions Contact Mr. John Christensen, Director of Admissions, St. John's College, PO Box 2800, 60 College Avenue, Annapolis, MD 21404. *Phone:* 410-626-2522. *Toll-free phone:* 800-727-9238. *Fax:* 410-269-7916. *E-mail:* admissions@sjca.edu.

■ *See page 2288 for a narrative description.*

ST. MARY'S COLLEGE OF MARYLAND
St. Mary's City, Maryland

- **State-supported** 4-year, founded 1840, part of Maryland State Colleges and Universities System
- **Calendar** semesters
- **Degree** bachelor's
- **Rural** 319-acre campus
- **Endowment** $26.6 million
- **Coed,** 1,922 undergraduate students, 92% full-time, 60% women, 40% men
- **Very difficult** entrance level, 55% of applicants were admitted

St. Mary's, with its distinctive identity as Maryland's Public Honors College, is one of the finest liberal arts and sciences colleges in the country. The lively academic atmosphere and stunning beauty of the riverfront campus create a challenging and memorable college experience; 50% of graduates go directly to graduate or professional school. Apartment-style residences opened in 2003 and athletic facilities will be completed in 2004.

Undergraduates 1,772 full-time, 150 part-time. Students come from 38 states and territories, 27 other countries, 17% are from out of state, 6% African American, 4% Asian American or Pacific Islander, 3% Hispanic American, 0.4% Native American, 0.7% international, 4% transferred in, 80% live on campus. *Retention:* 85% of 2002 full-time freshmen returned.

Freshmen *Admission:* 2,262 applied, 1,243 admitted, 421 enrolled. *Average high school GPA:* 3.50. *Test scores:* SAT verbal scores over 500: 96%; SAT math scores over 500: 96%; SAT verbal scores over 600: 72%; SAT math scores over 600: 66%; SAT verbal scores over 700: 20%; SAT math scores over 700: 15%.

Faculty *Total:* 197, 59% full-time, 79% with terminal degrees. *Student/faculty ratio:* 13:1.

Majors Anthropology; art; biochemistry; biological and physical sciences; biology/biological sciences; chemistry; computer and information sciences; dramatic/theatre arts; economics; English; foreign languages and literatures; history; mathematics; modern languages; multi-/interdisciplinary studies related; music; philosophy; physics; political science and government; psychology; psychology related; public policy analysis; religious studies; sociology.

Academic Programs *Special study options:* adult/continuing education programs, advanced placement credit, cooperative education, double majors, freshman honors college, honors programs, independent study, internships, off-campus study, part-time degree program, services for LD students, student-designed majors, study abroad, summer session for credit. *Unusual degree programs:* 3-2 engineering with University of Maryland, College Park.

Library Baltimore Hall with 153,827 titles, 1,797 serial subscriptions, 16,109 audiovisual materials, an OPAC, a Web page.

Computers on Campus 180 computers available on campus for general student use. A campuswide network can be accessed from student residence rooms and from off campus that provide access to e-mail. Internet access, online (class) registration, at least one staffed computer lab available.

Student Life *Housing options:* coed, men-only, women-only, disabled students. Campus housing is university owned. Freshman campus housing is guaranteed. *Activities and organizations:* drama/theater group, student-run newspaper, radio and television station, choral group, For Goodness Sake (community service), The Point News (student newspaper), FMLA (feminist group), Black Student Union, Dance Club. *Campus security:* 24-hour emergency response devices and patrols, student patrols, late-night transport/escort service, controlled dormitory access. *Student services:* health clinic, personal/psychological counseling.

Athletics Member NCAA. All Division III. *Intercollegiate sports:* baseball M, basketball M/W, crew M(c)/W(c), fencing M(c)/W(c), field hockey W, golf M(c)/W(c), lacrosse M/W, rugby M(c)/W(c), sailing M/W, soccer M/W, swimming M/W, tennis M/W, ultimate Frisbee M(c)/W(c), volleyball M(c)/W. *Intramural sports:* basketball M/W, bowling M/W, cross-country running M(c)/W(c), equestrian sports M(c)/W(c), football M/W, lacrosse M/W, sailing M/W, soccer M/W, softball M/W, swimming M/W, tennis M/W, track and field M(c)/W(c), volleyball M/W, water polo M/W.

Standardized Tests *Required:* SAT I or ACT (for admission).

Costs (2004–05) *Tuition:* state resident $8092 full-time, $150 per credit part-time; nonresident $15,572 full-time, $150 per credit part-time. Part-time tuition and fees vary according to course load. *Required fees:* $1588 full-time. *Room and board:* $7400; room only: $4165. Room and board charges vary according to board plan, housing facility, and student level. *Payment plan:* installment. *Waivers:* senior citizens and employees or children of employees.

Financial Aid Of all full-time matriculated undergraduates who enrolled in 2003, 1,457 applied for aid, 844 were judged to have need. 105 Federal Work-Study jobs (averaging $1164). In 2003, 535 non-need-based awards were made. *Average percent of need met:* 62%. *Average financial aid package:* $6755. *Average need-based loan:* $5500. *Average need-based gift aid:* $4000. *Average non-need-based aid:* $4500. *Average indebtedness upon graduation:* $17,125. *Financial aid deadline:* 3/1.

Applying *Options:* electronic application, early admission, early decision. *Application fee:* $40. *Required:* essay or personal statement, high school transcript, minimum 2.0 GPA. *Recommended:* 2 letters of recommendation, interview. *Application deadlines:* 1/15 (freshmen), 2/15 (transfers). *Early decision:* 12/1 (for plan 1), 1/15 (for plan 2). *Notification:* 4/1 (freshmen), 1/1 (early decision plan 1), 2/15 (early decision plan 2), 6/1 (transfers).

Admissions Contact Mr. Richard J. Edgar, Director of Admissions, St. Mary's College of Maryland, 18952 East Fisher Road, St. Mary's City, MD 20686-3001. *Phone:* 240-895-5000. *Toll-free phone:* 800-492-7181. *Fax:* 240-895-5001. *E-mail:* admissions@smcm.edu.

■ *See page 2316 for a narrative description.*

SALISBURY UNIVERSITY
Salisbury, Maryland

- **State-supported** comprehensive, founded 1925, part of University System of Maryland
- **Calendar** 4-1-4
- **Degrees** bachelor's and master's
- **Small-town** 144-acre campus
- **Endowment** $15.3 million
- **Coed,** 6,199 undergraduate students, 88% full-time, 57% women, 43% men
- **Moderately difficult** entrance level, 17% of applicants were admitted

Salisbury University has earned a national reputation for educating undergraduates, emphasizing undergraduate research, internships, community service, and study abroad. It has the highest graduation rates of all University System of Maryland institutions. SU vaulted into the top tier of its northern peers in the 2004 *U.S. News & World Report*'s "America's Best Colleges." Nationwide, Salisbury consistently ranks in the top 10 percent of public and private institutions, including the 2004 *Kiplinger's*, *Kaplan's*, and *Princeton Review* guides. Each of SU's 4 schools enjoy multimillion-dollar endowments.

Undergraduates 5,434 full-time, 765 part-time. Students come from 29 states and territories, 36 other countries, 14% are from out of state, 7% African American, 3% Asian American or Pacific Islander, 2% Hispanic American, 0.3% Native American, 0.8% international, 11% transferred in, 31% live on campus. *Retention:* 80% of 2002 full-time freshmen returned.

Freshmen *Admission:* 5,550 applied, 950 admitted, 950 enrolled. *Average high school GPA:* 3.48. *Test scores:* SAT verbal scores over 500: 84%; SAT math scores over 500: 90%; SAT verbal scores over 600: 25%; SAT math scores over 600: 38%; SAT verbal scores over 700: 2%; SAT math scores over 700: 4%.

Faculty *Total:* 498, 60% full-time, 54% with terminal degrees. *Student/faculty ratio:* 16:1.

Majors Accounting; art; athletic training; biology/biological sciences; business administration and management; chemistry; clinical laboratory science/medical technology; communication/speech communication and rhetoric; computer and information sciences; dramatic/theatre arts; economics; education; elementary education; English; environmental health; finance; fine arts related; French; geography; health and physical education; health/medical preparatory programs related; health teacher education; history; liberal arts and sciences/liberal studies; management information systems; management science; marketing/marketing management; mathematics; music; music performance; nursing (registered nurse training); peace studies and conflict resolution; philosophy; physical education teaching and coaching; physics; political science and government; psychology; respiratory care therapy; secondary education; social work; sociology; Spanish.

Academic Programs *Special study options:* academic remediation for entering students, adult/continuing education programs, advanced placement credit, double majors, English as a second language, honors programs, independent study, internships, off-campus study, part-time degree program, services for LD students, student-designed majors, study abroad, summer session for credit. *ROTC:* Army (c). *Unusual degree programs:* 3-2 engineering with University of Maryland College Park, Old Dominion University, Widener University; social work with University of Maryland Eastern Shore; environmental marine science with University of Maryland Eastern Shore.

Library Blackwell Library plus 1 other with 253,958 titles, 1,711 serial subscriptions, 10,690 audiovisual materials, an OPAC, a Web page.

Computers on Campus 226 computers available on campus for general student use. A campuswide network can be accessed from student residence rooms and from off campus. Internet access, online (class) registration, at least one staffed computer lab available. Computer purchase or lease plan available.

Student Life *Housing options:* coed, men-only, women-only. Campus housing is university owned. Freshman applicants given priority for college housing. *Activities and organizations:* drama/theater group, student-run newspaper, radio and television station, choral group, Student Government Association, campus radio station, Programming Board, Greek Council, Union of African-American Students, national fraternities, national sororities. *Campus security:* 24-hour emergency response devices and patrols, student patrols, late-night transport/escort service, controlled dormitory access. *Student services:* health clinic, personal/psychological counseling.

Athletics Member NCAA, NAIA. All NCAA Division III. *Intercollegiate sports:* baseball M, basketball M/W, cross-country running M/W, field hockey W, football M, lacrosse M/W, soccer M/W, softball W, swimming M/W, tennis M/W, track and field M/W, volleyball W. *Intramural sports:* basketball M/W, cross-country running M/W, fencing M(c)/W(c), field hockey W(c), football M/W, golf M(c)/W(c), ice hockey M(c), lacrosse M(c)/W, racquetball M/W, rugby M(c)/W(c), sailing M(c)/W(c), soccer M(c)/W(c), softball W, swimming M/W, tennis M/W, track and field M/W, volleyball W, water polo M/W.

Standardized Tests *Required:* SAT I or ACT (for admission).

Costs (2003–04) *Tuition:* state resident $5564 full-time, $171 per credit hour part-time; nonresident $12,452 full-time, $443 per credit hour part-time. *Required fees:* $1430 full-time, $8 per credit hour part-time. *Room and board:* $6900; room only: $3350. Room and board charges vary according to board plan and housing facility. *Payment plan:* installment. *Waivers:* senior citizens and employees or children of employees.

Financial Aid Of all full-time matriculated undergraduates who enrolled in 2002, 3,435 applied for aid, 2,252 were judged to have need, 499 had their need fully met. 96 Federal Work-Study jobs (averaging $1307). 96 state and other part-time jobs (averaging $365). In 2002, 379 non-need-based awards were made. *Average percent of need met:* 63%. *Average financial aid package:* $5629. *Average need-based loan:* $3433. *Average need-based gift aid:* $3467. *Average non-need-based aid:* $3129. *Average indebtedness upon graduation:* $14,759.

Applying *Options:* common application, electronic application, early admission, early action. *Application fee:* $45. *Required:* high school transcript, minimum 2.0 GPA. *Application deadline:* 1/15 (freshmen), rolling (transfers). *Notification:* 3/15 (freshmen), 1/15 (early action), continuous (transfers).

Salisbury University (continued)

Admissions Contact Mrs. Jane H. Dané, Dean of Admissions, Salisbury University, Admissions House, 1101 Camden Avenue, Salisbury, MD 21801. *Phone:* 410-543-6161. *Toll-free phone:* 888-543-0148. *Fax:* 410-546-6016. *E-mail:* admissions@salisbury.edu.

■ *See page 2338 for a narrative description.*

SOJOURNER-DOUGLASS COLLEGE
Baltimore, Maryland

Admissions Contact Ms. Diana Samuels, Manager, Office of Admissions, Sojourner-Douglass College, 500 North Caroline Street, Baltimore, MD 21205-1814. *Phone:* 410-276-0306 Ext. 251. *Fax:* 410-675-1810.

TOWSON UNIVERSITY
Towson, Maryland

- **State-supported** university, founded 1866, part of University System of Maryland
- **Calendar** semesters
- **Degrees** bachelor's, master's, doctoral, post-master's, and postbachelor's certificates
- **Suburban** 321-acre campus with easy access to Baltimore and Washington, DC
- **Endowment** $3.9 million
- **Coed,** 13,981 undergraduate students, 86% full-time, 61% women, 39% men
- **Moderately difficult** entrance level, 52% of applicants were admitted

Undergraduates 12,051 full-time, 1,930 part-time. Students come from 46 states and territories, 100 other countries, 19% are from out of state, 10% African American, 2% Asian American or Pacific Islander, 2% Hispanic American, 0.3% Native American, 3% international, 10% transferred in. *Retention:* 84% of 2002 full-time freshmen returned.

Freshmen *Admission:* 11,289 applied, 5,818 admitted, 1,754 enrolled. *Average high school GPA:* 3.54. *Test scores:* SAT verbal scores over 500: 75%; SAT math scores over 500: 80%; SAT verbal scores over 600: 21%; SAT math scores over 600: 27%; SAT verbal scores over 700: 2%; SAT math scores over 700: 2%.

Faculty *Total:* 1,282, 48% full-time, 51% with terminal degrees. *Student/faculty ratio:* 17:1.

Majors Accounting; art; art teacher education; athletic training; biochemistry, biophysics and molecular biology related; biology/biological sciences; business administration and management; business administration, management and operations related; chemistry; chemistry related; communication/speech communication and rhetoric; dance; dramatic/theatre arts; early childhood education; economics; education related; elementary education; English; family systems; forensic science and technology; French; geography; geological and earth sciences/geosciences related; geology/earth science; German; gerontology; health and physical education related; health/health care administration; health professions related; history; information science/studies; interdisciplinary studies; international relations and affairs; kinesiology and exercise science; mass communication/media; mathematics; music; music teacher education; nursing (registered nurse training); occupational therapy; philosophy; physical education teaching and coaching; physics; political science and government; psychology; psychology related; religious studies; social sciences; social sciences related; Spanish; special education; speech-language pathology; sport and fitness administration; women's studies.

Academic Programs *Special study options:* academic remediation for entering students, adult/continuing education programs, advanced placement credit, cooperative education, distance learning, double majors, English as a second language, freshman honors college, honors programs, independent study, internships, off-campus study, part-time degree program, services for LD students, student-designed majors, study abroad, summer session for credit. *ROTC:* Army (c). *Unusual degree programs:* 3-2 engineering with University of Maryland College Park; law with University of Baltimore.

Library Cook Library with 364,468 titles, 2,164 serial subscriptions, 14,174 audiovisual materials, an OPAC, a Web page.

Computers on Campus 1015 computers available on campus for general student use. A campuswide network can be accessed from student residence rooms and from off campus. Internet access, online (class) registration, at least one staffed computer lab available.

Student Life *Housing options:* coed, disabled students. Campus housing is university owned and is provided by a third party. Freshman campus housing is guaranteed. *Activities and organizations:* drama/theater group, student-run newspaper, radio and television station, choral group, marching band, Black Student Union, Student Government Association, Habitat for Humanity, Circle K, University Residence Government, national fraternities, national sororities. *Campus security:* 24-hour emergency response devices and patrols, late-night transport/escort service, controlled dormitory access. *Student services:* health clinic, personal/psychological counseling, women's center.

Athletics Member NCAA. All Division I except football (Division I-AA). *Intercollegiate sports:* baseball M(s), basketball M(s)/W(s), cheerleading M/W, cross-country running M(s)/W(s), field hockey W(s), golf M(s), gymnastics W(s), lacrosse M(s)/W(s), soccer M(s)/W(s), softball W(s), swimming M(s)/W(s), tennis M(s)/W(s), track and field M(s)/W(s), volleyball M/W(s). *Intramural sports:* badminton M(c)/W(c), basketball M/W, bowling M(c)/W(c), crew M(c)/W(c), equestrian sports M(c)/W(c), fencing M(c)/W(c), football M/W, golf M(c)/W(c), ice hockey M, lacrosse M/W, racquetball M(c)/W(c), rugby M, sailing M(c)/W(c), softball M/W, table tennis M/W, tennis M/W, ultimate Frisbee M(c)/W(c), volleyball M(c)/W(c), wrestling M.

Standardized Tests *Required:* SAT I or ACT (for admission).

Costs (2004–05) *Tuition:* state resident $4890 full-time, $212 per credit part-time; nonresident $13,570 full-time, $508 per credit part-time. Full-time tuition and fees vary according to course load. *Required fees:* $1782 full-time, $69 per credit part-time. *Room and board:* $6468; room only: $3816. Room and board charges vary according to board plan and housing facility. *Payment plan:* installment. *Waivers:* senior citizens and employees or children of employees.

Financial Aid Of all full-time matriculated undergraduates who enrolled in 2003, 5,944 applied for aid, 3,971 were judged to have need, 819 had their need fully met. In 2003, 693 non-need-based awards were made. *Average percent of need met:* 49%. *Average financial aid package:* $8090. *Average need-based loan:* $3845. *Average need-based gift aid:* $4363. *Average non-need-based aid:* $4006. *Average indebtedness upon graduation:* $15,750. *Financial aid deadline:* 3/1.

Applying *Options:* electronic application, deferred entrance. *Application fee:* $55. *Required:* high school transcript. *Required for some:* interview. *Recommended:* essay or personal statement, minimum 2.75 GPA, letters of recommendation, interview. *Application deadline:* 2/15 (freshmen). *Notification:* continuous (freshmen), continuous (transfers).

Admissions Contact Ms. Louise Shulack, Director of Admissions, Towson University, 8000 York Road, Towson, MD 21252. *Phone:* 410-704-3687. *Toll-free phone:* 888-4TOWSON. *Fax:* 410-830-3030. *E-mail:* admissions@towson.edu.

■ *See page 2514 for a narrative description.*

UNITED STATES NAVAL ACADEMY
Annapolis, Maryland

- **Federally supported** 4-year, founded 1845
- **Calendar** semesters
- **Degree** bachelor's
- **Small-town** 329-acre campus with easy access to Baltimore and Washington, DC
- **Coed, primarily men,** 4,335 undergraduate students, 100% full-time, 16% women, 84% men
- **Very difficult** entrance level, 10% of applicants were admitted

Undergraduates 4,335 full-time. Students come from 54 states and territories, 20 other countries, 96% are from out of state, 7% African American, 4% Asian American or Pacific Islander, 9% Hispanic American, 2% Native American, 0.9% international, 100% live on campus. *Retention:* 96% of 2002 full-time freshmen returned.

Freshmen *Admission:* 14,101 applied, 1,479 admitted, 1,178 enrolled. *Test scores:* SAT verbal scores over 500: 100%; SAT math scores over 500: 100%; SAT verbal scores over 600: 75%; SAT math scores over 600: 86%; SAT verbal scores over 700: 24%; SAT math scores over 700: 35%.

Faculty *Total:* 598, 94% full-time, 57% with terminal degrees. *Student/faculty ratio:* 7:1.

Majors Aerospace, aeronautical and astronautical engineering; chemistry; computer and information sciences; computer science; econometrics and quantitative economics; economics; electrical, electronics and communications engineering; engineering; English; history; mathematics; mechanical engineering; naval architecture and marine engineering; ocean engineering; oceanography (chemical and physical); physical sciences; physics; political science and government; systems engineering.

Academic Programs *Special study options:* academic remediation for entering students, advanced placement credit, double majors, English as a second language, honors programs, independent study, summer session for credit.

Library Nimitz Library plus 1 other with 800,000 titles, 1,892 serial subscriptions, an OPAC.

Computers on Campus 6100 computers available on campus for general student use. A campuswide network can be accessed from student residence rooms and from off campus. Internet access, online (class) registration, at least one staffed computer lab available. Computer purchase or lease plan available.

Student Life *Housing:* on-campus residence required through senior year. *Options:* coed. Campus housing is university owned. Freshman campus housing is guaranteed. *Activities and organizations:* drama/theater group, student-run radio station, choral group, marching band, Mountaineering Club, Semper Fi, Black Studies Club, Midshipmen Action Club, Martial Arts Club. *Campus security:* 24-hour emergency response devices and patrols, student patrols, front gate security. *Student services:* health clinic, personal/psychological counseling, legal services.

Athletics Member NCAA. All Division I except football (Division I-A). *Intercollegiate sports:* baseball M, basketball M/W, cheerleading M/W, crew M/W, cross-country running M/W, golf M, gymnastics M/W(c), ice hockey M(c), lacrosse M/W(c), riflery M/W, rugby M(c)/W(c), sailing M/W, skiing (downhill) M(c)/W(c), soccer M/W, softball W(c), squash M, swimming M/W, tennis M/W(c), track and field M/W, volleyball M(c)/W, water polo M, weight lifting M(c)/W(c), wrestling M. *Intramural sports:* basketball M/W, football M/W, lacrosse M(c), racquetball M/W, sailing M/W, skiing (cross-country) M(c)/W(c), soccer M/W, softball M/W, volleyball M/W, weight lifting M/W.

Standardized Tests *Required:* SAT I or ACT (for admission).

Costs (2004–05) *Tuition:* Tuition, room and board, and medical and dental care are provided by the U.S. government. Each midshipman receives a salary from which to pay for uniforms, books, supplies, and personal expenses. Entering freshmen are required to deposit $2500 to defray the initial cost of uniforms and equipment.

Applying *Required:* essay or personal statement, high school transcript, minimum 2.0 GPA, 2 letters of recommendation, interview, authorized nomination. *Application deadline:* 1/31 (freshmen). *Notification:* 4/15 (freshmen).

Admissions Contact Col. David A. Vetter, Dean of Admissions, United States Naval Academy, 117 Decatur Road, Annapolis, MD 21402-5000. *Phone:* 410-293-4361. *Fax:* 410-293-4348. *E-mail:* webmail@gwmail.usna.edu.

UNIVERSITY OF BALTIMORE

Baltimore, Maryland

- **State-supported** upper-level, founded 1925, part of University System of Maryland
- **Calendar** semesters
- **Degrees** certificates, bachelor's, master's, doctoral, first professional, post-master's, and postbachelor's certificates
- **Urban** 49-acre campus
- **Endowment** $18.9 million
- **Coed,** 2,059 undergraduate students, 51% full-time, 62% women, 38% men
- **Noncompetitive** entrance level, 82% of applicants were admitted

Undergraduates 1,048 full-time, 1,011 part-time. Students come from 14 states and territories, 50 other countries, 7% are from out of state, 34% African American, 3% Asian American or Pacific Islander, 2% Hispanic American, 0.7% Native American, 3% international, 97% transferred in.

Faculty *Total:* 306, 48% full-time, 85% with terminal degrees. *Student/faculty ratio:* 17:1.

Majors Accounting; business administration and management; community organization and advocacy; computer and information sciences; criminal justice/law enforcement administration; digital communication and media/multimedia; economics; English; finance; forensic science and technology; health and medical administrative services related; history; human resources management; human services; information science/studies; interdisciplinary studies; international business/trade/commerce; journalism; legal studies; liberal arts and sciences/liberal studies; literature; management information systems; marketing/marketing management; mass communication/media; non-profit management; political science and government; psychology; sales, distribution and marketing; technical and business writing.

Academic Programs *Special study options:* academic remediation for entering students, accelerated degree program, adult/continuing education programs, advanced placement credit, cooperative education, distance learning, honors programs, independent study, internships, off-campus study, part-time degree program, services for LD students, student-designed majors, summer session for credit. *ROTC:* Army (c). *Unusual degree programs:* 3-2 law school.

Library Langsdale Library plus 1 other with 258,747 titles, 10,738 serial subscriptions, 883 audiovisual materials, an OPAC, a Web page.

Computers on Campus 135 computers available on campus for general student use. A campuswide network can be accessed from off campus. Internet access, at least one staffed computer lab available.

Student Life *Housing:* college housing not available. *Options:* Campus housing is provided by a third party. *Activities and organizations:* student-run newspaper, Psi Chi, APALSA, International Student Association, African Student Association, Forensics Student Association. *Campus security:* 24-hour emergency response devices and patrols, late-night transport/escort service. *Student services:* health clinic, personal/psychological counseling.

Athletics *Intramural sports:* basketball M/W, golf M/W, racquetball M/W, soccer M, table tennis M/W, volleyball M/W, weight lifting M/W.

Costs (2003–04) *Tuition:* state resident $4613 full-time, $211 per credit part-time; nonresident $15,019 full-time, $626 per credit part-time. Full-time tuition and fees vary according to class time, course level, course load, and degree level. Part-time tuition and fees vary according to class time, course load, and degree level. *Required fees:* $1300 full-time, $50 per credit part-time, $60 per term part-time. *Payment plan:* deferred payment. *Waivers:* senior citizens and employees or children of employees.

Financial Aid *Average financial aid package:* $11,210. *Average indebtedness upon graduation:* $22,441.

Applying *Options:* electronic application. *Application fee:* $35. *Application deadline:* rolling (transfers). *Notification:* continuous (transfers).

Admissions Contact Mrs. Julia Pitman, Director of Admissions, University of Baltimore, 1420 North Charles Street, Baltimore, MD 21201-5779. *Phone:* 410-837-4777. *Toll-free phone:* 877-APPLYUB. *Fax:* 410-837-4793. *E-mail:* admissions@ubalt.edu.

■ *See page 2576 for a narrative description.*

UNIVERSITY OF MARYLAND, BALTIMORE COUNTY

Baltimore, Maryland

- **State-supported** university, founded 1963, part of University System of Maryland
- **Calendar** 4-1-4
- **Degrees** bachelor's, master's, doctoral, and postbachelor's certificates
- **Suburban** 530-acre campus with easy access to Washington, D.C.
- **Endowment** $19.7 million
- **Coed,** 9,646 undergraduate students, 83% full-time, 47% women, 53% men
- **Moderately difficult** entrance level, 58% of applicants were admitted

Some of the most exciting students and some of the best teaching talent anywhere are coming together at a university located in the suburbs of Baltimore, which has approximately 9,600 undergraduates. UMBC's leadership in technology and its friendly campus climate, business and industry partnerships, and ability to place students in leading graduate programs and promising careers are just a few of the reasons why students who could attend any college are choosing UMBC.

Undergraduates 8,024 full-time, 1,622 part-time. Students come from 45 states and territories, 108 other countries, 8% are from out of state, 15% African American, 20% Asian American or Pacific Islander, 3% Hispanic American, 0.4% Native American, 5% international, 11% transferred in, 33% live on campus. *Retention:* 82% of 2002 full-time freshmen returned.

Freshmen *Admission:* 5,501 applied, 3,167 admitted, 1,505 enrolled. *Average high school GPA:* 3.53. *Test scores:* SAT verbal scores over 500: 91%; SAT math scores over 500: 97%; ACT scores over 18: 98%; SAT verbal scores over 600: 47%; SAT math scores over 600: 65%; ACT scores over 24: 64%; SAT verbal scores over 700: 9%; SAT math scores over 700: 17%; ACT scores over 30: 12%.

Faculty *Total:* 702, 66% full-time, 70% with terminal degrees. *Student/faculty ratio:* 18:1.

Majors African-American/Black studies; American studies; ancient studies; anthropology; applied mathematics; art; art history, criticism and conservation; biochemistry; biochemistry/biophysics and molecular biology; bioinformatics; biology/biological sciences; chemical engineering; chemistry; classics and languages, literatures and linguistics; computer engineering; computer science; dance; dramatic/theatre arts; economics; emergency medical technology (EMT paramedic); engineering science; English; environmental science; environmental studies; film/cinema studies; French; geography; German; health/health care administration; health science; history; information science/studies; interdisciplinary studies; linguistics; mathematics; mechanical engineering; modern languages; music; philosophy; photography; physics; political science and government; pre-dentistry studies; pre-law studies; pre-medical studies; pre-veterinary studies; psychology; Russian; social work; sociology; Spanish; statistics; visual and performing arts.

Academic Programs *Special study options:* academic remediation for entering students, adult/continuing education programs, advanced placement credit, cooperative education, distance learning, double majors, English as a second language, external degree program, freshman honors college, honors programs, independent study, internships, off-campus study, part-time degree program, services for LD students, student-designed majors, study abroad, summer session for credit. *ROTC:* Army (c), Air Force (c).

Library Albin O. Kuhn Library and Gallery plus 1 other with 749,618 titles, 4,282 serial subscriptions, 39,007 audiovisual materials, an OPAC, a Web page.

University of Maryland, Baltimore County (continued)

Computers on Campus 673 computers available on campus for general student use. A campuswide network can be accessed from student residence rooms and from off campus that provide access to student account and grade information. Internet access, online (class) registration, at least one staffed computer lab available. Computer purchase or lease plan available.

Student Life *Housing options:* coed. Campus housing is university owned and is provided by a third party. Freshman campus housing is guaranteed. *Activities and organizations:* drama/theater group, student-run newspaper, radio and television station, choral group, marching band, Student Government Association, Student Events Board, Retriever Weekly, Resident Student Association, Black Student Union, national fraternities, national sororities. *Campus security:* 24-hour emergency response devices and patrols, late-night transport/escort service. *Student services:* health clinic, personal/psychological counseling, women's center, legal services.

Athletics Member NCAA. All Division I. *Intercollegiate sports:* baseball M(s), basketball M(s)/W(s), bowling M(c)/W(c), crew M(c)/W(c), cross-country running M(s)/W(s), fencing M(c)/W(c), field hockey W(c), ice hockey M(c), lacrosse M(s)/W(s), rugby M(c)/W(c), sailing M(c)/W(c), skiing (downhill) M(c)/W(c), soccer M(s)/W(s), softball W(s), swimming M(s)/W(s), tennis M(s)/W(s), track and field M(s)/W(s), volleyball M(c)/W(s), wrestling M(c). *Intramural sports:* badminton M/W, basketball M/W, cross-country running M/W, football M/W, lacrosse M/W, soccer M/W, softball M/W, swimming M/W, tennis M/W, track and field M/W, volleyball M/W.

Standardized Tests *Required:* SAT I or ACT (for admission). *Recommended:* SAT I (for admission).

Costs (2003–04) *Tuition:* state resident $7388 full-time, $232 per credit hour part-time; nonresident $14,240 full-time, $543 per credit hour part-time. *Required fees:* $250 per year part-time. *Room and board:* $7007; room only: $4714. Room and board charges vary according to board plan and housing facility. *Payment plan:* installment. *Waivers:* senior citizens and employees or children of employees.

Financial Aid Of all full-time matriculated undergraduates who enrolled in 2002, 6,219 applied for aid, 5,161 were judged to have need, 2,973 had their need fully met. In 2002, 1306 non-need-based awards were made. *Average percent of need met:* 60%. *Average financial aid package:* $6023. *Average need-based loan:* $4404. *Average need-based gift aid:* $3677. *Average non-need-based aid:* $6341. *Average indebtedness upon graduation:* $14,500.

Applying *Options:* common application, electronic application, early admission, early action, deferred entrance. *Required:* essay or personal statement, high school transcript. *Recommended:* minimum 3 GPA, 2 letters of recommendation. *Application deadlines:* 2/1 (freshmen), 5/31 (transfers). *Notification:* continuous (freshmen), 12/1 (early action).

Admissions Contact Ms. Yvette Mozie-Ross, Director of Admissions, University of Maryland, Baltimore County, 1000 Hilltop Circle, Baltimore, MD 21250. *Phone:* 410-455-3799. *Toll-free phone:* 800-UMBC-4U2 (in-state); 800-862-2402 (out-of-state). *Fax:* 410-455-1094. *E-mail:* admissions@umbc.edu.

■ *See page 2636 for a narrative description.*

UNIVERSITY OF MARYLAND, COLLEGE PARK

College Park, Maryland

- **State-supported** university, founded 1856, part of University System of Maryland
- **Calendar** semesters
- **Degrees** certificates, bachelor's, master's, doctoral, first professional, post-master's, and postbachelor's certificates
- **Suburban** 3688-acre campus with easy access to Baltimore and Washington, DC
- **Endowment** $247.1 million
- **Coed,** 25,379 undergraduate students, 91% full-time, 49% women, 51% men
- **Moderately difficult** entrance level, 43% of applicants were admitted

Undergraduates 22,979 full-time, 2,400 part-time. Students come from 54 states and territories, 159 other countries, 24% are from out of state, 12% African American, 14% Asian American or Pacific Islander, 6% Hispanic American, 0.3% Native American, 2% international, 8% transferred in, 39% live on campus. *Retention:* 93% of 2002 full-time freshmen returned.

Freshmen *Admission:* 25,028 applied, 10,679 admitted, 4,063 enrolled. *Average high school GPA:* 3.88. *Test scores:* SAT verbal scores over 500: 93%; SAT math scores over 500: 95%; SAT verbal scores over 600: 64%; SAT math scores over 600: 77%; SAT verbal scores over 700: 15%; SAT math scores over 700: 26%.

Faculty *Total:* 2,097, 75% full-time, 85% with terminal degrees. *Student/faculty ratio:* 13:1.

Majors Accounting; aerospace, aeronautical and astronautical engineering; African-American/Black studies; agricultural/biological engineering and bioengineering; agricultural economics; agriculture; agriculture and agriculture operations related; agronomy and crop science; American studies; animal sciences; anthropology; architecture; art history, criticism and conservation; art teacher education; astronomy; biochemistry; biology/biological sciences; business administration and management; business/commerce; business, management, and marketing related; chemical engineering; chemistry; Chinese; civil engineering; classics and languages, literatures and linguistics; communication/speech communication and rhetoric; computer and information sciences; computer engineering; criminology; dance; dietetics; dramatic/theatre arts; ecology; economics; education; electrical, electronics and communications engineering; elementary education; engineering; engineering related; English; English/language arts teacher education; family and community services; finance; food science; foods, nutrition, and wellness; foreign languages and literatures; foreign language teacher education; French; geography; geology/earth science; German; health teacher education; history; horticultural science; human resources management; information science/studies; Italian; Japanese; Jewish/Judaic studies; journalism; kindergarten/preschool education; landscape architecture; Latin; linguistics; management science; marketing/marketing management; materials engineering; mathematics; mathematics teacher education; mechanical engineering; medical microbiology and bacteriology; music; music performance; music teacher education; natural resources/conservation; nuclear engineering; philosophy; physical education teaching and coaching; physical sciences; physics; plant sciences; political science and government; psychology; Russian; Russian studies; science teacher education; secondary education; social studies teacher education; sociology; Spanish; special education; speech-language pathology; visual and performing arts; women's studies.

Academic Programs *Special study options:* academic remediation for entering students, accelerated degree program, adult/continuing education programs, advanced placement credit, cooperative education, distance learning, double majors, English as a second language, external degree program, honors programs, independent study, internships, off-campus study, part-time degree program, services for LD students, student-designed majors, study abroad, summer session for credit. *ROTC:* Army (b), Navy (c), Air Force (b).

Library McKeldin Library plus 6 others with 3.0 million titles, 33,858 serial subscriptions, 283,669 audiovisual materials, an OPAC, a Web page.

Computers on Campus 791 computers available on campus for general student use. A campuswide network can be accessed from student residence rooms and from off campus that provide access to student account information, financial aid summary. Internet access, online (class) registration, at least one staffed computer lab available. Computer purchase or lease plan available.

Student Life *Housing options:* coed, women-only, disabled students. Campus housing is university owned. Freshman campus housing is guaranteed. *Activities and organizations:* drama/theater group, student-run newspaper, radio and television station, choral group, marching band, Student Government Association, Residence Hall Association, Black Student Union, Asian-American Student Union/Jewish Student Union, Commuter Students Association, national fraternities, national sororities. *Campus security:* 24-hour emergency response devices and patrols, student patrols, late-night transport/escort service, controlled dormitory access, campus police, video camera surveillance. *Student services:* health clinic, personal/psychological counseling, women's center, legal services.

Athletics Member NCAA. All Division I except football (Division I-A). *Intercollegiate sports:* baseball M(s), basketball M(s)/W(s), cheerleading W(s), cross-country running M(s)/W(s), field hockey W(s), golf M(s)/W(s), gymnastics W(s), lacrosse M(s)/W(s), soccer M(s)/W(s), softball W(s), swimming M(s)/W(s), tennis M(s)/W(s), track and field M(s)/W(s), volleyball W(s), water polo W(s), wrestling M(s). *Intramural sports:* badminton M(c)/W(c), baseball M(c), basketball M/W, bowling M(c)/W(c), crew M(c)/W(c), cross-country running M/W, equestrian sports M(c)/W(c), fencing M(c)/W(c), field hockey W(c), football M/W, golf M/W, ice hockey M(c)/W(c), lacrosse M(c)/W(c), racquetball M(c)/W(c), rugby M(c)/W(c), sailing M(c)/W(c), soccer M(c)/W(c), softball W, swimming M(c)/W(c), table tennis M/W, tennis M/W, track and field M/W, ultimate Frisbee M/W, volleyball M(c)/W, water polo M(c)/W(c), weight lifting M/W, wrestling M.

Standardized Tests *Required:* SAT I or ACT (for admission).

Costs (2003–04) *Tuition:* state resident $5568 full-time, $232 per semester hour part-time; nonresident $16,242 full-time, $677 per semester hour part-time. *Required fees:* $1190 full-time. *Room and board:* $7608; room only: $4556. Room and board charges vary according to board plan. *Payment plans:* installment, deferred payment. *Waivers:* employees or children of employees.

Financial Aid Of all full-time matriculated undergraduates who enrolled in 2002, 12,856 applied for aid, 9,299 were judged to have need, 2,234 had their need fully met. 906 Federal Work-Study jobs (averaging $1340). In 2002, 1295 non-need-based awards were made. *Average percent of need met:* 68%. *Average financial aid package:* $8344. *Average need-based loan:* $3814. *Average need-based gift aid:* $4120. *Average non-need-based aid:* $3854. *Average indebtedness upon graduation:* $14,076.

Applying *Options:* early admission, early action. *Application fee:* $50. *Required:* essay or personal statement, high school transcript, 1 letter of recommendation. *Required for some:* resume of activities, auditions. *Recommended:* 2 letters of recommendation. *Application deadlines:* 1/20 (freshmen), 7/1 (transfers). *Notification:* continuous until 4/1 (freshmen), 2/15 (early action), continuous (transfers).

Admissions Contact Ms. Barbara Gill, Director of Undergraduate Admissions, University of Maryland, College Park, Mitchell Building, College Park, MD 20742-5235. *Phone:* 301-314-8385. *Toll-free phone:* 800-422-5867. *Fax:* 301-314-9693. *E-mail:* um-admit@uga.umd.edu.

■ *See page 2638 for a narrative description.*

UNIVERSITY OF MARYLAND EASTERN SHORE

Princess Anne, Maryland

- **State-supported** university, founded 1886, part of University System of Maryland
- **Calendar** semesters
- **Degrees** bachelor's, master's, and doctoral
- **Rural** 700-acre campus
- **Coed,** 3,326 undergraduate students, 87% full-time, 59% women, 41% men
- **Moderately difficult** entrance level, 58% of applicants were admitted

Undergraduates 2,902 full-time, 424 part-time. Students come from 30 states and territories, 50 other countries, 28% are from out of state, 76% African American, 2% Asian American or Pacific Islander, 0.9% Hispanic American, 0.4% Native American, 11% international, 4% transferred in, 52% live on campus. *Retention:* 69% of 2002 full-time freshmen returned.

Freshmen *Admission:* 3,714 applied, 2,165 admitted, 846 enrolled. *Test scores:* SAT verbal scores over 500: 19%; SAT math scores over 500: 17%; ACT scores over 18: 3%; SAT verbal scores over 600: 3%; SAT math scores over 600: 3%.

Faculty *Total:* 234, 77% full-time, 48% with terminal degrees. *Student/faculty ratio:* 17:1.

Majors Accounting; agricultural business and management; agricultural teacher education; agriculture; air traffic control; art teacher education; biology/biological sciences; business administration and management; business teacher education; chemistry; child development; clinical laboratory science/medical technology; clinical/medical laboratory technology; computer science; construction engineering technology; construction management; criminal justice/law enforcement administration; dietetics; ecology; education; electrical, electronic and communications engineering technology; elementary education; engineering technology; English; environmental studies; family and consumer economics related; family and consumer sciences/home economics teacher education; family and consumer sciences/human sciences; fashion/apparel design; fashion merchandising; history; hotel/motel administration; human ecology; industrial arts; industrial radiologic technology; kindergarten/preschool education; liberal arts and sciences/liberal studies; marine biology and biological oceanography; mass communication/media; mathematics; music teacher education; physical education teaching and coaching; physical therapy; poultry science; pre-dentistry studies; pre-law studies; pre-medical studies; rehabilitation therapy; social sciences; social work; sociology; special education; special products marketing.

Academic Programs *Special study options:* academic remediation for entering students, accelerated degree program, adult/continuing education programs, advanced placement credit, cooperative education, honors programs, internships, off-campus study, part-time degree program, services for LD students, student-designed majors, summer session for credit.

Library Frederick Douglass Library with 150,000 titles, 1,260 serial subscriptions, an OPAC, a Web page.

Computers on Campus 120 computers available on campus for general student use. A campuswide network can be accessed. At least one staffed computer lab available.

Student Life *Housing options:* coed, men-only, women-only. *Activities and organizations:* drama/theater group, student-run newspaper, choral group, national fraternities, national sororities. *Campus security:* 24-hour emergency response devices and patrols, student patrols, late-night transport/escort service, controlled dormitory access. *Student services:* health clinic, personal/psychological counseling.

Athletics Member NCAA. All Division I. *Intercollegiate sports:* baseball M(s), basketball M(s)/W(s), cross-country running M/W, softball W, tennis M(s)/W, track and field M/W, volleyball W, wrestling M. *Intramural sports:* basketball M/W, bowling W, cross-country running M/W, soccer M/W, softball W, swimming M/W, table tennis M/W, tennis M/W, track and field M/W, volleyball M/W, wrestling M.

Standardized Tests *Required:* SAT I or ACT (for admission).

Costs (2003–04) *Tuition:* state resident $3563 full-time, $148 per credit hour part-time; nonresident $8898 full-time, $321 per credit hour part-time. *Required fees:* $1542 full-time, $40 per term part-time. *Room and board:* $5630; room only: $3130. Room and board charges vary according to board plan and housing facility. *Payment plans:* installment, deferred payment. *Waivers:* senior citizens and employees or children of employees.

Financial Aid Of all full-time matriculated undergraduates who enrolled in 2002, 2,361 applied for aid, 1,888 were judged to have need, 342 had their need fully met. 252 Federal Work-Study jobs (averaging $786). In 2002, 317 non-need-based awards were made. *Average percent of need met:* 70%. *Average financial aid package:* $10,150. *Average need-based loan:* $4050. *Average need-based gift aid:* $6350. *Average non-need-based aid:* $2467. *Average indebtedness upon graduation:* $7350.

Applying *Options:* common application, electronic application, early admission, early action, deferred entrance. *Application fee:* $25. *Required:* essay or personal statement, high school transcript, minimum 2.5 GPA, 2 letters of recommendation. *Recommended:* interview. *Application deadline:* 7/15 (freshmen), rolling (transfers).

Admissions Contact Ms. Cheryll Collier-Mills, Director of Admissions and Recruitment, University of Maryland Eastern Shore, Princess Anne, MD 21853-1299. *Phone:* 410-651-8410. *Fax:* 410-651-7922. *E-mail:* umesadmissions@mail.umes.edu.

■ *See page 2640 for a narrative description.*

UNIVERSITY OF MARYLAND UNIVERSITY COLLEGE

Adelphi, Maryland

- **State-supported** comprehensive, founded 1947, part of University System of Maryland
- **Calendar** semesters
- **Degrees** certificates, associate, bachelor's, master's, doctoral, and postbachelor's certificates (offers primarily part-time evening and weekend degree programs at more than 30 off-campus locations in Maryland and the Washington, DC area, and more than 180 military communities in Europe and Asia with military enrollment not reflected in this profile; associate of arts program available to military students only)
- **Suburban** campus with easy access to Washington, DC
- **Coed,** 18,133 undergraduate students, 14% full-time, 58% women, 42% men
- **Noncompetitive** entrance level, 100% of applicants were admitted

Undergraduates 2,597 full-time, 15,536 part-time. Students come from 54 states and territories, 41 other countries, 31% are from out of state, 33% African American, 6% Asian American or Pacific Islander, 5% Hispanic American, 0.8% Native American, 2% international, 23% transferred in.

Freshmen *Admission:* 994 applied, 994 admitted, 529 enrolled.

Faculty *Total:* 1,023, 7% full-time, 63% with terminal degrees. *Student/faculty ratio:* 19:1.

Majors Accounting; business administration and management; communication/speech communication and rhetoric; computer and information sciences; computer science; criminal justice/law enforcement administration; English; environmental studies; fire science; history; humanities; human resources management; information science/studies; legal assistant/paralegal; management science; marketing/marketing management; multi-/interdisciplinary studies related; psychology; social sciences.

Academic Programs *Special study options:* accelerated degree program, adult/continuing education programs, advanced placement credit, cooperative education, distance learning, double majors, external degree program, off-campus study, part-time degree program, services for LD students, summer session for credit.

Library Information and Library Services plus 1 other with 5,807 titles, 31 serial subscriptions, an OPAC, a Web page.

Computers on Campus 375 computers available on campus for general student use. A campuswide network can be accessed from off campus. At least one staffed computer lab available.

Student Life *Housing:* college housing not available. *Campus security:* 24-hour emergency response devices and patrols, late-night transport/escort service.

Costs (2003–04) *Tuition:* state resident $5208 full-time, $217 per semester hour part-time; nonresident $9576 full-time, $399 per semester hour part-time. *Required fees:* $120 full-time. *Waivers:* senior citizens and employees or children of employees.

Financial Aid Of all full-time matriculated undergraduates who enrolled in 2001, 1,309 applied for aid, 1,157 were judged to have need, 36 had their need fully met. *Average percent of need met:* 29%. *Average financial aid package:* $1631. *Average need-based loan:* $1900. *Average need-based gift aid:* $1050. *Average indebtedness upon graduation:* $1977.

University of Maryland University College (continued)

Applying *Options:* electronic application, deferred entrance. *Application fee:* $30. *Required:* high school transcript. *Application deadline:* rolling (freshmen), rolling (transfers). *Notification:* continuous (freshmen), continuous (transfers).

Admissions Contact Ms. Anne Rahill, Technical Director, Admissions, University of Maryland University College, 3501 University Boulevard East, Adelphi, MD 20783. *Phone:* 301-985-7000. *Toll-free phone:* 800-888-8682. *Fax:* 301-985-7364. *E-mail:* umucinfo@nova.umuc.edu.

UNIVERSITY OF PHOENIX–MARYLAND CAMPUS

Columbia, Maryland

- **Proprietary** comprehensive
- **Calendar** continuous
- **Degrees** certificates, associate, bachelor's, master's, doctoral, post-master's, and postbachelor's certificates (courses conducted at 121 campuses and learning centers in 25 states)
- **Urban** campus
- **Coed,** 1,212 undergraduate students, 100% full-time, 53% women, 47% men
- **Noncompetitive** entrance level

Undergraduates 1,212 full-time. 32% African American, 2% Asian American or Pacific Islander, 3% Hispanic American, 0.6% Native American, 11% international.

Freshmen *Admission:* 78 enrolled.

Faculty *Total:* 153, 3% full-time, 38% with terminal degrees. *Student/faculty ratio:* 10:1.

Majors Accounting; business administration and management; information technology; management information systems; management science.

Academic Programs *Special study options:* accelerated degree program, adult/continuing education programs, advanced placement credit, distance learning, external degree program, independent study.

Library University Library with 27.1 million titles, 11,648 serial subscriptions, an OPAC, a Web page.

Computers on Campus A campuswide network can be accessed from off campus. Internet access, at least one staffed computer lab available.

Student Life *Housing:* college housing not available.

Costs (2003–04) *Tuition:* $10,200 full-time, $340 per credit part-time.

Financial Aid *Average financial aid package:* $1385.

Applying *Options:* deferred entrance. *Application fee:* $85. *Required:* 1 letter of recommendation, 2 years of work experience, 23 years of age. *Required for some:* high school transcript. *Application deadline:* rolling (freshmen), rolling (transfers).

Admissions Contact Ms. Beth Barilla, Director of Admissions, University of Phoenix–Maryland Campus, 4615 East Elwood Street, Mail Stop AA-K101, Phoenix, AZ 85040-1958. *Phone:* 480-317-6000. *Toll-free phone:* 800-228-7240. *Fax:* 480-894-1758. *E-mail:* beth.barilla@phoenix.edu.

VILLA JULIE COLLEGE

Stevenson, Maryland

- **Independent** comprehensive, founded 1952
- **Calendar** semesters
- **Degrees** certificates, associate, bachelor's, and master's
- **Suburban** 60-acre campus with easy access to Baltimore
- **Coed,** 2,656 undergraduate students, 78% full-time, 73% women, 27% men
- **Moderately difficult** entrance level, 63% of applicants were admitted

Undergraduates 2,060 full-time, 596 part-time. Students come from 14 states and territories, 6 other countries, 3% are from out of state, 13% African American, 3% Asian American or Pacific Islander, 1% Hispanic American, 0.3% Native American, 0.2% international, 8% transferred in, 18% live on campus. *Retention:* 84% of 2002 full-time freshmen returned.

Freshmen *Admission:* 2,195 applied, 1,382 admitted, 545 enrolled. *Average high school GPA:* 3.30. *Test scores:* SAT verbal scores over 500: 59%; SAT math scores over 500: 62%; SAT verbal scores over 600: 16%; SAT math scores over 600: 21%; SAT verbal scores over 700: 1%; SAT math scores over 700: 1%.

Faculty *Total:* 272, 31% full-time, 45% with terminal degrees. *Student/faculty ratio:* 13:1.

Majors Accounting; applied art; art; biological and physical sciences; biology/biological sciences; biology/biotechnology laboratory technician; business administration and management; chemistry; child development; cinematography and film/video production; clinical laboratory science/medical technology; clinical/medical laboratory technology; commercial and advertising art; computer and information sciences; computer graphics; computer programming; court reporting; developmental and child psychology; dramatic/theatre arts; elementary education; English; environmental studies; history; humanities; information science/studies; interdisciplinary studies; journalism; kindergarten/preschool education; legal assistant/paralegal; legal studies; liberal arts and sciences/liberal studies; management information systems; mass communication/media; medical laboratory technology; middle school education; nursing (registered nurse training); photography; physical sciences; physical therapy; political science and government; pre-dentistry studies; pre-law studies; pre-medical studies; pre-veterinary studies; psychology; science teacher education; social sciences; sociology.

Academic Programs *Special study options:* academic remediation for entering students, accelerated degree program, adult/continuing education programs, advanced placement credit, cooperative education, double majors, English as a second language, freshman honors college, honors programs, independent study, internships, off-campus study, part-time degree program, student-designed majors, summer session for credit. *ROTC:* Army (c). *Unusual degree programs:* 3-2 physical therapy with University of Maryland, Baltimore County.

Library Villa Julie College Library with 124,417 titles, 720 serial subscriptions, 2,288 audiovisual materials, an OPAC, a Web page.

Computers on Campus 250 computers available on campus for general student use. A campuswide network can be accessed from student residence rooms and from off campus. Internet access, at least one staffed computer lab available.

Student Life *Housing options:* coed. Campus housing is leased by the school. Freshman applicants given priority for college housing. *Activities and organizations:* drama/theater group, student-run newspaper, choral group, Student Government Association, wilderness club, Black Student Union, National Student Nurses Association, Phi Sigma, national sororities. *Campus security:* 24-hour emergency response devices, late-night transport/escort service, controlled dormitory access, patrols by trained security personnel during campus hours. *Student services:* personal/psychological counseling.

Athletics Member NCAA. All Division III. *Intercollegiate sports:* basketball M/W, cheerleading M/W, cross-country running M/W, field hockey W, golf M/W, lacrosse M/W, soccer M/W, tennis M/W, volleyball W. *Intramural sports:* badminton M/W, baseball M, basketball M/W, fencing M/W, field hockey W, football M/W, sailing M/W, skiing (cross-country) M/W, skiing (downhill) M/W, softball W, table tennis M/W, tennis M/W, volleyball M.

Standardized Tests *Required:* SAT I or ACT (for admission).

Costs (2003–04) *Tuition:* $12,816 full-time, $365 per credit part-time. *Required fees:* $877 full-time, $70 per term part-time. *Room only:* $4700. *Payment plan:* installment. *Waivers:* employees or children of employees.

Financial Aid Of all full-time matriculated undergraduates who enrolled in 2003, 1,496 applied for aid, 1,232 were judged to have need, 303 had their need fully met. 156 Federal Work-Study jobs (averaging $1775). In 2003, 383 non-need-based awards were made. *Average percent of need met:* 74%. *Average financial aid package:* $9343. *Average need-based loan:* $2164. *Average need-based gift aid:* $7262. *Average non-need-based aid:* $5387. *Average indebtedness upon graduation:* $16,832.

Applying *Options:* electronic application, early admission, deferred entrance. *Application fee:* $25. *Required:* essay or personal statement, high school transcript, 2 letters of recommendation. *Recommended:* minimum 3.0 GPA, interview. *Application deadlines:* 7/15 (freshmen), 7/15 (transfers). *Notification:* continuous (freshmen), continuous (transfers).

Admissions Contact Mr. Mark Hergan, Dean of Admissions, Villa Julie College, 1525 Greenspring Valley Road, Stevenson, MD 21153. *Phone:* 410-486-7001. *Toll-free phone:* 877-468-6852 (in-state); 877-468-3852 (out-of-state). *Fax:* 410-602-6600. *E-mail:* admissions@vjc.edu.

■ *See page 2760 for a narrative description.*

WASHINGTON BIBLE COLLEGE

Lanham, Maryland

- **Independent nondenominational** 4-year, founded 1938
- **Calendar** semesters
- **Degrees** certificates, associate, and bachelor's
- **Suburban** 63-acre campus with easy access to Washington, DC
- **Coed,** 331 undergraduate students, 56% full-time, 47% women, 53% men
- **Moderately difficult** entrance level, 65% of applicants were admitted

Since 1938, Washington Bible College has been preparing students for God-centered lives and careers through programs that include biblical, general, and professional studies. Located on a 63-acre campus in suburban Maryland, near Washington, D.C., WBC fosters an environment that enables students to grow spiritually, socially, and intellectually.

Undergraduates 187 full-time, 144 part-time. Students come from 14 states and territories, 9 other countries, 24% are from out of state, 39% African

American, 8% Asian American or Pacific Islander, 2% Hispanic American, 2% international, 28% live on campus. *Retention:* 70% of 2002 full-time freshmen returned.

Freshmen *Admission:* 167 applied, 108 admitted. *Average high school GPA:* 2.80.

Faculty *Total:* 14, 100% full-time, 14% with terminal degrees. *Student/faculty ratio:* 13:1.

Majors Biblical studies; elementary education; kindergarten/preschool education; music; music teacher education; religious education; religious studies; theology.

Academic Programs *Special study options:* academic remediation for entering students, accelerated degree program, adult/continuing education programs, advanced placement credit, cooperative education, double majors, English as a second language, internships, off-campus study, part-time degree program, summer session for credit.

Library Oyer Memorial Library plus 1 other with 78,000 titles, 525 serial subscriptions, 3,824 audiovisual materials, a Web page.

Computers on Campus 25 computers available on campus for general student use. Internet access, at least one staffed computer lab available.

Student Life *Housing:* on-campus residence required through senior year. *Options:* men-only, women-only. *Activities and organizations:* drama/theater group, choral group, Student Missions Fellowship, school choir and ensemble, Korean Student Fellowship. *Campus security:* 24-hour patrols, student patrols, late-night transport/escort service, secured campus entrances, trained guards on duty. *Student services:* health clinic, personal/psychological counseling.

Athletics Member NCCAA. *Intercollegiate sports:* basketball M/W, soccer M, volleyball W. *Intramural sports:* basketball M, football M, racquetball M/W, soccer M, table tennis M/W, tennis M/W, volleyball M/W.

Standardized Tests *Required:* SAT I or ACT (for admission).

Costs (2003–04) *Comprehensive fee:* $19,500 includes full-time tuition ($14,500) and room and board ($5000). Part-time tuition and fees vary according to course load and location. *College room only:* $3000. Room and board charges vary according to board plan. *Payment plans:* installment, deferred payment. *Waivers:* employees or children of employees.

Financial Aid Of all full-time matriculated undergraduates who enrolled in 2002, 160 applied for aid, 150 were judged to have need. 38 Federal Work-Study jobs (averaging $1290). In 2002, 29 non-need-based awards were made. *Average percent of need met:* 85%. *Average financial aid package:* $5000. *Average need-based loan:* $4625. *Average need-based gift aid:* $500. *Average non-need-based aid:* $2053. *Average indebtedness upon graduation:* $8000.

Applying *Options:* early admission, deferred entrance. *Application fee:* $25. *Required:* essay or personal statement, high school transcript, 2 letters of recommendation, Christian testimony. *Required for some:* interview. *Application deadline:* 1/9 (freshmen), rolling (transfers). *Notification:* continuous until 8/15 (freshmen), continuous until 1/15 (transfers).

Admissions Contact Stewart Bennett, Director of Admissions, Washington Bible College, 6511 Princess Garden Parkway, Lanham, MD 20706. *Phone:* 301-552-1400 Ext. 1221. *Toll-free phone:* 800-787-0256 Ext. 212. *Fax:* 301-552-2775. *E-mail:* admissions@bible.edu.

WASHINGTON COLLEGE
Chestertown, Maryland

- **Independent** comprehensive, founded 1782
- **Calendar** semesters
- **Degrees** bachelor's and master's
- **Small-town** 120-acre campus with easy access to Baltimore and Washington, DC
- **Endowment** $95.7 million
- **Coed,** 1,398 undergraduate students, 96% full-time, 63% women, 37% men
- **Moderately difficult** entrance level, 61% of applicants were admitted

Washington College (WC) has initiated a $40,000 scholarship program expressly for National Honor Society and Cum Laude Society members. Washington College NHS/CLS Scholarships are $10,000 annual awards renewable through the completion of 8 semesters. To be eligible for scholarship consideration, a student must be an honor society member prior to March 1 of the senior year. For more information, students should contact the Admissions Office or visit the WC Web site at http://www.washcoll.edu.

Undergraduates 1,349 full-time, 49 part-time. Students come from 36 states and territories, 40 other countries, 44% are from out of state, 4% African American, 1% Asian American or Pacific Islander, 0.8% Hispanic American, 0.2% Native American, 4% international, 2% transferred in, 80% live on campus. *Retention:* 88% of 2002 full-time freshmen returned.

Freshmen *Admission:* 2,114 applied, 1,290 admitted, 359 enrolled. *Average high school GPA:* 3.44. *Test scores:* SAT verbal scores over 500: 90%; SAT math scores over 500: 86%; ACT scores over 18: 97%; SAT verbal scores over 600: 44%; SAT math scores over 600: 33%; ACT scores over 24: 49%; SAT verbal scores over 700: 7%; SAT math scores over 700: 4%; ACT scores over 30: 3%.

Faculty *Total:* 143, 60% full-time, 64% with terminal degrees. *Student/faculty ratio:* 12:1.

Majors American studies; anthropology; art; biology/biological sciences; business administration and management; chemistry; computer science; dramatic/theatre arts; ecology; economics; English; environmental studies; foreign languages and literatures; French; German; history; humanities; international relations and affairs; Latin American studies; liberal arts and sciences/liberal studies; mathematics; multi-/interdisciplinary studies related; music; philosophy; physics; physiological psychology/psychobiology; political science and government; pre-dentistry studies; pre-law studies; pre-medical studies; pre-veterinary studies; psychology; sociology; Spanish.

Academic Programs *Special study options:* advanced placement credit, cooperative education, double majors, English as a second language, independent study, internships, off-campus study, part-time degree program, services for LD students, student-designed majors, study abroad. *Unusual degree programs:* 3-2 engineering with University of Maryland, College Park; nursing with Johns Hopkins University.

Library Clifton M. Miller Library with 243,030 titles, 4,667 serial subscriptions, 6,114 audiovisual materials, an OPAC, a Web page.

Computers on Campus 150 computers available on campus for general student use. A campuswide network can be accessed from student residence rooms and from off campus that provide access to e-mail. Internet access, at least one staffed computer lab available. Computer purchase or lease plan available.

Student Life *Housing:* on-campus residence required through sophomore year. *Options:* coed, men-only, women-only. Campus housing is university owned. Freshman campus housing is guaranteed. *Activities and organizations:* drama/theater group, student-run newspaper, choral group, Writers Union, Student Government Association, Hands Out, Omicron Delta Kappa, Dale Adams Society, national fraternities, national sororities. *Campus security:* 24-hour emergency response devices and patrols, student patrols, late-night transport/escort service, controlled dormitory access. *Student services:* health clinic, personal/psychological counseling.

Athletics Member NCAA. All Division III. *Intercollegiate sports:* baseball M, basketball M/W, crew M/W, equestrian sports M(c)/W(c), fencing M(c)/W(c), field hockey W, ice hockey M(c); lacrosse M/W, rugby M(c)/W(c), sailing M(c)/W(c), soccer M/W, softball W, swimming M/W, table tennis M(c)/W(c), tennis M/W, ultimate Frisbee M(c)/W(c), volleyball W. *Intramural sports:* basketball M/W, equestrian sports M/W, golf M, racquetball M/W, rugby M/W, sailing M/W, soccer M/W, softball M/W, squash M/W, tennis M/W, ultimate Frisbee M/W, volleyball M/W.

Standardized Tests *Required:* SAT I or ACT (for admission).

Costs (2003–04) *Comprehensive fee:* $30,040 includes full-time tuition ($23,740), mandatory fees ($560), and room and board ($5740). Full-time tuition and fees vary according to program and reciprocity agreements. Part-time tuition: $3957 per course. Part-time tuition and fees vary according to course load and program. *Required fees:* $92 per course part-time. *College room only:* $2600. Room and board charges vary according to board plan and housing facility. *Payment plans:* tuition prepayment, installment. *Waivers:* minority students and employees or children of employees.

Financial Aid Of all full-time matriculated undergraduates who enrolled in 2003, 793 applied for aid, 678 were judged to have need, 369 had their need fully met. 261 Federal Work-Study jobs (averaging $1497). In 2003, 454 non-need-based awards were made. *Average percent of need met:* 88%. *Average financial aid package:* $19,395. *Average need-based loan:* $3500. *Average need-based gift aid:* $15,023. *Average non-need-based aid:* $10,717. *Average indebtedness upon graduation:* $17,756.

Applying *Options:* common application, electronic application, early admission, early decision, early action, deferred entrance. *Application fee:* $40. *Required:* essay or personal statement, high school transcript, 1 letter of recommendation. *Required for some:* interview. *Recommended:* interview. *Application deadline:* 3/15 (freshmen), rolling (transfers). *Early decision:* 11/15. *Notification:* continuous until 4/1 (freshmen), 12/15 (early decision), 12/20 (early action), continuous (transfers).

Admissions Contact Mr. Kevin Coveney, Vice President for Admissions, Washington College, 300 Washington Avenue, Chestertown, MD 21620-1197. *Phone:* 410-778-7700. *Toll-free phone:* 800-422-1782. *E-mail:* admissions_office@washcoll.edu.

■ *See page 2788 for a narrative description.*

YESHIVA COLLEGE OF THE NATION'S CAPITAL
Silver Spring, Maryland

Admissions Contact 1216 Arcola Avenue, Silver Spring, MD 20902.

MASSACHUSETTS

AMERICAN INTERNATIONAL COLLEGE
Springfield, Massachusetts

- **Independent** comprehensive, founded 1885
- **Calendar** semesters
- **Degrees** certificates, associate, bachelor's, master's, doctoral, post-master's, and postbachelor's certificates
- **Urban** 58-acre campus
- **Endowment** $11.0 million
- **Coed,** 1,188 undergraduate students, 85% full-time, 53% women, 47% men
- **Moderately difficult** entrance level, 77% of applicants were admitted

Undergraduates 1,015 full-time, 173 part-time. Students come from 25 states and territories, 40 other countries, 41% are from out of state, 26% African American, 2% Asian American or Pacific Islander, 8% Hispanic American, 0.4% Native American, 4% international, 13% transferred in, 58% live on campus. *Retention:* 55% of 2002 full-time freshmen returned.

Freshmen *Admission:* 1,347 applied, 1,031 admitted, 331 enrolled. *Average high school GPA:* 2.90. *Test scores:* SAT verbal scores over 500: 51%; SAT math scores over 500: 52%; ACT scores over 18: 51%; SAT verbal scores over 600: 4%; SAT math scores over 600: 3%; ACT scores over 24: 2%.

Faculty *Total:* 158, 44% full-time, 54% with terminal degrees. *Student/faculty ratio:* 13:1.

Majors Accounting; adult and continuing education; biochemistry; biology/biological sciences; business administration and management; business/managerial economics; business teacher education; chemistry; clinical laboratory science/medical technology; criminal justice/law enforcement administration; criminal justice/police science; economics; education; elementary education; English; finance; history; human resources management; human services; information science/studies; international business/trade/commerce; international relations and affairs; kindergarten/preschool education; liberal arts and sciences/liberal studies; management information systems; marketing/marketing management; mass communication/media; mathematics; middle school education; nursing (registered nurse training); occupational therapy; philosophy; physical therapy; political science and government; pre-dentistry studies; pre-law studies; pre-medical studies; pre-veterinary studies; psychology; public administration; secondary education; social sciences; sociology; Spanish; special education.

Academic Programs *Special study options:* academic remediation for entering students, accelerated degree program, adult/continuing education programs, advanced placement credit, double majors, English as a second language, freshman honors college, honors programs, independent study, internships, off-campus study, part-time degree program, services for LD students, study abroad, summer session for credit. *ROTC:* Army (c), Air Force (c).

Library James J. Shea Jr. Library with 118,000 titles, 390 serial subscriptions, an OPAC, a Web page.

Computers on Campus 100 computers available on campus for general student use. A campuswide network can be accessed. Internet access, at least one staffed computer lab available.

Student Life *Housing:* on-campus residence required through sophomore year. *Options:* coed, men-only, women-only. Campus housing is university owned. Freshman campus housing is guaranteed. *Activities and organizations:* drama/theater group, student-run newspaper, radio station, choral group, Student Activities Committee, Golden Key Society, PRIDE (Persons Ready in Defense of Ebony), student government. *Campus security:* 24-hour emergency response devices and patrols, student patrols, late-night transport/escort service, controlled dormitory access. *Student services:* health clinic, personal/psychological counseling.

Athletics Member NCAA. All Division II except ice hockey (Division I). *Intercollegiate sports:* baseball M(s), basketball M(s)/W(s), field hockey W(s), football M(s), golf M, ice hockey M(s), lacrosse M/W(s), soccer M(s)/W(s), softball W(s), tennis M/W, volleyball W(s), wrestling M. *Intramural sports:* archery M/W, basketball M/W, cheerleading M/W, equestrian sports M/W, football M, golf M, skiing (cross-country) M/W, skiing (downhill) M/W, soccer M/W, swimming M/W, table tennis M/W, tennis M/W, volleyball M/W, wrestling W(c).

Standardized Tests *Required:* SAT I or ACT (for admission).

Costs (2004–05) *Comprehensive fee:* $26,300 includes full-time tuition ($17,800) and room and board ($8500). Full-time tuition and fees vary according to course load and program. Part-time tuition: $409 per credit. *College room only:* $4232. Room and board charges vary according to board plan. *Payment plans:* tuition prepayment, installment, deferred payment. *Waivers:* senior citizens and employees or children of employees.

Financial Aid Of all full-time matriculated undergraduates who enrolled in 2003, 1,060 applied for aid, 1,021 were judged to have need, 391 had their need fully met. 150 state and other part-time jobs (averaging $2400). In 2003, 34 non-need-based awards were made. *Average percent of need met:* 81%. *Average financial aid package:* $17,269. *Average need-based loan:* $4531. *Average need-based gift aid:* $9309. *Average non-need-based aid:* $2256. *Average indebtedness upon graduation:* $17,125.

Applying *Options:* common application, electronic application, early admission, deferred entrance. *Application fee:* $20. *Required:* high school transcript, 1 letter of recommendation. *Required for some:* interview. *Recommended:* essay or personal statement, interview. *Application deadline:* rolling (freshmen), rolling (transfers). *Notification:* continuous (freshmen), continuous (transfers).

Admissions Contact Dean of Admissions, American International College, 1000 State Street, Springfield, MA 01109-3189. *Phone:* 413-205-3201. *Fax:* 413-205-3051. *E-mail:* inquiry@acad.aic.edu.

■ See page 1166 for a narrative description.

AMHERST COLLEGE
Amherst, Massachusetts

- **Independent** 4-year, founded 1821
- **Calendar** semesters
- **Degree** bachelor's
- **Small-town** 1000-acre campus
- **Endowment** $877.2 million
- **Coed,** 1,623 undergraduate students, 100% full-time, 49% women, 51% men
- **Most difficult** entrance level, 18% of applicants were admitted

Undergraduates 1,618 full-time, 5 part-time. Students come from 50 states and territories, 31 other countries, 85% are from out of state, 10% African American, 12% Asian American or Pacific Islander, 8% Hispanic American, 0.2% Native American, 6% international, 0.6% transferred in, 98% live on campus. *Retention:* 96% of 2002 full-time freshmen returned.

Freshmen *Admission:* 5,631 applied, 1,001 admitted, 413 enrolled. *Test scores:* SAT verbal scores over 500: 100%; SAT math scores over 500: 100%; ACT scores over 18: 99%; SAT verbal scores over 600: 93%; SAT math scores over 600: 93%; ACT scores over 24: 99%; SAT verbal scores over 700: 64%; SAT math scores over 700: 65%; ACT scores over 30: 71%.

Faculty *Total:* 219, 83% full-time, 91% with terminal degrees. *Student/faculty ratio:* 8:1.

Majors African-American/Black studies; American studies; ancient/classical Greek; anthropology; art; Asian studies; astronomy; biology/biological sciences; chemistry; classics and languages, literatures and linguistics; computer science; dance; dramatic/theatre arts; economics; English; European studies; fine/studio arts; French; geology/earth science; German; history; interdisciplinary studies; Latin; legal studies; mathematics; music; neuroscience; philosophy; physics; political science and government; psychology; religious studies; Russian; sociology; Spanish; women's studies.

Academic Programs *Special study options:* double majors, honors programs, independent study, off-campus study, student-designed majors, study abroad.

Library Robert Frost Library plus 5 others with 977,379 titles, 5,348 serial subscriptions, 32,460 audiovisual materials, an OPAC, a Web page.

Computers on Campus 182 computers available on campus for general student use. A campuswide network can be accessed from student residence rooms and from off campus. Internet access, at least one staffed computer lab available. Computer purchase or lease plan available.

Student Life *Housing:* on-campus residence required for freshman year. *Options:* coed, cooperative. Campus housing is university owned. Freshman campus housing is guaranteed. *Activities and organizations:* drama/theater group, student-run newspaper, radio station, choral group, choral groups, WAMH (campus radio station), OUTREACH (community service), literary magazines, The Amherst Student (school newspaper). *Campus security:* 24-hour emergency response devices and patrols, student patrols, late-night transport/escort service, controlled dormitory access. *Student services:* health clinic, personal/psychological counseling, women's center.

Athletics Member NCAA. All Division III. *Intercollegiate sports:* baseball M, basketball M/W, crew M(c)/W(c), cross-country running M/W, equestrian sports M(c)/W(c), fencing M(c)/W(c), field hockey W, football M, golf M/W, ice hockey M/W, lacrosse M/W, rugby M(c)/W(c), sailing M(c)/W(c), skiing (downhill) M(c)/W(c), soccer M/W, softball W, squash M/W, swimming M/W, tennis M/W, track and field M/W, ultimate Frisbee M(c)/W(c), volleyball M(c)/W, water polo M(c)/W(c). *Intramural sports:* badminton M/W, basketball M/W, golf M/W, ice hockey M/W, soccer M/W, softball M/W, squash M/W, table tennis M/W, tennis M/W, track and field M/W, volleyball M/W.

Standardized Tests *Required:* SAT I and SAT II or ACT (for admission).

Costs (2003–04) *Comprehensive fee:* $37,470 includes full-time tuition ($29,170), mandatory fees ($560), and room and board ($7740). *College room only:* $4150. *Payment plans:* installment, deferred payment.

Financial Aid Of all full-time matriculated undergraduates who enrolled in 2003, 865 applied for aid, 773 were judged to have need, 773 had their need fully met. *Average percent of need met:* 100%. *Average financial aid package:* $25,366. *Average need-based loan:* $2233. *Average need-based gift aid:* $23,703. *Average indebtedness upon graduation:* $10,787.

Applying *Options:* common application, electronic application, early admission, early decision, deferred entrance. *Application fee:* $55. *Required:* essay or personal statement, high school transcript, 3 letters of recommendation. *Application deadlines:* 12/31 (freshmen), 2/1 (transfers). *Early decision:* 11/15. *Notification:* 4/5 (freshmen), 12/15 (early decision), 6/1 (transfers).

Admissions Contact Mr. Thomas Parker, Dean of Admission and Financial Aid, Amherst College, PO Box 5000, Amherst, MA 01002. *Phone:* 413-542-2328. *Fax:* 413-542-2040. *E-mail:* admission@amherst.edu.

ANNA MARIA COLLEGE
Paxton, Massachusetts

- **Independent Roman Catholic** comprehensive, founded 1946
- **Calendar** semesters
- **Degrees** associate, bachelor's, master's, post-master's, and postbachelor's certificates
- **Rural** 180-acre campus with easy access to Boston
- **Endowment** $1.4 million
- **Coed,** 731 undergraduate students, 75% full-time, 66% women, 34% men
- **Moderately difficult** entrance level, 88% of applicants were admitted

Undergraduates 547 full-time, 184 part-time. Students come from 11 states and territories, 7 other countries, 22% are from out of state, 1% African American, 0.7% Asian American or Pacific Islander, 2% Hispanic American, 0.3% Native American, 1% international, 2% transferred in, 60% live on campus. *Retention:* 69% of 2002 full-time freshmen returned.

Freshmen *Admission:* 568 applied, 500 admitted, 159 enrolled. *Average high school GPA:* 2.62. *Test scores:* SAT verbal scores over 500: 36%; SAT math scores over 500: 31%; SAT verbal scores over 600: 6%; SAT math scores over 600: 8%.

Faculty *Total:* 163, 23% full-time. *Student/faculty ratio:* 10:1.

Majors Art; art teacher education; art therapy; behavioral sciences; biology/biological sciences; business administration and management; computer and information sciences and support services related; criminal justice/law enforcement administration; elementary education; English; fine/studio arts; fire science; history; interdisciplinary studies; kindergarten/preschool education; legal assistant/paralegal; music; music teacher education; music therapy; nursing (registered nurse training); philosophy; piano and organ; political science and government; psychology; religious studies; social sciences; social work; voice and opera.

Academic Programs *Special study options:* academic remediation for entering students, accelerated degree program, adult/continuing education programs, advanced placement credit, cooperative education, double majors, English as a second language, internships, off-campus study, part-time degree program, services for LD students, student-designed majors, study abroad, summer session for credit. *ROTC:* Air Force (c).

Library Mondor-Eagen Library with 79,039 titles, 318 serial subscriptions, 895 audiovisual materials, an OPAC.

Computers on Campus 59 computers available on campus for general student use. A campuswide network can be accessed from student residence rooms and from off campus that provide access to on-line class schedules, student account information. Internet access available.

Student Life *Housing options:* coed, disabled students. Campus housing is university owned. Freshman campus housing is guaranteed. *Activities and organizations:* drama/theater group, student-run newspaper, choral group, Student Government Association, drama club, ski club, chorus, criminal justice club. *Campus security:* 24-hour emergency response devices and patrols, late-night transport/escort service, controlled dormitory access. *Student services:* health clinic, personal/psychological counseling.

Athletics Member NCAA. All Division III. *Intercollegiate sports:* baseball M, basketball M/W, cheerleading W, cross-country running M/W, field hockey W, golf M, soccer M/W, softball W, volleyball W. *Intramural sports:* basketball M/W, field hockey W, football M, softball M/W, volleyball M/W, weight lifting M.

Standardized Tests *Required:* SAT I or ACT (for admission).

Costs (2003–04) *Comprehensive fee:* $26,140 includes full-time tuition ($17,495), mandatory fees ($1650), and room and board ($6995). Part-time tuition: $1750 per course. *Room and board:* Room and board charges vary according to board plan. *Payment plan:* installment. *Waivers:* children of alumni, senior citizens, and employees or children of employees.

Financial Aid Of all full-time matriculated undergraduates who enrolled in 2002, 473 applied for aid, 436 were judged to have need, 134 had their need fully met. 113 Federal Work-Study jobs (averaging $1000). In 2002, 67 non-need-based awards were made. *Average percent of need met:* 80%. *Average financial aid package:* $14,378. *Average need-based loan:* $5548. *Average need-based gift aid:* $9385. *Average non-need-based aid:* $11,383. *Average indebtedness upon graduation:* $18,869.

Applying *Options:* common application, deferred entrance. *Application fee:* $40. *Required:* essay or personal statement, high school transcript, 2 letters of recommendation. *Required for some:* audition for music programs, portfolio for art programs. *Recommended:* minimum 2.0 GPA, interview. *Application deadline:* rolling (freshmen). *Notification:* continuous (freshmen), continuous (transfers).

Admissions Contact Ms. Wylie Culhane, Director of Admissions, Anna Maria College, Box O, Sunset Lane, Paxton, MA 01612. *Phone:* 508-849-3360. *Toll-free phone:* 800-344-4586 Ext. 360. *Fax:* 508-849-3362. *E-mail:* admission@annamaria.edu.

■ *See page 1176 for a narrative description.*

THE ART INSTITUTE OF BOSTON AT LESLEY UNIVERSITY
Boston, Massachusetts

- **Independent** comprehensive, founded 1912
- **Calendar** semesters
- **Degrees** certificates, diplomas, bachelor's, master's, and postbachelor's certificates
- **Urban** 1-acre campus
- **Endowment** $37.6 million
- **Coed,** 516 undergraduate students, 89% full-time, 57% women, 43% men
- **Moderately difficult** entrance level, 77% of applicants were admitted

Undergraduates 458 full-time, 58 part-time. Students come from 35 states and territories, 23 other countries, 43% are from out of state, 3% African American, 4% Asian American or Pacific Islander, 3% Hispanic American, 0.6% Native American, 11% international, 10% transferred in, 27% live on campus. *Retention:* 67% of 2002 full-time freshmen returned.

Freshmen *Admission:* 489 applied, 375 admitted, 95 enrolled. *Average high school GPA:* 3.00. *Test scores:* SAT verbal scores over 500: 68%; SAT math scores over 500: 54%; SAT verbal scores over 600: 21%; SAT math scores over 600: 13%; SAT verbal scores over 700: 4%.

Faculty *Total:* 113, 21% full-time, 51% with terminal degrees. *Student/faculty ratio:* 9:1.

Majors Fine/studio arts; graphic design; illustration; photography.

Academic Programs *Special study options:* academic remediation for entering students, accelerated degree program, adult/continuing education programs, advanced placement credit, distance learning, double majors, English as a second language, honors programs, independent study, internships, off-campus study, part-time degree program, services for LD students, study abroad, summer session for credit. *Unusual degree programs:* 3-2 art education, art therapy.

Library The Art Institute of Boston Library plus 2 others with 98,271 titles, 739 serial subscriptions, 47,312 audiovisual materials, an OPAC.

Computers on Campus 76 computers available on campus for general student use. A campuswide network can be accessed from student residence rooms and from off campus that provide access to graphics programs, software applications. Internet access, at least one staffed computer lab available.

Student Life *Housing options:* coed, women-only. Campus housing is university owned and leased by the school. Freshman applicants given priority for college housing. *Activities and organizations:* drama/theater group, choral group, Peer Advisors, Ski Club, International Student Association, Student Gallery Committee, Literary Journal. *Campus security:* 24-hour emergency response devices and patrols, late-night transport/escort service, controlled dormitory access, lighted walkways. *Student services:* health clinic, personal/psychological counseling.

Athletics Member NCAA. All Division III. *Intercollegiate sports:* basketball W, crew W, soccer W, softball W, volleyball W. *Intramural sports:* cross-country running W, swimming W, tennis W.

Standardized Tests *Required for some:* SAT I or ACT (for admission).

Costs (2004–05) *Comprehensive fee:* $28,080 includes full-time tuition ($18,000), mandatory fees ($710), and room and board ($9370). *College room only:* $5645. Room and board charges vary according to housing facility. *Payment plan:* installment. *Waivers:* employees or children of employees.

Applying *Options:* common application, deferred entrance. *Application fee:* $40. *Required:* essay or personal statement, high school transcript, interview, portfolio. *Recommended:* minimum 2.0 GPA. *Application deadline:* rolling (freshmen), rolling (transfers). *Notification:* continuous (freshmen), continuous (transfers).

The Art Institute of Boston at Lesley University (continued)

Admissions Contact Mr. Bradford White, Director of Admissions, The Art Institute of Boston at Lesley University, 700 Beacon Street, Boston, MA 02215-2598. *Phone:* 617-585-6700. *Toll-free phone:* 800-773-0494. *Fax:* 617-585-6720. *E-mail:* admissions@aiboston.edu.

■ *See page 1184 for a narrative description.*

ASSUMPTION COLLEGE
Worcester, Massachusetts

- **Independent Roman Catholic** comprehensive, founded 1904
- **Calendar** semesters
- **Degrees** bachelor's, master's, and post-master's certificates
- **Suburban** 145-acre campus with easy access to Boston
- **Endowment** $38.0 million
- **Coed,** 2,133 undergraduate students, 99% full-time, 62% women, 38% men
- **Moderately difficult** entrance level, 79% of applicants were admitted

Undergraduates 2,122 full-time, 11 part-time. Students come from 24 states and territories, 10 other countries, 32% are from out of state, 1% African American, 1% Asian American or Pacific Islander, 2% Hispanic American, 0.1% Native American, 0.7% international, 2% transferred in, 89% live on campus. *Retention:* 85% of 2002 full-time freshmen returned.

Freshmen *Admission:* 2,901 applied, 2,279 admitted, 640 enrolled. *Average high school GPA:* 3.20. *Test scores:* SAT verbal scores over 500: 74%; SAT math scores over 500: 74%; ACT scores over 18: 88%; SAT verbal scores over 600: 21%; SAT math scores over 600: 22%; ACT scores over 24: 30%; SAT verbal scores over 700: 1%; SAT math scores over 700: 1%.

Faculty *Total:* 180, 71% full-time, 83% with terminal degrees. *Student/faculty ratio:* 15:1.

Majors Accounting; biology/biological sciences; biotechnology; business administration and management; chemistry; classics and languages, literatures and linguistics; computer science; economics; economics related; elementary education; English; environmental science; foreign languages and literatures; French; history; human services; international business/trade/commerce; international economics; international/global studies; Latin American studies; marketing/marketing management; mathematics; molecular biology; organizational communication; philosophy; political science and government; psychology; rehabilitation and therapeutic professions related; secondary education; sociology; Spanish; theology; visual and performing arts.

Academic Programs *Special study options:* adult/continuing education programs, advanced placement credit, double majors, honors programs, independent study, internships, off-campus study, part-time degree program, services for LD students, student-designed majors, summer session for credit. *ROTC:* Air Force (c). *Unusual degree programs:* 3-2 engineering with Worcester Polytechnic Institute; special education, social rehabilitation counseling.

Library Emmanuel d'Alzon Library with 103,467 titles, 1,119 serial subscriptions, 1,450 audiovisual materials, an OPAC, a Web page.

Computers on Campus 190 computers available on campus for general student use. A campuswide network can be accessed from student residence rooms and from off campus. Internet access, at least one staffed computer lab available. Computer purchase or lease plan available.

Student Life *Housing options:* coed, women-only. Campus housing is university owned. Freshman campus housing is guaranteed. *Activities and organizations:* drama/theater group, student-run newspaper, television station, choral group, Volunteer Center, Campus Activities Board, student government, Campus Ministry, resident assistants. *Campus security:* 24-hour emergency response devices and patrols, student patrols, late-night transport/escort service, front gate security, well-lit pathways. *Student services:* health clinic, personal/psychological counseling.

Athletics Member NCAA. All Division II. *Intercollegiate sports:* baseball M, basketball M(s)/W(s), crew M/W, cross-country running M/W, field hockey W, football M, golf M, ice hockey M, lacrosse M/W, soccer M/W, softball W, tennis M/W, track and field M/W, volleyball W. *Intramural sports:* basketball M/W, football M, racquetball M/W, skiing (downhill) M/W, soccer M/W, softball M/W, volleyball M/W.

Standardized Tests *Required:* SAT I or ACT (for admission).

Costs (2003–04) *Comprehensive fee:* $26,255 includes full-time tuition ($21,000), mandatory fees ($165), and room and board ($5090). Full-time tuition and fees vary according to course load and reciprocity agreements. Part-time tuition: $700 per credit hour. Part-time tuition and fees vary according to course load. *Required fees:* $165 per year part-time. *College room only:* $3120. Room and board charges vary according to board plan and housing facility. *Payment plan:* installment. *Waivers:* minority students and employees or children of employees.

Financial Aid Of all full-time matriculated undergraduates who enrolled in 2003, 1,686 applied for aid, 1,476 were judged to have need, 421 had their need fully met. 522 Federal Work-Study jobs (averaging $1405). In 2003, 157 non-need-based awards were made. *Average percent of need met:* 76%. *Average financial aid package:* $14,955. *Average need-based loan:* $4953. *Average need-based gift aid:* $10,387. *Average non-need-based aid:* $7336. *Average indebtedness upon graduation:* $22,825.

Applying *Options:* common application, electronic application, early decision, deferred entrance. *Application fee:* $50. *Required:* essay or personal statement, high school transcript, 1 letter of recommendation. *Recommended:* interview. *Application deadlines:* 3/1 (freshmen), 5/1 (transfers). *Early decision:* 11/15. *Notification:* continuous until 5/1 (freshmen), 12/15 (early decision), continuous until 8/1 (transfers).

Admissions Contact Ms. Katherine Murphy, Dean of Enrollment, Assumption College, 500 Salisbury Street, Worcester, MA 01609-1296. *Phone:* 508-767-7110. *Toll-free phone:* 888-882-7786. *Fax:* 508-799-4412. *E-mail:* admiss@assumption.edu.

■ *See page 1192 for a narrative description.*

ATLANTIC UNION COLLEGE
South Lancaster, Massachusetts

- **Independent Seventh-day Adventist** comprehensive, founded 1882
- **Calendar** semesters
- **Degrees** certificates, associate, bachelor's, and master's
- **Small-town** 314-acre campus with easy access to Boston
- **Endowment** $2.0 million
- **Coed,** 398 undergraduate students
- **Moderately difficult** entrance level, 39% of applicants were admitted

Undergraduates Students come from 15 states and territories, 18 other countries, 45% are from out of state, 68% live on campus. *Retention:* 75% of 2002 full-time freshmen returned.

Freshmen *Admission:* 713 applied, 281 admitted.

Faculty *Total:* 46, 61% with terminal degrees. *Student/faculty ratio:* 13:1.

Majors Accounting; administrative assistant and secretarial science; adult and continuing education; art; art teacher education; biochemistry; biological and physical sciences; biology/biological sciences; business administration and management; business teacher education; chemistry; clinical laboratory science/medical technology; computer programming; computer science; divinity/ministry; education; elementary education; English; French; history; information science/studies; interior design; kindergarten/preschool education; kinesiology and exercise science; legal assistant/paralegal; mathematics; modern languages; music; music teacher education; natural sciences; nursing (registered nurse training); physical education teaching and coaching; pre-dentistry studies; pre-engineering; pre-law studies; pre-medical studies; pre-veterinary studies; psychology; religious/sacred music; religious studies; secondary education; social work; sociology; Spanish; theology.

Academic Programs *Special study options:* academic remediation for entering students, adult/continuing education programs, advanced placement credit, cooperative education, English as a second language, external degree program, freshman honors college, honors programs, internships, part-time degree program, study abroad, summer session for credit.

Library G. Eric Jones Library with 135,694 titles, 533 serial subscriptions, 4,544 audiovisual materials, an OPAC, a Web page.

Computers on Campus 74 computers available on campus for general student use. A campuswide network can be accessed. Internet access, at least one staffed computer lab available.

Student Life *Housing:* on-campus residence required through senior year. *Options:* coed, men-only, women-only. Campus housing is university owned. Freshman campus housing is guaranteed. *Activities and organizations:* drama/theater group, student-run newspaper, radio station, choral group, Student Association, Black Christian Union, choir, CHISPA (Hispanic group). *Campus security:* 24-hour patrols, late-night transport/escort service. *Student services:* health clinic, personal/psychological counseling.

Athletics *Intramural sports:* basketball M/W, football M/W, golf M/W, skiing (downhill) M/W, soccer M/W, softball M/W, volleyball M/W.

Standardized Tests *Required:* SAT I or ACT (for placement). *Recommended:* SAT I (for placement).

Costs (2003–04) *Comprehensive fee:* $18,348 includes full-time tuition ($13,000), mandatory fees ($780), and room and board ($4568). No tuition increase for student's term of enrollment. *College room only:* $2300. Room and board charges vary according to housing facility. *Waivers:* senior citizens and employees or children of employees.

Financial Aid In 2002, 168 non-need-based awards were made. *Average percent of need met:* 83%. *Average financial aid package:* $12,500. *Average indebtedness upon graduation:* $19,000.

Applying *Options:* common application. *Application fee:* $25. *Required:* high school transcript, minimum 2.0 GPA, 2 letters of recommendation. *Required for some:* essay or personal statement, interview. *Application deadlines:* 8/1 (freshmen), 8/1 (transfers).

Admissions Contact Mrs. Rosita Lashley, Associate Director for Admissions, Atlantic Union College, PO Box 1000, South Lancaster, MA 01561. *Phone:* 978-368-2239. *Toll-free phone:* 800-282-2030. *Fax:* 978-368-2015. *E-mail:* info@atlanticuc.edu.

BABSON COLLEGE
Wellesley, Massachusetts

- **Independent** comprehensive, founded 1919
- **Calendar** semesters
- **Degrees** bachelor's, master's, and post-master's certificates
- **Suburban** 370-acre campus with easy access to Boston
- **Endowment** $150.6 million
- **Coed,** 1,717 undergraduate students, 100% full-time, 40% women, 60% men
- **Very difficult** entrance level, 37% of applicants were admitted

Undergraduates 1,717 full-time. Students come from 46 states and territories, 62 other countries, 55% are from out of state, 3% African American, 8% Asian American or Pacific Islander, 4% Hispanic American, 0.4% Native American, 19% international, 3% transferred in, 85% live on campus. *Retention:* 93% of 2002 full-time freshmen returned.

Freshmen *Admission:* 2,991 applied, 1,110 admitted, 395 enrolled. *Test scores:* SAT verbal scores over 500: 98%; SAT math scores over 500: 100%; ACT scores over 18: 100%; SAT verbal scores over 600: 54%; SAT math scores over 600: 83%; ACT scores over 24: 100%; SAT verbal scores over 700: 7%; SAT math scores over 700: 19%; ACT scores over 30: 25%.

Faculty *Total:* 223, 74% full-time, 77% with terminal degrees. *Student/faculty ratio:* 14:1.

Majors Accounting; accounting and business/management; accounting and finance; auditing; business administration and management; business administration, management and operations related; business/corporate communications; economics; entrepreneurial and small business related; entrepreneurship; finance; finance and financial management services related; international business/trade/commerce; international finance; investments and securities; management information systems; marketing/marketing management; marketing related; office management; operations management; operations research; pre-law studies; sales, distribution and marketing; small business administration.

Academic Programs *Special study options:* accelerated degree program, advanced placement credit, freshman honors college, honors programs, independent study, internships, off-campus study, services for LD students, student-designed majors, study abroad, summer session for credit.

Library Horn Library plus 1 other with 131,844 titles, 680 serial subscriptions, 4,472 audiovisual materials, an OPAC, a Web page.

Computers on Campus 350 computers available on campus for general student use. A campuswide network can be accessed from student residence rooms and from off campus. Internet access, online (class) registration, at least one staffed computer lab available.

Student Life *Housing:* on-campus residence required for freshman year. *Options:* coed, men-only, disabled students. Campus housing is university owned. Freshman campus housing is guaranteed. *Activities and organizations:* drama/theater group, student-run newspaper, radio station, choral group, student government, Free Press, Dance Ensemble, Asian Pacific Student Association, college radio, national fraternities, national sororities. *Campus security:* 24-hour emergency response devices and patrols, late-night transport/escort service, controlled dormitory access. *Student services:* health clinic, personal/psychological counseling, women's center.

Athletics Member NCAA. All Division III. *Intercollegiate sports:* baseball M, basketball M/W, cheerleading W(c), cross-country running M/W, field hockey W, golf M/W(c), ice hockey M/W(c), lacrosse M/W, rugby M(c)/W(c), sailing M(c)/W(c), skiing (downhill) M/W, soccer M/W, softball W, squash M(c)/W(c), swimming M/W, tennis M/W, track and field M/W, volleyball M(c)/W. *Intramural sports:* basketball M/W, football M, golf M(c), ice hockey M/W, racquetball M/W, soccer M/W, softball M/W, squash M/W, swimming M/W, tennis M/W, volleyball M/W, water polo M/W, wrestling M(c).

Standardized Tests *Required:* SAT I or ACT (for admission). *Recommended:* SAT II: Writing Test (for admission), SAT II Subject Test in math.

Costs (2003–04) *Comprehensive fee:* $37,226 includes full-time tuition ($27,248) and room and board ($9978). *College room only:* $6438. Room and board charges vary according to board plan and housing facility. *Payment plan:* installment. *Waivers:* employees or children of employees.

Financial Aid Of all full-time matriculated undergraduates who enrolled in 2003, 808 applied for aid, 755 were judged to have need, 686 had their need fully met. 296 Federal Work-Study jobs (averaging $1458). 580 state and other part-time jobs (averaging $2384). In 2003, 85 non-need-based awards were made. *Average percent of need met:* 98%. *Average financial aid package:* $22,870. *Average need-based loan:* $4178. *Average need-based gift aid:* $17,461. *Average non-need-based aid:* $8559. *Average indebtedness upon graduation:* $20,531. *Financial aid deadline:* 2/15.

Applying *Options:* common application, electronic application, early decision, early action, deferred entrance. *Application fee:* $60. *Required:* essay or personal statement, high school transcript, 2 letters of recommendation. *Recommended:* interview. *Application deadlines:* 2/1 (freshmen), 4/1 (transfers). *Early decision:* 11/15. *Notification:* 4/1 (freshmen), 12/15 (early decision), 1/1 (early action), 5/15 (transfers).

Admissions Contact Mrs. Monica Inzer, Dean of Undergraduate Admission and Student Financial Services, Babson College, Mustard Hall, Babson Park, MA 02457-0310. *Phone:* 800-488-3696. *Toll-free phone:* 800-488-3696. *Fax:* 781-239-4135. *E-mail:* ugradadmission@babson.edu.

■ *See page 1204 for a narrative description.*

BAY PATH COLLEGE
Longmeadow, Massachusetts

- **Independent** comprehensive, founded 1897
- **Calendar** semesters
- **Degrees** certificates, associate, bachelor's, master's, and postbachelor's certificates
- **Suburban** 48-acre campus with easy access to Boston
- **Endowment** $17.0 million
- **Women only,** 1,242 undergraduate students, 82% full-time
- **Moderately difficult** entrance level, 82% of applicants were admitted

Undergraduates 1,016 full-time, 226 part-time. Students come from 15 states and territories, 10 other countries, 41% are from out of state, 11% African American, 1% Asian American or Pacific Islander, 7% Hispanic American, 0.5% Native American, 2% international, 3% transferred in, 40% live on campus. *Retention:* 70% of 2002 full-time freshmen returned.

Freshmen *Admission:* 263 enrolled. *Average high school GPA:* 3.00. *Test scores:* SAT verbal scores over 500: 57%; SAT math scores over 500: 46%; SAT verbal scores over 600: 11%; SAT math scores over 600: 8%.

Faculty *Total:* 127, 22% full-time, 21% with terminal degrees. *Student/faculty ratio:* 17:1.

Majors Biology/biological sciences; biotechnology; business/commerce; criminal justice/law enforcement administration; elementary education; international business/trade/commerce; kindergarten/preschool education; legal studies; liberal arts and sciences/liberal studies; occupational therapy; pre-law studies; psychology.

Academic Programs *Special study options:* academic remediation for entering students, adult/continuing education programs, advanced placement credit, English as a second language, freshman honors college, honors programs, independent study, internships, off-campus study, part-time degree program, services for LD students, student-designed majors, study abroad, summer session for credit. *ROTC:* Army (c), Air Force (c).

Library Frank and Marion Hatch Library with 42,375 titles, 200 serial subscriptions, 3,152 audiovisual materials, an OPAC, a Web page.

Computers on Campus 155 computers available on campus for general student use. A campuswide network can be accessed from student residence rooms and from off campus. Internet access, at least one staffed computer lab available.

Student Life *Housing options:* women-only. Campus housing is university owned. Freshman campus housing is guaranteed. *Activities and organizations:* drama/theater group, student-run radio and television station, choral group, student government, All Women Excel, Golden Z Service Club, Alliance, Women of Culture. *Campus security:* 24-hour emergency response devices and patrols, late-night transport/escort service, controlled dormitory access. *Student services:* health clinic, personal/psychological counseling.

Athletics Member NCAA. All Division III. *Intercollegiate sports:* basketball W, cross-country running W, soccer W, softball W, tennis W, volleyball W. *Intramural sports:* cheerleading W(c).

Standardized Tests *Required:* SAT I or ACT (for admission).

Costs (2003–04) *Comprehensive fee:* $24,910 includes full-time tuition ($16,890) and room and board ($8020). Part-time tuition: $433 per credit. *Room and board:* Room and board charges vary according to board plan. *Payment plans:* tuition prepayment, installment, deferred payment. *Waivers:* employees or children of employees.

Financial Aid Of all full-time matriculated undergraduates who enrolled in 2003, 868 applied for aid, 789 were judged to have need, 69 had their need fully

Bay Path College (continued)

met. 123 Federal Work-Study jobs (averaging $2000). In 2003, 119 non-need-based awards were made. *Average percent of need met:* 71%. *Average financial aid package:* $9267. *Average need-based loan:* $3231. *Average need-based gift aid:* $5990. *Average non-need-based aid:* $8574. *Average indebtedness upon graduation:* $17,000.

Applying *Options:* common application, electronic application, early admission, early action, deferred entrance. *Application fee:* $25. *Required:* essay or personal statement, high school transcript, 2 letters of recommendation. *Required for some:* minimum 3.0 GPA, interview. *Recommended:* minimum 2.0 GPA, interview. *Application deadline:* rolling (freshmen), rolling (transfers). *Notification:* continuous (freshmen), 1/2 (early action), continuous (transfers).

Admissions Contact Ms. Brenda Wishart, Director of Admissions, Bay Path College, 588 Longmeadow Street, Longmeadow, MA 01106-2292. *Phone:* 413-565-1000 Ext. 229. *Toll-free phone:* 800-782-7284 Ext. 331. *Fax:* 413-565-1105. *E-mail:* admiss@baypath.edu.

■ See page 1222 for a narrative description.

BECKER COLLEGE
Worcester, Massachusetts

- **Independent** 4-year, founded 1784
- **Calendar** semesters
- **Degrees** certificates, associate, and bachelor's (also includes Leicester, MA small town campus)
- **Urban** 100-acre campus with easy access to Boston
- **Coed,** 1,467 undergraduate students, 57% full-time, 79% women, 21% men
- **Minimally difficult** entrance level, 83% of applicants were admitted

Becker College's small classes and supportive academic atmosphere offer students the individual attention and recognition they deserve. The 2 campuses allow students the unique opportunity to choose the environment that best suits their personal tastes: an urban neighborhood setting or a small New England town.

Undergraduates 831 full-time, 636 part-time. Students come from 18 states and territories, 1 other country, 29% are from out of state, 5% African American, 2% Asian American or Pacific Islander, 3% Hispanic American, 0.3% Native American, 0.5% international, 10% transferred in, 40% live on campus. *Retention:* 61% of 2002 full-time freshmen returned.

Freshmen *Admission:* 1,146 applied, 947 admitted, 321 enrolled. *Average high school GPA:* 2.61. *Test scores:* SAT verbal scores over 500: 24%; SAT math scores over 500: 19%; ACT scores over 18: 43%; SAT verbal scores over 600: 2%; SAT math scores over 600: 1%; ACT scores over 24: 14%.

Faculty *Total:* 104, 38% full-time, 15% with terminal degrees. *Student/faculty ratio:* 15:1.

Majors Accounting; animal sciences; animal training; biology/biological sciences; business administration and management; business administration, management and operations related; commercial and advertising art; communications technology; computer and information sciences and support services related; criminal justice/law enforcement administration; criminal justice/police science; dog/pet/animal grooming; education; elementary education; graphic design; hospitality administration; hotel/motel administration; humanities; human resources management and services related; illustration; interior design; kindergarten/preschool education; kinesiology and exercise science; legal assistant/paralegal; legal studies; liberal arts and sciences/liberal studies; marketing/marketing management; mass communication/media; nursing (registered nurse training); physical therapist assistant; pre-law studies; psychology; sport and fitness administration; tourism and travel services management; veterinary/animal health technology; veterinary sciences; veterinary technology.

Academic Programs *Special study options:* academic remediation for entering students, accelerated degree program, adult/continuing education programs, advanced placement credit, cooperative education, distance learning, internships, off-campus study, part-time degree program, services for LD students, study abroad, summer session for credit. *ROTC:* Army (c), Air Force (c). *Unusual degree programs:* 3-2 law with Massachusetts School of Law.

Library Ruska Library plus 1 other with 65,000 titles, 400 serial subscriptions, 2,900 audiovisual materials, an OPAC.

Computers on Campus 155 computers available on campus for general student use. A campuswide network can be accessed from student residence rooms and from off campus. Internet access, at least one staffed computer lab available.

Student Life *Housing options:* coed, men-only, women-only. Campus housing is university owned. Freshman campus housing is guaranteed. *Activities and organizations:* drama/theater group, student-run newspaper, student government, Student Activities Committee, Black Student Union, Animal Health Club, drama club. *Campus security:* 24-hour emergency response devices and patrols, late-night transport/escort service, controlled dormitory access. *Student services:* health clinic, personal/psychological counseling.

Athletics Member NCAA. *Intercollegiate sports:* baseball M, basketball M/W, cross-country running M/W, equestrian sports M/W, field hockey W, golf M, ice hockey M(c)/W(c), soccer M/W, softball W, tennis M/W, volleyball W. *Intramural sports:* badminton M/W, basketball M/W, bowling M/W, skiing (downhill) M(c)/W(c), soccer M/W, table tennis M/W, volleyball M/W.

Standardized Tests *Required:* SAT I or ACT (for admission).

Costs (2004–05) *Comprehensive fee:* $25,670 includes full-time tuition ($17,200), mandatory fees ($470), and room and board ($8000). Full-time tuition and fees vary according to program. Part-time tuition: $595 per credit. *Payment plan:* installment. *Waivers:* senior citizens and employees or children of employees.

Financial Aid Of all full-time matriculated undergraduates who enrolled in 2003, 731 applied for aid, 676 were judged to have need, 70 had their need fully met. 321 Federal Work-Study jobs (averaging $1090). In 2003, 67 non-need-based awards were made. *Average percent of need met:* 52%. *Average financial aid package:* $9298. *Average need-based loan:* $3206. *Average need-based gift aid:* $5693. *Average non-need-based aid:* $11,697. *Average indebtedness upon graduation:* $22,262.

Applying *Options:* common application, electronic application, deferred entrance. *Application fee:* $30. *Required:* high school transcript, minimum 2.0 GPA. *Required for some:* minimum 2.5 GPA, interview. *Recommended:* essay or personal statement, letters of recommendation. *Application deadline:* rolling (freshmen), rolling (transfers). *Notification:* continuous (freshmen), continuous (transfers).

Admissions Contact Admissions Receptionist, Becker College, 61 Sever Street, Worcester, MA 01609. *Phone:* 508-791-9241 Ext. 245. *Toll-free phone:* 877-5BECKER Ext. 245. *Fax:* 508-890-1500. *E-mail:* admissions@beckercollege.edu.

■ See page 1224 for a narrative description.

BENJAMIN FRANKLIN INSTITUTE OF TECHNOLOGY
Boston, Massachusetts

- **Independent** primarily 2-year, founded 1908
- **Calendar** semesters
- **Degrees** certificates, associate, and bachelor's
- **Urban** 3-acre campus
- **Endowment** $8.0 million
- **Coed, primarily men**
- **Minimally difficult** entrance level

Faculty *Student/faculty ratio:* 11:1.

Student Life *Campus security:* 24-hour emergency response devices, student patrols.

Standardized Tests *Recommended:* SAT I or ACT (for admission).

Costs (2003–04) *Tuition:* $11,950 full-time, $498 per credit part-time. *Required fees:* $339 full-time. *Room only:* Room and board charges vary according to board plan and housing facility.

Applying *Options:* common application, electronic application, deferred entrance. *Application fee:* $20. *Required:* high school transcript. *Recommended:* essay or personal statement, minimum 2.0 GPA, letters of recommendation, interview.

Admissions Contact Mr. Will Arvelo, Dean of Enrollment Services, Benjamin Franklin Institute of Technology, 41 Berkeley Street, Boston, MA 02116-6296. *Phone:* 617-423-4630 Ext. 122. *Fax:* 617-482-3706. *E-mail:* fibadm@fib.edu.

BENTLEY COLLEGE
Waltham, Massachusetts

- **Independent** comprehensive, founded 1917
- **Calendar** semesters
- **Degrees** associate, bachelor's, master's, post-master's, and postbachelor's certificates
- **Suburban** 143-acre campus with easy access to Boston
- **Endowment** $136.7 million
- **Coed,** 4,344 undergraduate students, 91% full-time, 43% women, 57% men
- **Moderately difficult** entrance level, 46% of applicants were admitted

Undergraduates 3,932 full-time, 412 part-time. Students come from 40 states and territories, 62 other countries, 43% are from out of state, 3% African American, 7% Asian American or Pacific Islander, 4% Hispanic American, 0.1% Native American, 8% international, 4% transferred in, 79% live on campus. *Retention:* 93% of 2002 full-time freshmen returned.

Freshmen *Admission:* 5,474 applied, 2,529 admitted, 955 enrolled. *Test scores:* SAT verbal scores over 500: 87%; SAT math scores over 500: 98%; ACT scores over 18: 98%; SAT verbal scores over 600: 35%; SAT math scores over 600: 63%; ACT scores over 24: 62%; SAT verbal scores over 700: 3%; SAT math scores over 700: 11%; ACT scores over 30: 10%.

Faculty *Total:* 456, 57% full-time, 61% with terminal degrees. *Student/faculty ratio:* 13:1.

Majors Accounting; business administration and management; business/commerce; business/corporate communications; business/managerial economics; computer and information sciences; economics; English; finance; history; interdisciplinary studies; international economics; liberal arts and sciences/liberal studies; marketing/marketing management; mathematics; philosophy; public policy analysis.

Academic Programs *Special study options:* academic remediation for entering students, accelerated degree program, adult/continuing education programs, advanced placement credit, distance learning, English as a second language, honors programs, internships, off-campus study, part-time degree program, services for LD students, student-designed majors, study abroad, summer session for credit. *ROTC:* Army (c).

Library Soloman R. Baker Library with 212,573 titles, 1,993 serial subscriptions, 4,705 audiovisual materials, an OPAC, a Web page.

Computers on Campus A campuswide network can be accessed from student residence rooms and from off campus. Internet access, online (class) registration, at least one staffed computer lab available.

Student Life *Housing options:* coed. Campus housing is university owned. Freshman campus housing is guaranteed. *Activities and organizations:* drama/theater group, student-run newspaper, radio station, choral group, Student Government Association, Campus Activities Board, Hall Council Advisory Board, Greek Council, WBTY, national fraternities, national sororities. *Campus security:* 24-hour emergency response devices and patrols, late-night transport/escort service, controlled dormitory access, security cameras. *Student services:* health clinic, personal/psychological counseling.

Athletics Member NCAA. All Division II. *Intercollegiate sports:* baseball M(s), basketball M(s)/W(s), cross-country running M(s)/W(s), field hockey W(s), football M, ice hockey M(s), lacrosse M(s), soccer M(s)/W(s), softball W(s), swimming M(s)/W(s), tennis M/W, track and field M(s)/W(s), volleyball W(s). *Intramural sports:* basketball M/W, field hockey W, football M, racquetball M/W, soccer M/W, softball M/W, volleyball M/W.

Standardized Tests *Required:* SAT I or ACT (for admission).

Costs (2003–04) *Comprehensive fee:* $33,904 includes full-time tuition ($24,120), mandatory fees ($204), and room and board ($9580). Part-time tuition and fees vary according to class time. *College room only:* $5570. Room and board charges vary according to board plan and housing facility. *Payment plan:* installment. *Waivers:* employees or children of employees.

Financial Aid Of all full-time matriculated undergraduates who enrolled in 2003, 2,520 applied for aid, 2,015 were judged to have need, 751 had their need fully met. In 2003, 377 non-need-based awards were made. *Average percent of need met:* 95%. *Average financial aid package:* $22,573. *Average need-based loan:* $5029. *Average need-based gift aid:* $13,530. *Average non-need-based aid:* $10,551. *Average indebtedness upon graduation:* $19,560. *Financial aid deadline:* 2/1.

Applying *Options:* common application, electronic application, early admission, early decision, early action, deferred entrance. *Application fee:* $50. *Required:* essay or personal statement, high school transcript, 2 letters of recommendation. *Recommended:* interview. *Application deadlines:* 2/1 (freshmen), 5/15 (transfers). *Early decision:* 11/15. *Notification:* 4/1 (freshmen), 12/27 (early decision), 1/26 (early action), continuous (transfers).

Admissions Contact Director of Admission, Bentley College, 175 Forest Street, Waltham, MA 02452-4705. *Phone:* 781-891-2244. *Toll-free phone:* 800-523-2354. *Fax:* 781-891-3414. *E-mail:* ugadmission@bentley.edu.

■ *See page 1240 for a narrative description.*

BERKLEE COLLEGE OF MUSIC
Boston, Massachusetts

- **Independent** 4-year, founded 1945
- **Calendar** semesters
- **Degree** diplomas and bachelor's
- **Urban** campus
- **Endowment** $121.5 million
- **Coed,** 3,799 undergraduate students, 100% full-time, 24% women, 76% men
- **Moderately difficult** entrance level, 79% of applicants were admitted

Undergraduates 3,799 full-time. Students come from 54 states and territories, 73 other countries, 82% are from out of state, 4% African American, 3% Asian American or Pacific Islander, 4% Hispanic American, 0.4% Native American, 25% international, 8% transferred in, 20% live on campus.

Freshmen *Admission:* 2,123 applied, 1,680 admitted.

Faculty *Total:* 473, 41% full-time. *Student/faculty ratio:* 13:1.

Majors Audio engineering; jazz/jazz studies; music; music management and merchandising; music performance; music teacher education; music theory and composition; music therapy; piano and organ; violin, viola, guitar and other stringed instruments; voice and opera; wind/percussion instruments.

Academic Programs *Special study options:* accelerated degree program, advanced placement credit, double majors, English as a second language, internships, off-campus study, services for LD students, student-designed majors, summer session for credit.

Library The Stan Getz Media Center and Library with 30,208 titles, 77 serial subscriptions, 19,480 audiovisual materials, an OPAC, a Web page.

Computers on Campus 45 computers available on campus for general student use. A campuswide network can be accessed from student residence rooms. Internet access, at least one staffed computer lab available.

Student Life *Housing options:* coed. Campus housing is university owned. *Activities and organizations:* drama/theater group, student-run newspaper, choral group, Musical Theater at Berklee Club, Yoga Society, Black Student Union, Christian Fellowship. *Campus security:* 24-hour patrols. *Student services:* personal/psychological counseling.

Athletics *Intramural sports:* ice hockey M/W, rock climbing M/W, soccer M/W, table tennis M/W, ultimate Frisbee M/W.

Standardized Tests *Required for some:* SAT I or ACT (for admission).

Costs (2004–05) *Comprehensive fee:* $34,430 includes full-time tuition ($20,350), mandatory fees ($3180), and room and board ($10,900). *Payment plans:* tuition prepayment, installment. *Waivers:* employees or children of employees.

Financial Aid Of all full-time matriculated undergraduates who enrolled in 2002, 1,411 applied for aid, 1,411 were judged to have need. In 2002, 646 non-need-based awards were made. *Average percent of need met:* 61%. *Average financial aid package:* $14,402. *Average need-based loan:* $3785. *Average need-based gift aid:* $4125. *Average non-need-based aid:* $6608.

Applying *Options:* electronic application, deferred entrance. *Application fee:* $75. *Required:* essay or personal statement, high school transcript, 2 letters of recommendation, 2 years of formal music study. *Required for some:* interview. *Recommended:* interview. *Application deadline:* rolling (freshmen), rolling (transfers). *Notification:* continuous (freshmen), continuous (transfers).

Admissions Contact Mr. Damien Bracken, Director of Admissions, Berklee College of Music, 1140 Boyleston Street, Boston, MA 02215-3693. *Phone:* 617-747-2222. *Toll-free phone:* 800-BERKLEE. *Fax:* 617-747-2047. *E-mail:* admissions@berklee.edu.

■ *See page 1248 for a narrative description.*

BOSTON ARCHITECTURAL CENTER
Boston, Massachusetts

- **Independent** comprehensive, founded 1889
- **Calendar** semesters
- **Degrees** certificates, bachelor's, and master's
- **Urban** 1-acre campus
- **Endowment** $5.2 million
- **Coed,** 464 undergraduate students, 90% full-time, 36% women, 64% men
- **Noncompetitive** entrance level, 87% of applicants were admitted

Undergraduates 419 full-time, 45 part-time. Students come from 43 states and territories, 47% are from out of state, 3% African American, 3% Asian American or Pacific Islander, 3% Hispanic American, 0.6% Native American, 13% transferred in. *Retention:* 62% of 2002 full-time freshmen returned.

Freshmen *Admission:* 270 applied, 236 admitted, 69 enrolled. *Average high school GPA:* 2.90.

Faculty *Total:* 118, 53% with terminal degrees. *Student/faculty ratio:* 12:1.

Majors Architecture; interior design.

Academic Programs *Special study options:* adult/continuing education programs, advanced placement credit, distance learning, independent study, internships, off-campus study, summer session for credit.

Library Shaw and Stone Library with 25,000 titles, 140 serial subscriptions, a Web page.

Computers on Campus 50 computers available on campus for general student use. A campuswide network can be accessed. Internet access, at least one staffed computer lab available. Computer purchase or lease plan available.

Student Life *Housing:* college housing not available. *Activities and organizations:* student-run newspaper, student government. *Campus security:* 24-hour emergency response devices and patrols, electronically operated building access.

Boston Architectural Center (continued)

Costs (2004–05) *Tuition:* $8200 full-time. Full-time tuition and fees vary according to course load and program. Part-time tuition and fees vary according to course load, program, and reciprocity agreements. *Required fees:* $20 full-time. *Payment plan:* installment. *Waivers:* employees or children of employees.

Financial Aid Of all full-time matriculated undergraduates who enrolled in 2002, 176 applied for aid, 166 were judged to have need. In 2002, 15 non-need-based awards were made. *Average percent of need met:* 29%. *Average financial aid package:* $3602. *Average need-based loan:* $3163. *Average need-based gift aid:* $2858. *Average non-need-based aid:* $5675. *Average indebtedness upon graduation:* $25,387.

Applying *Options:* common application, electronic application. *Application fee:* $50. *Required:* high school transcript. *Application deadline:* rolling (freshmen), rolling (transfers).

Admissions Contact Mr. Will Dunfey, Director of Admission, Boston Architectural Center, 320 Newbury Street, Boston, MA 02115-2795. *Phone:* 617-585-0256. *Toll-free phone:* 877-585-0100. *Fax:* 617-585-0121. *E-mail:* admissions@the-bac.edu.

■ *See page 1270 for a narrative description.*

BOSTON BAPTIST COLLEGE

Boston, Massachusetts

- **Independent Baptist** primarily 2-year, founded 1976
- **Calendar** semesters
- **Degrees** certificates, diplomas, associate, and bachelor's
- **Suburban** 8-acre campus with easy access to Providence
- **Coed**
- **Moderately difficult** entrance level

Student Life *Campus security:* 24-hour emergency response devices, student patrols.

Standardized Tests *Required:* SAT I or ACT (for admission).

Costs (2003–04) *Comprehensive fee:* $9970 includes full-time tuition ($3850), mandatory fees ($1480), and room and board ($4640). Part-time tuition: $150 per credit hour. *Required fees:* $715 per term part-time. *College room only:* $2760.

Applying *Options:* common application. *Application fee:* $25. *Required:* essay or personal statement, high school transcript, letters of recommendation. *Recommended:* interview.

Admissions Contact Mr. James Thomasson, Director of Admissions and Records, Boston Baptist College, 950 Metropolitan Avenue, Boston, MA 02136. *Phone:* 617-364-3510 Ext. 215. *Toll-free phone:* 888-235-2014. *Fax:* 617-364-0723.

BOSTON COLLEGE

Chestnut Hill, Massachusetts

- **Independent Roman Catholic (Jesuit)** university, founded 1863
- **Calendar** semesters
- **Degrees** bachelor's, master's, doctoral, first professional, and post-master's certificates (also offers continuing education program with significant enrollment not reflected in profile)
- **Suburban** 240-acre campus with easy access to Boston
- **Endowment** $1.1 billion
- **Coed,** 8,851 undergraduate students, 100% full-time, 52% women, 48% men
- **Very difficult** entrance level, 31% of applicants were admitted

Boston College's international stature is strengthened by the more than 450-year tradition of Jesuit education. Students are challenged to fulfill their potential as scholars through honors programs, research with faculty members, independent study, study abroad, and service learning. Students are also challenged to fulfill their potential as caring, thoughtful individuals and future leaders in society with artistic, cultural, service, social, religious, and athletic opportunities that abound on campus and throughout Boston.

Undergraduates 8,851 full-time. Students come from 50 states and territories, 100 other countries, 72% are from out of state, 5% African American, 9% Asian American or Pacific Islander, 6% Hispanic American, 0.3% Native American, 2% international, 1% transferred in, 73% live on campus. *Retention:* 95% of 2002 full-time freshmen returned.

Freshmen *Admission:* 22,424 applied, 6,896 admitted, 1,839 enrolled. *Test scores:* SAT verbal scores over 500: 96%; SAT math scores over 500: 98%; SAT verbal scores over 600: 79%; SAT math scores over 600: 87%; SAT verbal scores over 700: 23%; SAT math scores over 700: 36%.

Faculty *Total:* 1,207, 53% full-time. *Student/faculty ratio:* 14:1.

Majors Accounting; art history, criticism and conservation; biochemistry; biology/biological sciences; business administration and management; chemistry; classics and languages, literatures and linguistics; computer science; dramatic/theatre arts; economics; elementary education; English; environmental studies; finance; fine/studio arts; French; geology/earth science; geophysics and seismology; German; Hispanic-American, Puerto Rican, and Mexican-American/Chicano studies; history; human development and family studies; human resources management; interdisciplinary studies; Italian; kindergarten/preschool education; management information systems; marketing/marketing management; mass communication/media; mathematics; music; nursing (registered nurse training); operations research; philosophy; physics; political science and government; pre-medical studies; psychology; Russian; Russian studies; secondary education; Slavic languages; sociology; special education; theology.

Academic Programs *Special study options:* accelerated degree program, adult/continuing education programs, advanced placement credit, double majors, freshman honors college, honors programs, independent study, internships, off-campus study, part-time degree program, services for LD students, student-designed majors, study abroad, summer session for credit. *ROTC:* Army (c), Air Force (c). *Unusual degree programs:* 3-2 engineering with Boston University; education.

Library Thomas P. O'Neill Library plus 6 others with 2.0 million titles, 21,121 serial subscriptions, 121,969 audiovisual materials, an OPAC, a Web page.

Computers on Campus 200 computers available on campus for general student use. A campuswide network can be accessed from student residence rooms and from off campus. At least one staffed computer lab available.

Student Life *Housing options:* coed, women-only. Campus housing is university owned. *Activities and organizations:* drama/theater group, student-run newspaper, radio and television station, choral group, marching band, ski club, The Bostonians, Boston College Bop. *Campus security:* 24-hour emergency response devices and patrols, late-night transport/escort service, controlled dormitory access. *Student services:* health clinic, personal/psychological counseling, women's center.

Athletics Member NCAA. All Division I except football (Division I-A). *Intercollegiate sports:* baseball M, basketball M(s)/W(s), crew M(c)/W(c), cross-country running M/W(s), fencing M/W, field hockey W(s), golf M/W, ice hockey M(s)/W, lacrosse M/W(s), rugby M(c)/W(c), sailing M/W, skiing (downhill) M/W, soccer M(s)/W(s), softball W(s), swimming M/W(s), tennis M/W(s), track and field M(s)/W(s), volleyball W(s), water polo M, wrestling M. *Intramural sports:* basketball M/W, cross-country running M/W, football M/W, ice hockey M/W, lacrosse M(c)/W(c), racquetball M/W, sailing M(c)/W(c), skiing (downhill) M(c)/W(c), softball M/W, squash M/W, swimming M/W, tennis M/W, track and field M/W, volleyball M/W, water polo M.

Standardized Tests *Required:* SAT I and SAT II or ACT (for admission), SAT II: Writing Test (for admission).

Costs (2003–04) *Comprehensive fee:* $36,842 includes full-time tuition ($27,080), mandatory fees ($462), and room and board ($9300). *College room only:* $5650. Room and board charges vary according to housing facility. *Payment plans:* tuition prepayment, installment. *Waivers:* employees or children of employees.

Financial Aid Of all full-time matriculated undergraduates who enrolled in 2002, 4,550 applied for aid, 3,424 were judged to have need, 3,314 had their need fully met. In 2002, 217 non-need-based awards were made. *Average percent of need met:* 100%. *Average financial aid package:* $22,859. *Average need-based loan:* $4769. *Average need-based gift aid:* $16,820. *Average non-need-based aid:* $7651. *Average indebtedness upon graduation:* $17,517.

Applying *Options:* common application, electronic application, early admission, early action, deferred entrance. *Application fee:* $60. *Required:* essay or personal statement, high school transcript, 2 letters of recommendation. *Application deadlines:* 1/2 (freshmen), 4/15 (transfers). *Notification:* 4/15 (freshmen), 12/24 (early action), 6/15 (transfers).

Admissions Contact Mr. John L. Mahoney Jr., Director of Undergraduate Admission, Boston College, 140 Commonwealth Avenue, Devlin Hall 208, Chestnut Hill, MA 02467-3809. *Phone:* 617-552-3100. *Toll-free phone:* 800-360-2522. *Fax:* 617-552-0798. *E-mail:* ugadmis@bc.edu.

■ *See page 1272 for a narrative description.*

THE BOSTON CONSERVATORY

Boston, Massachusetts

Admissions Contact Ms. Halley Shefler, Dean of Enrollment, The Boston Conservatory, 8 The Fenway, Boston, MA 02215. *Phone:* 617-912-9153. *Fax:* 617-536-3176. *E-mail:* admissions@bostonconservatory.edu.

BOSTON UNIVERSITY

Boston, Massachusetts

- **Independent** university, founded 1839
- **Calendar** semesters

- **Degrees** bachelor's, master's, doctoral, first professional, and post-master's certificates
- **Urban** 132-acre campus
- **Endowment** $630.0 million
- **Coed,** 17,681 undergraduate students, 92% full-time, 59% women, 41% men
- **Very difficult** entrance level, 52% of applicants were admitted

Boston University (BU) is a private teaching and research institution that strongly emphasizes undergraduate education. Throughout its 158-year history, the University has maintained a commitment to providing the highest level of teaching excellence, and fulfillment of this pledge is its highest priority. BU has 11 undergraduate schools and colleges offering 250 major and minor areas of concentration. Students may choose from programs of study in areas as diverse as biochemistry, theater arts, physical therapy, elementary education, broadcast journalism, international relations, business, and computer engineering. BU has an international student body, with students from every state and more than 100 countries. In addition, opportunities to study abroad exist through 29 different programs, spanning 16 countries on 6 continents.

Undergraduates 16,247 full-time, 1,434 part-time. Students come from 54 states and territories, 103 other countries, 78% are from out of state, 2% African American, 13% Asian American or Pacific Islander, 5% Hispanic American, 0.4% Native American, 7% international, 1% transferred in, 74% live on campus. *Retention:* 85% of 2002 full-time freshmen returned.

Freshmen *Admission:* 29,356 applied, 15,191 admitted, 3,961 enrolled. *Average high school GPA:* 3.5. *Test scores:* SAT verbal scores over 500: 100%; SAT math scores over 500: 100%; ACT scores over 18: 100%; SAT verbal scores over 600: 78%; SAT math scores over 600: 85%; ACT scores over 24: 96%; SAT verbal scores over 700: 21%; SAT math scores over 700: 25%; ACT scores over 30: 34%.

Faculty *Total:* 3,492, 72% full-time. *Student/faculty ratio:* 14:1.

Majors Accounting; acting; aerospace, aeronautical and astronautical engineering; American studies; ancient/classical Greek; animal physiology; anthropology; archeology; area studies related; art history, criticism and conservation; art teacher education; Asian studies (East); astronomy; astrophysics; athletic training; bilingual and multilingual education; biochemistry; biological and biomedical sciences related; biology/biological sciences; biomedical/medical engineering; business administration and management; chemistry; chemistry teacher education; cinematography and film/video production; classics and languages, literatures and linguistics; clinical laboratory science/medical technology; commercial and advertising art; communication disorders; communication/speech communication and rhetoric; computer engineering; computer science; dental laboratory technology; drama and dance teacher education; drawing; ecology; economics; education; education (specific levels and methods) related; electrical, electronics and communications engineering; elementary education; engineering; engineering related; English; English/language arts teacher education; environmental studies; ethnic, cultural minority, and gender studies related; finance; foreign languages and literatures; foreign language teacher education; French; geography; geology/earth science; German; health science; history; hospitality administration; hotel/motel administration; industrial engineering; information science/studies; interdisciplinary studies; international business/trade/commerce; international finance; international relations and affairs; Italian; journalism; journalism related; kindergarten/preschool education; kinesiology and exercise science; Latin; Latin American studies; legal assistant/paralegal; linguistics; management information systems; marine biology and biological oceanography; marketing/marketing management; marketing research; mass communication/media; mathematics; mathematics and computer science; mathematics teacher education; mechanical engineering; modern Greek; molecular biology; music history, literature, and theory; music performance; music teacher education; music theory and composition; neuroscience; nutrition sciences; occupational therapy; operations management; organizational behavior; painting; parks, recreation and leisure; philosophy; physical education teaching and coaching; physical therapy; physics; piano and organ; political science and government; pre-dentistry studies; psychology; public relations/image management; radio and television; rehabilitation therapy; religious studies; Russian; Russian studies; science teacher education; sculpture; social sciences related; social studies teacher education; sociology; Spanish; special education; special education (hearing impaired); speech/theater education; theatre design and technology; theatre literature, history and criticism; urban studies/affairs; voice and opera.

Academic Programs *Special study options:* accelerated degree program, adult/continuing education programs, advanced placement credit, cooperative education, double majors, English as a second language, honors programs, independent study, internships, off-campus study, part-time degree program, services for LD students, student-designed majors, study abroad, summer session for credit. *ROTC:* Army (b), Navy (b), Air Force (b). *Unusual degree programs:* 3-2 over 30 other programs.

Library Mugar Memorial Library plus 18 others with 2.2 million titles, 29,389 serial subscriptions, 71,067 audiovisual materials, an OPAC, a Web page.

Computers on Campus 750 computers available on campus for general student use. A campuswide network can be accessed from student residence rooms and from off campus that provide access to research and educational networks. Internet access, at least one staffed computer lab available. Computer purchase or lease plan available.

Student Life *Housing:* on-campus residence required for freshman year. *Options:* coed, women-only, cooperative. Campus housing is university owned. Freshman campus housing is guaranteed. *Activities and organizations:* drama/theater group, student-run newspaper, radio and television station, choral group, marching band, performing and acappella groups, cultural organizations, service organizations, student government, residence hall associations, national fraternities, national sororities. *Campus security:* 24-hour emergency response devices and patrols, late-night transport/escort service, controlled dormitory access, security personnel at residence hall entrances, self-defense education, well-lit sidewalks. *Student services:* health clinic, personal/psychological counseling, women's center.

Athletics Member NCAA. All Division I. *Intercollegiate sports:* badminton M(c)/W(c), baseball M(c), basketball M(s)/W(s), cheerleading M(c)/W(c), crew M(s)/W(s), cross-country running M(s)/W(s), equestrian sports M(c)/W(c), fencing M(c)/W(c), field hockey W(s), golf M/W, gymnastics M(c)/W(c), ice hockey M(s)/W(c), lacrosse M(c)/W(s), rugby M(c)/W(c), sailing M(c)/W(c), skiing (downhill) M(c)/W(c), soccer M(s)/W(s), softball W(s), swimming M(s)/W(s), tennis M/W(s), track and field M(s)/W(s), ultimate Frisbee M(c)/W(c), volleyball M(c)/W(c), water polo W(c), wrestling M(s). *Intramural sports:* basketball M/W, field hockey W, football M/W, ice hockey M, soccer M/W, softball M/W, swimming M/W, table tennis M/W, tennis M/W, volleyball M/W.

Standardized Tests *Required:* SAT I or ACT (for admission). *Required for some:* SAT II: Subject Tests (for admission), SAT II: Writing Test (for admission). *Recommended:* SAT II: Writing Test (for admission).

Costs (2003–04) *Comprehensive fee:* $38,194 includes full-time tuition ($28,512), mandatory fees ($394), and room and board ($9288). Part-time tuition: $891 per credit. *Required fees:* $40 per term part-time. *College room only:* $5930. Room and board charges vary according to board plan and housing facility. *Payment plans:* tuition prepayment, installment. *Waivers:* senior citizens and employees or children of employees.

Financial Aid Of all full-time matriculated undergraduates who enrolled in 2003, 7,865 applied for aid, 7,253 were judged to have need, 3,651 had their need fully met. 3,305 Federal Work-Study jobs (averaging $2246). 180 state and other part-time jobs (averaging $10,436). In 2003, 2065 non-need-based awards were made. *Average percent of need met:* 90%. *Average financial aid package:* $25,338. *Average need-based loan:* $4826. *Average need-based gift aid:* $16,953. *Average non-need-based aid:* $14,324. *Average indebtedness upon graduation:* $17,535.

Applying *Options:* common application, electronic application, early admission, early decision, deferred entrance. *Application fee:* $70. *Required:* essay or personal statement, high school transcript, 2 letters of recommendation. *Required for some:* interview, audition, portfolio. *Recommended:* minimum 3.0 GPA. *Application deadlines:* 1/1 (freshmen), 4/1 (transfers). *Early decision:* 11/1. *Notification:* continuous until 4/15 (freshmen), 12/15 (early decision).

Admissions Contact Ms. Kelly A. Walter, Director of Undergraduate Admissions, Boston University, 121 Bay State Road, Boston, MA 02215. *Phone:* 617-353-2300. *Fax:* 617-353-9695. *E-mail:* admissions@bu.edu.

■ *See page 1274 for a narrative description.*

BRANDEIS UNIVERSITY
Waltham, Massachusetts

- **Independent** university, founded 1948
- **Calendar** semesters
- **Degrees** bachelor's, master's, doctoral, and postbachelor's certificates
- **Suburban** 235-acre campus with easy access to Boston
- **Endowment** $397.0 million
- **Coed,** 3,175 undergraduate students, 99% full-time, 56% women, 44% men
- **Most difficult** entrance level, 44% of applicants were admitted

A recent major study ranked Brandeis 9th among all United States private research universities, based on the faculty's contribution to the generation of new knowledge. To assist students of exceptional scholarly achievement and promise to study with this teaching faculty, Brandeis offers a significant number of scholarships of up to 75% of tuition.

Undergraduates 3,137 full-time, 38 part-time. Students come from 46 states and territories, 57 other countries, 76% are from out of state, 2% African American, 8% Asian American or Pacific Islander, 3% Hispanic American, 0.2% Native American, 7% international, 1% transferred in, 82% live on campus. *Retention:* 94% of 2002 full-time freshmen returned.

Brandeis University (continued)

Freshmen *Admission:* 5,770 applied, 2,524 admitted, 824 enrolled. *Test scores:* SAT verbal scores over 500: 99%; SAT math scores over 500: 98%; ACT scores over 18: 100%; SAT verbal scores over 600: 86%; SAT math scores over 600: 83%; ACT scores over 24: 98%; SAT verbal scores over 700: 33%; SAT math scores over 700: 31%; ACT scores over 30: 50%.

Faculty *Total:* 441, 76% full-time, 94% with terminal degrees. *Student/faculty ratio:* 9:1.

Majors African-American/Black studies; African studies; American studies; ancient/classical Greek; anthropology; area, ethnic, cultural, and gender studies related; art; biochemistry; biological and biomedical sciences related; biology/biological sciences; biophysics; cell biology and anatomical sciences related; chemistry; classics and classical languages related; comparative literature; computer science; dramatic/theatre arts; economics; engineering physics; English; European studies; fine/studio arts; French; German; history; Islamic studies; Jewish/Judaic studies; Latin; Latin American studies; linguistics; mathematics; multi-/interdisciplinary studies related; music; Near and Middle Eastern studies; neuroscience; philosophy; physics; political science and government; psychology; Russian; Russian studies; sociology; Spanish.

Academic Programs *Special study options:* adult/continuing education programs, advanced placement credit, double majors, English as a second language, honors programs, independent study, internships, off-campus study, part-time degree program, services for LD students, student-designed majors, study abroad, summer session for credit. *ROTC:* Army (c), Air Force (c).

Library Goldfarb Library plus 2 others with 938,835 titles, 15,835 serial subscriptions, 35,287 audiovisual materials, an OPAC, a Web page.

Computers on Campus 104 computers available on campus for general student use. A campuswide network can be accessed from student residence rooms and from off campus that provide access to educational software. Internet access, online (class) registration, at least one staffed computer lab available. Computer purchase or lease plan available.

Student Life *Housing options:* coed, disabled students. Campus housing is university owned. Freshman campus housing is guaranteed. *Activities and organizations:* drama/theater group, student-run newspaper, radio and television station, choral group, Waltham Group, Student Programming Board, performing groups, student government. *Campus security:* 24-hour emergency response devices and patrols, late-night transport/escort service, controlled dormitory access. *Student services:* health clinic, personal/psychological counseling, women's center.

Athletics Member NCAA. All Division III. *Intercollegiate sports:* baseball M, basketball M/W, crew M(c), cross-country running M/W, fencing M/W, field hockey W(c), golf M, lacrosse M(c)/W(c), rugby M(c)/W(c), sailing M/W, skiing (downhill) M(c)/W(c), soccer W, softball W, squash M(c), swimming M/W, tennis M/W, track and field M/W, volleyball W. *Intramural sports:* basketball M/W, cheerleading W, equestrian sports M/W, football M, golf M/W, ice hockey M, lacrosse M, softball M/W, squash M/W, table tennis M/W, tennis M/W, volleyball M/W, water polo M/W, weight lifting M/W.

Standardized Tests *Required:* SAT I and SAT II or ACT (for admission).

Costs (2003–04) *Comprehensive fee:* $38,198 includes full-time tuition ($28,999), mandatory fees ($876), and room and board ($8323). Part-time tuition: $3625 per course. Part-time tuition and fees vary according to course load. *College room only:* $4675. Room and board charges vary according to board plan and housing facility. *Payment plans:* tuition prepayment, installment. *Waivers:* employees or children of employees.

Financial Aid Of all full-time matriculated undergraduates who enrolled in 2003, 1,805 applied for aid, 1,519 were judged to have need, 390 had their need fully met. 884 Federal Work-Study jobs (averaging $1561). 148 state and other part-time jobs (averaging $2804). In 2003, 720 non-need-based awards were made. *Average percent of need met:* 82%. *Average financial aid package:* $22,199. *Average need-based loan:* $6052. *Average need-based gift aid:* $16,420. *Average non-need-based aid:* $16,883.

Applying *Options:* common application, electronic application, early decision, deferred entrance. *Application fee:* $55. *Required:* essay or personal statement, high school transcript, 2 letters of recommendation. *Recommended:* minimum 3.0 GPA, interview. *Application deadlines:* 1/15 (freshmen), 4/1 (transfers). *Early decision:* 1/1. *Notification:* 4/15 (freshmen), 2/1 (early decision), 6/10 (transfers).

Admissions Contact Ms. Deena Whitfield, Director of Enrollment, Brandeis University, 415 South Street, Waltham, MA 02254-9110. *Phone:* 781-736-3500. *Toll-free phone:* 800-622-0622. *Fax:* 781-736-3536. *E-mail:* sendinfo@brandeis.edu.

■ *See page 1284 for a narrative description.*

BRIDGEWATER STATE COLLEGE

Bridgewater, Massachusetts

- **State-supported** comprehensive, founded 1840, part of Massachusetts Public Higher Education System
- **Calendar** semesters
- **Degrees** certificates, bachelor's, master's, post-master's, and postbachelor's certificates
- **Suburban** 235-acre campus with easy access to Boston
- **Endowment** $8.8 million
- **Coed,** 7,597 undergraduate students, 82% full-time, 61% women, 39% men
- **Moderately difficult** entrance level, 72% of applicants were admitted

Undergraduates 6,247 full-time, 1,350 part-time. Students come from 28 states and territories, 33 other countries, 3% are from out of state, 5% African American, 1% Asian American or Pacific Islander, 2% Hispanic American, 0.3% Native American, 2% international, 9% transferred in, 31% live on campus. *Retention:* 77% of 2002 full-time freshmen returned.

Freshmen *Admission:* 5,540 applied, 4,005 admitted, 1,304 enrolled. *Average high school GPA:* 2.90. *Test scores:* SAT verbal scores over 500: 55%; SAT math scores over 500: 56%; ACT scores over 18: 75%; SAT verbal scores over 600: 10%; SAT math scores over 600: 11%; ACT scores over 24: 15%; SAT verbal scores over 700: 1%; SAT math scores over 700: 1%.

Faculty *Total:* 494, 53% full-time, 51% with terminal degrees. *Student/faculty ratio:* 20:1.

Majors Accounting; airline pilot and flight crew; American government and politics; anthropology; archeology; area studies related; art; athletic training; aviation/airway management; biochemistry; biology/biological sciences; business administration and management; business/commerce; business, management, and marketing related; cell biology and anatomical sciences related; chemistry; chemistry related; city/urban, community and regional planning; clinical psychology; commercial and advertising art; communication disorders; computer science; crafts, folk art and artisanry; creative writing; criminal justice/safety; criminology; drama and dance teacher education; dramatic/theatre arts; economics; education; elementary education; English; entrepreneurship; environmental biology; finance; fine arts related; fine/studio arts; geochemistry; geography; geology/earth science; health and physical education; health and physical education related; health teacher education; history; industrial and organizational psychology; international business/trade/commerce; international relations and affairs; kindergarten/preschool education; kinesiology and exercise science; management information systems; marketing/marketing management; mathematics; middle school education; molecular biology; music; parks, recreation and leisure; philosophy; physical education teaching and coaching; physics; physics related; political science and government; pre-law studies; psychology; public relations, advertising, and applied communication related; science technologies related; social work; sociology; Spanish; special education; therapeutic recreation.

Academic Programs *Special study options:* academic remediation for entering students, accelerated degree program, adult/continuing education programs, advanced placement credit, distance learning, double majors, English as a second language, honors programs, independent study, internships, off-campus study, part-time degree program, services for LD students, study abroad, summer session for credit. *ROTC:* Army (c), Air Force (c).

Library Clement Maxwell Library with 326,662 titles, 1,100 serial subscriptions, 10,590 audiovisual materials, an OPAC, a Web page.

Computers on Campus 750 computers available on campus for general student use. A campuswide network can be accessed from student residence rooms and from off campus that provide access to student account information, application software. Internet access, online (class) registration, at least one staffed computer lab available.

Student Life *Housing options:* coed, women-only, disabled students. Campus housing is university owned. Freshman applicants given priority for college housing. *Activities and organizations:* drama/theater group, student-run newspaper, radio station, choral group, marching band, Greek life, Children's Developmental Clinic, Student Government Association, Afro-American/Latino club, Program Committee, national fraternities, national sororities. *Campus security:* 24-hour emergency response devices and patrols, late-night transport/escort service, controlled dormitory access. *Student services:* health clinic, personal/psychological counseling, women's center.

Athletics Member NCAA. All Division III. *Intercollegiate sports:* baseball M, basketball M/W, cross-country running M/W, field hockey W, football M, lacrosse M(c)/W, soccer M/W, softball W, swimming M/W, tennis M/W, track and field

M/W, volleyball W, water polo M(c)/W(c), wrestling M. *Intramural sports:* basketball M/W, football M/W, soccer M/W, softball M/W, tennis M/W, volleyball M/W.

Standardized Tests *Required:* SAT I or ACT (for admission).

Costs (2004–05) *Tuition:* state resident $910 full-time, $181 per credit hour part-time; nonresident $7050 full-time, $437 per credit hour part-time. *Required fees:* $3650 full-time. *Room and board:* $5922; room only: $3552. Room and board charges vary according to board plan and housing facility. *Payment plan:* installment. *Waivers:* employees or children of employees.

Financial Aid Of all full-time matriculated undergraduates who enrolled in 2002, 2,710 applied for aid, 1,902 were judged to have need, 987 had their need fully met. 455 Federal Work-Study jobs (averaging $1239). In 2002, 648 non-need-based awards were made. *Average percent of need met:* 75%. *Average financial aid package:* $7163. *Average need-based loan:* $3105. *Average need-based gift aid:* $3397. *Average non-need-based aid:* $5024. *Average indebtedness upon graduation:* $9243.

Applying *Options:* common application, electronic application, early admission, early action, deferred entrance. *Application fee:* $25. *Required:* essay or personal statement, high school transcript, minimum 2.7 GPA. *Recommended:* letters of recommendation. *Application deadlines:* 2/15 (freshmen), 6/1 (transfers). *Notification:* 4/1 (freshmen), 12/15 (early action).

Admissions Contact Mr. Gregg Meyer, Director of Admissions, Bridgewater State College, Gates House, Bridgewater, MA 02325. *Phone:* 508-531-1237. *Fax:* 508-531-1746. *E-mail:* admission@bridgew.edu.

■ *See page 1296 for a narrative description.*

CAMBRIDGE COLLEGE
Cambridge, Massachusetts

- **Independent** comprehensive, founded 1971
- **Calendar** trimesters
- **Degrees** certificates, bachelor's, and master's
- **Urban** campus with easy access to Boston
- **Coed,** 450 undergraduate students
- **Minimally difficult** entrance level

Cambridge College's innovative bachelor's programs are designed for working adults. They offer an empowering learning model, emphasize peer support and assessment, and encourage personal and professional development. Students may choose a BA in psychology, a BA in multidisciplinary studies, a BS in human services, or a BS in management studies.

Undergraduates Students come from 6 states and territories, 5 other countries, 2% are from out of state.

Faculty *Total:* 150, 20% full-time. *Student/faculty ratio:* 17:1.

Majors Psychology.

Academic Programs *Special study options:* accelerated degree program, adult/continuing education programs, English as a second language, independent study, internships, part-time degree program, study abroad, summer session for credit.

Library Gutman Library with an OPAC, a Web page.

Computers on Campus A campuswide network can be accessed. Internet access, at least one staffed computer lab available.

Student Life *Housing:* college housing not available.

Standardized Tests *Required:* ACCUPLACER (for placement).

Costs (2003–04) *One-time required fee:* $110. *Tuition:* $9000 full-time, $300 per credit part-time. *Required fees:* $150 full-time, $75 per term part-time. *Payment plan:* installment.

Financial Aid Of all full-time matriculated undergraduates who enrolled in 2002, 179 applied for aid, 155 were judged to have need. *Average financial aid package:* $8695. *Average need-based loan:* $3600. *Average need-based gift aid:* $5338. *Average indebtedness upon graduation:* $24,200.

Applying *Options:* deferred entrance. *Application fee:* $30. *Required:* essay or personal statement, high school transcript, letters of recommendation, interview. *Recommended:* 3 years of work experience. *Application deadline:* rolling (freshmen), rolling (transfers). *Notification:* continuous (freshmen), continuous (transfers).

Admissions Contact Ms. Joy King, Undergraduate Enrollment Manager, Cambridge College, 1000 Massachusetts Avenue, Cambridge, MA 02138. *Phone:* 617-868-1000. *Toll-free phone:* 800-877-4723. *Fax:* 617-349-3545. *E-mail:* admit@cambridgecollege.edu.

■ *See page 1336 for a narrative description.*

CLARK UNIVERSITY
Worcester, Massachusetts

- **Independent** university, founded 1887
- **Calendar** semesters
- **Degrees** bachelor's, master's, doctoral, post-master's, and postbachelor's certificates
- **Urban** 50-acre campus with easy access to Boston
- **Endowment** $150.8 million
- **Coed,** 2,190 undergraduate students, 91% full-time, 61% women, 39% men
- **Moderately difficult** entrance level, 63% of applicants were admitted

Undergraduates 2,002 full-time, 188 part-time. Students come from 47 states and territories, 56 other countries, 63% are from out of state, 3% African American, 4% Asian American or Pacific Islander, 3% Hispanic American, 0.2% Native American, 7% international, 2% transferred in, 77% live on campus. *Retention:* 85% of 2002 full-time freshmen returned.

Freshmen *Admission:* 3,950 applied, 2,488 admitted, 541 enrolled. *Average high school GPA:* 3.41. *Test scores:* SAT verbal scores over 500: 88%; SAT math scores over 500: 90%; ACT scores over 18: 96%; SAT verbal scores over 600: 49%; SAT math scores over 600: 54%; ACT scores over 24: 63%; SAT verbal scores over 700: 8%; SAT math scores over 700: 10%; ACT scores over 30: 14%.

Faculty *Total:* 275, 61% full-time. *Student/faculty ratio:* 10:1.

Majors Art; art history, criticism and conservation; Asian studies; biochemistry; biology/biological sciences; business administration and management; chemistry; classics and languages, literatures and linguistics; commercial and advertising art; comparative literature; computer science; cultural studies; development economics and international development; dramatic/theatre arts; ecology; economics; education; elementary education; engineering; English; environmental studies; film/cinema studies; fine/studio arts; French; geography; geology/earth science; history; interdisciplinary studies; international relations and affairs; Jewish/Judaic studies; literature; mass communication/media; mathematics; middle school education; modern languages; molecular biology; music; natural resources management and policy; neuroscience; peace studies and conflict resolution; philosophy; physics; political science and government; pre-dentistry studies; pre-law studies; pre-medical studies; pre-veterinary studies; psychology; secondary education; sociology; Spanish.

Academic Programs *Special study options:* academic remediation for entering students, accelerated degree program, adult/continuing education programs, advanced placement credit, double majors, English as a second language, honors programs, independent study, internships, off-campus study, part-time degree program, services for LD students, student-designed majors, study abroad, summer session for credit. *ROTC:* Army (c), Navy (c), Air Force (c). *Unusual degree programs:* 3-2 engineering with Columbia University, Washington University in St. Louis, Worcester Polytechnic Institute; environmental studies, international development, biology, chemistry, physics, economics, history, communication, public administration.

Library Robert Hutchings Goddard Library plus 4 others with 289,658 titles, 1,383 serial subscriptions, 1,007 audiovisual materials, an OPAC, a Web page.

Computers on Campus 200 computers available on campus for general student use. A campuswide network can be accessed from student residence rooms and from off campus that provide access to on-line course support. Internet access, at least one staffed computer lab available.

Student Life *Housing:* on-campus residence required through sophomore year. *Options:* coed, women-only, disabled students. Campus housing is university owned. Freshman campus housing is guaranteed. *Activities and organizations:* drama/theater group, student-run newspaper, radio and television station, choral group, Student Activities Board, Hillel, Pub Entertainment Committee, Massachusetts PIRG, Film Society. *Campus security:* 24-hour emergency response devices and patrols, student patrols, late-night transport/escort service, controlled dormitory access. *Student services:* health clinic, personal/psychological counseling.

Athletics Member NCAA. All Division III. *Intercollegiate sports:* baseball M, basketball M/W, cheerleading M/W, crew M/W, cross-country running M/W, field hockey W, lacrosse M, soccer M/W, softball W, swimming M/W, tennis M/W, volleyball W. *Intramural sports:* badminton M/W, basketball M/W, bowling M/W, equestrian sports M(c)/W(c), football M/W, golf M(c)/W(c), ice hockey M(c), lacrosse W(c), racquetball M/W, rock climbing M/W, rugby M(c)/W(c), sailing M(c)/W(c), soccer M/W, softball M/W, squash M/W, table tennis M/W, track and field M(c)/W(c), ultimate Frisbee M/W, volleyball M/W, water polo M/W, weight lifting M(c)/W(c).

Standardized Tests *Required:* SAT I or ACT (for admission).

Costs (2003–04) *Comprehensive fee:* $32,115 includes full-time tuition ($26,700), mandatory fees ($265), and room and board ($5150). Part-time tuition: $834 per credit hour. *College room only:* $3150. Room and board charges vary according to board plan and housing facility. *Payment plans:* tuition prepayment, installment. *Waivers:* employees or children of employees.

Clark University (continued)

Financial Aid Of all full-time matriculated undergraduates who enrolled in 2003, 1,560 applied for aid, 1,234 were judged to have need, 908 had their need fully met. In 2003, 159 non-need-based awards were made. *Average percent of need met:* 97%. *Average financial aid package:* $23,136. *Average need-based loan:* $3711. *Average need-based gift aid:* $18,012. *Average non-need-based aid:* $12,056. *Average indebtedness upon graduation:* $18,375.

Applying *Options:* common application, early admission, early decision, deferred entrance. *Application fee:* $50. *Required:* essay or personal statement, high school transcript, 2 letters of recommendation. *Recommended:* interview. *Application deadlines:* 2/1 (freshmen), 4/15 (transfers). *Early decision:* 11/15. *Notification:* 4/1 (freshmen), 12/15 (early decision), 6/1 (transfers).

Admissions Contact Mr. Harold M. Wingood, Dean of Admissions, Clark University, Admissions House, 950 Main Street, Worcester, MA 01610. *Phone:* 508-793-7431. *Toll-free phone:* 800-GO-CLARK. *Fax:* 508-793-8821. *E-mail:* admissions@clarku.edu.

COLLEGE OF THE HOLY CROSS

Worcester, Massachusetts

- **Independent Roman Catholic (Jesuit)** 4-year, founded 1843
- **Calendar** semesters
- **Degree** bachelor's
- **Suburban** 174-acre campus with easy access to Boston
- **Endowment** $358.1 million
- **Coed,** 2,773 undergraduate students, 99% full-time, 54% women, 46% men
- **Very difficult** entrance level, 42% of applicants were admitted

Undergraduates 2,748 full-time, 25 part-time. Students come from 48 states and territories, 18 other countries, 66% are from out of state, 3% African American, 4% Asian American or Pacific Islander, 5% Hispanic American, 0.3% Native American, 1% international, 0.8% transferred in, 87% live on campus. *Retention:* 98% of 2002 full-time freshmen returned.

Freshmen *Admission:* 5,035 applied, 2,131 admitted, 698 enrolled. *Test scores:* SAT verbal scores over 500: 98%; SAT math scores over 500: 98%; SAT verbal scores over 600: 71%; SAT math scores over 600: 79%; SAT verbal scores over 700: 19%; SAT math scores over 700: 14%.

Faculty *Total:* 287, 79% full-time. *Student/faculty ratio:* 11:1.

Majors Accounting; African-American/Black studies; African studies; American Sign Language (ASL); anthropology; art history, criticism and conservation; Asian studies; biology/biological sciences; chemistry; cinematography and film/video production; classics and languages, literatures and linguistics; dramatic/theatre arts; economics; English; environmental studies; fine/studio arts; French; German; German studies; gerontology; history; history related; Italian; Latin American studies; literature; mathematics; music; Near and Middle Eastern studies; peace studies and conflict resolution; philosophy; physics; political science and government; pre-dentistry studies; pre-medical studies; psychology; religious studies; Russian; Russian studies; sociology; Spanish; women's studies.

Academic Programs *Special study options:* accelerated degree program, advanced placement credit, double majors, honors programs, independent study, internships, off-campus study, student-designed majors, study abroad. *ROTC:* Army (c), Navy (b), Air Force (c). *Unusual degree programs:* 3-2 business administration with Clark University; engineering with Washington University in St. Louis, Columbia University, Dartmouth College.

Library Dinand Library plus 2 others with 584,883 titles, 1,921 serial subscriptions, 24,933 audiovisual materials, an OPAC, a Web page.

Computers on Campus 426 computers available on campus for general student use. A campuswide network can be accessed from student residence rooms and from off campus. Internet access, at least one staffed computer lab available.

Student Life *Housing:* on-campus residence required through sophomore year. *Options:* coed. Campus housing is university owned. Freshman campus housing is guaranteed. *Activities and organizations:* drama/theater group, student-run newspaper, radio station, choral group, marching band, SPUD (community service organization), choral and music groups, Campus Activities Board, Student Government Association, Purple Key Society. *Campus security:* 24-hour emergency response devices and patrols, late-night transport/escort service, controlled dormitory access. *Student services:* health clinic, personal/psychological counseling, women's center.

Athletics Member NCAA. All Division I except football (Division I-AA). *Intercollegiate sports:* baseball M, basketball M(s)/W(s), crew M/W, cross-country running M/W, field hockey W, golf M/W, ice hockey M/W, lacrosse M/W, soccer M/W, softball W, swimming M/W, tennis M/W, track and field M/W, volleyball W. *Intramural sports:* basketball M/W, cheerleading W, football M, ice hockey M(c), lacrosse M(c)/W(c), rugby M(c)/W(c), sailing M(c)/W(c), skiing (downhill) M(c)/W(c), soccer M(c)/W(c), softball M/W, ultimate Frisbee M(c)/W(c), volleyball M(c)/W, water polo M(c)/W(c).

Standardized Tests *Required:* SAT I and SAT II or ACT (for admission), SAT II: Writing Test (for admission).

Costs (2003–04) *Comprehensive fee:* $36,451 includes full-time tuition ($27,560), mandatory fees ($451), and room and board ($8440). *College room only:* $4220. Room and board charges vary according to board plan and housing facility. *Payment plans:* tuition prepayment, installment. *Waivers:* employees or children of employees.

Financial Aid Of all full-time matriculated undergraduates who enrolled in 2002, 1,654 applied for aid, 1,544 were judged to have need, 1,544 had their need fully met. 872 Federal Work-Study jobs (averaging $1488). In 2002, 60 non-need-based awards were made. *Average percent of need met:* 100%. *Average financial aid package:* $21,917. *Average need-based loan:* $6095. *Average need-based gift aid:* $14,858. *Average non-need-based aid:* $10,951. *Average indebtedness upon graduation:* $17,253. *Financial aid deadline:* 2/1.

Applying *Options:* common application, electronic application, early admission, early decision, deferred entrance. *Application fee:* $50. *Required:* essay or personal statement, high school transcript, 2 letters of recommendation. *Recommended:* interview. *Application deadlines:* 1/15 (freshmen), 5/1 (transfers). *Early decision:* 12/15. *Notification:* 4/1 (freshmen), 1/15 (early decision), 6/1 (transfers).

Admissions Contact Ms. Ann Bowe McDermott, Director of Admissions, College of the Holy Cross, 105 Fenwick Hall, 1 College Street, Worcester, MA 01610-2395. *Phone:* 508-793-2443. *Toll-free phone:* 800-442-2421. *Fax:* 508-793-3888. *E-mail:* admissions@holycross.edu.

CURRY COLLEGE

Milton, Massachusetts

- **Independent** comprehensive, founded 1879
- **Calendar** semesters
- **Degrees** certificates, bachelor's, and master's
- **Suburban** 131-acre campus with easy access to Boston
- **Endowment** $3.6 million
- **Coed,** 2,501 undergraduate students, 67% full-time, 55% women, 45% men
- **Moderately difficult** entrance level, 69% of applicants were admitted

Undergraduates 1,677 full-time, 824 part-time. Students come from 43 states and territories, 18 other countries, 31% are from out of state, 7% African American, 1% Asian American or Pacific Islander, 3% Hispanic American, 0.2% Native American, 1% international, 5% transferred in, 65% live on campus. *Retention:* 70% of 2002 full-time freshmen returned.

Freshmen *Admission:* 2,311 applied, 1,593 admitted, 473 enrolled. *Average high school GPA:* 2.70. *Test scores:* SAT verbal scores over 500: 30%; SAT math scores over 500: 20%; SAT verbal scores over 600: 7%; SAT math scores over 600: 3%; SAT verbal scores over 700: 1%; SAT math scores over 700: 1%.

Faculty *Total:* 399, 22% full-time. *Student/faculty ratio:* 12:1.

Majors Art; biology/biological sciences; business administration and management; commercial and advertising art; criminal justice/law enforcement administration; education; elementary education; English; environmental studies; film/cinema studies; health teacher education; history; information technology; journalism; kindergarten/preschool education; mass communication/media; nursing (registered nurse training); philosophy; physics; political science and government; pre-law studies; psychology; public relations/image management; radio and television; sociology; special education; women's studies.

Academic Programs *Special study options:* academic remediation for entering students, accelerated degree program, adult/continuing education programs, advanced placement credit, cooperative education, double majors, external degree program, honors programs, independent study, internships, off-campus study, part-time degree program, services for LD students, student-designed majors, study abroad, summer session for credit. *ROTC:* Army (c).

Library Levin Library plus 1 other with 90,000 titles, 675 serial subscriptions, 1,050 audiovisual materials, an OPAC, a Web page.

Computers on Campus 100 computers available on campus for general student use. A campuswide network can be accessed from student residence rooms and from off campus that provide access to library online catalog. Internet access, at least one staffed computer lab available.

Student Life *Housing options:* coed, men-only, women-only. *Activities and organizations:* drama/theater group, student-run newspaper, radio and television station, choral group, marching band, student radio station, student government, Community Campus Activities Board, student newspaper, drama club. *Campus security:* 24-hour emergency response devices and patrols, late-night transport/escort service, controlled dormitory access. *Student services:* health clinic, personal/psychological counseling.

Athletics Member NCAA. All Division III. *Intercollegiate sports:* baseball M, basketball M/W, cross-country running W, football M, ice hockey M, lacrosse M/W, soccer M/W, softball W, tennis M/W. *Intramural sports:* basketball M/W, rugby M/W, softball M/W, tennis M/W, volleyball M/W.

Standardized Tests *Required for some:* SAT I or ACT (for admission), Wechsler Adult Intelligence Scale-Revised for PAL candidates.

Costs (2004–05) *Comprehensive fee:* $30,520 includes full-time tuition ($21,530), mandatory fees ($810), and room and board ($8180). *College room only:* $4620.

Financial Aid Of all full-time matriculated undergraduates who enrolled in 2001, 1,000 applied for aid, 825 were judged to have need. *Average percent of need met:* 68%. *Average financial aid package:* $14,250. *Average need-based loan:* $4500. *Average need-based gift aid:* $5000. *Average indebtedness upon graduation:* $17,000.

Applying *Options:* common application, electronic application, early admission, early decision, deferred entrance. *Application fee:* $40. *Required:* essay or personal statement, high school transcript, minimum 2.0 GPA, 1 letter of recommendation. *Required for some:* interview. *Recommended:* interview. *Application deadlines:* 4/1 (freshmen), 7/1 (transfers). *Early decision:* 12/1. *Notification:* continuous until 5/1 (freshmen), 12/15 (early decision), continuous until 8/1 (transfers).

Admissions Contact Ms. Jane P. Fidler, Director of Admission, Curry College, 1071 Blue Hill Avenue, Milton, MA 02186. *Phone:* 617-333-2210. *Toll-free phone:* 800-669-0686. *Fax:* 617-333-2114. *E-mail:* curryadm@curry.edu.

■ *See page 1508 for a narrative description.*

EASTERN NAZARENE COLLEGE
Quincy, Massachusetts

- **Independent** comprehensive, founded 1918, affiliated with Church of the Nazarene
- **Calendar** 4-1-4
- **Degrees** associate, bachelor's, and master's
- **Suburban** 15-acre campus with easy access to Boston
- **Endowment** $8.0 million
- **Coed,** 1,069 undergraduate students, 98% full-time, 61% women, 39% men
- **Moderately difficult** entrance level, 62% of applicants were admitted

Undergraduates 1,043 full-time, 26 part-time. Students come from 32 states and territories, 18 other countries, 57% are from out of state, 10% African American, 2% Asian American or Pacific Islander, 4% Hispanic American, 0.6% Native American, 1% international, 3% transferred in, 82% live on campus. *Retention:* 77% of 2002 full-time freshmen returned.

Freshmen *Admission:* 552 applied, 342 admitted, 202 enrolled. *Average high school GPA:* 3.10. *Test scores:* SAT verbal scores over 500: 88%; SAT math scores over 500: 82%; ACT scores over 18: 99%; SAT verbal scores over 600: 48%; SAT math scores over 600: 39%; ACT scores over 24: 46%; SAT verbal scores over 700: 22%; SAT math scores over 700: 20%; ACT scores over 30: 15%.

Faculty *Total:* 48, 92% full-time, 71% with terminal degrees. *Student/faculty ratio:* 15:1.

Majors Advertising; aerospace, aeronautical and astronautical engineering; biological and physical sciences; biology/biological sciences; biomedical/medical engineering; business administration and management; business/commerce; chemistry; clinical psychology; computer engineering; computer science; dramatic/theatre arts; education; electrical, electronics and communications engineering; elementary education; engineering physics; English; general studies; health science; history; industrial engineering; journalism; kindergarten/preschool education; liberal arts and sciences/liberal studies; mass communication/media; mathematics; mechanical engineering; middle school education; music; music performance; music teacher education; pharmacy; physical education teaching and coaching; physical therapy; physics; pre-law studies; pre-medical studies; psychology; radio and television; religious education; religious/sacred music; religious studies; secondary education; social work; sociology; special education; systems engineering.

Academic Programs *Special study options:* academic remediation for entering students, accelerated degree program, adult/continuing education programs, advanced placement credit, double majors, English as a second language, honors programs, independent study, internships, off-campus study, part-time degree program, services for LD students, study abroad, summer session for credit. *ROTC:* Army (c). *Unusual degree programs:* 3-2 engineering with Boston University; nursing with Boston College; pharmacy with Massachusetts College of Pharmacy and Allied Health Sciences.

Library Nease Library with 117,540 titles, 466 serial subscriptions, 1,290 audiovisual materials, an OPAC.

Computers on Campus 98 computers available on campus for general student use. A campuswide network can be accessed from student residence rooms and from off campus. Internet access, at least one staffed computer lab available.

Student Life *Housing:* on-campus residence required through senior year. *Options:* men-only, women-only, disabled students. *Activities and organizations:* drama/theater group, student-run newspaper, radio station, choral group, AMS Associated Men Students, AWS Associated Women Students, gospel choir, ACTS Actors Christians Teachers Singers, Kid's Club. *Campus security:* 24-hour emergency response devices and patrols, student patrols, late-night transport/escort service, controlled dormitory access. *Student services:* health clinic, personal/psychological counseling.

Athletics Member NCAA. All Division III. *Intercollegiate sports:* baseball M, basketball M/W, cross-country running M/W, lacrosse M(c), soccer M/W, softball W, tennis M/W, volleyball M(c)/W. *Intramural sports:* baseball M, basketball M/W, cross-country running M/W, lacrosse M, skiing (downhill) M(c)/W(c), soccer M/W, softball W, tennis M/W, volleyball M/W.

Standardized Tests *Required:* SAT I or ACT (for admission).

Costs (2003–04) *Comprehensive fee:* $22,246 includes full-time tuition ($16,052), mandatory fees ($556), and room and board ($5638).

Financial Aid Of all full-time matriculated undergraduates who enrolled in 2000, 572 applied for aid, 456 were judged to have need, 110 had their need fully met. 179 Federal Work-Study jobs (averaging $1362). In 2000, 106 non-need-based awards were made. *Average percent of need met:* 69%. *Average financial aid package:* $10,394. *Average need-based loan:* $4122. *Average need-based gift aid:* $3144. *Average non-need-based aid:* $4275.

Applying *Options:* early admission, deferred entrance. *Application fee:* $25. *Required:* essay or personal statement, high school transcript, minimum 2.3 GPA, 2 letters of recommendation, interview. *Application deadline:* rolling (freshmen), rolling (transfers). *Notification:* continuous (freshmen), continuous (transfers).

Admissions Contact Ms. Doris Webb, Vice President of Admissions and Financial Aid, Eastern Nazarene College, 23 East Elm Avenue, Quincy, MA 02170. *Phone:* 617-745-3732. *Toll-free phone:* 800-88-ENC88. *Fax:* 617-745-3929. *E-mail:* admissions@enc.edu.

■ *See page 1560 for a narrative description.*

ELMS COLLEGE
Chicopee, Massachusetts

- **Independent Roman Catholic** comprehensive, founded 1928
- **Calendar** semesters
- **Degrees** associate, bachelor's, master's, and postbachelor's certificates
- **Suburban** 32-acre campus
- **Endowment** $6.4 million
- **Coed, primarily women,** 830 undergraduate students, 69% full-time, 80% women, 20% men
- **Moderately difficult** entrance level, 90% of applicants were admitted

Undergraduates 573 full-time, 257 part-time. Students come from 10 states and territories, 15% are from out of state, 5% African American, 1% Asian American or Pacific Islander, 4% Hispanic American, 0.1% Native American, 0.1% international, 5% transferred in, 39% live on campus. *Retention:* 90% of 2002 full-time freshmen returned.

Freshmen *Admission:* 420 applied, 376 admitted, 153 enrolled. *Average high school GPA:* 2.84. *Test scores:* SAT verbal scores over 500: 50%; SAT math scores over 500: 41%; SAT verbal scores over 600: 7%; SAT math scores over 600: 5%.

Faculty *Total:* 119, 41% full-time, 54% with terminal degrees. *Student/faculty ratio:* 12:1.

Majors Accounting; American studies; applied art; applied mathematics; art; art teacher education; art therapy; audiology and speech-language pathology; bilingual and multilingual education; biology/biological sciences; business administration and management; chemistry; clinical laboratory science/medical technology; commercial and advertising art; computer science; education; elementary education; English; English as a second/foreign language (teaching); English/language arts teacher education; French; history; interdisciplinary studies; international relations and affairs; kindergarten/preschool education; legal assistant/paralegal; legal studies; liberal arts and sciences/liberal studies; marketing/marketing management; mathematics; mathematics teacher education; molecular biology; natural sciences; nursing (registered nurse training); pre-dentistry studies; pre-law studies; pre-medical studies; pre-veterinary studies; psychology; religious studies; science teacher education; secondary education; social work; sociology; Spanish; special education; speech therapy.

Academic Programs *Special study options:* academic remediation for entering students, accelerated degree program, adult/continuing education programs, advanced placement credit, double majors, English as a second language, honors programs, internships, off-campus study, part-time degree program, student-designed majors, study abroad, summer session for credit. *ROTC:* Army (c), Air Force (c).

Library Alumnae Library with 111,379 titles, 529 serial subscriptions, 2,948 audiovisual materials, an OPAC.

Computers on Campus 70 computers available on campus for general student use. A campuswide network can be accessed from student residence rooms and from off campus. Internet access, at least one staffed computer lab available.

Elms College (continued)

Student Life *Housing options:* coed, women-only. Campus housing is university owned. Freshman campus housing is guaranteed. *Activities and organizations:* drama/theater group, student-run newspaper, choral group, Student Government Association, Zonta, Elmscript, Umoja, social work club. *Campus security:* 24-hour emergency response devices and patrols, late-night transport/escort service, controlled dormitory access. *Student services:* health clinic, personal/psychological counseling.

Athletics Member NCAA. All Division III. *Intercollegiate sports:* basketball M/W, cross-country running M/W, equestrian sports W, field hockey W, golf M, lacrosse W, soccer M/W, softball W, swimming M/W, volleyball M/W. *Intramural sports:* basketball M/W, bowling M/W, cross-country running M/W, equestrian sports W, field hockey W, golf W, lacrosse M/W, racquetball M/W, skiing (cross-country) M/W, soccer M/W, softball M/W, swimming M/W, volleyball M/W, water polo M/W, weight lifting M/W.

Standardized Tests *Required:* SAT I or ACT (for admission). *Recommended:* SAT II: Subject Tests (for admission).

Costs (2004–05) *Comprehensive fee:* $27,720 includes full-time tuition ($19,250), mandatory fees ($720), and room and board ($7750). Part-time tuition: $420 per credit. *Room and board:* Room and board charges vary according to board plan. *Waivers:* senior citizens and employees or children of employees.

Financial Aid Of all full-time matriculated undergraduates who enrolled in 2003, 402 applied for aid, 381 were judged to have need, 98 had their need fully met. 164 Federal Work-Study jobs (averaging $1328). In 2003, 37 non-need-based awards were made. *Average percent of need met:* 81%. *Average financial aid package:* $14,907. *Average need-based loan:* $5393. *Average need-based gift aid:* $9508. *Average non-need-based aid:* $8919. *Average indebtedness upon graduation:* $7138.

Applying *Options:* common application, early admission, deferred entrance. *Application fee:* $30. *Required:* essay or personal statement, high school transcript, minimum 2.0 GPA, 2 letters of recommendation. *Recommended:* interview. *Application deadline:* rolling (freshmen), rolling (transfers). *Notification:* continuous (freshmen), continuous (transfers).

Admissions Contact Mr. Joseph P. Wagner, Director of Admissions, Elms College, Chicopee, MA 01013-2839. *Phone:* 413-592-3189 Ext. 350. *Toll-free phone:* 800-255-ELMS. *Fax:* 413-594-2781. *E-mail:* admissions@elms.edu.

■ *See page 1582 for a narrative description.*

EMERSON COLLEGE
Boston, Massachusetts

- **Independent** comprehensive, founded 1880
- **Calendar** semesters
- **Degrees** bachelor's, master's, and doctoral
- **Urban** campus
- **Endowment** $33.6 million
- **Coed**, 3,401 undergraduate students, 87% full-time, 61% women, 39% men
- **Very difficult** entrance level, 48% of applicants were admitted

Founded in 1880, Emerson is one of the premier colleges in the U.S. for studying communication and the arts. Located on Boston Common in the city's Theatre District, the College's 2,800 students participate in internships, study abroad, and more than 60 student organizations, performance groups, 13 NCAA teams, student publications, and honor societies. More information can be found online at http://www.emerson.edu.

Undergraduates 2,947 full-time, 454 part-time. Students come from 48 states and territories, 59 other countries, 65% are from out of state, 2% African American, 4% Asian American or Pacific Islander, 5% Hispanic American, 0.3% Native American, 4% international, 6% transferred in, 45% live on campus. *Retention:* 83% of 2002 full-time freshmen returned.

Freshmen *Admission:* 4,321 applied, 2,090 admitted, 701 enrolled. *Average high school GPA:* 3.51. *Test scores:* SAT verbal scores over 500: 98%; SAT math scores over 500: 94%; ACT scores over 18: 100%; SAT verbal scores over 600: 64%; SAT math scores over 600: 46%; ACT scores over 24: 79%; SAT verbal scores over 700: 13%; SAT math scores over 700: 6%; ACT scores over 30: 21%.

Faculty *Total:* 345, 39% full-time, 57% with terminal degrees. *Student/faculty ratio:* 15:1.

Majors Acting; advertising; audiology and speech-language pathology; broadcast journalism; cinematography and film/video production; communication disorders; communication/speech communication and rhetoric; creative writing; drama and dance teacher education; dramatic/theatre arts; film/cinema studies; interdisciplinary studies; intermedia/multimedia; journalism; marketing/marketing management; mass communication/media; playwriting and screenwriting; political communication; public relations/image management; publishing; radio and television; radio and television broadcasting technology; radio, television, and digital communication related; special education (speech or language impaired); speech and rhetoric; speech-language pathology; speech therapy; theatre design and technology; visual and performing arts.

Academic Programs *Special study options:* adult/continuing education programs, advanced placement credit, double majors, honors programs, independent study, internships, off-campus study, part-time degree program, services for LD students, student-designed majors, study abroad, summer session for credit.

Library Emerson Library plus 1 other with 141,715 titles, 679 serial subscriptions, 8,597 audiovisual materials, an OPAC, a Web page.

Computers on Campus 296 computers available on campus for general student use. A campuswide network can be accessed from student residence rooms and from off campus. Internet access, online (class) registration, at least one staffed computer lab available.

Student Life *Housing options:* coed. Campus housing is university owned. Freshman applicants given priority for college housing. *Activities and organizations:* drama/theater group, student-run newspaper, radio and television station, choral group, EIV (Emerson Independent Video), WERS 88.9 FM, Musical Theatre Society, Berkeley Beacon, International Student Association, national fraternities, national sororities. *Campus security:* 24-hour emergency response devices and patrols, late-night transport/escort service, controlled dormitory access. *Student services:* health clinic, personal/psychological counseling.

Athletics Member NCAA. All Division III. *Intercollegiate sports:* baseball M, basketball M/W, cheerleading M/W(s), cross-country running M/W, lacrosse M/W, rock climbing W(c), soccer M/W, softball W, tennis M/W, volleyball W. *Intramural sports:* weight lifting M/W.

Standardized Tests *Required:* SAT I or ACT (for admission).

Costs (2003–04) *Comprehensive fee:* $32,521 includes full-time tuition ($22,144), mandatory fees ($549), and room and board ($9828). Part-time tuition: $692 per credit hour. *College room only:* $5850.

Financial Aid Of all full-time matriculated undergraduates who enrolled in 2002, 2,224 applied for aid, 1,792 were judged to have need, 1,337 had their need fully met. 506 Federal Work-Study jobs (averaging $2000). 33 state and other part-time jobs (averaging $7230). In 2002, 455 non-need-based awards were made. *Average percent of need met:* 76%. *Average financial aid package:* $11,820. *Average need-based loan:* $3998. *Average need-based gift aid:* $9631. *Average non-need-based aid:* $12,322. *Average indebtedness upon graduation:* $10,550.

Applying *Options:* electronic application, early admission, early action, deferred entrance. *Application fee:* $55. *Required:* essay or personal statement, high school transcript, 2 letters of recommendation. *Required for some:* interview, audition, essay, portfolio, or resume for performing arts applicants. *Application deadlines:* 1/15 (freshmen), 3/1 (transfers). *Notification:* 4/1 (freshmen), 12/15 (early action), 5/1 (transfers).

Admissions Contact Ms. Sara Ramirez, Director of Undergraduate Admission, Emerson College, 120 Boylston Street, Boston, MA 02116-4624. *Phone:* 617-824-8600. *Fax:* 617-824-8609. *E-mail:* admission@emerson.edu.

■ *See page 1590 for a narrative description.*

EMMANUEL COLLEGE
Boston, Massachusetts

- **Independent Roman Catholic** comprehensive, founded 1919
- **Calendar** semesters
- **Degrees** bachelor's and master's
- **Urban** 16-acre campus
- **Coed**
- **Moderately difficult** entrance level

Faculty *Student/faculty ratio:* 16:1.

Student Life *Campus security:* 24-hour emergency response devices and patrols, late-night transport/escort service, controlled dormitory access, 24-hour security personnel on duty at front desk in residence halls.

Athletics Member NCAA. All Division III.

Standardized Tests *Required:* SAT I or ACT (for admission).

Costs (2004–05) *Comprehensive fee:* $29,500 includes full-time tuition ($20,100), mandatory fees ($400), and room and board ($9000). Full-time tuition and fees vary according to degree level. Part-time tuition and fees vary according to degree level and program. *Payment plans:* installment, deferred payment.

Financial Aid Of all full-time matriculated undergraduates who enrolled in 2003, 978 applied for aid, 846 were judged to have need, 189 had their need fully met. 232 Federal Work-Study jobs (averaging $1112). 144 state and other part-time jobs (averaging $1056). In 2003, 80. *Average percent of need met:* 78. *Average financial aid package:* $16,474. *Average need-based loan:* $4108. *Average need-based gift aid:* $9973. *Average non-need-based aid:* $11,494. *Average indebtedness upon graduation:* $15,763.

Applying *Options:* common application, electronic application, early admission, early decision, deferred entrance. *Application fee:* $40. *Required:* essay or personal statement, high school transcript, minimum 2.0 GPA, 2 letters of recommendation. *Required for some:* interview.

Admissions Contact Ms. Sandra Robbins, Dean of Admissions, Emmanuel College, 400 The Fenway, Boston, MA 02115. *Phone:* 617-735-9715. *Fax:* 617-735-9801. *E-mail:* enroll@emmanuel.edu.

■ *See page 1592 for a narrative description.*

ENDICOTT COLLEGE
Beverly, Massachusetts

- **Independent** comprehensive, founded 1939
- **Calendar** semesters
- **Degrees** certificates, associate, bachelor's, and master's
- **Suburban** 240-acre campus with easy access to Boston
- **Endowment** $10.3 million
- **Coed,** 1,755 undergraduate students, 92% full-time, 63% women, 37% men
- **Moderately difficult** entrance level, 48% of applicants were admitted

Undergraduates 1,608 full-time, 147 part-time. Students come from 30 states and territories, 32 other countries, 53% are from out of state, 1% African American, 0.9% Asian American or Pacific Islander, 2% Hispanic American, 0.3% Native American, 5% international, 3% transferred in, 84% live on campus. *Retention:* 80% of 2002 full-time freshmen returned.

Freshmen *Admission:* 2,484 applied, 1,198 admitted, 457 enrolled. *Test scores:* SAT verbal scores over 500: 64%; SAT math scores over 500: 71%; ACT scores over 18: 87%; SAT verbal scores over 600: 10%; SAT math scores over 600: 13%; ACT scores over 24: 13%; SAT verbal scores over 700: 1%; SAT math scores over 700: 1%.

Faculty *Total:* 133, 43% full-time, 41% with terminal degrees. *Student/faculty ratio:* 15:1.

Majors Art therapy; athletic training; business administration and management; criminal justice/safety; design and visual communications; early childhood education; elementary education; English; environmental studies; fine/studio arts; hospitality administration; human services; information technology; international/global studies; liberal arts and sciences/liberal studies; mass communication/media; multi-/interdisciplinary studies related; nursing (registered nurse training); physical education teaching and coaching; psychology; sport and fitness administration.

Academic Programs *Special study options:* academic remediation for entering students, accelerated degree program, adult/continuing education programs, advanced placement credit, distance learning, English as a second language, honors programs, independent study, internships, off-campus study, part-time degree program, services for LD students, student-designed majors, study abroad, summer session for credit. *ROTC:* Army (c).

Library Endicott College Library with 121,000 titles, 3,500 serial subscriptions, 475 audiovisual materials, an OPAC, a Web page.

Computers on Campus 120 computers available on campus for general student use. A campuswide network can be accessed from student residence rooms and from off campus that provide access to e-mail. Internet access, online (class) registration, at least one staffed computer lab available.

Student Life *Housing:* on-campus residence required through senior year. *Options:* coed, women-only. Campus housing is university owned. Freshman campus housing is guaranteed. *Activities and organizations:* drama/theater group, student-run newspaper, radio and television station, choral group, Student Activities Committee, student government, yearbook, Admissions Ambassadors, Adventure Base Council. *Campus security:* 24-hour emergency response devices and patrols, late-night transport/escort service, controlled dormitory access. *Student services:* health clinic, personal/psychological counseling.

Athletics Member NCAA. All Division III. *Intercollegiate sports:* baseball M, basketball M/W, cross-country running M/W, equestrian sports M/W, field hockey W, football M, golf M/W, lacrosse M/W, soccer M/W, softball W, tennis M/W, volleyball M/W. *Intramural sports:* basketball M/W, football W, ice hockey M, racquetball M/W, soccer M/W, softball M/W, tennis M/W, ultimate Frisbee M/W, volleyball M/W.

Standardized Tests *Required:* SAT I or ACT (for admission).

Costs (2003–04) *Comprehensive fee:* $26,266 includes full-time tuition ($16,744), mandatory fees ($664), and room and board ($8858). Full-time tuition and fees vary according to student level. Part-time tuition: $514 per credit. Part-time tuition and fees vary according to program and student level. *Required fees:* $100 per term part-time. *College room only:* $6210. Room and board charges vary according to board plan and housing facility. *Payment plan:* installment. *Waivers:* employees or children of employees.

Financial Aid Of all full-time matriculated undergraduates who enrolled in 2003, 1,303 applied for aid, 1,007 were judged to have need, 129 had their need fully met. 237 Federal Work-Study jobs (averaging $1500). In 2003, 202 non-need-based awards were made. *Average percent of need met:* 62%. *Average financial aid package:* $12,062. *Average need-based loan:* $3990. *Average need-based gift aid:* $5411. *Average non-need-based aid:* $6845. *Average indebtedness upon graduation:* $17,125.

Applying *Options:* common application, electronic application, deferred entrance. *Application fee:* $40. *Required:* essay or personal statement, high school transcript, minimum 2.5 GPA. *Required for some:* interview. *Recommended:* interview. *Application deadlines:* 2/15 (freshmen), 2/15 (transfers). *Notification:* continuous (freshmen), continuous (transfers).

Admissions Contact Mr. Thomas J. Redman, Vice President of Admissions and Financial Aid, Endicott College, 376 Hale Street, Beverly, MA 01915. *Phone:* 978-921-1000. *Toll-free phone:* 800-325-1114. *Fax:* 978-232-2520. *E-mail:* admissio@endicott.edu.

FISHER COLLEGE
Boston, Massachusetts

- **Independent** primarily 2-year, founded 1903
- **Calendar** semesters
- **Degrees** associate and bachelor's
- **Urban** campus
- **Endowment** $12.9 million
- **Coed,** 556 undergraduate students, 100% full-time, 69% women, 31% men
- **Minimally difficult** entrance level, 66% of applicants were admitted

Undergraduates 556 full-time. Students come from 14 states and territories, 21 other countries, 21% are from out of state, 20% African American, 6% Asian American or Pacific Islander, 15% Hispanic American, 0.4% Native American, 10% international, 17% transferred in, 50% live on campus.

Freshmen *Admission:* 1,534 applied, 1,006 admitted, 314 enrolled. *Average high school GPA:* 2.52.

Faculty *Total:* 48, 50% full-time, 21% with terminal degrees.

Majors Accounting; business administration and management; data processing and data processing technology; fashion/apparel design; fashion merchandising; hospitality administration; humanities; kindergarten/preschool education; legal assistant/paralegal; liberal arts and sciences/liberal studies; office management; psychology; tourism and travel services management.

Academic Programs *Special study options:* academic remediation for entering students, adult/continuing education programs, advanced placement credit, English as a second language, internships, off-campus study, part-time degree program, summer session for credit.

Library Fisher College Library plus 1 other with 30,000 titles, 160 serial subscriptions, an OPAC.

Computers on Campus 112 computers available on campus for general student use. A campuswide network can be accessed from off campus. Internet access, at least one staffed computer lab available.

Student Life *Housing options:* coed, women-only. *Activities and organizations:* drama/theater group, choral group, Drama Club, student government, Student Activity Club, Intercultural Club. *Campus security:* 24-hour emergency response devices and patrols, controlled dormitory access. *Student services:* health clinic, personal/psychological counseling, women's center.

Athletics Member NAIA. *Intercollegiate sports:* baseball M, basketball M/W, softball W.

Costs (2004–05) *Comprehensive fee:* $27,550 includes full-time tuition ($15,975), mandatory fees ($1600), and room and board ($9975). Part-time tuition: $200 per credit. Part-time tuition and fees vary according to class time, course load, and program. *Payment plan:* installment. *Waivers:* employees or children of employees.

Applying *Options:* deferred entrance. *Application fee:* $25. *Required:* high school transcript. *Required for some:* essay or personal statement, letters of recommendation, interview. *Recommended:* minimum 2.0 GPA. *Application deadline:* rolling (freshmen), rolling (transfers). *Notification:* continuous (freshmen), continuous (transfers).

Admissions Contact Mr. William Graceffa, Director Admissions, Fisher College, 118 Beacon Street, Boston, MA 02116. *Phone:* 617-236-8800 Ext. 8822. *Toll-free phone:* 800-821-3050 (in-state); 800-446-1226 (out-of-state). *Fax:* 617-236-5473. *E-mail:* admissions@fisher.edu.

■ *See page 1620 for a narrative description.*

FITCHBURG STATE COLLEGE
Fitchburg, Massachusetts

- **State-supported** comprehensive, founded 1894, part of Massachusetts Public Higher Education System
- **Calendar** semesters

Fitchburg State College (continued)

- **Degrees** certificates, bachelor's, master's, post-master's, and postbachelor's certificates
- **Small-town** 45-acre campus with easy access to Boston
- **Coed**
- **Moderately difficult** entrance level

Faculty *Student/faculty ratio:* 13:1.

Student Life *Campus security:* 24-hour emergency response devices and patrols, student patrols, late-night transport/escort service, controlled dormitory access.

Athletics Member NCAA. All Division III.

Standardized Tests *Required:* SAT I or ACT (for admission).

Costs (2003–04) *Tuition:* state resident $970 full-time; nonresident $7050 full-time. Full-time tuition and fees vary according to class time, course load, location, and reciprocity agreements. Part-time tuition and fees vary according to class time, course load, location, and reciprocity agreements. *Required fees:* $3230 full-time. *Room and board:* $5506; room only: $3276. Room and board charges vary according to board plan and housing facility.

Financial Aid Of all full-time matriculated undergraduates who enrolled in 2003, 2,105 applied for aid, 1,342 were judged to have need, 1,020 had their need fully met. 225 Federal Work-Study jobs (averaging $1200). In 2003, 77. *Average percent of need met:* 99. *Average financial aid package:* $6135. *Average need-based loan:* $3060. *Average need-based gift aid:* $3620. *Average non-need-based aid:* $1910. *Average indebtedness upon graduation:* $8300.

Applying *Options:* common application, electronic application, deferred entrance. *Application fee:* $10. *Required:* essay or personal statement, high school transcript, minimum 3.0 GPA. *Required for some:* interview. *Recommended:* letters of recommendation.

Admissions Contact Ms. Lynn A. Petrillo, Director of Admissions, Fitchburg State College, 160 Pearl Street, Fitchburg, MA 01420-2697. *Phone:* 978-665-3140. *Toll-free phone:* 800-705-9692. *Fax:* 978-665-4540. *E-mail:* admissions@fsc.edu.

■ *See page 1622 for a narrative description.*

FRAMINGHAM STATE COLLEGE

Framingham, Massachusetts

- **State-supported** comprehensive, founded 1839, part of Massachusetts Public Higher Education System
- **Calendar** semesters
- **Degrees** bachelor's, master's, and postbachelor's certificates
- **Suburban** 73-acre campus with easy access to Boston
- **Coed,** 3,892 undergraduate students, 80% full-time, 66% women, 34% men
- **Moderately difficult** entrance level, 55% of applicants were admitted

Framingham State College has launched an initiative making it the first Massachusetts state college to provide wireless computing for all students. All entering students must purchase a laptop computer.

Undergraduates 3,132 full-time, 760 part-time. Students come from 15 states and territories, 20 other countries, 8% are from out of state, 3% African American, 3% Asian American or Pacific Islander, 3% Hispanic American, 0.5% Native American, 2% international, 8% transferred in, 45% live on campus. *Retention:* 72% of 2002 full-time freshmen returned.

Freshmen *Admission:* 4,214 applied, 2,319 admitted, 625 enrolled. *Average high school GPA:* 3.09. *Test scores:* SAT verbal scores over 500: 69%; SAT math scores over 500: 68%; SAT verbal scores over 600: 16%; SAT math scores over 600: 15%; SAT verbal scores over 700: 1%; SAT math scores over 700: 1%.

Faculty *Total:* 286, 56% full-time, 66% with terminal degrees. *Student/faculty ratio:* 15:1.

Majors Accounting; American government and politics; American history; anthropology; apparel and textiles related; art history, criticism and conservation; art teacher education; biology/biological sciences; biology teacher education; biomedical sciences; biotechnology; business administration and management; business/managerial economics; chemistry; chemistry teacher education; city/urban, community and regional planning; clinical nutrition; clothing/textiles; communication and journalism related; communication and media related; communication/speech communication and rhetoric; computer programming; computer science; creative writing; developmental and child psychology; dietetics; economics; education; elementary education; English; English/language arts teacher education; environmental biology; environmental science; environmental studies; European history; family and consumer economics related; family and consumer sciences/home economics teacher education; family and consumer sciences/human sciences; family and consumer sciences/human sciences communication; family and consumer sciences/human sciences related; fashion/apparel design; fashion merchandising; finance; fine/studio arts; foods and nutrition related; food science; food science and technology related; foods, nutrition, and wellness; foreign languages and literatures; geography; geology/earth science; graphic design; history; history teacher education; humanities; human nutrition; human resources management; human services; information technology; international business/trade/commerce; journalism; kindergarten/preschool education; liberal arts and sciences/liberal studies; literature; marketing/marketing management; mathematics; mathematics teacher education; middle school education; nursing administration; painting; physical sciences; political science and government; pre-dentistry studies; pre-law studies; pre-medical studies; pre-veterinary studies; printmaking; psychology; public administration; science teacher education; sculpture; secondary education; social sciences; sociology; Spanish; Spanish language teacher education; wildlife and wildlands science and management; wildlife biology.

Academic Programs *Special study options:* adult/continuing education programs, advanced placement credit, distance learning, double majors, English as a second language, honors programs, independent study, internships, off-campus study, part-time degree program, study abroad, summer session for credit. *ROTC:* Army (b).

Library Whittemore Library with 165,219 titles, 409 serial subscriptions, 3,313 audiovisual materials, an OPAC, a Web page.

Computers on Campus 575 computers available on campus for general student use. A campuswide network can be accessed from student residence rooms and from off campus that provide access to TELNET. Internet access, online (class) registration, at least one staffed computer lab available. Computer purchase or lease plan available.

Student Life *Housing options:* coed, women-only. Campus housing is university owned. Freshman applicants given priority for college housing. *Activities and organizations:* drama/theater group, student-run newspaper, radio station, choral group, Student Union Activities Board, Student Government Association, Gatepost (student newspaper), Hilltop Players, literary magazine. *Campus security:* 24-hour emergency response devices and patrols, student patrols, late-night transport/escort service, controlled dormitory access. *Student services:* health clinic, personal/psychological counseling.

Athletics Member NCAA. All Division III. *Intercollegiate sports:* baseball M, basketball M/W, cross-country running M/W, field hockey W, football M, ice hockey M, soccer M/W, softball W, volleyball W. *Intramural sports:* basketball M/W, cheerleading W, equestrian sports M/W, football M, rugby M/W, softball M/W, volleyball W.

Standardized Tests *Required:* SAT I or ACT (for admission).

Costs (2003–04) *Tuition:* state resident $970 full-time; nonresident $7050 full-time. Full-time tuition and fees vary according to class time. Part-time tuition and fees vary according to class time and course load. *Required fees:* $3354 full-time. *Room and board:* $5058. Room and board charges vary according to board plan and housing facility. *Payment plan:* installment. *Waivers:* senior citizens and employees or children of employees.

Financial Aid Of all full-time matriculated undergraduates who enrolled in 2001, 1,746 applied for aid, 1,117 were judged to have need, 751 had their need fully met. In 2001, 100 non-need-based awards were made. *Average percent of need met:* 89%. *Average financial aid package:* $6558. *Average need-based loan:* $2080. *Average need-based gift aid:* $3020. *Average non-need-based aid:* $1454. *Average indebtedness upon graduation:* $11,000.

Applying *Options:* electronic application, early admission, early action, deferred entrance. *Application fee:* $25. *Required:* high school transcript. *Required for some:* essay or personal statement, interview. *Recommended:* essay or personal statement, minimum 3.0 GPA, letters of recommendation. *Application deadlines:* 2/15 (freshmen), 2/15 (transfers). *Notification:* 3/31 (freshmen), 12/15 (early action), continuous until 4/1 (transfers).

Admissions Contact Ms. Elizabeth J. Canella, Associate Dean of Admissions, Framingham State College, PO Box 9101, Dwight Hall, Room 209, 100 State Street, Framingham, MA 01701-9101. *Phone:* 508-626-4500. *Fax:* 508-626-4017. *E-mail:* admiss@frc.mass.edu.

■ *See page 1644 for a narrative description.*

GORDON COLLEGE

Wenham, Massachusetts

- **Independent nondenominational** comprehensive, founded 1889
- **Calendar** semesters
- **Degrees** bachelor's and master's
- **Small-town** 500-acre campus with easy access to Boston
- **Endowment** $22.4 million
- **Coed,** 1,640 undergraduate students, 98% full-time, 65% women, 35% men
- **Moderately difficult** entrance level, 78% of applicants were admitted

Undergraduates 1,602 full-time, 38 part-time. Students come from 46 states and territories, 25 other countries, 72% are from out of state, 1% African

American, 2% Asian American or Pacific Islander, 2% Hispanic American, 0.2% Native American, 2% international, 4% transferred in, 88% live on campus. *Retention:* 87% of 2002 full-time freshmen returned.

Freshmen *Admission:* 1,080 applied, 845 admitted, 427 enrolled. *Average high school GPA:* 3.62. *Test scores:* SAT verbal scores over 500: 96%; SAT math scores over 500: 93%; SAT verbal scores over 600: 62%; SAT math scores over 600: 60%; SAT verbal scores over 700: 15%; SAT math scores over 700: 10%.

Faculty *Total:* 146, 64% full-time, 51% with terminal degrees. *Student/faculty ratio:* 14:1.

Majors Accounting; art; biology/biological sciences; business administration and management; chemistry; Christian studies; communication/speech communication and rhetoric; computer science; economics; elementary education; English; foreign languages and literatures; French; German; history; international relations and affairs; kinesiology and exercise science; mathematics; middle school education; music; music performance; music teacher education; parks, recreation and leisure; philosophy; physics; political science and government; psychology; social work; sociology; Spanish; special education; youth ministry.

Academic Programs *Special study options:* academic remediation for entering students, advanced placement credit, cooperative education, double majors, honors programs, independent study, internships, off-campus study, part-time degree program, services for LD students, student-designed majors, study abroad. *ROTC:* Army (c), Air Force (c). *Unusual degree programs:* 3-2 engineering with University of Massachusetts Lowell; nursing with Thomas Jefferson University.

Library Jenks Learning Resource Center with 142,688 titles, 8,555 serial subscriptions, 10,266 audiovisual materials, an OPAC.

Computers on Campus 141 computers available on campus for general student use. A campuswide network can be accessed from student residence rooms and from off campus. Internet access, online (class) registration, at least one staffed computer lab available.

Student Life *Housing:* on-campus residence required through senior year. *Options:* coed, men-only, women-only, disabled students. Campus housing is university owned. Freshman campus housing is guaranteed. *Activities and organizations:* drama/theater group, student-run newspaper, choral group, Student Government Association, student ministries, diverse music ensembles. *Campus security:* 24-hour emergency response devices and patrols, late-night transport/escort service, controlled dormitory access. *Student services:* health clinic, personal/psychological counseling.

Athletics Member NCAA. All Division III. *Intercollegiate sports:* baseball M, basketball M/W, cheerleading M/W, cross-country running M/W, field hockey W, golf M(c)/W(c), lacrosse M/W, soccer M/W, softball W, swimming M/W, tennis M/W, volleyball W. *Intramural sports:* basketball M/W, football M/W, ice hockey M(c)/W(c), racquetball M/W, rock climbing M/W, soccer M/W, softball M/W, table tennis M/W, tennis M/W, track and field M/W, ultimate Frisbee M/W.

Standardized Tests *Required:* SAT I or ACT (for admission).

Costs (2003–04) *Comprehensive fee:* $25,982 includes full-time tuition ($19,334), mandatory fees ($900), and room and board ($5748). Part-time tuition and fees vary according to course load. *College room only:* $3850. Room and board charges vary according to board plan and housing facility. *Payment plans:* tuition prepayment, installment. *Waivers:* employees or children of employees.

Financial Aid Of all full-time matriculated undergraduates who enrolled in 2003, 1,285 applied for aid, 1,133 were judged to have need, 184 had their need fully met. 642 Federal Work-Study jobs (averaging $1654). In 2003, 429 non-need-based awards were made. *Average percent of need met:* 75%. *Average financial aid package:* $14,375. *Average need-based loan:* $4598. *Average need-based gift aid:* $9609. *Average non-need-based aid:* $10,895. *Average indebtedness upon graduation:* $17,442.

Applying *Options:* electronic application, early admission, early decision, deferred entrance. *Application fee:* $40. *Required:* essay or personal statement, high school transcript, 2 letters of recommendation, interview, pastoral recommendation, statement of Christian faith. *Recommended:* minimum 3.0 GPA. *Application deadline:* rolling (freshmen), rolling (transfers). *Early decision:* 12/1. *Notification:* continuous (freshmen), 1/1 (early decision), continuous (transfers).

Admissions Contact Nancy Mering, Director of Admissions, Gordon College, 255 Grapevine Road, Wenham, MA 01984-1899. *Phone:* 978-867-4218. *Toll-free phone:* 800-343-1379. *Fax:* 978-867-4657. *E-mail:* admissions@hope.gordon.edu.

■ *See page 1674 for a narrative description.*

HAMPSHIRE COLLEGE
Amherst, Massachusetts

- **Independent** 4-year, founded 1965
- **Calendar** 4-1-4
- **Degree** bachelor's
- **Rural** 800-acre campus
- **Endowment** $28.1 million
- **Coed,** 1,332 undergraduate students, 100% full-time, 58% women, 42% men
- **Moderately difficult** entrance level, 55% of applicants were admitted

Hampshire College's bold, innovative approach to the liberal arts creates an academic atmosphere that energizes students to work hard and grow tremendously, both personally and intellectually. Students have the freedom to design an individualized course of study in a graduate school–like environment, culminating in original final projects such as science or social science research, academic study, or a body of work in writing, performing, visual, or media arts. Students work closely with faculty mentors, often integrating different disciplines. Independent thinking is expected. Hampshire students and faculty agree: if students incorporate what they love into their education, they will love their education.

Undergraduates 1,332 full-time. Students come from 46 states and territories, 25 other countries, 86% are from out of state, 3% African American, 4% Asian American or Pacific Islander, 5% Hispanic American, 0.8% Native American, 3% international, 2% transferred in, 92% live on campus. *Retention:* 79% of 2002 full-time freshmen returned.

Freshmen *Admission:* 2,270 applied, 1,246 admitted, 383 enrolled. *Average high school GPA:* 3.47. *Test scores:* SAT verbal scores over 500: 98%; SAT math scores over 500: 92%; ACT scores over 18: 100%; SAT verbal scores over 600: 78%; SAT math scores over 600: 56%; ACT scores over 24: 83%; SAT verbal scores over 700: 28%; SAT math scores over 700: 11%; ACT scores over 30: 23%.

Faculty *Total:* 141, 81% full-time, 80% with terminal degrees. *Student/faculty ratio:* 11:1.

Majors Acting; African-American/Black studies; African studies; agricultural economics; agriculture; American history; American Indian/Native American studies; American literature; American studies; anatomy; animal behavior and ethology; animal genetics; animal physiology; animal sciences; animation, interactive technology, video graphics and special effects; anthropology; applied mathematics; aquaculture; archeology; architectural history and criticism; architecture; area studies related; art; art history, criticism and conservation; artificial intelligence and robotics; Asian-American studies; Asian studies; Asian studies (East); Asian studies (South); Asian studies (Southeast); astronomy; astrophysics; behavioral sciences; biochemistry; biological and physical sciences; biology/biological sciences; biophysics; botany/plant biology; business/managerial economics; Canadian studies; cell biology and histology; chemistry; child development; cinematography and film/video production; city/urban, community and regional planning; classics and languages, literatures and linguistics; cognitive psychology and psycholinguistics; cognitive science; community organization and advocacy; comparative literature; computer and information sciences; computer graphics; computer programming; computer science; creative writing; cultural studies; dance; design and applied arts related; developmental and child psychology; digital communication and media/multimedia; directing and theatrical production; dramatic/theatre arts; dramatic/theatre arts and stagecraft related; drawing; ecology; economics; education; elementary education; English; English literature (British and Commonwealth); environmental biology; environmental design/architecture; environmental health; environmental science; environmental studies; ethnic, cultural minority, and gender studies related; European history; European studies; European studies (Central and Eastern); European studies (Western); evolutionary biology; family and consumer economics related; film/cinema studies; film/video and photographic arts related; fine/studio arts; foods, nutrition, and wellness; forest sciences and biology; genetics; geochemistry; geography; geology/earth science; geophysics and seismology; health science; Hispanic-American, Puerto Rican, and Mexican-American/Chicano studies; history; history and philosophy of science and technology; history of philosophy; history related; human development and family studies; humanities; interdisciplinary studies; intermedia/multimedia; international business/trade/commerce; international economics; international/global studies; international relations and affairs; Islamic studies; jazz/jazz studies; Jewish/Judaic studies; journalism; kindergarten/preschool education; kinesiology and exercise science; labor and industrial relations; Latin American studies; legal studies; liberal arts and sciences/liberal studies; linguistics; literature; marine biology and biological oceanography; mass communication/media; mathematics; medical microbiology and bacteriology; medieval and Renaissance studies; molecular biology; multi-/interdisciplinary studies related; music; music history, literature, and theory; musicology and ethnomusicology; music theory and composition; natural sciences; Near and Middle Eastern studies; neuroscience; oceanography (chemical and physical); painting; peace studies and conflict resolution; philosophy; photography; physical sciences; physics; physiological psychology/psychobiology; plant genetics; political science and government; pre-law studies; pre-medical studies; pre-veterinary studies; psychology; public health; public policy analysis; radio and television; religious studies; Russian studies; science, technology and society; sculpture; secondary education; social and philosophical foundations of education; social sciences; sociobiology; sociology; soil chemistry and physics; soil microbiology; solar energy technology; statistics; telecommunications; theatre design and tech-

Hampshire College (continued)
nology; theatre literature, history and criticism; theatre/theatre arts management; Tibetan studies; urban studies/affairs; women's studies.

Academic Programs *Special study options:* accelerated degree program, advanced placement credit, double majors, independent study, internships, off-campus study, services for LD students, student-designed majors, study abroad. *ROTC:* Army (c).

Library Harold F. Johnson Library with 124,710 titles, 731 serial subscriptions, 8,727 audiovisual materials, an OPAC, a Web page.

Computers on Campus 125 computers available on campus for general student use. A campuswide network can be accessed from student residence rooms and from off campus. At least one staffed computer lab available.

Student Life *Housing:* on-campus residence required through senior year. *Options:* coed, men-only, women-only, cooperative, disabled students. Campus housing is university owned. Freshman campus housing is guaranteed. *Activities and organizations:* drama/theater group, student-run newspaper, radio and television station, choral group, Alternative Music Collective, Jewish Student Union, Student Action for Radical Change, Theatre Board, Red Scare Ultimate Frisbee. *Campus security:* 24-hour emergency response devices and patrols, student patrols, late-night transport/escort service. *Student services:* health clinic, personal/psychological counseling, women's center.

Athletics *Intercollegiate sports:* basketball M(c)/W(c), fencing M(c)/W(c), soccer M(c)/W(c). *Intramural sports:* archery M(c)/W(c), lacrosse W(c), rock climbing M(c)/W(c), ultimate Frisbee M(c)/W(c).

Costs (2003–04) *Comprehensive fee:* $37,081 includes full-time tuition ($28,832), mandatory fees ($560), and room and board ($7689). *College room only:* $4904. Room and board charges vary according to board plan. *Payment plan:* installment. *Waivers:* employees or children of employees.

Financial Aid Of all full-time matriculated undergraduates who enrolled in 2003, 843 applied for aid, 723 were judged to have need, 649 had their need fully met. 584 Federal Work-Study jobs (averaging $2300). 281 state and other part-time jobs (averaging $2300). In 2003, 32 non-need-based awards were made. *Average percent of need met:* 100%. *Average financial aid package:* $24,615. *Average need-based loan:* $4030. *Average need-based gift aid:* $18,260. *Average non-need-based aid:* $4990. *Average indebtedness upon graduation:* $16,975.

Applying *Options:* common application, electronic application, early admission, early decision, early action, deferred entrance. *Application fee:* $55. *Required:* essay or personal statement, high school transcript, 2 letters of recommendation. *Recommended:* interview. *Application deadlines:* 1/15 (freshmen), 3/1 (transfers). *Early decision:* 11/15. *Notification:* 4/1 (freshmen), 12/15 (early decision), 2/1 (early action), 4/15 (transfers).

Admissions Contact Ms. Karen S. Parker, Director of Admissions, Hampshire College, 893 West Street, Amherst, MA 01002. *Phone:* 413-559-5471. *Toll-free phone:* 877-937-4267. *Fax:* 413-559-5631. *E-mail:* admissions@hampshire.edu.

■ *See page 1706 for a narrative description.*

HARVARD UNIVERSITY
Cambridge, Massachusetts

- **Independent** university, founded 1636
- **Calendar** semesters
- **Degrees** bachelor's, master's, doctoral, and first professional
- **Urban** 380-acre campus with easy access to Boston
- **Endowment** $19.3 billion
- **Coed,** 6,635 undergraduate students, 100% full-time, 47% women, 53% men
- **Most difficult** entrance level, 10% of applicants were admitted

Undergraduates 6,635 full-time. Students come from 53 states and territories, 82 other countries, 8% African American, 18% Asian American or Pacific Islander, 8% Hispanic American, 0.7% Native American, 7% international, 1% transferred in, 96% live on campus. *Retention:* 97% of 2002 full-time freshmen returned.

Freshmen *Admission:* 20,987 applied, 2,095 admitted, 1,635 enrolled.

Faculty *Total:* 760, 100% with terminal degrees. *Student/faculty ratio:* 8:1.

Majors African-American/Black studies; African languages; African studies; American studies; ancient Near Eastern and biblical languages; animal genetics; anthropology; applied mathematics; Arabic; archeology; architectural engineering; art; art history, criticism and conservation; artificial intelligence and robotics; Asian studies; Asian studies (East); Asian studies (South); Asian studies (Southeast); astronomy; astrophysics; atmospheric sciences and meteorology; behavioral sciences; biblical studies; biochemistry; biological and physical sciences; biology/biological sciences; biology/biotechnology laboratory technician; biomedical/medical engineering; biomedical sciences; biometry/biometrics; biophysics; cell biology and histology; chemical engineering; chemistry; Chinese; city/urban, community and regional planning; civil engineering; classics and languages, literatures and linguistics; cognitive psychology and psycholinguistics; cognitive science; comparative literature; computer and information sciences; computer engineering; computer engineering technology; computer graphics; computer programming; computer science; creative writing; cultural studies; dramatic/theatre arts; ecology; economics; electrical, electronics and communications engineering; engineering; engineering physics; engineering science; English; entomology; environmental biology; environmental design/architecture; environmental/environmental health engineering; environmental studies; European studies; European studies (Central and Eastern); evolutionary biology; film/cinema studies; fine/studio arts; fluid/thermal sciences; folklore; French; geochemistry; geological/geophysical engineering; geology/earth science; geophysics and seismology; German; Hebrew; Hispanic-American, Puerto Rican, and Mexican-American/Chicano studies; history; history and philosophy of science and technology; history of philosophy; human development and family studies; humanities; information science/studies; interdisciplinary studies; international economics; international relations and affairs; Islamic studies; Italian; Japanese; Jewish/Judaic studies; Latin; Latin American studies; liberal arts and sciences/liberal studies; linguistics; literature; marine biology and biological oceanography; materials engineering; materials science; mathematics; mathematics and computer science; mechanical engineering; medical microbiology and bacteriology; medieval and Renaissance studies; metallurgical engineering; modern Greek; modern languages; molecular biology; music; music history, literature, and theory; natural resources/conservation; Near and Middle Eastern studies; neuroscience; nuclear physics; philosophy; physical sciences; physics; physiological psychology/psychobiology; political science and government; polymer chemistry; Portuguese; pre-dentistry studies; pre-law studies; pre-medical studies; preveterinary studies; psychology; public policy analysis; religious studies; Romance languages; Russian; Russian studies; Scandinavian languages; Slavic languages; social sciences; sociobiology; sociology; Spanish; statistics; systems engineering; urban studies/affairs; western civilization; women's studies.

Academic Programs *Special study options:* academic remediation for entering students, accelerated degree program, adult/continuing education programs, advanced placement credit, double majors, English as a second language, honors programs, independent study, internships, off-campus study, services for LD students, student-designed majors, study abroad, summer session for credit. *ROTC:* Army (c), Air Force (c).

Library Widener Library plus 90 others with 14.0 million titles, 97,568 serial subscriptions.

Computers on Campus A campuswide network can be accessed from student residence rooms and from off campus. Internet access, at least one staffed computer lab available.

Student Life *Housing:* on-campus residence required for freshman year. *Options:* coed. *Activities and organizations:* drama/theater group, student-run newspaper, radio and television station, choral group, marching band, Phillips Brooks House, Asian-American Association, International Relations Council, Harvard Crimson (newspaper), Harvard/Radcliffe Chorus. *Campus security:* 24-hour emergency response devices and patrols, late-night transport/escort service, controlled dormitory access, required and optional safety courses. *Student services:* health clinic, personal/psychological counseling, women's center, legal services.

Athletics Member NCAA. All Division I except football (Division I-AA). *Intercollegiate sports:* baseball M, basketball M/W, crew M/W, cross-country running M/W, fencing M/W, field hockey W, golf M/W, ice hockey M/W, lacrosse M/W, sailing M/W, skiing (cross-country) M/W, skiing (downhill) M/W, soccer M/W, softball W, squash M/W, swimming M/W, tennis M/W, track and field M/W, volleyball M/W, water polo M/W, wrestling M. *Intramural sports:* badminton M(c)/W(c), baseball M, basketball M/W, crew M/W, cross-country running M/W, equestrian sports M(c)/W(c), fencing M/W, field hockey M/W, football M, gymnastics M(c)/W(c), ice hockey M/W, racquetball M/W, rugby M(c)/W(c), soccer M/W, softball W, squash M/W, swimming M/W, table tennis M(c)/W(c), tennis M/W, track and field M/W, volleyball M/W.

Standardized Tests *Required:* SAT I or ACT (for admission), SAT II: Subject Tests (for admission).

Costs (2003–04) *Comprehensive fee:* $37,928 includes full-time tuition ($26,066), mandatory fees ($2994), and room and board ($8868).

Financial Aid Of all full-time matriculated undergraduates who enrolled in 2002, 3,446 applied for aid, 3,220 were judged to have need, 3,220 had their need fully met. 643 Federal Work-Study jobs (averaging $1180). 3,546 state and other part-time jobs (averaging $1553). *Average percent of need met:* 100%. *Average financial aid package:* $25,299. *Average need-based loan:* $2467. *Average need-based gift aid:* $22,896. *Average indebtedness upon graduation:* $8830.

Applying *Options:* common application, early action, deferred entrance. *Application fee:* $60. *Required:* essay or personal statement, high school transcript, 2 letters of recommendation, interview. *Application deadlines:* 1/1 (freshmen), 2/1 (transfers). *Notification:* 4/1 (freshmen), 12/15 (early action), 6/1 (transfers).

Admissions Contact Office of Admissions and Financial Aid, Harvard University, Byerly Hall, 8 Garden Street, Cambridge, MA 02138. *Phone:* 617-495-1551. *E-mail:* college@harvard.edu.

■ *See page 1718 for a narrative description.*

HEBREW COLLEGE
Newton Centre, Massachusetts

Admissions Contact Melissa Roiter, Admissions, Hebrew College, 160 Herrick Road, Newton Centre, MA 02459. *Phone:* 617-559-8610. *Toll-free phone:* 800-866-4814. *Fax:* 617-559-8611. *E-mail:* admissions@lhebrewcollege.edu.

HELLENIC COLLEGE
Brookline, Massachusetts

- **Independent Greek Orthodox** 4-year, founded 1937
- **Calendar** semesters
- **Degrees** bachelor's (also offers graduate degree programs through Holy Cross Greek Orthodox School of Theology)
- **Suburban** 52-acre campus with easy access to Boston
- **Endowment** $19.4 million
- **Coed,** 92 undergraduate students, 98% full-time, 40% women, 60% men
- **Minimally difficult** entrance level, 39% of applicants were admitted

Undergraduates 90 full-time, 2 part-time. Students come from 39 states and territories, 8 other countries, 87% are from out of state, 2% African American, 1% Asian American or Pacific Islander, 16% international, 12% transferred in, 90% live on campus. *Retention:* 94% of 2002 full-time freshmen returned.

Freshmen *Admission:* 38 applied, 15 admitted, 15 enrolled. *Average high school GPA:* 3.00. *Test scores:* SAT verbal scores over 500: 60%; SAT math scores over 500: 60%; SAT verbal scores over 600: 20%; SAT math scores over 600: 20%; SAT verbal scores over 700: 20%.

Faculty *Total:* 22, 36% full-time. *Student/faculty ratio:* 9:1.

Majors Business administration and management; classics and languages, literatures and linguistics; elementary education; human development and family studies; religious studies; theology.

Academic Programs *Special study options:* academic remediation for entering students, advanced placement credit, double majors, independent study, internships, off-campus study, part-time degree program, summer session for credit.

Library Archbishop Iakoros Library with 116,533 titles, 747 serial subscriptions, 2,795 audiovisual materials, an OPAC, a Web page.

Computers on Campus 9 computers available on campus for general student use. At least one staffed computer lab available.

Student Life *Housing:* on-campus residence required through senior year. *Options:* coed. Campus housing is university owned. Freshman campus housing is guaranteed. *Activities and organizations:* drama/theater group, student-run newspaper, choral group. *Campus security:* controlled dormitory access. *Student services:* health clinic, personal/psychological counseling.

Athletics *Intramural sports:* baseball M, basketball M/W, football M, golf M, soccer M, table tennis M/W, ultimate Frisbee M/W, volleyball M/W.

Standardized Tests *Required:* SAT I or ACT (for admission). *Required for some:* SAT II: Subject Tests (for admission), SAT II: Writing Test (for admission).

Costs (2004–05) *Comprehensive fee:* $23,930 includes full-time tuition ($14,700), mandatory fees ($330), and room and board ($8900). Part-time tuition and fees vary according to course load. *Payment plan:* installment. *Waivers:* children of alumni and employees or children of employees.

Financial Aid Of all full-time matriculated undergraduates who enrolled in 2003, 69 applied for aid, 67 were judged to have need. In 2003, 3 non-need-based awards were made. *Average percent of need met:* 80%. *Average financial aid package:* $9200. *Average need-based loan:* $5500. *Average need-based gift aid:* $10,100. *Average non-need-based aid:* $1100. *Average indebtedness upon graduation:* $7300.

Applying *Options:* common application, electronic application, early action, deferred entrance. *Application fee:* $35. *Required:* essay or personal statement, high school transcript, minimum 2.0 GPA, letters of recommendation, interview, health certificate. *Application deadline:* rolling (freshmen), rolling (transfers). *Notification:* continuous (freshmen), continuous (transfers).

Admissions Contact Ms. Sonia Daly, Director of Admissions, Hellenic College, 50 Goddard Avenue, Brookline, MA 02445-7496. *Phone:* 617-731-3500 Ext. 1285. *Toll-free phone:* 866-424-2338. *Fax:* 617-850-1460. *E-mail:* admissions@hchc.edu.

LASELL COLLEGE
Newton, Massachusetts

- **Independent** comprehensive, founded 1851
- **Calendar** semesters
- **Degrees** bachelor's and master's
- **Suburban** 50-acre campus with easy access to Boston
- **Endowment** $12.1 million
- **Coed,** 1,081 undergraduate students, 98% full-time, 73% women, 27% men
- **Moderately difficult** entrance level, 68% of applicants were admitted

The Lasell Plan of Education is distinguished by a philosophy called Connected Learning. Connected Learning allows students to practice classroom theory in practical settings. In addition to using off-campus internship sites, students gain experience in on-campus labs that include 2 renowned child-study centers, a state-of-the-art business technology center, a fashion design and merchandising center, allied health labs, a CADD lab, and an art center.

Undergraduates 1,054 full-time, 27 part-time. Students come from 20 states and territories, 8 other countries, 34% are from out of state, 10% African American, 5% Asian American or Pacific Islander, 6% Hispanic American, 0.2% Native American, 3% international, 6% transferred in, 80% live on campus. *Retention:* 82% of 2002 full-time freshmen returned.

Freshmen *Admission:* 2,283 applied, 1,557 admitted, 367 enrolled. *Average high school GPA:* 2.75. *Test scores:* SAT verbal scores over 500: 41%; SAT math scores over 500: 36%; SAT verbal scores over 600: 4%; SAT math scores over 600: 5%.

Faculty *Total:* 130, 34% full-time, 15% with terminal degrees. *Student/faculty ratio:* 11:1.

Majors Accounting; business administration and management; child development; commercial and advertising art; communication/speech communication and rhetoric; consumer merchandising/retailing management; criminal justice/safety; education; elementary education; fashion/apparel design; fashion merchandising; finance; graphic design; history; hotel/motel administration; human services; information science/studies; interdisciplinary studies; international business/trade/commerce; kindergarten/preschool education; kinesiology and exercise science; legal studies; liberal arts and sciences/liberal studies; marketing/marketing management; pre-law studies; psychology; sociology; tourism and travel services management.

Academic Programs *Special study options:* advanced placement credit, cooperative education, double majors, English as a second language, honors programs, independent study, internships, part-time degree program, student-designed majors, study abroad.

Library Brennan Library with 51,219 titles, 521 serial subscriptions, 2,145 audiovisual materials, an OPAC.

Computers on Campus 150 computers available on campus for general student use. A campuswide network can be accessed from student residence rooms and from off campus. Internet access, at least one staffed computer lab available.

Student Life *Housing options:* coed, women-only. Campus housing is university owned. Freshman campus housing is guaranteed. *Activities and organizations:* drama/theater group, student-run newspaper, choral group, marching band, Center for Public Service, student government, Umoja-Nia, yearbook, Fashion Board. *Campus security:* 24-hour emergency response devices and patrols, late-night transport/escort service, controlled dormitory access. *Student services:* health clinic, personal/psychological counseling.

Athletics Member NCAA. All Division III. *Intercollegiate sports:* basketball M/W, cross-country running M/W, field hockey W, lacrosse M/W, soccer M/W, softball W, volleyball M/W. *Intramural sports:* basketball M/W, cheerleading M/W, crew M/W, soccer M/W, volleyball M/W.

Standardized Tests *Required:* SAT I (for admission).

Costs (2003–04) *Comprehensive fee:* $26,000 includes full-time tuition ($16,600), mandatory fees ($900), and room and board ($8500). *Room and board:* Room and board charges vary according to housing facility.

Financial Aid Of all full-time matriculated undergraduates who enrolled in 2003, 918 applied for aid, 836 were judged to have need, 106 had their need fully met. 751 Federal Work-Study jobs (averaging $2000). In 2003, 155 non-need-based awards were made. *Average percent of need met:* 75%. *Average financial aid package:* $15,200. *Average need-based loan:* $3500. *Average need-based gift aid:* $11,000. *Average non-need-based aid:* $4000. *Average indebtedness upon graduation:* $20,500.

Applying *Options:* electronic application, deferred entrance. *Application fee:* $40. *Required:* high school transcript, minimum 2.0 GPA, 1 letter of recommendation. *Recommended:* essay or personal statement, interview. *Application deadline:* rolling (freshmen), rolling (transfers). *Notification:* continuous (freshmen), continuous (transfers).

Lasell College (continued)

Admissions Contact Mr. James Tweed, Director of Admission, Lasell College, 1844 Commonwealth Avenue, Newton, MA 02466. *Phone:* 617-243-2225. *Toll-free phone:* 888-LASELL-4. *Fax:* 617-243-2380. *E-mail:* info@lasell.edu.

■ *See page 1848 for a narrative description.*

LESLEY UNIVERSITY
Cambridge, Massachusetts

- **Independent** comprehensive, founded 1909
- **Calendar** semesters
- **Degrees** certificates, diplomas, associate, bachelor's, master's, doctoral, post-master's, and postbachelor's certificates
- **Urban** 5 acre campus with easy access to Boston
- **Endowment** $37.6 million
- **Coed, primarily women,** 516 undergraduate students, 97% full-time, 100% women
- **Moderately difficult** entrance level, 77% of applicants were admitted

Located on Lesley University's main campus in Cambridge, Massachusetts, Lesley College offers a small, residential college experience to 550 undergraduate women. Academic programs in the areas of education, human services, management, and the arts integrate the liberal arts with professional course work and hands-on internship experience.

Undergraduates 498 full-time, 18 part-time. Students come from 21 states and territories, 8 other countries, 36% are from out of state, 9% African American, 5% Asian American or Pacific Islander, 4% Hispanic American, 0.2% Native American, 3% international, 9% transferred in, 66% live on campus. *Retention:* 72% of 2002 full-time freshmen returned.

Freshmen *Admission:* 365 applied, 281 admitted, 102 enrolled. *Average high school GPA:* 3.00. *Test scores:* SAT verbal scores over 500: 71%; SAT math scores over 500: 58%; SAT verbal scores over 600: 17%; SAT math scores over 600: 11%; SAT verbal scores over 700: 3%.

Faculty *Total:* 66, 52% full-time, 52% with terminal degrees. *Student/faculty ratio:* 11:1.

Majors American studies; art; art therapy; business administration and management; child development; communications technologies and support services related; counseling psychology; education; elementary education; English; environmental studies; human development and family studies; humanities; human services; kindergarten/preschool education; liberal arts and sciences/liberal studies; middle school education; natural sciences; secondary education; social sciences; special education.

Academic Programs *Special study options:* academic remediation for entering students, accelerated degree program, adult/continuing education programs, advanced placement credit, distance learning, double majors, English as a second language, external degree program, freshman honors college, honors programs, independent study, internships, off-campus study, part-time degree program, services for LD students, study abroad, summer session for credit. *Unusual degree programs:* 3-2 counseling psychology, clinical mental health counseling, elementary education, special education.

Library Eleanor DeWolfe Ludcke Library plus 2 others with 98,271 titles, 98,271 serial subscriptions, 47,312 audiovisual materials, an OPAC, a Web page.

Computers on Campus 170 computers available on campus for general student use. A campuswide network can be accessed from student residence rooms and from off campus. Internet access, at least one staffed computer lab available.

Student Life *Housing options:* women-only. Campus housing is university owned. Freshman campus housing is guaranteed. *Activities and organizations:* drama/theater group, student-run newspaper, choral group, Student Senate, Women for Social Justice, Hillel, Swim Club, Third Wave. *Campus security:* 24-hour emergency response devices and patrols, late-night transport/escort service, controlled dormitory access, self-defense education, lighted pathways. *Student services:* health clinic, personal/psychological counseling.

Athletics Member NCAA. All Division III. *Intercollegiate sports:* basketball W, crew W, soccer W, softball W, volleyball W. *Intramural sports:* cross-country running W, swimming W, tennis W.

Standardized Tests *Required:* SAT I or ACT (for admission).

Costs (2004–05) *Comprehensive fee:* $30,645 includes full-time tuition ($21,100), mandatory fees ($175), and room and board ($9370). Part-time tuition: $615 per credit. *College room only:* $5645. Room and board charges vary according to housing facility. *Payment plan:* installment. *Waivers:* employees or children of employees.

Financial Aid Of all full-time matriculated undergraduates who enrolled in 2002, 468 applied for aid, 360 were judged to have need, 26 had their need fully met. 169 Federal Work-Study jobs (averaging $1007). 136 state and other part-time jobs (averaging $1198). In 2002, 25 non-need-based awards were made. *Average percent of need met:* 93%. *Average financial aid package:* $16,079. *Average need-based loan:* $4794. *Average need-based gift aid:* $9936. *Average non-need-based aid:* $7550. *Average indebtedness upon graduation:* $14,125.

Applying *Options:* common application, electronic application, deferred entrance. *Application fee:* $35. *Required:* essay or personal statement, high school transcript, 2 letters of recommendation. *Recommended:* interview. *Application deadlines:* 3/1 (freshmen), 6/1 (transfers). *Notification:* continuous (freshmen), continuous (transfers).

Admissions Contact Ms. Jane A. Raley, Director of Lesley College Admissions, Lesley University, 29 Everett Street, Cambridge, MA 02138-2790. *Phone:* 617-349-8800. *Toll-free phone:* 800-999-1959 Ext. 8800. *Fax:* 617-349-8810. *E-mail:* ugadm@mail.lesley.edu.

■ *See page 1862 for a narrative description.*

MASSACHUSETTS COLLEGE OF ART
Boston, Massachusetts

- **State-supported** comprehensive, founded 1873, part of Massachusetts Public Higher Education System
- **Calendar** semesters
- **Degrees** certificates, bachelor's, master's, and postbachelor's certificates
- **Urban** 5-acre campus
- **Endowment** $1.4 million
- **Coed,** 1,947 undergraduate students, 67% full-time, 65% women, 35% men
- **Very difficult** entrance level, 53% of applicants were admitted

Undergraduates 1,304 full-time, 643 part-time. Students come from 23 states and territories, 48 other countries, 27% are from out of state, 3% African American, 5% Asian American or Pacific Islander, 4% Hispanic American, 0.1% Native American, 4% international, 6% transferred in, 28% live on campus. *Retention:* 90% of 2002 full-time freshmen returned.

Freshmen *Admission:* 1,149 applied, 608 admitted, 239 enrolled. *Average high school GPA:* 3.17. *Test scores:* SAT verbal scores over 500: 80%; SAT math scores over 500: 71%; SAT verbal scores over 600: 31%; SAT math scores over 600: 21%; SAT verbal scores over 700: 5%; SAT math scores over 700: 2%.

Faculty *Total:* 185, 39% full-time, 31% with terminal degrees. *Student/faculty ratio:* 13:1.

Majors Architecture; art history, criticism and conservation; art teacher education; ceramic arts and ceramics; cinematography and film/video production; commercial and advertising art; fashion/apparel design; fiber, textile and weaving arts; fine/studio arts; industrial design; intermedia/multimedia; metal and jewelry arts; painting; photography; printmaking; sculpture.

Academic Programs *Special study options:* double majors, external degree program, independent study, internships, off-campus study, part-time degree program, student-designed majors, study abroad, summer session for credit.

Library Morton R. Godine Library with 231,586 titles, 757 serial subscriptions, 125,000 audiovisual materials.

Computers on Campus 250 computers available on campus for general student use. A campuswide network can be accessed from off campus. At least one staffed computer lab available.

Student Life *Housing options:* coed. *Activities and organizations:* drama/theater group, student-run newspaper, radio station, international students, Design Research Unit, Spectrum, film society, Event Works. *Campus security:* 24-hour emergency response devices and patrols, late-night transport/escort service, security lighting, self-defense workshops. *Student services:* health clinic, personal/psychological counseling, women's center.

Athletics *Intramural sports:* basketball M/W, ice hockey M, table tennis M/W, volleyball M/W.

Standardized Tests *Required:* SAT I or ACT (for admission).

Costs (2003–04) *Tuition:* state resident $1030 full-time; nonresident $11,040 full-time. Part-time tuition and fees vary according to class time and course load. *Required fees:* $3938 full-time. *Room and board:* $9800. Room and board charges vary according to housing facility. *Payment plan:* installment. *Waivers:* senior citizens and employees or children of employees.

Financial Aid Of all full-time matriculated undergraduates who enrolled in 2002, 820 applied for aid, 619 were judged to have need. 142 Federal Work-Study jobs (averaging $887). *Average financial aid package:* $8459. *Average need-based loan:* $4058. *Average need-based gift aid:* $3588. *Average indebtedness upon graduation:* $18,337.

Applying *Options:* early admission, early decision, deferred entrance. *Application fee:* $30. *Required:* essay or personal statement, high school transcript, minimum 2.9 GPA, portfolio. *Recommended:* letters of recommendation. *Application deadlines:* 2/15 (freshmen), 4/1 (transfers). *Early decision:* 12/1. *Notification:* 4/20 (freshmen).

Admissions Contact Ms. Kay Ransdell, Dean of Admissions, Massachusetts College of Art, 621 Huntington Avenue, Boston, MA 02115. *Phone:* 617-232-1555 Ext. 235. *Fax:* 617-879-7250. *E-mail:* admissions@massart.edu.

MASSACHUSETTS COLLEGE OF LIBERAL ARTS
North Adams, Massachusetts

- **State-supported** comprehensive, founded 1894, part of Massachusetts Public Higher Education System
- **Calendar** semesters
- **Degrees** bachelor's, master's, and postbachelor's certificates
- **Small-town** 80-acre campus
- **Endowment** $3.9 million
- **Coed,** 1,401 undergraduate students, 79% full-time, 59% women, 41% men
- **Moderately difficult** entrance level, 100% of applicants were admitted

North Adams State College changed its name to Massachusetts College of Liberal Arts to officially recognize the institution's liberal arts character. With this new designation, Massachusetts College joins the 2 other specialized institutions in the public sector (Massachusetts College of Art and Massachusetts Maritime Academy) in providing a distinctive educational experience.

Undergraduates 1,109 full-time, 292 part-time. 17% are from out of state, 5% African American, 2% Asian American or Pacific Islander, 3% Hispanic American, 0.3% Native American, 0.7% international, 9% transferred in, 50% live on campus. *Retention:* 71% of 2002 full-time freshmen returned.

Freshmen *Admission:* 284 applied, 284 admitted, 277 enrolled. *Average high school GPA:* 2.98. *Test scores:* SAT verbal scores over 500: 73%; SAT math scores over 500: 54%; ACT scores over 18: 100%; SAT verbal scores over 600: 19%; SAT math scores over 600: 13%; ACT scores over 24: 100%; SAT verbal scores over 700: 4%; SAT math scores over 700: 1%.

Faculty *Total:* 126, 61% full-time. *Student/faculty ratio:* 13:1.

Majors Accounting; adult and continuing education; anthropology; art; athletic training; biological and physical sciences; biology/biological sciences; broadcast journalism; business administration and management; chemistry; clinical laboratory science/medical technology; clinical/medical laboratory technology; computer and information sciences; computer science; creative writing; dramatic/theatre arts; economics; education; elementary education; English; environmental studies; finance; history; interdisciplinary studies; journalism; kindergarten/preschool education; literature; marketing/marketing management; mass communication/media; mathematics; middle school education; multi-/interdisciplinary studies related; music; philosophy; physics; pre-law studies; psychology; secondary education; social work; sociology; visual and performing arts.

Academic Programs *Special study options:* academic remediation for entering students, advanced placement credit, distance learning, double majors, honors programs, independent study, internships, off-campus study, part-time degree program, services for LD students, student-designed majors, study abroad, summer session for credit.

Library Freel Library with 541 serial subscriptions, 4,567 audiovisual materials, an OPAC, a Web page.

Computers on Campus A campuswide network can be accessed from student residence rooms and from off campus. Internet access, at least one staffed computer lab available.

Student Life *Housing:* on-campus residence required through junior year. *Options:* coed, disabled students. *Activities and organizations:* drama/theater group, student-run newspaper, radio and television station, choral group, Student Activities Council, weightlifting club, Non-Traditional Student Organization, outing club, lacrosse club, national fraternities, national sororities. *Campus security:* 24-hour emergency response devices and patrols, late-night transport/escort service, controlled dormitory access. *Student services:* health clinic, personal/psychological counseling, women's center.

Athletics Member NCAA. All Division III. *Intercollegiate sports:* baseball M, basketball M/W, cross-country running M/W, golf M, ice hockey M/W, soccer M/W, softball W, tennis W. *Intramural sports:* basketball M/W, cross-country running M/W, football M, golf M/W, ice hockey M, lacrosse M(c)/W(c), racquetball M/W, rugby M(c)/W(c), skiing (cross-country) M(c)/W(c), skiing (downhill) M(c)/W(c), soccer M/W, softball M/W, squash M/W, swimming M/W, tennis M/W, volleyball M/W, water polo M/W, weight lifting M(c)/W(c), wrestling M(c)/W(c).

Standardized Tests *Required:* SAT I (for admission).

Costs (2003–04) *Tuition:* state resident $1030 full-time; nonresident $9975 full-time. *Required fees:* $4367 full-time. *Room and board:* $5620; room only: $2946. Room and board charges vary according to board plan and housing facility. *Payment plan:* installment. *Waivers:* senior citizens and employees or children of employees.

Financial Aid Of all full-time matriculated undergraduates who enrolled in 2002, 929 applied for aid, 739 were judged to have need, 220 had their need fully met. In 2002, 161 non-need-based awards were made. *Average percent of need met:* 69%. *Average financial aid package:* $6322. *Average need-based loan:* $3213. *Average need-based gift aid:* $3812. *Average non-need-based aid:* $3648. *Average indebtedness upon graduation:* $15,537.

Applying *Options:* common application, electronic application, early action, deferred entrance. *Application fee:* $10. *Required:* essay or personal statement, high school transcript, minimum 3.0 GPA. *Required for some:* interview. *Recommended:* letters of recommendation, interview. *Application deadline:* rolling (freshmen), rolling (transfers). *Notification:* continuous (freshmen), 12/15 (early action), continuous (transfers).

Admissions Contact Ms. Denise Richardello, Dean of Enrollment Management, Massachusetts College of Liberal Arts, 375 Church Street, North Adams, MA 01247-4100. *Phone:* 413-662-5410 Ext. 5416. *Toll-free phone:* 800-292-6632. *Fax:* 413-662-5179. *E-mail:* admissions@mcla.mass.edu.

■ *See page 1954 for a narrative description.*

MASSACHUSETTS COLLEGE OF PHARMACY AND HEALTH SCIENCES
Boston, Massachusetts

- **Independent** university, founded 1823
- **Calendar** semesters
- **Degrees** associate, bachelor's, master's, doctoral, first professional, and first professional certificates
- **Urban** 2-acre campus
- **Endowment** $25.0 million
- **Coed,** 444 undergraduate students, 85% full-time, 81% women, 19% men
- **Moderately difficult** entrance level, 76% of applicants were admitted

Dedicated solely to health education, the College is a highly respected institution in Boston's world-renowned Longwood Medical and Academic Area. A new $30 million Academic Student Center is scheduled to open in August 2004. It will house a professional pharmacy lab, expanded library and technical center, as well as four floors of apartment-style residences for 230 students. MCPHS offers a 6-year program leading to a Doctor of Pharmacy (PharmD) degree, along with the following undergraduate degrees and programs: Bachelor of Science degrees in pharmaceutical sciences, pharmaceutical marketing and management, pharmacy/chemistry (dual degree), chemistry, health psychology, premedical and health studies, physician assistant studies (6-year master's program), radiologic sciences (accelerated 3-year program in nuclear medicine, radiography, or radiation therapy), and dental hygiene (Forsyth Program for Dental Hygiene).

Undergraduates 379 full-time, 65 part-time. Students come from 36 states and territories, 31% are from out of state, 5% African American, 17% Asian American or Pacific Islander, 2% Hispanic American, 0.2% Native American, 0.5% international, 80% transferred in, 15% live on campus. *Retention:* 88% of 2002 full-time freshmen returned.

Freshmen *Admission:* 647 applied, 490 admitted, 85 enrolled. *Average high school GPA:* 3.31. *Test scores:* SAT verbal scores over 500: 47%; SAT math scores over 500: 78%; ACT scores over 18: 89%; SAT verbal scores over 600: 10%; SAT math scores over 600: 24%; ACT scores over 24: 17%; SAT math scores over 700: 4%.

Faculty *Total:* 146, 90% full-time, 58% with terminal degrees. *Student/faculty ratio:* 14:1.

Majors Chemistry; dental hygiene; health/medical psychology; health professions related; medical radiologic technology; nuclear medical technology; pharmacy; pharmacy, pharmaceutical sciences, and administration related; premedical studies; radiologic technology/science.

Academic Programs *Special study options:* adult/continuing education programs, advanced placement credit, double majors, English as a second language, independent study, internships, off-campus study, part-time degree program, services for LD students, summer session for credit. *ROTC:* Army (c), Air Force (c).

Library Shepard Library with 40,000 titles, 700 serial subscriptions, 750 audiovisual materials, an OPAC, a Web page.

Computers on Campus 100 computers available on campus for general student use. A campuswide network can be accessed from student residence rooms and from off campus. Internet access, at least one staffed computer lab available.

Student Life *Housing options:* coed. Campus housing is university owned and leased by the school. Freshman campus housing is guaranteed. *Activities and organizations:* student-run newspaper, choral group, Academy of Students of Pharmacy, Kappa Psi Fraternity, Vietnamese Student Association, Student Government Association, Students of American Dental Hygienists, national fraternities, national sororities. *Campus security:* 24-hour emergency response devices and patrols, controlled dormitory access, electronically operated academic area

Massachusetts College of Pharmacy and Health Sciences (continued)
entrances, security guards at entrance. *Student services:* health clinic, personal/psychological counseling, women's center.

Athletics *Intramural sports:* badminton M/W, baseball M, basketball M/W, bowling M/W, cross-country running M/W, field hockey W, golf M/W, skiing (downhill) M/W, soccer M, squash M/W, table tennis M/W, ultimate Frisbee M/W, volleyball M/W, weight lifting M/W.

Standardized Tests *Required:* SAT I or ACT (for admission).

Costs (2003–04) *Comprehensive fee:* $29,570 includes full-time tuition ($18,800), mandatory fees ($600), and room and board ($10,170). Part-time tuition: $690 per credit. *Required fees:* $150 per term part-time. *College room only:* $7100. *Waivers:* employees or children of employees.

Financial Aid Of all full-time matriculated undergraduates who enrolled in 2003, 1,203 applied for aid, 1,157 were judged to have need, 37 had their need fully met. In 2003, 62 non-need-based awards were made. *Average percent of need met:* 37%. *Average financial aid package:* $10,179. *Average need-based loan:* $5137. *Average need-based gift aid:* $6325. *Average non-need-based aid:* $16,866. *Average indebtedness upon graduation:* $28,660.

Applying *Options:* common application, electronic application, early admission, early decision, deferred entrance. *Application fee:* $70. *Required:* essay or personal statement, high school transcript, 2 letters of recommendation. *Required for some:* 3 letters of recommendation, interview. *Recommended:* interview. *Application deadlines:* 2/1 (freshmen), 3/1 (transfers). *Early decision:* 11/1. *Notification:* continuous until 8/1 (freshmen), 12/1 (early decision), continuous until 8/1 (transfers).

Admissions Contact Mr. Jim Zarakas, Admissions Assistant, Massachusetts College of Pharmacy and Health Sciences, 179 Longwood Avenue, Boston, MA 02115. *Phone:* 617-732-2846. *Toll-free phone:* 617-732-2850 (in-state); 800-225-5506 (out-of-state). *Fax:* 617-732-2801. *E-mail:* admissions@mcp.edu.

■ See page 1956 for a narrative description.

MASSACHUSETTS INSTITUTE OF TECHNOLOGY

Cambridge, Massachusetts

- **Independent** university, founded 1861
- **Calendar** 4-1-4
- **Degrees** bachelor's, master's, and doctoral
- **Urban** 154-acre campus with easy access to Boston
- **Endowment** $5.1 billion
- **Coed,** 4,112 undergraduate students, 99% full-time, 42% women, 58% men
- **Most difficult** entrance level, 16% of applicants were admitted

Undergraduates 4,070 full-time, 42 part-time. Students come from 55 states and territories, 79 other countries, 91% are from out of state, 6% African American, 28% Asian American or Pacific Islander, 12% Hispanic American, 2% Native American, 8% international, 0.1% transferred in, 94% live on campus. *Retention:* 98% of 2002 full-time freshmen returned.

Freshmen *Admission:* 10,549 applied, 1,735 admitted, 1,019 enrolled. *Average high school GPA:* 3.90. *Test scores:* SAT verbal scores over 500: 99%; SAT math scores over 500: 100%; ACT scores over 18: 100%; SAT verbal scores over 600: 95%; SAT math scores over 600: 100%; ACT scores over 24: 99%; SAT verbal scores over 700: 63%; SAT math scores over 700: 89%; ACT scores over 30: 76%.

Faculty *Total:* 2,182, 71% full-time, 93% with terminal degrees. *Student/faculty ratio:* 6:1.

Majors Aerospace, aeronautical and astronautical engineering; anthropology; architecture; biology/biological sciences; business administration and management; business/commerce; chemical engineering; chemistry; city/urban, community and regional planning; civil engineering; cognitive psychology and psycholinguistics; computer science; creative writing; economics; electrical, electronics and communications engineering; English; environmental/environmental health engineering; foreign languages and literatures; history; liberal arts and sciences/liberal studies; linguistics; mass communication/media; materials engineering; mathematics; mathematics and computer science; mechanical engineering; music; nuclear engineering; ocean engineering; philosophy; physics; political science and government; science, technology and society.

Academic Programs *Special study options:* accelerated degree program, advanced placement credit, cooperative education, English as a second language, internships, off-campus study, student-designed majors, summer session for credit. *ROTC:* Army (b), Navy (b), Air Force (b).

Library MIT Libraries plus 10 others with 2.7 million titles, 22,358 serial subscriptions, 603,605 audiovisual materials, an OPAC, a Web page.

Computers on Campus 950 computers available on campus for general student use. A campuswide network can be accessed from student residence rooms and from off campus. At least one staffed computer lab available. Computer purchase or lease plan available.

Student Life *Housing:* on-campus residence required for freshman year. *Options:* coed, women-only, cooperative, disabled students. Campus housing is university owned and is provided by a third party. Freshman campus housing is guaranteed. *Activities and organizations:* drama/theater group, student-run newspaper, radio and television station, choral group, marching band, Tech Catholic Community, outing club, Society of Women Engineers, Hillel, South Asian American Students, national fraternities, national sororities. *Campus security:* 24-hour emergency response devices and patrols, late-night transport/escort service, controlled dormitory access. *Student services:* health clinic, personal/psychological counseling.

Athletics Member NCAA. All Division III except men's and women's crew (Division I), sailing (Division I), skiing (cross-country) (Division I), skiing (downhill) (Division I). *Intercollegiate sports:* baseball M, basketball M/W, cheerleading M(c)/W(c), crew M/W, cross-country running M/W, fencing M/W, field hockey W, football M, golf M, gymnastics M/W, ice hockey M(c)/W, lacrosse M/W, riflery M/W, sailing M/W, skiing (cross-country) M/W, skiing (downhill) M/W, soccer M/W, softball W, squash M, swimming M/W, tennis M/W, track and field M/W, volleyball M/W, water polo M, wrestling M. *Intramural sports:* archery M(c)/W(c), badminton M(c)/W(c), basketball M/W, bowling M/W, cheerleading M(c)/W(c), crew M(c)/W(c), cross-country running M/W, equestrian sports M(c)/W(c), fencing M(c)/W(c), field hockey M(c)/W(c), football M/W, ice hockey M/W, rock climbing M/W, rugby M(c)/W(c), soccer M/W, softball M/W, squash M/W, table tennis M/W, tennis M/W, ultimate Frisbee M(c)/W(c), volleyball M(c)/W(c), water polo W(c).

Standardized Tests *Required:* SAT I or ACT (for admission), SAT II: Subject Tests (for admission).

Costs (2003–04) *Comprehensive fee:* $38,310 includes full-time tuition ($29,400), mandatory fees ($200), and room and board ($8710). Part-time tuition: $463 per unit. Part-time tuition and fees vary according to course load. *College room only:* $4560. Room and board charges vary according to board plan and housing facility. *Payment plan:* installment. *Waivers:* employees or children of employees.

Financial Aid Of all full-time matriculated undergraduates who enrolled in 2002, 3,184 applied for aid, 2,940 were judged to have need, 2,940 had their need fully met. 879 Federal Work-Study jobs (averaging $1375). In 2002, 664 non-need-based awards were made. *Average percent of need met:* 100%. *Average financial aid package:* $22,010. *Average need-based loan:* $3359. *Average need-based gift aid:* $20,823. *Average non-need-based aid:* $6948. *Average indebtedness upon graduation:* $20,580. *Financial aid deadline:* 2/1.

Applying *Options:* electronic application, early action, deferred entrance. *Application fee:* $65. *Required:* essay or personal statement, high school transcript, 2 letters of recommendation. *Recommended:* interview. *Application deadlines:* 1/1 (freshmen), 3/15 (transfers). *Notification:* 3/25 (freshmen), 12/15 (early action), 5/15 (transfers).

Admissions Contact Ms. Marilee Jones, Dean of Admissions, Massachusetts Institute of Technology, Room 3-108, 77 Massachusetts Avenue, Cambridge, MA 02139-4307. *Phone:* 617-253-4791. *Fax:* 617-258-8304.

■ See page 1958 for a narrative description.

MASSACHUSETTS MARITIME ACADEMY

Buzzards Bay, Massachusetts

- **State-supported** 4-year, founded 1891, part of Massachusetts Public Higher Education System
- **Calendar** semesters plus sea term
- **Degrees** certificates, bachelor's, master's, and first professional certificates
- **Small-town** 55-acre campus with easy access to Boston
- **Endowment** $4.1 million
- **Coed, primarily men,** 927 undergraduate students, 97% full-time, 12% women, 88% men
- **Moderately difficult** entrance level, 60% of applicants were admitted

Undergraduates 895 full-time, 32 part-time. Students come from 24 states and territories, 4 other countries, 28% are from out of state. *Retention:* 79% of 2002 full-time freshmen returned.

Freshmen *Admission:* 808 applied, 485 admitted, 275 enrolled. *Average high school GPA:* 2.80. *Test scores:* SAT verbal scores over 500: 52%; SAT math scores over 500: 64%; SAT verbal scores over 600: 10%; SAT math scores over 600: 17%; SAT verbal scores over 700: 1%; SAT math scores over 700: 1%.

Faculty *Total:* 70, 84% full-time, 61% with terminal degrees. *Student/faculty ratio:* 15:1.

Majors Engineering; engineering technology; environmental/environmental health engineering; environmental studies; international business/trade/commerce; marine science/merchant marine officer; maritime science; naval architecture and marine engineering.

Academic Programs *Special study options:* academic remediation for entering students, adult/continuing education programs, advanced placement credit, cooperative education, double majors, internships, services for LD students, summer session for credit. *ROTC:* Army (c), Navy (b).

Library Hurley Library with 42,000 titles, 505 serial subscriptions, a Web page.

Computers on Campus 70 computers available on campus for general student use. A campuswide network can be accessed from student residence rooms. Internet access, at least one staffed computer lab available.

Student Life *Housing:* on-campus residence required through senior year. *Options:* coed. *Activities and organizations:* drama/theater group, student-run newspaper, marching band, Club Hockey, water sports, sailing/cruising, rugby club, scuba club. *Campus security:* 24-hour emergency response devices and patrols, late-night transport/escort service. *Student services:* health clinic, personal/psychological counseling.

Athletics Member NCAA. All Division III. *Intercollegiate sports:* baseball M, crew M/W, cross-country running M/W, football M, lacrosse M, riflery M/W, sailing M/W, soccer M, softball W, volleyball W. *Intramural sports:* basketball M/W, crew M/W, cross-country running M/W, football M, golf M/W, ice hockey M, racquetball M/W, riflery M/W, rugby M, sailing M/W, soccer M/W, softball M/W, swimming M/W, table tennis M/W, tennis M/W, volleyball M/W, water polo M/W, weight lifting M(c)/W(c), wrestling M.

Standardized Tests *Required:* SAT I or ACT (for admission).

Costs (2004–05) *Tuition:* state resident $1030 full-time; nonresident $11,510 full-time. *Required fees:* $3633 full-time. *Room and board:* $5809; room only: $2884.

Financial Aid Of all full-time matriculated undergraduates who enrolled in 2003, 625 applied for aid, 383 were judged to have need, 169 had their need fully met. 223 Federal Work-Study jobs (averaging $1500). In 2003, 142 non-need-based awards were made. *Average percent of need met:* 27%. *Average financial aid package:* $7007. *Average need-based loan:* $3917. *Average need-based gift aid:* $1967. *Average non-need-based aid:* $1737. *Average indebtedness upon graduation:* $12,125.

Applying *Options:* early decision, deferred entrance. *Application fee:* $50. *Required:* essay or personal statement, high school transcript, 2 letters of recommendation, interview, physical examination. *Application deadline:* rolling (freshmen), rolling (transfers). *Early decision:* 11/1. *Notification:* continuous (freshmen), 12/15 (early decision), continuous (transfers).

Admissions Contact Roy Fulgueras, Director of Admissions, Massachusetts Maritime Academy, 101 Academy Drive, Buzzards Bay, MA 02532. *Phone:* 508-830-5031. *Toll-free phone:* 800-544-3411. *Fax:* 508-830-5077. *E-mail:* admissions@maritime.edu.

■ *See page 1960 for a narrative description.*

MERRIMACK COLLEGE
North Andover, Massachusetts

- **Independent Roman Catholic** comprehensive, founded 1947
- **Calendar** semesters
- **Degrees** certificates, associate, bachelor's, and master's
- **Suburban** 220-acre campus with easy access to Boston
- **Endowment** $24.8 million
- **Coed,** 2,389 undergraduate students, 86% full-time, 55% women, 45% men
- **Moderately difficult** entrance level, 60% of applicants were admitted

Undergraduates 2,046 full-time, 343 part-time. Students come from 36 states and territories, 18 other countries, 28% are from out of state, 0.8% African American, 1% Asian American or Pacific Islander, 1% Hispanic American, 0.1% Native American, 2% international, 4% transferred in, 73% live on campus. *Retention:* 81% of 2002 full-time freshmen returned.

Freshmen *Admission:* 3,353 applied, 2,000 admitted, 590 enrolled. *Average high school GPA:* 3.30. *Test scores:* SAT verbal scores over 500: 80%; SAT math scores over 500: 90%; ACT scores over 18: 99%; SAT verbal scores over 600: 16%; SAT math scores over 600: 21%; ACT scores over 24: 28%; SAT math scores over 700: 2%.

Faculty *Total:* 240, 59% full-time, 81% with terminal degrees. *Student/faculty ratio:* 13:1.

Majors Accounting; athletic training; biochemistry; biology/biological sciences; business administration and management; business/managerial economics; chemistry; civil engineering; communication/speech communication and rhetoric; computer engineering; computer science; economics; electrical, electronic and communications engineering technology; electrical, electronics and communications engineering; elementary education; engineering physics; engineering science; English; environmental studies; finance; fine/studio arts; French; health science; history; human services; interdisciplinary studies; international business/trade/commerce; legal assistant/paralegal; liberal arts and sciences/liberal studies; marketing/marketing management; mathematics; middle school education; modern languages; philosophy; physical therapy; physics; political science and government; pre-dentistry studies; pre-law studies; pre-medical studies; psychology; religious studies; secondary education; sociology; Spanish.

Academic Programs *Special study options:* academic remediation for entering students, adult/continuing education programs, advanced placement credit, cooperative education, double majors, English as a second language, honors programs, independent study, internships, off-campus study, part-time degree program, services for LD students, student-designed majors, study abroad, summer session for credit. *ROTC:* Air Force (c).

Library McQuade Library with 118,083 titles, 1,069 serial subscriptions, 1,970 audiovisual materials, an OPAC, a Web page.

Computers on Campus 175 computers available on campus for general student use. A campuswide network can be accessed from student residence rooms. Internet access, at least one staffed computer lab available.

Student Life *Housing options:* coed. Campus housing is university owned. Freshman applicants given priority for college housing. *Activities and organizations:* drama/theater group, student-run newspaper, television station, choral group, Merrimaction Community Outreach, MORE Retreat Program, Merrimack Marketing Association, Orientation Committee Coordinators, Developing Leaders Program, national fraternities, national sororities. *Campus security:* 24-hour emergency response devices and patrols, student patrols, late-night transport/escort service, controlled dormitory access. *Student services:* health clinic, personal/psychological counseling.

Athletics Member NCAA. All Division II except ice hockey (Division I). *Intercollegiate sports:* baseball M, basketball M(s)/W(s), cross-country running M/W(s), field hockey W(s), football M, ice hockey M(s), lacrosse M/W(s), soccer M/W(s), softball W(s), tennis M/W(s), track and field M(c)/W(c), volleyball M(c)/W(s). *Intramural sports:* basketball M/W, ice hockey M/W, lacrosse M/W, racquetball M/W, skiing (downhill) M(c)/W(c), softball M/W, tennis M/W, volleyball M/W.

Standardized Tests *Required:* SAT I or ACT (for admission).

Costs (2003–04) *Comprehensive fee:* $29,625 includes full-time tuition ($20,625), mandatory fees ($250), and room and board ($8750). Part-time tuition: $760 per credit. Part-time tuition and fees vary according to class time and course load. *Required fees:* $35 per term part-time. *College room only:* $4900. Room and board charges vary according to board plan and housing facility. *Payment plans:* installment, deferred payment. *Waivers:* senior citizens and employees or children of employees.

Financial Aid Of all full-time matriculated undergraduates who enrolled in 2003, 1,650 applied for aid, 1,550 were judged to have need, 1,100 had their need fully met. 175 Federal Work-Study jobs (averaging $1200). 350 state and other part-time jobs (averaging $2000). In 2003, 55 non-need-based awards were made. *Average percent of need met:* 70%. *Average financial aid package:* $17,000. *Average need-based loan:* $7000. *Average need-based gift aid:* $9000. *Average non-need-based aid:* $1657. *Average indebtedness upon graduation:* $21,125. *Financial aid deadline:* 2/1.

Applying *Options:* common application, electronic application, early admission, early action, deferred entrance. *Application fee:* $50. *Required:* essay or personal statement, high school transcript. *Required for some:* interview. *Recommended:* minimum 2.8 GPA, 1 letter of recommendation, interview. *Application deadline:* 2/1 (freshmen). *Notification:* continuous until 3/25 (freshmen), 12/15 (early action), continuous (transfers).

Admissions Contact Dr. John Craig, Director of Admissions, Merrimack College, Austin Hall, A22, North Andover, MA 01845. *Phone:* 978-837-5000 Ext. 4476. *Fax:* 978-837-5133. *E-mail:* admission@merrimack.edu.

■ *See page 1982 for a narrative description.*

MONTSERRAT COLLEGE OF ART
Beverly, Massachusetts

- **Independent** 4-year, founded 1970
- **Calendar** semesters
- **Degrees** diplomas, bachelor's, and postbachelor's certificates
- **Suburban** 10-acre campus with easy access to Boston
- **Endowment** $580,622
- **Coed,** 386 undergraduate students, 94% full-time, 60% women, 40% men
- **Moderately difficult** entrance level, 83% of applicants were admitted

Undergraduates 361 full-time, 25 part-time. Students come from 20 states and territories, 56% are from out of state, 0.8% African American, 3% Asian American or Pacific Islander, 1% Hispanic American, 1% international, 7% transferred in, 63% live on campus. *Retention:* 62% of 2002 full-time freshmen returned.

Freshmen *Admission:* 389 applied, 323 admitted, 93 enrolled. *Average high school GPA:* 2.70. *Test scores:* SAT verbal scores over 500: 62%; SAT math scores over 500: 46%; SAT verbal scores over 600: 24%; SAT math scores over 600: 12%; SAT verbal scores over 700: 3%; SAT math scores over 700: 1%.

Montserrat College of Art (continued)

Faculty *Total:* 65, 38% full-time, 75% with terminal degrees. *Student/faculty ratio:* 11:1.

Majors Art teacher education; drawing; fine arts related; fine/studio arts; graphic design; illustration; painting; photography; printmaking; sculpture.

Academic Programs *Special study options:* adult/continuing education programs, advanced placement credit, double majors, English as a second language, independent study, internships, off-campus study, part-time degree program, services for LD students, student-designed majors, study abroad. *ROTC:* Air Force (c).

Library Paul Scott Library plus 1 other with 12,134 titles, 78 serial subscriptions, 50,031 audiovisual materials, an OPAC.

Computers on Campus 98 computers available on campus for general student use. A campuswide network can be accessed. Internet access, at least one staffed computer lab available.

Student Life *Housing options:* coed. Campus housing is university owned and leased by the school. Freshman campus housing is guaranteed. *Activities and organizations:* student-run radio station, Student Council, Language Partners, peer leaders, Fashion Show Committee, coed intramural sports. *Campus security:* late-night transport/escort service. *Student services:* personal/psychological counseling.

Athletics *Intramural sports:* basketball M/W.

Standardized Tests *Required for some:* SAT I or ACT (for admission).

Costs (2003–04) *Tuition:* $17,200 full-time, $717 per credit part-time. Full-time tuition and fees vary according to course load. Part-time tuition and fees vary according to course load. *Required fees:* $640 full-time, $21 per credit part-time. *Room only:* $4950. Room and board charges vary according to housing facility. *Payment plan:* installment. *Waivers:* employees or children of employees.

Financial Aid Of all full-time matriculated undergraduates who enrolled in 2003, 301 applied for aid, 286 were judged to have need, 22 had their need fully met. 33 Federal Work-Study jobs (averaging $1000). In 2003, 38 non-need-based awards were made. *Average percent of need met:* 47%. *Average financial aid package:* $8780. *Average need-based loan:* $3762. *Average need-based gift aid:* $5862. *Average non-need-based aid:* $6864. *Average indebtedness upon graduation:* $24,007.

Applying *Options:* deferred entrance. *Application fee:* $40. *Required:* essay or personal statement, high school transcript, minimum 2.25 GPA, 2 letters of recommendation, portfolio. *Recommended:* minimum 2.5 GPA, interview. *Application deadlines:* 8/1 (freshmen), 8/1 (transfers). *Notification:* continuous until 8/20 (freshmen), continuous until 8/20 (transfers).

Admissions Contact Mr. Stephen M. Negron, Dean of Enrollment Management and Admissions, Montserrat College of Art, 23 Essex Street, PO Box 26, Beverly, MA 01915. *Phone:* 978-921-4242 Ext. 1153. *Toll-free phone:* 800-836-0487. *Fax:* 978-921-4241. *E-mail:* admiss@montserrat.edu.

■ *See page 2024 for a narrative description.*

MOUNT HOLYOKE COLLEGE
South Hadley, Massachusetts

- **Independent** comprehensive, founded 1837
- **Calendar** 4-1-4
- **Degrees** bachelor's, master's, and postbachelor's certificates
- **Small-town** 800-acre campus with easy access to Springfield
- **Endowment** $375.7 million
- **Women only,** 2,148 undergraduate students, 97% full-time
- **Very difficult** entrance level, 52% of applicants were admitted

Undergraduates 2,089 full-time, 59 part-time. Students come from 48 states and territories, 79 other countries, 64% are from out of state, 4% African American, 10% Asian American or Pacific Islander, 4% Hispanic American, 0.6% Native American, 15% international, 2% transferred in, 95% live on campus. *Retention:* 92% of 2002 full-time freshmen returned.

Freshmen *Admission:* 508 enrolled. *Average high school GPA:* 3.65. *Test scores:* SAT verbal scores over 500: 99%; SAT math scores over 500: 99%; ACT scores over 18: 100%; SAT verbal scores over 600: 86%; SAT math scores over 600: 74%; ACT scores over 24: 96%; SAT verbal scores over 700: 28%; SAT math scores over 700: 14%; ACT scores over 30: 33%.

Faculty *Total:* 254, 83% full-time, 88% with terminal degrees. *Student/faculty ratio:* 10:1.

Majors African-American/Black studies; American studies; anthropology; art history, criticism and conservation; Asian studies; astronomy; biochemistry; biology/biological sciences; chemistry; classics and languages, literatures and linguistics; computer science; dance; dramatic/theatre arts; economics; education; English; environmental studies; European studies; film/cinema studies; fine/studio arts; French; geography; geology/earth science; German; history; interdisciplinary studies; international relations and affairs; Italian; Jewish/Judaic studies; Latin; Latin American studies; mathematics; medieval and Renaissance studies; modern Greek; music; philosophy; physics; political science and government; psychology; religious studies; Romance languages; Russian; Russian studies; social sciences; sociology; Spanish; statistics; women's studies.

Academic Programs *Special study options:* adult/continuing education programs, advanced placement credit, double majors, honors programs, independent study, internships, off-campus study, part-time degree program, services for LD students, student-designed majors, study abroad. *ROTC:* Army (c), Air Force (c). *Unusual degree programs:* 3-2 engineering with Dartmouth College, California Institute of Technology, University of Massachusetts; nursing with Johns Hopkins University; public health with University of Massachusetts, Latin American studies with Georgetown University.

Library Williston Memorial Library plus 7 others with 670,304 titles, 1,537 serial subscriptions, 3,443 audiovisual materials, an OPAC, a Web page.

Computers on Campus 500 computers available on campus for general student use. A campuswide network can be accessed from student residence rooms and from off campus that provide access to personal web pages. Internet access, at least one staffed computer lab available.

Student Life *Housing:* on-campus residence required through senior year. *Options:* women-only, disabled students. Campus housing is university owned. Freshman campus housing is guaranteed. *Activities and organizations:* drama/theater group, student-run newspaper, radio station, choral group, Student Government Association, WMHC (radio station), Mount Holyoke News, cultural organizations, a cappella groups. *Campus security:* 24-hour emergency response devices and patrols, student patrols, late-night transport/escort service, controlled dormitory access, police officers on-campus. *Student services:* health clinic, personal/psychological counseling, women's center.

Athletics Member NCAA. All Division III. *Intercollegiate sports:* basketball W, cheerleading M(s)/W(s), crew W, cross-country running W, equestrian sports W, field hockey W, golf W, lacrosse W, soccer W, softball W, squash W, swimming W, tennis W, track and field W, ultimate Frisbee M(c)/W(c), volleyball W. *Intramural sports:* badminton W, basketball W, equestrian sports W, fencing W(c), ice hockey W(c), rock climbing W(c), rugby W(c), soccer W, tennis W, volleyball W, water polo W(c).

Standardized Tests *Required for some:* SAT II: Subject Tests (for admission), SAT II: Writing Test (for admission).

Costs (2003–04) *Comprehensive fee:* $37,918 includes full-time tuition ($29,170), mandatory fees ($168), and room and board ($8580). Part-time tuition: $860 per credit hour. *Required fees:* $168 per year part-time. *College room only:* $4200. Room and board charges vary according to board plan and housing facility. *Payment plans:* tuition prepayment, installment. *Waivers:* employees or children of employees.

Financial Aid Of all full-time matriculated undergraduates who enrolled in 2003, 1,695 applied for aid, 1,464 were judged to have need, 1,464 had their need fully met. 825 Federal Work-Study jobs (averaging $1650). 475 state and other part-time jobs (averaging $1600). In 2003, 100 non-need-based awards were made. *Average percent of need met:* 100%. *Average financial aid package:* $25,469. *Average need-based loan:* $4867. *Average need-based gift aid:* $20,062. *Average non-need-based aid:* $10,950. *Average indebtedness upon graduation:* $17,000. *Financial aid deadline:* 2/1.

Applying *Options:* common application, electronic application, early admission, early decision, deferred entrance. *Application fee:* $55. *Required:* essay or personal statement, high school transcript, 2 letters of recommendation. *Recommended:* interview. *Application deadlines:* 1/15 (freshmen), 5/15 (transfers). *Early decision:* 11/15 (for plan 1), 1/1 (for plan 2). *Notification:* 4/1 (freshmen), 1/1 (early decision plan 1), 2/1 (early decision plan 2), 6/15 (transfers).

Admissions Contact Ms. Diane Anci, Dean of Admission, Mount Holyoke College, 50 College Street, South Hadley, MA 01075. *Phone:* 413-538-2023. *Fax:* 413-538-2409. *E-mail:* admission@mtholyoke.edu.

■ *See page 2038 for a narrative description.*

MOUNT IDA COLLEGE
Newton Center, Massachusetts

- **Independent** 4-year, founded 1899
- **Calendar** semesters
- **Degrees** certificates, associate, and bachelor's
- **Suburban** 72-acre campus with easy access to Boston
- **Endowment** $9.4 million
- **Coed,** 1,076 undergraduate students
- **Moderately difficult** entrance level, 79% of applicants were admitted

Undergraduates Students come from 23 states and territories, 33 other countries, 38% live on campus.

Freshmen *Admission:* 2,203 applied, 1,736 admitted. *Average high school GPA:* 2.55. *Test scores:* SAT verbal scores over 500: 24%; SAT math scores over

500: 16%; SAT verbal scores over 600: 5%; SAT math scores over 600: 2%; SAT verbal scores over 700: 2%; SAT math scores over 700: 1%.

Faculty *Total:* 97, 58% full-time. *Student/faculty ratio:* 13:1.

Majors American studies; animal sciences; business administration and management; child development; commercial and advertising art; consumer merchandising/retailing management; criminal justice/law enforcement administration; dental hygiene; developmental and child psychology; equestrian studies; fashion/apparel design; fashion merchandising; funeral service and mortuary science; horse husbandry/equine science and management; hotel/motel administration; human services; interior design; kindergarten/preschool education; liberal arts and sciences/liberal studies; marketing/marketing management; psychology; social work; teacher assistant/aide; veterinary technology.

Academic Programs *Special study options:* academic remediation for entering students, accelerated degree program, adult/continuing education programs, cooperative education, English as a second language, freshman honors college, honors programs, internships, part-time degree program, services for LD students, student-designed majors, study abroad.

Library Wadsworth Learning Resource Center plus 1 other with 100,695 titles, 533 serial subscriptions, a Web page.

Computers on Campus 101 computers available on campus for general student use. A campuswide network can be accessed. Internet access, at least one staffed computer lab available.

Student Life *Housing options:* coed, men-only, women-only. *Activities and organizations:* drama/theater group, student-run newspaper, radio and television station, choral group, Leadership Students, student government, Phi Theta Kappa, Residence Council, Alpha Chi. *Campus security:* 24-hour emergency response devices and patrols, student patrols, late-night transport/escort service, controlled residence hall entrances, secured campus entrance. *Student services:* health clinic, personal/psychological counseling.

Athletics Member NCAA. except men's and women's basketball (Division III), men's and women's cross-country running (Division III), football (Division III), lacrosse (Division III), soccer (Division III), softball (Division III), men's and women's volleyball (Division III) *Intercollegiate sports:* baseball M, basketball M/W, cross-country running M/W, equestrian sports M/W, football M, lacrosse M, soccer M/W, softball W, volleyball M/W. *Intramural sports:* basketball M/W, football W, golf M/W, lacrosse W, skiing (downhill) M/W, soccer M/W, softball M/W, tennis M/W, volleyball M/W, weight lifting M/W.

Standardized Tests *Required:* SAT I or ACT (for admission).

Costs (2004–05) *Comprehensive fee:* $26,475 includes full-time tuition ($17,075) and room and board ($9400).

Financial Aid Of all full-time matriculated undergraduates who enrolled in 2002, 892 applied for aid, 846 were judged to have need, 45 had their need fully met. 320 Federal Work-Study jobs (averaging $1775). 17 state and other part-time jobs (averaging $1425). In 2002, 104 non-need-based awards were made. *Average percent of need met:* 51%. *Average financial aid package:* $11,023. *Average need-based loan:* $3399. *Average need-based gift aid:* $7458. *Average non-need-based aid:* $6286. *Average indebtedness upon graduation:* $26,346.

Applying *Options:* common application, electronic application, early action, deferred entrance. *Application fee:* $35. *Required:* high school transcript, 1 letter of recommendation. *Recommended:* essay or personal statement, minimum 2.0 GPA, interview. *Application deadline:* rolling (freshmen), rolling (transfers). *Notification:* continuous (freshmen), continuous (transfers).

Admissions Contact Ms. Nancy Lemelman, Director of Admissions, Mount Ida College, 777 Dedham Street, Newton, MA 02459. *Phone:* 617-928-4500 Ext. 4508. *E-mail:* admissions@mountida.edu.

■ See page 2040 for a narrative description.

NEWBURY COLLEGE
Brookline, Massachusetts

- **Independent** 4-year, founded 1962
- **Calendar** semesters
- **Degrees** certificates, associate, and bachelor's
- **Suburban** 10-acre campus with easy access to Boston
- **Endowment** $4.5 million
- **Coed,** 1,167 undergraduate students, 62% full-time, 62% women, 38% men
- **Minimally difficult** entrance level, 88% of applicants were admitted

Just minutes from Boston, Newbury College features an ideal collegiate setting in a safe, elite neighborhood with easy access to public transportation. Skilled and experienced faculty members, small classes, personalized attention, and hands-on training opportunities make Newbury graduates among the most employable. Students may pursue bachelor's and associate degrees.

Undergraduates 718 full-time, 449 part-time. Students come from 17 states and territories, 34 other countries, 18% are from out of state, 16% African American, 6% Asian American or Pacific Islander, 6% Hispanic American, 9% international, 4% transferred in, 35% live on campus. *Retention:* 80% of 2002 full-time freshmen returned.

Freshmen *Admission:* 964 applied, 850 admitted, 356 enrolled. *Average high school GPA:* 2.72. *Test scores:* SAT verbal scores over 500: 32%; SAT math scores over 500: 24%; ACT scores over 18: 75%; SAT verbal scores over 600: 7%; SAT math scores over 600: 6%; ACT scores over 24: 25%.

Faculty *Total:* 89, 39% full-time. *Student/faculty ratio:* 15:1.

Majors Accounting; business administration and management; commercial and advertising art; computer programming; computer science; consumer merchandising/retailing management; criminal justice/law enforcement administration; culinary arts; culinary arts related; fashion merchandising; finance; health/health care administration; hotel/motel administration; humanities; human resources management; interior design; international business/trade/commerce; legal assistant/paralegal; legal studies; marketing/marketing management; marketing research; mass communication/media; pre-law studies; psychology; radio and television; social sciences; sociology; special products marketing; tourism and travel services management.

Academic Programs *Special study options:* academic remediation for entering students, accelerated degree program, adult/continuing education programs, advanced placement credit, cooperative education, double majors, English as a second language, freshman honors college, honors programs, independent study, internships, off-campus study, part-time degree program, services for LD students, study abroad, summer session for credit.

Library Newbury College Library plus 1 other with 32,459 titles, 1,109 serial subscriptions, an OPAC.

Computers on Campus 75 computers available on campus for general student use. A campuswide network can be accessed from off campus. At least one staffed computer lab available.

Student Life *Housing options:* coed, women-only. *Activities and organizations:* student-run newspaper, radio and television station, student government, Newbury College Programming Board, Inn Keepers Club, Speech and Debate Team, International Student Organization. *Campus security:* 24-hour emergency response devices and patrols, late-night transport/escort service, controlled dormitory access. *Student services:* personal/psychological counseling.

Athletics Member NCAA. All Division III. *Intercollegiate sports:* basketball M/W, cross-country running M/W, golf M/W, soccer M, softball W, tennis M/W, volleyball M/W. *Intramural sports:* basketball M/W, football M/W, softball W, swimming M/W, volleyball M/W, weight lifting M/W.

Standardized Tests *Required for some:* SAT I or ACT (for admission). *Recommended:* SAT I or ACT (for admission).

Costs (2004–05) *One-time required fee:* $300. *Comprehensive fee:* $23,700 includes full-time tuition ($15,325), mandatory fees ($800), and room and board ($7575). Full-time tuition and fees vary according to class time, course load, and program. Part-time tuition and fees vary according to class time, course load, and program. *Room and board:* Room and board charges vary according to board plan and housing facility. *Payment plan:* installment. *Waivers:* employees or children of employees.

Financial Aid Of all full-time matriculated undergraduates who enrolled in 2002, 528 applied for aid, 459 were judged to have need. 147 Federal Work-Study jobs (averaging $2000). In 2002, 177 non-need-based awards were made. *Average percent of need met:* 76%. *Average financial aid package:* $3500. *Average need-based loan:* $3500. *Average non-need-based aid:* $7295.

Applying *Options:* electronic application, early admission, early action, deferred entrance. *Application fee:* $50. *Required:* essay or personal statement, high school transcript, letters of recommendation. *Recommended:* minimum 2.0 GPA, interview. *Application deadline:* rolling (freshmen), rolling (transfers). *Notification:* continuous until 8/1 (freshmen), 1/1 (early action), continuous until 9/1 (transfers).

Admissions Contact Ms. Jacqueline Giordano, Vice President of Enrollment, Newbury College, 129 Fisher Avenue, Brookline, MA 02445-5796. *Phone:* 617-730-7007. *Toll-free phone:* 800-NEWBURY. *Fax:* 617-731-9618. *E-mail:* info@newbury.edu.

■ See page 2066 for a narrative description.

NEW ENGLAND COLLEGE OF FINANCE
Boston, Massachusetts

- **Independent** primarily 2-year, founded 1909
- **Calendar** semesters
- **Degrees** certificates, associate, and bachelor's (offers primarily part-time evening degree programs; bachelor's degree offered jointly with Bentley College, Assumption College, Providence College, University of Hartford, and University System College for Lifelong Learning)
- **Urban** campus

New England College of Finance (continued)
- **Coed, primarily women**
- **Noncompetitive** entrance level

Student Life *Campus security:* reception desk in lobby of building.
Applying *Options:* common application. *Required:* essay or personal statement, high school transcript, 1 letter of recommendation, interview.
Admissions Contact Ms. Diane Monaghan, Vice President for Academic Affairs, New England College of Finance, 1 Lincoln Plaza, Boston, MA 02111-2645. *Phone:* 617-951-2350 Ext. 227. *Toll-free phone:* 888-696-NECF. *Fax:* 617-951-2533.

NEW ENGLAND CONSERVATORY OF MUSIC
Boston, Massachusetts

- **Independent** comprehensive, founded 1867
- **Calendar** semesters
- **Degrees** certificates, diplomas, bachelor's, master's, doctoral, and postbachelor's certificates
- **Urban** 2-acre campus
- **Endowment** $47.2 million
- **Coed,** 392 undergraduate students, 96% full-time, 47% women, 53% men
- **Very difficult** entrance level, 38% of applicants were admitted

Undergraduates 375 full-time, 17 part-time. Students come from 46 states and territories, 39 other countries, 85% are from out of state, 3% African American, 7% Asian American or Pacific Islander, 5% Hispanic American, 16% international, 5% transferred in, 40% live on campus. *Retention:* 96% of 2002 full-time freshmen returned.
Freshmen *Admission:* 838 applied, 316 admitted, 107 enrolled. *Average high school GPA:* 3.40.
Faculty *Total:* 208, 40% full-time. *Student/faculty ratio:* 3:1.
Majors Jazz/jazz studies; music history, literature, and theory; music pedagogy; music theory and composition; piano and organ; violin, viola, guitar and other stringed instruments; voice and opera; wind/percussion instruments.
Academic Programs *Special study options:* adult/continuing education programs, advanced placement credit, English as a second language, independent study, internships, off-campus study, part-time degree program, services for LD students, study abroad, summer session for credit.
Library Spaulding Library plus 1 other with 78,853 titles, 275 serial subscriptions, 46,384 audiovisual materials, an OPAC, a Web page.
Computers on Campus 48 computers available on campus for general student use. A campuswide network can be accessed. Internet access, at least one staffed computer lab available.
Student Life *Housing:* on-campus residence required for freshman year. *Options:* coed. Campus housing is university owned. Freshman campus housing is guaranteed. *Activities and organizations:* NEC Student Association, Chinese Student Association, Christian Fellowship, vegetarian club, soccer club. *Campus security:* 24-hour patrols, late-night transport/escort service. *Student services:* health clinic, personal/psychological counseling.
Standardized Tests *Required:* SAT I or ACT (for admission).
Costs (2003–04) *Comprehensive fee:* $35,000 includes full-time tuition ($24,500), mandatory fees ($250), and room and board ($10,250). *Payment plans:* installment, deferred payment. *Waivers:* employees or children of employees.
Financial Aid Of all full-time matriculated undergraduates who enrolled in 2003, 314 applied for aid, 311 were judged to have need, 25 had their need fully met. 299 Federal Work-Study jobs (averaging $2482). In 2003, 3 non-need-based awards were made. *Average percent of need met:* 62%. *Average financial aid package:* $16,438. *Average need-based loan:* $4316. *Average need-based gift aid:* $12,301. *Average non-need-based aid:* $6131. *Average indebtedness upon graduation:* $16,911.
Applying *Options:* deferred entrance. *Application fee:* $100. *Required:* essay or personal statement, high school transcript, minimum 2.75 GPA, 2 letters of recommendation, audition. *Application deadlines:* 12/1 (freshmen), 12/3 (transfers). *Notification:* 4/1 (freshmen), 4/1 (transfers).
Admissions Contact Mr. Tom Novak, Dean of Admissions, New England Conservatory of Music, 290 Huntington Avenue, Boston, MA 02115-5000. *Phone:* 617-585-1101. *Fax:* 617-585-1115. *E-mail:* admissions@newenglandconservatory.edu.

THE NEW ENGLAND INSTITUTE OF ART
Brookline, Massachusetts

- **Proprietary** 4-year, part of Education Management Corporation
- **Calendar** semesters
- **Degrees** associate and bachelor's
- **Urban** campus with easy access to Boston
- **Coed,** 1,045 undergraduate students
- **Minimally difficult** entrance level, 57% of applicants were admitted

Undergraduates Students come from 25 states and territories, 56 other countries, 14% are from out of state, 10% African American, 2% Asian American or Pacific Islander, 6% Hispanic American, 0.5% Native American.
Freshmen *Admission:* 1,411 applied, 800 admitted. *Average high school GPA:* 2.30.
Faculty *Total:* 89, 34% full-time, 12% with terminal degrees. *Student/faculty ratio:* 18:1.
Majors animation, interactive technology, video graphics and special effects; commercial and advertising art; communication/speech communication and rhetoric; computer graphics; design and applied arts related; digital communication and media/multimedia; graphic design; interior design; intermedia/multimedia; music management and merchandising; radio and television broadcasting technology; web/multimedia management and webmaster; web page, digital/multimedia and information resources design.
Academic Programs *Special study options:* academic remediation for entering students, adult/continuing education programs, distance learning, independent study, internships, services for LD students.
Library The New England Institute of Art Library with 6,500 titles, 140 serial subscriptions, 660 audiovisual materials, an OPAC.
Computers on Campus 250 computers available on campus for general student use. A campuswide network can be accessed. Internet access, at least one staffed computer lab available. Computer purchase or lease plan available.
Student Life *Housing options:* Campus housing is leased by the school. *Activities and organizations:* student-run newspaper, radio and television station, Graphic Design Club, Naked Truth, Naked Eye Video, Naked Ear Records, Web Raisers. *Campus security:* late-night transport/escort service, controlled dormitory access. *Student services:* personal/psychological counseling.
Costs (2004–05) *Comprehensive fee:* $26,797 includes full-time tuition ($16,947), mandatory fees ($250), and room and board ($9600). Full-time tuition and fees vary according to class time, degree level, and program. *College room only:* $7200. *Payment plans:* tuition prepayment, installment.
Applying *Options:* common application, electronic application. *Application fee:* $50. *Required:* essay or personal statement, high school transcript, minimum X GPA, interview. *Application deadline:* rolling (freshmen), rolling (transfers). *Notification:* continuous (freshmen), continuous (transfers).
Admissions Contact The New England Institute of Art, 10 Brookline Place West, Brookline, MA 02445. *Phone:* 617-582-4404. *Toll-free phone:* 800-903=4425. *Fax:* 617-582-4500. *E-mail:* aine_admissions@aii.edu.

■ See page 2074 for a narrative description.

NICHOLS COLLEGE
Dudley, Massachusetts

- **Independent** comprehensive, founded 1815
- **Calendar** semesters
- **Degrees** associate, bachelor's, and master's
- **Rural** 210-acre campus with easy access to Boston
- **Coed,** 1,327 undergraduate students, 62% full-time, 41% women, 59% men
- **Moderately difficult** entrance level, 83% of applicants were admitted

Undergraduates 825 full-time, 502 part-time. Students come from 20 states and territories, 3 other countries, 10% are from out of state, 4% transferred in, 80% live on campus. *Retention:* 76% of 2002 full-time freshmen returned.
Freshmen *Admission:* 1,017 applied, 845 admitted, 256 enrolled. *Average high school GPA:* 2.32. *Test scores:* SAT verbal scores over 500: 24%; SAT math scores over 500: 30%; SAT verbal scores over 600: 2%; SAT math scores over 600: 3%.
Faculty *Total:* 61, 54% full-time, 61% with terminal degrees. *Student/faculty ratio:* 20:1.
Majors Accounting; business administration and management; business/commerce; economics; English; finance; history; human resources management; management information systems; marketing/marketing management; mathematics; psychology; secondary education; sport and fitness administration.
Academic Programs *Special study options:* academic remediation for entering students, accelerated degree program, adult/continuing education programs, advanced placement credit, cooperative education, distance learning, double majors, independent study, internships, part-time degree program, study abroad, summer session for credit. *ROTC:* Army (c).
Library Conant Library plus 1 other with 60,000 titles, 450 serial subscriptions, an OPAC.
Computers on Campus 850 computers available on campus for general student use. A campuswide network can be accessed from student residence rooms and from off campus. Internet access, at least one staffed computer lab available.
Student Life *Housing:* on-campus residence required through senior year. *Options:* coed. Campus housing is university owned. Freshman campus housing

is guaranteed. *Activities and organizations:* drama/theater group, student-run newspaper, radio station, Rugby Club, Accounting Club, Racquetball Club, student publications, Theater Club. *Campus security:* 24-hour patrols, late-night transport/escort service. *Student services:* health clinic, personal/psychological counseling.

Athletics Member NCAA. All Division III. *Intercollegiate sports:* baseball M, basketball M/W, cheerleading M/W, field hockey W, football M, golf M/W, ice hockey M, lacrosse M/W, racquetball M(c)/W(c), rugby M(c)/W(c), skiing (downhill) M(c), soccer M/W, softball W, tennis M/W, volleyball W(c). *Intramural sports:* baseball M, basketball M/W, golf M/W, soccer M/W, softball W, tennis M/W, volleyball M, weight lifting M.

Standardized Tests *Required:* SAT I or ACT (for admission).

Costs (2003–04) *Comprehensive fee:* $27,533 includes full-time tuition ($19,223), mandatory fees ($500), and room and board ($7810). Part-time tuition: $420 per credit. Part-time tuition and fees vary according to course load. *Payment plan:* installment. *Waivers:* employees or children of employees.

Financial Aid Of all full-time matriculated undergraduates who enrolled in 2003, 712 applied for aid, 635 were judged to have need, 217 had their need fully met. 269 Federal Work-Study jobs (averaging $1864). In 2003, 177 non-need-based awards were made. *Average percent of need met:* 74%. *Average financial aid package:* $13,893. *Average need-based loan:* $6594. *Average need-based gift aid:* $7461. *Average non-need-based aid:* $9419. *Average indebtedness upon graduation:* $21,996.

Applying *Options:* electronic application, early admission, deferred entrance. *Application fee:* $25. *Required:* essay or personal statement, high school transcript, 1 letter of recommendation. *Required for some:* interview. *Application deadline:* rolling (freshmen), rolling (transfers). *Notification:* continuous (freshmen), continuous (transfers).

Admissions Contact Ms. Susan Montville, Admissions Assistant, Nichols College, PO Box 5000, Dudley, MA 01571. *Phone:* 508-943-2055. *Toll-free phone:* 800-470-3379. *Fax:* 508-943-9885. *E-mail:* admissions@nichols.edu.

NORTHEASTERN UNIVERSITY
Boston, Massachusetts

- **Independent** university, founded 1898
- **Calendar** semesters
- **Degrees** associate, bachelor's, master's, doctoral, first professional, post-master's, and postbachelor's certificates
- **Urban** 67-acre campus
- **Endowment** $420.6 million
- **Coed,** 14,492 undergraduate students, 100% full-time, 50% women, 50% men
- **Moderately difficult** entrance level, 47% of applicants were admitted

Northeastern University, a private research institution located in Boston, Massachusetts, is a world leader in cooperative education. Located in Boston's cultural district, Northeastern's beautiful 67-acre campus is within walking distance to the world-renowned Museum of Fine Arts, Symphony Hall, and stylish Newbury Street. Northeastern University offers more than 70 programs of study. The excellence of a Northeastern education is a result of the integration of classroom learning and real-world experience. Northeastern combines course work in the liberal arts and professional studies with its signature cooperative education program and other types of experiential learning to form the most complete education possible. *U.S. News & World Report*, in its 2003 guide "America's Best Colleges," ranked Northeastern University number one in the country among programs that "require or encourage students to apply what they're learning in the classroom out in the real world."

Undergraduates 14,492 full-time. Students come from 50 states and territories, 110 other countries, 64% are from out of state, 6% African American, 7% Asian American or Pacific Islander, 5% Hispanic American, 0.3% Native American, 5% international, 17% transferred in. *Retention:* 88% of 2002 full-time freshmen returned.

Freshmen *Admission:* 21,484 applied, 10,200 admitted, 3,194 enrolled. *Average high school GPA:* 3.18. *Test scores:* SAT verbal scores over 500: 90%; SAT math scores over 500: 94%; ACT scores over 18: 97%; SAT verbal scores over 600: 49%; SAT math scores over 600: 63%; ACT scores over 24: 74%; SAT verbal scores over 700: 6%; SAT math scores over 700: 11%; ACT scores over 30: 10%.

Faculty *Total:* 1,146, 72% full-time, 66% with terminal degrees. *Student/faculty ratio:* 16:1.

Majors Accounting; aeronautical/aerospace engineering technology; African-American/Black studies; anthropology; architecture; art; athletic training; audiology and speech-language pathology; behavioral sciences; biochemistry; biology/biological sciences; biology/biotechnology laboratory technician; business administration and management; business/commerce; chemical engineering; chemistry; civil engineering; clinical/medical laboratory technology; commercial and advertising art; communication/speech communication and rhetoric; computer engineering; computer engineering technology; computer science; corrections; criminal justice/police science; criminal justice/safety; dental hygiene; dramatic/theatre arts; economics; education; electrical, electronics and communications engineering; elementary education; engineering; English; entrepreneurship; environmental studies; finance; French; geology/earth science; German; health/health care administration; health science; history; human resources management; human services; industrial engineering; information science/studies; international business/trade/commerce; international relations and affairs; Italian; journalism; kindergarten/preschool education; liberal arts and sciences/liberal studies; linguistics; logistics and materials management; management information systems; management science; marine biology and biological oceanography; marketing/marketing management; mass communication/media; mathematics; mechanical engineering; mechanical engineering/mechanical technology; modern languages; music; music history, literature, and theory; music management and merchandising; nursing related; pharmacy; philosophy; physical therapy; physics; political science and government; psychology; public administration; radio and television; rehabilitation therapy; Russian; sign language interpretation and translation; sociology; Spanish; therapeutic recreation; toxicology; women's studies.

Academic Programs *Special study options:* academic remediation for entering students, accelerated degree program, adult/continuing education programs, advanced placement credit, cooperative education, distance learning, double majors, English as a second language, honors programs, independent study, internships, off-campus study, part-time degree program, services for LD students, student-designed majors, study abroad, summer session for credit. *ROTC:* Army (b), Navy (c), Air Force (c).

Library Snell Library plus 4 others with 710,843 titles, 7,798 serial subscriptions, 17,981 audiovisual materials, an OPAC, a Web page.

Computers on Campus A campuswide network can be accessed from student residence rooms and from off campus. Internet access, online (class) registration, at least one staffed computer lab available.

Student Life *Housing options:* coed, women-only, disabled students. Campus housing is university owned and leased by the school. Freshman campus housing is guaranteed. *Activities and organizations:* drama/theater group, student-run newspaper, radio station, choral group, Student Government Association, NU Hus-kiers and Outing Club, International Student Association, Council for University Programs, Resident Student Association, national fraternities, national sororities. *Campus security:* 24-hour emergency response devices and patrols, late-night transport/escort service, controlled dormitory access. *Student services:* health clinic, personal/psychological counseling, women's center.

Athletics Member NCAA. All Division I except football (Division I-AA). *Intercollegiate sports:* baseball M(s), basketball M(s)/W(s), crew M(s)/W(s), cross-country running M(s)/W(s), field hockey W(s), ice hockey M(s)/W(s), soccer M(s)/W(s), swimming W(s), track and field M(s)/W(s), volleyball W(s). *Intramural sports:* basketball M/W, cheerleading M(c)/W(c), fencing M(c)/W(c), football M/W, ice hockey M/W, lacrosse M(c)/W(c), racquetball M/W, rugby M(c)/W(c), sailing M(c)/W(c), skiing (downhill) M(c)/W(c), soccer M/W, softball M/W, tennis M(c)/W(c), ultimate Frisbee M(c)/W(c), volleyball M(c)/W, water polo M/W.

Standardized Tests *Required:* SAT I or ACT (for admission).

Costs (2003–04) *Comprehensive fee:* $35,650 includes full-time tuition ($25,600), mandatory fees ($240), and room and board ($9810). *College room only:* $5260. Room and board charges vary according to board plan and housing facility. *Payment plans:* installment, deferred payment. *Waivers:* senior citizens and employees or children of employees.

Financial Aid Of all full-time matriculated undergraduates who enrolled in 2003, 10,557 applied for aid, 9,342 were judged to have need, 1,401 had their need fully met. 5,338 Federal Work-Study jobs (averaging $1662). In 2003, 1728 non-need-based awards were made. *Average percent of need met:* 63%. *Average financial aid package:* $15,396. *Average need-based loan:* $4836. *Average need-based gift aid:* $11,050. *Average non-need-based aid:* $12,627.

Applying *Options:* electronic application, early admission, deferred entrance. *Application fee:* $50. *Required:* essay or personal statement, high school transcript. *Required for some:* interview. *Recommended:* minimum 2.0 GPA, 2 letters of recommendation. *Application deadlines:* 2/15 (freshmen), 2/15 (transfers).

Admissions Contact Ronne A. Patrick, Director of Admissions, Northeastern University, 150 Richards Hall, Boston, MA 02115. *Phone:* 617-373-2200. *Fax:* 617-373-8780. *E-mail:* admissions@neu.edu.

■ *See page 2098 for a narrative description.*

PINE MANOR COLLEGE
Chestnut Hill, Massachusetts

- **Independent** 4-year, founded 1911
- **Calendar** semesters

Pine Manor College (continued)

- **Degrees** certificates, associate, and bachelor's
- **Suburban** 65-acre campus with easy access to Boston
- **Endowment** $12.1 million
- **Women only,** 487 undergraduate students, 98% full-time
- **Moderately difficult** entrance level, 71% of applicants were admitted

Undergraduates 475 full-time, 12 part-time. Students come from 26 states and territories, 27 other countries, 33% are from out of state, 27% African American, 4% Asian American or Pacific Islander, 20% Hispanic American, 0.8% Native American, 10% international, 5% transferred in, 74% live on campus. *Retention:* 64% of 2002 full-time freshmen returned.

Freshmen *Admission:* 159 enrolled. *Average high school GPA:* 2.40. *Test scores:* SAT verbal scores over 500: 20%; SAT math scores over 500: 5%; ACT scores over 18: 37%; SAT verbal scores over 600: 4%; SAT math scores over 600: 2%; ACT scores over 24: 5%.

Faculty *Total:* 65, 48% full-time, 82% with terminal degrees. *Student/faculty ratio:* 10:1.

Majors American studies; art history, criticism and conservation; biology/biological sciences; business administration and management; communication/speech communication and rhetoric; creative writing; elementary education; English; fine/studio arts; history; kindergarten/preschool education; liberal arts and sciences/liberal studies; mass communication/media; political science and government; psychology; secondary education.

Academic Programs *Special study options:* academic remediation for entering students, adult/continuing education programs, advanced placement credit, double majors, English as a second language, external degree program, honors programs, independent study, internships, off-campus study, part-time degree program, services for LD students, student-designed majors, study abroad, summer session for credit.

Library Annenberg Library with 64,647 titles, 1,645 serial subscriptions, 4,085 audiovisual materials, an OPAC, a Web page.

Computers on Campus 135 computers available on campus for general student use. A campuswide network can be accessed from student residence rooms and from off campus. Internet access, at least one staffed computer lab available.

Student Life *Housing options:* women-only. Campus housing is university owned. Freshman campus housing is guaranteed. *Activities and organizations:* drama/theater group, student-run newspaper, radio station, choral group, Student Government Association, ALANA, LOVES (Ladies of Various Ebony Shades), CVSA (Cape Veraean Student Alliance), Campus Activities Board. *Campus security:* 24-hour emergency response devices and patrols, student patrols, late-night transport/escort service, controlled dormitory access. *Student services:* health clinic, personal/psychological counseling, women's center.

Athletics Member NCAA. All Division III. *Intercollegiate sports:* basketball W, cross-country running W, soccer W, softball W, tennis W, volleyball W. *Intramural sports:* basketball W, cross-country running W, soccer W, softball W, tennis W, track and field W(c), volleyball W.

Standardized Tests *Required:* SAT I or ACT (for admission).

Costs (2003–04) *Comprehensive fee:* $22,138 includes full-time tuition ($13,612) and room and board ($8526). Full-time tuition and fees vary according to course load. Part-time tuition: $400 per credit. Part-time tuition and fees vary according to course load. *Room and board:* Room and board charges vary according to housing facility. *Payment plan:* installment. *Waivers:* employees or children of employees.

Financial Aid Of all full-time matriculated undergraduates who enrolled in 2002, 360 applied for aid, 338 were judged to have need, 75 had their need fully met. In 2002, 44 non-need-based awards were made. *Average percent of need met:* 80%. *Average financial aid package:* $13,839. *Average need-based loan:* $3515. *Average need-based gift aid:* $9620. *Average non-need-based aid:* $8492. *Average indebtedness upon graduation:* $14,312.

Applying *Options:* electronic application, deferred entrance. *Application fee:* $25. *Required:* essay or personal statement, high school transcript, 1 letter of recommendation. *Recommended:* minimum 2.0 GPA, interview. *Application deadline:* rolling (freshmen), rolling (transfers). *Notification:* continuous (freshmen), continuous (transfers).

Admissions Contact Mr. Bill Nichols, Dean of Admissions, Pine Manor College, 400 Heath Street, Chestnut Hill, MA 02467-2332. *Phone:* 617-731-7104. *Toll-free phone:* 800-762-1357. *Fax:* 617-731-7102. *E-mail:* admission@pmc.edu.

■ *See page 2174 for a narrative description.*

REGIS COLLEGE
Weston, Massachusetts

- **Independent Roman Catholic** comprehensive, founded 1927
- **Calendar** semesters
- **Degrees** associate, bachelor's, master's, and post-master's certificates
- **Small-town** 168-acre campus with easy access to Boston
- **Endowment** $22.5 million
- **Women only,** 800 undergraduate students, 74% full-time
- **Moderately difficult** entrance level, 87% of applicants were admitted

Undergraduates 589 full-time, 211 part-time. Students come from 18 states and territories, 7 other countries, 12% are from out of state, 9% African American, 5% Asian American or Pacific Islander, 9% Hispanic American, 0.1% Native American, 1% international, 6% transferred in, 49% live on campus. *Retention:* 82% of 2002 full-time freshmen returned.

Freshmen *Admission:* 569 applied, 497 admitted, 156 enrolled. *Average high school GPA:* 3.00. *Test scores:* SAT verbal scores over 500: 41%; SAT math scores over 500: 35%; SAT verbal scores over 600: 8%; SAT math scores over 600: 8%; SAT verbal scores over 700: 1%; SAT math scores over 700: 1%.

Faculty *Total:* 126, 39% full-time, 49% with terminal degrees. *Student/faculty ratio:* 12:1.

Majors Art; biochemistry; biology/biological sciences; business/commerce; communication/speech communication and rhetoric; computer and information sciences; dramatic/theatre arts; English; history; mathematics; multi-/interdisciplinary studies related; museum studies; nursing (registered nurse training); political science and government; psychology; social work; sociology; Spanish.

Academic Programs *Special study options:* academic remediation for entering students, adult/continuing education programs, advanced placement credit, double majors, English as a second language, honors programs, independent study, internships, off-campus study, part-time degree program, services for LD students, student-designed majors, study abroad, summer session for credit. *ROTC:* Army (c). *Unusual degree programs:* 3-2 engineering with Worcester Polytechnic Institute.

Library Regis College Library with 133,565 titles, 951 serial subscriptions, 5,684 audiovisual materials, an OPAC, a Web page.

Computers on Campus 134 computers available on campus for general student use. A campuswide network can be accessed from student residence rooms. Internet access, at least one staffed computer lab available.

Student Life *Housing options:* women-only. Campus housing is university owned. Freshman campus housing is guaranteed. *Activities and organizations:* drama/theater group, student-run newspaper, radio station, choral group, Board of Programmers, student government, glee club, Amigos, AHANA Club. *Campus security:* 24-hour emergency response devices and patrols, late-night transport/escort service, controlled dormitory access. *Student services:* health clinic, personal/psychological counseling.

Athletics Member NCAA. All Division III. *Intercollegiate sports:* basketball W, cross-country running W, field hockey W, soccer W, softball W, swimming W, tennis W, track and field W, volleyball W. *Intramural sports:* basketball W, crew W, lacrosse W, softball W, ultimate Frisbee W, volleyball W, water polo W.

Standardized Tests *Required:* SAT I or ACT (for admission).

Costs (2003–04) *Comprehensive fee:* $29,000 includes full-time tuition ($19,910) and room and board ($9090). Part-time tuition: $2120 per course. *Payment plan:* installment. *Waivers:* employees or children of employees.

Financial Aid Of all full-time matriculated undergraduates who enrolled in 2003, 504 applied for aid, 466 were judged to have need, 70 had their need fully met. 383 Federal Work-Study jobs (averaging $2000). 32 state and other part-time jobs (averaging $1500). In 2003, 57 non-need-based awards were made. *Average percent of need met:* 36%. *Average financial aid package:* $17,940. *Average need-based loan:* $4874. *Average need-based gift aid:* $9242. *Average non-need-based aid:* $8985. *Average indebtedness upon graduation:* $20,174.

Applying *Options:* common application, electronic application, deferred entrance. *Application fee:* $30. *Required:* essay or personal statement, high school transcript, minimum 2.0 GPA, 2 letters of recommendation. *Required for some:* interview. *Recommended:* minimum 3.0 GPA, interview, rank in upper 50% of high school class. *Application deadline:* rolling (freshmen), rolling (transfers).

Admissions Contact Judith Dobai, Vice President, Enrollment and Marketing, Regis College, 235 Wellesley Street, Weston, MA 02493. *Phone:* 781-768-7100. *Toll-free phone:* 866-438-7344. *Fax:* 781-768-7071. *E-mail:* admission@regiscollege.edu.

■ *See page 2220 for a narrative description.*

SALEM STATE COLLEGE
Salem, Massachusetts

- **State-supported** comprehensive, founded 1854, part of Massachusetts Public Higher Education System
- **Calendar** semesters
- **Degrees** bachelor's, master's, and post-master's certificates
- **Small-town** 62-acre campus with easy access to Boston
- **Endowment** $5.2 million

■ **Coed,** 6,508 undergraduate students, 72% full-time, 64% women, 36% men
■ **Minimally difficult** entrance level, 82% of applicants were admitted

Undergraduates 4,696 full-time, 1,812 part-time. Students come from 18 states and territories, 4% African American, 2% Asian American or Pacific Islander, 4% Hispanic American, 0.5% Native American, 4% international, 22% live on campus. *Retention:* 72% of 2002 full-time freshmen returned.

Freshmen *Admission:* 4,018 applied, 3,313 admitted, 1,016 enrolled. *Average high school GPA:* 2.88. *Test scores:* SAT verbal scores over 500: 39%; SAT math scores over 500: 37%; SAT verbal scores over 600: 7%; SAT math scores over 600: 6%; SAT verbal scores over 700: 1%.

Faculty *Total:* 562, 49% full-time. *Student/faculty ratio:* 17:1.

Majors Accounting; administrative assistant and secretarial science; applied mathematics; art; art teacher education; aviation/airway management; biology/biological sciences; business administration and management; business/managerial economics; business teacher education; cartography; chemistry; city/urban, community and regional planning; clinical laboratory science/medical technology; commercial and advertising art; comparative literature; computer science; consumer merchandising/retailing management; criminal justice/law enforcement administration; dramatic/theatre arts; drawing; economics; education; elementary education; English; European studies; European studies (Central and Eastern); finance; geography; geology/earth science; health teacher education; history; journalism; kindergarten/preschool education; kinesiology and exercise science; liberal arts and sciences/liberal studies; literature; management information systems; marine biology and biological oceanography; marine science/merchant marine officer; marketing/marketing management; mass communication/media; mathematics; nuclear medical technology; nursing (registered nurse training); parks, recreation and leisure; photography; physical education teaching and coaching; political science and government; pre-dentistry studies; pre-law studies; pre-medical studies; pre-veterinary studies; psychology; public relations/image management; social sciences; social work; sociology; sport and fitness administration; tourism and travel services management.

Academic Programs *Special study options:* academic remediation for entering students, adult/continuing education programs, advanced placement credit, double majors, English as a second language, honors programs, independent study, internships, off-campus study, part-time degree program, services for LD students, student-designed majors, study abroad, summer session for credit.

Library Salem State College Library with 217,842 titles, 1,914 serial subscriptions, 79,000 audiovisual materials, an OPAC, a Web page.

Computers on Campus 426 computers available on campus for general student use. A campuswide network can be accessed from student residence rooms and from off campus. Internet access, at least one staffed computer lab available. Computer purchase or lease plan available.

Student Life *Housing options:* coed. Campus housing is university owned. Freshman applicants given priority for college housing. *Activities and organizations:* drama/theater group, student-run newspaper, radio and television station, choral group, Student Government Association, Program Council, Hispanic American Student Association, GLBT Alliance, WMWM Radio. *Campus security:* 24-hour emergency response devices and patrols, late-night transport/escort service. *Student services:* health clinic, personal/psychological counseling, women's center, legal services.

Athletics Member NCAA. All Division III. *Intercollegiate sports:* baseball M, basketball M/W, cross-country running M/W, field hockey W, golf M, ice hockey M, soccer M/W, softball W, swimming M/W, tennis M/W, track and field M/W, volleyball W. *Intramural sports:* archery M/W, badminton M/W, basketball M/W, cross-country running M/W, fencing M/W, field hockey W, football M, golf M/W, gymnastics M/W, ice hockey M/W, lacrosse M/W, racquetball M/W, skiing (cross-country) M/W, skiing (downhill) M/W, soccer M/W, squash M/W, swimming M/W, tennis M/W, volleyball M/W, water polo M/W, weight lifting M/W, wrestling M.

Standardized Tests *Required:* SAT I or ACT (for admission).

Costs (2003–04) *Tuition:* state resident $910 full-time; nonresident $7050 full-time. Full-time tuition and fees vary according to class time. Part-time tuition and fees vary according to class time. *Required fees:* $4128 full-time. *Room and board:* $5940. Room and board charges vary according to board plan and housing facility. *Payment plans:* installment, deferred payment. *Waivers:* senior citizens and employees or children of employees.

Financial Aid Of all full-time matriculated undergraduates who enrolled in 2002, 1,900 applied for aid, 1,842 were judged to have need, 733 had their need fully met. In 2002, 657 non-need-based awards were made. *Average percent of need met:* 75%. *Average financial aid package:* $3833. *Average need-based loan:* $1881. *Average need-based gift aid:* $5009. *Average non-need-based aid:* $783.

Applying *Options:* early admission. *Application fee:* $25. *Required:* high school transcript, minimum 2.9 GPA, letters of recommendation. *Required for some:* interview. *Recommended:* essay or personal statement. *Application deadline:* rolling (freshmen), rolling (transfers). *Notification:* continuous (freshmen), continuous (transfers).

Admissions Contact Mr. Nate Bryant, Director of Admissions, Salem State College, Admissions Office, 352 Lafayette Street, Salem, MA 01970. *Phone:* 978-542-6200.

SCHOOL OF THE MUSEUM OF FINE ARTS, BOSTON

Boston, Massachusetts

■ **Independent** comprehensive, founded 1876
■ **Calendar** semesters
■ **Degrees** certificates, diplomas, bachelor's, master's, and postbachelor's certificates
■ **Urban** 14-acre campus
■ **Endowment** $16.3 million
■ **Coed,** 640 undergraduate students, 88% full-time, 62% women, 38% men
■ **Moderately difficult** entrance level, 76% of applicants were admitted

Undergraduates 560 full-time, 80 part-time. Students come from 41 states and territories, 34 other countries, 50% are from out of state, 2% African American, 3% Asian American or Pacific Islander, 5% Hispanic American, 0.9% Native American, 8% international, 10% transferred in, 14% live on campus.

Freshmen *Admission:* 722 applied, 550 admitted, 114 enrolled. *Test scores:* SAT verbal scores over 500: 74%; SAT math scores over 500: 61%; ACT scores over 18: 100%; SAT verbal scores over 600: 28%; SAT math scores over 600: 15%; ACT scores over 24: 25%; SAT verbal scores over 700: 4%.

Faculty *Total:* 115, 43% full-time. *Student/faculty ratio:* 10:1.

Majors Applied art; art; art teacher education; ceramic arts and ceramics; cinematography and film/video production; commercial and advertising art; computer graphics; drawing; film/cinema studies; film/video and photographic arts related; fine arts related; fine/studio arts; graphic design; illustration; intermedia/multimedia; metal and jewelry arts; painting; photography; printmaking; sculpture; visual and performing arts related.

Academic Programs *Special study options:* adult/continuing education programs, double majors, independent study, internships, off-campus study, part-time degree program, student-designed majors, study abroad, summer session for credit. *ROTC:* Army (c), Navy (c), Air Force (c). *Unusual degree programs:* 3-2 fine arts, art education with Tufts University.

Library William Morris Hunt Memorial Library plus 1 other with 657 serial subscriptions, 220 audiovisual materials, an OPAC, a Web page.

Computers on Campus 46 computers available on campus for general student use. A campuswide network can be accessed from off campus. Internet access, at least one staffed computer lab available.

Student Life *Housing options:* coed, women-only. Campus housing is provided by a third party. Freshman applicants given priority for college housing. *Activities and organizations:* Gay/Lesbian/Bisexual Alliance, Student Body, Inc., Film, video and animation screening nights, Chess club, Animation club. *Campus security:* 24-hour emergency response devices and patrols. *Student services:* personal/psychological counseling.

Standardized Tests *Required for some:* SAT I or ACT (for admission).

Costs (2003–04) *Comprehensive fee:* $32,205 includes full-time tuition ($21,320), mandatory fees ($760), and room and board ($10,125). Full-time tuition and fees vary according to course load and program. Part-time tuition: $1335 per semester hour. Part-time tuition and fees vary according to course load and program. *Required fees:* $380 per semester part-time. *Room and board:* Room and board charges vary according to housing facility. *Payment plan:* installment. *Waivers:* employees or children of employees.

Financial Aid Of all full-time matriculated undergraduates who enrolled in 2003, 411 applied for aid, 411 were judged to have need, 30 had their need fully met. 184 Federal Work-Study jobs (averaging $1785). In 2003, 17 non-need-based awards were made. *Average percent of need met:* 50%. *Average financial aid package:* $12,242. *Average need-based loan:* $3870. *Average need-based gift aid:* $7315. *Average non-need-based aid:* $7135. *Average indebtedness upon graduation:* $20,554.

Applying *Options:* deferred entrance. *Application fee:* $50. *Required:* essay or personal statement, high school transcript, portfolio. *Required for some:* letters of recommendation, interview. *Application deadlines:* 2/1 (freshmen), 3/1 (transfers). *Notification:* continuous until 3/15 (freshmen), continuous (transfers).

Admissions Contact Any Assistant Director of Admissions, School of the Museum of Fine Arts, Boston, 230 The Fenway, Boston, MA 02115. *Phone:* 617-369-3626. *Toll-free phone:* 800-643-6078. *Fax:* 617-369-4264. *E-mail:* admissions@smfa.edu.

■ *See page 2358 for a narrative description.*

SIMMONS COLLEGE
Boston, Massachusetts

- **Independent** university, founded 1899
- **Calendar** semesters
- **Degrees** bachelor's, master's, doctoral, post-master's, and postbachelor's certificates
- **Urban** 12-acre campus
- **Endowment** $126.7 million
- **Women only,** 1,555 undergraduate students, 88% full-time
- **Moderately difficult** entrance level, 68% of applicants were admitted

Undergraduates 1,365 full-time, 190 part-time. Students come from 38 states and territories, 26 other countries, 40% are from out of state, 6% African American, 7% Asian American or Pacific Islander, 3% Hispanic American, 0.1% Native American, 4% international, 3% transferred in, 70% live on campus. *Retention:* 84% of 2002 full-time freshmen returned.

Freshmen *Admission:* 419 enrolled. *Average high school GPA:* 3.53. *Test scores:* SAT verbal scores over 500: 79%; SAT math scores over 500: 74%; SAT verbal scores over 600: 32%; SAT math scores over 600: 19%; SAT verbal scores over 700: 5%; SAT math scores over 700: 1%.

Faculty *Total:* 456, 40% full-time. *Student/faculty ratio:* 12:1.

Majors Accounting; advertising; African-American/Black studies; art; arts management; Asian studies (East); biochemistry; biology/biological sciences; business administration and management; chemistry; commercial and advertising art; comparative literature; computer science; consumer merchandising/retailing management; dietetics; economics; education; elementary education; English; English as a second/foreign language (teaching); environmental studies; finance; foods, nutrition, and wellness; French; history; human services; information technology; international relations and affairs; kindergarten/preschool education; management information systems; marketing/marketing management; mass communication/media; mathematics; music; music history, literature, and theory; nursing (registered nurse training); pharmacy; philosophy; physical therapy; physiological psychology/psychobiology; political science and government; pre-dentistry studies; pre-law studies; pre-medical studies; psychology; public policy analysis; public relations/image management; secondary education; sociology; Spanish; special education; women's studies.

Academic Programs *Special study options:* academic remediation for entering students, accelerated degree program, adult/continuing education programs, advanced placement credit, double majors, English as a second language, freshman honors college, honors programs, independent study, internships, off-campus study, part-time degree program, services for LD students, student-designed majors, study abroad, summer session for credit. *ROTC:* Army (c), Navy (c), Air Force (c). *Unusual degree programs:* 3-2 pharmacy with Massachusetts College of Pharmacy and Allied Health Sciences, nutrition with Boston University.

Library Beatley Library plus 4 others with 253,145 titles, 1,749 serial subscriptions, 4,843 audiovisual materials, an OPAC, a Web page.

Computers on Campus 420 computers available on campus for general student use. A campuswide network can be accessed from student residence rooms and from off campus. Internet access, online (class) registration, at least one staffed computer lab available.

Student Life *Housing options:* women-only, disabled students. Campus housing is university owned. *Activities and organizations:* drama/theater group, student-run newspaper, choral group, Student Government Association, Simmons Community Outreach, Campus Activities Board, class councils, Simmons Voice. *Campus security:* 24-hour emergency response devices and patrols, late-night transport/escort service, controlled dormitory access. *Student services:* health clinic, personal/psychological counseling, women's center.

Athletics Member NCAA. All Division III. *Intercollegiate sports:* basketball W, crew W, field hockey W, sailing W, soccer W, softball W, swimming W, tennis W, track and field W, volleyball W. *Intramural sports:* basketball W, golf W, racquetball W, skiing (cross-country) W, skiing (downhill) W, soccer W, softball W, tennis W, volleyball W.

Standardized Tests *Required:* SAT I or ACT (for admission).

Costs (2004–05) *Comprehensive fee:* $34,310 includes full-time tuition ($23,760), mandatory fees ($730), and room and board ($9820). Full-time tuition and fees vary according to course load. Part-time tuition: $745 per semester hour. Part-time tuition and fees vary according to course load. *Payment plan:* installment. *Waivers:* adult students, senior citizens, and employees or children of employees.

Financial Aid Of all full-time matriculated undergraduates who enrolled in 2003, 1,025 applied for aid, 942 were judged to have need, 34 had their need fully met. In 2003, 11 non-need-based awards were made. *Average percent of need met:* 56%. *Average financial aid package:* $15,175. *Average need-based loan:* $2880. *Average need-based gift aid:* $11,452. *Average non-need-based aid:* $12,454. *Average indebtedness upon graduation:* $25,025.

Applying *Options:* common application, electronic application, early admission, early action, deferred entrance. *Application fee:* $35. *Required:* essay or personal statement, high school transcript, 2 letters of recommendation. *Recommended:* minimum 3.0 GPA, interview. *Application deadlines:* 2/2 (freshmen), 4/1 (transfers). *Notification:* 4/15 (freshmen), 1/20 (early action), continuous (transfers).

Admissions Contact Ms. Jennifer O'Loughlin Hieber, Director of Undergraduate Admissions, Simmons College, 300 The Fenway, Boston, MA 02115. *Phone:* 617-521-2048. *Toll-free phone:* 800-345-8468. *Fax:* 617-521-3190. *E-mail:* ugadm@simmons.edu.

■ *See page 2388 for a narrative description.*

SIMON'S ROCK COLLEGE OF BARD
Great Barrington, Massachusetts

- **Independent** 4-year, founded 1964
- **Calendar** semesters
- **Degrees** associate and bachelor's
- **Rural** 275-acre campus with easy access to Albany and Springfield
- **Endowment** $6.6 million
- **Coed,** 399 undergraduate students, 97% full-time, 58% women, 42% men
- **Very difficult** entrance level, 46% of applicants were admitted

Undergraduates 386 full-time, 13 part-time. Students come from 44 states and territories, 80% are from out of state, 3% African American, 6% Asian American or Pacific Islander, 1% Hispanic American, 2% Native American, 0.5% international, 85% live on campus. *Retention:* 78% of 2002 full-time freshmen returned.

Freshmen *Admission:* 404 applied, 184 admitted, 143 enrolled. *Test scores:* SAT verbal scores over 500: 95%; SAT math scores over 500: 86%; ACT scores over 18: 100%; SAT verbal scores over 600: 75%; SAT math scores over 600: 56%; ACT scores over 24: 82%; SAT verbal scores over 700: 25%; SAT math scores over 700: 23%; ACT scores over 30: 27%.

Faculty *Total:* 66, 56% full-time, 83% with terminal degrees. *Student/faculty ratio:* 8:1.

Majors Acting; African-American/Black studies; agricultural business and management; American literature; American native/native American education; American studies; anthropology; applied mathematics; art history, criticism and conservation; Asian studies; biology/biological sciences; ceramic arts and ceramics; chemistry; Chinese; Chinese studies; cognitive psychology and psycholinguistics; computer and information sciences; computer graphics; computer science; creative writing; cultural studies; dance; developmental and child psychology; dramatic/theatre arts; drawing; ecology; economics related; English composition; environmental studies; ethnic, cultural minority, and gender studies related; European studies; fine/studio arts; foreign languages and literatures; French; French studies; geography; geology/earth science; German; German studies; interdisciplinary studies; jazz/jazz studies; Latin; Latin American studies; liberal arts and sciences/liberal studies; literature; mathematics; metal and jewelry arts; music; music theory and composition; natural sciences; painting; philosophy; photography; physics; playwriting and screenwriting; political science and government; pre-law studies; pre-medical studies; printmaking; psychology; religious studies; sculpture; sociology; Spanish; Spanish and Iberian studies; theatre design and technology; theatre literature, history and criticism; Ukraine studies; visual and performing arts; visual and performing arts related; women's studies.

Academic Programs *Special study options:* adult/continuing education programs, double majors, external degree program, independent study, internships, off-campus study, part-time degree program, services for LD students, student-designed majors, study abroad.

Library Alumni Library with 65,370 titles, 437 serial subscriptions, 4,032 audiovisual materials, an OPAC, a Web page.

Computers on Campus 50 computers available on campus for general student use. A campuswide network can be accessed from student residence rooms and from off campus. Internet access, at least one staffed computer lab available.

Student Life *Housing:* on-campus residence required through sophomore year. *Options:* coed. Campus housing is university owned. Freshman campus housing is guaranteed. *Activities and organizations:* drama/theater group, student-run newspaper, radio station, choral group, Women's Center, math and sciences club, multicultural student organization, Community Health Institute, Community Service Program. *Campus security:* 24-hour emergency response devices, late-night transport/escort service, controlled dormitory access, 24-hour weekend patrols by trained security personnel. *Student services:* health clinic, personal/psychological counseling, women's center.

Athletics *Intercollegiate sports:* basketball M/W, soccer M/W, water polo M/W. *Intramural sports:* basketball M/W, fencing M/W, racquetball M/W, rock climbing M/W, skiing (cross-country) M/W, skiing (downhill) M/W, soccer M/W, squash M/W, swimming M/W, table tennis M/W, tennis M/W, ultimate Frisbee M/W, volleyball M/W, weight lifting M/W.

Standardized Tests *Required:* SAT I (for admission), PSAT (for admission). *Recommended:* ACT (for admission).

Costs (2003–04) *Comprehensive fee:* $36,580 includes full-time tuition ($25,860), mandatory fees ($3090), and room and board ($7630). Full-time tuition and fees vary according to course load. Part-time tuition: $1000 per credit hour. Part-time tuition and fees vary according to course load. *Required fees:* $550 per course part-time. *College room only:* $3800. Room and board charges vary according to board plan and housing facility. *Payment plan:* installment. *Waivers:* employees or children of employees.

Financial Aid Of all full-time matriculated undergraduates who enrolled in 2003, 294 applied for aid, 239 were judged to have need, 52 had their need fully met. 155 Federal Work-Study jobs (averaging $1500). In 2003, 71 non-need-based awards were made. *Average percent of need met:* 68%. *Average financial aid package:* $17,723. *Average need-based loan:* $5212. *Average need-based gift aid:* $13,440. *Average non-need-based aid:* $17,009. *Average indebtedness upon graduation:* $13,525.

Applying *Options:* electronic application, early admission, deferred entrance. *Application fee:* $40. *Required:* essay or personal statement, high school transcript, minimum 2.0 GPA, 2 letters of recommendation, interview, parent application. *Recommended:* minimum 3.0 GPA. *Application deadlines:* 6/15 (freshmen), 7/15 (transfers). *Notification:* continuous (freshmen), continuous (transfers).

Admissions Contact Ms. Mary King Austin, Director of Admissions, Simon's Rock College of Bard, 84 Alford Road, Great Barrington, MA 01230. *Phone:* 413-528-7317. *Toll-free phone:* 800-235-7186. *Fax:* 413-528-7334. *E-mail:* admit@simons-rock.edu.

■ *See page 2390 for a narrative description.*

SMITH COLLEGE
Northampton, Massachusetts

- **Independent** comprehensive, founded 1871
- **Calendar** semesters
- **Degrees** bachelor's, master's, doctoral, post-master's, and postbachelor's certificates
- **Small-town** 125-acre campus with easy access to Hartford
- **Endowment** $823.9 million
- **Women only,** 2,682 undergraduate students, 98% full-time
- **Very difficult** entrance level, 52% of applicants were admitted

Undergraduates 2,641 full-time, 41 part-time. Students come from 53 states and territories, 62 other countries, 76% are from out of state, 6% African American, 10% Asian American or Pacific Islander, 6% Hispanic American, 1% Native American, 7% international, 3% transferred in, 91% live on campus. *Retention:* 92% of 2002 full-time freshmen returned.

Freshmen *Admission:* 635 enrolled. *Average high school GPA:* 3.80. *Test scores:* SAT verbal scores over 500: 94%; SAT math scores over 500: 96%; ACT scores over 18: 99%; SAT verbal scores over 600: 70%; SAT math scores over 600: 61%; ACT scores over 24: 82%; SAT verbal scores over 700: 27%; SAT math scores over 700: 15%; ACT scores over 30: 29%.

Faculty *Total:* 305, 93% full-time, 95% with terminal degrees. *Student/faculty ratio:* 9:1.

Majors African-American/Black studies; American studies; ancient/classical Greek; anthropology; architecture; art; art history, criticism and conservation; Asian studies (East); astronomy; biochemistry; biology/biological sciences; chemistry; classics and languages, literatures and linguistics; comparative literature; computer science; dance; dramatic/theatre arts; East Asian languages; economics; education; engineering science; English; fine/studio arts; French; French studies; geology/earth science; German; German studies; history; interdisciplinary studies; Italian; Latin; Latin American studies; mathematics; medieval and Renaissance studies; music; Near and Middle Eastern studies; neuroscience; philosophy; physics; political science and government; Portuguese; pre-law studies; premedical studies; psychology; religious studies; Russian; Russian studies; sociology; Spanish; women's studies.

Academic Programs *Special study options:* accelerated degree program, adult/continuing education programs, advanced placement credit, double majors, independent study, internships, off-campus study, part-time degree program, services for LD students, student-designed majors, study abroad. *ROTC:* Army (c), Air Force (c). *Unusual degree programs:* 3-2 engineering with Dartmouth College.

Library Neilson Library plus 3 others with 1.3 million titles, 6,530 serial subscriptions, 65,135 audiovisual materials, an OPAC, a Web page.

Computers on Campus 608 computers available on campus for general student use. A campuswide network can be accessed from student residence rooms and from off campus that provide access to e-mail. Internet access, online (class) registration, at least one staffed computer lab available. Computer purchase or lease plan available.

Student Life *Housing:* on-campus residence required through senior year. *Options:* women-only, cooperative. Campus housing is university owned. Freshman campus housing is guaranteed. *Activities and organizations:* drama/theater group, student-run newspaper, radio station, choral group, Recreation Council, Service Organizations of Smith, glee club and choirs, Athletic Association, Black Student Alliance. *Campus security:* 24-hour emergency response devices and patrols, late-night transport/escort service, self-defense workshops, emergency telephones, programs in crime and sexual assault prevention. *Student services:* health clinic, personal/psychological counseling, women's center.

Athletics Member NCAA. All Division III. *Intercollegiate sports:* basketball W, crew W, cross-country running W, equestrian sports W, field hockey W, lacrosse W, skiing (downhill) W, soccer W, softball W, squash W, swimming W, tennis W, track and field W, volleyball W. *Intramural sports:* badminton W(c), crew W, cross-country running W, equestrian sports W(c), fencing W(c), golf W(c), ice hockey W(c), rugby W(c), sailing W(c), skiing (cross-country) W(c), soccer W, softball W, squash W, swimming W, tennis W, track and field W, ultimate Frisbee W(c), volleyball W, water polo W.

Standardized Tests *Required:* SAT I or ACT (for admission). *Recommended:* SAT II: Subject Tests (for admission), SAT II: Writing Test (for admission).

Costs (2003–04) *Comprehensive fee:* $37,034 includes full-time tuition ($27,330), mandatory fees ($214), and room and board ($9490). *Room and board:* Room and board charges vary according to housing facility. *Payment plans:* tuition prepayment, installment. *Waivers:* employees or children of employees.

Financial Aid Of all full-time matriculated undergraduates who enrolled in 2003, 1,924 applied for aid, 1,583 were judged to have need, 1,583 had their need fully met. 219 state and other part-time jobs (averaging $1961). In 2003, 109 non-need-based awards were made. *Average percent of need met:* 100%. *Average financial aid package:* $27,378. *Average need-based loan:* $4401. *Average need-based gift aid:* $20,988. *Average non-need-based aid:* $8943. *Average indebtedness upon graduation:* $20,570. *Financial aid deadline:* 2/1.

Applying *Options:* common application, electronic application, early admission, early decision, deferred entrance. *Application fee:* $60. *Required:* essay or personal statement, high school transcript, 3 letters of recommendation. *Recommended:* interview. *Application deadlines:* 1/15 (freshmen), 6/1 (transfers). *Early decision:* 11/15 (for plan 1), 1/2 (for plan 2). *Notification:* 4/1 (freshmen), 12/15 (early decision plan 1), 2/1 (early decision plan 2), 6/15 (transfers).

Admissions Contact Ms. Debra Shaver, Director of Admissions, Smith College, 7 College Lane, Northampton, MA 01063. *Phone:* 413-585-2500. *Toll-free phone:* 800-383-3232. *Fax:* 413-585-2527. *E-mail:* admission@smith.edu.

■ *See page 2398 for a narrative description.*

SPRINGFIELD COLLEGE
Springfield, Massachusetts

- **Independent** comprehensive, founded 1885
- **Calendar** semesters
- **Degrees** bachelor's, master's, doctoral, and postbachelor's certificates
- **Suburban** 167-acre campus
- **Coed,** 2,238 undergraduate students, 96% full-time, 48% women, 52% men
- **Moderately difficult** entrance level, 74% of applicants were admitted

Founded in 1885, Springfield College emphasizes the education of leaders in the allied health sciences, human and social services, sports and movement activities, and the arts and sciences. Through its distinctive humanics philosophy—the education of the whole person, consisting of spirit, mind, and body—Springfield College prepares students for leadership in service to others.

Undergraduates 2,141 full-time, 97 part-time. Students come from 37 states and territories, 3% African American, 1% Asian American or Pacific Islander, 3% Hispanic American, 0.1% Native American, 0.5% international, 0.2% transferred in, 85% live on campus. *Retention:* 81% of 2002 full-time freshmen returned.

Freshmen *Admission:* 2,110 applied, 1,558 admitted, 553 enrolled. *Test scores:* SAT verbal scores over 500: 52%; SAT math scores over 500: 63%; SAT verbal scores over 600: 9%; SAT math scores over 600: 16%; SAT math scores over 700: 2%.

Faculty *Total:* 346, 61% full-time, 82% with terminal degrees. *Student/faculty ratio:* 12:1.

Majors Applied art; art therapy; athletic training; biology/biological sciences; business administration and management; chemistry; clinical laboratory science/medical technology; community organization and advocacy; computer graphics; computer science; ecology; education; elementary education; emergency medical technology (EMT paramedic); English; environmental health; environmental studies; general studies; gerontology; health/health care administration; health information/medical records administration; health teacher education; history; human resources management; human services; information science/studies; kindergarten/preschool education; kinesiology and exercise science; management information systems; mathematics; medical laboratory technology; mental health/

Springfield College (continued)
rehabilitation; middle school education; natural resources/conservation; parks, recreation and leisure; parks, recreation and leisure facilities management; physical education teaching and coaching; physical therapy; physician assistant; political science and government; pre-dentistry studies; pre-law studies; pre-medical studies; psychology; public health; rehabilitation therapy; science teacher education; secondary education; sociology; special education; sport and fitness administration; therapeutic recreation.

Academic Programs *Special study options:* accelerated degree program, adult/continuing education programs, advanced placement credit, cooperative education, double majors, English as a second language, independent study, internships, off-campus study, part-time degree program, services for LD students, study abroad, summer session for credit. *ROTC:* Army (c), Air Force (c). *Unusual degree programs:* 3-2 physical therapy, physician assistant, occupational therapy.

Library Babson Library with 125,000 titles, 850 serial subscriptions.

Computers on Campus 95 computers available on campus for general student use. A campuswide network can be accessed from student residence rooms and from off campus. Internet access available. Computer purchase or lease plan available.

Student Life *Housing:* on-campus residence required through junior year. *Options:* coed, men-only, women-only. Campus housing is university owned. Freshman campus housing is guaranteed. *Activities and organizations:* drama/theater group, student-run newspaper, radio station. *Student services:* health clinic, personal/psychological counseling.

Athletics Member NCAA. All Division III. *Intercollegiate sports:* baseball M, basketball M/W, cross-country running M/W, field hockey W, football M, golf M/W, gymnastics M/W, lacrosse M/W, soccer M/W, softball W, swimming M/W, tennis M/W, track and field M/W, volleyball M/W, wrestling M. *Intramural sports:* baseball M, basketball M/W, cheerleading M/W, crew M/W, equestrian sports M/W, field hockey W, football M, golf M/W, gymnastics M/W, ice hockey M/W, racquetball M/W, rock climbing M/W, rugby M/W, soccer M/W, softball M/W, swimming M/W, tennis M/W, track and field M/W, ultimate Frisbee M/W, volleyball M/W, water polo M/W, weight lifting M/W, wrestling M.

Standardized Tests *Required:* SAT I or ACT (for admission).

Costs (2003–04) *Comprehensive fee:* $27,130 includes full-time tuition ($19,410), mandatory fees ($200), and room and board ($7520). *College room only:* $3780. Room and board charges vary according to board plan and housing facility. *Payment plan:* installment. *Waivers:* employees or children of employees.

Financial Aid Of all full-time matriculated undergraduates who enrolled in 2002, 1,819 applied for aid, 1,612 were judged to have need, 331 had their need fully met. 1,080 Federal Work-Study jobs (averaging $1282). 80 state and other part-time jobs (averaging $5500). In 2002, 209 non-need-based awards were made. *Average percent of need met:* 81%. *Average financial aid package:* $14,600. *Average need-based loan:* $4000. *Average need-based gift aid:* $10,200. *Average non-need-based aid:* $11,650. *Average indebtedness upon graduation:* $24,000.

Applying *Options:* common application, electronic application, early admission, early decision, deferred entrance. *Required:* essay or personal statement, high school transcript, 1 letter of recommendation. *Required for some:* portfolio. *Recommended:* interview. *Application deadlines:* rolling (freshmen), 8/1 (transfers). *Early decision:* 12/1. *Notification:* continuous until 4/15 (freshmen), 2/1 (early decision), continuous until 8/15 (transfers).

Admissions Contact Ms. Mary N. DeAngelo, Director of Undergraduate Admissions, Springfield College, 263 Alden Street, Box M, Springfield, MA 01109. *Phone:* 413-748-3136. *Toll-free phone:* 800-343-1257. *Fax:* 413-748-3694. *E-mail:* admissions@spfldcol.edu.

■ *See page 2432 for a narrative description.*

STONEHILL COLLEGE
Easton, Massachusetts

- **Independent Roman Catholic** comprehensive, founded 1948
- **Calendar** semesters
- **Degrees** certificates, bachelor's, and master's
- **Suburban** 375-acre campus with easy access to Boston
- **Endowment** $90.1 million
- **Coed,** 2,567 undergraduate students, 87% full-time, 59% women, 41% men
- **Very difficult** entrance level, 49% of applicants were admitted

Located 20 miles south of Boston, Stonehill combines a community atmosphere and a beautiful 375-acre campus with easy access to America's premier college town. Exciting special programs, such as full-time international internships, study abroad, domestic internships, and Stonehill Undergraduate Research Experience (SURE), complement the College's rigorous education in the liberal arts, sciences, and business. More than 70% of graduating students take advantage of these enriching programs.

Undergraduates 2,225 full-time, 342 part-time. Students come from 29 states and territories, 16 other countries, 38% are from out of state, 3% African American, 3% Asian American or Pacific Islander, 2% Hispanic American, 0.2% Native American, 0.8% international, 1% transferred in, 76% live on campus. *Retention:* 89% of 2002 full-time freshmen returned.

Freshmen *Admission:* 4,808 applied, 2,366 admitted, 568 enrolled. *Average high school GPA:* 3.53. *Test scores:* SAT verbal scores over 500: 93%; SAT math scores over 500: 96%; ACT scores over 18: 99%; SAT verbal scores over 600: 48%; SAT math scores over 600: 54%; ACT scores over 24: 75%; SAT verbal scores over 700: 5%; SAT math scores over 700: 5%; ACT scores over 30: 6%.

Faculty *Total:* 239, 54% full-time, 63% with terminal degrees. *Student/faculty ratio:* 14:1.

Majors Accounting; American studies; biochemistry; biology/biological sciences; business administration and management; chemistry; communication/speech communication and rhetoric; computer engineering; computer science; criminal justice/safety; criminology; economics; elementary education; English; finance; fine/studio arts; foreign languages and literatures; health/health care administration; history; international relations and affairs; kindergarten/preschool education; marketing/marketing management; mathematics; multi-/interdisciplinary studies related; philosophy; political science and government; psychology; public administration; religious studies; sociology; speech and rhetoric.

Academic Programs *Special study options:* adult/continuing education programs, advanced placement credit, double majors, honors programs, independent study, internships, off-campus study, part-time degree program, services for LD students, student-designed majors, study abroad, summer session for credit. *ROTC:* Army (b). *Unusual degree programs:* 3-2 computer engineering with University of Notre Dame.

Library Bartley MacPhaidin, C.S.C. Library plus 1 other with 194,587 titles, 1,612 serial subscriptions, 4,588 audiovisual materials, an OPAC, a Web page.

Computers on Campus 287 computers available on campus for general student use. A campuswide network can be accessed from student residence rooms and from off campus that provide access to online schedules, assignments, grades and student accounts. Internet access, at least one staffed computer lab available.

Student Life *Housing options:* coed, women-only, disabled students. Campus housing is university owned and leased by the school. Freshman applicants given priority for college housing. *Activities and organizations:* drama/theater group, student-run newspaper, radio station, choral group, Into the Streets, student radio station, student government, Summit (student newspaper), sports clubs. *Campus security:* 24-hour emergency response devices and patrols, late-night transport/escort service. *Student services:* health clinic, personal/psychological counseling, women's center.

Athletics Member NCAA. All Division II. *Intercollegiate sports:* baseball M(s), basketball M(s)/W(s), cheerleading M(c)/W(c), cross-country running M(s)/W(s), equestrian sports W, field hockey W(s), football M(s), golf M(c)/W(c), ice hockey M, lacrosse M(c)/W(s), rugby M(c)/W(c), soccer M(s)/W(s), softball W(s), tennis M(s)/W(s), track and field M(s)/W(s), ultimate Frisbee M(c)/W(c), volleyball M(c)/W(s). *Intramural sports:* basketball M/W, field hockey M/W, football M/W, racquetball M/W, soccer M/W, softball M/W, tennis M/W, volleyball M/W.

Standardized Tests *Required:* SAT I or ACT (for admission).

Costs (2003–04) *Comprehensive fee:* $30,752 includes full-time tuition ($20,432), mandatory fees ($870), and room and board ($9450). Part-time tuition: $2044 per course. *Required fees:* $87 per course part-time. *Payment plans:* tuition prepayment, installment. *Waivers:* employees or children of employees.

Financial Aid Of all full-time matriculated undergraduates who enrolled in 2003, 1,738 applied for aid, 1,475 were judged to have need, 296 had their need fully met. 928 Federal Work-Study jobs (averaging $1874). 211 state and other part-time jobs (averaging $1120). In 2003, 486 non-need-based awards were made. *Average percent of need met:* 82%. *Average financial aid package:* $15,639. *Average need-based loan:* $4940. *Average need-based gift aid:* $10,995. *Average non-need-based aid:* $10,069. *Average indebtedness upon graduation:* $17,444.

Applying *Options:* common application, electronic application, early admission, early decision, deferred entrance. *Application fee:* $50. *Required:* essay or personal statement, high school transcript, 2 letters of recommendation. *Required for some:* interview. *Recommended:* campus visit. *Application deadlines:* 1/15 (freshmen), 4/1 (transfers). *Early decision:* 11/1. *Notification:* 4/1 (freshmen), 12/15 (early decision), 6/1 (transfers).

Admissions Contact Mr. Brian P. Murphy, Dean of Admissions and Enrollment, Stonehill College, 320 Washington Street, Easton, MA 02357-5610. *Phone:* 508-565-1373. *Fax:* 508-565-1545. *E-mail:* admissions@stonehill.edu.

■ *See page 2466 for a narrative description.*

SUFFOLK UNIVERSITY
Boston, Massachusetts

- **Independent** comprehensive, founded 1906
- **Calendar** semesters
- **Degrees** certificates, diplomas, associate, bachelor's, master's, doctoral, first professional, post-master's, postbachelor's, and first professional certificates (doctoral degree in law)
- **Urban** 2-acre campus
- **Endowment** $57.4 million
- **Coed,** 4,181 undergraduate students, 81% full-time, 59% women, 41% men
- **Moderately difficult** entrance level, 82% of applicants were admitted

Undergraduates 3,383 full-time, 798 part-time. Students come from 34 states and territories, 102 other countries, 16% are from out of state, 3% African American, 6% Asian American or Pacific Islander, 4% Hispanic American, 0.3% Native American, 11% international, 7% transferred in, 19% live on campus. *Retention:* 74% of 2002 full-time freshmen returned.

Freshmen *Admission:* 4,464 applied, 3,658 admitted, 925 enrolled. *Average high school GPA:* 2.90. *Test scores:* SAT verbal scores over 500: 56%; SAT math scores over 500: 53%; ACT scores over 18: 65%; SAT verbal scores over 600: 14%; SAT math scores over 600: 12%; ACT scores over 24: 15%; SAT verbal scores over 700: 1%; SAT math scores over 700: 1%.

Faculty *Total:* 632, 42% full-time, 63% with terminal degrees. *Student/faculty ratio:* 12:1.

Majors Accounting; administrative assistant and secretarial science; African-American/Black studies; art; biochemistry; biology/biological sciences; biology/biotechnology laboratory technician; biomedical sciences; biomedical technology; biophysics; broadcast journalism; business administration and management; business teacher education; chemistry; clinical laboratory science/medical technology; commercial and advertising art; computer and information sciences; computer engineering; computer science; criminal justice/law enforcement administration; developmental and child psychology; dramatic/theatre arts; economics; education; electrical, electronics and communications engineering; elementary education; English; environmental biology; environmental studies; finance; French; history; humanities; human services; information science/studies; interdisciplinary studies; interior design; international economics; journalism; legal assistant/paralegal; legal studies; liberal arts and sciences/liberal studies; management information systems; marine biology and biological oceanography; marine science/merchant marine officer; marketing/marketing management; mass communication/media; mathematics; modern languages; philosophy; physics; political science and government; pre-dentistry studies; pre-law studies; pre-medical studies; pre-veterinary studies; psychology; public administration; public policy analysis; public relations/image management; radiologic technology/science; secondary education; social sciences; social work; sociology; Spanish; speech and rhetoric; women's studies.

Academic Programs *Special study options:* academic remediation for entering students, accelerated degree program, adult/continuing education programs, advanced placement credit, cooperative education, distance learning, double majors, English as a second language, freshman honors college, honors programs, independent study, internships, off-campus study, part-time degree program, services for LD students, study abroad, summer session for credit. *ROTC:* Army (c). *Unusual degree programs:* 3-2 engineering with Boston University, Case Western Reserve University.

Library Mildred Sawyer Library plus 3 others with 300,900 titles, 5,330 serial subscriptions, 16,000 audiovisual materials, an OPAC, a Web page.

Computers on Campus 400 computers available on campus for general student use. A campuswide network can be accessed from student residence rooms and from off campus. Internet access, online (class) registration, at least one staffed computer lab available.

Student Life *Housing options:* coed. Campus housing is university owned and leased by the school. Freshman applicants given priority for college housing. *Activities and organizations:* drama/theater group, student-run newspaper, radio and television station, choral group, Student Government Association, Program Council, Black Student Union, Evening Student Association, International Student Association. *Campus security:* 24-hour emergency response devices, late-night transport/escort service, controlled dormitory access. *Student services:* health clinic, personal/psychological counseling, women's center.

Athletics Member NCAA. All Division III. *Intercollegiate sports:* baseball M, basketball M/W, cross-country running M/W, golf M, ice hockey M, soccer M, softball W, tennis M/W, volleyball W. *Intramural sports:* basketball M/W, soccer M/W, softball M/W, volleyball M/W.

Standardized Tests *Required:* SAT I or ACT (for admission).

Costs (2003–04) *Comprehensive fee:* $27,980 includes full-time tuition ($17,610), mandatory fees ($80), and room and board ($10,290). Part-time tuition: $492 per credit hour. *Room and board:* Room and board charges vary according to board plan and housing facility. *Payment plans:* installment, deferred payment. *Waivers:* senior citizens and employees or children of employees.

Financial Aid Of all full-time matriculated undergraduates who enrolled in 2003, 2,129 applied for aid, 1,800 were judged to have need, 244 had their need fully met. 834 Federal Work-Study jobs (averaging $2047). 211 state and other part-time jobs (averaging $1704). In 2003, 314 non-need-based awards were made. *Average percent of need met:* 67%. *Average financial aid package:* $12,457. *Average need-based loan:* $4666. *Average need-based gift aid:* $6417. *Average non-need-based aid:* $4450. *Average indebtedness upon graduation:* $18,821.

Applying *Options:* common application, electronic application, early action, deferred entrance. *Application fee:* $50. *Required:* essay or personal statement, high school transcript, 2 letters of recommendation. *Required for some:* interview. *Recommended:* minimum 2.5 GPA. *Application deadline:* 3/15 (freshmen), rolling (transfers). *Notification:* continuous (freshmen), 12/1 (early action), continuous (transfers).

Admissions Contact Mr. John Hamel, Director, Undergraduate Admissions, Suffolk University, 8 Ashburton Place, Boston, MA 02108. *Toll-free phone:* 800-6-SUFFOLK. *Fax:* 617-742-4291. *E-mail:* admission@suffolk.edu.

TUFTS UNIVERSITY
Medford, Massachusetts

- **Independent** university, founded 1852
- **Calendar** semesters
- **Degrees** bachelor's, master's, doctoral, first professional, and post-master's certificates
- **Suburban** 150-acre campus with easy access to Boston
- **Endowment** $697.2 million
- **Coed,** 4,892 undergraduate students, 98% full-time, 54% women, 46% men
- **Most difficult** entrance level, 26% of applicants were admitted

Undergraduates 4,800 full-time, 92 part-time. Students come from 51 states and territories, 67 other countries, 75% are from out of state, 7% African American, 13% Asian American or Pacific Islander, 8% Hispanic American, 0.4% Native American, 6% international, 2% transferred in, 75% live on campus. *Retention:* 96% of 2002 full-time freshmen returned.

Freshmen *Admission:* 14,528 applied, 3,830 admitted, 1,282 enrolled. *Test scores:* SAT verbal scores over 500: 98%; SAT math scores over 500: 99%; ACT scores over 18: 100%; SAT verbal scores over 600: 82%; SAT math scores over 600: 88%; ACT scores over 24: 92%; SAT verbal scores over 700: 31%; SAT math scores over 700: 44%; ACT scores over 30: 45%.

Faculty *Total:* 889, 66% full-time. *Student/faculty ratio:* 9:1.

Majors African-American/Black studies; American studies; anthropology; archeology; architectural engineering; art history, criticism and conservation; Asian studies; Asian studies (Southeast); astronomy; behavioral sciences; biology/biological sciences; chemical engineering; chemistry; child development; Chinese; civil engineering; classics and languages, literatures and linguistics; community health and preventive medicine; computer engineering; computer science; developmental and child psychology; dramatic/theatre arts; ecology; economics; electrical, electronics and communications engineering; elementary education; engineering; engineering physics; engineering related; engineering science; English; environmental/environmental health engineering; environmental studies; experimental psychology; French; geological/geophysical engineering; geology/earth science; German; history; industrial engineering; international relations and affairs; Jewish/Judaic studies; kindergarten/preschool education; Latin; mathematics; mechanical engineering; mental health/rehabilitation; modern Greek; music; philosophy; physics; political science and government; psychology; public health; Romance languages; Russian; Russian studies; secondary education; sociobiology; sociology; Spanish; special education; urban studies/affairs; women's studies.

Academic Programs *Special study options:* adult/continuing education programs, advanced placement credit, double majors, honors programs, independent study, internships, off-campus study, services for LD students, student-designed majors, study abroad, summer session for credit. *ROTC:* Army (c), Navy (c), Air Force (c). *Unusual degree programs:* 3-2 music with New England Conservatory of Music, fine arts with School of the Museum of Fine Arts.

Library Tisch Library plus 1 other with 1.6 million titles, 5,204 serial subscriptions, 33,731 audiovisual materials, an OPAC, a Web page.

Computers on Campus 254 computers available on campus for general student use. A campuswide network can be accessed from student residence rooms and from off campus. Internet access, online (class) registration, at least one staffed computer lab available.

Student Life *Housing:* on-campus residence required through sophomore year. *Options:* coed, women-only, cooperative. Campus housing is university owned. Freshman campus housing is guaranteed. *Activities and organizations:* drama/

Tufts University (continued)

theater group, student-run newspaper, radio and television station, choral group, marching band, Leonard Carmichael Society, mountain club, Environmental Consciousness Outreach, national fraternities, national sororities. *Campus security:* 24-hour emergency response devices and patrols, late-night transport/escort service, controlled dormitory access, security lighting, call boxes to campus police. *Student services:* health clinic, personal/psychological counseling, women's center, legal services.

Athletics Member NCAA. All Division III. *Intercollegiate sports:* baseball M, basketball M/W, crew M/W, cross-country running M/W, fencing W, field hockey W, football M, golf M, ice hockey M, lacrosse M/W, sailing M/W, soccer M/W, softball W, squash M/W, swimming M/W, tennis M/W, track and field M/W, volleyball W. *Intramural sports:* basketball M/W, cheerleading M/W, cross-country running M/W, equestrian sports M/W, fencing M, football M, racquetball M/W, rugby M/W, skiing (downhill) M/W, soccer M/W, softball M/W, squash M/W, tennis M/W, track and field M/W, ultimate Frisbee M/W, volleyball M, water polo M.

Standardized Tests *Required:* SAT I and SAT II or ACT (for admission). *Required for some:* SAT II: Writing Test (for admission).

Costs (2003–04) *Comprehensive fee:* $38,233 includes full-time tuition ($28,859), mandatory fees ($734), and room and board ($8640). *College room only:* $4420. Room and board charges vary according to board plan. *Payment plans:* tuition prepayment, installment. *Waivers:* employees or children of employees.

Financial Aid Of all full-time matriculated undergraduates who enrolled in 2003, 2,234 applied for aid, 1,953 were judged to have need, 1,953 had their need fully met. 1,597 Federal Work-Study jobs (averaging $1687). 43 state and other part-time jobs (averaging $1390). In 2003, 75 non-need-based awards were made. *Average percent of need met:* 100%. *Average financial aid package:* $24,084. *Average need-based loan:* $4202. *Average need-based gift aid:* $20,932. *Average non-need-based aid:* $500. *Average indebtedness upon graduation:* $14,925. *Financial aid deadline:* 2/15.

Applying *Options:* common application, electronic application, early admission, early decision, deferred entrance. *Application fee:* $60. *Required:* essay or personal statement, high school transcript, 1 letter of recommendation. *Recommended:* interview. *Application deadlines:* 1/1 (freshmen), 3/1 (transfers). *Early decision:* 11/15 (for plan 1), 1/1 (for plan 2). *Notification:* 4/1 (freshmen), 12/15 (early decision plan 1), 2/1 (early decision plan 2), 5/1 (transfers).

Admissions Contact Mr. Lee A. Coffin, Dean of Undergraduate Admissions, Tufts University, Bendetson Hall, Medford, MA 02155. *Phone:* 617-627-3170. *Fax:* 617-627-3860. *E-mail:* admissions.inquiry@ase.tufts.edu.

UNIVERSITY OF MASSACHUSETTS AMHERST

Amherst, Massachusetts

- **State-supported** university, founded 1863, part of University of Massachusetts
- **Calendar** semesters
- **Degrees** associate, bachelor's, master's, doctoral, and post-master's certificates
- **Small-town** 1463-acre campus with easy access to Hartford
- **Endowment** $66.0 million
- **Coed,** 18,718 undergraduate students, 93% full-time, 50% women, 50% men
- **Moderately difficult** entrance level, 82% of applicants were admitted

Commonwealth College, the honors college at the University of Massachusetts Amherst, combines an intellectually rigorous curriculum and opportunities for residential academic experiences, community service learning, and in-depth research through faculty mentoring relationships. The College encourages creativity, initiative, responsibility, collaboration, and independent thought. Profile of first-year honors students: median SAT, 1317; median weighted GPA, 4.1; on average in top 6% of their high school class.

Undergraduates 17,379 full-time, 1,339 part-time. Students come from 50 states and territories, 17% are from out of state, 4% African American, 7% Asian American or Pacific Islander, 3% Hispanic American, 0.4% Native American, 1% international, 6% transferred in, 59% live on campus. *Retention:* 84% of 2002 full-time freshmen returned.

Freshmen *Admission:* 16,427 applied, 13,461 admitted, 4,194 enrolled. *Average high school GPA:* 3.28. *Test scores:* SAT verbal scores over 500: 80%; SAT math scores over 500: 85%; SAT verbal scores over 600: 33%; SAT math scores over 600: 39%; SAT verbal scores over 700: 5%; SAT math scores over 700: 7%.

Faculty *Total:* 1,277, 84% full-time, 88% with terminal degrees. *Student/faculty ratio:* 18:1.

Majors Accounting; African-American/Black studies; animal sciences; anthropology; applied economics; applied horticulture/horticultural business services related; art history, criticism and conservation; astronomy; biochemistry/biophysics and molecular biology; biological and physical sciences; biology/biological sciences; business administration and management; chemical engineering; chemistry; Chinese; civil engineering; classics and languages, literatures and linguistics; clinical laboratory science/medical technology; communication disorders; communication/speech communication and rhetoric; comparative literature; computer engineering; computer science; crop production; dance; dramatic/theatre arts; economics; education; electrical, electronics and communications engineering; engineering; English; environmental design/architecture; environmental science; equestrian studies; finance; fine/studio arts; food science; forestry; French; general studies; geography; geology/earth science; German; history; hospitality administration; humanities; human nutrition; industrial engineering; interior design; Italian; Japanese; Jewish/Judaic studies; journalism; kinesiology and exercise science; landscape architecture; landscaping and groundskeeping; legal studies; liberal arts and sciences and humanities related; linguistics; marketing/marketing management; mathematics; mechanical engineering; microbiology; multi-/interdisciplinary studies related; music; music performance; natural resources management and policy; Near and Middle Eastern studies; nursing (registered nurse training); ornamental horticulture; philosophy; physics; plant sciences; political science and government; Portuguese; pre-dentistry studies; pre-medical studies; pre-veterinary studies; psychology; Russian studies; social sciences related; sociology; Spanish; sport and fitness administration; turf and turfgrass management; wildlife and wildlands science and management; women's studies; wood science and wood products/pulp and paper technology.

Academic Programs *Special study options:* academic remediation for entering students, adult/continuing education programs, advanced placement credit, cooperative education, distance learning, double majors, English as a second language, freshman honors college, honors programs, independent study, internships, off-campus study, part-time degree program, services for LD students, student-designed majors, study abroad, summer session for credit. *ROTC:* Army (b), Air Force (b).

Library W. E. B. Du Bois Library plus 3 others with 3.1 million titles, 14,022 serial subscriptions, 18,468 audiovisual materials, an OPAC, a Web page.

Computers on Campus 450 computers available on campus for general student use. A campuswide network can be accessed from student residence rooms and from off campus that provide access to on-line course and grade information. Internet access, online (class) registration, at least one staffed computer lab available.

Student Life *Housing:* on-campus residence required through sophomore year. *Options:* coed, men-only, women-only, disabled students. Campus housing is university owned. Freshman campus housing is guaranteed. *Activities and organizations:* drama/theater group, student-run newspaper, radio and television station, choral group, marching band, Minutemen Marching Band, Theater Guild, ski club, outing club, student newspaper, national fraternities, national sororities. *Campus security:* 24-hour emergency response devices and patrols, student patrols, controlled dormitory access, residence halls locked nights and weekends. *Student services:* health clinic, personal/psychological counseling, women's center, legal services.

Athletics Member NCAA. All Division I except football (Division I-AA). *Intercollegiate sports:* baseball M(s), basketball M(s)/W(s), cheerleading M/W, crew W(s), cross-country running M(s)/W(s), field hockey W(s), ice hockey M(s), lacrosse M(s)/W(s), skiing (downhill) M(s)/W(s), soccer M(s)/W(s), softball W(s), swimming M(s)/W(s), tennis M(s), track and field M(s)/W(s), volleyball W(s). *Intramural sports:* basketball M/W, crew M(c)/W(c), cross-country running M/W, equestrian sports M(c)/W(c), fencing M(c)/W(c), field hockey W, football M/W, ice hockey M/W, lacrosse M(c)/W, rugby M(c)/W(c), soccer M/W, softball M/W, swimming M/W, tennis M/W, ultimate Frisbee M/W, volleyball M/W, wrestling M/W.

Standardized Tests *Required:* SAT I or ACT (for admission).

Costs (2003–04) *Tuition:* state resident $1714 full-time, $72 per credit part-time; nonresident $9937 full-time, $414 per credit part-time. Full-time tuition and fees vary according to course load, reciprocity agreements, and student level. Part-time tuition and fees vary according to course load. *Required fees:* $6696 full-time, $1286 per term part-time. *Room and board:* $5748; room only: $3235. Room and board charges vary according to board plan and housing facility. *Payment plan:* installment. *Waivers:* senior citizens and employees or children of employees.

Financial Aid Of all full-time matriculated undergraduates who enrolled in 2002, 11,122 applied for aid, 8,163 were judged to have need, 2,979 had their need fully met. 4,854 Federal Work-Study jobs. In 2002, 649 non-need-based awards were made. *Average percent of need met:* 90%. *Average financial aid package:* $9422. *Average need-based loan:* $3692. *Average need-based gift aid:* $6167. *Average non-need-based aid:* $3526. *Average indebtedness upon graduation:* $15,374.

Applying *Options:* electronic application. *Application fee:* $40. *Required:* essay or personal statement, high school transcript. *Recommended:* minimum 3.0 GPA, letters of recommendation. *Application deadlines:* 1/15 (freshmen), 4/15 (transfers). *Notification:* continuous (freshmen), continuous (transfers).

Admissions Contact Mr. Michael Gargano, Vice Chancellor for Student Affairs, University of Massachusetts Amherst, 37 Mather Drive, Amherst, MA 01003-9291. *Fax:* 413-545-4312. *E-mail:* mail@admissions.umass.edu.

■ *See page 2642 for a narrative description.*

UNIVERSITY OF MASSACHUSETTS BOSTON

Boston, Massachusetts

- **State-supported** university, founded 1964, part of University of Massachusetts
- **Calendar** semesters
- **Degrees** certificates, bachelor's, master's, doctoral, post-master's, and postbachelor's certificates
- **Urban** 177-acre campus
- **Endowment** $9.3 million
- **Coed,** 9,650 undergraduate students, 60% full-time, 58% women, 42% men
- **Moderately difficult** entrance level, 55% of applicants were admitted

The University of Massachusetts Boston is a public university campus located on a picturesque peninsula south of downtown Boston, adjacent to the John F. Kennedy Library and Museum. Established in 1964, the University enrolls some 13,000 students in both undergraduate and graduate programs.

Undergraduates 5,772 full-time, 3,878 part-time. Students come from 35 states and territories, 89 other countries, 4% are from out of state, 15% African American, 11% Asian American or Pacific Islander, 7% Hispanic American, 0.4% Native American, 5% international, 14% transferred in. *Retention:* 70% of 2002 full-time freshmen returned.

Freshmen *Admission:* 2,834 applied, 1,561 admitted, 610 enrolled. *Average high school GPA:* 3.00. *Test scores:* SAT verbal scores over 500: 55%; SAT math scores over 500: 63%; SAT verbal scores over 600: 15%; SAT math scores over 600: 16%; SAT verbal scores over 700: 1%; SAT math scores over 700: 3%.

Faculty *Total:* 831, 52% full-time. *Student/faculty ratio:* 15:1.

Majors African-American/Black studies; American studies; anthropology; art; biochemistry; biology/biological sciences; business administration and management; chemistry; classics and languages, literatures and linguistics; clinical laboratory science/medical technology; community organization and advocacy; computer science; criminal justice/safety; dramatic/theatre arts; economics; engineering physics; English; French; geography; German; gerontology; history; human services; interdisciplinary studies; Italian; labor and industrial relations; legal studies; mathematics; music; nursing (registered nurse training); philosophy; physical education teaching and coaching; physics; political science and government; psychology; public policy analysis; sociology; Spanish; women's studies.

Academic Programs *Special study options:* academic remediation for entering students, accelerated degree program, adult/continuing education programs, advanced placement credit, cooperative education, distance learning, double majors, English as a second language, freshman honors college, honors programs, independent study, internships, off-campus study, part-time degree program, services for LD students, student-designed majors, study abroad, summer session for credit. *Unusual degree programs:* 3-2 engineering with University of Massachusetts Lowell, University of Massachusetts Amherst, Northeastern University.

Library Joseph P. Healey Library with 443,194 titles, 2,784 serial subscriptions, 1,885 audiovisual materials, an OPAC, a Web page.

Computers on Campus 260 computers available on campus for general student use. A campuswide network can be accessed from off campus. Internet access, online (class) registration, at least one staffed computer lab available. Computer purchase or lease plan available.

Student Life *Housing:* college housing not available. *Activities and organizations:* drama/theater group, student-run newspaper, radio station, choral group, Women's Center, Black Student Center, Asian Student Center, Veterans Student Center, Disabilities Student Center. *Campus security:* 24-hour emergency response devices and patrols, late-night transport/escort service, crime prevention program, bicycle patrols. *Student services:* health clinic, personal/psychological counseling, women's center, legal services.

Athletics Member NCAA. All Division III. *Intercollegiate sports:* baseball M, basketball M/W, cheerleading M(s)/W(s), cross-country running M/W, ice hockey M, lacrosse M, soccer M/W, softball W, tennis M/W, track and field M/W, volleyball W. *Intramural sports:* basketball M/W, ice hockey M, racquetball M/W, sailing M/W, soccer M/W, softball M/W, squash M/W, swimming M/W, tennis M/W, ultimate Frisbee M(c)/W(c), volleyball M/W, weight lifting M/W.

Standardized Tests *Required:* SAT I or ACT (for admission).

Costs (2003–04) *Tuition:* state resident $6977 full-time, $72 per credit hour part-time; nonresident $17,637 full-time, $407 per credit hour part-time. Part-time tuition and fees vary according to course load. *Required fees:* $263 per credit part-time. *Payment plan:* installment. *Waivers:* senior citizens and employees or children of employees.

Financial Aid Of all full-time matriculated undergraduates who enrolled in 2002, 3,831 applied for aid, 3,313 were judged to have need, 2,130 had their need fully met. In 2002, 34 non-need-based awards were made. *Average percent of need met:* 91%. *Average financial aid package:* $9552. *Average need-based loan:* $5393. *Average need-based gift aid:* $4729. *Average non-need-based aid:* $3026. *Average indebtedness upon graduation:* $17,213.

Applying *Options:* common application, electronic application, deferred entrance. *Application fee:* $40. *Required:* high school transcript, minimum 2.75 GPA. *Required for some:* essay or personal statement, letters of recommendation, interview. *Recommended:* essay or personal statement. *Application deadline:* rolling (freshmen), rolling (transfers). *Notification:* continuous (freshmen), continuous (transfers).

Admissions Contact Office of Admissions Information Service, University of Massachusetts Boston, 100 Morrissey Boulevard, Boston, MA 02125-3393. *Phone:* 617-287-6100. *Fax:* 617-287-5999. *E-mail:* undergrad@umb.edu.

■ *See page 2644 for a narrative description.*

UNIVERSITY OF MASSACHUSETTS DARTMOUTH

North Dartmouth, Massachusetts

- **State-supported** comprehensive, founded 1895, part of University of Massachusetts
- **Calendar** semesters
- **Degrees** certificates, bachelor's, master's, doctoral, post-master's, and postbachelor's certificates
- **Suburban** 710-acre campus with easy access to Boston and Providence
- **Endowment** $12.7 million
- **Coed,** 7,359 undergraduate students, 80% full-time, 52% women, 48% men
- **Moderately difficult** entrance level, 71% of applicants were admitted

The University of Massachusetts Dartmouth enrolls more than 8,500 students on its 710-acre campus in southeastern Massachusetts. Five colleges offer 42 undergraduate and 18 graduate programs. Publicly supported, the University provides affordable options in professional and preprofessional programs as well as in a variety of cocurricular activities, organizations, and teams.

Undergraduates 5,912 full-time, 1,447 part-time. Students come from 31 states and territories, 29 other countries, 5% are from out of state, 6% African American, 2% Asian American or Pacific Islander, 2% Hispanic American, 0.5% Native American, 0.9% international, 6% transferred in, 48% live on campus. *Retention:* 80% of 2002 full-time freshmen returned.

Freshmen *Admission:* 6,049 applied, 4,268 admitted, 1,523 enrolled. *Average high school GPA:* 3.06. *Test scores:* SAT verbal scores over 500: 67%; SAT math scores over 500: 70%; ACT scores over 18: 86%; SAT verbal scores over 600: 17%; SAT math scores over 600: 19%; ACT scores over 24: 30%; SAT verbal scores over 700: 1%; SAT math scores over 700: 2%; ACT scores over 30: 3%.

Faculty *Total:* 512, 64% full-time. *Student/faculty ratio:* 18:1.

Majors Accounting; art history, criticism and conservation; art teacher education; biology/biological sciences; business administration and management; ceramic arts and ceramics; chemistry; chemistry related; civil engineering; clinical laboratory science/medical technology; commercial and advertising art; computer and information sciences; computer engineering; design and applied arts related; design and visual communications; economics; electrical, electronic and communications engineering technology; electrical, electronics and communications engineering; English; fiber, textile and weaving arts; finance; fine arts related; French; history; interdisciplinary studies; intermedia/multimedia; liberal arts and sciences/liberal studies; management information systems; marketing/marketing management; mathematics; mechanical engineering; mechanical engineering/mechanical technology; metal and jewelry arts; music; nursing (registered nurse training); nursing related; painting; philosophy; photography; physics; political science and government; Portuguese; printmaking; psychology; sculpture; sociology; Spanish; textile sciences and engineering.

Academic Programs *Special study options:* academic remediation for entering students, adult/continuing education programs, advanced placement credit, cooperative education, distance learning, double majors, honors programs, independent study, internships, off-campus study, part-time degree program, services for LD students, student-designed majors, study abroad, summer session for credit. *ROTC:* Army (c).

Library University of Massachusetts Dartmouth Library with 947,000 titles, 2,925 serial subscriptions, 12,980 audiovisual materials, an OPAC, a Web page.

Computers on Campus 368 computers available on campus for general student use. A campuswide network can be accessed from student residence rooms and from off campus. Internet access, online (class) registration, at least one staffed computer lab available. Computer purchase or lease plan available.

University of Massachusetts Dartmouth (continued)

Student Life *Housing options:* coed, disabled students. Campus housing is university owned. *Activities and organizations:* drama/theater group, student-run newspaper, radio station, choral group, Student Activities Board, outing club, Phi Sigma Sigma, Portuguese language club, United Brothers and Sisters, national fraternities, national sororities. *Campus security:* 24-hour emergency response devices and patrols, student patrols, late-night transport/escort service, controlled dormitory access. *Student services:* health clinic, personal/psychological counseling, women's center, legal services.

Athletics Member NCAA. All Division III. *Intercollegiate sports:* baseball M, basketball M/W, cheerleading W, cross-country running M/W, equestrian sports M(c)/W(c), field hockey W, football M, golf M/W, ice hockey M, lacrosse M/W, soccer M/W, softball W, swimming M/W, tennis M/W, track and field M/W, volleyball W. *Intramural sports:* badminton M/W, basketball M/W, sailing M/W, soccer M/W, softball M/W, table tennis M/W, tennis M/W, ultimate Frisbee M/W, volleyball M/W.

Standardized Tests *Required:* SAT I or ACT (for admission).

Costs (2003–04) *Tuition:* state resident $1417 full-time, $59 per credit part-time; nonresident $8099 full-time, $337 per credit hour part-time. Part-time tuition and fees vary according to course load. *Required fees:* $4712 full-time, $196 per credit hour part-time. *Room and board:* $7099; room only: $4076. Room and board charges vary according to board plan and housing facility. *Payment plan:* installment. *Waivers:* employees or children of employees.

Financial Aid Of all full-time matriculated undergraduates who enrolled in 2002, 4,485 applied for aid, 3,483 were judged to have need, 1,967 had their need fully met. 755 Federal Work-Study jobs (averaging $990). In 2002, 241 non-need-based awards were made. *Average percent of need met:* 86%. *Average financial aid package:* $7031. *Average need-based loan:* $3601. *Average need-based gift aid:* $4261. *Average non-need-based aid:* $2184. *Average indebtedness upon graduation:* $14,939.

Applying *Options:* common application, early admission, early decision, deferred entrance. *Application fee:* $35. *Required:* essay or personal statement, high school transcript, minimum 3.0 GPA. *Recommended:* letters of recommendation. *Application deadline:* rolling (freshmen), rolling (transfers). *Early decision:* 11/15. *Notification:* continuous (freshmen), 12/15 (early decision), continuous (transfers).

Admissions Contact Mr. Steven Briggs, Director of Admissions, University of Massachusetts Dartmouth, 285 Old Westport Road, North Dartmouth, MA 02747-2300. *Phone:* 508-999-8605. *Fax:* 508-999-8755. *E-mail:* admissions@umassd.edu.

■ *See page 2646 for a narrative description.*

UNIVERSITY OF MASSACHUSETTS LOWELL

Lowell, Massachusetts

- **State-supported** university, founded 1894, part of University of Massachusetts
- **Calendar** semesters
- **Degrees** associate, bachelor's, master's, doctoral, and post-master's certificates
- **Urban** 100-acre campus with easy access to Boston
- **Endowment** $8.5 million
- **Coed,** 9,006 undergraduate students, 65% full-time, 41% women, 59% men
- **Moderately difficult** entrance level, 62% of applicants were admitted

Undergraduates 5,840 full-time, 3,166 part-time. Students come from 34 states and territories, 44 other countries, 11% are from out of state, 3% African American, 8% Asian American or Pacific Islander, 4% Hispanic American, 0.2% Native American, 2% international, 9% transferred in, 32% live on campus. *Retention:* 75% of 2002 full-time freshmen returned.

Freshmen *Admission:* 4,233 applied, 2,630 admitted, 1,020 enrolled. *Average high school GPA:* 3.09. *Test scores:* SAT verbal scores over 500: 71%; SAT math scores over 500: 82%; SAT verbal scores over 600: 21%; SAT math scores over 600: 29%; SAT verbal scores over 700: 3%; SAT math scores over 700: 3%.

Faculty *Total:* 361. *Student/faculty ratio:* 15:1.

Majors American studies; applied mathematics; biology/biological sciences; business administration and management; chemical engineering; chemistry; civil engineering; civil engineering technology; clinical laboratory science/medical technology; community health and preventive medicine; computer engineering; computer science; criminal justice/law enforcement administration; economics; electrical, electronic and communications engineering technology; electrical, electronics and communications engineering; engineering/industrial management; English; environmental science; fine/studio arts; foreign languages and literatures; history; industrial technology; information technology; kinesiology and exercise science; liberal arts and sciences/liberal studies; mathematics; mechanical engineering; mechanical engineering/mechanical technology; music; music performance; nursing (registered nurse training); philosophy; physics; political science and government; polymer/plastics engineering; psychology; sociology.

Academic Programs *Special study options:* accelerated degree program, adult/continuing education programs, advanced placement credit, cooperative education, distance learning, double majors, honors programs, internships, off-campus study, part-time degree program, services for LD students, study abroad, summer session for credit. *ROTC:* Air Force (b). *Unusual degree programs:* 3-2 engineering with Saint Anselm College.

Library O'Leary Library plus 2 others with 549,243 titles, an OPAC, a Web page.

Computers on Campus 4000 computers available on campus for general student use. A campuswide network can be accessed from student residence rooms and from off campus. At least one staffed computer lab available.

Student Life *Housing options:* coed, men-only, women-only. Campus housing is university owned. *Activities and organizations:* drama/theater group, student-run newspaper, radio station, choral group, marching band. *Campus security:* 24-hour emergency response devices and patrols, late-night transport/escort service, controlled dormitory access. *Student services:* health clinic, personal/psychological counseling, women's center.

Athletics Member NCAA. All Division II except ice hockey (Division I). *Intercollegiate sports:* basketball M(s)/W(s), crew M/W, cross-country running M(s)/W(s), field hockey W(s), football M, golf M, ice hockey M(s), soccer M, swimming M(s), tennis M(s)/W(s), track and field M(s)/W(s), volleyball W(s), wrestling M(s). *Intramural sports:* badminton M/W, basketball M/W, bowling M/W, golf M/W, ice hockey M/W, racquetball M/W, soccer M/W, squash M/W, table tennis M/W, tennis M/W, volleyball M/W, water polo M/W.

Standardized Tests *Required:* SAT I or ACT (for admission).

Costs (2003–04) *Tuition:* state resident $1454 full-time, $61 per credit part-time; nonresident $8567 full-time, $357 per credit part-time. Full-time required fee for out of state students: $8084. *Required fees:* $4759 full-time, $210 per credit part-time. *Room and board:* $5724; room only: $3486. Room and board charges vary according to board plan and housing facility. *Payment plan:* installment. *Waivers:* senior citizens and employees or children of employees.

Financial Aid Of all full-time matriculated undergraduates who enrolled in 2002, 3,700 applied for aid, 2,469 were judged to have need, 2,180 had their need fully met. 160 Federal Work-Study jobs (averaging $2688). 531 state and other part-time jobs (averaging $3008). In 2002, 279 non-need-based awards were made. *Average percent of need met:* 98%. *Average financial aid package:* $7184. *Average need-based loan:* $2833. *Average need-based gift aid:* $3797. *Average non-need-based aid:* $3194. *Average indebtedness upon graduation:* $15,258.

Applying *Options:* electronic application, deferred entrance. *Application fee:* $20. *Required:* essay or personal statement, high school transcript, minimum 3.0 GPA, 1 letter of recommendation. *Required for some:* interview. *Application deadline:* rolling (freshmen), rolling (transfers). *Notification:* continuous (freshmen), continuous (transfers).

Admissions Contact Ms. Lisa Johnson, Assistant Vice Chancellor of Enrollment Management, University of Massachusetts Lowell, 883 Broadway Street, Room 110, Lowell, MA 01854-5104. *Phone:* 978-934-3944. *Toll-free phone:* 800-410-4607. *Fax:* 978-934-3086. *E-mail:* admissions@uml.edu.

■ *See page 2648 for a narrative description.*

UNIVERSITY OF PHOENIX–BOSTON CAMPUS

Braintree, Massachusetts

- **Proprietary** comprehensive, founded 2001
- **Calendar** continuous
- **Degrees** certificates, associate, bachelor's, master's, doctoral, post-master's, and postbachelor's certificates (courses conducted at 121 campuses and learning centers in 25 states)
- **Coed,** 294 undergraduate students, 100% full-time, 49% women, 51% men
- **Noncompetitive** entrance level

Undergraduates 294 full-time. 13% African American, 2% Asian American or Pacific Islander, 2% Hispanic American, 0.7% Native American, 11% international.

Freshmen *Admission:* 28 enrolled.

Faculty *Total:* 26, 12% full-time, 23% with terminal degrees. *Student/faculty ratio:* 6:1.

Majors Business administration and management; management information systems; marketing/marketing management.

Academic Programs *Special study options:* accelerated degree program, adult/continuing education programs, advanced placement credit, distance learning, external degree program, independent study.

Library University Library with 27.1 million titles, 11,648 serial subscriptions, an OPAC, a Web page.

Computers on Campus A campuswide network can be accessed from off campus. At least one staffed computer lab available.
Student Life *Housing:* college housing not available.
Costs (2003–04) *Tuition:* $11,400 full-time, $380 per credit part-time. *Waivers:* employees or children of employees.
Financial Aid *Average financial aid package:* $1371.
Applying *Options:* deferred entrance. *Application fee:* $100. *Required:* essay or personal statement, 2 years of work experience, 23 years of age. *Required for some:* high school transcript. *Application deadline:* rolling (freshmen), rolling (transfers).
Admissions Contact Ms. Beth Barilla, Director of Admissions, University of Phoenix–Boston Campus, 4615 East Elwood Street, Mail Stop AA-K101, Phoenix, AZ 85040-1958. *Phone:* 480-317-6000. *Toll-free phone:* 800-228-7240. *Fax:* 480-594-1758. *E-mail:* beth.barilla@phoenix.edu.

UNIVERSITY OF PHOENIX–CENTRAL MASSACHUSETTS CAMPUS
Westborough, Massachusetts

Admissions Contact One Research Drive, Westborough, MA 01581.

WELLESLEY COLLEGE
Wellesley, Massachusetts

- **Independent** 4-year, founded 1870
- **Calendar** semesters
- **Degrees** bachelor's (double bachelor's degree with Massachusetts Institute of Technology)
- **Suburban** 500-acre campus with easy access to Boston
- **Endowment** $1.0 billion
- **Women only,** 2,312 undergraduate students, 96% full-time
- **Most difficult** entrance level, 41% of applicants were admitted

Undergraduates 2,219 full-time, 93 part-time. Students come from 52 states and territories, 79 other countries, 83% are from out of state, 6% African American, 25% Asian American or Pacific Islander, 5% Hispanic American, 0.4% Native American, 8% international, 0.5% transferred in, 93% live on campus. *Retention:* 95% of 2002 full-time freshmen returned.
Freshmen *Admission:* 3,434 applied, 1,394 admitted, 591 enrolled. *Test scores:* SAT verbal scores over 500: 99%; SAT math scores over 500: 99%; ACT scores over 18: 100%; SAT verbal scores over 600: 88%; SAT math scores over 600: 87%; ACT scores over 24: 94%; SAT verbal scores over 700: 45%; SAT math scores over 700: 41%; ACT scores over 30: 55%.
Faculty *Total:* 320, 69% full-time, 96% with terminal degrees. *Student/faculty ratio:* 9:1.
Majors African-American/Black studies; African studies; American studies; ancient/classical Greek; anthropology; archeology; architecture; art history, criticism and conservation; Asian studies (East); astronomy; astrophysics; biochemistry; biology/biological sciences; chemistry; Chinese; classics and languages, literatures and linguistics; cognitive psychology and psycholinguistics; comparative literature; computer science; dramatic/theatre arts; economics; English; environmental studies; ethnic, cultural minority, and gender studies related; film/cinema studies; fine/studio arts; French; geology/earth science; German; history; international relations and affairs; Islamic studies; Italian; Italian studies; Japanese; Jewish/Judaic studies; Latin; Latin American studies; linguistics; mathematics; medieval and Renaissance studies; music; neuroscience; peace studies and conflict resolution; philosophy; physics; political science and government; psychology; religious studies; Russian; Russian studies; sociology; Spanish; women's studies.
Academic Programs *Special study options:* adult/continuing education programs, advanced placement credit, double majors, independent study, internships, off-campus study, part-time degree program, services for LD students, student-designed majors, study abroad, summer session for credit. *ROTC:* Army (c), Air Force (c). *Unusual degree programs:* 3-2 in over 20 fields with Massachusetts Institute of Technology.
Library Margaret Clapp Library plus 3 others with 765,530 titles, 4,945 serial subscriptions, 22,777 audiovisual materials, an OPAC, a Web page.
Computers on Campus 200 computers available on campus for general student use. A campuswide network can be accessed from student residence rooms and from off campus that provide access to electronic bulletin boards. Internet access, online (class) registration, at least one staffed computer lab available. Computer purchase or lease plan available.
Student Life *Housing options:* women-only, cooperative, disabled students. Campus housing is university owned. Freshman campus housing is guaranteed. *Activities and organizations:* drama/theater group, student-run newspaper, radio station, choral group, student government, radio station, cultural clubs, rugby club, theater groups. *Campus security:* 24-hour emergency response devices and patrols, late-night transport/escort service, controlled dormitory access. *Student services:* health clinic, personal/psychological counseling, women's center.
Athletics Member NCAA. All Division III. *Intercollegiate sports:* basketball W, crew W, cross-country running W, fencing W, field hockey W, golf W, lacrosse W, rugby W(c), sailing W(c), skiing (downhill) W(c), soccer W, softball W, squash W, swimming W, tennis W, track and field W(c), ultimate Frisbee W(c), volleyball W. *Intramural sports:* archery W, badminton W, basketball W, crew W, cross-country running W, equestrian sports W, ice hockey W, racquetball W, sailing W(c), skiing (cross-country) W, soccer W, squash W, swimming W, table tennis W, tennis W, volleyball W, water polo W, weight lifting W.
Standardized Tests *Required:* SAT I and SAT II or ACT (for admission), SAT II: Subject Tests (for admission).
Costs (2003–04) *Comprehensive fee:* $36,336 includes full-time tuition ($27,134), mandatory fees ($590), and room and board ($8612). *College room only:* $4362. Room and board charges vary according to board plan. *Payment plans:* tuition prepayment, installment. *Waivers:* employees or children of employees.
Financial Aid Of all full-time matriculated undergraduates who enrolled in 2003, 1,467 applied for aid, 1,254 were judged to have need, 1,254 had their need fully met. 791 Federal Work-Study jobs (averaging $1156). 242 state and other part-time jobs (averaging $1228). *Average percent of need met:* 100%. *Average financial aid package:* $25,362. *Average need-based loan:* $3196. *Average need-based gift aid:* $22,554. *Average indebtedness upon graduation:* $11,913.
Applying *Options:* common application, electronic application, early admission, early decision, deferred entrance. *Application fee:* $50. *Required:* essay or personal statement, high school transcript, 3 letters of recommendation. *Required for some:* interview. *Recommended:* interview. *Application deadlines:* 1/15 (freshmen), 2/10 (transfers). *Early decision:* 11/1. *Notification:* 4/1 (freshmen), 12/15 (early decision), 4/1 (transfers).
Admissions Contact Ms. Jennifer Desjarlais, Director of Admission, Wellesley College, 106 Central Street, Green Hall 240, Wellesley, MA 02481-8203. *Phone:* 781-283-2270. *Fax:* 781-283-3678. *E-mail:* admission@wellesley.edu.

■ *See page 2796 for a narrative description.*

WENTWORTH INSTITUTE OF TECHNOLOGY
Boston, Massachusetts

- **Independent** 4-year, founded 1904
- **Calendar** semesters for freshmen and sophomores, trimesters for juniors and seniors
- **Degrees** certificates, associate, and bachelor's
- **Urban** 35-acre campus
- **Endowment** $74.8 million
- **Coed,** 3,273 undergraduate students, 77% full-time, 18% women, 82% men
- **Moderately difficult** entrance level, 70% of applicants were admitted

Founded in 1904, Wentworth Institute of Technology offers bachelor's degrees in architecture, computer science, design, engineering, engineering technology, and management of technology. Wentworth provides an education that balances classroom theory with laboratory/studio practice and work experience through its strong co-op program. Approximately 3,000 students attend this private coeducational institution, located on a 35-acre campus on Huntington Avenue, across from Boston's Museum of Fine Arts.

Undergraduates 2,535 full-time, 738 part-time. 5% African American, 6% Asian American or Pacific Islander, 4% Hispanic American, 0.3% Native American, 6% international, 4% transferred in, 50% live on campus.
Freshmen *Admission:* 3,623 applied, 2,548 admitted, 1,064 enrolled. *Test scores:* SAT verbal scores over 500: 42%; SAT math scores over 500: 61%; SAT verbal scores over 600: 10%; SAT math scores over 600: 17%; SAT verbal scores over 700: 1%; SAT math scores over 700: 2%.
Faculty *Total:* 239, 48% full-time. *Student/faculty ratio:* 24:1.
Majors Airframe mechanics and aircraft maintenance technology; architectural engineering technology; architecture; avionics maintenance technology; biomedical technology; business administration and management; civil engineering technology; computer engineering technology; computer science; construction engineering technology; construction management; electrical, electronic and communications engineering technology; electrical, electronics and communications engineering; engineering mechanics; engineering technology; environmental engineering technology; environmental/environmental health engineering; industrial design; industrial technology; interior design; mechanical engineering/mechanical technology.
Academic Programs *Special study options:* academic remediation for entering students, accelerated degree program, advanced placement credit, cooperative education, English as a second language, freshman honors college, internships,

Wentworth Institute of Technology (continued)
off-campus study, part-time degree program, services for LD students, study abroad, summer session for credit. *ROTC:* Army (c), Air Force (c).

Library Wentworth Alumni Library with 77,000 titles, 500 serial subscriptions, an OPAC, a Web page.

Computers on Campus 400 computers available on campus for general student use. A campuswide network can be accessed from student residence rooms and from off campus. At least one staffed computer lab available.

Student Life *Housing options:* coed. *Activities and organizations:* drama/theater group, student-run newspaper, radio station, intramural sports, Wentworth Events Board, Asian Students Association, ski and adventure club. *Campus security:* 24-hour emergency response devices and patrols, student patrols, late-night transport/escort service, controlled dormitory access. *Student services:* health clinic, personal/psychological counseling, women's center.

Athletics Member NCAA. All Division III. *Intercollegiate sports:* baseball M, basketball M/W, golf M/W, ice hockey M, lacrosse M, riflery M/W, rugby M(c), soccer M/W, softball W, tennis M/W, volleyball M/W. *Intramural sports:* archery M/W, badminton M/W, baseball M, basketball M/W, cross-country running M/W, golf M, ice hockey M, lacrosse M, riflery M/W, rugby M, skiing (downhill) M(c)/W(c), soccer M/W, softball W, tennis M/W, volleyball M/W, weight lifting M(c)/W(c).

Standardized Tests *Required:* SAT I or ACT (for admission).

Costs (2003–04) *Comprehensive fee:* $23,200 includes full-time tuition ($15,000) and room and board ($8200). Part-time tuition: $470 per credit.

Financial Aid Of all full-time matriculated undergraduates who enrolled in 2000, 2,276 applied for aid, 2,011 were judged to have need, 56 had their need fully met. *Average percent of need met:* 65%. *Average financial aid package:* $8146. *Average need-based loan:* $4957. *Average need-based gift aid:* $1814. *Average indebtedness upon graduation:* $6139.

Applying *Options:* common application, electronic application, deferred entrance. *Application fee:* $30. *Required:* high school transcript. *Recommended:* essay or personal statement, minimum 2.0 GPA, letters of recommendation, interview. *Application deadline:* rolling (freshmen), rolling (transfers). *Notification:* continuous (freshmen), continuous (transfers).

Admissions Contact Ms. Kathleen A. Lynch, Director of Admissions, Wentworth Institute of Technology, 550 Huntington Avenue, Boston, MA 02115-5998. *Phone:* 617-989-4009. *Toll-free phone:* 800-556-0610. *Fax:* 617-989-4010. *E-mail:* admissions@wit.edu.

■ *See page 2800 for a narrative description.*

WESTERN NEW ENGLAND COLLEGE
Springfield, Massachusetts

- **Independent** comprehensive, founded 1919
- **Calendar** semesters
- **Degrees** associate, bachelor's, master's, and first professional
- **Suburban** 215-acre campus
- **Endowment** $30.6 million
- **Coed,** 3,168 undergraduate students, 71% full-time, 37% women, 63% men
- **Moderately difficult** entrance level, 76% of applicants were admitted

Undergraduates 2,237 full-time, 931 part-time. Students come from 29 states and territories, 5 other countries, 44% are from out of state, 3% African American, 2% Asian American or Pacific Islander, 3% Hispanic American, 0.2% Native American, 0.4% international, 3% transferred in, 57% live on campus. *Retention:* 74% of 2002 full-time freshmen returned.

Freshmen *Admission:* 4,517 applied, 3,415 admitted, 704 enrolled. *Average high school GPA:* 3.06. *Test scores:* SAT verbal scores over 500: 64%; SAT math scores over 500: 70%; SAT verbal scores over 600: 15%; SAT math scores over 600: 24%; SAT verbal scores over 700: 1%; SAT math scores over 700: 2%.

Faculty *Total:* 339, 46% full-time, 62% with terminal degrees. *Student/faculty ratio:* 17:1.

Majors Accounting; advertising; biology/biological sciences; biomedical/medical engineering; business administration and management; chemistry; communication/speech communication and rhetoric; computer science; criminal justice/law enforcement administration; economics; electrical, electronics and communications engineering; engineering; English; finance; history; industrial engineering; information science/studies; international relations and affairs; liberal arts and sciences/liberal studies; marketing/marketing management; mathematics; mechanical engineering; political science and government; political science and government related; psychology; social work; sociology; sport and fitness administration.

Academic Programs *Special study options:* adult/continuing education programs, advanced placement credit, double majors, honors programs, independent study, internships, off-campus study, part-time degree program, services for LD students, student-designed majors, study abroad, summer session for credit. *ROTC:* Army (b), Air Force (b).

Library D'Amour Library plus 1 other with 151,896 titles, 352 serial subscriptions, 2,989 audiovisual materials, an OPAC, a Web page.

Computers on Campus 489 computers available on campus for general student use. A campuswide network can be accessed from student residence rooms and from off campus. Internet access, at least one staffed computer lab available.

Student Life *Housing options:* coed, men-only, women-only. Campus housing is university owned. Freshman campus housing is guaranteed. *Activities and organizations:* drama/theater group, student-run newspaper, radio station, choral group, Student Senate, Residence Hall Association, Campus Activities Board, student radio station, Management Association. *Campus security:* 24-hour emergency response devices and patrols, student patrols, controlled dormitory access, security cameras. *Student services:* health clinic, personal/psychological counseling.

Athletics Member NCAA. All Division III. *Intercollegiate sports:* baseball M, basketball M/W, bowling M/W, cross-country running M/W, field hockey W, football M, golf M, ice hockey M, lacrosse M/W, soccer M/W, softball W, swimming W, tennis M/W, volleyball W, wrestling M. *Intramural sports:* badminton M/W, basketball M/W, football M/W, racquetball M/W, soccer M/W, softball M/W, squash M/W, table tennis M/W, tennis M/W, volleyball M/W, water polo M/W.

Standardized Tests *Required:* SAT I or ACT (for admission).

Costs (2003–04) *Comprehensive fee:* $28,924 includes full-time tuition ($19,460), mandatory fees ($1364), and room and board ($8100). Full-time tuition and fees vary according to program and student level. Part-time tuition: $398 per credit hour. *Required fees:* $20 per term part-time. *Room and board:* Room and board charges vary according to board plan and housing facility. *Payment plans:* tuition prepayment, installment, deferred payment. *Waivers:* senior citizens and employees or children of employees.

Financial Aid Of all full-time matriculated undergraduates who enrolled in 2002, 1,965 applied for aid, 1,721 were judged to have need, 265 had their need fully met. In 2002, 153 non-need-based awards were made. *Average percent of need met:* 68%. *Average financial aid package:* $11,270. *Average need-based loan:* $3635. *Average need-based gift aid:* $6715. *Average non-need-based aid:* $5998.

Applying *Options:* common application, electronic application. *Application fee:* $50. *Required:* high school transcript, 1 letter of recommendation. *Recommended:* essay or personal statement, interview. *Application deadline:* rolling (freshmen), rolling (transfers). *Notification:* continuous (freshmen), continuous (transfers).

Admissions Contact Dr. Charles R. Pollock, Vice President of Enrollment Management, Western New England College, 1215 Wilbraham Road, Springfield, MA 01119. *Phone:* 413-782-1321. *Toll-free phone:* 800-325-1122 Ext. 1321. *Fax:* 413-782-1777. *E-mail:* ugradmis@wnec.edu.

■ *See page 2816 for a narrative description.*

WESTFIELD STATE COLLEGE
Westfield, Massachusetts

- **State-supported** comprehensive, founded 1838, part of Massachusetts Public Higher Education System
- **Calendar** semesters
- **Degrees** bachelor's, master's, post-master's, and postbachelor's certificates
- **Small-town** 227-acre campus
- **Endowment** $2.7 million
- **Coed,** 4,292 undergraduate students, 87% full-time, 56% women, 44% men
- **Moderately difficult** entrance level, 66% of applicants were admitted

Undergraduates 3,714 full-time, 578 part-time. Students come from 13 states and territories, 73% are from out of state, 3% African American, 0.6% Asian American or Pacific Islander, 3% Hispanic American, 0.3% Native American, 0.1% international, 7% transferred in, 59% live on campus. *Retention:* 76% of 2002 full-time freshmen returned.

Freshmen *Admission:* 3,838 applied, 2,521 admitted, 854 enrolled. *Average high school GPA:* 2.97. *Test scores:* SAT verbal scores over 500: 60%; SAT math scores over 500: 59%; ACT scores over 18: 83%; SAT verbal scores over 600: 10%; SAT math scores over 600: 10%; ACT scores over 24: 7%; SAT verbal scores over 700: 1%.

Faculty *Total:* 280, 61% full-time, 58% with terminal degrees. *Student/faculty ratio:* 18:1.

Majors Accounting; art; art teacher education; biology/biological sciences; business administration and management; business teacher education; city/urban, community and regional planning; clinical laboratory science/medical technology; commercial and advertising art; computer science; corrections; counselor education/school counseling and guidance; criminal justice/law enforcement administration; economics; education; elementary education; English; environmental biology; finance; geography; history; information science/studies; jazz/jazz studies; kindergarten/preschool education; liberal arts and sciences/liberal studies; literature; management information systems; marketing/marketing management; mass communication/media; mathematics; music; music history, literature, and theory; music management and merchandising; music teacher education; parks, recreation and leisure; physical education teaching and coaching; physical sciences; political science and government; pre-law studies; pre-medical studies; psychology; radio and television; reading teacher education; science teacher education; secondary education; social sciences; sociology; special education; voice and opera.

Academic Programs *Special study options:* adult/continuing education programs, advanced placement credit, cooperative education, distance learning, double majors, honors programs, independent study, internships, off-campus study, part-time degree program, services for LD students, student-designed majors, study abroad, summer session for credit. *ROTC:* Army (c), Air Force (c).

Library Ely Library with 124,363 titles, 819 serial subscriptions, 2,379 audiovisual materials, an OPAC, a Web page.

Computers on Campus 238 computers available on campus for general student use. A campuswide network can be accessed from student residence rooms and from off campus that provide access to on-line transcripts, grade reports, billing information. Internet access, online (class) registration, at least one staffed computer lab available.

Student Life *Housing options:* coed, disabled students. Campus housing is university owned. *Activities and organizations:* drama/theater group, student-run newspaper, radio and television station, choral group. *Campus security:* 24-hour emergency response devices and patrols, student patrols, late-night transport/escort service. *Student services:* health clinic, personal/psychological counseling, legal services.

Athletics Member NCAA. All Division III. *Intercollegiate sports:* baseball M, basketball M/W, cheerleading M/W, cross-country running M/W, field hockey W, football M, soccer M/W, softball W, swimming W, track and field M/W, volleyball W. *Intramural sports:* badminton M/W, basketball M/W, bowling M/W, football M/W, racquetball M/W, soccer M/W, softball M/W, tennis M/W, volleyball M/W, water polo M/W.

Standardized Tests *Required:* SAT I or ACT (for admission). *Recommended:* SAT I (for admission).

Costs (2003–04) *Tuition:* state resident $970 full-time; nonresident $7050 full-time. *Required fees:* $3587 full-time. *Room and board:* $5290; room only: $3250.

Financial Aid Of all full-time matriculated undergraduates who enrolled in 2002, 2,547 applied for aid, 1,617 were judged to have need, 517 had their need fully met. 339 Federal Work-Study jobs (averaging $1126). In 2002, 930 non-need-based awards were made. *Average percent of need met:* 80%. *Average financial aid package:* $5041. *Average need-based loan:* $2514. *Average need-based gift aid:* $3755. *Average non-need-based aid:* $4419. *Average indebtedness upon graduation:* $12,347.

Applying *Options:* deferred entrance. *Application fee:* $25. *Required:* high school transcript. *Recommended:* letters of recommendation. *Application deadlines:* 3/1 (freshmen), 4/1 (transfers).

Admissions Contact Ms. Emily Wilson, Assistant Director of Admissions, Westfield State College, 3577 Western Avenue, Westfield, MA 01086. *Phone:* 413-572-5218. *Toll-free phone:* 800-322-8401. *Fax:* 413-572-0520. *E-mail:* admission@wsc.ma.edu.

WHEATON COLLEGE

Norton, Massachusetts

- **Independent** 4-year, founded 1834
- **Calendar** semesters
- **Degree** bachelor's
- **Small-town** 385-acre campus with easy access to Boston
- **Endowment** $150.6 million
- **Coed,** 1,565 undergraduate students, 99% full-time, 64% women, 36% men
- **Moderately difficult** entrance level, 43% of applicants were admitted

Undergraduates 1,545 full-time, 20 part-time. Students come from 43 states and territories, 26 other countries, 67% are from out of state, 3% African American, 2% Asian American or Pacific Islander, 4% Hispanic American, 0.4% Native American, 2% international, 1% transferred in, 97% live on campus. *Retention:* 89% of 2002 full-time freshmen returned.

Freshmen *Admission:* 3,465 applied, 1,492 admitted, 445 enrolled. *Average high school GPA:* 3.45. *Test scores:* SAT verbal scores over 500: 97%; SAT math scores over 500: 97%; ACT scores over 18: 100%; SAT verbal scores over 600: 63%; SAT math scores over 600: 56%; ACT scores over 24: 91%; SAT verbal scores over 700: 11%; SAT math scores over 700: 6%; ACT scores over 30: 13%.

Faculty *Total:* 162, 75% full-time, 88% with terminal degrees. *Student/faculty ratio:* 11:1.

Majors American studies; anthropology; art; art history, criticism and conservation; Asian studies; astronomy; biochemistry; biology/biological sciences; chemistry; classics and languages, literatures and linguistics; computer science; dramatic/theatre arts; economics; English; environmental studies; fine/studio arts; French; German; Hispanic-American, Puerto Rican, and Mexican-American/Chicano studies; history; interdisciplinary studies; international relations and affairs; literature; mathematics; music; philosophy; physics; physiological psychology/psychobiology; political science and government; pre-medical studies; psychology; religious studies; Russian; Russian studies; sociology; women's studies.

Academic Programs *Special study options:* academic remediation for entering students, accelerated degree program, adult/continuing education programs, advanced placement credit, double majors, external degree program, honors programs, independent study, internships, off-campus study, part-time degree program, student-designed majors, study abroad. *ROTC:* Army (c). *Unusual degree programs:* 3-2 business administration with University of Rochester, Clark University; engineering with Dartmouth College, George Washington University, Worcester Polytechnic Institute; theology with Andover Newton Theological School, optometry with New England College of Optometry, communications with Emerson College, studio art with School of the Museum of Fine Arts.

Library Madeleine Clark Wallace Library plus 1 other with 381,749 titles, 2,046 serial subscriptions, 12,603 audiovisual materials, an OPAC, a Web page.

Computers on Campus 157 computers available on campus for general student use. A campuswide network can be accessed from student residence rooms and from off campus. Internet access, online (class) registration, at least one staffed computer lab available.

Student Life *Housing:* on-campus residence required through senior year. *Options:* coed, men-only, women-only, disabled students. *Activities and organizations:* drama/theater group, student-run newspaper, radio station, choral group, Student Government Association, Community Service Network, Amnesty International, a cappella singing groups, Programming Council. *Campus security:* 24-hour emergency response devices and patrols, student patrols, late-night transport/escort service, controlled dormitory access. *Student services:* health clinic, personal/psychological counseling, women's center.

Athletics Member NCAA. All Division III. *Intercollegiate sports:* baseball M, basketball M/W, cross-country running M/W, field hockey W, lacrosse M/W, soccer M/W, softball W, swimming M/W, tennis M/W, track and field M/W, volleyball W. *Intramural sports:* archery M/W, badminton M/W, basketball M/W, cross-country running M/W, equestrian sports M(c)/W(c), fencing M/W, field hockey W, golf M/W, ice hockey M(c)/W(c), lacrosse M/W, rugby M(c), sailing M(c)/W(c), skiing (cross-country) M/W, skiing (downhill) M(c)/W(c), soccer M/W, table tennis M/W, tennis M/W, track and field W(c), ultimate Frisbee M/W, volleyball M/W, water polo M/W, weight lifting M/W.

Costs (2003–04) *Comprehensive fee:* $36,330 includes full-time tuition ($28,675), mandatory fees ($225), and room and board ($7430). *College room only:* $3920.

Financial Aid Of all full-time matriculated undergraduates who enrolled in 2003, 983 applied for aid, 900 were judged to have need, 493 had their need fully met. 760 Federal Work-Study jobs (averaging $1728). 235 state and other part-time jobs (averaging $2199). In 2003, 169 non-need-based awards were made. *Average percent of need met:* 92%. *Average financial aid package:* $21,159. *Average need-based loan:* $4635. *Average need-based gift aid:* $16,164. *Average non-need-based aid:* $7625. *Average indebtedness upon graduation:* $20,188. *Financial aid deadline:* 2/1.

Applying *Options:* common application, electronic application, early admission, early decision, deferred entrance. *Application fee:* $55. *Required:* essay or personal statement, high school transcript, 2 letters of recommendation. *Recommended:* interview. *Application deadlines:* 1/15 (freshmen), 4/1 (transfers). *Early decision:* 11/15 (for plan 1), 1/15 (for plan 2). *Notification:* 4/1 (freshmen), 12/15 (early decision plan 1), 2/15 (early decision plan 2), 5/15 (transfers).

Admissions Contact Ms. Lynne M. Stack, Director of Admission, Wheaton College, 26 East Main Street, Norton, MA 02766. *Phone:* 508-286-8251. *Toll-free phone:* 800-394-6003. *Fax:* 508-286-8271. *E-mail:* admission@wheatoncollege.edu.

■ *See page 2836 for a narrative description.*

WHEELOCK COLLEGE

Boston, Massachusetts

- **Independent** comprehensive, founded 1888
- **Calendar** semesters
- **Degrees** associate, bachelor's, master's, post-master's, and postbachelor's certificates
- **Urban** 7-acre campus

Wheelock College (continued)

- **Endowment** $34.6 million
- **Coed, primarily women,** 587 undergraduate students, 98% full-time, 94% women, 6% men
- **Moderately difficult** entrance level, 67% of applicants were admitted

Undergraduates 577 full-time, 10 part-time. Students come from 20 states and territories, 46% are from out of state, 5% African American, 0.9% Asian American or Pacific Islander, 3% Hispanic American, 0.5% Native American, 0.9% international, 8% transferred in, 70% live on campus. *Retention:* 71% of 2002 full-time freshmen returned.

Freshmen *Admission:* 609 applied, 407 admitted, 139 enrolled. *Average high school GPA:* 3.09. *Test scores:* SAT verbal scores over 500: 68%; SAT math scores over 500: 57%; SAT verbal scores over 600: 23%; SAT math scores over 600: 15%; SAT verbal scores over 700: 4%.

Faculty *Total:* 116, 48% full-time, 59% with terminal degrees. *Student/faculty ratio:* 11:1.

Majors Child development; early childhood education; education; elementary education; human development and family studies; kindergarten/preschool education; social work; special education.

Academic Programs *Special study options:* academic remediation for entering students, advanced placement credit, double majors, honors programs, independent study, internships, off-campus study, part-time degree program, services for LD students, study abroad.

Library Wheelock College Library with 96,500 titles, 546 serial subscriptions, 5,058 audiovisual materials, an OPAC, a Web page.

Computers on Campus 120 computers available on campus for general student use. A campuswide network can be accessed from student residence rooms and from off campus. Internet access, at least one staffed computer lab available.

Student Life *Housing options:* coed, women-only, cooperative. Campus housing is university owned. Freshman campus housing is guaranteed. *Activities and organizations:* drama/theater group, choral group, Student Government Association, Campus Activities Board, AHANA Club, residence hall councils, class councils. *Campus security:* 24-hour patrols, late-night transport/escort service, controlled dormitory access, self-defense education. *Student services:* health clinic, personal/psychological counseling, women's center.

Athletics Member NCAA. All Division III. *Intercollegiate sports:* basketball W, field hockey W, soccer W, softball W, swimming W. *Intramural sports:* basketball M/W, racquetball M/W, soccer M, softball M/W, squash M/W, table tennis M/W, ultimate Frisbee M/W, volleyball M/W, water polo M/W.

Standardized Tests *Required:* SAT I or ACT (for admission).

Costs (2003–04) *Comprehensive fee:* $29,000 includes full-time tuition ($20,400) and room and board ($8600). Full-time tuition and fees vary according to location. Part-time tuition: $638 per credit. Part-time tuition and fees vary according to location. *Payment plan:* installment. *Waivers:* employees or children of employees.

Financial Aid Of all full-time matriculated undergraduates who enrolled in 2002, 489 applied for aid, 441 were judged to have need, 81 had their need fully met. 156 Federal Work-Study jobs (averaging $980). In 2002, 99 non-need-based awards were made. *Average percent of need met:* 76%. *Average financial aid package:* $14,176. *Average need-based loan:* $4939. *Average need-based gift aid:* $9464. *Average non-need-based aid:* $10,630. *Average indebtedness upon graduation:* $19,445.

Applying *Options:* common application, electronic application, early decision, deferred entrance. *Application fee:* $35. *Required:* essay or personal statement, high school transcript, 2 letters of recommendation. *Recommended:* minimum 2.0 GPA, interview. *Application deadlines:* 3/1 (freshmen), 4/15 (transfers). *Early decision:* 12/1. *Notification:* continuous until 4/15 (freshmen), 1/1 (early decision), continuous until 5/15 (transfers).

Admissions Contact Ms. Lynne E. Harding, Dean of Admissions, Wheelock College, 200 The Riverway, Boston, MA 02215. *Phone:* 617-879-2204. *Toll-free phone:* 800-734-5212. *Fax:* 617-566-4453. *E-mail:* undergrad@wheelock.edu.

■ *See page 2840 for a narrative description.*

WILLIAMS COLLEGE
Williamstown, Massachusetts

- **Independent** comprehensive, founded 1793
- **Calendar** 4-1-4
- **Degrees** bachelor's and master's
- **Small-town** 450-acre campus with easy access to Albany
- **Endowment** $980.2 million
- **Coed,** 2,045 undergraduate students, 98% full-time, 50% women, 50% men
- **Most difficult** entrance level, 21% of applicants were admitted

Undergraduates 1,995 full-time, 50 part-time. Students come from 51 states and territories, 32 other countries, 80% are from out of state, 9% African American, 9% Asian American or Pacific Islander, 8% Hispanic American, 0.2% Native American, 6% international, 0.2% transferred in, 96% live on campus. *Retention:* 97% of 2002 full-time freshmen returned.

Freshmen *Admission:* 5,341 applied, 1,133 admitted, 533 enrolled. *Test scores:* SAT verbal scores over 500: 100%; SAT math scores over 500: 99%; SAT verbal scores over 600: 92%; SAT math scores over 600: 93%; SAT verbal scores over 700: 60%; SAT math scores over 700: 60%.

Faculty *Total:* 278, 87% full-time, 95% with terminal degrees. *Student/faculty ratio:* 8:1.

Majors American studies; anthropology; art history, criticism and conservation; Asian studies; astronomy; astrophysics; biology/biological sciences; chemistry; Chinese; classics and languages, literatures and linguistics; computer science; dramatic/theatre arts; economics; English; fine/studio arts; French; geology/earth science; German; history; Japanese; literature; mathematics; music; philosophy; physics; political science and government; psychology; religious studies; Russian; sociology; Spanish.

Academic Programs *Special study options:* accelerated degree program, advanced placement credit, double majors, honors programs, independent study, internships, off-campus study, services for LD students, student-designed majors, study abroad. *Unusual degree programs:* 3-2 engineering with Columbia University, Washington University in St. Louis.

Library Sawyer Library plus 9 others with 888,504 titles, 1,904 serial subscriptions, 37,456 audiovisual materials, an OPAC, a Web page.

Computers on Campus 150 computers available on campus for general student use. A campuswide network can be accessed from student residence rooms and from off campus. At least one staffed computer lab available.

Student Life *Housing:* on-campus residence required through senior year. *Options:* coed. *Activities and organizations:* drama/theater group, student-run newspaper, radio station, choral group, marching band. *Campus security:* 24-hour emergency response devices and patrols, student patrols, late-night transport/escort service, controlled dormitory access. *Student services:* health clinic, personal/psychological counseling, women's center.

Athletics Member NCAA. All Division III except men's and women's skiing (cross-country) (Division I), men's and women's skiing (downhill) (Division I). *Intercollegiate sports:* baseball M, basketball M/W, crew M/W, cross-country running M/W, equestrian sports M(c)/W(c), field hockey W, football M, golf M/W(c), ice hockey M/W, lacrosse M/W, rugby M(c)/W(c), sailing M(c)/W(c), skiing (cross-country) M/W, skiing (downhill) M/W, soccer M/W, softball W, squash M/W, swimming M/W, tennis M/W, track and field M/W, volleyball M(c)/W, water polo M(c)/W(c), wrestling M. *Intramural sports:* badminton M/W, baseball M(c), basketball M/W, fencing M(c)/W(c), ice hockey M/W, skiing (cross-country) M/W, skiing (downhill) M/W, soccer M/W, softball M/W, volleyball M/W, water polo M/W.

Standardized Tests *Required:* SAT I and SAT II or ACT (for admission).

Costs (2003–04) *Comprehensive fee:* $35,750 includes full-time tuition ($27,890), mandatory fees ($200), and room and board ($7660). *College room only:* $3840.

Financial Aid Of all full-time matriculated undergraduates who enrolled in 2003, 972 applied for aid, 828 were judged to have need, 828 had their need fully met. 440 Federal Work-Study jobs (averaging $1656). 265 state and other part-time jobs (averaging $1664). *Average percent of need met:* 100%. *Average financial aid package:* $26,212. *Average need-based loan:* $2626. *Average need-based gift aid:* $23,665. *Average indebtedness upon graduation:* $10,627. *Financial aid deadline:* 2/1.

Applying *Options:* common application, electronic application, early admission, early decision, deferred entrance. *Application fee:* $50. *Required:* essay or personal statement, high school transcript, 2 letters of recommendation. *Application deadlines:* 1/1 (freshmen), 3/1 (transfers). *Early decision:* 11/10. *Notification:* 4/9 (freshmen), 12/15 (early decision), 5/1 (transfers).

Admissions Contact Mr. Richard L. Nesbitt, Director of Admission, Williams College, PO Box 487, Williamstown, MA 01267. *Phone:* 413-597-2211. *Fax:* 413-597-4052. *E-mail:* admission@williams.edu.

WORCESTER POLYTECHNIC INSTITUTE
Worcester, Massachusetts

- **Independent** university, founded 1865
- **Calendar** 4 7-week terms
- **Degrees** bachelor's, master's, doctoral, post-master's, and postbachelor's certificates
- **Suburban** 80-acre campus with easy access to Boston
- **Endowment** $213.3 million
- **Coed,** 2,785 undergraduate students, 97% full-time, 24% women, 76% men
- **Very difficult** entrance level, 71% of applicants were admitted

Undergraduates 2,711 full-time, 74 part-time. Students come from 45 states and territories, 70 other countries, 50% are from out of state, 1% African

American, 7% Asian American or Pacific Islander, 3% Hispanic American, 0.4% Native American, 4% international, 2% transferred in, 67% live on campus. *Retention:* 92% of 2002 full-time freshmen returned.

Freshmen *Admission:* 3,576 applied, 2,547 admitted, 633 enrolled. *Average high school GPA:* 3.60. *Test scores:* SAT verbal scores over 500: 96%; SAT math scores over 500: 100%; SAT verbal scores over 600: 61%; SAT math scores over 600: 87%; SAT verbal scores over 700: 15%; SAT math scores over 700: 32%.

Faculty *Total:* 338, 71% full-time, 89% with terminal degrees. *Student/faculty ratio:* 13:1.

Majors Actuarial science; aerospace, aeronautical and astronautical engineering; animal genetics; applied mathematics; biochemistry; biology/biological sciences; biology/biotechnology laboratory technician; biomedical/medical engineering; biomedical sciences; business administration and management; cell biology and histology; chemical engineering; chemistry; civil engineering; computer and information sciences; computer engineering; computer science; economics; electrical, electronics and communications engineering; engineering/industrial management; engineering mechanics; engineering physics; engineering related; environmental/environmental health engineering; environmental studies; fluid/thermal sciences; history; history and philosophy of science and technology; humanities; industrial engineering; information science/studies; interdisciplinary studies; management information systems; materials engineering; materials science; mathematics; mechanical engineering; medical microbiology and bacteriology; medicinal and pharmaceutical chemistry; molecular biology; music; nuclear engineering; philosophy; physical sciences related; physics; science, technology and society; social sciences; technical and business writing.

Academic Programs *Special study options:* accelerated degree program, adult/continuing education programs, advanced placement credit, cooperative education, double majors, English as a second language, independent study, off-campus study, part-time degree program, services for LD students, student-designed majors, study abroad, summer session for credit. *ROTC:* Army (b), Navy (c), Air Force (b).

Library Gordon Library with 146,372 titles, 982 serial subscriptions, 2,500 audiovisual materials, an OPAC, a Web page.

Computers on Campus 1000 computers available on campus for general student use. A campuswide network can be accessed from student residence rooms and from off campus. Internet access, online (class) registration, at least one staffed computer lab available.

Student Life *Housing options:* coed. Freshman campus housing is guaranteed. *Activities and organizations:* drama/theater group, student-run newspaper, radio station, choral group, student government, Masque (Drama Group), music groups, intramural sports, ethnic clubs, national fraternities, national sororities. *Campus security:* 24-hour emergency response devices and patrols, student patrols, late-night transport/escort service. *Student services:* health clinic, personal/psychological counseling, women's center.

Athletics Member NCAA. All Division III. *Intercollegiate sports:* baseball M, basketball M/W, bowling M(c)/W(c), cheerleading M(c)/W(c), crew M(c)/W(c), cross-country running M/W, fencing M(c)/W(c), field hockey W, football M, golf M, ice hockey M(c), lacrosse M(c)/W(c), rugby M(c)/W(c), sailing M(c)/W(c), skiing (downhill) M(c)/W(c), soccer M/W, softball W, swimming M/W, tennis M/W, track and field M/W, ultimate Frisbee M(c), volleyball M(c)/W, water polo M(c)/W(c), wrestling M. *Intramural sports:* basketball M/W, bowling M/W, cross-country running M/W, fencing M/W, football M, golf M/W, ice hockey M, lacrosse M/W, sailing M/W, skiing (downhill) M/W, soccer M/W, softball M/W, swimming M/W, table tennis M/W, track and field M/W, volleyball M/W, water polo M/W, wrestling M.

Standardized Tests *Required:* SAT I and SAT II or ACT (for admission).

Costs (2003–04) *Comprehensive fee:* $37,604 includes full-time tuition ($28,420), mandatory fees ($200), and room and board ($8984). Part-time tuition: $642 per credit hour. *College room only:* $5184. Room and board charges vary according to board plan and housing facility. *Waivers:* employees or children of employees.

Financial Aid Of all full-time matriculated undergraduates who enrolled in 2003, 2,112 applied for aid, 1,965 were judged to have need, 529 had their need fully met. 949 Federal Work-Study jobs (averaging $660). In 2003, 217 non-need-based awards were made. *Average percent of need met:* 90%. *Average financial aid package:* $21,030. *Average need-based loan:* $6104. *Average need-based gift aid:* $15,776. *Average non-need-based aid:* $17,352. *Average indebtedness upon graduation:* $25,609.

Applying *Options:* common application, electronic application, early admission, early decision, early action, deferred entrance. *Application fee:* $60. *Required:* essay or personal statement, high school transcript, 2 letters of recommendation. *Required for some:* interview. *Application deadlines:* 2/1 (freshmen), 4/15 (transfers). *Early decision:* 11/15 (for plan 1), 1/1 (for plan 2). *Notification:* 4/1 (freshmen), 12/15 (early decision plan 1), 2/1 (early decision plan 2), 12/15 (early action), 5/10 (transfers).

Admissions Contact Ms. Kristin Tichenor, Director of Admissions, Worcester Polytechnic Institute, 100 Institute Road, Worcester, MA 01609-2280. *Phone:* 508-831-5286. *Fax:* 508-831-5875. *E-mail:* admissions@wpi.edu.

WORCESTER STATE COLLEGE
Worcester, Massachusetts

- **State-supported** comprehensive, founded 1874, part of Massachusetts Public Higher Education System
- **Calendar** semesters
- **Degrees** certificates, bachelor's, master's, and postbachelor's certificates
- **Urban** 53-acre campus with easy access to Boston
- **Endowment** $7.8 million
- **Coed,** 4,665 undergraduate students, 66% full-time, 60% women, 40% men
- **Moderately difficult** entrance level, 56% of applicants were admitted

Undergraduates 3,101 full-time, 1,564 part-time. Students come from 19 states and territories, 41 other countries, 3% are from out of state, 4% African American, 3% Asian American or Pacific Islander, 4% Hispanic American, 0.3% Native American, 3% international, 8% transferred in, 15% live on campus. *Retention:* 72% of 2002 full-time freshmen returned.

Freshmen *Admission:* 2,939 applied, 1,634 admitted, 628 enrolled. *Average high school GPA:* 2.92. *Test scores:* SAT verbal scores over 500: 53%; SAT math scores over 500: 52%; ACT scores over 18: 69%; SAT verbal scores over 600: 8%; SAT math scores over 600: 11%; ACT scores over 24: 17%; SAT math scores over 700: 1%; ACT scores over 30: 3%.

Faculty *Total:* 369, 46% full-time. *Student/faculty ratio:* 15:1.

Majors Biological and physical sciences; biology/biological sciences; biotechnology; business administration and management; chemistry; communication disorders; computer and information sciences; criminal justice/safety; economics; elementary education; English; geography; health professions related; history; kindergarten/preschool education; mass communication/media; mathematics; nursing (registered nurse training); occupational therapy; psychology; sociology; Spanish; urban studies/affairs.

Academic Programs *Special study options:* accelerated degree program, adult/continuing education programs, advanced placement credit, double majors, honors programs, independent study, internships, off-campus study, part-time degree program, study abroad, summer session for credit. *ROTC:* Army (c), Navy (c), Air Force (c).

Library Learning Resources Center with 1,137 serial subscriptions, 11,963 audiovisual materials, an OPAC, a Web page.

Computers on Campus 250 computers available on campus for general student use. A campuswide network can be accessed from student residence rooms. Internet access, at least one staffed computer lab available.

Student Life *Housing options:* men-only, women-only, disabled students. *Activities and organizations:* drama/theater group, student-run newspaper, radio and television station, choral group, Senate, SEC (Student Events Committee), TWA (Third World Alliance), WSCW (Radio Station), Dance Company/Club. *Campus security:* 24-hour emergency response devices and patrols, late-night transport/escort service, controlled dormitory access, well-lit campus, limited access to campus at night. *Student services:* personal/psychological counseling, women's center.

Athletics Member NCAA, NAIA. All NCAA Division III. *Intercollegiate sports:* baseball M, basketball M/W, cheerleading M/W, crew M(c)/W(c), cross-country running M/W, equestrian sports M(c)/W(c), field hockey W, football M, golf M, ice hockey M, lacrosse W, soccer M/W, softball W, tennis M/W, track and field M/W, volleyball M/W. *Intramural sports:* baseball M, basketball M/W, cheerleading M/W, crew M/W, cross-country running M/W, field hockey W, football M, golf M, ice hockey M, lacrosse W, soccer M/W, softball W, tennis M/W, track and field M/W, volleyball M/W.

Standardized Tests *Required for some:* SAT I or ACT (for admission).

Costs (2003–04) *Tuition:* state resident $970 full-time, $40 per credit part-time; nonresident $7050 full-time, $294 per credit part-time. Full-time tuition and fees vary according to class time, course load, and reciprocity agreements. Part-time tuition and fees vary according to class time, course load, and reciprocity agreements. *Required fees:* $3153 full-time, $131 per credit part-time. *Room and board:* $5500. Room and board charges vary according to board plan and housing facility. *Payment plan:* deferred payment. *Waivers:* senior citizens and employees or children of employees.

Financial Aid Of all full-time matriculated undergraduates who enrolled in 2003, 1,920 applied for aid, 1,374 were judged to have need, 628 had their need fully met. In 2003, 40 non-need-based awards were made. *Average percent of need met:* 79%. *Average financial aid package:* $6868. *Average need-based loan:* $1532. *Average need-based gift aid:* $1836. *Average non-need-based aid:* $1541. *Average indebtedness upon graduation:* $11,843.

Applying *Options:* electronic application, early admission, deferred entrance. *Application fee:* $20. *Required:* high school transcript, minimum 2.0 GPA.

Worcester State College (continued)
Application deadlines: 8/1 (freshmen), 6/1 (out-of-state freshmen), 6/1 (transfers). *Notification:* continuous (freshmen), continuous (transfers).

Admissions Contact Mr. Alan Kines, Director of Admissions, Worcester State College, 486 Chandler Street, Administration Building, Room 204, Worcester, MA 01602-2597. *Phone:* 508-929-8758. *Toll-free phone:* 866-WSC-CALL. *Fax:* 508-929-8183. *E-mail:* admissions@worcester.edu.

■ *See page 2876 for a narrative description.*

MICHIGAN

ADRIAN COLLEGE
Adrian, Michigan

- **Independent** 4-year, founded 1859, affiliated with United Methodist Church
- **Calendar** semesters
- **Degrees** associate and bachelor's
- **Small-town** 100-acre campus with easy access to Detroit and Toledo
- **Endowment** $33.5 million
- **Coed,** 1,028 undergraduate students, 96% full-time, 56% women, 44% men
- **Moderately difficult** entrance level, 88% of applicants were admitted

Adrian College offers more than 40 majors and programs that are complemented by a liberal arts core. Academic and cocurricular opportunities develop students' fullest potential. Students have free Internet and e-mail access, internships, and study-abroad options, and there is a 90% placement record for graduates.

Undergraduates 986 full-time, 42 part-time. Students come from 18 states and territories, 8 other countries, 21% are from out of state, 5% African American, 0.8% Asian American or Pacific Islander, 1% Hispanic American, 0.4% Native American, 1% international, 4% transferred in, 75% live on campus. *Retention:* 66% of 2002 full-time freshmen returned.

Freshmen *Admission:* 1,300 applied, 1,143 admitted, 307 enrolled. *Average high school GPA:* 3.00. *Test scores:* ACT scores over 18: 81%; ACT scores over 24: 28%; ACT scores over 30: 1%.

Faculty *Total:* 107, 61% full-time, 58% with terminal degrees. *Student/faculty ratio:* 13:1.

Majors Accounting; art; arts management; art teacher education; bilingual and multilingual education; biology/biological sciences; broadcast journalism; business administration and management; business teacher education; chemistry; criminal justice/law enforcement administration; dramatic/theatre arts; economics; education; education (K-12); elementary education; English; environmental studies; French; geology/earth science; German; history; human services; interior design; international business/trade/commerce; international relations and affairs; kinesiology and exercise science; mass communication/media; mathematics; music; music teacher education; physical education teaching and coaching; physics; political science and government; pre-medical studies; pre-veterinary studies; psychology; religious studies; science teacher education; secondary education; social sciences; social work; sociology; Spanish.

Academic Programs *Special study options:* academic remediation for entering students, adult/continuing education programs, cooperative education, double majors, English as a second language, honors programs, independent study, internships, off-campus study, part-time degree program, services for LD students, student-designed majors, study abroad, summer session for credit. *Unusual degree programs:* 3-2 engineering with University of Detroit Mercy, Washington University in St. Louis.

Library Shipman Library with 143,484 titles, 610 serial subscriptions, 1,178 audiovisual materials, an OPAC, a Web page.

Computers on Campus 130 computers available on campus for general student use. A campuswide network can be accessed from student residence rooms and from off campus. Internet access, at least one staffed computer lab available.

Student Life *Housing:* on-campus residence required through junior year. *Options:* coed, disabled students. Campus housing is university owned. Freshman campus housing is guaranteed. *Activities and organizations:* drama/theater group, student-run newspaper, radio station, choral group, student government, volunteerism, Greek organizations, Adrian College Theatre, musical ensembles, national fraternities, national sororities. *Campus security:* 24-hour patrols, student patrols, late-night transport/escort service. *Student services:* health clinic, personal/psychological counseling.

Athletics Member NCAA. All Division III. *Intercollegiate sports:* baseball M, basketball M/W, cross-country running M/W, football M, golf M/W, soccer M/W, softball W, tennis M/W, track and field M/W, volleyball W. *Intramural sports:* badminton M/W, basketball M/W, cheerleading W, football M/W, golf M, racquetball M/W, soccer M/W, softball M/W, tennis M/W, volleyball M/W.

Standardized Tests *Required:* SAT I or ACT (for admission). *Recommended:* ACT (for admission).

Costs (2003–04) *Comprehensive fee:* $22,330 includes full-time tuition ($16,470), mandatory fees ($100), and room and board ($5760). *College room only:* $2460. Room and board charges vary according to board plan. *Payment plan:* installment. *Waivers:* children of alumni and employees or children of employees.

Financial Aid Of all full-time matriculated undergraduates who enrolled in 2003, 967 applied for aid, 765 were judged to have need, 626 had their need fully met. 654 Federal Work-Study jobs (averaging $988). In 2003, 193 non-need-based awards were made. *Average percent of need met:* 98%. *Average financial aid package:* $15,434. *Average need-based loan:* $4267. *Average need-based gift aid:* $8923. *Average non-need-based aid:* $7551. *Average indebtedness upon graduation:* $15,949.

Applying *Options:* common application, electronic application, deferred entrance. *Application fee:* $20. *Required:* high school transcript. *Required for some:* essay or personal statement. *Recommended:* interview. *Application deadlines:* 8/15 (freshmen), 8/15 (transfers). *Notification:* continuous (freshmen), continuous (transfers).

Admissions Contact Ms. Janel Sutkus, Director of Admissions, Adrian College, 110 South Madison Street, Adrian, MI 49221. *Phone:* 517-265-5161 Ext. 4326. *Toll-free phone:* 800-877-2246. *Fax:* 517-264-3331. *E-mail:* admissions@adrian.edu.

■ *See page 1134 for a narrative description.*

ALBION COLLEGE
Albion, Michigan

- **Independent Methodist** 4-year, founded 1835
- **Calendar** semesters
- **Degree** bachelor's
- **Small-town** 565-acre campus with easy access to Detroit
- **Endowment** $136.6 million
- **Coed,** 1,732 undergraduate students, 98% full-time, 57% women, 43% men
- **Moderately difficult** entrance level, 87% of applicants were admitted

Undergraduates 1,706 full-time, 26 part-time. Students come from 32 states and territories, 19 other countries, 6% are from out of state, 2% African American, 2% Asian American or Pacific Islander, 0.8% Hispanic American, 0.3% Native American, 1% international, 2% transferred in, 99% live on campus. *Retention:* 86% of 2002 full-time freshmen returned.

Freshmen *Admission:* 1,534 applied, 1,332 admitted, 487 enrolled. *Average high school GPA:* 3.54. *Test scores:* SAT verbal scores over 500: 84%; SAT math scores over 500: 86%; ACT scores over 18: 98%; SAT verbal scores over 600: 46%; SAT math scores over 600: 44%; ACT scores over 24: 66%; SAT verbal scores over 700: 7%; SAT math scores over 700: 9%; ACT scores over 30: 12%.

Faculty *Total:* 157, 78% full-time, 83% with terminal degrees. *Student/faculty ratio:* 13:1.

Majors American studies; anthropology; art; biology/biological sciences; business administration and management; chemistry; computer science; dramatic/theatre arts; economics; education; elementary education; English; environmental studies; French; geology/earth science; German; history; human services; international relations and affairs; mass communication/media; mathematics; modern languages; music; philosophy; physical education teaching and coaching; physics; political science and government; pre-law studies; pre-medical studies; pre-veterinary studies; psychology; public policy analysis; religious studies; secondary education; sociology; Spanish; women's studies.

Academic Programs *Special study options:* advanced placement credit, double majors, honors programs, independent study, internships, off-campus study, part-time degree program, services for LD students, student-designed majors, study abroad, summer session for credit. *Unusual degree programs:* 3-2 engineering with Columbia University, University of Michigan, Case Western Reserve University, Michigan Technological University, Washington University in St. Louis; forestry with Duke University, Washington University in St. Louis; nursing with Case Western Reserve University; public policy studies with University of Michigan, fine arts with Bank Street College of Education.

Library Stockwell Mudd Libraries with 363,000 titles, 2,016 serial subscriptions, 6,540 audiovisual materials, an OPAC, a Web page.

Computers on Campus 411 computers available on campus for general student use. A campuswide network can be accessed from student residence rooms and from off campus. Internet access, online (class) registration, at least one staffed computer lab available.

Student Life *Housing:* on-campus residence required through senior year. *Options:* coed, women-only, cooperative, disabled students. Campus housing is university owned. Freshman campus housing is guaranteed. *Activities and organizations:* drama/theater group, student-run newspaper, radio and television station, choral group, marching band, Alpha Phi Omega, Union Board, Inter-Varsity Christian Fellowship, Student Senate, national fraternities, national sororities. *Campus security:* 24-hour emergency response devices and patrols, student patrols, late-night transport/escort service, controlled dormitory access. *Student services:* health clinic, personal/psychological counseling, women's center.

Athletics Member NCAA. All Division III. *Intercollegiate sports:* baseball M, basketball M/W, cheerleading M/W, cross-country running M/W, football M, golf M/W, soccer M/W, softball W, swimming M/W, tennis M/W, track and field M/W, volleyball M(c)/W. *Intramural sports:* badminton M/W, basketball M/W, bowling M/W, equestrian sports M/W, field hockey W, football M, golf M/W, ice hockey M(c), lacrosse M/W, rugby M(c)/W(c), sailing M(c)/W(c), soccer M/W, softball M/W, swimming M/W, table tennis M/W, tennis M/W, track and field M/W, volleyball M/W, water polo M(c)/W(c).

Standardized Tests *Required:* SAT I or ACT (for admission). *Required for some:* SAT II: Subject Tests (for admission), SAT II: Writing Test (for admission).

Costs (2003–04) *Comprehensive fee:* $28,210 includes full-time tuition ($21,692), mandatory fees ($256), and room and board ($6262). *College room only:* $3062. Room and board charges vary according to housing facility. *Payment plan:* installment. *Waivers:* children of alumni and employees or children of employees.

Financial Aid Of all full-time matriculated undergraduates who enrolled in 2003, 1,242 applied for aid, 1,096 were judged to have need, 679 had their need fully met. 555 Federal Work-Study jobs (averaging $1190). In 2003, 563 non-need-based awards were made. *Average percent of need met:* 95%. *Average financial aid package:* $18,706. *Average need-based loan:* $4285. *Average need-based gift aid:* $14,791. *Average non-need-based aid:* $10,289. *Average indebtedness upon graduation:* $19,802.

Applying *Options:* common application, electronic application, early admission, deferred entrance. *Application fee:* $20. *Required:* essay or personal statement, high school transcript, 1 letter of recommendation. *Required for some:* interview. *Recommended:* minimum 3.0 GPA. *Application deadline:* 7/1 (freshmen), rolling (transfers). *Notification:* continuous (freshmen).

Admissions Contact Mr. Doug Kellar, Associate Vice President for Enrollment, Albion College, 611 East Porter Street, Albion, MI 49224. *Phone:* 517-629-0600. *Toll-free phone:* 800-858-6770. *E-mail:* admissions@albion.edu.

■ *See page 1144 for a narrative description.*

ALMA COLLEGE
Alma, Michigan

- **Independent Presbyterian** 4-year, founded 1886
- **Calendar** 4-4-1
- **Degree** bachelor's
- **Small-town** 125-acre campus
- **Endowment** $85.0 million
- **Coed,** 1,291 undergraduate students, 97% full-time, 58% women, 42% men
- **Moderately difficult** entrance level, 77% of applicants were admitted

Undergraduates 1,249 full-time, 42 part-time. Students come from 20 states and territories, 4% are from out of state, 2% African American, 1% Asian American or Pacific Islander, 2% Hispanic American, 0.8% Native American, 0.1% international, 2% transferred in, 86% live on campus. *Retention:* 85% of 2002 full-time freshmen returned.

Freshmen *Admission:* 1,497 applied, 1,155 admitted, 322 enrolled. *Average high school GPA:* 3.43. *Test scores:* ACT scores over 18: 98%; ACT scores over 24: 60%; ACT scores over 30: 10%.

Faculty *Total:* 135, 62% full-time, 67% with terminal degrees. *Student/faculty ratio:* 12:1.

Majors Accounting; anthropology; art; art teacher education; biochemistry; biological and physical sciences; biology/biological sciences; biology teacher education; business administration and management; chemistry; chemistry teacher education; communication and media related; computer science; computer teacher education; dance; design and visual communications; dramatic/theatre arts; early childhood education; economics; education; elementary education; English; English/language arts teacher education; fine/studio arts; French; French language teacher education; German; German language teacher education; gerontology; graphic design; health science; health teacher education; history; history teacher education; humanities; international business/trade/commerce; kindergarten/preschool education; kinesiology and exercise science; liberal arts and sciences/liberal studies; marketing/marketing management; mathematics; mathematics teacher education; medical illustration; modern languages; music; music performance; music teacher education; philosophy; physical education teaching and coaching; physics; physics teacher education; political science and government; pre-dentistry studies; pre-law studies; pre-medical studies; pre-theology/pre-ministerial studies; pre-veterinary studies; psychology; psychology teacher education; public health; religious studies; science teacher education; secondary education; social sciences; social science teacher education; social studies teacher education; sociology; Spanish; Spanish language teacher education.

Academic Programs *Special study options:* academic remediation for entering students, advanced placement credit, double majors, independent study, internships, off-campus study, services for LD students, student-designed majors, study abroad, summer session for credit. *ROTC:* Army (c). *Unusual degree programs:* 3-2 engineering with University of Michigan, Michigan Technological University, Washington University in St. Louis; occupational therapy with Washington University in St. Louis.

Library Kerhl Building-Monteith Library with 246,649 titles, 1,157 serial subscriptions, 7,962 audiovisual materials, an OPAC, a Web page.

Computers on Campus 684 computers available on campus for general student use. A campuswide network can be accessed from student residence rooms and from off campus. Internet access, at least one staffed computer lab available.

Student Life *Housing:* on-campus residence required through senior year. *Options:* coed, women-only. Campus housing is university owned. Freshman campus housing is guaranteed. *Activities and organizations:* drama/theater group, student-run newspaper, radio station, choral group, marching band, Ambassadors, Alma College Union Board, Trinity Baptist Fellowship, student government, SOS (Students Offering Service), national fraternities, national sororities. *Campus security:* 24-hour emergency response devices and patrols. *Student services:* health clinic, personal/psychological counseling, women's center.

Athletics Member NCAA. All Division III. *Intercollegiate sports:* baseball M, basketball M/W, cheerleading M(c)/W(c), cross-country running M/W, football M, golf M/W, soccer M/W, softball W, swimming M/W, tennis M/W, track and field M/W, volleyball W. *Intramural sports:* basketball M/W, football M/W, lacrosse M(c), rock climbing M(c)/W(c), soccer M/W, softball M/W, tennis M/W, ultimate Frisbee M/W, volleyball M/W.

Standardized Tests *Required:* SAT I or ACT (for admission).

Costs (2003–04) *Comprehensive fee:* $25,566 includes full-time tuition ($18,684), mandatory fees ($170), and room and board ($6712). Part-time tuition: $716 per credit. Part-time tuition and fees vary according to course load. *Required fees:* $716 per credit part-time. *College room only:* $3324. Room and board charges vary according to board plan and housing facility. *Payment plans:* installment, deferred payment. *Waivers:* employees or children of employees.

Financial Aid Of all full-time matriculated undergraduates who enrolled in 2003, 1,242 applied for aid, 984 were judged to have need, 326 had their need fully met. 140 Federal Work-Study jobs (averaging $950). 30 state and other part-time jobs (averaging $1000). In 2003, 251 non-need-based awards were made. *Average percent of need met:* 86%. *Average financial aid package:* $16,461. *Average need-based loan:* $5111. *Average need-based gift aid:* $12,568. *Average non-need-based aid:* $11,301. *Average indebtedness upon graduation:* $19,572.

Applying *Options:* electronic application, early admission, early action, deferred entrance. *Application fee:* $25. *Required:* high school transcript, minimum 3.0 GPA, minimum SAT score of 1030 or ACT score of 22. *Recommended:* essay or personal statement, interview. *Application deadline:* rolling (freshmen), rolling (transfers). *Notification:* continuous (freshmen), 11/15 (early action), continuous (transfers).

Admissions Contact Mr. Paul Pollatz, Director of Admissions, Alma College, Admissions Office, Alma, MI 48801-1599. *Phone:* 989-463-7139. *Toll-free phone:* 800-321-ALMA. *Fax:* 989-463-7057. *E-mail:* admissions@alma.edu.

■ *See page 1156 for a narrative description.*

ANDREWS UNIVERSITY
Berrien Springs, Michigan

- **Independent Seventh-day Adventist** university, founded 1874
- **Calendar** semesters
- **Degrees** associate, bachelor's, master's, doctoral, first professional, and post-master's certificates
- **Small-town** 1650-acre campus
- **Endowment** $15.9 million
- **Coed,** 1,687 undergraduate students, 86% full-time, 53% women, 47% men
- **Moderately difficult** entrance level, 58% of applicants were admitted

Undergraduates 1,455 full-time, 232 part-time. Students come from 48 states and territories, 49 other countries, 52% are from out of state, 20% African American, 9% Asian American or Pacific Islander, 10% Hispanic American, 0.2% Native American, 12% international, 8% transferred in, 58% live on campus. *Retention:* 76% of 2002 full-time freshmen returned.

Freshmen *Admission:* 1,009 applied, 585 admitted, 325 enrolled. *Average high school GPA:* 3.32. *Test scores:* SAT verbal scores over 500: 63%; SAT math scores over 500: 61%; ACT scores over 18: 88%; SAT verbal scores over 600: 27%; SAT math scores over 600: 27%; ACT scores over 24: 43%; SAT verbal scores over 700: 7%; SAT math scores over 700: 7%; ACT scores over 30: 7%.

Andrews University (continued)

Faculty *Total:* 234, 94% full-time, 66% with terminal degrees. *Student/faculty ratio:* 12:1.

Majors Accounting; agribusiness; agricultural business and management; agricultural mechanization; agricultural teacher education; agriculture; agronomy and crop science; airline pilot and flight crew; anatomy; animal sciences; architectural engineering; architecture; art; art history, criticism and conservation; art teacher education; audiology and speech-language pathology; automobile/automotive mechanics technology; avionics maintenance technology; behavioral sciences; biblical studies; biochemistry; biology/biological sciences; biomedical technology; biophysics; botany/plant biology; business administration and management; business/managerial economics; chemistry; clinical laboratory science/medical technology; clinical/medical laboratory technology; commercial and advertising art; computer and information sciences; computer engineering technology; computer programming; computer science; construction engineering; dietetics; economics; education; electrical, electronic and communications engineering technology; elementary education; engineering technology; English; family and community services; family and consumer economics related; foods, nutrition, and wellness; French; history; horticultural science; industrial arts; information science/studies; journalism; landscaping and groundskeeping; liberal arts and sciences/liberal studies; marketing/marketing management; mass communication/media; mathematics; mechanical engineering; mechanical engineering/mechanical technology; music; music teacher education; neurobiology and neurophysiology; nursing (registered nurse training); photography; physical therapy; physics; piano and organ; political science and government; pre-law studies; pre-medical studies; pre-veterinary studies; psychology; public relations/image management; religious education; religious studies; science teacher education; secondary education; social sciences; social work; sociology; Spanish; theology; voice and opera; youth ministry; zoology/animal biology.

Academic Programs *Special study options:* academic remediation for entering students, accelerated degree program, adult/continuing education programs, advanced placement credit, cooperative education, distance learning, double majors, English as a second language, external degree program, freshman honors college, honors programs, internships, off-campus study, part-time degree program, student-designed majors, study abroad, summer session for credit. *Unusual degree programs:* 3-2 physical therapy and architecture.

Library James White Library plus 2 others with 512,100 titles, 3,032 serial subscriptions, 41,503 audiovisual materials, an OPAC, a Web page.

Computers on Campus 130 computers available on campus for general student use. A campuswide network can be accessed from student residence rooms and from off campus. Internet access, at least one staffed computer lab available. Computer purchase or lease plan available.

Student Life *Housing:* on-campus residence required through senior year. *Options:* men-only, women-only. Campus housing is university owned. Freshman campus housing is guaranteed. *Activities and organizations:* drama/theater group, student-run newspaper, radio station, choral group. *Campus security:* 24-hour emergency response devices and patrols, controlled dormitory access. *Student services:* health clinic, personal/psychological counseling.

Athletics *Intramural sports:* basketball M/W, football M/W, golf M/W, gymnastics M/W, racquetball M/W, soccer M/W, softball M/W, volleyball M/W, water polo M/W.

Standardized Tests *Required:* SAT I or ACT (for admission). *Recommended:* ACT (for admission).

Costs (2004–05) *Comprehensive fee:* $20,566 includes full-time tuition ($15,050), mandatory fees ($396), and room and board ($5120). Full-time tuition and fees vary according to course load. Part-time tuition: $630 per credit hour. Part-time tuition and fees vary according to course load. *College room only:* $2430. Room and board charges vary according to board plan. *Payment plan:* installment. *Waivers:* senior citizens and employees or children of employees.

Financial Aid Of all full-time matriculated undergraduates who enrolled in 2002, 1,470 applied for aid, 975 were judged to have need, 364 had their need fully met. 398 Federal Work-Study jobs (averaging $1530). 187 state and other part-time jobs (averaging $1587). In 2002, 459 non-need-based awards were made. *Average percent of need met:* 92%. *Average financial aid package:* $17,675. *Average need-based loan:* $4523. *Average need-based gift aid:* $6012. *Average non-need-based aid:* $4704. *Average indebtedness upon graduation:* $21,376.

Applying *Options:* electronic application, deferred entrance. *Application fee:* $30. *Required:* essay or personal statement, high school transcript, minimum 2.25 GPA, 2 letters of recommendation. *Application deadline:* rolling (freshmen), rolling (transfers). *Notification:* continuous (freshmen), continuous (transfers).

Admissions Contact Ms. Charlotte Coy, Admissions Supervisor, Andrews University, Berrien Springs, MI 49104. *Toll-free phone:* 800-253-2874. *Fax:* 269-471-3228. *E-mail:* enroll@andrews.edu.

AQUINAS COLLEGE
Grand Rapids, Michigan

- **Independent Roman Catholic** comprehensive, founded 1886
- **Calendar** semesters
- **Degrees** associate, bachelor's, and master's
- **Suburban** 107-acre campus with easy access to Detroit
- **Endowment** $17.6 million
- **Coed,** 1,828 undergraduate students, 81% full-time, 66% women, 34% men
- **Moderately difficult** entrance level, 79% of applicants were admitted

Undergraduates 1,482 full-time, 346 part-time. Students come from 20 states and territories, 11 other countries, 6% are from out of state, 4% African American, 1% Asian American or Pacific Islander, 3% Hispanic American, 0.3% Native American, 0.7% international, 4% transferred in, 49% live on campus. *Retention:* 75% of 2002 full-time freshmen returned.

Freshmen *Admission:* 1,361 applied, 1,078 admitted, 284 enrolled. *Average high school GPA:* 3.40. *Test scores:* ACT scores over 18: 95%; ACT scores over 24: 46%; ACT scores over 30: 7%.

Faculty *Total:* 218, 45% full-time, 34% with terminal degrees. *Student/faculty ratio:* 16:1.

Majors Accounting; art; art history, criticism and conservation; arts management; art teacher education; athletic training; biology/biological sciences; business administration and management; business/corporate communications; chemistry; clinical laboratory science/medical technology; communication/speech communication and rhetoric; computer and information sciences; computer science; drawing; economics; education; elementary education; English; English as a second/foreign language (teaching); English/language arts teacher education; environmental science; environmental studies; fine/studio arts; French; geography; German; health teacher education; history; international business/trade/commerce; international relations and affairs; Japanese; liberal arts and sciences/liberal studies; mathematics; music; music performance; music teacher education; organizational communication; philosophy; physical education teaching and coaching; physics; political science and government; pre-dentistry studies; pre-law studies; pre-medical studies; pre-veterinary studies; psychology; reading teacher education; religious education; religious/sacred music; religious studies; science teacher education; sculpture; secondary education; social sciences; social studies teacher education; sociology; Spanish; special education (specific learning disabilities); urban studies/affairs.

Academic Programs *Special study options:* academic remediation for entering students, accelerated degree program, adult/continuing education programs, advanced placement credit, cooperative education, distance learning, double majors, honors programs, independent study, internships, off-campus study, part-time degree program, services for LD students, student-designed majors, study abroad, summer session for credit.

Library Woodhouse Library with 112,458 titles, 14,725 serial subscriptions, 4,907 audiovisual materials, an OPAC, a Web page.

Computers on Campus 176 computers available on campus for general student use. A campuswide network can be accessed from student residence rooms and from off campus. Internet access, at least one staffed computer lab available.

Student Life *Housing:* on-campus residence required through sophomore year. *Options:* coed. Campus housing is university owned. Freshman campus housing is guaranteed. *Activities and organizations:* drama/theater group, student-run newspaper, radio station, choral group, Community Senate Programming Board, Aquinas Times, JAMMIN (multicultural group). *Campus security:* 24-hour emergency response devices and patrols, student patrols, late-night transport/escort service, controlled dormitory access. *Student services:* health clinic, personal/psychological counseling, women's center.

Athletics Member NAIA. *Intercollegiate sports:* baseball M(s), basketball M(s)/W(s), cross-country running M(s)/W(s), golf M(s)/W(s), soccer M(s)/W(s), softball W(s), tennis M(s)/W(s), track and field M(s)/W(s), volleyball W(s). *Intramural sports:* basketball M/W, football M/W, golf M, ice hockey M, skiing (cross-country) M/W, skiing (downhill) M/W, soccer M/W, softball M/W, tennis M/W, volleyball M/W.

Standardized Tests *Required:* ACT (for admission).

Costs (2003–04) *Comprehensive fee:* $21,894 includes full-time tuition ($16,400) and room and board ($5494). Full-time tuition and fees vary according to course load. Part-time tuition: $330 per credit. Part-time tuition and fees vary according to course load. *College room only:* $2510. Room and board charges vary according to board plan and housing facility. *Payment plans:* installment, deferred payment. *Waivers:* children of alumni and employees or children of employees.

Financial Aid Of all full-time matriculated undergraduates who enrolled in 2003, 1,181 applied for aid, 1,056 were judged to have need, 430 had their need fully met. 134 Federal Work-Study jobs (averaging $700). In 2003, 416 non-need-based awards were made. *Average percent of need met:* 92%. *Average financial aid package:* $15,461. *Average need-based loan:* $2800. *Average need-based gift* *aid:* $12,661. *Average non-need-based aid:* $8266. *Average indebtedness upon graduation:* $13,638. *Financial aid deadline:* 8/15.

Applying *Options:* electronic application, early admission, deferred entrance. *Required:* high school transcript, minimum 2.5 GPA. *Required for some:* essay or personal statement, interview. *Application deadline:* rolling (freshmen), rolling (transfers).

Admissions Contact Ms. Amy Sprouse, Applications Specialist, Aquinas College, 1607 Robinson Road, SE, Grand Rapids, MI 49506-1799. *Phone:* 616-732-4460 Ext. 5150. *Toll-free phone:* 800-678-9593. *Fax:* 616-732-4469. *E-mail:* admissions@aquinas.edu.

■ *See page 1178 for a narrative description.*

AVE MARIA COLLEGE

Ypsilanti, Michigan

- **Independent Roman Catholic** 4-year, founded 1998
- **Calendar** semesters
- **Degree** bachelor's
- **Urban** campus with easy access to Detroit
- **Coed,** 308 undergraduate students
- **Very difficult** entrance level, 78% of applicants were admitted

Undergraduates Students come from 39 states and territories, 13 other countries, 72% are from out of state, 0.6% African American, 1% Asian American or Pacific Islander, 3% Hispanic American, 12% international, 95% live on campus. *Retention:* 72% of 2002 full-time freshmen returned.

Freshmen *Admission:* 214 applied, 167 admitted. *Average high school GPA:* 3.00.

Faculty *Total:* 27, 63% full-time. *Student/faculty ratio:* 15:1.

Majors Classics and languages, literatures and linguistics; economics; history; literature; mathematics; philosophy; political science and government; theology.

Academic Programs *Special study options:* study abroad.

Student Life *Housing:* on-campus residence required through senior year. *Options:* men-only, women-only, disabled students. Campus housing is university owned. *Activities and organizations:* drama/theater group, student-run newspaper, choral group, Pro-Life Organization, Student Government, Yearbook, Newspaper, Liturgical Ministries. *Campus security:* 24-hour emergency response devices, late-night transport/escort service, controlled dormitory access, 12-hour evening patrols by trained security personnel. *Student services:* personal/psychological counseling.

Standardized Tests *Required:* SAT I or ACT (for admission).

Costs (2003–04) *Comprehensive fee:* $15,000 includes full-time tuition ($9650), mandatory fees ($350), and room and board ($5000). Full-time tuition and fees vary according to program. Part-time tuition: $300 per credit. Part-time tuition and fees vary according to program. *Required fees:* $10 per credit part-time. *Payment plan:* installment. *Waivers:* employees or children of employees.

Financial Aid Of all full-time matriculated undergraduates who enrolled in 2002, 187 applied for aid, 141 were judged to have need, 34 had their need fully met. In 2002, 58 non-need-based awards were made. *Average percent of need met:* 72%. *Average financial aid package:* $6992. *Average need-based loan:* $3619. *Average need-based gift aid:* $8674. *Average non-need-based aid:* $4425. *Average indebtedness upon graduation:* $8105.

Applying *Application fee:* $25. *Required:* essay or personal statement, high school transcript, minimum 2.4 GPA, 2 letters of recommendation. *Required for some:* minimum SAT score of 1000 or ACT score of 21. *Recommended:* interview. *Notification:* continuous (transfers).

Admissions Contact Ms. Nicole Myshak, Admissions Counselor, Ave Maria College, 300 West Forest Avenue, Ypsilanti, MI 48197. *Phone:* 734-337-4527. *Toll-free phone:* 866-866-3030. *Fax:* 734-337-4140. *E-mail:* admissions@avemaria.edu.

BAKER COLLEGE OF ALLEN PARK

Allen Park, Michigan

- **Independent** 4-year, founded 2003, part of Baker College System
- **Calendar** quarters
- **Degree** certificates, diplomas, and bachelor's
- **Suburban** 13-acre campus with easy access to Detroit
- **Coed, primarily women,** 397 undergraduate students, 55% full-time, 78% women, 22% men
- 100% of applicants were admitted

Undergraduates 218 full-time, 179 part-time. Students come from 1 other state, 24% African American, 0.8% Asian American or Pacific Islander, 5% Hispanic American, 0.3% Native American.

Freshmen *Admission:* 428 applied, 428 admitted.

Majors Accounting; business administration and management; computer and information sciences; computer science; computer systems networking and telecommunications; data entry/microcomputer applications; data entry/microcomputer applications related; early childhood education; executive assistant/executive secretary; interior design; marketing/marketing management; medical/clinical assistant; medical insurance coding; medical insurance/medical billing; medical office computer specialist; receptionist; web page, digital/multimedia and information resources design; word processing.

Student Life *Housing:* college housing not available. *Campus security:* 24-hour patrols. *Student services:* personal/psychological counseling.

Costs (2003–04) *Tuition:* $5940 full-time, $165 per quarter hour part-time. Full-time tuition and fees vary according to program. *Waivers:* employees or children of employees.

Applying *Required:* high school transcript, interview. *Application deadline:* 9/24 (freshmen). *Notification:* continuous (transfers).

Admissions Contact Mr. Steve Peterson, Director of Admissions, Baker College of Allen Park, 4500 Enterprise Drive, Allen Park, MI 48101. *Phone:* 313-425-3700. *Toll-free phone:* 313-425-3700. *E-mail:* steve.peterson@baker.edu.

BAKER COLLEGE OF AUBURN HILLS

Auburn Hills, Michigan

- **Independent** 4-year, founded 1911, part of Baker College System
- **Calendar** quarters
- **Degrees** certificates, diplomas, associate, bachelor's, and postbachelor's certificates
- **Urban** 7-acre campus with easy access to Detroit
- **Coed,** 3,177 undergraduate students
- **Noncompetitive** entrance level, 100% of applicants were admitted

Undergraduates Students come from 1 other state, 22% African American, 3% Asian American or Pacific Islander, 4% Hispanic American, 0.5% Native American.

Freshmen *Admission:* 1,307 applied, 1,307 admitted.

Faculty *Total:* 115, 8% full-time, 10% with terminal degrees. *Student/faculty ratio:* 22:1.

Majors Accounting; administrative assistant and secretarial science; business administration and management; commercial and advertising art; computer typography and composition equipment operation; data processing and data processing technology; diagnostic medical sonography and ultrasound technology; drafting and design technology; education; health/health care administration; health information/medical records administration; interior design; legal administrative assistant/secretary; marketing/marketing management; medical administrative assistant and medical secretary; medical/clinical assistant; system, networking, and LAN/wan management.

Academic Programs *Special study options:* academic remediation for entering students, accelerated degree program, advanced placement credit, cooperative education, distance learning, double majors, external degree program, independent study, internships, part-time degree program, services for LD students, summer session for credit.

Library Baker College of Auburn Hills Library with 5,400 titles, 95 serial subscriptions, an OPAC, a Web page.

Computers on Campus 110 computers available on campus for general student use. A campuswide network can be accessed from off campus. Internet access, online (class) registration, at least one staffed computer lab available.

Student Life *Housing:* college housing not available. *Activities and organizations:* Baker Business Club, Interior Design Society, Students Action in Engineering, marketing club. *Campus security:* 24-hour emergency response devices.

Standardized Tests *Recommended:* SAT I or ACT (for placement).

Costs (2003–04) *Tuition:* $5940 full-time, $165 per quarter hour part-time. *Payment plan:* installment. *Waivers:* employees or children of employees.

Applying *Options:* early admission, deferred entrance. *Application fee:* $20. *Required:* high school transcript. *Application deadline:* rolling (freshmen), rolling (transfers).

Admissions Contact Ms. Jan Bohlen, Vice President for Admissions, Baker College of Auburn Hills, 1500 University Drive, Auburn Hills, MI 48326-1586. *Phone:* 248-340-0600. *Toll-free phone:* 888-429-0410. *Fax:* 248-340-0608. *E-mail:* jan.bohlen@baker.edu.

BAKER COLLEGE OF CADILLAC

Cadillac, Michigan

- **Independent** 4-year, founded 1986, part of Baker College System
- **Calendar** quarters

Baker College of Cadillac (continued)
- **Degrees** certificates, diplomas, associate, and bachelor's
- **Small-town** 40-acre campus
- **Coed,** 1,386 undergraduate students, 61% full-time, 77% women, 23% men
- **Noncompetitive** entrance level, 100% of applicants were admitted

Undergraduates 846 full-time, 540 part-time. Students come from 4 states and territories, 0.3% African American, 0.2% Asian American or Pacific Islander, 0.2% Hispanic American, 0.3% Native American. *Retention:* 69% of 2002 full-time freshmen returned.

Freshmen *Admission:* 600 applied, 600 admitted.

Faculty *Total:* 73, 5% full-time. *Student/faculty ratio:* 16:1.

Majors Accounting; administrative assistant and secretarial science; architectural engineering technology; business administration and management; computer graphics; computer typography and composition equipment operation; data processing and data processing technology; drafting and design technology; education; electrical, electronic and communications engineering technology; emergency medical technology (EMT paramedic); health information/medical records administration; information science/studies; marketing/marketing management; medical administrative assistant and medical secretary; medical/clinical assistant; quality control technology; veterinary/animal health technology.

Academic Programs *Special study options:* academic remediation for entering students, advanced placement credit, cooperative education, distance learning, double majors, external degree program, independent study, internships, part-time degree program, services for LD students, summer session for credit.

Library Baker College of Cadillac Library with 4,000 titles, 78 serial subscriptions, an OPAC, a Web page.

Computers on Campus 77 computers available on campus for general student use. A campuswide network can be accessed from off campus. Internet access, online (class) registration, at least one staffed computer lab available.

Student Life *Housing:* college housing not available. *Campus security:* 24-hour emergency response devices.

Standardized Tests *Recommended:* SAT I or ACT (for placement).

Costs (2003–04) *Tuition:* $5940 full-time, $165 per quarter hour part-time. Full-time tuition and fees vary according to program. Part-time tuition and fees vary according to program. *Waivers:* employees or children of employees.

Applying *Options:* early admission, deferred entrance. *Application fee:* $20. *Required:* high school transcript. *Recommended:* interview. *Application deadline:* rolling (freshmen), rolling (transfers).

Admissions Contact Mr. Mike Tisdale, Director of Admissions, Baker College of Cadillac, 9600 East 13th Street, Cadillac, MI 49601. *Phone:* 616-775-8458. *Toll-free phone:* 888-313-3463 (in-state); 231-876-3100 (out-of-state). *Fax:* 231-775-8505. *E-mail:* mike.tisdale@baker.edu.

BAKER COLLEGE OF CLINTON TOWNSHIP
Clinton Township, Michigan

- **Independent** 4-year, founded 1990, part of Baker College System
- **Calendar** quarters
- **Degrees** certificates, diplomas, associate, and bachelor's
- **Urban** 25-acre campus with easy access to Detroit
- **Coed,** 4,510 undergraduate students, 57% full-time, 79% women, 21% men
- **Noncompetitive** entrance level, 100% of applicants were admitted

Undergraduates 2,570 full-time, 1,940 part-time. Students come from 2 states and territories, 18% African American, 2% Asian American or Pacific Islander, 1% Hispanic American, 0.5% Native American.

Freshmen *Admission:* 2,415 applied, 2,415 admitted.

Faculty *Total:* 147, 8% full-time. *Student/faculty ratio:* 19:1.

Majors Accounting; administrative assistant and secretarial science; architectural engineering technology; business administration and management; business automation/technology/data entry; commercial and advertising art; computer typography and composition equipment operation; data processing and data processing technology; drafting and design technology; emergency medical technology (EMT paramedic); health information/medical records administration; human services; information science/studies; interior design; kindergarten/preschool education; legal administrative assistant/secretary; marketing/marketing management; medical administrative assistant and medical secretary; medical/clinical assistant; nursing (registered nurse training); radiologic technology/science; surgical technology.

Academic Programs *Special study options:* academic remediation for entering students, advanced placement credit, cooperative education, external degree program, internships, part-time degree program, services for LD students, summer session for credit.

Library Baker College of Mt. Clemens Library with 8,000 titles, 97 serial subscriptions, an OPAC, a Web page.

Computers on Campus 127 computers available on campus for general student use. A campuswide network can be accessed from off campus. Internet access, at least one staffed computer lab available.

Student Life *Housing:* college housing not available. *Campus security:* 24-hour emergency response devices and patrols, evening security guard. *Student services:* personal/psychological counseling.

Standardized Tests *Recommended:* SAT I or ACT (for placement).

Costs (2003–04) *Tuition:* $5940 full-time, $165 per quarter hour part-time. Full-time tuition and fees vary according to program. Part-time tuition and fees vary according to program. *Waivers:* employees or children of employees.

Applying *Options:* electronic application, early admission, deferred entrance. *Application fee:* $20. *Required:* high school transcript. *Application deadline:* rolling (freshmen), rolling (transfers).

Admissions Contact Ms. Annette M. Looser, Vice President for Admissions, Baker College of Clinton Township, 34950 Little Mack Avenue, Clinton Township, MI 48035. *Phone:* 810-791-6610. *Toll-free phone:* 888-272-2842. *Fax:* 810-791-6611. *E-mail:* annette.looser@baker.edu.

BAKER COLLEGE OF FLINT
Flint, Michigan

- **Independent** 4-year, founded 1911, part of Baker College System
- **Calendar** quarters
- **Degrees** certificates, diplomas, associate, and bachelor's
- **Urban** 30-acre campus with easy access to Detroit
- **Coed,** 5,639 undergraduate students, 58% full-time, 69% women, 31% men
- **Noncompetitive** entrance level, 100% of applicants were admitted

Undergraduates 3,271 full-time, 2,368 part-time. Students come from 5 states and territories, 1% are from out of state, 28% African American, 2% Asian American or Pacific Islander, 2% Hispanic American, 0.8% Native American, 2% live on campus.

Freshmen *Admission:* 2,790 applied, 2,790 admitted.

Faculty *Total:* 173, 15% full-time, 10% with terminal degrees. *Student/faculty ratio:* 37:1.

Majors Accounting; accounting technology and bookkeeping; administrative assistant and secretarial science; airline pilot and flight crew; architectural drafting and CAD/CADD; automobile/automotive mechanics technology; avionics maintenance technology; biomedical technology; business administration and management; business/commerce; commercial and advertising art; computer graphics; computer programming; computer systems analysis; computer systems networking and telecommunications; computer teacher education; computer typography and composition equipment operation; construction management; data processing and data processing technology; drafting and design technology; energy management and systems technology; entrepreneurship; environmental engineering technology; executive assistant/executive secretary; family and community services; health/health care administration; health information/medical records administration; health information/medical records technology; hospitality administration; human services; industrial technology; information science/studies; interior design; legal administrative assistant/secretary; management information systems; marketing/marketing management; mechanical drafting and CAD/CADD; mechanical engineering; mechanical engineering/mechanical technology; medical administrative assistant and medical secretary; medical/clinical assistant; medical transcription; nursing (registered nurse training); occupational therapy; office management; operations management; orthotics/prosthetics; pharmacy technician; physical therapist assistant; quality control technology; sales, distribution and marketing; surgical technology; tourism and travel services management; transportation technology; vehicle/equipment operation.

Academic Programs *Special study options:* academic remediation for entering students, accelerated degree program, advanced placement credit, cooperative education, distance learning, double majors, external degree program, independent study, internships, part-time degree program, services for LD students, summer session for credit.

Library Marianne Jewell Library with 168,700 titles, an OPAC, a Web page.

Computers on Campus 412 computers available on campus for general student use. A campuswide network can be accessed from off campus. At least one staffed computer lab available.

Student Life *Housing:* on-campus residence required for freshman year. *Options:* coed. Campus housing is university owned. *Activities and organizations:* Occupational Therapy Club, Interior Design Society, Medical Assistants Student Organization, Physical Therapist Assistant Club. *Campus security:* 24-hour patrols, late-night transport/escort service, controlled dormitory access, video monitoring of high traffic areas. *Student services:* personal/psychological counseling.

Standardized Tests *Recommended:* SAT I or ACT (for placement).

Costs (2003–04) *Tuition:* $5940 full-time, $165 per quarter hour part-time. Full-time tuition and fees vary according to program. Part-time tuition and fees vary according to program. *Room only:* $2600. *Waivers:* employees or children of employees.

Applying *Options:* early admission, deferred entrance. *Application fee:* $20. *Required:* high school transcript. *Application deadlines:* 9/20 (freshmen), 9/20 (transfers).

Admissions Contact Mr. Troy Crowe, Vice President for Admissions, Baker College of Flint, 1050 West Bristol Road, Flint, MI 48507-5508. *Phone:* 810-766-4015. *Toll-free phone:* 800-964-4299. *Fax:* 810-766-4049. *E-mail:* troy.crowe@baker.edu.

BAKER COLLEGE OF JACKSON

Jackson, Michigan

- **Independent** 4-year, founded 1994, part of Baker College System
- **Calendar** quarters
- **Degrees** certificates, diplomas, associate, and bachelor's
- **Urban** 42-acre campus with easy access to Lansing
- **Coed,** 1,593 undergraduate students, 51% full-time, 77% women, 23% men
- **Noncompetitive** entrance level, 100% of applicants were admitted

Undergraduates 813 full-time, 780 part-time. Students come from 2 states and territories, 1% are from out of state, 7% African American, 0.3% Asian American or Pacific Islander, 2% Hispanic American, 0.3% Native American.

Freshmen *Admission:* 721 applied, 721 admitted.

Faculty *Total:* 90, 10% full-time, 10% with terminal degrees. *Student/faculty ratio:* 13:1.

Majors Accounting; administrative assistant and secretarial science; business administration and management; business/commerce; communication/speech communication and rhetoric; computer typography and composition equipment operation; data processing and data processing technology; early childhood education; health information/medical records administration; health information/medical records technology; information science/studies; legal administrative assistant/secretary; marketing/marketing management; marketing research; medical administrative assistant and medical secretary; medical/clinical assistant; medical transcription; office management; pharmacy technician; sales, distribution and marketing; surgical technology; veterinary/animal health technology.

Academic Programs *Special study options:* academic remediation for entering students, accelerated degree program, advanced placement credit, cooperative education, distance learning, double majors, external degree program, independent study, internships, part-time degree program, services for LD students, summer session for credit.

Library Baker College of Jackson Library with 7,000 titles, 150 serial subscriptions, an OPAC, a Web page.

Computers on Campus 110 computers available on campus for general student use. A campuswide network can be accessed from off campus. Internet access, online (class) registration, at least one staffed computer lab available.

Student Life *Housing:* college housing not available. *Campus security:* 24-hour emergency response devices. *Student services:* personal/psychological counseling.

Standardized Tests *Recommended:* SAT I or ACT (for placement).

Costs (2003–04) *Tuition:* $5940 full-time, $165 per quarter hour part-time. Full-time tuition and fees vary according to program. Part-time tuition and fees vary according to program. *Waivers:* employees or children of employees.

Applying *Options:* electronic application, early admission, deferred entrance. *Application fee:* $20. *Required:* high school transcript. *Application deadline:* 9/19 (freshmen), rolling (transfers). *Notification:* continuous (freshmen).

Admissions Contact Ms. Kelli Stepka, Director of Admissions, Baker College of Jackson, 2800 Springport Road, Jackson, MI 49202. *Phone:* 517-788-7800. *Toll-free phone:* 888-343-3683. *Fax:* 517-789-7331. *E-mail:* kelli.stepka@baker.edu.

BAKER COLLEGE OF MUSKEGON

Muskegon, Michigan

- **Independent** 4-year, founded 1888, part of Baker College System
- **Calendar** quarters
- **Degrees** certificates, diplomas, associate, and bachelor's
- **Suburban** 40-acre campus with easy access to Grand Rapids
- **Coed,** 4,076 undergraduate students, 65% full-time, 69% women, 31% men
- **Noncompetitive** entrance level, 100% of applicants were admitted

Undergraduates 2,647 full-time, 1,429 part-time. Students come from 13 states and territories, 1% are from out of state, 15% African American, 0.8% Asian American or Pacific Islander, 4% Hispanic American, 0.4% Native American, 11% live on campus.

Freshmen *Admission:* 1,747 applied, 1,747 admitted.

Faculty *Total:* 145, 10% full-time, 6% with terminal degrees. *Student/faculty ratio:* 30:1.

Majors Accounting; administrative assistant and secretarial science; airline pilot and flight crew; architectural drafting and CAD/CADD; aviation/airway management; business administration and management; commercial and advertising art; computer and information sciences; computer programming; computer science; corrections; culinary arts; data processing and data processing technology; drafting and design technology; electrical, electronic and communications engineering technology; emergency medical technology (EMT paramedic); health/health care administration; hotel/motel administration; human services; industrial technology; information science/studies; interior design; kindergarten/preschool education; legal administrative assistant/secretary; marketing/marketing management; medical administrative assistant and medical secretary; medical/clinical assistant; nursing (registered nurse training); occupational therapist assistant; pharmacy technician; physical therapist assistant; quality control technology; radiologic technology/science; rehabilitation therapy; speech-language pathology; surgical technology; tourism and travel services management; veterinary/animal health technology.

Academic Programs *Special study options:* academic remediation for entering students, accelerated degree program, adult/continuing education programs, advanced placement credit, cooperative education, distance learning, double majors, external degree program, independent study, internships, part-time degree program, services for LD students, summer session for credit.

Library Marianne Jewell Library with 32,000 titles, 140 serial subscriptions, an OPAC, a Web page.

Computers on Campus 165 computers available on campus for general student use. A campuswide network can be accessed from student residence rooms and from off campus that provide access to e-mail. Internet access, at least one staffed computer lab available.

Student Life *Housing:* on-campus residence required for freshman year. *Options:* coed, disabled students. Campus housing is university owned. Freshman applicants given priority for college housing. *Activities and organizations:* accounting club, rehab club, travel club, culinary club. *Campus security:* 24-hour emergency response devices and patrols, late-night transport/escort service, controlled dormitory access, 24-hour security camera surveillance. *Student services:* personal/psychological counseling.

Standardized Tests *Recommended:* SAT I or ACT (for placement).

Costs (2003–04) *Tuition:* $5940 full-time, $165 per quarter hour part-time. Full-time tuition and fees vary according to program. Part-time tuition and fees vary according to program. *Room only:* $2400. *Waivers:* employees or children of employees.

Applying *Options:* electronic application, early admission, deferred entrance. *Application fee:* $20. *Required:* high school transcript. *Application deadline:* 9/24 (freshmen), rolling (transfers). *Notification:* continuous (freshmen).

Admissions Contact Ms. Kathy Jacobson, Vice President of Admissions, Baker College of Muskegon, 1903 Marquette Avenue, Muskegon, MI 49442-3497. *Phone:* 231-777-5207. *Toll-free phone:* 800-937-0337. *Fax:* 231-777-5201. *E-mail:* kathy.jacobson@baker.edu.

BAKER COLLEGE OF OWOSSO

Owosso, Michigan

- **Independent** 4-year, founded 1984, part of Baker College System
- **Calendar** quarters
- **Degrees** certificates, diplomas, associate, and bachelor's
- **Small-town** 32-acre campus
- **Coed,** 2,538 undergraduate students, 64% full-time, 68% women, 32% men
- **Noncompetitive** entrance level, 100% of applicants were admitted

Undergraduates 1,625 full-time, 913 part-time. Students come from 4 states and territories, 0.5% are from out of state, 2% African American, 0.1% Asian American or Pacific Islander, 1% Hispanic American, 0.6% Native American, 15% live on campus.

Freshmen *Admission:* 1,191 applied, 1,191 admitted.

Faculty *Total:* 103, 5% full-time, 11% with terminal degrees. *Student/faculty ratio:* 38:1.

Majors Accounting; administrative assistant and secretarial science; architectural engineering technology; business administration and management; clinical/medical laboratory technology; commercial and advertising art; computer engineering technology; computer programming; computer science; construction engineering technology; consumer merchandising/retailing management; data processing and data processing technology; diagnostic medical sonography and ultrasound technology; drafting and design technology; electrical, electronic and communications engineering technology; environmental engineering technology; health/health care administration; hospitality administration; hotel/motel admin-

Baker College of Owosso (continued)

istration; human resources management; industrial radiologic technology; information science/studies; interior design; kindergarten/preschool education; legal administrative assistant/secretary; marketing/marketing management; medical administrative assistant and medical secretary; medical/clinical assistant; nursing (registered nurse training).

Academic Programs *Special study options:* academic remediation for entering students, accelerated degree program, adult/continuing education programs, advanced placement credit, cooperative education, external degree program, internships, part-time degree program, services for LD students, summer session for credit.

Library Baker College of Owosso Library with 35,424 titles, 215 serial subscriptions, 344 audiovisual materials.

Computers on Campus 190 computers available on campus for general student use. A campuswide network can be accessed from off campus. Internet access, at least one staffed computer lab available.

Student Life *Housing options:* coed. *Activities and organizations:* student-run newspaper, accounting club, travel club, management club, Baker Health Information Management Club, RAD Club. *Campus security:* 24-hour emergency response devices and patrols, late-night transport/escort service, controlled dormitory access. *Student services:* personal/psychological counseling.

Standardized Tests *Recommended:* SAT I or ACT (for placement).

Costs (2003–04) *Tuition:* $5940 full-time, $165 per quarter hour part-time. Full-time tuition and fees vary according to program. *Room only:* $2175. *Waivers:* employees or children of employees.

Applying *Options:* common application, early admission, deferred entrance. *Application fee:* $20. *Required:* high school transcript. *Application deadline:* rolling (freshmen), rolling (transfers).

Admissions Contact Mr. Michael Konopacke, Vice President for Admissions, Baker College of Owosso, Owosso, MI 48867. *Phone:* 517-729-3353. *Toll-free phone:* 800-879-3797. *Fax:* 517-729-3359. *E-mail:* mike.konopacke@baker.edu.

BAKER COLLEGE OF PORT HURON
Port Huron, Michigan

- **Independent** 4-year, founded 1990, part of Baker College System
- **Calendar** quarters
- **Degrees** certificates, diplomas, associate, and bachelor's
- **Urban** 10-acre campus with easy access to Detroit
- **Coed,** 1,477 undergraduate students, 56% full-time, 78% women, 22% men
- **Noncompetitive** entrance level, 100% of applicants were admitted

Undergraduates 827 full-time, 650 part-time. 10% are from out of state, 4% African American, 0.2% Asian American or Pacific Islander, 1% Hispanic American, 1% Native American.

Freshmen *Admission:* 512 applied, 512 admitted.

Faculty *Total:* 95, 11% full-time, 9% with terminal degrees. *Student/faculty ratio:* 14:1.

Majors Accounting; administrative assistant and secretarial science; architectural engineering technology; business administration and management; commercial and advertising art; computer programming; data processing and data processing technology; dental hygiene; diagnostic medical sonography and ultrasound technology; drafting and design technology; environmental engineering technology; health/health care administration; health information/medical records administration; hotel/motel administration; information science/studies; interior design; legal administrative assistant/secretary; marketing/marketing management; medical administrative assistant and medical secretary; medical/clinical assistant.

Academic Programs *Special study options:* academic remediation for entering students, accelerated degree program, advanced placement credit, cooperative education, distance learning, double majors, external degree program, independent study, internships, part-time degree program, services for LD students, summer session for credit.

Library Baker College of Port Huron Library with 16,823 titles, 181 serial subscriptions, 135 audiovisual materials, an OPAC, a Web page.

Computers on Campus 145 computers available on campus for general student use. A campuswide network can be accessed from off campus that provide access to software. Internet access, online (class) registration, at least one staffed computer lab available.

Student Life *Housing:* college housing not available. *Activities and organizations:* travel club, Student Association Dental Hygienists of America. *Campus security:* 24-hour emergency response devices, late-night transport/escort service. *Student services:* personal/psychological counseling.

Costs (2003–04) *Tuition:* $5940 full-time, $165 per quarter hour part-time. Full-time tuition and fees vary according to program. *Waivers:* employees or children of employees.

Applying *Options:* early admission, deferred entrance. *Application fee:* $20. *Required:* high school transcript, interview. *Application deadline:* 9/24 (freshmen), rolling (transfers). *Notification:* continuous (freshmen), continuous (transfers).

Admissions Contact Mr. Daniel Kenny, Director of Admissions, Baker College of Port Huron, 3403 Lapeer Road, Port Huron, MI 48060-2597. *Phone:* 810-985-7000. *Toll-free phone:* 888-262-2442. *Fax:* 810-985-7066. *E-mail:* kenny_d@porthuron.baker.edu.

CALVIN COLLEGE
Grand Rapids, Michigan

- **Independent** comprehensive, founded 1876, affiliated with Christian Reformed Church
- **Calendar** 4-1-4
- **Degrees** bachelor's, master's, and postbachelor's certificates
- **Suburban** 370-acre campus
- **Endowment** $50.6 million
- **Coed,** 4,289 undergraduate students, 95% full-time, 56% women, 44% men
- **Moderately difficult** entrance level, 99% of applicants were admitted

Academic excellence, Christian commitment, reasonable cost, 4,300 students, 100 academic options. Calvin College receives high marks from *U.S. News & World Report's America's Best Colleges, The National Review College Guide*, the *Templeton Guide: Colleges that Encourage Character Development*, the *Fiske Guide to Colleges*, and *Barron's Best Buys in College Education*.

Undergraduates 4,092 full-time, 197 part-time. Students come from 48 states and territories, 44 other countries, 39% are from out of state, 0.8% African American, 3% Asian American or Pacific Islander, 0.9% Hispanic American, 0.5% Native American, 8% international, 3% transferred in, 56% live on campus. *Retention:* 87% of 2002 full-time freshmen returned.

Freshmen *Admission:* 1,933 applied, 1,906 admitted, 1,042 enrolled. *Average high school GPA:* 3.54. *Test scores:* SAT verbal scores over 500: 87%; SAT math scores over 500: 89%; ACT scores over 18: 99%; SAT verbal scores over 600: 53%; SAT math scores over 600: 52%; ACT scores over 24: 69%; SAT verbal scores over 700: 16%; SAT math scores over 700: 14%; ACT scores over 30: 16%.

Faculty *Total:* 382, 80% full-time, 70% with terminal degrees. *Student/faculty ratio:* 13:1.

Majors Accounting; American history; art; art history, criticism and conservation; art teacher education; athletic training; audiology and speech-language pathology; biblical studies; bilingual and multilingual education; biochemistry; biological and physical sciences; biology/biological sciences; biotechnology; business administration and management; business/corporate communications; chemical engineering; chemistry; civil engineering; classics and languages, literatures and linguistics; communication/speech communication and rhetoric; computer science; conducting; digital communication and media/multimedia; dramatic/theatre arts; economics; electrical, electronics and communications engineering; elementary education; engineering; English; English as a second/foreign language (teaching); environmental studies; European history; film/cinema studies; fine/studio arts; French; geography; geology/earth science; German; Germanic languages related; history; interdisciplinary studies; international relations and affairs; kinesiology and exercise science; Latin; management information systems; mass communication/media; mathematics; mechanical engineering; modern Greek; music; music history, literature, and theory; music performance; music teacher education; music theory and composition; natural sciences; nursing (registered nurse training); occupational therapy; parks, recreation and leisure; philosophy; physical education teaching and coaching; physical sciences; physics; piano and organ; political science and government; pre-dentistry studies; pre-law studies; pre-medical studies; pre-veterinary studies; psychology; public administration; religious/sacred music; religious studies; science teacher education; secondary education; social sciences; social work; sociology; Spanish; special education; speech and rhetoric; theology; voice and opera.

Academic Programs *Special study options:* academic remediation for entering students, accelerated degree program, adult/continuing education programs, advanced placement credit, double majors, honors programs, independent study, internships, off-campus study, part-time degree program, services for LD students, student-designed majors, study abroad, summer session for credit. *ROTC:* Army (c). *Unusual degree programs:* 3-2 occupational therapy with Washington University in St. Louis.

Library Hekman Library plus 1 other with 801,802 titles, 2,658 serial subscriptions, 22,394 audiovisual materials, an OPAC, a Web page.

Computers on Campus 700 computers available on campus for general student use. A campuswide network can be accessed from student residence rooms and from off campus. Internet access, online (class) registration, at least one staffed computer lab available. Computer purchase or lease plan available.

Student Life *Housing:* on-campus residence required through sophomore year. *Options:* men-only, women-only. Campus housing is university owned. Freshman campus housing is guaranteed. *Activities and organizations:* drama/theater group, student-run newspaper, radio station, choral group, Association for Supervision and Curriculum Development, Environmental Stewardship Coalition, China club, Young Life, Dance Guild. *Campus security:* 24-hour emergency response devices and patrols, student patrols, late-night transport/escort service, controlled dormitory access, crime prevention programs, crime alert bulletins. *Student services:* health clinic, personal/psychological counseling.

Athletics Member NCAA. All Division III. *Intercollegiate sports:* baseball M, basketball M/W, cross-country running M/W, golf M/W, ice hockey M(c), lacrosse M(c)/W(c), soccer M/W, softball W, swimming M/W, tennis M/W, track and field M/W, volleyball W. *Intramural sports:* badminton M/W, basketball M/W, cross-country running M/W, football M/W, golf M/W, racquetball M/W, soccer M/W, softball M/W, swimming M/W, tennis M/W, track and field M/W, volleyball M/W, water polo M/W.

Standardized Tests *Required:* SAT I or ACT (for admission).

Costs (2003–04) *Comprehensive fee:* $22,615 includes full-time tuition ($16,775) and room and board ($5840). Part-time tuition: $410 per credit hour. Part-time tuition and fees vary according to course load. *College room only:* $3180. Room and board charges vary according to board plan. *Payment plans:* tuition prepayment, installment. *Waivers:* employees or children of employees.

Financial Aid Of all full-time matriculated undergraduates who enrolled in 2002, 3,070 applied for aid, 2,605 were judged to have need, 634 had their need fully met. 660 Federal Work-Study jobs (averaging $1140). 1,250 state and other part-time jobs (averaging $1150). In 2002, 1048 non-need-based awards were made. *Average percent of need met:* 91%. *Average financial aid package:* $12,252. *Average need-based loan:* $4701. *Average need-based gift aid:* $7922. *Average non-need-based aid:* $3884. *Average indebtedness upon graduation:* $17,440.

Applying *Options:* common application, deferred entrance. *Application fee:* $50. *Required:* essay or personal statement, high school transcript, minimum 2.5 GPA, 1 letter of recommendation. *Recommended:* interview. *Application deadline:* 8/15 (freshmen), rolling (transfers). *Notification:* continuous (freshmen).

Admissions Contact Mr. Dale D. Kuiper, Director of Admissions, Calvin College, 3201 Burton Street, SE, Grand Rapids, MI 49546-4388. *Phone:* 616-526-6106. *Toll-free phone:* 800-688-0122. *Fax:* 616-526-6777. *E-mail:* admissions@calvin.edu.

■ *See page 1334 for a narrative description.*

CENTRAL MICHIGAN UNIVERSITY

Mount Pleasant, Michigan

- **State-supported** university, founded 1892
- **Calendar** semesters
- **Degrees** bachelor's, master's, doctoral, post-master's, and postbachelor's certificates
- **Small-town** 854-acre campus
- **Endowment** $42.8 million
- **Coed,** 19,642 undergraduate students, 87% full-time, 59% women, 41% men
- **Moderately difficult** entrance level, 70% of applicants were admitted

Undergraduates 17,090 full-time, 2,552 part-time. Students come from 45 states and territories, 40 other countries, 3% are from out of state, 6% African American, 1% Asian American or Pacific Islander, 2% Hispanic American, 0.7% Native American, 0.6% international, 5% transferred in, 35% live on campus. *Retention:* 77% of 2002 full-time freshmen returned.

Freshmen *Admission:* 13,489 applied, 9,490 admitted, 3,680 enrolled. *Average high school GPA:* 3.33. *Test scores:* SAT verbal scores over 500: 59%; SAT math scores over 500: 66%; ACT scores over 18: 91%; SAT verbal scores over 600: 25%; SAT math scores over 600: 23%; ACT scores over 24: 33%; SAT verbal scores over 700: 3%; SAT math scores over 700: 2%; ACT scores over 30: 3%.

Faculty *Total:* 1,118, 60% full-time, 57% with terminal degrees. *Student/faculty ratio:* 22:1.

Majors Accounting; accounting related; actuarial science; advertising; anthropology; art; art teacher education; astronomy; athletic training; audiology and speech-language pathology; automotive engineering technology; banking and financial support services; biology/biological sciences; biology teacher education; business administration and management; business administration, management and operations related; business/commerce; business, management, and marketing related; business teacher education; chemistry; chemistry teacher education; child care and support services management; clinical laboratory science/medical technology; commercial and advertising art; community organization and advocacy; computer and information sciences; computer and information sciences related; computer engineering technology; computer teacher education; construction engineering technology; creative writing; criminology; dietetics; dramatic/theatre arts; economics; education (specific subject areas) related; electrical, electronic and communications engineering technology; elementary education; English; English/language arts teacher education; environmental studies; European studies; family systems; fashion merchandising; finance; financial planning and services; foodservice systems administration; French; French language teacher education; geography; geology/earth science; German; German language teacher education; health teacher education; history; history teacher education; hospital and health care facilities administration; hospitality administration; human resources management; industrial engineering; industrial production technologies related; interior architecture; international business/trade/commerce; international relations and affairs; journalism; logistics and materials management; management information systems; marketing/marketing management; marketing related; mathematics; mathematics teacher education; mechanical engineering/mechanical technology; medical microbiology and bacteriology; music; music history, literature, and theory; music related; music teacher education; music theory and composition; natural resources/conservation; neuroscience; oceanography (chemical and physical); office management; operations management; parks, recreation and leisure; parks, recreation and leisure facilities management; philosophy; physical education teaching and coaching; physical sciences; physics; physics teacher education; political science and government; psychology; public health; public relations/image management; radio and television; rehabilitation and therapeutic professions related; religious studies; sales and marketing/marketing and distribution teacher education; sales, distribution and marketing; science teacher education; social sciences; social sciences related; social science teacher education; social studies teacher education; social work; sociology; Spanish; Spanish language teacher education; special education (emotionally disturbed); special education (mentally retarded); speech and rhetoric; speech teacher education; sport and fitness administration; statistics; technology/industrial arts teacher education; therapeutic recreation; women's studies.

Academic Programs *Special study options:* academic remediation for entering students, accelerated degree program, adult/continuing education programs, advanced placement credit, distance learning, double majors, English as a second language, external degree program, freshman honors college, honors programs, internships, part-time degree program, student-designed majors, study abroad, summer session for credit. *ROTC:* Army (b).

Library Park Library plus 1 other with 998,460 titles, 4,634 serial subscriptions, 24,630 audiovisual materials, an OPAC, a Web page.

Computers on Campus 1585 computers available on campus for general student use. A campuswide network can be accessed from student residence rooms and from off campus. Internet access, online (class) registration, at least one staffed computer lab available. Computer purchase or lease plan available.

Student Life *Housing options:* coed, men-only, women-only, disabled students. Campus housing is university owned and is provided by a third party. Freshman campus housing is guaranteed. *Activities and organizations:* drama/theater group, student-run newspaper, radio and television station, choral group, marching band, Residence Hall Assembly, Student Government Association, Panhellenic Council, Interfraternity Council, Program Board, national fraternities, national sororities. *Campus security:* 24-hour emergency response devices and patrols, student patrols, late-night transport/escort service, controlled dormitory access. *Student services:* health clinic, personal/psychological counseling, women's center.

Athletics Member NCAA. All Division I except football (Division I-A). *Intercollegiate sports:* baseball M(s), basketball M(s)/W(s), cross-country running M(s)/W(s), field hockey W(s), gymnastics W(s), soccer W(s), softball W(s), track and field M(s)/W(s), volleyball W(s), wrestling M(s). *Intramural sports:* baseball M(c), basketball M/W, bowling M/W, cross-country running M/W, football M/W, golf M/W, ice hockey M(c), lacrosse M(c)/W(c), rock climbing M(c)/W(c), rugby M(c)/W(c), skiing (downhill) M(c)/W(c), soccer M/W, softball M/W, table tennis M/W, tennis M/W, track and field M(c)/W(c), ultimate Frisbee M(c)/W(c), volleyball M(c)/W(c), wrestling M.

Standardized Tests *Required:* SAT I or ACT (for admission).

Costs (2003–04) *Tuition:* state resident $4463 full-time, $149 per credit part-time; nonresident $11,393 full-time, $380 per credit part-time. *Required fees:* $755 full-time, $213 per term part-time. *Room and board:* $5924; room only: $2962. Room and board charges vary according to board plan and housing facility. *Waivers:* children of alumni, senior citizens, and employees or children of employees.

Financial Aid Of all full-time matriculated undergraduates who enrolled in 2003, 11,617 applied for aid, 8,890 were judged to have need, 3,715 had their need fully met. 837 Federal Work-Study jobs (averaging $1839). 3,479 state and other part-time jobs (averaging $1837). In 2003, 3304 non-need-based awards were made. *Average percent of need met:* 95%. *Average financial aid package:* $8539. *Average need-based loan:* $3886. *Average need-based gift aid:* $3021. *Average non-need-based aid:* $3159. *Average indebtedness upon graduation:* $15,872.

Applying *Options:* electronic application, early admission, deferred entrance. *Application fee:* $35. *Required:* high school transcript. *Required for some:* essay or personal statement, letters of recommendation, interview. *Recommended:* minimum 3.0 GPA. *Application deadline:* rolling (freshmen), rolling (transfers).

Central Michigan University (continued)

Admissions Contact Mrs. Betty J. Wagner, Director of Admissions, Central Michigan University, 105 Warriner Hall, Mt. Pleasant, MI 48859. *Phone:* 989-774-3076. *Fax:* 989-774-7267. *E-mail:* cmuadmit@cmich.edu.

■ *See page 1378 for a narrative description.*

CLEARY UNIVERSITY

Ann Arbor, Michigan

- **Independent** comprehensive, founded 1883
- **Calendar** quarters
- **Degrees** associate, bachelor's, and master's
- **Suburban** 32-acre campus with easy access to Detroit and Lansing
- **Endowment** $2.1 million
- **Coed,** 908 undergraduate students, 94% full-time, 58% women, 42% men
- **Moderately difficult** entrance level, 97% of applicants were admitted

Undergraduates 858 full-time, 50 part-time. Students come from 2 states and territories, 4 other countries, 1% are from out of state, 10% African American, 1% Asian American or Pacific Islander, 2% Hispanic American, 1% Native American, 1% international. *Retention:* 67% of 2002 full-time freshmen returned.

Freshmen *Admission:* 29 applied, 28 admitted. *Average high school GPA:* 2.72. *Test scores:* ACT scores over 18: 77%; ACT scores over 24: 27%.

Faculty *Total:* 112, 10% full-time, 18% with terminal degrees. *Student/faculty ratio:* 10:1.

Majors Accounting; accounting technology and bookkeeping; business administration and management; computer and information sciences and support services related; finance; human resources management; management information systems; marketing/marketing management.

Academic Programs *Special study options:* accelerated degree program, adult/continuing education programs, advanced placement credit, cooperative education, distance learning, independent study, internships, summer session for credit.

Library Cleary University Library plus 1 other with 4,500 titles, 22 serial subscriptions, 100 audiovisual materials, an OPAC, a Web page.

Computers on Campus 56 computers available on campus for general student use. A campuswide network can be accessed from off campus. Internet access, at least one staffed computer lab available.

Student Life *Housing:* college housing not available. *Campus security:* 24-hour emergency response devices.

Standardized Tests *Required for some:* SAT I or ACT (for admission), SAT I and SAT II or ACT (for admission).

Costs (2004–05) *Tuition:* $11,760 full-time, $245 per quarter hour part-time. Full-time tuition and fees vary according to degree level. No tuition increase for student's term of enrollment. *Payment plans:* installment, deferred payment. *Waivers:* senior citizens and employees or children of employees.

Financial Aid Of all full-time matriculated undergraduates who enrolled in 2002, 228 applied for aid, 228 were judged to have need, 9 had their need fully met. 16 Federal Work-Study jobs (averaging $2985). In 2002, 35 non-need-based awards were made. *Average percent of need met:* 53%. *Average financial aid package:* $8568. *Average need-based loan:* $1264. *Average need-based gift aid:* $1061. *Average non-need-based aid:* $2450. *Average indebtedness upon graduation:* $10,500.

Applying *Options:* common application, electronic application, early admission, deferred entrance. *Application fee:* $25. *Required:* high school transcript, minimum 2.5 GPA, complete the Technology Skills Inventory (TSI). *Required for some:* essay or personal statement, 2 letters of recommendation. *Recommended:* interview. *Application deadlines:* 8/15 (freshmen), 8/15 (transfers).

Admissions Contact Ms. Charlotte Paquette, Admissions Representative, Cleary University, 3750 Cleary Drive, Howell, MI 48843. *Phone:* 517-548-3670 Ext. 2249. *Toll-free phone:* 888-5-CLEARY Ext. 2249. *Fax:* 517-552-7805. *E-mail:* admissions@cleary.edu.

COLLEGE FOR CREATIVE STUDIES

Detroit, Michigan

- **Independent** 4-year, founded 1926
- **Calendar** semesters
- **Degree** bachelor's
- **Urban** 11-acre campus
- **Coed,** 1,218 undergraduate students, 86% full-time, 42% women, 58% men
- **Moderately difficult** entrance level, 74% of applicants were admitted

Undergraduates 1,052 full-time, 166 part-time. Students come from 35 states and territories, 18 other countries, 17% are from out of state, 7% African American, 6% Asian American or Pacific Islander, 4% Hispanic American, 0.2% Native American, 4% international, 13% transferred in, 21% live on campus. *Retention:* 74% of 2002 full-time freshmen returned.

Freshmen *Admission:* 474 applied, 352 admitted, 190 enrolled. *Average high school GPA:* 3.02.

Faculty *Total:* 217, 20% full-time. *Student/faculty ratio:* 10:1.

Majors Applied art; art; ceramic arts and ceramics; cinematography and film/video production; commercial and advertising art; commercial photography; computer graphics; design and applied arts related; design and visual communications; drawing; environmental design/architecture; fiber, textile and weaving arts; film/video and photographic arts related; fine arts related; fine/studio arts; graphic design; illustration; industrial design; interior design; intermedia/multimedia; metal and jewelry arts; painting; photography; printmaking; sculpture.

Academic Programs *Special study options:* academic remediation for entering students, advanced placement credit, cooperative education, double majors, English as a second language, independent study, internships, off-campus study, part-time degree program, services for LD students, summer session for credit.

Library Center for Creative Studies Library with 24,000 titles, 75 serial subscriptions.

Computers on Campus A campuswide network can be accessed from student residence rooms and from off campus. Internet access, at least one staffed computer lab available.

Student Life *Housing options:* coed. Campus housing is university owned. *Campus security:* 24-hour patrols, late-night transport/escort service, controlled dormitory access. *Student services:* personal/psychological counseling.

Standardized Tests *Required:* SAT I or ACT (for admission).

Costs (2004–05) *Tuition:* $20,250 full-time, $675 per credit hour part-time. Part-time tuition and fees vary according to course load. *Required fees:* $1126 full-time, $563 per term part-time. *Room only:* $3500. Room and board charges vary according to housing facility. *Payment plans:* installment, deferred payment. *Waivers:* employees or children of employees.

Financial Aid *Average indebtedness upon graduation:* $26,482.

Applying *Options:* electronic application, deferred entrance. *Application fee:* $35. *Required:* essay or personal statement, high school transcript, portfolio. *Required for some:* letters of recommendation, interview. *Recommended:* minimum 2.5 GPA. *Application deadline:* rolling (freshmen), rolling (transfers).

Admissions Contact Office of Admissions, College for Creative Studies, 201 East Kirby, Detroit, MI 48202-4034. *Phone:* 313-664-7425. *Toll-free phone:* 800-952-ARTS. *Fax:* 313-872-2739. *E-mail:* admissions@ccscad.edu.

■ *See page 1432 for a narrative description.*

CONCORDIA UNIVERSITY

Ann Arbor, Michigan

- **Independent** comprehensive, founded 1963, affiliated with Lutheran Church–Missouri Synod, part of Concordia University System
- **Calendar** semesters
- **Degrees** associate, bachelor's, and master's
- **Suburban** 234-acre campus with easy access to Detroit
- **Endowment** $5.9 million
- **Coed,** 438 undergraduate students, 86% full-time, 57% women, 43% men
- **Moderately difficult** entrance level, 75% of applicants were admitted

Undergraduates 376 full-time, 62 part-time. Students come from 14 states and territories, 3 other countries, 19% are from out of state, 8% African American, 0.7% Asian American or Pacific Islander, 1% Hispanic American, 2% Native American, 1% international, 14% transferred in, 65% live on campus. *Retention:* 72% of 2002 full-time freshmen returned.

Freshmen *Admission:* 320 applied, 241 admitted, 72 enrolled. *Average high school GPA:* 3.36. *Test scores:* SAT verbal scores over 500: 100%; SAT math scores over 500: 33%; ACT scores over 18: 89%; SAT verbal scores over 600: 33%; ACT scores over 24: 41%; ACT scores over 30: 7%.

Faculty *Total:* 91, 44% full-time. *Student/faculty ratio:* 9:1.

Majors Ancient Near Eastern and biblical languages; art; art teacher education; biological and physical sciences; biology/biological sciences; biology teacher education; business administration and management; communication/speech communication and rhetoric; computer and information sciences; criminal justice/law enforcement administration; elementary education; English; English/language arts teacher education; general studies; human development and family studies; mathematics; mathematics teacher education; music; music teacher education; physical education teaching and coaching; pre-law studies; pre-medical studies; pre-theology/pre-ministerial studies; psychology; religious/sacred music; religious studies; science teacher education; secondary education; social sciences; social studies teacher education; Spanish; speech teacher education.

Academic Programs *Special study options:* academic remediation for entering students, accelerated degree program, adult/continuing education programs, advanced placement credit, distance learning, double majors, independent study, internships, off-campus study, part-time degree program, services for LD students, student-designed majors, study abroad, summer session for credit. *ROTC:* Army (c), Air Force (c).

Library Zimmerman Library with 120,000 titles, 3,950 serial subscriptions, 10,500 audiovisual materials, an OPAC, a Web page.

Computers on Campus 77 computers available on campus for general student use. A campuswide network can be accessed from student residence rooms and from off campus. Internet access, at least one staffed computer lab available.

Student Life *Housing:* on-campus residence required through sophomore year. *Options:* men-only, women-only. Campus housing is university owned. Freshman campus housing is guaranteed. *Activities and organizations:* drama/theater group, student-run newspaper, choral group, Student Activities Committee, drama club, Student Senate, Spiritual Life Committee, off-campus ministries. *Campus security:* student patrols, late-night transport/escort service. *Student services:* personal/psychological counseling.

Athletics Member NAIA, NCCAA. *Intercollegiate sports:* baseball M(s), basketball M(s)/W(s), soccer M(s)/W(s), softball W(s), volleyball W(s). *Intramural sports:* badminton M/W, basketball M/W, football M/W, golf M/W, softball M/W, tennis M/W, volleyball M/W.

Standardized Tests *Required:* SAT I or ACT (for admission). *Recommended:* ACT (for admission).

Costs (2003–04) *Comprehensive fee:* $23,995 includes full-time tuition ($16,900), mandatory fees ($350), and room and board ($6745). Part-time tuition: $565 per semester hour. *Payment plan:* installment. *Waivers:* employees or children of employees.

Financial Aid Of all full-time matriculated undergraduates who enrolled in 2003, 388 applied for aid, 355 were judged to have need, 104 had their need fully met. In 2003, 55 non-need-based awards were made. *Average percent of need met:* 86%. *Average financial aid package:* $14,769. *Average need-based loan:* $5038. *Average need-based gift aid:* $9233. *Average non-need-based aid:* $7733. *Average indebtedness upon graduation:* $19,846.

Applying *Options:* electronic application, deferred entrance. *Application fee:* $25. *Required:* high school transcript, minimum 2.5 GPA. *Required for some:* essay or personal statement, interview. *Recommended:* 1 letter of recommendation. *Application deadline:* rolling (freshmen), rolling (transfers).

Admissions Contact Ms. Sydney Wolf, Director of Admissions, Concordia University, 4090 Geddes Road, Ann Arbor, MI 48105. *Phone:* 734-995-7322 Ext. 7311. *Toll-free phone:* 800-253-0680. *Fax:* 734-995-7455. *E-mail:* admissions@cuaa.edu.

CORNERSTONE UNIVERSITY
Grand Rapids, Michigan

- **Independent nondenominational** comprehensive, founded 1941
- **Calendar** semesters
- **Degrees** diplomas, associate, bachelor's, master's, and first professional
- **Suburban** 132-acre campus
- **Endowment** $5.1 million
- **Coed,** 2,074 undergraduate students, 76% full-time, 62% women, 38% men
- **Moderately difficult** entrance level, 76% of applicants were admitted

Undergraduates 1,582 full-time, 492 part-time. Students come from 31 states and territories, 1 other country, 20% are from out of state, 14% African American, 0.8% Asian American or Pacific Islander, 4% Hispanic American, 0.3% Native American, 1% international, 6% transferred in, 56% live on campus. *Retention:* 74% of 2002 full-time freshmen returned.

Freshmen *Admission:* 1,285 applied, 973 admitted, 359 enrolled. *Average high school GPA:* 3.40. *Test scores:* ACT scores over 18: 91%; ACT scores over 24: 41%; ACT scores over 30: 5%.

Faculty *Total:* 143, 58% full-time, 27% with terminal degrees. *Student/faculty ratio:* 16:1.

Majors Accounting; airline pilot and flight crew; ancient Near Eastern and biblical languages; biblical studies; biology/biological sciences; biology teacher education; broadcast journalism; business administration and management; business administration, management and operations related; creative writing; early childhood education; education; elementary education; English; English/language arts teacher education; environmental biology; history; history teacher education; information science/studies; interdisciplinary studies; kinesiology and exercise science; management information systems; marketing/marketing management; mass communication/media; mathematics; mathematics teacher education; multi-/interdisciplinary studies related; music; music performance; music teacher education; music theory and composition; pastoral studies/counseling; philosophy; physical education teaching and coaching; political science and government; pre-dentistry studies; pre-law studies; pre-medical studies; pre-theology/pre-ministerial studies; pre-veterinary studies; psychology; religious education; religious studies; science teacher education; secondary education; social science teacher education; social studies teacher education; social work; sociology; Spanish; speech and rhetoric; sport and fitness administration.

Academic Programs *Special study options:* academic remediation for entering students, accelerated degree program, adult/continuing education programs, advanced placement credit, double majors, independent study, internships, off-campus study, part-time degree program, summer session for credit. *ROTC:* Army (c).

Library Miller Library with 109,376 titles, 1,073 serial subscriptions, 19,702 audiovisual materials, an OPAC, a Web page.

Computers on Campus 531 computers available on campus for general student use. A campuswide network can be accessed from student residence rooms and from off campus. Internet access, at least one staffed computer lab available.

Student Life *Housing:* on-campus residence required through junior year. *Options:* men-only, women-only, disabled students. Campus housing is university owned. Freshman campus housing is guaranteed. *Activities and organizations:* drama/theater group, student-run newspaper, choral group, student government, Student Education Association, Breakpoint, Student Activities Council. *Campus security:* 24-hour emergency response devices and patrols, student patrols, late-night transport/escort service, controlled dormitory access. *Student services:* health clinic, personal/psychological counseling.

Athletics Member NAIA. *Intercollegiate sports:* basketball M(s)/W(s), cross-country running M(s)/W(s), golf M(s), soccer M(s)/W(s), softball W(s), track and field M(s)/W(s), volleyball W(s). *Intramural sports:* basketball M/W, football M, soccer M/W, softball M/W, volleyball M/W.

Standardized Tests *Required:* SAT I or ACT (for admission).

Costs (2003–04) *Comprehensive fee:* $19,846 includes full-time tuition ($14,420) and room and board ($5426). Part-time tuition: $555 per credit. Part-time tuition and fees vary according to course load. *College room only:* $2476. Room and board charges vary according to board plan. *Payment plan:* installment. *Waivers:* employees or children of employees.

Financial Aid Of all full-time matriculated undergraduates who enrolled in 2003, 1,163 applied for aid, 918 were judged to have need, 138 had their need fully met. 134 Federal Work-Study jobs (averaging $1492). 26 state and other part-time jobs (averaging $1774). In 2003, 182 non-need-based awards were made. *Average percent of need met:* 80%. *Average financial aid package:* $12,302. *Average need-based loan:* $4102. *Average need-based gift aid:* $6225. *Average non-need-based aid:* $3004. *Average indebtedness upon graduation:* $17,218. *Financial aid deadline:* 2/1.

Applying *Options:* deferred entrance. *Application fee:* $25. *Required:* essay or personal statement, high school transcript, minimum 2.5 GPA, 1 letter of recommendation. *Recommended:* interview. *Application deadline:* rolling (freshmen), rolling (transfers). *Notification:* continuous (transfers).

Admissions Contact Mr. Brent Rudin, Director of Admissions, Cornerstone University, 1001 East Beltline Avenue, NE, Grand Rapids, MI 49525. *Phone:* 616-222-1426. *Toll-free phone:* 800-787-9778. *Fax:* 616-222-1400. *E-mail:* admissions@cornerstone.edu.

DAVENPORT UNIVERSITY
Dearborn, Michigan

- **Independent** comprehensive, founded 1985
- **Calendar** semesters
- **Degrees** certificates, associate, bachelor's, and master's
- **Suburban** 17-acre campus with easy access to Detroit
- **Coed,** 2,185 undergraduate students, 38% full-time, 75% women, 25% men
- **Noncompetitive** entrance level, 100% of applicants were admitted

Undergraduates 820 full-time, 1,365 part-time. Students come from 16 states and territories, 1% are from out of state, 59% African American, 1% Asian American or Pacific Islander, 2% Hispanic American, 0.5% Native American, 0.6% international.

Freshmen *Admission:* 625 applied, 625 admitted, 202 enrolled.

Faculty *Total:* 170, 12% full-time, 13% with terminal degrees. *Student/faculty ratio:* 23:1.

Majors Accounting; accounting technology and bookkeeping; administrative assistant and secretarial science; business administration and management; business administration, management and operations related; business/commerce; computer and information systems security; computer programming (vendor/product certification); computer systems analysis; computer systems networking and telecommunications; customer service support/call center/teleservice operation; desktop publishing and digital imaging design; entrepreneurship; executive assistant/executive secretary; finance; health/health care administration; health information/medical records technology; international business/trade/commerce;

Davenport University (continued)
legal administrative assistant/secretary; management information systems; marketing/marketing management; medical administrative assistant and medical secretary; medical/health management and clinical assistant; medical insurance coding; medical insurance/medical billing; non-profit management; nursing (licensed practical/vocational nurse training); nursing (registered nurse training); office management; operations management; web/multimedia management and webmaster.

Academic Programs *Special study options:* academic remediation for entering students, advanced placement credit, cooperative education, double majors, independent study, internships, part-time degree program, summer session for credit.

Library Dearborn Campus Library plus 1 other with 33,560 titles, 224 serial subscriptions, 299 audiovisual materials, an OPAC.

Computers on Campus 295 computers available on campus for general student use. A campuswide network can be accessed. Internet access, at least one staffed computer lab available.

Student Life *Activities and organizations:* student-run newspaper, Health Occupations Students of America (HOSA), student newspaper, Student Council, Allman Rafiki Society (ARS), President's Council. *Campus security:* late-night transport/escort service.

Athletics *Intramural sports:* bowling M/W, golf M, softball M/W.

Costs (2003–04) *Tuition:* $10,170 full-time, $339 per credit hour part-time. *Required fees:* $100 full-time. *Room only:* $3400.

Applying *Options:* early admission, deferred entrance. *Application fee:* $25. *Required:* high school transcript. *Recommended:* interview. *Application deadline:* rolling (freshmen), rolling (transfers). *Notification:* continuous (freshmen), continuous (transfers).

Admissions Contact Davenport University, 4801 Oakman Boulevard, Dearborn, MI 48126-3799. *Phone:* 313-581-4400. *Toll-free phone:* 800-815-8023. *Fax:* 313-581-1985. *E-mail:* jennifer.salloum@davenport.edu.

DAVENPORT UNIVERSITY
Gaylord, Michigan

- **Independent** 4-year, founded 1977
- **Calendar** semesters
- **Degrees** diplomas, associate, and bachelor's
- **Coed,** 126 undergraduate students, 21% full-time, 71% women, 29% men

Undergraduates 26 full-time, 100 part-time. Students come from 2 states and territories, 2% Hispanic American.

Freshmen *Admission:* 9 enrolled.

Faculty *Total:* 12, 8% full-time. *Student/faculty ratio:* 17:1.

Majors Business/commerce; computer programming (vendor/product certification); computer systems analysis; computer systems networking and telecommunications; entrepreneurship.

Costs (2003–04) *Tuition:* $10,170 full-time, $339 per credit hour part-time. *Required fees:* $100 full-time. *Room only:* $3400.

Applying *Application fee:* $25. *Application deadline:* rolling (freshmen). *Notification:* continuous (freshmen).

Admissions Contact Ms. Sheila Simpson, Career and Education Specialist, Davenport University, 80 Livingston Boulevard, Gaylord, MI 49735. *Phone:* 989-731-2966. *Toll-free phone:* 888-352-5791.

DAVENPORT UNIVERSITY
Grand Rapids, Michigan

- **Independent** comprehensive, founded 1866, part of Davenport University
- **Calendar** semesters
- **Degrees** certificates, diplomas, associate, bachelor's, master's, post-master's, and postbachelor's certificates
- **Urban** campus
- **Coed,** 1,751 undergraduate students, 37% full-time, 63% women, 37% men
- **Noncompetitive** entrance level, 65% of applicants were admitted

Undergraduates 649 full-time, 1,102 part-time. Students come from 15 states and territories, 11% African American, 2% Asian American or Pacific Islander, 4% Hispanic American, 0.5% Native American, 0.6% international, 10% live on campus. *Retention:* 51% of 2002 full-time freshmen returned.

Freshmen *Admission:* 452 applied, 295 admitted, 156 enrolled.

Faculty *Total:* 104, 25% full-time, 17% with terminal degrees. *Student/faculty ratio:* 25:1.

Majors Accounting; business administration and management; business administration, management and operations related; business/commerce; computer and information systems security; computer programming (vendor/product certification); computer systems analysis; computer systems networking and telecommunications; customer service support/call center/teleservice operation; entrepreneurship; finance; international business/trade/commerce; legal assistant/paralegal; marketing/marketing management; operations management; web/multimedia management and webmaster.

Academic Programs *Special study options:* academic remediation for entering students, accelerated degree program, adult/continuing education programs, advanced placement credit, cooperative education, distance learning, English as a second language, external degree program, independent study, internships, part-time degree program, study abroad, summer session for credit.

Library Sneden Library plus 1 other with 40,810 titles, 1,500 serial subscriptions, an OPAC.

Computers on Campus 122 computers available on campus for general student use. A campuswide network can be accessed from student residence rooms and from off campus. Internet access, at least one staffed computer lab available.

Student Life *Housing options:* coed. Campus housing is university owned. *Campus security:* 24-hour emergency response devices and patrols, late-night transport/escort service, controlled dormitory access. *Student services:* personal/psychological counseling.

Athletics *Intercollegiate sports:* basketball W, golf M, ice hockey M. *Intramural sports:* basketball M/W, golf M/W, soccer M/W, softball M/W, tennis M/W, volleyball M/W.

Standardized Tests *Recommended:* ACT (for placement).

Costs (2003–04) *Tuition:* $10,170 full-time, $339 per credit hour part-time. *Required fees:* $100 full-time. *Room only:* $3400.

Applying *Options:* common application, early admission, deferred entrance. *Application fee:* $25. *Required:* high school transcript. *Recommended:* essay or personal statement, interview. *Application deadlines:* rolling (freshmen), 9/15 (out-of-state freshmen), rolling (transfers). *Notification:* continuous (freshmen), continuous (out-of-state freshmen), continuous (transfers).

Admissions Contact Recruiter, Davenport University, 415 East Fulton Street, Administration Building, Fulton and Prospect, Grand Rapids, MI 49503. *Phone:* 616-451-3511. *Toll-free phone:* 800-724-7708.

DAVENPORT UNIVERSITY
Holland, Michigan

- **Independent** comprehensive, founded 1977
- **Calendar** semesters
- **Coed,** 706 undergraduate students, 21% full-time, 64% women, 36% men

Undergraduates 151 full-time, 555 part-time. Students come from 3 states and territories, 1 other country, 3% African American, 6% Asian American or Pacific Islander, 11% Hispanic American, 0.1% Native American, 0.1% international.

Freshmen *Admission:* 50 enrolled.

Faculty *Total:* 45, 11% full-time, 7% with terminal degrees. *Student/faculty ratio:* 23:1.

Majors Accounting technology and bookkeeping; business administration, management and operations related; business/commerce; computer systems analysis; computer systems networking and telecommunications; customer service support/call center/teleservice operation; desktop publishing and digital imaging design; executive assistant/executive secretary; health information/medical records technology; medical insurance coding; medical insurance/medical billing; medical transcription; web/multimedia management and webmaster.

Athletics *Intramural sports:* cheerleading M/W.

Costs (2003–04) *Tuition:* $10,170 full-time, $339 per credit hour part-time. *Required fees:* $100 full-time. *Room only:* $3400.

Applying *Application fee:* $25.

Admissions Contact Mr. Ken Moored, Financial Aid Coordinator, Davenport University, 643 Waverly Road, Holland, MI 49423. *Phone:* 616-395-4600. *Toll-free phone:* 800-643-4630.

DAVENPORT UNIVERSITY
Kalamazoo, Michigan

- **Independent** 4-year, founded 1977, part of Davenport Educational System
- **Calendar** semesters
- **Degrees** certificates, diplomas, associate, bachelor's, and postbachelor's certificates
- **Suburban** 5-acre campus
- **Endowment** $500,000
- **Coed,** 549 undergraduate students, 26% full-time, 72% women, 28% men
- **Noncompetitive** entrance level, 100% of applicants were admitted

Undergraduates 143 full-time, 406 part-time. Students come from 8 states and territories, 15% African American, 1% Asian American or Pacific Islander, 3% Hispanic American, 0.5% Native American, 0.4% international.
Freshmen *Admission:* 161 applied, 161 admitted, 43 enrolled.
Faculty *Total:* 56, 14% full-time, 13% with terminal degrees. *Student/faculty ratio:* 16:1.
Majors Accounting; accounting technology and bookkeeping; business administration and management; business/commerce; computer programming (vendor/product certification); computer systems analysis; computer systems networking and telecommunications; customer service support/call center/teleservice operation; data processing and data processing technology; desktop publishing and digital imaging design; executive assistant/executive secretary; health information/medical records administration; legal administrative assistant/secretary; legal assistant/paralegal; marketing/marketing management; medical insurance coding; medical insurance/medical billing; web/multimedia management and webmaster.
Academic Programs *Special study options:* academic remediation for entering students, adult/continuing education programs, cooperative education, distance learning, English as a second language, independent study, internships, off-campus study, part-time degree program, study abroad, summer session for credit.
Library T. F. Reed Library with 10,257 titles, 949 audiovisual materials.
Computers on Campus 100 computers available on campus for general student use. Internet access, at least one staffed computer lab available.
Student Life *Activities and organizations:* Management/Marketing Club, Institute of Management Accountants, Paralegal Association, Data Processing Management Association. *Campus security:* late-night transport/escort service. *Student services:* personal/psychological counseling.
Costs (2003–04) *Tuition:* $10,170 full-time, $339 per credit hour part-time. *Required fees:* $100 full-time. *Room only:* $3400.
Applying *Options:* common application, electronic application, early admission, deferred entrance. *Application fee:* $25. *Required:* essay or personal statement, high school transcript. *Application deadline:* rolling (freshmen), rolling (transfers). *Notification:* continuous (freshmen).
Admissions Contact Davenport University, 4123 West Main Street, Kalamazoo, MI 49006-2791. *Phone:* 269-382-2835. *Toll-free phone:* 800-632-8928. *Fax:* 616-382-2661.

DAVENPORT UNIVERSITY
Lansing, Michigan

- **Independent** 4-year, founded 1977, part of Davenport Educational System
- **Calendar** semesters
- **Degrees** certificates, diplomas, associate, bachelor's, and master's
- **Suburban** 2-acre campus with easy access to Detroit
- **Coed,** 718 undergraduate students, 24% full-time, 70% women, 30% men
- **Noncompetitive** entrance level

Undergraduates 175 full-time, 543 part-time. Students come from 11 states and territories, 5 other countries, 0.1% are from out of state, 19% African American, 2% Asian American or Pacific Islander, 5% Hispanic American, 1% Native American, 0.8% international. *Retention:* 43% of 2002 full-time freshmen returned.
Freshmen *Admission:* 85 enrolled.
Faculty *Total:* 53, 11% full-time, 15% with terminal degrees. *Student/faculty ratio:* 30:1.
Majors Accounting; business administration and management; business/commerce; computer and information systems security; computer management; computer systems analysis; computer systems networking and telecommunications; customer service support/call center/teleservice operation; desktop publishing and digital imaging design; executive assistant/executive secretary; health/health care administration; human resources management; marketing/marketing management; medical administrative assistant and medical secretary; medical/clinical assistant; medical insurance coding; medical insurance/medical billing; medical transcription; physical therapy.
Academic Programs *Special study options:* academic remediation for entering students, accelerated degree program, adult/continuing education programs, advanced placement credit, cooperative education, distance learning, external degree program, independent study, internships, part-time degree program, services for LD students, student-designed majors, summer session for credit. *ROTC:* Army (c).
Library 10,680 titles, 850 serial subscriptions, an OPAC, a Web page.
Computers on Campus 65 computers available on campus for general student use. At least one staffed computer lab available.
Student Life *Activities and organizations:* Student Accounting Society, Management Marketing Association, Student Leadership Council, Data Processing Management Association, Professional Secretaries International. *Campus security:* 24-hour emergency response devices, late-night transport/escort service.
Standardized Tests *Required for some:* ACT (for placement).
Costs (2003–04) *Tuition:* $10,170 full-time, $339 per credit hour part-time. *Required fees:* $100 full-time. *Room only:* $3400.
Financial Aid *Average indebtedness upon graduation:* $3280.
Applying *Options:* common application, electronic application, early admission, deferred entrance. *Application fee:* $25. *Required:* high school transcript. *Recommended:* interview. *Application deadlines:* rolling (freshmen), 9/15 (transfers). *Notification:* continuous (freshmen), continuous until 9/15 (transfers).
Admissions Contact Tonna Winks, Enrollment Manager, Davenport University, 220 East Kalamazoo, Lansing, MI 48933-2197. *Phone:* 517-484-2600. *Toll-free phone:* 800-686-1600. *Fax:* 517-484-9719. *E-mail:* laadmissions@davenport.edu.

DAVENPORT UNIVERSITY
Lapeer, Michigan

- **Independent** 4-year, founded 1985
- **Calendar** semesters
- **Degrees** diplomas, associate, and bachelor's
- **Coed,** 145 undergraduate students, 43% full-time, 81% women, 19% men

Undergraduates 63 full-time, 82 part-time. Students come from 1 other state, 2% African American, 3% Hispanic American, 0.7% Native American.
Freshmen *Admission:* 25 enrolled.
Faculty *Total:* 25, 4% with terminal degrees. *Student/faculty ratio:* 14:1.
Majors Accounting; accounting technology and bookkeeping; business administration and management; business administration, management and operations related; business/commerce; desktop publishing and digital imaging design; executive assistant/executive secretary; health information/medical records technology; medical administrative assistant and medical secretary; medical insurance coding.
Costs (2003–04) *Tuition:* $10,170 full-time, $339 per credit hour part-time. *Required fees:* $100 full-time. *Room only:* $3400.
Applying *Application fee:* $25. *Application deadline:* rolling (freshmen). *Notification:* continuous (freshmen).
Admissions Contact Mr. Jim Block, Executive Director, Davenport University, 550 Lake Drive, Lapeer, MI 48446. *Phone:* 810-664-9655.

DAVENPORT UNIVERSITY
Midland, Michigan

Admissions Contact Davenport University, 3555 East Patrick Road, Midland, MI 48642. *Toll-free phone:* 800-968-4860. *Fax:* 517-752-3453.

DAVENPORT UNIVERSITY
Traverse City, Michigan

- **Independent** comprehensive, founded 1977
- **Calendar** semesters
- **Coed,** 86 undergraduate students, 40% full-time, 62% women, 38% men

Undergraduates 34 full-time, 52 part-time. Students come from 6 states and territories.
Freshmen *Admission:* 10 enrolled.
Faculty *Total:* 13, 8% full-time. *Student/faculty ratio:* 13:1.
Majors Business/commerce; entrepreneurship.
Costs (2003–04) *Tuition:* $10,170 full-time, $339 per credit hour part-time. *Required fees:* $100 full-time. *Room only:* $3400.
Applying *Application fee:* $25. *Application deadline:* rolling (freshmen). *Notification:* continuous (freshmen).
Admissions Contact Career and Education Specialist, Davenport University, 2200 Dendrinos Drive, Suite 110, Traverse City, MI 49684. *Phone:* 213-995-1740. *Toll-free phone:* 231-995-1740.

DAVENPORT UNIVERSITY
Warren, Michigan

- **Independent** comprehensive, founded 1985
- **Calendar** semesters
- **Degrees** certificates, associate, bachelor's, and master's
- **Suburban** 9-acre campus with easy access to Detroit
- **Coed,** 1,250 undergraduate students, 30% full-time, 77% women, 23% men

Davenport University (continued)

■ **Noncompetitive** entrance level, 100% of applicants were admitted

Undergraduates 371 full-time, 879 part-time. Students come from 8 states and territories, 3 other countries, 1% are from out of state, 54% African American, 4% Asian American or Pacific Islander, 1% Hispanic American, 0.2% Native American, 0.2% international.

Freshmen *Admission:* 300 applied, 300 admitted, 90 enrolled.

Faculty *Total:* 86, 17% full-time, 19% with terminal degrees. *Student/faculty ratio:* 23:1.

Majors Accounting; accounting technology and bookkeeping; business administration and management; business administration, management and operations related; business/commerce; computer and information systems security; computer programming (vendor/product certification); computer systems analysis; computer systems networking and telecommunications; customer service support/call center/teleservice operation; desktop publishing and digital imaging design; entrepreneurship; executive assistant/executive secretary; finance; health information/medical records administration; health information/medical records technology; international business/trade/commerce; management information systems; marketing/marketing management; medical administrative assistant and medical secretary; medical insurance coding; medical insurance/medical billing; nursing (registered nurse training); office management; web/multimedia management and webmaster.

Academic Programs *Special study options:* academic remediation for entering students, advanced placement credit, cooperative education, double majors, internships, part-time degree program, summer session for credit.

Library Detroit College of Business-Warren Library plus 1 other with 95,000 titles, 185 serial subscriptions, 237 audiovisual materials, an OPAC.

Computers on Campus 110 computers available on campus for general student use. A campuswide network can be accessed. At least one staffed computer lab available.

Student Life *Activities and organizations:* student-run newspaper, Business Olympics, marketing club, management club, campus newspaper, accounting club. *Campus security:* late-night transport/escort service. *Student services:* personal/psychological counseling.

Athletics *Intramural sports:* bowling M/W.

Costs (2003–04) *Tuition:* $10,170 full-time, $339 per credit hour part-time. *Required fees:* $100 full-time. *Room only:* $3400.

Applying *Options:* early admission, deferred entrance. *Application fee:* $25. *Required:* high school transcript. *Application deadline:* rolling (freshmen), rolling (transfers). *Notification:* continuous (freshmen), continuous (transfers).

Admissions Contact Kash Richmonds, Assistant Director of Registration, Davenport University, 27650 Dequindre Road, Warren, MI 48092-5209. *Phone:* 586-558-8700. *Toll-free phone:* 800-724-7708. *Fax:* 810-558-7868.

Eastern Michigan University

Ypsilanti, Michigan

■ **State-supported** comprehensive, founded 1849
■ **Calendar** semesters
■ **Degrees** bachelor's, master's, doctoral, post-master's, and postbachelor's certificates
■ **Suburban** 460-acre campus with easy access to Detroit
■ **Endowment** $30.3 million
■ **Coed,** 19,577 undergraduate students, 69% full-time, 61% women, 39% men
■ **Moderately difficult** entrance level, 79% of applicants were admitted

Undergraduates 13,573 full-time, 6,004 part-time. Students come from 47 states and territories, 77 other countries, 6% are from out of state, 17% African American, 2% Asian American or Pacific Islander, 2% Hispanic American, 0.6% Native American, 2% international, 9% transferred in, 20% live on campus. *Retention:* 72% of 2002 full-time freshmen returned.

Freshmen *Admission:* 9,044 applied, 7,139 admitted, 2,577 enrolled. *Average high school GPA:* 3.00. *Test scores:* SAT verbal scores over 500: 56%; SAT math scores over 500: 54%; ACT scores over 18: 78%; SAT verbal scores over 600: 16%; SAT math scores over 600: 20%; ACT scores over 24: 24%; SAT verbal scores over 700: 2%; SAT math scores over 700: 3%; ACT scores over 30: 2%.

Faculty *Total:* 1,223, 62% full-time, 47% with terminal degrees. *Student/faculty ratio:* 19:1.

Majors Accounting; accounting and finance; accounting related; actuarial science; adult development and aging; aeronautics/aviation/aerospace science and technology; African-American/Black studies; anthropology; aquatic biology/limnology; architecture; area studies; area studies related; art; art history, criticism and conservation; artificial intelligence and robotics; arts management; art teacher education; athletic training; biochemistry; bioinformatics; biological and physical sciences; biology/biological sciences; biology teacher education; business administration and management; business/commerce; business/managerial economics; business teacher education; CAD/CADD drafting/design technology; cell and molecular biology; chemistry; chemistry teacher education; city/urban, community and regional planning; clinical laboratory science/medical technology; college student counseling and personnel services; communications technology; community college education; community organization and advocacy; computer and information sciences; computer engineering; computer teacher education; construction engineering technology; construction management; counselor education/school counseling and guidance; creative writing; criminology; cultural resource management and policy analysis; curriculum and instruction; dance; dietetics; dramatic/theatre arts; early childhood education; e-commerce; economics; economics related; educational/instructional media design; educational leadership and administration; educational psychology; education (specific subject areas) related; electrical, electronic and communications engineering technology; elementary and middle school administration/principalship; elementary education; engineering/industrial management; engineering related; engineering technology; English; English as a second/foreign language (teaching); English composition; English/language arts teacher education; English literature (British and Commonwealth); facilities planning and management; family and consumer sciences/human sciences; fashion merchandising; finance; fine/studio arts; foods, nutrition, and wellness; French; French language teacher education; funeral service and mortuary science; geography; geology/earth science; geophysics and seismology; German; Germanic languages; German language teacher education; gerontology; health and physical education; health/health care administration; health/medical preparatory programs related; health teacher education; higher education/higher education administration; historic preservation and conservation; history; history related; history teacher education; hospitality administration; human resources management; industrial technology; information science/studies; interdisciplinary studies; interior design; international business/trade/commerce; international economics; Japanese; journalism; labor studies; legal assistant/paralegal; linguistics; logistics and materials management; management information systems; manufacturing engineering; manufacturing technology; marketing/marketing management; mathematics; mathematics teacher education; mechanical drafting and CAD/CADD; mechanical engineering/mechanical technology; medieval and Renaissance studies; merchandising, sales, and marketing operations related (general); middle school education; multi-/interdisciplinary studies related; music; music history, literature, and theory; music pedagogy; music performance; music teacher education; music therapy; non-profit management; nursing (registered nurse training); occupational therapy; orthotics/prosthetics; parks, recreation and leisure facilities management; philosophy; physical education teaching and coaching; physical sciences related; physics; physics teacher education; physiology; political science and government; polymer/plastics engineering; pre-dentistry studies; pre-law studies; pre-medical studies; pre-pharmacy studies; pre-veterinary studies; psychology; public administration; public administration and social service professions related; public policy analysis; public relations/image management; quality control technology; radio and television broadcasting technology; reading teacher education; Romance languages; sales and marketing/marketing and distribution teacher education; science teacher education; science, technology and society; secondary education; secondary school administration/principalship; security and protective services related; social and philosophical foundations of education; social sciences; social sciences related; social science teacher education; social studies teacher education; social work; sociology; Spanish; Spanish language teacher education; special education; special education (emotionally disturbed); special education (hearing impaired); special education (mentally retarded); special education (orthopedic and other physical health impairments); special education (specific learning disabilities); special education (speech or language impaired); special education (vision impaired); speech and rhetoric; speech-language pathology; sport and fitness administration; statistics; technology/industrial arts teacher education; theatre/theatre arts management; therapeutic recreation; tourism/travel marketing; toxicology; voice and opera; women's studies.

Academic Programs *Special study options:* academic remediation for entering students, accelerated degree program, adult/continuing education programs, advanced placement credit, cooperative education, distance learning, double majors, English as a second language, honors programs, independent study, internships, part-time degree program, services for LD students, student-designed majors, study abroad, summer session for credit. *ROTC:* Army (b), Navy (c), Air Force (c).

Library Bruce T. Halle Library with 658,648 titles, 4,457 serial subscriptions, 11,524 audiovisual materials, an OPAC, a Web page.

Computers on Campus 1500 computers available on campus for general student use. A campuswide network can be accessed from student residence rooms and from off campus. Internet access, at least one staffed computer lab available. Computer purchase or lease plan available.

Student Life *Housing:* on-campus residence required through sophomore year. *Options:* coed, women-only, disabled students. Campus housing is university owned. *Activities and organizations:* drama/theater group, student-run newspaper, radio and television station, choral group, marching band, national fraternities, national sororities. *Campus security:* 24-hour emergency response devices and patrols, student patrols, late-night transport/escort service, controlled dormitory access, bicycle patrols, local police in dormitories, self-defense education, lighted pathways, bike lock lease program. *Student services:* health clinic, personal/psychological counseling, women's center.

Athletics Member NCAA. All Division I except football (Division I-A). *Intercollegiate sports:* baseball M(s), basketball M(s)/W(s), crew W(s), cross-country running M(s)/W(s), golf M(s)/W(s), gymnastics W(s), soccer W(s), softball W(s), swimming M(s)/W(s), tennis W(s), track and field M(s)/W(s), volleyball W(s), wrestling M(s). *Intramural sports:* badminton M/W, basketball M/W, bowling M/W, cross-country running M/W, fencing M(c)/W(c), golf M/W, gymnastics M(c)/W(c), ice hockey M(c), lacrosse M(c)/W(c), racquetball M/W, skiing (cross-country) M/W, soccer M/W, softball M/W, swimming M/W, table tennis M/W, tennis M/W, track and field M/W, ultimate Frisbee M(c)/W(c), volleyball M/W, water polo W(c), weight lifting M/W.

Standardized Tests *Required:* SAT I or ACT (for admission). *Recommended:* ACT (for admission).

Costs (2003–04) *Tuition:* state resident $4595 full-time, $153 per credit hour part-time; nonresident $14,013 full-time, $467 per credit hour part-time. Full-time tuition and fees vary according to reciprocity agreements. Part-time tuition and fees vary according to reciprocity agreements. *Required fees:* $1032 full-time, $32 per credit hour part-time, $40 per term part-time. *Room and board:* $5850; room only: $2748. Room and board charges vary according to housing facility and location. *Payment plan:* installment. *Waivers:* employees or children of employees.

Financial Aid Of all full-time matriculated undergraduates who enrolled in 2002, 11,151 applied for aid, 7,013 were judged to have need, 1,332 had their need fully met. 613 Federal Work-Study jobs (averaging $2800). 233 state and other part-time jobs (averaging $2800). In 2002, 1461 non-need-based awards were made. *Average percent of need met:* 55%. *Average financial aid package:* $9504. *Average need-based loan:* $6406. *Average need-based gift aid:* $3884. *Average non-need-based aid:* $2050. *Average indebtedness upon graduation:* $22,000.

Applying *Options:* deferred entrance. *Application fee:* $30. *Required:* high school transcript, minimum 2.0 GPA. *Required for some:* 1 letter of recommendation, interview. *Application deadline:* 6/30 (freshmen), rolling (transfers). *Notification:* continuous (freshmen), continuous (transfers).

Admissions Contact Ms. Judy Benfield-Tatum, Director of Admissions, Eastern Michigan University, 400 Pierce Hall, Ypsilanti, MI 48197. *Phone:* 734-487-3060. *Toll-free phone:* 800-GO TO EMU. *Fax:* 734-487-1484. *E-mail:* admissions@emich.edu.

■ *See page 1558 for a narrative description.*

FERRIS STATE UNIVERSITY

Big Rapids, Michigan

- **State-supported** comprehensive, founded 1884
- **Calendar** semesters
- **Degrees** certificates, associate, bachelor's, master's, and first professional
- **Small-town** 850-acre campus with easy access to Grand Rapids
- **Endowment** $18.5 million
- **Coed,** 10,767 undergraduate students, 79% full-time, 47% women, 53% men
- **Minimally difficult** entrance level, 73% of applicants were admitted

Undergraduates 8,481 full-time, 2,286 part-time. Students come from 43 states and territories, 55 other countries, 5% are from out of state, 7% African American, 2% Asian American or Pacific Islander, 1% Hispanic American, 0.7% Native American, 2% international, 12% transferred in, 36% live on campus. *Retention:* 65% of 2002 full-time freshmen returned.

Freshmen *Admission:* 12,184 applied, 8,951 admitted, 2,248 enrolled. *Average high school GPA:* 3.09. *Test scores:* ACT scores over 18: 75%; ACT scores over 24: 23%; ACT scores over 30: 2%.

Faculty *Total:* 1,023, 51% full-time, 92% with terminal degrees. *Student/faculty ratio:* 16:1.

Majors Accounting; advertising; applied mathematics; architectural engineering technology; automobile/automotive mechanics technology; biology/biological sciences; biology/biotechnology laboratory technician; business administration and management; business/managerial economics; business teacher education; chemical engineering; child development; civil engineering technology; clinical laboratory science/medical technology; clinical/medical laboratory technology; commercial and advertising art; communications technology; computer programming; construction engineering technology; construction management; consumer merchandising/retailing management; criminal justice/law enforcement administration; criminal justice/police science; dental hygiene; drafting and design technology; education; educational/instructional media design; electrical, electronic and communications engineering technology; energy management and systems technology; environmental health; family and consumer sciences/home economics teacher education; finance; fine/studio arts; furniture design and manufacturing; graphic and printing equipment operation/production; health/health care administration; health information/medical records administration; heating, air conditioning, ventilation and refrigeration maintenance technology; heavy equipment maintenance technology; hospitality administration; industrial design; industrial engineering; industrial radiologic technology; industrial technology; information science/studies; insurance; interior design; international business/trade/commerce; labor and industrial relations; legal administrative assistant/secretary; legal assistant/paralegal; liberal arts and sciences/liberal studies; machine tool technology; management information systems; marketing/marketing management; mass communication/media; mathematics; mechanical design technology; mechanical engineering/mechanical technology; music management and merchandising; nuclear medical technology; nursing (registered nurse training); occupational safety and health technology; opticianry; ornamental horticulture; parks, recreation and leisure; pharmacy, pharmaceutical sciences, and administration related; plastics engineering technology; polymer/plastics engineering; pre-engineering; public administration; public relations/image management; quality control technology; real estate; respiratory care therapy; science teacher education; secondary education; social work; special products marketing; speech and rhetoric; survey technology; technical and business writing; welding technology.

Academic Programs *Special study options:* academic remediation for entering students, accelerated degree program, adult/continuing education programs, advanced placement credit, cooperative education, distance learning, double majors, English as a second language, external degree program, freshman honors college, honors programs, internships, off-campus study, part-time degree program, study abroad, summer session for credit. *ROTC:* Army (c).

Library Ferris Library for Information, Technology and Education with 340,048 titles, 9,809 serial subscriptions, 10,199 audiovisual materials, an OPAC, a Web page.

Computers on Campus 1610 computers available on campus for general student use. A campuswide network can be accessed from student residence rooms and from off campus. Internet access, online (class) registration, at least one staffed computer lab available.

Student Life *Housing:* on-campus residence required through sophomore year. *Options:* coed. Campus housing is university owned. Freshman campus housing is guaranteed. *Activities and organizations:* drama/theater group, student-run newspaper, radio and television station, choral group, Student Government of Ferris State University, intramural sports club, University theatre, music club, forensics club, national fraternities, national sororities. *Campus security:* 24-hour emergency response devices, student patrols, late-night transport/escort service. *Student services:* health clinic, personal/psychological counseling.

Athletics Member NCAA. All Division II except ice hockey (Division I). *Intercollegiate sports:* basketball M(s)/W(s), cheerleading M/W, cross-country running M(s)/W(s), football M(s), golf M(s)/W(s), ice hockey M(s), soccer W(s), softball W(s), tennis M(s)/W(s), track and field M(s)/W(s), volleyball W(s). *Intramural sports:* badminton M/W, baseball M(c), basketball M/W, bowling M/W, cross-country running M/W, football M, golf M/W, ice hockey M, lacrosse M(c), racquetball M/W, rugby M(c)/W(c), skiing (downhill) M(c), softball M/W, swimming M/W, table tennis M/W, tennis M/W, track and field M/W, ultimate Frisbee M(c)/W(c), volleyball M/W, water polo M/W, wrestling M.

Standardized Tests *Required:* SAT I or ACT (for admission).

Costs (2003–04) *Tuition:* state resident $6044 full-time, $250 per credit hour part-time; nonresident $12,088 full-time, $500 per credit hour part-time. Full-time tuition and fees vary according to program and reciprocity agreements. Part-time tuition and fees vary according to course load. *Required fees:* $142 full-time, $71 per term part-time. *Room and board:* $6326; room only: $3118. Room and board charges vary according to board plan and housing facility. *Payment plans:* installment, deferred payment. *Waivers:* employees or children of employees.

Financial Aid Of all full-time matriculated undergraduates who enrolled in 2002, 6,283 applied for aid, 5,455 were judged to have need, 483 had their need fully met. 468 Federal Work-Study jobs (averaging $1372). 365 state and other part-time jobs (averaging $1016). In 2002, 259 non-need-based awards were made. *Average percent of need met:* 80%. *Average financial aid package:* $7900. *Average need-based loan:* $3300. *Average need-based gift aid:* $3500. *Average non-need-based aid:* $2000. *Average indebtedness upon graduation:* $14,500.

Applying *Options:* electronic application, deferred entrance. *Application fee:* $30. *Required:* high school transcript, minimum 2.25 GPA. *Required for some:* 3 letters of recommendation, interview. *Recommended:* interview. *Application deadlines:* 8/1 (freshmen), 8/1 (transfers). *Notification:* continuous (freshmen), continuous (transfers).

Admissions Contact Dr. Craig Westmann, Director Admissions Records/Associate Dean of Enrollment Services, Ferris State University, 1201 South State Street, CSS201, Big Rapids, MI 49307-2742. *Phone:* 231-591-2100. *Toll-free phone:* 800-433-7747. *Fax:* 616-592-2978. *E-mail:* admissions@ferris.edu.

■ *See page 1616 for a narrative description.*

FINLANDIA UNIVERSITY
Hancock, Michigan

- **Independent** 4-year, founded 1896, affiliated with Evangelical Lutheran Church in America
- **Calendar** semesters
- **Degrees** associate and bachelor's
- **Small-town** 25-acre campus
- **Endowment** $2.5 million
- **Coed**
- **Minimally difficult** entrance level

Faculty *Student/faculty ratio:* 11:1.

Student Life *Campus security:* 24-hour patrols, late-night transport/escort service.

Athletics Member NSCAA.

Standardized Tests *Recommended:* SAT I or ACT (for admission).

Costs (2003–04) *One-time required fee:* $75. *Comprehensive fee:* $18,620 includes full-time tuition ($13,750) and room and board ($4870). Full-time tuition and fees vary according to degree level. Part-time tuition: $460 per credit. Part-time tuition and fees vary according to course load and reciprocity agreements. *Room and board:* Room and board charges vary according to housing facility.

Financial Aid Of all full-time matriculated undergraduates who enrolled in 2002, 349 applied for aid, 333 were judged to have need. 195 Federal Work-Study jobs (averaging $1087). 16 state and other part-time jobs (averaging $1488). In 2002, 26. *Average percent of need met:* 90. *Average financial aid package:* $11,000. *Average non-need-based aid:* $3000. *Average indebtedness upon graduation:* $17,000.

Applying *Options:* common application, early admission. *Application fee:* $30. *Required:* high school transcript, minimum 2.5 GPA. *Required for some:* essay or personal statement, letters of recommendation, interview.

Admissions Contact Mr. Ben Larson, Executive Director of Admissions, Finlandia University, 601 Quincy Street, Hancock, MI 49930. *Phone:* 906-487-7311 Ext. 311. *Toll-free phone:* 877-202-5491. *Fax:* 906-487-7383. *E-mail:* admissions@finlandia.edu.

GRACE BIBLE COLLEGE
Grand Rapids, Michigan

- **Independent** 4-year, founded 1945, affiliated with Grace Gospel Fellowship
- **Calendar** semesters
- **Degrees** associate and bachelor's
- **Suburban** 16-acre campus
- **Endowment** $569,857
- **Coed,** 153 undergraduate students, 95% full-time, 51% women, 49% men
- **Minimally difficult** entrance level, 48% of applicants were admitted

Undergraduates 145 full-time, 8 part-time. Students come from 17 states and territories, 1 other country, 31% are from out of state, 0.7% African American, 0.7% Asian American or Pacific Islander, 0.7% Native American, 3% international, 12% transferred in, 58% live on campus. *Retention:* 74% of 2002 full-time freshmen returned.

Freshmen *Admission:* 188 applied, 90 admitted, 32 enrolled. *Average high school GPA:* 3.32. *Test scores:* SAT verbal scores over 500: 75%; ACT scores over 18: 72%; SAT verbal scores over 600: 50%; SAT math scores over 600: 50%; ACT scores over 24: 28%; ACT scores over 30: 4%.

Faculty *Total:* 29, 24% full-time, 14% with terminal degrees. *Student/faculty ratio:* 11:1.

Majors Accounting; biblical studies; business administration and management; computer and information sciences; digital communication and media/multimedia; early childhood education; elementary education; finance and financial management services related; human services; liberal arts and sciences/liberal studies; management science; marketing/marketing management; multi-/interdisciplinary studies related; music; music performance; music teacher education; pastoral studies/counseling; religious education; religious studies; secondary education; theology; youth ministry.

Academic Programs *Special study options:* academic remediation for entering students, advanced placement credit, English as a second language, independent study, internships, off-campus study.

Library Bultema Memorial Library with 32,291 titles, 192 serial subscriptions, 2,121 audiovisual materials, an OPAC.

Computers on Campus 25 computers available on campus for general student use. A campuswide network can be accessed from student residence rooms that provide access to library card catalog search. Internet access, at least one staffed computer lab available.

Student Life *Housing:* on-campus residence required through sophomore year. *Options:* men-only, women-only. Campus housing is university owned. Freshman campus housing is guaranteed. *Activities and organizations:* drama/theater group, choral group, Ambassador Fellowship, Student Activities Committee, Student Council, Ambassador Staff, Campus Ministry Team. *Campus security:* student patrols, controlled dormitory access. *Student services:* personal/psychological counseling.

Athletics Member NCCAA. *Intercollegiate sports:* basketball M/W, soccer M, volleyball W. *Intramural sports:* basketball M, football M, golf M, racquetball M/W, skiing (cross-country) M/W, skiing (downhill) M/W, soccer M/W, table tennis M/W, tennis M/W, volleyball M, weight lifting M/W.

Standardized Tests *Required:* ACT (for admission).

Costs (2003–04) *Comprehensive fee:* $15,890 includes full-time tuition ($9300), mandatory fees ($430), and room and board ($6160). Part-time tuition: $395 per semester hour. Part-time tuition and fees vary according to course load. *Room and board:* Room and board charges vary according to housing facility. *Payment plan:* installment. *Waivers:* employees or children of employees.

Financial Aid Of all full-time matriculated undergraduates who enrolled in 2002, 112 applied for aid, 103 were judged to have need, 15 had their need fully met. 34 Federal Work-Study jobs (averaging $875). 6 state and other part-time jobs (averaging $1042). In 2002, 9 non-need-based awards were made. *Average percent of need met:* 78%. *Average financial aid package:* $9169. *Average need-based loan:* $3092. *Average need-based gift aid:* $6069. *Average non-need-based aid:* $2325. *Average indebtedness upon graduation:* $3239.

Applying *Options:* early admission, deferred entrance. *Required:* high school transcript, 2 letters of recommendation. *Required for some:* interview. *Recommended:* minimum 2.5 GPA. *Application deadline:* 7/15 (freshmen). *Notification:* continuous until 8/1 (freshmen), continuous (transfers).

Admissions Contact Mr. Kevin Gilliam, Director of Enrollment, Grace Bible College, 1101 Aldon Street, SW, PO Box 910, Grand Rapids, MI 49509. *Phone:* 616-538-2330 Ext. 239. *Toll-free phone:* 800-968-1887. *Fax:* 616-538-0599. *E-mail:* gbc@gbcol.edu.

GRAND VALLEY STATE UNIVERSITY
Allendale, Michigan

- **State-supported** comprehensive, founded 1960
- **Calendar** semesters
- **Degrees** bachelor's, master's, post-master's, and postbachelor's certificates
- **Small-town** 900-acre campus with easy access to Grand Rapids
- **Endowment** $36.4 million
- **Coed,** 17,807 undergraduate students, 84% full-time, 60% women, 40% men
- **Moderately difficult** entrance level, 73% of applicants were admitted

Undergraduates 15,002 full-time, 2,805 part-time. Students come from 53 states and territories, 53 other countries, 4% are from out of state, 5% African American, 2% Asian American or Pacific Islander, 3% Hispanic American, 0.6% Native American, 0.6% international, 10% transferred in, 29% live on campus. *Retention:* 78% of 2002 full-time freshmen returned.

Freshmen *Admission:* 12,145 applied, 8,861 admitted, 3,288 enrolled. *Average high school GPA:* 3.42. *Test scores:* ACT scores over 18: 98%; ACT scores over 24: 46%; ACT scores over 30: 5%.

Faculty *Total:* 1,259, 68% full-time, 47% with terminal degrees. *Student/faculty ratio:* 17:1.

Majors Accounting; advertising; anthropology; applied mathematics; art; art history, criticism and conservation; art teacher education; athletic training; behavioral sciences; biochemistry; biological and physical sciences; biology/biological sciences; biomedical sciences; broadcast journalism; business administration and management; cell and molecular biology; ceramic arts and ceramics; chemistry; cinematography and film/video production; classics and languages, literatures and linguistics; clinical laboratory science/medical technology; commercial and advertising art; computer and information sciences; computer engineering; computer programming; computer science; creative writing; criminal justice/law enforcement administration; criminal justice/police science; dramatic/theatre arts; drawing; economics; education; electrical, electronics and communications engineering; elementary education; engineering; engineering/industrial management; English; film/cinema studies; finance; fine/studio arts; French; geology/earth science; German; health science; history; hotel/motel administration; humanities; human resources management; hydrology and water resources science; industrial engineering; information science/studies; interdisciplinary studies; international business/trade/commerce; international relations and affairs; journalism; labor and industrial relations; land use planning and management; legal assistant/paralegal; legal studies; liberal arts and sciences/liberal studies; literature; management information systems; marketing/marketing management; mass communication/media; mathematics; mechanical engineering; metal and jewelry arts; music; music teacher education; natural resources management and policy; natural sciences; nursing (registered nurse training); occupational safety and health technology; occupational therapist assistant; parks, recreation and leisure facilities management; philosophy; photography; physical education teaching and coaching; physical sciences; physical therapy; physician assistant; physics; physiological psychology/psychobiology; piano and organ; political science and government; pre-dentistry studies; pre-law studies; pre-medical studies; pre-veterinary studies; printmaking; psychology; public administration; public health; public policy analysis; public relations/image management; radiation biology; radio and television; reading teacher education; Russian studies; sanitation technology; science teacher education; sculpture; secondary education; social sciences; social studies teacher education; social work; sociology; Spanish; special education; statistics; technical and business writing; telecommunications; therapeutic recreation; tourism and travel services management; violin, viola, guitar and other stringed instruments; voice and opera; western civilization; wildlife and wildlands science and management; wildlife biology; wind/percussion instruments; women's studies.

Academic Programs *Special study options:* academic remediation for entering students, accelerated degree program, adult/continuing education programs, advanced placement credit, cooperative education, distance learning, double majors, English as a second language, freshman honors college, honors programs, independent study, internships, part-time degree program, services for LD students, study abroad, summer session for credit.

Library James H. Zumberge Library plus 2 others with 620,000 titles, 3,207 serial subscriptions, an OPAC, a Web page.

Computers on Campus 2600 computers available on campus for general student use. A campuswide network can be accessed from student residence rooms and from off campus that provide access to transcript, degree audit, credit card payments, grades. Internet access, online (class) registration, at least one staffed computer lab available.

Student Life *Housing options:* coed. Campus housing is university owned. Freshman campus housing is guaranteed. *Activities and organizations:* drama/theater group, student-run newspaper, radio and television station, choral group, marching band, Black Student Union, Residence Hall Association, crew club, student senate, Student Organization Network, national fraternities, national sororities. *Campus security:* 24-hour emergency response devices and patrols, student patrols, late-night transport/escort service, controlled dormitory access. *Student services:* health clinic, personal/psychological counseling, women's center.

Athletics Member NCAA. All Division II. *Intercollegiate sports:* baseball M(s), basketball M(s)/W(s), cheerleading M(c)/W(c), crew M(c)/W(c), cross-country running M(s)/W(s), football M(s), golf M(s)/W(s), ice hockey M(c), rugby M(c)/W(c), sailing M(c)/W(c), skiing (downhill) M(c)/W(c), soccer M(c)/W(s), softball W(s), swimming M(s)/W(s), tennis M(s)/W(s), track and field M(s)/W(s), volleyball M(c)/W(s), water polo M(c)/W(c), wrestling M(c). *Intramural sports:* archery M/W, badminton M/W, basketball M/W, bowling M/W, cheerleading M/W, crew M/W, cross-country running M/W, fencing M/W, field hockey M/W, football M/W, golf M/W, gymnastics M/W, racquetball M/W, skiing (cross-country) M/W, skiing (downhill) M/W, soccer M/W, softball M/W, squash M/W, swimming M/W, tennis M/W, volleyball M/W, water polo M/W, weight lifting M/W, wrestling M.

Standardized Tests *Required:* SAT I or ACT (for admission).

Costs (2003–04) *Tuition:* state resident $5648 full-time, $246 per semester hour part-time; nonresident $12,216 full-time, $520 per semester hour part-time. Full-time tuition and fees vary according to student level. Part-time tuition and fees vary according to course load and student level. *Room and board:* $5768. Room and board charges vary according to board plan, housing facility, and location. *Payment plans:* installment, deferred payment. *Waivers:* employees or children of employees.

Financial Aid Of all full-time matriculated undergraduates who enrolled in 2002, 11,205 applied for aid, 8,403 were judged to have need, 7,630 had their need fully met. 865 Federal Work-Study jobs (averaging $1200). 261 state and other part-time jobs (averaging $1340). In 2002, 1892 non-need-based awards were made. *Average percent of need met:* 92%. *Average financial aid package:* $6614. *Average need-based loan:* $3215. *Average need-based gift aid:* $3114. *Average non-need-based aid:* $1990. *Average indebtedness upon graduation:* $15,611.

Applying *Options:* electronic application. *Application fee:* $30. *Required:* high school transcript. *Required for some:* essay or personal statement, interview. *Application deadlines:* 5/1 (freshmen), 7/25 (transfers). *Notification:* continuous until 5/1 (freshmen), continuous until 7/25 (transfers).

Admissions Contact Ms. Jodi Chycinski, Director of Admissions, Grand Valley State University, 1 Campus Drive, Allendale, MI 49401. *Phone:* 616-331-2025. *Toll-free phone:* 800-748-0246. *Fax:* 616-331-2000. *E-mail:* go2gvsu@gvsu.edu.

■ See page 1686 for a narrative description.

GREAT LAKES CHRISTIAN COLLEGE
Lansing, Michigan

- **Independent** 4-year, founded 1949, affiliated with Christian Churches and Churches of Christ
- **Calendar** semesters
- **Degrees** associate and bachelor's
- **Suburban** 50-acre campus
- **Coed**
- **Moderately difficult** entrance level

Faculty *Student/faculty ratio:* 14:1.

Student Life *Campus security:* evening security patrols.

Standardized Tests *Required:* SAT I and SAT II or ACT (for admission).

Costs (2003–04) *Comprehensive fee:* $14,080 includes full-time tuition ($7680), mandatory fees ($1600), and room and board ($4800). Part-time tuition: $240 per hour.

Applying *Options:* early admission, deferred entrance. *Application fee:* $30. *Required:* essay or personal statement, high school transcript, minimum 2.25 GPA, 3 letters of recommendation.

Admissions Contact Mr. Mike Klauka, Dean of Student Affairs, Great Lakes Christian College, 6211 West Willow Highway, Lansing, MI 48917-1299. *Phone:* 517-321-0242 Ext. 221. *Toll-free phone:* 800-YES-GLCC. *Fax:* 517-321-5902.

HILLSDALE COLLEGE
Hillsdale, Michigan

- **Independent** 4-year, founded 1844
- **Calendar** semesters
- **Degree** bachelor's
- **Small-town** 200-acre campus
- **Endowment** $163.0 million
- **Coed,** 1,230 undergraduate students, 97% full-time, 53% women, 47% men
- **Very difficult** entrance level, 77% of applicants were admitted

Undergraduates 1,195 full-time, 35 part-time. Students come from 47 states and territories, 14 other countries, 53% are from out of state, 3% transferred in, 83% live on campus. *Retention:* 87% of 2002 full-time freshmen returned.

Freshmen *Admission:* 1,150 applied, 881 admitted, 360 enrolled. *Average high school GPA:* 3.63. *Test scores:* SAT verbal scores over 500: 97%; SAT math scores over 500: 93%; ACT scores over 18: 100%; SAT verbal scores over 600: 71%; SAT math scores over 600: 62%; ACT scores over 24: 78%; SAT verbal scores over 700: 25%; SAT math scores over 700: 14%; ACT scores over 30: 24%.

Faculty *Total:* 130, 74% full-time, 78% with terminal degrees. *Student/faculty ratio:* 11:1.

Majors Accounting; American studies; art; biology/biological sciences; business administration and management; chemistry; Christian studies; classics and languages, literatures and linguistics; comparative literature; computer science; drafting and design technology; dramatic/theatre arts; early childhood education; economics; education; education (K-12); elementary education; English; European studies; finance; French; German; history; interdisciplinary studies; international relations and affairs; kindergarten/preschool education; marketing/marketing management; mathematics; mathematics related; music; philosophy; physical education teaching and coaching; physics; political science and government; pre-dentistry studies; pre-medical studies; pre-veterinary studies; psychology; religious studies; secondary education; sociology; Spanish; speech and rhetoric.

Academic Programs *Special study options:* accelerated degree program, advanced placement credit, double majors, honors programs, independent study, internships, part-time degree program, study abroad, summer session for credit. *Unusual degree programs:* 3-2 engineering with Northwestern University, Tri-State University.

Library Mossey Learning Center plus 3 others with 205,000 titles, 1,625 serial subscriptions, 7,950 audiovisual materials, an OPAC, a Web page.

Computers on Campus 185 computers available on campus for general student use. A campuswide network can be accessed from student residence rooms and from off campus. Internet access, at least one staffed computer lab available.

Student Life *Housing:* on-campus residence required through sophomore year. *Options:* men-only, women-only. Campus housing is university owned. Freshman campus housing is guaranteed. *Activities and organizations:* drama/theater group, student-run newspaper, choral group, Inter-Varsity Christian Fellowship, Varsity H-Club, Student Federation, Young Life, College Republicans, national fraternities, national sororities. *Campus security:* 24-hour emergency response devices and patrols, late-night transport/escort service, controlled dormitory access. *Student services:* health clinic, personal/psychological counseling.

Athletics Member NCAA. All Division II. *Intercollegiate sports:* baseball M(s), basketball M(s)/W(s), cheerleading M/W, cross-country running M(s)/W(s),

Hillsdale College (continued)
equestrian sports W, football M(s), golf M(s), ice hockey M, lacrosse M, riflery M/W, soccer M/W, softball W(s), swimming W(s), tennis W(s), track and field M(s)/W(s), volleyball W(s). *Intramural sports:* basketball M/W, cross-country running M/W, equestrian sports W(c), football M/W, golf M/W, ice hockey M(c), lacrosse M(c), racquetball M/W, riflery M(c)/W(c), skiing (downhill) M(c)/W(c), soccer M(c)/W(c), softball M/W, squash M/W, swimming W, table tennis M/W, tennis W, track and field M/W, ultimate Frisbee M/W, volleyball M/W.

Standardized Tests *Required:* SAT I or ACT (for admission). *Recommended:* SAT II: Subject Tests (for admission), SAT II: Writing Test (for admission).

Costs (2003–04) *Comprehensive fee:* $22,450 includes full-time tuition ($15,750), mandatory fees ($300), and room and board ($6400). Part-time tuition: $610 per semester hour. *College room only:* $3140. Room and board charges vary according to board plan. *Payment plans:* tuition prepayment, installment, deferred payment. *Waivers:* children of alumni and employees or children of employees.

Financial Aid Of all full-time matriculated undergraduates who enrolled in 2002, 1,116 applied for aid, 1,080 were judged to have need, 486 had their need fully met. *Average percent of need met:* 80%. *Average financial aid package:* $12,714. *Average need-based loan:* $3500. *Average need-based gift aid:* $9971. *Average non-need-based aid:* $8500. *Average indebtedness upon graduation:* $16,370.

Applying *Options:* common application, electronic application, early admission, deferred entrance. *Application fee:* $15. *Required:* essay or personal statement, high school transcript, minimum 3.15 GPA, 1 letter of recommendation. *Required for some:* 2 letters of recommendation, interview. *Recommended:* 2 letters of recommendation, interview. *Application deadline:* rolling (freshmen), rolling (transfers). *Notification:* continuous until 7/1 (freshmen), continuous (transfers).

Admissions Contact Mr. Jeffrey S. Lantis, Director of Admissions, Hillsdale College, 33 East College Street, Hillsdale, MI 49242-1298. *Phone:* 517-607-2327 Ext. 2327. *Fax:* 517-607-2223. *E-mail:* admissions@hillsdale.edu.

■ *See page 1734 for a narrative description.*

HOPE COLLEGE
Holland, Michigan

- **Independent** 4-year, founded 1866, affiliated with Reformed Church in America
- **Calendar** semesters
- **Degree** bachelor's
- **Small-town** 45-acre campus with easy access to Grand Rapids
- **Endowment** $111.1 million
- **Coed,** 3,068 undergraduate students, 96% full-time, 62% women, 38% men
- **Moderately difficult** entrance level, 83% of applicants were admitted

Undergraduates 2,958 full-time, 110 part-time. Students come from 45 states and territories, 32 other countries, 24% are from out of state, 1% African American, 2% Asian American or Pacific Islander, 2% Hispanic American, 0.2% Native American, 1% international, 2% transferred in, 76% live on campus. *Retention:* 88% of 2002 full-time freshmen returned.

Freshmen *Admission:* 2,481 applied, 2,056 admitted, 811 enrolled. *Average high school GPA:* 3.72. *Test scores:* SAT verbal scores over 500: 88%; SAT math scores over 500: 89%; ACT scores over 18: 98%; SAT verbal scores over 600: 49%; SAT math scores over 600: 52%; ACT scores over 24: 67%; SAT verbal scores over 700: 13%; SAT math scores over 700: 13%; ACT scores over 30: 17%.

Faculty *Total:* 293, 69% full-time, 61% with terminal degrees. *Student/faculty ratio:* 13:1.

Majors Accounting; art history, criticism and conservation; art teacher education; athletic training; biology/biological sciences; biology teacher education; business administration and management; business/managerial economics; chemistry; chemistry teacher education; classics and languages, literatures and linguistics; communication/speech communication and rhetoric; computer science; dance; drama and dance teacher education; dramatic/theatre arts; economics; education (specific subject areas) related; elementary education; engineering; engineering physics; English; English/language arts teacher education; environmental studies; fine/studio arts; French; French language teacher education; geology/earth science; geophysics and seismology; German; German language teacher education; history; history teacher education; humanities; interdisciplinary studies; international/global studies; jazz/jazz studies; kinesiology and exercise science; Latin teacher education; mathematics; mathematics teacher education; multi-/interdisciplinary studies related; music; music performance; music teacher education; music theory and composition; nursing (registered nurse training); philosophy; physical education teaching and coaching; physics; physics teacher education; political science and government; psychology; religious studies; science teacher education; secondary education; social studies teacher education; social work; sociology; Spanish; Spanish language teacher education; special education (emotionally disturbed); special education (specific learning disabilities).

Academic Programs *Special study options:* advanced placement credit, double majors, English as a second language, independent study, internships, off-campus study, part-time degree program, services for LD students, student-designed majors, study abroad, summer session for credit.

Library Van Wylen Library plus 1 other with 343,865 titles, 2,250 serial subscriptions, 11,970 audiovisual materials, an OPAC, a Web page.

Computers on Campus 300 computers available on campus for general student use. A campuswide network can be accessed from student residence rooms and from off campus. Internet access, at least one staffed computer lab available. Computer purchase or lease plan available.

Student Life *Housing:* on-campus residence required through junior year. *Options:* coed, men-only, women-only, disabled students. Campus housing is university owned and leased by the school. Freshman campus housing is guaranteed. *Activities and organizations:* drama/theater group, student-run newspaper, radio and television station, choral group, Fellowship of Christian Athletes, Social Activities Committee. *Campus security:* 24-hour emergency response devices and patrols, late-night transport/escort service, controlled dormitory access. *Student services:* health clinic, personal/psychological counseling.

Athletics Member NCAA. All Division III. *Intercollegiate sports:* baseball M, basketball M/W, cheerleading M/W, cross-country running M/W, football M, golf M/W, ice hockey M(c), lacrosse M(c), soccer M/W, softball W, swimming M/W, tennis M/W, track and field M/W, volleyball M(c)/W, water polo M(c)/W(c). *Intramural sports:* basketball M/W, bowling M/W, cross-country running M/W, football M/W, lacrosse W, racquetball M/W, sailing M(c)/W(c), skiing (cross-country) M(c)/W(c), skiing (downhill) M(c)/W(c), soccer M/W, softball M/W, swimming M/W, tennis M/W, track and field M/W, ultimate Frisbee M, volleyball M/W, water polo M/W.

Standardized Tests *Required:* SAT I or ACT (for admission).

Costs (2003–04) *Comprehensive fee:* $25,340 includes full-time tuition ($19,212), mandatory fees ($110), and room and board ($6018). Full-time tuition and fees vary according to course load. *College room only:* $2744. Room and board charges vary according to board plan. *Payment plan:* installment.

Financial Aid Of all full-time matriculated undergraduates who enrolled in 2002, 1,972 applied for aid, 1,702 were judged to have need, 505 had their need fully met. 266 Federal Work-Study jobs (averaging $1138). 588 state and other part-time jobs (averaging $1786). In 2002, 721 non-need-based awards were made. *Average percent of need met:* 87%. *Average financial aid package:* $16,860. *Average need-based loan:* $4824. *Average need-based gift aid:* $11,360. *Average non-need-based aid:* $6662. *Average indebtedness upon graduation:* $19,705.

Applying *Options:* common application, electronic application, early admission, deferred entrance. *Application fee:* $35. *Required:* essay or personal statement, high school transcript. *Required for some:* 1 letter of recommendation. *Recommended:* interview. *Application deadline:* rolling (freshmen), rolling (transfers). *Notification:* continuous (freshmen), continuous (transfers).

Admissions Contact Dr. James R. Bekkering, Vice President for Admissions, Hope College, 69 East 10th Street, PO Box 9000, Holland, MI 49422-9000. *Phone:* 616-395-7955. *Toll-free phone:* 800-968-7850. *Fax:* 616-395-7130. *E-mail:* admissions@hope.edu.

■ *See page 1744 for a narrative description.*

KALAMAZOO COLLEGE
Kalamazoo, Michigan

- **Independent** 4-year, founded 1833, affiliated with American Baptist Churches in the U.S.A.
- **Calendar** quarters
- **Degree** bachelor's
- **Suburban** 60-acre campus
- **Endowment** $116.8 million
- **Coed,** 1,280 undergraduate students, 100% full-time, 56% women, 44% men
- **Very difficult** entrance level, 70% of applicants were admitted

Undergraduates 1,280 full-time. Students come from 35 states and territories, 14 other countries, 26% are from out of state, 3% African American, 4% Asian American or Pacific Islander, 1% Hispanic American, 0.2% Native American, 2% international, 0.3% transferred in, 74% live on campus. *Retention:* 86% of 2002 full-time freshmen returned.

Freshmen *Admission:* 1,603 applied, 1,127 admitted, 383 enrolled. *Average high school GPA:* 3.65. *Test scores:* SAT verbal scores over 500: 99%; SAT math scores over 500: 98%; ACT scores over 18: 99%; SAT verbal scores over 600: 83%; SAT math scores over 600: 81%; ACT scores over 24: 93%; SAT verbal scores over 700: 32%; SAT math scores over 700: 25%; ACT scores over 30: 26%.

Faculty *Total:* 117, 88% full-time, 85% with terminal degrees. *Student/faculty ratio:* 12:1.

Majors Anthropology; art; art history, criticism and conservation; biology/biological sciences; business/managerial economics; chemistry; classics and languages, literatures and linguistics; computer science; dramatic/theatre arts; English; French; German; health science; history; interdisciplinary studies; mathematics; music; philosophy; physics; political science and government; psychology; religious studies; sociology; Spanish.

Academic Programs *Special study options:* advanced placement credit, cooperative education, double majors, English as a second language, independent study, internships, off-campus study, services for LD students, study abroad. *ROTC:* Army (c). *Unusual degree programs:* 3-2 engineering with University of Michigan, Washington University in St. Louis; architecture with Washington University in St. Louis.

Library Upjohn Library plus 1 other with 342,939 titles, 1,495 serial subscriptions, 6,967 audiovisual materials, an OPAC, a Web page.

Computers on Campus 130 computers available on campus for general student use. A campuswide network can be accessed from student residence rooms and from off campus. Internet access, at least one staffed computer lab available.

Student Life *Housing:* on-campus residence required for freshman year. *Options:* coed. Campus housing is university owned. *Activities and organizations:* drama/theater group, student-run newspaper, radio station, choral group, Student Activities Committee, Student Commission, Index (college newspaper), Inter-Varsity Christian Fellowship, Project Brave Volunteer Organization. *Campus security:* 24-hour emergency response devices and patrols, late-night transport/escort service, controlled dormitory access. *Student services:* health clinic, personal/psychological counseling, women's center.

Athletics Member NCAA. All Division III. *Intercollegiate sports:* baseball M, basketball M/W, cross-country running M/W, football M, golf M/W, soccer M/W, softball W, swimming M/W, tennis M/W, volleyball W. *Intramural sports:* badminton M/W, basketball M/W, cheerleading M(c)/W(c), gymnastics W(c), racquetball M/W, rock climbing M(c)/W(c), rugby M(c)/W(c), skiing (downhill) M(c)/W(c), soccer M(c)/W(c), softball M/W, swimming M/W, table tennis M/W, tennis M/W, track and field M(c)/W(c), ultimate Frisbee M(c)/W(c), volleyball W, water polo M/W.

Standardized Tests *Required:* SAT I or ACT (for admission).

Costs (2003–04) *Comprehensive fee:* $29,388 includes full-time tuition ($22,908) and room and board ($6480). *College room only:* $3210. *Payment plan:* installment.

Financial Aid Of all full-time matriculated undergraduates who enrolled in 2003, 770 applied for aid, 638 were judged to have need, 451 had their need fully met. 430 Federal Work-Study jobs (averaging $1600). In 2003, 541 non-need-based awards were made. *Average financial aid package:* $19,556. *Average need-based loan:* $5080. *Average need-based gift aid:* $13,126. *Average non-need-based aid:* $8100. *Average indebtedness upon graduation:* $18,782.

Applying *Options:* common application, electronic application, early decision, early action, deferred entrance. *Required:* essay or personal statement, high school transcript, 2 letters of recommendation. *Recommended:* minimum 3.0 GPA, interview. *Application deadlines:* 2/15 (freshmen), 2/15 (transfers). *Early decision:* 11/15. *Notification:* 4/1 (freshmen), 12/1 (early decision), 12/20 (early action), 4/1 (transfers).

Admissions Contact Mrs. Linda Wirgau, Records Manager, Kalamazoo College, Mandelle Hall, 1200 Academy Street, Kalamazoo, MI 49006-3295. *Phone:* 269-337-7166. *Toll-free phone:* 800-253-3602. *E-mail:* admission@kzoo.edu.

KETTERING UNIVERSITY
Flint, Michigan

- **Independent** comprehensive, founded 1919
- **Calendar** semesters (11 weeks of full-time study plus 12 weeks of paid co-op experience per semester)
- **Degrees** bachelor's and master's
- **Suburban** 85-acre campus with easy access to Detroit
- **Endowment** $40.7 million
- **Coed,** 2,558 undergraduate students, 100% full-time, 17% women, 83% men
- **Very difficult** entrance level, 71% of applicants were admitted

Kettering University (formerly GMI Engineering & Management Institute) is prepared to jump-start a student's career in engineering, math, applied sciences, computers, or business. With Kettering's renowned professional co-op program, students alternate 3-month class terms with 3-month paid work experience terms with one of more than 700 corporate employers. Traditionally, 100% of Kettering seniors receive job offers or are accepted by graduate schools before they receive their diplomas. Kettering University provides an education for the real world.

Undergraduates 2,558 full-time. Students come from 52 states and territories, 24 other countries, 37% are from out of state, 7% African American, 5% Asian American or Pacific Islander, 2% Hispanic American, 0.3% Native American, 2% international, 2% transferred in, 48% live on campus. *Retention:* 88% of 2002 full-time freshmen returned.

Freshmen *Admission:* 2,365 applied, 1,669 admitted, 561 enrolled. *Average high school GPA:* 3.6. *Test scores:* SAT verbal scores over 500: 90%; SAT math scores over 500: 100%; ACT scores over 18: 99%; SAT verbal scores over 600: 48%; SAT math scores over 600: 78%; ACT scores over 24: 74%; SAT verbal scores over 700: 8%; SAT math scores over 700: 22%; ACT scores over 30: 12%.

Faculty *Total:* 153, 91% full-time, 86% with terminal degrees. *Student/faculty ratio:* 12:1.

Majors Accounting; accounting and finance; applied mathematics; biomedical/medical engineering; business administration and management; chemistry; computer engineering; computer/information technology services administration related; computer science; electrical, electronics and communications engineering; engineering/industrial management; finance; industrial engineering; information science/studies; management information systems; marketing/marketing management; mechanical engineering; operations management; physics; polymer/plastics engineering; statistics.

Academic Programs *Special study options:* accelerated degree program, advanced placement credit, cooperative education, distance learning, double majors, independent study, internships, services for LD students, study abroad.

Library Kettering University Library plus 1 other with 115,000 titles, 1,200 serial subscriptions, 778 audiovisual materials, an OPAC, a Web page.

Computers on Campus 300 computers available on campus for general student use. A campuswide network can be accessed from student residence rooms and from off campus. Internet access, online (class) registration, at least one staffed computer lab available.

Student Life *Housing:* on-campus residence required for freshman year. *Options:* coed. Campus housing is university owned and is provided by a third party. Freshman campus housing is guaranteed. *Activities and organizations:* drama/theater group, student-run newspaper, radio station, choral group, student government, Society of Automotive Engineers, National Society of Black Engineers, outdoors club, Christians in Action, national fraternities, national sororities. *Campus security:* 24-hour emergency response devices and patrols, late-night transport/escort service, controlled dormitory access. *Student services:* health clinic, personal/psychological counseling, women's center.

Athletics *Intercollegiate sports:* cheerleading M/W, ice hockey M(c), lacrosse M(c), soccer M(c), volleyball M(c). *Intramural sports:* basketball M/W, bowling M/W, cross-country running M/W, football M/W, golf M/W, ice hockey M/W, lacrosse M/W, racquetball M/W, rock climbing M(c)/W(c), soccer M/W, softball M/W, squash M/W, swimming M/W, table tennis M/W, tennis M/W, track and field M/W, ultimate Frisbee W, volleyball M/W, water polo M/W.

Standardized Tests *Required:* SAT I or ACT (for admission). *Recommended:* SAT II: Subject Tests (for admission).

Costs (2003–04) *Comprehensive fee:* $26,478 includes full-time tuition ($21,184), mandatory fees ($370), and room and board ($4924). Part-time tuition: $662 per credit. *College room only:* $3174. Room and board charges vary according to student level. *Payment plan:* installment. *Waivers:* employees or children of employees.

Financial Aid Of all full-time matriculated undergraduates who enrolled in 2003, 1,926 applied for aid, 1,823 were judged to have need, 74 had their need fully met. 336 Federal Work-Study jobs (averaging $593). In 2003, 351 non-need-based awards were made. *Average percent of need met:* 43%. *Average financial aid package:* $10,740. *Average need-based loan:* $4024. *Average need-based gift aid:* $6702. *Average non-need-based aid:* $5385. *Average indebtedness upon graduation:* $33,605.

Applying *Options:* electronic application, deferred entrance. *Application fee:* $35. *Required:* high school transcript. *Required for some:* essay or personal statement. *Recommended:* minimum 3.0 GPA, interview. *Application deadline:* rolling (freshmen), rolling (transfers). *Notification:* continuous (freshmen), continuous (transfers).

Admissions Contact Ms. Barbara Sosin, Director of Admissions, Kettering University, 1700 West Third Avenue, Flint, MI 48504-4898. *Phone:* 810-762-7865. *Toll-free phone:* 800-955-4464 Ext. 7865 (in-state); 800-955-4464 (out-of-state). *Fax:* 810-762-9837. *E-mail:* admissions@kettering.edu.

■ *See page 1818 for a narrative description.*

LAKE SUPERIOR STATE UNIVERSITY
Sault Sainte Marie, Michigan

- **State-supported** 4-year, founded 1946
- **Calendar** semesters
- **Degrees** certificates, associate, and bachelor's
- **Small-town** 121-acre campus
- **Endowment** $5.3 million

Lake Superior State University (continued)
- **Coed,** 3,258 undergraduate students, 76% full-time, 49% women, 51% men
- **Moderately difficult** entrance level, 89% of applicants were admitted

Undergraduates 2,474 full-time, 784 part-time. Students come from 20 states and territories, 12 other countries, 4% are from out of state, 0.5% African American, 0.5% Asian American or Pacific Islander, 0.7% Hispanic American, 9% Native American, 11% international, 9% transferred in, 29% live on campus. *Retention:* 70% of 2002 full-time freshmen returned.

Freshmen *Admission:* 1,557 applied, 1,388 admitted, 541 enrolled. *Average high school GPA:* 3.01. *Test scores:* ACT scores over 18: 80%; ACT scores over 24: 27%; ACT scores over 30: 2%.

Faculty *Total:* 232, 48% full-time. *Student/faculty ratio:* 17:1.

Majors Accounting; accounting technology and bookkeeping; administrative assistant and secretarial science; American Indian/Native American studies; athletic training; biology/biological sciences; business administration and management; business/managerial economics; chemistry; clinical laboratory science/medical technology; computer engineering technology; computer science; construction engineering technology; corrections; criminal justice/law enforcement administration; criminal justice/police science; data processing and data processing technology; drafting and design technology; economics; education; education (multiple levels); electrical, electronic and communications engineering technology; electrical, electronics and communications engineering; elementary education; engineering; engineering/industrial management; engineering technology; English; environmental engineering technology; environmental studies; finance; fire science; fish/game management; geology/earth science; history; human services; hydrology and water resources science; industrial technology; interdisciplinary studies; kindergarten/preschool education; kinesiology and exercise science; legal assistant/paralegal; legal studies; liberal arts and sciences/liberal studies; literature; machine tool technology; management information systems; mathematics; mathematics and computer science; mechanical engineering; mechanical engineering/mechanical technology; mental health/rehabilitation; middle school education; natural resources management and policy; nursing (registered nurse training); office management; parks, recreation and leisure; parks, recreation and leisure facilities management; political science and government; pre-dentistry studies; pre-law studies; pre-medical studies; pre-veterinary studies; psychiatric/mental health services technology; psychology; robotics technology; secondary education; social sciences; sociology; sport and fitness administration; therapeutic recreation; water quality and wastewater treatment management and recycling technology; wildlife and wildlands science and management.

Academic Programs *Special study options:* academic remediation for entering students, adult/continuing education programs, advanced placement credit, cooperative education, distance learning, double majors, freshman honors college, honors programs, independent study, internships, part-time degree program, services for LD students, student-designed majors, summer session for credit.

Library Kenneth Shouldice Library with 112,920 titles, 714 serial subscriptions, an OPAC.

Computers on Campus 350 computers available on campus for general student use. A campuswide network can be accessed from off campus. Internet access, at least one staffed computer lab available.

Student Life *Housing:* on-campus residence required through sophomore year. *Options:* coed, men-only, women-only. *Activities and organizations:* drama/theater group, student-run newspaper, radio station, choral group, national fraternities, national sororities. *Campus security:* 24-hour patrols, student patrols, late-night transport/escort service. *Student services:* health clinic, personal/psychological counseling.

Athletics Member NCAA. All Division II except ice hockey (Division I). *Intercollegiate sports:* basketball M(s)/W(s), cross-country running M(s)/W(s), golf M, ice hockey M(s), softball W, tennis M(s)/W(s), track and field M(s)/W(s), volleyball W(s). *Intramural sports:* basketball M/W, football M/W, ice hockey M, racquetball M/W, riflery M/W, tennis M/W, track and field M/W, volleyball M/W, water polo M/W, wrestling M.

Standardized Tests *Required:* ACT (for admission).

Costs (2003–04) *Tuition:* state resident $5136 full-time, $214 per credit hour part-time; nonresident $10,062 full-time, $419 per credit hour part-time. Full-time tuition and fees vary according to reciprocity agreements. Part-time tuition and fees vary according to reciprocity agreements. *Required fees:* $318 full-time. *Room and board:* $5993; room only: $5334. Room and board charges vary according to board plan. *Waivers:* minority students, children of alumni, senior citizens, and employees or children of employees.

Financial Aid Of all full-time matriculated undergraduates who enrolled in 2002, 2,231 applied for aid, 1,562 were judged to have need, 1,005 had their need fully met. In 2002, 213 non-need-based awards were made. *Average percent of need met:* 79%. *Average financial aid package:* $6700. *Average need-based loan:* $3765. *Average need-based gift aid:* $3103. *Average non-need-based aid:* $2381. *Average indebtedness upon graduation:* $17,948.

Applying *Options:* deferred entrance. *Application fee:* $20. *Required:* high school transcript. *Required for some:* minimum 2.0 GPA. *Application deadline:* 8/15 (freshmen), rolling (transfers). *Notification:* continuous (freshmen), continuous (transfers).

Admissions Contact Mr. Kevin Pollock, Director of Admissions, Lake Superior State University, 650 West Easterday Avenue, Sault Saint Marie, MI 49783-1699. *Phone:* 906-635-2670. *Toll-free phone:* 888-800-LSSU Ext. 2231. *Fax:* 906-635-6669. *E-mail:* admissions@gw.lssu.edu.

LAWRENCE TECHNOLOGICAL UNIVERSITY
Southfield, Michigan

- **Independent** university, founded 1932
- **Calendar** semesters
- **Degrees** associate, bachelor's, and master's
- **Suburban** 115-acre campus with easy access to Detroit
- **Endowment** $15.2 million
- **Coed,** 2,958 undergraduate students, 53% full-time, 24% women, 76% men
- **Moderately difficult** entrance level, 76% of applicants were admitted

Undergraduates 1,580 full-time, 1,378 part-time. Students come from 16 states and territories, 16 other countries, 1% are from out of state, 11% African American, 8% Asian American or Pacific Islander, 1% Hispanic American, 0.4% Native American, 4% international, 13% transferred in, 9% live on campus. *Retention:* 64% of 2002 full-time freshmen returned.

Freshmen *Admission:* 1,417 applied, 1,081 admitted, 470 enrolled. *Average high school GPA:* 3.24. *Test scores:* SAT verbal scores over 500: 54%; SAT math scores over 500: 75%; ACT scores over 18: 88%; SAT verbal scores over 600: 27%; SAT math scores over 600: 41%; ACT scores over 24: 48%; SAT verbal scores over 700: 7%; SAT math scores over 700: 16%; ACT scores over 30: 5%.

Faculty *Total:* 424, 27% full-time, 50% with terminal degrees. *Student/faculty ratio:* 13:1.

Majors Architecture; business administration and management; chemical technology; chemistry; chemistry related; civil engineering; communications technology; computer engineering; computer science; construction engineering technology; construction management; electrical and electronic engineering technologies related; electrical, electronic and communications engineering technology; electrical, electronics and communications engineering; engineering/industrial management; engineering technology; environmental design/architecture; general studies; humanities; illustration; industrial technology; information technology; interior architecture; manufacturing technology; mathematics; mathematics and computer science; mechanical engineering; mechanical engineering/mechanical technology; physics; physics related; psychology.

Academic Programs *Special study options:* academic remediation for entering students, adult/continuing education programs, advanced placement credit, cooperative education, distance learning, double majors, English as a second language, independent study, internships, off-campus study, part-time degree program, services for LD students, study abroad, summer session for credit. *ROTC:* Army (c), Air Force (c).

Library Lawrence Technological University Library plus 1 other with 110,250 titles, 700 serial subscriptions, 420 audiovisual materials, an OPAC, a Web page.

Computers on Campus 60 computers available on campus for general student use. A campuswide network can be accessed from student residence rooms that provide access to degree audit, black board, SCT Banner (student information). Internet access, online (class) registration, at least one staffed computer lab available.

Student Life *Housing options:* coed. Campus housing is university owned. Freshman applicants given priority for college housing. *Activities and organizations:* student-run newspaper, Society of Automotive Engineers, Institute of Electric and Electronic Engineers, American Institute of Architecture Students, American Society of Civil Engineers, Campus Crusade for Christ, national fraternities, national sororities. *Campus security:* 24-hour emergency response devices and patrols, late-night transport/escort service, controlled dormitory access. *Student services:* personal/psychological counseling.

Athletics *Intramural sports:* badminton M/W, basketball M/W, bowling M/W, football M, golf M/W, ice hockey M(c), racquetball M/W, skiing (cross-country) M/W, skiing (downhill) M/W, soccer M(c)/W, softball M/W, table tennis M/W, volleyball M/W.

Standardized Tests *Required:* ACT (for admission), SAT I or ACT (for admission). *Recommended:* SAT I (for admission).

Costs (2003–04) *Comprehensive fee:* $20,487 includes full-time tuition ($14,112), mandatory fees ($250), and room and board ($6125). Full-time tuition and fees vary according to degree level, program, and student level. Part-time tuition: $484 per hour. Part-time tuition and fees vary according to degree level, program, and student level. *Required fees:* $125 per term part-time. *College room* *only:* $4306. Room and board charges vary according to board plan and housing facility. *Payment plans:* tuition prepayment, installment. *Waivers:* employees or children of employees.

Financial Aid Of all full-time matriculated undergraduates who enrolled in 2002, 1,208 applied for aid, 814 were judged to have need, 177 had their need fully met. 74 Federal Work-Study jobs (averaging $1351). 86 state and other part-time jobs (averaging $688). In 2002, 328 non-need-based awards were made. *Average percent of need met:* 73%. *Average financial aid package:* $11,137. *Average need-based loan:* $4218. *Average need-based gift aid:* $6590. *Average non-need-based aid:* $6472. *Average indebtedness upon graduation:* $24,590.

Applying *Options:* electronic application, early admission, deferred entrance. *Application fee:* $30. *Required:* high school transcript, minimum 2.5 GPA. *Required for some:* essay or personal statement, letters of recommendation, interview. *Application deadlines:* 8/15 (freshmen), 8/15 (transfers). *Notification:* continuous until 8/26 (freshmen).

Admissions Contact Ms. Jane Rohrback, Director of Admissions, Lawrence Technological University, 21000 West Ten Mile Road, Southfield, MI 48075. *Phone:* 248-204-3180. *Toll-free phone:* 800-225-5588. *Fax:* 248-204-3188. *E-mail:* admissions@ltu.edu.

■ *See page 1850 for a narrative description.*

MADONNA UNIVERSITY
Livonia, Michigan

- **Independent Roman Catholic** comprehensive, founded 1947
- **Calendar** semesters
- **Degrees** certificates, diplomas, associate, bachelor's, master's, post-master's, and postbachelor's certificates
- **Suburban** 49-acre campus with easy access to Detroit
- **Endowment** $25.8 million
- **Coed,** 3,243 undergraduate students, 47% full-time, 74% women, 26% men
- **Moderately difficult** entrance level, 86% of applicants were admitted

Undergraduates 1,532 full-time, 1,711 part-time. Students come from 32 states and territories, 31 other countries, 4% are from out of state, 12% African American, 2% Asian American or Pacific Islander, 3% Hispanic American, 0.1% Native American, 5% international, 24% transferred in, 3% live on campus. *Retention:* 64% of 2002 full-time freshmen returned.

Freshmen *Admission:* 673 applied, 579 admitted, 241 enrolled. *Average high school GPA:* 3.3. *Test scores:* ACT scores over 18: 97%; ACT scores over 24: 70%; ACT scores over 30: 7%.

Faculty *Total:* 324, 33% full-time, 32% with terminal degrees. *Student/faculty ratio:* 17:1.

Majors Accounting; adult development and aging; American Sign Language (ASL); art; art teacher education; biochemistry; biological and physical sciences; biology/biological sciences; business administration and management; chemistry; child development; clinical laboratory science/medical technology; clinical/medical laboratory technology; computer and information sciences; computer and information sciences related; computer engineering technology; computer science; consumer merchandising/retailing management; criminal justice/safety; dietetics and clinical nutrition services related; education; education related; education (specific subject areas) related; elementary education; engineering related; English; family and consumer sciences/home economics teacher education; family and consumer sciences/human sciences; fine arts related; fire science; food services technology; foods, nutrition, and wellness; French; general studies; gerontology; health/health care administration; health/medical preparatory programs related; history; hospitality administration; human resources management; industrial and organizational psychology; industrial radiologic technology; information science/studies; international business/trade/commerce; journalism; legal assistant/paralegal; management information systems; management science; marketing/marketing management; mass communication/media; mathematics; mathematics teacher education; music; music management and merchandising; music teacher education; natural sciences; nursing (registered nurse training); nursing related; parks, recreation, and leisure related; pastoral studies/counseling; philosophy; Polish; pre-dentistry studies; pre-law studies; pre-medical studies; pre-pharmacy studies; pre-veterinary studies; psychology; psychology related; public relations, advertising, and applied communication related; public relations/image management; quality control and safety technologies related; radio, television, and digital communication related; religious studies; safety/security technology; science teacher education; science technologies related; secondary education; social studies teacher education; social work; sociology; Spanish; special education; special products marketing; speech and rhetoric; technical and business writing; trade and industrial teacher education.

Academic Programs *Special study options:* academic remediation for entering students, accelerated degree program, adult/continuing education programs, advanced placement credit, cooperative education, distance learning, double majors, English as a second language, independent study, internships, off-campus study, part-time degree program, services for LD students, study abroad, summer session for credit.

Library Madonna University Library with 199,144 titles, 1,679 serial subscriptions, an OPAC, a Web page.

Computers on Campus 175 computers available on campus for general student use. A campuswide network can be accessed from student residence rooms and from off campus. Internet access, at least one staffed computer lab available.

Student Life *Housing options:* coed. Campus housing is university owned. Freshman campus housing is guaranteed. *Activities and organizations:* student-run newspaper, radio station, choral group, Campus Ministry, Gerontology Association, Madonna University Nursing Student Association, Society of Future Teachers, national sororities. *Campus security:* 24-hour emergency response devices and patrols, late-night transport/escort service. *Student services:* personal/psychological counseling.

Athletics Member NAIA. *Intercollegiate sports:* baseball M(s), basketball M(s)/W(s), cheerleading W(c), golf M(s)/W(s), soccer M(s)/W(s), softball W(s), ultimate Frisbee M(c)/W(c), volleyball W(s). *Intramural sports:* baseball M/W, basketball W, rock climbing M/W, soccer M/W, weight lifting M/W.

Standardized Tests *Required:* ACT (for admission).

Costs (2004–05) *Comprehensive fee:* $15,412 includes full-time tuition ($9700), mandatory fees ($100), and room and board ($5612). *College room only:* $2550. Room and board charges vary according to board plan. *Payment plan:* deferred payment. *Waivers:* senior citizens and employees or children of employees.

Financial Aid Of all full-time matriculated undergraduates who enrolled in 2001, 2,575 applied for aid, 2,512 were judged to have need. *Average percent of need met:* 80%. *Average financial aid package:* $1800. *Average need-based gift aid:* $3000. *Average non-need-based aid:* $750.

Applying *Options:* early admission, deferred entrance. *Application fee:* $25. *Required:* high school transcript, minimum 2.75 GPA. *Required for some:* 2 letters of recommendation. *Application deadline:* rolling (freshmen), rolling (transfers). *Notification:* continuous (freshmen), continuous (transfers).

Admissions Contact Mr. Frank J. Hribar, Director of Enrollment Management, Madonna University, 36600 Schoolcraft Road, Livonia, MI 48150-1173. *Phone:* 734-432-5317. *Toll-free phone:* 800-852-4951. *Fax:* 734-432-5393. *E-mail:* muinfo@smtp.munet.edu.

MARYGROVE COLLEGE
Detroit, Michigan

- **Independent Roman Catholic** comprehensive, founded 1905
- **Calendar** semesters
- **Degrees** certificates, diplomas, associate, bachelor's, master's, and postbachelor's certificates
- **Urban** 50-acre campus
- **Endowment** $11.6 million
- **Coed, primarily women,** 858 undergraduate students, 49% full-time, 80% women, 20% men
- **Moderately difficult** entrance level, 60% of applicants were admitted

Undergraduates 421 full-time, 437 part-time. Students come from 2 states and territories, 3 other countries, 1% are from out of state, 72% African American, 0.1% Asian American or Pacific Islander, 2% Hispanic American, 0.3% Native American, 2% international, 11% transferred in, 4% live on campus. *Retention:* 65% of 2002 full-time freshmen returned.

Freshmen *Admission:* 117 applied, 70 admitted, 60 enrolled. *Average high school GPA:* 2.70. *Test scores:* ACT scores over 18: 48%.

Faculty *Total:* 74, 91% full-time, 58% with terminal degrees. *Student/faculty ratio:* 14:1.

Majors Accounting; applied art; art; art therapy; biological and physical sciences; biology/biological sciences; business administration and management; business/commerce; chemistry; computer and information sciences; corrections; dance; education; English; environmental biology; environmental studies; fine/studio arts; general studies; history; international business/trade/commerce; kindergarten/preschool education; liberal arts and sciences/liberal studies; marketing/marketing management; mathematics; music; music performance; political science and government; psychology; religious studies; social sciences; social work; special education (emotionally disturbed).

Academic Programs *Special study options:* academic remediation for entering students, advanced placement credit, cooperative education, distance learning, double majors, internships, off-campus study, part-time degree program, student-designed majors, summer session for credit.

Library 98,817 titles, 500 serial subscriptions, 1,559 audiovisual materials, an OPAC.

Marygrove College (continued)

Computers on Campus 115 computers available on campus for general student use. A campuswide network can be accessed from student residence rooms. Internet access, at least one staffed computer lab available. Computer purchase or lease plan available.

Student Life *Housing options:* coed. Campus housing is university owned. Freshman applicants given priority for college housing. *Activities and organizations:* choral group, Association of Black Social Workers, Council of Student Organization, political science club, United Brotherhood, Marygrove Business Association. *Campus security:* 24-hour emergency response devices and patrols, late-night transport/escort service. *Student services:* personal/psychological counseling.

Athletics *Intercollegiate sports:* basketball M/W.

Standardized Tests *Required:* ACT (for admission).

Costs (2003–04) *Comprehensive fee:* $17,550 includes full-time tuition ($11,500), mandatory fees ($250), and room and board ($5800). Part-time tuition: $418 per credit. *Required fees:* $10 per credit part-time. *Payment plan:* installment. *Waivers:* senior citizens and employees or children of employees.

Applying *Options:* early admission, deferred entrance. *Application fee:* $25. *Required:* high school transcript, minimum 2.7 GPA. *Required for some:* letters of recommendation, interview. *Application deadlines:* 8/15 (freshmen), 8/15 (transfers). *Notification:* continuous until 9/1 (freshmen), continuous until 9/1 (transfers).

Admissions Contact Mr. John Ambrose, Admission Counselor, Freshman, Marygrove College, Office of Admissions, Detroit, MI 48221-2599. *Phone:* 313-927-1236. *Toll-free phone:* 866-313-1297. *Fax:* 313-927-1345. *E-mail:* info@marygrove.edu.

■ *See page 1938 for a narrative description.*

MICHIGAN JEWISH INSTITUTE
Oak Park, Michigan

Admissions Contact Dr. T. Hershel Gardin, Vice President of Institutional Development and Dean of Academic Administration, Michigan Jewish Institute, 25401 Coolidge Highway, Oak Park, MI 48237-1304. *Phone:* 248-414-6900 Ext. 10.

MICHIGAN STATE UNIVERSITY
East Lansing, Michigan

- **State-supported** university, founded 1855
- **Calendar** semesters
- **Degrees** certificates, bachelor's, master's, doctoral, first professional, and post-master's certificates
- **Suburban** 5192-acre campus with easy access to Detroit
- **Endowment** $601.9 million
- **Coed,** 34,853 undergraduate students, 89% full-time, 54% women, 46% men
- **Moderately difficult** entrance level, 71% of applicants were admitted

Undergraduates 31,115 full-time, 3,738 part-time. Students come from 54 states and territories, 120 other countries, 7% are from out of state, 9% African American, 5% Asian American or Pacific Islander, 3% Hispanic American, 0.7% Native American, 3% international, 5% transferred in, 42% live on campus. *Retention:* 90% of 2002 full-time freshmen returned.

Freshmen *Admission:* 24,973 applied, 17,690 admitted, 7,122 enrolled. *Average high school GPA:* 3.58. *Test scores:* SAT verbal scores over 500: 76%; SAT math scores over 500: 83%; ACT scores over 18: 96%; SAT verbal scores over 600: 36%; SAT math scores over 600: 46%; ACT scores over 24: 61%; SAT verbal scores over 700: 7%; SAT math scores over 700: 11%; ACT scores over 30: 10%.

Faculty *Total:* 2,653, 87% full-time, 89% with terminal degrees. *Student/faculty ratio:* 18:1.

Majors Accounting; advertising; agricultural/biological engineering and bioengineering; agricultural business and management; agricultural communication/journalism; agricultural economics; agriculture and agriculture operations related; American studies; ancient studies; animal sciences; anthropology; apparel and textiles; applied economics; applied mathematics; art; art history, criticism and conservation; art teacher education; astrophysics; audiology and speech-language pathology; biochemistry; biochemistry/biophysics and molecular biology; biological and physical sciences; biology/biological sciences; biomedical/medical engineering; botany/plant biology; business administration and management; chemical engineering; chemical physics; chemistry; chemistry teacher education; child development; city/urban, community and regional planning; civil engineering; clinical laboratory science/medical technology; communication/speech communication and rhetoric; computational mathematics; computer and information sciences; computer engineering; construction management; criminal justice/law enforcement administration; criminal justice/safety; dietetics; dramatic/theatre arts; East Asian languages related; economics; education; electrical, electronics and communications engineering; elementary education; engineering; English; entomology; environmental biology; environmental science; environmental studies; family and community services; family and consumer sciences/home economics teacher education; family and consumer sciences/human sciences; fashion/apparel design; finance; food science; forestry; French; geography; geology/earth science; geophysics and seismology; German; history; horticultural science; hospitality administration; hotel/motel administration; humanities; human resources management; interior design; international/global studies; international relations and affairs; jazz/jazz studies; journalism; kinesiology and exercise science; landscape architecture; logistics and materials management; marketing/marketing management; mass communication/media; materials science; mathematics; mechanical engineering; merchandising; microbiology; music; music pedagogy; music performance; music teacher education; music theory and composition; music therapy; natural resource economics; nursing (registered nurse training); nutrition sciences; operations management; parks, recreation and leisure facilities management; philosophy; physical and theoretical chemistry; physical education teaching and coaching; physical sciences; physics; physiology; plant pathology/phytopathology; political science and government; pre-law studies; pre-medical studies; pre-veterinary studies; psychology; public administration; radio and television; religious studies; Russian; science, technology and society; social sciences; social science teacher education; social work; sociology; soil science and agronomy; Spanish; special education; special education (hearing impaired); special education (specific learning disabilities); statistics; technical and business writing; telecommunications; veterinary/animal health technology; veterinary technology; zoology/animal biology.

Academic Programs *Special study options:* academic remediation for entering students, accelerated degree program, adult/continuing education programs, advanced placement credit, cooperative education, distance learning, double majors, English as a second language, freshman honors college, honors programs, independent study, internships, off-campus study, part-time degree program, services for LD students, student-designed majors, study abroad, summer session for credit. *ROTC:* Army (b), Air Force (b).

Library Main Library plus 14 others with 4.4 million titles, 29,470 serial subscriptions, 290,206 audiovisual materials, an OPAC, a Web page.

Computers on Campus 2000 computers available on campus for general student use. A campuswide network can be accessed from student residence rooms and from off campus. Internet access, online (class) registration, at least one staffed computer lab available. Computer purchase or lease plan available.

Student Life *Housing:* on-campus residence required for freshman year. *Options:* coed, women-only, disabled students. Campus housing is university owned. Freshman campus housing is guaranteed. *Activities and organizations:* drama/theater group, student-run newspaper, radio and television station, choral group, marching band, national fraternities, national sororities. *Campus security:* 24-hour emergency response devices and patrols, late-night transport/escort service, self-defense workshops. *Student services:* health clinic, personal/psychological counseling, women's center, legal services.

Athletics Member NCAA. All Division I except football (Division I-A). *Intercollegiate sports:* baseball M, basketball M(s)/W(s), cheerleading M/W, crew W(s), cross-country running M(s)/W(s), equestrian sports M(c)/W(c), field hockey W(s), golf M(s)/W(s), gymnastics M(s)/W(s), ice hockey M(s)/W(c), lacrosse M(c), rugby M(c)/W(c), sailing M(c)/W(c), skiing (cross-country) M(c)/W(c), skiing (downhill) M(c), soccer M(s)/W(c), softball W, swimming M(s)/W(s), tennis M(s)/W(s), track and field M(s)/W(s), volleyball M(c)/W(s), water polo M(c)/W(c), wrestling M(s). *Intramural sports:* archery M/W, badminton M/W, baseball M, basketball M/W, crew M/W, cross-country running M/W, fencing M/W, football M/W, golf M/W, gymnastics M/W, ice hockey M/W, lacrosse M, racquetball M/W, rugby M/W, sailing M/W, skiing (cross-country) M/W, skiing (downhill) M/W, soccer M/W, softball W, squash M/W, swimming M/W, table tennis M/W, tennis M/W, track and field M/W, ultimate Frisbee M/W, volleyball M/W, water polo M/W, weight lifting M/W, wrestling M.

Standardized Tests *Required:* SAT I or ACT (for admission).

Costs (2003–04) *Tuition:* state resident $5925 full-time, $198 per semester hour part-time; nonresident $15,885 full-time, $530 per semester hour part-time. Full-time tuition and fees vary according to course load, degree level, program, and student level. Part-time tuition and fees vary according to course load, degree level, program, and student level. *Required fees:* $778 full-time, $778 per year part-time. *Room and board:* $5230; room only: $2250. Room and board charges vary according to housing facility. *Payment plan:* deferred payment. *Waivers:* employees or children of employees.

Financial Aid Of all full-time matriculated undergraduates who enrolled in 2003, 18,103 applied for aid, 12,849 were judged to have need, 4,209 had their need fully met. 1,607 Federal Work-Study jobs (averaging $1642). 474 state and other part-time jobs (averaging $1900). In 2003, 7172 non-need-based awards were made. *Average percent of need met:* 83%. *Average financial aid package:*

$8487. *Average need-based loan:* $4883. *Average need-based gift aid:* $3518. *Average non-need-based aid:* $4172. *Average indebtedness upon graduation:* $18,814. *Financial aid deadline:* 6/30.

Applying *Options:* electronic application, early action, deferred entrance. *Application fee:* $35. *Required:* high school transcript. *Application deadline:* rolling (freshmen). *Notification:* continuous until 9/1 (freshmen), 10/31 (early action), continuous until 8/15 (transfers).

Admissions Contact Ms. Pamela Horne, Assistant to the Provost for Enrollment and Director of Admissions, Michigan State University, 250 Administration Building, East Lansing, MI 48824. *Phone:* 517-355-8332. *Fax:* 517-353-1647. *E-mail:* admis@msu.edu.

MICHIGAN TECHNOLOGICAL UNIVERSITY
Houghton, Michigan

- **State-supported** university, founded 1885
- **Calendar** semesters
- **Degrees** certificates, associate, bachelor's, master's, and doctoral
- **Small-town** 240-acre campus
- **Endowment** $27.0 million
- **Coed,** 5,765 undergraduate students, 86% full-time, 24% women, 76% men
- **Moderately difficult** entrance level, 93% of applicants were admitted

Undergraduates 4,948 full-time, 817 part-time. Students come from 45 states and territories, 80 other countries, 21% are from out of state, 2% African American, 1% Asian American or Pacific Islander, 1% Hispanic American, 0.8% Native American, 6% international, 3% transferred in, 40% live on campus. *Retention:* 81% of 2002 full-time freshmen returned.

Freshmen *Admission:* 3,080 applied, 2,861 admitted, 1,187 enrolled. *Average high school GPA:* 3.54. *Test scores:* SAT verbal scores over 500: 83%; SAT math scores over 500: 92%; ACT scores over 18: 98%; SAT verbal scores over 600: 41%; SAT math scores over 600: 62%; ACT scores over 24: 70%; SAT verbal scores over 700: 10%; SAT math scores over 700: 14%; ACT scores over 30: 14%.

Faculty *Total:* 394, 88% full-time, 83% with terminal degrees. *Student/faculty ratio:* 12:1.

Majors Accounting; applied mathematics; biochemistry; biology/biological sciences; biology/biotechnology laboratory technician; business administration and management; business/managerial economics; chemical engineering; chemistry; civil engineering; civil engineering technology; clinical laboratory science/medical technology; communication/speech communication and rhetoric; computer engineering; computer programming; computer science; computer software engineering; construction engineering; ecology; electrical, electronic and communications engineering technology; electrical, electronics and communications engineering; electromechanical technology; engineering; engineering mechanics; engineering physics; English; environmental/environmental health engineering; finance; forestry; forestry technology; general studies; geological/geophysical engineering; geology/earth science; geophysics and seismology; humanities; industrial engineering; information science/studies; management information systems; marketing/marketing management; materials engineering; mathematics; mechanical engineering; mechanical engineering/mechanical technology; medical microbiology and bacteriology; metallurgical engineering; operations management; physical sciences; physics; pre-dentistry studies; pre-medical studies; pre-veterinary studies; science teacher education; secondary education; social sciences; statistics; survey technology; technical and business writing.

Academic Programs *Special study options:* advanced placement credit, cooperative education, distance learning, double majors, English as a second language, internships, off-campus study, part-time degree program, services for LD students, student-designed majors, study abroad, summer session for credit. *ROTC:* Army (b), Air Force (b).

Library J. R. Van Pelt Library with 820,414 titles, 10,369 serial subscriptions, 4,529 audiovisual materials, an OPAC, a Web page.

Computers on Campus 1555 computers available on campus for general student use. A campuswide network can be accessed from student residence rooms and from off campus. Internet access, online (class) registration, at least one staffed computer lab available.

Student Life *Housing:* on-campus residence required for freshman year. *Options:* coed, men-only, women-only. Campus housing is university owned. Freshman campus housing is guaranteed. *Activities and organizations:* drama/theater group, student-run newspaper, radio station, choral group, Film Board, Undergraduate Student Government, Inter-Residence Hall Council, Blue Key National Honor Fraternity, national fraternities, national sororities. *Campus security:* 24-hour emergency response devices and patrols, late-night transport/escort service. *Student services:* health clinic, personal/psychological counseling.

Athletics Member NCAA. All Division II except ice hockey (Division I). *Intercollegiate sports:* basketball M(s)/W(s), cross-country running M/W, fencing M(c)/W(c), football M(s), ice hockey M(s)/W(c), racquetball M(c)/W(c), riflery M(c)/W(c), skiing (cross-country) M/W, skiing (downhill) M(c)/W(c), soccer M(c)/W(c), squash M(c)/W(c), swimming M(c)/W(c), table tennis M(c)/W(c), tennis M/W(s), track and field M/W, volleyball W(s), water polo M(c)/W(c). *Intramural sports:* badminton M/W, basketball M/W, bowling M/W, cross-country running M/W, football M/W, golf M/W, ice hockey M/W, racquetball M/W, riflery M/W, skiing (cross-country) M(c)/W(c), soccer M/W, softball M/W, squash M/W, swimming M/W, table tennis M/W, tennis M/W, track and field M(c)/W(c), volleyball M/W(c), water polo M/W, weight lifting M/W, wrestling M.

Standardized Tests *Required:* SAT I or ACT (for admission).

Costs (2003–04) *Tuition:* state resident $6810 full-time, $227 per credit hour part-time; nonresident $17,700 full-time, $590 per credit hour part-time. Full-time tuition and fees vary according to course load and student level. Part-time tuition and fees vary according to course load and student level. *Required fees:* $630 full-time. *Room and board:* $5795; room only: $2759. Room and board charges vary according to board plan and housing facility. *Payment plan:* installment. *Waivers:* senior citizens and employees or children of employees.

Financial Aid Of all full-time matriculated undergraduates who enrolled in 2003, 3,618 applied for aid, 2,730 were judged to have need, 939 had their need fully met. 226 Federal Work-Study jobs (averaging $1387). 2,585 state and other part-time jobs (averaging $1583). In 2003, 1403 non-need-based awards were made. *Average percent of need met:* 76%. *Average financial aid package:* $8213. *Average need-based loan:* $4296. *Average need-based gift aid:* $5523. *Average non-need-based aid:* $3617. *Average indebtedness upon graduation:* $12,775.

Applying *Options:* common application, electronic application, deferred entrance. *Application fee:* $40. *Required:* high school transcript. *Recommended:* interview. *Application deadline:* rolling (freshmen), rolling (transfers).

Admissions Contact Ms. Nancy Rehling, Director of Undergraduate Admissions, Michigan Technological University, 1400 Townsend Drive, Houghton, MI 49931-1295. *Phone:* 906-487-2335. *Toll-free phone:* 888-MTU-1885. *Fax:* 906-487-2125. *E-mail:* mtu4u@mtu.edu.

■ *See page 1986 for a narrative description.*

NORTHERN MICHIGAN UNIVERSITY
Marquette, Michigan

- **State-supported** comprehensive, founded 1899, part of Autonomous
- **Calendar** semesters
- **Degrees** certificates, diplomas, associate, bachelor's, master's, post-master's, and postbachelor's certificates
- **Small-town** 300-acre campus with easy access to Sawyer International
- **Endowment** $26.6 million
- **Coed,** 8,536 undergraduate students, 88% full-time, 52% women, 48% men
- **Minimally difficult** entrance level, 84% of applicants were admitted

Undergraduates 7,479 full-time, 1,057 part-time. 16% are from out of state, 2% African American, 0.7% Asian American or Pacific Islander, 0.9% Hispanic American, 2% Native American, 30% live on campus. *Retention:* 72% of 2002 full-time freshmen returned.

Freshmen *Admission:* 4,460 applied, 3,762 admitted. *Average high school GPA:* 3.02. *Test scores:* ACT scores over 18: 85%; ACT scores over 24: 33%; ACT scores over 30: 3%.

Faculty *Total:* 428, 73% full-time, 64% with terminal degrees. *Student/faculty ratio:* 21:1.

Majors Accounting; administrative assistant and secretarial science; aircraft powerplant technology; animal physiology; applied art; applied mathematics; architectural engineering technology; art; art teacher education; athletic training; audiology and speech language pathology; autobody/collision and repair technology; automobile/automotive mechanics technology; avionics maintenance technology; behavioral sciences; biochemistry; biology/biological sciences; biology teacher education; botany/plant biology; broadcast journalism; business administration and management; business teacher education; carpentry; cartography; ceramic arts and ceramics; chemistry; chemistry teacher education; child development; cinematography and film/video production; city/urban, community and regional planning; clinical laboratory science/medical technology; clinical/medical laboratory assistant; clinical/medical laboratory technology; commercial and advertising art; communication/speech communication and rhetoric; computer and information sciences; computer graphics; computer programming; computer science; computer systems networking and telecommunications; computer teacher education; computer typography and composition equipment operation; construction engineering technology; consumer merchandising/retailing management; creative writing; criminal justice/law enforcement administration; criminal justice/police science; criminal justice/safety; culinary arts; cytotechnology; data processing and data processing technology; developmental and child psychology; dietetics; drafting and design technology; dramatic/theatre arts; drawing; early childhood education; ecology; economics; education; electrical,

Northern Michigan University (continued)
electronic and communications engineering technology; electromechanical technology; elementary education; English; English/language arts teacher education; entrepreneurship; environmental design/architecture; environmental science; environmental studies; experimental psychology; family and consumer economics related; fiber, textile and weaving arts; film/cinema studies; finance; fine/studio arts; French; French language teacher education; geography; geography teacher education; geology/earth science; health teacher education; heating, air conditioning, ventilation and refrigeration maintenance technology; histologic technology/histotechnologist; history; history teacher education; human development and family studies; hydrology and water resources science; industrial and organizational psychology; industrial design; industrial technology; information science/studies; international relations and affairs; kinesiology and exercise science; land use planning and management; legal administrative assistant/secretary; liberal arts and sciences/liberal studies, management information systems; manufacturing technology; marketing/marketing management; mass communication/media; mathematics; mathematics teacher education; mechanical engineering; medical administrative assistant and medical secretary; medical microbiology and bacteriology; metal and jewelry arts; microbiology; music; music teacher education; natural resources/conservation; nursing (licensed practical/vocational nurse training); nursing (registered nurse training); parks, recreation and leisure; philosophy; photography; physical education teaching and coaching; physics; physics teacher education; physiology; piano and organ; political science and government; pre-dentistry studies; pre-law studies; pre-medical studies; pre-veterinary studies; printmaking; psychology; public administration; public relations/image management; science teacher education; sculpture; secondary education; small business administration; social sciences; social science teacher education; social studies teacher education; social work; sociology; Spanish; Spanish language teacher education; special education; special education (mentally retarded); special products marketing; speech and rhetoric; speech-language pathology; sport and fitness administration; technical and business writing; technology/industrial arts teacher education; violin, viola, guitar and other stringed instruments; voice and opera; wildlife biology; wind/percussion instruments; zoology/animal biology.

Academic Programs *Special study options:* academic remediation for entering students, accelerated degree program, adult/continuing education programs, advanced placement credit, distance learning, double majors, honors programs, independent study, internships, off-campus study, part-time degree program, services for LD students, student-designed majors, study abroad, summer session for credit. *ROTC:* Army (b).

Library Lydia Olson Library plus 1 other with 1.1 million titles, 1,711 serial subscriptions, 19,167 audiovisual materials, an OPAC, a Web page.

Computers on Campus 9000 computers available on campus for general student use. A campuswide network can be accessed from student residence rooms and from off campus. Internet access, online (class) registration, at least one staffed computer lab available. Computer purchase or lease plan available.

Student Life *Housing:* on-campus residence required through sophomore year. *Options:* coed, disabled students. Campus housing is university owned. Freshman campus housing is guaranteed. *Activities and organizations:* drama/theater group, student-run newspaper, radio and television station, choral group, marching band, Associated Students of Northern Michigan University, Platform Personalities, campus cinema, Northern Arts and Entertainment, Student Leader Fellowship Program, national fraternities, national sororities. *Campus security:* 24-hour emergency response devices and patrols, student patrols, late-night transport/escort service. *Student services:* health clinic, personal/psychological counseling.

Athletics Member NCAA. All Division II except ice hockey (Division I). *Intercollegiate sports:* basketball M(s)/W(s), cheerleading M(c)/W(c), crew M(c)/W(c), cross-country running W(s), equestrian sports M(c)/W(c), football M(s), golf M(s), ice hockey M(s)/W(c), lacrosse M(c), rugby M(c)/W(c), skiing (cross-country) M(s)/W(s), skiing (downhill) M(c)/W(s)(c), soccer W(s), softball W(c), swimming W(s), track and field W(s), volleyball W(s). *Intramural sports:* basketball M/W, field hockey W, football M, ice hockey M, lacrosse M, skiing (downhill) M/W, soccer M/W, softball M/W, water polo M(c)/W(c), wrestling M(c).

Standardized Tests *Required:* SAT I or ACT (for admission).

Costs (2003–04) *One-time required fee:* $100. *Tuition:* state resident $4632 full-time, $193 per credit hour part-time; nonresident $7920 full-time, $330 per credit hour part-time. Full-time tuition and fees vary according to program. Part-time tuition and fees vary according to location. *Required fees:* $738 full-time, $30 per term part-time. *Room and board:* $5724. Room and board charges vary according to board plan and housing facility. *Payment plans:* installment, deferred payment. *Waivers:* senior citizens and employees or children of employees.

Financial Aid Of all full-time matriculated undergraduates who enrolled in 2002, 6,168 applied for aid, 3,823 were judged to have need, 574 had their need fully met. In 2002, 12 non-need-based awards were made. *Average percent of need met:* 82%. *Average financial aid package:* $7054. *Average need-based loan:* $3479. *Average need-based gift aid:* $3212. *Average non-need-based aid:* $1657. *Average indebtedness upon graduation:* $14,012.

Applying *Options:* common application, electronic application, deferred entrance. *Application fee:* $25. *Required:* high school transcript. *Required for some:* minimum 2.25 GPA. *Application deadline:* rolling (freshmen), rolling (transfers). *Notification:* continuous (freshmen), continuous (transfers).

Admissions Contact Ms. Gerri Daniels, Director of Admissions, Northern Michigan University, 1401 Presque Isle Avenue, Marquette, MI 49855. *Phone:* 906-227-2650. *Toll-free phone:* 800-682-9797 Ext. 1 (in-state); 800-682-9797 (out-of-state). *Fax:* 906-227-1747. *E-mail:* admiss@nmu.edu.

NORTHWOOD UNIVERSITY
Midland, Michigan

- **Independent** comprehensive, founded 1959
- **Calendar** quarters
- **Degrees** associate, bachelor's, and master's
- **Small-town** 434-acre campus
- **Endowment** $54.4 million
- **Coed,** 3,472 undergraduate students, 65% full-time, 46% women, 54% men
- **Moderately difficult** entrance level, 87% of applicants were admitted

Exciting programs: a new major in entrepreneurship; an honors program for the most capable students; automotive aftermarket management and hotel, restaurant, and resort management majors at the BBA and associate degree levels; new entertainment, sports and promotion management curriculum. Through the EXCEL Program, students participate in valuable, documentable activities and receive a Student Development Transcript in addition to an academic transcript. Potential employers of Northwood graduates see the experiences, attitudes, and leadership abilities gained by these students.

Undergraduates 2,241 full-time, 1,231 part-time. Students come from 35 states and territories, 27 other countries, 13% are from out of state, 15% African American, 1% Asian American or Pacific Islander, 2% Hispanic American, 0.1% Native American, 10% international, 6% transferred in, 37% live on campus. *Retention:* 72% of 2002 full-time freshmen returned.

Freshmen *Admission:* 1,387 applied, 1,200 admitted, 394 enrolled. *Average high school GPA:* 2.98. *Test scores:* SAT verbal scores over 500: 19%; SAT math scores over 500: 43%; ACT scores over 18: 80%; SAT verbal scores over 600: 4%; SAT math scores over 600: 11%; ACT scores over 24: 22%; ACT scores over 30: 1%.

Faculty *Total:* 75, 59% full-time, 21% with terminal degrees. *Student/faculty ratio:* 32:1.

Majors Accounting; advertising; banking and financial support services; business administration and management; business/managerial economics; computer and information sciences; computer management; entrepreneurship; fashion merchandising; hotel/motel administration; international business/trade/commerce; management information systems; marketing/marketing management; sport and fitness administration; vehicle and vehicle parts and accessories marketing.

Academic Programs *Special study options:* academic remediation for entering students, accelerated degree program, adult/continuing education programs, advanced placement credit, cooperative education, distance learning, double majors, English as a second language, external degree program, honors programs, independent study, internships, off-campus study, part-time degree program, study abroad, summer session for credit.

Library Strosacker Library with 40,140 titles, 402 serial subscriptions, an OPAC, a Web page.

Computers on Campus 156 computers available on campus for general student use. A campuswide network can be accessed from student residence rooms and from off campus. Internet access, at least one staffed computer lab available.

Student Life *Housing:* on-campus residence required for freshman year. *Options:* men-only, women-only. Campus housing is university owned. Freshman campus housing is guaranteed. *Activities and organizations:* drama/theater group, student-run newspaper, choral group, fraternities/sororities, Student Senate, intramural sports/club sports, campus art, Northwood University International Auto Show (NUTAS), national fraternities, national sororities. *Campus security:* 24-hour emergency response devices and patrols, late-night transport/escort service. *Student services:* health clinic, personal/psychological counseling.

Athletics Member NCAA. All Division II. *Intercollegiate sports:* baseball M(s), basketball M(s)/W(s), cheerleading M(s)/W(s), cross-country running M(s)/W(s), football M(s), golf M(s)/W(s), ice hockey M(c), soccer M(s)/W(s), softball W(s), tennis M(s)/W(s), track and field M(s)/W(s), volleyball W(s). *Intramural sports:* badminton M/W, baseball M(c), basketball M/W, field hockey M/W, football M, ice hockey M, lacrosse M(c), soccer M, softball M/W, table tennis M/W, ultimate Frisbee M/W, volleyball M/W.

Standardized Tests *Required:* SAT I or ACT (for admission).

Costs (2003–04) *Comprehensive fee:* $20,265 includes full-time tuition ($13,485), mandatory fees ($510), and room and board ($6270). Part-time tuition: $281 per credit. *Room and board:* Room and board charges vary according to board plan and location. *Payment plan:* installment. *Waivers:* children of alumni and employees or children of employees.

Financial Aid Of all full-time matriculated undergraduates who enrolled in 2003, 1,174 applied for aid, 1,010 were judged to have need, 176 had their need fully met. 138 Federal Work-Study jobs (averaging $1719). 60 state and other part-time jobs (averaging $1751). In 2003, 353 non-need-based awards were made. *Average percent of need met:* 76%. *Average financial aid package:* $11,175. *Average need-based loan:* $3664. *Average need-based gift aid:* $4525. *Average non-need-based aid:* $3959. *Average indebtedness upon graduation:* $11,229.

Applying *Options:* common application, electronic application, early admission, deferred entrance. *Application fee:* $25. *Required:* essay or personal statement, high school transcript. *Recommended:* minimum 2.0 GPA, 1 letter of recommendation, interview. *Application deadline:* rolling (freshmen), rolling (transfers). *Notification:* continuous (freshmen), continuous (transfers).

Admissions Contact Mr. Daniel F. Toland, Director of Admission, Northwood University, 4000 Whiting Drive, Midland, MI 48640. *Phone:* 989-837-4273. *Toll-free phone:* 800-457-7878. *Fax:* 989-837-4490. *E-mail:* admissions@northwood.edu.

■ *See page 2108 for a narrative description.*

OAKLAND UNIVERSITY

Rochester, Michigan

- **State-supported** university, founded 1957
- **Calendar** semesters
- **Degrees** bachelor's, master's, doctoral, post-master's, and postbachelor's certificates
- **Suburban** 1444-acre campus with easy access to Detroit
- **Endowment** $25.0 million
- **Coed,** 12,958 undergraduate students, 72% full-time, 62% women, 38% men
- **Moderately difficult** entrance level, 80% of applicants were admitted

Undergraduates 9,278 full-time, 3,680 part-time. Students come from 35 states and territories, 28 other countries, 1% are from out of state, 9% African American, 3% Asian American or Pacific Islander, 2% Hispanic American, 0.5% Native American, 0.8% international, 10% transferred in, 11% live on campus. *Retention:* 72% of 2002 full-time freshmen returned.

Freshmen *Admission:* 6,321 applied, 5,079 admitted, 2,101 enrolled. *Average high school GPA:* 3.14. *Test scores:* ACT scores over 18: 83%; ACT scores over 24: 28%; ACT scores over 30: 2%.

Faculty *Total:* 786, 54% full-time, 65% with terminal degrees. *Student/faculty ratio:* 19:1.

Majors Accounting; American studies; anthropology; applied mathematics; area studies related; art history, criticism and conservation; biochemistry; biology/biological sciences; business administration and management; business administration, management and operations related; chemistry; Chinese; classics and languages, literatures and linguistics; clinical laboratory science/medical technology; communication/speech communication and rhetoric; comparative literature; computer and information sciences; counselor education/school counseling and guidance; cytotechnology; dance; dramatic/theatre arts; early childhood education; economics; education; educational leadership and administration; education related; education (specific levels and methods) related; electrical, electronics and communications engineering; elementary education; engineering; English; English composition; environmental health; film/cinema studies; finance; fine/studio arts; foreign languages and literatures; foreign languages related; French; German; health professions related; health science; history; human resources development; interdisciplinary studies; Italian; Japanese; journalism; kinesiology and exercise science; liberal arts and sciences/liberal studies; linguistics; management information systems; management information systems and services related; management science; marketing/marketing management; mathematics; mathematics teacher education; mechanical engineering; medical laboratory technology; modern languages; music; music performance; music teacher education; music theory and composition; nuclear medical technology; nursing (registered nurse training); occupational health and industrial hygiene; operations management; organizational behavior; philosophy; physical sciences; physical therapy; physics; political science and government; psychology; public administration; reading teacher education; religious studies; Russian; science teacher education; secondary education; sociology; South Asian languages; Spanish; special education; statistics; systems engineering; visual and performing arts; women's studies.

Academic Programs *Special study options:* academic remediation for entering students, accelerated degree program, advanced placement credit, cooperative education, distance learning, double majors, English as a second language, honors programs, independent study, internships, off-campus study, part-time degree program, services for LD students, student-designed majors, study abroad, summer session for credit. *ROTC:* Air Force (c). *Unusual degree programs:* 3-2 physical therapy.

Library Kresge Library plus 1 other with 738,420 titles, 1,660 serial subscriptions, 5,340 audiovisual materials, an OPAC, a Web page.

Computers on Campus 640 computers available on campus for general student use. A campuswide network can be accessed from student residence rooms and from off campus. Internet access, online (class) registration, at least one staffed computer lab available.

Student Life *Housing:* on-campus residence required for freshman year. *Options:* coed, disabled students. Campus housing is university owned. Freshman applicants given priority for college housing. *Activities and organizations:* drama/theater group, student-run newspaper, radio station, choral group, Golden Key National Honor Society, Association of Black Students, SATE (Student Association for Teacher Education), Psi Chi Psychology Club, Student Nurses Association, national fraternities, national sororities. *Campus security:* 24-hour emergency response devices and patrols, student patrols, late-night transport/escort service, controlled dormitory access, security lighting, self-defense classes. *Student services:* health clinic, personal/psychological counseling.

Athletics Member NCAA. All Division I. *Intercollegiate sports:* baseball M(s), basketball M(s)/W(s), cross-country running M(s)/W(s), golf M(s)/W(s), ice hockey M(c)/W(c), soccer M(s)/W(s), softball W(s), swimming M(s)/W(s), tennis W(s), volleyball W(s). *Intramural sports:* badminton M/W, basketball M/W, football M/W, racquetball M/W, soccer M/W, softball M/W, table tennis M/W, tennis M/W, volleyball M/W, weight lifting M/W.

Standardized Tests *Required:* ACT (for placement).

Costs (2003–04) *Tuition:* state resident $4774 full-time, $159 per credit hour part-time; nonresident $11,468 full-time, $382 per credit hour part-time. Full-time tuition and fees vary according to program and student level. Part-time tuition and fees vary according to program and student level. *Required fees:* $486 full-time, $243 per term part-time. *Room and board:* $5540. Room and board charges vary according to housing facility. *Payment plans:* installment, deferred payment. *Waivers:* employees or children of employees.

Financial Aid Of all full-time matriculated undergraduates who enrolled in 2001, 3,872 applied for aid, 2,651 were judged to have need, 754 had their need fully met. 788 Federal Work-Study jobs (averaging $2150). In 2001, 1650 non-need-based awards were made. *Average percent of need met:* 90%. *Average financial aid package:* $5866. *Average need-based loan:* $3377. *Average need-based gift aid:* $2932.

Applying *Options:* electronic application, deferred entrance. *Application fee:* $35. *Required:* high school transcript, minimum 2.5 GPA. *Required for some:* minimum 3.0 GPA, letters of recommendation, interview, audition. *Application deadline:* rolling (freshmen), rolling (transfers). *Notification:* continuous (freshmen), continuous (transfers).

Admissions Contact Mr. Robert E. Johnson, Vice Provost for Enrollment Management, Oakland University, 101 North Foundation Hall, Rochester, MI 48309-4401. *Phone:* 248-370-3360. *Toll-free phone:* 800-OAK-UNIV. *Fax:* 248-370-4462. *E-mail:* ouinfo@oakland.edu.

■ *See page 2118 for a narrative description.*

OLIVET COLLEGE

Olivet, Michigan

- **Independent** comprehensive, founded 1844, affiliated with Congregational Christian Church
- **Calendar** 4-4-1
- **Degrees** bachelor's and master's
- **Small-town** 92-acre campus
- **Endowment** $11.5 million
- **Coed,** 1,042 undergraduate students, 90% full-time, 43% women, 57% men
- **Minimally difficult** entrance level, 59% of applicants were admitted

Undergraduates 940 full-time, 102 part-time. Students come from 15 states and territories, 16 other countries, 16% are from out of state, 16% African American, 0.6% Asian American or Pacific Islander, 2% Hispanic American, 1% Native American, 4% international, 11% transferred in, 59% live on campus. *Retention:* 78% of 2002 full-time freshmen returned.

Freshmen *Admission:* 972 applied, 574 admitted, 297 enrolled. *Average high school GPA:* 2.93. *Test scores:* ACT scores over 18: 89%; ACT scores over 24: 21%; ACT scores over 30: 5%.

Faculty *Total:* 79, 58% full-time, 51% with terminal degrees. *Student/faculty ratio:* 15:1.

Majors Accounting; applied art; art; art teacher education; biochemistry; biology/biological sciences; business administration and management; chemistry; commercial and advertising art; computer and information sciences; computer

Olivet College (continued)
science; criminal justice/safety; economics; education; elementary education; English; environmental studies; finance; fine/studio arts; health and physical education; history; insurance; journalism; liberal arts and sciences/liberal studies; marketing/marketing management; mass communication/media; mathematics; medical illustration; physical education teaching and coaching; pre-dentistry studies; pre-law studies; pre-medical studies; pre-veterinary studies; psychology; secondary education; social sciences; sociology; sport and fitness administration.

Academic Programs *Special study options:* accelerated degree program, advanced placement credit, cooperative education, double majors, honors programs, independent study, internships, part-time degree program, services for LD students, student-designed majors, study abroad, summer session for credit. *Unusual degree programs:* 3-2 engineering with Michigan Technological University.

Library Burrage Library with 90,000 titles, 415 serial subscriptions, an OPAC.

Computers on Campus 60 computers available on campus for general student use. A campuswide network can be accessed from student residence rooms and from off campus. Internet access, online (class) registration available.

Student Life *Housing:* on-campus residence required through junior year. *Options:* coed, men-only, women-only. Campus housing is university owned. *Activities and organizations:* drama/theater group, student-run newspaper, radio station, choral group, marching band, Campus Activities Board, Black Student Union, international club, non-traditional student organization, Omicron Delta Kappa. *Campus security:* 24-hour emergency response devices and patrols, late-night transport/escort service. *Student services:* health clinic, personal/psychological counseling, women's center.

Athletics Member NCAA. All Division III. *Intercollegiate sports:* baseball M, basketball M/W, cross-country running M/W, football M, golf M/W, soccer M/W, softball W, swimming M/W, tennis M/W, track and field M/W, volleyball W, wrestling M. *Intramural sports:* basketball M/W, bowling M/W, cheerleading M/W, football M/W, softball M/W, volleyball M/W.

Standardized Tests *Required:* SAT I or ACT (for admission).

Costs (2004–05) *Comprehensive fee:* $21,271 includes full-time tuition ($15,521), mandatory fees ($420), and room and board ($5330). Part-time tuition: $500 per credit. Part-time tuition and fees vary according to course load. *College room only:* $2901. Room and board charges vary according to board plan and housing facility. *Payment plan:* installment. *Waivers:* employees or children of employees.

Financial Aid Of all full-time matriculated undergraduates who enrolled in 2002, 789 applied for aid, 750 were judged to have need, 93 had their need fully met. 162 Federal Work-Study jobs (averaging $1018). 209 state and other part-time jobs (averaging $1151). In 2002, 89 non-need-based awards were made. *Average percent of need met:* 78%. *Average financial aid package:* $12,230. *Average need-based loan:* $3573. *Average need-based gift aid:* $8631. *Average non-need-based aid:* $8691. *Average indebtedness upon graduation:* $6329.

Applying *Options:* common application, electronic application, deferred entrance. *Application fee:* $25. *Required:* high school transcript. *Required for some:* essay or personal statement, letters of recommendation, interview. *Recommended:* minimum 2.6 GPA. *Application deadline:* rolling (freshmen), rolling (transfers). *Notification:* continuous (freshmen), continuous (transfers).

Admissions Contact Mr. Bernie McConnell, Director of Admissions, Olivet College, 320 South Main Street, Olivet, MI 49076. *Phone:* 269-749-7635 Ext. 7162. *Toll-free phone:* 800-456-7189. *Fax:* 269-749-6617. *E-mail:* admissions@olivetcollege.edu.

REFORMED BIBLE COLLEGE
Grand Rapids, Michigan

- **Independent religious** 4-year, founded 1939
- **Calendar** semesters
- **Degrees** certificates, associate, bachelor's, and postbachelor's certificates
- **Suburban** 34-acre campus
- **Endowment** $5.2 million
- **Coed,** 298 undergraduate students, 80% full-time, 52% women, 48% men
- **Moderately difficult** entrance level, 40% of applicants were admitted

Reformed Bible College (RBC) equips students with a biblical, Reformed worldview to effectively serve with a BA or AA in more than 17 fields of study, including social work, youth ministry, cross-cultural missions, education, and the ministry. With 22 denominations, a diverse student body, and a modern 34-acre residential campus, RBC students and alumni are found in 70 nations. For more information go to http://www.reformed.edu.

Undergraduates 237 full-time, 61 part-time. Students come from 14 states and territories, 8 other countries, 8% are from out of state, 4% African American, 3% Asian American or Pacific Islander, 4% Hispanic American, 6% international, 11% transferred in, 40% live on campus. *Retention:* 71% of 2002 full-time freshmen returned.

Freshmen *Admission:* 136 applied, 55 admitted, 56 enrolled. *Average high school GPA:* 3.09. *Test scores:* SAT verbal scores over 500: 25%; SAT math scores over 500: 25%; ACT scores over 18: 87%; SAT verbal scores over 600: 25%; ACT scores over 24: 32%; ACT scores over 30: 1%.

Faculty *Total:* 40, 43% full-time, 33% with terminal degrees. *Student/faculty ratio:* 17:1.

Majors Accounting; administrative assistant and secretarial science; biblical studies; broadcast journalism; business administration and management; child development; child guidance; communication/speech communication and rhetoric; computer and information sciences; cultural studies; divinity/ministry; elementary education; liberal arts and sciences/liberal studies; missionary studies and missiology; music teacher education; pastoral studies/counseling; pre-theology/pre-ministerial studies; religious education; secondary education; social work; theology.

Academic Programs *Special study options:* academic remediation for entering students, adult/continuing education programs, advanced placement credit, cooperative education, double majors, English as a second language, independent study, internships, off-campus study, part-time degree program, services for LD students, study abroad, summer session for credit. *Unusual degree programs:* 3-2 education.

Library Zondervan Library with 55,760 titles, 234 serial subscriptions, 3,855 audiovisual materials, an OPAC, a Web page.

Computers on Campus 27 computers available on campus for general student use. A campuswide network can be accessed from student residence rooms and from off campus. Internet access, at least one staffed computer lab available.

Student Life *Housing:* on-campus residence required through sophomore year. *Options:* Campus housing is university owned. Freshman campus housing is guaranteed. *Activities and organizations:* drama/theater group, choral group, bible study and prayer groups, Student Council, yearbook, student activities, Wellspring drama club. *Campus security:* student patrols, late-night transport/escort service, controlled dormitory access. *Student services:* health clinic, personal/psychological counseling.

Athletics *Intramural sports:* basketball M/W, football M/W, soccer M/W, softball M/W, volleyball M/W.

Standardized Tests *Required:* SAT I or ACT (for admission).

Costs (2003–04) *Comprehensive fee:* $15,240 includes full-time tuition ($9670), mandatory fees ($470), and room and board ($5100). Part-time tuition: $405 per credit hour. Part-time tuition and fees vary according to course load. *Required fees:* $80 per term part-time. *College room only:* $2300. Room and board charges vary according to board plan, housing facility, and student level. *Payment plan:* deferred payment. *Waivers:* employees or children of employees.

Financial Aid Of all full-time matriculated undergraduates who enrolled in 2003, 191 applied for aid, 153 were judged to have need, 38 had their need fully met. 57 Federal Work-Study jobs (averaging $1500). 4 state and other part-time jobs (averaging $1500). In 2003, 38 non-need-based awards were made. *Average percent of need met:* 53%. *Average financial aid package:* $9581. *Average need-based loan:* $4000. *Average need-based gift aid:* $5581. *Average non-need-based aid:* $500. *Average indebtedness upon graduation:* $17,125.

Applying *Options:* common application, electronic application, deferred entrance. *Application fee:* $25. *Required:* essay or personal statement, high school transcript, minimum 2.5 GPA, 2 letters of recommendation. *Recommended:* interview. *Application deadline:* rolling (freshmen). *Notification:* continuous (transfers).

Admissions Contact Reformed Bible College, 3333 East Beltline North East, Grand Rapids, MI 49525. *Phone:* 616-222-3000 Ext. 695. *Toll-free phone:* 800-511-3749. *Fax:* 616-222-3045. *E-mail:* admissions@reformed.edu.

ROCHESTER COLLEGE
Rochester Hills, Michigan

- **Independent** 4-year, founded 1959, affiliated with Church of Christ
- **Calendar** semesters
- **Degrees** associate and bachelor's
- **Suburban** 83-acre campus with easy access to Detroit
- **Endowment** $900,953
- **Coed,** 1,001 undergraduate students, 64% full-time, 59% women, 41% men
- **Minimally difficult** entrance level, 42% of applicants were admitted

Undergraduates 640 full-time, 361 part-time. Students come from 22 states and territories, 12 other countries, 13% are from out of state, 15% African American, 1% Asian American or Pacific Islander, 1% Hispanic American, 0.7% Native American, 2% international, 20% transferred in, 26% live on campus. *Retention:* 55% of 2002 full-time freshmen returned.

Freshmen *Admission:* 385 applied, 163 admitted, 119 enrolled. *Average high school GPA:* 2.79. *Test scores:* ACT scores over 18: 72%; ACT scores over 24: 23%; ACT scores over 30: 3%.

Faculty *Total:* 106, 36% full-time, 42% with terminal degrees. *Student/faculty ratio:* 13:1.

Majors Accounting; behavioral sciences; biblical studies; biological and physical sciences; business administration and management; business/corporate communications; child guidance; communication/speech communication and rhetoric; computer management; counseling psychology; English; English composition; history; interdisciplinary studies; liberal arts and sciences/liberal studies; literature; marketing/marketing management; mathematics; music; music teacher education; pastoral studies/counseling; psychology; sport and fitness administration; voice and opera.

Academic Programs *Special study options:* academic remediation for entering students, accelerated degree program, adult/continuing education programs, advanced placement credit, distance learning, double majors, external degree program, independent study, internships, off-campus study, part-time degree program, study abroad, summer session for credit.

Library Ennis and Nancy Ham Library with 45,000 titles, 325 serial subscriptions, 1,000 audiovisual materials, an OPAC, a Web page.

Computers on Campus 59 computers available on campus for general student use. A campuswide network can be accessed from student residence rooms and from off campus. Internet access, at least one staffed computer lab available.

Student Life *Housing:* on-campus residence required through sophomore year. *Options:* men-only, women-only, disabled students. Campus housing is university owned. Freshman campus housing is guaranteed. *Activities and organizations:* drama/theater group, student-run newspaper, choral group, Image, Student Government, American Marketing Association, Rotoact. *Campus security:* 24-hour emergency response devices, late-night transport/escort service, controlled dormitory access, evening security guards. *Student services:* personal/psychological counseling.

Athletics Member NCCAA. *Intercollegiate sports:* baseball M(s), basketball M(s)/W(s), soccer M(s)/W(s), softball W(s), volleyball W(s). *Intramural sports:* basketball M/W, football M/W, softball M/W, volleyball M/W.

Standardized Tests *Required:* SAT I or ACT (for admission).

Costs (2003–04) *Comprehensive fee:* $16,718 includes full-time tuition ($10,272), mandatory fees ($822), and room and board ($5624). Part-time tuition: $321 per credit hour. Part-time tuition and fees vary according to course load. *Required fees:* $142 per credit hour part-time. *Payment plan:* installment. *Waivers:* children of alumni, senior citizens, and employees or children of employees.

Financial Aid Of all full-time matriculated undergraduates who enrolled in 2002, 550 applied for aid, 394 were judged to have need, 84 had their need fully met. 100 Federal Work-Study jobs (averaging $1500). 130 state and other part-time jobs (averaging $1250). In 2002, 109 non-need-based awards were made. *Average percent of need met:* 78%. *Average financial aid package:* $9838. *Average need-based loan:* $3206. *Average need-based gift aid:* $4584. *Average non-need-based aid:* $2698. *Average indebtedness upon graduation:* $10,137.

Applying *Options:* electronic application, early admission, deferred entrance. *Application fee:* $25. *Required:* high school transcript. *Required for some:* interview. *Recommended:* essay or personal statement, minimum 2.25 GPA, 1 letter of recommendation. *Application deadline:* rolling (freshmen), rolling (transfers). *Notification:* continuous (freshmen), continuous (transfers).

Admissions Contact Mr. Larry Norman, Vice President for Enrollment Management, Rochester College, 800 West Avon Road, Rochester Hills, MI 48307-2764. *Phone:* 248-218-2032. *Toll-free phone:* 800-521-6010. *Fax:* 248-218-2005. *E-mail:* admissions@rc.edu.

SACRED HEART MAJOR SEMINARY
Detroit, Michigan

- **Independent Roman Catholic** comprehensive, founded 1919
- **Calendar** semesters
- **Degrees** certificates, associate, bachelor's, master's, first professional, and postbachelor's certificates
- **Urban** 24-acre campus
- **Endowment** $2.9 million
- **Coed,** 260 undergraduate students, 14% full-time, 41% women, 59% men
- **Moderately difficult** entrance level, 100% of applicants were admitted

Undergraduates 36 full-time, 224 part-time. Students come from 3 states and territories, 1 other country, 17% are from out of state, 3% African American, 8% Asian American or Pacific Islander, 5% Hispanic American, 4% transferred in. *Retention:* 100% of 2002 full-time freshmen returned.

Freshmen *Admission:* 3 applied, 3 admitted, 3 enrolled. *Average high school GPA:* 3.41.

Faculty *Total:* 42, 50% full-time, 79% with terminal degrees. *Student/faculty ratio:* 9:1.

Majors Liberal arts and sciences/liberal studies; philosophy; theology.

Academic Programs *Special study options:* academic remediation for entering students, advanced placement credit, independent study, off-campus study, part-time degree program, services for LD students.

Library Szoka Library with 160,000 titles, 510 serial subscriptions, an OPAC, a Web page.

Computers on Campus 23 computers available on campus for general student use. Internet access, at least one staffed computer lab available.

Student Life *Housing:* on-campus residence required through senior year. *Options:* men-only. Campus housing is university owned. Freshman campus housing is guaranteed. *Activities and organizations:* choral group. *Campus security:* 24-hour emergency response devices, late-night transport/escort service. *Student services:* personal/psychological counseling.

Standardized Tests *Required:* SAT I or ACT (for admission).

Costs (2003–04) *One-time required fee:* $100. *Comprehensive fee:* $14,380 includes full-time tuition ($8330), mandatory fees ($60), and room and board ($5990). Full-time tuition and fees vary according to course load. Part-time tuition: $213 per credit hour. Part-time tuition and fees vary according to course load. *Payment plans:* installment, deferred payment. *Waivers:* employees or children of employees.

Financial Aid *Average percent of need met:* 67%. *Average financial aid package:* $3000.

Applying *Options:* deferred entrance. *Application fee:* $30. *Required:* essay or personal statement, high school transcript, minimum 2.0 GPA, 1 letter of recommendation, interview. *Application deadlines:* 7/31 (freshmen), 7/31 (transfers). *Notification:* continuous until 8/15 (freshmen), continuous until 8/15 (transfers).

Admissions Contact Fr. Michael Byrnes, Vice Rector, Sacred Heart Major Seminary, 2701 Chicago Boulevard, Detroit, MI 48206. *Phone:* 313-883-8552.

SAGINAW VALLEY STATE UNIVERSITY
University Center, Michigan

- **State-supported** comprehensive, founded 1963
- **Calendar** semesters plus summer session
- **Degrees** bachelor's, master's, and post-master's certificates
- **Rural** 782-acre campus
- **Endowment** $22.0 million
- **Coed,** 7,580 undergraduate students, 73% full-time, 60% women, 40% men
- **Moderately difficult** entrance level, 90% of applicants were admitted

Undergraduates 5,505 full-time, 2,075 part-time. Students come from 18 states and territories, 41 other countries, 0.1% are from out of state, 6% African American, 0.7% Asian American or Pacific Islander, 2% Hispanic American, 0.3% Native American, 4% international, 8% transferred in, 14% live on campus. *Retention:* 63% of 2002 full-time freshmen returned.

Freshmen *Admission:* 3,324 applied, 2,985 admitted, 1,181 enrolled. *Average high school GPA:* 3.22. *Test scores:* ACT scores over 18: 41%; ACT scores over 24: 15%; ACT scores over 30: 1%.

Faculty *Total:* 243, 97% full-time. *Student/faculty ratio:* 28:1.

Majors Accounting; art; biochemistry; biological and physical sciences; biology/biological sciences; business administration and management; business/commerce; business/managerial economics; chemistry; clinical laboratory science/medical technology; communication/speech communication and rhetoric; computer and information sciences; computer systems analysis; criminal justice/safety; design and visual communications; dramatic/theatre arts; economics; electrical, electronics and communications engineering; elementary education; English; finance; fine/studio arts; French; general studies; history; industrial technology; international relations and affairs; marketing research; mathematics; mathematics and computer science; mechanical engineering; multi-/interdisciplinary studies related; music; nursing (registered nurse training); occupational therapy; operations management; optical sciences; physical education teaching and coaching; physics; political science and government; psychology; public administration; science teacher education; social work; sociology; Spanish; special education.

Academic Programs *Special study options:* academic remediation for entering students, accelerated degree program, adult/continuing education programs, advanced placement credit, cooperative education, distance learning, double majors, English as a second language, honors programs, independent study, internships, part-time degree program, services for LD students, student-designed majors, study abroad, summer session for credit.

Library Zahnow Library with 631,455 titles, 1,113 serial subscriptions, 22,713 audiovisual materials, an OPAC, a Web page.

Computers on Campus 851 computers available on campus for general student use. A campuswide network can be accessed from student residence rooms and from off campus. Internet access, at least one staffed computer lab available. Computer purchase or lease plan available.

Student Life *Housing options:* coed, disabled students. Campus housing is university owned. Freshman applicants given priority for college housing. *Activi-*

Saginaw Valley State University (continued)

ties and organizations: drama/theater group, student-run newspaper, choral group, marching band, Alpha Sigma Alpha, Sigma Pi, Organization of Black Unity, International Students Association, University Residence Association, national fraternities, national sororities. *Campus security:* 24-hour emergency response devices, late-night transport/escort service, controlled dormitory access, rape prevention program. *Student services:* health clinic, personal/psychological counseling.

Athletics Member NCAA. except baseball (Division II), men's and women's basketball (Division II), bowling (Division II), men's and women's cheerleading (Division II), men's and women's cross-country running (Division II), football (Division II), golf (Division II), men's and women's soccer (Division II), softball (Division II), tennis (Division II), men's and women's track and field (Division II), volleyball (Division II) *Intercollegiate sports:* baseball M(s), basketball M(s)/W(s), bowling M(s), cheerleading M/W, cross-country running M(s)/W(s), football M(s), golf M(s), soccer M(s)/W(s), softball W(s), tennis W(s), track and field M(s)/W(s), volleyball W(s). *Intramural sports:* archery M/W, badminton M/W, basketball M/W, bowling M/W, equestrian sports M(c)/W(c), football M/W, ice hockey M(c), racquetball M/W, skiing (cross-country) M/W, soccer M/W, softball M/W, table tennis M/W, tennis M/W, volleyball M/W.

Standardized Tests *Required:* ACT (for admission). *Required for some:* SAT II: Subject Tests (for placement).

Costs (2003–04) *Tuition:* $140 per credit hour part-time; state resident $4799 full-time, $140 per credit hour part-time; nonresident $10,398 full-time, $326 per credit hour part-time. Full-time tuition and fees vary according to course load, location, and program. Part-time tuition and fees vary according to course load, location, and program. *Required fees:* $611 full-time, $20 per credit hour part-time. *Room and board:* $5645; room only: $3530. Room and board charges vary according to board plan and housing facility. *Payment plan:* installment. *Waivers:* employees or children of employees.

Financial Aid Of all full-time matriculated undergraduates who enrolled in 2002, 4,584 applied for aid, 2,815 were judged to have need, 692 had their need fully met. In 2002, 1046 non-need-based awards were made. *Average percent of need met:* 90%. *Average financial aid package:* $5382. *Average need-based loan:* $3224. *Average need-based gift aid:* $2670. *Average non-need-based aid:* $3420. *Average indebtedness upon graduation:* $16,032.

Applying *Options:* electronic application, deferred entrance. *Application fee:* $25. *Required:* high school transcript. *Recommended:* minimum 2.5 GPA. *Application deadline:* rolling (freshmen), rolling (transfers). *Notification:* continuous (transfers).

Admissions Contact Mr. James P. Dwyer, Director of Admissions, Saginaw Valley State University, 7400 Bay Road, University Center, MI 48710-0001. *Phone:* 989-964-4200. *Toll-free phone:* 800-968-9500. *Fax:* 517-790-0180. *E-mail:* admissions@svsu.edu.

SIENA HEIGHTS UNIVERSITY
Adrian, Michigan

- **Independent Roman Catholic** comprehensive, founded 1919
- **Calendar** semesters
- **Degrees** associate, bachelor's, and master's
- **Small-town** 140-acre campus with easy access to Detroit
- **Coed,** 1,886 undergraduate students
- **Moderately difficult** entrance level, 64% of applicants were admitted

Siena Heights University students integrate liberal arts and career preparation. Siena has introduced a new field of study, sport management. The curriculum combines a strong business foundation with a specialized knowledge in sport. The program features an outstanding practicum experience along with great career opportunities.

Undergraduates Students come from 8 states and territories, 10% African American, 0.4% Asian American or Pacific Islander, 2% Hispanic American, 0.2% Native American, 0.7% international, 33% live on campus. *Retention:* 69% of 2002 full-time freshmen returned.

Freshmen *Admission:* 979 applied, 631 admitted. *Average high school GPA:* 3.25. *Test scores:* ACT scores over 18: 88%; ACT scores over 24: 25%; ACT scores over 30: 1%.

Faculty *Total:* 65. *Student/faculty ratio:* 14:1.

Majors Accounting; art; art teacher education; biology/biological sciences; business administration and management; business teacher education; chemistry; child guidance; community organization and advocacy; criminal justice/law enforcement administration; dramatic/theatre arts; elementary education; English; general studies; gerontology; history; hospitality administration; humanities; human services; information science/studies; kindergarten/preschool education; marketing/marketing management; mathematics; music; music teacher education; natural sciences; philosophy; pre-engineering; pre-law studies; psychology; public administration; religious studies; secondary education; social sciences; social work; Spanish.

Academic Programs *Special study options:* academic remediation for entering students, accelerated degree program, adult/continuing education programs, advanced placement credit, cooperative education, double majors, external degree program, independent study, internships, off-campus study, part-time degree program, services for LD students, student-designed majors, study abroad, summer session for credit.

Library 120,407 titles, 451 serial subscriptions.

Computers on Campus 75 computers available on campus for general student use. A campuswide network can be accessed from student residence rooms and from off campus. Internet access, at least one staffed computer lab available.

Student Life *Housing:* on-campus residence required through sophomore year. *Options:* coed. *Activities and organizations:* drama/theater group, student-run newspaper, choral group, Student Programming Association, Residence Hall Counsel, Student Senate, Siena Heights African American Knowledge Association, Greek Council, national fraternities, national sororities. *Campus security:* 24-hour patrols, student patrols, late-night transport/escort service. *Student services:* health clinic, personal/psychological counseling.

Athletics Member NAIA. *Intercollegiate sports:* baseball M(s), basketball M(s)/W(s), cross-country running M(s)/W(s), golf M(s), soccer M(s)/W(s), softball W(s), track and field M(s)/W(s), volleyball W(s). *Intramural sports:* basketball M/W, football M, softball M/W, volleyball M/W.

Standardized Tests *Required:* SAT I or ACT (for admission).

Costs (2004–05) *Comprehensive fee:* $20,975 includes full-time tuition ($15,020), mandatory fees ($500), and room and board ($5455). Part-time tuition: $415 per hour. *Required fees:* $100 per term part-time.

Financial Aid In 2002, 166 non-need-based awards were made. *Average percent of need met:* 66%. *Average financial aid package:* $12,200. *Average indebtedness upon graduation:* $13,500.

Applying *Options:* common application, electronic application, deferred entrance. *Application fee:* $25. *Required:* high school transcript. *Required for some:* essay or personal statement, letters of recommendation, interview. *Recommended:* minimum 2.3 GPA, interview. *Application deadline:* rolling (freshmen), rolling (transfers).

Admissions Contact Mr. Kevin Kucera, Dean of Admissions and Enrollment Services, Siena Heights University, 1247 East Siena Heights Drive, Adrian, MI 49221-1796. *Phone:* 517-264-7180. *Toll-free phone:* 800-521-0009. *Fax:* 517-264-7745. *E-mail:* admissions@sienahts.edu.

■ *See page 2386 for a narrative description.*

SPRING ARBOR UNIVERSITY
Spring Arbor, Michigan

- **Independent Free Methodist** comprehensive, founded 1873
- **Calendar** 4-1-4
- **Degrees** associate, bachelor's, and master's
- **Small-town** 123-acre campus
- **Endowment** $6.1 million
- **Coed,** 2,623 undergraduate students, 79% full-time, 69% women, 31% men
- **Moderately difficult** entrance level, 86% of applicants were admitted

Undergraduates 2,061 full-time, 562 part-time. Students come from 26 states and territories, 10 other countries, 13% are from out of state, 8% African American, 0.9% Asian American or Pacific Islander, 2% Hispanic American, 0.5% Native American, 1% international, 5% transferred in, 60% live on campus. *Retention:* 80% of 2002 full-time freshmen returned.

Freshmen *Admission:* 850 applied, 730 admitted, 312 enrolled. *Average high school GPA:* 3.36. *Test scores:* ACT scores over 18: 91%; ACT scores over 24: 45%; ACT scores over 30: 4%.

Faculty *Total:* 118, 58% full-time, 33% with terminal degrees. *Student/faculty ratio:* 15:1.

Majors Accounting; art; biochemistry; biology/biological sciences; business administration and management; chemistry; communication/speech communication and rhetoric; computer science; elementary education; English; family systems; health and physical education; health/health care administration; history; history of philosophy; human resources management; journalism; kindergarten/preschool education; liberal arts and sciences/liberal studies; management information systems; mathematics; music; music teacher education; philosophy; physical education teaching and coaching; piano and organ; psychology; radio and television; religious studies; secondary education; social sciences; social work; sociology; Spanish; sport and fitness administration.

Academic Programs *Special study options:* academic remediation for entering students, accelerated degree program, adult/continuing education programs,

advanced placement credit, double majors, English as a second language, external degree program, honors programs, independent study, internships, off-campus study, part-time degree program, services for LD students, student-designed majors, summer session for credit. *Unusual degree programs:* 3-2 engineering with University of Michigan, Michigan State University, Western Michigan University, Tri-State University.

Library Hugh A. White Library plus 1 other with 90,042 titles, 667 serial subscriptions, 2,025 audiovisual materials, a Web page.

Computers on Campus 147 computers available on campus for general student use. A campuswide network can be accessed from student residence rooms and from off campus. Internet access, at least one staffed computer lab available.

Student Life *Housing:* on-campus residence required for freshman year. *Options:* men-only, women-only, disabled students. Campus housing is university owned. *Activities and organizations:* drama/theater group, student-run newspaper, radio station, choral group, Action Jackson, Cougarettes, Multicultural Organization. *Campus security:* late-night transport/escort service. *Student services:* health clinic, personal/psychological counseling.

Athletics Member NAIA. *Intercollegiate sports:* baseball M(s), basketball M(s)/W(s), cross-country running M(s)/W(s), golf M(s), soccer M(s)/W(s), softball W(s), tennis M(s)/W(s), track and field M(s)/W(s), volleyball W(s). *Intramural sports:* basketball M/W, soccer M/W, softball M/W, tennis M/W, volleyball M/W.

Standardized Tests *Required:* SAT I or ACT (for admission). *Recommended:* ACT (for admission).

Costs (2003–04) *Comprehensive fee:* $20,206 includes full-time tuition ($14,700), mandatory fees ($216), and room and board ($5290). Part-time tuition: $290 per credit. Part-time tuition and fees vary according to course load. *College room only:* $2420. Room and board charges vary according to board plan, housing facility, and location. *Payment plans:* installment, deferred payment. *Waivers:* senior citizens and employees or children of employees.

Financial Aid Of all full-time matriculated undergraduates who enrolled in 2003, 1,336 applied for aid, 1,051 were judged to have need, 403 had their need fully met. 322 Federal Work-Study jobs (averaging $700). In 2003, 136 non-need-based awards were made. *Average percent of need met:* 78%. *Average financial aid package:* $11,773. *Average need-based loan:* $3875. *Average need-based gift aid:* $6283. *Average non-need-based aid:* $1668. *Average indebtedness upon graduation:* $11,169.

Applying *Options:* early admission, deferred entrance. *Application fee:* $30. *Required:* high school transcript, minimum 2.0 GPA. *Required for some:* letters of recommendation. *Recommended:* essay or personal statement, interview, guidance counselor's evaluation form. *Application deadline:* 8/1 (freshmen), rolling (transfers). *Notification:* continuous (freshmen), continuous (transfers).

Admissions Contact Mr. Randy Comfort, Director of Admissions, Spring Arbor University, 106 East Main Street, Spring Arbor, MI 49283-9799. *Phone:* 517-750-1200 Ext. 1475. *Toll-free phone:* 800-968-0011. *Fax:* 517-750-6620. *E-mail:* admissions@arbor.edu.

UNIVERSITY OF DETROIT MERCY

Detroit, Michigan

- **Independent Roman Catholic (Jesuit)** university, founded 1877
- **Calendar** semesters
- **Degrees** certificates, associate, bachelor's, master's, doctoral, first professional, post-master's, postbachelor's, and first professional certificates
- **Urban** 70-acre campus
- **Coed,** 3,383 undergraduate students, 56% full-time, 66% women, 34% men
- **Moderately difficult** entrance level, 81% of applicants were admitted

Undergraduates 1,886 full-time, 1,497 part-time. Students come from 27 states and territories, 19 other countries, 5% are from out of state, 32% African American, 2% Asian American or Pacific Islander, 2% Hispanic American, 0.9% Native American, 3% international, 7% transferred in, 21% live on campus. *Retention:* 76% of 2002 full-time freshmen returned.

Freshmen *Admission:* 2,181 applied, 1,768 admitted, 486 enrolled. *Average high school GPA:* 3.33. *Test scores:* ACT scores over 18: 85%; ACT scores over 24: 33%; ACT scores over 30: 3%.

Faculty *Total:* 655, 41% full-time. *Student/faculty ratio:* 15:1.

Majors Accounting; architecture; behavioral sciences; biochemistry; biology/biological sciences; broadcast journalism; business administration and management; chemistry; civil engineering; computer and information sciences; computer engineering; computer programming; computer science; criminal justice/law enforcement administration; dental hygiene; developmental and child psychology; dramatic/theatre arts; economics; education; electrical, electronics and communications engineering; elementary education; engineering; English; finance; health/health care administration; history; humanities; human resources management; human services; information science/studies; international business/trade/commerce; journalism; kindergarten/preschool education; labor and industrial relations; legal administrative assistant/secretary; legal studies; manufacturing engineering; marketing/marketing management; mass communication/media; mathematics; mechanical engineering; nursing (registered nurse training); philosophy; political science and government; pre-dentistry studies; pre-law studies; pre-medical studies; psychology; public relations/image management; radio and television; reading teacher education; religious studies; science teacher education; secondary education; social science teacher education; social studies teacher education; social work; sociology; special education; special education (emotionally disturbed); special education (multiply disabled); special education (specific learning disabilities); substance abuse/addiction counseling; systems engineering.

Academic Programs *Special study options:* academic remediation for entering students, accelerated degree program, adult/continuing education programs, advanced placement credit, cooperative education, double majors, English as a second language, honors programs, independent study, internships, off-campus study, part-time degree program, study abroad, summer session for credit. *ROTC:* Army (c).

Library McNichols Campus Library plus 3 others with 9,340 serial subscriptions, 32,053 audiovisual materials, an OPAC, a Web page.

Computers on Campus 250 computers available on campus for general student use. A campuswide network can be accessed from student residence rooms and from off campus. Internet access, at least one staffed computer lab available.

Student Life *Housing options:* coed. Freshman campus housing is guaranteed. *Activities and organizations:* drama/theater group, student-run newspaper, radio station, choral group, national sororities. *Campus security:* 24-hour emergency response devices and patrols, student patrols, late-night transport/escort service. *Student services:* health clinic, personal/psychological counseling, legal services.

Athletics Member NCAA. All Division I. *Intercollegiate sports:* baseball M(s), basketball M(s)/W(s), cross-country running M(s)/W(s), fencing M(s)/W(s), golf M(s)/W(s), soccer M(s)/W(s), softball W(s), tennis W(s), track and field M(s)/W(s). *Intramural sports:* basketball M/W, racquetball M, soccer M, softball M/W, volleyball M/W.

Standardized Tests *Required:* SAT I or ACT (for admission).

Costs (2004–05) *Comprehensive fee:* $28,010 includes full-time tuition ($20,400), mandatory fees ($570), and room and board ($7040). Part-time tuition: $500 per credit hour. *Required fees:* $185 per term part-time. *College room only:* $4128. Room and board charges vary according to housing facility. *Waivers:* employees or children of employees.

Financial Aid Of all full-time matriculated undergraduates who enrolled in 2003, 1,536 applied for aid, 1,415 were judged to have need, 228 had their need fully met. In 2003, 125 non-need-based awards were made. *Average percent of need met:* 80%. *Average financial aid package:* $18,195. *Average need-based loan:* $7500. *Average need-based gift aid:* $18,763. *Average non-need-based aid:* $11,476.

Applying *Options:* early admission, deferred entrance. *Application fee:* $25. *Required:* high school transcript, minimum 2.50 GPA. *Required for some:* 1 letter of recommendation, interview. *Recommended:* essay or personal statement, letters of recommendation, interview. *Application deadlines:* 7/1 (freshmen), 8/15 (transfers). *Notification:* continuous until 9/2 (freshmen), continuous until 9/2 (transfers).

Admissions Contact University of Detroit Mercy, PO Box 19900, Detroit, MI 48219-0900. *Phone:* 313-993-1245. *Toll-free phone:* 800-635-5020. *Fax:* 313-993-3326. *E-mail:* admissions@udmercy.edu.

UNIVERSITY OF MICHIGAN

Ann Arbor, Michigan

- **State-supported** university, founded 1817
- **Calendar** trimesters
- **Degrees** certificates, bachelor's, master's, doctoral, first professional, post-master's, and postbachelor's certificates
- **Suburban** 8070-acre campus with easy access to Detroit
- **Endowment** $3.5 billion
- **Coed,** 24,517 undergraduate students, 95% full-time, 51% women, 49% men
- **Very difficult** entrance level, 53% of applicants were admitted

Undergraduates 23,312 full-time, 1,205 part-time. Students come from 54 states and territories, 87 other countries, 32% are from out of state, 8% African American, 13% Asian American or Pacific Islander, 5% Hispanic American, 0.8% Native American, 5% international, 3% transferred in, 37% live on campus. *Retention:* 96% of 2002 full-time freshmen returned.

Freshmen *Admission:* 25,943 applied, 13,814 admitted, 5,551 enrolled. *Test scores:* SAT verbal scores over 500: 95%; SAT math scores over 500: 97%; ACT scores over 18: 99%; SAT verbal scores over 600: 70%; SAT math scores over 600: 84%; ACT scores over 24: 90%; SAT verbal scores over 700: 20%; SAT math scores over 700: 39%; ACT scores over 30: 34%.

University of Michigan (continued)

Faculty *Total:* 2,835, 78% full-time, 88% with terminal degrees. *Student/faculty ratio:* 15:1.

Majors Accounting; aerospace, aeronautical and astronautical engineering; African-American/Black studies; African studies; American studies; anthropology; applied art; applied mathematics; Arabic; archeology; architecture; art history, criticism and conservation; art teacher education; Asian studies; Asian studies (South); Asian studies (Southeast); astronomy; athletic training; atmospheric sciences and meteorology; biblical studies; biochemistry; biology/biological sciences; biomedical sciences; biometry/biometrics; biophysics; botany/plant biology; business administration and management; cell biology and histology; ceramic arts and ceramics; chemical engineering; chemistry; Chinese; civil engineering; classics and languages, literatures and linguistics; clinical laboratory science/medical technology; commercial and advertising art; comparative literature; computer engineering; computer science; creative writing; dance; dental hygiene; design and visual communications; dramatic/theatre arts; drawing; ecology; economics; education; electrical, electronics and communications engineering; elementary education; engineering; engineering physics; engineering science; English; environmental/environmental health engineering; environmental studies; European studies; fiber, textile and weaving arts; film/cinema studies; foods, nutrition, and wellness; French; general studies; geography; geology/earth science; German; Hebrew; Hispanic-American, Puerto Rican, and Mexican-American/Chicano studies; history; humanities; industrial design; industrial engineering; interdisciplinary studies; interior design; intermedia/multimedia; international relations and affairs; Islamic studies; Italian; Japanese; jazz/jazz studies; Jewish/Judaic studies; journalism; kinesiology and exercise science; landscape architecture; Latin; Latin American studies; liberal arts and sciences/liberal studies; linguistics; literature; mass communication/media; materials engineering; materials science; mathematics; mechanical engineering; medical microbiology and bacteriology; medieval and Renaissance studies; metal and jewelry arts; metallurgical engineering; modern Greek; molecular biology; music; music history, literature, and theory; music teacher education; music theory and composition; natural resources management and policy; naval architecture and marine engineering; Near and Middle Eastern studies; nuclear engineering; nursing (registered nurse training); oceanography (chemical and physical); painting; parks, recreation and leisure; pharmacy; philosophy; photography; physical education teaching and coaching; physics; piano and organ; playwriting and screenwriting; political science and government; printmaking; psychology; radiologic technology/science; religious studies; Romance languages; Russian; Russian studies; Scandinavian studies; sculpture; secondary education; social sciences; sociology; Spanish; speech and rhetoric; sport and fitness administration; statistics; theatre design and technology; violin, viola, guitar and other stringed instruments; visual and performing arts; voice and opera; wildlife biology; wind/percussion instruments; women's studies; zoology/animal biology.

Academic Programs *Special study options:* accelerated degree program, adult/continuing education programs, advanced placement credit, cooperative education, distance learning, double majors, English as a second language, honors programs, independent study, internships, off-campus study, part-time degree program, services for LD students, student-designed majors, study abroad, summer session for credit. *ROTC:* Army (b), Air Force (b). *Unusual degree programs:* 3-2 architecture, public policy.

Library University Library plus 20 others with 7.5 million titles, 69,849 serial subscriptions, 73,568 audiovisual materials, an OPAC, a Web page.

Computers on Campus 2600 computers available on campus for general student use. A campuswide network can be accessed from student residence rooms and from off campus. Internet access, online (class) registration, at least one staffed computer lab available. Computer purchase or lease plan available.

Student Life *Housing options:* coed, women-only, cooperative, disabled students. Campus housing is university owned and is provided by a third party. Freshman campus housing is guaranteed. *Activities and organizations:* drama/theater group, student-run newspaper, radio and television station, choral group, marching band, University Activities Center, Hillel, Project Serve, Residence Hall Association, Black Student Union, national fraternities, national sororities. *Campus security:* 24-hour emergency response devices and patrols, student patrols, late-night transport/escort service, controlled dormitory access, bicycle patrols. *Student services:* health clinic, personal/psychological counseling, women's center, legal services.

Athletics Member NCAA. All Division I except cheerleading (Division III), football (Division I-A). *Intercollegiate sports:* baseball M(s), basketball M(s)/W(s), cheerleading W, crew W, cross-country running M(s)/W(s), field hockey W(s), golf M(s)/W(s), gymnastics M(s)/W(s), ice hockey M(s), soccer M/W(s), softball W(s), swimming M(s)/W(s), tennis M(s)/W(s), track and field M(s)/W(s), volleyball W(s), water polo W, wrestling M(s). *Intramural sports:* archery M(c)/W(c), badminton M/W, basketball M/W, crew M(c)/W(c), cross-country running M/W, fencing M(c)/W(c), football M/W, golf M/W, ice hockey M/W, lacrosse M(c)/W(c), racquetball M/W, rugby M(c)/W(c), sailing M(c)/W(c), skiing (cross-country) M(c)/W(c), skiing (downhill) M(c)/W(c), soccer M/W, softball M/W, swimming M/W, table tennis M/W, tennis M/W, track and field M/W, ultimate Frisbee M/W, volleyball M/W, water polo M(c)/W(c), wrestling M/W.

Standardized Tests *Required:* SAT I or ACT (for admission). *Required for some:* SAT II: Subject Tests (for admission), SAT II: Writing Test (for admission).

Costs (2003–04) *Tuition:* state resident $7788 full-time, $299 per credit part-time; nonresident $24,590 full-time, $999 per credit part-time. *Required fees:* $187 full-time. *Room and board:* $6704.

Financial Aid Of all full-time matriculated undergraduates who enrolled in 2002, 12,246 applied for aid, 9,825 were judged to have need, 8,842 had their need fully met. 4,465 Federal Work-Study jobs (averaging $2677). 417 state and other part-time jobs (averaging $2417). In 2002, 5185 non-need-based awards were made. *Average percent of need met:* 90%. *Average financial aid package:* $11,375. *Average need-based loan:* $4780. *Average need-based gift aid:* $7512. *Average non-need-based aid:* $4744. *Average indebtedness upon graduation:* $19,407. *Financial aid deadline:* 4/30.

Applying *Options:* electronic application, deferred entrance. *Application fee:* $40. *Required:* essay or personal statement, high school transcript. *Required for some:* letters of recommendation, interview. *Application deadlines:* 2/1 (freshmen), 2/1 (transfers). *Notification:* continuous until 4/1 (freshmen), continuous until 4/1 (transfers).

Admissions Contact Mr. Ted Spencer, Director of Undergraduate Admissions, University of Michigan, 1220 Student Activities Building, 515 East Jefferson, Ann Arbor, MI 48109-1316. *Phone:* 734-764-7433. *Fax:* 734-936-0740. *E-mail:* ugadmiss@umich.edu.

UNIVERSITY OF MICHIGAN–DEARBORN
Dearborn, Michigan

- **State-supported** comprehensive, founded 1959, part of University of Michigan System
- **Calendar** semesters
- **Degrees** bachelor's, master's, and postbachelor's certificates
- **Suburban** 210-acre campus with easy access to Detroit
- **Coed,** 6,646 undergraduate students, 56% full-time, 53% women, 47% men
- **Moderately difficult** entrance level, 67% of applicants were admitted

Undergraduates 3,711 full-time, 2,935 part-time. Students come from 25 states and territories, 22 other countries, 4% are from out of state, 7% African American, 6% Asian American or Pacific Islander, 3% Hispanic American, 0.6% Native American, 2% international, 11% transferred in. *Retention:* 81% of 2002 full-time freshmen returned.

Freshmen *Admission:* 2,679 applied, 1,785 admitted, 767 enrolled. *Average high school GPA:* 3.52. *Test scores:* ACT scores over 18: 99%; ACT scores over 24: 50%; ACT scores over 30: 5%.

Faculty *Total:* 502, 53% full-time, 66% with terminal degrees. *Student/faculty ratio:* 16:1.

Majors American studies; anthropology; art history, criticism and conservation; arts management; art teacher education; behavioral sciences; bilingual and multilingual education; biochemistry; biological and physical sciences; biology/biological sciences; business administration and management; chemistry; child development; communications technology; comparative literature; computer and information sciences; computer science; developmental and child psychology; economics; education; electrical, electronics and communications engineering; elementary education; engineering; English; environmental studies; finance; French; German; health/health care administration; Hispanic-American, Puerto Rican, and Mexican-American/Chicano studies; history; humanities; industrial engineering; information science/studies; interdisciplinary studies; international relations and affairs; kindergarten/preschool education; liberal arts and sciences/liberal studies; marketing/marketing management; mathematics; mechanical engineering; medical microbiology and bacteriology; medieval and Renaissance studies; middle school education; music; music history, literature, and theory; natural sciences; philosophy; physical sciences; physics; political science and government; psychology; public administration; science teacher education; secondary education; social sciences; sociology; Spanish; speech and rhetoric; women's studies.

Academic Programs *Special study options:* academic remediation for entering students, accelerated degree program, adult/continuing education programs, cooperative education, double majors, honors programs, independent study, internships, off-campus study, part-time degree program, services for LD students, student-designed majors, study abroad, summer session for credit. *ROTC:* Army (c), Navy (c), Air Force (c).

Library Mardigian Library with 340,897 titles, 1,099 serial subscriptions, 4,734 audiovisual materials, an OPAC, a Web page.

Computers on Campus 350 computers available on campus for general student use. A campuswide network can be accessed from off campus. Internet access, at least one staffed computer lab available.

Student Life *Housing:* college housing not available. *Activities and organizations:* drama/theater group, student-run newspaper, radio and television station, Dearborn Campus Engineers, student radio station, Association for African-American Students, national fraternities, national sororities. *Campus security:* 24-hour emergency response devices and patrols, late-night transport/escort service. *Student services:* health clinic, personal/psychological counseling, women's center.

Athletics Member NAIA. *Intercollegiate sports:* basketball M(s)/W(s), volleyball W(s). *Intramural sports:* basketball M/W, cross-country running M(c)/W(c), fencing M(c)/W(c), ice hockey M(c), racquetball M/W, soccer M(c), table tennis M/W, tennis M/W, volleyball M/W.

Standardized Tests *Required:* SAT I or ACT (for admission). *Recommended:* ACT (for admission).

Costs (2003–04) *Tuition:* state resident $5839 full-time; nonresident $12,911 full-time. Full-time tuition and fees vary according to course level, course load, program, and student level. Part-time tuition and fees vary according to course level, course load, program, and student level. *Required fees:* $107 full-time. *Payment plan:* installment. *Waivers:* senior citizens and employees or children of employees.

Financial Aid Of all full-time matriculated undergraduates who enrolled in 2002, 2,616 applied for aid, 1,555 were judged to have need, 144 had their need fully met. 24 Federal Work-Study jobs (averaging $1067). 20 state and other part-time jobs (averaging $944). In 2002, 482 non-need-based awards were made. *Average percent of need met:* 29%. *Average financial aid package:* $7513. *Average need-based loan:* $4631. *Average need-based gift aid:* $3585. *Average non-need-based aid:* $2119. *Average indebtedness upon graduation:* $23,753.

Applying *Options:* deferred entrance. *Application fee:* $30. *Required:* high school transcript, minimum 3.0 GPA. *Required for some:* interview. *Application deadline:* rolling (freshmen), rolling (transfers). *Notification:* continuous (freshmen), continuous (transfers).

Admissions Contact Mr. David Placey, Director of Admissions, University of Michigan–Dearborn, 4901 Evergreen Road, Dearborn, MI 48128-1491. *Phone:* 313-593-5100. *Fax:* 313-436-9167. *E-mail:* admissions@umd.umich.edu.

UNIVERSITY OF MICHIGAN–FLINT
Flint, Michigan

- **State-supported** comprehensive, founded 1956, part of University of Michigan System
- **Calendar** semesters
- **Degrees** bachelor's, master's, and first professional
- **Urban** 72-acre campus with easy access to Detroit
- **Endowment** $41.8 million
- **Coed,** 5,578 undergraduate students, 61% full-time, 64% women, 36% men
- **Moderately difficult** entrance level, 81% of applicants were admitted

Undergraduates 3,392 full-time, 2,186 part-time. Students come from 23 states and territories, 17 other countries, 1% are from out of state, 10% African American, 1% Asian American or Pacific Islander, 2% Hispanic American, 0.6% Native American, 0.5% international, 11% transferred in. *Retention:* 69% of 2002 full-time freshmen returned.

Freshmen *Admission:* 1,113 applied, 902 admitted, 474 enrolled. *Average high school GPA:* 3.31. *Test scores:* SAT verbal scores over 500: 78%; SAT math scores over 500: 78%; ACT scores over 18: 86%; SAT verbal scores over 600: 33%; SAT math scores over 600: 45%; ACT scores over 24: 29%; ACT scores over 30: 3%.

Faculty *Total:* 367, 58% full-time, 49% with terminal degrees. *Student/faculty ratio:* 16:1.

Majors Accounting; actuarial science; African-American/Black studies; anthropology; art teacher education; biology/biological sciences; biology teacher education; business administration and management; ceramic arts and ceramics; chemistry; chemistry teacher education; clinical laboratory science/medical technology; clinical psychology; communication/speech communication and rhetoric; community health services counseling; computer science; corrections and criminal justice related; dramatic/theatre arts; early childhood education; ecology; economics; education; education (specific subject areas) related; elementary education; engineering science; English; English composition; environmental health; ethics; finance; fine/studio arts; foreign languages related; French; French language teacher education; geography; graphic design; health and medical administrative services related; health/health care administration; history; history teacher education; human resources management; information science/studies; information technology; kindergarten/preschool education; land use planning and management; liberal arts and sciences/liberal studies; marketing/marketing management; mass communication/media; mathematics; medical radiologic technology; music; music teacher education; natural resources and conservation related; natural resources/conservation; nursing (registered nurse training); operations management; organizational behavior; organizational communication; painting; philosophy; photography; physics; physics teacher education; political science and government; printmaking; psychology; psychology related; psychology teacher education; public administration; public health education and promotion; sculpture; social sciences; social work; sociology; Spanish; Spanish language teacher education; speech teacher education; technical and business writing; visual and performing arts; wildlife biology.

Academic Programs *Special study options:* academic remediation for entering students, advanced placement credit, cooperative education, distance learning, double majors, honors programs, independent study, internships, part-time degree program, services for LD students, student-designed majors, study abroad, summer session for credit.

Library Frances Willson Thompson Library with 267,062 titles, 1,111 serial subscriptions, 18,063 audiovisual materials, an OPAC, a Web page.

Computers on Campus 213 computers available on campus for general student use. A campuswide network can be accessed from off campus. Internet access, online (class) registration, at least one staffed computer lab available.

Student Life *Housing:* college housing not available. *Activities and organizations:* drama/theater group, student-run newspaper, television station, choral group, Business Club, International Student Organization, Muslim Student Association, Students Organizing Fun Activities Sober (SOFAS), Intervarsity Christian Fellowship, national fraternities, national sororities. *Campus security:* 24-hour emergency response devices and patrols, student patrols, late-night transport/escort service. *Student services:* health clinic, personal/psychological counseling, women's center.

Athletics *Intramural sports:* basketball M/W, football M/W, golf M/W, racquetball M/W, soccer M/W, table tennis M/W, volleyball M/W.

Standardized Tests *Recommended:* SAT I or ACT (for admission).

Costs (2003–04) *Tuition:* state resident $5274 full-time, $208 per credit part-time; nonresident $10,274 full-time, $417 per credit part-time. Full-time tuition and fees vary according to program and student level. Part-time tuition and fees vary according to program and student level. *Required fees:* $274 full-time, $137 per term part-time. *Waivers:* minority students, senior citizens, and employees or children of employees.

Financial Aid Of all full-time matriculated undergraduates who enrolled in 2002, 2,387 applied for aid, 1,925 were judged to have need, 459 had their need fully met. 403 Federal Work-Study jobs (averaging $2000). 106 state and other part-time jobs (averaging $2000). In 2002, 52 non-need-based awards were made. *Average financial aid package:* $6325. *Average need-based loan:* $3800. *Average need-based gift aid:* $3903. *Average non-need-based aid:* $1916. *Average indebtedness upon graduation:* $18,941.

Applying *Options:* deferred entrance. *Application fee:* $30. *Required:* high school transcript. *Recommended:* essay or personal statement. *Application deadlines:* 9/2 (freshmen), 8/19 (transfers). *Notification:* continuous (freshmen), continuous (transfers).

Admissions Contact Dr. Mary Jo Sekelsky, Assistant Vice Chancellor for Student services and Enrollment, University of Michigan–Flint, 303 East Kearsley Street, 245 UPAV, Flint, MI 48502-1950. *Phone:* 810-762-3434. *Toll-free phone:* 800-942-5636. *Fax:* 810-762-3272. *E-mail:* admissions@umflint.edu.

UNIVERSITY OF PHOENIX–METRO DETROIT CAMPUS
Troy, Michigan

- **Proprietary** comprehensive
- **Calendar** continuous
- **Degrees** certificates, associate, bachelor's, master's, doctoral, post-master's, and postbachelor's certificates (courses conducted at 121 campuses and learning centers in 25 states)
- **Urban** campus
- **Coed,** 2,255 undergraduate students, 100% full-time, 64% women, 36% men
- **Noncompetitive** entrance level

Undergraduates 2,255 full-time. 26% African American, 0.6% Asian American or Pacific Islander, 1% Hispanic American, 0.3% Native American, 2% international.

Freshmen *Admission:* 107 enrolled.

Faculty *Total:* 653, 1% full-time, 28% with terminal degrees. *Student/faculty ratio:* 11:1.

Majors Accounting; business administration and management; entrepreneurship; information technology; management information systems; management science; marketing/marketing management; nursing science.

Academic Programs *Special study options:* accelerated degree program, advanced placement credit, distance learning, external degree program, independent study.

Library University Library with 27.1 million titles, 11,648 serial subscriptions, an OPAC, a Web page.

University of Phoenix–Metro Detroit Campus (continued)

Computers on Campus A campuswide network can be accessed from off campus. Internet access, at least one staffed computer lab available.

Student Life *Housing:* college housing not available.

Costs (2003–04) *Tuition:* $10,110 full-time, $337 per credit part-time. *Waivers:* employees or children of employees.

Financial Aid *Average financial aid package:* $1246.

Applying *Options:* deferred entrance. *Application fee:* $100. *Required:* 1 letter of recommendation, 2 years of work experience, 23 years of age. *Required for some:* high school transcript. *Application deadline:* rolling (freshmen), rolling (transfers).

Admissions Contact Ms. Beth Barilla, Director of Admissions, University of Phoenix–Metro Detroit Campus, 4615 East Elwood Street, Mail Stop AA-K101, Phoenix, AZ 85040-1958. *Phone:* 480-317-6000. *Toll-free phone:* 800-834-2438. *Fax:* 480-594-1758. *E mail:* beth.barilla@phoenix.edu.

University of Phoenix–West Michigan Campus

Grand Rapids, Michigan

- **Proprietary** comprehensive, founded 2000
- **Calendar** continuous
- **Degrees** certificates, associate, bachelor's, master's, doctoral, post-master's, and postbachelor's certificates (courses conducted at 121 campuses and learning centers in 25 states)
- **Urban** campus
- **Coed,** 436 undergraduate students, 100% full-time, 53% women, 47% men
- **Noncompetitive** entrance level

Undergraduates 436 full-time. 7% African American, 0.2% Asian American or Pacific Islander, 2% Hispanic American, 0.5% Native American, 3% international.

Freshmen *Admission:* 18 enrolled.

Faculty *Total:* 99, 4% full-time, 14% with terminal degrees. *Student/faculty ratio:* 7:1.

Majors Accounting; business administration and management; corrections and criminal justice related; health/health care administration; information technology; management information systems; management science; nursing (registered nurse training); public administration and social service professions related.

Academic Programs *Special study options:* accelerated degree program, adult/continuing education programs, advanced placement credit, distance learning, external degree program, independent study.

Library University Library with 27.1 million titles, 11,648 serial subscriptions, an OPAC, a Web page.

Computers on Campus A campuswide network can be accessed from off campus. Internet access, at least one staffed computer lab available.

Student Life *Housing:* college housing not available.

Costs (2003–04) *Tuition:* $9870 full-time, $329 per credit part-time. *Waivers:* employees or children of employees.

Financial Aid *Average financial aid package:* $1355.

Applying *Options:* deferred entrance. *Application fee:* $85. *Required:* 1 letter of recommendation, 2 years of work experience, 23 years of age. *Required for some:* high school transcript. *Application deadline:* rolling (freshmen), rolling (transfers).

Admissions Contact Ms. Beth Barilla, Director of Admissions, University of Phoenix–West Michigan Campus, 4615 East Elwood Street, Mail Stop AA-K101, Phoenix, AZ 85040-1958. *Phone:* 480-317-6000. *Toll-free phone:* 800-228-7240. *E-mail:* beth.barilla@phoenix.edu.

Walsh College of Accountancy and Business Administration

Troy, Michigan

- **Independent** upper-level, founded 1922
- **Calendar** 4-11week terms
- **Degrees** bachelor's and master's
- **Suburban** 29-acre campus with easy access to Detroit
- **Endowment** $2.2 million
- **Coed,** 942 undergraduate students, 13% full-time, 61% women, 39% men
- **Noncompetitive** entrance level, 81% of applicants were admitted

Undergraduates 122 full-time, 820 part-time. Students come from 1 other state, 5% African American, 5% Asian American or Pacific Islander, 1% Hispanic American, 0.2% Native American, 6% international.

Faculty *Total:* 128, 11% full-time, 29% with terminal degrees. *Student/faculty ratio:* 20:1.

Majors Accounting; business administration and management; computer and information sciences; finance; marketing/marketing management.

Academic Programs *Special study options:* adult/continuing education programs, advanced placement credit, distance learning, double majors, independent study, internships, off-campus study, part-time degree program, services for LD students, summer session for credit.

Library Vollbrecht Library with 26,180 titles, 437 serial subscriptions, 121 audiovisual materials, an OPAC, a Web page.

Computers on Campus 298 computers available on campus for general student use. A campuswide network can be accessed from off campus. Internet access, at least one staffed computer lab available.

Student Life *Housing:* college housing not available. *Activities and organizations:* student government, American Marketing Association, economics/finance club, accounting club, National Association of Black Accountants. *Campus security:* 24-hour emergency response devices.

Athletics *Intercollegiate sports:* cheerleading M/W.

Costs (2003–04) *Tuition:* $7170 full-time, $239 per credit part-time. *Required fees:* $230 full-time, $115 per term part-time.

Financial Aid Of all full-time matriculated undergraduates who enrolled in 2003, 62 applied for aid, 60 were judged to have need. In 2003, 6 non-need-based awards were made. *Average percent of need met:* 48%. *Average financial aid package:* $10,012. *Average need-based loan:* $7021. *Average need-based gift aid:* $4204. *Average non-need-based aid:* $962. *Average indebtedness upon graduation:* $8908.

Applying *Options:* electronic application, deferred entrance. *Application fee:* $25. *Application deadline:* rolling (freshmen), rolling (transfers). *Notification:* continuous (transfers).

Admissions Contact Ms. Karen Mahaffy, Director of Admissions, Walsh College of Accountancy and Business Administration, 3838 Livernois Road, PO Box 7006, Troy, MI 48007-7006. *Phone:* 248-823-1610. *Toll-free phone:* 800-925-7401. *Fax:* 248-524-2520. *E-mail:* admissions@walshcollege.edu.

Wayne State University

Detroit, Michigan

- **State-supported** university, founded 1868
- **Calendar** semesters
- **Degrees** certificates, bachelor's, master's, doctoral, first professional, post-master's, and postbachelor's certificates
- **Urban** 203-acre campus
- **Coed,** 20,150 undergraduate students, 58% full-time, 60% women, 40% men
- **Moderately difficult** entrance level, 68% of applicants were admitted

Undergraduates 11,787 full-time, 8,363 part-time. Students come from 42 states and territories, 107 other countries, 1% are from out of state, 32% African American, 5% Asian American or Pacific Islander, 2% Hispanic American, 0.4% Native American, 5% international.

Freshmen *Admission:* 8,477 applied, 5,764 admitted. *Test scores:* ACT scores over 18: 70%; ACT scores over 24: 27%; ACT scores over 30: 2%.

Faculty *Total:* 1,805, 53% full-time. *Student/faculty ratio:* 11:1.

Majors Accounting; African-American/Black studies; allied health and medical assisting services related; American studies; anthropology; apparel and textile marketing management; art; art history, criticism and conservation; art teacher education; Asian studies; Asian studies (East); biology/biological sciences; business administration and management; chemical engineering; chemistry; civil engineering; classics and languages, literatures and linguistics; communication/speech communication and rhetoric; computer and information sciences; criminal justice/safety; dance; dietetics; dramatic/theatre arts; economics; electrical, electronic and communications engineering technology; electrical, electronics and communications engineering; electromechanical technology; elementary education; English; English/language arts teacher education; film/cinema studies; finance; foods, nutrition, and wellness; foreign languages and literatures; French; funeral service and mortuary science; geography; geology/earth science; German; health science; Hispanic-American, Puerto Rican, and Mexican-American/Chicano studies; history; industrial engineering; industrial production technologies related; industrial technology; information science/studies; interdisciplinary studies; international relations and affairs; Italian; journalism; labor and industrial relations; linguistics; logistics and materials management; management information systems; marketing/marketing management; mathematics; mathematics teacher education; mechanical engineering; mechanical engineering/mechanical technology; medical radiologic technology; music; nursing (registered nurse training); occupational therapy; organizational behavior; parks, recreation and leisure; peace studies and conflict resolution; pharmacy; philosophy; physical education teaching and coaching; physics; political science and government; psychology; public administration; public relations/image management; radio and television; Russian; science teacher education; Slavic languages; social studies teacher education; social work; sociology; Spanish; special education; special education (speech or language impaired); speech-language pathology; technical teacher education; urban studies/affairs; women's studies.

Academic Programs *Special study options:* academic remediation for entering students, accelerated degree program, adult/continuing education programs, advanced placement credit, cooperative education, distance learning, double majors, English as a second language, honors programs, independent study, internships, off-campus study, part-time degree program, services for LD students, student-designed majors, study abroad, summer session for credit. *ROTC:* Air Force (c).

Library David Adamany Undergraduate Library plus 6 others with 1.9 million titles, 18,645 serial subscriptions, 70,131 audiovisual materials, an OPAC, a Web page.

Computers on Campus 1800 computers available on campus for general student use. A campuswide network can be accessed from student residence rooms and from off campus. Internet access, online (class) registration, at least one staffed computer lab available.

Student Life *Housing options:* coed, disabled students. Campus housing is university owned. Freshman applicants given priority for college housing. *Activities and organizations:* drama/theater group, student-run newspaper, choral group, marching band, Indian Student Association, Golden Key Honor Society, Campus Crusade for Christ, Friendship Association of Chinese Students, Project Volunteer/Students of Service, national fraternities, national sororities. *Campus security:* 24-hour emergency response devices and patrols, late-night transport/escort service, controlled dormitory access. *Student services:* health clinic, personal/psychological counseling, women's center, legal services.

Athletics Member NCAA. All Division II. *Intercollegiate sports:* baseball M, basketball M(s)/W(s), cross-country running M(s)/W(s), fencing M(s)/W(s), football M(s), golf M(s), ice hockey M/W, softball W(s), swimming M(s)/W(s), tennis M(s)/W(s), volleyball W(s). *Intramural sports:* badminton M/W, basketball M/W, cross-country running M/W, fencing M/W, racquetball M/W, soccer M/W, softball M/W, squash M/W, swimming M/W, tennis M/W, volleyball M/W.

Standardized Tests *Required:* SAT I or ACT (for admission).

Costs (2003–04) *Tuition:* state resident $4662 full-time, $155 per semester hour part-time; nonresident $10,683 full-time, $356 per semester hour part-time. Full-time tuition and fees vary according to course level and student level. Part-time tuition and fees vary according to course level and student level. *Required fees:* $528 full-time, $14 per semester hour part-time, $96 per term part-time. *Room and board:* $6500. Room and board charges vary according to housing facility. *Payment plan:* installment. *Waivers:* senior citizens and employees or children of employees.

Financial Aid Of all full-time matriculated undergraduates who enrolled in 2002, 7,374 applied for aid, 5,015 were judged to have need, 220 had their need fully met. In 2002, 184 non-need-based awards were made. *Average percent of need met:* 56%. *Average financial aid package:* $6251. *Average need-based loan:* $4104. *Average need-based gift aid:* $3527. *Average non-need-based aid:* $5783. *Average indebtedness upon graduation:* $19,059.

Applying *Application fee:* $30. *Required:* high school transcript, minimum 2.0 GPA. *Required for some:* letters of recommendation, interview, portfolio. *Application deadlines:* 8/1 (freshmen), 8/1 (transfers). *Notification:* continuous until 9/1 (freshmen), continuous until 9/1 (transfers).

Admissions Contact Ms. Susan Zwieg, Director of University Admissions, Wayne State University, 3E HNJ, Detroit, MI 48202. *Phone:* 313-577-3581. *Fax:* 313-577-7536. *E-mail:* admissions@wayne.edu.

WESTERN MICHIGAN UNIVERSITY

Kalamazoo, Michigan

- **State-supported** university, founded 1903
- **Calendar** semesters
- **Degrees** bachelor's, master's, doctoral, and post-master's certificates
- **Urban** 1200-acre campus
- **Endowment** $110.5 million
- **Coed,** 23,309 undergraduate students, 87% full-time, 51% women, 49% men
- **Moderately difficult** entrance level, 86% of applicants were admitted

Undergraduates 20,248 full-time, 3,061 part-time. Students come from 54 states and territories, 110 other countries, 7% are from out of state, 5% African American, 1% Asian American or Pacific Islander, 2% Hispanic American, 0.4% Native American, 3% international, 7% transferred in, 30% live on campus. *Retention:* 76% of 2002 full-time freshmen returned.

Freshmen *Admission:* 15,100 applied, 12,923 admitted, 4,258 enrolled. *Average high school GPA:* 3.30. *Test scores:* ACT scores over 18: 93%; ACT scores over 24: 34%; ACT scores over 30: 3%.

Faculty *Total:* 1,189, 83% full-time. *Student/faculty ratio:* 16:1.

Majors Accounting; acting; aerospace, aeronautical and astronautical engineering; airline pilot and flight crew; American studies; anthropology; apparel and textiles; applied mathematics; architecture; art; art history, criticism and conservation; art teacher education; Asian studies; audiology and speech-language pathology; aviation/airway management; avionics maintenance technology; biochemistry; business administration and management; business/commerce; business/managerial economics; business statistics; business teacher education; chemical engineering; chemistry; chemistry related; chemistry teacher education; child development; civil engineering; commercial and advertising art; communication/speech communication and rhetoric; computer and information sciences; computer engineering; computer science; construction engineering; construction engineering technology; construction management; creative writing; criminal justice/safety; criminology; dance; dietetics; directing and theatrical production; dramatic/theatre arts; economics; electrical, electronics and communications engineering; elementary education; engineering; engineering/industrial management; engineering technologies related; English; English composition; English/French as a second/foreign language (teaching) related; English/language arts teacher education; environmental science; environmental studies; family and consumer sciences/home economics teacher education; family systems; finance; foodservice systems administration; foreign language teacher education; French; French as a second/foreign language (teaching); French language teacher education; general studies; geochemistry; geography; geography teacher education; geological and earth sciences/geosciences related; geology/earth science; geophysics and seismology; German; German language teacher education; health/health care administration; health teacher education; history; history teacher education; human resources management; industrial design; industrial engineering; interior design; journalism; kinesiology and exercise science; Latin; Latin teacher education; marketing/marketing management; marketing related; mathematics; mathematics teacher education; mechanical engineering; mechanical engineering/mechanical technology; music; music history, literature, and theory; music performance; music teacher education; music theory and composition; music therapy; nursing (registered nurse training); occupational therapy; parks, recreation and leisure; philosophy; physical education teaching and coaching; physics; physics teacher education; plastics engineering technology; political science and government; psychology; radio and television; religious studies; Russian studies; science teacher education; sculpture; social sciences; social science teacher education; social work; sociology; Spanish; Spanish language teacher education; special education (mentally retarded); special education (vision impaired); statistics; structural engineering; technology/industrial arts teacher education; telecommunications; theatre design and technology; theatre/theatre arts management; tourism and travel services management; tourism and travel services marketing; women's studies.

Academic Programs *Special study options:* academic remediation for entering students, accelerated degree program, adult/continuing education programs, advanced placement credit, cooperative education, distance learning, double majors, English as a second language, freshman honors college, honors programs, independent study, internships, off-campus study, part-time degree program, services for LD students, student-designed majors, study abroad, summer session for credit. *ROTC:* Army (b).

Library Waldo Library plus 4 others with 4.2 million titles, 6,707 serial subscriptions, 32,535 audiovisual materials, an OPAC, a Web page.

Computers on Campus 2000 computers available on campus for general student use. A campuswide network can be accessed from student residence rooms and from off campus. At least one staffed computer lab available.

Student Life *Housing options:* coed, men-only, women-only, disabled students. Campus housing is university owned. *Activities and organizations:* drama/theater group, student-run newspaper, radio station, choral group, marching band, Intrafraternity Council, National Panhellenic Conference, Golden Key, Inter-Varsity Christian Fellowship, Malaysian Student Organization, national fraternities, national sororities. *Campus security:* 24-hour emergency response devices and patrols, student patrols, late-night transport/escort service, controlled dormitory access. *Student services:* health clinic, personal/psychological counseling, women's center, legal services.

Athletics Member NCAA. All Division I except football (Division I-A). *Intercollegiate sports:* baseball M(s), basketball M(s)/W(s), cross-country running M(s)/W(s), golf W(s), gymnastics W(s), ice hockey M(s), soccer M(s)/W(s), softball W(s), tennis M(s)/W(s), track and field M(s)/W(s), volleyball W(s). *Intramural sports:* badminton M/W, basketball M/W, bowling M/W, equestrian sports M(c)/W(c), fencing M(c)/W(c), football M/W, golf M, ice hockey M(c)/W(c), lacrosse M(c)/W(c), racquetball M/W, rugby M(c)/W, sailing M(c)/W(c), soccer M/W, softball M/W, swimming M/W, table tennis M/W, tennis M/W, volleyball M/W.

Standardized Tests *Required:* SAT I or ACT (for admission).

Costs (2003–04) *Tuition:* state resident $4934 full-time, $164 per credit hour part-time; nonresident $12,446 full-time, $415 per credit hour part-time. Full-time

Western Michigan University (continued)

tuition and fees vary according to course load. Part-time tuition and fees vary according to course load. *Required fees:* $602 full-time, $162 per term part-time. *Room and board:* $6496; room only: $3350. Room and board charges vary according to board plan. *Payment plan:* installment. *Waivers:* senior citizens and employees or children of employees.

Financial Aid Of all full-time matriculated undergraduates who enrolled in 2003, 11,300 applied for aid, 10,800 were judged to have need, 2,500 had their need fully met. In 2003, 2600 non-need-based awards were made. *Average percent of need met:* 69%. *Average financial aid package:* $7300. *Average need-based loan:* $3800. *Average need-based gift aid:* $4100. *Average non-need-based aid:* $2400. *Average indebtedness upon graduation:* $16,100.

Applying *Options:* electronic application, early admission, deferred entrance. *Application fee:* $25. *Required:* high school transcript. *Required for some:* interview. *Application deadlines:* rolling (freshmen), 8/1 (transfers). *Notification:* continuous (freshmen), continuous (transfers).

Admissions Contact Mr. John Fraire, Dean, Office of Admissions and Orientation, Western Michigan University, 1903 West Michigan Avenue, Kalamazoo, MI 49008. *Phone:* 269-387-2000. *Toll-free phone:* 800-400-4968. *Fax:* 269-387-2096. *E-mail:* ask-wmu@wmich.edu.

■ *See page 2814 for a narrative description.*

WILLIAM TYNDALE COLLEGE
Farmington Hills, Michigan

- **Independent nondenominational** 4-year, founded 1945
- **Calendar** semesters
- **Degrees** certificates, associate, and bachelor's
- **Suburban** 28-acre campus with easy access to Detroit
- **Coed,** 292 undergraduate students, 41% full-time, 46% women, 54% men
- **Minimally difficult** entrance level, 50% of applicants were admitted

Undergraduates 121 full-time, 171 part-time. Students come from 3 states and territories, 6 other countries, 7% are from out of state, 30% African American, 1% Asian American or Pacific Islander, 0.3% Hispanic American, 1% Native American, 2% international, 27% transferred in, 7% live on campus. *Retention:* 66% of 1996 full-time freshmen returned.

Freshmen *Admission:* 40 applied, 20 admitted, 16 enrolled. *Average high school GPA:* 3.20. *Test scores:* ACT scores over 18: 83%; ACT scores over 24: 33%.

Faculty *Total:* 74, 5% full-time, 23% with terminal degrees. *Student/faculty ratio:* 8:1.

Majors Biblical studies; business administration and management; English; history; kindergarten/preschool education; liberal arts and sciences/liberal studies; mathematics; music; music performance; Near and Middle Eastern studies; pastoral studies/counseling; piano and organ; pre-law studies; psychology; religious education; religious/sacred music; social sciences; theology; voice and opera.

Academic Programs *Special study options:* academic remediation for entering students, accelerated degree program, adult/continuing education programs, advanced placement credit, double majors, independent study, internships, part-time degree program, summer session for credit.

Library Boll Mindlab with 63,500 titles, 230 serial subscriptions, 3,300 audiovisual materials.

Computers on Campus 21 computers available on campus for general student use. A campuswide network can be accessed from off campus. Internet access, at least one staffed computer lab available.

Student Life *Housing options:* coed. *Activities and organizations:* drama/theater group, choral group, choir, drama club, Student Executive Board. *Student services:* personal/psychological counseling.

Standardized Tests *Required:* SAT I or ACT (for admission).

Costs (2003–04) *Comprehensive fee:* $12,170 includes full-time tuition ($8550), mandatory fees ($100), and room and board ($3520). Part-time tuition: $285 per credit. *Room and board:* Room and board charges vary according to housing facility. *Payment plan:* deferred payment. *Waivers:* senior citizens and employees or children of employees.

Financial Aid Of all full-time matriculated undergraduates who enrolled in 2002, 114 applied for aid, 80 were judged to have need, 50 had their need fully met. 10 Federal Work-Study jobs (averaging $857). 9 state and other part-time jobs (averaging $983). In 2002, 39 non-need-based awards were made. *Average percent of need met:* 43%. *Average financial aid package:* $9500. *Average need-based loan:* $3928. *Average need-based gift aid:* $6520. *Average non-need-based aid:* $6275. *Average indebtedness upon graduation:* $8991. *Financial aid deadline:* 6/1.

Applying *Options:* electronic application, early admission, deferred entrance. *Required:* high school transcript, minimum 2.25 GPA. *Required for some:* essay or personal statement, letters of recommendation, interview. *Recommended:* minimum 3.0 GPA. *Application deadline:* rolling (freshmen), rolling (transfers). *Notification:* continuous until 9/1 (freshmen), continuous (transfers).

Admissions Contact Mr. Fred A. Schebor, Vice President for Enrollment Management, William Tyndale College, 37500 West Twelve Mile Road, Farmington Hills, MI 48331. *Phone:* 248-553-7200 Ext. 301. *Toll-free phone:* 800-483-0707. *Fax:* 248-553-5963. *E-mail:* admissions@williamtyndale.edu.

YESHIVA GEDDOLAH OF GREATER DETROIT RABBINICAL COLLEGE
Oak Park, Michigan

Admissions Contact Mr. Eric Krohner, Executive Director, Yeshiva Geddolah of Greater Detroit Rabbinical College, 24600 Greenfield, Oak Park, MI 48237-1544.

MINNESOTA

ACADEMY COLLEGE
Minneapolis, Minnesota

- **Proprietary** primarily 2-year
- **Calendar** quarters
- **Degrees** certificates, associate, and bachelor's
- **Urban** campus
- **Coed**
- **Minimally difficult** entrance level

Faculty *Student/faculty ratio:* 8:1.

Costs (2003–04) *Tuition:* $13,618 full-time, $270 per credit part-time. Full-time tuition and fees vary according to course level. Part-time tuition and fees vary according to course level. *Required fees:* $275 full-time, $270 per credit part-time.

Applying *Options:* common application, electronic application, early admission, deferred entrance. *Required:* high school transcript, interview.

Admissions Contact Mary Erickson, Director of Administration, Academy College, 1101 East 78th Street, Suite e100, Minneapolis, MN 55420. *Phone:* 952-851-0066. *Toll-free phone:* 800-292-9149. *Fax:* 952-851-0094. *E-mail:* admissions@academycollege.edu.

ARGOSY UNIVERSITY/TWIN CITIES
Eagan, Minnesota

- **Proprietary** upper-level, founded 1987, part of Education Management Corporation
- **Calendar** semesters
- **Degrees** bachelor's, master's, doctoral, and post-master's certificates
- **Suburban** campus with easy access to Minneapolis and St. Paul
- **Coed, primarily women,** 919 undergraduate students, 40% full-time, 85% women, 15% men
- 86% of applicants were admitted

Undergraduates 367 full-time, 552 part-time. Students come from 20 states and territories, 4% African American, 2% Asian American or Pacific Islander, 0.9% Hispanic American, 0.8% Native American.

Faculty *Total:* 140, 38% full-time, 38% with terminal degrees. *Student/faculty ratio:* 12:1.

Majors Cardiovascular technology; clinical/medical laboratory technology; dental hygiene; diagnostic medical sonography and ultrasound technology; histologic technician; medical/clinical assistant; psychology; radiation protection/health physics technology; radiologic technology/science; veterinary/animal health technology.

Student Life *Housing:* college housing not available. *Activities and organizations:* student-run newspaper, Student Senate. *Campus security:* 24-hour emergency response devices. *Student services:* personal/psychological counseling.

Costs (2003–04) *Tuition:* $360 per credit hour part-time. *Required fees:* $4 per term part-time.

Financial Aid Of all full-time matriculated undergraduates who enrolled in 2003, 8 Federal Work-Study jobs (averaging $2219).

Applying *Application fee:* $50. *Application deadline:* rolling (freshmen). *Notification:* continuous (transfers).

Admissions Contact Jeanne Stoneking, Vice President of Enrollment Services, Argosy University/Twin Cities, 1515 Central Parkway, Eagan, MN 55121. *Phone:* 651-846-3331. *Toll-free phone:* 888-844-2004. *Fax:* 651-994-7956. *E-mail:* tcadmissions@argosyu.edu.

THE ART INSTITUTES INTERNATIONAL MINNESOTA
Minneapolis, Minnesota

- **Proprietary** primarily 2-year, founded 1964, part of The Art Institute
- **Calendar** quarters
- **Degrees** certificates, associate, and bachelor's
- **Urban** campus
- **Coed**
- **Minimally difficult** entrance level

Faculty *Student/faculty ratio:* 20:1.
Student Life *Campus security:* security personnel during hours of operation.
Standardized Tests *Required:* Thurston Mental Alertness Test (for admission). *Recommended:* ACT (for admission).
Costs (2003–04) *Tuition:* $16,128 full-time, $336 per credit part-time. Full-time tuition and fees vary according to course load, degree level, and program. Part-time tuition and fees vary according to course load, degree level, and program. No tuition increase for student's term of enrollment. *Room only:* $6550. *Payment plans:* tuition prepayment, installment, deferred payment.
Financial Aid Of all full-time matriculated undergraduates who enrolled in 2001, 55 Federal Work-Study jobs (averaging $3200).
Applying *Options:* common application, electronic application, deferred entrance. *Application fee:* $50. *Required:* essay or personal statement, high school transcript, interview.
Admissions Contact Mr. Russ Gill, Director of Admissions, The Art Institutes International Minnesota, 15 South 9th Street, Minneapolis, MN 55402. *Phone:* 612-332-3361 Ext. 6820. *Toll-free phone:* 800-777-3643. *Fax:* 612-332-3934. *E-mail:* kozela@aii.edu.

AUGSBURG COLLEGE
Minneapolis, Minnesota

- **Independent Lutheran** comprehensive, founded 1869
- **Calendar** semesters for undergraduate programs; trimesters for graduate programs and weekend college
- **Degrees** certificates, bachelor's, master's, post-master's, and postbachelor's certificates
- **Urban** 23-acre campus
- **Endowment** $22.9 million
- **Coed,** 2,861 undergraduate students, 81% full-time, 58% women, 42% men
- **Moderately difficult** entrance level, 82% of applicants were admitted

Augsburg College, affiliated with the Evangelical Lutheran Church in America, is located in the heart of the Twin Cities and draws upon the cultural and corporate resources of both Minneapolis and St. Paul. Its challenging academic environment is enhanced by educational and service experiences that transform theory into action in preparing students as leaders for service in a global society. Students at Augsburg come from diverse religious, cultural, and ethnic backgrounds.

Undergraduates 2,326 full-time, 535 part-time. Students come from 45 states and territories, 29 other countries, 11% are from out of state, 5% African American, 3% Asian American or Pacific Islander, 1% Hispanic American, 1% Native American, 1% international, 12% transferred in, 53% live on campus. *Retention:* 80% of 2002 full-time freshmen returned.
Freshmen *Admission:* 935 applied, 765 admitted, 377 enrolled. *Average high school GPA:* 3.26. *Test scores:* SAT verbal scores over 500: 82%; SAT math scores over 500: 85%; ACT scores over 18: 96%; SAT verbal scores over 600: 39%; SAT math scores over 600: 30%; ACT scores over 24: 43%; SAT verbal scores over 700: 4%; SAT math scores over 700: 5%; ACT scores over 30: 6%.
Faculty *Total:* 289, 54% full-time, 64% with terminal degrees. *Student/faculty ratio:* 15:1.
Majors Accounting; aeronautics/aviation/aerospace science and technology; art; art history, criticism and conservation; art teacher education; Asian studies (East); astrophysics; athletic training; behavioral sciences; biological and physical sciences; biology/biological sciences; business administration and management; business/managerial economics; chemistry; computer science; criminal justice/safety; dramatic/theatre arts; economics; education; elementary education; English; finance; fine/studio arts; French; German; health teacher education; history; humanities; interdisciplinary studies; international business/trade/commerce; international relations and affairs; kindergarten/preschool education; liberal arts and sciences/liberal studies; management information systems; marketing/marketing management; mass communication/media; mathematics; music; music teacher education; music therapy; natural sciences; nursing (registered nurse training); philosophy; physical education teaching and coaching; physician assistant; physics; political science and government; pre-dentistry studies; pre-law studies; pre-medical studies; pre-veterinary studies; psychology; religious studies; Scandinavian languages; secondary education; social sciences; social work; sociology; Spanish; special education (emotionally disturbed); speech and rhetoric; theology; urban studies/affairs; women's studies.
Academic Programs *Special study options:* academic remediation for entering students, adult/continuing education programs, advanced placement credit, cooperative education, double majors, English as a second language, freshman honors college, honors programs, independent study, internships, off-campus study, part-time degree program, services for LD students, student-designed majors, study abroad, summer session for credit. *ROTC:* Army (c), Navy (c), Air Force (c). *Unusual degree programs:* 3-2 engineering with Michigan Technological University, University of Minnesota, Twin Cities Campus.
Library James G. Lindell Library with 146,166 titles, 754 serial subscriptions, 2,908 audiovisual materials, an OPAC, a Web page.
Computers on Campus 260 computers available on campus for general student use. A campuswide network can be accessed from student residence rooms and from off campus. Internet access, online (class) registration, at least one staffed computer lab available.
Student Life *Housing options:* coed, men-only, women-only, disabled students. Campus housing is university owned. Freshman applicants given priority for college housing. *Activities and organizations:* drama/theater group, student-run newspaper, radio station, choral group, Student Activities Council, student government, newspaper/yearbook, campus ministry, intramurals. *Campus security:* 24-hour emergency response devices and patrols, late-night transport/escort service, controlled dormitory access. *Student services:* health clinic, personal/psychological counseling.
Athletics Member NCAA. All Division III. *Intercollegiate sports:* baseball M, basketball M/W, cross-country running M/W, football M, golf M/W, ice hockey M/W, soccer M/W, softball W, track and field M/W, volleyball W, wrestling M. *Intramural sports:* basketball M/W, football M, skiing (cross-country) M(c)/W(c), skiing (downhill) M(c)/W(c), softball M/W, volleyball M/W, wrestling M.
Standardized Tests *Required:* SAT I or ACT (for admission).
Costs (2003–04) *Comprehensive fee:* $25,298 includes full-time tuition ($18,900), mandatory fees ($498), and room and board ($5900). Full-time tuition and fees vary according to location. Part-time tuition: $2300 per course. Part-time tuition and fees vary according to course load and location. *Required fees:* $66 per course part-time. *College room only:* $3010. Room and board charges vary according to board plan and housing facility. *Payment plans:* installment, deferred payment. *Waivers:* children of alumni, senior citizens, and employees or children of employees.
Financial Aid Of all full-time matriculated undergraduates who enrolled in 2002, 1,678 applied for aid, 1,478 were judged to have need, 344 had their need fully met. 241 Federal Work-Study jobs (averaging $1474). 235 state and other part-time jobs (averaging $2385). In 2002, 326 non-need-based awards were made. *Average percent of need met:* 72%. *Average financial aid package:* $12,491. *Average need-based loan:* $4317. *Average need-based gift aid:* $8999. *Average non-need-based aid:* $14,716. *Average indebtedness upon graduation:* $24,546. *Financial aid deadline:* 4/15.
Applying *Options:* electronic application, deferred entrance. *Application fee:* $25. *Required:* essay or personal statement, high school transcript, minimum 2.5 GPA, interview. *Required for some:* 2 letters of recommendation. *Application deadlines:* 8/15 (freshmen), 8/10 (transfers). *Notification:* continuous (freshmen), continuous (transfers).
Admissions Contact Ms. Sally Daniels, Director of Undergraduate Day Admissions, Augsburg College, 2211 Riverside Avenue, Minneapolis, MN 55454-1351. *Phone:* 612-330-1001. *Toll-free phone:* 800-788-5678. *Fax:* 612-330-1590. *E-mail:* admissions@augsburg.edu.

BEMIDJI STATE UNIVERSITY
Bemidji, Minnesota

- **State-supported** comprehensive, founded 1919, part of Minnesota State Colleges and Universities System
- **Calendar** semesters
- **Degrees** associate, bachelor's, and master's
- **Small-town** 89-acre campus
- **Endowment** $7.0 million
- **Coed,** 4,660 undergraduate students, 74% full-time, 53% women, 47% men
- **Moderately difficult** entrance level, 74% of applicants were admitted

Bemidji State University (continued)

Undergraduates 3,440 full-time, 1,220 part-time. Students come from 28 states and territories, 47 other countries, 5% are from out of state, 0.5% African American, 0.4% Asian American or Pacific Islander, 0.4% Hispanic American, 3% Native American, 6% international, 9% transferred in, 26% live on campus. *Retention:* 68% of 2002 full-time freshmen returned.

Freshmen *Admission:* 1,542 applied, 1,134 admitted, 692 enrolled. *Average high school GPA:* 3.33. *Test scores:* ACT scores over 18: 88%; ACT scores over 24: 26%; ACT scores over 30: 2%.

Faculty *Total:* 401, 53% full-time, 44% with terminal degrees. *Student/faculty ratio:* 19:1.

Majors Accounting; American Indian/Native American studies; American Native/Native American languages; applied art; art; art teacher education; behavioral sciences; biological and physical sciences; biology/biological sciences; broadcast journalism; business administration and management; chemistry; clinical laboratory science/medical technology; commercial and advertising art; community organization and advocacy; computer science; construction engineering technology; criminal justice/law enforcement administration; criminal justice/police science; data processing and data processing technology; dramatic/theatre arts; ecology; economics; education; elementary education; engineering physics; English; environmental studies; fine/studio arts; geography; geology/earth science; German; health teacher education; history; humanities; industrial arts; industrial technology; information science/studies; journalism; liberal arts and sciences/liberal studies; marine biology and biological oceanography; mass communication/media; mathematics; modern languages; music; music teacher education; natural sciences; nursing (registered nurse training); parks, recreation and leisure; philosophy; physical education teaching and coaching; physical sciences; physics; political science and government; pre-law studies; pre-medical studies; pre-veterinary studies; professional studies; psychology; radio and television; religious studies; science teacher education; secondary education; social sciences; social work; sociology; Spanish; speech and rhetoric; speech/theater education; sport and fitness administration; trade and industrial teacher education.

Academic Programs *Special study options:* academic remediation for entering students, adult/continuing education programs, advanced placement credit, cooperative education, distance learning, double majors, English as a second language, external degree program, honors programs, independent study, internships, off-campus study, part-time degree program, services for LD students, study abroad, summer session for credit.

Library A. C. Clark Library with 554,087 titles, 991 serial subscriptions, 5,521 audiovisual materials, an OPAC, a Web page.

Computers on Campus 600 computers available on campus for general student use. A campuswide network can be accessed from student residence rooms and from off campus. Internet access, online (class) registration, at least one staffed computer lab available.

Student Life *Housing options:* coed, men-only, women-only, disabled students. Campus housing is university owned. Freshman applicants given priority for college housing. *Activities and organizations:* drama/theater group, student-run newspaper, radio and television station, choral group, International Students Organization, Jazz Band Club, Madrigal Dinner Club, Student Senate, Council of Indian Students, national fraternities, national sororities. *Campus security:* 24-hour emergency response devices and patrols, late-night transport/escort service, controlled dormitory access. *Student services:* health clinic, personal/psychological counseling, women's center.

Athletics Member NCAA. All Division II. *Intercollegiate sports:* baseball M(s), basketball M(s)/W(s), cross-country running W, football M(s), golf M/W, ice hockey M(s)/W(s), soccer W(s), softball W(s), tennis W(s), track and field M(s)/W(s), volleyball W(s). *Intramural sports:* basketball M/W, football M, ice hockey M/W, racquetball M/W, soccer M/W, softball M/W, tennis M/W, track and field M/W, volleyball M/W, wrestling M.

Standardized Tests *Required:* ACT (for admission).

Costs (2003–04) *Tuition:* state resident $4338 full-time, $212 per credit part-time; nonresident $9200 full-time, $307 per credit part-time. Full-time tuition and fees vary according to reciprocity agreements. Part-time tuition and fees vary according to course load and reciprocity agreements. *Required fees:* $710 full-time, $78 per credit part-time. *Room and board:* $4597; room only: $2448. Room and board charges vary according to board plan and housing facility. *Payment plan:* installment. *Waivers:* senior citizens and employees or children of employees.

Financial Aid Of all full-time matriculated undergraduates who enrolled in 2003, 2,724 applied for aid, 2,177 were judged to have need, 777 had their need fully met. 253 Federal Work-Study jobs (averaging $1980). 525 state and other part-time jobs (averaging $1980). In 2003, 510 non-need-based awards were made. *Average percent of need met:* 79%. *Average financial aid package:* $7072. *Average need-based loan:* $3255. *Average need-based gift aid:* $3782. *Average non-need-based aid:* $6108. *Average indebtedness upon graduation:* $13,690.

Applying *Options:* common application, electronic application, deferred entrance. *Application fee:* $20. *Required:* high school transcript. *Required for some:* essay or personal statement, letters of recommendation, interview. *Application deadline:* rolling (freshmen), rolling (transfers). *Notification:* continuous (freshmen), continuous (transfers).

Admissions Contact Mr. Paul Muller, Director of Admissions, Bemidji State University, Deputy-102, Bemidji, MN 56601. *Phone:* 218-755-2040. *Toll-free phone:* 800-475-2001 (in-state); 800-652-9747 (out-of-state). *Fax:* 218-755-2074. *E-mail:* admissions@bemidjistate.edu.

BETHANY LUTHERAN COLLEGE

Mankato, Minnesota

- **Independent Lutheran** 4-year, founded 1927
- **Calendar** semesters
- **Degrees** associate and bachelor's
- **Small-town** 50-acre campus with easy access to Minneapolis–St. Paul
- **Endowment** $25.1 million
- **Coed,** 504 undergraduate students, 100% full-time, 57% women, 43% men
- **Moderately difficult** entrance level, 83% of applicants were admitted

Undergraduates 504 full-time. Students come from 25 states and territories, 14 other countries, 30% are from out of state, 2% African American, 2% Asian American or Pacific Islander, 0.4% Hispanic American, 0.4% Native American, 5% international, 4% transferred in, 85% live on campus. *Retention:* 68% of 2002 full-time freshmen returned.

Freshmen *Admission:* 370 applied, 308 admitted, 226 enrolled. *Average high school GPA:* 3.34. *Test scores:* ACT scores over 18: 90%; ACT scores over 24: 39%; ACT scores over 30: 3%.

Faculty *Total:* 64, 58% full-time, 30% with terminal degrees. *Student/faculty ratio:* 8:1.

Majors Art; biology/biological sciences; business administration and management; chemistry; communication/speech communication and rhetoric; dramatic/theatre arts; elementary education; English; history; liberal arts and sciences/liberal studies; music; psychology; religious/sacred music; social sciences; sociology.

Academic Programs *Special study options:* academic remediation for entering students, advanced placement credit, English as a second language, honors programs, services for LD students. *ROTC:* Army (c).

Library Memorial Library plus 1 other with 63,436 titles, 237 serial subscriptions, 4,002 audiovisual materials, an OPAC, a Web page.

Computers on Campus 70 computers available on campus for general student use. A campuswide network can be accessed from student residence rooms and from off campus. Internet access, at least one staffed computer lab available.

Student Life *Housing:* on-campus residence required through junior year. *Options:* men-only, women-only. Campus housing is university owned. Freshman campus housing is guaranteed. *Activities and organizations:* drama/theater group, student-run newspaper, television station, choral group, Student Senate, Paul Ylvisaker Center, BLC Scholastic Leadership Society, SIFE Students In Free Enterprise, Lutherans for Life. *Campus security:* 24-hour emergency response devices, late-night transport/escort service, controlled dormitory access. *Student services:* personal/psychological counseling.

Athletics Member NJCAA. *Intercollegiate sports:* baseball M, basketball M/W, cross-country running M/W, golf M/W, soccer M/W, softball W, tennis M/W, volleyball W. *Intramural sports:* basketball M/W, football M/W, racquetball M/W, soccer M/W, softball M/W, table tennis M/W, volleyball M/W.

Standardized Tests *Required:* SAT I or ACT (for admission).

Costs (2004–05) *Comprehensive fee:* $19,724 includes full-time tuition ($14,482), mandatory fees ($260), and room and board ($4982). Part-time tuition: $660 per credit. *Required fees:* $130 per term part-time. *College room only:* $1852. Room and board charges vary according to board plan. *Payment plan:* installment. *Waivers:* employees or children of employees.

Financial Aid Of all full-time matriculated undergraduates who enrolled in 2002, 393 applied for aid, 356 were judged to have need, 159 had their need fully met. 64 Federal Work-Study jobs (averaging $682). 181 state and other part-time jobs (averaging $579). In 2002, 75 non-need-based awards were made. *Average percent of need met:* 90%. *Average financial aid package:* $11,699. *Average need-based loan:* $3598. *Average need-based gift aid:* $8642. *Average non-need-based aid:* $5383. *Average indebtedness upon graduation:* $13,488.

Applying *Options:* common application, electronic application. *Application fee:* $20. *Required:* essay or personal statement, high school transcript, minimum 2.4 GPA. *Required for some:* interview. *Recommended:* minimum 3.2 GPA, interview. *Application deadline:* 7/15 (freshmen). *Notification:* continuous (transfers).

Admissions Contact Mr. Donald Westphal, Dean of Admissions, Bethany Lutheran College, 700 Luther Drive, Mankato, MN 56001. *Phone:* 507-344-7320. *Toll-free phone:* 800-944-3066. *Fax:* 507-344-7376. *E-mail:* admiss@blc.edu.

BETHEL UNIVERSITY
St. Paul, Minnesota

- **Independent comprehensive, founded 1871, affiliated with Baptist General Conference**
- **Calendar 4-1-4**
- **Degrees associate, bachelor's, and master's**
- **Suburban 231-acre campus with easy access to Twin Cities**
- **Endowment $15.1 million**
- **Coed, 2,911 undergraduate students, 89% full-time, 61% women, 39% men**
- **Moderately difficult entrance level, 91% of applicants were admitted**

Bethel University provides academic excellence in a dynamic Christian environment. *U.S. News & World Report* has recognized Bethel as one of the top Midwestern universities. Its beautiful lakeside, 231-acre campus provides the ideal background for the integration of faith and learning. Outstanding faculty, numerous extracurricular activities, and off-campus study opportunities make Bethel the place to be. Students are actively involved in their education, which prepares them both for life and a living. Bethel is committed to providing high-quality education to prepare tomorrow's leaders to make a difference in their community, the church, and the world.

Undergraduates 2,591 full-time, 320 part-time. Students come from 41 states and territories, 27% are from out of state, 2% African American, 3% Asian American or Pacific Islander, 1% Hispanic American, 0.4% Native American, 0.1% international, 5% transferred in, 37% live on campus. *Retention:* 87% of 2002 full-time freshmen returned.

Freshmen *Admission:* 1,512 applied, 1,370 admitted, 658 enrolled. *Average high school GPA:* 3.24. *Test scores:* SAT verbal scores over 500: 80%; SAT math scores over 500: 83%; ACT scores over 18: 91%; SAT verbal scores over 600: 46%; SAT math scores over 600: 48%; ACT scores over 24: 48%; SAT verbal scores over 700: 17%; SAT math scores over 700: 10%; ACT scores over 30: 9%.

Faculty *Total:* 255, 65% full-time, 54% with terminal degrees. *Student/faculty ratio:* 15:1.

Majors Area, ethnic, cultural, and gender studies related; art; art teacher education; athletic training; biblical studies; biology/biological sciences; biology teacher education; business administration and management; chemistry; chemistry teacher education; communication/speech communication and rhetoric; community health services counseling; computer and information sciences; dramatic/theatre arts; early childhood education; economics; elementary education; engineering science; English; English as a second/foreign language (teaching); English composition; English/language arts teacher education; environmental science; French; French language teacher education; health and physical education; health teacher education; history; international relations and affairs; kinesiology and exercise science; liberal arts and sciences/liberal studies; library science related; mass communication/media; mathematics; mathematics teacher education; molecular biology; multi-/interdisciplinary studies related; music; music performance; music teacher education; nursing (registered nurse training); philosophy; physical education teaching and coaching; physics; physics teacher education; political science and government; psychology; religious/sacred music; science teacher education; social sciences; social studies teacher education; social work; Spanish; Spanish language teacher education; youth ministry.

Academic Programs *Special study options:* accelerated degree program, adult/continuing education programs, advanced placement credit, double majors, English as a second language, external degree program, freshman honors college, honors programs, independent study, internships, off-campus study, part-time degree program, services for LD students, student-designed majors, study abroad, summer session for credit. *ROTC:* Army (c), Air Force (c). *Unusual degree programs:* 3-2 engineering with Washington University in St. Louis, Case Western Reserve University, University of Minnesota.

Library Bethel College Library plus 1 other with 173,000 titles, 14,678 serial subscriptions, 12,204 audiovisual materials, an OPAC, a Web page.

Computers on Campus 110 computers available on campus for general student use. A campuswide network can be accessed from student residence rooms and from off campus. Online (class) registration, at least one staffed computer lab available. Computer purchase or lease plan available.

Student Life *Housing:* on-campus residence required through sophomore year. *Options:* coed, disabled students. Campus housing is university owned. Freshman applicants given priority for college housing. *Activities and organizations:* drama/theater group, student-run newspaper, radio and television station, choral group, United Cultures, Student Senate, Student Association, Habitat for Humanity, Tri Beta. *Campus security:* 24-hour emergency response devices and patrols, student patrols, late-night transport/escort service, controlled dormitory access. *Student services:* health clinic, personal/psychological counseling.

Athletics Member NCAA. All Division III. *Intercollegiate sports:* baseball M, basketball M/W, cross-country running M/W, football M, golf M, ice hockey M/W, soccer M/W, softball W, tennis M/W, track and field M/W, volleyball M(c)/W. *Intramural sports:* badminton M/W, basketball M/W, football M/W, golf M/W, lacrosse M(c)/W(c), racquetball M/W, rugby M(c), softball M/W, table tennis M/W, tennis M/W, track and field M/W, ultimate Frisbee M/W, volleyball M/W, weight lifting M/W.

Standardized Tests *Required:* (for admission).

Costs (2004–05) *Comprehensive fee:* $26,560 includes full-time tuition ($19,880), mandatory fees ($110), and room and board ($6570). Part-time tuition: $755 per credit. Part-time tuition and fees vary according to course load. *College room only:* $3900. Room and board charges vary according to board plan. *Payment plan:* installment. *Waivers:* employees or children of employees.

Financial Aid Of all full-time matriculated undergraduates who enrolled in 2003, 2,425 applied for aid, 1,761 were judged to have need, 441 had their need fully met. 531 Federal Work-Study jobs (averaging $1600). 1,090 state and other part-time jobs (averaging $1605). In 2003, 586 non-need-based awards were made. *Average percent of need met:* 83%. *Average financial aid package:* $14,810. *Average need-based loan:* $4477. *Average need-based gift aid:* $8933. *Average non-need-based aid:* $3529. *Average indebtedness upon graduation:* $22,062.

Applying *Options:* electronic application, early admission, early action. *Application fee:* $25. *Required:* essay or personal statement, high school transcript, 2 letters of recommendation. *Required for some:* interview. *Recommended:* interview. *Application deadlines:* 3/1 (freshmen), 3/1 (transfers). *Notification:* 4/1 (freshmen), 1/15 (early action), 4/1 (transfers).

Admissions Contact Mr. Jay Fedje, Director of Admissions, Bethel University, 3900 Bethel Drive, St. Paul, MN 55112. *Phone:* 651-638-6242. *Toll-free phone:* 800-255-8706 Ext. 6242. *Fax:* 651-635-1490. *E-mail:* bcoll-admit@bethel.edu.

■ *See page 1258 for a narrative description.*

BROWN COLLEGE
Mendota Heights, Minnesota

- **Proprietary** primarily 2-year, founded 1946, part of Career Education Corporation
- **Calendar** quarters
- **Degrees** certificates, associate, and bachelor's
- **Suburban** 20-acre campus with easy access to Minneapolis–St. Paul
- **Coed**
- **Moderately difficult** entrance level

Faculty *Student/faculty ratio:* 24:1.

Student Life *Campus security:* 24-hour emergency response devices, student patrols, late-night transport/escort service.

Standardized Tests *Required:* CPAt, SAT I, or ACT (for admission).

Costs (2003–04) *Tuition:* $16,800 full-time. *Required fees:* $50 full-time.

Financial Aid Of all full-time matriculated undergraduates who enrolled in 2001, 20 Federal Work-Study jobs (averaging $2000).

Applying *Options:* deferred entrance. *Application fee:* $50. *Required:* high school transcript, interview. *Required for some:* minimum 2.0 GPA. *Recommended:* letters of recommendation.

Admissions Contact Mr. Mike Price, Director of Admissions, Brown College, 1440 Northland Drive, Mendota Heights, MN 55120. *Phone:* 651-905-3400. *Toll-free phone:* 800-6BROWN6. *Fax:* 651-905-3510.

CAPELLA UNIVERSITY
Minneapolis, Minnesota

- **Proprietary** upper-level, founded 1993
- **Calendar** quarters
- **Degrees** certificates, bachelor's, master's, doctoral, first professional, postbachelor's, and first professional certificates (offers only distance learning degree programs)
- **Coed**
- **Moderately difficult** entrance level

Undergraduates 85% are from out of state.

Faculty *Total:* 372. *Student/faculty ratio:* 20:1.

Majors Business/commerce; computer graphics; computer/information technology services administration related; computer systems networking and telecommunications; human resources management and services related; information technology; management science; marketing related; web page, digital/multimedia and information resources design.

Academic Programs *Special study options:* adult/continuing education programs, distance learning, double majors, external degree program, independent study, internships, off-campus study, part-time degree program, services for LD students, student-designed majors, summer session for credit.

Capella University (continued)

Library Sheridan Library System at Johns Hopkins University with an OPAC, a Web page.

Computers on Campus Online (class) registration available.

Student Life *Housing:* college housing not available.

Costs (2003–04) *Tuition:* $12,000 full-time. Full-time tuition and fees vary according to degree level and program. Part-time tuition and fees vary according to degree level and program.

Financial Aid *Average percent of need met:* 90%. *Average financial aid package:* $10,500. *Average indebtedness upon graduation:* $8000.

Applying *Options:* common application, electronic application. *Application fee:* $50. *Application deadline:* rolling (freshmen), rolling (transfers). *Notification:* continuous (transfers).

Admissions Contact Ms. Liz Hinz, Associate Director, Enrollment Services, Capella University, 222 South 9th Street, 20th Floor, Minneapolis, MN 55402. *Phone:* 612-659-5286. *Toll-free phone:* 888-CAPELLA. *Fax:* 612-339-8022. *E-mail:* info@capella.edu.

CARLETON COLLEGE
Northfield, Minnesota

- **Independent** 4-year, founded 1866
- **Calendar** three courses for each of three terms
- **Degree** bachelor's
- **Small-town** 955-acre campus with easy access to Minneapolis–St. Paul
- **Endowment** $451.9 million
- **Coed,** 1,943 undergraduate students, 99% full-time, 52% women, 48% men
- **Very difficult** entrance level, 30% of applicants were admitted

Undergraduates 1,927 full-time, 16 part-time. Students come from 49 states and territories, 30 other countries, 76% are from out of state, 5% African American, 9% Asian American or Pacific Islander, 4% Hispanic American, 0.6% Native American, 5% international, 0.1% transferred in, 89% live on campus. *Retention:* 97% of 2002 full-time freshmen returned.

Freshmen *Admission:* 4,737 applied, 1,414 admitted, 488 enrolled. *Test scores:* SAT verbal scores over 500: 100%; SAT math scores over 500: 100%; ACT scores over 18: 100%; SAT verbal scores over 600: 91%; SAT math scores over 600: 92%; ACT scores over 24: 94%; SAT verbal scores over 700: 52%; SAT math scores over 700: 44%; ACT scores over 30: 58%.

Faculty *Total:* 220, 89% full-time, 91% with terminal degrees. *Student/faculty ratio:* 9:1.

Majors African studies; American studies; ancient/classical Greek; anthropology; art history, criticism and conservation; Asian studies; biology/biological sciences; chemistry; classics and languages, literatures and linguistics; computer science; economics; English; fine/studio arts; French; French studies; geology/earth science; German; history; interdisciplinary studies; international relations and affairs; Latin; Latin American studies; mathematics; music; philosophy; physics; political science and government; psychology; religious studies; Romance languages; Russian; Russian studies; sociology; Spanish; women's studies.

Academic Programs *Special study options:* accelerated degree program, advanced placement credit, double majors, independent study, internships, off-campus study, services for LD students, student-designed majors, study abroad. *Unusual degree programs:* 3-2 engineering with Columbia University, Washington University in St. Louis; nursing with Rush University.

Library Laurence McKinley Gould Library plus 1 other with 662,871 titles, 10,964 serial subscriptions, 778 audiovisual materials, an OPAC, a Web page.

Computers on Campus 221 computers available on campus for general student use. A campuswide network can be accessed from student residence rooms and from off campus. Internet access, online (class) registration, at least one staffed computer lab available.

Student Life *Housing:* on-campus residence required through senior year. *Options:* coed, disabled students. Campus housing is university owned. Freshman campus housing is guaranteed. *Activities and organizations:* drama/theater group, student-run newspaper, radio station, choral group, CANOE (Carleton Association of Nature and Outdoor Enthusiasts), Farm Club, Amnesty International, WHIMS (Women in Math and Science), Ebony II. *Campus security:* 24-hour emergency response devices and patrols, student patrols, late-night transport/escort service, controlled dormitory access. *Student services:* health clinic, personal/psychological counseling, women's center.

Athletics Member NCAA. All Division III. *Intercollegiate sports:* badminton M(c)/W(c), baseball M, basketball M/W, crew M(c)/W(c), cross-country running M/W, equestrian sports M(c)/W(c), fencing M(c)/W(c), field hockey W(c), football M, golf M/W, gymnastics W(c), ice hockey M(c)/W(c), lacrosse M(c)/W(c), rugby M(c)/W(c), sailing M(c)/W(c), skiing (cross-country) M(c)/W(c), skiing (downhill) M(c)/W(c), soccer M/W, softball W, swimming M/W, tennis M/W, track and field M/W, ultimate Frisbee M(c)/W(c), volleyball M(c)/W, water polo M(c)/W(c), wrestling M(c). *Intramural sports:* badminton M/W, basketball M/W, soccer M/W, softball M/W, table tennis M/W, tennis M/W, ultimate Frisbee M/W, volleyball M/W.

Standardized Tests *Required:* SAT I or ACT (for admission). *Recommended:* SAT II: Subject Tests (for admission), SAT II: Writing Test (for admission).

Costs (2003–04) *Comprehensive fee:* $34,395 includes full-time tuition ($28,362), mandatory fees ($165), and room and board ($5868). *College room only:* $2547. *Payment plan:* tuition prepayment.

Financial Aid Of all full-time matriculated undergraduates who enrolled in 2002, 1,693 applied for aid, 1,041 were judged to have need, 1,041 had their need fully met. 460 Federal Work-Study jobs (averaging $2274). 1,089 state and other part-time jobs (averaging $1974). In 2002, 168 non-need-based awards were made. *Average percent of need met:* 100%. *Average financial aid package:* $19,933. *Average need-based loan:* $3283. *Average need-based gift aid:* $14,722. *Average non-need-based aid:* $2533. *Average indebtedness upon graduation:* $15,689.

Applying *Options:* common application, electronic application, early admission, early decision, deferred entrance. *Application fee:* $30. *Required:* essay or personal statement, high school transcript, 2 letters of recommendation. *Recommended:* interview. *Application deadlines:* 1/15 (freshmen), 3/31 (transfers). *Early decision:* 11/15 (for plan 1), 1/15 (for plan 2). *Notification:* 4/15 (freshmen), 12/15 (early decision plan 1), 2/15 (early decision plan 2), 5/15 (transfers).

Admissions Contact Mr. Paul Thiboutot, Dean of Admissions, Carleton College, 100 South College Street, Northfield, MN 55057. *Phone:* 507-646-4190. *Toll-free phone:* 800-995-2275. *Fax:* 507-646-4526. *E-mail:* admissions@acs.carleton.edu.

■ *See page 1348 for a narrative description.*

COLLEGE OF SAINT BENEDICT
Saint Joseph, Minnesota

- **Independent Roman Catholic** 4-year, founded 1887
- **Calendar** semesters
- **Degrees** certificates and bachelor's (coordinate with Saint John's University for men)
- **Small-town** 315-acre campus with easy access to Minneapolis–St. Paul
- **Endowment** $24.1 million
- **Coed, primarily women,** 2,054 undergraduate students, 97% full-time, 100% women
- **Moderately difficult** entrance level, 90% of applicants were admitted

Undergraduates 1,998 full-time, 56 part-time. Students come from 31 states and territories, 24 other countries, 14% are from out of state, 0.6% African American, 2% Asian American or Pacific Islander, 1% Hispanic American, 0.1% Native American, 4% international, 2% transferred in, 80% live on campus. *Retention:* 88% of 2002 full-time freshmen returned.

Freshmen *Admission:* 502 enrolled. *Average high school GPA:* 3.7. *Test scores:* SAT verbal scores over 500: 78%; SAT math scores over 500: 80%; ACT scores over 18: 99%; SAT verbal scores over 600: 39%; SAT math scores over 600: 40%; ACT scores over 24: 63%; SAT verbal scores over 700: 8%; SAT math scores over 700: 6%; ACT scores over 30: 10%.

Faculty *Total:* 174, 85% full-time, 66% with terminal degrees. *Student/faculty ratio:* 13:1.

Majors Accounting; art; art history, criticism and conservation; art teacher education; biochemistry; biological and physical sciences; biology/biological sciences; business administration and management; chemistry; classics and languages, literatures and linguistics; computer science; dietetics; dramatic/theatre arts; economics; education; elementary education; English; environmental studies; fine/studio arts; foods, nutrition, and wellness; forestry; French; German; history; humanities; liberal arts and sciences/liberal studies; mathematics; mathematics and computer science; mathematics and statistics related; music; music teacher education; natural sciences; nursing (registered nurse training); occupational therapy; peace studies and conflict resolution; philosophy; physical therapy; physics; political science and government; pre-dentistry studies; pre-law studies; pre-medical studies; pre-pharmacy studies; pre-theology/pre-ministerial studies; pre-veterinary studies; psychology; religious education; secondary education; social sciences; social work; sociology; Spanish; speech and rhetoric; theology.

Academic Programs *Special study options:* accelerated degree program, advanced placement credit, double majors, English as a second language, honors programs, independent study, internships, off-campus study, services for LD students, student-designed majors, study abroad. *ROTC:* Army (c). *Unusual degree programs:* 3-2 engineering with University of Minnesota, Twin Cities Campus.

Library Clemens Library plus 2 others with 805,376 titles, 5,735 serial subscriptions, 22,452 audiovisual materials, an OPAC, a Web page.

Computers on Campus 541 computers available on campus for general student use. A campuswide network can be accessed from student residence rooms and from off campus. Internet access, online (class) registration, at least one staffed computer lab available.

Student Life *Housing:* on-campus residence required through sophomore year. *Options:* women-only, disabled students. Campus housing is university owned. Freshman campus housing is guaranteed. *Activities and organizations:* drama/theater group, student-run newspaper, radio station, choral group, Volunteers in Service to Others, Ultimate Frisbee, Joint Events Council, Students in Free Enterprise, Cultural Affairs Board. *Campus security:* 24-hour emergency response devices and patrols, student patrols, late-night transport/escort service, controlled dormitory access, well-lit pathways. *Student services:* health clinic, personal/psychological counseling.

Athletics Member NCAA. All Division III. *Intercollegiate sports:* basketball W, cheerleading M/W, crew W(c), cross-country running W, golf W, ice hockey W, lacrosse W(c), rugby W(c), skiing (cross-country) W, soccer W, softball W, swimming W, tennis W, track and field W, volleyball W. *Intramural sports:* basketball W, bowling W(c), fencing W(c), football W, racquetball W, riflery W(c), rock climbing M(c)/W(c), skiing (cross-country) W(c), skiing (downhill) W(c), soccer W, softball W, ultimate Frisbee W, volleyball W, water polo W(c).

Standardized Tests *Required:* SAT I or ACT (for admission).

Costs (2003–04) *Comprehensive fee:* $26,672 includes full-time tuition ($20,335), mandatory fees ($350), and room and board ($5987). Part-time tuition: $847 per credit. Part-time tuition and fees vary according to course load. *Required fees:* $175 per term part-time. *College room only:* $3169. Room and board charges vary according to board plan and housing facility. *Payment plans:* tuition prepayment, installment. *Waivers:* employees or children of employees.

Financial Aid Of all full-time matriculated undergraduates who enrolled in 2003, 1,956 applied for aid, 1,329 were judged to have need, 1,180 had their need fully met. 600 Federal Work-Study jobs (averaging $2000). 300 state and other part-time jobs (averaging $2000). In 2003, 556 non-need-based awards were made. *Average percent of need met:* 88%. *Average financial aid package:* $17,223. *Average need-based loan:* $5009. *Average need-based gift aid:* $11,093. *Average non-need-based aid:* $5790. *Average indebtedness upon graduation:* $22,688.

Applying *Options:* common application, electronic application, early admission, early action, deferred entrance. *Application fee:* $30. *Required:* essay or personal statement, high school transcript, 1 letter of recommendation. *Recommended:* minimum 3.0 GPA, interview. *Application deadline:* 1/15 (freshmen), rolling (transfers). *Notification:* 1/15 (freshmen), 12/20 (early action), continuous (transfers).

Admissions Contact Ms. Karen Backes, Associate Dean of Admissions, College of Saint Benedict, PO Box 7155, Collegeville, MN 56321. *Phone:* 320-363-2196. *Toll-free phone:* 800-544-1489. *Fax:* 320-363-2750. *E-mail:* admissions@csbsju.edu.

COLLEGE OF ST. CATHERINE

St. Paul, Minnesota

- **Independent Roman Catholic** comprehensive, founded 1905
- **Calendar** 4-1-4
- **Degrees** certificates, associate, bachelor's, master's, doctoral, post-master's, and postbachelor's certificates
- **Urban** 110-acre campus with easy access to Minneapolis
- **Endowment** $33.2 million
- **Women only,** 3,681 undergraduate students, 65% full-time
- **Moderately difficult** entrance level, 77% of applicants were admitted

Undergraduates 2,393 full-time, 1,288 part-time. Students come from 31 states and territories, 30 other countries, 10% are from out of state, 7% African American, 5% Asian American or Pacific Islander, 2% Hispanic American, 0.6% Native American, 2% international, 22% transferred in, 38% live on campus. *Retention:* 78% of 2002 full-time freshmen returned.

Freshmen *Admission:* 1,170 applied, 904 admitted, 407 enrolled. *Average high school GPA:* 3.60. *Test scores:* SAT verbal scores over 500: 88%; SAT math scores over 500: 75%; ACT scores over 18: 97%; SAT verbal scores over 600: 59%; SAT math scores over 600: 47%; ACT scores over 24: 47%; SAT verbal scores over 700: 9%; SAT math scores over 700: 22%; ACT scores over 30: 5%.

Faculty *Total:* 528, 42% full-time, 42% with terminal degrees. *Student/faculty ratio:* 11:1.

Majors Accounting; art; art history, criticism and conservation; art teacher education; biochemistry; biology/biological sciences; biology teacher education; business administration and management; chemistry; chemistry teacher education; clinical laboratory science/medical technology; computer and information sciences; creative writing; diagnostic medical sonography and ultrasound technology; dietetics; drama and dance teacher education; dramatic/theatre arts; economics; education; elementary education; English; English/language arts teacher education; family and consumer sciences/home economics teacher education; family and consumer sciences/human sciences; fashion/apparel design; fashion merchandising; fine/studio arts; foods, nutrition, and wellness; French; French language teacher education; health and physical education; health information/medical records technology; history; intercultural/multicultural and diversity studies; international business/trade/commerce; international economics; international relations and affairs; journalism; kindergarten/preschool education; liberal arts and sciences/liberal studies; literature; management information systems; marketing/marketing management; mass communication/media; mathematics; mathematics teacher education; medical radiologic technology; music; music teacher education; nursing (registered nurse training); occupational therapist assistant; occupational therapy; philosophy; physical education teaching and coaching; physical therapist assistant; physics; political science and government; pre-dentistry studies; pre-law studies; pre-medical studies; pre-veterinary studies; psychology; respiratory care therapy; secondary education; sign language interpretation and translation; social sciences; social studies teacher education; social work; sociology; Spanish; Spanish language teacher education; speech and rhetoric; speech teacher education; substance abuse/addiction counseling; theology; women's studies.

Academic Programs *Special study options:* academic remediation for entering students, adult/continuing education programs, advanced placement credit, distance learning, double majors, English as a second language, external degree program, honors programs, independent study, internships, off-campus study, part-time degree program, services for LD students, student-designed majors, study abroad, summer session for credit. *ROTC:* Air Force (c). *Unusual degree programs:* 3-2 engineering with Washington University in St. Louis, University of Minnesota, Twin Cities Campus; optometry with Illinois College of Optometry.

Library St. Catherine Library plus 2 others with 263,495 titles, 1,141 serial subscriptions, 13,627 audiovisual materials, an OPAC, a Web page.

Computers on Campus 350 computers available on campus for general student use. A campuswide network can be accessed from student residence rooms and from off campus that provide access to transcript. Internet access, at least one staffed computer lab available. Computer purchase or lease plan available.

Student Life *Housing options:* women-only. Campus housing is university owned. Freshman campus housing is guaranteed. *Activities and organizations:* drama/theater group, student-run newspaper, choral group, student government, Residence Hall Association, Women Helping Women, Student Nursing Association, social work club. *Campus security:* 24-hour emergency response devices and patrols, student patrols, late-night transport/escort service, controlled dormitory access. *Student services:* health clinic, personal/psychological counseling, women's center.

Athletics Member NCAA. All Division III. *Intercollegiate sports:* basketball W, cross-country running W, ice hockey W, soccer W, softball W, swimming W, tennis W, track and field W, volleyball W. *Intramural sports:* basketball W, cross-country running W, football W, golf W, racquetball W, soccer W, softball W, swimming W, tennis W, track and field W, volleyball W.

Standardized Tests *Required:* SAT I or ACT (for admission).

Costs (2003–04) *Comprehensive fee:* $25,230 includes full-time tuition ($19,520), mandatory fees ($250), and room and board ($5460). Full-time tuition and fees vary according to class time. Part-time tuition: $610 per credit. Part-time tuition and fees vary according to class time. *College room only:* $3060. Room and board charges vary according to board plan and housing facility. *Waivers:* senior citizens and employees or children of employees.

Financial Aid Of all full-time matriculated undergraduates who enrolled in 2003, 1,287 applied for aid, 753 were judged to have need, 160 had their need fully met. 500 Federal Work-Study jobs. In 2003, 410 non-need-based awards were made. *Average percent of need met:* 77%. *Average financial aid package:* $18,319. *Average need-based loan:* $4752. *Average need-based gift aid:* $6954. *Average non-need-based aid:* $14,651. *Average indebtedness upon graduation:* $24,537.

Applying *Options:* common application, deferred entrance. *Application fee:* $20. *Required:* high school transcript, 1 letter of recommendation. *Required for some:* essay or personal statement, interview. *Recommended:* interview. *Application deadline:* 8/15 (freshmen), rolling (transfers). *Notification:* continuous (freshmen), continuous (transfers).

Admissions Contact Ms. Cory Piper-Hauswirth, Associate Director of Admission and Financial Aid, College of St. Catherine, 2004 Randolph Avenue, F-02, St. Paul, MN 55105. *Phone:* 651-690-6047. *Toll-free phone:* 800-945-4599. *Fax:* 651-690-8824. *E-mail:* admissions@stkate.edu.

THE COLLEGE OF ST. SCHOLASTICA

Duluth, Minnesota

- **Independent** comprehensive, founded 1912, affiliated with Roman Catholic Church

The College of St. Scholastica (continued)

- **Calendar** semesters
- **Degrees** bachelor's, master's, post-master's, and postbachelor's certificates
- **Suburban** 186-acre campus
- **Endowment** $16.4 million
- **Coed,** 2,308 undergraduate students, 89% full-time, 70% women, 30% men
- **Moderately difficult** entrance level, 88% of applicants were admitted

Undergraduates 2,052 full-time, 256 part-time. Students come from 19 states and territories, 10 other countries, 11% are from out of state, 3% African American, 1% Asian American or Pacific Islander, 0.5% Hispanic American, 2% Native American, 2% international, 9% transferred in, 39% live on campus. *Retention:* 82% of 2002 full-time freshmen returned.

Freshmen *Admission:* 1,206 applied, 1,062 admitted, 437 enrolled. *Average high school GPA:* 3.50. *Test scores:* SAT verbal scores over 500: 79%; SAT math scores over 500: 71%; ACT scores over 18: 97%; SAT verbal scores over 600: 33%; SAT math scores over 600: 29%; ACT scores over 24: 50%; SAT verbal scores over 700: 4%; SAT math scores over 700: 4%; ACT scores over 30: 5%.

Faculty *Total:* 209, 59% full-time, 45% with terminal degrees. *Student/faculty ratio:* 13:1.

Majors Accounting; applied economics; biochemistry; biology/biological sciences; biology teacher education; business administration and management; business, management, and marketing related; chemistry; chemistry teacher education; communication/speech communication and rhetoric; computer and information sciences; education (K-12); elementary education; English; English/language arts teacher education; health information/medical records administration; health science; health services/allied health/health sciences; history; history teacher education; humanities; international business/trade/commerce; international/global studies; kinesiology and exercise science; liberal arts and sciences/liberal studies; management science; mathematics; mathematics teacher education; music history, literature, and theory; music management and merchandising; music pedagogy; music performance; music teacher education; natural sciences; nursing (registered nurse training); organizational behavior; organizational communication; physical sciences related; psychology; religious studies; school librarian/school library media; science teacher education; social sciences; social science teacher education; social work.

Academic Programs *Special study options:* academic remediation for entering students, accelerated degree program, adult/continuing education programs, advanced placement credit, distance learning, double majors, external degree program, honors programs, independent study, internships, off-campus study, part-time degree program, services for LD students, student-designed majors, study abroad, summer session for credit. *ROTC:* Air Force (c).

Library College of St. Scholastica Library plus 1 other with 125,091 titles, 1,135 serial subscriptions, 15,262 audiovisual materials, an OPAC, a Web page.

Computers on Campus 145 computers available on campus for general student use. A campuswide network can be accessed from student residence rooms and from off campus. Internet access, at least one staffed computer lab available.

Student Life *Housing options:* coed. Campus housing is university owned. Freshman campus housing is guaranteed. *Activities and organizations:* drama/theater group, student-run newspaper, choral group, Campus Activity Board (CAB), Inter-Varsity, SOTA, SHIMA, social work club. *Campus security:* 24-hour emergency response devices and patrols, late-night transport/escort service, controlled dormitory access, student door monitor at night. *Student services:* health clinic, personal/psychological counseling.

Athletics Member NCAA, NAIA. All NCAA Division III. *Intercollegiate sports:* baseball M, basketball M/W, cross-country running M/W, ice hockey M, soccer M/W, softball W, tennis M/W, volleyball W. *Intramural sports:* basketball M/W, football M/W, ice hockey W(c), racquetball M/W, soccer M/W, track and field W, volleyball M/W.

Standardized Tests *Required:* SAT I or ACT (for admission). *Recommended:* PSAT.

Costs (2003–04) *Comprehensive fee:* $24,970 includes full-time tuition ($19,192), mandatory fees ($110), and room and board ($5668). Full-time tuition and fees vary according to class time. Part-time tuition: $601 per credit hour. Part-time tuition and fees vary according to class time and course load. *College room only:* $3228. Room and board charges vary according to board plan. *Payment plan:* installment. *Waivers:* employees or children of employees.

Financial Aid Of all full-time matriculated undergraduates who enrolled in 2003, 1,442 applied for aid, 1,331 were judged to have need, 1,138 had their need fully met. 253 Federal Work-Study jobs (averaging $1786). 249 state and other part-time jobs (averaging $2127). In 2003, 226 non-need-based awards were made. *Average percent of need met:* 85%. *Average financial aid package:* $15,945. *Average need-based loan:* $4639. *Average need-based gift aid:* $5510. *Average non-need-based aid:* $7253. *Average indebtedness upon graduation:* $25,474.

Applying *Options:* common application, electronic application, early admission, deferred entrance. *Application fee:* $25. *Required:* high school transcript. *Required for some:* minimum 2.0 GPA, interview. *Recommended:* essay or personal statement, letters of recommendation, interview. *Application deadline:* rolling (freshmen), rolling (transfers). *Notification:* continuous (freshmen), continuous (transfers).

Admissions Contact Mr. Brian Dalton, Vice President for Enrollment Management, The College of St. Scholastica, 1200 Kenwood Avenue, Duluth, MN 55811-4199. *Phone:* 218-723-6053. *Toll-free phone:* 800-249-6412. *Fax:* 218-723-5991. *E-mail:* admissions@css.edu.

■ *See page 1452 for a narrative description.*

COLLEGE OF VISUAL ARTS
St. Paul, Minnesota

- **Independent** 4-year, founded 1924
- **Calendar** semesters
- **Degree** bachelor's
- **Urban** 2-acre campus with easy access to Minneapolis
- **Endowment** $304,762
- **Coed,** 219 undergraduate students, 85% full-time, 55% women, 45% men
- **Moderately difficult** entrance level, 50% of applicants were admitted

Undergraduates 186 full-time, 33 part-time. Students come from 13 states and territories, 10% are from out of state, 2% African American, 3% Asian American or Pacific Islander, 0.9% Hispanic American, 0.5% Native American, 0.5% international, 6% transferred in. *Retention:* 61% of 2002 full-time freshmen returned.

Freshmen *Admission:* 142 applied, 71 admitted, 37 enrolled. *Average high school GPA:* 2.90. *Test scores:* SAT verbal scores over 500: 60%; SAT math scores over 500: 40%; ACT scores over 18: 81%; SAT verbal scores over 600: 20%; ACT scores over 24: 26%.

Faculty *Total:* 54, 17% full-time, 74% with terminal degrees. *Student/faculty ratio:* 8:1.

Majors Art; commercial and advertising art; drawing; painting; photography; printmaking; sculpture; visual and performing arts related.

Academic Programs *Special study options:* academic remediation for entering students, advanced placement credit, double majors, honors programs, independent study, internships, part-time degree program, study abroad, summer session for credit.

Library College of Visual Arts Library with 7,100 titles, 55 serial subscriptions, 30,370 audiovisual materials, an OPAC, a Web page.

Computers on Campus 60 computers available on campus for general student use. A campuswide network can be accessed. Internet access, at least one staffed computer lab available.

Student Life *Housing:* college housing not available. *Activities and organizations:* student-run newspaper, AIGA Student Chapter. *Campus security:* 24-hour emergency response devices, late-night transport/escort service. *Student services:* personal/psychological counseling.

Standardized Tests *Required:* SAT I or ACT (for admission).

Costs (2003–04) *Tuition:* $15,576 full-time, $780 per credit part-time. Full-time tuition and fees vary according to course load. Part-time tuition and fees vary according to course load. *Required fees:* $530 full-time, $53 per course part-time. *Payment plan:* installment. *Waivers:* children of alumni and employees or children of employees.

Financial Aid Of all full-time matriculated undergraduates who enrolled in 2003, 130 applied for aid, 127 were judged to have need. 29 Federal Work-Study jobs (averaging $1200). 33 state and other part-time jobs (averaging $2000). In 2003, 10 non-need-based awards were made. *Average financial aid package:* $7956. *Average need-based loan:* $3786. *Average need-based gift aid:* $5280. *Average non-need-based aid:* $2182. *Average indebtedness upon graduation:* $25,555.

Applying *Options:* common application, electronic application, deferred entrance. *Application fee:* $40. *Required:* essay or personal statement, high school transcript, minimum 2.7 GPA, interview, portfolio. *Recommended:* minimum 3.0 GPA, letters of recommendation. *Application deadline:* rolling (freshmen), rolling (transfers). *Notification:* continuous (freshmen), continuous (transfers).

Admissions Contact Ms. Elizabeth Catron, Associate Director of Admissions, College of Visual Arts, 344 Summit Avenue, St. Paul, MN 55102-2124. *Phone:* 651-224-3416. *Toll-free phone:* 800-224-1536. *Fax:* 651-224-8854. *E-mail:* info@cva.edu.

CONCORDIA COLLEGE
Moorhead, Minnesota

- **Independent** 4-year, founded 1891, affiliated with Evangelical Lutheran Church in America

- **Calendar** semesters
- **Degree** bachelor's
- **Suburban** 120-acre campus
- **Endowment** $58.6 million
- **Coed,** 2,856 undergraduate students, 97% full-time, 63% women, 37% men
- **Moderately difficult** entrance level, 86% of applicants were admitted

Undergraduates 2,766 full-time, 90 part-time. Students come from 39 states and territories, 42 other countries, 37% are from out of state, 0.6% African American, 2% Asian American or Pacific Islander, 0.9% Hispanic American, 0.3% Native American, 6% international, 3% transferred in, 60% live on campus. *Retention:* 80% of 2002 full-time freshmen returned.

Freshmen *Admission:* 2,444 applied, 2,098 admitted, 783 enrolled. *Test scores:* SAT verbal scores over 500: 85%; SAT math scores over 500: 83%; ACT scores over 18: 96%; SAT verbal scores over 600: 42%; SAT math scores over 600: 36%; ACT scores over 24: 54%; SAT verbal scores over 700: 5%; SAT math scores over 700: 4%; ACT scores over 30: 7%.

Faculty *Total:* 268, 65% full-time, 57% with terminal degrees. *Student/faculty ratio:* 14:1.

Majors Accounting; advertising; art; art history, criticism and conservation; art teacher education; biology/biological sciences; biology teacher education; broadcast journalism; business administration and management; business/commerce; business teacher education; chemistry; chemistry teacher education; child development; classics and classical languages related; clinical laboratory science/medical technology; communication/speech communication and rhetoric; computer science; creative writing; dietetics; dramatic/theatre arts; economics; education; elementary education; English; English/language arts teacher education; environmental studies; fine/studio arts; foods, nutrition, and wellness; French; French language teacher education; German; German language teacher education; health and physical education; health/health care administration; health teacher education; history; humanities; international business/trade/commerce; international/global studies; journalism; kindergarten/preschool education; kinesiology and exercise science; Latin; mass communication/media; mathematics; mathematics teacher education; music; music performance; music teacher education; music theory and composition; nursing (registered nurse training); occupational therapy; ophthalmic and optometric support services and allied professions related; philosophy; physical education teaching and coaching; physical therapy; physics; physics teacher education; piano and organ; political science and government; pre-dentistry studies; pre-law studies; pre-medical studies; pre-theology/pre-ministerial studies; pre-veterinary studies; psychology; public relations/image management; radio and television; religious studies; Russian studies; Scandinavian languages; science teacher education; secondary education; social studies teacher education; social work; sociology; Spanish; Spanish language teacher education; speech and rhetoric; voice and opera.

Academic Programs *Special study options:* adult/continuing education programs, advanced placement credit, cooperative education, double majors, English as a second language, honors programs, independent study, internships, off-campus study, part-time degree program, services for LD students, study abroad, summer session for credit. *ROTC:* Army (c), Air Force (c).

Library Carl B. Ylvisaker Library with 299,808 titles, 1,433 serial subscriptions, 20,778 audiovisual materials, an OPAC, a Web page.

Computers on Campus 303 computers available on campus for general student use. A campuswide network can be accessed from student residence rooms and from off campus. Internet access, at least one staffed computer lab available.

Student Life *Housing:* on-campus residence required through sophomore year. *Options:* coed, men-only, women-only. Campus housing is university owned. Freshman applicants given priority for college housing. *Activities and organizations:* drama/theater group, student-run newspaper, radio and television station, choral group, Sources of Service, Habitat for Humanity, Student Minnesota Education Association, language clubs, health professions interest club. *Campus security:* 24-hour emergency response devices and patrols, student patrols, late-night transport/escort service, well-lit campus, 24-hour locked wing doors. *Student services:* health clinic, personal/psychological counseling, women's center.

Athletics Member NCAA. All Division III. *Intercollegiate sports:* baseball M, basketball M/W, cheerleading W(c), cross-country running M/W, football M, golf M/W, ice hockey M/W, skiing (cross-country) M(c)/W(c), soccer M/W, softball W, swimming W, tennis M/W, track and field M/W, volleyball M(c)/W, wrestling M. *Intramural sports:* badminton M/W, baseball M/W, basketball M/W, bowling M/W, cross-country running M/W, football M/W, golf M/W, ice hockey M/W, racquetball M/W, rock climbing M/W, rugby M/W, skiing (cross-country) M/W, soccer M/W, softball M/W, swimming M/W, table tennis M/W, tennis M/W, track and field M/W, ultimate Frisbee M/W, volleyball M/W, water polo M/W, weight lifting M/W.

Standardized Tests *Required:* SAT I or ACT (for admission). *Recommended:* ACT (for admission).

Costs (2003–04) *Comprehensive fee:* $21,100 includes full-time tuition ($16,420), mandatory fees ($140), and room and board ($4540). Part-time tuition: $2580 per course. Part-time tuition and fees vary according to course load. *College room only:* $2040. Room and board charges vary according to board plan and housing facility. *Payment plan:* installment. *Waivers:* employees or children of employees.

Financial Aid Of all full-time matriculated undergraduates who enrolled in 2002, 2,229 applied for aid, 1,910 were judged to have need, 725 had their need fully met. 595 Federal Work-Study jobs (averaging $493). 1,478 state and other part-time jobs (averaging $1422). In 2002, 681 non-need-based awards were made. *Average percent of need met:* 91%. *Average financial aid package:* $12,737. *Average need-based loan:* $4465. *Average need-based gift aid:* $8115. *Average indebtedness upon graduation:* $19,546.

Applying *Options:* common application, electronic application, early admission, deferred entrance. *Application fee:* $20. *Required:* high school transcript, 2 letters of recommendation. *Application deadline:* rolling (freshmen), rolling (transfers).

Admissions Contact Mr. Scott E. Ellingson, Director of Admissions, Concordia College, 901 8th Street South, Moorhead, MN 56562. *Phone:* 218-299-3004. *Toll-free phone:* 800-699-9897. *Fax:* 218-299-3947. *E-mail:* admissions@cord.edu.

CONCORDIA UNIVERSITY, ST. PAUL
St. Paul, Minnesota

- **Independent** comprehensive, founded 1893, affiliated with Lutheran Church–Missouri Synod, part of Concordia University System
- **Calendar** semesters
- **Degrees** certificates, associate, bachelor's, master's, and postbachelor's certificates
- **Urban** 37-acre campus
- **Endowment** $11.5 million
- **Coed,** 1,741 undergraduate students, 86% full-time, 59% women, 41% men
- **Minimally difficult** entrance level, 64% of applicants were admitted

Undergraduates 1,505 full-time, 236 part-time. Students come from 39 states and territories, 6 other countries, 22% are from out of state, 6% African American, 5% Asian American or Pacific Islander, 1% Hispanic American, 0.6% Native American, 0.7% international, 19% transferred in. *Retention:* 71% of 2002 full-time freshmen returned.

Freshmen *Admission:* 728 applied, 465 admitted, 167 enrolled. *Average high school GPA:* 3.19. *Test scores:* SAT verbal scores over 500: 63%; SAT math scores over 500: 63%; ACT scores over 18: 82%; SAT verbal scores over 600: 27%; SAT math scores over 600: 27%; ACT scores over 24: 29%; SAT verbal scores over 700: 9%; SAT math scores over 700: 9%; ACT scores over 30: 4%.

Faculty *Total:* 382, 21% full-time. *Student/faculty ratio:* 11:1.

Majors Accounting; bilingual and multilingual education; biological and physical sciences; biology/biological sciences; biology teacher education; business administration and management; chemistry teacher education; child care and support services management; community organization and advocacy; criminal justice/safety; dramatic/theatre arts; early childhood education; education; education related; elementary education; English; English as a second/foreign language (teaching); environmental science; finance; fine/studio arts; general studies; health teacher education; history; human services; kindergarten/preschool education; kinesiology and exercise science; management information systems; mass communication/media; mathematics; mathematics teacher education; middle school education; missionary studies and missiology; music; music teacher education; natural sciences; organizational behavior; physical education teaching and coaching; psychology; religious education; religious/sacred music; science teacher education; secondary education; social studies teacher education; sociology; theology.

Academic Programs *Special study options:* academic remediation for entering students, accelerated degree program, adult/continuing education programs, advanced placement credit, cooperative education, distance learning, double majors, English as a second language, external degree program, independent study, internships, off-campus study, part-time degree program, services for LD students, student-designed majors, study abroad, summer session for credit. *ROTC:* Army (c), Air Force (c).

Library Buenger Memorial Library with 131,242 titles, 1,400 serial subscriptions, 6,843 audiovisual materials, an OPAC, a Web page.

Computers on Campus 1200 computers available on campus for general student use. A campuswide network can be accessed from student residence rooms and from off campus. Internet access, at least one staffed computer lab available. Computer purchase or lease plan available.

Student Life *Housing:* on-campus residence required for freshman year. *Options:* coed, men-only, women-only, disabled students. Campus housing is

Concordia University, St. Paul (continued)
university owned. Freshman campus housing is guaranteed. *Activities and organizations:* drama/theater group, student-run newspaper, television station, choral group, church vocations, minority students, ministry, Community Based Outreach. *Campus security:* 24-hour emergency response devices and patrols, student patrols, late-night transport/escort service. *Student services:* health clinic, personal/psychological counseling.

Athletics Member NCAA. All Division II. *Intercollegiate sports:* baseball M(s), basketball M(s)/W(s), cross-country running M(s)/W(s), football M(s), golf W(s), soccer M/W(s), softball W(s), track and field M(s)/W(s), volleyball W(s). *Intramural sports:* basketball M/W, cross-country running M/W, football M/W, racquetball M/W, skiing (cross-country) M/W, skiing (downhill) M/W, soccer M/W, table tennis M/W, tennis M/W, track and field M/W, volleyball M/W.

Standardized Tests *Required:* ACT (for admission).

Costs (2004–05) *Comprehensive fee:* $26,084 includes full-time tuition ($19,928) and room and board ($6156). Full-time tuition and fees vary according to program. Part-time tuition and fees vary according to course load. *Payment plan:* installment. *Waivers:* employees or children of employees.

Financial Aid Of all full-time matriculated undergraduates who enrolled in 2003, 1,245 applied for aid, 1,116 were judged to have need, 241 had their need fully met. 256 Federal Work-Study jobs (averaging $1611). 174 state and other part-time jobs (averaging $1647). In 2003, 79 non-need-based awards were made. *Average percent of need met:* 62%. *Average financial aid package:* $11,339. *Average need-based loan:* $4534. *Average need-based gift aid:* $8644. *Average non-need-based aid:* $5645. *Average indebtedness upon graduation:* $15,300.

Applying *Options:* common application, electronic application, early admission, deferred entrance. *Application fee:* $30. *Required:* high school transcript, 2 letters of recommendation. *Required for some:* essay or personal statement. *Recommended:* minimum 2.0 GPA, interview. *Application deadlines:* 8/1 (freshmen), 8/1 (transfers). *Notification:* continuous (freshmen), continuous (transfers).

Admissions Contact Concordia University, St. Paul, 275 Syndicate North, St. Paul, MN 55104-5494. *Phone:* 651-641-8230. *Toll-free phone:* 800-333-4705. *Fax:* 651-659-0207. *E-mail:* admiss@csp.edu.

CROSSROADS COLLEGE
Rochester, Minnesota

- **Independent** 4-year, founded 1913, affiliated with Christian Churches and Churches of Christ
- **Calendar** semesters
- **Degrees** associate and bachelor's
- **Urban** 40-acre campus with easy access to Minneapolis–St. Paul
- **Endowment** $707,100
- **Coed,** 133 undergraduate students, 86% full-time, 47% women, 53% men
- **Noncompetitive** entrance level, 67% of applicants were admitted

Undergraduates 114 full-time, 19 part-time. Students come from 11 states and territories, 6 other countries, 26% are from out of state, 6% African American, 4% Asian American or Pacific Islander, 5% international, 15% transferred in, 78% live on campus. *Retention:* 68% of 2002 full-time freshmen returned.

Freshmen *Admission:* 91 applied, 61 admitted, 31 enrolled. *Average high school GPA:* 3.30. *Test scores:* ACT scores over 18: 96%; ACT scores over 24: 39%; ACT scores over 30: 3%.

Faculty *Total:* 22, 36% full-time, 27% with terminal degrees. *Student/faculty ratio:* 10:1.

Majors Biblical studies; counseling psychology; liberal arts and sciences/liberal studies; missionary studies and missiology; religious education; religious/sacred music; theology; theology and religious vocations related; youth ministry.

Academic Programs *Special study options:* academic remediation for entering students, advanced placement credit, double majors, independent study, internships, student-designed majors.

Library G. H. Cachiaras Memorial Library with 31,059 titles, 300 serial subscriptions, 1,532 audiovisual materials.

Computers on Campus 15 computers available on campus for general student use. A campuswide network can be accessed from student residence rooms and from off campus. Internet access, at least one staffed computer lab available.

Student Life *Housing:* on-campus residence required through sophomore year. *Options:* men-only, women-only. Campus housing is university owned. Freshman campus housing is guaranteed. *Activities and organizations:* drama/theater group, student-run newspaper, choral group, Christian Outdoors, Musical Outreach, Ambassadors Mission Group. *Campus security:* student patrols, late-night transport/escort service. *Student services:* personal/psychological counseling.

Athletics *Intercollegiate sports:* baseball M, basketball M/W, golf M/W, softball W, tennis M/W, volleyball M/W. *Intramural sports:* basketball M/W, field hockey M/W, football M/W, golf M/W, racquetball M/W, skiing (cross-country) M/W, soccer M, softball M, swimming M/W, table tennis M/W, tennis M/W, volleyball M/W, weight lifting M/W.

Standardized Tests *Required:* SAT I or ACT (for admission).

Costs (2004–05) *Tuition:* $8310 full-time, $277 per semester hour part-time. Full-time tuition and fees vary according to course load. Part-time tuition and fees vary according to course load. *Required fees:* $130 full-time. *Room only:* $2158. Room and board charges vary according to housing facility. *Waivers:* senior citizens and employees or children of employees.

Financial Aid Of all full-time matriculated undergraduates who enrolled in 2002, 93 applied for aid, 58 were judged to have need, 34 had their need fully met. 16 Federal Work-Study jobs (averaging $1450). 9 state and other part-time jobs (averaging $3500). In 2002, 24 non-need-based awards were made. *Average percent of need met:* 83%. *Average financial aid package:* $7124. *Average need-based loan:* $4255. *Average need-based gift aid:* $4726. *Average non-need-based aid:* $3743. *Average indebtedness upon graduation:* $14,941.

Applying *Options:* deferred entrance. *Application fee:* $30. *Required:* essay or personal statement, high school transcript, 3 letters of recommendation. *Required for some:* interview. *Application deadlines:* 8/15 (freshmen), 8/15 (transfers). *Notification:* continuous until 9/1 (freshmen), continuous until 9/1 (transfers).

Admissions Contact Mr. Michael Golembiesky, Director of Admissions, Crossroads College, 920 Mayowood Road, SW, Rochester, MN 55902-2382. *Phone:* 507-288-4563 Ext. 313. *Toll-free phone:* 800-456-7651. *Fax:* 507-288-9046. *E-mail:* admissions@crossroadscollege.edu.

CROWN COLLEGE
St. Bonifacius, Minnesota

- **Independent** comprehensive, founded 1916, affiliated with The Christian and Missionary Alliance
- **Calendar** semesters
- **Degrees** certificates, associate, bachelor's, and master's
- **Suburban** 215-acre campus with easy access to Minneapolis–St. Paul
- **Endowment** $5.0 million
- **Coed,** 986 undergraduate students, 76% full-time, 57% women, 43% men
- **Minimally difficult** entrance level, 82% of applicants were admitted

Undergraduates 749 full-time, 237 part-time. Students come from 39 states and territories, 25% are from out of state, 3% African American, 5% Asian American or Pacific Islander, 3% Hispanic American, 0.5% Native American, 5% transferred in, 69% live on campus. *Retention:* 71% of 2002 full-time freshmen returned.

Freshmen *Admission:* 473 applied, 388 admitted, 118 enrolled. *Average high school GPA:* 3.10. *Test scores:* SAT verbal scores over 500: 55%; SAT math scores over 500: 72%; ACT scores over 18: 76%; SAT verbal scores over 600: 9%; SAT math scores over 600: 45%; ACT scores over 24: 22%; ACT scores over 30: 2%.

Faculty *Total:* 69, 48% full-time, 35% with terminal degrees. *Student/faculty ratio:* 22:1.

Majors Biblical studies; biological and physical sciences; biology/biological sciences; business administration and management; business/commerce; Christian studies; communication and media related; early childhood education; elementary education; English; English/language arts teacher education; general studies; history; history teacher education; kindergarten/preschool education; liberal arts and sciences/liberal studies; linguistics; missionary studies and missiology; music; music teacher education; pastoral studies/counseling; physical education teaching and coaching; pre-law studies; psychology; religious education; social sciences; social studies teacher education; sport and fitness administration; theology.

Academic Programs *Special study options:* academic remediation for entering students, adult/continuing education programs, advanced placement credit, distance learning, double majors, English as a second language, honors programs, independent study, internships, part-time degree program, services for LD students, study abroad, summer session for credit.

Library Peter Watne Memorial Library with 78,000 titles, 1,780 serial subscriptions, 2,400 audiovisual materials, an OPAC, a Web page.

Computers on Campus 52 computers available on campus for general student use. A campuswide network can be accessed from student residence rooms and from off campus. Internet access, at least one staffed computer lab available. Computer purchase or lease plan available.

Student Life *Housing:* on-campus residence required through senior year. *Options:* men-only, women-only. Campus housing is university owned. Freshman campus housing is guaranteed. *Activities and organizations:* drama/theater group, student-run newspaper, choral group, Global Impact Team, Hmong Student Fellowship, Married Student Fellowship, Senate/Student services Board, newspaper/yearbook staff. *Campus security:* 24-hour emergency response devices, late-night transport/escort service, controlled dormitory access. *Student services:* health clinic, personal/psychological counseling.

Athletics Member NAIA, NCCAA. *Intercollegiate sports:* baseball M, basketball M/W, cheerleading W, cross-country running M/W, football M, golf M/W, soccer M/W, softball W, volleyball W. *Intramural sports:* basketball M/W, football M, soccer M, table tennis M/W, tennis M/W, volleyball M/W, weight lifting M/W.

Standardized Tests *Required:* SAT I or ACT (for admission).

Costs (2003–04) *Comprehensive fee:* $18,720 includes full-time tuition ($13,168) and room and board ($5552). Part-time tuition: $550 per credit. Part-time tuition and fees vary according to course load. *College room only:* $2528. Room and board charges vary according to board plan. *Payment plan:* installment. *Waivers:* employees or children of employees.

Financial Aid Of all full-time matriculated undergraduates who enrolled in 2003, 548 applied for aid, 522 were judged to have need, 42 had their need fully met. 119 Federal Work-Study jobs (averaging $2113). 16 state and other part-time jobs (averaging $2445). In 2003, 25 non-need-based awards were made. *Average percent of need met:* 62%. *Average financial aid package:* $10,054. *Average need-based loan:* $4504. *Average need-based gift aid:* $4378. *Average non-need-based aid:* $2124. *Average indebtedness upon graduation:* $21,789.

Applying *Options:* early admission, deferred entrance. *Application fee:* $35. *Required:* essay or personal statement, high school transcript, minimum 2.0 GPA, 2 letters of recommendation. *Required for some:* interview. *Application deadline:* rolling (freshmen), rolling (transfers). *Notification:* continuous (transfers).

Admissions Contact Crown College, 6425 County Road 30, St. Bonifacius, MN 55375-9001. *Phone:* 952-446-4144. *Toll-free phone:* 800-68-CROWN. *Fax:* 952-446-4149. *E-mail:* info@crown.edu.

■ *See page 1500 for a narrative description.*

GLOBE COLLEGE
Oakdale, Minnesota

- **Private** primarily 2-year, founded 1885
- **Calendar** quarters
- **Degrees** diplomas, associate, and bachelor's
- 879 undergraduate students, 49% full-time
- **Noncompetitive** entrance level

Faculty *Student/faculty ratio:* 15:1.

Standardized Tests *Recommended:* SAT I or ACT (for admission).

Costs (2003–04) *Tuition:* $13,050 full-time, $290 per credit part-time. Full-time tuition and fees vary according to course load. Part-time tuition and fees vary according to course load. *Required fees:* $150 full-time, $10 per credit part-time.

Applying *Options:* common application, electronic application. *Required:* interview.

Admissions Contact Mr. Nathan Herrmann, Director of Admissions, Globe College, 7166 10th Street North, Oakdale, MN 55128. *Phone:* 651-730-5100 Ext. 315. *Fax:* 651-730-5151. *E-mail:* admissions@globecollege.edu.

GUSTAVUS ADOLPHUS COLLEGE
St. Peter, Minnesota

- **Independent** 4-year, founded 1862, affiliated with Evangelical Lutheran Church in America
- **Calendar** 4-1-4
- **Degree** bachelor's
- **Small-town** 330-acre campus with easy access to Minneapolis–St. Paul
- **Endowment** $68.0 million
- **Coed,** 2,574 undergraduate students, 98% full-time, 57% women, 43% men
- **Very difficult** entrance level, 77% of applicants were admitted

Additions to the 340-acre campus include an international education center and residence hall, a 9-lane outdoor track with access to an indoor track facility, an international soccer field, a 40-piece aerobic workout area, and state-of-the-art weightlifting equipment. A new residence hall will open by Fall 2005.

Undergraduates 2,533 full-time, 41 part-time. Students come from 38 states and territories, 18 other countries, 19% are from out of state, 0.8% African American, 4% Asian American or Pacific Islander, 1% Hispanic American, 0.3% Native American, 1% international, 1% transferred in, 85% live on campus. *Retention:* 89% of 2001 full-time freshmen returned.

Freshmen *Admission:* 2,317 applied, 1,790 admitted, 688 enrolled. *Average high school GPA:* 3.63. *Test scores:* SAT verbal scores over 500: 90%; SAT math scores over 500: 94%; ACT scores over 18: 100%; SAT verbal scores over 600: 58%; SAT math scores over 600: 63%; ACT scores over 24: 71%; SAT verbal scores over 700: 17%; SAT math scores over 700: 14%; ACT scores over 30: 14%.

Faculty *Total:* 247, 72% full-time, 66% with terminal degrees. *Student/faculty ratio:* 13:1.

Majors Accounting; anthropology; art; art history, criticism and conservation; art teacher education; athletic training; biochemistry; biology/biological sciences; biology teacher education; business administration and management; business/managerial economics; chemistry; chemistry teacher education; classics and languages, literatures and linguistics; computer science; criminal justice/law enforcement administration; dance; dramatic/theatre arts; economics; education; elementary education; English; environmental studies; French; geography; geology/earth science; German; health and physical education related; health teacher education; history; interdisciplinary studies; international business/trade/commerce; Japanese; Japanese studies; Latin American studies; mass communication/media; mathematics; mathematics teacher education; music; music teacher education; nursing (registered nurse training); philosophy; physical education teaching and coaching; physical therapy; physics; physics teacher education; political science and government; pre-dentistry studies; pre-law studies; pre-medical studies; pre-veterinary studies; psychology; religious/sacred music; religious studies; Russian; Russian studies; Scandinavian languages; Scandinavian studies; secondary education; social sciences; social studies teacher education; sociology; Spanish; speech and rhetoric.

Academic Programs *Special study options:* accelerated degree program, advanced placement credit, cooperative education, double majors, honors programs, independent study, internships, off-campus study, services for LD students, student-designed majors, study abroad, summer session for credit. *ROTC:* Army (c). *Unusual degree programs:* 3-2 engineering with Minnesota State University, Mankato; University of Minnesota; environmental studies with Duke University.

Library Folke Bernadotte Memorial Library plus 2 others with 287,761 titles, 1,001 serial subscriptions, 16,063 audiovisual materials, an OPAC, a Web page.

Computers on Campus 441 computers available on campus for general student use. A campuswide network can be accessed from student residence rooms and from off campus. Internet access, at least one staffed computer lab available.

Student Life *Housing:* on-campus residence required through senior year. *Options:* coed. Campus housing is university owned. Freshman campus housing is guaranteed. *Activities and organizations:* drama/theater group, student-run newspaper, radio station, choral group, Campus Activity Board, Gustavus Choir, Greens, Fellowship of Christian Athletes, Big Partner/Little Partner. *Campus security:* 24-hour emergency response devices and patrols, late-night transport/escort service, controlled dormitory access. *Student services:* health clinic, personal/psychological counseling, women's center.

Athletics Member NCAA. All Division III. *Intercollegiate sports:* baseball M, basketball M/W, cross-country running M/W, football M, golf M/W, gymnastics W, ice hockey M/W, lacrosse M(c), rugby M(c)/W(c), skiing (cross-country) M/W, soccer M/W, softball W, swimming M/W, tennis M/W, track and field M/W, ultimate Frisbee M(c)/W(c), volleyball M(c)/W. *Intramural sports:* basketball M/W, football M, ice hockey M, racquetball M/W, skiing (cross-country) M/W, skiing (downhill) M/W, soccer M/W, softball M/W, swimming M/W, tennis M/W, ultimate Frisbee M/W, volleyball W, water polo M/W, weight lifting M/W.

Standardized Tests *Required:* SAT I or ACT (for admission).

Costs (2003–04) *Comprehensive fee:* $27,120 includes full-time tuition ($21,300), mandatory fees ($360), and room and board ($5460). Full-time tuition and fees vary according to student level. Part-time tuition: $3000 per course. No tuition increase for student's term of enrollment. *Required fees:* $100 per course part-time. *College room only:* $3060. Room and board charges vary according to board plan, housing facility, and student level. *Payment plans:* tuition prepayment, installment. *Waivers:* employees or children of employees.

Financial Aid Of all full-time matriculated undergraduates who enrolled in 2002, 2,018 applied for aid, 1,654 were judged to have need. 949 Federal Work-Study jobs (averaging $1380). 565 state and other part-time jobs (averaging $1303). In 2002, 699 non-need-based awards were made. *Average percent of need met:* 88%. *Average financial aid package:* $14,765. *Average need-based loan:* $4041. *Average need-based gift aid:* $10,296. *Average non-need-based aid:* $5829. *Average indebtedness upon graduation:* $17,700.

Applying *Options:* common application, electronic application, early admission, early action, deferred entrance. *Required:* essay or personal statement, high school transcript, 2 letters of recommendation. *Recommended:* interview. *Application deadlines:* 4/1 (freshmen), 4/1 (transfers). *Notification:* continuous until 5/1 (freshmen), 11/20 (early action), 5/1 (transfers).

Gustavus Adolphus College (continued)

Admissions Contact Mr. Mark H. Anderson, Dean of Admission, Gustavus Adolphus College, 800 West College Avenue, St. Peter, MN 56082-1498. *Phone:* 507-933-7676. *Toll-free phone:* 800-GUSTAVU(S). *Fax:* 507-933-7474. *E-mail:* admission@gac.edu.

■ *See page 1698 for a narrative description.*

HAMLINE UNIVERSITY

St. Paul, Minnesota

- **Independent** comprehensive, founded 1854, affiliated with United Methodist Church
- **Calendar** 4-1-4
- **Degrees** certificates, bachelor's, master's, doctoral, first professional, post-master's, postbachelor's, and first professional certificates
- **Urban** 50-acre campus
- **Endowment** $50.3 million
- **Coed,** 1,980 undergraduate students, 95% full-time, 63% women, 37% men
- **Moderately difficult** entrance level, 75% of applicants were admitted

Undergraduates 1,872 full-time, 108 part-time. Students come from 27 states and territories, 21 other countries, 71% are from out of state, 4% African American, 6% Asian American or Pacific Islander, 2% Hispanic American, 0.8% Native American, 3% international, 7% transferred in, 45% live on campus. *Retention:* 84% of 2002 full-time freshmen returned.

Freshmen *Admission:* 1,815 applied, 1,353 admitted, 455 enrolled. *Average high school GPA:* 3.51. *Test scores:* SAT verbal scores over 500: 84%; SAT math scores over 500: 85%; ACT scores over 18: 94%; SAT verbal scores over 600: 53%; SAT math scores over 600: 42%; ACT scores over 24: 54%; SAT verbal scores over 700: 14%; SAT math scores over 700: 8%; ACT scores over 30: 10%.

Faculty *Total:* 344, 51% full-time, 77% with terminal degrees. *Student/faculty ratio:* 13:1.

Majors Anthropology; art; art history, criticism and conservation; Asian studies; Asian studies (East); athletic training; biochemistry; biology/biological sciences; business administration and management; chemistry; criminal justice/law enforcement administration; dramatic/theatre arts; economics; education; education (K-12); elementary education; English; environmental studies; European studies; European studies (Central and Eastern); fine/studio arts; French; German; health and physical education; health teacher education; history; international business/trade/commerce; international economics; international relations and affairs; Jewish/Judaic studies; kinesiology and exercise science; Latin American studies; legal assistant/paralegal; legal studies; mass communication/media; mathematics; music; music teacher education; occupational therapy; peace studies and conflict resolution; philosophy; physical education teaching and coaching; physical therapy; physics; political science and government; pre-dentistry studies; pre-law studies; pre-medical studies; pre-veterinary studies; psychology; public administration; religious studies; Russian studies; science teacher education; secondary education; social sciences; sociology; Spanish; speech/theater education; urban studies/affairs; women's studies.

Academic Programs *Special study options:* academic remediation for entering students, adult/continuing education programs, advanced placement credit, cooperative education, double majors, English as a second language, honors programs, independent study, internships, off-campus study, part-time degree program, services for LD students, student-designed majors, study abroad, summer session for credit. *ROTC:* Air Force (c). *Unusual degree programs:* 3-2 engineering with University of Minnesota, Washington University in St. Louis; occupational therapy with Washington University in St. Louis.

Library Bush Library plus 1 other with 556,450 titles, 3,858 serial subscriptions, 2,642 audiovisual materials, an OPAC, a Web page.

Computers on Campus A campuswide network can be accessed from student residence rooms and from off campus. Internet access, online (class) registration, at least one staffed computer lab available.

Student Life *Housing options:* coed. Campus housing is university owned. Freshman campus housing is guaranteed. *Activities and organizations:* drama/theater group, student-run newspaper, radio station, choral group, Student Congress (HUSC), Acting in the Community Together, Minnesota Public Interest Research Group, residential hall councils, Affordable Arts. *Campus security:* 24-hour emergency response devices and patrols, student patrols, late-night transport/escort service, controlled dormitory access. *Student services:* health clinic, personal/psychological counseling, women's center.

Athletics Member NCAA. All Division III except men's and women's cheerleading (Division I). *Intercollegiate sports:* baseball M, basketball M/W, cheerleading M/W, cross-country running M/W, football M, gymnastics W, ice hockey M, soccer M/W, softball W, swimming M/W, tennis M/W, track and field M/W, volleyball W. *Intramural sports:* basketball M/W, bowling M/W, football M/W, golf M/W, ice hockey W, lacrosse M, racquetball M/W, rock climbing M/W, skiing (cross-country) M/W, softball M/W, swimming M/W, table tennis M/W, tennis M/W, ultimate Frisbee M/W, volleyball M/W, water polo M/W, weight lifting M/W.

Standardized Tests *Required:* SAT I or ACT (for admission).

Costs (2003–04) *One-time required fee:* $100. *Comprehensive fee:* $27,052 includes full-time tuition ($20,582), mandatory fees ($250), and room and board ($6220). Full-time tuition and fees vary according to student level. Part-time tuition: $643 per credit. Part-time tuition and fees vary according to course load and student level. *Required fees:* $200 per term part-time. *College room only:* $3208. Room and board charges vary according to board plan and housing facility. *Payment plan:* installment. *Waivers:* employees or children of employees.

Financial Aid Of all full-time matriculated undergraduates who enrolled in 2003, 1,692 applied for aid, 1,334 were judged to have need, 652 had their need fully met. 860 Federal Work-Study jobs (averaging $1924). 916 state and other part-time jobs (averaging $1699). In 2003, 341 non-need-based awards were made. *Average percent of need met:* 87%. *Average financial aid package:* $21,606. *Average need-based loan:* $2636. *Average need-based gift aid:* $7203. *Average non-need-based aid:* $12,748. *Average indebtedness upon graduation:* $21,487.

Applying *Options:* electronic application, early admission, early action, deferred entrance. *Required:* essay or personal statement, high school transcript, 2 letters of recommendation. *Recommended:* interview, activity resume. *Application deadline:* rolling (freshmen), rolling (transfers). *Notification:* continuous (freshmen), 12/20 (early action), continuous (transfers).

Admissions Contact Mr. Steven Bjork, Director of Undergraduate Admission, Hamline University, 1536 Hewitt Avenue C1930, St. Paul, MN 55104-1284. *Phone:* 651-523-2207. *Toll-free phone:* 800-753-9753. *Fax:* 651-523-2458. *E-mail:* cla-admis@gw.hamline.edu.

HERZING COLLEGE, MINNEAPOLIS DRAFTING SCHOOL DIVISION

Minneapolis, Minnesota

- **Proprietary** primarily 2-year, part of Herzing College
- **Calendar** semesters
- **Degrees** certificates, diplomas, associate, and bachelor's
- **Suburban** 1-acre campus
- **Coed,** 346 undergraduate students, 59% full-time, 79% women, 21% men
- **Moderately difficult** entrance level, 75% of applicants were admitted

Undergraduates 205 full-time, 141 part-time. Students come from 3 states and territories, 1% are from out of state, 14% African American, 5% Asian American or Pacific Islander, 1% Hispanic American, 1% Native American.

Freshmen *Admission:* 128 applied, 96 admitted, 96 enrolled.

Faculty *Total:* 32, 66% full-time, 25% with terminal degrees. *Student/faculty ratio:* 14:1.

Majors Computer and information sciences; computer systems networking and telecommunications; dental assisting; dental hygiene; management information systems; massage therapy; medical/clinical assistant; medical insurance coding.

Academic Programs *Special study options:* adult/continuing education programs, part-time degree program.

Library Main Library plus 1 other.

Computers on Campus 50 computers available on campus for general student use. Internet access, at least one staffed computer lab available.

Student Life *Housing:* college housing not available. *Campus security:* 24-hour emergency response devices, late-night transport/escort service. *Student services:* personal/psychological counseling.

Standardized Tests *Required:* ACCUPLACER (for admission). *Recommended:* SAT I or ACT (for admission), SAT II: Subject Tests (for admission), SAT II: Writing Test (for admission).

Costs (2004–05) *Tuition:* $9680 full-time, $303 per credit part-time. Full-time tuition and fees vary according to course load and program. Part-time tuition and fees vary according to course load and program. *Required fees:* $25 full-time. *Payment plan:* installment. *Waivers:* employees or children of employees.

Applying *Required:* high school transcript, interview.

Admissions Contact Mr. James Decker, Director of Admissions, Herzing College, Minneapolis Drafting School Division, 5700 West Broadway, Minneapolis, MN 55428. *Phone:* 763-231-3152. *Toll-free phone:* 800-878-DRAW. *Fax:* 763-535-9205. *E-mail:* info@mpls.herzing.edu.

MACALESTER COLLEGE

St. Paul, Minnesota

- **Independent Presbyterian** 4-year, founded 1874
- **Calendar** semesters

- **Degree** bachelor's
- **Urban** 53-acre campus
- **Endowment** $436.0 million
- **Coed,** 1,884 undergraduate students, 97% full-time, 58% women, 42% men
- **Very difficult** entrance level, 44% of applicants were admitted

Undergraduates 1,835 full-time, 49 part-time. Students come from 50 states and territories, 86 other countries, 75% are from out of state, 3% African American, 5% Asian American or Pacific Islander, 3% Hispanic American, 1% Native American, 14% international, 1% transferred in, 69% live on campus. *Retention:* 92% of 2002 full-time freshmen returned.

Freshmen *Admission:* 4,341 applied, 1,920 admitted, 513 enrolled. *Test scores:* SAT verbal scores over 500: 100%; SAT math scores over 500: 100%; ACT scores over 18: 100%; SAT verbal scores over 600: 90%; SAT math scores over 600: 87%; ACT scores over 24: 98%; SAT verbal scores over 700: 50%; SAT math scores over 700: 30%; ACT scores over 30: 55%.

Faculty *Total:* 215, 69% full-time, 83% with terminal degrees. *Student/faculty ratio:* 11:1.

Majors Anthropology; art history, criticism and conservation; Asian studies; biology/biological sciences; chemistry; classics and languages, literatures and linguistics; communication/speech communication and rhetoric; computer science; dramatic/theatre arts; economics; English; environmental studies; fine/studio arts; French; geography; geology/earth science; history; humanities; interdisciplinary studies; international relations and affairs; Latin; Latin American studies; linguistics; mathematics; modern Greek; music; neuroscience; philosophy; physics; political science and government; psychology; religious studies; Russian; Russian studies; sociology; Spanish; urban studies/affairs; women's studies.

Academic Programs *Special study options:* double majors, honors programs, independent study, internships, off-campus study, part-time degree program, student-designed majors, study abroad. *ROTC:* Navy (c), Air Force (c). *Unusual degree programs:* 3-2 engineering with Washington University in St. Louis, University of Minnesota; nursing with Rush University; architecture with Washington University in St. Louis.

Library DeWitt Wallace Library with 407,321 titles, 2,119 serial subscriptions, 9,288 audiovisual materials, an OPAC, a Web page.

Computers on Campus 350 computers available on campus for general student use. A campuswide network can be accessed from student residence rooms and from off campus. Internet access, online (class) registration, at least one staffed computer lab available.

Student Life *Housing:* on-campus residence required through sophomore year. *Options:* coed, cooperative. Campus housing is university owned. Freshman campus housing is guaranteed. *Activities and organizations:* drama/theater group, student-run newspaper, radio and television station, choral group, Community Service Organization, student publications, multicultural organization, International Organization, outing club. *Campus security:* 24-hour emergency response devices and patrols, late-night transport/escort service, controlled dormitory access. *Student services:* health clinic, personal/psychological counseling.

Athletics Member NCAA. All Division III. *Intercollegiate sports:* baseball M, basketball M/W, crew M(c)/W(c), cross-country running M/W, fencing M(c)/W(c), football M, golf M/W, ice hockey M(c)/W(c), rugby M(c)/W(c), skiing (cross-country) M/W, soccer M/W, softball W, swimming M/W, tennis M/W, track and field M/W, ultimate Frisbee M(c)/W(c), volleyball M(c)/W, water polo M(c)/W. *Intramural sports:* badminton M/W, basketball M/W, bowling M/W, football M/W, golf M/W, racquetball M/W, soccer M/W, softball M/W, table tennis M/W, tennis M/W, volleyball M/W, water polo M/W, weight lifting M/W.

Standardized Tests *Required:* SAT I or ACT (for admission).

Costs (2004–05) *Comprehensive fee:* $34,156 includes full-time tuition ($26,638), mandatory fees ($168), and room and board ($7350). *College room only:* $3820. Room and board charges vary according to housing facility. *Payment plan:* installment. *Waivers:* employees or children of employees.

Financial Aid Of all full-time matriculated undergraduates who enrolled in 2003, 1,383 applied for aid, 1,265 were judged to have need, 1,265 had their need fully met. 406 Federal Work-Study jobs (averaging $1806). 788 state and other part-time jobs (averaging $2160). In 2003, 110 non-need-based awards were made. *Average percent of need met:* 100%. *Average financial aid package:* $21,386. *Average need-based loan:* $3483. *Average need-based gift aid:* $17,061. *Average non-need-based aid:* $5242.

Applying *Options:* common application, electronic application, early admission, early decision, deferred entrance. *Application fee:* $40. *Required:* essay or personal statement, high school transcript, 3 letters of recommendation. *Recommended:* interview. *Application deadlines:* 1/15 (freshmen), 4/1 (transfers). *Early decision:* 11/15 (for plan 1), 1/15 (for plan 2). *Notification:* 4/1 (freshmen), 12/15 (early decision plan 1), 2/7 (early decision plan 2), 5/15 (transfers).

Admissions Contact Mr. Lorne T. Robinson, Dean of Admissions and Financial Aid, Macalester College, 1600 Grand Avenue, St. Paul, MN 55105-1899. *Phone:* 651-696-6357. *Toll-free phone:* 800-231-7974. *Fax:* 651-696-6724. *E-mail:* admissions@macalester.edu.

MARTIN LUTHER COLLEGE

New Ulm, Minnesota

- **Independent** 4-year, founded 1995, affiliated with Wisconsin Evangelical Lutheran Synod
- **Calendar** semesters
- **Degree** bachelor's
- **Small-town** 50-acre campus
- **Coed,** 1,020 undergraduate students, 99% full-time, 49% women, 51% men
- **Moderately difficult** entrance level, 98% of applicants were admitted

Undergraduates 1,010 full-time, 10 part-time. Students come from 35 states and territories, 9 other countries, 86% are from out of state, 0.6% African American, 0.6% Asian American or Pacific Islander, 0.9% Hispanic American, 0.1% Native American, 1% international, 2% transferred in, 82% live on campus. *Retention:* 83% of 2002 full-time freshmen returned.

Freshmen *Admission:* 322 applied, 315 admitted, 222 enrolled. *Average high school GPA:* 3.00. *Test scores:* ACT scores over 18: 100%; ACT scores over 24: 55%; ACT scores over 30: 9%.

Faculty *Total:* 88, 86% full-time, 44% with terminal degrees. *Student/faculty ratio:* 14:1.

Majors Education (multiple levels); elementary education; interdisciplinary studies; kindergarten/preschool education; pre-theology/pre-ministerial studies; theology.

Academic Programs *Special study options:* academic remediation for entering students, advanced placement credit, double majors, English as a second language, independent study, internships, summer session for credit.

Library Martin Luther College Library with 115,309 titles, 519 serial subscriptions, 5,786 audiovisual materials, an OPAC.

Computers on Campus 125 computers available on campus for general student use. A campuswide network can be accessed from student residence rooms. At least one staffed computer lab available.

Student Life *Housing:* on-campus residence required through junior year. *Options:* men-only, women-only. *Activities and organizations:* drama/theater group, choral group, drama club, Color Guard, Pom Poms. *Campus security:* 24-hour emergency response devices, student patrols, controlled dormitory access. *Student services:* health clinic, personal/psychological counseling.

Athletics Member NCAA, NAIA. All NCAA Division III. *Intercollegiate sports:* baseball M, basketball M/W, cross-country running M/W, football M, golf M, soccer M/W, softball W, tennis M/W, track and field M/W, volleyball W. *Intramural sports:* badminton M/W, basketball M/W, bowling M/W, football M, soccer M/W, softball M/W, tennis M/W, volleyball M/W.

Standardized Tests *Required:* ACT (for admission).

Costs (2004–05) *Comprehensive fee:* $11,800 includes full-time tuition ($8500) and room and board ($3300). Part-time tuition: $190 per credit hour. *Payment plan:* installment.

Financial Aid Of all full-time matriculated undergraduates who enrolled in 2002, 909 applied for aid, 636 were judged to have need, 192 had their need fully met. In 2002, 152 non-need-based awards were made. *Average percent of need met:* 58%. *Average financial aid package:* $5324. *Average need-based loan:* $2020. *Average need-based gift aid:* $4173. *Average non-need-based aid:* $756. *Average indebtedness upon graduation:* $8782. *Financial aid deadline:* 4/15.

Applying *Options:* deferred entrance. *Application fee:* $25. *Required:* high school transcript, minimum 2.0 GPA, letters of recommendation. *Application deadline:* 4/15 (freshmen). *Notification:* continuous (freshmen), continuous (transfers).

Admissions Contact Prof. Ronald B. Brutlag, Associate Director of Admissions, Martin Luther College, 1995 Luther Court, New Ulm, MN 56073. *Phone:* 507-354-8221 Ext. 280. *Fax:* 507-354-8225. *E-mail:* mlcadmit@mlc-wels.edu.

METROPOLITAN STATE UNIVERSITY

St. Paul, Minnesota

- **State-supported** comprehensive, founded 1971, part of Minnesota State Colleges and Universities System
- **Calendar** semesters
- **Degrees** certificates, bachelor's, and master's (offers primarily part-time evening degree programs)
- **Urban** campus
- **Endowment** $992,712

Metropolitan State University (continued)

- **Coed,** 5,936 undergraduate students, 33% full-time, 59% women, 41% men
- **Minimally difficult** entrance level, 67% of applicants were admitted

Undergraduates 1,931 full-time, 4,005 part-time. Students come from 15 states and territories, 53 other countries, 2% are from out of state, 8% African American, 6% Asian American or Pacific Islander, 1% Hispanic American, 0.6% Native American, 3% international, 17% transferred in. *Retention:* 51% of 2002 full-time freshmen returned.

Freshmen *Admission:* 337 applied, 226 admitted, 88 enrolled. *Test scores:* ACT scores over 18: 65%; ACT scores over 24: 16%.

Faculty *Total:* 439, 26% full-time, 49% with terminal degrees. *Student/faculty ratio:* 16:1.

Majors Accounting; advertising; applied mathematics; biology/biological sciences; business administration and management; communication/speech communication and rhetoric; computer science; computer systems analysis; criminal justice/law enforcement administration; criminal justice/police science; criminal justice/safety; culinary arts; developmental and child psychology; dramatic/theatre arts; economics; English; English composition; ethnic, cultural minority, and gender studies related; finance; general studies; history; hospitality administration; human resources management; human services; information science/studies; international business/trade/commerce; kindergarten/preschool education; liberal arts and sciences/liberal studies; management information systems; marketing/marketing management; nursing (registered nurse training); office management; operations management; philosophy; playwriting and screenwriting; psychology; public administration; sales, distribution and marketing; social sciences; social work; substance abuse/addiction counseling; technical and business writing; women's studies.

Academic Programs *Special study options:* adult/continuing education programs, double majors, English as a second language, external degree program, independent study, internships, off-campus study, part-time degree program, student-designed majors, summer session for credit.

Library Library and Information Services with 9,856 titles, 235 serial subscriptions, 507 audiovisual materials, an OPAC, a Web page.

Computers on Campus 420 computers available on campus for general student use. A campuswide network can be accessed from off campus. Internet access, online (class) registration, at least one staffed computer lab available.

Student Life *Housing:* college housing not available. *Activities and organizations:* drama/theater group, student-run newspaper, Psychology Club, Lavender Bridge, International Student Organization, Student Senate, African-American Student Association. *Campus security:* late-night transport/escort service. *Student services:* personal/psychological counseling.

Standardized Tests *Required for some:* SAT I or ACT (for admission).

Costs (2003–04) *Tuition:* state resident $3600 full-time, $120 per credit part-time; nonresident $7980 full-time, $266 per credit part-time. Full-time tuition and fees vary according to reciprocity agreements. Part-time tuition and fees vary according to course load and reciprocity agreements. *Required fees:* $252 full-time, $8 per credit part-time. *Payment plan:* installment. *Waivers:* senior citizens and employees or children of employees.

Financial Aid Of all full-time matriculated undergraduates who enrolled in 2002, 1,220 applied for aid, 958 were judged to have need, 129 had their need fully met. 80 Federal Work-Study jobs (averaging $2616). In 2002, 47 non-need-based awards were made. *Average percent of need met:* 72%. *Average financial aid package:* $8671. *Average need-based loan:* $6525. *Average need-based gift aid:* $2181. *Average non-need-based aid:* $1235. *Average indebtedness upon graduation:* $22,700.

Applying *Options:* deferred entrance. *Application fee:* $20. *Required:* high school transcript, minimum 2.0 GPA. *Application deadlines:* 6/28 (freshmen), 6/28 (transfers).

Admissions Contact Rosa Rodriguez, Interim Director, Metropolitan State University, 700 East 7th Street, St. Paul, MN 55106-5000. *Phone:* 651-793-1303. *Fax:* 651-793-1310. *E-mail:* admissionsmetro@metrostate.edu.

MINNEAPOLIS COLLEGE OF ART AND DESIGN

Minneapolis, Minnesota

- **Independent** comprehensive, founded 1886
- **Calendar** semesters
- **Degrees** bachelor's, master's, and postbachelor's certificates
- **Urban** 7-acre campus
- **Endowment** $37.4 million
- **Coed,** 615 undergraduate students, 92% full-time, 46% women, 54% men
- **Moderately difficult** entrance level, 71% of applicants were admitted

Undergraduates 566 full-time, 49 part-time. Students come from 37 states and territories, 3% African American, 3% Asian American or Pacific Islander, 3% Hispanic American, 1% Native American, 10% transferred in, 45% live on campus. *Retention:* 75% of 2002 full-time freshmen returned.

Freshmen *Admission:* 407 applied, 287 admitted, 117 enrolled. *Average high school GPA:* 3.20. *Test scores:* SAT verbal scores over 500: 70%; SAT math scores over 500: 63%; ACT scores over 18: 89%; SAT verbal scores over 600: 57%; SAT math scores over 600: 25%; ACT scores over 24: 46%; SAT verbal scores over 700: 13%; ACT scores over 30: 3%.

Faculty *Total:* 95, 42% full-time, 24% with terminal degrees. *Student/faculty ratio:* 15:1.

Majors Advertising; cinematography and film/video production; commercial and advertising art; drawing; fine/studio arts; interdisciplinary studies; intermedia/multimedia; painting; photography; printmaking; sculpture.

Academic Programs *Special study options:* adult/continuing education programs, advanced placement credit, cooperative education, distance learning, independent study, internships, off-campus study, part-time degree program, services for LD students, study abroad, summer session for credit.

Library Minneapolis College of Art and Design Library with 47,166 titles, 196 serial subscriptions, 139,245 audiovisual materials, a Web page.

Computers on Campus 110 computers available on campus for general student use. A campuswide network can be accessed from off campus. Internet access, at least one staffed computer lab available.

Student Life *Housing options:* coed. Campus housing is university owned, leased by the school and is provided by a third party. Freshman applicants given priority for college housing. *Activities and organizations:* drama/theater group, student-run radio station. *Campus security:* 24-hour emergency response devices and patrols, late-night transport/escort service. *Student services:* personal/psychological counseling.

Athletics *Intercollegiate sports:* cheerleading M/W. *Intramural sports:* basketball M(c), rock climbing M/W, soccer M(c)/W(c), softball M(c)/W(c), ultimate Frisbee M/W.

Standardized Tests *Required:* SAT I or ACT (for admission).

Costs (2003–04) *Comprehensive fee:* $28,170 includes full-time tuition ($22,400), mandatory fees ($370), and room and board ($5400). Full-time tuition and fees vary according to student level. Part-time tuition: $747 per credit. Part-time tuition and fees vary according to course load and student level. *Required fees:* $185 per term part-time. *College room only:* $3600. Room and board charges vary according to housing facility. *Payment plan:* installment. *Waivers:* children of alumni and employees or children of employees.

Financial Aid Of all full-time matriculated undergraduates who enrolled in 2003, 428 applied for aid, 396 were judged to have need, 26 had their need fully met. 61 Federal Work-Study jobs (averaging $1843). 18 state and other part-time jobs (averaging $1753). In 2003, 56 non-need-based awards were made. *Average percent of need met:* 55%. *Average financial aid package:* $11,794. *Average need-based loan:* $3699. *Average need-based gift aid:* $8306. *Average non-need-based aid:* $10,736. *Average indebtedness upon graduation:* $41,153.

Applying *Options:* common application, early admission, deferred entrance. *Application fee:* $35. *Required:* essay or personal statement, high school transcript, 1 letter of recommendation. *Required for some:* portfolio. *Recommended:* interview. *Application deadline:* rolling (freshmen), rolling (transfers). *Notification:* 7/1 (freshmen), 7/1 (transfers).

Admissions Contact Mr. William Mullen, Director of Admissions, Minneapolis College of Art and Design, 2501 Stevens Avenue South, Minneapolis, MN 55404. *Phone:* 612-874-3762. *Toll-free phone:* 800-874-6223. *E-mail:* admissions@mn.mcad.edu.

■ *See page 1998 for a narrative description.*

MINNESOTA SCHOOL OF BUSINESS-RICHFIELD

Richfield, Minnesota

- **Proprietary** primarily 2-year, founded 1877
- **Calendar** quarters
- **Degrees** certificates, diplomas, associate, and bachelor's
- **Urban** 3-acre campus with easy access to Minneapolis–St. Paul
- **Coed**
- **Minimally difficult** entrance level

Faculty *Student/faculty ratio:* 12:1.

Standardized Tests *Required:* CPAt (for admission).

Costs (2003–04) *Tuition:* $290 per credit part-time.

Applying *Options:* common application. *Application fee:* $50. *Required:* high school transcript, interview. *Required for some:* essay or personal statement.

Admissions Contact Ms. Patricia Murray, Director of Marketing, Minnesota School of Business-Richfield, 1401 West 76th Street, Richfield, MN 55430. *Phone:* 612-861-2000 Ext. 712. *Toll-free phone:* 800-752-4223. *Fax:* 612-861-5548. *E-mail:* rkuhl@msbcollege.com.

MINNESOTA STATE UNIVERSITY MANKATO
Mankato, Minnesota

- **State-supported** comprehensive, founded 1868, part of Minnesota State Colleges and Universities System
- **Calendar** semesters
- **Degrees** associate, bachelor's, master's, and post-master's certificates
- **Small-town** 303-acre campus with easy access to Minneapolis–St. Paul
- **Coed,** 12,390 undergraduate students, 90% full-time, 53% women, 47% men
- **Moderately difficult** entrance level, 88% of applicants were admitted

Undergraduates 11,193 full-time, 1,197 part-time. Students come from 44 states and territories, 65 other countries, 13% are from out of state, 1% African American, 1% Asian American or Pacific Islander, 0.7% Hispanic American, 0.2% Native American, 4% international, 8% transferred in, 25% live on campus. *Retention:* 78% of 2002 full-time freshmen returned.

Freshmen *Admission:* 5,660 applied, 4,956 admitted, 2,287 enrolled. *Test scores:* ACT scores over 18: 90%; ACT scores over 24: 25%; ACT scores over 30: 1%.

Faculty *Total:* 633, 72% full-time, 57% with terminal degrees. *Student/faculty ratio:* 24:1.

Majors Accounting; anatomy; animal physiology; anthropology; applied art; Army R.O.T.C./military science; art; art history, criticism and conservation; art teacher education; astronomy; athletic training; audiology and speech-language pathology; automotive engineering technology; aviation/airway management; behavioral sciences; biochemistry; biological and physical sciences; biology/biological sciences; biology/biotechnology laboratory technician; botany/plant biology; business administration and management; ceramic arts and ceramics; chemistry; child development; city/urban, community and regional planning; civil engineering; clinical laboratory science/medical technology; clothing/textiles; commercial and advertising art; communication disorders; computer engineering; computer engineering technology; computer programming; computer science; construction management; corrections; creative writing; criminal justice/police science; cultural studies; data processing and data processing technology; dental hygiene; developmental and child psychology; dietetics; dramatic/theatre arts; drawing; ecology; economics; education; electrical, electronic and communications engineering technology; electrical, electronics and communications engineering; elementary education; English; environmental biology; environmental studies; family and consumer economics related; family and consumer sciences/home economics teacher education; family and consumer sciences/human sciences; fashion/apparel design; finance; fine/studio arts; foods, nutrition, and wellness; French; geography; geology/earth science; German; health science; health teacher education; history; humanities; industrial arts; industrial technology; information science/studies; insurance; interior design; international business/trade/commerce; international relations and affairs; journalism; kindergarten/preschool education; liberal arts and sciences/liberal studies; literature; management science; marketing/marketing management; mass communication/media; mathematics; mechanical engineering; medical microbiology and bacteriology; modern languages; music; music management and merchandising; music teacher education; natural sciences; nursing (registered nurse training); parks, recreation and leisure; parks, recreation and leisure facilities management; philosophy; physical education teaching and coaching; physical sciences; physics; piano and organ; political science and government; pre-dentistry studies; pre-engineering; pre-law studies; pre-medical studies; pre-theology/pre-ministerial studies; pre-veterinary studies; psychology; public administration; public health; public relations/image management; real estate; science teacher education; sculpture; secondary education; social sciences; social studies teacher education; social work; sociology; Spanish; speech and rhetoric; sport and fitness administration; therapeutic recreation; toxicology; urban studies/affairs; voice and opera; wind/percussion instruments; women's studies.

Academic Programs *Special study options:* academic remediation for entering students, adult/continuing education programs, advanced placement credit, distance learning, double majors, English as a second language, honors programs, independent study, internships, off-campus study, part-time degree program, services for LD students, student-designed majors, study abroad, summer session for credit. *ROTC:* Army (b).

Library Memorial Library with 468,567 titles, 3,275 serial subscriptions, 31,078 audiovisual materials, an OPAC, a Web page.

Computers on Campus 900 computers available on campus for general student use. A campuswide network can be accessed from student residence rooms and from off campus. Internet access, online (class) registration, at least one staffed computer lab available.

Student Life *Housing options:* coed. *Activities and organizations:* drama/theater group, student-run newspaper, radio station, choral group, marching band, national fraternities, national sororities. *Campus security:* 24-hour emergency response devices and patrols, student patrols, late-night transport/escort service, Night Owl security program in residence halls, closed circuit cameras in parking lots. *Student services:* health clinic, personal/psychological counseling, women's center, legal services.

Athletics Member NCAA. All Division II except men's and women's ice hockey (Division I). *Intercollegiate sports:* baseball M(s), basketball M(s)/W(s), cheerleading M/W, cross-country running M(s)/W(s), football M(s), golf M(s)/W(s), ice hockey M(s)/W(s), soccer W(s), softball W(s), swimming M(s)/W(s), tennis M(s)/W(s), track and field M(s)/W(s), volleyball W(s), wrestling M(s). *Intramural sports:* archery M/W, basketball M/W, bowling M/W, fencing M/W, football M, ice hockey M/W, lacrosse M/W, racquetball M/W, rugby M/W, sailing M/W, skiing (cross-country) M/W, skiing (downhill) M/W, soccer M, softball M/W, swimming M/W, tennis M/W, track and field M/W, volleyball M/W, wrestling M.

Standardized Tests *Required:* ACT (for admission).

Costs (2003–04) *Tuition:* state resident $3806 full-time, $152 per credit part-time; nonresident $8075 full-time, $322 per credit part-time. Full-time tuition and fees vary according to course load and reciprocity agreements. Part-time tuition and fees vary according to course load and reciprocity agreements. *Required fees:* $700 full-time, $29 per credit part-time. *Room and board:* $4297. Room and board charges vary according to board plan. *Payment plan:* installment. *Waivers:* senior citizens and employees or children of employees.

Financial Aid Of all full-time matriculated undergraduates who enrolled in 2003, 8,125 applied for aid, 5,807 were judged to have need, 2,682 had their need fully met. In 2003, 603 non-need-based awards were made. *Average percent of need met:* 81%. *Average financial aid package:* $6417. *Average need-based loan:* $3787. *Average need-based gift aid:* $3352. *Average non-need-based aid:* $1472. *Average indebtedness upon graduation:* $15,500.

Applying *Options:* electronic application, early admission, deferred entrance. *Application fee:* $20. *Required:* high school transcript. *Required for some:* essay or personal statement, 3 letters of recommendation. *Application deadline:* rolling (freshmen), rolling (transfers). *Notification:* continuous (freshmen), continuous (transfers).

Admissions Contact Mr. Walt Wolff, Director of Admissions, Minnesota State University Mankato, 122 Taylor Center, Mankato, MN 56001. *Phone:* 507-389-6670. *Toll-free phone:* 800-722-0544. *Fax:* 507-389-1511. *E-mail:* admissions@mnsu.edu.

MINNESOTA STATE UNIVERSITY MOORHEAD
Moorhead, Minnesota

- **State-supported** comprehensive, founded 1885, part of Minnesota State Colleges and Universities System
- **Calendar** semesters
- **Degrees** associate, bachelor's, master's, and post-master's certificates
- **Urban** 118-acre campus
- **Coed,** 7,282 undergraduate students, 86% full-time, 61% women, 39% men
- **Moderately difficult** entrance level, 86% of applicants were admitted

Undergraduates 6,277 full-time, 1,005 part-time. Students come from 34 states and territories, 32 other countries, 39% are from out of state, 0.8% African American, 1% Asian American or Pacific Islander, 1% Hispanic American, 1% Native American, 3% international, 9% transferred in, 27% live on campus. *Retention:* 67% of 2002 full-time freshmen returned.

Freshmen *Admission:* 2,764 applied, 2,375 admitted, 1,291 enrolled. *Test scores:* ACT scores over 18: 91%; ACT scores over 24: 29%; ACT scores over 30: 2%.

Faculty *Total:* 315, 79% with terminal degrees. *Student/faculty ratio:* 23:1.

Majors Accounting; advertising; American studies; anthropology; applied art; archeology; art; art history, criticism and conservation; art teacher education; audiology and speech-language pathology; biology/biological sciences; broadcast journalism; business administration and management; ceramic arts and ceramics; chemistry; clinical laboratory science/medical technology; commercial and advertising art; commercial photography; community health services counseling; computer and information sciences; computer science; construction engineering technology; criminal justice/safety; cytotechnology; drama and dance teacher education; dramatic/theatre arts; economics; elementary education; English; English/language arts teacher education; finance; fine/studio arts; foreign languages and literatures; health and physical education; health/health care administration; health teacher education; history; industrial technology; interdisciplinary studies; international business/trade/commerce; journalism; kindergarten/preschool education; legal assistant/paralegal; liberal arts and sciences/liberal studies; management information systems; marketing/marketing management; mass communication/media; mathematics; mathematics teacher education; middle school education; music; music management and merchandising; music teacher education; music theory and composition; nursing (registered nurse training); painting; philosophy; physical education teaching and coaching; physics; piano

Minnesota State University Moorhead (continued)
and organ; political science and government; pre-dentistry studies; pre-law studies; pre-medical studies; pre-veterinary studies; printmaking; psychology; public relations/image management; science teacher education; sculpture; secondary education; social studies teacher education; social work; sociology; Spanish; Spanish language teacher education; special education; special education (emotionally disturbed); special education (mentally retarded); special education (specific learning disabilities); speech and rhetoric; speech teacher education; sport and fitness administration; voice and opera; wind/percussion instruments.

Academic Programs *Special study options:* academic remediation for entering students, adult/continuing education programs, advanced placement credit, distance learning, double majors, external degree program, freshman honors college, honors programs, independent study, internships, off-campus study, part-time degree program, services for LD students, student-designed majors, study abroad, summer session for credit. *ROTC:* Army (c), Air Force (c).

Library Livingston Lord Library with 367,334 titles, 1,539 serial subscriptions, an OPAC, a Web page.

Computers on Campus 450 computers available on campus for general student use. A campuswide network can be accessed from student residence rooms and from off campus. Internet access, online (class) registration, at least one staffed computer lab available.

Student Life *Housing options:* coed, men-only, women-only. *Activities and organizations:* drama/theater group, student-run newspaper, radio station, choral group, residence hall associations, Campus Activities Board, Pi Sigma Epsilon, Campus Crusade for Christ, transfer club, national fraternities, national sororities. *Campus security:* 24-hour emergency response devices and patrols, student patrols, late-night transport/escort service, controlled dormitory access. *Student services:* health clinic, personal/psychological counseling, women's center.

Athletics Member NCAA. All Division II. *Intercollegiate sports:* basketball M(s)/W(s), cross-country running M/W, football M(s), golf M/W, soccer W(s), softball W(s), tennis W, track and field M(s)/W(s), volleyball W(s), wrestling M(s). *Intramural sports:* archery M/W, badminton M/W, basketball M/W, bowling M/W, football M/W, golf M/W, ice hockey M, racquetball M/W, skiing (cross-country) M/W, soccer M/W, softball W, swimming M/W, tennis W, track and field M/W, volleyball M/W, wrestling M.

Standardized Tests *Required:* SAT I or ACT (for admission), PSAT (for admission).

Costs (2003–04) *Tuition:* state resident $3628 full-time, $121 per credit hour part-time; nonresident $3628 full-time, $121 per credit hour part-time. *Required fees:* $626 full-time, $26 per credit part-time. *Room and board:* $4340; room only: $2560.

Financial Aid Of all full-time matriculated undergraduates who enrolled in 2003, 5,814 applied for aid, 3,826 were judged to have need. 205 Federal Work-Study jobs (averaging $1964). 1,467 state and other part-time jobs (averaging $1349). In 2003, 862 non-need-based awards were made. *Average financial aid package:* $4193. *Average need-based loan:* $3497. *Average need-based gift aid:* $3564. *Average non-need-based aid:* $779. *Average indebtedness upon graduation:* $18,228.

Applying *Options:* early admission, deferred entrance. *Application fee:* $20. *Required:* high school transcript. *Application deadlines:* 8/7 (freshmen), 8/7 (transfers). *Notification:* continuous (freshmen), continuous (transfers).

Admissions Contact Ms. Gina Monson, Director of Admissions, Minnesota State University Moorhead, Owens Hall, Moorhead, MN 56563-0002. *Phone:* 218-477-2161. *Toll-free phone:* 800-593-7246. *Fax:* 218-236-2168.

NATIONAL AMERICAN UNIVERSITY
Roseville, Minnesota

Admissions Contact Mr. Steve Grunlan, Director of Admissions, National American University, 1500 West Highway 36, Roseville, MN 55113. *Phone:* 651-644-1265.

NORTH CENTRAL UNIVERSITY
Minneapolis, Minnesota

- **Independent** 4-year, founded 1930, affiliated with Assemblies of God
- **Calendar** semesters plus January and May terms
- **Degrees** certificates, diplomas, associate, and bachelor's
- **Urban** 9-acre campus
- **Endowment** $969,948
- **Coed,** 1,227 undergraduate students, 100% full-time, 50% women, 50% men
- **Noncompetitive** entrance level, 55% of applicants were admitted

Undergraduates 1,227 full-time. Students come from 40 states and territories, 11 other countries, 50% are from out of state, 4% African American, 0.8% Asian American or Pacific Islander, 2% Hispanic American, 0.7% Native American, 1% international, 8% transferred in, 65% live on campus. *Retention:* 77% of 2002 full-time freshmen returned.

Freshmen *Admission:* 741 applied, 408 admitted, 275 enrolled. *Test scores:* SAT verbal scores over 500: 57%; ACT scores over 18: 80%; SAT verbal scores over 600: 17%; ACT scores over 24: 30%; SAT verbal scores over 700: 2%; ACT scores over 30: 10%.

Faculty *Total:* 97, 41% full-time. *Student/faculty ratio:* 18:1.

Majors Administrative assistant and secretarial science; American Sign Language (ASL); ancient Near Eastern and biblical languages; biblical studies; broadcast journalism; business administration and management; divinity/ministry; dramatic/theatre arts; elementary education; English; Hebrew; history; interdisciplinary studies; journalism; liberal arts and sciences/liberal studies; literature; mass communication/media; missionary studies and missiology; modern Greek; modern languages; music; music performance; music theory and composition; nursing (registered nurse training); pastoral studies/counseling; psychology; religious/sacred music; religious studies; secondary education; sign language interpretation and translation; youth ministry.

Academic Programs *Special study options:* academic remediation for entering students, adult/continuing education programs, advanced placement credit, cooperative education, external degree program, internships, off-campus study, part-time degree program, services for LD students, student-designed majors, study abroad, summer session for credit. *ROTC:* Army (c), Air Force (c).

Library T. J. Jones Information Resource Center with 70,041 titles, 384 serial subscriptions.

Computers on Campus 30 computers available on campus for general student use. A campuswide network can be accessed. Internet access, at least one staffed computer lab available.

Student Life *Housing:* on-campus residence required through senior year. *Options:* men-only, women-only. Campus housing is university owned. Freshman campus housing is guaranteed. *Activities and organizations:* drama/theater group, student-run newspaper, radio and television station, choral group, athletics, Mu Kappa, musical organizations, student government, student ministries. *Campus security:* 24-hour emergency response devices and patrols, late-night transport/escort service, controlled dormitory access. *Student services:* personal/psychological counseling.

Athletics Member NCAA, NCCAA. All NCAA Division III. *Intercollegiate sports:* basketball M/W, cross-country running M/W, soccer M/W, track and field M/W, volleyball W. *Intramural sports:* baseball M(c), football M/W, golf M(c), softball W(c), table tennis M/W, volleyball M/W.

Standardized Tests *Required:* SAT I or ACT (for admission).

Costs (2003–04) *Comprehensive fee:* $15,274 includes full-time tuition ($9840), mandatory fees ($754), and room and board ($4680). *College room only:* $1950. Room and board charges vary according to board plan and housing facility. *Payment plan:* installment. *Waivers:* senior citizens and employees or children of employees.

Applying *Options:* common application, deferred entrance. *Application fee:* $25. *Required:* essay or personal statement, high school transcript, minimum 2.2 GPA, letters of recommendation, Christian testimony. *Application deadlines:* 6/1 (freshmen), 6/1 (transfers). *Notification:* 6/15 (freshmen), 6/15 (transfers).

Admissions Contact Ms. Linda Kammerer, Admissions Secretary, North Central University, 910 Elliot Avenue, Minneapolis, MN 55404. *Phone:* 612-343-4460. *Toll-free phone:* 800-289-6222. *Fax:* 612-343-4146. *E-mail:* admissions@northcentral.edu.

NORTHWESTERN COLLEGE
St. Paul, Minnesota

- **Independent nondenominational** 4-year, founded 1902
- **Calendar** semesters
- **Degrees** certificates, associate, and bachelor's
- **Suburban** 100-acre campus
- **Endowment** $5.9 million
- **Coed,** 2,592 undergraduate students, 76% full-time, 63% women, 37% men
- **Moderately difficult** entrance level, 94% of applicants were admitted

Northwestern is a Christian liberal arts college of 2,000 undergraduate students. It offers 50 majors and is committed to educational excellence. Instruction from a biblical worldview integrates faith and learning. Benefits include strong music and athletic programs, study abroad opportunities, daily chapel, and outreach/missions opportunities. Northwestern rests on a beautiful lakeside campus just 15 minutes from downtown Minneapolis–St. Paul.

Undergraduates 1,982 full-time, 610 part-time. Students come from 32 states and territories, 28% are from out of state, 4% African American, 3% Asian

American or Pacific Islander, 1% Hispanic American, 0.3% Native American, 0.4% international, 5% transferred in, 57% live on campus. *Retention:* 75% of 2002 full-time freshmen returned.

Freshmen *Admission:* 980 applied, 919 admitted, 459 enrolled. *Average high school GPA:* 3.51. *Test scores:* SAT verbal scores over 500: 74%; SAT math scores over 500: 77%; ACT scores over 18: 99%; SAT verbal scores over 600: 48%; SAT math scores over 600: 39%; ACT scores over 24: 50%; SAT verbal scores over 700: 22%; SAT math scores over 700: 8%; ACT scores over 30: 7%.

Faculty *Total:* 156, 54% full-time, 46% with terminal degrees. *Student/faculty ratio:* 16:1.

Majors Accounting; art teacher education; biblical studies; biology/biological sciences; business administration and management; communication/speech communication and rhetoric; creative writing; criminal justice/safety; dramatic/theatre arts; early childhood education; elementary education; English; English as a second/foreign language (teaching); English/language arts teacher education; finance; fine/studio arts; graphic design; history; international business/trade/commerce; journalism; kindergarten/preschool education; kinesiology and exercise science; liberal arts and sciences/liberal studies; management information systems; marketing/marketing management; mathematics; mathematics teacher education; missionary studies and missiology; music; music performance; music teacher education; music theory and composition; physical education teaching and coaching; piano and organ; pre-theology/pre-ministerial studies; psychology; public relations/image management; radio and television; religious education; social sciences; social studies teacher education; Spanish; technical and business writing; theological and ministerial studies related; voice and opera; youth ministry.

Academic Programs *Special study options:* academic remediation for entering students, adult/continuing education programs, advanced placement credit, distance learning, double majors, English as a second language, honors programs, independent study, internships, off-campus study, part-time degree program, study abroad, summer session for credit. *ROTC:* Army (c), Air Force (c). *Unusual degree programs:* 3-2 engineering with University of Minnesota-Twin Cities.

Library Berntsen Library with 75,082 titles, 560 serial subscriptions, 3,716 audiovisual materials, an OPAC.

Computers on Campus 165 computers available on campus for general student use. A campuswide network can be accessed from student residence rooms and from off campus. Internet access, online (class) registration, at least one staffed computer lab available. Computer purchase or lease plan available.

Student Life *Housing:* on-campus residence required through sophomore year. *Options:* men-only, women-only, disabled students. Campus housing is university owned. Freshman campus housing is guaranteed. *Activities and organizations:* drama/theater group, student-run newspaper, radio station, choral group, NWSA (student government association), Edge (religious group), Transfer Connection, Guardian Angels, Mu Kappa. *Campus security:* 24-hour patrols, late-night transport/escort service, controlled dormitory access. *Student services:* health clinic, personal/psychological counseling.

Athletics Member NAIA, NCCAA. *Intercollegiate sports:* baseball M, basketball M/W, cheerleading W, cross-country running M/W, football M, golf M/W, ice hockey M(c), soccer M/W, softball W, tennis M/W, track and field M/W, volleyball W. *Intramural sports:* badminton M/W, basketball M/W, bowling M/W, cross-country running M/W, football M/W, golf M/W, racquetball M/W, skiing (cross-country) M/W, soccer W, softball M/W, table tennis M/W, tennis M/W, volleyball M/W, weight lifting M/W.

Standardized Tests *Required:* SAT I or ACT (for admission).

Costs (2004–05) *Comprehensive fee:* $24,390 includes full-time tuition ($18,370) and room and board ($6020). Full-time tuition and fees vary according to course load. Part-time tuition: $775 per credit. Part-time tuition and fees vary according to course load. *College room only:* $3300. Room and board charges vary according to board plan. *Payment plan:* installment. *Waivers:* children of alumni, senior citizens, and employees or children of employees.

Financial Aid Of all full-time matriculated undergraduates who enrolled in 2002, 1,585 applied for aid, 1,326 were judged to have need, 140 had their need fully met. 213 Federal Work-Study jobs (averaging $1938). 183 state and other part-time jobs (averaging $1845). In 2002, 255 non-need-based awards were made. *Average percent of need met:* 77%. *Average financial aid package:* $13,037. *Average need-based loan:* $4106. *Average need-based gift aid:* $9431. *Average non-need-based aid:* $3961. *Average indebtedness upon graduation:* $18,800. *Financial aid deadline:* 6/1.

Applying *Options:* electronic application, early admission, deferred entrance. *Application fee:* $25. *Required:* essay or personal statement, high school transcript, minimum 2.0 GPA, 2 letters of recommendation, lifestyle agreement, statement of Christian faith. *Required for some:* interview. *Recommended:* minimum 3.0 GPA. *Application deadlines:* 8/1 (freshmen), 8/1 (transfers). *Notification:* continuous until 8/15 (freshmen), continuous until 8/15 (transfers).

Admissions Contact Mr. Kenneth K. Faffler, Director of Admissions, Northwestern College, 3003 Snelling Avenue North, Nazareth Hall, Room 2122, St. Paul, MN 55113-1598. *Phone:* 651-631-5209. *Toll-free phone:* 800-827-6827. *Fax:* 651-631-5680. *E-mail:* admissions@nwc.edu.

OAK HILLS CHRISTIAN COLLEGE

Bemidji, Minnesota

- **Independent interdenominational** 4-year, founded 1946
- **Calendar** semesters
- **Degrees** certificates, diplomas, associate, and bachelor's
- **Rural** 180-acre campus
- **Endowment** $273,457
- **Coed,** 168 undergraduate students, 92% full-time, 48% women, 52% men
- **Minimally difficult** entrance level, 90% of applicants were admitted

Undergraduates 155 full-time, 13 part-time. Students come from 12 states and territories, 25% are from out of state, 0.6% African American, 2% Asian American or Pacific Islander, 1% Hispanic American, 4% Native American, 20% transferred in, 80% live on campus. *Retention:* 72% of 2002 full-time freshmen returned.

Freshmen *Admission:* 70 applied, 63 admitted, 31 enrolled. *Average high school GPA:* 2.91. *Test scores:* ACT scores over 18: 81%; ACT scores over 24: 28%; ACT scores over 30: 3%.

Faculty *Total:* 19, 37% full-time, 21% with terminal degrees. *Student/faculty ratio:* 18:1.

Majors Biblical studies; business administration and management; liberal arts and sciences/liberal studies; missionary studies and missiology; music; parks, recreation and leisure facilities management; psychology; religious/sacred music.

Academic Programs *Special study options:* academic remediation for entering students, advanced placement credit, double majors, honors programs, independent study, internships, off-campus study, part-time degree program, services for LD students.

Library Cummings Library with 25,079 titles, 99 serial subscriptions, 1,338 audiovisual materials, an OPAC, a Web page.

Computers on Campus 16 computers available on campus for general student use. Internet access, at least one staffed computer lab available.

Student Life *Housing:* on-campus residence required through sophomore year. *Options:* men-only, women-only. Campus housing is university owned. Freshman campus housing is guaranteed. *Activities and organizations:* drama/theater group, student-run newspaper, choral group, Student Council, Students Older Than Average. *Campus security:* 24-hour emergency response devices, student patrols, controlled dormitory access, evening patrols by trained security personnel. *Student services:* health clinic, personal/psychological counseling.

Athletics *Intercollegiate sports:* basketball M/W, volleyball M/W. *Intramural sports:* basketball M/W, football M/W, golf M/W, racquetball M/W, soccer M/W, softball M/W, table tennis M/W, tennis M/W, volleyball M/W, weight lifting M/W.

Standardized Tests *Required:* ACT (for admission).

Costs (2003–04) *Comprehensive fee:* $13,990 includes full-time tuition ($10,180) and room and board ($3810). Full-time tuition and fees vary according to course load. Part-time tuition: $125 per semester hour. Part-time tuition and fees vary according to course load. *College room only:* $1830. Room and board charges vary according to board plan and housing facility. *Payment plan:* installment. *Waivers:* employees or children of employees.

Financial Aid Of all full-time matriculated undergraduates who enrolled in 2002, 138 applied for aid, 131 were judged to have need, 9 had their need fully met. 22 Federal Work-Study jobs (averaging $1234). 54 state and other part-time jobs (averaging $2188). In 2002, 7 non-need-based awards were made. *Average percent of need met:* 73%. *Average financial aid package:* $9306. *Average need-based loan:* $3099. *Average need-based gift aid:* $6455. *Average non-need-based aid:* $2610. *Average indebtedness upon graduation:* $20,233.

Applying *Options:* deferred entrance. *Application fee:* $20. *Required:* essay or personal statement, high school transcript, 2 letters of recommendation. *Required for some:* minimum 2.0 GPA. *Application deadline:* rolling (freshmen), rolling (transfers). *Notification:* continuous (freshmen), continuous (transfers).

Admissions Contact Mr. Dan Hovestol, Admissions Director, Oak Hills Christian College, Bemidji, MN 56601. *Phone:* 218-751-8670 Ext. 1285. *Toll-free phone:* 888-751-8670 Ext. 285. *Fax:* 218-751-8825. *E-mail:* admissions@oakhills.edu.

PILLSBURY BAPTIST BIBLE COLLEGE

Owatonna, Minnesota

- **Independent Baptist** 4-year, founded 1957
- **Calendar** semesters
- **Degrees** certificates, associate, and bachelor's
- **Small-town** 14-acre campus with easy access to Minneapolis–St. Paul
- **Endowment** $389,149

Pillsbury Baptist Bible College (continued)

- **Coed,** 191 undergraduate students, 85% full-time, 55% women, 45% men
- **Noncompetitive** entrance level, 77% of applicants were admitted

Undergraduates 162 full-time, 29 part-time. Students come from 20 states and territories, 28% are from out of state, 2% African American, 0.5% Asian American or Pacific Islander, 0.5% Hispanic American, 4% transferred in, 83% live on campus. *Retention:* 72% of 2002 full-time freshmen returned.

Freshmen *Admission:* 90 applied, 69 admitted, 45 enrolled. *Test scores:* ACT scores over 18: 82%; ACT scores over 24: 26%.

Faculty *Total:* 27, 70% full-time, 4% with terminal degrees. *Student/faculty ratio:* 8:1.

Majors Administrative assistant and secretarial science; biblical studies; business administration and management; business teacher education; computer teacher education; education; elementary education; English/language arts teacher education; mathematics teacher education; missionary studies and missiology; music; music teacher education; pastoral studies/counseling; photography; physical education teaching and coaching; religious education; religious/sacred music; science teacher education; secondary education; social studies teacher education; speech teacher education; theological and ministerial studies related; youth ministry.

Academic Programs *Special study options:* academic remediation for entering students, accelerated degree program, advanced placement credit, double majors, independent study, internships, part-time degree program, services for LD students, summer session for credit.

Library Pillsbury College Library with 52,340 titles, 245 serial subscriptions, 817 audiovisual materials, an OPAC.

Computers on Campus 33 computers available on campus for general student use. A campuswide network can be accessed. Internet access, at least one staffed computer lab available.

Student Life *Housing:* on-campus residence required through senior year. *Options:* men-only, women-only. Campus housing is university owned. Freshman campus housing is guaranteed. *Activities and organizations:* drama/theater group, student-run newspaper, choral group. *Campus security:* student patrols. *Student services:* personal/psychological counseling.

Athletics Member NCCAA. *Intercollegiate sports:* baseball M, basketball M/W, golf M/W, soccer M, softball W, volleyball W. *Intramural sports:* basketball M/W, table tennis M/W, volleyball M/W.

Standardized Tests *Required:* ACT (for admission).

Costs (2003–04) *Comprehensive fee:* $11,720 includes full-time tuition ($6560), mandatory fees ($1560), and room and board ($3600). Part-time tuition: $205 per credit hour. Part-time tuition and fees vary according to course load. *Required fees:* $896 per year part-time. *Waivers:* employees or children of employees.

Financial Aid *Average percent of need met:* 50%.

Applying *Options:* deferred entrance. *Application fee:* $25. *Required:* essay or personal statement, high school transcript, 2 letters of recommendation, 2 photographs. *Recommended:* interview. *Application deadlines:* 8/20 (freshmen), 8/20 (transfers). *Notification:* continuous (freshmen), continuous (transfers).

Admissions Contact Mr. Steve Seidler, Director of Admissions, Pillsbury Baptist Bible College, 315 South Grove Avenue, Owatonna, MN 55060-3097. *Phone:* 507-451-2710 Ext. 279. *Toll-free phone:* 800-747-4557. *Fax:* 507-451-6459. *E-mail:* pbbc@pillsbury.edu.

Rochester Community and Technical College
Rochester, Minnesota

- **State-supported** primarily 2-year, founded 1915, part of Minnesota State Colleges and Universities System
- **Calendar** semesters
- **Degrees** certificates, diplomas, associate, and bachelor's (also offers 13 programs that lead to a bachelor's degree with Winona State University or University of Minnesota)
- **Small-town** 160-acre campus
- **Endowment** $437,000
- **Coed**
- **Noncompetitive** entrance level

Student Life *Campus security:* student patrols, late-night transport/escort service.

Athletics Member NJCAA.

Costs (2003–04) *Tuition:* state resident $2823 full-time, $118 per credit part-time; nonresident $5257 full-time, $219 per credit part-time.

Financial Aid Of all full-time matriculated undergraduates who enrolled in 2001, 500 Federal Work-Study jobs (averaging $3000). 300 state and other part-time jobs (averaging $3000).

Applying *Options:* early admission. *Application fee:* $20. *Required:* high school transcript.

Admissions Contact Mr. Troy Tynsky, Director of Admissions, Rochester Community and Technical College, 851 30th Avenue, SE, Rochester, MN 55904-4999. *Phone:* 507-280-3509. *Fax:* 507-285-7496.

St. Cloud State University
St. Cloud, Minnesota

- **State-supported** comprehensive, founded 1869, part of Minnesota State Colleges and Universities System
- **Calendar** semesters
- **Degrees** certificates, diplomas, associate, bachelor's, master's, postbachelor's, and first professional certificates
- **Suburban** 922-acre campus with easy access to Minneapolis–St. Paul
- **Endowment** $13.6 million
- **Coed,** 14,483 undergraduate students, 81% full-time, 55% women, 45% men
- **Moderately difficult** entrance level, 76% of applicants were admitted

Undergraduates 11,790 full-time, 2,693 part-time. Students come from 50 states and territories, 85 other countries, 9% are from out of state, 1% African American, 2% Asian American or Pacific Islander, 0.6% Hispanic American, 0.6% Native American, 5% international, 8% transferred in, 21% live on campus. *Retention:* 72% of 2002 full-time freshmen returned.

Freshmen *Admission:* 6,011 applied, 4,581 admitted, 2,298 enrolled. *Test scores:* ACT scores over 18: 89%; ACT scores over 24: 29%; ACT scores over 30: 2%.

Faculty *Total:* 793, 79% full-time, 69% with terminal degrees. *Student/faculty ratio:* 19:1.

Majors Accounting; acting; advertising; airline pilot and flight crew; air traffic control; American studies; anthropology; applied art; art; art history, criticism and conservation; art teacher education; atmospheric sciences and meteorology; audiology and speech-language pathology; aviation/airway management; behavioral sciences; biology/biological sciences; biology/biotechnology laboratory technician; biomedical sciences; botany/plant biology; broadcast journalism; business administration and management; ceramic arts and ceramics; chemistry; child development; city/urban, community and regional planning; clinical laboratory science/medical technology; communication disorders; communication disorders sciences and services related; comparative literature; computer engineering; computer science; counselor education/school counseling and guidance; creative writing; criminal justice/law enforcement administration; criminology; design and applied arts related; dramatic/theatre arts; dramatic/theatre arts and stagecraft related; drawing; ecology; economics; education; educational/instructional media design; educational leadership and administration; education (K-12); education (specific levels and methods) related; electrical, electronic and communications engineering technology; electrical, electronics and communications engineering; elementary education; engineering; engineering technologies related; engineering technology; English; environmental biology; film/cinema studies; finance; fine/studio arts; French; geography; geology/earth science; German; gerontology; health/medical preparatory programs related; health services/allied health/health sciences; health teacher education; history; human resources management; industrial arts; industrial engineering; information science/studies; insurance; interdisciplinary studies; international business/trade/commerce; international relations and affairs; jazz/jazz studies; journalism; kindergarten/preschool education; kinesiology and exercise science; Latin American studies; liberal arts and sciences/liberal studies; library science; linguistics; marketing/marketing management; mass communication/media; mathematics; mechanical engineering; medical microbiology and bacteriology; mental health/rehabilitation; middle school education; multi-/interdisciplinary studies related; music; music history, literature, and theory; music pedagogy; music performance; music teacher education; music theory and composition; natural sciences; nuclear medical technology; nursing (registered nurse training); optometric technician; painting; philosophy; physical education teaching and coaching; physical sciences; physical therapy; physics; piano and organ; political science and government; pre-dentistry studies; pre-law studies; pre-medical studies; pre-pharmacy studies; pre-veterinary studies; printmaking; psychoanalysis and psychotherapy; psychology; public administration; public policy analysis; public relations/image management; radio and television; reading teacher education; real estate; sales, distribution and marketing; science teacher education; sculpture; secondary education; social sciences; social work; sociology; Spanish; special education; speech and rhetoric; speech-language pathology; speech/theater education; speech therapy; statistics; substance abuse/addiction counseling; technology/industrial arts teacher education; theatre/theatre arts management; therapeutic recreation; tourism and travel services management; tourism promotion; urban studies/affairs; violin, viola, guitar and other stringed instruments; visual and performing arts related; voice and opera; wildlife biology.

Academic Programs *Special study options:* academic remediation for entering students, accelerated degree program, adult/continuing education programs,

advanced placement credit, distance learning, double majors, English as a second language, honors programs, independent study, internships, off-campus study, part-time degree program, services for LD students, student-designed majors, study abroad, summer session for credit. *ROTC:* Army (b).

Library James W. Miller Learning Resources Center with 560,251 titles, 1,487 serial subscriptions, 33,900 audiovisual materials, an OPAC, a Web page.

Computers on Campus 1244 computers available on campus for general student use. A campuswide network can be accessed from student residence rooms and from off campus. Internet access, online (class) registration, at least one staffed computer lab available. Computer purchase or lease plan available.

Student Life *Housing options:* coed. Campus housing is university owned. Freshman applicants given priority for college housing. *Activities and organizations:* drama/theater group, student-run newspaper, radio and television station, choral group, national fraternities, national sororities. *Campus security:* 24-hour emergency response devices and patrols, late-night transport/escort service. *Student services:* health clinic, personal/psychological counseling, women's center.

Athletics Member NCAA. All Division II except men's and women's ice hockey (Division I). *Intercollegiate sports:* baseball M(s), basketball M(s)/W(s), bowling M(c)/W(c), crew M(c)/W(c), cross-country running M(s)/W, fencing M(c)/W(c), football M(s), golf M/W(s), ice hockey M(s)/W(s), rugby M(c)/W(c), skiing (cross-country) M(c)/W(s), skiing (downhill) M(c)/W(c), soccer M(c)/W(s), softball W(s), swimming M(s)/W(s), tennis M(s)/W(s), track and field M(s)/W(s), volleyball M(c)/W(s), wrestling M(s). *Intramural sports:* badminton M/W, baseball M, basketball M/W, bowling M/W, crew M/W, field hockey M/W, football M/W, ice hockey M/W, lacrosse M/W, racquetball M/W, rugby W, sailing M/W, soccer M/W, softball W, squash M/W, swimming M/W, tennis M/W, volleyball M/W, water polo M/W, weight lifting M/W, wrestling M.

Standardized Tests *Required:* SAT I or ACT (for admission).

Costs (2003–04) *Tuition:* state resident $3980 full-time, $133 per credit part-time; nonresident $8639 full-time, $288 per credit part-time. Full-time tuition and fees vary according to course load and reciprocity agreements. Part-time tuition and fees vary according to course load and reciprocity agreements. *Required fees:* $570 full-time, $24 per credit part-time. *Room and board:* $3812; room only: $2548. Room and board charges vary according to board plan and housing facility. *Payment plan:* installment. *Waivers:* senior citizens and employees or children of employees.

Financial Aid Of all full-time matriculated undergraduates who enrolled in 2003, 7,378 applied for aid, 5,181 were judged to have need, 4,910 had their need fully met. 578 Federal Work-Study jobs (averaging $2452). 524 state and other part-time jobs (averaging $2671). In 2003, 2191 non-need-based awards were made. *Average percent of need met:* 96%. *Average financial aid package:* $6590. *Average need-based loan:* $2841. *Average need-based gift aid:* $1937. *Average non-need-based aid:* $478. *Average indebtedness upon graduation:* $17,112.

Applying *Options:* electronic application, early admission, deferred entrance. *Application fee:* $20. *Required:* high school transcript. *Required for some:* letters of recommendation. *Application deadlines:* 6/1 (freshmen), 7/11 (transfers). *Notification:* continuous (freshmen), continuous (transfers).

Admissions Contact Pat Krueger, Associate Director of Admissions, St. Cloud State University, 115 AS Building, 720 4th Avenue South, St. Cloud, MN 56301-4498. *Phone:* 320-308-2244. *Toll-free phone:* 877-654-7278. *Fax:* 320-308-2243. *E-mail:* scsu4u@stcloudstate.edu.

SAINT JOHN'S UNIVERSITY
Collegeville, Minnesota

- **Independent Roman Catholic** comprehensive, founded 1857
- **Calendar** semesters
- **Degrees** bachelor's, master's, and first professional (coordinate with College of Saint Benedict for women)
- **Rural** 2400-acre campus with easy access to Minneapolis–St. Paul
- **Endowment** $91.1 million
- **Coed, primarily men,** 1,940 undergraduate students, 98% full-time, 100% men
- **Moderately difficult** entrance level, 89% of applicants were admitted

Undergraduates 1,896 full-time, 44 part-time. Students come from 34 states and territories, 25 other countries, 14% are from out of state, 0.5% African American, 2% Asian American or Pacific Islander, 1% Hispanic American, 0.4% Native American, 3% international, 2% transferred in, 82% live on campus. *Retention:* 90% of 2002 full-time freshmen returned.

Freshmen *Admission:* 490 enrolled. *Average high school GPA:* 3.49. *Test scores:* SAT verbal scores over 500: 90%; SAT math scores over 500: 90%; ACT scores over 18: 99%; SAT verbal scores over 600: 45%; SAT math scores over 600: 53%; ACT scores over 24: 64%; SAT verbal scores over 700: 5%; SAT math scores over 700: 10%; ACT scores over 30: 14%.

Faculty *Total:* 167, 89% full-time, 83% with terminal degrees. *Student/faculty ratio:* 13:1.

Majors Accounting; art; art history, criticism and conservation; art teacher education; biochemistry; biology/biological sciences; business administration and management; chemistry; classics and languages, literatures and linguistics; computer science; dietetics; dramatic/theatre arts; economics; education; elementary education; English; environmental studies; fine/studio arts; foods, nutrition, and wellness; forestry; French; German; history; humanities; mathematics; mathematics and computer science; music; music teacher education; natural sciences; nursing (registered nurse training); occupational therapy; peace studies and conflict resolution; philosophy; physical therapy; physics; political science and government; pre-dentistry studies; pre-law studies; pre-medical studies; pre-pharmacy studies; pre-theology/pre-ministerial studies; pre-veterinary studies; psychology; religious education; secondary education; social sciences; social work; sociology; Spanish; speech and rhetoric; theology.

Academic Programs *Special study options:* accelerated degree program, advanced placement credit, double majors, English as a second language, honors programs, independent study, internships, off-campus study, services for LD students, student-designed majors, study abroad. *ROTC:* Army (b). *Unusual degree programs:* 3-2 engineering with University of Minnesota, Twin Cities Campus.

Library Alcuin Library plus 2 others with 805,376 titles, 5,735 serial subscriptions, 22,452 audiovisual materials, an OPAC, a Web page.

Computers on Campus 541 computers available on campus for general student use. A campuswide network can be accessed from student residence rooms and from off campus. Internet access, online (class) registration, at least one staffed computer lab available.

Student Life *Housing:* on-campus residence required through sophomore year. *Options:* men-only. Campus housing is university owned. Freshman campus housing is guaranteed. *Activities and organizations:* drama/theater group, student-run newspaper, radio station, choral group, Volunteers in Service to Others, Joint Events Council, Cultural Affairs Board, Students in Free Enterprise, ultimate frisbee. *Campus security:* 24-hour emergency response devices and patrols, late-night transport/escort service, well-lit pathways, 911 center on campus, closed circuit TV monitors. *Student services:* health clinic, personal/psychological counseling.

Athletics Member NCAA. All Division III. *Intercollegiate sports:* baseball M, basketball M, crew M(c), cross-country running M, football M, golf M, ice hockey M, lacrosse M(c), riflery M(c), rugby M(c), skiing (cross-country) M, soccer M, swimming M, tennis M, track and field M, volleyball M(c), water polo M(c), wrestling M. *Intramural sports:* basketball M, bowling M, fencing M(c), skiing (cross-country) M(c), skiing (downhill) M(c), soccer M, softball M, ultimate Frisbee M, volleyball M.

Standardized Tests *Required:* SAT I or ACT (for admission).

Costs (2003–04) *Comprehensive fee:* $26,473 includes full-time tuition ($20,335), mandatory fees ($350), and room and board ($5788). Part-time tuition: $847 per credit. Part-time tuition and fees vary according to course load. *Required fees:* $175 per term part-time. *College room only:* $2900. Room and board charges vary according to board plan and housing facility. *Payment plans:* tuition prepayment, installment. *Waivers:* employees or children of employees.

Financial Aid Of all full-time matriculated undergraduates who enrolled in 2003, 1,495 applied for aid, 1,160 were judged to have need, 649 had their need fully met. 308 Federal Work-Study jobs (averaging $2173). 805 state and other part-time jobs (averaging $2138). In 2003, 532 non-need-based awards were made. *Average percent of need met:* 86%. *Average financial aid package:* $17,585. *Average need-based loan:* $4547. *Average need-based gift aid:* $8242. *Average non-need-based aid:* $5849. *Average indebtedness upon graduation:* $21,598.

Applying *Options:* common application, electronic application, early admission, early action, deferred entrance. *Application fee:* $30. *Required:* essay or personal statement, high school transcript, 1 letter of recommendation. *Recommended:* minimum 3.0 GPA, interview. *Application deadline:* 1/15 (freshmen), rolling (transfers). *Notification:* continuous until 1/15 (freshmen), 12/20 (early action), continuous (transfers).

Admissions Contact Ms. Renee Miller, Director of Admission, Saint John's University, PO Box 7155, Collegeville, MN 56321-7155. *Phone:* 320-363-2196. *Toll-free phone:* 800-544-1489. *Fax:* 320-363-2750. *E-mail:* admissions@csbsju.edu.

SAINT MARY'S UNIVERSITY OF MINNESOTA
Winona, Minnesota

- **Independent Roman Catholic** comprehensive, founded 1912
- **Calendar** semesters
- **Degrees** certificates, diplomas, bachelor's, master's, doctoral, post-master's, and postbachelor's certificates

Saint Mary's University of Minnesota (continued)
- **Small-town** 350-acre campus
- **Endowment** $24.5 million
- **Coed,** 1,704 undergraduate students, 78% full-time, 55% women, 45% men
- **Moderately difficult** entrance level, 75% of applicants were admitted

Undergraduates 1,336 full-time, 368 part-time. Students come from 25 states and territories, 39% are from out of state, 3% African American, 2% Asian American or Pacific Islander, 2% Hispanic American, 0.5% Native American, 0.6% international, 5% transferred in, 78% live on campus. *Retention:* 75% of 2002 full-time freshmen returned.

Freshmen *Admission:* 1,312 applied, 981 admitted, 369 enrolled. *Average high school GPA:* 3.12. *Test scores:* SAT verbal scores over 500: 75%; SAT math scores over 500: 70%; ACT scores over 18: 91%; SAT verbal scores over 600: 27%; SAT math scores over 600: 29%; ACT scores over 24: 41%; SAT verbal scores over 700: 5%; SAT math scores over 700: 2%; ACT scores over 30: 4%.

Faculty *Total:* 553, 20% full-time, 69% with terminal degrees. *Student/faculty ratio:* 13:1.

Majors Accounting; American literature; atomic/molecular physics; biological and biomedical sciences related; biology/biological sciences; biophysics; business administration and management; business, management, and marketing related; chemistry; chemistry teacher education; clinical laboratory science/medical technology; commercial and advertising art; computer engineering; computer science; criminal justice/law enforcement administration; criminal justice/police science; cytotechnology; dramatic/theatre arts; e-commerce; elementary education; engineering physics; English; English language and literature related; English/language arts teacher education; fine/studio arts; foreign languages and literatures; French; French language teacher education; history; history related; human resources management; human services; industrial technology; information science/studies; international business/trade/commerce; marketing/marketing management; mathematics; mathematics and computer science; mathematics teacher education; music; music management and merchandising; music performance; music related; music teacher education; nuclear medical technology; philosophy; physical therapy; physics teacher education; political science and government; psychology; public relations/image management; publishing; religious education; science teacher education; social sciences; social sciences related; social science teacher education; sociology; Spanish; Spanish language teacher education; theology; youth ministry.

Academic Programs *Special study options:* academic remediation for entering students, accelerated degree program, adult/continuing education programs, advanced placement credit, double majors, English as a second language, honors programs, independent study, internships, off-campus study, part-time degree program, services for LD students, student-designed majors, study abroad, summer session for credit.

Library Fitzgerald Library with 130,944 titles, 708 serial subscriptions, 8,281 audiovisual materials, an OPAC, a Web page.

Computers on Campus 356 computers available on campus for general student use. A campuswide network can be accessed from student residence rooms and from off campus. Internet access, online (class) registration, at least one staffed computer lab available.

Student Life *Housing:* on-campus residence required through sophomore year. *Options:* coed, men-only, women-only, disabled students. Campus housing is university owned. Freshman campus housing is guaranteed. *Activities and organizations:* drama/theater group, student-run newspaper, radio station, choral group, Student Activity Committee, Habitat for Humanity, Volunteers in Service to Others, Serving Others United in Love (Soul), concert choir/chamber singers, national fraternities, national sororities. *Campus security:* 24-hour emergency response devices and patrols, late-night transport/escort service, controlled dormitory access. *Student services:* health clinic, personal/psychological counseling, women's center.

Athletics Member NCAA. All Division III. *Intercollegiate sports:* baseball M, basketball M/W, cross-country running M/W, golf M/W, ice hockey M/W, soccer M/W, softball W, swimming M/W, tennis M/W, track and field M/W, volleyball W. *Intramural sports:* basketball M/W, cheerleading W(c), field hockey M/W, football M/W, ice hockey M, lacrosse M(c)/W(c), rugby M(c)/W(c), skiing (downhill) M(c)/W(c), soccer M/W, softball M/W, tennis M/W, ultimate Frisbee M/W, volleyball W, water polo M(c)/W(c).

Standardized Tests *Required:* SAT I or ACT (for admission).

Costs (2004–05) *Comprehensive fee:* $23,375 includes full-time tuition ($17,480), mandatory fees ($445), and room and board ($5450). Full-time tuition and fees vary according to course load and program. Part-time tuition: $580 per credit. Part-time tuition and fees vary according to course load and program. *College room only:* $3050. Room and board charges vary according to housing facility. *Payment plan:* installment. *Waivers:* employees or children of employees.

Financial Aid Of all full-time matriculated undergraduates who enrolled in 2003, 1,103 applied for aid, 811 were judged to have need, 559 had their need fully met. 219 Federal Work-Study jobs (averaging $1339). 396 state and other part-time jobs (averaging $1377). In 2003, 310 non-need-based awards were made. *Average percent of need met:* 73%. *Average financial aid package:* $13,719. *Average need-based loan:* $4589. *Average need-based gift aid:* $5804. *Average non-need-based aid:* $4920. *Average indebtedness upon graduation:* $21,915.

Applying *Options:* common application, electronic application, early admission, deferred entrance. *Application fee:* $25. *Required:* essay or personal statement, high school transcript, minimum 2.5 GPA. *Required for some:* interview. *Recommended:* 2 letters of recommendation. *Application deadline:* 5/1 (freshmen), rolling (transfers). *Notification:* continuous (freshmen), continuous (transfers).

Admissions Contact Mr. Anthony M. Piscitiello, Vice President for Admission, Saint Mary's University of Minnesota, Admissions, 700 Terrace Heights, Winona, MN 55987-1399. *Phone:* 507 457-1700. *Toll-free phone:* 800-635-5987. *Fax:* 507-457-1722. *E-mail:* admissions@smumn.edu.

■ *See page 2318 for a narrative description.*

ST. OLAF COLLEGE
Northfield, Minnesota

- **Independent Lutheran** 4-year, founded 1874
- **Calendar** 4-1-4
- **Degree** bachelor's
- **Small-town** 300-acre campus with easy access to Minneapolis-St. Paul
- **Endowment** $151.3 million
- **Coed,** 2,994 undergraduate students, 98% full-time, 59% women, 41% men
- **Very difficult** entrance level, 75% of applicants were admitted

Undergraduates 2,929 full-time, 65 part-time. Students come from 49 states and territories, 22 other countries, 45% are from out of state, 1% African American, 4% Asian American or Pacific Islander, 2% Hispanic American, 0.2% Native American, 1% international, 1% transferred in, 96% live on campus. *Retention:* 92% of 2002 full-time freshmen returned.

Freshmen *Admission:* 2,517 applied, 1,894 admitted, 720 enrolled. *Average high school GPA:* 3.64. *Test scores:* SAT verbal scores over 500: 95%; SAT math scores over 500: 95%; ACT scores over 18: 98%; SAT verbal scores over 600: 70%; SAT math scores over 600: 72%; ACT scores over 24: 85%; SAT verbal scores over 700: 26%; SAT math scores over 700: 21%; ACT scores over 30: 28%.

Faculty *Total:* 334, 62% full-time, 76% with terminal degrees. *Student/faculty ratio:* 12:1.

Majors American studies; ancient/classical Greek; ancient studies; art; art history, criticism and conservation; Asian studies; biology/biological sciences; chemistry; classics and languages, literatures and linguistics; computer science; cultural studies; dance; dramatic/theatre arts; economics; English; environmental studies; ethnic, cultural minority, and gender studies related; French; German; Hispanic-American, Puerto Rican, and Mexican-American/Chicano studies; history; human development and family studies; kinesiology and exercise science; Latin; Latin American studies; liberal arts and sciences/liberal studies; mathematics; multi-/interdisciplinary studies related; music; music performance; music related; music teacher education; music theory and composition; nursing (registered nurse training); philosophy; physics; political science and government; psychology; religious studies; Russian; Russian studies; Scandinavian languages; social studies teacher education; social work; sociology; Spanish; visual and performing arts; women's studies.

Academic Programs *Special study options:* advanced placement credit, double majors, independent study, internships, off-campus study, part-time degree program, services for LD students, student-designed majors, study abroad, summer session for credit.

Library Rolvaag Memorial Library plus 3 others with 654,950 titles, 1,616 serial subscriptions, 16,194 audiovisual materials, an OPAC, a Web page.

Computers on Campus 805 computers available on campus for general student use. A campuswide network can be accessed from student residence rooms. Internet access, at least one staffed computer lab available.

Student Life *Housing:* on-campus residence required through senior year. *Options:* coed, disabled students. Campus housing is university owned. Freshman campus housing is guaranteed. *Activities and organizations:* drama/theater group, student-run newspaper, radio station, choral group, Student Government Association, Alpha Phi Omega, Habitat for Humanity, College Democrats, College Republicans. *Campus security:* 24-hour emergency response devices and patrols, late-night transport/escort service, controlled dormitory access, lighted pathways and sidewalks. *Student services:* health clinic, personal/psychological counseling.

Athletics Member NCAA. All Division III. *Intercollegiate sports:* baseball M, basketball M/W, cross-country running M/W, football M, golf M/W, ice hockey M/W, skiing (cross-country) M/W, skiing (downhill) M/W, soccer M/W, softball W, swimming M/W, tennis M/W, track and field M/W, volleyball W, wrestling M. *Intramural sports:* badminton M/W, basketball M/W, football M/W, lacrosse

M(c)/W(c), racquetball M/W, skiing (cross-country) M/W, skiing (downhill) M/W, soccer M/W, softball M/W, swimming M/W, table tennis M/W, tennis M/W, ultimate Frisbee M/W, volleyball M/W, water polo M/W.

Standardized Tests *Required:* SAT I or ACT (for admission).

Costs (2004–05) *Comprehensive fee:* $30,950 includes full-time tuition ($25,150) and room and board ($5800). Part-time tuition: $785 per credit hour. *College room only:* $2750. Room and board charges vary according to board plan. *Payment plans:* tuition prepayment, installment. *Waivers:* adult students, senior citizens, and employees or children of employees.

Financial Aid Of all full-time matriculated undergraduates who enrolled in 2003, 2,094 applied for aid, 1,843 were judged to have need, 1,843 had their need fully met. 1,223 Federal Work-Study jobs (averaging $1600). In 2003, 565 non-need-based awards were made. *Average percent of need met:* 100%. *Average financial aid package:* $18,172. *Average need-based loan:* $4707. *Average need-based gift aid:* $12,210. *Average non-need-based aid:* $5717. *Average indebtedness upon graduation:* $18,024.

Applying *Options:* common application, electronic application, early decision, early action, deferred entrance. *Application fee:* $35. *Required:* essay or personal statement, high school transcript, 2 letters of recommendation. *Recommended:* interview. *Application deadline:* rolling (freshmen). *Early decision:* 11/15. *Notification:* continuous (freshmen), 12/5 (early decision), 1/15 (early action), continuous (transfers).

Admissions Contact Mr. Jeff McLaughlin, Director of Admissions, St. Olaf College, 1520 St. Olaf Avenue, Northfield, MN 55057. *Phone:* 507-646-3025. *Toll-free phone:* 800-800-3025. *Fax:* 507-646-3832. *E-mail:* admiss@stolaf.edu.

SOUTHWEST MINNESOTA STATE UNIVERSITY

Marshall, Minnesota

- **State-supported** comprehensive, founded 1963, part of Minnesota State Colleges and Universities System
- **Calendar** semesters
- **Degrees** associate, bachelor's, and master's
- **Small-town** 216-acre campus
- **Endowment** $2.9 million
- **Coed**
- **Minimally difficult** entrance level

Faculty *Student/faculty ratio:* 18:1.

Student Life *Campus security:* 24-hour emergency response devices and patrols, student patrols, late-night transport/escort service.

Athletics Member NCAA. All Division II.

Standardized Tests *Required:* SAT I or ACT (for admission). *Recommended:* SAT I and SAT II or ACT (for admission).

Costs (2003–04) *Tuition:* state resident $3945 full-time; nonresident $3945 full-time. *Required fees:* $670 full-time. *Room and board:* $4491.

Financial Aid Of all full-time matriculated undergraduates who enrolled in 2003, 1,788 applied for aid, 1,425 were judged to have need, 637 had their need fully met. In 2003, 282. *Average percent of need met:* 68. *Average financial aid package:* $5926. *Average need-based loan:* $3231. *Average need-based gift aid:* $3178. *Average non-need-based aid:* $1319. *Average indebtedness upon graduation:* $14,420.

Applying *Options:* common application, electronic application, early admission, deferred entrance. *Application fee:* $20. *Required:* essay or personal statement, high school transcript, interview.

Admissions Contact Richard Shearer, Director of Enrollment Services, Southwest Minnesota State University, 1501 State Street, Marshall, MN 56258-1598. *Phone:* 507-537-6286. *Toll-free phone:* 800-642-0684. *Fax:* 507-537-7154. *E-mail:* shearerr@southwest.msus.edu.

UNIVERSITY OF MINNESOTA, CROOKSTON

Crookston, Minnesota

- **State-supported** 4-year, founded 1966, part of University of Minnesota System
- **Calendar** semesters
- **Degrees** certificates, associate, and bachelor's
- **Rural** 95-acre campus
- **Endowment** $1.5 million
- **Coed,** 2,320 undergraduate students, 47% full-time, 52% women, 48% men
- **Moderately difficult** entrance level, 89% of applicants were admitted

Undergraduates 1,084 full-time, 1,236 part-time. Students come from 38 states and territories, 13 other countries, 28% are from out of state, 3% African American, 1% Asian American or Pacific Islander, 2% Hispanic American, 0.8% Native American, 3% international, 7% transferred in. *Retention:* 67% of 2002 full-time freshmen returned.

Freshmen *Admission:* 487 applied, 431 admitted, 247 enrolled. *Average high school GPA:* 2.95.

Faculty *Total:* 100, 55% full-time, 42% with terminal degrees. *Student/faculty ratio:* 15:1.

Majors Accounting; agricultural business and management; agricultural power machinery operation; agricultural teacher education; agriculture; agronomy and crop science; animal sciences; aviation/airway management; avionics maintenance technology; business administration and management; dietetics; early childhood education; environmental studies; equestrian studies; farm and ranch management; health/health care administration; health services/allied health/health sciences; horticultural science; hospitality administration; hotel/motel administration; information science/studies; interdisciplinary studies; natural resources/conservation; natural resources management and policy; soil conservation; special products marketing; sport and fitness administration; system administration; system, networking, and LAN/wan management; turf and turfgrass management; water, wetlands, and marine resources management; wildlife and wildlands science and management.

Academic Programs *Special study options:* academic remediation for entering students, adult/continuing education programs, advanced placement credit, distance learning, double majors, independent study, internships, part-time degree program, services for LD students, study abroad, summer session for credit. *ROTC:* Air Force (c).

Library 30,000 titles, 700 serial subscriptions.

Computers on Campus 900 computers available on campus for general student use. A campuswide network can be accessed from student residence rooms and from off campus that provide access to e-mail. Internet access, at least one staffed computer lab available.

Student Life *Housing options:* coed. Campus housing is university owned. Freshman applicants given priority for college housing. *Activities and organizations:* drama/theater group, choral group, Students in Free Enterprise, Natural Resources Club, Horseman's Association, Multicultural and International Club, Ag-Arama Planning Club. *Campus security:* student patrols, controlled dormitory access. *Student services:* health clinic, personal/psychological counseling.

Athletics Member NCAA. All Division II. *Intercollegiate sports:* baseball M(s), basketball M(s)/W(s), football M(s), golf M(s)/W, ice hockey M(s), soccer W(s), softball W(s), tennis W(s), volleyball W(s). *Intramural sports:* basketball M/W, football M, racquetball M/W, softball M/W, table tennis M, tennis M/W, volleyball M/W.

Standardized Tests *Required:* ACT (for admission).

Costs (2003–04) *Tuition:* state resident $5471 full-time, $162 per credit part-time; nonresident $5471 full-time, $162 per credit part-time. Full-time tuition and fees vary according to reciprocity agreements. Part-time tuition and fees vary according to course load. No tuition increase for student's term of enrollment. *Required fees:* $1309 full-time. *Room and board:* $4684. Room and board charges vary according to board plan and housing facility. *Payment plan:* installment. *Waivers:* senior citizens.

Financial Aid Of all full-time matriculated undergraduates who enrolled in 2001, 821 applied for aid, 681 were judged to have need, 309 had their need fully met. In 2001, 51 non-need-based awards were made. *Average percent of need met:* 87%. *Average financial aid package:* $8069. *Average need-based loan:* $4163. *Average need-based gift aid:* $4453. *Average non-need-based aid:* $1982.

Applying *Options:* common application, electronic application, deferred entrance. *Application fee:* $25. *Required:* high school transcript. *Application deadlines:* 7/15 (freshmen), 7/15 (transfers). *Notification:* 9/1 (freshmen).

Admissions Contact Mr. Russell L. Kreager, Director of Admissions, University of Minnesota, Crookston, 2900 University Avenue, 170 Owen Hall, Crookston, MN 56716-5001. *Phone:* 218-281-8569. *Toll-free phone:* 800-862-6466. *Fax:* 218-281-8575. *E-mail:* info@mail.crk.umn.edu.

■ *See page 2652 for a narrative description.*

UNIVERSITY OF MINNESOTA, DULUTH

Duluth, Minnesota

- **State-supported** comprehensive, founded 1947, part of University of Minnesota System
- **Calendar** semesters
- **Degrees** bachelor's, master's, and first professional
- **Suburban** 250-acre campus
- **Endowment** $38.4 million
- **Coed,** 9,288 undergraduate students, 95% full-time, 49% women, 51% men
- **Moderately difficult** entrance level, 74% of applicants were admitted

Undergraduates 8,860 full-time, 428 part-time. Students come from 36 states and territories, 32 other countries, 12% are from out of state, 1% African American, 3% Asian American or Pacific Islander, 1% Hispanic American, 1%

University of Minnesota, Duluth (continued)
Native American, 2% international, 4% transferred in, 38% live on campus. *Retention:* 74% of 2002 full-time freshmen returned.

Freshmen *Admission:* 6,900 applied, 5,133 admitted, 2,194 enrolled. *Average high school GPA:* 3.22. *Test scores:* ACT scores over 18: 84%; ACT scores over 24: 30%; ACT scores over 30: 3%.

Faculty *Total:* 467, 78% full-time, 76% with terminal degrees. *Student/faculty ratio:* 22:1.

Majors Accounting; actuarial science; American Indian/Native American studies; anthropology; art; art history, criticism and conservation; art teacher education; audiology and speech-language pathology; biochemistry; biology/biological sciences; business administration and management; cell biology and histology; chemical engineering; chemistry; commercial and advertising art; computer engineering; computer science; criminology; dramatic/theatre arts; economics; education; electrical, electronics and communications engineering; elementary education; English; environmental studies; finance; fine/studio arts; fish/game management; French language teacher education; geography; geology/earth science; German language teacher education; health teacher education; history; human resources management; industrial engineering; interdisciplinary studies; international relations and affairs; jazz/jazz studies; kindergarten/preschool education; kinesiology and exercise science; marketing/marketing management; mathematics; mathematics teacher education; middle school education; molecular biology; music; music teacher education; parks, recreation and leisure; philosophy; physical education teaching and coaching; physics; piano and organ; political science and government; pre-dentistry studies; pre-law studies; pre-medical studies; pre-pharmacy studies; pre-veterinary studies; psychology; science teacher education; social studies teacher education; sociology; Spanish; Spanish language teacher education; special education; urban studies/affairs; women's studies.

Academic Programs *Special study options:* academic remediation for entering students, adult/continuing education programs, advanced placement credit, distance learning, double majors, English as a second language, honors programs, independent study, internships, off-campus study, part-time degree program, services for LD students, student-designed majors, study abroad, summer session for credit. *ROTC:* Air Force (b).

Library University of Minnesota Duluth Library with 709,145 titles, 4,500 serial subscriptions, 15,245 audiovisual materials, an OPAC, a Web page.

Computers on Campus 680 computers available on campus for general student use. A campuswide network can be accessed from student residence rooms and from off campus. Internet access, online (class) registration, at least one staffed computer lab available.

Student Life *Housing options:* coed, men-only, women-only. Campus housing is university owned. Freshman applicants given priority for college housing. *Activities and organizations:* drama/theater group, student-run newspaper, choral group, recreational sports, departmental clubs, outdoor recreation clubs, national fraternities, national sororities. *Campus security:* 24-hour emergency response devices and patrols, late-night transport/escort service. *Student services:* health clinic, personal/psychological counseling, women's center, legal services.

Athletics Member NCAA. All Division II except men's and women's ice hockey (Division I). *Intercollegiate sports:* baseball M(s), basketball M(s)/W(s), bowling M(c)/W(c), cheerleading W(c), cross-country running M(s)/W(s), football M(s), ice hockey M(s)/W, lacrosse M(c)/W(c), rugby M(c)/W(c), skiing (downhill) M(c)/W(c), soccer M(c)/W(s), softball W(s), tennis M(s)/W(s), track and field M(s)/W(s), volleyball M(c)/W(s), weight lifting M(c)/W(c). *Intramural sports:* basketball M/W, bowling M(c)/W(c), cross-country running M/W, field hockey M/W, football M/W, golf M/W, ice hockey M, riflery M/W, skiing (cross-country) M/W, skiing (downhill) M/W, soccer M/W, softball M/W, swimming M/W, tennis M/W, track and field M/W, volleyball M/W.

Standardized Tests *Required:* SAT I or ACT (for admission).

Costs (2003–04) *Tuition:* state resident $6047 full-time, $201 per credit part-time; nonresident $16,412 full-time, $547 per credit part-time. Full-time tuition and fees vary according to course load, degree level, program, and reciprocity agreements. Part-time tuition and fees vary according to course load, degree level, program, and reciprocity agreements. *Required fees:* $1323 full-time, $661 per term part-time. *Room and board:* $5100. *Payment plan:* installment. *Waivers:* children of alumni.

Financial Aid Of all full-time matriculated undergraduates who enrolled in 2003, 5,944 applied for aid, 4,463 were judged to have need, 3,593 had their need fully met. 243 Federal Work-Study jobs (averaging $1961). 185 state and other part-time jobs (averaging $2002). In 2003, 778 non-need-based awards were made. *Average percent of need met:* 52%. *Average financial aid package:* $7662. *Average need-based loan:* $3844. *Average need-based gift aid:* $5183. *Average non-need-based aid:* $2052. *Average indebtedness upon graduation:* $16,432.

Applying *Options:* electronic application. *Application fee:* $35. *Required:* high school transcript. *Application deadlines:* 2/1 (freshmen), 8/1 (transfers). *Notification:* continuous (freshmen), continuous (transfers).

Admissions Contact Ms. Beth Esselstrom, Director of Admissions, University of Minnesota, Duluth, 23 Solon Campus Center, 1117 University Drive, Duluth, MN 55812-3000. *Phone:* 218-726-7171. *Toll-free phone:* 800-232-1339. *Fax:* 218-726-7040. *E-mail:* umdadmis@d.umn.edu.

UNIVERSITY OF MINNESOTA, MORRIS
Morris, Minnesota

- **State-supported** 4-year, founded 1959, part of University of Minnesota System
- **Calendar** semesters
- **Degree** bachelor's
- **Small-town** 130-acre campus
- **Endowment** $5.3 million
- **Coed,** 1,861 undergraduate students, 93% full-time, 60% women, 40% men
- **Moderately difficult** entrance level, 83% of applicants were admitted

Undergraduates 1,727 full-time, 134 part-time. Students come from 31 states and territories, 18 other countries, 17% are from out of state, 3% African American, 3% Asian American or Pacific Islander, 2% Hispanic American, 7% Native American, 1% international, 5% transferred in, 51% live on campus. *Retention:* 83% of 2002 full-time freshmen returned.

Freshmen *Admission:* 1,117 applied, 922 admitted, 412 enrolled. *Test scores:* SAT verbal scores over 500: 87%; SAT math scores over 500: 80%; ACT scores over 18: 99%; SAT verbal scores over 600: 59%; SAT math scores over 600: 46%; ACT scores over 24: 60%; SAT verbal scores over 700: 14%; SAT math scores over 700: 6%; ACT scores over 30: 12%.

Faculty *Total:* 132, 94% with terminal degrees. *Student/faculty ratio:* 14:1.

Majors Anthropology; art history, criticism and conservation; biology/biological sciences; business administration and management; chemistry; computer science; dramatic/theatre arts; economics; education; education (K-12); elementary education; English; European studies; fine/studio arts; French; geology/earth science; German; history; human services; Latin American studies; liberal arts and sciences/liberal studies; management science; mathematics; music; philosophy; physical therapy; physics; political science and government; pre-dentistry studies; pre-law studies; pre-medical studies; pre-pharmacy studies; pre-veterinary studies; psychology; secondary education; social sciences; sociology; Spanish; speech and rhetoric; speech/theater education; statistics; women's studies.

Academic Programs *Special study options:* accelerated degree program, adult/continuing education programs, advanced placement credit, distance learning, double majors, English as a second language, external degree program, freshman honors college, honors programs, internships, off-campus study, part-time degree program, services for LD students, student-designed majors, study abroad, summer session for credit. *Unusual degree programs:* 3-2 engineering with University of Minnesota, Twin Cities Campus.

Library Rodney A. Briggs Library plus 1 other with 191,469 titles, 9,042 serial subscriptions, 2,140 audiovisual materials, an OPAC, a Web page.

Computers on Campus 133 computers available on campus for general student use. A campuswide network can be accessed from student residence rooms and from off campus. Internet access, online (class) registration, at least one staffed computer lab available.

Student Life *Housing options:* coed. Campus housing is university owned. Freshman campus housing is guaranteed. *Activities and organizations:* drama/theater group, student-run newspaper, radio and television station, choral group, student radio station, Inter-Varsity Christian Fellowship, jazz ensemble/concert choir, Big Friend, Little Friend, student newspaper. *Campus security:* 24-hour emergency response devices and patrols, late-night transport/escort service, controlled dormitory access. *Student services:* health clinic, personal/psychological counseling, women's center, legal services.

Athletics Member NCAA. All Division III. *Intercollegiate sports:* baseball M, basketball M/W, cross-country running W, football M, golf M/W, soccer W, softball W, swimming W, tennis M/W, track and field M/W, volleyball W. *Intramural sports:* baseball M, basketball M/W, bowling M/W, cheerleading M(c)/W(c), equestrian sports M(c)/W(c), fencing M(c)/W(c), football M/W, ice hockey M/W, racquetball M/W, rock climbing M(c)/W(c), rugby M(c)/W(c), skiing (cross-country) M/W, soccer M(c)/W(c), softball M/W, swimming M/W, table tennis M/W, ultimate Frisbee M(c)/W(c), volleyball M(c)/W(c).

Standardized Tests *Required:* SAT I or ACT (for admission).

Costs (2003–04) *Tuition:* state resident $6908 full-time, $230 per credit part-time; nonresident $6908 full-time, $230 per credit part-time. Full-time tuition and fees vary according to reciprocity agreements. Part-time tuition and fees vary according to course load and reciprocity agreements. *Required fees:* $1188 full-time. *Room and board:* $4800; room only: $2260. Room and board charges vary according to board plan and housing facility. *Payment plans:* installment, deferred payment.

Financial Aid Of all full-time matriculated undergraduates who enrolled in 2002, 1,418 applied for aid, 1,145 were judged to have need, 425 had their need

fully met. 610 Federal Work-Study jobs (averaging $710). 472 state and other part-time jobs (averaging $766). In 2002, 306 non-need-based awards were made. *Average percent of need met:* 81%. *Average financial aid package:* $9754. *Average need-based loan:* $5773. *Average need-based gift aid:* $5050. *Average non-need-based aid:* $2394. *Average indebtedness upon graduation:* $13,167.

Applying *Options:* electronic application, early admission, early action, deferred entrance. *Application fee:* $35. *Required:* essay or personal statement, high school transcript. *Required for some:* interview. *Recommended:* minimum 3.0 GPA. *Application deadlines:* 3/15 (freshmen), 5/1 (transfers). *Notification:* 4/1 (freshmen), 12/15 (early action), continuous (transfers).

Admissions Contact Dr. James Mootz, Associate Vice Chancellor for Enrollment, University of Minnesota, Morris, 600 East 4th Street, Morris, MN 56267-2199. *Phone:* 320-539-6035. *Toll-free phone:* 800-992-8863. *Fax:* 320-589-1673. *E-mail:* admissions@mrs.umn.edu.

University of Minnesota, Twin Cities Campus

Minneapolis, Minnesota

- **State-supported** university, founded 1851, part of University of Minnesota System
- **Calendar** semesters
- **Degrees** certificates, diplomas, bachelor's, master's, doctoral, first professional, post-master's, and postbachelor's certificates
- **Urban** 2000-acre campus
- **Coed,** 32,474 undergraduate students, 81% full-time, 53% women, 47% men
- **Moderately difficult** entrance level, 76% of applicants were admitted

Undergraduates 26,173 full-time, 6,301 part-time. Students come from 55 states and territories, 85 other countries, 26% are from out of state, 4% African American, 9% Asian American or Pacific Islander, 2% Hispanic American, 0.6% Native American, 2% international, 7% transferred in, 22% live on campus. *Retention:* 86% of 2002 full-time freshmen returned.

Freshmen *Admission:* 17,164 applied, 13,038 admitted, 5,186 enrolled. *Test scores:* SAT verbal scores over 500: 86%; SAT math scores over 500: 89%; ACT scores over 18: 95%; SAT verbal scores over 600: 56%; SAT math scores over 600: 61%; ACT scores over 24: 66%; SAT verbal scores over 700: 12%; SAT math scores over 700: 18%; ACT scores over 30: 13%.

Faculty *Total:* 3,079, 88% full-time, 95% with terminal degrees. *Student/faculty ratio:* 22:1.

Majors Accounting; actuarial science; aerospace, aeronautical and astronautical engineering; African-American/Black studies; African studies; agricultural/biological engineering and bioengineering; agricultural business and management; agricultural teacher education; agriculture; agronomy and crop science; American Indian/Native American studies; American studies; animal genetics; animal physiology; animal sciences; anthropology; architecture; art; art history, criticism and conservation; art teacher education; Asian studies (East); Asian studies (South); astronomy; astrophysics; audiology and speech-language pathology; biochemistry; biology/biological sciences; botany/plant biology; business teacher education; cell biology and histology; chemical engineering; chemistry; Chinese; civil engineering; clinical laboratory science/medical technology; clothing/textiles; commercial and advertising art; comparative literature; computer science; construction management; dance; dental hygiene; developmental and child psychology; dramatic/theatre arts; ecology; economics; education; electrical, electronics and communications engineering; elementary education; emergency medical technology (EMT paramedic); English; English/language arts teacher education; environmental studies; European studies; family and community services; family and consumer sciences/home economics teacher education; film/cinema studies; finance; fish/game management; foods, nutrition, and wellness; foreign language teacher education; forest/forest resources management; forestry; French; funeral service and mortuary science; geography; geological/geophysical engineering; geology/earth science; geophysics and seismology; German; health and physical education related; Hebrew; Hispanic-American, Puerto Rican, and Mexican-American/Chicano studies; history; industrial engineering; insurance; interior design; international business/trade/commerce; international relations and affairs; Italian; Japanese; Jewish/Judaic studies; journalism; kindergarten/preschool education; landscape architecture; Latin; Latin American studies; linguistics; management information systems; marketing/marketing management; mass communication/media; materials engineering; materials science; mathematics; mathematics teacher education; mechanical engineering; medical microbiology and bacteriology; modern Greek; music; music teacher education; music therapy; natural resources management and policy; Near and Middle Eastern studies; neuroscience; nursing (registered nurse training); occupational therapy; parks, recreation and leisure facilities management; philosophy; physical education teaching and coaching; physical therapy; physics; plant sciences; political science and government; Portuguese; pre-dentistry studies; pre-law studies; pre-medical studies; pre-veterinary studies; psychology; public health; religious studies; Russian; Russian studies; Scandinavian languages; science teacher education; social science teacher education; sociology; soil science and agronomy; Spanish; urban studies/affairs; women's studies; wood science and wood products/pulp and paper technology.

Academic Programs *Special study options:* academic remediation for entering students, accelerated degree program, adult/continuing education programs, advanced placement credit, cooperative education, distance learning, double majors, English as a second language, external degree program, freshman honors college, honors programs, independent study, internships, off-campus study, part-time degree program, services for LD students, student-designed majors, study abroad, summer session for credit. *ROTC:* Army (b), Navy (b), Air Force (b).

Library Wilson Library plus 17 others with 5.7 million titles, 45,000 serial subscriptions, 1.2 million audiovisual materials, an OPAC, a Web page.

Computers on Campus A campuswide network can be accessed from student residence rooms and from off campus that provide access to e-mail. At least one staffed computer lab available.

Student Life *Housing options:* coed, cooperative, disabled students. *Activities and organizations:* drama/theater group, student-run newspaper, radio and television station, choral group, marching band, sports clubs, student government, religious organizations, departmental/professional organizations, national fraternities, national sororities. *Campus security:* 24-hour emergency response devices and patrols, student patrols, late-night transport/escort service, controlled dormitory access, safety/security orientation, security lighting. *Student services:* health clinic, personal/psychological counseling, women's center, legal services.

Athletics Member NCAA. All Division I except football (Division I-A). *Intercollegiate sports:* baseball M(s), basketball M(s)/W(s), cross-country running M(s)/W(s), golf M(s)/W(s), gymnastics M(s)/W(s), ice hockey M(s)/W(s), soccer W(s), softball W(s), swimming M(s)/W(s), tennis M(s)/W(s), track and field M(s)/W(s), volleyball W(s), wrestling M(s). *Intramural sports:* baseball M/W, basketball M/W, bowling M/W, crew M/W, football M/W, golf M/W, ice hockey M/W, rugby M/W, skiing (cross-country) M/W, skiing (downhill) M/W, soccer M/W, softball M/W, tennis M/W, volleyball M/W, water polo M/W, wrestling M/W.

Standardized Tests *Required:* SAT I or ACT (for admission).

Costs (2003–04) *Tuition:* state resident $5962 full-time; nonresident $17,592 full-time. Full-time tuition and fees vary according to program. Part-time tuition and fees vary according to course load and program. No tuition increase for student's term of enrollment. *Required fees:* $1154 full-time. *Room and board:* $6044. Room and board charges vary according to board plan, housing facility, and location. *Payment plan:* installment.

Financial Aid Of all full-time matriculated undergraduates who enrolled in 2003, 16,775 applied for aid, 13,028 were judged to have need, 4,436 had their need fully met. In 2003, 2638 non-need-based awards were made. *Average percent of need met:* 76%. *Average financial aid package:* $9027. *Average need-based loan:* $5720. *Average need-based gift aid:* $6074. *Average non-need-based aid:* $4238.

Applying *Options:* electronic application, early admission, deferred entrance. *Application fee:* $35. *Required:* high school transcript. *Recommended:* minimum 2.0 GPA. *Application deadlines:* rolling (freshmen), 3/1 (transfers). *Notification:* continuous (freshmen), continuous (transfers).

Admissions Contact Ms. Patricia Jones Whyte, Associate Director of Admissions, University of Minnesota, Twin Cities Campus, 240 Williamson Hall, Minneapolis, MN 55455-0115. *Phone:* 612-625-2008. *Toll-free phone:* 800-752-1000. *Fax:* 612-626-1693. *E-mail:* admissions@tc.umn.edu.

University of St. Thomas

St. Paul, Minnesota

- **Independent Roman Catholic** university, founded 1885
- **Calendar** 4-1-4
- **Degrees** certificates, bachelor's, master's, doctoral, first professional, post-master's, and postbachelor's certificates
- **Urban** 78-acre campus with easy access to Minneapolis
- **Endowment** $258.8 million
- **Coed,** 5,236 undergraduate students, 88% full-time, 51% women, 49% men
- **Moderately difficult** entrance level, 87% of applicants were admitted

St. Thomas, a coeducational, Catholic liberal arts university with more than 11,000 undergraduate and graduate students—the largest independent university in Minnesota—has campuses in St. Paul and Minneapolis. St. Thomas offers more than 80 majors, including business administration, computer science, journalism, biology, engineering, and preprofessional programs. St. Thomas emphasizes values-centered, career-oriented education.

Undergraduates 4,623 full-time, 613 part-time. Students come from 44 states and territories, 36 other countries, 18% are from out of state, 2% African

University of St. Thomas (continued)
American, 5% Asian American or Pacific Islander, 2% Hispanic American, 0.6% Native American, 1% international, 5% transferred in, 43% live on campus. *Retention:* 85% of 2002 full-time freshmen returned.

Freshmen *Admission:* 2,979 applied, 2,583 admitted, 1,039 enrolled. *Average high school GPA:* 3.56. *Test scores:* SAT verbal scores over 500: 85%; SAT math scores over 500: 89%; ACT scores over 18: 99%; SAT verbal scores over 600: 38%; SAT math scores over 600: 43%; ACT scores over 24: 63%; SAT verbal scores over 700: 10%; SAT math scores over 700: 9%; ACT scores over 30: 9%.

Faculty *Total:* 800, 50% full-time, 60% with terminal degrees. *Student/faculty ratio:* 14:1.

Majors Accounting; actuarial science; ancient/classical Greek; art history, criticism and conservation; Asian studies (East); biochemistry; biology/biological sciences; biology teacher education; broadcast journalism; business administration and management; business administration, management and operations related; business/corporate communications; chemistry; chemistry teacher education; classics and classical languages related; classics and languages, literatures and linguistics; clinical/medical social work; communication/speech communication and rhetoric; computer and information sciences; creative writing; criminology; drama and dance teacher education; dramatic/theatre arts; econometrics and quantitative economics; economics; education (K-12); education (specific subject areas) related; electrical, electronics and communications engineering; elementary education; English; English/language arts teacher education; entrepreneurship; finance; foreign languages related; foreign language teacher education; French; geography; geology/earth science; German; health and physical education; health science; health teacher education; history; human resources management; interdisciplinary studies; international business/trade/commerce; international economics; international relations and affairs; Japanese; journalism; journalism related; Latin; legal professions and studies related; liberal arts and sciences and humanities related; marketing/marketing management; mathematics; mathematics teacher education; mechanical engineering; middle school education; multi-/interdisciplinary studies related; music; music teacher education; operations management; peace studies and conflict resolution; philosophy; physical education teaching and coaching; physics; physics teacher education; political science and government; psychology; psychology related; public administration; public health education and promotion; real estate; religious studies; Russian; Russian studies; science teacher education; social sciences; social studies teacher education; social work; sociology; Spanish; speech/theater education; women's studies.

Academic Programs *Special study options:* adult/continuing education programs, advanced placement credit, double majors, English as a second language, honors programs, independent study, internships, off-campus study, part-time degree program, services for LD students, student-designed majors, study abroad, summer session for credit. *ROTC:* Army (c), Navy (c), Air Force (b). *Unusual degree programs:* 3-2 engineering with University of Notre Dame; Washington University in St. Louis; University of Minnesota, Twin Cities Campus; Kettering University.

Library O'Shaughnessy-Frey Library plus 2 others with 440,023 titles, 4,168 serial subscriptions, 3,516 audiovisual materials, an OPAC, a Web page.

Computers on Campus 1249 computers available on campus for general student use. A campuswide network can be accessed from student residence rooms and from off campus. Internet access, online (class) registration, at least one staffed computer lab available.

Student Life *Housing options:* men-only, women-only, disabled students. Campus housing is university owned. *Activities and organizations:* drama/theater group, student-run newspaper, choral group. *Campus security:* 24-hour emergency response devices and patrols, late-night transport/escort service, controlled dormitory access. *Student services:* health clinic, personal/psychological counseling, women's center, legal services.

Athletics Member NCAA. All Division III. *Intercollegiate sports:* baseball M, basketball M/W, crew M(c)/W(c), cross-country running M/W, football M, golf M/W, ice hockey M/W, lacrosse M(c)/W(c), skiing (downhill) M(c)/W(c), soccer M/W, softball W, swimming M/W, tennis M/W, track and field M/W, volleyball W. *Intramural sports:* basketball M/W, racquetball M/W, soccer M/W, softball M/W, squash M/W, table tennis M/W, tennis M/W, volleyball M/W.

Standardized Tests *Required:* SAT I or ACT (for admission). *Recommended:* ACT (for admission).

Costs (2003–04) *Comprehensive fee:* $25,827 includes full-time tuition ($18,975), mandatory fees ($368), and room and board ($6484). Full-time tuition and fees vary according to course load. Part-time tuition and fees vary according to course load. *College room only:* $3774. Room and board charges vary according to board plan and housing facility. *Payment plans:* installment, deferred payment. *Waivers:* senior citizens and employees or children of employees.

Financial Aid Of all full-time matriculated undergraduates who enrolled in 2003, 3,175 applied for aid, 2,533 were judged to have need, 606 had their need fully met. 1,451 Federal Work-Study jobs (averaging $2461). 1,232 state and other part-time jobs (averaging $2388). In 2003, 514 non-need-based awards were made. *Average percent of need met:* 81%. *Average financial aid package:* $15,688. *Average need-based loan:* $3767. *Average need-based gift aid:* $8809. *Average non-need-based aid:* $6404. *Average indebtedness upon graduation:* $23,084.

Applying *Options:* electronic application, deferred entrance. *Required:* essay or personal statement, high school transcript. *Recommended:* letters of recommendation, interview. *Application deadlines:* rolling (freshmen), 8/1 (transfers). *Notification:* continuous (freshmen), continuous (transfers).

Admissions Contact Ms. Marla Friederichs, Associate Vice President of Enrollment Management, University of St. Thomas, 2115 Summit Avenue, Mail #32F-1, St. Paul, MN 55105-1096. *Phone:* 651-962-6150. *Toll-free phone:* 800-328-6819 Ext. 26150. *Fax:* 651-962-6160. *E-mail:* admissions@stthomas.edu.

■ *See page 2700 for a narrative description.*

WINONA STATE UNIVERSITY
Winona, Minnesota

- **State-supported** comprehensive, founded 1858, part of Minnesota State Colleges and Universities System
- **Calendar** semesters
- **Degrees** associate, bachelor's, master's, and post-master's certificates
- **Small-town** 40-acre campus
- **Endowment** $3.1 million
- **Coed,** 7,569 undergraduate students, 90% full-time, 63% women, 37% men
- **Moderately difficult** entrance level, 79% of applicants were admitted

Undergraduates 6,776 full-time, 793 part-time. Students come from 21 states and territories, 48 other countries, 34% are from out of state, 0.6% African American, 1% Asian American or Pacific Islander, 0.8% Hispanic American, 0.3% Native American, 4% international, 7% transferred in, 28% live on campus. *Retention:* 75% of 2002 full-time freshmen returned.

Freshmen *Admission:* 4,802 applied, 3,798 admitted, 1,552 enrolled. *Average high school GPA:* 3.30. *Test scores:* ACT scores over 18: 99%; ACT scores over 24: 59%; ACT scores over 30: 3%.

Faculty *Total:* 357, 88% full-time, 62% with terminal degrees. *Student/faculty ratio:* 19:1.

Majors Accounting; administrative assistant and secretarial science; advertising; airline pilot and flight crew; applied art; applied mathematics; art; art teacher education; athletic training; aviation/airway management; biological and physical sciences; biology/biological sciences; broadcast journalism; business administration and management; business/managerial economics; business teacher education; chemical engineering; chemistry; city/urban, community and regional planning; clinical laboratory science/medical technology; clinical/medical laboratory technology; commercial and advertising art; computer and information sciences; computer programming; computer science; consumer merchandising/retailing management; corrections; criminal justice/law enforcement administration; criminal justice/police science; cytotechnology; dramatic/theatre arts; drawing; ecology; economics; education; elementary education; engineering; English; environmental biology; finance; fine/studio arts; fish/game management; forestry; French; geology/earth science; German; gerontology; health/health care administration; health science; health teacher education; history; human resources management; information science/studies; international relations and affairs; Japanese; journalism; kindergarten/preschool education; kinesiology and exercise science; labor and industrial relations; legal assistant/paralegal; legal studies; liberal arts and sciences/liberal studies; management information systems; marketing/marketing management; mass communication/media; materials engineering; mathematics; mechanical engineering; middle school education; music; music management and merchandising; music teacher education; natural resources/conservation; natural sciences; nursing (registered nurse training); parks, recreation and leisure; parks, recreation and leisure facilities management; physical education teaching and coaching; physical sciences; physical therapy; physics; political science and government; polymer chemistry; polymer/plastics engineering; pre-dentistry studies; pre-engineering; pre-law studies; pre-medical studies; pre-veterinary studies; psychology; public administration; public health; public relations/image management; quality control technology; radio and television; reading teacher education; science teacher education; secondary education; social sciences; social work; sociology; Spanish; special education; speech and rhetoric; sport and fitness administration; statistics; telecommunications; therapeutic recreation; voice and opera; wildlife and wildlands science and management; wildlife biology; zoology/animal biology.

Academic Programs *Special study options:* academic remediation for entering students, accelerated degree program, adult/continuing education programs, advanced placement credit, distance learning, double majors, English as a second language, external degree program, honors programs, independent study, internships, off-campus study, part-time degree program, services for LD students, student-designed majors, study abroad, summer session for credit. *ROTC:* Army (c).

Library The Library with 243,500 titles, 1,950 serial subscriptions, an OPAC, a Web page.

Computers on Campus 1400 computers available on campus for general student use. A campuswide network can be accessed from student residence rooms and from off campus. Internet access, online (class) registration, at least one staffed computer lab available. Computer purchase or lease plan available.

Student Life *Housing options:* coed, men-only, women-only. Campus housing is university owned and leased by the school. Freshman campus housing is guaranteed. *Activities and organizations:* drama/theater group, student-run newspaper, radio station, choral group, marching band, University Program Activities Committee, Student Senate, Inter-Residence Hall Council, national fraternities, national sororities. *Campus security:* 24-hour emergency response devices and patrols, student patrols, late-night transport/escort service, controlled dormitory access, security cameras. *Student services:* health clinic, personal/psychological counseling, women's center, legal services.

Athletics Member NCAA. All Division II. *Intercollegiate sports:* baseball M(s), basketball M(s)/W(s), bowling M(c)/W(c), cross-country running M(c)/W(s), fencing M(c)/W(c), football M(s), golf M(s)/W(s), gymnastics W(s), ice hockey M(c), rugby M(c)/W(c), skiing (downhill) M(c)/W(c), soccer M(c)/W(s), softball W(s), tennis M(s)/W(s), track and field W(s), volleyball M(c)/W(s), wrestling M(c). *Intramural sports:* archery M/W, badminton M/W, baseball M, basketball M/W, bowling M/W, cross-country running M/W, fencing M/W, field hockey M/W, football M/W, golf M/W, gymnastics W, ice hockey M/W, racquetball M/W, riflery M/W, rugby M/W, skiing (cross-country) M/W, skiing (downhill) M/W, soccer M/W, softball M/W, swimming M/W, table tennis M/W, tennis M/W, track and field W, volleyball M/W, weight lifting M/W, wrestling M.

Standardized Tests *Required:* SAT I or ACT (for admission).

Costs (2003–04) *One-time required fee:* $1000. *Tuition:* state resident $4800 full-time; nonresident $9260 full-time. *Room and board:* $4640. Room and board charges vary according to board plan and housing facility.

Financial Aid Of all full-time matriculated undergraduates who enrolled in 2002, 4,603 applied for aid, 3,218 were judged to have need, 546 had their need fully met. 664 Federal Work-Study jobs (averaging $869). In 2002, 961 non-need-based awards were made. *Average percent of need met:* 57%. *Average financial aid package:* $5236. *Average need-based loan:* $2860. *Average need-based gift aid:* $3025. *Average non-need-based aid:* $1660. *Average indebtedness upon graduation:* $19,067.

Applying *Options:* common application, electronic application, early admission, early action, deferred entrance. *Application fee:* $20. *Required:* high school transcript, class rank. *Required for some:* essay or personal statement, letters of recommendation, interview. *Application deadlines:* rolling (freshmen), 8/1 (transfers). *Notification:* continuous (freshmen), continuous (transfers).

Admissions Contact Mr. Douglas Schacke, Director of Admissions, Winona State University, PO Box 5838, Winona, MN 55987. *Phone:* 507-457-5100. *Toll-free phone:* 800-DIAL WSU. *Fax:* 507-457-5620. *E-mail:* admissions@winona.edu.

MISSISSIPPI

ALCORN STATE UNIVERSITY

Alcorn State, Mississippi

- **State-supported** comprehensive, founded 1871, part of Mississippi Institutions of Higher Learning
- **Calendar** semesters
- **Degrees** associate, bachelor's, master's, and post-master's certificates
- **Rural** 1756-acre campus
- **Endowment** $209,871
- **Coed,** 2,662 undergraduate students, 89% full-time, 61% women, 39% men
- **Minimally difficult** entrance level, 22% of applicants were admitted

Undergraduates 2,358 full-time, 304 part-time. Students come from 34 states and territories, 11 other countries, 18% are from out of state, 92% African American, 0.1% Asian American or Pacific Islander, 0.2% Hispanic American, 0.1% Native American, 2% international, 8% transferred in, 66% live on campus. *Retention:* 70% of 2002 full-time freshmen returned.

Freshmen *Admission:* 4,619 applied, 1,008 admitted, 483 enrolled. *Average high school GPA:* 2.93. *Test scores:* ACT scores over 18: 53%; ACT scores over 24: 6%.

Faculty *Total:* 224, 83% full-time, 58% with terminal degrees. *Student/faculty ratio:* 14:1.

Majors Accounting; administrative assistant and secretarial science; agricultural business and management; agricultural economics; agriculture; agronomy and crop science; animal sciences; biology/biological sciences; business administration and management; chemistry; child guidance; clinical laboratory science/medical technology; computer and information sciences; criminal justice/safety; economics; educational psychology; elementary education; English; family and consumer sciences/human sciences; foods, nutrition, and wellness; health professions related; history; industrial technology; liberal arts and sciences/liberal studies; mass communication/media; mathematics; music performance; music teacher education; nursing (registered nurse training); parks, recreation and leisure; physical education teaching and coaching; physical therapy; political science and government; secondary education; sociology; special education; technology/industrial arts teacher education.

Academic Programs *Special study options:* academic remediation for entering students, advanced placement credit, cooperative education, distance learning, double majors, honors programs, independent study, internships, part-time degree program. *ROTC:* Army (b).

Library John Dewey Boyd Library with 195,433 titles, 1,046 serial subscriptions, 9,908 audiovisual materials, an OPAC.

Computers on Campus 500 computers available on campus for general student use. A campuswide network can be accessed from student residence rooms and from off campus. Online (class) registration, at least one staffed computer lab available.

Student Life *Housing options:* men-only, women-only. Campus housing is university owned. Freshman campus housing is guaranteed. *Activities and organizations:* drama/theater group, student-run newspaper, radio station, choral group, marching band, Panhellenic Council, intramural sports, marching band, gospel choir, interfaith choir, national fraternities, national sororities. *Campus security:* 24-hour patrols. *Student services:* health clinic, personal/psychological counseling.

Athletics Member NCAA. All Division I. *Intercollegiate sports:* baseball M(s), basketball M(s)/W(s), cross-country running M(s)/W(s), football M(s), golf M(s)/W(s), soccer W(s), softball W(s), tennis M(s)/W(s), track and field M(s)/W(s), volleyball W(s). *Intramural sports:* basketball M/W, football M, gymnastics M/W, softball W, swimming M/W, table tennis M/W, tennis M/W, track and field M/W, volleyball M/W, wrestling M/W.

Standardized Tests *Required:* SAT I or ACT (for admission).

Costs (2003–04) *Tuition:* state resident $3459 full-time; nonresident $7965 full-time. *Required fees:* $981 full-time. *Room and board:* $3821; room only: $2164. *Waivers:* employees or children of employees.

Financial Aid Of all full-time matriculated undergraduates who enrolled in 2003, 2,158 applied for aid, 1,558 were judged to have need, 1,461 had their need fully met. 321 Federal Work-Study jobs (averaging $1265). *Average percent of need met:* 79%. *Average financial aid package:* $9500. *Average need-based loan:* $5500. *Average need-based gift aid:* $4500. *Average non-need-based aid:* $4250. *Average indebtedness upon graduation:* $7500.

Applying *Options:* electronic application, early admission, deferred entrance. *Required:* high school transcript, minimum 2.0 GPA. *Application deadline:* rolling (freshmen), rolling (transfers). *Notification:* continuous (freshmen), continuous (transfers).

Admissions Contact Mr. Emanuel Barnes, Director of Admissions, Alcorn State University, 1000 ASU Drive #300, Alcorn State, MS 39096-7500. *Phone:* 601-877-6147. *Toll-free phone:* 800-222-6790. *Fax:* 601-877-6347. *E-mail:* ebarnes@loman.alcorn.edu.

BELHAVEN COLLEGE

Jackson, Mississippi

- **Independent Presbyterian** comprehensive, founded 1883
- **Calendar** semesters
- **Degrees** certificates, associate, bachelor's, and master's
- **Urban** 42-acre campus
- **Endowment** $2.3 million
- **Coed,** 2,023 undergraduate students, 94% full-time, 66% women, 34% men
- **Moderately difficult** entrance level, 56% of applicants were admitted

A nationally recognized leader in Christian higher education, Belhaven prepares students to serve Christ Jesus in their careers, in human relationships, and in the world of ideas. Majors are characterized by an intellectual foundation of a biblical world view. Scholarships are available, including a $1000 campus visit scholarship for full-time traditional freshmen who enroll. Apply online at www.belhaven.edu.

Undergraduates 1,910 full-time, 113 part-time. Students come from 35 states and territories, 11 other countries, 64% are from out of state, 33% African American, 0.3% Asian American or Pacific Islander, 1% Hispanic American, 0.7% Native American, 2% international, 8% transferred in, 32% live on campus. *Retention:* 59% of 2002 full-time freshmen returned.

Freshmen *Admission:* 595 applied, 333 admitted, 206 enrolled. *Average high school GPA:* 3.33. *Test scores:* SAT verbal scores over 500: 78%; SAT math scores over 500: 65%; ACT scores over 18: 100%; SAT verbal scores over 600: 45%;

Belhaven College (continued)

SAT math scores over 600: 36%; ACT scores over 24: 53%; SAT verbal scores over 700: 20%; SAT math scores over 700: 7%; ACT scores over 30: 10%.

Faculty *Total:* 211, 28% full-time, 39% with terminal degrees. *Student/faculty ratio:* 18:1.

Majors Accounting; art; athletic training; biblical studies; biology/biological sciences; business administration and management; chemistry; communication/speech communication and rhetoric; computer science; dance; dramatic/theatre arts; elementary education; English; history; humanities; information science/studies; mathematics; music; pastoral studies/counseling; philosophy; psychology; sport and fitness administration.

Academic Programs *Special study options:* academic remediation for entering students, accelerated degree program, adult/continuing education programs, advanced placement credit, double majors, English as a second language, honors programs, independent study, internships, off-campus study, part-time degree program, study abroad, summer session for credit. *Unusual degree programs:* 3-2 engineering with Mississippi State University.

Library Hood Library with 97,694 titles, 513 serial subscriptions, 12,311 audiovisual materials, an OPAC, a Web page.

Computers on Campus 50 computers available on campus for general student use. A campuswide network can be accessed from student residence rooms and from off campus that provide access to e-mail. Internet access, at least one staffed computer lab available.

Student Life *Housing:* on-campus residence required through sophomore year. *Options:* men-only, women-only. *Activities and organizations:* drama/theater group, student-run newspaper, choral group, Student Government Association, Reformed University Fellowship, Kappa Delta Epsilon, Black Student Association, math/computer science club. *Campus security:* 24-hour emergency response devices and patrols, late-night transport/escort service, controlled dormitory access. *Student services:* health clinic, personal/psychological counseling.

Athletics Member NAIA. *Intercollegiate sports:* baseball M(s), basketball M(s)/W(s), cross-country running M(s)/W(s), football M(s), golf M(s)/W(s), soccer M(s)/W(s), softball W(s), tennis M(s)/W(s), volleyball W(s). *Intramural sports:* basketball M/W, football M/W, soccer M/W, softball M/W, volleyball M/W.

Standardized Tests *Required:* SAT I or ACT (for admission).

Costs (2004–05) *Comprehensive fee:* $18,680 includes full-time tuition ($12,800), mandatory fees ($640), and room and board ($5240). Part-time tuition: $365 per semester hour. Part-time tuition and fees vary according to course load. *Required fees:* $70 per term part-time. *Room and board:* Room and board charges vary according to housing facility. *Payment plan:* installment. *Waivers:* employees or children of employees.

Financial Aid Of all full-time matriculated undergraduates who enrolled in 2001, 1,389 applied for aid, 1,292 were judged to have need, 121 had their need fully met. 124 Federal Work-Study jobs (averaging $1507). In 2001, 144 non-need-based awards were made. *Average percent of need met:* 58%. *Average financial aid package:* $9300. *Average need-based loan:* $4750. *Average need-based gift aid:* $3200. *Average non-need-based aid:* $4800. *Average indebtedness upon graduation:* $17,800.

Applying *Options:* early admission, deferred entrance. *Application fee:* $25. *Required:* high school transcript, minimum 2.0 GPA, 1 letter of recommendation, 1 academic reference. *Required for some:* essay or personal statement, interview. *Application deadline:* rolling (freshmen), rolling (transfers). *Notification:* continuous (freshmen), continuous (transfers).

Admissions Contact Ms. Suzanne T. Sullivan, Director of Admissions, Belhaven College, 150 Peachtree Street, Jackson, MS 39202. *Phone:* 601-968-5940. *Toll-free phone:* 800-960-5940. *Fax:* 601-968-8946. *E-mail:* admissions@belhaven.edu.

BLUE MOUNTAIN COLLEGE

Blue Mountain, Mississippi

- **Independent Southern Baptist** 4-year, founded 1873
- **Calendar** semesters
- **Degrees** bachelor's (also offers a coordinate academic program for men preparing for church-related vocations)
- **Rural** 44-acre campus with easy access to Memphis
- **Endowment** $6.1 million
- **Women only,** 431 undergraduate students, 77% full-time
- **Minimally difficult** entrance level, 64% of applicants were admitted

Undergraduates 334 full-time, 97 part-time. Students come from 7 states and territories, 2 other countries, 11% are from out of state, 10% African American, 0.3% Asian American or Pacific Islander, 0.5% Native American, 0.5% international, 14% transferred in, 34% live on campus. *Retention:* 80% of 2002 full-time freshmen returned.

Freshmen *Admission:* 129 applied, 83 admitted, 61 enrolled. *Average high school GPA:* 3.29. *Test scores:* ACT scores over 18: 75%; ACT scores over 24: 21%; ACT scores over 30: 4%.

Faculty *Total:* 37, 70% full-time, 43% with terminal degrees. *Student/faculty ratio:* 13:1.

Majors Biblical studies; biology/biological sciences; biology teacher education; business administration and management; business/commerce; business teacher education; chemistry; chemistry teacher education; clinical laboratory science/medical technology; dramatic/theatre arts; elementary education; English; English/language arts teacher education; history; mathematics; mathematics teacher education; music; music teacher education; natural sciences; physical education teaching and coaching; piano and organ; pre-dentistry studies; pre-law studies; pre-medical studies; pre-pharmacy studies; pre-theology/pre-ministerial studies; pre-veterinary studies; psychology; science teacher education; social sciences; social science teacher education; Spanish; Spanish language teacher education; speech and rhetoric; voice and opera.

Academic Programs *Special study options:* accelerated degree program, advanced placement credit, double majors, honors programs, internships, part-time degree program, summer session for credit.

Library Guyton Library with 61,297 titles, 186 serial subscriptions, 4,554 audiovisual materials.

Computers on Campus 59 computers available on campus for general student use. At least one staffed computer lab available.

Student Life *Housing:* on-campus residence required through senior year. *Options:* women-only. *Activities and organizations:* drama/theater group, choral group, Baptist Student Union, Student Government Association, Athletic Association, commuter club, Mississippi Association of Educators/Student Program. *Campus security:* 24-hour patrols.

Athletics Member NAIA. *Intercollegiate sports:* basketball W(s), tennis W(s). *Intramural sports:* basketball W, softball W, swimming W, table tennis W, tennis W, track and field W, ultimate Frisbee M/W, volleyball W.

Standardized Tests *Required:* SAT I or ACT (for admission).

Costs (2003–04) *Comprehensive fee:* $10,326 includes full-time tuition ($6300), mandatory fees ($500), and room and board ($3526). Full-time tuition and fees vary according to course load. Part-time tuition: $210 per semester hour. Part-time tuition and fees vary according to course load. *Required fees:* $70 per term part-time. *College room only:* $1300. Room and board charges vary according to board plan and housing facility. *Payment plan:* installment. *Waivers:* employees or children of employees.

Financial Aid Of all full-time matriculated undergraduates who enrolled in 2003, 323 applied for aid, 272 were judged to have need, 88 had their need fully met. 58 Federal Work-Study jobs (averaging $1400). 40 state and other part-time jobs (averaging $1400). In 2003, 35 non-need-based awards were made. *Average percent of need met:* 32%. *Average need-based loan:* $3752. *Average need-based gift aid:* $2511. *Average non-need-based aid:* $2526. *Average indebtedness upon graduation:* $9072.

Applying *Options:* early admission. *Application fee:* $10. *Required:* high school transcript. *Required for some:* essay or personal statement, 2 letters of recommendation, interview. *Recommended:* minimum 2.0 GPA. *Application deadline:* 9/3 (freshmen), rolling (transfers). *Notification:* continuous (freshmen), continuous (transfers).

Admissions Contact Ms. Tina Barkley, Director of Admissions, Blue Mountain College, PO Box 160, Blue Mountain, MS 38610-0160. *Phone:* 662-685-4161 Ext. 176. *Toll-free phone:* 800-235-0136. *E-mail:* tbarkley@bmc.edu.

DELTA STATE UNIVERSITY

Cleveland, Mississippi

- **State-supported** comprehensive, founded 1924, part of Mississippi Institutions of Higher Learning
- **Calendar** semesters
- **Degrees** bachelor's, master's, doctoral, and post-master's certificates
- **Small-town** 332-acre campus
- **Endowment** $10.3 million
- **Coed,** 3,156 undergraduate students, 81% full-time, 62% women, 38% men
- **Minimally difficult** entrance level, 26% of applicants were admitted

Undergraduates 2,550 full-time, 606 part-time. Students come from 27 states and territories, 9% are from out of state, 33% African American, 0.5% Asian American or Pacific Islander, 0.8% Hispanic American, 0.2% Native American, 14% transferred in, 38% live on campus. *Retention:* 71% of 2002 full-time freshmen returned.

Freshmen *Admission:* 1,289 applied, 330 admitted, 330 enrolled. *Average high school GPA:* 2.58. *Test scores:* ACT scores over 18: 77%; ACT scores over 24: 21%; ACT scores over 30: 2%.

Faculty *Total:* 277, 58% full-time, 58% with terminal degrees. *Student/faculty ratio:* 14:1.

Majors Accounting; aeronautics/aviation/aerospace science and technology; airline pilot and flight crew; art teacher education; audiology and speech-language pathology; biological and physical sciences; biology/biological sciences; biology teacher education; business administration and management; business/commerce; business teacher education; chemistry; chemistry teacher education; clinical laboratory science/medical technology; criminal justice/safety; education; elementary education; English; English/language arts teacher education; family and consumer sciences/home economics teacher education; family and consumer sciences/human sciences; fashion merchandising; finance; foreign languages and literatures; foreign language teacher education; history; hospitality administration; insurance; journalism; kindergarten/preschool education; management information systems; marketing/marketing management; mathematics; mathematics teacher education; music; music teacher education; nursing (registered nurse training); office management; physical education teaching and coaching; political science and government; psychology; science teacher education; secondary education; social sciences; social science teacher education; social work; special education; visual and performing arts.

Academic Programs *Special study options:* academic remediation for entering students, advanced placement credit, cooperative education, distance learning, double majors, honors programs, independent study, internships, part-time degree program, services for LD students, summer session for credit. *ROTC:* Air Force (b).

Library W. B. Roberts Library plus 1 other with 203,045 titles, 1,337 serial subscriptions, 15,523 audiovisual materials, an OPAC, a Web page.

Computers on Campus 300 computers available on campus for general student use. A campuswide network can be accessed from student residence rooms and from off campus that provide access to e-mail. Internet access, online (class) registration, at least one staffed computer lab available.

Student Life *Housing options:* men-only, women-only. Campus housing is university owned. *Activities and organizations:* drama/theater group, student-run newspaper, choral group, marching band, Student Government Association, Student Alumni Association, Baptist Student Union, Fellowship of Christian Athletes, Delta volunteers, national fraternities, national sororities. *Campus security:* 24-hour emergency response devices and patrols, late-night transport/escort service, controlled dormitory access. *Student services:* health clinic, personal/psychological counseling.

Athletics Member NCAA. All Division II. *Intercollegiate sports:* baseball M(s), basketball M(s)/W(s), cheerleading M/W, cross-country running W(s), football M(s), golf M(s), softball W, swimming M(s)/W(s), tennis M(s)/W(s). *Intramural sports:* archery M/W, badminton M/W, basketball M/W, bowling M/W, cross-country running M/W, football M/W, golf M/W, racquetball M/W, riflery M/W, rock climbing M/W, soccer M/W, softball M/W, swimming M/W, table tennis M/W, tennis M/W, track and field M/W, volleyball M/W.

Standardized Tests *Required:* SAT I or ACT (for admission).

Costs (2003–04) *Tuition:* state resident $3348 full-time, $119 per semester hour part-time; nonresident $7965 full-time, $311 per semester hour part-time. *Required fees:* $424 full-time. *Room and board:* $3270. *Payment plan:* installment. *Waivers:* children of alumni, senior citizens, and employees or children of employees.

Financial Aid Of all full-time matriculated undergraduates who enrolled in 2003, 2,150 applied for aid. 318 Federal Work-Study jobs (averaging $1650). *Average indebtedness upon graduation:* $8750.

Applying *Options:* electronic application, deferred entrance. *Required:* high school transcript. *Required for some:* interview for art, music majors. *Application deadlines:* 8/1 (freshmen), 8/1 (transfers). *Notification:* continuous (freshmen), continuous (transfers).

Admissions Contact Ms. Debbie Heslep, Associate Dean of Enrollment Services, Delta State University, Highway 8 West, Cleveland, MS 38733. *Phone:* 662-846-4018. *Toll-free phone:* 800-468-6378. *Fax:* 662-846-4683. *E-mail:* dheslep@deltastate.edu.

JACKSON STATE UNIVERSITY
Jackson, Mississippi

- **State-supported** university, founded 1877, part of Mississippi Institutions of Higher Learning
- **Calendar** semesters
- **Degrees** bachelor's, master's, doctoral, and post-master's certificates
- **Urban** 128-acre campus
- **Endowment** $5.1 million
- **Coed**
- **Minimally difficult** entrance level

Faculty *Student/faculty ratio:* 18:1.

Student Life *Campus security:* 24-hour emergency response devices and patrols, late-night transport/escort service, controlled dormitory access.

Athletics Member NCAA. All Division I except football (Division I-AA).

Standardized Tests *Required:* SAT I or ACT (for admission).

Costs (2003–04) *Tuition:* state resident $3612 full-time; nonresident $8116 full-time. *Room and board:* $4676; room only: $2670.

Applying *Options:* electronic application, early admission, deferred entrance. *Required:* high school transcript, minimum 3.0 GPA. *Required for some:* 3 letters of recommendation.

Admissions Contact Mrs. Linda Rush, Admissions Counselor, Jackson State University, PO Box 17330, 1400 John R. Lynch Street, Jackson, MS 39217. *Phone:* 601-968-2911. *Toll-free phone:* 800-682-5390 (in-state); 800-848-6817 (out-of-state). *E-mail:* schatman@ccaix.jsums.edu.

MAGNOLIA BIBLE COLLEGE
Kosciusko, Mississippi

- **Independent** 4-year, founded 1976, affiliated with Church of Christ
- **Calendar** semesters
- **Degree** bachelor's
- **Small-town** 5-acre campus
- **Endowment** $203,631
- **Coed, primarily men,** 52 undergraduate students, 65% full-time, 23% women, 77% men
- **Noncompetitive** entrance level, 100% of applicants were admitted

Undergraduates 34 full-time, 18 part-time. Students come from 12 states and territories, 1 other country, 33% are from out of state, 17% African American, 2% Hispanic American, 2% international, 17% transferred in, 48% live on campus. *Retention:* 75% of 2002 full-time freshmen returned.

Freshmen *Admission:* 11 applied, 11 admitted, 11 enrolled. *Average high school GPA:* 2.47.

Faculty *Total:* 9, 22% full-time, 22% with terminal degrees. *Student/faculty ratio:* 9:1.

Majors Biblical studies.

Academic Programs *Special study options:* academic remediation for entering students, independent study, internships, part-time degree program, summer session for credit.

Library John and Phillip Gaunt Library with 36,650 titles, 278 serial subscriptions, 1,403 audiovisual materials.

Computers on Campus 8 computers available on campus for general student use. At least one staffed computer lab available.

Student Life *Housing:* on-campus residence required through senior year. *Options:* coed. Campus housing is university owned. *Campus security:* 24-hour emergency response devices. *Student services:* personal/psychological counseling.

Standardized Tests *Recommended:* SAT I or ACT (for placement).

Costs (2003–04) *Tuition:* $5040 full-time, $165 per semester hour part-time. *Required fees:* $90 full-time, $90 per term part-time. *Room only:* $1120. Room and board charges vary according to housing facility. *Payment plan:* deferred payment. *Waivers:* employees or children of employees.

Financial Aid Of all full-time matriculated undergraduates who enrolled in 2003, 24 applied for aid, 20 were judged to have need, 3 had their need fully met. 3 Federal Work-Study jobs (averaging $2466). In 2003, 4 non-need-based awards were made. *Average percent of need met:* 57%. *Average financial aid package:* $4396. *Average need-based gift aid:* $4044. *Average indebtedness upon graduation:* $15,788.

Applying *Required:* essay or personal statement, high school transcript, 3 letters of recommendation. *Application deadlines:* 8/31 (freshmen), 8/31 (transfers). *Notification:* continuous (freshmen), continuous (transfers).

Admissions Contact Magnolia Bible College, PO Box 1109, 822 South Huntington Street, Kosciusko, MS 39090. *Phone:* 662-289-2896 Ext. 106. *Toll-free phone:* 800-748-8655. *Fax:* 662-289-1850. *E-mail:* mbcadmissions@hotmail.com.

MILLSAPS COLLEGE
Jackson, Mississippi

- **Independent United Methodist** comprehensive, founded 1890
- **Calendar** semesters
- **Degrees** bachelor's and master's
- **Urban** 100-acre campus
- **Endowment** $80.0 million
- **Coed,** 1,123 undergraduate students, 96% full-time, 54% women, 46% men
- **Moderately difficult** entrance level, 84% of applicants were admitted

Millsaps College (continued)

Undergraduates 1,083 full-time, 40 part-time. Students come from 30 states and territories, 5 other countries, 44% are from out of state, 10% African American, 3% Asian American or Pacific Islander, 1% Hispanic American, 0.6% Native American, 0.7% international, 5% transferred in, 76% live on campus. *Retention:* 83% of 2002 full-time freshmen returned.

Freshmen *Admission:* 1,045 applied, 880 admitted, 259 enrolled. *Average high school GPA:* 3.51. *Test scores:* SAT verbal scores over 500: 93%; SAT math scores over 500: 80%; ACT scores over 18: 100%; SAT verbal scores over 600: 48%; SAT math scores over 600: 38%; ACT scores over 24: 69%; SAT verbal scores over 700: 12%; SAT math scores over 700: 10%; ACT scores over 30: 14%.

Faculty *Total:* 97, 96% full-time, 93% with terminal degrees. *Student/faculty ratio:* 13:1.

Majors Accounting; anthropology; art; biology/biological sciences; business administration and management; chemistry; classics and languages, literatures and linguistics; computer science; dramatic/theatre arts; economics; education; English; European studies; French; geology/earth science; German; history; mathematics; music; philosophy; physics; political science and government; psychology; religious studies; sociology; Spanish.

Academic Programs *Special study options:* adult/continuing education programs, advanced placement credit, cooperative education, double majors, honors programs, independent study, internships, off-campus study, part-time degree program, study abroad, summer session for credit. *ROTC:* Army (c). *Unusual degree programs:* 3-2 engineering with Auburn University, Columbia University, Vanderbilt University, Washington University in St. Louis.

Library Millsaps Wilson Library with 136,937 titles, 3,434 serial subscriptions, 7,936 audiovisual materials, an OPAC, a Web page.

Computers on Campus 117 computers available on campus for general student use. A campuswide network can be accessed from student residence rooms. Internet access, at least one staffed computer lab available. Computer purchase or lease plan available.

Student Life *Housing:* on-campus residence required through sophomore year. *Options:* coed, men-only, women-only. Campus housing is university owned. Freshman campus housing is guaranteed. *Activities and organizations:* drama/theater group, student-run newspaper, choral group, Campus Ministry Team, Major Productions, Outdoors Club, Student Body Association, Black Student Association, national fraternities, national sororities. *Campus security:* 24-hour emergency response devices and patrols, student patrols, late-night transport/escort service, controlled dormitory access, self-defense education, lighted pathways. *Student services:* health clinic, personal/psychological counseling.

Athletics Member NCAA. All Division III. *Intercollegiate sports:* baseball M, basketball M/W, cheerleading M/W, cross-country running M/W, football M, golf M/W, soccer M/W, softball W, tennis M/W, volleyball W. *Intramural sports:* basketball M/W, football M/W, golf M/W, racquetball M/W, soccer M/W, softball M/W, table tennis M/W, tennis M/W, ultimate Frisbee M/W, volleyball M/W, weight lifting M/W.

Standardized Tests *Required:* SAT I or ACT (for admission).

Costs (2003–04) *Comprehensive fee:* $25,182 includes full-time tuition ($17,346), mandatory fees ($1068), and room and board ($6768). Part-time tuition: $540 per credit hour. Part-time tuition and fees vary according to course load. *Required fees:* $28 per credit hour part-time. *Room and board:* Room and board charges vary according to housing facility. *Payment plans:* installment, deferred payment. *Waivers:* employees or children of employees.

Financial Aid Of all full-time matriculated undergraduates who enrolled in 2003, 705 applied for aid, 607 were judged to have need, 174 had their need fully met. 286 Federal Work-Study jobs (averaging $1400). 307 state and other part-time jobs (averaging $665). In 2003, 425 non-need-based awards were made. *Average percent of need met:* 85%. *Average financial aid package:* $16,463. *Average need-based loan:* $4124. *Average need-based gift aid:* $12,572. *Average non-need-based aid:* $11,659. *Average indebtedness upon graduation:* $15,942.

Applying *Options:* common application, electronic application, early admission, early action, deferred entrance. *Application fee:* $25. *Required:* essay or personal statement, high school transcript, minimum 2.5 GPA, letters of recommendation. *Recommended:* interview. *Application deadline:* rolling (freshmen), rolling (transfers). *Notification:* 7/1 (freshmen), 12/20 (early action), continuous (transfers).

Admissions Contact Ms. Ann Hendrick, Dean of Admissions and Financial Aid, Millsaps College, 1701 North State Street, Jackson, MS 39210-0001. *Phone:* 601-974-1050. *Toll-free phone:* 800-352-1050. *Fax:* 601-974-1059. *E-mail:* admissions@millsaps.edu.

MISSISSIPPI COLLEGE
Clinton, Mississippi

- **Independent Southern Baptist** comprehensive, founded 1826
- **Calendar** semesters
- **Degrees** bachelor's, master's, first professional, and postbachelor's certificates
- **Suburban** 320-acre campus
- **Endowment** $34.1 million
- **Coed,** 2,367 undergraduate students, 91% full-time, 58% women, 42% men
- **Moderately difficult** entrance level, 58% of applicants were admitted

Undergraduates 2,143 full-time, 224 part-time. Students come from 28 states and territories, 19% are from out of state, 15% African American, 0.7% Asian American or Pacific Islander, 0.6% Hispanic American, 0.3% Native American, 14% transferred in, 92% live on campus. *Retention:* 82% of 2002 full-time freshmen returned.

Freshmen *Admission:* 1,646 applied, 949 admitted, 425 enrolled. *Average high school GPA:* 3.36. *Test scores:* ACT scores over 18: 97%; ACT scores over 24: 45%; ACT scores over 30: 6%.

Faculty *Total:* 263, 61% full-time, 59% with terminal degrees. *Student/faculty ratio:* 13:1.

Majors Accounting; art; art history, criticism and conservation; art teacher education; biochemistry; biology/biological sciences; business administration and management; business teacher education; chemistry; Christian studies; communication and journalism related; communication/speech communication and rhetoric; computer and information sciences; computer science; criminal justice/law enforcement administration; education; elementary education; English; foreign languages and literatures; foreign languages related; French; graphic design; health and physical education; history; interior design; kinesiology and exercise science; language interpretation and translation; legal assistant/paralegal; liberal arts and sciences/liberal studies; marketing/marketing management; mass communication/media; mathematics; music; music performance; music teacher education; music theory and composition; nursing (registered nurse training); physics; piano and organ; political science and government; pre-dentistry studies; pre-law studies; pre-medical studies; pre-pharmacy studies; pre-veterinary studies; psychology; public relations/image management; religious/sacred music; science teacher education; secondary education; social sciences; social sciences related; social science teacher education; social studies teacher education; social work; sociology; Spanish; special education; sport and fitness administration; voice and opera.

Academic Programs *Special study options:* academic remediation for entering students, adult/continuing education programs, advanced placement credit, cooperative education, double majors, freshman honors college, honors programs, independent study, internships, part-time degree program, services for LD students, study abroad, summer session for credit. *ROTC:* Army (c). *Unusual degree programs:* 3-2 engineering with Auburn University, University of Mississippi.

Library Leland Speed Library plus 1 other with 277,602 titles, 5,305 serial subscriptions, 14,800 audiovisual materials, an OPAC, a Web page.

Computers on Campus 207 computers available on campus for general student use. A campuswide network can be accessed from student residence rooms and from off campus. Internet access, at least one staffed computer lab available.

Student Life *Housing:* on-campus residence required through senior year. *Options:* men-only, women-only, disabled students. Campus housing is university owned. Freshman applicants given priority for college housing. *Activities and organizations:* drama/theater group, student-run newspaper, radio and television station, choral group, marching band, Baptist Student Union, Nenamoosha Social Tribe, Laguna Social Tribe, Civitan Service Club, Shawreth Service Club. *Campus security:* 24-hour emergency response devices and patrols, late-night transport/escort service, controlled dormitory access. *Student services:* health clinic, personal/psychological counseling.

Athletics Member NCAA. All Division III. *Intercollegiate sports:* baseball M, basketball M/W, cross-country running M/W, football M, soccer M/W, softball W, tennis M/W, volleyball W. *Intramural sports:* basketball M/W, football M/W, soccer M/W, softball M/W, tennis M/W, ultimate Frisbee M/W, volleyball M/W.

Standardized Tests *Required:* SAT I or ACT (for admission).

Costs (2003–04) *Comprehensive fee:* $16,925 includes full-time tuition ($10,888), mandatory fees ($641), and room and board ($5396). Full-time tuition and fees vary according to course load. Part-time tuition: $345 per credit hour. Part-time tuition and fees vary according to course load. *Required fees:* $73 per term part-time. *College room only:* $2830. Room and board charges vary according to board plan and housing facility. *Payment plans:* installment, deferred payment. *Waivers:* employees or children of employees.

Financial Aid Of all full-time matriculated undergraduates who enrolled in 2002, 1,747 applied for aid, 976 were judged to have need, 383 had their need fully met. 201 Federal Work-Study jobs (averaging $1016). In 2002, 752 non-need-based awards were made. *Average percent of need met:* 80%. *Average financial aid package:* $13,101. *Average need-based loan:* $5786. *Average need-based gift aid:* $8305. *Average non-need-based aid:* $9495. *Average indebtedness upon graduation:* $23,428.

Applying *Options:* common application, electronic application, early admission, early decision, deferred entrance. *Application fee:* $25. *Required:* high school transcript. *Recommended:* essay or personal statement, minimum 2.0 GPA, 1 letter of recommendation, interview. *Application deadline:* rolling (freshmen), rolling (transfers). *Early decision:* 12/15. *Notification:* continuous (freshmen), 12/31 (early decision), continuous (transfers).

Admissions Contact Mr. Chad Phillips, Director of Admissions, Mississippi College, PO Box 4026, 200 South Capitol Street, Clinton, MS 39058. *Phone:* 601-925-3800. *Toll-free phone:* 800-738-1236. *Fax:* 601-925-3804. *E-mail:* enrollment-services@mc.edu.

■ *See page 2000 for a narrative description.*

MISSISSIPPI STATE UNIVERSITY
Mississippi State, Mississippi

- **State-supported** university, founded 1878, part of Mississippi Board of Trustees of State Institutions of Higher Learning
- **Calendar** semesters
- **Degrees** bachelor's, master's, doctoral, first professional, and post-master's certificates
- **Small-town** 4200-acre campus
- **Endowment** $154.4 million
- **Coed,** 12,839 undergraduate students, 87% full-time, 47% women, 53% men
- **Moderately difficult** entrance level, 75% of applicants were admitted

Undergraduates 11,203 full-time, 1,636 part-time. Students come from 52 states and territories, 42 other countries, 20% are from out of state, 19% African American, 1% Asian American or Pacific Islander, 0.9% Hispanic American, 0.4% Native American, 1% international, 12% transferred in, 20% live on campus. *Retention:* 81% of 2002 full-time freshmen returned.

Freshmen *Admission:* 4,646 applied, 3,492 admitted, 1,688 enrolled. *Average high school GPA:* 3.23. *Test scores:* ACT scores over 18: 92%; ACT scores over 24: 47%; ACT scores over 30: 12%.

Faculty *Total:* 979, 87% full-time, 72% with terminal degrees. *Student/faculty ratio:* 16:1.

Majors Accounting; aerospace, aeronautical and astronautical engineering; agribusiness; agricultural/biological engineering and bioengineering; agricultural economics; agricultural teacher education; agriculture; agronomy and crop science; animal sciences; anthropology; architecture; biochemistry; biological and physical sciences; biology/biological sciences; biomedical/medical engineering; business administration and management; business/managerial economics; business teacher education; chemical engineering; chemistry; civil engineering; clinical laboratory science/medical technology; communication/speech communication and rhetoric; computer and information sciences; computer engineering; computer software engineering; construction management; economics; educational psychology; electrical, electronics and communications engineering; elementary education; English; family and consumer sciences/human sciences; finance; food science; foreign languages and literatures; forestry; geology/earth science; history; horticultural science; industrial engineering; industrial technology; insurance; landscape architecture; landscaping and groundskeeping; liberal arts and sciences/liberal studies; management information systems; marine biology and biological oceanography; marketing/marketing management; mathematics; mechanical engineering; medical microbiology and bacteriology; multi-/interdisciplinary studies related; music teacher education; philosophy; physical education teaching and coaching; physics; plant protection and integrated pest management; political science and government; poultry science; psychology; real estate; secondary education; social work; sociology; special education; technical teacher education; technology/industrial arts teacher education; visual and performing arts; wildlife and wildlands science and management; wood science and wood products/pulp and paper technology.

Academic Programs *Special study options:* academic remediation for entering students, accelerated degree program, adult/continuing education programs, advanced placement credit, cooperative education, distance learning, double majors, English as a second language, freshman honors college, honors programs, independent study, internships, off-campus study, part-time degree program, services for LD students, student-designed majors, study abroad, summer session for credit. *ROTC:* Army (b), Air Force (b).

Library Mitchell Memorial Library plus 2 others with 2.0 million titles, 17,722 serial subscriptions, 18,679 audiovisual materials, an OPAC, a Web page.

Computers on Campus 2000 computers available on campus for general student use. A campuswide network can be accessed from student residence rooms and from off campus that provide access to wireless network with partial campus coverage. Internet access, online (class) registration, at least one staffed computer lab available.

Student Life *Housing options:* coed, men-only, women-only, disabled students. Campus housing is university owned. Freshman applicants given priority for college housing. *Activities and organizations:* drama/theater group, student-run newspaper, radio and television station, choral group, marching band, Student Association, Black Student Alliance, Residence Hall Association, Fashion Board, Campus Activities Board, national fraternities, national sororities. *Campus security:* 24-hour emergency response devices and patrols, late-night transport/escort service, controlled dormitory access, bicycle patrols, crime prevention program, RAD program, general law enforcement services. *Student services:* health clinic, personal/psychological counseling.

Athletics Member NCAA. All Division I except football (Division I-A). *Intercollegiate sports:* baseball M(s), basketball M(s)/W(s), cross-country running W(s), golf M(s)/W(s), soccer W(s), softball W(s), tennis M(s)/W(s), track and field M(s)/W(s), ultimate Frisbee M(c)/W(c), volleyball W(s). *Intramural sports:* badminton M/W, basketball M/W, cheerleading M/W, fencing M(c)/W(c), football M/W, golf M/W, lacrosse M(c), racquetball M/W, rock climbing M/W, rugby M(c)/W(c), soccer M(c)/W(c), softball M/W, swimming M/W, table tennis M/W, tennis M/W, ultimate Frisbee M(c)/W(c), volleyball M(c)/W, water polo M/W, weight lifting M/W.

Standardized Tests *Required:* SAT I or ACT (for admission). *Required for some:* Placement testing and counseling for entering students with academic deficiencies.

Costs (2003–04) *Tuition:* state resident $3874 full-time, $162 per hour part-time; nonresident $8780 full-time, $366 per hour part-time. Full-time tuition and fees vary according to degree level and program. Part-time tuition and fees vary according to degree level and program. *Room and board:* $5265; room only: $2230. Room and board charges vary according to board plan and housing facility. *Waivers:* children of alumni, senior citizens, and employees or children of employees.

Financial Aid Of all full-time matriculated undergraduates who enrolled in 2002, 7,777 applied for aid, 6,608 were judged to have need, 2,998 had their need fully met. 1,042 Federal Work-Study jobs (averaging $2392). In 2002, 2589 non-need-based awards were made. *Average percent of need met:* 70%. *Average financial aid package:* $8184. *Average need-based loan:* $3706. *Average need-based gift aid:* $3317. *Average non-need-based aid:* $2018. *Average indebtedness upon graduation:* $17,109.

Applying *Options:* electronic application, early admission, deferred entrance. *Required:* high school transcript, minimum 2.0 GPA. *Required for some:* letters of recommendation. *Application deadlines:* 8/1 (freshmen), 8/1 (transfers). *Notification:* continuous (freshmen), continuous (transfers).

Admissions Contact Ms. Diane D. Wolfe, Director of Admissions, Mississippi State University, PO Box 6305, Mississippi State, MS 39762. *Phone:* 662-325-2224. *Fax:* 662-325-7360. *E-mail:* admit@admissions.msstate.edu.

MISSISSIPPI UNIVERSITY FOR WOMEN
Columbus, Mississippi

Admissions Contact Ms. Terri Heath, Director of Admissions, Mississippi University for Women, PO Box 1613, Columbus, MS 39701-9998. *Phone:* 601-329-7106. *Toll-free phone:* 877-GO 2 THE W. *Fax:* 601-241-7481. *E-mail:* admissions@muw.edu.

MISSISSIPPI VALLEY STATE UNIVERSITY
Itta Bena, Mississippi

- **State-supported** comprehensive, founded 1946, part of Mississippi Institutions of Higher Learning
- **Calendar** semesters
- **Degrees** bachelor's and master's
- **Small-town** 450-acre campus
- **Coed,** 3,259 undergraduate students, 89% full-time, 72% women, 28% men
- **Minimally difficult** entrance level, 99% of applicants were admitted

Undergraduates 2,904 full-time, 355 part-time. Students come from 25 states and territories, 3 other countries, 6% are from out of state, 96% African American, 0.1% Asian American or Pacific Islander, 0.1% Hispanic American, 7% transferred in, 53% live on campus. *Retention:* 73% of 2002 full-time freshmen returned.

Freshmen *Admission:* 3,486 applied, 3,447 admitted, 331 enrolled. *Average high school GPA:* 2.68. *Test scores:* ACT scores over 18: 77%; ACT scores over 24: 21%; ACT scores over 30: 1%.

Faculty *Total:* 155, 71% full-time. *Student/faculty ratio:* 23:1.

Majors Accounting; art; biology/biological sciences; business administration and management; chemistry; computer science; criminal justice/law enforcement administration; education; elementary education; English; English/language arts teacher education; history; industrial technology; kindergarten/preschool education; mass communication/media; mathematics; mathematics teacher education; music; music teacher education; office management; physical education teaching and coaching; political science and government; public administration; science

Mississippi Valley State University (continued)
teacher education; social science teacher education; social work; sociology; speech and rhetoric; water quality and wastewater treatment management and recycling technology.

Academic Programs *Special study options:* academic remediation for entering students, adult/continuing education programs, cooperative education, freshman honors college, honors programs, internships, part-time degree program, summer session for credit. *ROTC:* Army (b), Air Force (b).

Library James H. White Library with 130,918 titles, 599 serial subscriptions, 3,525 audiovisual materials, an OPAC, a Web page.

Computers on Campus 250 computers available on campus for general student use. A campuswide network can be accessed from student residence rooms and from off campus. Internet access, online (class) registration, at least one staffed computer lab available.

Student Life *Housing:* on-campus residence required through senior year. *Options:* men-only, women-only. Campus housing is university owned. *Activities and organizations:* drama/theater group, student-run newspaper, radio and television station, choral group, marching band, Student Government Association, Baptist Student Union, Black Student Fellowship, Panhellenic Council, National Education Association, national fraternities, national sororities. *Campus security:* 24-hour emergency response devices and patrols, controlled dormitory access. *Student services:* health clinic, personal/psychological counseling.

Athletics Member NCAA. All Division I except football (Division I-AA). *Intercollegiate sports:* baseball M(s), basketball M(s)/W(s), bowling W, cross-country running M(s)/W(s), golf M(s), tennis M(s), track and field M(s)/W(s). *Intramural sports:* baseball M, basketball M/W, cross-country running M/W, football M, golf M/W, softball M/W, tennis M/W, track and field M/W.

Standardized Tests *Required:* SAT I or ACT (for admission).

Costs (2003–04) *Tuition:* state resident $3411 full-time, $142 per semester hour part-time; nonresident $7965 full-time, $190 per semester hour part-time. *Room and board:* $3544. *Payment plans:* installment, deferred payment. *Waivers:* employees or children of employees.

Financial Aid *Average percent of need met:* 80%. *Average financial aid package:* $7000.

Applying *Options:* deferred entrance. *Required:* high school transcript. *Required for some:* 2.5 GPA for non-residents. *Recommended:* interview. *Application deadline:* rolling (freshmen), rolling (transfers). *Notification:* continuous (freshmen), continuous (transfers).

Admissions Contact Mr. Wilson Lee, Director of Admissions and Recruitment, Mississippi Valley State University, 14000 Highway 82 West, Itta Bena, MS 38941-1400. *Phone:* 662-254-3344. *Toll-free phone:* 800-844-6885. *Fax:* 662-254-7900.

RUST COLLEGE
Holly Springs, Mississippi

- **Independent United Methodist** 4-year, founded 1866
- **Calendar** semesters
- **Degrees** associate and bachelor's
- **Rural** 126-acre campus with easy access to Memphis
- **Endowment** $15.7 million
- **Coed**
- **Moderately difficult** entrance level

Faculty *Student/faculty ratio:* 19:1.

Student Life *Campus security:* 24-hour emergency response devices and patrols, late-night transport/escort service, controlled dormitory access.

Athletics Member NCAA. All Division III.

Standardized Tests *Required:* ACT (for admission).

Costs (2003–04) *Comprehensive fee:* $8535 includes full-time tuition ($5800), mandatory fees ($135), and room and board ($2600). Part-time tuition and fees vary according to class time and course load. *College room only:* $1162. *Payment plans:* installment, deferred payment.

Financial Aid Of all full-time matriculated undergraduates who enrolled in 2002, 835 applied for aid, 835 were judged to have need, 682 had their need fully met. 508 Federal Work-Study jobs (averaging $674). 136 state and other part-time jobs (averaging $795). In 2002, 121. *Average percent of need met:* 78. *Average financial aid package:* $4907. *Average need-based loan:* $1523. *Average need-based gift aid:* $3010. *Average non-need-based aid:* $2996. *Average indebtedness upon graduation:* $8434.

Applying *Options:* common application, deferred entrance. *Application fee:* $10. *Required:* high school transcript, minimum 2.0 GPA, 3 letters of recommendation. *Required for some:* essay or personal statement.

Admissions Contact Mr. Johnny McDonald, Director of Enrollment Services, Rust College, 150 Rust Avenue, Holly Springs, MS 38635-2328. *Phone:* 601-252-8000 Ext. 4065. *Toll-free phone:* 888-886-8492 Ext. 4065. *Fax:* 662-252-8895. *E-mail:* admissions@rustcollege.edu.

SOUTHEASTERN BAPTIST COLLEGE
Laurel, Mississippi

- **Independent Baptist** 4-year, founded 1949
- **Calendar** semesters
- **Degrees** associate and bachelor's
- **Small-town** 23-acre campus
- **Endowment** $177,930
- **Coed**
- **Noncompetitive** entrance level

Standardized Tests *Recommended:* ACT (for placement).

Costs (2003–04) *Tuition:* $4000 full-time, $125 per credit part-time.

Applying *Options:* early admission, deferred entrance. *Application fee:* $25. *Required:* high school transcript, 2 letters of recommendation. *Required for some:* interview.

Admissions Contact Mrs. Emma Bond, Director of Admissions, Southeastern Baptist College, 4229 Highway 15 North, Laurel, MS 39440-1096. *Phone:* 601-426-6346.

TOUGALOO COLLEGE
Tougaloo, Mississippi

- **Independent** 4-year, founded 1869, affiliated with United Church of Christ
- **Calendar** semesters
- **Degrees** associate and bachelor's
- **Suburban** 500-acre campus
- **Endowment** $4.7 million
- **Coed,** 940 undergraduate students, 94% full-time, 70% women, 30% men
- **Minimally difficult** entrance level, 99% of applicants were admitted

Undergraduates 883 full-time, 57 part-time. Students come from 24 states and territories, 1 other country, 14% are from out of state, 99% African American, 0.5% international, 5% transferred in. *Retention:* 78% of 2002 full-time freshmen returned.

Freshmen *Admission:* 627 applied, 621 admitted, 222 enrolled. *Average high school GPA:* 3.00. *Test scores:* ACT scores over 18: 58%; ACT scores over 24: 8%.

Faculty *Total:* 103, 68% full-time. *Student/faculty ratio:* 18:1.

Majors Accounting; African-American/Black studies; art; biology/biological sciences; business administration and management; chemistry; child guidance; computer science; economics; education; elementary education; English; history; interdisciplinary studies; kindergarten/preschool education; mathematics; music; physics; political science and government; pre-dentistry studies; psychology; secondary education; sociology.

Academic Programs *Special study options:* academic remediation for entering students, accelerated degree program, adult/continuing education programs, cooperative education, honors programs, internships, off-campus study, part-time degree program, student-designed majors, study abroad. *ROTC:* Army (b). *Unusual degree programs:* 3-2 engineering with Brown University, Georgia Institute of Technology.

Library L. Zenobiz Coleman Library with 137,000 titles, 432 serial subscriptions.

Computers on Campus 43 computers available on campus for general student use. Internet access, at least one staffed computer lab available.

Student Life *Housing options:* men-only, women-only. *Activities and organizations:* drama/theater group, student-run newspaper, choral group, concert choir, Student Government Association, gospel choir, NAACP, Pre-Alumni, national fraternities, national sororities. *Campus security:* 24-hour emergency response devices and patrols. *Student services:* health clinic, personal/psychological counseling.

Athletics Member NAIA. *Intercollegiate sports:* basketball M(s)/W(s), cross-country running M(s)/W(s), golf M, softball W. *Intramural sports:* basketball M/W, bowling M, cross-country running M/W, golf M/W, softball M/W, tennis M/W, volleyball M/W.

Standardized Tests *Required:* SAT I or ACT (for admission).

Costs (2004–05) *Comprehensive fee:* $13,780 includes full-time tuition ($8250), mandatory fees ($450), and room and board ($5080). Part-time tuition: $339 per credit hour. *College room only:* $3310. *Payment plans:* installment, deferred payment. *Waivers:* adult students, senior citizens, and employees or children of employees.

Financial Aid In 2002, 215 non-need-based awards were made. *Average percent of need met:* 85%. *Average financial aid package:* $10,000. *Average indebtedness upon graduation:* $25,000.

Applying *Options:* common application, early admission. *Application fee:* $5. *Required:* high school transcript, minimum 2.0 GPA. *Application deadline:* rolling (freshmen), rolling (transfers). *Notification:* continuous (freshmen), continuous (transfers).

Admissions Contact Ms. Adriene W. Walls, Data Entry Specialist, Tougaloo College, Student Enrollment Management Center, 500 West County Line Road, Tougaloo, MS 39174. *Phone:* 601-977-7768. *Toll-free phone:* 888-42GALOO. *E-mail:* carolyn.evans@tougaloo.edu.

UNIVERSITY OF MISSISSIPPI

Oxford, Mississippi

- **State-supported** university, founded 1844, part of Mississippi Institutions of Higher Learning
- **Calendar** semesters
- **Degrees** bachelor's, master's, doctoral, and first professional
- **Small-town** 2500-acre campus with easy access to Memphis
- **Endowment** $17.1 million
- **Coed,** 11,250 undergraduate students, 86% full-time, 53% women, 47% men
- **Moderately difficult** entrance level, 80% of applicants were admitted

Undergraduates 9,647 full-time, 1,603 part-time. Students come from 47 states and territories, 63 other countries, 32% are from out of state, 13% African American, 1% Asian American or Pacific Islander, 0.5% Hispanic American, 0.4% Native American, 1% international, 9% transferred in, 33% live on campus. *Retention:* 77% of 2002 full-time freshmen returned.

Freshmen *Admission:* 6,601 applied, 5,287 admitted, 2,380 enrolled. *Average high school GPA:* 3.34. *Test scores:* ACT scores over 18: 94%; ACT scores over 24: 46%; ACT scores over 30: 11%.

Faculty *Student/faculty ratio:* 19:1.

Majors Accounting; advertising; American studies; anthropology; art; art history, criticism and conservation; audiology and speech-language pathology; biology/biological sciences; biomedical sciences; business administration and management; business/commerce; business/managerial economics; chemical engineering; chemistry; civil engineering; classics and languages, literatures and linguistics; clinical laboratory science/medical technology; computer and information sciences; court reporting; dramatic/theatre arts; economics; electrical, electronics and communications engineering; elementary education; engineering; English; English/language arts teacher education; family and consumer sciences/human sciences; finance; forensic science and technology; French; geological/geophysical engineering; geology/earth science; German; history; insurance; international business/trade/commerce; international relations and affairs; journalism; kinesiology and exercise science; liberal arts and sciences/liberal studies; linguistics; management information systems; marketing/marketing management; mathematics; mathematics teacher education; mechanical engineering; music; parks, recreation and leisure; pharmacy; philosophy; physics; political science and government; psychology; public administration; radio and television; real estate; science teacher education; secondary education; social studies teacher education; social work; sociology; Spanish; special education.

Academic Programs *Special study options:* academic remediation for entering students, accelerated degree program, adult/continuing education programs, advanced placement credit, double majors, English as a second language, freshman honors college, honors programs, independent study, internships, part-time degree program, services for LD students, study abroad, summer session for credit. *ROTC:* Army (b), Air Force (b).

Library J. D. Williams Library plus 3 others with 951,259 titles, 8,495 serial subscriptions, 143,717 audiovisual materials, an OPAC, a Web page.

Computers on Campus 3500 computers available on campus for general student use. A campuswide network can be accessed from student residence rooms and from off campus. At least one staffed computer lab available.

Student Life *Housing:* on-campus residence required for freshman year. *Activities and organizations:* drama/theater group, student-run newspaper, radio and television station, choral group, marching band, Associated Student Body, School Spirit, sport clubs, Black Student Union, Student Programming Board, national fraternities, national sororities. *Campus security:* 24-hour emergency response devices and patrols, late-night transport/escort service, controlled dormitory access, crime prevention programs. *Student services:* health clinic, personal/psychological counseling, women's center, legal services.

Athletics Member NCAA. All Division I except football (Division I-A). *Intercollegiate sports:* baseball M(s), basketball M(s)/W(s), cross-country running M(s)/W(s), fencing M(c)/W(c), golf M(s)/W(s), lacrosse M(c), riflery W(s), rugby M(c), soccer M(c)/W(s), softball W(s), tennis M(s)/W(s), track and field M(s)/W(s), volleyball M(c)/W(s). *Intramural sports:* badminton M/W, basketball M/W, football M/W, golf M/W, racquetball M/W, riflery M(c), soccer M/W, softball M/W, swimming M/W, table tennis M(c)/W(c), tennis M/W, track and field M/W, volleyball M/W, water polo M/W.

Standardized Tests *Recommended:* SAT I or ACT (for admission).

Costs (2003–04) *Tuition:* state resident $3916 full-time; nonresident $8826 full-time. *Room and board:* $5300. *Payment plan:* tuition prepayment.

Financial Aid Of all full-time matriculated undergraduates who enrolled in 2001, 4,823 applied for aid, 3,522 were judged to have need, 1,438 had their need fully met. 482 Federal Work-Study jobs (averaging $1213). In 2001, 1260 non-need-based awards were made. *Average percent of need met:* 76%. *Average financial aid package:* $7374. *Average need-based loan:* $4065. *Average need-based gift aid:* $4650. *Average non-need-based aid:* $6308. *Average indebtedness upon graduation:* $14,459.

Applying *Options:* electronic application, early admission. *Required:* high school transcript, minimum 2.0 GPA. *Application deadlines:* 7/20 (freshmen), 7/24 (transfers). *Notification:* continuous until 8/16 (freshmen), continuous until 8/16 (transfers).

Admissions Contact Mr. Beckett Howorth, Director of Admissions, University of Mississippi, 145 Martindale Student services Center, University, MS 38677. *Phone:* 662-915-7226. *Toll-free phone:* 800-653-6477. *Fax:* 662-915-5869. *E-mail:* admissions@olemiss.edu.

UNIVERSITY OF MISSISSIPPI MEDICAL CENTER

Jackson, Mississippi

- **State-supported** upper-level, founded 1955
- **Calendar** semesters
- **Degrees** certificates, bachelor's, master's, doctoral, and first professional
- **Urban** 164-acre campus
- **Endowment** $31.7 million
- **Coed,** 483 undergraduate students, 96% full-time, 81% women, 19% men

Undergraduates 463 full-time, 20 part-time. Students come from 1 other state, 0.1% are from out of state, 17% African American, 0.6% Hispanic American, 0.2% Native American, 66% transferred in.

Faculty *Total:* 2,301, 26% full-time, 76% with terminal degrees. *Student/faculty ratio:* 2:1.

Majors Clinical laboratory science/medical technology; cytotechnology; dental hygiene; health information/medical records administration; nursing (registered nurse training).

Academic Programs *Special study options:* distance learning, internships, services for LD students, study abroad.

Library Rowland Medical Library with 291,435 titles, 2,371 serial subscriptions, 17,084 audiovisual materials, an OPAC, a Web page.

Computers on Campus 90 computers available on campus for general student use. A campuswide network can be accessed from off campus. Internet access, at least one staffed computer lab available. Computer purchase or lease plan available.

Student Life *Housing options:* women-only. Campus housing is university owned. *Activities and organizations:* student-run newspaper. *Campus security:* 24-hour emergency response devices and patrols, late-night transport/escort service, controlled dormitory access. *Student services:* health clinic, personal/psychological counseling.

Athletics *Intramural sports:* basketball M/W, football M/W, golf M, rugby M, soccer M/W, softball M/W, volleyball M/W.

Costs (2003–04) *Tuition:* state resident $3078 full-time, $128 per credit hour part-time; nonresident $6579 full-time, $273 per credit hour part-time. Full-time tuition and fees vary according to program. Part-time tuition and fees vary according to course load and program. *Room only:* $2080. Room and board charges vary according to housing facility. *Waivers:* employees or children of employees.

Financial Aid Of all full-time matriculated undergraduates who enrolled in 2001, 368 applied for aid, 191 were judged to have need, 41 had their need fully met. In 2001, 32 non-need-based awards were made. *Average percent of need met:* 47%. *Average financial aid package:* $6300. *Average need-based loan:* $4200. *Average need-based gift aid:* $2500. *Average non-need-based aid:* $1000. *Average indebtedness upon graduation:* $8000.

Applying *Application fee:* $10. *Application deadline:* 2/15 (transfers). *Notification:* continuous until 5/1 (transfers).

Admissions Contact Ms. Barbara Westerfield, Director of Student Records and Registrar, University of Mississippi Medical Center, 2500 North State Street, Jackson, MS 39216-4505. *Phone:* 601-984-1080. *Fax:* 601-984-1079.

University of Southern Mississippi
Hattiesburg, Mississippi

- **State-supported** university, founded 1910
- **Calendar** semesters
- **Degrees** bachelor's, master's, and doctoral
- **Suburban** 1090-acre campus with easy access to New Orleans
- **Coed**
- **Moderately difficult** entrance level

Faculty *Student/faculty ratio:* 19:1.

Student Life *Campus security:* 24-hour emergency response devices and patrols, late-night transport/escort service, controlled dormitory access.

Athletics Member NCAA. All Division I except football (Division I-A).

Standardized Tests *Required:* SAT I or ACT (for admission).

Costs (2003–04) *Tuition:* state resident $3874 full-time, $162 per credit hour part-time; nonresident $8752 full-time, $365 per credit hour part-time. Part-time tuition and fees vary according to course load. *Room and board:* $4785; room only: $3045. Room and board charges vary according to housing facility. *Payment plans:* tuition prepayment, installment.

Financial Aid Of all full-time matriculated undergraduates who enrolled in 2002, 7,892 applied for aid, 6,652 were judged to have need, 2,223 had their need fully met. 563 Federal Work-Study jobs (averaging $1302). In 2002, 912. *Average percent of need met:* 86. *Average financial aid package:* $7034. *Average need-based loan:* $4182. *Average need-based gift aid:* $3302. *Average non-need-based aid:* $1864. *Average indebtedness upon graduation:* $11,202.

Applying *Options:* common application, electronic application, early admission, deferred entrance. *Required:* high school transcript, minimum 2.0 GPA. *Required for some:* interview.

Admissions Contact Mr. Matthew Cox, Director of Admissions, University of Southern Mississippi, 118 college Drive, # 5166, Hattiesburg, MS 39406-1000. *Phone:* 601-266-5000. *Fax:* 601-266-5148. *E-mail:* admissions@usm.edu.

Wesley College
Florence, Mississippi

Admissions Contact Rev. Chris Lohrstorfer, Director of Admissions, Wesley College, PO Box 1070, Florence, MS 39073-1070. *Phone:* 601-845-2265 Ext. 21. *Toll-free phone:* 800-748-9972. *Fax:* 601-845-2266. *E-mail:* wcadmit@aol.com.

William Carey College
Hattiesburg, Mississippi

- **Independent Southern Baptist** comprehensive, founded 1906
- **Calendar** trimesters
- **Degrees** bachelor's and master's
- **Small-town** 64-acre campus with easy access to New Orleans
- **Endowment** $6.3 million
- **Coed,** 1,762 undergraduate students, 84% full-time, 70% women, 30% men
- **Moderately difficult** entrance level, 73% of applicants were admitted

Undergraduates 1,488 full-time, 274 part-time. Students come from 15 states and territories, 12 other countries, 22% are from out of state, 31% African American, 0.4% Asian American or Pacific Islander, 2% Hispanic American, 0.5% Native American, 2% international, 21% transferred in, 35% live on campus. *Retention:* 67% of 2002 full-time freshmen returned.

Freshmen *Admission:* 233 applied, 169 admitted, 168 enrolled. *Test scores:* SAT verbal scores over 500: 27%; SAT math scores over 500: 40%; ACT scores over 18: 85%; SAT verbal scores over 600: 7%; SAT math scores over 600: 7%; ACT scores over 24: 31%; ACT scores over 30: 3%.

Faculty *Total:* 193, 49% full-time, 56% with terminal degrees. *Student/faculty ratio:* 17:1.

Majors Art; art teacher education; biology/biological sciences; biology teacher education; business administration and management; chemistry; communication/speech communication and rhetoric; drama and dance teacher education; dramatic/theatre arts; elementary education; English; English/language arts teacher education; fine/studio arts; general studies; health and physical education; health professions related; history; journalism; mathematics; mathematics teacher education; music; music performance; music teacher education; music therapy; nursing (registered nurse training); physical education teaching and coaching; psychology; religious/sacred music; religious studies; social sciences; social studies teacher education; speech teacher education.

Academic Programs *Special study options:* academic remediation for entering students, accelerated degree program, adult/continuing education programs, advanced placement credit, distance learning, double majors, honors programs, independent study, internships, off-campus study, part-time degree program, services for LD students, summer session for credit. *ROTC:* Army (c), Air Force (c).

Library I. E. Rouse Library with 95,915 titles, 398 serial subscriptions, 150 audiovisual materials, an OPAC, a Web page.

Computers on Campus 30 computers available on campus for general student use. A campuswide network can be accessed from student residence rooms and from off campus. Internet access, at least one staffed computer lab available.

Student Life *Housing:* on-campus residence required through senior year. *Options:* men-only, women-only. Campus housing is university owned. Freshman campus housing is guaranteed. *Activities and organizations:* drama/theater group, student-run newspaper, choral group, Student Government Association, Baptist Student Union, Phi Beta Lambda, Intramural, Hope Project. *Campus security:* 24-hour patrols, controlled dormitory access. *Student services:* personal/psychological counseling.

Athletics Member NAIA. *Intercollegiate sports:* baseball M(s), basketball M(s)/W(s), cheerleading M/W, golf M, soccer M(s)/W(s), softball W(s). *Intramural sports:* badminton M/W, basketball M/W, football M/W, golf M, soccer M/W, softball M/W, table tennis M/W, volleyball M/W.

Standardized Tests *Required:* SAT I or ACT (for admission).

Costs (2003–04) *Comprehensive fee:* $11,205 includes full-time tuition ($7500), mandatory fees ($315), and room and board ($3390). Full-time tuition and fees vary according to degree level and location. Part-time tuition: $250 per hour. Part-time tuition and fees vary according to degree level and location. *Required fees:* $105 per term part-time. *College room only:* $1305. Room and board charges vary according to board plan and housing facility. *Payment plan:* deferred payment. *Waivers:* employees or children of employees.

Financial Aid Of all full-time matriculated undergraduates who enrolled in 2003, 1,296 applied for aid, 1,201 were judged to have need, 1,150 had their need fully met. 240 Federal Work-Study jobs (averaging $1500). 40 state and other part-time jobs (averaging $1500). In 2003, 95 non-need-based awards were made. *Average percent of need met:* 75%. *Average financial aid package:* $8000. *Average need-based loan:* $3500. *Average need-based gift aid:* $5500. *Average non-need-based aid:* $4000. *Average indebtedness upon graduation:* $15,000.

Applying *Options:* common application, early admission, deferred entrance. *Application fee:* $20. *Required:* high school transcript. *Required for some:* letters of recommendation. *Recommended:* minimum 2.0 GPA. *Application deadline:* rolling (freshmen), rolling (transfers). *Notification:* continuous until 8/15 (freshmen), continuous until 8/15 (transfers).

Admissions Contact Mr. William N. Curry, Director of Admissions, William Carey College, 498 Tuscan Avenue, Hattiesburg, MS 39401-5499. *Phone:* 601-318-6051 Ext. 103. *Toll-free phone:* 800-962-5991. *E-mail:* admissions@wmcarey.edu.

MISSOURI

Avila University
Kansas City, Missouri

- **Independent Roman Catholic** comprehensive, founded 1916
- **Calendar** semesters
- **Degrees** certificates, bachelor's, and master's
- **Suburban** 50-acre campus
- **Endowment** $5.3 million
- **Coed,** 1,160 undergraduate students, 76% full-time, 62% women, 38% men
- **Minimally difficult** entrance level, 42% of applicants were admitted

Undergraduates 884 full-time, 276 part-time. Students come from 23 states and territories, 26 other countries, 32% are from out of state, 27% transferred in, 17% live on campus. *Retention:* 80% of 2002 full-time freshmen returned.

Freshmen *Admission:* 936 applied, 395 admitted, 152 enrolled. *Average high school GPA:* 3.10. *Test scores:* SAT verbal scores over 500: 37%; SAT math scores over 500: 50%; ACT scores over 18: 85%; SAT verbal scores over 600: 12%; SAT math scores over 600: 12%; ACT scores over 24: 18%; ACT scores over 30: 3%.

Faculty *Total:* 202, 31% full-time, 40% with terminal degrees. *Student/faculty ratio:* 12:1.

Majors Accounting; biological and physical sciences; biology/biological sciences; business/commerce; chemistry; communication/speech communication and rhetoric; computer and information sciences; dramatic/theatre arts; education (specific subject areas) related; elementary education; English; finance; general studies; health and physical education related; health/medical preparatory programs related; history; hospital and health care facilities administration; international business/trade/commerce; legal assistant/paralegal; marketing/marketing management; mathematics; medical radiologic technology; middle school education; music performance; natural sciences; nursing related; political science and government; psychology; religious studies; social work; sociology; special education.

Academic Programs *Special study options:* academic remediation for entering students, accelerated degree program, adult/continuing education programs, advanced placement credit, cooperative education, distance learning, double majors, English as a second language, independent study, internships, off-campus study, part-time degree program, services for LD students, study abroad, summer session for credit. *ROTC:* Army (c). *Unusual degree programs:* 3-2 occupational therapy, physical therapy, law with Rockhurst University, University of Missouri-Kansas City.

Library Hooley Bundshu Library with 80,865 titles, 7,179 serial subscriptions, 3,265 audiovisual materials, an OPAC, a Web page.

Computers on Campus 68 computers available on campus for general student use. A campuswide network can be accessed from student residence rooms. Internet access, at least one staffed computer lab available.

Student Life *Housing:* on-campus residence required through sophomore year. *Options:* coed, men-only, women-only. Campus housing is university owned. Freshman campus housing is guaranteed. *Activities and organizations:* drama/theater group, student-run newspaper, television station, choral group, Group Activities Programming, Avila Student Nurses Association, Residence Hall Association, Student Senate, Black Student Union. *Campus security:* 24-hour emergency response devices, student patrols, late-night transport/escort service, controlled dormitory access. *Student services:* health clinic, personal/psychological counseling.

Athletics Member NAIA. *Intercollegiate sports:* baseball M(s), basketball M(s)/W(s), cheerleading W(s), football M(s), golf W(s), soccer M(s)/W(s), softball W(s), volleyball W(s). *Intramural sports:* basketball M/W, bowling M/W, football M/W, golf M/W, soccer M/W, softball M/W, table tennis M/W, tennis M/W, volleyball M/W, weight lifting M/W.

Standardized Tests *Required:* SAT I or ACT (for admission).

Costs (2004–05) *Comprehensive fee:* $21,270 includes full-time tuition ($15,500), mandatory fees ($370), and room and board ($5400). Full-time tuition and fees vary according to course load. Part-time tuition: $365 per credit hour. Part-time tuition and fees vary according to course load. No tuition increase for student's term of enrollment. *Required fees:* $12 per credit hour part-time. *Room and board:* Room and board charges vary according to board plan and housing facility. *Payment plans:* installment, deferred payment. *Waivers:* children of alumni, senior citizens, and employees or children of employees.

Financial Aid Of all full-time matriculated undergraduates who enrolled in 2003, 190 applied for aid. In 2003, 184 non-need-based awards were made. *Average indebtedness upon graduation:* $17,125.

Applying *Options:* common application, early admission. *Required:* high school transcript, minimum 2.5 GPA. *Required for some:* essay or personal statement, letters of recommendation. *Recommended:* interview. *Application deadline:* rolling (freshmen), rolling (transfers). *Notification:* continuous (freshmen), continuous (transfers).

Admissions Contact Ms. Paige Illum, Director of Admissions, Avila University, 11901 Wornall Rd, Kansas City, MO 64145. *Phone:* 816-501-3773. *Toll-free phone:* 800-GO-AVILA. *Fax:* 816-501-2453. *E-mail:* admissions@mail.avila.edu.

BAPTIST BIBLE COLLEGE
Springfield, Missouri

- **Independent Baptist** comprehensive, founded 1950
- **Calendar** semesters
- **Degrees** certificates, associate, bachelor's, master's, and first professional
- **Suburban** 38-acre campus
- **Coed,** 653 undergraduate students
- **Noncompetitive** entrance level, 76% of applicants were admitted

Undergraduates Students come from 46 states and territories, 5 other countries, 80% are from out of state, 0.9% African American, 0.3% Asian American or Pacific Islander, 3% Hispanic American, 0.6% Native American, 2% international, 61% live on campus.

Freshmen *Admission:* 264 applied, 200 admitted.

Faculty *Total:* 37, 73% full-time.

Majors Administrative assistant and secretarial science; business administration and management; divinity/ministry; elementary education; music; music teacher education; pastoral studies/counseling; religious education.

Academic Programs *Special study options:* academic remediation for entering students, internships, part-time degree program, summer session for credit. *ROTC:* Army (c).

Library 36,844 titles, 226 serial subscriptions.

Computers on Campus 50 computers available on campus for general student use. At least one staffed computer lab available.

Student Life *Housing:* on-campus residence required through senior year. *Options:* men-only, women-only. Campus housing is university owned. *Activities and organizations:* drama/theater group, student-run radio station, choral group. *Student services:* health clinic, personal/psychological counseling.

Athletics Member NAIA. *Intercollegiate sports:* basketball M/W, soccer M, volleyball W. *Intramural sports:* basketball M/W, soccer M, table tennis M/W, volleyball M/W.

Standardized Tests *Required:* ACT (for placement).

Costs (2003–04) *Comprehensive fee:* $8860 includes full-time tuition ($3562), mandatory fees ($574), and room and board ($4724). Full-time tuition and fees vary according to program.

Applying *Options:* early admission, deferred entrance. *Application fee:* $40. *Required:* high school transcript, 1 letter of recommendation. *Application deadline:* rolling (freshmen), rolling (transfers). *Notification:* continuous (freshmen), continuous (transfers).

Admissions Contact Dr. Joseph Gleason, Director of Admissions, Baptist Bible College, 628 East Kearney, Springfield, MO 65803-3498. *Phone:* 417-268-6000 Ext. 6013. *Fax:* 417-268-6694.

CALVARY BIBLE COLLEGE AND THEOLOGICAL SEMINARY
Kansas City, Missouri

- **Independent nondenominational** comprehensive, founded 1932
- **Calendar** semesters
- **Degrees** certificates, diplomas, associate, bachelor's, master's, and first professional
- **Suburban** 55-acre campus
- **Endowment** $154,365
- **Coed,** 266 undergraduate students, 83% full-time, 42% women, 58% men
- **Minimally difficult** entrance level, 76% of applicants were admitted

Undergraduates 220 full-time, 46 part-time. Students come from 22 states and territories, 4 other countries, 56% are from out of state, 8% African American, 3% Asian American or Pacific Islander, 2% Hispanic American, 0.8% Native American, 2% international. *Retention:* 69% of 2002 full-time freshmen returned.

Freshmen *Admission:* 58 applied, 44 admitted, 44 enrolled. *Average high school GPA:* 3.50. *Test scores:* SAT verbal scores over 500: 50%; SAT math scores over 500: 50%; ACT scores over 18: 91%; SAT verbal scores over 600: 25%; SAT math scores over 600: 25%; ACT scores over 24: 50%; ACT scores over 30: 6%.

Faculty *Total:* 34, 24% full-time, 32% with terminal degrees. *Student/faculty ratio:* 12:1.

Majors Biblical studies; broadcast journalism; elementary education; mass communication/media; missionary studies and missiology; music; music related; music teacher education; organizational behavior; pastoral counseling and specialized ministries related; pastoral studies/counseling; piano and organ; religious education; religious/sacred music; secondary education; urban studies/affairs; voice and opera; youth ministry.

Academic Programs *Special study options:* academic remediation for entering students, accelerated degree program, adult/continuing education programs, advanced placement credit, distance learning, double majors, independent study, off-campus study, part-time degree program, summer session for credit.

Library Hilda Kroeker Library with 59,000 titles, 307 serial subscriptions, an OPAC, a Web page.

Computers on Campus 10 computers available on campus for general student use. At least one staffed computer lab available.

Student Life *Housing:* on-campus residence required through senior year. *Options:* men-only, women-only. Campus housing is university owned. Freshman campus housing is guaranteed. *Activities and organizations:* drama/theater group, student-run radio station, choral group, Missions Encounter, Masterworks (Fine Arts). *Campus security:* late-night transport/escort service, night patrols by trained security personnel. *Student services:* health clinic, personal/psychological counseling.

Athletics Member NCCAA. *Intercollegiate sports:* basketball M/W, cheerleading W, soccer M, volleyball W. *Intramural sports:* badminton M/W, basketball M/W, bowling M/W, golf M/W, racquetball M/W, softball M/W, table tennis M/W, tennis M/W, volleyball M/W.

Standardized Tests *Required:* SAT I or ACT (for admission).

Costs (2004–05) *Comprehensive fee:* $10,312 includes full-time tuition ($6180), mandatory fees ($432), and room and board ($3700). Full-time tuition and fees vary according to course load. Part-time tuition: $230 per credit. Part-time tuition and fees vary according to course load. *Required fees:* $18 per credit part-time. *Room and board:* Room and board charges vary according to housing facility. *Payment plan:* installment. *Waivers:* employees or children of employees.

Financial Aid *Financial aid deadline:* 4/1.

Calvary Bible College and Theological Seminary (continued)

Applying *Options:* early admission, deferred entrance. *Application fee:* $25. *Required:* essay or personal statement, high school transcript, 2 letters of recommendation, statement of faith. *Required for some:* interview. *Application deadlines:* 8/11 (freshmen), 8/11 (transfers).

Admissions Contact Mr. Robert E. Crank, Director of Admissions and Financial Aid, Calvary Bible College and Theological Seminary, 15800 Calvary Road, Kansas City, MO 64147-1341. *Phone:* 816-322-0110 Ext. 1326. *Toll-free phone:* 800-326-3960. *Fax:* 816-331-4474. *E-mail:* admissions@calvary.edu.

CENTRAL BIBLE COLLEGE
Springfield, Missouri

- **Independent Assemblies of God** 4-year, founded 1922
- **Calendar** semesters
- **Degrees** certificates, diplomas, associate, and bachelor's
- **Suburban** 108-acre campus
- **Coed**
- **Moderately difficult** entrance level

Faculty *Student/faculty ratio:* 18:1.

Student Life *Campus security:* 24-hour emergency response devices and patrols, student patrols, controlled dormitory access.

Athletics Member NCCAA.

Standardized Tests *Required:* SAT I or ACT (for placement).

Costs (2003–04) *Comprehensive fee:* $11,478 includes full-time tuition ($6942), mandatory fees ($594), and room and board ($3942).

Financial Aid Of all full-time matriculated undergraduates who enrolled in 2003, 601 applied for aid, 541 were judged to have need. 137 Federal Work-Study jobs (averaging $1200). In 2003, 32. *Average percent of need met:* 48. *Average financial aid package:* $5482. *Average need-based loan:* $3846. *Average need-based gift aid:* $3618. *Average non-need-based aid:* $1117. *Average indebtedness upon graduation:* $28,959.

Applying *Options:* early admission, deferred entrance. *Application fee:* $25. *Required:* essay or personal statement, high school transcript, 3 letters of recommendation. *Required for some:* interview. *Recommended:* minimum 2.0 GPA.

Admissions Contact Mrs. Eunice A. Bruegman, Director of Admissions and Records, Central Bible College, 3000 North Grant Avenue, Springfield, MO 65803-1096. *Phone:* 417-833-2551 Ext. 1184. *Toll-free phone:* 800-831-4222 Ext. 1184. *Fax:* 417-833-5141. *E-mail:* info@cbcag.edu.

CENTRAL CHRISTIAN COLLEGE OF THE BIBLE
Moberly, Missouri

Admissions Contact Ms. Misty Rodda, Director of Admissions, Central Christian College of the Bible, 911 Urbandale Drive East, Moberly, MO 65270-1997. *Phone:* 660-263-3900. *Toll-free phone:* 888-263-3900. *Fax:* 660-263-3936. *E-mail:* iwant2be@cccb.edu.

CENTRAL METHODIST COLLEGE
Fayette, Missouri

- **Independent Methodist** comprehensive, founded 1854
- **Calendar** semesters
- **Degrees** associate, bachelor's, and master's
- **Small-town** 80-acre campus
- **Endowment** $19.3 million
- **Coed,** 850 undergraduate students, 93% full-time, 52% women, 48% men
- **Moderately difficult** entrance level, 73% of applicants were admitted

Undergraduates 791 full-time, 59 part-time. Students come from 17 states and territories, 10% are from out of state, 7% African American, 0.2% Asian American or Pacific Islander, 1% Hispanic American, 0.4% Native American, 2% international, 9% transferred in, 70% live on campus. *Retention:* 57% of 2002 full-time freshmen returned.

Freshmen *Admission:* 1,033 applied, 756 admitted, 224 enrolled. *Average high school GPA:* 3.21. *Test scores:* ACT scores over 18: 95%; ACT scores over 24: 24%; ACT scores over 30: 1%.

Faculty *Total:* 71, 76% full-time, 55% with terminal degrees. *Student/faculty ratio:* 14:1.

Majors Accounting; applied mathematics; athletic training; biology/biological sciences; biology teacher education; business administration and management; chemistry; chemistry teacher education; communication/speech communication and rhetoric; computer science; criminal justice/safety; dramatic/theatre arts; early childhood education; economics; education; elementary education; English; environmental biology; environmental science; foreign languages and literatures; foreign language teacher education; French; history; interdisciplinary studies; kindergarten/preschool education; management science; mathematics; middle school education; music; music performance; music teacher education; nursing administration; nursing (registered nurse training); philosophy; physical education teaching and coaching; physics; physics teacher education; political science and government; psychology; public administration; religious studies; science teacher education; secondary education; social science teacher education; sociology; Spanish; sport and fitness administration.

Academic Programs *Special study options:* academic remediation for entering students, accelerated degree program, advanced placement credit, distance learning, double majors, honors programs, independent study, internships, off-campus study, part-time degree program, services for LD students, student-designed majors, study abroad, summer session for credit. *ROTC:* Army (c), Air Force (c). *Unusual degree programs:* 3-2 engineering with University of Missouri-Rolla.

Library Smiley Library plus 1 other with 97,793 titles, 316 serial subscriptions, 379 audiovisual materials, an OPAC, a Web page.

Computers on Campus 72 computers available on campus for general student use. A campuswide network can be accessed from student residence rooms and from off campus. Internet access, at least one staffed computer lab available.

Student Life *Housing:* on-campus residence required through senior year. *Options:* coed, men-only, women-only. Campus housing is university owned. *Activities and organizations:* drama/theater group, student-run newspaper, radio and television station, choral group, marching band, Student Government Association, Wesley Foundation, Alpha Phi Omega, Christian Students United in Christ, Big Brothers/Big Sisters program. *Campus security:* 24-hour emergency response devices, late-night transport/escort service, controlled dormitory access. *Student services:* health clinic, personal/psychological counseling.

Athletics Member NAIA. *Intercollegiate sports:* baseball M(s), basketball M(s)/W(s), cross-country running M(s)/W(s), football M(s), golf M(s)/W(s), soccer M(s)/W(s), softball W(s), track and field M(s)/W(s), volleyball W(s). *Intramural sports:* basketball M/W, football M/W, golf M/W, racquetball M/W, soccer M/W, softball M/W, tennis M/W, track and field M/W, volleyball M/W, water polo M/W.

Standardized Tests *Required:* SAT I or ACT (for admission). *Recommended:* ACT (for admission).

Costs (2003–04) *Comprehensive fee:* $18,680 includes full-time tuition ($13,160), mandatory fees ($600), and room and board ($4920). Part-time tuition: $140 per credit hour. Part-time tuition and fees vary according to course load. *Required fees:* $26 per credit hour part-time. *College room only:* $2420. *Payment plan:* installment. *Waivers:* employees or children of employees.

Financial Aid Of all full-time matriculated undergraduates who enrolled in 2003, 635 applied for aid, 635 were judged to have need, 24 had their need fully met. 145 Federal Work-Study jobs (averaging $1000). 90 state and other part-time jobs (averaging $1619). In 2003, 23 non-need-based awards were made. *Average percent of need met:* 33%. *Average financial aid package:* $10,109. *Average need-based loan:* $2095. *Average need-based gift aid:* $3515. *Average non-need-based aid:* $5862. *Average indebtedness upon graduation:* $17,037.

Applying *Options:* common application, electronic application, early admission, deferred entrance. *Required:* high school transcript, minimum 2.0 GPA. *Required for some:* 2 letters of recommendation. *Application deadlines:* 8/1 (freshmen), 8/15 (transfers). *Notification:* continuous (freshmen), continuous (transfers).

Admissions Contact Mr. Edward J Lamm, Director of Admissions, Central Methodist College, 411 Central Methodist Square, Fayette, MO 65248-1198. *Phone:* 660-248-6247. *Toll-free phone:* 888-CMC-1854. *Fax:* 660-248-1872. *E-mail:* admissions@cmc.edu.

CENTRAL MISSOURI STATE UNIVERSITY
Warrensburg, Missouri

- **State-supported** comprehensive, founded 1871
- **Calendar** semesters
- **Degrees** associate, bachelor's, master's, post-master's, and postbachelor's certificates
- **Small-town** 1561-acre campus with easy access to Kansas City
- **Endowment** $68,018
- **Coed,** 8,707 undergraduate students, 82% full-time, 54% women, 46% men
- **Moderately difficult** entrance level, 76% of applicants were admitted

Central Missouri State University offers outstanding career-oriented programs in more than 150 areas of study within the arts and sciences, applied sciences and technology, business, and education and human services. A friendly environment, an excellent faculty, and state-of-the-art facilities make the 1,240-acre campus an exciting place to learn and live.

Undergraduates 7,128 full-time, 1,579 part-time. Students come from 44 states and territories, 59 other countries, 7% are from out of state, 5% African American, 1% Asian American or Pacific Islander, 1% Hispanic American, 0.6% Native American, 3% international, 9% transferred in, 32% live on campus. *Retention:* 71% of 2002 full-time freshmen returned.

Freshmen *Admission:* 3,544 applied, 2,709 admitted, 1,438 enrolled. *Test scores:* ACT scores over 18: 91%; ACT scores over 24: 28%; ACT scores over 30: 3%.

Faculty *Total:* 551, 78% full-time, 63% with terminal degrees. *Student/faculty ratio:* 18:1.

Majors Accounting; administrative assistant and secretarial science; aeronautical/aerospace engineering technology; agribusiness; agricultural business and management; agricultural economics; agricultural mechanization; agricultural teacher education; apparel and textiles; architectural engineering technology; art teacher education; automobile/automotive mechanics technology; automotive engineering technology; biology/biological sciences; biology teacher education; business administration and management; business statistics; business teacher education; chemistry; chemistry teacher education; child care and support services management; clinical laboratory science/medical technology; commercial and advertising art; communication and media related; computer and information sciences; construction engineering technology; criminal justice/law enforcement administration; dental laboratory technology; dietetics; drafting and design technology; dramatic/theatre arts; economics; education; electrical, electronic and communications engineering technology; elementary education; English; English/language arts teacher education; family and consumer sciences/home economics teacher education; family and consumer sciences/human sciences; finance; fine/studio arts; French; French language teacher education; geography; geology/earth science; German; German language teacher education; heating, air conditioning and refrigeration technology; history; hotel/motel administration; human resources management; industrial technology; interior architecture; interior design; journalism; legal support services related; management information systems; marketing/marketing management; mathematics; mathematics teacher education; merchandising, sales, and marketing operations related (specialized); middle school education; music; music teacher education; music theory and composition; nursing (registered nurse training); occupational safety and health technology; office management; parks, recreation and leisure; photography; physical education teaching and coaching; physics; physics teacher education; political science and government; pre-dentistry studies; pre-medical studies; pre-pharmacy studies; pre-veterinary studies; printing management; psychology; public relations/image management; radio and television; reading teacher education; science teacher education; secondary education; social studies teacher education; social work; sociology; Spanish; Spanish language teacher education; special education; speech and rhetoric; speech-language pathology; speech teacher education; technology/industrial arts teacher education; tourism and travel services marketing.

Academic Programs *Special study options:* academic remediation for entering students, adult/continuing education programs, advanced placement credit, cooperative education, distance learning, double majors, English as a second language, honors programs, internships, off-campus study, part-time degree program, services for LD students, student-designed majors, study abroad, summer session for credit. *ROTC:* Army (b), Air Force (c). *Unusual degree programs:* 3-2 engineering with University of Missouri-Columbia, University of Missouri-Rolla, University of Missouri-Kansas City.

Library James C. Kirkpatrick Library with 567,934 titles, 3,582 serial subscriptions, 23,690 audiovisual materials, an OPAC, a Web page.

Computers on Campus 1230 computers available on campus for general student use. A campuswide network can be accessed from student residence rooms and from off campus. Internet access, online (class) registration, at least one staffed computer lab available.

Student Life *Housing:* on-campus residence required for freshman year. *Options:* coed, men-only, women-only, disabled students. Campus housing is university owned. Freshman campus housing is guaranteed. *Activities and organizations:* drama/theater group, student-run newspaper, radio and television station, choral group, marching band, Student Government Association, Campus Activities Board, Association of Black Collegiates, Greek Associations, International Student Organization, national fraternities, national sororities. *Campus security:* 24-hour emergency response devices and patrols, student patrols, late-night transport/escort service, controlled dormitory access, canine patrol. *Student services:* health clinic, personal/psychological counseling, women's center.

Athletics Member NCAA. All Division II. *Intercollegiate sports:* baseball M(s), basketball M(s)/W(s), bowling M(c)/W(c), cross-country running M(s)/W(s), football M(s), golf M(s), rugby M(c)/W(c), soccer M(c)/W(s), softball W(s), track and field M(s)/W(s), volleyball W(s), wrestling M(s). *Intramural sports:* archery M, badminton M/W, basketball M/W, bowling M/W, cheerleading M/W, cross-country running M/W, football M/W, golf M/W, racquetball M/W, riflery M/W, rugby M/W, soccer M/W, softball M/W, swimming M/W, table tennis M/W, tennis M/W, track and field M/W, volleyball M/W, water polo M/W, weight lifting M, wrestling M.

Standardized Tests *Required:* ACT (for admission).

Costs (2003–04) *Tuition:* state resident $4980 full-time, $154 per credit part-time; nonresident $9600 full-time, $308 per credit part-time. Full-time tuition and fees vary according to course load and location. *Required fees:* $360 full-time, $12 per credit part-time. *Room and board:* $4796; room only: $2998. Room and board charges vary according to board plan and housing facility. *Payment plans:* installment, deferred payment. *Waivers:* children of alumni, senior citizens, and employees or children of employees.

Financial Aid Of all full-time matriculated undergraduates who enrolled in 2002, 5,693 applied for aid, 4,413 were judged to have need, 2,020 had their need fully met. 460 Federal Work-Study jobs (averaging $1235). 1,400 state and other part-time jobs (averaging $1175). In 2002, 2121 non-need-based awards were made. *Average percent of need met:* 92%. *Average financial aid package:* $6752. *Average need-based loan:* $3819. *Average need-based gift aid:* $3436. *Average non-need-based aid:* $2556. *Average indebtedness upon graduation:* $8827.

Applying *Options:* common application, electronic application, deferred entrance. *Application fee:* $25. *Required:* high school transcript, rank in upper two-thirds of high school class, minimum ACT score of 20. *Required for some:* letters of recommendation. *Application deadline:* rolling (freshmen), rolling (transfers). *Notification:* continuous (freshmen), continuous (transfers).

Admissions Contact Mr. Matt Melvin, Assistant Provost, Enrollment Management, Central Missouri State University, 1401 Ward Edwards, Warrensburg, MO 64093. *Phone:* 660-543-4290. *Toll-free phone:* 800-729-2678. *Fax:* 660-543-8517. *E-mail:* admit@cmsuvmb.cmsu.edu.

CLEVELAND CHIROPRACTIC COLLEGE-KANSAS CITY CAMPUS

Kansas City, Missouri

- **Independent** upper-level, founded 1922
- **Calendar** trimesters
- **Degrees** bachelor's and first professional
- **Urban** campus
- **Coed,** 71 undergraduate students, 86% full-time, 37% women, 63% men

Undergraduates 61 full-time, 10 part-time. Students come from 18 states and territories, 1 other country, 43% are from out of state, 4% African American, 1% Asian American or Pacific Islander, 1% international.

Faculty *Total:* 45. *Student/faculty ratio:* 15:1.

Majors Biology/biological sciences.

Academic Programs *Special study options:* academic remediation for entering students, accelerated degree program, cooperative education, internships, services for LD students, summer session for credit.

Library Ruth R. Cleveland Memorial Library with 14,000 titles, 268 serial subscriptions, 12,320 audiovisual materials, an OPAC, a Web page.

Computers on Campus 14 computers available on campus for general student use. A campuswide network can be accessed. Internet access available.

Student Life *Housing:* college housing not available.

Costs (2003–04) *Tuition:* $3670 full-time. *Required fees:* $150 full-time.

Applying *Options:* electronic application, deferred entrance. *Application fee:* $35.

Admissions Contact Ms. Melissa Denton, Director of Admissions, Cleveland Chiropractic College-Kansas City Campus, 6401 Rockhill Road, Kansas City, MO 64131. *Phone:* 816-501-0100. *Toll-free phone:* 800-467-2252. *Fax:* 816-501-0205. *E-mail:* kc.admissions@cleveland.edu.

COLLEGE OF THE OZARKS

Point Lookout, Missouri

- **Independent Presbyterian** 4-year, founded 1906
- **Calendar** semesters
- **Degree** bachelor's
- **Small-town** 1000-acre campus
- **Endowment** $255.6 million
- **Coed,** 1,348 undergraduate students, 95% full-time, 56% women, 44% men
- **Moderately difficult** entrance level, 14% of applicants were admitted

Undergraduates 1,278 full-time, 70 part-time. Students come from 26 states and territories, 22 other countries, 33% are from out of state, 0.4% African American, 0.6% Asian American or Pacific Islander, 1% Hispanic American, 0.4% Native American, 2% international, 2% transferred in, 68% live on campus. *Retention:* 76% of 2002 full-time freshmen returned.

College of the Ozarks (continued)

Freshmen *Admission:* 2,076 applied, 290 admitted, 254 enrolled. *Average high school GPA:* 2.89. *Test scores:* ACT scores over 18: 92%; ACT scores over 24: 34%; ACT scores over 30: 13%.

Faculty *Total:* 119, 73% full-time, 46% with terminal degrees. *Student/faculty ratio:* 15:1.

Majors Accounting; acting; agribusiness; agricultural mechanization; agricultural mechanization related; agricultural teacher education; agronomy and crop science; agronomy/crop science; animal sciences; apparel and textiles; applied horticulture; art; art teacher education; avionics maintenance technology; biology/biological sciences; biology teacher education; broadcast journalism; business administration and management; business/managerial economics; business teacher education; chemistry; chemistry teacher education; child care/guidance; child development; child guidance; clinical laboratory science/medical technology; communication and journalism related; computer and information sciences; computer science; consumer services and advocacy; corrections; criminal justice/law enforcement administration; criminal justice/police science; criminology; dietetics; dramatic/theatre arts; education; elementary education; engineering; English; English/language arts teacher education; family and consumer sciences/home economics teacher education; family and consumer sciences/human sciences; family/community studies; fine/studio arts; foods, nutrition, and wellness; forensic science and technology; French; French language teacher education; German; gerontology; graphic/printing equipment; health and physical education; health/medical preparatory programs related; health science; history; history related; history teacher education; horticultural science; hotel and restaurant management; hotel/motel administration; industrial arts; information technology; interdisciplinary studies; international business/trade/commerce; journalism; marketing/marketing management; mass communication/media; mathematics; mathematics teacher education; middle school education; multi-/interdisciplinary studies related; music; music management and merchandising; music related; music teacher education; parks, recreation and leisure facilities management; philosophy; philosophy and religious studies related; physical education teaching and coaching; political science and government; poultry science; pre-law studies; pre-medical studies; pre-pharmacy studies; pre-veterinary studies; psychology; public relations/image management; religious/sacred music; religious studies; science teacher education; science, technology and society; secondary education; social work; sociology; Spanish; speech and rhetoric; technology/industrial arts teacher education; wildlife and wildlands science and management.

Academic Programs *Special study options:* academic remediation for entering students, accelerated degree program, advanced placement credit, cooperative education, honors programs, internships, part-time degree program, student-designed majors, study abroad, summer session for credit. *ROTC:* Army (b). *Unusual degree programs:* 3-2 engineering with various colleges.

Library Lyons Memorial Library plus 1 other with 118,235 titles, 503 serial subscriptions, 5,193 audiovisual materials.

Computers on Campus 80 computers available on campus for general student use. A campuswide network can be accessed from student residence rooms and from off campus. Internet access, at least one staffed computer lab available.

Student Life *Housing:* on-campus residence required through senior year. *Options:* men-only, women-only. Campus housing is university owned. *Activities and organizations:* drama/theater group, student-run newspaper, radio station, choral group, aviation club, Student Senate, Baptist Student Union, Aggie Club, Business Undergraduate Society. *Campus security:* 24-hour emergency response devices and patrols, controlled dormitory access, front gate closed 1 a.m. to 6 a.m., gate security 5:30 p.m. to 1 a.m. *Student services:* health clinic, personal/psychological counseling.

Athletics Member NAIA. *Intercollegiate sports:* baseball M(s), basketball M(s)/W(s), volleyball W(s). *Intramural sports:* basketball M/W, fencing M/W, football M/W, golf M/W, racquetball M/W, soccer M, softball M/W, volleyball M/W, weight lifting M/W.

Standardized Tests *Required:* SAT I or ACT (for admission).

Costs (2004–05) *Comprehensive fee:* includes mandatory fees ($250) and room and board ($3550). Part-time tuition: $275 per credit. *Required fees:* $125 per term part-time. *College room only:* $1800. *Payment plan:* installment. *Waivers:* employees or children of employees.

Financial Aid Of all full-time matriculated undergraduates who enrolled in 2002, 1,253 applied for aid, 1,127 were judged to have need, 395 had their need fully met. 200 Federal Work-Study jobs (averaging $2884). 550 state and other part-time jobs (averaging $2884). In 2002, 126 non-need-based awards were made. *Average percent of need met:* 90%. *Average financial aid package:* $12,446. *Average need-based gift aid:* $7716. *Average non-need-based aid:* $12,466. *Average indebtedness upon graduation:* $6060.

Applying *Options:* early admission. *Required:* high school transcript, 2 letters of recommendation, interview, medical history, financial statement. *Recommended:* minimum 2.0 GPA. *Application deadlines:* 2/15 (freshmen), 2/1 (transfers). *Notification:* continuous (freshmen), continuous (transfers).

Admissions Contact Mrs. Gayle Groves, Admissions Secretary, College of the Ozarks, PO Box 17, Point Lookout, MO 65726. *Phone:* 417-334-6411 Ext. 4217. *Toll-free phone:* 800-222-0525. *Fax:* 417-335-2618. *E-mail:* admiss4@cofo.edu.

COLUMBIA COLLEGE

Columbia, Missouri

- **Independent** comprehensive, founded 1851, affiliated with Christian Church (Disciples of Christ)
- **Calendar** semesters
- **Degrees** associate, bachelor's, and master's (offers continuing education program with significant enrollment not reflected in profile)
- **Small-town** 29-acre campus
- **Endowment** $10.5 million
- **Coed,** 916 undergraduate students, 75% full-time, 62% women, 38% men
- **Minimally difficult** entrance level, 59% of applicants were admitted

Undergraduates 686 full-time, 230 part-time. Students come from 20 states and territories, 28 other countries, 5% are from out of state, 6% African American, 2% Asian American or Pacific Islander, 2% Hispanic American, 0.9% Native American, 5% international, 13% transferred in, 36% live on campus. *Retention:* 71% of 2002 full-time freshmen returned.

Freshmen *Admission:* 891 applied, 524 admitted, 157 enrolled. *Average high school GPA:* 3.15. *Test scores:* ACT scores over 18: 86%; ACT scores over 24: 37%; ACT scores over 30: 5%.

Faculty *Total:* 88, 67% full-time, 57% with terminal degrees. *Student/faculty ratio:* 11:1.

Majors Accounting; art; biology/biological sciences; business administration and management; chemistry; computer and information sciences; computer science; criminal justice/law enforcement administration; drawing; education; English; environmental studies; finance; forensic science and technology; graphic design; history; illustration; international business/trade/commerce; liberal arts and sciences/liberal studies; management science; marketing/marketing management; mathematics; multi-/interdisciplinary studies related; nursing (registered nurse training); painting; philosophy and religious studies related; photography; political science and government; pre-dentistry studies; pre-engineering; pre-law studies; pre-medical studies; pre-veterinary studies; printmaking; psychology; social work; sociology.

Academic Programs *Special study options:* academic remediation for entering students, accelerated degree program, adult/continuing education programs, advanced placement credit, cooperative education, distance learning, double majors, English as a second language, honors programs, independent study, internships, off-campus study, part-time degree program, student-designed majors, study abroad, summer session for credit. *ROTC:* Army (c), Navy (c), Air Force (c). *Unusual degree programs:* 3-2 education.

Library Stafford Library with 62,265 titles, 382 serial subscriptions, 3,613 audiovisual materials, an OPAC, a Web page.

Computers on Campus 137 computers available on campus for general student use. A campuswide network can be accessed from student residence rooms and from off campus. Internet access, at least one staffed computer lab available.

Student Life *Housing:* on-campus residence required through sophomore year. *Options:* coed, women-only. Campus housing is university owned. Freshman campus housing is guaranteed. *Activities and organizations:* drama/theater group, student-run newspaper, choral group, Students in Free Enterprise, Campus Community Government, Student Leaders Advocating Teaching Excellence, Spanish club, Criminal Justice Association. *Campus security:* 24-hour emergency response devices and patrols, late-night transport/escort service, controlled dormitory access. *Student services:* health clinic, personal/psychological counseling.

Athletics Member NAIA. *Intercollegiate sports:* basketball M(s)/W(s), cheerleading W, soccer M(s), softball W(s), volleyball W(s). *Intramural sports:* basketball M/W, softball M/W, table tennis M/W, volleyball M/W.

Standardized Tests *Required:* ACT (for admission). *Recommended:* SAT I (for admission).

Costs (2004–05) *Comprehensive fee:* $16,502 includes full-time tuition ($11,589) and room and board ($4913). Full-time tuition and fees vary according to class time and course load. Part-time tuition: $248 per credit hour. Part-time tuition and fees vary according to class time, course load, and location. *College room only:* $3090. Room and board charges vary according to board plan. *Payment plan:* deferred payment. *Waivers:* children of alumni and employees or children of employees.

Financial Aid Of all full-time matriculated undergraduates who enrolled in 2003, 529 applied for aid, 394 were judged to have need, 258 had their need fully met. 169 Federal Work-Study jobs (averaging $910). In 2003, 145 non-need-based awards were made. *Average percent of need met:* 85%. *Average financial aid package:* $7426. *Average need-based loan:* $3934. *Average need-based gift aid:* $3541. *Average non-need-based aid:* $8780. *Average indebtedness upon graduation:* $4479.

Applying *Options:* common application, early admission, deferred entrance. *Application fee:* $25. *Required:* high school transcript, minimum 2.0 GPA. *Required for some:* essay or personal statement, letters of recommendation, interview. *Recommended:* rank in upper 50% of high school class. *Application deadline:* rolling (freshmen), rolling (transfers). *Notification:* continuous (freshmen), continuous (transfers).

Admissions Contact Ms. Regina Morin, Director of Admissions, Columbia College, 1001 Rogers Street, Columbia, MO 65216. *Phone:* 573-875-7352. *Toll-free phone:* 800-231-2391 Ext. 7366. *Fax:* 573-875-7506. *E-mail:* admissions@ccis.edu.

■ *See page 1472 for a narrative description.*

CONCEPTION SEMINARY COLLEGE
Conception, Missouri

- **Independent Roman Catholic** 4-year, founded 1886
- **Calendar** semesters
- **Degree** certificates and bachelor's
- **Rural** 30-acre campus
- **Men only,** 100 undergraduate students, 90% full-time
- **Noncompetitive** entrance level, 100% of applicants were admitted

Undergraduates 90 full-time, 10 part-time. Students come from 18 states and territories, 5 other countries, 67% are from out of state, 1% African American, 10% Asian American or Pacific Islander, 6% Hispanic American, 8% international, 24% transferred in, 100% live on campus. *Retention:* 82% of 2002 full-time freshmen returned.

Freshmen *Admission:* 10 enrolled. *Average high school GPA:* 3.44. *Test scores:* ACT scores over 18: 88%; ACT scores over 24: 29%; ACT scores over 30: 11%.

Faculty *Total:* 26, 92% full-time, 77% with terminal degrees. *Student/faculty ratio:* 4:1.

Majors Liberal arts and sciences/liberal studies.

Academic Programs *Special study options:* academic remediation for entering students, advanced placement credit, double majors, English as a second language, independent study, off-campus study.

Library Conception Seminary College Library with 115,000 titles, 300 serial subscriptions, 5,000 audiovisual materials, a Web page.

Computers on Campus 12 computers available on campus for general student use. A campuswide network can be accessed from off campus. Internet access, at least one staffed computer lab available.

Student Life *Housing:* on-campus residence required through senior year. *Options:* men-only. Campus housing is university owned. *Activities and organizations:* drama/theater group, student-run newspaper, choral group, Vocation Committee, Drama Club, Apostolics, Fine Arts Committee, Social Concerns Committee. *Student services:* health clinic, personal/psychological counseling.

Athletics *Intramural sports:* basketball M, bowling M, cross-country running M, football M, golf M, gymnastics M, racquetball M, soccer M, softball M, swimming M, table tennis M, tennis M, track and field M, ultimate Frisbee M, volleyball M, weight lifting M.

Standardized Tests *Required:* ACT (for admission).

Costs (2004–05) *Comprehensive fee:* $18,406 includes full-time tuition ($11,432), mandatory fees ($180), and room and board ($6794). Part-time tuition: $150 per credit. *College room only:* $2874. Room and board charges vary according to board plan. *Payment plan:* installment.

Financial Aid Of all full-time matriculated undergraduates who enrolled in 2003, 42 applied for aid, 41 were judged to have need, 20 had their need fully met. 16 Federal Work-Study jobs (averaging $1350). 30 state and other part-time jobs (averaging $1144). In 2003, 35 non-need-based awards were made. *Average percent of need met:* 88%. *Average financial aid package:* $16,464. *Average need-based loan:* $4099. *Average need-based gift aid:* $9699. *Average non-need-based aid:* $17,044. *Average indebtedness upon graduation:* $10,815.

Applying *Options:* electronic application. *Required:* essay or personal statement, high school transcript, minimum 2.0 GPA, 2 letters of recommendation, church certificate, medical history. *Application deadlines:* 7/31 (freshmen), 7/31 (transfers). *Notification:* continuous until 8/15 (freshmen), continuous until 8/15 (transfers).

Admissions Contact Mr. Vincent Casper, Director of Recruitment and Admissions, Conception Seminary College, PO Box 502, Highway 136 & VV, 37174 State Highway VV, Conception, MO 64433. *Phone:* 660-944-2886. *E-mail:* vocations@conception.edu.

CULVER-STOCKTON COLLEGE
Canton, Missouri

- **Independent** 4-year, founded 1853, affiliated with Christian Church (Disciples of Christ)
- **Calendar** semesters
- **Degree** bachelor's
- **Rural** 143-acre campus
- **Endowment** $18.5 million
- **Coed,** 835 undergraduate students, 92% full-time, 57% women, 43% men
- **Moderately difficult** entrance level, 72% of applicants were admitted

Undergraduates 767 full-time, 68 part-time. Students come from 21 states and territories, 6 other countries, 45% are from out of state, 6% African American, 0.6% Asian American or Pacific Islander, 3% Hispanic American, 0.1% Native American, 0.8% international, 8% transferred in, 71% live on campus. *Retention:* 70% of 2002 full-time freshmen returned.

Freshmen *Admission:* 1,018 applied, 729 admitted, 219 enrolled. *Average high school GPA:* 3.26. *Test scores:* ACT scores over 18: 85%; ACT scores over 24: 30%; ACT scores over 30: 2%.

Faculty *Total:* 77, 74% full-time, 52% with terminal degrees. *Student/faculty ratio:* 12:1.

Majors Accounting; art; arts management; art teacher education; athletic training; biology/biological sciences; business administration and management; chemistry; clinical laboratory science/medical technology; criminal justice/law enforcement administration; dramatic/theatre arts; elementary education; English; English/language arts teacher education; finance; history; history teacher education; information science/studies; mass communication/media; mathematics; mathematics teacher education; music; music teacher education; nursing (registered nurse training); parks, recreation, and leisure related; physical education teaching and coaching; psychology; religious studies; science teacher education; sociology; special education; speech/theater education.

Academic Programs *Special study options:* advanced placement credit, double majors, honors programs, independent study, internships, off-campus study, part-time degree program, student-designed majors, study abroad, summer session for credit. *Unusual degree programs:* 3-2 engineering with Washington University in St. Louis; occupational therapy with Washington University in St. Louis.

Library Johann Memorial Library with 155,487 titles, 777 serial subscriptions, 4,327 audiovisual materials, an OPAC, a Web page.

Computers on Campus 70 computers available on campus for general student use. A campuswide network can be accessed from student residence rooms and from off campus. Internet access, at least one staffed computer lab available.

Student Life *Housing:* on-campus residence required through senior year. *Options:* coed, men-only, women-only. Campus housing is university owned. Freshman campus housing is guaranteed. *Activities and organizations:* drama/theater group, student-run newspaper, radio station, choral group, C-S Teachers Organization, Student Ambassadors, Christian Fellowship Group, Student Government Association, Student Nurses Organization, national fraternities, national sororities. *Campus security:* 24-hour emergency response devices, late-night transport/escort service. *Student services:* health clinic, personal/psychological counseling.

Athletics Member NAIA. *Intercollegiate sports:* baseball M(s), basketball M(s)/W(s), cheerleading M(s)/W(s), football M(s), golf M(s)/W(s), soccer M(s)/W(s), softball W(s), volleyball W(s). *Intramural sports:* basketball M/W, bowling M/W, racquetball M/W, soccer M/W, softball M/W, table tennis M/W, tennis M/W, volleyball M/W.

Standardized Tests *Required:* SAT I or ACT (for admission).

Costs (2003–04) *Comprehensive fee:* $17,850 includes full-time tuition ($12,400) and room and board ($5450). Part-time tuition: $340 per credit hour. *College room only:* $2525. Room and board charges vary according to board plan. *Payment plan:* installment. *Waivers:* senior citizens and employees or children of employees.

Financial Aid Of all full-time matriculated undergraduates who enrolled in 2003, 670 applied for aid, 620 were judged to have need, 189 had their need fully met. 103 Federal Work-Study jobs (averaging $914). 215 state and other part-time jobs (averaging $1242). In 2003, 101 non-need-based awards were made. *Average percent of need met:* 82%. *Average financial aid package:* $11,676. *Average need-based loan:* $3647. *Average need-based gift aid:* $8328. *Average non-need-based aid:* $8123. *Average indebtedness upon graduation:* $14,438. *Financial aid deadline:* 6/15.

Applying *Options:* electronic application, deferred entrance. *Application fee:* $25. *Required:* high school transcript, minimum 2.0 GPA, rank in top 50% of high school class. *Required for some:* interview. *Recommended:* essay or personal statement, letters of recommendation, interview. *Application deadline:* rolling (transfers). *Notification:* continuous (transfers).

Admissions Contact Ms. Karyn Bishoff, Director of Enrollment Services, Culver-Stockton College, One College Hill, Canton, MO 63435-1299. *Phone:* 800-537-1883. *Toll-free phone:* 800-537-1883. *Fax:* 217-231-6618. *E-mail:* enrollment@culver.edu.

■ *See page 1504 for a narrative description.*

DEACONESS COLLEGE OF NURSING
St. Louis, Missouri

- **Proprietary** 4-year, founded 1889
- **Calendar** semesters
- **Degrees** associate and bachelor's
- **Urban** 15-acre campus
- **Coed, primarily women**
- **Moderately difficult** entrance level

Faculty *Student/faculty ratio:* 12:1.
Student Life *Campus security:* 24-hour patrols, late-night transport/escort service, controlled dormitory access.
Standardized Tests *Required:* ACT (for admission).
Costs (2003–04) *Comprehensive fee:* $16,000 includes full-time tuition ($10,550), mandatory fees ($250), and room and board ($5200).
Financial Aid Of all full-time matriculated undergraduates who enrolled in 2002, 149 applied for aid, 117 were judged to have need, 19 had their need fully met. 22 Federal Work-Study jobs (averaging $1136). In 2002, 15. *Average percent of need met:* 60. *Average financial aid package:* $7081. *Average need-based loan:* $3950. *Average need-based gift aid:* $2013. *Average non-need-based aid:* $5638. *Average indebtedness upon graduation:* $20,900.
Applying *Options:* deferred entrance. *Application fee:* $30. *Required:* essay or personal statement, high school transcript. *Required for some:* letters of recommendation, interview. *Recommended:* minimum 2.5 GPA.
Admissions Contact Ms. Lisa Mancini, Dean of Enrollment and Student services, Deaconess College of Nursing, 6150 Oakland Avenue, St. Louis, MO 63139-3215. *Phone:* 314-768-3179. *Toll-free phone:* 800-942-4310. *Fax:* 314-768-5673.

DEVRY UNIVERSITY
Kansas City, Missouri

Admissions Contact City Center Square, 1100 Main Street, Suite 118, Kansas City, MO 64105-2112.

DEVRY UNIVERSITY
St. Louis, Missouri

Admissions Contact 1801 Park 270 Drive, Suite 260, St. Louis, MO 63146-4020.

DEVRY UNIVERSITY
Kansas City, Missouri

- **Proprietary** 4-year, founded 1931, part of DeVry University
- **Calendar** semesters
- **Degrees** associate, bachelor's, and postbachelor's certificates
- **Urban** 12-acre campus
- **Coed**
- **Minimally difficult** entrance level

Faculty *Student/faculty ratio:* 23:1.
Student Life *Campus security:* 24-hour emergency response devices and patrols, lighted pathways/sidewalks.
Standardized Tests *Recommended:* SAT I, ACT or CPT.
Costs (2003–04) *Tuition:* $9990 full-time, $355 per credit hour part-time. Full-time tuition and fees vary according to course load. Part-time tuition and fees vary according to course load. *Required fees:* $165 full-time. *Payment plans:* installment, deferred payment.
Financial Aid Of all full-time matriculated undergraduates who enrolled in 2002, 1,496 applied for aid, 1,413 were judged to have need, 49 had their need fully met. In 2002, 122. *Average percent of need met:* 42. *Average financial aid package:* $8714. *Average need-based loan:* $6437. *Average need-based gift aid:* $3982. *Average non-need-based aid:* $10,431.
Applying *Options:* electronic application, deferred entrance. *Application fee:* $50. *Required:* high school transcript, interview.
Admissions Contact Ms. Anna Diamond, New Student Coordinator, DeVry University, 11224 Holmes Road, Kansas City, MO 64131-3626. *Phone:* 816-941-0430. *Toll-free phone:* 800-821-3766. *E-mail:* ssmeed@kc.devry.edu.

DRURY UNIVERSITY
Springfield, Missouri

- **Independent** comprehensive, founded 1873
- **Calendar** semesters
- **Degrees** bachelor's (also offers evening program with significant enrollment not reflected in profile)
- **Urban** 80-acre campus
- **Endowment** $72.2 million
- **Coed,** 1,541 undergraduate students, 97% full-time, 56% women, 44% men
- **Moderately difficult** entrance level, 77% of applicants were admitted

Undergraduates 1,502 full-time, 39 part-time. Students come from 35 states and territories, 50 other countries, 19% are from out of state, 1% African American, 2% Asian American or Pacific Islander, 1% Hispanic American, 0.5% Native American, 5% international, 7% transferred in, 50% live on campus. *Retention:* 83% of 2002 full-time freshmen returned.
Freshmen *Admission:* 1,128 applied, 865 admitted, 365 enrolled. *Average high school GPA:* 3.67. *Test scores:* SAT verbal scores over 500: 85%; SAT math scores over 500: 90%; ACT scores over 18: 100%; SAT verbal scores over 600: 50%; SAT math scores over 600: 54%; ACT scores over 24: 67%; SAT verbal scores over 700: 18%; SAT math scores over 700: 11%; ACT scores over 30: 16%.
Faculty *Total:* 179, 67% full-time, 74% with terminal degrees. *Student/faculty ratio:* 11:1.
Majors Accounting; advertising; American government and politics; architecture; art; art history, criticism and conservation; arts management; behavioral sciences; biology/biological sciences; broadcast journalism; business administration and management; chemistry; computer and information sciences; computer science; creative writing; criminology; design and visual communications; dramatic/theatre arts; economics; education; elementary education; English; environmental studies; fine/studio arts; French; German; history; international business/trade/commerce; journalism; kinesiology and exercise science; mass communication/media; mathematics; music; music performance; music theory and composition; philosophy; physics; political science and government; pre-dentistry studies; pre-law studies; pre-medical studies; pre-veterinary studies; psychology; public relations/image management; religious studies; secondary education; Spanish.
Academic Programs *Special study options:* accelerated degree program, adult/continuing education programs, advanced placement credit, cooperative education, distance learning, double majors, English as a second language, honors programs, independent study, internships, off-campus study, part-time degree program, services for LD students, student-designed majors, study abroad, summer session for credit. *ROTC:* Army (c). *Unusual degree programs:* 3-2 engineering with Washington University in St. Louis; international management with American Graduate School of International Management, occupational therapy with Washington University in St. Louis.
Library F. W. Olin Library plus 1 other with 177,794 titles, 868 serial subscriptions, 60,098 audiovisual materials, an OPAC, a Web page.
Computers on Campus 323 computers available on campus for general student use. A campuswide network can be accessed from student residence rooms and from off campus that provide access to digital imaging lab. Internet access, online (class) registration, at least one staffed computer lab available.
Student Life *Housing:* on-campus residence required for freshman year. *Options:* coed, men-only, women-only. Campus housing is university owned and leased by the school. Freshman campus housing is guaranteed. *Activities and organizations:* drama/theater group, student-run newspaper, radio and television station, choral group, Student Union Board, Community Outreach/Taking a Stand for Kids, choral groups and bands, International Student Organization, academic department clubs, national fraternities, national sororities. *Campus security:* 24-hour emergency response devices and patrols, student patrols, late-night transport/escort service, controlled dormitory access, security cameras in parking areas. *Student services:* health clinic, personal/psychological counseling.
Athletics Member NCAA. All Division II. *Intercollegiate sports:* basketball M(s), cross-country running M(s)/W(s), golf M(s)/W(s), soccer M(s)/W(s), swimming M(s)/W(s), tennis M(s)/W(s), volleyball W(s). *Intramural sports:* basketball M/W, bowling M/W, football M/W, racquetball M/W, rugby W, soccer M/W, softball M/W, table tennis M/W, tennis M/W, ultimate Frisbee M/W, volleyball M/W.
Standardized Tests *Required:* SAT I or ACT (for admission).
Costs (2004–05) *Comprehensive fee:* $19,032 includes full-time tuition ($13,600), mandatory fees ($304), and room and board ($5128). Part-time tuition: $448 per semester hour. *Room and board:* Room and board charges vary according to board plan and housing facility. *Payment plans:* tuition prepayment, installment, deferred payment. *Waivers:* children of alumni, senior citizens, and employees or children of employees.
Financial Aid Of all full-time matriculated undergraduates who enrolled in 2003, 1,496 applied for aid, 1,388 were judged to have need, 1,249 had their need fully met. 421 Federal Work-Study jobs (averaging $2500). 106 state and other part-time jobs (averaging $1555). In 2003, 153 non-need-based awards were made. *Average percent of need met:* 83%. *Average financial aid package:* $7695. *Average need-based loan:* $5450. *Average need-based gift aid:* $6895. *Average non-need-based aid:* $2955. *Average indebtedness upon graduation:* $14,200.

Applying *Options:* electronic application, deferred entrance. *Application fee:* $25. *Required:* essay or personal statement, high school transcript, minimum 2.7 GPA, 1 letter of recommendation, minimum ACT score of 21. *Recommended:* interview. *Application deadline:* 3/15 (freshmen), rolling (transfers). *Notification:* continuous (freshmen), continuous (transfers).

Admissions Contact Mr. Chip Parker, Director of Admission, Drury University, 900 North Benton, Bay Hall, Springfield, MO 65802. *Phone:* 417-873-7205. *Toll-free phone:* 800-922-2274. *Fax:* 417-866-3873. *E-mail:* druryad@drury.edu.

EVANGEL UNIVERSITY
Springfield, Missouri

- **Independent** comprehensive, founded 1955, affiliated with Assemblies of God
- **Calendar** semesters
- **Degrees** associate, bachelor's, and master's
- **Urban** 80-acre campus
- **Endowment** $3.8 million
- **Coed,** 1,811 undergraduate students, 96% full-time, 59% women, 41% men
- **Moderately difficult** entrance level, 81% of applicants were admitted

Prominent Evangel University alumni include Admiral Vern Clerk, Chief of Naval Operations, U.S. Navy; Congressman Todd Tiahrt (R-KS); Dr. Fred Mihm, Professor of Anesthesiology, Director of ICU, Stanford University Medical School; Steve Poppen, VP/CFO, Minnesota Vikings (NFL); Beverly Lewis, best-selling author of inspirational fiction (*October Song, The Shunning*); and Phil Stanton, founding member of Blue Man Group.

Undergraduates 1,737 full-time, 74 part-time. Students come from 49 states and territories, 59% are from out of state, 3% African American, 1% Asian American or Pacific Islander, 2% Hispanic American, 1% Native American, 0.2% international, 8% transferred in, 82% live on campus. *Retention:* 75% of 2002 full-time freshmen returned.

Freshmen *Admission:* 862 applied, 696 admitted, 442 enrolled. *Average high school GPA:* 3.34. *Test scores:* ACT scores over 18: 90%; ACT scores over 24: 26%; ACT scores over 30: 7%.

Faculty *Total:* 147, 64% full-time, 41% with terminal degrees. *Student/faculty ratio:* 18:1.

Majors Accounting; administrative assistant and secretarial science; art; art teacher education; behavioral sciences; biblical studies; biology/biological sciences; biology teacher education; broadcast journalism; business administration and management; business teacher education; chemistry; chemistry teacher education; child development; clinical laboratory science/medical technology; computer science; criminal justice/law enforcement administration; early childhood education; education; elementary education; English; health and physical education; history; history teacher education; intercultural/multicultural and diversity studies; journalism; kindergarten/preschool education; marketing/marketing management; mass communication/media; mathematics; medical laboratory technology; mental health/rehabilitation; middle school education; music; music teacher education; parks, recreation and leisure; physical education teaching and coaching; political science and government; pre-dentistry studies; pre-law studies; pre-medical studies; pre-veterinary studies; psychology; public administration; radio and television; religious/sacred music; science teacher education; secondary education; social sciences; social work; sociology; Spanish; Spanish language teacher education; special education; speech and rhetoric; speech teacher education.

Academic Programs *Special study options:* academic remediation for entering students, accelerated degree program, adult/continuing education programs, advanced placement credit, double majors, internships, part-time degree program, services for LD students, summer session for credit. *ROTC:* Army (b). *Unusual degree programs:* 3-2 engineering with Washington University in St. Louis, University of Missouri-Rolla.

Library Claude Kendrick Library with 100,691 titles, 1,060 serial subscriptions, 6,962 audiovisual materials, an OPAC.

Computers on Campus 136 computers available on campus for general student use. At least one staffed computer lab available.

Student Life *Housing:* on-campus residence required through senior year. *Options:* coed. Campus housing is university owned. Freshman campus housing is guaranteed. *Activities and organizations:* drama/theater group, student-run newspaper, radio station, choral group, Evangel Student Government Association, Student Missouri State Teachers Association, Crosswalk, Students in Free Enterprise. *Campus security:* 24-hour emergency response devices and patrols, student patrols, late-night transport/escort service, controlled dormitory access. *Student services:* health clinic, personal/psychological counseling.

Athletics Member NAIA. *Intercollegiate sports:* baseball M(s), basketball M(s)/W(s), cross-country running M(s)/W(s), football M(s), golf M(s)/W(s), softball W(s), tennis M(s)/W(s), track and field M(s)/W(s), volleyball W(s). *Intramural sports:* baseball M, basketball M/W, football M, golf M/W, soccer M/W, softball W, tennis M/W, volleyball W.

Standardized Tests *Required:* SAT I or ACT (for admission).

Costs (2004–05) *Comprehensive fee:* $16,305 includes full-time tuition ($11,250), mandatory fees ($695), and room and board ($4360). Full-time tuition and fees vary according to course load. Part-time tuition: $438 per credit hour. *Required fees:* $274 per term part-time. *College room only:* $2100. Room and board charges vary according to board plan. *Payment plan:* installment. *Waivers:* employees or children of employees.

Financial Aid Of all full-time matriculated undergraduates who enrolled in 2002, 1,121 applied for aid, 1,016 were judged to have need, 93 had their need fully met. 315 Federal Work-Study jobs (averaging $929). 123 state and other part-time jobs (averaging $897). In 2002, 269 non-need-based awards were made. *Average percent of need met:* 56%. *Average financial aid package:* $8091. *Average need-based loan:* $4091. *Average need-based gift aid:* $4812. *Average non-need-based aid:* $5527. *Average indebtedness upon graduation:* $21,467.

Applying *Options:* electronic application, deferred entrance. *Application fee:* $25. *Required:* high school transcript. *Recommended:* minimum 2.0 GPA. *Application deadlines:* 8/1 (freshmen), 8/1 (transfers). *Notification:* continuous (freshmen), continuous (transfers).

Admissions Contact Ms. Charity Waltner, Director of Admissions, Evangel University, 1111 North Glenstone, Springfield, MO 65802. *Phone:* 417-865-2811 Ext. 7262. *Toll-free phone:* 800-382-6435. *Fax:* 417-865-9599. *E-mail:* admissions@evangel.edu.

FONTBONNE UNIVERSITY
St. Louis, Missouri

- **Independent Roman Catholic** comprehensive, founded 1917
- **Calendar** semesters
- **Degrees** certificates, bachelor's, master's, and postbachelor's certificates
- **Suburban** 13-acre campus
- **Endowment** $7.5 million
- **Coed,** 1,767 undergraduate students, 74% full-time, 77% women, 23% men
- **Moderately difficult** entrance level, 81% of applicants were admitted

Undergraduates 1,300 full-time, 467 part-time. Students come from 23 states and territories, 1 other country, 14% are from out of state, 29% African American, 0.6% Asian American or Pacific Islander, 1% Hispanic American, 0.6% Native American, 0.8% international, 16% transferred in, 16% live on campus. *Retention:* 74% of 2002 full-time freshmen returned.

Freshmen *Admission:* 505 applied, 409 admitted, 205 enrolled. *Average high school GPA:* 3.20. *Test scores:* ACT scores over 18: 81%; ACT scores over 24: 31%; ACT scores over 30: 3%.

Faculty *Total:* 294, 22% full-time, 38% with terminal degrees. *Student/faculty ratio:* 12:1.

Majors Accounting; advertising; art; arts management; art teacher education; audiology and speech-language pathology; biology/biological sciences; broadcast journalism; business administration and management; civil engineering technology; commercial and advertising art; communication/speech communication and rhetoric; computer science; consumer merchandising/retailing management; dietetics; dramatic/theatre arts; education; elementary education; engineering; English; family and consumer sciences/home economics teacher education; family and consumer sciences/human sciences; fashion merchandising; finance; fine/studio arts; history; human services; kindergarten/preschool education; liberal arts and sciences/liberal studies; management information systems; marketing/marketing management; mathematics; middle school education; pre-law studies; pre-medical studies; psychology; religious studies; secondary education; social sciences; special education; speech therapy.

Academic Programs *Special study options:* academic remediation for entering students, accelerated degree program, adult/continuing education programs, advanced placement credit, cooperative education, distance learning, double majors, English as a second language, honors programs, independent study, internships, off-campus study, services for LD students, student-designed majors, summer session for credit. *ROTC:* Army (c). *Unusual degree programs:* 3-2 engineering with Washington University in St. Louis; social work with Washington University in St. Louis.

Library Fontbonne Library with 102,552 titles, 333 serial subscriptions, 14,983 audiovisual materials, an OPAC, a Web page.

Computers on Campus 120 computers available on campus for general student use. A campuswide network can be accessed from student residence rooms and from off campus. Internet access, online (class) registration, at least one staffed computer lab available.

Student Life *Housing options:* coed, women-only. Campus housing is university owned. Freshman campus housing is guaranteed. *Activities and organizations:* drama/theater group, student-run newspaper, choral group, Future Teachers

Fontbonne University (continued)
Association, Students for the Enhancement of Black Awareness, Fontbonne Athletic Association, Fontbonne in Service and Humility, Student Government Association. *Campus security:* 24-hour patrols, late-night transport/escort service, controlled dormitory access. *Student services:* health clinic, personal/psychological counseling.

Athletics Member NCAA, NAIA. All NCAA Division III. *Intercollegiate sports:* baseball M, basketball M/W, cheerleading W, cross-country running M/W, golf M/W, soccer M/W, softball W, tennis M/W, volleyball W. *Intramural sports:* basketball M/W, soccer M, volleyball M/W.

Standardized Tests *Required:* SAT I or ACT (for admission).

Costs (2004–05) *Comprehensive fee:* $22,408 includes full-time tuition ($15,100), mandatory fees ($320), and room and board ($6988). Full-time tuition and fees vary according to program and reciprocity agreements. Part-time tuition: $410 per credit hour. Part-time tuition and fees vary according to course load, program, and reciprocity agreements. *Required fees:* $16 per credit hour part-time. *Room and board:* Room and board charges vary according to board plan and housing facility. *Payment plans:* installment, deferred payment. *Waivers:* senior citizens and employees or children of employees.

Financial Aid In 2002, 502 non-need-based awards were made. *Average percent of need met:* 86%. *Average financial aid package:* $15,600.

Applying *Options:* common application, electronic application, early admission, deferred entrance. *Application fee:* $25. *Required:* essay or personal statement, high school transcript, minimum 2.5 GPA. *Recommended:* 2 letters of recommendation, interview. *Application deadline:* 8/1 (freshmen), rolling (transfers). *Notification:* continuous (freshmen), continuous (transfers).

Admissions Contact Ms. Peggy Musen, Associate Dean for Enrollment Management, Fontbonne University, 6800 Wydown Boulevard, St. Louis, MO 63105-3098. *Phone:* 314-889-1400. *Fax:* 314-719-8021. *E-mail:* pmusen@fontbonne.edu.

GLOBAL UNIVERSITY OF THE ASSEMBLIES OF GOD
Springfield, Missouri

- **Independent** comprehensive, founded 1948, affiliated with Assemblies of God
- **Calendar** continuous
- **Degrees** certificates, diplomas, associate, bachelor's, master's, and postbachelor's certificates (offers only external degree programs)
- **Coed,** 6,503 undergraduate students, 23% full-time, 35% women, 65% men
- **Noncompetitive** entrance level

Undergraduates 1,511 full-time, 4,992 part-time. Students come from 50 states and territories, 127 other countries, 97% are from out of state.

Faculty *Total:* 498, 12% full-time, 46% with terminal degrees.

Majors Biblical studies; divinity/ministry; missionary studies and missiology; pastoral studies/counseling; religious education; religious studies; theology.

Academic Programs *Special study options:* academic remediation for entering students, accelerated degree program, adult/continuing education programs, advanced placement credit, cooperative education, distance learning, external degree program, honors programs, independent study, internships, part-time degree program.

Library Global University Library with 180 serial subscriptions, a Web page.

Student Life *Housing:* college housing not available. *Campus security:* 24-hour emergency response devices.

Costs (2003–04) *Tuition:* $2160 full-time, $90 per credit hour part-time. Full-time tuition and fees vary according to reciprocity agreements. Part-time tuition and fees vary according to course load and reciprocity agreements. *Payment plan:* installment. *Waivers:* employees or children of employees.

Applying *Application fee:* $35. *Required:* high school transcript. *Required for some:* 1 letter of recommendation. *Recommended:* essay or personal statement. *Application deadline:* rolling (freshmen), rolling (transfers).

Admissions Contact Ms. Jessica Dorn, Director of US Enrollments, Global University of the Assemblies of God, 1211 South Glenstone Avenue, Springfield, MO 65804. *Phone:* 800-443-1083. *Toll-free phone:* 800-443-1083. *E-mail:* studentinfo@globaluniversity.edu.

HANNIBAL-LAGRANGE COLLEGE
Hannibal, Missouri

- **Independent Southern Baptist** 4-year, founded 1858
- **Calendar** semesters
- **Degrees** associate and bachelor's
- **Small-town** 110-acre campus
- **Endowment** $4.0 million
- **Coed,** 1,133 undergraduate students, 65% full-time, 62% women, 38% men
- **Moderately difficult** entrance level, 94% of applicants were admitted

Undergraduates 731 full-time, 402 part-time. Students come from 24 states and territories, 17% are from out of state, 1% African American, 1% Asian American or Pacific Islander, 1% Hispanic American, 60% live on campus. *Retention:* 66% of 2002 full-time freshmen returned.

Freshmen *Admission:* 335 applied, 314 admitted. *Average high school GPA:* 2.98. *Test scores:* ACT scores over 18: 96%; ACT scores over 24: 35%; ACT scores over 30: 6%.

Faculty *Total:* 92, 58% full-time, 34% with terminal degrees. *Student/faculty ratio:* 14:1.

Majors Art; art teacher education; biblical studies; biology/biological sciences; business administration and management; business teacher education; chemistry; communication and journalism related; communication/speech communication and rhetoric; computer and information sciences; criminal justice/law enforcement administration; dramatic/theatre arts; early childhood education; education; elementary education; emergency medical technology (EMT paramedic); English; English/language arts teacher education; history; history teacher education; human services; kindergarten/preschool education; liberal arts and sciences/liberal studies; marketing/marketing management; mathematics; mathematics teacher education; medical administrative assistant and medical secretary; music; music teacher education; nursing (registered nurse training); parks, recreation and leisure facilities management; physical education teaching and coaching; piano and organ; pre-engineering; pre-law studies; psychology; religious education; religious/sacred music; science teacher education; secondary education; sociology; speech and rhetoric; voice and opera.

Academic Programs *Special study options:* academic remediation for entering students, accelerated degree program, adult/continuing education programs, advanced placement credit, cooperative education, double majors, freshman honors college, honors programs, independent study, internships, part-time degree program, services for LD students, student-designed majors, study abroad, summer session for credit.

Library L. A. Foster Library with 71,680 titles, 516 serial subscriptions, 6,605 audiovisual materials, an OPAC.

Computers on Campus 76 computers available on campus for general student use. A campuswide network can be accessed from student residence rooms and from off campus. Internet access, at least one staffed computer lab available.

Student Life *Housing options:* men-only, women-only. Campus housing is university owned. Freshman campus housing is guaranteed. *Activities and organizations:* drama/theater group, student-run newspaper, choral group, Phi Beta Lambda, Student Government, Student Teachers Organization, Phi Beta Delta, Association of Women Students. *Campus security:* 24-hour emergency response devices and patrols, late-night transport/escort service, controlled dormitory access. *Student services:* health clinic, personal/psychological counseling.

Athletics Member NAIA, NCCAA. *Intercollegiate sports:* baseball M(s), basketball M(s)/W(s), cheerleading M(s)/W(s), cross-country running M(s)/W(s), golf M(s), soccer M(s)/W(s), softball W(s), volleyball W(s). *Intramural sports:* basketball M/W, racquetball M/W, soccer M/W, softball M/W, tennis M/W, volleyball M/W.

Standardized Tests *Required:* SAT I or ACT (for admission).

Costs (2003–04) *Comprehensive fee:* $13,940 includes full-time tuition ($9840), mandatory fees ($320), and room and board ($3780). Full-time tuition and fees vary according to course load. Part-time tuition: $328 per credit hour. Part-time tuition and fees vary according to course load. *Required fees:* $70 per term part-time. *Room and board:* Room and board charges vary according to board plan and housing facility. *Payment plan:* deferred payment. *Waivers:* employees or children of employees.

Financial Aid Of all full-time matriculated undergraduates who enrolled in 2003, 676 applied for aid, 465 were judged to have need. 68 Federal Work-Study jobs (averaging $550). *Average financial aid package:* $8918. *Average need-based loan:* $3882. *Average need-based gift aid:* $3172. *Average indebtedness upon graduation:* $14,588.

Applying *Options:* early admission, deferred entrance. *Application fee:* $25. *Required:* high school transcript, minimum 2.0 GPA, 2 letters of recommendation. *Application deadline:* 8/26 (freshmen), rolling (transfers). *Notification:* continuous (freshmen).

Admissions Contact Mr. Raymond Carty, Dean of Enrollment Management, Hannibal-LaGrange College, 2800 Palmyra Road, Hannibal, MO 63401-1999. *Phone:* 573-221-3113. *Toll-free phone:* 800-HLG-1119. *E-mail:* admissio@hlg.edu.

HARRIS-STOWE STATE COLLEGE

St. Louis, Missouri

- **State-supported** 4-year, founded 1857, part of Missouri Coordinating Board for Higher Education
- **Calendar** semesters
- **Degree** bachelor's
- **Urban** 22-acre campus
- **Coed,** 1,911 undergraduate students, 31% full-time, 77% women, 23% men
- **Moderately difficult** entrance level, 47% of applicants were admitted

Undergraduates 591 full-time, 1,320 part-time. Students come from 3 states and territories, 13 other countries, 9% are from out of state, 7% transferred in. *Retention:* 62% of 2002 full-time freshmen returned.

Freshmen *Admission:* 433 applied, 204 admitted, 128 enrolled. *Average high school GPA:* 2.40. *Test scores:* ACT scores over 18: 45%; ACT scores over 24: 2%.

Faculty *Total:* 145, 38% full-time, 17% with terminal degrees. *Student/faculty ratio:* 17:1.

Majors Accounting; business administration and management; business/commerce; criminal justice/law enforcement administration; early childhood education; elementary education; health/health care administration; information science/studies; interdisciplinary studies; juvenile corrections; kindergarten/preschool education; marketing/marketing management; middle school education; public administration; secondary education; urban education and leadership; urban studies/affairs.

Academic Programs *Special study options:* academic remediation for entering students, advanced placement credit, cooperative education, internships, off-campus study, part-time degree program, services for LD students, student-designed majors, summer session for credit. *ROTC:* Air Force (c).

Library Southwestern Bell Library and Technology Center with 60,000 titles, 340 serial subscriptions, 15 audiovisual materials, an OPAC.

Computers on Campus 96 computers available on campus for general student use. A campuswide network can be accessed. Internet access, at least one staffed computer lab available.

Student Life *Housing:* college housing not available. *Activities and organizations:* drama/theater group, choral group, drama club, concert chorale, Student Government Association, Multicultural Council, Student Ambassadors, national fraternities, national sororities. *Campus security:* 24-hour emergency response devices, student patrols, late-night transport/escort service, 16-hour patrols by trained security personnel Monday through Friday, 24-hour weekend and holiday patrols. *Student services:* health clinic, personal/psychological counseling.

Athletics Member NAIA. *Intercollegiate sports:* baseball M(s), basketball M(s)/W(s), cheerleading M(s)/W(s), soccer M(s)/W(s), track and field W(s), volleyball W(s).

Standardized Tests *Required:* SAT I or ACT (for admission).

Costs (2003–04) *Tuition:* state resident $3120 full-time, $130 per credit hour part-time; nonresident $6146 full-time, $256 per credit hour part-time. Full-time tuition and fees vary according to course load. Part-time tuition and fees vary according to course load. *Required fees:* $160 full-time, $80 per term part-time. *Payment plans:* installment, deferred payment. *Waivers:* employees or children of employees.

Financial Aid Of all full-time matriculated undergraduates who enrolled in 2002, 348 applied for aid, 348 were judged to have need, 59 had their need fully met. 66 Federal Work-Study jobs (averaging $1878). 87 state and other part-time jobs (averaging $2279). In 2002, 7 non-need-based awards were made. *Average percent of need met:* 65%. *Average financial aid package:* $2890. *Average need-based loan:* $1905. *Average need-based gift aid:* $1779. *Average non-need-based aid:* $814. *Average indebtedness upon graduation:* $14,000.

Applying *Options:* early admission, deferred entrance. *Application fee:* $15. *Required:* high school transcript, minimum 2.0 GPA. *Application deadline:* rolling (freshmen), rolling (transfers). *Notification:* continuous (transfers).

Admissions Contact Ms. LaShanda Boone, Director of Admissions, Harris-Stowe State College, 3026 Laclede Avenue, St. Louis, MO 63103. *Phone:* 314-340-3301. *Fax:* 314-340-3555. *E-mail:* admissions@hssc.edu.

HICKEY COLLEGE

St. Louis, Missouri

- **Proprietary** 2-year, founded 1933
- **Calendar** semesters
- **Degree** diplomas, associate, bachelor's
- **Suburban** campus
- **Coed,** 450 undergraduate students

Founded in 1933, Hickey College provides business and technology programs that prepare students to enter the business world in the shortest possible time. Diploma, associate, and bachelor's degree programs are available. Programs are offered in accounting, administrative assistant studies, applied management, computer applications, computer programming, graphic design, legal administrative assistant studies, and paralegal studies.

Faculty *Total:* 17, 71% full-time. *Student/faculty ratio:* 30:1.

Majors Accounting technician; business administration and management; computer programming; executive assistant; graphic design; legal administrative assistant; paralegal/legal assistant.

Academic Programs *Special study options:* accelerated degree program.

Computers on Campus 109 computers available on campus for general student use.

Costs (2003–04) *Tuition:* $10480 full-time. *Room only:* $4840.

Applying *Application fee:* $50. *Required:* high school transcript, interview. *Application deadline:* rolling (freshmen), rolling (transfers).

Admissions Contact Ms. Michelle Hayes, Director of Admissions, Hickey College, 940 West Port Plaza Drive, St. Louis, MO 63146. *Phone:* 314-434-2212 Ext. 137. *Toll-free phone:* 800-777-1544. *Fax:* 314-434-1974. *E-mail:* admin@hickeycollege.com

ITT TECHNICAL INSTITUTE

Arnold, Missouri

- **Proprietary** primarily 2-year, part of ITT Educational Services, Inc.
- **Calendar** quarters
- **Degrees** associate and bachelor's
- **Coed**
- **Minimally difficult** entrance level

Standardized Tests *Required:* Wonderlic aptitude test (for admission).

Costs (2003–04) *Tuition:* $347 per credit hour part-time.

Applying *Options:* deferred entrance. *Application fee:* $100. *Required:* high school transcript, interview. *Recommended:* letters of recommendation.

Admissions Contact Mr. James R. Rowe, Director of Recruitment, ITT Technical Institute, 1930 Meyer Drury Drive, Arnold, MO 63010. *Phone:* 636-464-6600. *Toll-free phone:* 888-488-1082. *Fax:* 636-464-6611.

ITT TECHNICAL INSTITUTE

Earth City, Missouri

- **Proprietary** primarily 2-year, founded 1936, part of ITT Educational Services, Inc.
- **Calendar** quarters
- **Degrees** associate and bachelor's
- **Suburban** 2-acre campus with easy access to St. Louis
- **Coed**
- **Minimally difficult** entrance level

Standardized Tests *Required:* Wonderlic aptitude test (for admission).

Costs (2003–04) *Tuition:* $347 per credit hour part-time.

Applying *Options:* deferred entrance. *Application fee:* $100. *Required:* high school transcript, interview. *Recommended:* letters of recommendation.

Admissions Contact Mr. Randal Hayes, ITT Technical Institute, 13505 Lakefront Drive, Earth City, MO 63045. *Phone:* 314-298-7800. *Toll-free phone:* 800-235-5488. *Fax:* 314-298-0559.

JEWISH HOSPITAL COLLEGE OF NURSING AND ALLIED HEALTH

St. Louis, Missouri

- **Independent** comprehensive, founded 1902
- **Calendar** semesters
- **Degrees** associate, bachelor's, master's, post-master's, and postbachelor's certificates
- **Urban** campus
- **Endowment** $4.2 million
- **Coed, primarily women,** 686 undergraduate students, 29% full-time, 89% women, 11% men
- **Moderately difficult** entrance level, 91% of applicants were admitted

Undergraduates 200 full-time, 486 part-time. Students come from 7 states and territories, 14% are from out of state, 9% African American, 0.9% Asian American

Jewish Hospital College of Nursing and Allied Health (continued)
or Pacific Islander, 0.7% Hispanic American, 0.7% Native American, 16% transferred in, 1% live on campus. *Retention:* 72% of 2002 full-time freshmen returned.

Freshmen *Admission:* 310 applied, 282 admitted, 42 enrolled. *Average high school GPA:* 3.10. *Test scores:* ACT scores over 18: 100%; ACT scores over 24: 26%.

Faculty *Total:* 43, 77% full-time, 40% with terminal degrees. *Student/faculty ratio:* 10:1.

Majors Clinical laboratory science/medical technology; cytotechnology; nursing (registered nurse training).

Academic Programs *Special study options:* advanced placement credit, double majors, independent study, off-campus study, part-time degree program, services for LD students, summer session for credit.

Library George and Juanita Way Library plus 4 others with 3,765 titles, 232 serial subscriptions, 400 audiovisual materials, an OPAC, a Web page.

Computers on Campus 21 computers available on campus for general student use. A campuswide network can be accessed from off campus that provide access to software, research databases. Internet access, at least one staffed computer lab available.

Student Life *Housing options:* coed. Campus housing is university owned. *Activities and organizations:* Student Nurses Association. *Campus security:* 24-hour patrols, late-night transport/escort service, controlled dormitory access. *Student services:* personal/psychological counseling.

Athletics *Intramural sports:* soccer W, volleyball M/W.

Standardized Tests *Required:* SAT I or ACT (for admission).

Costs (2004–05) *Tuition:* $8808 full-time. Full-time tuition and fees vary according to course load. Part-time tuition and fees vary according to course load. *Required fees:* $300 full-time. *Room only:* $2550. *Payment plan:* installment.

Financial Aid Of all full-time matriculated undergraduates who enrolled in 2003, 150 applied for aid, 150 were judged to have need, 21 had their need fully met. 10 Federal Work-Study jobs (averaging $3300). In 2003, 21 non-need-based awards were made. *Average financial aid package:* $16,000. *Average need-based loan:* $4000. *Average need-based gift aid:* $4000. *Average non-need-based aid:* $9000. *Average indebtedness upon graduation:* $10,000.

Applying *Options:* common application. *Application fee:* $25. *Required:* high school transcript, minimum 2.0 GPA, 2 letters of recommendation. *Application deadline:* rolling (freshmen), rolling (transfers). *Notification:* continuous (transfers).

Admissions Contact Ms. Christie Schneider, Chief Admissions Officer, Jewish Hospital College of Nursing and Allied Health, 306 South Kingshighway Boulevard, St. Louis, MO 63110. *Phone:* 314-454-7538. *Toll-free phone:* 800-832-9009. *Fax:* 314-454-5239. *E-mail:* jhcollegeinquiry@bjc.org.

KANSAS CITY ART INSTITUTE
Kansas City, Missouri

- **Independent** 4-year, founded 1885
- **Calendar** semesters
- **Degree** bachelor's
- **Urban** 18-acre campus
- **Endowment** $17.4 million
- **Coed,** 571 undergraduate students, 98% full-time, 53% women, 47% men
- **Moderately difficult** entrance level, 81% of applicants were admitted

Undergraduates 559 full-time, 12 part-time. Students come from 37 states and territories, 36% are from out of state, 4% African American, 2% Asian American or Pacific Islander, 6% Hispanic American, 1% Native American, 1% international, 10% transferred in, 25% live on campus. *Retention:* 92% of 2002 full-time freshmen returned.

Freshmen *Admission:* 461 applied, 375 admitted, 114 enrolled. *Average high school GPA:* 3.55. *Test scores:* SAT verbal scores over 500: 70%; SAT math scores over 500: 59%; ACT scores over 18: 88%; SAT verbal scores over 600: 32%; SAT math scores over 600: 21%; ACT scores over 24: 42%; SAT verbal scores over 700: 6%; SAT math scores over 700: 3%; ACT scores over 30: 3%.

Faculty *Total:* 79, 53% full-time, 71% with terminal degrees. *Student/faculty ratio:* 9:1.

Majors Art history, criticism and conservation; ceramic arts and ceramics; commercial and advertising art; fiber, textile and weaving arts; industrial design; painting; photography; printmaking; sculpture.

Academic Programs *Special study options:* academic remediation for entering students, adult/continuing education programs, advanced placement credit, cooperative education, double majors, English as a second language, independent study, internships, off-campus study, services for LD students, study abroad, summer session for credit.

Library Charles T. and Marion M. Thompson Library with 30,000 titles, 125 serial subscriptions, an OPAC.

Computers on Campus 80 computers available on campus for general student use. A campuswide network can be accessed from student residence rooms and from off campus. Internet access, online (class) registration, at least one staffed computer lab available.

Student Life *Housing:* on-campus residence required for freshman year. *Options:* coed. Campus housing is university owned. Freshman applicants given priority for college housing. *Activities and organizations:* Student Union, Student Gallery Committee, Ethnic Student Association. *Campus security:* 24-hour emergency response devices and patrols, late-night transport/escort service, controlled dormitory access. *Student services:* personal/psychological counseling.

Standardized Tests *Required:* SAT I or ACT (for admission).

Costs (2004–05) *Comprehensive fee:* $28,126 includes full-time tuition ($21,326) and room and board ($6800). Part-time tuition: $850 per credit hour. *Room and board:* Room and board charges vary according to board plan and housing facility. *Waivers:* employees or children of employees.

Financial Aid Of all full-time matriculated undergraduates who enrolled in 2003, 451 applied for aid, 411 were judged to have need, 64 had their need fully met. 120 Federal Work-Study jobs (averaging $1000). 60 state and other part-time jobs (averaging $1000). In 2003, 119 non-need-based awards were made. *Average percent of need met:* 65%. *Average financial aid package:* $16,260. *Average need-based loan:* $6748. *Average need-based gift aid:* $9779. *Average non-need-based aid:* $10,003. *Average indebtedness upon graduation:* $17,125.

Applying *Options:* deferred entrance. *Application fee:* $35. *Required:* essay or personal statement, high school transcript, minimum 2.5 GPA, 2 letters of recommendation, portfolio, statement of purpose. *Recommended:* interview. *Application deadline:* rolling (freshmen), rolling (transfers). *Notification:* continuous until 8/1 (freshmen), continuous until 8/1 (transfers).

Admissions Contact Mr. Gerald Valet, Director of Admission Technology, Kansas City Art Institute, 4415 Warwick Boulevard, Kansas City, MO 64111-1874. *Phone:* 816-474-5224. *Toll-free phone:* 800-522-5224. *Fax:* 816-802-3309. *E-mail:* admiss@kcai.edu.

KANSAS CITY COLLEGE OF LEGAL STUDIES
Kansas City, Missouri

Admissions Contact Mrs. Rosemary Velez, Admissions Director, Kansas City College of Legal Studies, 402 East Bannister Road, Suite A, Kansas City, MO 64131. *Phone:* 816-444-2232. *Toll-free phone:* 816-444-2232 (in-state); 877-582-3963 (out-of-state).

LESTER L. COX COLLEGE OF NURSING AND HEALTH SCIENCES
Springfield, Missouri

- **Independent** 4-year, founded 1994
- **Calendar** semesters
- **Degrees** certificates, associate, and bachelor's
- **Urban** campus
- **Coed, primarily women,** 529 undergraduate students, 48% full-time, 92% women, 8% men
- 81% of applicants were admitted

Undergraduates 254 full-time, 275 part-time. Students come from 4 states and territories, 1% are from out of state, 1% African American, 1% Asian American or Pacific Islander, 1% Hispanic American, 0.6% Native American, 22% transferred in, 15% live on campus. *Retention:* 53% of 2002 full-time freshmen returned.

Freshmen *Admission:* 91 applied, 74 admitted, 53 enrolled. *Average high school GPA:* 3.48.

Faculty *Total:* 47, 45% full-time, 23% with terminal degrees. *Student/faculty ratio:* 9:1.

Majors Nursing (registered nurse training).

Academic Programs *Special study options:* academic remediation for entering students, accelerated degree program, part-time degree program, summer session for credit.

Library The Cox Health Systems Libraries.

Computers on Campus 48 computers available on campus for general student use. A campuswide network can be accessed from student residence rooms and from off campus. Internet access, at least one staffed computer lab available.

Student Life *Housing options:* coed. *Activities and organizations:* Student Nurses Association, National Student Nurses Association, Student Council, Residence Hall Council, Christian Fellowship. *Campus security:* 24-hour patrols, late-night transport/escort service. *Student services:* personal/psychological counseling.

Standardized Tests *Required:* ACT (for admission). *Recommended:* ACT (for admission), SAT I or ACT (for admission), SAT I and SAT II or ACT (for admission).

Costs (2004–05) *One-time required fee:* $100. *Tuition:* $8910 full-time, $297 per credit hour part-time. Full-time tuition and fees vary according to course load and program. Part-time tuition and fees vary according to course load and program. *Required fees:* $1050 full-time, $35 per credit hour part-time. *Room only:* $2000. *Payment plan:* deferred payment. *Waivers:* employees or children of employees.

Financial Aid Of all full-time matriculated undergraduates who enrolled in 2002, 11 Federal Work-Study jobs (averaging $2911). *Average financial aid package:* $8500.

Applying *Options:* common application, early decision. *Application fee:* $30. *Required:* high school transcript, minimum 2.5 GPA. *Application deadlines:* 2/1 (freshmen), 8/1 (transfers). *Early decision:* 11/1. *Notification:* 3/1 (freshmen), 12/1 (early decision), continuous (transfers).

Admissions Contact Ms. Jennifer Plimmer, Admission Coordinator, Lester L. Cox College of Nursing and Health Sciences, 1423 North Jefferson, Springfield, MO 65802. *Phone:* 417-269-3038. *Toll-free phone:* 866-898-5355. *Fax:* 417-269-3581. *E-mail:* admissions@coxcollege.edu.

LINCOLN UNIVERSITY

Jefferson City, Missouri

- **State-supported** comprehensive, founded 1866, part of Missouri Coordinating Board for Higher Education
- **Calendar** semesters
- **Degrees** associate, bachelor's, master's, and first professional certificates
- **Small-town** 152-acre campus
- **Coed,** 2,910 undergraduate students, 65% full-time, 61% women, 39% men
- **Noncompetitive** entrance level, 96% of applicants were admitted

Undergraduates 1,882 full-time, 1,028 part-time. 18% are from out of state, 40% African American, 0.8% Asian American or Pacific Islander, 1% Hispanic American, 0.9% Native American, 6% international, 6% transferred in, 24% live on campus. *Retention:* 54% of 2002 full-time freshmen returned.

Freshmen *Admission:* 1,155 applied, 1,109 admitted, 533 enrolled. *Test scores:* ACT scores over 18: 42%; ACT scores over 24: 6%.

Faculty *Total:* 224, 61% full-time, 36% with terminal degrees. *Student/faculty ratio:* 16:1.

Majors Accounting; administrative assistant and secretarial science; agricultural business and management; agriculture; art; art teacher education; biology/biological sciences; business administration and management; business teacher education; chemistry; clinical laboratory science/medical technology; computer science; criminal justice/law enforcement administration; data processing and data processing technology; drafting and design technology; economics; electrical, electronic and communications engineering technology; elementary education; English; fashion merchandising; French; history; industrial arts; information science/studies; journalism; marketing/marketing management; mathematics; mechanical design technology; music teacher education; nursing (registered nurse training); philosophy; physical education teaching and coaching; physics; political science and government; psychology; public administration; science teacher education; social sciences; sociology; special education.

Academic Programs *Special study options:* academic remediation for entering students, accelerated degree program, adult/continuing education programs, advanced placement credit, cooperative education, freshman honors college, honors programs, internships, part-time degree program, services for LD students, student-designed majors, summer session for credit. *ROTC:* Army (b).

Library Inman Page Library with 151,595 titles, 761 serial subscriptions.

Computers on Campus 175 computers available on campus for general student use. A campuswide network can be accessed from off campus. Internet access, at least one staffed computer lab available.

Student Life *Housing:* on-campus residence required through sophomore year. *Options:* coed, men-only, women-only. *Activities and organizations:* drama/theater group, student-run newspaper, radio and television station, choral group, marching band, national fraternities, national sororities. *Campus security:* 24-hour emergency response devices and patrols, student patrols, late-night transport/escort service, controlled dormitory access. *Student services:* health clinic, personal/psychological counseling.

Athletics Member NCAA. All Division II. *Intercollegiate sports:* baseball M(s), basketball M(s)/W(s), cross-country running M(s)/W(s), football M(s), golf M(s), soccer M(s), softball W(s), tennis W(s), track and field M(s)/W(s). *Intramural sports:* baseball M, basketball M/W, bowling M/W, track and field M/W, ultimate Frisbee M(c)/W(c).

Costs (2003–04) *Tuition:* state resident $3894 full-time, $135 per credit hour part-time; nonresident $7434 full-time, $253 per credit hour part-time. *Required fees:* $668 full-time. *Room and board:* $3790; room only: $1850.

Financial Aid Of all full-time matriculated undergraduates who enrolled in 2002, 1,500 applied for aid, 1,200 were judged to have need, 500 had their need fully met. 120 Federal Work-Study jobs (averaging $1200). 40 state and other part-time jobs (averaging $1000). In 2002, 100 non-need-based awards were made. *Average percent of need met:* 35%. *Average financial aid package:* $6000. *Average need-based loan:* $4000. *Average need-based gift aid:* $1000. *Average non-need-based aid:* $1000. *Average indebtedness upon graduation:* $10,000.

Applying *Options:* common application, early admission, deferred entrance. *Application fee:* $17. *Required:* high school transcript, 1 letter of recommendation. *Application deadline:* 8/1 (freshmen). *Notification:* 4/1 (freshmen), continuous (transfers).

Admissions Contact Executive Director of Enrollment Management, Lincoln University, 820 Chestnut Street, PO Box 29, Jefferson City, MO 62102-0029. *Phone:* 573-681-5599. *Toll-free phone:* 800-521-5052. *Fax:* 573-681-5889.

LINDENWOOD UNIVERSITY

St. Charles, Missouri

- **Independent Presbyterian** comprehensive, founded 1827
- **Calendar** 4-1-4 for daytime programs; quarters and trimesters for evening programs
- **Degrees** bachelor's, master's, and post-master's certificates
- **Suburban** 420-acre campus with easy access to St. Louis
- **Endowment** $24.1 million
- **Coed,** 4,923 undergraduate students, 89% full-time, 56% women, 44% men
- **Moderately difficult** entrance level, 46% of applicants were admitted

Undergraduates 4,365 full-time, 558 part-time. Students come from 38 states and territories, 61 other countries, 18% are from out of state, 11% African American, 0.7% Asian American or Pacific Islander, 1% Hispanic American, 0.3% Native American, 8% international, 14% transferred in, 48% live on campus. *Retention:* 64% of 2002 full-time freshmen returned.

Freshmen *Admission:* 2,428 applied, 1,112 admitted, 784 enrolled. *Average high school GPA:* 3.08. *Test scores:* ACT scores over 18: 100%; ACT scores over 24: 29%; ACT scores over 30: 4%.

Faculty *Total:* 426, 41% full-time. *Student/faculty ratio:* 17:1.

Majors Accounting; agribusiness; applied art; art; art history, criticism and conservation; art teacher education; athletic training; biology/biological sciences; biology teacher education; broadcast journalism; business administration and management; business teacher education; cell biology and histology; chemistry; chemistry teacher education; Christian studies; clinical laboratory science/medical technology; computer/information technology services administration related; computer science; consumer merchandising/retailing management; criminal justice/law enforcement administration; criminology; dance; digital communication and media/multimedia; dramatic/theatre arts; drawing; economics; education; educational/instructional media design; educational leadership and administration; education (K-12); elementary education; English; environmental science; fashion/apparel design; fashion merchandising; finance; fine/studio arts; French; French language teacher education; funeral service and mortuary science; gerontology; health and physical education; health/health care administration; history; history teacher education; human resources management; human services; international relations and affairs; journalism; kindergarten/preschool education; liberal arts and sciences/liberal studies; management information systems; marketing/marketing management; mass communication/media; mathematics; mathematics teacher education; middle school education; music; music teacher education; pastoral studies/counseling; physical education teaching and coaching; political science and government; pre-dentistry studies; pre-law studies; premedical studies; pre-nursing studies; pre-veterinary studies; psychology; public administration; public relations/image management; radio and television; religious studies; restaurant, culinary, and catering management; science teacher education; secondary education; social science teacher education; social work; sociology; Spanish; Spanish language teacher education; special education; special products marketing; sport and fitness administration; technology/industrial arts teacher education; voice and opera; youth ministry.

Academic Programs *Special study options:* academic remediation for entering students, accelerated degree program, adult/continuing education programs, advanced placement credit, cooperative education, double majors, external degree program, freshman honors college, honors programs, independent study, internships, off-campus study, part-time degree program, services for LD students, student-designed majors, study abroad, summer session for credit. *ROTC:* Army (b), Air Force (c). *Unusual degree programs:* 3-2 engineering with Washington University in St. Louis, University of Missouri–St. Louis, University of Missouri-Columbia.

Library Butler Library with 130,412 titles, 3,789 serial subscriptions, 2,748 audiovisual materials.

Computers on Campus 160 computers available on campus for general student use. A campuswide network can be accessed from student residence rooms

Lindenwood University (continued)

and from off campus. Internet access, at least one staffed computer lab available. Computer purchase or lease plan available.

Student Life *Housing options:* men-only, women-only. Campus housing is university owned. Freshman campus housing is guaranteed. *Activities and organizations:* drama/theater group, student-run newspaper, radio and television station, choral group, marching band, Lindenwood Student Government, American Humanics, Delta Zeta, Honors College, Intercultural Club, national fraternities, national sororities. *Campus security:* 24-hour emergency response devices and patrols, late-night transport/escort service, controlled dormitory access.

Athletics Member NAIA. *Intercollegiate sports:* baseball M(s), basketball M(s)/W(s), bowling M(s)/W(s), cheerleading M(s)/W(s), cross-country running M(s)/W(s), field hockey W(s), football M(s), golf M(s)/W(s), ice hockey M(s)/W(s), lacrosse M(s)/W(s), riflery M(s)/W(s), soccer M(s)/W(s), softball W(s), swimming M(s)/W(s), tennis M(s)/W(s), track and field M(s)/W(s), volleyball M(s)/W(s), water polo M(s)/W(s), wrestling M(s). *Intramural sports:* badminton M/W, basketball M/W, bowling M/W, cross-country running M/W, fencing M/W, football M/W, racquetball M/W, soccer M/W, softball M/W, swimming M/W, table tennis M/W, tennis M/W, track and field M/W, volleyball M/W, water polo M/W, weight lifting M/W, wrestling M.

Standardized Tests *Required:* SAT I or ACT (for admission).

Costs (2004–05) *Comprehensive fee:* $17,050 includes full-time tuition ($11,200), mandatory fees ($450), and room and board ($5400). Part-time tuition: $300 per credit hour. Part-time tuition and fees vary according to course load. *College room only:* $2700. *Payment plans:* installment, deferred payment. *Waivers:* senior citizens.

Applying *Options:* early admission, deferred entrance. *Application fee:* $25. *Required:* high school transcript, minimum ACT score of 20 or minimum SAT score of 900. *Required for some:* essay or personal statement, letters of recommendation, interview. *Recommended:* interview. *Application deadline:* rolling (freshmen), rolling (transfers). *Notification:* continuous (transfers).

Admissions Contact Ms. Kammie Kobyleski, Associate Director of Admissions, Lindenwood University, 209 South Kingshighway, St. Charles, MO 63301-1695. *Phone:* 636-949-4949. *Toll-free phone:* 636-949-4949. *Fax:* 636-949-4989.

■ *See page 1874 for a narrative description.*

LOGAN UNIVERSITY-COLLEGE OF CHIROPRACTIC

Chesterfield, Missouri

- **Independent** upper-level, founded 1935
- **Calendar** trimesters
- **Degrees** bachelor's and first professional
- **Suburban** 111-acre campus with easy access to St. Louis
- **Endowment** $8.0 million
- **Coed,** 115 undergraduate students, 77% full-time, 34% women, 66% men
- **Moderately difficult** entrance level

Undergraduates 88 full-time, 27 part-time. Students come from 26 states and territories, 1 other country, 57% are from out of state, 7% African American, 2% Hispanic American, 2% Native American, 0.9% international, 100% transferred in.

Faculty *Total:* 90, 56% full-time, 94% with terminal degrees. *Student/faculty ratio:* 12:1.

Majors Biology/biological sciences.

Academic Programs *Special study options:* adult/continuing education programs, advanced placement credit, distance learning, independent study, internships, services for LD students.

Library Learning Resources Center with 12,838 titles, 225 serial subscriptions, 2,078 audiovisual materials, an OPAC, a Web page.

Computers on Campus 70 computers available on campus for general student use. A campuswide network can be accessed. Internet access, at least one staffed computer lab available.

Student Life *Housing:* college housing not available. *Activities and organizations:* student-run newspaper, Pi Kappa Chi, Lambda Kappa Chi, Omega Sigma Pi, Student American Chiropractic Association, Student International Chiropractic Association, national fraternities, national sororities. *Campus security:* 24-hour patrols. *Student services:* health clinic, personal/psychological counseling.

Athletics *Intramural sports:* basketball M/W, bowling M/W, cheerleading M/W, football M, ice hockey M, soccer M, softball M/W, table tennis M/W, tennis M/W, volleyball M/W, weight lifting M/W.

Costs (2004–05) *Tuition:* $3090 full-time, $95 per credit hour part-time. Full-time tuition and fees vary according to program. Part-time tuition and fees vary according to program. *Required fees:* $220 full-time, $110 per semester part-time. *Waivers:* employees or children of employees.

Financial Aid Of all full-time matriculated undergraduates who enrolled in 1999, 160 applied for aid, 160 were judged to have need, 130 had their need fully met. 130 Federal Work-Study jobs (averaging $2693). *Average percent of need met:* 100%. *Average need-based loan:* $3500. *Average need-based gift aid:* $3000.

Applying *Options:* electronic application, deferred entrance. *Application fee:* $50. *Application deadline:* rolling (freshmen), rolling (transfers). *Notification:* continuous (transfers).

Admissions Contact Dr. Patrick Browne, Vice President of Enrollment, Logan University-College of Chiropractic, 1851 Schoettler Road, Chesterfield, MO 63006-1065. *Phone:* 636-227-2100 Ext. 149. *Toll-free phone:* 800-533-9210. *Fax:* 636-207-2425. *E-mail:* loganadm@logan.edu.

MARYVILLE UNIVERSITY OF SAINT LOUIS

St. Louis, Missouri

- **Independent** comprehensive, founded 1872
- **Calendar** semesters
- **Degrees** bachelor's and master's
- **Suburban** 130-acre campus
- **Endowment** $28.1 million
- **Coed,** 2,705 undergraduate students, 56% full-time, 76% women, 24% men
- **Moderately difficult** entrance level, 73% of applicants were admitted

At Maryville, students benefit from high-quality academic programs, small classes, professors who meet the highest standards of academic excellence, a diverse student-centered environment, and state-of-the-art facilities. Four campus facilities–the Anheuser-Busch Academic Center, the Art and Design Building, the University Auditorium, and University Center have been built since 1997. The campus is adjacent to Maryville Corporate Centre and St. Luke's Medical Center and is located just 20 minutes from downtown St. Louis, providing convenient access to internships.

Undergraduates 1,518 full-time, 1,187 part-time. Students come from 17 states and territories, 20 other countries, 9% are from out of state, 6% African American, 1% Asian American or Pacific Islander, 1% Hispanic American, 0.3% Native American, 2% international, 15% transferred in, 28% live on campus. *Retention:* 74% of 2002 full-time freshmen returned.

Freshmen *Admission:* 1,154 applied, 844 admitted, 335 enrolled. *Average high school GPA:* 3.51. *Test scores:* ACT scores over 18: 97%; ACT scores over 24: 50%; ACT scores over 30: 6%.

Faculty *Total:* 342, 26% full-time, 58% with terminal degrees. *Student/faculty ratio:* 13:1.

Majors Accounting; accounting related; actuarial science; applied mathematics; art teacher education; biological and physical sciences; biology/biological sciences; biology teacher education; business administration and management; business/commerce; chemistry; chemistry teacher education; clinical laboratory science/medical technology; computer science; criminology; e-commerce; elementary education; English; English/language arts teacher education; environmental science; environmental studies; fine/studio arts; graphic design; health/health care administration; health/medical preparatory programs related; health science; history; history teacher education; industrial and organizational psychology; interdisciplinary studies; interior design; kindergarten/preschool education; legal assistant/paralegal; liberal arts and sciences/liberal studies; management information systems; marketing/marketing management; mass communication/media; mathematics; mathematics teacher education; middle school education; music therapy; nursing (registered nurse training); psychology; public health; public health related; secondary education; social psychology; sociology.

Academic Programs *Special study options:* accelerated degree program, adult/continuing education programs, advanced placement credit, cooperative education, distance learning, double majors, English as a second language, freshman honors college, honors programs, independent study, internships, off-campus study, part-time degree program, services for LD students, student-designed majors, study abroad, summer session for credit. *ROTC:* Army (c). *Unusual degree programs:* 3-2 engineering with Washington University in St. Louis; social work with Saint Louis University; education.

Library Maryville University Library with 205,512 titles, 9,004 serial subscriptions, 10,933 audiovisual materials, an OPAC, a Web page.

Computers on Campus 250 computers available on campus for general student use. A campuswide network can be accessed from student residence rooms and from off campus that provide access to e-mail, specialized software, university catalog, schedules. Internet access, at least one staffed computer lab available.

Student Life *Housing options:* coed. Campus housing is university owned. *Activities and organizations:* drama/theater group, student-run newspaper, choral group, Campus Activity Board, physical therapy club, Maryville University Student Government, Community Service Club, Campus Crusade for Christ. *Campus security:* 24-hour emergency response devices and patrols, late-night transport/escort service, controlled dormitory access, video security system in residence halls, self-defense and education programs. *Student services:* health clinic, personal/psychological counseling.

Athletics Member NCAA. All Division III. *Intercollegiate sports:* baseball M, basketball M/W, cross-country running M/W, golf M, soccer M/W, softball W, tennis M/W, volleyball W. *Intramural sports:* basketball M/W, bowling M/W, cheerleading M(c)/W(c), football M/W, soccer M/W, softball M/W, table tennis M/W, ultimate Frisbee M(c)/W(c), volleyball M/W.

Standardized Tests *Required:* SAT I or ACT (for admission).

Costs (2004–05) *Comprehensive fee:* $23,300 includes full-time tuition ($16,000), mandatory fees ($300), and room and board ($7000). Part-time tuition: $485 per credit hour. Part-time tuition and fees vary according to class time. *Required fees:* $75 per term part-time. *Room and board:* Room and board charges vary according to housing facility. *Payment plan:* installment. *Waivers:* senior citizens and employees or children of employees.

Financial Aid Of all full-time matriculated undergraduates who enrolled in 2003, 1,301 applied for aid, 1,123 were judged to have need, 103 had their need fully met. 283 Federal Work-Study jobs (averaging $914). 102 state and other part-time jobs (averaging $2950). In 2003, 230 non-need-based awards were made. *Average percent of need met:* 42%. *Average financial aid package:* $10,822. *Average need-based loan:* $4591. *Average need-based gift aid:* $5999. *Average non-need-based aid:* $6687. *Average indebtedness upon graduation:* $11,167.

Applying *Options:* common application, electronic application, early admission, deferred entrance. *Application fee:* $25. *Required:* high school transcript, minimum 2.5 GPA. *Required for some:* essay or personal statement, letters of recommendation, interview, audition, portfolio. *Application deadline:* 8/15 (freshmen), rolling (transfers). *Notification:* continuous (freshmen), continuous (transfers).

Admissions Contact Ms. Lynn Jackson, Admissions Director, Maryville University of Saint Louis, 13550 Conway Road, St. Louis, MO 63141-7299. *Phone:* 314-529-9350. *Toll-free phone:* 800-627-9855. *Fax:* 314-529-9927. *E-mail:* admissions@maryville.edu.

■ *See page 1950 for a narrative description.*

MESSENGER COLLEGE
Joplin, Missouri

- **Independent Pentecostal** 4-year, founded 1987
- **Calendar** semesters
- **Degrees** associate and bachelor's
- **Suburban** 16-acre campus with easy access to Springfield
- **Endowment** $289,532
- **Coed,** 100 undergraduate students, 84% full-time, 47% women, 53% men
- **Moderately difficult** entrance level, 87% of applicants were admitted

Undergraduates 84 full-time, 16 part-time. Students come from 17 states and territories, 49% are from out of state, 4% African American, 8% Hispanic American, 6% Native American, 7% transferred in. *Retention:* 71% of 2002 full-time freshmen returned.

Freshmen *Admission:* 45 applied, 39 admitted, 31 enrolled. *Average high school GPA:* 3.00. *Test scores:* ACT scores over 18: 57%; ACT scores over 24: 21%.

Faculty *Total:* 14, 29% full-time, 29% with terminal degrees. *Student/faculty ratio:* 8:1.

Majors Biblical studies; business administration and management; divinity/ministry; education related; general studies; missionary studies and missiology; music; pastoral studies/counseling; religious education; religious/sacred music; religious studies; theological and ministerial studies related; youth ministry.

Academic Programs *Special study options:* academic remediation for entering students, cooperative education, distance learning, double majors, external degree program, honors programs, independent study, internships, part-time degree program.

Library McDole-McDonald Library with 28,874 titles, 114 serial subscriptions, 326 audiovisual materials, an OPAC.

Computers on Campus 5 computers available on campus for general student use. Internet access, at least one staffed computer lab available.

Student Life *Housing:* on-campus residence required through sophomore year. *Options:* men-only, women-only, disabled students. Campus housing is university owned. *Activities and organizations:* drama/theater group, choral group, Special Projects Team-Community Service, H.I.M Club-Heart in Missions Club. *Campus security:* 24-hour emergency response devices, student patrols. *Student services:* personal/psychological counseling.

Athletics Member NCCAA. *Intercollegiate sports:* basketball M/W, volleyball W.

Standardized Tests *Required:* SAT I or ACT (for admission).

Costs (2003–04) *Comprehensive fee:* $7970 includes full-time tuition ($4500), mandatory fees ($370), and room and board ($3100). Part-time tuition: $150 per credit hour. *Room and board:* Room and board charges vary according to housing facility. *Payment plan:* installment. *Waivers:* employees or children of employees.

Financial Aid Of all full-time matriculated undergraduates who enrolled in 2002, 116 applied for aid, 116 were judged to have need. 19 Federal Work-Study jobs (averaging $1485). *Average percent of need met:* 88%. *Average financial aid package:* $7000. *Average need-based loan:* $3034. *Average need-based gift aid:* $3600. *Average indebtedness upon graduation:* $21,521.

Applying *Options:* common application, electronic application. *Application fee:* $35. *Required:* essay or personal statement, high school transcript, minimum 2.0 GPA, 3 letters of recommendation, health form. *Required for some:* interview. *Application deadlines:* 8/1 (freshmen), 8/1 (transfers). *Notification:* continuous until 8/15 (freshmen), continuous until 8/15 (transfers).

Admissions Contact Tiffanny Stump, Director of Admissions, Messenger College, 300 East 50th, Joplin, MO 64804. *Phone:* 417-624-7070 Ext. 156. *Toll-free phone:* 800-385-8940. *Fax:* 417-624-5070. *E-mail:* info@messengercollege.edu.

METRO BUSINESS COLLEGE
Cape Girardeau, Missouri

- **Proprietary** primarily 2-year
- **Calendar** quarters
- **Degrees** certificates, diplomas, associate, and bachelor's
- **Coed**
- **Minimally difficult** entrance level

Admissions Contact Ms. Kyla Evans, Admissions Director, Metro Business College, 1732 North Kings Highway, Cape Girardeau, MO 63701. *Phone:* 573-334-9181.

MISSOURI BAPTIST UNIVERSITY
St. Louis, Missouri

- **Independent Southern Baptist** comprehensive, founded 1964
- **Calendar** semesters
- **Degrees** certificates, associate, bachelor's, master's, and postbachelor's certificates
- **Suburban** 65-acre campus
- **Endowment** $2.6 million
- **Coed,** 2,947 undergraduate students, 35% full-time, 61% women, 39% men
- **Moderately difficult** entrance level, 71% of applicants were admitted

Undergraduates 1,020 full-time, 1,927 part-time. Students come from 22 states and territories, 21 other countries, 11% are from out of state, 10% African American, 0.6% Asian American or Pacific Islander, 0.9% Hispanic American, 0.2% Native American, 3% international, 9% transferred in, 23% live on campus. *Retention:* 64% of 2002 full-time freshmen returned.

Freshmen *Admission:* 712 applied, 507 admitted, 210 enrolled. *Average high school GPA:* 3.05. *Test scores:* ACT scores over 18: 87%; ACT scores over 24: 33%; ACT scores over 30: 10%.

Faculty *Total:* 157, 29% full-time. *Student/faculty ratio:* 18:1.

Majors Accounting; biology/biological sciences; business administration and management; business administration, management and operations related; business teacher education; chemistry; child development; communication/speech communication and rhetoric; computer and information sciences; criminal justice/safety; elementary education; English; health teacher education; history; human services; kindergarten/preschool education; marketing/marketing management; mathematics; middle school education; multi-/interdisciplinary studies related; music performance; music teacher education; nursing science; operations management; physical education teaching and coaching; psychology; religious education; religious/sacred music; religious studies; science teacher education; social sciences; sport and fitness administration; theology and religious vocations related.

Academic Programs *Special study options:* accelerated degree program, adult/continuing education programs, advanced placement credit, distance learning, double majors, independent study, internships, off-campus study, part-time degree program, services for LD students, student-designed majors, study abroad, summer session for credit. *ROTC:* Army (c). *Unusual degree programs:* 3-2 engineering with University of Missouri-Columbia.

Library Jung-Kellogg Library with 90,387 titles, 610 serial subscriptions, 4,181 audiovisual materials, an OPAC.

Computers on Campus 78 computers available on campus for general student use. A campuswide network can be accessed from student residence rooms and from off campus. Internet access, at least one staffed computer lab available.

Missouri Baptist University (continued)

Student Life *Housing options:* men-only, women-only. *Activities and organizations:* drama/theater group, student-run newspaper, choral group, Baptist Collegiate Ministry, Students in Free Enterprise (SIFE), Missouri State Teacher's Association, Fellowship of Christian Athletes, Ministerial Alliance. *Campus security:* 24-hour patrols, late-night transport/escort service, controlled dormitory access, self-defense classes. *Student services:* personal/psychological counseling.

Athletics Member NAIA. *Intercollegiate sports:* baseball M(s), basketball M(s)/W(s), cross-country running M(s)/W(s), golf M(s), soccer M(s)/W(s), softball W(s), volleyball M(s)(c)/W(s), wrestling M(s). *Intramural sports:* basketball M/W, soccer M/W, softball M/W, volleyball M/W.

Standardized Tests *Required for some:* SAT I or ACT (for admission).

Costs (2003–04) *Comprehensive fee:* $18,080 includes full-time tuition ($11,770), mandatory fees ($510), and room and board ($5800). Full-time tuition and fees vary according to course load and location. Part-time tuition: $410 per credit. Part-time tuition and fees vary according to course load and location. *Room and board:* Room and board charges vary according to housing facility. *Payment plan:* installment. *Waivers:* children of alumni, senior citizens, and employees or children of employees.

Financial Aid Of all full-time matriculated undergraduates who enrolled in 2002, 1,011 applied for aid, 1,011 were judged to have need. 83 Federal Work-Study jobs (averaging $1096). 1 state and other part-time job (averaging $919). In 2002, 206 non-need-based awards were made. *Average percent of need met:* 40%. *Average financial aid package:* $7400. *Average need-based loan:* $3776. *Average need-based gift aid:* $6693. *Average non-need-based aid:* $707. *Average indebtedness upon graduation:* $15,435.

Applying *Options:* electronic application. *Application fee:* $25. *Required:* high school transcript, minimum 2.0 GPA, letters of recommendation, interview. *Application deadline:* rolling (freshmen), rolling (transfers). *Notification:* continuous (freshmen), continuous (transfers).

Admissions Contact Missouri Baptist University, One College Park Drive, St. Louis, MO 63141-8660. *Phone:* 314-392-2296. *Toll-free phone:* 877-434-1115 Ext. 2290. *Fax:* 314-434-7596. *E-mail:* admissions@mobap.edu.

MISSOURI SOUTHERN STATE UNIVERSITY

Joplin, Missouri

- **State-supported** 4-year, founded 1937
- **Calendar** semesters
- **Degrees** certificates, associate, and bachelor's
- **Small-town** 350-acre campus
- **Coed,** 5,410 undergraduate students, 65% full-time, 59% women, 41% men
- **Moderately difficult** entrance level, 74% of applicants were admitted

Undergraduates 3,531 full-time, 1,879 part-time. Students come from 28 states and territories, 35 other countries, 13% are from out of state, 3% African American, 1% Asian American or Pacific Islander, 2% Hispanic American, 3% Native American, 2% international, 6% transferred in, 8% live on campus. *Retention:* 65% of 2002 full-time freshmen returned.

Freshmen *Admission:* 1,771 applied, 1,317 admitted, 692 enrolled. *Test scores:* ACT scores over 18: 85%; ACT scores over 24: 32%; ACT scores over 30: 5%.

Faculty *Total:* 286, 69% full-time, 47% with terminal degrees. *Student/faculty ratio:* 18:1.

Majors Accounting; animal genetics; biology/biological sciences; biotechnology; business administration and management; chemistry; clinical laboratory science/medical technology; commercial and advertising art; communication/speech communication and rhetoric; computer and information sciences; computer science; criminal justice/law enforcement administration; criminal justice/police science; data processing and data processing technology; dental hygiene; drafting and design technology; dramatic/theatre arts; ecology; education; elementary education; English; environmental health; finance; French; German; history; information science/studies; international business/trade/commerce; international relations and affairs; kindergarten/preschool education; kinesiology and exercise science; machine tool technology; marine biology and biological oceanography; marketing/marketing management; mass communication/media; mathematics; medical microbiology and bacteriology; medical radiologic technology; middle school education; music; nursing (registered nurse training); physics; political science and government; pre-dentistry studies; pre-engineering; pre-medical studies; pre-pharmacy studies; pre-veterinary studies; professional studies; psychology; respiratory care therapy; secondary education; sociology; Spanish; special education; technology/industrial arts teacher education.

Academic Programs *Special study options:* academic remediation for entering students, accelerated degree program, adult/continuing education programs, advanced placement credit, cooperative education, distance learning, double majors, English as a second language, external degree program, honors programs, independent study, internships, off-campus study, part-time degree program, services for LD students, study abroad, summer session for credit.

Library Spiva Library with 157,362 titles, 1,574 serial subscriptions, 10,417 audiovisual materials, an OPAC, a Web page.

Computers on Campus 448 computers available on campus for general student use. A campuswide network can be accessed from student residence rooms and from off campus. Internet access, at least one staffed computer lab available.

Student Life *Housing:* on-campus residence required through sophomore year. *Options:* men-only, women-only, disabled students. Campus housing is university owned. *Activities and organizations:* drama/theater group, student-run newspaper, radio and television station, choral group, marching band, Koinonia, Campus Activities Board, Residence Hall Association, Baptist Student Union, Student Senate, national fraternities, national sororities. *Campus security:* 24-hour emergency response devices and patrols, late-night transport/escort service, controlled dormitory access, security at campus events, emergency vehicle assistance, safety awareness information to students. *Student services:* health clinic, personal/psychological counseling.

Athletics Member NCAA. All Division II. *Intercollegiate sports:* baseball M(s), basketball M(s)/W(s), cross-country running M(s)/W(s), football M(s), golf M(s), soccer M(s)/W(s), softball W(s), tennis W(s), track and field M(s)/W(s), volleyball W(s). *Intramural sports:* basketball M/W, bowling M/W, football M/W, golf M/W, racquetball M/W, soccer M/W, softball M/W, swimming M/W, table tennis M/W, tennis M/W, volleyball M/W.

Standardized Tests *Required:* SAT I or ACT (for admission), SAT I or ACT (for placement). *Required for some:* ACT (for admission), Michigan Test of English Language Proficiency. *Recommended:* ACT (for admission).

Costs (2003–04) *Tuition:* state resident $3810 full-time, $127 per credit part-time; nonresident $7620 full-time, $254 per credit part-time. Full-time tuition and fees vary according to course load. *Required fees:* $166 full-time. *Room and board:* $4480. Room and board charges vary according to housing facility. *Payment plan:* deferred payment. *Waivers:* employees or children of employees.

Financial Aid Of all full-time matriculated undergraduates who enrolled in 2003, 3,209 applied for aid, 2,804 were judged to have need. 149 Federal Work-Study jobs (averaging $1575). 438 state and other part-time jobs (averaging $1401). In 2003, 602 non-need-based awards were made. *Average percent of need met:* 69%. *Average financial aid package:* $6722. *Average need-based loan:* $3249. *Average need-based gift aid:* $4636. *Average non-need-based aid:* $2560. *Average indebtedness upon graduation:* $15,448.

Applying *Options:* common application, electronic application, deferred entrance. *Application fee:* $15. *Required:* high school transcript. *Application deadlines:* 8/3 (freshmen), 8/3 (transfers). *Notification:* continuous (freshmen), continuous (transfers).

Admissions Contact Mr. Derek Skaggs, Director of Enrollment Services, Missouri Southern State University, 3950 East Newman Road, Joplin, MO 64801-1595. *Phone:* 417-625-9537. *Toll-free phone:* 866-818-MSSU. *Fax:* 417-659-4429. *E-mail:* admissions@mssu.edu.

■ *See page 2002 for a narrative description.*

MISSOURI TECH

St. Louis, Missouri

- **Proprietary** 4-year, founded 1932
- **Calendar** semesters
- **Degrees** diplomas, associate, and bachelor's
- **Suburban** campus
- **Coed, primarily men,** 201 undergraduate students, 22% full-time, 11% women, 89% men
- **Moderately difficult** entrance level, 56% of applicants were admitted

Undergraduates 44 full-time, 157 part-time. Students come from 4 states and territories, 20% are from out of state, 17% African American, 1% Hispanic American, 3% international, 7% transferred in, 6% live on campus.

Freshmen *Admission:* 27 applied, 15 admitted, 11 enrolled. *Average high school GPA:* 2.9. *Test scores:* ACT scores over 18: 85%; ACT scores over 24: 23%.

Faculty *Total:* 11, 64% full-time, 9% with terminal degrees. *Student/faculty ratio:* 10:1.

Majors Computer engineering; computer engineering technology; electrical, electronic and communications engineering technology; electrical, electronics and communications engineering; engineering/industrial management; engineering technology; systems engineering.

Academic Programs *Special study options:* accelerated degree program, adult/continuing education programs, advanced placement credit, internships, part-time degree program, summer session for credit.

Computers on Campus 100 computers available on campus for general student use. A campuswide network can be accessed from off campus. Internet access, at least one staffed computer lab available.

Student Life *Housing options:* men-only, women-only. Campus housing is leased by the school. *Activities and organizations:* student council, President's Club. *Campus security:* 24-hour emergency response devices.

Standardized Tests *Recommended:* ACT (for admission).

Costs (2004–05) *Tuition:* $11,560 full-time, $370 per semester hour part-time. Full-time tuition and fees vary according to course load. Part-time tuition and fees vary according to course load. *Required fees:* $380 full-time. *Room only:* $3265. *Payment plan:* installment.

Applying *Options:* common application, electronic application. *Required:* high school transcript. *Required for some:* interview, minimum ACT score of 20. *Application deadline:* rolling (freshmen).

Admissions Contact Mr. Bob Honaker, Director of Admissions, Missouri Tech, 1167 Corporate Lake Drive, St. Louis, MO 63132. *Phone:* 314-569-3600 Ext. 363. *Fax:* 314-569-1167.

■ *See page 2004 for a narrative description.*

MISSOURI VALLEY COLLEGE

Marshall, Missouri

- **Independent** 4-year, founded 1889, affiliated with Presbyterian Church
- **Calendar** semesters plus 2 summer sessions
- **Degrees** associate and bachelor's
- **Small-town** 140-acre campus with easy access to Kansas City
- **Endowment** $3.4 million
- **Coed,** 1,623 undergraduate students, 85% full-time, 47% women, 53% men
- **Minimally difficult** entrance level, 67% of applicants were admitted

Founded in 1889, Missouri Valley is a private, liberal arts college located in Marshall, Missouri. The College prepares students for rewarding careers by personalizing education and focusing on scholarship, critical thinking, and academic excellence. Academic and athletic scholarships, as well as federal aid, are available to all qualified students.

Undergraduates 1,377 full-time, 246 part-time. Students come from 40 states and territories, 29 other countries, 34% are from out of state, 13% African American, 4% Asian American or Pacific Islander, 4% Hispanic American, 0.7% Native American, 8% international, 9% transferred in, 73% live on campus. *Retention:* 45% of 2002 full-time freshmen returned.

Freshmen *Admission:* 1,345 applied, 898 admitted, 405 enrolled. *Average high school GPA:* 2.90. *Test scores:* SAT verbal scores over 500: 20%; SAT math scores over 500: 35%; ACT scores over 18: 76%; SAT verbal scores over 600: 3%; SAT math scores over 600: 13%; ACT scores over 24: 13%.

Faculty *Total:* 113, 58% full-time, 43% with terminal degrees. *Student/faculty ratio:* 18:1.

Majors Accounting; art; athletic training; biology/biological sciences; business administration and management; computer science; criminal justice/law enforcement administration; dramatic/theatre arts; economics; education; elementary education; English; health teacher education; history; human services; liberal arts and sciences/liberal studies; marketing/marketing management; mass communication/media; mathematics; music; parks, recreation and leisure; parks, recreation and leisure facilities management; philosophy; physical education teaching and coaching; political science and government; pre-dentistry studies; pre-law studies; pre-medical studies; pre-nursing studies; pre-pharmacy studies; pre-veterinary studies; psychology; public administration; religious studies; science teacher education; secondary education; sociology; special education; speech and rhetoric; sport and fitness administration.

Academic Programs *Special study options:* adult/continuing education programs, advanced placement credit, cooperative education, double majors, English as a second language, independent study, internships, part-time degree program, services for LD students, summer session for credit. *ROTC:* Army (c).

Library Murrell Memorial Library plus 1 other with 61,907 titles, 391 serial subscriptions, 1,399 audiovisual materials, an OPAC, a Web page.

Computers on Campus 250 computers available on campus for general student use. A campuswide network can be accessed from student residence rooms and from off campus. Internet access, at least one staffed computer lab available.

Student Life *Housing options:* coed, men-only, women-only. Campus housing is university owned. Freshman campus housing is guaranteed. *Activities and organizations:* drama/theater group, student-run newspaper, radio and television station, choral group, student government, fraternities, sororities, Valley players, American Humanics, national fraternities, national sororities. *Campus security:* 24-hour emergency response devices, student patrols, controlled dormitory access. *Student services:* health clinic.

Athletics Member NAIA. *Intercollegiate sports:* baseball M(s), basketball M(s)/W(s), cheerleading M(s)/W(s), cross-country running M(s)/W(s), football M(s), golf M(s)/W(s), soccer M(s)/W(s), softball W(s), tennis M(s)/W(s), track and field M(s)/W(s), volleyball M(s)/W(s), wrestling M(s)/W(s). *Intramural sports:* badminton M/W, baseball M, basketball M/W, bowling M/W, football M/W, soccer M/W, softball M/W, table tennis M/W, tennis M/W, ultimate Frisbee M/W, volleyball M/W.

Standardized Tests *Required:* SAT I or ACT (for admission). *Recommended:* SAT II: Writing Test (for admission).

Costs (2004–05) *Comprehensive fee:* $18,700 includes full-time tuition ($13,000), mandatory fees ($500), and room and board ($5200). Part-time tuition: $350 per credit hour. *Payment plan:* installment. *Waivers:* children of alumni, senior citizens, and employees or children of employees.

Financial Aid Of all full-time matriculated undergraduates who enrolled in 2002, 1,298 applied for aid, 1,242 were judged to have need. 205 Federal Work-Study jobs (averaging $1860). 656 state and other part-time jobs. In 2002, 131 non-need-based awards were made. *Average percent of need met:* 80%. *Average financial aid package:* $12,141. *Average need-based loan:* $2455. *Average need-based gift aid:* $9999. *Average indebtedness upon graduation:* $11,900. *Financial aid deadline:* 9/15.

Applying *Options:* common application, electronic application, early admission, deferred entrance. *Application fee:* $15. *Required:* high school transcript. *Required for some:* essay or personal statement, 3 letters of recommendation, interview. *Recommended:* minimum 2.0 GPA, interview. *Application deadline:* rolling (freshmen), rolling (transfers). *Notification:* continuous (freshmen), continuous (transfers).

Admissions Contact Ms. Debi Bultmann, Admissions, Missouri Valley College, Admissions Office, 500 East College, Marshall, MO 65340. *Phone:* 660-831-4125. *Fax:* 660-831-4233. *E-mail:* admissions@moval.edu.

■ *See page 2006 for a narrative description.*

MISSOURI WESTERN STATE COLLEGE

St. Joseph, Missouri

- **State-supported** 4-year, founded 1915
- **Calendar** semesters
- **Degrees** certificates, associate, and bachelor's
- **Suburban** 744-acre campus with easy access to Kansas City
- **Endowment** $6.1 million
- **Coed,** 4,928 undergraduate students, 75% full-time, 60% women, 40% men
- 100% of applicants were admitted

Missouri Western State College affords quality instruction in a wide range of programs, reasonable costs, scholarships, and a well-rounded college experience. A friendly, personal atmosphere pervades both classroom and campus. The College serves a 4-state area and attracts students nationwide. Its small student-faculty ratio allows hands-on emphasis in all academic areas.

Undergraduates 3,704 full-time, 1,224 part-time. Students come from 31 states and territories, 7 other countries, 7% are from out of state, 11% African American, 0.7% Asian American or Pacific Islander, 2% Hispanic American, 0.8% Native American, 0.3% international, 6% transferred in, 20% live on campus. *Retention:* 55% of 2002 full-time freshmen returned.

Freshmen *Admission:* 2,421 applied, 2,421 admitted, 1,045 enrolled. *Test scores:* ACT scores over 18: 63%; ACT scores over 24: 14%; ACT scores over 30: 1%.

Faculty *Total:* 318, 57% full-time, 49% with terminal degrees. *Student/faculty ratio:* 18:1.

Majors Accounting; art; art teacher education; biology/biological sciences; business administration and management; chemistry; civil engineering technology; clinical laboratory science/medical technology; communication and media related; computer and information sciences; criminal justice/safety; economics; electrical, electronic and communications engineering technology; elementary education; English; English/language arts teacher education; finance; French; French language teacher education; graphic design; health information/medical records technology; history; information science/studies; kinesiology and exercise science; legal assistant/paralegal; manufacturing technology; marketing/marketing management; mathematics; multi-/interdisciplinary studies related; music; music teacher education; nursing (registered nurse training); parks, recreation and leisure facilities management; physical therapist assistant; political science and government; psychology; social work; Spanish; Spanish language teacher education; speech/theater education.

Academic Programs *Special study options:* academic remediation for entering students, accelerated degree program, advanced placement credit, distance learning, double majors, freshman honors college, honors programs, internships, part-time degree program, summer session for credit. *ROTC:* Army (b).

Library Warren E. Hearnes Library with 147,509 titles, 1,068 serial subscriptions, 13,705 audiovisual materials, an OPAC, a Web page.

Missouri Western State College (continued)

Computers on Campus 300 computers available on campus for general student use. A campuswide network can be accessed from student residence rooms and from off campus. Internet access, online (class) registration, at least one staffed computer lab available.

Student Life *Housing options:* coed. Campus housing is university owned. *Activities and organizations:* drama/theater group, student-run newspaper, choral group, marching band, national fraternities, national sororities. *Campus security:* 24-hour emergency response devices and patrols, student patrols, late-night transport/escort service, controlled dormitory access. *Student services:* health clinic, personal/psychological counseling, women's center.

Athletics Member NCAA. All Division II. *Intercollegiate sports:* baseball M(s), basketball M(s)/W(s), football M(s), golf M(s)/W, softball W(s), tennis W(s), volleyball W(s). *Intramural sports:* basketball M/W, bowling M/W, football M, golf M/W, ice hockey M, racquetball M/W, rugby M, soccer M, swimming M/W, table tennis M/W, tennis M/W, volleyball M/W.

Standardized Tests *Required:* ACT (for placement).

Costs (2003–04) *Tuition:* state resident $4098 full-time, $146 per credit part-time; nonresident $7674 full-time, $267 per credit part-time. *Required fees:* $366 full-time, $11 per credit part-time, $30 per term part-time. *Room and board:* $4058. Room and board charges vary according to board plan and housing facility. *Payment plans:* installment, deferred payment. *Waivers:* senior citizens and employees or children of employees.

Financial Aid Of all full-time matriculated undergraduates who enrolled in 2001, 2,418 applied for aid, 1,641 were judged to have need, 288 had their need fully met. 337 Federal Work-Study jobs (averaging $1192). In 2001, 311 non-need-based awards were made. *Average percent of need met:* 18%. *Average financial aid package:* $6677. *Average need-based gift aid:* $441. *Average indebtedness upon graduation:* $15,200.

Applying *Options:* early admission. *Application fee:* $15. *Required:* high school transcript. *Application deadlines:* 7/30 (freshmen), 7/30 (transfers). *Notification:* continuous until 8/10 (freshmen), continuous until 8/10 (transfers).

Admissions Contact Mr. Howard McCauley, Director of Admissions, Missouri Western State College, 4525 Downs Drive, St. Joseph, MO 64507-2294. *Phone:* 816-271-4267. *Toll-free phone:* 800-662-7041 Ext. 60. *Fax:* 816-271-5833. *E-mail:* admissn@mwsc.edu.

NATIONAL AMERICAN UNIVERSITY
Kansas City, Missouri

Admissions Contact Mr. Jerry D. Joy, Vice President, National American University, 4200 Blue Ridge Boulevard, Kansas City, MO 64133-1612. *Phone:* 816-353-4554. *Fax:* 816-353-1176.

NORTHWEST MISSOURI STATE UNIVERSITY
Maryville, Missouri

- **State-supported** comprehensive, founded 1905, part of Missouri Coordinating Board for Higher Education
- **Calendar** trimesters
- **Degrees** bachelor's and master's
- **Small-town** 240-acre campus with easy access to Kansas City
- **Coed**
- **Moderately difficult** entrance level

Faculty *Student/faculty ratio:* 24:1.

Student Life *Campus security:* 24-hour patrols, student patrols, late-night transport/escort service.

Athletics Member NCAA. All Division II.

Standardized Tests *Required:* SAT I or ACT (for admission).

Costs (2003–04) *Tuition:* state resident $4845 full-time; nonresident $8355 full-time. Full-time tuition and fees vary according to course load. Part-time tuition and fees vary according to course load. *Required fees:* $180 full-time. *Room and board:* $5042. Room and board charges vary according to board plan. *Payment plans:* installment, deferred payment.

Financial Aid Of all full-time matriculated undergraduates who enrolled in 2001, 3,320 applied for aid, 2,455 were judged to have need, 838 had their need fully met. 402 Federal Work-Study jobs (averaging $1374). 595 state and other part-time jobs (averaging $970). In 2001, 398. *Average percent of need met:* 82. *Average financial aid package:* $6047. *Average need-based loan:* $3252. *Average need-based gift aid:* $2560. *Average non-need-based aid:* $1706. *Average indebtedness upon graduation:* $13,799.

Applying *Options:* electronic application, deferred entrance. *Application fee:* $15. *Required:* high school transcript, minimum 2.0 GPA. *Required for some:* interview.

Admissions Contact Ms. Deb Powers, Associate Director of Admission, Northwest Missouri State University, Office of Admissions, 800 University Drive, Maryville, MO 64468. *Phone:* 660-562-1146. *Toll-free phone:* 800-633-1175. *Fax:* 660-562-1121. *E-mail:* admissions@acad.nwmissouri.edu.

OZARK CHRISTIAN COLLEGE
Joplin, Missouri

- **Independent Christian** 4-year, founded 1942
- **Calendar** semesters
- **Degrees** certificates, associate, and bachelor's
- **Suburban** 110-acre campus
- **Coed**
- **Noncompetitive** entrance level

Faculty *Student/faculty ratio:* 19:1.

Student Life *Campus security:* 24-hour emergency response devices, 12-hour patrols by trained security personnel.

Athletics Member NCCAA.

Standardized Tests *Required:* SAT I or ACT (for admission).

Costs (2003–04) *Comprehensive fee:* $10,265 includes full-time tuition ($5760), mandatory fees ($535), and room and board ($3970). *College room only:* $990. Room and board charges vary according to board plan. *Payment plans:* installment, deferred payment.

Financial Aid Of all full-time matriculated undergraduates who enrolled in 2001, 55 Federal Work-Study jobs (averaging $1078). *Financial aid deadline:* 4/1.

Applying *Options:* common application, electronic application. *Application fee:* $30. *Required:* essay or personal statement, high school transcript, 4 letters of recommendation. *Required for some:* interview.

Admissions Contact Mr. Troy B. Nelson, Executive Director of Admissions, Ozark Christian College, 1111 North Main Street, Joplin, MO 64801-4804. *Phone:* 417-624-2518 Ext. 2006. *Toll-free phone:* 800-299-4622. *Fax:* 417-624-0090. *E-mail:* occadmin@occ.edu.

PARK UNIVERSITY
Parkville, Missouri

- **Independent** comprehensive, founded 1875
- **Calendar** semesters
- **Degrees** associate, bachelor's, and master's
- **Suburban** 800-acre campus with easy access to Kansas City
- **Endowment** $31.5 million
- **Coed,** 11,520 undergraduate students, 10% full-time, 48% women, 52% men
- **Moderately difficult** entrance level

Undergraduates 1,182 full-time, 10,338 part-time. Students come from 49 states and territories, 90 other countries, 82% are from out of state, 21% African American, 2% Asian American or Pacific Islander, 15% Hispanic American, 0.6% Native American, 2% international, 18% transferred in, 12% live on campus. *Retention:* 74% of 2002 full-time freshmen returned.

Freshmen *Admission:* 100 enrolled. *Average high school GPA:* 3.00. *Test scores:* ACT scores over 18: 77%; ACT scores over 24: 24%; ACT scores over 30: 2%.

Faculty *Total:* 805, 12% full-time. *Student/faculty ratio:* 14:1.

Majors Accounting; accounting related; athletic training; aviation/airway management; biological and biomedical sciences related; biology/biological sciences; building/property maintenance and management; business administration and management; business, management, and marketing related; business/managerial economics; chemistry; commercial and advertising art; communication/speech communication and rhetoric; computer and information sciences; computer and information sciences and support services related; computer science; criminal justice/law enforcement administration; early childhood education; economics; education related; elementary education; engineering related; English; finance and financial management services related; fine/studio arts; health information/medical records administration; history; human resources management and services related; human services; interior design; legal studies; liberal arts and sciences/liberal studies; logistics and materials management; management information systems; marketing/marketing management; mathematics; multi-/interdisciplinary studies related; natural sciences; nursing (registered nurse training); office management; political science and government; psychology; public administration; social psychology; sociology; Spanish.

Academic Programs *Special study options:* academic remediation for entering students, adult/continuing education programs, advanced placement credit, distance learning, double majors, English as a second language, external degree program, honors programs, independent study, internships, off-campus study, part-time degree program, services for LD students, student-designed majors, summer session for credit. *ROTC:* Army (b).

Library McAfee Memorial Library with 144,870 titles, 775 serial subscriptions, 850 audiovisual materials, an OPAC.

Computers on Campus 143 computers available on campus for general student use. A campuswide network can be accessed from student residence rooms. Internet access, online (class) registration, at least one staffed computer lab available.

Student Life *Housing:* on-campus residence required through junior year. *Options:* coed. Campus housing is university owned. Freshman campus housing is guaranteed. *Activities and organizations:* drama/theater group, student-run newspaper, radio station, choral group, World Student Union, Student Senate, radio club, Latin American Student Organization, marketing club. *Campus security:* 24-hour patrols, student patrols, late-night transport/escort service. *Student services:* health clinic, personal/psychological counseling.

Athletics Member NAIA. *Intercollegiate sports:* baseball M(s), basketball M(s)/W(s), cross-country running M(s)/W(s), golf W, soccer M(s)/W(s), softball W(s), track and field M(s)/W(s), volleyball M(s)/W(s). *Intramural sports:* basketball M/W, softball M/W, volleyball M/W.

Standardized Tests *Required:* SAT I or ACT (for admission).

Costs (2003–04) *Comprehensive fee:* $10,780 includes full-time tuition ($5600) and room and board ($5180). Part-time tuition: $200 per credit hour. *Room and board:* Room and board charges vary according to board plan and housing facility. *Payment plan:* installment. *Waivers:* senior citizens and employees or children of employees.

Financial Aid Of all full-time matriculated undergraduates who enrolled in 2002, 5,289 applied for aid, 4,808 were judged to have need, 3,139 had their need fully met. 209 Federal Work-Study jobs (averaging $2875). 103 state and other part-time jobs (averaging $2675). In 2002, 483 non-need-based awards were made. *Average percent of need met:* 68%. *Average financial aid package:* $4800. *Average need-based loan:* $4120. *Average need-based gift aid:* $2812. *Average non-need-based aid:* $3590. *Average indebtedness upon graduation:* $12,800.

Applying *Options:* electronic application, early admission, deferred entrance. *Application fee:* $25. *Required:* high school transcript, minimum 2.0 GPA. *Required for some:* 2 letters of recommendation, interview. *Recommended:* essay or personal statement. *Application deadlines:* 8/1 (freshmen), 8/1 (transfers). *Notification:* continuous (freshmen), continuous (transfers).

Admissions Contact Jo Grove Henderson, Office of Admissions, Park University, 8700 NW River Park Drive, Campus Box 1, Parkville, MO 64152. *Phone:* 816-584-6215. *Toll-free phone:* 800-745-7275. *Fax:* 816-741-4462. *E-mail:* admissions@mail.park.edu.

RANKEN TECHNICAL COLLEGE
St. Louis, Missouri

- **Independent** primarily 2-year, founded 1907
- **Calendar** semesters
- **Degrees** certificates, associate, and bachelor's
- **Urban** 10-acre campus
- **Endowment** $39.0 million
- **Coed, primarily men**
- **Moderately difficult** entrance level

Faculty *Student/faculty ratio:* 15:1.

Student Life *Campus security:* 24-hour emergency response devices and patrols.

Costs (2003–04) *Tuition:* $9000 full-time. *Required fees:* $165 full-time.

Financial Aid Of all full-time matriculated undergraduates who enrolled in 2001, 30 Federal Work-Study jobs (averaging $2000).

Applying *Options:* common application, electronic application. *Application fee:* $95. *Required:* essay or personal statement, high school transcript, interview.

Admissions Contact Ms. Elizabeth Darr, Director of Admissions, Ranken Technical College, 4431 Finney Avenue, St. Louis, MO 63113. *Phone:* 314-371-0233 Ext. 4811. *Toll-free phone:* 866-4RANKEN. *Fax:* 314-371-0241. *E-mail:* admissions@ranken.edu.

RESEARCH COLLEGE OF NURSING
Kansas City, Missouri

- **Independent** comprehensive, founded 1980, part of Rockhurst University
- **Calendar** semesters
- **Degrees** bachelor's and master's (bachelor's degree offered jointly with Rockhurst College)
- **Urban** 66-acre campus
- **Coed, primarily women,** 197 undergraduate students, 99% full-time, 88% women, 12% men
- **Moderately difficult** entrance level, 77% of applicants were admitted

Undergraduates 196 full-time, 1 part-time. Students come from 7 states and territories, 5% African American, 2% Asian American or Pacific Islander, 3% Hispanic American, 5% transferred in.

Freshmen *Admission:* 94 applied, 72 admitted, 35 enrolled. *Average high school GPA:* 3.46. *Test scores:* ACT scores over 18: 100%; ACT scores over 24: 85%; ACT scores over 30: 35%.

Faculty *Total:* 35, 71% full-time. *Student/faculty ratio:* 7:1.

Majors Nursing (registered nurse training).

Academic Programs *Special study options:* accelerated degree program, advanced placement credit, double majors, honors programs, independent study, services for LD students, study abroad, summer session for credit. *ROTC:* Army (c).

Library Greenlease Library with 150,000 titles, 675 serial subscriptions, an OPAC, a Web page.

Computers on Campus 125 computers available on campus for general student use. A campuswide network can be accessed from student residence rooms and from off campus. Internet access, online (class) registration, at least one staffed computer lab available.

Student Life *Housing:* on-campus residence required for freshman year. *Options:* coed, men-only, women-only. Campus housing is university owned. Freshman campus housing is guaranteed. *Activities and organizations:* drama/theater group, student-run newspaper, radio station, choral group, national fraternities, national sororities. *Campus security:* 24-hour emergency response devices and patrols, late-night transport/escort service, controlled dormitory access. *Student services:* health clinic, personal/psychological counseling.

Athletics Member NCAA. All Division II. *Intercollegiate sports:* baseball M(s), basketball M(s)/W(s), golf M(s)/W(s), soccer M(s)/W(s), tennis M(s)/W(s), volleyball W(s). *Intramural sports:* badminton M/W, basketball M/W, cross-country running M/W, field hockey M/W, football M/W, golf M/W, lacrosse M/W, racquetball M/W, rock climbing M/W, rugby M/W, soccer M/W, softball M/W, table tennis M/W, tennis M/W, volleyball M/W, weight lifting M.

Standardized Tests *Required:* SAT I or ACT (for admission).

Costs (2003–04) *Comprehensive fee:* $22,850 includes full-time tuition ($16,950), mandatory fees ($450), and room and board ($5450). Full-time tuition and fees vary according to program. Part-time tuition: $575 per credit hour. Part-time tuition and fees vary according to class time and program. *Required fees:* $25 per term part-time. *Room and board:* Room and board charges vary according to board plan, housing facility, and location. *Payment plans:* installment, deferred payment. *Waivers:* senior citizens and employees or children of employees.

Financial Aid Of all full-time matriculated undergraduates who enrolled in 2003, 83 applied for aid, 83 were judged to have need, 17 had their need fully met. In 2003, 33 non-need-based awards were made. *Average percent of need met:* 60%. *Average financial aid package:* $18,933. *Average need-based loan:* $2900. *Average need-based gift aid:* $2000. *Average non-need-based aid:* $13,980. *Average indebtedness upon graduation:* $11,602.

Applying *Options:* common application, electronic application, deferred entrance. *Application fee:* $25. *Required:* high school transcript, 1 letter of recommendation. *Recommended:* minimum 2.8 GPA, interview, minimum ACT score of 20. *Application deadlines:* 6/30 (freshmen), 1/31 (transfers). *Notification:* continuous until 8/15 (freshmen), 3/15 (transfers).

Admissions Contact Ms. Amy Johnson, Rockhurst College Admission Office, Research College of Nursing, 1100 Rockhurst Road, Kansas City, MO 64110. *Phone:* 816-501-4100 Ext. 4654. *Toll-free phone:* 800-842-6776. *Fax:* 816-501-4588. *E-mail:* mendenhall@vax2.rockhurst.edu.

ROCKHURST UNIVERSITY
Kansas City, Missouri

- **Independent Roman Catholic (Jesuit)** comprehensive, founded 1910
- **Calendar** semesters
- **Degrees** certificates, bachelor's, master's, and postbachelor's certificates
- **Urban** 35-acre campus
- **Endowment** $38.3 million
- **Coed,** 1,957 undergraduate students, 55% full-time, 57% women, 43% men
- **Moderately difficult** entrance level, 80% of applicants were admitted

Undergraduates 1,084 full-time, 873 part-time. Students come from 24 states and territories, 10 other countries, 31% are from out of state, 9% African American, 3% Asian American or Pacific Islander, 5% Hispanic American, 1% Native American, 1% international, 5% transferred in, 53% live on campus. *Retention:* 79% of 2002 full-time freshmen returned.

Rockhurst University (continued)

Freshmen *Admission:* 960 applied, 766 admitted, 245 enrolled. *Average high school GPA:* 3.46. *Test scores:* SAT verbal scores over 500: 81%; SAT math scores over 500: 81%; ACT scores over 18: 98%; SAT verbal scores over 600: 48%; SAT math scores over 600: 38%; ACT scores over 24: 57%; SAT verbal scores over 700: 19%; SAT math scores over 700: 14%; ACT scores over 30: 14%.

Faculty *Total:* 208, 62% full-time, 63% with terminal degrees. *Student/faculty ratio:* 10:1.

Majors Accounting; biology/biological sciences; business administration and management; business/commerce; business/corporate communications; chemistry; communication/speech communication and rhetoric; community organization and advocacy; computer programming; computer science; computer systems analysis; creative writing; dramatic/theatre arts; economics; education; elementary education; English; finance; French; history; human resources management; information science/studies; international relations and affairs; labor and industrial relations; management science; marketing/marketing management; mathematics; medical laboratory technology; nursing (registered nurse training); philosophy; physics; political science and government; psychology; public relations/image management; secondary education; social sciences; sociology; Spanish; speech-language pathology; theology.

Academic Programs *Special study options:* academic remediation for entering students, accelerated degree program, adult/continuing education programs, advanced placement credit, cooperative education, distance learning, double majors, freshman honors college, honors programs, independent study, internships, off-campus study, part-time degree program, services for LD students, study abroad, summer session for credit. *ROTC:* Army (c). *Unusual degree programs:* 3-2 engineering with University of Missouri-Rolla, University of Detroit Mercy, Marquette University.

Library Greenlease Library with 597,800 titles, 750 serial subscriptions, 3,339 audiovisual materials, an OPAC, a Web page.

Computers on Campus 500 computers available on campus for general student use. A campuswide network can be accessed from student residence rooms and from off campus. Internet access, at least one staffed computer lab available.

Student Life *Housing:* on-campus residence required through sophomore year. *Options:* coed, men-only, women-only. Campus housing is university owned. *Activities and organizations:* drama/theater group, student-run newspaper, choral group, Student Activities Board, Organization of Collegiate Women, Black Student Union, Student Organization of Latinos, College Players, national fraternities, national sororities. *Campus security:* 24-hour emergency response devices and patrols, student patrols, late-night transport/escort service, controlled dormitory access, closed-circuit TV monitors. *Student services:* health clinic, personal/psychological counseling.

Athletics Member NCAA. All Division II. *Intercollegiate sports:* baseball M(s), basketball M(s)/W(s), golf M(s)/W(s), soccer M(s)/W(s), tennis M(s)/W(s), volleyball W(s). *Intramural sports:* badminton M/W, basketball M/W, cheerleading M/W, cross-country running M/W, field hockey M/W, football M/W, golf M/W, racquetball M/W, soccer M/W, softball M/W, tennis M/W, volleyball M/W, weight lifting M, wrestling M.

Standardized Tests *Required:* SAT I or ACT (for admission).

Costs (2003–04) *Comprehensive fee:* $23,160 includes full-time tuition ($16,950), mandatory fees ($460), and room and board ($5750). Full-time tuition and fees vary according to course load. Part-time tuition: $575 per semester hour. Part-time tuition and fees vary according to class time and course load. *Required fees:* $25 per term part-time. *Room and board:* Room and board charges vary according to board plan and housing facility. *Payment plans:* installment, deferred payment. *Waivers:* children of alumni, senior citizens, and employees or children of employees.

Financial Aid Of all full-time matriculated undergraduates who enrolled in 2002, 1,142 applied for aid, 915 were judged to have need, 8 had their need fully met. 219 Federal Work-Study jobs (averaging $1500). 131 state and other part-time jobs (averaging $1200). In 2002, 125 non-need-based awards were made. *Average percent of need met:* 86%. *Average financial aid package:* $16,299. *Average need-based loan:* $6037. *Average need-based gift aid:* $5653. *Average non-need-based aid:* $5819. *Average indebtedness upon graduation:* $14,556.

Applying *Options:* common application, electronic application, deferred entrance. *Application fee:* $25. *Required:* high school transcript, minimum 2.0 GPA, 1 letter of recommendation. *Required for some:* essay or personal statement, interview. *Application deadline:* 6/30 (freshmen), rolling (transfers). *Notification:* continuous (freshmen), continuous (transfers).

Admissions Contact Mr. Lane Ramey, Director of Freshman Admissions, Rockhurst University, 1100 Rockhurst Road, Kansas City, MO 64110-2561. *Phone:* 816-501-4100. *Toll-free phone:* 800-842-6776. *Fax:* 816-501-4142. *E-mail:* admission@rockhurst.edu.

■ See page 2252 for a narrative description.

St. Louis Christian College
Florissant, Missouri

- **Independent Christian** 4-year, founded 1956
- **Calendar** semesters
- **Degrees** associate and bachelor's
- **Suburban** 20-acre campus with easy access to St. Louis
- **Endowment** $577,910
- **Coed,** 213 undergraduate students, 67% full-time, 46% women, 54% men
- **Minimally difficult** entrance level, 76% of applicants were admitted

Undergraduates 143 full-time, 70 part-time. Students come from 11 states and territories, 3 other countries, 37% are from out of state, 27% African American, 0.9% Asian American or Pacific Islander, 2% Hispanic American, 1% Native American, 0.9% international, 6% transferred in, 38% live on campus. *Retention:* 65% of 2002 full-time freshmen returned.

Freshmen *Admission:* 55 applied, 42 admitted, 26 enrolled. *Average high school GPA:* 2.95. *Test scores:* ACT scores over 18: 90%; ACT scores over 24: 45%.

Faculty *Total:* 33, 27% full-time, 24% with terminal degrees. *Student/faculty ratio:* 12:1.

Majors Biblical studies; divinity/ministry; liberal arts and sciences/liberal studies; religious education; religious/sacred music; theology.

Academic Programs *Special study options:* academic remediation for entering students, accelerated degree program, adult/continuing education programs, advanced placement credit, internships, part-time degree program, services for LD students.

Library St. Louis Christian College Library with 39,728 titles, 144 serial subscriptions, a Web page.

Computers on Campus 11 computers available on campus for general student use. Internet access, at least one staffed computer lab available.

Student Life *Housing:* on-campus residence required through senior year. *Options:* men-only, women-only. Campus housing is university owned. *Activities and organizations:* drama/theater group, choral group, World Christians Unlimited, Drama Club, pep band. *Campus security:* 24-hour emergency response devices and patrols, controlled dormitory access, night security. *Student services:* personal/psychological counseling.

Athletics Member NCCAA. *Intercollegiate sports:* baseball M, basketball M, volleyball W. *Intramural sports:* basketball M/W, volleyball W.

Standardized Tests *Required:* ACT (for admission).

Costs (2004–05) *Comprehensive fee:* $12,860 includes full-time tuition ($7680) and room and board ($5180). Part-time tuition: $240 per hour. *Room and board:* Room and board charges vary according to housing facility. *Payment plan:* installment. *Waivers:* employees or children of employees.

Financial Aid Of all full-time matriculated undergraduates who enrolled in 2003, 120 applied for aid, 100 were judged to have need, 20 had their need fully met. 16 Federal Work-Study jobs (averaging $1308). 26 state and other part-time jobs (averaging $2600). In 2003, 13 non-need-based awards were made. *Average percent of need met:* 68%. *Average financial aid package:* $5104. *Average need-based loan:* $3522. *Average need-based gift aid:* $4931. *Average non-need-based aid:* $4547. *Average indebtedness upon graduation:* $11,598.

Applying *Options:* early admission. *Required:* essay or personal statement, high school transcript, 2 letters of recommendation. *Required for some:* interview. *Recommended:* minimum 2.0 GPA. *Application deadlines:* 8/15 (freshmen), 8/15 (transfers). *Notification:* continuous (freshmen), continuous (transfers).

Admissions Contact Mr. Richard Fordyce, Registrar, St. Louis Christian College, 1360 Grandview Drive, Florissant, MO 63033-6499. *Phone:* 314-837-6777 Ext. 1500. *Toll-free phone:* 800-887-SLCC. *Fax:* 314-837-8291. *E-mail:* questions@slcc4ministry.edu.

St. Louis College of Pharmacy
St. Louis, Missouri

- **Independent** comprehensive, founded 1864
- **Calendar** semesters
- **Degrees** bachelor's, master's, and first professional (bachelor of science degree program in pharmaceutical studies cannot be applied to directly; students have the option to transfer in after their second year in the PharmD program. Bachelor's degree candidates are not eligible to take the pharmacist's licensing examination)
- **Urban** 5-acre campus
- **Endowment** $50.4 million
- **Coed,** 170 undergraduate students, 98% full-time, 65% women, 35% men
- **Moderately difficult** entrance level, 44% of applicants were admitted

Undergraduates 166 full-time, 4 part-time. Students come from 10 states and territories, 48% are from out of state, 5% African American, 11% Asian American or Pacific Islander, 2% Hispanic American, 0.6% international, 29% transferred in, 40% live on campus. *Retention:* 84% of 2002 full-time freshmen returned.

Freshmen *Admission:* 514 applied, 228 admitted. *Average high school GPA:* 3.70. *Test scores:* ACT scores over 18: 100%; ACT scores over 24: 75%; ACT scores over 30: 11%.

Faculty *Total:* 125, 54% full-time. *Student/faculty ratio:* 12:1.

Majors Pharmacy.

Academic Programs *Special study options:* adult/continuing education programs, advanced placement credit, internships, summer session for credit. *ROTC:* Army (c), Air Force (c).

Library O. J. Cloughly Alumni Library with 59,012 titles, 234 serial subscriptions, 802 audiovisual materials, an OPAC, a Web page.

Computers on Campus 75 computers available on campus for general student use. A campuswide network can be accessed from student residence rooms and from off campus. Internet access, at least one staffed computer lab available. Computer purchase or lease plan available.

Student Life *Housing options:* coed. Campus housing is university owned. Freshman applicants given priority for college housing. *Activities and organizations:* drama/theater group, student-run newspaper, choral group, Gateway Academy of Student Pharmacists, Student Council, International Student Council, student ambassadors, Student Alumni Association, national fraternities, national sororities. *Campus security:* 24-hour emergency response devices and patrols, late-night transport/escort service, controlled dormitory access. *Student services:* personal/psychological counseling.

Athletics Member NAIA. *Intercollegiate sports:* basketball M/W, cross-country running M/W, ultimate Frisbee M(c)/W(c), volleyball W. *Intramural sports:* basketball M/W, cheerleading W, cross-country running M/W, football M/W, golf M/W, soccer M/W, softball M/W, table tennis M/W, tennis M/W, volleyball M/W, weight lifting M/W.

Standardized Tests *Required:* SAT I or ACT (for admission).

Costs (2004–05) *Comprehensive fee:* $24,610 includes full-time tuition ($17,010), mandatory fees ($250), and room and board ($7350). Full-time tuition and fees vary according to student level. Part-time tuition: $708 per credit. *Room and board:* Room and board charges vary according to housing facility. *Payment plan:* deferred payment. *Waivers:* employees or children of employees.

Financial Aid Of all full-time matriculated undergraduates who enrolled in 2000, 713 applied for aid, 650 were judged to have need, 2 had their need fully met. 111 Federal Work-Study jobs (averaging $1200). In 2000, 94 non-need-based awards were made. *Average percent of need met:* 31%. *Average financial aid package:* $11,324. *Average need-based loan:* $5340. *Average need-based gift aid:* $1498. *Average non-need-based aid:* $7279. *Average indebtedness upon graduation:* $64,500. *Financial aid deadline:* 11/15.

Applying *Options:* electronic application. *Application fee:* $35. *Required:* essay or personal statement, high school transcript, minimum 3.0 GPA, 2 letters of recommendation. *Required for some:* interview. *Application deadlines:* rolling (freshmen), 3/1 (transfers). *Notification:* continuous until 8/1 (freshmen), continuous (transfers).

Admissions Contact Ms. Patty Kulage, Admissions and Financial Aid Coordinator, St. Louis College of Pharmacy, 4588 Parkview Place, St. Louis, MO 63110-1088. *Phone:* 314-446-8328. *Toll-free phone:* 800-278-5267. *Fax:* 314-446-8310. *E-mail:* pkulage@stlcop.edu.

■ *See page 2306 for a narrative description.*

SAINT LOUIS UNIVERSITY

St. Louis, Missouri

- ■ **Independent Roman Catholic (Jesuit)** university, founded 1818
- ■ **Calendar** semesters
- ■ **Degrees** certificates, associate, bachelor's, master's, doctoral, first professional, post-master's, and postbachelor's certificates
- ■ **Urban** 373-acre campus
- ■ **Endowment** $648.7 million
- ■ **Coed,** 7,091 undergraduate students, 91% full-time, 55% women, 45% men
- ■ **Moderately difficult** entrance level, 70% of applicants were admitted

Undergraduates 6,461 full-time, 630 part-time. Students come from 48 states and territories, 78 other countries, 49% are from out of state, 7% African American, 4% Asian American or Pacific Islander, 2% Hispanic American, 0.4% Native American, 2% international, 5% transferred in, 54% live on campus. *Retention:* 88% of 2002 full-time freshmen returned.

Freshmen *Admission:* 6,405 applied, 4,500 admitted, 1,526 enrolled. *Average high school GPA:* 3.60. *Test scores:* SAT verbal scores over 500: 90%; SAT math scores over 500: 90%; ACT scores over 18: 99%; SAT verbal scores over 600: 48%; SAT math scores over 600: 55%; ACT scores over 24: 74%; SAT verbal scores over 700: 9%; SAT math scores over 700: 11%; ACT scores over 30: 18%.

Faculty *Total:* 933, 67% full-time, 75% with terminal degrees. *Student/faculty ratio:* 12:1.

Majors Accounting; aeronautical/aerospace engineering technology; aerospace, aeronautical and astronautical engineering; airline pilot and flight crew; American studies; applied mathematics; art history, criticism and conservation; atmospheric sciences and meteorology; aviation/airway management; biology/biological sciences; biomedical/medical engineering; business administration and management; chemistry; city/urban, community and regional planning; classics and classical languages related; clinical laboratory science/medical technology; clinical/medical laboratory science and allied professions related; communication and journalism related; communication/speech communication and rhetoric; computer and information sciences; computer and information sciences and support services related; corrections; criminal justice/law enforcement administration; criminal justice/police science; dramatic/theatre arts; economics; education; education (multiple levels); electrical, electronics and communications engineering; engineering/industrial management; English; environmental science; finance; fine/studio arts; foods, nutrition, and wellness; foreign languages and literatures; French; geology/earth science; geophysics and seismology; German; health/health care administration; health information/medical records administration; history; humanities; human resources management; international business/trade/commerce; international relations and affairs; kinesiology and exercise science; management information systems; management science; marketing/marketing management; mathematics; mechanical engineering; modern Greek; music; nuclear medical technology; nursing (registered nurse training); occupational therapy; organizational behavior; philosophy; physical therapy; physician assistant; physics; political science and government; psychology; Russian; social sciences; social work; sociology; Spanish; theology; urban studies/affairs; women's studies.

Academic Programs *Special study options:* academic remediation for entering students, accelerated degree program, adult/continuing education programs, advanced placement credit, cooperative education, distance learning, double majors, English as a second language, honors programs, independent study, internships, off-campus study, part-time degree program, services for LD students, student-designed majors, study abroad, summer session for credit. *ROTC:* Army (c), Air Force (b).

Library Pius XII Memorial Library plus 2 others with 1.3 million titles, 12,881 serial subscriptions, 195,651 audiovisual materials, a Web page.

Computers on Campus 6500 computers available on campus for general student use. A campuswide network can be accessed from student residence rooms and from off campus. Internet access, online (class) registration, at least one staffed computer lab available. Computer purchase or lease plan available.

Student Life *Housing options:* coed, disabled students. Campus housing is university owned. *Activities and organizations:* drama/theater group, student-run newspaper, radio and television station, choral group, Student Government Association, Student Activities Board, Black Student Alliance, International Student Federation, national fraternities, national sororities. *Campus security:* 24-hour emergency response devices and patrols, student patrols, late-night transport/escort service, controlled dormitory access, crime prevention program, bicycle patrols, pamphlets, posters, films. *Student services:* health clinic, personal/psychological counseling, legal services.

Athletics Member NCAA. All Division I. *Intercollegiate sports:* baseball M(s), basketball M(s)/W(s), crew M(c)/W(c), cross-country running M(s)/W(s), fencing M(c)/W(c), field hockey W(s), golf M(s), ice hockey M(c)/W(c), lacrosse M(c)/W(c), rugby M(c), soccer M(s)(c)/W(s)(c), softball W(s), swimming M(s)/W(s), tennis M(s)/W(s), ultimate Frisbee M(c)/W(c), volleyball M(c)/W(s)(c). *Intramural sports:* badminton M/W, basketball M/W, bowling M/W, cheerleading W, football M/W, golf M/W, racquetball M/W, soccer M/W, softball M/W, squash M/W, table tennis M/W, tennis M/W, ultimate Frisbee M/W, volleyball M/W.

Standardized Tests *Required:* SAT I or ACT (for admission).

Costs (2003–04) *Comprehensive fee:* $29,958 includes full-time tuition ($22,050), mandatory fees ($168), and room and board ($7740). Full-time tuition and fees vary according to location. Part-time tuition: $770 per credit hour. Part-time tuition and fees vary according to class time, location, and program. *Required fees:* $55 per term part-time. *College room only:* $4240. Room and board charges vary according to board plan, housing facility, and location. *Payment plan:* installment. *Waivers:* employees or children of employees.

Financial Aid Of all full-time matriculated undergraduates who enrolled in 2003, 4,949 applied for aid, 4,317 were judged to have need, 476 had their need fully met. 1,731 Federal Work-Study jobs (averaging $2748). In 2003, 1015 non-need-based awards were made. *Average percent of need met:* 62%. *Average financial aid package:* $18,526. *Average need-based loan:* $5222. *Average need-based gift aid:* $12,459. *Average non-need-based aid:* $8692. *Average indebtedness upon graduation:* $22,247.

Applying *Options:* common application, electronic application, deferred entrance. *Application fee:* $25. *Required:* essay or personal statement, high school transcript, secondary school report form. *Recommended:* minimum 2.5 GPA, 2 letters

Saint Louis University (continued)
of recommendation, interview. *Application deadline:* rolling (freshmen). *Notification:* continuous (freshmen), continuous (transfers).

Admissions Contact Ms. Shani Lenore, Director, Saint Louis University, 221 North Grand Boulevard, St. Louis, MO 63103-2097. *Phone:* 314-977-3415. *Toll-free phone:* 800-758-3678. *Fax:* 314-977-7136. *E-mail:* admitme@slu.edu.

SAINT LUKE'S COLLEGE
Kansas City, Missouri

- **Independent Episcopal** upper-level, founded 1903
- **Calendar** semesters
- **Degree** bachelor's
- **Urban** 3-acre campus
- **Endowment** $1.8 million
- **Coed, primarily women,** 110 undergraduate students, 85% full-time, 92% women, 8% men
- **Very difficult** entrance level

Undergraduates 93 full-time, 17 part-time. Students come from 5 states and territories, 9% African American, 5% Asian American or Pacific Islander, 0.9% Hispanic American, 49% transferred in.

Faculty *Total:* 16, 100% full-time, 13% with terminal degrees. *Student/faculty ratio:* 7:1.

Majors Nursing (registered nurse training).

Academic Programs *Special study options:* cooperative education, summer session for credit.

Library Health Sciences Library.

Computers on Campus 10 computers available on campus for general student use. At least one staffed computer lab available.

Student Life *Housing:* college housing not available. *Activities and organizations:* Saint Luke's Student Nurse Association. *Campus security:* 24-hour emergency response devices and patrols. *Student services:* health clinic, personal/psychological counseling.

Costs (2004–05) *Tuition:* $8250 full-time, $275 per credit hour part-time. *Required fees:* $510 full-time.

Financial Aid Of all full-time matriculated undergraduates who enrolled in 2003, 101 applied for aid, 86 were judged to have need, 13 had their need fully met. In 2003, 4 non-need-based awards were made. *Average percent of need met:* 76%. *Average financial aid package:* $6600. *Average need-based loan:* $5000. *Average need-based gift aid:* $2000. *Average non-need-based aid:* $1000. *Average indebtedness upon graduation:* $25,000.

Applying *Options:* common application. *Application fee:* $35. *Application deadline:* 12/31 (transfers). *Notification:* continuous until 3/1 (transfers).

Admissions Contact Ms. Christina Wood, Director of Admissions, Saint Luke's College, 8320 Wand parkway, Suite 300, Kansas City, MO 64114. *Phone:* 816-932-2073. *E-mail:* slc-admissions@saint-lukes.org.

SANFORD-BROWN COLLEGE
Fenton, Missouri

- **Proprietary** primarily 2-year, founded 1868
- **Calendar** quarters
- **Degrees** certificates, diplomas, associate, and bachelor's
- **Suburban** 6-acre campus with easy access to St. Louis
- **Coed**
- **Minimally difficult** entrance level

Faculty *Student/faculty ratio:* 9:1.

Student Life *Campus security:* late-night transport/escort service, trained security personnel from 7:30 p.m. to 10:30 p.m.

Standardized Tests *Required:* CPAt (for admission).

Applying *Options:* common application, deferred entrance. *Application fee:* $25. *Required:* high school transcript, interview.

Admissions Contact Ms. Judy Wilga, Director of Admissions, Sanford-Brown College, 1203 Smizer Mill Road, Fenton, MO 63026. *Phone:* 636-349-4900 Ext. 102. *Toll-free phone:* 800-456-7222. *Fax:* 636-349-9170.

SOUTHEAST MISSOURI STATE UNIVERSITY
Cape Girardeau, Missouri

- **State-supported** comprehensive, founded 1873, part of Missouri Coordinating Board for Higher Education
- **Calendar** semesters
- **Degrees** certificates, associate, bachelor's, master's, and post-master's certificates
- **Small-town** 693-acre campus with easy access to St. Louis
- **Endowment** $28.6 million
- **Coed,** 8,483 undergraduate students, 78% full-time, 58% women, 42% men
- **Moderately difficult** entrance level, 83% of applicants were admitted

Undergraduates 6,602 full-time, 1,881 part-time. Students come from 40 states and territories, 37 other countries, 13% are from out of state, 7% African American, 0.8% Asian American or Pacific Islander, 0.9% Hispanic American, 0.5% Native American, 2% international, 7% transferred in, 29% live on campus. *Retention:* 70% of 2002 full-time freshmen returned.

Freshmen *Admission:* 3,910 applied, 3,238 admitted, 1,495 enrolled. *Average high school GPA:* 3.29. *Test scores:* ACT scores over 18: 95%; ACT scores over 24: 35%; ACT scores over 30: 4%.

Faculty *Total:* 524, 74% full-time, 63% with terminal degrees. *Student/faculty ratio:* 18:1.

Majors Accounting; administrative assistant and secretarial science; agribusiness; agriculture; American studies; anthropology; art; art teacher education; biology/biological sciences; business administration and management; business/managerial economics; business teacher education; chemistry; child care and support services management; clinical laboratory science/medical technology; communication disorders; communication/speech communication and rhetoric; computer and information sciences; computer engineering technology; computer programming; computer technology/computer systems technology; construction engineering technology; corrections; dramatic/theatre arts; economics; elementary education; engineering physics; English; English/language arts teacher education; family and consumer sciences/home economics teacher education; family and consumer sciences/human sciences; finance; foreign language teacher education; French; general studies; geography; geological and earth sciences/geosciences related; German; health and physical education; history; humanities; industrial technology; interdisciplinary studies; kindergarten/preschool education; marketing/marketing management; mathematics; mathematics teacher education; middle school education; multi-/interdisciplinary studies related; music; music teacher education; nursing (registered nurse training); office management; parks, recreation and leisure; philosophy; physical education teaching and coaching; physics; political science and government; psychology; science teacher education; social studies teacher education; social work; sociology; Spanish; special education; speech and rhetoric; speech teacher education; sport and fitness administration; technology/industrial arts teacher education; visual and performing arts.

Academic Programs *Special study options:* academic remediation for entering students, adult/continuing education programs, advanced placement credit, cooperative education, distance learning, double majors, English as a second language, honors programs, independent study, internships, part-time degree program, services for LD students, student-designed majors, study abroad, summer session for credit. *ROTC:* Air Force (b).

Library Kent Library with 411,992 titles, 2,781 serial subscriptions, 9,400 audiovisual materials, an OPAC, a Web page.

Computers on Campus 650 computers available on campus for general student use. A campuswide network can be accessed from student residence rooms and from off campus. Internet access, online (class) registration, at least one staffed computer lab available. Computer purchase or lease plan available.

Student Life *Housing:* on-campus residence required through sophomore year. *Options:* coed. Campus housing is university owned. Freshman applicants given priority for college housing. *Activities and organizations:* drama/theater group, student-run newspaper, radio station, choral group, marching band, student government, Greek life, Residence Hall Association, marketing club, Student Activities Council, national fraternities, national sororities. *Campus security:* 24-hour emergency response devices and patrols, late-night transport/escort service, controlled dormitory access. *Student services:* health clinic, personal/psychological counseling.

Athletics Member NCAA. All Division I except football (Division I-AA). *Intercollegiate sports:* baseball M(s), basketball M(s)/W(s), cross-country running M(s)/W(s), golf M(s), gymnastics W(s), soccer W(s), softball W(s), tennis W(s), track and field M(s)/W(s), volleyball W(s). *Intramural sports:* badminton M/W, basketball M/W, bowling M/W, cross-country running M/W, fencing M/W, football M/W, golf M/W, lacrosse M/W, racquetball M/W, soccer M/W, softball M/W, swimming M/W, table tennis M/W, tennis M/W, track and field M/W, volleyball M/W, water polo M/W, weight lifting M/W, wrestling M/W.

Standardized Tests *Required:* SAT I or ACT (for admission).

Costs (2003–04) *Tuition:* state resident $4254 full-time, $153 per credit part-time; nonresident $7839 full-time, $272 per credit part-time. *Required fees:* $321 full-time, $11 per credit part-time. *Room and board:* $5450; room only: $3505. Room and board charges vary according to board plan and housing facility. *Payment plans:* installment, deferred payment. *Waivers:* senior citizens and employees or children of employees.

Financial Aid Of all full-time matriculated undergraduates who enrolled in 2002, 4,312 applied for aid, 3,173 were judged to have need, 549 had their need fully met. 230 Federal Work-Study jobs (averaging $2117). 1,250 state and other part-time jobs (averaging $1165). In 2002, 802 non-need-based awards were made. *Average percent of need met:* 70%. *Average financial aid package:* $6109. *Average need-based loan:* $3410. *Average need-based gift aid:* $3976. *Average non-need-based aid:* $3282. *Average indebtedness upon graduation:* $14,005.

Applying *Options:* common application, electronic application, deferred entrance. *Application fee:* $20. *Required:* high school transcript, minimum 2.0 GPA. *Application deadline:* 8/1 (freshmen). *Notification:* 10/1 (freshmen), continuous (transfers).

Admissions Contact Ms. Deborah Below, Director of Admissions, Southeast Missouri State University, MS 3550, Cape Girardeau, MO 63701. *Phone:* 573-651-2590. *Fax:* 573-651-5936. *E-mail:* admissions@semo.edu.

SOUTHWEST BAPTIST UNIVERSITY

Bolivar, Missouri

- **Independent Southern Baptist** comprehensive, founded 1878
- **Calendar** 4-1-4
- **Degrees** diplomas, associate, bachelor's, master's, and post-master's certificates
- **Small-town** 152-acre campus
- **Endowment** $13.3 million
- **Coed,** 2,746 undergraduate students, 66% full-time, 66% women, 34% men
- **Moderately difficult** entrance level, 86% of applicants were admitted

Southwest Baptist University (SBU) is a Christ-centered, caring academic community preparing students to be servant leaders in a global society. The University places priority on honoring God by inspiring excellence in the classroom. Through comprehensive opportunities, students discover extracurricular activities ranging from intramural athletics to an award-winning forensics program. SBU's learning environment is made up of energetic students and passionate instructors committed to achieving academic excellence. As an established leader in higher education, SBU has been named to *The Student Guide to America's 100 Best College Buys* since 1996 and to *America's Best Christian Colleges* since 1997.

Undergraduates 1,826 full-time, 920 part-time. Students come from 40 states and territories, 11 other countries, 51% are from out of state, 2% African American, 0.7% Asian American or Pacific Islander, 0.8% Hispanic American, 0.7% Native American, 0.7% international, 4% transferred in, 35% live on campus. *Retention:* 70% of 2002 full-time freshmen returned.

Freshmen *Admission:* 768 applied, 661 admitted, 470 enrolled. *Average high school GPA:* 3.36. *Test scores:* ACT scores over 18: 90%; ACT scores over 24: 46%; ACT scores over 30: 6%.

Faculty *Total:* 295, 35% full-time, 41% with terminal degrees. *Student/faculty ratio:* 21:1.

Majors Accounting; administrative assistant and secretarial science; art; art teacher education; athletic training; biblical studies; biology/biological sciences; business administration and management; business/commerce; business teacher education; chemistry; chemistry teacher education; clinical laboratory science/medical technology; commercial and advertising art; communication/speech communication and rhetoric; computer science; criminal justice/law enforcement administration; dramatic/theatre arts; education (K-12); education (specific subject areas) related; elementary education; emergency medical technology (EMT paramedic); English; English/language arts teacher education; general studies; history; history teacher education; human services; information science/studies; mathematics; mathematics teacher education; middle school education; music; music teacher education; nursing (registered nurse training); occupational safety and health technology; parks, recreation and leisure; pastoral studies/counseling; physical education teaching and coaching; political science and government; psychology; religious studies; science teacher education; secondary education; social sciences; social science teacher education; social studies teacher education; sociology; Spanish; Spanish language teacher education; speech teacher education; speech/theater education; sport and fitness administration; theological and ministerial studies related; youth ministry.

Academic Programs *Special study options:* academic remediation for entering students, accelerated degree program, advanced placement credit, cooperative education, double majors, English as a second language, honors programs, independent study, internships, part-time degree program, study abroad, summer session for credit. *ROTC:* Army (c). *Unusual degree programs:* 3-2 engineering with University of Missouri-Rolla.

Library Harriett K. Hutchens Library with 108,128 titles, 2,518 serial subscriptions, 9,370 audiovisual materials, an OPAC, a Web page.

Computers on Campus 130 computers available on campus for general student use. A campuswide network can be accessed from off campus. Internet access, at least one staffed computer lab available.

Student Life *Housing:* on-campus residence required through senior year. *Options:* men-only, women-only. Campus housing is university owned. Freshman campus housing is guaranteed. *Activities and organizations:* drama/theater group, student-run newspaper, choral group, small group ministries, Christian Service Organization, Student Government Association, Student Missouri State Teachers Association, revival teams. *Campus security:* 24-hour emergency response devices and patrols. *Student services:* health clinic, personal/psychological counseling.

Athletics Member NCAA. All Division II. *Intercollegiate sports:* baseball M(s), basketball M(s)/W(s), cheerleading M/W, cross-country running M(s)/W(s), football M(s), golf M(s), soccer M(s)/W(s), softball W(s), tennis M(s)/W(s), track and field M/W, volleyball W(s). *Intramural sports:* basketball M/W, bowling M/W, football M, golf M, softball M/W, table tennis M/W, volleyball M/W.

Standardized Tests *Required:* SAT I or ACT (for admission).

Costs (2004–05) *Comprehensive fee:* $16,220 includes full-time tuition ($11,800), mandatory fees ($532), and room and board ($3888). Part-time tuition: $500 per hour. Part-time tuition and fees vary according to course load. *Required fees:* $8 per hour part-time, $95 per term part-time. *College room only:* $2088. Room and board charges vary according to board plan and housing facility. *Payment plan:* installment. *Waivers:* employees or children of employees.

Financial Aid Of all full-time matriculated undergraduates who enrolled in 2003, 1,483 applied for aid, 1,323 were judged to have need, 267 had their need fully met. 542 Federal Work-Study jobs (averaging $1024). In 2003, 381 non-need-based awards were made. *Average percent of need met:* 70%. *Average financial aid package:* $9976. *Average need-based loan:* $4106. *Average need-based gift aid:* $3633. *Average non-need-based aid:* $4550. *Average indebtedness upon graduation:* $13,558.

Applying *Options:* electronic application. *Application fee:* $25. *Required:* essay or personal statement, high school transcript. *Required for some:* 3 letters of recommendation. *Recommended:* interview. *Application deadline:* rolling (freshmen), rolling (transfers). *Notification:* continuous (freshmen), continuous (transfers).

Admissions Contact Mr. Rob Harris, Director of Admissions, Southwest Baptist University, 1600 University Avenue, Bolivar, MO 65613-2597. *Phone:* 417-328-1809. *Toll-free phone:* 800-526-5859. *Fax:* 417-328-1514. *E-mail:* rharris@sbuniv.edu.

SOUTHWEST MISSOURI STATE UNIVERSITY

Springfield, Missouri

- **State-supported** comprehensive, founded 1905
- **Calendar** semesters
- **Degrees** bachelor's, master's, and postbachelor's certificates
- **Suburban** 225-acre campus
- **Endowment** $32.2 million
- **Coed,** 15,771 undergraduate students, 79% full-time, 56% women, 44% men
- **Moderately difficult** entrance level, 86% of applicants were admitted

Southwest Missouri State University (SMSU) is Missouri's second-largest university, with more than 18,000 students from 47 states and more than 80 countries. As Missouri's public affairs university, SMSU offers 140 undergraduate programs, 42 graduate programs, an Honors College, one of the largest cooperative education programs in the Midwest, NCAA Division I athletics, 250 student organizations, and much more. The compact SMSU campus, with a comfortable blend of traditional modern buildings and outstanding residence halls, is in Springfield, Missouri's third-largest city. Springfield and the surrounding Ozarks region offer abundant opportunities for recreation, entertainment, and employment.

Undergraduates 12,449 full-time, 3,322 part-time. Students come from 48 states and territories, 80 other countries, 8% are from out of state, 2% African American, 1% Asian American or Pacific Islander, 1% Hispanic American, 0.9% Native American, 2% international, 27% live on campus. *Retention:* 74% of 2002 full-time freshmen returned.

Freshmen *Admission:* 6,316 applied, 5,446 admitted, 2,695 enrolled. *Average high school GPA:* 3.50. *Test scores:* ACT scores over 18: 98%; ACT scores over 24: 46%; ACT scores over 30: 8%.

Faculty *Total:* 1,000, 73% full-time, 64% with terminal degrees. *Student/faculty ratio:* 18:1.

Majors Accounting; agribusiness; agricultural teacher education; agriculture; agronomy and crop science; ancient studies; animal sciences; anthropology; apparel and textiles; art; art teacher education; athletic training; audiology and speech-language pathology; biology/biological sciences; biology teacher education; business administration and management; business/commerce; business teacher education; cartography; cell and molecular biology; chemistry; chemistry teacher education; city/urban, community and regional planning; clinical laboratory science/medical technology; communication/speech communication and rhetoric; computer science; criminal justice/safety; dance; design and visual

Southwest Missouri State University (continued)
communications; dietetics; dramatic/theatre arts; early childhood education; economics; education (specific subject areas) related; elementary education; engineering physics; English; English/language arts teacher education; family and consumer sciences/home economics teacher education; finance; fine/studio arts; French; French language teacher education; geography; geology/earth science; German; German language teacher education; gerontology; history; history teacher education; horticultural science; hospitality administration; housing and human environments; human development and family studies; insurance; journalism; Latin; management information systems; marketing/marketing management; mass communication/media; mathematics; mathematics teacher education; medical radiologic technology; middle school education; molecular biology; music; music performance; music teacher education; music theory and composition; nursing (registered nurse training); parks, recreation and leisure; philosophy; physical education teaching and coaching; physical science technologies related; physics; physics teacher education; political science and government; psychology; public administration; radiologic technology/science; religious studies; respiratory care therapy; science teacher education; social work; sociology; Spanish; Spanish language teacher education; special education; technical and business writing; visual and performing arts; wildlife and wildlands science and management.

Academic Programs *Special study options:* accelerated degree program, adult/continuing education programs, advanced placement credit, cooperative education, distance learning, double majors, English as a second language, freshman honors college, honors programs, independent study, internships, off-campus study, part-time degree program, services for LD students, student-designed majors, study abroad, summer session for credit. *ROTC:* Army (b).

Library Meyer Library plus 3 others with 1.7 million titles, 4,238 serial subscriptions, 33,547 audiovisual materials, an OPAC, a Web page.

Computers on Campus 1800 computers available on campus for general student use. A campuswide network can be accessed from student residence rooms and from off campus. Internet access, at least one staffed computer lab available. Computer purchase or lease plan available.

Student Life *Housing:* on-campus residence required for freshman year. *Options:* coed, men-only, women-only, cooperative, disabled students. Campus housing is university owned. Freshman campus housing is guaranteed. *Activities and organizations:* drama/theater group, student-run newspaper, radio and television station, choral group, marching band, Residence Hall Association, Campus Crusade, Gamma Sigma Sigma, Student Government Association, national fraternities, national sororities. *Campus security:* 24-hour emergency response devices and patrols, late-night transport/escort service, controlled dormitory access, on-campus police substation. *Student services:* health clinic, personal/psychological counseling, legal services.

Athletics Member NCAA. All Division I except football (Division I-AA). *Intercollegiate sports:* baseball M(s), basketball M(s)/W(s), bowling M(c)/W(c), cross-country running M(s)/W(s), equestrian sports M(c)/W(c), field hockey W(s), golf M(s)/W(s), ice hockey M(c), lacrosse M(c), racquetball M(c)/W(c), riflery M(c)/W(c), soccer M(s)/W(s), softball W(s), swimming M(s)/W(s), tennis M(s)/W(s), track and field M(s)/W(s), ultimate Frisbee M(c)/W(c), volleyball M(c)/W(s), wrestling M(c). *Intramural sports:* badminton M/W, basketball M/W, bowling M/W, fencing M/W, football M/W, golf M/W, racquetball M/W, soccer M/W, softball M/W, table tennis M/W, tennis M/W, track and field M/W, ultimate Frisbee M/W, volleyball M/W, weight lifting M/W, wrestling M.

Standardized Tests *Required:* SAT I or ACT (for admission). *Recommended:* ACT (for admission).

Costs (2003–04) *Tuition:* state resident $4636 full-time, $138 per credit hour part-time; nonresident $8776 full-time, $276 per credit hour part-time. Full-time tuition and fees vary according to course load and degree level. Part-time tuition and fees vary according to course load and degree level. *Room and board:* $4282; room only: $2982. Room and board charges vary according to board plan and housing facility. *Payment plan:* deferred payment. *Waivers:* children of alumni, senior citizens, and employees or children of employees.

Financial Aid Of all full-time matriculated undergraduates who enrolled in 2003, 9,457 applied for aid, 6,024 were judged to have need, 445 had their need fully met. 449 Federal Work-Study jobs (averaging $1748). 1,336 state and other part-time jobs (averaging $2924). In 2003, 1057 non-need-based awards were made. *Average percent of need met:* 63%. *Average financial aid package:* $7253. *Average need-based loan:* $3722. *Average need-based gift aid:* $3034. *Average non-need-based aid:* $4527. *Average indebtedness upon graduation:* $12,993.

Applying *Options:* electronic application. *Application fee:* $25. *Required:* high school transcript. *Required for some:* essay or personal statement, interview. *Application deadlines:* 6/20 (freshmen), 12/20 (transfers). *Notification:* continuous (freshmen), continuous (transfers).

Admissions Contact Ms. Jill Duncan, Associate Director of Admissions, Southwest Missouri State University, 901 South National, Springfield, MO 65804. *Phone:* 417-836-5517. *Toll-free phone:* 800-492-7900. *Fax:* 417-836-6334. *E-mail:* smsuinfo@smsu.edu.

■ *See page 2428 for a narrative description.*

STEPHENS COLLEGE
Columbia, Missouri

- **Independent** comprehensive, founded 1833
- **Calendar** semesters
- **Degrees** bachelor's, master's, and postbachelor's certificates
- **Urban** 86-acre campus
- **Endowment** $19.7 million
- **Women only,** 577 undergraduate students, 77% full-time
- **Moderately difficult** entrance level, 79% of applicants were admitted

Undergraduates 447 full-time, 130 part-time. Students come from 41 states and territories, 3 other countries, 55% are from out of state, 8% African American, 1% Asian American or Pacific Islander, 3% Hispanic American, 0.7% Native American, 0.5% international, 5% transferred in, 75% live on campus. *Retention:* 73% of 2002 full-time freshmen returned.

Freshmen *Admission:* 393 applied, 311 admitted, 139 enrolled. *Average high school GPA:* 3.50. *Test scores:* SAT verbal scores over 500: 88%; SAT math scores over 500: 73%; ACT scores over 18: 99%; SAT verbal scores over 600: 34%; SAT math scores over 600: 24%; ACT scores over 24: 52%; SAT verbal scores over 700: 2%; SAT math scores over 700: 2%; ACT scores over 30: 4%.

Faculty *Total:* 77, 61% full-time, 69% with terminal degrees. *Student/faculty ratio:* 10:1.

Majors Accounting; advertising; biology/biological sciences; biomedical sciences; broadcast journalism; business administration and management; child development; creative writing; dance; dramatic/theatre arts; early childhood education; elementary education; English; environmental studies; equestrian studies; fashion/apparel design; fashion merchandising; horse husbandry/equine science and management; interdisciplinary studies; international relations and affairs; kindergarten/preschool education; liberal arts and sciences/liberal studies; marketing/marketing management; mass communication/media; modern languages; natural sciences; occupational therapy; philosophy; political science and government; pre-law studies; pre-medical studies; pre-veterinary studies; psychology; public relations/image management; radio and television.

Academic Programs *Special study options:* academic remediation for entering students, accelerated degree program, adult/continuing education programs, advanced placement credit, cooperative education, distance learning, double majors, English as a second language, external degree program, freshman honors college, honors programs, independent study, internships, off-campus study, part-time degree program, services for LD students, student-designed majors, study abroad. *ROTC:* Army (c), Air Force (c). *Unusual degree programs:* 3-2 animal science with University of Missouri–Columbia, occupational therapy with Washington University in St. Louis.

Library Hugh Stephens Library with 121,084 titles, 534 serial subscriptions, 4,764 audiovisual materials, an OPAC, a Web page.

Computers on Campus 64 computers available on campus for general student use. A campuswide network can be accessed from student residence rooms and from off campus. Internet access, at least one staffed computer lab available.

Student Life *Housing:* on-campus residence required through junior year. *Options:* women-only. Campus housing is university owned. Freshman campus housing is guaranteed. *Activities and organizations:* drama/theater group, student-run newspaper, radio and television station, choral group, Student Government Association, Martin Luther King Jr. Student Union, Stephens Ambassadors Association, Stephens Christian Fellowship, Young Women's Political Caucus, national sororities. *Campus security:* 24-hour emergency response devices and patrols, student patrols, late-night transport/escort service, controlled dormitory access. *Student services:* health clinic, personal/psychological counseling, women's center.

Athletics Member NCAA. All Division III. *Intercollegiate sports:* basketball W, soccer W, swimming W, tennis W, volleyball W.

Standardized Tests *Required:* SAT I or ACT (for admission).

Costs (2003–04) *Comprehensive fee:* $24,260 includes full-time tuition ($17,360) and room and board ($6900). *College room only:* $3050. Room and board charges vary according to board plan. *Payment plan:* installment. *Waivers:* employees or children of employees.

Financial Aid Of all full-time matriculated undergraduates who enrolled in 2003, 346 applied for aid, 323 were judged to have need, 100 had their need fully met. 40 Federal Work-Study jobs (averaging $1500). 238 state and other part-time jobs (averaging $1200). In 2003, 84 non-need-based awards were made. *Average percent of need met:* 82%. *Average financial aid package:* $16,576. *Average* *need-based loan:* $3885. *Average need-based gift aid:* $5477. *Average non-need-based aid:* $8532. *Average indebtedness upon graduation:* $6134.

Applying *Options:* common application, electronic application, early admission, deferred entrance. *Application fee:* $25. *Required:* essay or personal statement, high school transcript, minimum 2.5 GPA, 1 letter of recommendation. *Recommended:* interview. *Application deadline:* 7/31 (freshmen). *Notification:* continuous until 8/15 (freshmen), continuous until 8/15 (transfers).

Admissions Contact Ms. Amy Shaver, Director of Enrollment Services, Stephens College, 1200 East Broadway, Box 2121, Columbia, MO 65215-0002. *Phone:* 573-876-7207. *Toll-free phone:* 800-876-7207. *Fax:* 573-876-7237. *E-mail:* apply@stephens.edu.

■ See page 2458 for a narrative description.

TRUMAN STATE UNIVERSITY

Kirksville, Missouri

- **State-supported** comprehensive, founded 1867
- **Calendar** semesters
- **Degrees** bachelor's and master's
- **Small-town** 140-acre campus
- **Endowment** $14.3 million
- **Coed,** 5,479 undergraduate students, 97% full-time, 59% women, 41% men
- **Moderately difficult** entrance level, 84% of applicants were admitted

Undergraduates 5,338 full-time, 141 part-time. Students come from 37 states and territories, 48 other countries, 24% are from out of state, 4% African American, 2% Asian American or Pacific Islander, 2% Hispanic American, 0.5% Native American, 5% international, 1% transferred in, 46% live on campus. *Retention:* 85% of 2002 full-time freshmen returned.

Freshmen *Admission:* 4,334 applied, 3,622 admitted, 1,317 enrolled. *Average high school GPA:* 3.77. *Test scores:* SAT verbal scores over 500: 95%; SAT math scores over 500: 92%; ACT scores over 18: 100%; SAT verbal scores over 600: 59%; SAT math scores over 600: 58%; ACT scores over 24: 87%; SAT verbal scores over 700: 18%; SAT math scores over 700: 12%; ACT scores over 30: 32%.

Faculty *Total:* 377, 94% full-time, 82% with terminal degrees. *Student/faculty ratio:* 15:1.

Majors Accounting; agricultural business and management; agricultural economics; agriculture; agronomy and crop science; animal sciences; anthropology related; applied art; art; art history, criticism and conservation; biology/biological sciences; business administration and management; chemistry; classics and languages, literatures and linguistics; commercial and advertising art; communication disorders; communication/speech communication and rhetoric; computer science; criminal justice/law enforcement administration; criminal justice/police science; design and visual communications; dramatic/theatre arts; economics; economics related; English; equestrian studies; finance; fine/studio arts; French; German; health science; history; horticultural science; journalism; kinesiology and exercise science; mass communication/media; mathematics; music; music performance; nursing (registered nurse training); philosophy; physics; piano and organ; political science and government; pre-dentistry studies; pre-law studies; pre-medical studies; pre-pharmacy studies; pre-veterinary studies; psychology; public health; religious studies; Russian; sociology; Spanish; speech and rhetoric; voice and opera.

Academic Programs *Special study options:* accelerated degree program, advanced placement credit, double majors, English as a second language, honors programs, internships, off-campus study, part-time degree program, services for LD students, study abroad, summer session for credit. *ROTC:* Army (b).

Library Pickler Memorial Library with 481,424 titles, 3,197 serial subscriptions, 36,724 audiovisual materials, an OPAC, a Web page.

Computers on Campus 840 computers available on campus for general student use. A campuswide network can be accessed from student residence rooms and from off campus. Internet access, at least one staffed computer lab available. Computer purchase or lease plan available.

Student Life *Housing:* on-campus residence required for freshman year. *Options:* coed, women-only, disabled students. Campus housing is university owned. Freshman campus housing is guaranteed. *Activities and organizations:* drama/theater group, student-run newspaper, radio and television station, choral group, marching band, Campus Christian Fellowship, Alpha Phi Omega, Student Ambassadors, Alpha Sigma Gamma, Baptist Student Union, national fraternities, national sororities. *Campus security:* 24-hour emergency response devices and patrols, student patrols, late-night transport/escort service, patrols by commissioned officers. *Student services:* health clinic, personal/psychological counseling, women's center.

Athletics Member NCAA. All Division II. *Intercollegiate sports:* baseball M(s), basketball M(s)/W(s), cross-country running M(s)/W(s), equestrian sports M(c)/W(c), football M(s), golf M(s)/W(s), lacrosse M(c)/W(c), rugby M(c)/W(c), soccer M(s)/W(s), softball W(s), swimming M(s)/W(s), tennis M(s)/W(s), track and field M(s)/W(s), volleyball M(c)/W(s), wrestling M(s). *Intramural sports:* badminton M/W, basketball M/W, bowling M/W, cross-country running M/W, golf M/W, racquetball M/W, soccer M/W, softball M/W, swimming M/W, table tennis M/W, tennis M/W, track and field M/W, volleyball M/W, weight lifting M/W.

Standardized Tests *Required:* SAT I or ACT (for admission). *Recommended:* ACT (for admission).

Costs (2003–04) *Tuition:* state resident $4600 full-time, $192 per credit hour part-time; nonresident $8400 full-time, $350 per credit hour part-time. Part-time tuition and fees vary according to course load. *Required fees:* $56 full-time. *Room and board:* $5072. Room and board charges vary according to housing facility. *Payment plan:* installment. *Waivers:* senior citizens and employees or children of employees.

Financial Aid Of all full-time matriculated undergraduates who enrolled in 2002, 3,329 applied for aid, 2,692 were judged to have need, 1,485 had their need fully met. 371 Federal Work-Study jobs (averaging $1075). 1,849 state and other part-time jobs (averaging $980). In 2002, 2208 non-need-based awards were made. *Average percent of need met:* 83%. *Average financial aid package:* $5774. *Average need-based loan:* $3553. *Average need-based gift aid:* $3262. *Average non-need-based aid:* $4242. *Average indebtedness upon graduation:* $15,655.

Applying *Options:* common application, electronic application, early admission, early action, deferred entrance. *Required:* essay or personal statement, high school transcript. *Recommended:* minimum 3.0 GPA, interview. *Application deadline:* 3/1 (freshmen). *Notification:* continuous (freshmen), 12/15 (early action), continuous (transfers).

Admissions Contact Mr. Brad Chambers, Co-Director of Admissions, Truman State University, 205 McClain Hall, Kirksville, MO 63501-4221. *Phone:* 660-785-4114. *Toll-free phone:* 800-892-7792. *Fax:* 660-785-7456. *E-mail:* admissions@truman.edu.

■ See page 2534 for a narrative description.

UNIVERSITY OF MISSOURI–COLUMBIA

Columbia, Missouri

- **State-supported** university, founded 1839, part of University of Missouri System
- **Calendar** semesters
- **Degrees** bachelor's, master's, doctoral, first professional, and post-master's certificates
- **Small-town** 1358-acre campus
- **Endowment** $353.7 million
- **Coed,** 20,441 undergraduate students, 93% full-time, 52% women, 48% men
- **Moderately difficult** entrance level, 89% of applicants were admitted

Undergraduates 19,033 full-time, 1,408 part-time. Students come from 51 states and territories, 85 other countries, 12% are from out of state, 6% African American, 3% Asian American or Pacific Islander, 2% Hispanic American, 0.6% Native American, 1% international, 6% transferred in, 42% live on campus. *Retention:* 84% of 2002 full-time freshmen returned.

Freshmen *Admission:* 10,449 applied, 9,327 admitted, 4,669 enrolled. *Test scores:* ACT scores over 18: 99%; ACT scores over 24: 68%; ACT scores over 30: 16%.

Faculty *Total:* 1,545, 96% full-time, 94% with terminal degrees. *Student/faculty ratio:* 18:1.

Majors Accounting; advertising; agricultural business and management; agricultural communication/journalism; agricultural economics; agricultural mechanization; agricultural teacher education; agriculture; animal sciences; anthropology; apparel and textiles; archeology; art; art history, criticism and conservation; art teacher education; Asian studies (East); Asian studies (South); atmospheric sciences and meteorology; behavioral sciences; biochemistry; biology/biological sciences; biology teacher education; broadcast journalism; business administration and management; business/managerial economics; business teacher education; chemical engineering; chemistry; chemistry teacher education; civil engineering; classics and languages, literatures and linguistics; communication disorders sciences and services related; communication/speech communication and rhetoric; computer and information sciences; computer engineering; computer science; diagnostic medical sonography and ultrasound technology; dietetics; dramatic/theatre arts; early childhood education; economics; education; education related; electrical, electronics and communications engineering; elementary education; English; environmental studies; European studies; European studies (Central and Eastern); family and consumer economics related; finance; fish/game management; fishing and fisheries sciences and management; food science; foods, nutrition, and wellness; forestry; French; general studies; geography; geology/earth science; German; health/medical preparatory programs related; history; hotel/motel administration; housing and human environments; human development and family studies; human nutrition; industrial engineering; inter-

University of Missouri–Columbia (continued)
disciplinary studies; interior architecture; international agriculture; international business/trade/commerce; international economics; journalism; kindergarten/preschool education; Latin; Latin American studies; linguistics; management information systems; marketing/marketing management; mass communication/media; mathematics; mathematics teacher education; mechanical engineering; medical radiologic technology; microbiology; middle school education; modern Greek; music; music teacher education; natural resources/conservation; nuclear medical technology; nursing (registered nurse training); nutrition sciences; occupational therapy; parks, recreation and leisure; peace studies and conflict resolution; philosophy; photojournalism; physics; physics teacher education; plant sciences; political science and government; psychology; publishing; radio and television; radiologic technology/science; real estate; religious studies; respiratory care therapy; restaurant/food services management; Russian; Russian studies; science teacher education; secondary education; social studies teacher education; social work; sociology; Spanish; special education related; statistics; technical teacher education; tourism and travel services marketing; wildlife and wildlands science and management.

Academic Programs *Special study options:* academic remediation for entering students, accelerated degree program, adult/continuing education programs, advanced placement credit, cooperative education, distance learning, double majors, English as a second language, external degree program, freshman honors college, honors programs, independent study, internships, off-campus study, part-time degree program, services for LD students, student-designed majors, study abroad, summer session for credit. *ROTC:* Army (b), Navy (b), Air Force (b). *Unusual degree programs:* 3-2 accountancy.

Library Ellis Library plus 11 others with 3.1 million titles, 16,073 serial subscriptions, 19,383 audiovisual materials, an OPAC, a Web page.

Computers on Campus 1176 computers available on campus for general student use. A campuswide network can be accessed from student residence rooms and from off campus that provide access to telephone registration. Internet access, online (class) registration, at least one staffed computer lab available.

Student Life *Housing:* on-campus residence required for freshman year. *Options:* coed, men-only, women-only, disabled students. Campus housing is university owned, leased by the school and is provided by a third party. Freshman campus housing is guaranteed. *Activities and organizations:* drama/theater group, student-run newspaper, radio and television station, choral group, marching band, Students Association, Residence Hall Association, Honors International Organization, national fraternities, national sororities. *Campus security:* 24-hour emergency response devices and patrols, late-night transport/escort service, controlled dormitory access. *Student services:* health clinic, personal/psychological counseling, women's center, legal services.

Athletics Member NCAA. All Division I except football (Division I-A). *Intercollegiate sports:* baseball M(s), basketball M(s)/W(s), cross-country running M(s)/W(s), golf M(s)/W(s), gymnastics W(s), soccer W(s), softball W(s), swimming M(s)/W(s), tennis W(s), track and field M(s)/W(s), volleyball W(s), wrestling M(s). *Intramural sports:* basketball M/W, cheerleading M(c)/W(c), fencing M(c)/W(c), football M/W, golf M/W, ice hockey M(c)/W(c), lacrosse M(c)/W(c), racquetball M(c)/W(c), riflery M(c)/W(c), rugby M(c)/W(c), soccer W(c), softball M/W, ultimate Frisbee M(c)/W(c), volleyball M(c)/W(c), water polo M(c)/W(c).

Standardized Tests *Required:* SAT I or ACT (for admission).

Costs (2003–04) *Tuition:* state resident $5838 full-time, $195 per credit hour part-time; nonresident $15,285 full-time, $510 per credit hour part-time. *Required fees:* $720 full-time, $22 per credit hour part-time. *Room and board:* $5770. Room and board charges vary according to board plan and housing facility. *Waivers:* senior citizens and employees or children of employees.

Financial Aid Of all full-time matriculated undergraduates who enrolled in 2003, 11,706 applied for aid, 8,354 were judged to have need, 2,309 had their need fully met. 1,174 Federal Work-Study jobs (averaging $1764). In 2003, 4576 non-need-based awards were made. *Average percent of need met:* 86%. *Average financial aid package:* $9278. *Average need-based loan:* $3973. *Average need-based gift aid:* $5417. *Average non-need-based aid:* $4497. *Average indebtedness upon graduation:* $20,428.

Applying *Options:* electronic application, deferred entrance. *Application fee:* $35. *Required:* high school transcript, specific high school curriculum. *Application deadline:* rolling (freshmen), rolling (transfers). *Notification:* continuous (freshmen), continuous (transfers).

Admissions Contact Ms. Georgeanne Porter, Director of Admissions, University of Missouri–Columbia, 230 Jesse Hall, Columbia, MO 65211. *Phone:* 573-882-7786. *Toll-free phone:* 800-225-6075. *Fax:* 573-882-7887. *E-mail:* mu4u@missouri.edu.

UNIVERSITY OF MISSOURI–KANSAS CITY
Kansas City, Missouri

- **State-supported** university, founded 1929, part of University of Missouri System
- **Calendar** semesters
- **Degrees** bachelor's, master's, doctoral, first professional, post-master's, and first professional certificates
- **Urban** 191-acre campus
- **Coed,** 9,167 undergraduate students, 55% full-time, 60% women, 40% men
- **Moderately difficult** entrance level, 93% of applicants were admitted

Undergraduates 5,049 full-time, 4,118 part-time. Students come from 42 states and territories, 105 other countries, 23% are from out of state, 14% African American, 5% Asian American or Pacific Islander, 4% Hispanic American, 1% Native American, 4% international, 16% transferred in, 10% live on campus. *Retention:* 72% of 2002 full-time freshmen returned.

Freshmen *Admission:* 1,884 applied, 1,746 admitted, 785 enrolled. *Test scores:* ACT scores over 18: 88%; ACT scores over 24: 52%; ACT scores over 30: 12%.

Faculty *Total:* 910, 58% full-time, 65% with terminal degrees. *Student/faculty ratio:* 9:1.

Majors Accounting; American studies; art; art history, criticism and conservation; biology/biological sciences; business administration and management; chemistry; city/urban, community and regional planning; civil engineering; clinical/medical laboratory technology; computer science; criminal justice/law enforcement administration; dance; dental hygiene; dramatic/theatre arts; economics; education; electrical, electronics and communications engineering; elementary education; English; fine/studio arts; French; geography; geology/earth science; German; health and physical education; history; information technology; interdisciplinary studies; Jewish/Judaic studies; kindergarten/preschool education; liberal arts and sciences/liberal studies; mass communication/media; mathematics; mechanical engineering; music; music teacher education; music therapy; nursing (registered nurse training); pharmacy; philosophy; physical education teaching and coaching; physics; piano and organ; political science and government; psychology; secondary education; sociology; Spanish; statistics; urban education and leadership; urban studies/affairs; violin, viola, guitar and other stringed instruments; voice and opera; wind/percussion instruments.

Academic Programs *Special study options:* accelerated degree program, adult/continuing education programs, advanced placement credit, cooperative education, English as a second language, honors programs, internships, off-campus study, part-time degree program, services for LD students, student-designed majors, study abroad, summer session for credit. *ROTC:* Army (b). *Unusual degree programs:* 3-2 education.

Library Miller-Nichols Library plus 3 others with 1.2 million titles, 6,951 serial subscriptions, 449,074 audiovisual materials, an OPAC, a Web page.

Computers on Campus 400 computers available on campus for general student use. A campuswide network can be accessed from student residence rooms and from off campus. Internet access, online (class) registration, at least one staffed computer lab available.

Student Life *Housing options:* coed. Campus housing is university owned. *Activities and organizations:* drama/theater group, student-run newspaper, choral group, African-American Student Association, International Student Council, Alpha Phi Omega, Activities and Programs Council, national fraternities, national sororities. *Campus security:* 24-hour emergency response devices and patrols, late-night transport/escort service, controlled dormitory access. *Student services:* health clinic, personal/psychological counseling, women's center, legal services.

Athletics Member NCAA. All Division I. *Intercollegiate sports:* basketball M(s)/W(s), cheerleading W, cross-country running M(s)/W(s), golf M(s)/W(s), riflery M(s)/W(s), soccer M(s), softball W(s), tennis M(s)/W(s), track and field M(s)/W(s), volleyball W(s). *Intramural sports:* badminton M/W, basketball M/W, fencing M/W, football M/W, golf M/W, racquetball M/W, soccer M/W, softball M/W, squash M/W, swimming M/W, tennis M/W, track and field M/W, volleyball M/W, weight lifting M/W.

Standardized Tests *Required:* ACT (for admission).

Costs (2003–04) *Tuition:* state resident $5448 full-time; nonresident $14,266 full-time. Full-time tuition and fees vary according to course load, program, and student level. Part-time tuition and fees vary according to course load, program, and student level. *Required fees:* $698 full-time. *Room and board:* $7270; room only: $3170. Room and board charges vary according to board plan and housing facility. *Payment plan:* installment. *Waivers:* employees or children of employees.

Financial Aid Of all full-time matriculated undergraduates who enrolled in 2003, 4,308 applied for aid, 3,074 were judged to have need, 1,610 had their need fully met. 363 Federal Work-Study jobs (averaging $1192). In 2003, 676 non-need-based awards were made. *Average percent of need met:* 64%. *Average financial aid package:* $11,547. *Average need-based loan:* $6347. *Average need-based gift aid:* $4309. *Average non-need-based aid:* $3890. *Average indebtedness upon graduation:* $15,714.

Applying *Options:* deferred entrance. *Application fee:* $35. *Required:* high school transcript. *Application deadline:* rolling (freshmen), rolling (transfers). *Notification:* continuous (freshmen), continuous (transfers).

Admissions Contact Ms. Jennifer DeHaemers, Director of Admissions, University of Missouri–Kansas City, Office of Admissions, 5100 Rockhill Road, Kansas City, MO 64110-2499. *Phone:* 816-235-1111. *Toll-free phone:* 800-775-8652. *Fax:* 816-235-5544. *E-mail:* admit@umkc.edu.

■ *See page 2654 for a narrative description.*

UNIVERSITY OF MISSOURI–ROLLA
Rolla, Missouri

- **State-supported** university, founded 1870, part of University of Missouri System
- **Calendar** semesters
- **Degrees** bachelor's, master's, doctoral, and postbachelor's certificates
- **Small-town** 284-acre campus
- **Endowment** $63.8 million
- **Coed,** 4,089 undergraduate students, 90% full-time, 23% women, 77% men
- **Very difficult** entrance level, 90% of applicants were admitted

Undergraduates 3,677 full-time, 412 part-time. Students come from 45 states and territories, 34 other countries, 21% are from out of state, 5% African American, 3% Asian American or Pacific Islander, 2% Hispanic American, 0.6% Native American, 3% international, 6% transferred in, 56% live on campus. *Retention:* 83% of 2002 full-time freshmen returned.

Freshmen *Admission:* 1,942 applied, 1,753 admitted, 878 enrolled. *Average high school GPA:* 3.50. *Test scores:* ACT scores over 18: 100%; ACT scores over 24: 85%; ACT scores over 30: 32%.

Faculty *Total:* 392, 78% full-time, 85% with terminal degrees. *Student/faculty ratio:* 14:1.

Majors Aerospace, aeronautical and astronautical engineering; agricultural/biological engineering and bioengineering; applied mathematics; architectural engineering; biology/biological sciences; business administration and management; business/commerce; ceramic sciences and engineering; chemical engineering; chemistry; civil engineering; computer and information sciences and support services related; computer engineering; computer science; economics; electrical, electronics and communications engineering; engineering/industrial management; English; environmental/environmental health engineering; geological/geophysical engineering; geology/earth science; geophysics and seismology; history; industrial engineering; information science/studies; manufacturing engineering; materials engineering; mechanical engineering; metallurgical engineering; mining and mineral engineering; nuclear engineering; petroleum engineering; philosophy; physics; pre-dentistry studies; pre-law studies; pre-medical studies; psychology; secondary education; systems engineering.

Academic Programs *Special study options:* academic remediation for entering students, accelerated degree program, adult/continuing education programs, advanced placement credit, cooperative education, distance learning, double majors, English as a second language, freshman honors college, honors programs, independent study, internships, off-campus study, part-time degree program, services for LD students, study abroad, summer session for credit. *ROTC:* Army (b), Air Force (b).

Library Curtis Laws Wilson Library with 255,768 titles, 1,495 serial subscriptions, 6,353 audiovisual materials, an OPAC, a Web page.

Computers on Campus 800 computers available on campus for general student use. A campuswide network can be accessed from student residence rooms and from off campus. Internet access, online (class) registration, at least one staffed computer lab available.

Student Life *Housing:* on-campus residence required through sophomore year. *Options:* coed, men-only, women-only. *Activities and organizations:* drama/theater group, student-run newspaper, radio station, choral group, marching band, student government, service organizations, academic organizations, national fraternities, national sororities. *Campus security:* 24-hour emergency response devices and patrols, student patrols, late-night transport/escort service, controlled dormitory access, crime prevention programs. *Student services:* health clinic, personal/psychological counseling, legal services.

Athletics Member NCAA. All Division II except men's and women's cheerleading (Division I). *Intercollegiate sports:* baseball M(s), basketball M(s)/W(s), cheerleading M(s)/W(s), cross-country running M(s)/W(s), football M(s), soccer M(s)/W(s), softball W(s), swimming M(s), track and field M(s)/W(s). *Intramural sports:* badminton M/W, basketball M/W, bowling M/W, cross-country running M/W, football M, golf M/W, racquetball M/W, soccer M/W, softball M/W, swimming M/W, table tennis M/W, tennis M/W, track and field M/W, ultimate Frisbee M/W, volleyball M/W, water polo M, weight lifting M/W.

Standardized Tests *Required:* SAT I or ACT (for admission).

Costs (2003–04) *Tuition:* state resident $5838 full-time, $195 per credit hour part-time; nonresident $15,285 full-time, $510 per credit hour part-time. *Required fees:* $1001 full-time, $112 per credit hour part-time. *Room and board:* $5453.

Financial Aid Of all full-time matriculated undergraduates who enrolled in 2001, 2,175 applied for aid, 1,659 were judged to have need, 647 had their need fully met. 244 Federal Work-Study jobs (averaging $1220). 1,038 state and other part-time jobs (averaging $1145). In 2001, 1117 non-need-based awards were made. *Average percent of need met:* 87%. *Average financial aid package:* $8203. *Average need-based loan:* $4470. *Average need-based gift aid:* $4910. *Average non-need-based aid:* $5252. *Average indebtedness upon graduation:* $17,991.

Applying *Options:* common application, electronic application, early admission, deferred entrance. *Application fee:* $35. *Required:* high school transcript. *Application deadlines:* 7/1 (freshmen), 7/1 (transfers). *Notification:* continuous (freshmen), continuous (transfers).

Admissions Contact Ms. Lynn Stichnote, Director of Admissions, University of Missouri–Rolla, 106 Parker Hall, Rolla, MO 65409. *Phone:* 573-341-4164. *Toll-free phone:* 800-522-0938. *Fax:* 573-341-4082. *E-mail:* umrolla@umr.edu.

UNIVERSITY OF MISSOURI–ST. LOUIS
St. Louis, Missouri

- **State-supported** university, founded 1963, part of University of Missouri System
- **Calendar** semesters
- **Degrees** bachelor's, master's, doctoral, first professional, and postbachelor's certificates
- **Suburban** 350-acre campus
- **Endowment** $32.9 million
- **Coed,** 12,630 undergraduate students, 45% full-time, 61% women, 39% men
- **Moderately difficult** entrance level, 48% of applicants were admitted

Undergraduates 5,631 full-time, 6,999 part-time. Students come from 38 states and territories, 63 other countries, 5% are from out of state, 15% African American, 3% Asian American or Pacific Islander, 1% Hispanic American, 0.4% Native American, 2% international, 14% transferred in, 7% live on campus. *Retention:* 74% of 2002 full-time freshmen returned.

Freshmen *Admission:* 2,433 applied, 1,178 admitted, 534 enrolled. *Test scores:* SAT verbal scores over 500: 84%; SAT math scores over 500: 87%; ACT scores over 18: 97%; SAT verbal scores over 600: 46%; SAT math scores over 600: 32%; ACT scores over 24: 47%; SAT verbal scores over 700: 3%; SAT math scores over 700: 8%; ACT scores over 30: 4%.

Faculty *Total:* 679, 53% full-time, 55% with terminal degrees. *Student/faculty ratio:* 20:1.

Majors Accounting; anthropology; applied mathematics; art history, criticism and conservation; biology/biological sciences; biology teacher education; business administration and management; business/commerce; business teacher education; chemistry; chemistry teacher education; civil engineering; clinical laboratory science/medical technology; communication/speech communication and rhetoric; computer and information sciences; computer science; criminology; cytotechnology; drawing; early childhood education; economics; education; electrical, electronics and communications engineering; elementary education; English; English/language arts teacher education; finance; fine/studio arts; French; French language teacher education; general studies; German; German language teacher education; history; international business/trade/commerce; literature; management information systems; management science; marketing/marketing management; mass communication/media; mathematics; mathematics teacher education; mechanical engineering; music; music performance; music teacher education; nursing (registered nurse training); painting; philosophy; photography; physical education teaching and coaching; physics; physics teacher education; political science and government; pre-dentistry studies; pre-law studies; pre-medical studies; pre-pharmacy studies; pre-veterinary studies; printmaking; psychology; psychology teacher education; public administration; secondary education; social studies teacher education; social work; sociology; Spanish; Spanish language teacher education; special education.

Academic Programs *Special study options:* accelerated degree program, adult/continuing education programs, advanced placement credit, cooperative education, distance learning, double majors, English as a second language, freshman honors college, honors programs, independent study, internships, off-campus study, part-time degree program, services for LD students, student-designed majors, study abroad, summer session for credit. *ROTC:* Army (c), Air Force (c).

Library Thomas Jefferson Library plus 2 others with 782,431 titles, 3,570 serial subscriptions, 3,878 audiovisual materials, an OPAC, a Web page.

University of Missouri–St. Louis (continued)

Computers on Campus 750 computers available on campus for general student use. A campuswide network can be accessed from student residence rooms and from off campus. Internet access, online (class) registration, at least one staffed computer lab available. Computer purchase or lease plan available.

Student Life *Housing options:* coed. Campus housing is university owned and is provided by a third party. Freshman campus housing is guaranteed. *Activities and organizations:* drama/theater group, student-run newspaper, choral group, Student Government Association, Associated Black Collegians, Pierre laclede Honors College Student Association, Residence Hall Council, International Student Association, national fraternities, national sororities. *Campus security:* 24-hour emergency response devices and patrols, late-night transport/escort service, controlled dormitory access. *Student services:* health clinic, personal/psychological counseling, women's center.

Athletics Member NCAA, NCCAA. All NCAA Division II. *Intercollegiate sports:* baseball M(s), basketball M(s)/W(s), golf M(s)/W(s), ice hockey M(c), soccer M(s)/W(s), softball W(s), tennis M(s)/W(s), volleyball W(s). *Intramural sports:* badminton M/W, basketball M/W, bowling M/W, cheerleading M/W, cross-country running M/W, football M/W, golf M/W, ice hockey M, racquetball M/W, soccer M/W, softball M/W, swimming M/W, table tennis M/W, tennis M/W, volleyball M/W, weight lifting M/W.

Standardized Tests *Required:* SAT I or ACT (for admission).

Costs (2003–04) *Tuition:* state resident $5838 full-time, $195 per credit hour part-time; nonresident $15,285 full-time, $510 per credit hour part-time. Full-time tuition and fees vary according to program and reciprocity agreements. Part-time tuition and fees vary according to course load and program. *Required fees:* $1028 full-time, $40 per credit hour part-time. *Room and board:* $5600; room only: $4300. Room and board charges vary according to board plan and housing facility. *Payment plan:* installment. *Waivers:* employees or children of employees.

Financial Aid Of all full-time matriculated undergraduates who enrolled in 2003, 3,399 applied for aid, 2,886 were judged to have need, 56 had their need fully met. 195 Federal Work-Study jobs (averaging $3167). In 2003, 489 non-need-based awards were made. *Average percent of need met:* 68%. *Average financial aid package:* $9103. *Average need-based loan:* $4215. *Average need-based gift aid:* $3363. *Average non-need-based aid:* $4679. *Average indebtedness upon graduation:* $14,675.

Applying *Options:* electronic application, early admission, deferred entrance. *Application fee:* $25. *Required:* high school transcript, CBHE Core Requirements. *Application deadlines:* rolling (freshmen), 8/1 (transfers). *Notification:* continuous (freshmen), continuous (transfers).

Admissions Contact Ms. Melissa Hattman, Director of Admissions, University of Missouri–St. Louis, 351 Millennuim Student Center, 8001 National Bridge Road, St. Louis, MO 63121-4499. *Phone:* 314-516-5460. *Toll-free phone:* 888-GO2-UMSL. *Fax:* 314-516-5310. *E-mail:* admissions@umsl.edu.

■ *See page 2656 for a narrative description.*

University of Phoenix–Kansas City Campus

Kansas City, Missouri

- **Proprietary** comprehensive, founded 2002
- **Calendar** continuous
- **Degrees** certificates, associate, bachelor's, master's, doctoral, post-master's, and postbachelor's certificates (courses conducted at 121 campuses and learning centers in 25 states)
- **Coed,** 405 undergraduate students, 100% full-time, 52% women, 48% men
- **Noncompetitive** entrance level

Undergraduates 405 full-time. 20% African American, 4% Asian American or Pacific Islander, 3% Hispanic American, 0.5% Native American, 8% international.

Freshmen *Admission:* 29 enrolled.

Faculty *Total:* 25, 12% full-time, 20% with terminal degrees. *Student/faculty ratio:* 7:1.

Majors Accounting; business administration and management; business, management, and marketing related; computer and information sciences; entrepreneurship; health/health care administration; management science; public administration and social service professions related.

Academic Programs *Special study options:* accelerated degree program, adult/continuing education programs, advanced placement credit, distance learning, external degree program, independent study.

Library University Library with 27.1 million titles, 11,648 serial subscriptions, an OPAC, a Web page.

Computers on Campus A campuswide network can be accessed from off campus. At least one staffed computer lab available.

Student Life *Housing:* college housing not available.

Costs (2003–04) *Tuition:* $9990 full-time, $333 per credit part-time. *Waivers:* employees or children of employees.

Financial Aid *Average financial aid package:* $1314.

Applying *Options:* deferred entrance. *Application fee:* $100. *Required:* 1 letter of recommendation, 2 years of work experience, 23 years of age. *Required for some:* high school transcript. *Application deadline:* rolling (freshmen), rolling (transfers).

Admissions Contact Ms. Beth Barilla, Director of Admissions, University of Phoenix–Kansas City Campus, 4615 East Elwood Street, Mail Stop AA-K101, Phoenix, AZ 85040-1958. *Phone:* 480-317-6000. *Toll-free phone:* 800-228-7240. *Fax:* 480-594-1758. *E-mail:* beth.barilla@phoenix.edu.

University of Phoenix–St. Louis Campus

St. Louis, Missouri

- **Proprietary** comprehensive, founded 2000
- **Calendar** continuous
- **Degrees** certificates, associate, bachelor's, master's, doctoral, post-master's, and postbachelor's certificates (courses conducted at 121 campuses and learning centers in 25 states)
- **Urban** campus
- **Coed,** 1,327 undergraduate students, 100% full-time, 59% women, 41% men
- **Noncompetitive** entrance level

Undergraduates 1,327 full-time. 19% African American, 1% Asian American or Pacific Islander, 7% Hispanic American, 0.2% Native American, 24% international.

Freshmen *Admission:* 27 enrolled.

Faculty *Total:* 43, 9% full-time, 19% with terminal degrees. *Student/faculty ratio:* 7:1.

Majors Business administration and management; corrections and criminal justice related; management information systems; management science; marketing/marketing management; nursing (registered nurse training); public administration and social service professions related.

Academic Programs *Special study options:* accelerated degree program, adult/continuing education programs, advanced placement credit, distance learning, external degree program, independent study.

Library University Library with 27.1 million titles, 11,648 serial subscriptions, an OPAC, a Web page.

Computers on Campus A campuswide network can be accessed from off campus. Internet access, at least one staffed computer lab available.

Student Life *Housing:* college housing not available.

Costs (2003–04) *Tuition:* $10,500 full-time, $350 per credit part-time. *Waivers:* employees or children of employees.

Financial Aid *Average financial aid package:* $1271.

Applying *Options:* deferred entrance. *Application fee:* $85. *Required:* 1 letter of recommendation, 2 years of work experience, 23 years of age. *Required for some:* high school transcript. *Application deadline:* rolling (freshmen), rolling (transfers).

Admissions Contact Ms. Beth Barilla, Director of Admissions, University of Phoenix–St. Louis Campus, 4615 East Elwood Street, Mail Stop AA-K101, Phoenix, AZ 85040-1958. *Phone:* 480-317-6000. *Toll-free phone:* 888-326-7737 (in-state); 800-228-7240 (out-of-state). *Fax:* 480-594-1758. *E-mail:* beth.barilla@phoenix.edu.

Vatterott College

St. Ann, Missouri

- **Proprietary** primarily 2-year, founded 1969
- **Calendar** semesters
- **Degrees** diplomas, associate, and bachelor's
- **Suburban** campus with easy access to St. Louis
- **Coed**

Applying *Options:* common application.

Admissions Contact Ms. Michelle Tinsley, Co-Director of Admissions, Vatterott College, 3925 Industrial Drive, St. Ann, MO 63074-1807. *Phone:* 314-843-4200. *Toll-free phone:* 800-345-6018. *Fax:* 314-428-5956.

Vatterott College

Sunset Hills, Missouri

- **Proprietary** primarily 2-year
- **Calendar** semesters

■ **Degrees** diplomas, associate, and bachelor's
■ **Coed**

Admissions Contact Ms. Michelle Tinsley, Director of Admission, Vatterott College, 12970 Maurer Industrial Drive, St. Louis, MO 63127. *Phone:* 314-843-4200. *Fax:* 843-1709. *E-mail:* sunsethills@vatterott-college.edu.

WASHINGTON UNIVERSITY IN ST. LOUIS

St. Louis, Missouri

■ **Independent** university, founded 1853
■ **Calendar** semesters
■ **Degrees** certificates, bachelor's, master's, doctoral, first professional, and postbachelor's certificates
■ **Suburban** 169-acre campus
■ **Endowment** $3.6 billion
■ **Coed,** 7,188 undergraduate students, 82% full-time, 53% women, 47% men
■ **Most difficult** entrance level, 20% of applicants were admitted

Undergraduates 5,912 full-time, 1,276 part-time. Students come from 53 states and territories, 88 other countries, 89% are from out of state, 9% African American, 9% Asian American or Pacific Islander, 3% Hispanic American, 0.2% Native American, 4% international, 3% transferred in, 80% live on campus. *Retention:* 97% of 2002 full-time freshmen returned.

Freshmen *Admission:* 20,378 applied, 4,080 admitted, 1,367 enrolled. *Test scores:* SAT verbal scores over 500: 100%; SAT math scores over 500: 100%; ACT scores over 18: 100%; SAT verbal scores over 600: 94%; SAT math scores over 600: 98%; ACT scores over 24: 99%; SAT verbal scores over 700: 47%; SAT math scores over 700: 60%; ACT scores over 30: 70%.

Faculty *Total:* 1,100, 76% full-time, 75% with terminal degrees. *Student/faculty ratio:* 7:1.

Majors Accounting; advertising; aerospace, aeronautical and astronautical engineering; African-American/Black studies; African studies; American literature; American studies; ancient/classical Greek; anthropology; applied art; applied mathematics; Arabic; archeology; architectural engineering technology; architectural technology; architecture; architecture related; area, ethnic, cultural, and gender studies related; area studies related; art; art history, criticism and conservation; art teacher education; Asian studies; Asian studies (East); biochemistry; biological and biomedical sciences related; biological and physical sciences; biology/biological sciences; biology teacher education; biomedical/medical engineering; biophysics; biopsychology; business administration and management; business administration, management and operations related; business/commerce; business/managerial economics; ceramic arts and ceramics; chemical engineering; chemistry; chemistry related; chemistry teacher education; Chinese; civil engineering; civil engineering technology; classics and languages, literatures and linguistics; cognitive psychology and psycholinguistics; commercial and advertising art; communication and journalism related; communication/speech communication and rhetoric; comparative literature; computer and information sciences; computer and information sciences and support services related; computer engineering; computer/information technology services administration related; computer science; creative writing; cultural studies; dance; design and visual communications; drama and dance teacher education; dramatic/theatre arts; drawing; East Asian languages related; economics; education; education (K-12); education (specific levels and methods) related; electrical, electronics and communications engineering; elementary education; engineering; engineering physics; engineering science; English; English language and literature related; English/language arts teacher education; English literature (British and Commonwealth); entrepreneurship; environmental studies; ethnic, cultural minority, and gender studies related; European studies; fashion/apparel design; film/cinema studies; finance; fine/studio arts; French; French language teacher education; geology/earth science; German; Germanic languages; German language teacher education; graphic design; health professions related; Hebrew; history; history teacher education; humanities; human resources management; illustration; industrial and organizational psychology; information science/studies; interdisciplinary studies; international business/trade/commerce; international economics; international finance; international relations and affairs; Islamic studies; Italian; Japanese; Jewish/Judaic studies; Latin; Latin American studies; liberal arts and sciences/liberal studies; literature; marketing/marketing management; marketing related; mathematics; mathematics and computer science; mathematics teacher education; mechanical engineering; medieval and Renaissance studies; merchandising, sales, and marketing operations related (general); middle school education; modern languages; multi-/interdisciplinary studies related; music; music history, literature, and theory; music theory and composition; natural resources/conservation; natural sciences; Near and Middle Eastern studies; neuroscience; operations management; painting; philosophy; philosophy and religious studies related; photography; physical sciences; physics; physics teacher education; political science and government; pre-dentistry studies; pre-medical studies; pre-pharmacy studies; pre-veterinary studies; printmaking; psychology; religious studies; Romance languages; Russian; Russian studies; science teacher education; science, technology and society; sculpture; secondary education; social and philosophical foundations of education; social sciences; social sciences related; social science teacher education; social studies teacher education; Spanish; Spanish language teacher education; statistics; systems engineering; systems science and theory; theatre literature, history and criticism; urban studies/affairs; voice and opera; women's studies.

Academic Programs *Special study options:* accelerated degree program, adult/continuing education programs, advanced placement credit, cooperative education, double majors, English as a second language, independent study, internships, off-campus study, part-time degree program, services for LD students, student-designed majors, study abroad, summer session for credit. *ROTC:* Army (b), Air Force (c). *Unusual degree programs:* 3-2 art, occupational therapy, physical therapy, business, engineering, social work.

Library John M. Olin Library plus 13 others with 1.6 million titles, 18,316 serial subscriptions, 69,422 audiovisual materials, an OPAC, a Web page.

Computers on Campus 2500 computers available on campus for general student use. A campuswide network can be accessed from student residence rooms and from off campus that provide access to e-mail. Internet access, online (class) registration, at least one staffed computer lab available. Computer purchase or lease plan available.

Student Life *Housing:* on-campus residence required for freshman year. *Options:* coed, men-only, women-only. Campus housing is university owned. Freshman campus housing is guaranteed. *Activities and organizations:* drama/theater group, student-run newspaper, radio and television station, choral group, community service organizations, student government/programming groups, performing arts groups, multicultural interest groups, Greek organizations, national fraternities, national sororities. *Campus security:* 24-hour emergency response devices and patrols, student patrols, late-night transport/escort service, controlled dormitory access. *Student services:* health clinic, personal/psychological counseling, women's center.

Athletics Member NCAA. All Division III. *Intercollegiate sports:* badminton M(c)/W(c), baseball M, basketball M/W, crew M(c)/W(c), cross-country running M/W, equestrian sports M(c)/W(c), fencing M(c)/W(c), field hockey W(c), football M, gymnastics M(c)/W(c), ice hockey M(c), lacrosse M(c)/W(c), rugby M(c)/W(c), sailing M(c)/W(c), soccer M/W, softball W, swimming M/W, table tennis M(c)/W(c), tennis M(c)/W(c), track and field M/W, ultimate Frisbee M(c)/W(c), volleyball M(c)/W, water polo M(c)/W(c). *Intramural sports:* badminton M/W, basketball M/W, bowling M/W, cheerleading M/W, cross-country running M/W, football M/W, golf M/W, racquetball M/W, soccer M(c)/W(c), softball M/W, swimming M/W, table tennis M/W, tennis M/W, track and field M/W, ultimate Frisbee M/W, volleyball M/W, water polo M/W.

Standardized Tests *Required:* SAT I or ACT (for admission).

Costs (2004–05) *Comprehensive fee:* $40,186 includes full-time tuition ($29,700), mandatory fees ($846), and room and board ($9640). Part-time tuition and fees vary according to class time. *College room only:* $5750. Room and board charges vary according to board plan and housing facility. *Payment plans:* tuition prepayment, installment. *Waivers:* employees or children of employees.

Financial Aid Of all full-time matriculated undergraduates who enrolled in 2003, 4,207 applied for aid, 2,697 were judged to have need, 2,666 had their need fully met. 1,350 Federal Work-Study jobs (averaging $1892). In 2003, 820 non-need-based awards were made. *Average percent of need met:* 100%. *Average financial aid package:* $24,461. *Average need-based loan:* $6214. *Average need-based gift aid:* $19,641. *Average non-need-based aid:* $9231. *Financial aid deadline:* 2/15.

Applying *Options:* common application, electronic application, early admission, early decision, deferred entrance. *Application fee:* $55. *Required:* essay or personal statement, high school transcript, 2 letters of recommendation. *Recommended:* minimum 3.0 GPA, portfolio for art and architecture programs. *Application deadlines:* 1/15 (freshmen), 4/15 (transfers). *Early decision:* 11/15 (for plan 1), 1/1 (for plan 2). *Notification:* 4/1 (freshmen), 12/15 (early decision plan 1), 1/15 (early decision plan 2), continuous (transfers).

Admissions Contact Ms. Nanette Tarbouni, Director of Admissions, Washington University in St. Louis, Campus Box 1089, One Brookings Drive, St. Louis, MO 63130-4899. *Phone:* 314-935-6000. *Toll-free phone:* 800-638-0700. *Fax:* 314-935-4290. *E-mail:* admissions@wustl.edu.

WEBSTER UNIVERSITY

St. Louis, Missouri

■ **Independent** comprehensive, founded 1915
■ **Calendar** semesters
■ **Degrees** certificates, bachelor's, master's, doctoral, post-master's, and postbachelor's certificates
■ **Suburban** 47-acre campus

Webster University (continued)
- **Endowment** $34.1 million
- **Coed,** 3,559 undergraduate students, 70% full-time, 63% women, 37% men
- **Moderately difficult** entrance level, 58% of applicants were admitted

Undergraduates 2,483 full-time, 1,076 part-time. Students come from 44 states and territories, 46 other countries, 21% are from out of state, 12% African American, 2% Asian American or Pacific Islander, 2% Hispanic American, 0.3% Native American, 3% international, 15% transferred in, 25% live on campus. *Retention:* 79% of 2002 full-time freshmen returned.

Freshmen *Admission:* 1,282 applied, 738 admitted, 453 enrolled. *Average high school GPA:* 3.40. *Test scores:* SAT verbal scores over 500: 89%; SAT math scores over 500: 75%; ACT scores over 18: 96%; SAT verbal scores over 600: 54%; SAT math scores over 600: 35%; ACT scores over 24: 51%; SAT verbal scores over 700: 9%; SAT math scores over 700: 7%; ACT scores over 30: 8%.

Faculty *Total:* 842, 19% full-time, 37% with terminal degrees. *Student/faculty ratio:* 12:1.

Majors Accounting; advertising; anthropology; art; art history, criticism and conservation; art therapy; biology/biological sciences; broadcast journalism; business administration and management; business/commerce; cinematography and film/video production; communication and journalism related; computer management; computer science; dance; dramatic/theatre arts; economics; education; elementary education; English; English language and literature related; environmental studies; film/cinema studies; fine/studio arts; French; German; health/health care administration; history; human resources management; information science/studies; interdisciplinary studies; international business/trade/commerce; international relations and affairs; jazz/jazz studies; journalism; kindergarten/preschool education; legal studies; liberal arts and sciences/liberal studies; literature; management information systems; marketing/marketing management; mathematics; middle school education; music; music performance; music teacher education; music theory and composition; nurse anesthetist; nursing (registered nurse training); philosophy; photography; piano and organ; political science and government; psychology; public relations/image management; radio and television; religious studies; secondary education; social sciences; sociology; Spanish; special education; technical and business writing; theatre design and technology; voice and opera.

Academic Programs *Special study options:* academic remediation for entering students, accelerated degree program, adult/continuing education programs, advanced placement credit, cooperative education, distance learning, double majors, English as a second language, independent study, internships, off-campus study, part-time degree program, services for LD students, student-designed majors, study abroad, summer session for credit. *ROTC:* Army (c), Air Force (c). *Unusual degree programs:* 3-2 engineering with University of Missouri-Columbia, Washington University in St. Louis; architecture with Washington University in St. Louis.

Library Eden-Webster Library with 268,000 titles, 1,480 serial subscriptions, 14,800 audiovisual materials, an OPAC, a Web page.

Computers on Campus 330 computers available on campus for general student use. A campuswide network can be accessed. Internet access, online (class) registration, at least one staffed computer lab available.

Student Life *Housing:* on-campus residence required for freshman year. *Options:* coed. Campus housing is university owned. Freshman applicants given priority for college housing. *Activities and organizations:* drama/theater group, student-run newspaper, radio and television station, choral group, Student Government Association, Habitat for Humanity, Big Brothers Big Sisters, Marketing Communications Club, Residential Housing Association. *Campus security:* 24-hour emergency response devices and patrols, student patrols, late-night transport/escort service. *Student services:* health clinic, personal/psychological counseling, women's center.

Athletics Member NCAA. All Division III. *Intercollegiate sports:* baseball M, basketball M/W, cross-country running W, golf M, soccer M/W, softball W, swimming M/W, tennis M/W, volleyball W. *Intramural sports:* bowling M(c)/W(c), soccer M(c)/W(c), table tennis M(c)/W(c), volleyball M(c).

Standardized Tests *Required:* SAT I or ACT (for admission).

Costs (2003–04) *Comprehensive fee:* $21,848 includes full-time tuition ($15,480) and room and board ($6368). Full-time tuition and fees vary according to program. Part-time tuition: $430 per credit hour. Part-time tuition and fees vary according to location. *College room only:* $3140. Room and board charges vary according to board plan and housing facility. *Payment plan:* installment. *Waivers:* employees or children of employees.

Financial Aid Of all full-time matriculated undergraduates who enrolled in 2003, 1,954 applied for aid, 1,689 were judged to have need. 477 Federal Work-Study jobs (averaging $2167). 431 state and other part-time jobs (averaging $2446). In 2003, 341 non-need-based awards were made. *Average financial aid package:* $15,845. *Average need-based loan:* $4132. *Average need-based gift aid:* $4707. *Average non-need-based aid:* $8378. *Average indebtedness upon graduation:* $17,752.

Applying *Options:* common application, electronic application, early admission, deferred entrance. *Application fee:* $25. *Required:* essay or personal statement, high school transcript, minimum 2.5 GPA, 1 letter of recommendation. *Required for some:* audition. *Recommended:* minimum 3.0 GPA, interview. *Application deadlines:* 6/1 (freshmen), 8/1 (transfers). *Notification:* continuous (freshmen), continuous (transfers).

Admissions Contact Mr. Andrew Laue, Associate Director of Undergraduate Admission, Webster University, 470 East Lockwood Avenue, St. Louis, MO 63119-3194. *Phone:* 314-961-2660 Ext. 7712. *Toll-free phone:* 800-75-ENROL. *Fax:* 314-968-7115. *E-mail:* admit@webster.edu.

WESTMINSTER COLLEGE
Fulton, Missouri

- **Independent** 4-year, founded 1851, affiliated with Presbyterian Church
- **Calendar** semesters
- **Degree** bachelor's
- **Small-town** 65-acre campus
- **Endowment** $30.7 million
- **Coed,** 821 undergraduate students, 98% full-time, 42% women, 58% men
- **Moderately difficult** entrance level, 75% of applicants were admitted

Undergraduates 801 full-time, 20 part-time. Students come from 24 states and territories, 16 other countries, 27% are from out of state, 3% African American, 1% Asian American or Pacific Islander, 1% Hispanic American, 2% Native American, 6% international, 5% transferred in, 80% live on campus. *Retention:* 77% of 2002 full-time freshmen returned.

Freshmen *Admission:* 846 applied, 634 admitted, 240 enrolled. *Average high school GPA:* 3.40. *Test scores:* SAT verbal scores over 500: 78%; SAT math scores over 500: 75%; ACT scores over 18: 98%; SAT verbal scores over 600: 42%; SAT math scores over 600: 36%; ACT scores over 24: 50%; SAT verbal scores over 700: 6%; SAT math scores over 700: 9%; ACT scores over 30: 8%.

Faculty *Total:* 75, 69% full-time, 67% with terminal degrees. *Student/faculty ratio:* 14:1.

Majors Accounting; anthropology; biology/biological sciences; business administration and management; chemistry; computer science; economics; elementary education; English; environmental science; environmental studies; French; history; international business/trade/commerce; international relations and affairs; management information systems; mathematics; middle school education; philosophy; physical education teaching and coaching; physics; political science and government; pre-law studies; psychology; religious studies; secondary education; sociology; Spanish.

Academic Programs *Special study options:* academic remediation for entering students, advanced placement credit, cooperative education, double majors, honors programs, independent study, internships, off-campus study, part-time degree program, services for LD students, student-designed majors, study abroad, summer session for credit. *ROTC:* Army (c), Air Force (c). *Unusual degree programs:* 3-2 engineering with Washington University in St. Louis, University of Missouri-Columbia.

Library Reeves Memorial Library plus 1 other with 111,922 titles, 3,081 serial subscriptions, 9,082 audiovisual materials, an OPAC, a Web page.

Computers on Campus 140 computers available on campus for general student use. A campuswide network can be accessed from student residence rooms and from off campus. Internet access, online (class) registration, at least one staffed computer lab available. Computer purchase or lease plan available.

Student Life *Housing:* on-campus residence required through junior year. *Options:* coed, women-only. Campus housing is university owned. Freshman campus housing is guaranteed. *Activities and organizations:* drama/theater group, student-run newspaper, choral group, Student Government Association, Environmentally Concerned Students, international student club, Habitat for Humanity, Little Brother/Little Sister, national fraternities, national sororities. *Campus security:* 24-hour emergency response devices and patrols, late-night transport/escort service, controlled dormitory access, well-lit campus. *Student services:* health clinic, personal/psychological counseling, women's center.

Athletics Member NCAA. All Division III. *Intercollegiate sports:* baseball M, basketball M/W, football M, golf M/W, soccer M/W, softball W, tennis M/W, volleyball W. *Intramural sports:* basketball M/W, football M, softball M/W, table tennis M/W, volleyball M/W.

Standardized Tests *Required:* SAT I or ACT (for admission).

Costs (2004–05) *Comprehensive fee:* $19,060 includes full-time tuition ($12,990), mandatory fees ($420), and room and board ($5650). Part-time tuition: $710 per credit hour. *Required fees:* $210 per term part-time. *College room only:* $2880. Room and board charges vary according to board plan and housing facility. *Payment plan:* installment. *Waivers:* children of alumni and employees or children of employees.

Financial Aid Of all full-time matriculated undergraduates who enrolled in 2003, 592 applied for aid, 513 were judged to have need, 181 had their need fully

met. 152 Federal Work-Study jobs (averaging $474). 97 state and other part-time jobs (averaging $1186). In 2003, 258 non-need-based awards were made. *Average percent of need met:* 88%. *Average financial aid package:* $14,689. *Average need-based loan:* $2369. *Average need-based gift aid:* $11,329. *Average non-need-based aid:* $6573. *Average indebtedness upon graduation:* $15,597.

Applying *Options:* common application, electronic application, early admission, deferred entrance. *Required:* high school transcript, 1 letter of recommendation, minimum ACT score of 21 or minimum SAT score of 970. *Required for some:* interview. *Recommended:* essay or personal statement, minimum 2.5 GPA. *Notification:* continuous until 8/1 (freshmen), continuous (transfers).

Admissions Contact Dr. Patrick Kirby, Dean of Enrollment Services, Westminster College, 501 Westminster Avenue, Fulton, MO 65251-1299. *Phone:* 573-592-5251. *Toll-free phone:* 800-475-3361. *Fax:* 573-592-5255. *E-mail:* admissions@jaynet.wcmo.edu.

■ See page 2822 for a narrative description.

WILLIAM JEWELL COLLEGE

Liberty, Missouri

- **Independent Baptist** 4-year, founded 1849
- **Calendar** semesters
- **Degrees** bachelor's (also offers evening program with significant enrollment not reflected in profile)
- **Small-town** 200-acre campus with easy access to Kansas City
- **Endowment** $55.0 million
- **Coed,** 1,274 undergraduate students, 97% full-time, 59% women, 41% men
- **Moderately difficult** entrance level, 95% of applicants were admitted

The Oxbridge Honors Program, a program of tutorials and examinations through which a small number of academically outstanding students may pursue their areas of concentration, is available at William Jewell College. As its name implies, the program is an American adaptation of the educational method of the great English universities, Oxford and Cambridge.

Undergraduates 1,235 full-time, 39 part-time. Students come from 32 states and territories, 12 other countries, 22% are from out of state, 3% African American, 0.5% Asian American or Pacific Islander, 1% Hispanic American, 0.3% Native American, 1% international, 7% transferred in, 63% live on campus. *Retention:* 86% of 2002 full-time freshmen returned.

Freshmen *Admission:* 907 applied, 864 admitted, 358 enrolled. *Average high school GPA:* 3.66. *Test scores:* SAT verbal scores over 500: 80%; SAT math scores over 500: 87%; ACT scores over 18: 98%; SAT verbal scores over 600: 45%; SAT math scores over 600: 46%; ACT scores over 24: 56%; SAT verbal scores over 700: 7%; SAT math scores over 700: 10%; ACT scores over 30: 13%.

Faculty *Total:* 134, 56% full-time. *Student/faculty ratio:* 13:1.

Majors Accounting; art; biochemistry; biology/biological sciences; business administration and management; cell biology and histology; chemistry; clinical laboratory science/medical technology; computer science; drama and dance teacher education; dramatic/theatre arts; economics; education; elementary education; English; French; history; information science/studies; interdisciplinary studies; international business/trade/commerce; international relations and affairs; mathematics; molecular biology; music; music performance; music teacher education; music theory and composition; nursing (registered nurse training); philosophy; physics; political science and government; pre-dentistry studies; pre-law studies; pre-medical studies; pre-veterinary studies; psychology; religious/sacred music; religious studies; secondary education; Spanish; speech and rhetoric; speech teacher education.

Academic Programs *Special study options:* academic remediation for entering students, adult/continuing education programs, advanced placement credit, cooperative education, double majors, honors programs, independent study, internships, part-time degree program, student-designed majors, study abroad, summer session for credit. *Unusual degree programs:* 3-2 engineering with Columbia University, Washington University in St. Louis, University of Kansas; forestry with Duke University.

Library Charles F. Curry Library with 260,119 titles, 868 serial subscriptions, 27,617 audiovisual materials, an OPAC, a Web page.

Computers on Campus 160 computers available on campus for general student use. A campuswide network can be accessed from student residence rooms and from off campus. Internet access, at least one staffed computer lab available.

Student Life *Housing:* on-campus residence required through junior year. *Options:* coed, men-only, women-only. Campus housing is university owned. Freshman campus housing is guaranteed. *Activities and organizations:* drama/theater group, student-run newspaper, radio station, choral group, Christian student ministries, College Union activities, Fellowship of Christian Athletes, UNITY, Amnesty International, national fraternities, national sororities. *Campus security:* 24-hour emergency response devices and patrols, late-night transport/escort service, controlled dormitory access. *Student services:* health clinic, personal/psychological counseling.

Athletics Member NAIA. *Intercollegiate sports:* baseball M(s), basketball M(s)/W(s), cheerleading M(s)/W(s), cross-country running M(s)/W(s), football M(s), golf M(s)/W(s), soccer M(s)/W(s), softball W(s), tennis M(s)/W(s), track and field M(s)/W(s), volleyball W(s). *Intramural sports:* racquetball M/W, soccer M/W, softball M/W, tennis M/W, ultimate Frisbee M/W, volleyball M/W.

Standardized Tests *Required:* SAT I or ACT (for admission).

Costs (2003–04) *Comprehensive fee:* $21,320 includes full-time tuition ($16,500) and room and board ($4820). Full-time tuition and fees vary according to class time and course load. Part-time tuition and fees vary according to class time. *Room and board:* Room and board charges vary according to board plan and housing facility. *Payment plans:* tuition prepayment, installment. *Waivers:* minority students, children of alumni, senior citizens, and employees or children of employees.

Financial Aid Of all full-time matriculated undergraduates who enrolled in 2003, 987 applied for aid, 841 were judged to have need. 529 Federal Work-Study jobs (averaging $1629). 63 state and other part-time jobs (averaging $1224). *Average financial aid package:* $13,859. *Average need-based loan:* $4349. *Average need-based gift aid:* $9320. *Average indebtedness upon graduation:* $17,306.

Applying *Options:* common application, electronic application, early action, deferred entrance. *Application fee:* $25. *Required:* high school transcript, minimum 2.0 GPA. *Recommended:* essay or personal statement, minimum 2.5 GPA, 2 letters of recommendation, interview. *Application deadline:* 8/25 (freshmen), rolling (transfers). *Notification:* continuous until 10/1 (freshmen), 12/1 (early action), continuous (transfers).

Admissions Contact Mr. Chad Jolly, Dean of Enrollment Development, William Jewell College, 500 College Hill, Liberty, MO 64068. *Phone:* 816-781-7700. *Toll-free phone:* 800-753-7009. *Fax:* 816-415-5027. *E-mail:* admission@william.jewell.edu.

■ See page 2856 for a narrative description.

WILLIAM WOODS UNIVERSITY

Fulton, Missouri

- **Independent** comprehensive, founded 1870, affiliated with Christian Church (Disciples of Christ)
- **Calendar** semesters
- **Degrees** associate, bachelor's, and master's
- **Small-town** 170-acre campus with easy access to St. Louis
- **Endowment** $9.7 million
- **Coed,** 1,132 undergraduate students, 91% full-time, 72% women, 28% men
- **Moderately difficult** entrance level

Undergraduates 1,035 full-time, 97 part-time. Students come from 39 states and territories, 14 other countries, 29% are from out of state, 3% African American, 2% Hispanic American, 0.6% Native American, 5% international, 6% transferred in, 80% live on campus. *Retention:* 77% of 2002 full-time freshmen returned.

Freshmen *Admission:* 612 applied, 254 enrolled. *Average high school GPA:* 3.30. *Test scores:* SAT verbal scores over 500: 58%; SAT math scores over 500: 46%; ACT scores over 18: 85%; SAT verbal scores over 600: 20%; SAT math scores over 600: 8%; ACT scores over 24: 31%; SAT verbal scores over 700: 5%; ACT scores over 30: 2%.

Faculty *Total:* 92, 61% full-time. *Student/faculty ratio:* 12:1.

Majors Accounting; advertising; art; art teacher education; athletic training; biology/biological sciences; broadcast journalism; business administration and management; business/managerial economics; commercial and advertising art; communication/speech communication and rhetoric; comparative literature; computer and information sciences; design and visual communications; dramatic/theatre arts; education; elementary education; English; English composition; English/language arts teacher education; equestrian studies; fine/studio arts; French language teacher education; history; interdisciplinary studies; interior design; international business/trade/commerce; international relations and affairs; legal assistant/paralegal; management information systems; mathematics; mathematics teacher education; middle school education; physical education teaching and coaching; political science and government; psychology; public relations/image management; radio and television; science teacher education; secondary education; sign language interpretation and translation; social work; Spanish; special education; speech/theater education; theatre design and technology.

Academic Programs *Special study options:* academic remediation for entering students, accelerated degree program, adult/continuing education programs, advanced placement credit, double majors, honors programs, independent study, internships, off-campus study, part-time degree program, student-designed majors, study abroad, summer session for credit. *ROTC:* Army (c), Navy (c), Air Force (c).

William Woods University (continued)

Library Dulany Library with 93,917 titles, 26,773 audiovisual materials, an OPAC, a Web page.

Computers on Campus 105 computers available on campus for general student use. A campuswide network can be accessed from student residence rooms. Internet access, at least one staffed computer lab available. Computer purchase or lease plan available.

Student Life *Housing:* on-campus residence required through senior year. *Options:* coed, men-only, women-only. Campus housing is university owned. Freshman campus housing is guaranteed. *Activities and organizations:* drama/theater group, student-run newspaper, radio station, choral group, Campus Crusade for Christ, Panhellenic Council, Leader Scholars, Hunter Jumper Show Team, national fraternities, national sororities. *Campus security:* 24-hour patrols, controlled dormitory access. *Student services:* health clinic, personal/psychological counseling.

Athletics Member NAIA. *Intercollegiate sports:* baseball M(s), basketball W(s), cheerleading W(s), cross-country running M(s)/W(s), equestrian sports M/W, golf M(s)/W(s), soccer M(s)/W(s), softball W(s), track and field M/W, volleyball M(s)/W(s). *Intramural sports:* badminton M/W, baseball M, basketball M/W, bowling M/W, football M/W, rock climbing M/W, softball M/W, table tennis M/W, tennis M/W, ultimate Frisbee M/W, volleyball M/W, weight lifting M/W.

Standardized Tests *Required:* SAT I or ACT (for admission).

Costs (2004–05) *Comprehensive fee:* $20,120 includes full-time tuition ($14,000), mandatory fees ($420), and room and board ($5700). Full-time tuition and fees vary according to program. Part-time tuition: $465 per credit hour. *Required fees:* $15 per term part-time. *Room and board:* Room and board charges vary according to board plan. *Payment plan:* installment. *Waivers:* children of alumni, senior citizens, and employees or children of employees.

Financial Aid Of all full-time matriculated undergraduates who enrolled in 2003, 636 applied for aid, 390 were judged to have need, 118 had their need fully met. 281 Federal Work-Study jobs (averaging $958). 158 state and other part-time jobs (averaging $974). In 2003, 236 non-need-based awards were made. *Average percent of need met:* 84%. *Average financial aid package:* $13,532. *Average need-based loan:* $2547. *Average need-based gift aid:* $2034. *Average non-need-based aid:* $3554. *Average indebtedness upon graduation:* $9112.

Applying *Options:* electronic application, early admission, deferred entrance. *Application fee:* $25. *Required:* high school transcript. *Required for some:* essay or personal statement, 2 letters of recommendation. *Recommended:* interview. *Application deadline:* rolling (freshmen), rolling (transfers). *Notification:* continuous (transfers).

Admissions Contact Mr. Jimmy Clay, Executive Director of Enrollment Services, William Woods University, One University Avenue, Fulton, MO 65251. *Phone:* 573-592-4221. *Toll-free phone:* 800-995-3159 Ext. 4221. *Fax:* 573-592-1146. *E-mail:* admissions@williamwoods.edu.

■ *See page 2862 for a narrative description.*

MONTANA

CARROLL COLLEGE
Helena, Montana

- **Independent Roman Catholic** 4-year, founded 1909
- **Calendar** semesters
- **Degrees** associate and bachelor's
- **Small-town** 64-acre campus
- **Endowment** $20.5 million
- **Coed,** 1,411 undergraduate students, 87% full-time, 58% women, 42% men
- **Moderately difficult** entrance level, 83% of applicants were admitted

Undergraduates 1,230 full-time, 181 part-time. Students come from 27 states and territories, 8 other countries, 35% are from out of state, 0.3% African American, 0.8% Asian American or Pacific Islander, 1% Hispanic American, 0.9% Native American, 0.9% international, 6% transferred in, 56% live on campus. *Retention:* 80% of 2002 full-time freshmen returned.

Freshmen *Admission:* 899 applied, 742 admitted, 310 enrolled. *Average high school GPA:* 3.40. *Test scores:* SAT verbal scores over 500: 74%; SAT math scores over 500: 76%; ACT scores over 18: 91%; SAT verbal scores over 600: 27%; SAT math scores over 600: 23%; ACT scores over 24: 50%; SAT verbal scores over 700: 7%; SAT math scores over 700: 4%; ACT scores over 30: 5%.

Faculty *Total:* 126, 63% full-time, 45% with terminal degrees. *Student/faculty ratio:* 13:1.

Majors Accounting; acting; art; biology/biological sciences; biology teacher education; business administration and management; business/managerial economics; chemistry; civil engineering; clinical laboratory science/medical technology; communication/speech communication and rhetoric; computer science; dramatic/theatre arts; education; elementary education; engineering; English; English as a second/foreign language (teaching); English/language arts teacher education; environmental studies; finance; French; general studies; health information/medical records administration; history; history teacher education; international relations and affairs; Latin; mathematics; mathematics teacher education; nursing (registered nurse training); philosophy; physical education teaching and coaching; political science and government; pre-dentistry studies; pre-law studies; pre-medical studies; pre-pharmacy studies; pre-veterinary studies; psychology; public administration; public relations/image management; religious education; religious studies; secondary education; social sciences; social science teacher education; social work; sociology; Spanish; Spanish language teacher education; sport and fitness administration; technical and business writing; theatre design and technology; theology; visual and performing arts.

Academic Programs *Special study options:* accelerated degree program, adult/continuing education programs, advanced placement credit, cooperative education, double majors, English as a second language, freshman honors college, honors programs, independent study, internships, part-time degree program, student-designed majors, study abroad, summer session for credit. *ROTC:* Army (b). *Unusual degree programs:* 3-2 engineering with Columbia University, University of Southern California, University of Notre Dame, Montana State University, Gonzaga University, Montana College of Mineral Science and Technology.

Library Corette Library plus 1 other with 89,003 titles, 2,721 serial subscriptions, 3,890 audiovisual materials, an OPAC, a Web page.

Computers on Campus 91 computers available on campus for general student use. A campuswide network can be accessed from student residence rooms and from off campus that provide access to online book order. Internet access, at least one staffed computer lab available.

Student Life *Housing:* on-campus residence required through sophomore year. *Options:* coed, men-only, women-only. Campus housing is university owned. Freshman campus housing is guaranteed. *Activities and organizations:* drama/theater group, student-run newspaper, radio station, choral group, student government, drama club, Into the Streets, radio club, soccer club. *Campus security:* late-night transport/escort service, controlled dormitory access. *Student services:* health clinic, personal/psychological counseling.

Athletics Member NAIA. *Intercollegiate sports:* basketball M(s)/W(s), cheerleading M/W, football M(s), golf W(s), soccer W(s), swimming M/W, volleyball W(s). *Intramural sports:* badminton M/W, basketball M/W, bowling M/W, cross-country running M/W, football M/W, golf M/W, ice hockey M(c), racquetball M/W, rugby M(c), skiing (cross-country) M/W, skiing (downhill) M(c)/W(c), soccer M(c)/W(c), softball M/W, swimming M(c)/W(c), table tennis M/W, tennis M/W, track and field M/W, ultimate Frisbee M/W, volleyball M/W, water polo M/W, weight lifting M/W, wrestling M.

Standardized Tests *Required:* SAT I or ACT (for admission). *Required for some:* SAT II: Subject Tests (for admission), SAT II: Writing Test (for admission).

Costs (2003–04) *Comprehensive fee:* $20,476 includes full-time tuition ($14,466), mandatory fees ($200), and room and board ($5810). Part-time tuition: $483 per semester hour. *College room only:* $2720. Room and board charges vary according to board plan, housing facility, and student level. *Payment plan:* installment. *Waivers:* senior citizens and employees or children of employees.

Financial Aid Of all full-time matriculated undergraduates who enrolled in 2003, 1,212 applied for aid, 826 were judged to have need, 175 had their need fully met. 435 Federal Work-Study jobs (averaging $2164). 12 state and other part-time jobs (averaging $1719). In 2003, 333 non-need-based awards were made. *Average percent of need met:* 85%. *Average financial aid package:* $13,799. *Average need-based loan:* $4558. *Average need-based gift aid:* $8020. *Average non-need-based aid:* $5907. *Average indebtedness upon graduation:* $22,868.

Applying *Options:* common application, electronic application, deferred entrance. *Application fee:* $35. *Required:* essay or personal statement, high school transcript, minimum 2.0 GPA, 1 letter of recommendation. *Required for some:* interview. *Recommended:* minimum 3.0 GPA, interview. *Application deadlines:* 6/1 (freshmen), 6/1 (transfers). *Notification:* continuous (freshmen), continuous (transfers).

Admissions Contact Ms. Candace A. Cain, Director of Admission, Carroll College, 1601 North Benton Avenue, Helena, MT 59625-0002. *Phone:* 406-447-4384. *Toll-free phone:* 800-992-3648. *Fax:* 406-447-4533. *E-mail:* enroll@carroll.edu.

■ *See page 1356 for a narrative description.*

MONTANA STATE UNIVERSITY–BILLINGS
Billings, Montana

- **State-supported** comprehensive, founded 1927, part of Montana University System

- **Calendar** semesters
- **Degrees** certificates, associate, bachelor's, master's, post-master's, and postbachelor's certificates
- **Urban** 92-acre campus
- **Endowment** $10.0 million
- **Coed,** 4,139 undergraduate students, 77% full-time, 63% women, 37% men
- **Moderately difficult** entrance level, 96% of applicants were admitted

Undergraduates 3,178 full-time, 961 part-time. Students come from 33 states and territories, 19 other countries, 7% are from out of state, 0.5% African American, 1% Asian American or Pacific Islander, 3% Hispanic American, 6% Native American, 0.6% international, 9% transferred in, 11% live on campus. *Retention:* 54% of 2002 full-time freshmen returned.

Freshmen *Admission:* 996 applied, 956 admitted, 845 enrolled. *Average high school GPA:* 2.98. *Test scores:* SAT verbal scores over 500: 57%; SAT math scores over 500: 56%; ACT scores over 18: 76%; SAT verbal scores over 600: 15%; SAT math scores over 600: 21%; ACT scores over 24: 23%; SAT verbal scores over 700: 4%; SAT math scores over 700: 6%; ACT scores over 30: 1%.

Faculty *Total:* 244, 64% full-time. *Student/faculty ratio:* 20:1.

Majors Accounting; accounting related; administrative assistant and secretarial science; art; art teacher education; autobody/collision and repair technology; automobile/automotive mechanics technology; biology/biological sciences; biology teacher education; business administration and management; business automation/technology/data entry; business/commerce; business/managerial economics; chemistry; chemistry teacher education; community psychology; computer and information sciences; computer and information sciences and support services related; data processing and data processing technology; dental hygiene; diesel mechanics technology; drafting and design technology; dramatic/theatre arts; early childhood education; education; elementary education; emergency medical technology (EMT paramedic); engineering related; English; English/language arts teacher education; environmental studies; finance; fire protection and safety technology; health and physical education; health/health care administration; health information/medical records administration; health teacher education; heating, air conditioning, ventilation and refrigeration maintenance technology; history; history teacher education; human resources management; legal administrative assistant/secretary; liberal arts and sciences/liberal studies; marketing/marketing management; mass communication/media; mathematics; mathematics teacher education; medical administrative assistant and medical secretary; medical/clinical assistant; multi-/interdisciplinary studies related; music; music teacher education; nursing (licensed practical/vocational nurse training); petroleum technology; physical education teaching and coaching; pre-engineering; psychology; public relations/image management; rehabilitation and therapeutic professions related; rehabilitation therapy; science teacher education; secondary education; sheet metal technology; social science teacher education; sociology; Spanish; Spanish language teacher education; special education; sport and fitness administration; surgical technology.

Academic Programs *Special study options:* academic remediation for entering students, accelerated degree program, adult/continuing education programs, advanced placement credit, cooperative education, distance learning, double majors, English as a second language, external degree program, honors programs, independent study, internships, off-campus study, part-time degree program, services for LD students, study abroad, summer session for credit.

Library Montana State University-Billings Library with 488,004 titles, 3,276 serial subscriptions, 2,125 audiovisual materials, an OPAC, a Web page.

Computers on Campus 500 computers available on campus for general student use. A campuswide network can be accessed from student residence rooms and from off campus that provide access to on-line degree programs. Internet access, online (class) registration, at least one staffed computer lab available.

Student Life *Housing:* on-campus residence required for freshman year. *Options:* coed, men-only, women-only, disabled students. Campus housing is university owned. Freshman applicants given priority for college housing. *Activities and organizations:* drama/theater group, student-run newspaper, radio station, choral group, Art Student League, band club, Inter-Varsity Christian Fellowship, Residence Hall Association, Student Council for Exceptional Children. *Campus security:* 24-hour emergency response devices and patrols, late-night transport/escort service, controlled dormitory access. *Student services:* health clinic, personal/psychological counseling, women's center, legal services.

Athletics Member NCAA. All Division II. *Intercollegiate sports:* basketball M(s)/W(s), cross-country running M(s)/W(s), soccer M(s)/W(s), softball W, tennis M(s)/W(s), volleyball W(s). *Intramural sports:* baseball M/W, basketball M/W, bowling M/W, cheerleading M/W, cross-country running M/W, football M/W, golf M/W, racquetball M/W, skiing (cross-country) M/W, soccer M/W, softball M/W, swimming M/W, table tennis M/W, tennis M/W, track and field M/W, volleyball M/W.

Standardized Tests *Required:* SAT I or ACT (for admission).

Costs (2003–04) *Tuition:* state resident $4180 full-time, $116 per credit hour part-time; nonresident $11,540 full-time, $321 per credit hour part-time. Full-time tuition and fees vary according to course level, course load, degree level, location, reciprocity agreements, and student level. Part-time tuition and fees vary according to course level, course load, degree level, location, reciprocity agreements, and student level. *Room and board:* $4430. Room and board charges vary according to board plan and housing facility. *Payment plan:* installment. *Waivers:* minority students, senior citizens, and employees or children of employees.

Financial Aid Of all full-time matriculated undergraduates who enrolled in 2002, 2,614 applied for aid, 2,154 were judged to have need, 449 had their need fully met. 216 Federal Work-Study jobs (averaging $1053). 91 state and other part-time jobs (averaging $1153). In 2002, 117 non-need-based awards were made. *Average percent of need met:* 67%. *Average financial aid package:* $7109. *Average need-based loan:* $3145. *Average need-based gift aid:* $3937. *Average non-need-based aid:* $7918. *Average indebtedness upon graduation:* $13,250.

Applying *Options:* common application, early admission, deferred entrance. *Application fee:* $30. *Required:* high school transcript, minimum 2.5 GPA. *Application deadline:* 7/1 (freshmen), rolling (transfers). *Notification:* continuous (freshmen), continuous (transfers).

Admissions Contact Ms. Shelly Andersen, Associate Director of Admissions, Montana State University–Billings, 1500 University Drive, Billings, MT 59101. *Phone:* 406-657-2158. *Toll-free phone:* 800-565-6782. *Fax:* 406-657-2302. *E-mail:* keverett@msubillings.edu.

■ See page 2016 for a narrative description.

MONTANA STATE UNIVERSITY–BOZEMAN
Bozeman, Montana

- **State-supported** university, founded 1893, part of Montana University System
- **Calendar** semesters
- **Degrees** certificates, bachelor's, master's, doctoral, and post-master's certificates
- **Small-town** 1170-acre campus
- **Endowment** $56.2 million
- **Coed,** 10,750 undergraduate students, 86% full-time, 46% women, 54% men
- **Moderately difficult** entrance level, 81% of applicants were admitted

Undergraduates 9,284 full-time, 1,466 part-time. Students come from 50 states and territories, 60 other countries, 29% are from out of state, 0.4% African American, 1% Asian American or Pacific Islander, 1% Hispanic American, 2% Native American, 1% international, 7% transferred in, 25% live on campus. *Retention:* 70% of 2002 full-time freshmen returned.

Freshmen *Admission:* 4,380 applied, 3,547 admitted, 2,149 enrolled. *Average high school GPA:* 3.31. *Test scores:* SAT verbal scores over 500: 73%; SAT math scores over 500: 76%; ACT scores over 18: 92%; SAT verbal scores over 600: 27%; SAT math scores over 600: 34%; ACT scores over 24: 46%; SAT verbal scores over 700: 3%; SAT math scores over 700: 6%; ACT scores over 30: 5%.

Faculty *Total:* 808, 67% full-time, 67% with terminal degrees. *Student/faculty ratio:* 17:1.

Majors Agricultural business and management; agricultural mechanization; agricultural teacher education; animal sciences; anthropology; art; biology/biological sciences; biotechnology; business/commerce; chemical engineering; chemistry; cinematography and film/video production; civil engineering; computer engineering; computer science; construction engineering technology; economics; electrical, electronics and communications engineering; elementary education; English; environmental design/architecture; environmental studies; family and consumer sciences/human sciences; fine/studio arts; foreign languages and literatures; geology/earth science; health and physical education; health/health care administration; history; horticultural science; industrial engineering; mathematics; mechanical engineering; mechanical engineering/mechanical technology; medical microbiology and bacteriology; music; music teacher education; natural resources/conservation; nursing (registered nurse training); philosophy; physics; plant sciences; political science and government; psychology; range science and management; secondary education; sociology; sport and fitness administration; technology/industrial arts teacher education.

Academic Programs *Special study options:* academic remediation for entering students, adult/continuing education programs, advanced placement credit, distance learning, double majors, English as a second language, honors programs, independent study, internships, off-campus study, part-time degree program, services for LD students, student-designed majors, study abroad, summer session for credit. *ROTC:* Army (b), Air Force (b).

Library Renne Library plus 1 other with 574,634 titles, 6,643 serial subscriptions, 4,822 audiovisual materials, an OPAC, a Web page.

Computers on Campus 850 computers available on campus for general student use. A campuswide network can be accessed from student residence rooms and from off campus that provide access to e-mail. Internet access, online (class) registration, at least one staffed computer lab available.

Montana State University–Bozeman (continued)

Student Life *Housing:* on-campus residence required for freshman year. *Options:* coed, men-only, women-only, cooperative. Campus housing is university owned. Freshman campus housing is guaranteed. *Activities and organizations:* drama/theater group, student-run newspaper, radio and television station, choral group, marching band, Spurs, Intervarsity Christian Fellowship, Campus Crusade for Christ, Fangs, Mortar Board, national fraternities, national sororities. *Campus security:* 24-hour emergency response devices and patrols, student patrols, late-night transport/escort service, 24-hour residence hall monitoring. *Student services:* health clinic, personal/psychological counseling, women's center, legal services.

Athletics Member NCAA. All Division I except football (Division I-AA). *Intercollegiate sports:* basketball M(s)/W(s), cheerleading M(s)/W(s), cross-country running M(s)/W(s), golf W(s), skiing (cross-country) M(s)/W(s), skiing (downhill) M(s)/W(s), tennis M(s)/W(s), track and field M(s)/W(s), volleyball W(s). *Intramural sports:* archery M/W, badminton M/W, baseball M, basketball M/W, bowling M/W, cross-country running M/W, fencing M/W, football M, golf M/W, gymnastics M/W, racquetball M/W, rugby M/W, skiing (cross-country) M/W, skiing (downhill) M/W, soccer M/W, softball M/W, swimming M/W, table tennis M/W, tennis M/W, track and field M/W, ultimate Frisbee M/W, volleyball M/W, water polo M/W, weight lifting M/W, wrestling M.

Standardized Tests *Required:* SAT I or ACT (for admission).

Costs (2003–04) *Tuition:* state resident $4145 full-time; nonresident $12,707 full-time. Full-time tuition and fees vary according to course load. Part-time tuition and fees vary according to course load. *Room and board:* $5370. Room and board charges vary according to board plan and housing facility. *Payment plans:* installment, deferred payment. *Waivers:* minority students, senior citizens, and employees or children of employees.

Financial Aid Of all full-time matriculated undergraduates who enrolled in 2002, 6,976 applied for aid, 4,842 were judged to have need, 473 had their need fully met. 390 Federal Work-Study jobs (averaging $1086). 316 state and other part-time jobs (averaging $1124). In 2002, 588 non-need-based awards were made. *Average percent of need met:* 66%. *Average financial aid package:* $6919. *Average need-based loan:* $3914. *Average need-based gift aid:* $3569. *Average non-need-based aid:* $3255. *Average indebtedness upon graduation:* $18,000.

Applying *Options:* electronic application, early admission, deferred entrance. *Application fee:* $30. *Required:* high school transcript, minimum 2.5 GPA. *Application deadline:* rolling (freshmen), rolling (transfers). *Notification:* continuous (freshmen), continuous (transfers).

Admissions Contact Ms. Ronda Russell, Director of New Student services, Montana State University–Bozeman, PO Box 172190, Bozeman, MT 59717-2190. *Phone:* 406-994-2452. *Toll-free phone:* 888-MSU-CATS. *Fax:* 406-994-1923. *E-mail:* admissions@montana.edu.

■ *See page 2018 for a narrative description.*

MONTANA STATE UNIVERSITY–NORTHERN

Havre, Montana

- **State-supported** comprehensive, founded 1929, part of Montana University System
- **Calendar** semesters
- **Degrees** certificates, associate, bachelor's, and master's
- **Small-town** 105-acre campus
- **Endowment** $162,838
- **Coed**
- **Moderately difficult** entrance level

Faculty *Student/faculty ratio:* 15:1.

Athletics Member NAIA.

Standardized Tests *Required:* ACT (for placement).

Costs (2003–04) *Tuition:* state resident $4100 full-time; nonresident $11,220 full-time. *Room and board:* $5600.

Financial Aid Of all full-time matriculated undergraduates who enrolled in 2001, 1,020 applied for aid, 847 were judged to have need, 225 had their need fully met. 100 Federal Work-Study jobs (averaging $1500). 30 state and other part-time jobs (averaging $1500). In 2001, 49. *Average percent of need met:* 70. *Average financial aid package:* $8185. *Average need-based loan:* $3645. *Average need-based gift aid:* $4368. *Average non-need-based aid:* $3060. *Average indebtedness upon graduation:* $10,601.

Applying *Options:* early admission, deferred entrance. *Application fee:* $30. *Required:* high school transcript. *Required for some:* minimum 2.0 GPA.

Admissions Contact Ms. Rosalie Spinler, Director of Admissions, Montana State University–Northern, PO Box 7751, Havre, MT 59501-7751. *Phone:* 406-265-3704. *Toll-free phone:* 800-662-6132. *Fax:* 406-265-3777. *E-mail:* msunadmit@nmc1.nmclites.edu.

MONTANA TECH OF THE UNIVERSITY OF MONTANA

Butte, Montana

- **State-supported** comprehensive, founded 1895, part of Montana University System
- **Calendar** semesters
- **Degrees** certificates, diplomas, associate, bachelor's, master's, and postbachelor's certificates
- **Small-town** 56-acre campus
- **Endowment** $12.6 million
- **Coed,** 2,142 undergraduate students, 83% full-time, 46% women, 54% men
- **Moderately difficult** entrance level

Undergraduates 1,774 full-time, 368 part-time. Students come from 34 states and territories, 13 other countries, 11% are from out of state, 5% transferred in, 15% live on campus. *Retention:* 63% of 2002 full-time freshmen returned.

Freshmen *Admission:* 410 enrolled. *Average high school GPA:* 3.20. *Test scores:* SAT verbal scores over 500: 66%; SAT math scores over 500: 74%; ACT scores over 18: 88%; SAT verbal scores over 600: 20%; SAT math scores over 600: 28%; ACT scores over 24: 37%; SAT verbal scores over 700: 1%; SAT math scores over 700: 7%; ACT scores over 30: 4%.

Faculty *Total:* 156, 71% full-time, 35% with terminal degrees. *Student/faculty ratio:* 16:1.

Majors Accounting; administrative assistant and secretarial science; applied mathematics; architectural drafting and CAD/CADD; artificial intelligence and robotics; autobody/collision and repair technology; automobile/automotive mechanics technology; biological and physical sciences; biology/biological sciences; business administration and management; business automation/technology/data entry; business/commerce; chemistry; civil drafting and CAD/CADD; civil engineering; communication/speech communication and rhetoric; computer and information sciences; computer engineering; computer programming; computer science; computer systems analysis; data processing and data processing technology; drafting and design technology; engineering; engineering science; engineering technology; environmental/environmental health engineering; executive assistant/executive secretary; finance; geological/geophysical engineering; geotechnical engineering; health science; human resources management; information science/studies; legal administrative assistant/secretary; liberal arts and sciences/liberal studies; materials engineering; materials science; mathematics; mechanical drafting and CAD/CADD; mechanical engineering; medical administrative assistant and medical secretary; metallurgical engineering; mining and mineral engineering; nursing assistant/aide and patient care assistant; nursing (registered nurse training); occupational health and industrial hygiene; occupational safety and health technology; petroleum engineering; petroleum technology; systems engineering; technical and business writing; welding technology.

Academic Programs *Special study options:* academic remediation for entering students, adult/continuing education programs, advanced placement credit, cooperative education, distance learning, double majors, independent study, internships, part-time degree program, services for LD students, student-designed majors, summer session for credit.

Library Montana Tech Library plus 1 other with 161,187 titles, 495 serial subscriptions, 38 audiovisual materials, an OPAC, a Web page.

Computers on Campus 500 computers available on campus for general student use. A campuswide network can be accessed from student residence rooms and from off campus. Internet access, online (class) registration, at least one staffed computer lab available.

Student Life *Housing:* on-campus residence required for freshman year. *Options:* coed. Campus housing is university owned. Freshman campus housing is guaranteed. *Activities and organizations:* student-run newspaper, radio station, choral group, environmental engineering club, SH/IH Club, Petroleum Club SPE, Marcus Daly Mining, chemistry club. *Campus security:* 24-hour patrols, controlled dormitory access. *Student services:* health clinic, personal/psychological counseling.

Athletics Member NAIA. *Intercollegiate sports:* basketball M(s)/W(s), cross-country running M(c)/W(c), football M(s), golf M(s)/W(s), rugby M(c), soccer M(c)/W(c), swimming M(c)/W(c), volleyball W(s). *Intramural sports:* basketball M/W, football M/W, racquetball M/W, softball M/W, swimming M/W, tennis M/W, volleyball M/W, water polo M/W.

Standardized Tests *Required:* SAT I or ACT (for admission).

Costs (2003–04) *Tuition:* state resident $3350 full-time, $175 per credit part-time; nonresident $8060 full-time, $500 per credit part-time. Full-time tuition and fees vary according to course level, course load, degree level, and reciprocity agreements. Part-time tuition and fees vary according to course level, course load, degree level, location, and reciprocity agreements. *Required fees:* $1000 full-time, $36 per credit part-time, $482 per credit part-time. *Room and board:* $4980; room only: $2120. Room and board charges vary according to board plan and housing facility. *Payment plan:* deferred payment. *Waivers:* minority students, senior citizens, and employees or children of employees.

Financial Aid Of all full-time matriculated undergraduates who enrolled in 2003, 1,500 applied for aid, 1,300 were judged to have need, 700 had their need fully met. 75 state and other part-time jobs (averaging $2000). In 2003, 100 non-need-based awards were made. *Average percent of need met:* 60%. *Average financial aid package:* $7000. *Average need-based loan:* $5000. *Average need-based gift aid:* $1000. *Average non-need-based aid:* $4000. *Average indebtedness upon graduation:* $14,000.

Applying *Options:* common application, electronic application, early admission. *Application fee:* $30. *Required:* high school transcript, minimum 2.5 GPA, proof of immunization. *Application deadline:* rolling (freshmen), rolling (transfers). *Notification:* continuous (freshmen), continuous (transfers).

Admissions Contact Mr. Tony Campeau, Associate Director of Admissions, Montana Tech of The University of Montana, 1300 West Park Street, Butte, MT 59701-8997. *Phone:* 406-496-4178 Ext. 4632. *Toll-free phone:* 800-445-TECH Ext. 1. *Fax:* 406-496-4170. *E-mail:* admissions@mtech.edu.

Rocky Mountain College
Billings, Montana

- **Independent interdenominational** 4-year, founded 1878
- **Calendar** semesters
- **Degrees** diplomas, associate, bachelor's, and master's
- **Urban** 60-acre campus
- **Endowment** $11.2 million
- **Coed,** 919 undergraduate students, 94% full-time, 56% women, 44% men
- **Moderately difficult** entrance level, 85% of applicants were admitted

Undergraduates 860 full-time, 59 part-time. Students come from 39 states and territories, 23 other countries, 28% are from out of state, 1% African American, 1% Asian American or Pacific Islander, 3% Hispanic American, 8% Native American, 6% international, 12% transferred in, 38% live on campus. *Retention:* 75% of 2002 full-time freshmen returned.

Freshmen *Admission:* 720 applied, 611 admitted, 233 enrolled. *Average high school GPA:* 3.34. *Test scores:* SAT verbal scores over 500: 73%; SAT math scores over 500: 70%; ACT scores over 18: 89%; SAT verbal scores over 600: 22%; SAT math scores over 600: 15%; ACT scores over 24: 35%; SAT verbal scores over 700: 4%; SAT math scores over 700: 1%; ACT scores over 30: 4%.

Faculty *Total:* 104, 46% full-time, 44% with terminal degrees. *Student/faculty ratio:* 13:1.

Majors Accounting; accounting related; agricultural business and management; airline pilot and flight crew; art; art teacher education; athletic training; aviation/airway management; biology/biological sciences; biology teacher education; business administration and management; chemistry; chemistry teacher education; communication/speech communication and rhetoric; computer science; dramatic/theatre arts; economics; education; elementary education; English; English/language arts teacher education; environmental science; environmental studies; equestrian studies; geology/earth science; health and physical education related; health teacher education; history; history teacher education; information technology; interdisciplinary studies; kinesiology and exercise science; liberal arts and sciences/liberal studies; management information systems; management science; mathematics; mathematics teacher education; multi-/interdisciplinary studies related; music performance; music teacher education; philosophy; physical education teaching and coaching; physician assistant; political science and government; psychology; religious studies; secondary education; social studies teacher education; sociology; theatre design and technology.

Academic Programs *Special study options:* academic remediation for entering students, accelerated degree program, adult/continuing education programs, advanced placement credit, cooperative education, distance learning, double majors, English as a second language, honors programs, independent study, internships, part-time degree program, services for LD students, student-designed majors, study abroad, summer session for credit. *Unusual degree programs:* 3-2 engineering with Montana State University–Bozeman, Montana Tech of the University of Montana; occupational therapy with Washington University in St. Louis.

Library Paul Adams Library with 67,877 titles, 364 serial subscriptions, 782 audiovisual materials, an OPAC, a Web page.

Computers on Campus 193 computers available on campus for general student use. A campuswide network can be accessed from student residence rooms and from off campus. Internet access, at least one staffed computer lab available.

Student Life *Housing:* on-campus residence required through sophomore year. *Options:* coed. Campus housing is university owned. Freshman campus housing is guaranteed. *Activities and organizations:* drama/theater group, student-run newspaper, choral group, marching band, Sojourners, Equestrian Club, Oysters, STARs, Martial Arts Club. *Campus security:* 24-hour emergency response devices, student patrols, controlled dormitory access, security cameras. *Student services:* health clinic, personal/psychological counseling.

Athletics Member NAIA. *Intercollegiate sports:* basketball M(s)/W(s), football M(s), golf M/W(s), skiing (downhill) M(s)/W(s), soccer W(s), volleyball W(s). *Intramural sports:* basketball M/W, equestrian sports M/W, field hockey M/W, football M/W, golf M(c)/W(c), ice hockey M(c), skiing (downhill) M/W, swimming M/W.

Standardized Tests *Required:* SAT I or ACT (for admission). *Recommended:* ACT (for admission).

Costs (2003–04) *Comprehensive fee:* $19,015 includes full-time tuition ($13,950), mandatory fees ($165), and room and board ($4900). Full-time tuition and fees vary according to course load and program. Part-time tuition: $582 per credit. Part-time tuition and fees vary according to course load and program. *Required fees:* $35 per term part-time. *College room only:* $2112. Room and board charges vary according to board plan and housing facility. *Payment plan:* installment. *Waivers:* employees or children of employees.

Financial Aid Of all full-time matriculated undergraduates who enrolled in 2003, 661 applied for aid, 552 were judged to have need, 102 had their need fully met. 353 Federal Work-Study jobs (averaging $387). 216 state and other part-time jobs (averaging $1335). In 2003, 67 non-need-based awards were made. *Average percent of need met:* 74%. *Average financial aid package:* $13,276. *Average need-based loan:* $4233. *Average need-based gift aid:* $8476. *Average non-need-based aid:* $6869. *Average indebtedness upon graduation:* $20,571.

Applying *Options:* common application, electronic application, early admission, deferred entrance. *Application fee:* $25. *Required:* high school transcript, minimum 2.5 GPA. *Required for some:* essay or personal statement, interview. *Recommended:* 2 letters of recommendation. *Application deadline:* rolling (freshmen), rolling (transfers). *Notification:* continuous (freshmen), continuous (transfers).

Admissions Contact Ms. LynAnn Henderson, Director of Admissions, Rocky Mountain College, 1511 Poly Drive, Billings, MT 59102. *Phone:* 406-657-1026. *Toll-free phone:* 800-877-6259. *Fax:* 406-259-9751. *E-mail:* admissions@rocky.edu.

Salish Kootenai College
Pablo, Montana

- **Independent** primarily 2-year, founded 1977
- **Calendar** quarters
- **Degrees** certificates, associate, and bachelor's
- **Rural** 4-acre campus
- **Coed**
- **Noncompetitive** entrance level

Standardized Tests *Required:* TABE (for placement).

Financial Aid Of all full-time matriculated undergraduates who enrolled in 2001, 64 Federal Work-Study jobs (averaging $1387).

Applying *Options:* deferred entrance. *Required:* high school transcript, proof of immunization, tribal enrollment.

Admissions Contact Ms. Jackie Moran, Admissions Officer, Salish Kootenai College, PO 117, Highway 93, Pablo, MT 59855. *Phone:* 406-275-4866. *Fax:* 406-275-4810. *E-mail:* jackie_moran@skc.edu.

University of Great Falls
Great Falls, Montana

- **Independent Roman Catholic** comprehensive, founded 1932
- **Calendar** semesters
- **Degrees** certificates, associate, bachelor's, and master's
- **Urban** 40-acre campus
- **Endowment** $3.1 million
- **Coed,** 682 undergraduate students, 68% full-time, 71% women, 29% men
- **Noncompetitive** entrance level, 80% of applicants were admitted

Undergraduates 465 full-time, 217 part-time. Students come from 27 states and territories, 3 other countries, 11% are from out of state, 2% African American, 1% Asian American or Pacific Islander, 3% Hispanic American, 7% Native American, 1% international, 16% transferred in, 13% live on campus. *Retention:* 54% of 2002 full-time freshmen returned.

Freshmen *Admission:* 192 applied, 154 admitted, 84 enrolled. *Average high school GPA:* 2.93. *Test scores:* SAT verbal scores over 500: 55%; SAT math scores over 500: 37%; ACT scores over 18: 76%; SAT verbal scores over 600: 5%; SAT math scores over 600: 5%; ACT scores over 24: 17%; ACT scores over 30: 3%.

Faculty *Total:* 108, 33% full-time, 29% with terminal degrees. *Student/faculty ratio:* 8:1.

University of Great Falls (continued)

Majors Accounting; accounting and business/management; American literature; art; art teacher education; biology/biological sciences; biology teacher education; botany/plant biology; business administration and management; chemistry; chemistry teacher education; computer and information sciences; computer and information sciences and support services related; computer and information sciences related; computer and information systems security; computer graphics; computer/information technology services administration related; computer management; computer programming; computer science; computer software and media applications related; computer systems analysis; computer systems networking and telecommunications; corrections; corrections administration; corrections and criminal justice related; counseling psychology; creative writing; criminal justice/law enforcement administration; criminal justice/police science; criminal justice/safety; early childhood education; education (multiple levels); elementary education; English; English composition; English language and literature related; English/language arts teacher education; fine/studio arts; forensic science and technology; health and physical education; health/health care administration; health teacher education; history; history teacher education; human services; information science/studies; information technology; kindergarten/preschool education; legal assistant/paralegal; library science related; management science; marketing/marketing management; mathematics; mathematics teacher education; middle school education; physical education teaching and coaching; political science and government; psychology; reading teacher education; religious studies; school librarian/school library media; science teacher education; secondary education; social sciences; social science teacher education; social studies teacher education; sociology; special education; special education (gifted and talented); substance abuse/addiction counseling; system administration; system, networking, and LAN/wan management; theology; web/multimedia management and webmaster; web page, digital/multimedia and information resources design.

Academic Programs *Special study options:* academic remediation for entering students, adult/continuing education programs, advanced placement credit, cooperative education, distance learning, double majors, external degree program, independent study, internships, part-time degree program, services for LD students, summer session for credit.

Library University of Great Falls Library with 101,110 titles, 549 serial subscriptions, 4,069 audiovisual materials, an OPAC, a Web page.

Computers on Campus 110 computers available on campus for general student use. A campuswide network can be accessed from student residence rooms. Internet access, online (class) registration, at least one staffed computer lab available.

Student Life *Housing:* on-campus residence required through sophomore year. *Options:* coed, disabled students. Campus housing is university owned and leased by the school. Freshman campus housing is guaranteed. *Activities and organizations:* drama/theater group, student-run newspaper, choral group, Student Montana Education Association, Student Senate, international law and justice club, Students In Free Enterprise, Science club—medical, forensic and computer science students. *Campus security:* 24-hour emergency response devices and patrols, late-night transport/escort service, controlled dormitory access. *Student services:* personal/psychological counseling, women's center.

Athletics Member NAIA. *Intercollegiate sports:* basketball M(s)/W(s), cheerleading M/W, golf M/W, volleyball W(s). *Intramural sports:* basketball M/W, football M/W, golf M/W, skiing (downhill) M/W, soccer M/W, softball W, table tennis M/W, ultimate Frisbee M/W, volleyball M/W.

Standardized Tests *Recommended:* SAT I (for admission), ACT (for admission), SAT I or ACT (for admission), SAT I and SAT II or ACT (for admission).

Costs (2003–04) *Comprehensive fee:* $17,040 includes full-time tuition ($11,500), mandatory fees ($440), and room and board ($5100). Full-time tuition and fees vary according to course load, degree level, and reciprocity agreements. Part-time tuition: $365 per credit. Part-time tuition and fees vary according to course load, degree level, and reciprocity agreements. *Required fees:* $10 per credit part-time, $50 per term part-time. *College room only:* $2100. Room and board charges vary according to board plan and housing facility. *Payment plans:* installment, deferred payment. *Waivers:* senior citizens and employees or children of employees.

Financial Aid Of all full-time matriculated undergraduates who enrolled in 2003, 387 applied for aid, 354 were judged to have need, 63 had their need fully met. 62 Federal Work-Study jobs (averaging $2196). In 2003, 37 non-need-based awards were made. *Average percent of need met:* 77%. *Average financial aid package:* $9312. *Average need-based loan:* $4017. *Average need-based gift aid:* $3413. *Average non-need-based aid:* $2889. *Average indebtedness upon graduation:* $29,483.

Applying *Options:* common application, early admission, deferred entrance. *Application fee:* $35. *Required:* high school transcript. *Recommended:* interview. *Application deadlines:* 8/1 (freshmen), 8/1 (transfers). *Notification:* 9/1 (freshmen), 9/1 (transfers).

Admissions Contact Ms. Sarah Harris, Director of Admissions, University of Great Falls, 1301 20th Street South, Great Falls, MT 59405. *Phone:* 406-791-5200 Ext. 5203. *Toll-free phone:* 800-856-9544. *Fax:* 406-791-5209. *E-mail:* enroll@ugf.edu.

■ *See page 2608 for a narrative description.*

THE UNIVERSITY OF MONTANA–MISSOULA

Missoula, Montana

- **State-supported** university, founded 1893, part of Montana University System
- **Calendar** semesters
- **Degrees** certificates, associate, bachelor's, master's, doctoral, first professional, and post-master's certificates
- **Urban** 220-acre campus
- **Endowment** $78.3 million
- **Coed,** 11,343 undergraduate students, 84% full-time, 53% women, 47% men
- **Moderately difficult** entrance level, 93% of applicants were admitted

Undergraduates 9,547 full-time, 1,796 part-time. Students come from 52 states and territories, 61 other countries, 26% are from out of state, 0.5% African American, 1% Asian American or Pacific Islander, 1% Hispanic American, 4% Native American, 2% international, 26% transferred in, 23% live on campus. *Retention:* 71% of 2002 full-time freshmen returned.

Freshmen *Admission:* 4,112 applied, 3,813 admitted, 2,286 enrolled. *Average high school GPA:* 3.20. *Test scores:* SAT verbal scores over 500: 70%; SAT math scores over 500: 68%; ACT scores over 18: 90%; SAT verbal scores over 600: 28%; SAT math scores over 600: 25%; ACT scores over 24: 41%; SAT verbal scores over 700: 4%; SAT math scores over 700: 2%; ACT scores over 30: 4%.

Faculty *Total:* 658, 76% full-time, 69% with terminal degrees. *Student/faculty ratio:* 21:1.

Majors Accounting technology and bookkeeping; administrative assistant and secretarial science; African-American/Black studies; American government and politics; American Indian/Native American studies; anthropology; apparel and accessories marketing; applied mathematics; area studies; art; art history, criticism and conservation; art teacher education; Asian studies; Asian studies (East); astronomy; audiology and speech-language pathology; biochemistry; biology/biological sciences; botany/plant biology; business/commerce; business teacher education; chemistry; Chinese; city/urban, community and regional planning; classics and languages, literatures and linguistics; clinical laboratory science/medical technology; clinical/medical laboratory technology; communication/speech communication and rhetoric; computer and information sciences; computer science; creative writing; culinary arts; curriculum and instruction; dance; dramatic/theatre arts; drawing; economics; education; electrical, electronic and communications engineering technology; elementary education; English; English as a second/foreign language (teaching); environmental education; environmental studies; executive assistant/executive secretary; fashion merchandising; foreign languages and literatures; forest/forest resources management; forestry; French; geography; geology/earth science; German; health teacher education; heavy equipment maintenance technology; history; industrial arts; information science/studies; interdisciplinary studies; international business/trade/commerce; Japanese; journalism; Latin; legal administrative assistant/secretary; legal assistant/paralegal; legal studies; liberal arts and sciences/liberal studies; linguistics; marketing/marketing management; mathematics; mathematics teacher education; medical administrative assistant and medical secretary; medical microbiology and bacteriology; medical pharmacology and pharmaceutical sciences; music; music performance; music teacher education; natural resources/conservation; natural resources management and policy; nursing (licensed practical/vocational nurse training); parks, recreation and leisure; pharmacy; pharmacy technician; philosophy; physical education teaching and coaching; physical therapy; physics; pre-engineering; pre-law studies; pre-medical studies; pre-pharmacy studies; psychology; radio and television; reading teacher education; receptionist; respiratory care therapy; Russian; Russian studies; science teacher education; secondary education; small engine mechanics and repair technology; social sciences; social science teacher education; social work; sociology; Spanish; speech and rhetoric; statistics; surgical technology; technical and business writing; vehicle/equipment operation; welding technology; wildlife and wildlands science and management; women's studies; zoology/animal biology.

Academic Programs *Special study options:* academic remediation for entering students, adult/continuing education programs, advanced placement credit, cooperative education, distance learning, double majors, English as a second language, freshman honors college, honors programs, independent study, internships, off-campus study, part-time degree program, services for LD students, study abroad, summer session for credit. *ROTC:* Army (b).

Library Maureen and Mike Mansfield Library plus 2 others with 570,287 titles, 6,248 serial subscriptions, 118,190 audiovisual materials, an OPAC, a Web page.

Computers on Campus 545 computers available on campus for general student use. A campuswide network can be accessed from student residence rooms and from off campus. Internet access, online (class) registration, at least one staffed computer lab available.

Student Life *Housing:* on-campus residence required for freshman year. *Options:* coed, men-only, women-only, disabled students. Campus housing is university owned. *Activities and organizations:* drama/theater group, student-run newspaper, radio and television station, choral group, marching band, forestry club, Honors Student Association, Campus Outdoor Program, International Organization, Kyio Indian Club, national fraternities, national sororities. *Campus security:* 24-hour emergency response devices and patrols, student patrols, late-night transport/escort service, controlled dormitory access. *Student services:* health clinic, personal/psychological counseling, women's center, legal services.

Athletics Member NCAA. All Division I except football (Division I-AA). *Intercollegiate sports:* baseball M(c), basketball M(s)/W(s), crew M(c)/W(c), cross-country running M(s)/W(s), equestrian sports M(c)/W(c), fencing M(c)/W(c), field hockey W(c), golf W, ice hockey M(c)/W(c), lacrosse M(c)/W(c), rugby M(c)/W(c), skiing (downhill) M(c)/W(c), soccer M(c)/W, tennis M(s)/W(s), track and field M(s)/W(s), ultimate Frisbee M(c)/W(c), volleyball M(c)/W(s). *Intramural sports:* archery M/W, badminton M/W, baseball M, basketball M/W, bowling M/W, cross-country running M/W, football M/W, golf M, ice hockey M, racquetball M/W, rugby M/W, skiing (cross-country) M/W, soccer W, softball M/W, swimming M/W, table tennis M/W, tennis M/W, track and field M/W, volleyball M/W, water polo M/W, weight lifting M/W.

Standardized Tests *Required:* SAT I or ACT (for admission). *Required for some:* ACT ASSET or ACT COMPASS.

Costs (2004–05) *Tuition:* state resident $3221 full-time, $141 per credit part-time; nonresident $11,212 full-time, $485 per credit part-time. Full-time tuition and fees vary according to student level. Part-time tuition and fees vary according to course load. *Required fees:* $1156 full-time, $37 per credit part-time. *Room and board:* $5432; room only: $2448. Room and board charges vary according to board plan and housing facility. *Payment plan:* installment. *Waivers:* minority students and senior citizens.

Financial Aid Of all full-time matriculated undergraduates who enrolled in 2002, 6,834 applied for aid, 5,196 were judged to have need, 2,003 had their need fully met. 1,098 Federal Work-Study jobs (averaging $1977). In 2002, 1489 non-need-based awards were made. *Average percent of need met:* 79%. *Average financial aid package:* $8034. *Average need-based loan:* $4766. *Average need-based gift aid:* $3742. *Average non-need-based aid:* $3502. *Average indebtedness upon graduation:* $11,576.

Applying *Options:* common application, electronic application, early admission, deferred entrance. *Application fee:* $30. *Required:* high school transcript, minimum 2.5 GPA. *Application deadline:* 3/1 (freshmen), rolling (transfers). *Notification:* continuous (freshmen), continuous (transfers).

Admissions Contact Office of New Student services, The University of Montana–Missoula, Missoula, MT 59812-0002. *Phone:* 406-243-6266. *Toll-free phone:* 800-462-8636. *Fax:* 406-243-5711. *E-mail:* admiss@selway.umt.edu.

The University of Montana–Western

Dillon, Montana

- **State-supported** 4-year, founded 1893, part of Montana University System
- **Calendar** semesters
- **Degrees** associate and bachelor's
- **Small-town** 36-acre campus
- **Endowment** $5.0 million
- **Coed,** 1,160 undergraduate students, 75% full-time, 60% women, 40% men
- **Minimally difficult** entrance level, 100% of applicants were admitted

Undergraduates 869 full-time, 291 part-time. Students come from 12 states and territories, 2 other countries, 15% are from out of state, 0.8% African American, 2% Asian American or Pacific Islander, 2% Hispanic American, 3% Native American, 0.3% international, 11% transferred in, 35% live on campus. *Retention:* 60% of 2002 full-time freshmen returned.

Freshmen *Admission:* 291 applied, 291 admitted, 171 enrolled. *Average high school GPA:* 2.99. *Test scores:* SAT verbal scores over 500: 39%; SAT math scores over 500: 39%; ACT scores over 18: 63%; SAT verbal scores over 600: 2%; SAT math scores over 600: 9%; ACT scores over 24: 8%; SAT math scores over 700: 3%; ACT scores over 30: 1%.

Faculty *Total:* 69, 70% full-time, 57% with terminal degrees. *Student/faculty ratio:* 19:1.

Majors Administrative assistant and secretarial science; applied art; art teacher education; biology teacher education; business administration and management; business automation/technology/data entry; business/commerce; business/corporate communications; business teacher education; computer and information sciences; data processing and data processing technology; dramatic/theatre arts; education; education (K-12); elementary education; English; English/language arts teacher education; environmental studies; equestrian studies; health teacher education; history teacher education; human resources management; industrial arts; information science/studies; kindergarten/preschool education; liberal arts and sciences/liberal studies; literature; mathematics teacher education; music teacher education; physical education teaching and coaching; pre-dentistry studies; pre-law studies; pre-medical studies; pre-veterinary studies; science teacher education; secondary education; social sciences; social science teacher education; technology/industrial arts teacher education; tourism and travel services management; tourism/travel marketing.

Academic Programs *Special study options:* academic remediation for entering students, accelerated degree program, adult/continuing education programs, advanced placement credit, cooperative education, distance learning, double majors, honors programs, independent study, internships, part-time degree program, services for LD students, student-designed majors, summer session for credit.

Library Lucy Carson Memorial Library with 90,431 titles, 7,127 serial subscriptions, 3,718 audiovisual materials, an OPAC, a Web page.

Computers on Campus 140 computers available on campus for general student use. A campuswide network can be accessed from student residence rooms and from off campus. Internet access, online (class) registration, at least one staffed computer lab available.

Student Life *Housing:* on-campus residence required for freshman year. *Options:* coed, men-only, women-only, disabled students. Campus housing is university owned. Freshman campus housing is guaranteed. *Activities and organizations:* drama/theater group, student-run newspaper, radio station, choral group, soccer, IGNU-poetry club, admissions volunteers, rodeo club, Chi Alpha-Christian Fellowship. *Campus security:* 24-hour emergency response devices and patrols, late-night transport/escort service. *Student services:* personal/psychological counseling, legal services.

Athletics Member NAIA. *Intercollegiate sports:* basketball M(s)/W(s), football M(s), golf M(s)/W(s), volleyball W(s). *Intramural sports:* archery M(c)/W(c), basketball M/W, bowling M/W, cheerleading M/W, equestrian sports M/W, football M/W, golf M/W, racquetball M/W, skiing (cross-country) M/W, skiing (downhill) M/W, soccer M/W, softball M/W, table tennis M/W, tennis M/W, volleyball M/W, weight lifting M/W, wrestling M.

Standardized Tests *Required:* SAT I or ACT (for admission).

Costs (2004–05) *Tuition:* state resident $3030 full-time, $131 per credit part-time; nonresident $10,860 full-time, $458 per credit part-time. Full-time tuition and fees vary according to course load and student level. Part-time tuition and fees vary according to course load and student level. *Required fees:* $750 full-time, $114 per credit part-time, $370 per credit part-time. *Room and board:* $4600; room only: $1800. Room and board charges vary according to board plan and housing facility. *Payment plan:* deferred payment. *Waivers:* senior citizens.

Financial Aid Of all full-time matriculated undergraduates who enrolled in 2003, 650 applied for aid, 650 were judged to have need. 210 Federal Work-Study jobs (averaging $1178). 165 state and other part-time jobs (averaging $2480). In 2003, 11 non-need-based awards were made. *Average percent of need met:* 38%. *Average financial aid package:* $4991. *Average need-based loan:* $3742. *Average need-based gift aid:* $3557. *Average non-need-based aid:* $3167. *Average indebtedness upon graduation:* $13,510.

Applying *Options:* common application, electronic application, early admission, deferred entrance. *Application fee:* $30. *Required:* high school transcript, minimum 2.5 GPA. *Application deadlines:* 7/1 (freshmen), 7/1 (transfers). *Notification:* continuous (freshmen), continuous (transfers).

Admissions Contact Ms. Arlene Williams, Director of Admissions, The University of Montana–Western, 710 South Atlantic, Dillon, MT 59725. *Phone:* 406-683-7331. *Toll-free phone:* 866-869-6668. *Fax:* 406-683-7493. *E-mail:* admissions@umwestern.edu.

NEBRASKA

Bellevue University

Bellevue, Nebraska

- **Independent** comprehensive, founded 1965
- **Calendar** semesters for day division, trimesters for evening division
- **Degrees** bachelor's and master's
- **Suburban** 35-acre campus with easy access to Omaha
- **Endowment** $22.5 million
- **Coed,** 3,933 undergraduate students, 68% full-time, 50% women, 50% men
- **Noncompetitive** entrance level

Undergraduates 2,669 full-time, 1,264 part-time. Students come from 42 states and territories, 69 other countries, 20% are from out of state, 9% African American, 2% Asian American or Pacific Islander, 6% Hispanic American, 0.6% Native American, 8% international.

Bellevue University (continued)

Freshmen *Admission:* 327 enrolled.

Faculty *Total:* 264, 24% full-time, 25% with terminal degrees. *Student/faculty ratio:* 17:1.

Majors Accounting; business administration and management; communication and media related; computer and information sciences; computer and information sciences related; computer/information technology services administration related; criminal justice/law enforcement administration; health/health care administration; information science/studies; information technology; management information systems; marketing/marketing management; physical education teaching and coaching; web page, digital/multimedia and information resources design.

Academic Programs *Special study options:* academic remediation for entering students, accelerated degree program, adult/continuing education programs, advanced placement credit, cooperative education, distance learning, double majors, English as a second language, external degree program, independent study, internships, part-time degree program, summer session for credit. *ROTC:* Army (c), Air Force (c).

Library Freeman/Lozier Library plus 1 other with 87,000 titles, 7,564 serial subscriptions, 3,955 audiovisual materials, an OPAC, a Web page.

Computers on Campus 450 computers available on campus for general student use. A campuswide network can be accessed from off campus. Internet access, online (class) registration, at least one staffed computer lab available.

Student Life *Housing:* college housing not available. *Activities and organizations:* student-run newspaper. *Campus security:* 24-hour emergency response devices. *Student services:* personal/psychological counseling, women's center.

Athletics Member NAIA. *Intercollegiate sports:* baseball M(s), basketball M(s), soccer M(s)/W, softball W(s), volleyball W(s). *Intramural sports:* basketball M/W, football M/W, golf M/W, volleyball M.

Standardized Tests *Required:* ACT (for admission). *Required for some:* SAT I or ACT (for placement).

Costs (2004–05) *Tuition:* $4650 full-time, $155 per credit hour part-time. Full-time tuition and fees vary according to program. Part-time tuition and fees vary according to program. *Required fees:* $90 full-time, $45 per term part-time. *Payment plans:* installment, deferred payment. *Waivers:* employees or children of employees.

Financial Aid Of all full-time matriculated undergraduates who enrolled in 2002, 2,003 applied for aid, 2,003 were judged to have need. 46 Federal Work-Study jobs (averaging $1837). In 2002, 560 non-need-based awards were made. *Average need-based loan:* $2944. *Average need-based gift aid:* $2441. *Average non-need-based aid:* $956.

Applying *Options:* deferred entrance. *Application fee:* $25. *Required:* high school transcript. *Required for some:* 3 letters of recommendation. *Application deadline:* rolling (freshmen), rolling (transfers).

Admissions Contact Melinda Cruz, Associate Vice President of Enrollment Management, Bellevue University, 1000 Galvin Road South, Bellevue, NE 68005-3098. *Phone:* 402-293-2026. *Toll-free phone:* 800-756-7920. *Fax:* 402-293-3730. *E-mail:* set@scholars.bellevue.edu.

■ *See page 1226 for a narrative description.*

CHADRON STATE COLLEGE
Chadron, Nebraska

- **State-supported** comprehensive, founded 1911, part of Nebraska State College System
- **Calendar** semesters
- **Degrees** bachelor's and master's
- **Small-town** 281-acre campus
- **Endowment** $4.8 million
- **Coed,** 2,294 undergraduate students, 77% full-time, 60% women, 40% men
- **Noncompetitive** entrance level

The first year of college can be a rewarding experience, and Chadron State College (CSC) wants to make students feel at home. CSC students who take part in the Host Parent Program benefit from community members who donate their time to get to know CSC students and provide a network away from home.

Undergraduates 1,767 full-time, 527 part-time. Students come from 31 states and territories, 10 other countries, 26% are from out of state, 1% African American, 0.5% Asian American or Pacific Islander, 2% Hispanic American, 0.9% Native American, 1% international, 5% transferred in, 65% live on campus. *Retention:* 78% of 2002 full-time freshmen returned.

Freshmen *Admission:* 503 enrolled. *Average high school GPA:* 3.19. *Test scores:* SAT verbal scores over 500: 43%; SAT math scores over 500: 43%; ACT scores over 18: 84%; SAT verbal scores over 600: 29%; SAT math scores over 600: 29%; ACT scores over 24: 31%; ACT scores over 30: 3%.

Faculty *Total:* 118, 81% full-time, 53% with terminal degrees. *Student/faculty ratio:* 22:1.

Majors Art; art teacher education; biology/biological sciences; biology teacher education; business administration and management; business teacher education; chemistry; chemistry teacher education; corrections and criminal justice related; drama and dance teacher education; dramatic/theatre arts; education (specific subject areas) related; elementary education; English; English/language arts teacher education; family and consumer economics related; family and consumer sciences/home economics teacher education; health/medical preparatory programs related; history; history teacher education; industrial production technologies related; information science/studies; interdisciplinary studies; library science; mathematics; mathematics teacher education; middle school education; music; music teacher education; parks, recreation, and leisure related; physical education teaching and coaching; physics; physics teacher education; psychology; range science and management; science teacher education; secondary education; social science teacher education; social work; sociology; Spanish; Spanish language teacher education; special education; speech and rhetoric; speech teacher education; technology/industrial arts teacher education.

Academic Programs *Special study options:* adult/continuing education programs, advanced placement credit, cooperative education, distance learning, double majors, freshman honors college, honors programs, independent study, internships, part-time degree program, services for LD students, student-designed majors, study abroad, summer session for credit.

Library Reta King Library with 213,231 titles, 720 serial subscriptions, 5,596 audiovisual materials, an OPAC.

Computers on Campus 200 computers available on campus for general student use. A campuswide network can be accessed from student residence rooms and from off campus. Internet access, online (class) registration, at least one staffed computer lab available.

Student Life *Housing:* on-campus residence required for freshman year. *Options:* coed, men-only, women-only. Campus housing is university owned. Freshman campus housing is guaranteed. *Activities and organizations:* drama/theater group, student-run newspaper, radio station, choral group. *Campus security:* 24-hour emergency response devices and patrols, student patrols, late-night transport/escort service. *Student services:* health clinic, personal/psychological counseling.

Athletics Member NCAA. All Division II. *Intercollegiate sports:* basketball M(s)/W(s), equestrian sports M(c)/W(c), football M(s), golf W(s), track and field M(s)/W(s), volleyball W(s), wrestling M(s). *Intramural sports:* badminton M/W, basketball M/W, bowling M/W, golf M/W, racquetball M/W, rugby M(c), soccer M/W, softball M/W, track and field M/W, volleyball M/W, wrestling M.

Standardized Tests *Recommended:* SAT I or ACT (for admission).

Costs (2003–04) *Tuition:* state resident $2610 full-time; nonresident $5220 full-time. *Required fees:* $631 full-time. *Room and board:* $3862; room only: $1778.

Financial Aid Of all full-time matriculated undergraduates who enrolled in 2003, 1,316 applied for aid, 1,029 were judged to have need. *Average financial aid package:* $2615. *Average need-based loan:* $1273. *Average need-based gift aid:* $1934. *Average indebtedness upon graduation:* $11,000.

Applying *Options:* early admission. *Application fee:* $15. *Required:* high school transcript, health forms. *Application deadline:* rolling (freshmen), rolling (transfers). *Notification:* continuous (freshmen), continuous (transfers).

Admissions Contact Ms. Tena Cook Gould, Director of Admissions, Chadron State College, 1000 Main Street, Chadron, NE 69337-2690. *Phone:* 308-432-6263. *Toll-free phone:* 800-242-3766. *Fax:* 308-432-6229. *E-mail:* inquire@csc1.csc.edu.

■ *See page 1382 for a narrative description.*

CLARKSON COLLEGE
Omaha, Nebraska

- **Independent** comprehensive, founded 1888, part of Nebraska Health System
- **Calendar** semesters
- **Degrees** certificates, associate, bachelor's, and master's
- **Urban** 3-acre campus
- **Endowment** $2.2 million
- **Coed, primarily women**
- **Moderately difficult** entrance level

Faculty *Student/faculty ratio:* 12:1.

Student Life *Campus security:* 24-hour emergency response devices and patrols, late-night transport/escort service, controlled dormitory access.

Standardized Tests *Required for some:* SAT I or ACT (for admission).

Costs (2003–04) *Comprehensive fee:* $12,662 includes full-time tuition ($9300), mandatory fees ($462), and room and board ($2900). Part-time tuition: $310 per credit hour. *Required fees:* $18 per credit hour part-time, $15 per term part-time. *Room and board:* Room and board charges vary according to housing facility and location. *Payment plans:* installment, deferred payment.

Financial Aid Of all full-time matriculated undergraduates who enrolled in 2001, 109 applied for aid, 94 were judged to have need, 22 had their need fully met. 40 Federal Work-Study jobs (averaging $2500). In 2001, 15. *Average percent of need met:* 71. *Average financial aid package:* $8291. *Average need-based loan:* $3365. *Average need-based gift aid:* $5434. *Average non-need-based aid:* $4374. *Average indebtedness upon graduation:* $13,931.

Applying *Options:* electronic application, deferred entrance. *Application fee:* $15. *Required:* essay or personal statement, high school transcript, minimum 2.5 GPA. *Required for some:* 2 letters of recommendation. *Recommended:* minimum 3.0 GPA.

Admissions Contact Ms. Nicole Wegenast, Dean of Enrollment Services, Clarkson College, 101 South 42nd Street, Omaha, NE 68131-2739. *Phone:* 402-552-3100. *Toll-free phone:* 800-647-5500. *Fax:* 402-552-6057. *E-mail:* admiss@clarksoncollege.edu.

College of Saint Mary
Omaha, Nebraska

- **Independent Roman Catholic** 4-year, founded 1923
- **Calendar** semesters
- **Degrees** certificates, associate, and bachelor's
- **Suburban** 25-acre campus
- **Endowment** $7.5 million
- **Women only,** 915 undergraduate students, 66% full-time
- **Minimally difficult** entrance level, 70% of applicants were admitted

Undergraduates 605 full-time, 310 part-time. Students come from 16 states and territories, 7 other countries, 13% are from out of state, 6% African American, 0.7% Asian American or Pacific Islander, 3% Hispanic American, 0.9% Native American, 1% international, 23% transferred in, 37% live on campus. *Retention:* 72% of 2002 full-time freshmen returned.

Freshmen *Admission:* 218 applied, 153 admitted, 78 enrolled. *Average high school GPA:* 3.21. *Test scores:* ACT scores over 18: 84%; ACT scores over 24: 28%; ACT scores over 30: 3%.

Faculty *Total:* 51, 100% full-time, 37% with terminal degrees. *Student/faculty ratio:* 10:1.

Majors Accounting; art; biology/biological sciences; business administration and management; chemistry; clinical laboratory science/medical technology; computer management; early childhood education; education; education (K-12); elementary education; English; general studies; health information/medical records administration; humanities; human services; legal assistant/paralegal; management information systems; mathematics; natural sciences; nursing (registered nurse training); occupational therapy; pre-dentistry studies; pre-law studies; pre-medical studies; pre-veterinary studies; psychology; science teacher education; secondary education; social sciences; special education; telecommunications.

Academic Programs *Special study options:* academic remediation for entering students, accelerated degree program, adult/continuing education programs, advanced placement credit, double majors, independent study, internships, part-time degree program, services for LD students, study abroad, summer session for credit. *ROTC:* Army (c), Air Force (c).

Library College of Saint Mary Library with 70,514 titles, 12,675 serial subscriptions, 1,300 audiovisual materials, an OPAC, a Web page.

Computers on Campus 105 computers available on campus for general student use. A campuswide network can be accessed from student residence rooms. Internet access, online (class) registration, at least one staffed computer lab available.

Student Life *Housing:* on-campus residence required through sophomore year. *Options:* women-only. Campus housing is university owned. Freshman campus housing is guaranteed. *Activities and organizations:* choral group, Student Senate, Campus Activities Board, Student Education Association of Nebraska, Student Occupational Therapy Club, Sigma Rho Lambda. *Campus security:* 24-hour emergency response devices and patrols, late-night transport/escort service, controlled dormitory access, external cameras at residence hall entrances. *Student services:* personal/psychological counseling.

Athletics Member NAIA. *Intercollegiate sports:* basketball W(s), cross-country running W(s), golf W(s), soccer W(s), softball W(s), volleyball W(s). *Intramural sports:* racquetball W, tennis W, volleyball W.

Standardized Tests *Required:* SAT I or ACT (for admission).

Costs (2004–05) *Comprehensive fee:* $22,577 includes full-time tuition ($16,637), mandatory fees ($240), and room and board ($5700). Part-time tuition and fees vary according to class time. *Room and board:* Room and board charges vary according to housing facility. *Payment plans:* installment, deferred payment. *Waivers:* senior citizens and employees or children of employees.

Financial Aid Of all full-time matriculated undergraduates who enrolled in 2003, 569 applied for aid, 530 were judged to have need, 60 had their need fully met. 100 Federal Work-Study jobs (averaging $1250). In 2003, 83 non-need-based awards were made. *Average percent of need met:* 62%. *Average financial aid package:* $11,763. *Average need-based loan:* $4938. *Average need-based gift aid:* $7681. *Average non-need-based aid:* $8589. *Average indebtedness upon graduation:* $16,720.

Applying *Options:* common application, electronic application. *Application fee:* $30. *Required:* high school transcript, minimum 2.0 GPA. *Required for some:* minimum 3.0 GPA, 2 letters of recommendation, interview. *Recommended:* essay or personal statement. *Application deadline:* rolling (freshmen), rolling (transfers). *Notification:* continuous until 8/24 (freshmen), continuous until 8/24 (transfers).

Admissions Contact Ms. Natalie Vrbka, Senior Admissions Counselor, College of Saint Mary, 1901 South 72nd Street, Omaha, NE 68124-2377. *Phone:* 402-399-2405. *Toll-free phone:* 800-926-5534. *Fax:* 402-399-2412. *E-mail:* enroll@csm.edu.

Concordia University
Seward, Nebraska

- **Independent** comprehensive, founded 1894, affiliated with Lutheran Church–Missouri Synod, part of Concordia University System
- **Calendar** 4-4-1
- **Degrees** bachelor's and master's
- **Small-town** 120-acre campus with easy access to Omaha
- **Endowment** $15.0 million
- **Coed,** 1,202 undergraduate students, 93% full-time, 57% women, 43% men
- **Moderately difficult** entrance level, 89% of applicants were admitted

Undergraduates 1,122 full-time, 80 part-time. Students come from 38 states and territories, 59% are from out of state, 1% African American, 0.8% Asian American or Pacific Islander, 1% Hispanic American, 3% transferred in. *Retention:* 80% of 2002 full-time freshmen returned.

Freshmen *Admission:* 728 applied, 646 admitted, 222 enrolled. *Average high school GPA:* 3.50. *Test scores:* SAT verbal scores over 500: 71%; SAT math scores over 500: 64%; ACT scores over 18: 90%; SAT verbal scores over 600: 24%; SAT math scores over 600: 31%; ACT scores over 24: 52%; SAT verbal scores over 700: 10%; SAT math scores over 700: 10%; ACT scores over 30: 8%.

Faculty *Total:* 120, 52% full-time, 59% with terminal degrees. *Student/faculty ratio:* 14:1.

Majors Accounting; art; art teacher education; behavioral sciences; biology/biological sciences; biology teacher education; business administration and management; business/commerce; business teacher education; chemistry; chemistry teacher education; commercial and advertising art; communication/speech communication and rhetoric; computer and information sciences; computer science; computer teacher education; drama and dance teacher education; dramatic/theatre arts; early childhood education; education; elementary education; English; English as a second/foreign language (teaching); English/language arts teacher education; family and consumer sciences/home economics teacher education; fine/studio arts; geography; geography teacher education; health and physical education; health/medical preparatory programs related; health teacher education; history; history teacher education; kindergarten/preschool education; kinesiology and exercise science; management information systems; mass communication/media; mathematics; mathematics teacher education; middle school education; music; music teacher education; natural sciences; pastoral studies/counseling; physical education teaching and coaching; physical sciences; physics teacher education; piano and organ; pre-dentistry studies; pre-law studies; pre-medical studies; pre-nursing studies; pre-pharmacy studies; pre-theology/pre-ministerial studies; pre-veterinary studies; psychology; religious education; religious/sacred music; science teacher education; secondary education; social sciences; social science teacher education; sociology; Spanish; Spanish language teacher education; special education; speech and rhetoric; speech teacher education; sport and fitness administration; technology/industrial arts teacher education; theology; trade and industrial teacher education; voice and opera.

Academic Programs *Special study options:* academic remediation for entering students, accelerated degree program, adult/continuing education programs, advanced placement credit, cooperative education, distance learning, double majors, English as a second language, honors programs, independent study, internships, off-campus study, part-time degree program, services for LD students, study abroad, summer session for credit. *ROTC:* Army (c), Air Force (c).

Library Link Library with 171,688 titles, 575 serial subscriptions, 12,068 audiovisual materials, an OPAC, a Web page.

Computers on Campus 75 computers available on campus for general student use. A campuswide network can be accessed from student residence rooms and

Concordia University (continued)

from off campus that provide access to academic plans, human resource data. Internet access, online (class) registration, at least one staffed computer lab available.

Student Life *Housing:* on-campus residence required through senior year. *Options:* men-only, women-only, disabled students. Campus housing is university owned. Freshman campus housing is guaranteed. *Activities and organizations:* drama/theater group, student-run newspaper, choral group, Student Activities Council, musical groups, men's and women's C-club, Student Senate, Concordia Youth Ministry. *Campus security:* 24-hour emergency response devices and patrols, controlled dormitory access. *Student services:* health clinic, personal/psychological counseling.

Athletics Member NAIA. *Intercollegiate sports:* baseball M(s), basketball M(s)/W(s), cross-country running M(s)/W(s), football M(s), golf M(s)/W(s), soccer M(s)/W(s), softball W(s), tennis M(s)/W(s), track and field M(s)/W(s), volleyball W(s). *Intramural sports:* badminton M/W, basketball M/W, bowling M(c)/W(c), cross-country running M/W, soccer M/W, softball M/W, table tennis M/W, tennis M/W, volleyball M/W.

Standardized Tests *Required:* SAT I or ACT (for admission).

Costs (2003–04) *Comprehensive fee:* $20,480 includes full-time tuition ($16,000) and room and board ($4480). Part-time tuition: $500 per credit. Part-time tuition and fees vary according to course load. *College room only:* $1980. Room and board charges vary according to board plan. *Payment plan:* installment. *Waivers:* employees or children of employees.

Financial Aid Of all full-time matriculated undergraduates who enrolled in 2003, 907 applied for aid, 907 were judged to have need, 695 had their need fully met. 137 Federal Work-Study jobs (averaging $774). In 2003, 109 non-need-based awards were made. *Average percent of need met:* 92%. *Average financial aid package:* $14,099. *Average need-based loan:* $3733. *Average need-based gift aid:* $4932. *Average non-need-based aid:* $5488. *Average indebtedness upon graduation:* $14,280. *Financial aid deadline:* 5/1.

Applying *Options:* electronic application, deferred entrance. *Application fee:* $25. *Required:* high school transcript. *Required for some:* letters of recommendation. *Recommended:* minimum 2.0 GPA, interview. *Application deadlines:* 7/31 (freshmen), 8/1 (transfers).

Admissions Contact Mr. Pete Kenow, Director of Admissions, Concordia University, 800 North Columbia Avenue, Seward, NE 68434-1599. *Phone:* 402-643-7233. *Toll-free phone:* 800-535-5494. *Fax:* 402-643-4073. *E-mail:* admiss@cune.edu.

CREIGHTON UNIVERSITY

Omaha, Nebraska

- **Independent Roman Catholic (Jesuit)** university, founded 1878
- **Calendar** semesters
- **Degrees** certificates, associate, bachelor's, master's, doctoral, and first professional
- **Urban** 110-acre campus
- **Endowment** $182.6 million
- **Coed,** 3,736 undergraduate students, 92% full-time, 61% women, 39% men
- **Moderately difficult** entrance level, 88% of applicants were admitted

Undergraduates 3,444 full-time, 292 part-time. Students come from 44 states and territories, 52 other countries, 49% are from out of state, 3% African American, 7% Asian American or Pacific Islander, 3% Hispanic American, 1% Native American, 2% international, 5% transferred in, 48% live on campus. *Retention:* 86% of 2002 full-time freshmen returned.

Freshmen *Admission:* 3,199 applied, 2,813 admitted, 933 enrolled. *Average high school GPA:* 3.72. *Test scores:* SAT verbal scores over 500: 86%; SAT math scores over 500: 89%; ACT scores over 18: 99%; SAT verbal scores over 600: 47%; SAT math scores over 600: 52%; ACT scores over 24: 70%; SAT verbal scores over 700: 10%; SAT math scores over 700: 10%; ACT scores over 30: 17%.

Faculty *Total:* 860, 72% full-time, 92% with terminal degrees. *Student/faculty ratio:* 14:1.

Majors Accounting; American Indian/Native American studies; American studies; ancient/classical Greek; applied mathematics; art; athletic training; atmospheric sciences and meteorology; biology/biological sciences; chemistry; classical, ancient Mediterranean and Near Eastern studies and archaeology; communication/speech communication and rhetoric; computer programming; computer science; dramatic/theatre arts; economics; elementary education; emergency medical technology (EMT paramedic); English; environmental studies; finance; French; German; graphic design; health/health care administration; history; international business/trade/commerce; international relations and affairs; journalism; kinesiology and exercise science; Latin; management information systems; marketing/marketing management; mathematics; music; nursing (registered nurse training); organizational communication; philosophy; physics; political science and government; pre-law studies; psychology; social work; sociology; Spanish; speech and rhetoric; theology.

Academic Programs *Special study options:* academic remediation for entering students, accelerated degree program, adult/continuing education programs, advanced placement credit, double majors, English as a second language, honors programs, independent study, internships, off-campus study, part-time degree program, services for LD students, study abroad, summer session for credit. *ROTC:* Army (b), Air Force (c). *Unusual degree programs:* 3-2 engineering with Marquette University.

Library Reinert Alumni Memorial Library plus 2 others with 481,848 titles, 1,666 serial subscriptions, 2,500 audiovisual materials, an OPAC, a Web page.

Computers on Campus 520 computers available on campus for general student use. A campuswide network can be accessed from student residence rooms and from off campus that provide access to online grade information. Internet access, online (class) registration, at least one staffed computer lab available. Computer purchase or lease plan available.

Student Life *Housing:* on-campus residence required through sophomore year. *Options:* coed, women-only, disabled students. Campus housing is university owned. Freshman campus housing is guaranteed. *Activities and organizations:* drama/theater group, student-run newspaper, radio and television station, choral group, Bird Cage, Freshman Leadership Program, Alpha Pi Omega, Alpha Kappa Psi, Omecron Delta Kappa, national fraternities, national sororities. *Campus security:* 24-hour emergency response devices and patrols, student patrols, late-night transport/escort service, controlled dormitory access. *Student services:* health clinic, personal/psychological counseling, women's center, legal services.

Athletics Member NCAA. All Division I. *Intercollegiate sports:* baseball M(s), basketball M(s)/W(s), crew W(s), cross-country running M(s)/W(s), golf M(s)/W(s), soccer M(s)/W(s), softball W(s), tennis M(s)/W(s), ultimate Frisbee M(c)/W(c), volleyball W(s). *Intramural sports:* badminton M/W, basketball M/W, bowling M/W, crew M(c), football M/W, golf M/W, racquetball M/W, rugby M(c)/W(c), soccer M/W, softball M/W, tennis M/W, volleyball M/W, weight lifting M(c)/W(c).

Standardized Tests *Required:* SAT I or ACT (for admission).

Costs (2003–04) *Comprehensive fee:* $26,748 includes full-time tuition ($19,202), mandatory fees ($720), and room and board ($6826). Part-time tuition: $600 per credit hour. *Required fees:* $120 per semester part-time. *College room only:* $3870. Room and board charges vary according to board plan and housing facility. *Waivers:* adult students and employees or children of employees.

Financial Aid Of all full-time matriculated undergraduates who enrolled in 2002, 2,158 applied for aid, 1,775 were judged to have need, 602 had their need fully met. 657 Federal Work-Study jobs (averaging $1815). In 2002, 932 non-need-based awards were made. *Average percent of need met:* 85%. *Average financial aid package:* $17,937. *Average need-based loan:* $5666. *Average need-based gift aid:* $10,710. *Average non-need-based aid:* $8564. *Average indebtedness upon graduation:* $22,021.

Applying *Options:* common application, electronic application, deferred entrance. *Application fee:* $40. *Required:* essay or personal statement, high school transcript, minimum 2.75 GPA, 1 letter of recommendation. *Application deadline:* 8/1 (freshmen), rolling (transfers). *Notification:* continuous (freshmen), continuous (transfers).

Admissions Contact Ms. Mary Chase, Director of Admissions-Scholarships, Creighton University, 2500 California Plaza, Omaha, NE 68178-0001. *Phone:* 402-280-3105. *Toll-free phone:* 800-282-5835. *Fax:* 402-280-2685. *E-mail:* admissions@creighton.edu.

■ *See page 1498 for a narrative description.*

DANA COLLEGE

Blair, Nebraska

- **Independent** 4-year, founded 1884, affiliated with Evangelical Lutheran Church in America
- **Calendar** 4-1-4
- **Degree** bachelor's
- **Small-town** 150-acre campus with easy access to Omaha
- **Endowment** $9.1 million
- **Coed,** 581 undergraduate students, 97% full-time, 41% women, 59% men
- **Moderately difficult** entrance level, 98% of applicants were admitted

Undergraduates 563 full-time, 18 part-time. Students come from 38 states and territories, 2 other countries, 49% are from out of state, 6% African American, 2% Asian American or Pacific Islander, 3% Hispanic American, 0.5% Native American, 0.5% international, 7% transferred in, 63% live on campus. *Retention:* 60% of 2002 full-time freshmen returned.

Freshmen *Admission:* 583 applied, 572 admitted, 164 enrolled. *Average high school GPA:* 3.14. *Test scores:* SAT verbal scores over 500: 71%; SAT math scores over 500: 59%; ACT scores over 18: 92%; SAT verbal scores over 600: 29%; SAT math scores over 600: 18%; ACT scores over 24: 24%; SAT verbal scores over 700: 12%; ACT scores over 30: 1%.

Faculty *Total:* 71, 62% full-time, 41% with terminal degrees. *Student/faculty ratio:* 12:1.

Majors Accounting; art; art teacher education; biology/biological sciences; business administration and management; business teacher education; chemistry; communication/speech communication and rhetoric; computer science; criminal justice/law enforcement administration; drama and dance teacher education; education; elementary education; English; English/language arts teacher education; environmental studies; foreign language teacher education; German; health and physical education; history; history teacher education; interdisciplinary studies; mathematics; mathematics teacher education; music; music teacher education; organizational communication; physical education teaching and coaching; psychology; religious studies; science teacher education; secondary education; social sciences; social science teacher education; social work; sociology; Spanish; special education; speech teacher education; web/multimedia management and webmaster; web page, digital/multimedia and information resources design.

Academic Programs *Special study options:* accelerated degree program, adult/continuing education programs, advanced placement credit, double majors, English as a second language, honors programs, independent study, internships, off-campus study, part-time degree program, services for LD students, student-designed majors, study abroad, summer session for credit. *ROTC:* Army (c), Air Force (c).

Library C. A. Dana-Life Library plus 1 other with 157,860 titles, 27,150 serial subscriptions, 4,092 audiovisual materials, an OPAC, a Web page.

Computers on Campus 110 computers available on campus for general student use. A campuswide network can be accessed from student residence rooms and from off campus that provide access to student schedules, campus events, e-mail. Internet access, at least one staffed computer lab available.

Student Life *Housing:* on-campus residence required through junior year. *Options:* coed, women-only. Campus housing is university owned. Freshman campus housing is guaranteed. *Activities and organizations:* drama/theater group, student-run newspaper, radio and television station, choral group, Residence Hall Association, Social Awareness Organization, Fellowship of Christian Athletes, campus ministry, HOPE (Helping Our People Expand). *Campus security:* 24-hour emergency response devices and patrols, late-night transport/escort service, controlled dormitory access. *Student services:* health clinic, personal/psychological counseling.

Athletics Member NAIA. *Intercollegiate sports:* baseball M(s), basketball M(s)/W(s), cross-country running M(s)/W(s), football M(s), golf W(s), soccer M(s)/W(s), softball W(s), track and field M(s)/W(s), volleyball W(s), wrestling M(s). *Intramural sports:* basketball M/W, bowling M/W, football M/W, softball M/W, swimming M/W, table tennis M/W, volleyball M/W, weight lifting M/W.

Standardized Tests *Required:* SAT I or ACT (for admission). *Recommended:* ACT (for admission).

Costs (2003–04) *Comprehensive fee:* $20,630 includes full-time tuition ($15,200), mandatory fees ($550), and room and board ($4880). Part-time tuition: $465 per semester hour. Part-time tuition and fees vary according to course load. *Required fees:* $30 per term part-time. *College room only:* $1900. Room and board charges vary according to board plan and housing facility. *Payment plans:* installment, deferred payment. *Waivers:* children of alumni and employees or children of employees.

Financial Aid Of all full-time matriculated undergraduates who enrolled in 2003, 561 applied for aid, 464 were judged to have need, 116 had their need fully met. In 2003, 97 non-need-based awards were made. *Average percent of need met:* 85%. *Average financial aid package:* $14,622. *Average need-based loan:* $4619. *Average need-based gift aid:* $4077. *Average non-need-based aid:* $5186. *Average indebtedness upon graduation:* $16,182.

Applying *Options:* electronic application, deferred entrance. *Required:* high school transcript, minimum 2.0 GPA. *Required for some:* essay or personal statement, 1 letter of recommendation, interview. *Application deadline:* rolling (freshmen). *Notification:* continuous (freshmen), continuous (transfers).

Admissions Contact Mr. James Lynes, Director of Admissions, Dana College, 2848 College Drive, Blair, NE 68008-1099. *Phone:* 402-426-7220. *Toll-free phone:* 800-444-3262. *Fax:* 402-426-7386. *E-mail:* admissions@acad2.dana.edu.

DOANE COLLEGE
Crete, Nebraska

- **Independent** comprehensive, founded 1872, affiliated with United Church of Christ
- **Calendar** 4-1-4
- **Degrees** bachelor's and master's (nontraditional undergraduate programs and graduate programs offered at Lincoln campus)
- **Small-town** 300-acre campus with easy access to Omaha
- **Endowment** $65.5 million
- **Coed,** 1,610 undergraduate students, 85% full-time, 56% women, 44% men
- **Moderately difficult** entrance level, 84% of applicants were admitted

Undergraduates 1,367 full-time, 243 part-time. Students come from 23 states and territories, 7 other countries, 20% are from out of state, 0.6% transferred in, 74% live on campus. *Retention:* 80% of 2002 full-time freshmen returned.

Freshmen *Admission:* 1,097 applied, 922 admitted, 291 enrolled. *Average high school GPA:* 3.41. *Test scores:* ACT scores over 18: 87%; ACT scores over 24: 44%; ACT scores over 30: 1%.

Faculty *Total:* 127, 57% full-time, 39% with terminal degrees. *Student/faculty ratio:* 12:1.

Majors Accounting; art; biology/biological sciences; business administration and management; business teacher education; chemistry; communication/speech communication and rhetoric; computer and information sciences; computer science; dramatic/theatre arts; economics; elementary education; English; English as a second/foreign language (teaching); environmental studies; French; German; health and physical education; history; human services; international relations and affairs; mass communication/media; mathematics; music; natural sciences; philosophy; physical education teaching and coaching; physical sciences; physics; political science and government; psychology; public administration; public relations/image management; religious studies; secondary education; social sciences; sociology; Spanish; special education; speech and rhetoric.

Academic Programs *Special study options:* academic remediation for entering students, accelerated degree program, adult/continuing education programs, advanced placement credit, cooperative education, double majors, English as a second language, honors programs, independent study, internships, off-campus study, part-time degree program, student-designed majors, study abroad, summer session for credit. *ROTC:* Army (c), Air Force (c). *Unusual degree programs:* 3-2 engineering with Columbia University, Washington University in St. Louis; forestry with Duke University; environmental studies with Duke University.

Library Perkins Library with 257,560 titles, 3,500 serial subscriptions, 1,313 audiovisual materials, an OPAC, a Web page.

Computers on Campus 200 computers available on campus for general student use. A campuswide network can be accessed from student residence rooms and from off campus. Internet access, online (class) registration, at least one staffed computer lab available.

Student Life *Housing:* on-campus residence required through senior year. *Options:* coed. Campus housing is university owned. *Activities and organizations:* drama/theater group, student-run newspaper, radio and television station, choral group, marching band, Greek society, Student Activities Council, Hansen Leadership Program, band/choir, Doane Ambassadors. *Campus security:* student patrols, evening patrols by trained security personnel. *Student services:* health clinic, personal/psychological counseling.

Athletics Member NAIA. *Intercollegiate sports:* baseball M(s), basketball M(s)/W(s), cross-country running M(s)/W(s), football M(s), golf M(s)/W(s), soccer M(s)/W(s), softball W(s), tennis M/W, track and field M(s)/W(s), volleyball W(s). *Intramural sports:* baseball M(c)/W(c), basketball M/W, bowling M/W, football M/W, golf M/W, ice hockey M, racquetball M(c)/W(c), softball M/W, swimming M/W, table tennis M(c)/W(c), tennis M/W, volleyball M/W, water polo M/W.

Standardized Tests *Required:* SAT I or ACT (for admission).

Costs (2004–05) *Comprehensive fee:* $20,690 includes full-time tuition ($15,620), mandatory fees ($350), and room and board ($4720). Full-time tuition and fees vary according to location. Part-time tuition and fees vary according to course load and location. *Room and board:* Room and board charges vary according to board plan, housing facility, and location. *Payment plan:* installment. *Waivers:* senior citizens and employees or children of employees.

Financial Aid Of all full-time matriculated undergraduates who enrolled in 2003, 887 applied for aid, 803 were judged to have need, 587 had their need fully met. 462 Federal Work-Study jobs (averaging $829). 163 state and other part-time jobs (averaging $725). In 2003, 186 non-need-based awards were made. *Average percent of need met:* 99%. *Average financial aid package:* $12,953. *Average need-based loan:* $4149. *Average need-based gift aid:* $8872. *Average non-need-based aid:* $7159. *Average indebtedness upon graduation:* $12,539.

Applying *Options:* electronic application, early admission, deferred entrance. *Application fee:* $15. *Required:* high school transcript, 2 letters of recommendation. *Required for some:* interview. *Recommended:* minimum 2.0 GPA. *Application deadline:* rolling (freshmen), rolling (transfers). *Notification:* continuous (freshmen), continuous (transfers).

Admissions Contact Mr. Dan Kunzman, Dean of Admissions, Doane College, Crete, NE 68333. *Phone:* 402-826-8222. *Toll-free phone:* 800-333-6263. *Fax:* 402-826-8600. *E-mail:* admissions@doane.edu.

GRACE UNIVERSITY
Omaha, Nebraska

- **Independent interdenominational** comprehensive, founded 1943
- **Calendar** semesters
- **Degrees** certificates, associate, bachelor's, and master's
- **Urban** 15-acre campus
- **Endowment** $890,668
- **Coed,** 427 undergraduate students, 88% full-time, 57% women, 43% men
- **Moderately difficult** entrance level, 46% of applicants were admitted

Undergraduates 375 full-time, 52 part-time. Students come from 30 states and territories, 4 other countries, 36% are from out of state, 5% African American, 2% Hispanic American, 0.5% Native American, 11% transferred in, 61% live on campus. *Retention:* 68% of 2002 full-time freshmen returned.

Freshmen *Admission:* 325 applied, 150 admitted, 122 enrolled.

Faculty *Total:* 50, 50% full-time, 90% with terminal degrees. *Student/faculty ratio:* 18:1.

Majors Accounting; agricultural business and management; airline pilot and flight crew; avionics maintenance technology; biblical studies; broadcast journalism; business administration and management; business teacher education; communication/speech communication and rhetoric; computer and information sciences; computer and information sciences related; computer programming; computer science; divinity/ministry; education (K-12); elementary education; humanities; human resources management; liberal arts and sciences/liberal studies; marriage and family therapy/counseling; mass communication/media; middle school education; missionary studies and missiology; music; music teacher education; music theory and composition; nursing (licensed practical/vocational nurse training); nursing (registered nurse training); pastoral studies/counseling; piano and organ; pre-theology/pre-ministerial studies; psychology; religious education; religious/sacred music; secondary education; social science teacher education; voice and opera; web/multimedia management and webmaster; youth ministry.

Academic Programs *Special study options:* accelerated degree program, adult/continuing education programs, advanced placement credit, cooperative education, distance learning, double majors, external degree program, independent study, internships, off-campus study, part-time degree program, services for LD students, student-designed majors, study abroad, summer session for credit. *ROTC:* Army (c), Air Force (c). *Unusual degree programs:* 3-2 nursing with Clarkson College; social work with University of Nebraska at Omaha.

Library Grace University Library with 46,736 titles, 3,721 serial subscriptions, 3,882 audiovisual materials, an OPAC, a Web page.

Computers on Campus 45 computers available on campus for general student use. A campuswide network can be accessed. At least one staffed computer lab available.

Student Life *Housing:* on-campus residence required through sophomore year. *Options:* men-only, women-only. Campus housing is university owned. Freshman applicants given priority for college housing. *Activities and organizations:* student-run radio station, choral group, Choral, Band, Radio Station, Yearbook. *Campus security:* student patrols, late-night transport/escort service, controlled dormitory access. *Student services:* health clinic, personal/psychological counseling.

Athletics Member NCCAA. *Intercollegiate sports:* basketball M/W, soccer M, volleyball W. *Intramural sports:* basketball M/W, volleyball M/W.

Standardized Tests *Required:* ACT (for admission).

Costs (2003–04) *Comprehensive fee:* $15,680 includes full-time tuition ($10,500), mandatory fees ($180), and room and board ($5000). Part-time tuition: $350 per credit hour. Part-time tuition and fees vary according to course load. *Room and board:* Room and board charges vary according to board plan and housing facility. *Payment plan:* installment. *Waivers:* children of alumni, senior citizens, and employees or children of employees.

Financial Aid Of all full-time matriculated undergraduates who enrolled in 2002, 249 applied for aid, 232 were judged to have need, 25 had their need fully met. 66 Federal Work-Study jobs (averaging $1113). In 2002, 34 non-need-based awards were made. *Average percent of need met:* 55%. *Average financial aid package:* $6479. *Average need-based loan:* $3112. *Average need-based gift aid:* $4053. *Average non-need-based aid:* $4191. *Average indebtedness upon graduation:* $12,758.

Applying *Options:* electronic application, early admission, deferred entrance. *Application fee:* $35. *Required:* essay or personal statement, high school transcript, minimum 2.0 GPA, 3 letters of recommendation. *Required for some:* interview. *Application deadline:* rolling (freshmen), rolling (transfers).

Admissions Contact Ms. Diane V. Lee, Director of Admissions, Grace University, 1311 South Ninth Street, Omaha, NE 68108. *Phone:* 402-449-2831. *Toll-free phone:* 800-383-1422. *Fax:* 402-341-9587. *E-mail:* admissions@graceuniversity.com.

HASTINGS COLLEGE
Hastings, Nebraska

- **Independent Presbyterian** comprehensive, founded 1882
- **Calendar** 4-1-4
- **Degrees** bachelor's and master's
- **Small-town** 109-acre campus
- **Endowment** $43.2 million
- **Coed,** 1,074 undergraduate students, 98% full-time, 48% women, 52% men
- **Moderately difficult** entrance level, 80% of applicants were admitted

Undergraduates 1,054 full-time, 20 part-time. Students come from 25 states and territories, 5 other countries, 22% are from out of state, 2% African American, 1% Asian American or Pacific Islander, 2% Hispanic American, 0.3% Native American, 1% international, 3% transferred in, 55% live on campus. *Retention:* 73% of 2002 full-time freshmen returned.

Freshmen *Admission:* 1,553 applied, 1,236 admitted, 339 enrolled. *Average high school GPA:* 3.20. *Test scores:* SAT verbal scores over 500: 85%; SAT math scores over 500: 81%; ACT scores over 18: 87%; SAT verbal scores over 600: 41%; SAT math scores over 600: 44%; ACT scores over 24: 32%; SAT verbal scores over 700: 16%; SAT math scores over 700: 20%; ACT scores over 30: 14%.

Faculty *Total:* 117, 68% full-time, 56% with terminal degrees. *Student/faculty ratio:* 13:1.

Majors Accounting; advertising; art; art history, criticism and conservation; art teacher education; biology/biological sciences; biology teacher education; biopsychology; broadcast journalism; business administration and management; business teacher education; chemistry; chemistry teacher education; communication/speech communication and rhetoric; communications technology; computer and information sciences; computer science; corrections and criminal justice related; creative writing; drama and dance teacher education; dramatic/theatre arts; early childhood education; economics; education; education (K-12); elementary education; English; English/language arts teacher education; foreign languages and literatures; foreign language teacher education; German; health and physical education; health/health care administration; history; history teacher education; human resources management; human services; interdisciplinary studies; international relations and affairs; journalism; kinesiology and exercise science; liberal arts and sciences/liberal studies; literature; marketing/marketing management; mass communication/media; mathematics; mathematics teacher education; modern languages; multi-/interdisciplinary studies related; music; music history, literature, and theory; music pedagogy; music performance; music teacher education; parks, recreation and leisure facilities management; philosophy; physical education teaching and coaching; physics; physics teacher education; piano and organ; political science and government; pre-dentistry studies; pre-law studies; pre-medical studies; pre-veterinary studies; psychology; public relations/image management; radio and television; religious studies; science teacher education; secondary education; social science teacher education; social studies teacher education; sociology; Spanish; special education; speech and rhetoric; speech teacher education; speech/theater education; sport and fitness administration; violin, viola, guitar and other stringed instruments; voice and opera.

Academic Programs *Special study options:* adult/continuing education programs, advanced placement credit, double majors, independent study, internships, off-campus study, part-time degree program, services for LD students, student-designed majors, study abroad, summer session for credit. *Unusual degree programs:* 3-2 engineering with Columbia University, Georgia Institute of Technology, Washington University in St. Louis, University of Colorado at Boulder, Colorado State University; occupational therapy with Washington University in St. Louis, Boston University.

Library Perkins Library with 101,000 titles, 607 serial subscriptions, 714 audiovisual materials, an OPAC, a Web page.

Computers on Campus 168 computers available on campus for general student use. A campuswide network can be accessed from student residence rooms and from off campus that provide access to e-mail. Internet access, at least one staffed computer lab available. Computer purchase or lease plan available.

Student Life *Housing:* on-campus residence required through junior year. *Options:* coed, men-only, women-only. Campus housing is university owned. Freshman campus housing is guaranteed. *Activities and organizations:* drama/theater group, student-run newspaper, radio and television station, choral group, marching band, Student Association, Student Alumni Ambassadors, Fellowship of Christian Athletes, Phi Mu Alpha Sinfonia, Hastings College Singers. *Campus security:* 24-hour emergency response devices, student patrols, late-night transport/escort service, controlled dormitory access, security cameras at entrances and parking lots. *Student services:* health clinic, personal/psychological counseling.

Athletics Member NAIA. *Intercollegiate sports:* baseball M(s), basketball M(s)/W(s), cross-country running M(s)/W(s), football M(s), golf M(s)/W(s), soccer M(s)/W(s), softball W(s), tennis M(s)/W(s), track and field M(s)/W(s), volleyball W(s). *Intramural sports:* basketball M/W, bowling M/W, football M/W, racquetball M/W, softball M/W, table tennis M/W, ultimate Frisbee M/W, volleyball M/W.

Standardized Tests *Required:* SAT I or ACT (for admission).

Costs (2003–04) *Comprehensive fee:* $19,928 includes full-time tuition ($14,782), mandatory fees ($616), and room and board ($4530). Full-time tuition and fees vary according to degree level and program. Part-time tuition: $612 per semester hour. Part-time tuition and fees vary according to course load, degree level, and program. *Required fees:* $162 per term part-time. *College room only:* $1910. Room and board charges vary according to board plan. *Payment plans:* installment, deferred payment. *Waivers:* adult students and employees or children of employees.

Financial Aid Of all full-time matriculated undergraduates who enrolled in 2003, 909 applied for aid, 799 were judged to have need, 212 had their need fully met. In 2003, 261 non-need-based awards were made. *Average percent of need met:* 78%. *Average financial aid package:* $11,464. *Average need-based loan:* $3924. *Average need-based gift aid:* $8160. *Average non-need-based aid:* $7174. *Average indebtedness upon graduation:* $13,116. *Financial aid deadline:* 9/1.

Applying *Options:* common application. *Application fee:* $20. *Required:* high school transcript, minimum 2.0 GPA, counselor's recommendation. *Required for some:* essay or personal statement, 2 letters of recommendation, interview. *Application deadlines:* 8/1 (freshmen), 8/1 (transfers). *Notification:* continuous (freshmen), continuous (transfers).

Admissions Contact Ms. Mary Molliconi, Director of Admissions, Hastings College, 800 Turner Avenue, Hastings, NE 68901-7696. *Phone:* 402-461-7320. *Toll-free phone:* 800-532-7642. *Fax:* 402-461-7490. *E-mail:* mmolliconi@hastings.edu.

MIDLAND LUTHERAN COLLEGE

Fremont, Nebraska

- **Independent Lutheran** 4-year, founded 1883
- **Calendar** 4-1-4
- **Degrees** associate and bachelor's
- **Small-town** 27-acre campus with easy access to Omaha
- **Endowment** $28.9 million
- **Coed**
- **Moderately difficult** entrance level

Faculty *Student/faculty ratio:* 15:1.

Student Life *Campus security:* 24-hour emergency response devices, student patrols, late-night transport/escort service, controlled dormitory access.

Athletics Member NAIA.

Standardized Tests *Required:* SAT I or ACT (for admission).

Costs (2003–04) *Comprehensive fee:* $20,730 includes full-time tuition ($16,310) and room and board ($4420). *College room only:* $1950.

Financial Aid Of all full-time matriculated undergraduates who enrolled in 2003, 850 applied for aid, 789 were judged to have need, 338 had their need fully met. 212 Federal Work-Study jobs (averaging $1006). 108 state and other part-time jobs (averaging $1738). In 2003, 134. *Average percent of need met:* 91. *Average financial aid package:* $14,166. *Average need-based loan:* $4433. *Average need-based gift aid:* $10,191. *Average non-need-based aid:* $8994. *Average indebtedness upon graduation:* $18,915.

Applying *Options:* electronic application, early admission. *Application fee:* $30. *Required:* high school transcript. *Required for some:* interview. *Recommended:* essay or personal statement, minimum 3.0 GPA, letters of recommendation.

Admissions Contact Ms. Stacy Poggendorf, Assistant Vice President for Admissions, Midland Lutheran College, Admissions Office, Fremont, NE 68025-4200. *Phone:* 402-941-6508. *Toll-free phone:* 800-642-8382 Ext. 6501. *Fax:* 402-941-6513. *E-mail:* admissions@admin.mlc.edu.

NEBRASKA CHRISTIAN COLLEGE

Norfolk, Nebraska

- **Independent** 4-year, founded 1944, affiliated with Christian Churches and Churches of Christ
- **Calendar** semesters
- **Degrees** associate and bachelor's
- **Small-town** 85-acre campus
- **Endowment** $324,000
- **Coed**
- **Minimally difficult** entrance level

Faculty *Student/faculty ratio:* 17:1.

Athletics Member NCCAA.

Standardized Tests *Required:* ACT (for admission).

Costs (2003–04) *Comprehensive fee:* $9660 includes full-time tuition ($5380), mandatory fees ($580), and room and board ($3700). Part-time tuition: $180 per credit.

Financial Aid Of all full-time matriculated undergraduates who enrolled in 2003, 146 applied for aid, 134 were judged to have need. 15 Federal Work-Study jobs (averaging $970). In 2003, 10. *Average need-based loan:* $3585. *Average non-need-based aid:* $2535. *Average indebtedness upon graduation:* $11,868.

Applying *Application fee:* $25. *Required:* high school transcript, 2 letters of recommendation. *Required for some:* interview.

Admissions Contact Mr. Jason Epperson, Associate Director of Admissions, Nebraska Christian College, 1800 Syracuse Avenue, Norfolk, NE 68701. *Phone:* 402-378-5000 Ext. 413. *Fax:* 402-379-5100. *E-mail:* admissions@nechristian.edu.

NEBRASKA METHODIST COLLEGE

Omaha, Nebraska

- **Independent** comprehensive, founded 1891, affiliated with United Methodist Church
- **Calendar** semesters
- **Degrees** certificates, associate, bachelor's, master's, and post-master's certificates
- **Urban** 5-acre campus
- **Endowment** $30.2 million
- **Coed, primarily women,** 390 undergraduate students, 78% full-time, 87% women, 13% men
- **Moderately difficult** entrance level, 81% of applicants were admitted

Undergraduates 304 full-time, 86 part-time. Students come from 3 states and territories, 2 other countries, 20% are from out of state, 4% African American, 0.3% Asian American or Pacific Islander, 0.3% Native American, 0.5% international, 16% transferred in, 20% live on campus. *Retention:* 74% of 2002 full-time freshmen returned.

Freshmen *Admission:* 85 applied, 69 admitted, 37 enrolled. *Average high school GPA:* 3.51. *Test scores:* ACT scores over 18: 90%; ACT scores over 24: 20%.

Faculty *Total:* 57, 58% full-time, 23% with terminal degrees. *Student/faculty ratio:* 10:1.

Majors Cardiovascular technology; diagnostic medical sonography and ultrasound technology; emergency medical technology (EMT paramedic); nursing (registered nurse training); radiologic technology/science; respiratory care therapy.

Academic Programs *Special study options:* academic remediation for entering students, accelerated degree program, advanced placement credit, distance learning, independent study, internships, services for LD students, summer session for credit. *ROTC:* Army (c).

Library John Moritz Library plus 1 other with 8,656 titles, 475 serial subscriptions, 985 audiovisual materials, a Web page.

Computers on Campus 45 computers available on campus for general student use. A campuswide network can be accessed. Internet access, at least one staffed computer lab available.

Student Life *Housing options:* coed. Campus housing is university owned. Freshman applicants given priority for college housing. *Activities and organizations:* Student Senate, Student Nurses Association, Methodist Allied Health Student Association, Student Ambassadors, Residence Hall Council. *Campus security:* 24-hour emergency response devices, late-night transport/escort service, controlled dormitory access. *Student services:* health clinic, personal/psychological counseling.

Standardized Tests *Required:* SAT I or ACT (for admission).

Costs (2003–04) *Tuition:* $9600 full-time, $320 per credit hour part-time. *Required fees:* $600 full-time, $20 per credit hour part-time, $10 per term part-time. *Room only:* $1700. Room and board charges vary according to housing facility and location. *Payment plan:* installment. *Waivers:* employees or children of employees.

Financial Aid Of all full-time matriculated undergraduates who enrolled in 2003, 185 applied for aid, 154 were judged to have need, 40 had their need fully met. 3 state and other part-time jobs (averaging $1600). In 2003, 53 non-need-based awards were made. *Average percent of need met:* 75%. *Average financial aid package:* $8229. *Average need-based loan:* $3865. *Average need-based gift aid:* $5088. *Average non-need-based aid:* $7605. *Average indebtedness upon graduation:* $24,901.

Applying *Options:* electronic application, deferred entrance. *Application fee:* $25. *Required:* essay or personal statement, high school transcript, minimum 2.0 GPA, 3 letters of recommendation, interview. *Application deadlines:* 4/1 (freshmen), 4/1 (transfers). *Notification:* 4/15 (freshmen), 4/15 (transfers).

Nebraska Methodist College (continued)

Admissions Contact Ms. Deann Sterner, Director of Admissions, Nebraska Methodist College, Omaha, NE 68114. *Phone:* 402-354-4922. *Toll-free phone:* 800-335-5510. *Fax:* 402-354-8875. *E-mail:* dsterne@methodistcollege.edu.

NEBRASKA WESLEYAN UNIVERSITY
Lincoln, Nebraska

- **Independent United Methodist** comprehensive, founded 1887
- **Calendar** semesters
- **Degrees** certificates, bachelor's, and master's
- **Suburban** 50-acre campus with easy access to Omaha
- **Endowment** $28.7 million
- **Coed,** 1,687 undergraduate students, 91% full-time, 56% women, 44% men
- **Moderately difficult** entrance level, 93% of applicants were admitted

Undergraduates 1,530 full-time, 157 part-time. Students come from 25 states and territories, 8 other countries, 6% are from out of state, 1% African American, 2% Asian American or Pacific Islander, 2% Hispanic American, 0.3% Native American, 0.8% international, 5% transferred in, 61% live on campus. *Retention:* 82% of 2002 full-time freshmen returned.

Freshmen *Admission:* 1,312 applied, 1,214 admitted, 420 enrolled. *Test scores:* ACT scores over 18: 98%; ACT scores over 24: 59%; ACT scores over 30: 6%.

Faculty *Total:* 168, 60% full-time, 63% with terminal degrees. *Student/faculty ratio:* 14:1.

Majors Accounting; art; athletic training; biochemistry; biochemistry/biophysics and molecular biology; biology/biological sciences; biopsychology; business administration and management; business, management, and marketing related; chemistry; communication/speech communication and rhetoric; computer science; dramatic/theatre arts; dramatic/theatre arts and stagecraft related; economics; elementary education; English; English/language arts teacher education; French; German; health and physical education; history; industrial and organizational psychology; information science/studies; interdisciplinary studies; international business/trade/commerce; international/global studies; kinesiology and exercise science; mathematics; middle school education; music; music performance; music teacher education; nursing administration; nursing (registered nurse training); philosophy; physical education teaching and coaching; physics; political communication; political science and government; psychology; religious studies; science teacher education; social science teacher education; social work; sociology; Spanish; special education; speech and rhetoric; sport and fitness administration; web page, digital/multimedia and information resources design; women's studies.

Academic Programs *Special study options:* adult/continuing education programs, advanced placement credit, double majors, independent study, internships, off-campus study, part-time degree program, services for LD students, study abroad, summer session for credit. *ROTC:* Army (c), Air Force (c). *Unusual degree programs:* 3-2 engineering with Washington University in St. Louis, Columbia University, University of Nebraska-Lincoln; physical therapy with University of Nebraska Medical Center, Mayo Medical School.

Library Cochrane Woods Library with 178,531 titles, 743 serial subscriptions, 7,951 audiovisual materials, an OPAC, a Web page.

Computers on Campus 336 computers available on campus for general student use. A campuswide network can be accessed from student residence rooms and from off campus. Internet access, at least one staffed computer lab available. Computer purchase or lease plan available.

Student Life *Housing:* on-campus residence required through junior year. *Options:* coed, women-only. Campus housing is university owned and is provided by a third party. Freshman campus housing is guaranteed. *Activities and organizations:* drama/theater group, student-run newspaper, choral group, Student Affairs Senate, Union programs, Ambassadors, FCA, national fraternities, national sororities. *Campus security:* 24-hour emergency response devices, late-night transport/escort service, controlled dormitory access. *Student services:* health clinic, personal/psychological counseling, women's center.

Athletics Member NCAA, NAIA. All NCAA Division III. *Intercollegiate sports:* baseball M, basketball M/W, cheerleading W, cross-country running M/W, football M, golf M/W, soccer M/W, softball W, tennis M/W, track and field M/W, volleyball W. *Intramural sports:* basketball M/W, football M/W, racquetball M/W, soccer M/W, softball M/W, ultimate Frisbee M/W, volleyball M/W.

Standardized Tests *Required:* SAT I or ACT (for admission).

Costs (2003–04) *Comprehensive fee:* $20,960 includes full-time tuition ($16,140), mandatory fees ($290), and room and board ($4530). Part-time tuition: $609 per hour. Part-time tuition and fees vary according to class time and course load. *Room and board:* Room and board charges vary according to board plan and housing facility. *Payment plans:* installment, deferred payment. *Waivers:* adult students, senior citizens, and employees or children of employees.

Financial Aid Of all full-time matriculated undergraduates who enrolled in 2003, 1,221 applied for aid, 1,102 were judged to have need, 189 had their need fully met. In 2003, 323 non-need-based awards were made. *Average percent of need met:* 76%. *Average financial aid package:* $12,708. *Average need-based loan:* $4079. *Average need-based gift aid:* $8552. *Average non-need-based aid:* $4938. *Average indebtedness upon graduation:* $16,698.

Applying *Options:* common application, electronic application, early admission, early decision, deferred entrance. *Application fee:* $20. *Required:* minimum 2.0 GPA. *Required for some:* essay or personal statement, resume of activities. *Recommended:* interview. *Application deadlines:* 8/15 (freshmen), 8/15 (transfers). *Early decision:* 11/15. *Notification:* continuous (freshmen), 12/15 (early decision).

Admissions Contact Ms. Patty Karthauser, Vice President for Enrollment and Marketing, Nebraska Wesleyan University, 5000 Saint Paul Avenue, Lincoln, NE 68504. *Phone:* 402-465-2218. *Toll-free phone:* 800-541-3818. *Fax:* 402-465-2179. *E-mail:* admissions@nebrwesleyan.edu.

PERU STATE COLLEGE
Peru, Nebraska

- **State-supported** comprehensive, founded 1867, part of Nebraska State College System
- **Calendar** semesters
- **Degrees** certificates, bachelor's, and master's
- **Rural** 104-acre campus
- **Coed**
- **Noncompetitive** entrance level

Faculty *Student/faculty ratio:* 17:1.

Student Life *Campus security:* 24-hour patrols.

Athletics Member NAIA.

Standardized Tests *Required for some:* SAT I or ACT (for admission).

Costs (2003–04) *Tuition:* state resident $2610 full-time; nonresident $5220 full-time. Full-time tuition and fees vary according to course load, location, and reciprocity agreements. Part-time tuition and fees vary according to course load, location, and reciprocity agreements. *Required fees:* $674 full-time. *Room and board:* $4911; room only: $2361. Room and board charges vary according to board plan and housing facility.

Applying *Options:* common application, early admission, deferred entrance. *Required:* high school transcript. *Required for some:* minimum 2.0 GPA, letters of recommendation.

Admissions Contact Ms. Janelle Moran, Director of Recruitment and Admissions, Peru State College, PO Box 10, Peru, NE 68421. *Phone:* 402-872-2221. *Toll-free phone:* 800-742-4412. *Fax:* 402-872-2296. *E-mail:* jmoran@oakmail.peru.edu.

■ *See page 2168 for a narrative description.*

UNION COLLEGE
Lincoln, Nebraska

- **Independent Seventh-day Adventist** 4-year, founded 1891
- **Calendar** semesters
- **Degrees** associate and bachelor's
- **Suburban** 26-acre campus with easy access to Omaha
- **Endowment** $8.6 million
- **Coed,** 903 undergraduate students, 84% full-time, 59% women, 41% men
- **Moderately difficult** entrance level, 49% of applicants were admitted

Undergraduates 758 full-time, 145 part-time. Students come from 41 states and territories, 34 other countries, 77% are from out of state, 2% African American, 0.6% Asian American or Pacific Islander, 4% Hispanic American, 0.7% Native American, 12% international, 8% transferred in, 69% live on campus. *Retention:* 67% of 2002 full-time freshmen returned.

Freshmen *Admission:* 549 applied, 267 admitted, 165 enrolled. *Average high school GPA:* 3.27. *Test scores:* ACT scores over 18: 83%; ACT scores over 24: 32%; ACT scores over 30: 3%.

Faculty *Total:* 92, 57% full-time. *Student/faculty ratio:* 14:1.

Majors Accounting; art; art teacher education; biochemistry; biology/biological sciences; biology teacher education; business administration and management; business teacher education; chemistry; chemistry teacher education; clinical laboratory science/medical technology; commercial and advertising art; computer science; computer teacher education; education; elementary education; engineering; English; English/language arts teacher education; entrepreneurship; fine/studio arts; French; German; graphic design; health/medical preparatory programs related; health science; history; history teacher education; information science/studies; international relations and affairs; journalism; kinesiology and exercise science; mathematics; mathematics teacher education; music; music performance; music teacher education; nursing (registered nurse training); pastoral studies/counseling; physical education teaching and coaching; physician assistant; physics; physics teacher education; psychology; public relations/image management; religious education; religious studies; secondary education; social sciences; social science teacher education; social work; Spanish; sport and fitness administration; theology.

Academic Programs *Special study options:* accelerated degree program, adult/continuing education programs, advanced placement credit, cooperative education, double majors, English as a second language, honors programs, independent study, internships, off-campus study, part-time degree program, services for LD students, student-designed majors, study abroad, summer session for credit.

Library Ella Johnson Crandall Library with 147,813 titles, 1,357 serial subscriptions, 3,278 audiovisual materials, an OPAC, a Web page.

Computers on Campus 520 computers available on campus for general student use. A campuswide network can be accessed from student residence rooms and from off campus. Internet access, at least one staffed computer lab available. Computer purchase or lease plan available.

Student Life *Housing:* on-campus residence required through senior year. *Options:* men-only, women-only. Campus housing is university owned. Freshman applicants given priority for college housing. *Activities and organizations:* drama/theater group, student-run newspaper, choral group. *Campus security:* 24-hour emergency response devices, student patrols, late-night transport/escort service. *Student services:* health clinic, personal/psychological counseling.

Athletics *Intercollegiate sports:* basketball M/W, volleyball W. *Intramural sports:* badminton M/W, baseball M/W, basketball M/W, football M/W, golf M/W, gymnastics M/W, racquetball M/W, sailing M/W, soccer M/W, softball M/W, swimming M/W, tennis M/W, volleyball M/W.

Standardized Tests *Required:* ACT (for admission).

Costs (2003–04) *Comprehensive fee:* $16,508 includes full-time tuition ($12,750), mandatory fees ($128), and room and board ($3630). Part-time tuition: $532 per semester hour. *College room only:* $2490. *Payment plans:* tuition prepayment, installment. *Waivers:* employees or children of employees.

Financial Aid Of all full-time matriculated undergraduates who enrolled in 2002, 558 applied for aid, 558 were judged to have need, 109 had their need fully met. 172 Federal Work-Study jobs (averaging $1663). In 2002, 323 non-need-based awards were made. *Average percent of need met:* 44%. *Average financial aid package:* $8376. *Average need-based loan:* $4807. *Average need-based gift aid:* $5334. *Average non-need-based aid:* $3162. *Average indebtedness upon graduation:* $23,379.

Applying *Options:* common application, electronic application. *Required:* high school transcript, minimum 2.5 GPA, 3 letters of recommendation. *Required for some:* interview. *Recommended:* essay or personal statement. *Application deadline:* rolling (freshmen), rolling (transfers). *Notification:* continuous (freshmen), continuous (transfers).

Admissions Contact Huda McClelland, Director of Admissions, Union College, 3800 South 48th Street, Lincoln, NE 68506. *Phone:* 402-486-2504. *Toll-free phone:* 800-228-4600. *Fax:* 402-486-2895. *E-mail:* ucenrol@ucollege.edu.

■ *See page 2542 for a narrative description.*

UNIVERSITY OF NEBRASKA AT KEARNEY
Kearney, Nebraska

- **State-supported** comprehensive, founded 1903, part of University of Nebraska System
- **Calendar** semesters
- **Degrees** bachelor's and master's
- **Small-town** 235-acre campus
- **Coed**
- **Moderately difficult** entrance level

Faculty *Student/faculty ratio:* 16:1.

Student Life *Campus security:* 24-hour emergency response devices and patrols, late-night transport/escort service.

Athletics Member NCAA. All Division II except softball (Division III).

Standardized Tests *Required:* SAT I or ACT (for admission). *Recommended:* ACT (for admission).

Costs (2003–04) *Tuition:* state resident $3120 full-time; nonresident $6382 full-time. *Required fees:* $765 full-time. *Room and board:* $4436.

Financial Aid Of all full-time matriculated undergraduates who enrolled in 2002, 3,726 applied for aid, 2,810 were judged to have need, 1,271 had their need fully met. 325 Federal Work-Study jobs (averaging $1088). In 2002, 194. *Average percent of need met:* 77. *Average financial aid package:* $6035. *Average need-based loan:* $3084. *Average need-based gift aid:* $3085. *Average non-need-based aid:* $931. *Average indebtedness upon graduation:* $14,361.

Applying *Options:* electronic application. *Application fee:* $45. *Required:* high school transcript. *Required for some:* 3 letters of recommendation.

Admissions Contact Mr. John Kundel, Director of Admissions, University of Nebraska at Kearney, 905 West 25th Street, Kearney, NE 68849-0001. *Phone:* 308-865-8702. *Toll-free phone:* 800-532-7639. *Fax:* 308-865-8987. *E-mail:* admissionsug@unk.edu.

UNIVERSITY OF NEBRASKA AT OMAHA
Omaha, Nebraska

- **State-supported** university, founded 1908, part of University of Nebraska System
- **Calendar** semesters
- **Degrees** bachelor's, master's, doctoral, post-master's, and postbachelor's certificates
- **Urban** 158-acre campus
- **Endowment** $5.6 million
- **Coed,** 11,102 undergraduate students, 73% full-time, 53% women, 47% men
- **Minimally difficult** entrance level, 85% of applicants were admitted

Undergraduates 8,120 full-time, 2,982 part-time. Students come from 48 states and territories, 70 other countries, 11% are from out of state, 6% African American, 3% Asian American or Pacific Islander, 3% Hispanic American, 0.4% Native American, 2% international, 8% transferred in, 10% live on campus. *Retention:* 73% of 2002 full-time freshmen returned.

Freshmen *Admission:* 3,994 applied, 3,383 admitted, 1,537 enrolled. *Average high school GPA:* 3.33. *Test scores:* SAT verbal scores over 500: 63%; SAT math scores over 500: 58%; ACT scores over 18: 93%; SAT verbal scores over 600: 25%; SAT math scores over 600: 25%; ACT scores over 24: 42%; SAT verbal scores over 700: 5%; SAT math scores over 700: 5%; ACT scores over 30: 5%.

Faculty *Total:* 781, 60% full-time, 61% with terminal degrees. *Student/faculty ratio:* 18:1.

Majors Accounting; aeronautics/aviation/aerospace science and technology; African-American/Black studies; architectural engineering; art; art history, criticism and conservation; banking and financial support services; biology/biological sciences; biotechnology; broadcast journalism; business administration and management; business/commerce; business/managerial economics; chemistry; civil engineering; communication/speech communication and rhetoric; community health services counseling; computer engineering; computer science; construction engineering technology; creative writing; criminal justice/safety; dramatic/theatre arts; electrical, electronics and communications engineering; elementary education; engineering physics; English; environmental studies; family and consumer sciences/human sciences; family and consumer sciences/human sciences communication; family resource management; finance; fine/studio arts; French; general studies; geography; geology/earth science; German; gerontology; health and physical education; history; human resources management; industrial technology; international/global studies; journalism; Latin American studies; library science; management information systems; manufacturing technology; marketing/marketing management; mathematics; multi-/interdisciplinary studies related; music; music performance; music teacher education; music theory and composition; natural sciences; parks, recreation and leisure; philosophy; physical education teaching and coaching; physics; political science and government; psychology; real estate; religious studies; secondary education; social work; sociology; Spanish; special education (speech or language impaired); speech and rhetoric; voice and opera; women's studies.

Academic Programs *Special study options:* adult/continuing education programs, advanced placement credit, cooperative education, distance learning, double majors, English as a second language, honors programs, internships, off-campus study, part-time degree program, services for LD students, student-designed majors, study abroad, summer session for credit. *ROTC:* Army (c), Air Force (b).

Library University Library with 750,000 titles, 3,000 serial subscriptions, 7,000 audiovisual materials, a Web page.

Computers on Campus 64 computers available on campus for general student use. A campuswide network can be accessed from student residence rooms and from off campus. Internet access, online (class) registration, at least one staffed computer lab available.

Student Life *Housing options:* coed. Campus housing is leased by the school. *Activities and organizations:* drama/theater group, student-run newspaper, radio and television station, choral group, marching band, Student Programming Organization, fraternities/sororities, national fraternities, national sororities. *Campus security:* 24-hour emergency response devices and patrols, late-night transport/escort service, controlled dormitory access. *Student services:* health clinic, personal/psychological counseling, women's center, legal services.

Athletics Member NCAA. All Division II except ice hockey (Division I). *Intercollegiate sports:* baseball M(s), basketball M(s)/W(s), cross-country running W(s), football M(s), golf W, ice hockey M(s), soccer W, softball W(s), swimming W, tennis W, volleyball W(s), wrestling M(s). *Intramural sports:*

University of Nebraska at Omaha (continued)
basketball M/W, bowling M/W, football M, golf M/W, racquetball M/W, soccer M/W, softball M/W, squash M/W, swimming M/W, tennis M/W, volleyball M/W, wrestling M.

Standardized Tests *Required:* SAT I or ACT (for admission).

Costs (2003–04) *Tuition:* state resident $3518 full-time, $117 per semester hour part-time; nonresident $10,358 full-time, $345 per semester hour part-time. Full-time tuition and fees vary according to course load and student level. Part-time tuition and fees vary according to course load and student level. *Required fees:* $564 full-time, $16 per semester hour part-time, $72 per term part-time. *Room and board:* $3998; room only: $3078. Room and board charges vary according to board plan. *Payment plans:* installment, deferred payment. *Waivers:* employees or children of employees.

Financial Aid Of all full-time matriculated undergraduates who enrolled in 2002, 5,328 applied for aid, 3,827 were judged to have need. 373 Federal Work-Study jobs (averaging $1812). *Average indebtedness upon graduation:* $16,900.

Applying *Options:* deferred entrance. *Application fee:* $45. *Required:* high school transcript, minimum ACT score of 20 or rank in upper 50% of high school class. *Application deadlines:* 8/1 (freshmen), 8/1 (transfers). *Notification:* continuous (freshmen), continuous (transfers).

Admissions Contact Ms. Jolene Adams, Associate Director of Admissions, University of Nebraska at Omaha, 6001 Dodge Street, Omaha, NE 68182. *Phone:* 402-554-2416. *Toll-free phone:* 800-858-8648. *Fax:* 402-554-3472.

UNIVERSITY OF NEBRASKA–LINCOLN
Lincoln, Nebraska

- **State-supported** university, founded 1869, part of University of Nebraska System
- **Calendar** semesters
- **Degrees** associate, bachelor's, master's, doctoral, first professional, and post-master's certificates
- **Urban** 623-acre campus with easy access to Omaha
- **Endowment** $137.2 million
- **Coed,** 17,851 undergraduate students, 91% full-time, 48% women, 52% men
- **Moderately difficult** entrance level, 76% of applicants were admitted

Undergraduates 16,219 full-time, 1,632 part-time. Students come from 51 states and territories, 80 other countries, 12% are from out of state, 2% African American, 2% Asian American or Pacific Islander, 2% Hispanic American, 0.5% Native American, 3% international, 4% transferred in, 26% live on campus. *Retention:* 80% of 2002 full-time freshmen returned.

Freshmen *Admission:* 7,375 applied, 5,586 admitted, 3,679 enrolled. *Test scores:* SAT verbal scores over 500: 82%; SAT math scores over 500: 84%; ACT scores over 18: 97%; SAT verbal scores over 600: 45%; SAT math scores over 600: 51%; ACT scores over 24: 55%; SAT verbal scores over 700: 14%; SAT math scores over 700: 16%; ACT scores over 30: 13%.

Faculty *Total:* 1,022, 99% full-time, 96% with terminal degrees. *Student/faculty ratio:* 17:1.

Majors Accounting; actuarial science; advertising; agricultural/biological engineering and bioengineering; agricultural business and management; agricultural communication/journalism; agricultural economics; agricultural mechanization; agricultural teacher education; agriculture; agronomy and crop science; ancient/classical Greek; animal sciences; anthropology; apparel and textiles; architectural engineering; architecture; art history, criticism and conservation; art teacher education; athletic training; atmospheric sciences and meteorology; biochemistry; biology/biological sciences; biology teacher education; biomedical/medical engineering; broadcast journalism; business administration and management; business/managerial economics; business teacher education; chemical engineering; chemistry; chemistry teacher education; civil engineering; classics and languages, literatures and linguistics; communication/speech communication and rhetoric; community health services counseling; computer and information sciences; computer engineering; computer teacher education; construction engineering technology; dance; dramatic/theatre arts; economics; education (multiple levels); education (specific subject areas) related; electrical, electronic and communications engineering technology; electrical, electronics and communications engineering; elementary education; engineering related; English; English as a second/foreign language (teaching); English/language arts teacher education; environmental studies; European studies (Western); family and consumer economics related; film/cinema studies; finance; fine/studio arts; fire protection and safety technology; food science; foods, nutrition, and wellness; foreign language teacher education; French; French language teacher education; geography; geology/earth science; German; German language teacher education; health teacher education; history; history teacher education; horticultural science; housing and human environments; industrial engineering; industrial production technologies related; industrial technology; interior architecture; international business/trade/commerce; international relations and affairs; journalism related; kinesiology and exercise science; landscaping and groundskeeping; Latin; Latin American studies; law and legal studies related; legal professions and studies related; liberal arts and sciences and humanities related; liberal arts and sciences/liberal studies; management science; marketing/marketing management; mathematics; mathematics teacher education; mechanical engineering; medieval and Renaissance studies; middle school education; music; music teacher education; natural resources/conservation; natural resources management and policy; office management; philosophy; physical education teaching and coaching; physics; physics teacher education; plant protection and integrated pest management; political science and government; pre-dentistry studies; pre-medical studies; pre-pharmacy studies; pre-veterinary studies; psychology; range science and management; reading teacher education; Russian; sales and marketing/marketing and distribution teacher education; science teacher education; social science teacher education; sociology; soil science and agronomy; Spanish; Spanish language teacher education; special education (hearing impaired); special education related; speech-language pathology; technology/industrial arts teacher education; trade and industrial teacher education; veterinary/animal health technology; women's studies.

Academic Programs *Special study options:* accelerated degree program, adult/continuing education programs, advanced placement credit, cooperative education, distance learning, double majors, English as a second language, honors programs, independent study, internships, off-campus study, part-time degree program, services for LD students, student-designed majors, study abroad, summer session for credit. *ROTC:* Army (b), Navy (b), Air Force (b).

Library Love Memorial Library plus 10 others with 1.2 million titles, 21,309 serial subscriptions, 73,405 audiovisual materials, an OPAC, a Web page.

Computers on Campus 600 computers available on campus for general student use. A campuswide network can be accessed from student residence rooms and from off campus. Internet access, online (class) registration, at least one staffed computer lab available. Computer purchase or lease plan available.

Student Life *Housing:* on-campus residence required for freshman year. *Options:* coed, men-only, women-only, cooperative, disabled students. Campus housing is university owned. Freshman campus housing is guaranteed. *Activities and organizations:* drama/theater group, student-run newspaper, radio station, choral group, marching band, Student Alumni Association, University Ambassadors, University Program Council, Golden Key, national fraternities, national sororities. *Campus security:* 24-hour emergency response devices and patrols, student patrols, late-night transport/escort service, controlled dormitory access. *Student services:* health clinic, personal/psychological counseling, women's center, legal services.

Athletics Member NCAA. All Division I except football (Division I-A). *Intercollegiate sports:* baseball M(s), basketball M(s)/W(s), bowling M/W, cheerleading M/W, crew M(c)/W(c), cross-country running M(s)/W(s), fencing M(c)/W(c), golf M(s)/W(s), gymnastics M(s)/W(s), riflery W(s), soccer W(s), softball W(s), swimming W(s), tennis M(s)/W(s), track and field M(s)/W(s), volleyball W(s), wrestling M(s). *Intramural sports:* archery M/W, badminton M/W, basketball M/W, bowling M/W, crew M/W, cross-country running M/W, fencing M/W, football M/W, golf M/W, ice hockey M(c)/W(c), racquetball M/W, riflery M/W, rugby M(c)/W(c), soccer M/W, softball M/W, squash M/W, swimming W, table tennis M/W, tennis M/W, track and field M/W, ultimate Frisbee M/W, volleyball M/W, water polo M/W, weight lifting M/W, wrestling M/W.

Standardized Tests *Required:* SAT I or ACT (for admission).

Costs (2003–04) *Tuition:* state resident $3848 full-time, $128 per credit hour part-time; nonresident $11,430 full-time, $381 per credit hour part-time. Full-time tuition and fees vary according to course load. Part-time tuition and fees vary according to course load. *Required fees:* $863 full-time, $6 per credit hour part-time, $175 per term part-time. *Room and board:* $5204; room only: $2404. Room and board charges vary according to board plan and housing facility. *Waivers:* employees or children of employees.

Financial Aid Of all full-time matriculated undergraduates who enrolled in 2002, 10,036 applied for aid, 7,198 were judged to have need, 2,125 had their need fully met. 1,364 Federal Work-Study jobs (averaging $1881). In 2002, 977 non-need-based awards were made. *Average percent of need met:* 76%. *Average financial aid package:* $6947. *Average need-based loan:* $3680. *Average need-based gift aid:* $4142. *Average non-need-based aid:* $3102. *Average indebtedness upon graduation:* $16,376.

Applying *Options:* electronic application. *Application fee:* $25. *Required:* high school transcript. *Required for some:* rank in upper 50% of high school class. *Application deadlines:* 6/30 (freshmen), 6/30 (transfers). *Notification:* continuous (transfers).

Admissions Contact Pat McBride, Director, New Student Enrollment, University of Nebraska–Lincoln, 313 North 13th Street, Ross Van Brunt Building, Lincoln, NE 68588-0256. *Phone:* 402-472-8141. *Toll-free phone:* 800-742-8800. *Fax:* 402-472-0670. *E-mail:* nuhusker@unl.edu.

■ *See page 2660 for a narrative description.*

UNIVERSITY OF NEBRASKA MEDICAL CENTER

Omaha, Nebraska

- **State-supported** upper-level, founded 1869, part of University of Nebraska System
- **Calendar** semesters
- **Degrees** certificates, bachelor's, master's, doctoral, first professional, post-master's, postbachelor's, and first professional certificates
- **Urban** 51-acre campus
- **Endowment** $6.9 million
- **Coed,** 742 undergraduate students, 89% full-time, 93% women, 7% men
- **Moderately difficult** entrance level, 33% of applicants were admitted

Undergraduates 658 full-time, 84 part-time. Students come from 14 states and territories, 6 other countries, 9% are from out of state, 2% African American, 0.8% Asian American or Pacific Islander, 2% Hispanic American, 0.1% Native American, 0.9% international, 29% transferred in.

Faculty *Total:* 883, 80% full-time, 71% with terminal degrees.

Majors Clinical laboratory science/medical technology; dental hygiene; diagnostic medical sonography and ultrasound technology; medical radiologic technology; nuclear medical technology; nursing (registered nurse training); radiologic technology/science.

Academic Programs *Special study options:* distance learning, honors programs, internships, off-campus study, part-time degree program, services for LD students, summer session for credit. *ROTC:* Army (c), Air Force (c).

Library McGoogan Medical Library plus 1 other with 247,434 titles, 1,741 serial subscriptions, 849 audiovisual materials, an OPAC, a Web page.

Computers on Campus 65 computers available on campus for general student use. A campuswide network can be accessed from off campus that provide access to various software packages. Internet access, at least one staffed computer lab available.

Student Life *Housing:* college housing not available. *Activities and organizations:* student government, Toastmasters, Student Alliance for Global Health, Christian Medical Society, Student Research Group, national fraternities, national sororities. *Campus security:* 24-hour emergency response devices and patrols, late-night transport/escort service. *Student services:* health clinic, personal/psychological counseling.

Costs (2003–04) *Tuition:* state resident $4875 full-time, $163 per semester hour part-time; nonresident $14,280 full-time, $476 per semester hour part-time. Full-time tuition and fees vary according to program. Part-time tuition and fees vary according to program. *Required fees:* $353 full-time. *Payment plan:* installment. *Waivers:* children of alumni and employees or children of employees.

Financial Aid Of all full-time matriculated undergraduates who enrolled in 2002, 774 applied for aid, 774 were judged to have need. 38 Federal Work-Study jobs (averaging $1515). *Average percent of need met:* 60%. *Average need-based loan:* $5600. *Average need-based gift aid:* $3000.

Applying *Options:* electronic application. *Application fee:* $45. *Application deadline:* rolling (transfers).

Admissions Contact Ms. Crystal Oldham, Administrative Technician, University of Nebraska Medical Center, 984265 Nebraska Medical Center, Omaha, NE 68198-4230. *Phone:* 402-559-6468. *Toll-free phone:* 800-626-8431 Ext. 6468. *Fax:* 402-559-6796. *E-mail:* thorton@unmc.edu.

WAYNE STATE COLLEGE

Wayne, Nebraska

- **State-supported** comprehensive, founded 1910, part of Nebraska State College System
- **Calendar** semesters
- **Degrees** bachelor's, master's, and post-master's certificates
- **Small-town** 128-acre campus
- **Coed,** 2,769 undergraduate students, 93% full-time, 56% women, 44% men
- **Noncompetitive** entrance level, 100% of applicants were admitted

Undergraduates 2,565 full-time, 204 part-time. Students come from 25 states and territories, 22 other countries, 15% are from out of state, 3% African American, 0.5% Asian American or Pacific Islander, 2% Hispanic American, 1% Native American, 0.8% international, 8% transferred in, 42% live on campus. *Retention:* 70% of 2002 full-time freshmen returned.

Freshmen *Admission:* 1,321 applied, 1,321 admitted, 610 enrolled. *Average high school GPA:* 3.24. *Test scores:* ACT scores over 18: 78%; ACT scores over 24: 29%; ACT scores over 30: 2%.

Faculty *Total:* 191, 66% full-time, 57% with terminal degrees. *Student/faculty ratio:* 19:1.

Majors Accounting; advertising; agricultural business and management; applied mathematics; art; biology/biological sciences; business administration and management; business/managerial economics; business teacher education; chemistry; clinical laboratory science/medical technology; commercial and advertising art; computer science; counselor education/school counseling and guidance; creative writing; criminal justice/law enforcement administration; criminal justice/police science; dramatic/theatre arts; education; elementary education; English; family and consumer economics related; family and consumer sciences/home economics teacher education; family and consumer sciences/human sciences; fashion merchandising; finance; French; geography; German; history; information science/studies; interdisciplinary studies; interior design; international business/trade/commerce; journalism; kindergarten/preschool education; kinesiology and exercise science; literature; mass communication/media; mathematics; modern languages; music; music teacher education; natural sciences; parks, recreation and leisure; physical education teaching and coaching; physical sciences; political science and government; pre-medical studies; pre-veterinary studies; psychology; public administration; science teacher education; social sciences; sociology; Spanish; special education; special products marketing; speech and rhetoric; sport and fitness administration.

Academic Programs *Special study options:* adult/continuing education programs, cooperative education, distance learning, double majors, honors programs, independent study, internships, off-campus study, part-time degree program, services for LD students, student-designed majors, summer session for credit. *ROTC:* Army (c).

Library U. S. Conn Library plus 1 other with 147,205 titles, 656 serial subscriptions, 5,300 audiovisual materials, an OPAC, a Web page.

Computers on Campus 200 computers available on campus for general student use. A campuswide network can be accessed from student residence rooms and from off campus. Internet access, online (class) registration, at least one staffed computer lab available.

Student Life *Housing:* on-campus residence required for freshman year. *Options:* coed, women-only. Campus housing is university owned. Freshman campus housing is guaranteed. *Activities and organizations:* drama/theater group, student-run newspaper, radio and television station, choral group, marching band, national fraternities, national sororities. *Campus security:* 24-hour patrols, student patrols, late-night transport/escort service, controlled dormitory access. *Student services:* health clinic, personal/psychological counseling.

Athletics Member NCAA. All Division II. *Intercollegiate sports:* baseball M(s), basketball M(s)/W(s), cross-country running M(s)/W(s), football M(s), golf M(s)/W(s), soccer M(c)/W(s), softball W(s), track and field M(s)/W(s), volleyball W(s). *Intramural sports:* archery M/W, badminton M/W, basketball M/W, bowling M/W, football M/W, golf M/W, racquetball M/W, softball M/W, swimming M/W, table tennis M/W, tennis M/W, track and field M/W, volleyball M/W, weight lifting M/W, wrestling M.

Standardized Tests *Recommended:* SAT I or ACT (for placement).

Costs (2003–04) *Tuition:* state resident $2610 full-time; nonresident $5220 full-time. *Required fees:* $822 full-time. *Room and board:* $3920; room only: $1860. Room and board charges vary according to board plan and housing facility. *Payment plan:* installment. *Waivers:* employees or children of employees.

Financial Aid Of all full-time matriculated undergraduates who enrolled in 2002, 1,963 applied for aid, 1,547 were judged to have need, 787 had their need fully met. 196 Federal Work-Study jobs (averaging $1200). *Average percent of need met:* 41%. *Average financial aid package:* $3615. *Average need-based loan:* $1598. *Average need-based gift aid:* $1371.

Applying *Options:* common application, deferred entrance. *Application fee:* $30. *Required:* high school transcript. *Application deadline:* rolling (freshmen), rolling (transfers). *Notification:* continuous (freshmen), continuous (transfers).

Admissions Contact R. Lincoln Morris, Director of Admissions, Wayne State College, 1111 Main Street, Wayne, NE 68787. *Phone:* 402-375-7234. *Toll-free phone:* 800-228-9972. *Fax:* 402-375-7204. *E-mail:* admit1@wsc.edu.

YORK COLLEGE

York, Nebraska

- **Independent** 4-year, founded 1890, affiliated with Church of Christ
- **Calendar** semesters
- **Degrees** associate and bachelor's
- **Small-town** 44-acre campus
- **Endowment** $6.2 million
- **Coed,** 461 undergraduate students, 94% full-time, 52% women, 48% men
- **Moderately difficult** entrance level, 63% of applicants were admitted

York College, founded in 1890, is a private, liberal arts college offering bachelor's degrees in 29 fields to a student body of more than 500. York is one of the most affordable Christian colleges in America and is accredited by North Central Association of Colleges and Schools (NCA). The College offers NAIA sports and is located in one of the "top twenty best small towns in America."

Undergraduates 432 full-time, 29 part-time. Students come from 30 states and territories, 16 other countries, 71% are from out of state, 4% African American,

York College (continued)
3% Asian American or Pacific Islander, 3% Hispanic American, 0.2% Native American, 0.7% international, 8% transferred in, 61% live on campus. *Retention:* 68% of 2002 full-time freshmen returned.

Freshmen *Admission:* 344 applied, 216 admitted, 116 enrolled. *Average high school GPA:* 3.26. *Test scores:* SAT verbal scores over 500: 57%; SAT math scores over 500: 73%; ACT scores over 18: 89%; SAT verbal scores over 600: 10%; SAT math scores over 600: 26%; ACT scores over 24: 32%; SAT verbal scores over 700: 5%; ACT scores over 30: 2%.

Faculty *Total:* 51, 67% full-time, 25% with terminal degrees. *Student/faculty ratio:* 12:1.

Majors Accounting; ancient Near Eastern and biblical languages; art teacher education; biblical studies; biological and physical sciences; biology/biological sciences; biology teacher education; business administration and management; business teacher education; education; education (multiple levels); elementary education; English; English/language arts teacher education; general studies; history; history teacher education; human resources management; liberal arts and sciences/liberal studies; mathematics teacher education; middle school education; music; music teacher education; natural sciences; physical education teaching and coaching; physiological psychology/psychobiology; psychology; psychology teacher education; reading teacher education; religious education; religious studies; science teacher education; secondary education; social science teacher education; social studies teacher education; special education; speech teacher education; speech/theater education.

Academic Programs *Special study options:* academic remediation for entering students, adult/continuing education programs, advanced placement credit, cooperative education, double majors, external degree program, honors programs, independent study, internships, part-time degree program, services for LD students, study abroad, summer session for credit. *ROTC:* Army (c), Navy (c), Air Force (c). *Unusual degree programs:* 3-2 engineering with Oklahoma Christian University; nursing with Harding University.

Library Levitt Library with 49,891 titles, 339 serial subscriptions, 5,867 audiovisual materials, an OPAC, a Web page.

Computers on Campus 36 computers available on campus for general student use. A campuswide network can be accessed from off campus. At least one staffed computer lab available.

Student Life *Housing:* on-campus residence required through sophomore year. *Options:* men-only, women-only. Campus housing is university owned. Freshman campus housing is guaranteed. *Activities and organizations:* drama/theater group, student-run newspaper, choral group, concert choir, Student Association, Promethians, social organizations, Marksmen. *Campus security:* 24-hour patrols, student patrols, controlled dormitory access. *Student services:* personal/psychological counseling.

Athletics Member NAIA, NCCAA. *Intercollegiate sports:* baseball M(s), basketball M(s)/W(s), cross-country running M(s)/W(s), golf M(s)/W(s), soccer M(s)/W(s), softball W(s), track and field M(s)/W(s). *Intramural sports:* badminton M/W, basketball M/W, football M/W, soccer M/W, softball M/W, table tennis M/W, tennis M/W, volleyball M/W.

Standardized Tests *Required:* SAT I or ACT (for admission).

Costs (2003–04) *Comprehensive fee:* $14,975 includes full-time tuition ($10,400), mandatory fees ($1000), and room and board ($3575). Full-time tuition and fees vary according to course load. Part-time tuition: $325 per credit hour. Part-time tuition and fees vary according to course load. *Required fees:* $50 per hour part-time. *College room only:* $1375. Room and board charges vary according to board plan and housing facility. *Payment plan:* installment. *Waivers:* employees or children of employees.

Financial Aid In 2002, 74 non-need-based awards were made. *Average percent of need met:* 80%.

Applying *Options:* common application, electronic application, early admission, deferred entrance. *Application fee:* $20. *Required:* high school transcript, 2 letters of recommendation. *Required for some:* minimum 2.0 GPA. *Recommended:* minimum 2.0 GPA. *Application deadline:* rolling (freshmen), rolling (transfers). *Notification:* continuous (transfers).

Admissions Contact Ms. Kristin Mathews, Associate Director of Admissions, York College, 1125 East 8th Street, York, NE 68467-2699. *Phone:* 402-363-5629. *Toll-free phone:* 800-950-9675. *Fax:* 402-363-5623. *E-mail:* enroll@york.edu.

NEVADA

DeVry University
Henderson, Nevada

Admissions Contact 2490 Paseo Verde Parkway, Henderson, NV 89074-7120. *Toll-free phone:* 866-78DEVRY. *Fax:* 702-407-2950. *E-mail:* admissions@devry.edu.

Great Basin College
Elko, Nevada

- **State-supported** primarily 2-year, founded 1967, part of University and Community College System of Nevada
- **Calendar** semesters
- **Degrees** certificates, associate, and bachelor's
- **Rural** 58-acre campus
- **Endowment** $150,000
- **Coed**
- **Noncompetitive** entrance level

Faculty *Student/faculty ratio:* 18:1.

Student Life *Campus security:* evening patrols by trained security personnel.

Standardized Tests *Recommended:* SAT I or ACT (for placement).

Financial Aid Of all full-time matriculated undergraduates who enrolled in 2001, 35 Federal Work-Study jobs (averaging $1000).

Applying *Options:* common application, electronic application, early admission, deferred entrance. *Application fee:* $5. *Required:* high school transcript.

Admissions Contact Ms. Julie Byrnes, Director of Enrollment Management, Great Basin College, 1500 College Parkway, Elko, NV 89801-3348. *Phone:* 775-753-2271. *Fax:* 775-753-2311. *E-mail:* stdsvc@gbcnv.edu.

ITT Technical Institute
Henderson, Nevada

- **Proprietary** primarily 2-year, part of ITT Educational Services, Inc.
- **Degrees** associate and bachelor's
- **Coed**
- **Minimally difficult** entrance level

Standardized Tests *Required:* Wonderlic aptitude test (for admission).

Costs (2003–04) *Tuition:* $347 per credit hour part-time.

Financial Aid Of all full-time matriculated undergraduates who enrolled in 2001, 6 Federal Work-Study jobs (averaging $5000).

Applying *Options:* deferred entrance. *Application fee:* $100. *Required:* high school transcript, interview. *Recommended:* letters of recommendation.

Admissions Contact Ms. Sandra Turkington, Director of Recruitment, ITT Technical Institute, 168 North Gibson Road, Henderson, NV 89014. *Phone:* 702-558-5404. *Toll-free phone:* 800-488-8459. *Fax:* 702-558-5412.

Morrison University
Reno, Nevada

- **Proprietary** comprehensive, founded 1902
- **Calendar** 5 sessions per year
- **Degrees** certificates, diplomas, associate, bachelor's, and master's
- **Urban** 2-acre campus
- **Coed,** 110 undergraduate students, 100% full-time, 68% women, 32% men
- **Noncompetitive** entrance level

Undergraduates 110 full-time. Students come from 8 states and territories, 5 other countries, 4% African American, 5% Asian American or Pacific Islander, 7% Hispanic American, 8% Native American. *Retention:* 73% of 2002 full-time freshmen returned.

Freshmen *Average high school GPA:* 2.8.

Faculty *Total:* 25, 60% full-time.

Majors Accounting; administrative assistant and secretarial science; business administration and management; computer science; information science/studies; legal administrative assistant/secretary; legal assistant/paralegal; medical administrative assistant and medical secretary; tourism and travel services management.

Academic Programs *Special study options:* academic remediation for entering students, accelerated degree program, adult/continuing education programs, English as a second language, internships, part-time degree program, summer session for credit.

Library Morrison College Library with 6,000 titles, 20 serial subscriptions.

Computers on Campus 50 computers available on campus for general student use. A campuswide network can be accessed. At least one staffed computer lab available.

Student Life *Housing:* college housing not available. *Activities and organizations:* student-run newspaper, Phi Beta Lambda, national fraternities, national sororities. *Campus security:* 24-hour emergency response devices, late-night transport/escort service, evening patrols by security. *Student services:* personal/psychological counseling.

Costs (2003–04) *Tuition:* $12,000 full-time, $200 per credit part-time.

Applying *Options:* early admission, deferred entrance. *Application fee:* $25. *Required:* high school transcript, interview. *Required for some:* essay or personal statement. *Recommended:* CPAt of 160 for paralegal program. *Notification:* continuous (freshmen), continuous (transfers).

Admissions Contact Dr. Richard Carl Farmer, President, Morrison University, 10315 Professional Circle, Reno, NV 89521. *Phone:* 775-850-0700 Ext. 115. *Toll-free phone:* 800-369-6144.

NEVADA STATE COLLEGE AT HENDERSON
Henderson, Nevada

- **State-supported** 4-year, founded 2002, part of Nevada System of Higher Education
- **Calendar** semesters
- **Degree** bachelor's
- **Suburban** 520-acre campus with easy access to Las Vegas
- **Coed,** 535 undergraduate students, 46% full-time, 72% women, 28% men
- 58% of applicants were admitted

Undergraduates 248 full-time, 287 part-time. Students come from 8 states and territories, 9% are from out of state, 55% transferred in. *Retention:* 52% of 2002 full-time freshmen returned.

Freshmen *Admission:* 603 applied, 350 admitted, 89 enrolled. *Average high school GPA:* 2.80.

Faculty *Total:* 88, 17% full-time, 32% with terminal degrees. *Student/faculty ratio:* 9:1.

Majors Animation, interactive technology, video graphics and special effects; audiovisual communications technologies related; bilingual and multilingual education; biology/biological sciences; biology teacher education; business administration and management; computer programming; criminal justice/law enforcement administration; economics related; education; English; English/language arts teacher education; environmental science; history; history teacher education; liberal arts and sciences/liberal studies; mathematics teacher education; multi-/interdisciplinary studies related; nursing (registered nurse training); pre-nursing studies; psychology; public administration; science teacher education; social science teacher education; special education related; speech-language pathology.

Student Life *Housing:* college housing not available. *Activities and organizations:* student-run newspaper, Teachers of Principle, Nursing Club, Psychology Club, Running Team, Student Government. *Student services:* personal/psychological counseling.

Standardized Tests *Recommended:* SAT I or ACT (for admission).

Costs (2004–05) *Tuition:* state resident $2200 full-time, $74 per credit part-time; nonresident $6676 full-time, $74 per credit part-time. *Required fees:* $2200 full-time. *Payment plans:* installment, deferred payment. *Waivers:* senior citizens and employees or children of employees.

Applying *Application fee:* $30. *Required:* high school transcript, minimum 2.0 GPA. *Application deadlines:* 8/20 (freshmen), 8/20 (transfers). *Notification:* continuous (freshmen).

Admissions Contact Kathy Gonzales, Assistant Registrar, Nevada State College at Henderson, 1125 Nevada State Drive, Henderson, NV 89107. *Phone:* 702-992-2000. *Fax:* 702-992-2226. *E-mail:* students@nsc.nevada.edu.

SIERRA NEVADA COLLEGE
Incline Village, Nevada

- **Independent** comprehensive, founded 1969
- **Calendar** semesters
- **Degrees** bachelor's and postbachelor's certificates
- **Small-town** 20-acre campus with easy access to Reno
- **Endowment** $3.5 million
- **Coed,** 302 undergraduate students, 100% full-time, 51% women, 49% men
- **Moderately difficult** entrance level, 68% of applicants were admitted

Undergraduates 302 full-time. Students come from 32 states and territories, 5 other countries, 71% are from out of state, 1% African American, 3% Asian American or Pacific Islander, 3% Hispanic American, 1% Native American, 3% international, 12% transferred in, 45% live on campus. *Retention:* 70% of 2002 full-time freshmen returned.

Freshmen *Admission:* 383 applied, 262 admitted, 67 enrolled. *Average high school GPA:* 3.14. *Test scores:* SAT verbal scores over 500: 62%; SAT math scores over 500: 59%; SAT verbal scores over 600: 10%; SAT math scores over 600: 8%.

Faculty *Total:* 75, 25% full-time. *Student/faculty ratio:* 8:1.

Majors Art; biological and physical sciences; business administration and management; computer and information sciences; ecology; environmental studies; fine/studio arts; hotel/motel administration; humanities; music; sales, distribution and marketing.

Academic Programs *Special study options:* academic remediation for entering students, accelerated degree program, adult/continuing education programs, advanced placement credit, cooperative education, double majors, honors programs, independent study, internships, part-time degree program, services for LD students, study abroad, summer session for credit. *ROTC:* Army (c).

Library MacLean Library with 18,500 titles, 175 serial subscriptions, an OPAC, a Web page.

Computers on Campus 50 computers available on campus for general student use. A campuswide network can be accessed from student residence rooms and from off campus. Internet access available.

Student Life *Housing:* on-campus residence required through sophomore year. *Options:* coed. Campus housing is university owned. Freshman campus housing is guaranteed. *Activities and organizations:* drama/theater group, student-run newspaper, choral group, Recycling Club, Ski Club (NASIS), Enviroaction Club, Snowboard Club, Rotaract. *Campus security:* 24-hour emergency response devices and patrols. *Student services:* health clinic, personal/psychological counseling.

Athletics *Intercollegiate sports:* equestrian sports M/W, skiing (downhill) M(s)/W(s). *Intramural sports:* bowling M/W, fencing M/W, skiing (downhill) M/W, soccer M/W, softball M/W, volleyball M/W.

Standardized Tests *Required:* SAT I and SAT II or ACT (for admission).

Costs (2004–05) *Comprehensive fee:* $27,100 includes full-time tuition ($19,500), mandatory fees ($150), and room and board ($7450). Full-time tuition and fees vary according to course load, location, and program. Part-time tuition: $850 per hour. Part-time tuition and fees vary according to course load, location, and program. *Required fees:* $75 per term part-time. *Room and board:* Room and board charges vary according to gender and housing facility. *Payment plans:* installment, deferred payment. *Waivers:* employees or children of employees.

Financial Aid Of all full-time matriculated undergraduates who enrolled in 2002, 180 applied for aid, 180 were judged to have need. 63 Federal Work-Study jobs (averaging $2000). 2 state and other part-time jobs (averaging $2500). In 2002, 38 non-need-based awards were made. *Average percent of need met:* 60%. *Average financial aid package:* $14,000. *Average need-based gift aid:* $6000. *Average non-need-based aid:* $8000. *Average indebtedness upon graduation:* $18,000.

Applying *Options:* common application, electronic application, early admission, deferred entrance. *Required:* essay or personal statement, high school transcript, minimum 2.0 GPA. *Required for some:* letters of recommendation, school report form for high school seniors. *Recommended:* interview. *Application deadline:* rolling (freshmen), rolling (transfers). *Notification:* continuous (freshmen), continuous (transfers).

Admissions Contact Mr. Brett Schraeder, Dean of Enrollment, Sierra Nevada College, 999 Tahoe Boulevard, David Hall II, Incline Village, NV 89451. *Phone:* 775-831-7799 Ext. 4047. *Toll-free phone:* 775-831-1314. *Fax:* 775-831-1347. *E-mail:* admissions@sierranevada.edu.

UNIVERSITY OF NEVADA, LAS VEGAS
Las Vegas, Nevada

- **State-supported** university, founded 1957, part of University and Community College System of Nevada
- **Calendar** semesters
- **Degrees** certificates, bachelor's, master's, doctoral, first professional, post-master's, and postbachelor's certificates
- **Urban** 335-acre campus
- **Endowment** $90.0 million
- **Coed,** 20,680 undergraduate students, 70% full-time, 56% women, 44% men
- **Moderately difficult** entrance level, 80% of applicants were admitted

UNLV is a doctoral, research-intensive university that offers 180 undergraduate, master's, and doctoral degree programs to 25,000 students. A premier, metropolitan university, UNLV is located on a beautifully landscaped 335-acre enclosed campus that is just minutes from McCarran International Airport and the world-famous Las Vegas Strip.

Undergraduates 14,375 full-time, 6,305 part-time. Students come from 51 states and territories, 84 other countries, 22% are from out of state, 8% African American, 14% Asian American or Pacific Islander, 10% Hispanic American, 0.9% Native American, 4% international, 14% transferred in, 4% live on campus. *Retention:* 72% of 2002 full-time freshmen returned.

Freshmen *Admission:* 6,162 applied, 4,938 admitted, 2,976 enrolled. *Average high school GPA:* 3.23. *Test scores:* SAT verbal scores over 500: 55%; SAT math scores over 500: 59%; ACT scores over 18: 82%; SAT verbal scores over 600: 14%; SAT math scores over 600: 19%; ACT scores over 24: 27%; SAT verbal scores over 700: 1%; SAT math scores over 700: 2%; ACT scores over 30: 2%.

Faculty *Total:* 1,435, 54% full-time. *Student/faculty ratio:* 20:1.

Majors Accounting; adult and continuing education; African-American/Black studies; anthropology; applied mathematics; architecture; art; art history, criticism

University of Nevada, Las Vegas (continued)
and conservation; athletic training; biochemistry; biology/biological sciences; business administration and management; chemistry; city/urban, community and regional planning; civil engineering; clinical laboratory science/medical technology; communication/speech communication and rhetoric; comparative literature; computer engineering; computer science; construction engineering; criminal justice/law enforcement administration; culinary arts; cultural studies; dance; dramatic/theatre arts; dramatic/theatre arts and stagecraft related; economics; education; electrical, electronics and communications engineering; elementary education; English; environmental studies; film/cinema studies; finance; French; geological and earth sciences/geosciences related; geology/earth science; German; gerontology; health/health care administration; health/medical physics; health science; health teacher education; history; hospitality administration; human resources management; human services; interdisciplinary studies; interior architecture; international business/trade/commerce; jazz/jazz studies; kindergarten/preschool education; kinesiology and exercise science; landscape architecture; management information systems; marketing/marketing management; marriage and family therapy/counseling; mathematics; mechanical engineering; medical laboratory technology; medical radiologic technology; music; music theory and composition; nuclear medical technology; nursing (registered nurse training); nutrition sciences; parks, recreation and leisure; philosophy; physical education teaching and coaching; physics; physics related; political science and government; psychology; real estate; Romance languages; secondary education; social sciences; social work; sociology; Spanish; special education; sport and fitness administration; statistics; tourism and travel services management; women's studies.

Academic Programs *Special study options:* academic remediation for entering students, adult/continuing education programs, advanced placement credit, cooperative education, distance learning, double majors, English as a second language, honors programs, independent study, internships, off-campus study, part-time degree program, services for LD students, student-designed majors, study abroad, summer session for credit.

Library Lied Library with 1.0 million titles, 9,536 serial subscriptions, 120,128 audiovisual materials, an OPAC, a Web page.

Computers on Campus 1600 computers available on campus for general student use. A campuswide network can be accessed from student residence rooms and from off campus. Internet access, online (class) registration, at least one staffed computer lab available.

Student Life *Housing:* on-campus residence required for freshman year. *Options:* coed. Campus housing is university owned. Freshman applicants given priority for college housing. *Activities and organizations:* drama/theater group, student-run newspaper, radio and television station, choral group, marching band, Inter-Varsity Christian Fellowship, Rebel Ski Club, Student Organization of Latinos, Latter Day Saints, Hawaii club, national fraternities, national sororities. *Campus security:* 24-hour emergency response devices and patrols, late-night transport/escort service, controlled dormitory access. *Student services:* health clinic, personal/psychological counseling, women's center.

Athletics Member NCAA. All Division I except football (Division I-A). *Intercollegiate sports:* baseball M(s), basketball M(s)/W(s), cheerleading M(s)/W(s), cross-country running W(s), equestrian sports W, golf M(s), soccer M(s)/W(s), softball W(s), swimming M(s)/W(s), tennis M(s)/W(s), track and field W(s), volleyball W(s). *Intramural sports:* badminton M/W, basketball M/W, bowling M/W, cross-country running M/W, football M/W, golf M/W, racquetball M/W, soccer M/W, softball M/W, swimming M/W, tennis M/W, track and field W, volleyball M/W.

Standardized Tests *Required for some:* SAT I or ACT (for admission). *Recommended:* SAT I or ACT (for admission).

Costs (2004–05) *Tuition:* state resident $2850 full-time, $95 per credit hour part-time; nonresident $11,524 full-time, $95 per credit hour part-time. Full-time tuition and fees vary according to course load. Part-time tuition and fees vary according to course load. *Required fees:* $156 full-time. *Room and board:* $8258; room only: $5200. Room and board charges vary according to board plan. *Payment plan:* deferred payment. *Waivers:* children of alumni, senior citizens, and employees or children of employees.

Financial Aid Of all full-time matriculated undergraduates who enrolled in 2003, 7,594 applied for aid, 6,265 were judged to have need, 2,855 had their need fully met. In 2003, 3907 non-need-based awards were made. *Average percent of need met:* 74%. *Average financial aid package:* $6911. *Average need-based loan:* $3993. *Average need-based gift aid:* $3030. *Average non-need-based aid:* $2094. *Average indebtedness upon graduation:* $12,900.

Applying *Options:* deferred entrance. *Application fee:* $60. *Required:* high school transcript, minimum 2.5 GPA. *Required for some:* 2 letters of recommendation. *Application deadlines:* 4/2 (freshmen), 5/1 (transfers). *Notification:* continuous (freshmen), continuous (transfers).

Admissions Contact Ms. Kristi Rodriguez, Assistant Director for Undergraduate Recruitment, University of Nevada, Las Vegas, 4505 Maryland Parkway, Box 451021, Las Vegas, NV 89154-1021. *Phone:* 702-895-4678. *Fax:* 702-774-8008. *E-mail:* gounlv@ccmail.nevada.edu.

■ *See page 2662 for a narrative description.*

University of Nevada, Reno
Reno, Nevada

- **State-supported** university, founded 1874, part of University and Community College System of Nevada
- **Calendar** semesters
- **Degrees** bachelor's, master's, doctoral, first professional, post-master's, postbachelor's, and first professional certificates
- **Urban** 200-acre campus
- **Endowment** $86.4 million
- **Coed,** 12,118 undergraduate students, 78% full-time, 55% women, 45% men
- **Moderately difficult** entrance level, 88% of applicants were admitted

Undergraduates 9,457 full-time, 2,661 part-time. Students come from 54 states and territories, 73 other countries, 18% are from out of state, 2% African American, 7% Asian American or Pacific Islander, 7% Hispanic American, 1% Native American, 3% international, 8% transferred in, 14% live on campus. *Retention:* 76% of 2002 full-time freshmen returned.

Freshmen *Admission:* 4,024 applied, 3,551 admitted, 2,097 enrolled. *Average high school GPA:* 3.36. *Test scores:* SAT verbal scores over 500: 66%; SAT math scores over 500: 69%; ACT scores over 18: 92%; SAT verbal scores over 600: 23%; SAT math scores over 600: 26%; ACT scores over 24: 39%; SAT verbal scores over 700: 3%; SAT math scores over 700: 3%; ACT scores over 30: 5%.

Faculty *Total:* 1,134, 60% full-time, 65% with terminal degrees. *Student/faculty ratio:* 15:1.

Majors Accounting; advertising; agricultural animal breeding; agricultural economics; agricultural teacher education; animal sciences; anthropology; art; art history, criticism and conservation; art teacher education; biochemistry; biology/biological sciences; biotechnology; broadcast journalism; business/commerce; business/managerial economics; business teacher education; chemical engineering; chemistry; child development; civil engineering; communication/speech communication and rhetoric; computer and information sciences; computer engineering; computer science; construction engineering technology; criminology; dramatic/theatre arts; education (specific subject areas) related; electrical, electronics and communications engineering; elementary education; engineering physics; English; English composition; English language and literature related; English/language arts teacher education; entrepreneurship; environmental/environmental health engineering; family and consumer sciences/home economics teacher education; finance; foods, nutrition, and wellness; foreign language teacher education; forestry; French; general studies; geography; geological/geophysical engineering; geology/earth science; geophysics and seismology; German; health/medical preparatory programs related; health professions related; health teacher education; history; hospitality administration; housing and human environments related; human development and family studies; human resources management; international business/trade/commerce; international relations and affairs; journalism; logistics and materials management; marketing/marketing management; mathematics; mathematics teacher education; mechanical engineering; metallurgical engineering; mining and mineral engineering; music; music performance; music teacher education; natural resources/conservation; natural resources management and policy; nursing (registered nurse training); parks, recreation and leisure; philosophy; physical education teaching and coaching; physics; political science and government; pre-medical studies; pre-veterinary studies; psychology; science teacher education; science, technology and society; social psychology; social science teacher education; social studies teacher education; social work; sociology; Spanish; special education; speech-language pathology; technology/industrial arts teacher education; trade and industrial teacher education; water resources engineering; wildlife and wildlands science and management; women's studies.

Academic Programs *Special study options:* academic remediation for entering students, adult/continuing education programs, advanced placement credit, distance learning, double majors, English as a second language, honors programs, independent study, internships, off-campus study, part-time degree program, services for LD students, study abroad, summer session for credit. *ROTC:* Army (b). *Unusual degree programs:* 3-2 biotechnology.

Library Getchell Library plus 5 others with 1.1 million titles, 18,656 serial subscriptions, 460,751 audiovisual materials, an OPAC, a Web page.

Computers on Campus 200 computers available on campus for general student use. A campuswide network can be accessed from student residence rooms and from off campus. Internet access, online (class) registration, at least one staffed computer lab available. Computer purchase or lease plan available.

Student Life *Housing options:* coed, men-only, women-only, disabled students. Campus housing is university owned. Freshman applicants given priority for college housing. *Activities and organizations:* drama/theater group, student-run newspaper, radio station, choral group, marching band, Asian-American Student Association, Ambassadors, Non-Traditional Student Union, The Alliance, Orvis Nursing Student Association, national fraternities, national sororities. *Campus security:* 24-hour emergency response devices and patrols, late-night transport/escort service, controlled dormitory access. *Student services:* health clinic, personal/psychological counseling, women's center, legal services.

Athletics Member NCAA. All Division I except football (Division I-A). *Intercollegiate sports:* baseball M(s), basketball M(s)/W(s), cheerleading M/W, cross-country running W(s), golf M(s)/W(s), riflery M(s)/W(s), skiing (cross-country) M(s)/W(s), skiing (downhill) M(s)/W(s), soccer W(s), softball W, swimming W(s), tennis M(s)/W(s), track and field W(s), volleyball W(s). *Intramural sports:* basketball M/W, cross-country running M/W, equestrian sports M/W, golf M/W, racquetball M/W, rugby M/W, skiing (cross-country) M/W, skiing (downhill) M/W, soccer M/W, softball M/W, swimming M/W, table tennis M/W, tennis M/W, track and field M/W, volleyball M/W, water polo M/W.

Standardized Tests *Recommended:* SAT I or ACT (for placement).

Costs (2004–05) *Tuition:* state resident $91 per credit part-time; nonresident $191 per credit part-time. *Room and board:* Room and board charges vary according to housing facility.

Financial Aid Of all full-time matriculated undergraduates who enrolled in 2002, 3,791 applied for aid, 2,849 were judged to have need, 303 had their need fully met. 143 Federal Work-Study jobs (averaging $1939). 20 state and other part-time jobs (averaging $1965). In 2002, 3506 non-need-based awards were made. *Average percent of need met:* 61%. *Average financial aid package:* $7003. *Average need-based loan:* $3854. *Average need-based gift aid:* $3296. *Average non-need-based aid:* $2754. *Average indebtedness upon graduation:* $15,548.

Applying *Options:* early action, deferred entrance. *Application fee:* $40. *Required:* high school transcript, minimum 2.5 GPA. *Application deadline:* rolling (freshmen), rolling (transfers). *Notification:* continuous (freshmen), continuous (transfers).

Admissions Contact Office for Prospective Students, University of Nevada, Reno, Mail Stop 120, Reno, NV 89557. *Phone:* 775-784-4700. *Toll-free phone:* 866-263-8232. *Fax:* 775-784-4283. *E-mail:* asknevada@unr.edu.

■ *See page 2664 for a narrative description.*

UNIVERSITY OF PHOENIX–NEVADA CAMPUS

Las Vegas, Nevada

- **Proprietary** comprehensive, founded 1994
- **Calendar** continuous
- **Degrees** certificates, associate, bachelor's, master's, doctoral, post-master's, and postbachelor's certificates (courses conducted at 121 campuses and learning centers in 25 states)
- **Urban** campus
- **Coed,** 2,152 undergraduate students, 100% full-time, 57% women, 43% men
- **Noncompetitive** entrance level

Undergraduates 2,152 full-time. 10% African American, 4% Asian American or Pacific Islander, 7% Hispanic American, 0.9% Native American, 9% international.

Freshmen *Admission:* 119 enrolled.

Faculty *Total:* 495, 0.8% full-time, 24% with terminal degrees. *Student/faculty ratio:* 9:1.

Majors Accounting; business administration and management; business, management, and marketing related; computer and information sciences; health/health care administration; marketing/marketing management; public administration and social service professions related.

Academic Programs *Special study options:* accelerated degree program, adult/continuing education programs, advanced placement credit, distance learning, external degree program, independent study.

Library University Library with 27.1 million titles, 11,648 serial subscriptions, an OPAC, a Web page.

Computers on Campus A campuswide network can be accessed from off campus. Internet access, at least one staffed computer lab available.

Student Life *Housing:* college housing not available.

Costs (2003–04) *Tuition:* $8910 full-time, $297 per credit part-time. *Waivers:* employees or children of employees.

Financial Aid *Average financial aid package:* $1406.

Applying *Options:* deferred entrance. *Application fee:* $85. *Required:* 1 letter of recommendation, 2 years of work experience, 23 years of age. *Required for some:* high school transcript. *Application deadline:* rolling (freshmen), rolling (transfers).

Admissions Contact Ms. Beth Barilla, Director of Admissions, University of Phoenix–Nevada Campus, 4615 East Elwood Street, Mail Stop AA-K101, Phoenix, AZ 85040-1958. *Phone:* 480-317-6000. *Toll-free phone:* 800-228-7240. *Fax:* 480-594-1758. *E-mail:* beth.barilla@phoenix.edu.

NEW HAMPSHIRE

CHESTER COLLEGE OF NEW ENGLAND

Chester, New Hampshire

- **Independent** 4-year, founded 1965
- **Calendar** semesters
- **Degrees** associate and bachelor's
- **Rural** 75-acre campus with easy access to Boston
- **Endowment** $2.9 million
- **Coed,** 187 undergraduate students, 83% full-time, 60% women, 40% men
- **Moderately difficult** entrance level, 67% of applicants were admitted

Undergraduates 156 full-time, 31 part-time. Students come from 12 states and territories, 2 other countries, 40% are from out of state, 1% African American, 1% Asian American or Pacific Islander, 2% Hispanic American, 1% international, 5% transferred in, 48% live on campus. *Retention:* 64% of 2002 full-time freshmen returned.

Freshmen *Admission:* 131 applied, 88 admitted, 51 enrolled. *Average high school GPA:* 2.70. *Test scores:* SAT verbal scores over 500: 61%; SAT math scores over 500: 48%; ACT scores over 18: 60%; SAT verbal scores over 600: 23%; SAT math scores over 600: 7%; SAT verbal scores over 700: 2%.

Faculty *Total:* 33, 36% full-time, 70% with terminal degrees. *Student/faculty ratio:* 10:1.

Majors Creative writing; fine/studio arts; graphic design; journalism; liberal arts and sciences and humanities related; liberal arts and sciences/liberal studies; photography.

Academic Programs *Special study options:* academic remediation for entering students, adult/continuing education programs, advanced placement credit, cooperative education, double majors, English as a second language, honors programs, independent study, internships, part-time degree program, student-designed majors, study abroad, summer session for credit.

Library Wadleigh Library with 27,129 titles, 60 serial subscriptions, an OPAC, a Web page.

Computers on Campus 29 computers available on campus for general student use. A campuswide network can be accessed from student residence rooms. Internet access, at least one staffed computer lab available.

Student Life *Housing options:* coed. Campus housing is university owned. Freshman campus housing is guaranteed. *Activities and organizations:* drama/theater group, student government, Running Club, Green Life (Recycling), Filmmakers Club, Drama. *Campus security:* late-night transport/escort service, controlled dormitory access, regular patrols by trained security personnel.

Athletics *Intramural sports:* badminton M/W, basketball M/W, cross-country running M/W, football M/W, soccer M/W, softball M/W, table tennis M/W, volleyball M/W.

Standardized Tests *Recommended:* SAT I and SAT II or ACT (for admission).

Costs (2003–04) *Comprehensive fee:* $20,030 includes full-time tuition ($12,600), mandatory fees ($530), and room and board ($6900). Full-time tuition and fees vary according to course load and program. Part-time tuition: $420 per credit. Part-time tuition and fees vary according to course load and program. *Required fees:* $530 per year part-time. *Payment plan:* installment. *Waivers:* employees or children of employees.

Financial Aid Of all full-time matriculated undergraduates who enrolled in 2003, 150 applied for aid, 136 were judged to have need. 27 Federal Work-Study jobs (averaging $400). In 2003, 11 non-need-based awards were made. *Average percent of need met:* 40%. *Average financial aid package:* $7715. *Average need-based loan:* $3608. *Average need-based gift aid:* $1145. *Average non-need-based aid:* $3000. *Average indebtedness upon graduation:* $30,860.

Applying *Options:* common application, electronic application, deferred entrance. *Application fee:* $35. *Required:* essay or personal statement, high school transcript, 3 letters of recommendation, interview. *Recommended:* minimum 2.0 GPA, portfolio. *Application deadline:* rolling (freshmen), rolling (transfers). *Notification:* continuous (freshmen), continuous (transfers).

Admissions Contact Chester College of New England, 40 Chester Street, Chester, NH 03036. *Phone:* 603-887-7400. *Toll-free phone:* 800-974-6372. *Fax:* 603-887-1777. *E-mail:* admissions@chestercollege.edu.

■ *See page 1394 for a narrative description.*

COLBY-SAWYER COLLEGE

New London, New Hampshire

- **Independent** 4-year, founded 1837
- **Calendar** semesters
- **Degrees** associate and bachelor's
- **Small-town** 200-acre campus
- **Endowment** $17.5 million
- **Coed,** 986 undergraduate students, 97% full-time, 65% women, 35% men
- **Moderately difficult** entrance level, 82% of applicants were admitted

Undergraduates 953 full-time, 33 part-time. Students come from 25 states and territories, 7 other countries, 70% are from out of state, 0.3% African American, 0.8% Asian American or Pacific Islander, 0.4% Hispanic American, 0.1% Native American, 2% international, 2% transferred in, 87% live on campus. *Retention:* 75% of 2002 full-time freshmen returned.

Freshmen *Admission:* 1,434 applied, 1,178 admitted, 305 enrolled. *Average high school GPA:* 2.94. *Test scores:* SAT verbal scores over 500: 59%; SAT math scores over 500: 46%; ACT scores over 18: 78%; SAT verbal scores over 600: 12%; SAT math scores over 600: 10%; ACT scores over 24: 11%; SAT verbal scores over 700: 1%.

Faculty *Total:* 118, 40% full-time, 52% with terminal degrees. *Student/faculty ratio:* 12:1.

Majors Art; art teacher education; athletic training; biology/biological sciences; business administration and management; developmental and child psychology; early childhood education; English; English/language arts teacher education; environmental studies; fine/studio arts; graphic design; kinesiology and exercise science; liberal arts and sciences/liberal studies; mass communication/media; nursing (registered nurse training); psychology; social sciences related; social studies teacher education; sport and fitness administration.

Academic Programs *Special study options:* accelerated degree program, advanced placement credit, double majors, English as a second language, honors programs, independent study, internships, off-campus study, part-time degree program, services for LD students, student-designed majors, study abroad. *ROTC:* Army (c), Air Force (c).

Library Susan Colgate Cleveland Library Learning Center with 90,305 titles, 467 serial subscriptions, 3,512 audiovisual materials, an OPAC.

Computers on Campus 180 computers available on campus for general student use. A campuswide network can be accessed from student residence rooms that provide access to e-mail. Internet access available.

Student Life *Housing:* on-campus residence required for freshman year. *Options:* coed, women-only, disabled students. Campus housing is university owned. Freshman campus housing is guaranteed. *Activities and organizations:* drama/theater group, student-run newspaper, radio station, choral group, campus activities, Student Government Association, campus radio station, Alpha Chi Honor Society, outing club. *Campus security:* 24-hour emergency response devices and patrols, late-night transport/escort service, controlled dormitory access, awareness seminars. *Student services:* health clinic, personal/psychological counseling.

Athletics Member NCAA. All Division III. *Intercollegiate sports:* baseball M, basketball M/W, cheerleading M(c)/W(c), equestrian sports M/W, field hockey W(c), golf M(c)/W(c), ice hockey M(c)/W(c), lacrosse M(c)/W, rugby M(c)/W(c), skiing (cross-country) M(c)/W(c), skiing (downhill) M/W, soccer M/W, softball W(c), swimming M/W, tennis M/W, track and field M/W, volleyball W. *Intramural sports:* basketball M/W, golf M/W, soccer M/W, volleyball M/W.

Standardized Tests *Required:* SAT I or ACT (for admission).

Costs (2004–05) *Comprehensive fee:* $32,260 includes full-time tuition ($23,310) and room and board ($8950). Part-time tuition: $780 per credit hour. Part-time tuition and fees vary according to course load. *College room only:* $4980. *Payment plan:* installment. *Waivers:* employees or children of employees.

Financial Aid Of all full-time matriculated undergraduates who enrolled in 2002, 825 applied for aid, 658 were judged to have need, 26 had their need fully met. In 2002, 103 non-need-based awards were made. *Average percent of need met:* 80%. *Average financial aid package:* $14,086. *Average need-based loan:* $4105. *Average need-based gift aid:* $10,778. *Average non-need-based aid:* $3432. *Average indebtedness upon graduation:* $15,560. *Financial aid deadline:* 3/1.

Applying *Options:* common application, electronic application, early admission, early action, deferred entrance. *Application fee:* $40. *Required:* essay or personal statement, high school transcript, minimum 2.0 GPA, 2 letters of recommendation, minimum of 15 units of college preparatory work. *Recommended:* interview. *Application deadline:* rolling (freshmen). *Notification:* continuous (freshmen), 1/15 (early action), continuous (transfers).

Admissions Contact Ms. Wendy Beckemeyer, Vice President for Enrollment Management and Dean of Admissions, Colby-Sawyer College, 541 Main Street, New London, NH 03257-4648. *Phone:* 603-526-3700. *Toll-free phone:* 800-272-1015. *Fax:* 603-526-3452. *E-mail:* csadmiss@colby-sawyer.edu.

■ *See page 1428 for a narrative description.*

COLLEGE FOR LIFELONG LEARNING

Concord, New Hampshire

- **State and locally supported** 4-year, founded 1972, part of University System of New Hampshire
- **Calendar** semesters
- **Degrees** certificates, associate, bachelor's, and postbachelor's certificates (offers primarily part-time degree programs; courses offered at 50 locations in New Hampshire)
- **Rural** campus
- **Coed,** 1,794 undergraduate students
- **Noncompetitive** entrance level

Undergraduates Students come from 7 states and territories, 7% are from out of state, 0.5% African American, 0.6% Asian American or Pacific Islander, 1% Hispanic American, 0.7% Native American, 0.1% international.

Faculty *Total:* 223. *Student/faculty ratio:* 10:1.

Majors Behavioral sciences; business administration and management; computer management; computer programming; computer systems analysis; corrections and criminal justice related; criminal justice/law enforcement administration; early childhood education; finance; general studies; health/health care administration; human resources management; liberal arts and sciences/liberal studies.

Academic Programs *Special study options:* academic remediation for entering students, accelerated degree program, adult/continuing education programs, advanced placement credit, cooperative education, distance learning, double majors, independent study, internships, off-campus study, part-time degree program, services for LD students, student-designed majors, summer session for credit.

Library a Web page.

Computers on Campus 128 computers available on campus for general student use. A campuswide network can be accessed from off campus. Internet access, at least one staffed computer lab available.

Student Life *Housing:* college housing not available. *Activities and organizations:* Alumni Learner Association.

Costs (2003–04) *Tuition:* state resident $4368 full-time, $182 per credit part-time; nonresident $4848 full-time, $202 per credit part-time. Full-time tuition and fees vary according to course load. Part-time tuition and fees vary according to course load. *Required fees:* $195 full-time, $65 per term part-time. *Payment plan:* installment. *Waivers:* employees or children of employees.

Applying *Application fee:* $45. *Required for some:* ACCUPLACER. *Application deadline:* rolling (freshmen), rolling (transfers). *Notification:* continuous (freshmen), continuous (transfers).

Admissions Contact Ms. Teresa McDonnell, Associate Dean of Enrollment Management and Learner Services, College for Lifelong Learning, 125 North State Street, Concord, NH 03301. *Phone:* 603-228-3000 Ext. 308. *Toll-free phone:* 800-582-7248 Ext. 313. *Fax:* 603-229-0964. *E-mail:* ask.cll@cll.edu.

DANIEL WEBSTER COLLEGE

Nashua, New Hampshire

- **Independent** 4-year, founded 1965
- **Calendar** semesters
- **Degrees** certificates, associate, and bachelor's
- **Suburban** 50-acre campus with easy access to Boston
- **Endowment** $1.3 million
- **Coed,** 1,050 undergraduate students, 78% full-time, 27% women, 73% men
- **Moderately difficult** entrance level, 79% of applicants were admitted

Undergraduates 823 full-time, 227 part-time. Students come from 24 states and territories, 17 other countries, 46% are from out of state, 2% African American, 0.6% Asian American or Pacific Islander, 1% Hispanic American, 0.6% international, 3% transferred in, 80% live on campus. *Retention:* 56% of 2002 full-time freshmen returned.

Freshmen *Admission:* 642 applied, 506 admitted, 141 enrolled. *Average high school GPA:* 3.06. *Test scores:* SAT verbal scores over 500: 69%; SAT math scores over 500: 74%; ACT scores over 18: 87%; SAT verbal scores over 600: 18%; SAT math scores over 600: 30%; ACT scores over 24: 40%; SAT verbal scores over 700: 3%; SAT math scores over 700: 2%.

Faculty *Total:* 61, 56% full-time, 41% with terminal degrees. *Student/faculty ratio:* 13:1.

Majors Aeronautics/aviation/aerospace science and technology; airline pilot and flight crew; air traffic control; aviation/airway management; business administration and management; computer management; computer programming; computer science; engineering; engineering science; information science/studies; liberal arts and sciences/liberal studies; management information systems; marketing/marketing management; social sciences; sport and fitness administration.

Academic Programs *Special study options:* accelerated degree program, adult/continuing education programs, advanced placement credit, distance learning, double majors, independent study, internships, off-campus study, part-time degree program, study abroad, summer session for credit. *ROTC:* Army (c), Air Force (c).

Library Ann Bridge Baddour Library and Learning Center with 34,195 titles, 440 serial subscriptions, 1,439 audiovisual materials, an OPAC, a Web page.

Computers on Campus 137 computers available on campus for general student use. A campuswide network can be accessed from student residence rooms and from off campus. Internet access, at least one staffed computer lab available.

Student Life *Housing:* on-campus residence required through sophomore year. *Options:* coed, men-only, women-only, disabled students. Campus housing is university owned. Freshman campus housing is guaranteed. *Activities and organizations:* drama/theater group, student-run newspaper, choral group, Student Activities Board, Theatre Guild, ice hockey club, student government, jazz band. *Campus security:* 24-hour emergency response devices and patrols, student patrols, late-night transport/escort service, controlled dormitory access. *Student services:* health clinic, personal/psychological counseling.

Athletics Member NCAA. All Division III. *Intercollegiate sports:* baseball M, basketball M/W, cross-country running M/W, ice hockey M(c)/W(c), lacrosse M, soccer M/W, softball W, volleyball W. *Intramural sports:* basketball M/W, cross-country running M/W, football M/W, golf M/W, skiing (downhill) M(c)/W(c), soccer M/W, softball M/W, tennis M/W, volleyball M/W, weight lifting M/W.

Standardized Tests *Required:* SAT I or ACT (for admission).

Costs (2004–05) *Comprehensive fee:* $29,800 includes full-time tuition ($20,880), mandatory fees ($750), and room and board ($8170). Part-time tuition: $775 per credit. *College room only:* $4110. *Payment plan:* installment. *Waivers:* employees or children of employees.

Financial Aid Of all full-time matriculated undergraduates who enrolled in 2003, 545 applied for aid, 535 were judged to have need. 340 Federal Work-Study jobs (averaging $2000). In 2003, 21 non-need-based awards were made. *Average percent of need met:* 74%. *Average financial aid package:* $14,505. *Average need-based loan:* $3908. *Average need-based gift aid:* $5580. *Average non-need-based aid:* $7115. *Average indebtedness upon graduation:* $48,000.

Applying *Options:* common application, electronic application, early admission, deferred entrance. *Application fee:* $35. *Required:* high school transcript. *Recommended:* 1 letter of recommendation, interview. *Application deadline:* rolling (freshmen), rolling (transfers). *Notification:* continuous (freshmen), continuous (transfers).

Admissions Contact Mr. Sean J. Ryan, Director of Admissions, Daniel Webster College, 20 University Drive, Nashua, NH 03063. *Phone:* 603-577-6604. *Toll-free phone:* 800-325-6876. *Fax:* 603-577-6001. *E-mail:* admissions@dwc.edu.

■ See page 1514 for a narrative description.

DARTMOUTH COLLEGE

Hanover, New Hampshire

- **Independent** university, founded 1769
- **Calendar** quarters
- **Degrees** bachelor's, master's, doctoral, and first professional
- **Small-town** 265-acre campus
- **Endowment** $2.2 billion
- **Coed,** 4,098 undergraduate students, 99% full-time, 49% women, 51% men
- **Most difficult** entrance level, 18% of applicants were admitted

Undergraduates 4,039 full-time, 59 part-time. Students come from 52 states and territories, 64 other countries, 97% are from out of state, 6% African American, 12% Asian American or Pacific Islander, 6% Hispanic American, 3% Native American, 5% international, 0.5% transferred in, 82% live on campus. *Retention:* 97% of 2002 full-time freshmen returned.

Freshmen *Admission:* 11,855 applied, 2,155 admitted, 1,077 enrolled. *Average high school GPA:* 3.66. *Test scores:* SAT verbal scores over 500: 100%; SAT math scores over 500: 100%; SAT verbal scores over 600: 91%; SAT math scores over 600: 92%; SAT verbal scores over 700: 62%; SAT math scores over 700: 63%.

Faculty *Total:* 590, 81% full-time, 79% with terminal degrees. *Student/faculty ratio:* 8:1.

Majors African-American/Black studies; African studies; American Indian/Native American studies; ancient/classical Greek; animal genetics; anthropology; Arabic; archeology; art history, criticism and conservation; Asian studies; astronomy; biochemistry; biology/biological sciences; chemistry; chemistry related; Chinese; classics and languages, literatures and linguistics; cognitive psychology and psycholinguistics; comparative literature; computer science; creative writing; dramatic/theatre arts; East Asian languages related; ecology; economics; engineering; engineering physics; English; environmental studies; evolutionary biology; film/cinema studies; fine/studio arts; French; geography; geology/earth science; German; Hebrew; Hispanic-American, Puerto Rican, and Mexican-American/Chicano studies; history; Italian; Japanese; Latin; Latin American studies; linguistics; mathematics; molecular biology; multi-/interdisciplinary studies related; music; Near and Middle Eastern studies; philosophy; physics; political science and government; psychology; religious studies; Romance languages; Russian; Russian studies; sociology; Spanish; women's studies.

Academic Programs *Special study options:* advanced placement credit, double majors, honors programs, independent study, internships, off-campus study, services for LD students, student-designed majors, study abroad, summer session for credit. *ROTC:* Army (c).

Library Baker-Berry Library plus 10 others with 5.0 million titles, 20,834 serial subscriptions, 727,233 audiovisual materials, an OPAC, a Web page.

Computers on Campus 200 computers available on campus for general student use. A campuswide network can be accessed from student residence rooms and from off campus. Internet access, online (class) registration, at least one staffed computer lab available.

Student Life *Housing:* on-campus residence required for freshman year. *Options:* coed, cooperative. Freshman campus housing is guaranteed. *Activities and organizations:* drama/theater group, student-run newspaper, radio and television station, choral group, marching band, student government, outing club, intramural sports, community service, performing arts, national fraternities, national sororities. *Campus security:* 24-hour emergency response devices and patrols, student patrols, late-night transport/escort service, controlled dormitory access. *Student services:* health clinic, personal/psychological counseling, women's center.

Athletics Member NCAA. All Division I except football (Division I-AA). *Intercollegiate sports:* badminton M(c)/W(c), baseball M, basketball M/W, cheerleading M(c)/W(c), crew M/W, cross-country running M/W, equestrian sports M/W, fencing M(c)/W(c), field hockey W, golf M/W, gymnastics M(c)/W(c), ice hockey M/W, lacrosse M/W, rugby M(c)/W(c), sailing M/W, skiing (cross-country) M/W, skiing (downhill) M/W, soccer M/W, softball W, squash M/W, swimming M/W, table tennis M(c)/W(c), tennis M/W, track and field M/W, ultimate Frisbee M(c)/W(c), volleyball M(c)/W, water polo M(c)/W(c), wrestling M(c). *Intramural sports:* baseball M, basketball M/W, cross-country running M/W, football M/W, golf M/W, ice hockey M/W, lacrosse M/W, racquetball M/W, riflery M/W, rugby M/W, skiing (cross-country) M/W, skiing (downhill) M/W, soccer M/W, softball M/W, squash M/W, swimming M/W, table tennis M/W, tennis M/W, track and field M/W, volleyball M/W, water polo M/W, weight lifting M/W, wrestling M.

Standardized Tests *Required:* SAT I or ACT (for admission), SAT II: Subject Tests (for admission).

Costs (2003–04) *Comprehensive fee:* $37,995 includes full-time tuition ($28,965), mandatory fees ($291), and room and board ($8739). *College room only:* $5175.

Financial Aid Of all full-time matriculated undergraduates who enrolled in 2002, 2,373 applied for aid, 1,979 were judged to have need, 1,979 had their need fully met. 1,493 Federal Work-Study jobs (averaging $1902). 293 state and other part-time jobs (averaging $1206). In 2002, 12 non-need-based awards were made. *Average percent of need met:* 100%. *Average financial aid package:* $24,538. *Average need-based loan:* $4476. *Average need-based gift aid:* $20,563. *Average non-need-based aid:* $308. *Average indebtedness upon graduation:* $16,922. *Financial aid deadline:* 2/1.

Applying *Options:* common application, electronic application, early admission, early decision, deferred entrance. *Application fee:* $70. *Required:* essay or personal statement, high school transcript, 2 letters of recommendation, peer evaluation. *Recommended:* interview. *Application deadlines:* 1/1 (freshmen), 3/1 (transfers). *Early decision:* 11/1. *Notification:* 4/10 (freshmen), 12/15 (early decision), 4/15 (transfers).

Admissions Contact Mr. Karl M. Furstenberg, Dean of Admissions and Financial Aid, Dartmouth College, 6016 McNutt Hall, Hanover, NH 03755. *Phone:* 603-646-2875. *Toll-free phone:* 603-646 Ext. 2875. *E-mail:* admissions.office@dartmouth.edu.

■ See page 1516 for a narrative description.

FRANKLIN PIERCE COLLEGE

Rindge, New Hampshire

- **Independent** comprehensive, founded 1962
- **Calendar** semesters

Franklin Pierce College (continued)

- **Degrees** associate, bachelor's, and master's (profile does not reflect significant enrollment at 6 continuing education sites; master's degree is only offered at these sites)
- **Rural** 1000-acre campus
- **Endowment** $6.2 million
- **Coed,** 1,591 undergraduate students, 99% full-time, 49% women, 51% men
- **Moderately difficult** entrance level, 86% of applicants were admitted

Undergraduates 1,572 full-time, 19 part-time. Students come from 32 states and territories, 18 other countries, 84% are from out of state, 3% African American, 0.8% Asian American or Pacific Islander, 2% Hispanic American, 0.2% Native American, 3% international, 4% transferred in, 93% live on campus. *Retention:* 65% of 2002 full-time freshmen returned.

Freshmen *Admission:* 3,347 applied, 2,895 admitted, 514 enrolled. *Average high school GPA:* 2.79. *Test scores:* SAT verbal scores over 500: 55%; SAT math scores over 500: 48%; SAT verbal scores over 600: 12%; SAT math scores over 600: 11%; SAT verbal scores over 700: 1%.

Faculty *Total:* 142, 48% full-time, 54% with terminal degrees. *Student/faculty ratio:* 17:1.

Majors Accounting; adult and continuing education; advertising; American studies; anthropology; applied art; archeology; art; art teacher education; biology/biological sciences; business administration and management; ceramic arts and ceramics; clinical psychology; commercial and advertising art; computer programming; computer science; counselor education/school counseling and guidance; creative writing; criminal justice/law enforcement administration; dramatic/theatre arts; ecology; economics; education; elementary education; English; environmental biology; environmental studies; finance; fine/studio arts; history; journalism; kindergarten/preschool education; liberal arts and sciences/liberal studies; literature; marketing/marketing management; mass communication/media; mathematics; music; parks, recreation and leisure facilities management; political science and government; pre-dentistry studies; pre-law studies; pre-medical studies; pre-veterinary studies; psychology; radio and television; secondary education; social work; sociology; sport and fitness administration.

Academic Programs *Special study options:* academic remediation for entering students, adult/continuing education programs, advanced placement credit, double majors, English as a second language, honors programs, independent study, internships, off-campus study, part-time degree program, services for LD students, student-designed majors, study abroad, summer session for credit. *ROTC:* Air Force (c).

Library Franklin Pierce College Library plus 1 other with 110,210 titles, 10,985 serial subscriptions, 10,589 audiovisual materials, an OPAC, a Web page.

Computers on Campus 109 computers available on campus for general student use. A campuswide network can be accessed from student residence rooms. Internet access, at least one staffed computer lab available. Computer purchase or lease plan available.

Student Life *Housing:* on-campus residence required through senior year. *Options:* coed, disabled students. Campus housing is university owned. Freshman campus housing is guaranteed. *Activities and organizations:* drama/theater group, student-run newspaper, radio and television station, choral group, outing club, WFPR-Radio, Student Senate, law club, business club. *Campus security:* 24-hour emergency response devices and patrols, student patrols, late-night transport/escort service, controlled dormitory access. *Student services:* health clinic, personal/psychological counseling.

Athletics Member NCAA. All Division II. *Intercollegiate sports:* baseball M(s), basketball M(s)/W(s), crew M/W, cross-country running M/W, field hockey W(s), golf M/W, ice hockey M, lacrosse M/W, soccer M(s)/W(s), softball W(s), tennis M(s)/W(s), volleyball W(s). *Intramural sports:* baseball M, basketball M/W, cheerleading W, cross-country running M/W, field hockey W, football M/W, golf M/W, ice hockey M, lacrosse M/W, soccer M/W, softball W, table tennis M/W, tennis M/W, volleyball M/W.

Standardized Tests *Required:* SAT I or ACT (for admission).

Costs (2004–05) *Comprehensive fee:* $30,165 includes full-time tuition ($21,900), mandatory fees ($610), and room and board ($7655). Part-time tuition: $730 per credit. *College room only:* $4280. Room and board charges vary according to board plan and housing facility. *Payment plan:* installment. *Waivers:* senior citizens and employees or children of employees.

Financial Aid Of all full-time matriculated undergraduates who enrolled in 2003, 1,245 applied for aid, 1,139 were judged to have need, 90 had their need fully met. 758 Federal Work-Study jobs (averaging $1467). 183 state and other part-time jobs (averaging $2128). In 2003, 339 non-need-based awards were made. *Average percent of need met:* 71%. *Average financial aid package:* $16,719. *Average need-based loan:* $4802. *Average need-based gift aid:* $11,536. *Average non-need-based aid:* $10,460. *Average indebtedness upon graduation:* $20,815.

Applying *Options:* common application, electronic application, early admission, deferred entrance. *Required:* essay or personal statement, high school transcript, 1 letter of recommendation. *Recommended:* minimum 2.0 GPA, interview. *Application deadline:* rolling (freshmen). *Notification:* continuous (freshmen), continuous (transfers).

Admissions Contact Ms. Lucy C. Shonk, Dean of Admissions, Franklin Pierce College, Box 60, 20 College Road, Rindge, NH 03461. *Phone:* 603-899-4050. *Toll-free phone:* 800-437-0048. *Fax:* 603-899-4394. *E-mail:* admissions@fpc.edu.

■ *See page 1654 for a narrative description.*

HESSER COLLEGE
Manchester, New Hampshire

- **Proprietary** primarily 2-year, founded 1900, part of Quest Education Corporation
- **Calendar** semesters
- **Degrees** certificates, diplomas, associate, and bachelor's (also offers a graduate law program with Massachusetts School of Law at Andover)
- **Urban** 1-acre campus with easy access to Boston
- **Coed,** 2,860 undergraduate students, 66% full-time, 67% women, 33% men
- **Moderately difficult** entrance level, 91% of applicants were admitted

Undergraduates 1,880 full-time, 980 part-time. Students come from 12 states and territories, 3% African American, 1% Asian American or Pacific Islander, 7% Hispanic American, 0.2% Native American, 0.2% international, 50% live on campus.

Freshmen *Admission:* 1,725 applied, 1,562 admitted, 911 enrolled. *Average high school GPA:* 2.3.

Faculty *Total:* 215, 18% full-time. *Student/faculty ratio:* 18:1.

Majors Accounting; business administration and management; business and personal/financial services marketing; child care and support services management; commercial and advertising art; computer and information sciences; computer engineering technology; computer management; computer programming; computer science; computer systems analysis; corrections; criminal justice/law enforcement administration; criminal justice/police science; criminal justice/safety; human services; information science/studies; interior design; kindergarten/preschool education; legal assistant/paralegal; liberal arts and sciences/liberal studies; management information systems; marketing/marketing management; mass communication/media; medical administrative assistant and medical secretary; medical/clinical assistant; physical therapist assistant; psychology; radio and television; sales, distribution and marketing; security and loss prevention; social work; sport and fitness administration.

Academic Programs *Special study options:* accelerated degree program, adult/continuing education programs, advanced placement credit, cooperative education, double majors, internships, part-time degree program, student-designed majors, summer session for credit.

Library Kenneth W. Galeucia Memorial Library with 38,000 titles, 200 serial subscriptions, 60 audiovisual materials, an OPAC, a Web page.

Computers on Campus 60 computers available on campus for general student use. A campuswide network can be accessed from student residence rooms. Internet access, at least one staffed computer lab available.

Student Life *Housing options:* coed. Campus housing is university owned. Freshman campus housing is guaranteed. *Activities and organizations:* student-run radio and television station, student government, Ski Club, Amnesty International, yearbook, student ambassador. *Campus security:* 24-hour emergency response devices and patrols, student patrols, late-night transport/escort service, controlled dormitory access. *Student services:* health clinic, personal/psychological counseling.

Athletics *Intercollegiate sports:* basketball M(s)/W(s), soccer M(s)/W(s), volleyball M(s)/W(s). *Intramural sports:* baseball M, basketball M/W, bowling M/W, skiing (downhill) M/W, softball M/W, table tennis M/W, volleyball M/W.

Standardized Tests *Recommended:* SAT I (for admission).

Costs (2003–04) *Comprehensive fee:* $17,490 includes full-time tuition ($10,290), mandatory fees ($1000), and room and board ($6200). Full-time tuition and fees vary according to program. Part-time tuition: $373 per credit. Part-time tuition and fees vary according to program. *Required fees:* $250 per term part-time. *College room only:* $3400. *Payment plans:* tuition prepayment, installment, deferred payment. *Waivers:* children of alumni and employees or children of employees.

Financial Aid Of all full-time matriculated undergraduates who enrolled in 2001, 700 Federal Work-Study jobs (averaging $1000).

Applying *Options:* common application, electronic application, deferred entrance. *Application fee:* $10. *Required:* high school transcript, interview. *Required for some:* essay or personal statement, letters of recommendation. *Recommended:* minimum 2.0 GPA. *Application deadline:* rolling (freshmen), rolling (transfers). *Notification:* continuous (freshmen), continuous (transfers).

Admissions Contact Mr. Kevin Wilkenson, Director of Admissions, Hesser College, 3 Sundial Avenue, Manchester, NH 03103. *Phone:* 603-668-6660 Ext. 2101. *Toll-free phone:* 800-526-9231 Ext. 2110. *E-mail:* admissions@hesser.edu.

■ *See page 1728 for a narrative description.*

KEENE STATE COLLEGE
Keene, New Hampshire

- **State-supported** comprehensive, founded 1909, part of University System of New Hampshire
- **Calendar** semesters
- **Degrees** certificates, associate, bachelor's, master's, post-master's, and postbachelor's certificates
- **Small-town** 160-acre campus
- **Coed,** 4,756 undergraduate students, 87% full-time, 57% women, 43% men
- **Moderately difficult** entrance level, 71% of applicants were admitted

At Keene State College, students of all ages enrich their lives and careers through the arts, humanities, sciences, and professional studies. A member of the University System of New Hampshire, Keene State enrolls 5,000 undergraduate, graduate, and continuing education students in 35 academic areas, all grounded in the liberal arts.

Undergraduates 4,133 full-time, 623 part-time. Students come from 27 states and territories, 43% are from out of state, 0.2% African American, 0.9% Asian American or Pacific Islander, 0.9% Hispanic American, 0.2% Native American, 0.8% international, 51% transferred in, 56% live on campus. *Retention:* 77% of 2002 full-time freshmen returned.

Freshmen *Admission:* 4,207 applied, 2,997 admitted. *Average high school GPA:* 2.90. *Test scores:* SAT verbal scores over 500: 52%; SAT math scores over 500: 52%; SAT verbal scores over 600: 11%; SAT math scores over 600: 10%; SAT verbal scores over 700: 1%; SAT math scores over 700: 1%.

Faculty *Total:* 410, 48% full-time. *Student/faculty ratio:* 17:1.

Majors American studies; art; athletic training; biology/biological sciences; business administration and management; chemistry; commercial and advertising art; computer science; dietetics; drafting and design technology; dramatic/theatre arts; ecology; economics; education; electrical, electronic and communications engineering technology; elementary education; English; environmental studies; family and consumer sciences/home economics teacher education; family and consumer sciences/human sciences; film/cinema studies; foods, nutrition, and wellness; French; geography; geology/earth science; health teacher education; history; industrial arts; industrial technology; interdisciplinary studies; journalism; kindergarten/preschool education; liberal arts and sciences/liberal studies; mass communication/media; mathematics; music; music history, literature, and theory; music teacher education; occupational safety and health technology; physical education teaching and coaching; physics; political science and government; pre-engineering; psychology; safety/security technology; secondary education; social sciences; sociology; Spanish; special education; sport and fitness administration; substance abuse/addiction counseling; trade and industrial teacher education.

Academic Programs *Special study options:* advanced placement credit, cooperative education, double majors, English as a second language, honors programs, independent study, internships, off-campus study, part-time degree program, services for LD students, student-designed majors, study abroad, summer session for credit. *ROTC:* Air Force (c). *Unusual degree programs:* 3-2 engineering with Clarkson University, University of New Hampshire.

Library Mason Library with 958 serial subscriptions, an OPAC, a Web page.

Computers on Campus 386 computers available on campus for general student use. A campuswide network can be accessed from student residence rooms and from off campus that provide access to e-mail, personal web pages. Internet access, at least one staffed computer lab available. Computer purchase or lease plan available.

Student Life *Housing options:* coed, women-only, disabled students. Campus housing is university owned. Freshman campus housing is guaranteed. *Activities and organizations:* drama/theater group, student-run newspaper, radio and television station, choral group, Social Activities Council, Concerned Students Coalition, Pride, Habitat for Humanity, sports club, national fraternities, national sororities. *Campus security:* 24-hour emergency response devices and patrols, late-night transport/escort service, controlled dormitory access. *Student services:* health clinic, personal/psychological counseling, women's center.

Athletics Member NCAA. All Division III. *Intercollegiate sports:* baseball M, basketball M/W, cross-country running M/W, field hockey W, lacrosse M/W, rugby M(c)/W(c), skiing (downhill) M(c)/W(c), soccer M/W, softball W, swimming M/W, track and field M/W, volleyball W. *Intramural sports:* badminton M/W, basketball M/W, cheerleading M/W, football M/W, racquetball M/W, soccer W, softball M/W, squash M/W, tennis M/W, volleyball M/W, water polo M/W.

Standardized Tests *Required:* SAT I (for admission), SAT I or ACT (for admission).

Costs (2004–05) *Tuition:* state resident $4750 full-time, $198 per credit part-time; nonresident $10,800 full-time, $480 per credit part-time. Part-time tuition and fees vary according to course load. *Required fees:* $1780 full-time, $71 per credit part-time. *Room and board:* $5682; room only: $3870. Room and board charges vary according to board plan and housing facility. *Payment plan:* installment. *Waivers:* employees or children of employees.

Financial Aid Of all full-time matriculated undergraduates who enrolled in 2002, 3,073 applied for aid, 2,169 were judged to have need, 642 had their need fully met. 545 Federal Work-Study jobs (averaging $780). 487 state and other part-time jobs (averaging $838). In 2002, 357 non-need-based awards were made. *Average percent of need met:* 78%. *Average financial aid package:* $7085. *Average need-based loan:* $3662. *Average need-based gift aid:* $3926. *Average non-need-based aid:* $2218. *Average indebtedness upon graduation:* $18,529. *Financial aid deadline:* 3/1.

Applying *Options:* deferred entrance. *Application fee:* $25. *Required:* essay or personal statement, high school transcript, 1 letter of recommendation. *Required for some:* interview. *Recommended:* interview. *Application deadlines:* 4/1 (freshmen), 5/1 (transfers). *Notification:* continuous (freshmen), continuous (transfers).

Admissions Contact Ms. Margaret Richmond, Director of Admissions, Keene State College, 229 Main Street, Keene, NH 03435-2604. *Phone:* 603-358-2273. *Toll-free phone:* 800-572-1909. *Fax:* 603-358-2767. *E-mail:* admissions@keene.edu.

■ *See page 1808 for a narrative description.*

MAGDALEN COLLEGE
Warner, New Hampshire

- **Independent Roman Catholic** 4-year, founded 1973
- **Calendar** semesters
- **Degrees** associate and bachelor's
- **Small-town** 135-acre campus
- **Endowment** $1.0 million
- **Coed,** 74 undergraduate students, 100% full-time, 61% women, 39% men
- **Moderately difficult** entrance level, 67% of applicants were admitted

Undergraduates 74 full-time. Students come from 17 states and territories, 1 other country, 92% are from out of state, 4% Asian American or Pacific Islander, 8% Hispanic American, 3% international, 100% live on campus. *Retention:* 62% of 2002 full-time freshmen returned.

Freshmen *Admission:* 46 applied, 31 admitted, 26 enrolled. *Average high school GPA:* 3.30. *Test scores:* SAT verbal scores over 500: 84%; SAT math scores over 500: 73%; ACT scores over 18: 71%; SAT verbal scores over 600: 45%; SAT math scores over 600: 50%; ACT scores over 24: 28%; SAT verbal scores over 700: 17%.

Faculty *Total:* 9, 78% full-time, 22% with terminal degrees. *Student/faculty ratio:* 11:1.

Majors Liberal arts and sciences/liberal studies.

Academic Programs *Special study options:* academic remediation for entering students, cooperative education, part-time degree program.

Library St. Augustine Learning Center plus 1 other with 26,000 titles, 10 serial subscriptions.

Computers on Campus 6 computers available on campus for general student use. Internet access, at least one staffed computer lab available.

Student Life *Housing:* on-campus residence required through senior year. *Options:* men-only, women-only. Campus housing is university owned. Freshman campus housing is guaranteed. *Activities and organizations:* drama/theater group, student-run newspaper, choral group, performance choir, polophony choir, drama club, intramural sports, leisure activities programs. *Campus security:* 24-hour emergency response devices, student patrols. *Student services:* personal/psychological counseling.

Athletics *Intramural sports:* basketball M/W, skiing (cross-country) M/W, skiing (downhill) M/W, soccer M, softball M/W, table tennis M/W, tennis M/W, volleyball M/W.

Standardized Tests *Required:* SAT I or ACT (for admission).

Costs (2004–05) *Comprehensive fee:* $15,000 includes full-time tuition ($9000) and room and board ($6000). *Waivers:* employees or children of employees.

Financial Aid Of all full-time matriculated undergraduates who enrolled in 2003, 52 applied for aid, 52 were judged to have need, 26 had their need fully met. 11 state and other part-time jobs (averaging $1345). *Average percent of need met:* 100%. *Average financial aid package:* $9433. *Average need-based loan:* $4013. *Average need-based gift aid:* $2335. *Average indebtedness upon graduation:* $11,215.

Magdalen College (continued)

Applying *Options:* early admission, early decision. *Application fee:* $35. *Required:* essay or personal statement, high school transcript, 2 letters of recommendation, interview, medical examination form. *Application deadline:* 5/1 (freshmen). *Early decision:* 1/1.

Admissions Contact Mr. Paul V. Sullivan, Director of Admissions, Magdalen College, 511 Kearsarge Mountain Road, Warner, NH 03278. *Phone:* 603-456-2656. *Toll-free phone:* 877-498-1723. *Fax:* 603-456-2660. *E-mail:* admissions@magdalen.edu.

NEW ENGLAND COLLEGE

Henniker, New Hampshire

- **Independent** comprehensive, founded 1946
- **Calendar** semesters
- **Degrees** associate, bachelor's, and master's
- **Small-town** 225-acre campus with easy access to Boston
- **Endowment** $4.8 million
- **Coed**
- **Moderately difficult** entrance level

Faculty *Student/faculty ratio:* 12:1.

Student Life *Campus security:* 24-hour emergency response devices and patrols, student patrols, late-night transport/escort service.

Costs (2003–04) *Comprehensive fee:* $28,860 includes full-time tuition ($20,480), mandatory fees ($640), and room and board ($7740). Part-time tuition: $975 per credit. Part-time tuition and fees vary according to course load. *Required fees:* $215 per term part-time. *College room only:* $4026. Room and board charges vary according to board plan.

Financial Aid Of all full-time matriculated undergraduates who enrolled in 2003, 713 applied for aid, 661 were judged to have need, 292 had their need fully met. 432 Federal Work-Study jobs (averaging $1636). 33 state and other part-time jobs (averaging $1439). In 2003, 79. *Average percent of need met:* 85. *Average financial aid package:* $23,392. *Average need-based loan:* $8363. *Average need-based gift aid:* $11,567. *Average non-need-based aid:* $8195. *Average indebtedness upon graduation:* $28,167.

Applying *Options:* common application, electronic application, deferred entrance. *Application fee:* $30. *Required:* essay or personal statement, high school transcript, 1 letter of recommendation. *Recommended:* interview.

Admissions Contact Mr. Paul Miller, Director of Admission/Financial Aid, New England College, 26 Bridge Street, Henniker, NH 03242. *Phone:* 603-428-2223. *Toll-free phone:* 800-521-7642. *Fax:* 603-428-3155. *E-mail:* admission@nec.edu.

■ *See page 2072 for a narrative description.*

NEW HAMPSHIRE INSTITUTE OF ART

Manchester, New Hampshire

- **Proprietary** 4-year, founded 1898
- **Calendar** semesters
- **Degree** certificates and bachelor's
- **Urban** campus with easy access to Boston, MA
- **Coed,** 131 undergraduate students, 79% full-time, 75% women, 25% men
- **Minimally difficult** entrance level, 83% of applicants were admitted

Undergraduates 103 full-time, 28 part-time. Students come from 6 states and territories, 9% are from out of state, 21% transferred in.

Freshmen *Admission:* 75 applied, 62 admitted, 33 enrolled.

Faculty *Total:* 38, 11% full-time, 84% with terminal degrees. *Student/faculty ratio:* 15:1.

Majors Fine/studio arts.

Academic Programs *Special study options:* part-time degree program, summer session for credit.

Library New Hampshire Institute of Art Library with 5,000 titles, 55 serial subscriptions, 1,000 audiovisual materials, an OPAC, a Web page.

Computers on Campus 5 computers available on campus for general student use. Internet access available.

Student Life *Housing options:* coed, women-only. Campus housing is provided by a third party.

Standardized Tests *Required:* SAT I or ACT (for admission).

Costs (2003–04) *Tuition:* $8950 full-time, $298 per credit part-time. *Required fees:* $800 full-time, $400 per term part-time. *Room only:* Room and board charges vary according to housing facility. *Waivers:* employees or children of employees.

Applying *Application fee:* $25. *Required:* essay or personal statement, high school transcript, letters of recommendation, portfolio. *Recommended:* interview. *Notification:* continuous (transfers).

Admissions Contact Ms. Jane Langlois, Admissions Assistant, New Hampshire Institute of Art, 148 Concord Street, Manchester, NH 03104-4858. *Phone:* 603-623-0313 Ext. 576. *Toll-free phone:* 866-241-4918. *E-mail:* lsullivan@nhia.edu.

■ *See page 2076 for a narrative description.*

PLYMOUTH STATE UNIVERSITY

Plymouth, New Hampshire

- **State-supported** comprehensive, founded 1871, part of University System of New Hampshire
- **Calendar** semesters
- **Degrees** bachelor's, master's, post-master's, and postbachelor's certificates
- **Small-town** 170-acre campus
- **Endowment** $2.9 million
- **Coed,** 3,967 undergraduate students, 93% full-time, 51% women, 49% men
- **Moderately difficult** entrance level, 71% of applicants were admitted

Undergraduates 3,707 full-time, 260 part-time. Students come from 29 states and territories, 11 other countries, 43% are from out of state, 0.5% African American, 1% Asian American or Pacific Islander, 1% Hispanic American, 0.2% Native American, 0.3% international, 6% transferred in, 54% live on campus. *Retention:* 73% of 2002 full-time freshmen returned.

Freshmen *Admission:* 3,685 applied, 2,601 admitted, 903 enrolled. *Average high school GPA:* 2.78. *Test scores:* SAT verbal scores over 500: 43%; SAT math scores over 500: 43%; ACT scores over 18: 53%; SAT verbal scores over 600: 7%; SAT math scores over 600: 8%; ACT scores over 24: 14%; SAT verbal scores over 700: 1%; SAT math scores over 700: 1%.

Faculty *Total:* 340, 47% full-time, 54% with terminal degrees. *Student/faculty ratio:* 19:1.

Majors Accounting; applied economics; art; art teacher education; athletic training; atmospheric sciences and meteorology; biology/biological sciences; biotechnology; business administration and management; business/commerce; chemistry; city/urban, community and regional planning; commercial and advertising art; communication/speech communication and rhetoric; computer science; criminal justice/safety; demography and population; dramatic/theatre arts; early childhood education; education (specific subject areas) related; elementary education; English; environmental biology; fine/studio arts; French; geography; health and physical education; history; humanities; information technology; marketing/marketing management; mathematics; medieval and Renaissance studies; multi-/interdisciplinary studies related; music; music teacher education; parks, recreation, and leisure related; philosophy; political science and government; psychology; public administration; public health education and promotion; social sciences; social sciences related; social work; Spanish.

Academic Programs *Special study options:* accelerated degree program, advanced placement credit, double majors, honors programs, independent study, internships, off-campus study, part-time degree program, services for LD students, student-designed majors, study abroad, summer session for credit. *ROTC:* Army (c), Air Force (c).

Library Lamson Library with 296,479 titles, 1,071 serial subscriptions, 20,993 audiovisual materials, an OPAC, a Web page.

Computers on Campus 500 computers available on campus for general student use. A campuswide network can be accessed from student residence rooms and from off campus. Internet access, online (class) registration, at least one staffed computer lab available. Computer purchase or lease plan available.

Student Life *Housing:* on-campus residence required for freshman year. *Options:* coed. Campus housing is university owned. Freshman applicants given priority for college housing. *Activities and organizations:* drama/theater group, student-run newspaper, radio station, choral group, Programming Activities in College Environment, Student Senate, alternative spring break, Childhood Studies Club, Health, Physical Ed, & Recreation Club, national fraternities, national sororities. *Campus security:* 24-hour emergency response devices and patrols, student patrols, late-night transport/escort service, controlled dormitory access, shuttle bus service, crime prevention programs, self-defense education. *Student services:* health clinic, personal/psychological counseling, women's center.

Athletics Member NCAA. All Division III. *Intercollegiate sports:* baseball M, basketball M/W, cheerleading M(c)/W(c), field hockey W, football M, ice hockey M, lacrosse M/W, rugby M(c)/W(c), skiing (downhill) M/W, soccer M/W, softball W, swimming W, tennis W, volleyball M(c)/W, wrestling M. *Intramural sports:* basketball M/W, cheerleading M(c)/W(c), football M/W, golf M/W, racquetball M/W, soccer M/W, softball M/W, tennis M/W, ultimate Frisbee M/W, volleyball M/W.

Standardized Tests *Required:* SAT I or ACT (for admission).

Costs (2003–04) *Tuition:* state resident $4750 full-time, $266 per credit hour part-time; nonresident $10,800 full-time, $548 per credit hour part-time. *Required fees:* $1490 full-time, $64 per credit hour part-time. *Room and board:* $6058; room only: $4100. Room and board charges vary according to board plan and housing facility. *Payment plan:* installment. *Waivers:* senior citizens and employees or children of employees.

Financial Aid Of all full-time matriculated undergraduates who enrolled in 2003, 2,867 applied for aid, 2,146 were judged to have need, 122 had their need fully met. 1,133 Federal Work-Study jobs (averaging $1741). In 2003, 247 non-need-based awards were made. *Average percent of need met:* 68%. *Average financial aid package:* $6940. *Average need-based loan:* $3649. *Average need-based gift aid:* $4085. *Average non-need-based aid:* $1942. *Average indebtedness upon graduation:* $17,629.

Applying *Options:* electronic application, deferred entrance. *Application fee:* $35. *Required:* essay or personal statement, high school transcript, 1 letter of recommendation. *Required for some:* interview. *Application deadlines:* 4/1 (freshmen), 4/1 (transfers). *Notification:* continuous until 7/1 (freshmen), continuous until 11/1 (transfers).

Admissions Contact Mr. Eugene Fahey, Senior Associate Director of Admission, Plymouth State University, 17 High Street, MSC #52, Plymouth, NH 03264-1595. *Phone:* 800-842-6900. *Toll-free phone:* 800-842-6900. *Fax:* 603-535-2714. *E-mail:* plymouthadmit@plymouth.edu.

■ *See page 2178 for a narrative description.*

RIVIER COLLEGE
Nashua, New Hampshire

- **Independent Roman Catholic** comprehensive, founded 1933
- **Calendar** semesters
- **Degrees** certificates, associate, bachelor's, master's, post-master's, and postbachelor's certificates
- **Suburban** 64-acre campus with easy access to Boston
- **Endowment** $16.0 million
- **Coed,** 1,452 undergraduate students, 56% full-time, 82% women, 18% men
- **Moderately difficult** entrance level, 80% of applicants were admitted

Rivier's School of Undergraduate Studies enrolls approximately 800 full-time day students and 500 evening students. Rivier's programs combine academic achievement in the liberal arts and professional studies with hands-on preparation for the future. Special opportunities, such as the honors program, offer added challenges and enrichment.

Undergraduates 817 full-time, 635 part-time. Students come from 10 states and territories, 7 other countries, 35% are from out of state, 2% African American, 2% Asian American or Pacific Islander, 2% Hispanic American, 0.2% Native American, 0.1% international, 9% transferred in, 46% live on campus. *Retention:* 69% of 2002 full-time freshmen returned.

Freshmen *Admission:* 899 applied, 715 admitted, 221 enrolled. *Average high school GPA:* 3.0.

Faculty *Total:* 171, 41% full-time, 38% with terminal degrees. *Student/faculty ratio:* 14:1.

Majors American government and politics; art; biology/biological sciences; biology teacher education; business administration and management; chemistry; chemistry teacher education; commercial and advertising art; communication/speech communication and rhetoric; computer science; criminology; drawing; education; elementary education; English; English/language arts teacher education; fine/studio arts; foreign language teacher education; French; history; information science/studies; kindergarten/preschool education; legal studies; liberal arts and sciences/liberal studies; mathematics; mathematics teacher education; modern languages; nursing (registered nurse training); painting; photography; political science and government; pre-dentistry studies; pre-law studies; pre-medical studies; pre-veterinary studies; psychology; secondary education; social science teacher education; sociology; Spanish; special education.

Academic Programs *Special study options:* accelerated degree program, adult/continuing education programs, advanced placement credit, double majors, honors programs, independent study, internships, off-campus study, part-time degree program, services for LD students. *ROTC:* Air Force (c).

Library Regina Library plus 1 other with 105,000 titles, 1,802 serial subscriptions, 29,094 audiovisual materials, an OPAC, a Web page.

Computers on Campus 93 computers available on campus for general student use. A campuswide network can be accessed from student residence rooms and from off campus. At least one staffed computer lab available.

Student Life *Housing options:* coed. Campus housing is university owned. Freshman campus housing is guaranteed. *Activities and organizations:* drama/theater group, student-run newspaper, choral group, Student Government Association, Residence Hall Council, Student Business Organization, Student Admissions Committee, Behavioral Sciences Association. *Campus security:* 24-hour emergency response devices and patrols, late-night transport/escort service, controlled dormitory access. *Student services:* health clinic, personal/psychological counseling.

Athletics Member NCAA. except baseball (Division III), men's and women's basketball (Division III), men's and women's cheerleading (Division III), men's and women's cross-country running (Division III), men's and women's golf (Division III), men's and women's soccer (Division III), softball (Division III), men's and women's volleyball (Division III) *Intercollegiate sports:* baseball M, basketball M/W, cheerleading M/W, cross-country running M/W, golf M/W, soccer M/W, softball W, volleyball M/W. *Intramural sports:* basketball M/W, skiing (cross-country) M/W, skiing (downhill) M/W, soccer M/W, softball M/W, table tennis M/W, tennis M/W, volleyball M/W, weight lifting M/W.

Standardized Tests *Required:* SAT I or ACT (for admission). *Required for some:* nursing examination.

Costs (2003–04) *Comprehensive fee:* $25,542 includes full-time tuition ($18,450) and room and board ($7092). Part-time tuition: $615 per credit. Part-time tuition and fees vary according to class time. *Room and board:* Room and board charges vary according to board plan and housing facility. *Payment plans:* installment, deferred payment. *Waivers:* senior citizens and employees or children of employees.

Financial Aid Of all full-time matriculated undergraduates who enrolled in 2002, 749 applied for aid, 749 were judged to have need, 134 had their need fully met. 257 Federal Work-Study jobs (averaging $1926). 90 state and other part-time jobs (averaging $1849). In 2002, 74 non-need-based awards were made. *Average percent of need met:* 75%. *Average financial aid package:* $11,932. *Average need-based loan:* $4624. *Average need-based gift aid:* $8447. *Average non-need-based aid:* $6000. *Average indebtedness upon graduation:* $16,555.

Applying *Options:* common application, early action, deferred entrance. *Application fee:* $25. *Required:* essay or personal statement, high school transcript, 1 letter of recommendation. *Required for some:* interview, portfolio for art program. *Recommended:* minimum 2.3 GPA, interview. *Application deadline:* rolling (freshmen), rolling (transfers). *Notification:* continuous (freshmen), 12/1 (early action), continuous (transfers).

Admissions Contact Mr. David Boisvert, (Director of Undergraduate Admissions) Executive Assistant to President for Enrollment Management, Rivier College, 420 Main Street, Nashua, NH 03060. *Phone:* 603-897-8502. *Toll-free phone:* 800-44RIVIER. *Fax:* 603-891-1799. *E-mail:* rivadmit@rivier.edu.

■ *See page 2240 for a narrative description.*

SAINT ANSELM COLLEGE
Manchester, New Hampshire

- **Independent Roman Catholic** 4-year, founded 1889
- **Calendar** semesters
- **Degree** bachelor's
- **Suburban** 450-acre campus with easy access to Boston
- **Endowment** $48.6 million
- **Coed,** 2,008 undergraduate students, 97% full-time, 57% women, 43% men
- **Moderately difficult** entrance level, 71% of applicants were admitted

Undergraduates 1,939 full-time, 69 part-time. Students come from 28 states and territories, 15 other countries, 77% are from out of state, 0.3% African American, 0.5% Asian American or Pacific Islander, 1% Hispanic American, 0.2% Native American, 1% international, 1% transferred in, 88% live on campus. *Retention:* 86% of 2002 full-time freshmen returned.

Freshmen *Admission:* 3,033 applied, 2,140 admitted, 588 enrolled. *Average high school GPA:* 3.17. *Test scores:* SAT verbal scores over 500: 81%; SAT math scores over 500: 82%; SAT verbal scores over 600: 29%; SAT math scores over 600: 28%; SAT verbal scores over 700: 2%; SAT math scores over 700: 2%.

Faculty *Total:* 170, 71% full-time, 79% with terminal degrees. *Student/faculty ratio:* 14:1.

Majors Accounting; art; biochemistry; biological and physical sciences; biology/biological sciences; business/commerce; chemistry related; classics and languages, literatures and linguistics; computer science; criminal justice/safety; economics; engineering; English; environmental studies; finance; French; history; liberal arts and sciences and humanities related; mathematics; nursing related; philosophy; political science and government; pre-dentistry studies; pre-law studies; pre-medical studies; psychology; secondary education; sociology; Spanish; theology.

Academic Programs *Special study options:* advanced placement credit, honors programs, independent study, internships, off-campus study, part-time degree program, services for LD students, study abroad, summer session for credit. *ROTC:* Army (c), Air Force (c). *Unusual degree programs:* 3-2 engineering with University of Massachusetts Lowell, Catholic University of America, University of Notre Dame, Manhattan College.

Saint Anselm College (continued)

Library Geisel Library with 222,000 titles, 1,900 serial subscriptions, 8,000 audiovisual materials, an OPAC, a Web page.

Computers on Campus 400 computers available on campus for general student use. A campuswide network can be accessed from student residence rooms and from off campus. Internet access, at least one staffed computer lab available.

Student Life *Housing:* on-campus residence required for freshman year. *Options:* men-only, women-only, disabled students. Campus housing is university owned. Freshman campus housing is guaranteed. *Activities and organizations:* drama/theater group, student-run newspaper, choral group, Center for Volunteers, Anselmian Abbey Players, Knights of Columbus, spring break alternative, international relations club. *Campus security:* 24-hour emergency response devices and patrols, late-night transport/escort service, controlled dormitory access. *Student services:* health clinic, personal/psychological counseling.

Athletics Member NCAA. All Division II. *Intercollegiate sports:* baseball M, basketball M(s)/W(s), cheerleading W(c), field hockey W, football M, golf M, ice hockey M, lacrosse M/W, rugby M(c)/W(c), skiing (downhill) M/W, soccer M/W, softball W, tennis M/W, track and field M(c)/W(c), volleyball W. *Intramural sports:* basketball M/W, football M/W, ice hockey M/W, racquetball M/W, skiing (cross-country) M/W, soccer M/W, softball M/W, tennis M/W, ultimate Frisbee M/W, volleyball M/W, weight lifting M/W.

Standardized Tests *Required:* SAT I or ACT (for admission). *Required for some:* TOEFL.

Costs (2004–05) *Comprehensive fee:* $32,290 includes full-time tuition ($22,700), mandatory fees ($1010), and room and board ($8580). *Room and board:* Room and board charges vary according to housing facility. *Payment plans:* installment, deferred payment. *Waivers:* senior citizens and employees or children of employees.

Financial Aid Of all full-time matriculated undergraduates who enrolled in 2003, 1,743 applied for aid, 1,692 were judged to have need, 40 had their need fully met. 1,130 Federal Work-Study jobs (averaging $1304). 18 state and other part-time jobs (averaging $2806). In 2003, 226 non-need-based awards were made. *Average percent of need met:* 75%. *Average financial aid package:* $18,380. *Average need-based loan:* $3158. *Average need-based gift aid:* $13,108. *Average non-need-based aid:* $5602. *Average indebtedness upon graduation:* $19,111.

Applying *Options:* common application, electronic application, early admission, early decision, deferred entrance. *Application fee:* $50. *Required:* essay or personal statement, high school transcript, minimum 2.0 GPA, 2 letters of recommendation. *Recommended:* interview. *Application deadline:* rolling (freshmen), rolling (transfers). *Early decision:* 12/1. *Notification:* continuous (freshmen), 12/15 (early decision), continuous (transfers).

Admissions Contact Ms. Nancy Davis Griffin, Director of Admissions, Saint Anselm College, 100 Saint Anselm Drive, Manchester, NH 03102-1310. *Phone:* 603-641-7500. *Toll-free phone:* 888-4ANSELM. *Fax:* 603-641-7550. *E-mail:* admissions@anselm.edu.

■ *See page 2274 for a narrative description.*

SOUTHERN NEW HAMPSHIRE UNIVERSITY
Manchester, New Hampshire

- **Independent** comprehensive, founded 1932
- **Calendar** semesters
- **Degrees** certificates, associate, bachelor's, master's, doctoral, and postbachelor's certificates
- **Suburban** 280-acre campus with easy access to Boston
- **Endowment** $10.4 million
- **Coed**
- **Moderately difficult** entrance level

Southern New Hampshire University, formerly New Hampshire College, is enhanced by growth in response to the changing times. The University is a private institution that offers more than thirty-five majors in business, education, hospitality, and liberal arts disciplines. Master's and doctoral degrees are also awarded. The students and faculty members at SNHU enjoy the resources of a university with the personal approach of a small college.

Faculty *Student/faculty ratio:* 17:1.

Student Life *Campus security:* 24-hour emergency response devices and patrols, student patrols, late-night transport/escort service, controlled dormitory access.

Athletics Member NCAA. All Division II.

Standardized Tests *Required:* SAT I or ACT (for admission).

Costs (2004–05) *Comprehensive fee:* $27,180 includes full-time tuition ($18,984), mandatory fees ($330), and room and board ($7866). Full-time tuition and fees vary according to class time. Part-time tuition: $689 per credit. Part-time tuition and fees vary according to class time. *Room and board:* Room and board charges vary according to board plan and housing facility. *Payment plans:* installment, deferred payment.

Financial Aid Of all full-time matriculated undergraduates who enrolled in 2002, 363 Federal Work-Study jobs (averaging $1090).

Applying *Options:* common application, electronic application, early action, deferred entrance. *Application fee:* $35. *Required:* essay or personal statement, high school transcript, minimum 2.0 GPA, letters of recommendation, 1 letter of recommendation from guidance counselor. *Recommended:* interview.

Admissions Contact Mr. Steve Soba, Director of Admission, Southern New Hampshire University, 2500 North River Road, Manchester, NH 03106. *Phone:* 603-645-9611 Ext. 9633. *Toll-free phone:* 800-642-4968. *Fax:* 603-645-9693. *E-mail:* admission@snhu.edu.

■ *See page 2412 for a narrative description.*

THOMAS MORE COLLEGE OF LIBERAL ARTS
Merrimack, New Hampshire

- **Independent** 4-year, founded 1978, affiliated with Roman Catholic Church
- **Calendar** semesters
- **Degree** bachelor's
- **Small-town** 14-acre campus with easy access to Boston
- **Coed,** 89 undergraduate students, 99% full-time, 45% women, 55% men
- **Moderately difficult** entrance level, 100% of applicants were admitted

Now celebrating its 25th year, Thomas More College (TMC) initiates its students into a life-changing 4-year core curriculum grounded in the study of Western tradition. With an environment nurturing close friendships around classic books and a semester of study in Rome, Italy, for selected students, TMC is recognized as a top liberal arts college.

Undergraduates 88 full-time, 1 part-time. Students come from 26 states and territories, 3 other countries, 90% are from out of state, 7% transferred in, 97% live on campus. *Retention:* 85% of 2002 full-time freshmen returned.

Freshmen *Admission:* 40 applied, 40 admitted, 27 enrolled. *Average high school GPA:* 3.1. *Test scores:* SAT verbal scores over 500: 95%; SAT math scores over 500: 80%; ACT scores over 18: 100%; SAT verbal scores over 600: 70%; SAT math scores over 600: 30%; ACT scores over 24: 100%; SAT verbal scores over 700: 25%; SAT math scores over 700: 15%; ACT scores over 30: 25%.

Faculty *Total:* 10, 70% full-time, 50% with terminal degrees. *Student/faculty ratio:* 9:1.

Majors Biology/biological sciences; literature; philosophy; political science and government.

Academic Programs *Special study options:* independent study, study abroad.

Library Warren Memorial Library plus 1 other with 45,000 titles, 20 serial subscriptions, 1,000 audiovisual materials.

Computers on Campus 6 computers available on campus for general student use. Internet access, at least one staffed computer lab available.

Student Life *Housing:* on-campus residence required through senior year. *Options:* men-only, women-only. Campus housing is university owned. Freshman campus housing is guaranteed. *Activities and organizations:* choral group. *Campus security:* student patrols, late-night transport/escort service. *Student services:* personal/psychological counseling.

Standardized Tests *Required:* SAT I or ACT (for admission).

Costs (2003–04) *Comprehensive fee:* $18,150 includes full-time tuition ($10,400), mandatory fees ($50), and room and board ($7700). Part-time tuition: $125 per credit hour. *Payment plans:* installment, deferred payment. *Waivers:* employees or children of employees.

Financial Aid Of all full-time matriculated undergraduates who enrolled in 2003, 85 applied for aid, 75 were judged to have need. 49 state and other part-time jobs (averaging $1622). In 2003, 10 non-need-based awards were made. *Average percent of need met:* 80%. *Average financial aid package:* $14,627. *Average need-based loan:* $3759. *Average need-based gift aid:* $7567. *Average non-need-based aid:* $9069. *Average indebtedness upon graduation:* $14,505.

Applying *Options:* electronic application, early admission, deferred entrance. *Required:* essay or personal statement, high school transcript, 2 letters of recommendation. *Required for some:* interview. *Application deadline:* rolling (freshmen), rolling (transfers). *Notification:* continuous (freshmen), continuous (transfers).

Admissions Contact Ms. Catherine M. Alcarez, Director of Admissions, Thomas More College of Liberal Arts, 6 Manchester Street, Merrimack, NH 03054-4818. *Phone:* 800-880-8308. *Toll-free phone:* 800-880-8308. *Fax:* 603-880-9280. *E-mail:* admissions@thomasmorecollege.edu.

UNIVERSITY OF NEW HAMPSHIRE
Durham, New Hampshire

- **State-supported** university, founded 1866, part of University System of New Hampshire
- **Calendar** semesters
- **Degrees** associate, bachelor's, master's, doctoral, and post-master's certificates
- **Small-town** 2600-acre campus with easy access to Boston
- **Endowment** $145.9 million
- **Coed,** 11,516 undergraduate students, 93% full-time, 57% women, 43% men
- **Moderately difficult** entrance level, 69% of applicants were admitted

Undergraduates 10,700 full-time, 816 part-time. Students come from 42 states and territories, 26 other countries, 43% are from out of state, 1% African American, 2% Asian American or Pacific Islander, 1% Hispanic American, 0.4% Native American, 0.7% international, 3% transferred in, 56% live on campus. *Retention:* 85% of 2002 full-time freshmen returned.

Freshmen *Admission:* 10,798 applied, 7,502 admitted, 2,636 enrolled. *Test scores:* SAT verbal scores over 500: 78%; SAT math scores over 500: 81%; SAT verbal scores over 600: 26%; SAT math scores over 600: 33%; SAT verbal scores over 700: 3%; SAT math scores over 700: 4%.

Faculty *Total:* 694, 85% full-time, 84% with terminal degrees. *Student/faculty ratio:* 14:1.

Majors Accounting; adult and continuing education; agricultural business and management; agricultural teacher education; agriculture; agronomy and crop science; American studies; animal/livestock husbandry and production; animal sciences; anthropology; art; art history, criticism and conservation; art teacher education; athletic training; audiology and speech-language pathology; biochemistry; biological and physical sciences; biology/biological sciences; biomedical technology; botany/plant biology; business administration and management; cell biology and histology; chemical engineering; chemistry; child development; city/urban, community and regional planning; civil engineering; civil engineering technology; classics and languages, literatures and linguistics; clinical/medical laboratory technology; community organization and advocacy; computer engineering; computer science; computer software technology; construction engineering technology; construction management; criminal justice/law enforcement administration; culinary arts; dairy science; dietetics; dietetic technician; dramatic/theatre arts; ecology; economics; electrical, electronics and communications engineering; elementary education; English; English literature (British and Commonwealth); environmental/environmental health engineering; environmental studies; equestrian studies; European studies; evolutionary biology; family and consumer economics related; family and consumer sciences/human sciences; finance; fine/studio arts; foods, nutrition, and wellness; forestry; forestry technology; French; geography; geology/earth science; German; health/health care administration; history; horticultural science; hospitality administration; hotel/motel administration; humanities; hydrology and water resources science; interdisciplinary studies; international/global studies; international relations and affairs; journalism; kindergarten/preschool education; kinesiology and exercise science; landscape architecture; landscaping and groundskeeping; Latin; liberal arts and sciences/liberal studies; linguistics; literature; marine biology and biological oceanography; marine science/merchant marine officer; mass communication/media; materials science; mathematics; mathematics teacher education; mechanical engineering; medical microbiology and bacteriology; modern Greek; modern languages; molecular biology; music; music history, literature, and theory; music teacher education; natural resources/conservation; natural resources management and policy; natural sciences; nursing (registered nurse training); occupational therapy; ocean engineering; oceanography (chemical and physical); ornamental horticulture; parks, recreation and leisure; philosophy; physical education teaching and coaching; physics; piano and organ; political science and government; pre-engineering; pre-medical studies; pre-veterinary studies; psychology; restaurant, culinary, and catering management; restaurant/food services management; Romance languages; Russian; science teacher education; secondary education; social work; sociology; soil conservation; Spanish; speech therapy; statistics; survey technology; therapeutic recreation; tourism and travel services management; trade and industrial teacher education; violin, viola, guitar and other stringed instruments; voice and opera; wildlife and wildlands science and management; wildlife biology; wind/percussion instruments; women's studies; zoology/animal biology.

Academic Programs *Special study options:* accelerated degree program, adult/continuing education programs, advanced placement credit, double majors, English as a second language, external degree program, honors programs, independent study, internships, off-campus study, part-time degree program, services for LD students, student-designed majors, study abroad, summer session for credit. *ROTC:* Army (b), Air Force (b). *Unusual degree programs:* 3-2 liberal arts, French, botany.

Library Dimond Library plus 4 others with 1.1 million titles, 13,217 serial subscriptions, 24,247 audiovisual materials, an OPAC, a Web page.

Computers on Campus A campuswide network can be accessed from student residence rooms and from off campus. Internet access, online (class) registration, at least one staffed computer lab available.

Student Life *Housing options:* coed, women-only, disabled students. Campus housing is university owned. Freshman campus housing is guaranteed. *Activities and organizations:* drama/theater group, student-run newspaper, radio station, choral group, marching band, outing club, Student Committee on Popular Entertainment, Diversity Support Coalition, Campus Activities Board, Student Environmental Action Coalition, national fraternities, national sororities. *Campus security:* 24-hour emergency response devices and patrols, student patrols, late-night transport/escort service, controlled dormitory access, lighted pathways and sidewalks. *Student services:* health clinic, personal/psychological counseling, women's center, legal services.

Athletics Member NCAA. All Division I except football (Division I-AA). *Intercollegiate sports:* archery M(c)/W(c), baseball M(c), basketball M(s)/W(s), cheerleading W(s), crew M(c)/W, cross-country running M(s)/W(s), fencing M(c)/W(c), field hockey W(s), golf M(c), gymnastics W(s), ice hockey M(s)/W(s), lacrosse M(c)/W(s), rugby M(c)/W(c), sailing M(c)/W(c), skiing (cross-country) M(s)/W(s), skiing (downhill) M(s)/W(s), soccer M(s)/W(s), softball M(c), swimming M(s)/W(s), tennis M/W(s), track and field M(s)/W(s), volleyball M(c)/W(s), wrestling M(c). *Intramural sports:* badminton M(c)/W(c), basketball M/W, field hockey W, football M/W, golf M/W, ice hockey M/W, racquetball M/W, riflery M(c)/W(c), rock climbing M/W, soccer M/W, softball M/W, table tennis M/W, tennis M/W, ultimate Frisbee M/W, volleyball M/W.

Standardized Tests *Required:* SAT I or ACT (for admission).

Costs (2003–04) *Tuition:* state resident $6770 full-time, $282 per credit part-time; nonresident $17,130 full-time, $714 per credit part-time. Full-time tuition and fees vary according to program and reciprocity agreements. Part-time tuition and fees vary according to course load and reciprocity agreements. *Required fees:* $1894 full-time, $15 per term part-time. *Room and board:* $6234; room only: $3636. Room and board charges vary according to board plan and housing facility. *Payment plan:* installment. *Waivers:* senior citizens and employees or children of employees.

Financial Aid Of all full-time matriculated undergraduates who enrolled in 2003, 7,206 applied for aid, 5,878 were judged to have need, 1,156 had their need fully met. 3,146 Federal Work-Study jobs (averaging $1853). 2,811 state and other part-time jobs (averaging $1762). In 2003, 1984 non-need-based awards were made. *Average percent of need met:* 80%. *Average financial aid package:* $14,267. *Average need-based loan:* $3354. *Average need-based gift aid:* $2281. *Average non-need-based aid:* $5414. *Average indebtedness upon graduation:* $21,250.

Applying *Options:* common application, electronic application, early action, deferred entrance. *Application fee:* $45. *Required:* essay or personal statement, high school transcript, 1 letter of recommendation. *Recommended:* minimum 3.0 GPA. *Application deadlines:* 2/1 (freshmen), 3/1 (transfers). *Notification:* 4/15 (freshmen), 1/15 (early action), 4/15 (transfers).

Admissions Contact Mr. Robert McGann, Director of Admissions, University of New Hampshire, Grant House, 4 Garrison Avenue, Durham, NH 03824. *Phone:* 603-862-1360. *Fax:* 603-862-0077. *E-mail:* admissions@unh.edu.

■ *See page 2668 for a narrative description.*

UNIVERSITY OF NEW HAMPSHIRE AT MANCHESTER
Manchester, New Hampshire

- **State-supported** comprehensive, founded 1967, part of University System of New Hampshire
- **Calendar** semesters
- **Degrees** certificates, associate, bachelor's, and master's
- **Urban** 800-acre campus with easy access to Boston
- **Endowment** $18,851
- **Coed,** 1,078 undergraduate students, 51% full-time, 58% women, 42% men
- **Moderately difficult** entrance level, 72% of applicants were admitted

Undergraduates 554 full-time, 524 part-time. Students come from 4 states and territories, 1% African American, 2% Asian American or Pacific Islander, 1% Hispanic American, 0.2% Native American, 0.1% international, 11% transferred in.

Freshmen *Admission:* 580 applied, 420 admitted, 123 enrolled. *Test scores:* SAT verbal scores over 500: 66%; SAT math scores over 500: 54%; SAT verbal scores over 600: 11%; SAT math scores over 600: 14%; SAT verbal scores over 700: 2%; SAT math scores over 700: 1%.

Faculty *Total:* 88, 32% full-time, 42% with terminal degrees. *Student/faculty ratio:* 13:1.

University of New Hampshire at Manchester (continued)

Majors Biology/biological sciences; business administration and management; electrical, electronic and communications engineering technology; English; fine/studio arts; history; humanities; liberal arts and sciences/liberal studies; mass communication/media; mechanical engineering/mechanical technology; nursing science; psychology; sign language interpretation and translation.

Academic Programs *Special study options:* academic remediation for entering students, adult/continuing education programs, advanced placement credit, double majors, external degree program, independent study, internships, off-campus study, part-time degree program, services for LD students, student-designed majors, study abroad, summer session for credit. *ROTC:* Army (c), Air Force (c).

Library Norma K. Oudens Memorial Library with 25,000 titles, 550 serial subscriptions, 1,256 audiovisual materials, an OPAC, a Web page.

Computers on Campus 38 computers available on campus for general student use. A campuswide network can be accessed from off campus. Internet access, at least one staffed computer lab available.

Student Life *Housing:* college housing not available. *Activities and organizations:* Student Council. *Campus security:* late-night transport/escort service.

Standardized Tests *Required for some:* SAT I (for admission). *Recommended:* ACT (for admission).

Costs (2003–04) *Tuition:* state resident $5870 full-time, $245 per credit part-time; nonresident $14,850 full-time, $619 per credit part-time. Part-time tuition and fees vary according to program. *Required fees:* $177 full-time. *Payment plan:* installment. *Waivers:* senior citizens and employees or children of employees.

Financial Aid Of all full-time matriculated undergraduates who enrolled in 2003, 508 applied for aid, 380 were judged to have need, 36 had their need fully met. 97 Federal Work-Study jobs (averaging $1741). In 2003, 15 non-need-based awards were made. *Average percent of need met:* 64%. *Average financial aid package:* $8224. *Average need-based loan:* $3491. *Average need-based gift aid:* $502. *Average non-need-based aid:* $3874. *Average indebtedness upon graduation:* $21,250.

Applying *Options:* deferred entrance. *Application fee:* $35. *Required:* essay or personal statement, high school transcript, 1 letter of recommendation. *Recommended:* interview. *Application deadlines:* 6/15 (freshmen), 6/15 (transfers). *Notification:* continuous (freshmen), continuous (transfers).

Admissions Contact Ms. Susan Miller, Administrative Assistant, University of New Hampshire at Manchester, 400 Commercial Street, Manchester, NH 03101. *Phone:* 603-641-4150. *Toll-free phone:* 800-735-2964. *Fax:* 603-641-4125. *E-mail:* unhm@unh.edu.

NEW JERSEY

BERKELEY COLLEGE
West Paterson, New Jersey

- **Proprietary** primarily 2-year, founded 1931
- **Calendar** quarters
- **Degrees** certificates, associate, and bachelor's
- **Suburban** 25-acre campus with easy access to New York City
- **Coed,** 2,198 undergraduate students, 85% full-time, 77% women, 23% men
- **Minimally difficult** entrance level

Undergraduates 1,871 full-time, 327 part-time. Students come from 8 states and territories, 25 other countries, 16% African American, 5% Asian American or Pacific Islander, 34% Hispanic American, 0.3% Native American, 2% international, 1% live on campus.

Faculty *Total:* 158, 39% full-time. *Student/faculty ratio:* 24:1.

Majors Accounting; business administration and management; business/commerce; computer management; fashion merchandising; interior design; international business/trade/commerce; legal assistant/paralegal; marketing/marketing management; system administration; web page, digital/multimedia and information resources design.

Academic Programs *Special study options:* academic remediation for entering students, adult/continuing education programs, advanced placement credit, cooperative education, distance learning, English as a second language, internships, off-campus study, part-time degree program, study abroad, summer session for credit.

Library Walter A. Brower Library with 49,584 titles, 224 serial subscriptions, 2,659 audiovisual materials, an OPAC, a Web page.

Computers on Campus 300 computers available on campus for general student use. A campuswide network can be accessed from student residence rooms and from off campus. At least one staffed computer lab available.

Student Life *Housing options:* coed. Campus housing is university owned. *Activities and organizations:* student-run newspaper, Student Government Association, Athletics Club, Paralegal Student Association, International Club, Fashion and Marketing Club. *Campus security:* 24-hour emergency response devices, controlled dormitory access, security patrols. *Student services:* personal/psychological counseling.

Athletics *Intramural sports:* basketball M/W, football M/W, soccer M/W, softball M/W, volleyball M/W.

Standardized Tests *Required:* SAT I or ACT (for admission), institutional entrance exam (for admission).

Costs (2004–05) *One-time required fee:* $50. *Comprehensive fee:* $25,200 includes full-time tuition ($15,900) and room and board ($9300). Part-time tuition and fees vary according to class time. *Room and board:* Room and board charges vary according to housing facility. *Payment plan:* installment. *Waivers:* employees or children of employees.

Financial Aid Of all full-time matriculated undergraduates who enrolled in 2001, 150 Federal Work-Study jobs (averaging $1200).

Applying *Options:* electronic application, deferred entrance. *Application fee:* $40. *Required:* high school transcript. *Recommended:* interview. *Application deadline:* rolling (freshmen), rolling (transfers).

Admissions Contact Mrs. Carol Covino, Director of High School Admissions, Berkeley College, 44 Rifle Camp Road, West Paterson, NJ 07424. *Phone:* 973-278-5400 Ext. 1210. *Toll-free phone:* 800-446-5400. *E-mail:* info@berkeleycollege.edu.

■ *See page 1244 for a narrative description.*

BETH MEDRASH GOVOHA
Lakewood, New Jersey

Admissions Contact Rabbi Yehuda Jacobs, Director of Admissions, Beth Medrash Govoha, 617 Sixth Street, Lakewood, NJ 08701-2797. *Phone:* 908-367-1060.

BLOOMFIELD COLLEGE
Bloomfield, New Jersey

- **Independent** 4-year, founded 1868, affiliated with Presbyterian Church (U.S.A.)
- **Calendar** semesters
- **Degree** certificates and bachelor's
- **Suburban** 12-acre campus with easy access to New York City
- **Endowment** $7.1 million
- **Coed,** 2,083 undergraduate students
- **Minimally difficult** entrance level, 56% of applicants were admitted

Bloomfield College students come from a rich mixture of backgrounds and experiences. Reflecting the contemporary world, they learn together, share interests, build friendships to last a lifetime, and graduate fully prepared for careers and continued education. New programs include 2D/3D computer animation, allied health technology, bachelor of arts in internet technology, bachelor of arts in education, and an education certificate program.

Undergraduates Students come from 13 states and territories, 13 other countries, 2% are from out of state, 52% African American, 4% Asian American or Pacific Islander, 18% Hispanic American, 0.2% Native American, 2% international, 13% live on campus. *Retention:* 70% of 2002 full-time freshmen returned.

Freshmen *Admission:* 1,712 applied, 959 admitted. *Average high school GPA:* 2.54. *Test scores:* SAT verbal scores over 500: 12%; SAT math scores over 500: 14%; SAT verbal scores over 600: 3%; SAT math scores over 600: 3%; SAT verbal scores over 700: 1%; SAT math scores over 700: 1%.

Faculty *Total:* 228, 28% full-time, 30% with terminal degrees. *Student/faculty ratio:* 15:1.

Majors Accounting; allied health and medical assisting services related; applied mathematics; art teacher education; biochemistry; biology/biological sciences; biology teacher education; business administration and management; chemistry; chemistry teacher education; clinical laboratory science/medical technology; communication/speech communication and rhetoric; computer graphics; creative writing; criminal justice/law enforcement administration; cytotechnology; dramatic/theatre arts; economics; English; English/language arts teacher education; environmental biology; film/video and photographic arts related; finance; fine/studio arts; history; history teacher education; human resources management; human resources management and services related; information science/studies; marketing/marketing management; mathematics teacher education; multi-/interdisciplinary studies related; musical instrument fabrication and repair; nursing (registered nurse training); philosophy; political science and government; pre-dentistry studies; pre-medical studies; pre-veterinary studies; psychology; public administration; public policy analysis; purchasing, procurement/acquisitions and contracts management; religious studies; science teacher education; social studies teacher education; sociology; toxicology; web page, digital/multimedia and information resources design.

Academic Programs *Special study options:* academic remediation for entering students, accelerated degree program, advanced placement credit, cooperative education, distance learning, double majors, English as a second language, honors programs, independent study, internships, part-time degree program, services for LD students, student-designed majors, study abroad, summer session for credit. *ROTC:* Army (c). *Unusual degree programs:* 3-2 computer information systems with New Jersey Institute of Technology.

Library Bloomfield College Library plus 1 other with 60,000 titles, 375 serial subscriptions, 5,000 audiovisual materials, an OPAC, a Web page.

Computers on Campus 300 computers available on campus for general student use. A campuswide network can be accessed from student residence rooms and from off campus. Internet access, at least one staffed computer lab available. Computer purchase or lease plan available.

Student Life *Housing options:* coed. Campus housing is university owned. *Activities and organizations:* drama/theater group, student-run newspaper, radio station, choral group, Versatile Entertainment, Team Infinite, Residence Life Development, Haitian Student Organization, Sisters in Support, national fraternities, national sororities. *Campus security:* 24-hour emergency response devices and patrols, late-night transport/escort service, controlled dormitory access, security cameras in high-traffic areas. *Student services:* health clinic, personal/psychological counseling, women's center.

Athletics Member NCAA, NAIA. All NCAA Division II. *Intercollegiate sports:* baseball M(s), basketball M(s)/W(s), cross-country running M(s), soccer M(s)/W(s), softball W(s), volleyball W(s). *Intramural sports:* basketball M/W, bowling M/W, soccer M/W, softball M/W, volleyball M/W.

Standardized Tests *Required:* SAT I or ACT (for admission).

Costs (2004–05) *Comprehensive fee:* $20,650 includes full-time tuition ($13,700), mandatory fees ($200), and room and board ($6750). Part-time tuition: $1380 per course. *Required fees:* $25 per term part-time. *College room only:* $3375. Room and board charges vary according to housing facility. *Payment plans:* installment, deferred payment. *Waivers:* senior citizens and employees or children of employees.

Financial Aid In 2003, 22 non-need-based awards were made. *Average percent of need met:* 73%. *Average financial aid package:* $10,609. *Average indebtedness upon graduation:* $12,967.

Applying *Options:* common application, electronic application, early action, deferred entrance. *Application fee:* $35. *Required:* essay or personal statement, high school transcript, minimum 2.70 GPA, 2 letters of recommendation. *Recommended:* interview, graded essay/term paper. *Application deadlines:* 8/1 (freshmen), 8/1 (transfers). *Notification:* continuous (freshmen), 1/21 (early action), continuous (transfers).

Admissions Contact Ms. Mayten Sanchez, Director of Admissions, Bloomfield College, Office of Enrollment Management and Admission, Bloomfield, NJ 07003-9981. *Phone:* 973-748-9000 Ext. 3961. *Toll-free phone:* 800-848-4555 Ext. 230. *Fax:* 973-748-0916. *E-mail:* admission@bloomfield.edu.

■ *See page 1266 for a narrative description.*

CALDWELL COLLEGE
Caldwell, New Jersey

- **Independent Roman Catholic** comprehensive, founded 1939
- **Calendar** semesters
- **Degrees** bachelor's, master's, post-master's, and postbachelor's certificates
- **Suburban** 100-acre campus with easy access to New York City
- **Endowment** $2.6 million
- **Coed,** 1,836 undergraduate students, 59% full-time, 69% women, 31% men
- **Moderately difficult** entrance level, 69% of applicants were admitted

Funded by a $2 million federal grant, Caldwell College established the Center for Excellence in Teaching on campus. As a result, Caldwell recently renovated its biology, physics, and chemistry laboratories with a top priority of focusing on the teaching of math and science.

Undergraduates 1,091 full-time, 745 part-time. Students come from 19 states and territories, 27 other countries, 6% are from out of state, 18% African American, 2% Asian American or Pacific Islander, 10% Hispanic American, 0.2% Native American, 4% international, 8% transferred in, 23% live on campus. *Retention:* 68% of 2002 full-time freshmen returned.

Freshmen *Admission:* 1,164 applied, 806 admitted, 283 enrolled. *Average high school GPA:* 3.01. *Test scores:* SAT verbal scores over 500: 31%; SAT math scores over 500: 27%; SAT verbal scores over 600: 4%; SAT math scores over 600: 4%.

Faculty *Total:* 184, 43% full-time, 50% with terminal degrees. *Student/faculty ratio:* 13:1.

Majors Accounting; art; biology/biological sciences; business administration and management; chemistry; clinical laboratory science/medical technology; communication/speech communication and rhetoric; computer and information sciences; computer science; criminal justice/safety; elementary education; English; French; history; international business/trade/commerce; management science; marketing/marketing management; mathematics; multi-/interdisciplinary studies related; music; political science and government; psychology; social sciences; sociology; Spanish; theology.

Academic Programs *Special study options:* academic remediation for entering students, accelerated degree program, adult/continuing education programs, advanced placement credit, cooperative education, distance learning, double majors, English as a second language, external degree program, honors programs, independent study, internships, off-campus study, part-time degree program, services for LD students, student-designed majors, study abroad, summer session for credit. *ROTC:* Army (c).

Library Jennings Library with 140,714 titles, 428 serial subscriptions, 2,450 audiovisual materials, an OPAC, a Web page.

Computers on Campus 190 computers available on campus for general student use. A campuswide network can be accessed from student residence rooms. Internet access, at least one staffed computer lab available.

Student Life *Housing options:* coed. Campus housing is university owned. Freshman applicants given priority for college housing. *Activities and organizations:* drama/theater group, student-run newspaper, choral group, Student Government Association, International Students Organization, Caldwell College Education Association, Circle K, Black Student Cooperative Unit. *Campus security:* 24-hour patrols, late-night transport/escort service, controlled dormitory access, dusk-to-dawn patrols by trained security personnel. *Student services:* health clinic, personal/psychological counseling.

Athletics Member NCAA. All Division II. *Intercollegiate sports:* baseball M(s), basketball M(s)/W(s), cross-country running W(s), golf M(s), soccer M(s)/W(s), softball W(s), tennis M(s)/W(s). *Intramural sports:* basketball M/W, football M/W, soccer M/W, softball M/W, tennis M, volleyball W.

Standardized Tests *Required:* SAT I or ACT (for admission).

Costs (2003–04) *Comprehensive fee:* $24,060 includes full-time tuition ($16,960), mandatory fees ($100), and room and board ($7000). Part-time tuition: $408 per credit. Part-time tuition and fees vary according to course load. *Room and board:* Room and board charges vary according to board plan and housing facility. *Payment plans:* installment, deferred payment. *Waivers:* senior citizens and employees or children of employees.

Financial Aid Of all full-time matriculated undergraduates who enrolled in 2002, 955 applied for aid, 910 were judged to have need, 23 had their need fully met. 157 Federal Work-Study jobs (averaging $785). 13 state and other part-time jobs (averaging $5472). *Average percent of need met:* 71%. *Average financial aid package:* $9735. *Average need-based loan:* $3875. *Average need-based gift aid:* $6150. *Average indebtedness upon graduation:* $15,125.

Applying *Options:* common application, electronic application, early admission, early action, deferred entrance. *Application fee:* $40. *Required:* essay or personal statement, high school transcript, minimum 2.0 GPA, 1 letter of recommendation. *Required for some:* interview. *Application deadline:* 3/15 (freshmen), rolling (transfers). *Notification:* continuous (freshmen), 1/15 (early action), continuous (transfers).

Admissions Contact Ms. Kathryn Reilly, Director of Admissions, Caldwell College, 9 Ryerson Avenue, Caldwell, NJ 07006. *Phone:* 973-618-3226. *Toll-free phone:* 888-864-9516. *Fax:* 973-618-3600. *E-mail:* admissions@caldwell.edu.

■ *See page 1316 for a narrative description.*

CENTENARY COLLEGE
Hackettstown, New Jersey

- **Independent** comprehensive, founded 1867, affiliated with United Methodist Church
- **Calendar** semesters
- **Degrees** associate, bachelor's, master's, and postbachelor's certificates
- **Suburban** 42-acre campus with easy access to New York City
- **Endowment** $2.0 million
- **Coed,** 1,759 undergraduate students, 82% full-time, 67% women, 33% men
- **Moderately difficult** entrance level, 73% of applicants were admitted

Undergraduates 1,440 full-time, 319 part-time. Students come from 21 states and territories, 16 other countries, 15% are from out of state, 5% African American, 3% Asian American or Pacific Islander, 4% Hispanic American, 0.3% Native American, 4% international, 12% transferred in, 55% live on campus. *Retention:* 61% of 2002 full-time freshmen returned.

Freshmen *Admission:* 737 applied, 540 admitted, 350 enrolled. *Average high school GPA:* 2.50. *Test scores:* SAT verbal scores over 500: 33%; SAT math scores

Centenary College (continued)

over 500: 27%; ACT scores over 18: 50%; SAT verbal scores over 600: 6%; SAT math scores over 600: 8%; SAT verbal scores over 700: 1%; SAT math scores over 700: 1%.

Faculty *Total:* 121, 47% full-time, 40% with terminal degrees. *Student/faculty ratio:* 17:1.

Majors Accounting; biology/biological sciences; business administration and management; commercial and advertising art; criminology; education; elementary education; English; equestrian studies; fashion/apparel design; history; information science/studies; international relations and affairs; liberal arts and sciences/liberal studies; marketing/marketing management; mass communication/media; mathematics; political science and government; psychology; secondary education; sociology; special education; sport and fitness administration; theatre design and technology.

Academic Programs *Special study options:* academic remediation for entering students, accelerated degree program, advanced placement credit, double majors, English as a second language, honors programs, independent study, internships, off-campus study, part-time degree program, services for LD students, student-designed majors, study abroad, summer session for credit.

Library Taylor Memorial Learning Resource Center with 67,272 titles, 211 serial subscriptions, 4,965 audiovisual materials, an OPAC.

Computers on Campus 30 computers available on campus for general student use. A campuswide network can be accessed from student residence rooms and from off campus that provide access to laptop computer. Internet access, at least one staffed computer lab available.

Student Life *Housing options:* coed, women-only. Campus housing is university owned. Freshman applicants given priority for college housing. *Activities and organizations:* drama/theater group, student-run newspaper, radio and television station, Student Activities Council, equestrian teams, Quill, student government, Kappa Delta Epsilon. *Campus security:* late-night transport/escort service, controlled dormitory access, patrols by trained security personnel 4 p.m. to 8 a.m. *Student services:* health clinic, personal/psychological counseling, women's center.

Athletics Member NCAA, NSCAA. All NCAA Division III. *Intercollegiate sports:* baseball M, basketball M/W, cross-country running M/W, equestrian sports M/W, golf M/W, lacrosse M/W, soccer M/W, softball W, volleyball W, wrestling M.

Standardized Tests *Required:* SAT I or ACT (for admission).

Costs (2003–04) *Comprehensive fee:* $24,850 includes full-time tuition ($17,000), mandatory fees ($700), and room and board ($7150). Full-time tuition and fees vary according to location and program. Part-time tuition: $350 per credit. Part-time tuition and fees vary according to location and program. *Payment plan:* installment. *Waivers:* children of alumni, senior citizens, and employees or children of employees.

Financial Aid Of all full-time matriculated undergraduates who enrolled in 2003, 851 applied for aid, 684 were judged to have need, 211 had their need fully met. 231 Federal Work-Study jobs (averaging $1200). 226 state and other part-time jobs (averaging $1200). In 2003, 136 non-need-based awards were made. *Average percent of need met:* 69%. *Average financial aid package:* $11,862. *Average need-based loan:* $4907. *Average need-based gift aid:* $9082. *Average non-need-based aid:* $11,123. *Average indebtedness upon graduation:* $8900.

Applying *Options:* common application, electronic application, deferred entrance. *Application fee:* $30. *Required:* essay or personal statement, high school transcript. *Required for some:* interview, portfolio. *Recommended:* minimum 2.0 GPA, letters of recommendation, interview. *Application deadline:* rolling (freshmen), rolling (transfers). *Notification:* continuous (freshmen), continuous (transfers).

Admissions Contact Ms. Diane Finnan, Vice President for Enrollment Management, Centenary College, 400 Jefferson Street, Hackettstown, NJ 07840-2100. *Phone:* 908-852-1400 Ext. 2217. *Toll-free phone:* 800-236-8679. *Fax:* 908-852-3454. *E-mail:* admissions@centenarycollege.edu.

THE COLLEGE OF NEW JERSEY
Ewing, New Jersey

- **State-supported** comprehensive, founded 1855
- **Calendar** semesters
- **Degrees** certificates, bachelor's, master's, post-master's, and postbachelor's certificates
- **Suburban** 255-acre campus with easy access to Philadelphia
- **Endowment** $4.8 million
- **Coed,** 5,938 undergraduate students, 95% full-time, 60% women, 40% men
- **Very difficult** entrance level, 48% of applicants were admitted

The College of New Jersey (TCNJ) attracts New Jersey's highest-achieving students and students from other states who can meet its admissions requirements. With high expectations for both its students and itself, the College has created a culture of constant questioning. On an elegant campus, in small classes, students and faculty members collaborate in a transformative educational process.

Undergraduates 5,614 full-time, 324 part-time. Students come from 14 states and territories, 10 other countries, 5% are from out of state, 6% African American, 5% Asian American or Pacific Islander, 6% Hispanic American, 0.1% Native American, 0.1% international, 3% transferred in, 60% live on campus. *Retention:* 95% of 2002 full-time freshmen returned.

Freshmen *Admission:* 6,373 applied, 3,070 admitted, 1,178 enrolled. *Test scores:* SAT verbal scores over 500: 92%; SAT math scores over 500: 96%; SAT verbal scores over 600: 67%; SAT math scores over 600: 78%; SAT verbal scores over 700: 16%; SAT math scores over 700: 25%.

Faculty *Total:* 664, 49% full-time, 55% with terminal degrees. *Student/faculty ratio:* 12:1.

Majors Accounting; art; art history, criticism and conservation; art teacher education; biology/biological sciences; biology teacher education; biomedical/medical engineering; business administration and management; business/managerial economics; chemistry; chemistry teacher education; commercial and advertising art; computer and information sciences; computer engineering; criminal justice/law enforcement administration; economics; education; electrical, electronics and communications engineering; elementary education; engineering science; English; English/language arts teacher education; finance; fine/studio arts; history; history teacher education; intermedia/multimedia; international business/trade/commerce; international relations and affairs; kindergarten/preschool education; mathematics; mathematics teacher education; mechanical engineering; music; music teacher education; nursing (registered nurse training); philosophy; physical education teaching and coaching; physics; physics teacher education; political science and government; pre-law studies; pre-medical studies; psychology; secondary education; sociology; Spanish; Spanish language teacher education; special education; special education (hearing impaired); speech and rhetoric; statistics; technology/industrial arts teacher education; women's studies.

Academic Programs *Special study options:* academic remediation for entering students, advanced placement credit, double majors, honors programs, independent study, internships, off-campus study, part-time degree program, services for LD students, study abroad, summer session for credit. *ROTC:* Army (c), Air Force (c).

Library Roscoe L. West Library with 550,000 titles, 7,900 serial subscriptions, 4,000 audiovisual materials, an OPAC, a Web page.

Computers on Campus 800 computers available on campus for general student use. A campuswide network can be accessed from student residence rooms and from off campus. Internet access, online (class) registration, at least one staffed computer lab available.

Student Life *Housing options:* coed. Campus housing is university owned. *Activities and organizations:* drama/theater group, student-run newspaper, radio station, choral group, Student Government Association, College Union Board, The Signal, intramurals, national fraternities, national sororities. *Campus security:* 24-hour emergency response devices and patrols, student patrols, late-night transport/escort service, controlled dormitory access. *Student services:* health clinic, personal/psychological counseling, women's center, legal services.

Athletics Member NCAA. All Division III. *Intercollegiate sports:* baseball M, basketball M/W, cheerleading M/W, cross-country running M/W, field hockey W, football M, golf M, lacrosse W, soccer M/W, softball W, swimming M/W, tennis M/W, track and field M/W, wrestling M. *Intramural sports:* basketball M/W, bowling M(c)/W(c), fencing M(c)/W(c), field hockey M/W, football M/W, ice hockey M(c), lacrosse M(c), racquetball M/W, rock climbing M/W, rugby M/W, skiing (cross-country) M(c)/W(c), skiing (downhill) M(c)/W(c), soccer M/W, softball M/W, tennis M/W, ultimate Frisbee M(c)/W(c), volleyball M(c)/W(c), water polo M/W, weight lifting M(c)/W(c), wrestling M(c)/W(c).

Standardized Tests *Required:* SAT I or ACT (for admission).

Costs (2003–04) *Tuition:* state resident $6131 full-time, $288 per credit part-time; nonresident $10,706 full-time, $450 per credit part-time. Part-time tuition and fees vary according to course load. *Required fees:* $2075 full-time, $71 per credit part-time. *Room and board:* $7744; room only: $5565. Room and board charges vary according to board plan. *Payment plan:* installment. *Waivers:* senior citizens and employees or children of employees.

Financial Aid Of all full-time matriculated undergraduates who enrolled in 2003, 3,738 applied for aid, 2,566 were judged to have need, 361 had their need fully met. 217 Federal Work-Study jobs (averaging $995). In 2003, 552 non-need-based awards were made. *Average percent of need met:* 71%. *Average financial aid package:* $7658. *Average need-based loan:* $3847. *Average need-based gift aid:* $5984. *Average non-need-based aid:* $4554. *Average indebtedness upon graduation:* $11,157.

Applying *Options:* electronic application, early admission, early decision, deferred entrance. *Application fee:* $50. *Required:* essay or personal statement, high school transcript. *Required for some:* interview, art portfolio or music audition. *Application deadlines:* 2/15 (freshmen), 2/15 (transfers). *Early decision:* 11/15. *Notification:* continuous until 4/1 (freshmen), 12/15 (early decision), continuous (transfers).

Admissions Contact Ms. Lisa Angeloni, Dean of Admissions, The College of New Jersey, PO Box 7718, Ewing, NJ 08628. *Phone:* 609-771-2131. *Toll-free phone:* 800-624-0967. *Fax:* 609-637-5174. *E-mail:* admiss@tcnj.edu.

■ See page 1442 for a narrative description.

COLLEGE OF SAINT ELIZABETH

Morristown, New Jersey

- **Independent Roman Catholic** comprehensive, founded 1899
- **Calendar** semesters
- **Degrees** certificates, bachelor's, master's, and postbachelor's certificates (also offers co-ed adult undergraduate degree program and co-ed graduate programs)
- **Suburban** 188-acre campus with easy access to New York City
- **Endowment** $17.3 million
- **Women only,** 1,276 undergraduate students, 56% full-time
- **Moderately difficult** entrance level, 81% of applicants were admitted

An independent, four-year, Catholic liberal arts college founded in 1899 by the Sisters of Charity of Saint Elizabeth, CSE was one of the first colleges in New Jersey to award degrees to women. Today, the College plays a unique and critical role in higher education, not only as one of the preeminent Catholic colleges for women on the East Coast but also as a leader in the education of working adults, both men and women, at the undergraduate and graduate levels. CSE is also the regional center for theological and spiritual development of Catholic laity.

Undergraduates 716 full-time, 560 part-time. Students come from 8 states and territories, 46 other countries, 11% are from out of state, 12% African American, 5% Asian American or Pacific Islander, 13% Hispanic American, 0.2% Native American, 4% international, 2% transferred in, 70% live on campus. *Retention:* 83% of 2002 full-time freshmen returned.

Freshmen *Admission:* 456 applied, 369 admitted, 151 enrolled. *Average high school GPA:* 3.00. *Test scores:* SAT verbal scores over 500: 34%; SAT math scores over 500: 39%; SAT verbal scores over 600: 8%; SAT math scores over 600: 9%; SAT verbal scores over 700: 2%; SAT math scores over 700: 3%.

Faculty *Total:* 176, 34% full-time, 48% with terminal degrees. *Student/faculty ratio:* 10:1.

Majors Accounting; American studies; art; biochemistry; biology/biological sciences; business administration and management; chemistry; clinical laboratory science/medical technology; communication/speech communication and rhetoric; computer science; cytotechnology; dietetics; economics; education (multiple levels); English; history; human resources management; international relations and affairs; marketing/marketing management; mathematics; multi-/interdisciplinary studies related; music; nursing science; philosophy; pre-medical studies; pre-veterinary studies; psychology; sociology; Spanish; special education; theology; toxicology.

Academic Programs *Special study options:* academic remediation for entering students, accelerated degree program, advanced placement credit, distance learning, double majors, English as a second language, honors programs, independent study, internships, off-campus study, part-time degree program, services for LD students, student-designed majors, study abroad, summer session for credit.

Library Mahoney Library with 138,344 titles, 718 serial subscriptions, 1,737 audiovisual materials, an OPAC.

Computers on Campus 152 computers available on campus for general student use. A campuswide network can be accessed from student residence rooms and from off campus. Internet access, at least one staffed computer lab available.

Student Life *Housing options:* women-only. Campus housing is university owned and leased by the school. Freshman campus housing is guaranteed. *Activities and organizations:* drama/theater group, student-run newspaper, choral group, Student Government Association, Students Take Action Committee, International/Intercultural Club, College Activities Board, campus ministry. *Campus security:* 24-hour emergency response devices and patrols, late-night transport/escort service, controlled dormitory access. *Student services:* health clinic, personal/psychological counseling.

Athletics Member NCAA. All Division III. *Intercollegiate sports:* basketball W, equestrian sports W, soccer W, softball W, swimming W, tennis W, volleyball W. *Intramural sports:* volleyball W.

Standardized Tests *Required:* SAT I or ACT (for admission).

Costs (2003–04) *Comprehensive fee:* $25,580 includes full-time tuition ($16,450), mandatory fees ($1000), and room and board ($8130). Part-time tuition: $515 per credit hour. Part-time tuition and fees vary according to course load. *Required fees:* $110 per course part-time, $50 per term part-time. *Payment plan:* installment. *Waivers:* children of alumni, senior citizens, and employees or children of employees.

Financial Aid Of all full-time matriculated undergraduates who enrolled in 2002, 495 applied for aid, 456 were judged to have need, 106 had their need fully met. 74 Federal Work-Study jobs (averaging $289). In 2002, 124 non-need-based awards were made. *Average percent of need met:* 80%. *Average financial aid package:* $15,553. *Average need-based loan:* $3668. *Average need-based gift aid:* $13,069. *Average non-need-based aid:* $10,240. *Average indebtedness upon graduation:* $14,026.

Applying *Options:* electronic application, early admission, deferred entrance. *Application fee:* $35. *Required:* essay or personal statement, high school transcript, minimum 2.0 GPA, 2 letters of recommendation. *Recommended:* interview. *Application deadline:* 8/15 (freshmen), rolling (transfers). *Notification:* 11/15 (freshmen), continuous (transfers).

Admissions Contact Ms. Donna Tatarka, Dean of Admissions, College of Saint Elizabeth, 2 Convent Road, Morristown, NJ 07960-6989. *Phone:* 973-290-4700. *Toll-free phone:* 800-210-7900. *Fax:* 973-290-4710. *E-mail:* apply@cse.edu.

■ See page 1448 for a narrative description.

DEVRY UNIVERSITY

North Brunswick, New Jersey

- **Proprietary** 4-year, founded 1969, part of DeVry University
- **Calendar** semesters
- **Degrees** diplomas, associate, and bachelor's
- **Urban** 10-acre campus with easy access to New York City
- **Coed**
- **Minimally difficult** entrance level

Student Life *Campus security:* 24-hour emergency response devices and patrols, late-night transport/escort service.

Standardized Tests *Recommended:* SAT I, ACT or CPT.

Costs (2003–04) *Tuition:* $10,100 full-time, $420 per credit hour part-time. Full-time tuition and fees vary according to course load. Part-time tuition and fees vary according to course load. *Required fees:* $165 full-time. *Payment plans:* installment, deferred payment.

Financial Aid Of all full-time matriculated undergraduates who enrolled in 2003, 1,809 applied for aid, 1,695 were judged to have need, 43 had their need fully met. In 2003, 148. *Average percent of need met:* 45. *Average financial aid package:* $8488. *Average need-based loan:* $5111. *Average need-based gift aid:* $5448. *Average non-need-based aid:* $9674.

Applying *Options:* electronic application, deferred entrance. *Application fee:* $50. *Required:* high school transcript, interview.

Admissions Contact Ms. Kelley Taptich, Admissions, DeVry University, 630 US Highway One, North Brunswick, NJ 08902-3362. *Phone:* 732-435-4877. *Toll-free phone:* 800-333-3879. *E-mail:* ktaptich@devry.edu.

DREW UNIVERSITY

Madison, New Jersey

- **Independent** university, founded 1867, affiliated with United Methodist Church
- **Calendar** semesters
- **Degrees** bachelor's, master's, doctoral, first professional, and postbachelor's certificates
- **Suburban** 186-acre campus with easy access to New York City
- **Endowment** $193.0 million
- **Coed,** 1,606 undergraduate students, 96% full-time, 61% women, 39% men
- **Moderately difficult** entrance level, 69% of applicants were admitted

Drew is educating students to help shape the world of tomorrow. With its roots in the best traditions of the arts and sciences, Drew blends inspired teaching on a technologically integrated campus with numerous opportunities for academic internships in nearby corporate headquarters and research centers. Drew's innovative international seminars program and semesters in New York City on Wall Street and the United Nations, for example, provide students with an understanding of the issues that affect a global society.

Undergraduates 1,535 full-time, 71 part-time. Students come from 40 states and territories, 8 other countries, 43% are from out of state, 4% African American, 6% Asian American or Pacific Islander, 5% Hispanic American, 0.4% Native American, 0.7% international, 2% transferred in, 87% live on campus. *Retention:* 87% of 2002 full-time freshmen returned.

Drew University (continued)

Freshmen *Admission:* 2,746 applied, 1,894 admitted, 421 enrolled. *Test scores:* SAT verbal scores over 500: 95%; SAT math scores over 500: 90%; SAT verbal scores over 600: 57%; SAT math scores over 600: 53%; SAT verbal scores over 700: 18%; SAT math scores over 700: 9%.

Faculty *Total:* 166, 72% full-time. *Student/faculty ratio:* 12:1.

Majors Anthropology; art; behavioral sciences; biochemistry; biology/biological sciences; chemistry; classics and languages, literatures and linguistics; computer science; dramatic/theatre arts; economics; English; French; German; history; mathematics; mathematics and computer science; music; neuroscience; philosophy; physics; political science and government; psychology; religious studies; Russian; sociology; Spanish; women's studies.

Academic Programs *Special study options:* academic remediation for entering students, accelerated degree program, adult/continuing education programs, advanced placement credit, double majors, independent study, internships, off-campus study, part-time degree program, services for LD students, student-designed majors, study abroad, summer session for credit. *ROTC:* Army (c), Air Force (c). *Unusual degree programs:* 3-2 engineering with Washington University in St. Louis, Stevens Institute of Technology, Columbia University; forestry with Duke University.

Library Drew University Library with 491,489 titles, 2,589 serial subscriptions, 328 audiovisual materials.

Computers on Campus 200 computers available on campus for general student use. A campuswide network can be accessed from student residence rooms and from off campus. Internet access, online (class) registration, at least one staffed computer lab available. Computer purchase or lease plan available.

Student Life *Housing options:* coed, disabled students. Campus housing is university owned. Freshman campus housing is guaranteed. *Activities and organizations:* drama/theater group, student-run newspaper, radio and television station, choral group, The Acorn—Student Newspaper, Student Government Association, Volunteer Resource Center, University Program Board, WMNJ—Student Radio. *Campus security:* 24-hour emergency response devices and patrols, late-night transport/escort service, controlled dormitory access. *Student services:* health clinic, personal/psychological counseling.

Athletics Member NCAA. All Division III. *Intercollegiate sports:* baseball M, basketball M/W, cross-country running M/W, equestrian sports M/W, fencing M/W, field hockey W, lacrosse M/W, rugby M(c)/W(c), soccer M/W, softball W, swimming M/W, tennis M/W. *Intramural sports:* basketball M/W, football M/W, racquetball M/W, soccer M/W, softball M/W, squash M/W, table tennis M/W, ultimate Frisbee M/W, volleyball M/W.

Standardized Tests *Required:* SAT I or ACT (for admission).

Costs (2003–04) *Comprehensive fee:* $35,550 includes full-time tuition ($27,360), mandatory fees ($546), and room and board ($7644). Full-time tuition and fees vary according to course load. Part-time tuition: $1140 per credit. Part-time tuition and fees vary according to course load. *Required fees:* $23 per credit part-time. *College room only:* $4840. Room and board charges vary according to board plan and housing facility. *Payment plans:* tuition prepayment, installment. *Waivers:* senior citizens and employees or children of employees.

Financial Aid Of all full-time matriculated undergraduates who enrolled in 2002, 919 applied for aid, 753 were judged to have need, 231 had their need fully met. 309 Federal Work-Study jobs (averaging $1176). 38 state and other part-time jobs (averaging $5767). In 2002, 387 non-need-based awards were made. *Average percent of need met:* 82%. *Average financial aid package:* $19,955. *Average need-based loan:* $4834. *Average need-based gift aid:* $14,972. *Average non-need-based aid:* $11,421. *Average indebtedness upon graduation:* $16,381. *Financial aid deadline:* 2/15.

Applying *Options:* common application, early admission, early decision, deferred entrance. *Application fee:* $40. *Required:* essay or personal statement, high school transcript, 1 letter of recommendation. *Recommended:* interview. *Application deadlines:* 2/15 (freshmen), 8/1 (transfers). *Early decision:* 12/1 (for plan 1), 1/15 (for plan 2). *Notification:* 3/15 (freshmen), 12/24 (early decision plan 1), 2/15 (early decision plan 2), continuous until 4/1 (transfers).

Admissions Contact Ms. Mary Beth Carey, Dean of Admissions and Financial Assistance, Drew University, 36 Madison Avenue, Madison, NJ 07940-1493. *Phone:* 973-408-3739. *Fax:* 973-408-3068. *E-mail:* cadm@drew.edu.

■ *See page 1544 for a narrative description.*

FAIRLEIGH DICKINSON UNIVERSITY, COLLEGE AT FLORHAM

Madison, New Jersey

- **Independent** comprehensive, founded 1942
- **Calendar** semesters
- **Degrees** associate, bachelor's, master's, and post-master's certificates
- **Suburban** 178-acre campus with easy access to New York City
- **Endowment** $11.7 million
- **Coed,** 2,645 undergraduate students, 85% full-time, 54% women, 46% men
- **Moderately difficult** entrance level, 75% of applicants were admitted

Undergraduates 2,248 full-time, 397 part-time. Students come from 28 states and territories, 21 other countries, 14% are from out of state, 6% African American, 3% Asian American or Pacific Islander, 7% Hispanic American, 0.2% Native American, 1% international, 6% transferred in, 56% live on campus. *Retention:* 77% of 2002 full-time freshmen returned.

Freshmen *Admission:* 2,884 applied, 2,162 admitted, 616 enrolled. *Test scores:* SAT verbal scores over 500: 55%; SAT math scores over 500: 60%; SAT verbal scores over 600: 12%; SAT math scores over 600: 14%; SAT verbal scores over 700: 1%; SAT math scores over 700: 1%.

Faculty *Total:* 340, 34% full-time. *Student/faculty ratio:* 16:1.

Majors Accounting; allied health diagnostic, intervention, and treatment professions related; biological and biomedical sciences related; biology/biological sciences; business administration and management; business/managerial economics; chemistry; cinematography and film/video production; clinical laboratory science/medical technology; communication/speech communication and rhetoric; computer and information sciences; dramatic/theatre arts; economics; English; French; history; hotel/motel administration; humanities; marine biology and biological oceanography; marketing/marketing management; mathematics; medical radiologic technology; philosophy; physical therapist assistant; political science and government; psychology; sales, distribution and marketing; sociology; Spanish; visual and performing arts.

Academic Programs *Special study options:* academic remediation for entering students, accelerated degree program, adult/continuing education programs, advanced placement credit, cooperative education, distance learning, double majors, English as a second language, honors programs, independent study, internships, off-campus study, part-time degree program, services for LD students, study abroad, summer session for credit. *ROTC:* Army (c), Air Force (c). *Unusual degree programs:* 3-2 psychology, communications.

Library Friendship Library plus 1 other with 163,266 titles, 661 serial subscriptions, 681 audiovisual materials, an OPAC.

Computers on Campus 300 computers available on campus for general student use. A campuswide network can be accessed from student residence rooms and from off campus. At least one staffed computer lab available.

Student Life *Housing options:* coed. Campus housing is university owned. Freshman applicants given priority for college housing. *Activities and organizations:* drama/theater group, student-run newspaper, radio station, student government, Florham Programming Committee, Greek Council, Association of Black Collegians, "Metro" newspaper, national fraternities, national sororities. *Campus security:* 24-hour emergency response devices and patrols, late-night transport/escort service, trained law enforcement personnel on staff. *Student services:* health clinic, personal/psychological counseling, women's center.

Athletics Member NCAA. All Division III. *Intercollegiate sports:* baseball M, basketball M/W, cross-country running M/W, field hockey W, football M, golf M, lacrosse M/W, soccer M/W, softball W, swimming M/W, tennis M/W, volleyball W. *Intramural sports:* basketball M/W, bowling M/W, cheerleading W, cross-country running M/W, football M/W, golf M, racquetball M/W, soccer M/W, softball M/W, table tennis M/W, tennis M/W, volleyball M/W.

Standardized Tests *Required:* SAT I or ACT (for admission). *Recommended:* SAT II: Subject Tests (for admission).

Costs (2003–04) *Comprehensive fee:* $30,130 includes full-time tuition ($21,400), mandatory fees ($480), and room and board ($8250). Part-time tuition: $637 per credit. Part-time tuition and fees vary according to course load. *College room only:* $4832. Room and board charges vary according to board plan and housing facility. *Payment plans:* installment, deferred payment. *Waivers:* senior citizens and employees or children of employees.

Applying *Options:* common application, early admission, deferred entrance. *Application fee:* $40. *Required:* high school transcript, 2 letters of recommendation. *Required for some:* essay or personal statement, interview. *Application deadlines:* 3/1 (freshmen), 8/1 (transfers). *Notification:* continuous (freshmen), continuous (transfers).

Admissions Contact Mrs. Bernetta Millonde, Associate President for Enrollment Management, Fairleigh Dickinson University, College at Florham, 285 Madison Avenue, M-MS1-03, Madison, NJ 07940. *Phone:* 201-692-7304. *Toll-free phone:* 800-338-8803. *Fax:* 973-443-8088. *E-mail:* globaleducation@fdu.edu.

■ *See page 1606 for a narrative description.*

FAIRLEIGH DICKINSON UNIVERSITY, METROPOLITAN CAMPUS

Teaneck, New Jersey

- **Independent** comprehensive, founded 1942
- **Calendar** semesters
- **Degrees** associate, bachelor's, master's, doctoral, post-master's, and postbachelor's certificates
- **Suburban** 88-acre campus with easy access to New York City
- **Endowment** $14.7 million
- **Coed,** 5,036 undergraduate students, 42% full-time, 57% women, 43% men
- **Moderately difficult** entrance level, 68% of applicants were admitted

Undergraduates 2,101 full-time, 2,935 part-time. Students come from 25 states and territories, 52 other countries, 11% are from out of state, 21% African American, 6% Asian American or Pacific Islander, 16% Hispanic American, 0.2% Native American, 8% international, 8% transferred in, 29% live on campus. *Retention:* 70% of 2002 full-time freshmen returned.

Freshmen *Admission:* 2,645 applied, 1,787 admitted, 637 enrolled. *Test scores:* SAT verbal scores over 500: 41%; SAT math scores over 500: 47%; SAT verbal scores over 600: 9%; SAT math scores over 600: 11%; SAT math scores over 700: 1%.

Faculty *Total:* 604, 28% full-time. *Student/faculty ratio:* 13:1.

Majors Accounting; allied health diagnostic, intervention, and treatment professions related; biochemistry; biological and biomedical sciences related; biological and physical sciences; biology/biological sciences; business administration and management; business/managerial economics; chemistry; civil engineering technology; clinical laboratory science/medical technology; communication/speech communication and rhetoric; computer and information sciences; computer and information sciences and support services related; construction engineering technology; criminal justice/safety; dramatic/theatre arts; electrical, electronic and communications engineering technology; electrical, electronics and communications engineering; English; environmental studies; French; general studies; history; hotel/motel administration; humanities; international relations and affairs; liberal arts and sciences/liberal studies; marine biology and biological oceanography; marketing research; mathematics; mechanical engineering/mechanical technology; medical radiologic technology; multi-/interdisciplinary studies related; nursing science; philosophy; political science and government; psychology; sales, distribution and marketing; sociology; Spanish; visual and performing arts.

Academic Programs *Special study options:* academic remediation for entering students, accelerated degree program, adult/continuing education programs, advanced placement credit, cooperative education, distance learning, double majors, English as a second language, honors programs, independent study, internships, off-campus study, part-time degree program, services for LD students, student-designed majors, study abroad, summer session for credit. *ROTC:* Army (c), Air Force (c). *Unusual degree programs:* 3-2 psychology.

Library Weiner Library plus 2 others with 287,755 titles, 1,093 serial subscriptions, 1,052 audiovisual materials, an OPAC.

Computers on Campus 210 computers available on campus for general student use. A campuswide network can be accessed from student residence rooms and from off campus. At least one staffed computer lab available.

Student Life *Housing options:* coed, men-only, women-only. *Activities and organizations:* drama/theater group, student-run newspaper, radio station, choral group, Indian Cultural Experience, Student Program Board, Student Government Association, International Student Association, Multicultural Council, national fraternities, national sororities. *Campus security:* 24-hour emergency response devices and patrols, late-night transport/escort service, controlled dormitory access, trained law enforcement personnel on staff. *Student services:* health clinic, personal/psychological counseling.

Athletics Member NCAA. All Division I. *Intercollegiate sports:* baseball M(s), basketball M(s)/W(s), bowling W(s), cross-country running M(s)/W(s), fencing W(s), golf M(s), soccer M(s)/W(s), softball W(s), tennis M(s)/W(s), track and field M(s)/W(s), volleyball W(s). *Intramural sports:* basketball M/W, bowling M/W, cross-country running M/W, football M/W, racquetball M/W, skiing (downhill) M/W, softball M/W, table tennis M/W, tennis M/W, track and field M/W, volleyball M/W, weight lifting M/W.

Standardized Tests *Required:* SAT I or ACT (for admission). *Recommended:* SAT II: Writing Test (for admission).

Costs (2003–04) *Comprehensive fee:* $28,584 includes full-time tuition ($19,854), mandatory fees ($480), and room and board ($8250). Part-time tuition: $637 per credit. Part-time tuition and fees vary according to course load. *College room only:* $4832. Room and board charges vary according to board plan and housing facility. *Payment plans:* installment, deferred payment. *Waivers:* senior citizens and employees or children of employees.

Applying *Options:* common application, early admission, deferred entrance. *Application fee:* $40. *Required:* high school transcript, 2 letters of recommendation. *Required for some:* essay or personal statement, interview. *Application deadlines:* 3/1 (freshmen), 8/1 (transfers). *Notification:* continuous (freshmen), continuous (transfers).

Admissions Contact Fairleigh Dickinson University, Metropolitan Campus, 1000 River Road, H-DH3-10, Teaneck, NJ 07666. *Phone:* 201-692-7304. *Toll-free phone:* 800-338-8803. *Fax:* 201-692-7319. *E-mail:* globaleducation@fdu.edu.

■ See page 1606 for a narrative description.

FELICIAN COLLEGE

Lodi, New Jersey

- **Independent Roman Catholic** comprehensive, founded 1942
- **Calendar** semesters
- **Degrees** certificates, associate, bachelor's, master's, post-master's, and postbachelor's certificates
- **Suburban** 37-acre campus with easy access to New York City
- **Endowment** $716,953
- **Coed**
- **Moderately difficult** entrance level

Faculty *Student/faculty ratio:* 12:1.

Student Life *Campus security:* 24-hour patrols, student patrols, late-night transport/escort service.

Athletics Member NCAA, NAIA. All NCAA Division II.

Standardized Tests *Required:* SAT I and SAT II or ACT (for admission).

Costs (2004–05) *Comprehensive fee:* $24,625 includes full-time tuition ($15,900), mandatory fees ($1225), and room and board ($7500). Full-time tuition and fees vary according to course level, course load, degree level, and program. Part-time tuition: $530 per credit. Part-time tuition and fees vary according to course level, course load, degree level, and program. *Payment plans:* installment, deferred payment.

Financial Aid Of all full-time matriculated undergraduates who enrolled in 2002, 1,267 applied for aid, 1,267 were judged to have need, 200 had their need fully met. 108 Federal Work-Study jobs (averaging $1300). *Average percent of need met:* 85. *Average financial aid package:* $11,130. *Average need-based loan:* $6625. *Average indebtedness upon graduation:* $40,000.

Applying *Options:* deferred entrance. *Application fee:* $30. *Required:* high school transcript, minimum 2.0 GPA. *Required for some:* essay or personal statement, interview.

Admissions Contact College Admissions Office, Felician College, 262 South Main Street, Lodi, NJ 07644. *Phone:* 201-559-6131. *Fax:* 201-559-6188. *E-mail:* admissions@inet.felician.edu.

■ See page 1614 for a narrative description.

GEORGIAN COURT UNIVERSITY

Lakewood, New Jersey

- **Independent Roman Catholic** comprehensive, founded 1908
- **Calendar** semesters
- **Degrees** certificates, bachelor's, master's, post-master's, and postbachelor's certificates
- **Suburban** 150-acre campus with easy access to New York City and Philadelphia
- **Endowment** $32.8 million
- **Women only,** 1,956 undergraduate students, 65% full-time
- **Moderately difficult** entrance level, 86% of applicants were admitted

Georgian Court University is a Catholic comprehensive university with a strong liberal arts core and special concern for women. The Department of Art offers a BFA degree in Art, with concentrations in general fine arts and graphic design/illustration. The School of Business is accredited by the Association of Collegiate Business Schools and Programs. The Department of Social Work is accredited by the Council on Social Work Education. New majors include clinical laboratory sciences, criminal justice, and natural science.

Undergraduates 1,263 full-time, 693 part-time. Students come from 9 states and territories, 9 other countries, 5% are from out of state, 6% African American, 1% Asian American or Pacific Islander, 5% Hispanic American, 0.1% Native American, 1% international, 11% transferred in, 11% live on campus. *Retention:* 79% of 2002 full-time freshmen returned.

Freshmen *Admission:* 378 applied, 324 admitted, 138 enrolled. *Average high school GPA:* 3.07. *Test scores:* SAT verbal scores over 500: 34%; SAT math scores over 500: 29%; SAT verbal scores over 600: 4%; SAT math scores over 600: 4%.

Georgian Court University (continued)

Faculty *Total:* 261, 36% full-time, 46% with terminal degrees. *Student/faculty ratio:* 14:1.

Majors Accounting; allied health diagnostic, intervention, and treatment professions related; art; art history, criticism and conservation; art teacher education; bilingual and multilingual education; biochemistry; biology/biological sciences; biology teacher education; business administration and management; chemistry; computer and information sciences and support services related; computer science; criminal justice/law enforcement administration; elementary education; English; English as a second/foreign language (teaching); English/language arts teacher education; fine/studio arts; French; French language teacher education; history; humanities; liberal arts and sciences/liberal studies; mathematics; mathematics teacher education; music; music teacher education; physics; psychology; religious studies; social studies teacher education; social work; sociology; Spanish; Spanish language teacher education; special education.

Academic Programs *Special study options:* academic remediation for entering students, accelerated degree program, adult/continuing education programs, advanced placement credit, double majors, English as a second language, honors programs, independent study, internships, off-campus study, part-time degree program, services for LD students, study abroad, summer session for credit.

Library The Sister Mary Joseph Cunningham Library with 136,760 titles, 1,068 serial subscriptions, 2,188 audiovisual materials, an OPAC, a Web page.

Computers on Campus 172 computers available on campus for general student use. A campuswide network can be accessed from student residence rooms that provide access to intranet. Internet access, at least one staffed computer lab available.

Student Life *Housing options:* women-only. Campus housing is university owned. Freshman campus housing is guaranteed. *Activities and organizations:* student-run newspaper, choral group, social work club, athletic training club, Re-Entry Women, Commuter Life, Phi Alpha Theta. *Campus security:* 24-hour emergency response devices and patrols, late-night transport/escort service, controlled dormitory access. *Student services:* health clinic, personal/psychological counseling.

Athletics Member NCAA. All Division II. *Intercollegiate sports:* basketball W(s), cheerleading W, cross-country running W(s), soccer W(s), softball W(s), tennis W(s). *Intramural sports:* volleyball W.

Standardized Tests *Required:* SAT I or ACT (for admission).

Costs (2004–05) *Comprehensive fee:* $25,124 includes full-time tuition ($17,224), mandatory fees ($700), and room and board ($7200). Full-time tuition and fees vary according to program. Part-time tuition: $464 per credit. Part-time tuition and fees vary according to course load and program. *Required fees:* $175 per term part-time. *Room and board:* Room and board charges vary according to board plan. *Payment plans:* installment, deferred payment. *Waivers:* senior citizens and employees or children of employees.

Financial Aid Of all full-time matriculated undergraduates who enrolled in 2002, 1,188 applied for aid, 1,044 were judged to have need, 171 had their need fully met. 88 Federal Work-Study jobs (averaging $715). 166 state and other part-time jobs (averaging $991). In 2002, 171 non-need-based awards were made. *Average percent of need met:* 62%. *Average financial aid package:* $10,913. *Average need-based loan:* $4209. *Average need-based gift aid:* $8482. *Average non-need-based aid:* $9297. *Average indebtedness upon graduation:* $13,248.

Applying *Options:* early action. *Application fee:* $40. *Required:* high school transcript, minimum 2.0 GPA, letters of recommendation. *Recommended:* essay or personal statement, interview. *Application deadlines:* 8/1 (freshmen), 8/1 (transfers). *Notification:* 12/30 (early action), continuous (transfers).

Admissions Contact Ms. Kathie DeBona, Director of Admissions, Georgian Court University, Office of Admissions, 900 Lakewood Avenue, Lakewood, NJ 08701-2697. *Phone:* 732-364-2202 Ext. 2760. *Toll-free phone:* 800-458-8422. *Fax:* 732-364-4442. *E-mail:* admissions@georgian.edu.

■ *See page 1670 for a narrative description.*

KEAN UNIVERSITY
Union, New Jersey

- **State-supported** comprehensive, founded 1855, part of New Jersey State College System
- **Calendar** semesters
- **Degrees** certificates, diplomas, bachelor's, master's, post-master's, and postbachelor's certificates
- **Urban** 151-acre campus with easy access to New York City
- **Endowment** $3.8 million
- **Coed,** 10,179 undergraduate students, 73% full-time, 64% women, 36% men
- **Moderately difficult** entrance level, 64% of applicants were admitted

Undergraduates 7,387 full-time, 2,792 part-time. Students come from 17 states and territories, 79 other countries, 2% are from out of state, 20% African American, 6% Asian American or Pacific Islander, 20% Hispanic American, 0.2% Native American, 3% international, 12% transferred in, 12% live on campus. *Retention:* 80% of 2002 full-time freshmen returned.

Freshmen *Admission:* 4,225 applied, 2,723 admitted, 1,376 enrolled. *Test scores:* SAT verbal scores over 500: 36%; SAT math scores over 500: 44%; SAT verbal scores over 600: 5%; SAT math scores over 600: 5%.

Faculty *Total:* 1,000, 37% full-time. *Student/faculty ratio:* 16:1.

Majors Accounting; art; art history, criticism and conservation; biology/biological sciences; business administration and management; chemistry; clinical laboratory science/medical technology; communication/speech communication and rhetoric; computer and information sciences; computer systems networking and telecommunications; criminal justice/law enforcement administration; design and visual communications; dramatic/theatre arts; early childhood education; economics; elementary education; English; finance; fine/studio arts; geology/earth science; graphic communications; health information/medical records administration; history; industrial design; industrial production technologies related; industrial technology; interior design; liberal arts and sciences and humanities related; marketing/marketing management; mathematics; music; music teacher education; nursing (registered nurse training); nursing science; occupational therapy; parks, recreation and leisure facilities management; philosophy and religious studies related; physical education teaching and coaching; political science and government; psychology; psychology related; public administration; social work; sociology; Spanish; special education; speech teacher education; technology/industrial arts teacher education; telecommunications.

Academic Programs *Special study options:* academic remediation for entering students, accelerated degree program, adult/continuing education programs, advanced placement credit, cooperative education, distance learning, double majors, English as a second language, external degree program, freshman honors college, honors programs, independent study, internships, off-campus study, part-time degree program, services for LD students, study abroad, summer session for credit. *ROTC:* Army (c), Air Force (c).

Library Nancy Thompson Library plus 1 other with 270,000 titles, 11,164 serial subscriptions, an OPAC, a Web page.

Computers on Campus 2000 computers available on campus for general student use. A campuswide network can be accessed from student residence rooms and from off campus. Internet access, online (class) registration, at least one staffed computer lab available.

Student Life *Housing options:* coed. *Activities and organizations:* drama/theater group, student-run newspaper, radio station, choral group, Student Organization, Greek Cooperative Council, national fraternities, national sororities. *Campus security:* 24-hour emergency response devices and patrols, student patrols, late-night transport/escort service, controlled dormitory access, 24-hour patrols by campus police. *Student services:* health clinic, personal/psychological counseling, women's center, legal services.

Athletics Member NCAA, NAIA. All NCAA Division III. *Intercollegiate sports:* baseball M, basketball M/W, cross-country running M/W, fencing M/W, field hockey W, football M, lacrosse M/W, soccer M/W, softball W, swimming W, tennis M/W, track and field M/W, volleyball W. *Intramural sports:* basketball M/W, racquetball M/W, skiing (downhill) M/W, soccer M/W, swimming M/W, table tennis M/W, tennis M/W, track and field M/W, volleyball M/W, weight lifting M/W.

Standardized Tests *Required:* SAT I or ACT (for admission).

Costs (2003–04) *Tuition:* state resident $4448 full-time, $148 per credit part-time; nonresident $6810 full-time, $227 per credit part-time. Part-time tuition and fees vary according to course load. *Required fees:* $2276 full-time, $77 per credit part-time. *Room and board:* $7755; room only: $5355. Room and board charges vary according to board plan and housing facility. *Payment plans:* installment, deferred payment. *Waivers:* senior citizens and employees or children of employees.

Financial Aid Of all full-time matriculated undergraduates who enrolled in 2002, 4,552 applied for aid, 3,726 were judged to have need, 795 had their need fully met. 204 Federal Work-Study jobs (averaging $1201). In 2002, 68 non-need-based awards were made. *Average percent of need met:* 53%. *Average financial aid package:* $7613. *Average need-based loan:* $3585. *Average need-based gift aid:* $3820. *Average indebtedness upon graduation:* $14,409.

Applying *Options:* electronic application, early admission. *Application fee:* $50. *Required:* essay or personal statement, high school transcript, minimum 2.0 GPA. *Required for some:* interview. *Application deadlines:* 5/31 (freshmen), 7/15 (transfers). *Notification:* continuous until 8/1 (freshmen), continuous until 9/1 (transfers).

Admissions Contact Mr. Audley Bridges, Director of Admissions, Kean University, PO Box 411, Union, NJ 07083. *Phone:* 908-737-7100. *Fax:* 908-737-7105. *E-mail:* admitme@kean.edu.

■ *See page 1806 for a narrative description.*

MONMOUTH UNIVERSITY

West Long Branch, New Jersey

- **Independent** comprehensive, founded 1933
- **Calendar** semesters
- **Degrees** certificates, associate, bachelor's, master's, and post-master's certificates
- **Suburban** 153-acre campus with easy access to New York City and Philadelphia
- **Endowment** $29.6 million
- **Coed,** 4,381 undergraduate students, 89% full-time, 58% women, 42% men
- **Moderately difficult** entrance level, 66% of applicants were admitted

Undergraduates 3,903 full-time, 478 part-time. Students come from 24 states and territories, 11 other countries, 8% are from out of state, 5% African American, 2% Asian American or Pacific Islander, 4% Hispanic American, 0.2% Native American, 0.3% international, 8% transferred in, 45% live on campus. *Retention:* 74% of 2002 full-time freshmen returned.

Freshmen *Admission:* 5,772 applied, 3,785 admitted, 905 enrolled. *Average high school GPA:* 3.00. *Test scores:* SAT verbal scores over 500: 67%; SAT math scores over 500: 73%; ACT scores over 18: 100%; SAT verbal scores over 600: 11%; SAT math scores over 600: 17%; ACT scores over 24: 40%; SAT verbal scores over 700: 1%; SAT math scores over 700: 1%; ACT scores over 30: 5%.

Faculty *Total:* 517, 45% full-time, 45% with terminal degrees. *Student/faculty ratio:* 15:1.

Majors Anthropology; art; biology/biological sciences; business administration and management; chemistry; clinical laboratory science/medical technology; communication/speech communication and rhetoric; computer and information sciences; criminal justice/safety; cytotechnology; economics; education; engineering related; English; finance; fine arts related; foreign languages and literatures; general studies; history; interdisciplinary studies; marketing/marketing management; mathematics; multi-/interdisciplinary studies related; music; nursing related; nursing science; political science and government; psychology; secondary education; social sciences related; social work; special education; toxicology.

Academic Programs *Special study options:* academic remediation for entering students, accelerated degree program, advanced placement credit, cooperative education, double majors, honors programs, independent study, internships, part-time degree program, services for LD students, student-designed majors, study abroad, summer session for credit. *ROTC:* Air Force (c).

Library Murry and Leonie Guggenheim Memorial Library with 253,117 titles, 11,900 serial subscriptions, an OPAC, a Web page.

Computers on Campus 520 computers available on campus for general student use. A campuswide network can be accessed from student residence rooms and from off campus. Internet access, at least one staffed computer lab available.

Student Life *Housing options:* coed. Campus housing is university owned and leased by the school. Freshman applicants given priority for college housing. *Activities and organizations:* drama/theater group, student-run newspaper, radio and television station, choral group, student-run radio station, Student Government Association, student newspaper (Outlook), Student Activities Board, (Shadows) Yearbook, national fraternities, national sororities. *Campus security:* 24-hour emergency response devices and patrols, late-night transport/escort service, controlled dormitory access. *Student services:* health clinic, personal/psychological counseling, legal services.

Athletics Member NCAA. All Division I except football (Division I-AA). *Intercollegiate sports:* baseball M(s), basketball M(s)/W(s), cross-country running M(s)/W(s), field hockey W(s), golf M(s)/W(s), ice hockey M(c), lacrosse W(s), soccer M(s)/W(s), softball W(s), tennis M(s)/W(s), track and field M(s)/W(s). *Intramural sports:* badminton M/W, basketball M/W, cheerleading M/W, field hockey W(c), football M/W, rock climbing M/W, soccer M/W, softball M/W, volleyball M/W.

Standardized Tests *Required:* SAT I or ACT (for admission).

Costs (2003–04) *Comprehensive fee:* $26,334 includes full-time tuition ($18,198), mandatory fees ($568), and room and board ($7568). Part-time tuition: $527 per credit hour. *Required fees:* $142 per term part-time. *College room only:* $4028. Room and board charges vary according to board plan and housing facility. *Payment plan:* installment. *Waivers:* senior citizens and employees or children of employees.

Financial Aid Of all full-time matriculated undergraduates who enrolled in 2002, 3,739 applied for aid, 3,160 were judged to have need, 188 had their need fully met. *Average percent of need met:* 73%. *Average financial aid package:* $12,158. *Average need-based loan:* $4665. *Average need-based gift aid:* $6947. *Average non-need-based aid:* $4020. *Average indebtedness upon graduation:* $21,400.

Applying *Options:* early admission, early decision, early action, deferred entrance. *Application fee:* $35. *Required:* high school transcript. *Recommended:* essay or personal statement, letters of recommendation, interview. *Application deadlines:* 3/1 (freshmen), 1/1 (transfers). *Early decision:* 12/1. *Notification:* 4/1 (freshmen), 1/1 (early decision), 1/15 (early action), continuous (transfers).

Admissions Contact Ms. Deanna Campbell, Director of Admission Processing, Monmouth University, 400 Cedar Avenue, West Long Branch, NJ 07764-1898. *Phone:* 732-571-3456. *Toll-free phone:* 800-543-9671. *Fax:* 732-263-5166. *E-mail:* admission@monmouth.edu.

■ See page 2012 for a narrative description.

MONTCLAIR STATE UNIVERSITY

Upper Montclair, New Jersey

- **State-supported** comprehensive, founded 1908
- **Calendar** semesters
- **Degrees** certificates, bachelor's, master's, doctoral, post-master's, and postbachelor's certificates
- **Suburban** 275-acre campus with easy access to New York City
- **Coed,** 11,375 undergraduate students, 79% full-time, 62% women, 38% men
- **Moderately difficult** entrance level, 51% of applicants were admitted

Undergraduates 8,983 full-time, 2,392 part-time. Students come from 13 states and territories, 79 other countries, 1% are from out of state, 11% African American, 5% Asian American or Pacific Islander, 16% Hispanic American, 0.3% Native American, 4% international, 11% transferred in, 21% live on campus. *Retention:* 82% of 2002 full-time freshmen returned.

Freshmen *Admission:* 8,335 applied, 4,257 admitted, 1,647 enrolled. *Test scores:* SAT verbal scores over 500: 59%; SAT math scores over 500: 66%; SAT verbal scores over 600: 16%; SAT math scores over 600: 18%; SAT verbal scores over 700: 1%; SAT math scores over 700: 2%.

Faculty *Total:* 997, 46% full-time, 45% with terminal degrees. *Student/faculty ratio:* 18:1.

Majors Accounting; acting; anthropology; applied mathematics; art; art history, criticism and conservation; art teacher education; athletic training; biochemistry; biology/biological sciences; broadcast journalism; business administration and management; business/managerial economics; chemistry; child development; classics and languages, literatures and linguistics; communication/speech communication and rhetoric; computer and information sciences; computer science; consumer merchandising/retailing management; creative writing; dance; dietetics; dramatic/theatre arts; early childhood education; economics; English; environmental studies; family and consumer economics related; family and consumer sciences/home economics teacher education; family and consumer sciences/human sciences; fashion merchandising; finance; fine/studio arts; foods, nutrition, and wellness; French; geography; geology/earth science; health science; health teacher education; history; humanities; international business/trade/commerce; Italian; kindergarten/preschool education; Latin; linguistics; management information systems; marketing/marketing management; mathematics; molecular biology; music; music pedagogy; music performance; music teacher education; music theory and composition; music therapy; organizational communication; parks, recreation and leisure; parks, recreation and leisure facilities management; philosophy; physical education teaching and coaching; physics; political science and government; pre-dentistry studies; pre-law studies; pre-medical studies; pre-pharmacy studies; pre-veterinary studies; psychology; public relations/image management; religious studies; sociology; Spanish; tourism and travel services management; urban studies/affairs.

Academic Programs *Special study options:* academic remediation for entering students, accelerated degree program, adult/continuing education programs, advanced placement credit, cooperative education, double majors, English as a second language, freshman honors college, honors programs, independent study, internships, off-campus study, part-time degree program, services for LD students, study abroad, summer session for credit. *Unusual degree programs:* 3-2 practical anthropology.

Library Sprague Library with 368,830 titles, 2,195 serial subscriptions, 47,826 audiovisual materials, an OPAC, a Web page.

Computers on Campus 650 computers available on campus for general student use. A campuswide network can be accessed from student residence rooms and from off campus. Internet access, at least one staffed computer lab available.

Student Life *Housing options:* coed, women-only, disabled students. Campus housing is university owned. Freshman campus housing is guaranteed. *Activities and organizations:* drama/theater group, student-run newspaper, radio station, choral group, marching band, Latin American Student Organization, Campus Recreation, Players (A Theatrical Organization), WMSC-FM (The Student-Run Radio Station), Human Relations and Leadership Association, national fraternities, national sororities. *Campus security:* 24-hour emergency response devices and patrols, late-night transport/escort service, controlled dormitory access, video surveillance, student escorts. *Student services:* health clinic, personal/psychological counseling, women's center, legal services.

Athletics Member NCAA. All Division III. *Intercollegiate sports:* baseball M, basketball M/W, cross-country running M/W, field hockey W, football M, golf

Montclair State University (continued)
M/W, lacrosse M/W, soccer M/W, softball W, swimming M/W, tennis M/W, track and field M/W, volleyball W, wrestling M. *Intramural sports:* baseball M, basketball M/W, bowling M/W, football M/W, ice hockey M(c), skiing (downhill) M(c), soccer M, softball M/W, tennis M/W, volleyball M/W.

Standardized Tests *Required:* SAT I or ACT (for admission).

Costs (2003–04) *Tuition:* state resident $4785 full-time, $160 per credit part-time; nonresident $7784 full-time, $259 per credit part-time. *Required fees:* $1625 full-time, $53 per credit part-time, $15 per term part-time. *Room and board:* $7902; room only: $5442. Room and board charges vary according to board plan and housing facility. *Payment plan:* installment. *Waivers:* senior citizens and employees or children of employees.

Financial Aid Of all full-time matriculated undergraduates who enrolled in 2003, 5,875 applied for aid, 4,616 were judged to have need, 1,914 had their need fully met. 369 Federal Work Study jobs (averaging $1011). 1,012 state and other part-time jobs (averaging $2305). In 2003, 539 non-need-based awards were made. *Average percent of need met:* 83%. *Average financial aid package:* $8562. *Average need-based loan:* $3435. *Average need-based gift aid:* $2275. *Average non-need-based aid:* $2850. *Average indebtedness upon graduation:* $15,918.

Applying *Options:* electronic application, deferred entrance. *Application fee:* $55. *Required:* high school transcript. *Required for some:* essay or personal statement, interview. *Application deadlines:* 3/1 (freshmen), 6/15 (transfers). *Notification:* continuous (freshmen), continuous (transfers).

Admissions Contact Mr. Dennis Craig, Director of Admissions, Montclair State University, One Normal Avenue, Upper Montclair, NJ 07043-1624. *Phone:* 973-655-5116. *Toll-free phone:* 800-331-9205. *Fax:* 973-655-7700. *E-mail:* undergraduate.admissions@montclair.edu.

■ *See page 2020 for a narrative description.*

NEW JERSEY CITY UNIVERSITY

Jersey City, New Jersey

- **State-supported** comprehensive, founded 1927
- **Calendar** semesters
- **Degrees** bachelor's, master's, post-master's, and postbachelor's certificates
- **Urban** 46-acre campus with easy access to New York City
- **Coed,** 6,174 undergraduate students, 68% full-time, 62% women, 38% men
- **Moderately difficult** entrance level, 52% of applicants were admitted

Undergraduates 4,200 full-time, 1,974 part-time. Students come from 10 states and territories, 1% are from out of state, 20% African American, 9% Asian American or Pacific Islander, 34% Hispanic American, 0.1% Native American, 1% international, 11% transferred in, 4% live on campus. *Retention:* 69% of 2002 full-time freshmen returned.

Freshmen *Admission:* 2,689 applied, 1,400 admitted, 754 enrolled. *Test scores:* SAT verbal scores over 500: 21%; SAT math scores over 500: 24%; SAT verbal scores over 600: 2%; SAT math scores over 600: 1%.

Faculty *Total:* 582, 40% full-time. *Student/faculty ratio:* 15:1.

Majors Art; art teacher education; biology/biological sciences; business administration and management; chemistry; communication/speech communication and rhetoric; computer and information sciences; criminal justice/safety; economics; elementary education; English; geology/earth science; health science; history; kindergarten/preschool education; mathematics; music; music teacher education; nursing science; philosophy; physics; political science and government; psychology; sociology; Spanish; special education; urban studies/affairs.

Academic Programs *Special study options:* academic remediation for entering students, accelerated degree program, adult/continuing education programs, advanced placement credit, cooperative education, distance learning, double majors, English as a second language, honors programs, independent study, internships, off-campus study, part-time degree program, services for LD students, study abroad, summer session for credit. *ROTC:* Army (c), Air Force (c).

Library Congressman Frank J. Guarini Library with 212,786 titles, 1,260 serial subscriptions, 2,234 audiovisual materials, an OPAC.

Computers on Campus 1400 computers available on campus for general student use. At least one staffed computer lab available.

Student Life *Housing options:* coed. *Activities and organizations:* drama/theater group, student-run newspaper, radio station, choral group, International Student Association, Black Freedom Society, Latin Power Association, national fraternities. *Campus security:* 24-hour emergency response devices and patrols, late-night transport/escort service. *Student services:* health clinic, personal/psychological counseling, women's center, legal services.

Athletics Member NCAA. All Division III. *Intercollegiate sports:* baseball M, basketball M/W, cross-country running W, football M, golf M, soccer M/W, softball W, tennis M, volleyball M/W. *Intramural sports:* basketball M/W, bowling M/W, football M/W, golf M/W, soccer M/W, softball M/W, swimming M/W, table tennis M/W, tennis M/W, volleyball M/W, weight lifting M/W.

Standardized Tests *Required:* SAT I or ACT (for admission). *Recommended:* SAT I (for admission).

Costs (2003–04) *Tuition:* state resident $4560 full-time, $152 per credit hour part-time; nonresident $8868 full-time, $296 per credit hour part-time. *Required fees:* $1491 full-time. *Room and board:* $6586; room only: $4160.

Financial Aid Of all full-time matriculated undergraduates who enrolled in 2002, 2,488 applied for aid, 2,272 were judged to have need, 2,144 had their need fully met. In 2002, 748 non-need-based awards were made. *Average percent of need met:* 76%. *Average financial aid package:* $9858. *Average need-based loan:* $3406. *Average need-based gift aid:* $5740. *Average non-need-based aid:* $4215.

Applying *Options:* electronic application, deferred entrance. *Application fee:* $35. *Required:* essay or personal statement, high school transcript, minimum 2.0 GPA. *Required for some:* interview. *Recommended:* 1 letter of recommendation. *Application deadline:* 4/1 (freshmen), rolling (transfers). *Notification:* continuous (freshmen).

Admissions Contact Ms. Drusilla Blackman, Director of Admissions, New Jersey City University, 2039 Kennedy Boulevard, Jersey City, NJ 07305. *Phone:* 201-200-3234. *Toll-free phone:* 888-441-NJCU. *E-mail:* admissions@njcu.edu.

■ *See page 2078 for a narrative description.*

NEW JERSEY INSTITUTE OF TECHNOLOGY

Newark, New Jersey

- **State-supported** university, founded 1881
- **Calendar** semesters
- **Degrees** bachelor's, master's, doctoral, and postbachelor's certificates
- **Urban** 45-acre campus with easy access to New York City
- **Endowment** $60.0 million
- **Coed,** 5,712 undergraduate students, 74% full-time, 21% women, 79% men
- **Moderately difficult** entrance level, 68% of applicants were admitted

With nearly a century of experience in educating leaders in business and government, NJIT's Newark College of Engineering is also a pioneer in applying new technologies as learning tools. The College's curriculum emphasizes design, multidisciplinary teamwork, real-world experience, and computing as tools in every specialty area.

Undergraduates 4,239 full-time, 1,473 part-time. Students come from 27 states and territories, 53 other countries, 6% are from out of state, 10% African American, 23% Asian American or Pacific Islander, 12% Hispanic American, 0.2% Native American, 5% international, 9% transferred in, 27% live on campus. *Retention:* 85% of 2002 full-time freshmen returned.

Freshmen *Admission:* 2,566 applied, 1,747 admitted, 709 enrolled. *Test scores:* SAT verbal scores over 500: 69%; SAT math scores over 500: 96%; SAT verbal scores over 600: 23%; SAT math scores over 600: 54%; SAT verbal scores over 700: 2%; SAT math scores over 700: 12%.

Faculty *Total:* 634, 64% full-time. *Student/faculty ratio:* 13:1.

Majors Actuarial science; applied mathematics; architecture; biology/biological sciences; biomedical/medical engineering; business administration and management; chemical engineering; chemistry; civil engineering; computer and information sciences; computer and information sciences and support services related; computer engineering; electrical, electronics and communications engineering; engineering science; engineering technologies related; engineering technology; environmental/environmental health engineering; geological/geophysical engineering; history; industrial engineering; information science/studies; manufacturing engineering; mechanical engineering; natural resources/conservation; nursing (registered nurse training); nursing science; physics related; science, technology and society; technical and business writing.

Academic Programs *Special study options:* academic remediation for entering students, accelerated degree program, adult/continuing education programs, advanced placement credit, cooperative education, distance learning, double majors, English as a second language, freshman honors college, honors programs, independent study, internships, off-campus study, part-time degree program, services for LD students, study abroad, summer session for credit. *ROTC:* Air Force (b). *Unusual degree programs:* 3-2 engineering with Seton Hall University, Lincoln University (PA), Stockton State College.

Library Van Houten Library plus 1 other with 160,000 titles, 1,100 serial subscriptions, an OPAC, a Web page.

Computers on Campus 4500 computers available on campus for general student use. A campuswide network can be accessed from student residence rooms and from off campus. At least one staffed computer lab available.

Student Life *Housing options:* coed. Campus housing is university owned. *Activities and organizations:* drama/theater group, student-run newspaper, radio station, Student Senate, Student Activities Council, Microcomputers Users Group, chess club, national fraternities, national sororities. *Campus security:* 24-hour emergency response devices and patrols, late-night transport/escort service,

controlled dormitory access, bicycle patrols, sexual assault response team. *Student services:* health clinic, personal/psychological counseling, women's center.
Athletics Member NCAA. All Division II. *Intercollegiate sports:* baseball M, basketball M/W, cross-country running M/W, fencing M, golf M, soccer M, softball W, swimming W, tennis M/W, track and field W, volleyball M/W. *Intramural sports:* archery M/W, badminton M/W, basketball M/W, bowling M/W, football M, golf M/W, racquetball M/W, soccer M/W, softball M/W, swimming M/W, tennis M/W, track and field M/W, volleyball M/W, water polo M/W, weight lifting M/W.
Standardized Tests *Required:* SAT I or ACT (for admission). *Required for some:* SAT II: Subject Tests (for admission).
Costs (2003–04) *Tuition:* state resident $7332 full-time, $278 per credit part-time; nonresident $12,700 full-time, $544 per credit part-time. Full-time tuition and fees vary according to course load and degree level. Part-time tuition and fees vary according to course load and degree level. *Required fees:* $1168 full-time, $56 per credit part-time, $78 per term part-time. *Room and board:* $8076; room only: $5494. Room and board charges vary according to board plan and housing facility. *Payment plan:* installment. *Waivers:* employees or children of employees.
Financial Aid Of all full-time matriculated undergraduates who enrolled in 2002, 4,156 applied for aid, 2,505 were judged to have need, 825 had their need fully met. In 2002, 422 non-need-based awards were made. *Average percent of need met:* 90%. *Average financial aid package:* $5400. *Average need-based loan:* $1500. *Average need-based gift aid:* $3700. *Average non-need-based aid:* $2472. *Average indebtedness upon graduation:* $14,600. *Financial aid deadline:* 5/15.
Applying *Options:* electronic application, early admission, deferred entrance. *Application fee:* $35. *Required:* high school transcript. *Required for some:* essay or personal statement, interview. *Recommended:* 1 letter of recommendation. *Application deadlines:* 4/1 (freshmen), 6/1 (transfers). *Notification:* continuous (freshmen), continuous (transfers).
Admissions Contact Ms. Kathy Kelly, Director of Admissions, New Jersey Institute of Technology, University Heights, Newark, NJ 07102-1982. *Phone:* 973-596-3300. *Toll-free phone:* 800-925-NJIT. *Fax:* 973-596-3461. *E-mail:* admissions@njit.edu.

PRINCETON UNIVERSITY
Princeton, New Jersey

- **Independent** university, founded 1746
- **Calendar** semesters
- **Degrees** bachelor's, master's, and doctoral
- **Suburban** 600-acre campus with easy access to New York City and Philadelphia
- **Endowment** $7.5 billion
- **Coed,** 4,837 undergraduate students, 97% full-time, 48% women, 52% men
- **Most difficult** entrance level, 10% of applicants were admitted

Undergraduates 4,676 full-time, 161 part-time. Students come from 54 states and territories, 65 other countries, 86% are from out of state, 8% African American, 13% Asian American or Pacific Islander, 6% Hispanic American, 0.7% Native American, 8% international, 97% live on campus. *Retention:* 98% of 2002 full-time freshmen returned.
Freshmen *Admission:* 15,726 applied, 1,601 admitted, 1,168 enrolled. *Average high school GPA:* 3.83. *Test scores:* SAT verbal scores over 500: 100%; SAT math scores over 500: 100%; SAT verbal scores over 600: 96%; SAT math scores over 600: 98%; SAT verbal scores over 700: 71%; SAT math scores over 700: 73%.
Faculty *Total:* 1,015, 79% full-time, 83% with terminal degrees. *Student/faculty ratio:* 5:1.
Majors Anthropology; architecture; art history, criticism and conservation; Asian studies (East); astrophysics; chemical engineering; chemistry; civil engineering; classics and languages, literatures and linguistics; comparative literature; computer engineering; ecology; economics; electrical, electronics and communications engineering; English; French; geological and earth sciences/geosciences related; German; history; mathematics; mechanical engineering; molecular biology; multi-/interdisciplinary studies related; music; Near and Middle Eastern studies; operations research; philosophy; physics; political science and government; psychology; public policy analysis; religious studies; Slavic languages; sociology; Spanish.
Academic Programs *Special study options:* accelerated degree program, adult/continuing education programs, advanced placement credit, cooperative education, honors programs, independent study, internships, off-campus study, services for LD students, student-designed majors, study abroad. *ROTC:* Army (b), Air Force (c).
Library Harvey S. Firestone Memorial Library plus 14 others with 6.3 million titles, 32,446 serial subscriptions, 399,529 audiovisual materials, an OPAC, a Web page.
Computers on Campus 500 computers available on campus for general student use. A campuswide network can be accessed from student residence rooms and from off campus that provide access to academic applications and courseware. Internet access, online (class) registration, at least one staffed computer lab available. Computer purchase or lease plan available.
Student Life *Housing:* on-campus residence required through sophomore year. *Options:* coed, men-only, women-only, disabled students. Campus housing is university owned. Freshman campus housing is guaranteed. *Activities and organizations:* drama/theater group, student-run newspaper, radio station, choral group, marching band. *Campus security:* 24-hour emergency response devices and patrols, student patrols, late-night transport/escort service, controlled dormitory access. *Student services:* health clinic, personal/psychological counseling, women's center, legal services.
Athletics Member NCAA. All Division I except football (Division I-AA). *Intercollegiate sports:* baseball M, basketball M/W, crew M/W, cross-country running M/W, fencing M/W, field hockey W, golf M/W, ice hockey M/W, lacrosse M/W, soccer M/W, softball W, squash M/W, swimming M/W, tennis M/W, track and field M/W, volleyball M/W, water polo M/W, wrestling M. *Intramural sports:* badminton M/W, basketball M/W, equestrian sports M(c)/W(c), ice hockey M/W, lacrosse M(c)/W(c), riflery M(c)/W(c), rugby M(c)/W(c), sailing M(c)/W(c), skiing (downhill) M(c)/W(c), soccer M(c)/W(c), softball M/W, table tennis M/W, tennis M/W, track and field M/W, volleyball M/W.
Standardized Tests *Required:* SAT I or ACT (for admission), SAT II: Subject Tests (for admission).
Costs (2004–05) *Comprehensive fee:* $38,297 includes full-time tuition ($29,910) and room and board ($8387). *College room only:* $4315. *Payment plans:* installment, deferred payment. *Waivers:* employees or children of employees.
Financial Aid Of all full-time matriculated undergraduates who enrolled in 2002, 2,327 applied for aid, 2,127 were judged to have need, 2,127 had their need fully met. 165 Federal Work-Study jobs (averaging $1400). 640 state and other part-time jobs (averaging $1400). *Average percent of need met:* 100%. *Average financial aid package:* $24,078. *Average need-based gift aid:* $22,685. *Average indebtedness upon graduation:* $11,000.
Applying *Options:* early admission, early decision, deferred entrance. *Application fee:* $65. *Required:* essay or personal statement, high school transcript, 3 letters of recommendation. *Recommended:* interview. *Application deadline:* 1/2 (freshmen). *Early decision:* 11/1. *Notification:* 4/3 (freshmen), 12/15 (early decision).
Admissions Contact Ms. Janet Rapelye, Dean of Admission, Princeton University, PO Box 430, Princeton, NJ 08544. *Phone:* 609-258-3062. *Fax:* 609-258-6743.

■ *See page 2196 for a narrative description.*

RABBI JACOB JOSEPH SCHOOL
Edison, New Jersey

Admissions Contact One Plainfield Ave, Edison, NJ 08817.

RABBINICAL COLLEGE OF AMERICA
Morristown, New Jersey

Admissions Contact Rabbi Israel Teitelbaum, Registrar, Rabbinical College of America, Box 1996, Morristown, NJ 07962. *Phone:* 973-267-9404.

RAMAPO COLLEGE OF NEW JERSEY
Mahwah, New Jersey

- **State-supported** comprehensive, founded 1969, part of New Jersey State College System
- **Calendar** semesters
- **Degrees** certificates, bachelor's, and master's
- **Suburban** 300-acre campus with easy access to New York City
- **Endowment** $1.0 million
- **Coed,** 5,242 undergraduate students, 76% full-time, 60% women, 40% men
- **Moderately difficult** entrance level, 43% of applicants were admitted

As "the College of Choice for a Global Education," Ramapo College provides students with the opportunity to encounter the world beyond the campus through study-abroad and cooperative education programs and teleconferences. Undergraduate experiences through these programs have taken students to faraway countries such as China, Costa Rica, Czech Republic, England, Germany, Italy, and Kenya, and to corporate offices in the US and abroad.

Ramapo College of New Jersey (continued)

Undergraduates 3,978 full-time, 1,264 part-time. Students come from 20 states and territories, 65 other countries, 10% are from out of state, 7% African American, 4% Asian American or Pacific Islander, 8% Hispanic American, 0.4% Native American, 3% international, 10% transferred in, 57% live on campus. *Retention:* 87% of 2002 full-time freshmen returned.

Freshmen *Admission:* 4,028 applied, 1,746 admitted, 725 enrolled. *Average high school GPA:* 3.4. *Test scores:* SAT verbal scores over 500: 93%; SAT math scores over 500: 93%; SAT verbal scores over 600: 33%; SAT math scores over 600: 40%; SAT verbal scores over 700: 4%; SAT math scores over 700: 4%.

Faculty *Total:* 386, 44% full-time. *Student/faculty ratio:* 17:1.

Majors Accounting; allied health diagnostic, intervention, and treatment professions related; American studies; area studies related; biochemistry, biophysics and molecular biology related; bioinformatics; biological and biomedical sciences related; biology/biological sciences; business administration and management; chemistry; communication/speech communication and rhetoric; comparative literature; computer and information sciences; dramatic/theatre arts and stagecraft related; economics; English; environmental science; environmental studies; history; humanities; information science/studies; interdisciplinary studies; intermedia/multimedia; international business/trade/commerce; legal professions and studies related; legal studies; literature; mathematics; medical basic sciences related; multi-/interdisciplinary studies related; music; nursing (registered nurse training); physics; political science and government; psychology; social sciences; social work; sociology; Spanish; visual and performing arts.

Academic Programs *Special study options:* academic remediation for entering students, accelerated degree program, adult/continuing education programs, advanced placement credit, cooperative education, double majors, English as a second language, external degree program, freshman honors college, honors programs, independent study, internships, off-campus study, part-time degree program, services for LD students, student-designed majors, study abroad, summer session for credit. *ROTC:* Air Force (c). *Unusual degree programs:* 3-2 nursing with The University of Medicine and Dentistry of New Jersey; biology, chemistry with Rutgers, The State University of New Jersey.

Library George T. Potter Library plus 1 other with 158,633 titles, 670 serial subscriptions, 3,250 audiovisual materials, an OPAC.

Computers on Campus 400 computers available on campus for general student use. A campuswide network can be accessed from student residence rooms and from off campus. Internet access, online (class) registration, at least one staffed computer lab available.

Student Life *Housing options:* coed, disabled students. Campus housing is university owned. Freshman campus housing is guaranteed. *Activities and organizations:* drama/theater group, student-run newspaper, radio and television station, choral group, History Club, Organization for Latin Unity, Sci Fi Blub, Ramapo Pride, Future Educators of America, national fraternities, national sororities. *Campus security:* 24-hour emergency response devices and patrols, late-night transport/escort service, controlled dormitory access, surveillance cameras, patrols by trained security personnel. *Student services:* health clinic, personal/psychological counseling, women's center.

Athletics Member NCAA. All Division III. *Intercollegiate sports:* baseball M, basketball M/W, cheerleading W, cross-country running M/W, field hockey W, soccer M/W, softball W, tennis M/W, track and field M/W, volleyball M/W. *Intramural sports:* basketball M/W, bowling M/W, softball M/W, swimming M/W, volleyball M/W.

Standardized Tests *Required:* SAT I (for admission). *Required for some:* ACT (for admission).

Costs (2003–04) *Tuition:* state resident $5270 full-time, $165 per credit part-time; nonresident $9525 full-time, $298 per credit part-time. Part-time tuition and fees vary according to course load. *Required fees:* $2141 full-time, $67 per credit part-time, $1070 per term part-time. *Room and board:* $7792; room only: $5332. Room and board charges vary according to board plan and housing facility. *Payment plans:* installment, deferred payment. *Waivers:* minority students, senior citizens, and employees or children of employees.

Financial Aid Of all full-time matriculated undergraduates who enrolled in 2003, 2,564 applied for aid, 1,935 were judged to have need, 295 had their need fully met. 137 Federal Work-Study jobs (averaging $1703). 501 state and other part-time jobs (averaging $2105). In 2003, 826 non-need-based awards were made. *Average percent of need met:* 79%. *Average financial aid package:* $9351. *Average need-based loan:* $4026. *Average need-based gift aid:* $6721. *Average non-need-based aid:* $8468. *Average indebtedness upon graduation:* $15,183.

Applying *Options:* early admission, early action, deferred entrance. *Application fee:* $55. *Required:* essay or personal statement, high school transcript. *Recommended:* minimum 3.0 GPA, interview. *Application deadlines:* 3/1 (freshmen), 5/1 (transfers). *Notification:* continuous until 3/1 (freshmen), continuous until 7/1 (transfers).

Admissions Contact Mr. Peter Goetz, Vice President for Enrollment Management, Ramapo College of New Jersey, Office of Admissions, 505 Ramapo Valley Road, Mahwah, NJ 07430-1680. *Phone:* 201-684-7307 Ext. 7307. *Toll-free phone:* 800-9RAMAPO. *Fax:* 201-684-7964. *E-mail:* admissions@ramapo.edu.

■ *See page 2212 for a narrative description.*

THE RICHARD STOCKTON COLLEGE OF NEW JERSEY

Pomona, New Jersey

- **State-supported** comprehensive, founded 1969, part of New Jersey State College System
- **Calendar** semesters
- **Degrees** bachelor's, master's, and postbachelor's certificates
- **Suburban** 1600-acre campus with easy access to Philadelphia
- **Endowment** $2.9 million
- **Coed,** 6,540 undergraduate students, 83% full-time, 59% women, 41% men
- **Very difficult** entrance level, 43% of applicants were admitted

A state-assisted, 4-year coed institution, Richard Stockton College was founded in 1969. Located 12 miles from Atlantic City, Stockton is primarily an undergraduate arts and sciences college within the New Jersey system. Special educational experiences are encouraged, including study abroad, internships, field studies, and independent study. Admission is selective.

Undergraduates 5,439 full-time, 1,101 part-time. Students come from 24 states and territories, 26 other countries, 2% are from out of state, 8% African American, 4% Asian American or Pacific Islander, 6% Hispanic American, 0.5% Native American, 0.8% international, 14% transferred in, 32% live on campus. *Retention:* 83% of 2002 full-time freshmen returned.

Freshmen *Admission:* 3,795 applied, 1,624 admitted, 825 enrolled. *Average high school GPA:* 3.2. *Test scores:* SAT verbal scores over 500: 75%; SAT math scores over 500: 79%; SAT verbal scores over 600: 19%; SAT math scores over 600: 22%; SAT verbal scores over 700: 2%; SAT math scores over 700: 2%.

Faculty *Total:* 458, 46% full-time, 47% with terminal degrees. *Student/faculty ratio:* 19:1.

Majors Audiology and speech-language pathology; biochemistry; biology/biological sciences; business administration and management; chemistry; communication/speech communication and rhetoric; computer and information sciences; computer science; criminology; economics; education (multiple levels); English; environmental studies; foreign languages and literatures; geology/earth science; history; information science/studies; interdisciplinary studies; liberal arts and sciences/liberal studies; marine biology and biological oceanography; mathematics; nursing (registered nurse training); nursing science; philosophy; physics; political science and government; psychology; public health; social work; sociology; visual and performing arts.

Academic Programs *Special study options:* academic remediation for entering students, accelerated degree program, adult/continuing education programs, advanced placement credit, distance learning, freshman honors college, honors programs, independent study, internships, off-campus study, part-time degree program, services for LD students, student-designed majors, study abroad, summer session for credit. *ROTC:* Army (c). *Unusual degree programs:* 3-2 engineering with New Jersey Institute of Technology; Rutgers, The State University of New Jersey; public administration with Rutgers, The State University of New Jersey.

Library The Richard Stockton College of New Jersey Library with 287,769 titles, 7,682 audiovisual materials, an OPAC, a Web page.

Computers on Campus 450 computers available on campus for general student use. A campuswide network can be accessed from student residence rooms and from off campus. Internet access, at least one staffed computer lab available.

Student Life *Housing options:* coed. Campus housing is university owned. *Activities and organizations:* drama/theater group, student-run newspaper, radio and television station, choral group, Stockton Action Volunteers for the Environment, Board of Activities, Los Latinos Unidos, Unified Black Student Society, Stockton Residents Association, national fraternities, national sororities. *Campus security:* 24-hour emergency response devices and patrols, late-night transport/escort service, controlled dormitory access, on-campus sworn/commissioned police force. *Student services:* health clinic, personal/psychological counseling, women's center.

Athletics Member NCAA. All Division III. *Intercollegiate sports:* baseball M, basketball M/W, cheerleading M(s)/W(s), crew W, cross-country running M/W, field hockey W, lacrosse M, soccer M/W, softball W, tennis W, track and field M/W, volleyball W. *Intramural sports:* basketball M/W, bowling M(c)/W(c), crew M(c), fencing M(c)/W(c), football M/W, golf M(c)/W(c), skiing (downhill) M(c)/W(c), softball M/W, swimming M/W, table tennis M/W, tennis M/W, volleyball M/W, weight lifting M/W, wrestling M.

Standardized Tests *Required:* SAT I or ACT (for admission).

Costs (2003–04) *Tuition:* state resident $4736 full-time, $148 per credit part-time; nonresident $7680 full-time, $240 per credit part-time. *Required fees:*

$1488 full-time, $47 per credit part-time. *Room and board:* $6748; room only: $4300. Room and board charges vary according to board plan and housing facility. *Payment plan:* installment. *Waivers:* senior citizens and employees or children of employees.

Financial Aid Of all full-time matriculated undergraduates who enrolled in 2003, 3,879 applied for aid, 3,006 were judged to have need, 2,204 had their need fully met. 280 Federal Work-Study jobs (averaging $1675). 560 state and other part-time jobs (averaging $999). In 2003, 333 non-need-based awards were made. *Average percent of need met:* 61%. *Average financial aid package:* $9541. *Average need-based loan:* $3770. *Average need-based gift aid:* $5459. *Average non-need-based aid:* $1908. *Average indebtedness upon graduation:* $14,372.

Applying *Options:* electronic application, early admission, early action. *Application fee:* $50. *Required:* essay or personal statement, high school transcript, minimum 2.0 GPA. *Recommended:* minimum 3.0 GPA, letters of recommendation. *Application deadlines:* 5/1 (freshmen), 6/1 (transfers). *Notification:* continuous until 5/15 (freshmen), continuous until 6/15 (transfers).

Admissions Contact Mr. Salvatore Catalfamo, Dean of Enrollment Management, The Richard Stockton College of New Jersey, PO Box 195, Pomona, NJ 08240-0195. *Phone:* 609-652-4261. *Fax:* 609-748-5541. *E-mail:* admissions@stockton.edu.

■ *See page 2232 for a narrative description.*

RIDER UNIVERSITY

Lawrenceville, New Jersey

- **Independent** comprehensive, founded 1865
- **Calendar** semesters
- **Degrees** associate, bachelor's, master's, and post-master's certificates
- **Suburban** 340-acre campus with easy access to New York City and Philadelphia
- **Endowment** $46.1 million
- **Coed,** 4,329 undergraduate students, 82% full-time, 59% women, 41% men
- **Moderately difficult** entrance level, 78% of applicants were admitted

Rider University offers majors in business, education, liberal arts, sciences, and music. Rider's formula for career success includes a combination of small classes, personal advising, experiential learning, and use of modern facilities. Students enjoy activities ranging from social organizations to Division I athletics. More than 75 percent of the 3,100 full-time undergraduates receive financial assistance.

Undergraduates 3,553 full-time, 776 part-time. Students come from 36 states and territories, 16 other countries, 24% are from out of state, 8% African American, 3% Asian American or Pacific Islander, 4% Hispanic American, 0.3% Native American, 2% international, 4% transferred in, 56% live on campus. *Retention:* 79% of 2002 full-time freshmen returned.

Freshmen *Admission:* 4,329 applied, 3,394 admitted, 950 enrolled. *Test scores:* SAT verbal scores over 500: 60%; SAT math scores over 500: 64%; SAT verbal scores over 600: 15%; SAT math scores over 600: 19%; SAT verbal scores over 700: 1%; SAT math scores over 700: 1%.

Faculty *Total:* 490, 48% full-time, 71% with terminal degrees. *Student/faculty ratio:* 13:1.

Majors Accounting; actuarial science; advertising; American studies; bilingual and multilingual education; biochemistry; biology/biological sciences; biopsychology; business administration and management; business/managerial economics; business teacher education; chemistry; computer science; economics; education; elementary education; English; environmental studies; finance; French; general studies; geology/earth science; German; history; human resources management; information science/studies; international business/trade/commerce; journalism; kindergarten/preschool education; management science; marine science/merchant marine officer; marketing/marketing management; mathematics; music; music teacher education; music theory and composition; oceanography (chemical and physical); philosophy; physics; piano and organ; political science and government; psychology; public relations/image management; radio and television; religious/sacred music; Russian; science teacher education; secondary education; sociology; Spanish; speech and rhetoric; voice and opera.

Academic Programs *Special study options:* academic remediation for entering students, adult/continuing education programs, advanced placement credit, cooperative education, double majors, English as a second language, honors programs, independent study, internships, part-time degree program, services for LD students, study abroad, summer session for credit. *ROTC:* Army (c).

Library Franklin F. Moore Library plus 1 other with 460,574 titles, 3,031 serial subscriptions, 17,857 audiovisual materials, an OPAC, a Web page.

Computers on Campus 403 computers available on campus for general student use. A campuswide network can be accessed from student residence rooms and from off campus. Internet access, at least one staffed computer lab available. Computer purchase or lease plan available.

Student Life *Housing options:* coed, women-only. Campus housing is university owned. Freshman campus housing is guaranteed. *Activities and organizations:* drama/theater group, student-run newspaper, radio and television station, choral group, Student Government Association, Student Entertainment Council, Association of Commuter Students, Greek organizations, Latin American Student Organization, national fraternities, national sororities. *Campus security:* 24-hour emergency response devices and patrols, student patrols, late-night transport/escort service, controlled dormitory access. *Student services:* health clinic, personal/psychological counseling, women's center.

Athletics Member NCAA. All Division I. *Intercollegiate sports:* baseball M(s), basketball M(s)/W(s), cheerleading M/W, cross-country running M(s)/W(s), field hockey W(s), golf M(s), soccer M(s)/W(s), softball W(s), swimming M(s)/W(s), tennis M(s)/W(s), track and field M(s)/W(s), volleyball W(s), wrestling M(s). *Intramural sports:* basketball M/W, cheerleading M/W, equestrian sports W(c), golf M, ice hockey M(c), lacrosse M(c)/W, soccer M/W, softball M/W, track and field M/W, volleyball M/W, water polo M/W.

Standardized Tests *Required:* SAT I or ACT (for admission).

Costs (2003–04) *Comprehensive fee:* $29,110 includes full-time tuition ($20,590), mandatory fees ($460), and room and board ($8060). Full-time tuition and fees vary according to course load. Part-time tuition: $685 per credit. Part-time tuition and fees vary according to course load. *Required fees:* $35 per course part-time. *Room and board:* Room and board charges vary according to housing facility. *Payment plan:* installment. *Waivers:* employees or children of employees.

Financial Aid Of all full-time matriculated undergraduates who enrolled in 2003, 2,651 applied for aid, 2,318 were judged to have need, 237 had their need fully met. 1,711 Federal Work-Study jobs (averaging $2141). In 2003, 533 non-need-based awards were made. *Average percent of need met:* 79%. *Average financial aid package:* $17,733. *Average need-based loan:* $4564. *Average need-based gift aid:* $8196. *Average non-need-based aid:* $7427. *Average indebtedness upon graduation:* $27,113.

Applying *Options:* common application, electronic application, early admission, early action, deferred entrance. *Application fee:* $40. *Required:* essay or personal statement, high school transcript, minimum 2.0 GPA. *Required for some:* interview. *Recommended:* 2 letters of recommendation, interview. *Application deadline:* rolling (freshmen), rolling (transfers). *Notification:* continuous (freshmen), 12/15 (early action), continuous (transfers).

Admissions Contact Ms. Laurie Marie Kennedy, Director of Admissions, Rider University, 2083 Lawrenceville Road, Lawrenceville, NJ 08648-3099. *Phone:* 609-896-5177. *Toll-free phone:* 800-257-9026. *Fax:* 609-895-6645. *E-mail:* admissions@rider.edu.

■ *See page 2236 for a narrative description.*

ROWAN UNIVERSITY

Glassboro, New Jersey

- **State-supported** comprehensive, founded 1923, part of New Jersey State College System
- **Calendar** semesters
- **Degrees** bachelor's, master's, and doctoral
- **Small-town** 200-acre campus with easy access to Philadelphia
- **Coed,** 8,311 undergraduate students, 82% full-time, 57% women, 43% men
- **Moderately difficult** entrance level, 51% of applicants were admitted

Rowan University is a selective public university offering undergraduate majors plus graduate degrees and certificates. Included are nationally recognized programs in business, engineering, fine and performing arts, liberal arts and sciences, communication, and teacher education. The 200-acre campus hosts 6,500 full-time undergraduates in Glassboro, a southern New Jersey town.

Undergraduates 6,823 full-time, 1,488 part-time. Students come from 16 states and territories, 2% are from out of state, 9% African American, 3% Asian American or Pacific Islander, 6% Hispanic American, 0.3% Native American, 10% transferred in, 33% live on campus. *Retention:* 85% of 2002 full-time freshmen returned.

Freshmen *Admission:* 6,208 applied, 3,190 admitted, 1,239 enrolled. *Average high school GPA:* 3.39. *Test scores:* SAT verbal scores over 500: 77%; SAT math scores over 500: 82%; SAT verbal scores over 600: 22%; SAT math scores over 600: 33%; SAT verbal scores over 700: 2%; SAT math scores over 700: 4%.

Faculty *Total:* 780, 49% full-time, 50% with terminal degrees. *Student/faculty ratio:* 15:1.

Majors Accounting; art; biochemistry; biology/biological sciences; business administration and management; chemical engineering; chemistry; civil engineering; communication/speech communication and rhetoric; computer and information sciences; computer science; criminal justice/police science; dramatic/theatre arts; economics; education (specific levels and methods) related; electrical, electronics and communications engineering; elementary education; English;

Rowan University (continued)
environmental studies; fine/studio arts; geography; history; jazz/jazz studies; kindergarten/preschool education; liberal arts and sciences/liberal studies; mathematics; mechanical engineering; music performance; music theory and composition; nursing related; physical education teaching and coaching; physical sciences; political science and government; psychology; secondary education; sociology; Spanish; special education.

Academic Programs *Special study options:* academic remediation for entering students, adult/continuing education programs, advanced placement credit, double majors, English as a second language, honors programs, independent study, internships, part-time degree program, services for LD students, study abroad, summer session for credit. *ROTC:* Army (c). *Unusual degree programs:* 3-2 optometry with Pennsylvania College of Optometry, podiatry with Pennsylvania College of Podiatric Medicine, pharmacy with Philadelphia College of Pharmacy and Science.

Library Keith and Shirley Campbell Library plus 2 others with 316,500 titles, 1,858 serial subscriptions, 52,834 audiovisual materials, an OPAC, a Web page.

Computers on Campus 350 computers available on campus for general student use. A campuswide network can be accessed from student residence rooms and from off campus. Internet access, at least one staffed computer lab available.

Student Life *Housing:* on-campus residence required for freshman year. *Options:* coed, disabled students. Campus housing is university owned. Freshman campus housing is guaranteed. *Activities and organizations:* drama/theater group, student-run newspaper, radio and television station, choral group, marching band, Greek organizations, Student Government Association, Student Activities Board, national fraternities, national sororities. *Campus security:* 24-hour emergency response devices and patrols, late-night transport/escort service, controlled dormitory access. *Student services:* health clinic, personal/psychological counseling, women's center, legal services.

Athletics Member NCAA. All Division III. *Intercollegiate sports:* baseball M, basketball M/W, cross-country running M/W, field hockey W, football M, lacrosse W, soccer M/W, softball W, swimming M/W, tennis M/W, track and field M/W, volleyball W. *Intramural sports:* baseball M, basketball M/W, ice hockey M, wrestling M.

Costs (2003–04) *Tuition:* state resident $5396 full-time, $193 per semester hour part-time; nonresident $10,792 full-time, $385 per semester hour part-time. *Required fees:* $1826 full-time, $59 per credit part-time. *Room and board:* $7394; room only: $4478. Room and board charges vary according to board plan and housing facility. *Payment plan:* deferred payment. *Waivers:* employees or children of employees.

Financial Aid Of all full-time matriculated undergraduates who enrolled in 2002, 6,620 applied for aid, 5,283 were judged to have need, 1,990 had their need fully met. 481 Federal Work-Study jobs (averaging $1068). 414 state and other part-time jobs (averaging $1403). In 2002, 998 non-need-based awards were made. *Average percent of need met:* 91%. *Average financial aid package:* $7775. *Average need-based loan:* $3355. *Average need-based gift aid:* $4817. *Average non-need-based aid:* $1592.

Applying *Options:* deferred entrance. *Application fee:* $50. *Required:* high school transcript. *Required for some:* interview. *Recommended:* minimum 3.0 GPA, letters of recommendation, interview. *Application deadlines:* 3/15 (freshmen), 3/15 (transfers). *Notification:* 4/15 (freshmen), continuous (transfers).

Admissions Contact Mr. Marvin G. Sills, Director of Admissions, Rowan University, 201 Mullica Hill Road, Glassboro, NJ 08028. *Phone:* 856-256-4200. *Toll-free phone:* 800-447-1165. *Fax:* 856-256-4430. *E-mail:* admissions@rowan.edu.

■ *See page 2262 for a narrative description.*

RUTGERS, THE STATE UNIVERSITY OF NEW JERSEY, CAMDEN

Camden, New Jersey

- **State-supported** university, founded 1927, part of Rutgers, The State University of New Jersey
- **Calendar** semesters
- **Degrees** bachelor's, master's, and first professional
- **Endowment** $342.0 million
- **Coed,** 3,969 undergraduate students, 77% full-time, 58% women, 42% men
- **Moderately difficult** entrance level, 58% of applicants were admitted

Rutgers University at Camden is a vibrant intellectual community located on a tree-lined, 40-acre campus in the heart of the bustling metropolitan Philadelphia region. The closest university to the Liberty Bell, Rutgers-Camden offers 34 undergraduate majors, an Honors College, exceptional internship and clinical programs, and much more. As part of the internationally respected Rutgers system, Rutgers-Camden students enjoy a world-class faculty, libraries, technology, and more, all in an intimate campus setting.

Undergraduates 3,066 full-time, 903 part-time. 4% are from out of state, 14% African American, 8% Asian American or Pacific Islander, 6% Hispanic American, 0.3% Native American, 0.9% international, 10% transferred in, 13% live on campus. *Retention:* 82% of 2002 full-time freshmen returned.

Freshmen *Admission:* 4,697 applied, 2,717 admitted, 499 enrolled. *Test scores:* SAT verbal scores over 500: 74%; SAT math scores over 500: 78%; SAT verbal scores over 600: 22%; SAT math scores over 600: 33%; SAT verbal scores over 700: 4%; SAT math scores over 700: 6%.

Faculty *Total:* 378, 58% full-time, 99% with terminal degrees. *Student/faculty ratio:* 12:1.

Majors Accounting; African-American/Black studies; art; biology/biological sciences; biomedical technology; business administration and management; chemistry; clinical laboratory science/medical technology; computer and information sciences; criminal justice/safety; dramatic/theatre arts; economics; engineering; English; finance; French; German; history; hospitality administration; liberal arts and sciences/liberal studies; marketing/marketing management; mathematics; multi-/interdisciplinary studies related; music; nursing (registered nurse training); philosophy; physics; political science and government; psychology; social work; sociology; Spanish; urban studies/affairs.

Academic Programs *Special study options:* academic remediation for entering students, accelerated degree program, advanced placement credit, cooperative education, distance learning, double majors, English as a second language, freshman honors college, honors programs, independent study, part-time degree program, services for LD students, student-designed majors, study abroad, summer session for credit. *ROTC:* Army (c), Air Force (c).

Library Paul Robeson Library plus 2 others with 714,447 titles, 5,189 serial subscriptions, 326 audiovisual materials.

Computers on Campus 184 computers available on campus for general student use. A campuswide network can be accessed from student residence rooms and from off campus that provide access to online grade reports. Internet access, at least one staffed computer lab available.

Student Life *Housing options:* coed, disabled students. *Activities and organizations:* drama/theater group, student-run newspaper, radio station.

Standardized Tests *Required:* SAT I or ACT (for admission). *Required for some:* SAT II: Subject Tests (for admission).

Costs (2003–04) *Tuition:* state resident $6290 full-time, $203 per credit part-time; nonresident $12,804 full-time, $415 per credit part-time. *Required fees:* $1466 full-time, $292 per term part-time. *Room and board:* $7552; room only: $5152.

Financial Aid Of all full-time matriculated undergraduates who enrolled in 2003, 2,356 applied for aid, 1,966 were judged to have need, 805 had their need fully met. 355 Federal Work-Study jobs (averaging $1880). In 2003, 89 non-need-based awards were made. *Average percent of need met:* 86%. *Average financial aid package:* $9063. *Average need-based loan:* $3745. *Average need-based gift aid:* $6245. *Average non-need-based aid:* $4218. *Average indebtedness upon graduation:* $15,432.

Applying *Options:* electronic application, early admission. *Application fee:* $50. *Required:* high school transcript. *Application deadline:* rolling (freshmen). *Notification:* 2/28 (freshmen), 5/15 (transfers).

Admissions Contact Ms. Diane Williams Harris, Associate Director of University Undergraduate Admissions, Rutgers, The State University of New Jersey, Camden, 65 Davidson Road, Piscataway, NJ 08854-8097. *Phone:* 732-932-4636. *Fax:* 856-225-6498.

■ *See page 2264 for a narrative description.*

RUTGERS, THE STATE UNIVERSITY OF NEW JERSEY, NEWARK

Newark, New Jersey

- **State-supported** university, founded 1892, part of Rutgers, The State University of New Jersey
- **Calendar** semesters
- **Degrees** bachelor's, master's, doctoral, and first professional
- **Endowment** $342.0 million
- **Coed,** 6,784 undergraduate students, 75% full-time, 58% women, 42% men
- **Moderately difficult** entrance level, 47% of applicants were admitted

Rutgers-Newark offers high-quality and affordable education on a dynamic urban campus in New Jersey's largest city. A total of 99% of the faculty members hold a PhD or JD, and students enjoy a 14:1 student-teacher ratio. The campus is among the top national research universities, and *U.S. News & World Report* rates it as the nation's most diverse national university. This combination creates an academically challenging, rigorous learning environment that is also culturally stimulating, creating graduates well prepared for the demands of today's global society.

Undergraduates 5,094 full-time, 1,690 part-time. 8% are from out of state, 20% African American, 22% Asian American or Pacific Islander, 17% Hispanic American, 0.2% Native American, 3% international, 6% transferred in, 13% live on campus. *Retention:* 86% of 2002 full-time freshmen returned.

Freshmen *Admission:* 7,835 applied, 3,681 admitted, 987 enrolled. *Test scores:* SAT verbal scores over 500: 68%; SAT math scores over 500: 78%; SAT verbal scores over 600: 19%; SAT math scores over 600: 36%; SAT verbal scores over 700: 1%; SAT math scores over 700: 5%.

Faculty *Total:* 605, 64% full-time, 99% with terminal degrees. *Student/faculty ratio:* 12:1.

Majors Accounting; African-American/Black studies; allied health diagnostic, intervention, and treatment professions related; American studies; anthropology; applied mathematics; art; biological and biomedical sciences related; biology/biological sciences; botany/plant biology; business administration and management; chemistry; classics and classical languages related; classics and languages, literatures and linguistics; clinical laboratory science/medical technology; computer and information sciences; criminal justice/safety; cultural studies; dramatic/theatre arts; economics; engineering; English; environmental studies; finance; fine arts related; French; geological/geophysical engineering; geology/earth science; German; Hispanic-American, Puerto Rican, and Mexican-American/Chicano studies; history; information science/studies; Italian; journalism; marketing/marketing management; mathematics; multi-/interdisciplinary studies related; music; nursing (registered nurse training); philosophy; physics; physics related; political science and government; psychology; science, technology and society; Slavic, Baltic, and Albanian languages related; social work; sociology; Spanish; women's studies; zoology/animal biology.

Academic Programs *Special study options:* academic remediation for entering students, accelerated degree program, adult/continuing education programs, advanced placement credit, distance learning, double majors, English as a second language, freshman honors college, honors programs, independent study, internships, off-campus study, part-time degree program, services for LD students, student-designed majors, study abroad, summer session for credit. *ROTC:* Army (b), Air Force (b). *Unusual degree programs:* 3-2 criminal justice.

Library John Cotton Dana Library plus 4 others with 941,103 titles, 6,408 serial subscriptions, 34,994 audiovisual materials.

Computers on Campus 708 computers available on campus for general student use. A campuswide network can be accessed from student residence rooms and from off campus that provide access to online grade reports. Internet access, at least one staffed computer lab available.

Student Life *Housing options:* coed, disabled students. *Activities and organizations:* drama/theater group, student-run newspaper, radio station, choral group.

Standardized Tests *Required:* SAT I or ACT (for admission). *Required for some:* SAT II: Subject Tests (for admission).

Costs (2003–04) *Tuition:* state resident $6290 full-time, $203 per credit part-time; nonresident $12,804 full-time, $415 per credit part-time. *Required fees:* $1290 full-time. *Room and board:* $8140; room only: $5090.

Financial Aid Of all full-time matriculated undergraduates who enrolled in 2003, 3,680 applied for aid, 3,204 were judged to have need, 847 had their need fully met. 710 Federal Work-Study jobs (averaging $1944). In 2003, 185 non-need-based awards were made. *Average percent of need met:* 79%. *Average financial aid package:* $9164. *Average need-based loan:* $3432. *Average need-based gift aid:* $6769. *Average non-need-based aid:* $3590. *Average indebtedness upon graduation:* $14,757.

Applying *Options:* electronic application, early admission. *Application fee:* $50. *Required:* high school transcript. *Application deadline:* rolling (freshmen), rolling (transfers). *Notification:* 2/28 (freshmen), 5/15 (transfers).

Admissions Contact Ms. Diane William Harris, Associate Director of University Undergraduate Admissions, Rutgers, The State University of New Jersey, Newark, 65 Davidson Road, Piscataway, NJ 08854-8097. *Phone:* 732-932-4636. *Fax:* 973-353-1440.

■ *See page 2266 for a narrative description.*

RUTGERS, THE STATE UNIVERSITY OF NEW JERSEY, NEW BRUNSWICK/PISCATAWAY

New Brunswick, New Jersey

- **State-supported** university, founded 1766, part of Rutgers, The State University of New Jersey
- **Calendar** semesters
- **Degrees** bachelor's, master's, doctoral, and first professional
- **Endowment** $342.0 million
- **Coed,** 27,365 undergraduate students, 91% full-time, 52% women, 48% men
- **Moderately difficult** entrance level, 54% of applicants were admitted

Rutgers, The State University of New Jersey, New Brunswick, has grown from a small colonial college to a thriving university center. The largest of Rutgers University's three regional campuses, it is home to 12 schools offering undergraduate degrees in a variety of living and learning environments, from peaceful trails to a bustling downtown, and from "smart" classrooms to state-of-the-art laboratories. Rutgers has great people and offers an outstanding value, with myriad opportunities for personal growth.

Undergraduates 24,798 full-time, 2,567 part-time. Students come from 9 other countries, 11% are from out of state, 8% African American, 20% Asian American or Pacific Islander, 8% Hispanic American, 0.2% Native American, 2% international, 4% transferred in, 46% live on campus. *Retention:* 89% of 2002 full-time freshmen returned.

Freshmen *Admission:* 26,175 applied, 14,180 admitted, 4,717 enrolled. *Test scores:* SAT verbal scores over 500: 92%; SAT math scores over 500: 95%; SAT verbal scores over 600: 47%; SAT math scores over 600: 63%; SAT verbal scores over 700: 9%; SAT math scores over 700: 17%.

Faculty *Total:* 2,164, 69% full-time, 99% with terminal degrees. *Student/faculty ratio:* 15:1.

Majors Accounting; African studies; agricultural/biological engineering and bioengineering; agriculture; American studies; ancient/classical Greek; animal genetics; animal/livestock husbandry and production; animal physiology; animal sciences; anthropology; art; art history, criticism and conservation; Asian studies (East); astrophysics; atmospheric sciences and meteorology; biochemistry; biology/biological sciences; biomedical/medical engineering; biomedical sciences; biometry/biometrics; biotechnology; business administration and management; cell biology and anatomical sciences related; cell biology and histology; ceramic arts and ceramics; ceramic sciences and engineering; chemical engineering; chemistry; Chinese; civil engineering; classics and languages, literatures and linguistics; clinical laboratory science/medical technology; commercial and advertising art; communication/speech communication and rhetoric; comparative literature; computer engineering; computer science; criminal justice/law enforcement administration; cultural studies; dance; dramatic/theatre arts; drawing; ecology; economics; electrical, electronics and communications engineering; engineering science; English; environmental design/architecture; environmental studies; equestrian studies; European studies (Central and Eastern); evolutionary biology; film/cinema studies; finance; food science; foreign languages and literatures; French; geography; geology/earth science; German; Hispanic-American, Puerto Rican, and Mexican-American/Chicano studies; history; human ecology; industrial engineering; information science/studies; interdisciplinary studies; Italian; jazz/jazz studies; Jewish/Judaic studies; journalism; kinesiology and exercise science; labor and industrial relations; Latin; Latin American studies; liberal arts and sciences/liberal studies; linguistics; management science; management sciences and quantitative methods related; marine biology and biological oceanography; marketing/marketing management; mass communication/media; mathematics; mechanical engineering; medical microbiology and bacteriology; medieval and Renaissance studies; molecular biology; music; music teacher education; natural resources/conservation; natural resources management; Near and Middle Eastern studies; nursing (registered nurse training); nutrition sciences; painting; pharmacy; philosophy; photography; physics; plant sciences; political science and government; Portuguese; pre-dentistry studies; pre-law studies; pre-medical studies; printmaking; psychology; public health; religious studies; Russian; Russian studies; sculpture; social sciences related; social work; sociology; Spanish; statistics; turf and turfgrass management; urban studies/affairs; veterinary sciences; visual and performing arts; women's studies.

Academic Programs *Special study options:* academic remediation for entering students, accelerated degree program, advanced placement credit, cooperative education, distance learning, double majors, English as a second language, honors programs, independent study, student-designed majors, study abroad. *ROTC:* Army (b), Air Force (b). *Unusual degree programs:* 3-2 planning and public policy, education, criminal justice.

Library Archibald S. Alexander Library plus 14 others with 4.7 million titles, 17,182 serial subscriptions, 91,657 audiovisual materials, an OPAC, a Web page.

Computers on Campus 1450 computers available on campus for general student use. A campuswide network can be accessed from student residence rooms and from off campus that provide access to online grade reports. Internet access, at least one staffed computer lab available.

Student Life *Housing options:* coed, men-only, women-only, cooperative, disabled students. *Activities and organizations:* drama/theater group, student-run newspaper, radio and television station, choral group, marching band, national fraternities, national sororities. *Student services:* health clinic.

Athletics Member NCAA. All Division I except football (Division I-A). *Intercollegiate sports:* baseball M, basketball M/W, crew M/W, cross-country running M/W, fencing M/W, golf M/W, gymnastics W, lacrosse M/W, soccer M/W, softball W, swimming M/W, tennis M/W, track and field M/W, volleyball W, wrestling M. *Intramural sports:* badminton M/W, baseball M(c), basketball M/W, bowling M/W, cross-country running M/W, equestrian sports M(c)/W(c), field

Rutgers, The State University of New Jersey, New Brunswick/ Piscataway (continued)
hockey W(c), football M, golf M/W, ice hockey M(c), lacrosse M/W, racquetball M/W, rugby M(c)/W(c), sailing M(c)/W(c), skiing (cross-country) M(c)/W(c), skiing (downhill) M(c)/W(c), soccer M/W, softball M/W, squash M(c)/W(c), swimming M/W, table tennis M(c)/W(c), tennis M/W, track and field M/W, volleyball M/W, water polo M/W, wrestling M.

Standardized Tests *Required:* SAT I or ACT (for admission). *Required for some:* SAT II: Writing Test (for admission).

Costs (2003–04) *Tuition:* state resident $6290 full-time; nonresident $12,804 full-time. Full-time tuition and fees vary according to program. Part-time tuition and fees vary according to course level and program. *Required fees:* $1637 full-time. *Room and board:* $7711. Room and board charges vary according to board plan and housing facility. *Payment plan:* installment. *Waivers:* employees or children of employees.

Financial Aid Of all full-time matriculated undergraduates who enrolled in 2003, 15,599 applied for aid, 12,458 were judged to have need, 3,921 had their need fully met. 2,889 Federal Work-Study jobs (averaging $1934). In 2003, 2594 non-need-based awards were made. *Average percent of need met:* 82%. *Average financial aid package:* $10,288. *Average need-based loan:* $4064. *Average need-based gift aid:* $6738. *Average non-need-based aid:* $4954. *Average indebtedness upon graduation:* $15,018.

Applying *Options:* electronic application, early admission. *Application fee:* $50. *Required:* high school transcript. *Application deadline:* rolling (freshmen). *Notification:* 2/28 (freshmen), 5/15 (transfers).

Admissions Contact Ms. Diane Williams Harris, Associate Director of University Undergraduate Admissions, Rutgers, The State University of New Jersey, New Brunswick/Piscataway, 65 Davidson Road, Piscataway, NJ 08854-8097. *Phone:* 732-932-4636. *Fax:* 732-445-0237. *E-mail:* admissions@rutgers.edu.

■ *See page 2268 for a narrative description.*

SAINT PETER'S COLLEGE
Jersey City, New Jersey

- **Independent Roman Catholic (Jesuit)** comprehensive, founded 1872
- **Calendar** semesters
- **Degrees** certificates, associate, bachelor's, and master's
- **Urban** 15-acre campus with easy access to New York City
- **Endowment** $20.0 million
- **Coed**
- **Moderately difficult** entrance level

Faculty *Student/faculty ratio:* 15:1.

Student Life *Campus security:* 24-hour emergency response devices and patrols, late-night transport/escort service, controlled dormitory access, ID checks at residence halls and library.

Athletics Member NCAA. All Division I except football (Division I-AA).

Standardized Tests *Required:* SAT I or ACT (for admission).

Costs (2003–04) *Comprehensive fee:* $26,392 includes full-time tuition ($18,092), mandatory fees ($500), and room and board ($7800). Full-time tuition and fees vary according to course load and location. Part-time tuition: $604 per credit. Part-time tuition and fees vary according to class time and course load. *College room only:* $4933. Room and board charges vary according to board plan and housing facility. *Payment plans:* installment, deferred payment.

Financial Aid Of all full-time matriculated undergraduates who enrolled in 2001, 1,918 applied for aid, 1,608 were judged to have need, 242 had their need fully met. 214 Federal Work-Study jobs (averaging $1655). 219 state and other part-time jobs (averaging $2689). In 2001, 230. *Average percent of need met:* 78. *Average financial aid package:* $14,583. *Average need-based loan:* $3015. *Average need-based gift aid:* $5750. *Average non-need-based aid:* $9824. *Average indebtedness upon graduation:* $13,625.

Applying *Options:* common application, early admission, deferred entrance. *Application fee:* $40. *Required:* essay or personal statement, high school transcript, minimum 2.0 GPA, 2 letters of recommendation. *Required for some:* interview. *Recommended:* interview.

Admissions Contact Stephanie Decker, Director of Recruitment, Saint Peter's College, 2641 Kennedy Boulevard, Jersey City, NJ 07306-5944. *Phone:* 201-915-9213. *Toll-free phone:* 888-SPC-9933. *Fax:* 201-432-5860. *E-mail:* admissions@spc.edu.

■ *See page 2326 for a narrative description.*

SETON HALL UNIVERSITY
South Orange, New Jersey

- **Independent Roman Catholic** university, founded 1856
- **Calendar** semesters
- **Degrees** bachelor's, master's, doctoral, first professional, and post-master's certificates
- **Suburban** 58-acre campus with easy access to New York City
- **Endowment** $162.2 million
- **Coed,** 5,238 undergraduate students, 89% full-time, 52% women, 48% men
- **Moderately difficult** entrance level, 82% of applicants were admitted

Seton Hall University has been preparing students to assume leadership roles for nearly 150 years. A Catholic university founded with the purpose of "enriching the mind, the heart, and the spirit," Seton Hall offers more than 60 majors and concentrations, as well as honors and leadership programs. With a 14:1 student-faculty ratio and an average class size of 25, Seton Hall offers all the advantages of a big school but, with just 4,800 undergraduate students, the University also provides the personal attention of a small college. Seton Hall's mission of "preparing student leaders for a global society" is evidenced through its high academic standards, values-centered curriculum, and cutting-edge technology.

Undergraduates 4,683 full-time, 555 part-time. Students come from 45 states and territories, 49 other countries, 25% are from out of state, 11% African American, 8% Asian American or Pacific Islander, 9% Hispanic American, 0.1% Native American, 2% international, 6% transferred in, 42% live on campus. *Retention:* 80% of 2002 full-time freshmen returned.

Freshmen *Admission:* 5,750 applied, 4,707 admitted, 1,248 enrolled. *Average high school GPA:* 3.26. *Test scores:* SAT verbal scores over 500: 73%; SAT math scores over 500: 76%; SAT verbal scores over 600: 29%; SAT math scores over 600: 32%; SAT verbal scores over 700: 6%; SAT math scores over 700: 5%.

Faculty *Total:* 860, 47% full-time. *Student/faculty ratio:* 15:1.

Majors Accounting; African-American/Black studies; anthropology; art history, criticism and conservation; art teacher education; Asian studies; biochemistry; biology/biological sciences; business administration and management; business/managerial economics; chemistry; Christian studies; classics and languages, literatures and linguistics; commercial and advertising art; communication/speech communication and rhetoric; computer and information sciences; criminal justice/safety; economics; elementary education; English; finance; foreign languages and literatures; French; history; humanities; international relations and affairs; Italian; kindergarten/preschool education; labor and industrial relations; liberal arts and sciences/liberal studies; management information systems; marketing/marketing management; mathematics; music; music history, literature, and theory; music performance; nursing (registered nurse training); philosophy; physics; political science and government; psychology; religious education; religious studies; secondary education; social work; sociology; Spanish; special education; sport and fitness administration; visual and performing arts.

Academic Programs *Special study options:* academic remediation for entering students, accelerated degree program, advanced placement credit, cooperative education, distance learning, double majors, English as a second language, honors programs, independent study, internships, part-time degree program, services for LD students, study abroad, summer session for credit. *ROTC:* Army (b), Air Force (c). *Unusual degree programs:* 3-2 engineering with New Jersey Institute of Technology, Stevens Institute of Technology; occupational therapy.

Library Walsh Library plus 1 other with 506,042 titles, 1,475 serial subscriptions, 2,225 audiovisual materials, an OPAC, a Web page.

Computers on Campus 300 computers available on campus for general student use. A campuswide network can be accessed from student residence rooms and from off campus. Internet access, online (class) registration, at least one staffed computer lab available. Computer purchase or lease plan available.

Student Life *Housing options:* coed. Campus housing is university owned. *Activities and organizations:* drama/theater group, student-run newspaper, radio and television station, choral group, Martin Luther King Jr. Scholars Association, Adelante/Caribe, Black Student Union, National Council of Negro Women, national fraternities, national sororities. *Campus security:* 24-hour emergency response devices and patrols, late-night transport/escort service, controlled dormitory access. *Student services:* health clinic, personal/psychological counseling, women's center.

Athletics Member NCAA. All Division I. *Intercollegiate sports:* baseball M(s), basketball M(s)/W(s), cross-country running M(s)/W(s), golf M(s), ice hockey M(c), rugby M(c), soccer M(s)/W(s), softball W(s), swimming M(s)/W(s), tennis W(s), track and field M(s)/W(s), volleyball M(c)/W(s). *Intramural sports:* basketball M/W, football M/W, racquetball M/W, soccer M/W, softball M/W, tennis M/W, volleyball M/W.

Standardized Tests *Required:* SAT I or ACT (for admission).

Costs (2003–04) *Comprehensive fee:* $31,126 includes full-time tuition ($19,530), mandatory fees ($2050), and room and board ($9546). Full-time tuition and fees vary according to course load. Part-time tuition: $651 per credit. Part-time tuition and fees vary according to course load. *Required fees:* $185 per term part-time. *College room only:* $6068. Room and board charges vary according to board plan and housing facility. *Payment plans:* installment, deferred payment. *Waivers:* senior citizens and employees or children of employees.

Financial Aid Of all full-time matriculated undergraduates who enrolled in 2003, 3,434 applied for aid, 2,986 were judged to have need, 490 had their need fully met. 807 Federal Work-Study jobs (averaging $1930). 1,116 state and other part-time jobs (averaging $1289). In 2003, 692 non-need-based awards were made. *Average percent of need met:* 69%. *Average financial aid package:* $13,980. *Average need-based loan:* $3026. *Average need-based gift aid:* $4498. *Average non-need-based aid:* $11,763. *Average indebtedness upon graduation:* $16,763.

Applying *Options:* common application, electronic application, deferred entrance. *Application fee:* $45. *Required:* essay or personal statement, high school transcript, counselor report. *Required for some:* minimum 3.0 GPA, interview. *Recommended:* minimum 3.0 GPA, letters of recommendation, interview. *Application deadlines:* 3/1 (freshmen), 6/1 (transfers). *Notification:* continuous until 12/1 (freshmen), continuous until 1/1 (transfers).

Admissions Contact Mr. Darryl Jones, Director of Admissions, Seton Hall University, Enrollment Services, Bayley Hall, South Orange, NJ 07079-2697. *Phone:* 973-275-2576. *Toll-free phone:* 800-THE HALL. *Fax:* 973-275-2040. *E-mail:* thehall@shu.edu.

■ *See page 2368 for a narrative description.*

STEVENS INSTITUTE OF TECHNOLOGY
Hoboken, New Jersey

- **Independent** university, founded 1870
- **Calendar** semesters
- **Degrees** bachelor's, master's, doctoral, and postbachelor's certificates
- **Urban** 55-acre campus with easy access to New York City
- **Endowment** $113.1 million
- **Coed,** 1,707 undergraduate students, 100% full-time, 25% women, 75% men
- **Very difficult** entrance level, 51% of applicants were admitted

Stevens ranks in the top 5% of the nation's technological universities. A 9:1 student-faculty ratio and broad-based curricula in business, engineering, the sciences, and humanities fosters critical analysis and creativity, as well as hands-on research with world-renowned faculty members. Students also combine their classroom and laboratory experience with cooperative education and summer internship opportunities. Plus, the residential campus is located in Hoboken, just minutes from New York City and all of the excitement it offers.

Undergraduates 1,701 full-time, 6 part-time. Students come from 34 states and territories, 29 other countries, 35% are from out of state, 4% African American, 20% Asian American or Pacific Islander, 8% Hispanic American, 0.2% Native American, 5% international, 3% transferred in, 80% live on campus. *Retention:* 90% of 2002 full-time freshmen returned.

Freshmen *Admission:* 1,999 applied, 1,026 admitted, 395 enrolled. *Average high school GPA:* 3.80. *Test scores:* SAT verbal scores over 500: 95%; SAT math scores over 500: 100%; SAT verbal scores over 600: 56%; SAT math scores over 600: 88%; SAT verbal scores over 700: 12%; SAT math scores over 700: 34%.

Faculty *Total:* 300, 57% full-time, 90% with terminal degrees. *Student/faculty ratio:* 9:1.

Majors Asian studies (Ural-Altaic and Central); biochemistry; biomedical/medical engineering; business administration and management; chemical engineering; chemistry; civil engineering; computational mathematics; computer engineering; computer science; digital communication and media/multimedia; electrical, electronics and communications engineering; engineering/industrial management; engineering physics; English; environmental/environmental health engineering; history; history and philosophy of science and technology; humanities; intermedia/multimedia; mathematics; mechanical engineering; music performance; music theory and composition; Near and Middle Eastern studies; philosophy; physics; pre-dentistry studies; pre-law studies; pre-medical studies; statistics; systems engineering.

Academic Programs *Special study options:* accelerated degree program, advanced placement credit, cooperative education, distance learning, double majors, honors programs, independent study, internships, off-campus study, study abroad, summer session for credit. *ROTC:* Army (c), Air Force (c).

Library S. C. Williams Library with 59,489 titles, 162 serial subscriptions, an OPAC, a Web page.

Computers on Campus 1700 computers available on campus for general student use. A campuswide network can be accessed from student residence rooms and from off campus that provide access to online grade and account information. Internet access, online (class) registration, at least one staffed computer lab available. Computer purchase or lease plan available.

Student Life *Housing options:* coed, men-only, women-only. Campus housing is university owned. Freshman campus housing is guaranteed. *Activities and organizations:* drama/theater group, student-run newspaper, radio and television station, choral group, Drama Society, Student Council (including Ethnic Student Council), foreign student clubs, Interdormitory Council, student newspaper, national fraternities, national sororities. *Campus security:* 24-hour emergency response devices and patrols, late-night transport/escort service, controlled dormitory access. *Student services:* health clinic, personal/psychological counseling, women's center.

Athletics Member NCAA. All Division III. *Intercollegiate sports:* baseball M, basketball M/W, cross-country running M/W, equestrian sports W, fencing M/W, field hockey W, lacrosse M/W, soccer M/W, swimming M/W, tennis M/W, track and field M/W, volleyball M/W, wrestling M. *Intramural sports:* archery M(c)/W(c), badminton M/W, baseball M, basketball M/W, bowling M/W, equestrian sports M(c)/W(c), golf M(c)/W(c), racquetball M/W, rock climbing M(c)/W(c), sailing M(c)/W(c), skiing (cross-country) M(c)/W(c), soccer M/W, softball M/W, squash M/W, table tennis M/W, tennis M/W, volleyball M/W, weight lifting M(c)/W(c).

Standardized Tests *Required:* SAT I or ACT (for admission). *Required for some:* SAT I and SAT II or ACT (for admission), SAT II: Subject Tests (for admission), SAT II: Writing Test (for admission). *Recommended:* SAT II: Subject Tests (for admission), SAT II: Writing Test (for admission).

Costs (2003–04) *Comprehensive fee:* $35,460 includes full-time tuition ($26,000), mandatory fees ($960), and room and board ($8500). *College room only:* $4400. Room and board charges vary according to board plan and housing facility. *Payment plan:* installment. *Waivers:* employees or children of employees.

Financial Aid Of all full-time matriculated undergraduates who enrolled in 2003, 1,600 applied for aid, 1,417 were judged to have need, 196 had their need fully met. 818 Federal Work-Study jobs (averaging $1269). In 2003, 216 non-need-based awards were made. *Average percent of need met:* 85%. *Average financial aid package:* $18,336. *Average need-based loan:* $4298. *Average need-based gift aid:* $12,871. *Average non-need-based aid:* $9663. *Average indebtedness upon graduation:* $14,113.

Applying *Options:* electronic application, early admission, early decision, deferred entrance. *Application fee:* $45. *Required:* high school transcript, interview. *Recommended:* essay or personal statement, letters of recommendation. *Application deadlines:* 2/15 (freshmen), 7/1 (transfers). *Early decision:* 11/15. *Notification:* continuous until 5/1 (freshmen), 12/15 (early decision), continuous (transfers).

Admissions Contact Mr. Daniel Gallagher, Dean of University Admissions, Stevens Institute of Technology, Castle Point on Hudson, Hoboken, NJ 07030. *Phone:* 201-216-5197. *Toll-free phone:* 800-458-5323. *Fax:* 201-216-8348. *E-mail:* admissions@stevens-tech.edu.

■ *See page 2464 for a narrative description.*

TALMUDICAL ACADEMY OF NEW JERSEY
Adelphia, New Jersey

Admissions Contact Rabbi G. Finkel, Director of Admissions, Talmudical Academy of New Jersey, Route 524, Adelphia, NJ 07710. *Phone:* 201-431-1600.

THOMAS EDISON STATE COLLEGE
Trenton, New Jersey

- **State-supported** comprehensive, founded 1972
- **Calendar** continuous
- **Degrees** certificates, associate, bachelor's, and master's (offers only distance learning degree programs)
- **Urban** 2-acre campus with easy access to Philadelphia
- **Coed,** 10,011 undergraduate students, 47% women, 53% men
- **Noncompetitive** entrance level

Undergraduates 10,011 part-time. Students come from 55 states and territories, 83 other countries, 48% are from out of state, 10% African American, 2% Asian American or Pacific Islander, 4% Hispanic American, 1% Native American, 3% international.

Majors Accounting; advertising; aircraft powerplant technology; airline pilot and flight crew; air traffic control; anthropology; architectural engineering technology; art; banking and financial support services; biology/biological sciences; biomedical technology; business administration and management; chemistry; child guidance; civil engineering technology; communication/speech communication and rhetoric; community organization and advocacy; computer and information sciences; computer science; construction engineering technology; consumer merchandising/retailing management; criminal justice/law enforcement administration; cytotechnology; dance; dental hygiene; drafting and design technology; dramatic/theatre arts; economics; electrical, electronic and communications engineering technology; English; environmental studies; finance; fire protection and safety technology; foreign languages and literatures; forestry; gerontology; health/health care administration; history; horticultural science; hotel/motel administration; humanities; human resources management; industrial

Thomas Edison State College (continued)
technology; insurance; international business/trade/commerce; journalism; labor and industrial relations; legal assistant/paralegal; liberal arts and sciences/liberal studies; logistics and materials management; marine technology; marketing/marketing management; mathematics; mechanical engineering/mechanical technology; medical radiologic technology; mental health/rehabilitation; music; natural sciences; nuclear medical technology; nuclear/nuclear power technology; nursing science; operations management; organizational behavior; parks, recreation and leisure; perfusion technology; philosophy; photography; physics; political science and government; psychology; public administration; purchasing, procurement/acquisitions and contracts management; real estate; religious studies; respiratory care therapy; sales, distribution and marketing; social sciences; sociology; survey technology.

Academic Programs *Special study options:* adult/continuing education programs, advanced placement credit, distance learning, double majors, external degree program, independent study, part-time degree program, services for LD students, summer session for credit.

Computers on Campus A campuswide network can be accessed from off campus. Internet access, online (class) registration available.

Student Life *Housing:* college housing not available. *Campus security:* guard from 7 a.m. to 11 p.m., local police patrol.

Athletics *Intercollegiate sports:* ultimate Frisbee M(c)/W(c).

Costs (2003–04) *Tuition:* state resident $3325 per year part-time; nonresident $4775 per year part-time. *Waivers:* employees or children of employees.

Financial Aid Of all full-time matriculated undergraduates who enrolled in 2002, 1,807 applied for aid, 1,520 were judged to have need, 1,081 had their need fully met. *Average financial aid package:* $3831. *Average need-based loan:* $1425. *Average need-based gift aid:* $2050.

Applying *Options:* electronic application. *Application fee:* $75. *Required:* age 21 or over and a high school graduate. *Notification:* continuous (transfers).

Admissions Contact Mr. Gordon Holly, Director of Admissions Services, Thomas Edison State College, Trenton, NJ 08608-1176. *Phone:* 888-442-8372. *Toll-free phone:* 888-442-8372. *Fax:* 609-984-8447. *E-mail:* info@tesc.edu.

■ *See page 2504 for a narrative description.*

WESTMINSTER CHOIR COLLEGE OF RIDER UNIVERSITY

Princeton, New Jersey

- **Independent** comprehensive, founded 1926
- **Calendar** semesters
- **Degrees** bachelor's and master's
- **Small-town** 23-acre campus with easy access to New York City and Philadelphia
- **Coed,** 340 undergraduate students, 94% full-time, 62% women, 38% men
- **Moderately difficult** entrance level, 83% of applicants were admitted

Undergraduates 319 full-time, 21 part-time. Students come from 40 states and territories, 64% are from out of state, 9% African American, 3% Asian American or Pacific Islander, 5% Hispanic American, 4% international, 4% transferred in, 58% live on campus. *Retention:* 84% of 2002 full-time freshmen returned.

Freshmen *Admission:* 178 applied, 148 admitted, 97 enrolled. *Average high school GPA:* 3.41. *Test scores:* SAT verbal scores over 500: 75%; SAT math scores over 500: 58%; SAT verbal scores over 600: 33%; SAT math scores over 600: 35%; SAT verbal scores over 700: 6%; SAT math scores over 700: 8%.

Faculty *Total:* 85, 41% full-time, 48% with terminal degrees. *Student/faculty ratio:* 7:1.

Majors Conducting; liberal arts and sciences/liberal studies; music; music pedagogy; music related; music teacher education; music theory and composition; piano and organ; religious/sacred music; voice and opera.

Academic Programs *Special study options:* academic remediation for entering students, adult/continuing education programs, advanced placement credit, double majors, English as a second language, honors programs, independent study, internships, off-campus study, part-time degree program, services for LD students, summer session for credit.

Library Talbott Library-Learning Center with 55,000 titles, 160 serial subscriptions.

Computers on Campus 60 computers available on campus for general student use. At least one staffed computer lab available.

Student Life *Housing:* on-campus residence required through sophomore year. *Options:* coed. Campus housing is university owned. Freshman campus housing is guaranteed. *Activities and organizations:* drama/theater group, student-run newspaper, radio station, choral group, Westminster Choir, Westminster Singers, Westminster Handbell Choir, Black and Hispanic Alliance, Student Activities Committee. *Campus security:* 24-hour emergency response devices and patrols, late-night transport/escort service. *Student services:* health clinic, personal/psychological counseling.

Standardized Tests *Required:* SAT I or ACT (for admission).

Costs (2003–04) *Comprehensive fee:* $29,200 includes full-time tuition ($20,590), mandatory fees ($240), and room and board ($8370). Part-time tuition: $780 per credit. *College room only:* $3950. *Payment plan:* installment. *Waivers:* employees or children of employees.

Financial Aid Of all full-time matriculated undergraduates who enrolled in 2002, 246 applied for aid, 214 were judged to have need, 12 had their need fully met. 192 Federal Work-Study jobs (averaging $1860). In 2002, 37 non-need-based awards were made. *Average percent of need met:* 74%. *Average financial aid package:* $17,102. *Average need-based loan:* $4537. *Average need-based gift aid:* $6928. *Average non-need-based aid:* $5826. *Average indebtedness upon graduation:* $27,113.

Applying *Options:* deferred entrance. *Application fee:* $40. *Required:* essay or personal statement, high school transcript, 2 letters of recommendation, audition, music examination. *Recommended:* minimum 2.5 GPA, interview. *Application deadline:* rolling (freshmen), rolling (transfers). *Notification:* continuous (freshmen), continuous (transfers).

Admissions Contact Elizabeth S. Rush, Assistant Director of Admissions, Westminster Choir College of Rider University, 101 Walnut Lane, Princeton, NJ 08540-3899. *Phone:* 609-921-7144 Ext. 8221. *Toll-free phone:* 800-96-CHOIR. *Fax:* 609-921-2538. *E-mail:* wccadmission@rider.edu.

■ *See page 2820 for a narrative description.*

WILLIAM PATERSON UNIVERSITY OF NEW JERSEY

Wayne, New Jersey

- **State-supported** comprehensive, founded 1855, part of New Jersey State College System
- **Calendar** semesters
- **Degrees** bachelor's, master's, post-master's, and postbachelor's certificates
- **Suburban** 300-acre campus with easy access to New York City
- **Coed,** 9,302 undergraduate students, 79% full-time, 59% women, 41% men
- **Moderately difficult** entrance level, 61% of applicants were admitted

Committed to student success, William Paterson University seeks ambitious students who are up to its challenge. Small classes and a distinguished faculty; thirty majors; preprofessional programs in dentistry, engineering, law, medicine, pharmacy, physical therapy, speech/language pathology, and veterinary medicine; and eight distinctive honors programs provide a rewarding educational experience that far exceeds its cost.

Undergraduates 7,361 full-time, 1,941 part-time. Students come from 39 states and territories, 55 other countries, 2% are from out of state, 12% African American, 4% Asian American or Pacific Islander, 15% Hispanic American, 0.2% Native American, 1% international, 10% transferred in, 26% live on campus. *Retention:* 81% of 2002 full-time freshmen returned.

Freshmen *Admission:* 5,704 applied, 3,469 admitted, 1,365 enrolled. *Test scores:* SAT verbal scores over 500: 54%; SAT math scores over 500: 57%; SAT verbal scores over 600: 11%; SAT math scores over 600: 11%; SAT verbal scores over 700: 1%; SAT math scores over 700: 1%.

Faculty *Total:* 972, 36% full-time. *Student/faculty ratio:* 16:1.

Majors Accounting; African-American/Black studies; African studies; anthropology; applied art; applied mathematics; art; art history, criticism and conservation; art teacher education; behavioral sciences; biology/biological sciences; business administration and management; business/managerial economics; commercial and advertising art; computer science; dramatic/theatre arts; ecology; education; elementary education; English; environmental studies; fine/studio arts; geography; health science; health teacher education; history; humanities; international business/trade/commerce; jazz/jazz studies; kinesiology and exercise science; literature; mass communication/media; mathematics; music; music management and merchandising; music teacher education; nursing (registered nurse training); parks, recreation and leisure; philosophy; physical education teaching and coaching; physical sciences; political science and government; pre-dentistry studies; pre-law studies; pre-medical studies; psychology; public health; secondary education; social sciences; sociology; Spanish; special education; voice and opera.

Academic Programs *Special study options:* academic remediation for entering students, accelerated degree program, adult/continuing education programs, advanced placement credit, distance learning, double majors, English as a second language, honors programs, independent study, internships, off-campus study, part-time degree program, services for LD students, study abroad, summer session for credit.

Library David and Lorraine Cheng Library with 305,155 titles, 4,112 serial subscriptions, 19,661 audiovisual materials, an OPAC, a Web page.

Computers on Campus 700 computers available on campus for general student use. A campuswide network can be accessed from student residence rooms and from off campus. Internet access, online (class) registration, at least one staffed computer lab available.

Student Life *Housing options:* coed, disabled students. *Activities and organizations:* drama/theater group, student-run newspaper, radio and television station, choral group, Greek Senate, Caribbean Student Association, Organization of Latin American Students (OLAS), Sisters of Awareness, Student Activities Committee, national fraternities, national sororities. *Campus security:* 24-hour emergency response devices and patrols, controlled dormitory access. *Student services:* health clinic, personal/psychological counseling, women's center, legal services.

Athletics Member NCAA. All Division III. *Intercollegiate sports:* baseball M, basketball M/W, bowling M(c)/W(c), cheerleading M/W, cross-country running M/W, fencing M/W, field hockey W, football M, golf M, ice hockey M(c), skiing (downhill) M(c)/W(c), soccer M/W, softball W, swimming M/W, track and field M/W, volleyball W. *Intramural sports:* basketball M, equestrian sports M/W, football M, golf M, lacrosse M, racquetball M/W, softball M/W, tennis M(c)/W(c), volleyball M/W, wrestling M.

Standardized Tests *Required:* SAT I or ACT (for admission).

Costs (2003–04) *Tuition:* state resident $7120 full-time, $228 per credit part-time; nonresident $11,510 full-time, $372 per credit part-time. *Room and board:* $7630; room only: $4990. Room and board charges vary according to board plan and housing facility. *Payment plan:* installment. *Waivers:* senior citizens and employees or children of employees.

Financial Aid Of all full-time matriculated undergraduates who enrolled in 2003, 4,841 applied for aid, 3,747 were judged to have need, 997 had their need fully met. 265 Federal Work-Study jobs (averaging $1140). 184 state and other part-time jobs (averaging $1400). In 2003, 203 non-need-based awards were made. *Average percent of need met:* 84%. *Average financial aid package:* $8608. *Average need-based loan:* $3607. *Average need-based gift aid:* $5346. *Average non-need-based aid:* $3750. *Average indebtedness upon graduation:* $9981.

Applying *Options:* common application, electronic application, early action, deferred entrance. *Application fee:* $50. *Required:* essay or personal statement, high school transcript. *Required for some:* letters of recommendation, interview. *Recommended:* minimum 2.5 GPA. *Application deadlines:* 5/1 (freshmen), 5/1 (transfers). *Notification:* continuous (freshmen), continuous (transfers).

Admissions Contact Mr. Jonathan McCoy, Director of Admissions, William Paterson University of New Jersey, 300 Pompton Road, Wayne, NJ 07470. *Phone:* 973-720-2906. *Toll-free phone:* 877-WPU-EXCEL. *Fax:* 973-720-2910. *E-mail:* admissions@wpunj.edu.

■ *See page 2858 for a narrative description.*

NEW MEXICO

COLLEGE OF SANTA FE

Santa Fe, New Mexico

- **Independent** comprehensive, founded 1947
- **Calendar** semesters
- **Degrees** associate, bachelor's, and master's
- **Suburban** 100-acre campus with easy access to Albuquerque
- **Coed,** 1,389 undergraduate students, 49% full-time, 60% women, 40% men
- **Moderately difficult** entrance level, 81% of applicants were admitted

Undergraduates 683 full-time, 706 part-time. Students come from 45 states and territories, 5 other countries, 82% are from out of state, 3% African American, 2% Asian American or Pacific Islander, 25% Hispanic American, 3% Native American, 0.4% international, 6% transferred in, 56% live on campus. *Retention:* 68% of 2002 full-time freshmen returned.

Freshmen *Admission:* 503 applied, 407 admitted, 163 enrolled. *Average high school GPA:* 3.18. *Test scores:* SAT verbal scores over 500: 83%; SAT math scores over 500: 66%; ACT scores over 18: 89%; SAT verbal scores over 600: 45%; SAT math scores over 600: 17%; ACT scores over 24: 36%; SAT verbal scores over 700: 10%; SAT math scores over 700: 3%; ACT scores over 30: 6%.

Faculty *Total:* 251, 28% full-time. *Student/faculty ratio:* 9:1.

Majors Accounting; acting; art history, criticism and conservation; arts management; art therapy; business administration and management; business teacher education; computer science; counseling psychology; creative writing; criminal justice/law enforcement administration; dramatic/theatre arts; dramatic/theatre arts and stagecraft related; early childhood education; elementary education; English; English/language arts teacher education; environmental science; film/cinema studies; fine/studio arts; humanities; industrial and organizational psychology; intermedia/multimedia; international business/trade/commerce; management information systems; multi-/interdisciplinary studies related; music related; natural resources/conservation; natural resources management and policy; painting; pastoral studies/counseling; photography; political science and government; printmaking; psychology; public administration; regional studies; religious studies; science teacher education; sculpture; secondary education; social science teacher education; technical and business writing; theatre design and technology; theatre/theatre arts management.

Academic Programs *Special study options:* academic remediation for entering students, accelerated degree program, adult/continuing education programs, advanced placement credit, double majors, independent study, internships, off-campus study, part-time degree program, services for LD students, student-designed majors, study abroad, summer session for credit. *ROTC:* Air Force (c).

Library Fogelson Library Center plus 2 others with 128,982 titles, 421 serial subscriptions, 10,082 audiovisual materials, an OPAC, a Web page.

Computers on Campus 180 computers available on campus for general student use. A campuswide network can be accessed from student residence rooms and from off campus. Internet access, at least one staffed computer lab available.

Student Life *Housing:* on-campus residence required through sophomore year. *Options:* coed, men-only, women-only. Campus housing is university owned. Freshman campus housing is guaranteed. *Activities and organizations:* drama/theater group, student-run newspaper, choral group. *Campus security:* 24-hour patrols, late-night transport/escort service. *Student services:* health clinic, personal/psychological counseling.

Athletics Member NAIA. *Intercollegiate sports:* tennis M(s)/W(s). *Intramural sports:* basketball M/W, racquetball M/W, soccer M/W, volleyball M/W.

Standardized Tests *Required:* SAT I or ACT (for admission).

Costs (2003–04) *Comprehensive fee:* $25,293 includes full-time tuition ($18,980), mandatory fees ($525), and room and board ($5788). Part-time tuition: $632 per credit hour. *Required fees:* $5 per credit hour part-time. *College room only:* $2724. Room and board charges vary according to board plan and housing facility. *Payment plan:* installment. *Waivers:* senior citizens and employees or children of employees.

Financial Aid Of all full-time matriculated undergraduates who enrolled in 2003, 516 applied for aid, 465 were judged to have need, 71 had their need fully met. In 2003, 130 non-need-based awards were made. *Average percent of need met:* 82%. *Average financial aid package:* $18,190. *Average need-based loan:* $4363. *Average need-based gift aid:* $9879. *Average non-need-based aid:* $3427. *Average indebtedness upon graduation:* $22,641.

Applying *Options:* common application, electronic application, early admission, early decision, deferred entrance. *Application fee:* $35. *Required:* essay or personal statement, high school transcript, 2 letters of recommendation, interview, portfolio or audition for visual and performing arts programs. *Recommended:* minimum 3.0 GPA. *Application deadline:* rolling (freshmen), rolling (transfers). *Early decision:* 11/15. *Notification:* continuous (freshmen), 12/15 (early decision), continuous (transfers).

Admissions Contact Mr. Dale H. Reinhart, Director of Admissions and Enrollment Management, College of Santa Fe, 1600 Saint Michael's Drive, Santa Fe, NM 87505-7634. *Phone:* 505-473-6133. *Toll-free phone:* 800-456-2673. *Fax:* 505-473-6129. *E-mail:* admissions@csf.edu.

■ *See page 1454 for a narrative description.*

COLLEGE OF THE SOUTHWEST

Hobbs, New Mexico

- **Independent** comprehensive, founded 1962
- **Calendar** semesters
- **Degrees** bachelor's and master's
- **Small-town** 162-acre campus
- **Endowment** $433,655
- **Coed,** 696 undergraduate students, 68% full-time, 66% women, 34% men
- **Moderately difficult** entrance level, 16% of applicants were admitted

Undergraduates 470 full-time, 226 part-time. Students come from 11 states and territories, 6 other countries, 21% are from out of state, 3% African American, 0.4% Asian American or Pacific Islander, 28% Hispanic American, 2% Native American, 2% international, 19% transferred in, 18% live on campus. *Retention:* 63% of 1996 full-time freshmen returned.

Freshmen *Admission:* 592 applied, 93 admitted, 64 enrolled. *Average high school GPA:* 3.23. *Test scores:* SAT verbal scores over 500: 20%; SAT math scores over 500: 36%; ACT scores over 18: 53%; ACT scores over 24: 10%.

Faculty *Total:* 108, 24% full-time, 17% with terminal degrees. *Student/faculty ratio:* 12:1.

Majors Accounting; bilingual and multilingual education; biology/biological sciences; business administration and management; business teacher education; computer science; criminal justice/safety; dramatic/theatre arts; education; elemen-

College of the Southwest (continued)

tary education; English; environmental studies; history; marketing/marketing management; mathematics; middle school education; physical education teaching and coaching; psychology; science teacher education; secondary education; social sciences; special education.

Academic Programs *Special study options:* accelerated degree program, adult/continuing education programs, advanced placement credit, distance learning, external degree program, internships, part-time degree program, summer session for credit.

Library Scarborough Memorial Library plus 1 other with 73,876 titles, 302 serial subscriptions, 1,538 audiovisual materials.

Computers on Campus 35 computers available on campus for general student use. A campuswide network can be accessed. Internet access, at least one staffed computer lab available.

Student Life *Housing:* on-campus residence required through sophomore year. *Options:* coed. Campus housing is university owned. Freshman applicants given priority for college housing. *Activities and organizations:* drama/theater group, student-run newspaper, choral group, student government, Students in Free Enterprise, Southwest Association of Future Educators, Fellowship of Christian Athletes. *Campus security:* student patrols, night security. *Student services:* personal/psychological counseling.

Athletics Member NAIA. *Intercollegiate sports:* baseball M(s), golf M(s)/W(s), soccer M(s)/W(s), volleyball W(s). *Intramural sports:* badminton M/W, basketball M/W, football M, golf M, racquetball M/W, soccer M/W, volleyball M/W.

Standardized Tests *Required:* SAT I or ACT (for admission).

Costs (2004–05) *Comprehensive fee:* $13,015 includes full-time tuition ($8000), mandatory fees ($415), and room and board ($4600). Full-time tuition and fees vary according to course load. Part-time tuition: $250 per semester hour. Part-time tuition and fees vary according to course load. *Required fees:* $150 per term part-time. *Room and board:* Room and board charges vary according to housing facility. *Payment plan:* deferred payment. *Waivers:* employees or children of employees.

Financial Aid Of all full-time matriculated undergraduates who enrolled in 2003, 640 applied for aid, 502 were judged to have need, 12 had their need fully met. 43 Federal Work-Study jobs (averaging $1395). 50 state and other part-time jobs (averaging $1236). In 2003, 45 non-need-based awards were made. *Average percent of need met:* 62%. *Average financial aid package:* $3562. *Average need-based loan:* $2056. *Average need-based gift aid:* $2156. *Average non-need-based aid:* $1651. *Average indebtedness upon graduation:* $18,411.

Applying *Options:* electronic application, early admission, deferred entrance. *Application fee:* $25. *Required:* high school transcript, medical history. *Application deadline:* rolling (freshmen), rolling (transfers). *Notification:* continuous (freshmen), continuous (transfers).

Admissions Contact Ms. Karen Workentin, Director of Admissions, College of the Southwest, 6610 Lovington Highway, Hobbs, NM 88240. *Phone:* 505-392-6563. *Toll-free phone:* 800-530-4400. *Fax:* 505-392-6006.

EASTERN NEW MEXICO UNIVERSITY
Portales, New Mexico

- **State-supported** comprehensive, founded 1934, part of Eastern New Mexico University System
- **Calendar** semesters
- **Degrees** associate, bachelor's, and master's
- **Rural** 240-acre campus
- **Endowment** $5.5 million
- **Coed,** 3,015 undergraduate students, 81% full-time, 58% women, 42% men
- **Minimally difficult** entrance level, 74% of applicants were admitted

Undergraduates 2,457 full-time, 558 part-time. Students come from 42 states and territories, 17% are from out of state, 7% African American, 0.9% Asian American or Pacific Islander, 29% Hispanic American, 3% Native American, 0.4% international, 10% transferred in, 28% live on campus. *Retention:* 60% of 2002 full-time freshmen returned.

Freshmen *Admission:* 1,810 applied, 1,342 admitted, 558 enrolled. *Average high school GPA:* 3.15. *Test scores:* SAT verbal scores over 500: 40%; SAT math scores over 500: 37%; ACT scores over 18: 64%; SAT verbal scores over 600: 11%; SAT math scores over 600: 6%; ACT scores over 24: 14%; SAT verbal scores over 700: 3%; ACT scores over 30: 1%.

Faculty *Total:* 199, 71% full-time, 62% with terminal degrees. *Student/faculty ratio:* 17:1.

Majors Accounting; agricultural business and management; agricultural teacher education; anthropology; art; audiology and speech-language pathology; biology/biological sciences; business administration and management; business teacher education; chemistry; child care and support services management; clinical laboratory science/medical technology; communication/speech communication and rhetoric; computer and information sciences; criminal justice/safety; dramatic/theatre arts; elementary education; engineering technology; English; family and consumer sciences/human sciences; finance; general studies; geology/earth science; history; human resources management; kindergarten/preschool education; liberal arts and sciences/liberal studies; management information systems; marketing/marketing management; multi-/interdisciplinary studies related; music; music teacher education; nursing (registered nurse training); physical education teaching and coaching; physics; political science and government; psychology; religious studies; sales and marketing/marketing and distribution teacher education; social sciences; sociology; Spanish; special education; statistics; wildlife and wildlands science and management.

Academic Programs *Special study options:* academic remediation for entering students, accelerated degree program, adult/continuing education programs, advanced placement credit, cooperative education, distance learning, double majors, English as a second language, external degree program, honors programs, internships, part-time degree program, services for LD students, student-designed majors, study abroad, summer session for credit.

Library Golden Library with 240,163 titles, 1,903 serial subscriptions, 24,005 audiovisual materials, an OPAC, a Web page.

Computers on Campus 437 computers available on campus for general student use. A campuswide network can be accessed from student residence rooms and from off campus. Internet access, online (class) registration, at least one staffed computer lab available.

Student Life *Housing:* on-campus residence required through sophomore year. *Options:* coed, women-only, disabled students. Campus housing is university owned. Freshman campus housing is guaranteed. *Activities and organizations:* drama/theater group, student-run newspaper, radio and television station, choral group, marching band, Student Government Association, Student Activities Board, Residence Hall Association, IFC, Panhellenic Council, national fraternities, national sororities. *Campus security:* 24-hour emergency response devices and patrols, late-night transport/escort service, controlled dormitory access. *Student services:* health clinic, personal/psychological counseling.

Athletics Member NCAA. All Division II. *Intercollegiate sports:* baseball M(s), basketball M(s)/W(s), cross-country running M(s)/W(s), football M(s), soccer W(s), softball W(s), tennis W(s), track and field M(s)/W(s), volleyball W(s). *Intramural sports:* badminton M/W, basketball M/W, cross-country running M/W, football M/W, racquetball M/W, rugby M(c), soccer M/W, softball M/W, volleyball M/W, wrestling M(c).

Standardized Tests *Required:* SAT I or ACT (for admission).

Costs (2003–04) *Tuition:* state resident $1776 full-time, $103 per credit hour part-time; nonresident $7332 full-time, $335 per credit hour part-time. *Required fees:* $696 full-time, $29 per credit hour part-time. *Room and board:* $4290; room only: $1990. Room and board charges vary according to board plan and housing facility. *Payment plan:* installment. *Waivers:* senior citizens and employees or children of employees.

Financial Aid *Average financial aid package:* $5866.

Applying *Options:* electronic application, early admission, deferred entrance. *Required:* high school transcript, minimum 2.0 GPA. *Application deadline:* rolling (freshmen), rolling (transfers).

Admissions Contact Ms. Phyllis Seefeld, Interim Director, Eastern New Mexico University, Station #7 ENMU, Portales, NM 88130. *Phone:* 505-562-2178. *Toll-free phone:* 800-367-3668. *Fax:* 505-562-2118. *E-mail:* phyllis.seefeld@enmu.edu.

ITT TECHNICAL INSTITUTE
Albuquerque, New Mexico

- **Proprietary** primarily 2-year, founded 1989, part of ITT Educational Services, Inc.
- **Calendar** quarters
- **Degrees** associate and bachelor's
- **Coed**
- **Minimally difficult** entrance level

Standardized Tests *Required:* Wonderlic aptitude test (for admission).

Costs (2003–04) *Tuition:* $347 per credit hour part-time.

Applying *Options:* deferred entrance. *Application fee:* $100. *Required:* high school transcript, interview. *Recommended:* letters of recommendation.

Admissions Contact Mr. John Crooks, Director of Recruitment, ITT Technical Institute, 5100 Masthead Street NE, Albuquerque, NM 87109. *Phone:* 505-828-1114. *Toll-free phone:* 800-636-1114. *Fax:* 505-828-1849.

Metropolitan College of Court Reporting

Albuquerque, New Mexico

- **Proprietary** 4-year, founded 1980
- **Calendar** trimesters
- **Urban** campus
- **Coed**
- 80% of applicants were admitted

Costs (2003–04) *Tuition:* $6534 full-time.
Admissions Contact 8100 Mountain Road NE, Suite 200, Albuquerque, NM 87110-4129.

National American University

Albuquerque, New Mexico

- **Proprietary** 4-year, founded 1941
- **Calendar** quarters
- **Degrees** associate, bachelor's, and master's
- **Suburban** 5-acre campus
- **Coed,** 625 undergraduate students, 100% full-time, 49% women, 51% men
- **Noncompetitive** entrance level, 100% of applicants were admitted

Undergraduates 625 full-time. Students come from 1 other state, 2 other countries, 0.1% are from out of state. *Retention:* 60% of 2002 full-time freshmen returned.
Freshmen *Admission:* 105 applied, 105 admitted.
Faculty *Total:* 56, 9% with terminal degrees. *Student/faculty ratio:* 12:1.
Majors Accounting; applied art; business administration and management; engineering; hospitality administration; hotel/motel administration; information science/studies; management information systems.
Academic Programs *Special study options:* accelerated degree program, adult/continuing education programs, cooperative education, distance learning, double majors, external degree program, independent study, internships, off-campus study, part-time degree program, summer session for credit.
Library a Web page.
Computers on Campus 70 computers available on campus for general student use. A campuswide network can be accessed from off campus. Internet access, online (class) registration, at least one staffed computer lab available.
Student Life *Housing:* college housing not available. *Campus security:* 24-hour patrols, late-night transport/escort service.
Costs (2004–05) *Tuition:* $225 per credit hour part-time.
Applying *Application fee:* $25. *Required:* high school transcript. *Application deadline:* rolling (freshmen), rolling (transfers).
Admissions Contact Ms. Kim Hauser, Executive Admissions Representative, National American University, 4775 Indian School, NE, Albuquerque, NM 87110. *Phone:* 505-265-7517 Ext. 3019. *Toll-free phone:* 800-843-8892. *Fax:* 505-265-7542.

National College of Midwifery

Taos, New Mexico

- **Independent** comprehensive, founded 1989
- **Calendar** trimesters
- **Degrees** certificates, associate, bachelor's, master's, and doctoral
- **Women only,** 57 undergraduate students, 53% full-time
- 100% of applicants were admitted

Undergraduates 30 full-time, 27 part-time. 5% Hispanic American, 2% Native American.
Freshmen *Admission:* 30 applied, 30 admitted, 30 enrolled.
Faculty *Total:* 31, 100% full-time, 87% with terminal degrees. *Student/faculty ratio:* 2:1.
Student Life *Housing:* college housing not available.
Costs (2003–04) *One-time required fee:* $3000. *Tuition:* $6000 full-time, $3000 per year part-time. *Required fees:* $150 full-time.
Admissions Contact Ms. Beth Enson, Registrar, National College of Midwifery, 209 State Road 240, Taos, NM 87571. *Phone:* 505-758-8914.

New Mexico Highlands University

Las Vegas, New Mexico

- **State-supported** comprehensive, founded 1893
- **Calendar** semesters
- **Degrees** associate, bachelor's, and master's
- **Small-town** 120-acre campus
- **Endowment** $1.4 million
- **Coed,** 2,103 undergraduate students, 66% full-time, 59% women, 41% men
- **Minimally difficult** entrance level, 100% of applicants were admitted

Undergraduates 1,386 full-time, 717 part-time. Students come from 15 states and territories, 4 other countries, 6% are from out of state, 4% African American, 0.7% Asian American or Pacific Islander, 57% Hispanic American, 8% Native American, 0.7% international, 5% transferred in. *Retention:* 57% of 2002 full-time freshmen returned.
Freshmen *Admission:* 880 applied, 880 admitted, 255 enrolled. *Average high school GPA:* 2.94. *Test scores:* ACT scores over 18: 41%; ACT scores over 24: 7%.
Faculty *Total:* 241, 48% full-time, 42% with terminal degrees. *Student/faculty ratio:* 16:1.
Majors Accounting; anthropology; art; art teacher education; bilingual and multilingual education; biology/biological sciences; business administration and management; chemistry; commercial and advertising art; computer programming; computer science; criminal justice/safety; criminology; education; elementary education; engineering; English; environmental studies; health/health care administration; health teacher education; history; industrial arts; information science/studies; journalism; kindergarten/preschool education; management information systems; marketing/marketing management; mass communication/media; mathematics; music; music teacher education; natural resources management and policy; physical education teaching and coaching; political science and government; pre-law studies; pre-medical studies; psychology; science teacher education; secondary education; social work; sociology; Spanish; special education; teacher assistant/aide; tourism and travel services management.
Academic Programs *Special study options:* academic remediation for entering students, accelerated degree program, advanced placement credit, cooperative education, distance learning, double majors, honors programs, independent study, internships, off-campus study, part-time degree program, services for LD students, summer session for credit.
Library Donnelly Library with 429,533 titles, 850 serial subscriptions, 807 audiovisual materials, an OPAC, a Web page.
Computers on Campus 500 computers available on campus for general student use. A campuswide network can be accessed from student residence rooms and from off campus. Internet access, online (class) registration, at least one staffed computer lab available.
Student Life *Housing options:* coed, women-only. Campus housing is university owned. *Activities and organizations:* drama/theater group, student-run newspaper, radio station, choral group, marching band, BESO Club, Activities Board, Campus Crusade, AISES, Cowboy Cheerleaders. *Campus security:* 24-hour emergency response devices and patrols, late-night transport/escort service, controlled dormitory access. *Student services:* health clinic, personal/psychological counseling.
Athletics Member NCAA. All Division II. *Intercollegiate sports:* baseball M(s), basketball M(s)/W(s), cross-country running M(s)/W(s), football M(s), soccer W(s), softball W(s), track and field M/W, volleyball W(s). *Intramural sports:* badminton M/W, basketball M/W, football M, golf M/W, racquetball M/W, rugby M, skiing (cross-country) M/W, skiing (downhill) M/W, softball W, swimming M/W, table tennis M/W, tennis M/W, volleyball M/W, weight lifting M/W.
Standardized Tests *Required:* ACT (for placement).
Costs (2003–04) *Tuition:* state resident $2184 full-time, $91 per hour part-time; nonresident $9096 full-time, $379 per hour part-time. *Required fees:* $45 full-time. *Room and board:* $4085; room only: $1973. *Payment plan:* installment. *Waivers:* employees or children of employees.
Financial Aid Of all full-time matriculated undergraduates who enrolled in 2002, 1,056 applied for aid, 964 were judged to have need, 115 had their need fully met. 210 Federal Work-Study jobs (averaging $2752). 152 state and other part-time jobs (averaging $2870). In 2002, 18 non-need-based awards were made. *Average percent of need met:* 29%. *Average financial aid package:* $3830. *Average need-based loan:* $3446. *Average need-based gift aid:* $3223. *Average non-need-based aid:* $949. *Average indebtedness upon graduation:* $8792.
Applying *Options:* common application, electronic application, early admission, deferred entrance. *Application fee:* $15. *Required:* high school transcript, minimum 2.0 GPA. *Required for some:* 2 letters of recommendation, interview. *Application deadline:* rolling (freshmen), rolling (transfers). *Notification:* continuous (freshmen), continuous (transfers).
Admissions Contact Ms. Betsy Yost, Interim Dean of Students, New Mexico Highlands University, Box 9000, Las Vegas, NM 87701. *Phone:* 505-454-3020. *Toll-free phone:* 800-338-6648. *Fax:* 505-454-3311. *E-mail:* admission@venus.nmnu.edu.

NEW MEXICO INSTITUTE OF MINING AND TECHNOLOGY

Socorro, New Mexico

- **State-supported** university, founded 1889
- **Calendar** semesters
- **Degrees** associate, bachelor's, master's, and doctoral
- **Small-town** 320-acre campus with easy access to Albuquerque
- **Endowment** $20.4 million
- **Coed,** 1,365 undergraduate students, 80% full-time, 32% women, 68% men
- **Moderately difficult** entrance level, 98% of applicants were admitted

Undergraduates 1,091 full-time, 274 part-time. Students come from 52 states and territories, 14 other countries, 16% are from out of state, 1% African American, 3% Asian American or Pacific Islander, 19% Hispanic American, 3% Native American, 3% international, 4% transferred in, 49% live on campus. *Retention:* 72% of 2002 full-time freshmen returned.

Freshmen *Admission:* 363 applied, 356 admitted, 285 enrolled. *Average high school GPA:* 3.6. *Test scores:* SAT verbal scores over 500: 93%; SAT math scores over 500: 98%; ACT scores over 18: 99%; SAT verbal scores over 600: 66%; SAT math scores over 600: 70%; ACT scores over 24: 69%; SAT verbal scores over 700: 12%; SAT math scores over 700: 17%; ACT scores over 30: 17%.

Faculty *Total:* 148, 82% full-time, 84% with terminal degrees. *Student/faculty ratio:* 12:1.

Majors Applied mathematics; astrophysics; atmospheric sciences and meteorology; behavioral sciences; biological and physical sciences; biology/biological sciences; business administration and management; chemical engineering; chemistry; civil engineering; clinical laboratory science/medical technology; computer programming; computer science; electrical, electronics and communications engineering; engineering; engineering mechanics; environmental biology; environmental/environmental health engineering; environmental studies; experimental psychology; geochemistry; geology/earth science; geophysics and seismology; information technology; interdisciplinary studies; liberal arts and sciences/liberal studies; materials engineering; mathematics; mechanical engineering; metallurgical engineering; mining and mineral engineering; petroleum engineering; physics; pre-dentistry studies; pre-medical studies; pre-veterinary studies; psychology; technical and business writing.

Academic Programs *Special study options:* accelerated degree program, advanced placement credit, cooperative education, distance learning, double majors, independent study, internships, part-time degree program, services for LD students, student-designed majors, summer session for credit.

Library New Mexico Tech Library plus 1 other with 318,429 titles, 833 serial subscriptions, 2,410 audiovisual materials, a Web page.

Computers on Campus 225 computers available on campus for general student use. A campuswide network can be accessed from student residence rooms and from off campus. Internet access, online (class) registration, at least one staffed computer lab available.

Student Life *Housing options:* coed, men-only, women-only. Campus housing is university owned. *Activities and organizations:* drama/theater group, student-run newspaper, radio station, choral group, Search and Rescue, Society for Creative Anachronism, Amateur Astronomers, ski club. *Campus security:* 24-hour emergency response devices and patrols, late-night transport/escort service. *Student services:* health clinic, personal/psychological counseling.

Athletics *Intercollegiate sports:* golf M(c)/W(c), rugby M(c)/W(c), soccer M(c)/W(c). *Intramural sports:* badminton M/W, basketball M/W, cheerleading M/W, cross-country running M/W, fencing M/W, racquetball M/W, riflery M/W, skiing (downhill) M/W, softball M/W, squash M/W, table tennis M/W, tennis M/W, ultimate Frisbee M(c)/W(c), volleyball M/W, weight lifting M/W.

Standardized Tests *Required:* SAT I or ACT (for admission).

Costs (2003–04) *Tuition:* state resident $2156 full-time, $90 per credit hour part-time; nonresident $8677 full-time, $362 per credit hour part-time. Part-time tuition and fees vary according to course load. *Required fees:* $924 full-time, $27 per credit hour part-time, $107 per term part-time. *Room and board:* $4200; room only: $1850. Room and board charges vary according to board plan and housing facility. *Payment plan:* deferred payment. *Waivers:* senior citizens and employees or children of employees.

Financial Aid Of all full-time matriculated undergraduates who enrolled in 2003, 932 applied for aid, 449 were judged to have need, 229 had their need fully met. In 2003, 352 non-need-based awards were made. *Average percent of need met:* 90%. *Average financial aid package:* $7641. *Average need-based loan:* $7170. *Average need-based gift aid:* $7689. *Average non-need-based aid:* $3853. *Average indebtedness upon graduation:* $9161.

Applying *Options:* electronic application, deferred entrance. *Application fee:* $15. *Required:* high school transcript, minimum 2.5 GPA. *Required for some:* 2 letters of recommendation. *Recommended:* interview. *Application deadlines:* 8/1 (freshmen), 8/1 (transfers). *Notification:* continuous (freshmen), continuous (transfers).

Admissions Contact Mr. Mike Kloeppel, Director of Admissions, New Mexico Institute of Mining and Technology, 801 Leroy Place, Socorro, NM 87801. *Phone:* 505-835-5424. *Toll-free phone:* 800-428-TECH. *Fax:* 505-835-5989. *E-mail:* admission@admin.nmt.edu.

■ *See page 2080 for a narrative description.*

NEW MEXICO STATE UNIVERSITY

Las Cruces, New Mexico

- **State-supported** university, founded 1888, part of New Mexico State University System
- **Calendar** semesters
- **Degrees** associate, bachelor's, master's, doctoral, and post-master's certificates
- **Suburban** 900-acre campus with easy access to El Paso
- **Endowment** $50.4 million
- **Coed,** 12,797 undergraduate students, 82% full-time, 55% women, 45% men
- **Moderately difficult** entrance level, 84% of applicants were admitted

Undergraduates 10,531 full-time, 2,266 part-time. Students come from 53 states and territories, 42 other countries, 17% are from out of state, 3% African American, 1% Asian American or Pacific Islander, 45% Hispanic American, 3% Native American, 0.9% international, 4% transferred in, 18% live on campus. *Retention:* 72% of 2002 full-time freshmen returned.

Freshmen *Admission:* 5,630 applied, 4,739 admitted, 2,067 enrolled. *Average high school GPA:* 3.35. *Test scores:* ACT scores over 18: 76%; ACT scores over 24: 23%; ACT scores over 30: 1%.

Faculty *Total:* 977, 71% full-time, 69% with terminal degrees. *Student/faculty ratio:* 19:1.

Majors Accounting; aerospace, aeronautical and astronautical engineering; agricultural economics; agricultural teacher education; agriculture; agronomy and crop science; animal sciences; anthropology; apparel and textiles; athletic training; biochemistry; biology/biological sciences; business administration and management; business/commerce; chemical engineering; chemistry; city/urban, community and regional planning; civil engineering; clothing/textiles; community organization and advocacy; computer and information sciences; criminal justice/safety; dance; dramatic/theatre arts; early childhood education; economics; electrical, electronics and communications engineering; elementary education; engineering technology; English; environmental health; environmental studies; family and consumer sciences/home economics teacher education; finance; fine/studio arts; foods, nutrition, and wellness; foreign languages and literatures; general studies; geography; geology/earth science; history; horticultural science; human development and family studies; industrial engineering; information science/studies; interdisciplinary studies; international business/trade/commerce; journalism; kindergarten/preschool education; marketing/marketing management; mathematics; mechanical engineering; medical microbiology and bacteriology; microbiology; music performance; music teacher education; nursing (registered nurse training); parks, recreation and leisure facilities management; philosophy; physical education teaching and coaching; physics; plant pathology/phytopathology; political science and government; psychology; public health; public health education and promotion; range science and management; secondary education; social work; sociology; soil science and agronomy; special education; special education (speech or language impaired); speech and rhetoric; survey technology; teacher assistant/aide; tourism promotion; visual and performing arts; wildlife and wildlands science and management; wildlife biology.

Academic Programs *Special study options:* academic remediation for entering students, accelerated degree program, adult/continuing education programs, advanced placement credit, cooperative education, distance learning, double majors, honors programs, independent study, internships, off-campus study, part-time degree program, services for LD students, student-designed majors, study abroad, summer session for credit. *ROTC:* Army (b), Air Force (b).

Library New Mexico State University Library plus 1 other with 2.6 million titles, 6,747 serial subscriptions, 1,066 audiovisual materials, an OPAC, a Web page.

Computers on Campus 500 computers available on campus for general student use. A campuswide network can be accessed from student residence rooms and from off campus. Internet access, online (class) registration, at least one staffed computer lab available.

Student Life *Housing options:* coed, men-only, women-only, disabled students. *Activities and organizations:* drama/theater group, student-run newspaper, radio and television station, choral group, marching band, national fraternities, national sororities. *Campus security:* 24-hour emergency response devices and patrols, late-night transport/escort service, controlled dormitory access. *Student services:* health clinic, personal/psychological counseling, women's center, legal services.

Athletics Member NCAA. All Division I except football (Division I-A). *Intercollegiate sports:* baseball M(s), basketball M(s)/W(s), cross-country running M(s)/W(s), equestrian sports M/W, golf M(s)/W(s), softball W(s), swimming W(s), tennis M(s)/W(s), track and field W(s), volleyball W(s). *Intramural sports:* archery M/W, badminton M/W, baseball M, basketball M/W, bowling M(c)/W(c), cheerleading M/W, football M/W, golf M/W, racquetball M/W, rock climbing M(c)/W(c), rugby M(c)/W(c), skiing (downhill) M(c)/W(c), soccer M(c)/W(c), softball M/W, tennis M/W, ultimate Frisbee M(c)/W(c), volleyball M(c)/W(c), water polo M/W, weight lifting M(c)/W(c), wrestling M.

Standardized Tests *Required:* SAT I or ACT (for admission).

Costs (2003–04) *Tuition:* state resident $2418 full-time, $141 per credit part-time; nonresident $10,296 full-time, $469 per credit part-time. *Required fees:* $954 full-time. *Room and board:* $4560; room only: $2440. Room and board charges vary according to board plan and gender. *Payment plans:* installment, deferred payment. *Waivers:* senior citizens and employees or children of employees.

Financial Aid Of all full-time matriculated undergraduates who enrolled in 2003, 7,432 applied for aid, 6,437 were judged to have need, 1,300 had their need fully met. In 2003, 2244 non-need-based awards were made. *Average percent of need met:* 73%. *Average financial aid package:* $8292. *Average need-based loan:* $3882. *Average need-based gift aid:* $5697. *Average non-need-based aid:* $2727.

Applying *Options:* electronic application, early admission, deferred entrance. *Application fee:* $15. *Required:* high school transcript, minimum 2.0 GPA. *Application deadlines:* 8/19 (freshmen), 8/14 (transfers). *Notification:* continuous (freshmen), continuous (transfers).

Admissions Contact Ms. Angela Mora-Riley, Director of Admissions, New Mexico State University, Box 30001, MSC, Las Cruces, NM 88003-8001. *Phone:* 505-646-3121. *Toll-free phone:* 800-662-6678. *Fax:* 505-646-6330. *E-mail:* admssions@nmsu.edu.

■ *See page 2082 for a narrative description.*

ST. JOHN'S COLLEGE
Santa Fe, New Mexico

- **Independent** comprehensive, founded 1964
- **Calendar** semesters
- **Degrees** bachelor's and master's
- **Small-town** 250-acre campus
- **Endowment** $18.0 million
- **Coed,** 434 undergraduate students, 100% full-time, 46% women, 54% men
- **Very difficult** entrance level, 81% of applicants were admitted

Undergraduates 432 full-time, 2 part-time. Students come from 57 states and territories, 8 other countries, 88% are from out of state, 0.7% African American, 3% Asian American or Pacific Islander, 6% Hispanic American, 2% Native American, 2% international, 6% transferred in, 71% live on campus. *Retention:* 69% of 2002 full-time freshmen returned.

Freshmen *Admission:* 338 applied, 275 admitted, 138 enrolled. *Test scores:* SAT verbal scores over 500: 99%; SAT math scores over 500: 94%; ACT scores over 18: 100%; SAT verbal scores over 600: 86%; SAT math scores over 600: 63%; ACT scores over 24: 87%; SAT verbal scores over 700: 31%; SAT math scores over 700: 13%; ACT scores over 30: 36%.

Faculty *Total:* 70, 97% full-time, 79% with terminal degrees. *Student/faculty ratio:* 8:1.

Majors Ancient/classical Greek; classics and languages, literatures and linguistics; English; ethics; foreign languages and literatures; French; general studies; history; history of philosophy; humanities; liberal arts and sciences and humanities related; liberal arts and sciences/liberal studies; literature; mathematics; philosophy; philosophy and religious studies related; philosophy related; physical sciences; physics; pre-medical studies; religious studies; western civilization.

Academic Programs *Special study options:* off-campus study, summer session for credit.

Library Meem Library with 65,000 titles, 140 serial subscriptions, an OPAC, a Web page.

Computers on Campus 20 computers available on campus for general student use. A campuswide network can be accessed. At least one staffed computer lab available.

Student Life *Housing:* on-campus residence required for freshman year. *Options:* coed, men-only, disabled students. Campus housing is university owned. Freshman campus housing is guaranteed. *Activities and organizations:* drama/theater group, student-run newspaper, choral group, student government, film society, Search and Rescue Team, student newspaper, theatre group. *Campus security:* 24-hour emergency response devices and patrols, student patrols, late-night transport/escort service. *Student services:* health clinic, personal/psychological counseling.

Athletics *Intercollegiate sports:* fencing M/W, soccer M/W. *Intramural sports:* badminton M/W, basketball M/W, cross-country running M/W, fencing M/W, football M/W, golf M/W, racquetball M/W, rock climbing M/W, skiing (cross-country) M/W, skiing (downhill) M/W, soccer M/W, softball M/W, squash M/W, swimming M/W, table tennis M/W, tennis M/W, track and field M/W, ultimate Frisbee M/W, volleyball M/W, water polo M/W, weight lifting M/W.

Standardized Tests *Required for some:* SAT I or ACT (for admission).

Costs (2003–04) *Comprehensive fee:* $36,360 includes full-time tuition ($28,840), mandatory fees ($200), and room and board ($7320). *College room only:* $4164. Room and board charges vary according to board plan and housing facility. *Payment plan:* installment. *Waivers:* employees or children of employees.

Financial Aid Of all full-time matriculated undergraduates who enrolled in 2002, 342 applied for aid, 329 were judged to have need, 316 had their need fully met. 193 Federal Work-Study jobs (averaging $2350). 14 state and other part-time jobs (averaging $2290). In 2002, 5 non-need-based awards were made. *Average percent of need met:* 93%. *Average financial aid package:* $19,898. *Average need-based loan:* $4248. *Average need-based gift aid:* $13,053. *Average non-need-based aid:* $2850. *Average indebtedness upon graduation:* $22,140.

Applying *Options:* common application, early admission, deferred entrance. *Required:* essay or personal statement, high school transcript, 2 letters of recommendation. *Required for some:* interview. *Recommended:* 3 letters of recommendation, interview. *Application deadline:* rolling (freshmen), rolling (transfers). *Notification:* continuous (freshmen), continuous (transfers).

Admissions Contact Mr. Larry Clendenin, Director of Admissions, St. John's College, 1160 Camino Cruz Blanca, Santa Fe, NM 87505. *Phone:* 505-984-6060. *Toll-free phone:* 800-331-5232. *Fax:* 505-984-6162. *E-mail:* admissions@sjcsf.edu.

UNIVERSITY OF NEW MEXICO
Albuquerque, New Mexico

- **State-supported** university, founded 1889
- **Calendar** semesters
- **Degrees** associate, bachelor's, master's, doctoral, first professional, and post-master's certificates
- **Urban** 875-acre campus with easy access to Albuquerque
- **Endowment** $195.7 million
- **Coed,** 17,932 undergraduate students, 79% full-time, 57% women, 43% men
- **Moderately difficult** entrance level, 75% of applicants were admitted

Undergraduates 14,130 full-time, 3,802 part-time. Students come from 51 states and territories, 90 other countries, 19% are from out of state, 3% African American, 3% Asian American or Pacific Islander, 34% Hispanic American, 7% Native American, 0.7% international, 6% transferred in, 11% live on campus. *Retention:* 73% of 2002 full-time freshmen returned.

Freshmen *Admission:* 6,752 applied, 5,095 admitted, 3,004 enrolled. *Average high school GPA:* 3.31. *Test scores:* SAT verbal scores over 500: 80%; SAT math scores over 500: 71%; ACT scores over 18: 86%; SAT verbal scores over 600: 44%; SAT math scores over 600: 26%; ACT scores over 24: 32%; SAT verbal scores over 700: 9%; SAT math scores over 700: 4%; ACT scores over 30: 3%.

Faculty *Total:* 1,372, 64% full-time, 72% with terminal degrees. *Student/faculty ratio:* 16:1.

Majors African-American/Black studies; American studies; anthropology; architecture; art; art history, criticism and conservation; artificial intelligence and robotics; art teacher education; Asian studies; astrophysics; audiology and speech-language pathology; biochemistry; biology/biological sciences; business administration and management; business teacher education; chemical engineering; chemistry; civil engineering; classics and languages, literatures and linguistics; community organization and advocacy; comparative literature; computer and information sciences; computer engineering; computer science; construction engineering technology; corrections; creative writing; dance; dental hygiene; dramatic/theatre arts; economics; education; electrical, electronics and communications engineering; elementary education; engineering; engineering science; English; environmental design/architecture; European studies; family and consumer sciences/home economics teacher education; family and consumer sciences/human sciences; film/cinema studies; foods, nutrition, and wellness; foreign languages and literatures; French; general studies; geography; geology/earth science; German; health teacher education; history; humanities; industrial engineering; information science/studies; journalism; kindergarten/preschool education; Latin American studies; liberal arts and sciences/liberal studies; linguistics; mass communication/media; mathematics; mechanical engineering; medical radiologic technology; music performance; music teacher education; nuclear engineering; nursing (registered nurse training); parks, recreation and leisure; pharmacy; philosophy; physical education teaching and coaching; physician assistant; physics; political science and government; Portuguese; psychology; religious studies; Russian; Russian studies; secondary education; sign language interpretation and

University of New Mexico (continued)
translation; sociology; Spanish; special education; speech and rhetoric; teacher assistant/aide; technology/industrial arts teacher education; women's studies.

Academic Programs *Special study options:* academic remediation for entering students, accelerated degree program, adult/continuing education programs, advanced placement credit, cooperative education, distance learning, double majors, English as a second language, honors programs, independent study, internships, off-campus study, part-time degree program, services for LD students, student-designed majors, study abroad, summer session for credit. *ROTC:* Army (b), Air Force (b). *Unusual degree programs:* 3-2 Latin American studies, business.

Library The University of New Mexico General Library plus 7 others with 2.5 million titles, 339,266 serial subscriptions, 1.9 million audiovisual materials, an OPAC, a Web page.

Computers on Campus 382 computers available on campus for general student use. A campuswide network can be accessed from student residence rooms and from off campus. Internet access, online (class) registration, at least one staffed computer lab available.

Student Life *Housing options:* coed, women-only, disabled students. *Activities and organizations:* drama/theater group, student-run newspaper, radio and television station, choral group, marching band, Associated Students of UNM, Graduate and Professional Students Association, Golden Key National Honor Society, national fraternities, national sororities. *Campus security:* 24-hour emergency response devices and patrols, student patrols, late-night transport/escort service, controlled dormitory access. *Student services:* health clinic, personal/psychological counseling, women's center.

Athletics Member NCAA. All Division I except football (Division I-A). *Intercollegiate sports:* baseball M, basketball M(s)/W(s), cross-country running M(s)/W(s), golf M(s)/W(s), skiing (cross-country) M(s)/W(s), skiing (downhill) M(s)/W(s), soccer M(s)/W(s), softball W(s), swimming W(s), tennis M(s)/W(s), track and field M(s)/W(s), volleyball W(s). *Intramural sports:* archery M/W, badminton M/W, basketball M/W, bowling M/W, cross-country running M/W, fencing M/W, football M/W, golf M/W, ice hockey M(c), racquetball M/W, rugby M(c), skiing (downhill) M/W, soccer M/W, softball M/W, swimming W, table tennis M/W, tennis M/W, volleyball M/W, water polo M/W.

Standardized Tests *Required:* SAT I or ACT (for admission). *Required for some:* SAT II: Subject Tests (for admission), SAT II: Writing Test (for admission).

Costs (2003–04) *Tuition:* state resident $3313 full-time; nonresident $11,954 full-time. Part-time tuition and fees vary according to course load. *Room and board:* $5910; room only: $3410. Room and board charges vary according to board plan and housing facility. *Waivers:* senior citizens and employees or children of employees.

Financial Aid Of all full-time matriculated undergraduates who enrolled in 2001, 7,598 applied for aid, 6,570 were judged to have need, 1,051 had their need fully met. 1,521 Federal Work-Study jobs, 865 state and other part-time jobs. In 2001, 4124 non-need-based awards were made. *Average percent of need met:* 75%. *Average financial aid package:* $7829. *Average need-based loan:* $3261. *Average need-based gift aid:* $4796. *Average non-need-based aid:* $3173. *Average indebtedness upon graduation:* $16,595.

Applying *Options:* electronic application, early admission, deferred entrance. *Application fee:* $20. *Required:* high school transcript, minimum 2.25 GPA. *Required for some:* essay or personal statement, letters of recommendation. *Application deadline:* 6/15 (freshmen). *Notification:* continuous (freshmen), continuous (transfers).

Admissions Contact Ms. Robin Ryan, Associate Director of Admissions, University of New Mexico, Student Service Center Room 140, MSC063720, 1 University of New Mexico, Albuquerque, NM 87131-0001. *Phone:* 505-277-2446. *Toll-free phone:* 800-CALLUNM. *Fax:* 505-277-6686. *E-mail:* apply@unm.edu.

UNIVERSITY OF NEW MEXICO–GALLUP

Gallup, New Mexico

- **State-supported** primarily 2-year, founded 1968, part of New Mexico Commission on Higher Education
- **Calendar** semesters
- **Degrees** certificates, diplomas, associate, and bachelor's
- **Small-town** 80-acre campus
- **Coed**
- **Noncompetitive** entrance level

Faculty *Student/faculty ratio:* 25:1.

Student Life *Campus security:* late-night transport/escort service.

Standardized Tests *Required for some:* SAT I (for admission), ACT (for admission).

Costs (2003–04) *Tuition:* state resident $1032 full-time, $43 per credit hour part-time; nonresident $2436 full-time, $87 per credit hour part-time.

Applying *Options:* early admission. *Application fee:* $15. *Required for some:* high school transcript.

Admissions Contact Ms. Pearl A. Morris, Admissions Representative, University of New Mexico–Gallup, 200 College Road, Gallup, NM 87301-5603. *Phone:* 505-863-7576. *Fax:* 505-863-7610. *E-mail:* pmorris@gallup.unm.edu.

UNIVERSITY OF PHOENIX–NEW MEXICO CAMPUS

Albuquerque, New Mexico

- **Proprietary** comprehensive
- **Calendar** continuous
- **Degrees** certificates, associate, bachelor's, master's, doctoral, post-master's, and postbachelor's certificates (courses conducted at 121 campuses and learning centers in 25 states)
- **Urban** campus
- **Coed,** 2,767 undergraduate students, 100% full-time, 59% women, 41% men
- **Noncompetitive** entrance level

Undergraduates 2,767 full-time. 2% African American, 0.6% Asian American or Pacific Islander, 44% Hispanic American, 1% Native American, 11% international.

Freshmen *Admission:* 156 enrolled.

Faculty *Total:* 507, 0.4% full-time, 25% with terminal degrees. *Student/faculty ratio:* 11:1.

Majors Accounting; business administration and management; criminal justice/law enforcement administration; health/health care administration; information technology; management information systems; management science; marketing/marketing management; nursing (registered nurse training); nursing science; public administration and social service professions related.

Academic Programs *Special study options:* accelerated degree program, adult/continuing education programs, advanced placement credit, distance learning, external degree program, independent study.

Library University Library with 27.1 million titles, 11,648 serial subscriptions, an OPAC, a Web page.

Computers on Campus A campuswide network can be accessed from off campus. Internet access, at least one staffed computer lab available.

Student Life *Housing:* college housing not available.

Costs (2003–04) *Tuition:* $8550 full-time, $285 per credit part-time. *Waivers:* employees or children of employees.

Financial Aid *Average financial aid package:* $1375.

Applying *Options:* deferred entrance. *Application fee:* $85. *Required:* 1 letter of recommendation, 2 years of work experience, 23 years of age. *Required for some:* high school transcript. *Application deadline:* rolling (freshmen), rolling (transfers).

Admissions Contact Ms. Beth Barilla, Director of Admissions, University of Phoenix–New Mexico Campus, 4615 East Elwood Street, Mail Stop AA-K101, Phoenix, AZ 85040-1958. *Phone:* 480-317-6000. *Toll-free phone:* 800-228-7240. *Fax:* 480-594-1758. *E-mail:* beth.barilla@phoenix.edu.

WESTERN NEW MEXICO UNIVERSITY

Silver City, New Mexico

- **State-supported** comprehensive, founded 1893
- **Calendar** semesters
- **Degrees** certificates, diplomas, associate, bachelor's, and master's
- **Rural** 83-acre campus
- **Endowment** $2.2 million
- **Coed**
- **Noncompetitive** entrance level

Faculty *Student/faculty ratio:* 17:1.

Student Life *Campus security:* 24-hour emergency response devices and patrols, student patrols, late-night transport/escort service.

Standardized Tests *Required:* ACT COMPASS (for placement). *Recommended:* ACT (for admission).

Costs (2003–04) *Tuition:* state resident $2371 full-time; nonresident $8923 full-time. *Required fees:* $80 full-time. *Room and board:* $4280; room only: $1550.

Financial Aid Of all full-time matriculated undergraduates who enrolled in 2002, 1,438 applied for aid, 1,170 were judged to have need, 230 had their need fully met. 160 Federal Work-Study jobs (averaging $1617). 301 state and other part-time jobs (averaging $1166). In 2002, 109. *Average percent of need met:* 75. *Average financial aid package:* $5249. *Average need-based loan:* $2546. *Average need-based gift aid:* $3638. *Average non-need-based aid:* $666. *Average indebtedness upon graduation:* $12,000.

Applying *Options:* common application, early admission, deferred entrance. *Application fee:* $10. *Required:* high school transcript.

Admissions Contact Mr. Michael Alecksen, Director of Admissions, Western New Mexico University, College Avenue, Silver City, NM 88062-0680. *Phone:* 505-538-6106. *Toll-free phone:* 800-872-WNMU. *Fax:* 505-538-6155.

NEW YORK

ADELPHI UNIVERSITY

Garden City, New York

- **Independent** university, founded 1896
- **Calendar** semesters
- **Degrees** associate, bachelor's, master's, doctoral, post-master's, postbachelor's, and first professional certificates
- **Suburban** 75-acre campus with easy access to New York City
- **Endowment** $53.4 million
- **Coed,** 4,157 undergraduate students, 82% full-time, 71% women, 29% men
- **Moderately difficult** entrance level, 71% of applicants were admitted

Adelphi is a private, coeducational university offering degrees in the liberal arts and the professions at the bachelor's, master's, and doctoral levels. Undergraduate student–faculty ratio is 15:1. Entrance difficulty level is competitive and is highly competitive for the Honors College. Merit and talent scholarships as well as need-based aid are available.

Undergraduates 3,428 full-time, 729 part-time. Students come from 37 states and territories, 51 other countries, 9% are from out of state, 12% African American, 4% Asian American or Pacific Islander, 9% Hispanic American, 0.1% Native American, 3% international, 16% transferred in, 25% live on campus. *Retention:* 79% of 2002 full-time freshmen returned.

Freshmen *Admission:* 4,379 applied, 3,089 admitted, 792 enrolled. *Average high school GPA:* 3.30. *Test scores:* SAT verbal scores over 500: 69%; SAT math scores over 500: 78%; ACT scores over 18: 99%; SAT verbal scores over 600: 24%; SAT math scores over 600: 27%; ACT scores over 24: 44%; SAT verbal scores over 700: 3%; SAT math scores over 700: 4%; ACT scores over 30: 6%.

Faculty *Total:* 698, 33% full-time. *Student/faculty ratio:* 15:1.

Majors Accounting; anthropology; art history, criticism and conservation; art teacher education; audiology and speech-language pathology; biochemistry; biology/biological sciences; business administration and management; business, management, and marketing related; chemistry; communication/speech communication and rhetoric; computer and information sciences; criminal justice/law enforcement administration; dance; dramatic/theatre arts; ecology; economics; education; English; finance; fine arts related; French; history; humanities; international/global studies; Latin American studies; liberal arts and sciences/liberal studies; mathematics; multi-/interdisciplinary studies related; music; nursing (registered nurse training); nursing related; philosophy; physical education teaching and coaching; physics; political science and government; psychology; social sciences; social sciences related; social work; sociology; Spanish; speech and rhetoric; visual and performing arts related.

Academic Programs *Special study options:* accelerated degree program, advanced placement credit, distance learning, double majors, freshman honors college, honors programs, independent study, internships, part-time degree program, services for LD students, student-designed majors, study abroad, summer session for credit. *ROTC:* Army (c), Air Force (c). *Unusual degree programs:* 3-2 engineering with Columbia University, Polytechnic University, Rensselaer Polytechnic Institute, Stevens Institute of Technology; physical therapy with New York Medical College; dentistry with Tufts; law with NYU; optometry with SUNY College of Optometry; environmental studies with Columbia.

Library Swirbul Library plus 1 other with 631,023 titles, 1,642 serial subscriptions, 44,191 audiovisual materials, an OPAC, a Web page.

Computers on Campus 525 computers available on campus for general student use. A campuswide network can be accessed from student residence rooms and from off campus that provide access to payment, grades, drop/add classes, check application status. Internet access, online (class) registration, at least one staffed computer lab available. Computer purchase or lease plan available.

Student Life *Housing options:* coed, disabled students. Campus housing is university owned. Freshman campus housing is guaranteed. *Activities and organizations:* drama/theater group, student-run newspaper, radio station, choral group, Student Activities Board, Student Government Association, Caliber, Caribbean Cultural Awareness Club, Umoja, national fraternities, national sororities. *Campus security:* 24-hour emergency response devices and patrols, late-night transport/escort service, controlled dormitory access. *Student services:* health clinic, personal/psychological counseling.

Athletics Member NCAA. All Division II except soccer (Division I). *Intercollegiate sports:* baseball M(s), basketball M(s)/W(s), cross-country running M(s)/W(s), golf M(s), lacrosse M(s)/W(s), soccer M(s)/W(s), softball W(s), swimming M(s)/W(s), tennis M(s)/W(s), track and field M(s)/W(s), volleyball W(s). *Intramural sports:* badminton M/W, basketball M/W, football M/W, racquetball M/W, soccer M/W, softball M/W, volleyball M/W, water polo M/W.

Standardized Tests *Required:* SAT I or ACT (for admission).

Costs (2003–04) *Comprehensive fee:* $26,300 includes full-time tuition ($16,800), mandatory fees ($1000), and room and board ($8500). Full-time tuition and fees vary according to course level, location, and program. Part-time tuition: $545 per credit. Part-time tuition and fees vary according to course level, location, and program. *Required fees:* $520 per year part-time. *Room and board:* Room and board charges vary according to board plan and housing facility. *Payment plans:* tuition prepayment, installment, deferred payment. *Waivers:* employees or children of employees.

Financial Aid Of all full-time matriculated undergraduates who enrolled in 2003, 2,491 applied for aid, 2,339 were judged to have need. 1,817 Federal Work-Study jobs (averaging $2000). 693 state and other part-time jobs (averaging $1217). In 2003, 701 non-need-based awards were made. *Average financial aid package:* $13,500. *Average need-based loan:* $4239. *Average need-based gift aid:* $5043. *Average non-need-based aid:* $6971. *Average indebtedness upon graduation:* $24,528.

Applying *Options:* common application, electronic application, early admission, early action, deferred entrance. *Application fee:* $35. *Required:* essay or personal statement, high school transcript, 1 letter of recommendation. *Required for some:* 2 letters of recommendation, interview, auditions/portfolios for performing and fine arts. *Recommended:* minimum 3.0 GPA, interview. *Application deadline:* rolling (freshmen), rolling (transfers). *Notification:* continuous (freshmen), 12/31 (early action), continuous (transfers).

Admissions Contact Ms. Christine Murphy, Acting Director of Admissions, Adelphi University, Levermore Hall 114, 1 South Avenue, Garden City, NY 11530. *Phone:* 516-877-3056. *Toll-free phone:* 800-ADELPHI. *Fax:* 516-877-3039. *E-mail:* admissions@adelphi.edu.

■ *See page 1132 for a narrative description.*

ALBANY COLLEGE OF PHARMACY OF UNION UNIVERSITY

Albany, New York

- **Independent** comprehensive, founded 1881, part of Union University (Albany Law School, Albany Medical College, Union College, NY)
- **Calendar** semesters
- **Degrees** certificates, bachelor's, and first professional
- **Urban** 1-acre campus
- **Endowment** $6.6 million
- **Coed,** 701 undergraduate students, 100% full-time, 61% women, 39% men
- **Moderately difficult** entrance level, 64% of applicants were admitted

Undergraduates 699 full-time, 2 part-time. Students come from 10 states and territories, 7 other countries, 12% are from out of state, 2% African American, 8% Asian American or Pacific Islander, 1% Hispanic American, 0.4% Native American, 4% international, 10% transferred in, 30% live on campus. *Retention:* 93% of 2002 full-time freshmen returned.

Freshmen *Admission:* 741 applied, 474 admitted, 206 enrolled. *Average high school GPA:* 3.40. *Test scores:* SAT verbal scores over 500: 88%; SAT math scores over 500: 98%; SAT verbal scores over 600: 34%; SAT math scores over 600: 49%; SAT verbal scores over 700: 3%; SAT math scores over 700: 6%.

Faculty *Total:* 69, 91% full-time, 75% with terminal degrees. *Student/faculty ratio:* 14:1.

Majors Biomedical sciences; health professions related; pharmacy; pharmacy, pharmaceutical sciences, and administration related.

Academic Programs *Special study options:* academic remediation for entering students, accelerated degree program, advanced placement credit, internships, off-campus study, services for LD students, summer session for credit. *ROTC:* Army (c), Air Force (c).

Library George and Leona Lewis Library with 16,124 titles, 3,576 serial subscriptions, 319 audiovisual materials, an OPAC, a Web page.

Computers on Campus 47 computers available on campus for general student use. A campuswide network can be accessed from student residence rooms and from off campus. Internet access, at least one staffed computer lab available. Computer purchase or lease plan available.

Student Life *Housing:* on-campus residence required through sophomore year. *Options:* coed. Campus housing is university owned and is provided by a third party. Freshman campus housing is guaranteed. *Activities and organizations:* student-run newspaper, choral group, national fraternities, national sororities. *Campus security:* 24-hour emergency response devices and patrols, controlled dormitory access. *Student services:* health clinic, personal/psychological counseling.

Albany College of Pharmacy of Union University (continued)

Athletics *Intercollegiate sports:* basketball M/W, soccer M/W. *Intramural sports:* basketball M/W, cross-country running M/W, football M/W, volleyball M/W, weight lifting M/W.

Standardized Tests *Required:* SAT I or ACT (for admission).

Costs (2003–04) *Comprehensive fee:* $22,162 includes full-time tuition ($16,100), mandatory fees ($562), and room and board ($5500). *College room only:* $4100. Room and board charges vary according to board plan and housing facility. *Payment plan:* installment. *Waivers:* employees or children of employees.

Financial Aid Of all full-time matriculated undergraduates who enrolled in 2002, 567 applied for aid, 498 were judged to have need, 186 had their need fully met. 202 Federal Work-Study jobs (averaging $450). 12 state and other part-time jobs (averaging $432). In 2002, 74 non-need-based awards were made. *Average percent of need met:* 78%. *Average financial aid package:* $12,320. *Average need-based loan:* $8238. *Average need-based gift aid:* $5247. *Average non-need-based aid:* $8933. *Average indebtedness upon graduation:* $9397.

Applying *Options:* electronic application, early decision. *Application fee:* $50. *Required:* essay or personal statement, high school transcript, 2 letters of recommendation. *Required for some:* interview. *Recommended:* minimum 2.0 GPA. *Application deadline:* 2/1 (freshmen). *Early decision:* 11/1. *Notification:* continuous until 8/1 (freshmen), 12/15 (early decision).

Admissions Contact Mr. Robert Gould, Director of Admissions, Albany College of Pharmacy of Union University, 106 New Scotland Avenue, Albany, NY 12208-3425. *Phone:* 518-445-7221. *Toll-free phone:* 888-203-8010. *Fax:* 518-445-7202. *E-mail:* admissions@acp.edu.

ALFRED UNIVERSITY
Alfred, New York

- **Independent** university, founded 1836
- **Calendar** semesters
- **Degrees** bachelor's, master's, doctoral, and post-master's certificates
- **Rural** 232-acre campus with easy access to Rochester
- **Endowment** $68.7 million
- **Coed,** 2,055 undergraduate students, 95% full-time, 52% women, 48% men
- **Moderately difficult** entrance level, 69% of applicants were admitted

Through the Colleges of Business and Liberal Arts & Sciences and Design and Engineering, Alfred University offers more than 60 majors and programs of study, high-technology opportunities, top-notch facilities, and an outstanding academic experience in an up-close and personal learning environment. Research, co-op and internship opportunities, active learning, and study abroad allow students to gain extensive knowledge that makes them more marketable for graduate or professional school placement or for securing employment. All students are encouraged to value diversity, tolerance, and interdisciplinary work.

Undergraduates 1,944 full-time, 111 part-time. Students come from 38 states and territories, 32 other countries, 30% are from out of state, 5% African American, 2% Asian American or Pacific Islander, 4% Hispanic American, 0.7% Native American, 2% international, 4% transferred in, 67% live on campus. *Retention:* 82% of 2002 full-time freshmen returned.

Freshmen *Admission:* 2,169 applied, 1,493 admitted, 474 enrolled. *Test scores:* SAT verbal scores over 500: 80%; SAT math scores over 500: 78%; SAT verbal scores over 600: 32%; SAT math scores over 600: 30%; SAT verbal scores over 700: 6%; SAT math scores over 700: 5%.

Faculty *Total:* 214, 87% full-time. *Student/faculty ratio:* 12:1.

Majors Accounting; applied art; art; art teacher education; athletic training; biological and physical sciences; biology/biological sciences; biomedical technology; business administration and management; business teacher education; ceramic arts and ceramics; ceramic sciences and engineering; chemistry; clinical/medical laboratory technology; communication and journalism related; computer and information sciences; criminal justice/law enforcement administration; dramatic/theatre arts; economics; electrical, electronics and communications engineering; elementary education; English; environmental studies; fine/studio arts; French; general studies; geology/earth science; German; gerontology; health/health care administration; history; interdisciplinary studies; literature; materials science; mathematics; mathematics and computer science; mechanical engineering; modern languages; philosophy; physics; political science and government; psychology; public administration; science teacher education; secondary education; sociology; Spanish.

Academic Programs *Special study options:* academic remediation for entering students, accelerated degree program, advanced placement credit, cooperative education, double majors, honors programs, independent study, internships, off-campus study, part-time degree program, services for LD students, student-designed majors, study abroad, summer session for credit. *ROTC:* Army (c). *Unusual degree programs:* 3-2 engineering with Columbia University; forestry with Duke University; dentistry with New York University.

Library Herrick Memorial Library plus 1 other with 288,137 titles, 1,478 serial subscriptions, 166,301 audiovisual materials, an OPAC, a Web page.

Computers on Campus A campuswide network can be accessed from student residence rooms and from off campus. Internet access, at least one staffed computer lab available. Computer purchase or lease plan available.

Student Life *Housing:* on-campus residence required through sophomore year. *Options:* coed. Campus housing is university owned. Freshman campus housing is guaranteed. *Activities and organizations:* drama/theater group, student-run newspaper, radio and television station, choral group, Student Activities Board, Spectrum, WALF, Student Senate, Fiat Lux. *Campus security:* 24-hour emergency response devices, student patrols, late-night transport/escort service. *Student services:* health clinic, personal/psychological counseling, women's center.

Athletics Member NCAA. All Division III. *Intercollegiate sports:* basketball M/W, cross-country running M/W, equestrian sports M/W, football M, lacrosse M/W, skiing (cross-country) M(c)/W(c), skiing (downhill) M/W, soccer M/W, softball W, swimming M/W, tennis M/W, track and field M/W, volleyball W. *Intramural sports:* baseball M(c), basketball M/W, cheerleading W(c), football M/W, ice hockey M(c), lacrosse M/W, racquetball M/W, rugby M(c)/W(c), soccer M/W, softball M/W, squash M/W, tennis M/W, ultimate Frisbee M(c)/W(c), volleyball M/W.

Standardized Tests *Required:* SAT I or ACT (for admission). *Recommended:* SAT II: Writing Test (for admission).

Costs (2003–04) *Comprehensive fee:* $28,290 includes full-time tuition ($18,498), mandatory fees ($780), and room and board ($9012). Full-time tuition and fees vary according to program and student level. Part-time tuition and fees vary according to course load and program. New York State College of Ceramics at Alfred University tuition: instate, $10,785; out-of-state, $14,868. *College room only:* $4696. Room and board charges vary according to board plan and housing facility. *Payment plans:* tuition prepayment, installment, deferred payment. *Waivers:* employees or children of employees.

Financial Aid Of all full-time matriculated undergraduates who enrolled in 2003, 1,714 applied for aid, 1,563 were judged to have need, 1,328 had their need fully met. 1,064 Federal Work-Study jobs (averaging $1328). In 2003, 234 non-need-based awards were made. *Average percent of need met:* 92%. *Average financial aid package:* $19,352. *Average need-based loan:* $4906. *Average need-based gift aid:* $14,264. *Average non-need-based aid:* $6300. *Average indebtedness upon graduation:* $18,000.

Applying *Options:* common application, electronic application, early admission, early decision, deferred entrance. *Application fee:* $40. *Required:* high school transcript, 1 letter of recommendation. *Required for some:* essay or personal statement, interview, portfolio. *Recommended:* interview. *Application deadlines:* 2/1 (freshmen), 8/1 (transfers). *Early decision:* 12/1. *Notification:* 3/15 (freshmen), 12/15 (early decision), continuous (transfers).

Admissions Contact Mr. Scott Hooker, Director of Admissions, Alfred University, Alumni Hall, Alfred, NY 14802-1205. *Phone:* 607-871-2115. *Toll-free phone:* 800-541-9229. *Fax:* 607-871-2198. *E-mail:* admwww@alfred.edu.

■ *See page 1150 for a narrative description.*

BARD COLLEGE
Annandale-on-Hudson, New York

- **Independent** comprehensive, founded 1860
- **Calendar** 4-1-4
- **Degrees** associate, bachelor's, master's, and doctoral
- **Rural** 600-acre campus
- **Endowment** $150.8 million
- **Coed,** 1,382 undergraduate students, 96% full-time, 58% women, 42% men
- **Very difficult** entrance level, 39% of applicants were admitted

Undergraduates 1,324 full-time, 58 part-time. Students come from 50 states and territories, 43 other countries, 70% are from out of state, 3% African American, 5% Asian American or Pacific Islander, 5% Hispanic American, 0.5% Native American, 6% international, 3% transferred in, 81% live on campus. *Retention:* 86% of 2002 full-time freshmen returned.

Freshmen *Admission:* 3,367 applied, 1,310 admitted, 382 enrolled. *Average high school GPA:* 3.5. *Test scores:* SAT verbal scores over 500: 100%; SAT math scores over 500: 99%; SAT verbal scores over 600: 88%; SAT math scores over 600: 68%; SAT verbal scores over 700: 31%; SAT math scores over 700: 15%.

Faculty *Total:* 224, 55% full-time, 100% with terminal degrees. *Student/faculty ratio:* 9:1.

Majors Acting; African studies; American government and politics; American history; American studies; ancient/classical Greek; anthropology; archeology; area studies; art; art history, criticism and conservation; Asian history; Asian studies; biochemistry; biological and physical sciences; biology/biological sciences; chemistry; Chinese; cinematography and film/video production; classics and languages, literatures and linguistics; comparative literature; computer science; creative writing; cultural studies; dance; dramatic/theatre arts; drawing; ecology; economics; English; environmental biology; environmental studies; European history; European studies; European studies (Central and Eastern); film/cinema studies; fine/studio arts; French; German; Hebrew; history; history and philosophy of science and technology; history of philosophy; history related; humanities; interdisciplinary studies; international economics; international relations and affairs; Italian; jazz/jazz studies; Jewish/Judaic studies; Latin; Latin American studies; literature; mathematics; medieval and Renaissance studies; modern Greek; modern languages; molecular biology; music; music history, literature, and theory; music performance; music theory and composition; natural sciences; painting; philosophy; photography; physical sciences; physics; playwriting and screenwriting; political science and government; pre-dentistry studies; pre-law studies; pre-medical studies; pre-veterinary studies; psychology; religious studies; Romance languages; Russian; Russian studies; sculpture; social sciences; sociology; Spanish; theatre literature, history and criticism; visual and performing arts; voice and opera; western civilization.

Academic Programs *Special study options:* accelerated degree program, adult/continuing education programs, advanced placement credit, double majors, English as a second language, independent study, internships, off-campus study, part-time degree program, services for LD students, student-designed majors, study abroad. *Unusual degree programs:* 3-2 business administration with University of Rochester; engineering with Columbia University, Washington University in St. Louis, Dartmouth College; forestry with Duke University; social work with Adelphi University; public administration with Syracuse University, public health with Yale University, environmental policy with Bard College.

Library Stevenson Library plus 3 others with 275,000 titles, 1,400 serial subscriptions, 5,800 audiovisual materials, an OPAC, a Web page.

Computers on Campus 400 computers available on campus for general student use. A campuswide network can be accessed from student residence rooms and from off campus. Internet access, at least one staffed computer lab available. Computer purchase or lease plan available.

Student Life *Housing:* on-campus residence required for freshman year. *Options:* coed, women-only. Campus housing is university owned. Freshman campus housing is guaranteed. *Activities and organizations:* drama/theater group, student-run newspaper, radio station, choral group, student government, Social Action Workshop, Model United Nations, student newspaper, International Student Organization. *Campus security:* 24-hour emergency response devices and patrols, student patrols, late-night transport/escort service, controlled dormitory access. *Student services:* health clinic, personal/psychological counseling, women's center, legal services.

Athletics Member NCAA, NAIA. All NCAA Division III. *Intercollegiate sports:* basketball M/W, cross-country running M/W, rugby M, soccer M/W, squash M/W, tennis M/W, volleyball M/W. *Intramural sports:* badminton M/W, basketball M/W, fencing M(c)/W(c), football M(c)/W(c), golf M/W, rugby M/W, skiing (cross-country) M(c)/W(c), skiing (downhill) M(c)/W(c), soccer M/W, softball M/W, squash M/W, swimming M(c)/W(c), table tennis M/W, tennis M/W, ultimate Frisbee M(c)/W(c), volleyball M/W, water polo M/W.

Standardized Tests *Recommended:* SAT I or ACT (for admission), SAT II: Subject Tests (for admission).

Costs (2003–04) *One-time required fee:* $490. *Comprehensive fee:* $37,582 includes full-time tuition ($28,244), mandatory fees ($794), and room and board ($8544). Part-time tuition: $883 per credit. *Required fees:* $180 per term part-time. *College room only:* $4282. *Payment plans:* tuition prepayment, installment. *Waivers:* employees or children of employees.

Financial Aid Of all full-time matriculated undergraduates who enrolled in 2003, 854 applied for aid, 817 were judged to have need, 400 had their need fully met. 569 Federal Work-Study jobs (averaging $1612). 79 state and other part-time jobs (averaging $2779). In 2003, 24 non-need-based awards were made. *Average percent of need met:* 90%. *Average financial aid package:* $22,828. *Average need-based loan:* $4330. *Average need-based gift aid:* $18,336. *Average non-need-based aid:* $12,905. *Average indebtedness upon graduation:* $16,000. *Financial aid deadline:* 3/1.

Applying *Options:* common application, electronic application, early admission, early action, deferred entrance. *Application fee:* $50. *Required:* essay or personal statement, high school transcript, 3 letters of recommendation. *Required for some:* interview. *Recommended:* minimum 3.0 GPA, interview. *Application deadlines:* 1/15 (freshmen), 1/15 (transfers). *Notification:* 4/1 (freshmen), 1/1 (early action), 4/1 (transfers).

Admissions Contact Ms. Mary Inga Backlund, Director of Admissions, Bard College, PO Box 5000, 51 Ravine Road, Annandale-on-Hudson, NY 12504-5000. *Phone:* 845-758-7472. *Fax:* 845-758-5208. *E-mail:* admission@bard.edu.

BARNARD COLLEGE

New York, New York

- **Independent** 4-year, founded 1889, part of Columbia University
- **Calendar** semesters
- **Degree** bachelor's
- **Urban** 4-acre campus
- **Endowment** $127.7 million
- **Women only,** 2,281 undergraduate students, 98% full-time
- **Most difficult** entrance level, 31% of applicants were admitted

Undergraduates 2,232 full-time, 49 part-time. Students come from 50 states and territories, 35 other countries, 64% are from out of state, 5% African American, 19% Asian American or Pacific Islander, 6% Hispanic American, 0.7% Native American, 3% international, 4% transferred in, 89% live on campus. *Retention:* 93% of 2002 full-time freshmen returned.

Freshmen *Admission:* 554 enrolled. *Average high school GPA:* 3.86. *Test scores:* SAT verbal scores over 500: 98%; SAT math scores over 500: 99%; ACT scores over 18: 100%; SAT verbal scores over 600: 91%; SAT math scores over 600: 89%; ACT scores over 24: 95%; SAT verbal scores over 700: 47%; SAT math scores over 700: 29%; ACT scores over 30: 47%.

Faculty *Total:* 293, 63% full-time, 90% with terminal degrees. *Student/faculty ratio:* 10:1.

Majors African studies; American studies; ancient/classical Greek; ancient studies; anthropology; applied mathematics; architectural history and criticism; architecture; area studies related; art history, criticism and conservation; Asian studies; astronomy; astrophysics; biochemistry; biology/biological sciences; biophysics; biopsychology; chemical physics; chemistry; classics and languages, literatures and linguistics; comparative literature; computer and information sciences; dance; dramatic/theatre arts; economics; economics related; English; environmental biology; environmental science; environmental studies; European studies; film/cinema studies; French; French studies; geography; geology/earth science; German; German studies; history; Italian; jazz/jazz studies; Latin; Latin American studies; linguistics; mathematics; mathematics and statistics related; medieval and Renaissance studies; modern Greek; multi-/interdisciplinary studies related; music; Near and Middle Eastern studies; philosophy; physics; political science and government; psychology; religious studies; Russian; Russian studies; Slavic studies; sociology; Spanish; Spanish and Iberian studies; statistics; urban studies/affairs; visual and performing arts; women's studies.

Academic Programs *Special study options:* accelerated degree program, advanced placement credit, double majors, honors programs, independent study, internships, off-campus study, services for LD students, student-designed majors, study abroad. *Unusual degree programs:* 3-2 engineering with Columbia University, The Fu Foundation School of Engineering and Applied Science; international affairs with Columbia University, School of International and Public Affairs.

Library Wollman Library with 201,566 titles, 544 serial subscriptions, 16,403 audiovisual materials, an OPAC, a Web page.

Computers on Campus 150 computers available on campus for general student use. A campuswide network can be accessed from student residence rooms and from off campus. Internet access, online (class) registration, at least one staffed computer lab available.

Student Life *Housing options:* women-only, disabled students. Campus housing is university owned and leased by the school. Freshman campus housing is guaranteed. *Activities and organizations:* drama/theater group, student-run newspaper, radio and television station, choral group, marching band, Community Impact, Student Government Association, Student Activities Council, WBAR Radio, Asian-American Alliance. *Campus security:* 24-hour emergency response devices and patrols, late-night transport/escort service, 4 permanent security posts. *Student services:* health clinic, personal/psychological counseling, women's center.

Athletics Member NCAA. All Division I. *Intercollegiate sports:* archery W, basketball W, cheerleading M(c)/W(c), crew W, cross-country running W, equestrian sports W(c), fencing W, field hockey W, golf W, ice hockey W(c), lacrosse W, rugby W(c), sailing W(c), skiing (downhill) W(c), soccer W, softball W, squash W(c), swimming W, tennis W, track and field W, ultimate Frisbee M(c)/W(c), volleyball W. *Intramural sports:* archery W, badminton W, basketball W, bowling W, equestrian sports W, fencing W, field hockey W, ice hockey W, lacrosse W, racquetball W, rugby W, sailing W, soccer W, squash W, tennis W, ultimate Frisbee M/W, volleyball W.

Standardized Tests *Required:* SAT I and SAT II or ACT (for admission).

Costs (2003–04) *Comprehensive fee:* $36,990 includes full-time tuition ($25,294), mandatory fees ($1234), and room and board ($10,462). Part-time tuition: $843 per credit. *College room only:* $6352. Room and board charges vary

Barnard College (continued)

according to board plan and housing facility. *Payment plans:* tuition prepayment, installment, deferred payment. *Waivers:* employees or children of employees.

Financial Aid Of all full-time matriculated undergraduates who enrolled in 2003, 1,083 applied for aid, 937 were judged to have need, 937 had their need fully met. 449 Federal Work-Study jobs (averaging $1610). 586 state and other part-time jobs (averaging $1490). *Average percent of need met:* 100%. *Average financial aid package:* $26,045. *Average need-based loan:* $3951. *Average need-based gift aid:* $21,533. *Average indebtedness upon graduation:* $16,275. *Financial aid deadline:* 2/1.

Applying *Options:* common application, early admission, early decision, deferred entrance. *Application fee:* $45. *Required:* essay or personal statement, high school transcript, 3 letters of recommendation. *Recommended:* interview. *Application deadlines:* 1/1 (freshmen), 4/1 (transfers). *Early decision:* 11/15. *Notification:* 4/1 (freshmen), 12/15 (early decision), 5/15 (transfers).

Admissions Contact Ms. Jennifer Gill Fondiller, Dean of Admissions, Barnard College, 3009 Broadway, New York, NY 10027. *Phone:* 212-854-2014. *Fax:* 212-854-6220. *E-mail:* admissions@barnard.edu.

■ See page 1212 for a narrative description.

BERKELEY COLLEGE-NEW YORK CITY CAMPUS

New York, New York

- **Proprietary** primarily 2-year, founded 1936
- **Calendar** quarters
- **Degrees** certificates, associate, and bachelor's
- **Urban** campus
- **Coed,** 1,807 undergraduate students, 88% full-time, 72% women, 28% men
- **Minimally difficult** entrance level, 87% of applicants were admitted

Undergraduates 1,598 full-time, 209 part-time. Students come from 14 states and territories, 66 other countries, 9% are from out of state, 29% African American, 5% Asian American or Pacific Islander, 32% Hispanic American, 0.4% Native American, 13% international, 7% transferred in.

Freshmen *Admission:* 1,295 applied, 1,123 admitted, 411 enrolled.

Faculty *Total:* 140, 29% full-time. *Student/faculty ratio:* 24:1.

Majors Accounting; business administration and management; business/commerce; fashion merchandising; international business/trade/commerce; legal assistant/paralegal; marketing/marketing management; office management.

Academic Programs *Special study options:* academic remediation for entering students, adult/continuing education programs, advanced placement credit, cooperative education, distance learning, English as a second language, internships, off-campus study, part-time degree program, study abroad, summer session for credit.

Library 13,164 titles, 138 serial subscriptions, 949 audiovisual materials, an OPAC, a Web page.

Computers on Campus 200 computers available on campus for general student use. A campuswide network can be accessed from off campus. Internet access, at least one staffed computer lab available.

Student Life *Housing:* college housing not available. *Activities and organizations:* student-run newspaper, student government, International Club, Paralegal Club, Accounting Club. *Campus security:* 24-hour emergency response devices. *Student services:* personal/psychological counseling.

Standardized Tests *Required:* SAT I or ACT (for admission), institutional entrance exam (for admission).

Costs (2003–04) *Tuition:* $14,685 full-time, $380 per credit part-time. *Required fees:* $450 full-time, $75 per term part-time. *Payment plan:* installment. *Waivers:* employees or children of employees.

Financial Aid Of all full-time matriculated undergraduates who enrolled in 2001, 120 Federal Work-Study jobs (averaging $1500).

Applying *Options:* electronic application, deferred entrance. *Application fee:* $40. *Required:* high school transcript. *Recommended:* interview. *Application deadline:* rolling (freshmen), rolling (transfers).

Admissions Contact Mr. Stuart Siegman, Director, High School Admissions, Berkeley College-New York City Campus, 3 East 43rd Street, New York, NY 10017. *Phone:* 212-986-4343 Ext. 123. *Toll-free phone:* 800-446-5400. *Fax:* 212-818-1079. *E-mail:* info@berkeleycollege.edu.

■ See page 1246 for a narrative description.

BERKELEY COLLEGE-WESTCHESTER CAMPUS

White Plains, New York

- **Proprietary** primarily 2-year, founded 1945
- **Calendar** quarters
- **Degrees** certificates, associate, and bachelor's
- **Suburban** 10-acre campus with easy access to New York City
- **Coed,** 629 undergraduate students, 87% full-time, 70% women, 30% men
- **Minimally difficult** entrance level, 88% of applicants were admitted

Undergraduates 547 full-time, 82 part-time. Students come from 9 states and territories, 28 other countries, 14% are from out of state, 28% African American, 3% Asian American or Pacific Islander, 23% Hispanic American, 0.2% Native American, 6% international, 14% transferred in, 10% live on campus.

Freshmen *Admission:* 517 applied, 455 admitted, 198 enrolled.

Faculty *Total:* 53, 32% full-time. *Student/faculty ratio:* 24:1.

Majors Accounting; business administration and management; business/commerce; fashion merchandising; international business/trade/commerce; legal assistant/paralegal; marketing/marketing management; office management.

Academic Programs *Special study options:* academic remediation for entering students, adult/continuing education programs, advanced placement credit, cooperative education, distance learning, English as a second language, internships, off-campus study, part-time degree program, services for LD students, study abroad, summer session for credit.

Library 9,526 titles, 66 serial subscriptions, 777 audiovisual materials, an OPAC, a Web page.

Computers on Campus 175 computers available on campus for general student use. A campuswide network can be accessed from off campus. Internet access, at least one staffed computer lab available.

Student Life *Housing options:* coed. Campus housing is university owned. *Activities and organizations:* student-run newspaper, student government, Paralegal Club, Fashion Club, Phi Theta Kappa. *Campus security:* monitored entrance with front desk security guard. *Student services:* personal/psychological counseling.

Standardized Tests *Required:* SAT I or ACT (for admission), institutional entrance exam (for admission).

Costs (2003–04) *One-time required fee:* $50. *Comprehensive fee:* $24,435 includes full-time tuition ($14,685), mandatory fees ($450), and room and board ($9300). Part-time tuition: $380 per credit. *Required fees:* $75 per term part-time. *College room only:* $6000. Room and board charges vary according to board plan. *Payment plan:* installment. *Waivers:* employees or children of employees.

Financial Aid Of all full-time matriculated undergraduates who enrolled in 2001, 40 Federal Work-Study jobs (averaging $1100).

Applying *Options:* electronic application, deferred entrance. *Application fee:* $40. *Required:* high school transcript. *Recommended:* interview. *Application deadline:* rolling (freshmen), rolling (transfers).

Admissions Contact Mr. David Bertrone, Director of High School Admissions, Berkeley College-Westchester Campus, 99 Church Street, White Plains, NY 10601. *Phone:* 914-694-1122 Ext. 3110. *Toll-free phone:* 800-446-5400. *Fax:* 914-328-9469. *E-mail:* info@berkeleycollege.edu.

■ See page 1246 for a narrative description.

BERNARD M. BARUCH COLLEGE OF THE CITY UNIVERSITY OF NEW YORK

New York, New York

- **State and locally supported** comprehensive, founded 1919, part of City University of New York System
- **Calendar** semesters
- **Degrees** bachelor's, master's, doctoral, and post-master's certificates
- **Urban** campus
- **Coed,** 12,462 undergraduate students, 72% full-time, 57% women, 43% men
- **Very difficult** entrance level, 36% of applicants were admitted

Undergraduates 8,993 full-time, 3,469 part-time. Students come from 7 states and territories, 103 other countries, 4% are from out of state, 15% African American, 26% Asian American or Pacific Islander, 18% Hispanic American, 0.1% Native American, 9% international, 8% transferred in. *Retention:* 89% of 2002 full-time freshmen returned.

Freshmen *Admission:* 9,446 applied, 3,425 admitted, 1,674 enrolled. *Test scores:* SAT verbal scores over 500: 61%; SAT math scores over 500: 86%; SAT verbal scores over 600: 18%; SAT math scores over 600: 41%; SAT verbal scores over 700: 2%; SAT math scores over 700: 7%.

Faculty *Total:* 995, 48% full-time. *Student/faculty ratio:* 17:1.

Majors Accounting; actuarial science; advertising; arts management; business administration and management; business/managerial economics; creative writing; economics; education; English; finance; history; human resources management; information science/studies; interdisciplinary studies; international business/trade/commerce; journalism; literature; management information systems; marketing/marketing management; mathematics; music; natural sciences; operations research;

philosophy; political science and government; psychology; public administration; public policy analysis; Romance languages; sociology; Spanish; statistics.

Academic Programs *Special study options:* accelerated degree program, adult/continuing education programs, advanced placement credit, distance learning, double majors, English as a second language, honors programs, independent study, internships, part-time degree program, services for LD students, student-designed majors, study abroad, summer session for credit.

Library The William and Anita Newman Library plus 1 other with 297,959 titles, 4,038 serial subscriptions, 1,044 audiovisual materials, an OPAC.

Computers on Campus 1294 computers available on campus for general student use. A campuswide network can be accessed. Internet access, online (class) registration, at least one staffed computer lab available.

Student Life *Housing:* college housing not available. *Activities and organizations:* drama/theater group, student-run newspaper, radio station, choral group, Accounting Society, Computer Information Systems Society, Association of Latino Professionals in Finance and Accounting, Golden Key International Society, Helpline, national fraternities, national sororities. *Campus security:* 24-hour emergency response devices and patrols, late-night transport/escort service, controlled access by ID card. *Student services:* health clinic, personal/psychological counseling, legal services.

Athletics Member NCAA. All Division III. *Intercollegiate sports:* baseball M, basketball M/W, cheerleading W, cross-country running W, soccer M, softball W, tennis M/W, volleyball M/W. *Intramural sports:* archery M/W, badminton M/W, basketball M/W, table tennis M/W, volleyball M/W, weight lifting M/W.

Standardized Tests *Required:* SAT I or ACT (for admission).

Costs (2004–05) *Tuition:* state resident $4000 full-time, $170 per credit part-time; nonresident $8640 full-time, $360 per credit part-time. Full-time tuition and fees vary according to class time and course load. Part-time tuition and fees vary according to class time and course load. *Required fees:* $300 full-time, $38 per term part-time. *Payment plans:* installment, deferred payment. *Waivers:* senior citizens.

Financial Aid Of all full-time matriculated undergraduates who enrolled in 2003, 7,945 applied for aid, 7,640 were judged to have need, 1,830 had their need fully met. 520 Federal Work-Study jobs. In 2003, 590 non-need-based awards were made. *Average percent of need met:* 64%. *Average financial aid package:* $4930. *Average need-based loan:* $2860. *Average need-based gift aid:* $4300. *Average non-need-based aid:* $1800. *Average indebtedness upon graduation:* $10,100. *Financial aid deadline:* 4/30.

Applying *Options:* early admission, early decision, early action. *Application fee:* $40. *Required:* high school transcript, minimum 2.5 GPA, 16 academic units. *Required for some:* letters of recommendation. *Application deadlines:* 4/1 (freshmen), 5/1 (transfers). *Early decision:* 12/13. *Notification:* continuous until 7/1 (freshmen), 1/7 (early decision), 1/7 (early action), continuous until 6/1 (transfers).

Admissions Contact Mr. James F. Murphy, Director of Undergraduate Admissions and Financial Aid, Bernard M. Baruch College of the City University of New York, Box H-0720, New York, NY 10010-5585. *Phone:* 212-312-1400. *E-mail:* admissions@baruch.cuny.edu.

■ *See page 1250 for a narrative description.*

BETH HAMEDRASH SHAAREI YOSHER INSTITUTE
Brooklyn, New York

Admissions Contact Mr. Menachem Steinberg, Director of Admissions, Beth HaMedrash Shaarei Yosher Institute, 4102-10 Sixteenth Avenue, Brooklyn, NY 11204. *Phone:* 718-854-2290.

BETH HATALMUD RABBINICAL COLLEGE
Brooklyn, New York

Admissions Contact Rabbi Osina, Director of Admissions, Beth Hatalmud Rabbinical College, 2127 Eighty-second Street, Brooklyn, NY 11214. *Phone:* 718-259-2525.

BORICUA COLLEGE
New York, New York

Admissions Contact Dr. Alicea Mercedes, Director of Registration and Assessment, Boricua College, 3755 Broadway, New York, NY 10032-1560. *Phone:* 212-694-1000 Ext. 525.

BRIARCLIFFE COLLEGE
Bethpage, New York

- **Proprietary** 4-year, founded 1966, part of Career Education Corporation
- **Calendar** semesters
- **Degrees** diplomas, associate, and bachelor's
- **Suburban** 18-acre campus with easy access to New York City
- **Coed,** 2,911 undergraduate students, 77% full-time, 50% women, 50% men
- **Moderately difficult** entrance level, 80% of applicants were admitted

Undergraduates 2,240 full-time, 671 part-time. Students come from 10 states and territories, 7 other countries, 0.1% are from out of state, 5% African American, 0.7% Asian American or Pacific Islander, 5% Hispanic American, 0.3% Native American, 0.3% international, 11% transferred in. *Retention:* 65% of 2002 full-time freshmen returned.

Freshmen *Admission:* 1,167 applied, 934 admitted, 593 enrolled. *Average high school GPA:* 2.5.

Faculty *Total:* 203, 25% full-time, 13% with terminal degrees. *Student/faculty ratio:* 16:1.

Majors Accounting; administrative assistant and secretarial science; business administration and management; business administration, management and operations related; commercial and advertising art; computer programming; electrical, electronic and communications engineering technology; information science/studies; legal assistant/paralegal; telecommunications; visual and performing arts.

Academic Programs *Special study options:* academic remediation for entering students, accelerated degree program, adult/continuing education programs, advanced placement credit, cooperative education, distance learning, external degree program, independent study, internships, part-time degree program, services for LD students, summer session for credit.

Library Briarcliffe Library with 11,834 titles, 191 serial subscriptions.

Computers on Campus 350 computers available on campus for general student use. A campuswide network can be accessed. Internet access, at least one staffed computer lab available.

Student Life *Housing:* college housing not available. *Activities and organizations:* student-run newspaper, radio station, Student Government Association, telecommunication club, graphic design club, law club. *Campus security:* late-night transport/escort service. *Student services:* personal/psychological counseling.

Athletics Member NJCAA. *Intercollegiate sports:* baseball M(s), bowling M(s)/W(s), soccer W(s), softball W(s). *Intramural sports:* football M/W, tennis M/W, volleyball M/W.

Standardized Tests *Recommended:* SAT I and SAT II or ACT (for admission).

Costs (2003–04) *Tuition:* $12,720 full-time. Full-time tuition and fees vary according to course load. Part-time tuition and fees vary according to course load. *Required fees:* $1400 full-time. *Payment plans:* installment, deferred payment. *Waivers:* senior citizens and employees or children of employees.

Applying *Options:* electronic application, deferred entrance. *Application fee:* $35. *Required:* high school transcript, interview. *Application deadline:* rolling (freshmen), rolling (transfers). *Notification:* continuous (freshmen), continuous (transfers).

Admissions Contact Ms. Theresa Donohue, Vice President of Marketing and Admissions, Briarcliffe College, Bethpage, NY 11714. *Phone:* 516-918-3705. *Toll-free phone:* 888-333-1150. *Fax:* 516-470-6020. *E-mail:* info@bcl.edu.

■ *See page 1292 for a narrative description.*

BROOKLYN COLLEGE OF THE CITY UNIVERSITY OF NEW YORK
Brooklyn, New York

- **State and locally supported** comprehensive, founded 1930, part of City University of New York System
- **Calendar** semesters
- **Degrees** certificates, bachelor's, master's, post-master's, and postbachelor's certificates
- **Urban** 26-acre campus
- **Coed,** 10,960 undergraduate students, 70% full-time, 60% women, 40% men
- **Moderately difficult** entrance level, 36% of applicants were admitted

Undergraduates 7,699 full-time, 3,261 part-time. Students come from 25 states and territories, 75 other countries, 1% are from out of state, 28% African American, 10% Asian American or Pacific Islander, 11% Hispanic American, 0.1% Native American, 5% international, 13% transferred in. *Retention:* 84% of 2002 full-time freshmen returned.

Freshmen *Admission:* 7,128 applied, 2,595 admitted, 1,349 enrolled. *Average high school GPA:* 3.00. *Test scores:* SAT verbal scores over 500: 56%; SAT math

Brooklyn College of the City University of New York (continued)
scores over 500: 67%; SAT verbal scores over 600: 16%; SAT math scores over 600: 21%; SAT verbal scores over 700: 3%; SAT math scores over 700: 3%.

Faculty *Total:* 953, 53% full-time, 48% with terminal degrees. *Student/faculty ratio:* 13:1.

Majors Accounting; African studies; American studies; anthropology; art; art history, criticism and conservation; art teacher education; audiology and speech-language pathology; bilingual and multilingual education; biology/biological sciences; biology teacher education; broadcast journalism; Caribbean studies; chemistry; chemistry teacher education; Chinese; cinematography and film/video production; classics and languages, literatures and linguistics; communication/speech communication and rhetoric; comparative literature; computational mathematics; computer and information sciences; computer graphics; creative writing; developmental and child psychology; early childhood education; economics; education; elementary education; English; English/language arts teacher education; environmental studies; film/cinema studies; fine/studio arts; foods, nutrition, and wellness; French; French language teacher education; geology/earth science; German; health teacher education; Hebrew; Hispanic-American, Puerto Rican, and Mexican-American/Chicano studies; history; industrial and organizational psychology; information science/studies; Italian; Jewish/Judaic studies; journalism; Latin; linguistics; mathematics; mathematics teacher education; modern Greek; music; music performance; music teacher education; music theory and composition; philosophy; physical education teaching and coaching; physics; physics teacher education; political science and government; Portuguese; psychology; radio and television; religious studies; Russian; social studies teacher education; sociology; Spanish; Spanish language teacher education; special education (speech or language impaired); speech-language pathology; speech teacher education; theatre/theatre arts management; women's studies.

Academic Programs *Special study options:* adult/continuing education programs, advanced placement credit, distance learning, double majors, English as a second language, freshman honors college, honors programs, independent study, internships, off-campus study, part-time degree program, services for LD students, study abroad, summer session for credit.

Library Brooklyn College Library plus 1 other with 1.3 million titles, 13,500 serial subscriptions, 21,731 audiovisual materials, an OPAC, a Web page.

Computers on Campus 800 computers available on campus for general student use. A campuswide network can be accessed from off campus. Internet access, online (class) registration, at least one staffed computer lab available.

Student Life *Housing:* college housing not available. *Activities and organizations:* drama/theater group, student-run newspaper, radio and television station, choral group, Academic Club Association, Kingsman and Excelsior Newspaper, NY Public Interest Group (NYPIRG), Student Government CIAS, SGS, and GSO, Student Forensics, national fraternities, national sororities. *Campus security:* 24-hour emergency response devices and patrols, late-night transport/escort service. *Student services:* health clinic, personal/psychological counseling, women's center.

Athletics Member NCAA. All Division III. *Intercollegiate sports:* basketball M/W, cheerleading M/W, cross-country running M/W, soccer M, softball W, swimming M/W, tennis M/W, track and field M/W, volleyball M/W. *Intramural sports:* badminton M/W, basketball M/W, bowling M/W, football M/W, racquetball M/W, soccer M/W, softball M/W, swimming M/W, table tennis M/W, tennis M/W, track and field M/W, volleyball M/W.

Standardized Tests *Required:* SAT I or ACT (for admission). *Recommended:* SAT II: Subject Tests (for admission).

Costs (2004–05) *Tuition:* state resident $4000 full-time, $170 per credit part-time; nonresident $8640 full-time, $360 per credit part-time. *Required fees:* $353 full-time, $139 per term part-time. *Payment plan:* installment. *Waivers:* senior citizens.

Financial Aid Of all full-time matriculated undergraduates who enrolled in 2003, 6,300 applied for aid, 5,977 were judged to have need, 5,800 had their need fully met. 1,100 Federal Work-Study jobs (averaging $1200). In 2003, 750 non-need-based awards were made. *Average percent of need met:* 99%. *Average financial aid package:* $5400. *Average need-based loan:* $2850. *Average need-based gift aid:* $3300. *Average non-need-based aid:* $4000. *Average indebtedness upon graduation:* $13,750.

Applying *Options:* early admission, deferred entrance. *Application fee:* $50. *Required:* high school transcript, minimum 3.0 GPA. *Required for some:* essay or personal statement, letters of recommendation, interview. *Application deadline:* rolling (freshmen). *Notification:* continuous (freshmen), continuous (transfers).

Admissions Contact Ms. Marianne Booufall-Tynan, Director of Admissions, Brooklyn College of the City University of New York, 2900 Bedford Avenue, 1203 Plaza, Brooklyn, NY 11210-2889. *Phone:* 718-951-5001. *Fax:* 718-951-4506. *E-mail:* admingry@brooklyn.cuny.edu.

■ *See page 1300 for a narrative description.*

BUFFALO STATE COLLEGE, STATE UNIVERSITY OF NEW YORK

Buffalo, New York

- **State-supported** comprehensive, founded 1867
- **Calendar** semesters
- **Degrees** bachelor's, master's, and post-master's certificates
- **Urban** 115-acre campus
- **Endowment** $11.2 million
- **Coed,** 9,003 undergraduate students, 86% full-time, 60% women, 40% men
- **Moderately difficult** entrance level, 53% of applicants were admitted

Undergraduates 7,745 full-time, 1,258 part-time. Students come from 27 states and territories, 23 other countries, 1% are from out of state, 11% African American, 1% Asian American or Pacific Islander, 3% Hispanic American, 0.6% Native American, 0.5% international, 10% transferred in, 19% live on campus. *Retention:* 72% of 2002 full-time freshmen returned.

Freshmen *Admission:* 7,820 applied, 4,118 admitted, 1,365 enrolled. *Test scores:* SAT verbal scores over 500: 48%; SAT math scores over 500: 50%; SAT verbal scores over 600: 8%; SAT math scores over 600: 10%; SAT verbal scores over 700: 1%; SAT math scores over 700: 1%.

Faculty *Total:* 698, 55% full-time, 54% with terminal degrees. *Student/faculty ratio:* 18:1.

Majors Anthropology; applied art; art; art history, criticism and conservation; art teacher education; audiology and speech-language pathology; biology/biological sciences; broadcast journalism; business administration and management; business teacher education; chemistry; city/urban, community and regional planning; commercial and advertising art; communication/speech communication and rhetoric; criminal justice/law enforcement administration; design and visual communications; dietetics; dramatic/theatre arts; drawing; economics; electrical, electronic and communications engineering technology; electromechanical technology; elementary education; engineering; engineering technology; English; English/language arts teacher education; fashion/apparel design; fashion merchandising; fine/studio arts; foreign language teacher education; forensic science and technology; French; general studies; geography; geology/earth science; history; hospitality administration; hotel/motel administration; humanities; industrial arts; industrial technology; information science/studies; journalism; kindergarten/preschool education; kinesiology and exercise science; liberal arts and sciences/liberal studies; mass communication/media; mathematics; mathematics teacher education; mechanical engineering/mechanical technology; multi-/interdisciplinary studies related; music; painting; philosophy; photography; physics; political science and government; pre-dentistry studies; pre-law studies; pre-medical studies; pre-veterinary studies; printmaking; psychology; public relations/image management; radio and television; science teacher education; sculpture; secondary education; social studies teacher education; social work; sociology; Spanish; special education; special education (speech or language impaired); special products marketing; technology/industrial arts teacher education; trade and industrial teacher education; urban studies/affairs.

Academic Programs *Special study options:* academic remediation for entering students, adult/continuing education programs, advanced placement credit, cooperative education, distance learning, double majors, English as a second language, freshman honors college, honors programs, independent study, internships, off-campus study, part-time degree program, services for LD students, study abroad, summer session for credit. *ROTC:* Army (c). *Unusual degree programs:* 3-2 engineering with State University of New York at Binghamton, Clarkson University, State University of New York at Buffalo.

Library E. H. Butler Library with 489,069 titles, 2,847 serial subscriptions, 22,189 audiovisual materials, an OPAC, a Web page.

Computers on Campus 900 computers available on campus for general student use. A campuswide network can be accessed from student residence rooms and from off campus. Internet access, at least one staffed computer lab available.

Student Life *Housing:* on-campus residence required through sophomore year. *Options:* coed. Campus housing is university owned. Freshman campus housing is guaranteed. *Activities and organizations:* drama/theater group, student-run newspaper, radio station, choral group, United Student Government, African-American Student Organization, Caribbean Student Organization, The Record, WBNY radio, national fraternities, national sororities. *Campus security:* 24-hour emergency response devices and patrols, student patrols, late-night transport/escort service, controlled dormitory access. *Student services:* health clinic, personal/psychological counseling, women's center, legal services.

Athletics Member NCAA. All Division III. *Intercollegiate sports:* baseball M(c), basketball M/W, bowling M(c)/W(c), cross-country running M/W, fencing M(c), football M, ice hockey M/W, lacrosse M(c)/W, rugby M(c), skiing (cross-country) M(c)/W(c), skiing (downhill) M(c)/W(c), soccer M/W, softball W, swimming M/W, tennis W, track and field M/W, volleyball M(c)/W. *Intramural sports:* basketball M, football M, racquetball M/W, softball M/W, volleyball M/W.

Standardized Tests *Required:* SAT I or ACT (for admission).

Costs (2003–04) *Tuition:* state resident $4350 full-time, $181 per semester hour part-time; nonresident $10,300 full-time, $429 per semester hour part-time. *Required fees:* $709 full-time, $30 per credit hour part-time. *Room and board:* $5866; room only: $3734. Room and board charges vary according to board plan, housing facility, and student level. *Payment plan:* installment. *Waivers:* employees or children of employees.

Financial Aid Of all full-time matriculated undergraduates who enrolled in 2001, 6,439 applied for aid, 5,241 were judged to have need, 903 had their need fully met. In 2001, 3295 non-need-based awards were made. *Average percent of need met:* 62%. *Average financial aid package:* $3037. *Average need-based loan:* $1558. *Average need-based gift aid:* $889. *Average non-need-based aid:* $1429. *Average indebtedness upon graduation:* $13,430.

Applying *Options:* early admission, early decision, deferred entrance. *Application fee:* $30. *Required:* high school transcript, minimum 3.0 GPA. *Required for some:* essay or personal statement, letters of recommendation, interview. *Application deadline:* rolling (freshmen), rolling (transfers). *Early decision:* 11/15. *Notification:* continuous (freshmen), 12/15 (early decision), continuous (transfers).

Admissions Contact Ms. Lesa Loritts, Director of Admissions, Buffalo State College, State University of New York, 1300 Elmwood Avenue, Buffalo, NY 14222-1095. *Phone:* 716-878-5519. *Fax:* 716-878-6100. *E-mail:* admissio@buffalostate.edu.

■ *See page 1310 for a narrative description.*

CANISIUS COLLEGE

Buffalo, New York

- **Independent Roman Catholic (Jesuit)** comprehensive, founded 1870
- **Calendar** semesters
- **Degrees** bachelor's, master's, and post-master's certificates
- **Urban** 36-acre campus
- **Endowment** $40.9 million
- **Coed,** 3,535 undergraduate students, 88% full-time, 55% women, 45% men
- **Moderately difficult** entrance level, 83% of applicants were admitted

Undergraduates 3,107 full-time, 428 part-time. Students come from 23 states and territories, 38 other countries, 6% are from out of state, 7% African American, 1% Asian American or Pacific Islander, 3% Hispanic American, 0.5% Native American, 2% international, 4% transferred in, 41% live on campus. *Retention:* 83% of 2002 full-time freshmen returned.

Freshmen *Admission:* 3,437 applied, 2,868 admitted, 836 enrolled. *Average high school GPA:* 3.45. *Test scores:* SAT verbal scores over 500: 77%; SAT math scores over 500: 78%; ACT scores over 18: 92%; SAT verbal scores over 600: 27%; SAT math scores over 600: 32%; ACT scores over 24: 50%; SAT verbal scores over 700: 4%; SAT math scores over 700: 4%; ACT scores over 30: 8%.

Faculty *Total:* 468, 45% full-time, 60% with terminal degrees. *Student/faculty ratio:* 14:1.

Majors Accounting; accounting technology and bookkeeping; anthropology; art history, criticism and conservation; athletic training; biochemistry; bioinformatics; biological and physical sciences; business administration and management; business administration, management and operations related; chemistry; communication and media related; computer science; criminal justice/law enforcement administration; digital communication and media/multimedia; early childhood education; economics; engineering related; English; entrepreneurship; environmental science; European studies; finance; forest sciences and biology; French; general studies; Germanic languages; history; information technology; international business/trade/commerce; international relations and affairs; marketing related; mathematics and statistics related; philosophy; physical education teaching and coaching; physics; political science and government; psychology; religious studies; science teacher education; secondary education; sociology; Spanish; special education (early childhood); urban studies/affairs.

Academic Programs *Special study options:* academic remediation for entering students, advanced placement credit, English as a second language, external degree program, honors programs, independent study, internships, off-campus study, part-time degree program, services for LD students, student-designed majors, study abroad, summer session for credit. *ROTC:* Army (b). *Unusual degree programs:* 3-2 engineering with State University of New York at Buffalo, Cornell University, Clarkson University, Rensselaer Polytechnic Institute.

Library Andrew L. Bouwhuis Library plus 1 other with 328,278 titles, 1,637 serial subscriptions, 7,710 audiovisual materials, an OPAC, a Web page.

Computers on Campus 325 computers available on campus for general student use. A campuswide network can be accessed from student residence rooms and from off campus that provide access to online accounts. Internet access, online (class) registration, at least one staffed computer lab available. Computer purchase or lease plan available.

Student Life *Housing options:* coed. Campus housing is university owned. Freshman applicants given priority for college housing. *Activities and organizations:* drama/theater group, student-run newspaper, radio station, choral group, Campus Programming Board, Undergraduate Student Association, Afro-American Society, Residence Hall Association, Student Association, national fraternities, national sororities. *Campus security:* 24-hour emergency response devices and patrols, late-night transport/escort service, controlled dormitory access, crime prevention programs, closed-circuit television monitors. *Student services:* health clinic, personal/psychological counseling.

Athletics Member NCAA. All Division I. *Intercollegiate sports:* baseball M(s), basketball M(s)/W(s), cross-country running M(s)/W(s), golf M(s), ice hockey M(s), lacrosse M(s)/W(s), rugby M(c), soccer M(s)/W(s), softball W(s), swimming W(s), volleyball M(c)/W(s). *Intramural sports:* basketball M/W, cheerleading M(c)/W(c), crew M(c)/W(c), field hockey W, racquetball M/W, riflery M(c)/W(c), soccer M/W, softball M(c)/W(c), tennis M/W, ultimate Frisbee M/W, volleyball M/W.

Standardized Tests *Required:* SAT I or ACT (for admission).

Costs (2003–04) *Comprehensive fee:* $28,163 includes full-time tuition ($19,542), mandatory fees ($651), and room and board ($7970). Part-time tuition: $557 per credit. *Required fees:* $21 per credit part-time, $21 per term part-time. *College room only:* $3430. Room and board charges vary according to board plan, housing facility, and student level. *Payment plans:* tuition prepayment, installment, deferred payment. *Waivers:* employees or children of employees.

Financial Aid Of all full-time matriculated undergraduates who enrolled in 2003, 2,592 applied for aid, 2,337 were judged to have need, 634 had their need fully met. 550 Federal Work-Study jobs. In 2003, 578 non-need-based awards were made. *Average percent of need met:* 80%. *Average financial aid package:* $16,917. *Average need-based loan:* $4030. *Average need-based gift aid:* $11,650. *Average non-need-based aid:* $8787. *Average indebtedness upon graduation:* $18,938.

Applying *Options:* common application, electronic application, early admission, deferred entrance. *Application fee:* $25. *Required:* high school transcript. *Required for some:* interview. *Recommended:* letters of recommendation, interview. *Application deadline:* rolling (freshmen), rolling (transfers). *Notification:* continuous (freshmen), continuous (transfers).

Admissions Contact Miss Penelope H. Lips, Director of Admissions, Canisius College, 2001 Main Street, Buffalo, NY 14208-1098. *Phone:* 716-888-2200. *Toll-free phone:* 800-843-1517. *Fax:* 716-888-3230. *E-mail:* admissions@canisius.edu.

■ *See page 1340 for a narrative description.*

CAZENOVIA COLLEGE

Cazenovia, New York

- **Independent** 4-year, founded 1824
- **Calendar** semesters
- **Degrees** associate and bachelor's
- **Small-town** 40-acre campus with easy access to Syracuse
- **Endowment** $30.6 million
- **Coed,** 997 undergraduate students, 80% full-time, 75% women, 25% men
- **Minimally difficult** entrance level, 84% of applicants were admitted

A state-of-the-art, $4-million, 24,000-square-foot art and design center will open in 2004. The College also offers an outstanding academic achievement scholarship program, with awards ranging from $10,000 to full tuition.

Undergraduates 802 full-time, 195 part-time. Students come from 17 states and territories, 2 other countries, 12% are from out of state, 4% African American, 0.3% Asian American or Pacific Islander, 3% Hispanic American, 1% Native American, 0.2% international, 5% transferred in, 71% live on campus. *Retention:* 68% of 2002 full-time freshmen returned.

Freshmen *Admission:* 1,053 applied, 889 admitted, 273 enrolled. *Average high school GPA:* 3.12. *Test scores:* SAT verbal scores over 500: 64%; SAT math scores over 500: 41%; ACT scores over 18: 72%; SAT verbal scores over 600: 26%; SAT math scores over 600: 5%; ACT scores over 24: 6%.

Faculty *Total:* 109, 42% full-time, 38% with terminal degrees. *Student/faculty ratio:* 13:1.

Majors Accounting; business administration and management; community organization and advocacy; criminal justice/safety; design and visual communications; early childhood education; educational administration and supervision related; English; environmental studies; equestrian studies; fashion/apparel design; fine/studio arts; human services; interior design; liberal arts and sciences/liberal studies; literature; photography; psychology; social sciences; special education (early childhood); sport and fitness administration; visual and performing arts; youth services.

Academic Programs *Special study options:* academic remediation for entering students, adult/continuing education programs, advanced placement credit, coop-

Cazenovia College (continued)

erative education, distance learning, honors programs, independent study, internships, off-campus study, part-time degree program, services for LD students, student-designed majors, study abroad, summer session for credit. *ROTC:* Army (c), Air Force (c).

Library Witheral Library with 61,694 titles, 526 serial subscriptions, an OPAC, a Web page.

Computers on Campus 75 computers available on campus for general student use. A campuswide network can be accessed from student residence rooms and from off campus. Internet access, at least one staffed computer lab available.

Student Life *Housing:* on-campus residence required through sophomore year. *Options:* coed. Campus housing is university owned. Freshman applicants given priority for college housing. *Activities and organizations:* drama/theater group, student-run newspaper, radio station, choral group, Activities Board, Multicultural Student Group, performing arts, student radio station, yearbook. *Campus security:* 24-hour emergency response devices and patrols, late-night transport/escort service, controlled dormitory access. *Student services:* health clinic, personal/psychological counseling, women's center.

Athletics Member NCAA. *Intercollegiate sports:* cross-country running M, lacrosse M/W. *Intramural sports:* archery M.

Standardized Tests *Recommended:* SAT I and SAT II or ACT (for admission).

Costs (2003–04) *Comprehensive fee:* $23,930 includes full-time tuition ($16,730), mandatory fees ($240), and room and board ($6960). Full-time tuition and fees vary according to course load. Part-time tuition: $353 per credit. Part-time tuition and fees vary according to class time and course load. *College room only:* $3740. Room and board charges vary according to board plan. *Payment plan:* installment. *Waivers:* employees or children of employees.

Financial Aid Of all full-time matriculated undergraduates who enrolled in 2003, 737 applied for aid, 635 were judged to have need, 146 had their need fully met. 200 Federal Work-Study jobs (averaging $1000). In 2003, 75 non-need-based awards were made. *Average percent of need met:* 80%. *Average financial aid package:* $14,600. *Average need-based loan:* $3750. *Average need-based gift aid:* $10,000. *Average non-need-based aid:* $4520. *Average indebtedness upon graduation:* $16,466.

Applying *Options:* common application, early admission, deferred entrance. *Application fee:* $25. *Required:* high school transcript. *Application deadline:* rolling (freshmen), rolling (transfers). *Notification:* continuous (freshmen), continuous (transfers).

Admissions Contact Mr. Robert A. Croot, Dean for Enrollment Management, Cazenovia College, Cazenovia, NY 13035. *Phone:* 315-655-7208. *Toll-free phone:* 800-654-3210. *Fax:* 315-655-4860. *E-mail:* admission@cazenovia.edu.

■ *See page 1370 for a narrative description.*

CENTRAL YESHIVA TOMCHEI TMIMIM-LUBAVITCH

Brooklyn, New York

Admissions Contact Moses Gluckowsky, Director of Admissions, Central Yeshiva Tomchei Tmimim-Lubavitch, 841-853 Ocean Parkway, Brooklyn, NY 11230. *Phone:* 718-859-7600.

CITY COLLEGE OF THE CITY UNIVERSITY OF NEW YORK

New York, New York

- **State and locally supported** university, founded 1847, part of City University of New York System
- **Calendar** semesters
- **Degrees** bachelor's, master's, first professional, and post-master's certificates
- **Urban** 35-acre campus
- **Coed,** 8,838 undergraduate students, 67% full-time, 49% women, 51% men
- **Moderately difficult** entrance level, 35% of applicants were admitted

For more than 150 years, the City College of New York (CUNY) has provided an excellent higher education to generations of New Yorkers. City College offers degree programs in architecture, the arts, biomedical education, computer science, education, engineering, humanities, sciences, and social sciences. Conveniently located in New York City, students can take advantage of an environment that is diverse, politically and socially active, and artistically and intellectually stimulating. For more information, students can visit the Web site at http://www.ccny.cuny.edu.

Undergraduates 5,915 full-time, 2,923 part-time. Students come from 130 other countries, 4% are from out of state, 28% African American, 16% Asian American or Pacific Islander, 33% Hispanic American, 0.1% Native American, 11% international, 14% transferred in.

Freshmen *Admission:* 6,584 applied, 2,329 admitted, 1,173 enrolled. *Test scores:* SAT verbal scores over 500: 38%; SAT math scores over 500: 50%; SAT verbal scores over 600: 12%; SAT math scores over 600: 20%; SAT verbal scores over 700: 2%; SAT math scores over 700: 4%.

Faculty *Total:* 966, 51% full-time. *Student/faculty ratio:* 11:1.

Majors African-American/Black studies; anthropology; architecture; art; art history, criticism and conservation; art teacher education; Asian studies; biochemistry; biology/biological sciences; biology teacher education; biomedical/medical engineering; biomedical sciences; business administration and management; chemical engineering; chemistry; chemistry teacher education; cinematography and film/video production; civil engineering; computer science; creative writing; dramatic/theatre arts; early childhood education; economics; education; electrical, electronics and communications engineering; elementary education; English; French; geography; geology/earth science; graphic design; history; intermedia/multimedia; international/global studies; international relations and affairs; jazz/jazz studies; Jewish/Judaic studies; landscape architecture; Latin American studies; linguistics; literature; mass communication/media; mathematics; mathematics teacher education; mechanical engineering; music; music performance; music teacher education; music theory and composition; philosophy; physician assistant; physics; physics teacher education; political science and government; pre-dentistry studies; pre-law studies; pre-medical studies; pre-veterinary studies; psychology; reading teacher education; Romance languages; science teacher education; secondary education; social studies teacher education; sociology; Spanish; women's studies.

Academic Programs *Special study options:* academic remediation for entering students, accelerated degree program, adult/continuing education programs, advanced placement credit, cooperative education, English as a second language, freshman honors college, honors programs, independent study, internships, off-campus study, part-time degree program, services for LD students, student-designed majors, study abroad, summer session for credit. *ROTC:* Army (c), Air Force (c).

Library Morris Raphael Cohen Library plus 3 others with 1.4 million titles, 5,156 serial subscriptions, 21,174 audiovisual materials, an OPAC, a Web page.

Computers on Campus 3000 computers available on campus for general student use. A campuswide network can be accessed from off campus. Internet access, at least one staffed computer lab available.

Student Life *Housing:* college housing not available. *Activities and organizations:* drama/theater group, student-run newspaper, radio station, LAESA-SHPE, NSBE, BSA, Salsa-Mambo, IVCF, national fraternities. *Campus security:* 24-hour patrols. *Student services:* health clinic, personal/psychological counseling.

Athletics Member NCAA. All Division III. *Intercollegiate sports:* basketball M/W, cross-country running M/W, fencing W, lacrosse M, soccer M, softball W, tennis M/W, track and field M/W, volleyball W. *Intramural sports:* basketball M/W, fencing W, soccer M, softball W, tennis M/W, track and field M/W, volleyball M/W.

Standardized Tests *Required:* SAT I or ACT (for admission).

Costs (2003–04) *Tuition:* $2000 per semester hour part-time; state resident $4080 full-time, $170 per credit part-time; nonresident $8640 full-time, $360 per credit part-time. Full-time tuition and fees vary according to class time and program. Part-time tuition and fees vary according to class time and program. *Required fees:* $259 full-time. *Payment plan:* deferred payment. *Waivers:* senior citizens.

Financial Aid Of all full-time matriculated undergraduates who enrolled in 2003, 5,060 applied for aid, 4,301 were judged to have need, 690 had their need fully met. 1,635 Federal Work-Study jobs (averaging $1303). In 2003, 375 non-need-based awards were made. *Average percent of need met:* 70%. *Average financial aid package:* $5342. *Average need-based loan:* $2020. *Average need-based gift aid:* $4850. *Average non-need-based aid:* $2500. *Average indebtedness upon graduation:* $16,800.

Applying *Options:* early admission, deferred entrance. *Application fee:* $50. *Required:* high school transcript. *Application deadline:* 3/1 (freshmen), rolling (transfers). *Notification:* continuous until 8/1 (freshmen), continuous until 8/1 (transfers).

Admissions Contact Celia Lloyd, Interim Director of Admissions, City College of the City University of New York, Convent Avenue at 138th Street, New York, NY 10031-9198. *Phone:* 212-650-6977. *Fax:* 212-650-6417. *E-mail:* admissions@ccny.cuny.edu.

■ *See page 1404 for a narrative description.*

CLARKSON UNIVERSITY

Potsdam, New York

- **Independent** university, founded 1896
- **Calendar** semesters
- **Degrees** bachelor's, master's, and doctoral

■ **Small-town** 640-acre campus
■ **Endowment** $84.4 million
■ **Coed,** 2,723 undergraduate students, 99% full-time, 24% women, 76% men
■ **Very difficult** entrance level, 81% of applicants were admitted

Undergraduates 2,696 full-time, 27 part-time. Students come from 39 states and territories, 33 other countries, 23% are from out of state, 3% African American, 2% Asian American or Pacific Islander, 2% Hispanic American, 0.5% Native American, 3% international, 3% transferred in, 80% live on campus. *Retention:* 86% of 2002 full-time freshmen returned.

Freshmen *Admission:* 2,698 applied, 2,189 admitted, 721 enrolled. *Average high school GPA:* 3.49. *Test scores:* SAT verbal scores over 500: 84%; SAT math scores over 500: 96%; ACT scores over 18: 99%; SAT verbal scores over 600: 34%; SAT math scores over 600: 61%; ACT scores over 24: 67%; SAT verbal scores over 700: 5%; SAT math scores over 700: 13%; ACT scores over 30: 11%.

Faculty *Total:* 199, 90% full-time, 84% with terminal degrees. *Student/faculty ratio:* 17:1.

Majors Accounting; aerospace, aeronautical and astronautical engineering; applied mathematics; biochemistry; biology/biological sciences; biophysics; biotechnology; business administration and management; cell biology and histology; chemical engineering; chemistry; civil engineering; communication/speech communication and rhetoric; computer and information sciences; computer engineering; computer science; computer software engineering; construction engineering; digital communication and media/multimedia; ecology; electrical, electronics and communications engineering; engineering; environmental/environmental health engineering; environmental health; environmental studies; finance; history; humanities; human resources management; industrial and organizational psychology; information resources management; interdisciplinary studies; international business/trade/commerce; liberal arts and sciences/liberal studies; logistics and materials management; management information systems; manufacturing engineering; marketing/marketing management; materials engineering; materials science; mathematics; mechanical engineering; molecular biology; non-profit management; occupational health and industrial hygiene; operations management; physics; political science and government; pre-dentistry studies; pre-law studies; premedical studies; pre-veterinary studies; psychology; social sciences; sociology; statistics; structural engineering; technical and business writing; toxicology.

Academic Programs *Special study options:* accelerated degree program, advanced placement credit, cooperative education, double majors, English as a second language, honors programs, independent study, internships, off-campus study, part-time degree program, services for LD students, student-designed majors, study abroad, summer session for credit. *ROTC:* Army (b), Air Force (b).

Library Andrew S. Schuler Educational Resources Center plus 1 other with 272,204 titles, 1,656 serial subscriptions, 2,004 audiovisual materials, an OPAC, a Web page.

Computers on Campus 400 computers available on campus for general student use. A campuswide network can be accessed from student residence rooms and from off campus. Internet access available. Computer purchase or lease plan available.

Student Life *Housing:* on-campus residence required through senior year. *Options:* coed, men-only, women-only. Campus housing is university owned. Freshman campus housing is guaranteed. *Activities and organizations:* drama/theater group, student-run newspaper, radio and television station, choral group, Ski Club, Outing Club, Pep Band, Crew Club, Racquetball Club, national fraternities, national sororities. *Campus security:* 24-hour emergency response devices and patrols, late-night transport/escort service, controlled dormitory access. *Student services:* health clinic, personal/psychological counseling, legal services.

Athletics Member NCAA. All Division III except men's and women's ice hockey (Division I). *Intercollegiate sports:* baseball M, basketball M/W, bowling M(c)/W(c), cross-country running M/W, golf M, ice hockey M(s)/W(s), lacrosse M/W, rugby M(c)/W(c), skiing (cross-country) M/W, skiing (downhill) M/W, soccer M/W, swimming M/W, tennis M/W, volleyball M(c)/W. *Intramural sports:* archery M(c)/W(c), basketball M/W, bowling M(c)/W(c), crew M(c), football M, ice hockey M/W, lacrosse M/W, racquetball M(c)/W(c), soccer M/W, softball M/W, swimming M/W, tennis M/W, ultimate Frisbee M(c)/W(c), volleyball M/W.

Standardized Tests *Required:* SAT I or ACT (for admission). *Recommended:* SAT II: Subject Tests (for admission).

Costs (2004–05) *Comprehensive fee:* $33,208 includes full-time tuition ($24,100), mandatory fees ($40), and room and board ($9068). Full-time tuition and fees vary according to course load. Part-time tuition: $803 per credit. Part-time tuition and fees vary according to course load. *College room only:* $4728. Room and board charges vary according to housing facility. *Payment plans:* tuition prepayment, installment. *Waivers:* employees or children of employees.

Financial Aid Of all full-time matriculated undergraduates who enrolled in 2003, 2,285 applied for aid, 2,191 were judged to have need, 4 had their need fully met. 702 Federal Work-Study jobs (averaging $922). 249 state and other part-time jobs (averaging $954). In 2003, 194 non-need-based awards were made. *Average percent of need met:* 88%. *Average financial aid package:* $16,730. *Average need-based loan:* $8000. *Average need-based gift aid:* $8469. *Average non-need-based aid:* $6909. *Average indebtedness upon graduation:* $18,148.

Applying *Options:* common application, early admission, early decision, deferred entrance. *Application fee:* $30. *Required:* high school transcript, 1 letter of recommendation. *Recommended:* interview. *Application deadline:* 3/15 (freshmen). *Early decision:* 12/1 (for plan 1), 1/15 (for plan 2). *Notification:* continuous (freshmen), 12/15 (early decision plan 1), 2/1 (early decision plan 2), continuous (transfers).

Admissions Contact Mr. Brian T. Grant, Director of Admission, Clarkson University, Holcroft House, Potsdam, NY 13699-5605. *Phone:* 315-268-6479. *Toll-free phone:* 800-527-6577. *Fax:* 315-268-7647. *E-mail:* admission@clarkson.edu.

■ See page 1412 for a narrative description.

COLGATE UNIVERSITY
Hamilton, New York

■ **Independent** comprehensive, founded 1819
■ **Calendar** semesters
■ **Degrees** bachelor's and master's
■ **Rural** 515-acre campus
■ **Endowment** $423.4 million
■ **Coed,** 2,796 undergraduate students, 99% full-time, 50% women, 50% men
■ **Very difficult** entrance level, 31% of applicants were admitted

Undergraduates 2,769 full-time, 27 part-time. Students come from 50 states and territories, 35 other countries, 69% are from out of state, 0.7% transferred in, 84% live on campus. *Retention:* 96% of 2002 full-time freshmen returned.

Freshmen *Admission:* 6,789 applied, 2,126 admitted, 725 enrolled. *Average high school GPA:* 3.54. *Test scores:* SAT verbal scores over 500: 98%; SAT math scores over 500: 99%; ACT scores over 18: 100%; SAT verbal scores over 600: 82%; SAT math scores over 600: 90%; ACT scores over 24: 94%; SAT verbal scores over 700: 33%; SAT math scores over 700: 40%; ACT scores over 30: 62%.

Faculty *Total:* 290, 83% full-time, 91% with terminal degrees. *Student/faculty ratio:* 10:1.

Majors African-American/Black studies; African studies; American Indian/Native American studies; anthropology; art; art history, criticism and conservation; Asian studies; Asian studies (East); astronomy; astrophysics; biochemistry; biology/biological sciences; chemistry; Chinese; classics and languages, literatures and linguistics; computer science; dramatic/theatre arts; economics; education; English; environmental biology; environmental studies; French; geography; geology/earth science; German; history; humanities; international relations and affairs; Japanese; Latin; Latin American studies; mathematics; modern Greek; molecular biology; music; natural sciences; neuroscience; peace studies and conflict resolution; philosophy; physical sciences; physics; political science and government; psychology; religious studies; Romance languages; Russian; Russian studies; social sciences; sociology; Spanish; women's studies.

Academic Programs *Special study options:* advanced placement credit, double majors, honors programs, independent study, internships, off-campus study, services for LD students, student-designed majors, study abroad. *Unusual degree programs:* 3-2 engineering with Rensselaer Polytechnic Institute, Columbia University, Washington University in St. Louis.

Library Everett Needham Case Library plus 1 other with 1.1 million titles, 2,315 serial subscriptions, 8,805 audiovisual materials, an OPAC, a Web page.

Computers on Campus 181 computers available on campus for general student use. A campuswide network can be accessed from student residence rooms and from off campus that provide access to software applications. Internet access, online (class) registration, at least one staffed computer lab available. Computer purchase or lease plan available.

Student Life *Housing:* on-campus residence required through senior year. *Options:* coed, men-only, women-only, cooperative. Campus housing is university owned. Freshman campus housing is guaranteed. *Activities and organizations:* drama/theater group, student-run newspaper, radio and television station, choral group, Volunteer Colgate, student government, cultural/ethnic interest groups, student publications, Outdoor Education, national fraternities, national sororities. *Campus security:* 24-hour emergency response devices and patrols, student patrols, late-night transport/escort service, controlled dormitory access. *Student services:* health clinic, personal/psychological counseling, women's center, legal services.

Athletics Member NCAA. All Division I except football (Division I-AA). *Intercollegiate sports:* baseball M(c), basketball M(s)/W(s), cheerleading M(c)/W(c), crew M/W, cross-country running M/W, equestrian sports M(c)/W(c), fencing M(c)/W(c), field hockey W(s), golf M/W(c), ice hockey M(s)/W(s), lacrosse M(s)/W(s), rugby M(c)/W(c), sailing M(c)/W(c), skiing (downhill)

Colgate University (continued)
M(c)/W(c), soccer M(s)/W(s), softball W(s), squash M(c)/W(c), swimming M/W, table tennis M(c)/W(c), tennis M/W, track and field M/W, volleyball M(c)/W(s), water polo M(c)/W(c), wrestling M(c)/W(c). *Intramural sports:* basketball M/W, bowling M/W, football M/W, golf M/W, ice hockey M/W, racquetball M/W, riflery M/W, soccer M/W, softball M/W, squash M/W, tennis M/W, ultimate Frisbee M/W, volleyball M/W.

Standardized Tests *Required:* SAT I and SAT II or ACT (for admission).

Costs (2003–04) *Comprehensive fee:* $37,095 includes full-time tuition ($29,740), mandatory fees ($200), and room and board ($7155). Full-time tuition and fees vary according to course load. Part-time tuition and fees vary according to course load. *College room only:* $3455. Room and board charges vary according to board plan and housing facility. *Payment plans:* tuition prepayment, installment, deferred payment. *Waivers:* employees or children of employees.

Financial Aid Of all full-time matriculated undergraduates who enrolled in 2003, 1,281 applied for aid, 1,218 were judged to have need, 1,218 had their need fully met. 650 Federal Work-Study jobs (averaging $1397). 163 state and other part-time jobs (averaging $1484). *Average percent of need met:* 100%. *Average financial aid package:* $25,421. *Average need-based loan:* $2772. *Average need-based gift aid:* $22,956. *Average indebtedness upon graduation:* $11,104. *Financial aid deadline:* 2/1.

Applying *Options:* common application, electronic application, early decision, deferred entrance. *Application fee:* $55. *Required:* essay or personal statement, high school transcript, 3 letters of recommendation. *Application deadlines:* 1/15 (freshmen), 3/15 (transfers). *Early decision:* 11/15 (for plan 1), 1/15 (for plan 2). *Notification:* 4/1 (freshmen), 12/15 (early decision plan 1), 2/15 (early decision plan 2), 5/1 (transfers).

Admissions Contact Mr. Gary L. Ross, Dean of Admission, Colgate University, 13 Oak Drive, Hamilton, NY 13346-1383. *Phone:* 315-228-7401. *Fax:* 315-228-7544. *E-mail:* admission@mail.colgate.edu.

■ *See page 1430 for a narrative description.*

COLLEGE OF AERONAUTICS

Flushing, New York

- **Independent** 4-year, founded 1932
- **Calendar** semesters
- **Degrees** associate and bachelor's
- **Urban** 6-acre campus
- **Endowment** $31.2 million
- **Coed, primarily men**
- **Minimally difficult** entrance level

Faculty *Student/faculty ratio:* 11:1.

Student Life *Campus security:* 24-hour emergency response devices and patrols.

Standardized Tests *Required for some:* SAT I (for admission).

Costs (2003–04) *Tuition:* $9400 full-time, $340 per credit part-time. Full-time tuition and fees vary according to course load and program. *Required fees:* $250 full-time, $125 per term part-time.

Financial Aid Of all full-time matriculated undergraduates who enrolled in 2001, 769 applied for aid, 769 were judged to have need, 195 had their need fully met. 78 Federal Work-Study jobs (averaging $2628). In 2001, 157. *Average percent of need met:* 50. *Average financial aid package:* $1950. *Average need-based loan:* $2625. *Average need-based gift aid:* $1875. *Average non-need-based aid:* $1250. *Average indebtedness upon graduation:* $15,000.

Applying *Options:* deferred entrance. *Application fee:* $35. *Required:* high school transcript. *Required for some:* interview. *Recommended:* interview.

Admissions Contact Thomas Bracken, Associate Director, Admissions, College of Aeronautics, La Guardia Airport, 86-01 23rd Avenue, Flushing, NY 11369. *Phone:* 718-429-6600 Ext. 167. *Toll-free phone:* 800-776-2376 Ext. 145. *Fax:* 718-779-2231. *E-mail:* admissions@aero.edu.

COLLEGE OF MOUNT SAINT VINCENT

Riverdale, New York

- **Independent** comprehensive, founded 1911
- **Calendar** semesters
- **Degrees** certificates, associate, bachelor's, master's, and post-master's certificates
- **Suburban** 70-acre campus with easy access to New York City
- **Endowment** $3.7 million
- **Coed,** 1,281 undergraduate students, 87% full-time, 79% women, 21% men
- **Moderately difficult** entrance level, 75% of applicants were admitted

Undergraduates 1,117 full-time, 164 part-time. Students come from 20 states and territories, 11% are from out of state, 12% African American, 11% Asian American or Pacific Islander, 33% Hispanic American, 0.2% Native American, 0.5% international, 6% transferred in, 47% live on campus. *Retention:* 75% of 2002 full-time freshmen returned.

Freshmen *Admission:* 1,609 applied, 1,202 admitted, 336 enrolled. *Average high school GPA:* 3.0. *Test scores:* SAT verbal scores over 500: 44%; SAT math scores over 500: 40%; SAT verbal scores over 600: 10%; SAT math scores over 600: 5%; SAT verbal scores over 700: 1%.

Faculty *Total:* 158, 44% full-time, 51% with terminal degrees. *Student/faculty ratio:* 12:1.

Majors Biochemistry; biology/biological sciences; business administration and management; business/managerial economics; chemistry; computer science; economics; education; elementary education; English; French; health science; health teacher education; history; hospital and health care facilities administration; interdisciplinary studies; kinesiology and exercise science; liberal arts and sciences/liberal studies; mass communication/media; mathematics; middle school education; modern languages; nursing (registered nurse training); philosophy; physical education teaching and coaching; physics; pre-dentistry studies; pre-law studies; pre-medical studies; psychology; religious studies; science teacher education; secondary education; social sciences; sociology; Spanish; special education; urban studies/affairs.

Academic Programs *Special study options:* academic remediation for entering students, accelerated degree program, adult/continuing education programs, advanced placement credit, double majors, English as a second language, freshman honors college, honors programs, independent study, internships, off-campus study, part-time degree program, services for LD students, student-designed majors, study abroad, summer session for credit. *ROTC:* Army (c), Air Force (c). *Unusual degree programs:* 3-2 engineering with Manhattan College; occupational therapy with Columbia University, physical therapy with New York Medical College.

Library Elizabeth Seton Library with 169,529 titles, 616 serial subscriptions, 6,642 audiovisual materials, an OPAC, a Web page.

Computers on Campus A campuswide network can be accessed from student residence rooms and from off campus that provide access to e-mail. At least one staffed computer lab available.

Student Life *Housing options:* coed. Campus housing is university owned. Freshman campus housing is guaranteed. *Activities and organizations:* drama/theater group, student-run newspaper, radio and television station, choral group, Latino club, Players, dance club, Student Nurse Association, Black Student Union. *Campus security:* 24-hour emergency response devices and patrols, late-night transport/escort service, controlled dormitory access, emergency call boxes. *Student services:* health clinic, personal/psychological counseling.

Athletics Member NCAA. All Division III. *Intercollegiate sports:* baseball M, basketball M/W, cheerleading W, cross-country running M/W, lacrosse M/W, soccer M/W, softball W, swimming W, tennis M/W, track and field W, volleyball M/W. *Intramural sports:* basketball M/W, soccer M/W, track and field M/W, volleyball M/W.

Standardized Tests *Required:* SAT I or ACT (for admission).

Costs (2003–04) *Comprehensive fee:* $26,850 includes full-time tuition ($18,600), mandatory fees ($450), and room and board ($7800). *Payment plan:* installment. *Waivers:* senior citizens and employees or children of employees.

Financial Aid Of all full-time matriculated undergraduates who enrolled in 2002, 968 applied for aid, 850 were judged to have need. *Average percent of need met:* 74%. *Average financial aid package:* $15,000. *Average need-based loan:* $4100. *Average need-based gift aid:* $7000. *Average indebtedness upon graduation:* $14,000.

Applying *Options:* common application, electronic application, early admission, early decision, deferred entrance. *Application fee:* $35. *Required:* essay or personal statement, high school transcript, minimum 2.0 GPA, 1 letter of recommendation. *Required for some:* interview. *Recommended:* 2 letters of recommendation, interview. *Application deadline:* rolling (freshmen), rolling (transfers). *Early decision:* 11/15. *Notification:* continuous (freshmen), 12/15 (early decision), continuous (transfers).

Admissions Contact Mr. Timothy Nash, Dean of Admissions and Financial Aid, College of Mount Saint Vincent, 6301 Riverdale Avenue, Riverdale, NY 10471-1093. *Phone:* 718-405-3268. *Toll-free phone:* 800-665-CMSV. *Fax:* 718-549-7945. *E-mail:* admissns@mountsaintvincent.edu.

■ *See page 1440 for a narrative description.*

THE COLLEGE OF NEW ROCHELLE

New Rochelle, New York

- **Independent** comprehensive, founded 1904
- **Calendar** semesters

■ **Degrees** bachelor's, master's, post-master's, and postbachelor's certificates (also offers a non-traditional adult program with significant enrollment not reflected in profile)
■ **Suburban** 20-acre campus with easy access to New York City
■ **Endowment** $15.0 million
■ **Coed, primarily women,** 967 undergraduate students, 64% full-time, 94% women, 6% men
■ **Moderately difficult** entrance level, 51% of applicants were admitted

Undergraduates 622 full-time, 345 part-time. Students come from 16 states and territories, 10 other countries, 14% are from out of state, 26% African American, 4% Asian American or Pacific Islander, 10% Hispanic American, 0.1% Native American, 1% international, 6% transferred in, 37% live on campus. *Retention:* 77% of 2002 full-time freshmen returned.

Freshmen *Admission:* 1,210 applied, 619 admitted, 117 enrolled. *Average high school GPA:* 2.80. *Test scores:* SAT verbal scores over 500: 47%; SAT math scores over 500: 33%; SAT verbal scores over 600: 12%; SAT math scores over 600: 8%; SAT verbal scores over 700: 2%.

Faculty *Total:* 162, 45% full-time. *Student/faculty ratio:* 7:1.

Majors Art history, criticism and conservation; art teacher education; art therapy; biology/biological sciences; broadcast journalism; business administration and management; chemistry; classics and languages, literatures and linguistics; economics; education; elementary education; English; environmental studies; fine/studio arts; foreign languages related; French; history; international/global studies; Latin; liberal arts and sciences/liberal studies; mass communication/media; mathematics; multi-/interdisciplinary studies related; nursing (registered nurse training); philosophy; physics; political science and government; pre-law studies; pre-medical studies; psychology; religious studies; social work; sociology; Spanish; special education; women's studies.

Academic Programs *Special study options:* academic remediation for entering students, accelerated degree program, adult/continuing education programs, advanced placement credit, cooperative education, double majors, honors programs, independent study, internships, off-campus study, part-time degree program, services for LD students, student-designed majors, study abroad, summer session for credit.

Library Gill Library with 220,000 titles, 1,450 serial subscriptions, 4,350 audiovisual materials, an OPAC.

Computers on Campus 120 computers available on campus for general student use. A campuswide network can be accessed from off campus. Internet access, online (class) registration, at least one staffed computer lab available. Computer purchase or lease plan available.

Student Life *Housing options:* women-only. Campus housing is university owned. Freshman campus housing is guaranteed. *Activities and organizations:* drama/theater group, student-run newspaper, choral group, drama club, science and math society, Latin-American Women's Society. *Campus security:* 24-hour emergency response devices and patrols, late-night transport/escort service, controlled dormitory access, 24-hour monitored security cameras at residence hall entrances. *Student services:* health clinic, personal/psychological counseling, women's center.

Athletics Member NCAA. All Division III. *Intercollegiate sports:* basketball W, cross-country running W, softball W, swimming W, tennis W, volleyball W.

Standardized Tests *Required:* SAT I or ACT (for admission).

Costs (2004–05) *Comprehensive fee:* $26,750 includes full-time tuition ($19,100), mandatory fees ($250), and room and board ($7400). Full-time tuition and fees vary according to course load and program. Part-time tuition: $643 per credit. Part-time tuition and fees vary according to course load. *Required fees:* $30 per term part-time. *Room and board:* Room and board charges vary according to housing facility. *Payment plan:* installment. *Waivers:* employees or children of employees.

Financial Aid Of all full-time matriculated undergraduates who enrolled in 2003, 570 applied for aid, 570 were judged to have need, 570 had their need fully met. 300 Federal Work-Study jobs (averaging $3916). 10 state and other part-time jobs (averaging $4500). In 2003, 251 non-need-based awards were made. *Average percent of need met:* 100%. *Average financial aid package:* $16,020. *Average need-based loan:* $5222. *Average need-based gift aid:* $7460. *Average non-need-based aid:* $5000. *Average indebtedness upon graduation:* $23,000.

Applying *Options:* common application, early admission, early decision, deferred entrance. *Application fee:* $20. *Required:* high school transcript. *Recommended:* essay or personal statement, 1 letter of recommendation, interview. *Application deadline:* rolling (freshmen), rolling (transfers). *Early decision:* 11/1. *Notification:* continuous (freshmen), 12/15 (early decision), continuous (transfers).

Admissions Contact Ms. Stephanie Decker, Director of Admission, The College of New Rochelle, 29 Castle Place, New Rochelle, NY 10805-2339. *Phone:* 914-654-5452. *Toll-free phone:* 800-933-5923. *Fax:* 914-654-5464. *E-mail:* admission@cnr.edu.

■ *See page 1444 for a narrative description.*

THE COLLEGE OF SAINT ROSE

Albany, New York

■ **Independent** comprehensive, founded 1920
■ **Calendar** semesters
■ **Degrees** bachelor's, master's, post-master's, and postbachelor's certificates
■ **Urban** 28-acre campus
■ **Endowment** $18.8 million
■ **Coed,** 2,898 undergraduate students, 88% full-time, 74% women, 26% men
■ **Moderately difficult** entrance level, 74% of applicants were admitted

Undergraduates 2,547 full-time, 351 part-time. Students come from 20 states and territories, 6% are from out of state, 2% African American, 1% Asian American or Pacific Islander, 3% Hispanic American, 0.2% Native American, 0.3% international, 12% transferred in, 30% live on campus. *Retention:* 86% of 2002 full-time freshmen returned.

Freshmen *Admission:* 1,917 applied, 1,414 admitted, 535 enrolled. *Average high school GPA:* 3.50. *Test scores:* SAT verbal scores over 500: 64%; SAT math scores over 500: 36%; ACT scores over 18: 95%; SAT verbal scores over 600: 16%; SAT math scores over 600: 3%; ACT scores over 24: 38%; SAT verbal scores over 700: 1%; ACT scores over 30: 3%.

Faculty *Total:* 425, 39% full-time. *Student/faculty ratio:* 15:1.

Majors Accounting; American studies; art teacher education; audiology and speech-language pathology; biochemistry; biology/biological sciences; biology teacher education; business administration and management; cell biology and histology; chemistry; chemistry teacher education; clinical laboratory science/medical technology; commercial and advertising art; communication disorders; communication/speech communication and rhetoric; communications technology; computer and information sciences; criminal justice/law enforcement administration; cytotechnology; elementary education; English; English/language arts teacher education; environmental studies; fine/studio arts; history; information science/studies; interdisciplinary studies; liberal arts and sciences/liberal studies; mathematics; mathematics teacher education; music; music teacher education; political science and government; psychology; religious studies; social studies teacher education; social work; sociology; Spanish; Spanish language teacher education; special education; trade and industrial teacher education.

Academic Programs *Special study options:* academic remediation for entering students, accelerated degree program, adult/continuing education programs, advanced placement credit, double majors, external degree program, independent study, internships, off-campus study, part-time degree program, services for LD students, student-designed majors, study abroad, summer session for credit. *Unusual degree programs:* 3-2 engineering with Alfred University, Clarkson University, Union College (NY), Rensselaer Polytechnic Institute.

Library Neil Hellman Library plus 1 other with 205,938 titles, 925 serial subscriptions, 1,513 audiovisual materials, an OPAC, a Web page.

Computers on Campus 322 computers available on campus for general student use. A campuswide network can be accessed from student residence rooms and from off campus. Internet access, online (class) registration, at least one staffed computer lab available.

Student Life *Housing options:* coed, men-only, women-only. Campus housing is university owned. Freshman applicants given priority for college housing. *Activities and organizations:* drama/theater group, student-run newspaper, choral group, Student Association, Student Events Board, Circle K, Student Education Association, Student Speech, Hearing and Language Association. *Campus security:* 24-hour emergency response devices and patrols, student patrols, late-night transport/escort service, controlled dormitory access. *Student services:* health clinic, personal/psychological counseling.

Athletics Member NCAA. All Division II. *Intercollegiate sports:* baseball M(s), basketball M(s)/W(s), cross-country running M(s)/W(s), soccer M(s)/W(s), softball W(s), swimming M(s)/W(s), volleyball W(s). *Intramural sports:* basketball M/W, soccer M/W, softball W, volleyball M/W.

Standardized Tests *Required:* SAT I or ACT (for admission).

Costs (2003–04) *Comprehensive fee:* $22,864 includes full-time tuition ($15,242), mandatory fees ($396), and room and board ($7226). Full-time tuition and fees vary according to course load and program. Part-time tuition and fees vary according to class time. *College room only:* $3374. Room and board charges vary according to board plan. *Waivers:* employees or children of employees.

Financial Aid Of all full-time matriculated undergraduates who enrolled in 2002, 2,366 applied for aid, 2,075 were judged to have need, 60 had their need fully met. 406 Federal Work-Study jobs (averaging $815). 83 state and other part-time jobs (averaging $892). In 2002, 237 non-need-based awards were made. *Average percent of need met:* 37%. *Average financial aid package:* $7031. *Average need-based loan:* $1172. *Average need-based gift aid:* $3254. *Average non-need-based aid:* $1786. *Average indebtedness upon graduation:* $16,595.

Applying *Options:* electronic application, deferred entrance. *Application fee:* $35. *Required:* essay or personal statement, high school transcript, 1 letter of

The College of Saint Rose (continued)
recommendation. *Required for some:* interview. *Recommended:* minimum 3.0 GPA, interview. *Application deadlines:* 5/1 (freshmen), 5/1 (transfers). *Notification:* continuous (freshmen), continuous (transfers).

Admissions Contact Ms. Mary Elizabeth Amico, Director of Undergraduate Admissions, The College of Saint Rose, 432 Western Avenue, Albany, NY 12203. *Phone:* 518-454-5150. *Toll-free phone:* 800-637-8556. *Fax:* 518-454-2013. *E-mail:* admit@strose.edu.

■ See page 1450 for a narrative description.

College of Staten Island of the City University of New York

Staten Island, New York

- **State and locally supported** comprehensive, founded 1955, part of City University of New York System
- **Calendar** semesters
- **Degrees** certificates, associate, bachelor's, master's, and post-master's certificates
- **Urban** 204-acre campus with easy access to New York City
- **Endowment** $4.1 million
- **Coed,** 11,101 undergraduate students, 65% full-time, 59% women, 41% men
- **Moderately difficult** entrance level, 100% of applicants were admitted

Undergraduates 7,258 full-time, 3,843 part-time. Students come from 8 states and territories, 112 other countries, 1% are from out of state, 9% African American, 7% Asian American or Pacific Islander, 9% Hispanic American, 0.1% Native American, 3% international, 6% transferred in. *Retention:* 80% of 2002 full-time freshmen returned.

Freshmen *Admission:* 6,487 applied, 6,487 admitted, 2,127 enrolled. *Average high school GPA:* 2.94. *Test scores:* SAT verbal scores over 500: 52%; SAT math scores over 500: 57%; SAT verbal scores over 600: 11%; SAT math scores over 600: 13%; SAT verbal scores over 700: 2%; SAT math scores over 700: 1%.

Faculty *Total:* 770, 44% full-time, 53% with terminal degrees. *Student/faculty ratio:* 19:1.

Majors Accounting; African-American/Black studies; American studies; architecture; biochemistry; biology/biological sciences; business/commerce; chemistry; cinematography and film/video production; clinical laboratory science/medical technology; clinical/medical laboratory technology; communication/speech communication and rhetoric; computer and information sciences; computer and information sciences and support services related; computer programming; construction engineering technology; dramatic/theatre arts; economics; engineering; English; fine arts related; history; information science/studies; international relations and affairs; liberal arts and sciences/liberal studies; mathematics; music; nursing (registered nurse training); nursing related; philosophy; physical therapy; physician assistant; physics; political science and government; psychology; social work; Spanish.

Academic Programs *Special study options:* accelerated degree program, adult/continuing education programs, advanced placement credit, cooperative education, double majors, English as a second language, freshman honors college, honors programs, independent study, internships, off-campus study, part-time degree program, services for LD students, study abroad, summer session for credit. *Unusual degree programs:* 3-2 physical therapy, physicians assistant, medical technology.

Library College of Staten Island Library with 212,554 titles, 1,425 serial subscriptions, 14,500 audiovisual materials, an OPAC, a Web page.

Computers on Campus 140 computers available on campus for general student use. A campuswide network can be accessed from off campus. Internet access, online (class) registration, at least one staffed computer lab available.

Student Life *Housing:* college housing not available. *Activities and organizations:* drama/theater group, student-run newspaper, radio station, choral group, Latin club, Spanish club, Southasian Cultural Club, Apostolic Christian Life Center. *Campus security:* 24-hour emergency response devices and patrols, late-night transport/escort service, emergency call boxes, blue light system, bicycle patrols, radar-controlled traffic monitoring, lighted pathways. *Student services:* health clinic, personal/psychological counseling, women's center.

Athletics Member NCAA. All Division III. *Intercollegiate sports:* baseball M, basketball M/W, cheerleading M(c)/W(c), soccer M/W, softball W, swimming M/W, tennis M/W, volleyball W. *Intramural sports:* badminton M/W, basketball M/W, football M/W, racquetball M/W, soccer M/W, softball M/W, table tennis M/W, tennis M/W, track and field M/W, volleyball M/W.

Standardized Tests *Required for some:* SAT I (for admission), SAT I (for placement). *Recommended:* SAT I (for placement).

Costs (2003–04) *Tuition:* state resident $4000 full-time, $170 per credit part-time; nonresident $8640 full-time, $360 per credit part-time. Full-time tuition and fees vary according to course load. Part-time tuition and fees vary according to course load. *Required fees:* $308 full-time, $91 per semester part-time. *Payment plan:* installment. *Waivers:* senior citizens.

Financial Aid Of all full-time matriculated undergraduates who enrolled in 2003, 5,112 applied for aid, 4,059 were judged to have need, 230 had their need fully met. 1,028 Federal Work-Study jobs (averaging $1155). *Average percent of need met:* 52%. *Average financial aid package:* $5225. *Average need-based loan:* $3348. *Average need-based gift aid:* $5016.

Applying *Options:* deferred entrance. *Application fee:* $50. *Required:* high school transcript, minimum 2.0 GPA. *Application deadline:* rolling (freshmen), rolling (transfers). *Notification:* 12/15 (freshmen), continuous (transfers).

Admissions Contact Ms. Mary-Beth Riley, Director of Admissions and Recruitment, College of Staten Island of the City University of New York, 2800 Victory Boulevard, Building 2A Room 404, Staten Island, NY 10314. *Phone:* 718-982-2011. *Fax:* 718-982-2500. *E-mail:* recruitment@postbox.csi.cuny.edu.

■ See page 1458 for a narrative description.

Columbia College

New York, New York

- **Independent** 4-year, founded 1754, part of Columbia University
- **Calendar** semesters
- **Degree** bachelor's
- **Urban** 35-acre campus
- **Coed,** 4,181 undergraduate students, 100% full-time, 51% women, 49% men
- **Most difficult** entrance level, 11% of applicants were admitted

Undergraduates 4,181 full-time. Students come from 54 states and territories, 72 other countries, 75% are from out of state, 8% African American, 12% Asian American or Pacific Islander, 8% Hispanic American, 0.3% Native American, 6% international, 1% transferred in, 98% live on campus. *Retention:* 97% of 2002 full-time freshmen returned.

Freshmen *Admission:* 14,648 applied, 1,643 admitted, 1,010 enrolled. *Average high school GPA:* 3.80. *Test scores:* SAT verbal scores over 500: 99%; SAT math scores over 500: 100%; ACT scores over 18: 100%; SAT verbal scores over 600: 89%; SAT math scores over 600: 93%; ACT scores over 24: 96%; SAT verbal scores over 700: 60%; SAT math scores over 700: 59%; ACT scores over 30: 47%.

Faculty *Total:* 689. *Student/faculty ratio:* 7:1.

Majors African-American/Black studies; American studies; ancient/classical Greek; ancient studies; anthropology; archeology; architecture; architecture related; art history, criticism and conservation; Asian-American studies; Asian studies (East); astronomy; astrophysics; atomic/molecular physics; biochemistry; biology/biological sciences; biophysics; biopsychology; chemistry; classical, ancient Mediterranean and Near Eastern studies and archaeology; classics and languages, literatures and linguistics; comparative literature; computer science; creative writing; dance; dramatic/theatre arts; East Asian languages; economics; education (K-12); English; environmental biology; environmental studies; film/cinema studies; French; French studies; geochemistry; geology/earth science; German; German studies; Hispanic-American, Puerto Rican, and Mexican-American/Chicano studies; history; Italian; Italian studies; Latin American studies; linguistics; mathematics; medieval and Renaissance studies; modern Greek; music; Near and Middle Eastern studies; philosophy; physics; political science and government; psychology; religious studies; Russian; Russian studies; Slavic languages; sociology; Spanish; statistics; urban studies/affairs; visual and performing arts; women's studies.

Academic Programs *Special study options:* accelerated degree program, advanced placement credit, double majors, internships, off-campus study, services for LD students, student-designed majors, study abroad, summer session for credit. *ROTC:* Army (c), Navy (c), Air Force (c). *Unusual degree programs:* 3-2 engineering with Columbia University, The Fu Foundation School of Engineering and Applied Science; music with The Juilliard School, law with Columbia University, international affairs with Columbia University.

Library Butler Library plus 20 others with 7.2 million titles, 66,000 serial subscriptions, an OPAC, a Web page.

Computers on Campus 400 computers available on campus for general student use. A campuswide network can be accessed from student residence rooms and from off campus. Internet access, online (class) registration, at least one staffed computer lab available. Computer purchase or lease plan available.

Student Life *Housing:* on-campus residence required for freshman year. *Options:* coed, men-only, women-only, disabled students. Campus housing is university owned. Freshman campus housing is guaranteed. *Activities and organizations:* drama/theater group, student-run newspaper, radio and television station, choral group, marching band, community service, cultural organizations, performing arts, national fraternities, national sororities. *Campus security:* 24-hour emergency response devices and patrols, student patrols, late-night transport/escort service, 24-hour ID check at door. *Student services:* health clinic, personal/psychological counseling, women's center.

Athletics Member NCAA. All Division I except football (Division I-AA). *Intercollegiate sports:* archery M(c)/W, badminton M(c)/W(c), baseball M, basketball M/W, crew M/W, cross-country running M/W, fencing M/W, field hockey W, golf M, ice hockey M(c), lacrosse M(c)/W, racquetball M(c)/W(c), riflery M(c)/W(c), rugby M(c)/W(c), skiing (cross-country) M(c)/W(c), skiing (downhill) M(c)/W(c), soccer M(c)/W(c), softball W, squash M(c)/W(c), swimming M/W, table tennis M(c)/W(c), tennis M(c)/W(c), track and field M/W, ultimate Frisbee M(c)/W(c), volleyball M(c)/W(c), water polo M(c)/W(c), wrestling M. *Intramural sports:* archery W(c), badminton M/W, basketball M(c)/W(c), cross-country running M(c)/W(c), field hockey W, lacrosse W(c), racquetball M/W, soccer M/W, softball M/W, squash M/W, swimming M/W, tennis M/W, volleyball M/W, water polo W.

Standardized Tests *Required:* SAT I or ACT (for admission), SAT II: Subject Tests (for admission), SAT II: Writing Test (for admission).

Costs (2003–04) *Comprehensive fee:* $38,590 includes full-time tuition ($28,686), mandatory fees ($1102), and room and board ($8802). *College room only:* $5136. *Payment plans:* tuition prepayment, installment.

Financial Aid Of all full-time matriculated undergraduates who enrolled in 2003, 2,035 applied for aid, 1,764 were judged to have need, 1,764 had their need fully met. *Average percent of need met:* 100%. *Average financial aid package:* $27,079. *Average need-based loan:* $4626. *Average need-based gift aid:* $23,555. *Average indebtedness upon graduation:* $16,085. *Financial aid deadline:* 2/10.

Applying *Options:* electronic application, early admission, early decision, deferred entrance. *Application fee:* $65. *Required:* essay or personal statement, high school transcript, 3 letters of recommendation. *Application deadlines:* 1/2 (freshmen), 3/15 (transfers). *Early decision:* 11/1. *Notification:* 4/4 (freshmen), 12/15 (early decision), 5/15 (transfers).

Admissions Contact Mr. Eric Furda, Director of Undergraduate Admissions, Columbia College, 212 Hamilton Hall MC 2807, 1130 Amsterdam Avenue, New York, NY 10027. *Phone:* 212-854-2522. *Fax:* 212-854-1209.

■ *See page 1470 for a narrative description.*

COLUMBIA UNIVERSITY, SCHOOL OF GENERAL STUDIES

New York, New York

- **Independent** 4-year, founded 1754, part of Columbia University
- **Calendar** semesters
- **Degrees** bachelor's and postbachelor's certificates
- **Urban** 36-acre campus
- **Endowment** $12.1 million
- **Coed,** 1,085 undergraduate students, 54% full-time, 52% women, 48% men
- **Most difficult** entrance level, 47% of applicants were admitted

Undergraduates 586 full-time, 499 part-time. Students come from 36 states and territories, 38% are from out of state, 8% African American, 10% Asian American or Pacific Islander, 11% Hispanic American, 0.5% Native American. *Retention:* 96% of 2002 full-time freshmen returned.

Freshmen *Admission:* 752 applied, 352 admitted.

Faculty *Total:* 632, 100% full-time, 100% with terminal degrees. *Student/faculty ratio:* 7:1.

Majors African-American/Black studies; anthropology; applied art; applied mathematics; architecture; art history, criticism and conservation; Asian studies (East); astronomy; biology/biological sciences; chemistry; classics and languages, literatures and linguistics; comparative literature; computer science; dance; dramatic/theatre arts; economics; English; film/cinema studies; French; geology/earth science; German; Hispanic-American, Puerto Rican, and Mexican-American/Chicano studies; history; Italian; literature; mathematics; music; Near and Middle Eastern studies; philosophy; physics; political science and government; psychology; religious studies; Russian; Slavic languages; sociology; Spanish; statistics; urban studies/affairs; women's studies.

Academic Programs *Special study options:* academic remediation for entering students, accelerated degree program, adult/continuing education programs, advanced placement credit, double majors, English as a second language, honors programs, internships, off-campus study, part-time degree program, services for LD students, student-designed majors, study abroad, summer session for credit. *Unusual degree programs:* 3-2 business administration with Columbia University, Graduate School of Business; engineering with Columbia University, School of Engineering and Applied Science; social work with Columbia University, School of Social Work; international affairs, public policy and administration with Columbia University, School of International and Public Affairs; public health with Columbia University, School of Public Health.

Library Butler Library plus 21 others with 5.6 million titles, 59,400 serial subscriptions, a Web page.

Computers on Campus 250 computers available on campus for general student use. A campuswide network can be accessed from student residence rooms.

Student Life *Housing options:* coed. Campus housing is university owned, leased by the school and is provided by a third party. *Activities and organizations:* drama/theater group, student-run newspaper, radio and television station, choral group, Columbia Dramatists, writers club, General Studies Student Council, The Observer, national fraternities, national sororities. *Campus security:* 24-hour emergency response devices and patrols, late-night transport/escort service. *Student services:* health clinic, personal/psychological counseling, women's center.

Athletics Member NCAA. All Division I except football (Division I-AA). *Intercollegiate sports:* baseball M, basketball M/W, crew M/W, cross-country running M/W, fencing M/W, field hockey W(c), golf M, gymnastics W, soccer M/W, swimming M/W, tennis M/W, track and field M/W, volleyball M/W, wrestling M. *Intramural sports:* racquetball M/W, rugby M, softball W, squash M/W, volleyball M/W, weight lifting M/W.

Standardized Tests *Required for some:* SAT I or ACT (for admission).

Costs (2004–05) *Tuition:* $29,280 full-time, $976 per credit part-time. Full-time tuition and fees vary according to course load. Part-time tuition and fees vary according to course load. *Required fees:* $1118 full-time, $221 per term part-time. *Room only:* $6240. Room and board charges vary according to housing facility. *Payment plans:* tuition prepayment, deferred payment. *Waivers:* employees or children of employees.

Financial Aid Of all full-time matriculated undergraduates who enrolled in 1999, 457 Federal Work-Study jobs (averaging $1975).

Applying *Options:* electronic application, deferred entrance. *Application fee:* $50. *Required:* essay or personal statement, high school transcript, letters of recommendation, General Studies Admissions Exam. *Required for some:* interview. *Application deadlines:* 7/1 (freshmen), 7/1 (transfers). *Notification:* continuous (freshmen), continuous (transfers).

Admissions Contact Mr. Carlos A. Porro, Director of Admissions, Columbia University, School of General Studies, Mail Code 4101, Lewisohn Hall, 2970 Broadway, New York, NY 10027-9829. *Phone:* 212-854-2772. *Toll-free phone:* 800-895-1169. *Fax:* 212-854-6316. *E-mail:* gsdegree@columbia.edu.

■ *See page 1480 for a narrative description.*

COLUMBIA UNIVERSITY, THE FU FOUNDATION SCHOOL OF ENGINEERING AND APPLIED SCIENCE

New York, New York

- **Independent** university, founded 1864, part of Columbia University
- **Calendar** semesters
- **Degrees** bachelor's, master's, and doctoral
- **Urban** campus
- **Coed,** 1,360 undergraduate students, 100% full-time, 26% women, 74% men
- **Most difficult** entrance level, 29% of applicants were admitted

Undergraduates 1,360 full-time. Students come from 44 states and territories, 59 other countries, 70% are from out of state, 3% African American, 34% Asian American or Pacific Islander, 6% Hispanic American, 12% international, 1% transferred in, 99% live on campus. *Retention:* 96% of 2002 full-time freshmen returned.

Freshmen *Admission:* 2,219 applied, 649 admitted, 314 enrolled. *Average high school GPA:* 3.80. *Test scores:* SAT verbal scores over 500: 98%; SAT math scores over 500: 99%; ACT scores over 18: 100%; SAT verbal scores over 600: 91%; SAT math scores over 600: 89%; ACT scores over 24: 96%; SAT verbal scores over 700: 52%; SAT math scores over 700: 60%; ACT scores over 30: 89%.

Faculty *Total:* 130. *Student/faculty ratio:* 8:1.

Majors Applied mathematics; biomedical/medical engineering; chemical engineering; civil engineering; computer engineering; computer science; electrical, electronics and communications engineering; engineering/industrial management; engineering mechanics; engineering physics; environmental/environmental health engineering; industrial engineering; materials science; mechanical engineering; operations research.

Academic Programs *Special study options:* academic remediation for entering students, adult/continuing education programs, advanced placement credit, internships, services for LD students, study abroad, summer session for credit. *ROTC:* Army (c), Navy (c), Air Force (c).

Library Butler Library plus 20 others with 7.2 million titles, 66,000 serial subscriptions, an OPAC, a Web page.

Computers on Campus 400 computers available on campus for general student use. A campuswide network can be accessed from student residence rooms

Columbia University, The Fu Foundation School of Engineering and Applied Science (continued)

and from off campus. Internet access, online (class) registration, at least one staffed computer lab available. Computer purchase or lease plan available.

Student Life *Housing:* on-campus residence required for freshman year. *Options:* coed, men-only, women-only, disabled students. Campus housing is university owned. Freshman campus housing is guaranteed. *Activities and organizations:* drama/theater group, student-run newspaper, radio and television station, choral group, marching band, community service, cultural organizations, performing arts, national fraternities, national sororities. *Campus security:* 24-hour emergency response devices and patrols, late-night transport/escort service, 24-hour ID check at door. *Student services:* health clinic, personal/psychological counseling, women's center.

Athletics Member NCAA. All Division I except football (Division I-AA). *Intercollegiate sports:* archery M(c)/W, badminton M(c)/W(c), baseball M, basketball M/W, crew M/W, cross-country running M/W, fencing M/W, field hockey W, golf M, ice hockey M(c), lacrosse M(c)/W, riflery M(c)/W(c), rugby M(c)/W(c), skiing (cross-country) M(c)/W(c), skiing (downhill) M(c)/W(c), soccer M(c)/W(c), softball W, squash M(c)/W(c), swimming M/W, table tennis M(c)/W(c), tennis M(c)/W(c), track and field M/W, ultimate Frisbee M(c)/W(c), volleyball M(c)/W(c), water polo M(c)/W(c), wrestling M. *Intramural sports:* archery W(c), badminton M/W, basketball M(c)/W(c), cross-country running M(c)/W(c), field hockey W, lacrosse W(c), racquetball M/W, soccer M/W, softball M/W, squash M/W, swimming M/W, tennis M/W, volleyball M/W, water polo W.

Standardized Tests *Required:* SAT I or ACT (for admission), SAT II: Subject Tests (for admission), SAT II: Writing Test (for admission).

Costs (2003–04) *Comprehensive fee:* $38,590 includes full-time tuition ($28,686), mandatory fees ($1102), and room and board ($8802). *College room only:* $5136. *Payment plans:* tuition prepayment, installment.

Financial Aid Of all full-time matriculated undergraduates who enrolled in 2003, 751 applied for aid, 648 were judged to have need, 648 had their need fully met. *Average percent of need met:* 100%. *Average financial aid package:* $26,470. *Average need-based loan:* $4833. *Average need-based gift aid:* $22,393. *Average indebtedness upon graduation:* $15,391. *Financial aid deadline:* 2/10.

Applying *Options:* electronic application, early admission, early decision, deferred entrance. *Application fee:* $65. *Required:* essay or personal statement, high school transcript, 3 letters of recommendation. *Recommended:* interview. *Application deadlines:* 1/2 (freshmen), 3/15 (transfers). *Early decision:* 11/1. *Notification:* 4/4 (freshmen), 12/15 (early decision), 5/15 (transfers).

Admissions Contact Mr. Eric J. Furda, Director of Undergraduate Admissions, Columbia University, The Fu Foundation School of Engineering and Applied Science, 212 Hamilton Hall MC 2807, 1130 Amsterdam Avenue, New York, NY 10027. *Phone:* 212-854-2522. *Fax:* 212-854-1209.

CONCORDIA COLLEGE

Bronxville, New York

- **Independent Lutheran** 4-year, founded 1881, part of Concordia University System
- **Calendar** semesters
- **Degrees** associate and bachelor's
- **Suburban** 33-acre campus with easy access to New York City
- **Endowment** $6.4 million
- **Coed,** 666 undergraduate students, 87% full-time, 60% women, 40% men
- **Moderately difficult** entrance level, 74% of applicants were admitted

Undergraduates 581 full-time, 85 part-time. Students come from 23 states and territories, 32% are from out of state, 11% African American, 2% Asian American or Pacific Islander, 9% Hispanic American, 9% international, 5% transferred in, 68% live on campus. *Retention:* 78% of 2002 full-time freshmen returned.

Freshmen *Admission:* 658 applied, 485 admitted, 137 enrolled. *Average high school GPA:* 2.90. *Test scores:* SAT verbal scores over 500: 39%; SAT math scores over 500: 39%; ACT scores over 18: 37%; SAT verbal scores over 600: 9%; SAT math scores over 600: 8%; ACT scores over 24: 16%; SAT verbal scores over 700: 1%; SAT math scores over 700: 1%; ACT scores over 30: 5%.

Faculty *Total:* 66, 38% full-time, 47% with terminal degrees. *Student/faculty ratio:* 16:1.

Majors Administrative assistant and secretarial science; arts management; biology/biological sciences; business administration and management; business teacher education; ecology; education; elementary education; English; history; international relations and affairs; liberal arts and sciences/liberal studies; mathematics; middle school education; music; music teacher education; pre-law studies; religious/sacred music; religious studies; science teacher education; secondary education; social sciences; social work.

Academic Programs *Special study options:* academic remediation for entering students, accelerated degree program, adult/continuing education programs, advanced placement credit, distance learning, double majors, English as a second language, honors programs, independent study, internships, off-campus study, part-time degree program, services for LD students, student-designed majors, study abroad. *Unusual degree programs:* 3-2 physical therapy with New York Medical College.

Library Scheele Memorial Library with 71,500 titles, 467 serial subscriptions, 7,660 audiovisual materials, an OPAC, a Web page.

Computers on Campus 50 computers available on campus for general student use. A campuswide network can be accessed from student residence rooms and from off campus. Internet access, at least one staffed computer lab available.

Student Life *Housing options:* men-only, women-only. Campus housing is university owned. Freshman campus housing is guaranteed. *Activities and organizations:* drama/theater group, student-run newspaper, choral group, Campus Christian Ministries, drama club, Student Government Association, International and Afro/Latin American club, yearbook and newspaper, national fraternities, national sororities. *Campus security:* 24-hour emergency response devices and patrols, late-night transport/escort service, controlled dormitory access. *Student services:* health clinic, personal/psychological counseling.

Athletics Member NCAA. All Division II. *Intercollegiate sports:* baseball M(s), basketball M(s)/W(s), soccer M(s)/W(s), softball W(s), tennis M(s)/W(s), volleyball W(s). *Intramural sports:* basketball M/W, racquetball M/W, squash M/W, table tennis M/W, tennis M/W, volleyball W.

Standardized Tests *Required:* SAT I or ACT (for admission).

Costs (2004–05) *Comprehensive fee:* $26,300 includes full-time tuition ($18,700) and room and board ($7600). Part-time tuition: $504 per credit hour. Part-time tuition and fees vary according to course load. *Room and board:* Room and board charges vary according to board plan. *Payment plan:* installment. *Waivers:* senior citizens and employees or children of employees.

Applying *Options:* electronic application, early admission, early decision, deferred entrance. *Application fee:* $30. *Required:* high school transcript, 1 letter of recommendation. *Required for some:* interview. *Recommended:* essay or personal statement, minimum 2.5 GPA. *Application deadlines:* 3/15 (freshmen), 7/15 (transfers). *Early decision:* 11/15. *Notification:* continuous until 6/15 (freshmen), 12/1 (early decision), continuous until 8/15 (transfers).

Admissions Contact Ms. Amy M. Becher, Director of Admission, Concordia College, Bronxville, NY 10708. *Phone:* 914-337-9300 Ext. 2149. *Toll-free phone:* 800-YES-COLLEGE. *Fax:* 914-395-4636. *E-mail:* admission@concordia-ny.edu.

■ *See page 1486 for a narrative description.*

COOPER UNION FOR THE ADVANCEMENT OF SCIENCE AND ART

New York, New York

- **Independent** 4-year, founded 1859
- **Calendar** semesters
- **Degrees** certificates and bachelor's (also offers master's program with enrollment generally made up of currently-enrolled students)
- **Urban** campus
- **Endowment** $220.0 million
- **Coed,** 918 undergraduate students, 99% full-time, 35% women, 65% men
- **Most difficult** entrance level, 12% of applicants were admitted

Undergraduates 908 full-time, 10 part-time. Students come from 41 states and territories, 41% are from out of state, 5% African American, 25% Asian American or Pacific Islander, 8% Hispanic American, 0.7% Native American, 9% international, 4% transferred in, 19% live on campus. *Retention:* 94% of 2002 full-time freshmen returned.

Freshmen *Admission:* 2,414 applied, 295 admitted, 207 enrolled. *Average high school GPA:* 3.20. *Test scores:* SAT verbal scores over 500: 99%; SAT math scores over 500: 98%; SAT verbal scores over 600: 85%; SAT math scores over 600: 86%; SAT verbal scores over 700: 30%; SAT math scores over 700: 54%.

Faculty *Total:* 252, 22% full-time, 38% with terminal degrees. *Student/faculty ratio:* 7:1.

Majors Architecture; chemical engineering; civil engineering; electrical, electronics and communications engineering; engineering; fine/studio arts; mechanical engineering; visual and performing arts.

Academic Programs *Special study options:* advanced placement credit, honors programs, independent study, internships, off-campus study, student-designed majors, study abroad, summer session for credit.

Library Cooper Union Library with 97,000 titles, 370 serial subscriptions, 200,000 audiovisual materials, an OPAC, a Web page.

Computers on Campus 400 computers available on campus for general student use. A campuswide network can be accessed from student residence rooms and from off campus. Internet access, at least one staffed computer lab available.

Student Life *Housing options:* coed. Campus housing is university owned. Freshman applicants given priority for college housing. *Activities and organiza-*

tions: drama/theater group, student-run newspaper, Campus Crusade for Christ, Chinese Students Association, Kesher, Athletic Association, Muslim Students Organization, national fraternities, national sororities. *Campus security:* 24-hour emergency response devices and patrols, controlled dormitory access, security guards. *Student services:* personal/psychological counseling.

Athletics *Intercollegiate sports:* basketball M, soccer M, table tennis M/W, tennis M/W, volleyball M/W. *Intramural sports:* basketball M/W, bowling M/W, soccer M, softball M/W, table tennis M/W, tennis M/W, ultimate Frisbee M/W, volleyball M/W.

Standardized Tests *Required:* SAT I or ACT (for admission). *Required for some:* SAT II: Subject Tests (for admission).

Costs (2004–05) *Comprehensive fee:* includes mandatory fees ($1400) and room and board ($13,000). All students are awarded full-tuition scholarships. Living expenses are subsidized by college-administered financial aid. *College room only:* $9000.

Financial Aid Of all full-time matriculated undergraduates who enrolled in 2002, 423 applied for aid, 296 were judged to have need, 245 had their need fully met. 43 Federal Work-Study jobs (averaging $893). 498 state and other part-time jobs (averaging $1065). *Average percent of need met:* 91%. *Average financial aid package:* $26,000. *Average need-based loan:* $3170. *Average need-based gift aid:* $4431. *Average non-need-based aid:* $26,000. *Average indebtedness upon graduation:* $11,030.

Applying *Options:* electronic application, early admission, early decision, deferred entrance. *Application fee:* $50. *Required:* high school transcript, minimum 2.0 GPA. *Required for some:* essay or personal statement, 3 letters of recommendation, portfolio, home examination. *Recommended:* minimum 3.0 GPA. *Application deadlines:* 1/1 (freshmen), 1/1 (transfers). *Early decision:* 12/1 (for plan 1), 12/1 (for plan 2). *Notification:* 4/1 (freshmen), 12/24 (early decision plan 1), 2/1 (early decision plan 2), 5/1 (transfers).

Admissions Contact Mr. Richard Bory, Dean of Admissions and Records and Registrar, Cooper Union for the Advancement of Science and Art, 30 Cooper Square, New York, NY 10003. *Phone:* 212-353-4120. *Fax:* 212-353-4342. *E-mail:* admission@cooper.edu.

CORNELL UNIVERSITY

Ithaca, New York

- **Independent** university, founded 1865
- **Calendar** semesters
- **Degrees** bachelor's, master's, doctoral, and first professional
- **Small-town** 745-acre campus with easy access to Syracuse
- **Endowment** $2.9 billion
- **Coed,** 13,655 undergraduate students, 100% full-time, 50% women, 50% men
- **Most difficult** entrance level, 31% of applicants were admitted

Undergraduates 13,655 full-time. Students come from 56 states and territories, 107 other countries, 62% are from out of state, 5% African American, 16% Asian American or Pacific Islander, 5% Hispanic American, 0.5% Native American, 7% international, 4% transferred in, 58% live on campus. *Retention:* 96% of 2002 full-time freshmen returned.

Freshmen *Admission:* 20,441 applied, 6,334 admitted, 3,135 enrolled. *Test scores:* SAT verbal scores over 500: 98%; SAT math scores over 500: 98%; ACT scores over 18: 100%; SAT verbal scores over 600: 85%; SAT math scores over 600: 91%; ACT scores over 24: 95%; SAT verbal scores over 700: 37%; SAT math scores over 700: 58%; ACT scores over 30: 51%.

Faculty *Total:* 1,796, 91% full-time, 90% with terminal degrees. *Student/faculty ratio:* 9:1.

Majors Accounting; acting; aerospace, aeronautical and astronautical engineering; African-American/Black studies; agricultural and extension education; agricultural and horticultural plant breeding; agricultural animal breeding; agricultural/biological engineering and bioengineering; agricultural business and management; agricultural economics; agricultural teacher education; agriculture; agronomy and crop science; American government and politics; American history; American Indian/Native American studies; American literature; American studies; analysis and functional analysis; analytical chemistry; animal genetics; animal nutrition; animal physiology; animal sciences; animal sciences related; anthropology; apparel and textiles; applied art; applied economics; applied mathematics; archeology; architectural history and criticism; architecture; architecture related; art; art history, criticism and conservation; Asian history; Asian studies; Asian studies (East); astronomy; astrophysics; atmospheric sciences and meteorology; biochemistry; biochemistry/biophysics and molecular biology; biological and biomedical sciences related; biology/biological sciences; biomathematics and bioinformatics related; biomedical/medical engineering; biometry/biometrics; biophysics; biopsychology; botany/plant biology; business administration and management; business/commerce; business family and consumer sciences/human sciences; cell biology and histology; chemical engineering; chemistry; chemistry related; Chinese; city/urban, community and regional planning; civil engineering; classics and languages, literatures and linguistics; cognitive science; communication/speech communication and rhetoric; community organization and advocacy; comparative literature; computer and information sciences; computer science; consumer economics; counselor education/school counseling and guidance; creative writing; crop production; dairy science; dance; demography and population; design and visual communications; developmental and child psychology; dramatic/theatre arts; East Asian languages; ecology; economics; education; educational leadership and administration; educational psychology; educational statistics and research methods; electrical, electronics and communications engineering; engineering; engineering physics; English; English as a second/foreign language (teaching); English/language arts teacher education; English literature (British and Commonwealth); entomology; environmental design/architecture; environmental/environmental health engineering; environmental studies; environmental toxicology; epidemiology; European history; evolutionary biology; family and consumer sciences/home economics teacher education; family and consumer sciences/human sciences; family resource management; farm and ranch management; fashion/apparel design; fiber, textile and weaving arts; film/cinema studies; finance; fine/studio arts; food science; foodservice systems administration; foods, nutrition, and wellness; food technology and processing; foreign language teacher education; French; gay/lesbian studies; genetics; geochemistry; geography related; geological and earth sciences/geosciences related; geological/geophysical engineering; geology/earth science; geophysics and seismology; geotechnical engineering; German; German studies; Hispanic-American, Puerto Rican, and Mexican-American/Chicano studies; historic preservation and conservation; history; history and philosophy of science and technology; history related; horticultural science; hospitality administration; hospitality administration related; hotel/motel administration; housing and human environments; human development and family studies; human ecology; humanities; human nutrition; hydrology and water resources science; immunology; industrial engineering; information science/studies; inorganic chemistry; interdisciplinary studies; international agriculture; international relations and affairs; Italian; labor and industrial relations; landscape architecture; Latin American studies; liberal arts and sciences/liberal studies; linguistics; management science; marketing/marketing management; materials engineering; materials science; mathematics; mathematics teacher education; mechanical engineering; medical microbiology and bacteriology; medieval and Renaissance studies; meteorology; microbiology; molecular biology; multi-/interdisciplinary studies related; music; music history, literature, and theory; musicology and ethnomusicology; music theory and composition; mycology; natural resource economics; natural resources/conservation; Near and Middle Eastern studies; neuroscience; nuclear engineering; nutrition sciences; operations research; organic chemistry; ornamental horticulture; painting; peace studies and conflict resolution; personality psychology; philosophy; photography; physical and theoretical chemistry; physical sciences; physics; physics related; physics teacher education; physiology; planetary astronomy and science; plant genetics; plant pathology/phytopathology; plant sciences; political science and government; political science and government related; pre-law studies; pre-medical studies; pre-veterinary studies; psychology; public administration; public administration and social service professions related; public policy analysis; religious studies; Romance languages; Russian studies; science, technology and society; sculpture; Semitic languages; Slavic languages; Slavic studies; social psychology; social sciences related; sociobiology; sociology; soil science and agronomy; soil sciences related; Spanish; statistics; structural engineering; surveying engineering; systems engineering; textile science; theatre literature, history and criticism; toxicology; transportation and highway engineering; urban studies/affairs; visual and performing arts; women's studies; zoology/animal biology.

Academic Programs *Special study options:* academic remediation for entering students, accelerated degree program, advanced placement credit, cooperative education, distance learning, double majors, English as a second language, honors programs, independent study, internships, off-campus study, services for LD students, student-designed majors, study abroad, summer session for credit. *ROTC:* Army (b), Navy (b), Air Force (b). *Unusual degree programs:* 3-2 law.

Library Olin Library plus 17 others with 7.2 million titles, 64,760 serial subscriptions, 427,798 audiovisual materials, an OPAC, a Web page.

Computers on Campus 2500 computers available on campus for general student use. A campuswide network can be accessed from student residence rooms and from off campus. Internet access, online (class) registration, at least one staffed computer lab available. Computer purchase or lease plan available.

Student Life *Housing options:* coed, men-only, women-only, cooperative, disabled students. Campus housing is university owned. Freshman campus housing is guaranteed. *Activities and organizations:* drama/theater group, student-run newspaper, radio station, choral group, marching band, Student Assembly, Residence Hall Association, Catholic Community, Hillel, Concert Commission, national fraternities, national sororities. *Campus security:* 24-hour emergency response devices and patrols, late-night transport/escort service, controlled dormitory access, escort service. *Student services:* health clinic, personal/psychological counseling, women's center.

Cornell University (continued)

Athletics Member NCAA. All Division I except football (Division I-AA). *Intercollegiate sports:* baseball M, basketball M/W, crew M/W, cross-country running M/W, equestrian sports W, fencing W, field hockey W, golf M, gymnastics W, ice hockey M/W(c), lacrosse M/W, soccer M/W, softball W(c), squash M/W, swimming M/W, tennis M/W, track and field M/W, volleyball W, wrestling M. *Intramural sports:* badminton M/W, basketball M/W, bowling M/W, crew M(c)/W(c), cross-country running M/W, football M/W, golf M/W, ice hockey M/W, rugby M(c), skiing (downhill) M/W, soccer M/W, softball M/W, squash M/W, table tennis M/W, tennis M/W, track and field M/W, volleyball M/W, water polo M/W, wrestling M/W.

Standardized Tests *Required:* SAT I or ACT (for admission). *Required for some:* SAT II: Subject Tests (for admission). *Recommended:* SAT II: Subject Tests (for admission).

Costs (2003–04) *Comprehensive fee:* $38,334 includes full-time tuition ($28,630), mandatory fees ($124), and room and board ($9580). *College room only:* $5675. Room and board charges vary according to board plan and housing facility. *Payment plans:* tuition prepayment, installment. *Waivers:* employees or children of employees.

Financial Aid Of all full-time matriculated undergraduates who enrolled in 2003, 7,220 applied for aid, 6,580 were judged to have need, 6,580 had their need fully met. 5,262 Federal Work-Study jobs (averaging $1881). *Average percent of need met:* 100%. *Average financial aid package:* $24,500. *Average need-based loan:* $7000. *Average need-based gift aid:* $17,100. *Average indebtedness upon graduation:* $20,277. *Financial aid deadline:* 2/10.

Applying *Options:* electronic application, early admission, early decision, deferred entrance. *Application fee:* $65. *Required:* essay or personal statement, high school transcript, 1 letter of recommendation. *Required for some:* interview. *Application deadlines:* 1/1 (freshmen), 3/15 (transfers). *Early decision:* 11/10. *Notification:* 4/3 (freshmen), 12/11 (early decision), continuous until 6/15 (transfers).

Admissions Contact Mr. Jason Locke, Director of Undergraduate Admissions, Cornell University, 410 Thurston Avenue, Ithaca, NY 14850. *Phone:* 607-255-5241. *Fax:* 607-255-0659. *E-mail:* admissions@cornell.edu.

■ *See page 1496 for a narrative description.*

THE CULINARY INSTITUTE OF AMERICA

Hyde Park, New York

- **Independent** 4-year, founded 1946
- **Calendar** semesters plus 18 or 21 week externship program
- **Degrees** associate and bachelor's
- **Small-town** 150-acre campus
- **Coed,** 2,404 undergraduate students, 100% full-time, 35% women, 65% men
- **Moderately difficult** entrance level, 67% of applicants were admitted

Undergraduates 2,404 full-time. Students come from 50 states and territories, 30 other countries, 71% are from out of state, 2% African American, 3% Asian American or Pacific Islander, 5% Hispanic American, 0.5% Native American, 7% international, 70% live on campus.

Freshmen *Admission:* 1,173 applied, 788 admitted, 532 enrolled. *Average high school GPA:* 2.98.

Faculty *Total:* 190, 69% full-time. *Student/faculty ratio:* 18:1.

Majors Baking and pastry arts; culinary arts; culinary arts related.

Academic Programs *Special study options:* academic remediation for entering students, adult/continuing education programs, cooperative education, distance learning, internships, off-campus study, services for LD students.

Library Conrad N. Hilton Library with 67,008 titles, 300 serial subscriptions, 4,195 audiovisual materials, an OPAC.

Computers on Campus 154 computers available on campus for general student use. A campuswide network can be accessed from student residence rooms and from off campus. Internet access, at least one staffed computer lab available.

Student Life *Housing options:* coed. Campus housing is university owned. Freshman campus housing is guaranteed. *Activities and organizations:* student-run newspaper, Epicures of Wine, Baker's Club, Food Art Club, Oye Me, Gourmet Society. *Campus security:* 24-hour emergency response devices and patrols, late-night transport/escort service, controlled dormitory access. *Student services:* health clinic, personal/psychological counseling.

Athletics *Intercollegiate sports:* ice hockey M(c), soccer M(c). *Intramural sports:* basketball M/W, bowling M/W, fencing M/W, softball M/W, tennis M/W, volleyball M/W.

Standardized Tests *Recommended:* SAT I or ACT (for admission).

Costs (2003–04) *Comprehensive fee:* $24,085 includes full-time tuition ($17,640), mandatory fees ($175), and room and board ($6270). *College room only:* $4100.

Financial Aid Of all full-time matriculated undergraduates who enrolled in 2002, 2,000 applied for aid, 1,858 were judged to have need, 10 had their need fully met. 806 Federal Work-Study jobs (averaging $764). In 2002, 100 non-need-based awards were made. *Average percent of need met:* 50%. *Average financial aid package:* $8500. *Average need-based loan:* $4100. *Average need-based gift aid:* $2000. *Average non-need-based aid:* $2000. *Average indebtedness upon graduation:* $18,000. *Financial aid deadline:* 2/15.

Applying *Options:* common application, electronic application, deferred entrance. *Application fee:* $30. *Required:* essay or personal statement, high school transcript, 2 letters of recommendation. *Required for some:* interview, an Affidavit of Support. *Application deadline:* 1/15 (freshmen). *Notification:* continuous until 4/1 (freshmen), continuous (transfers).

Admissions Contact Ms. Rachel Birchwood, Assistant Director of Recruitment, The Culinary Institute of America, 1946 Campus Drive, Hudson Hall, Hyde Park, NY 12538. *Phone:* 845-451-1459. *Toll-free phone:* 800-CULINARY. *Fax:* 845-451-1068. *E-mail:* admissions@culinary.edu.

■ *See page 1502 for a narrative description.*

DAEMEN COLLEGE

Amherst, New York

- **Independent** comprehensive, founded 1947
- **Calendar** semesters
- **Degrees** certificates, bachelor's, master's, first professional, post-master's, and postbachelor's certificates
- **Suburban** 35-acre campus with easy access to Buffalo
- **Endowment** $1.8 million
- **Coed,** 1,761 undergraduate students, 80% full-time, 76% women, 24% men
- **Moderately difficult** entrance level, 70% of applicants were admitted

Undergraduates 1,408 full-time, 353 part-time. Students come from 21 states and territories, 15 other countries, 5% are from out of state, 15% African American, 1% Asian American or Pacific Islander, 2% Hispanic American, 0.9% Native American, 1% international, 7% transferred in, 42% live on campus. *Retention:* 73% of 2002 full-time freshmen returned.

Freshmen *Admission:* 1,800 applied, 1,252 admitted, 355 enrolled. *Average high school GPA:* 3.45. *Test scores:* SAT verbal scores over 500: 54%; SAT math scores over 500: 57%; ACT scores over 18: 80%; SAT verbal scores over 600: 9%; SAT math scores over 600: 9%; ACT scores over 24: 19%.

Faculty *Total:* 199, 37% full-time, 42% with terminal degrees. *Student/faculty ratio:* 16:1.

Majors Accounting; applied art; art; art teacher education; biochemistry; biology/biological sciences; biology teacher education; business administration and management; design and applied arts related; early childhood education; elementary education; English; English/language arts teacher education; fine/studio arts; French; French language teacher education; graphic design; health services/allied health/health sciences; history; mathematics; mathematics teacher education; natural sciences; nursing (registered nurse training); physical therapy; physician assistant; political science and government; psychology; religious studies; social studies teacher education; social work; Spanish; Spanish language teacher education; special education.

Academic Programs *Special study options:* academic remediation for entering students, adult/continuing education programs, advanced placement credit, cooperative education, double majors, honors programs, independent study, internships, off-campus study, part-time degree program, services for LD students, student-designed majors, study abroad, summer session for credit. *ROTC:* Army (c).

Library Marian Library plus 1 other with 128,029 titles, 915 serial subscriptions, 14,029 audiovisual materials, an OPAC, a Web page.

Computers on Campus 80 computers available on campus for general student use. A campuswide network can be accessed from student residence rooms and from off campus. Internet access, at least one staffed computer lab available.

Student Life *Housing:* on-campus residence required for freshman year. *Options:* coed. Campus housing is university owned. Freshman campus housing is guaranteed. *Activities and organizations:* drama/theater group, student-run newspaper, choral group, Students Without Borders, Student Physical Therapy Association, Physician Assistant Student Society, Step Team, Cheerleaders. *Campus security:* 24-hour emergency response devices and patrols, late-night transport/escort service, 24-hour security cameras. *Student services:* personal/psychological counseling.

Athletics Member NAIA. *Intercollegiate sports:* basketball M(s)/W(s), cross-country running M(s)/W(s), golf M(s), rugby M(c), soccer M(s)/W(s), volleyball W(s). *Intramural sports:* basketball M/W, cheerleading W(c), softball M/W.

Standardized Tests *Required:* SAT I or ACT (for admission).

Costs (2003–04) *Comprehensive fee:* $22,120 includes full-time tuition ($14,700), mandatory fees ($420), and room and board ($7000). Part-time tuition:

$490 per credit. Part-time tuition and fees vary according to course load. *Required fees:* $3 per credit part-time, $68 per term part-time. *Room and board:* Room and board charges vary according to board plan and housing facility. *Payment plans:* installment, deferred payment. *Waivers:* children of alumni, senior citizens, and employees or children of employees.

Financial Aid Of all full-time matriculated undergraduates who enrolled in 2002, 1,175 applied for aid, 1,061 were judged to have need, 252 had their need fully met. 294 Federal Work-Study jobs (averaging $1027). 15 state and other part-time jobs (averaging $1130). In 2002, 96 non-need-based awards were made. *Average percent of need met:* 86%. *Average financial aid package:* $13,465. *Average need-based loan:* $4166. *Average need-based gift aid:* $5983. *Average non-need-based aid:* $5130. *Average indebtedness upon graduation:* $11,250.

Applying *Options:* common application, electronic application, early admission, early action, deferred entrance. *Application fee:* $25. *Required:* high school transcript, minimum 2.0 GPA. *Required for some:* essay or personal statement, 3 letters of recommendation, interview, portfolio for art program, supplemental application for physician's assistant program. *Application deadline:* rolling (freshmen), rolling (transfers). *Notification:* continuous (freshmen), 9/1 (early action), continuous (transfers).

Admissions Contact Mr. Cecil Foster, Director of Admissions, Daemen College, 4380 Main Street, Amherst, NY 14226-3592. *Phone:* 716-839-8225. *Toll-free phone:* 800-462-7652. *Fax:* 716-839-8229. *E-mail:* admissions@daemen.edu.

■ See page 1510 for a narrative description.

DARKEI NOAM RABBINICAL COLLEGE
Brooklyn, New York

Admissions Contact Rabbi Pinchas Horowitz, Director of Admissions, Darkei Noam Rabbinical College, 2822 Avenue J, Brooklyn, NY 11210. *Phone:* 718-338-6464.

DEVRY INSTITUTE OF TECHNOLOGY
Long Island City, New York

- **Proprietary** 4-year, founded 1998, part of DeVry University
- **Calendar** semesters
- **Degrees** associate, bachelor's, and master's
- **Urban** 4-acre campus
- **Coed**
- **Minimally difficult** entrance level

Student Life *Campus security:* 24-hour emergency response devices and patrols, student patrols, late-night transport/escort service, lighted pathways/sidewalks.

Standardized Tests *Recommended:* SAT I, ACT or CPT.

Costs (2003–04) *Tuition:* $11,100 full-time, $395 per credit hour part-time. Full-time tuition and fees vary according to course load. Part-time tuition and fees vary according to course load. *Required fees:* $165 full-time. *Payment plans:* installment, deferred payment.

Financial Aid Of all full-time matriculated undergraduates who enrolled in 2003, 1,596 applied for aid, 1,571 were judged to have need, 24 had their need fully met. In 2003, 63. *Average percent of need met:* 48. *Average financial aid package:* $10,384. *Average need-based loan:* $5123. *Average need-based gift aid:* $6127. *Average non-need-based aid:* $8252.

Applying *Options:* electronic application, deferred entrance. *Application fee:* $50. *Required:* high school transcript, interview.

Admissions Contact Ms. Edith Bolanos, New Student Coordinator, DeVry Institute of Technology, 30-20 Thomson Avenue, Long Island City, NY 11101-3051. *Phone:* 718-472-2728. *Toll-free phone:* 888-71-Devry. *Fax:* 718-269-4288. *E-mail:* nyemailleads@ny.devry.edu.

DOMINICAN COLLEGE
Orangeburg, New York

- **Independent** comprehensive, founded 1952
- **Calendar** semesters
- **Degrees** certificates, associate, bachelor's, and master's
- **Suburban** 26-acre campus with easy access to New York City
- **Endowment** $312,000
- **Coed,** 1,303 undergraduate students, 71% full-time, 67% women, 33% men
- **Moderately difficult** entrance level, 88% of applicants were admitted

Undergraduates 927 full-time, 376 part-time. Students come from 18 states and territories, 18% are from out of state, 15% African American, 5% Asian American or Pacific Islander, 15% Hispanic American, 0.1% Native American, 9% transferred in, 20% live on campus. *Retention:* 66% of 2002 full-time freshmen returned.

Freshmen *Admission:* 847 applied, 743 admitted, 257 enrolled. *Average high school GPA:* 2.39. *Test scores:* SAT verbal scores over 500: 28%; SAT math scores over 500: 28%; ACT scores over 18: 100%; SAT verbal scores over 600: 4%; SAT math scores over 600: 4%.

Faculty *Total:* 165, 32% full-time, 49% with terminal degrees. *Student/faculty ratio:* 12:1.

Majors Accounting; American studies; athletic training; biology/biological sciences; biology teacher education; business administration and management; computer and information sciences; economics; education; elementary education; English; English/language arts teacher education; finance; health/health care administration; history; history teacher education; humanities; human resources management; international business/trade/commerce; liberal arts and sciences/liberal studies; management information systems; marketing/marketing management; mathematics; mathematics teacher education; nursing (registered nurse training); occupational therapy; pre-law studies; psychology; secondary education; social sciences; social science teacher education; social work; Spanish; special education; special education (multiply disabled).

Academic Programs *Special study options:* academic remediation for entering students, accelerated degree program, adult/continuing education programs, advanced placement credit, cooperative education, honors programs, independent study, internships, part-time degree program, services for LD students, summer session for credit. *Unusual degree programs:* 3-2 engineering with Manhattan College.

Library Pius X Hall plus 1 other with 103,350 titles, 650 serial subscriptions, an OPAC.

Computers on Campus 38 computers available on campus for general student use. A campuswide network can be accessed from student residence rooms and from off campus. Internet access, at least one staffed computer lab available.

Student Life *Housing options:* coed. Campus housing is university owned, leased by the school and is provided by a third party. *Activities and organizations:* drama/theater group, student-run newspaper, choral group, Student Government Association, Business Club, Aquin Players, school newspaper, Nursing Association. *Campus security:* 24-hour emergency response devices and patrols, student patrols, late-night transport/escort service, controlled dormitory access. *Student services:* health clinic, personal/psychological counseling.

Athletics Member NCAA, NAIA. All NCAA Division II. *Intercollegiate sports:* baseball M(s), basketball M(s)/W(s), cross-country running M(s)/W(s), golf M(s), lacrosse M(s), soccer M(s)/W(s), softball W(s), volleyball W(s). *Intramural sports:* football M, volleyball M/W.

Standardized Tests *Required:* SAT I or ACT (for admission).

Costs (2003–04) *Comprehensive fee:* $24,810 includes full-time tuition ($16,000), mandatory fees ($650), and room and board ($8160). Part-time tuition: $490 per credit. *Required fees:* $150 per term part-time. *Payment plans:* installment, deferred payment. *Waivers:* employees or children of employees.

Financial Aid Of all full-time matriculated undergraduates who enrolled in 2003, 815 applied for aid, 718 were judged to have need, 130 had their need fully met. 95 Federal Work-Study jobs (averaging $1989). 25 state and other part-time jobs (averaging $2102). In 2003, 126 non-need-based awards were made. *Average percent of need met:* 68%. *Average financial aid package:* $12,090. *Average need-based loan:* $3864. *Average need-based gift aid:* $8674. *Average non-need-based aid:* $12,824. *Average indebtedness upon graduation:* $30,625.

Applying *Options:* common application, deferred entrance. *Application fee:* $35. *Required:* high school transcript. *Application deadline:* rolling (freshmen), rolling (transfers). *Notification:* continuous (freshmen), continuous (transfers).

Admissions Contact Ms. Joyce Elbe, Director of Admissions, Dominican College, Orangeburg, NY 10962-1210. *Phone:* 845-359-7800 Ext. 271. *Toll-free phone:* 866-432-4636. *Fax:* 845-365-3150. *E-mail:* admissions@dc.edu.

■ See page 1536 for a narrative description.

DOWLING COLLEGE
Oakdale, New York

- **Independent** comprehensive, founded 1955
- **Calendar** semesters
- **Degrees** bachelor's, master's, doctoral, post-master's, and postbachelor's certificates
- **Suburban** 157-acre campus with easy access to New York City
- **Endowment** $10.3 million
- **Coed,** 3,095 undergraduate students, 69% full-time, 61% women, 39% men
- **Moderately difficult** entrance level, 97% of applicants were admitted

Undergraduates 2,136 full-time, 959 part-time. Students come from 28 states and territories, 56 other countries, 9% are from out of state, 10% African

Dowling College (continued)
American, 2% Asian American or Pacific Islander, 11% Hispanic American, 0.3% Native American, 0.4% international, 13% transferred in, 17% live on campus. *Retention:* 69% of 2002 full-time freshmen returned.

Freshmen *Admission:* 2,465 applied, 2,384 admitted, 487 enrolled. *Average high school GPA:* 2.76. *Test scores:* SAT verbal scores over 500: 53%; SAT math scores over 500: 43%; SAT verbal scores over 600: 8%; SAT math scores over 600: 11%; SAT verbal scores over 700: 1%; SAT math scores over 700: 1%.

Faculty *Total:* 502, 26% full-time, 46% with terminal degrees. *Student/faculty ratio:* 18:1.

Majors Accounting; aerospace, aeronautical and astronautical engineering; anthropology; applied art; art teacher education; biological and physical sciences; biology/biological sciences; biology teacher education; business administration and management; business, management, and marketing related; business teacher education; commercial and advertising art; communication/speech communication and rhetoric; computer and information sciences; computer and information sciences and support services related; economics; education; elementary education; engineering related; English; English/language arts teacher education; finance; fine arts related; fine/studio arts; foreign languages and literatures; health professions related; history; humanities; interdisciplinary studies; international business/trade/commerce; liberal arts and sciences/liberal studies; marine biology and biological oceanography; mathematics; mathematics teacher education; music; music teacher education; natural sciences; philosophy; political science and government; psychology; Romance languages; sales, distribution and marketing; secondary education; social sciences; social studies teacher education; sociology; Spanish language teacher education; special education; speech and rhetoric; tourism and travel services management; transportation and materials moving related; transportation technology.

Academic Programs *Special study options:* academic remediation for entering students, accelerated degree program, advanced placement credit, cooperative education, double majors, English as a second language, honors programs, independent study, internships, off-campus study, part-time degree program, services for LD students, student-designed majors, summer session for credit. *ROTC:* Army (c), Navy (c), Air Force (c).

Library Dowling College Library with 118,830 titles, 3,131 serial subscriptions, an OPAC.

Computers on Campus 118 computers available on campus for general student use. A campuswide network can be accessed. Internet access, online (class) registration, at least one staffed computer lab available.

Student Life *Housing options:* coed. Campus housing is university owned and leased by the school. *Activities and organizations:* drama/theater group, student-run newspaper, radio station, choral group, Student Government Association, Residence Hall Council, Pan African-American-Caribbean Club, aeronautics club, Lion's Voice: (student newspaper). *Campus security:* 24-hour emergency response devices and patrols, late-night transport/escort service. *Student services:* health clinic, personal/psychological counseling.

Athletics Member NCAA. All Division II. *Intercollegiate sports:* baseball M(s), basketball M(s)/W(s), crew M(c)/W(c), equestrian sports W, lacrosse M, soccer M(s), softball W(s), tennis M(s)/W(s), volleyball W(s). *Intramural sports:* bowling M/W, cross-country running M/W, track and field M/W, weight lifting M/W.

Standardized Tests *Recommended:* SAT I or ACT (for admission).

Costs (2004–05) *Tuition:* $14,490 full-time, $483 per credit part-time. Part-time tuition and fees vary according to course load and degree level. *Required fees:* $840 full-time, $275 per term part-time. *Room only:* $5300. Room and board charges vary according to housing facility and location. *Payment plans:* installment, deferred payment. *Waivers:* minority students, children of alumni, adult students, senior citizens, and employees or children of employees.

Financial Aid Of all full-time matriculated undergraduates who enrolled in 2002, 2,082 applied for aid, 1,758 were judged to have need, 379 had their need fully met. 350 Federal Work-Study jobs (averaging $2000). In 2002, 256 non-need-based awards were made. *Average percent of need met:* 74%. *Average financial aid package:* $14,107. *Average need-based loan:* $5500. *Average need-based gift aid:* $5215. *Average non-need-based aid:* $4063. *Average indebtedness upon graduation:* $16,200.

Applying *Options:* common application, electronic application, deferred entrance. *Application fee:* $25. *Required:* high school transcript. *Application deadline:* rolling (freshmen), rolling (transfers). *Notification:* continuous (freshmen), continuous (transfers).

Admissions Contact Ms. Bridget Masturzo, Director of Enrollment Services/Recruitment, Dowling College, 150 Idle Hour Boulevard, Oakdale, NY 11769. *Phone:* 631-244-3436. *Toll-free phone:* 800-DOWLING. *Fax:* 631-563-3827. *E-mail:* admissions@dowling.edu.

D'YOUVILLE COLLEGE
Buffalo, New York

- **Independent** comprehensive, founded 1908
- **Calendar** semesters plus summer session
- **Degrees** bachelor's, master's, doctoral, first professional, post-master's, and postbachelor's certificates
- **Urban** 7-acre campus
- **Endowment** $13.4 million
- **Coed,** 976 undergraduate students, 80% full-time, 75% women, 25% men
- **Moderately difficult** entrance level, 69% of applicants were admitted

The College offers a new chiropractic program and a new physical therapy program in both bachelor's and doctoral degrees and a new exercise and sports studies (BS) program. The 5-year combined bachelor's/master's degree is offered in occupational therapy, international business, nursing, education, and dietetics. All dual-degree students pay undergraduate full-time tuition all 5 years. The Instant Scholarship Program offers scholarships with total values up to $43,500. D'Youville automatically rewards applicants in recognition of their high school or college accomplishments. The Honors Scholarship requiremes a minimum 1100 SAT/24 ACT and gives 50% off tuition, 25% off total room and board. The Academic Scholarship requiremes 1000 SAT/21 ACT and 85% average grades and gives 25% off tuition and 50% off total room and board. Other scholarships are available. All scholarships are renewable annually and are not based on financial need.

Undergraduates 783 full-time, 193 part-time. Students come from 26 states and territories, 29 other countries, 7% are from out of state, 16% African American, 2% Asian American or Pacific Islander, 5% Hispanic American, 1% Native American, 13% international, 47% transferred in, 20% live on campus. *Retention:* 71% of 2002 full-time freshmen returned.

Freshmen *Admission:* 860 applied, 597 admitted, 139 enrolled. *Average high school GPA:* 2.88. *Test scores:* SAT verbal scores over 500: 39%; SAT math scores over 500: 51%; ACT scores over 18: 90%; SAT verbal scores over 600: 5%; SAT math scores over 600: 8%; ACT scores over 24: 29%.

Faculty *Total:* 196, 51% full-time, 34% with terminal degrees. *Student/faculty ratio:* 14:1.

Majors Accounting; biology/biological sciences; business administration and management; business teacher education; dietetics; education; education (K-12); elementary education; English; health/health care administration; health professions related; health services/allied health/health sciences; history; history related; information technology; interdisciplinary studies; international business/trade/commerce; liberal arts and sciences/liberal studies; marketing/marketing management; nursing (registered nurse training); occupational therapy; philosophy; physical therapy; physician assistant; pre-dentistry studies; pre-law studies; pre-medical studies; pre-veterinary studies; psychology; science teacher education; secondary education; sociology; special education.

Academic Programs *Special study options:* academic remediation for entering students, accelerated degree program, adult/continuing education programs, distance learning, double majors, independent study, internships, off-campus study, part-time degree program, services for LD students, study abroad, summer session for credit. *ROTC:* Army (c). *Unusual degree programs:* 3-2 education, dietetics, international business, occupational therapy, physical therapy.

Library D'Youville College Library with 95,995 titles, 1,235 serial subscriptions, 3,280 audiovisual materials, an OPAC, a Web page.

Computers on Campus 70 computers available on campus for general student use. A campuswide network can be accessed from student residence rooms and from off campus. Internet access, at least one staffed computer lab available.

Student Life *Housing:* on-campus residence required for freshman year. *Options:* coed, men-only, women-only, disabled students. Campus housing is university owned. Freshman campus housing is guaranteed. *Activities and organizations:* drama/theater group, student-run newspaper, choral group, Student Association, Occupational Therapy Student Association, Physical Therapy Student Association, Student Nurses Association, Black Student Union. *Campus security:* 24-hour emergency response devices and patrols, late-night transport/escort service, controlled dormitory access. *Student services:* health clinic, personal/psychological counseling.

Athletics Member NCAA, NSCAA. All NCAA Division III. *Intercollegiate sports:* baseball M, basketball M/W, cross-country running W, golf M/W, soccer M/W, softball W, volleyball M/W. *Intramural sports:* basketball M/W, cheerleading W, crew W, cross-country running M, football M/W, golf M/W, ice hockey M, skiing (downhill) M/W, soccer M/W, softball M, swimming M/W, table tennis M/W, tennis M/W, volleyball M/W.

Standardized Tests *Required:* SAT I or ACT (for admission).

Costs (2003–04) *Comprehensive fee:* $21,120 includes full-time tuition ($13,960), mandatory fees ($200), and room and board ($6960). Part-time tuition: $400 per credit. Part-time tuition and fees vary according to course load. No tuition increase for student's term of enrollment. *Required fees:* $100 per term part-time. *Room and board:* Room and board charges vary according to housing facility. *Payment plans:* tuition prepayment, installment, deferred payment. *Waivers:* minority students, children of alumni, adult students, senior citizens, and employees or children of employees.

Financial Aid Of all full-time matriculated undergraduates who enrolled in 2003, 610 applied for aid, 562 were judged to have need, 146 had their need fully met. 72 state and other part-time jobs (averaging $2000). In 2003, 592 non-need-based awards were made. *Average percent of need met:* 76%. *Average financial aid package:* $12,735. *Average need-based loan:* $4764. *Average need-based gift aid:* $7854. *Average non-need-based aid:* $4378.

Applying *Options:* common application, electronic application. *Application fee:* $25. *Required:* high school transcript, minimum 2.0 GPA. *Required for some:* essay or personal statement, minimum 3.0 GPA, letters of recommendation, interview. *Application deadline:* rolling (freshmen), rolling (transfers). *Notification:* continuous (freshmen), continuous (transfers).

Admissions Contact Mr. Ron Dannecker, Director of Admissions, D'Youville College, 320 Porter Avenue, Buffalo, NY 14201-1084. *Phone:* 716-881-7600. *Toll-free phone:* 800-777-3921. *Fax:* 716-881-7790. *E-mail:* admiss@dyc.edu.

■ *See page 1550 for a narrative description.*

ELMIRA COLLEGE
Elmira, New York

- **Independent** 4-year, founded 1855
- **Calendar** 4-4-1
- **Degrees** bachelor's (also offers master's degree in education mainly for local students)
- **Small-town** 42-acre campus
- **Endowment** $32.5 million
- **Coed,** 1,533 undergraduate students, 82% full-time, 72% women, 28% men
- **Moderately difficult** entrance level, 67% of applicants were admitted

Undergraduates 1,262 full-time, 271 part-time. Students come from 35 states and territories, 23 other countries, 48% are from out of state, 2% African American, 0.6% Asian American or Pacific Islander, 1% Hispanic American, 0.2% Native American, 4% international, 5% transferred in, 95% live on campus. *Retention:* 79% of 2002 full-time freshmen returned.

Freshmen *Admission:* 1,895 applied, 1,274 admitted, 339 enrolled. *Average high school GPA:* 3.50. *Test scores:* SAT verbal scores over 500: 74%; SAT math scores over 500: 70%; ACT scores over 18: 99%; SAT verbal scores over 600: 25%; SAT math scores over 600: 23%; ACT scores over 24: 58%; SAT verbal scores over 700: 4%; SAT math scores over 700: 4%; ACT scores over 30: 7%.

Faculty *Total:* 97, 89% full-time, 85% with terminal degrees. *Student/faculty ratio:* 12:1.

Majors Accounting; American studies; anthropology; art; art teacher education; audiology and speech-language pathology; biochemistry; biology/biological sciences; biology teacher education; business administration and management; business/managerial economics; chemistry; chemistry teacher education; classics and languages, literatures and linguistics; clinical laboratory science/medical technology; criminal justice/law enforcement administration; dramatic/theatre arts; economics; education; elementary education; English; English/language arts teacher education; environmental studies; European studies; fine/studio arts; foreign languages and literatures; foreign language teacher education; French; French language teacher education; history; history teacher education; humanities; human services; information science/studies; interdisciplinary studies; international business/trade/commerce; international relations and affairs; liberal arts and sciences/liberal studies; literature; marketing/marketing management; mathematics; mathematics teacher education; mental health/rehabilitation; middle school education; modern languages; music; nursing (registered nurse training); nursing science; philosophy; political science and government; pre-dentistry studies; pre-law studies; pre-medical studies; pre-veterinary studies; psychology; religious studies; Romance languages; science teacher education; secondary education; social sciences; social science teacher education; social studies teacher education; social work; sociology; Spanish; Spanish language teacher education; speech teacher education.

Academic Programs *Special study options:* accelerated degree program, adult/continuing education programs, advanced placement credit, English as a second language, independent study, internships, off-campus study, part-time degree program, student-designed majors, study abroad, summer session for credit. *ROTC:* Army (c), Air Force (c). *Unusual degree programs:* 3-2 chemical engineering with Clarkson University.

Library Gannet-Tripp Library with 389,036 titles, 859 serial subscriptions, 45,691 audiovisual materials, an OPAC, a Web page.

Computers on Campus 90 computers available on campus for general student use. A campuswide network can be accessed from student residence rooms. Internet access, at least one staffed computer lab available. Computer purchase or lease plan available.

Student Life *Housing:* on-campus residence required through senior year. *Options:* coed, women-only. Campus housing is university owned. Freshman campus housing is guaranteed. *Activities and organizations:* drama/theater group, student-run newspaper, radio station, choral group, student radio station, Student Activities Board, psychology club, ski club, Pal Program. *Campus security:* 24-hour patrols, late-night transport/escort service, 24-hour locked residence hall entrances. *Student services:* health clinic, personal/psychological counseling.

Athletics Member NCAA. All Division III. *Intercollegiate sports:* basketball M/W, cheerleading W, field hockey W, golf M/W, ice hockey M/W, lacrosse M/W, soccer M/W, softball W, tennis M/W, volleyball W. *Intramural sports:* badminton M/W, basketball M/W, bowling M/W, football M, golf M/W, ice hockey M/W, lacrosse M/W, racquetball M/W, skiing (downhill) M/W, soccer M/W, softball M/W, squash M/W, swimming M/W, table tennis M/W, tennis M/W, volleyball M/W.

Standardized Tests *Required:* SAT I or ACT (for admission).

Costs (2004–05) *Comprehensive fee:* $35,360 includes full-time tuition ($26,130), mandatory fees ($900), and room and board ($8330). Part-time tuition: $250 per credit. *Payment plans:* tuition prepayment, installment. *Waivers:* employees or children of employees.

Financial Aid Of all full-time matriculated undergraduates who enrolled in 2003, 1,046 applied for aid, 988 were judged to have need, 161 had their need fully met. 425 Federal Work-Study jobs (averaging $1000). 185 state and other part-time jobs (averaging $1200). In 2003, 217 non-need-based awards were made. *Average percent of need met:* 85%. *Average financial aid package:* $20,384. *Average need-based loan:* $5647. *Average need-based gift aid:* $15,038. *Average non-need-based aid:* $15,850. *Average indebtedness upon graduation:* $19,480.

Applying *Options:* common application, electronic application, early admission, early decision, deferred entrance. *Application fee:* $50. *Required:* essay or personal statement, high school transcript, minimum 2.0 GPA, 2 letters of recommendation. *Required for some:* interview. *Recommended:* interview. *Application deadline:* 4/15 (freshmen). *Early decision:* 11/15 (for plan 1), 1/15 (for plan 2). *Notification:* continuous until 4/30 (freshmen), 12/15 (early decision plan 1), 2/1 (early decision plan 2), continuous (transfers).

Admissions Contact Mr. William S. Neal, Dean of Admissions, Elmira College, Office of Admissions, Elmira, NY 14901. *Phone:* 607-735-1724. *Toll-free phone:* 800-935-6472. *Fax:* 607-735-1718. *E-mail:* admissions@elmira.edu.

■ *See page 1580 for a narrative description.*

EUGENE LANG COLLEGE, NEW SCHOOL UNIVERSITY
New York, New York

- **Independent** 4-year, founded 1978, part of New School University
- **Calendar** semesters
- **Degree** bachelor's
- **Urban** 5-acre campus
- **Endowment** $114.9 million
- **Coed,** 742 undergraduate students, 97% full-time, 68% women, 32% men
- **Moderately difficult** entrance level, 65% of applicants were admitted

Eugene Lang offers undergraduates a seminar style of learning that emphasizes interdisciplinary liberal arts courses in discussion-based classes of no more than 20 students. The internship program encourages students to extend their learning beyond the classroom. The Greenwich location means that all the cultural treasures of New York City—museums, theater, dance, and music—are at a student's doorstep.

Undergraduates 719 full-time, 23 part-time. Students come from 36 states and territories, 15 other countries, 55% are from out of state, 5% African American, 4% Asian American or Pacific Islander, 5% Hispanic American, 3% international, 13% transferred in, 34% live on campus. *Retention:* 71% of 2002 full-time freshmen returned.

Freshmen *Admission:* 862 applied, 560 admitted, 188 enrolled. *Average high school GPA:* 2.99. *Test scores:* SAT verbal scores over 500: 97%; SAT math scores over 500: 82%; ACT scores over 18: 95%; SAT verbal scores over 600: 65%; SAT math scores over 600: 32%; ACT scores over 24: 59%; SAT verbal scores over 700: 17%; SAT math scores over 700: 4%; ACT scores over 30: 14%.

Faculty *Total:* 114, 31% full-time. *Student/faculty ratio:* 12:1.

Majors Anthropology; creative writing; dramatic/theatre arts; economics; education; English; history; humanities; interdisciplinary studies; international relations and affairs; liberal arts and sciences/liberal studies; literature; music history,

Eugene Lang College, New School University (continued)
literature, and theory; philosophy; political science and government; psychology; religious studies; social sciences; sociology; urban studies/affairs; women's studies.

Academic Programs *Special study options:* accelerated degree program, adult/continuing education programs, advanced placement credit, distance learning, independent study, internships, off-campus study, part-time degree program, student-designed majors, study abroad, summer session for credit. *Unusual degree programs:* 3-2 media studies, education, social science, management and urban policy.

Library Raymond Fogelman Library plus 2 others with 4.1 million titles, 22,150 serial subscriptions, 48,379 audiovisual materials, an OPAC, a Web page.

Computers on Campus 934 computers available on campus for general student use. A campuswide network can be accessed from student residence rooms and from off campus. At least one staffed computer lab available.

Student Life *Housing options:* coed, disabled students. Campus housing is university owned and leased by the school. Freshman campus housing is guaranteed. *Activities and organizations:* drama/theater group, choral group, Student Union, theater club, student newspaper, literary journal, ethnic organizations. *Campus security:* 24-hour emergency response devices, controlled dormitory access, 24-hour desk attendants in residence halls. *Student services:* health clinic, personal/psychological counseling.

Standardized Tests *Required:* SAT I or ACT (for admission).

Costs (2003–04) *Comprehensive fee:* $34,940 includes full-time tuition ($23,620), mandatory fees ($510), and room and board ($10,810). Part-time tuition: $868 per credit. *Required fees:* $115 per term part-time. *College room only:* $8100. *Payment plan:* installment.

Financial Aid Of all full-time matriculated undergraduates who enrolled in 2003, 533 applied for aid, 496 were judged to have need, 34 had their need fully met. In 2003, 14 non-need-based awards were made. *Average percent of need met:* 69%. *Average financial aid package:* $17,793. *Average need-based loan:* $3254. *Average need-based gift aid:* $14,857. *Average non-need-based aid:* $6610. *Average indebtedness upon graduation:* $20,093.

Applying *Options:* common application, early admission, early decision, deferred entrance. *Application fee:* $40. *Required:* essay or personal statement, high school transcript, minimum 2.0 GPA, 2 letters of recommendation, interview. *Recommended:* minimum 3.0 GPA. *Application deadlines:* 2/1 (freshmen), 5/15 (transfers). *Early decision:* 11/15. *Notification:* 4/1 (freshmen), 12/15 (early decision), 6/1 (transfers).

Admissions Contact Mr. Terence Peavy, Director of Admissions, Eugene Lang College, New School University, 65 West 11th Street, New York, NY 10011-8601. *Phone:* 212-229-5665. *Toll-free phone:* 877-528-3321. *Fax:* 212-229-5166. *E-mail:* lang@newschool.edu.

■ *See page 1598 for a narrative description.*

EXCELSIOR COLLEGE
Albany, New York

- **Independent** comprehensive, founded 1970
- **Calendar** continuous
- **Degrees** associate, bachelor's, master's, and postbachelor's certificates (offers only external degree programs)
- **Urban** campus
- **Coed,** 25,880 undergraduate students
- **Noncompetitive** entrance level

Undergraduates Students come from 50 states and territories, 51 other countries, 90% are from out of state, 14% African American, 9% Asian American or Pacific Islander, 6% Hispanic American, 0.9% Native American, 1% international.

Majors Accounting; area studies; biology/biological sciences; business administration and management; chemical engineering; chemistry; computer engineering technology; computer science; economics; electrical, electronic and communications engineering technology; electromechanical technology; finance; foreign languages and literatures; geography; geology/earth science; history; human resources management; industrial technology; information science/studies; insurance; international business/trade/commerce; laser and optical technology; liberal arts and sciences/liberal studies; literature; management information systems; marketing/marketing management; mass communication/media; mathematics; mechanical engineering/mechanical technology; music; nuclear engineering technology; nursing (registered nurse training); operations management; philosophy; physics; political science and government; psychology; sociology; welding technology.

Academic Programs *Special study options:* accelerated degree program, adult/continuing education programs, advanced placement credit, distance learning, external degree program, independent study, part-time degree program, student-designed majors.

Library Excelsior College Virtual Library with a Web page.

Computers on Campus A campuswide network can be accessed from off campus.

Student Life *Housing:* college housing not available.

Costs (2003–04) *Tuition:* $225 per credit part-time. Part-time tuition and fees vary according to course load. *Required fees:* $975 full-time, $455 per year part-time. *Payment plan:* installment. *Waivers:* employees or children of employees.

Financial Aid *Average indebtedness upon graduation:* $7192.

Applying *Application fee:* $50. *Application deadline:* rolling (freshmen), rolling (transfers). *Notification:* continuous (transfers).

Admissions Contact Ms. Chari Leader, Vice President for Enrollment Management, Excelsior College, 7 Columbia Circle, Albany, NY 12203-5159. *Phone:* 518-464-8500. *Toll-free phone:* 888-647-2388. *Fax:* 518-464-8777. *E-mail:* info@excelsior.edu.

FARMINGDALE STATE UNIVERSITY OF NEW YORK
Farmingdale, New York

- **State-supported** 4-year, founded 1912, part of State University of New York System
- **Calendar** semesters
- **Degrees** certificates, associate, and bachelor's
- **Small-town** 380-acre campus with easy access to New York City
- **Endowment** $444,187
- **Coed,** 5,949 undergraduate students, 61% full-time, 43% women, 57% men
- **Moderately difficult** entrance level, 55% of applicants were admitted

Undergraduates 3,644 full-time, 2,305 part-time. Students come from 12 states and territories, 11 other countries, 0.3% are from out of state, 13% African American, 5% Asian American or Pacific Islander, 10% Hispanic American, 0.2% Native American, 0.7% international, 7% transferred in, 11% live on campus. *Retention:* 77% of 2002 full-time freshmen returned.

Freshmen *Admission:* 3,739 applied, 2,063 admitted, 876 enrolled. *Average high school GPA:* 2.80. *Test scores:* SAT verbal scores over 500: 36%; SAT math scores over 500: 46%; SAT verbal scores over 600: 4%; SAT math scores over 600: 8%; SAT math scores over 700: 1%.

Faculty *Total:* 416, 36% full-time, 24% with terminal degrees. *Student/faculty ratio:* 20:1.

Majors Airline pilot and flight crew; applied mathematics; architectural engineering technology; automotive engineering technology; aviation/airway management; biological and biomedical sciences related; business administration and management; clinical/medical laboratory technology; computer engineering technology; computer programming; computer programming related; computer science; construction engineering technology; construction management; criminal justice/law enforcement administration; data processing and data processing technology; dental hygiene; design and visual communications; electrical, electronic and communications engineering technology; engineering/industrial management; information science/studies; landscaping and groundskeeping; liberal arts and sciences/liberal studies; manufacturing technology; mechanical engineering/mechanical technology; nursing (registered nurse training); operations management; ornamental horticulture; safety/security technology; security and loss prevention; technical and business writing.

Academic Programs *Special study options:* academic remediation for entering students, advanced placement credit, distance learning, double majors, internships, part-time degree program, services for LD students, study abroad, summer session for credit. *ROTC:* Army (c), Air Force (c).

Library Greenley Hall with 132,049 titles, 1,185 serial subscriptions, 18,021 audiovisual materials, an OPAC, a Web page.

Computers on Campus 305 computers available on campus for general student use. A campuswide network can be accessed from off campus. Internet access, online (class) registration, at least one staffed computer lab available.

Student Life *Housing options:* coed. Campus housing is university owned. *Activities and organizations:* drama/theater group, student-run newspaper, radio station, choral group, Liberal Arts Club, Campus Activities Board, Farmingdale Student Government, student radio station, Rambler Newspaper. *Campus security:* 24-hour emergency response devices and patrols, controlled dormitory access. *Student services:* health clinic, personal/psychological counseling.

Athletics Member NCAA. All Division III. *Intercollegiate sports:* baseball M, basketball M/W, cross-country running M/W, golf M, lacrosse M, soccer M/W, softball W, track and field M/W, volleyball W. *Intramural sports:* basketball M/W, football M, golf M/W, racquetball M/W, soccer M/W, softball M/W, squash M/W, swimming M/W, tennis M/W, volleyball M/W, weight lifting M/W.

Standardized Tests *Required:* SAT I or ACT (for admission).

Costs (2003–04) *Tuition:* state resident $4350 full-time, $181 per credit part-time; nonresident $10,300 full-time, $429 per credit part-time. *Required fees:* $861 full-time, $29 per credit part-time. *Room and board:* $7680; room only: $4300. Room and board charges vary according to board plan. *Payment plan:* installment.

Financial Aid Of all full-time matriculated undergraduates who enrolled in 2000, 1,872 applied for aid, 1,480 were judged to have need, 257 had their need fully met. 134 Federal Work-Study jobs, 78 state and other part-time jobs. In 2000, 213 non-need-based awards were made. *Average percent of need met:* 63%. *Average financial aid package:* $5127. *Average need-based gift aid:* $3786. *Average non-need-based aid:* $3198.

Applying *Options:* electronic application, early admission. *Application fee:* $40. *Required:* high school transcript, minimum 2.0 GPA. *Required for some:* portfolio. *Application deadline:* rolling (freshmen), rolling (transfers). *Notification:* continuous (freshmen).

Admissions Contact Mr. Jim Hall, Director of Admissions, Farmingdale State University of New York, 2350 Broadhollow Road, Farmingdale, NY 11735-1021. *Phone:* 631-420-2457. *Toll-free phone:* 877-4-FARMINGDALE. *Fax:* 631-420-2633. *E-mail:* admissions@farmingdale.edu.

■ *See page 1610 for a narrative description.*

Fashion Institute of Technology

New York, New York

- **State and locally supported** comprehensive, founded 1944, part of State University of New York System
- **Calendar** 4-1-4
- **Degrees** certificates, associate, bachelor's, and master's
- **Urban** 5-acre campus
- **Coed, primarily women,** 10,653 undergraduate students, 62% full-time, 83% women, 17% men
- **Moderately difficult** entrance level, 47% of applicants were admitted

Undergraduates 6,593 full-time, 4,060 part-time. Students come from 53 states and territories, 89 other countries, 29% are from out of state, 7% African American, 11% Asian American or Pacific Islander, 10% Hispanic American, 0.2% Native American, 12% international, 9% transferred in, 16% live on campus. *Retention:* 82% of 2002 full-time freshmen returned.

Freshmen *Admission:* 3,187 applied, 1,482 admitted, 883 enrolled. *Average high school GPA:* 3.42.

Faculty *Total:* 967, 22% full-time. *Student/faculty ratio:* 17:1.

Majors Advertising; apparel and textiles; art; art history, criticism and conservation; commercial and advertising art; design and applied arts related; fashion/apparel design; fashion merchandising; industrial design; industrial production technologies related; interior architecture; machine tool technology; visual and performing arts related; watchmaking and jewelrymaking.

Academic Programs *Special study options:* academic remediation for entering students, adult/continuing education programs, advanced placement credit, cooperative education, distance learning, English as a second language, honors programs, internships, part-time degree program, services for LD students, study abroad, summer session for credit.

Library Gladys Marcus Library with 154,015 titles, 244,335 audiovisual materials.

Computers on Campus 450 computers available on campus for general student use. A campuswide network can be accessed from student residence rooms and from off campus. Internet access, online (class) registration, at least one staffed computer lab available.

Student Life *Housing options:* coed, women-only. Campus housing is university owned and is provided by a third party. Freshman applicants given priority for college housing. *Activities and organizations:* drama/theater group, student-run newspaper, radio station, choral group, Public Relations Student Society of America, Delta Epsilon Chi, Merchandising Society, Student Government. *Campus security:* 24-hour emergency response devices and patrols. *Student services:* health clinic, personal/psychological counseling.

Athletics Member NJCAA. *Intercollegiate sports:* basketball M/W, bowling M/W, cross-country running M/W, table tennis M/W, tennis M/W, volleyball W. *Intramural sports:* basketball M/W, bowling M/W, table tennis M/W, tennis M/W, volleyball M/W.

Standardized Tests *Recommended:* SAT I or ACT (for placement).

Costs (2003–04) *Tuition:* state resident $4350 full-time, $181 per credit part-time; nonresident $10,300 full-time, $429 per credit part-time. Full-time tuition and fees vary according to degree level and program. Part-time tuition and fees vary according to degree level and program. *Required fees:* $270 full-time, $5 per term part-time. *Room and board:* $6549. Room and board charges vary according to board plan and housing facility. *Payment plan:* installment. *Waivers:* employees or children of employees.

Financial Aid Of all full-time matriculated undergraduates who enrolled in 2003, 4,554 applied for aid, 2,962 were judged to have need, 454 had their need fully met. 560 Federal Work-Study jobs (averaging $2056). In 2003, 151 non-need-based awards were made. *Average percent of need met:* 70%. *Average financial aid package:* $6936. *Average need-based loan:* $3759. *Average need-based gift aid:* $3915. *Average non-need-based aid:* $1069. *Average indebtedness upon graduation:* $10,205.

Applying *Options:* electronic application, early action, deferred entrance. *Application fee:* $40. *Required:* essay or personal statement, high school transcript, portfolio for art and design programs. *Application deadlines:* 1/1 (freshmen), 1/1 (transfers). *Notification:* continuous (freshmen), 1/31 (early action), continuous (transfers).

Admissions Contact Ms. Dolores Lombardi, Director of Admissions, Fashion Institute of Technology, Seventh Avenue at 27th Street, New York, NY 10001-5992. *Phone:* 212-217-7675. *Toll-free phone:* 800-GOTOFIT. *Fax:* 212-217-7481. *E-mail:* fitinfo@fitnyc.edu.

■ *See page 1612 for a narrative description.*

Five Towns College

Dix Hills, New York

- **Independent** comprehensive, founded 1972
- **Calendar** semesters
- **Degrees** associate, bachelor's, master's, and doctoral
- **Suburban** 40-acre campus with easy access to New York City
- **Coed,** 1,002 undergraduate students, 96% full-time, 30% women, 70% men
- **Moderately difficult** entrance level, 51% of applicants were admitted

Five Towns College offers associate, bachelor's, master's, and doctoral degree programs. Students may select from nearly 40 different majors, including audio recording technology, broadcasting, journalism, music business, jazz/commercial music, music teacher education, elementary education, theater arts, and film/video. The College is accredited by the Middle States Association and the New York State Board of Regents.

Undergraduates 962 full-time, 40 part-time. Students come from 10 states and territories, 7 other countries, 17% African American, 2% Asian American or Pacific Islander, 17% Hispanic American, 0.4% Native American, 1% international, 10% live on campus. *Retention:* 74% of 2002 full-time freshmen returned.

Freshmen *Admission:* 535 applied, 273 admitted, 273 enrolled. *Average high school GPA:* 2.30. *Test scores:* SAT verbal scores over 500: 44%; SAT math scores over 500: 39%; ACT scores over 18: 86%; SAT verbal scores over 600: 4%; SAT math scores over 600: 3%.

Faculty *Total:* 110, 52% full-time, 32% with terminal degrees. *Student/faculty ratio:* 13:1.

Majors Audio engineering; broadcast journalism; business administration and management; cinematography and film/video production; computer management; data processing and data processing technology; dramatic/theatre arts; elementary education; jazz/jazz studies; liberal arts and sciences/liberal studies; marketing/marketing management; mass communication/media; music; music management and merchandising; music teacher education; theatre design and technology; violin, viola, guitar and other stringed instruments; voice and opera; wind/percussion instruments.

Academic Programs *Special study options:* academic remediation for entering students, advanced placement credit, cooperative education, distance learning, independent study, internships, off-campus study, part-time degree program, services for LD students, summer session for credit.

Library Five Towns College Library with 35,000 titles, 565 serial subscriptions, 6,500 audiovisual materials, an OPAC.

Computers on Campus 110 computers available on campus for general student use. A campuswide network can be accessed. Internet access, at least one staffed computer lab available. Computer purchase or lease plan available.

Student Life *Housing options:* coed. Campus housing is university owned. Freshman applicants given priority for college housing. *Activities and organizations:* drama/theater group, student-run newspaper, choral group, concert choir, live audio club, dance club, musical theatre, yearbook. *Campus security:* 24-hour emergency response devices and patrols, late-night transport/escort service, controlled dormitory access. *Student services:* health clinic, personal/psychological counseling.

Standardized Tests *Required:* SAT I and SAT II or ACT (for admission).

Costs (2004–05) *Comprehensive fee:* $22,800 includes full-time tuition ($13,200), mandatory fees ($600), and room and board ($9000). Part-time tuition: $550 per credit. *Room and board:* Room and board charges vary according to board plan and location.

Financial Aid Of all full-time matriculated undergraduates who enrolled in 2003, 913 applied for aid, 867 were judged to have need, 95 had their need fully

Five Towns College (continued)
met. 80 Federal Work-Study jobs (averaging $1550). In 2003, 35 non-need-based awards were made. *Average percent of need met:* 60%. *Average financial aid package:* $5000. *Average need-based loan:* $2300. *Average need-based gift aid:* $5000. *Average non-need-based aid:* $1000. *Average indebtedness upon graduation:* $17,000.

Applying *Options:* common application, electronic application, early admission, deferred entrance. *Application fee:* $25. *Required:* essay or personal statement, high school transcript, minimum 2.3 GPA, letters of recommendation. *Required for some:* interview. *Application deadline:* rolling (freshmen), rolling (transfers). *Notification:* continuous (freshmen), continuous (transfers).

Admissions Contact Mr. Jerry Cohen, Dean of Enrollment, Five Towns College, 305 North Service Road, Dix Hills, NY 11746-6055. *Phone:* 631-424-7000 Ext. 2110. *Fax:* 631-656-2172.

■ *See page 1624 for a narrative description.*

FORDHAM UNIVERSITY
New York, New York

- **Independent Roman Catholic (Jesuit)** university, founded 1841
- **Calendar** semesters
- **Degrees** bachelor's, master's, doctoral, first professional, and post-master's certificates (branch locations: an 85-acre campus at Rose Hill and an 8-acre campus at Lincoln Center)
- **Urban** 85-acre campus
- **Endowment** $241.1 million
- **Coed,** 7,403 undergraduate students, 90% full-time, 60% women, 40% men
- **Very difficult** entrance level, 54% of applicants were admitted

Fordham, New York City's Jesuit University, has two residential campuses in New York City. The 85-acre Rose Hill campus is the largest green campus in New York City. The Lincoln Center campus, with a new 20-story residence hall, is in the cultural heart of Manhattan. Fordham's third campus, Marymount, is located on the Hudson River in historic Tarrytown, New York.

Undergraduates 6,690 full-time, 713 part-time. Students come from 53 states and territories, 50 other countries, 41% are from out of state, 6% African American, 6% Asian American or Pacific Islander, 11% Hispanic American, 0.2% Native American, 1% international, 3% transferred in, 60% live on campus. *Retention:* 90% of 2002 full-time freshmen returned.

Freshmen *Admission:* 12,801 applied, 6,862 admitted, 1,728 enrolled. *Average high school GPA:* 3.64. *Test scores:* SAT verbal scores over 500: 90%; SAT math scores over 500: 91%; ACT scores over 18: 98%; SAT verbal scores over 600: 50%; SAT math scores over 600: 50%; ACT scores over 24: 72%; SAT verbal scores over 700: 9%; SAT math scores over 700: 6%; ACT scores over 30: 14%.

Faculty *Total:* 1,132, 53% full-time. *Student/faculty ratio:* 11:1.

Majors Accounting; accounting and computer science; African-American/Black studies; African studies; American studies; anthropology; art; art history, criticism and conservation; bilingual and multilingual education; biological and physical sciences; biology/biological sciences; broadcast journalism; business administration and management; business/managerial economics; chemistry; classics and languages, literatures and linguistics; commercial and advertising art; comparative literature; computer and information sciences; computer management; computer science; creative writing; criminal justice/law enforcement administration; dance; dramatic/theatre arts; economics; education; elementary education; English; entrepreneurship; European studies (Central and Eastern); film/cinema studies; finance; fine/studio arts; French; French studies; German; German studies; health/medical preparatory programs related; Hispanic-American, Puerto Rican, and Mexican-American/Chicano studies; history; human resources management; information science/studies; interdisciplinary studies; international business/trade/commerce; international economics; international relations and affairs; Italian; Italian studies; journalism; Latin; Latin American studies; liberal arts and sciences/liberal studies; literature; management information systems; management information systems and services related; marketing/marketing management; mass communication/media; mathematics; medieval and Renaissance studies; modern Greek; modern languages; music; music history, literature, and theory; natural sciences; Near and Middle Eastern studies; peace studies and conflict resolution; philosophy; photography; physical sciences; physics; playwriting and screenwriting; political science and government; pre-dentistry studies; pre-law studies; pre-medical studies; pre-pharmacy studies; pre-veterinary studies; psychology; public administration; radio and television; religious studies; Romance languages; Russian; Russian studies; secondary education; social sciences; social work; sociology; Spanish; Spanish and Iberian studies; theology; urban studies/affairs; women's studies.

Academic Programs *Special study options:* accelerated degree program, adult/continuing education programs, advanced placement credit, double majors, English as a second language, honors programs, independent study, internships, off-campus study, part-time degree program, services for LD students, student-designed majors, study abroad, summer session for credit. *ROTC:* Army (b), Navy (c), Air Force (c). *Unusual degree programs:* 3-2 engineering with Columbia University, Case Western Reserve University.

Library Walsh Library plus 3 others with 1.8 million titles, 14,094 serial subscriptions, 13,318 audiovisual materials, an OPAC, a Web page.

Computers on Campus 617 computers available on campus for general student use. A campuswide network can be accessed from student residence rooms and from off campus. Internet access, online (class) registration, at least one staffed computer lab available.

Student Life *Housing options:* coed. Campus housing is university owned. *Activities and organizations:* drama/theater group, student-run newspaper, radio station, choral group, marching band, United Student Government, Commuting Student Association, Residence Hall Association, Ambassador Program. *Campus security:* 24-hour emergency response devices and patrols, student patrols, late-night transport/escort service, controlled dormitory access, security at each campus entrance and at residence halls. *Student services:* health clinic, personal/psychological counseling.

Athletics Member NCAA. All Division I except football (Division I-AA). *Intercollegiate sports:* baseball M(s), basketball M(s)/W(s), cheerleading W(c), crew M(c)/W(s), cross-country running M(s)/W(s), golf M, ice hockey M(c), lacrosse M(c)/W(c), rugby M(c)/W(c), sailing M(c)/W(c), soccer M(s)/W(s), softball W(s), squash M, swimming M(s)/W(s), tennis M(s)/W(s), track and field M(s)/W(s), ultimate Frisbee M(c)/W(c), volleyball W(s), water polo M(s). *Intramural sports:* badminton M/W, baseball M, basketball M/W, fencing M/W, field hockey M/W, football M, golf W, racquetball M/W, rock climbing M(c)/W(c), skiing (cross-country) M/W, skiing (downhill) M/W, soccer M/W, softball M/W, squash M/W, swimming M/W, tennis M/W, volleyball W.

Standardized Tests *Required:* SAT I or ACT (for admission). *Recommended:* SAT II: Subject Tests (for admission).

Costs (2003–04) *Comprehensive fee:* $34,420 includes full-time tuition ($24,720) and room and board ($9700). Part-time tuition: $801 per credit. *Required fees:* $40 per term part-time. *Room and board:* Room and board charges vary according to board plan, housing facility, and location. *Payment plans:* tuition prepayment, installment.

Financial Aid Of all full-time matriculated undergraduates who enrolled in 2002, 4,676 applied for aid, 4,120 were judged to have need, 999 had their need fully met. In 2002, 564 non-need-based awards were made. *Average percent of need met:* 77%. *Average financial aid package:* $17,427. *Average need-based loan:* $4154. *Average need-based gift aid:* $12,974. *Average non-need-based aid:* $7824. *Average indebtedness upon graduation:* $16,274.

Applying *Options:* common application, electronic application, early admission, early decision. *Application fee:* $50. *Required:* essay or personal statement, high school transcript, 1 letter of recommendation. *Required for some:* interview. *Recommended:* minimum 3.0 GPA, interview. *Application deadlines:* 2/1 (freshmen), 7/1 (transfers). *Early decision:* 11/1. *Notification:* 4/1 (freshmen), 12/25 (early decision), continuous (transfers).

Admissions Contact Ms. Karen Pellegrino, Director of Admission, Fordham University, Theband Hall, 441 East Fordham Road, New York, NY 10458. *Phone:* 718-817-4000. *Toll-free phone:* 800-FORDHAM. *Fax:* 718-367-9404. *E-mail:* enroll@fordham.edu.

■ *See page 1640 for a narrative description.*

GLOBE INSTITUTE OF TECHNOLOGY
New York, New York

- **Proprietary** 4-year
- **Calendar** semesters
- **Degrees** certificates, associate, and bachelor's
- **Urban** campus
- **Coed,** 844 undergraduate students, 95% full-time, 69% women, 31% men

Undergraduates 801 full-time, 43 part-time. Students come from 7 states and territories, 51 other countries, 11% are from out of state, 11% African American, 51% Asian American or Pacific Islander, 8% Hispanic American, 0.1% Native American, 6% international.

Freshmen *Admission:* 508 enrolled.

Faculty *Student/faculty ratio:* 18:1.

Majors Accounting; banking and financial support services; business administration and management; computer and information sciences; computer programming; finance; management information systems.

Academic Programs *Special study options:* academic remediation for entering students, accelerated degree program, advanced placement credit, English as a second language, internships, part-time degree program, services for LD students.

Library Globe Institute of Technology's Library with 6,678 titles, 1,237 serial subscriptions, 60 audiovisual materials, a Web page.

Computers on Campus 140 computers available on campus for general student use. A campuswide network can be accessed from off campus. Internet access, at least one staffed computer lab available.

Student Life *Housing options:* Campus housing is provided by a third party.

Athletics Member NJCAA. *Intercollegiate sports:* baseball M, basketball M(s)/W(s), bowling M/W, soccer M(s), volleyball M/W.

Standardized Tests *Recommended:* SAT I or ACT (for placement).

Costs (2004–05) *One-time required fee:* $50. *Tuition:* $8950 full-time, $370 per credit part-time. *Required fees:* $136 full-time, $136 per year part-time. *Room only:* $3500.

Applying *Options:* common application, electronic application. *Application fee:* $50. *Required:* interview.

Admissions Contact Ms. Tanya Garelik, Admissions Director, Globe Institute of Technology, 291 Broadway, New York, NY 10007. *Phone:* 212-349-4330 Ext. 117. *Toll-free phone:* 877-394-5623. *Fax:* 212-227-5920. *E-mail:* admissions@globe.edu.

HAMILTON COLLEGE

Clinton, New York

- **Independent** 4-year, founded 1812
- **Calendar** semesters
- **Degree** bachelor's
- **Small-town** 1200-acre campus
- **Endowment** $456.0 million
- **Coed,** 1,797 undergraduate students, 99% full-time, 51% women, 49% men
- **Very difficult** entrance level, 33% of applicants were admitted

Undergraduates 1,775 full-time, 22 part-time. Students come from 41 states and territories, 40 other countries, 63% are from out of state, 4% African American, 5% Asian American or Pacific Islander, 3% Hispanic American, 0.4% Native American, 5% international, 0.1% transferred in, 97% live on campus. *Retention:* 94% of 2002 full-time freshmen returned.

Freshmen *Admission:* 4,405 applied, 1,457 admitted, 467 enrolled. *Test scores:* SAT verbal scores over 500: 97%; SAT math scores over 500: 97%; SAT verbal scores over 600: 80%; SAT math scores over 600: 88%; SAT verbal scores over 700: 30%; SAT math scores over 700: 28%.

Faculty *Total:* 209, 88% full-time, 88% with terminal degrees. *Student/faculty ratio:* 9:1.

Majors African studies; American studies; anthropology; archeology; art; art history, criticism and conservation; Asian studies; Asian studies (East); biochemistry; biology/biological sciences; chemistry; classics and languages, literatures and linguistics; comparative literature; computer science; creative writing; dance; dramatic/theatre arts; economics; English; fine/studio arts; French; geology/earth science; German; history; history related; international relations and affairs; Latin; literature; mass communication/media; mathematics; medieval and Renaissance studies; modern Greek; modern languages; molecular biology; music; neuroscience; philosophy; physics; physiological psychology/psychobiology; political science and government; psychology; public policy analysis; religious studies; Russian studies; sociology; Spanish; women's studies.

Academic Programs *Special study options:* accelerated degree program, adult/continuing education programs, advanced placement credit, double majors, English as a second language, independent study, internships, off-campus study, part-time degree program, services for LD students, student-designed majors, study abroad. *ROTC:* Army (c), Air Force (c). *Unusual degree programs:* 3-2 engineering with Columbia University, Rensselaer Polytechnic Institute, Washington University in St. Louis; public policy analysis with University of Rochester.

Library Burke Library plus 3 others with 538,377 titles, 3,585 serial subscriptions, 52,051 audiovisual materials, an OPAC, a Web page.

Computers on Campus 475 computers available on campus for general student use. A campuswide network can be accessed from student residence rooms and from off campus. Internet access, online (class) registration, at least one staffed computer lab available.

Student Life *Housing:* on-campus residence required through senior year. *Options:* coed, disabled students. Campus housing is university owned. Freshman campus housing is guaranteed. *Activities and organizations:* drama/theater group, student-run newspaper, radio station, choral group, community service groups, outing club, student newspaper, club/intramural sports, performing arts groups, national fraternities. *Campus security:* 24-hour emergency response devices and patrols, late-night transport/escort service, controlled dormitory access, student safety program. *Student services:* health clinic, personal/psychological counseling, women's center.

Athletics Member NCAA. All Division III. *Intercollegiate sports:* baseball M, basketball M/W, crew W, cross-country running M/W, fencing M(c)/W(c), field hockey W, football M, golf M/W(c), ice hockey M/W, lacrosse M/W, rugby M(c)/W(c), sailing M(c)/W(c), skiing (downhill) M(c)/W(c), soccer M/W, softball W, squash M/W, swimming M/W, tennis M/W, track and field M/W, ultimate Frisbee M(c)/W(c), volleyball M(c)/W, water polo M(c)/W(c). *Intramural sports:* basketball M/W, bowling M/W, cross-country running M/W, equestrian sports M/W, field hockey W, football M, golf M/W, ice hockey M/W, lacrosse M/W, racquetball M/W, skiing (cross-country) M/W, skiing (downhill) M/W, soccer M/W, softball M, squash M/W, table tennis M/W, tennis M/W, volleyball M/W, water polo M/W.

Standardized Tests *Required:* SAT I, SAT II or ACT (for admission).

Costs (2003–04) *Comprehensive fee:* $37,560 includes full-time tuition ($30,000), mandatory fees ($200), and room and board ($7360). Part-time tuition: $2800 per unit. *College room only:* $3800. *Payment plan:* installment. *Waivers:* employees or children of employees.

Financial Aid Of all full-time matriculated undergraduates who enrolled in 2003, 1,160 applied for aid, 1,022 were judged to have need, 1,022 had their need fully met. In 2003, 65 non-need-based awards were made. *Average percent of need met:* 99%. *Average financial aid package:* $22,980. *Average need-based loan:* $3952. *Average need-based gift aid:* $19,451. *Average non-need-based aid:* $9665. *Average indebtedness upon graduation:* $16,894.

Applying *Options:* common application, electronic application, early admission, early decision, deferred entrance. *Application fee:* $50. *Required:* essay or personal statement, high school transcript, 1 letter of recommendation, sample of expository prose. *Recommended:* interview. *Application deadlines:* 1/1 (freshmen), 4/15 (transfers). *Early decision:* 11/15 (for plan 1), 1/1 (for plan 2). *Notification:* 4/1 (freshmen), 12/15 (early decision plan 1), 2/20 (early decision plan 2), 6/1 (transfers).

Admissions Contact Ms. Lora Schilder, Dean of Admission and Financial Aid, Hamilton College, 198 College Hill Road, Clinton, NY 13323. *Phone:* 315-859-4421. *Toll-free phone:* 800-843-2655. *Fax:* 315-859-4457. *E-mail:* admission@hamilton.edu.

■ *See page 1702 for a narrative description.*

HARTWICK COLLEGE

Oneonta, New York

- **Independent** 4-year, founded 1797
- **Calendar** 4-1-4
- **Degree** bachelor's
- **Small-town** 425-acre campus with easy access to Albany
- **Endowment** $61.6 million
- **Coed,** 1,466 undergraduate students, 96% full-time, 58% women, 42% men
- **Moderately difficult** entrance level, 89% of applicants were admitted

Undergraduates 1,412 full-time, 54 part-time. Students come from 30 states and territories, 34 other countries, 36% are from out of state, 4% African American, 0.8% Asian American or Pacific Islander, 4% Hispanic American, 0.9% Native American, 4% international, 3% transferred in, 86% live on campus. *Retention:* 78% of 2002 full-time freshmen returned.

Freshmen *Admission:* 1,853 applied, 1,654 admitted, 447 enrolled. *Test scores:* SAT verbal scores over 500: 82%; SAT math scores over 500: 84%; ACT scores over 18: 97%; SAT verbal scores over 600: 29%; SAT math scores over 600: 32%; ACT scores over 24: 53%; SAT verbal scores over 700: 3%; SAT math scores over 700: 4%; ACT scores over 30: 8%.

Faculty *Total:* 144, 70% full-time, 65% with terminal degrees. *Student/faculty ratio:* 12:1.

Majors Accounting; anthropology; art; art history, criticism and conservation; biochemistry; biology/biological sciences; business administration and management; chemistry; clinical laboratory science/medical technology; computer and information sciences; computer science; dramatic/theatre arts; economics; English; French; geology/earth science; German; history; mathematics; music; music teacher education; nursing (registered nurse training); philosophy; physics; political science and government; pre-law studies; pre-medical studies; pre-veterinary studies; psychology; religious studies; sociology; Spanish.

Academic Programs *Special study options:* accelerated degree program, advanced placement credit, double majors, honors programs, independent study, internships, off-campus study, part-time degree program, services for LD students, student-designed majors, study abroad. *ROTC:* Army (c), Air Force (c). *Unusual degree programs:* 3-2 engineering with Clarkson University, Columbia University.

Library Stevens-German Library plus 1 other with 353,776 titles, 571 serial subscriptions, 6,171 audiovisual materials, an OPAC, a Web page.

Computers on Campus 80 computers available on campus for general student use. A campuswide network can be accessed from student residence rooms and from off campus that provide access to students receive notebook computer, printers and software. Internet access, at least one staffed computer lab available. Computer purchase or lease plan available.

Hartwick College (continued)

Student Life *Housing:* on-campus residence required through junior year. *Options:* coed, men-only, women-only. Campus housing is university owned. *Activities and organizations:* drama/theater group, student-run newspaper, radio and television station, choral group, Student Union, student radio station, Student Senate, Hilltops, Cardboard Alley Players, national fraternities, national sororities. *Campus security:* 24-hour emergency response devices and patrols, late-night transport/escort service. *Student services:* health clinic, personal/psychological counseling, women's center.

Athletics Member NCAA. All Division III except soccer (Division I), water polo (Division I). *Intercollegiate sports:* baseball M, basketball M/W, cross-country running M/W, equestrian sports W, field hockey W, football M, golf M/W, ice hockey M(c), lacrosse M/W, rugby M(c), soccer M(s)/W, softball W, swimming M/W, tennis M/W, track and field M/W, volleyball W, water polo M(c)/W(s). *Intramural sports:* archery M/W, badminton M/W, basketball M/W, cross-country running M/W, equestrian sports M/W, football M/W, golf M/W, racquetball M/W, soccer M/W, squash M/W, swimming M/W, table tennis M/W, tennis M/W, track and field M/W, volleyball M/W, water polo M/W.

Standardized Tests *Recommended:* SAT I or ACT (for admission).

Costs (2004–05) *Comprehensive fee:* $33,840 includes full-time tuition ($25,830), mandatory fees ($730), and room and board ($7280). *College room only:* $3840.

Financial Aid Of all full-time matriculated undergraduates who enrolled in 2002, 1,086 applied for aid, 989 were judged to have need, 742 had their need fully met. In 2002, 298 non-need-based awards were made. *Average percent of need met:* 82%. *Average financial aid package:* $20,000. *Average need-based loan:* $4110. *Average need-based gift aid:* $10,718. *Average non-need-based aid:* $12,440. *Average indebtedness upon graduation:* $19,400. *Financial aid deadline:* 2/1.

Applying *Options:* common application, electronic application, early admission, early decision, early action, deferred entrance. *Application fee:* $35. *Required:* essay or personal statement, high school transcript, 2 letters of recommendation, audition for music program. *Recommended:* minimum 3.0 GPA, interview. *Application deadlines:* 2/15 (freshmen), 8/1 (transfers). *Early decision:* 1/15. *Notification:* 3/5 (freshmen), 2/22 (early action).

Admissions Contact Ms. Patricia Maben, Director of Admissions, Hartwick College, PO Box 4022, Oneonta, NY 13820-4022. *Phone:* 607-431-4150. *Toll-free phone:* 888-HARTWICK. *Fax:* 607-431-4102. *E-mail:* admissions@hartwick.edu.

■ See page 1716 for a narrative description.

HILBERT COLLEGE
Hamburg, New York

- **Independent** 4-year, founded 1957
- **Calendar** semesters
- **Degrees** associate and bachelor's
- **Small-town** 40-acre campus with easy access to Buffalo
- **Endowment** $2.9 million
- **Coed,** 1,055 undergraduate students, 68% full-time, 63% women, 37% men
- **Minimally difficult** entrance level, 94% of applicants were admitted

Hilbert College's pioneering Economic Crime Investigation degree is one of only two baccalaureate programs in the country offering students career education in the fields of computer investigation and forensic accounting. Through a new grant, Hilbert has the unique distinction of being the only western New York college to have a modern psychology computer lab dedicated exclusively to undergraduate research.

Undergraduates 714 full-time, 341 part-time. Students come from 5 states and territories, 3 other countries, 0.7% are from out of state, 4% African American, 0.5% Asian American or Pacific Islander, 2% Hispanic American, 1% Native American, 0.5% international, 13% transferred in, 10% live on campus. *Retention:* 74% of 2002 full-time freshmen returned.

Freshmen *Admission:* 380 applied, 357 admitted, 164 enrolled. *Average high school GPA:* 2.20. *Test scores:* SAT verbal scores over 500: 34%; SAT math scores over 500: 39%; ACT scores over 18: 83%; SAT verbal scores over 600: 4%; SAT math scores over 600: 5%; SAT math scores over 700: 1%.

Faculty *Total:* 95, 41% full-time, 35% with terminal degrees. *Student/faculty ratio:* 16:1.

Majors Accounting; banking and financial support services; business administration and management; criminal justice/law enforcement administration; criminal justice/police science; English; finance; human services; legal assistant/paralegal; legal studies; liberal arts and sciences/liberal studies; management information systems; psychology.

Academic Programs *Special study options:* academic remediation for entering students, advanced placement credit, cooperative education, honors programs, independent study, internships, part-time degree program, services for LD students, summer session for credit.

Library McGrath Library with 40,127 titles, 4,845 serial subscriptions, 940 audiovisual materials, an OPAC, a Web page.

Computers on Campus 82 computers available on campus for general student use. A campuswide network can be accessed from student residence rooms. At least one staffed computer lab available.

Student Life *Housing options:* coed. Campus housing is university owned and leased by the school. Freshman campus housing is guaranteed. *Activities and organizations:* student-run newspaper, choral group, Student Government Association, Student Business and Accounting Association, SADD, Students in Free Enterprise (SIFE), criminal justice association. *Campus security:* 24-hour emergency response devices and patrols, student patrols, late-night transport/escort service, controlled dormitory access. *Student services:* personal/psychological counseling.

Athletics Member NCAA. All Division III. *Intercollegiate sports:* baseball M, basketball M/W, cross-country running W, golf M, lacrosse W, soccer M/W, softball W, volleyball M/W. *Intramural sports:* baseball M, basketball M/W, bowling M/W, cheerleading W, cross-country running M/W, football M/W, golf M, ice hockey M(c), lacrosse M(c)/W, soccer M/W, softball W, table tennis M/W, ultimate Frisbee M/W, volleyball M/W.

Standardized Tests *Recommended:* SAT I or ACT (for admission).

Costs (2004–05) *Comprehensive fee:* $19,670 includes full-time tuition ($13,500), mandatory fees ($500), and room and board ($5670). Full-time tuition and fees vary according to course load. Part-time tuition: $312 per credit hour. *Required fees:* $12 per credit hour part-time, $30 per term part-time. *College room only:* $2200. Room and board charges vary according to board plan and housing facility. *Payment plans:* installment, deferred payment. *Waivers:* children of alumni, senior citizens, and employees or children of employees.

Financial Aid Of all full-time matriculated undergraduates who enrolled in 2003, 709 applied for aid, 633 were judged to have need, 153 had their need fully met. 63 Federal Work-Study jobs (averaging $1530). In 2003, 108 non-need-based awards were made. *Average percent of need met:* 76%. *Average financial aid package:* $10,135. *Average need-based loan:* $4084. *Average need-based gift aid:* $6446. *Average non-need-based aid:* $7378. *Average indebtedness upon graduation:* $16,110. *Financial aid deadline:* 5/1.

Applying *Options:* electronic application, early admission, deferred entrance. *Application fee:* $20. *Required:* high school transcript. *Required for some:* interview. *Recommended:* letters of recommendation, interview. *Application deadlines:* 9/1 (freshmen), 8/1 (transfers). *Notification:* continuous (freshmen), continuous (transfers).

Admissions Contact Admissions Counselor, Hilbert College, 5200 South Park Avenue, Hamburg, NY 14075-1597. *Phone:* 716-649-7900 Ext. 211. *Fax:* 716-649-0702.

■ See page 1732 for a narrative description.

HOBART AND WILLIAM SMITH COLLEGES
Geneva, New York

- **Independent** 4-year, founded 1822
- **Calendar** semesters
- **Degree** bachelor's
- **Small-town** 200-acre campus with easy access to Rochester and Syracuse
- **Endowment** $126.6 million
- **Coed,** 1,873 undergraduate students, 100% full-time, 55% women, 45% men
- **Very difficult** entrance level, 62% of applicants were admitted

Hobart and William Smith Colleges are dedicated to providing a liberal arts education that is not merely informative but also transformative, by emphasizing ideals as well as knowledge. In other words, they are committed to nurturing the whole person, not just the academic student. To achieve this goal, HWS melds an interdisciplinary curriculum with a world view of learning, the highlights of which are an extensive and vibrant study-abroad program; local, national, and global internships; and a strong community service component.

Undergraduates 1,866 full-time, 7 part-time. Students come from 40 states and territories, 18 other countries, 54% are from out of state, 3% African American, 2% Asian American or Pacific Islander, 4% Hispanic American, 0.3% Native American, 2% international, 2% transferred in, 92% live on campus. *Retention:* 84% of 2002 full-time freshmen returned.

Freshmen *Admission:* 3,277 applied, 2,045 admitted, 516 enrolled. *Average high school GPA:* 3.30. *Test scores:* SAT verbal scores over 500: 89%; SAT math scores over 500: 93%; SAT verbal scores over 600: 41%; SAT math scores over 600: 46%; SAT verbal scores over 700: 5%; SAT math scores over 700: 5%.

Faculty *Total:* 189, 83% full-time, 92% with terminal degrees. *Student/faculty ratio:* 11:1.

Majors African-American/Black studies; African studies; American studies; ancient/classical Greek; anthropology; architecture; art; art history, criticism and conservation; Asian studies; biochemistry; biology/biological sciences; chemistry; Chinese; classics and languages, literatures and linguistics; comparative literature; computer science; dance; dramatic/theatre arts; economics; English; environmental studies; European studies; fine/studio arts; French; gay/lesbian studies; geology/earth science; history; interdisciplinary studies; international relations and affairs; Japanese; Latin; Latin American studies; liberal arts and sciences/liberal studies; mass communication/media; mathematics; medieval and Renaissance studies; modern languages; music; philosophy; physics; political science and government; pre-dentistry studies; pre-law studies; pre-medical studies; pre-veterinary studies; psychology; public policy analysis; religious studies; Russian; Russian studies; sociology; Spanish; urban studies/affairs; women's studies.

Academic Programs *Special study options:* accelerated degree program, adult/continuing education programs, advanced placement credit, double majors, English as a second language, honors programs, independent study, internships, off-campus study, services for LD students, student-designed majors, study abroad. *Unusual degree programs:* 3-2 business administration with Clarkson University, Rochester Institute of Technology; engineering with Columbia University, University of Rochester, Rensselaer Polytechnic Institute, Dartmouth College; architecture with Washington University in St. Louis.

Library Warren Hunting Smith Library plus 1 other with 370,770 titles, 1,153 serial subscriptions, 8,712 audiovisual materials, an OPAC, a Web page.

Computers on Campus 250 computers available on campus for general student use. A campuswide network can be accessed from student residence rooms and from off campus. Internet access, online (class) registration, at least one staffed computer lab available. Computer purchase or lease plan available.

Student Life *Housing:* on-campus residence required through senior year. *Options:* coed, men-only, women-only, cooperative. Campus housing is university owned. Freshman campus housing is guaranteed. *Activities and organizations:* drama/theater group, student-run newspaper, radio station, choral group, Student Life and Leadership, student government, African-American Student Coalition, Service Network, sports clubs, national fraternities. *Campus security:* 24-hour emergency response devices and patrols, late-night transport/escort service, controlled dormitory access. *Student services:* health clinic, personal/psychological counseling, women's center, legal services.

Athletics Member NCAA. All Division III except lacrosse (Division I). *Intercollegiate sports:* basketball M/W, cheerleading M/W, crew M/W, cross-country running M/W, field hockey W, football M, golf M/W, ice hockey M/W(c), lacrosse M/W, rugby M(c)/W(c), sailing M/W, skiing (downhill) M(c)/W(c), soccer M/W, squash M/W, swimming W, tennis M/W. *Intramural sports:* archery M/W, badminton M/W, baseball M, basketball M/W, equestrian sports M/W, fencing M/W, football M, golf M/W, ice hockey M/W, lacrosse M/W, racquetball M/W, rugby M, sailing M(c)/W(c), skiing (cross-country) M/W, skiing (downhill) M/W, soccer M/W, softball M/W, squash M, swimming W, table tennis M/W, tennis W, track and field M, ultimate Frisbee M/W, volleyball M/W, water polo M, weight lifting M/W.

Standardized Tests *Required:* SAT I or ACT (for admission). *Recommended:* SAT II: Subject Tests (for admission).

Costs (2003–04) *Comprehensive fee:* $36,536 includes full-time tuition ($28,400), mandatory fees ($548), and room and board ($7588). Part-time tuition: $3550 per course. *College room only:* $4000. *Payment plans:* tuition prepayment, installment. *Waivers:* employees or children of employees.

Financial Aid Of all full-time matriculated undergraduates who enrolled in 2003, 1,322 applied for aid, 1,166 were judged to have need, 879 had their need fully met. 956 Federal Work-Study jobs (averaging $1462). 218 state and other part-time jobs (averaging $1690). In 2003, 288 non-need-based awards were made. *Average percent of need met:* 90%. *Average financial aid package:* $22,903. *Average need-based loan:* $3833. *Average need-based gift aid:* $18,731. *Average non-need-based aid:* $16,640. *Average indebtedness upon graduation:* $20,508. *Financial aid deadline:* 3/15.

Applying *Options:* common application, electronic application, early admission, early decision, deferred entrance. *Application fee:* $45. *Required:* essay or personal statement, high school transcript, 2 letters of recommendation. *Recommended:* interview. *Application deadlines:* 2/1 (freshmen), 7/1 (transfers). *Early decision:* 11/15 (for plan 1), 1/1 (for plan 2). *Notification:* 4/1 (freshmen), 12/15 (early decision plan 1), 2/1 (early decision plan 2), continuous (transfers).

Admissions Contact Ms. Mara O'Laughlin, Director of Admissions, Hobart and William Smith Colleges, 629 South Main Street, Geneva, NY 14456-3397. *Phone:* 315-781-3472. *Toll-free phone:* 800-245-0100. *Fax:* 315-781-5471. *E-mail:* admissions@hws.edu.

■ *See page 1738 for a narrative description.*

HOFSTRA UNIVERSITY
Hempstead, New York

- **Independent** university, founded 1935
- **Calendar** 4-1-4
- **Degrees** bachelor's, master's, doctoral, first professional, post-master's, and postbachelor's certificates
- **Suburban** 240-acre campus with easy access to New York City
- **Endowment** $109.1 million
- **Coed,** 9,387 undergraduate students, 89% full-time, 53% women, 47% men
- **Moderately difficult** entrance level, 68% of applicants were admitted

Hofstra University is an independent, dynamic, and private university offering more than 130 undergraduate and 140 graduate programs in liberal arts and sciences, business, communications, education and allied human services, law, and honors studies. With a student-faculty ratio of 14:1, University professors teach small classes that emphasize interaction, critical thinking, and development of judgment. At Hofstra, students have the resources they need—high-speed, readily available access to the Internet, excellent library resources, and state-of-the-art classrooms and learning and laboratory facilities. With a diverse mix of students, Hofstra University's vibrant campus hosts a wide selection of cultural, social, and recreational activities, providing students with the full college experience. Hofstra offers students the opportunity to live and learn on its beautiful 240-acre campus on Long Island that is an accredited arboretum and museum and have easy access to the theater and cultural life of New York City.

Undergraduates 8,369 full-time, 1,018 part-time. Students come from 45 states and territories, 61 other countries, 25% are from out of state, 9% African American, 4% Asian American or Pacific Islander, 8% Hispanic American, 0.2% Native American, 2% international, 8% transferred in, 43% live on campus. *Retention:* 74% of 2002 full-time freshmen returned.

Freshmen *Admission:* 11,691 applied, 8,000 admitted, 1,877 enrolled. *Average high school GPA:* 3.08. *Test scores:* SAT verbal scores over 500: 83%; SAT math scores over 500: 88%; ACT scores over 18: 99%; SAT verbal scores over 600: 29%; SAT math scores over 600: 35%; ACT scores over 24: 59%; SAT verbal scores over 700: 2%; SAT math scores over 700: 3%; ACT scores over 30: 2%.

Faculty *Total:* 1,294, 39% full-time, 54% with terminal degrees. *Student/faculty ratio:* 14:1.

Majors Accounting; actuarial science; administrative assistant and secretarial science; African studies; American studies; anthropology; applied mathematics; area studies related; art history, criticism and conservation; art teacher education; Asian studies; athletic training; audiology and speech-language pathology; audiovisual communications technologies related; bilingual and multilingual education; biochemistry; biology/biological sciences; biology teacher education; biomedical/medical engineering; broadcast journalism; business administration and management; business/commerce; business/managerial economics; business teacher education; Caribbean studies; ceramic arts and ceramics; chemistry; chemistry related; chemistry teacher education; cinematography and film/video production; civil engineering; classics and languages, literatures and linguistics; communication/speech communication and rhetoric; communications technologies and support services related; community health and preventive medicine; comparative literature; computer engineering; computer science; creative writing; dance; dramatic/theatre arts; early childhood education; economics; education; education (specific subject areas) related; electrical, electronics and communications engineering; elementary education; engineering science; English; English/language arts teacher education; English literature (British and Commonwealth); entrepreneurship; environmental/environmental health engineering; environmental science; film/cinema studies; finance; fine/studio arts; foreign languages related; foreign language teacher education; French; French language teacher education; geography; geology/earth science; German; German language teacher education; health professions related; health teacher education; Hebrew; Hispanic-American, Puerto Rican, and Mexican-American/Chicano studies; history; humanities; industrial engineering; information science/studies; interdisciplinary studies; international business/trade/commerce; Italian; jazz/jazz studies; Jewish/Judaic studies; journalism; kindergarten/preschool education; kinesiology and exercise science; labor studies; Latin American studies; legal professions and studies related; liberal arts and sciences/liberal studies; management information systems; manufacturing engineering; marketing/marketing management; mass communication/media; mathematics; mathematics and computer science; mathematics and statistics related; mathematics teacher education; mechanical engineering; metal and jewelry arts; multi-/interdisciplinary studies related; music; music history, literature, and theory; music management and merchandising; music performance; music teacher education; music theory and composition; natural sciences; painting; philosophy; photography; physical education teaching and coaching; physical sciences related; physician assistant; physics; physics teacher education; political science and government; pre-dentistry studies; pre-law studies; pre-medical studies; pre-veterinary studies; psychology; public

Hofstra University (continued)

relations/image management; radio and television; radio and television broadcasting technology; Russian; science teacher education; sculpture; secondary education; social sciences; social studies teacher education; sociology; Spanish; Spanish language teacher education; speech and rhetoric.

Academic Programs *Special study options:* accelerated degree program, adult/continuing education programs, advanced placement credit, double majors, English as a second language, freshman honors college, honors programs, independent study, internships, part-time degree program, services for LD students, student-designed majors, study abroad, summer session for credit. *ROTC:* Army (b).

Library Axinn Library plus 1 other with 1.6 million titles, 7,017 serial subscriptions, 7,016 audiovisual materials, an OPAC, a Web page.

Computers on Campus 1130 computers available on campus for general student use. A campuswide network can be accessed from student residence rooms. Internet access, online (class) registration, at least one staffed computer lab available. Computer purchase or lease plan available.

Student Life *Housing options:* coed, women-only, disabled students. Campus housing is university owned. Freshman applicants given priority for college housing. *Activities and organizations:* drama/theater group, student-run newspaper, radio and television station, choral group, Student Government Association, Hillel, Interfraternity/Sorority Council, Entertainment Unlimited, Danceworks, national fraternities, national sororities. *Campus security:* 24-hour emergency response devices and patrols, student patrols, late-night transport/escort service, controlled dormitory access, security booths and cameras at each residence hall entrance. *Student services:* health clinic, personal/psychological counseling.

Athletics Member NCAA. All Division I except football (Division I-AA). *Intercollegiate sports:* baseball M(s), basketball M(s)/W(s), cross-country running M(s)/W(s), field hockey W(s), golf M(s)/W(s), lacrosse M(s)/W(s), soccer M(s)/W(s), softball W(s), tennis M(s)/W(s), volleyball W(s), wrestling M(s). *Intramural sports:* badminton M/W, baseball M, basketball M/W, cheerleading M(c)/W(c), crew M(c)/W(c), equestrian sports M(c)/W(c), fencing M(c)/W(c), football M/W, ice hockey M(c)/W(c), rugby M(c)/W(c), soccer M/W, softball W, table tennis M(c)/W(c), volleyball M/W, weight lifting M(c)/W(c), wrestling M/W.

Standardized Tests *Required for some:* SAT I or ACT (for admission). *Recommended:* SAT II: Subject Tests (for admission), SAT II: Writing Test (for admission).

Costs (2003–04) *Comprehensive fee:* $27,112 includes full-time tuition ($17,410), mandatory fees ($1002), and room and board ($8700). Full-time tuition and fees vary according to course load and program. Part-time tuition: $560 per semester hour. Part-time tuition and fees vary according to course load and program. *Required fees:* $155 per term part-time. *College room only:* $5600. Room and board charges vary according to board plan and housing facility. *Payment plans:* installment, deferred payment. *Waivers:* senior citizens and employees or children of employees.

Financial Aid Of all full-time matriculated undergraduates who enrolled in 2003, 5,904 applied for aid, 4,706 were judged to have need, 1,525 had their need fully met. 600 Federal Work-Study jobs (averaging $1850). 139 state and other part-time jobs (averaging $720). In 2003, 574 non-need-based awards were made. *Average financial aid package:* $10,649. *Average need-based loan:* $4105. *Average need-based gift aid:* $6897. *Average non-need-based aid:* $5400. *Average indebtedness upon graduation:* $17,763.

Applying *Options:* common application, electronic application, early admission, early action, deferred entrance. *Application fee:* $40. *Required:* essay or personal statement, high school transcript, 1 letter of recommendation. *Required for some:* interview, proof of degree required for all; TOEFL required for international students. *Application deadline:* rolling (freshmen). *Notification:* 2/1 (freshmen), 12/15 (early action), continuous (transfers).

Admissions Contact Ms. Gigi Lamens, Vice President for Enrollment Management, Hofstra University, 100 Hofstra University, Hempstead, NY 11549. *Phone:* 516-463-6700. *Toll-free phone:* 800-HOFSTRA. *Fax:* 516-560-7660. *E-mail:* admitme@hofstra.edu.

■ *See page 1740 for a narrative description.*

HOLY TRINITY ORTHODOX SEMINARY
Jordanville, New York

- **Independent Russian Orthodox** 5-year, founded 1948
- **Calendar** semesters
- **Degree** certificates and bachelor's
- **Rural** 900-acre campus
- **Men only,** 28 undergraduate students, 100% full-time
- **Noncompetitive** entrance level, 64% of applicants were admitted

Undergraduates 28 full-time. Students come from 6 states and territories, 8 other countries, 0.1% are from out of state, 50% international, 95% live on campus. *Retention:* 100% of 2002 full-time freshmen returned.

Freshmen *Admission:* 14 applied, 9 admitted, 6 enrolled.

Faculty *Total:* 19, 32% full-time. *Student/faculty ratio:* 4:1.

Majors Theology.

Academic Programs *Special study options:* accelerated degree program, English as a second language.

Library Holy Trinity Orthodox Seminary Library plus 1 other with 25,000 titles, 200 serial subscriptions.

Computers on Campus 5 computers available on campus for general student use. At least one staffed computer lab available.

Student Life *Housing:* on-campus residence required through senior year. *Options:* men-only. Campus housing is university owned. Freshman campus housing is guaranteed. *Activities and organizations:* student-run newspaper, choral group, Student Union. *Campus security:* 24-hour emergency response devices. *Student services:* health clinic, personal/psychological counseling.

Costs (2003–04) *Comprehensive fee:* $4025 includes full-time tuition ($2000), mandatory fees ($25), and room and board ($2000). Part-time tuition: $100 per term.

Applying *Required:* essay or personal statement, high school transcript, letters of recommendation, special examination, proficiency in Russian, Eastern Orthodox baptism. *Recommended:* minimum 3.0 GPA. *Application deadlines:* 5/1 (freshmen), 5/1 (transfers).

Admissions Contact Fr. Vladimir Tsurikov, Assistant Dean, Holy Trinity Orthodox Seminary, PO Box 36, Jordanville, NY 13361. *Phone:* 315-858-0945. *Fax:* 315-858-0945. *E-mail:* info@hts.edu.

HOUGHTON COLLEGE
Houghton, New York

- **Independent Wesleyan** 4-year, founded 1883
- **Calendar** semesters
- **Degrees** associate, bachelor's, and master's
- **Rural** 1300-acre campus with easy access to Buffalo and Rochester
- **Endowment** $25.5 million
- **Coed,** 1,458 undergraduate students, 94% full-time, 65% women, 35% men
- **Moderately difficult** entrance level, 85% of applicants were admitted

Houghton College is a selective, residential Christian liberal arts college of more than 1,200 undergraduates. Located on 1,300 acres in western New York, the College attracts talented students from around the world. Small classes in a traditional liberal arts curriculum of 49 majors and programs characterize Houghton's academic life. More than 90 percent of students receive financial aid.

Undergraduates 1,373 full-time, 85 part-time. Students come from 43 states and territories, 18 other countries, 39% are from out of state, 3% African American, 1% Asian American or Pacific Islander, 0.6% Hispanic American, 0.4% Native American, 4% international, 8% transferred in, 79% live on campus. *Retention:* 83% of 2002 full-time freshmen returned.

Freshmen *Admission:* 1,071 applied, 911 admitted, 304 enrolled. *Average high school GPA:* 3.48. *Test scores:* SAT verbal scores over 500: 84%; SAT math scores over 500: 82%; ACT scores over 18: 99%; SAT verbal scores over 600: 48%; SAT math scores over 600: 37%; ACT scores over 24: 64%; SAT verbal scores over 700: 13%; SAT math scores over 700: 6%; ACT scores over 30: 9%.

Faculty *Total:* 103, 81% full-time, 74% with terminal degrees. *Student/faculty ratio:* 14:1.

Majors Accounting; art; art teacher education; biblical studies; biological and physical sciences; biology/biological sciences; business administration and management; chemistry; clinical laboratory science/medical technology; computer science; creative writing; cultural studies; elementary education; English; French; health and physical education; history; humanities; international relations and affairs; liberal arts and sciences/liberal studies; literature; mathematics; music; music teacher education; music theory and composition; parks, recreation and leisure; pastoral studies/counseling; philosophy; physical education teaching and coaching; physics; piano and organ; political science and government; predentistry studies; pre-law studies; pre-medical studies; pre-veterinary studies; psychology; religious education; religious studies; secondary education; sociology; Spanish; theology; violin, viola, guitar and other stringed instruments; voice and opera; wind/percussion instruments.

Academic Programs *Special study options:* adult/continuing education programs, advanced placement credit, double majors, honors programs, independent study, internships, off-campus study, part-time degree program, services for LD students, study abroad, summer session for credit. *ROTC:* Army (c). *Unusual degree programs:* 3-2 engineering with Clarkson University, Washington University in St. Louis.

Library Willard J. Houghton Library plus 1 other with 238,300 titles, 4,102 serial subscriptions, 2,547 audiovisual materials, an OPAC, a Web page.

Computers on Campus 50 computers available on campus for general student use. A campuswide network can be accessed from student residence rooms and from off campus. Internet access, at least one staffed computer lab available.

Student Life *Housing:* on-campus residence required through sophomore year. *Options:* men-only, women-only. Campus housing is university owned. Freshman campus housing is guaranteed. *Activities and organizations:* drama/theater group, student-run newspaper, radio station, choral group, One Thing, Allegany County Outreach, World Mission Fellowship, Campus Activities Board, International Student Organization. *Campus security:* 24-hour patrols, late-night transport/escort service, controlled dormitory access, phone connection to security patrols. *Student services:* health clinic, personal/psychological counseling.

Athletics Member NAIA. *Intercollegiate sports:* basketball M(s)/W(s), cheerleading M/W, cross-country running M(s)/W(s), field hockey W(s), soccer M(s)/W(s), track and field M(s)/W(s), volleyball W(s). *Intramural sports:* basketball M/W, equestrian sports M/W, football M, golf M, racquetball M/W, rock climbing M/W, skiing (cross-country) M/W, skiing (downhill) M/W, soccer M/W, softball M/W, swimming M/W, table tennis M/W, tennis M/W, volleyball M/W, water polo M/W, weight lifting M/W.

Standardized Tests *Required:* SAT I or ACT (for admission).

Costs (2003–04) *Comprehensive fee:* $23,984 includes full-time tuition ($17,984) and room and board ($6000). Full-time tuition and fees vary according to course load and program. Part-time tuition: $750 per hour. *College room only:* $3000. Room and board charges vary according to board plan and housing facility. *Payment plan:* installment. *Waivers:* senior citizens and employees or children of employees.

Financial Aid Of all full-time matriculated undergraduates who enrolled in 2003, 1,091 applied for aid, 1,007 were judged to have need, 290 had their need fully met. 225 Federal Work-Study jobs (averaging $1500). 66 state and other part-time jobs (averaging $1500). In 2003, 230 non-need-based awards were made. *Average percent of need met:* 77%. *Average financial aid package:* $15,078. *Average need-based loan:* $4625. *Average need-based gift aid:* $9667. *Average non-need-based aid:* $7293. *Average indebtedness upon graduation:* $20,768.

Applying *Options:* electronic application, deferred entrance. *Application fee:* $40. *Required:* essay or personal statement, high school transcript, 1 letter of recommendation, pastoral recommendation. *Recommended:* minimum 2.5 GPA, interview. *Application deadline:* rolling (freshmen), rolling (transfers). *Notification:* continuous (freshmen), continuous (transfers).

Admissions Contact Mr. Bruce Campbell, Director of Admission, Houghton College, PO Box 128, Houghton, NY 14744. *Phone:* 585-567-9353. *Toll-free phone:* 800-777-2556. *Fax:* 585-567-9522. *E-mail:* admission@houghton.edu.

■ *See page 1746 for a narrative description.*

HUNTER COLLEGE OF THE CITY UNIVERSITY OF NEW YORK

New York, New York

- **State and locally supported** comprehensive, founded 1870, part of City University of New York System
- **Calendar** semesters
- **Degrees** bachelor's, master's, and post-master's certificates
- **Urban** campus
- **Coed,** 15,906 undergraduate students, 66% full-time, 70% women, 30% men
- **Moderately difficult** entrance level, 30% of applicants were admitted

Undergraduates 10,489 full-time, 5,417 part-time. Students come from 29 states and territories, 3% are from out of state, 17% African American, 15% Asian American or Pacific Islander, 21% Hispanic American, 0.2% Native American, 6% international, 9% transferred in, 1% live on campus. *Retention:* 81% of 2002 full-time freshmen returned.

Freshmen *Admission:* 12,345 applied, 3,659 admitted, 1,691 enrolled. *Average high school GPA:* 2.90. *Test scores:* SAT verbal scores over 500: 63%; SAT math scores over 500: 72%; SAT verbal scores over 600: 19%; SAT math scores over 600: 23%; SAT verbal scores over 700: 4%; SAT math scores over 700: 4%.

Faculty *Total:* 1,365, 45% full-time. *Student/faculty ratio:* 17:1.

Majors Accounting; African-American/Black studies; ancient/classical Greek; anthropology; archeology; art; art history, criticism and conservation; audiology and speech-language pathology; biology/biological sciences; biology teacher education; biotechnology research; chemistry; Chinese; cinematography and film/video production; classics; classics and languages, literatures and linguistics; clinical/medical laboratory science and allied professions related; comparative literature; computer science; dance; dramatic/theatre arts; economics; elementary education; English; English literature (British and Commonwealth); environmental science; film/cinema studies; fine/studio arts; foods, nutrition, and wellness; French; geography; German; German language teacher education; health teacher education; Hebrew; Hispanic-American, Puerto Rican, and Mexican-American/Chicano studies; history; humanities; Italian; Jewish/Judaic studies; kindergarten/preschool education; Latin; Latin American studies; literature; mass communication/media; mathematics; mathematics teacher education; music; nursing (registered nurse training); pharmacology; philosophy; physical education teaching and coaching; physical therapy; physics; political science and government; psychology; public health; religious studies; Romance languages; Russian; science teacher education; secondary education; sociology; Spanish; statistics; urban studies/affairs; women's studies.

Academic Programs *Special study options:* academic remediation for entering students, advanced placement credit, distance learning, double majors, English as a second language, freshman honors college, honors programs, independent study, internships, off-campus study, part-time degree program, services for LD students, student-designed majors, study abroad, summer session for credit. *Unusual degree programs:* 3-2 anthropology, economics, english, history, math, music, physics, sociology.

Library Hunter College Library with 534,283 titles, 2,160 serial subscriptions, 13,137 audiovisual materials, an OPAC, a Web page.

Computers on Campus 600 computers available on campus for general student use. A campuswide network can be accessed. Internet access, at least one staffed computer lab available.

Student Life *Housing options:* coed. *Activities and organizations:* drama/theater group, student-run newspaper, radio and television station, choral group. *Campus security:* 24-hour emergency response devices and patrols. *Student services:* personal/psychological counseling, women's center.

Athletics Member NCAA. All Division III. *Intercollegiate sports:* basketball M/W, cross-country running M/W, fencing M/W, gymnastics W, soccer M, swimming W, tennis M/W, track and field M/W, volleyball M/W, wrestling M. *Intramural sports:* basketball M/W, cross-country running M/W, gymnastics M/W, racquetball M/W, rugby M, soccer M/W, swimming M/W, tennis M/W, volleyball M/W.

Standardized Tests *Required:* SAT I or ACT (for admission).

Costs (2003–04) *Tuition:* state resident $4000 full-time, $170 per credit part-time; nonresident $360 per credit part-time. *Required fees:* $165 full-time, $96 per term part-time. *Room and board:* Room and board charges vary according to housing facility. *Payment plan:* deferred payment. *Waivers:* senior citizens.

Financial Aid *Average financial aid package:* $4809. *Average indebtedness upon graduation:* $7200.

Applying *Options:* early admission. *Application fee:* $50. *Required:* high school transcript. *Application deadlines:* 10/1 (freshmen), 3/1 (transfers). *Notification:* continuous until 1/3 (freshmen), continuous (transfers).

Admissions Contact Office of Admissions, Hunter College of the City University of New York, 695 Park Avenue, New York, NY 10021-5085. *Phone:* 212-772-4490. *Fax:* 212-650-3472.

■ *See page 1752 for a narrative description.*

IONA COLLEGE

New Rochelle, New York

- **Independent** comprehensive, founded 1940, affiliated with Roman Catholic Church
- **Calendar** semesters
- **Degrees** certificates, bachelor's, master's, post-master's, and postbachelor's certificates
- **Suburban** 35-acre campus with easy access to New York City
- **Endowment** $14.9 million
- **Coed,** 3,395 undergraduate students, 88% full-time, 53% women, 47% men
- **Moderately difficult** entrance level, 64% of applicants were admitted

Founded in 1940, Iona College is dedicated to personal teaching in the tradition of American Catholic higher education and the Christian Brothers. The College endeavors to develop informed, critical, and responsible individuals who are equipped to participate actively in culture and society. At Iona College, students are the first priority.

Undergraduates 3,000 full-time, 395 part-time. Students come from 37 states and territories, 30 other countries, 17% are from out of state, 8% African American, 1% Asian American or Pacific Islander, 11% Hispanic American, 0.1% Native American, 2% international, 5% transferred in, 28% live on campus. *Retention:* 79% of 2002 full-time freshmen returned.

Freshmen *Admission:* 4,196 applied, 2,696 admitted, 860 enrolled. *Average high school GPA:* 3.30. *Test scores:* SAT verbal scores over 500: 74%; SAT math scores over 500: 75%; SAT verbal scores over 600: 25%; SAT math scores over 600: 25%; SAT verbal scores over 700: 2%; SAT math scores over 700: 1%.

Faculty *Total:* 381, 46% full-time. *Student/faculty ratio:* 15:1.

Iona College (continued)

Majors Accounting; advertising; applied mathematics; audiology and speech-language pathology; behavioral sciences; biochemistry; biology/biological sciences; biology teacher education; business administration and management; chemistry; clinical laboratory science/medical technology; communication/speech communication and rhetoric; computer science; criminal justice/law enforcement administration; dramatic/theatre arts; early childhood education; ecology; economics; education; education (multiple levels); elementary education; English; English/language arts teacher education; finance; French; French language teacher education; health/health care administration; health/medical psychology; history; humanities; interdisciplinary studies; international business/trade/commerce; international/global studies; Italian; journalism; management information systems; marketing/marketing management; mass communication/media; mathematics; mathematics teacher education; philosophy; physics; political science and government; psychology; public relations/image management; radio and television; radio and television broadcasting technology; religious studies; science teacher education; secondary education; social sciences; social studies teacher education; social work; sociology; Spanish; Spanish language teacher education; speech and rhetoric; speech therapy.

Academic Programs *Special study options:* accelerated degree program, adult/continuing education programs, advanced placement credit, distance learning, double majors, honors programs, internships, off-campus study, part-time degree program, services for LD students, study abroad, summer session for credit. *ROTC:* Army (c). *Unusual degree programs:* 3-2 psychology.

Library Ryan Library plus 2 others with 270,731 titles, 738 serial subscriptions, 3,022 audiovisual materials, an OPAC, a Web page.

Computers on Campus 500 computers available on campus for general student use. A campuswide network can be accessed from student residence rooms and from off campus. Internet access, online (class) registration, at least one staffed computer lab available. Computer purchase or lease plan available.

Student Life *Housing options:* coed. Campus housing is university owned and leased by the school. Freshman applicants given priority for college housing. *Activities and organizations:* drama/theater group, student-run newspaper, radio station, choral group, marching band, Council of Multicultural Leaders, student government, The Ionian, LASO, WICR, national fraternities, national sororities. *Campus security:* 24-hour emergency response devices and patrols, controlled dormitory access. *Student services:* health clinic, personal/psychological counseling.

Athletics Member NCAA. All Division I except football (Division I-AA). *Intercollegiate sports:* baseball M(s), basketball M(s)/W(s), crew M/W, cross-country running M(s)/W(s), golf M(s), lacrosse W(s), soccer M(s)/W(s), softball W(s), swimming M(s)/W(s), track and field M(s)/W(s), volleyball W(s), water polo M(s)/W(s). *Intramural sports:* basketball M/W, cheerleading M(c)/W(c), football M, rugby M/W, softball M/W, ultimate Frisbee M/W.

Standardized Tests *Required:* SAT I or ACT (for admission). *Recommended:* SAT II: Subject Tests (for admission), SAT II: Writing Test (for admission).

Costs (2003–04) *Comprehensive fee:* $27,988 includes full-time tuition ($17,750), mandatory fees ($540), and room and board ($9698). Full-time tuition and fees vary according to class time. Part-time tuition: $590 per credit. Part-time tuition and fees vary according to class time and course load. *Required fees:* $185 per term part-time. *College room only:* $6826. Room and board charges vary according to housing facility. *Payment plan:* installment. *Waivers:* senior citizens and employees or children of employees.

Financial Aid Of all full-time matriculated undergraduates who enrolled in 2003, 2,783 applied for aid, 2,234 were judged to have need, 446 had their need fully met. 314 Federal Work-Study jobs (averaging $1614). 257 state and other part-time jobs (averaging $1379). In 2003, 519 non-need-based awards were made. *Average percent of need met:* 27%. *Average financial aid package:* $13,144. *Average need-based loan:* $3116. *Average need-based gift aid:* $2925. *Average non-need-based aid:* $9051. *Average indebtedness upon graduation:* $18,646.

Applying *Options:* common application, early admission, early action, deferred entrance. *Application fee:* $40. *Required:* high school transcript. *Recommended:* essay or personal statement, minimum 2.5 GPA, letters of recommendation, interview. *Application deadlines:* 3/15 (freshmen), 8/15 (transfers). *Notification:* continuous (freshmen), 12/20 (early action), continuous (transfers).

Admissions Contact Mr. Thomas Weede, Director of Admissions, Iona College, Admissions, 715 North Avenue, New Rochelle, NY 10801. *Phone:* 914-633-2502. *Toll-free phone:* 800-231-IONA (in-state); 914-633-2502 (out-of-state). *Fax:* 914-637-2778. *E-mail:* icad@iona.edu.

■ *See page 1774 for a narrative description.*

ITHACA COLLEGE

Ithaca, New York

- **Independent** comprehensive, founded 1892
- **Calendar** semesters
- **Degrees** certificates, bachelor's, and master's
- **Small-town** 757-acre campus with easy access to Syracuse
- **Endowment** $100.0 million
- **Coed,** 6,260 undergraduate students, 98% full-time, 57% women, 43% men
- **Moderately difficult** entrance level, 63% of applicants were admitted

Undergraduates 6,113 full-time, 147 part-time. Students come from 48 states and territories, 66 other countries, 51% are from out of state, 2% African American, 3% Asian American or Pacific Islander, 3% Hispanic American, 0.3% Native American, 3% international, 2% transferred in, 70% live on campus. *Retention:* 88% of 2002 full-time freshmen returned.

Freshmen *Admission:* 10,650 applied, 6,756 admitted, 1,585 enrolled. *Test scores:* SAT verbal scores over 500: 90%; SAT math scores over 500: 93%; SAT verbal scores over 600: 46%; SAT math scores over 600: 49%; SAT verbal scores over 700: 8%; SAT math scores over 700: 7%.

Faculty *Total:* 633, 72% full-time, 81% with terminal degrees. *Student/faculty ratio:* 12:1.

Majors Accounting; acting; anthropology; applied economics; applied mathematics; art; art history, criticism and conservation; arts management; art teacher education; athletic training; audiology and speech-language pathology; biochemistry; biology/biological sciences; biology teacher education; broadcast journalism; business administration and management; business/commerce; business/managerial economics; chemistry; chemistry teacher education; cinematography and film/video production; communication and journalism related; computer and information sciences; computer science; creative writing; dance; dramatic/theatre arts; economics; educational/instructional media design; education (K-12); education (multiple levels); English; English/language arts teacher education; environmental studies; film/cinema studies; finance; fine/studio arts; foods, nutrition, and wellness; French; French language teacher education; German; German language teacher education; gerontology; health and physical education; health and physical education related; health/health care administration; health/medical preparatory programs related; health teacher education; history; history teacher education; hospital and health care facilities administration; industrial and organizational psychology; interdisciplinary studies; international business/trade/commerce; jazz/jazz studies; journalism; kinesiology and exercise science; labor and industrial relations; liberal arts and sciences/liberal studies; marketing/marketing management; marketing research; mass communication/media; mathematics; mathematics and computer science; mathematics teacher education; middle school education; multi-/interdisciplinary studies related; music; music performance; music teacher education; music theory and composition; occupational therapy; parks, recreation and leisure; philosophy; photography; physical education teaching and coaching; physical therapy; physics; physics teacher education; piano and organ; political science and government; pre-law studies; pre-medical studies; psychology; public health education and promotion; public relations/image management; radio and television; rehabilitation therapy; science teacher education; secondary education; social sciences; social studies teacher education; sociology; Spanish; Spanish language teacher education; special education (speech or language impaired); speech and rhetoric; sport and fitness administration; telecommunications; theatre design and technology; therapeutic recreation; visual and performing arts; voice and opera.

Academic Programs *Special study options:* accelerated degree program, adult/continuing education programs, advanced placement credit, double majors, freshman honors college, honors programs, independent study, internships, off-campus study, part-time degree program, services for LD students, student-designed majors, study abroad, summer session for credit. *ROTC:* Army (c), Air Force (c). *Unusual degree programs:* 3-2 engineering with Cornell University, Rensselaer Polytechnic Institute, Clarkson University, State University of New York at Binghamton.

Library Ithaca College Library with 246,545 titles, 2,305 serial subscriptions, 25,547 audiovisual materials, an OPAC, a Web page.

Computers on Campus 624 computers available on campus for general student use. A campuswide network can be accessed from student residence rooms and from off campus. Internet access, online (class) registration, at least one staffed computer lab available. Computer purchase or lease plan available.

Student Life *Housing:* on-campus residence required through junior year. *Options:* coed, women-only, disabled students. Campus housing is university owned and leased by the school. Freshman campus housing is guaranteed. *Activities and organizations:* drama/theater group, student-run newspaper, radio and television station, choral group, student government, Student Activities

Board, African-Latino Society, Residence Hall Association, Community Service Network, national fraternities, national sororities. *Campus security:* 24-hour emergency response devices, student patrols, late-night transport/escort service, controlled dormitory access, patrols by trained security personnel 11 p.m. to 7 a.m. *Student services:* health clinic, personal/psychological counseling.

Athletics Member NCAA. All Division III. *Intercollegiate sports:* baseball M, basketball M/W, crew M/W, cross-country running M/W, field hockey W, football M, gymnastics W, lacrosse M/W, soccer M/W, softball W, swimming M/W, tennis M/W, track and field M/W, volleyball W, wrestling M. *Intramural sports:* basketball M/W, bowling M(c)/W(c), crew M(c)/W(c), football M, golf M/W, ice hockey M(c), rugby W(c), skiing (downhill) M(c)/W(c), soccer M/W, softball M/W, tennis M/W, volleyball M/W.

Standardized Tests *Required:* SAT I or ACT (for admission).

Costs (2003–04) *Comprehensive fee:* $31,730 includes full-time tuition ($22,264) and room and board ($9466). Part-time tuition: $696 per credit hour. *College room only:* $4802. Room and board charges vary according to board plan and housing facility. *Payment plan:* installment. *Waivers:* employees or children of employees.

Financial Aid Of all full-time matriculated undergraduates who enrolled in 2003, 4,682 applied for aid, 4,212 were judged to have need, 1,900 had their need fully met. In 2003, 540 non-need-based awards were made. *Average percent of need met:* 89%. *Average financial aid package:* $20,381. *Average need-based loan:* $5237. *Average need-based gift aid:* $13,112. *Average non-need-based aid:* $8111.

Applying *Options:* common application, electronic application, early admission, early decision, deferred entrance. *Application fee:* $55. *Required:* essay or personal statement, high school transcript, 1 letter of recommendation. *Required for some:* audition. *Recommended:* minimum 3.0 GPA, interview. *Application deadlines:* 3/1 (freshmen), 3/1 (transfers). *Early decision:* 11/1. *Notification:* continuous until 4/15 (freshmen), 12/15 (early decision), continuous (transfers).

Admissions Contact Ms. Paula J. Mitchell, Director of Admission, Ithaca College, 100 Job Hall, Ithaca, NY 14850-7020. *Phone:* 607-274-3124. *Toll-free phone:* 800-429-4274. *Fax:* 607-274-1900. *E-mail:* admission@ithaca.edu.

■ *See page 1778 for a narrative description.*

JEWISH THEOLOGICAL SEMINARY OF AMERICA

New York, New York

- **Independent Jewish** university, founded 1886
- **Calendar** semesters
- **Degrees** bachelor's, master's, doctoral, and first professional (double bachelor's degree with Barnard College, Columbia University, joint bachelor's degree with Columbia University)
- **Urban** 1-acre campus
- **Coed,** 191 undergraduate students, 85% full-time, 62% women, 38% men
- **Very difficult** entrance level, 53% of applicants were admitted

The Albert A. List College of Jewish Studies, the undergraduate school of the Jewish Theological Seminary, offers students a unique opportunity to pursue 2 bachelor's degrees simultaneously. Students earn a degree from List in one of a dozen areas of Jewish study and a second degree in the liberal arts field of their choice from Columbia University or Barnard College. This exciting 4-year program enables students to experience an intimate and supportive Jewish community as well as a diverse and dynamic campus life.

Undergraduates 162 full-time, 29 part-time. Students come from 23 states and territories, 2 other countries, 60% are from out of state, 77% live on campus. *Retention:* 92% of 2002 full-time freshmen returned.

Freshmen *Admission:* 135 applied, 72 admitted, 52 enrolled. *Average high school GPA:* 3.80.

Faculty *Total:* 115. *Student/faculty ratio:* 5:1.

Majors Ancient Near Eastern and biblical languages; biblical studies; cultural studies; Hebrew; history; Jewish/Judaic studies; literature; music; philosophy; religious education; religious studies; talmudic studies; women's studies.

Academic Programs *Special study options:* academic remediation for entering students, adult/continuing education programs, advanced placement credit, distance learning, double majors, freshman honors college, honors programs, internships, off-campus study, part-time degree program, services for LD students, student-designed majors, study abroad, summer session for credit.

Library Library of the Jewish Theological Seminary with 271,000 titles, 720 serial subscriptions, an OPAC, a Web page.

Computers on Campus 20 computers available on campus for general student use. A campuswide network can be accessed from student residence rooms and from off campus. Internet access available.

Student Life *Housing options:* coed. Campus housing is university owned and leased by the school. Freshman campus housing is guaranteed. *Activities and organizations:* drama/theater group, student-run newspaper, radio station, choral group. *Campus security:* 24-hour emergency response devices and patrols, late-night transport/escort service, controlled dormitory access. *Student services:* health clinic, personal/psychological counseling, women's center.

Athletics *Intramural sports:* basketball M, rock climbing M/W, softball M/W.

Standardized Tests *Required:* SAT I and SAT II or ACT (for admission), SAT II: Writing Test (for admission).

Costs (2003–04) *Tuition:* $10,100 full-time. *Required fees:* $500 full-time. *Room only:* $7270. Room and board charges vary according to housing facility. *Waivers:* senior citizens and employees or children of employees.

Financial Aid Of all full-time matriculated undergraduates who enrolled in 1999, 97 applied for aid, 91 were judged to have need, 81 had their need fully met. In 1999, 38 non-need-based awards were made. *Average percent of need met:* 75%. *Average non-need-based aid:* $2411. *Average indebtedness upon graduation:* $12,325. *Financial aid deadline:* 3/1.

Applying *Options:* early admission, early decision, deferred entrance. *Application fee:* $65. *Required:* essay or personal statement, high school transcript, 2 letters of recommendation. *Recommended:* minimum 3.0 GPA, interview. *Application deadlines:* 2/15 (freshmen), 5/1 (transfers). *Early decision:* 11/15 (for plan 1), 1/15 (for plan 2). *Notification:* continuous until 4/15 (freshmen), 12/15 (early decision plan 1), 2/15 (early decision plan 2), continuous until 6/1 (transfers).

Admissions Contact Director of Admissions, Jewish Theological Seminary of America, 3080 Broadway, New York, NY 10027. *Phone:* 212-678-8832. *Fax:* 212-280-6022. *E-mail:* lcadmissions@jtsa.edu.

■ *See page 1782 for a narrative description.*

JOHN JAY COLLEGE OF CRIMINAL JUSTICE OF THE CITY UNIVERSITY OF NEW YORK

New York, New York

- **State and locally supported** comprehensive, founded 1964, part of City University of New York System
- **Calendar** semesters
- **Degrees** certificates, diplomas, associate, bachelor's, master's, doctoral, and postbachelor's certificates
- **Urban** campus
- **Endowment** $221,000
- **Coed,** 11,515 undergraduate students, 100% full-time, 61% women, 39% men
- **Moderately difficult** entrance level, 73% of applicants were admitted

Undergraduates 11,515 full-time. Students come from 52 states and territories. *Retention:* 72% of 2002 full-time freshmen returned.

Freshmen *Admission:* 3,144 applied, 2,299 admitted.

Faculty *Total:* 585, 49% full-time. *Student/faculty ratio:* 20:1.

Majors Behavioral sciences; corrections; corrections and criminal justice related; criminal justice/law enforcement administration; criminal justice/police science; fire science; fire services administration; forensic psychology; forensic science and technology; information science/studies; legal studies; pre-law studies; public administration; safety/security technology; security and loss prevention.

Academic Programs *Special study options:* academic remediation for entering students, advanced placement credit, cooperative education, English as a second language, honors programs, internships, off-campus study, part-time degree program, services for LD students, summer session for credit. *ROTC:* Navy (c), Air Force (c).

Library Lloyd George Sealy Library with 310,000 titles, 1,325 serial subscriptions, an OPAC.

Computers on Campus 250 computers available on campus for general student use. A campuswide network can be accessed from off campus. Internet access, at least one staffed computer lab available.

Student Life *Housing:* college housing not available. *Activities and organizations:* drama/theater group, student-run newspaper, radio station, choral group, Organization of Black Students, Latino Diversity Club, Lex Review, Women's Awareness Club, Forensic Psychology Society. *Campus security:* 24-hour emergency response devices and patrols. *Student services:* health clinic, personal/psychological counseling, women's center, legal services.

Athletics Member NCAA. All Division III. *Intercollegiate sports:* basketball M/W, cross-country running M/W, tennis M/W, volleyball W. *Intramural sports:* basketball M/W, bowling M/W, football M/W, golf M/W, riflery M/W, swimming M/W, tennis M/W, track and field M/W, volleyball M/W, weight lifting M/W, wrestling M/W.

Standardized Tests *Required:* SAT I or ACT (for admission).

Costs (2003–04) *Tuition:* state resident $4000 full-time, $170 per credit part-time; nonresident $8640 full-time, $360 per credit part-time. Full-time tuition and fees vary according to course level and course load. Part-time tuition and fees

John Jay College of Criminal Justice of the City University of New York (continued)

vary according to course level and course load. *Required fees:* $259 full-time, $82 per term part-time. *Payment plan:* installment.

Financial Aid Of all full-time matriculated undergraduates who enrolled in 2002, 10,448 applied for aid, 10,448 were judged to have need. 339 Federal Work-Study jobs (averaging $1064). 190 state and other part-time jobs (averaging $10,000). In 2002, 14 non-need-based awards were made. *Average percent of need met:* 70%. *Average financial aid package:* $5100. *Average need-based loan:* $2400. *Average non-need-based aid:* $500. *Average indebtedness upon graduation:* $10,000.

Applying *Options:* early admission, deferred entrance. *Application fee:* $50. *Required:* high school transcript, minimum 1.7 GPA. *Application deadline:* 3/15 (freshmen), rolling (transfers). *Notification:* continuous (freshmen), continuous (transfers).

Admissions Contact Mr. Richard Saulnier, Acting Dean for Admissions and Registration, John Jay College of Criminal Justice of the City University of New York, 445 West 59th Street, Room 4205, New York, NY 10019. *Phone:* 212-237-8878. *Toll-free phone:* 877-JOHNJAY.

■ *See page 1788 for a narrative description.*

THE JUILLIARD SCHOOL
New York, New York

- **Independent** comprehensive, founded 1905
- **Calendar** semesters
- **Degrees** diplomas, bachelor's, master's, doctoral, post-master's, and postbachelor's certificates
- **Urban** campus
- **Endowment** $478.1 million
- **Coed,** 495 undergraduate students, 100% full-time, 52% women, 48% men
- **Most difficult** entrance level, 7% of applicants were admitted

Undergraduates 494 full-time, 1 part-time. Students come from 43 states and territories, 41 other countries, 85% are from out of state, 13% African American, 11% Asian American or Pacific Islander, 5% Hispanic American, 0.4% Native American, 24% international, 6% transferred in, 48% live on campus. *Retention:* 93% of 2002 full-time freshmen returned.

Freshmen *Admission:* 1,824 applied, 124 admitted, 97 enrolled.

Faculty *Total:* 272, 44% full-time. *Student/faculty ratio:* 3:1.

Majors Acting; dance; jazz/jazz studies; music; piano and organ; violin, viola, guitar and other stringed instruments; voice and opera; wind/percussion instruments.

Academic Programs *Special study options:* accelerated degree program, adult/continuing education programs, double majors, English as a second language, off-campus study, study abroad. *Unusual degree programs:* 3-2 music/liberal arts with Columbia University.

Library Lila Acheson Wallace Library with 80,793 titles, 220 serial subscriptions, 21,867 audiovisual materials, an OPAC, a Web page.

Computers on Campus 34 computers available on campus for general student use. A campuswide network can be accessed from off campus. Internet access, at least one staffed computer lab available.

Student Life *Housing:* on-campus residence required for freshman year. *Options:* coed, men-only, women-only. Campus housing is university owned. Freshman campus housing is guaranteed. *Activities and organizations:* drama/theater group, student-run newspaper, choral group, ArtREACH, Korean Campus Crusade for Christ, Juilliard Christian Fellowship, The Forum, Artists Inspired. *Campus security:* 24-hour emergency response devices and patrols, controlled dormitory access, electronically operated main building entrances. *Student services:* health clinic, personal/psychological counseling, legal services.

Costs (2003–04) *Comprehensive fee:* $30,290 includes full-time tuition ($21,250), mandatory fees ($600), and room and board ($8440). *Room and board:* Room and board charges vary according to board plan and housing facility. *Payment plan:* installment. *Waivers:* employees or children of employees.

Financial Aid Of all full-time matriculated undergraduates who enrolled in 2003, 465 applied for aid, 378 were judged to have need, 82 had their need fully met. 204 Federal Work-Study jobs (averaging $1936). 265 state and other part-time jobs (averaging $2147). In 2003, 57 non-need-based awards were made. *Average percent of need met:* 83%. *Average financial aid package:* $21,298. *Average need-based loan:* $5473. *Average need-based gift aid:* $15,760. *Average non-need-based aid:* $4698. *Average indebtedness upon graduation:* $21,447. *Financial aid deadline:* 3/1.

Applying *Application fee:* $100. *Required:* essay or personal statement, high school transcript, audition. *Application deadlines:* 12/1 (freshmen), 12/1 (transfers). *Notification:* 4/1 (freshmen), 4/1 (transfers).

Admissions Contact Ms. Lee Cioppa, Associate Dean for Admissions, The Juilliard School, 60 Lincoln Center Plaza, New York, NY 10023-6588. *Phone:* 212-799-5000 Ext. 223. *Fax:* 212-724-0263. *E-mail:* admissions@juilliard.edu.

KEHILATH YAKOV RABBINICAL SEMINARY
Brooklyn, New York

Admissions Contact Rabbi Zalman Gombo, Admissions Officer, Kehilath Yakov Rabbinical Seminary, 206 Wilson Street, Brooklyn, NY 11211-7207. *Phone:* 718-963-1212.

KEUKA COLLEGE
Keuka Park, New York

- **Independent** comprehensive, founded 1890, affiliated with American Baptist Churches in the U.S.A.
- **Calendar** 4-1-4
- **Degrees** bachelor's and master's
- **Rural** 173-acre campus with easy access to Rochester
- **Endowment** $5.1 million
- **Coed,** 1,148 undergraduate students, 93% full-time, 70% women, 30% men
- **Moderately difficult** entrance level, 82% of applicants were admitted

Undergraduates 1,071 full-time, 77 part-time. Students come from 15 states and territories, 8% are from out of state, 3% African American, 0.6% Asian American or Pacific Islander, 1% Hispanic American, 0.7% Native American, 6% transferred in, 68% live on campus. *Retention:* 70% of 2002 full-time freshmen returned.

Freshmen *Admission:* 777 applied, 639 admitted, 266 enrolled. *Average high school GPA:* 3.00. *Test scores:* SAT verbal scores over 500: 41%; SAT math scores over 500: 42%; ACT scores over 18: 60%; SAT verbal scores over 600: 7%; SAT math scores over 600: 6%; ACT scores over 24: 20%; SAT verbal scores over 700: 1%.

Faculty *Total:* 88, 59% full-time, 40% with terminal degrees. *Student/faculty ratio:* 16:1.

Majors Accounting; biochemistry; biology/biological sciences; biology teacher education; biomedical sciences; business administration and management; clinical laboratory science/medical technology; communication/speech communication and rhetoric; criminal justice/law enforcement administration; elementary education; English; English/language arts teacher education; environmental science; history; hotel/motel administration; interdisciplinary studies; liberal arts and sciences/liberal studies; marketing/marketing management; mathematics; mathematics teacher education; nursing (registered nurse training); occupational therapy; pre-dentistry studies; pre-law studies; pre-medical studies; pre-veterinary studies; psychology; secondary education; social sciences; social studies teacher education; social work; sociology; special education; special education (early childhood).

Academic Programs *Special study options:* academic remediation for entering students, accelerated degree program, adult/continuing education programs, advanced placement credit, cooperative education, double majors, independent study, internships, off-campus study, part-time degree program, services for LD students, student-designed majors, study abroad, summer session for credit.

Library Lightner Library with 83,882 titles, 3,005 audiovisual materials, an OPAC.

Computers on Campus 85 computers available on campus for general student use. A campuswide network can be accessed from student residence rooms and from off campus. Internet access, at least one staffed computer lab available.

Student Life *Housing:* on-campus residence required through senior year. *Options:* coed, women-only, cooperative. *Activities and organizations:* drama/theater group, student-run newspaper, radio station, choral group, Student Senate, Campus Activities Board, OTTERS (occupational therapy club), education club, BAKU. *Campus security:* 24-hour emergency response devices and patrols, late-night transport/escort service. *Student services:* health clinic, personal/psychological counseling.

Athletics Member NCAA. All Division III. *Intercollegiate sports:* baseball M, basketball M/W, cross-country running M/W, lacrosse M, soccer M/W, softball W, swimming W, volleyball W. *Intramural sports:* badminton M/W, basketball M/W, cheerleading M/W, crew M/W, lacrosse W, rock climbing M/W, skiing (cross-country) M/W, skiing (downhill) M/W, soccer M/W, softball M/W, table tennis M/W, tennis M/W, ultimate Frisbee M/W, volleyball M/W, water polo M/W.

Standardized Tests *Required:* SAT I or ACT (for admission).

Costs (2004–05) *Comprehensive fee:* $24,460 includes full-time tuition ($16,400), mandatory fees ($260), and room and board ($7800). Full-time tuition and fees vary according to program. Part-time tuition: $525 per credit hour. Part-time tuition and fees vary according to program. *College room only:* $3700.

Room and board charges vary according to board plan and housing facility. *Payment plan:* installment. *Waivers:* employees or children of employees.

Financial Aid Of all full-time matriculated undergraduates who enrolled in 2002, 1,009 applied for aid, 949 were judged to have need, 217 had their need fully met. 401 Federal Work-Study jobs (averaging $1365). 261 state and other part-time jobs (averaging $1083). In 2002, 67 non-need-based awards were made. *Average percent of need met:* 80%. *Average financial aid package:* $14,560. *Average need-based loan:* $5230. *Average need-based gift aid:* $9413. *Average non-need-based aid:* $11,505. *Average indebtedness upon graduation:* $18,645.

Applying *Options:* common application, electronic application, early admission, deferred entrance. *Application fee:* $30. *Required:* essay or personal statement, high school transcript, letters of recommendation. *Required for some:* interview. *Recommended:* minimum 2.75 GPA, interview. *Application deadline:* rolling (freshmen), rolling (transfers).

Admissions Contact Ms. Claudine Ninestine, Director of Admissions, Keuka College, Wagner House. *Phone:* 315-279-5413. *Toll-free phone:* 800-33-KEUKA. *Fax:* 315-279-5386. *E-mail:* admissions@mail.keuka.edu.

THE KING'S COLLEGE

New York, New York

- **Independent religious** 4-year
- **Calendar** semesters
- **Degrees** associate and bachelor's
- **Urban** campus
- **Coed,** 186 undergraduate students, 70% full-time, 54% women, 46% men
- 71% of applicants were admitted

Undergraduates 131 full-time, 55 part-time. Students come from 24 states and territories, 50% are from out of state, 10% African American, 9% Asian American or Pacific Islander, 28% Hispanic American, 2% Native American, 7% international, 40% live on campus. *Retention:* 62% of 2002 full-time freshmen returned.

Freshmen *Admission:* 112 applied, 79 admitted, 61 enrolled. *Average high school GPA:* 3.10. *Test scores:* SAT verbal scores over 500: 50%; SAT math scores over 500: 65%; ACT scores over 18: 100%; SAT verbal scores over 600: 25%; SAT math scores over 600: 20%; ACT scores over 24: 72%; SAT verbal scores over 700: 11%; ACT scores over 30: 11%.

Faculty *Total:* 29, 41% full-time, 55% with terminal degrees. *Student/faculty ratio:* 8:1.

Majors Business administration and management; education; elementary education; finance; marketing/marketing management.

Student Life *Housing options:* coed. Campus housing is leased by the school. *Activities and organizations:* drama/theater group, student-run newspaper, radio station, choral group, Student Newspaper, E-teams, Student Radio, Business Club, Freshman Small Groups. *Campus security:* 24-hour emergency response devices, late-night transport/escort service, controlled dormitory access.

Athletics *Intercollegiate sports:* cheerleading M/W. *Intramural sports:* rock climbing M/W, ultimate Frisbee M(c)/W(c), volleyball M/W, weight lifting M/W.

Standardized Tests *Required:* SAT I or ACT (for admission).

Costs (2004–05) *Tuition:* $16,000 full-time, $625 per credit part-time. Full-time tuition and fees vary according to course load and program. Part-time tuition and fees vary according to course load and program. *Required fees:* $950 full-time, $262 per term part-time. *Room only:* $7400. *Payment plan:* installment. *Waivers:* employees or children of employees.

Applying *Options:* early action. *Application fee:* $30. *Required:* high school transcript, interview. *Required for some:* essay or personal statement. *Recommended:* minimum 3.0 GPA, letters of recommendation. *Application deadlines:* 2/1 (freshmen), 2/1 (transfers). *Notification:* 3/7 (freshmen), 12/15 (early action), 3/7 (transfers).

Admissions Contact Mr. Brian T. Bell, Vice President of Enrollment Management, The King's College, Empire State Building, 350 Fifth Avenue, Lower Lobby, New York, NY 10118. *Phone:* 888-969-7200. *Toll-free phone:* 888-969-7200 Ext. 3610. *Fax:* 212-659-3611. *E-mail:* info@tkc.edu.

KOL YAAKOV TORAH CENTER

Monsey, New York

Admissions Contact Assistant Director of Admissions, Kol Yaakov Torah Center, 29 West Maple Avenue, Monsey, NY 10952-2954. *Phone:* 914-425-3871. *E-mail:* horizonss@aol.com.

LABORATORY INSTITUTE OF MERCHANDISING

New York, New York

- **Proprietary** 4-year, founded 1939
- **Calendar** semesters
- **Degrees** associate and bachelor's
- **Urban** campus
- **Coed, primarily women,** 493 undergraduate students, 99% full-time, 96% women, 4% men
- **Moderately difficult** entrance level, 66% of applicants were admitted

A private, Middle States–accredited 4-year college offering bachelor's and associate degrees in fashion merchandising, marketing, and visual merchandising. Distinctive educational opportunity through a combination of academics and industry work-study/co-ops. Prepares students for careers in fashion marketing, buying, product development, retail management, production, cosmetics, magazines, and more. Experience broadened by weekly field trips and guest lectures. Campus setting is in the finest area of New York City near business, fashion, and cultural centers. Summer sessions available for high school and college students.

Undergraduates 486 full-time, 7 part-time. Students come from 27 states and territories, 49% are from out of state, 11% African American, 6% Asian American or Pacific Islander, 18% Hispanic American, 0.2% Native American, 15% transferred in, 8% live on campus. *Retention:* 70% of 2002 full-time freshmen returned.

Freshmen *Admission:* 356 applied, 235 admitted, 129 enrolled. *Average high school GPA:* 3.34. *Test scores:* SAT verbal scores over 500: 34%; SAT math scores over 500: 26%; SAT verbal scores over 600: 4%; SAT math scores over 600: 2%; SAT math scores over 700: 2%.

Faculty *Total:* 55, 16% full-time, 15% with terminal degrees. *Student/faculty ratio:* 9:1.

Majors Fashion merchandising; marketing/marketing management.

Academic Programs *Special study options:* academic remediation for entering students, advanced placement credit, internships, part-time degree program, study abroad, summer session for credit.

Library LIM Library with 11,550 titles, 100 serial subscriptions, 462 audiovisual materials.

Computers on Campus 75 computers available on campus for general student use. A campuswide network can be accessed from off campus. Internet access, at least one staffed computer lab available.

Student Life *Housing options:* coed. Campus housing is leased by the school. *Activities and organizations:* student government, LIMlight Club (yearbook), fashion club, Latin Cultures Club, marketing club/SIFE. *Student services:* personal/psychological counseling.

Standardized Tests *Required:* SAT I or ACT (for admission).

Costs (2004–05) *Tuition:* $15,800 full-time, $495 per credit part-time. *Required fees:* $250 full-time, $100 per term part-time. *Room only:* $11,000. Room and board charges vary according to housing facility. *Payment plan:* installment. *Waivers:* employees or children of employees.

Financial Aid Of all full-time matriculated undergraduates who enrolled in 2002, 341 applied for aid, 306 were judged to have need, 83 had their need fully met. 20 Federal Work-Study jobs (averaging $2800). In 2002, 33 non-need-based awards were made. *Average percent of need met:* 87%. *Average financial aid package:* $11,500. *Average need-based loan:* $3500. *Average need-based gift aid:* $1000. *Average non-need-based aid:* $1000. *Average indebtedness upon graduation:* $14,500.

Applying *Options:* electronic application, deferred entrance. *Application fee:* $40. *Required:* essay or personal statement, high school transcript, 2 letters of recommendation, interview. *Recommended:* minimum 2.5 GPA. *Application deadline:* rolling (freshmen), rolling (transfers). *Notification:* continuous (freshmen), continuous (transfers).

Admissions Contact Ms. Karen Hamill Iglio, Director of Admissions, Laboratory Institute of Merchandising, 12 East 53rd Street, New York, NY 10022. *Phone:* 212-752-1530 Ext. 213. *Toll-free phone:* 800-677-1323. *Fax:* 212-317-8602. *E-mail:* admissions@limcollege.edu.

■ *See page 1830 for a narrative description.*

LEHMAN COLLEGE OF THE CITY UNIVERSITY OF NEW YORK

Bronx, New York

- **State and locally supported** comprehensive, founded 1931, part of City University of New York System
- **Calendar** semesters
- **Degrees** certificates, bachelor's, and master's
- **Urban** 37-acre campus
- **Coed,** 7,594 undergraduate students, 60% full-time, 72% women, 28% men
- **Moderately difficult** entrance level, 30% of applicants were admitted

Undergraduates 4,584 full-time, 3,010 part-time. Students come from 5 states and territories, 110 other countries, 0.1% are from out of state, 35% African

Lehman College of the City University of New York (continued)
American, 4% Asian American or Pacific Islander, 46% Hispanic American, 0.1% Native American, 3% international, 14% transferred in. *Retention:* 76% of 2002 full-time freshmen returned.

Freshmen *Admission:* 4,553 applied, 1,370 admitted, 819 enrolled. *Average high school GPA:* 2.7. *Test scores:* SAT verbal scores over 500: 19%; SAT math scores over 500: 20%; SAT verbal scores over 600: 3%; SAT math scores over 600: 4%; SAT verbal scores over 700: 1%; SAT math scores over 700: 1%.

Faculty *Total:* 709, 43% full-time, 50% with terminal degrees. *Student/faculty ratio:* 14:1.

Majors Accounting; African-American/Black studies; American studies; anthropology; art; art history, criticism and conservation; art teacher education; audiology and speech-language pathology; biochemistry; biology/biological sciences; business administration and management; business teacher education; chemistry; classics and languages, literatures and linguistics; communication and journalism related; computer and information sciences; computer management; computer science; creative writing; dance; dietetics; dramatic/theatre arts; economics; English; foods, nutrition, and wellness; French; geography; geology/earth science; health/health care administration; health teacher education; Hebrew; history; interdisciplinary studies; Italian; Jewish/Judaic studies; Latin; Latin American studies; linguistics; mass communication/media; mathematics; modern Greek; music; nursing (registered nurse training); philosophy; physics; political science and government; psychology; Russian; social work; sociology; Spanish; speech and rhetoric; speech-language pathology.

Academic Programs *Special study options:* adult/continuing education programs, advanced placement credit, cooperative education, distance learning, double majors, English as a second language, freshman honors college, honors programs, independent study, internships, off-campus study, part-time degree program, services for LD students, student-designed majors, study abroad, summer session for credit. *ROTC:* Army (c). *Unusual degree programs:* 3-2 mathematics.

Library Lehman College Library plus 1 other with 541,944 titles, 1,350 serial subscriptions, an OPAC, a Web page.

Computers on Campus 600 computers available on campus for general student use. Internet access, at least one staffed computer lab available.

Student Life *Housing:* college housing not available. *Activities and organizations:* drama/theater group, student-run newspaper, radio and television station, choral group, Club Mac, African Students Association, Dominican Student Association, The Sociology Club, Club Live. *Campus security:* 24-hour emergency response devices and patrols, student patrols, late-night transport/escort service. *Student services:* health clinic, personal/psychological counseling, women's center.

Athletics Member NCAA. All Division III. *Intercollegiate sports:* baseball M, basketball M/W, cross-country running M/W, soccer M, softball W, swimming M/W, tennis M/W, track and field M/W, volleyball M/W, water polo M, wrestling M. *Intramural sports:* baseball M/W, basketball M, racquetball M/W, soccer M, softball M/W, tennis M/W, volleyball M/W, wrestling M.

Standardized Tests *Required:* SAT I or ACT (for admission).

Costs (2003–04) *Tuition:* state resident $4000 full-time, $170 per credit part-time; nonresident $8640 full-time, $360 per credit part-time. Full-time tuition and fees vary according to course load and program. Part-time tuition and fees vary according to course load and program. *Required fees:* $270 full-time, $35 per term part-time. *Payment plan:* installment. *Waivers:* senior citizens.

Financial Aid Of all full-time matriculated undergraduates who enrolled in 2002, 3,939 applied for aid, 3,809 were judged to have need, 322 had their need fully met. 1,199 Federal Work-Study jobs (averaging $670). *Average percent of need met:* 70%. *Average financial aid package:* $7825. *Average need-based loan:* $3380. *Average need-based gift aid:* $6678. *Average indebtedness upon graduation:* $11,521.

Applying *Options:* deferred entrance. *Application fee:* $50. *Required:* high school transcript, minimum 3.0 GPA. *Required for some:* essay or personal statement, letters of recommendation, interview. *Application deadline:* rolling (freshmen), rolling (transfers). *Notification:* continuous (freshmen), continuous (transfers).

Admissions Contact Lehman College of the City University of New York, 250 Bedford Park Boulevard West, Bronx, NY 10468. *Phone:* 718-960-8706. *Toll-free phone:* 877-Lehman1. *Fax:* 718-960-8712. *E-mail:* enroll@lehman.cuny.edu.

■ *See page 1858 for a narrative description.*

LE MOYNE COLLEGE
Syracuse, New York

- **Independent Roman Catholic (Jesuit)** comprehensive, founded 1946
- **Calendar** semesters
- **Degrees** bachelor's, master's, and postbachelor's certificates
- **Suburban** 151-acre campus
- **Endowment** $30.3 million
- **Coed,** 2,691 undergraduate students, 84% full-time, 63% women, 37% men
- **Moderately difficult** entrance level, 72% of applicants were admitted

Le Moyne is a coeducational, residential college founded in the Jesuit tradition of academic excellence. Offering a comprehensive program rooted in the liberal arts and sciences, Le Moyne's shared mission of learning and services stresses education of the whole person. Strong academic programs, committed faculty members, a reassuring Jesuit presence, and career advisement/internship opportunities prepare Le Moyne students for leadership and service in their personal and professional lives. Le Moyne is consistently recognized for outstanding value in *U.S. News & World Report*'s annual college rankings.

Undergraduates 2,266 full-time, 425 part-time. Students come from 24 states and territories, 4 other countries, 7% are from out of state, 4% African American, 2% Asian American or Pacific Islander, 4% Hispanic American, 0.6% Native American, 0.9% international, 6% transferred in, 64% live on campus. *Retention:* 90% of 2002 full-time freshmen returned.

Freshmen *Admission:* 2,940 applied, 2,118 admitted, 503 enrolled. *Average high school GPA:* 3.37. *Test scores:* SAT verbal scores over 500: 79%; SAT math scores over 500: 84%; ACT scores over 18: 99%; SAT verbal scores over 600: 26%; SAT math scores over 600: 29%; ACT scores over 24: 46%; SAT verbal scores over 700: 3%; SAT math scores over 700: 3%; ACT scores over 30: 6%.

Faculty *Total:* 287, 53% full-time, 64% with terminal degrees. *Student/faculty ratio:* 13:1.

Majors Accounting; applied mathematics; biochemistry; biological and physical sciences; biology/biological sciences; biology teacher education; business administration and management; business teacher education; chemistry; chemistry teacher education; communication/speech communication and rhetoric; creative writing; criminology; dramatic/theatre arts; economics; elementary education; English; English/language arts teacher education; foreign language teacher education; French; French language teacher education; history; information science/studies; international relations and affairs; labor and industrial relations; management information systems; mathematics; mathematics teacher education; peace studies and conflict resolution; philosophy; physician assistant; physics; physics teacher education; political science and government; pre-dentistry studies; pre-law studies; pre-medical studies; pre-pharmacy studies; pre-veterinary studies; psychology; religious studies; science teacher education; secondary education; social studies teacher education; sociology; Spanish; Spanish language teacher education.

Academic Programs *Special study options:* academic remediation for entering students, accelerated degree program, adult/continuing education programs, advanced placement credit, double majors, honors programs, independent study, internships, off-campus study, part-time degree program, services for LD students, study abroad, summer session for credit. *ROTC:* Army (c), Air Force (c). *Unusual degree programs:* 3-2 engineering with Manhattan College, Clarkson University, University of Detroit Mercy; forestry with State University of New York College of Environmental Science and Forestry.

Library Noreen Reale Falcone Library with 159,159 titles, 1,448 serial subscriptions, 10,129 audiovisual materials, an OPAC, a Web page.

Computers on Campus 325 computers available on campus for general student use. A campuswide network can be accessed from student residence rooms and from off campus that provide access to ECHO (campus-wide portal). Internet access, online (class) registration, at least one staffed computer lab available.

Student Life *Housing:* on-campus residence required through senior year. *Options:* coed, men-only, women-only, disabled students. Campus housing is university owned. Freshman campus housing is guaranteed. *Activities and organizations:* drama/theater group, student-run newspaper, radio station, choral group, Student Programming Board, outing club, performing arts groups, Student Dancers, New Student Orientation Committee. *Campus security:* 24-hour emergency response devices and patrols, late-night transport/escort service, controlled dormitory access, self-defense education, lighted pathways, closed-circuit security cameras. *Student services:* health clinic, personal/psychological counseling.

Athletics Member NCAA. All Division II except baseball (Division I), lacrosse (Division I). *Intercollegiate sports:* baseball M(s), basketball M(s)/W(s), cross-country running M(s)/W(s), golf M(s), lacrosse M(s)/W(s), soccer M(s)/W(s), softball W(s), swimming M/W, tennis M(s)/W(s), volleyball W(s). *Intramural sports:* basketball M/W, cheerleading M(c)/W(c), cross-country running M/W, field hockey W(c), football M, ice hockey M(c), racquetball M/W, rugby M(c)/W(c), soccer M/W, softball M/W, volleyball M/W.

Standardized Tests *Required:* SAT I or ACT (for admission).

Costs (2003–04) *Comprehensive fee:* $26,400 includes full-time tuition ($18,440), mandatory fees ($510), and room and board ($7450). Part-time tuition: $392 per credit hour. Part-time tuition and fees vary according to class time. *College room only:* $4710. Room and board charges vary according to board plan and housing facility. *Payment plans:* installment, deferred payment. *Waivers:* employees or children of employees.

Financial Aid Of all full-time matriculated undergraduates who enrolled in 2002, 1,984 applied for aid, 1,814 were judged to have need, 729 had their need fully met. 336 Federal Work-Study jobs (averaging $1067). In 2002, 205 non-need-based awards were made. *Average percent of need met:* 86%. *Average financial aid package:* $16,702. *Average need-based loan:* $4203. *Average need-based gift aid:* $12,999. *Average non-need-based aid:* $7518. *Average indebtedness upon graduation:* $19,490.

Applying *Options:* common application, electronic application, early admission, early decision, deferred entrance. *Application fee:* $35. *Required:* essay or personal statement, high school transcript, 2 letters of recommendation. *Recommended:* interview. *Application deadlines:* 2/1 (freshmen), 6/1 (transfers). *Early decision:* 12/1. *Notification:* continuous until 5/1 (freshmen), 12/15 (early decision), continuous (transfers).

Admissions Contact Mr. Dennis J. Nicholson, Director of Admission, Le Moyne College, 1419 Salt Spring Road, Syracuse, NY 13214-1399. *Phone:* 315-445-4300. *Toll-free phone:* 800-333-4733. *Fax:* 315-445-4711. *E-mail:* admission@lemoyne.edu.

■ *See page 1860 for a narrative description.*

LONG ISLAND UNIVERSITY, BRENTWOOD CAMPUS

Brentwood, New York

- **Independent** upper-level, founded 1959, part of Long Island University
- **Calendar** semesters
- **Degrees** certificates, bachelor's, master's, and post-master's certificates
- **Suburban** 172-acre campus
- **Coed,** 62 undergraduate students, 27% full-time, 68% women, 32% men

Undergraduates 17 full-time, 45 part-time. Students come from 1 other state, 1% are from out of state, 3% African American, 16% Hispanic American, 29% transferred in.

Faculty *Total:* 110, 18% full-time, 86% with terminal degrees. *Student/faculty ratio:* 7:1.

Majors Accounting; business administration and management; criminal justice/safety; finance; marketing/marketing management.

Academic Programs *Special study options:* advanced placement credit, honors programs, independent study, internships, part-time degree program, services for LD students, summer session for credit.

Library Brentwood Campus Library with 55,000 titles, 285 serial subscriptions, 12 audiovisual materials, a Web page.

Computers on Campus 42 computers available on campus for general student use. A campuswide network can be accessed. Internet access, at least one staffed computer lab available. Computer purchase or lease plan available.

Student Life *Housing:* college housing not available. *Campus security:* evening security guard. *Student services:* health clinic, personal/psychological counseling.

Costs (2003–04) *Tuition:* $19,510 full-time, $609 per credit part-time. Part-time tuition and fees vary according to course load. *Required fees:* $850 full-time, $180 per term part-time. *Payment plans:* installment, deferred payment. *Waivers:* senior citizens.

Applying *Application deadline:* 9/14 (transfers).

Admissions Contact Mr. John P. Metcalfe, Director of Admissions, Long Island University, Brentwood Campus, 100 Second Avenue, Brentwood, NY 11717. *Phone:* 631-273-5112 Ext. 26. *E-mail:* information@brentwood.liu.edu.

LONG ISLAND UNIVERSITY, BROOKLYN CAMPUS

Brooklyn, New York

- **Independent** university, founded 1926, part of Long Island University
- **Calendar** semesters
- **Degrees** certificates, associate, bachelor's, master's, doctoral, first professional, post-master's, postbachelor's, and first professional certificates
- **Urban** 10-acre campus
- **Endowment** $40.0 million
- **Coed,** 5,380 undergraduate students, 82% full-time, 73% women, 27% men
- **Minimally difficult** entrance level, 69% of applicants were admitted

Undergraduates 4,397 full-time, 983 part-time. Students come from 42 states and territories, 9% are from out of state, 44% African American, 12% Asian American or Pacific Islander, 15% Hispanic American, 0.3% Native American, 2% international, 11% live on campus. *Retention:* 55% of 2002 full-time freshmen returned.

Freshmen *Admission:* 3,604 applied, 2,479 admitted, 967 enrolled. *Average high school GPA:* 3.00. *Test scores:* SAT verbal scores over 500: 67%; SAT math scores over 500: 73%; SAT verbal scores over 600: 26%; SAT math scores over 600: 35%; SAT verbal scores over 700: 4%; SAT math scores over 700: 13%.

Faculty *Total:* 965, 27% full-time. *Student/faculty ratio:* 17:1.

Majors Accounting; art; art teacher education; athletic training; bilingual and multilingual education; biological and physical sciences; biology/biological sciences; business administration and management; chemistry; chemistry teacher education; clinical laboratory science/medical technology; communication disorders sciences and services related; communication/speech communication and rhetoric; community health services counseling; computer and information sciences; computer science; computer teacher education; cytotechnology; dance; data processing and data processing technology; economics; education; education related; elementary education; English; English/language arts teacher education; finance; fine arts related; foreign languages and literatures; health professions related; health science; history; humanities; interdisciplinary studies; jazz/jazz studies; journalism; kinesiology and exercise science; liberal arts and sciences/liberal studies; mathematics; mathematics teacher education; modern languages; multi-/interdisciplinary studies related; music performance; music related; music teacher education; music theory and composition; nuclear medical technology; nursing (registered nurse training); nursing related; occupational therapy; operations research; pharmacy; pharmacy, pharmaceutical sciences, and administration related; philosophy; physical education teaching and coaching; physical sciences; physical therapy; physician assistant; physics; political science and government; pre-medical studies; psychology; respiratory care therapy; sales, distribution and marketing; secondary education; social sciences; social studies teacher education; social work; sociology; Spanish language teacher education; special education; special education (speech or language impaired); speech and rhetoric.

Academic Programs *Special study options:* academic remediation for entering students, adult/continuing education programs, advanced placement credit, cooperative education, double majors, English as a second language, honors programs, internships, part-time degree program, services for LD students, student-designed majors, summer session for credit. *Unusual degree programs:* 3-2 physical therapy, pharmacy.

Library Salena Library with 149,455 titles, 1,667 serial subscriptions, 23,794 audiovisual materials, an OPAC.

Computers on Campus 345 computers available on campus for general student use. A campuswide network can be accessed from student residence rooms and from off campus. At least one staffed computer lab available.

Student Life *Housing options:* coed, disabled students. Campus housing is university owned. Freshman applicants given priority for college housing. *Activities and organizations:* student-run newspaper, radio and television station, Caribbean Students Movement, Hillel, Muslim Student Organization, Student Government Association, WLIU-BK Radio (campus radio station), national fraternities, national sororities. *Campus security:* 24-hour emergency response devices and patrols. *Student services:* health clinic, personal/psychological counseling.

Athletics Member NCAA. All Division I. *Intercollegiate sports:* baseball M(s), basketball M(s)/W(s), cross-country running M(s)/W(s), golf M(s)/W(s), lacrosse W(s), soccer M(s)/W(s), softball W(s), tennis W(s), track and field M(s)/W(s), volleyball W(s). *Intramural sports:* baseball M, basketball M, cheerleading W, softball W, tennis M/W.

Standardized Tests *Required for some:* SAT I or ACT (for admission).

Costs (2003–04) *Comprehensive fee:* $23,602 includes full-time tuition ($17,052), mandatory fees ($70), and room and board ($6480). Part-time tuition: $609 per credit. Part-time tuition and fees vary according to course load. *Required fees:* $214 per term part-time. *College room only:* $4200. Room and board charges vary according to board plan. *Payment plan:* deferred payment. *Waivers:* employees or children of employees.

Financial Aid Of all full-time matriculated undergraduates who enrolled in 2003, 3,781 applied for aid, 3,668 were judged to have need, 1,921 had their need fully met. 355 Federal Work-Study jobs (averaging $4143). In 2003, 106 non-need-based awards were made. *Average percent of need met:* 48%. *Average financial aid package:* $13,159. *Average need-based loan:* $4105. *Average need-based gift aid:* $8213. *Average non-need-based aid:* $14,105. *Average indebtedness upon graduation:* $20,921.

Applying *Options:* common application, electronic application, deferred entrance. *Application fee:* $30. *Required:* high school transcript, minimum 2.0 GPA. *Required for some:* minimum 3.0 GPA, 2 letters of recommendation, interview. *Recommended:* essay or personal statement, minimum 2.5 GPA. *Application deadline:* rolling (freshmen), rolling (transfers).

Admissions Contact Mr. Richard Sunday, Interim Dean of Admissions, Long Island University, Brooklyn Campus, 1 University Plaza, Brooklyn, NY 11201. *Phone:* 718-488-1011. *Toll-free phone:* 800-LIU-PLAN. *Fax:* 718-797-2399. *E-mail:* admissions@brooklyn.liu.edu.

■ *See page 1880 for a narrative description.*

LONG ISLAND UNIVERSITY, C.W. POST CAMPUS

Brookville, New York

- **Independent** comprehensive, founded 1954, part of Long Island University
- **Calendar** semesters
- **Degrees** certificates, bachelor's, master's, doctoral, post-master's, and postbachelor's certificates
- **Suburban** 308-acre campus with easy access to New York City
- **Endowment** $40.0 million
- **Coed,** 4,716 undergraduate students, 85% full-time, 61% women, 39% men
- **Moderately difficult** entrance level, 77% of applicants were admitted

Undergraduates 3,991 full-time, 725 part-time. Students come from 30 states and territories, 8% are from out of state, 4% African American, 1% Asian American or Pacific Islander, 4% Hispanic American, 0.2% Native American, 2% international, 13% transferred in, 34% live on campus. *Retention:* 69% of 2002 full-time freshmen returned.

Freshmen *Admission:* 4,418 applied, 3,382 admitted, 806 enrolled. *Average high school GPA:* 3.36. *Test scores:* SAT verbal scores over 500: 48%; SAT math scores over 500: 48%; SAT verbal scores over 600: 11%; SAT math scores over 600: 12%; SAT verbal scores over 700: 1%; SAT math scores over 700: 1%.

Faculty *Total:* 1,186, 27% full-time. *Student/faculty ratio:* 14:1.

Majors Accounting; acting; American studies; applied mathematics; art history, criticism and conservation; arts management; art teacher education; art therapy; audiology and speech-language pathology; biology/biological sciences; biology teacher education; broadcast journalism; business administration and management; chemistry; chemistry teacher education; cinematography and film/video production; clinical laboratory science/medical technology; clinical/medical laboratory technology; communication/speech communication and rhetoric; computer and information sciences; computer and information sciences and support services related; computer science; criminal justice/law enforcement administration; criminal justice/safety; cytotechnology; dance; dramatic/theatre arts; economics; education; elementary education; English; English/language arts teacher education; environmental science; environmental studies; finance; fine arts related; fine/studio arts; foreign languages and literatures; foreign language teacher education; forensic science and technology; French; French language teacher education; general studies; geography; geology/earth science; German; health information/medical records administration; health professions related; health teacher education; history; hospital and health care facilities administration; information science/studies; information technology; interdisciplinary studies; intermedia/multimedia; international business/trade/commerce; international relations and affairs; Italian; journalism; kindergarten/preschool education; liberal arts and sciences/liberal studies; management information systems; marketing/marketing management; mathematics; mathematics and computer science; mathematics teacher education; medical radiologic technology; molecular biology; multi-/interdisciplinary studies related; music; music performance; music teacher education; nuclear medical technology; nursing (registered nurse training); nursing related; nursing science; philosophy; photography; physical education teaching and coaching; physics; political science and government; pre-medical studies; pre-pharmacy studies; psychology; public administration; public relations/image management; secondary education; social studies teacher education; social work; sociology; Spanish; Spanish language teacher education; special education (speech or language impaired); visual and performing arts; visual and performing arts related; voice and opera.

Academic Programs *Special study options:* academic remediation for entering students, accelerated degree program, adult/continuing education programs, advanced placement credit, cooperative education, double majors, English as a second language, honors programs, independent study, internships, off-campus study, part-time degree program, services for LD students, student-designed majors, study abroad, summer session for credit. *ROTC:* Army (c), Air Force (c). *Unusual degree programs:* 3-2 engineering with Polytechnic University, Arizona State University, Stevens Institute of Technology; respiratory therapy and pharmacy with Long Island University, Brooklyn Campus.

Library B. Davis Schwartz Memorial Library with 859,212 titles, 11,446 serial subscriptions, 34,530 audiovisual materials, an OPAC, a Web page.

Computers on Campus 357 computers available on campus for general student use. A campuswide network can be accessed from student residence rooms and from off campus. Internet access, at least one staffed computer lab available.

Student Life *Housing options:* coed. Campus housing is university owned. Freshman campus housing is guaranteed. *Activities and organizations:* drama/theater group, student-run newspaper, radio and television station, choral group, Student Government Association, Association for Campus Programming, African People's Organization, Resident Student Association, Post TV and Newman, national fraternities, national sororities. *Campus security:* 24-hour emergency response devices and patrols, late-night transport/escort service, controlled dormitory access. *Student services:* health clinic, personal/psychological counseling.

Athletics Member NCAA. All Division II. *Intercollegiate sports:* baseball M(s), basketball M(s)/W(s), crew M(c)/W(c), cross-country running M(s)/W(s), equestrian sports M(c)/W(c), field hockey W(s), football M, lacrosse M(s)/W(s), soccer M(s)/W(s), softball W(s), swimming W(s), tennis W(s), track and field M(s)/W(s), volleyball W(s).

Standardized Tests *Required:* SAT I or ACT (for admission).

Costs (2003–04) *Comprehensive fee:* $28,220 includes full-time tuition ($19,510), mandatory fees ($980), and room and board ($7730). Part-time tuition: $609 per credit. Part-time tuition and fees vary according to course load. *College room only:* $5150. Room and board charges vary according to board plan. *Payment plan:* deferred payment. *Waivers:* employees or children of employees.

Financial Aid Of all full-time matriculated undergraduates who enrolled in 2002, 3,390 applied for aid, 2,881 were judged to have need, 430 had their need fully met. 823 Federal Work-Study jobs (averaging $1620). In 2002, 960 non-need-based awards were made. *Average percent of need met:* 75%. *Average financial aid package:* $8500. *Average need-based loan:* $4000. *Average need-based gift aid:* $4500. *Average non-need-based aid:* $7000. *Average indebtedness upon graduation:* $12,500. *Financial aid deadline:* 3/1.

Applying *Options:* common application, electronic application, deferred entrance. *Application fee:* $30. *Required:* high school transcript, minimum 2.5 GPA. *Recommended:* essay or personal statement. *Application deadline:* rolling (freshmen). *Notification:* continuous (freshmen), continuous (transfers).

Admissions Contact Office of Admissions/Enrollment Services, Long Island University, C.W. Post Campus, 720 Northern Boulevard, Brookville, NY 11548-1300. *Phone:* 516-299-2900. *Toll-free phone:* 800-LIU-PLAN. *Fax:* 516-299-2137. *E-mail:* enroll@cwpost.liu.edu.

■ *See page 1882 for a narrative description.*

LONG ISLAND UNIVERSITY, FRIENDS WORLD PROGRAM

Southampton, New York

- **Independent** 4-year, founded 1965, part of Long Island University
- **Calendar** semesters
- **Degree** bachelor's
- **Rural** 110-acre campus
- **Coed,** 160 undergraduate students, 96% full-time, 68% women, 33% men
- **Noncompetitive** entrance level, 92% of applicants were admitted

Friends World is committed to a uniquely international education with an emphasis on deeper understanding of current world issues. Dedicated faculty members serve at all international centers and programs, assisting students with individual study programs and core curriculum. In 1991, the academic programs of Friends World College were affiliated with Long Island University and became Friends World Program. See Long Island University, Friends World Program, in the In-Depth Descriptions section of this guide.

Undergraduates 153 full-time, 7 part-time. Students come from 29 states and territories, 5 other countries, 80% are from out of state, 3% African American, 1% Asian American or Pacific Islander, 3% Hispanic American, 2% Native American, 1% international, 16% transferred in, 20% live on campus. *Retention:* 66% of 2002 full-time freshmen returned.

Freshmen *Admission:* 52 applied, 48 admitted, 28 enrolled. *Average high school GPA:* 3.25.

Faculty *Total:* 29, 62% full-time, 100% with terminal degrees. *Student/faculty ratio:* 10:1.

Majors Interdisciplinary studies; liberal arts and sciences/liberal studies; multi-/interdisciplinary studies related.

Academic Programs *Special study options:* advanced placement credit, external degree program, independent study, internships, off-campus study, student-designed majors, study abroad.

Library Southampton College with 115,380 titles, 665 serial subscriptions, 886 audiovisual materials.

Computers on Campus 175 computers available on campus for general student use. A campuswide network can be accessed from student residence rooms and from off campus that provide access to online center registration. Internet access, at least one staffed computer lab available. Computer purchase or lease plan available.

Student Life *Housing:* on-campus residence required through sophomore year. *Options:* coed. Campus housing is provided by a third party. Freshman campus housing is guaranteed. *Activities and organizations:* drama/theater group, student-run newspaper, radio station, Activist Club, P.E.A.C.E., LaFuenza Latina, Caribbean Student Association, Women's Issues Collective. *Student services:* health clinic, personal/psychological counseling.

Costs (2003–04) *Comprehensive fee:* $32,400 includes full-time tuition ($20,400), mandatory fees ($6000), and room and board ($6000). Full-time tuition and fees vary according to location. Part-time tuition: $609 per credit. Part-time tuition and fees vary according to course load. *Room and board:* Room and board charges vary according to board plan, housing facility, and location. *Payment plans:* installment, deferred payment. *Waivers:* senior citizens and employees or children of employees.
Applying *Options:* electronic application, early admission, deferred entrance. *Application fee:* $30. *Required:* essay or personal statement, high school transcript, interview. *Recommended:* minimum 3.0 GPA. *Application deadline:* rolling (freshmen), rolling (transfers). *Notification:* continuous (freshmen), continuous (transfers).
Admissions Contact Long Island University, Friends World Program, Friends World Program, 239 Montauk Highway, Southampton, NY 11968. *Phone:* 631-287-8465. *Toll-free phone:* 631-287-8474 (in-state); 800-287-8093 (out-of-state). *Fax:* 631-287-8093. *E-mail:* fw@liu.edu.

■ *See page 1884 for a narrative description.*

LONG ISLAND UNIVERSITY, SOUTHAMPTON COLLEGE
Southampton, New York

- **Independent** comprehensive, founded 1963, part of Long Island University
- **Calendar** semesters
- **Degrees** bachelor's, master's, and postbachelor's certificates
- **Small-town** 110-acre campus
- **Endowment** $40.0 million
- **Coed,** 1,196 undergraduate students, 89% full-time, 67% women, 33% men
- **Moderately difficult** entrance level, 63% of applicants were admitted

Undergraduates 1,070 full-time, 126 part-time. Students come from 46 states and territories, 35% are from out of state, 5% African American, 1% Asian American or Pacific Islander, 5% Hispanic American, 0.8% Native American, 5% international, 8% transferred in, 37% live on campus. *Retention:* 68% of 2002 full-time freshmen returned.
Freshmen *Admission:* 1,354 applied, 856 admitted, 224 enrolled. *Average high school GPA:* 3.20. *Test scores:* SAT verbal scores over 500: 64%; SAT math scores over 500: 60%; ACT scores over 18: 100%; SAT verbal scores over 600: 21%; SAT math scores over 600: 21%; ACT scores over 24: 63%; SAT verbal scores over 700: 2%; SAT math scores over 700: 2%; ACT scores over 30: 21%.
Faculty *Total:* 240, 28% full-time. *Student/faculty ratio:* 18:1.
Majors Accounting; art teacher education; biology/biological sciences; biology teacher education; business administration and management; chemistry; communication/speech communication and rhetoric; elementary education; English; English/language arts teacher education; environmental science; environmental studies; fine/studio arts; liberal arts and sciences/liberal studies; marine biology and biological oceanography; mass communication/media; psychology; psychology related; reading teacher education; social sciences related; social studies teacher education; sociology.
Academic Programs *Special study options:* academic remediation for entering students, accelerated degree program, adult/continuing education programs, advanced placement credit, cooperative education, distance learning, double majors, English as a second language, external degree program, honors programs, independent study, internships, off-campus study, part-time degree program, student-designed majors, study abroad, summer session for credit.
Library Southampton Campus Library plus 1 other with 147,496 titles, 678 serial subscriptions, 903 audiovisual materials, an OPAC, a Web page.
Computers on Campus 150 computers available on campus for general student use. A campuswide network can be accessed from student residence rooms and from off campus. Internet access, at least one staffed computer lab available. Computer purchase or lease plan available.
Student Life *Housing:* on-campus residence required for freshman year. *Options:* coed, women-only. Campus housing is university owned. Freshman campus housing is guaranteed. *Activities and organizations:* drama/theater group, student-run newspaper, radio station, choral group, Program Board, Marine Mammals Society, Film Committee, Campus Storm, Southampton Player. *Campus security:* 24-hour patrols, controlled dormitory access. *Student services:* health clinic, personal/psychological counseling.
Athletics Member NCAA. All Division II. *Intercollegiate sports:* basketball M(s)/W(s), cross-country running W(s), lacrosse M(s), soccer M(s)/W(s), softball W(s), tennis M(s), volleyball M(s)/W(s). *Intramural sports:* basketball M/W, sailing M(c)/W(c), soccer M/W, softball M/W, tennis M/W, ultimate Frisbee M/W, volleyball M/W, weight lifting M/W.
Standardized Tests *Required:* SAT I or ACT (for admission).
Costs (2003–04) *Comprehensive fee:* $29,370 includes full-time tuition ($19,510), mandatory fees ($1050), and room and board ($8810). Part-time tuition: $609 per credit. Part-time tuition and fees vary according to course load. *College room only:* $5030. Room and board charges vary according to board plan and housing facility. *Payment plan:* deferred payment. *Waivers:* employees or children of employees.
Financial Aid Of all full-time matriculated undergraduates who enrolled in 2002, 995 applied for aid, 917 were judged to have need, 248 had their need fully met. 600 Federal Work-Study jobs (averaging $3000). *Average percent of need met:* 74%. *Average financial aid package:* $22,800. *Average need-based loan:* $8770. *Average need-based gift aid:* $13,750. *Average non-need-based aid:* $9000. *Average indebtedness upon graduation:* $19,800.
Applying *Options:* common application, electronic application, early action, deferred entrance. *Application fee:* $30. *Required:* essay or personal statement, high school transcript, minimum 2.0 GPA, 1 letter of recommendation. *Required for some:* 2 letters of recommendation, interview. *Application deadline:* rolling (freshmen). *Notification:* continuous (freshmen), continuous (transfers).
Admissions Contact Ms. Rory Shaffer-Walsh, Director of Admissions, Long Island University, Southampton College, 239 Montauk Highway, Southampton, NY 11968-9822. *Phone:* 631-287-8000. *Toll-free phone:* 800-LIU PLAN Ext. 2. *Fax:* 631-287-8130. *E-mail:* admissions@southampton.liu.edu.

■ *See page 1886 for a narrative description.*

MACHZIKEI HADATH RABBINICAL COLLEGE
Brooklyn, New York

- **Independent Jewish** comprehensive, founded 1956
- **Calendar** semesters
- **Degrees** bachelor's and master's
- **Men only**
- **Moderately difficult** entrance level

Costs (2003–04) *Comprehensive fee:* $7300 includes full-time tuition ($5500) and room and board ($1800). *Payment plans:* installment, deferred payment.
Applying *Required:* interview.
Admissions Contact Rabbi Abraham M. Lezerowitz, Director of Admissions, Machzikei Hadath Rabbinical College, 5407 Sixteenth Avenue, Brooklyn, NY 11204-1805. *Phone:* 718-854-8777.

MANHATTAN COLLEGE
Riverdale, New York

- **Independent** comprehensive, founded 1853, affiliated with Roman Catholic Church
- **Calendar** semesters
- **Degrees** bachelor's, master's, and post-master's certificates
- **Urban** 31-acre campus with easy access to New York City
- **Endowment** $27.4 million
- **Coed,** 2,879 undergraduate students, 94% full-time, 50% women, 50% men
- **Moderately difficult** entrance level, 53% of applicants were admitted

Radiation therapy is commonly used in hospitals to help cancer patients and ease pain in others. The program at Manhattan College includes 24 credits of clinical internship courses, equal to about 275 days in a Radiation Therapy Department in 1 of 8 hospitals, such as New York University Hospital, St. Vincent's Hospital, and Westchester Medical Center.

Undergraduates 2,697 full-time, 182 part-time. Students come from 42 states and territories, 27 other countries, 28% are from out of state, 5% African American, 5% Asian American or Pacific Islander, 10% Hispanic American, 0.1% Native American, 1% international, 5% transferred in, 54% live on campus. *Retention:* 83% of 2002 full-time freshmen returned.
Freshmen *Admission:* 4,414 applied, 2,332 admitted, 651 enrolled. *Average high school GPA:* 3.35. *Test scores:* SAT verbal scores over 500: 73%; SAT math scores over 500: 79%; SAT verbal scores over 600: 18%; SAT math scores over 600: 27%; SAT verbal scores over 700: 2%; SAT math scores over 700: 3%.
Faculty *Total:* 282, 59% full-time, 68% with terminal degrees. *Student/faculty ratio:* 14:1.
Majors Accounting; biochemistry; biology/biological sciences; biotechnology; chemical engineering; chemistry; civil engineering; classics and languages, literatures and linguistics; computer engineering; computer science; economics; education; education (multiple levels); electrical, electronics and communications engineering; elementary education; engineering; English; environmental/environmental health engineering; finance; French; history; international relations and affairs; liberal arts and sciences/liberal studies; management science; marketing/marketing management; mathematics; mechanical engineering; middle school education; nuclear medical technology; organizational behavior; philosophy; physical education teaching and coaching; physics; political science and

Manhattan College (continued)
government; psychology; radiologic technology/science; religious studies; sociology; Spanish; special education; urban studies/affairs.

Academic Programs *Special study options:* academic remediation for entering students, accelerated degree program, adult/continuing education programs, advanced placement credit, cooperative education, double majors, English as a second language, honors programs, independent study, internships, off-campus study, part-time degree program, services for LD students, study abroad, summer session for credit. *ROTC:* Army (c), Air Force (b). *Unusual degree programs:* 3-2 education.

Library O'Malley Library plus 1 other with 211,376 titles, 1,190 serial subscriptions, 1,122 audiovisual materials, an OPAC, a Web page.

Computers on Campus 375 computers available on campus for general student use. A campuswide network can be accessed from student residence rooms and from off campus. Internet access, online (class) registration, at least one staffed computer lab available.

Student Life *Housing options:* coed. Campus housing is university owned and leased by the school. *Activities and organizations:* drama/theater group, student-run newspaper, radio station, choral group, marching band, Minority Student Union, student government, student radio station, Manhattan College Singers, Resident/Commuter Student Association, national fraternities, national sororities. *Campus security:* 24-hour patrols, late-night transport/escort service, controlled dormitory access. *Student services:* health clinic, personal/psychological counseling.

Athletics Member NCAA. All Division I. *Intercollegiate sports:* baseball M(s), basketball M(s)/W(s), cheerleading M(s)/W(s), crew M(c)/W(c), cross-country running M(s)/W(s), golf M(s), lacrosse M(s)/W(s), rugby M(c), soccer M(s)/W(s), softball W(s), swimming W(s), tennis M(s)/W(s), track and field M(s)/W(s), volleyball M/W(s). *Intramural sports:* baseball M, basketball M/W, cross-country running M/W, equestrian sports M/W, soccer M/W, softball M/W, swimming W, track and field M/W, volleyball M/W.

Standardized Tests *Required:* SAT I or ACT (for admission).

Costs (2003–04) *Comprehensive fee:* $27,400 includes full-time tuition ($17,800), mandatory fees ($1500), and room and board ($8100). Full-time tuition and fees vary according to program. Part-time tuition: $500 per credit. *Required fees:* $125 per term part-time. *Room and board:* Room and board charges vary according to board plan. *Payment plan:* installment. *Waivers:* employees or children of employees.

Financial Aid Of all full-time matriculated undergraduates who enrolled in 2002, 2,121 applied for aid, 1,858 were judged to have need, 27 had their need fully met. 520 Federal Work-Study jobs (averaging $1240). 249 state and other part-time jobs (averaging $1506). In 2002, 325 non-need-based awards were made. *Average percent of need met:* 70%. *Average financial aid package:* $14,185. *Average need-based loan:* $3582. *Average need-based gift aid:* $5395. *Average non-need-based aid:* $7184. *Average indebtedness upon graduation:* $15,715.

Applying *Options:* common application, early admission, early decision, deferred entrance. *Application fee:* $40. *Required:* essay or personal statement, high school transcript, minimum 2.5 GPA, 1 letter of recommendation. *Required for some:* interview. *Recommended:* minimum 3.0 GPA, interview. *Application deadlines:* 3/1 (freshmen), 7/1 (transfers). *Early decision:* 11/15. *Notification:* continuous until 8/15 (freshmen), 12/1 (early decision), continuous until 8/15 (transfers).

Admissions Contact Mr. William J. Bisset Jr., Assistant Vice President for Enrollment Management, Manhattan College, 4513 Manhattan College Parkway, Riverdale, NY 10471. *Phone:* 718-862-7200. *Toll-free phone:* 800-622-9235. *Fax:* 718-862-8019. *E-mail:* admit@manhattan.edu.

■ *See page 1916 for a narrative description.*

MANHATTAN SCHOOL OF MUSIC
New York, New York

- **Independent** comprehensive, founded 1917
- **Calendar** semesters
- **Degrees** diplomas, bachelor's, master's, doctoral, post-master's, and postbachelor's certificates
- **Urban** 1-acre campus
- **Endowment** $12.1 million
- **Coed,** 400 undergraduate students, 93% full-time, 46% women, 54% men
- **Very difficult** entrance level, 32% of applicants were admitted

Undergraduates 370 full-time, 30 part-time. Students come from 38 states and territories, 42 other countries, 67% are from out of state, 3% African American, 10% Asian American or Pacific Islander, 7% Hispanic American, 1% Native American, 29% international, 3% transferred in, 55% live on campus. *Retention:* 84% of 2002 full-time freshmen returned.

Freshmen *Admission:* 727 applied, 230 admitted, 71 enrolled.

Faculty *Total:* 363, 21% full-time, 26% with terminal degrees. *Student/faculty ratio:* 7:1.

Majors Jazz/jazz studies; music; piano and organ; violin, viola, guitar and other stringed instruments; voice and opera; wind/percussion instruments.

Academic Programs *Special study options:* academic remediation for entering students, advanced placement credit, English as a second language, off-campus study, services for LD students.

Library Francis Hall Ballard Library with 60,000 titles, 110 serial subscriptions, 20,100 audiovisual materials, an OPAC, a Web page.

Computers on Campus 14 computers available on campus for general student use. A campuswide network can be accessed from student residence rooms that provide access to word processing. Internet access, at least one staffed computer lab available.

Student Life *Housing:* on-campus residence required through sophomore year. *Options:* coed. Campus housing is university owned. *Activities and organizations:* choral group, Pan-African Student Union, International Student Association, Student Council, Resident Community Council, Gay/Lesbian/Bisexual Students Association. *Campus security:* 24-hour patrols, controlled dormitory access.

Athletics *Intramural sports:* basketball M/W.

Standardized Tests *Recommended:* SAT I or ACT (for admission).

Costs (2003–04) *Tuition:* $23,300 full-time, $950 per credit part-time. Full-time tuition and fees vary according to course load. Part-time tuition and fees vary according to course load. *Required fees:* $1648 full-time. *Room only:* $7600. Room and board charges vary according to housing facility. *Payment plans:* installment, deferred payment. *Waivers:* employees or children of employees.

Financial Aid Of all full-time matriculated undergraduates who enrolled in 2002, 306 applied for aid, 306 were judged to have need, 14 had their need fully met. 73 Federal Work-Study jobs (averaging $1585). In 2002, 25 non-need-based awards were made. *Average percent of need met:* 45%. *Average financial aid package:* $16,350. *Average need-based loan:* $4092. *Average need-based gift aid:* $10,839. *Average non-need-based aid:* $3067. *Average indebtedness upon graduation:* $15,965.

Applying *Options:* deferred entrance. *Application fee:* $100. *Required:* essay or personal statement, high school transcript, minimum 2.8 GPA, 1 letter of recommendation, audition. *Recommended:* minimum 3.0 GPA, interview. *Application deadlines:* 12/1 (freshmen), 12/1 (transfers). *Notification:* 4/1 (freshmen), 4/1 (transfers).

Admissions Contact Mrs. Amy Anderson, Director of Admission and Financial Aid, Manhattan School of Music, 120 Claremont Avenue, New York, NY 10027. *Phone:* 212-749-2802 Ext. 4501. *Fax:* 212-749-3025. *E-mail:* admission@msmnyc.edu.

■ *See page 1918 for a narrative description.*

MANHATTANVILLE COLLEGE
Purchase, New York

- **Independent** comprehensive, founded 1841
- **Calendar** semesters
- **Degrees** bachelor's and master's
- **Suburban** 100-acre campus with easy access to New York City
- **Endowment** $13.5 million
- **Coed,** 1,671 undergraduate students, 91% full-time, 68% women, 32% men
- **Moderately difficult** entrance level, 55% of applicants were admitted

Manhattanville College, founded in 1841, is a private, coeducational, 4-year, comprehensive liberal arts institution. Its location in scenic Westchester County, NY, is approximately 30 minutes northeast of New York City. The College offers more than 40 academic areas of concentration. An active social life involves nearly 50 student organizations, 14 Division III varsity teams, intramurals, and sports clubs.

Undergraduates 1,528 full-time, 143 part-time. Students come from 35 states and territories, 49 other countries, 34% are from out of state, 5% African American, 3% Asian American or Pacific Islander, 14% Hispanic American, 0.3% Native American, 9% international, 4% transferred in, 73% live on campus. *Retention:* 77% of 2002 full-time freshmen returned.

Freshmen *Admission:* 2,450 applied, 1,348 admitted, 420 enrolled. *Average high school GPA:* 3. *Test scores:* SAT verbal scores over 500: 65%; SAT math scores over 500: 63%; ACT scores over 18: 100%; SAT verbal scores over 600: 20%; SAT math scores over 600: 15%; ACT scores over 24: 58%; SAT verbal scores over 700: 2%; SAT math scores over 700: 1%; ACT scores over 30: 3%.

Faculty *Total:* 196, 45% full-time, 42% with terminal degrees. *Student/faculty ratio:* 12:1.

Majors American studies; art history, criticism and conservation; art teacher education; Asian studies; biochemistry; biology/biological sciences; biology teacher education; business administration and management; chemistry; chemistry teacher education; classics and languages, literatures and linguistics; computer science; dance; economics; education; elementary education; English; English/language arts teacher education; finance; fine/studio arts; French; French language teacher education; German studies; history; international relations and affairs; legal studies; mathematics; mathematics teacher education; music; music teacher education; philosophy; physics; political science and government; pre-medical studies; psychology; religious studies; Romance languages; secondary education; social studies teacher education; sociology; Spanish; Spanish language teacher education.

Academic Programs *Special study options:* academic remediation for entering students, accelerated degree program, adult/continuing education programs, advanced placement credit, distance learning, double majors, English as a second language, freshman honors college, honors programs, independent study, internships, off-campus study, part-time degree program, services for LD students, student-designed majors, study abroad, summer session for credit. *Unusual degree programs:* 3-2 education.

Library Manhattanville College Library with 281,949 titles, 13,697 serial subscriptions, 3,921 audiovisual materials, an OPAC, a Web page.

Computers on Campus 155 computers available on campus for general student use. A campuswide network can be accessed from student residence rooms and from off campus. Internet access, online (class) registration, at least one staffed computer lab available. Computer purchase or lease plan available.

Student Life *Housing options:* coed, disabled students. Campus housing is university owned. Freshman campus housing is guaranteed. *Activities and organizations:* drama/theater group, student-run newspaper, radio and television station, choral group, Latin American Student Organization (LASO), International Student Organization (ISO), Black Student Union, WMVL (radio station), Connie Hogarth Center. *Campus security:* 24-hour emergency response devices and patrols, late-night transport/escort service, controlled dormitory access. *Student services:* health clinic, personal/psychological counseling, women's center.

Athletics Member NCAA. All Division III. *Intercollegiate sports:* baseball M, basketball M/W, field hockey W, golf M, ice hockey M/W, lacrosse M/W, soccer M/W, softball W, swimming W, tennis M/W, volleyball W. *Intramural sports:* basketball M/W, cheerleading M/W.

Standardized Tests *Required:* SAT I or ACT (for admission). *Required for some:* SAT I (for admission), ACT (for admission), SAT I and SAT II or ACT (for admission), SAT II: Subject Tests (for admission), SAT II: Writing Test (for admission).

Costs (2004–05) *Comprehensive fee:* $34,700 includes full-time tuition ($23,620), mandatory fees ($950), and room and board ($10,130). Part-time tuition: $540 per credit. Part-time tuition and fees vary according to program. *Required fees:* $35 per term part-time. *College room only:* $6020. Room and board charges vary according to board plan. *Payment plans:* installment, deferred payment. *Waivers:* senior citizens and employees or children of employees.

Financial Aid Of all full-time matriculated undergraduates who enrolled in 2003, 1,100 applied for aid, 992 were judged to have need, 209 had their need fully met. 282 Federal Work-Study jobs (averaging $1056). 219 state and other part-time jobs (averaging $1323). In 2003, 338 non-need-based awards were made. *Average percent of need met:* 80%. *Average financial aid package:* $19,872. *Average need-based loan:* $4133. *Average need-based gift aid:* $9137. *Average non-need-based aid:* $8271. *Average indebtedness upon graduation:* $21,160.

Applying *Options:* common application, electronic application, early admission, early decision, deferred entrance. *Application fee:* $50. *Required:* essay or personal statement, high school transcript, minimum 2.0 GPA, 2 letters of recommendation. *Recommended:* minimum 3.0 GPA, interview. *Application deadlines:* 3/1 (freshmen), 3/1 (transfers). *Early decision:* 12/1. *Notification:* continuous (freshmen), 12/31 (early decision), continuous (transfers).

Admissions Contact Mr. Jose Flores, Director of Admissions, Manhattanville College, 2900 Purchase Street, Purchase, NY 10577. *Phone:* 914-323-5124. *Toll-free phone:* 800-328-4553. *Fax:* 914-694-1732. *E-mail:* admissions@mville.edu.

■ *See page 1920 for a narrative description.*

MANNES COLLEGE OF MUSIC, NEW SCHOOL UNIVERSITY

New York, New York

- **Independent** comprehensive, founded 1916, part of New School University
- **Calendar** semesters
- **Degrees** diplomas, bachelor's, master's, and postbachelor's certificates
- **Urban** campus
- **Endowment** $114.9 million
- **Coed,** 446 undergraduate students, 33% full-time, 57% women, 43% men
- **Very difficult** entrance level, 32% of applicants were admitted

A small, distinguished conservatory in the heart of New York City, Mannes College of Music features faculty who are members of New York City's most prominent and internationally known ensembles. Students receive rigorous professional training as members of a friendly, supportive community dedicated to the highest artistic achievement.

Undergraduates 149 full-time, 297 part-time. Students come from 16 states and territories, 14 other countries, 65% are from out of state, 5% African American, 4% Asian American or Pacific Islander, 4% Hispanic American, 0.6% Native American, 35% international, 4% transferred in, 13% live on campus. *Retention:* 89% of 2002 full-time freshmen returned.

Freshmen *Admission:* 355 applied, 112 admitted, 34 enrolled.

Faculty *Total:* 183, 3% full-time. *Student/faculty ratio:* 7:1.

Majors Conducting; music; music theory and composition; piano and organ; violin, viola, guitar and other stringed instruments; voice and opera; wind/percussion instruments.

Academic Programs *Special study options:* academic remediation for entering students, adult/continuing education programs, advanced placement credit, double majors, English as a second language, summer session for credit.

Library Harry Scherman Library plus 2 others with 4.1 million titles, 22,150 serial subscriptions, 48,379 audiovisual materials, an OPAC, a Web page.

Computers on Campus 934 computers available on campus for general student use. A campuswide network can be accessed from student residence rooms and from off campus that provide access to e-mail. Internet access, at least one staffed computer lab available.

Student Life *Housing options:* coed, disabled students. Campus housing is university owned and leased by the school. Freshman applicants given priority for college housing. *Activities and organizations:* choral group. *Campus security:* 24-hour emergency response devices, controlled dormitory access. *Student services:* health clinic, personal/psychological counseling.

Costs (2003–04) *Comprehensive fee:* $33,320 includes full-time tuition ($22,000), mandatory fees ($510), and room and board ($10,810). Part-time tuition: $724 per credit. *College room only:* $8100. Room and board charges vary according to board plan. *Payment plan:* installment. *Waivers:* employees or children of employees.

Financial Aid Of all full-time matriculated undergraduates who enrolled in 2003, 94 applied for aid, 59 were judged to have need, 3 had their need fully met. 19 Federal Work-Study jobs (averaging $1911). In 2003, 51 non-need-based awards were made. *Average percent of need met:* 68%. *Average financial aid package:* $10,880. *Average need-based loan:* $4574. *Average need-based gift aid:* $9085. *Average non-need-based aid:* $8715. *Average indebtedness upon graduation:* $26,052.

Applying *Options:* deferred entrance. *Application fee:* $100. *Required:* high school transcript, minimum 2.5 GPA, 1 letter of recommendation, audition. *Application deadlines:* 12/1 (freshmen), 12/1 (transfers). *Notification:* 4/15 (freshmen), 4/15 (transfers).

Admissions Contact Ms. Allison Scola, Director of Enrollment, Mannes College of Music, New School University, 150 West 85th Street, New York, NY 10024-4402. *Phone:* 212-580-0210 Ext. 247. *Toll-free phone:* 800-292-3040. *Fax:* 212-580-1738. *E-mail:* mannesadmissions@newschool.edu.

■ *See page 1922 for a narrative description.*

MARIST COLLEGE

Poughkeepsie, New York

- **Independent** comprehensive, founded 1929
- **Calendar** semesters
- **Degrees** certificates, bachelor's, and master's
- **Small-town** 150-acre campus with easy access to Albany and New York City
- **Endowment** $15.9 million
- **Coed,** 4,773 undergraduate students, 88% full-time, 57% women, 43% men
- **Moderately difficult** entrance level, 71% of applicants were admitted

Undergraduates 4,219 full-time, 554 part-time. Students come from 37 states and territories, 19 other countries, 35% are from out of state, 3% African American, 2% Asian American or Pacific Islander, 5% Hispanic American, 0.2% Native American, 0.2% international, 3% transferred in, 70% live on campus. *Retention:* 89% of 2002 full-time freshmen returned.

Freshmen *Admission:* 6,606 applied, 4,664 admitted, 1,125 enrolled. *Average high school GPA:* 3.30. *Test scores:* SAT verbal scores over 500: 91%; SAT math scores over 500: 95%; SAT verbal scores over 600: 37%; SAT math scores over 600: 44%; SAT verbal scores over 700: 2%; SAT math scores over 700: 3%.

Faculty *Total:* 601, 33% full-time. *Student/faculty ratio:* 15:1.

Marist College (continued)

Majors Accounting; advertising; American studies; art; athletic training; behavioral sciences; biochemistry; biology/biological sciences; broadcast journalism; business administration and management; chemistry; clinical laboratory science/medical technology; communication/speech communication and rhetoric; computer engineering technology; computer science; criminal justice/law enforcement administration; digital communication and media/multimedia; dramatic/theatre arts; economics; elementary education; English; environmental biology; environmental studies; fashion/apparel design; fashion merchandising; fine/studio arts; French; history; humanities; information science/studies; information technology; journalism; legal assistant/paralegal; literature; mass communication/media; mathematics; political science and government; pre-dentistry studies; pre-law studies; pre-medical studies; pre-veterinary studies; psychology; public administration; public relations/image management; radio and television; secondary education; social work; Spanish; special education.

Academic Programs *Special study options:* academic remediation for entering students, accelerated degree program, adult/continuing education programs, advanced placement credit, cooperative education, distance learning, double majors, English as a second language, honors programs, independent study, internships, off-campus study, part-time degree program, services for LD students, study abroad, summer session for credit. *Unusual degree programs:* 3-2 psychology, computer science.

Library Marist College Library with 167,033 titles, 10,702 serial subscriptions, 4,438 audiovisual materials, an OPAC, a Web page.

Computers on Campus 501 computers available on campus for general student use. A campuswide network can be accessed from student residence rooms and from off campus. Internet access, at least one staffed computer lab available. Computer purchase or lease plan available.

Student Life *Housing options:* coed. Campus housing is university owned. Freshman campus housing is guaranteed. *Activities and organizations:* drama/theater group, student-run newspaper, radio and television station, choral group, marching band, outback club, student newspaper, student government, theater club, community service and campus ministry, national fraternities. *Campus security:* 24-hour emergency response devices and patrols, student patrols, late-night transport/escort service, controlled dormitory access, night residence hall monitors. *Student services:* health clinic, personal/psychological counseling.

Athletics Member NCAA. All Division I except football (Division I-AA). *Intercollegiate sports:* baseball M(s), basketball M(s)/W(s), crew M/W, cross-country running M(s)/W(s), equestrian sports M(c)/W(c), fencing M(c)/W(c), field hockey W(c), ice hockey M(c), lacrosse M/W, rugby M(c)/W(c), sailing M(c)/W(c), skiing (cross-country) M(c)/W(c), skiing (downhill) M(c)/W(c), soccer M(s)/W(s), softball W(s), swimming M(s)/W(s), tennis M(s)/W(s), track and field M(s)/W(s), volleyball M(c)/W(s), water polo W(s). *Intramural sports:* baseball M, basketball M/W, bowling M/W, fencing M/W, football M, golf M/W, ice hockey M, racquetball M/W, skiing (downhill) M/W, soccer M/W, softball W, swimming M/W, table tennis M/W, tennis M/W, track and field M/W, volleyball M/W, water polo M/W.

Standardized Tests *Required:* SAT I or ACT (for admission).

Costs (2003–04) *One-time required fee:* $25. *Comprehensive fee:* $27,596 includes full-time tuition ($18,432), mandatory fees ($530), and room and board ($8634). Part-time tuition: $420 per credit. *Required fees:* $65 per term part-time. *College room only:* $5460. Room and board charges vary according to board plan and housing facility. *Payment plan:* installment. *Waivers:* employees or children of employees.

Financial Aid Of all full-time matriculated undergraduates who enrolled in 2003, 3,300 applied for aid, 2,729 were judged to have need, 495 had their need fully met. In 2003, 269 non-need-based awards were made. *Average percent of need met:* 70%. *Average financial aid package:* $12,126. *Average need-based loan:* $4560. *Average need-based gift aid:* $6342. *Average non-need-based aid:* $5272. *Average indebtedness upon graduation:* $20,124.

Applying *Options:* electronic application, early admission, early action, deferred entrance. *Application fee:* $40. *Required:* essay or personal statement, high school transcript, 2 letters of recommendation. *Application deadlines:* 2/15 (freshmen), 6/1 (transfers). *Notification:* 3/15 (freshmen), 1/15 (early action), continuous (transfers).

Admissions Contact Mr. Jay Murray, Director of Admissions, Marist College, 3399 North Road. *Phone:* 845-575-3226 Ext. 2190. *Toll-free phone:* 800-436-5483. *E-mail:* admissions@marist.edu.

■ *See page 1930 for a narrative description.*

MARYMOUNT COLLEGE OF FORDHAM UNIVERSITY

Tarrytown, New York

- **Independent** 4-year, founded 1907, part of Fordham University
- **Calendar** semesters
- **Degrees** certificates, associate, and bachelor's
- **Suburban** 25-acre campus with easy access to New York City
- **Endowment** $5.3 million
- **Women only,** 1,083 undergraduate students, 88% full-time
- **Moderately difficult** entrance level, 82% of applicants were admitted

Marymount College consolidated with Fordham University on July 1, 2002, to create a new model of a Catholic women's college—with the academic and administrative resources of a major university and the character of a small, liberal arts college. The new school is known as Marymount College of Fordham University.

Undergraduates 956 full-time, 127 part-time. Students come from 30 states and territories, 15 other countries, 24% are from out of state, 16% African American, 5% Asian American or Pacific Islander, 13% Hispanic American, 2% international, 8% transferred in, 51% live on campus. *Retention:* 69% of 2002 full-time freshmen returned.

Freshmen *Admission:* 1,496 applied, 1,228 admitted, 285 enrolled. *Average high school GPA:* 2.89. *Test scores:* SAT verbal scores over 500: 57%; SAT math scores over 500: 38%; ACT scores over 18: 94%; SAT verbal scores over 600: 14%; SAT math scores over 600: 7%; ACT scores over 24: 25%; SAT verbal scores over 700: 2%; SAT math scores over 700: 2%; ACT scores over 30: 6%.

Faculty *Total:* 167, 34% full-time, 41% with terminal degrees. *Student/faculty ratio:* 11:1.

Majors Accounting; American studies; area studies; art; art history, criticism and conservation; art teacher education; art therapy; biological and physical sciences; biology/biological sciences; biology teacher education; business administration and management; business/commerce; business/managerial economics; chemistry; chemistry teacher education; clinical laboratory science/medical technology; clothing/textiles; community health services counseling; computer and information sciences; creative writing; dietetics; dramatic/theatre arts; economics; education; elementary education; English; family and consumer sciences/home economics teacher education; family and consumer sciences/human sciences; fashion/apparel design; fashion merchandising; finance; fine/studio arts; food science; foods, nutrition, and wellness; French; French language teacher education; history; human ecology; information science/studies; interdisciplinary studies; interior design; international business/trade/commerce; international relations and affairs; journalism; legal studies; liberal arts and sciences/liberal studies; literature; marketing/marketing management; mass communication/media; mathematics; mathematics teacher education; middle school education; modern languages; political science and government; pre-law studies; pre-medical studies; psychology; science teacher education; secondary education; social studies teacher education; social work; sociology; Spanish; Spanish language teacher education; special education; speech and rhetoric.

Academic Programs *Special study options:* academic remediation for entering students, adult/continuing education programs, advanced placement credit, double majors, English as a second language, honors programs, independent study, internships, off-campus study, part-time degree program, services for LD students, student-designed majors, study abroad, summer session for credit. *Unusual degree programs:* 3-2 business administration with Fordham University, Pace University, St. Thomas Aquinas College, Richmond University in London; social work with Fordham University; education with Fordham University, optometry with State University of New York State College of Optometry, physical therapy, occupational therapy, physician assistant with Touro College.

Library Gloria Gaines Memorial Library plus 1 other with 2.5 million titles, 16,224 serial subscriptions, 17,756 audiovisual materials, an OPAC, a Web page.

Computers on Campus 135 computers available on campus for general student use. A campuswide network can be accessed from student residence rooms and from off campus. Internet access, at least one staffed computer lab available.

Student Life *Housing options:* women-only. Campus housing is university owned. Freshman campus housing is guaranteed. *Activities and organizations:* drama/theater group, student-run newspaper, television station, choral group, Campus Activities Board, Student Government Association, Latin Unity, Black Student Union, Residence Hall Association. *Campus security:* 24-hour emergency response devices and patrols, late-night transport/escort service, controlled dormitory access. *Student services:* health clinic, personal/psychological counseling.

Athletics *Intercollegiate sports:* basketball W, equestrian sports W, softball W, swimming W, tennis W, volleyball W. *Intramural sports:* badminton W, basketball W, soccer W, table tennis W, tennis W.

Standardized Tests *Required:* SAT I or ACT (for admission). *Recommended:* SAT I (for admission).

Costs (2003–04) *Comprehensive fee:* $27,686 includes full-time tuition ($17,850), mandatory fees ($576), and room and board ($9260). Full-time tuition and fees vary according to student level. Part-time tuition: $565 per credit hour. Part-time tuition and fees vary according to class time. *Room and board:* Room and board charges vary according to board plan and housing facility. *Payment plans:* installment, deferred payment. *Waivers:* employees or children of employees.

Financial Aid Of all full-time matriculated undergraduates who enrolled in 2002, 667 applied for aid, 599 were judged to have need, 114 had their need fully met. 219 Federal Work-Study jobs (averaging $1289). In 2002, 221 non-need-based awards were made. *Average percent of need met:* 70%. *Average financial aid package:* $14,606. *Average need-based loan:* $5360. *Average need-based gift aid:* $9598. *Average non-need-based aid:* $6286. *Average indebtedness upon graduation:* $11,006.

Applying *Options:* common application, early action, deferred entrance. *Application fee:* $30. *Required:* essay or personal statement, high school transcript, minimum 2.0 GPA. *Recommended:* minimum 3.0 GPA, 1 letter of recommendation, interview. *Application deadline:* 8/31 (freshmen), rolling (transfers). *Notification:* continuous (freshmen), 11/30 (early action), continuous (transfers).

Admissions Contact Ms. Barbara Seyter, Director of Admissions, Marymount College of Fordham University, 100 Marymount Avenue, Tarrytown, NY 10591-3796. *Phone:* 914-332-8295. *Toll-free phone:* 800-724-4312. *Fax:* 914-332-7442. *E-mail:* mcenroll@fordham.edu.

■ See page 1942 for a narrative description.

MARYMOUNT MANHATTAN COLLEGE

New York, New York

- **Independent** 4-year, founded 1936
- **Calendar** semesters plus summer and January mini-semesters
- **Degree** certificates and bachelor's
- **Urban** 3-acre campus
- **Endowment** $8.5 million
- **Coed,** 2,183 undergraduate students, 73% full-time, 79% women, 21% men
- **Moderately difficult** entrance level, 80% of applicants were admitted

Undergraduates 1,600 full-time, 583 part-time. Students come from 47 states and territories, 37 other countries, 35% are from out of state, 17% African American, 4% Asian American or Pacific Islander, 14% Hispanic American, 0.2% Native American, 4% international, 5% transferred in, 21% live on campus. *Retention:* 69% of 2002 full-time freshmen returned.

Freshmen *Admission:* 1,588 applied, 1,264 admitted, 410 enrolled. *Average high school GPA:* 3.20. *Test scores:* SAT verbal scores over 500: 71%; SAT math scores over 500: 57%; ACT scores over 18: 100%; SAT verbal scores over 600: 26%; SAT math scores over 600: 17%; ACT scores over 24: 42%; SAT verbal scores over 700: 3%; SAT math scores over 700: 1%.

Faculty *Total:* 309, 28% full-time, 56% with terminal degrees. *Student/faculty ratio:* 11:1.

Majors Accounting; acting; art; art history, criticism and conservation; audiology and speech-language pathology; biology/biological sciences; business administration and management; dance; dramatic/theatre arts; English; fine/studio arts; history; international relations and affairs; liberal arts and sciences/liberal studies; mass communication/media; political science and government; psychology; sociology; theatre literature, history and criticism.

Academic Programs *Special study options:* academic remediation for entering students, accelerated degree program, adult/continuing education programs, advanced placement credit, double majors, English as a second language, honors programs, independent study, internships, off-campus study, part-time degree program, services for LD students, study abroad, summer session for credit. *Unusual degree programs:* 3-2 computer science with Polytechnic University.

Library Shanahan Library with 100,535 titles, 600 serial subscriptions, 13,285 audiovisual materials, an OPAC, a Web page.

Computers on Campus 150 computers available on campus for general student use. A campuswide network can be accessed from off campus. Internet access, at least one staffed computer lab available.

Student Life *Housing options:* coed. Campus housing is university owned and leased by the school. Freshman applicants given priority for college housing. *Activities and organizations:* drama/theater group, student-run newspaper, radio station, education club, African-American Heritage Club, Asian-American Heritage Club, Latino Heritage Club, business club. *Campus security:* 24-hour emergency response devices and patrols, student patrols, 24-hour security in residence halls. *Student services:* personal/psychological counseling.

Athletics *Intramural sports:* softball M/W.

Standardized Tests *Required:* SAT I or ACT (for admission).

Costs (2004–05) *Comprehensive fee:* $29,718 includes full-time tuition ($16,606), mandatory fees ($746), and room and board ($12,366). Full-time tuition and fees vary according to course load. Part-time tuition: $490 per credit. Part-time tuition and fees vary according to course load. *Required fees:* $325 per term part-time. *College room only:* $9066. Room and board charges vary according to housing facility. *Payment plan:* installment. *Waivers:* children of alumni, adult students, senior citizens, and employees or children of employees.

Financial Aid Of all full-time matriculated undergraduates who enrolled in 2002, 1,383 applied for aid, 1,116 were judged to have need. In 2002, 208 non-need-based awards were made. *Average percent of need met:* 56%. *Average financial aid package:* $8695. *Average need-based loan:* $4581. *Average need-based gift aid:* $8752. *Average non-need-based aid:* $3802. *Average indebtedness upon graduation:* $21,000.

Applying *Options:* electronic application, early decision, deferred entrance. *Application fee:* $50. *Required:* essay or personal statement, high school transcript, minimum 2 GPA, 2 letters of recommendation. *Required for some:* audition for dance and theater programs. *Recommended:* interview. *Application deadline:* rolling (freshmen), rolling (transfers). *Early decision:* 11/1. *Notification:* continuous (freshmen), 12/15 (early decision), continuous (transfers).

Admissions Contact Mr. Thomas Friebel, Associate Vice President for Enrollment Services, Marymount Manhattan College, 221 East 71st Street, New York, NY 10021. *Phone:* 212-517-0430. *Toll-free phone:* 800-MARYMOUNT. *Fax:* 212-517-0448. *E-mail:* admissions@mmm.edu.

■ See page 1944 for a narrative description.

MEDAILLE COLLEGE

Buffalo, New York

- **Independent** comprehensive, founded 1875
- **Calendar** semesters (modular courses available for evening studies and weekend college program)
- **Degrees** certificates, associate, bachelor's, and master's
- **Urban** 13-acre campus
- **Endowment** $407,346
- **Coed,** 1,655 undergraduate students, 91% full-time, 67% women, 33% men
- **Moderately difficult** entrance level, 66% of applicants were admitted

Undergraduates 1,503 full-time, 152 part-time. Students come from 4 states and territories, 2 other countries, 1% are from out of state, 16% African American, 0.5% Asian American or Pacific Islander, 3% Hispanic American, 0.6% Native American, 3% international, 14% transferred in, 18% live on campus. *Retention:* 70% of 2002 full-time freshmen returned.

Freshmen *Admission:* 772 applied, 508 admitted, 288 enrolled. *Average high school GPA:* 2.80. *Test scores:* SAT verbal scores over 500: 32%; SAT math scores over 500: 32%; SAT verbal scores over 600: 5%; SAT math scores over 600: 5%.

Faculty *Total:* 279, 25% full-time, 21% with terminal degrees. *Student/faculty ratio:* 15:1.

Majors Accounting; art; biology/biological sciences; business administration and management; computer and information sciences; computer programming; creative writing; criminal justice/safety; education; elementary education; English; financial planning and services; human resources management; human services; kindergarten/preschool education; liberal arts and sciences/liberal studies; marketing/marketing management; mass communication/media; middle school education; physiological psychology/psychobiology; pre-law studies; psychology; social sciences; sport and fitness administration; technical and business writing; veterinary/animal health technology; veterinary technology; web page, digital/multimedia and information resources design; youth services.

Academic Programs *Special study options:* academic remediation for entering students, accelerated degree program, adult/continuing education programs, advanced placement credit, double majors, honors programs, independent study, internships, off-campus study, part-time degree program, services for LD students, student-designed majors, summer session for credit. *ROTC:* Army (c).

Library Medaille College Library with 55,225 titles, 209 serial subscriptions, 3,563 audiovisual materials, an OPAC, a Web page.

Computers on Campus 105 computers available on campus for general student use. A campuswide network can be accessed from student residence rooms and from off campus. Internet access, at least one staffed computer lab available.

Student Life *Housing options:* coed, men-only, women-only, disabled students. Campus housing is university owned. *Activities and organizations:* drama/theater group, student-run newspaper, radio and television station, student government,

Medaille College (continued)
radio station, ASRA (Admissions Club), Student Activities Board, Teach. *Campus security:* 24-hour emergency response devices, late-night transport/escort service, controlled dormitory access. *Student services:* health clinic, personal/psychological counseling.

Athletics Member NCAA, NSCAA. All NCAA Division III. *Intercollegiate sports:* baseball M, basketball M/W, cheerleading M/W, cross-country running W, lacrosse M/W, soccer M/W, softball W, volleyball M/W. *Intramural sports:* basketball M/W, skiing (downhill) M/W, soccer M/W, softball M/W, table tennis M/W, tennis M/W, volleyball M/W, weight lifting M/W.

Standardized Tests *Required:* SAT I or ACT (for admission). *Recommended:* SAT I (for admission).

Costs (2003–04) *Comprehensive fee:* $20,060 includes full-time tuition ($13,350), mandatory fees ($310), and room and board ($6400). Full-time tuition and fees vary according to location. Part-time tuition: $445 per credit hour. Part-time tuition and fees vary according to course load. *Required fees:* $90 per term part-time. *Room and board:* Room and board charges vary according to housing facility. *Payment plan:* installment. *Waivers:* adult students, senior citizens, and employees or children of employees.

Financial Aid Of all full-time matriculated undergraduates who enrolled in 2003, 1,322 applied for aid, 1,225 were judged to have need, 125 had their need fully met. 140 Federal Work-Study jobs (averaging $1500). In 2003, 29 non-need-based awards were made. *Average percent of need met:* 75%. *Average financial aid package:* $10,000. *Average need-based loan:* $4100. *Average need-based gift aid:* $4200. *Average non-need-based aid:* $1000. *Average indebtedness upon graduation:* $18,000.

Applying *Options:* common application, electronic application, early admission, deferred entrance. *Application fee:* $25. *Required:* high school transcript, interview. *Required for some:* essay or personal statement, 2.5 high school GPA for veterinary technology and elementary teacher education majors. *Recommended:* essay or personal statement, minimum 2.0 GPA, 1 letter of recommendation. *Application deadline:* 8/1 (freshmen), rolling (transfers). *Notification:* continuous (freshmen), continuous (transfers).

Admissions Contact Mrs. Jacqueline S. Matheny, Director of Enrollment Management, Medaille College, Medaille College, Office of Admissions, Buffalo, NY 14214. *Phone:* 716-884-3281 Ext. 203. *Toll-free phone:* 800-292-1582. *Fax:* 716-884-0291. *E-mail:* jmatheny@medaille.edu.

MEDGAR EVERS COLLEGE OF THE CITY UNIVERSITY OF NEW YORK
Brooklyn, New York

- **State and locally supported** 4-year, founded 1969, part of City University of New York System
- **Calendar** semesters
- **Degrees** certificates, associate, and bachelor's
- **Urban** 1-acre campus
- **Coed,** 4,722 undergraduate students, 55% full-time, 78% women, 22% men
- **Noncompetitive** entrance level, 76% of applicants were admitted

Undergraduates 2,598 full-time, 2,124 part-time. Students come from 3 states and territories, 50 other countries, 1% are from out of state, 86% African American, 1% Asian American or Pacific Islander, 4% Hispanic American, 0.1% Native American, 6% international, 7% transferred in. *Retention:* 61% of 2002 full-time freshmen returned.

Freshmen *Admission:* 1,701 applied, 1,299 admitted, 671 enrolled. *Average high school GPA:* 1.66.

Faculty *Total:* 401, 42% full-time. *Student/faculty ratio:* 13:1.

Majors Accounting; applied mathematics; biological and physical sciences; biology/biological sciences; business administration and management; computer/information technology services administration related; computer science; education; environmental studies; information science/studies; liberal arts and sciences/liberal studies; natural sciences; nursing (licensed practical/vocational nurse training); nursing (registered nurse training); pre-engineering; pre-medical studies; psychology; public administration; special education.

Academic Programs *Special study options:* academic remediation for entering students, adult/continuing education programs, advanced placement credit, cooperative education, English as a second language, external degree program, honors programs, independent study, internships, off-campus study, part-time degree program, services for LD students, study abroad, summer session for credit.

Library Charles Innis Memorial Library with 111,000 titles, 430 serial subscriptions, 20,000 audiovisual materials, an OPAC.

Computers on Campus 550 computers available on campus for general student use. A campuswide network can be accessed from off campus. Internet access, online (class) registration, at least one staffed computer lab available.

Student Life *Housing:* college housing not available. *Activities and organizations:* drama/theater group, student-run newspaper, radio and television station, choral group, Caribbean American Student Association, African Heritage, Phi Beta Sigma, Black Social Worker, Latino club. *Campus security:* 24-hour patrols. *Student services:* women's center, legal services.

Athletics Member NCAA. All Division III except men's and women's cheerleading (Division II). *Intercollegiate sports:* basketball M, cheerleading M/W, cross-country running M/W, soccer M, track and field M/W, volleyball W. *Intramural sports:* basketball M, bowling M/W, swimming M/W, table tennis M/W, tennis M/W, ultimate Frisbee M/W, volleyball M/W.

Standardized Tests *Required for some:* SAT I and SAT II or ACT (for admission).

Costs (2003–04) *Tuition:* state resident $4000 full-time, $170 per credit part-time; nonresident $8640 full-time, $360 per credit part-time. *Required fees:* $230 full-time, $78 per term part-time. *Payment plans:* installment, deferred payment.

Financial Aid Of all full-time matriculated undergraduates who enrolled in 2002, 516 Federal Work-Study jobs (averaging $1300).

Applying *Options:* common application, deferred entrance. *Application fee:* $40. *Required:* high school transcript, GED. *Application deadline:* rolling (freshmen), rolling (transfers). *Notification:* continuous (freshmen), continuous (transfers).

Admissions Contact Mr. Warren Heusner, Director of Admissions, Medgar Evers College of the City University of New York, 1665 Bedford Avenue, Brooklyn, NY 11225. *Phone:* 718-270-6025. *Fax:* 718-270-6198. *E-mail:* enroll@mec.cuny.edu.

MERCY COLLEGE
Dobbs Ferry, New York

- **Independent** comprehensive, founded 1951
- **Calendar** semesters
- **Degrees** certificates, associate, bachelor's, and master's
- **Suburban** 60-acre campus with easy access to New York City
- **Endowment** $24.0 million
- **Coed,** 6,208 undergraduate students, 29% full-time, 35% women, 65% men

Undergraduates 1,787 full-time, 4,421 part-time. Students come from 6 states and territories, 49 other countries, 27% African American, 3% Asian American or Pacific Islander, 30% Hispanic American, 0.3% Native American, 2% international, 19% transferred in.

Freshmen *Admission:* 2,708 applied, 693 enrolled.

Faculty *Total:* 989, 24% full-time. *Student/faculty ratio:* 17:1.

Majors Accounting; actuarial science; art; audiology and speech-language pathology; behavioral sciences; bilingual and multilingual education; biology/biological sciences; business administration and management; business/managerial economics; child care provision; clinical laboratory science/medical technology; commercial and advertising art; computer science; criminal justice/law enforcement administration; education; elementary education; English; English as a second/foreign language (teaching); finance; fire science; French; gerontology; health/health care administration; history; human services; information science/studies; interdisciplinary studies; Italian; journalism; kindergarten/preschool education; legal assistant/paralegal; liberal arts and sciences/liberal studies; marketing/marketing management; mathematics; music; music teacher education; nursing (registered nurse training); occupational safety and health technology; operations research; political science and government; pre-dentistry studies; pre-law studies; pre-medical studies; psychology; radio and television; safety/security technology; secondary education; social work; sociology; Spanish; special education; speech and rhetoric; veterinary sciences; veterinary technology.

Academic Programs *Special study options:* academic remediation for entering students, accelerated degree program, adult/continuing education programs, advanced placement credit, cooperative education, distance learning, double majors, English as a second language, honors programs, independent study, internships, off-campus study, part-time degree program, services for LD students, student-designed majors, study abroad, summer session for credit. *ROTC:* Air Force (c). *Unusual degree programs:* 3-2 pharmacy.

Library Mercy College Library with 322,610 titles, 1,765 serial subscriptions, an OPAC, a Web page.

Computers on Campus 138 computers available on campus for general student use. A campuswide network can be accessed from off campus. Internet access, at least one staffed computer lab available.

Student Life *Housing options:* coed. *Activities and organizations:* student-run newspaper, Latin American Student Association, African Descendants of One Mind, Veterinarian Technology, The Reporters Impact, Resident Student Association. *Campus security:* 24-hour patrols. *Student services:* personal/psychological counseling.

Athletics Member NCAA. All Division II. *Intercollegiate sports:* badminton M(s), baseball M(s), basketball M(s)/W(s), cross-country running M(s)/W(s), equestrian sports M(c)/W(c), golf M(s), soccer M(s)/W(s), softball W(s), tennis M(s), volleyball W(s). *Intramural sports:* basketball M/W, volleyball M/W.

Standardized Tests *Recommended:* SAT I (for admission).

Costs (2003–04) *Comprehensive fee:* $19,024 includes full-time tuition ($10,700), mandatory fees ($144), and room and board ($8180). Full-time tuition and fees vary according to course load and degree level. Part-time tuition: $450 per credit. *Required fees:* $6 per credit part-time. *Room and board:* Room and board charges vary according to board plan and housing facility. *Payment plans:* installment, deferred payment. *Waivers:* children of alumni, senior citizens, and employees or children of employees.

Financial Aid Of all full-time matriculated undergraduates who enrolled in 2003, 8,950 applied for aid, 5,513 were judged to have need.

Applying *Options:* electronic application, early admission, deferred entrance. *Application fee:* $35. *Required:* high school transcript, 1 letter of recommendation. *Recommended:* interview. *Application deadline:* rolling (freshmen), rolling (transfers). *Notification:* continuous (freshmen), continuous (transfers).

Admissions Contact Mrs. Sharon Handelson, Director of Admissions and Recruitment, Mercy College, 555 Broadway, Dobbs Ferry, NY 10522-1189. *Phone:* 800-Mercy-NY Ext. 7499. *Toll-free phone:* 800-MERCY-NY. *Fax:* 914-674-7382. *E-mail:* admissions@mercy.edu.

■ *See page 1976 for a narrative description.*

MESIVTA OF EASTERN PARKWAY RABBINICAL SEMINARY
Brooklyn, New York

Admissions Contact Rabbi Joseph Halberstadt, Dean, Mesivta of Eastern Parkway Rabbinical Seminary, 510 Dahill Road, Brooklyn, NY 11218-5559. *Phone:* 718-438-1002.

MESIVTA TIFERETH JERUSALEM OF AMERICA
New York, New York

Admissions Contact Rabbi Fishellis, Director of Admissions, Mesivta Tifereth Jerusalem of America, 141 East Broadway, New York, NY 10002-6301. *Phone:* 212-964-2830.

MESIVTA TORAH VODAATH RABBINICAL SEMINARY
Brooklyn, New York

Admissions Contact Rabbi Issac Braun, Administrator, Mesivta Torah Vodaath Rabbinical Seminary, 425 East Ninth Street, Brooklyn, NY 11218-5209. *Phone:* 718-941-8000. *Fax:* 718-941-8032.

METROPOLITAN COLLEGE OF NEW YORK
New York, New York

- **Independent** comprehensive, founded 1964
- **Calendar** 3 15-week semesters
- **Degrees** certificates, associate, bachelor's, and master's
- **Urban** campus
- **Endowment** $4.6 million
- **Coed, primarily women**
- **Moderately difficult** entrance level

Faculty *Student/faculty ratio:* 20:1.

Student Life *Campus security:* 24-hour patrols.

Standardized Tests *Required:* TABE (for admission). *Required for some:* TABE. *Recommended:* SAT I (for admission), SAT I or ACT (for admission).

Costs (2003–04) *Tuition:* $16,380 full-time, $341 per credit part-time. No tuition increase for student's term of enrollment. *Required fees:* $255 full-time. *Payment plans:* installment, deferred payment.

Financial Aid Of all full-time matriculated undergraduates who enrolled in 2000, 1,066 applied for aid, 1,062 were judged to have need. 52 Federal Work-Study jobs (averaging $1969). 30 state and other part-time jobs (averaging $1920). *Average financial aid package:* $6337. *Average need-based loan:* $3377. *Average need-based gift aid:* $3650. *Average indebtedness upon graduation:* $20,130.

Applying *Options:* electronic application, deferred entrance. *Application fee:* $30. *Required:* essay or personal statement, high school transcript, 2 letters of recommendation, interview. *Required for some:* college entrance exam. *Recommended:* minimum 3.0 GPA.

Admissions Contact Ms. Sabrina Badal-Mohammed, Director of Admissions, Metropolitan College of New York, 75 Varick Street, 12th Floor, New York, NY 10013. *Phone:* 212-343-1234 Ext. 2711. *Toll-free phone:* 800-33-THINK Ext. 5001. *Fax:* 212-343-8470.

MIRRER YESHIVA
Brooklyn, New York

Admissions Contact Director of Admissions, Mirrer Yeshiva, 1795 Ocean Parkway, Brooklyn, NY 11223-2010. *Phone:* 718-645-0536.

MOLLOY COLLEGE
Rockville Centre, New York

- **Independent** comprehensive, founded 1955
- **Calendar** 4-1-4
- **Degrees** associate, bachelor's, master's, and post-master's certificates
- **Suburban** 30-acre campus with easy access to New York City
- **Coed,** 2,311 undergraduate students, 70% full-time, 77% women, 23% men
- **Moderately difficult** entrance level, 67% of applicants were admitted

Undergraduates 1,622 full-time, 689 part-time. Students come from 4 states and territories, 9 other countries, 19% African American, 4% Asian American or Pacific Islander, 8% Hispanic American, 0.1% Native American, 0.8% international, 22% transferred in. *Retention:* 76% of 2002 full-time freshmen returned.

Freshmen *Admission:* 918 applied, 617 admitted, 275 enrolled. *Average high school GPA:* 3.0. *Test scores:* SAT verbal scores over 500: 62%; SAT math scores over 500: 63%; SAT verbal scores over 600: 15%; SAT math scores over 600: 17%; SAT verbal scores over 700: 1%; SAT math scores over 700: 2%.

Faculty *Total:* 357, 39% full-time, 34% with terminal degrees. *Student/faculty ratio:* 11:1.

Majors Accounting; art; audiology and speech-language pathology; biology/biological sciences; biology teacher education; business administration and management; cardiovascular technology; communication/speech communication and rhetoric; computer science; criminal justice/safety; education; elementary education; English; English/language arts teacher education; environmental studies; French; French language teacher education; health information/medical records technology; history; interdisciplinary studies; liberal arts and sciences/liberal studies; mathematics; mathematics teacher education; music; music therapy; nuclear medical technology; nursing (registered nurse training); peace studies and conflict resolution; philosophy; political science and government; pre-dentistry studies; pre-law studies; pre-medical studies; pre-veterinary studies; psychology; religious studies; respiratory care therapy; secondary education; social studies teacher education; social work; sociology; Spanish; Spanish language teacher education; special education.

Academic Programs *Special study options:* academic remediation for entering students, adult/continuing education programs, advanced placement credit, cooperative education, double majors, English as a second language, honors programs, internships, part-time degree program, services for LD students, student-designed majors, study abroad, summer session for credit. *ROTC:* Army (c), Navy (c), Air Force (c).

Library James Edward Tobin Library with 135,000 titles, 9,675 audiovisual materials, an OPAC.

Computers on Campus 246 computers available on campus for general student use. A campuswide network can be accessed. Internet access, at least one staffed computer lab available.

Student Life *Housing:* college housing not available. *Activities and organizations:* drama/theater group, student-run newspaper, choral group, Nursing Student Association, African-American Caribbean Organization, Gaelic Society, education club, International Society. *Campus security:* 24-hour emergency response devices and patrols, late-night transport/escort service. *Student services:* health clinic, personal/psychological counseling, women's center.

Athletics Member NCAA. All Division II. *Intercollegiate sports:* baseball M(s), basketball M(s)/W(s), cross-country running M(s)/W(s), equestrian sports M(s)/W(s), lacrosse M(s), soccer M(s)/W(s), softball W(s), tennis W(s), volleyball W(s).

Standardized Tests *Required:* SAT I or ACT (for admission).

Costs (2003–04) *Tuition:* $14,430 full-time, $480 per credit part-time. *Required fees:* $700 full-time. *Payment plan:* installment. *Waivers:* employees or children of employees.

Molloy College (continued)

Financial Aid Of all full-time matriculated undergraduates who enrolled in 2002, 1,518 applied for aid. 386 Federal Work-Study jobs. In 2002, 243 non-need-based awards were made. *Average percent of need met:* 75%. *Average indebtedness upon graduation:* $17,500.

Applying *Options:* common application, electronic application, early admission, early decision, deferred entrance. *Application fee:* $30. *Required:* essay or personal statement, high school transcript. *Required for some:* 1 letter of recommendation. *Recommended:* interview. *Application deadline:* rolling (freshmen), rolling (transfers). *Early decision:* 11/1. *Notification:* continuous (freshmen), 12/1 (early decision), continuous (transfers).

Admissions Contact Molloy College, 1000 Hempstead Avenue, PO Box 5002, Rockville Centre, NY 11571-5002. *Phone:* 516-678-5000 Ext. 6240. *Toll-free phone:* 888-4MOLLOY. *Fax:* 516-256-2247. *E-mail:* admissions@molloy.edu.

■ *See page 2010 for a narrative description.*

MONROE COLLEGE
Bronx, New York

- **Proprietary** primarily 2-year, founded 1933
- **Calendar** trimesters
- **Degrees** associate and bachelor's
- **Urban** campus
- **Coed**
- **Moderately difficult** entrance level

Faculty *Student/faculty ratio:* 21:1.

Student Life *Campus security:* late-night transport/escort service.

Athletics Member NJCAA.

Standardized Tests *Required:* ACT ASSET (for placement).

Costs (2003–04) *Comprehensive fee:* $18,480 includes full-time tuition ($7960), mandatory fees ($500), and room and board ($10,020). Part-time tuition: $332 per credit. *Required fees:* $125 per term part-time.

Financial Aid Of all full-time matriculated undergraduates who enrolled in 2001, 132 Federal Work-Study jobs (averaging $3100).

Applying *Options:* early admission, deferred entrance. *Application fee:* $25. *Required:* high school transcript, interview.

Admissions Contact Ms. Lauren Rosenthal, Director of Admissions, Monroe College, Monroe College Way, 2501 Jerome Avenue, Bronx, NY 10468. *Phone:* 718-933-6700 Ext. 536. *Toll-free phone:* 800-55MONROE.

■ *See page 2014 for a narrative description.*

MONROE COLLEGE
New Rochelle, New York

- **Proprietary** primarily 2-year, founded 1983
- **Calendar** trimesters
- **Degrees** associate and bachelor's
- **Urban** campus with easy access to New York City
- **Coed**
- **Moderately difficult** entrance level

Faculty *Student/faculty ratio:* 18:1.

Student Life *Campus security:* late-night transport/escort service.

Athletics Member NJCAA.

Standardized Tests *Required:* ACT ASSET (for placement).

Financial Aid Of all full-time matriculated undergraduates who enrolled in 2001, 50 Federal Work-Study jobs (averaging $4000).

Applying *Options:* common application, electronic application, early admission, deferred entrance. *Application fee:* $25. *Required:* high school transcript, interview.

Admissions Contact Ms. Lisa Scorca, High School Admissions, Monroe College, Monroe College Way, 2468 Jerome Avenue, Bronx, NY 10468. *Phone:* 914-632-5400 Ext. 407. *Toll-free phone:* 800-55MONROE. *E-mail:* ejerome@monroecollege.edu.

MOUNT SAINT MARY COLLEGE
Newburgh, New York

- **Independent** comprehensive, founded 1960
- **Calendar** semesters
- **Degrees** certificates, bachelor's, and master's
- **Suburban** 72-acre campus with easy access to New York City
- **Endowment** $6.5 million
- **Coed,** 2,130 undergraduate students, 73% full-time, 73% women, 27% men
- **Moderately difficult** entrance level, 82% of applicants were admitted

Undergraduates 1,563 full-time, 567 part-time. Students come from 14 states and territories, 11% are from out of state, 12% African American, 2% Asian American or Pacific Islander, 8% Hispanic American, 0.2% Native American, 10% transferred in, 39% live on campus. *Retention:* 71% of 2002 full-time freshmen returned.

Freshmen *Admission:* 1,404 applied, 1,154 admitted, 349 enrolled. *Average high school GPA:* 2.85. *Test scores:* SAT verbal scores over 500: 53%; SAT math scores over 500: 54%; SAT verbal scores over 600: 11%; SAT math scores over 600: 12%; SAT verbal scores over 700: 1%; SAT math scores over 700: 1%.

Faculty *Total:* 200, 34% full-time, 43% with terminal degrees. *Student/faculty ratio:* 18:1.

Majors Accounting; biology/biological sciences; business administration and management; chemistry; clinical laboratory science/medical technology; clinical/medical laboratory technology; computer and information sciences; computer science; criminal justice/safety; education; education (K-12); elementary education; English; Hispanic-American, Puerto Rican, and Mexican-American/Chicano studies; history; human services; interdisciplinary studies; international business/trade/commerce; international relations and affairs; liberal arts and sciences/liberal studies; marketing related; mass communication/media; mathematics; nursing (registered nurse training); physical therapy; political science and government; pre-law studies; psychology; public relations/image management; secondary education; social sciences; sociology; special education.

Academic Programs *Special study options:* academic remediation for entering students, accelerated degree program, adult/continuing education programs, advanced placement credit, cooperative education, distance learning, double majors, freshman honors college, honors programs, independent study, internships, off-campus study, part-time degree program, study abroad, summer session for credit. *ROTC:* Army (c). *Unusual degree programs:* 3-2 engineering with The Catholic University of America; social work with Fordam University; physical therapy with New York Medical College.

Library Curtin Memorial Library plus 1 other with 105,683 titles, 860 serial subscriptions, 23,524 audiovisual materials.

Computers on Campus 286 computers available on campus for general student use. A campuswide network can be accessed from student residence rooms and from off campus that provide access to intranet. Internet access, online (class) registration, at least one staffed computer lab available.

Student Life *Housing options:* men-only, women-only. Campus housing is university owned. Freshman campus housing is guaranteed. *Activities and organizations:* drama/theater group, student-run newspaper, radio station, choral group, Student Government Association, Different Stages, Big Brothers/Big Sisters, Black and Latin Student Unions, Habitat for Humanity. *Campus security:* 24-hour emergency response devices and patrols, student patrols, late-night transport/escort service, controlled dormitory access, monitored surveillance cameras in all residence halls. *Student services:* health clinic, personal/psychological counseling.

Athletics Member NCAA. All Division III. *Intercollegiate sports:* baseball M, basketball M/W, soccer M/W, softball W, swimming M/W, tennis M/W, volleyball W. *Intramural sports:* baseball M, basketball M/W, football M, skiing (cross-country) M(c)/W(c), soccer M/W, softball W, swimming M/W, table tennis M/W, tennis M/W, volleyball W.

Standardized Tests *Required:* SAT I or ACT (for admission).

Costs (2003–04) *Comprehensive fee:* $21,270 includes full-time tuition ($13,830), mandatory fees ($460), and room and board ($6980). Full-time tuition and fees vary according to degree level. Part-time tuition: $461 per credit hour. Part-time tuition and fees vary according to degree level. *Required fees:* $30 per term part-time. *College room only:* $3940. Room and board charges vary according to board plan, gender, housing facility, location, and student level. *Payment plan:* installment. *Waivers:* minority students and employees or children of employees.

Financial Aid Of all full-time matriculated undergraduates who enrolled in 2003, 1,360 applied for aid, 1,163 were judged to have need, 307 had their need fully met. 192 Federal Work-Study jobs (averaging $1500). 49 state and other part-time jobs (averaging $1500). *Average percent of need met:* 71%. *Average financial aid package:* $12,303. *Average need-based loan:* $4017. *Average need-based gift aid:* $5065. *Average indebtedness upon graduation:* $20,000.

Applying *Options:* common application, deferred entrance. *Application fee:* $35. *Required:* high school transcript. *Required for some:* essay or personal statement, 3 letters of recommendation, interview. *Recommended:* essay or personal statement, minimum 3.0 GPA, 3 letters of recommendation, interview. *Application deadline:* rolling (freshmen), rolling (transfers). *Notification:* continuous (freshmen), continuous (transfers).

Admissions Contact Mr. J. Randall Ognibene, Director of Admissions, Mount Saint Mary College, 330 Powell Avenue, Newburgh, NY 12550. *Phone:* 845-569-3248. *Toll-free phone:* 888-937-6762. *Fax:* 845-562-6762. *E-mail:* admissions@msmc.edu.

■ *See page 2048 for a narrative description.*

NAZARETH COLLEGE OF ROCHESTER

Rochester, New York

- **Independent** comprehensive, founded 1924
- **Calendar** semesters
- **Degrees** bachelor's, master's, and post-master's certificates
- **Suburban** 150-acre campus
- **Endowment** $39.7 million
- **Coed,** 1,997 undergraduate students, 88% full-time, 76% women, 24% men
- **Moderately difficult** entrance level, 83% of applicants were admitted

Undergraduates 1,767 full-time, 230 part-time. Students come from 23 states and territories, 6% are from out of state, 4% African American, 2% Asian American or Pacific Islander, 2% Hispanic American, 0.2% Native American, 0.4% international, 8% transferred in, 57% live on campus. *Retention:* 83% of 2002 full-time freshmen returned.

Freshmen *Admission:* 1,627 applied, 1,352 admitted, 383 enrolled. *Average high school GPA:* 3.39. *Test scores:* SAT verbal scores over 500: 81%; SAT math scores over 500: 84%; ACT scores over 18: 98%; SAT verbal scores over 600: 37%; SAT math scores over 600: 33%; ACT scores over 24: 51%; SAT verbal scores over 700: 5%; SAT math scores over 700: 4%; ACT scores over 30: 8%.

Faculty *Total:* 230, 59% full-time, 68% with terminal degrees. *Student/faculty ratio:* 13:1.

Majors Accounting; American studies; anthropology; art; art history, criticism and conservation; art teacher education; art therapy; audiology and speech-language pathology; biochemistry; biology/biological sciences; biology teacher education; business administration and management; business teacher education; ceramic arts and ceramics; chemistry; chemistry teacher education; commercial and advertising art; creative writing; dramatic/theatre arts; drawing; economics; education; elementary education; English; English/language arts teacher education; environmental science; environmental studies; fine/studio arts; foreign language teacher education; French; German; gerontology; history; history teacher education; human resources management; information science/studies; information technology; interdisciplinary studies; international relations and affairs; Italian; literature; management information systems; marketing/marketing management; mathematics; mathematics teacher education; modern languages; music; music history, literature, and theory; music teacher education; music therapy; nursing (registered nurse training); philosophy; photography; physical therapy; political science and government; pre-dentistry studies; pre-law studies; premedical studies; pre-veterinary studies; psychology; religious studies; science teacher education; secondary education; social sciences; social studies teacher education; social work; sociology; Spanish; special education; women's studies.

Academic Programs *Special study options:* academic remediation for entering students, adult/continuing education programs, advanced placement credit, cooperative education, double majors, honors programs, independent study, internships, off-campus study, part-time degree program, services for LD students, study abroad, summer session for credit. *ROTC:* Army (c), Air Force (c).

Library Lorette Wilmot Library with 162,593 titles, 1,888 serial subscriptions, 12,236 audiovisual materials, an OPAC, a Web page.

Computers on Campus 150 computers available on campus for general student use. A campuswide network can be accessed from student residence rooms and from off campus. Internet access, at least one staffed computer lab available.

Student Life *Housing options:* coed, women-only, disabled students. Campus housing is university owned. Freshman campus housing is guaranteed. *Activities and organizations:* drama/theater group, student-run newspaper, radio station, choral group, Student Activities Council, French club, theater club, Campus Ministry Council, Coffeehouse, Arts, Lecture, Entertainment Board (CALEB). *Campus security:* 24-hour emergency response devices and patrols, student patrols, late-night transport/escort service, controlled dormitory access, alarm system, security beeper, lighted pathways. *Student services:* health clinic, personal/psychological counseling.

Athletics Member NCAA. All Division III. *Intercollegiate sports:* basketball M/W, cheerleading W, cross-country running M/W, equestrian sports M/W, field hockey W, golf M/W, lacrosse M/W, soccer M/W, softball W, swimming M/W, tennis M/W, track and field M/W, volleyball M/W. *Intramural sports:* basketball M/W, golf M/W, soccer M/W, swimming M/W, tennis M/W, track and field M/W, ultimate Frisbee M/W, volleyball M/W.

Standardized Tests *Required:* SAT I or ACT (for admission).

Costs (2004–05) *Comprehensive fee:* $26,274 includes full-time tuition ($18,040), mandatory fees ($534), and room and board ($7700). *College room only:* $4400. Room and board charges vary according to board plan and housing facility. *Payment plan:* installment. *Waivers:* minority students, children of alumni, and employees or children of employees.

Financial Aid Of all full-time matriculated undergraduates who enrolled in 2003, 1,565 applied for aid, 1,401 were judged to have need. 607 Federal Work-Study jobs (averaging $1621). In 2003, 227 non-need-based awards were made. *Average percent of need met:* 80%. *Average financial aid package:* $14,497. *Average need-based loan:* $4670. *Average need-based gift aid:* $9354. *Average non-need-based aid:* $6046. *Average indebtedness upon graduation:* $21,307.

Applying *Options:* common application, electronic application, early admission, early decision, early action, deferred entrance. *Application fee:* $40. *Required:* essay or personal statement, high school transcript, 1 letter of recommendation. *Required for some:* audition/portfolio review. *Recommended:* 2 letters of recommendation, interview. *Application deadlines:* 2/15 (freshmen), 3/15 (transfers). *Early decision:* 11/15. *Notification:* continuous (freshmen), 12/15 (early decision), 1/15 (early action), 4/15 (transfers).

Admissions Contact Nazareth College of Rochester, 4245 East Avenue, Rochester, NY 14618-3790. *Phone:* 585-389-2860. *Toll-free phone:* 800-462-3944. *Fax:* 585-389-2826. *E-mail:* admissions@naz.edu.

■ *See page 2060 for a narrative description.*

NEW SCHOOL BACHELOR OF ARTS, NEW SCHOOL UNIVERSITY

New York, New York

- **Independent** upper-level, founded 1919, part of New School University
- **Calendar** semesters
- **Degrees** certificates, bachelor's, master's, and doctoral
- **Urban** campus
- **Endowment** $114.9 million
- **Coed,** 989 undergraduate students, 30% full-time, 65% women, 35% men
- **Moderately difficult** entrance level, 63% of applicants were admitted

The New School offers an individualized undergraduate program in the liberal arts designed for adults. Students select their curriculum from nearly 1,000 courses offered each semester. Special features include the New School OnLine University, which offers courses at a distance via computer conferencing; accelerated bachelor's/master's options, which enable undergraduates to begin graduate study; and credit for prior experiential learning through portfolio assessment.

Undergraduates 301 full-time, 688 part-time. Students come from 28 states and territories, 25 other countries, 20% are from out of state, 13% African American, 3% Asian American or Pacific Islander, 7% Hispanic American, 0.5% Native American, 5% international, 18% transferred in.

Faculty *Total:* 515, 0.2% full-time.

Majors Liberal arts and sciences/liberal studies.

Academic Programs *Special study options:* accelerated degree program, adult/continuing education programs, advanced placement credit, distance learning, English as a second language, independent study, internships, part-time degree program, student-designed majors, summer session for credit.

Library Raymond Fogelman Library plus 2 others with 368,890 titles, 1,155 serial subscriptions, 433,123 audiovisual materials.

Computers on Campus 705 computers available on campus for general student use. A campuswide network can be accessed from off campus. Internet access, at least one staffed computer lab available.

Student Life *Housing options:* coed. *Activities and organizations:* university committees, B.A. program committees, student advisory committees, publications. *Campus security:* 24-hour emergency response devices, controlled dormitory access, trained security personnel in central buildings. *Student services:* health clinic, personal/psychological counseling.

Costs (2003–04) *Comprehensive fee:* $27,064 includes full-time tuition ($15,744), mandatory fees ($510), and room and board ($10,810). Part-time tuition: $656 per credit. *College room only:* $8100. Room and board charges vary according to board plan. *Payment plan:* installment. *Waivers:* employees or children of employees.

Financial Aid Of all full-time matriculated undergraduates who enrolled in 2003, 180 applied for aid, 171 were judged to have need, 22 had their need fully met. In 2003, 2 non-need-based awards were made. *Average percent of need met:* 58%. *Average financial aid package:* $9046. *Average need-based loan:* $3978. *Average need-based gift aid:* $5264. *Average non-need-based aid:* $3125. *Average indebtedness upon graduation:* $18,407.

Applying *Options:* deferred entrance. *Application fee:* $40. *Notification:* continuous (transfers).

New School Bachelor of Arts, New School University (continued)

Admissions Contact Ms. Gerianne Brusati, Director of Educational Advising and Admissions, New School Bachelor of Arts, New School University, 66 West 12th Street, New York, NY 10011-8603. *Phone:* 212-229-5630. *Fax:* 212-989-3887. *E-mail:* admissions@dialnsa.edu.

■ *See page 2084 for a narrative description.*

NEW YORK CITY COLLEGE OF TECHNOLOGY OF THE CITY UNIVERSITY OF NEW YORK

Brooklyn, New York

- **State and locally supported** primarily 2-year, founded 1946, part of City University of New York System
- **Calendar** semesters
- **Degrees** certificates, associate, and bachelor's
- **Urban** campus
- **Endowment** $11.6 million
- **Coed**
- **Noncompetitive** entrance level

Faculty *Student/faculty ratio:* 25:1.

Student Life *Campus security:* 24-hour emergency response devices and patrols.

Athletics Member NCAA. All Division III.

Costs (2003–04) *Tuition:* state resident $3400 full-time, $150 per credit hour part-time; nonresident $7000 full-time, $375 per credit hour part-time. *Required fees:* $150 full-time.

Applying *Application fee:* $40. *Required:* high school transcript.

Admissions Contact Mr. Joseph Lento, Director of Admissions, New York City College of Technology of the City University of New York, 300 Jay Street, Brooklyn, NY 11201-2983. *Phone:* 718-260-5500. *E-mail:* jlento@nyctc.cuny.edu.

NEW YORK COLLEGE OF HEALTH PROFESSIONS

Syosset, New York

- **Independent** founded 1981
- **Calendar** trimesters
- **Degrees** certificates, diplomas, associate, incidental bachelor's, and master's
- **Suburban** campus with easy access to New York City
- **Coed**
- **Moderately difficult** entrance level

Student Life *Campus security:* 24-hour patrols, security guard during certain evening and weekend hours.

Standardized Tests *Required:* Wonderlic aptitude test (for admission).

Costs (2003–04) *Tuition:* $9900 full-time, $275 per credit part-time. *Required fees:* $400 full-time.

Financial Aid Of all full-time matriculated undergraduates who enrolled in 2001, 15 Federal Work-Study jobs.

Applying *Options:* common application, electronic application, deferred entrance. *Application fee:* $85. *Required:* essay or personal statement, high school transcript, minimum 2.5 GPA, 2 letters of recommendation, interview.

Admissions Contact Mr. Phil Giuliano, Director of Admissions, New York College of Health Professions, 6801 Jericho Turnpike, Syosset, NY 11791. *Phone:* 800-922-7337 Ext. 296. *Toll-free phone:* 800-922-7337 Ext. 351. *E-mail:* admission@nycollege.edu.

NEW YORK INSTITUTE OF TECHNOLOGY

Old Westbury, New York

- **Independent** university, founded 1955
- **Calendar** semesters
- **Degrees** certificates, associate, bachelor's, master's, doctoral, first professional, post-master's, and postbachelor's certificates
- **Suburban** 1050-acre campus with easy access to New York City
- **Endowment** $37.3 million
- **Coed,** 5,602 undergraduate students, 74% full-time, 39% women, 61% men
- **Moderately difficult** entrance level, 76% of applicants were admitted

Undergraduates 4,167 full-time, 1,435 part-time. Students come from 30 states and territories, 92 other countries, 10% are from out of state, 11% African American, 10% Asian American or Pacific Islander, 10% Hispanic American, 0.2% Native American, 7% international, 10% transferred in, 9% live on campus. *Retention:* 71% of 2002 full-time freshmen returned.

Freshmen *Admission:* 3,511 applied, 2,678 admitted, 874 enrolled. *Average high school GPA:* 3.10. *Test scores:* SAT verbal scores over 500: 69%; SAT math scores over 500: 86%; ACT scores over 18: 97%; SAT verbal scores over 600: 24%; SAT math scores over 600: 42%; ACT scores over 24: 43%; SAT verbal scores over 700: 2%; SAT math scores over 700: 8%; ACT scores over 30: 7%.

Faculty *Total:* 866, 25% full-time. *Student/faculty ratio:* 16:1.

Majors Accounting; accounting technology and bookkeeping; administrative assistant and secretarial science; advertising; aeronautical/aerospace engineering technology; architecture; architecture related; art teacher education; biology/biological sciences; biology teacher education; biomedical technology; business administration and management; business teacher education; chemistry; chemistry teacher education; commercial and advertising art; community psychology; computer and information sciences; criminal justice/law enforcement administration; culinary arts related; data processing and data processing technology; design and applied arts related; economics; education; electrical and electronic engineering technologies related; electrical, electronic and communications engineering technology; electrical, electronics and communications engineering; elementary education; English; English/language arts teacher education; environmental control technologies related; environmental engineering technology; finance; fine/studio arts; health occupations teacher education; hotel/motel administration; human resources management; industrial engineering; information science/studies; interior design; international business/trade/commerce; management information systems; marketing/marketing management; mathematics teacher education; mechanical engineering; mechanical engineering/mechanical technology; mechanical engineering technologies related; multi-/interdisciplinary studies related; nursing (registered nurse training); nursing related; nutrition sciences; occupational therapy; physical therapy; physician assistant; physics; physics teacher education; political science and government; pre-medical studies; psychology; radio and television; radio and television broadcasting technology; sales and marketing/marketing and distribution teacher education; social sciences; social studies teacher education; sociology; technical and business writing; technical teacher education; technology/industrial arts teacher education; telecommunications; trade and industrial teacher education.

Academic Programs *Special study options:* academic remediation for entering students, accelerated degree program, adult/continuing education programs, advanced placement credit, cooperative education, distance learning, double majors, English as a second language, external degree program, honors programs, independent study, internships, off-campus study, part-time degree program, services for LD students, student-designed majors, study abroad, summer session for credit. *ROTC:* Army (b), Air Force (b). *Unusual degree programs:* 3-2 business administration with architectural technology/MBA; engineering with mechanical engineering/energy management; occupational therapy, physical therapy, communication arts, architectural technology/energy management.

Library George and Gertrude Wisser Memorial Library plus 4 others with 412,406 titles, 3,212 serial subscriptions, 40,958 audiovisual materials, an OPAC, a Web page.

Computers on Campus 815 computers available on campus for general student use. A campuswide network can be accessed from student residence rooms and from off campus that provide access to e-mail. Internet access, at least one staffed computer lab available.

Student Life *Housing options:* coed. Campus housing is university owned and is provided by a third party. Freshman campus housing is guaranteed. *Activities and organizations:* drama/theater group, student-run newspaper, radio and television station, choral group, Physical Therapy Society, Occupational Therapy Association, ASHRAM, Bio-Medical Society, National Society of Black Engineers, national fraternities, national sororities. *Campus security:* 24-hour emergency response devices and patrols, late-night transport/escort service, controlled dormitory access. *Student services:* health clinic, personal/psychological counseling, women's center.

Athletics Member NCAA. All Division II except baseball (Division I). *Intercollegiate sports:* baseball M(s), basketball M(s)/W(s), cross-country running M(s)/W(s), lacrosse M(s), soccer M(s)/W(s), softball W(s), track and field M(s)/W(s), volleyball W(s). *Intramural sports:* basketball M/W, football M/W, golf M/W, soccer M/W, softball W, swimming M/W, tennis M/W, volleyball M/W, weight lifting M/W.

Standardized Tests *Required:* SAT I or ACT (for admission).

Costs (2003–04) *Comprehensive fee:* $25,006 includes full-time tuition ($16,926), mandatory fees ($300), and room and board ($7780). Full-time tuition and fees vary according to course load and program. Part-time tuition: $564 per credit. Part-time tuition and fees vary according to course load. *Required fees:* $125 per term part-time. *College room only:* $4080. Room and board charges vary according to board plan, housing facility, and location. *Payment plan:* installment. *Waivers:* senior citizens and employees or children of employees.

Financial Aid Of all full-time matriculated undergraduates who enrolled in 2002, 4,353 applied for aid, 3,806 were judged to have need. In 2002, 155 non-need-based awards were made. *Average financial aid package:* $10,050.

Average need-based gift aid: $4767. *Average non-need-based aid:* $6590. *Average indebtedness upon graduation:* $17,125.

Applying *Options:* electronic application, deferred entrance. *Application fee:* $50. *Required:* essay or personal statement, high school transcript. *Required for some:* minimum X GPA, letters of recommendation, interview, proof of volunteer or work experience required for physical therapy, physician assistant and occupational therapy programs; portfolio for fine arts programs. *Application deadline:* rolling (freshmen), rolling (transfers). *Notification:* continuous (freshmen), continuous (transfers).

Admissions Contact Ms. Robbie de Leur, Director of Financial Aid, New York Institute of Technology, PO Box 8000, Old Westbury, NY 11568. *Phone:* 516-686-7680. *Toll-free phone:* 800-345-NYIT. *Fax:* 516-686-7613. *E-mail:* admissions@nyit.edu.

NEW YORK SCHOOL OF INTERIOR DESIGN
New York, New York

- **Independent** comprehensive, founded 1916
- **Calendar** semesters
- **Degrees** certificates, associate, bachelor's, and master's
- **Urban** 1-acre campus
- **Coed, primarily women,** 760 undergraduate students, 21% full-time, 92% women, 8% men
- **Moderately difficult** entrance level, 62% of applicants were admitted

The New York School of Interior Design is an NASAD-accredited private college devoted to interior design education. The Bachelor of Fine Arts degree is FIDER-accredited. Located on Manhattan's Upper East Side, the School is surrounded by world-famous museums, showrooms, and architectural landmarks.

Undergraduates 162 full-time, 598 part-time. Students come from 16 states and territories, 30 other countries, 17% are from out of state, 1% African American, 10% Asian American or Pacific Islander, 5% Hispanic American, 11% international, 8% transferred in. *Retention:* 50% of 2002 full-time freshmen returned.

Freshmen *Admission:* 107 applied, 66 admitted, 66 enrolled. *Average high school GPA:* 3.00. *Test scores:* SAT verbal scores over 500: 47%; SAT math scores over 500: 47%; SAT verbal scores over 600: 8%; SAT math scores over 600: 8%; SAT verbal scores over 700: 8%; SAT math scores over 700: 8%.

Faculty *Total:* 79, 3% full-time, 33% with terminal degrees. *Student/faculty ratio:* 10:1.

Majors Interior design.

Academic Programs *Special study options:* advanced placement credit, English as a second language, independent study, internships, part-time degree program, services for LD students, study abroad, summer session for credit.

Library NYSID Library with 10,000 titles, 88 serial subscriptions, 100 audiovisual materials, an OPAC, a Web page.

Computers on Campus 70 computers available on campus for general student use. A campuswide network can be accessed from off campus. Internet access, at least one staffed computer lab available.

Student Life *Housing:* college housing not available. *Activities and organizations:* American Society of Interior Designers. *Campus security:* security during school hours.

Standardized Tests *Required:* SAT I or ACT (for admission).

Costs (2004–05) *Tuition:* $19,470 full-time, $590 per credit part-time. *Required fees:* $150 full-time, $75 per term part-time. *Payment plan:* installment. *Waivers:* employees or children of employees.

Financial Aid Of all full-time matriculated undergraduates who enrolled in 2003, 59 applied for aid, 59 were judged to have need. 15 Federal Work-Study jobs (averaging $3000). *Average percent of need met:* 50%. *Average financial aid package:* $8500. *Average need-based loan:* $3000. *Average need-based gift aid:* $5000. *Average indebtedness upon graduation:* $13,250.

Applying *Options:* common application, deferred entrance. *Application fee:* $50. *Required:* essay or personal statement, high school transcript, minimum 2.7 GPA, 2 letters of recommendation, portfolio. *Required for some:* interview. *Recommended:* interview. *Application deadline:* rolling (freshmen), rolling (transfers). *Notification:* continuous (freshmen), continuous (transfers).

Admissions Contact Ms. Briana Cristantiello, Admissions Associate, New York School of Interior Design, 170 East 70th Street, New York, NY 10021-5110. *Phone:* 212-472-1500 Ext. 204. *Toll-free phone:* 800-336-9743. *Fax:* 212-472-1867. *E-mail:* admissions@nysid.edu.

■ *See page 2086 for a narrative description.*

NEW YORK UNIVERSITY
New York, New York

- **Independent** university, founded 1831
- **Calendar** semesters
- **Degrees** certificates, diplomas, associate, bachelor's, master's, doctoral, first professional, post-master's, postbachelor's, and first professional certificates
- **Urban** campus
- **Endowment** $1.3 billion
- **Coed,** 19,506 undergraduate students, 91% full-time, 60% women, 40% men
- **Most difficult** entrance level, 32% of applicants were admitted

Undergraduates 17,718 full-time, 1,788 part-time. Students come from 52 states and territories, 91 other countries, 58% are from out of state, 5% African American, 14% Asian American or Pacific Islander, 7% Hispanic American, 0.2% Native American, 4% international, 5% transferred in, 55% live on campus. *Retention:* 92% of 2002 full-time freshmen returned.

Freshmen *Admission:* 33,776 applied, 10,843 admitted, 4,254 enrolled. *Average high school GPA:* 3.65. *Test scores:* SAT verbal scores over 500: 99%; SAT math scores over 500: 99%; ACT scores over 18: 100%; SAT verbal scores over 600: 81%; SAT math scores over 600: 83%; ACT scores over 24: 98%; SAT verbal scores over 700: 29%; SAT math scores over 700: 32%; ACT scores over 30: 52%.

Faculty *Total:* 4,302, 44% full-time. *Student/faculty ratio:* 12:1.

Majors Accounting; actuarial science; African-American/Black studies; anthropology; archeology; area, ethnic, cultural, and gender studies related; art; art history, criticism and conservation; Asian studies (East); biochemistry; biology/biological sciences; biology teacher education; business administration and management; business, management, and marketing related; business/managerial economics; chemistry; chemistry teacher education; cinematography and film/video production; city/urban, community and regional planning; classics and languages, literatures and linguistics; communication/speech communication and rhetoric; comparative literature; computer and information sciences; computer programming; computer science; dance; dental hygiene; diagnostic medical sonography and ultrasound technology; digital communication and media/multimedia; dramatic/theatre arts; economics; education; elementary education; engineering related; English; English/language arts teacher education; European studies; film/cinema studies; finance; fine/studio arts; foods, nutrition, and wellness; foreign language teacher education; French; French language teacher education; general studies; German; graphic communications; health/health care administration; health information/medical records technology; Hebrew; history; hospitality administration; hotel/motel administration; humanities; human services; information science/studies; interdisciplinary studies; international business/trade/commerce; international relations and affairs; Italian; Jewish/Judaic studies; journalism; kindergarten/preschool education; Latin; Latin American studies; liberal arts and sciences/liberal studies; linguistics; management information systems; marketing/marketing management; mass communication/media; mathematics; mathematics and statistics related; mathematics teacher education; medieval and Renaissance studies; middle school education; modern Greek; music; music management and merchandising; music performance; music teacher education; music theory and composition; Near and Middle Eastern studies; neuroscience; nursing (registered nurse training); operations research; philosophy; photography; physical therapist assistant; physics; physics teacher education; piano and organ; playwriting and screenwriting; political science and government; Portuguese; pre-dentistry studies; pre-medical studies; psychology; radio and television; real estate; religious studies; Romance languages; Russian; secondary education; social sciences; social studies teacher education; social work; sociology; Spanish; special education; special education (speech or language impaired); sport and fitness administration; statistics; theatre literature, history and criticism; tourism and travel services management; urban studies/affairs; voice and opera.

Academic Programs *Special study options:* accelerated degree program, adult/continuing education programs, advanced placement credit, distance learning, double majors, English as a second language, freshman honors college, honors programs, independent study, internships, off-campus study, part-time degree program, services for LD students, student-designed majors, study abroad, summer session for credit. *Unusual degree programs:* 3-2 engineering with Stevens Institute of Technology.

Library Elmer H. Bobst Library plus 11 others with 4.2 million titles, 33,405 serial subscriptions, 92,989 audiovisual materials, an OPAC, a Web page.

Computers on Campus 1400 computers available on campus for general student use. A campuswide network can be accessed from student residence rooms and from off campus. Internet access, online (class) registration, at least one staffed computer lab available. Computer purchase or lease plan available.

Student Life *Housing options:* coed, disabled students. Campus housing is university owned and leased by the school. Freshman campus housing is guaranteed. *Activities and organizations:* drama/theater group, student-run newspaper, radio and television station, choral group, Inter-Varsity Christian Fellowship,

New York University (continued)
Asian Cultural Union, Hillel, Latinos Unidos Con Honor y Amistad (LUCHA), South Asian Student Association (SHRUTI), national fraternities, national sororities. *Campus security:* 24-hour emergency response devices and patrols, student patrols, late-night transport/escort service, controlled dormitory access, 24-hour security in residence halls. *Student services:* health clinic, personal/psychological counseling, women's center.

Athletics Member NCAA. All Division III. *Intercollegiate sports:* badminton M(c)/W(c), baseball M(c), basketball M/W, crew M(c)/W(c), cross-country running M/W, equestrian sports M(c)/W(c), fencing M/W, golf M, ice hockey M(c), lacrosse M(c)/W(c), racquetball M(c)/W(c), soccer M/W, softball W(c), squash M(c)/W(c), swimming M/W, tennis M/W, track and field M(c)/W(c), ultimate Frisbee M(c)/W(c), volleyball M/W, water polo M(c)/W(c), wrestling M. *Intramural sports:* basketball M/W, bowling M/W, football M/W, soccer M/W, softball M/W, tennis M/W, volleyball M/W.

Standardized Tests *Required:* SAT I or ACT (for admission). *Required for some:* SAT II: Subject Tests (for admission). *Recommended:* SAT II: Subject Tests (for admission), SAT II: Writing Test (for admission).

Costs (2003–04) *Comprehensive fee:* $39,406 includes full-time tuition ($26,766), mandatory fees ($1730), and room and board ($10,910). Full-time tuition and fees vary according to program. Part-time tuition: $782 per credit. Part-time tuition and fees vary according to program. *Required fees:* $51 per credit part-time, $257 per term part-time. *Room and board:* Room and board charges vary according to board plan and housing facility. *Payment plans:* tuition prepayment, installment, deferred payment. *Waivers:* employees or children of employees.

Financial Aid Of all full-time matriculated undergraduates who enrolled in 2003, 11,359 applied for aid, 9,834 were judged to have need. 3,324 Federal Work-Study jobs (averaging $2319). In 2003, 2168 non-need-based awards were made. *Average percent of need met:* 67%. *Average financial aid package:* $18,686. *Average need-based loan:* $5068. *Average need-based gift aid:* $12,371. *Average non-need-based aid:* $6497. *Average indebtedness upon graduation:* $24,620.

Applying *Options:* common application, electronic application, early decision, deferred entrance. *Application fee:* $60. *Required:* essay or personal statement, high school transcript, minimum 3.0 GPA, 2 letters of recommendation. *Required for some:* interview, audition, portfolio. *Application deadlines:* 1/15 (freshmen), 4/1 (transfers). *Early decision:* 11/1. *Notification:* 4/1 (freshmen), 12/15 (early decision), 5/1 (transfers).

Admissions Contact Ms. Barbara Hall, Associate Provost for Admissions and Financial Aid, New York University, 22 Washington Square North, New York, NY 10011. *Phone:* 212-998-4500. *Fax:* 212-995-4902.

■ *See page 2088 for a narrative description.*

NIAGARA UNIVERSITY
Niagara Falls, New York

- **Independent** comprehensive, founded 1856, affiliated with Roman Catholic Church
- **Calendar** semesters
- **Degrees** associate, bachelor's, master's, and post-master's certificates
- **Suburban** 160-acre campus with easy access to Buffalo and Toronto
- **Endowment** $38.0 million
- **Coed,** 2,734 undergraduate students, 95% full-time, 61% women, 39% men
- **Moderately difficult** entrance level, 80% of applicants were admitted

Niagara University offers an extensive merit scholarship and grant program. Students, regardless of need, may be eligible to receive an academic award ranging from $5000 up to full tuition. These merit-based grants, awards, and scholarships are renewable. To be considered, students must meet certain academic criteria and other NU guidelines.

Undergraduates 2,594 full-time, 140 part-time. Students come from 31 states and territories, 16 other countries, 8% are from out of state, 4% African American, 1% Asian American or Pacific Islander, 2% Hispanic American, 1% Native American, 4% international, 6% transferred in, 55% live on campus. *Retention:* 80% of 2002 full-time freshmen returned.

Freshmen *Admission:* 2,658 applied, 2,130 admitted, 686 enrolled. *Average high school GPA:* 3.0. *Test scores:* SAT verbal scores over 500: 58%; SAT math scores over 500: 63%; ACT scores over 18: 91%; SAT verbal scores over 600: 14%; SAT math scores over 600: 18%; ACT scores over 24: 33%; SAT verbal scores over 700: 1%; SAT math scores over 700: 2%; ACT scores over 30: 4%.

Faculty *Total:* 307, 43% full-time. *Student/faculty ratio:* 16:1.

Majors Accounting; biochemistry; biology/biological sciences; biology/biotechnology laboratory technician; biology teacher education; business administration and management; business/commerce; business/managerial economics; business teacher education; chemistry; chemistry teacher education; computer science; criminal justice/law enforcement administration; criminology; dramatic/theatre arts; economics; education; elementary education; English; French; French language teacher education; history; hospitality administration related; hotel/motel administration; human resources management; human resources management and services related; information science/studies; international business/trade/commerce; international relations and affairs; liberal arts and sciences/liberal studies; logistics and materials management; marketing/marketing management; mass communication/media; mathematics; mathematics teacher education; philosophy; political science and government; pre-dentistry studies; pre-engineering; pre-law studies; pre-medical studies; pre-veterinary studies; psychology; religious studies; restaurant/food services management; science teacher education; secondary education; social sciences; social studies teacher education; social work; sociology; Spanish; Spanish language teacher education; special education; tourism and travel services management; transportation technology.

Academic Programs *Special study options:* academic remediation for entering students, accelerated degree program, adult/continuing education programs, advanced placement credit, cooperative education, double majors, English as a second language, freshman honors college, honors programs, internships, off-campus study, part-time degree program, services for LD students, study abroad, summer session for credit. *ROTC:* Army (b).

Library Our Lady of Angels Library with 275,871 titles, 7,500 serial subscriptions, an OPAC.

Computers on Campus 150 computers available on campus for general student use. A campuswide network can be accessed from student residence rooms. Internet access, at least one staffed computer lab available.

Student Life *Housing:* on-campus residence required through sophomore year. *Options:* coed, women-only. Campus housing is university owned. Freshman campus housing is guaranteed. *Activities and organizations:* drama/theater group, student-run newspaper, radio station, choral group, Niagara University Community Action Program, student government, Programming Board, national fraternities. *Campus security:* 24-hour emergency response devices and patrols, late-night transport/escort service, controlled dormitory access, 24-hour escort service. *Student services:* health clinic, personal/psychological counseling.

Athletics Member NCAA. All Division I. *Intercollegiate sports:* baseball M(s), basketball M(s)/W(s), cross-country running M(s)/W(s), golf M(s), ice hockey M(s)/W(s), lacrosse M/W(s), soccer M(s)/W(s), softball W(s), swimming M(s)/W(s), tennis M(s)/W(s), volleyball W(s). *Intramural sports:* basketball M/W, ice hockey M/W, lacrosse M/W, racquetball M/W, rugby M(c)/W(c), skiing (downhill) M(c)/W(c), soccer M/W, softball M/W, volleyball M/W, water polo M/W.

Standardized Tests *Required:* SAT I or ACT (for admission).

Costs (2003–04) *Comprehensive fee:* $25,050 includes full-time tuition ($16,700), mandatory fees ($680), and room and board ($7670). *Payment plans:* installment, deferred payment. *Waivers:* senior citizens and employees or children of employees.

Financial Aid Of all full-time matriculated undergraduates who enrolled in 2003, 2,271 applied for aid, 2,188 were judged to have need, 630 had their need fully met. 466 Federal Work-Study jobs (averaging $2078). 30 state and other part-time jobs (averaging $2833). In 2003, 385 non-need-based awards were made. *Average percent of need met:* 84%. *Average financial aid package:* $15,400. *Average need-based loan:* $4505. *Average need-based gift aid:* $10,355. *Average non-need-based aid:* $7039. *Average indebtedness upon graduation:* $15,402.

Applying *Options:* electronic application, early admission, deferred entrance. *Application fee:* $30. *Required:* high school transcript. *Recommended:* minimum 3.0 GPA, 3 letters of recommendation, interview. *Application deadlines:* 8/1 (freshmen), 8/15 (transfers).

Admissions Contact Ms. Christine M. McDermott, Associate Director of Admissions, Niagara University, Office of Admissions, Niagara, NY 14109. *Phone:* 716-286-8700 Ext. 8715. *Toll-free phone:* 800-462-2111. *Fax:* 716-286-8733. *E-mail:* admissions@niagara.edu.

■ *See page 2090 for a narrative description.*

NYACK COLLEGE
Nyack, New York

- **Independent** comprehensive, founded 1882, affiliated with The Christian and Missionary Alliance
- **Calendar** semesters
- **Degrees** certificates, associate, bachelor's, master's, and first professional
- **Suburban** 102-acre campus with easy access to New York City
- **Endowment** $3.9 million
- **Coed,** 2,069 undergraduate students, 86% full-time, 60% women, 40% men
- **Moderately difficult** entrance level

Undergraduates 1,774 full-time, 295 part-time. Students come from 41 states and territories, 43 other countries, 36% are from out of state, 31% African

American, 6% Asian American or Pacific Islander, 21% Hispanic American, 0.2% Native American, 4% international, 16% transferred in, 42% live on campus. *Retention:* 64% of 2002 full-time freshmen returned.

Freshmen *Admission:* 295 enrolled. *Average high school GPA:* 2.73. *Test scores:* SAT verbal scores over 500: 40%; SAT math scores over 500: 36%; ACT scores over 18: 89%; SAT verbal scores over 600: 14%; SAT math scores over 600: 9%; ACT scores over 24: 32%; SAT verbal scores over 700: 1%; SAT math scores over 700: 1%; ACT scores over 30: 7%.

Faculty *Total:* 233, 31% full-time, 40% with terminal degrees. *Student/faculty ratio:* 15:1.

Majors Accounting; biblical studies; business administration and management; communication/speech communication and rhetoric; computer science; elementary education; English; English as a second/foreign language (teaching); general studies; history; interdisciplinary studies; liberal arts and sciences/liberal studies; mathematics; missionary studies and missiology; music; music teacher education; music theory and composition; pastoral studies/counseling; philosophy; piano and organ; psychology; religious education; religious/sacred music; religious studies; secondary education; social sciences; social work; theology; voice and opera.

Academic Programs *Special study options:* academic remediation for entering students, accelerated degree program, advanced placement credit, distance learning, double majors, English as a second language, honors programs, independent study, internships, off-campus study, part-time degree program, study abroad, summer session for credit.

Library The Bailey Library plus 2 others with 127,271 titles, 958 serial subscriptions, 4,739 audiovisual materials, an OPAC, a Web page.

Computers on Campus 180 computers available on campus for general student use. A campuswide network can be accessed. Internet access, at least one staffed computer lab available.

Student Life *Housing options:* men-only, women-only. Campus housing is university owned. Freshman campus housing is guaranteed. *Activities and organizations:* drama/theater group, student-run newspaper, radio station, choral group, gospel teams, drama club, Student Government Association. *Campus security:* 24-hour emergency response devices and patrols, student patrols, late-night transport/escort service. *Student services:* health clinic, personal/psychological counseling.

Athletics Member NCAA, NAIA, NCCAA. All NCAA Division II. *Intercollegiate sports:* baseball M(s), basketball M(s)/W(s), cheerleading M(s)/W(s), cross-country running M(s)/W(s), golf M(s), soccer M(s)/W(s), softball W(s), volleyball W(s). *Intramural sports:* basketball M, football M, volleyball M/W.

Standardized Tests *Required for some:* SAT I or ACT (for admission).

Costs (2004–05) *Comprehensive fee:* $22,040 includes full-time tuition ($13,990), mandatory fees ($800), and room and board ($7250). Full-time tuition and fees vary according to program. Part-time tuition: $580 per credit. Part-time tuition and fees vary according to course load and program. *Required fees:* $200 per semester part-time. *Room and board:* Room and board charges vary according to housing facility. *Payment plan:* installment. *Waivers:* employees or children of employees.

Financial Aid Of all full-time matriculated undergraduates who enrolled in 2002, 1,404 applied for aid, 1,334 were judged to have need, 212 had their need fully met. 240 Federal Work-Study jobs (averaging $998). 40 state and other part-time jobs (averaging $1852). In 2002, 219 non-need-based awards were made. *Average percent of need met:* 55%. *Average financial aid package:* $12,860. *Average need-based loan:* $4463. *Average need-based gift aid:* $8351. *Average non-need-based aid:* $6348. *Average indebtedness upon graduation:* $14,563.

Applying *Options:* electronic application, early admission, deferred entrance. *Application fee:* $15. *Required:* essay or personal statement, high school transcript, 2 letters of recommendation. *Required for some:* interview, evidence of faith commitment. *Application deadline:* rolling (freshmen), rolling (transfers). *Notification:* continuous (freshmen), continuous (transfers).

Admissions Contact Ms. Bethany Ilsley, Director of Admissions, Nyack College, 1 South Boulevard, Nyack, NY 10960-3698. *Phone:* 845-358-1710 Ext. 350. *Toll-free phone:* 800-33-NYACK. *Fax:* 845-353-1297. *E-mail:* enroll@nyack.edu.

OHR HAMEIR THEOLOGICAL SEMINARY

Peekskill, New York

Admissions Contact Rabbi M. Z. Weisverg, Director of Admissions, Ohr Hameir Theological Seminary, Furnace Woods Road, Peekskill, NY 10566. *Phone:* 914-736-1500.

OHR SOMAYACH/JOSEPH TANENBAUM EDUCATIONAL CENTER

Monsey, New York

- **Independent Jewish** 5-year, founded 1979
- **Calendar** semesters
- **Degrees** bachelor's and first professional
- **Small-town** 7-acre campus with easy access to New York City
- **Men only,** 114 undergraduate students, 100% full-time
- **Moderately difficult** entrance level, 65% of applicants were admitted

Undergraduates 114 full-time. Students come from 10 states and territories, 4 other countries, 39% are from out of state, 22% international, 5% transferred in.

Freshmen *Admission:* 100 applied, 65 admitted, 18 enrolled.

Faculty *Total:* 10, 60% full-time.

Majors Rabbinical studies.

Academic Programs *Special study options:* academic remediation for entering students, adult/continuing education programs, honors programs, internships, part-time degree program, services for LD students, summer session for credit.

Library Finer Library with 2,300 titles.

Student Life *Campus security:* 24-hour emergency response devices and patrols, controlled dormitory access. *Student services:* personal/psychological counseling.

Costs (2003–04) *Tuition:* $10,500 full-time.

Applying *Options:* early admission. *Required:* letters of recommendation, interview. *Required for some:* essay or personal statement. *Recommended:* high school transcript. *Application deadline:* rolling (freshmen), rolling (transfers).

Admissions Contact Rabbi Avrohom Braun, Dean of Students, Ohr Somayach/Joseph Tanenbaum Educational Center, PO Box 334, Monsey, NY 10952-0334. *Phone:* 914-425-1370 Ext. 22.

PACE UNIVERSITY

New York, New York

- **Independent** university, founded 1906
- **Calendar** semesters
- **Degrees** certificates, diplomas, associate, bachelor's, master's, doctoral, first professional, post-master's, postbachelor's, and first professional certificates
- **Endowment** $71.5 million
- **Coed,** 8,871 undergraduate students, 78% full-time, 61% women, 39% men
- **Moderately difficult** entrance level, 74% of applicants were admitted

Undergraduates 6,893 full-time, 1,978 part-time. Students come from 41 states and territories, 34 other countries, 17% are from out of state, 10% African American, 12% Asian American or Pacific Islander, 12% Hispanic American, 0.2% Native American, 4% international, 7% transferred in, 23% live on campus. *Retention:* 77% of 2002 full-time freshmen returned.

Freshmen *Admission:* 7,973 applied, 5,906 admitted, 1,657 enrolled. *Average high school GPA:* 3.20. *Test scores:* SAT verbal scores over 500: 71%; SAT math scores over 500: 75%; ACT scores over 18: 98%; SAT verbal scores over 600: 21%; SAT math scores over 600: 25%; ACT scores over 24: 44%; SAT verbal scores over 700: 2%; SAT math scores over 700: 3%; ACT scores over 30: 2%.

Faculty *Total:* 1,138, 38% full-time, 53% with terminal degrees. *Student/faculty ratio:* 15:1.

Majors Accounting; accounting technology and bookkeeping; advertising; art; art history, criticism and conservation; biochemistry; biology/biological sciences; biology teacher education; business administration and management; business automation/technology/data entry; business teacher education; chemistry; chemistry teacher education; child guidance; clinical laboratory science/medical technology; commercial and advertising art; communication and journalism related; communication disorders; communication/speech communication and rhetoric; community organization and advocacy; computer and information sciences; criminal justice/law enforcement administration; design and visual communications; ecology; economics; education related; elementary education; English; English/language arts teacher education; entrepreneurship; fine/studio arts; foreign languages and literatures; French; French language teacher education; geology/earth science; health information/medical records administration; history; hotel/motel administration; human resources management; information science/studies; interdisciplinary studies; international business/trade/commerce; international marketing; international relations and affairs; liberal arts and sciences/liberal studies; literature; marketing/marketing management; marketing related; mathematics; mathematics teacher education; modern languages; multi-/interdisciplinary studies related; nursing (registered nurse training); philosophy and religious studies related; physician assistant; physics; physics teacher education; political science and government; psychology; social sciences; social studies

Pace University (continued)
teacher education; Spanish; Spanish language teacher education; special education (speech or language impaired); speech and rhetoric; speech-language pathology.

Academic Programs *Special study options:* academic remediation for entering students, accelerated degree program, adult/continuing education programs, advanced placement credit, cooperative education, distance learning, double majors, English as a second language, freshman honors college, honors programs, independent study, internships, part-time degree program, study abroad, summer session for credit. *ROTC:* Air Force (c). *Unusual degree programs:* 3-2 engineering with Manhattan College, Rensselaer Polytechnic Institute; occupational therapy with Columbia University College of Physicians and Surgeons.

Library Henry Birnbaum Library plus 3 others with 811,957 titles, 2,303 serial subscriptions, an OPAC, a Web page.

Computers on Campus 234 computers available on campus for general student use. A campuswide network can be accessed from student residence rooms and from off campus. At least one staffed computer lab available.

Student Life *Housing options:* coed. Campus housing is university owned and leased by the school. *Activities and organizations:* drama/theater group, student-run newspaper, radio and television station, choral group, student government, Pace Press Newspaper, United Chinese Students Association, Alianza Latina, National Association of Black Accountants, national fraternities, national sororities. *Campus security:* 24-hour emergency response devices and patrols, late-night transport/escort service, controlled dormitory access. *Student services:* health clinic, personal/psychological counseling.

Athletics Member NCAA. All Division II except baseball (Division I). *Intercollegiate sports:* baseball M(s), basketball M(s)/W(s), cross-country running M(s)/W(s), equestrian sports M/W, football M, golf M(s)/W(s), lacrosse M(s), soccer W(s), softball W(s), swimming M/W, tennis M(s)/W(s), track and field M(s)/W(s), volleyball W(s). *Intramural sports:* basketball M/W, football M, soccer M/W, volleyball M/W.

Standardized Tests *Required:* SAT I or ACT (for admission).

Costs (2003–04) *Comprehensive fee:* $28,754 includes full-time tuition ($20,540), mandatory fees ($564), and room and board ($7650). Full-time tuition and fees vary according to student level. Part-time tuition: $590 per credit. Part-time tuition and fees vary according to course load. No tuition increase for student's term of enrollment. *Required fees:* $136 per term part-time. *Room and board:* Room and board charges vary according to board plan and housing facility. *Payment plan:* installment. *Waivers:* senior citizens and employees or children of employees.

Financial Aid Of all full-time matriculated undergraduates who enrolled in 2003, 6,248 applied for aid, 5,798 were judged to have need, 382 had their need fully met. 1,018 Federal Work-Study jobs (averaging $3585). In 2003, 345 non-need-based awards were made. *Average percent of need met:* 87%. *Average financial aid package:* $12,919. *Average need-based loan:* $4120. *Average need-based gift aid:* $4780. *Average non-need-based aid:* $5644. *Average indebtedness upon graduation:* $20,670.

Applying *Options:* common application, electronic application, early action, deferred entrance. *Application fee:* $45. *Required:* essay or personal statement, high school transcript, 2 letters of recommendation. *Recommended:* minimum 3.0 GPA, interview. *Application deadline:* rolling (freshmen), rolling (transfers). *Notification:* continuous (freshmen), 12/15 (early action), continuous (transfers).

Admissions Contact Ms. Joanna Broda, Director of Admission, NY and Westchester, Pace University, One Pace Plaza, New York, NY 10038. *Phone:* 212-346-1323. *Toll-free phone:* 800-874-7223. *Fax:* 212-346-1040. *E-mail:* infoctr@pace.edu.

■ *See page 2144 for a narrative description.*

Parsons School of Design, New School University

New York, New York

- **Independent** comprehensive, founded 1896, part of New School University
- **Calendar** semesters
- **Degrees** certificates, associate, bachelor's, and master's
- **Urban** 2-acre campus
- **Endowment** $114.9 million
- **Coed,** 2,502 undergraduate students, 93% full-time, 76% women, 24% men
- **Very difficult** entrance level, 42% of applicants were admitted

Undergraduates 2,331 full-time, 171 part-time. Students come from 48 states and territories, 66 other countries, 47% are from out of state, 3% African American, 18% Asian American or Pacific Islander, 6% Hispanic American, 0.1% Native American, 32% international, 18% transferred in, 21% live on campus. *Retention:* 86% of 2002 full-time freshmen returned.

Freshmen *Admission:* 1,630 applied, 690 admitted, 309 enrolled. *Average high school GPA:* 3.10. *Test scores:* SAT verbal scores over 500: 74%; SAT math scores over 500: 80%; SAT verbal scores over 600: 44%; SAT math scores over 600: 34%; SAT verbal scores over 700: 14%; SAT math scores over 700: 10%.

Faculty *Total:* 759, 6% full-time. *Student/faculty ratio:* 10:1.

Majors Architecture; art; art teacher education; commercial and advertising art; drawing; environmental design/architecture; fashion/apparel design; fashion merchandising; industrial design; interior design; photography; sculpture.

Academic Programs *Special study options:* accelerated degree program, adult/continuing education programs, advanced placement credit, cooperative education, distance learning, English as a second language, honors programs, independent study, internships, off-campus study, services for LD students, student-designed majors, study abroad, summer session for credit.

Library Adam and Sophie Gimbel Design Library plus 2 others with 4.1 million titles, 22,150 serial subscriptions, 48,379 audiovisual materials, an OPAC, a Web page.

Computers on Campus 934 computers available on campus for general student use. A campuswide network can be accessed from student residence rooms and from off campus that provide access to e-mail. Internet access, at least one staffed computer lab available.

Student Life *Housing options:* coed, disabled students. Campus housing is university owned and leased by the school. Freshman applicants given priority for college housing. *Activities and organizations:* gallery committees, Latino/Latina Student Group, Chinese Student Association, American Institute of Architectural Students. *Campus security:* 24-hour emergency response devices, controlled dormitory access. *Student services:* health clinic, personal/psychological counseling.

Standardized Tests *Required:* SAT I or ACT (for admission).

Costs (2003–04) *Comprehensive fee:* $36,735 includes full-time tuition ($25,330), mandatory fees ($595), and room and board ($10,810). Part-time tuition: $864 per credit hour. *College room only:* $8100. *Payment plan:* installment. *Waivers:* employees or children of employees.

Financial Aid Of all full-time matriculated undergraduates who enrolled in 2003, 1,702 applied for aid, 1,637 were judged to have need, 92 had their need fully met. In 2003, 94 non-need-based awards were made. *Average percent of need met:* 55%. *Average financial aid package:* $11,495. *Average need-based loan:* $3425. *Average need-based gift aid:* $8512. *Average non-need-based aid:* $2972. *Average indebtedness upon graduation:* $25,226.

Applying *Options:* early admission. *Application fee:* $40. *Required:* high school transcript, minimum 2.0 GPA, portfolio, home examination. *Required for some:* essay or personal statement, interview. *Recommended:* minimum 3.0 GPA. *Application deadline:* rolling (transfers). *Notification:* continuous (freshmen), continuous (transfers).

Admissions Contact Ms. Heather Ward, Director of Admissions, Parsons School of Design, New School University, 66 Fifth Avenue, New York, NY 10011-8878. *Phone:* 212-229-8910. *Toll-free phone:* 877-528-3321. *Fax:* 212-229-5166. *E-mail:* customer@newschool.edu.

Paul Smith's College of Arts and Sciences

Paul Smiths, New York

- **Independent** 4-year, founded 1937
- **Calendar** semesters
- **Degrees** certificates, associate, and bachelor's
- **Rural** 14,200-acre campus
- **Endowment** $11.8 million
- **Coed,** 862 undergraduate students
- **Minimally difficult** entrance level, 80% of applicants were admitted

Undergraduates Students come from 29 states and territories, 11 other countries, 40% are from out of state, 3% African American, 0.7% Asian American or Pacific Islander, 2% Hispanic American, 0.5% Native American, 0.5% international, 95% live on campus.

Freshmen *Admission:* 1,173 applied, 933 admitted. *Average high school GPA:* 3.24. *Test scores:* SAT verbal scores over 500: 39%; SAT math scores over 500: 33%; ACT scores over 18: 59%; SAT verbal scores over 600: 6%; SAT math scores over 600: 8%; ACT scores over 24: 7%; SAT verbal scores over 700: 1%.

Faculty *Total:* 65, 98% full-time, 18% with terminal degrees. *Student/faculty ratio:* 14:1.

Majors American studies; business administration and management; culinary arts; ecology; environmental studies; forestry; forestry technology; hospitality administration; hotel/motel administration; liberal arts and sciences/liberal studies; natural resources management and policy; parks, recreation and leisure facilities management; survey technology; technical and business writing; tourism and travel services management.

Academic Programs *Special study options:* academic remediation for entering students, adult/continuing education programs, advanced placement credit, cooperative education, double majors, English as a second language, honors programs, internships, services for LD students, student-designed majors, study abroad, summer session for credit.

Library Frank C. Cubley Library with 56,000 titles, 504 serial subscriptions, an OPAC, a Web page.

Computers on Campus 65 computers available on campus for general student use. A campuswide network can be accessed from student residence rooms and from off campus. Internet access, at least one staffed computer lab available.

Student Life *Housing:* on-campus residence required through sophomore year. *Options:* coed. *Activities and organizations:* drama/theater group, student-run newspaper, radio station, Forestry Club, Adirondack Experience Club, student radio station, Emergency Wilderness Response Team, Junior American Culinary. *Campus security:* 24-hour emergency response devices and patrols, late-night transport/escort service. *Student services:* health clinic, personal/psychological counseling.

Athletics Member NJCAA. *Intercollegiate sports:* basketball M(s)/W(s), ice hockey M(s), skiing (downhill) M(s)/W(s), soccer M(s)/W(s). *Intramural sports:* basketball M/W, cross-country running M(c)/W(c), football M, golf M, ice hockey M(c), riflery M(c)/W(c), rugby M(c), soccer M/W, softball M/W, swimming M/W, table tennis M/W, tennis M/W, volleyball M/W.

Standardized Tests *Required:* SAT I or ACT (for admission).

Costs (2004–05) *Comprehensive fee:* $23,060 includes full-time tuition ($15,330), mandatory fees ($1010), and room and board ($6720). Full-time tuition and fees vary according to program. Part-time tuition: $505 per credit hour. Part-time tuition and fees vary according to course load and program. No tuition increase for student's term of enrollment. *College room only:* $3360. Room and board charges vary according to board plan. *Payment plan:* installment. *Waivers:* employees or children of employees.

Financial Aid Of all full-time matriculated undergraduates who enrolled in 2003, 861 applied for aid, 809 were judged to have need, 40 had their need fully met. 814 Federal Work-Study jobs (averaging $1588). In 2003, 75 non-need-based awards were made. *Average percent of need met:* 85%. *Average financial aid package:* $5300. *Average need-based loan:* $6625. *Average need-based gift aid:* $3034. *Average non-need-based aid:* $2525. *Average indebtedness upon graduation:* $6625.

Applying *Options:* common application, electronic application, early admission, deferred entrance. *Application fee:* $30. *Required:* essay or personal statement, high school transcript, 1 letter of recommendation. *Required for some:* interview. *Application deadline:* rolling (freshmen), rolling (transfers).

Admissions Contact Mr. Scott Allan, Director of Admissions, Paul Smith's College of Arts and Sciences, PO Box 265, Paul Smiths, NY 12970-0265. *Phone:* 518-327-6227. *Toll-free phone:* 800-421-2605. *Fax:* 518-327-6016.

■ *See page 2154 for a narrative description.*

POLYTECHNIC UNIVERSITY, BROOKLYN CAMPUS
Brooklyn, New York

- **Independent** university, founded 1854
- **Calendar** semesters
- **Degrees** certificates, bachelor's, master's, doctoral, and postbachelor's certificates
- **Urban** 3-acre campus
- **Endowment** $117.9 million
- **Coed,** 1,559 undergraduate students, 95% full-time, 18% women, 82% men
- **Very difficult** entrance level, 73% of applicants were admitted

Undergraduates 1,488 full-time, 71 part-time. Students come from 18 states and territories, 31 other countries, 4% are from out of state, 10% African American, 38% Asian American or Pacific Islander, 8% Hispanic American, 0.3% Native American, 8% international, 5% transferred in, 13% live on campus. *Retention:* 81% of 2002 full-time freshmen returned.

Freshmen *Admission:* 1,307 applied, 959 admitted, 396 enrolled. *Average high school GPA:* 3.20. *Test scores:* SAT verbal scores over 500: 75%; SAT math scores over 500: 97%; SAT verbal scores over 600: 25%; SAT math scores over 600: 69%; SAT verbal scores over 700: 3%; SAT math scores over 700: 20%.

Faculty *Total:* 292, 52% full-time. *Student/faculty ratio:* 12:1.

Majors Chemical engineering; chemistry; civil engineering; computer engineering; computer science; construction management; electrical, electronics and communications engineering; journalism; liberal arts and sciences/liberal studies; management information systems; mathematics; mechanical engineering; molecular biochemistry; physics.

Academic Programs *Special study options:* academic remediation for entering students, accelerated degree program, advanced placement credit, cooperative education, double majors, English as a second language, honors programs, internships, part-time degree program, summer session for credit. *ROTC:* Air Force (c).

Library Bern Dibner Library plus 1 other with 148,000 titles, 613 serial subscriptions, 235 audiovisual materials, an OPAC, a Web page.

Computers on Campus 1330 computers available on campus for general student use. A campuswide network can be accessed from student residence rooms and from off campus. Internet access, at least one staffed computer lab available. Computer purchase or lease plan available.

Student Life *Housing options:* coed. Campus housing is university owned. Freshman applicants given priority for college housing. *Activities and organizations:* student-run newspaper, National Society of Black Engineers, Society of Hispanic Professional Engineers, Association for Computing Machinery, Alpha Phi Omega, Chinese Student Society, national fraternities, national sororities. *Campus security:* 24-hour patrols, controlled dormitory access. *Student services:* health clinic, personal/psychological counseling, women's center.

Athletics Member NCAA. All Division III. *Intercollegiate sports:* baseball M, basketball M/W, cross-country running M/W, soccer M/W, softball W, tennis M/W, track and field M/W, volleyball M/W. *Intramural sports:* badminton M/W, basketball M/W, bowling M/W, football M/W, golf M(c)/W(c), soccer M/W, table tennis M(c)/W(c), track and field M(c)/W(c), volleyball M/W, weight lifting M(c)/W(c).

Standardized Tests *Required:* SAT I or ACT (for admission). *Recommended:* SAT II: Subject Tests (for admission), SAT II: Writing Test (for admission).

Costs (2003–04) *Comprehensive fee:* $33,772 includes full-time tuition ($24,802), mandatory fees ($970), and room and board ($8000). Full-time tuition and fees vary according to course load. Part-time tuition: $791 per credit. Part-time tuition and fees vary according to course load. *Required fees:* $300 per term part-time. *College room only:* $6500. Room and board charges vary according to housing facility. *Payment plans:* installment, deferred payment. *Waivers:* minority students and employees or children of employees.

Financial Aid Of all full-time matriculated undergraduates who enrolled in 2003, 1,460 applied for aid, 1,233 were judged to have need, 457 had their need fully met. 176 Federal Work-Study jobs (averaging $2306). In 2003, 228 non-need-based awards were made. *Average percent of need met:* 87%. *Average financial aid package:* $20,600. *Average need-based loan:* $5062. *Average need-based gift aid:* $8407. *Average non-need-based aid:* $16,341. *Average indebtedness upon graduation:* $20,219.

Applying *Options:* common application, electronic application, deferred entrance. *Application fee:* $50. *Required:* essay or personal statement, high school transcript, 2 letters of recommendation. *Recommended:* interview. *Application deadline:* 2/1 (freshmen), rolling (transfers).

Admissions Contact Jonathan D. Wexlar, Dean of Undergraduate Admissions, Polytechnic University, Brooklyn Campus, Six Metrotech Center, Brooklyn, NY 11201-2990. *Phone:* 718-260-3100. *Toll-free phone:* 800-POLYTECH. *Fax:* 718-260-3446. *E-mail:* admitme@poly.edu.

■ *See page 2184 for a narrative description.*

PRACTICAL BIBLE COLLEGE
Bible School Park, New York

- **Independent nondenominational** 4-year, founded 1900
- **Calendar** semesters
- **Degrees** certificates, diplomas, associate, and bachelor's
- **Suburban** 22-acre campus with easy access to Syracuse
- **Coed,** 293 undergraduate students, 78% full-time, 50% women, 50% men
- **Minimally difficult** entrance level, 53% of applicants were admitted

Undergraduates 229 full-time, 64 part-time. Students come from 13 states and territories, 4 other countries, 23% are from out of state, 1% African American, 0.3% Asian American or Pacific Islander, 0.7% Hispanic American, 2% international, 61% live on campus. *Retention:* 84% of 2002 full-time freshmen returned.

Freshmen *Admission:* 98 applied, 52 admitted. *Average high school GPA:* 3.38. *Test scores:* ACT scores over 18: 62%; ACT scores over 24: 26%; ACT scores over 30: 5%.

Faculty *Total:* 24, 29% full-time, 42% with terminal degrees. *Student/faculty ratio:* 17:1.

Majors Biblical studies.

Academic Programs *Special study options:* academic remediation for entering students, adult/continuing education programs, advanced placement credit, cooperative education, English as a second language, independent study, internships, part-time degree program, services for LD students, summer session for credit.

Library Alice E. Chatlos Library with 77,000 titles, 644 serial subscriptions, 8,500 audiovisual materials, an OPAC, a Web page.

Practical Bible College (continued)

Computers on Campus 12 computers available on campus for general student use. A campuswide network can be accessed. Internet access, at least one staffed computer lab available.

Student Life *Housing:* on-campus residence required through senior year. *Options:* men-only, women-only. Campus housing is university owned. *Activities and organizations:* drama/theater group, choral group, Student Missionary Fellowship, Student Wives Fellowship, Student Life Committee, Married Couples Fellowship. *Campus security:* 24-hour emergency response devices and patrols, student patrols, late-night transport/escort service. *Student services:* health clinic, personal/psychological counseling.

Athletics Member NCCAA. *Intercollegiate sports:* basketball M/W, soccer M, volleyball W. *Intramural sports:* skiing (downhill) M/W, soccer M/W, table tennis M/W, volleyball M/W, weight lifting M/W.

Standardized Tests *Required:* SAT I or ACT (for admission). *Recommended:* ACT (for admission).

Costs (2003–04) *Comprehensive fee:* $13,410 includes full-time tuition ($8060), mandatory fees ($700), and room and board ($4650).

Financial Aid Of all full-time matriculated undergraduates who enrolled in 2002, 182 applied for aid, 175 were judged to have need, 27 had their need fully met. 77 Federal Work-Study jobs (averaging $898). In 2002, 10 non-need-based awards were made. *Average percent of need met:* 37%. *Average financial aid package:* $5120. *Average need-based loan:* $4893. *Average need-based gift aid:* $4360. *Average non-need-based aid:* $610. *Average indebtedness upon graduation:* $5360.

Applying *Options:* common application, electronic application, deferred entrance. *Application fee:* $25. *Required:* high school transcript, 2 letters of recommendation, references. *Required for some:* essay or personal statement. *Recommended:* minimum 2.0 GPA, interview. *Application deadline:* rolling (freshmen), rolling (transfers). *Notification:* continuous (freshmen), continuous (transfers).

Admissions Contact Mr. Brian J. Murphy, Director of Admissions, Practical Bible College, PO Box 601, Bible School Park, NY 13737-0601. *Phone:* 607-729-1581 Ext. 406. *Toll-free phone:* 800-331-4137 Ext. 406. *Fax:* 607-729-2962. *E-mail:* admissions@practical.edu.

PRATT INSTITUTE

Brooklyn, New York

- **Independent** comprehensive, founded 1887
- **Calendar** semesters plus optional May term and summer session
- **Degrees** associate, bachelor's, master's, and first professional
- **Urban** 25-acre campus
- **Endowment** $41.1 million
- **Coed,** 2,994 undergraduate students, 95% full-time, 57% women, 43% men
- **Very difficult** entrance level, 47% of applicants were admitted

Pratt Institute, one of the premier art, design, writing, and architecture schools nationwide, is located in the historic Clinton Hill section of Brooklyn, just 25 minutes from downtown Manhattan. The majority of Pratt's freshmen live on the Institute's 25-acre tree-lined campus. Pratt offers 4-year bachelor's, 2-year associate, and combined bachelor's and master's degrees.

Undergraduates 2,835 full-time, 159 part-time. Students come from 46 states and territories, 38 other countries, 47% are from out of state, 7% African American, 13% Asian American or Pacific Islander, 8% Hispanic American, 9% international, 7% transferred in, 55% live on campus. *Retention:* 87% of 2002 full-time freshmen returned.

Freshmen *Admission:* 3,469 applied, 1,646 admitted, 558 enrolled. *Average high school GPA:* 3.38. *Test scores:* SAT verbal scores over 500: 84%; SAT math scores over 500: 86%; SAT verbal scores over 600: 30%; SAT math scores over 600: 38%; SAT verbal scores over 700: 5%; SAT math scores over 700: 8%.

Faculty *Total:* 802, 14% full-time. *Student/faculty ratio:* 11:1.

Majors Adult and continuing education; applied art; architecture; area, ethnic, cultural, and gender studies related; art; art history, criticism and conservation; art teacher education; ceramic arts and ceramics; cinematography and film/video production; city/urban, community and regional planning; commercial and advertising art; computer graphics; construction management; creative writing; design and applied arts related; drawing; fashion/apparel design; film/video and photographic arts related; fine arts related; fine/studio arts; graphic design; illustration; industrial design; interior design; metal and jewelry arts; painting; photography; printmaking; sculpture.

Academic Programs *Special study options:* advanced placement credit, English as a second language, independent study, internships, off-campus study, part-time degree program, services for LD students, study abroad, summer session for credit. *ROTC:* Army (c).

Library Pratt Institute Library with 172,000 titles, 540 serial subscriptions, 2,851 audiovisual materials, an OPAC, a Web page.

Computers on Campus 250 computers available on campus for general student use. A campuswide network can be accessed from student residence rooms and from off campus. Internet access, online (class) registration, at least one staffed computer lab available.

Student Life *Housing options:* coed. Campus housing is university owned. Freshman campus housing is guaranteed. *Activities and organizations:* drama/theater group, student-run newspaper, radio and television station, travel and recreation, student newspaper, athletic clubs, Performing Arts Committee, national fraternities. *Campus security:* 24-hour emergency response devices and patrols, late-night transport/escort service. *Student services:* health clinic, personal/psychological counseling.

Athletics Member NCAA. All Division III. *Intercollegiate sports:* basketball M, cross-country running M/W, soccer M/W, tennis M/W, track and field M/W, volleyball W. *Intramural sports:* badminton M/W, basketball M, field hockey M, football M, golf M, lacrosse M/W, volleyball M, weight lifting M/W.

Standardized Tests *Required:* SAT I or ACT (for admission). *Required for some:* SAT II: Subject Tests (for admission), SAT II: Writing Test (for admission).

Costs (2004–05) *Comprehensive fee:* $34,000 includes full-time tuition ($25,000), mandatory fees ($680), and room and board ($8320). Part-time tuition: $860 per credit. *College room only:* $5120. Room and board charges vary according to board plan, housing facility, and student level. *Payment plans:* installment, deferred payment. *Waivers:* employees or children of employees.

Financial Aid Of all full-time matriculated undergraduates who enrolled in 2003, 2,594 applied for aid, 2,278 were judged to have need. 468 Federal Work-Study jobs (averaging $1300). In 2003, 266 non-need-based awards were made. *Average percent of need met:* 58%. *Average financial aid package:* $14,605. *Average need-based loan:* $3780. *Average need-based gift aid:* $5870. *Average non-need-based aid:* $6960.

Applying *Options:* common application, electronic application, early decision. *Application fee:* $40. *Required:* essay or personal statement, high school transcript, 1 letter of recommendation. *Required for some:* interview, portfolio. *Recommended:* minimum 3.38 GPA. *Application deadlines:* 2/1 (freshmen), 2/11 (transfers). *Early decision:* 11/15. *Notification:* continuous until 4/11 (freshmen), 12/15 (early decision), 4/1 (transfers).

Admissions Contact Mrs. Micah Moody, Visit Coordinator, Pratt Institute, DeKalb Hall, 200 Willoughby Avenue, Brooklyn, NY 11205-3899. *Phone:* 718-636-3669 Ext. 3779. *Toll-free phone:* 800-331-0834. *Fax:* 718-636-3670. *E-mail:* admissions@pratt.edu.

■ *See page 2190 for a narrative description.*

PURCHASE COLLEGE, STATE UNIVERSITY OF NEW YORK

Purchase, New York

- **State-supported** comprehensive, founded 1967, part of State University of New York System
- **Calendar** semesters
- **Degrees** certificates, bachelor's, master's, and post-master's certificates
- **Small-town** 500-acre campus with easy access to New York City
- **Endowment** $28.3 million
- **Coed**
- **Moderately difficult** entrance level

Purchase College combines selective liberal arts and sciences programs with professional conservatory programs in the visual and performing arts. Purchase offers undergraduate degree programs in music, film, acting, dramatic writing, stage design/technology (including costume design), dance, visual arts, humanities, social sciences, and natural sciences. New programs in cinema studies, new media, creative writing, and journalism are very successful. Purchase is a small college community that offers students the opportunity to enter into apprentice relationships with artists, performers, scholars, and scientists who are making significant contributions to their fields. Residential learning communities are provided for select students. Purchase is committed to fostering educational creativity in a climate of artistic and intellectual freedom.

Faculty *Student/faculty ratio:* 17:1.

Student Life *Campus security:* 24-hour emergency response devices and patrols, late-night transport/escort service, controlled dormitory access, 24-hour patrols by police officers.

Standardized Tests *Required:* SAT I or ACT (for admission).

Costs (2003–04) *Tuition:* state resident $4350 full-time, $137 per credit part-time; nonresident $10,300 full-time, $346 per credit part-time. *Required fees:* $1186 full-time, $1 per credit part-time, $29 per term part-time. *Room and board:* $7122; room only: $5009. Room and board charges vary according to board plan and housing facility.

Financial Aid Of all full-time matriculated undergraduates who enrolled in 2002, 1,980 applied for aid, 1,519 were judged to have need, 267 had their need fully met. 210 Federal Work-Study jobs (averaging $1150). In 2002, 454. *Average percent of need met:* 69. *Average financial aid package:* $7235. *Average need-based loan:* $3643. *Average need-based gift aid:* $3975. *Average non-need-based aid:* $11,242. *Average indebtedness upon graduation:* $13,873.

Applying *Options:* early admission, early decision, deferred entrance. *Application fee:* $40. *Required:* high school transcript, minimum 3.0 GPA. *Required for some:* essay or personal statement, 1 letter of recommendation, interview, audition, portfolio.

Admissions Contact Ms. Betsy Immergut, Director of Admissions, Purchase College, State University of New York, 735 Anderson Hill Road, Purchase, NY 10577-1400. *Phone:* 914-251-6300. *Fax:* 914-251-6314. *E-mail:* admissn@purchase.edu.

■ *See page 2200 for a narrative description.*

QUEENS COLLEGE OF THE CITY UNIVERSITY OF NEW YORK

Flushing, New York

- **State and locally supported** comprehensive, founded 1937, part of City University of New York System
- **Calendar** semesters
- **Degrees** bachelor's, master's, post-master's, and postbachelor's certificates
- **Urban** 76-acre campus
- **Endowment** $15,000
- **Coed,** 12,346 undergraduate students, 66% full-time, 63% women, 37% men
- **Very difficult** entrance level, 99% of applicants were admitted

Queens College offers students a rigorous education in the liberal arts and sciences under the guidance of a faculty dedicated to teaching and research. Students graduate with a real competitive advantage—the ability to think critically, explore cultures, and use modern technologies. With a student population that reflects the diversity of New York City, Queens College provides an unusually rich education.

Undergraduates 8,169 full-time, 4,177 part-time. Students come from 18 states and territories, 118 other countries, 1% are from out of state, 10% African American, 19% Asian American or Pacific Islander, 16% Hispanic American, 0.1% Native American, 6% international, 13% transferred in. *Retention:* 87% of 2002 full-time freshmen returned.

Freshmen *Admission:* 2,503 applied, 2,468 admitted, 1,330 enrolled. *Average high school GPA:* 3.30. *Test scores:* SAT verbal scores over 500: 52%; SAT math scores over 500: 70%; SAT verbal scores over 600: 14%; SAT math scores over 600: 22%; SAT verbal scores over 700: 3%; SAT math scores over 700: 2%.

Faculty *Total:* 1,190, 48% full-time, 59% with terminal degrees. *Student/faculty ratio:* 17:1.

Majors Accounting; actuarial science; African studies; American studies; ancient/classical Greek; anthropology; applied mathematics; art; art history, criticism and conservation; art teacher education; Asian studies (East); biochemistry; biology/biological sciences; chemistry; communication disorders; communication/speech communication and rhetoric; comparative literature; computer science; dance; dramatic/theatre arts; economics; elementary education; English; English as a second/foreign language (teaching); English/language arts teacher education; environmental science; environmental studies; family and consumer sciences/home economics teacher education; family and consumer sciences/human sciences; film/cinema studies; finance; fine/studio arts; foreign language teacher education; French; geology/earth science; German; health and physical education; Hebrew; history; interdisciplinary studies; international business/trade/commerce; Italian; Jewish/Judaic studies; kindergarten/preschool education; kinesiology and exercise science; labor and industrial relations; Latin; Latin American studies; linguistics; mass communication/media; mathematics; mathematics teacher education; multi-/interdisciplinary studies related; music; music performance; music teacher education; Near and Middle Eastern studies; philosophy; physical education teaching and coaching; physics; political science and government; psychology; religious studies; Russian; science teacher education; social sciences related; social studies teacher education; sociology; Spanish; speech therapy; urban studies/affairs; women's studies.

Academic Programs *Special study options:* accelerated degree program, adult/continuing education programs, advanced placement credit, cooperative education, double majors, English as a second language, freshman honors college, honors programs, independent study, internships, off-campus study, part-time degree program, services for LD students, student-designed majors, study abroad, summer session for credit. *ROTC:* Army (c), Navy (c). *Unusual degree programs:* 3-2 BA/MA chemistry, biochemistry, computer science, music, philosophy, physics, political science.

Library Benjamin S. Rosenthal Library plus 1 other with 985,550 titles, 2,756 serial subscriptions, 30,505 audiovisual materials, an OPAC, a Web page.

Computers on Campus 1000 computers available on campus for general student use. A campuswide network can be accessed from off campus. Internet access, at least one staffed computer lab available.

Student Life *Housing:* college housing not available. *Activities and organizations:* drama/theater group, student-run newspaper, radio station, choral group, Alliance of Latin American Students, Black Student Union, Caribbean Student Association, Hillel-Jewish Student Organization, India Cultural Exchange, national fraternities, national sororities. *Campus security:* 24-hour emergency response devices and patrols. *Student services:* health clinic, personal/psychological counseling, women's center, legal services.

Athletics Member NCAA. All Division II. *Intercollegiate sports:* baseball M(s), basketball M(s)/W(s), fencing W(s), golf M(s), soccer W(s), softball M(s), swimming M(s)/W(s), tennis M(s)/W(s), volleyball M(s)/W(s), water polo M(s)/W(s). *Intramural sports:* basketball M/W, fencing M, ice hockey M, racquetball M/W, soccer M/W, softball M/W, tennis M/W, volleyball M/W, water polo M/W.

Standardized Tests *Required:* SAT I (for admission). *Recommended:* SAT II: Subject Tests (for admission).

Costs (2004–05) *Tuition:* state resident $4000 full-time, $170 per credit part-time; nonresident $8640 full-time, $360 per credit part-time. Full-time tuition and fees vary according to program. Part-time tuition and fees vary according to course load and program. *Required fees:* $361 full-time, $112 per term part-time. *Payment plan:* installment. *Waivers:* senior citizens.

Financial Aid Of all full-time matriculated undergraduates who enrolled in 2001, 4,993 applied for aid, 3,744 were judged to have need, 2,700 had their need fully met. 1,253 Federal Work-Study jobs (averaging $1300). In 2001, 292 non-need-based awards were made. *Average percent of need met:* 90%. *Average financial aid package:* $5000. *Average need-based gift aid:* $3400. *Average indebtedness upon graduation:* $12,000.

Applying *Options:* electronic application, deferred entrance. *Application fee:* $40. *Required:* high school transcript, minimum 3.0 GPA. *Application deadlines:* 1/1 (freshmen), 2/1 (transfers). *Notification:* continuous (freshmen), continuous (transfers).

Admissions Contact Undergraduate Admissions Office, Queens College of the City University of New York, Undergraduate Admissions, Kiely Hall 217, 65-30 Kissena Boulevard, Flushing, NY 11367. *Phone:* 718-997-5600. *Fax:* 718-997-5617. *E-mail:* admissions@qc.edu.

■ *See page 2202 for a narrative description.*

RABBINICAL ACADEMY MESIVTA RABBI CHAIM BERLIN

Brooklyn, New York

Admissions Contact Mr. Mayer Weinberger, Executive Administrator, Office of Admissions, Rabbinical Academy Mesivta Rabbi Chaim Berlin, 1605 Coney Island Avenue, Brooklyn, NY 11230-4715. *Phone:* 718-377-0777.

RABBINICAL COLLEGE BETH SHRAGA

Monsey, New York

- **Independent Jewish** comprehensive, founded 1965
- **Calendar** semesters
- **Degrees** bachelor's and master's
- **Small-town** campus
- **Men only**

Costs (2003–04) *Tuition:* $6750 full-time.

Admissions Contact Rabbi Schiff, Director of Admissions, Rabbinical College Beth Shraga, 28 Saddle River Road, Monsey, NY 10952-3035.

RABBINICAL COLLEGE BOBOVER YESHIVA B'NEI ZION

Brooklyn, New York

Admissions Contact Mr. Israel Licht, Director of Admissions, Rabbinical College Bobover Yeshiva B'nei Zion, 1577 Forty-eighth Street, Brooklyn, NY 11219. *Phone:* 718-438-2018.

RABBINICAL COLLEGE CH'SAN SOFER

Brooklyn, New York

Admissions Contact Director of Admissions, Rabbinical College Ch'san Sofer, 1876 Fiftieth Street, Brooklyn, NY 11204. *Phone:* 718-236-1171.

Rabbinical College of Long Island
Long Beach, New York

Admissions Contact Director of Admissions, Rabbinical College of Long Island, 201 Magnolia Boulevard, Long Beach, NY 11561-3305. *Phone:* 516-431-7414.

Rabbinical College of Ohr Shimon Yisroel
Brooklyn, New York

Admissions Contact 215-217 Hewes Street, Brooklyn, NY 11211.

Rabbinical Seminary Adas Yereim
Brooklyn, New York

Admissions Contact Mr. Hersch Greenschweig, Director of Admissions, Rabbinical Seminary Adas Yereim, 185 Wilson Street, Brooklyn, NY 11211-7206. *Phone:* 718-388-1751.

Rabbinical Seminary M'kor Chaim
Brooklyn, New York

Admissions Contact Rabbi Benjamin Paler, Director of Admissions, Rabbinical Seminary M'kor Chaim, 1571 Fifty-fifth Street, Brooklyn, NY 11219. *Phone:* 718-851-0183.

Rabbinical Seminary of America
Flushing, New York

Admissions Contact Rabbi Abraham Semmel, Director of Admissions, Rabbinical Seminary of America, 76-01 147th Street, Flushing, NY 11367. *Phone:* 718-268-4700.

Rensselaer Polytechnic Institute
Troy, New York

- **Independent** university, founded 1824
- **Calendar** semesters
- **Degrees** bachelor's, master's, and doctoral
- **Suburban** 260-acre campus with easy access to Albany
- **Endowment** $510.9 million
- **Coed,** 5,210 undergraduate students, 99% full-time, 25% women, 75% men
- **Very difficult** entrance level, 80% of applicants were admitted

Hands-on programs emphasize the practical and responsible application of technology and prepare students for meaningful careers in a global society. Tomorrow's leaders are educated in the fields of architecture, engineering, humanities and social sciences, information technology, management, and science. The 5,100 undergraduate students come from all 50 states and 71 countries.

Undergraduates 5,170 full-time, 40 part-time. Students come from 51 states and territories, 37 other countries, 54% are from out of state, 4% African American, 12% Asian American or Pacific Islander, 5% Hispanic American, 0.4% Native American, 4% international, 2% transferred in, 55% live on campus. *Retention:* 93% of 2002 full-time freshmen returned.

Freshmen *Admission:* 5,252 applied, 4,216 admitted, 1,341 enrolled. *Test scores:* SAT verbal scores over 500: 95%; SAT math scores over 500: 99%; ACT scores over 18: 100%; SAT verbal scores over 600: 70%; SAT math scores over 600: 90%; ACT scores over 24: 79%; SAT verbal scores over 700: 19%; SAT math scores over 700: 44%; ACT scores over 30: 9%.

Faculty *Total:* 479, 80% full-time, 89% with terminal degrees. *Student/faculty ratio:* 15:1.

Majors Aerospace, aeronautical and astronautical engineering; Air Force R.O.T.C./air science; applied mathematics; architecture; architecture related; Army R.O.T.C./military science; biochemistry; bioinformatics; biological and biomedical sciences related; biological and physical sciences; biology/biological sciences; biomedical/medical engineering; biophysics; business administration and management; chemical engineering; chemistry; civil engineering; communication/speech communication and rhetoric; computer and information sciences; computer engineering; computer science; economics; electrical, electronics and communications engineering; engineering; engineering physics; engineering science; entrepreneurship; environmental/environmental health engineering; finance; geology/earth science; hydrology and water resources science; industrial engineering; information technology; interdisciplinary studies; management information systems; management information systems and services related; manufacturing engineering; marketing/marketing management; materials engineering; mathematics; mechanical engineering; Navy/Marine Corps R.O.T.C./naval science; nuclear engineering; philosophy; physical sciences; physics; pre-dentistry studies; pre-law studies; pre-medical studies; psychology; science, technology and society; social sciences; systems engineering; visual and performing arts related.

Academic Programs *Special study options:* accelerated degree program, adult/continuing education programs, advanced placement credit, cooperative education, distance learning, double majors, English as a second language, independent study, internships, off-campus study, part-time degree program, services for LD students, student-designed majors, study abroad, summer session for credit. *ROTC:* Army (b), Navy (b), Air Force (b).

Library Folsom Library plus 1 other with 309,171 titles, 10,210 serial subscriptions, 91,435 audiovisual materials, an OPAC, a Web page.

Computers on Campus 500 computers available on campus for general student use. A campuswide network can be accessed from student residence rooms and from off campus. Internet access, online (class) registration, at least one staffed computer lab available. Computer purchase or lease plan available.

Student Life *Housing:* on-campus residence required for freshman year. *Options:* coed, disabled students. Campus housing is university owned. Freshman campus housing is guaranteed. *Activities and organizations:* drama/theater group, student-run newspaper, radio station, choral group, ski club, musical organizations, weightlifting, ballroom dance, campus radio station, national fraternities, national sororities. *Campus security:* 24-hour emergency response devices and patrols, late-night transport/escort service, controlled dormitory access, campus foot patrols at night. *Student services:* health clinic, personal/psychological counseling, legal services.

Athletics Member NCAA. All Division III except ice hockey (Division I). *Intercollegiate sports:* archery M(c)/W(c), badminton M(c)/W(c), baseball M, basketball M/W, cheerleading M(c)/W(c), crew M(c)/W(c), cross-country running M/W, equestrian sports M(c)/W(c), fencing M(c)/W(c), field hockey W, football M, golf M, gymnastics M(c)/W(c), ice hockey M(s)/W, lacrosse M/W, racquetball M(c)/W(c), riflery M(c)/W(c), rock climbing M(c)/W(c), rugby M(c)/W(c), sailing M(c)/W(c), skiing (cross-country) M(c)/W(c), skiing (downhill) M(c)/W(c), soccer M/W, softball W, squash M(c)/W(c), swimming M/W, table tennis M(c)/W(c), tennis M/W, track and field M/W, volleyball M(c)/W, water polo M(c)/W(c), weight lifting M(c)/W(c). *Intramural sports:* badminton M/W, basketball M/W, bowling M/W, cheerleading M/W, football M/W, golf M/W, ice hockey M/W, rock climbing M/W, soccer M/W, softball M/W, swimming M/W, table tennis M/W, tennis M/W, track and field M/W, ultimate Frisbee M/W, volleyball M/W, water polo M/W, wrestling M.

Standardized Tests *Required:* SAT I or ACT (for admission). *Required for some:* SAT II: Subject Tests (for admission).

Costs (2003–04) *Comprehensive fee:* $37,579 includes full-time tuition ($27,700), mandatory fees ($796), and room and board ($9083). Part-time tuition: $865 per credit hour. *College room only:* $5101. Room and board charges vary according to board plan and housing facility. *Payment plan:* installment. *Waivers:* employees or children of employees.

Financial Aid Of all full-time matriculated undergraduates who enrolled in 2002, 4,016 applied for aid, 3,627 were judged to have need, 2,310 had their need fully met. 1,337 Federal Work-Study jobs (averaging $1088). In 2002, 726 non-need-based awards were made. *Average percent of need met:* 90%. *Average financial aid package:* $22,791. *Average need-based loan:* $5810. *Average need-based gift aid:* $16,840. *Average non-need-based aid:* $10,789. *Average indebtedness upon graduation:* $23,725.

Applying *Options:* common application, electronic application, early admission, early decision, deferred entrance. *Application fee:* $50. *Required:* essay or personal statement, high school transcript, 1 letter of recommendation. *Required for some:* portfolio for architecture and electronic arts programs. *Application deadlines:* 1/1 (freshmen), 7/1 (transfers). *Early decision:* 11/15. *Notification:* 3/31 (freshmen), 12/31 (early decision), continuous until 8/15 (transfers).

Admissions Contact Ms. Teresa Duffy, Dean of Enrollment Management, Rensselaer Polytechnic Institute, 110 8th Street, Troy, NY 12180-3590. *Phone:* 518-276-6216. *Toll-free phone:* 800-448-6562. *Fax:* 518-276-4072. *E-mail:* admissions@rpi.edu.

■ See page 2224 for a narrative description.

Roberts Wesleyan College
Rochester, New York

- **Independent** comprehensive, founded 1866, affiliated with Free Methodist Church of North America
- **Calendar** semesters

- **Degrees** associate, bachelor's, and master's
- **Suburban** 75-acre campus
- **Endowment** $10.0 million
- **Coed,** 1,292 undergraduate students, 91% full-time, 66% women, 34% men
- **Moderately difficult** entrance level, 80% of applicants were admitted

Academic life continues to flourish at Roberts Wesleyan, with new master's programs in education, psychology, and counseling. Several divisions, graduate and undergraduate, recently have earned professional accreditation or reaccreditation. Roberts Wesleyan recently established a Center for Christian Social Ministries and an Institute for Social Entrepreneurship, which benefit students and the Rochester community.

Undergraduates 1,173 full-time, 119 part-time. Students come from 24 states and territories, 19 other countries, 18% are from out of state, 6% African American, 1% Asian American or Pacific Islander, 2% Hispanic American, 0.1% Native American, 4% international, 8% transferred in, 69% live on campus. *Retention:* 82% of 2002 full-time freshmen returned.

Freshmen *Admission:* 689 applied, 554 admitted, 253 enrolled. *Average high school GPA:* 3.32. *Test scores:* SAT verbal scores over 500: 71%; SAT math scores over 500: 66%; ACT scores over 18: 66%; SAT verbal scores over 600: 29%; SAT math scores over 600: 27%; ACT scores over 24: 34%; SAT verbal scores over 700: 2%; SAT math scores over 700: 3%; ACT scores over 30: 13%.

Faculty *Total:* 196, 46% full-time. *Student/faculty ratio:* 17:1.

Majors Accounting; art; art teacher education; biochemistry; biological and physical sciences; biology/biological sciences; biology teacher education; business administration and management; chemistry; chemistry teacher education; clinical laboratory science/medical technology; communication/speech communication and rhetoric; computer and information sciences and support services related; computer science; criminal justice/law enforcement administration; divinity/ministry; education; elementary education; English; English/language arts teacher education; fine/studio arts; history; humanities; human resources management; management information systems; marketing/marketing management; mathematics; mathematics teacher education; music; music teacher education; natural sciences; nursing (registered nurse training); nursing related; pastoral studies/counseling; philosophy; philosophy and religious studies related; physical sciences; physics; physics teacher education; piano and organ; pre-dentistry studies; pre-engineering; pre-law studies; pre-medical studies; pre-pharmacy studies; pre-theology/pre-ministerial studies; pre-veterinary studies; psychology; science teacher education; secondary education; social studies teacher education; social work; sociology; special education; voice and opera.

Academic Programs *Special study options:* academic remediation for entering students, adult/continuing education programs, advanced placement credit, cooperative education, double majors, English as a second language, freshman honors college, honors programs, independent study, internships, off-campus study, services for LD students, study abroad, summer session for credit. *ROTC:* Army (c), Air Force (c). *Unusual degree programs:* 3-2 engineering with Clarkson University, Rensselaer Polytechnic Institute, Rochester Institute of Technology.

Library Ora A. Sprague Library with 118,464 titles, 971 serial subscriptions, 3,701 audiovisual materials, an OPAC, a Web page.

Computers on Campus 160 computers available on campus for general student use. A campuswide network can be accessed from student residence rooms and from off campus that provide access to campus Intranet. Internet access, online (class) registration, at least one staffed computer lab available.

Student Life *Housing:* on-campus residence required through senior year. *Options:* men-only, women-only. Campus housing is university owned. Freshman campus housing is guaranteed. *Activities and organizations:* drama/theater group, student-run newspaper, radio station, choral group, Habitat for Humanity, Foot of the Cross, Radiant Light, nursing club, drama club. *Campus security:* 24 hour emergency response devices and patrols, late-night transport/escort service, controlled dormitory access, 24-hour Resident Life staff on-call. *Student services:* health clinic, personal/psychological counseling.

Athletics Member NCAA, NAIA, NCCAA. All NCAA Division II. *Intercollegiate sports:* basketball M(s)/W(s), cross-country running M(s)/W(s), golf M(s)/W(s), soccer M(s)/W(s), tennis M(s)/W(s), track and field M(s)/W(s), volleyball W(s). *Intramural sports:* basketball M/W, racquetball M/W, soccer M/W, softball M/W, table tennis M/W, tennis M/W, volleyball M/W.

Standardized Tests *Required:* SAT I or ACT (for admission).

Costs (2003–04) *Comprehensive fee:* $22,952 includes full-time tuition ($16,134), mandatory fees ($618), and room and board ($6200). Part-time tuition: $334 per credit. Part-time tuition and fees vary according to course load. *College room only:* $4420. Room and board charges vary according to board plan. *Payment plan:* installment. *Waivers:* employees or children of employees.

Financial Aid Of all full-time matriculated undergraduates who enrolled in 2002, 840 applied for aid, 796 were judged to have need, 188 had their need fully met. 610 Federal Work-Study jobs (averaging $1048). 50 state and other part-time jobs (averaging $1988). In 2002, 110 non-need-based awards were made. *Average percent of need met:* 83%. *Average financial aid package:* $14,346. *Average need-based loan:* $5138. *Average need-based gift aid:* $8923. *Average non-need-based aid:* $8409.

Applying *Options:* electronic application, early admission, deferred entrance. *Application fee:* $35. *Required:* essay or personal statement, high school transcript, 2 letters of recommendation. *Recommended:* minimum 2.5 GPA, interview. *Application deadline:* 2/1 (freshmen), rolling (transfers).

Admissions Contact Ms. Linda Kurtz, Vice President for Admissions and Marketing, Roberts Wesleyan College, 2301 Westside Drive, Rochester, NY 14624. *Phone:* 585-594-6400. *Toll-free phone:* 800-777-4RWC. *Fax:* 585-594-6371. *E-mail:* admissions@roberts.edu.

■ *See page 2246 for a narrative description.*

ROCHESTER INSTITUTE OF TECHNOLOGY

Rochester, New York

- **Independent** comprehensive, founded 1829
- **Calendar** quarters
- **Degrees** certificates, diplomas, associate, bachelor's, master's, doctoral, post-master's, and postbachelor's certificates
- **Suburban** 1300-acre campus with easy access to Buffalo
- **Endowment** $414.9 million
- **Coed,** 12,381 undergraduate students, 86% full-time, 31% women, 69% men
- **Moderately difficult** entrance level, 70% of applicants were admitted

Undergraduates 10,652 full-time, 1,729 part-time. Students come from 50 states and territories, 85 other countries, 45% are from out of state, 5% African American, 7% Asian American or Pacific Islander, 3% Hispanic American, 0.4% Native American, 5% international, 7% transferred in, 60% live on campus. *Retention:* 88% of 2002 full-time freshmen returned.

Freshmen *Admission:* 8,317 applied, 5,784 admitted, 2,203 enrolled. *Average high school GPA:* 3.70. *Test scores:* SAT verbal scores over 500: 89%; SAT math scores over 500: 96%; ACT scores over 18: 99%; SAT verbal scores over 600: 46%; SAT math scores over 600: 65%; ACT scores over 24: 76%; SAT verbal scores over 700: 8%; SAT math scores over 700: 16%; ACT scores over 30: 19%.

Faculty *Total:* 1,145, 61% full-time, 83% with terminal degrees. *Student/faculty ratio:* 13:1.

Majors Accounting; advertising; aerospace, aeronautical and astronautical engineering; American Sign Language (ASL); animation, interactive technology, video graphics and special effects; applied art; applied mathematics; art; biochemistry; bioinformatics; biological and biomedical sciences related; biology/biological sciences; biomedical/medical engineering; biopsychology; biotechnology; business administration and management; ceramic arts and ceramics; chemistry; cinematography and film/video production; civil engineering technology; clinical laboratory science/medical technology; commercial photography; communication and media related; computer and information sciences; computer and information systems security; computer engineering; computer engineering technology; computer graphics; computer hardware engineering; computer programming (specific applications); computer science; computer software engineering; computer systems analysis; computer systems networking and telecommunications; crafts, folk art and artisanry; criminal justice/law enforcement administration; criminal justice/safety; data modeling/warehousing and database administration; design and visual communications; diagnostic medical sonography and ultrasound technology; dietetics; economics; electrical, electronic and communications engineering technology; electrical, electronics and communications engineering; electromechanical technology; engineering; engineering related; engineering-related technologies; engineering science; engineering technology; environmental science; finance; fine/studio arts; foodservice systems administration; furniture design and manufacturing; general studies; genetics; graphic communications; graphic design; hazardous materials management and waste technology; hospitality administration; hospitality/recreation marketing; hotel/motel administration; human nutrition; illustration; industrial design; industrial engineering; industrial safety technology; information technology; interdisciplinary studies; interior design; international business/trade/commerce; international relations and affairs; management information systems; manufacturing technology; marketing/marketing management; marketing research; mathematics; mathematics and computer science; mechanical engineering; mechanical engineering/mechanical technology; medical illustration; metal and jewelry arts; natural resources management and policy; nuclear medical technology; occupational safety and health technology; ophthalmic laboratory technology; photographic and film/video technology; photography; photojournalism; physician assistant; physics; polymer chemistry; pre-dentistry studies; pre-law studies; pre-medical studies; pre-veterinary studies; psychology; public policy analysis; public relations, advertising, and applied communication related; public relations/image management; publishing; resort management; restaurant/food services management; sculpture; sign language interpretation and translation; social work; special products marketing; statistics; system administration; system, networking, and

Rochester Institute of Technology (continued)

LAN/wan management; systems engineering; telecommunications; telecommunications technology; tourism and travel services management; tourism/travel marketing; web/multimedia management and webmaster; web page, digital/multimedia and information resources design.

Academic Programs *Special study options:* accelerated degree program, adult/continuing education programs, advanced placement credit, cooperative education, distance learning, English as a second language, honors programs, independent study, internships, off-campus study, part-time degree program, services for LD students, student-designed majors, study abroad, summer session for credit. *ROTC:* Army (b), Air Force (b).

Library Wallace Memorial Library with 350,000 titles, 4,305 serial subscriptions, 8,215 audiovisual materials, an OPAC, a Web page.

Computers on Campus 2500 computers available on campus for general student use. A campuswide network can be accessed from student residence rooms and from off campus that provide access to student account information. Internet access, online (class) registration, at least one staffed computer lab available.

Student Life *Housing:* on-campus residence required for freshman year. *Options:* coed, men-only, women-only, disabled students. Campus housing is university owned. Freshman campus housing is guaranteed. *Activities and organizations:* drama/theater group, student-run newspaper, radio station, choral group, campus radio station, campus weekly magazine, student government, Off-Campus Student Association, Music Association, national fraternities, national sororities. *Campus security:* 24-hour emergency response devices and patrols, student patrols, late-night transport/escort service. *Student services:* health clinic, personal/psychological counseling, women's center, legal services.

Athletics Member NCAA. All Division III. *Intercollegiate sports:* baseball M, basketball M/W, bowling M(c)/W(c), cheerleading M(c)/W(c), crew M/W, cross-country running M/W, equestrian sports M(c)/W(c), field hockey W(c), ice hockey M/W, lacrosse M/W, rugby M(c)/W(c), skiing (downhill) M(c)/W(c), soccer M/W, softball W, swimming M/W, tennis M/W, track and field M/W, ultimate Frisbee M(c)/W(c), volleyball M(c)/W, water polo M(c), wrestling M. *Intramural sports:* badminton M/W, basketball M/W, bowling M/W, football M, golf M/W, ice hockey M/W, lacrosse M(c), racquetball M/W, soccer M/W, softball M/W, table tennis M/W, tennis M/W, volleyball M/W.

Standardized Tests *Required:* SAT I or ACT (for admission).

Costs (2003–04) *Comprehensive fee:* $29,217 includes full-time tuition ($21,027), mandatory fees ($357), and room and board ($7833). Full-time tuition and fees vary according to course load, program, and student level. Part-time tuition: $468 per credit hour. Part-time tuition and fees vary according to class time, course level, course load, and program. *Required fees:* $29 per term part-time. *College room only:* $4452. Room and board charges vary according to board plan and housing facility. *Payment plans:* tuition prepayment, installment, deferred payment. *Waivers:* employees or children of employees.

Financial Aid Of all full-time matriculated undergraduates who enrolled in 2002, 7,940 applied for aid, 7,020 were judged to have need, 6,320 had their need fully met. 1,850 Federal Work-Study jobs (averaging $1360). 4,500 state and other part-time jobs (averaging $1860). In 2002, 900 non-need-based awards were made. *Average percent of need met:* 90%. *Average financial aid package:* $16,000. *Average need-based loan:* $4500. *Average need-based gift aid:* $9700. *Average non-need-based aid:* $5300.

Applying *Options:* common application, electronic application, early admission, early decision, deferred entrance. *Application fee:* $50. *Required:* essay or personal statement, high school transcript. *Required for some:* portfolio. *Recommended:* minimum 3.0 GPA, 1 letter of recommendation, interview. *Application deadline:* 3/15 (freshmen). *Early decision:* 12/1. *Notification:* continuous (freshmen), 1/15 (early decision), continuous (transfers).

Admissions Contact Dr. Daniel Shelley, Director of Undergraduate Admissions, Rochester Institute of Technology, 60 Lomb Memorial Drive, Rochester, NY 14623-5604. *Phone:* 585-475-6631. *Fax:* 585-475-7424. *E-mail:* admissions@rit.edu.

■ See page 2248 for a narrative description.

RUSSELL SAGE COLLEGE

Troy, New York

- **Independent** 4-year, founded 1916, part of The Sage Colleges
- **Calendar** semesters
- **Degree** bachelor's
- **Urban** 8-acre campus
- **Endowment** $21.3 million
- **Women only,** 824 undergraduate students, 92% full-time
- **Moderately difficult** entrance level, 82% of applicants were admitted

Russell Sage College is a small college devoted to women of influence—where individuals count and are consistently challenged to think differently and ultimately succeed. The College offers a wide selection of academic opportunities in the liberal arts in addition to the latest professional-degree programs in fields such as the health sciences, humanities, natural sciences and mathematics, and social and professional sciences. To schedule a visit to its beautiful Victorian campus in the heart of New York's "Tech Valley" and capital region, students should call 518-244-2217 or 888-VERY-SAGE (toll-free). E-mail: rscadm@sage.edu; Web site: http://www.rsc.admission.sage.edu.

Undergraduates 759 full-time, 65 part-time. Students come from 13 states and territories, 2 other countries, 8% are from out of state, 5% African American, 2% Asian American or Pacific Islander, 3% Hispanic American, 0.2% international, 11% transferred in, 46% live on campus. *Retention:* 80% of 2002 full-time freshmen returned.

Freshmen *Admission:* 130 enrolled. *Average high school GPA:* 3.30. *Test scores:* SAT verbal scores over 500: 69%; SAT math scores over 500: 63%; ACT scores over 18: 100%; SAT verbal scores over 600: 20%; SAT math scores over 600: 14%; ACT scores over 24: 53%; SAT verbal scores over 700: 2%; ACT scores over 30: 12%.

Faculty *Total:* 103, 56% full-time, 60% with terminal degrees. *Student/faculty ratio:* 11:1.

Majors Art therapy; athletic training; biochemistry; biology/biological sciences; biopsychology; business administration and management; chemistry; criminal justice/law enforcement administration; dramatic/theatre arts; elementary education; engineering; English; history; interdisciplinary studies; international relations and affairs; mass communication/media; mathematics; nursing (registered nurse training); nutrition sciences; occupational therapy; physical therapy; political science and government; psychology; sociology; Spanish.

Academic Programs *Special study options:* academic remediation for entering students, accelerated degree program, adult/continuing education programs, advanced placement credit, cooperative education, double majors, English as a second language, freshman honors college, honors programs, independent study, internships, off-campus study, part-time degree program, services for LD students, student-designed majors, study abroad, summer session for credit. *ROTC:* Army (c), Air Force (c). *Unusual degree programs:* 3-2 business administration with Sage Graduate School; engineering with Rensselaer Polytechnic Institute; nursing with Sage Graduate School; occupational therapy, physical therapy, public administration with Sage Graduate School.

Library James Wheelock Clark Library plus 1 other with 350,466 titles, 15,771 serial subscriptions, 34,485 audiovisual materials, an OPAC.

Computers on Campus 121 computers available on campus for general student use. A campuswide network can be accessed from student residence rooms and from off campus. Internet access, at least one staffed computer lab available.

Student Life *Housing:* on-campus residence required through senior year. *Options:* women-only. Campus housing is university owned. Freshman campus housing is guaranteed. *Activities and organizations:* drama/theater group, student-run newspaper, choral group, student government, Sage Recreation Association, physical therapy club, crew club, Black-Latin Student Alliance. *Campus security:* 24-hour emergency response devices and patrols, late-night transport/escort service, controlled dormitory access. *Student services:* health clinic, personal/psychological counseling, women's center.

Athletics Member NCAA. All Division III. *Intercollegiate sports:* basketball W, soccer W, softball W, tennis W, volleyball W. *Intramural sports:* badminton W, basketball W, cheerleading W(c), crew W(c), equestrian sports W(c), field hockey W(c), ice hockey W(c), lacrosse W(c), skiing (cross-country) W(c), skiing (downhill) W(c), soccer W, softball W, tennis W, track and field W(c), ultimate Frisbee W, volleyball W, water polo W.

Standardized Tests *Required:* SAT I or ACT (for admission).

Costs (2003–04) *Comprehensive fee:* $26,811 includes full-time tuition ($19,200), mandatory fees ($745), and room and board ($6866). Part-time tuition: $640 per credit hour. *College room only:* $3316.

Financial Aid Of all full-time matriculated undergraduates who enrolled in 2002, 699 applied for aid, 673 were judged to have need. 274 Federal Work-Study jobs (averaging $1500). 124 state and other part-time jobs (averaging $1200). In 2002, 43 non-need-based awards were made. *Average non-need-based aid:* $9600. *Average indebtedness upon graduation:* $19,200.

Applying *Options:* common application, electronic application, early admission, early decision, deferred entrance. *Application fee:* $30. *Required:* essay or personal statement, high school transcript, minimum 2.0 GPA, 2 letters of recommendation. *Recommended:* interview. *Application deadline:* 8/1 (freshmen), rolling (transfers). *Early decision:* 12/1. *Notification:* continuous (freshmen), 12/15 (early decision), continuous (transfers).

Admissions Contact Ms. Beth Robertson, Director of Undergraduate Admission, Russell Sage College, 45 Ferry Street, Troy, NY 12180. *Phone:* 518-244-2444. *Toll-free phone:* 888-VERY-SAGE (in-state); 888-VERY SAGE (out-of-state). *Fax:* 518-244-6880. *E-mail:* rscadm@sage.edu.

SAGE COLLEGE OF ALBANY
Albany, New York

- **Independent** 4-year, founded 1957, part of The Sage Colleges
- **Calendar** semesters
- **Degrees** certificates, associate, and bachelor's
- **Urban** 15-acre campus
- **Endowment** $21.3 million
- **Coed,** 998 undergraduate students, 54% full-time, 70% women, 30% men
- **Minimally difficult** entrance level, 32% of applicants were admitted

The newest four-year college in New York's capital region, Sage College of Albany, works closely with each student to design an individualized education leading to a successful and enjoyable career. Sage offers mind-changing educational pathways from associate through bachelor's degrees in applied studies, a 2+2 model, and part-time bachelor's degree-completion programs.

Undergraduates 537 full-time, 461 part-time. Students come from 6 states and territories, 4 other countries, 2% are from out of state, 11% African American, 1% Asian American or Pacific Islander, 3% Hispanic American, 0.7% Native American, 0.4% international, 14% transferred in, 31% live on campus. *Retention:* 54% of 2002 full-time freshmen returned.

Freshmen *Admission:* 352 applied, 113 admitted, 113 enrolled. *Average high school GPA:* 2.75. *Test scores:* SAT verbal scores over 500: 45%; SAT math scores over 500: 30%; ACT scores over 18: 67%; SAT verbal scores over 600: 6%; SAT math scores over 600: 3%; ACT scores over 24: 13%.

Faculty *Total:* 102, 41% full-time, 36% with terminal degrees. *Student/faculty ratio:* 11:1.

Majors Accounting; business administration and management; commercial and advertising art; communication/speech communication and rhetoric; computer and information sciences; computer systems networking and telecommunications; criminal justice/law enforcement administration; fine/studio arts; humanities; interior design; legal assistant/paralegal; legal studies; liberal arts and sciences/liberal studies; marketing/marketing management; photography; psychology; social sciences.

Academic Programs *Special study options:* academic remediation for entering students, adult/continuing education programs, advanced placement credit, cooperative education, English as a second language, external degree program, freshman honors college, honors programs, independent study, internships, off-campus study, part-time degree program, services for LD students, student-designed majors, summer session for credit.

Library Troy and Albany Campus Libraries with 371,686 titles, 15,771 serial subscriptions, 34,485 audiovisual materials, an OPAC.

Computers on Campus 165 computers available on campus for general student use. A campuswide network can be accessed from student residence rooms and from off campus. At least one staffed computer lab available.

Student Life *Housing options:* coed, women-only. Freshman applicants given priority for college housing. *Activities and organizations:* student-run newspaper, student government, Phi Theta Kappa, psychology club, ski club, "Vernacular" (art and literary publication). *Campus security:* 24-hour emergency response devices and patrols, late-night transport/escort service, controlled dormitory access, 24-hour security cameras. *Student services:* health clinic, personal/psychological counseling.

Athletics *Intramural sports:* badminton M/W, basketball M/W, cheerleading W(c), field hockey M(c)/W(c), football M/W, ice hockey M(c)/W(c), lacrosse M(c)/W(c), skiing (downhill) M(c)/W(c), soccer M/W, volleyball W, water polo M/W.

Standardized Tests *Required:* SAT I or ACT (for admission).

Costs (2003–04) *Comprehensive fee:* $22,061 includes full-time tuition ($14,500), mandatory fees ($695), and room and board ($6866). Part-time tuition: $490 per credit hour. *College room only:* $3316. Room and board charges vary according to board plan and location. *Payment plans:* installment, deferred payment. *Waivers:* employees or children of employees.

Financial Aid Of all full-time matriculated undergraduates who enrolled in 2002, 406 applied for aid, 379 were judged to have need. 220 Federal Work-Study jobs (averaging $1500). 86 state and other part-time jobs (averaging $1200). In 2002, 24 non-need-based awards were made. *Average non-need-based aid:* $3600. *Average indebtedness upon graduation:* $8600.

Applying *Options:* common application, electronic application, deferred entrance. *Application fee:* $30. *Required:* high school transcript, 1 letter of recommendation, portfolio for fine arts program. *Recommended:* essay or personal statement, interview. *Application deadlines:* 8/1 (freshmen), 8/1 (transfers). *Notification:* continuous until 8/15 (freshmen), continuous until 8/15 (transfers).

Admissions Contact Ms. Elizabeth Robertson, Director of Undergraduate Admission, Sage College of Albany, 140 New Scotland Avenue, Albany, NY 12208. *Phone:* 518-292-1730. *Toll-free phone:* 888-VERY-SAGE. *Fax:* 518-292-1912. *E-mail:* scaadm@sage.edu.

ST. BONAVENTURE UNIVERSITY
St. Bonaventure, New York

- **Independent comprehensive, founded 1858, affiliated with Roman Catholic Church**
- **Calendar semesters**
- **Degrees bachelor's, master's, post-master's, and postbachelor's certificates**
- **Small-town 600-acre campus**
- **Endowment $33.0 million**
- **Coed, 2,291 undergraduate students, 95% full-time, 51% women, 49% men**
- **Moderately difficult entrance level, 87% of applicants were admitted**

Offering more than 30 majors and a 4+1 program enabling undergraduates to obtain a master's degree in one year, St. Bonaventure University attracts exceptional students from 34 states and 12 countries. Adding to the Bonaventure experience are broadcast journalism and modern language laboratories, an expanded fiber-optic computer network, an endowed visiting professorship, a regional arts center, Division I athletics, and a dynamic intramural program. *U.S. News & World Report* repeatedly ranks St. Bonaventure in its top tier of regional universities.

Undergraduates 2,177 full-time, 114 part-time. Students come from 36 states and territories, 25% are from out of state, 1% African American, 0.7% Asian American or Pacific Islander, 1% Hispanic American, 0.1% Native American, 0.3% international, 3% transferred in, 77% live on campus. *Retention:* 82% of 2002 full-time freshmen returned.

Freshmen *Admission:* 1,990 applied, 1,728 admitted, 596 enrolled. *Average high school GPA:* 3.1. *Test scores:* SAT verbal scores over 500: 67%; SAT math scores over 500: 65%; ACT scores over 18: 91%; SAT verbal scores over 600: 18%; SAT math scores over 600: 19%; ACT scores over 24: 30%; SAT verbal scores over 700: 2%; SAT math scores over 700: 2%; ACT scores over 30: 5%.

Faculty *Total:* 229, 68% full-time. *Student/faculty ratio:* 14:1.

Majors Accounting; art teacher education; biochemistry; biology/biological sciences; biology teacher education; biophysics; business administration and management; business/commerce; business/managerial economics; chemistry; chemistry teacher education; classics and classical languages related; classics and languages, literatures and linguistics; computer science; early childhood education; elementary education; engineering physics; English; English/language arts teacher education; environmental studies; finance; foreign language teacher education; French; French language teacher education; German language teacher education; history; interdisciplinary studies; international business/trade/commerce; journalism; kindergarten/preschool education; management information systems and services related; management science; marketing/marketing management; mass communication/media; mathematics; mathematics teacher education; middle school education; modern languages; philosophy; physical education teaching and coaching; physical sciences; physics; physics teacher education; political science and government; pre-dentistry studies; pre-law studies; pre-medical studies; pre-veterinary studies; psychology; religious education; secondary education; social sciences; social studies teacher education; sociology; Spanish; Spanish language teacher education; special education; visual and performing arts.

Academic Programs *Special study options:* advanced placement credit, double majors, freshman honors college, honors programs, independent study, internships, off-campus study, part-time degree program, services for LD students, student-designed majors, study abroad, summer session for credit. *ROTC:* Army (b). *Unusual degree programs:* 3-2 English, physics, psychology.

Library Friedsam Library with 287,622 titles, 1,584 serial subscriptions, 8,891 audiovisual materials, an OPAC, a Web page.

Computers on Campus 200 computers available on campus for general student use. A campuswide network can be accessed from student residence rooms and from off campus. Internet access, online (class) registration, at least one staffed computer lab available.

Student Life *Housing:* on-campus residence required through junior year. *Options:* coed, men-only, women-only, disabled students. Campus housing is university owned. Freshman campus housing is guaranteed. *Activities and organizations:* drama/theater group, student-run newspaper, radio and television station, choral group, student government, Student Programming Board, campus media, Bonaventure Business Association, Student Ambassadors. *Campus security:* 24-hour emergency response devices and patrols, student patrols, late-night transport/escort service. *Student services:* health clinic, personal/psychological counseling.

Athletics Member NCAA. All Division I. *Intercollegiate sports:* baseball M(s), basketball M(s)/W(s), cheerleading M(c)/W(c), cross-country running M(s)/W(s), field hockey W(c), golf M(s), lacrosse M(c)/W, rugby M(c)/W(c), soccer M(s)/W(s), softball W(s), swimming M(s)/W(s), tennis M(s)/W(s), volleyball M(c)/W(s). *Intramural sports:* basketball M/W, bowling M/W, football M/W,

St. Bonaventure University (continued)
racquetball M/W, skiing (cross-country) M/W, skiing (downhill) M/W, soccer M/W, softball M/W, squash M/W, swimming M/W, table tennis M/W, tennis M/W, volleyball M/W, water polo M/W, weight lifting M/W.

Standardized Tests *Required:* SAT I or ACT (for admission). *Required for some:* SAT I or ACT (for placement).

Costs (2003–04) *Comprehensive fee:* $24,455 includes full-time tuition ($17,190), mandatory fees ($735), and room and board ($6530). Part-time tuition: $560 per hour. *College room only:* $3300. Room and board charges vary according to board plan and housing facility. *Payment plans:* tuition prepayment, installment, deferred payment. *Waivers:* senior citizens and employees or children of employees.

Financial Aid Of all full-time matriculated undergraduates who enrolled in 2002, 1,737 applied for aid, 1,499 were judged to have need, 542 had their need fully met. In 2002, 339 non-need-based awards were made. *Average percent of need met:* 87%. *Average financial aid package:* $14,448. *Average need-based loan:* $4195. *Average need-based gift aid:* $9753. *Average non-need-based aid:* $6155. *Average indebtedness upon graduation:* $16,900.

Applying *Options:* common application, early admission, deferred entrance. *Application fee:* $30. *Required:* high school transcript, 1 letter of recommendation. *Required for some:* essay or personal statement. *Recommended:* essay or personal statement, minimum 3.0 GPA, 3 letters of recommendation, interview. *Application deadlines:* 4/15 (freshmen), 8/15 (transfers). *Notification:* continuous (freshmen), continuous (transfers).

Admissions Contact Mr. James M. DiRisio, Director of Admissions, St. Bonaventure University, PO Box D, St. Bonaventure, NY 14778. *Phone:* 716-375-2400. *Toll-free phone:* 800-462-5050. *Fax:* 716-375-4005. *E-mail:* admissions@sbu.edu.

■ *See page 2278 for a narrative description.*

St. Francis College
Brooklyn Heights, New York

- **Independent Roman Catholic** 4-year, founded 1884
- **Calendar** semesters
- **Degrees** associate and bachelor's
- **Urban** 1-acre campus with easy access to New York City
- **Endowment** $62.3 million
- **Coed,** 2,468 undergraduate students, 80% full-time, 58% women, 42% men
- **Moderately difficult** entrance level, 88% of applicants were admitted

Undergraduates 1,976 full-time, 492 part-time. Students come from 6 states and territories, 42 other countries, 1% are from out of state, 20% African American, 2% Asian American or Pacific Islander, 14% Hispanic American, 0.2% Native American, 13% international, 7% transferred in. *Retention:* 76% of 2002 full-time freshmen returned.

Freshmen *Admission:* 1,304 applied, 1,149 admitted, 434 enrolled. *Average high school GPA:* 3.1. *Test scores:* SAT verbal scores over 500: 41%; SAT math scores over 500: 35%; SAT verbal scores over 600: 10%; SAT math scores over 600: 5%; SAT verbal scores over 700: 1%.

Faculty *Total:* 220, 31% full-time, 40% with terminal degrees. *Student/faculty ratio:* 18:1.

Majors Accounting; aeronautics/aviation/aerospace science and technology; area studies related; aviation/airway management; biology/biological sciences; biology teacher education; biomedical sciences; business administration and management; business teacher education; chemistry; chemistry teacher education; clinical laboratory science/medical technology; communication/speech communication and rhetoric; criminal justice/safety; data processing and data processing technology; economics; English; English/language arts teacher education; ethnic, cultural minority, and gender studies related; French; French language teacher education; health/health care administration; health professions related; history; information technology; liberal arts and sciences/liberal studies; mathematics; mathematics teacher education; medical radiologic technology; nursing related; philosophy; physical education teaching and coaching; physician assistant; political science and government; psychology; religious studies; social studies teacher education; sociology; Spanish; Spanish language teacher education; special education (vision impaired).

Academic Programs *Special study options:* academic remediation for entering students, accelerated degree program, adult/continuing education programs, advanced placement credit, double majors, English as a second language, external degree program, honors programs, independent study, internships, part-time degree program, study abroad, summer session for credit. *ROTC:* Army (c), Air Force (c). *Unusual degree programs:* 3-2 podiatric medicine with New York College of Podiatric Medicine.

Library McGarry Library with 120,000 titles, 571 serial subscriptions, 2,150 audiovisual materials, an OPAC, a Web page.

Computers on Campus 300 computers available on campus for general student use. Internet access, at least one staffed computer lab available.

Student Life *Housing:* college housing not available. *Activities and organizations:* drama/theater group, student-run newspaper, radio and television station, choral group, Fine Arts Society, Latin American Society, Physical Education Club, Arab American Society, History and Political Science Society, national fraternities, national sororities. *Campus security:* ID checks, crime awareness workshops, pamphlets, posters, films. *Student services:* personal/psychological counseling.

Athletics Member NCAA. All Division I. *Intercollegiate sports:* baseball M(s), basketball M(s)/W(s), cross-country running M(s)/W(s), soccer M(s), softball W(s), swimming M(s)/W(s), tennis M(s)/W(s), track and field M(s)/W(s), volleyball W(s), water polo M(s)/W(s). *Intramural sports:* basketball M/W, football M, soccer M/W, softball M/W, table tennis M/W, volleyball M/W.

Standardized Tests *Required:* SAT I (for admission).

Costs (2003–04) *Tuition:* $10,620 full-time, $365 per credit part-time. Full-time tuition and fees vary according to course level, course load, degree level, program, and student level. Part-time tuition and fees vary according to course level, course load, degree level, program, and student level. *Required fees:* $260 full-time, $20 per term part-time. *Payment plans:* installment, deferred payment. *Waivers:* employees or children of employees.

Financial Aid Of all full-time matriculated undergraduates who enrolled in 2001, 2,272 applied for aid, 1,842 were judged to have need, 156 had their need fully met. 98 Federal Work-Study jobs (averaging $1998). In 2001, 325 non-need-based awards were made. *Average percent of need met:* 68%. *Average financial aid package:* $6940. *Average need-based loan:* $3439. *Average need-based gift aid:* $3400. *Average non-need-based aid:* $6752.

Applying *Options:* electronic application, deferred entrance. *Application fee:* $35. *Required:* essay or personal statement, high school transcript, minimum 2.0 GPA, 1 letter of recommendation. *Required for some:* interview. *Recommended:* interview. *Application deadline:* rolling (freshmen), rolling (transfers). *Notification:* continuous (freshmen), continuous (transfers).

Admissions Contact Br. George Larkin OSF, Dean of Admissions, St. Francis College, Brooklyn Heights, NY 11201. *Phone:* 718-489-5200. *Fax:* 718-802-0453. *E-mail:* glarkin@stfranciscolleg.edu.

St. John Fisher College
Rochester, New York

- **Independent** comprehensive, founded 1948, affiliated with Roman Catholic Church
- **Calendar** semesters
- **Degrees** bachelor's, master's, and postbachelor's certificates
- **Suburban** 136-acre campus
- **Endowment** $29.4 million
- **Coed,** 2,496 undergraduate students, 88% full-time, 58% women, 42% men
- **Moderately difficult** entrance level, 71% of applicants were admitted

St. John Fisher College's newest academic building, the Ralph C. Wilson Jr. Building, opened in September 2003. Ralph Wilson, owner of the Buffalo Bills, is an active supporter of community affairs, particularly in the areas of education and medical research. This multi-level structure expands Fisher's classroom capacity by 20% and provides for additional faculty offices, seminar rooms, and meeting space. It is used primarily for the teaching of math, science, and technology courses and houses the College's newly-created School of Education.

Undergraduates 2,190 full-time, 306 part-time. Students come from 17 states and territories, 3 other countries, 2% are from out of state, 4% African American, 2% Asian American or Pacific Islander, 3% Hispanic American, 0.4% Native American, 0.1% international, 9% transferred in. *Retention:* 84% of 2002 full-time freshmen returned.

Freshmen *Admission:* 2,263 applied, 1,617 admitted, 540 enrolled. *Average high school GPA:* 3.33. *Test scores:* SAT verbal scores over 500: 68%; SAT math scores over 500: 75%; ACT scores over 18: 94%; SAT verbal scores over 600: 15%; SAT math scores over 600: 19%; ACT scores over 24: 34%; SAT verbal scores over 700: 2%; SAT math scores over 700: 1%; ACT scores over 30: 2%.

Faculty *Total:* 295, 42% full-time. *Student/faculty ratio:* 10:1.

Majors Accounting; American studies; anthropology; biochemistry; biology/biological sciences; business administration and management; chemistry; computer science; economics; elementary education; English; finance; French; German; health and physical education related; history; human resources management; international business/trade/commerce; international relations and affairs; Italian; management information systems; marketing/marketing management; mass communication/media; mathematics; mathematics teacher education; multi-/interdisciplinary studies related; nursing (registered nurse training); philosophy;

physics; political science and government; psychology; religious studies; science teacher education; sociology; Spanish; special education; technology/industrial arts teacher education.

Academic Programs *Special study options:* academic remediation for entering students, accelerated degree program, adult/continuing education programs, advanced placement credit, double majors, honors programs, independent study, internships, off-campus study, part-time degree program, services for LD students, student-designed majors, study abroad, summer session for credit. *ROTC:* Army (c), Navy (c), Air Force (c). *Unusual degree programs:* 3-2 engineering with Clarkson University, Manhattan College, State University of New York at Buffalo, Columbia University, University of Detroit Mercy, Rensselaer Polytechnic Institute, University of Rochester.

Library Charles V. Lavery Library plus 1 other with 207,343 titles, 1,214 serial subscriptions, 29,052 audiovisual materials, an OPAC, a Web page.

Computers on Campus 260 computers available on campus for general student use. A campuswide network can be accessed from student residence rooms and from off campus. Internet access, online (class) registration, at least one staffed computer lab available.

Student Life *Housing options:* coed, women-only. Campus housing is university owned and leased by the school. Freshman campus housing is guaranteed. *Activities and organizations:* drama/theater group, student-run newspaper, radio and television station, choral group, student government, Student Activities Board, Commuter Council, resident student association. *Campus security:* 24-hour emergency response devices and patrols, late-night transport/escort service, controlled dormitory access. *Student services:* health clinic, personal/psychological counseling.

Athletics Member NCAA. All Division III. *Intercollegiate sports:* baseball M, basketball M/W, cheerleading W, football M, golf M, lacrosse M/W, soccer M/W, softball W, tennis M/W, volleyball W. *Intramural sports:* basketball M/W, ice hockey M(c)/W(c), rugby M(c)/W(c), skiing (cross-country) M(c)/W(c), skiing (downhill) M(c)/W(c), soccer M/W, softball M/W, volleyball M/W.

Standardized Tests *Required:* SAT I or ACT (for admission).

Costs (2003–04) *One-time required fee:* $300. *Comprehensive fee:* $24,870 includes full-time tuition ($17,200), mandatory fees ($250), and room and board ($7420). Part-time tuition: $477 per credit hour. *College room only:* $4780. Room and board charges vary according to board plan. *Payment plans:* installment, deferred payment. *Waivers:* employees or children of employees.

Financial Aid Of all full-time matriculated undergraduates who enrolled in 2003, 2,060 applied for aid, 1,855 were judged to have need, 992 had their need fully met. 1,585 Federal Work-Study jobs (averaging $1636). In 2003, 278 non-need-based awards were made. *Average percent of need met:* 80%. *Average financial aid package:* $13,000. *Average need-based loan:* $5861. *Average need-based gift aid:* $9417. *Average non-need-based aid:* $4478. *Average indebtedness upon graduation:* $18,400.

Applying *Options:* common application, electronic application, early admission, early decision, deferred entrance. *Application fee:* $25. *Required:* high school transcript, minimum 2.0 GPA, 1 letter of recommendation. *Recommended:* interview. *Application deadline:* rolling (freshmen). *Early decision:* 12/1. *Notification:* continuous until 9/1 (freshmen), 12/15 (early decision), continuous (transfers).

Admissions Contact Mrs. Stacy A. Ledermann, Director of Freshmen Admissions, St. John Fisher College, 3690 East Avenue, Rochester, NY 14618. *Phone:* 585-385-8064. *Toll-free phone:* 800-444-4640. *Fax:* 585-385-8386. *E-mail:* admissions@sjfc.edu.

■ *See page 2286 for a narrative description.*

St. John's University

Jamaica, New York

- **Independent** university, founded 1870, affiliated with Roman Catholic Church
- **Calendar** semesters
- **Degrees** certificates, diplomas, associate, bachelor's, master's, doctoral, first professional, post-master's, and postbachelor's certificates
- **Urban** 98-acre campus with easy access to New York City
- **Endowment** $118.7 million
- **Coed,** 14,908 undergraduate students, 79% full-time, 59% women, 41% men
- **Moderately difficult** entrance level, 68% of applicants were admitted

Founded in 1870, St. John's University prepares students for personal and professional success. St. John's combines a rigorous academic program, a close-knit campus environment, and nationally renowned athletic teams with the vast business and cultural opportunities of New York City. With magnificent new residence halls and the latest academic technologies, a St. John's education is the right step toward a bright future.

Undergraduates 11,841 full-time, 3,067 part-time. Students come from 47 states and territories, 109 other countries, 10% are from out of state, 16% African American, 15% Asian American or Pacific Islander, 15% Hispanic American, 0.2% Native American, 3% international, 4% transferred in, 16% live on campus. *Retention:* 82% of 2002 full-time freshmen returned.

Freshmen *Admission:* 15,383 applied, 10,515 admitted, 2,976 enrolled. *Average high school GPA:* 3.50. *Test scores:* SAT verbal scores over 500: 55%; SAT math scores over 500: 64%; SAT verbal scores over 600: 15%; SAT math scores over 600: 23%; SAT verbal scores over 700: 1%; SAT math scores over 700: 5%.

Faculty *Total:* 1,304, 43% full-time, 58% with terminal degrees. *Student/faculty ratio:* 19:1.

Majors Accounting; actuarial science; anthropology; area, ethnic, cultural, and gender studies related; area studies related; art teacher education; Asian studies; Asian studies (East); audiology and speech-language pathology; bilingual, multilingual, and multicultural education related; biology/biological sciences; biology teacher education; business administration and management; business/managerial economics; chemistry; chemistry teacher education; clinical child psychology; clinical laboratory science/medical technology; commercial and advertising art; communication/speech communication and rhetoric; computer and information sciences; counselor education/school counseling and guidance; criminal justice/law enforcement administration; criminology; curriculum and instruction; cytotechnology; data processing and data processing technology; divinity/ministry; early childhood education; ecology; economics; educational leadership and administration; elementary education; English; English as a second/foreign language (teaching); English/language arts teacher education; environmental studies; experimental psychology; finance; fine arts related; fine/studio arts; foreign language teacher education; French; French language teacher education; funeral service and mortuary science; graphic design; health/health care administration; history; hospital and health care facilities administration; hospitality administration; hotel/motel administration; human services; illustration; information science/studies; insurance; international business/trade/commerce; international relations and affairs; Italian; journalism; legal assistant/paralegal; legal studies; liberal arts and sciences/liberal studies; library science; logistics and materials management; management information systems; marketing/marketing management; mathematics; mathematics teacher education; middle school education; nursing (registered nurse training); pastoral counseling and specialized ministries related; pathologist assistant; pharmacy; pharmacy, pharmaceutical sciences, and administration related; philosophy; philosophy and religious studies related; photographic and film/video technology; photography; physical sciences; physician assistant; physics; physics teacher education; political science and government; psychology; public administration; purchasing, procurement/acquisitions and contracts management; reading teacher education; real estate; school psychology; science teacher education; secondary education; social sciences; social studies teacher education; sociology; Spanish; Spanish language teacher education; special education; speech and rhetoric; sport and fitness administration; taxation; telecommunications; telecommunications technology; theology; toxicology; transportation and materials moving related.

Academic Programs *Special study options:* accelerated degree program, adult/continuing education programs, advanced placement credit, distance learning, double majors, English as a second language, honors programs, independent study, internships, off-campus study, part-time degree program, services for LD students, study abroad, summer session for credit. *ROTC:* Army (b). *Unusual degree programs:* 3-2 engineering with Manhattan College.

Library St. John's University Library plus 2 others with 1.2 million titles, 16,014 serial subscriptions, 22,376 audiovisual materials, an OPAC, a Web page.

Computers on Campus 950 computers available on campus for general student use. A campuswide network can be accessed from student residence rooms and from off campus that provide access to various software packages. Internet access, online (class) registration, at least one staffed computer lab available.

Student Life *Housing options:* coed. Campus housing is university owned. *Activities and organizations:* drama/theater group, student-run newspaper, radio and television station, choral group, Student Government, Incorporated, Student Programming Board, Community and University Services in Education, Haraya, American Pharmaceutical Association, national fraternities, national sororities. *Campus security:* 24-hour emergency response devices and patrols, student patrols, late-night transport/escort service, controlled dormitory access. *Student services:* health clinic, personal/psychological counseling.

Athletics Member NCAA. All Division I. *Intercollegiate sports:* baseball M(s), basketball M(s)/W(s), cross-country running W(s), fencing M(s)/W(s), golf M(s)/W(s), lacrosse M(s)/W(s), soccer M(s)/W(s), softball W(s), tennis M(s)/W(s), volleyball W(s). *Intramural sports:* basketball M/W, bowling M(c)/W(c), cheerleading M/W, equestrian sports M/W(c), racquetball M/W, softball M/W, table tennis M(c)/W(c), volleyball M/W, weight lifting M/W.

Standardized Tests *Required:* SAT I or ACT (for admission).

Costs (2003–04) *Comprehensive fee:* $30,180 includes full-time tuition ($19,600), mandatory fees ($480), and room and board ($10,100). Full-time

St. John's University (continued)
tuition and fees vary according to class time, course level, course load, program, and student level. Part-time tuition: $653 per credit. Part-time tuition and fees vary according to class time, course level, course load, program, and student level. No tuition increase for student's term of enrollment. *Required fees:* $165 per term part-time. *College room only:* $6300. Room and board charges vary according to board plan and housing facility. *Payment plans:* installment, deferred payment. *Waivers:* senior citizens and employees or children of employees.

Financial Aid Of all full-time matriculated undergraduates who enrolled in 2002, 10,305 applied for aid, 9,542 were judged to have need, 1,102 had their need fully met. 1,039 Federal Work-Study jobs (averaging $3034). *Average percent of need met:* 72%. *Average financial aid package:* $15,763. *Average need-based loan:* $4222. *Average need-based gift aid:* $6993. *Average non-need-based aid:* $8000. *Average indebtedness upon graduation:* $18,037.

Applying *Options:* common application, electronic application, deferred entrance. *Application fee:* $30. *Required:* essay or personal statement, high school transcript, letters of recommendation. *Application deadline:* rolling (freshmen), rolling (transfers). *Notification:* continuous (freshmen).

Admissions Contact Mr. Matthew Whelan, Director, Office of Admission, St. John's University, 8000 Utopia Parkway, Jamaica, NY 11439. *Phone:* 718-990-2000. *Toll-free phone:* 888-9STJOHNS (in-state); 888-9ST JOHNS (out-of-state). *Fax:* 718-990-1677. *E-mail:* admissions@stjohns.edu.

■ *See page 2290 for a narrative description.*

St. Joseph's College, New York

Brooklyn, New York

- **Independent** 4-year, founded 1916
- **Calendar** semesters
- **Degrees** bachelor's and master's
- **Urban** campus
- **Endowment** $23.4 million
- **Coed,** 1,126 undergraduate students, 51% full-time, 79% women, 21% men
- **Moderately difficult** entrance level, 66% of applicants were admitted

Since 1916, thousands of students have made St. Joseph's their college of choice. Here, young men and women have found academic excellence, real-life learning, a vibrant community, and an unrivaled degree of personal attention. Students can choose from a variety of career-oriented majors, such as business administration and education as well as preprofessional programs in law and medicine. St. Joseph's College provides an invigorating learning experience that challenges, inspires, and helps students reach their goals.

Undergraduates 572 full-time, 554 part-time. Students come from 4 states and territories, 8 other countries, 1% are from out of state, 40% African American, 5% Asian American or Pacific Islander, 11% Hispanic American, 0.8% international, 13% transferred in. *Retention:* 80% of 2002 full-time freshmen returned.

Freshmen *Admission:* 513 applied, 337 admitted, 123 enrolled. *Average high school GPA:* 3.0. *Test scores:* SAT verbal scores over 500: 55%; SAT math scores over 500: 51%; ACT scores over 18: 60%; SAT verbal scores over 600: 8%; SAT math scores over 600: 18%; ACT scores over 24: 20%.

Faculty *Total:* 134, 40% full-time. *Student/faculty ratio:* 12:1.

Majors Accounting; biology/biological sciences; business administration and management; chemistry; child guidance; developmental and child psychology; education; English; general studies; health/health care administration; history; human resources management; human services; mathematics; mathematics and computer science; nursing (registered nurse training); pre-law studies; psychology; public health; social sciences; Spanish; speech and rhetoric.

Academic Programs *Special study options:* adult/continuing education programs, advanced placement credit, honors programs, internships, part-time degree program, summer session for credit. *Unusual degree programs:* 3-2 podiatry with New York College of Podiatric Medicine.

Library McEntegart Hall Library with 100,000 titles, 432 serial subscriptions, 4,482 audiovisual materials.

Computers on Campus 90 computers available on campus for general student use. Internet access, at least one staffed computer lab available.

Student Life *Housing:* college housing not available. *Activities and organizations:* drama/theater group, student-run newspaper, choral group, admissions club, science club, dramatics, child study club, dance team. *Campus security:* late-night transport/escort service. *Student services:* personal/psychological counseling.

Athletics *Intercollegiate sports:* basketball M/W, cross-country running M/W, softball W, volleyball M/W. *Intramural sports:* basketball M/W, bowling M/W, table tennis M/W, volleyball M/W.

Standardized Tests *Required:* SAT I or ACT (for admission).

Costs (2003–04) *Tuition:* $10,955 full-time. *Required fees:* $342 full-time.

Financial Aid Of all full-time matriculated undergraduates who enrolled in 2002, 518 applied for aid, 350 were judged to have need, 300 had their need fully met. 42 Federal Work-Study jobs (averaging $1700). 3 state and other part-time jobs (averaging $1700). In 2002, 120 non-need-based awards were made. *Average percent of need met:* 85%. *Average financial aid package:* $11,764. *Average need-based loan:* $3351. *Average need-based gift aid:* $7476. *Average non-need-based aid:* $4000. *Average indebtedness upon graduation:* $15,639.

Applying *Options:* early admission, deferred entrance. *Application fee:* $25. *Required:* high school transcript, minimum 3.0 GPA. *Required for some:* interview. *Recommended:* essay or personal statement, 2 letters of recommendation. *Application deadlines:* 8/15 (freshmen), 8/15 (transfers). *Notification:* continuous until 8/30 (freshmen), continuous until 8/30 (transfers).

Admissions Contact Ms. Theresa LaRocca-Meyer, Director of Admissions, St. Joseph's College, New York, 245 Clinton Avenue, Brooklyn, NY 11205-3688. *Phone:* 718-636-6868. *E-mail:* asinfob@sjcny.edu.

■ *See page 2296 for a narrative description.*

St. Joseph's College, Suffolk Campus

Patchogue, New York

- **Independent** comprehensive, founded 1916
- **Calendar** 4-1-4
- **Degrees** certificates, bachelor's, and master's (master's degree in education only)
- **Small-town** 28-acre campus with easy access to New York City
- **Coed,** 3,692 undergraduate students, 71% full-time, 75% women, 25% men
- **Moderately difficult** entrance level, 77% of applicants were admitted

Undergraduates 2,636 full-time, 1,056 part-time. Students come from 4 states and territories, 0.1% are from out of state, 3% African American, 1% Asian American or Pacific Islander, 5% Hispanic American, 0.2% Native American, 0.2% international, 12% transferred in. *Retention:* 86% of 2002 full-time freshmen returned.

Freshmen *Admission:* 1,050 applied, 810 admitted, 421 enrolled. *Average high school GPA:* 3.60. *Test scores:* SAT verbal scores over 500: 70%; SAT math scores over 500: 78%; SAT verbal scores over 600: 17%; SAT math scores over 600: 25%; SAT verbal scores over 700: 1%; SAT math scores over 700: 1%.

Faculty *Total:* 298, 34% full-time, 29% with terminal degrees. *Student/faculty ratio:* 15:1.

Majors Accounting; adult and continuing education; behavioral sciences; biology/biological sciences; business administration and management; computer science; developmental and child psychology; early childhood education; economics; education; elementary education; English; health/health care administration; history; human resources management; kindergarten/preschool education; liberal arts and sciences/liberal studies; mathematics; nursing (registered nurse training); parks, recreation and leisure; political science and government; pre-dentistry studies; pre-law studies; pre-medical studies; pre-veterinary studies; psychology; secondary education; social sciences; sociology; special education; speech and rhetoric; therapeutic recreation.

Academic Programs *Special study options:* adult/continuing education programs, advanced placement credit, off-campus study, part-time degree program, services for LD students, summer session for credit. *ROTC:* Army (c), Air Force (c). *Unusual degree programs:* 3-2 biology with New York College of Podiatric Medicine; BA/BS and MS Program computer science with Polytechnic University, Farmingdale Campus.

Library Callahan Library with 75,646 titles, 307 serial subscriptions, 1,213 audiovisual materials, an OPAC, a Web page.

Computers on Campus 223 computers available on campus for general student use. A campuswide network can be accessed from off campus. Internet access, online (class) registration, at least one staffed computer lab available.

Student Life *Housing:* college housing not available. *Activities and organizations:* drama/theater group, student-run newspaper, choral group, Council for Exceptional Children, Child Study Club, Campus Activities Board, Society of Human Resources Management, National Student Speech Language Hearing Association. *Campus security:* 24-hour patrols, late-night transport/escort service. *Student services:* personal/psychological counseling.

Athletics Member NCAA. All Division III. *Intercollegiate sports:* baseball M, basketball M/W, cross-country running M/W, equestrian sports M/W, soccer M/W, softball W, swimming W, tennis M/W, volleyball W. *Intramural sports:* cheerleading M(c)/W(c).

Standardized Tests *Required:* SAT I or ACT (for admission).

Costs (2003–04) *Tuition:* $10,955 full-time, $355 per credit part-time. Part-time tuition and fees vary according to course load. *Required fees:* $342 full-time, $118 per term part-time. *Payment plan:* installment. *Waivers:* senior citizens and employees or children of employees.

Financial Aid Of all full-time matriculated undergraduates who enrolled in 2003, 1,719 applied for aid, 1,335 were judged to have need, 754 had their need fully met. 57 Federal Work-Study jobs (averaging $1975). 68 state and other part-time jobs (averaging $1955). In 2003, 479 non-need-based awards were made. *Average percent of need met:* 64%. *Average financial aid package:* $9975. *Average need-based loan:* $3890. *Average need-based gift aid:* $5576. *Average non-need-based aid:* $4984. *Average indebtedness upon graduation:* $15,086.

Applying *Options:* early admission, deferred entrance. *Application fee:* $25. *Required:* high school transcript, minimum 3.0 GPA. *Required for some:* 2 letters of recommendation. *Recommended:* essay or personal statement, interview. *Application deadline:* rolling (freshmen), rolling (transfers). *Notification:* continuous (freshmen), continuous (transfers).

Admissions Contact Mrs. Marion E. Salgado, Director of Admissions, St. Joseph's College, Suffolk Campus, 155 West Roe Boulevard, Patchogue, NY 11772. *Phone:* 631-447-3219. *Toll-free phone:* 866-AT ST JOE. *Fax:* 631-447-1734. *E-mail:* admissions_patchogue@sjcny.edu.

St. Lawrence University

Canton, New York

- **Independent** comprehensive, founded 1856
- **Calendar** semesters
- **Degrees** bachelor's, master's, and post-master's certificates
- **Small-town** 1000-acre campus with easy access to Ottawa
- **Endowment** $170.4 million
- **Coed,** 2,148 undergraduate students, 98% full-time, 53% women, 47% men
- **Very difficult** entrance level, 57% of applicants were admitted

Undergraduates 2,114 full-time, 34 part-time. Students come from 41 states and territories, 21 other countries, 48% are from out of state, 2% African American, 1% Asian American or Pacific Islander, 3% Hispanic American, 0.6% Native American, 4% international, 1% transferred in, 95% live on campus. *Retention:* 86% of 2002 full-time freshmen returned.

Freshmen *Admission:* 3,082 applied, 1,767 admitted, 566 enrolled. *Average high school GPA:* 3.37. *Test scores:* SAT verbal scores over 500: 83%; SAT math scores over 500: 87%; ACT scores over 18: 100%; SAT verbal scores over 600: 38%; SAT math scores over 600: 40%; ACT scores over 24: 65%; SAT verbal scores over 700: 5%; SAT math scores over 700: 4%; ACT scores over 30: 7%.

Faculty *Total:* 203, 79% full-time, 84% with terminal degrees. *Student/faculty ratio:* 12:1.

Majors African studies; anthropology; art; art history, criticism and conservation; Asian studies; biochemistry; biology/biological sciences; biophysics; Canadian studies; chemistry; computer science; creative writing; dramatic/theatre arts; economics; English; environmental studies; foreign languages and literatures; French; geology/earth science; geophysics and seismology; German; history; mathematics; modern languages; music; neuroscience; philosophy; physics; political science and government; psychology; religious studies; sociology; Spanish.

Academic Programs *Special study options:* advanced placement credit, double majors, independent study, internships, off-campus study, part-time degree program, services for LD students, student-designed majors, study abroad, summer session for credit. *ROTC:* Army (c), Air Force (c). *Unusual degree programs:* 3-2 business administration with Clarkson University; engineering with Columbia University, Clarkson University, Rensselaer Polytechnic Institute, University of Rochester, University of Southern California, Washington University in St. Louis, Worcester Polytechnic Institute.

Library Owen D. Young Library plus 1 other with 533,463 titles, 2,065 serial subscriptions, 4,242 audiovisual materials, an OPAC, a Web page.

Computers on Campus 600 computers available on campus for general student use. A campuswide network can be accessed from student residence rooms and from off campus. Internet access, at least one staffed computer lab available.

Student Life *Housing:* on-campus residence required through senior year. *Options:* coed. Campus housing is university owned. Freshman campus housing is guaranteed. *Activities and organizations:* drama/theater group, student-run newspaper, radio and television station, choral group, outing club, student newspaper, student government, Circle K, Habitat for Humanity, national fraternities, national sororities. *Campus security:* 24-hour emergency response devices and patrols, student patrols, late-night transport/escort service, controlled dormitory access. *Student services:* health clinic, personal/psychological counseling, women's center.

Athletics Member NCAA. All Division III except men's and women's ice hockey (Division I). *Intercollegiate sports:* baseball M, basketball M/W, crew M/W, cross-country running M/W, equestrian sports M/W, field hockey W, football M, golf M/W, ice hockey M(s)/W(s), lacrosse M/W, skiing (cross-country) M/W, skiing (downhill) M/W, soccer M/W, softball W, squash M/W, swimming M/W, tennis M/W, track and field M/W, volleyball W. *Intramural sports:* basketball M/W, crew M/W, football M, ice hockey M/W, rugby M/W, skiing (cross-country) M/W, soccer M/W, softball W, ultimate Frisbee M/W, volleyball M/W, wrestling M.

Standardized Tests *Required:* SAT I or ACT (for admission). *Recommended:* SAT II: Subject Tests (for admission).

Costs (2003–04) *Comprehensive fee:* $35,945 includes full-time tuition ($27,985), mandatory fees ($205), and room and board ($7755). Part-time tuition: $3500 per course. *College room only:* $4170. Room and board charges vary according to board plan. *Payment plans:* installment, deferred payment. *Waivers:* employees or children of employees.

Financial Aid Of all full-time matriculated undergraduates who enrolled in 2003, 1,620 applied for aid, 1,493 were judged to have need, 548 had their need fully met. 931 Federal Work-Study jobs (averaging $1402). 483 state and other part-time jobs (averaging $1366). In 2003, 204 non-need-based awards were made. *Average percent of need met:* 90%. *Average financial aid package:* $26,013. *Average need-based loan:* $6134. *Average need-based gift aid:* $18,585. *Average non-need-based aid:* $9151. *Average indebtedness upon graduation:* $23,091. *Financial aid deadline:* 2/15.

Applying *Options:* common application, electronic application, early decision, deferred entrance. *Application fee:* $50. *Required:* essay or personal statement, high school transcript, 2 letters of recommendation. *Recommended:* minimum 2.0 GPA, interview. *Application deadlines:* 2/15 (freshmen), 4/1 (transfers). *Early decision:* 11/15 (for plan 1), 1/15 (for plan 2). *Notification:* 3/31 (freshmen), 12/15 (early decision plan 1), 2/15 (early decision plan 2), 5/1 (transfers).

Admissions Contact Ms. Terry Cowdrey, Dean of Admissions and Financial Aid, St. Lawrence University, Payson Hall, Canton, NY 13617-1455. *Phone:* 315-229-5261. *Toll-free phone:* 800-285-1856. *Fax:* 315-229-5818. *E-mail:* admissions@stlawu.edu.

■ *See page 2302 for a narrative description.*

St. Thomas Aquinas College

Sparkill, New York

- **Independent** comprehensive, founded 1952
- **Calendar** semesters
- **Degrees** associate, bachelor's, master's, and postbachelor's certificates
- **Suburban** 46-acre campus with easy access to New York City
- **Endowment** $8.4 million
- **Coed,** 2,148 undergraduate students, 63% full-time, 58% women, 42% men
- **Moderately difficult** entrance level, 75% of applicants were admitted

Undergraduates 1,345 full-time, 803 part-time. Students come from 17 states and territories, 10 other countries, 37% are from out of state, 6% African American, 3% Asian American or Pacific Islander, 15% Hispanic American, 0.1% Native American, 2% international, 8% transferred in, 34% live on campus. *Retention:* 74% of 2002 full-time freshmen returned.

Freshmen *Admission:* 1,269 applied, 947 admitted, 343 enrolled. *Average high school GPA:* 2.8. *Test scores:* SAT verbal scores over 500: 35%; SAT math scores over 500: 33%; ACT scores over 18: 36%; SAT verbal scores over 600: 8%; SAT math scores over 600: 8%; ACT scores over 24: 4%; SAT verbal scores over 700: 1%; SAT math scores over 700: 1%.

Faculty *Total:* 132, 49% full-time, 86% with terminal degrees. *Student/faculty ratio:* 17:1.

Majors Accounting; applied art; applied mathematics; art; art teacher education; art therapy; biology/biological sciences; business administration and management; clinical laboratory science/medical technology; clinical/medical laboratory technology; commercial and advertising art; criminal justice/law enforcement administration; education; elementary education; engineering science; English; finance; fine/studio arts; history; humanities; information science/studies; journalism; kindergarten/preschool education; marketing/marketing management; mass communication/media; mathematics; modern languages; natural sciences; parks, recreation and leisure; philosophy; pre-medical studies; psychology; religious studies; Romance languages; secondary education; social sciences; Spanish; special education.

Academic Programs *Special study options:* academic remediation for entering students, accelerated degree program, adult/continuing education programs, advanced placement credit, English as a second language, freshman honors college, honors programs, internships, off-campus study, part-time degree program, services for LD students, summer session for credit. *ROTC:* Air Force (c). *Unusual degree programs:* 3-2 engineering with George Washington University, Manhattan College; physical therapy with New York Medical College.

Library Lougheed Library plus 1 other with 176,000 titles, 940 serial subscriptions, an OPAC.

Computers on Campus 200 computers available on campus for general student use. A campuswide network can be accessed from student residence rooms and from off campus. Internet access, at least one staffed computer lab available.

St. Thomas Aquinas College (continued)

Student Life *Housing options:* coed. *Activities and organizations:* drama/theater group, student-run newspaper, radio station. *Campus security:* 24-hour emergency response devices and patrols, late-night transport/escort service, controlled dormitory access. *Student services:* personal/psychological counseling.

Athletics Member NAIA. *Intercollegiate sports:* baseball M(s), basketball M(s)/W(s), cross-country running M(s)/W(s), golf M/W, soccer M(s)/W(s), softball W(s), volleyball W(s). *Intramural sports:* basketball M/W, volleyball M/W.

Standardized Tests *Required:* SAT I or ACT (for admission).

Costs (2004–05) *Comprehensive fee:* $24,290 includes full-time tuition ($15,300), mandatory fees ($400), and room and board ($8590). Part-time tuition: $510 per credit hour. *Required fees:* $100 per term part-time. *College room only:* $4640.

Applying *Options:* common application, electronic application, early admission, early decision, early action, deferred entrance. *Application fee:* $30. *Required:* high school transcript, minimum 2.0 GPA. *Required for some:* 3 letters of recommendation. *Recommended:* essay or personal statement, interview. *Application deadline:* rolling (freshmen), rolling (transfers). *Early decision:* 12/1. *Notification:* continuous (freshmen), 1/15 (early decision), 1/15 (early action), continuous (transfers).

Admissions Contact Mr. John Edel, Dean of Enrollment Management, St. Thomas Aquinas College, 125 Route 340, Sparkill, NY 10976. *Phone:* 845-398-4100. *Toll-free phone:* 800-999-STAC.

■ *See page 2328 for a narrative description.*

SARAH LAWRENCE COLLEGE

Bronxville, New York

- **Independent** comprehensive, founded 1926
- **Calendar** semesters
- **Degrees** bachelor's and master's
- **Suburban** 40-acre campus with easy access to New York City
- **Endowment** $42.2 million
- **Coed,** 1,292 undergraduate students, 95% full-time, 74% women, 26% men
- **Very difficult** entrance level, 41% of applicants were admitted

At the heart of the Sarah Lawrence learning experience is the seminar and conference system. Every course has 2 parts: a seminar limited to 15 students and an individual meeting held every 2 weeks between student and teacher, during which they create a project that extends the seminar material and connects it to the student's academic goals and aspirations. Through dialogue, reading, and research, students work with their teachers to create an individualized education.

Undergraduates 1,222 full-time, 70 part-time. Students come from 46 states and territories, 25 other countries, 81% are from out of state, 5% African American, 5% Asian American or Pacific Islander, 3% Hispanic American, 0.5% Native American, 2% international, 4% transferred in, 87% live on campus. *Retention:* 93% of 2002 full-time freshmen returned.

Freshmen *Admission:* 2,672 applied, 1,107 admitted, 326 enrolled. *Average high school GPA:* 3.60. *Test scores:* SAT verbal scores over 500: 96%; SAT math scores over 500: 88%; ACT scores over 18: 100%; SAT verbal scores over 600: 77%; SAT math scores over 600: 47%; ACT scores over 24: 86%; SAT verbal scores over 700: 27%; SAT math scores over 700: 7%; ACT scores over 30: 21%.

Faculty *Total:* 236, 76% full-time. *Student/faculty ratio:* 6:1.

Majors Acting; African-American/Black studies; African studies; American history; American literature; American studies; animal genetics; anthropology; archeology; architectural history and criticism; art; art history, criticism and conservation; Asian history; Asian studies; Asian studies (East); Asian studies (South); astronomy; biological and physical sciences; biology/biological sciences; chemistry; Chinese studies; cinematography and film/video production; classics and languages, literatures and linguistics; comparative literature; computer science; creative writing; dance; dance related; developmental and child psychology; directing and theatrical production; dramatic/theatre arts; drawing; early childhood education; ecology; economics; education; elementary education; English; English language and literature related; English literature (British and Commonwealth); environmental studies; European history; European studies; European studies (Central and Eastern); film/cinema studies; fine/studio arts; foreign languages and literatures; French; gay/lesbian studies; geology/earth science; German; history; history and philosophy of science and technology; history related; human development and family studies; humanities; human/medical genetics; interdisciplinary studies; international relations and affairs; Italian; Japanese; jazz/jazz studies; kindergarten/preschool education; Latin; Latin American studies; liberal arts and sciences and humanities related; liberal arts and sciences/liberal studies; literature; marine biology and biological oceanography; mathematics; Middle/ Near Eastern and Semitic languages related; modern languages; molecular biology; music; music history, literature, and theory; music performance; music theory and composition; natural sciences; Near and Middle Eastern studies; organic chemistry; painting; philosophy; philosophy and religious studies related; photography; physics; piano and organ; playwriting and screenwriting; political science and government; pre-dentistry studies; pre-law studies; pre-medical studies; pre-veterinary studies; printmaking; psychology; public policy analysis; religious studies; religious studies related; Romance languages; Russian; sculpture; social sciences; social sciences related; sociology; Spanish; urban studies/affairs; violin, viola, guitar and other stringed instruments; visual and performing arts; visual and performing arts related; voice and opera; western civilization; wind/percussion instruments; women's studies.

Academic Programs *Special study options:* adult/continuing education programs, advanced placement credit, independent study, internships, off-campus study, part-time degree program, services for LD students, student-designed majors, study abroad.

Library Esther Rauschenbush Library plus 2 others with 193,581 titles, 1,260 serial subscriptions, 8,674 audiovisual materials, an OPAC, a Web page.

Computers on Campus 110 computers available on campus for general student use. A campuswide network can be accessed from student residence rooms and from off campus. Internet access, at least one staffed computer lab available.

Student Life *Housing:* on-campus residence required for freshman year. *Options:* coed, men-only, women-only, cooperative. Campus housing is university owned. Freshman campus housing is guaranteed. *Activities and organizations:* drama/theater group, student-run newspaper, radio station, choral group, Student Senate, APICAD, UNIDAD, Harambe, Amnesty International. *Campus security:* 24-hour emergency response devices and patrols, student patrols, late-night transport/escort service, controlled dormitory access. *Student services:* health clinic, personal/psychological counseling.

Athletics *Intercollegiate sports:* crew M/W, cross-country running M/W, equestrian sports M/W, swimming W, tennis M/W, volleyball W. *Intramural sports:* bowling M/W, fencing M/W, soccer M/W, softball M/W, squash M/W, swimming M/W, tennis M/W, volleyball M/W.

Costs (2003–04) *Comprehensive fee:* $41,218 includes full-time tuition ($30,120), mandatory fees ($704), and room and board ($10,394). Full-time tuition and fees vary according to course load. Part-time tuition: $1004 per credit. Part-time tuition and fees vary according to course load. *Required fees:* $352 per term part-time. *College room only:* $6894. Room and board charges vary according to board plan. *Payment plan:* installment. *Waivers:* employees or children of employees.

Financial Aid Of all full-time matriculated undergraduates who enrolled in 2003, 685 applied for aid, 666 were judged to have need, 396 had their need fully met. 472 Federal Work-Study jobs (averaging $1655). 87 state and other part-time jobs (averaging $1794). In 2003, 138 non-need-based awards were made. *Average percent of need met:* 95%. *Average financial aid package:* $25,826. *Average need-based loan:* $3080. *Average need-based gift aid:* $21,014. *Average non-need-based aid:* $6418. *Average indebtedness upon graduation:* $15,023. *Financial aid deadline:* 2/1.

Applying *Options:* common application, electronic application, early admission, early decision, deferred entrance. *Application fee:* $50. *Required:* essay or personal statement, high school transcript, 3 letters of recommendation. *Recommended:* minimum 3.0 GPA, interview. *Application deadlines:* 1/1 (freshmen), 3/1 (transfers). *Early decision:* 11/15 (for plan 1), 1/1 (for plan 2). *Notification:* 4/1 (freshmen), 12/15 (early decision plan 1), 2/15 (early decision plan 2), continuous (transfers).

Admissions Contact Ms. Thyra L. Briggs, Dean of Admission, Sarah Lawrence College, 1 Mead Way, Bronxville, NY 10708-5999. *Phone:* 914-395-2510. *Toll-free phone:* 800-888-2858. *Fax:* 914-395-2515. *E-mail:* slcadmit@slc.edu.

■ *See page 2348 for a narrative description.*

SCHOOL OF VISUAL ARTS

New York, New York

- **Proprietary** comprehensive, founded 1947
- **Calendar** semesters
- **Degrees** certificates, bachelor's, and master's
- **Urban** 1-acre campus
- **Coed**
- **Moderately difficult** entrance level

Faculty *Student/faculty ratio:* 8:1.

Student Life *Campus security:* 24-hour patrols.

Standardized Tests *Required:* SAT I or ACT (for admission).

Costs (2003–04) *Comprehensive fee:* $28,700 includes full-time tuition ($18,200), mandatory fees ($500), and room and board ($10,000). *College room only:* $6500.

Financial Aid Of all full-time matriculated undergraduates who enrolled in 2003, 1,861 applied for aid, 1,708 were judged to have need, 11 had their need fully met. 120 Federal Work-Study jobs (averaging $2056). In 2003, 241. *Average percent of need met:* 46. *Average financial aid package:* $11,622. *Average need-based loan:* $4327. *Average need-based gift aid:* $5921. *Average non-need-based aid:* $3360. *Average indebtedness upon graduation:* $18,105.

Applying *Options:* early decision, deferred entrance. *Application fee:* $50. *Required:* essay or personal statement, high school transcript, minimum 2.3 GPA, portfolio. *Required for some:* 1 letter of recommendation. *Recommended:* interview.

Admissions Contact Mr. Richard M. Longo, Executive Director of Admissions, School of Visual Arts, 209 East 23rd Street, New York, NY 10010. *Phone:* 212-592-2100 Ext. 2182. *Toll-free phone:* 800-436-4204. *Fax:* 212-592-2116. *E-mail:* admissions@sva.edu.

■ See page 2360 for a narrative description.

SH'OR YOSHUV RABBINICAL COLLEGE
Lawrence, New York

Admissions Contact Rabbi Avrohom Halpern, Executive Director, Sh'or Yoshuv Rabbinical College, 1284 Central Avenue, Far Rockaway, NY 11691-4002. *Phone:* 718-327-7244.

SIENA COLLEGE
Loudonville, New York

- **Independent Roman Catholic** 4-year, founded 1937
- **Calendar** semesters
- **Degree** certificates and bachelor's
- **Suburban** 163-acre campus
- **Endowment** $96.4 million
- **Coed,** 3,379 undergraduate students, 90% full-time, 56% women, 44% men
- **Moderately difficult** entrance level, 63% of applicants were admitted

One of the Northeast's premier small, private liberal arts colleges, Siena offers a broad, time-tested liberal arts curriculum that is a journey taken with mentoring, thoughtful faculty members, friars, and friends. It is a journey that empowers students with competence, character, and compassion, buttressing classwork with real-world experience. The curriculum includes 25 majors in business, liberal arts, and sciences. In addition, there are more than 15 preprofessional and special academic programs. Siena's 152-acre campus is located in Loudonville, a suburb of Albany, New York, the state capital.

Undergraduates 3,025 full-time, 354 part-time. Students come from 30 states and territories, 6 other countries, 20% are from out of state, 2% African American, 3% Asian American or Pacific Islander, 3% Hispanic American, 0.2% Native American, 0.4% international, 4% transferred in, 76% live on campus. *Retention:* 91% of 2002 full-time freshmen returned.

Freshmen *Admission:* 4,112 applied, 2,599 admitted, 759 enrolled. *Average high school GPA:* 3.50. *Test scores:* SAT verbal scores over 500: 81%; SAT math scores over 500: 88%; ACT scores over 18: 99%; SAT verbal scores over 600: 25%; SAT math scores over 600: 36%; ACT scores over 24: 48%; SAT verbal scores over 700: 2%; SAT math scores over 700: 3%; ACT scores over 30: 5%.

Faculty *Total:* 324, 52% full-time, 61% with terminal degrees. *Student/faculty ratio:* 14:1.

Majors Accounting; American studies; biology/biological sciences; chemistry; classics and languages, literatures and linguistics; computer and information sciences; ecology; economics; English; finance; fine/studio arts; French; history; marketing/marketing management; mathematics; philosophy; physics; political science and government; pre-dentistry studies; pre-law studies; pre-medical studies; psychology; religious studies; secondary education; social work; sociology; Spanish.

Academic Programs *Special study options:* academic remediation for entering students, accelerated degree program, adult/continuing education programs, advanced placement credit, double majors, honors programs, independent study, internships, off-campus study, part-time degree program, services for LD students, study abroad, summer session for credit. *ROTC:* Army (b), Air Force (c). *Unusual degree programs:* 3-2 engineering with Clarkson University, Manhattan College, Catholic University of America, Western New England College, Rensselaer Polytechnic Institute, State University of New York at Binghamton; forestry with State University of New York College of Environmental Science and Forestry; Pace University Law School, Western New England College of Law.

Library J. Spencer and Patricia Standish Library with 314,942 titles, 1,063 serial subscriptions, 5,179 audiovisual materials, an OPAC, a Web page.

Computers on Campus 650 computers available on campus for general student use. A campuswide network can be accessed from student residence rooms and from off campus. Internet access, at least one staffed computer lab available.

Student Life *Housing:* on-campus residence required through senior year. *Options:* coed. Campus housing is university owned. Freshman applicants given priority for college housing. *Activities and organizations:* drama/theater group, student-run newspaper, radio station, choral group, Student Senate, Student Events Board, Big Brothers/Big Sisters, Gaelic Society, outing club. *Campus security:* 24-hour emergency response devices and patrols, late-night transport/escort service, controlled dormitory access, call boxes in parking lots and on roadways. *Student services:* health clinic, personal/psychological counseling, legal services.

Athletics Member NCAA. All Division I. *Intercollegiate sports:* baseball M(s), basketball M(s)/W(s), cross-country running M/W, equestrian sports M(c)/W(c), field hockey W, golf M/W, ice hockey M(c), lacrosse M/W, rugby M(c)/W(c), soccer M(s)/W(s), softball W(s), swimming W(s), tennis M(s)/W(s), track and field M(c)/W(c), volleyball W(s), water polo W(s). *Intramural sports:* basketball M/W, bowling M/W, cheerleading W, golf M/W, racquetball M/W, soccer M/W, softball M/W, volleyball M/W.

Standardized Tests *Required:* SAT I or ACT (for admission).

Costs (2004–05) *Comprehensive fee:* $26,705 includes full-time tuition ($18,590), mandatory fees ($540), and room and board ($7575). Part-time tuition: $370 per credit hour. *Required fees:* $25 per term part-time. *College room only:* $4750. Room and board charges vary according to board plan and housing facility. *Payment plan:* installment. *Waivers:* senior citizens and employees or children of employees.

Financial Aid Of all full-time matriculated undergraduates who enrolled in 2002, 2,359 applied for aid, 1,960 were judged to have need, 328 had their need fully met. 391 Federal Work-Study jobs (averaging $675). In 2002, 365 non-need-based awards were made. *Average percent of need met:* 80%. *Average financial aid package:* $12,655. *Average need-based loan:* $4192. *Average need-based gift aid:* $9030. *Average non-need-based aid:* $5581. *Average indebtedness upon graduation:* $12,700.

Applying *Options:* electronic application, early admission, early decision, early action, deferred entrance. *Application fee:* $40. *Required:* essay or personal statement, high school transcript, 1 letter of recommendation. *Required for some:* interview. *Application deadlines:* 3/1 (freshmen), 6/1 (transfers). *Early decision:* 12/1. *Notification:* 3/15 (freshmen), 12/15 (early decision), 1/1 (early action), continuous (transfers).

Admissions Contact Mr. Edward Jones, Director of Admissions, Siena College, 515 Loudon Road, Loudonville, NY 12211-1462. *Phone:* 518-783-2423. *Toll-free phone:* 888-AT-SIENA. *Fax:* 518-783-2436. *E-mail:* admit@siena.edu.

■ See page 2384 for a narrative description.

SKIDMORE COLLEGE
Saratoga Springs, New York

- **Independent** comprehensive, founded 1903
- **Calendar** semesters plus optional 6-week internship period
- **Degrees** bachelor's and master's
- **Small-town** 800-acre campus with easy access to Albany
- **Endowment** $156.7 million
- **Coed,** 2,532 undergraduate students, 90% full-time, 59% women, 41% men
- **Very difficult** entrance level, 46% of applicants were admitted

Undergraduates 2,286 full-time, 246 part-time. Students come from 44 states and territories, 25 other countries, 70% are from out of state, 3% African American, 5% Asian American or Pacific Islander, 4% Hispanic American, 0.6% Native American, 1% international, 2% transferred in, 77% live on campus. *Retention:* 90% of 2002 full-time freshmen returned.

Freshmen *Admission:* 5,903 applied, 2,724 admitted, 642 enrolled. *Average high school GPA:* 3.29. *Test scores:* SAT verbal scores over 500: 95%; SAT math scores over 500: 97%; ACT scores over 18: 100%; SAT verbal scores over 600: 67%; SAT math scores over 600: 69%; ACT scores over 24: 84%; SAT verbal scores over 700: 16%; SAT math scores over 700: 12%; ACT scores over 30: 12%.

Faculty *Total:* 201, 96% full-time, 84% with terminal degrees. *Student/faculty ratio:* 11:1.

Majors Agriculture; anthropology; area, ethnic, cultural, and gender studies related; art history, criticism and conservation; Asian studies; biochemistry; biological and biomedical sciences related; biology/biological sciences; business/commerce; business, management, and marketing related; chemistry; classics and languages, literatures and linguistics; computer and information sciences; dance; dramatic/theatre arts; economics; elementary education; English language and literature related; environmental science; environmental studies; fine arts related; French; geology/earth science; German; history; kinesiology and exercise science; liberal arts and sciences/liberal studies; literature; mathematics; music history, literature, and theory; neuroscience; philosophy; physics; political science and government; psychology; psychology related; religious studies; social sciences related; social work; sociology; Spanish; women's studies.

Skidmore College (continued)

Academic Programs *Special study options:* accelerated degree program, adult/continuing education programs, advanced placement credit, double majors, external degree program, honors programs, independent study, internships, off-campus study, student-designed majors, study abroad, summer session for credit. *ROTC:* Army (c), Air Force (c). *Unusual degree programs:* 3-2 business administration with Rensselaer Polytechnic Institute; engineering with Dartmouth College, Clarkson University.

Library Scribner Library with 372,769 titles, 1,983 serial subscriptions, 137,110 audiovisual materials, an OPAC, a Web page.

Computers on Campus 173 computers available on campus for general student use. A campuswide network can be accessed from student residence rooms and from off campus. Internet access, at least one staffed computer lab available.

Student Life *Housing:* on-campus residence required through sophomore year. *Options:* coed, women-only, disabled students. Campus housing is university owned. Freshman campus housing is guaranteed. *Activities and organizations:* drama/theater group, student-run newspaper, radio and television station, choral group, Student Government Association, student radio station, Student Volunteer Bureau, outing club, Skidmore News. *Campus security:* 24-hour emergency response devices and patrols, late-night transport/escort service, controlled dormitory access, well-lit campus. *Student services:* health clinic, personal/psychological counseling.

Athletics Member NCAA. All Division III. *Intercollegiate sports:* baseball M, basketball M/W, crew M/W, equestrian sports M/W, field hockey W, golf M, ice hockey M/W(c), lacrosse M/W, skiing (downhill) M(c)/W(c), soccer M/W, softball W, swimming M/W, tennis M/W, volleyball W. *Intramural sports:* basketball M/W, football M/W, racquetball M/W, soccer M/W, softball W, swimming M/W, tennis M/W, volleyball M/W.

Standardized Tests *Required:* SAT I or ACT (for admission).

Costs (2003–04) *Comprehensive fee:* $37,930 includes full-time tuition ($29,350), mandatory fees ($280), and room and board ($8300). Full-time tuition and fees vary according to course load. Part-time tuition: $980 per credit hour. Part-time tuition and fees vary according to course load. *Required fees:* $25 per term part-time. *College room only:* $4630. Room and board charges vary according to board plan and housing facility. *Payment plans:* tuition prepayment, installment. *Waivers:* employees or children of employees.

Financial Aid Of all full-time matriculated undergraduates who enrolled in 2003, 1,025 applied for aid, 948 were judged to have need, 827 had their need fully met. In 2003, 14 non-need-based awards were made. *Average percent of need met:* 94%. *Average financial aid package:* $24,114. *Average need-based loan:* $3608. *Average need-based gift aid:* $18,765. *Average non-need-based aid:* $10,000. *Average indebtedness upon graduation:* $16,228. *Financial aid deadline:* 1/15.

Applying *Options:* common application, early admission, early decision, deferred entrance. *Application fee:* $60. *Required:* essay or personal statement, high school transcript, 2 letters of recommendation. *Recommended:* interview. *Application deadlines:* 1/15 (freshmen), 4/1 (transfers). *Early decision:* 12/1 (for plan 1), 1/15 (for plan 2). *Notification:* 4/1 (freshmen), 1/1 (early decision plan 1), 2/15 (early decision plan 2).

Admissions Contact John W. Young, Director of Admissions, Skidmore College, 815 North Broadway, Saratoga Springs, NY 12866-1632. *Phone:* 518-580-5570. *Toll-free phone:* 800-867-6007. *Fax:* 518-580-5584. *E-mail:* admissions@skidmore.edu.

■ *See page 2394 for a narrative description.*

STATE UNIVERSITY OF NEW YORK AT BINGHAMTON

Binghamton, New York

- **State-supported** university, founded 1946, part of State University of New York System
- **Calendar** semesters
- **Degrees** bachelor's, master's, doctoral, and post-master's certificates
- **Suburban** 887-acre campus
- **Endowment** $38.7 million
- **Coed,** 10,563 undergraduate students, 97% full-time, 52% women, 48% men
- **Very difficult** entrance level, 45% of applicants were admitted

Undergraduates 10,292 full-time, 271 part-time. Students come from 39 states and territories, 56 other countries, 5% are from out of state, 5% African American, 16% Asian American or Pacific Islander, 6% Hispanic American, 0.2% Native American, 3% international, 7% transferred in, 57% live on campus. *Retention:* 92% of 2002 full-time freshmen returned.

Freshmen *Admission:* 19,076 applied, 8,521 admitted, 2,291 enrolled. *Average high school GPA:* 3.60. *Test scores:* SAT verbal scores over 500: 95%; SAT math scores over 500: 98%; ACT scores over 18: 100%; SAT verbal scores over 600: 53%; SAT math scores over 600: 73%; ACT scores over 24: 87%; SAT verbal scores over 700: 7%; SAT math scores over 700: 17%; ACT scores over 30: 15%.

Faculty *Total:* 704, 72% full-time. *Student/faculty ratio:* 22:1.

Majors Accounting; African-American/Black studies; African studies; anthropology; Arabic; art; art history, criticism and conservation; Asian-American studies; biochemistry; biology/biological sciences; biomedical/medical engineering; chemistry; classics and languages, literatures and linguistics; comparative literature; computer engineering; computer science; dramatic/theatre arts; drawing; economics; electrical, electronics and communications engineering; English; environmental studies; film/cinema studies; fine/studio arts; French; geography; geology/earth science; German; Hebrew; history; industrial engineering; information science/studies; interdisciplinary studies; Italian; Jewish/Judaic studies; Latin American studies; linguistics; literature, management science; mathematics; mechanical engineering; medieval and Renaissance studies; music; music performance; nursing (registered nurse training); philosophy; physics; physiological psychology/psychobiology; political science and government; pre-law studies; psychology; sociology; Spanish.

Academic Programs *Special study options:* academic remediation for entering students, accelerated degree program, adult/continuing education programs, advanced placement credit, distance learning, double majors, English as a second language, honors programs, independent study, internships, off-campus study, part-time degree program, services for LD students, student-designed majors, summer session for credit. *ROTC:* Air Force (c). *Unusual degree programs:* 3-2 business administration with Hanour College; management, engineering and physics with Columbia University, Clarkson University, Rochester Institute of Technology, State University of New York at Buffalo, State University of New York at Stony Brook, University of Rochester, chemistry and materials science, biology, computer science.

Library Glenn G. Bartle Library plus 1 other with 1.8 million titles, 8,630 serial subscriptions, 121,251 audiovisual materials, an OPAC, a Web page.

Computers on Campus 6228 computers available on campus for general student use. A campuswide network can be accessed from student residence rooms and from off campus. Internet access, online (class) registration, at least one staffed computer lab available. Computer purchase or lease plan available.

Student Life *Housing:* on-campus residence required for freshman year. *Options:* coed, disabled students. Campus housing is university owned. *Activities and organizations:* drama/theater group, student-run newspaper, radio and television station, choral group, student radio station, Student Association, student newspaper, cultural organizations, Peer Counseling/Mentoring/Volunteering Program, national fraternities, national sororities. *Campus security:* 24-hour emergency response devices and patrols, student patrols, late-night transport/escort service, controlled dormitory access, safety awareness programs, well-lit campus, self-defense education, secured campus entrance 12 a.m. to 5 a.m., emergency telephones. *Student services:* health clinic, personal/psychological counseling, women's center, legal services.

Athletics Member NCAA. All Division I. *Intercollegiate sports:* badminton M(c)/W(c), baseball M(s), basketball M(s)/W(s), bowling M(c)/W(c), crew M(c)/W(c), cross-country running M(s)/W(s), equestrian sports M(c)/W(c), fencing M(c)/W(c), golf M(s), ice hockey M(c), lacrosse M(s)/W(s), racquetball M(c)/W(c), rugby M(c)/W(c), skiing (downhill) M(c)/W(c), soccer M(s)/W(s), softball W(s), swimming M(s)/W(s), table tennis M(c)/W(c), tennis M(s)/W(s), track and field M(s)/W(s), volleyball M(c)/W(s). *Intramural sports:* badminton M/W, basketball M/W, bowling M/W, cross-country running M/W, football M/W, golf M/W, racquetball M/W, soccer M/W, squash M/W, table tennis M/W, tennis M/W, volleyball M/W, water polo M/W.

Standardized Tests *Required:* SAT I or ACT (for admission).

Costs (2003–04) *Tuition:* state resident $4350 full-time, $181 per credit part-time; nonresident $10,300 full-time, $429 per credit part-time. *Required fees:* $1337 full-time. *Room and board:* $7100; room only: $4384. Room and board charges vary according to board plan and housing facility. *Payment plan:* installment. *Waivers:* employees or children of employees.

Financial Aid Of all full-time matriculated undergraduates who enrolled in 2003, 7,105 applied for aid, 5,139 were judged to have need, 3,678 had their need fully met. 1,478 Federal Work-Study jobs (averaging $1427). In 2003, 207 non-need-based awards were made. *Average percent of need met:* 84%. *Average financial aid package:* $10,629. *Average need-based loan:* $4214. *Average need-based gift aid:* $4752. *Average non-need-based aid:* $2471. *Average indebtedness upon graduation:* $14,531.

Applying *Options:* common application, electronic application, early admission, early action, deferred entrance. *Application fee:* $40. *Required:* essay or personal statement, high school transcript. *Required for some:* 1 letter of recommendation, portfolio, audition. *Application deadlines:* 1/15 (freshmen), 2/15 (transfers). *Notification:* continuous (freshmen), 12/22 (early action), continuous (transfers).

Admissions Contact Ms. Cheryl S. Brown, Director of Admissions, State University of New York at Binghamton, PO Box 6001, Binghamton, NY 13902-6001. *Phone:* 607-777-2171. *Fax:* 607-777-4445. *E-mail:* admit@binghamton.edu.

■ *See page 2436 for a narrative description.*

STATE UNIVERSITY OF NEW YORK AT NEW PALTZ

New Paltz, New York

- **State-supported** comprehensive, founded 1828, part of State University of New York System
- **Calendar** semesters
- **Degrees** bachelor's, master's, and post-master's certificates
- **Small-town** 216-acre campus
- **Endowment** $4.4 million
- **Coed,** 6,292 undergraduate students, 87% full-time, 64% women, 36% men
- **Moderately difficult** entrance level, 34% of applicants were admitted

Undergraduates 5,469 full-time, 823 part-time. Students come from 25 states and territories, 30 other countries, 5% are from out of state, 7% African American, 4% Asian American or Pacific Islander, 10% Hispanic American, 0.3% Native American, 2% international, 12% transferred in, 52% live on campus. *Retention:* 84% of 2002 full-time freshmen returned.

Freshmen *Admission:* 10,942 applied, 3,768 admitted, 916 enrolled. *Average high school GPA:* 3.20. *Test scores:* SAT verbal scores over 500: 78%; SAT math scores over 500: 80%; SAT verbal scores over 600: 29%; SAT math scores over 600: 25%; SAT verbal scores over 700: 3%; SAT math scores over 700: 3%.

Faculty *Total:* 689, 43% full-time, 46% with terminal degrees. *Student/faculty ratio:* 17:1.

Majors Accounting; African-American/Black studies; anthropology; applied mathematics; art; art history, criticism and conservation; art teacher education; audiology and speech-language pathology; biochemistry; biology/biological sciences; broadcast journalism; business administration and management; business/managerial economics; ceramic arts and ceramics; chemistry; city/urban, community and regional planning; commercial and advertising art; comparative literature; computer engineering; computer science; creative writing; dramatic/theatre arts; drawing; economics; education; electrical, electronics and communications engineering; elementary education; engineering physics; English; environmental studies; finance; fine/studio arts; French; geography; geology/earth science; German; history; international business/trade/commerce; international economics; international relations and affairs; jazz/jazz studies; Jewish/Judaic studies; journalism; kindergarten/preschool education; Latin American studies; marketing/marketing management; mass communication/media; mathematics; metal and jewelry arts; music; music history, literature, and theory; music therapy; nursing (registered nurse training); ophthalmic/optometric services; philosophy; photography; physics; physiological psychology/psychobiology; political science and government; pre-dentistry studies; pre-law studies; pre-medical studies; psychology; radio and television; science teacher education; sculpture; secondary education; social work; sociology; Spanish; special education; speech and rhetoric; speech therapy; women's studies.

Academic Programs *Special study options:* academic remediation for entering students, adult/continuing education programs, advanced placement credit, distance learning, double majors, English as a second language, honors programs, independent study, internships, off-campus study, part-time degree program, services for LD students, study abroad, summer session for credit. *Unusual degree programs:* 3-2 forestry with State University of New York College of Environmental Science and Forestry.

Library Sojourner Truth Library with 507,300 titles, 1,434 serial subscriptions, 1,100 audiovisual materials, an OPAC, a Web page.

Computers on Campus 600 computers available on campus for general student use. A campuswide network can be accessed from student residence rooms and from off campus that provide access to e-mail. Internet access, online (class) registration, at least one staffed computer lab available.

Student Life *Housing:* on-campus residence required for freshman year. *Options:* coed, disabled students. Freshman campus housing is guaranteed. *Activities and organizations:* drama/theater group, student-run newspaper, radio and television station, choral group, outing club, Greek letter organizations, intramurals, Residence Hall Student Association, Student Art Alliance, national fraternities, national sororities. *Campus security:* 24-hour emergency response devices and patrols, late-night transport/escort service, controlled dormitory access, safety seminars. *Student services:* health clinic, personal/psychological counseling, women's center, legal services.

Athletics Member NCAA. All Division III. *Intercollegiate sports:* baseball M, basketball M/W, cross-country running M/W, equestrian sports W(c), field hockey W, ice hockey M(c), lacrosse M(c)/W, rugby M(c)/W(c), soccer M/W, softball W, swimming M/W, tennis M/W, track and field M/W, volleyball M/W. *Intramural sports:* badminton M/W, basketball M/W, football M, golf M/W, racquetball M/W, softball M/W, track and field M/W, volleyball M/W.

Standardized Tests *Required:* SAT I or ACT (for admission).

Costs (2003–04) *Tuition:* state resident $4350 full-time, $181 per credit part-time; nonresident $10,300 full-time, $429 per credit part-time. *Required fees:* $795 full-time, $24 per credit part-time, $103 per term part-time. *Room and board:* $6420; room only: $3880. Room and board charges vary according to board plan. *Payment plan:* installment.

Financial Aid Of all full-time matriculated undergraduates who enrolled in 2002, 4,006 applied for aid, 2,759 were judged to have need, 1,008 had their need fully met. 656 Federal Work-Study jobs (averaging $800). 478 state and other part-time jobs (averaging $1000). In 2002, 182 non-need-based awards were made. *Average percent of need met:* 78%. *Average financial aid package:* $2189. *Average need-based loan:* $891. *Average need-based gift aid:* $1893. *Average non-need-based aid:* $891. *Average indebtedness upon graduation:* $15,000.

Applying *Options:* electronic application, early admission, early action, deferred entrance. *Application fee:* $40. *Required:* high school transcript. *Required for some:* essay or personal statement, letters of recommendation, interview, portfolio for art program, audition for music and theater programs. *Recommended:* minimum 3.0 GPA. *Application deadlines:* 3/31 (freshmen), 5/1 (transfers). *Notification:* continuous (freshmen), 1/1 (early action).

Admissions Contact Ms. Kimberly A. Lavoie, Director of Freshmen and International Admissions, State University of New York at New Paltz, 75 South Manheim Boulevard, Suite 1, New Paltz, NY 12561-2499. *Phone:* 845-257-3200. *Toll-free phone:* 888-639-7589. *Fax:* 845-257-3209. *E-mail:* admissions@newpaltz.edu.

STATE UNIVERSITY OF NEW YORK AT OSWEGO

Oswego, New York

- **State-supported** comprehensive, founded 1861, part of State University of New York System
- **Calendar** semesters
- **Degrees** bachelor's, master's, and post-master's certificates
- **Small-town** 696-acre campus with easy access to Syracuse
- **Endowment** $4.1 million
- **Coed,** 7,181 undergraduate students, 91% full-time, 54% women, 46% men
- **Moderately difficult** entrance level, 57% of applicants were admitted

Undergraduates 6,537 full-time, 644 part-time. Students come from 29 states and territories, 22 other countries, 2% are from out of state, 4% African American, 2% Asian American or Pacific Islander, 3% Hispanic American, 0.5% Native American, 0.9% international, 10% transferred in, 51% live on campus. *Retention:* 75% of 2002 full-time freshmen returned.

Freshmen *Admission:* 7,438 applied, 4,223 admitted, 1,336 enrolled. *Average high school GPA:* 3.22. *Test scores:* SAT verbal scores over 500: 75%; SAT math scores over 500: 80%; ACT scores over 18: 100%; SAT verbal scores over 600: 17%; SAT math scores over 600: 20%; ACT scores over 24: 37%; SAT verbal scores over 700: 2%; SAT math scores over 700: 1%; ACT scores over 30: 4%.

Faculty *Total:* 528, 57% full-time, 77% with terminal degrees. *Student/faculty ratio:* 20:1.

Majors Accounting; accounting related; agricultural teacher education; American studies; anthropology; applied mathematics; art; atmospheric sciences and meteorology; biology/biological sciences; business administration and management; chemistry; cognitive psychology and psycholinguistics; cognitive science; commercial and advertising art; computer science; creative writing; criminal justice/law enforcement administration; dramatic/theatre arts; econometrics and quantitative economics; economics; education; elementary education; English; finance; French; geochemistry; geology/earth science; German; health teacher education; history; human development and family studies; human resources management; industrial arts; information science/studies; international economics; international relations and affairs; journalism; linguistics; management science; marketing/marketing management; mass communication/media; mathematics; music; philosophy; philosophy and religious studies related; physics; political science and government; pre-dentistry studies; pre-law studies; pre-medical studies; pre-veterinary studies; psychology; psychology related; public relations/image management; sales and marketing/marketing and distribution teacher education; science teacher education; secondary education; sociology; Spanish; sport and fitness administration; technology/industrial arts teacher education; trade and industrial teacher education; women's studies; zoology/animal biology.

Academic Programs *Special study options:* accelerated degree program, adult/continuing education programs, advanced placement credit, cooperative education, distance learning, double majors, English as a second language, freshman honors college, honors programs, independent study, internships, off-

State University of New York at Oswego (continued)
campus study, part-time degree program, services for LD students, student-designed majors, study abroad, summer session for credit. *ROTC:* Army (c). *Unusual degree programs:* 3-2 engineering with Clarkson University, Case Western Reserve University, State University of New York at Binghamton.

Library Penfield Library plus 1 other with 467,346 titles, 1,070 serial subscriptions, 38,066 audiovisual materials, an OPAC, a Web page.

Computers on Campus 600 computers available on campus for general student use. A campuswide network can be accessed from student residence rooms and from off campus. Internet access, online (class) registration, at least one staffed computer lab available. Computer purchase or lease plan available.

Student Life *Housing:* on-campus residence required through sophomore year. *Options:* coed, disabled students. Campus housing is university owned. Freshman campus housing is guaranteed. *Activities and organizations:* drama/theater group, student-run newspaper, radio and television station, choral group, club/intramural sports, student radio/television stations, outing/recreation club, student government, programming boards, national fraternities, national sororities. *Campus security:* 24-hour emergency response devices and patrols, controlled dormitory access. *Student services:* health clinic, personal/psychological counseling, women's center, legal services.

Athletics Member NCAA. All Division III. *Intercollegiate sports:* baseball M, basketball M/W, crew M(c)/W(c), cross-country running M/W, field hockey W, golf M/W, ice hockey M, lacrosse M/W, soccer M/W, softball W, swimming M/W, tennis M/W, track and field M/W, volleyball W, wrestling M. *Intramural sports:* basketball M/W, cheerleading W(c), equestrian sports M(c)/W(c), fencing M(c)/W(c), field hockey W(c), football M/W, golf M/W, ice hockey M(c), lacrosse M/W, racquetball M/W, rock climbing M/W, rugby M(c)/W(c), sailing M(c)/W(c), skiing (cross-country) M(c)/W(c), skiing (downhill) M(c)/W(c), soccer M/W, softball M/W, swimming M/W, tennis M/W, volleyball M(c)/W, weight lifting M, wrestling M.

Standardized Tests *Required:* SAT I or ACT (for admission).

Costs (2003–04) *Tuition:* state resident $4350 full-time, $181 per credit hour part-time; nonresident $10,300 full-time, $429 per credit hour part-time. *Required fees:* $826 full-time, $33 per credit hour part-time. *Room and board:* $7540; room only: $4490. Room and board charges vary according to board plan. *Payment plans:* installment, deferred payment.

Financial Aid Of all full-time matriculated undergraduates who enrolled in 2003, 5,539 applied for aid, 4,487 were judged to have need, 1,404 had their need fully met. 450 Federal Work-Study jobs (averaging $1294). 1,131 state and other part-time jobs (averaging $1081). In 2003, 929 non-need-based awards were made. *Average percent of need met:* 85%. *Average financial aid package:* $8550. *Average need-based loan:* $4835. *Average need-based gift aid:* $3665. *Average non-need-based aid:* $5370. *Average indebtedness upon graduation:* $16,086.

Applying *Options:* electronic application, early admission, early decision, deferred entrance. *Application fee:* $40. *Required:* high school transcript. *Required for some:* letters of recommendation. *Recommended:* essay or personal statement, interview. *Application deadline:* rolling (freshmen), rolling (transfers). *Early decision:* 11/15. *Notification:* 1/15 (freshmen), 12/15 (early decision), continuous until 1/15 (transfers).

Admissions Contact Dr. Joseph F. Grant Jr., Vice President for Student Affairs and Enrollment, State University of New York at Oswego, 7060 State Route 104, Oswego, NY 13126. *Phone:* 315-312-2250. *Fax:* 315-312-3260. *E-mail:* admiss@oswego.edu.

■ See page 2438 for a narrative description.

STATE UNIVERSITY OF NEW YORK AT PLATTSBURGH
Plattsburgh, New York

- **State-supported** comprehensive, founded 1889, part of State University of New York System
- **Calendar** semesters plus 2 5-week summer sessions and 1 winter session
- **Degrees** bachelor's, master's, and post-master's certificates
- **Small-town** 265-acre campus with easy access to Montreal
- **Endowment** $8.7 million
- **Coed,** 5,403 undergraduate students, 92% full-time, 58% women, 42% men
- **Moderately difficult** entrance level, 62% of applicants were admitted

Plattsburgh State students benefit from close connection with faculty and a campus set in one of America's best college locations. The curriculum focuses on preparing undergraduates to become thoughtful, educated persons and successful career professionals. Plattsburgh State offers a comprehensive selection of majors, and provides students with opportunities for merit scholarships, internships, and exchange programs.

Undergraduates 4,994 full-time, 409 part-time. Students come from 17 states and territories, 54 other countries, 4% are from out of state, 5% African American, 2% Asian American or Pacific Islander, 3% Hispanic American, 0.3% Native American, 7% international, 10% transferred in, 46% live on campus. *Retention:* 75% of 2002 full-time freshmen returned.

Freshmen *Admission:* 6,798 applied, 4,232 admitted, 967 enrolled. *Average high school GPA:* 3.00. *Test scores:* SAT verbal scores over 500: 61%; SAT math scores over 500: 65%; ACT scores over 18: 93%; SAT verbal scores over 600: 13%; SAT math scores over 600: 15%; ACT scores over 24: 26%; SAT verbal scores over 700: 1%; SAT math scores over 700: 1%; ACT scores over 30: 2%.

Faculty *Total:* 434, 58% full-time, 57% with terminal degrees. *Student/faculty ratio:* 18:1.

Majors Accounting; anthropology; art history, criticism and conservation; audiology and speech-language pathology; biochemistry; biology/biological sciences; broadcast journalism; business administration and management; business/managerial economics; Canadian studies; chemistry; child development; clinical laboratory science/medical technology; communication disorders; communication/speech communication and rhetoric; computer science; criminology; dramatic/theatre arts; economics; education; elementary education; English; environmental studies; fine/studio arts; foods, nutrition, and wellness; French; geography; geology/earth science; history; hotel/motel administration; interdisciplinary studies; international business/trade/commerce; Latin American studies; marketing/marketing management; mass communication/media; mathematics; music; nursing (registered nurse training); philosophy; physics; political science and government; psychology; secondary education; social work; sociology; Spanish; special education.

Academic Programs *Special study options:* academic remediation for entering students, accelerated degree program, adult/continuing education programs, advanced placement credit, cooperative education, distance learning, double majors, English as a second language, honors programs, independent study, internships, off-campus study, part-time degree program, services for LD students, student-designed majors, study abroad, summer session for credit. *Unusual degree programs:* 3-2 engineering with Clarkson University, State University of New York at Stony Brook, Syracuse University, University of Vermont, McGill University, State University of New York at Binghamton; international policy studies with Monterey Institute of International Studies in French and Spanish.

Library Feinberg Library with 378,020 titles, 1,407 serial subscriptions, 19,714 audiovisual materials, an OPAC, a Web page.

Computers on Campus 450 computers available on campus for general student use. A campuswide network can be accessed from student residence rooms and from off campus. Internet access, online (class) registration, at least one staffed computer lab available. Computer purchase or lease plan available.

Student Life *Housing:* on-campus residence required through sophomore year. *Options:* coed, disabled students. Campus housing is university owned. Freshman campus housing is guaranteed. *Activities and organizations:* drama/theater group, student-run newspaper, radio and television station, choral group, Student Association, honor societies, student media organizations, service/leadership organizations, intramural and recreational sports, national fraternities, national sororities. *Campus security:* 24-hour emergency response devices and patrols, late-night transport/escort service, controlled dormitory access, enhanced 911 system. *Student services:* health clinic, personal/psychological counseling, women's center, legal services.

Athletics Member NCAA. All Division III. *Intercollegiate sports:* basketball M/W, cross-country running M/W, golf M/W, ice hockey M, lacrosse M, soccer M/W, softball W, swimming M/W, tennis W, track and field M/W, volleyball W. *Intramural sports:* basketball M/W, football M, golf M/W, ice hockey M(c), lacrosse M, racquetball M(c)/W(c), rugby M(c)/W(c), soccer M/W, softball W, tennis W, volleyball M/W, weight lifting M(c)/W(c).

Standardized Tests *Required:* SAT I or ACT (for admission).

Costs (2003–04) *Tuition:* state resident $4350 full-time, $181 per credit hour part-time; nonresident $10,300 full-time, $429 per credit hour part-time. Part-time tuition and fees vary according to course load. *Required fees:* $850 full-time, $34 per credit hour part-time. *Room and board:* $6448; room only: $4040. Room and board charges vary according to board plan. *Payment plans:* installment, deferred payment. *Waivers:* employees or children of employees.

Financial Aid Of all full-time matriculated undergraduates who enrolled in 2003, 3,870 applied for aid, 3,051 were judged to have need, 1,485 had their need fully met. 393 Federal Work-Study jobs (averaging $1606). In 2003, 1185 non-need-based awards were made. *Average percent of need met:* 88%. *Average financial aid package:* $8519. *Average need-based loan:* $5399. *Average need-based gift aid:* $4177. *Average non-need-based aid:* $4621. *Average indebtedness upon graduation:* $16,158.

Applying *Options:* electronic application, early admission, early decision, deferred entrance. *Application fee:* $40. *Required:* high school transcript, minimum 2.5 GPA. *Recommended:* essay or personal statement, minimum 3.4 GPA, letters of recommendation, interview. *Application deadline:* 8/1 (freshmen), rolling (transfers). *Early decision:* 11/15. *Notification:* continuous (freshmen), 12/15 (early decision), continuous (transfers).

Admissions Contact Mr. Richard Higgins, Director of Admissions, State University of New York at Plattsburgh, 101 Broad Street, Plattsburgh, NY 12901-2681. *Phone:* 518-564-2040. *Toll-free phone:* 888-673-0012. *Fax:* 518-564-2045. *E-mail:* admissions@plattsburgh.edu.

■ *See page 2440 for a narrative description.*

STATE UNIVERSITY OF NEW YORK COLLEGE AT BROCKPORT

Brockport, New York

- **State-supported** comprehensive, founded 1867, part of State University of New York System
- **Calendar** semesters
- **Degrees** bachelor's, master's, post-master's, and postbachelor's certificates
- **Small-town** 435-acre campus with easy access to Rochester
- **Endowment** $2.7 million
- **Coed,** 6,962 undergraduate students, 88% full-time, 57% women, 43% men
- **Moderately difficult** entrance level, 51% of applicants were admitted

Undergraduates 6,095 full-time, 867 part-time. Students come from 35 states and territories, 23 other countries, 1% are from out of state, 5% African American, 1% Asian American or Pacific Islander, 2% Hispanic American, 0.4% Native American, 0.9% international, 13% transferred in, 38% live on campus. *Retention:* 80% of 2002 full-time freshmen returned.

Freshmen *Admission:* 7,214 applied, 3,701 admitted, 1,046 enrolled. *Average high school GPA:* 3.06. *Test scores:* SAT verbal scores over 500: 74%; SAT math scores over 500: 68%; ACT scores over 18: 95%; SAT verbal scores over 600: 20%; SAT math scores over 600: 16%; ACT scores over 24: 35%; SAT verbal scores over 700: 2%; SAT math scores over 700: 2%; ACT scores over 30: 2%.

Faculty *Total:* 555, 54% full-time, 55% with terminal degrees. *Student/faculty ratio:* 18:1.

Majors Accounting; acting; African-American/Black studies; African studies; American literature; anthropology; art; Asian studies; astronomy; athletic training; atmospheric sciences and meteorology; bilingual, multilingual, and multicultural education related; biochemistry; biology/biological sciences; biology/biotechnology laboratory technician; biology teacher education; biotechnology; broadcast journalism; business administration and management; cell and molecular biology; cell biology and histology; ceramic arts and ceramics; chemistry; chemistry teacher education; clinical laboratory science/medical technology; communication and journalism related; communication and media related; communication/speech communication and rhetoric; computer science; corrections; corrections and criminal justice related; creative writing; criminal justice/law enforcement administration; criminal justice/police science; criminology; dance; dramatic/theatre arts; drawing; early childhood education; economics; education; elementary education; English; English/language arts teacher education; environmental biology; environmental studies; European studies; exercise physiology; finance; fine/studio arts; foreign language teacher education; French; French language teacher education; geological and earth sciences/geosciences related; geology/earth science; health and physical education; health and physical education related; health/health care administration; health science; health teacher education; history; history teacher education; hydrology and water resources science; interdisciplinary studies; international business/trade/commerce; international relations and affairs; journalism; kinesiology and exercise science; Latin American studies; literature; marketing/marketing management; mass communication/media; mathematics; mathematics teacher education; metal and jewelry arts; meteorology; middle school education; molecular biology; nursing (registered nurse training); organizational communication; painting; parks, recreation and leisure; parks, recreation, and leisure related; philosophy; physical education teaching and coaching; physics; physics related; physics teacher education; political science and government; pre-dentistry studies; pre-law studies; pre-medical studies; pre-veterinary studies; psychology; public relations, advertising, and applied communication related; public relations/image management; radio and television; radio, television, and digital communication related; science teacher education; sculpture; secondary education; securities services administration; social studies teacher education; social work; sociology; Spanish; Spanish language teacher education; speech and rhetoric; sport and fitness administration; substance abuse/addiction counseling; therapeutic recreation; women's studies.

Academic Programs *Special study options:* academic remediation for entering students, accelerated degree program, advanced placement credit, cooperative education, distance learning, double majors, freshman honors college, honors programs, independent study, internships, off-campus study, part-time degree program, services for LD students, student-designed majors, study abroad, summer session for credit. *ROTC:* Army (b), Air Force (c). *Unusual degree programs:* 3-2 environmental science with State University of New York College of Environmental Science and Forestry.

Library Drake Memorial Library with 584,687 titles, 1,800 serial subscriptions, 8,228 audiovisual materials, an OPAC, a Web page.

Computers on Campus 750 computers available on campus for general student use. A campuswide network can be accessed from student residence rooms and from off campus. Internet access, online (class) registration, at least one staffed computer lab available.

Student Life *Housing:* on-campus residence required for freshman year. *Options:* coed, disabled students. Campus housing is university owned. Freshman campus housing is guaranteed. *Activities and organizations:* drama/theater group, student-run newspaper, radio and television station, choral group, fine arts clubs, Organization for Students of African Descent, communication club, student radio station, sports clubs, national fraternities, national sororities. *Campus security:* 24-hour emergency response devices and patrols, student patrols, late-night transport/escort service, controlled dormitory access. *Student services:* health clinic, personal/psychological counseling, women's center, legal services.

Athletics Member NCAA. All Division III. *Intercollegiate sports:* baseball M, basketball M/W, cross-country running M/W, field hockey W, football M, gymnastics W, ice hockey M, lacrosse M/W, soccer M/W, softball W, swimming M/W, tennis W, track and field M/W, volleyball W, wrestling M. *Intramural sports:* badminton M/W, basketball M/W, bowling M/W, cheerleading M/W, cross-country running M/W, football M/W, ice hockey M/W, lacrosse M/W, racquetball M/W, rugby M/W, skiing (downhill) M/W, soccer M/W, softball M/W, squash M/W, tennis M/W, volleyball M/W, water polo M/W, weight lifting M/W.

Standardized Tests *Required:* SAT I or ACT (for admission).

Costs (2004–05) *Tuition:* state resident $4350 full-time, $181 per credit hour part-time; nonresident $10,300 full-time, $429 per credit hour part-time. Part-time tuition and fees vary according to course load. *Required fees:* $871 full-time, $36 per credit hour part-time. *Room and board:* $6890; room only: $4240. Room and board charges vary according to board plan and housing facility. *Payment plans:* installment, deferred payment. *Waivers:* senior citizens and employees or children of employees.

Financial Aid Of all full-time matriculated undergraduates who enrolled in 2003, 5,868 applied for aid, 4,628 were judged to have need, 2,815 had their need fully met. 750 Federal Work-Study jobs (averaging $1054). 1,526 state and other part-time jobs (averaging $1797). In 2003, 684 non-need-based awards were made. *Average percent of need met:* 98%. *Average financial aid package:* $8062. *Average need-based loan:* $3537. *Average need-based gift aid:* $3730. *Average non-need-based aid:* $2882. *Average indebtedness upon graduation:* $16,902.

Applying *Options:* electronic application, deferred entrance. *Application fee:* $40. *Required:* high school transcript. *Required for some:* essay or personal statement, letters of recommendation, interview. *Recommended:* minimum 2.6 GPA, letters of recommendation. *Application deadline:* rolling (freshmen). *Notification:* continuous (freshmen), continuous (transfers).

Admissions Contact Mr. Bernard S. Valento, Associate Director of Undergraduate Admissions, State University of New York College at Brockport, 350 New Campus Drive, Brockport, NY 14420-2997. *Phone:* 585-395-2751. *Toll-free phone:* 585-395-2751. *Fax:* 585-395-5452. *E-mail:* admit@brockport.edu.

STATE UNIVERSITY OF NEW YORK COLLEGE AT CORTLAND

Cortland, New York

- **State-supported** comprehensive, founded 1868, part of State University of New York System
- **Calendar** semesters
- **Degrees** bachelor's, master's, post-master's, and postbachelor's certificates
- **Small-town** 191-acre campus with easy access to Syracuse
- **Coed,** 5,796 undergraduate students, 95% full-time, 58% women, 42% men
- **Moderately difficult** entrance level, 49% of applicants were admitted

Undergraduates 5,511 full-time, 285 part-time. Students come from 26 states and territories, 2% are from out of state, 3% African American, 1% Asian American or Pacific Islander, 3% Hispanic American, 0.3% Native American, 0.2% international, 11% transferred in, 49% live on campus. *Retention:* 77% of 2002 full-time freshmen returned.

Freshmen *Admission:* 9,327 applied, 4,532 admitted, 1,134 enrolled. *Average high school GPA:* 3.20. *Test scores:* SAT verbal scores over 500: 80%; SAT math scores over 500: 67%; SAT verbal scores over 600: 17%; SAT math scores over 600: 11%; SAT verbal scores over 700: 1%; SAT math scores over 700: 1%.

Faculty *Total:* 512, 52% full-time, 50% with terminal degrees. *Student/faculty ratio:* 16:1.

Majors African-American/Black studies; anthropology; art history, criticism and conservation; athletic training; audiology and speech-language pathology; biology/biological sciences; biology teacher education; chemistry; chemistry teacher education; communication/speech communication and rhetoric; criminology; economics; elementary education; English; environmental biology; environmental science; environmental studies; fine/studio arts; French; French language teacher education; geochemistry; geography; geology/earth science; German;

State University of New York College at Cortland (continued)
health science; health teacher education; history; human services; international/global studies; international relations and affairs; kindergarten/preschool education; kinesiology and exercise science; mathematics; mathematics teacher education; middle school education; parks, recreation and leisure; parks, recreation and leisure facilities management; philosophy; physical education teaching and coaching; physics; physics teacher education; political science and government; pre-dentistry studies; pre-law studies; pre-medical studies; psychology; reading teacher education; science teacher education; secondary education; social studies teacher education; social work; sociology; Spanish; Spanish language teacher education; special education (speech or language impaired); speech and rhetoric; therapeutic recreation.

Academic Programs *Special study options:* academic remediation for entering students, adult/continuing education programs, advanced placement credit, cooperative education, distance learning, double majors, honors programs, independent study, internships, off-campus study, part-time degree program, services for LD students, student-designed majors, study abroad, summer session for credit. *ROTC:* Army (c), Air Force (c). *Unusual degree programs:* 3-2 engineering with State University of New York at Buffalo, State University of New York at Stony Brook, Alfred University, Clarkson University, State University of New York at Binghamton, Case Western Reserve University; forestry with Duke University, State University of New York College of Environmental Science and Forestry.

Library Memorial Library with 82,257 titles, an OPAC, a Web page.

Computers on Campus 832 computers available on campus for general student use. A campuswide network can be accessed from student residence rooms and from off campus. At least one staffed computer lab available.

Student Life *Housing:* on-campus residence required through sophomore year. *Options:* coed. *Activities and organizations:* drama/theater group, student-run newspaper, radio and television station, choral group, national fraternities, national sororities. *Campus security:* 24-hour emergency response devices and patrols, late-night transport/escort service. *Student services:* health clinic, personal/psychological counseling, women's center, legal services.

Athletics Member NCAA. All Division III. *Intercollegiate sports:* baseball M, basketball M/W, cross-country running M/W, field hockey W, football M/W(c), golf W, gymnastics W, ice hockey M/W(c), lacrosse M/W, racquetball M(c)/W(c), rugby M(c)/W(c), soccer M/W, softball W, swimming M/W, tennis W, track and field M/W, volleyball M(c)/W, wrestling M. *Intramural sports:* archery M/W, badminton M/W, baseball M, basketball M/W, bowling M/W, cross-country running M/W, fencing M/W, field hockey W, football M/W, golf M/W, gymnastics W, ice hockey M, lacrosse M/W, racquetball M/W, rugby M/W, skiing (cross-country) M/W, skiing (downhill) M/W, soccer M/W, softball M/W, squash M/W, swimming M/W, table tennis M/W, tennis M/W, track and field M/W, volleyball M/W, weight lifting M/W, wrestling M.

Standardized Tests *Required:* SAT I or ACT (for admission).

Costs (2003–04) *Tuition:* state resident $4350 full-time, $181 per credit part-time; nonresident $10,300 full-time, $429 per credit part-time. *Required fees:* $885 full-time. *Room and board:* $6860; room only: $3960.

Financial Aid Of all full-time matriculated undergraduates who enrolled in 2002, 4,557 applied for aid, 3,416 were judged to have need, 781 had their need fully met. In 2002, 942 non-need-based awards were made. *Average percent of need met:* 79%. *Average financial aid package:* $8091. *Average need-based loan:* $3709. *Average need-based gift aid:* $3234. *Average non-need-based aid:* $5760. *Financial aid deadline:* 3/31.

Applying *Options:* electronic application, early admission, early decision, deferred entrance. *Application fee:* $40. *Required:* essay or personal statement, high school transcript, minimum 2.3 GPA, 1 letter of recommendation. *Recommended:* minimum 3.0 GPA, 3 letters of recommendation, interview. *Application deadline:* rolling (freshmen). *Early decision:* 11/15. *Notification:* continuous (freshmen), 12/15 (early decision), continuous (transfers).

Admissions Contact Mr. Gradin Avery, Director of Admission, State University of New York College at Cortland, PO Box 2000, Cortland, NY 13045. *Phone:* 607-753-4711. *Fax:* 607-753-5998. *E-mail:* admssn_info@snycorva.cortland.edu.

STATE UNIVERSITY OF NEW YORK COLLEGE AT FREDONIA

Fredonia, New York

- **State-supported** comprehensive, founded 1826, part of State University of New York System
- **Calendar** semesters
- **Degrees** bachelor's and master's
- **Small-town** 266-acre campus with easy access to Buffalo
- **Endowment** $10.0 million
- **Coed,** 4,852 undergraduate students, 96% full-time, 59% women, 41% men
- **Moderately difficult** entrance level, 57% of applicants were admitted

Undergraduates 4,650 full-time, 202 part-time. Students come from 27 states and territories, 9 other countries, 2% are from out of state, 1% African American, 1% Asian American or Pacific Islander, 2% Hispanic American, 0.7% Native American, 0.6% international, 9% transferred in, 53% live on campus. *Retention:* 81% of 2002 full-time freshmen returned.

Freshmen *Admission:* 5,961 applied, 3,377 admitted, 1,074 enrolled. *Average high school GPA:* 3.33. *Test scores:* SAT verbal scores over 500: 81%; SAT math scores over 500: 83%; ACT scores over 18: 100%; SAT verbal scores over 600: 22%; SAT math scores over 600: 24%; ACT scores over 24: 54%; SAT verbal scores over 700: 4%; SAT math scores over 700: 3%; ACT scores over 30: 3%.

Faculty *Total:* 432, 59% full-time, 50% with terminal degrees. *Student/faculty ratio:* 18:1.

Majors Accounting; American studies; applied art; art; art history, criticism and conservation; arts management; audio engineering; audiology and speech-language pathology; biochemistry; biological and physical sciences; biology/biological sciences; biology/biotechnology laboratory technician; biomedical sciences; broadcast journalism; business administration and management; chemistry; clinical laboratory science/medical technology; commercial and advertising art; communication disorders; computer graphics; computer science; criminal justice/law enforcement administration; dance; dramatic/theatre arts; drawing; economics; education; elementary education; English; environmental studies; film/cinema studies; finance; fine/studio arts; French; geochemistry; geology/earth science; geophysics and seismology; gerontology; health/health care administration; history; information science/studies; interdisciplinary studies; intermedia/multimedia; kindergarten/preschool education; labor and industrial relations; legal studies; liberal arts and sciences/liberal studies; marketing/marketing management; mass communication/media; mathematics; music; music history, literature, and theory; music management and merchandising; music teacher education; music therapy; philosophy; physics; piano and organ; political science and government; pre-law studies; pre-medical studies; pre-veterinary studies; psychology; radio and television; science teacher education; secondary education; social work; sociology; Spanish; speech therapy; violin, viola, guitar and other stringed instruments; voice and opera; wind/percussion instruments; women's studies.

Academic Programs *Special study options:* accelerated degree program, adult/continuing education programs, advanced placement credit, distance learning, double majors, honors programs, independent study, internships, off-campus study, part-time degree program, services for LD students, student-designed majors, study abroad, summer session for credit. *Unusual degree programs:* 3-2 business administration with Clarkson University, State University of New York at Buffalo, University of Pittsburgh; engineering with Clarkson University, State University of New York at Buffalo, Case Western Reserve, Columbia University, Cornell University, Louisiana Technical University, New York State College of Ceramics at Alfred, Ohio State University.

Library Reed Library with 396,000 titles, 2,270 serial subscriptions, 17,607 audiovisual materials, an OPAC, a Web page.

Computers on Campus 500 computers available on campus for general student use. A campuswide network can be accessed from student residence rooms and from off campus. At least one staffed computer lab available.

Student Life *Housing:* on-campus residence required through sophomore year. *Options:* coed, men-only, women-only. Campus housing is university owned. Freshman campus housing is guaranteed. *Activities and organizations:* drama/theater group, student-run newspaper, radio and television station, choral group, Student Association, Undergraduate Alumni Council, communication club, Greek organizations, ethnic organizations, national fraternities, national sororities. *Campus security:* 24-hour emergency response devices and patrols, late-night transport/escort service, controlled dormitory access. *Student services:* health clinic, personal/psychological counseling, legal services.

Athletics Member NCAA. All Division III. *Intercollegiate sports:* baseball M, basketball M/W, cheerleading M/W, cross-country running M/W, field hockey M(c)/W(c), ice hockey M, lacrosse W, soccer M/W, softball W, swimming M/W, tennis M/W, track and field M/W, volleyball M/W. *Intramural sports:* basketball M/W, cross-country running M/W, field hockey W, football M, golf M, lacrosse M, racquetball M/W, rock climbing M/W, rugby M(c)/W(c), skiing (cross-country) M/W, skiing (downhill) M/W, soccer M/W, softball W, squash M/W, table tennis M/W, tennis M/W, ultimate Frisbee M/W, volleyball M(c)/W, water polo M/W.

Standardized Tests *Required:* SAT I or ACT (for admission).

Costs (2004–05) *Tuition:* state resident $4350 full-time, $181 per credit hour part-time; nonresident $10,300 full-time, $429 per credit hour part-time. *Required fees:* $1012 full-time, $42 per credit hour part-time. *Room and board:* $6120; room only: $4050. Room and board charges vary according to board plan and housing facility. *Payment plan:* installment.

Financial Aid Of all full-time matriculated undergraduates who enrolled in 2003, 3,890 applied for aid, 2,952 were judged to have need, 2,373 had their need fully met. 230 Federal Work-Study jobs (averaging $1186). In 2003, 747 non-need-based awards were made. *Average percent of need met:* 74%. *Average* *financial aid package:* $7165. *Average need-based loan:* $4063. *Average need-based gift aid:* $3279. *Average non-need-based aid:* $1447. *Average indebtedness upon graduation:* $13,125.

Applying *Options:* electronic application, early admission, early decision, deferred entrance. *Application fee:* $40. *Required:* high school transcript, minimum 2.5 GPA. *Required for some:* essay or personal statement, interview, audition for music and theater programs, portfolio for art and media arts program. *Recommended:* letters of recommendation. *Application deadline:* rolling (freshmen), rolling (transfers). *Early decision:* 11/1. *Notification:* continuous (freshmen), 12/1 (early decision), continuous (transfers).

Admissions Contact Mr. Daniel Tramuta, Director of Admissions, State University of New York College at Fredonia, Fredonia, NY 14063-1136. *Phone:* 716-673-3251. *Toll-free phone:* 800-252-1212. *Fax:* 716-673-3249. *E-mail:* admissions.office@fredonia.edu.

■ *See page 2442 for a narrative description.*

State University of New York College at Geneseo

Geneseo, New York

- **State-supported** comprehensive, founded 1871, part of State University of New York System
- **Calendar** semesters
- **Degrees** bachelor's and master's
- **Small-town** 220-acre campus with easy access to Rochester
- **Endowment** $5.3 million
- **Coed,** 5,307 undergraduate students, 98% full-time, 63% women, 37% men
- **Very difficult** entrance level, 42% of applicants were admitted

Undergraduates 5,201 full-time, 106 part-time. Students come from 20 states and territories, 23 other countries, 1% are from out of state, 2% African American, 5% Asian American or Pacific Islander, 3% Hispanic American, 0.2% Native American, 2% international, 19% transferred in, 54% live on campus. *Retention:* 92% of 2002 full-time freshmen returned.

Freshmen *Admission:* 8,783 applied, 3,684 admitted, 996 enrolled. *Average high school GPA:* 3.70. *Test scores:* SAT verbal scores over 500: 97%; SAT math scores over 500: 99%; ACT scores over 18: 100%; SAT verbal scores over 600: 70%; SAT math scores over 600: 77%; ACT scores over 24: 94%; SAT verbal scores over 700: 12%; SAT math scores over 700: 9%; ACT scores over 30: 12%.

Faculty *Total:* 349, 70% full-time, 66% with terminal degrees. *Student/faculty ratio:* 19:1.

Majors Accounting; African-American/Black studies; American studies; anthropology; art; art history, criticism and conservation; audiology and speech-language pathology; biochemistry; biology/biological sciences; biophysics; business administration and management; chemistry; communication/speech communication and rhetoric; comparative literature; computer science; dramatic/theatre arts; economics; education; elementary education; English; fine/studio arts; French; geochemistry; geography; geology/earth science; geophysics and seismology; history; international relations and affairs; kindergarten/preschool education; mathematics; music; natural sciences; philosophy; physics; political science and government; pre-dentistry studies; pre-law studies; pre-medical studies; pre-veterinary studies; psychology; sociology; Spanish; special education; speech therapy; visual and performing arts related.

Academic Programs *Special study options:* academic remediation for entering students, advanced placement credit, double majors, English as a second language, honors programs, independent study, internships, off-campus study, part-time degree program, services for LD students, study abroad, summer session for credit. *ROTC:* Army (c), Air Force (c). *Unusual degree programs:* 3-2 business administration with Pace University, Syracuse University, State University of New York at Buffalo; engineering with Columbia University, Case Western Reserve University, Alfred University, Clarkson University, Syracuse University, The Pennsylvania State University, University of Rochester, SUNY Binghamton, SUNY Buffalo; forestry with State University of New York College of Environmental Science and Forestry; dentistry with State University of New York at Buffalo.

Library Milne Library plus 1 other with 524,692 titles, 2,048 serial subscriptions, 21,463 audiovisual materials, an OPAC, a Web page.

Computers on Campus 900 computers available on campus for general student use. A campuswide network can be accessed from student residence rooms and from off campus. Internet access, online (class) registration, at least one staffed computer lab available. Computer purchase or lease plan available.

Student Life *Housing:* on-campus residence required for freshman year. *Options:* coed. Campus housing is university owned. Freshman campus housing is guaranteed. *Activities and organizations:* drama/theater group, student-run newspaper, radio and television station, choral group, national fraternities, national sororities. *Campus security:* 24-hour emergency response devices and patrols, student patrols, late-night transport/escort service, controlled dormitory access. *Student services:* health clinic, personal/psychological counseling, women's center, legal services.

Athletics Member NCAA. All Division III. *Intercollegiate sports:* basketball M/W, crew M(c)/W(c), cross-country running M/W, equestrian sports M(c)/W(c), field hockey W, ice hockey M, lacrosse M/W, racquetball M(c)/W(c), rugby M(c)/W(c), sailing M(c)/W(c), soccer M/W, softball W, squash M(c)/W(c), swimming M/W, tennis W, track and field M/W, ultimate Frisbee M(c)/W(c), volleyball M(c)/W. *Intramural sports:* badminton M/W, basketball M/W, cross-country running M/W, football M/W, golf M/W, ice hockey M/W, racquetball M/W, rugby M/W, skiing (cross-country) M/W, skiing (downhill) M/W, soccer M/W, softball M/W, squash M/W, table tennis M/W, tennis M/W, water polo M/W.

Standardized Tests *Required:* SAT I or ACT (for admission).

Costs (2003–04) *Tuition:* state resident $4350 full-time, $181 per credit hour part-time; nonresident $10,300 full-time, $429 per credit hour part-time. Part-time tuition and fees vary according to course load. *Required fees:* $1040 full-time. *Room and board:* $6750; room only: $3700. Room and board charges vary according to board plan and housing facility. *Payment plans:* installment, deferred payment. *Waivers:* senior citizens.

Financial Aid Of all full-time matriculated undergraduates who enrolled in 2003, 4,695 applied for aid, 2,520 were judged to have need, 2,190 had their need fully met. 425 Federal Work-Study jobs (averaging $1400). 640 state and other part-time jobs (averaging $2100). In 2003, 550 non-need-based awards were made. *Average percent of need met:* 87%. *Average financial aid package:* $8555. *Average need-based loan:* $3845. *Average need-based gift aid:* $3340. *Average non-need-based aid:* $1060. *Average indebtedness upon graduation:* $15,500.

Applying *Options:* electronic application, early admission, early decision, deferred entrance. *Application fee:* $30. *Required:* essay or personal statement, high school transcript. *Recommended:* letters of recommendation, interview. *Application deadlines:* 1/15 (freshmen), 1/15 (transfers). *Early decision:* 11/15. *Notification:* continuous until 3/15 (freshmen), 12/15 (early decision), 3/15 (transfers).

Admissions Contact Kris Shay, Associate Director of Admissions, State University of New York College at Geneseo, 1 College Circle, Geneseo, NY 14454-1401. *Phone:* 585-245-5571. *Toll-free phone:* 866-245-5211. *Fax:* 585-245-5550. *E-mail:* admissions@geneseo.edu.

State University of New York College at Old Westbury

Old Westbury, New York

- **State-supported** comprehensive, founded 1965, part of State University of New York System
- **Calendar** semesters
- **Degree** certificates and bachelor's
- **Suburban** 605-acre campus with easy access to New York City
- **Coed,** 3,227 undergraduate students, 76% full-time, 59% women, 41% men
- **Moderately difficult** entrance level, 57% of applicants were admitted

SUNY Old Westbury has exchange programs with colleges and universities in the Far East, South Africa, and Europe. SUNY tuition, room and board costs, and fees are paid to the College at Old Westbury. Travel is the only additional expense. Exchange faculty members from China and Korea are regularly on campus.

Undergraduates 2,467 full-time, 760 part-time. Students come from 7 states and territories, 37 other countries, 1% are from out of state, 27% African American, 8% Asian American or Pacific Islander, 14% Hispanic American, 0.2% Native American, 2% international, 21% transferred in, 25% live on campus. *Retention:* 74% of 2002 full-time freshmen returned.

Freshmen *Admission:* 2,844 applied, 1,635 admitted, 334 enrolled. *Average high school GPA:* 2.60. *Test scores:* SAT verbal scores over 500: 28%; SAT math scores over 500: 39%; SAT verbal scores over 600: 4%; SAT math scores over 600: 4%.

Faculty *Total:* 214, 57% full-time. *Student/faculty ratio:* 18:1.

Majors Accounting; American studies; art; bilingual and multilingual education; biology/biological sciences; biology teacher education; business administration and management; chemistry; chemistry teacher education; communication/speech communication and rhetoric; computer and information sciences; criminology; early childhood education; elementary education; finance; foreign language teacher education; humanities; information science/studies; labor and industrial relations; literature; marketing/marketing management; mathematics; mathematics teacher education; middle school education; philosophy; psychology; religious studies; science teacher education; secondary education; social sciences; social studies teacher education; sociology; Spanish; special education; visual and performing arts.

State University of New York College at Old Westbury (continued)

Academic Programs *Special study options:* academic remediation for entering students, advanced placement credit, double majors, English as a second language, independent study, internships, off-campus study, part-time degree program, services for LD students, study abroad, summer session for credit. *ROTC:* Army (c), Air Force (c). *Unusual degree programs:* 3-2 engineering with State University of New York at Stony Brook.

Library SUNY College at Old Westbury Library plus 1 other with 216,289 titles, 850 serial subscriptions, an OPAC, a Web page.

Computers on Campus 245 computers available on campus for general student use. A campuswide network can be accessed from student residence rooms and from off campus. Internet access, online (class) registration, at least one staffed computer lab available.

Student Life *Housing options:* coed. Campus housing is university owned. *Activities and organizations:* drama/theater group, student-run newspaper, radio station, choral group, Alianza Latina, Caribbean Student Association, Asian club, finance/accounting society, national fraternities, national sororities. *Campus security:* 24-hour emergency response devices and patrols, student patrols, late-night transport/escort service, controlled dormitory access. *Student services:* health clinic, personal/psychological counseling, women's center.

Athletics Member NCAA. All Division III. *Intercollegiate sports:* baseball M, basketball M/W, cheerleading M(s)/W(s), cross-country running M/W, soccer M, softball W, tennis M/W, volleyball W. *Intramural sports:* badminton M/W, racquetball M/W, soccer M/W, softball M/W, swimming M/W, volleyball M/W.

Standardized Tests *Required:* SAT I or ACT (for admission).

Costs (2003–04) *Tuition:* state resident $4350 full-time, $181 per credit part-time; nonresident $10,300 full-time, $429 per credit part-time. Part-time tuition and fees vary according to course load. *Required fees:* $691 full-time, $13 per credit part-time, $106 per term part-time. *Room and board:* $7749; room only: $5459. Room and board charges vary according to board plan and housing facility. *Payment plan:* installment. *Waivers:* senior citizens.

Financial Aid Of all full-time matriculated undergraduates who enrolled in 2003, 1,808 applied for aid, 1,639 were judged to have need, 362 had their need fully met. 234 Federal Work-Study jobs (averaging $778). 50 state and other part-time jobs (averaging $1704). *Average percent of need met:* 58%. *Average financial aid package:* $7080. *Average need-based loan:* $2602. *Average need-based gift aid:* $5022. *Average indebtedness upon graduation:* $13,335.

Applying *Options:* electronic application, early admission, early action, deferred entrance. *Application fee:* $40. *Required:* high school transcript. *Required for some:* essay or personal statement, 2 letters of recommendation, interview. *Application deadlines:* rolling (freshmen), 12/15 (transfers). *Notification:* continuous (freshmen), 12/15 (early action), continuous (transfers).

Admissions Contact Ms. Mary Marquez Bell, Vice President, State University of New York College at Old Westbury, PO Box 307, Old Westbury, NY 11568. *Phone:* 516-876-3073. *Fax:* 516-876-3307. *E-mail:* enroll@oldwestbury.edu.

■ *See page 2444 for a narrative description.*

STATE UNIVERSITY OF NEW YORK COLLEGE AT ONEONTA

Oneonta, New York

- **State-supported** comprehensive, founded 1889, part of State University of New York System
- **Calendar** semesters
- **Degrees** bachelor's, master's, and post-master's certificates
- **Small-town** 250-acre campus
- **Endowment** $17.6 million
- **Coed,** 5,506 undergraduate students, 97% full-time, 59% women, 41% men
- **Moderately difficult** entrance level, 48% of applicants were admitted

The College at Oneonta is a comprehensive college with studies that include the arts and sciences, elementary and secondary education, business, criminal justice, computer science, music industry, computer art, and prelaw as well as premedicine. An exceptional library, outstanding campuswide computing facilities, and a distinctive student center for volunteering enhance students' intellectual and personal development in a safe, scenic, and convenient campus environment.

Undergraduates 5,341 full-time, 165 part-time. Students come from 12 states and territories, 23 other countries, 3% are from out of state, 3% African American, 2% Asian American or Pacific Islander, 4% Hispanic American, 0.1% Native American, 1% international, 9% transferred in, 56% live on campus. *Retention:* 75% of 2002 full-time freshmen returned.

Freshmen *Admission:* 10,200 applied, 4,880 admitted, 1,201 enrolled. *Average high school GPA:* 3.46. *Test scores:* SAT verbal scores over 500: 76%; SAT math scores over 500: 84%; ACT scores over 18: 98%; SAT verbal scores over 600: 16%; SAT math scores over 600: 19%; ACT scores over 24: 38%; SAT verbal scores over 700: 1%; SAT math scores over 700: 1%.

Faculty *Total:* 426, 58% full-time, 51% with terminal degrees. *Student/faculty ratio:* 18:1.

Majors Accounting; African-American/Black studies; anthropology; art; art history, criticism and conservation; atmospheric sciences and meteorology; biochemistry; biology/biological sciences; biology/biotechnology laboratory technician; biology teacher education; business/managerial economics; cartography; chemistry; chemistry teacher education; child development; computer graphics; computer science; consumer services and advocacy; criminal justice/safety; dietetics; dramatic/theatre arts; early childhood education; economics; education; elementary education; engineering science; English; English/language arts teacher education; environmental studies; family and consumer sciences/home economics teacher education; family and consumer sciences/human sciences; fashion merchandising; fine/studio arts; foodservice systems administration; French; French language teacher education; geography; geology/earth science; gerontology; Hispanic-American, Puerto Rican, and Mexican-American/Chicano studies; history; human ecology; hydrology and water resources science; interdisciplinary studies; international relations and affairs; liberal arts and sciences/liberal studies; mass communication/media; mathematics; mathematics teacher education; middle school education; music; music management and merchandising; ophthalmic/optometric services; philosophy; physics; physics teacher education; political science and government; pre-dentistry studies; pre-law studies; pre-medical studies; pre-veterinary studies; psychology; reading teacher education; science teacher education; secondary education; social science teacher education; sociology; Spanish; Spanish language teacher education; speech and rhetoric; statistics.

Academic Programs *Special study options:* academic remediation for entering students, adult/continuing education programs, advanced placement credit, distance learning, double majors, English as a second language, honors programs, independent study, internships, off-campus study, part-time degree program, services for LD students, study abroad, summer session for credit. *Unusual degree programs:* 3-2 business administration with State University of New York at Binghamton, University of Rochester; engineering with Georgia Institute of Technology, State University of New York at Buffalo, Clarkson University; forestry with State University of New York College of Environmental Science and Forestry; nursing with Johns Hopkins University; accounting with State University of New York at Binghamton, fashion with American Intercontinental University in London.

Library Milne Library with 549,243 titles, 14,452 serial subscriptions, 30,772 audiovisual materials, an OPAC, a Web page.

Computers on Campus 600 computers available on campus for general student use. A campuswide network can be accessed from student residence rooms and from off campus. Internet access, online (class) registration, at least one staffed computer lab available. Computer purchase or lease plan available.

Student Life *Housing:* on-campus residence required through sophomore year. *Options:* coed. Campus housing is university owned. Freshman campus housing is guaranteed. *Activities and organizations:* drama/theater group, student-run newspaper, radio and television station, choral group, Center for Social Responsibility and Community, Mask and Hammer, Terpsichorean, student government, WONY radio station, national sororities. *Campus security:* 24-hour emergency response devices and patrols, late-night transport/escort service, controlled dormitory access. *Student services:* health clinic, personal/psychological counseling, women's center.

Athletics Member NCAA. All Division III except soccer (Division I). *Intercollegiate sports:* baseball M, basketball M/W, cheerleading W(c), cross-country running M/W, field hockey W, ice hockey M(c), lacrosse M/W, rugby M(c)/W(c), soccer M(s)/W, softball W, swimming M/W, tennis M/W, track and field M/W, volleyball M(c)/W, wrestling M. *Intramural sports:* basketball M/W, football M, lacrosse M, skiing (downhill) M/W, soccer M/W, softball M/W, ultimate Frisbee M/W, volleyball M/W.

Standardized Tests *Required:* SAT I or ACT (for admission).

Costs (2003–04) *Tuition:* state resident $4350 full-time, $181 per semester hour part-time; nonresident $10,300 full-time, $429 per semester hour part-time. Part-time tuition and fees vary according to course load. *Required fees:* $906 full-time, $29 per semester hour part-time. *Room and board:* $6458; room only: $3688. Room and board charges vary according to board plan and housing facility. *Payment plan:* installment. *Waivers:* employees or children of employees.

Financial Aid Of all full-time matriculated undergraduates who enrolled in 2003, 4,111 applied for aid, 3,145 were judged to have need, 563 had their need fully met. 454 Federal Work-Study jobs (averaging $1045). In 2003, 390 non-need-based awards were made. *Average percent of need met:* 68%. *Average financial aid package:* $8004. *Average need-based loan:* $4006. *Average need-based gift aid:* $3209. *Average non-need-based aid:* $680. *Average indebtedness upon graduation:* $5815.

Applying *Options:* electronic application, early admission, early decision, early action, deferred entrance. *Application fee:* $40. *Required:* essay or personal statement, high school transcript. *Recommended:* minimum 3.0 GPA, 3 letters of recommendation. *Application deadline:* rolling (freshmen), rolling (transfers). *Notification:* continuous (freshmen), 11/15 (early action), continuous (transfers).

Admissions Contact Ms. Karen A. Brown, Director of Admissions, State University of New York College at Oneonta, Alumni Hall 116, Oneonta, NY 13820-4015. *Phone:* 607-436-2524. *Toll-free phone:* 800-SUNY-123. *Fax:* 607-436-3074. *E-mail:* admissions@oneonta.edu.

■ *See page 2446 for a narrative description.*

STATE UNIVERSITY OF NEW YORK COLLEGE AT POTSDAM

Potsdam, New York

- **State-supported** comprehensive, founded 1816, part of State University of New York System
- **Calendar** semesters
- **Degrees** bachelor's and master's
- **Small-town** 240-acre campus
- **Endowment** $10.6 million
- **Coed,** 3,484 undergraduate students, 96% full-time, 59% women, 41% men
- **Moderately difficult** entrance level, 69% of applicants were admitted

Potsdam, the oldest liberal arts college of SUNY, has strong programs in the arts and sciences, teacher education, and the Crane School of Music. With more than 325 faculty members, the student-faculty ratio is 18:1. Within the Crane School of Music, the ratio is 10:1. Potsdam is within an easy drive of Interstates 81 and 87, Lake Placid, Ottawa, Syracuse, and Montreal. Potsdam offers more than 42 majors, including new programs in education, archeological studies, business administration, community health, computer and information science, criminal justice, and the business of music.

Undergraduates 3,338 full-time, 146 part-time. Students come from 23 states and territories, 28 other countries, 3% are from out of state, 2% African American, 1% Asian American or Pacific Islander, 2% Hispanic American, 2% Native American, 3% international, 10% transferred in, 52% live on campus. *Retention:* 73% of 2002 full-time freshmen returned.

Freshmen *Admission:* 3,418 applied, 2,366 admitted, 677 enrolled. *Average high school GPA:* 3.20. *Test scores:* SAT verbal scores over 500: 69%; SAT math scores over 500: 70%; ACT scores over 18: 95%; SAT verbal scores over 600: 22%; SAT math scores over 600: 24%; ACT scores over 24: 44%; SAT verbal scores over 700: 3%; SAT math scores over 700: 3%; ACT scores over 30: 6%.

Faculty *Total:* 362, 64% full-time, 56% with terminal degrees. *Student/faculty ratio:* 18:1.

Majors Anthropology; archeology; art; art history, criticism and conservation; biology/biological sciences; biology teacher education; business administration and management; business/managerial economics; ceramic arts and ceramics; chemistry; chemistry teacher education; computer and information sciences; criminal justice/safety; dance; dramatic/theatre arts; economics; education related; elementary education; English; English/language arts teacher education; environmental studies; foreign language teacher education; French; French language teacher education; geography; geology/earth science; history; labor and industrial relations; mathematics; mathematics teacher education; multi-/interdisciplinary studies related; music; music management and merchandising; music performance; music related; music teacher education; music theory and composition; painting; philosophy; photography; physical education teaching and coaching; physics; physics teacher education; political science and government; printmaking; psychology; science teacher education; sculpture; social studies teacher education; sociology; Spanish; Spanish language teacher education; speech and rhetoric.

Academic Programs *Special study options:* adult/continuing education programs, advanced placement credit, distance learning, double majors, honors programs, independent study, internships, off-campus study, part-time degree program, services for LD students, student-designed majors, study abroad, summer session for credit. *ROTC:* Army (c), Air Force (c). *Unusual degree programs:* 3-2 engineering with Clarkson University, State University of New York at Binghamton; management, accounting with State University of New York Institute of Technology at Utica/Rome, applied science with State University of New York College of Technology at Canton.

Library F. W. Crumb Memorial Library plus 1 other with 407,491 titles, 1,080 serial subscriptions, 17,631 audiovisual materials, an OPAC, a Web page.

Computers on Campus 400 computers available on campus for general student use. A campuswide network can be accessed from student residence rooms and from off campus that provide access to online access to grades and financial aid status. Internet access, online (class) registration, at least one staffed computer lab available. Computer purchase or lease plan available.

Student Life *Housing:* on-campus residence required through sophomore year. *Options:* coed, women-only, disabled students. Campus housing is university owned. Freshman campus housing is guaranteed. *Activities and organizations:* drama/theater group, student-run newspaper, radio station, choral group, Student Government Association, Crane Student Association, Student Entertainment Services (Programming Board), Caribbean-Latin American Student Society, The Racquette Student Newspaper, national fraternities, national sororities. *Campus security:* 24-hour emergency response devices and patrols, late-night transport/escort service, controlled dormitory access, self-defense education, pamphlets/posters/films. *Student services:* health clinic, personal/psychological counseling, women's center, legal services.

Athletics Member NCAA. All Division III. *Intercollegiate sports:* basketball M/W, cross-country running M/W, equestrian sports W(c), golf M, ice hockey M, lacrosse M/W, rugby W(c), soccer M/W, softball W, swimming M/W, tennis W, track and field M(c)/W(c), volleyball W. *Intramural sports:* badminton M/W, basketball M/W, equestrian sports M/W, racquetball M/W, skiing (cross-country) M/W, skiing (downhill) M/W, squash M/W, tennis M/W, volleyball M/W, water polo M/W.

Standardized Tests *Required:* SAT I or ACT (for admission).

Costs (2003–04) *Tuition:* state resident $4350 full-time, $181 per credit hour part-time; nonresident $10,300 full-time, $429 per credit hour part-time. *Required fees:* $840 full-time, $39 per credit hour part-time. *Room and board:* $6970; room only: $4070. Room and board charges vary according to board plan and housing facility. *Payment plan:* installment.

Financial Aid Of all full-time matriculated undergraduates who enrolled in 2003, 2,785 applied for aid, 2,284 were judged to have need, 1,886 had their need fully met. 366 Federal Work-Study jobs (averaging $1000). In 2003, 131 non-need-based awards were made. *Average percent of need met:* 83%. *Average financial aid package:* $11,203. *Average need-based loan:* $4115. *Average need-based gift aid:* $4231. *Average non-need-based aid:* $6660. *Average indebtedness upon graduation:* $17,601. *Financial aid deadline:* 5/1.

Applying *Options:* electronic application, early admission, deferred entrance. *Application fee:* $40. *Required:* high school transcript, minimum 3.0 GPA. *Required for some:* essay or personal statement, letters of recommendation, audition for music program. *Recommended:* interview. *Application deadline:* rolling (freshmen). *Notification:* continuous (freshmen), continuous (transfers).

Admissions Contact Mr. Thomas Nesbitt, Director of Admissions, State University of New York College at Potsdam, 44 Pierrepont Avenue, Potsdam, NY 13676. *Phone:* 315-267-2180. *Toll-free phone:* 877-POTSDAM. *Fax:* 315-267-2163. *E-mail:* admissions@potsdam.edu.

STATE UNIVERSITY OF NEW YORK COLLEGE OF AGRICULTURE AND TECHNOLOGY AT COBLESKILL

Cobleskill, New York

- **State-supported** 4-year, founded 1916, part of State University of New York System
- **Calendar** semesters
- **Degrees** certificates, associate, and bachelor's
- **Rural** 750-acre campus
- **Endowment** $1.7 million
- **Coed,** 2,443 undergraduate students, 93% full-time, 47% women, 53% men
- **Moderately difficult** entrance level, 92% of applicants were admitted

Undergraduates 2,270 full-time, 173 part-time. Students come from 16 states and territories, 8 other countries, 8% are from out of state, 6% African American, 1% Asian American or Pacific Islander, 4% Hispanic American, 0.5% Native American, 2% international, 14% transferred in, 62% live on campus. *Retention:* 80% of 2002 full-time freshmen returned.

Freshmen *Admission:* 2,966 applied, 2,731 admitted, 991 enrolled. *Average high school GPA:* 2.43. *Test scores:* SAT verbal scores over 500: 29%; SAT math scores over 500: 31%; ACT scores over 18: 59%; SAT verbal scores over 600: 4%; SAT math scores over 600: 5%; ACT scores over 24: 13%; ACT scores over 30: 1%.

Faculty *Total:* 163, 66% full-time, 28% with terminal degrees. *Student/faculty ratio:* 19:1.

Majors Accounting; agricultural/biological engineering and bioengineering; agricultural business and management; agricultural mechanization; agriculture; agronomy and crop science; animal sciences; biological and physical sciences; biology/biotechnology laboratory technician; business administration and management; business/corporate communications; chemical technology; clinical/medical laboratory technology; computer programming; computer science; computer technology/computer systems technology; culinary arts; dairy science; data processing and data processing technology; engineering technology; environmental studies; equestrian studies; family and community services; fish/game management; fishing and fisheries sciences and management; food services

State University of New York College of Agriculture and Technology at Cobleskill (continued)

technology; horticultural science; hotel/motel administration; information science/studies; institutional food workers; international business/trade/commerce; kindergarten/preschool education; landscape architecture; landscaping and groundskeeping; liberal arts and sciences/liberal studies; ornamental horticulture; parks, recreation and leisure facilities management; plant nursery management; plant sciences; pre-medical studies; telecommunications; tourism/travel marketing; turf and turfgrass management; wildlife and wildlands science and management.

Academic Programs *Special study options:* academic remediation for entering students, adult/continuing education programs, advanced placement credit, distance learning, English as a second language, freshman honors college, honors programs, internships, off-campus study, part-time degree program, services for LD students, study abroad, summer session for credit.

Library Jared van Wagenen Library with 76,919 titles, 327 serial subscriptions, 12,601 audiovisual materials, an OPAC, a Web page.

Computers on Campus 200 computers available on campus for general student use. A campuswide network can be accessed from student residence rooms and from off campus. Internet access, at least one staffed computer lab available.

Student Life *Housing:* on-campus residence required for freshman year. *Options:* coed, men-only, women-only. *Activities and organizations:* drama/theater group, student-run newspaper, choral group, Orange Key, American Animal Producers Club, outing club, Phi Theta Kappa, Little Theater. *Campus security:* 24-hour emergency response devices and patrols, late-night transport/escort service, controlled dormitory access, bicycle patrols. *Student services:* health clinic, personal/psychological counseling.

Athletics Member NJCAA. *Intercollegiate sports:* baseball M, basketball M/W, cross-country running M/W, golf M/W, lacrosse M, soccer M/W, softball W, swimming M/W, tennis M/W, track and field M/W, volleyball W, wrestling M. *Intramural sports:* archery M/W, badminton M/W, basketball M/W, bowling M/W, football M/W, racquetball M/W, rock climbing M/W, soccer M/W, softball M/W, table tennis M/W, tennis M/W, volleyball M/W, weight lifting M/W.

Standardized Tests *Required for some:* SAT I or ACT (for admission). *Recommended:* SAT I or ACT (for admission).

Costs (2003–04) *Tuition:* state resident $4350 full-time; nonresident $10,300 full-time. Full-time tuition and fees vary according to course level and degree level. Part-time tuition and fees vary according to course level and degree level. *Required fees:* $911 full-time. *Room and board:* $6880; room only: $3960. Room and board charges vary according to board plan and housing facility. *Payment plan:* installment. *Waivers:* employees or children of employees.

Financial Aid Of all full-time matriculated undergraduates who enrolled in 2001, 1,698 applied for aid, 1,662 were judged to have need, 531 had their need fully met. 160 Federal Work-Study jobs (averaging $750). *Average percent of need met:* 78%. *Average financial aid package:* $4792. *Average need-based loan:* $2902. *Average need-based gift aid:* $1236. *Financial aid deadline:* 3/15.

Applying *Options:* electronic application, early admission, deferred entrance. *Application fee:* $40. *Required:* high school transcript, minimum 2.0 GPA. *Required for some:* interview. *Application deadline:* rolling (freshmen), rolling (transfers). *Notification:* continuous (freshmen), continuous (transfers).

Admissions Contact Mr. Clayton Smith, Director of Admissions, State University of New York College of Agriculture and Technology at Cobleskill, Office of Admissions, Cobleskill, NY 12043. *Phone:* 518-255-5525. *Toll-free phone:* 800-295-8988. *Fax:* 518-255-6769. *E-mail:* admissions@cobleskill.edu.

State University of New York College of Agriculture and Technology at Morrisville

Morrisville, New York

- **State-supported** primarily 2-year, founded 1908, part of State University of New York System
- **Calendar** semesters
- **Degrees** certificates, associate, and bachelor's
- **Rural** 740-acre campus with easy access to Syracuse
- **Endowment** $681,026
- **Coed**
- **Moderately difficult** entrance level

Faculty *Student/faculty ratio:* 14:1.

Student Life *Campus security:* 24-hour emergency response devices and patrols, late-night transport/escort service, controlled dormitory access.

Athletics Member NJCAA.

Standardized Tests *Required for some:* SAT I (for admission). *Recommended:* SAT I and SAT II or ACT (for admission).

Costs (2003–04) *Tuition:* state resident $3200 full-time, $128 per credit hour part-time; nonresident $5000 full-time, $208 per credit hour part-time. Full-time tuition and fees vary according to degree level, program, and student level. Part-time tuition and fees vary according to course load, degree level, program, and student level. *Required fees:* $835 full-time, $25 per credit hour part-time. *Room and board:* $6070; room only: $3310. Room and board charges vary according to board plan and housing facility. *Payment plans:* installment, deferred payment.

Financial Aid Of all full-time matriculated undergraduates who enrolled in 2001, 300 Federal Work-Study jobs (averaging $1500).

Applying *Options:* electronic application, early admission, deferred entrance. *Application fee:* $40. *Required:* high school transcript. *Required for some:* essay or personal statement, letters of recommendation. *Recommended:* minimum 2.0 GPA, letters of recommendation, interview.

Admissions Contact Mr. Thomas VerDow, Interim Dean of Enrollment Management, State University of New York College of Agriculture and Technology at Morrisville, Box 901, Morrisville, NY 13408. *Phone:* 315-684-6046. *Toll-free phone:* 800-258-0111. *Fax:* 315-684-6427. *E-mail:* admissions@morrisville.edu.

State University of New York College of Environmental Science and Forestry

Syracuse, New York

- **State-supported** university, founded 1911, part of State University of New York System
- **Calendar** semesters
- **Degrees** associate, bachelor's, master's, and doctoral
- **Urban** 12-acre campus
- **Endowment** $7.0 million
- **Coed,** 1,486 undergraduate students, 82% full-time, 43% women, 57% men
- **Very difficult** entrance level, 63% of applicants were admitted

Undergraduates 1,217 full-time, 269 part-time. Students come from 28 states and territories, 7 other countries, 11% are from out of state, 2% African American, 1% Asian American or Pacific Islander, 3% Hispanic American, 0.4% Native American, 0.6% international, 15% transferred in, 40% live on campus. *Retention:* 89% of 2002 full-time freshmen returned.

Freshmen *Admission:* 796 applied, 499 admitted, 228 enrolled. *Average high school GPA:* 3.50. *Test scores:* SAT verbal scores over 500: 85%; SAT math scores over 500: 81%; ACT scores over 18: 100%; SAT verbal scores over 600: 33%; SAT math scores over 600: 34%; ACT scores over 24: 49%; SAT verbal scores over 700: 4%; SAT math scores over 700: 2%; ACT scores over 30: 4%.

Faculty *Total:* 147, 79% full-time, 87% with terminal degrees. *Student/faculty ratio:* 8:1.

Majors Biochemistry; biological and physical sciences; biology/biological sciences; biology teacher education; biotechnology; botany/plant biology; chemical engineering; chemistry; chemistry teacher education; city/urban, community and regional planning; construction engineering; ecology; entomology; environmental biology; environmental design/architecture; environmental education; environmental/environmental health engineering; environmental studies; fish/game management; fishing and fisheries sciences and management; forest engineering; forest/forest resources management; forestry; hydrology and water resources science; landscape architecture; land use planning and management; natural resources/conservation; natural resources management and policy; parks, recreation and leisure; plant pathology/phytopathology; plant physiology; plant protection and integrated pest management; plant sciences; polymer chemistry; pre-dentistry studies; pre-law studies; pre-medical studies; pre-veterinary studies; science teacher education; water resources engineering; wildlife and wildlands science and management; wildlife biology; wood science and wood products/pulp and paper technology; zoology/animal biology.

Academic Programs *Special study options:* academic remediation for entering students, accelerated degree program, adult/continuing education programs, advanced placement credit, cooperative education, distance learning, double majors, English as a second language, freshman honors college, honors programs, independent study, internships, off-campus study, part-time degree program, services for LD students, study abroad. *ROTC:* Army (c), Air Force (c). *Unusual degree programs:* 3-2 landscape architecture.

Library F. Franklin Moon Library plus 1 other with 130,305 titles, 2,001 serial subscriptions, an OPAC, a Web page.

Computers on Campus 150 computers available on campus for general student use. A campuswide network can be accessed from student residence rooms and from off campus. Internet access, online (class) registration, at least one staffed computer lab available.

Student Life *Housing:* on-campus residence required for freshman year. *Options:* coed, men-only, women-only, disabled students. Campus housing is

university owned, leased by the school and is provided by a third party. Freshman campus housing is guaranteed. *Activities and organizations:* drama/theater group, student-run newspaper, radio station, choral group, marching band, Bob Marshall/outing club, forestry Club, Student Environmental Action Coalition, national fraternities, national sororities. *Campus security:* 24-hour emergency response devices and patrols, late-night transport/escort service, controlled dormitory access. *Student services:* health clinic, personal/psychological counseling, women's center, legal services.

Athletics *Intramural sports:* archery M/W, badminton M/W, baseball M/W, basketball M/W, bowling M/W, crew M/W, cross-country running M/W, equestrian sports M/W, fencing M/W, field hockey W, football M, golf M/W, gymnastics M/W, ice hockey M/W, lacrosse M/W, racquetball M/W, riflery M, rugby M/W, sailing M/W, skiing (cross-country) M/W, skiing (downhill) M/W, soccer M/W, softball M/W, squash M/W, swimming M/W, table tennis M/W, tennis M/W, track and field M/W, ultimate Frisbee M/W, volleyball M/W, weight lifting M/W.

Standardized Tests *Required:* SAT I or ACT (for admission).

Costs (2004–05) *Tuition:* state resident $4350 full-time, $181 per credit hour part-time; nonresident $10,300 full-time, $429 per credit hour part-time. Full-time tuition and fees vary according to location. Part-time tuition and fees vary according to course load and location. *Required fees:* $641 full-time, $16 per credit hour part-time, $19 per year part-time. *Room and board:* $9790; room only: $4890. Room and board charges vary according to board plan, housing facility, and location. *Payment plans:* installment, deferred payment.

Financial Aid Of all full-time matriculated undergraduates who enrolled in 2003, 1,064 applied for aid, 878 were judged to have need, 878 had their need fully met. 310 Federal Work-Study jobs (averaging $1200). 118 state and other part-time jobs (averaging $1000). In 2003, 150 non-need-based awards were made. *Average percent of need met:* 100%. *Average financial aid package:* $8300. *Average need-based loan:* $5500. *Average need-based gift aid:* $5300. *Average non-need-based aid:* $2500. *Average indebtedness upon graduation:* $19,000.

Applying *Options:* electronic application, early admission, early decision, deferred entrance. *Application fee:* $40. *Required:* essay or personal statement, high school transcript, minimum 3.3 GPA, inventory of courses-in-progress form. *Recommended:* 3 letters of recommendation, interview. *Application deadline:* rolling (freshmen), rolling (transfers). *Early decision:* 11/15. *Notification:* continuous (freshmen), 12/15 (early decision), continuous (transfers).

Admissions Contact Ms. Susan Sanford, Director of Admissions, State University of New York College of Environmental Science and Forestry, 1 Forestry Drive, Syracuse, NY 13210-2779. *Phone:* 315-470-6600. *Toll-free phone:* 800-777-7373. *Fax:* 315-470-6933. *E-mail:* esfinfo@esf.edu.

STATE UNIVERSITY OF NEW YORK COLLEGE OF TECHNOLOGY AT ALFRED

Alfred, New York

- **State-supported** primarily 2-year, founded 1908, part of State University of New York System
- **Calendar** semesters
- **Degrees** certificates, associate, and bachelor's
- **Rural** 175-acre campus
- **Endowment** $2.6 million
- **Coed,** 3,471 undergraduate students, 89% full-time, 35% women, 65% men
- **Moderately difficult** entrance level, 67% of applicants were admitted

Undergraduates 3,074 full-time, 397 part-time. Students come from 29 states and territories, 1% are from out of state, 5% African American, 1% Asian American or Pacific Islander, 3% Hispanic American, 0.3% Native American, 70% live on campus. *Retention:* 96% of 2002 full-time freshmen returned.

Freshmen *Admission:* 4,300 applied, 2,867 admitted.

Faculty *Total:* 191, 77% full-time, 14% with terminal degrees. *Student/faculty ratio:* 19:1.

Majors Accounting; agricultural business and management; agriculture; animal sciences; architectural engineering technology; autobody/collision and repair technology; automobile/automotive mechanics technology; biological and physical sciences; biology/biotechnology laboratory technician; business administration and management; carpentry; civil engineering technology; computer and information sciences; computer engineering technology; computer graphics; computer hardware engineering; computer/information technology services administration related; computer installation and repair technology; computer science; computer/technical support; computer typography and composition equipment operation; construction engineering; construction engineering technology; court reporting; culinary arts; dairy science; data processing and data processing technology; drafting and design technology; electrical, electronic and communications engineering technology; electrical/electronics equipment installation and repair; electromechanical technology; engineering science; environmental studies; finance; health information/medical records administration; heating, air conditioning, ventilation and refrigeration maintenance technology; heavy equipment maintenance technology; humanities; human services; industrial electronics technology; landscaping and groundskeeping; liberal arts and sciences/liberal studies; machine tool technology; marketing/marketing management; masonry; mathematics; mechanical design technology; mechanical engineering/mechanical technology; medical/clinical assistant; nursing (registered nurse training); pipefitting and sprinkler fitting; restaurant, culinary, and catering management; sales, distribution and marketing; social sciences; sport and fitness administration; survey technology; system administration; veterinary sciences; welding technology.

Academic Programs *Special study options:* academic remediation for entering students, adult/continuing education programs, advanced placement credit, distance learning, external degree program, honors programs, independent study, off-campus study, part-time degree program, services for LD students, student-designed majors, summer session for credit. *ROTC:* Army (c).

Library Walter C. Hinkle Memorial Library plus 1 other with 71,243 titles, 594 serial subscriptions, 8,148 audiovisual materials, an OPAC, a Web page.

Computers on Campus 1600 computers available on campus for general student use. A campuswide network can be accessed from student residence rooms and from off campus. Internet access, online (class) registration, at least one staffed computer lab available.

Student Life *Housing options:* coed, disabled students. Campus housing is university owned. Freshman campus housing is guaranteed. *Activities and organizations:* drama/theater group, student-run newspaper, radio station, choral group, Outdoor Activity Club, BACCHUS, Sondai Society, Drama Club, choir. *Campus security:* 24-hour emergency response devices and patrols, late-night transport/escort service, residence hall entrance guards. *Student services:* health clinic, personal/psychological counseling.

Athletics Member NJCAA. *Intercollegiate sports:* baseball M, basketball M(s)/W(s), cheerleading M/W, cross-country running M(s)/W(s), football M(s), lacrosse M(s), soccer M(s)/W(s), softball W(s), swimming M/W, track and field M(s)/W(s), volleyball W, wrestling M. *Intramural sports:* basketball M/W, bowling M/W, cross-country running M/W, football M, golf M/W, lacrosse M/W, racquetball M/W, rugby M/W, skiing (cross-country) M/W, soccer M/W, softball M/W, table tennis M/W, tennis M/W, volleyball M/W, water polo M/W.

Standardized Tests *Recommended:* SAT I or ACT (for admission).

Costs (2003–04) *Tuition:* state resident $4350 full-time; nonresident $7000 full-time. Full-time tuition and fees vary according to degree level. *Required fees:* $930 full-time. *Room and board:* $6376. Room and board charges vary according to board plan and housing facility. *Payment plan:* installment.

Financial Aid Of all full-time matriculated undergraduates who enrolled in 2001, 350 Federal Work-Study jobs (averaging $1000).

Applying *Options:* common application, electronic application, deferred entrance. *Application fee:* $40. *Required:* high school transcript. *Required for some:* minimum 2.0 GPA. *Recommended:* essay or personal statement, letters of recommendation, interview. *Application deadline:* rolling (freshmen), rolling (transfers). *Notification:* continuous (freshmen), continuous (transfers).

Admissions Contact Ms. Deborah J. Goodrich, Director of Admissions, State University of New York College of Technology at Alfred, Huntington Administration Building, 10 Upper College Drive, Alfred, NY 14802. *Phone:* 607-587-4215. *Toll-free phone:* 800-4-ALFRED. *Fax:* 607-587-4299. *E-mail:* admissions@alfredstate.edu.

STATE UNIVERSITY OF NEW YORK COLLEGE OF TECHNOLOGY AT CANTON

Canton, New York

- **State-supported** primarily 2-year, founded 1906, part of State University of New York System
- **Calendar** semesters
- **Degrees** certificates, associate, and bachelor's
- **Small-town** 555-acre campus
- **Endowment** $5.0 million
- **Coed**
- **Minimally difficult** entrance level

Faculty *Student/faculty ratio:* 23:1.

Student Life *Campus security:* 24-hour emergency response devices and patrols, late-night transport/escort service, controlled dormitory access.

Athletics Member NJCAA.

Costs (2003–04) *Tuition:* state resident $4350 full-time; nonresident $10,300 full-time. Full-time tuition and fees vary according to degree level, location, and program. Part-time tuition and fees vary according to degree level, location, and program. *Required fees:* $925 full-time. *Room and board:* $6910; room only: $3980. Room and board charges vary according to housing facility. *Payment plans:* installment, deferred payment.

State University of New York College of Technology at Canton (continued)

Financial Aid Of all full-time matriculated undergraduates who enrolled in 2001, 250 Federal Work-Study jobs (averaging $1200). 10 state and other part-time jobs (averaging $1200).

Applying *Options:* electronic application, early admission, deferred entrance. *Application fee:* $40. *Required:* high school transcript. *Required for some:* interview. *Recommended:* minimum 2.0 GPA.

Admissions Contact Mr. David M. Gerlach, Dean of Enrollment Management, State University of New York College of Technology at Canton, Canton, NY 13617. *Phone:* 315-386-7123. *Toll-free phone:* 800-388-7123. *Fax:* 315-386-7929. *E-mail:* williama@scanva.canton.edu.

STATE UNIVERSITY OF NEW YORK COLLEGE OF TECHNOLOGY AT DELHI

Delhi, New York

- **State-supported** primarily 2-year, founded 1913, part of State University of New York System
- **Calendar** semesters
- **Degrees** certificates, associate, and bachelor's
- **Small-town** 1100-acre campus
- **Endowment** $1.2 million
- **Coed**
- **Moderately difficult** entrance level

Faculty *Student/faculty ratio:* 16:1.

Student Life *Campus security:* 24-hour emergency response devices and patrols.

Athletics Member NAIA, NJCAA.

Costs (2004–05) *Tuition:* state resident $4350 full-time; nonresident $10,300 full-time. *Required fees:* $975 full-time. *Room and board:* $6390.

Financial Aid Of all full-time matriculated undergraduates who enrolled in 2001, 150 Federal Work-Study jobs (averaging $1050).

Applying *Options:* electronic application, early admission, deferred entrance. *Application fee:* $30. *Required:* high school transcript. *Required for some:* minimum 2.0 GPA.

Admissions Contact Mr. Larry Barrett, Director of Enrollment Services, State University of New York College of Technology at Delhi, 2 Main Street, Delhi, NY 13753. *Phone:* 607-746-4558. *Toll-free phone:* 800-96-DELHI. *Fax:* 607-746-4104. *E-mail:* enroll@delhi.edu.

■ *See page 2448 for a narrative description.*

STATE UNIVERSITY OF NEW YORK DOWNSTATE MEDICAL CENTER

Brooklyn, New York

- **State-supported** upper-level, founded 1858, part of State University of New York System
- **Calendar** semesters
- **Degrees** bachelor's, master's, doctoral, first professional, post-master's, and postbachelor's certificates
- **Urban** campus
- **Coed,** 352 undergraduate students, 53% full-time, 85% women, 15% men
- **Moderately difficult** entrance level

Undergraduates 187 full-time, 165 part-time. 2% are from out of state, 61% African American, 6% Asian American or Pacific Islander, 5% Hispanic American, 0.6% international, 44% transferred in.

Majors Diagnostic medical sonography and ultrasound technology; health information/medical records administration; nursing (registered nurse training); occupational therapy; physical therapy; physician assistant.

Academic Programs *Special study options:* accelerated degree program, adult/continuing education programs, advanced placement credit, independent study, internships, off-campus study, part-time degree program, services for LD students, summer session for credit.

Library The Medical Research Library of Brooklyn with 357,209 titles, 2,104 serial subscriptions, 812 audiovisual materials, an OPAC, a Web page.

Computers on Campus 183 computers available on campus for general student use. A campuswide network can be accessed from student residence rooms and from off campus. Internet access, at least one staffed computer lab available.

Student Life *Housing options:* coed. Campus housing is university owned. *Campus security:* late-night transport/escort service. *Student services:* health clinic, personal/psychological counseling, women's center.

Costs (2003–04) *Tuition:* state resident $4350 full-time, $181 per credit part-time; nonresident $10,300 full-time, $429 per credit part-time. Full-time tuition and fees vary according to degree level and program. Part-time tuition and fees vary according to degree level and program. *Required fees:* $1877 full-time. *Room and board:* $10,514; room only: $6948. Room and board charges vary according to housing facility. *Waivers:* employees or children of employees.

Financial Aid Of all full-time matriculated undergraduates who enrolled in 2002, 56 applied for aid, 53 were judged to have need. 40 Federal Work-Study jobs (averaging $1000). In 2002, 4 non-need-based awards were made. *Average percent of need met:* 55%. *Average financial aid package:* $10,332. *Average need-based loan:* $4642. *Average need-based gift aid:* $7188. *Average non-need-based aid:* $10,992. *Average indebtedness upon graduation:* $11,800. *Financial aid deadline:* 2/15.

Applying *Application fee:* $30. *Application deadline:* 5/1 (transfers). *Notification:* continuous until 8/31 (transfers).

Admissions Contact Mr. Tom Sabia, Assistant Dean of Admissions, State University of New York Downstate Medical Center, 450 Clarkson Avenue, Box 60, Brooklyn, NY 11203. *Phone:* 718-270-2446. *Fax:* 718-270-7592.

STATE UNIVERSITY OF NEW YORK EMPIRE STATE COLLEGE

Saratoga Springs, New York

- **State-supported** comprehensive, founded 1971, part of State University of New York System
- **Calendar** continuous
- **Degrees** associate, bachelor's, and master's (branch locations at 7 regional centers with 35 auxiliary units)
- **Small-town** campus
- **Coed,** 9,872 undergraduate students, 30% full-time, 55% women, 45% men
- **Minimally difficult** entrance level, 62% of applicants were admitted

Empire State College is an international leader in adult higher education. Students design their own individualized associate, bachelor's, and master's degree programs based on their academic and professional goals. Students benefit from flexible, guided independent study; credit earned for learning gained in work and life; and low SUNY tuition. Empire State College, accredited by the Middle States Association of Colleges and Schools, has more than 30 locations throughout New York State as well as distance learning options.

Undergraduates 2,949 full-time, 6,923 part-time. Students come from 52 states and territories, 23 other countries, 10% are from out of state, 12% African American, 2% Asian American or Pacific Islander, 7% Hispanic American, 0.4% Native American, 7% international. *Retention:* 41% of 2002 full-time freshmen returned.

Freshmen *Admission:* 453 applied, 281 admitted.

Faculty *Total:* 487, 31% full-time, 47% with terminal degrees. *Student/faculty ratio:* 30:1.

Majors Art; biological and physical sciences; business administration and management; community organization and advocacy; economics; education; history; human development and family studies; humanities; human services; interdisciplinary studies; labor and industrial relations; mathematics; social sciences.

Academic Programs *Special study options:* adult/continuing education programs, advanced placement credit, cooperative education, distance learning, external degree program, independent study, off-campus study, part-time degree program, services for LD students, student-designed majors, study abroad.

Library 5,300 titles, 209 serial subscriptions.

Computers on Campus 100 computers available on campus for general student use. A campuswide network can be accessed from off campus. Internet access, online (class) registration, at least one staffed computer lab available.

Student Life *Housing:* college housing not available.

Costs (2004–05) *Tuition:* state resident $4555 full-time, $181 per credit part-time; nonresident $10,505 full-time, $429 per credit part-time. *Required fees:* $159 full-time, $5 per credit part-time, $75 per term part-time. *Payment plan:* installment. *Waivers:* children of alumni and adult students.

Applying *Options:* electronic application, early admission. *Required:* essay or personal statement. *Required for some:* interview. *Application deadline:* rolling (freshmen), rolling (transfers). *Notification:* continuous (transfers).

Admissions Contact Ms. Jennifer Riley, Assistant Director of Admissions, State University of New York Empire State College, One Union Avenue, Saratoga Springs, NY 12866. *Phone:* 518-587-2100 Ext. 214. *Toll-free phone:* 800-847-3000. *Fax:* 518-580-0105. *E-mail:* admissions@esc.edu.

■ *See page 2450 for a narrative description.*

STATE UNIVERSITY OF NEW YORK INSTITUTE OF TECHNOLOGY AT UTICA/ROME

Utica, New York

- **State-supported** comprehensive, founded 1966, part of State University of New York System
- **Calendar** semesters
- **Degrees** bachelor's, master's, and post-master's certificates
- **Suburban** 850-acre campus
- **Endowment** $1.2 million
- **Coed,** 2,059 undergraduate students, 62% full-time, 50% women, 50% men
- **Minimally difficult** entrance level, 23% of applicants were admitted

SUNY Institute of Technology (SUNYIT) primarily serves 2-year college transfer and graduate students. In fall 2003, freshmen are admitted to select programs. Residence halls feature town house–style suites. Distinctive programs include computer science, engineering technologies, health-information management, health-services management, professional and technical communications, and telecommunications. A variety of scholarships are available to reward academic excellence.

Undergraduates 1,285 full-time, 774 part-time. Students come from 10 states and territories, 14 other countries, 1% are from out of state, 6% African American, 2% Asian American or Pacific Islander, 3% Hispanic American, 0.4% Native American, 3% international, 25% transferred in, 18% live on campus.

Freshmen *Admission:* 868 applied, 200 admitted, 105 enrolled. *Test scores:* SAT verbal scores over 500: 93%; SAT math scores over 500: 97%; ACT scores over 18: 100%; SAT verbal scores over 600: 36%; SAT math scores over 600: 61%; ACT scores over 24: 75%; SAT verbal scores over 700: 5%; SAT math scores over 700: 6%.

Faculty *Total:* 170, 55% full-time. *Student/faculty ratio:* 19:1.

Majors Accounting; applied mathematics; business administration and management; civil engineering technology; communication and journalism related; computer and information sciences; computer engineering technology; computer science; electrical, electronic and communications engineering technology; finance; general studies; health/health care administration; health information/medical records administration; industrial technology; information science/studies; mechanical engineering/mechanical technology; nursing (registered nurse training); psychology; sociology.

Academic Programs *Special study options:* academic remediation for entering students, accelerated degree program, adult/continuing education programs, advanced placement credit, distance learning, double majors, English as a second language, independent study, internships, part-time degree program, services for LD students, summer session for credit. *ROTC:* Army (c), Air Force (c). *Unusual degree programs:* 3-2 computer information science.

Library SUNY Institute of Technology at Utica/Rome Library with 193,682 titles, 1,090 serial subscriptions, 11,818 audiovisual materials, an OPAC, a Web page.

Computers on Campus 250 computers available on campus for general student use. A campuswide network can be accessed from student residence rooms and from off campus that provide access to various other software applications. Internet access, online (class) registration, at least one staffed computer lab available.

Student Life *Housing options:* coed. Campus housing is university owned. *Activities and organizations:* student-run newspaper, radio station, telecommunications Ccub, snowmobile club, Phi Beta Lambda, Black Student Union, American Society of Mechanical Engineers. *Campus security:* 24-hour emergency response devices and patrols, late-night transport/escort service, controlled dormitory access, closed-circuit TV monitors. *Student services:* health clinic, personal/psychological counseling, legal services.

Athletics Member NCAA. All Division III. *Intercollegiate sports:* baseball M, basketball M/W, bowling M/W, cross-country running W, golf M/W, lacrosse M, soccer M/W, softball W, volleyball W. *Intramural sports:* badminton M/W, basketball M/W, bowling M/W, golf M/W, racquetball M/W, soccer M/W, softball M/W, tennis M/W, volleyball M/W.

Costs (2003–04) *Tuition:* state resident $4350 full-time, $181 per credit hour part-time; nonresident $10,300 full-time, $429 per credit hour part-time. *Required fees:* $804 full-time, $31 per credit hour part-time. *Room and board:* $6800.

Financial Aid Of all full-time matriculated undergraduates who enrolled in 2002, 1,277 applied for aid, 1,138 were judged to have need, 210 had their need fully met. 132 Federal Work-Study jobs (averaging $1124). *Average percent of need met:* 81%. *Average financial aid package:* $7672. *Average need-based loan:* $3662. *Average need-based gift aid:* $1500. *Average indebtedness upon graduation:* $5718.

Applying *Options:* electronic application, deferred entrance. *Application fee:* $30. *Application deadline:* rolling (freshmen), rolling (transfers). *Notification:* continuous (freshmen), continuous (transfers).

Admissions Contact Ms. Marybeth Lyons, Director of Admissions, State University of New York Institute of Technology at Utica/Rome, PO Box 3050, Utica, NY 13504-3050. *Phone:* 315-792-7500. *Toll-free phone:* 800-SUNYTEC. *Fax:* 315-792-7837. *E-mail:* admissions@sunyit.edu.

■ *See page 2452 for a narrative description.*

STATE UNIVERSITY OF NEW YORK MARITIME COLLEGE

Throggs Neck, New York

- **State-supported** comprehensive, founded 1874, part of State University of New York System
- **Calendar** semesters plus 2-month summer sea term
- **Degrees** associate, bachelor's, and master's
- **Suburban** 56-acre campus
- **Endowment** $1.0 million
- **Coed, primarily men**
- **Moderately difficult** entrance level

Faculty *Student/faculty ratio:* 12:1.

Student Life *Campus security:* 24-hour emergency response devices and patrols, student patrols, late-night transport/escort service.

Athletics Member NCAA. All Division III.

Standardized Tests *Required:* SAT I or ACT (for admission). *Recommended:* SAT II: Subject Tests (for admission).

Costs (2003–04) *One-time required fee:* $2100. *Tuition:* state resident $4350 full-time; nonresident $10,300 full-time. Full-time tuition and fees vary according to reciprocity agreements. Part-time tuition and fees vary according to reciprocity agreements. *Required fees:* $1500 full-time. *Room and board:* $7046. Room and board charges vary according to board plan.

Applying *Options:* electronic application, early admission, early decision, deferred entrance. *Application fee:* $30. *Required:* high school transcript, minimum 2.5 GPA, medical history. *Recommended:* essay or personal statement, 1 letter of recommendation, interview.

Admissions Contact Ms. Deirdre Whitman, Vice President of Enrollment and Campus Life, State University of New York Maritime College, 6 Pennyfield Avenue, Throggs Neck, NY 10465. *Phone:* 718-409-7220 Ext. 7222. *Toll-free phone:* 800-654-1874 (in-state); 800-642-1874 (out-of-state). *Fax:* 718-409-7465. *E-mail:* admissions@sunymaritime.edu.

■ *See page 2454 for a narrative description.*

STATE UNIVERSITY OF NEW YORK UPSTATE MEDICAL UNIVERSITY

Syracuse, New York

- **State-supported** upper-level, founded 1950, part of State University of New York System
- **Calendar** semesters
- **Degrees** bachelor's, master's, doctoral, and first professional
- **Urban** 25-acre campus
- **Coed,** 271 undergraduate students, 64% full-time, 73% women, 27% men
- **Moderately difficult** entrance level

Undergraduates 174 full-time, 97 part-time. Students come from 4 states and territories, 2 other countries, 2% are from out of state, 4% African American, 3% Asian American or Pacific Islander, 2% Hispanic American, 0.8% Native American, 2% international, 50% live on campus.

Faculty *Total:* 695, 69% full-time. *Student/faculty ratio:* 10:1.

Majors Cardiovascular technology; clinical laboratory science/medical technology; cytotechnology; medical radiologic technology; nursing science; perfusion technology; physical therapy; radiologic technology/science; respiratory care therapy.

Academic Programs *Special study options:* advanced placement credit, internships, off-campus study, part-time degree program, services for LD students, summer session for credit. *Unusual degree programs:* 3-2 physical therapy.

Library Weiskotten Library with 132,500 titles, 1,800 serial subscriptions, 29,515 audiovisual materials, an OPAC, a Web page.

Computers on Campus 130 computers available on campus for general student use. A campuswide network can be accessed from student residence rooms and from off campus. Internet access, at least one staffed computer lab available.

Student Life *Housing options:* coed. Campus housing is university owned. *Activities and organizations:* Undergraduate Student Council, Diversity in Allied Health. *Campus security:* late-night transport/escort service, controlled dormitory access. *Student services:* health clinic, personal/psychological counseling.

State University of New York Upstate Medical University (continued)

Athletics *Intramural sports:* basketball M/W, football M, golf M/W, racquetball M/W, skiing (cross-country) M/W, skiing (downhill) M/W, softball M, squash M/W, swimming M/W, table tennis M/W, tennis M/W, volleyball M/W, water polo M/W, weight lifting M/W.

Costs (2003–04) *Tuition:* state resident $4350 full-time, $181 per credit hour part-time; nonresident $10,300 full-time, $429 per credit hour part-time. *Required fees:* $500 full-time. *Room and board:* $7785; room only: $5175. *Payment plan:* installment.

Financial Aid *Financial aid deadline:* 4/1.

Applying *Options:* early admission, deferred entrance. *Application fee:* $30. *Application deadline:* rolling (transfers).

Admissions Contact Ms. Donna L. Vavonese, Associate Director of Admissions, State University of New York Upstate Medical University, Weiskotten Hall, 766 Irving Avenue, Syracuse, NY 13210. *Phone:* 315-464-4570. *Toll-free phone:* 800-736-2171. *Fax:* 315-464-8867. *E-mail:* stuadmis@upstate.edu.

STONY BROOK UNIVERSITY, STATE UNIVERSITY OF NEW YORK

Stony Brook, New York

- **State-supported** university, founded 1957, part of State University of New York System
- **Calendar** semesters
- **Degrees** bachelor's, master's, doctoral, first professional, post-master's, postbachelor's, and first professional certificates
- **Small-town** 1100-acre campus with easy access to New York City
- **Endowment** $43.7 million
- **Coed,** 14,072 undergraduate students, 90% full-time, 49% women, 51% men
- **Very difficult** entrance level, 51% of applicants were admitted

Since its founding in 1957, Stony Brook University has grown tremendously and is now recognized as one of the nation's leading centers of learning and scholarship, as demonstrated by its recent invitation to join the Association of American Universities. Stony Brook is at the forefront of integrating research and education at the undergraduate level and prides itself on the quality of its academic programs and outstanding faculty.

Undergraduates 12,710 full-time, 1,362 part-time. Students come from 39 states and territories, 62 other countries, 2% are from out of state, 10% African American, 24% Asian American or Pacific Islander, 8% Hispanic American, 0.1% Native American, 4% international, 11% transferred in, 56% live on campus. *Retention:* 87% of 2002 full-time freshmen returned.

Freshmen *Admission:* 16,909 applied, 8,564 admitted, 2,181 enrolled. *Average high school GPA:* 3.60. *Test scores:* SAT verbal scores over 500: 93%; SAT math scores over 500: 99%; SAT verbal scores over 600: 40%; SAT math scores over 600: 62%; SAT verbal scores over 700: 5%; SAT math scores over 700: 13%.

Faculty *Total:* 1,339, 65% full-time, 95% with terminal degrees. *Student/faculty ratio:* 18:1.

Majors African-American/Black studies; American studies; anthropology; applied mathematics; art history, criticism and conservation; astronomy; athletic training; biochemistry; biology/biological sciences; biomedical/medical engineering; business administration and management; chemistry; chemistry related; clinical laboratory science/medical technology; comparative literature; computer hardware engineering; computer science; cytotechnology; dramatic/theatre arts; economics; electrical, electronics and communications engineering; engineering; English; environmental studies; fine/studio arts; French; geology/earth science; German; health professions related; history; humanities; information science/studies; Italian; linguistics; mathematics; mechanical engineering; multi-/interdisciplinary studies related; music; nursing (registered nurse training); pharmacology; philosophy; physical sciences related; physician assistant; physics; political science and government; psychology; religious studies; respiratory care therapy; Russian; social sciences; social work; sociology; Spanish; women's studies.

Academic Programs *Special study options:* academic remediation for entering students, adult/continuing education programs, advanced placement credit, distance learning, double majors, English as a second language, freshman honors college, honors programs, independent study, internships, off-campus study, part-time degree program, services for LD students, student-designed majors, study abroad, summer session for credit.

Library Frank Melville, Jr. Building Library plus 6 others with 3.2 million titles, 10,018 serial subscriptions, 40,192 audiovisual materials, an OPAC, a Web page.

Computers on Campus 2587 computers available on campus for general student use. A campuswide network can be accessed from student residence rooms and from off campus. Internet access, online (class) registration, at least one staffed computer lab available.

Student Life *Housing options:* coed. Campus housing is university owned. Freshman campus housing is guaranteed. *Activities and organizations:* drama/theater group, student-run newspaper, radio station, choral group, Carribbean Student Organization, Muslim Student Association, Commuter Student Association, Inter-Fraternity and Sorority Council, Student Activities Board, national fraternities, national sororities. *Campus security:* 24-hour emergency response devices and patrols, late-night transport/escort service, controlled dormitory access. *Student services:* health clinic, personal/psychological counseling, women's center, legal services.

Athletics Member NCAA, NAIA. All NCAA Division I. *Intercollegiate sports:* baseball M(s), basketball M(s)/W(s), cross-country running M(s)/W(s), football M(s), lacrosse M(s)/W(s), soccer M(s)/W(s), softball W(s), swimming M(s)/W(s), tennis M(s)/W(s), track and field M(s)/W(s), volleyball W(s). *Intramural sports:* badminton M/W, basketball M/W, bowling M/W, cheerleading W, crew M(c)/W(c), equestrian sports M(c)/W(c), golf M, ice hockey M(c), racquetball M/W, rugby M(c)/W(c), soccer M/W, softball M/W, table tennis M/W, tennis M/W, ultimate Frisbee M(c)/W(c), volleyball M/W.

Standardized Tests *Required:* SAT I or ACT (for admission). *Recommended:* SAT II: Subject Tests (for admission).

Costs (2003–04) *Tuition:* state resident $4350 full-time, $181 per credit part-time; nonresident $10,300 full-time, $429 per credit part-time. *Required fees:* $966 full-time, $46 per credit part-time. *Room and board:* $7458. Room and board charges vary according to board plan and housing facility. *Payment plan:* installment.

Financial Aid Of all full-time matriculated undergraduates who enrolled in 2003, 8,919 applied for aid, 7,433 were judged to have need, 1,837 had their need fully met. 683 Federal Work-Study jobs (averaging $2114). 1,922 state and other part-time jobs (averaging $1756). In 2003, 455 non-need-based awards were made. *Average percent of need met:* 77%. *Average financial aid package:* $9281. *Average need-based loan:* $3903. *Average need-based gift aid:* $2638. *Average non-need-based aid:* $3188. *Average indebtedness upon graduation:* $16,080.

Applying *Options:* electronic application, early action, deferred entrance. *Application fee:* $40. *Required:* essay or personal statement, high school transcript, minimum 3.0 GPA. *Required for some:* audition. *Recommended:* 2 letters of recommendation, interview. *Application deadlines:* 3/1 (freshmen), 4/15 (transfers). *Notification:* continuous (freshmen), 1/1 (early action), continuous (transfers).

Admissions Contact Ms. Judith Burke-Berhanan, Acting Dean of Admissions and Enrollment Services, Stony Brook University, State University of New York, Stony Brook, NY 11794. *Phone:* 631-632-6868. *Toll-free phone:* 800-872-7869. *Fax:* 631-632-9898. *E-mail:* ugadmissions@notes.cc.sunysb.edu.

■ *See page 2468 for a narrative description.*

SWEDISH INSTITUTE, COLLEGE OF HEALTH SCIENCES

New York, New York

Admissions Contact Ms. Leslie Kielson, Dean of Admissions, Swedish Institute, College of Health Sciences, 226 West 26th Street, New York, NY 10001-6700. *Phone:* 212-924-5900.

SYRACUSE UNIVERSITY

Syracuse, New York

- **Independent** university, founded 1870
- **Calendar** semesters
- **Degrees** bachelor's, master's, doctoral, first professional, and post-master's certificates
- **Urban** 200-acre campus
- **Endowment** $674.8 million
- **Coed,** 10,840 undergraduate students, 99% full-time, 56% women, 44% men
- **Very difficult** entrance level, 62% of applicants were admitted

Undergraduates 10,746 full-time, 94 part-time. Students come from 51 states and territories, 63 other countries, 60% are from out of state, 6% African American, 6% Asian American or Pacific Islander, 4% Hispanic American, 0.3% Native American, 3% international, 2% transferred in, 73% live on campus. *Retention:* 91% of 2000 full-time freshmen returned.

Freshmen *Admission:* 14,144 applied, 8,718 admitted, 2,650 enrolled. *Average high school GPA:* 3.60. *Test scores:* SAT verbal scores over 500: 96%; SAT math scores over 500: 95%; SAT verbal scores over 600: 55%; SAT math scores over 600: 63%; SAT verbal scores over 700: 9%; SAT math scores over 700: 14%.

Faculty *Total:* 1,362, 63% full-time. *Student/faculty ratio:* 12:1.

Majors Accounting; acting; advertising; aerospace, aeronautical and astronautical engineering; African-American/Black studies; American studies; anthropology; apparel and textiles; applied art; architecture; area, ethnic, cultural, and gender studies related; art; art history, criticism and conservation; art teacher education; Asian studies (South); audiology and speech-language pathology; biochemistry; biology/biological sciences; biology teacher education; biomedical/medical engineering; broadcast journalism; business administration and management; ceramic arts and ceramics; chemical engineering; chemistry; chemistry teacher education; child development; cinematography and film/video production; civil engineering; classics and languages, literatures and linguistics; clothing/textiles; commercial and advertising art; communication and journalism related; communication disorders sciences and services related; communication/speech communication and rhetoric; computer and information sciences; computer engineering; computer graphics; consumer merchandising/retailing management; consumer services and advocacy; design and visual communications; dietetics; dramatic/theatre arts; economics; education (K-12); education related; education (specific subject areas) related; electrical, electronics and communications engineering; engineering physics; engineering related; English; English/language arts teacher education; English literature (British and Commonwealth); entrepreneurship; environmental/environmental health engineering; family and community services; family and consumer sciences/home economics teacher education; family systems; fashion/apparel design; fiber, textile and weaving arts; finance; fine arts related; fine/studio arts; foods, nutrition, and wellness; foreign languages and literatures; French; geography; geology/earth science; German; health science; history; hospitality administration; housing and human environments; human development and family studies; humanities; illustration; industrial design; information science/studies; interdisciplinary studies; interior architecture; interior design; international relations and affairs; Italian; journalism; kindergarten/preschool education; kinesiology and exercise science; Latin American studies; liberal arts and sciences/liberal studies; linguistics; literature; logistics and materials management; marketing/marketing management; mathematics; mathematics teacher education; mechanical engineering; medieval and Renaissance studies; metal and jewelry arts; modern languages; music; music management and merchandising; music performance; music teacher education; music theory and composition; painting; philosophy; philosophy and religious studies related; photography; physical education teaching and coaching; physics; physics teacher education; piano and organ; political science and government; pre-dentistry studies; pre-law studies; pre-medical studies; pre-veterinary studies; printmaking; psychology; public administration; public relations/image management; radio and television; religious studies; restaurant/food services management; retailing; Russian; Russian studies; sales, distribution and marketing; sculpture; social studies teacher education; social work; sociology; Spanish; special education; speech and rhetoric; telecommunications; theatre design and technology; transportation and materials moving related; violin, viola, guitar and other stringed instruments; voice and opera; wind/percussion instruments; women's studies.

Academic Programs *Special study options:* accelerated degree program, adult/continuing education programs, advanced placement credit, cooperative education, distance learning, double majors, English as a second language, external degree program, honors programs, independent study, internships, off-campus study, part-time degree program, services for LD students, student-designed majors, study abroad, summer session for credit. *ROTC:* Army (b), Air Force (b). *Unusual degree programs:* 3-2 public administration, law.

Library E. S. Bird Library plus 6 others with 3.1 million titles, 14,462 serial subscriptions, 858,500 audiovisual materials, an OPAC, a Web page.

Computers on Campus 1200 computers available on campus for general student use. A campuswide network can be accessed from student residence rooms and from off campus that provide access to online services, networked client and server computing. Internet access, online (class) registration, at least one staffed computer lab available.

Student Life *Housing:* on-campus residence required through sophomore year. *Options:* coed, disabled students. Campus housing is university owned. Freshman campus housing is guaranteed. *Activities and organizations:* drama/theater group, student-run newspaper, radio and television station, choral group, marching band, Student Government Association, Programming Council, First Year Players, Student African-American Society, national fraternities, national sororities. *Campus security:* 24-hour emergency response devices and patrols, late-night transport/escort service, controlled dormitory access, crime prevention and neighborhood outreach programs. *Student services:* health clinic, personal/psychological counseling, women's center, legal services.

Athletics Member NCAA. All Division I except football (Division I-A). *Intercollegiate sports:* archery M(c)/W(c), badminton M(c)/W(c), baseball M(c), basketball M(s)/W(s), bowling M(c)/W(c), cheerleading M/W, crew M(s)/W(s), cross-country running M(s)/W(s), equestrian sports M(c)/W(c), fencing M(c)/W(c), field hockey W(s), gymnastics M(c)/W(c), ice hockey M(c)/W(c), lacrosse M(s)/W(s), racquetball M(c)/W(c), riflery M(c)/W(c), rugby M(c)/W(c), sailing M(c)/W(c), skiing (downhill) M(c)/W(c), soccer M(s)/W(s), softball M(c)/W(s), squash M(c)/W(c), swimming M(s)/W(s), table tennis M(c)/W(c), tennis M(c)/W(s), track and field M(s)/W(s), volleyball M(c)/W(s), water polo M(c)/W(c), weight lifting M(c)/W(c). *Intramural sports:* badminton M/W, basketball M/W, cross-country running M/W, football M/W, golf M/W, lacrosse M(c)/W(c), racquetball M/W, soccer M/W, softball M/W, squash M/W, swimming M/W, table tennis M/W, tennis M/W, track and field M/W, ultimate Frisbee M/W, volleyball M/W.

Standardized Tests *Required:* SAT I or ACT (for admission).

Costs (2003–04) *Comprehensive fee:* $34,420 includes full-time tuition ($24,170), mandatory fees ($660), and room and board ($9590). Part-time tuition: $1053 per credit hour. Part-time tuition and fees vary according to course load, location, and program. *Room and board:* Room and board charges vary according to board plan and housing facility. *Payment plan:* installment. *Waivers:* employees or children of employees.

Financial Aid Of all full-time matriculated undergraduates who enrolled in 2003, 7,134 applied for aid, 6,276 were judged to have need, 1,567 had their need fully met. In 2003, 1853 non-need-based awards were made. *Average percent of need met:* 80%. *Average financial aid package:* $18,720. *Average need-based loan:* $5200. *Average need-based gift aid:* $12,793. *Average non-need-based aid:* $7240. *Average indebtedness upon graduation:* $19,000.

Applying *Options:* common application, early admission, early decision, deferred entrance. *Application fee:* $60. *Required:* essay or personal statement, high school transcript, 2 letters of recommendation. *Required for some:* audition for drama and music programs, portfolio for art and architecture programs. *Recommended:* interview. *Application deadlines:* 1/1 (freshmen), 1/1 (transfers). *Early decision:* 11/15. *Notification:* 3/15 (freshmen), 12/31 (early decision), continuous (transfers).

Admissions Contact Office of Admissions, Syracuse University, 201 Tolley Administration Building, Syracuse, NY 13244-1100. *Phone:* 315-443-3611. *E-mail:* orange@syr.edu.

■ *See page 2480 for a narrative description.*

TALMUDICAL INSTITUTE OF UPSTATE NEW YORK

Rochester, New York

Admissions Contact Director of Admissions, Talmudical Institute of Upstate New York, 769 Park Avenue, Rochester, NY 14607-3046. *Phone:* 716-473-2810.

TALMUDICAL SEMINARY OHOLEI TORAH

Brooklyn, New York

Admissions Contact Rabbi E. Piekarski, Director of Academic Affairs, Talmudical Seminary Oholei Torah, 667 Eastern Parkway, Brooklyn, NY 11213-3310. *Phone:* 718-363-2034.

TORAH TEMIMAH TALMUDICAL SEMINARY

Brooklyn, New York

Admissions Contact Rabbi I. Hisiger, Principal, Torah Temimah Talmudical Seminary, 555 Ocean Parkway, Brooklyn, NY 11218-5913. *Phone:* 718-853-8500.

TOURO COLLEGE

New York, New York

- **Independent** comprehensive, founded 1971
- **Calendar** semesters
- **Degrees** certificates, diplomas, associate, bachelor's, master's, doctoral, first professional, and post-master's certificates
- **Urban** campus
- **Coed**
- **Moderately difficult** entrance level

Faculty *Student/faculty ratio:* 16:1.

Student Life *Campus security:* 24-hour emergency response devices and patrols.

Standardized Tests *Recommended:* SAT I or ACT (for admission).

Costs (2003–04) *Comprehensive fee:* $15,400 includes full-time tuition ($10,400) and room and board ($5000).

Financial Aid Of all full-time matriculated undergraduates who enrolled in 2002, 5,940 applied for aid, 5,940 were judged to have need. *Average percent of need met:* 90. *Average financial aid package:* $9000. *Average need-based loan:* $4275. *Average non-need-based aid:* $1500. *Average indebtedness upon graduation:* $17,000.

Touro College (continued)

Applying *Options:* early admission, deferred entrance. *Application fee:* $50. *Required:* high school transcript. *Required for some:* 2 letters of recommendation, interview. *Recommended:* essay or personal statement, 1 letter of recommendation.

Admissions Contact Mr. Andre Baron, Director of Admissions, Touro College, 27-33 West 23rd Street, New York, NY 10010. *Phone:* 212-463-0400 Ext. 665.

UNION COLLEGE

Schenectady, New York

- **Independent** 4-year, founded 1795
- **Calendar** trimesters
- **Degree** bachelor's
- **Suburban** 100-acre campus
- **Endowment** $246.1 million
- **Coed,** 2,174 undergraduate students, 99% full-time, 47% women, 53% men
- **Very difficult** entrance level, 44% of applicants were admitted

Union's new house system is designed to create more opportunities for students to interact with teachers and each other. All students and faculty members have house affiliations, and each house contributes intellectual, cultural, and social events to the campus.

Undergraduates 2,154 full-time, 20 part-time. Students come from 37 states and territories, 17 other countries, 55% are from out of state, 3% African American, 5% Asian American or Pacific Islander, 4% Hispanic American, 2% international, 1% transferred in, 80% live on campus. *Retention:* 93% of 2002 full-time freshmen returned.

Freshmen *Admission:* 4,159 applied, 1,822 admitted, 559 enrolled. *Average high school GPA:* 3.49. *Test scores:* SAT verbal scores over 500: 97%; SAT math scores over 500: 99%; SAT verbal scores over 600: 60%; SAT math scores over 600: 72%; SAT verbal scores over 700: 12%; SAT math scores over 700: 22%.

Faculty *Total:* 218, 88% full-time, 88% with terminal degrees. *Student/faculty ratio:* 11:1.

Majors American studies; anthropology; biochemistry; biological and physical sciences; biology/biological sciences; chemistry; classics and languages, literatures and linguistics; computer and information sciences; economics; electrical, electronics and communications engineering; English; fine/studio arts; foreign languages and literatures; geology/earth science; history; humanities; liberal arts and sciences/liberal studies; mathematics; mechanical engineering; neuroscience; philosophy; physics; political science and government; psychology; social sciences; sociology.

Academic Programs *Special study options:* accelerated degree program, advanced placement credit, cooperative education, double majors, English as a second language, honors programs, independent study, internships, off-campus study, part-time degree program, student-designed majors, study abroad, summer session for credit. *ROTC:* Army (c), Navy (c), Air Force (c).

Library Schaffer Library with 301,101 titles, 1,988 serial subscriptions, 8,450 audiovisual materials, an OPAC, a Web page.

Computers on Campus 435 computers available on campus for general student use. A campuswide network can be accessed from student residence rooms and from off campus. Internet access, at least one staffed computer lab available. Computer purchase or lease plan available.

Student Life *Housing:* on-campus residence required through senior year. *Options:* coed, cooperative. Campus housing is university owned and leased by the school. Freshman campus housing is guaranteed. *Activities and organizations:* drama/theater group, student-run newspaper, radio station, choral group, U-Program (Programming Board), student radio station, student newspaper, Concert Committee, national fraternities, national sororities. *Campus security:* 24-hour emergency response devices and patrols, late-night transport/escort service, controlled dormitory access, awareness programs, bicycle patrol, shuttle service. *Student services:* health clinic, personal/psychological counseling, women's center.

Athletics Member NCAA. All Division III except men's and women's ice hockey (Division I). *Intercollegiate sports:* baseball M, basketball M/W, crew M/W, cross-country running M/W, fencing M(c)/W(c), field hockey W, football M, golf M(c)/W(c), ice hockey M/W, lacrosse M/W, rugby M(c)/W(c), skiing (downhill) M(c)/W(c), soccer M/W, softball W, swimming M/W, tennis M/W, track and field M/W, ultimate Frisbee M(c)/W(c), volleyball W, water polo M(c)/W(c). *Intramural sports:* basketball M/W, football M/W, ice hockey M/W, lacrosse M/W, soccer M/W, softball M/W, volleyball M/W.

Standardized Tests *Required:* SAT I or ACT (for admission), 3 SAT II Subject Tests (including SAT II: Writing Test) (for admission). *Required for some:* SAT II: Subject Tests (for admission).

Costs (2003–04) *Comprehensive fee:* $36,005 includes full-time tuition ($28,608), mandatory fees ($320), and room and board ($7077). Part-time tuition: $3180 per course. *College room only:* $3882. Room and board charges vary according to board plan. *Payment plan:* installment. *Waivers:* senior citizens and employees or children of employees.

Financial Aid Of all full-time matriculated undergraduates who enrolled in 2002, 1,135 applied for aid, 1,091 were judged to have need, 1,015 had their need fully met. 639 Federal Work-Study jobs (averaging $1200). 29 state and other part-time jobs (averaging $1515). In 2002, 7 non-need-based awards were made. *Average percent of need met:* 100%. *Average financial aid package:* $22,601. *Average need-based loan:* $4221. *Average need-based gift aid:* $18,007. *Average non-need-based aid:* $20,000. *Average indebtedness upon graduation:* $14,673. *Financial aid deadline:* 2/1.

Applying *Options:* common application, electronic application, early admission, early decision, deferred entrance. *Application fee:* $50. *Required:* essay or personal statement, high school transcript, 2 letters of recommendation. *Recommended:* interview. *Application deadlines:* 1/15 (freshmen), 5/1 (transfers). *Early decision:* 11/15 (for plan 1), 1/15 (for plan 2). *Notification:* 4/1 (freshmen), 12/15 (early decision plan 1), 2/1 (early decision plan 2), continuous (transfers).

Admissions Contact Ms. Dianne Crozier, Director of Admissions, Union College, Grant Hall, Schenectady, NY 12308. *Phone:* 518-388-6112. *Toll-free phone:* 888-843-6688. *Fax:* 518-388-6986. *E-mail:* admissions@union.edu.

■ *See page 2544 for a narrative description.*

UNITED STATES MERCHANT MARINE ACADEMY

Kings Point, New York

- **Federally supported** 4-year, founded 1943
- **Calendar** trimesters
- **Degree** bachelor's
- **Suburban** 82-acre campus with easy access to New York City
- **Coed,** 971 undergraduate students, 100% full-time, 13% women, 87% men
- **Very difficult** entrance level, 16% of applicants were admitted

Undergraduates 971 full-time. Students come from 49 states and territories, 3 other countries, 86% are from out of state, 100% live on campus. *Retention:* 92% of 2002 full-time freshmen returned.

Freshmen *Admission:* 1,919 applied, 303 admitted, 303 enrolled. *Average high school GPA:* 3.60. *Test scores:* SAT verbal scores over 500: 100%; SAT math scores over 500: 100%; SAT verbal scores over 600: 64%; SAT math scores over 600: 61%; SAT verbal scores over 700: 22%; SAT math scores over 700: 8%.

Faculty *Total:* 95, 89% full-time. *Student/faculty ratio:* 11:1.

Majors Engineering/industrial management; engineering-related technologies; marine science/merchant marine officer; marine transportation related; maritime science; naval architecture and marine engineering; nuclear engineering technology; transportation and materials moving related.

Academic Programs *Special study options:* honors programs, internships.

Library Schuyler Otis Bland Memorial Library with 185,000 titles, 950 serial subscriptions, 3,389 audiovisual materials, an OPAC, a Web page.

Computers on Campus 1200 computers available on campus for general student use. A campuswide network can be accessed from student residence rooms that provide access to engineering and economics software. Internet access, at least one staffed computer lab available. Computer purchase or lease plan available.

Student Life *Housing:* on-campus residence required through senior year. *Options:* coed. Campus housing is university owned. Freshman campus housing is guaranteed. *Activities and organizations:* drama/theater group, student-run newspaper, choral group, marching band, Regimental Band. *Campus security:* 24-hour patrols. *Student services:* health clinic, personal/psychological counseling.

Athletics Member NCAA. All Division III. *Intercollegiate sports:* baseball M, basketball M/W, crew M/W, cross-country running M/W, football M, golf M/W, lacrosse M, rugby M(c), sailing M/W, soccer M, softball W, swimming M/W, tennis M/W, track and field M/W, volleyball W, wrestling M. *Intramural sports:* basketball M/W, bowling M/W, crew M/W, cross-country running M/W, football M, golf M/W, lacrosse M, racquetball M/W, riflery M/W, rugby M, sailing M/W, skiing (cross-country) M/W, skiing (downhill) M/W, soccer M/W, softball M/W, swimming M/W, tennis M/W, track and field M/W, volleyball M/W, water polo M, wrestling M.

Standardized Tests *Required:* SAT I or ACT (for admission).

Costs (2003–04) *Tuition:* Full-time tuition and fees vary according to program and student level. Tuition, room and board, and medical and dental care provided by the U.S. government. Each midshipman receives a monthly salary while assigned aboard ship for training. Entering freshmen are required to deposit $6250 to defray the initial cost of computer equipment and activities fees.

Applying *Options:* electronic application, early decision. *Required:* essay or personal statement, high school transcript, 3 letters of recommendation. *Recom-*

mended: interview. *Application deadlines:* 3/1 (freshmen), 3/1 (transfers). *Early decision:* 11/1. *Notification:* continuous until 4/1 (freshmen), 12/15 (early decision), continuous until 4/1 (transfers).

Admissions Contact Capt. James M. Skinner, Director of Admissions, United States Merchant Marine Academy, 300 Steamboat Road, Kings Point, NY 11024-1699. *Phone:* 516-773-5391. *Toll-free phone:* 866-546-4778. *Fax:* 516-773-5390. *E-mail:* admissions@usmma.edu.

■ *See page 2552 for a narrative description.*

UNITED STATES MILITARY ACADEMY
West Point, New York

- **Federally supported** 4-year, founded 1802
- **Calendar** semesters
- **Degree** bachelor's
- **Small-town** 16,080-acre campus with easy access to New York City
- **Coed, primarily men,** 4,242 undergraduate students, 100% full-time, 15% women, 85% men
- **Most difficult** entrance level, 10% of applicants were admitted

If you want to lead and make a difference as our nation faces the challenges of the 21st century, consider West Point as a college option. The U.S. Military Academy offers this outstanding opportunity, challenging young men and women in academics, leadership, and physical development. The West Point experience builds a foundation for career success as an Army officer; it is tough but rewarding. Graduates earn a Bachelor of Science degree and a commission as a second lieutenant in the U.S. Army.

Undergraduates 4,242 full-time. Students come from 53 states and territories, 25 other countries, 92% are from out of state, 8% African American, 7% Asian American or Pacific Islander, 7% Hispanic American, 0.7% Native American, 0.8% international, 100% live on campus. *Retention:* 92% of 2002 full-time freshmen returned.

Freshmen *Admission:* 12,688 applied, 1,314 admitted, 1,314 enrolled. *Test scores:* SAT verbal scores over 500: 98%; SAT math scores over 500: 100%; ACT scores over 18: 100%; SAT verbal scores over 600: 69%; SAT math scores over 600: 82%; ACT scores over 24: 97%; SAT verbal scores over 700: 18%; SAT math scores over 700: 25%; ACT scores over 30: 34%.

Faculty *Total:* 598, 100% full-time, 51% with terminal degrees. *Student/faculty ratio:* 7:1.

Majors Aerospace, aeronautical and astronautical engineering; American studies; applied mathematics; Arabic; Army R.O.T.C./military science; Asian studies (East); behavioral sciences; biological and physical sciences; biology/biological sciences; business administration and management; chemical engineering; chemistry; Chinese; civil engineering; computer engineering; computer science; economics; electrical, electronics and communications engineering; engineering; engineering/industrial management; engineering physics; environmental/environmental health engineering; environmental studies; European studies; European studies (Central and Eastern); French; geography; German; history; humanities; information science/studies; interdisciplinary studies; Latin American studies; literature; mathematics; mechanical engineering; modern languages; Near and Middle Eastern studies; nuclear engineering; operations research; philosophy; physics; political science and government; Portuguese; pre-law studies; pre-medical studies; psychology; public policy analysis; Russian; Spanish; systems engineering.

Academic Programs *Special study options:* academic remediation for entering students, advanced placement credit, double majors, off-campus study, summer session for credit.

Library United States Military Academy Library plus 1 other with 457,340 titles, 2,220 serial subscriptions, 8,000 audiovisual materials, an OPAC, a Web page.

Computers on Campus 5500 computers available on campus for general student use. A campuswide network can be accessed from student residence rooms and from off campus. Internet access, online (class) registration, at least one staffed computer lab available. Computer purchase or lease plan available.

Student Life *Housing:* on-campus residence required through senior year. *Options:* coed. Campus housing is university owned. Freshman campus housing is guaranteed. *Activities and organizations:* drama/theater group, student-run radio station, choral group, rugby club, chapel choirs, Big Brothers/Big Sisters, Orienteering Team, Spirit Support Group. *Campus security:* 24-hour emergency response devices and patrols, student patrols, late-night transport/escort service. *Student services:* health clinic, personal/psychological counseling, legal services.

Athletics Member NCAA. All Division I except football (Division I-A). *Intercollegiate sports:* baseball M, basketball M/W, bowling M(c)/W(c), crew M(c)/W(c), cross-country running M/W, equestrian sports M(c)/W(c), fencing M(c)/W(c), golf M, gymnastics M, ice hockey M, lacrosse M/W(c), racquetball M(c)/W(c), riflery M(c)/W(c), rugby M(c), sailing M(c)/W(c), skiing (cross-country) M(c)/W(c), skiing (downhill) M(c)/W(c), soccer M/W, softball W, squash M(c)/W(c), swimming M/W, tennis M/W, track and field M/W, volleyball M(c)/W, water polo M(c), weight lifting M(c)/W(c), wrestling M. *Intramural sports:* basketball M/W, cross-country running M/W, football M, lacrosse M, soccer M/W, softball M/W, swimming M/W.

Standardized Tests *Required:* SAT I or ACT (for admission).

Costs (2003–04) *Tuition:* Tuition, room and board, and medical and dental care are provided by the U.S. government. Each cadet receives a salary from which to pay for personal computer, uniforms, activities, books, services, and personal expenses. Entering freshmen are required to pay a $2400 deposit to defray the initial cost of uniforms, books, supplies, equipment and fees.

Applying *Options:* early action. *Required:* essay or personal statement, high school transcript, 4 letters of recommendation, medical examination, authorized nomination. *Recommended:* interview. *Application deadlines:* 3/21 (freshmen), 3/21 (transfers). *Notification:* continuous until 6/1 (freshmen), 1/5 (early action), continuous until 6/1 (transfers).

Admissions Contact Col. Michael C. Jones, Director of Admissions, United States Military Academy, Building 606, West Point, NY 10996. *Phone:* 845-938-4041. *E-mail:* 8dad@sunams.usma.army.mil.

■ *See page 2554 for a narrative description.*

UNITED TALMUDICAL SEMINARY
Brooklyn, New York

Admissions Contact Director of Admissions, United Talmudical Seminary, 82 Lee Avenue, Brooklyn, NY 11211-7900. *Phone:* 718-963-9770.

UNIVERSITY AT ALBANY, STATE UNIVERSITY OF NEW YORK
Albany, New York

- **State-supported** university, founded 1844, part of State University of New York System
- **Calendar** semesters
- **Degrees** bachelor's, master's, doctoral, and post-master's certificates
- **Suburban** 560-acre campus
- **Endowment** $14.8 million
- **Coed,** 11,796 undergraduate students, 91% full-time, 50% women, 50% men
- **Moderately difficult** entrance level, 56% of applicants were admitted

Undergraduates 10,718 full-time, 1,078 part-time. Students come from 38 states and territories, 51 other countries, 5% are from out of state, 8% African American, 6% Asian American or Pacific Islander, 7% Hispanic American, 0.3% Native American, 2% international, 10% transferred in, 58% live on campus. *Retention:* 84% of 2002 full-time freshmen returned.

Freshmen *Admission:* 17,328 applied, 9,672 admitted, 2,161 enrolled. *Average high school GPA:* 3.34. *Test scores:* SAT verbal scores over 500: 82%; SAT math scores over 500: 87%; SAT verbal scores over 600: 31%; SAT math scores over 600: 39%; SAT verbal scores over 700: 3%; SAT math scores over 700: 5%.

Faculty *Total:* 937, 64% full-time. *Student/faculty ratio:* 20:1.

Majors Accounting; actuarial science; African-American/Black studies; anthropology; applied mathematics; art; art history, criticism and conservation; Asian studies; Asian studies (East); atmospheric sciences and meteorology; biochemistry; biology/biological sciences; biology teacher education; business administration and management; chemistry; chemistry teacher education; Chinese; classics and languages, literatures and linguistics; computer and information sciences; computer science; criminal justice/law enforcement administration; dramatic/theatre arts; economics; English; English/language arts teacher education; environmental science; European studies (Central and Eastern); foreign language teacher education; French; French language teacher education; geography; geology/earth science; Hispanic-American, Puerto Rican, and Mexican-American/Chicano studies; history; information science/studies; interdisciplinary studies; Italian; Japanese studies; Jewish/Judaic studies; Latin; Latin American studies; linguistics; mass communication/media; mathematics; mathematics and computer science; mathematics teacher education; medieval and Renaissance studies; molecular biology; music; philosophy; physics; political science and government; psychology; public administration; public policy analysis; religious studies; Romance languages; Russian; Russian studies; science teacher education; Slavic languages; social science teacher education; social work; sociology; Spanish; Spanish language teacher education; speech and rhetoric; urban studies/affairs; women's studies.

Academic Programs *Special study options:* advanced placement credit, double majors, English as a second language, freshman honors college, honors programs, independent study, internships, off-campus study, services for LD students, student-designed majors, study abroad, summer session for credit. *ROTC:* Army (b), Air Force (c). *Unusual degree programs:* 3-2 engineering with Rensselaer

University at Albany, State University of New York (continued)
Polytechnic Institute, State University of New York at Binghamton, State University of New York at New Paltz, Clarkson University; library science, law.

Library University Library plus 2 others with 1.2 million titles, 28,055 serial subscriptions, 10,115 audiovisual materials, an OPAC, a Web page.

Computers on Campus 500 computers available on campus for general student use. A campuswide network can be accessed from student residence rooms and from off campus. Internet access, at least one staffed computer lab available.

Student Life *Housing:* on-campus residence required through sophomore year. *Options:* coed, men-only, women-only. Campus housing is university owned. *Activities and organizations:* drama/theater group, student-run newspaper, radio station, choral group, intramural athletics, cultural organizations, political organizations, community service, national fraternities, national sororities. *Campus security:* 24-hour emergency response devices and patrols, late-night transport/escort service, controlled dormitory access, crime prevention unit. *Student services:* health clinic, personal/psychological counseling, legal services.

Athletics Member NCAA. All Division I. *Intercollegiate sports:* baseball M(s), basketball M(s)/W(s), crew M/W, cross-country running M(s)/W(s), field hockey W(s), football M(s), golf W(s), lacrosse M(s)/W(s), rugby M/W, soccer M(s)/W(s), softball W(s), tennis W(s), track and field M(s)/W(s), volleyball W(s). *Intramural sports:* basketball M/W, fencing M/W, ice hockey M, racquetball M/W, skiing (cross-country) M/W, skiing (downhill) M/W, soccer M/W, softball M/W, squash M/W, track and field M/W, ultimate Frisbee M/W, volleyball M/W, water polo M/W, wrestling M.

Standardized Tests *Required:* SAT I or ACT (for admission).

Costs (2003–04) *Tuition:* state resident $4350 full-time, $181 per credit part-time; nonresident $10,300 full-time, $429 per credit part-time. Part-time tuition and fees vary according to course load. *Required fees:* $1420 full-time. *Room and board:* $7181; room only: $4417. Room and board charges vary according to board plan and housing facility. *Payment plan:* installment. *Waivers:* senior citizens.

Financial Aid Of all full-time matriculated undergraduates who enrolled in 2003, 7,887 applied for aid, 6,075 were judged to have need, 1,137 had their need fully met. 1,135 Federal Work-Study jobs (averaging $1601). In 2003, 548 non-need-based awards were made. *Average percent of need met:* 71%. *Average financial aid package:* $8251. *Average need-based loan:* $4283. *Average need-based gift aid:* $4456. *Average non-need-based aid:* $3534. *Average indebtedness upon graduation:* $16,700.

Applying *Options:* common application, electronic application, early admission, early action, deferred entrance. *Application fee:* $40. *Required:* high school transcript. *Required for some:* portfolio, audition. *Recommended:* essay or personal statement, letters of recommendation. *Application deadlines:* 3/1 (freshmen), 7/1 (transfers). *Notification:* continuous (freshmen), 1/1 (early action), continuous (transfers).

Admissions Contact Mr. Robert Andrea, Director of Undergraduate Admissions, University at Albany, State University of New York, 1400 Washington Avenue, University Administration Building 101, Albany, NY 12222. *Phone:* 518-442-5435. *Toll-free phone:* 800-293-7869. *E-mail:* ugadmissions@albany.edu.

■ See page 2558 for a narrative description.

UNIVERSITY AT BUFFALO, THE STATE UNIVERSITY OF NEW YORK

Buffalo, New York

- **State-supported** university, founded 1846, part of State University of New York System
- **Calendar** semesters
- **Degrees** associate, bachelor's, master's, doctoral, first professional, post-master's, and first professional certificates
- **Suburban** 1350-acre campus
- **Endowment** $378.4 million
- **Coed,** 17,818 undergraduate students, 91% full-time, 45% women, 55% men
- **Moderately difficult** entrance level, 62% of applicants were admitted

The University at Buffalo (UB) attracts highly qualified students with its University Honors Program—the largest in the SUNY system—and the University at Buffalo Scholars Program. UB offers a growing number of combined bachelor's and master's programs. The University is dedicated to providing the latest in educational technology, exposing students to computer-enhanced classwork and training them for the demands of the 21st century. UB is also committed to enhancing student life by offering new on-campus apartment housing options, NCAA Division I athletics and intramural and club sports.

Undergraduates 16,219 full-time, 1,599 part-time. Students come from 42 states and territories, 78 other countries, 2% are from out of state, 7% African American, 9% Asian American or Pacific Islander, 3% Hispanic American, 0.3% Native American, 6% international, 9% transferred in, 38% live on campus. *Retention:* 85% of 2002 full-time freshmen returned.

Freshmen *Admission:* 17,448 applied, 10,890 admitted, 3,593 enrolled. *Average high school GPA:* 3.10. *Test scores:* SAT verbal scores over 500: 77%; SAT math scores over 500: 88%; ACT scores over 18: 99%; SAT verbal scores over 600: 28%; SAT math scores over 600: 42%; ACT scores over 24: 74%; SAT verbal scores over 700: 4%; SAT math scores over 700: 6%; ACT scores over 30: 14%.

Faculty *Total:* 1,711, 66% full-time. *Student/faculty ratio:* 15:1.

Majors Adult health nursing; aerospace, aeronautical and astronautical engineering; African-American/Black studies; American studies; anthropology; architecture; art; art history, criticism and conservation; Asian studies; audiology and speech-language pathology; biochemical technology; biochemistry; bioinformatics; biology/biological sciences; biophysics; biotechnology; business administration and management; chemical engineering; chemistry; civil engineering; classics and languages, literatures and linguistics; clinical laboratory science/medical technology; communication/speech communication and rhetoric; computer engineering; computer science; critical care nursing; dance; dramatic/theatre arts; dramatic/theatre arts and stagecraft related; economics; economics related; electrical, electronics and communications engineering; engineering physics; English; environmental design/architecture; environmental/environmental health engineering; family practice nursing/nurse practitioner; film/cinema studies; fine/studio arts; French; geography; geology/earth science; German; history; industrial engineering; Italian; kinesiology and exercise science; linguistics; mass communication/media; maternal/child health and neonatal nursing; mathematics; mathematics related; mechanical engineering; medicinal and pharmaceutical chemistry; multi-/interdisciplinary studies related; music; music performance; nuclear medical technology; nurse anesthetist; nursing (registered nurse training); nursing related; nutrition sciences; occupational therapy; pediatric nursing; pharmacology; pharmacy administration/pharmaceutics; pharmacy, pharmaceutical sciences, and administration related; philosophy; physics; physics related; political science and government; psychiatric/mental health nursing; psychology; social work; sociology; Spanish; structural engineering; theoretical and mathematical physics; women's studies.

Academic Programs *Special study options:* academic remediation for entering students, accelerated degree program, adult/continuing education programs, advanced placement credit, distance learning, double majors, English as a second language, freshman honors college, honors programs, independent study, internships, off-campus study, part-time degree program, services for LD students, student-designed majors, study abroad, summer session for credit. *ROTC:* Army (c). *Unusual degree programs:* 3-2 law.

Library Lockwood Library plus 7 others with 2.0 million titles, 32,179 serial subscriptions, 5.3 million audiovisual materials, an OPAC, a Web page.

Computers on Campus 2391 computers available on campus for general student use. A campuswide network can be accessed from student residence rooms and from off campus. Internet access, online (class) registration, at least one staffed computer lab available.

Student Life *Housing options:* coed. Campus housing is university owned. Freshman campus housing is guaranteed. *Activities and organizations:* drama/theater group, student-run newspaper, radio and television station, choral group, marching band, PODER-Latinos Unidos, Black Student Union, Caribbean Student Association, Crew, LaCross, national fraternities, national sororities. *Campus security:* 24-hour emergency response devices and patrols, student patrols, late-night transport/escort service, controlled dormitory access, self-defense and awareness programs. *Student services:* health clinic, personal/psychological counseling, women's center, legal services.

Athletics Member NCAA. All Division I except football (Division I-A). *Intercollegiate sports:* baseball M(s), basketball M(s)/W(s), crew W(s), cross-country running M(s)/W(s), soccer M(s)/W(s), softball W(s), swimming M(s)/W(s), tennis M(s)/W(s), track and field M(s)/W(s), volleyball W(s), wrestling M(s). *Intramural sports:* badminton M/W, baseball M(c), basketball M/W, crew M(c), cross-country running M/W, field hockey W(c), football M, gymnastics M(c)/W(c), ice hockey M(c)/W(c), lacrosse M(c)/W(c), racquetball M/W, rugby M(c)/W(c), skiing (downhill) M(c)/W(c), soccer M/W, softball M/W, squash M/W, tennis M(c)/W, ultimate Frisbee M(c)/W(c), volleyball M/W, weight lifting M(c)/W(c), wrestling M(c)/W(c).

Standardized Tests *Required:* SAT I or ACT (for admission).

Costs (2003–04) *Tuition:* state resident $4350 full-time, $181 per credit hour part-time; nonresident $10,300 full-time, $429 per credit hour part-time. Part-time tuition and fees vary according to course load. *Required fees:* $1501 full-time. *Room and board:* $6816; room only: $4036. Room and board charges vary according to board plan and housing facility. *Payment plan:* installment. *Waivers:* minority students.

Financial Aid Of all full-time matriculated undergraduates who enrolled in 2003, 11,777 applied for aid, 11,430 were judged to have need, 7,671 had their need fully met. 2,185 Federal Work-Study jobs (averaging $992). 913 state and other part-time jobs (averaging $5428). In 2003, 395 non-need-based awards were made. *Average percent of need met:* 71%. *Average financial aid package:* $7520. *Average need-based loan:* $3040. *Average need-based gift aid:* $3573. *Average non-need-based aid:* $2930. *Average indebtedness upon graduation:* $16,418.

Applying *Options:* electronic application, early admission, early decision. *Application fee:* $40. *Required:* high school transcript. *Required for some:* letters of recommendation, portfolio, audition. *Application deadline:* rolling (freshmen), rolling (transfers). *Early decision:* 11/1. *Notification:* 12/10 (early decision).

Admissions Contact Ms. Patricia Armstrong, Director of Admissions, University at Buffalo, The State University of New York, Capen Hall, Room 15, North Campus, Buffalo, NY 14260-1660. *Phone:* 716-645-6900. *Toll-free phone:* 888-UB-ADMIT. *Fax:* 716-645-6411. *E-mail:* ub-admissions@buffalo.edu.

■ See page 2560 for a narrative description.

UNIVERSITY OF ROCHESTER

Rochester, New York

- **Independent** university, founded 1850
- **Calendar** semesters plus optional summer term
- **Degrees** certificates, bachelor's, master's, doctoral, first professional, post-master's, and postbachelor's certificates
- **Suburban** 534-acre campus
- **Endowment** $1.1 billion
- **Coed,** 4,581 undergraduate students, 95% full-time, 47% women, 53% men
- **Very difficult** entrance level, 49% of applicants were admitted

Rochester is a world-class private university, offering the diversity of a major university but with a small student body, allowing plenty of individual attention from faculty members. The flexible curriculum gives students the freedom to shape their own paths and take advantage of such distinctive educational opportunities as Take Five—a tuition-free 5th year—and music studies at renowned Eastman School.

Undergraduates 4,359 full-time, 222 part-time. Students come from 52 states and territories, 36 other countries, 50% are from out of state, 5% African American, 12% Asian American or Pacific Islander, 4% Hispanic American, 0.4% Native American, 3% international, 2% transferred in, 80% live on campus. *Retention:* 94% of 2002 full-time freshmen returned.

Freshmen *Admission:* 10,486 applied, 5,096 admitted, 1,091 enrolled. *Average high school GPA:* 3.70. *Test scores:* SAT verbal scores over 500: 95%; SAT math scores over 500: 99%; ACT scores over 18: 100%; SAT verbal scores over 600: 73%; SAT math scores over 600: 84%; ACT scores over 24: 91%; SAT verbal scores over 700: 22%; SAT math scores over 700: 35%; ACT scores over 30: 35%.

Faculty *Total:* 532, 96% full-time, 88% with terminal degrees. *Student/faculty ratio:* 9:1.

Majors African-American/Black studies; American Sign Language (ASL); anthropology; applied mathematics; art history, criticism and conservation; biological and physical sciences; biology/biological sciences; biomedical/medical engineering; chemical engineering; chemistry; classics and languages, literatures and linguistics; cognitive science; comparative literature; computer science; economics; electrical, electronics and communications engineering; engineering science; English; environmental science; environmental studies; film/cinema studies; fine/studio arts; French; geological/geophysical engineering; geology/earth science; German; history; Japanese; jazz/jazz studies; linguistics; mathematics; mathematics and statistics related; mechanical engineering; music; music teacher education; music theory and composition; nursing (registered nurse training); optical sciences; philosophy; physics; physics related; political science and government; psychology; religious studies; Russian; Russian studies; social sciences related; Spanish; statistics; women's studies.

Academic Programs *Special study options:* advanced placement credit, double majors, English as a second language, independent study, internships, off-campus study, part-time degree program, services for LD students, student-designed majors, study abroad, summer session for credit. *ROTC:* Army (c), Air Force (c). *Unusual degree programs:* 3-2 public health, optics, public policy, human development, computer science, medical statistics, applied mathematics, elementary teacher education, music education, materials science.

Library Rush Rhees Library plus 5 others with 3.0 million titles, 11,254 serial subscriptions, 78,600 audiovisual materials, an OPAC, a Web page.

Computers on Campus 260 computers available on campus for general student use. A campuswide network can be accessed from student residence rooms and from off campus. At least one staffed computer lab available.

Student Life *Housing:* on-campus residence required through sophomore year. *Options:* coed, men-only, women-only. Campus housing is university owned. Freshman campus housing is guaranteed. *Activities and organizations:* drama/theater group, student-run newspaper, radio station, choral group, student radio station, cinema group, Debate Union, Campus Board Program, national fraternities, national sororities. *Campus security:* 24-hour emergency response devices and patrols, late-night transport/escort service, controlled dormitory access. *Student services:* health clinic, personal/psychological counseling, women's center, legal services.

Athletics Member NCAA. All Division III. *Intercollegiate sports:* baseball M, basketball M/W, crew M(c)/W(c), cross-country running M/W, equestrian sports M(c)/W(c), field hockey W, football M, golf M, ice hockey M(c)/W(c), lacrosse M(c)/W, rugby M(c)/W(c), skiing (downhill) M(c)/W(c), soccer M/W, softball W, squash M, swimming M/W, tennis M/W, track and field M/W, ultimate Frisbee M(c)/W(c), volleyball M(c)/W. *Intramural sports:* basketball M/W, cheerleading M/W, fencing M(c)/W(c), football M/W, gymnastics M(c)/W(c), sailing M(c)/W(c), soccer M/W, softball M/W, tennis M/W, volleyball M/W, water polo M/W.

Standardized Tests *Required:* SAT I or ACT (for admission).

Costs (2003–04) *Comprehensive fee:* $36,343 includes full-time tuition ($26,900), mandatory fees ($673), and room and board ($8770). Part-time tuition: $470 per credit hour. Part-time tuition and fees vary according to course load. *College room only:* $5250. Room and board charges vary according to board plan. *Payment plans:* tuition prepayment, installment. *Waivers:* children of alumni and employees or children of employees.

Financial Aid Of all full-time matriculated undergraduates who enrolled in 2003, 2,564 applied for aid, 2,199 were judged to have need, 2,199 had their need fully met. 1,232 Federal Work-Study jobs (averaging $1960). In 2003, 1217 non-need-based awards were made. *Average percent of need met:* 100%. *Average financial aid package:* $22,854. *Average need-based loan:* $4981. *Average need-based gift aid:* $17,801. *Average non-need-based aid:* $10,022.

Applying *Options:* common application, electronic application, early admission, early decision, deferred entrance. *Application fee:* $50. *Required:* essay or personal statement, high school transcript, 1 letter of recommendation. *Required for some:* audition, portfolio. *Recommended:* 2 letters of recommendation, interview. *Application deadline:* 1/20 (freshmen), rolling (transfers). *Early decision:* 11/15 (for plan 1), 1/20 (for plan 2). *Notification:* 4/1 (freshmen), 12/15 (early decision plan 1), 4/1 (early decision plan 2), continuous (transfers).

Admissions Contact Mr. Gregory MacDonald, Director of Admissions, University of Rochester, PO Box 270251, W. Allen Wallis Hall, 300 Wilson Boulevard, Rochester, NY 14627-0251. *Phone:* 585-275-3221. *Toll-free phone:* 888-822-2256. *Fax:* 585-461-4595. *E-mail:* admit@admissions.rochester.edu.

■ See page 2696 for a narrative description.

U.T.A. MESIVTA OF KIRYAS JOEL

Monroe, New York

Admissions Contact 55 Forest Road, Suite 101, Monroe, NY 10950.

UTICA COLLEGE

Utica, New York

- **Independent** comprehensive, founded 1946
- **Calendar** semesters
- **Degrees** bachelor's and master's
- **Suburban** 128-acre campus
- **Endowment** $12.8 million
- **Coed,** 2,170 undergraduate students, 86% full-time, 59% women, 41% men
- **Moderately difficult** entrance level, 77% of applicants were admitted

Utica College offers a warm, friendly atmosphere with small classes and a dedicated faculty. Students choose from 31 majors in both the liberal arts and professional career programs. Extensive cooperative education and internship opportunities provide students with valuable experience in the workplace. Upon graduation, Utica College students receive the internationally recognized Syracuse University degree.

Undergraduates 1,869 full-time, 301 part-time. Students come from 30 states and territories, 20 other countries, 16% are from out of state, 8% African American, 1% Asian American or Pacific Islander, 4% Hispanic American, 0.4% Native American, 1% international, 10% transferred in, 49% live on campus. *Retention:* 69% of 2002 full-time freshmen returned.

Freshmen *Admission:* 2,946 applied, 2,273 admitted, 449 enrolled. *Average high school GPA:* 3.2. *Test scores:* SAT verbal scores over 500: 45%; SAT math scores over 500: 49%; SAT verbal scores over 600: 8%; SAT math scores over 600: 13%; SAT verbal scores over 700: 1%; SAT math scores over 700: 1%.

Faculty *Total:* 223, 48% full-time, 46% with terminal degrees. *Student/faculty ratio:* 17:1.

Majors Accounting; biology/biological sciences; biology teacher education; business administration and management; business, management, and marketing related; business/managerial economics; business teacher education; chemistry; chemistry teacher education; communication/speech communication and rhetoric; computer and information sciences; computer teacher education; criminal

Utica College (continued)
justice/law enforcement administration; developmental and child psychology; economics; elementary education; English; English/language arts teacher education; health/medical preparatory programs related; history; history teacher education; international business/trade/commerce; international relations and affairs; journalism; liberal arts and sciences/liberal studies; mathematics; mathematics teacher education; nursing (registered nurse training); occupational therapy; philosophy; physical therapy; physics; physics teacher education; political science and government; pre-dentistry studies; pre-law studies; pre-medical studies; pre-veterinary studies; psychology; public relations/image management; secondary education; social sciences; social science teacher education; social studies teacher education; sociology; therapeutic recreation.

Academic Programs *Special study options:* academic remediation for entering students, accelerated degree program, adult/continuing education programs, advanced placement credit, cooperative education, distance learning, double majors, English as a second language, freshman honors college, honors programs, independent study, internships, off-campus study, part-time degree program, services for LD students, study abroad, summer session for credit. *ROTC:* Army (b), Air Force (c). *Unusual degree programs:* 3-2 engineering with Syracuse University.

Library Gannett Memorial Library with 181,558 titles, 1,311 serial subscriptions, 1,682 audiovisual materials, an OPAC, a Web page.

Computers on Campus 203 computers available on campus for general student use. A campuswide network can be accessed from student residence rooms and from off campus. Internet access, at least one staffed computer lab available.

Student Life *Housing:* on-campus residence required through sophomore year. *Options:* coed. Campus housing is university owned. Freshman campus housing is guaranteed. *Activities and organizations:* drama/theater group, student-run newspaper, radio station, choral group, Honor Association, Double Up, Outing Club, Student Senate, CJ Student Association, national fraternities, national sororities. *Campus security:* 24-hour emergency response devices and patrols, late-night transport/escort service, controlled dormitory access. *Student services:* health clinic, personal/psychological counseling, women's center.

Athletics Member NCAA. All Division III. *Intercollegiate sports:* baseball M, basketball M/W, field hockey W, football M, golf M/W, ice hockey M/W, lacrosse M/W, soccer M/W, softball W, swimming M/W, tennis M/W, volleyball W, water polo W. *Intramural sports:* badminton M/W, baseball M, basketball M/W, bowling M/W, cheerleading W(c), fencing M(c)/W(c), golf M/W, racquetball M/W, soccer M/W, softball W, swimming M/W, table tennis M/W, tennis M/W, volleyball M/W.

Standardized Tests *Recommended:* SAT I or ACT (for admission).

Costs (2003–04) *Comprehensive fee:* $28,340 includes full-time tuition ($19,980), mandatory fees ($290), and room and board ($8070). Full-time tuition and fees vary according to class time, course load, and reciprocity agreements. Part-time tuition: $669 per credit. Part-time tuition and fees vary according to class time, course load, and reciprocity agreements. *College room only:* $4200. Room and board charges vary according to board plan and housing facility. *Waivers:* employees or children of employees.

Financial Aid Of all full-time matriculated undergraduates who enrolled in 2003, 1,833 applied for aid, 1,704 were judged to have need, 289 had their need fully met. 802 Federal Work-Study jobs (averaging $1478). 410 state and other part-time jobs (averaging $1820). In 2003, 26 non-need-based awards were made. *Average need-based loan:* $4107. *Average need-based gift aid:* $12,477. *Average non-need-based aid:* $8038.

Applying *Options:* common application. *Application fee:* $35. *Required:* essay or personal statement, high school transcript, minimum 2.0 GPA. *Required for some:* minimum 3.0 GPA. *Recommended:* letters of recommendation, interview. *Application deadline:* rolling (freshmen), rolling (transfers). *Notification:* continuous (transfers).

Admissions Contact Mr. Patrick Quinn, Vice President for Enrollment Management, Utica College, 1600 Burrstone Road, Utica, NY 13502. *Phone:* 315-792-3006. *Toll-free phone:* 800-782-8884. *Fax:* 315-792-3003. *E-mail:* admiss@utica.edu.

■ *See page 2748 for a narrative description.*

VASSAR COLLEGE

Poughkeepsie, New York

- **Independent** 4-year, founded 1861
- **Calendar** semesters
- **Degrees** bachelor's and master's
- **Suburban** 1000-acre campus with easy access to New York City
- **Endowment** $546.9 million
- **Coed,** 2,444 undergraduate students, 98% full-time, 60% women, 40% men
- **Very difficult** entrance level, 29% of applicants were admitted

Undergraduates 2,395 full-time, 49 part-time. Students come from 53 states and territories, 49 other countries, 72% are from out of state, 5% African American, 9% Asian American or Pacific Islander, 5% Hispanic American, 0.4% Native American, 4% international, 0.7% transferred in, 95% live on campus. *Retention:* 95% of 2002 full-time freshmen returned.

Freshmen *Admission:* 6,207 applied, 1,806 admitted, 632 enrolled. *Average high school GPA:* 3.60. *Test scores:* SAT verbal scores over 500: 100%; SAT math scores over 500: 100%; SAT verbal scores over 600: 96%; SAT math scores over 600: 92%; SAT verbal scores over 700: 50%; SAT math scores over 700: 37%.

Faculty *Total:* 293, 87% full-time, 91% with terminal degrees. *Student/faculty ratio:* 9:1.

Majors African studies; American studies; ancient/classical Greek; anthropology; art history, criticism and conservation; Asian studies; astronomy; biochemistry; biology/biological sciences; chemistry; classics and languages, literatures and linguistics; cognitive psychology and psycholinguistics; computer and information sciences; dramatic/theatre arts; economics; English; environmental science; environmental studies; film/cinema studies; fine/studio arts; French; geography; geology/earth science; German; history; interdisciplinary studies; international relations and affairs; Italian; Jewish/Judaic studies; Latin; Latin American studies; liberal arts and sciences and humanities related; mathematics; medieval and Renaissance studies; multi-/interdisciplinary studies related; music; philosophy; physics; physiological psychology/psychobiology; political science and government; psychology; religious studies; Russian; science, technology and society; sociology; Spanish; urban studies/affairs; visual and performing arts; women's studies.

Academic Programs *Special study options:* advanced placement credit, cooperative education, double majors, independent study, internships, off-campus study, part-time degree program, services for LD students, student-designed majors, study abroad. *Unusual degree programs:* 3-2 engineering with Dartmouth College.

Library Vassar College Libraries plus 1 other with 830,235 titles, 5,028 serial subscriptions, 19,396 audiovisual materials, an OPAC, a Web page.

Computers on Campus 300 computers available on campus for general student use. A campuswide network can be accessed from student residence rooms and from off campus that provide access to Ethernet. Internet access, online (class) registration, at least one staffed computer lab available.

Student Life *Housing:* on-campus residence required for freshman year. *Options:* coed, women-only, cooperative. Campus housing is university owned. Freshman campus housing is guaranteed. *Activities and organizations:* drama/theater group, student-run newspaper, radio and television station, choral group, Student Association, Black Students Union, VICE (programming social events), Student Activists' Union, Poder Latino. *Campus security:* 24-hour emergency response devices and patrols, student patrols, late-night transport/escort service, controlled dormitory access. *Student services:* health clinic, personal/psychological counseling, women's center.

Athletics Member NCAA. All Division III. *Intercollegiate sports:* baseball M, basketball M/W, crew M/W, cross-country running M/W, fencing M/W, field hockey W, lacrosse M/W, rugby M(c)/W(c), sailing M(c)/W(c), soccer M/W, squash M/W, swimming M/W, tennis M/W, track and field M(c)/W(c), volleyball M/W. *Intramural sports:* badminton M(c)/W(c), basketball M/W, bowling M/W, equestrian sports M(c)/W(c), golf M/W, skiing (cross-country) M(c)/W(c), skiing (downhill) M(c)/W(c), soccer M/W, softball M/W, squash M/W, tennis M/W, volleyball M/W, water polo M/W.

Standardized Tests *Required:* SAT I and SAT II or ACT (for admission).

Costs (2003–04) *Comprehensive fee:* $37,030 includes full-time tuition ($29,095), mandatory fees ($445), and room and board ($7490). Part-time tuition: $3430 per course. Part-time tuition and fees vary according to course load. *Required fees:* $220 per year part-time. *College room only:* $3980. Room and board charges vary according to board plan and housing facility. *Payment plan:* installment. *Waivers:* employees or children of employees.

Financial Aid Of all full-time matriculated undergraduates who enrolled in 2003, 1,542 applied for aid, 1,268 were judged to have need, 1,268 had their need fully met. 933 Federal Work-Study jobs (averaging $1682). 282 state and other part-time jobs (averaging $1658). *Average percent of need met:* 100%. *Average financial aid package:* $24,305. *Average need-based loan:* $3009. *Average need-based gift aid:* $19,511. *Average indebtedness upon graduation:* $18,729. *Financial aid deadline:* 2/1.

Applying *Options:* common application, electronic application, early decision, deferred entrance. *Application fee:* $60. *Required:* essay or personal statement, high school transcript, 2 letters of recommendation. *Application deadlines:* 1/1 (freshmen), 4/1 (transfers). *Early decision:* 11/15 (for plan 1), 1/1 (for plan 2). *Notification:* 4/1 (freshmen), 12/15 (early decision plan 1), 2/1 (early decision plan 2), 5/10 (transfers).

Admissions Contact Dr. David M. Borus, Dean of Admission and Financial Aid, Vassar College, 124 Raymond Avenue, Poughkeepsie, NY 12604. *Phone:* 845-437-7300. *Toll-free phone:* 800-827-7270. *Fax:* 914-437-7063. *E-mail:* admissions@vassar.edu.

■ *See page 2756 for a narrative description.*

WAGNER COLLEGE

Staten Island, New York

- **Independent** comprehensive, founded 1883
- **Calendar** semesters
- **Degrees** bachelor's and master's
- **Urban** 105-acre campus with easy access to New York City
- **Endowment** $9.0 million
- **Coed,** 1,826 undergraduate students, 97% full-time, 60% women, 40% men
- **Moderately difficult** entrance level, 50% of applicants were admitted

Undergraduates 1,780 full-time, 46 part-time. Students come from 38 states and territories, 14 other countries, 48% are from out of state, 5% African American, 2% Asian American or Pacific Islander, 5% Hispanic American, 0.1% Native American, 2% international, 3% transferred in, 70% live on campus. *Retention:* 85% of 2002 full-time freshmen returned.

Freshmen *Admission:* 2,425 applied, 1,209 admitted, 540 enrolled. *Average high school GPA:* 3.50. *Test scores:* SAT verbal scores over 500: 79%; SAT math scores over 500: 78%; ACT scores over 18: 100%; SAT verbal scores over 600: 24%; SAT math scores over 600: 25%; ACT scores over 24: 58%; SAT verbal scores over 700: 3%; SAT math scores over 700: 4%; ACT scores over 30: 2%.

Faculty *Total:* 188, 51% full-time. *Student/faculty ratio:* 16:1.

Majors Accounting; anthropology; art; arts management; biology/biological sciences; business administration and management; chemistry; computer science; dramatic/theatre arts; education; elementary education; English; finance; gerontology; history; kindergarten/preschool education; mathematics; medical microbiology and bacteriology; middle school education; music; nursing (registered nurse training); physician assistant; physics; physiological psychology/psychobiology; political science and government; pre-dentistry studies; pre-law studies; pre-medical studies; psychology; public administration; secondary education; sociology; Spanish; veterinary sciences.

Academic Programs *Special study options:* academic remediation for entering students, accelerated degree program, advanced placement credit, double majors, English as a second language, honors programs, internships, off-campus study, part-time degree program, services for LD students, student-designed majors, study abroad, summer session for credit. *ROTC:* Army (c), Air Force (c).

Library August Horrmann Library with 310,000 titles, 1,000 serial subscriptions, a Web page.

Computers on Campus 150 computers available on campus for general student use. A campuswide network can be accessed from student residence rooms and from off campus. Internet access, at least one staffed computer lab available.

Student Life *Housing options:* coed. Freshman campus housing is guaranteed. *Activities and organizations:* drama/theater group, student-run newspaper, radio station, choral group, Student Government Association, Student Activities Board, Wagner College Theatre, Wagner College Choir, student newspaper, national fraternities, national sororities. *Campus security:* 24-hour emergency response devices and patrols, late-night transport/escort service, controlled dormitory access. *Student services:* health clinic, personal/psychological counseling.

Athletics Member NCAA. All Division I except football (Division I-AA). *Intercollegiate sports:* baseball M(s), basketball M(s)/W(s), cross-country running M(s)/W(s), golf M(s)/W(s), ice hockey M(c), lacrosse M(s)/W(s), soccer W(s), softball W(s), swimming W(s), tennis M(s)/W(s), track and field M(s)/W(s), volleyball W(s), water polo W(s), wrestling M(s). *Intramural sports:* basketball M/W, bowling M/W, football M, racquetball M/W, rugby M, soccer M/W, softball M/W, tennis M/W, volleyball M/W.

Standardized Tests *Required:* SAT I or ACT (for admission). *Required for some:* SAT II: Subject Tests (for admission). *Recommended:* SAT II: Subject Tests (for admission), SAT II: Writing Test (for admission).

Costs (2004–05) *Comprehensive fee:* $31,400 includes full-time tuition ($23,900) and room and board ($7500). Part-time tuition: $2650 per course.

Financial Aid Of all full-time matriculated undergraduates who enrolled in 2003, 1,341 applied for aid, 1,125 were judged to have need, 277 had their need fully met. 670 Federal Work-Study jobs (averaging $1176). In 2003, 471 non-need-based awards were made. *Average percent of need met:* 73%. *Average financial aid package:* $14,768. *Average need-based loan:* $4542. *Average need-based gift aid:* $10,955. *Average non-need-based aid:* $7439. *Average indebtedness upon graduation:* $23,144.

Applying *Options:* common application, electronic application, early admission, early decision, deferred entrance. *Application fee:* $50. *Required:* essay or personal statement, high school transcript, minimum 2.7 GPA, 2 letters of recommendation. *Required for some:* interview. *Recommended:* minimum 3.0 GPA, interview. *Application deadlines:* 2/15 (freshmen), 5/1 (transfers). *Early decision:* 12/1. *Notification:* 3/1 (freshmen), 1/1 (early decision), 6/1 (transfers).

Admissions Contact Mr. Angelo Araimo, Vice President for Enrollment, Wagner College, One Campus Road, Staten Island, NY 10301. *Phone:* 718-390-3411 Ext. 3412. *Toll-free phone:* 800-221-1010. *Fax:* 718-390-3105. *E-mail:* admissions@wagner.edu.

■ *See page 2776 for a narrative description.*

WEBB INSTITUTE

Glen Cove, New York

- **Independent** 4-year, founded 1889
- **Calendar** semesters
- **Degree** bachelor's
- **Suburban** 26-acre campus with easy access to New York City
- **Endowment** $44.6 million
- **Coed,** 72 undergraduate students, 100% full-time, 21% women, 79% men
- **Most difficult** entrance level, 31% of applicants were admitted

Webb Institute is a private engineering college, where all undergraduate students receive a full tuition scholarship. BS degrees in naval architecture and marine engineering are offered. There is a cooperative work term in each year and a 100% employment record. Competitive selection of students is based on academic record, standardized test scores, and motivation for the program. The Institute's programs are fully accredited.

Undergraduates 72 full-time. Students come from 20 states and territories, 68% are from out of state, 1% African American, 3% Asian American or Pacific Islander, 100% live on campus. *Retention:* 95% of 2002 full-time freshmen returned.

Freshmen *Admission:* 106 applied, 33 admitted, 26 enrolled. *Average high school GPA:* 3.90. *Test scores:* SAT verbal scores over 500: 100%; SAT math scores over 500: 100%; SAT verbal scores over 600: 88%; SAT math scores over 600: 100%; SAT verbal scores over 700: 38%; SAT math scores over 700: 85%.

Faculty *Total:* 15, 53% full-time, 73% with terminal degrees. *Student/faculty ratio:* 7:1.

Majors Naval architecture and marine engineering.

Academic Programs *Special study options:* cooperative education, double majors, independent study, internships, off-campus study.

Library Livingston Library with 43,104 titles, 262 serial subscriptions, 1,860 audiovisual materials, an OPAC, a Web page.

Computers on Campus 75 computers available on campus for general student use. A campuswide network can be accessed from student residence rooms and from off campus. Internet access available.

Student Life *Housing:* on-campus residence required through senior year. *Options:* coed, men-only, women-only. Campus housing is university owned. Freshman campus housing is guaranteed. *Activities and organizations:* drama/theater group, student-run newspaper, choral group, Student Organization, Society of Naval Architects and Marine Engineers, American Society of Naval Engineers, Society of Women Engineers. *Campus security:* 24-hour emergency response devices and patrols, controlled dormitory access. *Student services:* personal/psychological counseling.

Athletics *Intercollegiate sports:* basketball M/W, cross-country running M/W, sailing M/W, soccer M/W, tennis M/W, volleyball M/W. *Intramural sports:* baseball M/W, ultimate Frisbee M/W, volleyball M/W.

Standardized Tests *Required:* SAT I (for admission), SAT II: Writing Test (for admission), SAT II Subject Tests in math and either physics or chemistry (for admission).

Costs (2004–05) *Comprehensive fee:* includes room and board ($7550). All students are awarded full tuition scholarships.

Financial Aid Of all full-time matriculated undergraduates who enrolled in 2003, 11 applied for aid, 11 were judged to have need, 1 had their need fully met. *Average percent of need met:* 90%. *Average financial aid package:* $4650. *Average need-based loan:* $4230. *Average need-based gift aid:* $1850. *Average indebtedness upon graduation:* $14,450.

Applying *Options:* early decision. *Application fee:* $25. *Required:* high school transcript, minimum 3.5 GPA, 2 letters of recommendation, interview, proof of U.S. citizenship. *Application deadlines:* 2/15 (freshmen), 2/15 (transfers). *Early decision:* 10/15. *Notification:* continuous until 4/30 (freshmen), 12/15 (early decision), continuous until 4/30 (transfers).

Admissions Contact Mr. William G. Murray, Executive Director of Student Administrative Services, Webb Institute, Crescent Beach Road, Glen Cove, NY 11542-1398. *Phone:* 516-671-2213. *Fax:* 516-674-9838. *E-mail:* admissions@webb-institute.edu.

■ *See page 2794 for a narrative description.*

WELLS COLLEGE
Aurora, New York

- **Independent** 4-year, founded 1868
- **Calendar** semesters
- **Degree** bachelor's
- **Rural** 365-acre campus with easy access to Syracuse
- **Endowment** $53.9 million
- **Women only,** 420 undergraduate students, 95% full-time
- **Moderately difficult** entrance level, 84% of applicants were admitted

Wells College believes that the 21st century needs women who have the ability, self-confidence, and vision to contribute to an ever-changing world. Wells offers an outstanding classroom experience and an innovative liberal arts curriculum that prepare students for leadership in a variety of fields, including business, government, the arts, sciences, medicine, and education. By directly connecting the liberal arts curriculum to experience and career development through internships, off-campus study, study abroad, research with professors, and community service, each student is prepared both for graduate and professional school as well as for life in the 21st century.

Undergraduates 398 full-time, 22 part-time. Students come from 35 states and territories, 6 other countries, 31% are from out of state, 6% African American, 4% Asian American or Pacific Islander, 3% Hispanic American, 0.3% Native American, 2% international, 8% transferred in, 80% live on campus. *Retention:* 78% of 2002 full-time freshmen returned.

Freshmen *Admission:* 410 applied, 345 admitted, 100 enrolled. *Average high school GPA:* 3.50. *Test scores:* SAT verbal scores over 500: 83%; SAT math scores over 500: 67%; ACT scores over 18: 95%; SAT verbal scores over 600: 43%; SAT math scores over 600: 27%; ACT scores over 24: 54%; SAT verbal scores over 700: 4%; SAT math scores over 700: 1%; ACT scores over 30: 11%.

Faculty *Total:* 66, 73% full-time, 83% with terminal degrees. *Student/faculty ratio:* 8:1.

Majors African-American/Black studies; American studies; anthropology; art; art history, criticism and conservation; biochemistry; biology/biological sciences; business administration and management; chemistry; computer science; creative writing; dance; dramatic/theatre arts; economics; education; elementary education; engineering; English; environmental studies; fine/studio arts; French; history; international relations and affairs; mathematics; molecular biology; music; philosophy; physics; political science and government; pre-dentistry studies; pre-law studies; pre-medical studies; pre-veterinary studies; psychology; public policy analysis; religious studies; secondary education; sociology; Spanish; women's studies.

Academic Programs *Special study options:* accelerated degree program, adult/continuing education programs, advanced placement credit, double majors, English as a second language, independent study, internships, off-campus study, part-time degree program, services for LD students, student-designed majors, study abroad. *ROTC:* Air Force (c). *Unusual degree programs:* 3-2 business administration with University of Rochester; engineering with Columbia University, Clarkson University, Cornell University, Case Western Reserve University; community health with University of Rochester.

Library Louis Jefferson Long Library with 250,893 titles, 407 serial subscriptions, 924 audiovisual materials, an OPAC, a Web page.

Computers on Campus 89 computers available on campus for general student use. A campuswide network can be accessed from student residence rooms and from off campus. Internet access, at least one staffed computer lab available.

Student Life *Housing:* on-campus residence required through senior year. *Options:* women-only. Campus housing is university owned. Freshman campus housing is guaranteed. *Activities and organizations:* drama/theater group, student-run newspaper, choral group, creative and performing arts groups, POWER, Amnesty International, Athletic Association, choral groups. *Campus security:* 24-hour emergency response devices and patrols, late-night transport/escort service, controlled dormitory access. *Student services:* health clinic, personal/psychological counseling, women's center.

Athletics Member NCAA. All Division III. *Intercollegiate sports:* field hockey W, lacrosse W, soccer W, softball W, swimming W, tennis W. *Intramural sports:* basketball W, field hockey W, football W, golf W, rugby W, sailing W, skiing (cross-country) W, skiing (downhill) W, soccer W, tennis W, volleyball W.

Standardized Tests *Required:* SAT I or ACT (for admission).

Costs (2003–04) *Comprehensive fee:* $21,122 includes full-time tuition ($13,592), mandatory fees ($700), and room and board ($6830). Part-time tuition: $570 per credit hour. *College room only:* $3415. *Payment plan:* installment. *Waivers:* children of alumni, senior citizens, and employees or children of employees.

Financial Aid Of all full-time matriculated undergraduates who enrolled in 2003, 344 applied for aid, 302 were judged to have need, 109 had their need fully met. 78 Federal Work-Study jobs (averaging $1400). 222 state and other part-time jobs (averaging $1400). In 2003, 48 non-need-based awards were made. *Average percent of need met:* 91%. *Average financial aid package:* $15,475. *Average need-based loan:* $4775. *Average need-based gift aid:* $10,235. *Average non-need-based aid:* $4756. *Average indebtedness upon graduation:* $17,125.

Applying *Options:* common application, electronic application, early admission, early decision, early action, deferred entrance. *Application fee:* $40. *Required:* essay or personal statement, high school transcript, 2 letters of recommendation. *Recommended:* interview. *Application deadline:* 3/1 (freshmen), rolling (transfers). *Early decision:* 12/15. *Notification:* 4/1 (freshmen), 1/15 (early decision), 2/1 (early action), continuous (transfers).

Admissions Contact Ms. Susan Raith Sloan, Director of Admissions, Wells College, 170 Main Street, Aurora, NY 13026. *Phone:* 315-364-3264. *Toll-free phone:* 800-952-9355. *Fax:* 315-364-3227. *E-mail:* admissions@wells.edu

■ *See page 2798 for a narrative description.*

YESHIVA AND KOLEL BAIS MEDRASH ELYON
Monsey, New York

Admissions Contact 73 Main Street, Monsey, NY 10952.

YESHIVA AND KOLLEL HARBOTZAS TORAH
Brooklyn, New York

Admissions Contact 1049 East 15th Street, Brooklyn, NY 11230.

YESHIVA DERECH CHAIM
Brooklyn, New York

Admissions Contact Mr. Y. Borchardt, Administrator, Yeshiva Derech Chaim, 4907 18th Avenue, Brooklyn, NY 11218. *Phone:* 718-438-5476.

YESHIVA D'MONSEY RABBINICAL COLLEGE
Monsey, New York

Admissions Contact 2 Roman Boulevard, Monsey, NY 10952.

YESHIVA GEDOLAH IMREI YOSEF D'SPINKA
Brooklyn, New York

Admissions Contact 1466 56th Street, Brooklyn, NY 11219.

YESHIVA KARLIN STOLIN RABBINICAL INSTITUTE
Brooklyn, New York

Admissions Contact Mr. Aryeh L. Wolpin, Director of Admissions, Yeshiva Karlin Stolin Rabbinical Institute, 1818 Fifty-fourth Street, Brooklyn, NY 11204. *Phone:* 718-232-7800 Ext. 26. *Fax:* 718-331-4833.

YESHIVA OF NITRA RABBINICAL COLLEGE
Mount Kisco, New York

Admissions Contact Mr. Ernest Schwartz, Administrator, Yeshiva of Nitra Rabbinical College, Pines Bridge Road, Mount Kisco, NY 10549. *Phone:* 718-384-5460.

YESHIVA OF THE TELSHE ALUMNI
Riverdale, New York

Admissions Contact 4904 Independence Avenue, Riverdale, NY 10471.

YESHIVA SHAAREI TORAH OF ROCKLAND
Suffern, New York

Admissions Contact 91 West Carlton Road, Suffern, NY 10901.

YESHIVA SHAAR HATORAH TALMUDIC RESEARCH INSTITUTE
Kew Gardens, New York

Admissions Contact Rabbi Kalman Epstein, Assistant Dean, Yeshiva Shaar Hatorah Talmudic Research Institute, 83-96 117th Street, Kew Gardens, NY 11418-1469. *Phone:* 718-846-1940.

YESHIVAS NOVOMINSK
Brooklyn, New York

Admissions Contact Yeshivas Novominsk, 1569 47th Street, Brooklyn, NY 11219.

YESHIVATH VIZNITZ
Monsey, New York

Admissions Contact Rabbi Bernard Rosenfeld, Registrar, Yeshivath Viznitz, Phyllis Terrace, PO Box 446, Monsey, NY 10952. *Phone:* 914-356-1010.

YESHIVATH ZICHRON MOSHE
South Fallsburg, New York

Admissions Contact Rabbi Abba Gorelick, Dean, Yeshivath Zichron Moshe, Laurel Park Road, South Fallsburg, NY 12779. *Phone:* 914-434-5240.

YESHIVAT MIKDASH MELECH
Brooklyn, New York

Admissions Contact Rabbi S. Churba, Director of Admissions, Yeshivat Mikdash Melech, 1326 Ocean Parkway, Brooklyn, NY 11230-5601. *Phone:* 718-339-1090.

YESHIVA UNIVERSITY
New York, New York

Admissions Contact Mr. Michael Kranzler, Director of Undergraduate Admissions, Yeshiva University, 500 West 185th Street, New York, NY 10033-3201. *Phone:* 212-960-5277. *Fax:* 212-960-0086. *E-mail:* yuadmit@ymail.yu.edu.

YORK COLLEGE OF THE CITY UNIVERSITY OF NEW YORK
Jamaica, New York

- **State and locally supported** 4-year, founded 1967, part of City University of New York System
- **Calendar** semesters
- **Degree** bachelor's
- **Urban** 50-acre campus with easy access to New York City
- **Coed,** 5,672 undergraduate students, 60% full-time, 70% women, 30% men
- **Moderately difficult** entrance level, 31% of applicants were admitted

Undergraduates 3,416 full-time, 2,256 part-time. Students come from 4 states and territories, 100 other countries, 0.1% are from out of state, 58% African American, 11% Asian American or Pacific Islander, 16% Hispanic American, 0.4% Native American, 7% international, 12% transferred in. *Retention:* 88% of 2002 full-time freshmen returned.

Freshmen *Admission:* 2,389 applied, 738 admitted, 599 enrolled. *Test scores:* SAT verbal scores over 500: 14%; SAT math scores over 500: 16%; SAT verbal scores over 600: 1%; SAT math scores over 600: 2%.

Faculty *Total:* 400, 40% full-time, 54% with terminal degrees. *Student/faculty ratio:* 15:1.

Majors Accounting; African-American/Black studies; anthropology; art; biology/biological sciences; biology/biotechnology laboratory technician; business administration and management; chemistry; clinical laboratory science/medical technology; computer management; dramatic/theatre arts; economics; English; environmental health; French; geology/earth science; gerontology; health teacher education; history; information science/studies; Italian; liberal arts and sciences/liberal studies; marketing/marketing management; mathematics; music; nursing (registered nurse training); occupational therapy; philosophy; physical education teaching and coaching; physics; political science and government; psychology; social work; sociology; Spanish; speech and rhetoric.

Academic Programs *Special study options:* adult/continuing education programs, advanced placement credit, cooperative education, double majors, English as a second language, honors programs, independent study, internships, off-campus study, part-time degree program, services for LD students, summer session for credit. *ROTC:* Army (c), Air Force (c).

Library 178,047 titles, 1,121 serial subscriptions, an OPAC, a Web page.

Computers on Campus 530 computers available on campus for general student use. A campuswide network can be accessed from off campus. At least one staffed computer lab available.

Student Life *Housing:* college housing not available. *Activities and organizations:* drama/theater group, student-run newspaper, television station, choral group, Haitian Students Association, Caribbean Students Association, Haitian Cultural Association, Latin Caucus. *Campus security:* 24-hour emergency response devices and patrols, late-night transport/escort service. *Student services:* health clinic, personal/psychological counseling, women's center.

Athletics Member NCAA. All Division III. *Intercollegiate sports:* baseball M/W, basketball M/W, crew M/W, cross-country running M/W, equestrian sports M/W, soccer M/W, softball W, swimming M/W, tennis M/W, track and field M/W, volleyball M/W, weight lifting M/W. *Intramural sports:* basketball M/W, soccer M/W, softball W, swimming M/W, table tennis M/W, tennis M/W, track and field M/W, volleyball M/W, weight lifting M/W.

Standardized Tests *Required:* SAT I or ACT (for admission).

Costs (2004–05) *Tuition:* state resident $4000 full-time; nonresident $8640 full-time. *Required fees:* $242 full-time. *Payment plan:* deferred payment. *Waivers:* senior citizens and employees or children of employees.

Applying *Options:* deferred entrance. *Application fee:* $40. *Required:* high school transcript, minimum 2.0 GPA. *Required for some:* minimum 2.5 GPA. *Recommended:* minimum 3.0 GPA. *Application deadline:* rolling (freshmen), rolling (transfers). *Notification:* continuous (freshmen), continuous (transfers).

Admissions Contact Ms. Sally Nelson, Director of Admissions, York College of the City University of New York, 94-20 Guy R. Brewer Boulevard, Jamaica, NY 11451. *Phone:* 718-262-2165. *Fax:* 718-262-2601.

■ *See page 2884 for a narrative description.*

NORTH CAROLINA

APEX SCHOOL OF THEOLOGY
Durham, North Carolina

- **Independent interdenominational** comprehensive, founded 1995
- **Calendar** semesters
- **Degrees** bachelor's and master's
- **Suburban** campus
- **Coed,** 36 undergraduate students, 28% full-time, 58% women, 42% men
- 75% of applicants were admitted

Undergraduates 10 full-time, 26 part-time. 97% African American. *Retention:* 100% of 2002 full-time freshmen returned.

Freshmen *Admission:* 8 applied, 6 admitted.

Faculty *Total:* 15, 20% full-time, 47% with terminal degrees. *Student/faculty ratio:* 2:1.

Majors Religious education; theology.

Costs (2004–05) *Tuition:* $825 full-time, $325 per course part-time. *Required fees:* $100 full-time.

Admissions Contact Dr. Joseph E. Perkins, President, Apex School of Theology, 5104 Revere Road, Durham, NC 27713. *Phone:* 919-572-1625.

APPALACHIAN STATE UNIVERSITY
Boone, North Carolina

- **State-supported** comprehensive, founded 1899, part of University of North Carolina System
- **Calendar** semesters
- **Degrees** bachelor's, master's, doctoral, and post-master's certificates
- **Small-town** 340-acre campus
- **Endowment** $40.7 million
- **Coed,** 12,934 undergraduate students, 91% full-time, 51% women, 49% men
- **Moderately difficult** entrance level, 66% of applicants were admitted

Undergraduates 11,833 full-time, 1,101 part-time. Students come from 46 states and territories, 11% are from out of state, 3% African American, 1% Asian American or Pacific Islander, 1% Hispanic American, 0.4% Native American, 0.3% international, 6% transferred in, 36% live on campus. *Retention:* 83% of 2002 full-time freshmen returned.

Appalachian State University (continued)

Freshmen *Admission:* 9,598 applied, 6,293 admitted, 2,473 enrolled. *Average high school GPA:* 3.65. *Test scores:* SAT verbal scores over 500: 74%; SAT math scores over 500: 79%; ACT scores over 18: 89%; SAT verbal scores over 600: 23%; SAT math scores over 600: 27%; ACT scores over 24: 30%; SAT verbal scores over 700: 3%; SAT math scores over 700: 2%; ACT scores over 30: 2%.

Faculty *Total:* 934, 71% full-time, 63% with terminal degrees. *Student/faculty ratio:* 17:1.

Majors Accounting; advertising; anthropology; apparel and textiles; art; arts management; art teacher education; athletic training; audiology and speech-language pathology; biology/biological sciences; biology teacher education; business administration and management; business teacher education; chemistry; chemistry teacher education; child development; city/urban, community and regional planning; clinical laboratory science/medical technology; communication disorders; computer science; criminal justice/safety; drama and dance teacher education; dramatic/theatre arts; ecology; economics; education (specific subject areas) related; electrical, electronic and communications engineering technology; elementary education; English; English/language arts teacher education; family and consumer sciences/home economics teacher education; finance; fine/studio arts; foods, nutrition, and wellness; French; French language teacher education; geography; geology/earth science; gerontology; graphic and printing equipment operation/production; graphic design; health/health care administration; health teacher education; history; history teacher education; hospitality administration; industrial design; industrial production technologies related; industrial technology; insurance; international business/trade/commerce; journalism; kindergarten/preschool education; kinesiology and exercise science; liberal arts and sciences/liberal studies; library science; management information systems; marketing/marketing management; mathematics; mathematics teacher education; middle school education; music management and merchandising; music performance; music teacher education; music therapy; parks, recreation and leisure facilities management; philosophy and religious studies related; physical education teaching and coaching; physics; physics teacher education; political science and government; psychology; public health education and promotion; public relations/image management; radio and television; social studies teacher education; social work; sociology; Spanish; Spanish language teacher education; special education (specific learning disabilities); speech and rhetoric; statistics; technology/industrial arts teacher education.

Academic Programs *Special study options:* academic remediation for entering students, accelerated degree program, adult/continuing education programs, advanced placement credit, distance learning, double majors, English as a second language, honors programs, independent study, internships, off-campus study, part-time degree program, services for LD students, student-designed majors, study abroad, summer session for credit. *ROTC:* Army (b). *Unusual degree programs:* 3-2 engineering with Auburn University; forestry with North Carolina State University.

Library Carol Grotnes Belk Library plus 1 other with 533,391 titles, 5,313 serial subscriptions, 75,571 audiovisual materials, an OPAC, a Web page.

Computers on Campus 500 computers available on campus for general student use. A campuswide network can be accessed from student residence rooms. Internet access, at least one staffed computer lab available.

Student Life *Housing:* on-campus residence required for freshman year. *Options:* coed, men-only, women-only, cooperative, disabled students. Campus housing is university owned. Freshman campus housing is guaranteed. *Activities and organizations:* drama/theater group, student-run newspaper, radio and television station, choral group, marching band, Baptist Student Union, Inter-University Christian Fellowship, Campus Crusade for Christ, Circle K, Criminal Justice Association, national fraternities, national sororities. *Campus security:* 24-hour emergency response devices and patrols, late-night transport/escort service, controlled dormitory access. *Student services:* health clinic, personal/psychological counseling, women's center, legal services.

Athletics Member NCAA, NAIA. All NCAA Division I except football (Division I-AA). *Intercollegiate sports:* baseball M(s), basketball M(s)/W(s), cross-country running M(s)/W(s), field hockey W(s), golf M(s)/W(s), soccer M(s)/W(s), tennis M(s)/W(s), track and field M(s)/W(s), volleyball W(s), wrestling M(s). *Intramural sports:* archery M/W, badminton M/W, basketball M/W, bowling M/W, cross-country running M/W, fencing M/W, field hockey W, football M/W, golf M/W, gymnastics M/W, racquetball M/W, rugby M, skiing (cross-country) M/W, skiing (downhill) M/W, soccer M/W, squash M/W, swimming M/W, table tennis M/W, tennis M/W, track and field M/W, volleyball M/W, water polo M/W, weight lifting M/W, wrestling M.

Standardized Tests *Required:* SAT I or ACT (for admission).

Costs (2003–04) *Tuition:* state resident $1596 full-time; nonresident $10,963 full-time. Part-time tuition and fees vary according to course load. *Required fees:* $1331 full-time. *Room and board:* $4435; room only: $2770. Room and board charges vary according to board plan and housing facility. *Payment plan:* installment. *Waivers:* employees or children of employees.

Financial Aid Of all full-time matriculated undergraduates who enrolled in 2003, 6,939 applied for aid, 4,165 were judged to have need, 1,571 had their need fully met. 431 Federal Work-Study jobs (averaging $1800). In 2003, 1085 non-need-based awards were made. *Average percent of need met:* 76%. *Average financial aid package:* $5778. *Average need-based loan:* $3328. *Average need-based gift aid:* $3399. *Average non-need-based aid:* $2751. *Average indebtedness upon graduation:* $14,000.

Applying *Options:* common application, early admission, deferred entrance. *Application fee:* $45. *Required:* high school transcript. *Application deadline:* rolling (freshmen), rolling (transfers). *Notification:* continuous (freshmen), continuous (transfers).

Admissions Contact Mr. Joe Watts, Associate Vice Chancellor, Appalachian State University, Boone, NC 28608. *Phone:* 828-262-2120. *Fax:* 828-262-3296. *E-mail:* admissions@appstate.edu.

BARBER-SCOTIA COLLEGE

Concord, North Carolina

- **Independent** 4-year, founded 1867, affiliated with Presbyterian Church (U.S.A.)
- **Calendar** semesters
- **Degree** bachelor's
- **Small-town** 23-acre campus with easy access to Charlotte
- **Endowment** $4.3 million
- **Coed,** 742 undergraduate students, 99% full-time, 43% women, 57% men
- **Minimally difficult** entrance level, 70% of applicants were admitted

Undergraduates 737 full-time, 5 part-time. Students come from 20 states and territories, 32% are from out of state, 86% African American, 0.4% Hispanic American, 12% international, 10% transferred in, 90% live on campus. *Retention:* 62% of 2002 full-time freshmen returned.

Freshmen *Admission:* 1,502 applied, 1,058 admitted, 294 enrolled. *Average high school GPA:* 2.00.

Faculty *Total:* 42, 81% full-time, 48% with terminal degrees. *Student/faculty ratio:* 19:1.

Majors Accounting; biology/biological sciences; business administration and management; computer science; criminal justice/law enforcement administration; elementary education; English; finance; hotel/motel administration; marketing/marketing management; mass communication/media; mathematics; political science and government; pre-law studies; sociology; sport and fitness administration.

Academic Programs *Special study options:* academic remediation for entering students, advanced placement credit, cooperative education, double majors, honors programs, internships, off-campus study, summer session for credit. *ROTC:* Army (c), Air Force (b). *Unusual degree programs:* 3-2 nursing with University of North Carolina at Charlotte; law with St. John's University.

Library Sage Memorial Library with 24,270 titles, 193 serial subscriptions.

Computers on Campus 125 computers available on campus for general student use. A campuswide network can be accessed from off campus. Internet access, at least one staffed computer lab available.

Student Life *Housing:* on-campus residence required through senior year. *Options:* Campus housing is university owned. *Activities and organizations:* drama/theater group, student-run newspaper, choral group, SGA (Student Government Association), Student Christian Association, Pre-Alumni Council, Scotia Express, yearbook, national fraternities, national sororities. *Campus security:* 24-hour emergency response devices and patrols. *Student services:* health clinic, personal/psychological counseling.

Athletics Member NAIA. *Intercollegiate sports:* basketball M(s)/W(s), cross-country running M(s)/W(s), softball W(s), tennis M(s), track and field M(s)/W(s), volleyball W(s). *Intramural sports:* basketball M/W, football M, golf M, tennis M.

Standardized Tests *Required:* SAT I or ACT (for admission).

Costs (2004–05) *Comprehensive fee:* $15,070 includes full-time tuition ($8970), mandatory fees ($1648), and room and board ($4452). Full-time tuition and fees vary according to course load. Part-time tuition: $374 per credit. Part-time tuition and fees vary according to course load. *Payment plan:* installment. *Waivers:* employees or children of employees.

Applying *Options:* common application, electronic application, early admission. *Application fee:* $15. *Required:* high school transcript, letters of recommendation. *Required for some:* minimum 2.0 GPA. *Recommended:* essay or personal statement, minimum 3.0 GPA, interview. *Application deadline:* rolling (freshmen), rolling (transfers). *Notification:* continuous (freshmen), continuous (transfers).

Admissions Contact Dr. Alexander Erwin, Academic Dean, Barber-Scotia College, 145 Cabarrus Avenue, West, Concord, NC 28025-5187. *Phone:* 704-789-2948. *Toll-free phone:* 800-610-0778. *Fax:* 704-784-3817.

BARTON COLLEGE
Wilson, North Carolina

- **Independent** 4-year, founded 1902, affiliated with Christian Church (Disciples of Christ)
- **Calendar** 4-1-4
- **Degree** bachelor's
- **Small-town** 62-acre campus with easy access to Raleigh-Durham, NC
- **Endowment** $17.0 million
- **Coed,** 1,188 undergraduate students, 80% full-time, 71% women, 29% men
- **Minimally difficult** entrance level, 74% of applicants were admitted

Undergraduates 949 full-time, 239 part-time. Students come from 30 states and territories, 16 other countries, 24% are from out of state, 20% African American, 0.9% Asian American or Pacific Islander, 1% Hispanic American, 0.4% Native American, 2% international, 12% transferred in, 40% live on campus. *Retention:* 63% of 2002 full-time freshmen returned.

Freshmen *Admission:* 930 applied, 692 admitted, 249 enrolled. *Average high school GPA:* 2.94. *Test scores:* SAT verbal scores over 500: 40%; SAT math scores over 500: 44%; SAT verbal scores over 600: 5%; SAT math scores over 600: 9%; SAT math scores over 700: 2%.

Faculty *Total:* 104, 77% full-time, 38% with terminal degrees. *Student/faculty ratio:* 12:1.

Majors Accounting; art teacher education; athletic training; biology/biological sciences; business administration and management; chemistry; computer and information sciences; criminal justice/law enforcement administration; dramatic/theatre arts; economics; elementary education; English; environmental studies; fine/studio arts; history; human resources management; liberal arts and sciences and humanities related; marketing/marketing management; mass communication/media; mathematics; middle school education; musical instrument fabrication and repair; nursing (registered nurse training); philosophy and religious studies related; physical education teaching and coaching; political science and government; psychology; social work; Spanish; special education; special education (hearing impaired); sport and fitness administration.

Academic Programs *Special study options:* academic remediation for entering students, adult/continuing education programs, advanced placement credit, cooperative education, double majors, independent study, internships, part-time degree program, services for LD students, study abroad, summer session for credit. *Unusual degree programs:* 3-2 engineering with North Carolina State University, North Carolina Agricultural and Technical State University.

Library Willis N. Hackney Library with 336,836 titles, 437 serial subscriptions, 3,445 audiovisual materials, an OPAC, a Web page.

Computers on Campus 125 computers available on campus for general student use. A campuswide network can be accessed from student residence rooms and from off campus that provide access to online class schedules and student picture directory. Internet access, at least one staffed computer lab available.

Student Life *Housing:* on-campus residence required through sophomore year. *Options:* coed, women-only. Campus housing is university owned. Freshman campus housing is guaranteed. *Activities and organizations:* drama/theater group, student-run newspaper, television station, choral group, Barton College Association of Nurses, Students in Free Enterprise, Stage and Script, Campus Activities Board, College Habitat for Humanity, national fraternities, national sororities. *Campus security:* 24-hour emergency response devices, late-night transport/escort service, controlled dormitory access, city police substation on campus. *Student services:* health clinic, personal/psychological counseling.

Athletics Member NCAA. All Division II. *Intercollegiate sports:* baseball M(s), basketball M(s)/W(s), cheerleading W, cross-country running M(s)/W(s), golf M(s), soccer M(s)/W(s), softball W(s), tennis M(s)/W(s), volleyball W(s). *Intramural sports:* badminton M/W, basketball M/W, bowling M/W, football M/W, golf M/W, racquetball M/W, soccer M/W, softball M/W, tennis M/W, volleyball M/W.

Standardized Tests *Required:* SAT I or ACT (for admission).

Costs (2003–04) *Comprehensive fee:* $19,314 includes full-time tuition ($13,368), mandatory fees ($910), and room and board ($5036). Full-time tuition and fees vary according to course load. Part-time tuition: $525 per hour. Part-time tuition and fees vary according to course load and program. *College room only:* $2408. Room and board charges vary according to housing facility. *Payment plan:* installment. *Waivers:* children of alumni, adult students, senior citizens, and employees or children of employees.

Financial Aid Of all full-time matriculated undergraduates who enrolled in 2003, 707 applied for aid, 642 were judged to have need, 125 had their need fully met. 430 Federal Work-Study jobs (averaging $1113). In 2003, 224 non-need-based awards were made. *Average percent of need met:* 76%. *Average financial aid package:* $13,185. *Average need-based loan:* $4120. *Average need-based gift aid:* $4634. *Average non-need-based aid:* $3482. *Average indebtedness upon graduation:* $17,110.

Applying *Options:* electronic application, deferred entrance. *Application fee:* $25. *Required:* high school transcript. *Recommended:* minimum 2.5 GPA, interview. *Application deadline:* rolling (freshmen), rolling (transfers).

Admissions Contact Ms. Amy Denton, Director of Admissions, Barton College, Box 5000, College Station, Wilson, NC 27893. *Phone:* 252-399-6314. *Toll-free phone:* 800-345-4973. *Fax:* 252-399-6572. *E-mail:* enroll@barton.edu.

■ *See page 1216 for a narrative description.*

BELMONT ABBEY COLLEGE
Belmont, North Carolina

- **Independent Roman Catholic** 4-year, founded 1876
- **Calendar** semesters
- **Degree** bachelor's
- **Small-town** 650-acre campus with easy access to Charlotte
- **Endowment** $14.2 million
- **Coed,** 863 undergraduate students, 89% full-time, 60% women, 40% men
- **Moderately difficult** entrance level, 69% of applicants were admitted

Undergraduates 765 full-time, 98 part-time. Students come from 33 states and territories, 21 other countries, 11% African American, 0.8% Asian American or Pacific Islander, 4% Hispanic American, 0.1% Native American, 5% international, 15% transferred in, 49% live on campus. *Retention:* 60% of 2002 full-time freshmen returned.

Freshmen *Admission:* 811 applied, 558 admitted, 147 enrolled. *Average high school GPA:* 2.99. *Test scores:* SAT verbal scores over 500: 50%; SAT math scores over 500: 43%; ACT scores over 18: 78%; SAT verbal scores over 600: 13%; SAT math scores over 600: 13%; ACT scores over 24: 17%; SAT verbal scores over 700: 1%; SAT math scores over 700: 1%.

Faculty *Total:* 84, 52% full-time, 50% with terminal degrees. *Student/faculty ratio:* 14:1.

Majors Accounting; biology/biological sciences; business administration and management; clinical laboratory science/medical technology; economics; education; elementary education; English; history; information science/studies; international business/trade/commerce; philosophy; political science and government; pre-dentistry studies; pre-law studies; pre-medical studies; pre-pharmacy studies; pre-veterinary studies; psychology; secondary education; sociology; theology; therapeutic recreation.

Academic Programs *Special study options:* accelerated degree program, adult/continuing education programs, advanced placement credit, cooperative education, double majors, external degree program, freshman honors college, honors programs, independent study, internships, off-campus study, part-time degree program, services for LD students, study abroad, summer session for credit. *ROTC:* Army (c), Air Force (c).

Library Abbot Vincent Taylor Library plus 1 other with 110,050 titles, 630 serial subscriptions, an OPAC.

Computers on Campus 125 computers available on campus for general student use. A campuswide network can be accessed from student residence rooms and from off campus. Internet access, at least one staffed computer lab available.

Student Life *Housing:* on-campus residence required through senior year. *Options:* coed, men-only. Campus housing is university owned. Freshman campus housing is guaranteed. *Activities and organizations:* drama/theater group, student-run newspaper, radio station, choral group, Greek system, College Union, WABY (student radio station), Abbey Players, national fraternities, national sororities. *Campus security:* 24-hour emergency response devices and patrols, late-night transport/escort service. *Student services:* health clinic, personal/psychological counseling.

Athletics Member NCAA. All Division II. *Intercollegiate sports:* baseball M(s), basketball M(s)/W(s), cheerleading M/W, cross-country running M(s)/W(s), golf M(s), soccer M(s)/W(s), softball W(s), tennis M(s)/W(s), volleyball W. *Intramural sports:* basketball M/W, crew M/W, cross-country running M/W, football M/W, rock climbing M/W, rugby M(c), soccer M/W, softball M/W, table tennis M/W, tennis M/W, ultimate Frisbee M/W, weight lifting M, wrestling M.

Standardized Tests *Required:* SAT I or ACT (for admission).

Costs (2004–05) *One-time required fee:* $672. *Comprehensive fee:* $23,878 includes full-time tuition ($15,010), mandatory fees ($768), and room and board ($8100). Full-time tuition and fees vary according to class time, course level, course load, location, program, reciprocity agreements, and student level. Part-time tuition: $471 per credit. Part-time tuition and fees vary according to class time, course level, course load, location, reciprocity agreements, and student level. *Required fees:* $190 per hour part-time. *College room only:* $4556. Room and board charges vary according to board plan, housing facility, location, and student level. *Payment plans:* installment, deferred payment. *Waivers:* senior citizens and employees or children of employees.

Financial Aid Of all full-time matriculated undergraduates who enrolled in 2003, 658 applied for aid, 581 were judged to have need, 71 had their need fully

Belmont Abbey College (continued)
met. 174 Federal Work-Study jobs (averaging $951). In 2003, 224 non-need-based awards were made. *Average percent of need met:* 68%. *Average financial aid package:* $11,476. *Average need-based loan:* $3233. *Average need-based gift aid:* $8581. *Average non-need-based aid:* $7986. *Average indebtedness upon graduation:* $15,500.

Applying *Options:* common application, electronic application, deferred entrance. *Application fee:* $35. *Required:* high school transcript, minimum 2.0 GPA. *Required for some:* essay or personal statement, 2 letters of recommendation. *Recommended:* interview. *Application deadlines:* 8/1 (freshmen), 8/15 (transfers). *Notification:* continuous (freshmen), continuous (transfers).

Admissions Contact Mr. Michael Poll, Director of Admission, Belmont Abbey College, 100 Belmont-Mt. Holly Road, Belmont, NC 28012-1802. *Phone:* 704-825-6884. *Toll-free phone:* 888-BAC-0110. *Fax:* 704-825-6220. *E-mail:* admissions@bac.edu.

■ See page 1228 for a narrative description.

BENNETT COLLEGE
Greensboro, North Carolina

- **Independent United Methodist** 4-year, founded 1873
- **Calendar** semesters
- **Degree** bachelor's
- **Urban** 55-acre campus
- **Women only**
- **Moderately difficult** entrance level

Faculty *Student/faculty ratio:* 9:1.

Student Life *Campus security:* 24-hour patrols, late-night transport/escort service.

Athletics Member NCAA. All Division III.

Standardized Tests *Required:* SAT I or ACT (for admission).

Costs (2003–04) *Comprehensive fee:* $16,050 includes full-time tuition ($9978), mandatory fees ($1000), and room and board ($5072). *College room only:* $2526.

Financial Aid *Average percent of need met:* 81.

Applying *Options:* deferred entrance. *Application fee:* $20. *Required:* essay or personal statement, high school transcript, minimum 2.0 GPA, letters of recommendation. *Required for some:* interview.

Admissions Contact Ms. Ulisa Bowles, Director of Admissions, Bennett College, Campus Box H, Greensboro, NC 27401. *Phone:* 336-517-8624. *E-mail:* admiss@bennett.edu.

BREVARD COLLEGE
Brevard, North Carolina

- **Independent United Methodist** 4-year, founded 1853
- **Calendar** semesters
- **Degree** bachelor's
- **Small-town** 120-acre campus
- **Endowment** $16.9 million
- **Coed,** 604 undergraduate students, 94% full-time, 46% women, 54% men
- **Minimally difficult** entrance level, 82% of applicants were admitted

Undergraduates 565 full-time, 39 part-time. Students come from 36 states and territories, 11 other countries, 52% are from out of state, 7% African American, 0.3% Asian American or Pacific Islander, 2% Hispanic American, 1% Native American, 2% international, 10% transferred in, 64% live on campus. *Retention:* 50% of 2002 full-time freshmen returned.

Freshmen *Admission:* 534 applied, 436 admitted, 157 enrolled. *Average high school GPA:* 2.98. *Test scores:* SAT verbal scores over 500: 49%; SAT math scores over 500: 41%; ACT scores over 18: 76%; SAT verbal scores over 600: 11%; SAT math scores over 600: 8%; ACT scores over 24: 22%; SAT verbal scores over 700: 3%; ACT scores over 30: 4%.

Faculty *Total:* 87, 68% full-time, 45% with terminal degrees. *Student/faculty ratio:* 9:1.

Majors Art; business administration and management; dramatic/theatre arts and stagecraft related; ecology; education; elementary education; English; environmental studies; health services/allied health/health sciences; history; interdisciplinary studies; kinesiology and exercise science; mathematics; middle school education; multi-/interdisciplinary studies related; music; parks, recreation and leisure; psychology; religious studies; secondary education.

Academic Programs *Special study options:* academic remediation for entering students, adult/continuing education programs, advanced placement credit, double majors, English as a second language, honors programs, independent study, internships, part-time degree program, services for LD students, student-designed majors, study abroad.

Library Jones Library plus 1 other with 42,275 titles, 322 serial subscriptions, 3,742 audiovisual materials, an OPAC, a Web page.

Computers on Campus 119 computers available on campus for general student use. A campuswide network can be accessed from student residence rooms and from off campus. Internet access, at least one staffed computer lab available.

Student Life *Housing:* on-campus residence required through sophomore year. *Options:* coed, men-only, women-only. Campus housing is university owned. Freshman campus housing is guaranteed. *Activities and organizations:* drama/theater group, student-run newspaper, choral group, fine arts organizations, Omicron Delta Kappa, Fellowship of Christian Athletes, BC Recycles, Campus Coalition for Service. *Campus security:* 24-hour emergency response devices and patrols. *Student services:* health clinic, personal/psychological counseling.

Athletics Member NAIA. *Intercollegiate sports:* baseball M(s), basketball M(s)/W(s), cheerleading M(s)/W(s), cross-country running M(s)/W(s), golf M(s), soccer M(s)/W(s), softball W(s), tennis M(s)/W(s), track and field M(s)/W(s), volleyball W(s). *Intramural sports:* archery M/W, badminton M/W, basketball M/W, bowling M/W, cross-country running M/W, equestrian sports M/W, football M/W, golf W, skiing (cross-country) M/W, skiing (downhill) M/W, soccer M/W, softball M/W, swimming M/W, tennis M/W, track and field M/W, ultimate Frisbee M/W, volleyball M/W, weight lifting M/W.

Standardized Tests *Required:* SAT I or ACT (for admission).

Costs (2003–04) *Comprehensive fee:* $19,190 includes full-time tuition ($13,480), mandatory fees ($200), and room and board ($5510). Full-time tuition and fees vary according to course load. Part-time tuition: $550 per credit. Part-time tuition and fees vary according to course load. *Required fees:* $15 per term part-time. *Room and board:* Room and board charges vary according to board plan and housing facility. *Payment plan:* installment. *Waivers:* senior citizens and employees or children of employees.

Financial Aid Of all full-time matriculated undergraduates who enrolled in 2003, 447 applied for aid, 382 were judged to have need, 73 had their need fully met. 85 Federal Work-Study jobs (averaging $1160). 35 state and other part-time jobs (averaging $1250). In 2003, 88 non-need-based awards were made. *Average percent of need met:* 79%. *Average financial aid package:* $12,400. *Average need-based loan:* $3840. *Average need-based gift aid:* $9975. *Average non-need-based aid:* $3415. *Average indebtedness upon graduation:* $16,950.

Applying *Options:* common application, electronic application, deferred entrance. *Application fee:* $30. *Required:* essay or personal statement, high school transcript, minimum 2.0 GPA. *Required for some:* 3 letters of recommendation, students in music-auditions, music tests; students in art-portfolio of ten slides. *Recommended:* interview. *Application deadline:* rolling (freshmen), rolling (transfers). *Notification:* continuous (freshmen), continuous (transfers).

Admissions Contact Ms. Joretta Nelson, Vice President for Enrollment Management, Brevard College, 400 North Broad Street, Brevard, NC 28712-3306. *Phone:* 828-884-8300. *Toll-free phone:* 800-527-9090. *Fax:* 828-884-3790. *E-mail:* admissions@brevard.edu.

■ See page 1290 for a narrative description.

CABARRUS COLLEGE OF HEALTH SCIENCES
Concord, North Carolina

Admissions Contact Ms. Deborah D. Bowman, Director of Admissions, Cabarrus College of Health Sciences, 431 Copperfield Boulevard, NE, Concord, NC 28025-2405. *Phone:* 704-783-1616. *Fax:* 704-783-1764. *E-mail:* dbowman@northeastmedical.org.

CAMPBELL UNIVERSITY
Buies Creek, North Carolina

- **Independent** university, founded 1887, affiliated with North Carolina Baptist State Convention
- **Calendar** semesters
- **Degrees** associate, bachelor's, master's, doctoral, and first professional
- **Rural** 850-acre campus with easy access to Raleigh
- **Endowment** $79.5 million
- **Coed,** 2,535 undergraduate students, 94% full-time, 55% women, 45% men
- **Moderately difficult** entrance level, 58% of applicants were admitted

Undergraduates 2,391 full-time, 144 part-time. Students come from 50 states and territories, 46 other countries, 25% are from out of state, 9% African American, 2% Hispanic American, 1% Native American, 3% international, 9% transferred in, 70% live on campus. *Retention:* 87% of 2002 full-time freshmen returned.

Freshmen *Admission:* 1,780 applied, 1,032 admitted, 679 enrolled. *Average high school GPA:* 3.50. *Test scores:* SAT verbal scores over 500: 77%; SAT math

scores over 500: 76%; SAT verbal scores over 600: 31%; SAT math scores over 600: 30%; SAT verbal scores over 700: 3%; SAT math scores over 700: 2%.

Faculty *Total:* 316, 67% full-time, 65% with terminal degrees. *Student/faculty ratio:* 12:1.

Majors Accounting; accounting and business/management; accounting and finance; acting; advertising; Army R.O.T.C./military science; art; athletic training; biochemistry; biology/biological sciences; biology teacher education; broadcast journalism; business administration and management; business/commerce; chemistry; child development; commercial and advertising art; communication and journalism related; communication and media related; communication/speech communication and rhetoric; computer and information sciences; computer and information sciences related; criminal justice/law enforcement administration; directing and theatrical production; divinity/ministry; dramatic/theatre arts; economics; education; educational leadership and administration; education (K-12); education (multiple levels); education related; elementary and middle school administration/principalship; elementary education; engineering; English; family and consumer sciences/home economics teacher education; family and consumer sciences/human sciences; finance; fine/studio arts; foreign languages and literatures; French; French as a second/foreign language (teaching); general studies; graphic design; health and physical education; health and physical education related; history; history teacher education; international business/trade/commerce; international relations and affairs; journalism; journalism related; kinesiology and exercise science; liberal arts and sciences/liberal studies; marketing/marketing management; mass communication/media; mathematics; mathematics teacher education; medical pharmacology and pharmaceutical sciences; middle school education; music; music pedagogy; music performance; music teacher education; music theory and composition; pastoral studies/counseling; pharmacology; pharmacy; pharmacy, pharmaceutical sciences, and administration related; physical education teaching and coaching; piano and organ; political science and government; pre-dentistry studies; pre-engineering; pre-law studies; pre-medical studies; pre-pharmacy studies; pre-theology/pre-ministerial studies; pre-veterinary studies; psychology; public administration; public relations, advertising, and applied communication related; public relations/image management; radio and television; radio, television, and digital communication related; religious studies; religious studies related; science teacher education; secondary education; social sciences; social studies teacher education; social work; Spanish; Spanish language teacher education; sport and fitness administration; theatre/theatre arts management; youth ministry.

Academic Programs *Special study options:* accelerated degree program, adult/continuing education programs, advanced placement credit, cooperative education, distance learning, double majors, freshman honors college, honors programs, independent study, internships, part-time degree program, study abroad, summer session for credit. *ROTC:* Army (b).

Library Carrie Rich Memorial Library plus 3 others with 208,000 titles, 9,211 serial subscriptions, 4,064 audiovisual materials, an OPAC, a Web page.

Computers on Campus 256 computers available on campus for general student use. A campuswide network can be accessed from student residence rooms and from off campus. Internet access, at least one staffed computer lab available.

Student Life *Housing:* on-campus residence required through sophomore year. *Options:* men-only, women-only. Campus housing is university owned. Freshman campus housing is guaranteed. *Activities and organizations:* drama/theater group, student-run newspaper, radio station, choral group, Student Government Association, Baptist Student Union, Campbell Catholic Community, Presidential Scholars Club, Pre-pharmacy club. *Campus security:* 24-hour emergency response devices and patrols, late-night transport/escort service, controlled dormitory access. *Student services:* health clinic, personal/psychological counseling.

Athletics Member NCAA. All Division I. *Intercollegiate sports:* baseball M(s), basketball M(s)/W(s), cheerleading W(s), cross-country running M(s)/W(s), golf M(s)/W(s), soccer M(s)/W(s), softball W(s), swimming W, tennis M(s)/W(s), track and field M(s)/W(s), volleyball W(s), wrestling M(s). *Intramural sports:* basketball M/W, football M/W, golf M/W, soccer M/W, softball M/W, swimming M/W, table tennis M/W, tennis M/W, track and field M/W, ultimate Frisbee M/W, volleyball M/W, water polo M/W, wrestling M.

Standardized Tests *Required:* SAT I or ACT (for admission).

Costs (2003–04) *Comprehensive fee:* $18,268 includes full-time tuition ($13,260), mandatory fees ($252), and room and board ($4756). Full-time tuition and fees vary according to course load and location. Part-time tuition and fees vary according to location and program. *Room and board:* Room and board charges vary according to board plan and housing facility. *Payment plan:* installment. *Waivers:* employees or children of employees.

Financial Aid Of all full-time matriculated undergraduates who enrolled in 2003, 2,709 applied for aid, 2,363 were judged to have need, 2,363 had their need fully met. 925 Federal Work-Study jobs (averaging $1058). 560 state and other part-time jobs (averaging $1000). In 2003, 1092 non-need-based awards were made. *Average percent of need met:* 100%. *Average financial aid package:* $18,024. *Average need-based loan:* $4187. *Average need-based gift aid:* $4997. *Average non-need-based aid:* $6534. *Average indebtedness upon graduation:* $10,438.

Applying *Options:* common application, electronic application, early admission, deferred entrance. *Application fee:* $25. *Required:* high school transcript, minimum 2.7 GPA. *Required for some:* 3 letters of recommendation. *Recommended:* essay or personal statement, interview. *Application deadline:* rolling (freshmen), rolling (transfers). *Notification:* continuous (freshmen), continuous (transfers).

Admissions Contact Ms. Peggy Mason, Director of Admissions, Campbell University, PO Box 546, 56 Main Street, Buies Creek, NC 27506. *Phone:* 910-893-1290. *Toll-free phone:* 800-334-4111. *Fax:* 910-893-1288. *E-mail:* adm@mailcenter.campbell.edu.

■ *See page 1338 for a narrative description.*

CATAWBA COLLEGE
Salisbury, North Carolina

- **Independent** comprehensive, founded 1851, affiliated with United Church of Christ
- **Calendar** semesters
- **Degrees** bachelor's and master's
- **Small-town** 210-acre campus with easy access to Charlotte
- **Endowment** $27.6 million
- **Coed,** 1,452 undergraduate students, 96% full-time, 55% women, 45% men
- **Moderately difficult** entrance level, 64% of applicants were admitted

Undergraduates 1,389 full-time, 63 part-time. Students come from 31 states and territories, 14 other countries, 28% are from out of state, 15% African American, 0.8% Asian American or Pacific Islander, 1% Hispanic American, 0.6% Native American, 2% international, 8% transferred in, 43% live on campus. *Retention:* 63% of 2002 full-time freshmen returned.

Freshmen *Admission:* 933 applied, 597 admitted, 252 enrolled. *Average high school GPA:* 3.22. *Test scores:* SAT verbal scores over 500: 55%; SAT math scores over 500: 67%; ACT scores over 18: 89%; SAT verbal scores over 600: 14%; SAT math scores over 600: 19%; ACT scores over 24: 26%; SAT verbal scores over 700: 2%; SAT math scores over 700: 1%; ACT scores over 30: 6%.

Faculty *Total:* 126, 60% full-time, 57% with terminal degrees. *Student/faculty ratio:* 16:1.

Majors Athletic training; biology/biological sciences; business administration and management; business/managerial economics; chemistry; clinical laboratory science/medical technology; computer science; dramatic/theatre arts; education; elementary education; English; environmental studies; French; history; humanities; information science/studies; interdisciplinary studies; international relations and affairs; marketing/marketing management; mass communication/media; mathematics; middle school education; music; music teacher education; parks, recreation and leisure; philosophy; physical education teaching and coaching; physician assistant; piano and organ; political science and government; pre-dentistry studies; pre-law studies; pre-medical studies; pre-veterinary studies; psychology; reading teacher education; religious studies; secondary education; sociology; Spanish; therapeutic recreation; voice and opera.

Academic Programs *Special study options:* adult/continuing education programs, advanced placement credit, double majors, honors programs, independent study, internships, part-time degree program, services for LD students, student-designed majors, study abroad, summer session for credit. *ROTC:* Army (c).

Library Corriher-Linn-Black Memorial Library plus 1 other with 112,447 titles, 24,542 audiovisual materials, an OPAC.

Computers on Campus 97 computers available on campus for general student use. A campuswide network can be accessed. Internet access, at least one staffed computer lab available.

Student Life *Housing:* on-campus residence required through sophomore year. *Options:* coed, men-only, women-only. Campus housing is university owned. Freshman campus housing is guaranteed. *Activities and organizations:* drama/theater group, student-run newspaper, choral group, United In Service, Catawba Guides, Blue Masque (drama), L'il Chiefs, Wigwam Productions. *Campus security:* 24-hour emergency response devices and patrols, late-night transport/escort service, controlled dormitory access. *Student services:* health clinic, personal/psychological counseling.

Athletics Member NCAA. All Division II. *Intercollegiate sports:* baseball M(s), basketball M(s)/W(s), cross-country running M(s)/W(s), field hockey W(s), football M(s), golf M(s), lacrosse M, soccer M(s)/W(s), softball W(s), swimming W(s), tennis M(s)/W(s), volleyball W(s). *Intramural sports:* archery M/W, basketball M/W, football M/W, golf M/W, ice hockey M, lacrosse M, racquetball M/W, skiing (downhill) M/W, soccer M/W, swimming M/W, table tennis M/W, tennis M/W, volleyball M/W, weight lifting M/W, wrestling M.

Standardized Tests *Required:* SAT I or ACT (for admission).

Catawba College (continued)

Costs (2003–04) *Comprehensive fee:* $22,000 includes full-time tuition ($16,400) and room and board ($5600). Full-time tuition and fees vary according to class time. Part-time tuition: $450 per semester hour. Part-time tuition and fees vary according to class time, course load, degree level, and student level. *Payment plan:* installment. *Waivers:* employees or children of employees.

Financial Aid Of all full-time matriculated undergraduates who enrolled in 2002, 1,054 applied for aid, 961 were judged to have need, 278 had their need fully met. 230 Federal Work-Study jobs (averaging $1200). 205 state and other part-time jobs (averaging $1138). In 2002, 157 non-need-based awards were made. *Average percent of need met:* 67%. *Average financial aid package:* $13,705. *Average need-based loan:* $3890. *Average need-based gift aid:* $3952. *Average non-need-based aid:* $6848. *Average indebtedness upon graduation:* $25,000.

Applying *Options:* common application, electronic application, early admission, deferred entrance. *Application fee:* $25. *Required:* high school transcript, minimum 2.0 GPA. *Recommended:* essay or personal statement, letters of recommendation, interview. *Application deadline:* rolling (freshmen), rolling (transfers). *Notification:* continuous (freshmen), continuous (transfers).

Admissions Contact Mr. Gordon Kirkland, Chief Enrollment Officer, Catawba College, 2300 West Innes Street, Salisbury, NC 28144-2488. *Phone:* 800-CATAWBA. *Toll-free phone:* 800-CATAWBA. *Fax:* 704-637-4222. *E-mail:* gakirkla@catawba.edu.

■ *See page 1366 for a narrative description.*

CHOWAN COLLEGE
Murfreesboro, North Carolina

- **Independent Baptist** 4-year, founded 1848
- **Calendar** semesters
- **Degrees** associate and bachelor's
- **Rural** 300-acre campus with easy access to Norfolk and Hampton Roads
- **Endowment** $12.0 million
- **Coed,** 790 undergraduate students, 95% full-time, 43% women, 57% men
- **Minimally difficult** entrance level, 67% of applicants were admitted

Undergraduates 753 full-time, 37 part-time. Students come from 23 states and territories, 3 other countries, 51% are from out of state, 26% African American, 0.6% Asian American or Pacific Islander, 2% Hispanic American, 0.8% Native American, 0.4% international, 6% transferred in, 79% live on campus. *Retention:* 54% of 2002 full-time freshmen returned.

Freshmen *Admission:* 1,464 applied, 979 admitted, 254 enrolled. *Average high school GPA:* 2.70. *Test scores:* SAT verbal scores over 500: 20%; SAT math scores over 500: 21%; ACT scores over 18: 34%; SAT verbal scores over 600: 2%; SAT math scores over 600: 2%; ACT scores over 24: 1%.

Faculty *Total:* 79, 62% full-time, 33% with terminal degrees. *Student/faculty ratio:* 14:1.

Majors Accounting; art; athletic training; biological and physical sciences; biology/biological sciences; business administration and management; commercial and advertising art; criminal justice/safety; elementary education; English; English/language arts teacher education; environmental biology; fine/studio arts; graphic and printing equipment operation/production; history; information science/studies; kinesiology and exercise science; liberal arts and sciences/liberal studies; marketing/marketing management; mathematics; mathematics teacher education; music; music management and merchandising; music teacher education; physical education teaching and coaching; physical sciences; pre-dentistry studies; pre-law studies; pre-medical studies; pre-veterinary studies; psychology; religious studies; sport and fitness administration.

Academic Programs *Special study options:* advanced placement credit, double majors, independent study, internships, part-time degree program, student-designed majors, study abroad, summer session for credit. *Unusual degree programs:* 3-2 engineering with North Carolina State University.

Library Whitaker Library plus 1 other with 93,676 titles, 1,113 serial subscriptions, 4,569 audiovisual materials, an OPAC.

Computers on Campus 100 computers available on campus for general student use. A campuswide network can be accessed from student residence rooms and from off campus. Internet access, online (class) registration, at least one staffed computer lab available. Computer purchase or lease plan available.

Student Life *Housing:* on-campus residence required through sophomore year. *Options:* men-only, women-only. Campus housing is university owned. Freshman campus housing is guaranteed. *Activities and organizations:* drama/theater group, choral group, Christian Student Union, Student Government Association, Habitat for Humanity, Phi Kappa Tau, SNCAE (Students of North Carolina Association of Educators), national fraternities. *Campus security:* 24-hour emergency response devices and patrols, late-night transport/escort service, controlled dormitory access. *Student services:* health clinic, personal/psychological counseling.

Athletics Member NCAA. All Division III. *Intercollegiate sports:* baseball M, basketball M/W, cross-country running W, football M, golf M/W, soccer M/W, softball W, tennis M/W, volleyball W. *Intramural sports:* basketball M/W, football M/W, racquetball M/W, soccer M/W, softball M/W, table tennis M/W, tennis M/W, ultimate Frisbee M/W, volleyball M/W.

Standardized Tests *Required:* SAT I or ACT (for admission).

Costs (2004–05) *Comprehensive fee:* $20,200 includes full-time tuition ($14,000), mandatory fees ($100), and room and board ($6100). Part-time tuition: $210 per hour. Part-time tuition and fees vary according to course load. *College room only:* $2900. Room and board charges vary according to board plan. *Payment plans:* installment, deferred payment. *Waivers:* senior citizens and employees or children of employees.

Financial Aid Of all full-time matriculated undergraduates who enrolled in 2002, 674 applied for aid, 624 were judged to have need, 77 had their need fully met. 230 Federal Work-Study jobs (averaging $882). 55 state and other part-time jobs (averaging $2580). In 2002, 99 non-need-based awards were made. *Average percent of need met:* 70%. *Average financial aid package:* $10,595. *Average need-based loan:* $3507. *Average need-based gift aid:* $7361. *Average non-need-based aid:* $10,007. *Average indebtedness upon graduation:* $17,953.

Applying *Options:* electronic application, early admission, deferred entrance. *Application fee:* $20. *Required:* high school transcript. *Required for some:* essay or personal statement, interview. *Recommended:* minimum 2.0 GPA, 2 letters of recommendation. *Application deadline:* rolling (freshmen), rolling (transfers). *Notification:* continuous (freshmen), continuous (transfers).

Admissions Contact Associate Vice President for Enrollment Management, Chowan College, 200 Jones Drive, Murfreesboro, NC 27855. *Phone:* 252-398-6314. *Toll-free phone:* 800-488-4101. *Fax:* 252-398-1190. *E-mail:* admissions@chowan.edu.

DAVIDSON COLLEGE
Davidson, North Carolina

- **Independent Presbyterian** 4-year, founded 1837
- **Calendar** semesters
- **Degree** bachelor's
- **Small-town** 556-acre campus with easy access to Charlotte
- **Endowment** $283.9 million
- **Coed,** 1,712 undergraduate students, 100% full-time, 50% women, 50% men
- **Very difficult** entrance level, 32% of applicants were admitted

Undergraduates 1,711 full-time, 1 part-time. Students come from 46 states and territories, 34 other countries, 78% are from out of state, 6% African American, 2% Asian American or Pacific Islander, 3% Hispanic American, 0.3% Native American, 3% international, 0.3% transferred in, 91% live on campus. *Retention:* 96% of 2002 full-time freshmen returned.

Freshmen *Admission:* 3,927 applied, 1,249 admitted, 490 enrolled. *Test scores:* SAT verbal scores over 500: 99%; SAT math scores over 500: 100%; ACT scores over 18: 100%; SAT verbal scores over 600: 87%; SAT math scores over 600: 91%; ACT scores over 24: 95%; SAT verbal scores over 700: 38%; SAT math scores over 700: 39%; ACT scores over 30: 47%.

Faculty *Total:* 170, 95% full-time, 98% with terminal degrees. *Student/faculty ratio:* 11:1.

Majors Anthropology; art; biology/biological sciences; chemistry; classics and languages, literatures and linguistics; dramatic/theatre arts; economics; English; French; German; history; mathematics; multi-/interdisciplinary studies related; music; philosophy; physics; political science and government; psychology; religious studies; sociology; Spanish.

Academic Programs *Special study options:* advanced placement credit, double majors, honors programs, independent study, off-campus study, services for LD students, student-designed majors, study abroad. *ROTC:* Army (b), Air Force (c). *Unusual degree programs:* 3-2 engineering with Columbia University, Washington University in St. Louis, North Carolina State University, Georgia Institute of Technology, Duke University.

Library E. H. Little Library plus 1 other with 422,035 titles, 2,767 serial subscriptions, 9,497 audiovisual materials, an OPAC, a Web page.

Computers on Campus 142 computers available on campus for general student use. A campuswide network can be accessed from student residence rooms and from off campus. Internet access, online (class) registration, at least one staffed computer lab available.

Student Life *Housing:* on-campus residence required through senior year. *Options:* coed, men-only, women-only. Campus housing is university owned. Freshman campus housing is guaranteed. *Activities and organizations:* drama/theater group, student-run newspaper, radio station, choral group, Inter-Varsity Christian Fellowship, Dean Rusk Program Student Advisory Council, music organizations, Community Service Council, Student Government Association, national fraternities. *Campus security:* 24-hour emergency response devices and patrols, late-night transport/escort service, controlled dormitory access. *Student services:* health clinic, personal/psychological counseling, women's center.

Athletics Member NCAA. All Division I except football (Division I-AA). *Intercollegiate sports:* baseball M(s), basketball M(s)/W(s), crew M(c)/W(c), cross-country running M(s)/W(s), fencing M(c)/W(c), field hockey W(s), golf M(s), lacrosse M(c)/W(s), rugby M(c), sailing M(c)/W(c), soccer M(s)/W(s), swimming M(s)/W(s), tennis M(s)/W(s), track and field M(s)/W(s), ultimate Frisbee M(c)/W(c), volleyball W(s), weight lifting M(c), wrestling M(s). *Intramural sports:* basketball M/W, field hockey M(c)/W(c), football M/W, soccer M(c)/W(c), softball M/W, tennis M(c)/W(c), volleyball M/W(c).

Standardized Tests *Required:* SAT I or ACT (for admission). *Recommended:* SAT II: Subject Tests (for admission), SAT II: Writing Test (for admission).

Costs (2003–04) *Comprehensive fee:* $33,274 includes full-time tuition ($24,987), mandatory fees ($916), and room and board ($7371). *College room only:* $3892.

Financial Aid Of all full-time matriculated undergraduates who enrolled in 2002, 683 applied for aid, 544 were judged to have need, 544 had their need fully met. 265 Federal Work-Study jobs (averaging $1595). 142 state and other part-time jobs (averaging $1445). In 2002, 390 non-need-based awards were made. *Average percent of need met:* 100%. *Average financial aid package:* $17,432. *Average need-based loan:* $4093. *Average need-based gift aid:* $14,710. *Average non-need-based aid:* $6652. *Average indebtedness upon graduation:* $21,530.

Applying *Options:* common application, early admission, early decision, deferred entrance. *Application fee:* $50. *Required:* essay or personal statement, high school transcript, 3 letters of recommendation. *Recommended:* interview. *Application deadlines:* 1/2 (freshmen), 3/15 (transfers). *Early decision:* 11/15 (for plan 1), 1/2 (for plan 2). *Notification:* 4/1 (freshmen), 12/15 (early decision plan 1), 2/1 (early decision plan 2), 5/15 (transfers).

Admissions Contact Dr. Nancy J. Cable, Dean of Admission and Financial Aid, Davidson College, Box 7156, Davidson, NC 28035-7156. *Phone:* 704-894-2230. *Toll-free phone:* 800-768-0380. *Fax:* 704-894-2016. *E-mail:* admission@davidson.edu.

■ *See page 1518 for a narrative description.*

DEVRY UNIVERSITY
Charlotte, North Carolina

Admissions Contact 4521 Sharon Road, Suite 145, Charlotte, NC 28211-3627. *Fax:* 704-362-2668. *E-mail:* tgordon@keller.edu.

DUKE UNIVERSITY
Durham, North Carolina

- **Independent** university, founded 1838, affiliated with United Methodist Church
- **Calendar** semesters
- **Degrees** bachelor's, master's, doctoral, first professional, post-master's, and postbachelor's certificates
- **Suburban** 8500-acre campus
- **Endowment** $2.6 billion
- **Coed,** 6,248 undergraduate students, 99% full-time, 49% women, 51% men
- **Most difficult** entrance level, 23% of applicants were admitted

Undergraduates 6,169 full-time, 79 part-time. Students come from 53 states and territories, 84 other countries, 85% are from out of state, 10% African American, 12% Asian American or Pacific Islander, 7% Hispanic American, 0.3% Native American, 5% international, 0.6% transferred in, 82% live on campus. *Retention:* 96% of 2002 full-time freshmen returned.

Freshmen *Admission:* 16,729 applied, 3,873 admitted, 1,619 enrolled. *Average high school GPA:* 3.93. *Test scores:* SAT verbal scores over 500: 99%; SAT math scores over 500: 100%; ACT scores over 18: 99%; SAT verbal scores over 600: 91%; SAT math scores over 600: 94%; ACT scores over 24: 96%; SAT verbal scores over 700: 51%; SAT math scores over 700: 66%; ACT scores over 30: 61%.

Faculty *Total:* 958. *Student/faculty ratio:* 11:1.

Majors African-American/Black studies; anatomy; ancient/classical Greek; anthropology; art; art history, criticism and conservation; Asian studies; biology/biological sciences; biomedical/medical engineering; Canadian studies; chemistry; civil engineering; classics and languages, literatures and linguistics; computer science; design and visual communications; dramatic/theatre arts; economics; electrical, electronics and communications engineering; English; environmental studies; French; geology/earth science; German; history; international relations and affairs; Italian; Latin; linguistics; literature; materials science; mathematics; mechanical engineering; medieval and Renaissance studies; music; philosophy; physics; political science and government; psychology; public policy analysis; religious studies; Russian; Slavic languages; sociology; Spanish; women's studies.

Academic Programs *Special study options:* accelerated degree program, adult/continuing education programs, advanced placement credit, distance learning, English as a second language, honors programs, independent study, internships, off-campus study, part-time degree program, services for LD students, student-designed majors, study abroad, summer session for credit. *ROTC:* Army (b), Air Force (b). *Unusual degree programs:* 3-2 law.

Library Perkins Library plus 11 others with 5.1 million titles, 28,274 serial subscriptions, 472,618 audiovisual materials, an OPAC, a Web page.

Computers on Campus 600 computers available on campus for general student use. A campuswide network can be accessed from student residence rooms and from off campus. Internet access, online (class) registration, at least one staffed computer lab available. Computer purchase or lease plan available.

Student Life *Housing:* on-campus residence required through junior year. *Options:* coed, men-only, women-only. Campus housing is university owned. Freshman campus housing is guaranteed. *Activities and organizations:* drama/theater group, student-run newspaper, radio and television station, choral group, marching band, national fraternities, national sororities. *Campus security:* 24-hour emergency response devices and patrols, late-night transport/escort service, controlled dormitory access. *Student services:* health clinic, personal/psychological counseling, women's center, legal services.

Athletics Member NCAA. All Division I except football (Division I-A). *Intercollegiate sports:* badminton M(c)/W(c), baseball M(s), basketball M(s)/W(s), crew M(c)/W(s), cross-country running M/W, equestrian sports M(c)/W(c), fencing M/W, field hockey M(c)/W(s), football M(s)/W(c), golf M(s)/W(s), ice hockey M(c)/W(c), lacrosse M(s)/W(s), racquetball M(c)/W(c), rugby M(c)/W(c), sailing M(c)/W(c), skiing (cross-country) M(c)/W(c), skiing (downhill) M(c)/W(c), soccer M(s)/W(s), softball M(c)/W(c), squash M(c)/W(c), swimming M/W, table tennis M(c)/W(c), tennis M(s)/W(s), track and field M/W, ultimate Frisbee M(c)/W(c), volleyball M(c)/W(s), water polo M(c)/W(c), wrestling M. *Intramural sports:* badminton M/W, baseball M/W, basketball M/W, football M, golf M/W, soccer M/W, softball M/W, squash M/W, swimming M/W, table tennis M/W, tennis M/W, volleyball M/W.

Standardized Tests *Required:* SAT I or ACT (for admission). *Required for some:* SAT II: Subject Tests (for admission), SAT II: Writing Test (for admission).

Costs (2003–04) *Comprehensive fee:* $37,555 includes full-time tuition ($28,475), mandatory fees ($870), and room and board ($8210). Full-time tuition and fees vary according to program. Part-time tuition: $3560 per course. Part-time tuition and fees vary according to program. *College room only:* $4430. Room and board charges vary according to board plan and housing facility. *Payment plans:* tuition prepayment, installment, deferred payment. *Waivers:* employees or children of employees.

Financial Aid Of all full-time matriculated undergraduates who enrolled in 2003, 2,719 applied for aid, 2,486 were judged to have need, 2,486 had their need fully met. 1,965 Federal Work-Study jobs (averaging $1839). 396 state and other part-time jobs (averaging $1480). In 2003, 874 non-need-based awards were made. *Average percent of need met:* 100%. *Average financial aid package:* $26,250. *Average need-based loan:* $5075. *Average need-based gift aid:* $20,700. *Average non-need-based aid:* $9321. *Average indebtedness upon graduation:* $19,737. *Financial aid deadline:* 2/1.

Applying *Options:* common application, electronic application, early admission, early decision, deferred entrance. *Application fee:* $70. *Required:* essay or personal statement, high school transcript, 3 letters of recommendation. *Recommended:* minimum 3.0 GPA, interview, audition tape for applicants with outstanding dance, dramatic, or musical talent; slides of artwork. *Application deadlines:* 1/2 (freshmen), 3/15 (transfers). *Early decision:* 11/1. *Notification:* 4/15 (freshmen), 12/15 (early decision), 5/1 (transfers).

Admissions Contact Mr. Christoph Guttentag, Director of Admissions, Duke University, 2138 Campus Drive, Durham, NC 27708. *Phone:* 919-684-3214. *Fax:* 919-684-8941. *E-mail:* askduke@admiss.duke.edu.

■ *See page 1548 for a narrative description.*

EAST CAROLINA UNIVERSITY
Greenville, North Carolina

- **State-supported** university, founded 1907, part of The University of North Carolina
- **Calendar** semesters
- **Degrees** bachelor's, master's, doctoral, first professional, and post-master's certificates
- **Urban** 1000-acre campus
- **Endowment** $9.0 million
- **Coed,** 16,935 undergraduate students, 91% full-time, 59% women, 41% men
- **Moderately difficult** entrance level, 77% of applicants were admitted

East Carolina University (continued)

Undergraduates 15,348 full-time, 1,587 part-time. Students come from 42 states and territories, 28 other countries, 15% are from out of state, 15% African American, 2% Asian American or Pacific Islander, 2% Hispanic American, 0.7% Native American, 0.3% international, 8% transferred in, 30% live on campus. *Retention:* 77% of 2002 full-time freshmen returned.

Freshmen *Admission:* 11,005 applied, 8,423 admitted, 3,534 enrolled. *Average high school GPA:* 3.38. *Test scores:* SAT verbal scores over 500: 60%; SAT math scores over 500: 68%; ACT scores over 18: 78%; SAT verbal scores over 600: 14%; SAT math scores over 600: 16%; ACT scores over 24: 14%; SAT verbal scores over 700: 1%; SAT math scores over 700: 1%; ACT scores over 30: 1%.

Faculty *Total:* 1,225, 85% full-time, 68% with terminal degrees. *Student/faculty ratio:* 17:1.

Majors Accounting; accounting related; anthropology; apparel and textiles; art; art history, criticism and conservation; art teacher education; athletic training; audiology and speech-language pathology; biochemistry; biology/biological sciences; broadcast journalism; business administration and management; business automation/technology/data entry; business teacher education; chemistry; child development; city/urban, community and regional planning; clinical laboratory science/medical technology; communication/speech communication and rhetoric; computer engineering technology; computer science; criminal justice/safety; dance; dietetics; drama and dance teacher education; dramatic/theatre arts; economics; electrical, electronic and communications engineering technology; elementary education; engineering technologies related; English; English/language arts teacher education; environmental engineering technology; environmental health; family and consumer sciences/home economics teacher education; finance; fine/studio arts; French; French language teacher education; geography; geology/earth science; German; German language teacher education; health and physical education related; health information/medical records administration; health professions related; health teacher education; history; hotel/motel administration; human development and family studies; industrial production technologies related; industrial technology; interior design; kindergarten/preschool education; kinesiology and exercise science; liberal arts and sciences/liberal studies; management information systems; manufacturing technology; marketing/marketing management; mathematics; mathematics teacher education; middle school education; music performance; music teacher education; music theory and composition; music therapy; nursing (registered nurse training); occupational therapy; parks, recreation and leisure facilities management; philosophy; physical education teaching and coaching; physician assistant; physics; political science and government; psychology; public/applied history and archival administration; public health education and promotion; sales and marketing/marketing and distribution teacher education; science teacher education; social studies teacher education; social work; sociology; Spanish; Spanish language teacher education; special education (emotionally disturbed); special education (mentally retarded); special education (specific learning disabilities); therapeutic recreation; vocational rehabilitation counseling; women's studies.

Academic Programs *Special study options:* academic remediation for entering students, accelerated degree program, adult/continuing education programs, advanced placement credit, cooperative education, distance learning, double majors, honors programs, independent study, internships, off-campus study, part-time degree program, services for LD students, student-designed majors, study abroad, summer session for credit. *ROTC:* Army (b), Air Force (b). *Unusual degree programs:* 3-2 accounting.

Library J. Y. Joyner Library plus 1 other with 1.3 million titles, 4,453 serial subscriptions, 27,816 audiovisual materials, an OPAC, a Web page.

Computers on Campus 1425 computers available on campus for general student use. A campuswide network can be accessed from student residence rooms and from off campus. Internet access, online (class) registration, at least one staffed computer lab available. Computer purchase or lease plan available.

Student Life *Housing options:* coed, men-only, women-only. Campus housing is university owned. *Activities and organizations:* drama/theater group, student-run newspaper, radio station, choral group, marching band, Student Government Association, Pan Hellenic Association, Student Union, Interfraternity Council, Residence Hall Association, national fraternities, national sororities. *Campus security:* 24-hour emergency response devices and patrols, student patrols, late-night transport/escort service, controlled dormitory access, Operation ID, Staff and Faculty Eyes, Campus Community Watch program. *Student services:* health clinic, personal/psychological counseling, legal services.

Athletics Member NCAA. All Division I except football (Division I-A). *Intercollegiate sports:* baseball M(s), basketball M(s)/W(s), cross-country running M(s)/W(s), golf M(s)/W(s), soccer M(s)/W(s), softball W(s), swimming M(s)/W(s), tennis M(s)/W(s), track and field M(s)/W(s), volleyball W(s). *Intramural sports:* badminton M(c)/W(c), basketball M/W, bowling M(c)/W(c), cross-country running M/W, equestrian sports M(c)/W(c), fencing M(c)/W(c), field hockey W(c), football M/W, golf M/W, lacrosse M(c)/W(c), racquetball M/W, rugby M(c)/W(c), skiing (downhill) M(c)/W(c), soccer M(c)/W(c), softball M/W(c), swimming M(c)/W(c), table tennis M/W, tennis M/W, ultimate Frisbee M(c)/W(c), volleyball M(c)/W(c), water polo M(c)/W(c).

Standardized Tests *Required:* SAT I or ACT (for admission).

Costs (2003–04) *Tuition:* state resident $1910 full-time; nonresident $12,049 full-time. Part-time tuition and fees vary according to course load. *Required fees:* $1221 full-time. *Room and board:* $5540; room only: $2640. Room and board charges vary according to board plan and housing facility. *Payment plans:* installment, deferred payment. *Waivers:* senior citizens and employees or children of employees.

Financial Aid Of all full-time matriculated undergraduates who enrolled in 2003, 10,105 applied for aid, 5,039 were judged to have need, 2,306 had their need fully met. 316 Federal Work-Study jobs (averaging $1745). 126 state and other part-time jobs (averaging $5655). In 2003, 3747 non-need-based awards were made. *Average need-based loan:* $3511. *Average need-based gift aid:* $3072. *Average non-need-based aid:* $5659. *Average indebtedness upon graduation:* $18,318.

Applying *Options:* electronic application, early admission, deferred entrance. *Application fee:* $50. *Required:* high school transcript, minimum 2.0 GPA. *Application deadline:* 3/15 (freshmen). *Notification:* continuous (freshmen), continuous (transfers).

Admissions Contact Dr. Thomas E. Powell, Director of Admissions, East Carolina University, Undergraduate Admission, Whichard Building 106, East 5th Street, Greenville, NC 27858-4353. *Phone:* 252-328-6640. *Fax:* 252-328-6945. *E-mail:* admis@mail.ecu.edu.

ELIZABETH CITY STATE UNIVERSITY

Elizabeth City, North Carolina

- **State-supported** comprehensive, founded 1891, part of University of North Carolina System
- **Calendar** semesters
- **Degrees** bachelor's and master's
- **Small-town** 125-acre campus with easy access to Norfolk
- **Coed,** 2,282 undergraduate students, 84% full-time, 63% women, 37% men
- **Moderately difficult** entrance level, 76% of applicants were admitted

Undergraduates 1,918 full-time, 364 part-time. Students come from 25 states and territories, 2 other countries, 12% are from out of state, 78% African American, 0.4% Asian American or Pacific Islander, 0.6% Hispanic American, 0.2% Native American, 0.1% international, 56% live on campus. *Retention:* 75% of 2002 full-time freshmen returned.

Freshmen *Admission:* 1,383 applied, 1,046 admitted, 464 enrolled. *Average high school GPA:* 2.79. *Test scores:* SAT verbal scores over 500: 10%; SAT math scores over 500: 10%; ACT scores over 18: 30%; SAT verbal scores over 600: 2%; SAT math scores over 600: 1%.

Faculty *Total:* 201, 70% full-time, 49% with terminal degrees. *Student/faculty ratio:* 15:1.

Majors Accounting; aeronautics/aviation/aerospace science and technology; applied art; art; art teacher education; avionics maintenance technology; biology/biological sciences; biology/biotechnology laboratory technician; biology teacher education; business administration and management; business teacher education; chemistry; chemistry teacher education; computer science; criminal justice/law enforcement administration; criminal justice/safety; education; elementary education; English; English/language arts teacher education; fine/studio arts; geology/earth science; history; history teacher education; industrial arts; industrial technology; kindergarten/preschool education; mathematics; mathematics teacher education; middle school education; music; music management and merchandising; music teacher education; oceanography (chemical and physical); physical education teaching and coaching; physics; political science and government; psychology; secondary education; social sciences; social work; sociology; special education; special education (specific learning disabilities); technology/industrial arts teacher education.

Academic Programs *Special study options:* academic remediation for entering students, adult/continuing education programs, advanced placement credit, double majors, honors programs, independent study, internships, off-campus study, part-time degree program, services for LD students, summer session for credit. *ROTC:* Army (b).

Library G. R. Little Library with 147,479 titles, 1,665 serial subscriptions.

Computers on Campus 300 computers available on campus for general student use. A campuswide network can be accessed from student residence rooms. Internet access, at least one staffed computer lab available.

Student Life *Housing options:* coed, men-only, women-only. Campus housing is university owned. *Activities and organizations:* drama/theater group, student-run newspaper, radio and television station, choral group, marching band, national fraternities, national sororities. *Campus security:* 24-hour emergency response devices and patrols. *Student services:* health clinic, personal/psychological counseling.

Athletics Member NCAA. All Division II. *Intercollegiate sports:* basketball M(s)/W(s), football M(s), tennis M/W, track and field M/W, volleyball M/W. *Intramural sports:* basketball M/W, football M, golf M/W, gymnastics M/W, tennis M/W, volleyball M/W.

Standardized Tests *Required:* SAT I or ACT (for admission).

Costs (2003–04) *Tuition:* state resident $1118 full-time; nonresident $8989 full-time. Part-time tuition and fees vary according to course load. *Required fees:* $1525 full-time. *Room and board:* $4608. *Waivers:* senior citizens.

Applying *Options:* electronic application, deferred entrance. *Application fee:* $30. *Required:* high school transcript, minimum 2.0 GPA. *Application deadline:* rolling (freshmen), rolling (transfers). *Notification:* continuous (freshmen), continuous (transfers).

Admissions Contact Mr. Grady Deese, Director of Admissions, Elizabeth City State University, Campus Box 901, Elizabeth City, NC 27909-7806. *Phone:* 252-335-3305. *Toll-free phone:* 800-347-3278. *Fax:* 252-335-3537. *E-mail:* admissions@mail.ecsu.edu.

■ *See page 1574 for a narrative description.*

ELON UNIVERSITY
Elon, North Carolina

- **Independent** comprehensive, founded 1889, affiliated with United Church of Christ
- **Calendar** 4-1-4
- **Degrees** bachelor's, master's, doctoral, and first professional
- **Suburban** 580-acre campus with easy access to Raleigh
- **Endowment** $50.6 million
- **Coed,** 4,431 undergraduate students, 97% full-time, 62% women, 38% men
- **Moderately difficult** entrance level, 45% of applicants were admitted

Elon is a small, selective private university located in central North Carolina. Elon specializes in the undergraduate student experience, offering 49 majors as well as exceptional programs in study abroad, undergraduate research, career preparation, service learning, and leadership. Outstanding facilities and a campus well-known for its friendly atmosphere characterize Elon.

Undergraduates 4,309 full-time, 122 part-time. Students come from 45 states and territories, 36 other countries, 70% are from out of state, 6% African American, 0.8% Asian American or Pacific Islander, 0.8% Hispanic American, 0.1% Native American, 1% international, 2% transferred in, 61% live on campus. *Retention:* 87% of 2002 full-time freshmen returned.

Freshmen *Admission:* 7,052 applied, 3,205 admitted, 1,227 enrolled. *Average high school GPA:* 3.60. *Test scores:* SAT verbal scores over 500: 89%; SAT math scores over 500: 92%; SAT verbal scores over 600: 37%; SAT math scores over 600: 43%; SAT verbal scores over 700: 4%; SAT math scores over 700: 5%.

Faculty *Total:* 324, 78% full-time, 73% with terminal degrees. *Student/faculty ratio:* 15:1.

Majors Accounting; art; athletic training; biology/biological sciences; broadcast journalism; business administration and management; business/corporate communications; chemistry; clinical laboratory science/medical technology; communication/speech communication and rhetoric; computer science; dramatic/theatre arts; economics; education; elementary education; engineering; English; environmental studies; foreign languages and literatures; French; health teacher education; history; human services; international relations and affairs; journalism; mathematics; middle school education; music; music performance; music teacher education; parks, recreation and leisure; philosophy; physical education teaching and coaching; physics; political science and government; pre-dentistry studies; pre-law studies; pre-medical studies; pre-veterinary studies; psychology; public administration; religious studies; science teacher education; secondary education; social science teacher education; social studies teacher education; sociology; Spanish; special education; sport and fitness administration.

Academic Programs *Special study options:* accelerated degree program, advanced placement credit, double majors, English as a second language, honors programs, independent study, internships, off-campus study, part-time degree program, services for LD students, student-designed majors, study abroad, summer session for credit. *ROTC:* Army (b), Air Force (c). *Unusual degree programs:* 3-2 engineering with North Carolina State University, North Carolina Agricultural and Technical State University, Virginia Polytechnic Institute and State University, Washington University, Columbia University.

Library Carol Grotnes Belk with 214,979 titles, 1,214 serial subscriptions, 12,164 audiovisual materials, an OPAC, a Web page.

Computers on Campus 500 computers available on campus for general student use. A campuswide network can be accessed from student residence rooms and from off campus that provide access to e-mail. Internet access, online (class) registration, at least one staffed computer lab available. Computer purchase or lease plan available.

Student Life *Housing:* on-campus residence required through sophomore year. *Options:* coed, men-only, women-only. Campus housing is university owned and leased by the school. Freshman campus housing is guaranteed. *Activities and organizations:* drama/theater group, student-run newspaper, radio and television station, choral group, marching band, Elon volunteers, student media, Greek affairs, intramural athletics, religious life, national fraternities, national sororities. *Campus security:* 24-hour emergency response devices and patrols, late-night transport/escort service, controlled dormitory access. *Student services:* health clinic, personal/psychological counseling, women's center.

Athletics Member NCAA. All Division I except football (Division I-AA). *Intercollegiate sports:* baseball M(s), basketball M(s)/W(s), cheerleading M/W, cross-country running M(s)/W(s), golf M(s)/W(s), lacrosse M(c)/W(c), rugby M(c), soccer M(s)/W(s), softball W(s), swimming M(c)/W(c), tennis M(s)/W(s), track and field W(s), volleyball W(s). *Intramural sports:* basketball M/W, bowling M/W, equestrian sports M/W, field hockey W(c), football M/W, golf M/W, racquetball M/W, soccer M/W, softball M/W, table tennis M/W, tennis M/W, ultimate Frisbee M(c)/W(c), volleyball M/W, weight lifting M/W.

Standardized Tests *Required:* SAT I or ACT (for admission).

Costs (2003–04) *Comprehensive fee:* $22,240 includes full-time tuition ($16,325), mandatory fees ($245), and room and board ($5670). Part-time tuition: $513 per hour. Part-time tuition and fees vary according to course load. *College room only:* $2770. Room and board charges vary according to board plan and housing facility. *Payment plan:* installment. *Waivers:* employees or children of employees.

Financial Aid Of all full-time matriculated undergraduates who enrolled in 2003, 2,034 applied for aid, 1,525 were judged to have need. 816 Federal Work-Study jobs (averaging $2400). In 2003, 806 non-need-based awards were made. *Average percent of need met:* 71%. *Average financial aid package:* $11,368. *Average need-based loan:* $4031. *Average need-based gift aid:* $5779. *Average non-need-based aid:* $3512. *Average indebtedness upon graduation:* $18,102.

Applying *Options:* common application, electronic application, early admission, early decision, early action, deferred entrance. *Application fee:* $40. *Required:* essay or personal statement, high school transcript, minimum 2.5 GPA, 1 letter of recommendation. *Application deadline:* 1/10 (freshmen), rolling (transfers). *Early decision:* 11/1. *Notification:* 3/15 (freshmen), 12/1 (early decision), 12/20 (early action), continuous (transfers).

Admissions Contact Ms. Staci Powell, Director of Admissions Records, Elon University, 2700 Campus Box, Elon, NC 27244. *Phone:* 336-278-3566. *Toll-free phone:* 800-334-8448. *Fax:* 336-278-7699. *E-mail:* admissions@elon.edu.

■ *See page 1584 for a narrative description.*

FAYETTEVILLE STATE UNIVERSITY
Fayetteville, North Carolina

- **State-supported** comprehensive, founded 1867, part of University of North Carolina System
- **Calendar** semesters
- **Degrees** associate, bachelor's, master's, and doctoral
- **Urban** 156-acre campus with easy access to Raleigh
- **Coed,** 4,359 undergraduate students, 81% full-time, 63% women, 37% men
- **Minimally difficult** entrance level, 85% of applicants were admitted

Undergraduates 3,550 full-time, 809 part-time. Students come from 41 states and territories, 8 other countries, 11% are from out of state, 79% African American, 1% Asian American or Pacific Islander, 4% Hispanic American, 1% Native American, 0.3% international, 10% transferred in, 30% live on campus. *Retention:* 73% of 2002 full-time freshmen returned.

Freshmen *Admission:* 1,914 applied, 1,629 admitted, 802 enrolled. *Average high school GPA:* 2.77. *Test scores:* SAT verbal scores over 500: 18%; SAT math scores over 500: 17%; SAT verbal scores over 600: 2%; SAT math scores over 600: 2%; SAT verbal scores over 700: 1%.

Faculty *Total:* 255, 86% full-time, 65% with terminal degrees. *Student/faculty ratio:* 21:1.

Majors Accounting; art; biology/biological sciences; biology teacher education; business administration and management; business/managerial economics; business teacher education; chemistry; computer science; criminal justice/law enforcement administration; dramatic/theatre arts and stagecraft related; education; elementary education; English; English/language arts teacher education; finance; geography; health teacher education; history; kindergarten/preschool education; marketing/marketing management; mathematics; mathematics teacher education; middle school education; music teacher education; nursing (registered nurse training); physical education teaching and coaching; political science and government; psychology; sales and marketing/marketing and distribution teacher education; social science teacher education; sociology; Spanish; Spanish language teacher education.

Fayetteville State University (continued)

Academic Programs *Special study options:* academic remediation for entering students, accelerated degree program, adult/continuing education programs, cooperative education, distance learning, double majors, honors programs, independent study, internships, part-time degree program, summer session for credit. *ROTC:* Army (c), Air Force (b). *Unusual degree programs:* 3-2 engineering with North Carolina State University.

Library Charles W. Chestnut Library with 241,000 titles, 3,600 serial subscriptions, 6,600 audiovisual materials, an OPAC, a Web page.

Computers on Campus 325 computers available on campus for general student use. A campuswide network can be accessed from student residence rooms and from off campus that provide access to access to student information. Internet access, online (class) registration, at least one staffed computer lab available.

Student Life *Housing options:* Campus housing is university owned. Freshman campus housing is guaranteed. *Activities and organizations:* drama/theater group, student-run newspaper, choral group, marching band, national fraternities, national sororities. *Campus security:* 24-hour emergency response devices and patrols, late-night transport/escort service, controlled dormitory access. *Student services:* health clinic, personal/psychological counseling.

Athletics Member NCAA. All Division II. *Intercollegiate sports:* basketball M(s)/W, bowling M/W, cheerleading M/W, cross-country running M/W, football M(s), golf M/W, tennis M/W, track and field M/W, volleyball W. *Intramural sports:* basketball M/W, golf M/W, gymnastics M/W, tennis M/W, volleyball M/W.

Standardized Tests *Required:* SAT I or ACT (for admission).

Costs (2004–05) *One-time required fee:* $50. *Tuition:* state resident $1621 full-time; nonresident $10,982 full-time. Full-time tuition and fees vary according to location. Part-time tuition and fees vary according to course load and location. *Required fees:* $733 full-time. *Room and board:* $4120; room only: $2320. Room and board charges vary according to board plan and housing facility. *Payment plan:* installment. *Waivers:* senior citizens.

Financial Aid Of all full-time matriculated undergraduates who enrolled in 2001, 2,508 applied for aid, 2,174 were judged to have need, 1,423 had their need fully met. In 2001, 247 non-need-based awards were made. *Average percent of need met:* 69%. *Average financial aid package:* $6690. *Average need-based loan:* $9341. *Average need-based gift aid:* $7976. *Average non-need-based aid:* $4106. *Average indebtedness upon graduation:* $9225. *Financial aid deadline:* 3/1.

Applying *Options:* electronic application, early admission, early decision, early action, deferred entrance. *Application fee:* $25. *Required:* high school transcript, minimum 2.00 GPA. *Recommended:* essay or personal statement, letters of recommendation. *Application deadlines:* 8/1 (freshmen), 8/1 (transfers). *Notification:* continuous (freshmen), continuous (transfers).

Admissions Contact Mrs. Carol Hogan, Director of Admissions, Fayetteville State University, 1200 Murchison Road, Fayetteville, NC 28301. *Phone:* 910-486-1371. *Toll-free phone:* 800-222-2594.

GARDNER-WEBB UNIVERSITY

Boiling Springs, North Carolina

- **Independent Baptist** comprehensive, founded 1905
- **Calendar** semesters
- **Degrees** associate, bachelor's, master's, doctoral, and first professional
- **Small-town** 250-acre campus with easy access to Charlotte
- **Endowment** $25.0 million
- **Coed,** 2,682 undergraduate students, 85% full-time, 64% women, 36% men
- **Moderately difficult** entrance level, 74% of applicants were admitted

Undergraduates 2,286 full-time, 396 part-time. Students come from 36 states and territories, 34 other countries, 24% are from out of state, 15% African American, 0.7% Asian American or Pacific Islander, 1% Hispanic American, 0.2% Native American, 0.1% international, 19% transferred in, 42% live on campus. *Retention:* 73% of 2002 full-time freshmen returned.

Freshmen *Admission:* 1,753 applied, 1,303 admitted, 369 enrolled. *Average high school GPA:* 3.41. *Test scores:* SAT verbal scores over 500: 55%; SAT math scores over 500: 56%; ACT scores over 18: 80%; SAT verbal scores over 600: 17%; SAT math scores over 600: 17%; ACT scores over 24: 28%; SAT verbal scores over 700: 4%; SAT math scores over 700: 1%.

Faculty *Total:* 131, 92% full-time, 77% with terminal degrees. *Student/faculty ratio:* 15:1.

Majors Accounting; art; athletic training; biology/biological sciences; business administration and management; chemistry; clinical laboratory science/medical technology; clinical/medical laboratory technology; computer science; criminal justice/law enforcement administration; data processing and data processing technology; dramatic/theatre arts; early childhood education; education; elementary education; English; English/language arts teacher education; fine/studio arts; foreign language teacher education; French; French language teacher education; health and physical education; health teacher education; history; journalism; kindergarten/preschool education; liberal arts and sciences/liberal studies; management information systems; mass communication/media; mathematics; mathematics teacher education; missionary studies and missiology; music; music performance; music teacher education; nursing (registered nurse training); pastoral studies/counseling; physical education teaching and coaching; physician assistant; political science and government; pre-dentistry studies; pre-law studies; pre-medical studies; pre-pharmacy studies; pre-veterinary studies; psychology; radio and television broadcasting technology; religious education; religious/sacred music; religious studies; secondary education; sign language interpretation and translation; social sciences; sociology; Spanish; sport and fitness administration; youth ministry.

Academic Programs *Special study options:* academic remediation for entering students, accelerated degree program, adult/continuing education programs, advanced placement credit, English as a second language, honors programs, internships, off-campus study, part-time degree program, services for LD students, study abroad, summer session for credit. *ROTC:* Air Force (c). *Unusual degree programs:* 3-2 engineering with Auburn University, University of North Carolina at Charlotte.

Library Dover Memorial Library with 210,000 titles, 5,600 serial subscriptions, 9,065 audiovisual materials, an OPAC.

Computers on Campus 150 computers available on campus for general student use. A campuswide network can be accessed from student residence rooms and from off campus. Internet access, online (class) registration, at least one staffed computer lab available.

Student Life *Housing:* on-campus residence required for freshman year. *Options:* men-only, women-only, disabled students. Campus housing is university owned. Freshman campus housing is guaranteed. *Activities and organizations:* drama/theater group, student-run newspaper, radio and television station, choral group, Student Volunteer Corps, The Verge, Fellowship of Christian Athletes, Student Government Association, Student Alumni Council. *Campus security:* 24-hour patrols, student patrols, controlled dormitory access. *Student services:* personal/psychological counseling.

Athletics Member NCAA. All Division I except football (Division I-AA). *Intercollegiate sports:* baseball M(s), basketball M(s)/W(s), cheerleading M(s)/W(s), cross-country running M(s)/W(s), golf M(s)/W(s), soccer M(s)/W(s), softball W(s), swimming W(s), tennis M(s)/W(s), track and field M(s)/W(s), volleyball W(s), wrestling M(s). *Intramural sports:* basketball M/W, football M/W, racquetball M/W, soccer M/W, softball M/W, table tennis M/W, tennis M/W, ultimate Frisbee M/W, volleyball M/W.

Standardized Tests *Required:* SAT I or ACT (for admission).

Costs (2003–04) *Comprehensive fee:* $19,480 includes full-time tuition ($14,160), mandatory fees ($180), and room and board ($5140). Part-time tuition: $270 per credit hour. Part-time tuition and fees vary according to course load. *College room only:* $2140. Room and board charges vary according to board plan and housing facility. *Payment plan:* installment. *Waivers:* senior citizens and employees or children of employees.

Financial Aid Of all full-time matriculated undergraduates who enrolled in 2001, 1,611 applied for aid, 1,373 were judged to have need, 470 had their need fully met. 235 Federal Work-Study jobs (averaging $1113). 611 state and other part-time jobs (averaging $1061). In 2001, 590 non-need-based awards were made. *Average percent of need met:* 85%. *Average financial aid package:* $9921. *Average need-based loan:* $3936. *Average need-based gift aid:* $5467. *Average non-need-based aid:* $4848. *Average indebtedness upon graduation:* $6059.

Applying *Options:* common application, electronic application, early admission, deferred entrance. *Application fee:* $25. *Required:* essay or personal statement, high school transcript, minimum 2.4 GPA. *Required for some:* letters of recommendation. *Application deadline:* rolling (freshmen), rolling (transfers).

Admissions Contact Mr. Nathan Alexander, Director of Admissions and Enrollment Management, Gardner-Webb University, PO Box 817, 110 South Main Street, Boiling Springs, NC 28017. *Phone:* 704-406-4491. *Toll-free phone:* 800-253-6472. *Fax:* 704-406-4488. *E-mail:* admissions@gardner-webb.edu.

■ *See page 1662 for a narrative description.*

GREENSBORO COLLEGE

Greensboro, North Carolina

- **Independent United Methodist** comprehensive, founded 1838
- **Calendar** semesters
- **Degrees** certificates, bachelor's, master's, and postbachelor's certificates
- **Urban** 75-acre campus with easy access to Charlotte
- **Endowment** $28.4 million
- **Coed,** 1,176 undergraduate students, 75% full-time, 56% women, 44% men
- **Moderately difficult** entrance level, 74% of applicants were admitted

Undergraduates 885 full-time, 291 part-time. Students come from 27 states and territories, 26% are from out of state, 18% African American, 0.6% Asian

American or Pacific Islander, 1% Hispanic American, 0.3% Native American, 0.7% international, 8% transferred in, 48% live on campus. *Retention:* 69% of 2002 full-time freshmen returned.

Freshmen *Admission:* 875 applied, 648 admitted, 229 enrolled. *Average high school GPA:* 3.00. *Test scores:* SAT verbal scores over 500: 43%; SAT math scores over 500: 45%; ACT scores over 18: 44%; SAT verbal scores over 600: 10%; SAT math scores over 600: 9%; ACT scores over 24: 24%; SAT verbal scores over 700: 2%; ACT scores over 30: 4%.

Faculty *Total:* 123, 49% full-time, 50% with terminal degrees. *Student/faculty ratio:* 14:1.

Majors Accounting; acting; art; art teacher education; athletic training; biology/biological sciences; biology teacher education; business administration and management; business/managerial economics; chemistry; clinical laboratory science/medical technology; communication/speech communication and rhetoric; drama and dance teacher education; dramatic/theatre arts; early childhood education; education; elementary education; English; English/language arts teacher education; foreign language teacher education; French; health and physical education related; history; interdisciplinary studies; kindergarten/preschool education; kinesiology and exercise science; mathematics; mathematics teacher education; middle school education; music; music performance; music teacher education; physical education teaching and coaching; political science and government; psychology; religious studies; science teacher education; secondary education; social studies teacher education; sociology; Spanish; Spanish language teacher education; special education; special education (emotionally disturbed); special education (mentally retarded); special education (specific learning disabilities); sport and fitness administration; theatre design and technology.

Academic Programs *Special study options:* academic remediation for entering students, accelerated degree program, adult/continuing education programs, advanced placement credit, double majors, English as a second language, freshman honors college, honors programs, independent study, internships, off-campus study, part-time degree program, services for LD students, student-designed majors, study abroad, summer session for credit. *ROTC:* Army (c), Air Force (c).

Library James Addison Jones Library with 108,350 titles, 290 serial subscriptions, 2,686 audiovisual materials, an OPAC, a Web page.

Computers on Campus 140 computers available on campus for general student use. A campuswide network can be accessed from student residence rooms and from off campus that provide access to online course support. Internet access, at least one staffed computer lab available.

Student Life *Housing:* on-campus residence required through sophomore year. *Options:* coed, men-only, women-only. Campus housing is university owned. Freshman campus housing is guaranteed. *Activities and organizations:* drama/theater group, student-run newspaper, choral group, marching band, Student Christian Fellowship, Campus Activities Board, student government, Choir, United African American Society, national fraternities. *Campus security:* 24-hour patrols, late-night transport/escort service, controlled dormitory access. *Student services:* health clinic, personal/psychological counseling.

Athletics Member NCAA. All Division III. *Intercollegiate sports:* baseball M, basketball M/W, cheerleading M/W, cross-country running M/W, football M, golf M, lacrosse M/W, soccer M/W, softball W, swimming W, tennis M/W, volleyball W. *Intramural sports:* basketball M/W, bowling M/W, football M/W, racquetball M/W, skiing (downhill) M/W, ultimate Frisbee M/W.

Standardized Tests *Required:* SAT I or ACT (for admission).

Costs (2003–04) *Comprehensive fee:* $21,750 includes full-time tuition ($15,500), mandatory fees ($220), and room and board ($6030). Full-time tuition and fees vary according to course load. Part-time tuition: $415 per hour. Part-time tuition and fees vary according to course load. *Room and board:* Room and board charges vary according to board plan and housing facility. *Payment plan:* installment. *Waivers:* adult students, senior citizens, and employees or children of employees.

Financial Aid Of all full-time matriculated undergraduates who enrolled in 2002, 718 applied for aid, 574 were judged to have need, 234 had their need fully met. 162 Federal Work-Study jobs (averaging $1100). 23 state and other part-time jobs (averaging $1100). In 2002, 238 non-need-based awards were made. *Average percent of need met:* 71%. *Average financial aid package:* $9395. *Average need-based loan:* $4011. *Average need-based gift aid:* $3824. *Average non-need-based aid:* $4473. *Average indebtedness upon graduation:* $11,802.

Applying *Options:* common application, electronic application, early admission, early action, deferred entrance. *Application fee:* $35. *Required:* high school transcript. *Required for some:* 2 letters of recommendation, interview. *Recommended:* essay or personal statement, interview. *Application deadline:* rolling (freshmen), rolling (transfers). *Notification:* continuous (freshmen), 1/15 (early action), continuous (transfers).

Admissions Contact Mr. Timothy L. Jackson, Director of Admissions, Greensboro College, 815 West Market Street, Greensboro, NC 27401. *Phone:* 336-272-7102 Ext. 211. *Toll-free phone:* 800-346-8226. *Fax:* 336-378-0154. *E-mail:* admissions@gborocollege.edu.

■ *See page 1690 for a narrative description.*

GUILFORD COLLEGE
Greensboro, North Carolina

- **Independent** 4-year, founded 1837, affiliated with Society of Friends
- **Calendar** semesters
- **Degree** certificates and bachelor's
- **Suburban** 340-acre campus
- **Endowment** $45.5 million
- **Coed,** 2,101 undergraduate students, 83% full-time, 61% women, 39% men
- **Moderately difficult** entrance level, 69% of applicants were admitted

Undergraduates 1,734 full-time, 367 part-time. Students come from 42 states and territories, 21 other countries, 34% are from out of state, 19% African American, 2% Asian American or Pacific Islander, 2% Hispanic American, 0.9% Native American, 2% international, 3% transferred in, 78% live on campus. *Retention:* 71% of 2002 full-time freshmen returned.

Freshmen *Admission:* 1,647 applied, 1,137 admitted, 334 enrolled. *Average high school GPA:* 3.06. *Test scores:* SAT verbal scores over 500: 81%; SAT math scores over 500: 79%; ACT scores over 18: 95%; SAT verbal scores over 600: 44%; SAT math scores over 600: 35%; ACT scores over 24: 57%; SAT verbal scores over 700: 13%; SAT math scores over 700: 5%; ACT scores over 30: 12%.

Faculty *Total:* 165, 55% full-time, 58% with terminal degrees. *Student/faculty ratio:* 16:1.

Majors Accounting; African-American/Black studies; art; athletic training; biological and biomedical sciences related; biology/biological sciences; business administration and management; chemistry; computer and information sciences; criminal justice/safety; dramatic/theatre arts; economics; elementary education; English; environmental studies; French; geology/earth science; German; health and physical education; health/medical preparatory programs related; history; information science/studies; interdisciplinary studies; international relations and affairs; mathematics; music; peace studies and conflict resolution; philosophy; physics; political science and government; psychology; religious studies; secondary education; sociology; Spanish; sport and fitness administration; women's studies.

Academic Programs *Special study options:* academic remediation for entering students, accelerated degree program, adult/continuing education programs, advanced placement credit, double majors, honors programs, independent study, internships, off-campus study, part-time degree program, student-designed majors, study abroad, summer session for credit. *Unusual degree programs:* 3-2 forestry with Duke University.

Library Hege Library with 157,054 titles, 829 serial subscriptions, 10,151 audiovisual materials, an OPAC, a Web page.

Computers on Campus 283 computers available on campus for general student use. A campuswide network can be accessed from student residence rooms and from off campus. Internet access, online (class) registration, at least one staffed computer lab available.

Student Life *Housing:* on-campus residence required through junior year. *Options:* coed, men-only, women-only, cooperative. Campus housing is university owned. Freshman campus housing is guaranteed. *Activities and organizations:* drama/theater group, student-run newspaper, radio station, choral group, student government, student radio station, student newspaper, Project Community, African-American Cultural Society. *Campus security:* 24-hour emergency response devices and patrols, student patrols, late-night transport/escort service, controlled dormitory access. *Student services:* health clinic, personal/psychological counseling, women's center.

Athletics Member NCAA. All Division III. *Intercollegiate sports:* baseball M, basketball M/W, cross-country running M/W, football M, golf M, lacrosse M/W, rugby M(c)/W(c), soccer M/W, softball W, swimming W, tennis M/W, ultimate Frisbee M(c)/W(c), volleyball W. *Intramural sports:* cheerleading W(c), tennis M/W.

Standardized Tests *Required:* SAT I or ACT (for admission).

Costs (2004–05) *Tuition:* $615 per credit hour part-time. Part-time tuition and fees vary according to course load. *Required fees:* $330 per year part-time. *Room only:* Room and board charges vary according to board plan, housing facility, and location. *Payment plan:* installment. *Waivers:* employees or children of employees.

Financial Aid Of all full-time matriculated undergraduates who enrolled in 2003, 1,269 applied for aid, 1,113 were judged to have need, 287 had their need

Guilford College (continued)
fully met. 114 Federal Work-Study jobs (averaging $1290). 126 state and other part-time jobs (averaging $1185). In 2003, 403 non-need-based awards were made. *Average percent of need met:* 75%. *Average financial aid package:* $12,795. *Average need-based loan:* $4691. *Average need-based gift aid:* $9105. *Average non-need-based aid:* $7112. *Average indebtedness upon graduation:* $17,380.

Applying *Options:* common application, electronic application, early admission, early decision, early action, deferred entrance. *Application fee:* $25. *Required:* essay or personal statement, high school transcript, minimum 2.0 GPA. *Recommended:* minimum 3.0 GPA, 2 letters of recommendation, interview. *Application deadlines:* 2/15 (freshmen), 5/1 (transfers). *Early decision:* 11/15. *Notification:* 4/1 (freshmen), 12/15 (early decision), 2/15 (early action), continuous (transfers).

Admissions Contact Mr. Randy Doss, Vice President of Enrollment, Guilford College, 5800 West Friendly Avenue, Greensboro, NC 27410. *Phone:* 336-316-2100. *Toll-free phone:* 800-992-7759. *Fax:* 336-316-2954. *E-mail:* admission@guilford.edu.

■ *See page 1696 for a narrative description.*

HERITAGE BIBLE COLLEGE
Dunn, North Carolina

- **Independent Pentecostal Free Will Baptist** 4-year, founded 1971
- **Calendar** semesters
- **Degrees** associate and bachelor's
- **Small-town** 82-acre campus with easy access to Raleigh-Durham
- **Endowment** $6000
- **Coed,** 108 undergraduate students, 73% full-time, 45% women, 55% men
- **Minimally difficult** entrance level

Undergraduates 79 full-time, 29 part-time. Students come from 1 other state, 1 other country, 5% are from out of state, 27% African American, 8% Hispanic American, 0.9% Native American, 0.9% international, 6% transferred in, 2% live on campus. *Retention:* 60% of 2002 full-time freshmen returned.

Freshmen *Admission:* 34 enrolled.

Faculty *Total:* 17, 35% full-time, 18% with terminal degrees. *Student/faculty ratio:* 13:1.

Majors Buddhist studies; Christian studies; theology.

Academic Programs *Special study options:* adult/continuing education programs, external degree program, independent study, internships, off-campus study, summer session for credit.

Library Alphin Learning Center with 18,455 titles, 110 serial subscriptions, 1,364 audiovisual materials, an OPAC, a Web page.

Computers on Campus 25 computers available on campus for general student use. Internet access, at least one staffed computer lab available.

Student Life *Housing options:* coed. Campus housing is university owned. *Activities and organizations:* drama/theater group, choral group.

Standardized Tests *Required:* ACT ASSET (for placement).

Costs (2003–04) *Comprehensive fee:* $6600 includes full-time tuition ($3600), mandatory fees ($600), and room and board ($2400). Full-time tuition and fees vary according to course level. Part-time tuition: $150 per credit. Part-time tuition and fees vary according to course level. *Required fees:* $150 per term part-time. *College room only:* $1440. Room and board charges vary according to board plan and housing facility. *Payment plans:* installment, deferred payment.

Financial Aid Of all full-time matriculated undergraduates who enrolled in 2003, 60 applied for aid, 60 were judged to have need. 3 Federal Work-Study jobs. *Average financial aid package:* $4330. *Average need-based loan:* $3500. *Average indebtedness upon graduation:* $15,152.

Applying *Options:* common application. *Application fee:* $25. *Required:* essay or personal statement, high school transcript, letters of recommendation. *Application deadline:* rolling (freshmen), rolling (transfers).

Admissions Contact Heritage Bible College, PO Box 1628, Dunn, NC 28335. *Phone:* 910-892-3178 Ext. 230. *Toll-free phone:* 800-297-6351 Ext. 230. *Fax:* 910-892-1809. *E-mail:* dwallace@heritagebiblecollege.org.

HIGH POINT UNIVERSITY
High Point, North Carolina

- **Independent United Methodist** comprehensive, founded 1924
- **Calendar** semesters
- **Degrees** bachelor's, master's, and postbachelor's certificates
- **Suburban** 77-acre campus with easy access to Charlotte
- **Endowment** $44.8 million
- **Coed,** 2,684 undergraduate students, 91% full-time, 61% women, 39% men
- **Moderately difficult** entrance level, 87% of applicants were admitted

Undergraduates 2,449 full-time, 235 part-time. Students come from 38 states and territories, 55% are from out of state, 21% African American, 1% Asian American or Pacific Islander, 2% Hispanic American, 0.3% Native American, 4% international, 10% transferred in, 60% live on campus. *Retention:* 76% of 2002 full-time freshmen returned.

Freshmen *Admission:* 1,709 applied, 1,491 admitted, 550 enrolled. *Average high school GPA:* 2.80. *Test scores:* SAT verbal scores over 500: 56%; SAT math scores over 500: 59%; SAT verbal scores over 600: 16%; SAT math scores over 600: 15%; SAT verbal scores over 700: 2%; SAT math scores over 700: 2%.

Faculty *Total:* 210, 57% full-time, 48% with terminal degrees. *Student/faculty ratio:* 15:1.

Majors Accounting; American studies; art teacher education; athletic training; biology/biological sciences; business administration and management; chemistry; clinical laboratory science/medical technology; community organization and advocacy; computer and information sciences; computer science; creative writing; criminal justice/safety; dramatic/theatre arts; education; elementary education; English; fine/studio arts; French; history; human services; information science/studies; interior design; international business/trade/commerce; international relations and affairs; kindergarten/preschool education; kinesiology and exercise science; literature; marketing/marketing management; mass communication/media; mathematics; middle school education; parks, recreation and leisure; parks, recreation and leisure facilities management; philosophy; physical education teaching and coaching; physician assistant; political science and government; pre-dentistry studies; pre-law studies; pre-medical studies; pre-veterinary studies; psychology; religious studies; secondary education; sociology; Spanish; special education; sport and fitness administration.

Academic Programs *Special study options:* academic remediation for entering students, accelerated degree program, adult/continuing education programs, advanced placement credit, cooperative education, double majors, English as a second language, honors programs, independent study, internships, off-campus study, part-time degree program, student-designed majors, study abroad, summer session for credit. *ROTC:* Army (c), Air Force (c). *Unusual degree programs:* 3-2 forestry with Duke University; medical technology with Wake Forest University.

Library Herman and Louise Smith Library with 205,000 titles, 30,000 serial subscriptions, 15,000 audiovisual materials, an OPAC, a Web page.

Computers on Campus 176 computers available on campus for general student use. A campuswide network can be accessed from student residence rooms and from off campus. Internet access, at least one staffed computer lab available.

Student Life *Housing options:* coed, men-only, women-only, cooperative, disabled students. *Activities and organizations:* drama/theater group, student-run newspaper, radio and television station, choral group, student government, Habitat for Humanity, international club, Student Activities Board, honors club, national fraternities, national sororities. *Campus security:* 24-hour emergency response devices and patrols, student patrols, late-night transport/escort service, controlled dormitory access. *Student services:* health clinic, personal/psychological counseling.

Athletics Member NCAA. All Division I. *Intercollegiate sports:* baseball M(s), basketball M(s)/W(s), cross-country running M(s)/W(s), golf M(s), soccer M(s)/W(s), tennis M(s)/W(s), track and field M/W(s), volleyball W(s). *Intramural sports:* basketball M/W, bowling M/W, football M/W, racquetball M/W, soccer M/W, softball M/W, swimming M/W, table tennis M/W, tennis M/W, track and field M/W, volleyball M/W.

Standardized Tests *Required:* SAT I or ACT (for admission). *Recommended:* SAT I or ACT (for admission), SAT II: Subject Tests (for admission), SAT II: Writing Test (for admission).

Costs (2004–05) *Comprehensive fee:* $22,480 includes full-time tuition ($14,290), mandatory fees ($1410), and room and board ($6780). Full-time tuition and fees vary according to class time. Part-time tuition: $246 per credit hour. *College room only:* $2890. Room and board charges vary according to board plan. *Waivers:* employees or children of employees.

Financial Aid Of all full-time matriculated undergraduates who enrolled in 2002, 2,237 applied for aid, 1,859 were judged to have need, 129 had their need fully met. 111 Federal Work-Study jobs (averaging $1500). In 2002, 110 non-need-based awards were made. *Average percent of need met:* 87%. *Average financial aid package:* $11,400. *Average need-based loan:* $5200. *Average need-based gift aid:* $4000. *Average non-need-based aid:* $3000. *Average indebtedness upon graduation:* $15,000.

Applying *Options:* common application, electronic application, deferred entrance. *Application fee:* $25. *Required:* high school transcript, minimum 2.0 GPA, 2 letters of recommendation. *Recommended:* essay or personal statement, minimum

3.0 GPA, interview. *Application deadlines:* 8/15 (freshmen), 8/15 (transfers). *Notification:* continuous until 8/15 (freshmen), continuous (transfers).

Admissions Contact Mr. James L. Schlimmer, Dean of Enrollment Management, High Point University, University Station 3187, High Point, NC 27262-3598. *Phone:* 336-841-9216. *Toll-free phone:* 800-345-6993. *Fax:* 336-888-6382. *E-mail:* admiss@highpoint.edu.

■ See page 1730 for a narrative description.

JOHNSON & WALES UNIVERSITY

Charlotte, North Carolina

Admissions Contact 901 West Trade Street, Suite 175, Charlotte, NC 28202. *Toll-free phone:* 866-598-2427.

JOHNSON C. SMITH UNIVERSITY

Charlotte, North Carolina

- **Independent** 4-year, founded 1867
- **Calendar** semesters
- **Degree** bachelor's
- **Urban** 105-acre campus
- **Endowment** $31.0 million
- **Coed,** 1,474 undergraduate students, 95% full-time, 58% women, 42% men
- **Minimally difficult** entrance level, 48% of applicants were admitted

Johnson C. Smith University is committed to academic excellence. While developing new programs that are responsive to the needs of communities, the University is also committed to maintaining its rich liberal arts heritage by infusing information technology into the curriculum through the IBM ThinkPad Initiative.

Undergraduates 1,399 full-time, 75 part-time. Students come from 37 states and territories, 72% are from out of state, 100% African American, 0.1% Asian American or Pacific Islander, 2% transferred in, 80% live on campus. *Retention:* 58% of 2002 full-time freshmen returned.

Freshmen *Admission:* 3,171 applied, 1,532 admitted, 461 enrolled. *Average high school GPA:* 2.72. *Test scores:* SAT verbal scores over 500: 12%; SAT math scores over 500: 8%; ACT scores over 18: 25%.

Faculty *Total:* 115, 76% full-time, 67% with terminal degrees. *Student/faculty ratio:* 15:1.

Majors Applied mathematics; biological and physical sciences; biology/biological sciences; business administration and management; chemistry; computer engineering; computer science; criminal justice/law enforcement administration; early childhood education; economics; education; elementary education; engineering; English; French; general studies; health and physical education; health teacher education; history; information science/studies; liberal arts and sciences/liberal studies; mass communication/media; mathematics; mathematics teacher education; music; music related; physical education teaching and coaching; physics; political science and government; pre-medical studies; psychology; science teacher education; secondary education; social sciences; social work; sociology; Spanish.

Academic Programs *Special study options:* accelerated degree program, adult/continuing education programs, advanced placement credit, cooperative education, double majors, freshman honors college, honors programs, independent study, internships, off-campus study, part-time degree program, services for LD students, study abroad, summer session for credit. *ROTC:* Army (b), Air Force (b). *Unusual degree programs:* 3-2 engineering with University of North Carolina at Charlotte, Florida Agricultural and Mechanical University.

Library James B. Duke Library plus 1 other with 112,477 titles, 800 serial subscriptions, 1,993 audiovisual materials, an OPAC, a Web page.

Computers on Campus 250 computers available on campus for general student use. A campuswide network can be accessed from off campus. Internet access, at least one staffed computer lab available.

Student Life *Housing:* on-campus residence required for freshman year. *Options:* coed, men-only, women-only. Campus housing is university owned. Freshman campus housing is guaranteed. *Activities and organizations:* drama/theater group, student-run newspaper, choral group, marching band, Union Program Board, Royal Golden Bull Pep Squad, health and physical education club, Delta Sigma Theta, Alpha Kappa Alpha, national fraternities, national sororities. *Campus security:* 24-hour emergency response devices and patrols, late-night transport/escort service, controlled dormitory access. *Student services:* health clinic, personal/psychological counseling.

Athletics Member NCAA. All Division II. *Intercollegiate sports:* basketball M(s)/W(s), cheerleading W, cross-country running M(s)/W(s), football M(s), golf M(s), softball W(s), tennis M(s)/W(s), track and field M(s)/W(s), volleyball W(s). *Intramural sports:* basketball M/W, track and field M/W, volleyball M/W.

Standardized Tests *Required:* SAT I or ACT (for admission).

Costs (2003–04) *Comprehensive fee:* $18,108 includes full-time tuition ($10,992), mandatory fees ($2070), and room and board ($5046). Part-time tuition: $242 per credit hour. Part-time tuition and fees vary according to course load. *College room only:* $2904. Room and board charges vary according to board plan, housing facility, and location. *Payment plan:* installment. *Waivers:* employees or children of employees.

Financial Aid Of all full-time matriculated undergraduates who enrolled in 2002, 1,530 applied for aid, 1,530 were judged to have need, 36 had their need fully met. 460 Federal Work-Study jobs (averaging $1200). *Average percent of need met:* 83%. *Average financial aid package:* $6200. *Average need-based gift aid:* $2000. *Average indebtedness upon graduation:* $22,000.

Applying *Options:* common application, electronic application, early admission, deferred entrance. *Application fee:* $25. *Required:* high school transcript. *Required for some:* letters of recommendation. *Recommended:* essay or personal statement, interview. *Application deadlines:* 8/1 (freshmen), 8/1 (transfers). *Notification:* continuous (freshmen), continuous (transfers).

Admissions Contact Mr. Jeffrey Smith, Director of Admissions, Johnson C. Smith University, 100 Beatties Ford Road, Charlotte, NC 28216. *Phone:* 704-378-1010. *Toll-free phone:* 800-782-7303.

■ See page 1796 for a narrative description.

JOHN WESLEY COLLEGE

High Point, North Carolina

- **Independent interdenominational** 4-year, founded 1932
- **Calendar** semesters
- **Degrees** associate and bachelor's
- **Urban** 24-acre campus
- **Coed,** 142 undergraduate students, 79% full-time, 42% women, 58% men
- **Minimally difficult** entrance level, 72% of applicants were admitted

Undergraduates 112 full-time, 30 part-time. Students come from 7 states and territories, 5% are from out of state, 24% African American, 1% Asian American or Pacific Islander, 0.7% Hispanic American, 0.7% Native American, 35% transferred in, 16% live on campus. *Retention:* 80% of 2002 full-time freshmen returned.

Freshmen *Admission:* 18 applied, 13 admitted, 13 enrolled. *Average high school GPA:* 2.5.

Faculty *Total:* 18, 61% full-time, 44% with terminal degrees. *Student/faculty ratio:* 12:1.

Majors Biblical studies; business administration and management; divinity/ministry; elementary education; liberal arts and sciences/liberal studies; pastoral studies/counseling; psychology; religious education; religious studies; theology.

Academic Programs *Special study options:* academic remediation for entering students, adult/continuing education programs, advanced placement credit, internships, off-campus study, part-time degree program, summer session for credit.

Library Temple Library with 43,305 titles, 146 serial subscriptions, 2,886 audiovisual materials.

Computers on Campus 5 computers available on campus for general student use. Internet access, at least one staffed computer lab available.

Student Life *Activities and organizations:* student-run newspaper, choral group.

Standardized Tests *Recommended:* SAT I and SAT II or ACT (for placement), SAT II: Writing Test (for placement).

Costs (2003–04) *Tuition:* $7166 full-time, $330 per semester hour part-time. Part-time tuition and fees vary according to course load. *Required fees:* $376 full-time, $188 per term part-time. *Room only:* $1990. Room and board charges vary according to housing facility. *Payment plan:* installment. *Waivers:* employees or children of employees.

Financial Aid Of all full-time matriculated undergraduates who enrolled in 2003, 114 applied for aid, 114 were judged to have need. 7 Federal Work-Study jobs (averaging $3000). In 2003, 2 non-need-based awards were made. *Average percent of need met:* 52%. *Average financial aid package:* $8600. *Average need-based loan:* $4000. *Average need-based gift aid:* $2025. *Average non-need-based aid:* $500. *Average indebtedness upon graduation:* $15,000.

Applying *Options:* early admission, deferred entrance. *Application fee:* $30. *Required:* high school transcript, 2 letters of recommendation, interview. *Recommended:* minimum 2.0 GPA. *Application deadlines:* 8/1 (freshmen), 8/1 (transfers). *Notification:* continuous until 8/10 (freshmen), continuous until 8/10 (transfers).

Admissions Contact Mr. Greg Workman, Admissions Officer, John Wesley College, 2314 North Centennial Street, High Point, NC 27265-3197. *Phone:* 336-889-2262 Ext. 127. *Fax:* 336-889-2261. *E-mail:* admissions@johnwesley.edu.

LEES-MCRAE COLLEGE
Banner Elk, North Carolina

- **Independent** 4-year, founded 1900, affiliated with Presbyterian Church (U.S.A.)
- **Calendar** semesters
- **Degree** bachelor's
- **Rural** 400-acre campus
- **Endowment** $15.4 million
- **Coed**
- **Minimally difficult** entrance level

Faculty *Student/faculty ratio:* 14:1.

Student Life *Campus security:* 24-hour patrols.

Athletics Member NCAA. All Division II.

Standardized Tests *Required:* SAT I or ACT (for admission).

Costs (2003–04) *Comprehensive fee:* $19,940 includes full-time tuition ($14,340), mandatory fees ($160), and room and board ($5440). Part-time tuition: $431 per hour. *College room only:* $2550. Room and board charges vary according to board plan.

Financial Aid Of all full-time matriculated undergraduates who enrolled in 2002, 826 applied for aid, 508 were judged to have need, 90 had their need fully met. 240 Federal Work-Study jobs (averaging $1400). 200 state and other part-time jobs (averaging $1400). In 2002, 366. *Average percent of need met:* 91. *Average financial aid package:* $9871. *Average need-based loan:* $3574. *Average need-based gift aid:* $4185. *Average non-need-based aid:* $4500. *Average indebtedness upon graduation:* $9234.

Applying *Options:* common application, electronic application, early admission, deferred entrance. *Application fee:* $25. *Required:* high school transcript, minimum 2.0 GPA. *Required for some:* letters of recommendation, interview. *Recommended:* essay or personal statement.

Admissions Contact Mr. Brad Parrish, Assistant Dean of Students for Admissions, Lees-McRae College, PO Box 128, Banner Elk, NC 28604-0128. *Phone:* 828-898-3432. *Toll-free phone:* 800-280-4562. *Fax:* 828-898-8707. *E-mail:* admissions@lmc.edu.

LENOIR-RHYNE COLLEGE
Hickory, North Carolina

- **Independent Lutheran** comprehensive, founded 1891
- **Calendar** semesters
- **Degrees** bachelor's and master's
- **Small-town** 100-acre campus with easy access to Charlotte
- **Coed,** 1,348 undergraduate students, 92% full-time, 64% women, 36% men
- **Moderately difficult** entrance level, 81% of applicants were admitted

Undergraduates 1,239 full-time, 109 part-time. Students come from 28 states and territories, 4 other countries, 26% are from out of state, 8% African American, 2% Asian American or Pacific Islander, 1% Hispanic American, 0.4% Native American, 0.1% international, 10% transferred in, 60% live on campus. *Retention:* 75% of 2002 full-time freshmen returned.

Freshmen *Admission:* 1,563 applied, 1,261 admitted, 310 enrolled. *Average high school GPA:* 3.39. *Test scores:* SAT verbal scores over 500: 52%; SAT math scores over 500: 58%; ACT scores over 18: 78%; SAT verbal scores over 600: 14%; SAT math scores over 600: 18%; ACT scores over 24: 17%; SAT verbal scores over 700: 1%; SAT math scores over 700: 2%.

Faculty *Total:* 154, 56% full-time, 47% with terminal degrees. *Student/faculty ratio:* 13:1.

Majors Accounting; adult and continuing education; art teacher education; athletic training; biology/biological sciences; business administration and management; business teacher education; chemistry; classics and languages, literatures and linguistics; clinical laboratory science/medical technology; computer science; dramatic/theatre arts; ecology; economics; education; elementary education; English; environmental studies; French; German; history; human services; international business/trade/commerce; international relations and affairs; kindergarten/preschool education; kinesiology and exercise science; Latin; mass communication/media; mathematics; modern languages; music; music teacher education; nursing (registered nurse training); occupational therapy; pastoral studies/counseling; philosophy; physical education teaching and coaching; physical sciences; physician assistant; physics; political science and government; pre-dentistry studies; pre-law studies; pre-medical studies; pre-veterinary studies; psychology; religious education; religious/sacred music; religious studies; science teacher education; secondary education; sociology; Spanish; theology.

Academic Programs *Special study options:* academic remediation for entering students, accelerated degree program, adult/continuing education programs, advanced placement credit, cooperative education, distance learning, double majors, English as a second language, honors programs, independent study, internships, part-time degree program, services for LD students, student-designed majors, study abroad, summer session for credit. *ROTC:* Army (c). *Unusual degree programs:* 3-2 engineering with North Carolina State University, University of North Carolina at Charlotte, Clemson University, North Carolina Agricultural and Technical State University; forestry with Duke University.

Library Carl Rudisill Library plus 3 others with 275,961 titles, 445 serial subscriptions, 40,379 audiovisual materials, an OPAC, a Web page.

Computers on Campus 100 computers available on campus for general student use. A campuswide network can be accessed from student residence rooms and from off campus. Internet access, at least one staffed computer lab available.

Student Life *Housing:* on-campus residence required through junior year. *Options:* coed, men-only, women-only, disabled students. Campus housing is university owned. Freshman campus housing is guaranteed. *Activities and organizations:* drama/theater group, student-run newspaper, radio and television station, choral group, Student Government Association, religious clubs, outdoors and service club, Playmakers, Bear Trackers (Student Recruitment Organization), national fraternities, national sororities. *Campus security:* 24-hour emergency response devices and patrols, late-night transport/escort service, controlled dormitory access. *Student services:* health clinic, personal/psychological counseling, women's center.

Athletics Member NCAA. All Division II. *Intercollegiate sports:* baseball M(s), basketball M(s)/W(s), cross-country running M(s)/W(s), football M(s), golf M(s)/W(s), soccer M(s)/W(s), softball W(s), volleyball W(s). *Intramural sports:* basketball M/W, football M/W, soccer M/W, softball M/W, ultimate Frisbee M/W.

Standardized Tests *Required:* SAT I or ACT (for admission).

Costs (2004–05) *Comprehensive fee:* $24,150 includes full-time tuition ($17,120), mandatory fees ($730), and room and board ($6300). Part-time tuition: $430 per credit. Part-time tuition and fees vary according to class time. *Room and board:* Room and board charges vary according to board plan and housing facility. *Payment plans:* installment, deferred payment. *Waivers:* employees or children of employees.

Financial Aid Of all full-time matriculated undergraduates who enrolled in 2001, 1,156 applied for aid, 1,156 were judged to have need, 391 had their need fully met. In 2001, 350 non-need-based awards were made. *Average percent of need met:* 73%. *Average financial aid package:* $10,277. *Average need-based loan:* $3321. *Average need-based gift aid:* $7650. *Average non-need-based aid:* $15,182. *Average indebtedness upon graduation:* $21,125.

Applying *Options:* electronic application, early action, deferred entrance. *Application fee:* $25. *Required:* high school transcript, minimum 2.5 GPA. *Recommended:* interview. *Application deadlines:* rolling (freshmen), 9/1 (transfers). *Notification:* continuous (freshmen), 9/1 (early action), continuous (transfers).

Admissions Contact Mrs. Rachel Nichols, Dean of Admissions and Financial Aid, Lenoir-Rhyne College, PO Box 7227, Hickory, NC 28603. *Phone:* 828-328-7300. *Toll-free phone:* 800-277-5721. *Fax:* 828-328-7378. *E-mail:* admission@lrc.edu.

LIVINGSTONE COLLEGE
Salisbury, North Carolina

- **Independent** 4-year, founded 1879, affiliated with African Methodist Episcopal Zion Church
- **Calendar** semesters
- **Degree** bachelor's
- **Small-town** 272-acre campus
- **Coed,** 1,005 undergraduate students, 98% full-time, 52% women, 48% men
- **Minimally difficult** entrance level, 45% of applicants were admitted

Undergraduates 987 full-time, 18 part-time. Students come from 16 states and territories, 30 other countries, 36% are from out of state, 92% African American, 0.1% Asian American or Pacific Islander, 0.4% Hispanic American, 3% international, 1% transferred in, 65% live on campus. *Retention:* 68% of 2002 full-time freshmen returned.

Freshmen *Admission:* 1,792 applied, 802 admitted, 286 enrolled. *Average high school GPA:* 2.6. *Test scores:* SAT verbal scores over 500: 9%; SAT math scores over 500: 7%; ACT scores over 18: 13%; SAT verbal scores over 600: 2%; SAT math scores over 600: 1%; ACT scores over 24: 1%; SAT math scores over 700: 1%.

Faculty *Total:* 67, 81% full-time, 46% with terminal degrees. *Student/faculty ratio:* 18:1.

Majors Accounting; biology/biological sciences; business administration and management; chemistry; computer science; education; elementary education; English; history; human services; information science/studies; kindergarten/preschool education; mathematics; music; music teacher education; music therapy; physical education teaching and coaching; political science and government;

psychology; reading teacher education; social sciences; social work; sociology; sport and fitness administration; therapeutic recreation.

Academic Programs *Special study options:* academic remediation for entering students, adult/continuing education programs, advanced placement credit, cooperative education, double majors, honors programs, internships, part-time degree program, summer session for credit. *ROTC:* Army (b). *Unusual degree programs:* 3-2 engineering with North Carolina Agricultural and Technical State University; law, history, political science with St. John's University.

Library Carnegie Library plus 2 others with 135,000 titles, 235 serial subscriptions, 1,003 audiovisual materials.

Computers on Campus 62 computers available on campus for general student use. A campuswide network can be accessed from student residence rooms. Internet access, at least one staffed computer lab available.

Student Life *Housing options:* Campus housing is university owned. Freshman applicants given priority for college housing. *Activities and organizations:* drama/theater group, choral group, marching band, national fraternities, national sororities. *Campus security:* 24-hour emergency response devices and patrols, late-night transport/escort service, controlled dormitory access. *Student services:* health clinic, personal/psychological counseling.

Athletics Member NCAA. All Division II. *Intercollegiate sports:* basketball M(s)/W(s), bowling M(s)/W(s), football M(s), softball W, track and field M/W. *Intramural sports:* softball W, track and field M/W.

Standardized Tests *Recommended:* SAT I or ACT (for admission).

Costs (2003–04) *One-time required fee:* $3078. *Comprehensive fee:* $18,101 includes full-time tuition ($10,383), mandatory fees ($1915), and room and board ($5803). Part-time tuition: $405 per semester hour. *College room only:* $2725. *Payment plan:* installment. *Waivers:* minority students, children of alumni, adult students, and employees or children of employees.

Applying *Options:* deferred entrance. *Application fee:* $25. *Required:* high school transcript, minimum 2.0 GPA. *Recommended:* essay or personal statement, 3 letters of recommendation, interview. *Application deadlines:* 8/2 (freshmen), 8/2 (out-of-state freshmen). *Notification:* 8/31 (freshmen), 8/31 (out-of-state freshmen), 8/31 (early action), continuous (transfers).

Admissions Contact Mr. Anthony Brooks, Assistant Vice President of Enrollment Management, Livingstone College, 701 West Monroe Street, Salisbury, NC 28144. *Phone:* 704-216-6005. *Toll-free phone:* 800-835-3435. *Fax:* 704-216-6215. *E-mail:* admissions@livingstone.edu.

MARS HILL COLLEGE

Mars Hill, North Carolina

- **Independent Baptist** 4-year, founded 1856
- **Calendar** semesters
- **Degree** bachelor's
- **Small-town** 194-acre campus
- **Endowment** $34.0 million
- **Coed,** 1,351 undergraduate students
- **Moderately difficult** entrance level, 85% of applicants were admitted

Undergraduates Students come from 29 states and territories, 16 other countries, 33% are from out of state, 11% African American, 0.4% Asian American or Pacific Islander, 1% Hispanic American, 1% Native American, 2% international, 56% live on campus. *Retention:* 73% of 2002 full-time freshmen returned.

Freshmen *Admission:* 1,006 applied, 856 admitted. *Average high school GPA:* 3.4. *Test scores:* SAT verbal scores over 500: 47%; SAT math scores over 500: 46%; ACT scores over 18: 100%; SAT verbal scores over 600: 13%; SAT math scores over 600: 11%; ACT scores over 24: 35%; SAT verbal scores over 700: 1%; SAT math scores over 700: 2%; ACT scores over 30: 6%.

Faculty *Total:* 150, 54% full-time. *Student/faculty ratio:* 14:1.

Majors Accounting; adult and continuing education; art; art history, criticism and conservation; art teacher education; athletic training; behavioral sciences; biological and physical sciences; biology/biological sciences; botany/plant biology; business administration and management; business/managerial economics; chemistry; computer science; criminal justice/law enforcement administration; dental hygiene; dramatic/theatre arts; education; elementary education; English; fashion merchandising; finance; gerontology; history; industrial radiologic technology; interdisciplinary studies; international business/trade/commerce; international relations and affairs; journalism; kindergarten/preschool education; liberal arts and sciences/liberal studies; marketing/marketing management; mass communication/media; mathematics; music; music teacher education; nursing (registered nurse training); parks, recreation and leisure; physical education teaching and coaching; physician assistant; political science and government; pre-dentistry studies; pre-law studies; pre-medical studies; pre-veterinary studies; psychology; religious education; religious/sacred music; religious studies; science teacher education; secondary education; social sciences; social work; sociology; Spanish; sport and fitness administration; therapeutic recreation; violin, viola, guitar and other stringed instruments; voice and opera; wind/percussion instruments; zoology/animal biology.

Academic Programs *Special study options:* academic remediation for entering students, accelerated degree program, adult/continuing education programs, advanced placement credit, cooperative education, double majors, English as a second language, honors programs, independent study, internships, part-time degree program, services for LD students, student-designed majors, study abroad, summer session for credit. *Unusual degree programs:* 3-2 physician's assistant, medical technology with Wake Forest University.

Library Renfro Library plus 1 other with 98,150 titles, 700 serial subscriptions, an OPAC, a Web page.

Computers on Campus 188 computers available on campus for general student use. A campuswide network can be accessed from student residence rooms and from off campus. Internet access, at least one staffed computer lab available.

Student Life *Housing:* on-campus residence required through sophomore year. *Options:* men-only, women-only. *Activities and organizations:* drama/theater group, student-run newspaper, radio station, choral group, marching band, Student Government Association, Fellowship of Christian Athletes, Christian Student Movement, Student Union Board, Inter-Greek Council, national fraternities, national sororities. *Campus security:* 24-hour emergency response devices and patrols, late-night transport/escort service, controlled dormitory access. *Student services:* health clinic, personal/psychological counseling.

Athletics Member NCAA. All Division II. *Intercollegiate sports:* baseball M, basketball M(s)/W(s), cross-country running M(s)/W(s), football M(s), golf M(s)/W, lacrosse M(s), soccer M(s)/W(s), softball W(s), tennis M(s)/W(s), track and field M/W, volleyball W(s). *Intramural sports:* basketball M/W, football M/W, skiing (downhill) M(c)/W(c), soccer M/W, track and field M(c)/W(c), volleyball M/W, water polo M/W.

Standardized Tests *Required:* SAT I or ACT (for admission).

Costs (2003–04) *Comprehensive fee:* $22,218 includes full-time tuition ($14,204), mandatory fees ($1254), and room and board ($6760). Full-time tuition and fees vary according to student level. Part-time tuition and fees vary according to student level. *Room and board:* Room and board charges vary according to board plan and housing facility. *Payment plan:* installment. *Waivers:* employees or children of employees.

Financial Aid Of all full-time matriculated undergraduates who enrolled in 2003, 784 applied for aid, 706 were judged to have need, 189 had their need fully met. 278 Federal Work-Study jobs (averaging $1033). 4 state and other part-time jobs (averaging $1750). *Average percent of need met:* 72%. *Average financial aid package:* $11,609. *Average need-based loan:* $3575. *Average need-based gift aid:* $8749. *Average non-need-based aid:* $6884. *Average indebtedness upon graduation:* $10,395.

Applying *Options:* early admission, deferred entrance. *Application fee:* $25. *Required:* high school transcript, minimum 2.0 GPA. *Required for some:* interview. *Recommended:* minimum 3.0 GPA. *Application deadline:* rolling (freshmen), rolling (transfers).

Admissions Contact Mr. Ryan C. Holt, Dean of Enrollment Services, Mars Hill College, PO Box 370, Mars Hill, NC 28754. *Phone:* 828-689-1201. *Toll-free phone:* 866-MHC-4-YOU. *Fax:* 828-689-1473. *E-mail:* admissions@mhc.edu.

■ See page 1936 for a narrative description.

MEREDITH COLLEGE

Raleigh, North Carolina

- **Independent** comprehensive, founded 1891
- **Calendar** semesters
- **Degrees** bachelor's, master's, and postbachelor's certificates
- **Urban** 225-acre campus
- **Endowment** $54.2 million
- **Women only,** 2,000 undergraduate students, 78% full-time
- **Moderately difficult** entrance level, 87% of applicants were admitted

Undergraduates 1,564 full-time, 436 part-time. Students come from 30 states and territories, 9% are from out of state, 7% African American, 1% Asian American or Pacific Islander, 2% Hispanic American, 0.4% Native American, 0.8% international, 5% transferred in, 46% live on campus. *Retention:* 79% of 2002 full-time freshmen returned.

Freshmen *Admission:* 344 enrolled. *Average high school GPA:* 2.97. *Test scores:* SAT verbal scores over 500: 61%; SAT math scores over 500: 60%; ACT scores over 18: 87%; SAT verbal scores over 600: 19%; SAT math scores over 600: 17%; ACT scores over 24: 27%; SAT verbal scores over 700: 2%; SAT math scores over 700: 1%; ACT scores over 30: 5%.

Faculty *Total:* 278, 49% full-time, 56% with terminal degrees. *Student/faculty ratio:* 9:1.

Meredith College (continued)

Majors Accounting; American studies; art history, criticism and conservation; art teacher education; biology/biological sciences; business administration and management; business/managerial economics; chemistry; child development; commercial and advertising art; communication/speech communication and rhetoric; computer and information sciences; computer science; dance; dietetics; drama and dance teacher education; dramatic/theatre arts; economics; English; environmental science; environmental studies; family and consumer sciences/human sciences; fashion/apparel design; fashion merchandising; finance; fine/studio arts; French; health/medical preparatory programs related; history; human resources management; interior design; international business/trade/commerce; international relations and affairs; kinesiology and exercise science; marketing/marketing management; mass communication/media; mathematics; molecular biology; multi-/interdisciplinary studies related; music; music pedagogy; music performance; music teacher education; music theory and composition; physical education teaching and coaching; piano and organ; political science and government; pre-dentistry studies; pre-medical studies; pre-pharmacy studies; pre-veterinary studies; psychology; public/applied history and archival administration; religious studies; social work; sociology; Spanish; sport and fitness administration; violin, viola, guitar and other stringed instruments; visual and performing arts related; voice and opera; wind/percussion instruments.

Academic Programs *Special study options:* academic remediation for entering students, accelerated degree program, adult/continuing education programs, advanced placement credit, cooperative education, double majors, honors programs, independent study, internships, off-campus study, part-time degree program, services for LD students, student-designed majors, study abroad, summer session for credit. *ROTC:* Army (c), Air Force (c).

Library Carlyle Campbell Library plus 1 other with 116,974 titles, 2,680 serial subscriptions, 12,085 audiovisual materials, an OPAC, a Web page.

Computers on Campus 140 computers available on campus for general student use. A campuswide network can be accessed from student residence rooms that provide access to wireless connectivity in most buildings. Internet access, at least one staffed computer lab available. Computer purchase or lease plan available.

Student Life *Housing:* on-campus residence required through sophomore year. *Options:* women-only. Campus housing is university owned. Freshman campus housing is guaranteed. *Activities and organizations:* drama/theater group, student-run newspaper, choral group, Student Government Association, Entertainment Association, Recreation Association, Class Organizations, choral groups. *Campus security:* 24-hour emergency response devices and patrols, late-night transport/escort service, controlled dormitory access, self-defense instruction. *Student services:* health clinic, personal/psychological counseling.

Athletics Member NCAA. All Division III. *Intercollegiate sports:* basketball W, cross-country running W(c), soccer W, softball W, tennis W, volleyball W. *Intramural sports:* swimming W(c).

Standardized Tests *Required:* SAT I or ACT (for admission). *Required for some:* SAT II: Subject Tests (for admission).

Costs (2004–05) *Comprehensive fee:* $24,350 includes full-time tuition ($19,000) and room and board ($5350). Part-time tuition: $500 per credit hour. *Payment plan:* installment. *Waivers:* employees or children of employees.

Financial Aid Of all full-time matriculated undergraduates who enrolled in 2003, 1,059 applied for aid, 894 were judged to have need, 87 had their need fully met. 352 Federal Work-Study jobs. In 2003, 432 non-need-based awards were made. *Average percent of need met:* 76%. *Average financial aid package:* $13,574. *Average need-based loan:* $3636. *Average need-based gift aid:* $9935. *Average non-need-based aid:* $4397. *Average indebtedness upon graduation:* $14,840.

Applying *Options:* common application, electronic application, early admission, early decision, deferred entrance. *Application fee:* $35. *Required:* high school transcript, minimum 2.0 GPA, 2 letters of recommendation. *Required for some:* essay or personal statement, interview. *Application deadlines:* 2/15 (freshmen), 2/15 (transfers). *Early decision:* 10/15. *Notification:* continuous (freshmen), 11/1 (early decision), continuous (transfers).

Admissions Contact Ms. Carol R. Kercheval, Director of Admissions, Meredith College, 3800 Hillsborough Street, Raleigh, NC 27607-5298. *Phone:* 919-760-8581. *Toll-free phone:* 800-MEREDITH. *Fax:* 919-760-2348. *E-mail:* admissions@meredith.edu.

■ *See page 1980 for a narrative description.*

METHODIST COLLEGE
Fayetteville, North Carolina

- **Independent United Methodist** comprehensive, founded 1956
- **Calendar** semesters
- **Degrees** associate, bachelor's, and master's
- **Suburban** 600-acre campus with easy access to Raleigh-Durham
- **Endowment** $8.1 million
- **Coed,** 2,210 undergraduate students, 75% full-time, 42% women, 58% men
- **Moderately difficult** entrance level, 76% of applicants were admitted

Undergraduates 1,655 full-time, 555 part-time. Students come from 48 states and territories, 30 other countries, 48% are from out of state, 22% African American, 2% Asian American or Pacific Islander, 5% Hispanic American, 0.9% Native American, 3% international, 9% transferred in, 50% live on campus. *Retention:* 63% of 2002 full-time freshmen returned.

Freshmen *Admission:* 1,935 applied, 1,465 admitted, 430 enrolled. *Average high school GPA:* 3.11. *Test scores:* SAT verbal scores over 500: 44%; SAT math scores over 500: 54%; ACT scores over 18: 67%; SAT verbal scores over 600: 7%; SAT math scores over 600: 15%; ACT scores over 24: 13%; SAT math scores over 700: 1%.

Faculty *Total:* 171, 60% full-time, 59% with terminal degrees. *Student/faculty ratio:* 16:1.

Majors Accounting; Army R.O.T.C./military science; art; art teacher education; athletic training; behavioral sciences; biblical studies; biological and physical sciences; biology/biological sciences; business administration and management; chemistry; computer science; creative writing; criminal justice/law enforcement administration; dramatic/theatre arts; economics; education; education (K-12); elementary education; English; finance; French; German; health/health care administration; history; hospitality and recreation marketing; international relations and affairs; kindergarten/preschool education; legal studies; liberal arts and sciences/liberal studies; marketing research; mass communication/media; mathematics; music; music management and merchandising; music teacher education; parks, recreation and leisure facilities management; philosophy; physical education teaching and coaching; physician assistant; political science and government; pre-dentistry studies; pre-engineering; pre-law studies; pre-medical studies; pre-veterinary studies; psychology; religious education; religious studies; science teacher education; secondary education; social work; sociology; Spanish; special education; sport and fitness administration.

Academic Programs *Special study options:* academic remediation for entering students, accelerated degree program, adult/continuing education programs, advanced placement credit, cooperative education, double majors, English as a second language, honors programs, independent study, internships, part-time degree program, services for LD students, study abroad, summer session for credit. *ROTC:* Army (b), Air Force (c). *Unusual degree programs:* 3-2 engineering with North Carolina State University, Georgia Institute of Technology.

Library Davis Memorial Library plus 1 other with 86,259 titles, 571 serial subscriptions, 13,208 audiovisual materials, an OPAC, a Web page.

Computers on Campus 175 computers available on campus for general student use. A campuswide network can be accessed from student residence rooms and from off campus. Internet access, at least one staffed computer lab available.

Student Life *Housing:* on-campus residence required for freshman year. *Options:* coed, men-only, women-only. Campus housing is university owned. Freshman campus housing is guaranteed. *Activities and organizations:* drama/theater group, student-run newspaper, choral group, Student Activities Committee, Student Government Association, Student Education Association, Fellowship of Christian Athletes, Residence Hall Association, national sororities. *Campus security:* 24-hour emergency response devices and patrols, late-night transport/escort service, controlled dormitory access, regular patrol by county sheriff department. *Student services:* health clinic, personal/psychological counseling.

Athletics Member NCAA. All Division III. *Intercollegiate sports:* baseball M, basketball M/W, cheerleading M(s)/W(s), cross-country running M/W, football M, golf M/W, lacrosse W, soccer M/W, softball W, tennis M/W, track and field M/W, volleyball W. *Intramural sports:* basketball M/W, bowling M/W, football M/W, golf M/W, racquetball M/W, soccer M/W, softball M/W, table tennis M/W, tennis M/W, volleyball M/W, weight lifting M/W.

Standardized Tests *Required:* SAT I or ACT (for admission).

Costs (2004–05) *Comprehensive fee:* $23,130 includes full-time tuition ($16,500), mandatory fees ($260), and room and board ($6370). Full-time tuition and fees vary according to class time and program. Part-time tuition and fees vary according to class time and program. *Room and board:* Room and board charges vary according to board plan and housing facility. *Payment plans:* installment, deferred payment. *Waivers:* senior citizens and employees or children of employees.

Financial Aid Of all full-time matriculated undergraduates who enrolled in 2002, 1,422 applied for aid, 1,204 were judged to have need, 234 had their need fully met. 788 Federal Work-Study jobs (averaging $693). 268 state and other part-time jobs (averaging $621). In 2002, 111 non-need-based awards were made. *Average percent of need met:* 64%. *Average financial aid package:* $10,696. *Average need-based loan:* $2477. *Average need-based gift aid:* $5682. *Average non-need-based aid:* $4299. *Average indebtedness upon graduation:* $11,414.

Applying *Options:* common application, deferred entrance. *Application fee:* $25. *Required:* high school transcript. *Required for some:* essay or personal statement, 2 letters of recommendation, interview. *Recommended:* 2 letters of recommendation, interview. *Application deadline:* rolling (freshmen), rolling (transfers). *Notification:* continuous until 8/15 (freshmen), continuous until 8/15 (transfers).

Admissions Contact Mr. Jamie Legg, Director of Admissions, Methodist College, 5400 Ramsey Street, Fayetteville, NC 28311. *Phone:* 910-630-7027. *Toll-free phone:* 800-488-7110. *Fax:* 910-630-7285. *E-mail:* admissions@methodist.edu.

MONTREAT COLLEGE
Montreat, North Carolina

- **Independent** comprehensive, founded 1916, affiliated with Presbyterian Church (U.S.A.)
- **Calendar** semesters
- **Degrees** associate, bachelor's, and master's
- **Small-town** 112-acre campus
- **Endowment** $9.7 million
- **Coed,** 943 undergraduate students, 99% full-time, 62% women, 38% men
- **Moderately difficult** entrance level, 78% of applicants were admitted

Undergraduates 935 full-time, 8 part-time. Students come from 28 states and territories, 8 other countries, 20% are from out of state, 18% African American, 0.6% Asian American or Pacific Islander, 0.6% Hispanic American, 7% Native American, 1% international, 6% transferred in, 34% live on campus. *Retention:* 66% of 2002 full-time freshmen returned.

Freshmen *Admission:* 409 applied, 320 admitted, 126 enrolled. *Average high school GPA:* 3.12. *Test scores:* SAT verbal scores over 500: 59%; SAT math scores over 500: 56%; ACT scores over 18: 89%; SAT verbal scores over 600: 25%; SAT math scores over 600: 13%; ACT scores over 24: 35%; SAT verbal scores over 700: 4%; SAT math scores over 700: 3%; ACT scores over 30: 4%.

Faculty *Total:* 120, 26% full-time, 31% with terminal degrees. *Student/faculty ratio:* 17:1.

Majors American studies; biblical studies; biology/biological sciences; business administration and management; computer and information sciences; education; elementary education; English; environmental studies; history; human services; music management and merchandising; music performance; parks, recreation and leisure.

Academic Programs *Special study options:* accelerated degree program, adult/continuing education programs, advanced placement credit, cooperative education, double majors, independent study, internships, off-campus study, part-time degree program, study abroad.

Library L. Nelson Bell Library with 68,100 titles, 426 serial subscriptions, an OPAC.

Computers on Campus 60 computers available on campus for general student use. A campuswide network can be accessed from student residence rooms and from off campus. Internet access, at least one staffed computer lab available.

Student Life *Housing:* on-campus residence required through sophomore year. *Options:* men-only, women-only. Campus housing is university owned. Freshman campus housing is guaranteed. *Activities and organizations:* drama/theater group, student-run newspaper, choral group, student government, Student Christian Association, Inter-Varsity Missions Fellowship, paint ball club, business club. *Campus security:* 24-hour emergency response devices and patrols, controlled dormitory access. *Student services:* health clinic, personal/psychological counseling.

Athletics Member NAIA. *Intercollegiate sports:* baseball M(s), basketball M(s)/W(s), cross-country running M(s)/W(s), golf M(s), soccer M(s)/W(s), softball W(s), tennis M(s)/W(s), volleyball W(s). *Intramural sports:* basketball M/W, football M, softball M/W, table tennis M/W, tennis M/W, ultimate Frisbee M/W, volleyball M/W.

Standardized Tests *Required:* SAT I or ACT (for admission).

Costs (2004–05) *Comprehensive fee:* $19,970 includes full-time tuition ($15,108) and room and board ($4862). Part-time tuition: $350 per credit hour. *Room and board:* Room and board charges vary according to board plan. *Payment plan:* installment. *Waivers:* employees or children of employees.

Financial Aid Of all full-time matriculated undergraduates who enrolled in 2002, 878 applied for aid, 647 were judged to have need, 111 had their need fully met. 104 Federal Work-Study jobs (averaging $1447). 21 state and other part-time jobs (averaging $1700). In 2002, 229 non-need-based awards were made. *Average percent of need met:* 76%. *Average financial aid package:* $10,343. *Average need-based loan:* $4960. *Average need-based gift aid:* $5836. *Average non-need-based aid:* $4981. *Average indebtedness upon graduation:* $17,877.

Applying *Options:* early admission, deferred entrance. *Application fee:* $15. *Required:* essay or personal statement, high school transcript, minimum 2.25 GPA, 1 letter of recommendation. *Required for some:* interview. *Application deadlines:* 8/15 (freshmen), 8/15 (transfers). *Notification:* continuous (freshmen), continuous (transfers).

Admissions Contact Ms. Anita Darby, Director of Admissions, Montreat College, PO Box 1267, 310 Gaither Circle, Montreat, NC 28757-1267. *Phone:* 828-669-8012 Ext. 3784. *Toll-free phone:* 800-622-6968. *Fax:* 828-669-0120. *E-mail:* admissions@montreat.edu.

■ *See page 2022 for a narrative description.*

MOUNT OLIVE COLLEGE
Mount Olive, North Carolina

- **Independent Free Will Baptist** 4-year, founded 1951
- **Calendar** semester or continuous accelerated programs
- **Degrees** associate and bachelor's
- **Small-town** 123-acre campus with easy access to Raleigh
- **Endowment** $7.3 million
- **Coed**
- **Minimally difficult** entrance level

Faculty *Student/faculty ratio:* 20:1.

Student Life *Campus security:* overnight security patrols; weekend patrols.

Athletics Member NCAA. All Division II.

Standardized Tests *Required:* SAT I or ACT (for admission). *Required for some:* TOEFL for foreign students. *Recommended:* SAT I (for admission).

Costs (2004–05) *Comprehensive fee:* $15,820 includes full-time tuition ($10,950), mandatory fees ($270), and room and board ($4600). Full-time tuition and fees vary according to location. Part-time tuition and fees vary according to course load and location. *College room only:* $2000. Room and board charges vary according to board plan and housing facility.

Financial Aid Of all full-time matriculated undergraduates who enrolled in 2002, 1,282 applied for aid, 1,130 were judged to have need, 229 had their need fully met. 120 Federal Work-Study jobs (averaging $719). In 2002, 228. *Average percent of need met:* 72. *Average financial aid package:* $6460. *Average need-based loan:* $2658. *Average need-based gift aid:* $4458. *Average non-need-based aid:* $4180.

Applying *Options:* common application, early admission, deferred entrance. *Application fee:* $20. *Required:* high school transcript, minimum 2.0 GPA. *Recommended:* 2 letters of recommendation, interview.

Admissions Contact Mr. Tim Woodard, Director of Admissions, Mount Olive College, 634 Henderson Street, Mount Olive, NC 28365. *Phone:* 919-658-2502 Ext. 3009. *Toll-free phone:* 800-653-0854. *Fax:* 919-658-9816. *E-mail:* admissions@moc.edu.

NEW LIFE THEOLOGICAL SEMINARY
Charlotte, North Carolina

Admissions Contact PO Box 790106, Charlotte, NC 28206-7901.

NORTH CAROLINA AGRICULTURAL AND TECHNICAL STATE UNIVERSITY
Greensboro, North Carolina

- **State-supported** university, founded 1891, part of University of North Carolina System
- **Calendar** semesters
- **Degrees** bachelor's, master's, and doctoral
- **Urban** 191-acre campus
- **Endowment** $10.4 million
- **Coed**
- **Moderately difficult** entrance level

Faculty *Student/faculty ratio:* 17:1.

Student Life *Campus security:* 24-hour emergency response devices and patrols, late-night transport/escort service, controlled dormitory access.

Athletics Member NCAA. All Division I except football (Division I-AA).

Standardized Tests *Recommended:* SAT I or ACT (for admission).

Costs (2003–04) *Tuition:* state resident $1544 full-time, $64 per credit part-time; nonresident $10,911 full-time, $455 per credit part-time. *Required fees:* $1178 full-time. *Room and board:* $4968; room only $2768.

Financial Aid Of all full-time matriculated undergraduates who enrolled in 2003, 5,538 applied for aid, 4,597 were judged to have need, 243 had their need fully met. In 2003, 278. *Average percent of need met:* 53. *Average financial aid package:* $5098. *Average need-based loan:* $5579. *Average need-based gift aid:* $1265. *Average non-need-based aid:* $3873. *Average indebtedness upon graduation:* $15,008.

Applying *Options:* early admission, deferred entrance. *Application fee:* $35. *Required:* high school transcript, minimum 2.0 GPA.

North Carolina Agricultural and Technical State University (continued)

Admissions Contact Mr. John Smith, Director of Admissions, North Carolina Agricultural and Technical State University, 1601 East Market Street, Webb Hall, Greensboro, NC 27411. *Phone:* 336-334-7946. *Toll-free phone:* 800-443-8964. *Fax:* 336-334-7478. *E-mail:* uadmit@ncat.edu.

■ *See page 2092 for a narrative description.*

NORTH CAROLINA CENTRAL UNIVERSITY

Durham, North Carolina

- **State-supported** comprehensive, founded 1910, part of University of North Carolina System
- **Calendar** semesters
- **Degrees** bachelor's, master's, and first professional
- **Urban** 103-acre campus
- **Coed,** 5,362 undergraduate students, 79% full-time, 67% women, 33% men
- **Minimally difficult** entrance level, 89% of applicants were admitted

A historically black constituent institution of the UNC System, NCCU is located in Durham, near Research Triangle, NC. Raleigh, Durham, and Chapel Hill are a hotbed of academic institutions. Both major private grant and federal funding support opportunities for undergraduate involvement in meaningful research activity under the guidance of a faculty mentor.

Undergraduates 4,223 full-time, 1,139 part-time. Students come from 35 states and territories, 20 other countries, 11% are from out of state, 90% African American, 0.7% Asian American or Pacific Islander, 1% Hispanic American, 0.4% Native American, 0.6% international, 7% transferred in. *Retention:* 78% of 2002 full-time freshmen returned.

Freshmen *Admission:* 2,423 applied, 2,146 admitted, 1,053 enrolled. *Average high school GPA:* 2.67. *Test scores:* SAT verbal scores over 500: 16%; SAT math scores over 500: 15%; ACT scores over 18: 27%; SAT verbal scores over 600: 3%; SAT math scores over 600: 2%; ACT scores over 24: 2%; SAT verbal scores over 700: 1%.

Faculty *Total:* 349, 74% full-time, 64% with terminal degrees. *Student/faculty ratio:* 13:1.

Majors Accounting; art; art teacher education; athletic training; biology/biological sciences; biology teacher education; business administration and management; chemistry; chemistry teacher education; computer science; criminal justice/law enforcement administration; dramatic/theatre arts; elementary education; English; English/language arts teacher education; environmental studies; family and consumer economics related; family and consumer sciences/home economics teacher education; family and consumer sciences/human sciences; fine/studio arts; French; French language teacher education; geography; health and physical education; health teacher education; history; history teacher education; hospitality administration; information science/studies; jazz/jazz studies; kindergarten/preschool education; mathematics; mathematics teacher education; middle school education; music; music teacher education; nursing (registered nurse training); parks, recreation and leisure facilities management; physical education teaching and coaching; physics; physics teacher education; political science and government; psychology; public health education and promotion; religious/sacred music; social work; sociology; Spanish; Spanish language teacher education.

Academic Programs *Special study options:* academic remediation for entering students, adult/continuing education programs, advanced placement credit, cooperative education, distance learning, double majors, English as a second language, honors programs, independent study, internships, off-campus study, part-time degree program, services for LD students, study abroad, summer session for credit. *ROTC:* Army (c), Air Force (c). *Unusual degree programs:* 3-2 engineering with Georgia Institute of Technology, North Carolina State University.

Library Shepherd Library plus 1 other with an OPAC.

Computers on Campus 450 computers available on campus for general student use. A campuswide network can be accessed from student residence rooms and from off campus. Internet access, online (class) registration, at least one staffed computer lab available. Computer purchase or lease plan available.

Student Life *Housing options:* coed. Campus housing is university owned. Freshman applicants given priority for college housing. *Activities and organizations:* drama/theater group, student-run newspaper, choral group, marching band, national fraternities, national sororities. *Campus security:* 24-hour emergency response devices and patrols, controlled dormitory access. *Student services:* health clinic, personal/psychological counseling.

Athletics Member NCAA, NAIA. All NCAA Division II. *Intercollegiate sports:* basketball M(s)/W(s), bowling M/W, cross-country running M, football M(s), golf M(s)/W(s), softball W, tennis M/W, track and field M/W, volleyball W.

Standardized Tests *Required:* SAT I or ACT (for admission).

Costs (2003–04) *Tuition:* state resident $1653 full-time; nonresident $11,022 full-time. Part-time tuition and fees vary according to course load. *Required fees:* $1565 full-time. *Room and board:* $4311; room only: $2464. Room and board charges vary according to board plan. *Waivers:* employees or children of employees.

Financial Aid Of all full-time matriculated undergraduates who enrolled in 2001, 2,894 applied for aid, 2,429 were judged to have need, 862 had their need fully met. In 2001, 410 non-need-based awards were made. *Average percent of need met:* 72%. *Average financial aid package:* $6621. *Average need-based loan:* $3487. *Average need-based gift aid:* $3348. *Average non-need-based aid:* $7144.

Applying *Application fee:* $30. *Required:* high school transcript. *Recommended:* 3 letters of recommendation. *Application deadlines:* 7/1 (freshmen), 7/1 (transfers). *Notification:* continuous (freshmen), continuous (transfers).

Admissions Contact Ms. Jocelyn L. Foy, Undergraduate Director of Admissions, North Carolina Central University, PO Box 19717, Durham, NC 27707. *Phone:* 919-530-6298. *Toll-free phone:* 877-667-7533. *Fax:* 919-530-7625. *E-mail:* athorpe@wpo.nccu.edu.

■ *See page 2094 for a narrative description.*

NORTH CAROLINA SCHOOL OF THE ARTS

Winston-Salem, North Carolina

- **State-supported** comprehensive, founded 1963, part of University of North Carolina System
- **Calendar** trimesters
- **Degrees** diplomas, bachelor's, master's, and post-master's certificates
- **Urban** 57-acre campus
- **Endowment** $16.8 million
- **Coed,** 738 undergraduate students, 98% full-time, 41% women, 59% men
- **Very difficult** entrance level, 46% of applicants were admitted

Undergraduates 723 full-time, 15 part-time. Students come from 44 states and territories, 52% are from out of state, 10% African American, 3% Asian American or Pacific Islander, 2% Hispanic American, 0.1% Native American, 1% international, 9% transferred in, 55% live on campus. *Retention:* 74% of 2002 full-time freshmen returned.

Freshmen *Admission:* 744 applied, 339 admitted, 200 enrolled. *Average high school GPA:* 3.48. *Test scores:* SAT verbal scores over 500: 93%; SAT math scores over 500: 78%; ACT scores over 18: 100%; SAT verbal scores over 600: 45%; SAT math scores over 600: 34%; ACT scores over 24: 38%; SAT verbal scores over 700: 11%; SAT math scores over 700: 6%; ACT scores over 30: 9%.

Faculty *Total:* 139, 97% full-time. *Student/faculty ratio:* 8:1.

Majors Cinematography and film/video production; dance; dramatic/theatre arts; film/cinema studies; music performance; piano and organ; theatre design and technology; visual and performing arts; voice and opera.

Academic Programs *Special study options:* academic remediation for entering students, services for LD students.

Library Semans Library plus 1 other with 87,917 titles, 490 serial subscriptions, 73,025 audiovisual materials.

Computers on Campus 60 computers available on campus for general student use. Internet access, online (class) registration, at least one staffed computer lab available.

Student Life *Housing:* on-campus residence required through sophomore year. *Options:* coed. Campus housing is university owned and is provided by a third party. Freshman campus housing is guaranteed. *Activities and organizations:* drama/theater group, choral group, Pride (gay/lesbian organization), Appreciation of Black Artists. *Campus security:* 24-hour emergency response devices and patrols, controlled dormitory access. *Student services:* health clinic, personal/psychological counseling.

Standardized Tests *Required:* SAT I or ACT (for admission).

Costs (2003–04) *Tuition:* state resident $2305 full-time; nonresident $13,435 full-time. Full-time tuition and fees vary according to program. Part-time tuition and fees vary according to course load. *Required fees:* $1360 full-time. *Room and board:* $5530; room only: $2865. Room and board charges vary according to board plan and housing facility.

Financial Aid Of all full-time matriculated undergraduates who enrolled in 2002, 459 applied for aid, 367 were judged to have need, 44 had their need fully met. 126 Federal Work-Study jobs (averaging $397). In 2002, 71 non-need-based awards were made. *Average percent of need met:* 77%. *Average financial aid package:* $9381. *Average need-based loan:* $3332. *Average need-based gift aid:* $4270. *Average non-need-based aid:* $2994. *Average indebtedness upon graduation:* $15,832.

Applying *Options:* electronic application. *Application fee:* $50. *Required:* high school transcript, 2 letters of recommendation, audition. *Required for some:* essay or personal statement, interview. *Application deadline:* 3/1 (freshmen), rolling (transfers). *Notification:* continuous (freshmen), continuous (transfers).

Admissions Contact Ms. Sheeler Lawson, Director of Admissions, North Carolina School of the Arts, 1533 South Main Street, PO Box 12189, Winston-Salem, NC 27127-2188. *Phone:* 336-770-3290. *Fax:* 336-770-3370. *E-mail:* admissions@ncarts.edu.

NORTH CAROLINA STATE UNIVERSITY

Raleigh, North Carolina

- **State-supported** university, founded 1887, part of University of North Carolina System
- **Calendar** semesters
- **Degrees** associate, bachelor's, master's, doctoral, first professional, and first professional certificates
- **Suburban** 1623-acre campus
- **Endowment** $314.3 million
- **Coed,** 22,971 undergraduate students, 82% full-time, 42% women, 58% men
- **Very difficult** entrance level, 62% of applicants were admitted

Undergraduates 18,904 full-time, 4,067 part-time. Students come from 51 states and territories, 65 other countries, 8% are from out of state, 10% African American, 5% Asian American or Pacific Islander, 2% Hispanic American, 0.7% Native American, 1% international, 5% transferred in, 32% live on campus. *Retention:* 90% of 2002 full-time freshmen returned.

Freshmen *Admission:* 12,852 applied, 7,947 admitted, 3,931 enrolled. *Average high school GPA:* 4.00. *Test scores:* SAT verbal scores over 500: 88%; SAT math scores over 500: 95%; ACT scores over 18: 99%; SAT verbal scores over 600: 42%; SAT math scores over 600: 60%; ACT scores over 24: 68%; SAT verbal scores over 700: 6%; SAT math scores over 700: 14%; ACT scores over 30: 21%.

Faculty *Total:* 1,823, 90% full-time, 89% with terminal degrees. *Student/faculty ratio:* 15:1.

Majors Accounting; aerospace, aeronautical and astronautical engineering; agribusiness; agricultural and extension education; agricultural and food products processing; agricultural/biological engineering and bioengineering; agricultural business and management; agricultural economics; agricultural teacher education; agriculture; agronomy and crop science; American government and politics; animal sciences; anthropology; apparel and textile manufacturing; apparel and textile marketing management; applied mathematics; architecture; arts management; biochemistry; biology/biological sciences; biology teacher education; biomedical/medical engineering; botany/plant biology; business administration and management; chemical engineering; chemistry; chemistry teacher education; civil engineering; communication/speech communication and rhetoric; computer engineering; computer science; construction engineering; construction management; creative writing; criminology; design and applied arts related; design and visual communications; ecology; economics; education; electrical, electronics and communications engineering; engineering; English; English/language arts teacher education; environmental design/architecture; environmental/environmental health engineering; environmental science; environmental studies; film/cinema studies; finance; fishing and fisheries sciences and management; food science; foreign language teacher education; forest/forest resources management; French; French language teacher education; geology/earth science; graphic design; health occupations teacher education; history; history teacher education; horticultural science; human resources management; hydrology and water resources science; industrial design; industrial engineering; information technology; landscape architecture; landscaping and groundskeeping; liberal arts and sciences/liberal studies; marketing/marketing management; mass communication/media; materials engineering; materials science; mathematics; mathematics teacher education; mechanical engineering; meteorology; microbiology; middle school education; natural resources/conservation; natural resources management and policy; nuclear engineering; oceanography (chemical and physical); paleontology; parks, recreation and leisure facilities management; parks, recreation, and leisure related; philosophy; physics; physics related; physics teacher education; plant protection and integrated pest management; political science and government; political science and government related; poultry science; psychology; psychology related; public policy analysis; public relations/image management; religious studies; sales and marketing/marketing and distribution teacher education; science teacher education; science, technology and society; secondary education; social studies teacher education; social work; sociology; soil science and agronomy; Spanish; Spanish language teacher education; sport and fitness administration; statistics; technology/industrial arts teacher education; textile science; textile sciences and engineering; tourism and travel services management; turf and turfgrass management; wildlife and wildlands science and management; wood science and wood products/pulp and paper technology; zoology/animal biology.

Academic Programs *Special study options:* academic remediation for entering students, accelerated degree program, adult/continuing education programs, advanced placement credit, cooperative education, distance learning, double majors, freshman honors college, honors programs, independent study, internships, off-campus study, part-time degree program, services for LD students, student-designed majors, study abroad, summer session for credit. *ROTC:* Army (b), Navy (b), Air Force (b).

Library D. H. Hill Library plus 4 others with 986,993 titles, 17,050 serial subscriptions, 164,821 audiovisual materials, an OPAC, a Web page.

Computers on Campus 4600 computers available on campus for general student use. A campuswide network can be accessed from student residence rooms and from off campus. Internet access, at least one staffed computer lab available. Computer purchase or lease plan available.

Student Life *Housing options:* coed, men-only, women-only, disabled students. Campus housing is university owned. Freshman applicants given priority for college housing. *Activities and organizations:* drama/theater group, student-run newspaper, radio and television station, choral group, marching band, student government, student media, student musical groups, intramural sports, national fraternities, national sororities. *Campus security:* 24-hour emergency response devices and patrols, student patrols, late-night transport/escort service, controlled dormitory access. *Student services:* health clinic, personal/psychological counseling, women's center, legal services.

Athletics Member NCAA. All Division I except football (Division I-A). *Intercollegiate sports:* baseball M(s), basketball M(s)/W(s), cheerleading M/W, cross-country running M(s)/W(s), fencing M/W, golf M(s)/W, gymnastics M/W(s), ice hockey M(c), lacrosse M(c), racquetball M(c)/W(c), riflery M/W, rugby M(c)/W(c), sailing M(c)/W(c), skiing (downhill) M(c)/W(c), soccer M(s)/W(s), softball W(s), swimming M(s)/W(s), tennis M(s)/W(s), track and field M(s)/W(s), volleyball M(c)/W(s), water polo M(c)/W(c), weight lifting M(c)/W(c), wrestling M(s). *Intramural sports:* archery M/W, badminton M/W, baseball M, basketball M/W, bowling M/W, crew M/W, cross-country running M/W, equestrian sports M/W, fencing M/W, field hockey W, football M/W, golf M/W, gymnastics M/W, ice hockey M, lacrosse M/W, racquetball M/W, riflery M/W, rugby M/W, sailing M/W, skiing (downhill) M/W, soccer M/W, softball M/W, squash M/W, swimming M/W, table tennis M/W, tennis M/W, track and field M/W, volleyball M/W, water polo M/W, weight lifting M, wrestling M.

Standardized Tests *Required:* SAT I or ACT (for admission). *Recommended:* SAT II: Subject Tests (for admission).

Costs (2004–05) *Tuition:* state resident $3255 full-time; nonresident $15,103 full-time. Part-time tuition and fees vary according to course load. *Required fees:* $1089 full-time. *Room and board:* $6496; room only: $3920. Room and board charges vary according to board plan and housing facility. *Payment plans:* installment, deferred payment. *Waivers:* senior citizens and employees or children of employees.

Financial Aid Of all full-time matriculated undergraduates who enrolled in 2003, 9,564 applied for aid, 7,628 were judged to have need, 1,827 had their need fully met. 579 Federal Work-Study jobs (averaging $1028). 10 state and other part-time jobs (averaging $2030). In 2003, 4061 non-need-based awards were made. *Average percent of need met:* 84%. *Average financial aid package:* $7497. *Average need-based loan:* $2763. *Average need-based gift aid:* $5356. *Average non-need-based aid:* $6852. *Average indebtedness upon graduation:* $16,897.

Applying *Options:* electronic application, early admission, early action, deferred entrance. *Application fee:* $55. *Required:* high school transcript. *Required for some:* interview. *Recommended:* essay or personal statement, minimum 3.0 GPA. *Application deadlines:* 2/1 (freshmen), 4/1 (transfers). *Notification:* continuous (freshmen), 1/15 (early action), continuous (transfers).

Admissions Contact Mr. Thomas H. Griffin, Director of Undergraduate Admissions, North Carolina State University, Box 7103, 112 Peele Hall, Raleigh, NC 27695. *Phone:* 919-515-2434. *Fax:* 919-515-5039. *E-mail:* undergrad_admissions@ncsu.edu.

NORTH CAROLINA WESLEYAN COLLEGE

Rocky Mount, North Carolina

- **Independent** 4-year, founded 1956, affiliated with United Methodist Church
- **Calendar** semesters
- **Degrees** bachelor's (also offers adult part-time degree program with significant enrollment not reflected in profile)
- **Suburban** 200-acre campus
- **Endowment** $8.2 million
- **Coed,** 1,695 undergraduate students, 66% full-time, 59% women, 41% men
- **Moderately difficult** entrance level, 83% of applicants were admitted

Undergraduates 1,124 full-time, 571 part-time. Students come from 22 states and territories, 12% are from out of state, 40% African American, 0.8% Asian American or Pacific Islander, 1% Hispanic American, 0.9% Native American, 0.1% international, 5% transferred in, 28% live on campus. *Retention:* 57% of 2002 full-time freshmen returned.

North Carolina Wesleyan College (continued)

Freshmen *Admission:* 651 applied, 542 admitted, 200 enrolled. *Average high school GPA:* 2.79. *Test scores:* SAT verbal scores over 500: 26%; SAT math scores over 500: 26%; SAT verbal scores over 600: 6%; SAT math scores over 600: 6%; SAT verbal scores over 700: 1%.

Faculty *Total:* 194, 23% full-time, 51% with terminal degrees. *Student/faculty ratio:* 15:1.

Majors Accounting; anthropology; biology/biological sciences; business administration and management; chemistry; criminal justice/law enforcement administration; dramatic/theatre arts; education; elementary education; English; environmental studies; history; hotel/motel administration; information science/studies; legal studies; mathematics; middle school education; philosophy; physical education teaching and coaching; political science and government; pre-medical studies; psychology; religious studies; secondary education; sociology; special products marketing.

Academic Programs *Special study options:* academic remediation for entering students, accelerated degree program, adult/continuing education programs, advanced placement credit, cooperative education, distance learning, double majors, honors programs, independent study, internships, part-time degree program, services for LD students, summer session for credit.

Library Elizabeth Braswell Pearsall Library with 88,975 titles, 11,245 serial subscriptions, 1,810 audiovisual materials, an OPAC, a Web page.

Computers on Campus 43 computers available on campus for general student use. A campuswide network can be accessed. At least one staffed computer lab available.

Student Life *Housing:* on-campus residence required through sophomore year. *Options:* coed, men-only, disabled students. *Activities and organizations:* drama/theater group, student-run newspaper, choral group, Club Dramatica, Student Government Association, gospel choir, Wesleyan Singers, pep band, national fraternities, national sororities. *Campus security:* 24-hour emergency response devices and patrols, student patrols, late-night transport/escort service, controlled dormitory access. *Student services:* health clinic, personal/psychological counseling.

Athletics Member NCAA. All Division III. *Intercollegiate sports:* baseball M, basketball M/W, golf M, soccer M/W, softball W, tennis M/W, volleyball W. *Intramural sports:* basketball M/W, football M/W, lacrosse M/W, softball M/W, table tennis M/W, tennis M/W, volleyball M/W.

Standardized Tests *Required:* SAT I or ACT (for admission).

Costs (2003–04) *Comprehensive fee:* $18,834 includes full-time tuition ($11,225), mandatory fees ($1054), and room and board ($6555). Part-time tuition: $317 per credit hour. *Required fees:* $97 per credit hour part-time. *College room only:* $3000.

Financial Aid Of all full-time matriculated undergraduates who enrolled in 2002, 292 had their need fully met. *Average percent of need met:* 93%. *Average financial aid package:* $8480. *Average need-based loan:* $3690. *Average need-based gift aid:* $2977.

Applying *Options:* common application, electronic application. *Application fee:* $25. *Required:* high school transcript. *Recommended:* minimum 2.0 GPA, 2 letters of recommendation, interview. *Application deadlines:* rolling (freshmen), 7/15 (transfers). *Notification:* continuous (freshmen), continuous (transfers).

Admissions Contact Ms. Cecelia Summers, Associate Director of Admissions, North Carolina Wesleyan College, 3400 North Wesleyan Boulevard, Rocky Mount, NC 27804. *Phone:* 800-488-6292 Ext. 5202. *Toll-free phone:* 800-488-6292. *Fax:* 252-985-5295. *E-mail:* adm@ncwc.edu.

PEACE COLLEGE
Raleigh, North Carolina

- **Independent** 4-year, founded 1857, affiliated with Presbyterian Church (U.S.A.)
- **Calendar** semesters
- **Degree** bachelor's
- **Urban** 19-acre campus
- **Endowment** $43.3 million
- **Women only,** 701 undergraduate students, 95% full-time
- **Moderately difficult** entrance level, 35% of applicants were admitted

Undergraduates 668 full-time, 33 part-time. 63% are from out of state, 13% African American, 2% Asian American or Pacific Islander, 2% Hispanic American, 0.6% Native American, 1% international, 1% transferred in, 82% live on campus. *Retention:* 71% of 2002 full-time freshmen returned.

Freshmen *Admission:* 251 enrolled. *Average high school GPA:* 3.03. *Test scores:* SAT verbal scores over 500: 44%; SAT math scores over 500: 40%; ACT scores over 18: 56%; SAT verbal scores over 600: 9%; SAT math scores over 600: 6%; ACT scores over 24: 22%; SAT verbal scores over 700: 2%; ACT scores over 30: 11%.

Faculty *Total:* 78, 53% full-time, 58% with terminal degrees. *Student/faculty ratio:* 14:1.

Majors Biology/biological sciences; business administration and management; communication/speech communication and rhetoric; design and visual communications; English; human resources management; liberal arts and sciences/liberal studies; music; music performance; psychology; Spanish.

Academic Programs *Special study options:* academic remediation for entering students, adult/continuing education programs, advanced placement credit, double majors, English as a second language, freshman honors college, honors programs, independent study, internships, off-campus study, services for LD students, study abroad. *ROTC:* Army (c), Navy (c), Air Force (c).

Library Lucy Cooper Finch Library with 51,118 titles, 3,900 serial subscriptions, 1,200 audiovisual materials, an OPAC, a Web page.

Computers on Campus 45 computers available on campus for general student use. A campuswide network can be accessed. Internet access, at least one staffed computer lab available.

Student Life *Housing:* on-campus residence required through sophomore year. *Options:* women-only. Campus housing is university owned. Freshman campus housing is guaranteed. *Activities and organizations:* drama/theater group, student-run newspaper, choral group, Student Government Association, Peace Student Christian Association, Recreation Association, Human Resources Society, psychology club. *Campus security:* 24-hour emergency response devices and patrols, late-night transport/escort service, controlled dormitory access. *Student services:* health clinic, personal/psychological counseling.

Athletics Member NCAA. All Division III. *Intercollegiate sports:* basketball W, tennis W, volleyball W. *Intramural sports:* badminton W, basketball W, equestrian sports W, soccer W, softball W, swimming W, table tennis W, tennis W, volleyball W.

Standardized Tests *Required:* SAT I or ACT (for admission).

Costs (2004–05) *Comprehensive fee:* $23,407 includes full-time tuition ($16,881) and room and board ($6526). Part-time tuition: $400 per credit hour. *Payment plans:* installment, deferred payment. *Waivers:* employees or children of employees.

Financial Aid Of all full-time matriculated undergraduates who enrolled in 2003, 513 applied for aid, 434 were judged to have need, 70 had their need fully met. 89 Federal Work-Study jobs. In 2003, 223 non-need-based awards were made. *Average percent of need met:* 72%. *Average financial aid package:* $12,086. *Average need-based loan:* $2897. *Average need-based gift aid:* $9015. *Average non-need-based aid:* $7483. *Average indebtedness upon graduation:* $9938.

Applying *Options:* early admission, deferred entrance. *Application fee:* $25. *Required:* essay or personal statement, high school transcript, minimum 2.0 GPA, 2 letters of recommendation. *Recommended:* interview. *Application deadline:* rolling (freshmen), rolling (transfers). *Notification:* continuous (freshmen), continuous (transfers).

Admissions Contact Mrs. R. Lizzie Wahab, Interim Director of Admissions, Peace College, 15 East Peace Street, Raleigh, NC 27604-1194. *Phone:* 919-508-2023. *Toll-free phone:* 800-PEACE-47. *Fax:* 919-508-2306. *E-mail:* chill@peace.edu.

■ *See page 2156 for a narrative description.*

PFEIFFER UNIVERSITY
Misenheimer, North Carolina

- **Independent United Methodist** comprehensive, founded 1885
- **Calendar** semesters
- **Degrees** bachelor's and master's
- **Rural** 300-acre campus with easy access to Charlotte
- **Endowment** $12.5 million
- **Coed,** 1,188 undergraduate students, 84% full-time, 58% women, 42% men
- **Moderately difficult** entrance level, 72% of applicants were admitted

Undergraduates 992 full-time, 196 part-time. Students come from 33 states and territories, 11 other countries, 19% are from out of state, 20% African American, 0.7% Asian American or Pacific Islander, 1% Hispanic American, 0.3% Native American, 5% international, 9% transferred in, 41% live on campus. *Retention:* 77% of 2002 full-time freshmen returned.

Freshmen *Admission:* 586 applied, 419 admitted, 170 enrolled. *Average high school GPA:* 3.10. *Test scores:* SAT verbal scores over 500: 49%; SAT math scores over 500: 57%; ACT scores over 18: 90%; SAT verbal scores over 600: 9%; SAT math scores over 600: 13%; ACT scores over 24: 25%; SAT verbal scores over 700: 1%; SAT math scores over 700: 1%.

Faculty *Total:* 134, 49% full-time, 58% with terminal degrees. *Student/faculty ratio:* 13:1.

Majors Accounting; arts management; athletic training; biology/biological sciences; business administration and management; business/managerial economics; chemistry; communication/speech communication and rhetoric; criminal justice/law enforcement administration; economics; education; elementary education; engineering; English; environmental science; environmental studies; exercise physiology; finance; history; human services; international business/trade/commerce; journalism; management information systems; marketing/marketing management; mathematics; mathematics and computer science; music; music teacher education; organizational communication; physical education teaching and coaching; political science and government; pre-law studies; pre-medical studies; psychology; public relations/image management; religious education; religious/sacred music; religious studies; science teacher education; social sciences; social studies teacher education; sociology; special education; sport and fitness administration; youth ministry.

Academic Programs *Special study options:* academic remediation for entering students, accelerated degree program, advanced placement credit, cooperative education, double majors, English as a second language, honors programs, independent study, internships, part-time degree program, services for LD students, study abroad, summer session for credit. *ROTC:* Army (c). *Unusual degree programs:* 3-2 engineering with Auburn University.

Library Gustavus A. Pfeiffer Library with 117,000 titles, 415 serial subscriptions, 2,963 audiovisual materials, an OPAC, a Web page.

Computers on Campus 90 computers available on campus for general student use. A campuswide network can be accessed from student residence rooms and from off campus that provide access to e-mail. Internet access, at least one staffed computer lab available.

Student Life *Housing:* on-campus residence required through senior year. *Options:* coed, men-only, women-only. Campus housing is university owned. Freshman applicants given priority for college housing. *Activities and organizations:* drama/theater group, student-run newspaper, choral group, Student Government Association, Religious Life Council, Commuter Student Association, Programming Activities Council, Residence Hall Association. *Campus security:* 24-hour emergency response devices and patrols, late-night transport/escort service, controlled dormitory access. *Student services:* health clinic, personal/psychological counseling, women's center.

Athletics Member NCAA. All Division II. *Intercollegiate sports:* baseball M(s), basketball M(s)/W(s), cheerleading M(s)/W(s), cross-country running M(s)/W(s), golf M(s)/W(s), lacrosse M(s)/W(s), soccer M(s)/W(s), softball W(s), swimming W(s), tennis M(s)/W(s), volleyball W(s). *Intramural sports:* badminton M/W, basketball M/W, football M/W, soccer M/W, softball M/W, tennis M/W, ultimate Frisbee M/W, volleyball M/W, water polo M/W.

Standardized Tests *Required:* SAT I or ACT (for admission).

Costs (2004–05) *Comprehensive fee:* $20,400 includes full-time tuition ($14,570) and room and board ($5830). Full-time tuition and fees vary according to course load. Part-time tuition: $330 per credit hour. Part-time tuition and fees vary according to course load. *College room only:* $3030. Room and board charges vary according to housing facility. *Payment plan:* installment. *Waivers:* employees or children of employees.

Financial Aid Of all full-time matriculated undergraduates who enrolled in 2002, 835 applied for aid, 716 were judged to have need, 370 had their need fully met. 406 Federal Work-Study jobs (averaging $458). In 2002, 313 non-need-based awards were made. *Average percent of need met:* 80%. *Average financial aid package:* $10,324. *Average need-based loan:* $2892. *Average need-based gift aid:* $7825. *Average non-need-based aid:* $5400. *Average indebtedness upon graduation:* $17,125.

Applying *Options:* common application, electronic application, early admission, deferred entrance. *Application fee:* $25. *Required:* high school transcript. *Required for some:* 2 letters of recommendation. *Recommended:* minimum 2.0 GPA, interview. *Application deadline:* rolling (freshmen), rolling (transfers). *Notification:* continuous (freshmen), continuous (transfers).

Admissions Contact Ms. Jennifer Pate, Admissions Counselor, Pfeiffer University, PO Box 960, Highway 52 North, Misenheimer, NC 28109. *Phone:* 704-463-1360 Ext. 2066. *Toll-free phone:* 800-338-2060. *Fax:* 704-463-1363. *E-mail:* admiss@pfeiffer.edu.

PIEDMONT BAPTIST COLLEGE

Winston-Salem, North Carolina

- **Independent Baptist** comprehensive, founded 1947
- **Calendar** semesters
- **Degrees** certificates, associate, bachelor's, and master's
- **Urban** 12-acre campus
- **Endowment** $288,000
- **Coed**
- **Noncompetitive** entrance level

Faculty *Student/faculty ratio:* 11:1.

Student Life *Campus security:* student patrols, late-night transport/escort service, controlled dormitory access, security guards on duty during evening hours.

Athletics Member NCCAA.

Standardized Tests *Required:* ACT (for admission), ACT (for placement).

Costs (2003–04) *Comprehensive fee:* $12,900 includes full-time tuition ($7780), mandatory fees ($600), and room and board ($4520). Full-time tuition and fees vary according to course load and program. Part-time tuition: $325 per hour. Part-time tuition and fees vary according to class time and course load. *Room and board:* Room and board charges vary according to housing facility.

Financial Aid *Financial aid deadline:* 8/31.

Applying *Options:* common application, electronic application, early admission, early action, deferred entrance. *Application fee:* $50. *Required:* essay or personal statement, high school transcript, 2 letters of recommendation, medical history, proof of immunization. *Recommended:* minimum 2.0 GPA, interview.

Admissions Contact Troy Crain, Assistant Director of Admissions, Piedmont Baptist College, 716 Franklin Street, Winston-Salem, NC 27101-5197. *Phone:* 336-725-8344 Ext. 2327. *Toll-free phone:* 800-937-5097. *Fax:* 336-725-5522. *E-mail:* admissions@pbc.edu.

QUEENS UNIVERSITY OF CHARLOTTE

Charlotte, North Carolina

- **Independent Presbyterian** comprehensive, founded 1857
- **Calendar** semesters
- **Degrees** bachelor's, master's, and postbachelor's certificates
- **Suburban** 25-acre campus
- **Endowment** $36.6 million
- **Coed,** 1,411 undergraduate students, 61% full-time, 77% women, 23% men
- **Moderately difficult** entrance level, 74% of applicants were admitted

Undergraduates 861 full-time, 550 part-time. Students come from 32 states and territories, 21 other countries, 20% African American, 1% Asian American or Pacific Islander, 3% Hispanic American, 0.7% Native American, 3% international, 5% transferred in, 75% live on campus. *Retention:* 79% of 2002 full-time freshmen returned.

Freshmen *Admission:* 839 applied, 619 admitted, 252 enrolled. *Average high school GPA:* 3.30. *Test scores:* SAT verbal scores over 500: 69%; SAT math scores over 500: 67%; ACT scores over 18: 94%; SAT verbal scores over 600: 24%; SAT math scores over 600: 21%; ACT scores over 24: 36%; SAT verbal scores over 700: 3%; SAT math scores over 700: 1%.

Faculty *Total:* 113, 68% full-time, 65% with terminal degrees. *Student/faculty ratio:* 12:1.

Majors Accounting; American literature; American studies; applied mathematics; art; biochemistry; biology/biological sciences; business administration and management; computer/information technology services administration related; dramatic/theatre arts; education; elementary education; English; English/language arts teacher education; environmental biology; fine/studio arts; foreign languages and literatures; history; information science/studies; international relations and affairs; journalism; mass communication/media; mathematics; mathematics teacher education; music; music therapy; nursing science; philosophy; piano and organ; political science and government; pre-law studies; pre-medical studies; pre-veterinary studies; psychology; religious studies; secondary education; voice and opera.

Academic Programs *Special study options:* adult/continuing education programs, advanced placement credit, double majors, honors programs, independent study, internships, off-campus study, part-time degree program, study abroad, summer session for credit. *ROTC:* Army (c), Air Force (c).

Library Everett Library plus 1 other with 130,798 titles, 592 serial subscriptions, 1,369 audiovisual materials, an OPAC, a Web page.

Computers on Campus 125 computers available on campus for general student use. A campuswide network can be accessed from student residence rooms. Internet access, online (class) registration, at least one staffed computer lab available. Computer purchase or lease plan available.

Student Life *Housing:* on-campus residence required for freshman year. *Options:* coed, women-only. Campus housing is university owned. Freshman campus housing is guaranteed. *Activities and organizations:* drama/theater group, student-run newspaper, choral group, Senate, College Union Board, Admissions Ambassadors, Students for Black Awareness, International club, national fraternities, national sororities. *Campus security:* 24-hour emergency response devices and patrols, late-night transport/escort service, controlled dormitory access. *Student services:* health clinic, personal/psychological counseling.

Athletics Member NCAA. All Division II. *Intercollegiate sports:* basketball M(s)/W(s), cross-country running M(s)/W(s), golf M(s)/W(s), lacrosse M(s)/

Queens University of Charlotte (continued)
W(s), soccer M(s)/W(s), softball W(s), tennis M(s)/W(s), volleyball W(s). *Intramural sports:* basketball M/W, soccer M/W, softball M/W, table tennis M/W, tennis M/W, volleyball M/W.

Standardized Tests *Required:* SAT I or ACT (for admission).

Costs (2004–05) *Comprehensive fee:* $23,198 includes full-time tuition ($17,008) and room and board ($6190). Part-time tuition: $260 per credit hour. *Room and board:* Room and board charges vary according to board plan. *Payment plan:* installment. *Waivers:* employees or children of employees.

Financial Aid Of all full-time matriculated undergraduates who enrolled in 2002, 510 applied for aid, 382 were judged to have need, 110 had their need fully met. 134 Federal Work-Study jobs (averaging $879). 4 state and other part-time jobs (averaging $999). In 2002, 266 non-need-based awards were made. *Average percent of need met:* 74%. *Average financial aid package:* $10,198. *Average need-based loan:* $2962. *Average need-based gift aid:* $7790. *Average non-need-based aid:* $7426. *Average indebtedness upon graduation:* $15,874.

Applying *Options:* common application, deferred entrance. *Application fee:* $40. *Required:* essay or personal statement, high school transcript, minimum 2.0 GPA, 1 letter of recommendation. *Recommended:* interview. *Application deadline:* rolling (freshmen). *Notification:* continuous (freshmen), continuous (transfers).

Admissions Contact Mr. William Lee, Director of Admissions, Queens University of Charlotte, 1900 Selwyn Avenue, Charlotte, NC 28274. *Phone:* 704-337-2212. *Toll-free phone:* 800-849-0202. *Fax:* 704-337-2403. *E-mail:* admissions@queens.edu.

ROANOKE BIBLE COLLEGE
Elizabeth City, North Carolina

- **Independent Christian** 4-year, founded 1948
- **Calendar** semesters
- **Degrees** certificates, associate, and bachelor's
- **Small-town** 19-acre campus with easy access to Norfolk
- **Endowment** $2.2 million
- **Coed**
- **Minimally difficult** entrance level

Faculty *Student/faculty ratio:* 13:1.

Student Life *Campus security:* 24-hour emergency response devices, controlled dormitory access.

Standardized Tests *Required:* SAT I or ACT (for admission), SAT I or ACT (for placement).

Costs (2003–04) *Comprehensive fee:* $11,800 includes full-time tuition ($6400), mandatory fees ($800), and room and board ($4600). Part-time tuition: $200 per semester hour. *Required fees:* $51 per term part-time. *College room only:* $2400. Room and board charges vary according to board plan.

Financial Aid Of all full-time matriculated undergraduates who enrolled in 2002, 150 applied for aid, 130 were judged to have need, 53 had their need fully met. 15 Federal Work-Study jobs (averaging $811). In 2002, 20. *Average financial aid package:* $5888. *Average need-based loan:* $2450. *Average need-based gift aid:* $3323. *Average non-need-based aid:* $5414. *Average indebtedness upon graduation:* $16,110.

Applying *Options:* electronic application, early admission, deferred entrance. *Application fee:* $25. *Required:* essay or personal statement, high school transcript, reference from church. *Required for some:* interview.

Admissions Contact Mrs. Julie Fields, Director of Admissions and Financial Aid, Roanoke Bible College, 715 North Poindexter Street, Elizabeth City, NC 27909-4054. *Phone:* 252-334-2019. *Toll-free phone:* 800-RBC-8980. *Fax:* 252-334-2071. *E-mail:* admissions@roanokebible.edu.

ST. ANDREWS PRESBYTERIAN COLLEGE
Laurinburg, North Carolina

- **Independent Presbyterian** 4-year, founded 1958
- **Calendar** semesters
- **Degree** bachelor's
- **Small-town** 600-acre campus
- **Endowment** $12.0 million
- **Coed,** 693 undergraduate students, 91% full-time, 60% women, 40% men
- **Moderately difficult** entrance level, 84% of applicants were admitted

Undergraduates 629 full-time, 64 part-time. Students come from 35 states and territories, 14 other countries, 45% are from out of state, 13% African American, 2% Asian American or Pacific Islander, 2% Hispanic American, 1% Native American, 6% international, 7% transferred in, 76% live on campus. *Retention:* 72% of 2002 full-time freshmen returned.

Freshmen *Admission:* 668 applied, 562 admitted, 196 enrolled. *Average high school GPA:* 3.03. *Test scores:* SAT verbal scores over 500: 45%; SAT math scores over 500: 46%; SAT verbal scores over 600: 15%; SAT math scores over 600: 8%; SAT verbal scores over 700: 2%.

Faculty *Total:* 89, 42% full-time, 45% with terminal degrees. *Student/faculty ratio:* 10:1.

Majors Art; Asian studies; biology/biological sciences; business administration and management; chemistry; counseling psychology; creative writing; elementary education; English; equestrian studies; fine/studio arts; history; interdisciplinary studies; international business/trade/commerce; liberal arts and sciences/liberal studies; mass communication/media; mathematics; philosophy; physical education teaching and coaching; political science and government; pre-law studies; pre-medical studies; pre-veterinary studies; psychology; religious studies; sport and fitness administration.

Academic Programs *Special study options:* accelerated degree program, adult/continuing education programs, advanced placement credit, double majors, honors programs, independent study, internships, part-time degree program, services for LD students, student-designed majors, study abroad, summer session for credit. *Unusual degree programs:* 3-2 engineering with North Carolina State University; accounting with University of Georgia.

Library DeTamble Library with 108,734 titles, 436 serial subscriptions, 4,405 audiovisual materials, an OPAC, a Web page.

Computers on Campus 100 computers available on campus for general student use. A campuswide network can be accessed from student residence rooms and from off campus. Internet access, at least one staffed computer lab available.

Student Life *Housing:* on-campus residence required through senior year. *Options:* coed, men-only, women-only, disabled students. Campus housing is university owned. *Activities and organizations:* drama/theater group, student-run newspaper, choral group, Business Club, Breaking the Mirror (women's group), Writer's Forum, Student Activities Union, Eco-Action. *Campus security:* 24-hour emergency response devices and patrols, late-night transport/escort service. *Student services:* health clinic, personal/psychological counseling.

Athletics Member NCAA. All Division II. *Intercollegiate sports:* baseball M(s), basketball M(s)/W(s), cross-country running M(s)/W(s), equestrian sports M(s)/W(s), golf M(s)/W(s), lacrosse M(s)/W(s), rugby M(c)/W(c), soccer M(s)/W(s), softball W(s), tennis M(s)/W(s), volleyball W(s). *Intramural sports:* basketball M/W, football M/W, rugby M(c)/W(c), softball M/W, table tennis M/W, tennis M/W, volleyball M/W.

Standardized Tests *Required:* SAT I or ACT (for admission).

Costs (2003–04) *Comprehensive fee:* $20,525 includes full-time tuition ($14,540), mandatory fees ($575), and room and board ($5410). Full-time tuition and fees vary according to location. Part-time tuition: $410 per credit. Part-time tuition and fees vary according to location. *College room only:* $2200. *Payment plan:* installment. *Waivers:* adult students, senior citizens, and employees or children of employees.

Financial Aid Of all full-time matriculated undergraduates who enrolled in 2003, 507 applied for aid, 422 were judged to have need, 123 had their need fully met. 220 Federal Work-Study jobs (averaging $1800). 75 state and other part-time jobs (averaging $1800). In 2003, 226 non-need-based awards were made. *Average percent of need met:* 81%. *Average financial aid package:* $12,835. *Average need-based loan:* $3243. *Average need-based gift aid:* $9793. *Average non-need-based aid:* $9723. *Average indebtedness upon graduation:* $14,162.

Applying *Options:* common application, electronic application, early admission, early decision, deferred entrance. *Application fee:* $30. *Required:* high school transcript, 1 letter of recommendation. *Required for some:* essay or personal statement, interview. *Recommended:* minimum 2.0 GPA. *Application deadline:* rolling (freshmen), rolling (transfers). *Early decision:* 12/1. *Notification:* continuous (freshmen), 1/1 (early decision), continuous (transfers).

Admissions Contact Rev. Glenn Batten, Dean for Student Affairs and Enrollment, St. Andrews Presbyterian College, 1700 Dogwood Mile, Laurinburg, NC 28352. *Phone:* 910-277-5555. *Toll-free phone:* 800-763-0198. *Fax:* 910-277-5087. *E-mail:* admission@sapc.edu.

SAINT AUGUSTINE'S COLLEGE
Raleigh, North Carolina

- **Independent Episcopal** 4-year, founded 1867
- **Calendar** semesters
- **Degree** bachelor's
- **Urban** 105-acre campus
- **Endowment** $17.2 million
- **Coed,** 1,635 undergraduate students, 95% full-time, 49% women, 51% men
- **Minimally difficult** entrance level, 60% of applicants were admitted

Undergraduates 1,558 full-time, 77 part-time. Students come from 33 states and territories, 17 other countries, 94% African American, 1% Hispanic American, 4% international, 3% transferred in, 62% live on campus. *Retention:* 66% of 2002 full-time freshmen returned.

Freshmen *Admission:* 1,957 applied, 1,181 admitted, 548 enrolled. *Average high school GPA:* 2.60. *Test scores:* SAT verbal scores over 500: 10%; SAT math scores over 500: 11%; ACT scores over 18: 23%.

Faculty *Total:* 121, 64% full-time, 45% with terminal degrees. *Student/faculty ratio:* 17:1.

Majors Accounting; African-American/Black studies; art; biology/biological sciences; biology teacher education; business administration and management; business teacher education; chemistry; communication/speech communication and rhetoric; computer and information sciences; computer/information technology services administration related; computer science; criminal justice/law enforcement administration; dramatic/theatre arts and stagecraft related; early childhood education; education (K-12); elementary education; English; English/language arts teacher education; film/cinema studies; forensic science and technology; health and physical education related; history; international business/trade/commerce; international relations and affairs; mathematics; mathematics teacher education; music performance; music teacher education; occupational health and industrial hygiene; organizational behavior; physical education teaching and coaching; political science and government; pre-law studies; pre-medical studies; psychology; real estate; social studies teacher education; sociology; special education; visual and performing arts.

Academic Programs *Special study options:* academic remediation for entering students, accelerated degree program, adult/continuing education programs, cooperative education, double majors, honors programs, independent study, internships, off-campus study, part-time degree program, summer session for credit. *ROTC:* Army (b), Air Force (c).

Library Prezell R. Robinson Library with 76,000 titles, 415 serial subscriptions, 300 audiovisual materials, an OPAC, a Web page.

Computers on Campus 130 computers available on campus for general student use. A campuswide network can be accessed from student residence rooms that provide access to online course enhancement via blackboard.com. Internet access, at least one staffed computer lab available.

Student Life *Housing:* on-campus residence required for freshman year. *Options:* men-only, women-only. Campus housing is university owned. Freshman campus housing is guaranteed. *Activities and organizations:* drama/theater group, student-run newspaper, radio and television station, choral group, chorale group, jazz band, International Student Organization, national fraternities, national sororities. *Campus security:* 24-hour emergency response devices and patrols. *Student services:* health clinic, personal/psychological counseling.

Athletics Member NCAA. All Division II. *Intercollegiate sports:* baseball M(s), basketball M(s)/W(s), bowling W(s), cheerleading W(s), cross-country running M(s)/W(s), football M(s), golf M(s), softball W(s), tennis M(s)/W(s), track and field M(s)/W(s), volleyball W(s).

Standardized Tests *Required:* SAT I or ACT (for admission).

Costs (2003–04) *Comprehensive fee:* $14,490 includes full-time tuition ($7280), mandatory fees ($2250), and room and board ($4960). Full-time tuition and fees vary according to course load and program. Part-time tuition: $260 per credit. Part-time tuition and fees vary according to course load, program, and reciprocity agreements. *Required fees:* $95 per credit part-time. *College room only:* $2084. Room and board charges vary according to housing facility and location. *Payment plan:* installment. *Waivers:* senior citizens and employees or children of employees.

Financial Aid Of all full-time matriculated undergraduates who enrolled in 2002, 1,400 applied for aid, 1,147 were judged to have need, 530 had their need fully met. 318 Federal Work-Study jobs (averaging $1623). 33 state and other part-time jobs (averaging $1065). In 2002, 214 non-need-based awards were made. *Average percent of need met:* 69%. *Average financial aid package:* $11,387. *Average need-based loan:* $3094. *Average non-need-based aid:* $8906. *Average indebtedness upon graduation:* $10,416.

Applying *Options:* electronic application, deferred entrance. *Application fee:* $25. *Required:* essay or personal statement, high school transcript, 3 letters of recommendation, medical history. *Recommended:* minimum 2.0 GPA. *Application deadline:* 7/1 (freshmen), rolling (transfers). *Notification:* continuous (freshmen), continuous (transfers).

Admissions Contact Ms. Sadiya Wims, Assistant Director, Admissions, Saint Augustine's College, 1315 Oakwood Avenue, Raleigh, NC 27610-2298. *Phone:* 919-516-4012. *Toll-free phone:* 800-948-1126. *Fax:* 919-516-5805. *E-mail:* admissions@es.st-aug.edu.

■ See page 2276 for a narrative description.

SALEM COLLEGE
Winston-Salem, North Carolina

- **Independent Moravian** comprehensive, founded 1772
- **Calendar** 4-1-4
- **Degrees** bachelor's and master's (only students 23 or over are eligible to enroll part-time; men may attend evening program only)
- **Urban** 57-acre campus
- **Endowment** $44.5 million
- **Women only,** 910 undergraduate students, 80% full-time
- **Moderately difficult** entrance level, 70% of applicants were admitted

Undergraduates 726 full-time, 184 part-time. Students come from 25 states and territories, 17 other countries, 42% are from out of state, 20% African American, 1% Asian American or Pacific Islander, 3% Hispanic American, 0.6% Native American, 6% international, 2% transferred in, 89% live on campus. *Retention:* 79% of 2002 full-time freshmen returned.

Freshmen *Admission:* 164 enrolled. *Average high school GPA:* 3.50. *Test scores:* SAT verbal scores over 500: 81%; SAT math scores over 500: 76%; SAT verbal scores over 600: 40%; SAT math scores over 600: 34%; SAT verbal scores over 700: 7%; SAT math scores over 700: 4%.

Faculty *Total:* 95, 55% full-time, 61% with terminal degrees. *Student/faculty ratio:* 13:1.

Majors Accounting; American studies; art history, criticism and conservation; arts management; biology/biological sciences; business administration and management; chemistry; clinical laboratory science/medical technology; economics; education; English; fine/studio arts; French; German; history; interdisciplinary studies; interior design; international business/trade/commerce; international relations and affairs; mass communication/media; mathematics; music; music performance; philosophy; physician assistant; psychology; religious studies; sociology; Spanish.

Academic Programs *Special study options:* adult/continuing education programs, advanced placement credit, double majors, external degree program, honors programs, independent study, internships, off-campus study, part-time degree program, student-designed majors, study abroad, summer session for credit. *ROTC:* Army (c). *Unusual degree programs:* 3-2 engineering with Duke University, Vanderbilt University.

Library Gramley Library plus 1 other with 128,072 titles, 427 serial subscriptions, 13,735 audiovisual materials, an OPAC, a Web page.

Computers on Campus 54 computers available on campus for general student use. A campuswide network can be accessed from student residence rooms and from off campus that provide access to e-mail. Internet access, at least one staffed computer lab available.

Student Life *Housing:* on-campus residence required through senior year. *Options:* Campus housing is university owned. Freshman campus housing is guaranteed. *Activities and organizations:* drama/theater group, student-run newspaper, choral group, marching band, Student Government Association, Onua, Campus Activities Council, international club, Ambassadors. *Campus security:* 24-hour emergency response devices and patrols, late-night transport/escort service, controlled dormitory access. *Student services:* health clinic, personal/psychological counseling.

Athletics *Intercollegiate sports:* basketball W, cross-country running W, equestrian sports W, field hockey W, soccer W, softball W, swimming W, tennis W, volleyball W. *Intramural sports:* badminton W, basketball W, fencing W, football W, golf W, rock climbing M/W, softball W, volleyball W, water polo W.

Standardized Tests *Required:* SAT I or ACT (for admission).

Costs (2003–04) *Comprehensive fee:* $24,585 includes full-time tuition ($15,500), mandatory fees ($215), and room and board ($8870). *Payment plan:* installment. *Waivers:* employees or children of employees.

Financial Aid *Average financial aid package:* $12,300.

Applying *Options:* common application, electronic application, early admission, deferred entrance. *Application fee:* $25. *Required:* essay or personal statement, high school transcript, 2 letters of recommendation. *Recommended:* interview. *Application deadline:* rolling (freshmen), rolling (transfers). *Notification:* continuous (freshmen), continuous (transfers).

Admissions Contact Ms. Dana E. Evans, Dean of Admissions and Financial Aid, Salem College, PO Box 10548, Shober House, Winston-Salem, NC 27108. *Phone:* 336-721-2621. *Toll-free phone:* 800-327-2536. *Fax:* 336-724-7102. *E-mail:* admissions@salem.edu.

■ See page 2336 for a narrative description.

SHAW UNIVERSITY
Raleigh, North Carolina

- **Independent Baptist** comprehensive, founded 1865
- **Calendar** semesters

Shaw University (continued)
- **Degrees** certificates, associate, bachelor's, master's, and first professional
- **Urban** 30-acre campus
- **Endowment** $11.0 million
- **Coed,** 2,446 undergraduate students, 87% full-time, 63% women, 37% men
- **Minimally difficult** entrance level, 44% of applicants were admitted

Undergraduates 2,120 full-time, 326 part-time. Students come from 32 states and territories, 15 other countries, 25% are from out of state, 84% African American, 0.2% Hispanic American, 0.1% Native American, 3% international, 6% transferred in, 39% live on campus. *Retention:* 62% of 2002 full-time freshmen returned.

Freshmen *Admission:* 3,854 applied, 1,707 admitted, 509 enrolled. *Average high school GPA:* 2.45. *Test scores:* SAT verbal scores over 500: 13%; SAT math scores over 500: 14%; SAT verbal scores over 600: 1%; SAT math scores over 600: 3%.

Faculty *Total:* 238, 37% full-time, 50% with terminal degrees. *Student/faculty ratio:* 15:1.

Majors Accounting; African studies; audiology and speech-language pathology; biology/biological sciences; business administration and management; chemistry; computer and information sciences; computer science; criminal justice/safety; dramatic/theatre arts; elementary education; English; English/language arts teacher education; environmental studies; gerontology; international business/trade/commerce; international relations and affairs; liberal arts and sciences/liberal studies; mass communication/media; mathematics; mathematics teacher education; music; parks, recreation and leisure; philosophy; physics; political science and government; psychology; public administration; religious studies; social work; sociology; special education (mentally retarded); therapeutic recreation.

Academic Programs *Special study options:* academic remediation for entering students, accelerated degree program, adult/continuing education programs, advanced placement credit, distance learning, double majors, honors programs, independent study, internships, off-campus study, part-time degree program, services for LD students, student-designed majors, study abroad, summer session for credit. *ROTC:* Army (c), Air Force (c). *Unusual degree programs:* 3-2 engineering with North Carolina State University, North Carolina Agricultural and Technical State University.

Library James E. Cheek Learning Resources Center plus 1 other with 152,132 titles, 6,910 serial subscriptions, 840 audiovisual materials, an OPAC, a Web page.

Computers on Campus 150 computers available on campus for general student use. A campuswide network can be accessed. Internet access, online (class) registration, at least one staffed computer lab available.

Student Life *Housing:* on-campus residence required for freshman year. *Options:* men-only, women-only. Campus housing is university owned. *Activities and organizations:* drama/theater group, student-run newspaper, radio station, choral group, marching band, Student Government Association, choir, University band, Shaw Players, academic clubs, national fraternities, national sororities. *Campus security:* 24-hour emergency response devices and patrols, late-night transport/escort service, 24-hour electronic surveillance cameras. *Student services:* health clinic, personal/psychological counseling.

Athletics Member NCAA. All Division II. *Intercollegiate sports:* baseball M(s), basketball M(s)/W(s), bowling W(s), cross-country running M(s)/W(s), football M, softball W(s), tennis M(s)/W(s), track and field M(s)/W(s), volleyball W(s). *Intramural sports:* basketball M/W, tennis M/W, volleyball M/W.

Standardized Tests *Required:* SAT I or ACT (for admission).

Costs (2003–04) *Comprehensive fee:* $14,832 includes full-time tuition ($7800), mandatory fees ($1378), and room and board ($5654). *College room only:* $2448. *Payment plans:* installment, deferred payment. *Waivers:* employees or children of employees.

Financial Aid Of all full-time matriculated undergraduates who enrolled in 2002, 2,173 applied for aid, 2,033 were judged to have need. 337 Federal Work-Study jobs (averaging $1237). In 2002, 35 non-need-based awards were made. *Average financial aid package:* $8145. *Average need-based loan:* $3708. *Average need-based gift aid:* $5019. *Average non-need-based aid:* $9581. *Average indebtedness upon graduation:* $17,125. *Financial aid deadline:* 6/1.

Applying *Options:* common application, electronic application, early admission, deferred entrance. *Application fee:* $25. *Required:* essay or personal statement, high school transcript, minimum 2.0 GPA. *Application deadlines:* 7/30 (freshmen), 7/30 (transfers). *Notification:* continuous until 8/25 (freshmen).

Admissions Contact Mr. Paul Vandergrift, Director of Admissions and Recruitment, Shaw University, 118 East South Street, Raleigh, NC 27601-2399. *Phone:* 919-546-8275. *Toll-free phone:* 800-214-6683. *Fax:* 919-546-8271. *E-mail:* paulv@shawu.edu.

Southeastern Baptist Theological Seminary

Wake Forest, North Carolina

- **Independent Southern Baptist** comprehensive, founded 1950
- **Calendar** semesters
- **Degrees** certificates, associate, bachelor's, master's, doctoral, and first professional
- **Small-town** 450-acre campus with easy access to Raleigh
- **Coed**
- **Noncompetitive** entrance level

Student Life *Campus security:* 24-hour emergency response devices and patrols, late-night transport/escort service.

Standardized Tests *Recommended:* SAT I and SAT II or ACT (for placement).

Costs (2003–04) *Tuition:* Contact college for tuition, fees, and room and board expenses.

Applying *Options:* common application. *Application fee:* $25. *Required:* essay or personal statement, high school transcript, 3 letters of recommendation. *Required for some:* interview.

Admissions Contact Southeastern Baptist Theological Seminary, PO Box 1889, Wake Forest, NC 27588. *Phone:* 919-761-2280. *Toll-free phone:* 800-284-6317. *E-mail:* admissions@sebts.edu.

The University of North Carolina at Asheville

Asheville, North Carolina

- **State-supported** comprehensive, founded 1927, part of University of North Carolina System
- **Calendar** semesters
- **Degrees** certificates, bachelor's, master's, and postbachelor's certificates
- **Suburban** 265-acre campus
- **Endowment** $13.1 million
- **Coed,** 3,410 undergraduate students, 80% full-time, 57% women, 43% men
- **Moderately difficult** entrance level, 73% of applicants were admitted

Undergraduates 2,727 full-time, 683 part-time. Students come from 40 states and territories, 24 other countries, 13% are from out of state, 2% African American, 2% Asian American or Pacific Islander, 2% Hispanic American, 0.4% Native American, 1% international, 9% transferred in, 37% live on campus. *Retention:* 78% of 2002 full-time freshmen returned.

Freshmen *Admission:* 2,293 applied, 1,663 admitted, 599 enrolled. *Average high school GPA:* 3.70. *Test scores:* SAT verbal scores over 500: 84%; SAT math scores over 500: 86%; ACT scores over 18: 97%; SAT verbal scores over 600: 38%; SAT math scores over 600: 38%; ACT scores over 24: 58%; SAT verbal scores over 700: 5%; SAT math scores over 700: 3%; ACT scores over 30: 9%.

Faculty *Total:* 309, 57% full-time, 65% with terminal degrees. *Student/faculty ratio:* 13:1.

Majors Accounting; art; atmospheric sciences and meteorology; biology/biological sciences; business administration and management; chemistry; classics and languages, literatures and linguistics; computer science; dramatic/theatre arts; economics; English; environmental studies; fine/studio arts; French; German; history; journalism related; liberal arts and sciences/liberal studies; mathematics; music; music related; operations management; philosophy; physics; political science and government; psychology; sociology; Spanish.

Academic Programs *Special study options:* academic remediation for entering students, adult/continuing education programs, advanced placement credit, distance learning, double majors, honors programs, independent study, internships, off-campus study, part-time degree program, student-designed majors, study abroad, summer session for credit.

Library D. Hidden Ramsey Library with 254,179 titles, 2,014 serial subscriptions, 9,816 audiovisual materials, an OPAC, a Web page.

Computers on Campus 350 computers available on campus for general student use. A campuswide network can be accessed from student residence rooms and from off campus that provide access to online grade reports. Internet access, online (class) registration, at least one staffed computer lab available. Computer purchase or lease plan available.

Student Life *Housing:* on-campus residence required for freshman year. *Options:* coed, men-only, women-only, disabled students. Campus housing is university owned and leased by the school. Freshman campus housing is guaranteed. *Activities and organizations:* drama/theater group, student-run newspaper, radio station, choral group, Student Government Association, Underdog Productions, Residence Hall Association, African-American Association, International Student Association, national fraternities, national sororities. *Campus security:* 24-hour emergency response devices and patrols, late-night transport/escort service, dorm entrances secured at night. *Student services:* health clinic, personal/psychological counseling, women's center.

Athletics Member NCAA. All Division I. *Intercollegiate sports:* baseball M(s), basketball M(s)/W(s), cheerleading M/W, cross-country running M(s)/W(s), soccer M(s)/W(s), tennis M(s)/W(s), track and field M(s)/W(s), volleyball W(s). *Intramural sports:* badminton M/W, basketball M/W, football M, golf M/W, racquetball M/W, soccer M/W, softball M/W, tennis M/W, ultimate Frisbee M/W, volleyball M/W, water polo M/W.

Standardized Tests *Required:* SAT I or ACT (for admission).

Costs (2003–04) *Tuition:* state resident $1672 full-time; nonresident $10,497 full-time. Part-time tuition and fees vary according to course load. *Required fees:* $1429 full-time. *Room and board:* $4978; room only: $2548. Room and board charges vary according to housing facility. *Payment plan:* installment. *Waivers:* senior citizens and employees or children of employees.

Financial Aid Of all full-time matriculated undergraduates who enrolled in 2002, 1,689 applied for aid, 1,070 were judged to have need, 439 had their need fully met. 119 Federal Work-Study jobs (averaging $1227). 579 state and other part-time jobs (averaging $1335). In 2002, 280 non-need-based awards were made. *Average percent of need met:* 83%. *Average financial aid package:* $7758. *Average need-based loan:* $3906. *Average need-based gift aid:* $3499. *Average non-need-based aid:* $2925. *Average indebtedness upon graduation:* $13,961.

Applying *Options:* deferred entrance. *Application fee:* $50. *Required:* high school transcript. *Required for some:* interview. *Recommended:* essay or personal statement, minimum 3.0 GPA. *Application deadlines:* 3/12 (freshmen), 4/16 (transfers). *Notification:* continuous (freshmen), continuous (transfers).

Admissions Contact Mr. Scot Schaeffer, Director of Admissions and Financial Aid, The University of North Carolina at Asheville, 117 Lipinsky Hall, CPO 2210, One University Heights, Asheville, NC 28804-8510. *Phone:* 828-251-6481. *Toll-free phone:* 800-531-9842. *Fax:* 828-251-6482. *E-mail:* admissions@unca.edu.

■ *See page 2674 for a narrative description.*

THE UNIVERSITY OF NORTH CAROLINA AT CHAPEL HILL

Chapel Hill, North Carolina

- **State-supported** university, founded 1789, part of University of North Carolina System
- **Calendar** semesters
- **Degrees** certificates, diplomas, bachelor's, master's, doctoral, first professional, and post-master's certificates
- **Suburban** 729-acre campus with easy access to Raleigh-Durham
- **Endowment** $1.1 billion
- **Coed,** 16,144 undergraduate students, 95% full-time, 59% women, 41% men
- **Very difficult** entrance level, 37% of applicants were admitted

Undergraduates 15,355 full-time, 789 part-time. Students come from 54 states and territories, 105 other countries, 18% are from out of state, 11% African American, 6% Asian American or Pacific Islander, 2% Hispanic American, 0.8% Native American, 1% international, 5% transferred in, 59% live on campus. *Retention:* 95% of 2002 full-time freshmen returned.

Freshmen *Admission:* 17,591 applied, 6,441 admitted, 3,516 enrolled. *Test scores:* SAT verbal scores over 500: 96%; SAT math scores over 500: 98%; ACT scores over 18: 99%; SAT verbal scores over 600: 72%; SAT math scores over 600: 78%; ACT scores over 24: 83%; SAT verbal scores over 700: 21%; SAT math scores over 700: 26%; ACT scores over 30: 26%.

Faculty *Total:* 1,408, 92% full-time, 82% with terminal degrees. *Student/faculty ratio:* 14:1.

Majors Accounting; African-American/Black studies; American studies; anthropology; applied mathematics; area, ethnic, cultural, and gender studies related; art history, criticism and conservation; Asian studies; biology/biological sciences; biostatistics; business administration and management; chemistry; classics and languages, literatures and linguistics; clinical laboratory science/medical technology; communication/speech communication and rhetoric; comparative literature; computer science; dental hygiene; dramatic/theatre arts; early childhood education; economics; elementary education; English; English/language arts teacher education; environmental health; environmental science; environmental studies; fine/studio arts; foods, nutrition, and wellness; French language teacher education; geography; geology/earth science; German; German language teacher education; health and physical education; health/health care administration; health teacher education; history; human resources management; information science/studies; Latin American studies; liberal arts and sciences/liberal studies; linguistics; mass communication/media; mathematics; mathematics teacher education; medical radiologic technology; middle school education; music; music performance; music teacher education; nursing (registered nurse training); parks, recreation and leisure facilities management; peace studies and conflict resolution; philosophy; physical sciences related; physics; political science and government; psychology; public health education and promotion; public policy analysis; religious studies; Romance languages; Russian; Russian studies; social studies teacher education; sociology; Spanish language teacher education; speech teacher education; women's studies.

Academic Programs *Special study options:* advanced placement credit, distance learning, double majors, freshman honors college, honors programs, independent study, internships, off-campus study, services for LD students, student-designed majors, study abroad, summer session for credit. *ROTC:* Army (b), Navy (b), Air Force (b).

Library Davis Library plus 14 others with 2.6 million titles, 42,635 serial subscriptions, 225,151 audiovisual materials, an OPAC, a Web page.

Computers on Campus 600 computers available on campus for general student use. A campuswide network can be accessed from student residence rooms and from off campus that provide access to online grade reports. Internet access, online (class) registration, at least one staffed computer lab available. Computer purchase or lease plan available.

Student Life *Housing options:* coed, men-only, women-only, disabled students. Campus housing is university owned. Freshman applicants given priority for college housing. *Activities and organizations:* drama/theater group, student-run newspaper, radio and television station, choral group, marching band, Campus Y, Newman Catholic Student Center Parish, Friendship Association of Chinese Students and Scholars, Residence Hall Association, North Carolina Hillel, national fraternities, national sororities. *Campus security:* 24-hour emergency response devices and patrols, student patrols, late-night transport/escort service, controlled dormitory access, crime prevention programs. *Student services:* health clinic, personal/psychological counseling, women's center, legal services.

Athletics Member NCAA. All Division I except football (Division I-A). *Intercollegiate sports:* baseball M(s)/W(c), basketball M(s)/W(s), crew M(c)/W(s), cross-country running M(s)/W(s), equestrian sports M(c)/W(c), fencing M/W, field hockey W(s), golf M(s)/W(s), gymnastics W(s), lacrosse M(s)/W(s), racquetball M(c)/W(c), rugby M(c)/W(c), sailing M(c)/W(c), soccer M(s)/W(s), softball W(s), swimming M(s)/W(s), tennis M(s)/W(s), track and field M(s)/W(s), ultimate Frisbee M(c)/W(c), volleyball M(c)/W(s), wrestling M(s). *Intramural sports:* badminton M/W, basketball M/W, bowling M/W, cross-country running M/W, field hockey M(c)/W(c), football M/W, golf M(c)/W(c), gymnastics M(c)/W(c), ice hockey M(c)/W(c), lacrosse M(c)/W(c), racquetball M/W, soccer M/W, softball M/W, squash M(c)/W(c), swimming M/W, table tennis M/W, tennis M/W, track and field M/W, ultimate Frisbee M/W, volleyball M/W, water polo M/W, weight lifting M/W, wrestling M(c).

Standardized Tests *Required:* SAT I or ACT (for admission).

Costs (2003–04) *Tuition:* state resident $2955 full-time; nonresident $14,803 full-time. Full-time tuition and fees vary according to program. Part-time tuition and fees vary according to course load, program, and student level. *Required fees:* $1117 full-time. *Room and board:* $6045; room only: $3220. Room and board charges vary according to board plan, housing facility, and location. *Payment plans:* installment, deferred payment. *Waivers:* employees or children of employees.

Financial Aid Of all full-time matriculated undergraduates who enrolled in 2002, 9,045 applied for aid, 4,624 were judged to have need, 3,219 had their need fully met. 824 Federal Work-Study jobs (averaging $1691). In 2002, 2170 non-need-based awards were made. *Average percent of need met:* 100%. *Average financial aid package:* $8983. *Average need-based loan:* $3719. *Average need-based gift aid:* $5325. *Average non-need-based aid:* $5451. *Average indebtedness upon graduation:* $12,314.

Applying *Options:* electronic application, early action, deferred entrance. *Application fee:* $60. *Required:* essay or personal statement, high school transcript, 1 letter of recommendation, counselor's statement. *Application deadlines:* 1/15 (freshmen), 3/1 (transfers). *Notification:* 3/31 (freshmen), 1/31 (early action), 4/15 (transfers).

Admissions Contact The University of North Carolina at Chapel Hill, Campus Box # 2200, Jackson Hall, Chapel Hill, NC 27599-2200. *Phone:* 919-966-3621. *Fax:* 919-962-3045. *E-mail:* uadm@email.unc.edu.

THE UNIVERSITY OF NORTH CAROLINA AT CHARLOTTE

Charlotte, North Carolina

- **State-supported** university, founded 1946, part of University of North Carolina System
- **Calendar** semesters

The University of North Carolina at Charlotte (continued)

- **Degrees** bachelor's, master's, doctoral, and post-master's certificates
- **Suburban** 1000-acre campus
- **Endowment** $67.7 million
- **Coed,** 15,694 undergraduate students, 78% full-time, 54% women, 46% men
- **Moderately difficult** entrance level, 72% of applicants were admitted

Undergraduates 12,191 full-time, 3,503 part-time. Students come from 49 states and territories, 78 other countries, 9% are from out of state, 16% African American, 5% Asian American or Pacific Islander, 2% Hispanic American, 0.5% Native American, 2% international, 11% transferred in, 20% live on campus. *Retention:* 76% of 2002 full-time freshmen returned.

Freshmen *Admission:* 8,478 applied, 6,085 admitted, 2,519 enrolled. *Average high school GPA:* 3.50. *Test scores:* SAT verbal scores over 500: 64%; SAT math scores over 500: 73%; ACT scores over 18: 87%; SAT verbal scores over 600: 15%; SAT math scores over 600: 23%; ACT scores over 24: 25%; SAT verbal scores over 700: 2%; SAT math scores over 700: 2%; ACT scores over 30: 1%.

Faculty *Total:* 1,074, 72% full-time, 71% with terminal degrees. *Student/faculty ratio:* 16:1.

Majors Accounting; African-American/Black studies; anthropology; architecture; area, ethnic, cultural, and gender studies related; art; art teacher education; athletic training/sports medicine; biology/biological sciences; business administration and management; business/managerial economics; chemistry; chemistry teacher education; civil engineering; civil engineering technology; clinical laboratory science/medical technology; communication/speech communication and rhetoric; computer engineering; computer science; criminal justice/safety; dance; drama and dance teacher education; dramatic/theatre arts; earth sciences; economics; electrical, electronic and communications engineering technology; electrical, electronics and communications engineering; elementary education; English; English/language arts teacher education; finance; fine/studio arts; fire services administration; French; French language teacher education; geography; geology/earth science; German; German language teacher education; health and physical education; history; history teacher education; human development and family studies; industrial technology; international business/trade/commerce; kindergarten/preschool education; management information systems; marketing/marketing management; mathematics; mathematics teacher education; mechanical engineering; mechanical engineering/mechanical technology; middle school education; music; music performance; music teacher education; nursing (registered nurse training); operations management; philosophy; physics; political science and government; psychology; religious studies; social work; sociology; Spanish; Spanish language teacher education; special education (mentally retarded).

Academic Programs *Special study options:* adult/continuing education programs, advanced placement credit, cooperative education, distance learning, double majors, English as a second language, freshman honors college, honors programs, internships, off-campus study, part-time degree program, services for LD students, study abroad, summer session for credit. *ROTC:* Army (b), Air Force (b).

Library J. Murrey Atkins Library with 1.7 million titles, 11,084 serial subscriptions, 10,481 audiovisual materials, an OPAC, a Web page.

Computers on Campus 1100 computers available on campus for general student use. A campuswide network can be accessed from student residence rooms and from off campus. Internet access, online (class) registration, at least one staffed computer lab available. Computer purchase or lease plan available.

Student Life *Housing options:* coed, men-only, women-only, disabled students. Campus housing is university owned. *Activities and organizations:* drama/theater group, student-run newspaper, choral group, University Program Board, Student Government Association, Resident Student Association, Black Student Union, Greek Council, national fraternities, national sororities. *Campus security:* 24-hour emergency response devices and patrols, late-night transport/escort service, controlled dormitory access. *Student services:* health clinic, personal/psychological counseling.

Athletics Member NCAA. All Division I. *Intercollegiate sports:* baseball M(s), basketball M(s)/W(s), cross-country running M(s)/W(s), golf M(s), soccer M(s)/W(s), softball W(s), tennis M(s)/W(s), track and field M(s)/W(s), volleyball W(s). *Intramural sports:* archery M(c)/W(c), badminton M(c)/W(c), baseball M(c)/W(c), basketball M/W, bowling M(c)/W(c), fencing M(c)/W(c), football M/W, golf M/W, ice hockey M(c)/W(c), lacrosse M(c)/W(c), racquetball M(c)/W(c), rock climbing M/W, rugby M(c)/W(c), soccer M(c)/W(c), softball M(c)/W(c), swimming M(c)/W(c), table tennis M/W, tennis M(c)/W(c), track and field M/W, volleyball M(c)/W(c), water polo M/W, wrestling M(c)/W(c).

Standardized Tests *Required:* SAT I or ACT (for admission).

Costs (2003–04) *Tuition:* state resident $1904 full-time, $476 per term part-time; nonresident $11,941 full-time, $2986 per term part-time. Full-time tuition and fees vary according to course load. Part-time tuition and fees vary according to course load. *Required fees:* $1201 full-time, $321 per term part-time. *Room and board:* $5076; room only: $2596. Room and board charges vary according to board plan and housing facility. *Waivers:* senior citizens.

Financial Aid Of all full-time matriculated undergraduates who enrolled in 2003, 7,362 applied for aid, 5,744 were judged to have need, 1,814 had their need fully met. 410 Federal Work-Study jobs (averaging $1209). 1,804 state and other part-time jobs (averaging $1630). In 2003, 1935 non-need-based awards were made. *Average percent of need met:* 81%. *Average financial aid package:* $8210. *Average need-based loan:* $3779. *Average need-based gift aid:* $3829. *Average non-need-based aid:* $1691. *Average indebtedness upon graduation:* $17,250.

Applying *Options:* common application, electronic application, early admission, deferred entrance. *Application fee:* $35. *Required:* high school transcript, minimum 2.0 GPA, 1 letter of recommendation, medical history. *Required for some:* interview. *Application deadlines:* 7/1 (freshmen), 7/1 (transfers). *Notification:* continuous (transfers).

Admissions Contact Mr. Craig Fulton, Director of Admissions, The University of North Carolina at Charlotte, 9201 University City Boulevard, New Admissions Building, 1st Floor, Charlotte, NC 28223-0001. *Phone:* 704-687-2213. *Fax:* 704-687-6483. *E-mail:* unccadm@email.uncc.edu.

THE UNIVERSITY OF NORTH CAROLINA AT GREENSBORO

Greensboro, North Carolina

- **State-supported** university, founded 1891, part of University of North Carolina System
- **Calendar** semesters
- **Degrees** bachelor's, master's, and doctoral
- **Urban** 200-acre campus
- **Coed,** 11,106 undergraduate students, 84% full-time, 68% women, 32% men
- **Moderately difficult** entrance level, 47% of applicants were admitted

Undergraduates 9,317 full-time, 1,789 part-time. Students come from 41 states and territories, 55 other countries, 8% are from out of state, 20% African American, 3% Asian American or Pacific Islander, 1% Hispanic American, 0.3% Native American, 0.9% international, 9% transferred in, 34% live on campus. *Retention:* 76% of 2002 full-time freshmen returned.

Freshmen *Admission:* 6,968 applied, 3,297 admitted, 2,056 enrolled. *Average high school GPA:* 3.45. *Test scores:* SAT verbal scores over 500: 60%; SAT math scores over 500: 62%; SAT verbal scores over 600: 18%; SAT math scores over 600: 18%; SAT verbal scores over 700: 2%; SAT math scores over 700: 2%.

Faculty *Total:* 947, 75% full-time, 71% with terminal degrees. *Student/faculty ratio:* 14:1.

Majors Accounting; African-American/Black studies; anthropology; apparel and textiles; applied mathematics; archeology; art; art history, criticism and conservation; art teacher education; audiology and speech-language pathology; biochemistry; biology/biological sciences; biology teacher education; business administration and management; business/managerial economics; business teacher education; chemistry; child development; cinematography and film/video production; classics; classics and languages, literatures and linguistics; clinical laboratory science/medical technology; clothing/textiles; computer and information sciences; computer science; dance; dietetics; drama and dance teacher education; dramatic/theatre arts; early childhood education; economics; elementary education; English; English/language arts teacher education; European studies; family and community services; family and consumer sciences/human sciences; finance; fine/studio arts; foodservice systems administration; foods, nutrition, and wellness; French; French language teacher education; geography; German; German language teacher education; gerontology; health teacher education; history; human development and family studies; interdisciplinary studies; interior design; kinesiology and exercise science; Latin; Latin American studies; liberal arts and sciences/liberal studies; linguistics; management information systems; marketing/marketing management; marriage and family therapy/counseling; mass communication/media; mass communications; mathematics; mathematics teacher education; middle school education; museum studies; music; music history, literature, and theory; music performance; music teacher education; music theory and composition; nursing (registered nurse training); parks, recreation and leisure; parks, recreation and leisure facilities management; philosophy; physical education teaching and coaching; physics; piano and organ; political science and government; pre-dentistry studies; pre-law studies; pre-medical studies; pre-veterinary studies; psychology; public health education and promotion; radio and television; religious studies; Russian; sculpture; sign language interpretation and translation; social science teacher education; social studies teacher education; social work; sociology; Spanish; Spanish language teacher education; special education; special education (hearing impaired); speech and rhetoric; speech teacher education; statistics; urban studies/affairs; voice and opera; women's studies.

Academic Programs *Special study options:* academic remediation for entering students, accelerated degree program, adult/continuing education programs, advanced placement credit, distance learning, double majors, English as a second language, freshman honors college, honors programs, independent study, internships, off-campus study, part-time degree program, services for LD students, student-designed majors, study abroad, summer session for credit. *ROTC:* Army (c), Air Force (c). *Unusual degree programs:* 3-2 business administration with North Carolina State University, University of North Carolina at Charlotte.

Library Jackson Library plus 1 other with 844,448 titles, 8,714 serial subscriptions, 59,027 audiovisual materials, an OPAC, a Web page.

Computers on Campus 500 computers available on campus for general student use. A campuswide network can be accessed from student residence rooms and from off campus. Internet access, online (class) registration, at least one staffed computer lab available. Computer purchase or lease plan available.

Student Life *Housing options:* coed, women-only. Campus housing is university owned. Freshman applicants given priority for college housing. *Activities and organizations:* drama/theater group, student-run newspaper, radio station, choral group, Campus Activities Board, Neo-Black Society, religious organizations, International Students Association, national fraternities, national sororities. *Campus security:* 24-hour emergency response devices and patrols, late-night transport/escort service, controlled dormitory access. *Student services:* health clinic, personal/psychological counseling.

Athletics Member NCAA. All Division I. *Intercollegiate sports:* baseball M(s), basketball M(s)/W(s), cheerleading M/W, cross-country running M(s)/W(s), golf M(s)/W(s), soccer M(s)/W(s), softball W(s), tennis M(s)/W(s), volleyball W(s), wrestling M(s). *Intramural sports:* badminton M/W, basketball M/W, bowling M/W, equestrian sports M(c)/W(c), fencing M(c)/W(c), football M/W, golf M/W, ice hockey M(c), lacrosse M(c)/W(c), racquetball M/W, rugby M(c)/W(c), soccer M/W, softball M/W, swimming M/W, table tennis M/W, tennis M/W, track and field M/W, volleyball M/W.

Standardized Tests *Required:* SAT I or ACT (for admission).

Costs (2003–04) *Tuition:* state resident $1717 full-time; nonresident $12,091 full-time. Part-time tuition and fees vary according to course load. *Required fees:* $1321 full-time. *Room and board:* $4760. Room and board charges vary according to board plan and housing facility. *Waivers:* employees or children of employees.

Financial Aid Of all full-time matriculated undergraduates who enrolled in 2003, 6,571 applied for aid, 4,421 were judged to have need, 2,731 had their need fully met. 299 Federal Work-Study jobs (averaging $1925). In 2003, 3582 non-need-based awards were made. *Average percent of need met:* 88%. *Average financial aid package:* $9269. *Average need-based loan:* $1257. *Average need-based gift aid:* $6721. *Average non-need-based aid:* $3437. *Average indebtedness upon graduation:* $16,942.

Applying *Options:* early admission. *Application fee:* $35. *Required:* high school transcript, minimum 2.0 GPA. *Application deadlines:* 8/1 (freshmen), 8/1 (transfers). *Notification:* continuous (freshmen), continuous (transfers).

Admissions Contact Associate Director of Admissions, The University of North Carolina at Greensboro, 1000 Spring Garden Street, Greensboro, NC 27412-5001. *Phone:* 336-334-5243. *Fax:* 336-334-4180. *E-mail:* undergrad_admissions@uncg.edu.

THE UNIVERSITY OF NORTH CAROLINA AT PEMBROKE

Pembroke, North Carolina

- **State-supported** comprehensive, founded 1887, part of University of North Carolina System
- **Calendar** semesters
- **Degrees** bachelor's and master's
- **Rural** 152-acre campus
- **Endowment** $2.3 million
- **Coed,** 4,253 undergraduate students, 77% full-time, 64% women, 36% men
- **Moderately difficult** entrance level, 43% of applicants were admitted

Undergraduates 3,292 full-time, 961 part-time. Students come from 32 states and territories, 20 other countries, 4% are from out of state, 22% African American, 2% Asian American or Pacific Islander, 2% Hispanic American, 21% Native American, 0.8% international, 11% transferred in, 32% live on campus. *Retention:* 67% of 2002 full-time freshmen returned.

Freshmen *Admission:* 1,902 applied, 809 admitted, 809 enrolled. *Average high school GPA:* 3.02. *Test scores:* SAT verbal scores over 500: 33%; SAT math scores over 500: 38%; ACT scores over 18: 61%; SAT verbal scores over 600: 6%; SAT math scores over 600: 7%; ACT scores over 24: 16%; SAT verbal scores over 700: 1%; SAT math scores over 700: 1%; ACT scores over 30: 7%.

Faculty *Total:* 294, 69% full-time, 60% with terminal degrees. *Student/faculty ratio:* 17:1.

Majors Accounting; American Indian/Native American studies; American studies; art teacher education; athletic training/sports medicine; biology/biological sciences; biology teacher education; business administration and management; chemistry; computer science; criminal justice/safety; dramatic/theatre arts; early childhood education; elementary education; English; English/language arts teacher education; fine/studio arts; health and physical education; history; mass communications; mathematics; mathematics teacher education; middle school education; music; music teacher education; nursing (registered nurse training); parks, recreation and leisure facilities management; philosophy and religious studies related; physical education teaching and coaching; physics; political science and government; psychology; public administration; public health education and promotion; science teacher education; social studies teacher education; social work; sociology; special education (mentally retarded); special education (specific learning disabilities).

Academic Programs *Special study options:* academic remediation for entering students, accelerated degree program, adult/continuing education programs, advanced placement credit, cooperative education, distance learning, double majors, English as a second language, honors programs, independent study, internships, off-campus study, part-time degree program, services for LD students, summer session for credit. *ROTC:* Army (b), Air Force (b).

Library Sampson-Livermore Library with 296,080 titles, 1,561 serial subscriptions, 1,856 audiovisual materials, an OPAC, a Web page.

Computers on Campus 380 computers available on campus for general student use. A campuswide network can be accessed from student residence rooms and from off campus. Internet access, at least one staffed computer lab available.

Student Life *Housing options:* coed, men-only, women-only. Campus housing is university owned and is provided by a third party. *Activities and organizations:* drama/theater group, student-run newspaper, television station, choral group, Phi Kappa Tau, Zeta Tau Alpha, Tau Kappa Epsilon, Sigma Sigma Sigma, Pi Lambda Upsilon, national fraternities, national sororities. *Campus security:* 24-hour emergency response devices and patrols, late-night transport/escort service, controlled dormitory access. *Student services:* health clinic, personal/psychological counseling.

Athletics Member NCAA. All Division II. *Intercollegiate sports:* baseball M(s), basketball M(s)/W(s), cross-country running M(s)/W(s), golf M(s), soccer M(s)/W(s), softball W(s), tennis W(s), track and field M(s), volleyball W(s), wrestling M(s). *Intramural sports:* basketball M/W, bowling M/W, football M/W, golf M/W, racquetball M/W, soccer M/W, softball M/W, tennis M/W, track and field M/W, volleyball M/W, water polo M/W, weight lifting M/W, wrestling M/W.

Standardized Tests *Required:* SAT I or ACT (for admission).

Costs (2003–04) *Tuition:* state resident $1464 full-time; nonresident $10,828 full-time. *Required fees:* $1101 full-time. *Room and board:* $4364; room only: $2510. *Payment plan:* installment.

Financial Aid Of all full-time matriculated undergraduates who enrolled in 2003, 2,679 applied for aid, 2,235 were judged to have need, 520 had their need fully met. 247 Federal Work-Study jobs (averaging $1500). 41 state and other part-time jobs (averaging $1500). In 2003, 88 non-need-based awards were made. *Average percent of need met:* 78%. *Average financial aid package:* $6433. *Average need-based loan:* $3424. *Average need-based gift aid:* $4106. *Average non-need-based aid:* $1465. *Average indebtedness upon graduation:* $11,764.

Applying *Options:* common application, early admission, deferred entrance. *Application fee:* $40. *Required:* high school transcript. *Required for some:* letters of recommendation, interview. *Recommended:* essay or personal statement, minimum 2.0 GPA. *Application deadline:* rolling (freshmen), rolling (transfers). *Notification:* continuous (freshmen), continuous (transfers).

Admissions Contact Mr. John McMillian, Associate Director of Admissions, The University of North Carolina at Pembroke, PO Box 1510, Pembroke, NC 28372-1510. *Phone:* 910-521-6262. *Toll-free phone:* 800-949-UNCP (in-state); 800-949-UNCP (out-of-state). *Fax:* 910-521-6497.

■ *See page 2676 for a narrative description.*

THE UNIVERSITY OF NORTH CAROLINA AT WILMINGTON

Wilmington, North Carolina

- **State-supported** comprehensive, founded 1947, part of University of North Carolina System
- **Calendar** semesters
- **Degrees** bachelor's, master's, and doctoral
- **Urban** 650-acre campus
- **Endowment** $23.4 million
- **Coed,** 9,974 undergraduate students, 90% full-time, 60% women, 40% men
- **Moderately difficult** entrance level, 54% of applicants were admitted

Undergraduates 8,970 full-time, 1,004 part-time. Students come from 46 states and territories, 22 other countries, 13% are from out of state, 5% African American, 2% Asian American or Pacific Islander, 2% Hispanic American, 0.8% Native American, 0.5% international, 10% transferred in, 23% live on campus. *Retention:* 86% of 2002 full-time freshmen returned.

The University of North Carolina at Wilmington (continued)

Freshmen *Admission:* 8,325 applied, 4,522 admitted, 1,772 enrolled. *Average high school GPA:* 3.67. *Test scores:* SAT verbal scores over 500: 71%; SAT math scores over 500: 80%; ACT scores over 18: 93%; SAT verbal scores over 600: 17%; SAT math scores over 600: 26%; ACT scores over 24: 32%; SAT verbal scores over 700: 1%; SAT math scores over 700: 2%; ACT scores over 30: 2%.

Faculty *Total:* 650, 72% full-time, 70% with terminal degrees. *Student/faculty ratio:* 16:1.

Majors Accounting; anthropology; art history, criticism and conservation; athletic training; biology/biological sciences; biology teacher education; business administration and management; business/managerial economics; chemistry; chemistry teacher education; cinematography and film/video production; clinical laboratory science/medical technology; computer science; creative writing; criminal justice/safety; dramatic/theatre arts; economics; education (specific subject areas) related; elementary education; English; English/language arts teacher education; environmental science; environmental studies; finance; fine/studio arts; French; French language teacher education; geography; geology/earth science; health and physical education; history; history teacher education; kindergarten/preschool education; management information systems; marine biology and biological oceanography; marketing/marketing management; mathematics; mathematics teacher education; middle school education; music; music performance; music teacher education; nursing (registered nurse training); parks, recreation and leisure facilities management; philosophy and religious studies related; physical education teaching and coaching; physics; physics teacher education; political science and government; psychology; social work; sociology; Spanish; Spanish language teacher education; special education (emotionally disturbed); special education (mentally retarded); special education (specific learning disabilities); speech and rhetoric; statistics; therapeutic recreation.

Academic Programs *Special study options:* academic remediation for entering students, accelerated degree program, adult/continuing education programs, advanced placement credit, cooperative education, distance learning, double majors, English as a second language, freshman honors college, honors programs, independent study, internships, part-time degree program, services for LD students, study abroad, summer session for credit.

Library William M. Randall Library with 503,093 titles, 3,626 serial subscriptions, 10,901 audiovisual materials, an OPAC, a Web page.

Computers on Campus 778 computers available on campus for general student use. A campuswide network can be accessed from student residence rooms and from off campus. Internet access, online (class) registration, at least one staffed computer lab available. Computer purchase or lease plan available.

Student Life *Housing options:* coed, women-only. Campus housing is university owned. Freshman applicants given priority for college housing. *Activities and organizations:* drama/theater group, student-run newspaper, radio and television station, choral group, Student Government Association, Association of Campus Entertainment, Residence Hall Association, Greek governing bodies, sailing club, national fraternities, national sororities. *Campus security:* 24-hour emergency response devices and patrols, late-night transport/escort service, controlled dormitory access, escort service. *Student services:* health clinic, personal/psychological counseling, legal services.

Athletics Member NCAA. All Division I. *Intercollegiate sports:* baseball M(s), basketball M(s)/W(s), cheerleading M/W, cross-country running M(s)/W(s), golf M(s)/W(s), soccer M(s)/W(s), softball W(s), swimming M(s)/W(s), tennis M(s)/W(s), track and field M(s)/W(s), volleyball W(s). *Intramural sports:* badminton M/W, baseball M(c), basketball M/W, crew M(c)/W(c), field hockey W(c), gymnastics M(c)/W(c), lacrosse M(c)/W(c), rugby M(c), sailing M(c)/W(c), soccer M/W, softball M/W(c), table tennis M/W, tennis M(c)/W(c), ultimate Frisbee M(c)/W(c), volleyball M/W, wrestling M(c)/W(c).

Standardized Tests *Required:* SAT I or ACT (for admission).

Costs (2003–04) *Tuition:* state resident $1703 full-time; nonresident $11,278 full-time. Part-time tuition and fees vary according to course load and program. *Required fees:* $1659 full-time. *Room and board:* $5578. Room and board charges vary according to board plan and housing facility. *Payment plan:* installment. *Waivers:* senior citizens and employees or children of employees.

Financial Aid Of all full-time matriculated undergraduates who enrolled in 2003, 5,234 applied for aid, 3,409 were judged to have need, 2,089 had their need fully met. 279 Federal Work-Study jobs (averaging $3000). *Average percent of need met:* 87%. *Average financial aid package:* $6466. *Average need-based loan:* $3982. *Average need-based gift aid:* $3551. *Average indebtedness upon graduation:* $15,176.

Applying *Options:* common application, electronic application. *Application fee:* $45. *Required:* essay or personal statement, high school transcript. *Application deadlines:* 2/1 (freshmen), 3/15 (transfers). *Notification:* 4/1 (freshmen), 1/19 (early action), continuous (transfers).

Admissions Contact Dr. Roxie Shabazz, Assistant Vice Chancellor for Admissions, The University of North Carolina at Wilmington, 601 South College Road, Wilmington, NC 28403-3297. *Phone:* 910-962-4198. *Toll-free phone:* 800-228-5571. *Fax:* 910-962-3038. *E-mail:* admissions@uncwil.edu.

UNIVERSITY OF PHOENIX–CHARLOTTE CAMPUS

Charlotte, North Carolina

Admissions Contact 3800 Arco Corporate Drive, Suite 100, Charlotte, NC 28273.

WAKE FOREST UNIVERSITY

Winston-Salem, North Carolina

- **Independent** university, founded 1834
- **Calendar** semesters
- **Degrees** bachelor's, master's, doctoral, and first professional
- **Suburban** 340-acre campus
- **Endowment** $725.2 million
- **Coed,** 4,031 undergraduate students, 99% full-time, 51% women, 49% men
- **Very difficult** entrance level, 45% of applicants were admitted

Undergraduates 3,984 full-time, 47 part-time. Students come from 50 states and territories, 26 other countries, 74% are from out of state, 7% African American, 3% Asian American or Pacific Islander, 2% Hispanic American, 0.2% Native American, 0.9% international, 1% transferred in, 75% live on campus. *Retention:* 93% of 2002 full-time freshmen returned.

Freshmen *Admission:* 5,752 applied, 2,599 admitted, 1,004 enrolled. *Test scores:* SAT verbal scores over 500: 97%; SAT math scores over 500: 98%; SAT verbal scores over 600: 83%; SAT math scores over 600: 87%; SAT verbal scores over 700: 24%; SAT math scores over 700: 31%.

Faculty *Total:* 552, 81% full-time, 86% with terminal degrees. *Student/faculty ratio:* 10:1.

Majors Accounting; ancient/classical Greek; anthropology; art history, criticism and conservation; biology/biological sciences; business/commerce; chemistry; classics and languages, literatures and linguistics; clinical laboratory science/medical technology; communication/speech communication and rhetoric; computer and information sciences; dramatic/theatre arts; econometrics and quantitative economics; economics; education (multiple levels); engineering; English; finance; fine/studio arts; French; German; history; kinesiology and exercise science; Latin; management information systems; management science; mathematics; music; philosophy; physician assistant; physics; political science and government; psychology; religious studies; Russian; sociology; Spanish.

Academic Programs *Special study options:* academic remediation for entering students, accelerated degree program, advanced placement credit, double majors, honors programs, independent study, internships, off-campus study, part-time degree program, services for LD students, study abroad, summer session for credit. *ROTC:* Army (b). *Unusual degree programs:* 3-2 engineering with North Carolina State University; forestry with Duke University; dentistry with University of North Carolina at Chapel Hill; physician's assistant, accounting, medical technology, Latin American studies with Georgetown University.

Library Z. Smith Reynolds Library plus 3 others with 923,123 titles, 16,448 serial subscriptions, 21,055 audiovisual materials, an OPAC, a Web page.

Computers on Campus 150 computers available on campus for general student use. A campuswide network can be accessed from student residence rooms and from off campus that provide access to personal computer. Internet access, online (class) registration, at least one staffed computer lab available. Computer purchase or lease plan available.

Student Life *Housing:* on-campus residence required through sophomore year. *Options:* coed, women-only. Campus housing is university owned. Freshman campus housing is guaranteed. *Activities and organizations:* drama/theater group, student-run newspaper, radio and television station, choral group, marching band, Student Union Network, Volunteer Service Corps, Inter-Varsity Christian Fellowship, student government, sororities/fraternities, national fraternities, national sororities. *Campus security:* 24-hour emergency response devices and patrols, late-night transport/escort service, controlled dormitory access. *Student services:* health clinic, personal/psychological counseling.

Athletics Member NCAA. All Division I except football (Division I-A). *Intercollegiate sports:* baseball M(s), basketball M(s)/W(s), cross-country running M(s)/W(s), field hockey W(s), golf M(s)/W(s), soccer M(s)/W(s), tennis M(s)/W(s), track and field M(s)/W(s), volleyball W(s). *Intramural sports:* baseball M(c), basketball M/W, bowling M/W, cheerleading M(c)/W(c), crew M(c)/W(c), cross-country running M(c)/W(c), equestrian sports M(c)/W(c), fencing M(c)/W(c), field hockey W(c), football M/W, golf M(c)/W, ice hockey M(c), lacrosse M(c)/W(c), racquetball M/W, rugby M(c), skiing (downhill) M(c)/W(c), soccer M(c)/W(c), softball M/W(c), swimming M/W, table tennis M/W, tennis M/W, ultimate Frisbee M/W, volleyball M/W, water polo M/W, wrestling M(c).

Standardized Tests *Required:* SAT I (for admission). *Recommended:* SAT II: Subject Tests (for admission).

Costs (2004–05) *Comprehensive fee:* $36,310 includes full-time tuition ($28,210), mandatory fees ($100), and room and board ($8000). *College room only:* $4900. Room and board charges vary according to board plan and housing facility. *Payment plan:* installment. *Waivers:* employees or children of employees.

Financial Aid Of all full-time matriculated undergraduates who enrolled in 2003, 1,592 applied for aid, 1,304 were judged to have need, 524 had their need fully met. 872 Federal Work-Study jobs (averaging $1818). In 2003, 1171 non-need-based awards were made. *Average percent of need met:* 91%. *Average financial aid package:* $21,413. *Average need-based loan:* $6380. *Average need-based gift aid:* $15,699. *Average non-need-based aid:* $10,201. *Average indebtedness upon graduation:* $24,549.

Applying *Options:* common application, electronic application, early admission, early decision, deferred entrance. *Application fee:* $40. *Required:* essay or personal statement, high school transcript, 1 letter of recommendation. *Application deadlines:* 1/15 (freshmen), 2/15 (transfers). *Early decision:* 11/15. *Notification:* 4/1 (freshmen), 12/15 (early decision), continuous until 8/1 (transfers).

Admissions Contact Ms. Martha Allman, Director of Admissions, Wake Forest University, PO Box 7305, Winston-Salem, NC 27109. *Phone:* 336-758-5201. *E-mail:* admissions@wfu.edu.

WARREN WILSON COLLEGE

Swannanoa, North Carolina

- **Independent** comprehensive, founded 1894, affiliated with Presbyterian Church (U.S.A.)
- **Calendar** semesters
- **Degrees** bachelor's and master's
- **Small-town** 1135-acre campus
- **Endowment** $26.5 million
- **Coed,** 781 undergraduate students, 99% full-time, 61% women, 39% men
- **Moderately difficult** entrance level, 79% of applicants were admitted

Warren Wilson College isn't for everyone. Some colleges treat prospective students as if they're all alike. There are very few "alike" students at Warren Wilson College. Balancing academics, working on campus, and performing community service may not be the experience many are looking for. But that's the point—Warren Wilson College is not for everyone. Solid academic students who want to make a difference in the world and who are environmentally aware may want to consider applying to Warren Wilson College.

Undergraduates 773 full-time, 8 part-time. Students come from 38 states and territories, 23 other countries, 79% are from out of state, 1% African American, 0.7% Asian American or Pacific Islander, 2% Hispanic American, 5% international, 88% live on campus. *Retention:* 62% of 2002 full-time freshmen returned.

Freshmen *Admission:* 753 applied, 595 admitted. *Average high school GPA:* 3.33. *Test scores:* SAT verbal scores over 500: 91%; SAT math scores over 500: 81%; ACT scores over 18: 100%; SAT verbal scores over 600: 57%; SAT math scores over 600: 36%; ACT scores over 24: 89%; SAT verbal scores over 700: 15%; SAT math scores over 700: 5%; ACT scores over 30: 17%.

Faculty *Total:* 75, 79% full-time, 80% with terminal degrees. *Student/faculty ratio:* 10:1.

Majors Art; Asian studies; biology/biological sciences; business administration and management; chemistry; creative writing; economics; education; elementary education; English; entrepreneurial and small business related; environmental studies; history; humanities; interdisciplinary studies; international business/trade/commerce; international/global studies; Latin American studies; mathematics; non-profit management; philosophy; psychology; secondary education; social work; sociology; Spanish; women's studies.

Academic Programs *Special study options:* advanced placement credit, cooperative education, double majors, English as a second language, honors programs, independent study, internships, off-campus study, part-time degree program, services for LD students, student-designed majors, study abroad. *Unusual degree programs:* 3-2 engineering with Washington University in St. Louis; forestry with Duke University.

Library Pew Learning Center and Ellison Library with 90,393 titles, 2,392 audiovisual materials, an OPAC, a Web page.

Computers on Campus 68 computers available on campus for general student use. A campuswide network can be accessed from student residence rooms and from off campus that provide access to word processing, software. Internet access, at least one staffed computer lab available.

Student Life *Housing:* on-campus residence required for freshman year. *Options:* coed, men-only, women-only. Campus housing is university owned. Freshman campus housing is guaranteed. *Activities and organizations:* drama/theater group, student-run newspaper, radio station, choral group, Collective Conscience/Social Justice/Student Caucus, Resistance and Peacemaking (RAP), yoga, outing club, African Dance. *Campus security:* 24-hour emergency response devices and patrols, student patrols, late-night transport/escort service, controlled dormitory access. *Student services:* health clinic, personal/psychological counseling.

Athletics Member NSCAA. *Intercollegiate sports:* basketball M/W, cross-country running M/W, rock climbing M/W, soccer M/W, swimming M/W. *Intramural sports:* fencing M/W, lacrosse M/W, soccer M/W, softball M/W, table tennis M/W, tennis M/W, ultimate Frisbee M/W, volleyball M/W, weight lifting M/W.

Standardized Tests *Required:* SAT I or ACT (for admission).

Costs (2004–05) *Comprehensive fee:* $23,266 includes full-time tuition ($17,738), mandatory fees ($250), and room and board ($5278). Full-time tuition and fees vary according to course load. Part-time tuition and fees vary according to course load. *Room and board:* Room and board charges vary according to board plan. *Payment plan:* installment. *Waivers:* employees or children of employees.

Financial Aid Of all full-time matriculated undergraduates who enrolled in 2003, 525 applied for aid, 443 were judged to have need, 75 had their need fully met. 300 Federal Work-Study jobs (averaging $2258). 400 state and other part-time jobs (averaging $1875). In 2003, 117 non-need-based awards were made. *Average percent of need met:* 73%. *Average financial aid package:* $12,695. *Average need-based loan:* $3430. *Average need-based gift aid:* $7372. *Average non-need-based aid:* $3014. *Average indebtedness upon graduation:* $14,407.

Applying *Options:* common application, electronic application, early admission, early decision, deferred entrance. *Required:* essay or personal statement, high school transcript, minimum 2.5 GPA, 2 letters of recommendation. *Recommended:* interview. *Application deadlines:* 3/15 (freshmen), 3/15 (transfers). *Early decision:* 11/15. *Notification:* continuous (freshmen), 12/1 (early decision), continuous until 4/1 (transfers).

Admissions Contact Mr. Richard Blomgren, Dean of Admission, Warren Wilson College, PO Box 9000, Asheville, NC 28815-9000. *Phone:* 828-771-2073. *Toll-free phone:* 800-934-3536. *Fax:* 828-298-1440. *E-mail:* admit@warren-wilson.edu.

■ *See page 2782 for a narrative description.*

WESTERN CAROLINA UNIVERSITY

Cullowhee, North Carolina

- **State-supported** comprehensive, founded 1889, part of University of North Carolina System
- **Calendar** semesters
- **Degrees** bachelor's, master's, doctoral, and post-master's certificates
- **Rural** 260-acre campus
- **Endowment** $24.0 million
- **Coed,** 6,087 undergraduate students, 87% full-time, 52% women, 48% men
- **Moderately difficult** entrance level, 74% of applicants were admitted

Undergraduates 5,292 full-time, 795 part-time. Students come from 41 states and territories, 41 other countries, 7% are from out of state, 6% African American, 0.7% Asian American or Pacific Islander, 0.9% Hispanic American, 2% Native American, 3% international, 10% transferred in, 45% live on campus. *Retention:* 69% of 2002 full-time freshmen returned.

Freshmen *Admission:* 4,606 applied, 3,392 admitted, 1,495 enrolled. *Average high school GPA:* 3.25. *Test scores:* SAT verbal scores over 500: 53%; SAT math scores over 500: 57%; ACT scores over 18: 79%; SAT verbal scores over 600: 13%; SAT math scores over 600: 15%; ACT scores over 24: 13%; SAT verbal scores over 700: 2%; SAT math scores over 700: 1%; ACT scores over 30: 1%.

Faculty *Total:* 537, 62% full-time, 63% with terminal degrees. *Student/faculty ratio:* 16:1.

Majors Accounting; anthropology; art; art teacher education; biology/biological sciences; business administration and management; chemistry; clinical laboratory science/medical technology; communication disorders; communication/speech communication and rhetoric; computer science; construction engineering technology; criminal justice/safety; dietetics; dramatic/theatre arts; early childhood education; electrical and electronic engineering technologies related; electrical, electronic and communications engineering technology; electrical, electronics and communications engineering; elementary education; emergency medical technology (EMT paramedic); English; English/language arts teacher education; environmental health; environmental science; finance; fine/studio arts; French language teacher education; geography; geology/earth science; German; German language teacher education; health information/medical records administration; history; hospitality administration; interior design; international business/trade/commerce; liberal arts and sciences/liberal studies; management information systems; manufacturing technology; marketing/marketing management; marketing related; mathematics; mathematics teacher education; middle school education; music; music performance; music teacher education; natural resources

Western Carolina University (continued)
management and policy; nursing (registered nurse training); parks, recreation and leisure facilities management; philosophy; physical education teaching and coaching; political science and government; psychology; public administration; science teacher education; social sciences; social studies teacher education; social work; sociology; Spanish; Spanish language teacher education; special education; sport and fitness administration; therapeutic recreation.

Academic Programs *Special study options:* academic remediation for entering students, accelerated degree program, adult/continuing education programs, advanced placement credit, cooperative education, distance learning, double majors, English as a second language, honors programs, independent study, internships, part-time degree program, services for LD students, student-designed majors, study abroad, summer session for credit.

Library Hunter Library with 675,929 titles, 2,472 serial subscriptions, 24,514 audiovisual materials, an OPAC, a Web page.

Computers on Campus 575 computers available on campus for general student use. A campuswide network can be accessed from student residence rooms and from off campus that provide access to e-mail. Internet access, online (class) registration, at least one staffed computer lab available.

Student Life *Housing:* on-campus residence required for freshman year. *Options:* coed, men-only, women-only. Campus housing is university owned. Freshman campus housing is guaranteed. *Activities and organizations:* drama/theater group, student-run newspaper, radio station, choral group, marching band, Inter-Fraternity Council, Student Government Association, Panhellenic Council, Organization of Ebony Students, Resident Student Association, national fraternities, national sororities. *Campus security:* 24-hour emergency response devices and patrols, controlled dormitory access. *Student services:* health clinic, personal/psychological counseling, women's center.

Athletics Member NCAA. All Division I except football (Division I-AA). *Intercollegiate sports:* baseball M(s), basketball M(s)/W(s), cheerleading M/W, cross-country running M(s)/W(s), golf M(s)/W(s), soccer W(s), tennis W(s), track and field M(s)/W(s), volleyball W(s). *Intramural sports:* badminton M/W, basketball M/W, bowling M/W, cross-country running M/W, football M/W, lacrosse M/W, racquetball M/W, rugby M, soccer M/W, softball M/W, swimming M/W, table tennis M/W, tennis M/W, track and field M/W, ultimate Frisbee M/W, volleyball M/W, water polo M/W, weight lifting M/W, wrestling M.

Standardized Tests *Required:* SAT I or ACT (for admission). *Recommended:* SAT I (for admission).

Costs (2003–04) *Tuition:* state resident $1426 full-time; nonresident $10,787 full-time. Part-time tuition and fees vary according to course load. *Required fees:* $1380 full-time. *Room and board:* $3826; room only: $2026. Room and board charges vary according to board plan and housing facility. *Payment plan:* installment. *Waivers:* senior citizens and employees or children of employees.

Financial Aid Of all full-time matriculated undergraduates who enrolled in 2003, 3,541 applied for aid, 2,567 were judged to have need, 1,467 had their need fully met. 395 Federal Work-Study jobs (averaging $1266). In 2003, 650 non-need-based awards were made. *Average percent of need met:* 79%. *Average financial aid package:* $6229. *Average need-based loan:* $3319. *Average need-based gift aid:* $3549. *Average non-need-based aid:* $2325. *Average indebtedness upon graduation:* $16,249.

Applying *Options:* electronic application, early admission. *Application fee:* $40. *Required:* high school transcript, minimum 2.5 GPA. *Application deadlines:* 8/1 (freshmen), 8/1 (transfers). *Notification:* continuous (freshmen), continuous (transfers).

Admissions Contact Mr. Philip Cauley, Director of Admissions, Western Carolina University, Cullowhee, NC 28723. *Phone:* 828-227-7317. *Toll-free phone:* 877-WCU4YOU. *Fax:* 828-227-7319. *E-mail:* admiss@email.wcu.edu.

■ *See page 2808 for a narrative description.*

WINGATE UNIVERSITY
Wingate, North Carolina

- **Independent Baptist** comprehensive, founded 1896
- **Calendar** semesters
- **Degrees** bachelor's, master's, and first professional
- **Small-town** 330-acre campus with easy access to Charlotte
- **Coed,** 1,324 undergraduate students, 96% full-time, 54% women, 46% men
- **Moderately difficult** entrance level, 82% of applicants were admitted

Undergraduates 1,277 full-time, 47 part-time. Students come from 35 states and territories, 17 other countries, 44% are from out of state, 11% African American, 0.8% Asian American or Pacific Islander, 1% Hispanic American, 0.3% Native American, 3% international, 4% transferred in, 81% live on campus. *Retention:* 68% of 2002 full-time freshmen returned.

Freshmen *Admission:* 1,235 applied, 1,011 admitted, 372 enrolled. *Average high school GPA:* 3.35. *Test scores:* SAT verbal scores over 500: 59%; SAT math scores over 500: 63%; ACT scores over 18: 94%; SAT verbal scores over 600: 16%; SAT math scores over 600: 20%; ACT scores over 24: 40%; SAT verbal scores over 700: 1%; SAT math scores over 700: 1%; ACT scores over 30: 6%.

Faculty *Total:* 122, 72% full-time, 68% with terminal degrees. *Student/faculty ratio:* 14:1.

Majors Accounting; American studies; art; art teacher education; athletic training; biology/biological sciences; business administration and management; business/managerial economics; chemistry; computer graphics; drawing; economics; education; elementary education; English; environmental biology; finance; fine/studio arts; history; human services; information science/studies; interdisciplinary studies; journalism; kindergarten/preschool education; liberal arts and sciences/liberal studies; management information systems; marketing/marketing management; mass communication/media; mathematics; middle school education; music; music management and merchandising; music teacher education; parks, recreation and leisure; philosophy; physical education teaching and coaching; piano and organ; pre-law studies; pre-medical studies; pre-veterinary studies; psychology; public relations/image management; reading teacher education; religious studies; science teacher education; secondary education; social sciences; sociology; Spanish; speech and rhetoric; sport and fitness administration; telecommunications; voice and opera.

Academic Programs *Special study options:* accelerated degree program, adult/continuing education programs, advanced placement credit, double majors, honors programs, independent study, internships, off-campus study, part-time degree program, services for LD students, study abroad, summer session for credit. *ROTC:* Army (c), Air Force (c).

Library Ethel K. Smith Library with 107,187 titles, 15,325 serial subscriptions, 6,925 audiovisual materials, an OPAC, a Web page.

Computers on Campus 75 computers available on campus for general student use. A campuswide network can be accessed from student residence rooms and from off campus. Internet access, at least one staffed computer lab available.

Student Life *Housing:* on-campus residence required through senior year. *Options:* men-only, women-only. Campus housing is university owned. Freshman campus housing is guaranteed. *Activities and organizations:* drama/theater group, student-run newspaper, television station, choral group, Student Community Service Organization, Fellowship of Christian Athletes, Student Government Association, Christian Student Union, national fraternities, national sororities. *Campus security:* 24-hour emergency response devices and patrols, late-night transport/escort service, controlled dormitory access. *Student services:* health clinic, personal/psychological counseling.

Athletics Member NCAA. All Division II. *Intercollegiate sports:* baseball M(s), basketball M(s)/W(s), cross-country running M(s)/W, football M(s), golf M(s)/W(s), lacrosse M(s), soccer M(s)/W, softball W(s), swimming W(s), tennis M(s)/W(s), volleyball W(s). *Intramural sports:* basketball M/W, bowling M/W, cross-country running M, football M/W, golf M/W, racquetball M/W, swimming M/W, table tennis M/W, tennis M/W, track and field M/W, volleyball M/W, water polo M/W, weight lifting M/W.

Standardized Tests *Required:* SAT I or ACT (for admission). *Recommended:* SAT I (for admission).

Costs (2004–05) *Comprehensive fee:* $22,200 includes full-time tuition ($15,000), mandatory fees ($1000), and room and board ($6200). Part-time tuition: $495 per credit hour. *Payment plan:* installment. *Waivers:* employees or children of employees.

Financial Aid Of all full-time matriculated undergraduates who enrolled in 2003, 1,273 applied for aid, 861 were judged to have need, 5 had their need fully met. 373 state and other part-time jobs (averaging $560). In 2003, 25 non-need-based awards were made. *Average percent of need met:* 56%. *Average financial aid package:* $12,748. *Average need-based loan:* $3359. *Average need-based gift aid:* $4134. *Average non-need-based aid:* $4918. *Average indebtedness upon graduation:* $24,000.

Applying *Options:* common application, electronic application, early admission, early decision, deferred entrance. *Application fee:* $25. *Required:* high school transcript, minimum 2.0 GPA. *Required for some:* letters of recommendation, interview. *Recommended:* essay or personal statement, minimum 3.0 GPA. *Application deadline:* rolling (freshmen), rolling (transfers). *Early decision:* 12/1. *Notification:* continuous (freshmen), 12/15 (early decision), continuous (transfers).

Admissions Contact Mr. Walter P. Crutchfield III, Dean of Admissions, Wingate University, PO Box 159, Wingate, NC 28174. *Phone:* 704-233-8000. *Toll-free phone:* 800-755-5550. *Fax:* 704-233-8110. *E-mail:* admit@wingate.edu.

■ *See page 2868 for a narrative description.*

WINSTON-SALEM BIBLE COLLEGE
Winston-Salem, North Carolina

- **Independent nondenominational** 4-year, founded 1949
- **Calendar** semesters

- **Degrees** associate and bachelor's
- **Coed**

Costs (2003–04) *Tuition:* $4500 full-time.

Admissions Contact Admissions Office, Winston-Salem Bible College, 4117 Northampton Drive, PO Box 777, Winston-Salem, NC 27102-0777. *Phone:* 336-744-0900.

WINSTON-SALEM STATE UNIVERSITY

Winston-Salem, North Carolina

- **State-supported** comprehensive, founded 1892, part of University of North Carolina System
- **Calendar** semesters
- **Degrees** certificates, bachelor's, and master's
- **Urban** 94-acre campus
- **Endowment** $14.7 million
- **Coed,** 3,929 undergraduate students, 84% full-time, 68% women, 32% men
- **Minimally difficult** entrance level, 77% of applicants were admitted

Undergraduates 3,312 full-time, 617 part-time. Students come from 30 states and territories, 8% are from out of state, 85% African American, 0.6% Asian American or Pacific Islander, 0.7% Hispanic American, 0.2% Native American, 0.1% international, 9% transferred in, 40% live on campus. *Retention:* 68% of 2002 full-time freshmen returned.

Freshmen *Admission:* 2,597 applied, 1,994 admitted, 897 enrolled. *Average high school GPA:* 2.84.

Faculty *Total:* 333, 59% full-time, 46% with terminal degrees. *Student/faculty ratio:* 15:1.

Majors Accounting; art; art teacher education; biology/biological sciences; business administration and management; chemistry; clinical laboratory science/ medical technology; computer science; economics; education; elementary education; English; English/language arts teacher education; general studies; gerontology; history; kindergarten/preschool education; kinesiology and exercise science; management information systems; mass communication/media; mathematics; mathematics teacher education; middle school education; molecular biology; music; music teacher education; nursing (registered nurse training); occupational therapy; physical education teaching and coaching; political science and government; psychology; social sciences; social studies teacher education; sociology; Spanish; Spanish language teacher education; special education; special education (specific learning disabilities); sport and fitness administration; therapeutic recreation; vocational rehabilitation counseling.

Academic Programs *Special study options:* academic remediation for entering students, accelerated degree program, adult/continuing education programs, advanced placement credit, cooperative education, distance learning, double majors, freshman honors college, honors programs, independent study, internships, part-time degree program, services for LD students, summer session for credit. *ROTC:* Army (b), Air Force (b).

Library O'Kelly Library with 197,765 titles, 1,010 serial subscriptions, 2,198 audiovisual materials, an OPAC, a Web page.

Computers on Campus 100 computers available on campus for general student use. A campuswide network can be accessed from student residence rooms and from off campus. Internet access, online (class) registration, at least one staffed computer lab available.

Student Life *Housing options:* coed, men-only, women-only. Campus housing is university owned and is provided by a third party. Freshman applicants given priority for college housing. *Activities and organizations:* drama/theater group, student-run newspaper, radio station, choral group, marching band, national fraternities, national sororities. *Campus security:* 24-hour emergency response devices and patrols. *Student services:* health clinic, personal/psychological counseling.

Athletics Member NCAA. All Division II. *Intercollegiate sports:* basketball M(s)/W(s), bowling M(s)/W(s), cheerleading M, cross-country running M(s)/ W(s), football M(s), softball W(s), tennis M(s)/W(s), volleyball W(s). *Intramural sports:* basketball M/W, softball M/W, swimming M/W, table tennis M/W, tennis M/W, track and field M/W, volleyball W, weight lifting M/W.

Standardized Tests *Required:* SAT I or ACT (for admission).

Costs (2003–04) *Tuition:* state resident $1226 full-time; nonresident $9491 full-time. Full-time tuition and fees vary according to course load. Part-time tuition and fees vary according to course load. *Required fees:* $1168 full-time. *Room and board:* $5306; room only: $3300. Room and board charges vary according to board plan and housing facility. *Payment plan:* installment. *Waivers:* senior citizens and employees or children of employees.

Financial Aid Of all full-time matriculated undergraduates who enrolled in 2002, 2,467 applied for aid, 2,346 were judged to have need, 413 had their need fully met. 238 Federal Work-Study jobs (averaging $1025). 133 state and other part-time jobs (averaging $1481). In 2002, 116 non-need-based awards were made. *Average percent of need met:* 80%. *Average financial aid package:* $3969. *Average need-based loan:* $2852. *Average need-based gift aid:* $3386. *Average non-need-based aid:* $3108. *Average indebtedness upon graduation:* $10,600. *Financial aid deadline:* 4/1.

Applying *Options:* early admission, deferred entrance. *Application fee:* $30. *Required:* high school transcript. *Recommended:* 1 letter of recommendation. *Application deadline:* rolling (freshmen), rolling (transfers).

Admissions Contact Mr. Daniel Lovett, Vice Chancellor, Enrollment Management, Winston-Salem State University, 601 Martin Luther King Jr Drive, Winston-Salem, NC 27110-0003. *Phone:* 336-750-2070. *Toll-free phone:* 800-257-4052. *Fax:* 336-750-2079. *E-mail:* admissions@wssu.edu.

NORTH DAKOTA

DICKINSON STATE UNIVERSITY

Dickinson, North Dakota

- **State-supported** 4-year, founded 1918, part of North Dakota University System
- **Calendar** semesters
- **Degrees** certificates, associate, and bachelor's
- **Small-town** 100-acre campus
- **Endowment** $3.8 million
- **Coed,** 2,461 undergraduate students, 70% full-time, 57% women, 43% men
- **Noncompetitive** entrance level, 99% of applicants were admitted

Dickinson State, with an enrollment of approximately 2,000 students, offers Bachelor of Arts and Bachelor of Science degrees. Programs include liberal arts and specialized programs in education, business, nursing, agriculture, and computer science. There is opportunity for preprofessional study and vocational training in selected areas as well.

Undergraduates 1,726 full-time, 735 part-time. Students come from 26 states and territories, 28 other countries, 28% are from out of state, 1% African American, 0.4% Asian American or Pacific Islander, 2% Hispanic American, 2% Native American, 5% international, 10% transferred in, 30% live on campus. *Retention:* 56% of 2002 full-time freshmen returned.

Freshmen *Admission:* 717 applied, 712 admitted, 684 enrolled. *Average high school GPA:* 3.12. *Test scores:* SAT verbal scores over 500: 43%; SAT math scores over 500: 91%; ACT scores over 18: 76%; SAT verbal scores over 600: 12%; SAT math scores over 600: 36%; ACT scores over 24: 23%; SAT verbal scores over 700: 6%; SAT math scores over 700: 18%; ACT scores over 30: 2%.

Faculty *Total:* 146, 51% full-time, 30% with terminal degrees. *Student/faculty ratio:* 19:1.

Majors Accounting; administrative assistant and secretarial science; agricultural business and management; art; art teacher education; biology/biological sciences; business administration and management; business teacher education; chemistry; computer science; dramatic/theatre arts; education; education (K-12); elementary education; English; environmental studies; finance; geography; geology/ earth science; history; international business/trade/commerce; liberal arts and sciences/liberal studies; marketing/marketing management; mathematics; medical administrative assistant and medical secretary; music; music teacher education; nursing (licensed practical/vocational nurse training); nursing (registered nurse training); physical education teaching and coaching; political science and government; pre-dentistry studies; pre-law studies; pre-medical studies; preveterinary studies; psychology; science teacher education; secondary education; social sciences; social work; Spanish; speech and rhetoric; speech/theater education.

Academic Programs *Special study options:* academic remediation for entering students, accelerated degree program, adult/continuing education programs, advanced placement credit, cooperative education, distance learning, double majors, external degree program, honors programs, independent study, internships, off-campus study, part-time degree program, services for LD students, student-designed majors, study abroad, summer session for credit.

Library Stoxen Library with 87,324 titles, 5,450 serial subscriptions, 4,668 audiovisual materials, an OPAC, a Web page.

Computers on Campus 216 computers available on campus for general student use. A campuswide network can be accessed from student residence rooms and from off campus. Internet access, online (class) registration, at least one staffed computer lab available.

Student Life *Housing:* on-campus residence required through sophomore year. *Options:* coed. Campus housing is university owned. Freshman campus housing is guaranteed. *Activities and organizations:* drama/theater group, student-run

Dickinson State University (continued)

newspaper, choral group, marching band, rodeo club, Blue Hawk Brigade, chorale, business club, Navigators. *Campus security:* late-night transport/escort service. *Student services:* health clinic.

Athletics Member NAIA. *Intercollegiate sports:* badminton M/W, baseball M(s), basketball M(s)/W(s), cross-country running M(s)/W(s), football M(s), golf M(s)/W(s), softball W(s), track and field M(s)/W(s), volleyball W(s), wrestling M(s). *Intramural sports:* badminton M/W, basketball M/W, football M/W, soccer M/W, softball W, squash M/W, table tennis M/W, tennis M/W, volleyball M/W, water polo M/W.

Standardized Tests *Required:* SAT I or ACT (for admission).

Costs (2003–04) *Tuition:* state resident $3139 full-time; nonresident $7406 full-time. Full-time tuition and fees vary according to location, program, and reciprocity agreements. Part-time tuition and fees vary according to course load, location, program, and reciprocity agreements. *Room and board:* $3350; room only: $1200. Room and board charges vary according to board plan. *Waivers:* minority students, senior citizens, and employees or children of employees.

Financial Aid Of all full-time matriculated undergraduates who enrolled in 2002, 203 Federal Work-Study jobs (averaging $1083). 206 state and other part-time jobs (averaging $1119).

Applying *Options:* electronic application, early admission, deferred entrance. *Application fee:* $35. *Required:* high school transcript, medical history, proof of measles-rubella shot. *Application deadline:* rolling (freshmen), rolling (transfers). *Notification:* continuous (freshmen), continuous (transfers).

Admissions Contact Ms. Deb Dazell, Director of Student Recruitment, Dickinson State University, Campus Box 169, Dickinson, ND 58601. *Phone:* 701-483-2175. *Toll-free phone:* 800-279-4295. *Fax:* 701-483-2409. *E-mail:* dsu.hawks@dsu.nodak.edu.

■ *See page 1534 for a narrative description.*

JAMESTOWN COLLEGE

Jamestown, North Dakota

- **Independent Presbyterian** 4-year, founded 1883
- **Calendar** semesters
- **Degree** bachelor's
- **Small-town** 107-acre campus
- **Endowment** $16.0 million
- **Coed,** 1,152 undergraduate students, 94% full-time, 55% women, 45% men
- **Minimally difficult** entrance level, 98% of applicants were admitted

Undergraduates 1,087 full-time, 65 part-time. Students come from 30 states and territories, 16 other countries, 38% are from out of state, 2% African American, 1% Asian American or Pacific Islander, 2% Hispanic American, 1% Native American, 4% international, 5% transferred in, 61% live on campus. *Retention:* 68% of 2002 full-time freshmen returned.

Freshmen *Admission:* 781 applied, 762 admitted, 293 enrolled. *Average high school GPA:* 3.24.

Faculty *Total:* 70, 83% full-time, 44% with terminal degrees. *Student/faculty ratio:* 18:1.

Majors Accounting; actuarial science; applied mathematics; art; biochemistry; biology/biological sciences; biology teacher education; business administration and management; business/managerial economics; chemistry; clinical laboratory science/medical technology; communication/speech communication and rhetoric; computer science; counseling psychology; criminal justice/safety; dramatic/theatre arts; educational leadership and administration; education (K-12); elementary education; English; English composition; English/language arts teacher education; financial planning and services; fine/studio arts; history; history teacher education; industrial radiologic technology; international business/trade/commerce; management information systems; marketing/marketing management; mathematics; mathematics teacher education; music; music performance; music teacher education; nursing (registered nurse training); philosophy; physical education teaching and coaching; political science and government; psychology; radiologic technology/science; religious studies; secondary education.

Academic Programs *Special study options:* advanced placement credit, cooperative education, double majors, honors programs, independent study, internships, off-campus study, part-time degree program, services for LD students, student-designed majors, study abroad, summer session for credit. *Unusual degree programs:* 3-2 engineering with North Dakota State University, University of North Dakota, South Dakota State University, Washington University in St. Louis.

Library Raugust Library with 128,915 titles, 675 serial subscriptions, 5,219 audiovisual materials, an OPAC, a Web page.

Computers on Campus 440 computers available on campus for general student use. A campuswide network can be accessed from student residence rooms and from off campus. Internet access, online (class) registration, at least one staffed computer lab available.

Student Life *Housing:* on-campus residence required through sophomore year. *Options:* coed, disabled students. Campus housing is university owned. Freshman campus housing is guaranteed. *Activities and organizations:* drama/theater group, student-run newspaper, choral group, Jimmie Ambassadors, Student Activities Committee, Nursing Students Association, Students of Service, Student Senate. *Campus security:* late-night transport/escort service, controlled dormitory access. *Student services:* personal/psychological counseling.

Athletics Member NAIA. *Intercollegiate sports:* baseball M(s), basketball M(s)/W(s), cross-country running M(s)/W(s), football M(s), golf M(s)/W(s), soccer W(s), softball W(s), track and field M(s)/W(s), volleyball W(s), wrestling M(s). *Intramural sports:* basketball M/W, bowling M(c)/W(c), football M/W, racquetball M(c)/W(c), soccer M(c)/W(c), softball M(c)/W(c), volleyball M/W.

Standardized Tests *Required for some:* SAT I or ACT (for admission). *Recommended:* SAT I or ACT (for admission).

Costs (2004–05) *One-time required fee:* $50. *Comprehensive fee:* $13,370 includes full-time tuition ($9400) and room and board ($3970). Part-time tuition: $270 per credit hour. Part-time tuition and fees vary according to course load and program. *College room only:* $1700. Room and board charges vary according to board plan. *Payment plan:* installment. *Waivers:* employees or children of employees.

Financial Aid Of all full-time matriculated undergraduates who enrolled in 2003, 1,073 applied for aid, 945 were judged to have need, 170 had their need fully met. 308 Federal Work-Study jobs (averaging $816). 124 state and other part-time jobs (averaging $729). In 2003, 138 non-need-based awards were made. *Average percent of need met:* 68%. *Average financial aid package:* $7775. *Average need-based loan:* $4064. *Average need-based gift aid:* $4149. *Average non-need-based aid:* $7449. *Average indebtedness upon graduation:* $16,986.

Applying *Options:* common application, electronic application, deferred entrance. *Application fee:* $20. *Required:* high school transcript. *Required for some:* letters of recommendation, minimum ACT score of 18 or minimum SAT score of 850. *Recommended:* minimum 2.5 GPA, minimum ACT score of 18 or minimum SAT score of 850. *Application deadline:* rolling (freshmen), rolling (transfers).

Admissions Contact Ms. Judy Erickson, Director of Admissions, Jamestown College, 6081 College Lane, Jamestown, ND 58405. *Phone:* 701-252-3467 Ext. 2548. *Toll-free phone:* 800-336-2554. *Fax:* 701-253-4318. *E-mail:* admissions@jc.edu.

MAYVILLE STATE UNIVERSITY

Mayville, North Dakota

- **State-supported** 4-year, founded 1889, part of North Dakota University System
- **Calendar** semesters
- **Degrees** associate and bachelor's
- **Rural** 60-acre campus
- **Coed,** 817 undergraduate students, 75% full-time, 57% women, 43% men
- **Noncompetitive** entrance level

Undergraduates 613 full-time, 204 part-time. Students come from 21 states and territories, 9 other countries, 28% are from out of state, 3% African American, 0.4% Asian American or Pacific Islander, 1% Hispanic American, 2% Native American, 3% international, 14% transferred in, 43% live on campus. *Retention:* 57% of 2002 full-time freshmen returned.

Freshmen *Admission:* 222 enrolled. *Average high school GPA:* 3.05. *Test scores:* ACT scores over 18: 67%; ACT scores over 24: 11%; ACT scores over 30: 2%.

Faculty *Total:* 62, 56% full-time, 31% with terminal degrees. *Student/faculty ratio:* 15:1.

Majors Administrative assistant and secretarial science; biology/biological sciences; biology teacher education; business administration and management; business administration, management and operations related; business teacher education; chemistry; chemistry teacher education; child care provision; computer and information sciences; computer and information sciences and support services related; education; elementary education; English; English/language arts teacher education; general studies; health and physical education; health and physical education related; health teacher education; mathematics; mathematics teacher education; office management; physical education teaching and coaching; physical sciences; physics teacher education; pre-dentistry studies; pre-law studies; pre-medical studies; pre-pharmacy studies; pre-veterinary studies; social sciences; social science teacher education.

Academic Programs *Special study options:* academic remediation for entering students, accelerated degree program, adult/continuing education programs,

advanced placement credit, cooperative education, distance learning, double majors, internships, part-time degree program, services for LD students, student-designed majors, summer session for credit. *ROTC:* Air Force (c).

Library Byrnes-Quanbeck Library plus 1 other with 71,595 titles, 599 serial subscriptions, 20,679 audiovisual materials, an OPAC.

Computers on Campus A campuswide network can be accessed from student residence rooms and from off campus that provide access to laptop for each student. Internet access, online (class) registration, at least one staffed computer lab available. Computer purchase or lease plan available.

Student Life *Housing:* on-campus residence required through sophomore year. *Options:* coed, men-only, women-only. Campus housing is university owned and is provided by a third party. Freshman campus housing is guaranteed. *Activities and organizations:* drama/theater group, student-run newspaper, choral group, Student Activities Council, Student Education Association, health and physical education club, Campus Crusade, Student Ambassadors. *Campus security:* controlled dormitory access. *Student services:* health clinic, personal/psychological counseling.

Athletics Member NAIA. *Intercollegiate sports:* baseball M(s), basketball M(s)/W(s), cheerleading W, football M(s), soccer M(s)/W(s), softball W(s), volleyball W(s). *Intramural sports:* basketball M/W, bowling M/W, football M/W, golf M/W, ice hockey M, racquetball M/W, soccer M/W, softball M/W, table tennis M/W, tennis M/W, track and field M/W, volleyball M/W.

Standardized Tests *Required:* SAT I or ACT (for admission).

Costs (2004–05) *Tuition:* state resident $3014 full-time; nonresident $7535 full-time. Full-time tuition and fees vary according to reciprocity agreements. Part-time tuition and fees vary according to reciprocity agreements. *Required fees:* $1342 full-time. *Room and board:* $3508; room only: $1452. Room and board charges vary according to board plan and housing facility. *Waivers:* minority students, senior citizens, and employees or children of employees.

Financial Aid Of all full-time matriculated undergraduates who enrolled in 2002, 483 applied for aid, 395 were judged to have need, 172 had their need fully met. 86 Federal Work-Study jobs (averaging $860). 178 state and other part-time jobs (averaging $665). In 2002, 52 non-need-based awards were made. *Average percent of need met:* 72%. *Average financial aid package:* $5782. *Average need-based loan:* $3584. *Average need-based gift aid:* $2752. *Average non-need-based aid:* $1095. *Average indebtedness upon graduation:* $15,835.

Applying *Options:* electronic application, deferred entrance. *Application fee:* $35. *Required:* high school transcript. *Recommended:* interview. *Application deadline:* rolling (freshmen), rolling (transfers). *Notification:* 1/1 (freshmen), 1/1 (transfers).

Admissions Contact Mr. Brian Larson, Director of Enrollment Services, Mayville State University, 330 3rd Street, NE, Mayville, ND 58257-1299. *Phone:* 701-788-4768 Ext. 34768. *Toll-free phone:* 800-437-4104. *Fax:* 701-788-4748. *E-mail:* admit@mail.masu.nodak.edu.

MEDCENTER ONE COLLEGE OF NURSING
Bismarck, North Dakota

- **Independent** upper-level, founded 1988
- **Calendar** semesters
- **Degree** bachelor's
- **Small-town** 15-acre campus
- **Endowment** $100,500
- **Coed, primarily women,** 83 undergraduate students, 94% full-time, 96% women, 4% men
- **Moderately difficult** entrance level, 51% of applicants were admitted

Undergraduates 78 full-time, 5 part-time. Students come from 6 states and territories, 7% are from out of state, 4% Native American, 61% transferred in, 4% live on campus.

Faculty *Total:* 12, 83% full-time. *Student/faculty ratio:* 9:1.

Majors Nursing (registered nurse training).

Academic Programs *Special study options:* honors programs, independent study, internships.

Library Q & R/Medcenter One Health Sciences Library plus 1 other with 28,470 titles, 331 serial subscriptions, 1,467 audiovisual materials, an OPAC, a Web page.

Computers on Campus 13 computers available on campus for general student use. Internet access available.

Student Life *Housing options:* coed. Campus housing is university owned. *Activities and organizations:* student-run newspaper, Student Body Organization, Student Nurses Association. *Campus security:* late-night transport/escort service. *Student services:* health clinic, personal/psychological counseling.

Costs (2003–04) *Tuition:* $8000 full-time, $334 per credit part-time. Full-time tuition and fees vary according to student level. Part-time tuition and fees vary according to course load and student level. *Required fees:* $620 full-time, $5 per credit part-time, $190 per term part-time. *Room only:* $900.

Financial Aid Of all full-time matriculated undergraduates who enrolled in 2003, 64 applied for aid, 56 were judged to have need, 41 had their need fully met. 7 Federal Work-Study jobs (averaging $990). In 2003, 4 non-need-based awards were made. *Average percent of need met:* 97%. *Average financial aid package:* $8405. *Average need-based loan:* $4291. *Average need-based gift aid:* $3195. *Average non-need-based aid:* $300. *Average indebtedness upon graduation:* $9776.

Applying *Application fee:* $40. *Application deadline:* 11/7 (transfers). *Notification:* continuous (transfers).

Admissions Contact Ms. Mary Smith, Director of Student services, Medcenter One College of Nursing, 512 North 7th Street, Bismarck, ND 58501-4494. *Phone:* 701-323-6271. *Fax:* 701-323-6967.

MINOT STATE UNIVERSITY
Minot, North Dakota

- **State-supported** comprehensive, founded 1913, part of North Dakota University System
- **Calendar** semesters
- **Degrees** certificates, associate, bachelor's, master's, and post-master's certificates
- **Small-town** 103-acre campus
- **Endowment** $2.0 million
- **Coed,** 3,594 undergraduate students, 70% full-time, 62% women, 38% men
- **Minimally difficult** entrance level, 86% of applicants were admitted

Undergraduates 2,512 full-time, 1,082 part-time. Students come from 44 states and territories, 18 other countries, 12% are from out of state, 3% African American, 1% Asian American or Pacific Islander, 2% Hispanic American, 4% Native American, 5% international, 12% transferred in, 15% live on campus. *Retention:* 58% of 2002 full-time freshmen returned.

Freshmen *Admission:* 720 applied, 619 admitted, 568 enrolled. *Average high school GPA:* 3.17. *Test scores:* ACT scores over 18: 89%; ACT scores over 24: 30%; ACT scores over 30: 2%.

Faculty *Total:* 221, 72% full-time, 46% with terminal degrees. *Student/faculty ratio:* 16:1.

Majors Accounting; art; art teacher education; biology/biological sciences; biology teacher education; business administration and management; business teacher education; chemistry; chemistry teacher education; clinical laboratory science/medical technology; communication disorders; computer science; criminal justice/safety; digital communication and media/multimedia; economics; education (specific subject areas) related; elementary education; English; English/language arts teacher education; finance; French; French language teacher education; general studies; geology/earth science; German; German language teacher education; history; history teacher education; international business/trade/commerce; management information systems; marketing/marketing management; mathematics; mathematics teacher education; medical radiologic technology; music; music teacher education; nursing (registered nurse training); nursing related; physical education teaching and coaching; physical sciences; physics; physics teacher education; psychology; radio and television; science teacher education; social sciences; social science teacher education; social work; sociology; Spanish; Spanish language teacher education; special education (hearing impaired); special education (mentally retarded); special education related; special education (speech or language impaired); speech and rhetoric; sport and fitness administration; substance abuse/addiction counseling.

Academic Programs *Special study options:* academic remediation for entering students, accelerated degree program, adult/continuing education programs, advanced placement credit, cooperative education, distance learning, double majors, honors programs, independent study, internships, part-time degree program, services for LD students, student-designed majors, study abroad, summer session for credit.

Library Gordon B. Olson Library with 240,395 titles, 805 serial subscriptions, 11,073 audiovisual materials, an OPAC, a Web page.

Computers on Campus 400 computers available on campus for general student use. A campuswide network can be accessed from student residence rooms and from off campus. Internet access, online (class) registration, at least one staffed computer lab available.

Student Life *Housing options:* coed, men-only, women-only. Campus housing is university owned. Freshman campus housing is guaranteed. *Activities and organizations:* drama/theater group, student-run newspaper, radio and television station, choral group, Student ND Education Association, Minot State Club of Physical Education, Inter-Varsity Christian Fellowship, Residence Hall Association, National Student Speech and Hearing Association. *Campus security:* controlled dormitory access, patrols by trained security personnel. *Student services:* health clinic, personal/psychological counseling, women's center.

Minot State University (continued)

Athletics Member NAIA. *Intercollegiate sports:* baseball M(s), basketball M(s)/W(s), cheerleading W, cross-country running M(s)/W(s), football M(s), golf M/W, ice hockey M(c), softball W(s), track and field M(s)/W(s), volleyball W(s). *Intramural sports:* basketball M/W, racquetball M/W, softball M/W, volleyball M/W.

Standardized Tests *Required:* SAT I or ACT (for admission).

Costs (2003–04) *Tuition:* state resident $2730 full-time, $114 per semester hour part-time; nonresident $7289 full-time, $304 per semester hour part-time. Full-time tuition and fees vary according to course load, location, and reciprocity agreements. Part-time tuition and fees vary according to location and reciprocity agreements. *Required fees:* $498 full-time, $21 per semester hour part-time. *Room and board:* $3274; room only: $1200. Room and board charges vary according to board plan and housing facility. *Payment plan:* installment. *Waivers:* employees or children of employees.

Financial Aid Of all full-time matriculated undergraduates who enrolled in 2003, 2,527 applied for aid, 2,100 were judged to have need, 2,100 had their need fully met. 215 Federal Work-Study jobs (averaging $1970). *Average percent of need met:* 95%. *Average financial aid package:* $6372. *Average need-based loan:* $2398. *Average need-based gift aid:* $2310. *Average indebtedness upon graduation:* $13,709.

Applying *Options:* electronic application, deferred entrance. *Application fee:* $35. *Required:* high school transcript. *Required for some:* minimum 2.75 GPA. *Application deadline:* rolling (freshmen), rolling (transfers). *Notification:* continuous (freshmen), continuous (transfers).

Admissions Contact Ms. Mariah Huizenga, Admissions Specialist, Minot State University, 500 University Avenue West, Minot, ND 58707-0002. *Phone:* 701-858-3346. *Toll-free phone:* 800-777-0750 Ext. 3350. *Fax:* 701-839-6933. *E-mail:* askmsu@misu.nodak.edu.

NORTH DAKOTA STATE COLLEGE OF SCIENCE
Wahpeton, North Dakota

- **State-supported** primarily 2-year, founded 1903, part of North Dakota University System
- **Calendar** semesters
- **Degrees** bachelor's, master's, doctoral, and first professional
- **Rural** 125-acre campus
- **Endowment** $4000
- **Coed,** 2,398 undergraduate students
- **Noncompetitive** entrance level

Undergraduates Students come from 21 states and territories, 8 other countries, 27% are from out of state, 2% African American, 0.3% Asian American or Pacific Islander, 0.6% Hispanic American, 2% Native American, 1% international, 56% live on campus.

Freshmen *Average high school GPA:* 2.73. *Test scores:* ACT scores over 18: 58%; ACT scores over 24: 10%.

Faculty *Total:* 140, 91% full-time, 1% with terminal degrees. *Student/faculty ratio:* 15:1.

Majors Administrative assistant and secretarial science; agricultural business and management related; agricultural/farm supplies retailing and wholesaling; agricultural mechanization; agricultural production; architectural engineering technology; autobody/collision and repair technology; automobile/automotive mechanics technology; business/commerce; civil engineering technology; computer programming (specific applications); construction engineering technology; dental hygiene; diesel mechanics technology; electrical, electronic and communications engineering technology; foodservice systems administration; health information/medical records technology; heating, air conditioning and refrigeration technology; heating, air conditioning, ventilation and refrigeration maintenance technology; industrial electronics technology; industrial technology; liberal arts and sciences/liberal studies; machine shop technology; nursing (licensed practical/vocational nurse training); occupational therapist assistant; pharmacy technician; psychiatric/mental health services technology; small engine mechanics and repair technology; technical teacher education; vehicle maintenance and repair technologies related; welding technology.

Academic Programs *Special study options:* academic remediation for entering students, accelerated degree program, adult/continuing education programs, advanced placement credit, cooperative education, distance learning, English as a second language, internships, part-time degree program, services for LD students, student-designed majors, summer session for credit.

Library Mildred Johnson Library with 124,508 titles, 852 serial subscriptions, 4,178 audiovisual materials, an OPAC, a Web page.

Computers on Campus 450 computers available on campus for general student use. A campuswide network can be accessed from student residence rooms and from off campus. Internet access, at least one staffed computer lab available.

Student Life *Housing:* on-campus residence required for freshman year. *Options:* coed, men-only, women-only. Campus housing is university owned. *Activities and organizations:* drama/theater group, choral group, marching band, Student Health Advisory Club, Drama Club, Intervarsity Christian Fellowship, Cultural Diversity, Habitat for Humanity. *Campus security:* 24-hour emergency response devices and patrols, student patrols, late-night transport/escort service, controlled dormitory access. *Student services:* health clinic, personal/psychological counseling, legal services.

Athletics Member NJCAA. *Intercollegiate sports:* basketball M(s)/W(s), football M(s), volleyball W(s). *Intramural sports:* basketball M/W, football M, racquetball M/W, softball M/W, volleyball M/W.

Standardized Tests *Required:* ACT (for placement).

Costs (2003–04) *Tuition:* state resident $2052 full-time; nonresident $5478 full-time. Full-time tuition and fees vary according to reciprocity agreements. Part-time tuition and fees vary according to reciprocity agreements. *Required fees:* $450 full-time. *Room and board:* $4066; room only: $1269. *Payment plans:* installment, deferred payment. *Waivers:* employees or children of employees.

Financial Aid Of all full-time matriculated undergraduates who enrolled in 2001, 90 Federal Work-Study jobs (averaging $1500).

Applying *Options:* common application, electronic application, early admission. *Application fee:* $35. *Required:* high school transcript. *Application deadline:* rolling (freshmen), rolling (transfers). *Notification:* continuous (freshmen), continuous (transfers).

Admissions Contact Mr. Keath Borchert, Director of Enrollment Services, North Dakota State College of Science, 800 North 6th Street, Wahpeton, ND 58076. *Phone:* 701-671-2189 Ext. 2189. *Toll-free phone:* 800-342-4325 Ext. 2202. *Fax:* 701-671-2332.

NORTH DAKOTA STATE UNIVERSITY
Fargo, North Dakota

- **State-supported** university, founded 1890, part of North Dakota University System
- **Calendar** semesters
- **Degrees** certificates, bachelor's, master's, doctoral, first professional, and post-master's certificates
- **Urban** 2100-acre campus
- **Endowment** $53.7 million
- **Coed,** 10,148 undergraduate students, 89% full-time, 44% women, 56% men
- **Moderately difficult** entrance level, 61% of applicants were admitted

Undergraduates 8,981 full-time, 1,167 part-time. Students come from 36 states and territories, 62 other countries, 40% are from out of state, 1% African American, 1% Asian American or Pacific Islander, 0.6% Hispanic American, 1% Native American, 1% international, 8% transferred in, 29% live on campus. *Retention:* 72% of 2002 full-time freshmen returned.

Freshmen *Admission:* 3,245 applied, 1,986 admitted, 1,974 enrolled. *Average high school GPA:* 3.37. *Test scores:* SAT verbal scores over 500: 76%; SAT math scores over 500: 87%; ACT scores over 18: 93%; SAT verbal scores over 600: 42%; SAT math scores over 600: 54%; ACT scores over 24: 45%; SAT verbal scores over 700: 11%; SAT math scores over 700: 13%; ACT scores over 30: 6%.

Faculty *Total:* 596, 84% full-time, 85% with terminal degrees. *Student/faculty ratio:* 19:1.

Majors Accounting; agribusiness; agricultural/biological engineering and bioengineering; agricultural business and management; agricultural economics; agricultural mechanization; agricultural teacher education; agriculture; animal sciences; apparel and textiles; architecture; art; athletic training; biochemistry/biophysics and molecular biology; biology/biological sciences; biology teacher education; biotechnology; botany/plant biology; business administration and management; chemistry; chemistry teacher education; civil engineering; classics and languages, literatures and linguistics; clinical laboratory science/medical technology; computer engineering; computer science; construction engineering; construction management; corrections and criminal justice related; crop production; dietetics; dramatic/theatre arts; economics; electrical, electronics and communications engineering; elementary education; engineering; English; English/language arts teacher education; environmental design/architecture; equestrian studies; facilities planning and management; family and consumer sciences/home economics teacher education; food science; French; French language teacher education; geology/earth science; health teacher education; history; history teacher education; horticultural science; hospitality administration; human development and family studies; humanities; industrial engineering; interior design; international/global studies; landscape architecture; manufacturing engineering; mass communication/media; mathematics; mathematics teacher education; mechanical engineering; microbiology; multi-/interdisciplinary studies related; music; music teacher education; natural resources management and policy; nursing (registered nurse training); parks, recreation and leisure; pharmacy; philosophy; physical education teaching and coaching; physics; physics teacher education; plant protection and integrated pest management; political science and government; polymer/plastics engineering; psychology; psychometrics and quantitative psychology; radiologic technology/science; respiratory care therapy; science teacher education; security and protective services related; social sciences; social science teacher education; sociology; soil science and agronomy; Spanish; Spanish language teacher education; speech and rhetoric; speech teacher education; sport and fitness administration; statistics; turf and turfgrass management; veterinary/animal health technology; zoology/animal biology.

Academic Programs *Special study options:* academic remediation for entering students, advanced placement credit, cooperative education, distance learning, double majors, English as a second language, honors programs, independent study, internships, off-campus study, part-time degree program, services for LD students, student-designed majors, study abroad, summer session for credit. *ROTC:* Army (b), Air Force (b).

Library North Dakota State University Library plus 3 others with 303,274 titles, 4,497 serial subscriptions, 2,757 audiovisual materials, an OPAC, a Web page.

Computers on Campus 500 computers available on campus for general student use. A campuswide network can be accessed from student residence rooms and from off campus. Internet access, at least one staffed computer lab available.

Student Life *Housing:* on-campus residence required for freshman year. *Options:* coed, men-only, women-only, disabled students. Campus housing is university owned. Freshman campus housing is guaranteed. *Activities and organizations:* drama/theater group, student-run newspaper, radio station, choral group, marching band, Saddle and Sirloin, Habitat for Humanity, Residence Hall Association, juggling club, national fraternities, national sororities. *Campus security:* 24-hour emergency response devices and patrols, student patrols, late-night transport/escort service, controlled dormitory access. *Student services:* health clinic, personal/psychological counseling, legal services.

Athletics Member NCAA. All Division II. *Intercollegiate sports:* archery M(c)/W(c), baseball M(s), basketball M(s)/W(s), bowling M(c)/W(c), cheerleading M(c)/W(c), cross-country running M(s)/W(s), football M(s), golf M/W(s), ice hockey M(c), riflery M(c)/W(c), rugby M(c)/W(c), soccer M(c)/W(s), softball W(s), track and field M(s)/W(s), volleyball M(c)/W(s), wrestling M(s). *Intramural sports:* basketball M/W, football M/W, softball M/W, volleyball M/W, wrestling M.

Standardized Tests *Required:* SAT I or ACT (for admission).

Costs (2003–04) *One-time required fee:* $45. *Tuition:* area resident $3374 full-time; state resident $3600 full-time, $141 per credit part-time; nonresident $9009 full-time, $375 per credit part-time. Full-time tuition and fees vary according to reciprocity agreements. Part-time tuition and fees vary according to course load and reciprocity agreements. *Required fees:* $590 full-time, $25 per credit part-time. *Room and board:* $4471; room only: $1711. Room and board charges vary according to board plan and housing facility. *Payment plan:* installment. *Waivers:* minority students, children of alumni, senior citizens, and employees or children of employees.

Financial Aid Of all full-time matriculated undergraduates who enrolled in 2002, 6,471 applied for aid, 4,790 were judged to have need, 1,617 had their need fully met. 845 Federal Work-Study jobs (averaging $1848). In 2002, 987 non-need-based awards were made. *Average percent of need met:* 75%. *Average financial aid package:* $5367. *Average need-based loan:* $3661. *Average need-based gift aid:* $2986. *Average non-need-based aid:* $1709. *Average indebtedness upon graduation:* $20,498.

Applying *Options:* electronic application. *Application fee:* $35. *Required:* high school transcript, minimum 2.5 GPA. *Application deadlines:* 8/15 (freshmen), 8/15 (transfers). *Notification:* continuous (freshmen), continuous (transfers).

Admissions Contact Dr. Kate Haugen, Director of Admission, North Dakota State University, PO Box 5454, Fargo, ND 58105-5454. *Phone:* 701-231-8643. *Toll-free phone:* 800-488-NDSU. *Fax:* 701-231-8802. *E-mail:* ndsu.admission@ndsu.nodak.edu.

TRINITY BIBLE COLLEGE
Ellendale, North Dakota

- **Independent Assemblies of God** 4-year, founded 1948
- **Calendar** semesters
- **Degrees** certificates, associate, and bachelor's
- **Rural** 28-acre campus
- **Endowment** $539,057
- **Coed,** 307 undergraduate students, 89% full-time, 54% women, 46% men
- **Noncompetitive** entrance level, 50% of applicants were admitted

Undergraduates 272 full-time, 35 part-time. Students come from 29 states and territories, 77% are from out of state, 2% African American, 0.7% Asian American or Pacific Islander, 3% Hispanic American, 3% Native American, 7% transferred in, 69% live on campus. *Retention:* 81% of 2002 full-time freshmen returned.

Freshmen *Admission:* 234 applied, 117 admitted, 73 enrolled. *Average high school GPA:* 3.20.

Faculty *Total:* 38, 76% full-time, 13% with terminal degrees. *Student/faculty ratio:* 8:1.

Majors Administrative assistant and secretarial science; biblical studies; business administration and management; elementary education; finance; liberal arts and sciences/liberal studies; music; pastoral studies/counseling.

Academic Programs *Special study options:* academic remediation for entering students, accelerated degree program, advanced placement credit, distance learning, double majors, internships, part-time degree program, summer session for credit.

Library Graham Library with 67,868 titles, 227 serial subscriptions, 2,258 audiovisual materials.

Computers on Campus 40 computers available on campus for general student use. At least one staffed computer lab available.

Student Life *Housing:* on-campus residence required through junior year. *Options:* men-only, women-only. Campus housing is university owned. Freshman campus housing is guaranteed. *Activities and organizations:* drama/theater group, student-run radio station, choral group, GAP, Youth Ministry, Inner City Ministry, fine arts club, Children's Ministry. *Campus security:* 24-hour emergency response devices, student patrols, late-night transport/escort service. *Student services:* personal/psychological counseling.

Athletics Member NCCAA. *Intercollegiate sports:* baseball M, basketball M/W, football M, volleyball W, wrestling M(c). *Intramural sports:* basketball M/W, football M, golf M/W, softball M/W, tennis M/W, volleyball W, weight lifting M(c)/W(c).

Standardized Tests *Required:* ACT (for admission). *Required for some:* SAT I (for admission).

Costs (2004–05) *Comprehensive fee:* $15,280 includes full-time tuition ($8880), mandatory fees ($2178), and room and board ($4222). Full-time tuition and fees vary according to course load. Part-time tuition: $296 per credit. Part-time tuition and fees vary according to course load. *Required fees:* $350 per term part-time. *College room only:* $1986. Room and board charges vary according to housing facility. *Payment plans:* installment, deferred payment. *Waivers:* employees or children of employees.

Financial Aid Of all full-time matriculated undergraduates who enrolled in 2003, 269 applied for aid, 263 were judged to have need. 162 Federal Work-Study jobs (averaging $1073). In 2003, 10 non-need-based awards were made. *Average need-based loan:* $4391. *Average need-based gift aid:* $6187. *Average non-need-based aid:* $3451. *Financial aid deadline:* 9/1.

Applying *Options:* common application, deferred entrance. *Application fee:* $25. *Required:* essay or personal statement, high school transcript, minimum 2.0 GPA, 2 letters of recommendation, health form, evidence of Christian conversion. *Required for some:* interview. *Application deadline:* rolling (freshmen), rolling (transfers). *Notification:* continuous (freshmen), continuous (transfers).

Admissions Contact Rev. Steve Tvedt, Vice President of College Relations, Trinity Bible College, 50 South Sixth Avenue, Ellendale, ND 58436. *Phone:* 701-349-3621 Ext. 2045. *Toll-free phone:* 888-TBC-2DAY. *Fax:* 701-349-5443. *E-mail:* admissions@trinitybiblecollege.edu.

UNIVERSITY OF MARY
Bismarck, North Dakota

- **Independent Roman Catholic** comprehensive, founded 1959
- **Calendar** 4-4-1
- **Degrees** associate, bachelor's, and master's
- **Suburban** 107-acre campus
- **Endowment** $9.7 million
- **Coed,** 2,152 undergraduate students, 90% full-time, 61% women, 39% men
- **Moderately difficult** entrance level, 90% of applicants were admitted

Undergraduates 1,935 full-time, 217 part-time. Students come from 25 states and territories, 21 other countries, 27% are from out of state, 1% African American, 0.8% Asian American or Pacific Islander, 0.9% Hispanic American, 6% Native American, 2% international, 11% transferred in, 41% live on campus. *Retention:* 71% of 2002 full-time freshmen returned.

Freshmen *Admission:* 890 applied, 804 admitted, 391 enrolled. *Average high school GPA:* 3.29. *Test scores:* ACT scores over 18: 89%; ACT scores over 24: 32%; ACT scores over 30: 2%.

Faculty *Total:* 218, 43% full-time, 31% with terminal degrees. *Student/faculty ratio:* 16:1.

Majors Accounting; athletic training; behavioral sciences; biology/biological sciences; biology teacher education; business administration and management; business/corporate communications; clinical laboratory science/medical technology; criminal justice/police science; early childhood education; elementary education; English; English/language arts teacher education; general studies; health

University of Mary (continued)
and physical education; history; information science/studies; interdisciplinary studies; kinesiology and exercise science; management science; mass communication/media; mathematics; mathematics teacher education; music performance; music teacher education; natural sciences; nursing (registered nurse training); pastoral counseling and specialized ministries related; physical education teaching and coaching; psychology; radiologic technology/science; religious studies; respiratory care therapy; social sciences; social science teacher education; social work; special education (mentally retarded); substance abuse/addiction counseling; theology.

Academic Programs *Special study options:* academic remediation for entering students, accelerated degree program, adult/continuing education programs, advanced placement credit, cooperative education, distance learning, double majors, external degree program, independent study, internships, off-campus study, part-time degree program, services for LD students, study abroad, summer session for credit. *Unusual degree programs:* 3-2 engineering with University of Minnesota; pharmacy with North Dakota State University.

Library University of Mary Library with 74,205 titles, 597 serial subscriptions, 5,382 audiovisual materials, an OPAC.

Computers on Campus 250 computers available on campus for general student use. A campuswide network can be accessed from student residence rooms. Internet access, online (class) registration, at least one staffed computer lab available.

Student Life *Housing:* on-campus residence required through sophomore year. *Options:* men-only, women-only. Campus housing is university owned. Freshman applicants given priority for college housing. *Activities and organizations:* drama/theater group, student-run newspaper, radio station, choral group, Student Senate, Student Social Workers Association, Nursing Student Organization, Student Education Association, Fellowship of Christian Athletes. *Student services:* health clinic, personal/psychological counseling.

Athletics Member NAIA. *Intercollegiate sports:* baseball M(s), basketball M(s)/W(s), cross-country running M(s)/W(s), football M(s), golf M(s)/W(s), soccer M(s)/W(s), softball W(s), tennis M(s)/W(s), track and field M(s)/W(s), volleyball W(s), wrestling M(s). *Intramural sports:* badminton M/W, basketball M/W, bowling M/W, cheerleading M/W, football M/W, golf M/W, racquetball M/W, soccer M/W, softball M/W, swimming M/W, table tennis M/W, tennis M/W, volleyball M/W, water polo M/W, weight lifting M/W.

Standardized Tests *Required:* SAT I and SAT II or ACT (for admission).

Costs (2004–05) *Comprehensive fee:* $14,370 includes full-time tuition ($9990), mandatory fees ($300), and room and board ($4080). Full-time tuition and fees vary according to course load and program. Part-time tuition and fees vary according to degree level. *College room only:* $1940. Room and board charges vary according to board plan, housing facility, and location. *Waivers:* senior citizens and employees or children of employees.

Financial Aid Of all full-time matriculated undergraduates who enrolled in 2002, 366 Federal Work-Study jobs (averaging $930).

Applying *Options:* common application, electronic application, early admission, deferred entrance. *Application fee:* $25. *Required:* high school transcript, 1 letter of recommendation. *Required for some:* essay or personal statement, interview. *Recommended:* minimum 2.5 GPA. *Application deadline:* rolling (freshmen), rolling (transfers).

Admissions Contact Dr. Dave Hebinger, Vice President for Enrollment Services, University of Mary, 7500 University Drive, Bismarck, ND 58504-9652. *Phone:* 701-355-81910. *Toll-free phone:* 800-288-6279. *Fax:* 701-255-7687. *E-mail:* marauder@umary.edu.

UNIVERSITY OF NORTH DAKOTA

Grand Forks, North Dakota

- **State-supported** university, founded 1883, part of North Dakota University System
- **Calendar** semesters
- **Degrees** diplomas, bachelor's, master's, doctoral, first professional, and post-master's certificates
- **Small-town** 543-acre campus
- **Endowment** $9.6 million
- **Coed,** 10,711 undergraduate students, 90% full-time, 47% women, 53% men
- **Minimally difficult** entrance level, 76% of applicants were admitted

Undergraduates 9,647 full-time, 1,064 part-time. Students come from 54 states and territories, 32 other countries, 47% are from out of state, 0.7% African American, 1% Asian American or Pacific Islander, 0.9% Hispanic American, 3% Native American, 2% international, 8% transferred in, 33% live on campus. *Retention:* 75% of 2002 full-time freshmen returned.

Freshmen *Admission:* 4,066 applied, 3,096 admitted, 2,233 enrolled. *Average high school GPA:* 3.36. *Test scores:* ACT scores over 18: 95%; ACT scores over 24: 41%; ACT scores over 30: 5%.

Faculty *Total:* 897, 64% full-time. *Student/faculty ratio:* 18:1.

Majors Accounting; accounting and finance; aeronautics/aviation/aerospace science and technology; air traffic control; American Indian/Native American studies; anthropology; art; art teacher education; athletic training/sports medicine; atmospheric sciences and meteorology; audiology and speech-language pathology; aviation/airway management; biological and biomedical sciences related; biology/biological sciences; business/commerce; business/managerial economics; business systems analysis/design; business teacher education; chemical engineering; chemistry; civil engineering; clinical laboratory science/medical technology; communication/speech communication and rhetoric; computer and information sciences; criminal justice/safety; cytotechnology; dietetics; dramatic/theatre arts; early childhood education; economics; elementary education; English; entrepreneurship; environmental/environmental health engineering; finance; foreign languages and literatures; forensic science and technology; French; geography; geological engineering; geology/earth science; German; history; industrial technology; liberal arts and sciences and humanities related; marketing/marketing management; mathematics; mathematics teacher education; mechanical engineering; middle school education; multi-/interdisciplinary studies related; music; music performance; music teacher education; nursing (registered nurse training); occupational safety and health technology; parks, recreation and leisure facilities management; philosophy; physical education teaching and coaching; physical therapy; physics; political science and government; psychology; religious studies; sales and marketing/marketing and distribution teacher education; Scandinavian languages; science teacher education; social sciences; social work; sociology; Spanish.

Academic Programs *Special study options:* accelerated degree program, adult/continuing education programs, advanced placement credit, cooperative education, distance learning, double majors, honors programs, independent study, internships, off-campus study, part-time degree program, services for LD students, student-designed majors, study abroad, summer session for credit. *ROTC:* Army (b), Air Force (b).

Library Chester Fritz Library plus 2 others with 658,957 titles, 10,438 serial subscriptions, 14,306 audiovisual materials, an OPAC, a Web page.

Computers on Campus 1000 computers available on campus for general student use. A campuswide network can be accessed from student residence rooms and from off campus. Internet access, at least one staffed computer lab available. Computer purchase or lease plan available.

Student Life *Housing options:* coed, men-only, women-only, disabled students. Campus housing is university owned. Freshman campus housing is guaranteed. *Activities and organizations:* drama/theater group, student-run newspaper, radio and television station, choral group, marching band, student government, National Society of Collegiate Scholars, Association of Residence Halls, University of North Dakota Indian Association, Sioux Crew, national fraternities, national sororities. *Campus security:* 24-hour emergency response devices and patrols, student patrols, late-night transport/escort service, controlled dormitory access, emergency telephones. *Student services:* health clinic, personal/psychological counseling, women's center, legal services.

Athletics Member NCAA. All Division II except men's and women's ice hockey (Division I). *Intercollegiate sports:* baseball M(s), basketball M(s)/W(s), cross-country running M/W, football M(s), golf M/W, ice hockey M(s)/W(s), softball W(s), swimming M/W(s), tennis W, track and field M(s)/W(s), volleyball W(s). *Intramural sports:* badminton M/W, baseball M, basketball M/W, cross-country running M/W, football M, golf M/W, ice hockey M/W, racquetball M/W, softball M/W, swimming M/W, table tennis M/W, tennis M/W, track and field M/W, ultimate Frisbee M/W, volleyball M/W.

Standardized Tests *Required:* SAT I or ACT (for admission). *Recommended:* ACT (for admission).

Costs (2003–04) *Tuition:* state resident $3441 full-time, $143 per credit hour part-time; nonresident $9187 full-time, $383 per credit hour part-time. Full-time tuition and fees vary according to degree level, program, and reciprocity agreements. Part-time tuition and fees vary according to course load, degree level, program, and reciprocity agreements. *Required fees:* $715 full-time. *Room and board:* $4234; room only: $1706. Room and board charges vary according to board plan and housing facility. *Payment plan:* deferred payment. *Waivers:* minority students, senior citizens, and employees or children of employees.

Financial Aid Of all full-time matriculated undergraduates who enrolled in 2003, 6,936 applied for aid, 4,769 were judged to have need, 2,427 had their need fully met. 972 Federal Work-Study jobs (averaging $1313). In 2003, 381 non-need-based awards were made. *Average percent of need met:* 87%. *Average financial aid package:* $8150. *Average need-based loan:* $4036. *Average need-based gift aid:* $3087. *Average non-need-based aid:* $2300. *Average indebtedness upon graduation:* $22,733.

Applying *Options:* electronic application, deferred entrance. *Application fee:* $35. *Required:* high school transcript. *Recommended:* minimum 2.25 GPA. *Application deadline:* 7/1 (freshmen), rolling (transfers). *Notification:* continuous (freshmen), continuous (transfers).

Admissions Contact Ms. Heidi Kippenhan, Director of Admissions, University of North Dakota, PO Box 8135, Grand Forks, ND 58202. *Phone:* 701-777-3821. *Toll-free phone:* 800-CALL UND. *Fax:* 701-777-4857. *E-mail:* enrolser@sage.und.nodak.edu.

VALLEY CITY STATE UNIVERSITY
Valley City, North Dakota

- **State-supported** 4-year, founded 1890, part of North Dakota University System
- **Calendar** semesters
- **Degree** bachelor's
- **Small-town** 55-acre campus
- **Endowment** $541,200
- **Coed,** 998 undergraduate students, 74% full-time, 55% women, 45% men
- **Noncompetitive** entrance level, 91% of applicants were admitted

Undergraduates 742 full-time, 256 part-time. Students come from 22 states and territories, 7 other countries, 25% are from out of state, 3% African American, 0.4% Asian American or Pacific Islander, 0.4% Hispanic American, 2% Native American, 4% international, 12% transferred in, 32% live on campus. *Retention:* 71% of 2002 full-time freshmen returned.

Freshmen *Admission:* 264 applied, 240 admitted, 166 enrolled. *Average high school GPA:* 2.98. *Test scores:* ACT scores over 18: 88%; ACT scores over 24: 18%; ACT scores over 30: 2%.

Faculty *Total:* 86, 71% full-time, 31% with terminal degrees. *Student/faculty ratio:* 12:1.

Majors Art; art teacher education; biology/biological sciences; biology teacher education; business administration and management; business teacher education; chemistry; chemistry teacher education; computer and information sciences; computer and information sciences and support services related; education; elementary education; English; English/language arts teacher education; health teacher education; history; history teacher education; human resources management; mass communication/media; mathematics; mathematics teacher education; music; music teacher education; office management; physical education teaching and coaching; pre-dentistry studies; pre-engineering; pre-law studies; pre-medical studies; pre-pharmacy studies; pre-veterinary studies; psychology; science teacher education; secondary education; social sciences; social science teacher education; Spanish; Spanish language teacher education; technical teacher education; technology/industrial arts teacher education.

Academic Programs *Special study options:* academic remediation for entering students, cooperative education, distance learning, double majors, internships, off-campus study, part-time degree program, services for LD students, student-designed majors, summer session for credit.

Library Allen Memorial Library with 94,236 titles, 392 serial subscriptions, 15,305 audiovisual materials, an OPAC, a Web page.

Computers on Campus 925 computers available on campus for general student use. A campuswide network can be accessed from student residence rooms and from off campus. Internet access, online (class) registration, at least one staffed computer lab available. Computer purchase or lease plan available.

Student Life *Housing:* on-campus residence required through sophomore year. *Options:* coed, men-only, women-only. Campus housing is university owned. Freshman campus housing is guaranteed. *Activities and organizations:* drama/theater group, student-run newspaper, choral group, departmental clubs, Greek organizations, Fellowship of Christian Athletes. *Campus security:* controlled dormitory access. *Student services:* health clinic, personal/psychological counseling.

Athletics Member NAIA. *Intercollegiate sports:* baseball M(s), basketball M(s)/W(s), football M(s), softball W(s), volleyball W(s). *Intramural sports:* basketball M/W, bowling M/W, football M, golf M/W, ice hockey M/W, racquetball M/W, skiing (cross-country) M/W, softball M/W, volleyball M/W.

Standardized Tests *Required:* SAT I or ACT (for placement).

Costs (2003–04) *Tuition:* state resident $2652 full-time, $111 per semester hour part-time; nonresident $7080 full-time, $295 per semester hour part-time. *Required fees:* $597 full-time, $57 per semester hour part-time. *Room and board:* $3254; room only: $1230. Room and board charges vary according to board plan. *Waivers:* children of alumni and employees or children of employees.

Financial Aid Of all full-time matriculated undergraduates who enrolled in 2002, 638 applied for aid, 518 were judged to have need, 125 had their need fully met. 71 Federal Work-Study jobs (averaging $1106). 165 state and other part-time jobs (averaging $1123). In 2002, 120 non-need-based awards were made. *Average percent of need met:* 94%. *Average financial aid package:* $5838. *Average need-based loan:* $3431. *Average need-based gift aid:* $3129. *Average non-need-based aid:* $1563. *Average indebtedness upon graduation:* $15,800.

Applying *Options:* electronic application, early admission, deferred entrance. *Application fee:* $35. *Required:* high school transcript. *Application deadline:* rolling (freshmen), rolling (transfers). *Notification:* continuous (freshmen), continuous (transfers).

Admissions Contact Mr. Dan Klein, Director of Enrollment Services, Valley City State University, 101 College Street Southwest, Valley City, ND 58072. *Phone:* 701-845-7101 Ext. 37204. *Toll-free phone:* 800-532-8641 Ext. 37101. *Fax:* 701-845-7299. *E-mail:* enrollment.services@vcsu.edu.

OHIO

ALLEGHENY WESLEYAN COLLEGE
Salem, Ohio

- **Independent religious** 4-year
- **Calendar** semesters
- **Degree** bachelor's
- **Coed**

Costs (2003–04) *Tuition:* $6060 full-time.

Admissions Contact Admissions Office, Allegheny Wesleyan College, 2161 Woodsdale Road, Salem, OH 44460. *Phone:* 330-337-6403. *Toll-free phone:* 800-292-3153.

ANTIOCH COLLEGE
Yellow Springs, Ohio

- **Independent** 4-year, founded 1852, part of Antioch University
- **Calendar** trimesters
- **Degree** bachelor's
- **Small-town** 100-acre campus with easy access to Dayton
- **Endowment** $28.4 million
- **Coed,** 571 undergraduate students, 100% full-time, 62% women, 38% men
- **Moderately difficult** entrance level, 75% of applicants were admitted

Undergraduates 571 full-time. Students come from 43 states and territories, 2 other countries, 76% are from out of state, 5% African American, 1% Asian American or Pacific Islander, 4% Hispanic American, 0.7% Native American, 0.3% international, 6% transferred in, 97% live on campus. *Retention:* 69% of 2002 full-time freshmen returned.

Freshmen *Admission:* 467 applied, 348 admitted, 142 enrolled. *Average high school GPA:* 3.0. *Test scores:* SAT verbal scores over 500: 94%; SAT math scores over 500: 79%; SAT verbal scores over 600: 62%; SAT math scores over 600: 36%; SAT verbal scores over 700: 15%; SAT math scores over 700: 8%.

Faculty *Total:* 60, 95% full-time, 100% with terminal degrees. *Student/faculty ratio:* 10:1.

Majors African-American/Black studies; African studies; anthropology; behavioral sciences; biological and physical sciences; biology/biological sciences; biomedical sciences; business administration and management; chemistry; cinematography and film/video production; communication/speech communication and rhetoric; comparative literature; computer science; creative writing; dance; dramatic/theatre arts; drawing; economics; education; English; environmental biology; environmental studies; European studies; French; geology/earth science; German; history; human development and family studies; humanities; interdisciplinary studies; international relations and affairs; Japanese; literature; mass communication/media; mathematics; middle school education; music; natural sciences; peace studies and conflict resolution; philosophy; physical sciences; physics; political science and government; pre-law studies; pre-medical studies; pre-veterinary studies; psychology; religious studies; science teacher education; sculpture; secondary education; social sciences; sociology; Spanish; visual and performing arts; women's studies.

Academic Programs *Special study options:* academic remediation for entering students, advanced placement credit, cooperative education, double majors, independent study, internships, off-campus study, services for LD students, student-designed majors, study abroad, summer session for credit.

Library Olive Kettering Memorial Library with 300,000 titles, 10,504 serial subscriptions, 6,259 audiovisual materials, an OPAC, a Web page.

Computers on Campus 68 computers available on campus for general student use. A campuswide network can be accessed from student residence rooms and from off campus. Internet access, at least one staffed computer lab available.

Student Life *Housing:* on-campus residence required through senior year. *Options:* coed, men-only, women-only. Campus housing is university owned. *Activities and organizations:* drama/theater group, student-run newspaper, radio station, choral group, Third World Alliance, Women's Center, Lesbian/Gay/Bisexual Center, Uni-Dad, Alternative Library. *Campus security:* 24-hour emer-

Antioch College (continued)
gency response devices and patrols, late-night transport/escort service. *Student services:* health clinic, personal/psychological counseling, women's center.
Athletics *Intramural sports:* badminton M/W, basketball M/W, rugby W, soccer M/W, softball M/W.
Costs (2003–04) *Comprehensive fee:* $29,589 includes full-time tuition ($22,673), mandatory fees ($922), and room and board ($5994). Part-time tuition: $400 per credit hour. *College room only:* $2932. Room and board charges vary according to board plan. *Payment plan:* installment. *Waivers:* employees or children of employees.
Financial Aid Of all full-time matriculated undergraduates who enrolled in 2003, 522 applied for aid, 384 were judged to have need, 191 had their need fully met. 373 Federal Work-Study jobs (averaging $1970). In 2003, 138 non-need-based awards were made. *Average percent of need met:* 82%. *Average financial aid package:* $19,214. *Average need-based loan:* $3424. *Average need-based gift aid:* $11,293. *Average non-need-based aid:* $7520. *Average indebtedness upon graduation:* $18,034.
Applying *Options:* common application, electronic application, early action, deferred entrance. *Application fee:* $35. *Required:* essay or personal statement, high school transcript, minimum 2.5 GPA, 2 letters of recommendation. *Recommended:* interview. *Application deadline:* 2/1 (freshmen), rolling (transfers). *Notification:* continuous until 4/1 (freshmen), 12/15 (early action), continuous (transfers).
Admissions Contact Ms. Cathy Paige, Information Manager, Antioch College, 795 Livermore Street, Yellow Springs, OH 45387-1697. *Phone:* 937-769-1100 Ext. 1119. *Toll-free phone:* 800-543-9436. *Fax:* 937-769-1111. *E-mail:* admissions@antioch-college.edu.

ANTIOCH UNIVERSITY MCGREGOR
Yellow Springs, Ohio

- **Independent** upper-level, founded 1988, part of Antioch University
- **Calendar** quarters (predominantly Saturdays)
- **Degrees** certificates, bachelor's, and master's
- **Small-town** 100-acre campus with easy access to Dayton
- **Coed**
- **Noncompetitive** entrance level

Faculty *Student/faculty ratio:* 7:1.
Student Life *Campus security:* 24-hour emergency response devices and patrols.
Costs (2003–04) *Tuition:* $10,755 full-time. *Required fees:* $225 full-time.
Financial Aid Of all full-time matriculated undergraduates who enrolled in 2002, 62 applied for aid, 59 were judged to have need. 2 Federal Work-Study jobs. In 2002, 2. *Average percent of need met:* 30. *Average financial aid package:* $10,500. *Average need-based loan:* $5000. *Average need-based gift aid:* $1500. *Average non-need-based aid:* $10,500. *Average indebtedness upon graduation:* $28,500.
Applying *Options:* deferred entrance. *Application fee:* $45.
Admissions Contact Mr. Oscar Robinson, Enrollment Services Manager, Antioch University McGregor, Student and Alumni Services Division, Enrollment Services, 800 Livermore Street, Yellow Springs, OH 45387. *Phone:* 937-769-1823. *Toll-free phone:* 937-769-1818. *Fax:* 937-769-1805. *E-mail:* sas@mcgregor.edu.

ART ACADEMY OF CINCINNATI
Cincinnati, Ohio

- **Independent** comprehensive, founded 1887
- **Calendar** semesters
- **Degrees** associate, bachelor's, and master's
- **Urban** 184-acre campus
- **Endowment** $12.5 million
- **Coed,** 193 undergraduate students, 93% full-time, 53% women, 47% men
- **Moderately difficult** entrance level, 69% of applicants were admitted

Undergraduates 180 full-time, 13 part-time. Students come from 14 states and territories, 3 other countries, 25% are from out of state, 4% African American, 1% Asian American or Pacific Islander, 2% Hispanic American, 2% international, 14% transferred in. *Retention:* 81% of 2002 full-time freshmen returned.
Freshmen *Admission:* 149 applied, 103 admitted, 43 enrolled. *Average high school GPA:* 3.10. *Test scores:* SAT verbal scores over 500: 67%; SAT math scores over 500: 58%; ACT scores over 18: 76%; SAT verbal scores over 600: 34%; SAT math scores over 600: 8%; ACT scores over 24: 24%; SAT verbal scores over 700: 8%; SAT math scores over 700: 8%; ACT scores over 30: 4%.
Faculty *Total:* 51, 33% full-time, 84% with terminal degrees. *Student/faculty ratio:* 12:1.
Majors Art; art history, criticism and conservation; drawing; fine/studio arts; graphic design; illustration; intermedia/multimedia; painting; photography; printmaking; sculpture.
Academic Programs *Special study options:* adult/continuing education programs, advanced placement credit, double majors, independent study, internships, off-campus study, part-time degree program, services for LD students, student-designed majors, study abroad, summer session for credit.
Library Mary Schiff Library with 66,404 titles, 150 serial subscriptions, 588 audiovisual materials.
Computers on Campus 40 computers available on campus for general student use. Internet access, at least one staffed computer lab available.
Student Life *Housing:* college housing not available. *Options:* Campus housing is provided by a third party. *Campus security:* 24-hour emergency response devices and patrols. *Student services:* health clinic, personal/psychological counseling.
Standardized Tests *Required:* SAT I or ACT (for admission).
Costs (2004–05) *Tuition:* $17,700 full-time, $740 per credit hour part-time. Part-time tuition and fees vary according to course load. *Required fees:* $350 full-time, $175 per term part-time. *Payment plan:* installment. *Waivers:* employees or children of employees.
Financial Aid Of all full-time matriculated undergraduates who enrolled in 2002, 139 applied for aid, 118 were judged to have need, 23 had their need fully met. 22 Federal Work-Study jobs. In 2002, 53 non-need-based awards were made. *Average percent of need met:* 67%. *Average financial aid package:* $10,735. *Average need-based loan:* $5116. *Average need-based gift aid:* $6922. *Average non-need-based aid:* $6673. *Average indebtedness upon graduation:* $11,290.
Applying *Options:* deferred entrance. *Application fee:* $25. *Required:* essay or personal statement, high school transcript, minimum 2.0 GPA, 1 letter of recommendation, portfolio. *Application deadlines:* 6/30 (freshmen), 6/30 (transfers). *Notification:* continuous (freshmen), continuous (transfers).
Admissions Contact Ms. Mary Jane Zumwalde, Director of Admissions, Art Academy of Cincinnati, 1125 Saint Gregory Street, Cincinnati, OH 45202. *Phone:* 513-562-8744. *Toll-free phone:* 800-323-5692. *Fax:* 513-562-8778. *E-mail:* admissions@artacademy.edu.

■ *See page 1182 for a narrative description.*

ASHLAND UNIVERSITY
Ashland, Ohio

- **Independent** comprehensive, founded 1878, affiliated with Brethren Church
- **Calendar** semesters
- **Degrees** associate, bachelor's, master's, doctoral, and first professional
- **Small-town** 98-acre campus with easy access to Cleveland
- **Endowment** $33.7 million
- **Coed,** 2,782 undergraduate students, 86% full-time, 61% women, 39% men
- **Moderately difficult** entrance level, 86% of applicants were admitted

Ashland University provides a liberal arts and science curriculum that prepares students for various professions and careers with such distinctive programs as environmental science and toxicology. AU's philosophy of "Accent on the Individual" is evident both in and out of the classroom. The spring 2004 opening of a new 60,000-square-foot College of Business and Economics building as well as the planned construction of an $18 million Sport Sciences/Recreation Center, an $11 million renovation and addition to the Kettering Science Center, and a new $10 million College of Education building are examples of AU's commitment to the future.

Undergraduates 2,401 full-time, 381 part-time. Students come from 27 states and territories, 14 other countries, 5% are from out of state, 8% African American, 0.5% Asian American or Pacific Islander, 1% Hispanic American, 0.3% Native American, 2% international, 5% transferred in, 72% live on campus. *Retention:* 76% of 2002 full-time freshmen returned.
Freshmen *Admission:* 2,102 applied, 1,811 admitted, 610 enrolled. *Average high school GPA:* 3.40. *Test scores:* SAT verbal scores over 500: 61%; SAT math scores over 500: 59%; ACT scores over 18: 91%; SAT verbal scores over 600: 21%; SAT math scores over 600: 19%; ACT scores over 24: 37%; SAT verbal scores over 700: 1%; SAT math scores over 700: 3%; ACT scores over 30: 3%.
Faculty *Total:* 553, 39% full-time, 51% with terminal degrees. *Student/faculty ratio:* 15:1.
Majors Accounting; American studies; art; art teacher education; athletic training; biology/biological sciences; business administration and management; chemistry; child development; commercial and advertising art; computer science; creative writing; criminal justice/law enforcement administration; dietetics; dramatic/theatre arts; economics; education; elementary education; English;

environmental studies; family and consumer economics related; family and consumer sciences/home economics teacher education; family and consumer sciences/human sciences; fashion merchandising; finance; fine/studio arts; foods, nutrition, and wellness; French; geology/earth science; health teacher education; history; hotel/motel administration; human development and family studies; information science/studies; international relations and affairs; journalism; kindergarten/preschool education; liberal arts and sciences/liberal studies; marketing/marketing management; marketing research; mass communication/media; mathematics; middle school education; music; music teacher education; parks, recreation and leisure; philosophy; physical education teaching and coaching; physics; political science and government; pre-dentistry studies; pre-law studies; pre-medical studies; pre-pharmacy studies; pre-theology/pre-ministerial studies; pre-veterinary studies; psychology; radio and television; religious education; religious studies; science teacher education; secondary education; social sciences; social work; sociology; Spanish; special education; speech and rhetoric; therapeutic recreation; toxicology.

Academic Programs *Special study options:* academic remediation for entering students, adult/continuing education programs, advanced placement credit, double majors, English as a second language, honors programs, independent study, internships, off-campus study, part-time degree program, services for LD students, student-designed majors, study abroad, summer session for credit. *Unusual degree programs:* 3-2 dietetics with University of Akron.

Library Ashland Library plus 2 others with 205,200 titles, 1,625 serial subscriptions, 3,550 audiovisual materials, an OPAC, a Web page.

Computers on Campus 90 computers available on campus for general student use. A campuswide network can be accessed from student residence rooms and from off campus. At least one staffed computer lab available.

Student Life *Housing:* on-campus residence required through senior year. *Options:* coed, men-only, women-only. Campus housing is university owned. Freshman campus housing is guaranteed. *Activities and organizations:* drama/theater group, student-run newspaper, radio and television station, choral group, marching band, Campus Activity Board, Fellowship of Christian Athletes, Hope Fellowship, intramurals, Community Care, national fraternities, national sororities. *Campus security:* 24-hour emergency response devices and patrols, student patrols, late-night transport/escort service, controlled dormitory access. *Student services:* health clinic, personal/psychological counseling.

Athletics Member NCAA. All Division II. *Intercollegiate sports:* baseball M(s), basketball M(s)/W(s), cross-country running M(s)/W(s), football M(s), golf M(s)/W(s), soccer M(s)/W(s), softball M/W(s), swimming M(s)/W(s), tennis M/W, track and field M(s)/W(s), volleyball W(s), wrestling M(s). *Intramural sports:* badminton M/W, baseball M(c), basketball M/W, bowling M/W, cross-country running M/W, football M, golf M/W, racquetball M/W, skiing (downhill) M(c)/W(c), soccer M/W, softball M(c)/W(c), swimming M/W, table tennis M/W, tennis M/W, track and field M/W, volleyball M(c)/W(c), wrestling M.

Standardized Tests *Required:* SAT I or ACT (for admission).

Costs (2004–05) *Comprehensive fee:* $25,822 includes full-time tuition ($18,394), mandatory fees ($464), and room and board ($6964). Full-time tuition and fees vary according to location and reciprocity agreements. Part-time tuition: $565 per credit hour. Part-time tuition and fees vary according to location and program. *Required fees:* $14 per credit hour part-time. *College room only:* $3740. Room and board charges vary according to board plan and housing facility. *Payment plan:* installment. *Waivers:* senior citizens and employees or children of employees.

Financial Aid Of all full-time matriculated undergraduates who enrolled in 2003, 2,022 applied for aid, 1,736 were judged to have need. 1,143 Federal Work-Study jobs (averaging $1842). 43 state and other part-time jobs (averaging $6055). In 2003, 305 non-need-based awards were made. *Average percent of need met:* 90%. *Average financial aid package:* $16,446. *Average need-based loan:* $4055. *Average need-based gift aid:* $11,333. *Average non-need-based aid:* $5680. *Average indebtedness upon graduation:* $18,250. *Financial aid deadline:* 3/15.

Applying *Options:* common application, electronic application, deferred entrance. *Application fee:* $25. *Required:* essay or personal statement, high school transcript, minimum 2.5 GPA. *Required for some:* letters of recommendation, interview. *Recommended:* interview. *Application deadline:* rolling (freshmen), rolling (transfers). *Notification:* continuous (freshmen), continuous (transfers).

Admissions Contact Mr. Thomas Mansperger, Director of Admission, Ashland University, 401 College Avenue, Ashland, OH 44805. *Phone:* 419-289-5052. *Toll-free phone:* 800-882-1548. *Fax:* 419-289-5999. *E-mail:* auadmsn@ashland.edu.

■ *See page 1190 for a narrative description.*

BALDWIN-WALLACE COLLEGE

Berea, Ohio

- **Independent Methodist** comprehensive, founded 1845
- **Calendar** semesters
- **Degrees** bachelor's and master's
- **Suburban** 100-acre campus with easy access to Cleveland
- **Endowment** $109.7 million
- **Coed,** 3,862 undergraduate students, 79% full-time, 61% women, 39% men
- **Moderately difficult** entrance level, 82% of applicants were admitted

Undergraduates 3,054 full-time, 808 part-time. Students come from 30 states and territories, 14 other countries, 9% are from out of state, 4% African American, 1% Asian American or Pacific Islander, 1% Hispanic American, 0.3% Native American, 1% international, 4% transferred in, 61% live on campus. *Retention:* 85% of 2002 full-time freshmen returned.

Freshmen *Admission:* 2,211 applied, 1,820 admitted, 702 enrolled. *Average high school GPA:* 3.52. *Test scores:* SAT verbal scores over 500: 75%; SAT math scores over 500: 75%; ACT scores over 18: 94%; SAT verbal scores over 600: 33%; SAT math scores over 600: 31%; ACT scores over 24: 47%; SAT verbal scores over 700: 5%; SAT math scores over 700: 6%; ACT scores over 30: 8%.

Faculty *Total:* 389, 42% full-time, 44% with terminal degrees. *Student/faculty ratio:* 14:1.

Majors Art history, criticism and conservation; art teacher education; athletic training; biology/biological sciences; broadcast journalism; business administration and management; business teacher education; chemistry; clinical/medical laboratory technology; communication disorders; communication/speech communication and rhetoric; computer science; computer software and media applications related; computer systems analysis; computer systems networking and telecommunications; criminal justice/law enforcement administration; dance; dramatic/theatre arts and stagecraft related; early childhood education; economics; education; educational leadership and administration; elementary education; engineering; English; exercise physiology; family and consumer economics related; fine/studio arts; French; geology/earth science; German; health and physical education; health professions related; health teacher education; history; human services; information science/studies; international/global studies; liberal arts and sciences and humanities related; mass communication/media; mathematics; middle school education; multi-/interdisciplinary studies related; music; music history, literature, and theory; music performance; music teacher education; music theory and composition; music therapy; neuroscience; philosophy; physical education teaching and coaching; physics; physics teacher education; piano and organ; political science and government; pre-dentistry studies; pre-law studies; pre-medical studies; pre-veterinary studies; psychology; religious studies; science teacher education; secondary education; sociology; Spanish; special education (specific learning disabilities); sport and fitness administration; visual and performing arts related.

Academic Programs *Special study options:* academic remediation for entering students, accelerated degree program, adult/continuing education programs, advanced placement credit, distance learning, double majors, English as a second language, honors programs, independent study, internships, off-campus study, part-time degree program, services for LD students, student-designed majors, study abroad, summer session for credit. *ROTC:* Army (c), Air Force (c). *Unusual degree programs:* 3-2 engineering with Case Western Reserve University, Columbia University, Washington University in St. Louis; forestry with Duke University; social work with Case Western Reserve University; biology with Case Western Reserve University, ecology/environmental studies with Duke University.

Library Ritter Library plus 2 others with 200,000 titles, 883 serial subscriptions, an OPAC, a Web page.

Computers on Campus 450 computers available on campus for general student use. A campuswide network can be accessed from student residence rooms. Internet access, at least one staffed computer lab available. Computer purchase or lease plan available.

Student Life *Housing options:* coed, men-only, women-only, disabled students. Campus housing is university owned. *Activities and organizations:* drama/theater group, student-run newspaper, radio station, choral group, campus entertainment productions, Student Senate, Dance Marathon, Campus Crusade, Black Student Alliance, national fraternities, national sororities. *Campus security:* 24-hour emergency response devices and patrols, student patrols, late-night transport/escort service, controlled dormitory access. *Student services:* health clinic, personal/psychological counseling, women's center.

Athletics Member NCAA. All Division III. *Intercollegiate sports:* baseball M, basketball M/W, cross-country running M/W, football M, golf M/W, soccer M/W,

Baldwin-Wallace College (continued)
softball W, swimming M/W, tennis M/W, track and field M/W, volleyball W, wrestling M. *Intramural sports:* badminton M, basketball M/W, bowling M/W, football M/W, golf M/W, ice hockey M(c), lacrosse M(c)/W(c), racquetball M(c)/W(c), rugby M(c), skiing (cross-country) M(c)/W(c), skiing (downhill) M(c)/W(c), softball M/W, swimming M/W, table tennis M, tennis M/W, track and field M/W, volleyball M(c)/W, weight lifting M(c)/W(c), wrestling M.

Standardized Tests *Required:* SAT I or ACT (for admission).

Costs (2003–04) *Comprehensive fee:* $23,880 includes full-time tuition ($18,478) and room and board ($5402). Part-time tuition: $588 per hour. Part-time tuition and fees vary according to class time. *College room only:* $3042. *Payment plans:* installment, deferred payment. *Waivers:* children of alumni and employees or children of employees.

Financial Aid Of all full-time matriculated undergraduates who enrolled in 2003, 2,669 applied for aid, 2,281 were judged to have need, 1,711 had their need fully met. 2,234 Federal Work-Study jobs (averaging $1330). 728 state and other part-time jobs (averaging $1864). In 2003, 758 non-need-based awards were made. *Average percent of need met:* 95%. *Average financial aid package:* $13,257. *Average need-based loan:* $3778. *Average need-based gift aid:* $9733. *Average non-need-based aid:* $7181. *Average indebtedness upon graduation:* $14,099. *Financial aid deadline:* 9/1.

Applying *Options:* common application, electronic application, deferred entrance. *Application fee:* $15. *Required:* essay or personal statement, high school transcript, minimum 2.6 GPA, 1 letter of recommendation. *Recommended:* minimum 3.2 GPA, interview. *Application deadline:* rolling (freshmen), rolling (transfers). *Notification:* continuous until 5/1 (freshmen), 6/1 (transfers).

Admissions Contact Ms. Grace B. Chalker, Interim Associate Director of Admissions, Baldwin-Wallace College, 275 Eastland Road, Berea, OH 44017-2088. *Phone:* 440-826-2222. *Toll-free phone:* 877-BWAPPLY. *Fax:* 440-826-3830. *E-mail:* admission@bw.edu.

BLUFFTON COLLEGE
Bluffton, Ohio

- **Independent Mennonite** comprehensive, founded 1899
- **Calendar** semesters
- **Degrees** bachelor's and master's
- **Small-town** 65-acre campus with easy access to Toledo
- **Endowment** $15.3 million
- **Coed,** 1,056 undergraduate students, 92% full-time, 60% women, 40% men
- **Moderately difficult** entrance level, 77% of applicants were admitted

Undergraduates 971 full-time, 85 part-time. Students come from 21 states and territories, 16 other countries, 11% are from out of state, 3% African American, 0.4% Asian American or Pacific Islander, 2% Hispanic American, 0.2% Native American, 2% international, 8% transferred in, 81% live on campus. *Retention:* 79% of 2002 full-time freshmen returned.

Freshmen *Admission:* 901 applied, 691 admitted, 236 enrolled. *Average high school GPA:* 3.42. *Test scores:* SAT verbal scores over 500: 59%; SAT math scores over 500: 63%; ACT scores over 18: 92%; SAT verbal scores over 600: 27%; SAT math scores over 600: 17%; ACT scores over 24: 46%; SAT verbal scores over 700: 3%; SAT math scores over 700: 3%; ACT scores over 30: 2%.

Faculty *Total:* 117, 54% full-time, 44% with terminal degrees. *Student/faculty ratio:* 14:1.

Majors Accounting; apparel and accessories marketing; art; biology/biological sciences; business administration and management; chemistry; clothing/textiles; communication/speech communication and rhetoric; computer science; creative writing; criminal justice/safety; economics; elementary education; English; family and consumer sciences/home economics teacher education; family and consumer sciences/human sciences; foods, nutrition, and wellness; health and physical education; history; information science/studies; information technology; kindergarten/preschool education; mathematics; middle school education; multi-/interdisciplinary studies related; music; music teacher education; organizational behavior; parks, recreation and leisure; physics; pre-medical studies; psychology; religious studies; social sciences; social work; sociology; Spanish; sport and fitness administration; youth ministry.

Academic Programs *Special study options:* academic remediation for entering students, adult/continuing education programs, advanced placement credit, honors programs, independent study, internships, off-campus study, part-time degree program, student-designed majors, study abroad, summer session for credit.

Library Musselman Library with 163,448 titles, 385 serial subscriptions, 1,259 audiovisual materials, an OPAC.

Computers on Campus 125 computers available on campus for general student use. A campuswide network can be accessed from student residence rooms and from off campus. Internet access, online (class) registration, at least one staffed computer lab available. Computer purchase or lease plan available.

Student Life *Housing:* on-campus residence required through senior year. *Options:* coed, men-only, women-only. Campus housing is university owned. Freshman campus housing is guaranteed. *Activities and organizations:* drama/theater group, student-run newspaper, radio station, choral group, Brothers and Sisters in Christ, Campus Government, Student Union Board, music groups/chorale, chapel service. *Campus security:* late-night transport/escort service, controlled dormitory access, night security guards. *Student services:* health clinic, personal/psychological counseling, women's center.

Athletics Member NCAA. All Division III. *Intercollegiate sports:* baseball M, basketball M/W, cross-country running M/W, football M, golf M, soccer M/W, softball W, tennis M/W, track and field M/W, volleyball W. *Intramural sports:* basketball M/W, bowling M/W, football M/W, golf M, softball M/W, volleyball M/W.

Standardized Tests *Required:* SAT I or ACT (for admission).

Costs (2004–05) *Comprehensive fee:* $24,620 includes full-time tuition ($17,950), mandatory fees ($400), and room and board ($6270). Full-time tuition and fees vary according to course load and program. Part-time tuition: $748 per credit hour. Part-time tuition and fees vary according to course load and program. *College room only:* $2868. Room and board charges vary according to board plan and housing facility. *Payment plan:* installment. *Waivers:* employees or children of employees.

Financial Aid Of all full-time matriculated undergraduates who enrolled in 2003, 727 applied for aid, 688 were judged to have need, 359 had their need fully met. 518 Federal Work-Study jobs (averaging $1588). 300 state and other part-time jobs (averaging $1698). In 2003, 99 non-need-based awards were made. *Average percent of need met:* 93%. *Average financial aid package:* $16,776. *Average need-based loan:* $4777. *Average need-based gift aid:* $10,829. *Average non-need-based aid:* $7030. *Average indebtedness upon graduation:* $20,039. *Financial aid deadline:* 10/1.

Applying *Options:* deferred entrance. *Application fee:* $20. *Required:* high school transcript, 2 letters of recommendation, rank in upper 50% of high school class or 2.3 high school GPA. *Required for some:* essay or personal statement. *Recommended:* interview. *Application deadline:* 5/31 (freshmen), rolling (transfers). *Notification:* 6/1 (freshmen), continuous (transfers).

Admissions Contact Mr. Eric Fulcomer, Director of Admissions, Vice President for Enrollment Management, Bluffton College, 280 West College Avenue, Bluffton, OH 45817. *Phone:* 419-358-3254. *Toll-free phone:* 800-488-3257. *Fax:* 419-358-3232. *E-mail:* admissions@bluffton.edu.

■ *See page 1268 for a narrative description.*

BOWLING GREEN STATE UNIVERSITY
Bowling Green, Ohio

- **State-supported** university, founded 1910
- **Calendar** semesters
- **Degrees** bachelor's, master's, doctoral, and post-master's certificates
- **Small-town** 1230-acre campus with easy access to Toledo
- **Endowment** $92.5 million
- **Coed,** 15,481 undergraduate students, 93% full-time, 56% women, 44% men
- **Moderately difficult** entrance level, 90% of applicants were admitted

BGSU offers a small college atmosphere with major university opportunities. A residential campus, BGSU emphasizes values exploration and character development, nationally known academic programs, first-year student programs, leadership development, and an appreciation for diversity. Award-winning career center and nationally ranked cooperative education program are part of BGSU's distinctive environment; 65% of students receive financial aid.

Undergraduates 14,462 full-time, 1,019 part-time. Students come from 47 states and territories, 41 other countries, 7% are from out of state, 6% African American, 0.7% Asian American or Pacific Islander, 3% Hispanic American, 0.3% Native American, 0.7% international, 4% transferred in, 44% live on campus. *Retention:* 74% of 2002 full-time freshmen returned.

Freshmen *Admission:* 10,281 applied, 9,283 admitted, 3,541 enrolled. *Average high school GPA:* 3.17. *Test scores:* SAT verbal scores over 500: 53%; SAT math scores over 500: 53%; ACT scores over 18: 95%; SAT verbal scores over 600: 16%; SAT math scores over 600: 17%; ACT scores over 24: 26%; SAT verbal scores over 700: 3%; SAT math scores over 700: 3%; ACT scores over 30: 4%.

Faculty *Total:* 1,026, 80% full-time. *Student/faculty ratio:* 19:1.

Majors Accounting; adult development and aging; African studies; airline pilot and flight crew; American studies; art history, criticism and conservation; art teacher education; art therapy; Asian studies; athletic training; aviation/airway management; biology/biological sciences; biology teacher education; broadcast journalism; business/commerce; business, management, and marketing related; business/managerial economics; business teacher education; ceramic arts and ceramics; chemistry; child development; classics and languages, literatures and linguistics; clinical laboratory science/medical technology; clothing/textiles; communication and journalism related; communication disorders; communication/speech communication and rhetoric; computer and information sciences; construction engineering technology; crafts, folk art and artisanry; creative writing; criminal justice/safety; dance; design and visual communications; dietetics; drama and dance teacher education; dramatic/theatre arts; dramatic/theatre arts and stagecraft related; drawing; economics; education; education related; education (specific levels and methods) related; education (specific subject areas) related; electrical, electronic and communications engineering technology; elementary education; English; English/language arts teacher education; environmental design/architecture; environmental health; ethnic, cultural minority, and gender studies related; family and consumer sciences/home economics teacher education; fashion merchandising; fiber, textile and weaving arts; film/cinema studies; finance; fine arts related; fine/studio arts; foods, nutrition, and wellness; foreign language teacher education; French; geography; geology/earth science; German; gerontology; health and physical education related; health/health care administration; health professions related; health teacher education; history; hospitality administration; human resources management; industrial technology; international business/trade/commerce; international relations and affairs; journalism; kindergarten/preschool education; labor and industrial relations; Latin teacher education; liberal arts and sciences/liberal studies; logistics and materials management; management information systems; management information systems and services related; marketing related; mathematics; mathematics teacher education; mechanical design technology; mechanical engineering/mechanical technology; medical microbiology and bacteriology; metal and jewelry arts; middle school education; multi-/interdisciplinary studies related; music; musicology and ethnomusicology; music performance; music related; music teacher education; music theory and composition; natural resources management and policy; neuroscience; nursing (registered nurse training); operations management; painting; parks, recreation and leisure; philosophy; photography; physical education teaching and coaching; physical therapy; physics; piano and organ; political science and government; pre-law studies; psychology; public administration; public relations/image management; quality control technology; Russian; sales and marketing/marketing and distribution teacher education; science teacher education; sculpture; social studies teacher education; social work; sociology; Spanish; special education; special education (hearing impaired); special education (mentally retarded); special education (multiply disabled); special education (specific learning disabilities); speech and rhetoric; sport and fitness administration; statistics; technical and business writing; technical teacher education; telecommunications; tourism promotion; voice and opera; wind/percussion instruments; women's studies.

Academic Programs *Special study options:* academic remediation for entering students, accelerated degree program, adult/continuing education programs, advanced placement credit, cooperative education, distance learning, double majors, English as a second language, honors programs, independent study, internships, off-campus study, part-time degree program, services for LD students, student-designed majors, study abroad, summer session for credit. *ROTC:* Army (b), Air Force (b).

Library Jerome Library plus 7 others with 2.4 million titles, 4,833 serial subscriptions, 718,734 audiovisual materials, an OPAC, a Web page.

Computers on Campus 6240 computers available on campus for general student use. A campuswide network can be accessed from student residence rooms and from off campus. Internet access, online (class) registration, at least one staffed computer lab available.

Student Life *Housing:* on-campus residence required through sophomore year. *Options:* coed, disabled students. Campus housing is university owned. Freshman campus housing is guaranteed. *Activities and organizations:* drama/theater group, student-run newspaper, radio station, choral group, marching band, University Activities Organization, Undergraduate Student Government, Latino Student Union, H20 (Religious/Spiritual Group), national fraternities, national sororities. *Campus security:* 24-hour emergency response devices and patrols, student patrols, late-night transport/escort service, controlled dormitory access. *Student services:* health clinic, personal/psychological counseling, women's center, legal services.

Athletics Member NCAA. All Division I except football (Division I-A). *Intercollegiate sports:* baseball M(s), basketball M(s)/W(s), crew M(c), cross-country running M(s)/W(s), golf M(s)/W(s), gymnastics W(s), ice hockey M(s), soccer M(s), softball W(s), swimming M(s)/W(s), tennis M(s)/W(s), track and field M(s)/W(s), volleyball M(c)/W(s), water polo M(c)/W(c), weight lifting M(c)/W(c). *Intramural sports:* basketball M/W, bowling M/W, cross-country running M/W, football M/W, golf M/W, ice hockey M/W, lacrosse M(c)/W(c), racquetball M/W, rugby M(c)/W(c), skiing (cross-country) M(c)/W(c), skiing (downhill) M(c)/W(c), soccer M/W, softball M/W, tennis M/W, track and field M/W, ultimate Frisbee M/W, volleyball M/W, water polo M(c)/W(c).

Standardized Tests *Required:* SAT I or ACT (for admission).

Costs (2003–04) *Tuition:* state resident $5940 full-time, $292 per credit hour part-time; nonresident $12,900 full-time, $624 per credit hour part-time. Part-time tuition and fees vary according to course load. *Required fees:* $1204 full-time, $60 per credit hour part-time. *Room and board:* $5892; room only: $3642. Room and board charges vary according to board plan and housing facility. *Payment plan:* installment. *Waivers:* senior citizens and employees or children of employees.

Financial Aid Of all full-time matriculated undergraduates who enrolled in 2002, 11,150 applied for aid, 8,813 were judged to have need, 832 had their need fully met. 1,073 Federal Work-Study jobs (averaging $1134). In 2002, 2116 non-need-based awards were made. *Average percent of need met:* 76%. *Average financial aid package:* $8536. *Average need-based loan:* $3441. *Average need-based gift aid:* $3583. *Average non-need-based aid:* $2642. *Average indebtedness upon graduation:* $17,967.

Applying *Options:* electronic application, deferred entrance. *Application fee:* $35. *Required:* high school transcript, minimum 2.5 GPA. *Recommended:* interview. *Application deadlines:* 7/15 (freshmen), 7/15 (transfers). *Notification:* continuous (freshmen), continuous (transfers).

Admissions Contact Mr. Gary Swegan, Director of Admissions, Bowling Green State University, 110 McFall, Bowling Green, OH 43403. *Phone:* 419-372-2086. *Fax:* 419-372-6955. *E-mail:* admissions@bgnet.bgsu.edu.

■ *See page 1280 for a narrative description.*

BRYANT AND STRATTON COLLEGE
Cleveland, Ohio

- **Proprietary** 4-year, founded 1929, part of Bryant and Stratton Business Institute, Inc.
- **Calendar** semesters
- **Degrees** associate and bachelor's
- **Urban** campus
- **Coed**
- **Minimally difficult** entrance level

Faculty *Student/faculty ratio:* 10:1.

Student Life *Campus security:* controlled dormitory access.

Standardized Tests *Required:* TABE (for admission). *Recommended:* SAT I or ACT (for admission).

Costs (2003–04) *Tuition:* $10,410 full-time, $347 per credit hour part-time. *Required fees:* $200 full-time. *Room only:* $3887.

Financial Aid Of all full-time matriculated undergraduates who enrolled in 2001, 110 applied for aid, 108 were judged to have need, 90 had their need fully met. 8 Federal Work-Study jobs (averaging $3000). *Average percent of need met:* 89. *Average financial aid package:* $6200. *Average need-based loan:* $3065. *Average need-based gift aid:* $1500. *Average indebtedness upon graduation:* $12,000.

Applying *Options:* deferred entrance. *Application fee:* $25. *Required:* essay or personal statement, high school transcript, interview.

Admissions Contact Ms. Marilyn Scheaffer, Director of Admissions, Bryant and Stratton College, 1700 East 13th Street, Cleveland, OH 44114-3203. *Phone:* 216-771-1700. *Fax:* 216-771-7787.

CAPITAL UNIVERSITY
Columbus, Ohio

- **Independent** comprehensive, founded 1830, affiliated with Evangelical Lutheran Church in America
- **Calendar** semesters
- **Degrees** certificates, bachelor's, master's, and first professional
- **Suburban** 48-acre campus
- **Endowment** $35.6 million
- **Coed,** 2,830 undergraduate students, 76% full-time, 64% women, 36% men
- **Moderately difficult** entrance level, 84% of applicants were admitted

Recognition as one of the top universities–master's in *U.S. News & World Report*, a Center for Academic Achievement to help each student succeed academically, and the construction of the new Capital Center, a 126,000-square-foot recreational, educational, and athletic complex, are just a few reasons Capital University is a leader in the Midwest.

Undergraduates 2,153 full-time, 677 part-time. Students come from 24 states and territories, 10 other countries, 1% are from out of state, 14% African American, 2% Asian American or Pacific Islander, 1% Hispanic American, 0.1% Native American, 0.5% international, 3% transferred in, 48% live on campus. *Retention:* 79% of 2002 full-time freshmen returned.

Freshmen *Admission:* 2,216 applied, 1,871 admitted, 577 enrolled. *Average high school GPA:* 3.40. *Test scores:* SAT verbal scores over 500: 70%; SAT math scores over 500: 72%; ACT scores over 18: 96%; SAT verbal scores over 600: 28%; SAT math scores over 600: 27%; ACT scores over 24: 45%; SAT verbal scores over 700: 4%; SAT math scores over 700: 5%; ACT scores over 30: 8%.

Capital University (continued)

Faculty *Total:* 445, 47% full-time, 60% with terminal degrees. *Student/faculty ratio:* 9:1.

Majors Accounting; agricultural business and management; art; art teacher education; art therapy; athletic training; biochemistry; biological and biomedical sciences related; biology/biological sciences; biology teacher education; business administration and management; business administration, management and operations related; business/commerce; business/managerial economics; chemistry; chemistry teacher education; communication/speech communication and rhetoric; computer engineering; computer science; computer teacher education; creative writing; criminal justice/safety; criminology; drama and dance teacher education; dramatic/theatre arts; early childhood education; economics; education; educational/instructional media design; elementary education; English; English/language arts teacher education; environmental science; finance; fine/studio arts; French; health and physical education; health and physical education related; health teacher education; history; human resources management; interdisciplinary studies; international relations and affairs; jazz/jazz studies; kinesiology and exercise science; liberal arts and sciences/liberal studies; literature; marketing/marketing management; mathematics; mathematics teacher education; middle school education; multi-/interdisciplinary studies related; music; music management and merchandising; music performance; music related; music teacher education; music theory and composition; nursing (registered nurse training); nursing related; organizational communication; philosophy; philosophy and religious studies related; physical education teaching and coaching; piano and organ; political science and government; political science and government related; pre-dentistry studies; pre-medical studies; pre-veterinary studies; psychology; public administration; public health/community nursing; public relations/image management; radio, television, and digital communication related; religious education; religious studies; science teacher education; secondary education; social studies teacher education; social work; sociology; Spanish; special education; speech and rhetoric; speech teacher education; taxation; violin, viola, guitar and other stringed instruments; voice and opera; wind/percussion instruments.

Academic Programs *Special study options:* adult/continuing education programs, advanced placement credit, double majors, English as a second language, freshman honors college, independent study, internships, off-campus study, part-time degree program, services for LD students, student-designed majors, study abroad, summer session for credit. *ROTC:* Army (b), Air Force (c). *Unusual degree programs:* 3-2 engineering with Washington University in St. Louis, Case Western Reserve University; occupational therapy with Washington University in St. Louis, University of Indianapolis.

Library Blackmore Library with 187,281 titles, 3,741 serial subscriptions, 6,048 audiovisual materials, an OPAC.

Computers on Campus 100 computers available on campus for general student use. A campuswide network can be accessed from student residence rooms and from off campus. Internet access, at least one staffed computer lab available.

Student Life *Housing:* on-campus residence required through sophomore year. *Options:* coed. Campus housing is university owned. Freshman campus housing is guaranteed. *Activities and organizations:* drama/theater group, student-run newspaper, radio and television station, choral group, national fraternities, national sororities. *Campus security:* 24-hour patrols, late-night transport/escort service, controlled dormitory access. *Student services:* health clinic, personal/psychological counseling.

Athletics Member NCAA. All Division III. *Intercollegiate sports:* baseball M, basketball M/W, cheerleading M(s)/W(s), cross-country running M/W, football M, golf M/W, soccer M/W, softball W, tennis M/W, track and field M/W, volleyball W. *Intramural sports:* basketball M/W, bowling M/W, football M/W, soccer M/W, softball M/W, table tennis M/W, tennis M/W, track and field M/W, ultimate Frisbee M(c)/W(c), volleyball M/W.

Standardized Tests *Required:* SAT I or ACT (for admission).

Costs (2003–04) *One-time required fee:* $200. *Comprehensive fee:* $26,550 includes full-time tuition ($20,500) and room and board ($6050). Full-time tuition and fees vary according to program. *Room and board:* Room and board charges vary according to board plan and housing facility. *Payment plan:* installment. *Waivers:* senior citizens and employees or children of employees.

Financial Aid Of all full-time matriculated undergraduates who enrolled in 2003, 1,880 applied for aid, 1,736 were judged to have need, 400 had their need fully met. In 2003, 365 non-need-based awards were made. *Average percent of need met:* 80%. *Average financial aid package:* $16,856. *Average need-based loan:* $4589. *Average need-based gift aid:* $9890. *Average non-need-based aid:* $8628. *Average indebtedness upon graduation:* $25,171.

Applying *Options:* common application, early action, deferred entrance. *Application fee:* $25. *Required:* high school transcript, minimum 2.6 GPA. *Required for some:* 1 letter of recommendation, audition. *Recommended:* interview. *Application deadline:* 4/15 (freshmen), rolling (transfers). *Notification:* 9/1 (freshmen), 10/2 (early action), continuous (transfers).

Admissions Contact Mrs. Kimberly V. Ebbrecht, Director of Admission, Capital University, 2199 East Main Street, Columbus, OH 43209. *Phone:* 614-236-6101. *Toll-free phone:* 800-289-6289. *Fax:* 614-236-6926. *E-mail:* admissions@capital.edu.

■ *See page 1342 for a narrative description.*

CASE WESTERN RESERVE UNIVERSITY
Cleveland, Ohio

- **Independent** university, founded 1826
- **Calendar** semesters
- **Degrees** bachelor's, master's, doctoral, first professional, and postbachelor's certificates
- **Urban** 150-acre campus
- **Endowment** $1.3 billion
- **Coed,** 3,587 undergraduate students, 92% full-time, 39% women, 61% men
- **Very difficult** entrance level, 75% of applicants were admitted

College-bound students most often list diversity of academic programs as the most important factor in choosing a college. They understand that their academic interests are not fully tested in high school and that a high-quality college education should offer them the opportunity to explore more varied academic offerings. Case has long recognized the importance of academic diversity. At Case, regardless of their tentative interest in engineering, liberal arts, management, sciences, or nursing, students apply through a single admission process; admission is not based on academic interest. Once enrolled, students can choose from more than 60 available majors and can double major across disciplinary lines (engineering and music is a popular combination).

Undergraduates 3,314 full-time, 273 part-time. Students come from 50 states and territories, 24 other countries, 45% are from out of state, 5% African American, 15% Asian American or Pacific Islander, 2% Hispanic American, 0.4% Native American, 5% international, 2% transferred in, 73% live on campus. *Retention:* 93% of 2001 full-time freshmen returned.

Freshmen *Admission:* 4,680 applied, 3,525 admitted, 878 enrolled. *Test scores:* SAT verbal scores over 500: 94%; SAT math scores over 500: 99%; ACT scores over 18: 100%; SAT verbal scores over 600: 73%; SAT math scores over 600: 84%; ACT scores over 24: 90%; SAT verbal scores over 700: 29%; SAT math scores over 700: 44%; ACT scores over 30: 43%.

Faculty *Total:* 600, 100% full-time, 96% with terminal degrees. *Student/faculty ratio:* 8:1.

Majors Accounting; aerospace, aeronautical and astronautical engineering; American studies; anthropology; applied mathematics; art history, criticism and conservation; art teacher education; Asian studies; astronomy; biochemistry; biology/biological sciences; biomedical/medical engineering; business administration and management; chemical engineering; chemistry; civil engineering; classics and languages, literatures and linguistics; communication disorders; comparative literature; computer engineering; computer science; dietetics; dramatic/theatre arts; economics; electrical, electronics and communications engineering; engineering; engineering physics; engineering science; English; environmental studies; evolutionary biology; French; French studies; geology/earth science; German; German studies; gerontology; history; history and philosophy of science and technology; human nutrition; international/global studies; international relations and affairs; Japanese studies; materials engineering; materials science; mathematics; mechanical engineering; music; music teacher education; natural sciences; nursing (registered nurse training); nutrition sciences; philosophy; physics; political science and government; polymer/plastics engineering; psychology; religious studies; sociology; Spanish; statistics; systems engineering; women's studies.

Academic Programs *Special study options:* accelerated degree program, adult/continuing education programs, advanced placement credit, cooperative education, double majors, English as a second language, honors programs, independent study, internships, off-campus study, part-time degree program, services for LD students, student-designed majors, study abroad, summer session for credit. *ROTC:* Army (c), Air Force (c). *Unusual degree programs:* 3-2 astronomy, biochemistry.

Library University Library plus 6 others with 2.2 million titles, 17,506 serial subscriptions, 49,889 audiovisual materials, an OPAC, a Web page.

Computers on Campus 100 computers available on campus for general student use. A campuswide network can be accessed from student residence rooms and from off campus that provide access to software library, CD-ROM databases. Internet access, online (class) registration, at least one staffed computer lab available. Computer purchase or lease plan available.

Student Life *Housing:* on-campus residence required through senior year. *Options:* coed. Campus housing is university owned. Freshman campus housing is guaranteed. *Activities and organizations:* drama/theater group, student-run newspaper, radio station, choral group, marching band, student radio station, Habitat for Humanity, international student groups, music/dance groups, national fraternities, national sororities. *Campus security:* 24-hour emergency response devices and patrols, student patrols, late-night transport/escort service, controlled dormitory access, crime prevention programs. *Student services:* health clinic, personal/psychological counseling, women's center, legal services.

Athletics Member NCAA. All Division III. *Intercollegiate sports:* archery M(c)/W(c), baseball M, basketball M/W, crew M(c)/W(c), cross-country running M/W, fencing M(c)/W(c), football M, ice hockey M(c)/W(c), soccer M/W, softball W, swimming M/W, tennis M/W, track and field M/W, ultimate Frisbee M(c)/W(c), volleyball M(c)/W, wrestling M. *Intramural sports:* badminton M/W, basketball M/W, bowling M/W, cross-country running M/W, football M/W, golf M/W, racquetball M/W, soccer M/W, softball M/W, squash M/W, swimming M/W, table tennis M/W, tennis M/W, track and field M/W, ultimate Frisbee M/W, volleyball M/W, water polo M/W, weight lifting M/W, wrestling M.

Standardized Tests *Required:* SAT I or ACT (for admission). *Recommended:* SAT II: Subject Tests (for admission).

Costs (2003–04) *Comprehensive fee:* $32,002 includes full-time tuition ($24,100), mandatory fees ($242), and room and board ($7660). Part-time tuition and fees vary according to course load. *College room only:* $4770. Room and board charges vary according to board plan and housing facility. *Payment plans:* tuition prepayment, installment. *Waivers:* employees or children of employees.

Financial Aid Of all full-time matriculated undergraduates who enrolled in 2003, 2,205 applied for aid, 1,811 were judged to have need, 1,661 had their need fully met. 1,790 Federal Work-Study jobs (averaging $1310). In 2003, 1138 non-need-based awards were made. *Average percent of need met:* 94%. *Average financial aid package:* $23,571. *Average need-based loan:* $5908. *Average need-based gift aid:* $15,695. *Average non-need-based aid:* $12,352. *Average indebtedness upon graduation:* $23,534.

Applying *Options:* common application, electronic application, early admission, early action, deferred entrance. *Application fee:* $35. *Required:* essay or personal statement, high school transcript, 1 letter of recommendation. *Recommended:* interview. *Application deadlines:* 1/15 (freshmen), 5/15 (transfers). *Notification:* 3/1 (freshmen), 1/15 (early action), continuous until 6/15 (transfers).

Admissions Contact Ms. Elizabeth H. Woyczynski, Director of Undergraduate Admission, Case Western Reserve University, 10900 Euclid Avenue, Cleveland, OH 44106. *Phone:* 216-368-4450. *Fax:* 216-368-5111. *E-mail:* admission@case.edu.

■ *See page 1362 for a narrative description.*

CEDARVILLE UNIVERSITY

Cedarville, Ohio

- **Independent Baptist** comprehensive, founded 1887
- **Calendar** semesters
- **Degrees** certificates, bachelor's, and master's
- **Rural** 400-acre campus with easy access to Columbus and Dayton
- **Endowment** $10.3 million
- **Coed,** 2,996 undergraduate students, 94% full-time, 54% women, 46% men
- **Moderately difficult** entrance level, 81% of applicants were admitted

Undergraduates 2,830 full-time, 166 part-time. Students come from 49 states and territories, 16 other countries, 67% are from out of state, 1% African American, 1% Asian American or Pacific Islander, 1% Hispanic American, 0.1% Native American, 0.5% international, 4% transferred in, 82% live on campus. *Retention:* 81% of 2002 full-time freshmen returned.

Freshmen *Admission:* 2,174 applied, 1,762 admitted, 787 enrolled. *Average high school GPA:* 3.60. *Test scores:* SAT verbal scores over 500: 91%; SAT math scores over 500: 87%; ACT scores over 18: 100%; SAT verbal scores over 600: 49%; SAT math scores over 600: 45%; ACT scores over 24: 67%; SAT verbal scores over 700: 12%; SAT math scores over 700: 9%; ACT scores over 30: 14%.

Faculty *Total:* 271, 74% full-time, 49% with terminal degrees. *Student/faculty ratio:* 14:1.

Majors Accounting; American studies; athletic training; biblical studies; biological and physical sciences; biology/biological sciences; biology teacher education; broadcast journalism; business administration and management; chemistry; clinical laboratory science/medical technology; communication/speech communication and rhetoric; computer engineering; computer science; criminal justice/law enforcement administration; dramatic/theatre arts; early childhood education; electrical, electronics and communications engineering; English; English/language arts teacher education; environmental biology; finance; graphic design; health and physical education; health teacher education; history; information science/studies; international business/trade/commerce; international relations and affairs; kinesiology and exercise science; marketing/marketing management; mathematics; mathematics teacher education; mechanical engineering; missionary studies and missiology; music; music pedagogy; music performance; music teacher education; music theory and composition; nursing (registered nurse training); pastoral studies/counseling; philosophy; physical education teaching and coaching; physics; physics teacher education; piano and organ; political science and government; pre-dentistry studies; pre-law studies; pre-medical studies; pre-veterinary studies; psychology; public administration; religious education; religious/sacred music; science teacher education; secondary education; social studies teacher education; social work; sociology; Spanish; Spanish language teacher education; special education; speech and rhetoric; sport and fitness administration; technical and business writing; theology; voice and opera; youth ministry.

Academic Programs *Special study options:* academic remediation for entering students, accelerated degree program, advanced placement credit, distance learning, double majors, honors programs, independent study, internships, off-campus study, part-time degree program, services for LD students, study abroad, summer session for credit. *ROTC:* Army (c), Air Force (c).

Library Centennial Library with 149,164 titles, 4,932 serial subscriptions, 15,452 audiovisual materials, an OPAC, a Web page.

Computers on Campus 1600 computers available on campus for general student use. A campuswide network can be accessed from student residence rooms and from off campus that provide access to software packages. Internet access, online (class) registration, at least one staffed computer lab available.

Student Life *Housing:* on-campus residence required through senior year. *Options:* men-only, women-only. Campus housing is university owned. Freshman campus housing is guaranteed. *Activities and organizations:* drama/theater group, student-run newspaper, radio station, choral group, Student Government Association, College Republicans, ASME, Chi Theta Pi, MENC. *Campus security:* 24-hour emergency response devices and patrols, student patrols, late-night transport/escort service, controlled dormitory access. *Student services:* health clinic, personal/psychological counseling.

Athletics Member NAIA, NCCAA. *Intercollegiate sports:* baseball M(s), basketball M(s)/W(s), cheerleading M/W, cross-country running M(s)/W(s), golf M(s), soccer M(s)/W(s), softball W(s), tennis M(s)/W(s), track and field M(s)/W(s), volleyball W(s). *Intramural sports:* badminton M/W, basketball M/W, bowling M/W, football M/W, golf M/W, racquetball M/W, rock climbing M(c)/W(c), skiing (downhill) M/W, soccer M/W, softball M/W, table tennis M/W, tennis M/W, ultimate Frisbee M(c)/W(c), volleyball M/W.

Standardized Tests *Required:* SAT I or ACT (for admission).

Costs (2003–04) *Comprehensive fee:* $19,954 includes full-time tuition ($14,944) and room and board ($5010). Part-time tuition: $467 per semester hour. Part-time tuition and fees vary according to course load. *College room only:* $2684. Room and board charges vary according to board plan. *Payment plan:* installment. *Waivers:* senior citizens and employees or children of employees.

Financial Aid Of all full-time matriculated undergraduates who enrolled in 2002, 2,008 applied for aid, 1,651 were judged to have need, 761 had their need fully met. 340 Federal Work-Study jobs (averaging $994). 1,298 state and other part-time jobs (averaging $1014). In 2002, 635 non-need-based awards were made. *Average percent of need met:* 40%. *Average financial aid package:* $12,738. *Average need-based loan:* $3845. *Average need-based gift aid:* $1644. *Average non-need-based aid:* $6995. *Average indebtedness upon graduation:* $16,633.

Applying *Options:* electronic application, early admission, deferred entrance. *Application fee:* $30. *Required:* essay or personal statement, high school transcript, minimum 3.0 GPA, 2 letters of recommendation. *Required for some:* interview. *Application deadline:* rolling (freshmen). *Notification:* continuous (freshmen).

Admissions Contact Mr. Roscoe Smith, Director of Admissions, Cedarville University, 251 North Main Street, Cedarville, OH 45314-0601. *Phone:* 937-766-7700. *Toll-free phone:* 800-CEDARVILLE. *Fax:* 937-766-7575. *E-mail:* admiss@cedarville.edu.

■ *See page 1374 for a narrative description.*

CENTRAL STATE UNIVERSITY

Wilberforce, Ohio

- **State-supported** comprehensive, founded 1887, part of Ohio Board of Regents
- **Calendar** quarters
- **Degrees** bachelor's, master's, and postbachelor's certificates
- **Rural** 60-acre campus with easy access to Dayton
- **Endowment** $732,439
- **Coed,** 1,611 undergraduate students, 92% full-time, 54% women, 46% men
- **Minimally difficult** entrance level, 49% of applicants were admitted

Undergraduates 1,483 full-time, 128 part-time. Students come from 26 states and territories, 5 other countries, 25% are from out of state, 86% African American, 0.1% Asian American or Pacific Islander, 0.3% Hispanic American, 0.1% Native American, 0.7% international, 8% transferred in, 50% live on campus. *Retention:* 53% of 2002 full-time freshmen returned.

Central State University (continued)

Freshmen *Admission:* 3,691 applied, 1,814 admitted, 550 enrolled. *Average high school GPA:* 2.51. *Test scores:* ACT scores over 18: 22%; ACT scores over 24: 1%.

Faculty *Total:* 143, 61% full-time, 38% with terminal degrees. *Student/faculty ratio:* 14:1.

Majors Accounting; art; art teacher education; biology/biological sciences; business administration and management; chemistry; computer and information sciences; economics; English; English/language arts teacher education; finance; health teacher education; history; hotel/motel administration; industrial engineering; industrial technology; jazz/jazz studies; journalism related; kindergarten/preschool education; management information systems; marketing/marketing management; mathematics; mathematics teacher education; middle school education; music; music teacher education; parks, recreation and leisure; physical education teaching and coaching; political science and government; psychology; radio and television; science teacher education; social studies teacher education; social work; sociology; special education; water resources engineering.

Academic Programs *Special study options:* adult/continuing education programs, cooperative education, double majors, honors programs, independent study, internships, off-campus study, part-time degree program, services for LD students, study abroad, summer session for credit. *ROTC:* Army (b).

Library Hallie Q. Brown Memorial Library plus 1 other with 280,470 titles, 26,066 serial subscriptions, 497 audiovisual materials, an OPAC.

Computers on Campus 338 computers available on campus for general student use. A campuswide network can be accessed. Internet access, at least one staffed computer lab available.

Student Life *Housing:* on-campus residence required for freshman year. *Options:* men-only, women-only. Campus housing is university owned. Freshman campus housing is guaranteed. *Activities and organizations:* drama/theater group, student-run radio station, choral group, marching band, Student Ambassadors, student government, national fraternities, national sororities. *Campus security:* 24-hour emergency response devices and patrols, controlled dormitory access. *Student services:* health clinic, personal/psychological counseling.

Athletics Member NAIA. *Intercollegiate sports:* basketball M(s)/W(s), cheerleading M(s)/W(s), cross-country running M(s)/W(s), golf M(s)/W(s), tennis M(s)/W(s), track and field M(s)/W(s), volleyball W(s). *Intramural sports:* basketball M/W, bowling M/W, softball M/W, tennis M/W.

Standardized Tests *Required:* SAT I or ACT (for admission). *Recommended:* ACT (for admission).

Costs (2003–04) *Tuition:* state resident $2340 full-time; nonresident $7335 full-time. Full-time tuition and fees vary according to course load. *Required fees:* $1947 full-time. *Room and board:* $6069; room only: $3198. *Payment plans:* installment, deferred payment. *Waivers:* senior citizens and employees or children of employees.

Financial Aid Of all full-time matriculated undergraduates who enrolled in 2002, 1,340 applied for aid. *Average percent of need met:* 85%.

Applying *Options:* common application. *Application fee:* $20. *Required:* high school transcript. *Required for some:* minimum 2.0 GPA, 2 letters of recommendation, 2.5 high school GPA for nonresidents. *Recommended:* interview. *Application deadlines:* 6/15 (freshmen), 6/15 (transfers). *Notification:* continuous (freshmen), continuous (transfers).

Admissions Contact Dr. Eric V. Hilton, Director, Admissions, Central State University, PO Box 1004, 1400 Blush Row Road, Wilberforce, OH 45384. *Phone:* 937-376-6348. *Toll-free phone:* 800-388-CSU1. *Fax:* 937-376-6648. *E-mail:* admissions@csu.ces.edu.

CINCINNATI BIBLE COLLEGE AND SEMINARY
Cincinnati, Ohio

- **Independent** comprehensive, founded 1924, affiliated with Church of Christ
- **Calendar** semesters
- **Degrees** associate, bachelor's, master's, and first professional
- **Urban** 40-acre campus
- **Endowment** $988,063
- **Coed**
- **Minimally difficult** entrance level

Faculty *Student/faculty ratio:* 16:1.

Student Life *Campus security:* 24-hour emergency response devices and patrols, student patrols.

Athletics Member NCCAA.

Standardized Tests *Required:* SAT I or ACT (for admission).

Costs (2003–04) *Comprehensive fee:* $13,730 includes full-time tuition ($8320), mandatory fees ($570), and room and board ($4840).

Financial Aid Of all full-time matriculated undergraduates who enrolled in 2003, 421 applied for aid, 322 were judged to have need, 47 had their need fully met. 128 Federal Work-Study jobs (averaging $628). In 2003, 98. *Average percent of need met:* 60. *Average financial aid package:* $7702. *Average need-based loan:* $3454. *Average need-based gift aid:* $4360. *Average non-need-based aid:* $8005. *Average indebtedness upon graduation:* $16,000.

Applying *Options:* early admission, deferred entrance. *Application fee:* $35. *Required:* essay or personal statement, high school transcript, 3 letters of recommendation. *Recommended:* minimum 2.0 GPA, interview.

Admissions Contact Mr. Alex Eady, Director of Undergraduate Admissions, Cincinnati Bible College and Seminary, 2700 Glenway Avenue, Cincinnati, OH 45204-1799. *Phone:* 800-949-4222 Ext. 8610. *Toll-free phone:* 800-949-4CBC. *Fax:* 513-244-8140. *E-mail:* admissions@cincybible.edu.

CINCINNATI COLLEGE OF MORTUARY SCIENCE
Cincinnati, Ohio

- **Independent** primarily 2-year, founded 1882
- **Calendar** quarters
- **Degrees** associate and bachelor's
- **Urban** 10-acre campus
- **Coed**
- **Minimally difficult** entrance level

Faculty *Student/faculty ratio:* 5:1.

Applying *Options:* deferred entrance. *Application fee:* $25. *Required:* high school transcript. *Recommended:* letters of recommendation.

Admissions Contact Ms. Pat Leon, Director of Financial Aid, Cincinnati College of Mortuary Science, 645 West North Bend Road, Cincinnati, OH 45224-1462. *Phone:* 513-761-2020. *Fax:* 513-761-3333.

CIRCLEVILLE BIBLE COLLEGE
Circleville, Ohio

- **Independent** 4-year, founded 1948, affiliated with Churches of Christ in Christian Union
- **Calendar** semesters
- **Degrees** associate and bachelor's
- **Small-town** 40-acre campus with easy access to Columbus
- **Coed**
- **Minimally difficult** entrance level

Faculty *Student/faculty ratio:* 13:1.

Student Life *Campus security:* security checks after midnight.

Athletics Member NCCAA.

Standardized Tests *Required for some:* ACT (for admission). *Recommended:* SAT I (for admission).

Costs (2003–04) *Comprehensive fee:* $14,394 includes full-time tuition ($8460), mandatory fees ($844), and room and board ($5090). Full-time tuition and fees vary according to course load, location, and reciprocity agreements. Part-time tuition and fees vary according to course load, location, and reciprocity agreements. *Room and board:* Room and board charges vary according to board plan.

Financial Aid Of all full-time matriculated undergraduates who enrolled in 2003, 280 applied for aid, 265 were judged to have need, 175 had their need fully met. 60 Federal Work-Study jobs (averaging $1100). *Average percent of need met:* 85. *Average financial aid package:* $10,000. *Average need-based loan:* $4500. *Average indebtedness upon graduation:* $17,500.

Applying *Options:* common application, electronic application, early admission. *Application fee:* $25. *Required:* essay or personal statement, high school transcript, 4 letters of recommendation, medical form. *Required for some:* interview.

Admissions Contact Rev. James Schroeder, Acting Director of Enrollment, Circleville Bible College, PO Box 458, Circleville, OH 43113-9487. *Phone:* 740-477-7741. *Toll-free phone:* 800-701-0222. *Fax:* 740-477-7755. *E-mail:* enroll@biblecollege.edu.

THE CLEVELAND INSTITUTE OF ART
Cleveland, Ohio

- **Independent** comprehensive, founded 1882
- **Calendar** semesters
- **Degrees** bachelor's and master's
- **Urban** 488-acre campus
- **Endowment** $16.9 million
- **Coed,** 618 undergraduate students, 96% full-time, 50% women, 50% men
- **Moderately difficult** entrance level, 65% of applicants were admitted

Undergraduates 592 full-time, 26 part-time. Students come from 30 states and territories, 9 other countries, 31% are from out of state, 4% African American, 3% Asian American or Pacific Islander, 3% Hispanic American, 0.3% Native American, 3% international, 12% transferred in, 21% live on campus. *Retention:* 82% of 2002 full-time freshmen returned.

Freshmen *Admission:* 423 applied, 277 admitted, 92 enrolled. *Average high school GPA:* 3.14. *Test scores:* SAT verbal scores over 500: 95%; SAT math scores over 500: 89%; ACT scores over 18: 100%; SAT verbal scores over 600: 76%; SAT math scores over 600: 17%; ACT scores over 24: 60%; SAT verbal scores over 700: 12%; ACT scores over 30: 3%.

Faculty *Total:* 99, 47% full-time, 62% with terminal degrees. *Student/faculty ratio:* 10:1.

Majors Ceramic arts and ceramics; commercial and advertising art; crafts, folk art and artisanry; drawing; fiber, textile and weaving arts; graphic design; illustration; industrial design; interior design; intermedia/multimedia; medical illustration; metal and jewelry arts; painting; photography; printmaking; sculpture; web page, digital/multimedia and information resources design.

Academic Programs *Special study options:* academic remediation for entering students, advanced placement credit, honors programs, independent study, internships, off-campus study, part-time degree program, services for LD students, study abroad.

Library Jessica R. Gund Memorial Library with 42,000 titles, 250 serial subscriptions, 95,000 audiovisual materials.

Computers on Campus 80 computers available on campus for general student use. A campuswide network can be accessed from off campus. At least one staffed computer lab available.

Student Life *Housing:* on-campus residence required for freshman year. *Options:* coed. Campus housing is leased by the school. Freshman applicants given priority for college housing. *Activities and organizations:* student-run newspaper, Photo Club, PUMA, Artist for Christ, GIBT, Student Artist Association. *Campus security:* 24-hour emergency response devices and patrols, late-night transport/escort service, controlled dormitory access. *Student services:* health clinic, personal/psychological counseling.

Athletics *Intramural sports:* basketball M/W, bowling M/W, cross-country running M/W, football M/W, golf M/W, ice hockey M/W, racquetball M/W, soccer M/W, softball M/W, swimming M/W, tennis M/W, track and field M/W, ultimate Frisbee M/W, volleyball M/W, wrestling M.

Standardized Tests *Required:* SAT I or ACT (for admission).

Costs (2003–04) *Comprehensive fee:* $30,875 includes full-time tuition ($21,975), mandatory fees ($1360), and room and board ($7540). Part-time tuition: $920 per credit. Part-time tuition and fees vary according to course load. *Required fees:* $80 per credit part-time. *College room only:* $4600. Room and board charges vary according to board plan and housing facility. *Payment plan:* installment. *Waivers:* employees or children of employees.

Financial Aid Of all full-time matriculated undergraduates who enrolled in 2003, 512 applied for aid, 478 were judged to have need, 74 had their need fully met. In 2003, 35 non-need-based awards were made. *Average percent of need met:* 63%. *Average financial aid package:* $13,424. *Average need-based loan:* $4052. *Average need-based gift aid:* $4902. *Average non-need-based aid:* $9844. *Average indebtedness upon graduation:* $22,775.

Applying *Options:* electronic application, deferred entrance. *Application fee:* $30. *Required:* essay or personal statement, high school transcript, minimum 2.0 GPA, 2 letters of recommendation, portfolio. *Recommended:* interview. *Application deadline:* rolling (freshmen), rolling (transfers). *Notification:* continuous (freshmen), continuous (transfers).

Admissions Contact Office of Admissions, The Cleveland Institute of Art, 11141 East Boulevard, Cleveland, OH 44106. *Phone:* 216-421-7418. *Toll-free phone:* 800-223-4700. *Fax:* 216-754-3634. *E-mail:* admiss@gate.cia.edu.

■ *See page 1418 for a narrative description.*

CLEVELAND INSTITUTE OF MUSIC
Cleveland, Ohio

- **Independent** comprehensive, founded 1920
- **Calendar** semesters
- **Degrees** bachelor's, master's, doctoral, and postbachelor's certificates
- **Urban** 488-acre campus
- **Endowment** $21.6 million
- **Coed,** 245 undergraduate students, 100% full-time, 59% women, 41% men
- **Very difficult** entrance level, 40% of applicants were admitted

Ranked as one of the foremost schools of music in the US, CIM's curriculum is based upon solid, traditional musical values, while incorporating liberal arts instruction and new technologies that equip students to meet the challenges of the 21st century. Graduates are routinely admitted to leading graduate schools, are winners of major competitions, and occupy important performance and teaching positions throughout the world.

Undergraduates 245 full-time. Students come from 38 states and territories, 15 other countries, 82% are from out of state, 0.4% African American, 9% Asian American or Pacific Islander, 4% Hispanic American, 0.4% Native American, 12% international, 5% transferred in, 40% live on campus. *Retention:* 96% of 2002 full-time freshmen returned.

Freshmen *Admission:* 349 applied, 141 admitted, 67 enrolled.

Faculty *Total:* 96, 33% full-time, 4% with terminal degrees. *Student/faculty ratio:* 7:1.

Majors Audio engineering; music; music teacher education; piano and organ; violin, viola, guitar and other stringed instruments; voice and opera; wind/percussion instruments.

Academic Programs *Special study options:* academic remediation for entering students, accelerated degree program, advanced placement credit, English as a second language, internships, off-campus study, summer session for credit. *ROTC:* Army (c), Air Force (c).

Library Cleveland Institute of Music Library with 48,128 titles, 115 serial subscriptions, 19,633 audiovisual materials, an OPAC, a Web page.

Computers on Campus 25 computers available on campus for general student use. A campuswide network can be accessed from student residence rooms and from off campus. Internet access, at least one staffed computer lab available. Computer purchase or lease plan available.

Student Life *Housing:* on-campus residence required through sophomore year. *Options:* coed. Campus housing is leased by the school. Freshman campus housing is guaranteed. *Activities and organizations:* choral group. *Campus security:* 24-hour emergency response devices and patrols, late-night transport/escort service, controlled dormitory access. *Student services:* health clinic, personal/psychological counseling.

Standardized Tests *Required:* SAT I or ACT (for placement).

Costs (2003–04) *Comprehensive fee:* $30,028 includes full-time tuition ($21,866), mandatory fees ($902), and room and board ($7260). Part-time tuition: $1004 per credit hour. *Required fees:* $610 per term part-time. *College room only:* $4370. Room and board charges vary according to board plan. *Payment plan:* installment. *Waivers:* employees or children of employees.

Financial Aid Of all full-time matriculated undergraduates who enrolled in 2002, 191 applied for aid, 134 were judged to have need, 30 had their need fully met. 83 Federal Work-Study jobs (averaging $1228). 43 state and other part-time jobs (averaging $869). In 2002, 83 non-need-based awards were made. *Average percent of need met:* 80%. *Average financial aid package:* $15,299. *Average need-based loan:* $5504. *Average need-based gift aid:* $10,061. *Average non-need-based aid:* $9720. *Average indebtedness upon graduation:* $9000. *Financial aid deadline:* 2/15.

Applying *Options:* early admission, deferred entrance. *Application fee:* $100. *Required:* essay or personal statement, high school transcript, 2 letters of recommendation, audition. *Recommended:* interview. *Application deadlines:* 12/1 (freshmen), 12/1 (transfers). *Notification:* 4/1 (freshmen), 4/1 (transfers).

Admissions Contact Mr. William Fay, Director of Admission, Cleveland Institute of Music, 11021 East Boulevard, Cleveland, OH 44106-1776. *Phone:* 216-795-3107. *Fax:* 216-791-1530. *E-mail:* cimadmission@po.cwru.edu.

■ *See page 1420 for a narrative description.*

CLEVELAND STATE UNIVERSITY
Cleveland, Ohio

- **State-supported** university, founded 1964
- **Calendar** semesters
- **Degrees** certificates, bachelor's, master's, doctoral, first professional, post-master's, postbachelor's, and first professional certificates
- **Urban** 70-acre campus with easy access to Akron
- **Endowment** $17.5 million
- **Coed,** 10,054 undergraduate students, 69% full-time, 54% women, 46% men
- **Noncompetitive** entrance level, 78% of applicants were admitted

Undergraduates 6,931 full-time, 3,123 part-time. Students come from 21 states and territories, 63 other countries, 1% are from out of state, 21% African American, 3% Asian American or Pacific Islander, 3% Hispanic American, 0.2% Native American, 2% international, 13% transferred in, 4% live on campus. *Retention:* 59% of 2002 full-time freshmen returned.

Freshmen *Admission:* 2,813 applied, 2,205 admitted, 987 enrolled. *Average high school GPA:* 2.73. *Test scores:* SAT verbal scores over 500: 39%; SAT math scores over 500: 39%; ACT scores over 18: 60%; SAT verbal scores over 600: 9%; SAT math scores over 600: 11%; ACT scores over 24: 13%; SAT verbal scores over 700: 1%; SAT math scores over 700: 2%.

Faculty *Total:* 920, 59% full-time, 58% with terminal degrees. *Student/faculty ratio:* 16:1.

Cleveland State University (continued)

Majors Accounting; anthropology; applied art; art; audiology and hearing sciences; bioethics/medical ethics; biology/biological sciences; biology/biotechnology laboratory technician; business administration and management; business administration, management and operations related; business/managerial economics; business statistics; chemical engineering; chemistry; civil engineering; communication/speech communication and rhetoric; community health services counseling; community organization and advocacy; computer and information sciences; computer engineering; computer science; dance; dramatic/theatre arts; early childhood education; economics; education; educational leadership and administration; education related; electrical, electronic and communications engineering technology; electrical, electronics and communications engineering; elementary education; engineering; engineering mechanics; engineering related; engineering science; engineering technology; English; environmental studies; finance; French; general studies; geology/earth science; Germanic languages; gerontology; health professions related; industrial engineering; industrial technology; information science/studies; interdisciplinary studies; international relations and affairs; kinesiology and exercise science; labor and industrial relations; liberal arts and sciences/liberal studies; linguistics; marketing/marketing management; mathematics; mechanical engineering; mechanical engineering technologies related; metallurgical engineering; middle school education; multi-/interdisciplinary studies related; music; nursing (registered nurse training); occupational therapy; philosophy; physical education teaching and coaching; physical therapy; physics; political science and government; pre-nursing studies; psychology; public administration; public relations/image management; religious studies; science, technology and society; social sciences; social sciences related; social work; sociology; Spanish; special education; sport and fitness administration; urban studies/affairs.

Academic Programs *Special study options:* academic remediation for entering students, accelerated degree program, adult/continuing education programs, advanced placement credit, cooperative education, English as a second language, freshman honors college, honors programs, independent study, internships, off-campus study, part-time degree program, student-designed majors, study abroad, summer session for credit. *ROTC:* Army (c), Air Force (c).

Library University Library plus 1 other with 484,914 titles, 6,186 serial subscriptions, 101,376 audiovisual materials, an OPAC, a Web page.

Computers on Campus 600 computers available on campus for general student use. A campuswide network can be accessed. Internet access, online (class) registration, at least one staffed computer lab available. Computer purchase or lease plan available.

Student Life *Housing options:* coed. Campus housing is university owned. Freshman campus housing is guaranteed. *Activities and organizations:* drama/theater group, student-run newspaper, radio station, choral group, honor societies, sororities, fraternities, International Student Association, Chinese Student Association, national fraternities, national sororities. *Campus security:* 24-hour emergency response devices and patrols, student patrols, late-night transport/escort service, controlled dormitory access. *Student services:* health clinic, personal/psychological counseling, women's center.

Athletics Member NCAA. All Division I. *Intercollegiate sports:* baseball M(s), basketball M(s)/W(s), cross-country running W(s), fencing M(s)/W(s), golf M(s), soccer M(s), softball W(s), swimming M(s)/W(s), tennis W(s), track and field W(s), volleyball W(s), wrestling M(s). *Intramural sports:* badminton M/W, basketball M/W, bowling M/W, cross-country running M/W, fencing M/W, field hockey M/W, football M, golf M/W, racquetball M/W, sailing M/W, soccer M/W, swimming M/W, tennis M/W, track and field M/W, volleyball M/W, water polo M/W, weight lifting M(c)/W(c), wrestling M.

Standardized Tests *Required:* SAT I or ACT (for admission).

Costs (2003–04) *Tuition:* state resident $6072 full-time, $253 per semester hour part-time; nonresident $11,940 full-time, $498 per semester hour part-time. Full-time tuition and fees vary according to program and student level. Part-time tuition and fees vary according to program and student level. *Room and board:* $7805; room only: $5316. Room and board charges vary according to board plan and housing facility. *Payment plan:* installment. *Waivers:* senior citizens and employees or children of employees.

Financial Aid Of all full-time matriculated undergraduates who enrolled in 2003, 5,058 applied for aid, 4,660 were judged to have need, 385 had their need fully met. In 2003, 599 non-need-based awards were made. *Average percent of need met:* 54%. *Average financial aid package:* $6893. *Average need-based loan:* $3954. *Average need-based gift aid:* $4663. *Average non-need-based aid:* $7054.

Applying *Options:* common application, deferred entrance. *Application fee:* $30. *Required:* high school transcript. *Application deadlines:* rolling (freshmen), 7/15 (transfers). *Notification:* continuous (freshmen), continuous (transfers).

Admissions Contact Ms. Bonnie Jones, Office of Admissions, Cleveland State University, Rhodes Tower West, Room 204, 1983 East 24th Street, Cleveland, OH 44115. *Phone:* 216-523-5139. *Toll-free phone:* 888-CSU-OHIO. *Fax:* 216-687-9210. *E-mail:* admissions@csuohio.edu.

College of Mount St. Joseph

Cincinnati, Ohio

- **Independent Roman Catholic** comprehensive, founded 1920
- **Calendar** semesters
- **Degrees** certificates, associate, bachelor's, master's, and postbachelor's certificates
- **Suburban** 88-acre campus
- **Endowment** $16.6 million
- **Coed,** 1,876 undergraduate students, 68% full-time, 69% women, 31% men
- **Moderately difficult** entrance level, 76% of applicants were admitted

Undergraduates 1,282 full-time, 594 part-time. Students come from 17 states and territories, 11% are from out of state, 9% African American, 0.7% Asian American or Pacific Islander, 0.5% Hispanic American, 0.3% Native American, 0.1% international, 9% transferred in, 21% live on campus. *Retention:* 74% of 2002 full-time freshmen returned.

Freshmen *Admission:* 863 applied, 655 admitted, 309 enrolled. *Average high school GPA:* 3.19. *Test scores:* SAT verbal scores over 500: 52%; SAT math scores over 500: 56%; ACT scores over 18: 79%; SAT verbal scores over 600: 13%; SAT math scores over 600: 14%; ACT scores over 24: 24%; SAT verbal scores over 700: 1%; SAT math scores over 700: 2%; ACT scores over 30: 1%.

Faculty *Total:* 193, 60% full-time, 49% with terminal degrees. *Student/faculty ratio:* 12:1.

Majors Accounting; applied mathematics; art teacher education; athletic training; biochemistry; biology/biological sciences; business administration and management; business, management, and marketing related; chemistry; chemistry related; clinical laboratory science/medical technology; communication/speech communication and rhetoric; computer and information sciences and support services related; computer science; criminology; English; fine/studio arts; gerontology; graphic design; history; interior design; kindergarten/preschool education; legal assistant/paralegal; liberal arts and sciences/liberal studies; management information systems and services related; mathematics; mathematics and statistics related; middle school education; music; natural sciences; nursing (registered nurse training); pastoral counseling and specialized ministries related; physical education teaching and coaching; physical therapy; psychology; public administration and social service professions related; religious education; religious studies; social work; sociology; special education; theology and religious vocations related; therapeutic recreation.

Academic Programs *Special study options:* academic remediation for entering students, accelerated degree program, adult/continuing education programs, advanced placement credit, cooperative education, distance learning, double majors, English as a second language, external degree program, freshman honors college, honors programs, independent study, internships, off-campus study, part-time degree program, services for LD students, study abroad, summer session for credit. *ROTC:* Army (c), Air Force (c).

Library Archbishop Alter Library with 98,849 titles, 429 serial subscriptions, 3,109 audiovisual materials, an OPAC, a Web page.

Computers on Campus 251 computers available on campus for general student use. A campuswide network can be accessed from student residence rooms and from off campus that provide access to computer-aided instruction. Internet access, online (class) registration, at least one staffed computer lab available. Computer purchase or lease plan available.

Student Life *Housing options:* coed. Campus housing is university owned. Freshman applicants given priority for college housing. *Activities and organizations:* drama/theater group, student-run newspaper, choral group, marching band, Student Government Association, Black Student Union, peer educators, Campus Activities Board, Campus Ambassadors. *Campus security:* 24-hour emergency response devices and patrols, late-night transport/escort service. *Student services:* health clinic, personal/psychological counseling, women's center.

Athletics Member NCAA. All Division III. *Intercollegiate sports:* baseball M, basketball M/W, cross-country running M/W, football M, golf M/W, soccer W, softball W, tennis M/W, track and field M/W, volleyball W, wrestling M. *Intramural sports:* basketball M/W, racquetball M/W, soccer M(c), softball M/W, table tennis M/W, tennis M/W, volleyball M/W.

Standardized Tests *Required:* SAT I or ACT (for admission).

Costs (2004–05) *Comprehensive fee:* $24,285 includes full-time tuition ($17,200), mandatory fees ($1240), and room and board ($5845). Full-time tuition and fees vary according to course load, program, reciprocity agreements, and student level. Part-time tuition: $420 per semester hour. Part-time tuition and fees vary according to course load, location, and reciprocity agreements. *Required fees:* $65 per term part-time. *College room only:* $2875. Room and board charges vary according to board plan and housing facility. *Payment plan:* installment. *Waivers:* senior citizens and employees or children of employees.

Financial Aid Of all full-time matriculated undergraduates who enrolled in 2002, 1,250 applied for aid, 962 were judged to have need, 333 had their need fully met. 121 Federal Work-Study jobs (averaging $1344). 95 state and other part-time jobs (averaging $1067). In 2002, 176 non-need-based awards were made. *Average percent of need met:* 90%. *Average financial aid package:* $13,332. *Average need-based loan:* $4156. *Average need-based gift aid:* $8000. *Average non-need-based aid:* $3800. *Average indebtedness upon graduation:* $13,400.

Applying *Options:* common application, electronic application. *Application fee:* $25. *Required:* high school transcript, minimum 2.25 GPA, minimum SAT score of 960 or ACT score of 19. *Required for some:* essay or personal statement, 1 letter of recommendation, interview. *Application deadlines:* 8/15 (freshmen), 8/15 (transfers). *Notification:* continuous (freshmen), continuous (transfers).

Admissions Contact Ms. Peggy Minnich, Director of Admission, College of Mount St. Joseph, 5701 Delhi Road, Cincinnati, OH 45233-1672. *Phone:* 513-244-4814. *Toll-free phone:* 800-654-9314. *Fax:* 513-244-4629. *E-mail:* peggy_minnich@mail.msj.edu.

■ See page 1438 for a narrative description.

THE COLLEGE OF WOOSTER

Wooster, Ohio

- **Independent** 4-year, founded 1866, affiliated with Presbyterian Church (U.S.A.)
- **Calendar** semesters
- **Degree** bachelor's
- **Small-town** 240-acre campus with easy access to Cleveland
- **Endowment** $184.3 million
- **Coed,** 1,871 undergraduate students, 98% full-time, 53% women, 47% men
- **Moderately difficult** entrance level, 70% of applicants were admitted

Wooster encourages students to be active participants in their education. First-year seminars; small classes; internships; a required Independent Study (IS) program, which enables each student to work with a faculty mentor on a student-designed research project and which is supported by an IS library with computer-ready study carrels for each senior; and the Copeland Fund, which allows students to travel or purchase relevant research materials, are central to the curriculum. Wooster also encourages students to be active in areas such as music, theater, student government, athletics, and community service organizations.

Undergraduates 1,838 full-time, 33 part-time. Students come from 39 states and territories, 21 other countries, 42% are from out of state, 5% African American, 2% Asian American or Pacific Islander, 1% Hispanic American, 0.3% Native American, 7% international, 0.5% transferred in, 97% live on campus. *Retention:* 87% of 2002 full-time freshmen returned.

Freshmen *Admission:* 2,560 applied, 1,780 admitted, 552 enrolled. *Average high school GPA:* 3.58. *Test scores:* SAT verbal scores over 500: 90%; SAT math scores over 500: 91%; ACT scores over 18: 100%; SAT verbal scores over 600: 53%; SAT math scores over 600: 53%; ACT scores over 24: 73%; SAT verbal scores over 700: 15%; SAT math scores over 700: 9%; ACT scores over 30: 16%.

Faculty *Total:* 179, 75% full-time, 91% with terminal degrees. *Student/faculty ratio:* 12:1.

Majors African-American/Black studies; archeology; area, ethnic, cultural, and gender studies related; art history, criticism and conservation; biochemistry; biology/biological sciences; business/managerial economics; chemistry; classics and languages, literatures and linguistics; communication/speech communication and rhetoric; comparative literature; computer science; dramatic/theatre arts; economics; English; fine/studio arts; French; geology/earth science; German; German studies; history; interdisciplinary studies; international relations and affairs; Latin; mass communication/media; mathematics; molecular biology; multi-/interdisciplinary studies related; music; music history, literature, and theory; music performance; music teacher education; music theory and composition; music therapy; philosophy; physics; physics related; political science and government; psychology; religious studies; Russian studies; sociology; Spanish; urban studies/affairs; women's studies.

Academic Programs *Special study options:* advanced placement credit, double majors, independent study, internships, off-campus study, services for LD students, student-designed majors, study abroad, summer session for credit. *Unusual degree programs:* 3-2 engineering with Case Western Reserve University, Washington University in St. Louis, University of Michigan; forestry with Duke University; nursing with Case Western Reserve University; social work with Case Western Reserve University; dentistry with Case Western Reserve University, architecture with Washington University in St. Louis.

Library The College of Wooster Libraries plus 3 others with 581,518 titles, 12,416 audiovisual materials, an OPAC, a Web page.

Computers on Campus 275 computers available on campus for general student use. A campuswide network can be accessed from student residence rooms and from off campus. Internet access, at least one staffed computer lab available. Computer purchase or lease plan available.

Student Life *Housing:* on-campus residence required through senior year. *Options:* coed, men-only, women-only. Campus housing is university owned. Freshman campus housing is guaranteed. *Activities and organizations:* drama/theater group, student-run newspaper, radio station, choral group, marching band, Volunteer Network, Christian Fellowship, National Student Speech, Hearing, and Language Association, Gay, Lesbian, Bisexual, Transgendered and Allies, Let's Dance. *Campus security:* 24-hour emergency response devices and patrols, student patrols, late-night transport/escort service, controlled dormitory access. *Student services:* health clinic, personal/psychological counseling, women's center.

Athletics Member NCAA. All Division III. *Intercollegiate sports:* badminton M(c)/W(c), baseball M, basketball M/W, cheerleading W(c), cross-country running M/W, field hockey W, football M, golf M, lacrosse M/W, rugby M(c)/W(c), soccer M/W, softball W, swimming M/W, tennis M/W, track and field M/W, volleyball M(c)/W. *Intramural sports:* badminton M/W, basketball M/W, bowling M/W, football M, golf M/W, soccer M/W, table tennis M/W, tennis M/W, track and field M/W, ultimate Frisbee M/W, volleyball M/W.

Standardized Tests *Required:* SAT I or ACT (for admission).

Costs (2003–04) *Comprehensive fee:* $31,300 includes full-time tuition ($25,040) and room and board ($6260). Full-time tuition and fees vary according to course load and reciprocity agreements. Part-time tuition and fees vary according to course load. *College room only:* $2850. *Payment plan:* installment. *Waivers:* employees or children of employees.

Financial Aid Of all full-time matriculated undergraduates who enrolled in 2003, 1,296 applied for aid, 1,157 were judged to have need, 808 had their need fully met. 690 Federal Work-Study jobs (averaging $1342). 118 state and other part-time jobs (averaging $1931). In 2003, 621 non-need-based awards were made. *Average percent of need met:* 95%. *Average financial aid package:* $21,812. *Average need-based loan:* $4664. *Average need-based gift aid:* $15,970. *Average non-need-based aid:* $10,643. *Average indebtedness upon graduation:* $19,494.

Applying *Options:* common application, electronic application, early admission, early decision, deferred entrance. *Application fee:* $40. *Required:* essay or personal statement, high school transcript, 2 letters of recommendation. *Recommended:* interview. *Application deadlines:* 2/15 (freshmen), 6/1 (transfers). *Early decision:* 12/1 (for plan 1), 1/15 (for plan 2). *Notification:* 4/1 (freshmen), 12/15 (early decision plan 1), 2/1 (early decision plan 2), continuous (transfers).

Admissions Contact Mr. Paul Deutsch, Dean of Admissions, The College of Wooster, 847 College Avenue, Wooster, OH 44691. *Phone:* 330-263-2270 Ext. 2118. *Toll-free phone:* 800-877-9905. *Fax:* 330-263-2621. *E-mail:* admissions@wooster.edu.

■ See page 1462 for a narrative description.

COLUMBUS COLLEGE OF ART & DESIGN

Columbus, Ohio

- **Independent** 4-year, founded 1879
- **Calendar** semesters
- **Degree** bachelor's
- **Urban** 10-acre campus
- **Endowment** $4.8 million
- **Coed,** 1,634 undergraduate students, 79% full-time, 51% women, 49% men
- **Moderately difficult** entrance level, 64% of applicants were admitted

CCAD, a private, 4-year BFA-degree-granting institution, prepares tomorrow's creative leaders for professional careers. CCAD advances a distinct, challenging, and inclusive learning culture in art, design, and the humanities.

Undergraduates 1,291 full-time, 343 part-time. Students come from 41 states and territories, 31 other countries, 22% are from out of state, 8% African American, 3% Asian American or Pacific Islander, 2% Hispanic American, 0.4% Native American, 7% international, 4% transferred in, 18% live on campus. *Retention:* 87% of 2002 full-time freshmen returned.

Freshmen *Admission:* 799 applied, 512 admitted, 186 enrolled. *Average high school GPA:* 2.90. *Test scores:* SAT verbal scores over 500: 59%; SAT math scores over 500: 53%; ACT scores over 18: 78%; SAT verbal scores over 600: 23%; SAT math scores over 600: 12%; ACT scores over 24: 22%; SAT verbal scores over 700: 3%; ACT scores over 30: 4%.

Faculty *Total:* 187, 43% full-time, 40% with terminal degrees. *Student/faculty ratio:* 12:1.

Majors Fashion/apparel design; fine/studio arts; graphic design; illustration; industrial design; interior design; photography.

Academic Programs *Special study options:* academic remediation for entering students, advanced placement credit, double majors, English as a second language, independent study, internships, off-campus study, part-time degree program, services for LD students, summer session for credit.

Library Packard Library with 45,257 titles, 275 serial subscriptions, 126,726 audiovisual materials, an OPAC, a Web page.

Columbus College of Art & Design (continued)

Computers on Campus 150 computers available on campus for general student use. A campuswide network can be accessed. Internet access, at least one staffed computer lab available.

Student Life *Housing:* on-campus residence required for freshman year. *Options:* coed. Campus housing is university owned. Freshman applicants given priority for college housing. *Activities and organizations:* Student Government Interest Group, International Student Group, Student Art Critique, Anime Club, Environmental Awareness Society. *Campus security:* 24-hour emergency response devices and patrols, late-night transport/escort service, controlled dormitory access. *Student services:* personal/psychological counseling, legal services.

Athletics *Intramural sports:* basketball M/W, soccer M/W, volleyball M/W.

Standardized Tests *Required:* SAT I or ACT (for admission).

Costs (2003–04) *Comprehensive fee:* $24,720 includes full-time tuition ($17,880), mandatory fees ($540), and room and board ($6300). Part-time tuition: $745 per credit. Part-time tuition and fees vary according to course load. *Required fees:* $180 per term part-time. *Room and board:* Room and board charges vary according to housing facility and student level. *Payment plans:* installment, deferred payment. *Waivers:* employees or children of employees.

Financial Aid Of all full-time matriculated undergraduates who enrolled in 2003, 1,210 applied for aid, 1,056 were judged to have need, 195 had their need fully met. 130 Federal Work-Study jobs (averaging $3250). 240 state and other part-time jobs (averaging $3000). In 2003, 245 non-need-based awards were made. *Average percent of need met:* 64%. *Average financial aid package:* $12,897. *Average need-based loan:* $5117. *Average need-based gift aid:* $8613. *Average non-need-based aid:* $10,034. *Average indebtedness upon graduation:* $9601.

Applying *Options:* deferred entrance. *Application fee:* $25. *Required:* essay or personal statement, high school transcript, minimum 2.0 GPA, portfolio. *Required for some:* letters of recommendation. *Recommended:* interview. *Application deadline:* rolling (freshmen), rolling (transfers). *Notification:* continuous (freshmen), continuous (transfers).

Admissions Contact Mr. Thomas E. Green, Director of Admissions, Columbus College of Art & Design, 107 North Ninth Street, Columbus, OH 43215-1758. *Phone:* 614-224-9101. *Toll-free phone:* 877-997-2223. *Fax:* 614-232-8344. *E-mail:* admissions@ccad.edu.

■ *See page 1482 for a narrative description.*

DAVID N. MYERS UNIVERSITY
Cleveland, Ohio

Admissions Contact Ms. Tiffiney Payton, Interim Director of Admissions, David N. Myers University, 112 Prospect Avenue, Cleveland, OH 44115. *Phone:* 216-523-3806 Ext. 805. *Toll-free phone:* 800-424-3953. *Fax:* 216-696-6430. *E-mail:* tpayton@dnmyers.edu.

DEFIANCE COLLEGE
Defiance, Ohio

- **Independent** comprehensive, founded 1850, affiliated with United Church of Christ
- **Calendar** semesters
- **Degrees** associate, bachelor's, and master's
- **Small-town** 150-acre campus with easy access to Toledo
- **Endowment** $11.6 million
- **Coed,** 938 undergraduate students, 76% full-time, 57% women, 43% men
- **Moderately difficult** entrance level, 75% of applicants were admitted

Undergraduates 717 full-time, 221 part-time. Students come from 11 states and territories, 4 other countries, 15% are from out of state, 3% African American, 0.4% Asian American or Pacific Islander, 3% Hispanic American, 0.3% Native American, 0.4% international, 7% transferred in, 50% live on campus. *Retention:* 69% of 2002 full-time freshmen returned.

Freshmen *Admission:* 796 applied, 597 admitted, 216 enrolled. *Average high school GPA:* 3.03. *Test scores:* SAT verbal scores over 500: 53%; SAT math scores over 500: 47%; ACT scores over 18: 83%; SAT verbal scores over 600: 18%; SAT math scores over 600: 15%; ACT scores over 24: 23%; SAT math scores over 700: 5%; ACT scores over 30: 2%.

Faculty *Total:* 93, 48% full-time, 27% with terminal degrees. *Student/faculty ratio:* 14:1.

Majors Accounting; art; art teacher education; athletic training; biology/biological sciences; business administration and management; business teacher education; chemistry; clinical laboratory science/medical technology; computer science; criminal justice/law enforcement administration; criminal justice/police science; ecology; education; elementary education; English; environmental studies; finance; health teacher education; history; kinesiology and exercise science; liberal arts and sciences/liberal studies; literature; marketing/marketing management; mass communication/media; mathematics; natural sciences; physical education teaching and coaching; physical sciences; pre-dentistry studies; pre-law studies; pre-medical studies; pre-veterinary studies; psychology; public relations/image management; religious education; religious studies; science teacher education; secondary education; social sciences; social work; special education; speech and rhetoric; sport and fitness administration.

Academic Programs *Special study options:* academic remediation for entering students, adult/continuing education programs, advanced placement credit, cooperative education, distance learning, double majors, external degree program, honors programs, independent study, internships, off-campus study, part-time degree program, student-designed majors, study abroad, summer session for credit.

Library Pilgrim Library with 88,000 titles, 424 serial subscriptions, 25,000 audiovisual materials, an OPAC.

Computers on Campus 125 computers available on campus for general student use. A campuswide network can be accessed from student residence rooms and from off campus. Internet access, at least one staffed computer lab available.

Student Life *Housing:* on-campus residence required through junior year. *Options:* coed, men-only, women-only. Campus housing is university owned. Freshman campus housing is guaranteed. *Activities and organizations:* drama/theater group, student-run newspaper, choral group, Campus Activities Board, Criminal Justice Society, Greek life, Student Senate, Fellowship of Christian Athletes, national fraternities, national sororities. *Campus security:* late-night transport/escort service, controlled dormitory access. *Student services:* health clinic, personal/psychological counseling.

Athletics Member NCAA. All Division III. *Intercollegiate sports:* baseball M, basketball M/W, cross-country running M/W, football M, golf M/W, soccer M/W, softball W, tennis M/W, track and field M/W, volleyball W. *Intramural sports:* baseball M, basketball M/W, bowling M/W, field hockey M/W, football M/W, racquetball M/W, soccer M/W, softball M/W, table tennis M/W, volleyball M/W, weight lifting M.

Standardized Tests *Required:* SAT I or ACT (for admission).

Costs (2003–04) *Comprehensive fee:* $22,615 includes full-time tuition ($16,950), mandatory fees ($415), and room and board ($5250). Part-time tuition: $300 per credit hour. *College room only:* $2650. Room and board charges vary according to board plan and housing facility. *Payment plan:* installment. *Waivers:* senior citizens and employees or children of employees.

Financial Aid Of all full-time matriculated undergraduates who enrolled in 2002, 680 applied for aid. 149 Federal Work-Study jobs (averaging $601). 151 state and other part-time jobs (averaging $689). In 2002, 50 non-need-based awards were made. *Average percent of need met:* 85%. *Average financial aid package:* $13,294. *Average non-need-based aid:* $8802. *Average indebtedness upon graduation:* $14,726.

Applying *Options:* common application, electronic application, early admission, deferred entrance. *Application fee:* $25. *Required:* high school transcript, minimum 2.25 GPA. *Required for some:* essay or personal statement, interview. *Recommended:* letters of recommendation, interview. *Application deadlines:* 8/15 (freshmen), 8/15 (transfers). *Notification:* continuous (freshmen), continuous (transfers).

Admissions Contact Mr. Mark Thompson, Dean of Admissions, Defiance College, 701 North Clinton Street, Defiance, OH 43512-1610. *Phone:* 419-783-2361. *Toll-free phone:* 800-520-4632 Ext. 2359. *Fax:* 419-783-2468. *E-mail:* admissions@defiance.edu.

■ *See page 1522 for a narrative description.*

DENISON UNIVERSITY
Granville, Ohio

- **Independent** 4-year, founded 1831
- **Calendar** semesters plus optional May term
- **Degree** bachelor's
- **Small-town** 1200-acre campus with easy access to Columbus
- **Endowment** $422.2 million
- **Coed,** 2,232 undergraduate students, 95% full-time, 56% women, 44% men
- **Moderately difficult** entrance level, 68% of applicants were admitted

Denison University attracts intellectually serious, well-rounded students from throughout the U.S. and 34 other countries. Its Environmental Studies Center, model Honors Program, exceptional collaborative research opportunities with faculty members, state-of-the-art science facilities, and leadership training through more than 150 campus organizations provide its students with a challenging and enriching college experience.

Undergraduates 2,121 full-time, 111 part-time. Students come from 48 states and territories, 31 other countries, 55% are from out of state, 5% African

American, 2% Asian American or Pacific Islander, 3% Hispanic American, 0.1% Native American, 4% international, 0.9% transferred in, 98% live on campus. *Retention:* 89% of 2002 full-time freshmen returned.

Freshmen *Admission:* 3,141 applied, 2,125 admitted, 629 enrolled. *Average high school GPA:* 3.60. *Test scores:* SAT verbal scores over 500: 97%; SAT math scores over 500: 96%; ACT scores over 18: 100%; SAT verbal scores over 600: 57%; SAT math scores over 600: 59%; ACT scores over 24: 81%; SAT verbal scores over 700: 12%; SAT math scores over 700: 11%; ACT scores over 30: 22%.

Faculty *Total:* 191, 94% full-time, 92% with terminal degrees. *Student/faculty ratio:* 11:1.

Majors African-American/Black studies; anthropology; area studies; art; art history, criticism and conservation; Asian studies (East); biochemistry; biology/biological sciences; chemistry; classics and languages, literatures and linguistics; computer science; creative writing; dance; dramatic/theatre arts; economics; English; environmental studies; film/cinema studies; fine/studio arts; French; geology/earth science; German; history; international relations and affairs; Latin American studies; mass communication/media; mathematics; music; organizational behavior; philosophy; physical education teaching and coaching; physics; political science and government; psychology; religious studies; sociology; Spanish; speech and rhetoric; women's studies.

Academic Programs *Special study options:* advanced placement credit, cooperative education, double majors, honors programs, independent study, internships, off-campus study, part-time degree program, services for LD students, student-designed majors, study abroad. *ROTC:* Army (c). *Unusual degree programs:* 3-2 engineering with Case Western Reserve University, Columbia University, Rensselaer Polytechnic Institute, Washington University in St. Louis; forestry with Duke University; natural resources with University of Michigan; occupational therapy with Washington University in St. Louis; environmental management, dentistry with Case Western Reserve University; medical technology with Rochester General Hospital.

Library William Howard Doane Library with 728,949 titles, 4,445 serial subscriptions, 25,452 audiovisual materials, an OPAC, a Web page.

Computers on Campus 460 computers available on campus for general student use. A campuswide network can be accessed from student residence rooms and from off campus. Internet access, at least one staffed computer lab available. Computer purchase or lease plan available.

Student Life *Housing:* on-campus residence required through senior year. *Options:* coed, men-only, women-only. Campus housing is university owned. Freshman campus housing is guaranteed. *Activities and organizations:* drama/theater group, student-run newspaper, radio and television station, choral group, Community Association, Black Student Union, International Student Association, Student Activities Committee, national fraternities, national sororities. *Campus security:* 24-hour emergency response devices and patrols, student patrols, late-night transport/escort service, controlled dormitory access, security lighting, escort service. *Student services:* health clinic, personal/psychological counseling, women's center.

Athletics Member NCAA. All Division III. *Intercollegiate sports:* baseball M, basketball M/W, crew M(c), cross-country running M/W, equestrian sports M(c)/W(c), field hockey W, football M, golf M, ice hockey M(c), lacrosse M/W, riflery M(c)/W(c), rugby M(c)/W(c), sailing M(c)/W(c), skiing (downhill) M(c)/W(c), soccer M/W, softball W, squash M(c)/W(c), swimming M/W, tennis M/W, track and field M/W, volleyball W. *Intramural sports:* badminton M(c)/W(c), basketball M/W, cheerleading M/W, crew W(c), fencing M(c)/W(c), football M/W, golf M/W, lacrosse M(c), racquetball M/W, soccer M/W, softball M/W, squash M/W, table tennis M/W, tennis M/W, ultimate Frisbee M/W, volleyball M(c)/W, water polo M/W, weight lifting M/W.

Standardized Tests *Required:* SAT I or ACT (for admission). *Recommended:* SAT II: Subject Tests (for admission).

Costs (2003–04) *Comprehensive fee:* $33,050 includes full-time tuition ($25,090), mandatory fees ($670), and room and board ($7290). Part-time tuition and fees vary according to course load. *College room only:* $3980. Room and board charges vary according to housing facility. *Payment plans:* tuition prepayment, installment. *Waivers:* employees or children of employees.

Financial Aid Of all full-time matriculated undergraduates who enrolled in 2002, 1,219 applied for aid, 1,041 were judged to have need, 619 had their need fully met. 569 Federal Work-Study jobs (averaging $1794). 858 state and other part-time jobs (averaging $1954). In 2002, 1078 non-need-based awards were made. *Average percent of need met:* 98%. *Average financial aid package:* $22,756. *Average need-based loan:* $4495. *Average need-based gift aid:* $16,876. *Average non-need-based aid:* $10,732. *Average indebtedness upon graduation:* $15,009.

Applying *Options:* common application, early admission, early decision, deferred entrance. *Application fee:* $40. *Required:* essay or personal statement, high school transcript, 2 letters of recommendation. *Recommended:* interview. *Application deadlines:* 2/1 (freshmen), 7/1 (transfers). *Early decision:* 11/15 (for plan 1), 1/15 (for plan 2). *Notification:* 4/1 (freshmen), 12/1 (early decision plan 1), 2/1 (early decision plan 2), continuous (transfers).

Admissions Contact Mr. Perry Robinson, Director of Admissions, Denison University, Box H, Granville, OH 43023. *Phone:* 740-587-6276. *Toll-free phone:* 800-DENISON. *E-mail:* admissions@denison.edu.

■ *See page 1526 for a narrative description.*

DeVRY UNIVERSITY
Cleveland, Ohio

Admissions Contact 200 Public Square, Suite 150, Cleveland, OH 44114-2301.

DeVRY UNIVERSITY
Seven Hills, Ohio

Admissions Contact The Genesis Building, 6000 Lombardo Center, Seven Hills, OH 44131-6907. *Toll-free phone:* 866-453-3879.

DeVRY UNIVERSITY
Columbus, Ohio

- **Proprietary** comprehensive, founded 1952, part of DeVry University
- **Calendar** semesters
- **Degrees** diplomas, associate, bachelor's, master's, and postbachelor's certificates
- **Urban** 21-acre campus
- **Coed**
- **Minimally difficult** entrance level

Student Life *Campus security:* late-night transport/escort service, security at evening activities.

Standardized Tests *Recommended:* SAT I, ACT or CPT.

Costs (2003–04) *Tuition:* $9990 full-time, $355 per credit hour part-time. Full-time tuition and fees vary according to course load. Part-time tuition and fees vary according to course load. *Required fees:* $165 full-time. *Payment plans:* installment, deferred payment.

Financial Aid Of all full-time matriculated undergraduates who enrolled in 2002, 2,500 applied for aid, 2,392 were judged to have need, 99 had their need fully met. In 2002, 230. *Average percent of need met:* 45. *Average financial aid package:* $9184. *Average need-based loan:* $5820. *Average need-based gift aid:* $4181. *Average non-need-based aid:* $6932.

Applying *Options:* electronic application, deferred entrance. *Application fee:* $50. *Required:* high school transcript, interview.

Admissions Contact Ms. Shelia Brown, New Student Coordinator, DeVry University, 1350 Alum Creek Drive, Columbus, OH 43209-2705. *Phone:* 614-253-1850. *Toll-free phone:* 800-426-2206. *Fax:* 614-253-0843. *E-mail:* admissions@devry.edu.

FRANCISCAN UNIVERSITY OF STEUBENVILLE
Steubenville, Ohio

- **Independent Roman Catholic** comprehensive, founded 1946
- **Calendar** semesters
- **Degrees** associate, bachelor's, and master's
- **Suburban** 124-acre campus with easy access to Pittsburgh
- **Endowment** $16.5 million
- **Coed,** 1,844 undergraduate students, 92% full-time, 60% women, 40% men
- **Moderately difficult** entrance level, 84% of applicants were admitted

Undergraduates 1,690 full-time, 154 part-time. Students come from 52 states and territories, 24 other countries, 76% are from out of state, 0.4% African American, 2% Asian American or Pacific Islander, 4% Hispanic American, 0.5% Native American, 2% international, 11% transferred in, 64% live on campus. *Retention:* 84% of 2002 full-time freshmen returned.

Freshmen *Admission:* 846 applied, 714 admitted, 357 enrolled. *Average high school GPA:* 3.53. *Test scores:* SAT verbal scores over 500: 88%; SAT math scores over 500: 82%; ACT scores over 18: 99%; SAT verbal scores over 600: 47%; SAT math scores over 600: 35%; ACT scores over 24: 54%; SAT verbal scores over 700: 10%; SAT math scores over 700: 4%; ACT scores over 30: 7%.

Faculty *Total:* 172, 60% full-time, 48% with terminal degrees. *Student/faculty ratio:* 16:1.

Franciscan University of Steubenville (continued)

Majors Accounting; anthropology; biology/biological sciences; business administration and management; chemistry; child development; classics and languages, literatures and linguistics; communication/speech communication and rhetoric; computer and information sciences; computer science; economics; elementary education; engineering science; English; French; general studies; German; history; humanities; legal studies; mathematics; nursing (registered nurse training); philosophy; political science and government; psychiatric/mental health services technology; psychology; religious education; social work; sociology; Spanish; theology.

Academic Programs *Special study options:* accelerated degree program, adult/continuing education programs, advanced placement credit, distance learning, double majors, honors programs, independent study, internships, part-time degree program, services for LD students, study abroad, summer session for credit.

Library John Paul II Library with 231,176 titles, 578 serial subscriptions, 1,260 audiovisual materials, an OPAC, a Web page.

Computers on Campus 126 computers available on campus for general student use. A campuswide network can be accessed. Internet access, at least one staffed computer lab available.

Student Life *Housing:* on-campus residence required through junior year. *Options:* men-only, women-only. Campus housing is university owned and leased by the school. *Activities and organizations:* drama/theater group, student-run newspaper, radio station, choral group, Franciscan University Student Association, Student Activities Board, Human Life Concerns, Works of Mercy, Troubadour, national fraternities, national sororities. *Campus security:* 24-hour emergency response devices and patrols, student patrols, late-night transport/escort service. *Student services:* health clinic, personal/psychological counseling.

Athletics *Intramural sports:* baseball M(c), basketball M/W, cheerleading M/W, racquetball M/W, rock climbing M(c)/W(c), rugby M(c), soccer M(c)/W(c), softball W(c), tennis M/W, ultimate Frisbee M/W, volleyball M/W, weight lifting M/W, wrestling M.

Standardized Tests *Required:* SAT I or ACT (for admission).

Costs (2003–04) *Comprehensive fee:* $20,300 includes full-time tuition ($14,670), mandatory fees ($380), and room and board ($5250). Part-time tuition: $485 per credit. Part-time tuition and fees vary according to class time. *Required fees:* $10 per credit part-time. *Room and board:* Room and board charges vary according to board plan. *Payment plan:* installment. *Waivers:* employees or children of employees.

Financial Aid Of all full-time matriculated undergraduates who enrolled in 2003, 1,380 applied for aid, 1,134 were judged to have need, 171 had their need fully met. 300 Federal Work-Study jobs (averaging $795). 577 state and other part-time jobs (averaging $1729). In 2003, 350 non-need-based awards were made. *Average percent of need met:* 62%. *Average financial aid package:* $10,631. *Average need-based loan:* $3066. *Average need-based gift aid:* $6565. *Average non-need-based aid:* $6930. *Average indebtedness upon graduation:* $21,616.

Applying *Options:* common application, early admission, deferred entrance. *Application fee:* $20. *Required:* essay or personal statement, high school transcript, minimum 2.4 GPA, letters of recommendation. *Recommended:* interview. *Application deadlines:* 5/1 (freshmen), 5/1 (transfers). *Notification:* 9/1 (freshmen), 8/30 (transfers).

Admissions Contact Mrs. Margaret Weber, Director of Admissions, Franciscan University of Steubenville, 1235 University Boulevard, Steubenville, OH 43952-1763. *Phone:* 740-283-6226. *Toll-free phone:* 800-783-6220. *Fax:* 740-284-5456. *E-mail:* admissions@franciscan.edu.

■ *See page 1646 for a narrative description.*

FRANKLIN UNIVERSITY
Columbus, Ohio

- **Independent** comprehensive, founded 1902
- **Calendar** trimesters
- **Degrees** associate, bachelor's, and master's
- **Urban** 14-acre campus
- **Endowment** $21.4 million
- **Coed,** 5,318 undergraduate students, 35% full-time, 55% women, 45% men
- **Noncompetitive** entrance level, 100% of applicants were admitted

Undergraduates 1,853 full-time, 3,465 part-time. Students come from 42 states and territories, 94 other countries, 22% are from out of state, 18% African American, 3% Asian American or Pacific Islander, 2% Hispanic American, 0.5% Native American, 7% international, 38% transferred in.

Freshmen *Admission:* 268 applied, 268 admitted, 92 enrolled.

Faculty *Total:* 429, 9% full-time, 21% with terminal degrees. *Student/faculty ratio:* 19:1.

Majors Accounting; business administration and management; computer and information sciences; finance; health/health care administration; human resources management; interdisciplinary studies; management information systems; management science; marketing/marketing management; operations management; security and protective services related; web page, digital/multimedia and information resources design.

Academic Programs *Special study options:* academic remediation for entering students, accelerated degree program, adult/continuing education programs, advanced placement credit, cooperative education, distance learning, English as a second language, independent study, internships, off-campus study, part-time degree program, services for LD students, student-designed majors, study abroad, summer session for credit. *ROTC:* Army (c), Air Force (c).

Library Franklin University Library with 73,702 titles, 432 serial subscriptions, 220 audiovisual materials, an OPAC.

Computers on Campus 358 computers available on campus for general student use. A campuswide network can be accessed. Internet access, online (class) registration, at least one staffed computer lab available.

Student Life *Housing:* college housing not available. *Activities and organizations:* American Marketing Association, International Student Association, Human Resources Society, Accounting Association. *Campus security:* security personnel during operating hours.

Costs (2003–04) *Tuition:* $6720 full-time, $224 per credit hour part-time. Full-time tuition and fees vary according to program. Part-time tuition and fees vary according to program. *Payment plans:* installment, deferred payment. *Waivers:* employees or children of employees.

Financial Aid Of all full-time matriculated undergraduates who enrolled in 2003, 1,135 applied for aid, 1,071 were judged to have need. 29 Federal Work-Study jobs (averaging $7702). In 2003, 108 non-need-based awards were made. *Average need-based loan:* $5091. *Average need-based gift aid:* $4436. *Average non-need-based aid:* $2211.

Applying *Options:* deferred entrance. *Required for some:* high school transcript. *Application deadline:* rolling (freshmen), rolling (transfers). *Notification:* continuous (transfers).

Admissions Contact Ms. Tracy Austin, Director of Student services, Franklin University, 201 South Grant Avenue, Columbus, OH 43215. *Phone:* 614-797-4700 Ext. 7501. *Toll-free phone:* 877-341-6300. *Fax:* 614-224-8027. *E-mail:* info@franklin.edu.

GOD'S BIBLE SCHOOL AND COLLEGE
Cincinnati, Ohio

- **Independent interdenominational** 4-year, founded 1900
- **Calendar** semesters
- **Degrees** associate and bachelor's
- **Urban** 14-acre campus
- **Coed,** 252 undergraduate students, 83% full-time, 49% women, 51% men
- **Minimally difficult** entrance level, 100% of applicants were admitted

Undergraduates 209 full-time, 43 part-time. Students come from 25 states and territories, 13 other countries, 0.9% African American, 0.9% Asian American or Pacific Islander, 0.4% Hispanic American, 0.4% Native American, 9% international, 10% transferred in. *Retention:* 76% of 2002 full-time freshmen returned.

Freshmen *Admission:* 59 applied, 59 admitted, 59 enrolled. *Average high school GPA:* 3.32.

Faculty *Total:* 20, 55% full-time, 30% with terminal degrees. *Student/faculty ratio:* 14:1.

Majors Administrative assistant and secretarial science; biblical studies; business/commerce; Christian studies; elementary education; family and community services; general studies; missionary studies and missiology; music teacher education; office management; pastoral studies/counseling; religious/sacred music; theological and ministerial studies related.

Academic Programs *Special study options:* academic remediation for entering students, advanced placement credit, independent study, internships, part-time degree program, summer session for credit.

Library R. G. Flexon Memorial Library with 28,452 titles, 240 serial subscriptions.

Computers on Campus 14 computers available on campus for general student use. At least one staffed computer lab available.

Student Life *Housing:* on-campus residence required through senior year. *Options:* men-only, women-only. *Activities and organizations:* student-run newspaper, choral group. *Campus security:* 24-hour patrols. *Student services:* health clinic.

Standardized Tests *Required:* SAT I or ACT (for placement).

Costs (2004–05) *Comprehensive fee:* $7780 includes full-time tuition ($4030), mandatory fees ($600), and room and board ($3150). Part-time tuition: $155 per credit. *College room only:* $1300. *Payment plan:* installment. *Waivers:* employees or children of employees.

Applying *Options:* common application. *Application fee:* $50. *Required:* high school transcript, 3 letters of recommendation, interview. *Application deadline:* 8/18 (freshmen), rolling (transfers). *Notification:* continuous (transfers).

Admissions Contact Mrs. Lori Waggoner, Director of Admissions, God's Bible School and College, 1810 Young Street, Cincinnati, OH 45202-6838. *Phone:* 513-721-7944 Ext. 205. *Toll-free phone:* 800-486-4637. *Fax:* 513-721-3971. *E-mail:* admissions@gbs.edu.

HEIDELBERG COLLEGE
Tiffin, Ohio

- **Independent** comprehensive, founded 1850, affiliated with United Church of Christ
- **Calendar** semesters
- **Degrees** bachelor's and master's
- **Small-town** 110-acre campus
- **Endowment** $28.5 million
- **Coed,** 1,054 undergraduate students, 92% full-time, 52% women, 48% men
- **Moderately difficult** entrance level, 98% of applicants were admitted

Undergraduates 969 full-time, 85 part-time. Students come from 22 states and territories, 10 other countries, 20% are from out of state, 31% transferred in, 87% live on campus. *Retention:* 68% of 2002 full-time freshmen returned.

Freshmen *Admission:* 1,649 applied, 1,610 admitted, 319 enrolled. *Average high school GPA:* 3.10. *Test scores:* SAT verbal scores over 500: 45%; SAT math scores over 500: 40%; ACT scores over 18: 79%; SAT verbal scores over 600: 15%; SAT math scores over 600: 7%; ACT scores over 24: 24%; ACT scores over 30: 6%.

Faculty *Total:* 118, 56% full-time, 54% with terminal degrees. *Student/faculty ratio:* 12:1.

Majors Accounting; anthropology; athletic training; biology/biological sciences; business administration and management; chemistry; computer science; dramatic/theatre arts; economics; education; elementary education; English; environmental biology; environmental science; environmental studies; German; health/health care administration; health teacher education; history; hydrology and water resources science; information science/studies; international relations and affairs; mass communication/media; mathematics; music; music management and merchandising; music teacher education; philosophy; physical education teaching and coaching; physics; piano and organ; political science and government; pre-dentistry studies; pre-law studies; pre-medical studies; pre-veterinary studies; psychology; public administration; public relations/image management; religious studies; science teacher education; secondary education; Spanish; special education; violin, viola, guitar and other stringed instruments; voice and opera.

Academic Programs *Special study options:* academic remediation for entering students, accelerated degree program, adult/continuing education programs, advanced placement credit, double majors, English as a second language, honors programs, internships, off-campus study, part-time degree program, services for LD students, study abroad, summer session for credit. *ROTC:* Army (c), Air Force (c). *Unusual degree programs:* 3-2 engineering with Case Western Reserve University; nursing with Case Western Reserve University; environmental management with Duke University.

Library Beeghly Library plus 1 other with 260,055 titles, 829 serial subscriptions, an OPAC, a Web page.

Computers on Campus 125 computers available on campus for general student use. A campuswide network can be accessed from student residence rooms and from off campus. Internet access, online (class) registration, at least one staffed computer lab available.

Student Life *Housing:* on-campus residence required through junior year. *Options:* coed, women-only, cooperative. Campus housing is university owned. Freshman campus housing is guaranteed. *Activities and organizations:* drama/theater group, student-run newspaper, radio and television station, choral group, Alpha Phi Omega, BERG Events Council, Student Senate, Campus Fellowship, Black Student Union/World Student Union. *Campus security:* 24-hour emergency response devices and patrols, student patrols, late-night transport/escort service. *Student services:* health clinic, personal/psychological counseling.

Athletics Member NCAA. except baseball (Division III), men's and women's basketball (Division III), men's and women's cross-country running (Division III), football (Division III), men's and women's golf (Division III), men's and women's soccer (Division III), softball (Division III), men's and women's tennis (Division III), men's and women's track and field (Division III), men's and women's volleyball (Division III), wrestling (Division III) *Intercollegiate sports:* baseball M, basketball M/W, cross-country running M/W, football M, golf M/W, soccer M/W, softball W, tennis M/W, track and field M/W, volleyball M/W, wrestling M. *Intramural sports:* archery M/W, badminton M/W, cheerleading M/W, football M, golf M/W, racquetball M/W, skiing (cross-country) M/W, softball W, table tennis M/W.

Standardized Tests *Required:* SAT I or ACT (for admission).

Costs (2004–05) *Comprehensive fee:* $21,610 includes full-time tuition ($14,575), mandatory fees ($325), and room and board ($6710). Full-time tuition and fees vary according to course load and location. *Room and board:* Room and board charges vary according to board plan. *Payment plan:* installment. *Waivers:* minority students, children of alumni, and employees or children of employees.

Financial Aid Of all full-time matriculated undergraduates who enrolled in 2003, 881 applied for aid, 810 were judged to have need, 379 had their need fully met. 509 Federal Work-Study jobs (averaging $860). 32 state and other part-time jobs (averaging $2573). In 2003, 155 non-need-based awards were made. *Average percent of need met:* 95%. *Average financial aid package:* $16,974. *Average need-based loan:* $4300. *Average need-based gift aid:* $10,089. *Average non-need-based aid:* $5553. *Average indebtedness upon graduation:* $22,032.

Applying *Options:* common application, electronic application, deferred entrance. *Application fee:* $25. *Required:* high school transcript, minimum 2.0 GPA. *Recommended:* 2 letters of recommendation, interview. *Notification:* continuous until 8/31 (freshmen).

Admissions Contact Director of Admission, Heidelberg College, 310 East Market Street, Tiffin, OH 44883. *Phone:* 419-448-2342. *Toll-free phone:* 800-434-3352. *Fax:* 419-448-2334. *E-mail:* adminfo@heidelberg.edu.

■ *See page 1726 for a narrative description.*

HIRAM COLLEGE
Hiram, Ohio

- **Independent** 4-year, founded 1850, affiliated with Christian Church (Disciples of Christ)
- **Calendar** semesters
- **Degree** bachelor's
- **Rural** 110-acre campus with easy access to Cleveland
- **Endowment** $60.4 million
- **Coed,** 1,110 undergraduate students, 80% full-time, 58% women, 42% men
- **Very difficult** entrance level, 88% of applicants were admitted

Each of Hiram's 15-week semesters is divided into 12- and 3-week terms. During the 3-week terms, students take only 1 course. Hiram supplements classroom study through an extensive study-abroad program. More than 50 percent of students participate, with all courses taught by Hiram faculty members. Hiram opened a $7.2-million library in 1995, and the $6.2-million Esther and Carl Gerstacker Science Hall opened in January 2000.

Undergraduates 886 full-time, 224 part-time. Students come from 31 states and territories, 20 other countries, 20% are from out of state, 11% African American, 1% Asian American or Pacific Islander, 1% Hispanic American, 0.3% Native American, 3% international, 2% transferred in, 95% live on campus. *Retention:* 73% of 2002 full-time freshmen returned.

Freshmen *Admission:* 888 applied, 778 admitted, 236 enrolled. *Average high school GPA:* 3.37. *Test scores:* SAT verbal scores over 500: 79%; SAT math scores over 500: 71%; ACT scores over 18: 95%; SAT verbal scores over 600: 42%; SAT math scores over 600: 32%; ACT scores over 24: 50%; SAT verbal scores over 700: 11%; SAT math scores over 700: 3%; ACT scores over 30: 7%.

Faculty *Total:* 121, 60% full-time, 64% with terminal degrees. *Student/faculty ratio:* 11:1.

Majors Art; art history, criticism and conservation; biology/biological sciences; business administration and management; chemistry; classics and languages, literatures and linguistics; computer science; dramatic/theatre arts; economics; elementary education; English; environmental studies; fine/studio arts; French; German; health science; history; international business/trade/commerce; international economics; mass communication/media; mathematics; music; philosophy; physics; physiological psychology/psychobiology; political science and government; pre-dentistry studies; pre-law studies; pre-medical studies; pre-veterinary studies; psychology; religious studies; secondary education; sociology; Spanish.

Academic Programs *Special study options:* accelerated degree program, adult/continuing education programs, advanced placement credit, double majors, English as a second language, independent study, internships, off-campus study, part-time degree program, services for LD students, student-designed majors, study abroad, summer session for credit. *Unusual degree programs:* 3-2 engineering with Case Western Reserve University, Washington University in St. Louis.

Library Hiram College Library with 187,451 titles, 3,993 serial subscriptions, 10,351 audiovisual materials, an OPAC, a Web page.

Computers on Campus A campuswide network can be accessed from student residence rooms and from off campus. Internet access, at least one staffed computer lab available.

Hiram College (continued)

Student Life *Housing:* on-campus residence required through junior year. *Options:* coed, women-only, disabled students. Campus housing is university owned. Freshman campus housing is guaranteed. *Activities and organizations:* drama/theater group, student-run newspaper, radio station, choral group, Student Senate, African American Students United, outdoors club, Resident Student Association, Christian Outreach. *Campus security:* 24-hour emergency response devices and patrols, late-night transport/escort service, controlled dormitory access. *Student services:* health clinic, personal/psychological counseling.

Athletics Member NCAA. All Division III. *Intercollegiate sports:* baseball M, basketball M/W, cross-country running M/W, equestrian sports M(c)/W(c), football M, golf M/W, rugby M(c)/W(c), sailing M(c)/W(c), soccer M/W, softball W, swimming M/W, table tennis M(c)/W(c), tennis M/W, track and field M/W, volleyball W. *Intramural sports:* basketball M/W, football M/W, racquetball M/W, rock climbing M/W, soccer M/W, softball M/W, tennis M/W, ultimate Frisbee M/W, volleyball M/W.

Standardized Tests *Required:* SAT I or ACT (for admission).

Costs (2003–04) *Comprehensive fee:* $28,234 includes full-time tuition ($20,440), mandatory fees ($694), and room and board ($7100). Part-time tuition: $682 per credit hour. *College room only:* $3160.

Financial Aid Of all full-time matriculated undergraduates who enrolled in 2002, 790 applied for aid, 736 were judged to have need, 699 had their need fully met. 587 Federal Work-Study jobs (averaging $1600). 18 state and other part-time jobs (averaging $1580). In 2002, 114 non-need-based awards were made. *Average percent of need met:* 95%. *Average financial aid package:* $21,218. *Average need-based loan:* $6960. *Average need-based gift aid:* $8163. *Average non-need-based aid:* $8635. *Average indebtedness upon graduation:* $17,125.

Applying *Options:* common application, electronic application, early admission, early decision, deferred entrance. *Application fee:* $35. *Required:* essay or personal statement, high school transcript, 2 letters of recommendation. *Required for some:* interview. *Recommended:* 3 letters of recommendation, interview. *Application deadlines:* 2/1 (freshmen), 7/15 (transfers). *Early decision:* 12/1. *Notification:* continuous (freshmen), 12/15 (early decision), continuous (transfers).

Admissions Contact Ms. Brenda Swihart Meyer, Director of Admission, Hiram College, PO Box 96, Hiram, OH 44234. *Phone:* 330-569-5169. *Toll-free phone:* 800-362-5280. *Fax:* 330-569-5944. *E-mail:* admission@hiram.edu.

■ *See page 1736 for a narrative description.*

JOHN CARROLL UNIVERSITY
University Heights, Ohio

- **Independent Roman Catholic (Jesuit)** comprehensive, founded 1886
- **Calendar** semesters
- **Degrees** bachelor's and master's
- **Suburban** 60-acre campus with easy access to Cleveland
- **Endowment** $122.4 million
- **Coed,** 3,279 undergraduate students
- **Moderately difficult** entrance level, 86% of applicants were admitted

The beautiful front lawn of John Carroll University is now a new academic quad. The new Dolan Center for Science and Technology, which opened for classes in fall 2003, houses the biology, chemistry, computer science, mathematics, physics, and psychology departments.

Undergraduates Students come from 35 states and territories, 27% are from out of state, 59% live on campus. *Retention:* 86% of 2002 full-time freshmen returned.

Freshmen *Admission:* 2,764 applied, 2,387 admitted. *Average high school GPA:* 3.27. *Test scores:* SAT verbal scores over 500: 84%; SAT math scores over 500: 88%; ACT scores over 18: 96%; SAT verbal scores over 600: 32%; SAT math scores over 600: 43%; ACT scores over 24: 48%; SAT verbal scores over 700: 6%; SAT math scores over 700: 4%; ACT scores over 30: 6%.

Faculty *Total:* 411, 59% full-time. *Student/faculty ratio:* 15:1.

Majors Accounting; art history, criticism and conservation; Asian studies; Asian studies (East); biological and physical sciences; biology/biological sciences; business administration and management; chemistry; classics and languages, literatures and linguistics; computer science; economics; education; education (K-12); elementary education; engineering physics; English; environmental studies; finance; French; German; gerontology; history; humanities; interdisciplinary studies; international economics; international relations and affairs; kindergarten/preschool education; Latin; literature; marketing/marketing management; mass communication/media; mathematics; modern Greek; neuroscience; philosophy; physical education teaching and coaching; physics; political science and government; pre-dentistry studies; pre-law studies; pre-medical studies; pre-veterinary studies; psychology; public administration; religious education; religious studies; secondary education; sociology; Spanish; special education.

Academic Programs *Special study options:* accelerated degree program, adult/continuing education programs, advanced placement credit, cooperative education, double majors, honors programs, independent study, internships, off-campus study, part-time degree program, student-designed majors, study abroad, summer session for credit. *ROTC:* Army (b). *Unusual degree programs:* 3-2 engineering with Case Western Reserve University, University of Detroit Mercy; nursing with Case Western Reserve University.

Library Grasselli Library with 620,000 titles, 2,198 serial subscriptions, 5,820 audiovisual materials, an OPAC, a Web page.

Computers on Campus 210 computers available on campus for general student use. A campuswide network can be accessed from student residence rooms and from off campus. Internet access, online (class) registration, at least one staffed computer lab available.

Student Life *Housing:* on-campus residence required for freshman year. *Options:* coed, men-only, women-only. *Activities and organizations:* drama/theater group, student-run newspaper, radio station, choral group, Volunteer Service Organization, Student Union, Carroll News, band, University Concert Choir, national fraternities, national sororities. *Campus security:* 24-hour emergency response devices and patrols, late-night transport/escort service. *Student services:* health clinic, personal/psychological counseling.

Athletics Member NCAA. All Division III. *Intercollegiate sports:* baseball M, basketball M/W, crew M(c)/W(c), cross-country running M/W, football M, golf M/W, ice hockey M(c), lacrosse M(c)/W(c), rugby M(c)/W(c), sailing M(c)/W(c), skiing (downhill) M(c)/W(c), soccer M/W, softball W, swimming M/W, tennis M/W, track and field M/W, volleyball M(c)/W, wrestling M. *Intramural sports:* basketball M/W, football M/W, racquetball M/W, softball M/W, swimming M/W, tennis M/W, volleyball M/W, water polo M/W.

Standardized Tests *Required:* SAT I or ACT (for admission).

Costs (2003–04) *Comprehensive fee:* $27,658 includes full-time tuition ($20,566), mandatory fees ($200), and room and board ($6892). Part-time tuition and fees vary according to course load. *Room and board:* Room and board charges vary according to board plan. *Payment plan:* installment. *Waivers:* employees or children of employees.

Financial Aid *Average financial aid package:* $14,104. *Average indebtedness upon graduation:* $12,695.

Applying *Options:* early admission, deferred entrance. *Application fee:* $25. *Required:* high school transcript, 1 letter of recommendation. *Required for some:* interview. *Recommended:* essay or personal statement, interview. *Application deadline:* 2/1 (freshmen), rolling (transfers). *Notification:* continuous (freshmen).

Admissions Contact Mr. Thomas P. Fanning, Director of Admission, John Carroll University, 20700 North Park Boulevard, University Heights, OH 44118. *Phone:* 216-397-4294. *Fax:* 216-397-4981. *E-mail:* admission@jcu.edu.

■ *See page 1786 for a narrative description.*

KENT STATE UNIVERSITY
Kent, Ohio

- **State-supported** university, founded 1910, part of Kent State University System
- **Calendar** semesters
- **Degrees** certificates, associate, bachelor's, master's, doctoral, post-master's, and postbachelor's certificates
- **Suburban** 1347-acre campus with easy access to Cleveland
- **Endowment** $47.9 million
- **Coed,** 19,173 undergraduate students, 83% full-time, 59% women, 41% men
- **Moderately difficult** entrance level, 89% of applicants were admitted

Undergraduates 15,982 full-time, 3,191 part-time. Students come from 51 states and territories, 61 other countries, 8% are from out of state, 8% African American, 1% Asian American or Pacific Islander, 1% Hispanic American, 0.3% Native American, 0.9% international, 5% transferred in, 33% live on campus. *Retention:* 73% of 2002 full-time freshmen returned.

Freshmen *Admission:* 11,098 applied, 9,922 admitted, 3,822 enrolled. *Average high school GPA:* 3.15. *Test scores:* SAT verbal scores over 500: 58%; SAT math scores over 500: 57%; ACT scores over 18: 86%; SAT verbal scores over 600: 18%; SAT math scores over 600: 18%; ACT scores over 24: 27%; SAT verbal scores over 700: 2%; SAT math scores over 700: 1%; ACT scores over 30: 3%.

Faculty *Total:* 1,335, 61% full-time, 47% with terminal degrees. *Student/faculty ratio:* 20:1.

Majors Accounting; accounting technology and bookkeeping; administrative assistant and secretarial science; advertising; aeronautics/aviation/aerospace science and technology; African-American/Black studies; allied health diagnostic, intervention, and treatment professions related; American studies; animation, interactive technology, video graphics and special effects; anthropology; applied horticulture; applied mathematics; architecture; area, ethnic, cultural, and gender studies related; area studies related; art history, criticism and conservation; art teacher education; athletic training; audiology and speech-language pathology; biological and biomedical sciences related; biological specializations related; biology/biological sciences; biotechnology; botany/plant biology; business administration and management; business automation/technology/data entry; business/commerce; business/managerial economics; business teacher education; CAD/CADD drafting/design technology; chemistry; chemistry teacher education; classics and languages, literatures and linguistics; clinical laboratory science/medical technology; commercial and advertising art; computer graphics; computer programming; computer programming (specific applications); computer science; computer systems analysis; computer technology/computer systems technology; crafts, folk art and artisanry; criminal justice/safety; cultural studies; dance; digital communication and media/multimedia; dramatic/theatre arts; ecology; economics; education; education related; electrical and electronic engineering technologies related; emergency care attendant (EMT ambulance); emergency medical technology (EMT paramedic); engineering technologies related; English; English/language arts teacher education; environmental control technologies related; environmental design/architecture; environmental studies; European studies (Central and Eastern); family and consumer sciences/home economics teacher education; family and consumer sciences/human sciences; fashion/apparel design; fashion merchandising; finance; fine/studio arts; foods and nutrition related; foods, nutrition, and wellness; foreign language teacher education; French; French language teacher education; general studies; geography; geology/earth science; German; health and medical administrative services related; health services/allied health/health sciences; health teacher education; history; hospitality administration related; human development and family studies; human development and family studies related; human nutrition; human services; industrial engineering; industrial production technologies related; industrial technology; interior design; international relations and affairs; journalism; journalism related; kindergarten/preschool education; kinesiology and exercise science; Latin; Latin American studies; Latin teacher education; legal assistant/paralegal; liberal arts and sciences/liberal studies; linguistics of ASL and other sign languages; manufacturing technology; marketing/marketing management; mass communication/media; mathematics; mechanical engineering/mechanical technology; medical radiologic technology; middle school education; multi-/interdisciplinary studies related; music; music performance; music teacher education; natural resources/conservation; nuclear medical technology; nursing (licensed practical/vocational nurse training); nursing (registered nurse training); occupational therapist assistant; operations management; parks, recreation and leisure facilities management; peace studies and conflict resolution; philosophy; photographic and film/video technology; physical education teaching and coaching; physical therapist assistant; physics; plastics engineering technology; political science and government; pre-dentistry studies; professional studies; psychology; public relations/image management; radio and television; radiologic technology/science; real estate; Russian; Russian studies; sales and marketing/marketing and distribution teacher education; science teacher education; social sciences; social studies teacher education; sociology; Spanish; Spanish language teacher education; special education; speech and rhetoric; technology/industrial arts teacher education; trade and industrial teacher education; zoology/animal biology.

Academic Programs *Special study options:* academic remediation for entering students, accelerated degree program, adult/continuing education programs, advanced placement credit, cooperative education, distance learning, double majors, English as a second language, freshman honors college, honors programs, independent study, internships, off-campus study, part-time degree program, services for LD students, student-designed majors, study abroad, summer session for credit. *ROTC:* Army (b), Air Force (b). *Unusual degree programs:* 3-2 international relations.

Library Kent Library plus 5 others with 1.1 million titles, 8,771 serial subscriptions, 27,447 audiovisual materials, an OPAC, a Web page.

Computers on Campus 1680 computers available on campus for general student use. A campuswide network can be accessed from student residence rooms and from off campus. Internet access, at least one staffed computer lab available.

Student Life *Housing:* on-campus residence required through sophomore year. *Options:* coed, men-only, women-only, disabled students. Campus housing is university owned. Freshman campus housing is guaranteed. *Activities and organizations:* drama/theater group, student-run newspaper, radio and television station, choral group, marching band, Kent Interhall Council, Black United Students, All Campus Programming Board, Delta Sigma PI, Late Night Christian Fellowship, national fraternities, national sororities. *Campus security:* 24-hour emergency response devices and patrols, student patrols, late-night transport/escort service, controlled dormitory access, campus police and fire department, electronic locks on computer labs, studios and laboratory research areas. *Student services:* health clinic, personal/psychological counseling, women's center, legal services.

Athletics Member NCAA. All Division I except football (Division I-A). *Intercollegiate sports:* baseball M(s), basketball M(s)/W(s), cross-country running M(s)/W(s), field hockey W(s), golf M(s)/W(s), gymnastics W(s), soccer W(s), softball W(s), track and field M(s)/W(s), volleyball W(s), wrestling M(s). *Intramural sports:* badminton M(c)/W(c), baseball M(c), basketball M/W, bowling M(c)/W(c), equestrian sports M(c)/W(c), fencing M(c)/W(c), field hockey W(c), football M/W, golf M(c)/W(c), ice hockey M(c), lacrosse M(c), racquetball M(c)/W(c), rugby M(c)/W(c), sailing M(c)/W(c), skiing (downhill) M(c)/W(c), soccer M(c)/W(c), softball M/W, swimming M(c)/W(c), table tennis M/W, tennis M/W, ultimate Frisbee M/W, volleyball M(c)/W(c), water polo M/W, wrestling M.

Standardized Tests *Required:* SAT I or ACT (for admission).

Costs (2003–04) *One-time required fee:* $100. *Tuition:* state resident $6882 full-time, $314 per credit hour part-time; nonresident $13,314 full-time, $607 per credit hour part-time. Full-time tuition and fees vary according to course level, course load, degree level, location, reciprocity agreements, and student level. Part-time tuition and fees vary according to course level, course load, degree level, location, program, reciprocity agreements, and student level. *Room and board:* $7920; room only: $3540. Room and board charges vary according to board plan and housing facility. *Payment plans:* tuition prepayment, installment, deferred payment. *Waivers:* employees or children of employees.

Financial Aid Of all full-time matriculated undergraduates who enrolled in 2003, 10,898 applied for aid, 9,192 were judged to have need, 1,444 had their need fully met. 1,042 Federal Work-Study jobs (averaging $2316). In 2003, 1219 non-need-based awards were made. *Average percent of need met:* 62%. *Average financial aid package:* $7151. *Average need-based loan:* $3925. *Average need-based gift aid:* $4614. *Average non-need-based aid:* $3455. *Average indebtedness upon graduation:* $19,439.

Applying *Options:* electronic application, early admission. *Application fee:* $30. *Required:* high school transcript, minimum 2.5 GPA. *Application deadline:* 5/1 (freshmen). *Notification:* continuous (transfers).

Admissions Contact Mr. Christopher Buttenschon, Assistant Director of Admissions, Kent State University, 161 Michael Schwartz Center, Kent, OH 44242-0001. *Phone:* 330-672-2444. *Toll-free phone:* 800-988-KENT. *Fax:* 330-672-2499. *E-mail:* admissions@kent.edu.

■ *See page 1812 for a narrative description.*

KENT STATE UNIVERSITY, ASHTABULA CAMPUS
Ashtabula, Ohio

- **State-supported** primarily 2-year, founded 1958, part of Kent State University System
- **Calendar** semesters
- **Degrees** certificates, associate, and bachelor's (also offers some upper-level and graduate courses)
- **Small-town** 120-acre campus with easy access to Cleveland
- **Coed**
- **Noncompetitive** entrance level

Student Life *Campus security:* 24-hour emergency response devices.

Standardized Tests *Recommended:* SAT I or ACT (for placement).

Financial Aid Of all full-time matriculated undergraduates who enrolled in 2001, 1,042 Federal Work-Study jobs (averaging $2316).

Applying *Options:* early admission, deferred entrance.

Admissions Contact Ms. Kelly Sanford, Director, Enrollment Management and Student services, Kent State University, Ashtabula Campus, 3325 West 13th Street, Ashtabula, OH 44004-2299. *Phone:* 440-964-4217. *E-mail:* robinson@ashtabula.kent.edu.

KENT STATE UNIVERSITY, GEAUGA CAMPUS
Burton, Ohio

- **State-supported** founded 1964, part of Kent State University System
- **Calendar** semesters
- **Degrees** associate, bachelor's, and master's
- **Rural** 87-acre campus with easy access to Cleveland
- **Coed**
- **Noncompetitive** entrance level

Faculty *Student/faculty ratio:* 14:1.

Student Life *Campus security:* 24-hour emergency response devices.

Standardized Tests *Recommended:* ACT (for placement).

Costs (2003–04) *Tuition:* state resident $3968 full-time; nonresident $10,400 full-time.

Financial Aid Of all full-time matriculated undergraduates who enrolled in 2001, 189 applied for aid, 157 were judged to have need, 17 had their need fully met. 11 Federal Work-Study jobs (averaging $1554). In 2001, 3. *Average percent of need met:* 56. *Average financial aid package:* $5391. *Average need-based loan:* $3147. *Average need-based gift aid:* $3785. *Average non-need-based aid:* $2415. *Average indebtedness upon graduation:* $19,489.

Kent State University, Geauga Campus (continued)

Applying *Options:* early admission, deferred entrance. *Application fee:* $30. *Required:* high school transcript, interview. *Recommended:* minimum 2.0 GPA.

Admissions Contact Ms. Betty Landrus, Admissions and Records Secretary, Kent State University, Geauga Campus, 14111 Claridon-Troy Road, Burton, OH 44021. *Phone:* 440-834-4187. *Fax:* 440-834-8846. *E-mail:* cbaker@geauga.kent.edu.

KENT STATE UNIVERSITY, SALEM CAMPUS

Salem, Ohio

- **State-supported** primarily 2-year, founded 1966, part of Kent State University System
- **Calendar** semesters
- **Degrees** associate and bachelor's (also offers some upper-level and graduate courses)
- **Rural** 98-acre campus
- **Coed**
- **Noncompetitive** entrance level

Faculty *Student/faculty ratio:* 13:1.

Student Life *Campus security:* late-night transport/escort service.

Standardized Tests *Required for some:* ACT (for admission), SAT I or ACT (for placement). *Recommended:* SAT I or ACT (for placement).

Costs (2003–04) *Tuition:* state resident $3968 full-time; nonresident $10,400 full-time. Full-time tuition and fees vary according to course level. Part-time tuition and fees vary according to course level. *Payment plans:* installment, deferred payment.

Financial Aid Of all full-time matriculated undergraduates who enrolled in 2001, 16 Federal Work-Study jobs (averaging $3021).

Applying *Options:* early admission, deferred entrance. *Application fee:* $30. *Required:* high school transcript. *Required for some:* essay or personal statement, minimum X GPA, letters of recommendation.

Admissions Contact Ms. Malinda Shean, Admissions Secretary, Kent State University, Salem Campus, 2491 State Route 45 South, Salem, OH 44460-9412. *Phone:* 330-332-0361 Ext. 74208.

KENT STATE UNIVERSITY, STARK CAMPUS

Canton, Ohio

- **State-supported** primarily 2-year, founded 1967, part of Kent State University System
- **Calendar** semesters
- **Degrees** associate and bachelor's (also offers some graduate courses)
- **Suburban** 200-acre campus with easy access to Cleveland
- **Coed**
- **Noncompetitive** entrance level

Faculty *Student/faculty ratio:* 19:1.

Student Life *Campus security:* 24-hour emergency response devices, late-night transport/escort service.

Standardized Tests *Required for some:* SAT I or ACT (for admission).

Financial Aid Of all full-time matriculated undergraduates who enrolled in 2001, 54 Federal Work-Study jobs (averaging $2389).

Applying *Options:* early admission, deferred entrance. *Application fee:* $30. *Required:* high school transcript. *Required for some:* interview.

Admissions Contact Mrs. Deborah Ann Speck, Director of Admissions, Kent State University, Stark Campus, 6000 Frank Avenue NW, Canton, OH 44720-7599. *Phone:* 330-499-9600 Ext. 53259. *Fax:* 330-499-0301. *E-mail:* aspeck@stark.kent.edu.

KENT STATE UNIVERSITY, TUSCARAWAS CAMPUS

New Philadelphia, Ohio

- **State-supported** primarily 2-year, founded 1962, part of Kent State University System
- **Calendar** semesters
- **Degrees** certificates, diplomas, associate, bachelor's, and master's (also offers some upper-level and graduate courses)
- **Small-town** 172-acre campus with easy access to Cleveland
- **Coed**
- **Noncompetitive** entrance level

Faculty *Student/faculty ratio:* 16:1.

Standardized Tests *Required for some:* SAT I or ACT (for placement).

Costs (2003–04) *Tuition:* state resident $207 per credit part-time; nonresident $500 per credit part-time. Full-time tuition and fees vary according to course level, course load, and location. Part-time tuition and fees vary according to course level, course load, and location.

Financial Aid Of all full-time matriculated undergraduates who enrolled in 2001, 26 Federal Work-Study jobs (averaging $2699).

Applying *Options:* common application, early admission, deferred entrance. *Application fee:* $30. *Required:* high school transcript.

Admissions Contact Ms. Denise L. Testa, Director of Admissions, Kent State University, Tuscarawas Campus, 330 University Drive NE, New Philadelphia, OH 44663-9403. *Phone:* 330-339-3391 Ext. 47425. *Fax:* 330-339-3321.

KENYON COLLEGE

Gambier, Ohio

- **Independent** 4-year, founded 1824
- **Calendar** semesters
- **Degree** bachelor's
- **Rural** 1200-acre campus with easy access to Columbus
- **Endowment** $125.5 million
- **Coed,** 1,612 undergraduate students, 99% full-time, 55% women, 45% men
- **Very difficult** entrance level, 46% of applicants were admitted

Undergraduates 1,592 full-time, 20 part-time. Students come from 24 other countries, 78% are from out of state, 3% African American, 3% Asian American or Pacific Islander, 2% Hispanic American, 0.1% Native American, 2% international, 1% transferred in, 99% live on campus. *Retention:* 92% of 2002 full-time freshmen returned.

Freshmen *Admission:* 3,360 applied, 1,534 admitted, 454 enrolled. *Average high school GPA:* 3.76. *Test scores:* SAT verbal scores over 500: 99%; SAT math scores over 500: 99%; ACT scores over 18: 100%; SAT verbal scores over 600: 86%; SAT math scores over 600: 78%; ACT scores over 24: 99%; SAT verbal scores over 700: 40%; SAT math scores over 700: 23%; ACT scores over 30: 57%.

Faculty *Total:* 168, 86% full-time, 93% with terminal degrees. *Student/faculty ratio:* 10:1.

Majors African-American/Black studies; African studies; American studies; ancient/classical Greek; anthropology; art; art history, criticism and conservation; Asian studies; biochemistry; biology/biological sciences; chemistry; classics and languages, literatures and linguistics; creative writing; dance; dramatic/theatre arts; economics; English; environmental studies; ethnic, cultural minority, and gender studies related; fine/studio arts; foreign languages and literatures; French; German; history; humanities; interdisciplinary studies; international/global studies; international relations and affairs; Latin; legal studies; literature; mathematics; modern Greek; modern languages; molecular biology; multi-/interdisciplinary studies related; music; natural sciences; neuroscience; philosophy; physics; political science and government; pre-dentistry studies; pre-law studies; premedical studies; pre-veterinary studies; psychology; public policy analysis; religious studies; Romance languages; sociology; Spanish; statistics; women's studies.

Academic Programs *Special study options:* accelerated degree program, advanced placement credit, double majors, honors programs, independent study, internships, off-campus study, services for LD students, student-designed majors, study abroad. *Unusual degree programs:* 3-2 engineering with Washington University in St. Louis, Case Western Reserve University, Rensselaer Polytechnic Institute; environmental science with Duke University, education with The Bank Street College of Education.

Library Olin Library plus 1 other with 858,000 titles, 5,300 serial subscriptions, 171,230 audiovisual materials, an OPAC, a Web page.

Computers on Campus 300 computers available on campus for general student use. A campuswide network can be accessed from student residence rooms and from off campus that provide access to commercial databases. Internet access, at least one staffed computer lab available.

Student Life *Housing:* on-campus residence required through senior year. *Options:* coed, women-only, cooperative, disabled students. Campus housing is university owned. Freshman campus housing is guaranteed. *Activities and organizations:* drama/theater group, student-run newspaper, radio station, choral group, music groups, Student Theater Organization, writing organizations, student radio station, ballroom dance club, national fraternities. *Campus security:* 24-hour emergency response devices and patrols, student patrols, late-night transport/escort service. *Student services:* health clinic, personal/psychological counseling, women's center.

Athletics Member NCAA. All Division III. *Intercollegiate sports:* baseball M, basketball M/W, cheerleading M(c)/W(c), cross-country running M/W, equestrian sports M(c)/W(c), fencing M(c)/W(c), field hockey W, football M, golf M, ice hockey M(c)/W(c), lacrosse M/W, rugby M(c)/W(c), soccer M/W, softball W, squash M(c)/W(c), swimming M/W, tennis M/W, track and field M/W, ultimate Frisbee M(c)/W(c), volleyball W. *Intramural sports:* basketball M/W, bowling M(c)/W(c), crew M(c)/W(c), football M, racquetball M/W, sailing M(c)/W(c), skiing (downhill) M(c)/W(c), soccer M(c)/W(c), softball M/W, tennis M/W, wrestling M(c)/W(c).

Standardized Tests *Required:* SAT I or ACT (for admission).

Costs (2003–04) *Comprehensive fee:* $35,370 includes full-time tuition ($29,500), mandatory fees ($830), and room and board ($5040). *College room only:* $2340. Room and board charges vary according to housing facility. *Payment plan:* installment. *Waivers:* employees or children of employees.

Financial Aid Of all full-time matriculated undergraduates who enrolled in 2003, 829 applied for aid, 695 were judged to have need, 389 had their need fully met. 224 Federal Work-Study jobs (averaging $600). In 2003, 400 non-need-based awards were made. *Average percent of need met:* 98%. *Average financial aid package:* $22,151. *Average need-based loan:* $3644. *Average need-based gift aid:* $18,731. *Average non-need-based aid:* $12,502. *Average indebtedness upon graduation:* $19,587.

Applying *Options:* common application, electronic application, early admission, early decision, deferred entrance. *Application fee:* $45. *Required:* essay or personal statement, high school transcript, minimum 2.0 GPA, 1 letter of recommendation. *Recommended:* minimum 3.0 GPA, 2 letters of recommendation, interview. *Application deadlines:* 2/1 (freshmen), 6/1 (transfers). *Early decision:* 12/1 (for plan 1), 1/15 (for plan 2). *Notification:* 4/1 (freshmen), 12/15 (early decision plan 1), 2/1 (early decision plan 2), continuous (transfers).

Admissions Contact Ms. Jennifer Britz, Dean of Admissions, Kenyon College, Ransom Hall, Gambier, OH 43022. *Phone:* 740-427-5776. *Toll-free phone:* 800-848-2468. *Fax:* 740-427-5770. *E-mail:* admissions@kenyon.edu.

KETTERING COLLEGE OF MEDICAL ARTS
Kettering, Ohio

- **Independent Seventh-day Adventist** primarily 2-year, founded 1967
- **Calendar** semesters
- **Degrees** certificates, associate, and bachelor's
- **Suburban** 35-acre campus
- **Coed**
- **Moderately difficult** entrance level

Student Life *Campus security:* 24-hour emergency response devices and patrols, late-night transport/escort service.

Standardized Tests *Required:* ACT (for admission). *Recommended:* SAT I (for admission).

Applying *Options:* early admission. *Application fee:* $25. *Required:* high school transcript, minimum 2.0 GPA, 3 letters of recommendation. *Recommended:* minimum 3.0 GPA, interview.

Admissions Contact Mr. David Lofthouse, Director of Enrollment Services, Kettering College of Medical Arts, 3737 Southern Boulevard, Kettering, OH 45429-1299. *Phone:* 937-296-7228. *Toll-free phone:* 800-433-5262. *Fax:* 937-296-4238.

LAKE ERIE COLLEGE
Painesville, Ohio

- **Independent** comprehensive, founded 1856
- **Calendar** semesters
- **Degrees** bachelor's and master's
- **Small-town** 57-acre campus with easy access to Cleveland
- **Endowment** $25.0 million
- **Coed,** 720 undergraduate students, 78% full-time, 76% women, 24% men
- **Minimally difficult** entrance level, 55% of applicants were admitted

Undergraduates 565 full-time, 155 part-time. Students come from 22 states and territories, 5 other countries, 16% are from out of state, 13% transferred in, 56% live on campus. *Retention:* 61% of 2002 full-time freshmen returned.

Freshmen *Admission:* 509 applied, 281 admitted, 121 enrolled. *Average high school GPA:* 3.03. *Test scores:* SAT verbal scores over 500: 52%; SAT math scores over 500: 42%; ACT scores over 18: 63%; SAT verbal scores over 600: 16%; SAT math scores over 600: 7%; ACT scores over 24: 12%; SAT verbal scores over 700: 1%; ACT scores over 30: 1%.

Faculty *Total:* 81, 37% full-time, 43% with terminal degrees. *Student/faculty ratio:* 12:1.

Majors Accounting; art; biology/biological sciences; business administration and management; chemistry; dance; dramatic/theatre arts; education (K-12); elementary education; English; environmental studies; equestrian studies; fine/studio arts; French; German; international business/trade/commerce; Italian; legal assistant/paralegal; mathematics; modern languages; music; pre-dentistry studies; pre-law studies; pre-medical studies; pre-veterinary studies; psychology; social sciences; sociology; Spanish.

Academic Programs *Special study options:* academic remediation for entering students, accelerated degree program, adult/continuing education programs, advanced placement credit, cooperative education, double majors, external degree program, independent study, internships, off-campus study, part-time degree program, services for LD students, student-designed majors, study abroad, summer session for credit.

Library Lincoln Library plus 2 others with 86,600 titles, 6,020 serial subscriptions, 1,093 audiovisual materials, an OPAC, a Web page.

Computers on Campus 104 computers available on campus for general student use. A campuswide network can be accessed from student residence rooms and from off campus. Internet access, online (class) registration, at least one staffed computer lab available.

Student Life *Housing:* on-campus residence required through sophomore year. *Options:* coed, men-only, women-only. Campus housing is university owned. Freshman campus housing is guaranteed. *Activities and organizations:* drama/theater group, student-run newspaper, radio station, choral group, Delta Kappa Psi, Student Government Association, Mortar Board, IHSA, Activities Council. *Campus security:* 24-hour emergency response devices and patrols, late-night transport/escort service. *Student services:* personal/psychological counseling, legal services.

Athletics Member NCAA. All Division III. *Intercollegiate sports:* baseball M, basketball M/W, cross-country running M/W, golf M, soccer M/W, softball W, volleyball W. *Intramural sports:* basketball M/W, cheerleading W, equestrian sports M/W, fencing M/W, skiing (downhill) M/W, soccer M/W, softball W, tennis M/W, volleyball W.

Standardized Tests *Required:* SAT I or ACT (for admission).

Costs (2003–04) *Comprehensive fee:* $23,550 includes full-time tuition ($16,880), mandatory fees ($840), and room and board ($5830). Full-time tuition and fees vary according to course load and program. Part-time tuition: $460 per credit hour. *Required fees:* $25 per credit hour part-time. *College room only:* $3120. Room and board charges vary according to board plan. *Payment plan:* installment. *Waivers:* senior citizens and employees or children of employees.

Financial Aid Of all full-time matriculated undergraduates who enrolled in 2003, 565 applied for aid. 151 Federal Work-Study jobs (averaging $1211). 76 state and other part-time jobs (averaging $951). *Average percent of need met:* 90%. *Average indebtedness upon graduation:* $17,125.

Applying *Options:* common application, electronic application, early admission. *Application fee:* $25. *Required:* high school transcript, minimum 2.0 GPA. *Recommended:* interview. *Notification:* continuous (freshmen), continuous (transfers).

Admissions Contact Lake Erie College, 391 West Washington Street, Painesville, OH 44077-3389. *Phone:* 440-375-7055. *Toll-free phone:* 800-916-0904. *Fax:* 440-375-7005. *E-mail:* admissions@lec.edu.

■ *See page 1838 for a narrative description.*

LAURA AND ALVIN SIEGAL COLLEGE OF JUDAIC STUDIES
Beachwood, Ohio

- **Independent** comprehensive, founded 1963
- **Calendar** semesters
- **Degrees** bachelor's and master's
- **Suburban** 2-acre campus with easy access to Cleveland
- **Coed,** 17 undergraduate students, 18% full-time, 88% women, 12% men
- **Noncompetitive** entrance level, 80% of applicants were admitted

Undergraduates 3 full-time, 14 part-time. Students come from 1 other state, 0.1% are from out of state. *Retention:* 100% of 2002 full-time freshmen returned.

Freshmen *Admission:* 5 applied, 4 admitted, 4 enrolled.

Faculty *Total:* 40, 28% full-time, 53% with terminal degrees. *Student/faculty ratio:* 8:1.

Majors Ancient Near Eastern and biblical languages; biblical studies; Hebrew; history; Jewish/Judaic studies; religious studies; theology.

Academic Programs *Special study options:* adult/continuing education programs, cooperative education, distance learning, double majors, external degree program, independent study, internships, off-campus study, part-time degree program, summer session for credit.

Library Aaron Garber Library with 28,000 titles, 100 serial subscriptions, an OPAC.

Computers on Campus 8 computers available on campus for general student use.

Laura and Alvin Siegal College of Judaic Studies (continued)

Student Life *Housing:* college housing not available. *Activities and organizations:* "YES"-Young Educators and Scholars. *Campus security:* 24-hour emergency response devices, 24-hour ID check at all doors.

Costs (2003–04) *Tuition:* $9750 full-time, $325 per credit part-time. Full-time tuition and fees vary according to course load. Part-time tuition and fees vary according to course load. *Required fees:* $25 full-time, $25 per year part-time. *Payment plan:* installment. *Waivers:* employees or children of employees.

Financial Aid Of all full-time matriculated undergraduates who enrolled in 2003, 3 applied for aid, 3 were judged to have need. *Average financial aid package:* $500. *Average need-based gift aid:* $500.

Applying *Options:* common application, deferred entrance. *Application fee:* $50. *Required:* essay or personal statement, high school transcript, 2 letters of recommendation, interview. *Application deadline:* rolling (freshmen), rolling (transfers). *Notification:* continuous (freshmen), continuous (transfers).

Admissions Contact Ms. Linda L. Rosen, Director of Student services, Laura and Alvin Siegal College of Judaic Studies, 26500 Shaker Boulevard, Beachwood, OH 44122-7116. *Phone:* 216-464-4050 Ext. 101. *Toll-free phone:* 888-336-2257. *Fax:* 216-464-5827. *E-mail:* admissions@siegalcollege.edu.

LOURDES COLLEGE

Sylvania, Ohio

- **Independent Roman Catholic** comprehensive, founded 1958
- **Calendar** semesters
- **Degrees** certificates, associate, bachelor's, and master's
- **Suburban** 90-acre campus with easy access to Toledo
- **Endowment** $2.9 million
- **Coed,** 1,202 undergraduate students, 41% full-time, 84% women, 16% men
- **Moderately difficult** entrance level, 25% of applicants were admitted

Undergraduates 495 full-time, 707 part-time. Students come from 2 states and territories, 1 other country, 9% are from out of state, 14% African American, 0.4% Asian American or Pacific Islander, 2% Hispanic American, 0.8% Native American, 0.1% international, 12% transferred in. *Retention:* 56% of 2002 full-time freshmen returned.

Freshmen *Admission:* 283 applied, 70 admitted, 62 enrolled. *Average high school GPA:* 2.83. *Test scores:* SAT math scores over 500: 50%; ACT scores over 18: 74%; SAT math scores over 600: 50%; ACT scores over 24: 9%.

Faculty *Total:* 125, 48% full-time, 26% with terminal degrees. *Student/faculty ratio:* 14:1.

Majors Accounting; art; art history, criticism and conservation; biology/biological sciences; business administration and management; chemistry; criminal justice/law enforcement administration; English; history; kindergarten/preschool education; liberal arts and sciences/liberal studies; management science; middle school education; music; natural sciences; nursing (registered nurse training); pre-medical studies; psychology; religious studies; social work; sociology.

Academic Programs *Special study options:* academic remediation for entering students, accelerated degree program, adult/continuing education programs, advanced placement credit, cooperative education, double majors, independent study, internships, part-time degree program, services for LD students, student-designed majors, study abroad, summer session for credit. *ROTC:* Army (c).

Library Duns Scotus Library plus 1 other with 57,730 titles, 448 serial subscriptions, 1,571 audiovisual materials, an OPAC, a Web page.

Computers on Campus 125 computers available on campus for general student use. A campuswide network can be accessed from off campus. Internet access, at least one staffed computer lab available. Computer purchase or lease plan available.

Student Life *Housing:* college housing not available. *Activities and organizations:* drama/theater group, student-run newspaper, choral group, Future Educators Association, Student Leader Advisory Council, Lourdes College Chorus, Student Nurse Association, Campus Ministry Organization. *Campus security:* 24-hour emergency response devices, late-night transport/escort service, evening patrols by trained security personnel. *Student services:* personal/psychological counseling.

Athletics *Intramural sports:* badminton M, baseball M/W, basketball M/W, bowling M/W, football M, golf M/W, soccer M/W, table tennis M/W, tennis M/W, volleyball M/W.

Standardized Tests *Required:* SAT I or ACT (for admission).

Costs (2003–04) *Tuition:* $14,200 full-time, $330 per credit hour part-time. Full-time tuition and fees vary according to course load and program. Part-time tuition and fees vary according to course load and program. *Required fees:* $900 full-time, $40 per credit hour part-time. *Payment plans:* installment, deferred payment. *Waivers:* senior citizens and employees or children of employees.

Financial Aid Of all full-time matriculated undergraduates who enrolled in 2003, 495 applied for aid, 403 were judged to have need, 321 had their need fully met. *Average percent of need met:* 89%. *Average financial aid package:* $13,596.

Applying *Options:* common application, early admission, deferred entrance. *Application fee:* $25. *Required:* high school transcript. *Required for some:* interview. *Application deadline:* rolling (freshmen), rolling (transfers). *Notification:* continuous (freshmen), continuous (transfers).

Admissions Contact Ms. Amy Mergen, Office of Admissions, Lourdes College, 6832 Convent Boulevard, Sylvania, OH 43560. *Phone:* 419-885-5291. *Toll-free phone:* 800-878-3210 Ext. 1299. *Fax:* 419-882-3987. *E-mail:* lcadmits@lourdes.edu.

MALONE COLLEGE

Canton, Ohio

- **Independent** comprehensive, founded 1892, affiliated with Evangelical Friends Church–Eastern Region
- **Calendar** semesters
- **Degrees** bachelor's and master's
- **Suburban** 78-acre campus with easy access to Cleveland
- **Endowment** $5.5 million
- **Coed,** 1,937 undergraduate students, 86% full-time, 61% women, 39% men
- **Moderately difficult** entrance level, 85% of applicants were admitted

Malone College is a Christian college committed to offering an education of the highest quality in a setting that encourages a solid devotion to God. The combination of strong academics, great location, and spiritual development makes Malone an attractive and challenging opportunity for students.

Undergraduates 1,660 full-time, 277 part-time. Students come from 24 states and territories, 12 other countries, 10% are from out of state, 6% African American, 0.4% Asian American or Pacific Islander, 0.8% Hispanic American, 0.1% Native American, 0.7% international, 4% transferred in, 49% live on campus. *Retention:* 75% of 2002 full-time freshmen returned.

Freshmen *Admission:* 992 applied, 842 admitted, 401 enrolled. *Average high school GPA:* 3.35. *Test scores:* SAT verbal scores over 500: 69%; SAT math scores over 500: 61%; ACT scores over 18: 90%; SAT verbal scores over 600: 30%; SAT math scores over 600: 22%; ACT scores over 24: 35%; SAT verbal scores over 700: 3%; SAT math scores over 700: 5%; ACT scores over 30: 4%.

Faculty *Total:* 199, 50% full-time, 39% with terminal degrees. *Student/faculty ratio:* 14:1.

Majors Accounting; art teacher education; biblical studies; biology/biological sciences; business administration and management; business administration, management and operations related; chemistry; clinical laboratory science/medical technology; communication and journalism related; computer science; early childhood education; English; English/language arts teacher education; fine/studio arts; health and physical education; health teacher education; history; kinesiology and exercise science; liberal arts and sciences and humanities related; mathematics; middle school education; music; music related; music teacher education; nursing (registered nurse training); parks, recreation, and leisure related; pastoral counseling and specialized ministries related; physical education teaching and coaching; political science and government; psychology; public health education and promotion; public health related; religious education; religious/sacred music; science teacher education; social studies teacher education; social work; Spanish; Spanish language teacher education; special education (specific learning disabilities); sport and fitness administration; youth ministry.

Academic Programs *Special study options:* academic remediation for entering students, accelerated degree program, adult/continuing education programs, advanced placement credit, cooperative education, distance learning, double majors, honors programs, independent study, internships, off-campus study, part-time degree program, services for LD students, student-designed majors, study abroad, summer session for credit. *ROTC:* Army (c), Air Force (c).

Library Everett L. Cattell Library with 158,974 titles, 1,517 serial subscriptions, 9,693 audiovisual materials, an OPAC.

Computers on Campus 197 computers available on campus for general student use. A campuswide network can be accessed from student residence rooms and from off campus. Internet access, at least one staffed computer lab available.

Student Life *Housing:* on-campus residence required through junior year. *Options:* men-only, women-only. Campus housing is university owned. Freshman applicants given priority for college housing. *Activities and organizations:* drama/theater group, student-run newspaper, radio station, choral group, marching band, Spiritual Life Committee, Student Activities Council, Student Senate, Woolman-Whittier-Fox Hall Council, intramural athletics. *Campus security:* 24-hour emergency response devices and patrols, late-night transport/escort service. *Student services:* health clinic, personal/psychological counseling.

Athletics Member NAIA, NCCAA. *Intercollegiate sports:* baseball M(s), basketball M(s)/W(s), cheerleading M/W, cross-country running M(s)/W(s), football M(s), golf M(s)/W(s), soccer M(s)/W(s), softball W(s), tennis M(s)/W(s), track and field M(s)/W(s), volleyball W(s). *Intramural sports:* badminton M/W, basketball M/W, bowling M/W, cross-country running M/W, football M, racquetball M/W, skiing (cross-country) M/W, soccer M/W, softball M/W, table tennis M/W, tennis M/W, ultimate Frisbee M/W, volleyball M/W, weight lifting M/W.

Standardized Tests *Required:* SAT I or ACT (for admission).

Costs (2003–04) *Comprehensive fee:* $20,995 includes full-time tuition ($14,745), mandatory fees ($250), and room and board ($6000). Part-time tuition: $315 per semester hour. Part-time tuition and fees vary according to course load. *Required fees:* $63 per term part-time. *College room only:* $3200. Room and board charges vary according to board plan. *Payment plan:* installment. *Waivers:* senior citizens and employees or children of employees.

Financial Aid Of all full-time matriculated undergraduates who enrolled in 2003, 1,379 applied for aid, 1,231 were judged to have need, 242 had their need fully met. 324 Federal Work-Study jobs (averaging $1796). 68 state and other part-time jobs (averaging $2213). In 2003, 150 non-need-based awards were made. *Average percent of need met:* 75%. *Average financial aid package:* $11,365. *Average need-based loan:* $3517. *Average need-based gift aid:* $7708. *Average non-need-based aid:* $3995. *Average indebtedness upon graduation:* $16,465. *Financial aid deadline:* 7/31.

Applying *Options:* common application, electronic application, early admission, deferred entrance. *Application fee:* $20. *Required:* essay or personal statement, high school transcript, minimum 2.5 GPA. *Required for some:* interview. *Application deadlines:* 7/1 (freshmen), 7/1 (transfers). *Notification:* continuous (freshmen), continuous (transfers).

Admissions Contact Mr. John Russell, Director of Admissions, Malone College, 515 25th Street, NW, Canton, OH 44709-3897. *Phone:* 330-471-8145 Ext. 8139. *Toll-free phone:* 800-521-1146. *Fax:* 330-471-8149. *E-mail:* admissions@malone.edu.

■ *See page 1912 for a narrative description.*

MARIETTA COLLEGE
Marietta, Ohio

- **Independent** comprehensive, founded 1835
- **Calendar** semesters
- **Degrees** certificates, associate, bachelor's, and master's
- **Small-town** 120-acre campus
- **Endowment** $37.5 million
- **Coed,** 1,222 undergraduate students, 94% full-time, 49% women, 51% men
- **Moderately difficult** entrance level, 78% of applicants were admitted

Undergraduates 1,144 full-time, 78 part-time. Students come from 42 states and territories, 13 other countries, 50% are from out of state, 2% African American, 4% Asian American or Pacific Islander, 1% Hispanic American, 0.7% Native American, 6% international, 5% transferred in, 85% live on campus. *Retention:* 77% of 2002 full-time freshmen returned.

Freshmen *Admission:* 1,912 applied, 1,486 admitted, 378 enrolled. *Average high school GPA:* 3.30. *Test scores:* SAT verbal scores over 500: 70%; SAT math scores over 500: 62%; ACT scores over 18: 96%; SAT verbal scores over 600: 24%; SAT math scores over 600: 21%; ACT scores over 24: 41%; SAT verbal scores over 700: 3%; SAT math scores over 700: 3%; ACT scores over 30: 5%.

Faculty *Total:* 116, 67% full-time, 66% with terminal degrees. *Student/faculty ratio:* 12:1.

Majors Accounting; art; athletic training; biochemistry; biology/biological sciences; business administration and management; business/corporate communications; chemistry; commercial and advertising art; communication/speech communication and rhetoric; computer science; dramatic/theatre arts; economics; education; elementary education; English; environmental science; environmental studies; fine/studio arts; geology/earth science; graphic design; history; human resources management; information science/studies; international business/trade/commerce; journalism; liberal arts and sciences/liberal studies; marketing/marketing management; mathematics; music; petroleum engineering; philosophy; physics; political science and government; psychology; public relations, advertising, and applied communication related; radio and television; secondary education; Spanish; speech and rhetoric.

Academic Programs *Special study options:* academic remediation for entering students, accelerated degree program, adult/continuing education programs, advanced placement credit, double majors, English as a second language, honors programs, independent study, internships, off-campus study, part-time degree program, services for LD students, student-designed majors, study abroad, summer session for credit. *Unusual degree programs:* 3-2 engineering with University of Pennsylvania, Columbia University, Case Western Reserve University, Washington University in St. Louis.

Library Dawes Memorial Library with 250,000 titles, 7,100 serial subscriptions, 5,800 audiovisual materials, an OPAC, a Web page.

Computers on Campus 200 computers available on campus for general student use. A campuswide network can be accessed from student residence rooms and from off campus. Internet access, at least one staffed computer lab available.

Student Life *Housing:* on-campus residence required through senior year. *Options:* coed, men-only, women-only. Campus housing is university owned and is provided by a third party. Freshman campus housing is guaranteed. *Activities and organizations:* drama/theater group, student-run newspaper, radio and television station, choral group, Student Programming Board, student government, Great Outdoors Club, Inter-Varsity Christian Fellowship, Arts and Humanities Council, national fraternities, national sororities. *Campus security:* 24-hour emergency response devices and patrols, student patrols, late-night transport/escort service, controlled dormitory access. *Student services:* health clinic, personal/psychological counseling.

Athletics Member NCAA. All Division III. *Intercollegiate sports:* baseball M, basketball M/W, cheerleading W(c), crew M/W, cross-country running M/W, football M, lacrosse M(c), soccer M/W, softball W, tennis M/W, track and field M/W, volleyball W. *Intramural sports:* badminton M/W, basketball M/W, bowling M/W, cross-country running M/W, football M/W, racquetball M/W, rock climbing M/W, rugby M(c)/W(c), soccer M/W, softball M/W, swimming M/W, tennis M/W, ultimate Frisbee M/W, volleyball M/W, weight lifting M.

Standardized Tests *Required:* SAT I or ACT (for admission). *Recommended:* SAT II: Subject Tests (for admission).

Costs (2003–04) *Comprehensive fee:* $26,838 includes full-time tuition ($20,356), mandatory fees ($536), and room and board ($5946). Part-time tuition: $676 per credit. Part-time tuition and fees vary according to class time. *College room only:* $3176. Room and board charges vary according to board plan. *Payment plan:* installment. *Waivers:* employees or children of employees.

Financial Aid Of all full-time matriculated undergraduates who enrolled in 2003, 998 applied for aid, 890 were judged to have need, 438 had their need fully met. 431 Federal Work-Study jobs (averaging $928). In 2003, 179 non-need-based awards were made. *Average percent of need met:* 91%. *Average financial aid package:* $17,671. *Average need-based loan:* $3258. *Average need-based gift aid:* $6200. *Average non-need-based aid:* $6400. *Average indebtedness upon graduation:* $17,643.

Applying *Options:* common application, electronic application, early admission, deferred entrance. *Application fee:* $25. *Required:* essay or personal statement, high school transcript, minimum 2.0 GPA, 2 letters of recommendation. *Recommended:* minimum 3.0 GPA, interview. *Application deadline:* 4/15 (freshmen), rolling (transfers). *Notification:* continuous until 5/1 (freshmen), continuous (transfers).

Admissions Contact Ms. Marke Vickers, Director of Admission, Marietta College, 215 Fifth Street, Marietta, OH 45750. *Phone:* 740-376-4600. *Toll-free phone:* 800-331-7896. *Fax:* 740-376-8888. *E-mail:* admit@marietta.edu.

■ *See page 1928 for a narrative description.*

MEDCENTRAL COLLEGE OF NURSING
Mansfield, Ohio

- **Independent** 4-year, founded 1996
- **Calendar** quarters
- **Degree** bachelor's
- **Coed, primarily women,** 153 undergraduate students, 72% full-time, 90% women, 10% men
- 58% of applicants were admitted

Undergraduates 110 full-time, 43 part-time. Students come from 1 other state, 0.1% are from out of state, 1% Asian American or Pacific Islander, 0.7% Native American, 13% live on campus.

Freshmen *Admission:* 101 applied, 59 admitted, 59 enrolled. *Average high school GPA:* 3.32.

Faculty *Total:* 8, 88% full-time. *Student/faculty ratio:* 15:1.

Majors Nursing (registered nurse training).

Student Life *Housing options:* coed. Campus housing is university owned. Freshman applicants given priority for college housing. *Student services:* health clinic.

Standardized Tests *Required:* SAT I or ACT (for admission).

Costs (2003–04) *Tuition:* $6658 full-time.

Applying *Application fee:* $50. *Required:* high school transcript, minimum 2.6 GPA. *Required for some:* essay or personal statement, interview. *Recommended:* minimum 3.0 GPA. *Application deadlines:* 8/1 (freshmen), 8/1 (transfers). *Notification:* continuous until 8/15 (freshmen), continuous (transfers).

Admissions Contact Mr. Mark A. Fegley, Associate Director for Enrollment Services, MedCentral College of Nursing, 335 Glessner Avenue, Mansfield, OH 44903. *Phone:* 877-656-4360. *Toll-free phone:* 877-656-4360. *Fax:* 419-520-2610. *E-mail:* mfegley@medcentral.edu.

Mercy College of Northwest Ohio
Toledo, Ohio

- **Independent** primarily 2-year, founded 1993, affiliated with Roman Catholic Church
- **Calendar** semesters
- **Degrees** certificates, associate, and bachelor's
- **Urban** campus with easy access to Detroit
- **Endowment** $2.2 million
- **Coed, primarily women**
- **Moderately difficult** entrance level

Faculty *Student/faculty ratio:* 13:1.

Student Life *Campus security:* 24-hour patrols, late-night transport/escort service, controlled dormitory access.

Standardized Tests *Required for some:* SAT I or ACT (for admission). *Recommended:* SAT I or ACT (for admission).

Costs (2003–04) *One-time required fee:* $60. *Tuition:* $6234 full-time, $242 per credit hour part-time. Full-time tuition and fees vary according to course load. Part-time tuition and fees vary according to course load. *Required fees:* $160 full-time, $5 per credit hour part-time. *Room only:* $2800. Room and board charges vary according to housing facility.

Financial Aid Of all full-time matriculated undergraduates who enrolled in 2001, 18 Federal Work-Study jobs.

Applying *Application fee:* $25. *Required:* high school transcript. *Required for some:* minimum 2.3 GPA.

Admissions Contact Ms. Janice Bernard, Secretary, Mercy College of Northwest Ohio, 2221 Madison Avenue, Toledo, OH 43624-1197. *Phone:* 419-251-1313 Ext. 11723. *Toll-free phone:* 888-80-Mercy. *Fax:* 419-251-1462. *E-mail:* admissions@mercycollege.edu.

Miami University
Oxford, Ohio

- **State-related** university, founded 1809, part of Miami University System
- **Calendar** semesters
- **Degrees** associate, bachelor's, master's, doctoral, and post-master's certificates
- **Small-town** 2000-acre campus with easy access to Cincinnati
- **Endowment** $223.4 million
- **Coed,** 15,174 undergraduate students, 97% full-time, 54% women, 46% men
- **Moderately difficult** entrance level, 71% of applicants were admitted

Undergraduates 14,786 full-time, 388 part-time. Students come from 48 states and territories, 59 other countries, 28% are from out of state, 4% African American, 2% Asian American or Pacific Islander, 2% Hispanic American, 0.5% Native American, 0.8% international, 2% transferred in, 45% live on campus. *Retention:* 90% of 2001 full-time freshmen returned.

Freshmen *Admission:* 13,859 applied, 9,842 admitted, 3,309 enrolled. *Test scores:* SAT verbal scores over 500: 97%; SAT math scores over 500: 98%; ACT scores over 18: 99%; SAT verbal scores over 600: 55%; SAT math scores over 600: 70%; ACT scores over 24: 87%; SAT verbal scores over 700: 8%; SAT math scores over 700: 11%; ACT scores over 30: 18%.

Faculty *Total:* 1,137, 73% full-time, 73% with terminal degrees. *Student/faculty ratio:* 18:1.

Majors Accounting; aerospace, aeronautical and astronautical engineering; African-American/Black studies; American studies; ancient/classical Greek; anthropology; architecture; art; art history, criticism and conservation; art teacher education; athletic training; audiology and speech-language pathology; biochemistry; biology/biological sciences; biology teacher education; botany/plant biology; business administration and management; business/commerce; business/managerial economics; chemistry; child development; city/urban, community and regional planning; classics and languages, literatures and linguistics; clinical laboratory science/medical technology; computer and information sciences; computer systems analysis; creative writing; dietetics; dramatic/theatre arts; economics; electrical, electronics and communications engineering; elementary education; engineering/industrial management; engineering physics; engineering technology; English; English/language arts teacher education; environmental design/architecture; family and consumer economics related; family and consumer sciences/home economics teacher education; family and consumer sciences/human sciences; finance; fine/studio arts; French; geography; geology/earth science; German; health and physical education; health teacher education; history; human development and family studies; human resources management; industrial engineering; interdisciplinary studies; interior design; international relations and affairs; journalism; kindergarten/preschool education; kinesiology and exercise science; Latin; linguistics; management information systems; management science; marketing/marketing management; mass communication/media; mathematics; mechanical engineering; medical microbiology and bacteriology; middle school education; multi-/interdisciplinary studies related; music; music performance; music teacher education; nursing (registered nurse training); operations management; operations research; organizational behavior; philosophy; physical education teaching and coaching; physics; political science and government; pre-dentistry studies; pre-law studies; pre-medical studies; pre-veterinary studies; psychology; public administration; purchasing, procurement/acquisitions and contracts management; religious studies; Russian; science teacher education; secondary education; social studies teacher education; social work; sociology; Spanish; special education; speech and rhetoric; speech-language pathology; sport and fitness administration; statistics; systems science and theory; technical and business writing; wood science and wood products/pulp and paper technology; zoology/animal biology.

Academic Programs *Special study options:* adult/continuing education programs, advanced placement credit, cooperative education, double majors, honors programs, independent study, internships, off-campus study, services for LD students, student-designed majors, study abroad, summer session for credit. *ROTC:* Army (c), Navy (b), Air Force (b). *Unusual degree programs:* 3-2 engineering with Case Western Reserve University, Columbia University; forestry with Duke University.

Library King Library plus 3 others with 2.7 million titles, 14,089 serial subscriptions, 143,868 audiovisual materials, an OPAC, a Web page.

Computers on Campus 1000 computers available on campus for general student use. A campuswide network can be accessed from student residence rooms and from off campus. Internet access, online (class) registration, at least one staffed computer lab available.

Student Life *Housing:* on-campus residence required for freshman year. *Options:* coed, men-only, women-only, disabled students. Campus housing is university owned. Freshman campus housing is guaranteed. *Activities and organizations:* drama/theater group, student-run newspaper, radio and television station, choral group, marching band, student government, Alpha Phi Omega, Miami Marketing Enterprises, Campus Crusade for Christ, national fraternities, national sororities. *Campus security:* 24-hour emergency response devices and patrols, student patrols, late-night transport/escort service, controlled dormitory access. *Student services:* health clinic, personal/psychological counseling, women's center.

Athletics Member NCAA. All Division I except football (Division I-A). *Intercollegiate sports:* archery M(c)/W(c), baseball M(s), basketball M(s)/W(s), cross-country running M(s)/W(s), equestrian sports M(c)/W(c), fencing M(c)/W(c), field hockey W(s), golf M(s), gymnastics M(c)/W(c), ice hockey M(s), lacrosse M(c), racquetball M(c)/W(c), rugby M(c), sailing M(c)/W(c), soccer M(c)/W(s), softball W(s), swimming M(s)/W(s), tennis M(c)/W(s), track and field M(s)/W(s), volleyball M(c)/W(s), wrestling M(c). *Intramural sports:* archery M/W, badminton M(c)/W(c), basketball M/W, cheerleading M(c)/W(c), crew M(c)/W(c), cross-country running M(c)/W(c), equestrian sports M(c)/W(c), fencing M(c)/W(c), field hockey W, football M/W, golf M(c)/W(c), gymnastics M(c)/W(c), ice hockey M(c)/W(c), lacrosse M(c)/W(c), racquetball M(c)/W(c), rugby M(c), sailing M/W, skiing (cross-country) M/W, skiing (downhill) M(c)/W(c), soccer M(c)/W(c), softball M/W, squash M(c)/W(c), swimming M/W, table tennis M(c)/W(c), tennis M(c)/W(c), track and field M/W, ultimate Frisbee M(c)/W(c), volleyball M(c)/W(c), water polo M(c)/W(c), weight lifting M(c)/W(c), wrestling M(c).

Standardized Tests *Required:* SAT I or ACT (for admission).

Costs (2003–04) *Tuition:* state resident $7019 full-time; nonresident $16,789 full-time. *Required fees:* $1334 full-time. *Room and board:* $6680; room only: $3340. *Payment plans:* tuition prepayment, installment. *Waivers:* employees or children of employees.

Financial Aid Of all full-time matriculated undergraduates who enrolled in 2003, 7,115 applied for aid, 4,886 were judged to have need, 1,088 had their need fully met. 1,136 Federal Work-Study jobs (averaging $1603). In 2003, 2138 non-need-based awards were made. *Average percent of need met:* 67%. *Average financial aid package:* $7090. *Average need-based loan:* $3723. *Average need-based gift aid:* $4217. *Average non-need-based aid:* $4539. *Average indebtedness upon graduation:* $18,302.

Applying *Options:* common application, electronic application, early decision. *Application fee:* $45. *Required:* high school transcript. *Recommended:* essay or personal statement, 1 letter of recommendation. *Application deadlines:* 1/31 (freshmen), 5/1 (transfers). *Early decision:* 11/1. *Notification:* 3/15 (freshmen), 12/15 (early decision), continuous (transfers).

Admissions Contact Mr. Michael E. Mills, Director of Undergraduate Admissions, Miami University, 301 South Campus Avenue, Oxford, OH 45056. *Phone:* 513-529-2531. *Fax:* 513-529-1550. *E-mail:* admission@muohio.edu.

MIAMI UNIVERSITY HAMILTON
Hamilton, Ohio

- **State-supported** founded 1968, part of Miami University System
- **Calendar** semesters plus summer sessions
- **Degrees** certificates, associate, bachelor's, and master's (degrees awarded by Miami University main campus)
- **Suburban** 78-acre campus with easy access to Cincinnati
- **Coed,** 3,322 undergraduate students, 43% full-time, 57% women, 43% men
- **Noncompetitive** entrance level, 99% of applicants were admitted

Undergraduates 1,427 full-time, 1,895 part-time. 6% African American, 2% Asian American or Pacific Islander, 1% Hispanic American, 0.3% Native American, 4% transferred in.

Freshmen *Admission:* 968 applied, 962 admitted, 649 enrolled.

Faculty *Total:* 222, 41% full-time. *Student/faculty ratio:* 15:1.

Majors Accounting; American studies; anthropology; architectural history and criticism; architecture; art; art teacher education; athletic training; audiology and speech-language pathology; biochemistry; botany/plant biology related; business administration and management; business administration, management and operations related; business/commerce; business/managerial economics; chemistry; chemistry teacher education; city/urban, community and regional planning; classics and languages, literatures and linguistics; clinical laboratory science/medical technology; communication/speech communication and rhetoric; computer and information sciences related; computer engineering; computer science; computer systems analysis; computer technology/computer systems technology; creative writing; dietetics; early childhood education; econometrics and quantitative economics; economics; education (multiple levels); electrical and electronic engineering technologies related; electromechanical technology; engineering/industrial management; engineering physics; engineering technology; English; English composition; English/language arts teacher education; environmental science; environmental studies; ethnic, cultural minority, and gender studies related; exercise physiology; finance; French; French language teacher education; general studies; geography; geology/earth science; German; German language teacher education; gerontology; graphic design; health teacher education; history; human resources management and services related; interior design; international/global studies; journalism; Latin; Latin teacher education; linguistics; management information systems; marketing/marketing management; marketing related; mass communication/media; mathematics; mathematics and statistics related; mathematics teacher education; mechanical engineering/mechanical technology; microbiology; multi-/interdisciplinary studies related; music; music teacher education; office management; philosophy; physical education teaching and coaching; physics; physics teacher education; political science and government; psychology; public administration; purchasing, procurement/acquisitions and contracts management; real estate; Russian; science teacher education; social studies teacher education; social work related; sociology; Spanish; Spanish language teacher education; special education; speech-language pathology; statistics; technical and business writing; theatre/theatre arts management; work and family studies; zoology/animal biology.

Academic Programs *Special study options:* academic remediation for entering students, adult/continuing education programs, advanced placement credit, cooperative education, double majors, English as a second language, honors programs, internships, part-time degree program, services for LD students, student-designed majors, study abroad, summer session for credit. *ROTC:* Navy (c), Air Force (c).

Library Rentschler Library with 68,000 titles, 400 serial subscriptions, an OPAC, a Web page.

Computers on Campus 250 computers available on campus for general student use. A campuswide network can be accessed from off campus. Internet access, online (class) registration, at least one staffed computer lab available.

Student Life *Housing:* college housing not available. *Activities and organizations:* drama/theater group, choral group, student government, Campus Activities Committee, Ski Club, Student Nursing Association, Minority Action Committee. *Campus security:* 24-hour emergency response devices and patrols, late-night transport/escort service. *Student services:* personal/psychological counseling.

Athletics *Intercollegiate sports:* baseball M, basketball M/W, cheerleading W, golf M, tennis M/W, volleyball W. *Intramural sports:* basketball M/W, bowling M/W, skiing (cross-country) M/W, soccer M/W, softball M/W, tennis M/W, volleyball M/W, weight lifting M/W.

Standardized Tests *Required for some:* SAT I or ACT (for placement).

Costs (2003–04) *Tuition:* state resident $3150 full-time, $131 per credit part-time; nonresident $12,901 full-time, $538 per credit part-time. *Required fees:* $382 full-time, $15 per credit part-time, $17 per term part-time. *Payment plan:* installment. *Waivers:* employees or children of employees.

Applying *Options:* electronic application. *Application fee:* $25. *Required:* high school transcript. *Application deadline:* rolling (freshmen). *Notification:* continuous (freshmen), continuous (transfers).

Admissions Contact Ms. Triana Adlon, Director of Admission and Financial Aid, Miami University Hamilton, 1601 Peck Boulevard, Hamilton, OH 45011-3399. *Phone:* 513-785-3111. *Fax:* 513-785-3148. *E-mail:* adlontm@muohio.edu.

MIAMI UNIVERSITY–MIDDLETOWN CAMPUS
Middletown, Ohio

- **State-supported** primarily 2-year, founded 1966, part of Miami University System
- **Calendar** semesters
- **Degrees** certificates, diplomas, associate, and bachelor's (also offers up to 2 years of most bachelor's degree programs offered at Miami University main campus)
- **Small-town** 141-acre campus with easy access to Cincinnati and Dayton
- **Endowment** $779,742
- **Coed**
- **Noncompetitive** entrance level

Faculty *Student/faculty ratio:* 13:1.

Student Life *Campus security:* 24-hour patrols, late-night transport/escort service.

Standardized Tests *Recommended:* SAT I or ACT (for placement).

Costs (2003–04) *Tuition:* state resident $3498 full-time, $146 per credit hour part-time; nonresident $13,248 full-time, $552 per credit hour part-time. Full-time tuition and fees vary according to student level. Part-time tuition and fees vary according to student level. *Required fees:* $201 full-time.

Applying *Options:* electronic application, early admission, deferred entrance. *Application fee:* $25. *Required:* high school transcript.

Admissions Contact Mrs. Mary Lou Flynn, Director of Enrollment Services, Miami University–Middletown Campus, 4200 East University Boulevard, Middletown, OH 45042. *Phone:* 513-727-3346. *Toll-free phone:* 800-622-2262. *Fax:* 513-727-3223. *E-mail:* flynnml@muohio.edu.

MOUNT CARMEL COLLEGE OF NURSING
Columbus, Ohio

- **Independent** comprehensive
- **Degree** bachelor's
- **Coed, primarily women**
- 71% of applicants were admitted

Faculty *Student/faculty ratio:* 11:1.

Costs (2003–04) *Tuition:* $11,173 full-time. Full-time tuition and fees vary according to student level. Part-time tuition and fees vary according to student level. *Required fees:* $292 full-time. *Room only:* $1870.

Financial Aid Of all full-time matriculated undergraduates who enrolled in 2003, 380 applied for aid, 365 were judged to have need, 100 had their need fully met. 27 state and other part-time jobs (averaging $1930). In 2003, 20. *Average percent of need met:* 70. *Average financial aid package:* $9000. *Average need-based loan:* $7500. *Average need-based gift aid:* $1500. *Average non-need-based aid:* $2000. *Average indebtedness upon graduation:* $25,000.

Applying *Application fee:* $30.

Admissions Contact Ms. Merschel Menefield, Director of Admissions, Mount Carmel College of Nursing, 127 South Davis Avenue, Columbus, OH 43222. *Phone:* 614-234-5800.

MOUNT UNION COLLEGE
Alliance, Ohio

- **Independent United Methodist** 4-year, founded 1846
- **Calendar** semesters
- **Degree** bachelor's
- **Suburban** 105-acre campus with easy access to Cleveland
- **Endowment** $124.3 million
- **Coed,** 2,425 undergraduate students, 87% full-time, 55% women, 45% men
- **Moderately difficult** entrance level, 75% of applicants were admitted

There are numerous international educational opportunities at Mount Union College. In addition to the cultural interaction with students from approximately twelve countries who study at the College, many students take advantage of the study-abroad program, which currently places students in more than 26 countries. The College makes grants available for study overseas, regardless of the student's major.

Mount Union College (continued)

Undergraduates 2,110 full-time, 315 part-time. Students come from 26 states and territories, 12 other countries, 9% are from out of state, 4% African American, 0.3% Asian American or Pacific Islander, 0.5% Hispanic American, 0.2% Native American, 1% international, 8% transferred in, 67% live on campus. *Retention:* 80% of 2002 full-time freshmen returned.

Freshmen *Admission:* 2,177 applied, 1,632 admitted, 586 enrolled. *Average high school GPA:* 3.26. *Test scores:* ACT scores over 18: 94%; ACT scores over 24: 32%; ACT scores over 30: 3%.

Faculty *Total:* 211, 60% full-time, 55% with terminal degrees. *Student/faculty ratio:* 14:1.

Majors Accounting; American studies; art; Asian studies; astronomy; athletic training; biochemistry, biophysics and molecular biology related; biology/biological sciences; business administration and management; chemistry; communication/speech communication and rhetoric; computer science; design and visual communications; dramatic/theatre arts; early childhood education; economics; English; English composition; environmental biology; French; geology/earth science; German; history; information science/studies; interdisciplinary studies; international business/trade/commerce; Japanese; kindergarten/preschool education; kinesiology and exercise science; mass communication/media; mathematics; middle school education; music; music performance; music teacher education; philosophy; physical education teaching and coaching; physics; political science and government; psychology; religious studies; sociology; Spanish; sport and fitness administration.

Academic Programs *Special study options:* accelerated degree program, adult/continuing education programs, advanced placement credit, cooperative education, double majors, English as a second language, external degree program, honors programs, independent study, internships, off-campus study, part-time degree program, services for LD students, student-designed majors, study abroad, summer session for credit. *ROTC:* Army (c), Air Force (c).

Library Mount Union College Library plus 2 others with 228,850 titles, 972 serial subscriptions, 500 audiovisual materials, an OPAC, a Web page.

Computers on Campus 200 computers available on campus for general student use. A campuswide network can be accessed from student residence rooms and from off campus. Internet access, online (class) registration, at least one staffed computer lab available. Computer purchase or lease plan available.

Student Life *Housing:* on-campus residence required through sophomore year. *Options:* coed, men-only, women-only, disabled students. Campus housing is university owned and is provided by a third party. Freshman campus housing is guaranteed. *Activities and organizations:* drama/theater group, student-run newspaper, radio station, choral group, marching band, Association of Women Students, Student Senate, Black Student Union, Student Activities Council, Association of International Students, national fraternities, national sororities. *Campus security:* 24-hour emergency response devices and patrols, 24-hour locked residence hall entrances, outside phones. *Student services:* health clinic, personal/psychological counseling.

Athletics Member NCAA. All Division III. *Intercollegiate sports:* baseball M, basketball M/W, cheerleading W, cross-country running M/W, football M, golf M/W, soccer M/W, softball W, swimming M/W, tennis M/W, track and field M/W, volleyball W, wrestling M. *Intramural sports:* archery M/W, badminton M/W, basketball M/W, bowling M/W, football M, golf M/W, gymnastics M/W, racquetball M/W, soccer M/W, softball M/W, swimming M/W, tennis M/W, track and field M/W, volleyball M/W, weight lifting M/W.

Standardized Tests *Required:* SAT I or ACT (for admission).

Costs (2004–05) *Comprehensive fee:* $24,440 includes full-time tuition ($18,560), mandatory fees ($250), and room and board ($5630). Part-time tuition: $775 per semester hour. *Required fees:* $50 per term part-time. *College room only:* $2360. Room and board charges vary according to housing facility. *Payment plans:* tuition prepayment, installment. *Waivers:* children of alumni, adult students, and employees or children of employees.

Financial Aid Of all full-time matriculated undergraduates who enrolled in 2003, 1,761 applied for aid, 1,636 were judged to have need, 296 had their need fully met. 1,256 Federal Work-Study jobs (averaging $1173). 144 state and other part-time jobs (averaging $1620). In 2003, 374 non-need-based awards were made. *Average percent of need met:* 85%. *Average financial aid package:* $15,324. *Average need-based loan:* $4438. *Average need-based gift aid:* $10,617. *Average non-need-based aid:* $7428. *Average indebtedness upon graduation:* $15,999.

Applying *Options:* electronic application, early admission, deferred entrance. *Application fee:* $20. *Required:* essay or personal statement, high school transcript, minimum 2.0 GPA, 1 letter of recommendation. *Recommended:* interview. *Application deadline:* rolling (freshmen), rolling (transfers). *Notification:* continuous (freshmen), continuous (transfers).

Admissions Contact Mr. Vince Heslop, Director of Admissions, Mount Union College, 1972 Clark Avenue, Alliance, OH 44601. *Phone:* 330-823-2590. *Toll-free phone:* 800-334-6682 (in-state); 800-992-6682 (out-of-state). *Fax:* 330-823-3487. *E-mail:* admissn@muc.edu.

■ *See page 2052 for a narrative description.*

MOUNT VERNON NAZARENE UNIVERSITY

Mount Vernon, Ohio

- **Independent Nazarene** comprehensive, founded 1964
- **Calendar** 4-1-4
- **Degrees** associate, bachelor's, and master's
- **Small-town** 401-acre campus with easy access to Columbus
- **Endowment** $8.3 million
- **Coed,** 2,206 undergraduate students, 88% full-time, 57% women, 43% men
- **Moderately difficult** entrance level, 86% of applicants were admitted

Undergraduates 1,944 full-time, 262 part-time. Students come from 24 states and territories, 10% are from out of state, 3% African American, 0.6% Asian American or Pacific Islander, 0.9% Hispanic American, 0.3% Native American, 0.2% international, 3% transferred in, 75% live on campus. *Retention:* 77% of 2002 full-time freshmen returned.

Freshmen *Admission:* 699 applied, 602 admitted, 375 enrolled. *Average high school GPA:* 3.30. *Test scores:* SAT verbal scores over 500: 70%; SAT math scores over 500: 71%; ACT scores over 18: 89%; SAT verbal scores over 600: 34%; SAT math scores over 600: 28%; ACT scores over 24: 38%; SAT verbal scores over 700: 4%; SAT math scores over 700: 3%; ACT scores over 30: 5%.

Faculty *Total:* 214, 41% full-time, 40% with terminal degrees. *Student/faculty ratio:* 17:1.

Majors Accounting; administrative assistant and secretarial science; applied art; art; art teacher education; biblical studies; biological and physical sciences; biology/biological sciences; broadcast journalism; business/commerce; business teacher education; chemistry; child care and support services management; clinical laboratory science/medical technology; communication/speech communication and rhetoric; computer and information sciences; criminal justice/law enforcement administration; data processing and data processing technology; design and visual communications; dramatic/theatre arts; early childhood education; education; elementary education; English; English/language arts teacher education; family and consumer sciences/home economics teacher education; family and consumer sciences/human sciences; fine arts related; general studies; health and physical education; health teacher education; history; human services; journalism; kindergarten/preschool education; kinesiology and exercise science; literature; marketing/marketing management; mass communication/media; mathematics; mathematics teacher education; middle school education; music; music teacher education; natural resources/conservation; philosophy; physical education teaching and coaching; physical therapy; pre-dentistry studies; pre-law studies; pre-medical studies; pre-pharmacy studies; pre-veterinary studies; psychology; religious education; religious/sacred music; science teacher education; secondary education; social sciences; social studies teacher education; social work; sociology; Spanish; special education; sport and fitness administration; theology.

Academic Programs *Special study options:* academic remediation for entering students, adult/continuing education programs, advanced placement credit, double majors, freshman honors college, honors programs, independent study, internships, off-campus study, part-time degree program, services for LD students, study abroad, summer session for credit.

Library Thorne Library/Learning Resource Center with 92,169 titles, 586 serial subscriptions, 4,744 audiovisual materials, an OPAC, a Web page.

Computers on Campus 217 computers available on campus for general student use. A campuswide network can be accessed from student residence rooms and from off campus. Internet access, at least one staffed computer lab available.

Student Life *Housing:* on-campus residence required through senior year. *Options:* men-only, women-only, disabled students. Campus housing is university owned. Freshman campus housing is guaranteed. *Activities and organizations:* drama/theater group, student-run newspaper, radio station, choral group, campus ministry groups, Student Government Association, Student Education Association, drama club, music department ensembles. *Campus security:* 24-hour emergency response devices and patrols, late-night transport/escort service, controlled dormitory access. *Student services:* health clinic, personal/psychological counseling.

Athletics Member NAIA, NCCAA. *Intercollegiate sports:* baseball M(s), basketball M(s)/W(s), golf M(s), soccer M(s)/W(s), softball W(s), volleyball W(s). *Intramural sports:* basketball M/W, bowling M/W, cheerleading M/W, football M/W, skiing (downhill) M/W, soccer M/W, softball M/W, table tennis M/W, ultimate Frisbee M(c)/W(c), volleyball M/W.

Standardized Tests *Required:* SAT I or ACT (for admission).

Costs (2004–05) *Comprehensive fee:* $19,710 includes full-time tuition ($14,482), mandatory fees ($494), and room and board ($4734). Full-time tuition and fees vary according to course load and program. Part-time tuition and fees vary according to course load and program. *College room only:* $2619. Room and board charges vary according to board plan and housing facility. *Payment plan:* installment. *Waivers:* senior citizens and employees or children of employees.

Financial Aid Of all full-time matriculated undergraduates who enrolled in 2003, 1,325 applied for aid, 1,038 were judged to have need, 275 had their need fully met. 180 Federal Work-Study jobs (averaging $1472). 317 state and other part-time jobs (averaging $1534). In 2003, 815 non-need-based awards were made. *Average percent of need met:* 83%. *Average financial aid package:* $10,581. *Average need-based loan:* $831. *Average need-based gift aid:* $5355. *Average non-need-based aid:* $1406. *Average indebtedness upon graduation:* $17,796.

Applying *Options:* electronic application, early admission, deferred entrance. *Application fee:* $25. *Required:* essay or personal statement, high school transcript, minimum 2.5 GPA, 2 letters of recommendation. *Recommended:* interview. *Application deadline:* 5/31 (freshmen). *Notification:* continuous until 9/1 (freshmen), continuous (transfers).

Admissions Contact Mr. Tim Eades, Director of Admissions and Student Recruitment, Mount Vernon Nazarene University, 800 Martinsburg Road, Mount Vernon, OH 43050. *Phone:* 740-392-6868 Ext. 4511. *Toll-free phone:* 866-462-6868. *Fax:* 740-393-0511. *E-mail:* admissions@mvnu.edu.

MUSKINGUM COLLEGE
New Concord, Ohio

- **Independent** comprehensive, founded 1837, affiliated with Presbyterian Church (U.S.A.)
- **Calendar** semesters
- **Degrees** bachelor's and master's
- **Small-town** 215-acre campus with easy access to Columbus
- **Endowment** $55.7 million
- **Coed**
- **Moderately difficult** entrance level

Faculty *Student/faculty ratio:* 16:1.

Student Life *Campus security:* 24-hour emergency response devices and patrols, student patrols, late-night transport/escort service.

Athletics Member NCAA. All Division III.

Standardized Tests *Required:* SAT I or ACT (for admission).

Costs (2004–05) *Comprehensive fee:* $21,830 includes full-time tuition ($14,920), mandatory fees ($710), and room and board ($6200). Part-time tuition: $280 per credit hour. Part-time tuition and fees vary according to course load. *Room and board:* Room and board charges vary according to board plan and housing facility.

Financial Aid Of all full-time matriculated undergraduates who enrolled in 2003, 1,298 applied for aid, 1,195 were judged to have need, 462 had their need fully met. 620 state and other part-time jobs (averaging $1000). In 2003, 260. *Average percent of need met:* 86. *Average financial aid package:* $13,767. *Average need-based loan:* $4065. *Average need-based gift aid:* $9809. *Average non-need-based aid:* $4649. *Average indebtedness upon graduation:* $18,036.

Applying *Options:* electronic application, early admission, deferred entrance. *Required:* high school transcript, minimum 2.0 GPA, 1 letter of recommendation. *Recommended:* essay or personal statement, minimum 3.0 GPA, interview.

Admissions Contact Mrs. Beth DaLonzo, Director of Admission, Muskingum College, 163 Stormont Street, New Concord, OH 43762. *Phone:* 740-825-8137. *Toll-free phone:* 800-752-6082. *Fax:* 740-826-8100. *E-mail:* adminfo@muskingum.edu.

NOTRE DAME COLLEGE
South Euclid, Ohio

- **Independent Roman Catholic** comprehensive, founded 1922
- **Calendar** semesters
- **Degrees** certificates, associate, bachelor's, master's, and postbachelor's certificates
- **Suburban** 53-acre campus with easy access to Cleveland
- **Endowment** $4.5 million
- **Coed,** 766 undergraduate students, 43% full-time, 76% women, 24% men
- **Moderately difficult** entrance level, 47% of applicants were admitted

NDC is a special place. The focus is on helping students of all ages develop confidence and build self-esteem through a rigorous, yet supportive, career-oriented liberal arts environment. NDC is large enough to provide many of the opportunities of a large college, yet small enough to give students the individual attention important to their development.

Undergraduates 332 full-time, 434 part-time. Students come from 4 states and territories, 17 other countries, 10% are from out of state, 24% African American, 0.7% Asian American or Pacific Islander, 2% Hispanic American, 5% international, 4% transferred in, 34% live on campus. *Retention:* 62% of 2002 full-time freshmen returned.

Freshmen *Admission:* 138 applied, 65 admitted, 64 enrolled. *Average high school GPA:* 2.92. *Test scores:* SAT verbal scores over 500: 80%; SAT math scores over 500: 75%; ACT scores over 18: 95%; SAT verbal scores over 600: 30%; SAT math scores over 600: 25%; ACT scores over 24: 23%; ACT scores over 30: 2%.

Faculty *Total:* 84, 29% full-time. *Student/faculty ratio:* 14:1.

Majors Accounting; art; art teacher education; biochemistry; biology/biological sciences; business administration and management; chemistry; communication/speech communication and rhetoric; early childhood education; elementary education; English; environmental science; fine/studio arts; graphic communications; history; human resources management; information science/studies; kindergarten/preschool education; marketing/marketing management; mathematics; middle school education; multi-/interdisciplinary studies related; pastoral studies/counseling; political science and government; pre-law studies; premedical studies; psychology; public administration; public relations, advertising, and applied communication related; Spanish language teacher education; special education (specific learning disabilities); sport and fitness administration; theology.

Academic Programs *Special study options:* academic remediation for entering students, accelerated degree program, adult/continuing education programs, advanced placement credit, cooperative education, double majors, independent study, internships, off-campus study, part-time degree program, student-designed majors, study abroad, summer session for credit.

Library Clara Fritzsche Library with 9,983 audiovisual materials, an OPAC.

Computers on Campus A campuswide network can be accessed. Internet access, at least one staffed computer lab available.

Student Life *Housing:* on-campus residence required through sophomore year. *Options:* coed, men-only, women-only. Campus housing is university owned. Freshman applicants given priority for college housing. *Activities and organizations:* drama/theater group, student-run newspaper, choral group, Undergraduate Student Senate, Resident Association Board, International Students/Multicultural Club, IHOP (I Help Other People), Bowling Club. *Campus security:* 24-hour emergency response devices and patrols, late-night transport/escort service, controlled dormitory access. *Student services:* personal/psychological counseling.

Athletics Member NAIA. *Intercollegiate sports:* basketball M(s)/W(s), cross-country running M(s)/W(s), soccer M(s)/W(s), softball W(s), tennis M(s), track and field M(s)/W(s), volleyball W(s). *Intramural sports:* basketball M/W, football M/W, soccer M/W, softball M/W, volleyball M/W, water polo M/W.

Standardized Tests *Required:* SAT I or ACT (for admission).

Costs (2003–04) *Comprehensive fee:* $23,690 includes full-time tuition ($16,990), mandatory fees ($500), and room and board ($6200). Full-time tuition and fees vary according to class time. Part-time tuition: $405 per credit. Part-time tuition and fees vary according to class time. *College room only:* $3114. Room and board charges vary according to board plan. *Payment plan:* installment. *Waivers:* employees or children of employees.

Financial Aid Of all full-time matriculated undergraduates who enrolled in 2002, 325 applied for aid, 273 were judged to have need, 210 had their need fully met. 150 Federal Work-Study jobs (averaging $2700). In 2002, 24 non-need-based awards were made. *Average percent of need met:* 97%. *Average financial aid package:* $15,336. *Average need-based loan:* $4281. *Average need-based gift aid:* $7211. *Average non-need-based aid:* $4280. *Average indebtedness upon graduation:* $15,000.

Applying *Options:* common application, electronic application, deferred entrance. *Application fee:* $30. *Required:* essay or personal statement, high school transcript, minimum 2.0 GPA, interview. *Recommended:* minimum 2.5 GPA, interview. *Application deadline:* rolling (freshmen), rolling (transfers). *Notification:* continuous (freshmen), continuous (transfers).

Admissions Contact Mr. David Armstrong Esq., Dean of Admissions, Notre Dame College, 4545 College Road, South Euclid, OH 44121-4293. *Phone:* 216-373-5214. *Toll-free phone:* 800-632-1680. *Fax:* 216-381-3802. *E-mail:* admissions@ndc.edu.

■ *See page 2112 for a narrative description.*

OBERLIN COLLEGE
Oberlin, Ohio

- **Independent** comprehensive, founded 1833
- **Calendar** 4-1-4
- **Degrees** diplomas, bachelor's, master's, and postbachelor's certificates
- **Small-town** 440-acre campus with easy access to Cleveland

Oberlin College (continued)
■ **Endowment** $550.0 million
■ **Coed,** 2,883 undergraduate students, 97% full-time, 55% women, 45% men
■ **Very difficult** entrance level, 36% of applicants were admitted

Oberlin College is an independent, coeducational liberal arts college of approximately 2,900 students. It comprises 2 divisions, the College of Arts and Sciences and the Conservatory of Music. Oberlin has a history of progressive thinking, a supportive academic community, and a diverse, active student body.

Undergraduates 2,809 full-time, 74 part-time. Students come from 50 states and territories, 44 other countries, 90% are from out of state, 7% African American, 7% Asian American or Pacific Islander, 5% Hispanic American, 0.9% Native American, 6% international, 1% transferred in, 70% live on campus. *Retention:* 90% of 2002 full-time freshmen returned.

Freshmen *Admission:* 5,983 applied, 2,159 admitted, 764 enrolled. *Average high school GPA:* 3.52. *Test scores:* SAT verbal scores over 500: 98%; SAT math scores over 500: 97%; ACT scores over 18: 100%; SAT verbal scores over 600: 86%; SAT math scores over 600: 79%; ACT scores over 24: 93%; SAT verbal scores over 700: 43%; SAT math scores over 700: 30%; ACT scores over 30: 38%.

Faculty *Total:* 292, 93% full-time. *Student/faculty ratio:* 10:1.

Majors African-American/Black studies; anthropology; archeology; art; art history, criticism and conservation; Asian studies (East); biochemistry; biology/biological sciences; chemistry; classics and languages, literatures and linguistics; comparative literature; computer science; creative writing; dance; dramatic/theatre arts; ecology; economics; English; environmental studies; fine/studio arts; French; geology/earth science; German; history; interdisciplinary studies; jazz/jazz studies; Jewish/Judaic studies; Latin; Latin American studies; legal studies; mathematics; modern Greek; music; music history, literature, and theory; music teacher education; music theory and composition; Near and Middle Eastern studies; neuroscience; philosophy; physics; physiological psychology/psychobiology; piano and organ; political science and government; psychology; religious studies; Romance languages; Russian; Russian studies; sociology; Spanish; violin, viola, guitar and other stringed instruments; voice and opera; wind/percussion instruments; women's studies.

Academic Programs *Special study options:* advanced placement credit, double majors, English as a second language, honors programs, independent study, internships, off-campus study, part-time degree program, services for LD students, student-designed majors, study abroad. *Unusual degree programs:* 3-2 engineering with Washington University in St. Louis, Case Western Reserve University, California Institute of Technology.

Library Mudd Center Library plus 3 others with 1.5 million titles, 4,560 serial subscriptions, 59,186 audiovisual materials, an OPAC.

Computers on Campus 340 computers available on campus for general student use. A campuswide network can be accessed from student residence rooms and from off campus. Internet access, online (class) registration, at least one staffed computer lab available.

Student Life *Housing:* on-campus residence required through sophomore year. *Options:* coed, women-only, cooperative, disabled students. Campus housing is university owned. Freshman campus housing is guaranteed. *Activities and organizations:* drama/theater group, student-run newspaper, radio station, choral group, marching band, Experimental College, Community Outreach, Black Students Organization, Students Cooperative Association, student radio station. *Campus security:* 24-hour emergency response devices and patrols, student patrols, late-night transport/escort service, controlled dormitory access, crime prevention programs. *Student services:* health clinic, personal/psychological counseling, women's center.

Athletics Member NCAA. All Division III. *Intercollegiate sports:* baseball M, basketball M/W, cheerleading W(c), cross-country running M/W, equestrian sports M(c)/W(c), fencing M(c)/W(c), field hockey W, football M, golf M/W, ice hockey M(c)/W(c), lacrosse M/W, rugby M(c)/W(c), soccer M/W, softball W(c), swimming M/W, tennis M/W, track and field M/W, ultimate Frisbee M(c)/W(c), volleyball M(c)/W, water polo M(c)/W(c). *Intramural sports:* baseball M, basketball M/W, bowling M/W, cross-country running M/W, football M, golf M/W, racquetball M/W, rock climbing M/W, soccer M/W, softball M/W, squash M/W, table tennis M/W, tennis M/W, track and field M/W, volleyball M/W, water polo M/W, weight lifting M/W.

Standardized Tests *Required:* SAT I or ACT (for admission). *Recommended:* SAT II: Subject Tests (for admission), SAT II: Writing Test (for admission).

Costs (2003–04) *Comprehensive fee:* $36,938 includes full-time tuition ($29,500), mandatory fees ($188), and room and board ($7250). Part-time tuition: $1230 per credit. Part-time tuition and fees vary according to course load. *College room only:* $3800. Room and board charges vary according to housing facility. *Payment plan:* installment. *Waivers:* employees or children of employees.

Financial Aid Of all full-time matriculated undergraduates who enrolled in 2003, 1,857 applied for aid, 1,640 were judged to have need, 1,157 had their need fully met. In 2003, 283 non-need-based awards were made. *Average percent of need met:* 100%. *Average financial aid package:* $22,576. *Average need-based loan:* $4013. *Average need-based gift aid:* $17,488. *Average non-need-based aid:* $11,472. *Average indebtedness upon graduation:* $17,000.

Applying *Options:* common application, electronic application, early admission, early decision, deferred entrance. *Application fee:* $35. *Required:* essay or personal statement, high school transcript, 2 letters of recommendation. *Required for some:* interview. *Application deadlines:* 1/15 (freshmen), 3/15 (transfers). *Early decision:* 11/15 (for plan 1), 1/2 (for plan 2). *Notification:* 4/1 (freshmen), 12/15 (early decision plan 1), 2/1 (early decision plan 2), 5/1 (transfers).

Admissions Contact Ms. Debra Chermonte, Dean of Admissions and Financial Aid, Oberlin College, Admissions Office, Carnegie Building, Oberlin, OH 44074-1090. *Phone:* 440-775-8411. *Toll-free phone:* 800-622-OBIE. *Fax:* 440-775-6905. *E-mail:* college.admissions@oberlin.edu.

■ *See page 2120 for a narrative description.*

OHIO DOMINICAN UNIVERSITY

Columbus, Ohio

■ **Independent Roman Catholic** comprehensive, founded 1911
■ **Calendar** semesters
■ **Degrees** certificates, associate, bachelor's, and master's
■ **Urban** 62-acre campus
■ **Endowment** $11.7 million
■ **Coed,** 2,308 undergraduate students, 73% full-time, 70% women, 30% men
■ **Moderately difficult** entrance level, 76% of applicants were admitted

Undergraduates 1,678 full-time, 630 part-time. Students come from 15 states and territories, 16 other countries, 1% are from out of state, 26% African American, 1% Asian American or Pacific Islander, 2% Hispanic American, 0.3% Native American, 1% international, 10% transferred in, 17% live on campus. *Retention:* 58% of 2002 full-time freshmen returned.

Freshmen *Admission:* 1,193 applied, 902 admitted, 312 enrolled. *Average high school GPA:* 3.08. *Test scores:* ACT scores over 18: 83%; ACT scores over 24: 19%.

Faculty *Total:* 160, 38% full-time, 51% with terminal degrees. *Student/faculty ratio:* 16:1.

Majors Accounting; art teacher education; biology/biological sciences; business administration and management; business/corporate communications; chemistry; chemistry teacher education; communication/speech communication and rhetoric; computer programming; computer science; criminal justice/law enforcement administration; early childhood education; economics; education (K-12); English; English as a second/foreign language (teaching); finance; fine/studio arts; foreign language teacher education; general studies; gerontology; graphic design; history; information science/studies; interdisciplinary studies; international business/trade/commerce; kindergarten/preschool education; legal studies; liberal arts and sciences/liberal studies; library assistant; mathematics; mathematics teacher education; middle school education; peace studies and conflict resolution; philosophy; physics teacher education; political science and government; psychology; public relations/image management; school librarian/school library media; science teacher education; secondary education; social studies teacher education; social work; sociology; special education; theology.

Academic Programs *Special study options:* academic remediation for entering students, adult/continuing education programs, advanced placement credit, English as a second language, honors programs, independent study, internships, off-campus study, part-time degree program, student-designed majors, study abroad, summer session for credit. *ROTC:* Army (c).

Library Spangler Library with 110,953 titles, 553 serial subscriptions, 4,302 audiovisual materials, an OPAC, a Web page.

Computers on Campus 198 computers available on campus for general student use. A campuswide network can be accessed from student residence rooms and from off campus that provide access to laptop for each student, intranet. Internet access, at least one staffed computer lab available. Computer purchase or lease plan available.

Student Life *Housing:* on-campus residence required through junior year. *Options:* coed. Campus housing is university owned. *Activities and organizations:* drama/theater group, student-run newspaper, radio station, choral group, Campus Ministry, honors program, College Choir, Black Student Union, American-International Membership. *Campus security:* 24-hour emergency response devices and patrols, late-night transport/escort service, controlled dormitory access. *Student services:* health clinic, personal/psychological counseling.

Athletics Member NAIA. *Intercollegiate sports:* baseball M(s), basketball M(s)/W(s), cheerleading M/W, football M(s), golf M(s)/W(s), soccer M(s)/W(s), softball W(s), tennis M(s)/W(s), volleyball W(s). *Intramural sports:* badminton M/W, basketball M/W, golf M/W, rock climbing M/W, soccer M/W, softball M/W, table tennis M/W, tennis M/W, volleyball M/W.

Standardized Tests *Required for some:* SAT I and SAT II or ACT (for admission).

Costs (2004–05) *Comprehensive fee:* $23,900 includes full-time tuition ($18,000) and room and board ($5900). Part-time tuition: $370 per credit hour. *Required fees:* $100 per term part-time. *Room and board:* Room and board charges vary according to housing facility. *Payment plan:* installment. *Waivers:* senior citizens and employees or children of employees.

Financial Aid Of all full-time matriculated undergraduates who enrolled in 2002, 200 Federal Work-Study jobs (averaging $2000). *Average percent of need met:* 92%. *Average financial aid package:* $12,467. *Average indebtedness upon graduation:* $13,500.

Applying *Options:* deferred entrance. *Application fee:* $25. *Required:* essay or personal statement, high school transcript, minimum 2.0 GPA, interview. *Required for some:* letters of recommendation. *Application deadline:* rolling (freshmen), rolling (transfers). *Notification:* continuous (freshmen), continuous (transfers).

Admissions Contact Ms. Vicki Thompson-Campbell, Director of Admissions, Ohio Dominican University, 1216 Sunbury Road, Columbus, OH 43219-2099. *Phone:* 614-251-4500. *Toll-free phone:* 800-854-2670. *Fax:* 614-251-0156. *E-mail:* admissions@ohiodominican.edu.

■ See page 2124 for a narrative description.

OHIO NORTHERN UNIVERSITY

Ada, Ohio

- **Independent** comprehensive, founded 1871, affiliated with United Methodist Church
- **Calendar** quarters
- **Degrees** bachelor's, master's, first professional, and postbachelor's certificates
- **Small-town** 285-acre campus
- **Endowment** $94.6 million
- **Coed,** 2,214 undergraduate students, 93% full-time, 47% women, 53% men
- **Moderately difficult** entrance level, 80% of applicants were admitted

Undergraduates 2,049 full-time, 165 part-time. Students come from 37 states and territories, 13% are from out of state, 1% African American, 0.6% Asian American or Pacific Islander, 0.7% Hispanic American, 0.1% Native American, 0.6% international, 3% transferred in, 64% live on campus. *Retention:* 85% of 2002 full-time freshmen returned.

Freshmen *Admission:* 2,841 applied, 2,277 admitted, 554 enrolled. *Average high school GPA:* 3.57. *Test scores:* SAT verbal scores over 500: 81%; SAT math scores over 500: 89%; ACT scores over 18: 97%; SAT verbal scores over 600: 37%; SAT math scores over 600: 51%; ACT scores over 24: 63%; SAT verbal scores over 700: 6%; SAT math scores over 700: 9%; ACT scores over 30: 10%.

Faculty *Total:* 275, 75% full-time, 72% with terminal degrees. *Student/faculty ratio:* 13:1.

Majors Accounting; art; art teacher education; athletic training; biochemistry; biology/biological sciences; biology teacher education; business administration and management; business/commerce; ceramic arts and ceramics; chemistry; chemistry related; chemistry teacher education; civil engineering; civil engineering related; clinical laboratory science/medical technology; commercial and advertising art; communication and journalism related; communication/speech communication and rhetoric; computer engineering; computer engineering related; computer science; creative writing; criminal justice/law enforcement administration; criminal justice/police science; criminal justice/safety; design and visual communications; dramatic/theatre arts; early childhood education; education; education (multiple levels); education related; electrical, electronics and communications engineering; elementary education; engineering; engineering related; English; English/language arts teacher education; environmental studies; fine/studio arts; foreign language teacher education; French; French language teacher education; general studies; Germanic languages related; German language teacher education; graphic design; health and physical education; health and physical education related; health teacher education; history; history teacher education; industrial arts; industrial technology; international business/trade/commerce; international relations and affairs; journalism; kindergarten/preschool education; kinesiology and exercise science; management science; management sciences and quantitative methods related; mass communication/media; mathematics; mathematics related; mathematics teacher education; mechanical engineering; medicinal and pharmaceutical chemistry; middle school education; molecular biology; music; music management and merchandising; music performance; music related; music teacher education; organizational communication; painting; pharmacy; pharmacy, pharmaceutical sciences, and administration related; philosophy; philosophy related; physical education teaching and coaching; physics; physics related; physics teacher education; political science and government; pre-dentistry studies; pre-law studies; pre-medical studies; pre-theology/pre-ministerial studies; pre-veterinary studies; printmaking; psychology; psychology related; public relations/image management; radio and television; religious studies; religious studies related; science teacher education; sculpture; secondary education; social studies teacher education; sociology; Spanish; Spanish language teacher education; sport and fitness administration; statistics; statistics related; technical and business writing; theatre/theatre arts management; visual and performing arts; visual and performing arts related.

Academic Programs *Special study options:* academic remediation for entering students, advanced placement credit, cooperative education, distance learning, double majors, honors programs, independent study, internships, off-campus study, part-time degree program, services for LD students, study abroad, summer session for credit. *ROTC:* Army (c), Air Force (c).

Library Heterick Memorial Library plus 1 other with 250,231 titles, 9,220 serial subscriptions, 9,776 audiovisual materials, an OPAC, a Web page.

Computers on Campus 550 computers available on campus for general student use. A campuswide network can be accessed from student residence rooms and from off campus. Internet access, online (class) registration, at least one staffed computer lab available.

Student Life *Housing:* on-campus residence required through junior year. *Options:* coed, men-only, women-only. Campus housing is university owned. Freshman campus housing is guaranteed. *Activities and organizations:* drama/theater group, student-run newspaper, radio and television station, choral group, marching band, Good News Bears, Student Planning Committee, Student Senate, President's Club, national fraternities, national sororities. *Campus security:* 24-hour emergency response devices and patrols, late-night transport/escort service, controlled dormitory access. *Student services:* health clinic, personal/psychological counseling, legal services.

Athletics Member NCAA. All Division III. *Intercollegiate sports:* baseball M, basketball M/W, cross-country running M/W, football M, golf M/W, soccer M/W, softball W, swimming M/W, tennis M/W, track and field M/W, volleyball W, wrestling M. *Intramural sports:* badminton M/W, basketball M/W, bowling M/W, cheerleading M(c)/W(c), football M, golf M, racquetball M/W, rugby M(c)/W(c), skiing (downhill) M(c)/W(c), soccer M/W, softball M/W, swimming M/W, table tennis M/W, tennis M/W, ultimate Frisbee M(c)/W(c), volleyball M(c)/W, water polo M(c)/W(c), wrestling M.

Standardized Tests *Required:* SAT I or ACT (for admission).

Costs (2003–04) *Comprehensive fee:* $30,675 includes full-time tuition ($24,435), mandatory fees ($210), and room and board ($6030). Full-time tuition and fees vary according to program and student level. Part-time tuition: $679 per quarter hour. Part-time tuition and fees vary according to course load, program, and student level. *Required fees:* $210 per term part-time. *College room only:* $3015. Room and board charges vary according to board plan and housing facility. *Payment plan:* installment. *Waivers:* employees or children of employees.

Financial Aid Of all full-time matriculated undergraduates who enrolled in 2003, 1,865 applied for aid, 1,707 were judged to have need, 492 had their need fully met. 1,224 Federal Work-Study jobs (averaging $2031). 169 state and other part-time jobs (averaging $1338). In 2003, 358 non-need-based awards were made. *Average percent of need met:* 88%. *Average financial aid package:* $20,347. *Average need-based loan:* $4842. *Average need-based gift aid:* $14,487. *Average non-need-based aid:* $10,438. *Average indebtedness upon graduation:* $29,713. *Financial aid deadline:* 6/1.

Applying *Options:* common application, electronic application, early admission, deferred entrance. *Application fee:* $30. *Required:* high school transcript. *Required for some:* 2 letters of recommendation. *Recommended:* essay or personal statement, minimum 2.5 GPA, interview. *Application deadlines:* 8/15 (freshmen), 9/1 (transfers). *Notification:* continuous (freshmen), continuous (transfers).

Admissions Contact Mrs. Karen Condeni, Vice President of Admissions and Financial Aid, Ohio Northern University, 525 South Main, Ada, OH 45810-1599. *Phone:* 419-772-2260. *Toll-free phone:* 888-408-4ONU. *Fax:* 419-772-2313. *E-mail:* admissions-ug@onu.edu.

■ See page 2126 for a narrative description.

THE OHIO STATE UNIVERSITY

Columbus, Ohio

- **State-supported** university, founded 1870
- **Calendar** quarters
- **Degrees** associate, bachelor's, master's, doctoral, first professional, post-master's, and postbachelor's certificates
- **Urban** 3117-acre campus
- **Endowment** $956.0 million
- **Coed,** 37,605 undergraduate students, 89% full-time, 48% women, 52% men
- **Moderately difficult** entrance level, 72% of applicants were admitted

Undergraduates 33,421 full-time, 4,184 part-time. Students come from 53 states and territories, 85 other countries, 11% are from out of state, 8% African American, 6% Asian American or Pacific Islander, 2% Hispanic American, 0.4%

The Ohio State University (continued)
Native American, 4% international, 4% transferred in, 24% live on campus. *Retention:* 88% of 2002 full-time freshmen returned.

Freshmen *Admission:* 20,122 applied, 14,488 admitted, 6,390 enrolled. *Test scores:* SAT verbal scores over 500: 86%; SAT math scores over 500: 90%; ACT scores over 18: 98%; SAT verbal scores over 600: 43%; SAT math scores over 600: 53%; ACT scores over 24: 70%; SAT verbal scores over 700: 8%; SAT math scores over 700: 12%; ACT scores over 30: 12%.

Faculty *Total:* 3,657, 75% full-time. *Student/faculty ratio:* 14:1.

Majors Accounting; actuarial science; aerospace, aeronautical and astronautical engineering; African-American/Black studies; African studies; agricultural and food products processing; agricultural/biological engineering and bioengineering; agricultural business and management; agricultural economics; agricultural teacher education; agronomy and crop science; animal genetics; animal sciences; anthropology; apparel and textiles; Arabic; architecture; art; art history, criticism and conservation; art teacher education; Asian-American studies; Asian studies (East); astronomy; athletic training; audiology and speech-language pathology; aviation/airway management; avionics maintenance technology; biochemistry; biology/biological sciences; biotechnology; botany/plant biology; business administration and management; business family and consumer sciences/human sciences; business/managerial economics; ceramic arts and ceramics; ceramic sciences and engineering; chemical engineering; chemistry; Chinese; city/urban, community and regional planning; civil engineering; classics and languages, literatures and linguistics; clinical laboratory science/medical technology; clothing/textiles; commercial and advertising art; communication and journalism related; communication/speech communication and rhetoric; comparative literature; computer and information sciences; computer engineering; computer science; creative writing; criminal justice/safety; criminology; cultural studies; dance; dental hygiene; design and visual communications; development economics and international development; dietetics; drama and dance teacher education; dramatic/theatre arts; drawing; economics; electrical, electronics and communications engineering; engineering physics; English; entomology; environmental education; environmental studies; European studies (Western); family resource management; finance; fine/studio arts; fishing and fisheries sciences and management; folklore; food science; foods, nutrition, and wellness; forestry; French; geography; geology/earth science; German; health information/medical records administration; health professions related; Hebrew; history; history related; horticultural science; hospitality administration; human development and family studies; humanities; human resources management; industrial design; industrial engineering; information science/studies; insurance; interior design; international business/trade/commerce; international relations and affairs; Islamic studies; Italian; Japanese; jazz/jazz studies; Jewish/Judaic studies; journalism; kinesiology and exercise science; landscape architecture; Latin American studies; linguistics; logistics and materials management; management information systems; marketing/marketing management; materials engineering; materials science; mathematics; mathematics and statistics related; mechanical engineering; medical microbiology and bacteriology; medical radiologic technology; metallurgical engineering; modern Greek; music; music history, literature, and theory; music performance; music teacher education; music theory and composition; natural resources management; natural resources management and policy; Near and Middle Eastern studies; nursing (registered nurse training); nursing science; occupational therapy; operations management; painting; peace studies and conflict resolution; pharmacy; philosophy; physical education teaching and coaching; physical therapy; physics; piano and organ; plant pathology/phytopathology; plant sciences; political science and government; Portuguese; printmaking; psychology; radiologic technology/science; real estate; religious studies; respiratory care therapy; Russian; Russian studies; sculpture; social sciences; social work; sociology; soil conservation; Spanish; special education; survey technology; systems engineering; technical teacher education; technology/industrial arts teacher education; turf and turfgrass management; voice and opera; wildlife and wildlands science and management; women's studies; zoology/animal biology.

Academic Programs *Special study options:* academic remediation for entering students, accelerated degree program, adult/continuing education programs, advanced placement credit, cooperative education, distance learning, double majors, English as a second language, freshman honors college, honors programs, independent study, internships, off-campus study, part-time degree program, services for LD students, student-designed majors, study abroad, summer session for credit. *ROTC:* Army (b), Air Force (b).

Library Main Library plus 12 others with 5.6 million titles, 43,086 serial subscriptions, 46,705 audiovisual materials, an OPAC, a Web page.

Computers on Campus 1000 computers available on campus for general student use. A campuswide network can be accessed from student residence rooms and from off campus. Internet access, online (class) registration, at least one staffed computer lab available.

Student Life *Housing:* on-campus residence required for freshman year. *Options:* coed, women-only, cooperative, disabled students. Campus housing is university owned. Freshman campus housing is guaranteed. *Activities and organizations:* drama/theater group, student-run newspaper, radio and television station, choral group, marching band, African Student Union, Bisexual, Gay and Lesbian Alliance, Campus Crusade for Christ, University Wide Council of Hispanic Organizations, Asian American Association, national fraternities, national sororities. *Campus security:* 24-hour emergency response devices and patrols, student patrols, late-night transport/escort service, controlled dormitory access, dorm entrances locked after 9 p.m, lighted pathways and sidewalks, self-defense education. *Student services:* health clinic, personal/psychological counseling, women's center, legal services.

Athletics Member NCAA. All Division I except football (Division I-A). *Intercollegiate sports:* baseball M(s), basketball M(s)/W(s), cross-country running M(s)/W(s), fencing M(s)/W(s), field hockey W(s), golf M(s)/W(s), gymnastics M(s)/W(s), ice hockey M(s)/W(s), lacrosse M(s)/W(s), riflery M/W, soccer M(s)/W(s), softball W(s), swimming M(s)/W(s), tennis M(s)/W(s), track and field M(s)/W(s), volleyball M(s)/W(s), wrestling M(s). *Intramural sports:* badminton M(c)/W(c), baseball M(c), basketball M/W, bowling M(c)/W(c), crew M(c)/W, cross-country running M/W, equestrian sports M(c)/W(c), fencing M(c)/W(c), field hockey W, football M/W, golf M/W, gymnastics M(c)/W(c), ice hockey M(c)/W(c), lacrosse M(c)/W(c), racquetball M(c)/W(c), riflery M(c)/W(c), rugby M(c)/W(c), sailing M(c)/W(c), skiing (downhill) M(c)/W(c), soccer M(c)/W(c), softball W(c), squash M(c)/W(c), swimming M(c)/W(c), table tennis M/W, tennis M/W, track and field M(c)/W(c), ultimate Frisbee M(c)/W(c), volleyball M(c)/W(c), water polo M(c)/W(c), weight lifting M(c), wrestling M/W.

Standardized Tests *Required:* SAT I or ACT (for admission).

Costs (2003–04) *Tuition:* state resident $6651 full-time; nonresident $16,638 full-time. Full-time tuition and fees vary according to course load, program, and reciprocity agreements. Part-time tuition and fees vary according to course load, program, and reciprocity agreements. *Room and board:* $6429. Room and board charges vary according to board plan and housing facility. *Payment plan:* installment. *Waivers:* senior citizens and employees or children of employees.

Financial Aid Of all full-time matriculated undergraduates who enrolled in 2003, 21,154 applied for aid, 16,713 were judged to have need, 3,899 had their need fully met. 3,667 Federal Work-Study jobs (averaging $3365). In 2003, 2198 non-need-based awards were made. *Average percent of need met:* 71%. *Average financial aid package:* $8897. *Average need-based loan:* $4361. *Average need-based gift aid:* $3321. *Average non-need-based aid:* $3741. *Average indebtedness upon graduation:* $14,869.

Applying *Options:* common application, electronic application. *Application fee:* $40. *Required:* essay or personal statement, high school transcript. *Application deadlines:* 2/1 (freshmen), 6/25 (transfers). *Notification:* continuous (freshmen), continuous (transfers).

Admissions Contact Dr. Mabel G. Freeman, Assistant Vice President for Undergraduate Admissions and First Year Experience, The Ohio State University, Enarson Hall, 154 West 12th Avenue, Columbus, OH 43210. *Phone:* 614-247-6281. *Fax:* 614-292-4818. *E-mail:* askabuckeye@osu.edu.

THE OHIO STATE UNIVERSITY AT LIMA
Lima, Ohio

- **State-supported** comprehensive, founded 1960, part of Ohio State University
- **Calendar** quarters
- **Degrees** associate, bachelor's, and master's
- **Small-town** 565-acre campus
- **Coed,** 1,248 undergraduate students, 80% full-time, 57% women, 43% men
- **Noncompetitive** entrance level, 99% of applicants were admitted

Undergraduates 1,001 full-time, 247 part-time. Students come from 1 other state, 1% are from out of state, 3% African American, 1% Asian American or Pacific Islander, 1% Hispanic American, 0.1% Native American. *Retention:* 61% of 2002 full-time freshmen returned.

Freshmen *Admission:* 621 applied, 617 admitted, 364 enrolled. *Test scores:* SAT verbal scores over 500: 50%; SAT math scores over 500: 70%; ACT scores over 18: 80%; SAT verbal scores over 600: 10%; ACT scores over 24: 22%.

Faculty *Total:* 83, 47% full-time. *Student/faculty ratio:* 15:1.

Majors Biology/biological sciences; business administration and management; elementary education; English; financial planning and services; health services/allied health/health sciences; history; hospitality administration; liberal arts and sciences/liberal studies; mathematics; psychology.

Academic Programs *Special study options:* academic remediation for entering students, accelerated degree program, adult/continuing education programs, advanced placement credit, English as a second language, honors programs, part-time degree program, services for LD students, summer session for credit. *ROTC:* Army (c), Navy (c), Air Force (c).

Library Ohio State University-Lima Campus Library with 74,619 titles, 592 serial subscriptions, an OPAC.

Computers on Campus 104 computers available on campus for general student use.

Financial Aid Of all full-time matriculated undergraduates who enrolled in 2003, 11,258 applied for aid, 7,942 were judged to have need, 838 had their need fully met. In 2003, 1302 non-need-based awards were made. *Average percent of need met:* 54%. *Average financial aid package:* $6823. *Average need-based loan:* $3927. *Average need-based gift aid:* $3487. *Average non-need-based aid:* $3813. *Average indebtedness upon graduation:* $16,307.

Applying *Options:* early admission, deferred entrance. *Application fee:* $45. *Required:* high school transcript. *Required for some:* essay or personal statement, interview. *Recommended:* 2 letters of recommendation. *Application deadlines:* 2/1 (freshmen), 5/15 (transfers). *Notification:* continuous (freshmen), continuous (transfers).

Admissions Contact Mr. N. Kip Howard Jr., Director of Admissions, Ohio University, Athens, OH 45701-2979. *Phone:* 740-593-4100. *E-mail:* admissions.freshmen@ohiou.edu.

OHIO UNIVERSITY–CHILLICOTHE

Chillicothe, Ohio

- **State-supported** 4-year, founded 1946, part of Ohio Board of Regents
- **Calendar** quarters
- **Degrees** certificates, associate, bachelor's, and master's (offers first 2 years of most bachelor's degree programs available at the main campus in Athens; also offers several bachelor's degree programs that can be completed at this campus and several programs exclusive to this campus; also offers some graduate programs)
- **Small-town** 124-acre campus with easy access to Columbus
- **Coed,** 1,960 undergraduate students
- **Noncompetitive** entrance level, 52% of applicants were admitted

Undergraduates Students come from 2 states and territories, 2% African American, 0.3% Asian American or Pacific Islander, 0.4% Hispanic American, 0.3% Native American, 0.2% international. *Retention:* 55% of 2002 full-time freshmen returned.

Freshmen *Admission:* 775 applied, 400 admitted.

Faculty *Total:* 106, 39% full-time.

Majors Administrative assistant and secretarial science; biological and physical sciences; business administration and management; criminal justice/law enforcement administration; criminal justice/police science; elementary education; environmental/environmental health engineering; environmental studies; human services; legal assistant/paralegal; liberal arts and sciences/liberal studies; nursing (registered nurse training); safety/security technology; special education (hearing impaired).

Academic Programs *Special study options:* academic remediation for entering students, accelerated degree program, adult/continuing education programs, advanced placement credit, distance learning, double majors, independent study, internships, part-time degree program, services for LD students, student-designed majors, summer session for credit. *ROTC:* Army (c), Air Force (c).

Library Quinn Library with 47,900 titles, 418 serial subscriptions.

Computers on Campus 215 computers available on campus for general student use. A campuswide network can be accessed from off campus. Internet access, online (class) registration, at least one staffed computer lab available.

Student Life *Housing:* college housing not available. *Activities and organizations:* drama/theater group, Nursing Student Association, Students In Free Enterprise Club, drama club, Phi Theta Kappa, Gamma Phi Delta. *Campus security:* 24-hour emergency response devices, patrols by city police. *Student services:* personal/psychological counseling.

Athletics *Intercollegiate sports:* baseball M(c), basketball M(c)/W(c), golf M/W, volleyball W(c).

Standardized Tests *Required:* SAT I or ACT (for placement).

Costs (2003–04) *Tuition:* state resident $4008 full-time, $121 per hour part-time; nonresident $10,146 full-time, $325 per hour part-time. *Payment plan:* installment. *Waivers:* senior citizens and employees or children of employees.

Financial Aid Of all full-time matriculated undergraduates who enrolled in 2003, 903 applied for aid, 785 were judged to have need, 67 had their need fully met. In 2003, 41 non-need-based awards were made. *Average percent of need met:* 54%. *Average financial aid package:* $6689. *Average need-based loan:* $3412. *Average need-based gift aid:* $4348. *Average non-need-based aid:* $2484.

Applying *Options:* early admission. *Application fee:* $20. *Required:* high school transcript. *Application deadlines:* 9/1 (freshmen), 9/1 (transfers). *Notification:* continuous (freshmen), continuous (transfers).

Admissions Contact Mr. Doug Henning, Coordinator, Admissions Office, Ohio University–Chillicothe, 571 West Fifth Street, Chillicothe, OH 45601. *Phone:* 740-774-7200 Ext. 242. *Toll-free phone:* 877-462-6824. *Fax:* 740-774-7295.

OHIO UNIVERSITY–EASTERN

St. Clairsville, Ohio

Admissions Contact Assistant VP for Enrollment Services/Director of Admissions, Ohio University–Eastern, 45425 National Road, St. Clairsville, OH 43950-9724. *Phone:* 740-593-4120. *Toll-free phone:* 800-648-3331. *E-mail:* chenowet@ohio.edu.

OHIO UNIVERSITY–LANCASTER

Lancaster, Ohio

- **State-supported** comprehensive, founded 1968, part of Ohio Board of Regents
- **Calendar** quarters
- **Degrees** associate, bachelor's, and master's
- **Small-town** 360-acre campus with easy access to Columbus
- **Endowment** $75,000
- **Coed**
- **Noncompetitive** entrance level

Faculty *Student/faculty ratio:* 30:1.

Standardized Tests *Required:* SAT I or ACT (for placement).

Costs (2003–04) *Tuition:* state resident $4008 full-time; nonresident $10,146 full-time.

Financial Aid Of all full-time matriculated undergraduates who enrolled in 2003, 767 applied for aid, 599 were judged to have need, 57 had their need fully met. In 2003, 39. *Average percent of need met:* 55. *Average financial aid package:* $6269. *Average need-based loan:* $3507. *Average need-based gift aid:* $4099. *Average non-need-based aid:* $2863.

Applying *Options:* common application, electronic application, early admission, deferred entrance. *Application fee:* $20. *Required:* high school transcript. *Recommended:* interview.

Admissions Contact Mr. Nathan Thomas, Admissions Officer, Ohio University–Lancaster, 1570 Granville Pike, Lancaster, OH 43130-1097. *Phone:* 740-654-6711 Ext. 215. *Toll-free phone:* 888-446-4468 Ext. 215. *Fax:* 740-687-9497. *E-mail:* fox@ohio.edu.

OHIO UNIVERSITY–SOUTHERN CAMPUS

Ironton, Ohio

- **State-supported** comprehensive, founded 1956, part of Ohio Board of Regents
- **Calendar** quarters
- **Degrees** associate, bachelor's, and master's
- **Small-town** 9-acre campus
- **Coed,** 1,630 undergraduate students, 68% full-time, 63% women, 37% men
- **Noncompetitive** entrance level, 100% of applicants were admitted

Undergraduates 1,110 full-time, 520 part-time. Students come from 4 states and territories, 14% are from out of state, 3% African American, 0.2% Asian American or Pacific Islander, 0.3% Hispanic American, 0.7% Native American, 0.1% international.

Freshmen *Admission:* 482 applied, 482 admitted, 348 enrolled.

Faculty *Total:* 155, 10% full-time.

Majors Accounting and business/management; accounting technology and bookkeeping; biological and physical sciences; business administration and management; computer science; criminal justice/law enforcement administration; early childhood education; education; health/health care administration; health services administration; human services; interdisciplinary studies; kindergarten/preschool education; liberal arts and sciences/liberal studies; multi-/interdisciplinary studies related; nursing (registered nurse training); office occupations and clerical services; organizational communication; radio and television broadcasting technology; tourism and travel services marketing.

Academic Programs *Special study options:* academic remediation for entering students, adult/continuing education programs, part-time degree program, student-designed majors, summer session for credit.

Library Ohio University-Southern Campus Library with 26,000 titles, 275 serial subscriptions, 524 audiovisual materials, an OPAC, a Web page.

Computers on Campus 147 computers available on campus for general student use. A campuswide network can be accessed from off campus. Internet access, online (class) registration, at least one staffed computer lab available.

Student Life *Housing:* college housing not available. *Activities and organizations:* choral group. *Student services:* legal services.

Athletics *Intercollegiate sports:* basketball M/W, cheerleading M/W. *Intramural sports:* archery M/W, skiing (downhill) M/W, tennis M/W, volleyball M/W.

Ohio University–Southern Campus (continued)

Standardized Tests *Recommended:* SAT I or ACT (for placement).

Costs (2003–04) *Tuition:* state resident $3693 full-time; nonresident $5013 full-time. Full-time tuition and fees vary according to student level. Part-time tuition and fees vary according to student level. *Waivers:* senior citizens and employees or children of employees.

Financial Aid Of all full-time matriculated undergraduates who enrolled in 2003, 1,084 applied for aid, 989 were judged to have need, 58 had their need fully met. In 2003, 32 non-need-based awards were made. *Average percent of need met:* 55%. *Average financial aid package:* $6807. *Average need-based loan:* $3369. *Average need-based gift aid:* $4156. *Average non-need-based aid:* $1223.

Applying *Options:* early admission, deferred entrance. *Application fee:* $20. *Required for some:* high school transcript. *Application deadline:* rolling (freshmen), rolling (transfers).

Admissions Contact Dr. Kim K. Lawson, Coordinator of Admissions, Ohio University–Southern Campus, 1804 Liberty Avenue, Ironton, OH 45638. *Phone:* 740-533-4612. *Toll-free phone:* 800-626-0513. *Fax:* 740-593-4632.

OHIO UNIVERSITY–ZANESVILLE

Zanesville, Ohio

- **State-supported** comprehensive, founded 1946, part of Ohio Board of Regents
- **Calendar** quarters
- **Degrees** associate, bachelor's, and master's (offers first 2 years of most bachelor's degree programs available at the main campus in Athens; also offers several bachelor's degree programs that can be completed at this campus; also offers some graduate courses)
- **Rural** 179-acre campus with easy access to Columbus
- **Coed,** 1,709 undergraduate students, 70% full-time, 69% women, 31% men
- **Noncompetitive** entrance level, 100% of applicants were admitted

Undergraduates 1,190 full-time, 519 part-time. Students come from 4 states and territories, 1% are from out of state, 2% African American, 0.3% Asian American or Pacific Islander, 0.2% Hispanic American, 0.2% Native American, 0.1% international. *Retention:* 62% of 2002 full-time freshmen returned.

Freshmen *Admission:* 582 applied, 582 admitted, 388 enrolled. *Test scores:* ACT scores over 18: 74%; ACT scores over 24: 21%.

Faculty *Total:* 130, 24% full-time, 25% with terminal degrees. *Student/faculty ratio:* 23:1.

Majors Biological and physical sciences; broadcast journalism; criminal justice/law enforcement administration; elementary education; liberal arts and sciences/liberal studies; nursing (registered nurse training); public relations/image management; radio and television; social sciences.

Academic Programs *Special study options:* academic remediation for entering students, adult/continuing education programs, advanced placement credit, external degree program, off-campus study, part-time degree program, services for LD students, student-designed majors, summer session for credit.

Library Zanesville Campus Library plus 1 other with 64,227 titles, 489 serial subscriptions, an OPAC.

Computers on Campus 42 computers available on campus for general student use. A campuswide network can be accessed from off campus. Internet access, at least one staffed computer lab available.

Student Life *Housing:* college housing not available. *Activities and organizations:* drama/theater group, student-run newspaper, radio station, Student Senate, Student Nurses Association, drama club, chess club. *Campus security:* night security.

Athletics *Intercollegiate sports:* baseball M, basketball M/W, golf M/W, softball W, tennis M/W, volleyball W. *Intramural sports:* basketball M/W, bowling M/W, football M, golf M/W, skiing (downhill) M/W, soccer M/W, softball M/W, table tennis M/W, tennis M/W, volleyball M/W.

Standardized Tests *Required for some:* SAT I or ACT (for placement), nursing examination.

Costs (2003–04) *Tuition:* state resident $4008 full-time; nonresident $10,146 full-time.

Financial Aid Of all full-time matriculated undergraduates who enrolled in 2003, 1,069 applied for aid, 842 were judged to have need, 104 had their need fully met. In 2003, 135 non-need-based awards were made. *Average percent of need met:* 58%. *Average financial aid package:* $6417. *Average need-based loan:* $3377. *Average need-based gift aid:* $3963. *Average non-need-based aid:* $3253.

Applying *Options:* common application, early admission, deferred entrance. *Application fee:* $20. *Required:* high school transcript. *Application deadline:* rolling (freshmen), rolling (transfers).

Admissions Contact Mrs. Karen Ragsdale, Student services Secretary, Ohio University–Zanesville, 1425 Newark Road, Zanesville, OH 43701-2695. *Phone:* 740-588-1440. *Fax:* 740-453-6161.

OHIO WESLEYAN UNIVERSITY

Delaware, Ohio

- **Independent United Methodist** 4-year, founded 1842
- **Calendar** semesters
- **Degree** bachelor's
- **Small-town** 200-acre campus with easy access to Columbus
- **Endowment** $113.9 million
- **Coed,** 1,929 undergraduate students, 99% full-time, 54% women, 46% men
- **Very difficult** entrance level, 74% of applicants were admitted

Personalized honors study offers unusual opportunities to talented students as early as freshman year. Internships and research are encouraged. The University's distinctive commitment to public service and civic involvement is reflected in annual student work trips to South America and other states in the U.S., the acclaimed Sagan National Colloquium, and extensive volunteer and community service opportunities.

Undergraduates 1,904 full-time, 25 part-time. Students come from 44 states and territories, 45 other countries, 41% are from out of state, 5% African American, 2% Asian American or Pacific Islander, 1% Hispanic American, 0.1% Native American, 10% international, 1% transferred in, 85% live on campus. *Retention:* 78% of 2002 full-time freshmen returned.

Freshmen *Admission:* 2,580 applied, 1,910 admitted, 567 enrolled. *Average high school GPA:* 3.33. *Test scores:* SAT verbal scores over 500: 88%; SAT math scores over 500: 90%; ACT scores over 18: 100%; SAT verbal scores over 600: 55%; SAT math scores over 600: 53%; ACT scores over 24: 84%; SAT verbal scores over 700: 14%; SAT math scores over 700: 11%; ACT scores over 30: 20%.

Faculty *Total:* 188, 69% full-time, 81% with terminal degrees. *Student/faculty ratio:* 13:1.

Majors Accounting; African-American/Black studies; animal genetics; anthropology; art history, criticism and conservation; art teacher education; art therapy; Asian studies (East); astronomy; biology/biological sciences; biology teacher education; botany/plant biology; broadcast journalism; business administration and management; business/managerial economics; chemistry; chemistry teacher education; classics and languages, literatures and linguistics; computer science; creative writing; cultural studies; drama and dance teacher education; dramatic/theatre arts; early childhood education; economics; education; education (K-12); education (multiple levels); elementary education; engineering related; engineering science; English; environmental studies; fine/studio arts; foreign language teacher education; French; French language teacher education; general studies; genetics; geography; geology/earth science; German; German language teacher education; health teacher education; history; history teacher education; humanities; international business/trade/commerce; international relations and affairs; journalism; kindergarten/preschool education; Latin teacher education; literature; mathematics; mathematics teacher education; medical microbiology and bacteriology; medieval and Renaissance studies; middle school education; multi-/interdisciplinary studies related; music; music performance; music teacher education; neuroscience; philosophy; physical education teaching and coaching; physics; physics teacher education; political science and government; pre-dentistry studies; pre-law studies; pre-medical studies; pre-theology/pre-ministerial studies; pre-veterinary studies; psychology; psychology teacher education; public administration; religious studies; secondary education; social studies teacher education; sociology; Spanish; Spanish language teacher education; statistics; urban studies/affairs; women's studies; zoology/animal biology.

Academic Programs *Special study options:* advanced placement credit, double majors, freshman honors college, honors programs, independent study, internships, off-campus study, part-time degree program, services for LD students, student-designed majors, study abroad, summer session for credit. *ROTC:* Army (c). *Unusual degree programs:* 3-2 engineering with Rensselaer Polytechnic Institute, California Institute of Technology, Case Western Reserve University, New York State College of Ceramics at Alfred University, Polytechnic Institute of New York, Washington University in St. Louis; medical technology, optometry, physical therapy.

Library L. A. Beeghly Library plus 3 others with 420,936 titles, 1,084 serial subscriptions, 2,980 audiovisual materials, an OPAC, a Web page.

Computers on Campus 295 computers available on campus for general student use. A campuswide network can be accessed from student residence rooms and from off campus. Internet access, at least one staffed computer lab available.

Student Life *Housing:* on-campus residence required through senior year. *Options:* coed, men-only, women-only. Campus housing is university owned. Freshman campus housing is guaranteed. *Activities and organizations:* drama/theater group, student-run newspaper, radio station, choral group, community services, student government, Campus Programming Board, religious organizations, ethnic organizations, national fraternities, national sororities. *Campus security:* 24-hour emergency response devices and patrols, late-night transport/escort service, controlled dormitory access. *Student services:* health clinic, personal/psychological counseling, women's center.

Athletics Member NCAA. All Division III. *Intercollegiate sports:* baseball M, basketball M/W, cross-country running M/W, equestrian sports M(c)/W(c), field hockey W, football M, golf M, ice hockey M(c), lacrosse M/W, rugby M(c)/W(c), sailing M(c)/W(c), soccer M/W, softball W, swimming M/W, tennis M/W, track and field M/W, ultimate Frisbee M(c)/W(c), volleyball M(c)/W. *Intramural sports:* badminton M/W, basketball M/W, cross-country running M/W, football M/W, golf M/W, lacrosse M/W, racquetball M/W, skiing (cross-country) M/W, skiing (downhill) M/W, soccer M/W, softball M/W, squash M/W, swimming M/W, tennis M/W, track and field M/W, volleyball M/W, water polo M/W.

Standardized Tests *Required:* SAT I or ACT (for admission). *Recommended:* SAT II: Subject Tests (for admission).

Costs (2003–04) *Comprehensive fee:* $32,550 includes full-time tuition ($25,080), mandatory fees ($360), and room and board ($7110). Part-time tuition: $2730 per course. *College room only:* $3530. Room and board charges vary according to board plan. *Payment plan:* installment. *Waivers:* children of alumni and employees or children of employees.

Financial Aid Of all full-time matriculated undergraduates who enrolled in 2003, 1,223 applied for aid, 1,106 were judged to have need, 351 had their need fully met. 804 Federal Work-Study jobs (averaging $1598). In 2003, 730 non-need-based awards were made. *Average percent of need met:* 90%. *Average financial aid package:* $22,149. *Average need-based loan:* $4497. *Average need-based gift aid:* $16,141. *Average non-need-based aid:* $11,847. *Average indebtedness upon graduation:* $22,166. *Financial aid deadline:* 5/15.

Applying *Options:* common application, electronic application, early admission, early decision, early action, deferred entrance. *Application fee:* $35. *Required:* essay or personal statement, high school transcript, 1 letter of recommendation. *Recommended:* minimum 2.5 GPA, 2 letters of recommendation, interview. *Application deadlines:* 3/1 (freshmen), 5/15 (transfers). *Early decision:* 12/1. *Notification:* continuous (freshmen), 12/30 (early decision), 1/15 (early action), continuous (transfers).

Admissions Contact Ms. Carol Wheatley, Director of Admission, Ohio Wesleyan University, 61 South Sandusky Street, Delaware, OH 43015. *Phone:* 740-368-3020. *Toll-free phone:* 800-922-8953. *Fax:* 740-368-3314. *E-mail:* owuadmit@owu.edu.

■ *See page 2128 for a narrative description.*

OTTERBEIN COLLEGE
Westerville, Ohio

- **Independent United Methodist** comprehensive, founded 1847
- **Calendar** quarters
- **Degrees** bachelor's and master's
- **Suburban** 142-acre campus with easy access to Columbus
- **Endowment** $61.0 million
- **Coed,** 2,673 undergraduate students, 78% full-time, 66% women, 34% men
- **Moderately difficult** entrance level, 84% of applicants were admitted

Otterbein continues to offer an excellent combination of a broad-based liberal arts education with professional/career preparation. Its campus in Westerville provides access to Ohio's capital city, Columbus, for internships as well as cultural and social activities. A student-faculty ratio of 13:1 ensures individual attention for students pursuing one of 49 majors offered. More than $11 million in grants and scholarships was awarded last year. Students graduate in 4 years.

Undergraduates 2,088 full-time, 585 part-time. Students come from 34 states and territories, 8% are from out of state, 7% African American, 1% Asian American or Pacific Islander, 1% Hispanic American, 0.2% Native American, 3% transferred in, 52% live on campus. *Retention:* 92% of 2002 full-time freshmen returned.

Freshmen *Admission:* 2,305 applied, 1,929 admitted, 632 enrolled. *Average high school GPA:* 3.30. *Test scores:* SAT verbal scores over 500: 71%; SAT math scores over 500: 64%; ACT scores over 18: 93%; SAT verbal scores over 600: 24%; SAT math scores over 600: 20%; ACT scores over 24: 40%; SAT verbal scores over 700: 3%; SAT math scores over 700: 2%; ACT scores over 30: 3%.

Faculty *Total:* 249, 58% full-time. *Student/faculty ratio:* 13:1.

Majors Accounting; art; art teacher education; athletic training; audiology and speech-language pathology; biochemistry; biology/biological sciences; business administration and management; business/managerial economics; chemistry; computer science; dramatic/theatre arts; economics; education; elementary education; English; environmental biology; environmental science; equestrian studies; finance; French; health teacher education; history; international business/trade/commerce; international relations and affairs; journalism; literature; marketing/marketing management; mathematics; middle school education; molecular biology; multi-/interdisciplinary studies related; music; music history, literature, and theory; music management and merchandising; music performance; music teacher education; nursing (registered nurse training); philosophy; physical education teaching and coaching; physical sciences; physics; piano and organ; political science and government; pre-dentistry studies; pre-law studies; pre-medical studies; pre-veterinary studies; psychology; public relations/image management; radio and television; religious studies; science teacher education; secondary education; sociology; Spanish; sport and fitness administration; violin, viola, guitar and other stringed instruments; voice and opera; wind/percussion instruments.

Academic Programs *Special study options:* academic remediation for entering students, adult/continuing education programs, advanced placement credit, double majors, honors programs, internships, off-campus study, part-time degree program, services for LD students, student-designed majors, study abroad, summer session for credit. *ROTC:* Army (c), Air Force (c). *Unusual degree programs:* 3-2 engineering with Case Western Reserve University, Washington University in St. Louis.

Library Courtright Memorial Library with 182,629 titles, 1,012 serial subscriptions, 8,971 audiovisual materials, an OPAC, a Web page.

Computers on Campus 146 computers available on campus for general student use. A campuswide network can be accessed from student residence rooms and from off campus. Internet access, at least one staffed computer lab available.

Student Life *Housing:* on-campus residence required through sophomore year. *Options:* men-only, women-only. Campus housing is university owned. Freshman campus housing is guaranteed. *Activities and organizations:* drama/theater group, student-run newspaper, radio and television station, choral group, marching band, musical groups, Greek organizations, honoraries, academic interest clubs, Governance, national fraternities. *Campus security:* 24-hour emergency response devices and patrols, student patrols, late-night transport/escort service, controlled dormitory access, 24-hour locked residence hall entrances. *Student services:* health clinic, personal/psychological counseling.

Athletics Member NCAA. All Division III. *Intercollegiate sports:* baseball M, basketball M/W, cheerleading M/W, cross-country running M/W, equestrian sports M/W, football M, golf M/W, soccer M/W, softball W, tennis M/W, track and field M/W, volleyball W. *Intramural sports:* basketball M/W, football M, racquetball M/W, soccer M/W, softball M/W, volleyball M/W.

Standardized Tests *Required:* SAT I or ACT (for admission).

Costs (2003–04) *Comprehensive fee:* $26,085 includes full-time tuition ($20,133) and room and board ($5952). Full-time tuition and fees vary according to course load and program. Part-time tuition: $242 per credit hour. Part-time tuition and fees vary according to course load and program. *College room only:* $2712. Room and board charges vary according to housing facility. *Payment plan:* installment. *Waivers:* employees or children of employees.

Applying *Options:* common application, electronic application, deferred entrance. *Application fee:* $25. *Required:* high school transcript. *Recommended:* minimum 2.5 GPA, interview. *Application deadline:* 3/1 (freshmen), rolling (transfers). *Notification:* continuous (freshmen), continuous (transfers).

Admissions Contact Dr. Cass Johnson, Director of Admissions, Otterbein College, One Otterbein College, Westerville, OH 43081-9924. *Phone:* 614-823-1500. *Toll-free phone:* 800-488-8144. *Fax:* 614-823-1200. *E-mail:* uotterb@otterbein.edu.

■ *See page 2140 for a narrative description.*

PONTIFICAL COLLEGE JOSEPHINUM
Columbus, Ohio

- **Independent Roman Catholic** comprehensive, founded 1888
- **Calendar** semesters
- **Degrees** bachelor's, master's, and first professional
- **Suburban** 100-acre campus
- **Endowment** $22.1 million
- **Coed, primarily men,** 80 undergraduate students, 100% full-time, 100% men
- **Minimally difficult** entrance level, 90% of applicants were admitted

Undergraduates 80 full-time. Students come from 19 states and territories, 3 other countries, 49% are from out of state, 8% Hispanic American, 7% international, 16% transferred in. *Retention:* 67% of 2002 full-time freshmen returned.

Freshmen *Admission:* 8 enrolled.

Faculty *Total:* 19, 47% full-time. *Student/faculty ratio:* 6:1.

Majors English; humanities; Latin American studies; philosophy.

Academic Programs *Special study options:* academic remediation for entering students, advanced placement credit, double majors, English as a second language, honors programs, internships, off-campus study, services for LD students.

Library Wehrle Memorial Library with 124,742 titles, 520 serial subscriptions.

Computers on Campus 10 computers available on campus for general student use. A campuswide network can be accessed. Internet access, at least one staffed computer lab available.

Student Life *Housing:* on-campus residence required through senior year. *Options:* Campus housing is university owned. *Activities and organizations:*

Pontifical College Josephinum (continued)
drama/theater group, choral group. *Campus security:* 24-hour emergency response devices, controlled dormitory access. *Student services:* health clinic, personal/psychological counseling.

Athletics *Intramural sports:* basketball M, bowling M, football M, golf M, soccer M, softball M, swimming M, table tennis M, tennis M, volleyball M, weight lifting M.

Standardized Tests *Recommended:* SAT I and SAT II or ACT (for admission).

Costs (2003–04) *Comprehensive fee:* $16,320 includes full-time tuition ($10,220), mandatory fees ($100), and room and board ($6000). *Payment plans:* installment, deferred payment.

Financial Aid Of all full-time matriculated undergraduates who enrolled in 2003, 49 applied for aid, 21 were judged to have need, 17 had their need fully met. 4 Federal Work-Study jobs (averaging $507). In 2003, 5 non-need-based awards were made. *Average percent of need met:* 86%. *Average financial aid package:* $14,084. *Average need-based loan:* $6637. *Average need-based gift aid:* $4367. *Average non-need-based aid:* $1990. *Average indebtedness upon graduation:* $13,698.

Applying *Options:* deferred entrance. *Application fee:* $25. *Required:* essay or personal statement, high school transcript, 3 letters of recommendation. *Recommended:* interview. *Application deadline:* 7/31 (freshmen), rolling (transfers).

Admissions Contact Arminda Crawford, Secretary for Admissions, Pontifical College Josephinum, Columbus, OH 43235. *Phone:* 614-985-2241. *Toll-free phone:* 888-252-5812. *Fax:* 614-885-2307. *E-mail:* acrawford@pcj.edu.

Rabbinical College of Telshe

Wickliffe, Ohio

Admissions Contact 28400 Euclid Avenue, Wickliffe, OH 44092-2523.

Shawnee State University

Portsmouth, Ohio

- **State-supported** 4-year, founded 1986, part of Ohio Board of Regents
- **Calendar** quarters
- **Degrees** certificates, associate, and bachelor's
- **Small-town** 52-acre campus
- **Endowment** $8.5 million
- **Coed,** 3,693 undergraduate students, 83% full-time, 60% women, 40% men
- **Noncompetitive** entrance level, 100% of applicants were admitted

Shawnee State University (SSU) offers baccalaureate and associate degrees through the College of Arts and Sciences and the College of Professional Studies. Programs are available in business, health sciences, engineering technologies, arts and sciences, and teacher education. With distinctive student housing and a beautiful new campus, SSU offers a high-quality education with individualized attention.

Undergraduates 3,047 full-time, 646 part-time. Students come from 13 states and territories, 10 other countries, 9% are from out of state, 3% African American, 0.1% Asian American or Pacific Islander, 0.6% Hispanic American, 1% Native American, 0.7% international, 5% transferred in, 11% live on campus. *Retention:* 58% of 2002 full-time freshmen returned.

Freshmen *Admission:* 2,610 applied, 2,610 admitted, 709 enrolled. *Test scores:* ACT scores over 18: 64%; ACT scores over 24: 9%.

Faculty *Total:* 276, 45% full-time. *Student/faculty ratio:* 18:1.

Majors Accounting; applied mathematics; art; art teacher education; athletic training; biological and physical sciences; biology/biological sciences; business administration and management; CAD/CADD drafting/design technology; ceramic arts and ceramics; chemistry; clinical/medical laboratory technology; computer engineering technology; dental hygiene; dramatic/theatre arts; drawing; early childhood education; education; education (multiple levels); electromechanical technology; elementary education; emergency medical technology (EMT paramedic); English; English/language arts teacher education; environmental engineering technology; fine/studio arts; general studies; geography teacher education; graphic design; history; history teacher education; humanities; international relations and affairs; kindergarten/preschool education; legal administrative assistant/secretary; legal assistant/paralegal; management information systems; mathematics; mathematics teacher education; medical radiologic technology; middle school education; music; natural sciences; nursing (registered nurse training); occupational therapy; office management; painting; photography; physical sciences; physical therapy; physics teacher education; plastics engineering technology; pre-engineering; pre-law studies; pre-medical studies; pre-veterinary studies; psychology; psychology teacher education; respiratory care therapy; science teacher education; secondary education; social sciences; social studies teacher education; sociology; special education; sport and fitness administration.

Academic Programs *Special study options:* academic remediation for entering students, adult/continuing education programs, advanced placement credit, distance learning, double majors, honors programs, independent study, internships, off-campus study, part-time degree program, services for LD students, study abroad, summer session for credit.

Library Shawnee State University Library with 152,961 titles, 6,909 serial subscriptions, 19,316 audiovisual materials, an OPAC, a Web page.

Computers on Campus 400 computers available on campus for general student use. A campuswide network can be accessed from off campus. Internet access, online (class) registration, at least one staffed computer lab available.

Student Life *Housing:* on-campus residence required through sophomore year. *Options:* coed. Campus housing is university owned. *Activities and organizations:* drama/theater group, student-run newspaper, choral group, campus ministry, Health Executives and Administrators Learning Society, Greek sororities and fraternities, Student Programming Board, SGA, national fraternities. *Campus security:* 24-hour emergency response devices and patrols. *Student services:* personal/psychological counseling, women's center.

Athletics Member NAIA. *Intercollegiate sports:* baseball M, basketball M/W, cross-country running M/W, golf M, soccer M/W, softball W, tennis W, volleyball W. *Intramural sports:* basketball M/W, bowling M/W, golf M/W, racquetball M/W, softball M, swimming M/W, table tennis M/W, tennis M/W, volleyball M/W.

Standardized Tests *Recommended:* ACT (for placement).

Costs (2003–04) *Tuition:* state resident $4212 full-time, $117 per credit hour part-time; nonresident $7497 full-time, $208 per credit hour part-time. Full-time tuition and fees vary according to reciprocity agreements and student level. Part-time tuition and fees vary according to reciprocity agreements and student level. *Required fees:* $522 full-time, $15 per credit hour part-time. *Room and board:* $6297; room only: $4155. Room and board charges vary according to board plan and housing facility. *Payment plan:* installment. *Waivers:* senior citizens and employees or children of employees.

Financial Aid Of all full-time matriculated undergraduates who enrolled in 1999, 2,591 applied for aid, 1,806 were judged to have need, 1,751 had their need fully met. 104 Federal Work-Study jobs (averaging $2018). *Average percent of need met:* 70%. *Average financial aid package:* $3972. *Average need-based gift aid:* $2620. *Average indebtedness upon graduation:* $10,944.

Applying *Options:* electronic application, deferred entrance. *Required:* high school transcript. *Required for some:* letters of recommendation, interview. *Application deadline:* rolling (freshmen), rolling (transfers). *Notification:* continuous (freshmen), continuous (transfers).

Admissions Contact Mr. Bob Trusz, Director of Admission, Shawnee State University, 940 Second Street, Commons Building, Portsmouth, OH 45662. *Phone:* 740-351-3610 Ext. 610. *Toll-free phone:* 800-959-2SSU. *Fax:* 740-351-3111. *E-mail:* to_ssu@shawnee.edu.

■ *See page 2372 for a narrative description.*

Temple Baptist College

Cincinnati, Ohio

Admissions Contact 11965 Kenn Road, Cincinnati, OH 45240.

Tiffin University

Tiffin, Ohio

- **Independent** comprehensive, founded 1888
- **Calendar** semesters
- **Degrees** associate, bachelor's, and master's
- **Small-town** 110-acre campus with easy access to Toledo
- **Endowment** $2.6 million
- **Coed,** 1,026 undergraduate students, 85% full-time, 54% women, 46% men
- **Minimally difficult** entrance level, 91% of applicants were admitted

Undergraduates 870 full-time, 156 part-time. Students come from 14 states and territories, 10 other countries, 9% are from out of state, 11% African American, 0.3% Asian American or Pacific Islander, 2% Hispanic American, 3% international, 4% transferred in, 40% live on campus. *Retention:* 61% of 2002 full-time freshmen returned.

Freshmen *Admission:* 1,000 applied, 911 admitted, 262 enrolled. *Average high school GPA:* 2.95. *Test scores:* SAT verbal scores over 500: 32%; SAT math scores over 500: 32%; ACT scores over 18: 75%; SAT math scores over 600: 4%; ACT scores over 24: 14%; SAT math scores over 700: 1%.

Faculty *Total:* 147, 33% full-time, 39% with terminal degrees. *Student/faculty ratio:* 10:1.

Majors Accounting; business administration and management; communication/speech communication and rhetoric; computer and information sciences and support services related; computer programming; corrections; criminal justice/law enforcement administration; criminal justice/police science; criminal justice/safety; English; finance; forensic psychology; human services; information science/studies; international relations and affairs; management information systems; marketing/marketing management; office management; pre-law studies; psychology.

Academic Programs *Special study options:* accelerated degree program, adult/continuing education programs, advanced placement credit, distance learning, double majors, independent study, internships, study abroad, summer session for credit. *ROTC:* Army (c), Air Force (c).

Library Pfeiffer Library with 29,779 titles, 250 serial subscriptions, 544 audiovisual materials, an OPAC.

Computers on Campus 60 computers available on campus for general student use. A campuswide network can be accessed from student residence rooms and from off campus. Internet access, online (class) registration, at least one staffed computer lab available.

Student Life *Housing:* on-campus residence required through sophomore year. *Options:* coed, men-only, women-only, disabled students. Campus housing is university owned. Freshman campus housing is guaranteed. *Activities and organizations:* drama/theater group, student-run newspaper, choral group, marching band, Student Government Association, Greek organizations, Black United Students, International Student Association, Gay, Lesbian and Straight Supporters (GLASS), national fraternities, national sororities. *Campus security:* student patrols, late-night transport/escort service. *Student services:* personal/psychological counseling.

Athletics Member NCAA, NAIA. All NCAA Division II. *Intercollegiate sports:* baseball M(s), basketball M(s)/W(s), cheerleading M(s)/W(s), cross-country running M(s)/W(s), football M(s), golf M(s)/W(s), soccer M(s)/W(s), softball W(s), tennis M(s)/W(s), track and field M(s)/W(s), volleyball W(s). *Intramural sports:* basketball M/W, bowling M/W, football M, rugby M(c), soccer M/W, softball M/W, table tennis M/W, tennis M/W, volleyball M/W, weight lifting M/W.

Standardized Tests *Required:* SAT I or ACT (for admission).

Costs (2004–05) *Comprehensive fee:* $20,365 includes full-time tuition ($14,290) and room and board ($6075). Part-time tuition: $473 per credit hour. *College room only:* $3075. Room and board charges vary according to board plan and housing facility. *Payment plan:* installment. *Waivers:* senior citizens and employees or children of employees.

Financial Aid Of all full-time matriculated undergraduates who enrolled in 2002, 959 applied for aid, 848 were judged to have need, 52 had their need fully met. 128 Federal Work-Study jobs (averaging $875). In 2002, 48 non-need-based awards were made. *Average percent of need met:* 6%. *Average financial aid package:* $10,415. *Average need-based loan:* $3854. *Average need-based gift aid:* $3077. *Average non-need-based aid:* $1353. *Average indebtedness upon graduation:* $17,125.

Applying *Options:* common application, electronic application, deferred entrance. *Application fee:* $20. *Required:* essay or personal statement, high school transcript. *Required for some:* essay or personal statement, letters of recommendation, interview. *Recommended:* minimum 3.00 GPA, interview, 19 on ACT or 890 on SAT. *Application deadline:* rolling (freshmen). *Notification:* continuous (transfers).

Admissions Contact Mr. Cameron Cruickshank, Director of Admissions, Tiffin University, 155 Miami Street, Tiffin, OH 44883. *Phone:* 419-448-3368. *Toll-free phone:* 800-968-6446. *Fax:* 419-443-5006. *E-mail:* admiss@tiffin.edu.

■ *See page 2510 for a narrative description.*

TRI-STATE BIBLE COLLEGE
South Point, Ohio

Admissions Contact Mr. Dale Cook, Admissions Director, Tri-State Bible College, 506 Margaret Street, PO Box 445, South Point, OH 45680-8402. *Phone:* 740-377-2520.

UNION INSTITUTE & UNIVERSITY
Cincinnati, Ohio

- **Independent** university, founded 1969
- **Calendar** semesters
- **Degrees** bachelor's, master's, doctoral, and post-master's certificates
- **Urban** 5-acre campus
- **Coed,** 1,288 undergraduate students, 64% full-time, 71% women, 29% men
- **Moderately difficult** entrance level

Undergraduates 826 full-time, 462 part-time. Students come from 45 states and territories, 6 other countries, 23% are from out of state, 26% African American, 1% Asian American or Pacific Islander, 8% Hispanic American, 0.5% Native American, 0.5% international. *Retention:* 79% of 2002 full-time freshmen returned.

Freshmen *Admission:* 38 enrolled.

Faculty *Total:* 240, 47% full-time, 77% with terminal degrees. *Student/faculty ratio:* 15:1.

Majors Business/commerce; communication/speech communication and rhetoric; criminal justice/law enforcement administration; education; health science; history; humanities; liberal arts and sciences/liberal studies; psychology; public administration; social sciences; social work.

Academic Programs *Special study options:* accelerated degree program, adult/continuing education programs, advanced placement credit, distance learning, double majors, external degree program, independent study, part-time degree program, services for LD students, student-designed majors, summer session for credit.

Library Gary Library plus 1 other with 50,000 titles, 300 audiovisual materials, an OPAC, a Web page.

Computers on Campus A campuswide network can be accessed from off campus. Internet access, at least one staffed computer lab available.

Student Life *Housing:* college housing not available. *Campus security:* late-night transport/escort service, security during class hours.

Costs (2003–04) *Tuition:* $7776 full-time, $324 per semester hour part-time. Full-time tuition and fees vary according to course load and program. *Required fees:* $72 full-time, $36 per term part-time. *Room only:* Room and board charges vary according to location. *Payment plan:* installment. *Waivers:* employees or children of employees.

Financial Aid Of all full-time matriculated undergraduates who enrolled in 2000, 587 applied for aid, 507 were judged to have need, 75 had their need fully met. 14 Federal Work-Study jobs (averaging $4500). *Average percent of need met:* 70%. *Average financial aid package:* $8000. *Average need-based loan:* $8000. *Average indebtedness upon graduation:* $26,250.

Applying *Options:* electronic application, deferred entrance. *Application fee:* $50. *Required:* essay or personal statement, high school transcript, 2 letters of recommendation, interview.

Admissions Contact Dr. Emily Harbold, Associate Vice President-Academic Affairs, Union Institute & University, 440 East McMillan Street, Cincinnati, OH 45206. *Phone:* 800-486-3116. *Toll-free phone:* 800-486-3116. *E-mail:* admissions@tui.edu.

THE UNIVERSITY OF AKRON
Akron, Ohio

- **State-supported** university, founded 1870
- **Calendar** semesters
- **Degrees** certificates, associate, bachelor's, master's, doctoral, and first professional
- **Urban** 170-acre campus with easy access to Cleveland
- **Endowment** $152.0 million
- **Coed,** 20,111 undergraduate students, 69% full-time, 54% women, 46% men
- **Minimally difficult** entrance level, 87% of applicants were admitted

Undergraduates 13,926 full-time, 6,185 part-time. Students come from 42 states and territories, 86 other countries, 2% are from out of state, 14% African American, 2% Asian American or Pacific Islander, 0.8% Hispanic American, 0.5% Native American, 0.8% international, 6% transferred in, 9% live on campus. *Retention:* 67% of 2002 full-time freshmen returned.

Freshmen *Admission:* 7,113 applied, 6,216 admitted, 3,715 enrolled. *Average high school GPA:* 2.78. *Test scores:* SAT verbal scores over 500: 50%; SAT math scores over 500: 52%; ACT scores over 18: 70%; SAT verbal scores over 600: 16%; SAT math scores over 600: 21%; ACT scores over 24: 20%; SAT verbal scores over 700: 2%; SAT math scores over 700: 4%; ACT scores over 30: 2%.

Faculty *Total:* 1,721, 47% full-time, 56% with terminal degrees. *Student/faculty ratio:* 19:1.

Majors Accounting; accounting related; accounting technology and bookkeeping; acting; administrative assistant and secretarial science; agricultural teacher education; airline flight attendant; allied health diagnostic, intervention, and treatment professions related; American government and politics; animal physiology; apparel and textiles; applied art; applied mathematics; applied mathematics related; art; art history, criticism and conservation; art teacher education; athletic training; atomic/molecular physics; audiology and hearing sciences; audiology and speech-language pathology; automotive engineering technology; aviation/airway management; banking and financial support services; behavioral sciences; bilingual and multilingual education; biological and physical sciences; biology/biological sciences; biology teacher education; biomedical/medical engineering; botany/plant biology; broadcast journalism; business administration and management; business automation/technology/data entry; business/commerce; business,

The University of Akron (continued)
management, and marketing related; business operations support and secretarial services related; business teacher education; cartography; ceramic arts and ceramics; chemical engineering; chemical technology; chemistry; chemistry teacher education; child development; civil engineering; classics and languages, literatures and linguistics; clinical laboratory science/medical technology; clinical/medical laboratory science and allied professions related; clothing/textiles; commercial and advertising art; commercial photography; communication and journalism related; communication disorders; communication/speech communication and rhetoric; community organization and advocacy; computer engineering; computer/information technology services administration related; computer science; computer systems analysis; computer teacher education; construction engineering technology; corrections; crafts, folk art and artisanry; criminal justice/law enforcement administration; criminal justice/police science; criminal justice/safety; culinary arts; cytotechnology; dance; data processing and data processing technology; design and applied arts related; developmental and child psychology; dietetics; drafting and design technology; drafting/design engineering technologies related; drama and dance teacher education; dramatic/theatre arts; dramatic/theatre arts and stagecraft related; drawing; ecology; economics; economics related; education; education (multiple levels); education related; education (specific levels and methods) related; education (specific subject areas) related; electrical, electronic and communications engineering technology; electrical, electronics and communications engineering; electromechanical technology; elementary education; engineering; engineering physics; engineering technologies related; engineering technology; English; English/language arts teacher education; entrepreneurship; environmental health; executive assistant/executive secretary; family and consumer economics related; family and consumer sciences/home economics teacher education; family and consumer sciences/human sciences; family systems; fashion merchandising; finance; finance and financial management services related; fine arts related; fine/studio arts; fire protection and safety technology; fire protection related; food science; foods, nutrition, and wellness; foreign language teacher education; French; French language teacher education; geography; geological and earth sciences/geosciences related; geological/geophysical engineering; geology/earth science; geophysics and seismology; German; German language teacher education; gerontology; health and medical administrative services related; health and physical education related; health/medical preparatory programs related; health teacher education; history; history teacher education; hospitality administration; hospitality and recreation marketing; hotel/motel administration; housing and human environments; humanities; human resources management; industrial production technologies related; industrial technology; insurance; interdisciplinary studies; interior design; international business/trade/commerce; international finance; international marketing; kindergarten/preschool education; labor and industrial relations; legal administrative assistant/secretary; legal assistant/paralegal; liberal arts and sciences and humanities related; liberal arts and sciences/liberal studies; literature; logistics and materials management; management information systems; marketing/marketing management; marketing related; mass communication/media; mathematics; mathematics and computer science; mathematics and statistics related; mathematics teacher education; mechanical engineering; mechanical engineering/mechanical technology; medical administrative assistant and medical secretary; medical/clinical assistant; medical microbiology and bacteriology; medical office management; medical radiologic technology; merchandising; merchandising, sales, and marketing operations related (general); merchandising, sales, and marketing operations related (specialized); metal and jewelry arts; middle school education; multi-/interdisciplinary studies related; music; music history, literature, and theory; musicology and ethnomusicology; music performance; music teacher education; music theory and composition; natural sciences; nursing (registered nurse training); nursing related; nursing science; opticianry; painting; philosophy; photography; physical education teaching and coaching; physical science technologies related; physics; physics related; physics teacher education; piano and organ; political science and government; political science and government related; polymer chemistry; polymer/plastics engineering; predentistry studies; pre-law studies; pre-medical studies; pre-pharmacy studies; pre-veterinary studies; printmaking; psychology; public administration and social service professions related; public relations, advertising, and applied communication related; respiratory care therapy; restaurant, culinary, and catering management; retailing; science teacher education; sculpture; secondary education; selling skills and sales; social sciences; social sciences related; social science teacher education; social studies teacher education; social work; sociology; Spanish; Spanish language teacher education; special education (mentally retarded); special education (multiply disabled); special education related; special education (specific learning disabilities); special education (speech or language impaired); speech and rhetoric; speech-language pathology; speech teacher education; statistics; substance abuse/addiction counseling; surgical technology; survey technology; teacher assistant/aide; technical teacher education; theatre design and technology; tourism and travel services management; violin, viola, guitar and other stringed instruments; visual and performing arts related; voice and opera; wind/percussion instruments; zoology/animal biology.

Academic Programs *Special study options:* academic remediation for entering students, accelerated degree program, adult/continuing education programs, advanced placement credit, cooperative education, distance learning, double majors, English as a second language, honors programs, independent study, internships, part-time degree program, services for LD students, student-designed majors, study abroad, summer session for credit. *ROTC:* Army (b), Air Force (b).

Library Bierce Library plus 3 others with 1.2 million titles, 12,849 serial subscriptions, 43,448 audiovisual materials, an OPAC, a Web page.

Computers on Campus 2450 computers available on campus for general student use. A campuswide network can be accessed from student residence rooms and from off campus that provide access to wireless campus, library has laptops for student checkout. Internet access, online (class) registration, at least one staffed computer lab available.

Student Life *Housing:* on-campus residence required for freshman year. *Options:* coed, men-only, women-only. Campus housing is university owned. Freshman campus housing is guaranteed. *Activities and organizations:* drama/theater group, student-run newspaper, radio station, choral group, marching band, Inter-Fraternity Council, Panhellenic Council, Associated Student Government, Residence Hall Program Board, American Society of Mechanical Engineers, national fraternities, national sororities. *Campus security:* 24-hour emergency response devices and patrols, student patrols, late-night transport/escort service, controlled dormitory access. *Student services:* health clinic, personal/psychological counseling, women's center, legal services.

Athletics Member NCAA. All Division I except football (Division I-A). *Intercollegiate sports:* baseball M(s), basketball M(s)/W(s), cheerleading M/W, cross-country running M(s)/W(s), golf M(s), riflery M/W, soccer M(s)/W, softball W(s), tennis M(s)/W(s), track and field M(s)/W(s), volleyball W(s). *Intramural sports:* archery M/W, basketball M/W, bowling M/W, cross-country running M/W, football M, golf M/W, lacrosse M/W, racquetball M/W, riflery M(c)/W(c), skiing (cross-country) M(c)/W(c), skiing (downhill) M(c)/W(c), soccer M/W, softball M/W, swimming W, table tennis M/W, tennis M/W, track and field M/W, volleyball M/W, weight lifting M, wrestling M.

Standardized Tests *Required:* SAT I or ACT (for admission).

Costs (2003–04) *One-time required fee:* $300. *Tuition:* state resident $5846 full-time, $244 per credit part-time; nonresident $13,335 full-time, $494 per credit part-time. Full-time tuition and fees vary according to course load, degree level, location, and student level. Part-time tuition and fees vary according to course load, degree level, location, and student level. *Required fees:* $966 full-time, $40 per credit part-time. *Room and board:* $6326; room only: $4000. Room and board charges vary according to board plan and housing facility. *Payment plan:* installment. *Waivers:* senior citizens and employees or children of employees.

Financial Aid Of all full-time matriculated undergraduates who enrolled in 2003, 9,849 applied for aid, 9,819 were judged to have need, 838 had their need fully met. 492 Federal Work-Study jobs (averaging $2582). 2,368 state and other part-time jobs (averaging $1730). In 2003, 759 non-need-based awards were made. *Average percent of need met:* 49%. *Average financial aid package:* $1988. *Average need-based loan:* $2509. *Average need-based gift aid:* $1528. *Average non-need-based aid:* $2105. *Average indebtedness upon graduation:* $15,363. *Financial aid deadline:* 3/1.

Applying *Options:* electronic application, early admission, early action, deferred entrance. *Application fee:* $30. *Required:* high school transcript. *Required for some:* essay or personal statement, 3 letters of recommendation, interview. *Application deadlines:* 8/15 (freshmen), 8/15 (transfers). *Notification:* continuous (freshmen), 3/15 (early action), continuous (transfers).

Admissions Contact Ms. Diane Raybuck, Director of Admissions, The University of Akron, 381 Buchtel Common, Akron, OH 44325-2001. *Phone:* 330-972-6425. *Toll-free phone:* 800-655-4884. *Fax:* 330-972-7676. *E-mail:* admissions@uakron.edu.

UNIVERSITY OF CINCINNATI

Cincinnati, Ohio

- **State-supported** university, founded 1819, part of University of Cincinnati System
- **Calendar** quarters
- **Degrees** certificates, associate, bachelor's, master's, doctoral, first professional, and postbachelor's certificates
- **Urban** 137-acre campus
- **Endowment** $890.9 million
- **Coed,** 19,159 undergraduate students, 82% full-time, 48% women, 52% men
- **Moderately difficult** entrance level, 88% of applicants were admitted

Undergraduates 15,725 full-time, 3,434 part-time. Students come from 48 states and territories, 93 other countries, 7% are from out of state, 14% African American, 3% Asian American or Pacific Islander, 1% Hispanic American, 0.4%

Native American, 1% international, 6% transferred in, 18% live on campus. *Retention:* 76% of 2002 full-time freshmen returned.

Freshmen *Admission:* 10,958 applied, 9,673 admitted, 3,820 enrolled. *Average high school GPA:* 3.09. *Test scores:* SAT verbal scores over 500: 63%; SAT math scores over 500: 65%; ACT scores over 18: 83%; SAT verbal scores over 600: 24%; SAT math scores over 600: 30%; ACT scores over 24: 38%; SAT verbal scores over 700: 3%; SAT math scores over 700: 5%; ACT scores over 30: 6%.

Faculty *Total:* 1,173, 95% full-time, 62% with terminal degrees. *Student/faculty ratio:* 15:1.

Majors Accounting; administrative assistant and secretarial science; aerospace, aeronautical and astronautical engineering; African-American/Black studies; anthropology; architectural engineering; architectural engineering technology; architecture; art; art history, criticism and conservation; artificial intelligence and robotics; art teacher education; Asian studies; audiology and speech-language pathology; biochemistry; biological and physical sciences; biology/biological sciences; broadcast journalism; business administration and management; chemical engineering; chemistry; child development; city/urban, community and regional planning; civil engineering; civil engineering technology; classics and languages, literatures and linguistics; clinical laboratory science/medical technology; clinical/medical laboratory technology; commercial and advertising art; comparative literature; computer and information sciences; computer engineering; computer engineering technology; computer management; computer programming; computer science; construction engineering; construction engineering technology; construction management; court reporting; criminal justice/law enforcement administration; criminal justice/police science; dance; data processing and data processing technology; drafting and design technology; dramatic/theatre arts; economics; education; electrical, electronic and communications engineering technology; electrical, electronics and communications engineering; elementary education; energy management and systems technology; engineering; engineering mechanics; engineering science; English; environmental engineering technology; environmental studies; fashion/apparel design; finance; fire protection and safety technology; fire science; foods, nutrition, and wellness; French; geography; geology/earth science; German; health/health care administration; health teacher education; heating, air conditioning, ventilation and refrigeration maintenance technology; history; humanities; human services; industrial arts; industrial design; industrial engineering; industrial radiologic technology; industrial technology; information science/studies; insurance; interior design; international relations and affairs; jazz/jazz studies; Jewish/Judaic studies; kindergarten/preschool education; Latin American studies; legal administrative assistant/secretary; legal assistant/paralegal; liberal arts and sciences/liberal studies; linguistics; literature; management information systems; marketing/marketing management; mass communication/media; mathematics; mechanical engineering; mechanical engineering/mechanical technology; medical administrative assistant and medical secretary; medical laboratory technology; medical microbiology and bacteriology; metallurgical engineering; metallurgical technology; music; music history, literature, and theory; music teacher education; natural sciences; nuclear engineering; nuclear medical technology; nursing (registered nurse training); occupational safety and health technology; operations research; pharmacology; pharmacy; philosophy; physical education teaching and coaching; physical therapy; physics; piano and organ; political science and government; pre-law studies; pre-medical studies; pre-veterinary studies; psychology; public health; public policy analysis; quality control technology; radio and television; real estate; Romance languages; safety/security technology; science teacher education; secondary education; social sciences; social work; sociology; Spanish; special education; transportation technology; urban studies/affairs; violin, viola, guitar and other stringed instruments; voice and opera; wind/percussion instruments.

Academic Programs *Special study options:* academic remediation for entering students, accelerated degree program, adult/continuing education programs, advanced placement credit, cooperative education, distance learning, double majors, English as a second language, honors programs, independent study, internships, off-campus study, part-time degree program, services for LD students, study abroad, summer session for credit. *ROTC:* Army (b), Air Force (b).

Library Langsam Library plus 7 others with 16,560 serial subscriptions, 51,224 audiovisual materials, an OPAC, a Web page.

Computers on Campus 325 computers available on campus for general student use. A campuswide network can be accessed from student residence rooms and from off campus. Internet access, online (class) registration, at least one staffed computer lab available.

Student Life *Housing:* on-campus residence required for freshman year. *Options:* coed, men-only, women-only. Freshman campus housing is guaranteed. *Activities and organizations:* drama/theater group, student-run newspaper, radio station, choral group, marching band, national fraternities, national sororities. *Campus security:* 24-hour emergency response devices and patrols, late-night transport/escort service, controlled dormitory access. *Student services:* health clinic, personal/psychological counseling, women's center, legal services.

Athletics Member NCAA. All Division I except football (Division I-A). *Intercollegiate sports:* basketball M(s)/W(s), cheerleading M/W, crew M(c)/W(c), cross-country running M(s)/W(s), golf M(s), rugby M(c), soccer M(s)/W(s), swimming M(s)/W(s), tennis M(s)/W(s), track and field M(s)/W, volleyball W(s). *Intramural sports:* archery W, badminton M/W, basketball M/W, bowling M/W, crew M(c)/W(c), football M, golf M/W, gymnastics W, ice hockey M, racquetball M/W, soccer M/W, squash M/W, swimming M/W, tennis M/W, track and field M/W, volleyball M/W, weight lifting M, wrestling M.

Standardized Tests *Required:* SAT I (for admission), SAT II: Subject Tests (for admission).

Costs (2003–04) *Tuition:* state resident $6336 full-time, $212 per credit hour part-time; nonresident $17,943 full-time, $535 per credit hour part-time. Full-time tuition and fees vary according to location. Part-time tuition and fees vary according to location. *Required fees:* $1287 full-time. *Room and board:* $7113. Room and board charges vary according to board plan and housing facility. *Payment plan:* installment. *Waivers:* employees or children of employees.

Financial Aid Of all full-time matriculated undergraduates who enrolled in 2003, 9,166 applied for aid, 7,601 were judged to have need, 819 had their need fully met. In 2003, 625 non-need-based awards were made. *Average percent of need met:* 56%. *Average financial aid package:* $7524. *Average need-based loan:* $3011. *Average need-based gift aid:* $3325. *Average non-need-based aid:* $4111.

Applying *Options:* electronic application. *Application fee:* $35. *Required:* high school transcript. *Required for some:* 2 letters of recommendation, audition. *Recommended:* interview. *Application deadline:* rolling (freshmen), rolling (transfers). *Notification:* continuous until 11/1 (freshmen), continuous (transfers).

Admissions Contact University of Cincinnati, 340 University Pavillion, Cincinnati, OH 45221-0091. *Phone:* 513-556-6999. *Toll-free phone:* 513-556-4100. *Fax:* 513-556-1105. *E-mail:* admissions@uc.edu.

■ *See page 2586 for a narrative description.*

UNIVERSITY OF DAYTON

Dayton, Ohio

- **Independent Roman Catholic** university, founded 1850
- **Calendar** semesters plus 2 6-week summer terms
- **Degrees** bachelor's, master's, doctoral, first professional, and post-master's certificates
- **Suburban** 110-acre campus with easy access to Cincinnati
- **Endowment** $254.8 million
- **Coed,** 7,103 undergraduate students, 93% full-time, 50% women, 50% men
- **Moderately difficult** entrance level, 97% of applicants were admitted

A Catholic leader in higher education, the University of Dayton offers the resources and diversity of a comprehensive university and the attention and accessibility of a small college. The impressive campus, challenging academic programs, advanced research facilities, NCAA Division I athletic programs, wired campus, and access to the Dayton metropolitan community are big-school advantages. Small classes, undergraduate emphasis, student-centered faculty and staff members, residential campus, and friendliness are small-school qualities.

Undergraduates 6,582 full-time, 521 part-time. Students come from 48 states and territories, 29 other countries, 34% are from out of state, 4% African American, 1% Asian American or Pacific Islander, 2% Hispanic American, 0.2% Native American, 0.6% international, 2% transferred in, 79% live on campus. *Retention:* 86% of 2002 full-time freshmen returned.

Freshmen *Admission:* 7,052 applied, 6,821 admitted, 1,858 enrolled. *Test scores:* SAT verbal scores over 500: 80%; SAT math scores over 500: 82%; ACT scores over 18: 99%; SAT verbal scores over 600: 34%; SAT math scores over 600: 45%; ACT scores over 24: 62%; SAT verbal scores over 700: 6%; SAT math scores over 700: 10%; ACT scores over 30: 14%.

Faculty *Total:* 822, 49% full-time. *Student/faculty ratio:* 15:1.

Majors Accounting; American studies; applied art; applied mathematics related; art; art history, criticism and conservation; art teacher education; biochemistry; biology/biological sciences; broadcast journalism; business administration and management; business/managerial economics; chemical engineering; chemistry; civil engineering; commercial and advertising art; computer engineering; computer engineering technology; computer science; criminal justice/law enforcement administration; dietetics; dramatic/theatre arts; economics; education; electrical, electronic and communications engineering technology; electrical, electronics and communications engineering; elementary education; English; environmental biology; environmental studies; finance; fine/studio arts; foods, nutrition, and wellness; French; general studies; geology/earth science; German; health teacher education; history; industrial technology; information science/studies; international business/trade/commerce; international relations and affairs; journalism; kindergarten/preschool education; kinesiology and exercise science; management information systems; marketing/marketing management; mass communication/media; mathematics; mechanical engineering; mechanical engineering/mechanical technology; music; music teacher education; music therapy; philoso-

University of Dayton (continued)

phy; photography; physical education teaching and coaching; physical sciences; physics; political science and government; pre-dentistry studies; pre-law studies; pre-medical studies; psychology; public relations/image management; radio and television; religious education; religious studies; science teacher education; secondary education; sociology; Spanish; special education; sport and fitness administration.

Academic Programs *Special study options:* academic remediation for entering students, accelerated degree program, adult/continuing education programs, advanced placement credit, cooperative education, double majors, English as a second language, honors programs, independent study, internships, off-campus study, part-time degree program, services for LD students, study abroad, summer session for credit. *ROTC:* Army (b), Air Force (c).

Library Roesch Library plus 1 other with 849,244 titles, 7,318 serial subscriptions, 1,763 audiovisual materials, an OPAC, a Web page.

Computers on Campus 1000 computers available on campus for general student use. A campuswide network can be accessed from student residence rooms and from off campus. Internet access, online (class) registration, at least one staffed computer lab available. Computer purchase or lease plan available.

Student Life *Housing:* on-campus residence required through sophomore year. *Options:* coed, men-only, women-only, disabled students. Campus housing is university owned. Freshman campus housing is guaranteed. *Activities and organizations:* drama/theater group, student-run newspaper, radio and television station, choral group, marching band, Student Government Association, marching band, Red Scare (basketball student cheering section), Campus Connection, Chi Omega, national fraternities, national sororities. *Campus security:* 24-hour emergency response devices and patrols, student patrols, late-night transport/escort service, controlled dormitory access. *Student services:* health clinic, personal/psychological counseling.

Athletics Member NCAA. All Division I except football (Division I-AA). *Intercollegiate sports:* baseball M(s), basketball M(s)/W(s), crew W, cross-country running M(s)/W(s), golf M(s)/W(s), soccer M(s)/W(s), softball W(s), tennis M(s)/W(s), track and field W(s), volleyball W(s). *Intramural sports:* archery M(c)/W(c), baseball M(c), basketball M/W, crew M(c), football M/W, golf M/W, ice hockey M(c), lacrosse M(c)/W(c), racquetball M/W, rugby M(c)/W(c), soccer M(c)/W(c), softball M/W, swimming M/W, tennis M/W, track and field M(c)/W(c), ultimate Frisbee M(c)/W(c), volleyball M(c)/W(c), water polo M(c).

Standardized Tests *Required:* SAT I or ACT (for admission).

Costs (2004–05) *Comprehensive fee:* $26,930 includes full-time tuition ($19,950), mandatory fees ($680), and room and board ($6300). Full-time tuition and fees vary according to program. Part-time tuition: $652 per credit hour. Part-time tuition and fees vary according to course load and program. *College room only:* $2700. Room and board charges vary according to board plan, housing facility, and student level. *Payment plan:* deferred payment. *Waivers:* senior citizens and employees or children of employees.

Financial Aid Of all full-time matriculated undergraduates who enrolled in 2002, 4,913 applied for aid, 3,928 were judged to have need, 2,430 had their need fully met. 955 Federal Work-Study jobs (averaging $920). 2,709 state and other part-time jobs (averaging $1465). In 2002, 2059 non-need-based awards were made. *Average percent of need met:* 81%. *Average financial aid package:* $13,258. *Average need-based loan:* $4567. *Average need-based gift aid:* $8254. *Average non-need-based aid:* $4399. *Average indebtedness upon graduation:* $21,467.

Applying *Options:* electronic application, deferred entrance. *Required:* high school transcript, 1 letter of recommendation. *Required for some:* audition required for music, music therapy, music education programs. *Recommended:* essay or personal statement, interview. *Application deadlines:* rolling (freshmen), 6/15 (transfers). *Notification:* continuous (freshmen), continuous (transfers).

Admissions Contact Mr. Robert F. Durkle, Director of Admission, University of Dayton, 300 College Park, Dayton, OH 45469-1300. *Phone:* 937-229-4411. *Toll-free phone:* 800-837-7433. *Fax:* 937-229-4729. *E-mail:* admission@udayton.edu.

■ **See pages 2596 and 2598 for narrative descriptions.**

THE UNIVERSITY OF FINDLAY

Findlay, Ohio

- **Independent** comprehensive, founded 1882, affiliated with Church of God
- **Calendar** semesters
- **Degrees** certificates, associate, bachelor's, and master's
- **Small-town** 200-acre campus with easy access to Toledo
- **Endowment** $16.4 million
- **Coed,** 3,432 undergraduate students, 78% full-time, 58% women, 42% men
- **Moderately difficult** entrance level, 74% of applicants were admitted

Neither a mega-university nor a small college, the University of Findlay (UF) is just the right size. It offers students options and opportunities without sacrificing personal attention. Total enrollment is more than 4,700. Some of UF's more innovative degree programs include 10 majors in the health professions, equestrian studies, pre-veterinary medicine, technology management, and hospitality management.

Undergraduates 2,669 full-time, 763 part-time. Students come from 45 states and territories, 34 other countries, 14% are from out of state, 3% African American, 2% Asian American or Pacific Islander, 2% Hispanic American, 0.5% Native American, 2% international, 5% transferred in, 38% live on campus. *Retention:* 73% of 2002 full-time freshmen returned.

Freshmen *Admission:* 2,682 applied, 1,980 admitted, 998 enrolled. *Average high school GPA:* 3.4. *Test scores:* SAT verbal scores over 500: 60%; SAT math scores over 500: 61%; ACT scores over 18: 89%; SAT verbal scores over 600: 19%; SAT math scores over 600: 16%; ACT scores over 24: 28%; SAT verbal scores over 700: 2%; ACT scores over 30: 1%.

Faculty *Total:* 336, 46% full-time. *Student/faculty ratio:* 19:1.

Majors Accounting; administrative assistant and secretarial science; art; art teacher education; athletic training; bilingual and multilingual education; biological and physical sciences; biology/biological sciences; broadcast journalism; business administration and management; business/corporate communications; business teacher education; clinical laboratory science/medical technology; community organization and advocacy; computer science; computer systems networking and telecommunications; creative writing; criminal justice/law enforcement administration; dramatic/theatre arts; economics; education; elementary education; English; English as a second/foreign language (teaching); environmental studies; equestrian studies; farm and ranch management; history; hotel/motel administration; humanities; human resources management; international business/trade/commerce; Japanese; journalism; logistics and materials management; marketing/marketing management; mathematics; natural sciences; nuclear medical technology; occupational therapy; philosophy; physical education teaching and coaching; physical therapy; physician assistant; political science and government; pre-law studies; pre-medical studies; pre-veterinary studies; psychology; public relations/image management; radiologic technology/science; religious studies; sales, distribution and marketing; science teacher education; secondary education; social sciences; social work; sociology; Spanish; special education; therapeutic recreation.

Academic Programs *Special study options:* academic remediation for entering students, accelerated degree program, adult/continuing education programs, advanced placement credit, cooperative education, distance learning, double majors, English as a second language, honors programs, independent study, internships, off-campus study, part-time degree program, services for LD students, student-designed majors, study abroad, summer session for credit. *ROTC:* Army (c), Air Force (c). *Unusual degree programs:* 3-2 engineering with University of Toledo, Washington University in St. Louis, Ohio Northern University; nursing with Mount Carmel College of Nursing.

Library Shafer Library with 135,000 titles, 1,050 serial subscriptions, 2,000 audiovisual materials, an OPAC.

Computers on Campus 200 computers available on campus for general student use. A campuswide network can be accessed from student residence rooms and from off campus. Internet access, online (class) registration, at least one staffed computer lab available. Computer purchase or lease plan available.

Student Life *Housing:* on-campus residence required through junior year. *Options:* coed, men-only, women-only, disabled students. Campus housing is university owned. Freshman campus housing is guaranteed. *Activities and organizations:* drama/theater group, student-run newspaper, radio and television station, choral group, marching band, Campus Program Board, pre-vet club, horse club, Circle K, international club, national fraternities, national sororities. *Campus security:* 24-hour emergency response devices and patrols, late-night transport/escort service. *Student services:* health clinic, personal/psychological counseling, women's center.

Athletics Member NCAA. All Division II. *Intercollegiate sports:* baseball M(s), basketball M(s)/W(s), cross-country running M(s)/W(s), football M(s), golf M(s)/W(s), ice hockey M(s)/W(s), soccer M(s)/W(s), softball W(s), swimming M(s)/W(s), tennis M(s)/W(s), track and field M(s)/W(s), volleyball M(s)/W(s), water polo M(c)/W(c), wrestling M(s). *Intramural sports:* basketball M/W, volleyball M/W.

Standardized Tests *Required:* SAT I or ACT (for admission).

Costs (2003–04) *Comprehensive fee:* $27,014 includes full-time tuition ($19,052), mandatory fees ($900), and room and board ($7062). Full-time tuition and fees vary according to location and program. Part-time tuition and fees vary according to location and program. *College room only:* $3540. Room and board charges vary according to housing facility. *Payment plan:* installment. *Waivers:* children of alumni, senior citizens, and employees or children of employees.

Financial Aid Of all full-time matriculated undergraduates who enrolled in 2003, 1,875 applied for aid, 1,830 were judged to have need, 355 had their need

fully met. 300 Federal Work-Study jobs (averaging $830). In 2003, 400 non-need-based awards were made. *Average percent of need met:* 84%. *Average financial aid package:* $14,150. *Average need-based loan:* $4000. *Average need-based gift aid:* $9100. *Average non-need-based aid:* $7200. *Average indebtedness upon graduation:* $17,000.

Applying *Options:* common application, electronic application, deferred entrance. *Required:* high school transcript, minimum 2.3 GPA. *Required for some:* essay or personal statement, letters of recommendation, interview. *Application deadlines:* rolling (freshmen), 8/1 (transfers). *Notification:* continuous (freshmen), continuous (transfers).

Admissions Contact Mr. Michael Momany, Executive Director of Enrollment Services, The University of Findlay, 1000 North Main Street, Findlay, OH 45840-3653. *Phone:* 419-434-4732. *Toll-free phone:* 800-548-0932. *Fax:* 419-434-4898. *E-mail:* admissions@findlay.edu.

■ *See page 2604 for a narrative description.*

UNIVERSITY OF NORTHWESTERN OHIO
Lima, Ohio

- **Independent** primarily 2-year, founded 1920
- **Calendar** quarters
- **Degrees** diplomas, associate, and bachelor's
- **Small-town** 35-acre campus with easy access to Dayton and Toledo
- **Coed,** 2,665 undergraduate students, 89% full-time, 22% women, 78% men
- **Noncompetitive** entrance level, 93% of applicants were admitted

Undergraduates 2,370 full-time, 295 part-time. Students come from 37 states and territories, 15% are from out of state, 0.6% African American, 0.2% Hispanic American, 3% transferred in, 45% live on campus.

Freshmen *Admission:* 3,000 applied, 2,800 admitted, 1,875 enrolled. *Average high school GPA:* 2.5.

Faculty *Total:* 95, 72% full-time, 9% with terminal degrees. *Student/faculty ratio:* 24:1.

Majors Accounting; administrative assistant and secretarial science; agricultural business and management; automobile/automotive mechanics technology; business administration and management; computer programming; diesel mechanics technology; health/health care administration; heating, air conditioning, ventilation and refrigeration maintenance technology; legal administrative assistant/secretary; legal assistant/paralegal; marketing/marketing management; medical administrative assistant and medical secretary; medical/clinical assistant; pharmacy technician; tourism and travel services management.

Academic Programs *Special study options:* academic remediation for entering students, accelerated degree program, adult/continuing education programs, advanced placement credit, cooperative education, distance learning, double majors, part-time degree program, summer session for credit.

Library University of Northwestern Ohio Library with 8,857 titles, 117 serial subscriptions, 10 audiovisual materials.

Computers on Campus 149 computers available on campus for general student use. A campuswide network can be accessed from off campus. Internet access, at least one staffed computer lab available.

Student Life *Housing options:* men-only, women-only, disabled students. Campus housing is university owned and leased by the school. Freshman campus housing is guaranteed. *Activities and organizations:* student-run newspaper, Students in Free Enterprise. *Campus security:* 24-hour emergency response devices and patrols, late-night transport/escort service. *Student services:* personal/psychological counseling.

Athletics *Intramural sports:* basketball M, bowling M/W, volleyball M/W.

Costs (2003–04) *Tuition:* $10,200 full-time, $175 per credit part-time. No tuition increase for student's term of enrollment. *Room only:* $2520. *Payment plan:* installment. *Waivers:* employees or children of employees.

Financial Aid Of all full-time matriculated undergraduates who enrolled in 2001, 40 Federal Work-Study jobs (averaging $2000).

Applying *Options:* electronic application, early admission, deferred entrance. *Application fee:* $50. *Required:* high school transcript. *Application deadline:* rolling (freshmen), rolling (transfers).

Admissions Contact Mr. Dan Klopp, Vice President for Enrollment Management, University of Northwestern Ohio, 1441 North Cable Road, Lima, OH 45805-1498. *Phone:* 419-227-3141. *Fax:* 419-229-6926. *E-mail:* info@nc.edu.

■ *See page 2678 for a narrative description.*

UNIVERSITY OF PHOENIX–CINCINNATI CAMPUS
Cincinnati, Ohio

Admissions Contact 110 Boggs Lane, Suite 149, Cincinnati, OH 45246.

UNIVERSITY OF PHOENIX–CLEVELAND CAMPUS
Independence, Ohio

- **Proprietary** comprehensive, founded 2000
- **Calendar** continuous
- **Degrees** certificates, associate, bachelor's, master's, doctoral, post-master's, and postbachelor's certificates (courses conducted at 121 campuses and learning centers in 25 states)
- **Urban** campus
- **Coed,** 457 undergraduate students, 100% full-time, 56% women, 44% men
- **Noncompetitive** entrance level

Undergraduates 457 full-time. 0.1% are from out of state, 25% African American, 0.2% Asian American or Pacific Islander, 1% Hispanic American, 5% international.

Freshmen *Admission:* 32 enrolled.

Faculty *Total:* 44, 7% full-time, 14% with terminal degrees. *Student/faculty ratio:* 5:1.

Majors Business administration and management; computer and information sciences; health/health care administration; management information systems; marketing/marketing management.

Academic Programs *Special study options:* accelerated degree program, adult/continuing education programs, advanced placement credit, distance learning, external degree program, independent study.

Library University Library with 27.1 million titles, 11,648 serial subscriptions, an OPAC, a Web page.

Computers on Campus A campuswide network can be accessed from off campus. Internet access, at least one staffed computer lab available.

Student Life *Housing:* college housing not available.

Costs (2003–04) *Tuition:* $11,250 full-time, $375 per credit part-time. *Waivers:* employees or children of employees.

Financial Aid *Average financial aid package:* $1473.

Applying *Options:* deferred entrance. *Application fee:* $100. *Required:* 1 letter of recommendation, 2 years of work experience, 23 years of age. *Required for some:* high school transcript. *Application deadline:* rolling (freshmen), rolling (transfers).

Admissions Contact Ms. Beth Barilla, Director of Admissions, University of Phoenix–Cleveland Campus, 4615 East Elwood Street, Mail Stop AA-K101, Phoenix, AZ 85040-1958. *Phone:* 480-317-6000. *Fax:* 480-594-1758. *E-mail:* beth.barilla@phoenix.edu.

UNIVERSITY OF PHOENIX–COLUMBUS OHIO CAMPUS
Columbus, Ohio

Admissions Contact 8425 Pulsar Place, Columbus, OH 43240.

UNIVERSITY OF RIO GRANDE
Rio Grande, Ohio

- **Independent** comprehensive, founded 1876
- **Calendar** semesters
- **Degrees** associate, bachelor's, and master's
- **Rural** 170-acre campus
- **Endowment** $22.6 million
- **Coed**
- **Noncompetitive** entrance level

Faculty *Student/faculty ratio:* 18:1.

Student Life *Campus security:* 24-hour emergency response devices and patrols, late-night transport/escort service, controlled dormitory access.

Athletics Member NAIA.

Standardized Tests *Required:* ACT (for placement).

Costs (2003–04) *Tuition:* area resident $9514 full-time; state resident $9718 full-time; nonresident $10,532 full-time. *Required fees:* $520 full-time. *Room and board:* $5768. Room and board charges vary according to board plan.

Financial Aid Of all full-time matriculated undergraduates who enrolled in 2002, 1,626 applied for aid, 1,219 were judged to have need, 613 had their need fully met. In 2002, 366. *Average percent of need met:* 73. *Average financial aid package:* $7835. *Average need-based loan:* $4281. *Average need-based gift aid:* $3755. *Average indebtedness upon graduation:* $13,750.

Applying *Options:* common application. *Application fee:* $15. *Required:* high school transcript, medical history.

University of Rio Grande (continued)

Admissions Contact Mr. Mark F. Abell, Executive Director of Admissions, University of Rio Grande, PO Box 500, Rio Grande, OH 45674. *Phone:* 740-245-7208. *Toll-free phone:* 800-282-7201. *Fax:* 740-245-7260. *E-mail:* elambert@rio.edu.

■ *See page 2694 for a narrative description.*

UNIVERSITY OF TOLEDO
Toledo, Ohio

- **State-supported** university, founded 1872
- **Calendar** semesters
- **Degrees** certificates, associate, bachelor's, master's, doctoral, first professional, post-master's, and postbachelor's certificates
- **Suburban** 407-acre campus with easy access to Detroit
- **Endowment** $29.6 million
- **Coed,** 17,388 undergraduate students, 79% full-time, 51% women, 49% men
- **Noncompetitive** entrance level, 97% of applicants were admitted

Undergraduates 13,773 full-time, 3,615 part-time. Students come from 36 states and territories, 93 other countries, 8% are from out of state, 12% African American, 2% Asian American or Pacific Islander, 2% Hispanic American, 0.3% Native American, 2% international, 7% transferred in, 18% live on campus. *Retention:* 72% of 2002 full-time freshmen returned.

Freshmen *Admission:* 8,877 applied, 8,650 admitted, 3,884 enrolled. *Average high school GPA:* 3.02. *Test scores:* SAT verbal scores over 500: 69%; SAT math scores over 500: 60%; ACT scores over 18: 82%; SAT verbal scores over 600: 29%; SAT math scores over 600: 25%; ACT scores over 24: 31%; SAT verbal scores over 700: 4%; SAT math scores over 700: 4%; ACT scores over 30: 4%.

Faculty *Total:* 1,180, 58% full-time, 57% with terminal degrees. *Student/faculty ratio:* 18:1.

Majors Accounting; administrative assistant and secretarial science; adult and continuing education; adult development and aging; African-American/Black studies; allied health diagnostic, intervention, and treatment professions related; American studies; anthropology; applied art; architectural drafting and CAD/CADD; art; art history, criticism and conservation; art teacher education; Asian studies; astronomy; audiology and speech-language pathology; biological and physical sciences; biology/biological sciences; biomedical/medical engineering; business administration and management; business administration, management and operations related; business automation/technology/data entry; business/commerce; business, management, and marketing related; business/managerial economics; business teacher education; cardiovascular technology; chemical engineering; chemical technology; chemistry; civil engineering; civil engineering technology; classics and languages, literatures and linguistics; clinical laboratory science/medical technology; communication/speech communication and rhetoric; community organization and advocacy; computer engineering; computer programming; computer programming (specific applications); computer science; computer systems analysis; computer typography and composition equipment operation; construction engineering technology; consumer merchandising/retailing management; corrections; criminal justice/police science; criminal justice/safety; data processing and data processing technology; developmental and child psychology; drafting and design technology; dramatic/theatre arts; drawing; economics; education; educational/instructional media design; education (specific levels and methods) related; education (specific subject areas) related; electrical, electronic and communications engineering technology; electrical, electronics and communications engineering; electromechanical technology; elementary education; emergency medical technology (EMT paramedic); engineering; engineering physics; English; English/language arts teacher education; entrepreneurship; environmental engineering technology; environmental studies; European studies; experimental psychology; film/cinema studies; finance; fine/studio arts; fire protection and safety technology; French; French language teacher education; general studies; geography; geology/earth science; German; German language teacher education; gerontology; health information/medical records administration; health teacher education; history; hospital and health care facilities administration; human development and family studies related; humanities; human resources management; industrial engineering; industrial technology; information science/studies; international business/trade/commerce; international relations and affairs; journalism; kindergarten/preschool education; kinesiology and exercise science; Latin American studies; legal administrative assistant/secretary; legal assistant/paralegal; liberal arts and sciences/liberal studies; linguistics; literature; logistics and materials management; management information systems; management sciences and quantitative methods related; marketing/marketing management; marketing research; mass communication/media; mathematics; mathematics teacher education; mechanical engineering; mechanical engineering/mechanical technology; medical/clinical assistant; medieval and Renaissance studies; mental and social health services and allied professions related; mental health/rehabilitation; multi-/interdisciplinary studies related; music; music teacher education; natural sciences; Near and Middle Eastern studies; nursing (registered nurse training); nursing related; operations management; organizational behavior; parks, recreation and leisure; parks, recreation, and leisure related; pharmacy; pharmacy, pharmaceutical sciences, and administration related; philosophy; physical education teaching and coaching; physical sciences; physical therapy; physics; political science and government; pre-dentistry studies; pre-law studies; pre-medical studies; pre-veterinary studies; psychiatric/mental health services technology; psychology; psychology related; public health education and promotion; public policy analysis; religious studies; respiratory care therapy; science teacher education; secondary education; social sciences; social studies teacher education; social work; sociology; Spanish; Spanish language teacher education; special education; special education (emotionally disturbed); special education (hearing impaired); special education (multiply disabled); special education related; special education (specific learning disabilities); special education (speech or language impaired); special education (vision impaired); speech-language pathology; speech therapy; structural engineering; substance abuse/addiction counseling; trade and industrial teacher education; transportation technology; urban studies/affairs; welding technology; women's studies.

Academic Programs *Special study options:* academic remediation for entering students, adult/continuing education programs, advanced placement credit, cooperative education, distance learning, double majors, honors programs, independent study, internships, off-campus study, part-time degree program, services for LD students, student-designed majors, study abroad, summer session for credit. *ROTC:* Army (b), Air Force (c).

Library Carlson Library plus 3 others with 1.3 million titles, 4,754 serial subscriptions, 4,695 audiovisual materials, an OPAC, a Web page.

Computers on Campus 2800 computers available on campus for general student use. A campuswide network can be accessed from student residence rooms and from off campus that provide access to online transcripts, student account and grade information. Internet access, online (class) registration, at least one staffed computer lab available.

Student Life *Housing:* on-campus residence required for freshman year. *Options:* coed, women-only, disabled students. Campus housing is university owned. *Activities and organizations:* drama/theater group, student-run newspaper, radio station, choral group, marching band, student government, University YMCA, Newman Club, International Student Association, Campus Activities and Programming, national fraternities, national sororities. *Campus security:* 24-hour emergency response devices and patrols, student patrols, late-night transport/escort service, controlled dormitory access, bicycle patrols by security staff, crime prevention officer. *Student services:* health clinic, personal/psychological counseling, women's center, legal services.

Athletics Member NCAA. All Division I except football (Division I-A). *Intercollegiate sports:* baseball M(s), basketball M(s)/W(s), cross-country running M(s)/W(s), golf M(s)/W(s), soccer W(s), softball W(s), swimming M(s)/W(s), tennis M(s)/W(s), track and field M(s)/W(s), volleyball W(s). *Intramural sports:* badminton M/W, basketball M/W, bowling M/W, crew M(c)/W(c), fencing M(c)/W(c), football M/W, golf M/W, lacrosse M/W, racquetball M/W, sailing M(c)/W(c), skiing (cross-country) M(c)/W(c), skiing (downhill) M(c)/W(c), soccer M(c)/W(c), softball M/W, swimming M/W, table tennis M/W, tennis M/W, track and field M/W, volleyball M/W, water polo M/W, weight lifting M/W.

Standardized Tests *Required for some:* SAT I or ACT (for admission). *Recommended:* SAT I (for admission), ACT (for admission).

Costs (2003–04) *Tuition:* state resident $5410 full-time, $267 per semester hour part-time; nonresident $14,048 full-time, $627 per semester hour part-time. *Required fees:* $1004 full-time. *Room and board:* $6834. Room and board charges vary according to board plan, housing facility, and location. *Payment plan:* installment. *Waivers:* employees or children of employees.

Financial Aid Of all full-time matriculated undergraduates who enrolled in 2003, 9,930 applied for aid, 7,827 were judged to have need, 866 had their need fully met. 434 Federal Work-Study jobs (averaging $2338). In 2003, 2001 non-need-based awards were made. *Average percent of need met:* 56%. *Average financial aid package:* $6881. *Average need-based loan:* $3770. *Average need-based gift aid:* $4372. *Average non-need-based aid:* $3130. *Average indebtedness upon graduation:* $21,272.

Applying *Options:* electronic application, deferred entrance. *Application fee:* $40. *Required:* high school transcript. *Required for some:* minimum 2.0 GPA. *Application deadline:* rolling (freshmen), rolling (transfers). *Notification:* continuous (freshmen), continuous (transfers).

Admissions Contact Ms. Nancy Hintz, Assistant Director, University of Toledo, 2801 West Bancroft, Toledo, OH 43606-3398. *Phone:* 419-530-5728. *Toll-free phone:* 800-5TOLEDO. *Fax:* 419-530-5872. *E-mail:* enroll@utnet.utoledo.edu.

URBANA UNIVERSITY
Urbana, Ohio

- **Independent** comprehensive, founded 1850, affiliated with Church of the New Jerusalem
- **Calendar** semesters
- **Degrees** associate, bachelor's, and master's
- **Small-town** 128-acre campus with easy access to Columbus and Dayton
- **Coed,** 1,441 undergraduate students, 61% full-time, 55% women, 45% men
- **Moderately difficult** entrance level, 58% of applicants were admitted

Founded in 1850, Urbana University is located on 128 acres in Urbana, Ohio. Urbana offers a liberal arts education in a small-university environment while emphasizing individual attention in the academic and social aspects of campus life. Degrees are awarded within 6 academic divisions at the associate, bachelor's, and master's level. Scholarships are available for academics, athletics, and special-interest activities.

Undergraduates 883 full-time, 558 part-time. 14% African American, 0.4% Asian American or Pacific Islander, 0.5% Hispanic American, 0.6% Native American, 0.1% international, 8% transferred in. *Retention:* 76% of 2002 full-time freshmen returned.

Freshmen *Admission:* 538 applied, 312 admitted, 261 enrolled.

Faculty *Total:* 115, 43% full-time, 39% with terminal degrees. *Student/faculty ratio:* 16:1.

Majors Accounting; adult and continuing education; athletic training; biology/biological sciences; business administration and management; business/managerial economics; chemistry; criminal justice/law enforcement administration; education; elementary education; English; health teacher education; history; human resources management; liberal arts and sciences/liberal studies; marketing/marketing management; mass communication/media; middle school education; philosophy; pre-dentistry studies; pre-law studies; pre-medical studies; pre-veterinary studies; psychology; religious studies; science teacher education; secondary education; sociology.

Academic Programs *Special study options:* academic remediation for entering students, accelerated degree program, adult/continuing education programs, advanced placement credit, cooperative education, double majors, honors programs, independent study, internships, off-campus study, part-time degree program, services for LD students, student-designed majors, summer session for credit.

Library Swedenborg Memorial Library with 61,600 titles, 800 serial subscriptions, 22,036 audiovisual materials, an OPAC, a Web page.

Computers on Campus 75 computers available on campus for general student use. A campuswide network can be accessed from student residence rooms. Internet access, at least one staffed computer lab available.

Student Life *Housing:* on-campus residence required through junior year. *Options:* coed, men-only, women-only. Campus housing is university owned. *Activities and organizations:* drama/theater group, student-run newspaper, radio station, choral group, Student Government Association, business club, education club, drama club, Student Activities Planning Committee. *Campus security:* 24-hour emergency response devices and patrols, late-night transport/escort service. *Student services:* health clinic, personal/psychological counseling.

Athletics Member NAIA. *Intercollegiate sports:* baseball M(s), basketball M(s)/W(s), football M(s), golf M(s), soccer M(s)/W(s), softball W(s), volleyball W(s). *Intramural sports:* basketball M/W, football M, racquetball M/W, soccer M/W, swimming M/W, table tennis M/W, track and field M/W, volleyball M/W, water polo M/W, weight lifting M.

Standardized Tests *Required:* SAT I or ACT (for admission).

Costs (2004–05) *Comprehensive fee:* $19,900 includes full-time tuition ($14,220) and room and board ($5680). Full-time tuition and fees vary according to location. Part-time tuition: $295 per semester hour. Part-time tuition and fees vary according to location. *Required fees:* $90 per term part-time. *College room only:* $1920. Room and board charges vary according to board plan, housing facility, location, and student level. *Payment plans:* installment, deferred payment. *Waivers:* children of alumni, senior citizens, and employees or children of employees.

Financial Aid Of all full-time matriculated undergraduates who enrolled in 2003, 727 applied for aid, 727 were judged to have need, 640 had their need fully met. 328 Federal Work-Study jobs (averaging $1000). *Average percent of need met:* 46%. *Average financial aid package:* $13,121. *Average need-based loan:* $4833. *Average need-based gift aid:* $2336. *Average indebtedness upon graduation:* $17,125.

Applying *Options:* electronic application, deferred entrance. *Application fee:* $25. *Required:* essay or personal statement, high school transcript, minimum 2.0 GPA. *Required for some:* 2 letters of recommendation, interview. *Recommended:* interview. *Application deadline:* rolling (freshmen), rolling (transfers). *Notification:* 8/15 (freshmen), 8/15 (transfers).

Admissions Contact Ms. Melissa Tolle, Associate Director of Admissions, Urbana University, 579 College Way, Urbana, OH 93078. *Phone:* 937-484-1356. *Toll-free phone:* 800-7-URBANA. *Fax:* 937-484-1389. *E-mail:* admiss@urbana.edu.

URSULINE COLLEGE
Pepper Pike, Ohio

- **Independent Roman Catholic** comprehensive, founded 1871
- **Calendar** semesters
- **Degrees** bachelor's, master's, and post-master's certificates (applications from men are also accepted)
- **Suburban** 112-acre campus with easy access to Cleveland
- **Endowment** $17.1 million
- **Women only,** 1,095 undergraduate students, 60% full-time
- **Minimally difficult** entrance level, 70% of applicants were admitted

Undergraduates 661 full-time, 434 part-time. Students come from 9 states and territories, 7 other countries, 1% are from out of state, 24% African American, 1% Asian American or Pacific Islander, 2% Hispanic American, 0.4% Native American, 1% international, 17% transferred in, 11% live on campus. *Retention:* 69% of 2002 full-time freshmen returned.

Freshmen *Admission:* 351 applied, 244 admitted, 118 enrolled. *Average high school GPA:* 3.13. *Test scores:* SAT verbal scores over 500: 41%; SAT math scores over 500: 39%; ACT scores over 18: 66%; SAT verbal scores over 600: 10%; SAT math scores over 600: 6%; ACT scores over 24: 13%; ACT scores over 30: 1%.

Faculty *Total:* 185, 32% full-time, 39% with terminal degrees. *Student/faculty ratio:* 10:1.

Majors Accounting; American studies; art history, criticism and conservation; art teacher education; behavioral sciences; biological and biomedical sciences related; biology/biological sciences; biotechnology; business administration and management; business administration, management and operations related; Christian studies; early childhood education; English; English/language arts teacher education; environmental biology; fashion/apparel design; fashion merchandising; fine/studio arts; graphic design; health and medical administrative services related; health/health care administration; health services administration; health services/allied health/health sciences; historic preservation and conservation; history; hospital and health care facilities administration; humanities; human resources management; interior design; legal assistant/paralegal; management information systems; marketing/marketing management; mathematics; mathematics teacher education; middle school education; multi-/interdisciplinary studies related; nursing (registered nurse training); philosophy; psychology; public relations/image management; religious studies related; science teacher education; social studies teacher education; social work; sociology; special education; work and family studies.

Academic Programs *Special study options:* academic remediation for entering students, accelerated degree program, adult/continuing education programs, advanced placement credit, cooperative education, distance learning, double majors, independent study, internships, off-campus study, part-time degree program, services for LD students, summer session for credit.

Library Ralph M. Besse Library with 126,491 titles, 332 serial subscriptions, 6,926 audiovisual materials, an OPAC, a Web page.

Computers on Campus 107 computers available on campus for general student use. A campuswide network can be accessed from student residence rooms. Internet access, at least one staffed computer lab available.

Student Life *Housing options:* Campus housing is university owned. Freshman applicants given priority for college housing. *Activities and organizations:* drama/theater group, student-run newspaper, Student Government Association, Student Nurses of Ursuline College, Fashion Focus, Students United for Black Awareness, drama club. *Campus security:* 24-hour emergency response devices and patrols, late-night transport/escort service, controlled dormitory access. *Student services:* health clinic, personal/psychological counseling.

Athletics Member NAIA. *Intercollegiate sports:* basketball W(s), golf W(s), soccer W(s), softball W(s), tennis W(s), volleyball W(s).

Standardized Tests *Required:* SAT I or ACT (for admission).

Costs (2003–04) *Comprehensive fee:* $22,728 includes full-time tuition ($17,100), mandatory fees ($170), and room and board ($5458). *Room and board:* Room and board charges vary according to board plan. *Payment plan:* installment. *Waivers:* employees or children of employees.

Financial Aid Of all full-time matriculated undergraduates who enrolled in 2003, 540 applied for aid, 509 were judged to have need, 115 had their need fully

Ursuline College (continued)
met. In 2003, 44 non-need-based awards were made. *Average percent of need met:* 78%. *Average financial aid package:* $15,872. *Average non-need-based aid:* $4212. *Average indebtedness upon graduation:* $22,111.

Applying *Options:* early action, deferred entrance. *Application fee:* $25. *Required:* high school transcript. *Recommended:* essay or personal statement, minimum 2.0 GPA, letters of recommendation, interview. *Application deadline:* rolling (freshmen), rolling (transfers). *Notification:* continuous (freshmen), 2/15 (early action), continuous (transfers).

Admissions Contact Ms. Sarah Carr, Director of Admissions, Ursuline College, 2550 Lander Road, Pepper Pike, OH 44124. *Phone:* 440-449-4203. *Toll-free phone:* 888-URSULINE. *Fax:* 440-684-6138. *E-mail:* admission@ursuline.edu.

WALSH UNIVERSITY
North Canton, Ohio

- **Independent Roman Catholic** comprehensive, founded 1958
- **Calendar** semesters
- **Degrees** certificates, associate, bachelor's, and master's
- **Small-town** 107-acre campus with easy access to Cleveland
- **Endowment** $5.0 million
- **Coed,** 1,573 undergraduate students, 73% full-time, 60% women, 40% men
- **Moderately difficult** entrance level, 82% of applicants were admitted

Undergraduates 1,149 full-time, 424 part-time. Students come from 20 states and territories, 16 other countries, 1% are from out of state, 6% African American, 0.4% Asian American or Pacific Islander, 0.7% Hispanic American, 0.3% Native American, 2% international, 8% transferred in, 50% live on campus. *Retention:* 70% of 2002 full-time freshmen returned.

Freshmen *Admission:* 970 applied, 792 admitted, 294 enrolled. *Average high school GPA:* 3.22. *Test scores:* ACT scores over 18: 89%; ACT scores over 24: 30%; ACT scores over 30: 2%.

Faculty *Total:* 196, 37% full-time, 40% with terminal degrees. *Student/faculty ratio:* 14:1.

Majors Accounting; athletic training; behavioral sciences; biological and physical sciences; biology/biological sciences; business administration and management; chemistry; communication and media related; computer science; education; elementary education; English; finance; French; history; human services; kindergarten/preschool education; liberal arts and sciences/liberal studies; marketing/marketing management; mathematics; modern languages; nursing (registered nurse training); pastoral studies/counseling; philosophy; physical education teaching and coaching; political science and government; pre-dentistry studies; pre-medical studies; pre-veterinary studies; psychology; religious studies; science teacher education; secondary education; sociology; Spanish; special education; theology.

Academic Programs *Special study options:* academic remediation for entering students, accelerated degree program, adult/continuing education programs, advanced placement credit, double majors, English as a second language, freshman honors college, honors programs, internships, off-campus study, part-time degree program, services for LD students, student-designed majors, summer session for credit. *Unusual degree programs:* 3-2 forestry with University of Michigan.

Library Walsh University Library with 132,957 titles, 663 serial subscriptions, 1,434 audiovisual materials, an OPAC, a Web page.

Computers on Campus 115 computers available on campus for general student use. A campuswide network can be accessed from student residence rooms and from off campus. Internet access, at least one staffed computer lab available.

Student Life *Housing:* on-campus residence required through senior year. *Options:* coed, men-only, women-only. Campus housing is university owned. Freshman campus housing is guaranteed. *Activities and organizations:* drama/theater group, student-run newspaper, radio station, choral group, Walsh University Student Government, Circle K, Business & Communication Club, Behavioral Science Club, Education Club. *Campus security:* 24-hour emergency response devices and patrols, controlled dormitory access. *Student services:* health clinic, personal/psychological counseling.

Athletics Member NAIA. *Intercollegiate sports:* baseball M(s), basketball M(s)/W(s), cheerleading W, cross-country running M(s)/W(s), football M(s), golf M(s)/W(s), soccer M(s)/W(s), softball W(s), tennis M(s)/W(s), track and field M(s)/W(s), volleyball W(s). *Intramural sports:* basketball M/W, bowling M/W, football M/W, soccer M/W, softball M/W, table tennis M/W, volleyball M/W.

Standardized Tests *Required:* SAT I or ACT (for admission).

Costs (2004–05) *One-time required fee:* $165. *Comprehensive fee:* $23,310 includes full-time tuition ($15,100), mandatory fees ($510), and room and board ($7700). Full-time tuition and fees vary according to course load. Part-time tuition: $500 per credit. *Required fees:* $17 per credit part-time. *College room only:* $4500. Room and board charges vary according to board plan and housing facility. *Payment plans:* installment, deferred payment. *Waivers:* children of alumni and employees or children of employees.

Financial Aid Of all full-time matriculated undergraduates who enrolled in 2003, 969 applied for aid, 843 were judged to have need, 657 had their need fully met. 182 Federal Work-Study jobs (averaging $1480). 30 state and other part-time jobs (averaging $1418). In 2003, 157 non-need-based awards were made. *Average percent of need met:* 81%. *Average financial aid package:* $10,364. *Average need-based loan:* $2424. *Average need-based gift aid:* $5602. *Average non-need-based aid:* $4312. *Average indebtedness upon graduation:* $18,200.

Applying *Options:* common application, electronic application, early admission, deferred entrance. *Application fee:* $25. *Required:* high school transcript, minimum 2.1 GPA. *Required for some:* essay or personal statement, minimum 3.0 GPA, 2 letters of recommendation. *Recommended:* interview. *Application deadline:* rolling (freshmen), rolling (transfers). *Notification:* continuous (freshmen), continuous (transfers).

Admissions Contact Mr. Brett Freshour, Dean of Enrollment Management, Walsh University, 2020 East Maple. *Phone:* 330-490-7171. *Toll-free phone:* 800-362-9846 (in-state); 800-362-8846 (out-of-state). *Fax:* 330-490-7165. *E-mail:* admissions@walsh.edu.

■ *See page 2778 for a narrative description.*

WILBERFORCE UNIVERSITY
Wilberforce, Ohio

- **Independent** 4-year, founded 1856, affiliated with African Methodist Episcopal Church
- **Calendar** semesters
- **Degree** bachelor's
- **Rural** 125-acre campus with easy access to Dayton
- **Endowment** $9.3 million
- **Coed,** 1,180 undergraduate students, 99% full-time, 60% women, 40% men
- **Minimally difficult** entrance level, 22% of applicants were admitted

Founded in 1856, Wilberforce University is the first predominantly African-American private university in the nation. Students of all faiths, races, colors, and national and ethnic origins are welcome. Wilberforce University is accredited by the North Central Association and is a member of the United Negro College Fund.

Undergraduates 1,166 full-time, 14 part-time. Students come from 30 states and territories, 3 other countries, 38% are from out of state, 90% African American, 0.3% Asian American or Pacific Islander, 0.9% Hispanic American, 0.4% Native American, 0.3% international, 3% transferred in, 85% live on campus.

Freshmen *Admission:* 2,405 applied, 521 admitted, 190 enrolled. *Average high school GPA:* 2.5.

Faculty *Total:* 74, 66% full-time. *Student/faculty ratio:* 17:1.

Majors Accounting; accounting and finance; biology/biological sciences; business administration and management; business/managerial economics; chemistry; computer engineering; computer science; economics; electrical, electronics and communications engineering; engineering physics; finance; fine/studio arts; health/health care administration; information science/studies; liberal arts and sciences/liberal studies; literature; marketing/marketing management; mass communication/media; mathematics; music theory and composition; political science and government; psychology; rehabilitation therapy; sociology; voice and opera.

Academic Programs *Special study options:* academic remediation for entering students, advanced placement credit, cooperative education, external degree program, freshman honors college, honors programs, off-campus study, study abroad. *ROTC:* Army (c), Air Force (c). *Unusual degree programs:* 3-2 engineering with University of Dayton, University of Cincinnati; computer science with University of Dayton.

Library Rembert E. Stokes Library with 63,000 titles, 650 serial subscriptions, 500 audiovisual materials, an OPAC, a Web page.

Computers on Campus 77 computers available on campus for general student use. A campuswide network can be accessed from student residence rooms and from off campus. Internet access, at least one staffed computer lab available.

Student Life *Housing:* on-campus residence required through junior year. *Options:* coed, men-only, women-only. *Activities and organizations:* drama/theater group, student-run newspaper, radio station, choral group, yearbook staff, campus radio station, National Student Business League, Student Government Association, national fraternities, national sororities. *Campus security:* 24-hour emergency response devices and patrols, controlled dormitory access. *Student services:* health clinic, personal/psychological counseling.

Athletics Member NAIA. *Intercollegiate sports:* basketball M/W, cross-country running M/W, golf M/W. *Intramural sports:* basketball M/W, soccer M/W, softball M/W, tennis M/W, volleyball M/W.

Standardized Tests *Required:* SAT I or ACT (for admission).
Costs (2003–04) *Comprehensive fee:* $16,090 includes full-time tuition ($9720), mandatory fees ($1050), and room and board ($5320). Part-time tuition: $376 per credit hour. *College room only:* $2820. *Payment plans:* installment, deferred payment. *Waivers:* employees or children of employees.
Financial Aid *Financial aid deadline:* 6/1.
Applying *Options:* common application, electronic application, early admission, deferred entrance. *Application fee:* $20. *Required:* essay or personal statement, high school transcript, minimum 2.0 GPA, 2 letters of recommendation. *Recommended:* interview. *Application deadlines:* 7/1 (freshmen), 7/1 (transfers). *Notification:* continuous until 8/1 (freshmen), continuous until 8/1 (transfers).
Admissions Contact Mr. Kenneth C. Christmon, Director of Admissions, Wilberforce University, PO Box 1001, Wilberforce, OH 45384-1001. *Phone:* 937-708-5789. *Toll-free phone:* 800-367-8568. *Fax:* 937-376-4751. *E-mail:* kchristm@wilberforce.edu.

■ *See page 2848 for a narrative description.*

WILMINGTON COLLEGE
Wilmington, Ohio

- **Independent Friends** comprehensive, founded 1870
- **Calendar** semesters
- **Degrees** bachelor's and master's
- **Small-town** 1465-acre campus with easy access to Cincinnati and Columbus
- **Endowment** $19.0 million
- **Coed**
- **Moderately difficult** entrance level

Faculty *Student/faculty ratio:* 16:1.
Student Life *Campus security:* 24-hour emergency response devices and patrols, late-night transport/escort service, controlled dormitory access.
Athletics Member NCAA. All Division III.
Standardized Tests *Required:* SAT I or ACT (for admission).
Costs (2003–04) *Comprehensive fee:* $24,172 includes full-time tuition ($17,256), mandatory fees ($426), and room and board ($6490). Part-time tuition and fees vary according to course load. *College room only:* $3080. Room and board charges vary according to board plan and housing facility.
Financial Aid Of all full-time matriculated undergraduates who enrolled in 2003, 1,065 applied for aid, 1,000 were judged to have need, 311 had their need fully met. 518 Federal Work-Study jobs (averaging $1342). In 2003, 119. *Average percent of need met:* 87. *Average financial aid package:* $16,395. *Average need-based loan:* $4864. *Average need-based gift aid:* $11,185. *Average non-need-based aid:* $6490. *Average indebtedness upon graduation:* $21,235.
Applying *Options:* deferred entrance. *Application fee:* $25. *Required:* high school transcript. *Recommended:* minimum 2.5 GPA, 1 letter of recommendation, interview.
Admissions Contact Ms. Tina Garland, Interim Director of Admission and Financial Aid, Wilmington College, Pyle Center Box 1325, 251 Ludovic Street, Wilmington, OH 45177. *Phone:* 937-382-6661 Ext. 260. *Toll-free phone:* 800-341-9318 Ext. 260. *Fax:* 937-382-7077. *E-mail:* admission@wilmington.edu.

WITTENBERG UNIVERSITY
Springfield, Ohio

- **Independent** comprehensive, founded 1845, affiliated with Evangelical Lutheran Church
- **Calendar** semesters
- **Degrees** bachelor's and master's
- **Suburban** 71-acre campus with easy access to Columbus and Dayton
- **Endowment** $88.4 million
- **Coed,** 2,152 undergraduate students, 95% full-time, 58% women, 42% men
- **Moderately difficult** entrance level, 74% of applicants were admitted

Undergraduates 2,055 full-time, 97 part-time. Students come from 40 states and territories, 23 other countries, 46% are from out of state, 6% African American, 1% Asian American or Pacific Islander, 0.6% Hispanic American, 0.2% Native American, 3% international, 2% transferred in, 86% live on campus. *Retention:* 82% of 2002 full-time freshmen returned.
Freshmen *Admission:* 3,048 applied, 2,263 admitted, 549 enrolled. *Average high school GPA:* 3.40. *Test scores:* SAT verbal scores over 500: 85%; SAT math scores over 500: 85%; ACT scores over 18: 97%; SAT verbal scores over 600: 39%; SAT math scores over 600: 39%; ACT scores over 24: 49%; SAT verbal scores over 700: 7%; SAT math scores over 700: 5%; ACT scores over 30: 7%.
Faculty *Total:* 200, 74% full-time, 78% with terminal degrees. *Student/faculty ratio:* 14:1.
Majors American studies; art; Asian studies (East); biochemistry; biology/biological sciences; business administration and management; business/managerial economics; chemistry; communication/speech communication and rhetoric; computer science; dramatic/theatre arts; economics; education; elementary education; English; environmental studies; French; geography; geology/earth science; German; history; liberal arts and sciences/liberal studies; marketing/marketing management; mathematics; music; philosophy; physical sciences; physics; political science and government; pre-dentistry studies; pre-law studies; pre-medical studies; pre-veterinary studies; psychology; religious studies; Russian studies; social sciences; sociology; Spanish; urban studies/affairs.
Academic Programs *Special study options:* academic remediation for entering students, accelerated degree program, adult/continuing education programs, advanced placement credit, cooperative education, double majors, English as a second language, external degree program, freshman honors college, honors programs, independent study, internships, off-campus study, part-time degree program, student-designed majors, study abroad, summer session for credit. *ROTC:* Army (c), Air Force (c). *Unusual degree programs:* 3-2 engineering with Georgia Institute of Technology, Washington University in St. Louis, Case Western Reserve University; forestry with Duke University; nursing with Case Western Reserve University, Johns Hopkins University; occupational therapy with Washington University in St. Louis.
Library Thomas Library plus 2 others with 350,000 titles, 1,300 serial subscriptions, an OPAC, a Web page.
Computers on Campus 750 computers available on campus for general student use. A campuswide network can be accessed from student residence rooms and from off campus. Internet access, online (class) registration, at least one staffed computer lab available.
Student Life *Housing:* on-campus residence required through sophomore year. *Options:* coed, women-only. Campus housing is university owned, leased by the school and is provided by a third party. Freshman campus housing is guaranteed. *Activities and organizations:* drama/theater group, student-run newspaper, radio station, choral group, Student Senate, Union Board, Choirs, Weaver Chapel Association, national fraternities, national sororities. *Campus security:* 24-hour emergency response devices and patrols, student patrols, late-night transport/escort service, controlled dormitory access, crime prevention programs. *Student services:* health clinic, personal/psychological counseling, women's center.
Athletics Member NCAA. All Division III. *Intercollegiate sports:* baseball M, basketball M/W, cheerleading M/W, crew M(c)/W(c), cross-country running M/W, equestrian sports W(c), field hockey W, football M, golf M/W, ice hockey M(c), lacrosse M/W, rugby M(c)/W(c), soccer M/W, softball W, swimming M/W, tennis M/W, track and field M/W, volleyball M(c)/W. *Intramural sports:* archery M/W, badminton M/W, basketball M/W, fencing M/W, football M/W, golf M/W, racquetball M/W, sailing M/W, skiing (downhill) M/W, soccer M/W, softball M/W, swimming M/W, table tennis M/W, tennis M/W, track and field M/W, ultimate Frisbee M/W, volleyball M/W, water polo M/W, weight lifting M/W.
Standardized Tests *Required:* SAT I or ACT (for admission).
Costs (2004–05) *Comprehensive fee:* $32,882 includes full-time tuition ($26,040), mandatory fees ($156), and room and board ($6686). Part-time tuition: $826 per hour. Part-time tuition and fees vary according to course load. *College room only:* $3454. Room and board charges vary according to board plan. *Payment plan:* installment. *Waivers:* minority students, children of alumni, adult students, senior citizens, and employees or children of employees.
Financial Aid Of all full-time matriculated undergraduates who enrolled in 2002, 1,802 applied for aid, 1,594 were judged to have need, 651 had their need fully met. In 2002, 594 non-need-based awards were made. *Average percent of need met:* 91%. *Average financial aid package:* $21,286. *Average need-based loan:* $3551. *Average need-based gift aid:* $15,646. *Average non-need-based aid:* $7904. *Average indebtedness upon graduation:* $18,623. *Financial aid deadline:* 3/15.
Applying *Options:* common application, electronic application, early admission, early decision, early action, deferred entrance. *Application fee:* $40. *Required:* essay or personal statement, high school transcript. *Recommended:* letters of recommendation, interview. *Application deadline:* rolling (transfers). *Early decision:* 11/15. *Notification:* continuous (freshmen), 1/1 (early decision), 2/1 (early action), continuous (transfers).
Admissions Contact Mr. Kenneth G. Benne, Dean of Admissions and Financial Aid, Wittenberg University, PO Box 720, Springfield, OH 45501-0720. *Phone:* 937-327-6314 Ext. 6366. *Toll-free phone:* 800-677-7558 Ext. 6314. *Fax:* 937-327-6379. *E-mail:* admission@wittenberg.edu.

■ *See page 2872 for a narrative description.*

WRIGHT STATE UNIVERSITY
Dayton, Ohio

- **State-supported** university, founded 1964
- **Calendar** quarters

Wright State University (continued)

- **Degrees** certificates, associate, bachelor's, master's, doctoral, first professional, and post-master's certificates
- **Suburban** 557-acre campus with easy access to Cincinnati
- **Endowment** $5.7 million
- **Coed,** 11,787 undergraduate students, 85% full-time, 57% women, 43% men
- **Minimally difficult** entrance level, 91% of applicants were admitted

Undergraduates 10,000 full-time, 1,787 part-time. Students come from 49 states and territories, 60 other countries, 3% are from out of state, 11% African American, 2% Asian American or Pacific Islander, 1% Hispanic American, 0.4% Native American, 1% international, 7% transferred in, 21% live on campus. *Retention:* 73% of 2002 full-time freshmen returned.

Freshmen *Admission:* 5,104 applied, 4,650 admitted, 2,282 enrolled. *Average high school GPA:* 2.99. *Test scores:* SAT verbal scores over 500: 52%; SAT math scores over 500: 51%; ACT scores over 18: 78%; SAT verbal scores over 600: 15%; SAT math scores over 600: 16%; ACT scores over 24: 25%; SAT verbal scores over 700: 1%; SAT math scores over 700: 2%; ACT scores over 30: 3%.

Faculty *Total:* 864, 61% full-time. *Student/faculty ratio:* 20:1.

Majors Accounting; accounting technology and bookkeeping; administrative assistant and secretarial science; adult health nursing; African-American/Black studies; anatomy; anthropology; applied mathematics; area studies related; art; art history, criticism and conservation; arts management; art teacher education; art therapy; biochemistry; biological and physical sciences; biology/biological sciences; biomedical/medical engineering; biomedical technology; business administration and management; business/commerce; business/managerial economics; business statistics; business teacher education; chemistry; city/urban, community and regional planning; classics and languages, literatures and linguistics; clinical laboratory science/medical technology; communication/speech communication and rhetoric; community psychology; computer and information sciences; computer engineering; computer science; computer teacher education; construction engineering technology; counselor education/school counseling and guidance; criminal justice/police science; criminology; curriculum and instruction; dance; data processing and data processing technology; drafting and design technology; dramatic/theatre arts; drawing; economics; economics related; education; educational, instructional, and curriculum supervision; educational leadership and administration; education (multiple levels); education related; education (specific levels and methods) related; education (specific subject areas) related; electrical, electronic and communications engineering technology; electrical, electronics and communications engineering; electromechanical technology; elementary education; engineering; engineering physics; engineering related; engineering science; English; English as a second/foreign language (teaching); English/language arts teacher education; environmental engineering technology; environmental health; environmental science; film/cinema studies; finance; foreign languages and literatures; foreign language teacher education; French; geography; geology/earth science; geophysics and seismology; German; health and physical education; health/health care administration; health/medical preparatory programs related; health teacher education; higher education/higher education administration; history; humanities; human resources management; hydrology and water resources science; industrial and organizational psychology; industrial technology; information science/studies; international business/trade/commerce; international relations and affairs; kindergarten/preschool education; legal administrative assistant/secretary; liberal arts and sciences and humanities related; liberal arts and sciences/liberal studies; linguistics; logistics and materials management; management information systems; management science; marketing/marketing management; mass communication/media; materials engineering; mathematics; mathematics teacher education; mechanical engineering; medical administrative assistant and medical secretary; mental and social health services and allied professions related; mental health/rehabilitation; microbiological sciences and immunology related; middle school education; military technologies; modern Greek; modern languages; multi-/interdisciplinary studies related; music; music history, literature, and theory; music performance; music teacher education; music theory and composition; nursing (registered nurse training); nursing related; occupational safety and health technology; office management; office occupations and clerical services; operations management; organizational communication; pharmacology and toxicology; philosophy; photography; physical education teaching and coaching; physics; physics related; political science and government; pre-dentistry studies; pre-law studies; pre-medical studies; pre-pharmacy studies; pre-veterinary studies; psychology; public administration; public health/community nursing; purchasing, procurement/acquisitions and contracts management; reading teacher education; religious studies; sales and marketing/marketing and distribution teacher education; science teacher education; secondary education; social studies teacher education; social work; sociology; Spanish; special education (administration); special education (emotionally disturbed); special education (gifted and talented); special education (mentally retarded); special education (multiply disabled); special education (orthopedic and other physical health impairments); special education related; special education (specific learning disabilities); statistics; systems engineering; systems science and theory; technical teacher education; theatre design and technology; trade and industrial teacher education; urban studies/affairs; vocational rehabilitation counseling; water quality and wastewater treatment management and recycling technology; women's studies.

Academic Programs *Special study options:* academic remediation for entering students, adult/continuing education programs, advanced placement credit, cooperative education, English as a second language, honors programs, internships, off-campus study, part-time degree program, services for LD students, student-designed majors, study abroad, summer session for credit. *ROTC:* Army (b), Air Force (b).

Library Paul Laurence Dunbar Library plus 2 others with 695,805 titles, 5,312 serial subscriptions, an OPAC, a Web page.

Computers on Campus 450 computers available on campus for general student use. A campuswide network can be accessed from student residence rooms and from off campus. At least one staffed computer lab available.

Student Life *Housing options:* coed, disabled students. Campus housing is university owned and leased by the school. *Activities and organizations:* drama/theater group, student-run newspaper, radio station, choral group, national fraternities, national sororities. *Campus security:* 24-hour emergency response devices and patrols, student patrols, late-night transport/escort service, controlled dormitory access. *Student services:* health clinic, personal/psychological counseling, women's center, legal services.

Athletics Member NCAA. All Division I. *Intercollegiate sports:* baseball M(s), basketball M(s)/W(s), cross-country running M(s)/W(s), golf M(s), soccer M(s)/W(s), softball W(s), swimming M(s)/W(s), tennis M(s)/W(s), track and field W(s), volleyball W(s). *Intramural sports:* baseball M, basketball M/W, cheerleading M/W, cross-country running M/W, football M/W, golf M/W, racquetball M(c)/W(c), rugby M(c)/W(c), skiing (downhill) M(c)/W(c), soccer M/W, softball M/W, squash M/W, table tennis M(c)/W(c), tennis M/W, volleyball M(c)/W.

Standardized Tests *Required:* SAT I or ACT (for admission).

Costs (2003–04) *Tuition:* state resident $5892 full-time, $170 per hour part-time; nonresident $10,524 full-time, $340 per hour part-time. *Room and board:* $6019. Room and board charges vary according to board plan and housing facility. *Payment plans:* tuition prepayment, installment. *Waivers:* senior citizens and employees or children of employees.

Financial Aid In 2002, 4027 non-need-based awards were made. *Average financial aid package:* $7857.

Applying *Options:* electronic application, early admission, deferred entrance. *Application fee:* $30. *Required:* high school transcript. *Recommended:* minimum 2.0 GPA. *Application deadline:* rolling (freshmen), rolling (transfers). *Notification:* continuous (freshmen), continuous (transfers).

Admissions Contact Ms. Cathy Davis, Director of Undergraduate Admissions, Wright State University, 3640 Colonel Glenn Highway, Dayton, OH 45435. *Phone:* 937-775-5700. *Toll-free phone:* 800-247-1770. *Fax:* 937-775-5795. *E-mail:* admissions@wright.edu.

■ *See page 2878 for a narrative description.*

XAVIER UNIVERSITY
Cincinnati, Ohio

- **Independent Roman Catholic** comprehensive, founded 1831
- **Calendar** semesters
- **Degrees** certificates, associate, bachelor's, master's, doctoral, post-master's, and postbachelor's certificates
- **Suburban** 130-acre campus
- **Endowment** $81.7 million
- **Coed,** 3,915 undergraduate students, 84% full-time, 56% women, 44% men
- **Moderately difficult** entrance level, 78% of applicants were admitted

Founded in 1831, Xavier University is a Jesuit university that seeks to educate the whole person. The Jesuit tradition is evident in Xavier's love of ideas and rigorous intellectual inquiry, respect for life, passion for justice, sense of community, and working together for the common good. With 70 majors and 40 minors, numerous scholarships, and opportunities for leadership and service, Xavier is more than a degree—it's an education for life.

Undergraduates 3,304 full-time, 611 part-time. Students come from 46 states and territories, 53 other countries, 34% are from out of state, 10% African American, 2% Asian American or Pacific Islander, 2% Hispanic American, 0.2% Native American, 3% international, 2% transferred in, 48% live on campus. *Retention:* 89% of 2002 full-time freshmen returned.

Freshmen *Admission:* 4,364 applied, 3,420 admitted, 786 enrolled. *Average high school GPA:* 3.54. *Test scores:* SAT verbal scores over 500: 88%; SAT math scores over 500: 90%; ACT scores over 18: 99%; SAT verbal scores over 600: 44%; SAT math scores over 600: 44%; ACT scores over 24: 71%; SAT verbal scores over 700: 8%; SAT math scores over 700: 8%; ACT scores over 30: 18%.

Faculty *Total:* 591, 47% full-time, 52% with terminal degrees. *Student/faculty ratio:* 13:1.

Majors Accounting; advertising; art; athletic training; biological and physical sciences; biology/biological sciences; biology teacher education; business administration and management; business/commerce; business/managerial economics; chemical engineering; chemistry; chemistry teacher education; classics and languages, literatures and linguistics; clinical laboratory science/medical technology; computer science; corrections; criminal justice/safety; economics; education; education (specific levels and methods) related; elementary education; English; finance; fine/studio arts; French; German; history; human resources management; international relations and affairs; liberal arts and sciences/liberal studies; management information systems; marketing/marketing management; mathematics; middle school education; music; music teacher education; nursing science; occupational therapy; philosophy; physics; physics teacher education; political science and government; psychology; public relations/image management; radio and television; science teacher education; social work; sociology; Spanish; special education; sport and fitness administration; theology.

Academic Programs *Special study options:* academic remediation for entering students, adult/continuing education programs, advanced placement credit, cooperative education, double majors, English as a second language, honors programs, independent study, internships, off-campus study, part-time degree program, services for LD students, study abroad, summer session for credit. *ROTC:* Army (b), Air Force (c). *Unusual degree programs:* 3-2 engineering with University of Cincinnati; forestry with Duke University; environmental management, accounting.

Library McDonald Library plus 1 other with 191,923 titles, 1,633 serial subscriptions, 8,371 audiovisual materials, an OPAC, a Web page.

Computers on Campus 200 computers available on campus for general student use. A campuswide network can be accessed from student residence rooms and from off campus. Internet access, online (class) registration, at least one staffed computer lab available.

Student Life *Housing:* on-campus residence required through sophomore year. *Options:* coed. Campus housing is university owned. Freshman campus housing is guaranteed. *Activities and organizations:* drama/theater group, student-run newspaper, radio and television station, choral group, Student Government Association, Student Activities Council, performing arts group, Xavier Action (service organization), Residence Hall Association. *Campus security:* 24-hour emergency response devices and patrols, late-night transport/escort service, campus-wide shuttle service. *Student services:* health clinic, personal/psychological counseling.

Athletics Member NCAA. All Division I except men's and women's cheerleading (Division II). *Intercollegiate sports:* baseball M(s), basketball M(s)/W(s), cheerleading M/W, crew M(c)/W(c), cross-country running M(s)/W(s), fencing M(c)/W(c), golf M(s)/W(s), lacrosse M(c)/W(c), riflery M(s)/W(s), rugby M(c)/W(c), soccer M(s)/W(s), swimming M(s)/W(s), tennis M(s)/W(s), volleyball M(c)/W(s), wrestling M(c). *Intramural sports:* baseball M(c), basketball M/W, racquetball M/W, soccer M(c)/W(c), tennis M/W, ultimate Frisbee M/W, volleyball M/W.

Standardized Tests *Required:* SAT I or ACT (for admission).

Costs (2003–04) *Comprehensive fee:* $27,150 includes full-time tuition ($18,850), mandatory fees ($300), and room and board ($8000). Full-time tuition and fees vary according to program. Part-time tuition: $395 per credit hour. Part-time tuition and fees vary according to course load. *College room only:* $4400. Room and board charges vary according to board plan and housing facility. *Payment plans:* installment, deferred payment. *Waivers:* senior citizens and employees or children of employees.

Financial Aid Of all full-time matriculated undergraduates who enrolled in 2003, 1,973 applied for aid, 1,603 were judged to have need, 352 had their need fully met. 689 Federal Work-Study jobs (averaging $1923). 84 state and other part-time jobs (averaging $1759). In 2003, 1149 non-need-based awards were made. *Average percent of need met:* 75%. *Average financial aid package:* $13,616. *Average need-based loan:* $4118. *Average need-based gift aid:* $9759. *Average non-need-based aid:* $8237. *Average indebtedness upon graduation:* $17,981.

Applying *Options:* common application, electronic application, early admission, deferred entrance. *Application fee:* $35. *Required:* essay or personal statement, high school transcript, 1 letter of recommendation. *Recommended:* interview. *Application deadline:* 2/1 (freshmen), rolling (transfers). *Notification:* continuous (transfers).

Admissions Contact Mr. Marc Camille, Dean of Admission, Xavier University, 3800 Victory Parkway, Cincinnati, OH 45207-5311. *Phone:* 513-745-3301. *Toll-free phone:* 800-344-4698. *Fax:* 513-745-4319. *E-mail:* xuadmit@xavier.edu.

■ *See page 2880 for a narrative description.*

YOUNGSTOWN STATE UNIVERSITY
Youngstown, Ohio

- **State-supported** comprehensive, founded 1908
- **Calendar** semesters
- **Degrees** certificates, diplomas, associate, bachelor's, master's, doctoral, and postbachelor's certificates
- **Urban** 200-acre campus with easy access to Cleveland and Pittsburgh
- **Endowment** $4.4 million
- **Coed,** 11,592 undergraduate students, 79% full-time, 55% women, 45% men
- **Noncompetitive** entrance level, 99% of applicants were admitted

Located on a beautiful campus in northeast Ohio, YSU offers more than 100 major programs at 2-year, 4-year, and graduate levels. A 19:1 student-faculty ratio, flexible curriculum planning, simplified transfer options, and an expanding honors program characterize YSU's academics. A comprehensive scholarship and financial aid program is available. Prospective students are invited to tour the campus and meet with professors in their major.

Undergraduates 9,158 full-time, 2,434 part-time. Students come from 39 states and territories, 52 other countries, 9% are from out of state, 10% African American, 0.7% Asian American or Pacific Islander, 2% Hispanic American, 0.3% Native American, 0.7% international, 5% transferred in, 10% live on campus. *Retention:* 71% of 2002 full-time freshmen returned.

Freshmen *Admission:* 3,760 applied, 3,738 admitted, 2,029 enrolled. *Average high school GPA:* 2.80. *Test scores:* ACT scores over 18: 75%; ACT scores over 24: 23%; ACT scores over 30: 2%.

Faculty *Total:* 951, 43% full-time, 49% with terminal degrees. *Student/faculty ratio:* 18:1.

Majors Accounting; accounting technology and bookkeeping; acting; administrative assistant and secretarial science; advertising; African-American/Black studies; African studies; American studies; anthropology; apparel and accessories marketing; apparel and textiles; art; art history, criticism and conservation; art teacher education; astronomy; athletic training; banking and financial support services; biological and physical sciences; biology/biological sciences; biology teacher education; business administration and management; business automation/technology/data entry; business/commerce; business/managerial economics; business teacher education; chemical engineering; chemistry; chemistry teacher education; child care and support services management; child development; civil engineering; civil engineering technology; clinical laboratory science/medical technology; clinical/medical laboratory assistant; clinical/medical laboratory technology; commercial and advertising art; communication/speech communication and rhetoric; community health services counseling; computer and information sciences; computer programming; computer science; computer teacher education; consumer merchandising/retailing management; corrections; criminal justice/law enforcement administration; criminal justice/police science; criminal justice/safety; data processing and data processing technology; dental hygiene; dietetics; dietitian assistant; drafting and design technology; drama and dance teacher education; dramatic/theatre arts; econometrics and quantitative economics; economics; education; education (multiple levels); electrical, electronic and communications engineering technology; electrical, electronics and communications engineering; elementary education; emergency medical technology (EMT paramedic); engineering; engineering technology; English; English/language arts teacher education; environmental/environmental health engineering; environmental studies; executive assistant/executive secretary; family and community services; family and consumer sciences/home economics teacher education; family and consumer sciences/human sciences; fashion merchandising; finance; fine/studio arts; foods, nutrition, and wellness; foreign languages and literatures; foreign language teacher education; French; French language teacher education; geography; geology/earth science; German language teacher education; health and physical education; health science; health teacher education; history; history teacher education; hospitality administration; hotel/motel administration; human development and family studies; industrial engineering; information science/studies; international economics; Italian; journalism; kindergarten/preschool education; kinesiology and exercise science; labor and industrial relations; legal administrative assistant/secretary; management information systems; marketing/marketing management; mathematics; mathematics teacher education; mechanical engineering; mechanical engineering/mechanical technology; medical administrative assistant and medical secretary; medical/clinical assistant; medical office management; merchandising; middle school education; music; music history, literature, and theory; music performance; music teacher education; music theory and composition; nursing (registered nurse training); office management; office occupations and clerical services; operations management; painting; philosophy; photography; physical education teaching and coaching; physics; physics teacher education; piano and organ; political science and government; pre-dentistry studies; pre-law studies; pre-medical studies; pre-pharmacy studies; pre-veterinary studies; printmaking; psychology; public administration; public relations/image management; radio and television; religious studies; respiratory care therapy;

Youngstown State University (continued)
retailing; sales, distribution and marketing; science teacher education; secondary education; security and loss prevention; selling skills and sales; social sciences; social science teacher education; social studies teacher education; social work; sociology; Spanish; Spanish language teacher education; special education; special education (specific learning disabilities); speech and rhetoric; speech teacher education; sport and fitness administration; technical and business writing; telecommunications; theatre design and technology; tourism and travel services management; violin, viola, guitar and other stringed instruments; voice and opera.

Academic Programs *Special study options:* academic remediation for entering students, accelerated degree program, adult/continuing education programs, advanced placement credit, cooperative education, distance learning, double majors, English as a second language, honors programs, internships, off-campus study, part-time degree program, services for LD students, student-designed majors, study abroad, summer session for credit. *ROTC:* Army (b), Air Force (c). *Unusual degree programs:* 3-2 chemistry, physical therapy.

Library Maag Library with 991,501 titles, 2,908 serial subscriptions, 16,976 audiovisual materials, an OPAC, a Web page.

Computers on Campus 1619 computers available on campus for general student use. A campuswide network can be accessed from student residence rooms and from off campus. Internet access, online (class) registration, at least one staffed computer lab available.

Student Life *Housing options:* coed, women-only. Campus housing is university owned, leased by the school and is provided by a third party. *Activities and organizations:* drama/theater group, student-run newspaper, choral group, marching band, student government, Panhellenic Council, Inter-Fraternity Council, Omicron Delta Kappa, Golden Key, national fraternities, national sororities. *Campus security:* 24-hour emergency response devices and patrols, student patrols, late-night transport/escort service, controlled dormitory access, residence hall patrols. *Student services:* health clinic, personal/psychological counseling, women's center.

Athletics Member NCAA. All Division I except football (Division I-AA). *Intercollegiate sports:* baseball M(s), basketball M(s)/W(s), cross-country running M(s)/W(s), golf M(s)/W, soccer W, softball W(s), swimming W, tennis M(s)/W(s), track and field M(s)/W(s), volleyball W(s). *Intramural sports:* badminton M/W, basketball M/W, bowling M/W, golf M/W, ice hockey M/W, lacrosse M/W, racquetball M/W, soccer M/W, softball M/W, swimming M/W, table tennis M/W, tennis M/W, ultimate Frisbee M/W, volleyball M/W, water polo M/W.

Standardized Tests *Required:* SAT I or ACT (for admission).

Costs (2003–04) *Tuition:* state resident $5328 full-time, $180 per credit part-time; nonresident $10,536 full-time, $397 per credit part-time. Full-time tuition and fees vary according to course load. Part-time tuition and fees vary according to course load. *Required fees:* $150 full-time, $5 per credit part-time. *Room and board:* $5700. Room and board charges vary according to board plan and housing facility. *Payment plan:* installment. *Waivers:* senior citizens and employees or children of employees.

Financial Aid Of all full-time matriculated undergraduates who enrolled in 2002, 447 Federal Work-Study jobs (averaging $1722).

Applying *Options:* common application, electronic application, early admission, early action, deferred entrance. *Application fee:* $30. *Required:* high school transcript. *Required for some:* interview. *Application deadlines:* 8/15 (freshmen), 8/15 (transfers). *Notification:* continuous (freshmen), 2/15 (early action), continuous (transfers).

Admissions Contact Ms. Sue Davis, Director of Undergraduate Admissions, Youngstown State University, One University Plaza, Youngstown, OH 44555-0001. *Phone:* 330-941-2000. *Toll-free phone:* 877-468-6978 (in-state); 877-466-6978 (out-of-state). *Fax:* 330-941-3674. *E-mail:* enroll@ysu.edu.

■ *See page 2888 for a narrative description.*

OKLAHOMA

AMERICAN CHRISTIAN COLLEGE AND SEMINARY
Oklahoma City, Oklahoma

- **Independent interdenominational** comprehensive, founded 1976
- **Calendar** semesters
- **Degrees** associate, bachelor's, master's, doctoral, and first professional
- **Small-town** 1-acre campus with easy access to Oklahoma City
- **Endowment** $10,000
- **Coed**
- **Noncompetitive** entrance level

Faculty *Student/faculty ratio:* 8:1.

Costs (2003–04) *Tuition:* $3360 full-time, $420 per course part-time. *Required fees:* $140 per semester hour part-time.

Applying *Options:* common application, electronic application. *Application fee:* $50. *Required:* high school transcript.

Admissions Contact Dr. Mitchel Beville, Vice President of Business Affairs/Admissions, American Christian College and Seminary, 4300 Highline Boulevard #202, Oklahoma City, OK 73108. *Phone:* 405-945-0100 Ext. 120. *Toll-free phone:* 800-488-2528. *Fax:* 405-945-0311. *E-mail:* info@accs.edu.

BACONE COLLEGE
Muskogee, Oklahoma

- **Independent** 4-year, founded 1880, affiliated with American Baptist Churches in the U.S.A.
- **Calendar** semesters
- **Degrees** diplomas, associate, and bachelor's
- **Small-town** 220-acre campus with easy access to Tulsa
- **Endowment** $1.4 million
- **Coed,** 914 undergraduate students, 76% full-time, 54% women, 46% men
- **Minimally difficult** entrance level, 58% of applicants were admitted

Undergraduates 697 full-time, 217 part-time. Students come from 24 states and territories, 10 other countries, 15% are from out of state, 20% African American, 4% Hispanic American, 39% Native American, 3% international, 10% transferred in, 48% live on campus. *Retention:* 50% of 2002 full-time freshmen returned.

Freshmen *Admission:* 819 applied, 479 admitted, 231 enrolled. *Average high school GPA:* 2.83. *Test scores:* SAT verbal scores over 500: 41%; SAT math scores over 500: 24%; ACT scores over 18: 44%; SAT verbal scores over 600: 6%; ACT scores over 24: 5%.

Faculty *Total:* 32.

Majors Accounting; administrative assistant and secretarial science; American Indian/Native American studies; art; business administration and management; cardiopulmonary technology; computer science; dramatic/theatre arts; early childhood education; education; elementary education; entrepreneurship; finance; general studies; history; horticultural science; humanities; journalism; liberal arts and sciences/liberal studies; mass communication/media; mathematics; medical radiologic technology; natural resources management and policy; nursing (registered nurse training); physical education teaching and coaching; physical sciences; political science and government; sales, distribution and marketing; sociology; substance abuse/addiction counseling; theological and ministerial studies related.

Academic Programs *Special study options:* academic remediation for entering students, accelerated degree program, adult/continuing education programs, advanced placement credit, cooperative education, internships, part-time degree program, services for LD students, student-designed majors, summer session for credit.

Library Bacone College Library with 34,564 titles, 121 serial subscriptions, 185 audiovisual materials, an OPAC.

Computers on Campus 46 computers available on campus for general student use. A campuswide network can be accessed from off campus. Internet access, at least one staffed computer lab available.

Student Life *Housing:* on-campus residence required through sophomore year. *Options:* men-only, women-only. Campus housing is university owned. Freshman applicants given priority for college housing. *Activities and organizations:* drama/theater group, student-run newspaper, choral group, Native American Club, Phi Beta Kappa, Christian Nurses Fellowship. *Campus security:* 24-hour emergency response devices, controlled dormitory access, 8-hour patrols by trained security personnel. *Student services:* health clinic, personal/psychological counseling.

Athletics Member NAIA. *Intercollegiate sports:* baseball M(s), basketball M(s)/W(s), cheerleading M(s)/W(s), cross-country running M(s)/W(s), football M(s), golf M(s)/W(s), soccer M(s)/W(s), softball W(s), track and field M(s)/W(s), volleyball M(s)/W(s), wrestling M(s). *Intramural sports:* badminton M/W, basketball M/W, bowling M/W, football M/W, golf M/W, racquetball M/W, softball M/W, table tennis M/W, tennis M/W, volleyball M/W, weight lifting M/W.

Standardized Tests *Required:* SAT I or ACT (for admission). *Recommended:* ACT (for admission).

Costs (2004–05) *Comprehensive fee:* $14,230 includes full-time tuition ($7900), mandatory fees ($630), and room and board ($5700). Part-time tuition: $350 per credit hour. Part-time tuition and fees vary according to course load. *Required fees:* $240 per term part-time. *College room only:* $3000. *Payment plan:* installment. *Waivers:* employees or children of employees.

Financial Aid Of all full-time matriculated undergraduates who enrolled in 2001, 200 Federal Work-Study jobs (averaging $2000).

Applying *Options:* common application, electronic application, early admission, deferred entrance. *Application fee:* $25. *Required:* high school transcript, minimum 2.0 GPA, minimum ACT score of 14. *Application deadline:* rolling (freshmen), rolling (transfers). *Notification:* continuous (freshmen), continuous (transfers).

Admissions Contact Ms. Carla Green, Admissions Counselor, Bacone College, 2299 Old Bacone Road, Muskogee, OK 74403. *Phone:* 918-781-7340. *Toll-free phone:* 888-682-5514 Ext. 7340. *Fax:* 918-781-7416. *E-mail:* admissions@bacone.edu.

CAMERON UNIVERSITY
Lawton, Oklahoma

- **State-supported** comprehensive, founded 1908, part of Oklahoma State Regents for Higher Education
- **Calendar** semesters
- **Degrees** bachelor's and master's
- **Small-town** 160-acre campus
- **Endowment** $4.6 million
- **Coed,** 5,193 undergraduate students, 60% full-time, 57% women, 43% men
- **Minimally difficult** entrance level, 100% of applicants were admitted

Undergraduates 3,092 full-time, 2,101 part-time. Students come from 22 states and territories, 21 other countries, 2% are from out of state, 20% African American, 3% Asian American or Pacific Islander, 8% Hispanic American, 6% Native American, 3% international, 6% transferred in, 1% live on campus. *Retention:* 56% of 2002 full-time freshmen returned.

Freshmen *Admission:* 888 applied, 888 admitted, 888 enrolled. *Average high school GPA:* 3.20. *Test scores:* ACT scores over 18: 77%; ACT scores over 24: 23%; ACT scores over 30: 2%.

Faculty *Total:* 267, 69% full-time, 42% with terminal degrees. *Student/faculty ratio:* 23:1.

Majors Accounting; agricultural sciences; allied health diagnostic, intervention, and treatment professions related; art; art teacher education; biological and physical sciences; biology/biological sciences; business administration and management; chemistry; child care services management; clinical laboratory science/medical technology; communication/speech communication and rhetoric; computer and information sciences; criminal justice/police science; criminology; education; education (specific subject areas) related; electrical, electronic and communications engineering technology; engineering technologies related; English; family and consumer sciences/human sciences; foreign languages and literatures; general studies; history; industrial technology; management information systems; mathematics; mechanical drafting; music; physics; political science and government; psychology; sociology; visual and performing arts related.

Academic Programs *Special study options:* academic remediation for entering students, accelerated degree program, adult/continuing education programs, advanced placement credit, distance learning, double majors, honors programs, independent study, off-campus study, part-time degree program, services for LD students, summer session for credit. *ROTC:* Army (b).

Library Cameron University Library with 258,000 titles, 3,840 serial subscriptions, 7,053 audiovisual materials.

Computers on Campus 350 computers available on campus for general student use. A campuswide network can be accessed. At least one staffed computer lab available.

Student Life *Housing options:* men-only, women-only. *Activities and organizations:* drama/theater group, student-run newspaper, radio and television station, choral group, Student Government Association, Aggie Club, intramural club, Baptist Student Union, sociology club, national fraternities, national sororities. *Campus security:* 24-hour emergency response devices and patrols, student patrols, late-night transport/escort service. *Student services:* personal/psychological counseling.

Athletics Member NCAA. All Division II. *Intercollegiate sports:* baseball M(s), basketball M(s)/W(s), golf M(s), softball W(s), tennis M(s)/W(s), volleyball W(s). *Intramural sports:* badminton M/W, basketball M/W, bowling M/W, racquetball M/W, table tennis M/W, volleyball M/W, water polo M/W.

Standardized Tests *Required:* SAT I or ACT (for admission).

Costs (2004–05) *Tuition:* state resident $2778 full-time, $93 per semester hour part-time; nonresident $6678 full-time, $223 per semester hour part-time. Full-time tuition and fees vary according to course level, course load, degree level, and student level. Part-time tuition and fees vary according to course level, course load, degree level, and student level. *Required fees:* $165 full-time, $80 per term part-time. *Room and board:* $2854. Room and board charges vary according to board plan. *Payment plan:* installment. *Waivers:* senior citizens and employees or children of employees.

Financial Aid Of all full-time matriculated undergraduates who enrolled in 2002, 132 Federal Work-Study jobs (averaging $1311). 240 state and other part-time jobs (averaging $1596). *Average indebtedness upon graduation:* $6300.

Applying *Options:* common application, electronic application, early admission, deferred entrance. *Application fee:* $15. *Required:* high school transcript. *Application deadline:* rolling (freshmen), rolling (transfers). *Notification:* continuous until 8/10 (freshmen), continuous until 8/10 (transfers).

Admissions Contact Ms. Brenda Dally, Coordinator of Student Recruitment, Cameron University, Cameron University, Attention: Admissions, 2800 West Gore Boulevard, Lawton, OK 73505. *Phone:* 580-581-2837. *Toll-free phone:* 888-454-7600. *Fax:* 580-581-5514. *E-mail:* admiss@cua.cameron.edu.

EAST CENTRAL UNIVERSITY
Ada, Oklahoma

- **State-supported** comprehensive, founded 1909, part of Oklahoma State Regents for Higher Education
- **Calendar** semesters
- **Degrees** bachelor's and master's
- **Small-town** 140-acre campus with easy access to Oklahoma City
- **Endowment** $847,022
- **Coed,** 3,685 undergraduate students, 86% full-time, 59% women, 41% men
- **Moderately difficult** entrance level

Undergraduates 3,159 full-time, 526 part-time. Students come from 19 states and territories, 32 other countries, 3% are from out of state, 5% African American, 1% Asian American or Pacific Islander, 2% Hispanic American, 19% Native American, 17% live on campus. *Retention:* 62% of 2002 full-time freshmen returned.

Freshmen *Admission:* 704 enrolled. *Average high school GPA:* 3.41. *Test scores:* ACT scores over 18: 78%; ACT scores over 24: 21%; ACT scores over 30: 2%.

Faculty *Total:* 265, 72% full-time. *Student/faculty ratio:* 19:1.

Majors Accounting; administrative assistant and secretarial science; advertising; art; art teacher education; biology/biological sciences; biology teacher education; business administration and management; business automation/technology/data entry; business/managerial economics; business teacher education; cartography; chemistry; chemistry teacher education; clinical/medical laboratory technology; computer science; consumer merchandising/retailing management; corrections; counselor education/school counseling and guidance; criminal justice/law enforcement administration; criminal justice/police science; drafting and design technology; early childhood education; ecology; education; electrical, electronic and communications engineering technology; elementary education; English; English/language arts teacher education; entrepreneurship; environmental health; environmental science; environmental studies; family and consumer sciences/home economics teacher education; family and consumer sciences/human sciences; fashion merchandising; finance; general studies; health information/medical records administration; health teacher education; history; history teacher education; human resources management; hydrology and water resources science; juvenile corrections; kindergarten/preschool education; legal studies; literature; management information systems; marketing/marketing management; mass communication/media; mathematics; mathematics teacher education; medical staff services technology; music; music teacher education; nursing (registered nurse training); physical education teaching and coaching; physics; physics teacher education; piano and organ; political science and government; pre-dentistry studies; pre-law studies; pre-medical studies; pre-pharmacy studies; pre-veterinary studies; psychology; public relations/image management; radio and television; science teacher education; secondary education; social work; sociology; special education; special education (administration); speech and rhetoric; speech teacher education; theatre/theatre arts management; voice and opera.

Academic Programs *Special study options:* academic remediation for entering students, accelerated degree program, adult/continuing education programs, advanced placement credit, distance learning, double majors, honors programs, internships, off-campus study, part-time degree program, services for LD students, summer session for credit.

Library Linscheid Library with 213,000 titles, 800 serial subscriptions, an OPAC, a Web page.

Computers on Campus 40 computers available on campus for general student use. A campuswide network can be accessed. At least one staffed computer lab available.

Student Life *Housing options:* coed, men-only, women-only, disabled students. Campus housing is university owned. *Activities and organizations:* drama/theater group, student-run newspaper, choral group, marching band, Panhellenic Council, Interfraternity Council, BACCHUS, Fellowship of Christian Athletes, Human Resources, national fraternities, national sororities. *Campus security:* 24-hour patrols, controlled dormitory access. *Student services:* health clinic, personal/psychological counseling.

Athletics Member NCAA, NAIA. All NCAA Division II. *Intercollegiate sports:* baseball M(s), basketball M(s)/W(s), cheerleading M/W, cross-country

East Central University (continued)
running M(s)/W(s), football M(s), golf M(s)/W, soccer W(s), softball W(s), tennis M(s)/W(s), track and field M/W. *Intramural sports:* basketball M/W, football M/W, racquetball M/W, soccer M/W, softball M/W, tennis M/W, volleyball M/W.
Standardized Tests *Required:* SAT I or ACT (for admission). *Recommended:* ACT (for admission).
Costs (2003–04) *Tuition:* state resident $2685 full-time, $89 per semester hour part-time; nonresident $6585 full-time, $219 per semester hour part-time. Full-time tuition and fees vary according to course level, course load, and student level. Part-time tuition and fees vary according to course level, course load, and student level. *Required fees:* $773 full-time. *Room and board:* $2774; room only: $960. Room and board charges vary according to board plan and housing facility. *Waivers:* senior citizens and employees or children of employees.
Financial Aid Of all full-time matriculated undergraduates who enrolled in 2003, 1,971 applied for aid, 1,752 were judged to have need, 634 had their need fully met. 181 Federal Work-Study jobs (averaging $1888). 377 state and other part-time jobs (averaging $2274). In 2003, 263 non-need-based awards were made. *Average percent of need met:* 63%. *Average financial aid package:* $7444. *Average need-based loan:* $1842. *Average need-based gift aid:* $3640. *Average non-need-based aid:* $3040. *Average indebtedness upon graduation:* $13,199.
Applying *Options:* early admission. *Required:* high school transcript. *Required for some:* minimum 2.7 GPA, rank in upper 50% of high school class. *Application deadlines:* 9/1 (freshmen), 9/1 (transfers). *Notification:* continuous (transfers).
Admissions Contact Pam Denny, Freshman Admissions Officer, East Central University, PMBJ8, 1100 East 14th Street, Ada, OK 74820-6999. *Phone:* 580-332-8000 Ext. 233. *Fax:* 580-310-5432. *E-mail:* parmstro@mailclerk.ecok.edu.

HILLSDALE FREE WILL BAPTIST COLLEGE
Moore, Oklahoma

- **Independent Free Will Baptist** comprehensive, founded 1959
- **Calendar** semesters
- **Degrees** associate, bachelor's, and master's
- **Suburban** 41-acre campus with easy access to Oklahoma City
- **Endowment** $277,141
- **Coed,** 265 undergraduate students, 78% full-time, 45% women, 55% men
- **Noncompetitive** entrance level, 100% of applicants were admitted

Undergraduates 208 full-time, 57 part-time. Students come from 15 states and territories, 13 other countries, 19% are from out of state, 7% African American, 0.4% Asian American or Pacific Islander, 4% Hispanic American, 11% Native American, 7% international, 13% transferred in, 45% live on campus. *Retention:* 47% of 2002 full-time freshmen returned.
Freshmen *Admission:* 72 applied, 72 admitted, 71 enrolled. *Average high school GPA:* 3.09. *Test scores:* ACT scores over 18: 54%; ACT scores over 24: 13%.
Faculty *Total:* 48, 38% full-time, 33% with terminal degrees. *Student/faculty ratio:* 9:1.
Majors Biblical studies; business/commerce; elementary education; English; general studies; interdisciplinary studies; liberal arts and sciences/liberal studies; mathematics; missionary studies and missiology; music; nursing (registered nurse training); physical education teaching and coaching; psychology; religious education; religious/sacred music; theology.
Academic Programs *Special study options:* academic remediation for entering students, accelerated degree program, adult/continuing education programs, advanced placement credit, double majors, English as a second language, independent study, internships, part-time degree program, summer session for credit.
Library Geri Ann Hull Learning Resource Center with 20,102 titles, 363 serial subscriptions, 1,800 audiovisual materials, an OPAC.
Computers on Campus 22 computers available on campus for general student use. A campuswide network can be accessed. Internet access, at least one staffed computer lab available.
Student Life *Housing:* on-campus residence required through sophomore year. *Options:* men-only, women-only. Campus housing is university owned. *Activities and organizations:* drama/theater group, choral group, Student Mission Fellowship, Ironmen Fellowship, society organizations, Fellowship of Christian Athletes. *Campus security:* 24-hour emergency response devices, controlled dormitory access. *Student services:* personal/psychological counseling.
Athletics Member NCCAA. *Intercollegiate sports:* baseball M, basketball M/W, softball W. *Intramural sports:* baseball M/W, football M, table tennis M/W.
Standardized Tests *Required:* SAT I or ACT (for placement).
Costs (2004–05) *Comprehensive fee:* $11,490 includes full-time tuition ($6400), mandatory fees ($890), and room and board ($4200). Part-time tuition: $240 per credit hour. *Payment plan:* deferred payment. *Waivers:* senior citizens.
Applying *Options:* common application, early admission, deferred entrance. *Application fee:* $20. *Required:* essay or personal statement, high school transcript, 1 letter of recommendation, Biblical foundation statement, student conduct pledge; medical form required for some. *Required for some:* 1 letter of recommendation, interview. *Recommended:* minimum 2.0 GPA, 2 letters of recommendation. *Application deadline:* rolling (freshmen), rolling (transfers).
Admissions Contact Ms. Sue Chaffin, Registrar/Assistant Director of Admissions, Hillsdale Free Will Baptist College, PO Box 7208, Moore, OK 73153-1208. *Phone:* 405-912-9005. *Fax:* 405-912-9050. *E-mail:* hillsdale@hc.edu.

LANGSTON UNIVERSITY
Langston, Oklahoma

- **State-supported** comprehensive, founded 1897, part of Oklahoma State Regents for Higher Education
- **Calendar** semesters
- **Degrees** associate, bachelor's, and master's
- **Rural** 40-acre campus with easy access to Oklahoma City
- **Coed**
- **Minimally difficult** entrance level

Faculty *Student/faculty ratio:* 30:1.
Athletics Member NAIA.
Standardized Tests *Required:* SAT I or ACT (for admission), SAT I or ACT (for placement).
Costs (2003–04) *Tuition:* state resident $1818 full-time; nonresident $5430 full-time. *Required fees:* $969 full-time. *Room and board:* $4380; room only: $2400.
Financial Aid Of all full-time matriculated undergraduates who enrolled in 2002, 2,604 applied for aid, 2,030 were judged to have need, 1,055 had their need fully met. *Average percent of need met:* 74. *Average financial aid package:* $7738. *Average need-based loan:* $4016. *Average need-based gift aid:* $969. *Average non-need-based aid:* $2226.
Applying *Options:* electronic application. *Required:* high school transcript, minimum 2.70 GPA. *Required for some:* letters of recommendation.
Admissions Contact Brent Russell, Assistant Director of Admission, Langston University, Langston University, PO Box 728, Langston, OK 73120. *Phone:* 405-466-2984. *Toll-free phone:* 405-466-3428. *Fax:* 405-466-3391.

METROPOLITAN COLLEGE
Oklahoma City, Oklahoma

- **Proprietary** 4-year, part of Wyandotte Collegiate Systems
- **Calendar** trimesters
- **Degrees** certificates, associate, and bachelor's
- **Coed, primarily women**
- **Minimally difficult** entrance level

Standardized Tests *Required:* Wonderlic aptitude test (for admission).
Costs (2003–04) *Tuition:* $7710 full-time.
Applying *Application fee:* $50. *Required:* high school transcript, interview.
Admissions Contact Ms. Pamela Picken, Admissions Director, Metropolitan College, 1900 NW Expressway R-302, Oklahoma City, OK 73118. *Phone:* 405-843-1000.

METROPOLITAN COLLEGE
Tulsa, Oklahoma

- **Proprietary** 4-year
- **Calendar** trimesters
- **Degrees** diplomas, associate, and bachelor's
- **Urban** campus
- **Coed, primarily women,** 223 undergraduate students, 100% full-time, 91% women, 9% men
- **Minimally difficult** entrance level

Undergraduates 223 full-time. Students come from 3 states and territories, 1% are from out of state, 17% African American, 5% Asian American or Pacific Islander, 3% Hispanic American, 4% transferred in. *Retention:* 71% of 2002 full-time freshmen returned.
Freshmen *Admission:* 87 enrolled. *Average high school GPA:* 2.75.
Faculty *Total:* 16, 25% full-time, 50% with terminal degrees. *Student/faculty ratio:* 15:1.
Majors Court reporting; legal assistant/paralegal.
Academic Programs *Special study options:* academic remediation for entering students, accelerated degree program, adult/continuing education programs, internships, part-time degree program.

Library Learning Resource Center.
Computers on Campus 25 computers available on campus for general student use. A campuswide network can be accessed. Internet access, at least one staffed computer lab available.
Student Life *Housing:* college housing not available. *Activities and organizations:* student-run newspaper.
Standardized Tests *Required:* Wonderlic aptitude test (for admission).
Costs (2004–05) *Tuition:* $6535 full-time. Full-time tuition and fees vary according to course load and program. *Required fees:* $1200 full-time. *Payment plan:* installment.
Financial Aid *Average percent of need met:* 99%.
Applying *Application fee:* $50. *Required:* high school transcript, interview.
Admissions Contact Ms. Vicki Angelo, Admissions Director, Metropolitan College, 4528 South Sheridan Road, Suite 105, Tulsa, OK 74145-1011. *Phone:* 918-627-9300 Ext. 213.

MID-AMERICA CHRISTIAN UNIVERSITY
Oklahoma City, Oklahoma

Admissions Contact Ms. Dianna Rea, Director of College Relations, Mid-America Christian University, 3500 Southwest 119th Street, Oklahoma City, OK 73170. *Phone:* 405-692-3180. *Fax:* 405-692-3165. *E-mail:* mbcinfo@mabc.edu.

NORTHEASTERN STATE UNIVERSITY
Tahlequah, Oklahoma

- **State-supported** comprehensive, founded 1846, part of Oklahoma State Regents for Higher Education
- **Calendar** semesters
- **Degrees** bachelor's, master's, and first professional
- **Small-town** 160-acre campus with easy access to Tulsa
- **Endowment** $780,030
- **Coed,** 8,313 undergraduate students, 78% full-time, 59% women, 41% men
- **Moderately difficult** entrance level, 89% of applicants were admitted

Undergraduates 6,505 full-time, 1,808 part-time. Students come from 27 states and territories, 44 other countries, 0.1% are from out of state, 6% African American, 0.6% Asian American or Pacific Islander, 1% Hispanic American, 28% Native American, 2% international, 17% transferred in. *Retention:* 60% of 2002 full-time freshmen returned.
Freshmen *Admission:* 2,223 applied, 1,976 admitted, 1,294 enrolled. *Average high school GPA:* 3.23.
Faculty *Total:* 446. *Student/faculty ratio:* 24:1.
Majors Accounting; American Indian/Native American studies; art; art teacher education; audiology and speech-language pathology; biology/biological sciences; business administration and management; business teacher education; cell biology and histology; chemistry; clinical laboratory science/medical technology; commercial and advertising art; computer science; criminal justice/law enforcement administration; criminal justice/police science; dramatic/theatre arts; education; electrical, electronic and communications engineering technology; elementary education; engineering physics; English; family and consumer sciences/home economics teacher education; family and consumer sciences/human sciences; fashion merchandising; finance; fine/studio arts; foods, nutrition, and wellness; geography; health/health care administration; health teacher education; history; human resources management; industrial arts; industrial technology; journalism; kindergarten/preschool education; library science; marketing/marketing management; mathematics; medical microbiology and bacteriology; music; music teacher education; nursing (registered nurse training); ophthalmic/optometric services; physical education teaching and coaching; physics; piano and organ; political science and government; pre-dentistry studies; pre-law studies; pre-medical studies; pre-veterinary studies; psychology; reading teacher education; secondary education; social work; sociology; Spanish; special education; speech therapy; tourism and travel services management; trade and industrial teacher education; voice and opera; wildlife biology; zoology/animal biology.
Academic Programs *Special study options:* academic remediation for entering students, adult/continuing education programs, advanced placement credit, distance learning, double majors, English as a second language, honors programs, internships, part-time degree program, services for LD students, summer session for credit. *ROTC:* Army (b).
Library John Vaughn Library with 424,818 titles, 3,983 serial subscriptions, 6,804 audiovisual materials, an OPAC, a Web page.
Computers on Campus 534 computers available on campus for general student use. A campuswide network can be accessed from student residence rooms and from off campus. Internet access, at least one staffed computer lab available.
Student Life *Housing:* on-campus residence required through sophomore year. *Options:* coed. Campus housing is university owned. Freshman applicants given priority for college housing. *Activities and organizations:* drama/theater group, student-run newspaper, television station, choral group, marching band, national fraternities, national sororities. *Campus security:* 24-hour emergency response devices and patrols, late-night transport/escort service, controlled dormitory access. *Student services:* health clinic, personal/psychological counseling.
Athletics Member NCAA. All Division II. *Intercollegiate sports:* baseball M(s), basketball M(s)/W(s), cheerleading M/W, football M(s), golf M(s)/W(s), soccer M(s)/W(s), softball W(s), tennis W(s). *Intramural sports:* basketball M/W, bowling M/W, football M, golf M/W, racquetball M/W, soccer M/W, softball M/W, swimming M/W, tennis W, track and field M, volleyball M/W, water polo M/W, weight lifting M, wrestling M.
Standardized Tests *Required:* ACT (for admission).
Costs (2003–04) *Tuition:* state resident $2664 full-time, $89 per credit hour part-time; nonresident $6564 full-time, $219 per credit hour part-time. Full-time tuition and fees vary according to course level, course load, location, and student level. Part-time tuition and fees vary according to course level, course load, and student level. *Required fees:* $36 full-time. *Room and board:* $3080. Room and board charges vary according to board plan and housing facility. *Waivers:* senior citizens and employees or children of employees.
Financial Aid Of all full-time matriculated undergraduates who enrolled in 2002, 4,847 applied for aid, 4,662 were judged to have need, 4,016 had their need fully met. 314 Federal Work-Study jobs (averaging $2600). 761 state and other part-time jobs (averaging $3000). In 2002, 1080 non-need-based awards were made. *Average percent of need met:* 69%. *Average financial aid package:* $8100. *Average need-based loan:* $4100. *Average need-based gift aid:* $4050. *Average non-need-based aid:* $900. *Average indebtedness upon graduation:* $7500.
Applying *Required:* high school transcript. *Required for some:* letters of recommendation, interview. *Application deadlines:* 8/5 (freshmen), 8/5 (transfers). *Notification:* continuous (freshmen), continuous (transfers).
Admissions Contact Mr. Todd Essary, Director of High School and College Relations, Northeastern State University, 601 North Grand, Tahlequah, OK 74464. *Phone:* 918-456-5511 Ext. 4675. *Toll-free phone:* 800-722-9614. *Fax:* 918-458-2342. *E-mail:* nsuadmis@nsuok.edu.

NORTHWESTERN OKLAHOMA STATE UNIVERSITY
Alva, Oklahoma

- **State-supported** comprehensive, founded 1897, part of Oklahoma State Regents for Higher Education
- **Calendar** semesters
- **Degrees** bachelor's, master's, post-master's, and postbachelor's certificates
- **Small-town** 70-acre campus
- **Endowment** $12.9 million
- **Coed,** 1,874 undergraduate students, 73% full-time, 54% women, 46% men
- **Moderately difficult** entrance level, 99% of applicants were admitted

Undergraduates 1,366 full-time, 508 part-time. Students come from 33 states and territories, 28 other countries, 17% are from out of state, 4% African American, 0.3% Asian American or Pacific Islander, 3% Hispanic American, 3% Native American, 2% international, 13% transferred in, 20% live on campus. *Retention:* 67% of 2002 full-time freshmen returned.
Freshmen *Admission:* 525 applied, 522 admitted, 313 enrolled. *Average high school GPA:* 3.28. *Test scores:* ACT scores over 18: 80%; ACT scores over 24: 19%; ACT scores over 30: 1%.
Faculty *Total:* 142, 49% full-time, 35% with terminal degrees. *Student/faculty ratio:* 16:1.
Majors Accounting; agricultural business and management; agriculture; biology/biological sciences; business administration and management; business teacher education; chemistry; computer science; computer systems networking and telecommunications; criminal justice/police science; elementary education; English; health teacher education; history; information science/studies; kindergarten/preschool education; mass communication/media; mathematics; music; music teacher education; nursing (registered nurse training); physical education teaching and coaching; physics; political science and government; pre-dentistry studies; pre-law studies; pre-medical studies; psychology; science teacher education; secondary education; social sciences; social work; sociology; Spanish; special education; speech and rhetoric; speech teacher education.
Academic Programs *Special study options:* academic remediation for entering students, adult/continuing education programs, advanced placement credit, distance learning, double majors, independent study, internships, off-campus study, part-time degree program, services for LD students, study abroad, summer session for credit.

Northwestern Oklahoma State University (continued)

Library J. W. Martin Library plus 1 other with 299,974 titles, 1,411 serial subscriptions, 3,466 audiovisual materials, an OPAC, a Web page.

Computers on Campus 131 computers available on campus for general student use. A campuswide network can be accessed from off campus. Internet access, online (class) registration, at least one staffed computer lab available.

Student Life *Housing options:* men-only, women-only. Campus housing is university owned. Freshman campus housing is guaranteed. *Activities and organizations:* drama/theater group, student-run newspaper, radio and television station, choral group, marching band, Student Government Association, Aggie Club, Phi Beta Lambda, Baptist Student Union. *Campus security:* 24-hour emergency response devices and patrols, late-night transport/escort service. *Student services:* health clinic, personal/psychological counseling.

Athletics Member NAIA. *Intercollegiate sports:* baseball M(s), basketball M(s)/W(s), cheerleading M(s)/W(s), cross-country running M(s)/W(s), football M(s), soccer W(s), softball W(s). *Intramural sports:* basketball M/W, football M, softball M/W, ultimate Frisbee M/W, volleyball M/W.

Standardized Tests *Required:* SAT I or ACT (for admission).

Costs (2003–04) *Tuition:* state resident $2697 full-time, $90 per credit hour part-time; nonresident $6597 full-time, $219 per credit hour part-time. Full-time tuition and fees vary according to course load, location, and student level. Part-time tuition and fees vary according to course load, location, and student level. *Required fees:* $31 full-time, $16 per term part-time. *Room and board:* $2720; room only: $860. Room and board charges vary according to board plan. *Waivers:* senior citizens and employees or children of employees.

Financial Aid Of all full-time matriculated undergraduates who enrolled in 2002, 934 applied for aid, 722 were judged to have need, 296 had their need fully met. 187 Federal Work-Study jobs (averaging $1075). 188 state and other part-time jobs (averaging $1012). In 2002, 252 non-need-based awards were made. *Average percent of need met:* 77%. *Average financial aid package:* $4660. *Average need-based loan:* $2256. *Average need-based gift aid:* $3316. *Average non-need-based aid:* $1853. *Average indebtedness upon graduation:* $9577.

Applying *Options:* early admission. *Application fee:* $15. *Required:* high school transcript. *Required for some:* essay or personal statement, minimum 2.7 GPA, 3 letters of recommendation. *Application deadline:* rolling (freshmen), rolling (transfers). *Notification:* continuous (freshmen), continuous (transfers).

Admissions Contact Mrs. Shirley Murrow, Registrar, Northwestern Oklahoma State University, 709 Oklahoma Boulevard, Alva, OK 73717-2799. *Phone:* 580-327-8550. *Fax:* 580-327-8699. *E-mail:* smmurrow@nwosu.edu.

OKLAHOMA BAPTIST UNIVERSITY

Shawnee, Oklahoma

- **Independent Southern Baptist** comprehensive, founded 1910
- **Calendar** 4-1-4
- **Degrees** bachelor's and master's
- **Small-town** 125-acre campus with easy access to Oklahoma City
- **Endowment** $68.2 million
- **Coed,** 1,866 undergraduate students, 81% full-time, 56% women, 44% men
- **Moderately difficult** entrance level, 85% of applicants were admitted

Undergraduates 1,511 full-time, 355 part-time. Students come from 42 states and territories, 17 other countries, 39% are from out of state, 5% transferred in, 72% live on campus. *Retention:* 74% of 2000 full-time freshmen returned.

Freshmen *Admission:* 1,098 applied, 938 admitted, 411 enrolled. *Average high school GPA:* 3.65. *Test scores:* SAT verbal scores over 500: 84%; SAT math scores over 500: 79%; ACT scores over 18: 96%; SAT verbal scores over 600: 48%; SAT math scores over 600: 38%; ACT scores over 24: 55%; SAT verbal scores over 700: 12%; SAT math scores over 700: 9%; ACT scores over 30: 10%.

Faculty *Total:* 119. *Student/faculty ratio:* 15:1.

Majors Accounting; advertising; ancient Near Eastern and biblical languages; applied art; art; art teacher education; athletic training; biblical studies; biological and physical sciences; biology/biological sciences; biology teacher education; broadcast journalism; business administration and management; chemistry; chemistry teacher education; child development; child guidance; computer and information sciences; computer management; computer programming (specific applications); computer science; computer systems analysis; developmental and child psychology; divinity/ministry; drama and dance teacher education; dramatic/theatre arts; education; elementary education; English; English composition; English/language arts teacher education; finance; fine/studio arts; French; French language teacher education; German; German language teacher education; health and physical education; history; history teacher education; humanities; human resources management; information science/studies; interdisciplinary studies; international business/trade/commerce; international marketing; journalism; kindergarten/preschool education; kinesiology and exercise science; management information systems; marketing/marketing management; marriage and family therapy/counseling; mass communication/media; mathematics; mathematics teacher education; missionary studies and missiology; museum studies; music; music teacher education; music theory and composition; natural sciences; nursing (registered nurse training); parks, recreation and leisure; pastoral studies/counseling; philosophy; physical education teaching and coaching; physical sciences; physics; piano and organ; political science and government; pre-dentistry studies; pre-law studies; pre-medical studies; pre-pharmacy studies; pre-veterinary studies; psychology; public relations/image management; radio and television; religious education; religious/sacred music; religious studies; science teacher education; secondary education; social sciences; social science teacher education; social studies teacher education; social work; sociology; Spanish; Spanish language teacher education; special education; special education (emotionally disturbed); special education (mentally retarded); special education (specific learning disabilities); speech and rhetoric; speech teacher education; telecommunications; theology; voice and opera; wind/percussion instruments.

Academic Programs *Special study options:* academic remediation for entering students, advanced placement credit, cooperative education, double majors, honors programs, independent study, internships, off-campus study, part-time degree program, services for LD students, student-designed majors, study abroad, summer session for credit. *ROTC:* Air Force (c).

Library Mabee Learning Center with 230,000 titles, 1,800 serial subscriptions, 1,600 audiovisual materials, an OPAC, a Web page.

Computers on Campus 170 computers available on campus for general student use. A campuswide network can be accessed from student residence rooms. Internet access, at least one staffed computer lab available.

Student Life *Housing:* on-campus residence required through junior year. *Options:* men-only, women-only. *Activities and organizations:* drama/theater group, student-run newspaper, television station, choral group, Campus Activities Board, Student Ambassadors, Student Government Association, Baptist Student Union, University Concert Series. *Campus security:* 24-hour emergency response devices and patrols, late-night transport/escort service, controlled dormitory access. *Student services:* health clinic, personal/psychological counseling.

Athletics Member NAIA. *Intercollegiate sports:* baseball M(s), basketball M(s)/W(s), cross-country running M(s)/W(s), golf M(s)/W(s), softball W(s), tennis M(s)/W(s), track and field M(s)/W(s). *Intramural sports:* badminton M/W, basketball M/W, bowling M/W, football M/W, racquetball M/W, soccer M/W, softball M/W, swimming M/W, table tennis M/W, tennis M/W, volleyball M/W.

Standardized Tests *Required:* SAT I or ACT (for admission).

Costs (2003–04) *Comprehensive fee:* $15,220 includes full-time tuition ($10,800), mandatory fees ($780), and room and board ($3640). Full-time tuition and fees vary according to course load. Part-time tuition: $340 per credit hour. Part-time tuition and fees vary according to course load. *College room only:* $1690. Room and board charges vary according to board plan and housing facility. *Payment plan:* installment. *Waivers:* senior citizens and employees or children of employees.

Financial Aid Of all full-time matriculated undergraduates who enrolled in 2003, 1,398 applied for aid, 966 were judged to have need, 489 had their need fully met. 303 Federal Work-Study jobs (averaging $834). In 2003, 432 non-need-based awards were made. *Average percent of need met:* 70%. *Average financial aid package:* $10,644. *Average need-based loan:* $3834. *Average need-based gift aid:* $3301. *Average non-need-based aid:* $4398. *Average indebtedness upon graduation:* $14,510.

Applying *Options:* early admission, deferred entrance. *Application fee:* $25. *Required:* high school transcript, minimum 2.5 GPA. *Required for some:* essay or personal statement, letters of recommendation, interview. *Application deadlines:* rolling (freshmen), 8/1 (transfers). *Notification:* continuous until 9/1 (freshmen), continuous until 9/1 (transfers).

Admissions Contact Mr. Trent Argo, Dean of Enrollment Management, Oklahoma Baptist University, Box 61174, Shawnee, OK 74804. *Phone:* 405-878-2033. *Toll-free phone:* 800-654-3285. *Fax:* 405-878-2046. *E-mail:* admissions@mail.okbu.edu.

OKLAHOMA CHRISTIAN UNIVERSITY

Oklahoma City, Oklahoma

- **Independent** comprehensive, founded 1950, affiliated with Church of Christ
- **Calendar** semesters
- **Degrees** bachelor's and master's
- **Suburban** 200-acre campus
- **Endowment** $32.0 million
- **Coed,** 1,553 undergraduate students, 96% full-time, 51% women, 49% men
- **Noncompetitive** entrance level, 30% of applicants were admitted

Undergraduates 1,491 full-time, 62 part-time. 52% are from out of state, 6% African American, 1% Asian American or Pacific Islander, 2% Hispanic American, 2% Native American, 16% transferred in, 71% live on campus. *Retention:* 66% of 2002 full-time freshmen returned.

Freshmen *Admission:* 1,271 applied, 386 admitted, 386 enrolled. *Test scores:* ACT scores over 18: 85%; ACT scores over 24: 48%; ACT scores over 30: 9%.
Faculty *Total:* 153, 58% full-time, 49% with terminal degrees. *Student/faculty ratio:* 14:1.
Majors Accounting; advertising; American government and politics; art; biblical studies; biochemistry; biology/biological sciences; broadcast journalism; business administration and management; business/commerce; chemistry; child development; clinical laboratory science/medical technology; commercial and advertising art; computer engineering; computer science; creative writing; dramatic/theatre arts; early childhood education; electrical, electronics and communications engineering; elementary education; engineering; English; English as a second/foreign language (teaching); English/language arts teacher education; family and community services; history; information science/studies; interior design; journalism; kindergarten/preschool education; liberal arts and sciences/liberal studies; marketing/marketing management; mass communication/media; mathematics; mathematics teacher education; mechanical engineering; missionary studies and missiology; music; music teacher education; physical education teaching and coaching; pre-law studies; psychology; public relations/image management; radio and television; religious education; religious studies; science teacher education; secondary education; social studies teacher education; Spanish; speech and rhetoric; voice and opera; wind/percussion instruments.
Academic Programs *Special study options:* academic remediation for entering students, accelerated degree program, adult/continuing education programs, advanced placement credit, distance learning, double majors, English as a second language, honors programs, internships, off-campus study, services for LD students, study abroad, summer session for credit. *ROTC:* Army (c), Air Force (c).
Library Tom and Ada Beam Library with 99,916 titles, 990 serial subscriptions, 10,232 audiovisual materials, an OPAC, a Web page.
Computers on Campus 101 computers available on campus for general student use. A campuswide network can be accessed from student residence rooms and from off campus that provide access to each student has a laptop computer. Internet access, at least one staffed computer lab available. Computer purchase or lease plan available.
Student Life *Housing:* on-campus residence required through senior year. *Options:* men-only, women-only, disabled students. Campus housing is university owned. Freshman campus housing is guaranteed. *Activities and organizations:* drama/theater group, student-run newspaper, radio station, choral group, Outreach, Agape, College Women for Christ, Young Republicans, College Democrats. *Campus security:* 24-hour emergency response devices and patrols, late-night transport/escort service. *Student services:* health clinic, personal/psychological counseling.
Athletics Member NAIA. *Intercollegiate sports:* basketball M(s)/W(s), cross-country running M(s)/W(s), golf M(s), soccer M(s)/W(s), softball W(s), tennis M(s)/W(s), track and field M(s)/W(s). *Intramural sports:* basketball M/W, bowling M/W, cheerleading M/W, cross-country running M/W, football M/W, soccer M/W, softball M/W, swimming M/W, table tennis M/W, tennis M/W, track and field M/W, volleyball M/W.
Standardized Tests *Required:* SAT I or ACT (for admission).
Costs (2004–05) *Comprehensive fee:* $17,980 includes full-time tuition ($11,780), mandatory fees ($1380), and room and board ($4820). Full-time tuition and fees vary according to course load. Part-time tuition and fees vary according to course load. *Room and board:* Room and board charges vary according to housing facility. *Payment plans:* tuition prepayment, installment. *Waivers:* employees or children of employees.
Financial Aid Of all full-time matriculated undergraduates who enrolled in 2003, 1,546 applied for aid, 1,049 were judged to have need, 237 had their need fully met. 200 Federal Work-Study jobs (averaging $1500). In 2003, 347 non-need-based awards were made. *Average percent of need met:* 57%. *Average financial aid package:* $11,748. *Average need-based loan:* $3841. *Average need-based gift aid:* $1737. *Average non-need-based aid:* $2233. *Average indebtedness upon graduation:* $25,100. *Financial aid deadline:* 8/31.
Applying *Options:* early admission, deferred entrance. *Application fee:* $25. *Required:* high school transcript. *Application deadline:* rolling (freshmen), rolling (transfers). *Notification:* continuous (freshmen), continuous (transfers).
Admissions Contact Ms. Risa Forrester, Director of Admissions, Oklahoma Christian University, Box 11000, Oklahoma City, OK 73136-1100. *Phone:* 405-425-5050. *Toll-free phone:* 800-877-5010. *Fax:* 405-425-5208. *E-mail:* info@oc.edu.

OKLAHOMA CITY UNIVERSITY
Oklahoma City, Oklahoma

- **Independent United Methodist** comprehensive, founded 1904
- **Calendar** semesters
- **Degrees** bachelor's, master's, and first professional
- **Urban** 68-acre campus
- **Endowment** $57.8 million
- **Coed,** 1,793 undergraduate students, 75% full-time, 62% women, 38% men
- **Moderately difficult** entrance level, 78% of applicants were admitted

Undergraduates 1,344 full-time, 449 part-time. Students come from 48 states and territories, 67 other countries, 31% are from out of state, 7% African American, 2% Asian American or Pacific Islander, 4% Hispanic American, 4% Native American, 23% international, 9% transferred in, 36% live on campus. *Retention:* 73% of 2002 full-time freshmen returned.
Freshmen *Admission:* 822 applied, 639 admitted, 319 enrolled. *Average high school GPA:* 3.51. *Test scores:* SAT verbal scores over 500: 82%; SAT math scores over 500: 72%; ACT scores over 18: 97%; SAT verbal scores over 600: 33%; SAT math scores over 600: 37%; ACT scores over 24: 54%; SAT verbal scores over 700: 1%; SAT math scores over 700: 4%; ACT scores over 30: 18%.
Faculty *Total:* 270, 56% full-time. *Student/faculty ratio:* 11:1.
Majors Accounting; advertising; American studies; art; art history, criticism and conservation; arts management; art teacher education; biochemistry; biological and physical sciences; biology/biological sciences; biophysics; broadcast journalism; business administration and management; business/commerce; business/managerial economics; chemistry; cinematography and film/video production; commercial and advertising art; computer science; corrections; criminal justice/law enforcement administration; criminal justice/police science; dance; dramatic/theatre arts; education; elementary education; English; finance; fine/studio arts; French; German; history; humanities; international business/trade/commerce; journalism; kindergarten/preschool education; kinesiology and exercise science; liberal arts and sciences/liberal studies; management information systems; marketing/marketing management; mass communication/media; mathematics; Montessori teacher education; music; music management and merchandising; music teacher education; music theory and composition; nursing (registered nurse training); philosophy; physical education teaching and coaching; physics; piano and organ; political science and government; pre-dentistry studies; pre-law studies; pre-medical studies; pre-nursing studies; pre-pharmacy studies; pre-veterinary studies; psychology; public relations/image management; radio and television; religious education; religious/sacred music; religious studies; science teacher education; secondary education; sociology; Spanish; speech and rhetoric; speech/theater education; theatre design and technology; violin, viola, guitar and other stringed instruments; voice and opera; wind/percussion instruments.
Academic Programs *Special study options:* academic remediation for entering students, accelerated degree program, adult/continuing education programs, advanced placement credit, cooperative education, double majors, English as a second language, external degree program, honors programs, independent study, internships, off-campus study, part-time degree program, services for LD students, student-designed majors, study abroad, summer session for credit. *ROTC:* Army (c), Air Force (c).
Library Dulaney Browne Library plus 1 other with 321,093 titles, 5,498 serial subscriptions, 10,132 audiovisual materials, an OPAC, a Web page.
Computers on Campus 264 computers available on campus for general student use. A campuswide network can be accessed from student residence rooms and from off campus. Internet access, online (class) registration, at least one staffed computer lab available.
Student Life *Housing:* on-campus residence required through senior year. *Options:* men-only, women-only. Campus housing is university owned and is provided by a third party. Freshman applicants given priority for college housing. *Activities and organizations:* drama/theater group, student-run newspaper, television station, choral group, national fraternities, national sororities. *Campus security:* 24-hour emergency response devices and patrols, student patrols, late-night transport/escort service, Operation ID. *Student services:* health clinic, personal/psychological counseling.
Athletics Member NAIA. *Intercollegiate sports:* baseball M(s), basketball M(s)/W(s), cheerleading M(s)/W(s), crew M/W, golf M(s)/W(s), soccer M(s)/W(s), softball W(s). *Intramural sports:* badminton M/W, basketball M/W, bowling M/W, crew M/W, fencing M/W, football M, golf M/W, softball M/W, table tennis M/W, volleyball M/W.
Standardized Tests *Required:* SAT I or ACT (for admission).
Costs (2003–04) *Comprehensive fee:* $19,580 includes full-time tuition ($13,340), mandatory fees ($690), and room and board ($5550). Full-time tuition and fees vary according to program. Part-time tuition: $455 per semester hour. Part-time tuition and fees vary according to program. *Required fees:* $100 per term part-time. *Room and board:* Room and board charges vary according to board plan and housing facility. *Payment plans:* installment, deferred payment. *Waivers:* employees or children of employees.
Financial Aid Of all full-time matriculated undergraduates who enrolled in 2002, 753 applied for aid, 609 were judged to have need, 124 had their need fully met. 221 Federal Work-Study jobs (averaging $1684). 44 state and other part-time jobs (averaging $1997). In 2002, 116 non-need-based awards were made. *Average percent of need met:* 82%. *Average financial aid package:* $10,680. *Average*

Oklahoma City University (continued)
need-based loan: $3313. *Average need-based gift aid:* $7037. *Average non-need-based aid:* $5567. *Average indebtedness upon graduation:* $18,669.
Applying *Options:* common application, electronic application, deferred entrance. *Application fee:* $30. *Required:* high school transcript, minimum 3.0 GPA. *Required for some:* interview, audition for music and dance programs. *Application deadline:* 8/20 (freshmen), rolling (transfers). *Notification:* continuous (freshmen), continuous until 8/15 (transfers).
Admissions Contact Ms. Shery Boyles, Director of Admissions, Oklahoma City University, 2501 North Blackwelder, Oklahoma City, OK 73106. *Phone:* 405-521-5050. *Toll-free phone:* 800-633-7242. *Fax:* 405-521-5916. *E-mail:* uadmissions@okcu.edu.

■ *See page 2130 for a narrative description.*

OKLAHOMA PANHANDLE STATE UNIVERSITY
Goodwell, Oklahoma

- **State-supported** 4-year, founded 1909, part of Oklahoma State Regents for Higher Education
- **Calendar** semesters
- **Degrees** certificates, associate, and bachelor's
- **Rural** 40-acre campus
- **Endowment** $4.0 million
- **Coed,** 1,226 undergraduate students, 67% full-time, 53% women, 47% men
- **Noncompetitive** entrance level

Undergraduates 826 full-time, 400 part-time. Students come from 36 states and territories, 26 other countries, 52% are from out of state, 7% African American, 0.4% Asian American or Pacific Islander, 11% Hispanic American, 2% Native American, 5% international, 13% transferred in, 17% live on campus. *Retention:* 50% of 2002 full-time freshmen returned.
Freshmen *Admission:* 222 enrolled. *Test scores:* ACT scores over 18: 65%; ACT scores over 24: 15%; ACT scores over 30: 3%.
Faculty *Total:* 65, 82% full-time, 31% with terminal degrees. *Student/faculty ratio:* 22:1.
Majors Accounting; agricultural business and management; agricultural teacher education; agriculture; agronomy and crop science; animal sciences; biological and physical sciences; biology/biological sciences; business administration and management; business teacher education; chemistry; clinical laboratory science/medical technology; computer and information sciences; elementary education; English; farm and ranch management; general studies; history; humanities; industrial arts; industrial technology; information science/studies; mathematics; natural sciences; nursing (registered nurse training); parks, recreation and leisure; physical education teaching and coaching; psychology; science teacher education; secondary education; social sciences; technology/industrial arts teacher education.
Academic Programs *Special study options:* academic remediation for entering students, accelerated degree program, adult/continuing education programs, advanced placement credit, cooperative education, distance learning, double majors, English as a second language, internships, part-time degree program, summer session for credit.
Library McKee Library with 106,000 titles, 308 serial subscriptions, 2,079 audiovisual materials, an OPAC.
Computers on Campus 50 computers available on campus for general student use. A campuswide network can be accessed from off campus. Internet access, at least one staffed computer lab available.
Student Life *Housing:* on-campus residence required for freshman year. *Options:* coed. Campus housing is university owned. Freshman campus housing is guaranteed. *Activities and organizations:* drama/theater group, student-run newspaper, radio station, choral group, marching band. *Campus security:* 24-hour emergency response devices and patrols, student patrols, safety bars over door latches. *Student services:* health clinic, personal/psychological counseling.
Athletics Member NCAA. except football (Division II) *Intercollegiate sports:* baseball M(s), basketball M(s)/W(s), cross-country running W(s), equestrian sports M(s)/W(s), football M(s), golf M(s), softball W(s). *Intramural sports:* basketball M/W, bowling M/W, equestrian sports M/W, football M/W, softball M/W, volleyball M/W.
Standardized Tests *Required:* SAT I or ACT (for placement).
Costs (2004–05) *Tuition:* state resident $1800 full-time; nonresident $3300 full-time. Full-time tuition and fees vary according to course level. Part-time tuition and fees vary according to course level. *Required fees:* $1170 full-time. *Room and board:* $2810; room only: $930. Room and board charges vary according to board plan, housing facility, and student level. *Waivers:* employees or children of employees.
Financial Aid Of all full-time matriculated undergraduates who enrolled in 2002, 1,001 applied for aid, 1,001 were judged to have need. 21 Federal Work-Study jobs, 297 state and other part-time jobs. *Average percent of need met:* 70%. *Average financial aid package:* $9200. *Average need-based loan:* $4411. *Average need-based gift aid:* $3683. *Average indebtedness upon graduation:* $4315.
Applying *Options:* common application. *Required:* high school transcript. *Application deadline:* rolling (freshmen), rolling (transfers).
Admissions Contact Mr. Vic Shrock, Registrar and Director of Admissions, Oklahoma Panhandle State University, PO Box 430, 323 Eagle Boulevard, Goodwell, OK 73939-0430. *Phone:* 580-349-1376. *Toll-free phone:* 800-664-6778. *Fax:* 580-349-2302. *E-mail:* opsu@opsu.edu.

OKLAHOMA STATE UNIVERSITY
Stillwater, Oklahoma

- **State-supported** university, founded 1890, part of Oklahoma State University
- **Calendar** semesters
- **Degrees** diplomas, bachelor's, master's, doctoral, and first professional
- **Small-town** 840-acre campus with easy access to Oklahoma City and Tulsa
- **Endowment** $149.3 million
- **Coed,** 18,689 undergraduate students, 88% full-time, 49% women, 51% men
- **Moderately difficult** entrance level, 89% of applicants were admitted

Undergraduates 16,408 full-time, 2,281 part-time. Students come from 50 states and territories, 122 other countries, 13% are from out of state, 3% African American, 2% Asian American or Pacific Islander, 2% Hispanic American, 9% Native American, 5% international, 10% transferred in, 39% live on campus. *Retention:* 80% of 2002 full-time freshmen returned.
Freshmen *Admission:* 6,629 applied, 5,930 admitted, 3,490 enrolled. *Average high school GPA:* 3.49. *Test scores:* SAT verbal scores over 500: 75%; SAT math scores over 500: 76%; ACT scores over 18: 96%; SAT verbal scores over 600: 26%; SAT math scores over 600: 31%; ACT scores over 24: 47%; SAT verbal scores over 700: 4%; SAT math scores over 700: 5%; ACT scores over 30: 8%.
Faculty *Total:* 1,060, 85% full-time, 82% with terminal degrees. *Student/faculty ratio:* 21:1.
Majors Accounting; advertising; aerospace, aeronautical and astronautical engineering; agricultural business and management; agricultural communication/journalism; agricultural economics; agricultural teacher education; agriculture; airline pilot and flight crew; American studies; animal sciences; apparel and textiles; architectural engineering; architecture; art; athletic training; aviation/airway management; avionics maintenance technology; biochemistry; biochemistry, biophysics and molecular biology related; biology/biological sciences; biomedical/medical engineering; botany/plant biology; broadcast journalism; business/commerce; business/managerial economics; cell biology and histology; chemical engineering; chemistry; child development; civil engineering; clinical laboratory science/medical technology; clothing/textiles; commercial and advertising art; communication and journalism related; communication disorders; computer and information sciences; computer engineering; computer management; computer science; construction engineering technology; construction/heavy equipment/earthmoving equipment operation; construction management; creative writing; dietetics; dramatic/theatre arts; economics; education; education (specific subject areas) related; electrical, electronic and communications engineering technology; electrical, electronics and communications engineering; elementary education; engineering; engineering technology; English; entomology; environmental studies; family and community services; family and consumer economics related; family and consumer sciences/human sciences; fashion/apparel design; fashion merchandising; finance; fine/studio arts; fire protection and safety technology; foods, nutrition, and wellness; forestry; French; geography; geology/earth science; German; graphic design; health and physical education; health science; history; horticultural science; hotel/motel administration; human development and family studies; human resources management; industrial arts; industrial engineering; industrial technology; information science/studies; interior design; international business/trade/commerce; journalism; landscape architecture; landscaping and groundskeeping; liberal arts and sciences/liberal studies; management information systems; management science; marketing/marketing management; mathematics; mechanical engineering; mechanical engineering/mechanical technology; medical microbiology and bacteriology; music; music management and merchandising; music pedagogy; music related; music teacher education; philosophy; physical education teaching and coaching; physics; physics related; plant sciences; political science and government; predentistry studies; pre-law studies; pre-medical studies; pre-nursing studies; pre-pharmacy studies; pre-veterinary studies; psychology; restaurant/food services management; Russian; secondary education; sociology; Spanish; speech and rhetoric; statistics; technical and business writing; trade and industrial teacher education; wildlife and wildlands science and management; zoology/animal biology; zoology/animal biology related.
Academic Programs *Special study options:* academic remediation for entering students, accelerated degree program, adult/continuing education programs,

advanced placement credit, cooperative education, distance learning, double majors, English as a second language, freshman honors college, honors programs, independent study, internships, off-campus study, part-time degree program, services for LD students, student-designed majors, study abroad, summer session for credit. *ROTC:* Army (b), Air Force (b). *Unusual degree programs:* 3-2 accounting.

Library Edmon Low Library plus 4 others with 2.4 million titles, 24,806 serial subscriptions, 510,548 audiovisual materials, an OPAC, a Web page.

Computers on Campus 2000 computers available on campus for general student use. A campuswide network can be accessed from student residence rooms and from off campus. Internet access, online (class) registration, at least one staffed computer lab available.

Student Life *Housing:* on-campus residence required for freshman year. *Options:* coed, men-only, women-only, disabled students. Campus housing is university owned and is provided by a third party. Freshman campus housing is guaranteed. *Activities and organizations:* drama/theater group, student-run newspaper, radio and television station, choral group, marching band, Student Government Association, Campus Crusade for Christ, Flying Aggies, Block and Bridle Club, OSU ski club, national fraternities, national sororities. *Campus security:* 24-hour emergency response devices and patrols, student patrols, controlled dormitory access. *Student services:* health clinic, personal/psychological counseling, women's center, legal services.

Athletics Member NCAA. All Division I except football (Division I-A). *Intercollegiate sports:* baseball M(s), basketball M(s)/W(s), cross-country running M(s)/W(s), equestrian sports W(s), golf M(s)/W(s), soccer W, softball W(s), tennis M(s)/W(s), track and field M(s)/W(s), wrestling M(s). *Intramural sports:* archery M/W, badminton M/W, basketball M/W, bowling M/W, crew M(c)/W(c), cross-country running M/W, football M/W, golf M/W, ice hockey M(c)/W(c), lacrosse M(c), racquetball M/W, riflery M(c)/W(c), rugby M(c)/W(c), sailing M(c)/W(c), soccer M/W, softball M/W, squash M/W, swimming M/W, table tennis M/W, tennis M/W, track and field M/W, volleyball M/W, water polo M/W, weight lifting M/W, wrestling M.

Standardized Tests *Required:* SAT I or ACT (for admission). *Recommended:* ACT (for admission).

Costs (2003–04) *Tuition:* state resident $2513 full-time, $84 per credit hour part-time; nonresident $8459 full-time, $282 per credit hour part-time. Full-time tuition and fees vary according to course level. Part-time tuition and fees vary according to course level. *Required fees:* $1152 full-time, $40 per credit part-time, $115 per term part-time. *Room and board:* $5468; room only: $2468. Room and board charges vary according to board plan, housing facility, and location. *Payment plan:* installment. *Waivers:* children of alumni.

Financial Aid Of all full-time matriculated undergraduates who enrolled in 2002, 10,299 applied for aid, 7,909 were judged to have need, 1,844 had their need fully met. 600 Federal Work-Study jobs (averaging $1750). 2,750 state and other part-time jobs (averaging $2205). In 2002, 3894 non-need-based awards were made. *Average percent of need met:* 79%. *Average financial aid package:* $7671. *Average need-based loan:* $3791. *Average need-based gift aid:* $3324. *Average non-need-based aid:* $2685. *Average indebtedness upon graduation:* $16,268.

Applying *Options:* electronic application, early admission. *Application fee:* $25. *Required:* high school transcript, minimum 3.0 GPA, class rank. *Required for some:* interview. *Application deadline:* rolling (freshmen), rolling (transfers). *Notification:* continuous (freshmen), continuous (transfers).

Admissions Contact Ms. Paulette Cundiff, Coordinator of Admissions Processing, Oklahoma State University, 324 Student Union, Stillwater, OK 74078. *Phone:* 405-744-6858. *Toll-free phone:* 800-233-5019 (in-state); 800-852-1255 (out-of-state). *Fax:* 405-744-5285. *E-mail:* admit@okstate.edu.

Oklahoma Wesleyan University

Bartlesville, Oklahoma

- **Independent** comprehensive, founded 1909, affiliated with Wesleyan Church
- **Calendar** semesters
- **Degrees** certificates, diplomas, associate, bachelor's, and master's
- **Small-town** 127-acre campus with easy access to Tulsa
- **Coed**
- **Minimally difficult** entrance level

Faculty *Student/faculty ratio:* 14:1.

Student Life *Campus security:* 24-hour emergency response devices and patrols, controlled dormitory access.

Athletics Member NAIA, NCCAA.

Standardized Tests *Required:* SAT I or ACT (for admission).

Costs (2003–04) *Comprehensive fee:* $16,850 includes full-time tuition ($11,550), mandatory fees ($700), and room and board ($4600). *College room only:* $2300. Room and board charges vary according to board plan and housing facility. *Payment plans:* installment, deferred payment.

Financial Aid Of all full-time matriculated undergraduates who enrolled in 2002, 671 applied for aid, 601 were judged to have need, 151 had their need fully met. 130 Federal Work-Study jobs (averaging $1596). 13 state and other part-time jobs (averaging $1550). In 2002, 49. *Average percent of need met:* 59. *Average financial aid package:* $6651. *Average need-based loan:* $4286. *Average need-based gift aid:* $4019. *Average non-need-based aid:* $2341. *Average indebtedness upon graduation:* $15,123.

Applying *Options:* early admission, deferred entrance. *Application fee:* $25. *Required:* high school transcript, letters of recommendation, minimum ACT of 18 or SAT 860. *Recommended:* minimum 2.0 GPA.

Admissions Contact Mr. Jim Weidman, Director of Enrollment Services, Oklahoma Wesleyan University, 2201 Silver Lake Road, Bartlesville, OK 74006-6299. *Phone:* 800-468-6292. *Toll-free phone:* 800-468-6292. *Fax:* 918-335-6229. *E-mail:* admissions@okwu.edu.

Oral Roberts University

Tulsa, Oklahoma

- **Independent interdenominational** comprehensive, founded 1963
- **Calendar** semesters
- **Degrees** bachelor's, master's, doctoral, and first professional
- **Urban** 263-acre campus
- **Endowment** $66.4 million
- **Coed,** 3,363 undergraduate students, 91% full-time, 61% women, 39% men
- **Moderately difficult** entrance level, 64% of applicants were admitted

Undergraduates 3,059 full-time, 304 part-time. Students come from 41 other countries, 64% are from out of state, 16% African American, 2% Asian American or Pacific Islander, 5% Hispanic American, 2% Native American, 3% international, 7% transferred in, 71% live on campus. *Retention:* 82% of 2002 full-time freshmen returned.

Freshmen *Admission:* 1,363 applied, 867 admitted, 644 enrolled. *Average high school GPA:* 3.90. *Test scores:* SAT verbal scores over 500: 64%; SAT math scores over 500: 62%; SAT verbal scores over 600: 25%; SAT math scores over 600: 22%; SAT verbal scores over 700: 5%; SAT math scores over 700: 3%.

Faculty *Total:* 282, 70% full-time, 47% with terminal degrees. *Student/faculty ratio:* 16:1.

Majors Accounting; art teacher education; biblical studies; biochemistry; biology/biological sciences; biomedical/medical engineering; biomedical technology; business administration and management; chemistry; commercial and advertising art; communication/speech communication and rhetoric; computer engineering; computer science; dramatic/theatre arts; education; educational leadership and administration; education (multiple levels); electrical, electronics and communications engineering; elementary education; engineering mechanics; English as a second/foreign language (teaching); English/language arts teacher education; English literature (British and Commonwealth); finance; fine/studio arts; French; French language teacher education; German; German language teacher education; history; international relations and affairs; journalism; kindergarten/preschool education; kinesiology and exercise science; liberal arts and sciences/liberal studies; management information systems; management science; marketing/marketing management; mathematics; mathematics teacher education; mechanical engineering; missionary studies and missiology; music; music performance; music teacher education; music theory and composition; nursing (registered nurse training); pastoral studies/counseling; philosophy; physical education teaching and coaching; physics; political science and government; pre-dentistry studies; pre-medical studies; psychology; public relations/image management; radio and television; religious/sacred music; religious studies; science teacher education; social studies teacher education; social work; Spanish; Spanish language teacher education; special education; theology.

Academic Programs *Special study options:* academic remediation for entering students, adult/continuing education programs, advanced placement credit, distance learning, double majors, English as a second language, external degree program, freshman honors college, honors programs, independent study, internships, off-campus study, part-time degree program, services for LD students, student-designed majors, study abroad, summer session for credit. *ROTC:* Air Force (c). *Unusual degree programs:* 3-2 education.

Library John D. Messick Resources Center plus 1 other with 216,691 titles, 600 serial subscriptions, 25,445 audiovisual materials, an OPAC, a Web page.

Computers on Campus 253 computers available on campus for general student use. A campuswide network can be accessed from student residence rooms and from off campus. Internet access, at least one staffed computer lab available.

Student Life *Housing:* on-campus residence required through senior year. *Options:* men-only, women-only. *Activities and organizations:* drama/theater group, student-run newspaper, radio and television station, choral group, missions, Student Nurse Association, American Management Society, Accounting

Oral Roberts University (continued)
Society. *Campus security:* 24-hour emergency response devices and patrols, late-night transport/escort service. *Student services:* health clinic, personal/psychological counseling.

Athletics Member NCAA. All Division I. *Intercollegiate sports:* baseball M(s), basketball M(s)/W(s), cross-country running M(s)/W(s), golf M(s)/W(s), soccer M(s)/W(s), tennis M(s)/W(s), track and field M(s)/W(s), volleyball W(s). *Intramural sports:* badminton M/W, basketball M/W, bowling M/W, football M/W, racquetball M/W, soccer M/W, softball M/W, table tennis M/W, tennis M/W, volleyball M/W.

Standardized Tests *Required:* SAT I or ACT (for admission).

Costs (2003–04) *Comprehensive fee:* $19,870 includes full-time tuition ($13,550), mandatory fees ($420), and room and board ($5900). Part-time tuition: $565 per credit hour. *College room only:* $2880. Room and board charges vary according to board plan. *Payment plan:* installment. *Waivers:* children of alumni and employees or children of employees.

Financial Aid Of all full-time matriculated undergraduates who enrolled in 2002, 2,110 applied for aid, 1,922 were judged to have need, 746 had their need fully met. 313 Federal Work-Study jobs (averaging $1590). 750 state and other part-time jobs (averaging $1500). In 2002, 491 non-need-based awards were made. *Average percent of need met:* 87%. *Average financial aid package:* $13,998. *Average need-based loan:* $7725. *Average need-based gift aid:* $7444. *Average non-need-based aid:* $7152. *Average indebtedness upon graduation:* $25,836.

Applying *Options:* early admission, early action, deferred entrance. *Application fee:* $35. *Required:* essay or personal statement, high school transcript, minimum 2.0 GPA, 1 letter of recommendation, proof of immunization. *Required for some:* interview. *Application deadline:* rolling (freshmen), rolling (transfers). *Notification:* continuous (freshmen), 9/1 (early action), continuous (transfers).

Admissions Contact Chris Miller, Director of Undergraduate Admissions, Oral Roberts University, 7777 South Lewis Avenue, Tulsa, OK 74171. *Phone:* 918-495-6518. *Toll-free phone:* 800-678-8876. *Fax:* 918-495-6222. *E-mail:* admissions@oru.edu.

ROGERS STATE UNIVERSITY
Claremore, Oklahoma

- **State-supported** 4-year, founded 1909, part of Oklahoma State Regents for Higher Education
- **Calendar** semesters
- **Degrees** certificates, diplomas, associate, and bachelor's
- **Small-town** 40-acre campus with easy access to Tulsa
- **Endowment** $4.0 million
- **Coed**
- **Noncompetitive** entrance level

Faculty *Student/faculty ratio:* 19:1.

Student Life *Campus security:* 24-hour patrols, late-night transport/escort service.

Standardized Tests *Required for some:* ACT (for admission), ACT COMPASS (for students over 21).

Costs (2003–04) *Tuition:* state resident $2140 full-time, $89 per credit part-time; nonresident $5261 full-time, $219 per credit part-time. *Required fees:* $30 full-time, $15 per term part-time. *Room and board:* $5481; room only: $3321.

Financial Aid Of all full-time matriculated undergraduates who enrolled in 2002, 2,464 applied for aid, 2,464 were judged to have need, 2,464 had their need fully met. 73 Federal Work-Study jobs (averaging $1331). 233 state and other part-time jobs (averaging $2043). *Average percent of need met:* 76. *Average financial aid package:* $8200. *Average need-based loan:* $2755. *Average need-based gift aid:* $5550. *Average indebtedness upon graduation:* $12,250.

Applying *Options:* electronic application. *Required:* high school transcript. *Required for some:* minimum 2.7 GPA.

Admissions Contact Ms. Becky Noah, Director of Enrollment Management, Rogers State University, Roger's State University, Office of Admissions, 1701 West Will Rogers Boulevard, Claremore, OK 74017. *Phone:* 918-343-7545. *Toll-free phone:* 800-256-7511. *Fax:* 918-343-7595. *E-mail:* shunter@rsu.edu.

ST. GREGORY'S UNIVERSITY
Shawnee, Oklahoma

- **Independent Roman Catholic** 4-year, founded 1875
- **Calendar** semesters
- **Degrees** associate and bachelor's
- **Small-town** 640-acre campus with easy access to Oklahoma City
- **Endowment** $6.9 million
- **Coed,** 705 undergraduate students, 75% full-time, 54% women, 46% men
- **Minimally difficult** entrance level, 62% of applicants were admitted

Undergraduates 530 full-time, 175 part-time. Students come from 15 states and territories, 22 other countries, 18% are from out of state, 5% African American, 1% Asian American or Pacific Islander, 9% Hispanic American, 8% Native American, 10% international, 14% transferred in, 65% live on campus. *Retention:* 63% of 2002 full-time freshmen returned.

Freshmen *Admission:* 473 applied, 292 admitted, 120 enrolled. *Average high school GPA:* 3.21. *Test scores:* ACT scores over 18: 75%; ACT scores over 24: 25%.

Faculty *Total:* 60, 48% full-time, 33% with terminal degrees. *Student/faculty ratio:* 10:1.

Majors Accounting; art; biology/biological sciences; biology teacher education; biomedical sciences; broadcast journalism; business administration and management; chemistry; communication and media related; conservation biology; criminal justice/police science; criminal justice/safety; dance; English; English language and literature related; English/language arts teacher education; fine/studio arts; history; humanities; journalism; liberal arts and sciences/liberal studies; management information systems; management science; marketing/marketing management; mathematics; mathematics and computer science; mathematics teacher education; natural resources and conservation related; natural sciences; pastoral studies/counseling; philosophy; photojournalism; political science and government; pre-dentistry studies; pre-engineering; pre-law studies; pre-medical studies; pre-nursing studies; pre-pharmacy studies; pre-theology/pre-ministerial studies; psychology; social sciences; social studies teacher education; sociology; theology; visual and performing arts.

Academic Programs *Special study options:* academic remediation for entering students, adult/continuing education programs, advanced placement credit, double majors, English as a second language, external degree program, honors programs, independent study, internships, off-campus study, part-time degree program, services for LD students, student-designed majors, study abroad, summer session for credit. *ROTC:* Army (c), Navy (c), Air Force (c).

Library James J. Kelly Library plus 1 other with 55,500 titles, 284 serial subscriptions.

Computers on Campus 60 computers available on campus for general student use. A campuswide network can be accessed from student residence rooms and from off campus. Online (class) registration, at least one staffed computer lab available.

Student Life *Housing:* on-campus residence required through senior year. *Options:* men-only, women-only, disabled students. Campus housing is university owned. Freshman campus housing is guaranteed. *Activities and organizations:* drama/theater group, student-run newspaper, choral group, Student Government Association, Delta Epsilon Sigma Homer Society, Campus Ministry, ITEST-Institute for Theological Encounter with Science and Technology, Drama Club. *Campus security:* 24-hour emergency response devices and patrols, late-night transport/escort service, controlled dormitory access. *Student services:* health clinic, personal/psychological counseling.

Athletics Member NAIA. *Intercollegiate sports:* baseball M(s), basketball M(s)/W(s), cross-country running M(s)/W(s), golf M(s)/W(s), soccer M(s)/W(s), softball W(s), track and field M(s)/W(s). *Intramural sports:* basketball M/W, football M, racquetball M/W, soccer M/W, softball M/W, swimming M/W, tennis M/W, volleyball M/W.

Standardized Tests *Required:* SAT I or ACT (for admission).

Costs (2004–05) *Comprehensive fee:* $15,964 includes full-time tuition ($10,260), mandatory fees ($816), and room and board ($4888). Part-time tuition: $342 per hour.

Financial Aid Of all full-time matriculated undergraduates who enrolled in 2002, 542 applied for aid, 365 were judged to have need, 82 had their need fully met. 43 Federal Work-Study jobs (averaging $1078). 34 state and other part-time jobs (averaging $1808). In 2002, 101 non-need-based awards were made. *Average percent of need met:* 87%. *Average financial aid package:* $9652. *Average need-based loan:* $3536. *Average need-based gift aid:* $5391. *Average non-need-based aid:* $3953. *Average indebtedness upon graduation:* $15,396.

Applying *Options:* common application, electronic application, deferred entrance. *Application fee:* $25. *Required:* high school transcript, minimum 2.0 GPA. *Required for some:* essay or personal statement, letters of recommendation, interview. *Application deadline:* rolling (freshmen), rolling (transfers). *Notification:* continuous (freshmen), continuous (transfers).

Admissions Contact Mrs. Kay Stith, Director of Admissions, St. Gregory's University, 1900 West MacArthur Drive, Shawnee, OK 74804. *Phone:* 405-878-5447. *Toll-free phone:* 888-STGREGS. *Fax:* 405-878-5198. *E-mail:* admissions@stgregorys.edu.

SOUTHEASTERN OKLAHOMA STATE UNIVERSITY
Durant, Oklahoma

- **State-supported** comprehensive, founded 1909, part of Oklahoma State Regents for Higher Education
- **Calendar** semesters
- **Degrees** bachelor's, master's, and post-master's certificates
- **Small-town** 177-acre campus
- **Endowment** $9.2 million
- **Coed,** 3,738 undergraduate students, 79% full-time, 54% women, 46% men
- **Moderately difficult** entrance level, 80% of applicants were admitted

Undergraduates 2,966 full-time, 772 part-time. Students come from 34 states and territories, 25 other countries, 22% are from out of state, 5% African American, 0.6% Asian American or Pacific Islander, 2% Hispanic American, 29% Native American, 2% international, 12% transferred in, 20% live on campus. *Retention:* 58% of 2002 full-time freshmen returned.

Freshmen *Admission:* 1,067 applied, 856 admitted, 646 enrolled. *Average high school GPA:* 3.27. *Test scores:* ACT scores over 18: 71%; ACT scores over 24: 17%.

Faculty *Total:* 223, 69% full-time, 54% with terminal degrees. *Student/faculty ratio:* 20:1.

Majors Accounting; airline pilot and flight crew; art; art teacher education; aviation/airway management; biology/biological sciences; biotechnology; botany/plant biology; business administration and management; business teacher education; chemistry; clinical laboratory science/medical technology; communication and journalism related; communication/speech communication and rhetoric; computer and information sciences; criminal justice/safety; dramatic/theatre arts; economics; education; electrical, electronic and communications engineering technology; elementary education; English; English/language arts teacher education; environmental science; finance; fish/game management; general studies; gerontology; health teacher education; history; industrial technology; information science/studies; kindergarten/preschool education; management information systems and services related; management science; marketing/marketing management; mathematics; mathematics teacher education; medical laboratory technology; music; music performance; music teacher education; natural resources/conservation; occupational safety and health technology; office management; parks, recreation and leisure; physical education teaching and coaching; physics; political science and government; psychology; science teacher education; secondary education; social studies teacher education; sociology; Spanish language teacher education; special education related; wildlife and wildlands science and management; zoology/animal biology.

Academic Programs *Special study options:* academic remediation for entering students, accelerated degree program, adult/continuing education programs, advanced placement credit, distance learning, double majors, honors programs, independent study, internships, off-campus study, part-time degree program, services for LD students, summer session for credit.

Library Henry G. Bennett Memorial Library with 187,971 titles, 671 serial subscriptions, 5,291 audiovisual materials, an OPAC, a Web page.

Computers on Campus 398 computers available on campus for general student use. A campuswide network can be accessed. Internet access, online (class) registration, at least one staffed computer lab available.

Student Life *Housing options:* coed, men-only, women-only, disabled students. Campus housing is university owned. *Activities and organizations:* drama/theater group, student-run newspaper, radio station, choral group, marching band, Baptist Collegiate Ministries, Fellowship of Christian Athletes, Wesley Foundation, Resident Hall Association, Panhellenic, national fraternities, national sororities. *Campus security:* 24-hour patrols, late-night transport/escort service. *Student services:* health clinic, personal/psychological counseling.

Athletics Member NCAA. All Division II. *Intercollegiate sports:* baseball M(s), basketball M(s)/W(s), cross-country running W(s), football M(s), softball W(s), tennis M(s)/W(s), volleyball W(s). *Intramural sports:* basketball M/W, football M, softball M/W, volleyball M/W.

Standardized Tests *Required for some:* ACT (for admission), SAT II: Subject Tests (for admission).

Costs (2003–04) *Tuition:* state resident $1950 full-time, $65 per credit hour part-time; nonresident $5850 full-time, $195 per credit hour part-time. Full-time tuition and fees vary according to course level. Part-time tuition and fees vary according to course level and course load. *Required fees:* $997 full-time, $21 per semester hour part-time, $51 per term part-time. *Room and board:* $3200; room only: $1400. Room and board charges vary according to board plan and housing facility. *Waivers:* minority students, children of alumni, senior citizens, and employees or children of employees.

Financial Aid Of all full-time matriculated undergraduates who enrolled in 2002, 1,858 applied for aid, 1,584 were judged to have need, 834 had their need fully met. 186 Federal Work-Study jobs (averaging $1130). 557 state and other part-time jobs (averaging $1591). In 2002, 427 non-need-based awards were made. *Average percent of need met:* 65%. *Average financial aid package:* $3631. *Average need-based loan:* $1885. *Average need-based gift aid:* $1403. *Average non-need-based aid:* $781. *Average indebtedness upon graduation:* $6579.

Applying *Application fee:* $20. *Required:* high school transcript. *Required for some:* interview. *Application deadline:* rolling (freshmen), rolling (transfers). *Notification:* continuous (freshmen), continuous (transfers).

Admissions Contact Mr. Kyle Stafford, Director of Admissions and Enrollment Services, Southeastern Oklahoma State University, 1405 North 4th Avenue PMB 4225, Durant, OK 74701-0609. *Phone:* 580-745-2060. *Toll-free phone:* 800-435-1327. *Fax:* 580-745-4502. *E-mail:* admissions@sosu.edu.

SOUTHERN NAZARENE UNIVERSITY
Bethany, Oklahoma

- **Independent Nazarene** comprehensive, founded 1899
- **Calendar** semesters
- **Degrees** associate, bachelor's, and master's
- **Suburban** 40-acre campus with easy access to Oklahoma City
- **Endowment** $13.0 million
- **Coed,** 1,803 undergraduate students, 96% full-time, 53% women, 47% men
- **Noncompetitive** entrance level, 41% of applicants were admitted

Undergraduates 1,723 full-time, 80 part-time. Students come from 34 states and territories, 47% are from out of state, 8% African American, 2% Asian American or Pacific Islander, 3% Hispanic American, 3% Native American, 0.3% international, 6% transferred in, 63% live on campus. *Retention:* 73% of 2002 full-time freshmen returned.

Freshmen *Admission:* 735 applied, 304 admitted, 304 enrolled. *Average high school GPA:* 3.4. *Test scores:* ACT scores over 18: 78%; ACT scores over 24: 33%; ACT scores over 30: 4%.

Faculty *Total:* 204, 34% full-time, 48% with terminal degrees. *Student/faculty ratio:* 18:1.

Majors Accounting; American studies; art teacher education; athletic training; aviation/airway management; biochemistry; biology/biological sciences; broadcast journalism; business administration and management; business/commerce; business teacher education; chemistry; communication/speech communication and rhetoric; computer science; criminal justice/safety; early childhood education; education; elementary education; English; English/language arts teacher education; environmental studies; finance; foreign language teacher education; general studies; history; human development and family studies; information science/studies; interdisciplinary studies; international relations and affairs; journalism; kinesiology and exercise science; literature; management information systems; management science; marketing/marketing management; mass communication/media; mathematics; mathematics teacher education; middle school education; missionary studies and missiology; music management and merchandising; music performance; music teacher education; nursing (registered nurse training); philosophy; physical education teaching and coaching; physics; piano and organ; political science and government; pre-dentistry studies; pre-law studies; premedical studies; pre-pharmacy studies; psychology; religious education; science teacher education; secondary education; social science teacher education; social studies teacher education; social work; sociology; Spanish; Spanish language teacher education; speech and rhetoric; speech teacher education; sport and fitness administration; system, networking, and LAN/wan management; theology; urban studies/affairs; voice and opera.

Academic Programs *Special study options:* academic remediation for entering students, accelerated degree program, adult/continuing education programs, advanced placement credit, double majors, external degree program, honors programs, internships, off-campus study, part-time degree program, services for LD students, student-designed majors, study abroad, summer session for credit. *ROTC:* Army (c), Air Force (c).

Library R. T. Williams Learning Resources Center with 115,564 titles, 2,748 audiovisual materials, an OPAC, a Web page.

Computers on Campus 55 computers available on campus for general student use. A campuswide network can be accessed from student residence rooms and from off campus. Internet access, at least one staffed computer lab available.

Student Life *Housing:* on-campus residence required through senior year. *Options:* men-only, women-only. Campus housing is university owned. Freshman campus housing is guaranteed. *Activities and organizations:* drama/theater group, student-run newspaper, television station, choral group, Business Gaming Team,

Southern Nazarene University (continued)
Campus Social Life Committee, intramural sports societies, Choral Society, Inter-Club. *Campus security:* 24-hour emergency response devices, student patrols, late-night transport/escort service, controlled dormitory access. *Student services:* health clinic, personal/psychological counseling.

Athletics Member NAIA. *Intercollegiate sports:* baseball M(s), basketball M(s)/W(s), cross-country running M(s)/W(s), football M(s), golf M(s)/W(s), soccer M(s)/W(s), softball W(s), tennis M(s)/W(s), track and field M(s)/W(s), volleyball W(s). *Intramural sports:* basketball M/W, football M/W, golf M/W, racquetball M/W, skiing (downhill) M/W, soccer M/W, softball M/W, swimming M/W, table tennis M/W, tennis M/W, volleyball M/W, weight lifting M/W.

Standardized Tests *Required:* SAT I or ACT (for placement). *Recommended:* ACT (for placement).

Costs (2004–05) *Comprehensive fee:* $17,944 includes full-time tuition ($12,090), mandatory fees ($744), and room and board ($5110). Part-time tuition: $403 per credit hour. Part-time tuition and fees vary according to course load. *Required fees:* $21 per credit hour part-time. *College room only:* $2410. Room and board charges vary according to board plan and housing facility. *Payment plans:* installment, deferred payment. *Waivers:* employees or children of employees.

Financial Aid Of all full-time matriculated undergraduates who enrolled in 2000, 1,521 applied for aid, 1,437 were judged to have need.

Applying *Options:* deferred entrance. *Application fee:* $25. *Required:* high school transcript, 2 letters of recommendation. *Recommended:* interview. *Application deadlines:* 8/15 (freshmen), 8/15 (transfers). *Notification:* continuous (freshmen), continuous (transfers).

Admissions Contact Mr. Larry Hess, Director of Admissions, Southern Nazarene University, 6729 Northwest 39th Expressway, Bethany, OK 73008. *Phone:* 405-491-6324. *Toll-free phone:* 800-648-9899. *Fax:* 405-491-6320. *E-mail:* admiss@snu.edu.

SOUTHWESTERN CHRISTIAN UNIVERSITY
Bethany, Oklahoma

Admissions Contact Rev. Johnny Upton, Director of Admissions, Southwestern Christian University, PO Box 340, Bethany, OK 73008-0340. *Phone:* 405-789-7661 Ext. 3449. *E-mail:* admissions@sccm.edu.

SOUTHWESTERN OKLAHOMA STATE UNIVERSITY
Weatherford, Oklahoma

- **State-supported** comprehensive, founded 1901, part of Southwestern Oklahoma State University
- **Calendar** semesters
- **Degrees** bachelor's, master's, and first professional
- **Small-town** 73-acre campus with easy access to Oklahoma City
- **Endowment** $9.1 million
- **Coed,** 4,181 undergraduate students, 89% full-time, 54% women, 46% men
- **Moderately difficult** entrance level, 93% of applicants were admitted

Undergraduates 3,737 full-time, 444 part-time. Students come from 32 states and territories, 32 other countries, 10% are from out of state, 4% African American, 1% Asian American or Pacific Islander, 4% Hispanic American, 6% Native American, 3% international, 7% transferred in, 27% live on campus. *Retention:* 69% of 2002 full-time freshmen returned.

Freshmen *Admission:* 1,470 applied, 1,362 admitted, 964 enrolled. *Average high school GPA:* 3.42. *Test scores:* ACT scores over 18: 75%; ACT scores over 24: 25%; ACT scores over 30: 3%.

Faculty *Total:* 229, 86% full-time, 58% with terminal degrees. *Student/faculty ratio:* 20:1.

Majors Accounting; art teacher education; biology/biological sciences; biophysics; business administration and management; chemistry; clinical laboratory science/medical technology; commercial and advertising art; computer and information sciences; computer science; criminal justice/law enforcement administration; education; elementary education; engineering physics; engineering technology; English; English/language arts teacher education; finance; health/health care administration; health information/medical records administration; history; history teacher education; industrial arts; industrial technology; marketing/marketing management; mass communication/media; mathematics; music; music management and merchandising; music teacher education; music therapy; nursing (registered nurse training); parks, recreation and leisure; pharmacy; physical education teaching and coaching; physics; piano and organ; political science and government; pre-dentistry studies; pre-law studies; pre-medical studies; pre-veterinary studies; psychology; religious/sacred music; science teacher education; secondary education; social science teacher education; social work; special education; technology/industrial arts teacher education; therapeutic recreation; voice and opera; wind/percussion instruments.

Academic Programs *Special study options:* academic remediation for entering students, accelerated degree program, adult/continuing education programs, advanced placement credit, cooperative education, distance learning, double majors, independent study, internships, off-campus study, part-time degree program, services for LD students, student-designed majors, summer session for credit.

Library Al Harris Library with 217,051 titles, 1,230 serial subscriptions, 6,718 audiovisual materials, an OPAC, a Web page.

Computers on Campus 270 computers available on campus for general student use. A campuswide network can be accessed from student residence rooms and from off campus. Internet access, at least one staffed computer lab available.

Student Life *Housing options:* men-only, women-only. Campus housing is university owned. Freshman campus housing is guaranteed. *Activities and organizations:* drama/theater group, student-run newspaper, choral group, marching band, Student Education Association, Baptist Student Union, Southwestern Pharmaceutical Association, Gamma Delta Kappa, Bible Chair Student Union, national fraternities. *Campus security:* late-night transport/escort service, controlled dormitory access, 20-hour campus emergency security. *Student services:* health clinic, personal/psychological counseling.

Athletics Member NCAA. All Division II. *Intercollegiate sports:* baseball M(s), basketball M(s)/W(s), cheerleading M/W, cross-country running W(s), equestrian sports M(s)/W(s), football M(s), golf M(s)/W(s), soccer W(s), softball W(s). *Intramural sports:* basketball M/W, bowling M/W, football M/W, softball M/W, volleyball M/W, weight lifting M.

Standardized Tests *Required:* ACT (for admission).

Costs (2003–04) *Tuition:* state resident $1950 full-time, $65 per hour part-time; nonresident $5850 full-time, $195 per hour part-time. *Required fees:* $808 full-time, $31 per hour part-time, $17 per term part-time. *Room and board:* $2910; room only: $1230. Room and board charges vary according to board plan. *Payment plan:* installment. *Waivers:* children of alumni and employees or children of employees.

Financial Aid Of all full-time matriculated undergraduates who enrolled in 2002, 2,545 applied for aid, 2,119 were judged to have need, 1,077 had their need fully met. In 2002, 680 non-need-based awards were made. *Average percent of need met:* 87%. *Average financial aid package:* $3377. *Average need-based loan:* $1293. *Average need-based gift aid:* $1028. *Average non-need-based aid:* $875. *Average indebtedness upon graduation:* $12,222. *Financial aid deadline:* 3/1.

Applying *Options:* deferred entrance. *Application fee:* $15. *Required:* high school transcript, minimum 2.0 GPA. *Notification:* continuous (freshmen), continuous (transfers).

Admissions Contact Ms. Connie Phillips, Admission Counselor, Southwestern Oklahoma State University, 100 Campus Drive, Weatherford, OK 73096. *Phone:* 580-774-3009. *Fax:* 580-774-3795. *E-mail:* phillic@swosu.edu.

SPARTAN SCHOOL OF AERONAUTICS
Tulsa, Oklahoma

- **Proprietary** primarily 2-year, founded 1928
- **Calendar** calendar terms
- **Degrees** certificates, associate, and bachelor's
- **Urban** 26-acre campus
- **Coed, primarily men**
- **Noncompetitive** entrance level

Standardized Tests *Required:* ACT ASSET (for placement).

Costs (2003–04) *Tuition:* Full-time tuition varies with program. Single student housing available from $290 to $350 per month.

Financial Aid Of all full-time matriculated undergraduates who enrolled in 2001, 15 Federal Work-Study jobs (averaging $5739).

Applying *Options:* deferred entrance. *Application fee:* $100. *Required:* high school transcript. *Recommended:* interview.

Admissions Contact Mr. Mark Fowler, Vice President of Student Records and Finance, Spartan School of Aeronautics, 8820 East Pine Street, PO Box 582833, Tulsa, OK 74158-2833. *Phone:* 918-836-6886.

UNIVERSITY OF CENTRAL OKLAHOMA
Edmond, Oklahoma

- **State-supported** comprehensive, founded 1890, part of Oklahoma State Regents for Higher Education
- **Calendar** semesters
- **Degrees** certificates, bachelor's, and master's

■ **Suburban** 200-acre campus with easy access to Oklahoma City
■ **Endowment** $453,079
■ **Coed**
■ **Minimally difficult** entrance level

Faculty *Student/faculty ratio:* 23:1.
Student Life *Campus security:* 24-hour emergency response devices and patrols, late-night transport/escort service.
Athletics Member NCAA. All Division II.
Standardized Tests *Required:* SAT I or ACT (for admission). *Recommended:* ACT (for admission).
Costs (2003–04) *Tuition:* state resident $1950 full-time, $90 per semester hour part-time; nonresident $5850 full-time, $220 per semester hour part-time. Full-time tuition and fees vary according to course level, course load, program, and student level. Part-time tuition and fees vary according to course level, course load, program, and student level. *Required fees:* $699 full-time. *Room and board:* $3670. Room and board charges vary according to board plan and housing facility.
Financial Aid Of all full-time matriculated undergraduates who enrolled in 2001, 4,906 applied for aid, 4,121 were judged to have need, 1,833 had their need fully met. In 2001, 1809. *Average percent of need met:* 75. *Average financial aid package:* $5000. *Average need-based loan:* $3500. *Average need-based gift aid:* $1350. *Average indebtedness upon graduation:* $10,500.
Applying *Options:* deferred entrance. *Application fee:* $25. *Required:* high school transcript, minimum 2.7 GPA, rank in upper 50% of high school class.
Admissions Contact Ms. Linda Lofton, Director, Admissions and Records Processing, University of Central Oklahoma, Office of Enrollment Services, 100 North University Drive, Box 151, Edmond, OK 73034-5209. *Phone:* 405-974-2338 Ext. 2338. *Toll-free phone:* 800-254-4215. *Fax:* 405-341-4964. *E-mail:* admituco@ucok.edu.

UNIVERSITY OF OKLAHOMA
Norman, Oklahoma

■ **State-supported** university, founded 1890
■ **Calendar** semesters
■ **Degrees** certificates, bachelor's, master's, doctoral, first professional, and post-master's certificates
■ **Suburban** 3500-acre campus with easy access to Oklahoma City
■ **Endowment** $410.3 million
■ **Coed,** 20,254 undergraduate students, 87% full-time, 49% women, 51% men
■ **Moderately difficult** entrance level, 82% of applicants were admitted

Undergraduates 17,647 full-time, 2,607 part-time. Students come from 50 states and territories, 85 other countries, 19% are from out of state, 6% African American, 5% Asian American or Pacific Islander, 4% Hispanic American, 8% Native American, 3% international, 8% transferred in, 20% live on campus. *Retention:* 83% of 2002 full-time freshmen returned.
Freshmen *Admission:* 8,140 applied, 6,638 admitted, 3,808 enrolled. *Average high school GPA:* 3.59. *Test scores:* ACT scores over 18: 98%; ACT scores over 24: 76%; ACT scores over 30: 17%.
Faculty *Total:* 1,191, 82% full-time, 80% with terminal degrees. *Student/faculty ratio:* 21:1.
Majors Accounting; advertising; aeronautics/aviation/aerospace science and technology; aerospace, aeronautical and astronautical engineering; African-American/Black studies; American Indian/Native American studies; anthropology; architecture; architecture related; area studies; area studies related; art; art history, criticism and conservation; astronomy; astrophysics; atmospheric sciences and meteorology; biomedical/medical engineering; botany/plant biology; broadcast journalism; business administration and management; business/managerial economics; chemical engineering; chemistry; cinematography and film/video production; civil engineering; classics and languages, literatures and linguistics; clinical/medical laboratory technology; communication and journalism related; communication/speech communication and rhetoric; computer and information sciences; computer engineering; criminology; dance; design and visual communications; dramatic/theatre arts; early childhood education; economics; education (specific subject areas) related; electrical, electronics and communications engineering; elementary education; engineering; engineering physics; English; English language and literature related; English/language arts teacher education; entrepreneurship; environmental design/architecture; environmental/environmental health engineering; environmental science; finance; fine/studio arts; foreign language teacher education; French; geography; geological and earth sciences/geosciences related; geology/earth science; geophysics and seismology; German; health and physical education; history; human resources management and services related; industrial engineering; interior design; international business/trade/commerce; journalism; liberal arts and sciences/liberal studies; library science; linguistics; management information systems; marketing/marketing management; mathematics; mathematics teacher education; mechanical engineering; medical laboratory technology; microbiology; multi-/interdisciplinary studies related; music; music performance; music theory and composition; petroleum engineering; philosophy; photography; physics; piano and organ; political science and government; professional studies; psychology; public administration; public relations/image management; religious studies; Russian; science teacher education; social studies teacher education; social work; sociology; Spanish; special education; violin, viola, guitar and other stringed instruments; visual and performing arts related; voice and opera; wind/percussion instruments; women's studies; zoology/animal biology.
Academic Programs *Special study options:* academic remediation for entering students, accelerated degree program, adult/continuing education programs, advanced placement credit, cooperative education, distance learning, double majors, English as a second language, external degree program, freshman honors college, honors programs, independent study, internships, off-campus study, part-time degree program, services for LD students, student-designed majors, study abroad, summer session for credit. *ROTC:* Army (b), Air Force (b).
Library Bizzell Memorial Library plus 8 others with 4.0 million titles, 26,696 serial subscriptions, 7,647 audiovisual materials, an OPAC, a Web page.
Computers on Campus 2187 computers available on campus for general student use. A campuswide network can be accessed from student residence rooms and from off campus. Internet access, online (class) registration, at least one staffed computer lab available. Computer purchase or lease plan available.
Student Life *Housing:* on-campus residence required for freshman year. *Options:* coed, men-only, women-only, disabled students. Campus housing is university owned. Freshman campus housing is guaranteed. *Activities and organizations:* drama/theater group, student-run newspaper, radio and television station, choral group, marching band, Campus Activities Council, international student organizations, OU Cousins, American Indian Student Association, Black Student Association, national fraternities, national sororities. *Campus security:* 24-hour emergency response devices and patrols, student patrols, late-night transport/escort service, controlled dormitory access, crime prevention programs, police bicycle patrols, self-defense classes. *Student services:* health clinic, personal/psychological counseling, women's center, legal services.
Athletics Member NCAA. All Division I except football (Division I-A). *Intercollegiate sports:* baseball M(s), basketball M(s)/W(s), cross-country running M(s)/W(s), golf M(s)/W(s), gymnastics M(s)/W(s), soccer W(s), softball W(s), tennis M(s)/W(s), track and field M(s)/W(s), volleyball W(s), wrestling M(s). *Intramural sports:* badminton M/W, basketball M/W, bowling M/W, crew M(c)/W(c), cross-country running M/W, football M/W, golf M/W, ice hockey M(c)/W(c), lacrosse M, racquetball M/W, rock climbing M/W, rugby M(c)/W(c), sailing M(c)/W(c), soccer M/W, softball M/W, squash M/W, swimming M/W, table tennis M/W, tennis M/W, track and field M/W, ultimate Frisbee M(c)/W(c), volleyball M/W, water polo M/W.
Standardized Tests *Required:* SAT I or ACT (for admission).
Costs (2003–04) *Tuition:* state resident $2541 full-time, $85 per credit hour part-time; nonresident $9054 full-time, $302 per credit hour part-time. Full-time tuition and fees vary according to course level, course load, location, program, and reciprocity agreements. Part-time tuition and fees vary according to course level, course load, location, program, and reciprocity agreements. *Required fees:* $1200 full-time, $33 per credit hour part-time, $107 per term part-time. *Room and board:* $5485; room only: $2797. Room and board charges vary according to board plan and housing facility. *Payment plan:* installment. *Waivers:* children of alumni, senior citizens, and employees or children of employees.
Financial Aid Of all full-time matriculated undergraduates who enrolled in 2002, 8,777 applied for aid, 7,926 were judged to have need, 4,547 had their need fully met. 733 Federal Work-Study jobs (averaging $2061). In 2002, 1731 non-need-based awards were made. *Average percent of need met:* 84%. *Average financial aid package:* $7421. *Average need-based loan:* $4181. *Average need-based gift aid:* $3591. *Average non-need-based aid:* $1073. *Average indebtedness upon graduation:* $17,444.
Applying *Options:* electronic application. *Application fee:* $25. *Required:* high school transcript, minimum 3.0 GPA. *Required for some:* essay or personal statement. *Application deadline:* 6/1 (freshmen). *Notification:* continuous (freshmen), continuous (transfers).
Admissions Contact Ms. Karen Renfroe, Executive Director of Recruitment Services, University of Oklahoma, 1000 Asp Avenue, Norman, OK 73019. *Phone:* 405-325-2151. *Toll-free phone:* 800-234-6868. *Fax:* 405-325-7124. *E-mail:* admrec@ou.edu.

UNIVERSITY OF OKLAHOMA HEALTH SCIENCES CENTER
Oklahoma City, Oklahoma

■ **State-supported** upper-level, founded 1890, part of University of Oklahoma
■ **Calendar** semesters

University of Oklahoma Health Sciences Center (continued)

- **Degrees** bachelor's, master's, doctoral, first professional, post-master's, postbachelor's, and first professional certificates
- **Urban** 200-acre campus with easy access to Oklahoma City
- **Endowment** $97.0 million
- **Coed,** 712 undergraduate students, 88% full-time, 89% women, 11% men
- **Moderately difficult** entrance level

Undergraduates 624 full-time, 88 part-time. Students come from 14 states and territories, 11 other countries, 7% are from out of state, 5% African American, 3% Asian American or Pacific Islander, 2% Hispanic American, 9% Native American, 0.9% international, 51% transferred in.

Faculty *Total:* 361, 68% full-time, 82% with terminal degrees.

Majors Audiology and hearing sciences; audiology and speech-language pathology; communication disorders sciences and services related; dental hygiene; dietetics; nuclear medical technology; nursing (registered nurse training); radiologic technology/science; speech-language pathology; speech therapy.

Academic Programs *Special study options:* advanced placement credit, distance learning, honors programs, internships, part-time degree program, summer session for credit. *ROTC:* Army (c), Air Force (c).

Library Robert M. Bird Health Sciences Library with 234,000 titles, 2,658 serial subscriptions.

Computers on Campus 120 computers available on campus for general student use. A campuswide network can be accessed from off campus. Internet access, at least one staffed computer lab available.

Student Life *Housing:* college housing not available. *Activities and organizations:* student-run newspaper, Student Government Association, Public Health Student Association, Student National Medical Association, Graduate Student Council, Student Medical Association. *Campus security:* 24-hour emergency response devices and patrols, late-night transport/escort service. *Student services:* health clinic, personal/psychological counseling.

Costs (2003–04) *Tuition:* state resident $2098 full-time, $87 per credit part-time; nonresident $7615 full-time, $317 per credit part-time. Full-time tuition and fees vary according to program. Part-time tuition and fees vary according to program. *Required fees:* $959 full-time, $40 per credit part-time. *Payment plan:* installment.

Applying *Options:* electronic application, deferred entrance. *Application fee:* $25. *Application deadline:* rolling (freshmen). *Notification:* continuous (transfers).

Admissions Contact Ms. Leslie Wilbourn, Director of Admissions and Records, University of Oklahoma Health Sciences Center, BSE-200, PO Box 26901, 941 S. L. Young Boulevard, Oklahoma City, OK 73190. *Phone:* 405-271-2359 Ext. 48902. *Fax:* 405-271-2480. *E-mail:* admissions@ouhsc.edu.

UNIVERSITY OF PHOENIX–OKLAHOMA CITY CAMPUS

Oklahoma City, Oklahoma

- **Proprietary** comprehensive, founded 1976
- **Calendar** continuous
- **Degrees** certificates, associate, bachelor's, master's, doctoral, post-master's, and postbachelor's certificates (courses conducted at 121 campuses and learning centers in 25 states)
- **Urban** campus
- **Coed,** 659 undergraduate students, 100% full-time, 56% women, 44% men
- **Noncompetitive** entrance level

Undergraduates 659 full-time. 15% African American, 2% Asian American or Pacific Islander, 3% Hispanic American, 4% Native American, 1% international.

Freshmen *Admission:* 51 enrolled.

Faculty *Total:* 103, 3% full-time, 20% with terminal degrees. *Student/faculty ratio:* 6:1.

Majors Accounting; business administration and management; health/health care administration; information technology; management information systems; management science; nursing (registered nurse training); public administration and social service professions related.

Academic Programs *Special study options:* accelerated degree program, adult/continuing education programs, advanced placement credit, distance learning, external degree program, independent study.

Library University Library with 27.1 million titles, 11,648 serial subscriptions, an OPAC, a Web page.

Computers on Campus A campuswide network can be accessed from off campus. Internet access, at least one staffed computer lab available.

Student Life *Housing:* college housing not available.

Costs (2003–04) *Tuition:* $8550 full-time, $285 per credit part-time. *Waivers:* employees or children of employees.

Financial Aid *Average financial aid package:* $1392.

Applying *Options:* deferred entrance. *Application fee:* $85. *Required:* 1 letter of recommendation, 2 years of work experience, 23 years of age. *Required for some:* high school transcript. *Application deadline:* rolling (freshmen), rolling (transfers).

Admissions Contact Ms. Beth Barilla, Director of Admissions, University of Phoenix–Oklahoma City Campus, 4615 East Elwood Street, Mail Stop AA-K101, Phoenix, AZ 85040-1958. *Phone:* 480-317-6000. *Toll-free phone:* 800-228-7240. *Fax:* 480-594-1758. *E-mail:* beth.barilla@phoenix.edu.

UNIVERSITY OF PHOENIX–TULSA CAMPUS

Tulsa, Oklahoma

- **Proprietary** comprehensive, founded 1998
- **Calendar** continuous
- **Degrees** certificates, associate, bachelor's, master's, doctoral, post-master's, and postbachelor's certificates (courses conducted at 121 campuses and learning centers in 25 states)
- **Urban** campus
- **Coed,** 610 undergraduate students, 100% full-time, 58% women, 42% men
- **Noncompetitive** entrance level

Undergraduates 610 full-time. 7% African American, 0.2% Asian American or Pacific Islander, 1% Hispanic American, 3% Native American, 38% international.

Freshmen *Admission:* 26 enrolled.

Faculty *Total:* 93, 5% full-time, 15% with terminal degrees. *Student/faculty ratio:* 8:1.

Majors Accounting; business administration and management; computer and information sciences; corrections and criminal justice related; health/health care administration; management information systems; management science; marketing/marketing management; nursing (registered nurse training).

Academic Programs *Special study options:* accelerated degree program, adult/continuing education programs, advanced placement credit, distance learning, external degree program, independent study.

Library University Library with 27.1 million titles, 11,648 serial subscriptions, an OPAC, a Web page.

Computers on Campus A campuswide network can be accessed from off campus. Internet access, at least one staffed computer lab available.

Student Life *Housing:* college housing not available.

Costs (2003–04) *Tuition:* $8550 full-time, $285 per credit part-time. *Waivers:* employees or children of employees.

Financial Aid *Average financial aid package:* $1343.

Applying *Options:* deferred entrance. *Application fee:* $85. *Required:* 1 letter of recommendation, 2 years of work experience, 23 years of age. *Required for some:* high school transcript. *Application deadline:* rolling (freshmen), rolling (transfers).

Admissions Contact Ms. Beth Barilla, Director of Admissions, University of Phoenix–Tulsa Campus, 4615 East Elwood Street, Mail Stop AA-K101, Phoenix, AZ 85040-1958. *Phone:* 480-317-6000. *Toll-free phone:* 800-228-7240. *Fax:* 480-594-1758. *E-mail:* beth.barilla@phoenix.edu.

UNIVERSITY OF SCIENCE AND ARTS OF OKLAHOMA

Chickasha, Oklahoma

- **State-supported** 4-year, founded 1908, part of Oklahoma State Regents for Higher Education
- **Calendar** trimesters
- **Degree** bachelor's
- **Small-town** 75-acre campus with easy access to Oklahoma City
- **Endowment** $272,327
- **Coed,** 1,449 undergraduate students, 73% full-time, 64% women, 36% men
- **Moderately difficult** entrance level, 86% of applicants were admitted

Undergraduates 1,059 full-time, 390 part-time. Students come from 16 states and territories, 14 other countries, 5% are from out of state, 6% African American, 1% Asian American or Pacific Islander, 2% Hispanic American, 14% Native American, 2% international, 7% transferred in, 32% live on campus. *Retention:* 56% of 2002 full-time freshmen returned.

Freshmen *Admission:* 523 applied, 448 admitted, 296 enrolled. *Average high school GPA:* 3.25. *Test scores:* ACT scores over 18: 65%; ACT scores over 24: 21%; ACT scores over 30: 1%.

Faculty *Total:* 91, 53% full-time, 57% with terminal degrees. *Student/faculty ratio:* 19:1.

Majors American Indian/Native American studies; art; biology/biological sciences; business/commerce; chemistry; clinical/medical laboratory technology; communication/speech communication and rhetoric; computer and information sciences; dramatic/theatre arts; early childhood education; economics; elementary education; English; fine arts related; health and physical education; history; mathematics; music; natural sciences; physics; political science and government; psychology; sociology; special education (hearing impaired); speech-language pathology.

Academic Programs *Special study options:* academic remediation for entering students, accelerated degree program, adult/continuing education programs, advanced placement credit, distance learning, double majors, independent study, internships, off-campus study, part-time degree program, services for LD students, student-designed majors, summer session for credit.

Library Nash Library with 72,395 titles, 137 serial subscriptions, 4,187 audiovisual materials, an OPAC, a Web page.

Computers on Campus 125 computers available on campus for general student use. A campuswide network can be accessed from student residence rooms and from off campus. Internet access, at least one staffed computer lab available.

Student Life *Housing:* on-campus residence required for freshman year. *Options:* men-only, women-only. Campus housing is university owned and is provided by a third party. Freshman campus housing is guaranteed. *Activities and organizations:* drama/theater group, student-run newspaper, television station, choral group, Student Activities Council, Volunteer Action Council, Baptist Student Union, Intertribal Heritage Club, Psychology Club. *Campus security:* 24-hour emergency response devices and patrols, controlled dormitory access. *Student services:* health clinic, personal/psychological counseling.

Athletics Member NAIA. *Intercollegiate sports:* baseball M(s), basketball M(s)/W(s), cheerleading M(s)/W(s), soccer M(s)/W(s), softball W(s). *Intramural sports:* basketball M/W, football M/W, softball M/W, ultimate Frisbee M/W, volleyball M/W.

Standardized Tests *Required:* SAT I or ACT (for admission).

Costs (2003–04) *Tuition:* state resident $2100 full-time, $70 per hour part-time; nonresident $6000 full-time, $200 per hour part-time. Full-time tuition and fees vary according to course load. Part-time tuition and fees vary according to course load. *Required fees:* $791 full-time, $26 per hour part-time. *Room and board:* $3530. Room and board charges vary according to board plan and housing facility. *Payment plan:* installment. *Waivers:* senior citizens and employees or children of employees.

Financial Aid Of all full-time matriculated undergraduates who enrolled in 2003, 816 applied for aid, 776 were judged to have need, 120 had their need fully met. 248 Federal Work-Study jobs (averaging $1160). In 2003, 113 non-need-based awards were made. *Average percent of need met:* 69%. *Average financial aid package:* $6413. *Average need-based loan:* $2756. *Average need-based gift aid:* $4671. *Average non-need-based aid:* $1887. *Average indebtedness upon graduation:* $12,268.

Applying *Options:* common application, electronic application, early admission, deferred entrance. *Application fee:* $15. *Required:* high school transcript. *Recommended:* minimum 2.7 GPA, graduated in top half of high school class. *Application deadlines:* 9/3 (freshmen), 6/1 (transfers). *Notification:* 2/10 (freshmen).

Admissions Contact Mr. Joseph Evans, Registrar and Director of Admissions and Records, University of Science and Arts of Oklahoma, 1727 West Alabama, Chickasha, OK 73018-5322. *Phone:* 405-574-1204. *Toll-free phone:* 800-933-8726 Ext. 1204. *Fax:* 405-574-1220. *E-mail:* jwevans@usao.edu.

UNIVERSITY OF TULSA
Tulsa, Oklahoma

- **Independent** university, founded 1894, affiliated with Presbyterian Church (U.S.A.)
- **Calendar** semesters
- **Degrees** bachelor's, master's, doctoral, first professional, postbachelor's, and first professional certificates
- **Urban** 200-acre campus with easy access to Tulsa
- **Endowment** $640.0 million
- **Coed,** 2,672 undergraduate students, 92% full-time, 50% women, 50% men
- **Very difficult** entrance level, 76% of applicants were admitted

Undergraduates 2,461 full-time, 211 part-time. Students come from 37 states and territories, 48 other countries, 28% are from out of state, 7% African American, 2% Asian American or Pacific Islander, 3% Hispanic American, 5% Native American, 10% international, 7% transferred in, 61% live on campus. *Retention:* 78% of 2002 full-time freshmen returned.

Freshmen *Admission:* 2,292 applied, 1,747 admitted, 590 enrolled. *Average high school GPA:* 3.70. *Test scores:* SAT verbal scores over 500: 83%; SAT math scores over 500: 83%; ACT scores over 18: 99%; SAT verbal scores over 600: 54%; SAT math scores over 600: 51%; ACT scores over 24: 67%; SAT verbal scores over 700: 22%; SAT math scores over 700: 18%; ACT scores over 30: 23%.

Faculty *Total:* 412, 74% full-time, 96% with terminal degrees. *Student/faculty ratio:* 11:1.

Majors Accounting; anthropology; applied mathematics; art history, criticism and conservation; arts management; athletic training; audiology and speech-language pathology; biochemistry; biology/biological sciences; business administration and management; chemical engineering; chemistry; communication/speech communication and rhetoric; computer science; dramatic/theatre arts; economics; education; electrical, electronics and communications engineering; elementary education; engineering physics; English; environmental studies; film/cinema studies; finance; fine/studio arts; French; geology/earth science; geophysics and seismology; German; history; information science/studies; international business/trade/commerce; kinesiology and exercise science; legal professions and studies related; liberal arts and sciences/liberal studies; management information systems; marketing/marketing management; mathematics; mechanical engineering; music; music related; music teacher education; nursing (registered nurse training); petroleum engineering; philosophy; physics; piano and organ; political science and government; psychology; religious studies; sociology; Spanish; sport and fitness administration; voice and opera.

Academic Programs *Special study options:* accelerated degree program, adult/continuing education programs, advanced placement credit, double majors, English as a second language, honors programs, independent study, internships, part-time degree program, services for LD students, student-designed majors, study abroad, summer session for credit. *ROTC:* Air Force (c). *Unusual degree programs:* 3-2 law.

Library McFarlin Library plus 1 other with 940,105 titles, 6,317 serial subscriptions, 13,320 audiovisual materials, an OPAC, a Web page.

Computers on Campus 900 computers available on campus for general student use. A campuswide network can be accessed from student residence rooms and from off campus. Internet access, at least one staffed computer lab available. Computer purchase or lease plan available.

Student Life *Housing:* on-campus residence required through sophomore year. *Options:* coed, men-only, women-only, disabled students. Campus housing is university owned. Freshman campus housing is guaranteed. *Activities and organizations:* drama/theater group, student-run newspaper, radio and television station, choral group, marching band, Student Association, Residence Hall Association, honor societies, intramural sports, pre-professional clubs, national fraternities, national sororities. *Campus security:* 24-hour emergency response devices and patrols, late-night transport/escort service, controlled dormitory access. *Student services:* health clinic, personal/psychological counseling, women's center.

Athletics Member NCAA. All Division I except football (Division I-A). *Intercollegiate sports:* basketball M(s)/W(s), crew W(s), cross-country running M(s)/W(s), golf M(s)/W(s), soccer M(s)/W(s), softball W(s), tennis M(s)/W(s), track and field M(s)/W(s), volleyball W(s). *Intramural sports:* badminton M/W, basketball M/W, bowling M/W, crew M(c), cross-country running M/W, fencing M(c)/W(c), football M/W, golf M/W, racquetball M/W, rugby M(c), soccer M/W, softball M/W, squash M/W, swimming M/W, table tennis M/W, tennis M/W, track and field M/W, ultimate Frisbee M/W, volleyball M/W, water polo M/W, weight lifting M/W.

Standardized Tests *Required:* SAT I or ACT (for admission).

Costs (2003–04) *Comprehensive fee:* $21,346 includes full-time tuition ($15,656), mandatory fees ($80), and room and board ($5610). Part-time tuition: $562 per credit hour. *Required fees:* $3 per credit hour part-time. *College room only:* $3060. Room and board charges vary according to board plan and housing facility. *Payment plans:* tuition prepayment, installment. *Waivers:* employees or children of employees.

Financial Aid Of all full-time matriculated undergraduates who enrolled in 2003, 2,075 applied for aid, 1,205 were judged to have need, 795 had their need fully met. 576 Federal Work-Study jobs (averaging $1625). 13 state and other part-time jobs (averaging $1200). In 2003, 604 non-need-based awards were made. *Average percent of need met:* 91%. *Average financial aid package:* $13,737. *Average need-based loan:* $5248. *Average need-based gift aid:* $4234. *Average non-need-based aid:* $8285. *Average indebtedness upon graduation:* $17,622.

Applying *Options:* common application, electronic application, early admission, deferred entrance. *Application fee:* $35. *Required:* high school transcript, 1 letter of recommendation. *Recommended:* essay or personal statement, minimum 3.0 GPA, interview. *Application deadline:* rolling (freshmen), rolling (transfers). *Notification:* continuous (freshmen), continuous (transfers).

Admissions Contact Mr. John C. Corso, Associate Vice President for Administration/Dean of Admission, University of Tulsa, 600 South College Avenue, Tulsa, OK 74104. *Phone:* 918-631-2307. *Toll-free phone:* 800-331-3050. *Fax:* 918-631-5003. *E-mail:* admission@utulsa.edu.

■ *See page 2734 for a narrative description.*

OREGON

THE ART INSTITUTE OF PORTLAND
Portland, Oregon

- **Proprietary** 4-year, founded 1963, part of Education Management Corporation
- **Calendar** quarters
- **Degrees** associate and bachelor's
- **Urban** 1-acre campus
- **Coed,** 1,327 undergraduate students, 67% full-time, 54% women, 46% men
- **Minimally difficult** entrance level

Undergraduates 890 full-time, 437 part-time. Students come from 25 other countries, 1% African American, 6% Asian American or Pacific Islander, 5% Hispanic American, 0.8% Native American, 2% international, 9% live on campus. *Retention:* 55% of 2002 full-time freshmen returned.

Freshmen *Admission:* 137 enrolled.

Faculty *Total:* 118, 25% full-time, 28% with terminal degrees. *Student/faculty ratio:* 19:1.

Majors Advertising; animation, interactive technology, video graphics and special effects; fashion/apparel design; graphic design; interior design; intermedia/multimedia; web page, digital/multimedia and information resources design.

Academic Programs *Special study options:* academic remediation for entering students, advanced placement credit, independent study, internships, part-time degree program, services for LD students, study abroad, summer session for credit.

Library AIPD Learning Resource Center with 19,831 titles, 200 serial subscriptions, 400 audiovisual materials, an OPAC.

Computers on Campus 160 computers available on campus for general student use. Internet access, at least one staffed computer lab available.

Student Life *Housing options:* coed. Campus housing is leased by the school. *Activities and organizations:* student-run newspaper, Fashion Group International, Interior Design Student Chapter, International Student Group. *Campus security:* 24-hour emergency response devices, security patrol from 4 p.m. to midnight, electronically operated building entrances. *Student services:* personal/psychological counseling.

Costs (2003–04) *Comprehensive fee:* $23,445 includes full-time tuition ($15,750) and room and board ($7695). Full-time tuition and fees vary according to student level. Part-time tuition: $350 per credit. Part-time tuition and fees vary according to student level. No tuition increase for student's term of enrollment. *Payment plan:* installment. *Waivers:* employees or children of employees.

Financial Aid Of all full-time matriculated undergraduates who enrolled in 2003, 943 applied for aid, 849 were judged to have need, 15 had their need fully met. 36 Federal Work-Study jobs (averaging $2432). In 2003, 10 non-need-based awards were made. *Average percent of need met:* 15%. *Average financial aid package:* $4765. *Average need-based loan:* $3766. *Average need-based gift aid:* $1749. *Average non-need-based aid:* $3817. *Average indebtedness upon graduation:* $21,500.

Applying *Options:* electronic application, deferred entrance. *Application fee:* $50. *Required:* essay or personal statement, high school transcript, interview. *Recommended:* letters of recommendation. *Application deadline:* rolling (freshmen), rolling (transfers). *Notification:* continuous (freshmen), continuous (transfers).

Admissions Contact Ms. Lori Murray, Director of Admissions, The Art Institute of Portland, 1122 NW Davis Street, Portland, OR 97209-2911. *Phone:* 503-228-6528 Ext. 4794. *Toll-free phone:* 888-228-6528. *Fax:* 503-227-1945. *E-mail:* aipdadm@aii.edu.

CASCADE COLLEGE
Portland, Oregon

- **Independent** 4-year, founded 1994, affiliated with Church of Christ
- **Calendar** semesters
- **Degree** bachelor's
- **Urban** 13-acre campus
- **Endowment** $358,467
- **Coed,** 280 undergraduate students, 94% full-time, 51% women, 49% men
- **Noncompetitive** entrance level, 100% of applicants were admitted

Undergraduates 264 full-time, 16 part-time. Students come from 20 states and territories, 6 other countries, 64% are from out of state, 5% African American, 3% Asian American or Pacific Islander, 6% Hispanic American, 0.4% Native American, 2% international, 9% transferred in, 73% live on campus. *Retention:* 54% of 2002 full-time freshmen returned.

Freshmen *Admission:* 232 applied, 232 admitted, 74 enrolled. *Test scores:* SAT verbal scores over 500: 65%; SAT math scores over 500: 46%; ACT scores over 18: 76%; SAT verbal scores over 600: 19%; SAT math scores over 600: 8%; ACT scores over 24: 43%; SAT verbal scores over 700: 2%; ACT scores over 30: 5%.

Faculty *Total:* 33, 39% full-time, 30% with terminal degrees. *Student/faculty ratio:* 14:1.

Majors Biblical studies; business administration and management; early childhood education; elementary education; English; liberal arts and sciences/liberal studies; missionary studies and missiology; psychology; youth ministry.

Academic Programs *Special study options:* academic remediation for entering students, accelerated degree program, advanced placement credit, double majors, independent study, internships, off-campus study, part-time degree program, services for LD students, study abroad, summer session for credit. *ROTC:* Army (c), Air Force (c).

Library E.W. McMillan Library with 28,050 titles, 104 serial subscriptions, an OPAC, a Web page.

Computers on Campus 26 computers available on campus for general student use. A campuswide network can be accessed from student residence rooms and from off campus. Internet access, at least one staffed computer lab available.

Student Life *Housing:* on-campus residence required through senior year. *Options:* coed, men-only, women-only. Campus housing is university owned. Freshman campus housing is guaranteed. *Activities and organizations:* drama/theater group, choral group, choir, service clubs, student government. *Campus security:* 24-hour emergency response devices, late-night transport/escort service, controlled dormitory access, 12-hour patrols by trained security personnel. *Student services:* health clinic, personal/psychological counseling.

Athletics Member NAIA, NCCAA. *Intercollegiate sports:* basketball M(s)/W(s), cross-country running M(s)/W(s), soccer M(s)/W(s), track and field M(s)/W(s), volleyball W(s). *Intramural sports:* basketball M/W, football M/W, soccer M/W, softball M/W, table tennis M/W, tennis M/W, volleyball M/W.

Standardized Tests *Required:* SAT I or ACT (for placement).

Costs (2004–05) *Comprehensive fee:* $16,990 includes full-time tuition ($10,790), mandatory fees ($400), and room and board ($5800). Full-time tuition and fees vary according to course load. *Payment plan:* installment. *Waivers:* children of alumni and employees or children of employees.

Financial Aid Of all full-time matriculated undergraduates who enrolled in 2003, 264 applied for aid, 217 were judged to have need, 45 had their need fully met. 35 Federal Work-Study jobs (averaging $1256). 52 state and other part-time jobs (averaging $1269). In 2003, 37 non-need-based awards were made. *Average percent of need met:* 55%. *Average financial aid package:* $10,972. *Average need-based loan:* $3683. *Average need-based gift aid:* $1638. *Average non-need-based aid:* $2357. *Average indebtedness upon graduation:* $16,438. *Financial aid deadline:* 7/31.

Applying *Options:* common application, early admission, deferred entrance. *Application fee:* $25. *Required:* high school transcript. *Recommended:* essay or personal statement, 1 letter of recommendation. *Application deadline:* rolling (freshmen), rolling (transfers). *Notification:* continuous (transfers).

Admissions Contact Mr. Clint La Rue, Director of Admissions, Cascade College, 9101 East Burnside, Portland, OR 97216-1515. *Phone:* 503-257-1202. *Toll-free phone:* 800-550-7678. *E-mail:* admissions@cascade.edu.

CONCORDIA UNIVERSITY
Portland, Oregon

- **Independent** comprehensive, founded 1905, affiliated with Lutheran Church–Missouri Synod, part of Concordia University System
- **Calendar** semesters
- **Degrees** certificates, associate, bachelor's, master's, and postbachelor's certificates
- **Urban** 13-acre campus
- **Endowment** $6.3 million
- **Coed,** 905 undergraduate students, 82% full-time, 62% women, 38% men
- **Moderately difficult** entrance level, 72% of applicants were admitted

Undergraduates 745 full-time, 160 part-time. Students come from 24 states and territories, 5% African American, 4% Asian American or Pacific Islander, 2% Hispanic American, 1% Native American, 2% international, 17% transferred in. *Retention:* 75% of 2002 full-time freshmen returned.

Freshmen *Admission:* 631 applied, 452 admitted, 128 enrolled. *Average high school GPA:* 3.33. *Test scores:* SAT verbal scores over 500: 59%; SAT math scores over 500: 58%; ACT scores over 18: 86%; SAT verbal scores over 600: 14%; SAT math scores over 600: 17%; ACT scores over 24: 32%; SAT verbal scores over 700: 3%; SAT math scores over 700: 1%; ACT scores over 30: 5%.

Faculty *Total:* 103, 41% full-time, 48% with terminal degrees. *Student/faculty ratio:* 18:1.

Majors Biological and physical sciences; biology/biological sciences; business administration and management; chemistry; dramatic/theatre arts; education; elementary education; English; English/language arts teacher education; environmental studies; health/health care administration; humanities; interdisciplinary studies; kindergarten/preschool education; liberal arts and sciences/liberal studies; mathematics teacher education; natural sciences; physical education teaching and coaching; physical sciences; pre-medical studies; pre-theology/pre-ministerial studies; psychology; religious education; religious studies; science teacher education; secondary education; social sciences; social studies teacher education; social work; sport and fitness administration; theology.

Academic Programs *Special study options:* academic remediation for entering students, accelerated degree program, adult/continuing education programs, advanced placement credit, double majors, English as a second language, internships, off-campus study, part-time degree program, student-designed majors, study abroad, summer session for credit. *ROTC:* Air Force (c).

Library Concordia Library plus 1 other with 61,000 titles, 374 serial subscriptions, 9,178 audiovisual materials, an OPAC.

Computers on Campus 60 computers available on campus for general student use. A campuswide network can be accessed from student residence rooms and from off campus. Internet access, at least one staffed computer lab available.

Student Life *Housing:* on-campus residence required through sophomore year. *Options:* coed. Campus housing is university owned. Freshman applicants given priority for college housing. *Activities and organizations:* drama/theater group, student-run newspaper, choral group, drama club, business club, Christian Life Ministry, Service Organization, The Promethean. *Campus security:* 24-hour emergency response devices and patrols, student patrols, late-night transport/escort service, controlled dormitory access. *Student services:* health clinic, personal/psychological counseling.

Athletics Member NAIA. *Intercollegiate sports:* baseball M(s), basketball M(s)/W(s), soccer M(s)/W(s), softball W(s), volleyball W(s). *Intramural sports:* basketball M/W, volleyball M/W.

Standardized Tests *Required:* SAT I or ACT (for admission).

Costs (2003–04) *Comprehensive fee:* $22,540 includes full-time tuition ($17,400), mandatory fees ($90), and room and board ($5050). Full-time tuition and fees vary according to program. Part-time tuition: $535 per credit. Part-time tuition and fees vary according to course load and program. *Required fees:* $20 per term part-time. *Room and board:* Room and board charges vary according to housing facility. *Payment plan:* installment. *Waivers:* employees or children of employees.

Financial Aid Of all full-time matriculated undergraduates who enrolled in 2003, 798 applied for aid, 599 were judged to have need, 240 had their need fully met. In 2003, 50 non-need-based awards were made. *Average percent of need met:* 60%. *Average financial aid package:* $13,500. *Average need-based loan:* $4500. *Average need-based gift aid:* $9000. *Average non-need-based aid:* $5000. *Average indebtedness upon graduation:* $20,000.

Applying *Options:* electronic application, deferred entrance. *Application fee:* $20. *Required:* essay or personal statement, high school transcript, minimum 2.5 GPA, 1 letter of recommendation. *Required for some:* interview. *Recommended:* interview. *Application deadline:* rolling (freshmen), rolling (transfers). *Notification:* continuous (freshmen), continuous (transfers).

Admissions Contact Bobi L. Swan, Dean of Admission, Concordia University, 2811 Northeast Holman, Portland, OR 97211-6099. *Phone:* 503-493-6526. *Toll-free phone:* 800-321-9371. *Fax:* 503-280-8531. *E-mail:* admissions@portland.edu.

■ *See page 1488 for a narrative description.*

DeVry University
Portland, Oregon

Admissions Contact 9755 SW Barnes Road, Suite 150, Portland, OR 97225-6651.

Eastern Oregon University
La Grande, Oregon

- **State-supported** comprehensive, founded 1929, part of Oregon University System
- **Calendar** quarters
- **Degrees** bachelor's and master's
- **Rural** 121-acre campus
- **Endowment** $1.7 million
- **Coed,** 3,041 undergraduate students, 64% full-time, 58% women, 42% men
- **Moderately difficult** entrance level, 99% of applicants were admitted

Undergraduates 1,945 full-time, 1,096 part-time. Students come from 42 states and territories, 25 other countries, 30% are from out of state, 2% African American, 4% Asian American or Pacific Islander, 3% Hispanic American, 1% Native American, 2% international, 15% transferred in, 15% live on campus. *Retention:* 68% of 2002 full-time freshmen returned.

Freshmen *Admission:* 714 applied, 709 admitted, 339 enrolled. *Average high school GPA:* 3.36. *Test scores:* SAT verbal scores over 500: 50%; SAT math scores over 500: 49%; ACT scores over 18: 82%; SAT verbal scores over 600: 14%; SAT math scores over 600: 14%; ACT scores over 24: 20%; SAT verbal scores over 700: 2%; SAT math scores over 700: 2%.

Faculty *Total:* 114, 82% full-time. *Student/faculty ratio:* 15:1.

Majors Accounting; administrative assistant and secretarial science; agricultural business and management; agricultural economics; agronomy and crop science; anthropology; art; biological and physical sciences; biology/biological sciences; business/managerial economics; chemistry; city/urban, community and regional planning; computer science; dramatic/theatre arts; economics; education; English; fire science; history; liberal arts and sciences/liberal studies; mathematics; music; natural resources management and policy; physical education teaching and coaching; physics; pre-dentistry studies; pre-law studies; pre-medical studies; pre-veterinary studies; psychology; sociology; special education.

Academic Programs *Special study options:* adult/continuing education programs, advanced placement credit, cooperative education, distance learning, double majors, English as a second language, external degree program, honors programs, independent study, internships, off-campus study, part-time degree program, services for LD students, student-designed majors, study abroad, summer session for credit. *ROTC:* Army (b). *Unusual degree programs:* 3-2 engineering with Oregon State University; nursing with Oregon Health Sciences University; agriculture with Oregon State University.

Library Pierce Library plus 1 other with 329,942 titles, 998 serial subscriptions, 35,556 audiovisual materials, an OPAC, a Web page.

Computers on Campus 125 computers available on campus for general student use. A campuswide network can be accessed from student residence rooms and from off campus. Internet access, online (class) registration, at least one staffed computer lab available. Computer purchase or lease plan available.

Student Life *Housing:* on-campus residence required for freshman year. *Options:* coed, men-only, women-only. Campus housing is university owned. *Activities and organizations:* drama/theater group, student-run newspaper, radio station, choral group, outdoor club, Island Magic, student radio station, intramurals, student government. *Campus security:* 24-hour emergency response devices and patrols, late-night transport/escort service, controlled dormitory access. *Student services:* health clinic, personal/psychological counseling, women's center.

Athletics Member NCAA, NAIA. All NCAA Division III. *Intercollegiate sports:* baseball M, basketball M/W, cross-country running M/W, football M, skiing (cross-country) M(c)/W(c), skiing (downhill) M(c)/W(c), soccer W, softball W, track and field M/W, volleyball M(c)/W. *Intramural sports:* baseball M/W, basketball M/W, cheerleading M/W, football M/W, racquetball M/W, soccer M/W, softball M/W, volleyball M/W, weight lifting M/W.

Standardized Tests *Required:* SAT I or ACT (for admission).

Costs (2004–05) *Tuition:* state resident $4257 full-time, $95 per credit hour part-time; nonresident $4257 full-time. Full-time tuition and fees vary according to course load. Part-time tuition and fees vary according to course load. *Required fees:* $1260 full-time. *Room and board:* $6100; room only: $3250. Room and board charges vary according to board plan and housing facility.

Financial Aid Of all full-time matriculated undergraduates who enrolled in 2003, 1,589 applied for aid, 1,300 were judged to have need, 439 had their need fully met. 245 Federal Work-Study jobs (averaging $1553). In 2003, 26 non-need-based awards were made. *Average percent of need met:* 64%. *Average financial aid package:* $9461. *Average need-based loan:* $3667. *Average need-based gift aid:* $3264. *Average non-need-based aid:* $1656. *Average indebtedness upon graduation:* $14,185.

Applying *Options:* electronic application, early action, deferred entrance. *Application fee:* $50. *Required:* high school transcript, minimum 3.0 GPA. *Required for some:* essay or personal statement, 2 letters of recommendation. *Application deadline:* 9/24 (freshmen). *Notification:* continuous (freshmen), 1/15 (early action), continuous (transfers).

Admissions Contact Ms. Sherri Edvalson, Director, Admissions, Eastern Oregon University, One University Boulevard, La Grande, OR 97850. *Phone:* 541-962-3393. *Toll-free phone:* 800-452-8639 (in-state); 800-452-3393 (out-of-state). *Fax:* 541-962-3418. *E-mail:* admissions@eou.edu.

■ *See page 1562 for a narrative description.*

Eugene Bible College
Eugene, Oregon

- **Independent** 4-year, founded 1925, affiliated with Open Bible Standard Churches
- **Calendar** quarters

Eugene Bible College (continued)
- **Degree** certificates and bachelor's
- **Suburban** 40-acre campus
- **Endowment** $546,055
- **Coed,** 163 undergraduate students, 78% full-time, 56% women, 44% men
- **Minimally difficult** entrance level, 73% of applicants were admitted

Since 1925, Eugene Bible College has been fulfilling the Great Commission by equipping students for spirit-empowered leadership and ministry. In addition to the bachelor degree programs, Eugene Bible College offers students opportunities for community ministry, music, drama, athletics, and other activities that open doors to spiritual growth, fellowship, and lifelong friendships.

Undergraduates 127 full-time, 36 part-time. Students come from 18 states and territories, 4 other countries, 49% are from out of state, 2% African American, 2% Asian American or Pacific Islander, 4% Hispanic American, 2% international, 53% live on campus. *Retention:* 51% of 2002 full-time freshmen returned.

Freshmen *Admission:* 100 applied, 73 admitted, 67 enrolled. *Average high school GPA:* 2.83. *Test scores:* SAT verbal scores over 500: 70%; SAT math scores over 500: 70%; ACT scores over 18: 75%; SAT verbal scores over 600: 14%; SAT math scores over 600: 9%; ACT scores over 24: 28%; ACT scores over 30: 2%.

Faculty *Total:* 25, 48% full-time, 28% with terminal degrees. *Student/faculty ratio:* 14:1.

Majors Biblical studies; divinity/ministry; missionary studies and missiology; pastoral studies/counseling; religious education; religious/sacred music; youth ministry.

Academic Programs *Special study options:* academic remediation for entering students, advanced placement credit, distance learning, double majors, independent study, internships, part-time degree program, summer session for credit.

Library Flint Memorial Library with 34,000 titles, 260 serial subscriptions, 350 audiovisual materials.

Computers on Campus 16 computers available on campus for general student use. A campuswide network can be accessed. Internet access, at least one staffed computer lab available.

Student Life *Housing:* on-campus residence required through junior year. *Options:* men-only, women-only. Campus housing is university owned. Freshman campus housing is guaranteed. *Activities and organizations:* drama/theater group, choral group, Element X. *Campus security:* 24-hour emergency response devices, student patrols, controlled dormitory access. *Student services:* personal/psychological counseling.

Athletics *Intercollegiate sports:* basketball M. *Intramural sports:* basketball M/W, football M, golf M, soccer M/W, ultimate Frisbee M/W, volleyball M/W.

Standardized Tests *Required:* SAT I or ACT (for admission).

Costs (2003–04) *Comprehensive fee:* $11,586 includes full-time tuition ($6855), mandatory fees ($651), and room and board ($4080). Part-time tuition: $195 per credit. Part-time tuition and fees vary according to class time and course load. *Required fees:* $138 per term part-time. *Room and board:* Room and board charges vary according to housing facility. *Payment plans:* tuition prepayment, installment. *Waivers:* senior citizens and employees or children of employees.

Financial Aid Of all full-time matriculated undergraduates who enrolled in 2003, 100 applied for aid, 100 were judged to have need, 11 had their need fully met. 8 Federal Work-Study jobs (averaging $2089). In 2003, 11 non-need-based awards were made. *Average financial aid package:* $6300. *Average need-based loan:* $3100. *Average need-based gift aid:* $3700. *Average non-need-based aid:* $310. *Average indebtedness upon graduation:* $10,550. *Financial aid deadline:* 9/1.

Applying *Options:* common application, electronic application. *Application fee:* $30. *Required:* essay or personal statement, high school transcript, minimum 2.0 GPA, 2 letters of recommendation. *Application deadlines:* 9/1 (freshmen), 9/1 (transfers). *Notification:* continuous until 9/1 (freshmen), continuous until 9/1 (transfers).

Admissions Contact Mr. Trent Combs, Director of Admissions, Eugene Bible College, 2155 Bailey Hill Road, Eugene, OR 97405. *Phone:* 541-485-1780 Ext. 135. *Toll-free phone:* 800-322-2638. *Fax:* 541-343-5801. *E-mail:* admissions@ebc.edu.

GEORGE FOX UNIVERSITY
Newberg, Oregon

- **Independent Friends** university, founded 1891
- **Calendar** semesters
- **Degrees** bachelor's, master's, doctoral, and first professional
- **Small-town** 73-acre campus with easy access to Portland
- **Endowment** $16.9 million
- **Coed,** 1,717 undergraduate students, 78% full-time, 59% women, 41% men
- **Moderately difficult** entrance level, 93% of applicants were admitted

George Fox University in Newberg, Oregon, is a Christian university ranked by *U.S. News & World Report* as a "Best Value" and as a top-tier master's university in the West. Innovative offerings include a personal computer for each undergraduate, subsidized international study trips, and a campuswide community service day.

Undergraduates 1,334 full-time, 383 part-time. Students come from 25 states and territories, 16 other countries, 36% are from out of state, 0.8% African American, 3% Asian American or Pacific Islander, 3% Hispanic American, 1% Native American, 3% international, 7% transferred in, 59% live on campus. *Retention:* 83% of 2001 full-time freshmen returned.

Freshmen *Admission:* 876 applied, 815 admitted, 337 enrolled. *Average high school GPA:* 4.00. *Test scores:* SAT verbal scores over 500: 74%; SAT math scores over 500: 74%; ACT scores over 18: 98%; SAT verbal scores over 600: 36%; SAT math scores over 600: 32%; ACT scores over 24: 63%; SAT verbal scores over 700: 6%; SAT math scores over 700: 4%; ACT scores over 30: 18%.

Faculty *Total:* 361, 37% full-time, 29% with terminal degrees. *Student/faculty ratio:* 15:1.

Majors Art; athletic training; biblical studies; biology/biological sciences; biology teacher education; business administration and management; business/managerial economics; chemistry; chemistry teacher education; clinical psychology; cognitive psychology and psycholinguistics; communication/speech communication and rhetoric; computer and information sciences; education (multiple levels); elementary education; engineering; English; English/language arts teacher education; family and consumer sciences/home economics teacher education; family and consumer sciences/human sciences; family resource management; fashion merchandising; health teacher education; history; human resources management; interdisciplinary studies; international relations and affairs; management information systems; mathematics; mathematics teacher education; missionary studies and missiology; music; music teacher education; nursing related; pastoral studies/counseling; physical education teaching and coaching; psychology; public relations/image management; radio and television; religious education; religious studies; social studies teacher education; social work; sociology; Spanish; sport and fitness administration.

Academic Programs *Special study options:* academic remediation for entering students, accelerated degree program, adult/continuing education programs, advanced placement credit, cooperative education, distance learning, double majors, English as a second language, external degree program, honors programs, independent study, internships, off-campus study, part-time degree program, services for LD students, student-designed majors, study abroad. *ROTC:* Air Force (c).

Library Murdock Learning Resource Center plus 1 other with 123,734 titles, 1,323 serial subscriptions, 2,687 audiovisual materials, an OPAC, a Web page.

Computers on Campus 1300 computers available on campus for general student use. A campuswide network can be accessed from student residence rooms and from off campus. Internet access, online (class) registration, at least one staffed computer lab available.

Student Life *Housing:* on-campus residence required through junior year. *Options:* men-only, women-only, disabled students. *Activities and organizations:* drama/theater group, student-run newspaper, radio station, choral group, student government, student activities, Christian ministries, Orientation Committee, Chaplain's Committee. *Campus security:* 24-hour emergency response devices and patrols, student patrols, late-night transport/escort service, controlled dormitory access. *Student services:* health clinic, personal/psychological counseling.

Athletics Member NCAA. All Division III. *Intercollegiate sports:* baseball M, basketball M/W, cross-country running M/W, soccer M/W, softball W, tennis M/W, track and field M/W, volleyball W. *Intramural sports:* badminton M/W, basketball M/W, football M/W, golf M/W, racquetball M/W, soccer M/W, table tennis M/W, tennis W, volleyball M/W, weight lifting M/W.

Standardized Tests *Required:* SAT I or ACT (for admission).

Costs (2003–04) *Comprehensive fee:* $26,110 includes full-time tuition ($19,500), mandatory fees ($310), and room and board ($6300). Full-time tuition and fees vary according to program. Part-time tuition: $600 per semester hour. Part-time tuition and fees vary according to course load. *College room only:* $3500. Room and board charges vary according to housing facility and location. *Payment plan:* installment.

Financial Aid Of all full-time matriculated undergraduates who enrolled in 2003, 1,305 applied for aid, 1,184 were judged to have need, 166 had their need fully met. 797 Federal Work-Study jobs (averaging $1881). In 2003, 217 non-need-based awards were made. *Average percent of need met:* 78%. *Average financial aid package:* $14,902. *Average need-based loan:* $3642. *Average need-based gift aid:* $10,967. *Average non-need-based aid:* $8584. *Average indebtedness upon graduation:* $16,912.

Applying *Options:* common application, electronic application, early admission, deferred entrance. *Application fee:* $40. *Required:* essay or personal statement, high school transcript, 2 letters of recommendation. *Required for some:*

interview. *Recommended:* interview. *Application deadlines:* 6/1 (freshmen), 4/1 (transfers). *Notification:* continuous until 10/1 (freshmen), continuous (transfers).

Admissions Contact Mr. Dale Seipp, Director of Admissions, George Fox University, 414 North Meridian Street, Newberg, OR 97132. *Phone:* 503-554-2240. *Toll-free phone:* 800-765-4369. *Fax:* 503-554-3110. *E-mail:* admissions@georgefox.edu.

■ See page 1664 for a narrative description.

ITT TECHNICAL INSTITUTE
Portland, Oregon

- **Proprietary** primarily 2-year, founded 1971, part of ITT Educational Services, Inc.
- **Calendar** quarters
- **Degrees** associate and bachelor's
- **Urban** 4-acre campus
- **Coed**
- **Minimally difficult** entrance level

Standardized Tests *Required:* Wonderlic aptitude test (for admission).

Costs (2003–04) *Tuition:* $347 per credit hour part-time.

Financial Aid Of all full-time matriculated undergraduates who enrolled in 2001, 15 Federal Work-Study jobs (averaging $4000).

Applying *Options:* deferred entrance. *Application fee:* $100. *Required:* high school transcript, interview. *Recommended:* letters of recommendation.

Admissions Contact Mr. Ed Yakimchick, Director of Recruitment, ITT Technical Institute, 6035 Northeast 78th Court, Portland, OR 97218. *Phone:* 503-255-6500. *Toll-free phone:* 800-234-5488. *Fax:* 503-255-8381.

LEWIS & CLARK COLLEGE
Portland, Oregon

- **Independent** comprehensive, founded 1867
- **Calendar** semesters
- **Degrees** bachelor's, master's, first professional, and first professional certificates
- **Suburban** 137-acre campus
- **Endowment** $120.8 million
- **Coed,** 1,792 undergraduate students, 98% full-time, 61% women, 39% men
- **Very difficult** entrance level, 68% of applicants were admitted

Lewis & Clark combines a solid foundation in the liberal arts and sciences with a reputation as a national college with a global reach. Students come from 49 states and 41 countries. More than 60% participate in overseas and off-campus study programs. Portland provides many internship and community service opportunities. Lewis & Clark also offers one of the top-rated outdoors programs in the country.

Undergraduates 1,757 full-time, 35 part-time. Students come from 51 states and territories, 40 other countries, 80% are from out of state, 1% African American, 6% Asian American or Pacific Islander, 3% Hispanic American, 2% Native American, 5% international, 4% transferred in, 64% live on campus. *Retention:* 84% of 2002 full-time freshmen returned.

Freshmen *Admission:* 3,405 applied, 2,310 admitted, 493 enrolled. *Average high school GPA:* 3.66. *Test scores:* SAT verbal scores over 500: 99%; SAT math scores over 500: 99%; ACT scores over 18: 100%; SAT verbal scores over 600: 78%; SAT math scores over 600: 68%; ACT scores over 24: 85%; SAT verbal scores over 700: 30%; SAT math scores over 700: 17%; ACT scores over 30: 25%.

Faculty *Total:* 331, 59% full-time, 77% with terminal degrees. *Student/faculty ratio:* 12:1.

Majors Anthropology; art; Asian studies (East); biochemistry; biology/biological sciences; chemistry; communication/speech communication and rhetoric; computer science; dramatic/theatre arts; economics; English; environmental studies; foreign languages and literatures; French; German; Hispanic-American, Puerto Rican, and Mexican-American/Chicano studies; history; international relations and affairs; mathematics; modern languages; music; philosophy; physics; political science and government; pre-engineering; psychology; religious studies; sociology; Spanish.

Academic Programs *Special study options:* accelerated degree program, advanced placement credit, double majors, English as a second language, honors programs, independent study, internships, off-campus study, part-time degree program, services for LD students, student-designed majors, study abroad, summer session for credit. *Unusual degree programs:* 3-2 engineering with Columbia University, Washington University in St. Louis, University of Southern California, Oregon Health Sciences University.

Library Aubrey Watzek Library plus 1 other with 227,609 titles, 7,477 serial subscriptions, 11,586 audiovisual materials, an OPAC, a Web page.

Computers on Campus 158 computers available on campus for general student use. A campuswide network can be accessed from student residence rooms and from off campus. Internet access, at least one staffed computer lab available. Computer purchase or lease plan available.

Student Life *Housing:* on-campus residence required through sophomore year. *Options:* coed. Campus housing is university owned. Freshman campus housing is guaranteed. *Activities and organizations:* drama/theater group, student-run newspaper, radio and television station, choral group, College Outdoors, Associated Students, Center for Service and Work, musical groups, student radio station. *Campus security:* 24-hour emergency response devices and patrols, student patrols, late-night transport/escort service, controlled dormitory access. *Student services:* health clinic, personal/psychological counseling, women's center.

Athletics Member NCAA, NAIA. All NCAA Division III. *Intercollegiate sports:* baseball M, basketball M/W, crew M/W, cross-country running M/W, football M, golf M/W, lacrosse M(c)/W(c), rugby M(c)/W(c), soccer M(c)/W, softball W, swimming M/W, tennis M/W, track and field M/W, volleyball W. *Intramural sports:* badminton M/W, basketball M/W, cross-country running M/W, fencing M(c)/W(c), football M/W, sailing M(c)/W(c), skiing (cross-country) M(c)/W(c), skiing (downhill) M(c)/W(c), softball M/W, swimming M/W, table tennis M/W, tennis M/W, ultimate Frisbee M/W, volleyball M/W, water polo M/W.

Standardized Tests *Required:* SAT I, ACT, or academic portfolio (for admission).

Costs (2003–04) *Comprehensive fee:* $31,700 includes full-time tuition ($23,886), mandatory fees ($784), and room and board ($7030). *College room only:* $3710. Room and board charges vary according to board plan and housing facility. *Payment plan:* installment. *Waivers:* employees or children of employees.

Financial Aid Of all full-time matriculated undergraduates who enrolled in 2003, 1,193 applied for aid, 1,101 were judged to have need, 393 had their need fully met. 734 Federal Work-Study jobs (averaging $1832). In 2003, 84 non-need-based awards were made. *Average percent of need met:* 79%. *Average financial aid package:* $18,654. *Average need-based loan:* $4600. *Average need-based gift aid:* $17,314. *Average non-need-based aid:* $7229. *Average indebtedness upon graduation:* $17,055.

Applying *Options:* common application, electronic application, early admission, early action, deferred entrance. *Application fee:* $50. *Required:* essay or personal statement, high school transcript, minimum 2.0 GPA, 2 letters of recommendation. *Required for some:* 4 letters of recommendation, portfolio applicants must submit samples of graded work. *Recommended:* minimum 3.0 GPA, interview. *Application deadline:* 2/1 (freshmen). *Notification:* 4/1 (freshmen), 1/15 (early action).

Admissions Contact Mr. Michael Sexton, Dean of Admissions, Lewis & Clark College, 0615 SW Palatine Hill Road, Portland, OR 97219-7899. *Phone:* 503-768-7040. *Toll-free phone:* 800-444-4111. *Fax:* 503-768-7055. *E-mail:* admissions@lclark.edu.

■ See page 1864 for a narrative description.

LINFIELD COLLEGE
McMinnville, Oregon

- **Independent American Baptist Churches in the USA** 4-year, founded 1849
- **Calendar** 4-1-4
- **Degree** bachelor's
- **Small-town** 193-acre campus with easy access to Portland
- **Endowment** $39.5 million
- **Coed,** 1,659 undergraduate students, 97% full-time, 55% women, 45% men
- **Moderately difficult** entrance level, 78% of applicants were admitted

Linfield College, tracing its roots back to 1858, is an independent, 4-year institution nationally recognized for its strong teaching faculty, outstanding science programs, and extensive study-abroad opportunities. More than 50 percent of graduating students have spent a January term, a semester, or an academic year in another country. Linfield is located in the heart of the Willamette Valley.

Undergraduates 1,609 full-time, 50 part-time. Students come from 30 states and territories, 19 other countries, 45% are from out of state, 2% African American, 6% Asian American or Pacific Islander, 2% Hispanic American, 1% Native American, 2% international, 3% transferred in, 74% live on campus. *Retention:* 83% of 2002 full-time freshmen returned.

Freshmen *Admission:* 1,903 applied, 1,482 admitted, 453 enrolled. *Average high school GPA:* 3.56. *Test scores:* SAT verbal scores over 500: 75%; SAT math scores over 500: 82%; ACT scores over 18: 94%; SAT verbal scores over 600: 29%; SAT math scores over 600: 35%; ACT scores over 24: 51%; SAT verbal scores over 700: 5%; SAT math scores over 700: 5%; ACT scores over 30: 5%.

Faculty *Total:* 164, 63% full-time, 68% with terminal degrees. *Student/faculty ratio:* 13:1.

Linfield College (continued)

Majors Accounting; anthropology; area, ethnic, cultural, and gender studies related; art; athletic training; biology/biological sciences; business/commerce; chemistry; communication/speech communication and rhetoric; computer science; creative writing; dramatic/theatre arts; economics; elementary education; English; environmental studies; finance; French; German; health and physical education; history; international business/trade/commerce; Japanese; kinesiology and exercise science; mathematics; music; philosophy; physical sciences; physics; political science and government; psychology; religious studies; sociology; Spanish.

Academic Programs *Special study options:* accelerated degree program, adult/continuing education programs, advanced placement credit, cooperative education, distance learning, double majors, English as a second language, external degree program, honors programs, independent study, internships, off-campus study, part-time degree program, services for LD students, student-designed majors, study abroad, summer session for credit. *ROTC:* Army (c), Air Force (c). *Unusual degree programs:* 3-2 engineering with Washington State University, Oregon State University, University of Southern California.

Library Emanuel Northup Library with 163,744 titles, 1,296 serial subscriptions, 19,549 audiovisual materials, an OPAC, a Web page.

Computers on Campus 189 computers available on campus for general student use. A campuswide network can be accessed from student residence rooms and from off campus. Internet access, at least one staffed computer lab available. Computer purchase or lease plan available.

Student Life *Housing:* on-campus residence required through junior year. *Options:* coed, men-only, women-only. Campus housing is university owned. Freshman campus housing is guaranteed. *Activities and organizations:* drama/theater group, student-run newspaper, radio station, choral group, Fellowship of Christian Athletes, Linfield Ultimate Players Association, Hawaiian Club, International Club, Lacrosse Club, national fraternities, national sororities. *Campus security:* 24-hour emergency response devices and patrols, late-night transport/escort service, controlled dormitory access. *Student services:* health clinic, personal/psychological counseling.

Athletics Member NCAA. All Division III. *Intercollegiate sports:* baseball M, basketball M/W, cross-country running M/W, football M, golf M/W, lacrosse W, soccer M/W, softball W, swimming M/W, tennis M/W, track and field M/W, volleyball W. *Intramural sports:* basketball M/W, bowling M/W, football M/W, lacrosse M, racquetball M/W, soccer M/W, softball M/W, ultimate Frisbee M/W, volleyball M/W, water polo M/W.

Standardized Tests *Required:* SAT I or ACT (for admission).

Costs (2003–04) *Comprehensive fee:* $27,090 includes full-time tuition ($20,770), mandatory fees ($200), and room and board ($6120). Part-time tuition: $650 per credit. Part-time tuition and fees vary according to course load. *Required fees:* $60 per term part-time. *College room only:* $3200. Room and board charges vary according to board plan and housing facility. *Payment plan:* installment. *Waivers:* senior citizens and employees or children of employees.

Financial Aid Of all full-time matriculated undergraduates who enrolled in 2003, 1,115 applied for aid, 1,115 were judged to have need, 336 had their need fully met. 750 Federal Work-Study jobs (averaging $1707). 475 state and other part-time jobs (averaging $1113). In 2003, 304 non-need-based awards were made. *Average percent of need met:* 83%. *Average financial aid package:* $16,638. *Average need-based loan:* $4617. *Average need-based gift aid:* $4400. *Average non-need-based aid:* $8902. *Average indebtedness upon graduation:* $29,926.

Applying *Options:* common application, electronic application, early action, deferred entrance. *Application fee:* $40. *Required:* essay or personal statement, high school transcript, 1 letter of recommendation. *Recommended:* interview. *Application deadlines:* 2/15 (freshmen), 4/15 (transfers). *Notification:* 4/1 (freshmen), 1/15 (early action), 5/15 (transfers).

Admissions Contact Ms. Lisa Knodle-Bragiel, Director of Admissions, Linfield College, 900 SE Baker Street, McMinnville, OR 97128-6894. *Phone:* 503-883-2213. *Toll-free phone:* 800-640-2287. *Fax:* 503-883-2472. *E-mail:* admission@linfield.edu.

■ *See page 1876 for a narrative description.*

MARYLHURST UNIVERSITY

Marylhurst, Oregon

- **Independent Roman Catholic** comprehensive, founded 1893
- **Calendar** quarters
- **Degrees** bachelor's, master's, and postbachelor's certificates
- **Suburban** 73-acre campus with easy access to Portland
- **Endowment** $10.0 million
- **Coed,** 804 undergraduate students, 28% full-time, 75% women, 25% men
- **Noncompetitive** entrance level, 50% of applicants were admitted

Undergraduates 228 full-time, 576 part-time. Students come from 9 states and territories, 22 other countries, 12% are from out of state, 1% African American, 1% Asian American or Pacific Islander, 0.7% Hispanic American, 0.7% Native American, 4% international, 68% transferred in, 3% live on campus. *Retention:* 52% of 2002 full-time freshmen returned.

Freshmen *Admission:* 28 applied, 14 admitted, 11 enrolled. *Test scores:* SAT verbal scores over 500: 83%; SAT math scores over 500: 67%; ACT scores over 18: 50%; SAT verbal scores over 600: 50%; SAT math scores over 600: 17%; SAT math scores over 700: 17%.

Faculty *Total:* 184, 17% full-time, 33% with terminal degrees. *Student/faculty ratio:* 7:1.

Majors Art; biological and physical sciences; business administration and management; creative writing; divinity/ministry; education related; English literature (British and Commonwealth); environmental studies; ethnic, cultural minority, and gender studies related; history related; interdisciplinary studies; interior design; mass communication/media; music; music related; pastoral studies/counseling; psychology; public relations/image management; real estate; religious studies; social sciences.

Academic Programs *Special study options:* accelerated degree program, adult/continuing education programs, advanced placement credit, distance learning, double majors, English as a second language, independent study, internships, off-campus study, part-time degree program, services for LD students, student-designed majors, summer session for credit.

Library Shoen Library with 1,449 audiovisual materials, an OPAC, a Web page.

Computers on Campus 40 computers available on campus for general student use. A campuswide network can be accessed. Internet access, online (class) registration, at least one staffed computer lab available.

Student Life *Housing options:* coed. *Activities and organizations:* choral group, Toastmasters, environmental science club, Student Ambassadors, Bahia club, student government. *Campus security:* 24-hour emergency response devices and patrols, late-night transport/escort service, controlled dormitory access. *Student services:* personal/psychological counseling.

Costs (2004–05) *Tuition:* $13,185 full-time, $293 per credit hour part-time. Full-time tuition and fees vary according to course load. Part-time tuition and fees vary according to course load. *Required fees:* $270 full-time, $6 per credit hour part-time. *Room only:* Room and board charges vary according to housing facility. *Payment plans:* installment, deferred payment. *Waivers:* employees or children of employees.

Financial Aid Of all full-time matriculated undergraduates who enrolled in 2003, 120 applied for aid, 116 were judged to have need, 5 had their need fully met. 45 Federal Work-Study jobs. In 2003, 5 non-need-based awards were made. *Average percent of need met:* 58%. *Average financial aid package:* $12,933. *Average need-based loan:* $5456. *Average need-based gift aid:* $7015. *Average indebtedness upon graduation:* $17,906.

Applying *Options:* deferred entrance. *Application fee:* $20. *Required:* high school transcript. *Application deadline:* rolling (freshmen), rolling (transfers). *Notification:* continuous (freshmen), continuous (transfers).

Admissions Contact Mr. John French, Academic Advising Specialist, Marylhurst University, 17600 Pacific Highway (Hwy 43), PO Box 261, Marylhurst, OR 97036. *Phone:* 503-699-6268 Ext. 3325. *Toll-free phone:* 800-634-9982. *Fax:* 503-635-6585. *E-mail:* admissions@marylhurst.edu.

MOUNT ANGEL SEMINARY

Saint Benedict, Oregon

Admissions Contact Mount Angel Seminary, Saint Benedict, OR 97373. *Phone:* 503-845-3951.

MULTNOMAH BIBLE COLLEGE AND BIBLICAL SEMINARY

Portland, Oregon

- **Independent interdenominational** comprehensive, founded 1936
- **Calendar** early semesters
- **Degrees** bachelor's, master's, first professional, and postbachelor's certificates
- **Urban** 22-acre campus
- **Endowment** $5.8 million
- **Coed,** 564 undergraduate students, 89% full-time, 45% women, 55% men
- **Moderately difficult** entrance level, 80% of applicants were admitted

Undergraduates 501 full-time, 63 part-time. Students come from 34 states and territories, 55% are from out of state, 2% African American, 5% Asian American or Pacific Islander, 3% Hispanic American, 0.4% Native American, 0.4% international, 16% transferred in, 56% live on campus. *Retention:* 58% of 2002 full-time freshmen returned.

Freshmen *Admission:* 167 applied, 134 admitted, 85 enrolled. *Average high school GPA:* 3.30. *Test scores:* SAT verbal scores over 500: 80%; SAT math scores over 500: 61%; ACT scores over 18: 95%; SAT verbal scores over 600: 46%; SAT math scores over 600: 24%; ACT scores over 24: 15%; SAT verbal scores over 700: 11%; SAT math scores over 700: 1%.

Faculty *Total:* 51, 47% full-time, 35% with terminal degrees. *Student/faculty ratio:* 16:1.

Majors Ancient/classical Greek; biblical studies; communication/speech communication and rhetoric; Hebrew; history; journalism; missionary studies and missiology; pastoral counseling and specialized ministries related; pastoral studies/counseling; religious education; religious/sacred music; theology; youth ministry.

Academic Programs *Special study options:* academic remediation for entering students, adult/continuing education programs, advanced placement credit, double majors, internships, part-time degree program, services for LD students, summer session for credit.

Library John Mitchell Library with 73,591 titles, 369 serial subscriptions, 11,693 audiovisual materials, an OPAC.

Computers on Campus 42 computers available on campus for general student use. A campuswide network can be accessed from student residence rooms and from off campus. Internet access, online (class) registration, at least one staffed computer lab available.

Student Life *Housing:* on-campus residence required through senior year. *Options:* men-only, women-only. Campus housing is university owned. Freshman campus housing is guaranteed. *Activities and organizations:* drama/theater group, student-run newspaper, choral group. *Campus security:* 24-hour emergency response devices and patrols, late-night transport/escort service, controlled dormitory access. *Student services:* health clinic, personal/psychological counseling.

Athletics Member NCCAA. *Intercollegiate sports:* basketball M/W(c), volleyball W. *Intramural sports:* basketball M/W, tennis M/W, ultimate Frisbee M/W, volleyball M/W.

Standardized Tests *Required:* SAT I or ACT (for admission).

Costs (2003–04) *Comprehensive fee:* $15,310 includes full-time tuition ($10,560) and room and board ($4750). Part-time tuition: $440 per semester hour. Part-time tuition and fees vary according to course load. *Room and board:* Room and board charges vary according to board plan and housing facility. *Payment plan:* installment. *Waivers:* employees or children of employees.

Financial Aid Of all full-time matriculated undergraduates who enrolled in 2002, 455 applied for aid, 406 were judged to have need, 16 had their need fully met. 85 Federal Work-Study jobs (averaging $1660). In 2002, 92 non-need-based awards were made. *Average percent of need met:* 58%. *Average financial aid package:* $7328. *Average need-based loan:* $3499. *Average need-based gift aid:* $3966. *Average non-need-based aid:* $7010. *Average indebtedness upon graduation:* $19,651.

Applying *Options:* deferred entrance. *Application fee:* $40. *Required:* essay or personal statement, high school transcript, minimum 2.5 GPA, 4 letters of recommendation. *Application deadlines:* 7/15 (freshmen), 7/15 (transfers). *Notification:* continuous until 8/15 (freshmen), continuous (transfers).

Admissions Contact Ms. Nancy Gerecz, Admissions Assistant, Multnomah Bible College and Biblical Seminary, 8435 Northeast Glisan Street, Portland, OR 97220-5898. *Phone:* 503-255-0332 Ext. 373. *Toll-free phone:* 800-275-4672. *Fax:* 503-254-1268. *E-mail:* admiss@multnomah.edu.

NORTHWEST CHRISTIAN COLLEGE
Eugene, Oregon

- **Independent Christian** comprehensive, founded 1895
- **Calendar** quarters
- **Degrees** certificates, associate, bachelor's, master's, and postbachelor's certificates
- **Urban** 8-acre campus with easy access to Portland
- **Endowment** $5.3 million
- **Coed,** 392 undergraduate students, 91% full-time, 59% women, 41% men
- **Moderately difficult** entrance level, 65% of applicants were admitted

Undergraduates 356 full-time, 36 part-time. Students come from 14 states and territories, 2 other countries, 11% are from out of state, 1% African American, 2% Asian American or Pacific Islander, 3% Hispanic American, 0.3% Native American, 0.8% international, 14% transferred in. *Retention:* 63% of 2002 full-time freshmen returned.

Freshmen *Admission:* 168 applied, 109 admitted, 53 enrolled. *Average high school GPA:* 3.41. *Test scores:* SAT verbal scores over 500: 45%; SAT math scores over 500: 58%; ACT scores over 18: 79%; SAT verbal scores over 600: 13%; SAT math scores over 600: 13%; ACT scores over 24: 32%; SAT verbal scores over 700: 3%.

Faculty *Total:* 56, 41% full-time, 41% with terminal degrees. *Student/faculty ratio:* 13:1.

Majors Area, ethnic, cultural, and gender studies related; biblical studies; business administration, management and operations related; communication/speech communication and rhetoric; computer and information sciences; education (multiple levels); health services administration; human services; liberal arts and sciences and humanities related; management information systems; music management and merchandising; music related; psychology related; social sciences related; theological and ministerial studies related.

Academic Programs *Special study options:* academic remediation for entering students, accelerated degree program, adult/continuing education programs, advanced placement credit, cooperative education, distance learning, double majors, English as a second language, independent study, internships, off-campus study, part-time degree program, services for LD students, study abroad, summer session for credit. *ROTC:* Army (c).

Library Kellenberger Library with 62,220 titles, 261 serial subscriptions, 8,677 audiovisual materials, an OPAC.

Computers on Campus 40 computers available on campus for general student use. A campuswide network can be accessed from student residence rooms and from off campus. Internet access, at least one staffed computer lab available.

Student Life *Housing:* on-campus residence required for freshman year. *Options:* coed, men-only, women-only. Campus housing is university owned and leased by the school. Freshman applicants given priority for college housing. *Activities and organizations:* drama/theater group, student-run newspaper, choral group, Praise Gathering, Spirit Club, Teachers for Tomorrow, environmental club, drama club. *Campus security:* 24-hour emergency response devices, late-night transport/escort service, controlled dormitory access, late-night patrols by trained security personnel. *Student services:* personal/psychological counseling.

Athletics Member NSCAA. *Intercollegiate sports:* basketball M(s)/W(s), cheerleading W, softball W(s). *Intramural sports:* basketball M/W, volleyball M/W.

Standardized Tests *Required:* SAT I or ACT (for admission). *Required for some:* SAT II: Subject Tests (for admission).

Costs (2003–04) *Comprehensive fee:* $21,710 includes full-time tuition ($16,200) and room and board ($5510). Full-time tuition and fees vary according to course load and program. Part-time tuition: $360 per credit. Part-time tuition and fees vary according to course load. *College room only:* $2300. Room and board charges vary according to board plan and housing facility. *Payment plans:* installment, deferred payment. *Waivers:* employees or children of employees.

Financial Aid Of all full-time matriculated undergraduates who enrolled in 2003, 319 applied for aid, 300 were judged to have need, 65 had their need fully met. 150 Federal Work-Study jobs (averaging $2466). 15 state and other part-time jobs (averaging $2560). In 2003, 26 non-need-based awards were made. *Average percent of need met:* 75%. *Average financial aid package:* $13,790. *Average need-based loan:* $4055. *Average need-based gift aid:* $9365. *Average non-need-based aid:* $8601. *Average indebtedness upon graduation:* $14,992.

Applying *Options:* common application, electronic application, deferred entrance. *Application fee:* $25. *Required:* essay or personal statement, high school transcript, minimum 2.5 GPA, 2 letters of recommendation. *Recommended:* interview. *Application deadline:* rolling (freshmen), rolling (transfers). *Notification:* continuous (freshmen), continuous (transfers).

Admissions Contact Ms. Cheryl Brelsford, Interim Director of Admissions, Northwest Christian College, 828 East 11th Avenue, Eugene, OR 97401-3745. *Phone:* 541-684-7247. *Toll-free phone:* 877-463-6622. *Fax:* 541-684-7317. *E-mail:* admissions@nwcc.edu.

OREGON COLLEGE OF ART & CRAFT
Portland, Oregon

- **Independent** 4-year, founded 1907
- **Calendar** semesters
- **Degrees** certificates, bachelor's, and postbachelor's certificates
- **Urban** 11-acre campus
- **Endowment** $3.8 million
- **Coed,** 120 undergraduate students, 73% full-time, 73% women, 28% men
- **Minimally difficult** entrance level

Undergraduates 88 full-time, 32 part-time. Students come from 21 states and territories, 2 other countries, 38% are from out of state, 0.9% African American, 3% Asian American or Pacific Islander, 4% Hispanic American, 0.9% Native American, 3% international, 23% transferred in. *Retention:* 75% of 2002 full-time freshmen returned.

Freshmen *Admission:* 15 enrolled. *Average high school GPA:* 3.26.

Faculty *Total:* 18, 44% full-time, 89% with terminal degrees. *Student/faculty ratio:* 8:1.

Majors Crafts, folk art and artisanry; fine arts related.

Academic Programs *Special study options:* adult/continuing education programs, advanced placement credit, double majors, independent study, internships, off-campus study, part-time degree program.

Oregon College of Art & Craft (continued)

Library Oregon College of Art and Craft Library plus 1 other with 6,500 titles, 90 serial subscriptions, 24,000 audiovisual materials, an OPAC.

Computers on Campus 4 computers available on campus for general student use. Internet access, at least one staffed computer lab available.

Student Life *Housing:* college housing not available. *Activities and organizations:* Student Life Committee. *Campus security:* 24-hour emergency response devices, late-night transport/escort service. *Student services:* personal/psychological counseling.

Costs (2004–05) *Tuition:* $14,800 full-time, $1935 per course part-time. Part-time tuition and fees vary according to course load. *Required fees:* $1050 full-time. *Payment plans:* installment, deferred payment.

Financial Aid Of all full-time matriculated undergraduates who enrolled in 2002, 58 applied for aid, 54 were judged to have need, 1 had their need fully met. 26 Federal Work-Study jobs (averaging $406). 41 state and other part-time jobs (averaging $614). *Average percent of need met:* 68%. *Average financial aid package:* $12,100. *Average need-based loan:* $3500. *Average need-based gift aid:* $8550. *Average indebtedness upon graduation:* $25,000.

Applying *Options:* deferred entrance. *Application fee:* $35. *Required:* essay or personal statement, high school transcript, minimum 2.5 GPA, 2 letters of recommendation, interview, portfolio. *Application deadline:* rolling (freshmen), rolling (transfers). *Notification:* continuous (freshmen), continuous (transfers).

Admissions Contact Mr. Barry Beach, Director of Admissions, Oregon College of Art & Craft, 8245 Southwest Barnes Road, Portland, OR 97225. *Phone:* 503-297-5544. *Toll-free phone:* 800-390-0632. *Fax:* 503-297-9651. *E-mail:* admissions@ocac.edu.

OREGON HEALTH & SCIENCE UNIVERSITY

Portland, Oregon

Admissions Contact Ms. Cherie Honnell, Registrar and Director of Financial Aid, Oregon Health & Science University, 3181 Southwest Sam Jackson Park Road, Portland, OR 97201-3098. *Phone:* 503-494-7800.

OREGON INSTITUTE OF TECHNOLOGY

Klamath Falls, Oregon

- **State-supported** 4-year, founded 1947, part of Oregon University System
- **Calendar** quarters
- **Degrees** associate and bachelor's
- **Small-town** 173-acre campus
- **Endowment** $13.6 million
- **Coed,** 3,235 undergraduate students, 63% full-time, 46% women, 54% men
- **Moderately difficult** entrance level, 54% of applicants were admitted

Undergraduates 2,047 full-time, 1,188 part-time. Students come from 35 states and territories, 10 other countries, 1% African American, 5% Asian American or Pacific Islander, 4% Hispanic American, 2% Native American, 1% international, 9% transferred in, 17% live on campus. *Retention:* 72% of 2002 full-time freshmen returned.

Freshmen *Admission:* 877 applied, 473 admitted, 354 enrolled. *Average high school GPA:* 3.40. *Test scores:* SAT verbal scores over 500: 58%; SAT math scores over 500: 67%; ACT scores over 18: 78%; SAT verbal scores over 600: 20%; SAT math scores over 600: 23%; ACT scores over 24: 22%; SAT verbal scores over 700: 4%; SAT math scores over 700: 3%; ACT scores over 30: 3%.

Faculty *Total:* 130, 88% full-time. *Student/faculty ratio:* 15:1.

Majors Accounting; business administration and management; civil engineering; communication/speech communication and rhetoric; computer and information sciences; computer engineering technology; computer programming; counseling psychology; dental hygiene; electrical, electronic and communications engineering technology; environmental studies; industrial radiologic technology; laser and optical technology; liberal arts and sciences/liberal studies; management information systems; mechanical engineering/mechanical technology; premedical studies; radiologic technology/science; survey technology.

Academic Programs *Special study options:* academic remediation for entering students, adult/continuing education programs, advanced placement credit, cooperative education, distance learning, double majors, English as a second language, internships, off-campus study, part-time degree program, services for LD students, study abroad, summer session for credit.

Library Center for Learning and Teaching plus 2 others with 90,389 titles, 1,764 serial subscriptions, 1,905 audiovisual materials, an OPAC, a Web page.

Computers on Campus 700 computers available on campus for general student use. A campuswide network can be accessed from off campus that provide access to online grade information. Internet access, online (class) registration, at least one staffed computer lab available.

Student Life *Housing options:* coed. Campus housing is university owned. *Activities and organizations:* student-run newspaper, radio and television station, choral group, Phi Delta Theta, Christian Fellowship, international club, Society of Women Engineers, Association of Student Mechanical Engineers, national fraternities. *Campus security:* 24-hour emergency response devices and patrols, late-night transport/escort service. *Student services:* health clinic, personal/psychological counseling.

Athletics Member NAIA. *Intercollegiate sports:* baseball M, basketball M(s)/W, cross-country running M(s)/W(s), soccer M/W, softball W(s), track and field M(s)/W(s), volleyball W(s). *Intramural sports:* basketball M/W, bowling M/W, cheerleading M/W, cross-country running M/W, football M/W, golf M/W, lacrosse M, rugby M/W, soccer M/W, softball W, track and field M/W, volleyball M/W, water polo M/W.

Standardized Tests *Required:* SAT I or ACT (for admission).

Costs (2003–04) *Tuition:* state resident $3348 full-time, $93 per credit part-time; nonresident $12,528 full-time, $93 per credit part-time. Full-time tuition and fees vary according to course load. *Required fees:* $1095 full-time. *Room and board:* $6135. Room and board charges vary according to board plan. *Waivers:* senior citizens and employees or children of employees.

Financial Aid Of all full-time matriculated undergraduates who enrolled in 2002, 1,913 applied for aid, 1,796 were judged to have need, 647 had their need fully met. In 2002, 2 non-need-based awards were made. *Average percent of need met:* 17%. *Average financial aid package:* $5791. *Average need-based loan:* $4308. *Average need-based gift aid:* $3951. *Average non-need-based aid:* $9563. *Average indebtedness upon graduation:* $21,620.

Applying *Options:* common application, electronic application, deferred entrance. *Application fee:* $50. *Required:* high school transcript, minimum 2.5 GPA. *Required for some:* letters of recommendation. *Application deadlines:* 6/1 (freshmen), 6/1 (transfers). *Notification:* continuous until 9/1 (freshmen), continuous (transfers).

Admissions Contact Mr. Palmer Muntz, Director of Admissions, Oregon Institute of Technology, 3201 Campus Drive, Klamath Falls, OR 97601. *Phone:* 541-885-1150. *Toll-free phone:* 800-422-2017 (in-state); 800-343-6653 (out-of-state). *Fax:* 541-885-1115. *E-mail:* oit@oit.edu.

OREGON STATE UNIVERSITY

Corvallis, Oregon

- **State-supported** university, founded 1868, part of Oregon University System
- **Calendar** quarters
- **Degrees** bachelor's, master's, doctoral, and first professional
- **Small-town** 422-acre campus with easy access to Portland
- **Coed,** 15,599 undergraduate students, 90% full-time, 47% women, 53% men
- **Moderately difficult** entrance level, 88% of applicants were admitted

Small classes, motivated students, honors-level instruction, and close interaction with some of Oregon State University's finest faculty members create an exciting, challenging University Honors College atmosphere. In honors classes, colloquia, and other innovative ways, Honors College students explore their majors with an interdisciplinary approach. Students also work with faculty mentors to prepare honors theses. Graduates receive an honors baccalaureate degree in their major, conferred jointly by the Honors College and their academic college. Honors College graduates enjoy virtually 100% placement into graduate and professional programs.

Undergraduates 13,987 full-time, 1,612 part-time. Students come from 50 states and territories, 91 other countries, 11% are from out of state, 1% African American, 8% Asian American or Pacific Islander, 3% Hispanic American, 1% Native American, 2% international, 7% transferred in, 22% live on campus. *Retention:* 87% of 2002 full-time freshmen returned.

Freshmen *Admission:* 7,410 applied, 6,529 admitted, 2,949 enrolled. *Average high school GPA:* 3.45. *Test scores:* SAT verbal scores over 500: 65%; SAT math scores over 500: 72%; ACT scores over 18: 91%; SAT verbal scores over 600: 24%; SAT math scores over 600: 30%; ACT scores over 24: 41%; SAT verbal scores over 700: 3%; SAT math scores over 700: 5%; ACT scores over 30: 5%.

Faculty *Total:* 789, 80% full-time, 64% with terminal degrees. *Student/faculty ratio:* 21:1.

Majors Accounting; actuarial science; agricultural business and management; agricultural economics; agriculture; agronomy and crop science; American studies; animal sciences; anthropology; applied art; applied mathematics; archeology; art; art history, criticism and conservation; athletic training; biochemistry; biological and physical sciences; biology/biological sciences; biophysics; botany/plant biology; business administration and management; cell biology and histology; chemical engineering; chemistry; child development; civil engineering; clinical laboratory science/medical technology; clothing/textiles; comparative literature; computer engineering; computer science; construction engineering; construction management; cultural studies; dairy science; dietetics; dramatic/theatre arts;

economics; electrical, electronics and communications engineering; engineering; engineering physics; English; entomology; environmental biology; environmental/environmental health engineering; environmental health; environmental studies; equestrian studies; evolutionary biology; family and community services; family and consumer economics related; family and consumer sciences/human sciences; fashion/apparel design; fashion merchandising; fiber, textile and weaving arts; finance; fine/studio arts; fish/game management; food science; foods, nutrition, and wellness; forest engineering; forestry; French; geography; geological/geophysical engineering; geology/earth science; geophysics and seismology; German; health/health care administration; health science; history; history and philosophy of science and technology; horticultural science; human development and family studies; industrial engineering; information science/studies; interdisciplinary studies; interior design; international business/trade/commerce; international relations and affairs; kindergarten/preschool education; kinesiology and exercise science; landscaping and groundskeeping; liberal arts and sciences/liberal studies; literature; management information systems; marine science/merchant marine officer; marketing/marketing management; mass communication/media; materials science; mathematics; mechanical engineering; medical microbiology and bacteriology; metallurgical engineering; mining and mineral engineering; music; natural resources management and policy; nuclear engineering; occupational safety and health technology; parks, recreation and leisure; parks, recreation and leisure facilities management; pharmacy; philosophy; physical education teaching and coaching; physical sciences; physics; political science and government; pre-dentistry studies; pre-medical studies; pre-veterinary studies; psychology; public health; range science and management; sociology; Spanish; special products marketing; speech and rhetoric; technical and business writing; wildlife and wildlands science and management; wood science and wood products/pulp and paper technology; zoology/animal biology.

Academic Programs *Special study options:* academic remediation for entering students, advanced placement credit, cooperative education, distance learning, double majors, English as a second language, freshman honors college, honors programs, internships, off-campus study, part-time degree program, services for LD students, student-designed majors, study abroad, summer session for credit. *ROTC:* Army (b), Air Force (b).

Library Valley Library with 689,119 titles, 12,254 serial subscriptions, 6,225 audiovisual materials, an OPAC, a Web page.

Computers on Campus 2251 computers available on campus for general student use. A campuswide network can be accessed from student residence rooms and from off campus. Internet access, online (class) registration, at least one staffed computer lab available.

Student Life *Housing options:* coed, cooperative, disabled students. Campus housing is university owned. *Activities and organizations:* drama/theater group, student-run newspaper, radio and television station, choral group, marching band, Associated Students of OSU, International Students of OSU, Graduate Students Organization, Campus Crusade, MECHA, national fraternities, national sororities. *Campus security:* 24-hour emergency response devices and patrols, student patrols, late-night transport/escort service, controlled dormitory access, crime prevention office. *Student services:* health clinic, personal/psychological counseling, women's center, legal services.

Athletics Member NCAA. All Division I except football (Division I-A). *Intercollegiate sports:* baseball M(s), basketball M(s)/W(s), crew M/W, golf M(s)/W(s), gymnastics W(s), soccer M(s)/W(s), softball W(s), swimming W(s), volleyball W(s), wrestling M(s). *Intramural sports:* archery M/W, badminton M/W, basketball M/W, bowling M/W, crew M/W, cross-country running M/W, equestrian sports M(c)/W(c), fencing M(c)/W(c), football M, golf M/W, lacrosse M(c)/W(c), racquetball M/W, riflery M(c)/W(c), rugby M(c)/W(c), sailing M(c)/W(c), skiing (cross-country) M(c)/W(c), skiing (downhill) M(c)/W(c), soccer M/W, softball M/W, squash M(c), swimming M/W, table tennis M(c)/W(c), tennis M/W, track and field M/W, volleyball M/W, water polo M/W, wrestling M.

Standardized Tests *Required:* SAT I or ACT (for admission). *Required for some:* SAT II: Subject Tests (for admission).

Costs (2003–04) *Tuition:* state resident $3642 full-time, $97 per credit part-time; nonresident $16,398 full-time, $451 per credit part-time. Part-time tuition and fees vary according to course load. *Required fees:* $1227 full-time. *Room and board:* $6336. Room and board charges vary according to board plan and housing facility. *Payment plan:* deferred payment.

Financial Aid *Financial aid deadline:* 5/1.

Applying *Options:* common application, electronic application, early admission, early action, deferred entrance. *Application fee:* $50. *Required:* high school transcript, minimum 3.0 GPA. *Application deadlines:* 3/1 (freshmen), 5/1 (transfers). *Notification:* continuous (freshmen), continuous (transfers).

Admissions Contact Ms. Michele Sandlin, Director of Admissions, Oregon State University, Corvallis, OR 97331. *Phone:* 541-737-4411. *Toll-free phone:* 800-291-4192. *E-mail:* osuadmit@orst.edu.

■ *See page 2136 for a narrative description.*

PACIFIC NORTHWEST COLLEGE OF ART
Portland, Oregon

- **Independent** 4-year, founded 1909
- **Calendar** semesters
- **Degree** certificates and bachelor's
- **Urban** 2-acre campus
- **Endowment** $2.8 million
- **Coed,** 308 undergraduate students, 87% full-time, 53% women, 47% men
- **Moderately difficult** entrance level, 91% of applicants were admitted

Undergraduates 268 full-time, 40 part-time. Students come from 20 states and territories, 4 other countries, 20% are from out of state, 1% African American, 6% Asian American or Pacific Islander, 3% Hispanic American, 1% Native American, 1% international, 22% transferred in. *Retention:* 63% of 2002 full-time freshmen returned.

Freshmen *Admission:* 91 applied, 83 admitted, 30 enrolled. *Average high school GPA:* 3.13. *Test scores:* SAT verbal scores over 500: 59%; SAT math scores over 500: 50%; ACT scores over 18: 65%; SAT verbal scores over 600: 17%; SAT math scores over 600: 33%.

Faculty *Total:* 53, 26% full-time, 47% with terminal degrees. *Student/faculty ratio:* 12:1.

Majors Graphic design; illustration; intermedia/multimedia; painting; photography; printmaking; sculpture.

Academic Programs *Special study options:* adult/continuing education programs, advanced placement credit, cooperative education, independent study, internships, off-campus study, part-time degree program, services for LD students, student-designed majors, study abroad, summer session for credit.

Library Charles Vorhies Fine Arts Library plus 1 other with 12,716 titles, 65 serial subscriptions, 62,300 audiovisual materials, an OPAC, a Web page.

Computers on Campus 60 computers available on campus for general student use. A campuswide network can be accessed from off campus. Internet access, at least one staffed computer lab available.

Student Life *Housing:* college housing not available. *Campus security:* entrance security guards during open hours. *Student services:* personal/psychological counseling.

Costs (2003–04) *Tuition:* $14,270 full-time, $615 per semester hour part-time. Part-time tuition and fees vary according to course load. *Required fees:* $530 full-time, $157 per term part-time. *Payment plan:* installment. *Waivers:* employees or children of employees.

Financial Aid Of all full-time matriculated undergraduates who enrolled in 2001, 257 applied for aid, 257 were judged to have need, 23 had their need fully met. 26 Federal Work-Study jobs (averaging $1200). 21 state and other part-time jobs (averaging $1200). In 2001, 7 non-need-based awards were made. *Average percent of need met:* 72%. *Average financial aid package:* $6240. *Average need-based loan:* $5320. *Average need-based gift aid:* $3856. *Average non-need-based aid:* $1245. *Average indebtedness upon graduation:* $18,917.

Applying *Options:* common application, electronic application, deferred entrance. *Application fee:* $35. *Required:* essay or personal statement, high school transcript, minimum 2.5 GPA, 1 letter of recommendation, portfolio of artwork. *Recommended:* interview.

Admissions Contact Ms. Rebecca Haas, Director of Admissions, Pacific Northwest College of Art, 1241 NW Johnson Street, Portland, OR 97209. *Phone:* 503-821-8972. *Fax:* 503-821-8972. *E-mail:* admissions@pnca.edu.

PACIFIC UNIVERSITY
Forest Grove, Oregon

- **Independent** comprehensive, founded 1849
- **Calendar** 4-1-4
- **Degrees** bachelor's, master's, doctoral, and first professional
- **Small-town** 55-acre campus with easy access to Portland
- **Endowment** $31.7 million
- **Coed,** 1,203 undergraduate students, 93% full-time, 61% women, 39% men
- **Moderately difficult** entrance level, 84% of applicants were admitted

Undergraduates 1,113 full-time, 90 part-time. Students come from 35 states and territories, 6 other countries, 47% are from out of state, 0.9% African American, 19% Asian American or Pacific Islander, 3% Hispanic American, 0.9% Native American, 0.4% international, 6% transferred in, 64% live on campus. *Retention:* 81% of 2002 full-time freshmen returned.

Freshmen *Admission:* 1,214 applied, 1,020 admitted, 303 enrolled. *Average high school GPA:* 3.55. *Test scores:* SAT verbal scores over 500: 78%; SAT math scores over 500: 79%; ACT scores over 18: 96%; SAT verbal scores over 600: 32%; SAT math scores over 600: 31%; ACT scores over 24: 51%; SAT verbal scores over 700: 1%; SAT math scores over 700: 3%; ACT scores over 30: 6%.

Pacific University (continued)

Faculty *Total:* 140, 60% full-time, 62% with terminal degrees. *Student/faculty ratio:* 11:1.

Majors Accounting; art; art teacher education; athletic training; biology/biological sciences; broadcast journalism; business administration and management; chemistry; Chinese; computer science; creative writing; dramatic/theatre arts; economics; education; elementary education; English; environmental studies; finance; French; German; health science; history; humanities; international relations and affairs; Japanese; journalism; kindergarten/preschool education; kinesiology and exercise science; liberal arts and sciences/liberal studies; literature; marketing/marketing management; mass communication/media; mathematics; modern languages; music; music teacher education; philosophy; physics; political science and government; pre-dentistry studies; pre-medical studies; psychology; radio and television; secondary education; social work; sociology; Spanish; telecommunications.

Academic Programs *Special study options:* accelerated degree program, advanced placement credit, double majors, English as a second language, honors programs, independent study, internships, off-campus study, services for LD students, study abroad, summer session for credit. *ROTC:* Army (c), Air Force (c). *Unusual degree programs:* 3-2 engineering with Washington State University, Washington University in St. Louis, Oregon Graduate Institute of Science and Technology, Oregon State University; medical technology, computer science, environmental science with Oregon Graduate Institute of Science and Technology.

Library Scott Memorial Library with 244,691 titles, 1,180 serial subscriptions, 5,715 audiovisual materials, an OPAC, a Web page.

Computers on Campus 150 computers available on campus for general student use. A campuswide network can be accessed from student residence rooms and from off campus that provide access to email, web space. Internet access, at least one staffed computer lab available. Computer purchase or lease plan available.

Student Life *Housing:* on-campus residence required through sophomore year. *Options:* coed, disabled students. Freshman campus housing is guaranteed. *Activities and organizations:* drama/theater group, student-run newspaper, radio station, choral group, Pacific Outback activities, Hawaiian club, Big Buddy Program, business and economics club, exercise science club. *Campus security:* 24-hour emergency response devices and patrols, late-night transport/escort service. *Student services:* health clinic, personal/psychological counseling.

Athletics Member NCAA. All Division III. *Intercollegiate sports:* baseball M, basketball M/W, cross-country running M/W, golf M/W, soccer M/W, softball W, swimming M(c)/W, tennis M/W, track and field M/W, volleyball M(c)/W, wrestling M/W. *Intramural sports:* basketball M/W, golf M/W, racquetball M/W, soccer M/W, softball M/W, tennis M/W, volleyball M/W.

Standardized Tests *Required:* SAT I or ACT (for admission).

Costs (2003–04) *Comprehensive fee:* $25,430 includes full-time tuition ($19,330), mandatory fees ($560), and room and board ($5540). Part-time tuition and fees vary according to course load. *College room only:* $2680. Room and board charges vary according to board plan and housing facility. *Payment plans:* installment, deferred payment. *Waivers:* employees or children of employees.

Financial Aid Of all full-time matriculated undergraduates who enrolled in 2003, 1,086 applied for aid, 848 were judged to have need, 398 had their need fully met. 593 Federal Work-Study jobs (averaging $1708). 167 state and other part-time jobs (averaging $1534). In 2003, 205 non-need-based awards were made. *Average percent of need met:* 89%. *Average financial aid package:* $17,369. *Average need-based loan:* $4892. *Average need-based gift aid:* $11,834. *Average non-need-based aid:* $8259. *Average indebtedness upon graduation:* $21,465.

Applying *Options:* common application, electronic application, deferred entrance. *Application fee:* $30. *Required:* essay or personal statement, high school transcript, minimum 3.0 GPA, 1 letter of recommendation. *Recommended:* interview. *Application deadlines:* 8/15 (freshmen), 8/15 (transfers). *Notification:* continuous (freshmen), continuous (transfers).

Admissions Contact Mr. Ian Symmonds, Executive Director of Admissions, Pacific University, 2043 College Way, Forest Grove, OR 97116-1797. *Phone:* 503-352-2218. *Toll-free phone:* 877-722-8648. *Fax:* 503-352-2975. *E-mail:* admissions@pacificu.edu.

■ *See page 2146 for a narrative description.*

PIONEER PACIFIC COLLEGE
Wilsonville, Oregon

- **Proprietary** primarily 2-year, founded 1981
- **Calendar** continuous
- **Degrees** diplomas, associate, and bachelor's
- **Suburban** campus with easy access to Portland
- **Coed**
- **Noncompetitive** entrance level

Faculty *Student/faculty ratio:* 15:1.

Standardized Tests *Required:* CPAt (for admission).

Costs (2004–05) *Tuition:* $7200 full-time, $160 per credit hour part-time. *Required fees:* $150 full-time.

Applying *Application fee:* $50. *Required:* high school transcript, interview.

Admissions Contact Pioneer Pacific College, 27501 Southwest Parkway Avenue, Wilsonville, OR 97070. *Phone:* 503-682-3903. *Toll-free phone:* 866-772-4636. *Fax:* 503-682-1514. *E-mail:* inquiries@pioneerpacific.edu.

PORTLAND STATE UNIVERSITY
Portland, Oregon

- **State-supported** university, founded 1946, part of Oregon University System
- **Calendar** quarters
- **Degrees** certificates, bachelor's, master's, doctoral, and postbachelor's certificates
- **Urban** 49-acre campus
- **Endowment** $17.1 million
- **Coed,** 16,906 undergraduate students, 62% full-time, 54% women, 46% men
- **Minimally difficult** entrance level, 85% of applicants were admitted

Undergraduates 10,401 full-time, 6,505 part-time. Students come from 47 states and territories, 67 other countries, 13% are from out of state, 3% African American, 10% Asian American or Pacific Islander, 4% Hispanic American, 1% Native American, 3% international, 15% transferred in, 10% live on campus. *Retention:* 65% of 2002 full-time freshmen returned.

Freshmen *Admission:* 3,344 applied, 2,832 admitted, 1,538 enrolled. *Average high school GPA:* 3.16. *Test scores:* SAT verbal scores over 500: 59%; SAT math scores over 500: 61%; ACT scores over 18: 82%; SAT verbal scores over 600: 20%; SAT math scores over 600: 20%; ACT scores over 24: 31%; SAT verbal scores over 700: 3%; SAT math scores over 700: 2%; ACT scores over 30: 2%.

Faculty *Total:* 1,138, 57% full-time. *Student/faculty ratio:* 20:1.

Majors Accounting; advertising; African studies; American Indian/Native American studies; anthropology; applied art; architecture; art; art history, criticism and conservation; Asian studies (East); biochemistry; biological and physical sciences; biology/biological sciences; business administration and management; chemistry; child development; Chinese; city/urban, community and regional planning; civil engineering; commercial and advertising art; computer and information sciences; computer engineering; computer science; criminal justice/law enforcement administration; dramatic/theatre arts; drawing; economics; electrical, electronics and communications engineering; English; environmental studies; European studies (Central and Eastern); finance; French; geography; geology/earth science; German; health teacher education; history; humanities; human resources management; international relations and affairs; Japanese; Latin American studies; liberal arts and sciences/liberal studies; linguistics; logistics and materials management; marketing/marketing management; mathematics; mechanical engineering; music; Near and Middle Eastern studies; philosophy; physics; political science and government; psychology; Russian; sculpture; social sciences; sociology; Spanish; speech and rhetoric; urban studies/affairs; women's studies.

Academic Programs *Special study options:* academic remediation for entering students, accelerated degree program, adult/continuing education programs, advanced placement credit, cooperative education, distance learning, double majors, English as a second language, honors programs, independent study, internships, off-campus study, part-time degree program, services for LD students, student-designed majors, study abroad, summer session for credit. *ROTC:* Army (b), Air Force (c).

Library Branford P. Millar Library with 1.8 million titles, 8,698 serial subscriptions, 91,912 audiovisual materials, an OPAC, a Web page.

Computers on Campus 425 computers available on campus for general student use. A campuswide network can be accessed from student residence rooms and from off campus. Internet access, online (class) registration, at least one staffed computer lab available.

Student Life *Housing options:* coed, disabled students. Campus housing is provided by a third party. Freshman applicants given priority for college housing. *Activities and organizations:* drama/theater group, student-run newspaper, radio station, choral group, radio station, Women's Union, Association of African Students, Queers and Allies, OSPERG, national fraternities, national sororities. *Campus security:* 24-hour emergency response devices and patrols, late-night transport/escort service, controlled dormitory access, self-defense education. *Student services:* health clinic, personal/psychological counseling, women's center, legal services.

Athletics Member NCAA. All Division I except football (Division I-AA). *Intercollegiate sports:* baseball M(s), basketball M(s)/W(s), cross-country running M(s)/W(s), golf M(s)/W(s), soccer W(s), softball W(s), tennis M(s)/W(s), track and field M(s)/W(s), volleyball W(s), wrestling M(s). *Intramural sports:* archery M/W, basketball M/W, bowling M(c)/W(c), crew M(c)/W(c), fencing M(c)/W(c), football M, golf M/W, racquetball M/W, sailing M(c)/W(c), skiing (downhill) M(c)/W(c), soccer M(c)/W, softball M/W, table tennis M(c)/W(c), tennis M(c)/W(c), volleyball M/W, water polo M(c)/W(c).

Standardized Tests *Required:* SAT I or ACT (for admission).

Costs (2003–04) *Tuition:* state resident $3240 full-time, $107 per credit part-time; nonresident $12,636 full-time, $107 per credit part-time. Part-time tuition and fees vary according to course load. *Required fees:* $1038 full-time, $17 per credit part-time, $35 per term part-time. *Room and board:* $8175; room only: $6075. Room and board charges vary according to board plan and housing facility. *Payment plans:* installment, deferred payment. *Waivers:* minority students, senior citizens, and employees or children of employees.

Financial Aid Of all full-time matriculated undergraduates who enrolled in 2002, 6,003 applied for aid, 4,983 were judged to have need, 895 had their need fully met. 696 Federal Work-Study jobs (averaging $3476). In 2002, 246 non-need-based awards were made. *Average percent of need met:* 67%. *Average financial aid package:* $7712. *Average need-based loan:* $6982. *Average need-based gift aid:* $3755. *Average non-need-based aid:* $2378. *Average indebtedness upon graduation:* $17,456.

Applying *Options:* electronic application, early admission, deferred entrance. *Application fee:* $50. *Required:* high school transcript, minimum 3.0 GPA. *Application deadline:* rolling (freshmen), rolling (transfers). *Notification:* continuous (freshmen), continuous (transfers).

Admissions Contact Ms. Agnes A. Hoffman, Director of Admissions and Records, Portland State University, PO Box 751, Portland, OR 97207-0751. *Phone:* 503-725-3511. *Toll-free phone:* 800-547-8887. *Fax:* 503-725-5525. *E-mail:* admissions@pdx.edu.

REED COLLEGE
Portland, Oregon

- **Independent** comprehensive, founded 1908
- **Calendar** semesters
- **Degrees** bachelor's and master's
- **Suburban** 98-acre campus
- **Endowment** $295.5 million
- **Coed,** 1,312 undergraduate students, 96% full-time, 54% women, 46% men
- **Most difficult** entrance level, 46% of applicants were admitted

Undergraduates 1,266 full-time, 46 part-time. Students come from 49 states and territories, 38 other countries, 82% are from out of state, 0.9% African American, 5% Asian American or Pacific Islander, 4% Hispanic American, 1% Native American, 3% international, 2% transferred in, 65% live on campus. *Retention:* 87% of 2002 full-time freshmen returned.

Freshmen *Admission:* 2,282 applied, 1,044 admitted, 301 enrolled. *Average high school GPA:* 3.80. *Test scores:* SAT verbal scores over 500: 99%; SAT math scores over 500: 99%; ACT scores over 18: 100%; SAT verbal scores over 600: 93%; SAT math scores over 600: 84%; ACT scores over 24: 99%; SAT verbal scores over 700: 55%; SAT math scores over 700: 31%; ACT scores over 30: 60%.

Faculty *Total:* 133, 90% full-time, 86% with terminal degrees. *Student/faculty ratio:* 10:1.

Majors American studies; anthropology; art; biochemistry; biology/biological sciences; chemistry; Chinese; classics and languages, literatures and linguistics; dance; dramatic/theatre arts; economics; English; fine/studio arts; French; German; history; international relations and affairs; linguistics; literature; mathematics; music; philosophy; physics; political science and government; psychology; religious studies; Russian; sociology; Spanish.

Academic Programs *Special study options:* accelerated degree program, advanced placement credit, double majors, independent study, off-campus study, part-time degree program, services for LD students, study abroad. *Unusual degree programs:* 3-2 engineering with California Institute of Technology, Rensselaer Polytechnic Institute, Columbia University; forestry with Duke University; computer science with University of Washington; studio art with Pacific Northwest College of Art; applied physics, electronic science with Oregon Graduate Institute.

Library Hauser Library with 5.0 million titles, 2,300 serial subscriptions, 16,596 audiovisual materials, an OPAC, a Web page.

Computers on Campus 324 computers available on campus for general student use. A campuswide network can be accessed from student residence rooms and from off campus. Internet access, online (class) registration, at least one staffed computer lab available. Computer purchase or lease plan available.

Student Life *Housing:* on-campus residence required for freshman year. *Options:* coed, women-only, cooperative, disabled students. Campus housing is university owned. Freshman campus housing is guaranteed. *Activities and organizations:* drama/theater group, student-run newspaper, radio station, choral group, Reed Recycling, movie board, outdoor club. *Campus security:* 24-hour emergency response devices and patrols, student patrols, late-night transport/escort service, controlled dormitory access, 24-hour emergency dispatch. *Student services:* health clinic, personal/psychological counseling, women's center.

Athletics *Intercollegiate sports:* basketball M(c), crew M(c)/W(c), fencing M(c)/W(c), rock climbing M(c)/W(c), sailing M(c)/W(c), skiing (downhill) M(c)/W(c), soccer M(c)/W(c), squash M(c)/W(c), weight lifting M(c)/W(c). *Intramural sports:* archery M/W, badminton M/W, basketball M/W, racquetball M/W, skiing (downhill) M/W, soccer M/W, softball M/W, squash M/W, swimming M/W, tennis M/W, ultimate Frisbee M/W, volleyball M/W, weight lifting M/W.

Standardized Tests *Required:* SAT I or ACT (for admission). *Recommended:* SAT II: Subject Tests (for admission), SAT II: Writing Test (for admission).

Costs (2003–04) *Comprehensive fee:* $36,950 includes full-time tuition ($29,000), mandatory fees ($200), and room and board ($7750). Full-time tuition and fees vary according to degree level. Part-time tuition: $4900 per course. Part-time tuition and fees vary according to course load and degree level. *College room only:* $4020. Room and board charges vary according to board plan and housing facility. *Payment plan:* installment. *Waivers:* employees or children of employees.

Financial Aid Of all full-time matriculated undergraduates who enrolled in 2003, 846 applied for aid, 686 were judged to have need, 649 had their need fully met. 478 Federal Work-Study jobs (averaging $677). 29 state and other part-time jobs (averaging $674). *Average percent of need met:* 100%. *Average financial aid package:* $24,309. *Average need-based loan:* $4119. *Average need-based gift aid:* $20,880. *Average indebtedness upon graduation:* $13,692. *Financial aid deadline:* 2/1.

Applying *Options:* common application, electronic application, early admission, early decision, deferred entrance. *Application fee:* $40. *Required:* essay or personal statement, high school transcript, 2 letters of recommendation. *Recommended:* minimum 3.0 GPA, interview. *Application deadlines:* 1/15 (freshmen), 3/1 (transfers). *Early decision:* 11/15 (for plan 1), 1/2 (for plan 2). *Notification:* 4/1 (freshmen), 12/15 (early decision plan 1), 2/1 (early decision plan 2), 5/1 (transfers).

Admissions Contact Mr. Paul Marthers, Dean of Admission, Reed College, 3203 Southeast Woodstock Boulevard, Portland, OR 97202-8199. *Phone:* 503-777-7511. *Toll-free phone:* 800-547-4750. *Fax:* 503-777-7553. *E-mail:* admission@reed.edu.

■ *See page 2218 for a narrative description.*

SOUTHERN OREGON UNIVERSITY
Ashland, Oregon

- **State-supported** comprehensive, founded 1926, part of Oregon University System
- **Calendar** quarters
- **Degrees** bachelor's, master's, and postbachelor's certificates
- **Small-town** 175-acre campus
- **Endowment** $10.3 million
- **Coed,** 4,964 undergraduate students, 78% full-time, 55% women, 45% men
- **Moderately difficult** entrance level, 90% of applicants were admitted

Undergraduates 3,863 full-time, 1,101 part-time. Students come from 45 states and territories, 33 other countries, 20% are from out of state, 0.9% African American, 4% Asian American or Pacific Islander, 4% Hispanic American, 2% Native American, 2% international, 10% transferred in, 25% live on campus. *Retention:* 69% of 2002 full-time freshmen returned.

Freshmen *Admission:* 2,176 applied, 1,960 admitted, 968 enrolled. *Average high school GPA:* 3.18. *Test scores:* SAT verbal scores over 500: 61%; SAT math scores over 500: 59%; ACT scores over 18: 89%; SAT verbal scores over 600: 22%; SAT math scores over 600: 17%; ACT scores over 24: 29%; SAT verbal scores over 700: 3%; SAT math scores over 700: 2%; ACT scores over 30: 2%.

Faculty *Total:* 337, 56% full-time. *Student/faculty ratio:* 19:1.

Majors Accounting; anthropology; art; biochemistry; biology/biological sciences; business administration and management; business statistics; chemistry; communication/speech communication and rhetoric; computer science; criminology; dramatic/theatre arts; economics; English; environmental studies; French; geography; geology/earth science; German; health teacher education; history; hotel/motel administration; interdisciplinary studies; international relations and affairs; liberal arts and sciences/liberal studies; marketing/marketing management; mathematics; mathematics and computer science; music; music management and merchandising; nursing (registered nurse training); physical education teaching and coaching; physics; political science and government; pre-law studies; pre-medical studies; psychology; social sciences; sociology; Spanish.

Academic Programs *Special study options:* academic remediation for entering students, accelerated degree program, adult/continuing education programs,

Southern Oregon University (continued)
advanced placement credit, cooperative education, distance learning, double majors, English as a second language, freshman honors college, honors programs, independent study, internships, off-campus study, part-time degree program, services for LD students, student-designed majors, study abroad, summer session for credit.

Library Southern Oregon University Library with 272,319 titles, 2,040 serial subscriptions, 20,241 audiovisual materials, an OPAC, a Web page.

Computers on Campus 400 computers available on campus for general student use. A campuswide network can be accessed. At least one staffed computer lab available.

Student Life *Housing:* on-campus residence required for freshman year. *Options:* coed, disabled students. Campus housing is university owned. *Activities and organizations:* drama/theater group, student-run newspaper, radio and television station, choral group, Native American Student Union, International Student Association, Impact (religious club), Ho'opa'a Hawaii Club, Omicron Delta Kappa. *Campus security:* 24-hour emergency response devices and patrols, student patrols, late-night transport/escort service. *Student services:* health clinic, personal/psychological counseling, women's center, legal services.

Athletics Member NAIA. *Intercollegiate sports:* basketball M(s)/W(s), cross-country running M(s)/W(s), football M(s), skiing (downhill) M/W, soccer W(s), softball W(s), tennis W(s), track and field M(s)/W(s), volleyball W(s), wrestling M(s). *Intramural sports:* basketball M/W, bowling M/W, cheerleading M/W, crew M/W, football M/W, golf M/W, racquetball M/W, rugby M/W, sailing M/W, skiing (cross-country) M/W, soccer M/W, softball M/W, swimming M/W, table tennis M/W, tennis M/W, track and field M/W, ultimate Frisbee M/W, volleyball M/W, water polo M/W.

Standardized Tests *Required:* SAT I or ACT (for admission). *Required for some:* SAT II: Subject Tests (for admission).

Costs (2003–04) *Tuition:* state resident $3138 full-time; nonresident $11,808 full-time. Full-time tuition and fees vary according to course load, location, and reciprocity agreements. Part-time tuition and fees vary according to course load, location, and reciprocity agreements. *Required fees:* $1015 full-time. *Room and board:* $6039. Room and board charges vary according to board plan and housing facility. *Payment plan:* deferred payment. *Waivers:* senior citizens and employees or children of employees.

Financial Aid Of all full-time matriculated undergraduates who enrolled in 2002, 4,282 applied for aid, 3,913 were judged to have need, 221 had their need fully met. 410 Federal Work-Study jobs (averaging $830). In 2002, 370 non-need-based awards were made. *Average percent of need met:* 44%. *Average financial aid package:* $5118. *Average need-based loan:* $3703. *Average need-based gift aid:* $3652. *Average non-need-based aid:* $7237. *Average indebtedness upon graduation:* $14,617.

Applying *Options:* common application, early admission, deferred entrance. *Application fee:* $50. *Required:* high school transcript, 2.75 high school GPA or minimum SAT score of 1010. *Application deadline:* rolling (freshmen), rolling (transfers). *Notification:* continuous (freshmen), continuous (transfers).

Admissions Contact Ms. Mara A. Affre, Director of Admissions, Southern Oregon University, 1250 Siskiyou Boulevard, Ashland, OR 97520. *Phone:* 541-552-6411. *Toll-free phone:* 800-482-7672. *Fax:* 541-552-6614. *E-mail:* admissions@sou.edu.

■ *See page 2414 for a narrative description.*

UNIVERSITY OF OREGON
Eugene, Oregon

- **State-supported** university, founded 1872, part of Oregon University System
- **Calendar** quarters
- **Degrees** bachelor's, master's, doctoral, and first professional
- **Urban** 295-acre campus
- **Endowment** $234.8 million
- **Coed,** 15,983 undergraduate students, 90% full-time, 53% women, 47% men
- **Moderately difficult** entrance level, 84% of applicants were admitted

Undergraduates 14,452 full-time, 1,531 part-time. Students come from 54 states and territories, 86 other countries, 24% are from out of state, 2% African American, 6% Asian American or Pacific Islander, 3% Hispanic American, 1% Native American, 5% international, 9% transferred in, 21% live on campus. *Retention:* 83% of 2002 full-time freshmen returned.

Freshmen *Admission:* 10,193 applied, 8,602 admitted, 2,865 enrolled. *Average high school GPA:* 3.54. *Test scores:* SAT verbal scores over 500: 74%; SAT math scores over 500: 77%; SAT verbal scores over 600: 30%; SAT math scores over 600: 33%; SAT verbal scores over 700: 5%; SAT math scores over 700: 5%.

Faculty *Total:* 1,131, 70% full-time, 94% with terminal degrees. *Student/faculty ratio:* 19:1.

Majors Accounting; advertising; anthropology; applied art; architecture; art; art history, criticism and conservation; Asian studies; Asian studies (East); audiology and speech-language pathology; biochemistry; biological and physical sciences; biology/biological sciences; broadcast journalism; business administration and management; ceramic arts and ceramics; chemistry; Chinese; city/urban, community and regional planning; classics and languages, literatures and linguistics; commercial and advertising art; community organization and advocacy; comparative literature; computer and information sciences; computer science; cultural studies; dance; dramatic/theatre arts; drawing; East Asian languages; economics; education; educational leadership and administration; English; environmental science; environmental studies; ethnic, cultural minority, and gender studies related; European studies (Central and Eastern); fiber, textile and weaving arts; finance; fine/studio arts; folklore; French; geography; geology/earth science; German; Hebrew; history; humanities; human services; interior architecture; interior design; intermedia/multimedia; international business/trade/commerce; international relations and affairs; Italian; Japanese; jazz/jazz studies; Jewish/Judaic studies; journalism; kinesiology and exercise science; landscape architecture; Latin; liberal arts and sciences/liberal studies; linguistics; marketing/marketing management; mass communication/media; mathematics; mathematics and computer science; metal and jewelry arts; modern Greek; music; musicology and ethnomusicology; music performance; music teacher education; painting; philosophy; photography; physics; political science and government; pre-dentistry studies; pre-medical studies; printmaking; psychology; public administration; public policy analysis; public relations/image management; radio and television; religious studies; Romance languages; Russian; sculpture; sociology; Spanish; statistics; voice and opera; women's studies.

Academic Programs *Special study options:* academic remediation for entering students, accelerated degree program, adult/continuing education programs, advanced placement credit, distance learning, double majors, English as a second language, freshman honors college, honors programs, independent study, internships, off-campus study, part-time degree program, services for LD students, student-designed majors, study abroad, summer session for credit. *ROTC:* Army (b), Air Force (c). *Unusual degree programs:* 3-2 engineering with Oregon State University; nursing with Oregon Health Sciences University.

Library Knight Library plus 6 others with 2.5 million titles, 17,840 serial subscriptions, 1.2 million audiovisual materials, an OPAC, a Web page.

Computers on Campus 1250 computers available on campus for general student use. A campuswide network can be accessed from student residence rooms and from off campus. Internet access, online (class) registration, at least one staffed computer lab available.

Student Life *Housing options:* coed, men-only, women-only, disabled students. Campus housing is university owned. Freshman applicants given priority for college housing. *Activities and organizations:* drama/theater group, student-run newspaper, radio station, choral group, marching band, Political and Environment Action, cultural organizations, student newspaper, Frat Council/Panhellenic, club sports, national fraternities, national sororities. *Campus security:* 24-hour emergency response devices and patrols, student patrols, late-night transport/escort service, controlled dormitory access. *Student services:* health clinic, personal/psychological counseling, women's center, legal services.

Athletics Member NCAA. All Division I except football (Division I-A). *Intercollegiate sports:* badminton M(c)/W(c), basketball M(s)/W(s), bowling M(c)/W(c), cheerleading M(c)/W(c), crew M(c)/W(c), cross-country running M(s)/W(s), fencing M(c)/W(c), field hockey W(c), golf M(s)/W(s), ice hockey M(c)/W(c), lacrosse M(c)/W(c), racquetball M(c)/W(c), rugby M(c), sailing M(c)/W(c), skiing (cross-country) M(c)/W(c), skiing (downhill) M(c)/W(c), soccer M(c)/W(s), softball W(s), squash M(c)/W(c), swimming M(c)/W(c), table tennis M(c)/W(c), tennis M(s)/W(s), track and field M(s)/W(s), volleyball M(c)/W(s), water polo M(c)/W(c), wrestling M(s). *Intramural sports:* badminton M/W, basketball M/W, bowling M/W, crew M/W, cross-country running M/W, fencing M/W, field hockey W, football M, golf M/W, gymnastics M/W, ice hockey M/W, lacrosse M/W, racquetball M/W, rugby M, sailing M/W, skiing (cross-country) M/W, skiing (downhill) M/W, soccer M/W, softball W, squash M/W, swimming M/W, tennis M/W, track and field M/W, ultimate Frisbee M(c)/W(c), volleyball M/W, water polo M/W, weight lifting M/W, wrestling M.

Standardized Tests *Required:* SAT I or ACT (for admission).

Costs (2003–04) *Tuition:* state resident $3543 full-time, $92 per credit hour part-time; nonresident $14,979 full-time, $393 per credit hour part-time. Part-time tuition and fees vary according to course load. *Required fees:* $1371 full-time, $305 per credit hour part-time. *Room and board:* $6981. Room and board charges vary according to board plan and housing facility. *Payment plan:* installment. *Waivers:* minority students and employees or children of employees.

Financial Aid Of all full-time matriculated undergraduates who enrolled in 2003, 8,794 applied for aid, 6,596 were judged to have need, 1,993 had their need fully met. In 2003, 816 non-need-based awards were made. *Average percent of need met:* 77%. *Average financial aid package:* $8054. *Average need-based loan:*

$4243. *Average need-based gift aid:* $3779. *Average non-need-based aid:* $1753. *Average indebtedness upon graduation:* $17,111.

Applying *Options:* electronic application, early admission. *Application fee:* $50. *Required:* high school transcript, minimum 3.25 GPA. *Required for some:* essay or personal statement, 2 letters of recommendation. *Application deadlines:* 1/15 (freshmen), 5/15 (transfers). *Notification:* 3/15 (freshmen), continuous (transfers).

Admissions Contact Ms. Martha Pitts, Assistant Vice President for Enrollment Services and Director of Admissions, University of Oregon, Eugene, OR 97403. *Phone:* 541-346-3201. *Toll-free phone:* 800-232-3825. *Fax:* 541-346-5815. *E-mail:* uoadmit@uoregon.edu.

■ *See page 2680 for a narrative description.*

UNIVERSITY OF PHOENIX–OREGON CAMPUS

Portland, Oregon

- **Proprietary** comprehensive, founded 1976
- **Calendar** continuous
- **Degrees** certificates, associate, bachelor's, master's, doctoral, post-master's, and postbachelor's certificates (courses conducted at 121 campuses and learning centers in 25 states)
- **Urban** campus
- **Coed,** 1,241 undergraduate students, 100% full-time, 44% women, 56% men
- **Noncompetitive** entrance level

Undergraduates 1,241 full-time. 2% African American, 3% Asian American or Pacific Islander, 2% Hispanic American, 0.7% Native American, 2% international.

Freshmen *Admission:* 30 enrolled.

Faculty *Total:* 355, 1% full-time, 18% with terminal degrees. *Student/faculty ratio:* 7:1.

Majors Accounting; business administration and management; information technology; management information systems; management science; marketing/marketing management; public administration and social service professions related.

Academic Programs *Special study options:* accelerated degree program, adult/continuing education programs, advanced placement credit, distance learning, external degree program, independent study.

Library University Library with 27.1 million titles, 11,648 serial subscriptions, an OPAC, a Web page.

Computers on Campus A campuswide network can be accessed from off campus. Internet access, at least one staffed computer lab available.

Student Life *Housing:* college housing not available.

Costs (2003–04) *Tuition:* $9540 full-time, $318 per credit part-time. *Waivers:* employees or children of employees.

Financial Aid *Average financial aid package:* $1243.

Applying *Options:* deferred entrance. *Application fee:* $85. *Required:* 1 letter of recommendation, 2 years of work experience, 23 years of age. *Required for some:* high school transcript. *Application deadline:* rolling (freshmen), rolling (transfers).

Admissions Contact Ms. Beth Barilla, Director of Admissions, University of Phoenix–Oregon Campus, 4615 East Elwood Street, Mail Stop AA-K101, Phoenix, AZ 85040-1958. *Phone:* 480-317*6000. *Toll-free phone:* 800-228-7240. *Fax:* 480-594-1758. *E-mail:* beth.barilla@phoenix.edu.

UNIVERSITY OF PORTLAND

Portland, Oregon

- **Independent Roman Catholic** comprehensive, founded 1901
- **Calendar** semesters
- **Degrees** bachelor's, master's, and post-master's certificates
- **Urban** 125-acre campus
- **Endowment** $72.7 million
- **Coed,** 2,739 undergraduate students, 96% full-time, 60% women, 40% men
- **Moderately difficult** entrance level, 72% of applicants were admitted

Undergraduates 2,629 full-time, 110 part-time. Students come from 42 states and territories, 19 other countries, 56% are from out of state, 2% African American, 10% Asian American or Pacific Islander, 3% Hispanic American, 0.4% Native American, 2% international, 4% transferred in, 59% live on campus. *Retention:* 84% of 2002 full-time freshmen returned.

Freshmen *Admission:* 2,964 applied, 2,136 admitted, 674 enrolled. *Average high school GPA:* 3.62. *Test scores:* SAT verbal scores over 500: 86%; SAT math scores over 500: 90%; SAT verbal scores over 600: 47%; SAT math scores over 600: 47%; SAT verbal scores over 700: 8%; SAT math scores over 700: 8%.

Faculty *Total:* 275, 64% full-time. *Student/faculty ratio:* 13:1.

Majors Accounting; arts management; biology/biological sciences; business administration and management; chemistry; civil engineering; computer engineering; computer science; criminal justice/safety; dramatic/theatre arts; education; electrical, electronics and communications engineering; elementary education; engineering; engineering/industrial management; engineering science; English; environmental studies; finance; history; interdisciplinary studies; international business/trade/commerce; journalism; marketing/marketing management; mass communication/media; mathematics; mechanical engineering; music; music teacher education; nursing (registered nurse training); philosophy; physics; political science and government; pre-dentistry studies; pre-law studies; pre-medical studies; psychology; secondary education; social work; sociology; Spanish; theology.

Academic Programs *Special study options:* adult/continuing education programs, advanced placement credit, double majors, honors programs, independent study, internships, off-campus study, part-time degree program, services for LD students, study abroad, summer session for credit. *ROTC:* Army (b), Air Force (b).

Library Wilson M. Clark Library plus 1 other with 350,000 titles, 1,400 serial subscriptions, 11,044 audiovisual materials, an OPAC, a Web page.

Computers on Campus 200 computers available on campus for general student use. A campuswide network can be accessed from student residence rooms and from off campus. Internet access, online (class) registration, at least one staffed computer lab available.

Student Life *Housing options:* coed, men-only, women-only. Campus housing is university owned. Freshman campus housing is guaranteed. *Activities and organizations:* drama/theater group, student-run newspaper, radio station, choral group, English Society, international club, Hawaiian club, rugby club, social science club. *Campus security:* 24-hour patrols, student patrols, late-night transport/escort service, controlled dormitory access. *Student services:* health clinic, personal/psychological counseling.

Athletics Member NCAA. All Division I. *Intercollegiate sports:* baseball M(s), basketball M(s)/W(s), cross-country running M(s)/W(s), golf M(s)/W(s), rugby M(c), soccer M(s)/W(s), tennis M(s)/W(s), track and field M(s)/W(s), volleyball W(s). *Intramural sports:* basketball M/W, crew M/W, cross-country running M/W, football M/W, rugby M, skiing (cross-country) M/W, skiing (downhill) M/W, soccer M(c)/W, softball M/W, swimming M/W, tennis M/W, track and field M/W, ultimate Frisbee M/W, volleyball M/W, water polo M/W, weight lifting M/W.

Standardized Tests *Required:* SAT I or ACT (for admission).

Costs (2003–04) *Comprehensive fee:* $28,810 includes full-time tuition ($21,800), mandatory fees ($340), and room and board ($6670). Full-time tuition and fees vary according to program. Part-time tuition: $690 per credit hour. Part-time tuition and fees vary according to program. *Room and board:* Room and board charges vary according to board plan and housing facility. *Payment plans:* installment, deferred payment. *Waivers:* employees or children of employees.

Financial Aid Of all full-time matriculated undergraduates who enrolled in 2003, 1,895 applied for aid, 1,555 were judged to have need, 511 had their need fully met. 994 Federal Work-Study jobs (averaging $1724). 31 state and other part-time jobs (averaging $1837). In 2003, 876 non-need-based awards were made. *Average percent of need met:* 83%. *Average financial aid package:* $19,304. *Average need-based loan:* $5213. *Average need-based gift aid:* $12,719. *Average non-need-based aid:* $16,102. *Average indebtedness upon graduation:* $18,909.

Applying *Options:* common application, electronic application, deferred entrance. *Application fee:* $45. *Required:* essay or personal statement, high school transcript, 1 letter of recommendation. *Application deadlines:* 6/1 (freshmen), 6/1 (transfers). *Notification:* continuous (freshmen), continuous (transfers).

Admissions Contact Mr. James C. Lyons, Dean of Admissions, University of Portland, 5000 North Willamette Boulevard, Portland, OR 97203. *Phone:* 503-943-7147. *Toll-free phone:* 888-627-5601. *Fax:* 503-943-7315. *E-mail:* admissio@up.edu.

WARNER PACIFIC COLLEGE

Portland, Oregon

- **Independent** comprehensive, founded 1937, affiliated with Church of God
- **Calendar** semesters
- **Degrees** associate, bachelor's, master's, and postbachelor's certificates
- **Urban** 15-acre campus
- **Coed,** 504 undergraduate students, 83% full-time, 61% women, 39% men
- **Moderately difficult** entrance level, 44% of applicants were admitted

Undergraduates 417 full-time, 87 part-time. Students come from 20 states and territories, 25% are from out of state, 3% African American, 3% Asian American or Pacific Islander, 3% Hispanic American, 2% Native American, 0.6% international, 13% transferred in, 32% live on campus. *Retention:* 66% of 2002 full-time freshmen returned.

Warner Pacific College (continued)

Freshmen *Admission:* 802 applied, 355 admitted, 68 enrolled. *Average high school GPA:* 3.32.

Faculty *Total:* 35, 100% full-time. *Student/faculty ratio:* 14:1.

Majors American studies; biblical studies; biological and physical sciences; biology/biological sciences; business administration and management; divinity/ministry; education; elementary education; English; health science; history; human development and family studies; kindergarten/preschool education; kinesiology and exercise science; liberal arts and sciences/liberal studies; middle school education; music; music management and merchandising; music teacher education; nursing (registered nurse training); pastoral studies/counseling; physical education teaching and coaching; physical sciences; pre-law studies; premedical studies; pre-veterinary studies; psychology; religious education; religious studies; science teacher education; secondary education; social sciences; social work; theology.

Academic Programs *Special study options:* academic remediation for entering students, adult/continuing education programs, advanced placement credit, cooperative education, double majors, honors programs, independent study, internships, off-campus study, part-time degree program, services for LD students, student-designed majors, study abroad, summer session for credit. *ROTC:* Army (c), Air Force (c).

Library Otto F. Linn Library with 54,000 titles, 400 serial subscriptions, an OPAC.

Computers on Campus 30 computers available on campus for general student use. A campuswide network can be accessed from student residence rooms and from off campus. Internet access available.

Student Life *Housing:* on-campus residence required through sophomore year. *Options:* men-only, women-only. Campus housing is university owned. *Activities and organizations:* drama/theater group, student-run newspaper, choral group, Associated Students of Warner Pacific College, yearbook, College Activities Board, Fellowship of Christian Athletes. *Campus security:* 24-hour emergency response devices and patrols, student patrols, late-night transport/escort service, controlled dormitory access. *Student services:* health clinic, personal/psychological counseling.

Athletics Member NAIA, NCCAA. *Intercollegiate sports:* basketball M(s)/W(s), cross-country running M(s)/W(s), soccer M/W, track and field M/W, volleyball W(s). *Intramural sports:* basketball M/W, football M/W, skiing (cross-country) M/W, skiing (downhill) M/W, soccer M/W, softball M/W, table tennis M/W, volleyball M/W.

Standardized Tests *Required:* SAT I or ACT (for admission). *Recommended:* SAT II: Subject Tests (for admission), SAT II: Writing Test (for admission).

Costs (2003–04) *Comprehensive fee:* $21,900 includes full-time tuition ($16,510), mandatory fees ($400), and room and board ($4990). Part-time tuition: $365 per credit. Part-time tuition and fees vary according to course load. *Room and board:* Room and board charges vary according to board plan and housing facility. *Payment plan:* installment. *Waivers:* children of alumni and employees or children of employees.

Financial Aid Of all full-time matriculated undergraduates who enrolled in 2002, 392 applied for aid, 360 were judged to have need, 20 had their need fully met. 238 Federal Work-Study jobs (averaging $882). 1 state and other part-time job (averaging $3000). In 2002, 30 non-need-based awards were made. *Average percent of need met:* 66%. *Average financial aid package:* $16,830. *Average need-based loan:* $4461. *Average need-based gift aid:* $4371. *Average non-need-based aid:* $6198.

Applying *Options:* electronic application. *Application fee:* $25. *Required:* essay or personal statement, high school transcript, minimum 2.5 GPA. *Required for some:* 1 letter of recommendation, interview. *Recommended:* minimum 3.0 GPA, interview. *Application deadline:* rolling (freshmen), rolling (transfers). *Notification:* continuous (freshmen), continuous (transfers).

Admissions Contact Dr. Jack P. Powell, Dean of Enrollment Management, Warner Pacific College, 2219 Southeast 68th Avenue, Portland, OR 97215. *Phone:* 503-517-1020. *Toll-free phone:* 800-582-7885 (in-state); 800-804-1510 (out-of-state). *Fax:* 503-517-1352. *E-mail:* admiss@warnerpacific.edu.

■ *See page 2780 for a narrative description.*

WESTERN BAPTIST COLLEGE

Salem, Oregon

- **Independent religious** 4-year, founded 1935
- **Calendar** semesters
- **Degrees** associate and bachelor's
- **Suburban** 107-acre campus with easy access to Portland
- **Endowment** $1.4 million
- **Coed,** 737 undergraduate students, 84% full-time, 59% women, 41% men
- **Moderately difficult** entrance level, 84% of applicants were admitted

Undergraduates 618 full-time, 119 part-time. Students come from 30 states and territories, 5 other countries, 31% are from out of state, 0.6% African American, 1% Asian American or Pacific Islander, 3% Hispanic American, 2% Native American, 0.7% international, 13% transferred in, 56% live on campus. *Retention:* 76% of 2002 full-time freshmen returned.

Freshmen *Admission:* 550 applied, 460 admitted, 167 enrolled. *Average high school GPA:* 3.51. *Test scores:* SAT verbal scores over 500: 76%; SAT math scores over 500: 69%; ACT scores over 18: 74%; SAT verbal scores over 600: 31%; SAT math scores over 600: 26%; ACT scores over 24: 34%; SAT verbal scores over 700: 3%; SAT math scores over 700: 3%; ACT scores over 30: 7%.

Faculty *Total:* 66, 52% full-time, 29% with terminal degrees. *Student/faculty ratio:* 15:1.

Majors Accounting; biblical studies; biology teacher education; business administration and management; business, management, and marketing related; business teacher education; communication/speech communication and rhetoric; community organization and advocacy; computer science; divinity/ministry; education; elementary education; English; English/language arts teacher education; family psychology; finance; health science; health services/allied health/health sciences; humanities; industrial and organizational psychology; interdisciplinary studies; journalism; liberal arts and sciences/liberal studies; management information systems; mathematics; mathematics teacher education; missionary studies and missiology; music; music performance; music teacher education; pastoral studies/counseling; physical education teaching and coaching; pre-law studies; pre-theology/pre-ministerial studies; psychology; religious education; religious/sacred music; religious studies; secondary education; social sciences; social science teacher education; social studies teacher education; sport and fitness administration; theology; voice and opera; youth ministry.

Academic Programs *Special study options:* accelerated degree program, adult/continuing education programs, advanced placement credit, distance learning, double majors, freshman honors college, honors programs, independent study, internships, off-campus study, services for LD students, study abroad, summer session for credit. *ROTC:* Army (c), Air Force (c).

Library 85,000 titles, 600 serial subscriptions, 4,500 audiovisual materials, an OPAC, a Web page.

Computers on Campus 34 computers available on campus for general student use. A campuswide network can be accessed from student residence rooms and from off campus. Internet access, at least one staffed computer lab available.

Student Life *Housing:* on-campus residence required through sophomore year. *Options:* men-only, women-only. Campus housing is university owned. Freshman campus housing is guaranteed. *Activities and organizations:* drama/theater group, student-run newspaper, choral group, Student Fellowship Groups, Poetry Club, Worship Teams, Drama Club, Westrek Hiking Club. *Campus security:* 24-hour emergency response devices, student patrols, late-night transport/escort service. *Student services:* health clinic, personal/psychological counseling.

Athletics Member NAIA, NCCAA. *Intercollegiate sports:* baseball M(s), basketball M(s)/W(s), cross-country running M(s)/W(s), golf M, soccer M(s)/W(s), softball W(s), volleyball W(s). *Intramural sports:* basketball M/W, football M, soccer M/W, softball W, ultimate Frisbee M/W, volleyball M/W, weight lifting M/W.

Standardized Tests *Required:* SAT I or ACT (for admission).

Costs (2004–05) *One-time required fee:* $200. *Comprehensive fee:* $23,100 includes full-time tuition ($16,825), mandatory fees ($210), and room and board ($6065). Part-time tuition: $700 per credit. Part-time tuition and fees vary according to course load. *Required fees:* $30 per term part-time. *Room and board:* Room and board charges vary according to board plan. *Payment plan:* installment. *Waivers:* employees or children of employees.

Financial Aid Of all full-time matriculated undergraduates who enrolled in 2003, 551 applied for aid, 507 were judged to have need, 127 had their need fully met. 106 Federal Work-Study jobs (averaging $1500). In 2003, 81 non-need-based awards were made. *Average percent of need met:* 71%. *Average financial aid package:* $12,689. *Average need-based loan:* $5741. *Average need-based gift aid:* $7978. *Average non-need-based aid:* $8192. *Average indebtedness upon graduation:* $17,500.

Applying *Options:* electronic application, early admission. *Application fee:* $35. *Required:* essay or personal statement, high school transcript, minimum 2.5 GPA, 3 letters of recommendation. *Application deadlines:* 8/1 (freshmen), 8/1 (transfers).

Admissions Contact Mr. Marty Ziesemer, Director of Admissions, Western Baptist College, 5000 Deer Park Drive, SE, Salem, OR 97301-9392. *Phone:* 503-375-7115. *Toll-free phone:* 800-845-3005. *E-mail:* admissions@wbc.edu.

WESTERN OREGON UNIVERSITY

Monmouth, Oregon

- **State-supported** comprehensive, founded 1856, part of Oregon University System

■ **Calendar** quarters
■ **Degrees** associate, bachelor's, master's, and postbachelor's certificates
■ **Rural** 157-acre campus with easy access to Portland
■ **Endowment** $3.2 million
■ **Coed,** 4,470 undergraduate students, 90% full-time, 59% women, 41% men
■ **Moderately difficult** entrance level, 94% of applicants were admitted

Undergraduates 4,016 full-time, 454 part-time. Students come from 23 states and territories, 19 other countries, 9% are from out of state, 2% African American, 3% Asian American or Pacific Islander, 5% Hispanic American, 1% Native American, 2% international, 10% transferred in, 20% live on campus. *Retention:* 71% of 2002 full-time freshmen returned.

Freshmen *Admission:* 1,809 applied, 1,694 admitted, 926 enrolled. *Average high school GPA:* 3.26. *Test scores:* SAT verbal scores over 500: 48%; SAT math scores over 500: 45%; ACT scores over 18: 77%; SAT verbal scores over 600: 11%; SAT math scores over 600: 10%; ACT scores over 24: 27%; SAT math scores over 700: 1%; ACT scores over 30: 2%.

Faculty *Total:* 323, 56% full-time, 60% with terminal degrees. *Student/faculty ratio:* 21:1.

Majors Anthropology; art; biology/biological sciences; business/commerce; chemistry; computer science; corrections; criminal justice/law enforcement administration; criminal justice/police science; dance; dramatic/theatre arts; economics; educational/instructional media design; English; fire services administration; geography; history; humanities; interdisciplinary studies; international relations and affairs; liberal arts and sciences/liberal studies; mathematics; music; natural sciences; philosophy; political science and government; psychology; public administration; secondary education; sign language interpretation and translation; social sciences; sociology; Spanish.

Academic Programs *Special study options:* academic remediation for entering students, adult/continuing education programs, advanced placement credit, distance learning, double majors, English as a second language, freshman honors college, honors programs, independent study, internships, off-campus study, part-time degree program, services for LD students, student-designed majors, study abroad, summer session for credit. *ROTC:* Army (b), Air Force (c).

Library Wayne and Lynn Hamersly Library with 157,186 titles, 3,680 serial subscriptions, 3,169 audiovisual materials, an OPAC, a Web page.

Computers on Campus 277 computers available on campus for general student use. A campuswide network can be accessed from student residence rooms and from off campus. Internet access, at least one staffed computer lab available.

Student Life *Housing:* on-campus residence required for freshman year. *Options:* coed. Campus housing is university owned. Freshman applicants given priority for college housing. *Activities and organizations:* drama/theater group, student-run newspaper, television station, choral group, Model United Nations, Multicultural Student Union, Oregon Student Association. *Campus security:* 24-hour emergency response devices and patrols, student patrols, late-night transport/escort service, controlled dormitory access. *Student services:* health clinic, personal/psychological counseling, women's center.

Athletics Member NCAA. All Division II. *Intercollegiate sports:* baseball M, basketball M/W, cross-country running M/W, football M, soccer W, softball W, track and field M/W, volleyball W. *Intramural sports:* badminton M/W, basketball M/W, bowling M/W, cross-country running M(c)/W(c), football M/W, golf M/W, racquetball M(c)/W(c), riflery M/W, skiing (downhill) M/W, soccer M(c)/W(c), softball M/W, table tennis M/W, tennis M/W, track and field M/W, volleyball M(c)/W(c), water polo M(c)/W(c), weight lifting M/W, wrestling M.

Standardized Tests *Required:* SAT I or ACT (for admission). *Recommended:* SAT I and SAT II or ACT (for admission), SAT II: Subject Tests (for admission).

Costs (2003–04) *Tuition:* state resident $3240 full-time, $90 per credit part-time; nonresident $11,505 full-time, $320 per credit part-time. *Required fees:* $1065 full-time. *Room and board:* $5976. Room and board charges vary according to board plan and housing facility. *Payment plan:* deferred payment. *Waivers:* employees or children of employees.

Financial Aid Of all full-time matriculated undergraduates who enrolled in 2003, 2,961 applied for aid, 2,421 were judged to have need, 264 had their need fully met. 343 Federal Work-Study jobs (averaging $756). In 2003, 646 non-need-based awards were made. *Average percent of need met:* 69%. *Average financial aid package:* $6447. *Average need-based loan:* $3536. *Average need-based gift aid:* $4002. *Average non-need-based aid:* $7045. *Average indebtedness upon graduation:* $12,563.

Applying *Options:* electronic application, deferred entrance. *Application fee:* $50. *Required:* high school transcript, minimum 2.75 GPA. *Application deadline:* rolling (freshmen), rolling (transfers). *Notification:* continuous (freshmen).

Admissions Contact Mr. Rob Kvidt, Director of Admissions, Western Oregon University, 345 North Monmouth Avenue, Monmouth, OR 97361. *Phone:* 503-838-8211. *Toll-free phone:* 877-877-1593. *Fax:* 503-838-8067. *E-mail:* wolfgram@wou.edu.

WILLAMETTE UNIVERSITY
Salem, Oregon

■ **Independent United Methodist** comprehensive, founded 1842
■ **Calendar** semesters
■ **Degrees** bachelor's, master's, first professional, postbachelor's, and first professional certificates
■ **Urban** 72-acre campus with easy access to Portland
■ **Endowment** $192.5 million
■ **Coed,** 1,945 undergraduate students, 93% full-time, 55% women, 45% men
■ **Very difficult** entrance level, 74% of applicants were admitted

Undergraduates 1,808 full-time, 137 part-time. Students come from 36 states and territories, 12 other countries, 59% are from out of state, 2% African American, 7% Asian American or Pacific Islander, 5% Hispanic American, 1% Native American, 0.7% international, 3% transferred in, 69% live on campus. *Retention:* 87% of 2002 full-time freshmen returned.

Freshmen *Admission:* 2,164 applied, 1,603 admitted, 541 enrolled. *Average high school GPA:* 3.74. *Test scores:* SAT verbal scores over 500: 94%; SAT math scores over 500: 96%; ACT scores over 18: 100%; SAT verbal scores over 600: 64%; SAT math scores over 600: 65%; ACT scores over 24: 86%; SAT verbal scores over 700: 17%; SAT math scores over 700: 14%; ACT scores over 30: 21%.

Faculty *Total:* 269, 69% full-time, 77% with terminal degrees. *Student/faculty ratio:* 11:1.

Majors Anthropology; art; art history, criticism and conservation; biology/biological sciences; chemistry; classics and languages, literatures and linguistics; comparative literature; computer science; dramatic/theatre arts; economics; English; environmental science; fine/studio arts; French; German; history; humanities; international/global studies; Japanese studies; kinesiology and exercise science; Latin American studies; mathematics; music; music pedagogy; music performance; music theory and composition; philosophy; physics; piano and organ; political science and government; psychology; religious studies; sociology; Spanish; speech and rhetoric; violin, viola, guitar and other stringed instruments; voice and opera.

Academic Programs *Special study options:* accelerated degree program, advanced placement credit, cooperative education, double majors, independent study, internships, off-campus study, part-time degree program, services for LD students, student-designed majors, study abroad. *ROTC:* Air Force (c). *Unusual degree programs:* 3-2 engineering with University of Southern California, Washington University in St. Louis, Columbia University; forestry with Duke University.

Library Mark O. Hatfield Library plus 1 other with 317,000 titles, 1,400 serial subscriptions, 8,800 audiovisual materials, an OPAC, a Web page.

Computers on Campus 400 computers available on campus for general student use. A campuswide network can be accessed from student residence rooms and from off campus. At least one staffed computer lab available.

Student Life *Housing:* on-campus residence required through sophomore year. *Options:* coed. Campus housing is university owned. Freshman campus housing is guaranteed. *Activities and organizations:* drama/theater group, student-run newspaper, radio station, choral group, Hawaii club, Bush Mentor Program, outdoors club, Campus Ambassadors, Associated Students, national fraternities, national sororities. *Campus security:* 24-hour emergency response devices and patrols, student patrols, late-night transport/escort service, controlled dormitory access. *Student services:* health clinic, personal/psychological counseling, women's center.

Athletics Member NCAA. All Division III. *Intercollegiate sports:* baseball M, basketball M/W, crew M/W, cross-country running M/W, football M, golf M/W, lacrosse M(c), soccer M/W, softball W, swimming M/W, tennis M/W, track and field M/W, volleyball W. *Intramural sports:* badminton M/W, basketball M/W, bowling M/W, cross-country running M/W, football M/W, golf M/W, racquetball M/W, skiing (cross-country) M(c)/W(c), skiing (downhill) M(c)/W(c), soccer M/W, softball M/W, table tennis M/W, tennis M/W, ultimate Frisbee M/W, volleyball M/W, water polo M/W, weight lifting M/W.

Standardized Tests *Required:* SAT I or ACT (for admission).

Costs (2003–04) *Comprehensive fee:* $32,062 includes full-time tuition ($25,300), mandatory fees ($162), and room and board ($6600). Full-time tuition and fees vary according to course load. Part-time tuition: $3162 per course. Part-time tuition and fees vary according to course load. *Room and board:* Room and board charges vary according to board plan and housing facility. *Payment plans:* tuition prepayment, installment. *Waivers:* employees or children of employees.

Financial Aid Of all full-time matriculated undergraduates who enrolled in 2002, 1,192 applied for aid, 1,054 were judged to have need, 468 had their need fully met. 688 Federal Work-Study jobs (averaging $1885). In 2002, 488 non-need-based awards were made. *Average percent of need met:* 93%. *Average financial aid package:* $21,886. *Average need-based loan:* $3836. *Average*

Willamette University (continued)
need-based gift aid: $16,823. *Average non-need-based aid:* $10,866. *Average indebtedness upon graduation:* $17,660.

Applying *Options:* common application, electronic application, early admission, early action, deferred entrance. *Application fee:* $50. *Required:* essay or personal statement, high school transcript, minimum 2.0 GPA, 1 letter of recommendation. *Required for some:* interview. *Recommended:* interview. *Application deadlines:* 2/1 (freshmen), 2/1 (transfers). *Notification:* 4/1 (freshmen), 1/15 (early action), 4/1 (transfers).

Admissions Contact Dr. Robin Brown, Vice President for Enrollment, Willamette University, 900 State Street, Salem, OR 97301-3931. *Phone:* 503-370-6303. *Toll-free phone:* 877-542-2787. *Fax:* 503-375-5363. *E-mail:* libarts@willamette.edu.

■ *See page 2852 for a narrative description.*

PENNSYLVANIA

ALBRIGHT COLLEGE
Reading, Pennsylvania

- **Independent** comprehensive, founded 1856, affiliated with United Methodist Church
- **Calendar** 4-1-4
- **Degrees** certificates, bachelor's, and master's
- **Suburban** 118-acre campus with easy access to Philadelphia
- **Endowment** $31.8 million
- **Coed,** 2,046 undergraduate students, 97% full-time, 56% women, 44% men
- **Moderately difficult** entrance level, 72% of applicants were admitted

Undergraduates 1,992 full-time, 54 part-time. Students come from 20 states and territories, 26 other countries, 31% are from out of state, 9% African American, 2% Asian American or Pacific Islander, 4% Hispanic American, 0.3% Native American, 4% international, 2% transferred in, 69% live on campus. *Retention:* 81% of 2002 full-time freshmen returned.

Freshmen *Admission:* 2,967 applied, 2,137 admitted, 456 enrolled. *Average high school GPA:* 3.27. *Test scores:* SAT verbal scores over 500: 56%; SAT math scores over 500: 56%; SAT verbal scores over 600: 16%; SAT math scores over 600: 18%; SAT verbal scores over 700: 1%; SAT math scores over 700: 2%.

Faculty *Total:* 150, 69% full-time, 63% with terminal degrees. *Student/faculty ratio:* 13:1.

Majors Accounting; American studies; apparel and textiles; art; art teacher education; biochemistry; biology/biological sciences; business administration and management; chemistry; communication/speech communication and rhetoric; computer science; criminology; design and visual communications; dramatic/theatre arts; economics; elementary education; English; environmental science; finance; forestry; French; history; industrial and organizational psychology; information science/studies; interdisciplinary studies; international business/trade/commerce; kindergarten/preschool education; Latin American studies; marketing/marketing management; mathematics; multi-/interdisciplinary studies related; music; natural resources management and policy; philosophy; physics; physiological psychology/psychobiology; political science and government; pre-law studies; psychology; religious studies; secondary education; sociology; Spanish; special education; women's studies.

Academic Programs *Special study options:* academic remediation for entering students, accelerated degree program, advanced placement credit, double majors, English as a second language, honors programs, independent study, internships, off-campus study, part-time degree program, services for LD students, student-designed majors, study abroad, summer session for credit. *Unusual degree programs:* 3-2 forestry with Duke University; natural resource management with University of Michigan.

Library F. W. Gingrich Library plus 1 other with 218,232 titles, 8,190 serial subscriptions, 8,166 audiovisual materials, an OPAC, a Web page.

Computers on Campus 326 computers available on campus for general student use. A campuswide network can be accessed from student residence rooms and from off campus. Internet access, at least one staffed computer lab available. Computer purchase or lease plan available.

Student Life *Housing:* on-campus residence required for freshman year. *Options:* coed. Campus housing is university owned. Freshman campus housing is guaranteed. *Activities and organizations:* drama/theater group, student-run newspaper, radio and television station, choral group, Campus Center Board, Student Government Association, yearbook, newspaper, radio station, national fraternities, national sororities. *Campus security:* 24-hour emergency response devices and patrols, student patrols, late-night transport/escort service, controlled dormitory access. *Student services:* health clinic, personal/psychological counseling, women's center.

Athletics Member NCAA. All Division III. *Intercollegiate sports:* badminton W, baseball M, basketball M/W, cheerleading W, cross-country running M/W, field hockey W, football M, golf M, lacrosse M(c)/W(c), rugby M(c)/W(c), soccer M/W, softball W, swimming M/W, tennis M/W, track and field M/W, volleyball W, wrestling M. *Intramural sports:* basketball M/W, football M, softball M/W, volleyball M/W, water polo M/W.

Standardized Tests *Required:* SAT I or ACT (for admission).

Costs (2004–05) *Comprehensive fee:* $32,090 includes full-time tuition ($24,030), mandatory fees ($550), and room and board ($7510). Full-time tuition and fees vary according to program. Part-time tuition: $2860 per course. Part-time tuition and fees vary according to class time. *College room only:* $4275. Room and board charges vary according to board plan and housing facility. *Payment plan:* installment. *Waivers:* children of alumni, senior citizens, and employees or children of employees.

Financial Aid Of all full-time matriculated undergraduates who enrolled in 2003, 1,585 applied for aid, 1,444 were judged to have need, 235 had their need fully met. 750 Federal Work-Study jobs (averaging $1390). 300 state and other part-time jobs (averaging $1300). In 2003, 231 non-need-based awards were made. *Average percent of need met:* 76%. *Average financial aid package:* $16,536. *Average need-based loan:* $4206. *Average need-based gift aid:* $12,748. *Average non-need-based aid:* $11,053. *Average indebtedness upon graduation:* $24,876.

Applying *Options:* common application, electronic application, early admission, deferred entrance. *Application fee:* $25. *Required:* essay or personal statement, high school transcript, 1 letter of recommendation, secondary school report (guidance department). *Recommended:* interview. *Application deadlines:* 3/1 (freshmen), 8/15 (transfers). *Notification:* continuous (freshmen), continuous (transfers).

Admissions Contact Mr. Gregory E. Eichhorn, Vice President for Enrollment Management, Albright College, PO Box 15234, 13th and Bern Streets, Reading, PA 19612-5234. *Phone:* 610-921-7260. *Toll-free phone:* 800-252-1856. *Fax:* 610-921-7294. *E-mail:* admission@albright.edu.

■ *See page 1146 for a narrative description.*

ALLEGHENY COLLEGE
Meadville, Pennsylvania

- **Independent** 4-year, founded 1815
- **Calendar** semesters
- **Degree** bachelor's
- **Small-town** 254-acre campus
- **Endowment** $103.7 million
- **Coed,** 1,849 undergraduate students, 98% full-time, 52% women, 48% men
- **Very difficult** entrance level, 82% of applicants were admitted

Allegheny College attracts students with varied interests, skills, and talents. Its nationally recognized Center for Experiential Learning, which offers an enormous variety of opportunities for internships, off-campus study (both in the US and abroad), service learning, and leadership development, makes Allegheny College a perfect fit for students.

Undergraduates 1,809 full-time, 40 part-time. Students come from 33 states and territories, 33% are from out of state, 2% African American, 2% Asian American or Pacific Islander, 1% Hispanic American, 0.3% Native American, 0.8% international, 1% transferred in, 73% live on campus. *Retention:* 85% of 2002 full-time freshmen returned.

Freshmen *Admission:* 2,438 applied, 2,002 admitted, 481 enrolled. *Average high school GPA:* 3.68. *Test scores:* SAT verbal scores over 500: 89%; SAT math scores over 500: 93%; ACT scores over 18: 99%; SAT verbal scores over 600: 53%; SAT math scores over 600: 52%; ACT scores over 24: 73%; SAT verbal scores over 700: 9%; SAT math scores over 700: 9%; ACT scores over 30: 10%.

Faculty *Total:* 147, 91% full-time, 84% with terminal degrees. *Student/faculty ratio:* 13:1.

Majors Applied economics; art; art history, criticism and conservation; biochemistry; biology/biological sciences; business/managerial economics; chemistry; communication/speech communication and rhetoric; computer science; computer software engineering; creative writing; dramatic/theatre arts; economics; education; English; environmental science; environmental studies; fine arts related; fine/studio arts; French; geology/earth science; German; health/medical preparatory programs related; history; international/global studies; international relations and affairs; journalism; mass communication/media; mathematics; multi-/interdisciplinary studies related; music; music performance; neuroscience; philosophy; physics; political science and government; pre-dentistry studies; pre-law studies; pre-medical studies; pre-nursing studies; pre-pharmacy studies; pre-veterinary studies; psychology; religious studies; Spanish; technical and business writing; women's studies.

Academic Programs *Special study options:* advanced placement credit, double majors, independent study, internships, off-campus study, part-time degree program, services for LD students, student-designed majors, study abroad. *Unusual degree programs:* 3-2 engineering with Columbia University, Case Western Reserve University, Duke University, Washington University, University of Pittsburgh; nursing with Case Western Reserve University.

Library Lawrence Lee Pelletier Library with 279,648 titles, 3,500 serial subscriptions, 7,051 audiovisual materials, an OPAC, a Web page.

Computers on Campus 336 computers available on campus for general student use. A campuswide network can be accessed from student residence rooms and from off campus. Internet access, online (class) registration, at least one staffed computer lab available. Computer purchase or lease plan available.

Student Life *Housing:* on-campus residence required through junior year. *Options:* coed, men-only, women-only, disabled students. Campus housing is university owned. Freshman campus housing is guaranteed. *Activities and organizations:* drama/theater group, student-run newspaper, radio and television station, choral group, student government, Gators Activity Programming, Orchesis Dance Company, Greek Life, Up'til Dawn, national fraternities, national sororities. *Campus security:* 24-hour emergency response devices and patrols, student patrols, late-night transport/escort service, controlled dormitory access, local police patrol. *Student services:* health clinic, personal/psychological counseling, women's center.

Athletics Member NCAA. All Division III. *Intercollegiate sports:* baseball M, basketball M/W, cheerleading M(c)/W(c), cross-country running M/W, equestrian sports W(c), fencing M(c)/W(c), football M, golf M/W(c), ice hockey M(c), lacrosse M(c)/W, rugby M(c)/W(c), soccer M/W, softball W, swimming M/W, tennis M/W, track and field M/W, ultimate Frisbee M(c)/W(c), volleyball M(c)/W. *Intramural sports:* basketball M/W, football M/W, golf M/W, racquetball M/W, soccer M/W, softball M/W, table tennis M/W, tennis M/W, volleyball M/W.

Standardized Tests *Required:* SAT I or ACT (for admission). *Recommended:* SAT II: Subject Tests (for admission), SAT II: Writing Test (for admission).

Costs (2003–04) *Comprehensive fee:* $30,280 includes full-time tuition ($24,100), mandatory fees ($300), and room and board ($5880). Part-time tuition: $1004 per credit hour. Part-time tuition and fees vary according to course load. *Required fees:* $150 per term part-time. *College room only:* $3000. Room and board charges vary according to board plan and housing facility. *Payment plans:* tuition prepayment, installment. *Waivers:* employees or children of employees.

Financial Aid Of all full-time matriculated undergraduates who enrolled in 2003, 1,485 applied for aid, 1,330 were judged to have need, 615 had their need fully met. 1,055 Federal Work-Study jobs (averaging $1554). 311 state and other part-time jobs (averaging $1632). In 2003, 401 non-need-based awards were made. *Average percent of need met:* 94%. *Average financial aid package:* $19,624. *Average need-based loan:* $4538. *Average need-based gift aid:* $13,733. *Average non-need-based aid:* $8883. *Average indebtedness upon graduation:* $23,735.

Applying *Options:* common application, electronic application, early admission, early decision, deferred entrance. *Application fee:* $35. *Required:* essay or personal statement, high school transcript, 2 letters of recommendation. *Recommended:* interview. *Application deadlines:* 2/15 (freshmen), 7/1 (transfers). *Early decision:* 1/15. *Notification:* 4/1 (freshmen), 10/15 (early decision), 8/1 (transfers).

Admissions Contact Dr. W. Scott Friedhoff, Vice President for Enrollment, Allegheny College, 520 North Main Street, Box 5, Meadville, PA 16335. *Phone:* 814-332-4351. *Toll-free phone:* 800-521-5293. *Fax:* 814-337-0431. *E-mail:* admissions@allegheny.edu.

■ *See page 1152 for a narrative description.*

ALVERNIA COLLEGE
Reading, Pennsylvania

- **Independent Roman Catholic** comprehensive, founded 1958
- **Calendar** semesters
- **Degrees** associate, bachelor's, master's, post-master's, and postbachelor's certificates
- **Suburban** 85-acre campus with easy access to Philadelphia
- **Endowment** $10.2 million
- **Coed,** 1,848 undergraduate students, 75% full-time, 67% women, 33% men
- **Moderately difficult** entrance level, 80% of applicants were admitted

Alvernia College, a private Catholic college, blends traditional liberal arts with professional programs. Alvernia offers 27 bachelor's degree programs as well as 5-year master's programs in business, education, liberal studies, and occupational therapy. All programs are geared to meet the needs of students and the community.

Undergraduates 1,384 full-time, 464 part-time. Students come from 13 states and territories, 4 other countries, 8% are from out of state, 10% African American, 2% Asian American or Pacific Islander, 5% Hispanic American, 1% international, 4% transferred in, 26% live on campus. *Retention:* 79% of 2002 full-time freshmen returned.

Freshmen *Admission:* 692 applied, 556 admitted, 292 enrolled. *Average high school GPA:* 3.16. *Test scores:* SAT verbal scores over 500: 33%; SAT math scores over 500: 33%; SAT verbal scores over 600: 8%; SAT math scores over 600: 6%; SAT verbal scores over 700: 1%.

Faculty *Total:* 133, 49% full-time. *Student/faculty ratio:* 18:1.

Majors Accounting; biochemistry; biological and physical sciences; biology/biological sciences; biology teacher education; biomedical technology; business administration and management; chemistry; chemistry teacher education; clinical laboratory science/medical technology; communication/speech communication and rhetoric; criminal justice/law enforcement administration; education; elementary education; English; English/language arts teacher education; forensic science and technology; health/health care administration; history; information science/studies; kindergarten/preschool education; liberal arts and sciences/liberal studies; marketing/marketing management; mathematics; mathematics teacher education; nursing (registered nurse training); occupational therapy; philosophy; physical therapy; political science and government; pre-law studies; pre-medical studies; psychology; religious studies; science teacher education; social sciences; social work; sport and fitness administration; substance abuse/addiction counseling; theology.

Academic Programs *Special study options:* academic remediation for entering students, accelerated degree program, adult/continuing education programs, advanced placement credit, double majors, honors programs, independent study, internships, off-campus study, part-time degree program, services for LD students, summer session for credit. *ROTC:* Army (c). *Unusual degree programs:* 3-2 occupational therapy.

Library Franco Library with 89,399 titles, 378 serial subscriptions, 7,766 audiovisual materials, an OPAC, a Web page.

Computers on Campus 60 computers available on campus for general student use. A campuswide network can be accessed from student residence rooms. Internet access, at least one staffed computer lab available.

Student Life *Housing options:* coed, women-only, disabled students. Campus housing is university owned. Freshman applicants given priority for college housing. *Activities and organizations:* drama/theater group, student-run newspaper, choral group, Student Government Association, Ice Hockey Club, Science Association, Sigma Tau Delta, Criminal Justice Association. *Campus security:* 24-hour patrols, late-night transport/escort service, controlled dormitory access. *Student services:* health clinic, personal/psychological counseling.

Athletics Member NCAA. All Division III. *Intercollegiate sports:* baseball M, basketball M/W, cross-country running M/W, field hockey W, golf M, lacrosse M/W, soccer M/W, softball W, tennis M/W, volleyball W. *Intramural sports:* basketball M/W, ice hockey M(c)/W(c), lacrosse M/W, skiing (downhill) M(c)/W(c), volleyball M(c).

Standardized Tests *Required:* SAT I or ACT (for admission). *Recommended:* SAT I (for admission).

Costs (2003–04) *Comprehensive fee:* $23,312 includes full-time tuition ($16,200), mandatory fees ($162), and room and board ($6950). Part-time tuition: $490 per credit. Part-time tuition and fees vary according to class time and course load. *College room only:* $3490. Room and board charges vary according to board plan and housing facility. *Payment plans:* installment, deferred payment. *Waivers:* senior citizens and employees or children of employees.

Financial Aid Of all full-time matriculated undergraduates who enrolled in 2003, 1,191 applied for aid, 1,089 were judged to have need, 263 had their need fully met. 399 Federal Work-Study jobs (averaging $1801). 56 state and other part-time jobs. In 2003, 122 non-need-based awards were made. *Average percent of need met:* 77%. *Average financial aid package:* $12,444. *Average need-based loan:* $4175. *Average need-based gift aid:* $8611. *Average non-need-based aid:* $10,275. *Average indebtedness upon graduation:* $6749.

Applying *Options:* common application, electronic application, deferred entrance. *Application fee:* $25. *Required:* essay or personal statement, high school transcript. *Required for some:* 2 letters of recommendation, interview. *Recommended:* minimum 2.0 GPA, 1 letter of recommendation. *Application deadline:* rolling (freshmen), rolling (transfers).

Admissions Contact Mr. John Diamond, Dean of Enrollment Management, Alvernia College, 400 Saint Bernardine Street, Reading, PA 19607. *Phone:* 610-796-3005. *Toll-free phone:* 888-ALVERNIA. *Fax:* 610-796-8336. *E-mail:* admissions@alvernia.edu.

■ *See page 1158 for a narrative description.*

ARCADIA UNIVERSITY
Glenside, Pennsylvania

- **Independent** comprehensive, founded 1853, affiliated with Presbyterian Church (U.S.A.)

Arcadia University (continued)
- **Calendar** semesters
- **Degrees** bachelor's, master's, and doctoral
- **Suburban** 60-acre campus with easy access to Philadelphia
- **Endowment** $27.0 million
- **Coed,** 1,840 undergraduate students, 85% full-time, 74% women, 26% men
- **Moderately difficult** entrance level, 75% of applicants were admitted

Undergraduates 1,570 full-time, 270 part-time. Students come from 22 states and territories, 10 other countries, 27% are from out of state, 11% African American, 2% Asian American or Pacific Islander, 2% Hispanic American, 0.1% Native American, 1% international, 7% transferred in, 68% live on campus. *Retention:* 83% of 2002 full-time freshmen returned.

Freshmen *Admission:* 2,691 applied, 2,014 admitted, 507 enrolled. *Test scores:* SAT verbal scores over 500: 69%; SAT math scores over 500: 65%; SAT verbal scores over 600: 26%; SAT math scores over 600: 22%; SAT verbal scores over 700: 1%; SAT math scores over 700: 2%.

Faculty *Total:* 332, 29% full-time. *Student/faculty ratio:* 12:1.

Majors Accounting; acting; art; art history, criticism and conservation; art teacher education; biology/biological sciences; business administration and management; ceramic arts and ceramics; chemistry; commercial and advertising art; computer and information sciences; computer programming; computer science; dramatic/theatre arts; drawing; early childhood education; education; elementary education; English; environmental biology; finance; fine/studio arts; health/health care administration; history; human resources management; human services; interior design; international business/trade/commerce; kindergarten/preschool education; liberal arts and sciences/liberal studies; literature; management information systems; marketing/marketing management; mass communication/media; mathematics; medical illustration; metal and jewelry arts; natural sciences; philosophy; photography; physiological psychology/psychobiology; political science and government; pre-dentistry studies; pre-law studies; pre-medical studies; pre-veterinary studies; psychology; secondary education; sociology; Spanish.

Academic Programs *Special study options:* adult/continuing education programs, advanced placement credit, cooperative education, distance learning, double majors, English as a second language, honors programs, independent study, internships, off-campus study, part-time degree program, services for LD students, student-designed majors, study abroad, summer session for credit. *ROTC:* Army (c). *Unusual degree programs:* 3-2 engineering with Columbia University; environmental studies; optometry with Pennsylvania College of Optometry.

Library Landman Library with 139,903 titles, 798 serial subscriptions, 2,861 audiovisual materials, an OPAC, a Web page.

Computers on Campus 110 computers available on campus for general student use. A campuswide network can be accessed from student residence rooms and from off campus. Internet access, at least one staffed computer lab available. Computer purchase or lease plan available.

Student Life *Housing options:* coed, women-only. Campus housing is university owned and leased by the school. Freshman applicants given priority for college housing. *Activities and organizations:* drama/theater group, student-run newspaper, radio station, choral group, Student Program Board, Residence Hall Council, student government, Arcadia Christian Fellowship, Student Alumni Association. *Campus security:* 24-hour emergency response devices and patrols, student patrols, late-night transport/escort service, controlled dormitory access. *Student services:* health clinic, personal/psychological counseling.

Athletics Member NCAA. All Division III. *Intercollegiate sports:* baseball M, basketball M/W, cross-country running M/W, equestrian sports M/W, field hockey W, golf M/W, lacrosse W, soccer M/W, softball W, swimming M/W, tennis M/W, volleyball W. *Intramural sports:* basketball M/W, cheerleading W(c), equestrian sports M/W, field hockey W, soccer M/W, swimming M, tennis M/W, volleyball M/W, weight lifting M/W.

Standardized Tests *Required:* SAT I or ACT (for admission).

Costs (2004–05) *Comprehensive fee:* $31,680 includes full-time tuition ($22,440), mandatory fees ($280), and room and board ($8960). Full-time tuition and fees vary according to course load, degree level, and program. Part-time tuition: $400 per credit. *Room and board:* Room and board charges vary according to board plan. *Payment plans:* installment, deferred payment. *Waivers:* employees or children of employees.

Financial Aid Of all full-time matriculated undergraduates who enrolled in 2003, 1,532 applied for aid, 1,447 were judged to have need, 98 had their need fully met. 843 Federal Work-Study jobs (averaging $1326). 207 state and other part-time jobs (averaging $1061). In 2003, 110 non-need-based awards were made. *Average percent of need met:* 92%. *Average financial aid package:* $18,164. *Average need-based loan:* $5133. *Average need-based gift aid:* $7715. *Average non-need-based aid:* $6607. *Average indebtedness upon graduation:* $29,145.

Applying *Options:* common application, electronic application, early admission, early decision, deferred entrance. *Application fee:* $30. *Required:* essay or personal statement, high school transcript, 2 letters of recommendation. *Required for some:* portfolio. *Recommended:* minimum 3.0 GPA, interview. *Application deadline:* rolling (freshmen), rolling (transfers). *Early decision:* 11/1. *Notification:* continuous until 9/1 (freshmen), 12/1 (early decision), continuous until 9/1 (transfers).

Admissions Contact Mr. Mark Lapreziosa, Director of Enrollment Management, Arcadia University, 450 South Easton Road, Glenside, PA 19038. *Phone:* 215-572-2910. *Toll-free phone:* 877-ARCADIA. *Fax:* 215-572-4049. *E-mail:* admiss@arcadia.edu.

■ *See page 1180 for a narrative description.*

THE ART INSTITUTE OF PHILADELPHIA
Philadelphia, Pennsylvania

- **Proprietary** primarily 2-year, founded 1966, part of The Art Institutes
- **Calendar** quarters
- **Degrees** associate and bachelor's
- **Urban** campus
- **Coed**
- **Moderately difficult** entrance level

Faculty *Student/faculty ratio:* 20:1.

Student Life *Campus security:* controlled dormitory access.

Standardized Tests *Recommended:* SAT I or ACT (for placement).

Applying *Options:* common application, electronic application, deferred entrance. *Application fee:* $50. *Required:* essay or personal statement, high school transcript, interview. *Recommended:* minimum 2.5 GPA, letters of recommendation.

Admissions Contact Mr. Tim Howard, Director of Admissions, The Art Institute of Philadelphia, 1622 Chestnut Street, Philadelphia, PA 19103. *Phone:* 215-567-7080 Ext. 6337. *Toll-free phone:* 800-275-2474. *Fax:* 215-405-6399.

THE ART INSTITUTE OF PITTSBURGH
Pittsburgh, Pennsylvania

- **Proprietary** primarily 2-year, founded 1921, part of The Art Institutes International
- **Calendar** quarters
- **Degrees** diplomas, associate, and bachelor's
- **Urban** campus
- **Coed**
- **Minimally difficult** entrance level

Faculty *Student/faculty ratio:* 20:1.

Student Life *Campus security:* 24-hour emergency response devices and patrols, controlled dormitory access.

Standardized Tests *Required:* ACT ASSET (for placement). *Recommended:* SAT I or ACT (for placement).

Costs (2003–04) *Tuition:* $345 per credit part-time. Full-time tuition and fees vary according to course load. Part-time tuition and fees vary according to course load. *Required fees:* $150 full-time. *Room only:* Room and board charges vary according to board plan and housing facility. *Payment plans:* installment, deferred payment.

Financial Aid Of all full-time matriculated undergraduates who enrolled in 2001, 100 Federal Work-Study jobs (averaging $3000).

Applying *Options:* common application, deferred entrance. *Application fee:* $50. *Required:* essay or personal statement, high school transcript, minimum 2.0 GPA. *Recommended:* interview.

Admissions Contact Mrs. Janet Stevens, Vice President and Director of Enrollment Services, The Art Institute of Pittsburgh, 420 Boulevard of the Allies, Pittsburgh, PA 15219. *Phone:* 800-275-2470 Ext. 6315. *Toll-free phone:* 800-275-2470. *Fax:* 412-263-6667. *E-mail:* admissions@aii.edu.

BAPTIST BIBLE COLLEGE OF PENNSYLVANIA
Clarks Summit, Pennsylvania

Admissions Contact Ms. Chris Hansen, Applications Coordinator, Baptist Bible College of Pennsylvania, PO Box 800, Clarks Summit, PA 18411-1297. *Phone:* 570-586-2400 Ext. 9370. *Toll-free phone:* 800-451-7664. *Fax:* 570-585-9400. *E-mail:* gamos@bbc.edu.

BLOOMSBURG UNIVERSITY OF PENNSYLVANIA
Bloomsburg, Pennsylvania

- **State-supported** comprehensive, founded 1839, part of Pennsylvania State System of Higher Education

■ **Calendar** semesters
■ **Degrees** associate, bachelor's, master's, and postbachelor's certificates
■ **Small-town** 282-acre campus
■ **Coed,** 7,520 undergraduate students, 93% full-time, 61% women, 39% men
■ **Moderately difficult** entrance level, 70% of applicants were admitted

Undergraduates 6,974 full-time, 546 part-time. Students come from 25 states and territories, 34 other countries, 10% are from out of state, 4% African American, 0.8% Asian American or Pacific Islander, 2% Hispanic American, 0.2% Native American, 0.7% international, 5% transferred in, 45% live on campus. *Retention:* 81% of 2002 full-time freshmen returned.

Freshmen *Admission:* 7,274 applied, 5,123 admitted, 1,671 enrolled. *Average high school GPA:* 3.00. *Test scores:* SAT verbal scores over 500: 56%; SAT math scores over 500: 60%; SAT verbal scores over 600: 10%; SAT math scores over 600: 11%; SAT verbal scores over 700: 1%; SAT math scores over 700: 1%.

Faculty *Total:* 384, 92% full-time, 76% with terminal degrees. *Student/faculty ratio:* 20:1.

Majors Accounting; allied health and medical assisting services related; anthropology; art history, criticism and conservation; audiology and speech-language pathology; biological and physical sciences; biology/biological sciences; business administration and management; business/commerce; business/managerial economics; chemistry; clinical laboratory science/medical technology; clinical/medical laboratory technology; communication/speech communication and rhetoric; computer and information sciences; computer science; criminal justice/safety; dramatic/theatre arts; early childhood education; economics; economics related; electrical, electronics and communications engineering; elementary education; English; fine/studio arts; French; geography; geology/earth science; German; health and physical education related; health/medical physics; history; humanities; mass communication/media; mathematics; medical radiologic technology; multi-/interdisciplinary studies related; music; nursing (registered nurse training); philosophy; physical sciences; physics; political science and government; psychology; sign language interpretation and translation; social sciences; social sciences related; social work; sociology; Spanish; special education; special education (speech or language impaired); speech and rhetoric.

Academic Programs *Special study options:* academic remediation for entering students, adult/continuing education programs, advanced placement credit, cooperative education, distance learning, double majors, freshman honors college, honors programs, independent study, internships, off-campus study, part-time degree program, services for LD students, study abroad, summer session for credit. *ROTC:* Army (b), Air Force (c). *Unusual degree programs:* 3-2 engineering with Pennsylvania State University, Wilkes University.

Library Andruss Library with 430,815 titles, 2,386 serial subscriptions, 7,961 audiovisual materials, an OPAC, a Web page.

Computers on Campus 800 computers available on campus for general student use. A campuswide network can be accessed from student residence rooms and from off campus. Internet access, online (class) registration, at least one staffed computer lab available.

Student Life *Housing:* on-campus residence required for freshman year. *Options:* coed, women-only. Campus housing is university owned. Freshman campus housing is guaranteed. *Activities and organizations:* drama/theater group, student-run newspaper, radio and television station, choral group, marching band, national fraternities, national sororities. *Campus security:* 24-hour emergency response devices and patrols, late-night transport/escort service, controlled dormitory access, monitored surveillance cameras. *Student services:* health clinic, personal/psychological counseling, women's center, legal services.

Athletics Member NCAA. All Division II except wrestling (Division I). *Intercollegiate sports:* baseball M, basketball M(s)/W(s), bowling M(c)/W(c), cheerleading M/W, cross-country running M/W(s), field hockey W(s), football M(s), lacrosse W, soccer M/W(s), softball W(s), swimming M(s)/W(s), tennis M(s)/W(s), track and field M(s)/W(s), wrestling M(s). *Intramural sports:* badminton W, baseball M, basketball M/W, bowling M(c)/W, cross-country running M, fencing M(c)/W(c), field hockey W, football M/W, golf M/W, gymnastics M/W, ice hockey M(c), lacrosse M(c), racquetball M/W, rugby M(c)/W(c), skiing (downhill) M(c)/W(c), soccer M, softball M/W, table tennis M(c)/W(c), tennis M/W, track and field M, volleyball M/W, water polo M(c)/W(c), weight lifting M, wrestling M.

Standardized Tests *Required:* SAT I or ACT (for admission).

Costs (2003–04) *Tuition:* state resident $4598 full-time, $192 per credit part-time; nonresident $11,496 full-time, $479 per credit part-time. Full-time tuition and fees vary according to course load. Part-time tuition and fees vary according to course load. *Required fees:* $1246 full-time. *Room and board:* $5000. Room and board charges vary according to board plan and housing facility. *Waivers:* minority students and employees or children of employees.

Financial Aid Of all full-time matriculated undergraduates who enrolled in 2003, 5,552 applied for aid, 4,442 were judged to have need, 3,798 had their need fully met. 1,067 Federal Work-Study jobs (averaging $2454). 1,116 state and other part-time jobs (averaging $2794). *Average percent of need met:* 65%. *Average financial aid package:* $10,026. *Average need-based loan:* $3470. *Average need-based gift aid:* $3570. *Average indebtedness upon graduation:* $15,743.

Applying *Options:* common application, electronic application, early admission, early decision, deferred entrance. *Application fee:* $30. *Required:* high school transcript, letters of recommendation. *Application deadline:* rolling (freshmen), rolling (transfers). *Early decision:* 11/15. *Notification:* 10/1 (freshmen), 12/1 (early decision), continuous (transfers).

Admissions Contact Mr. Christopher Keller, Director of Admissions, Bloomsburg University of Pennsylvania, 104 Student services Center, Bloomsburg, PA 17815-1905. *Phone:* 570-389-4316. *E-mail:* buadmiss@bloomu.edu.

BRYN ATHYN COLLEGE OF THE NEW CHURCH

Bryn Athyn, Pennsylvania

■ **Independent Swedenborgian** comprehensive, founded 1876, part of The Academy of the New Church
■ **Calendar** trimesters
■ **Degrees** associate, bachelor's, master's, first professional, and first professional certificates
■ **Suburban** 130-acre campus with easy access to Philadelphia
■ **Endowment** $260.0 million
■ **Coed,** 129 undergraduate students, 93% full-time, 56% women, 44% men
■ **Minimally difficult** entrance level, 98% of applicants were admitted

Undergraduates 120 full-time, 9 part-time. Students come from 17 states and territories, 10 other countries, 36% are from out of state, 4% Asian American or Pacific Islander, 0.9% Hispanic American, 20% international, 7% transferred in, 72% live on campus. *Retention:* 66% of 2002 full-time freshmen returned.

Freshmen *Admission:* 40 applied, 39 admitted, 35 enrolled. *Test scores:* SAT verbal scores over 500: 77%; SAT math scores over 500: 81%; SAT verbal scores over 600: 50%; SAT math scores over 600: 35%; SAT verbal scores over 700: 15%; SAT math scores over 700: 8%.

Faculty *Total:* 47, 32% full-time, 45% with terminal degrees. *Student/faculty ratio:* 5:1.

Majors Biology/biological sciences; elementary education; English; history; liberal arts and sciences/liberal studies; religious studies related; theology and religious vocations related.

Academic Programs *Special study options:* academic remediation for entering students, advanced placement credit, cooperative education, English as a second language, independent study, internships, part-time degree program, services for LD students, student-designed majors, study abroad.

Library Swedenborg Library plus 1 other with 97,561 titles, 180 serial subscriptions, 559 audiovisual materials, an OPAC.

Computers on Campus 44 computers available on campus for general student use. A campuswide network can be accessed from student residence rooms. Internet access, at least one staffed computer lab available.

Student Life *Housing:* on-campus residence required for freshman year. *Options:* men-only, women-only. Campus housing is university owned. Freshman campus housing is guaranteed. *Activities and organizations:* drama/theater group, student-run newspaper, choral group, C.A.R.E. Community Service, business club, International Student Organization, Peer Advisory Council, outing club. *Campus security:* 24-hour emergency response devices, controlled dormitory access, 18-hour patrols by trained personnel. *Student services:* health clinic, personal/psychological counseling.

Athletics *Intercollegiate sports:* badminton M/W, ice hockey M, lacrosse M/W, soccer M/W, volleyball W.

Standardized Tests *Required:* SAT I or ACT (for admission).

Costs (2004–05) *Comprehensive fee:* $13,958 includes full-time tuition ($7410), mandatory fees ($1394), and room and board ($5154). Part-time tuition: $289 per credit. *Required fees:* $50 per credit part-time. *Payment plan:* installment. *Waivers:* senior citizens and employees or children of employees.

Financial Aid Of all full-time matriculated undergraduates who enrolled in 2003, 64 applied for aid, 57 were judged to have need, 57 had their need fully met. In 2003, 9 non-need-based awards were made. *Average percent of need met:* 100%. *Average financial aid package:* $7248. *Average need-based loan:* $2000. *Average need-based gift aid:* $7248. *Average non-need-based aid:* $1037. *Average indebtedness upon graduation:* $2000.

Applying *Options:* electronic application, deferred entrance. *Application fee:* $30. *Required:* essay or personal statement, high school transcript, minimum 2.2 GPA, 2 letters of recommendation. *Required for some:* 3 letters of recommendation, interview. *Application deadlines:* 7/1 (freshmen), 7/1 (transfers). *Notification:* continuous (freshmen), continuous (transfers).

Admissions Contact Ms. Dee Smith-Johns, Admissions Coordinator, Bryn Athyn College of the New Church, Box 717, Bryn Athyn, PA 19009. *Phone:* 215-938-2511. *Toll-free phone:* 215-938-2511. *Fax:* 215-938-2658. *E-mail:* dsjohns@newchurch.edu.

BRYN MAWR COLLEGE

Bryn Mawr, Pennsylvania

- **Independent** university, founded 1885
- **Calendar** semesters
- **Degrees** bachelor's, master's, and doctoral
- **Suburban** 135-acre campus with easy access to Philadelphia
- **Endowment** $443.6 million
- **Women only,** 1,334 undergraduate students, 96% full-time
- **Most difficult** entrance level, 51% of applicants were admitted

Bryn Mawr, a liberal arts college for women located in suburban Philadelphia, is a diverse community of individuals who share an intense intellectual commitment, a self-directed and purposeful vision of their lives, and a desire to make a meaningful contribution to the world. Bryn Mawr benefits from its proximity to Philadelphia with its rich cultural and social resources, as well as an active academic and social consortium with neighboring Haverford College, nearby Swarthmore College, and the University of Pennsylvania.

Undergraduates 1,284 full-time, 50 part-time. Students come from 48 states and territories, 44 other countries, 80% are from out of state, 4% African American, 12% Asian American or Pacific Islander, 3% Hispanic American, 8% international, 1% transferred in, 95% live on campus. *Retention:* 95% of 2002 full-time freshmen returned.

Freshmen *Admission:* 352 enrolled. *Test scores:* SAT verbal scores over 500: 98%; SAT math scores over 500: 99%; SAT verbal scores over 600: 82%; SAT math scores over 600: 68%; SAT verbal scores over 700: 38%; SAT math scores over 700: 15%.

Faculty *Total:* 198, 74% full-time, 90% with terminal degrees. *Student/faculty ratio:* 8:1.

Majors Ancient/classical Greek; anthropology; archeology; art; art history, criticism and conservation; Asian studies (East); astronomy; biology/biological sciences; chemistry; classics and languages, literatures and linguistics; comparative literature; economics; English; French; geology/earth science; German; history; Italian; Latin; mathematics; music; philosophy; physics; political science and government; psychology; religious studies; Romance languages; Russian; sociology; Spanish; urban studies/affairs.

Academic Programs *Special study options:* academic remediation for entering students, accelerated degree program, adult/continuing education programs, advanced placement credit, double majors, honors programs, independent study, off-campus study, services for LD students, student-designed majors, study abroad, summer session for credit. *ROTC:* Air Force (c). *Unusual degree programs:* 3-2 engineering with University of Pennsylvania; city and regional planning with University of Pennsylvania.

Library Miriam Coffin Canaday Library plus 2 others with an OPAC, a Web page.

Computers on Campus 200 computers available on campus for general student use. A campuswide network can be accessed from student residence rooms and from off campus. Internet access, at least one staffed computer lab available. Computer purchase or lease plan available.

Student Life *Housing:* on-campus residence required for freshman year. *Options:* women-only, cooperative. Campus housing is university owned. Freshman campus housing is guaranteed. *Activities and organizations:* drama/theater group, student-run newspaper, choral group, musical and theater groups, community service, Student Government Association, International Students Association, cultural groups. *Campus security:* 24-hour emergency response devices and patrols, late-night transport/escort service, controlled dormitory access, shuttle bus service, awareness programs, bicycle registration, security Website. *Student services:* health clinic, personal/psychological counseling, women's center.

Athletics Member NCAA. All Division III. *Intercollegiate sports:* badminton W, basketball W, crew W, cross-country running W, field hockey W, lacrosse W, rugby W(c), soccer W, swimming W, tennis W, track and field W, volleyball W. *Intramural sports:* archery W, badminton W, cross-country running W, equestrian sports W, field hockey W, lacrosse W, rugby W, soccer W, softball W, swimming W, tennis W, track and field W, volleyball W, weight lifting W.

Standardized Tests *Required:* SAT I and SAT II or ACT (for admission).

Costs (2003–04) *Comprehensive fee:* $36,890 includes full-time tuition ($26,830), mandatory fees ($690), and room and board ($9370). Part-time tuition: $3360 per course. Part-time tuition and fees vary according to course load. *College room only:* $5400. Room and board charges vary according to board plan. *Payment plans:* tuition prepayment, installment. *Waivers:* senior citizens and employees or children of employees.

Financial Aid Of all full-time matriculated undergraduates who enrolled in 2003, 818 applied for aid, 751 were judged to have need, 743 had their need fully met. 502 Federal Work-Study jobs (averaging $1727). 103 state and other part-time jobs (averaging $1706). *Average percent of need met:* 99%. *Average financial aid package:* $25,139. *Average need-based loan:* $4421. *Average need-based gift aid:* $21,583. *Average indebtedness upon graduation:* $17,827. *Financial aid deadline:* 2/2.

Applying *Options:* common application, electronic application, early admission, early decision, deferred entrance. *Application fee:* $50. *Required:* essay or personal statement, high school transcript, 3 letters of recommendation. *Recommended:* interview. *Application deadlines:* 1/15 (freshmen), 3/15 (transfers). *Early decision:* 11/15 (for plan 1), 1/1 (for plan 2). *Notification:* 3/15 (freshmen), 12/15 (early decision plan 1), 2/1 (early decision plan 2), 5/15 (transfers).

Admissions Contact Ms. Jennifer Rickard, Dean of Admissions and Financial Aid, Bryn Mawr College, 101 North Merion Avenue, Bryn Mawr, PA 19010. *Phone:* 610-526-5152. *Toll-free phone:* 800-BMC-1885. *E-mail:* admissions@brynmawr.edu.

■ *See page 1306 for a narrative description.*

BUCKNELL UNIVERSITY

Lewisburg, Pennsylvania

- **Independent** comprehensive, founded 1846
- **Calendar** semesters
- **Degrees** bachelor's and master's
- **Small-town** 445-acre campus
- **Endowment** $355.9 million
- **Coed,** 3,486 undergraduate students, 99% full-time, 50% women, 50% men
- **Very difficult** entrance level, 38% of applicants were admitted

Bucknell University is a top-ranked institution that gives students broad choices of academic programs and activities and the intense personal support of faculty members who help students make the most of their college education. The University's 3,350 undergraduates and 150 graduate students are high achievers who enjoy becoming active members of the close-knit Bucknell community.

Undergraduates 3,449 full-time, 37 part-time. Students come from 48 states and territories, 46 other countries, 68% are from out of state, 3% African American, 6% Asian American or Pacific Islander, 2% Hispanic American, 0.4% Native American, 2% international, 0.9% transferred in, 89% live on campus. *Retention:* 94% of 2002 full-time freshmen returned.

Freshmen *Admission:* 7,706 applied, 2,961 admitted, 906 enrolled. *Test scores:* SAT verbal scores over 500: 99%; SAT math scores over 500: 100%; SAT verbal scores over 600: 77%; SAT math scores over 600: 88%; SAT verbal scores over 700: 15%; SAT math scores over 700: 29%.

Faculty *Total:* 310, 94% full-time, 93% with terminal degrees. *Student/faculty ratio:* 12:1.

Majors Accounting; anthropology; area studies; art; art history, criticism and conservation; Asian studies (East); biology/biological sciences; biomedical/medical engineering; biopsychology; business administration and management; chemical engineering; chemistry; civil engineering; classics and languages, literatures and linguistics; computer and information sciences; computer engineering; dramatic/theatre arts; economics; education; educational statistics and research methods; electrical, electronics and communications engineering; elementary education; English; environmental studies; fine/studio arts; French; geography; geological and earth sciences/geosciences related; geology/earth science; German; history; humanities; interdisciplinary studies; international relations and affairs; kindergarten/preschool education; Latin American studies; mathematics; mechanical engineering; multi-/interdisciplinary studies related; music; music history, literature, and theory; music performance; music teacher education; music theory and composition; philosophy; physics; political science and government; psychology; religious studies; Russian; secondary education; sociology; Spanish; women's studies.

Academic Programs *Special study options:* advanced placement credit, double majors, honors programs, independent study, internships, off-campus study, part-time degree program, services for LD students, student-designed majors, study abroad, summer session for credit. *ROTC:* Army (b). *Unusual degree programs:* 3-2 chemistry, biology, mathematics.

Library Ellen Clarke Bertrand Library with 710,985 titles, 5,853 serial subscriptions, 15,300 audiovisual materials, an OPAC, a Web page.

Computers on Campus 610 computers available on campus for general student use. A campuswide network can be accessed from student residence rooms and from off campus. Internet access, at least one staffed computer lab available.

Student Life *Housing:* on-campus residence required through senior year. *Options:* coed, women-only, disabled students. Campus housing is university owned. Freshman campus housing is guaranteed. *Activities and organizations:* drama/theater group, student-run newspaper, radio station, choral group, Alpha Phi Omega, outing club, C.A.L.V.I.N. & H.O.B.B.E.S., Activities Council, Catholic Campus Ministries, national fraternities, national sororities. *Campus security:* 24-hour emergency response devices and patrols, student patrols, late-night transport/escort service, well-lit pathways, self-defense education, safety/security orientation. *Student services:* health clinic, personal/psychological counseling, women's center.

Athletics Member NCAA. All Division I except football (Division I-AA). *Intercollegiate sports:* baseball M, basketball M(s)/W(s), cheerleading M(c)/W(c), crew M(c)/W, cross-country running M/W, equestrian sports M(c)/W(c), field hockey W, golf M/W, ice hockey M(c), lacrosse M/W, rugby M(c)/W(c), skiing (downhill) M(c)/W(c), soccer M/W, softball W, swimming M/W, tennis M/W, track and field M/W, ultimate Frisbee M(c)/W(c), volleyball M(c)/W, water polo M/W, wrestling M(c). *Intramural sports:* basketball M/W, bowling M/W, cross-country running M/W, golf M/W, racquetball M/W, soccer M/W, softball M/W, squash M/W, table tennis M/W, tennis M/W, ultimate Frisbee M/W, volleyball M/W, weight lifting M.

Standardized Tests *Required:* SAT I or ACT (for admission).

Costs (2003–04) *Comprehensive fee:* $35,262 includes full-time tuition ($28,764), mandatory fees ($196), and room and board ($6302). Part-time tuition: $3290 per course. *College room only:* $3365. Room and board charges vary according to board plan and housing facility. *Payment plan:* installment. *Waivers:* employees or children of employees.

Financial Aid Of all full-time matriculated undergraduates who enrolled in 2003, 1,785 applied for aid, 1,740 were judged to have need, 1,740 had their need fully met. 1,000 Federal Work-Study jobs (averaging $1504). 54 state and other part-time jobs (averaging $1500). In 2003, 9 non-need-based awards were made. *Average percent of need met:* 100%. *Average financial aid package:* $19,000. *Average need-based loan:* $5200. *Average need-based gift aid:* $16,500. *Average non-need-based aid:* $6777. *Average indebtedness upon graduation:* $16,695. *Financial aid deadline:* 1/1.

Applying *Options:* common application, electronic application, early decision. *Application fee:* $60. *Required:* essay or personal statement, high school transcript, 2 letters of recommendation. *Recommended:* interview. *Application deadlines:* 1/1 (freshmen), 4/1 (transfers). *Early decision:* 11/15 (for plan 1), 1/1 (for plan 2). *Notification:* 4/1 (freshmen), 12/15 (early decision plan 1), 2/1 (early decision plan 2), 6/1 (transfers).

Admissions Contact Mr. Mark D. Davies, Dean of Admissions, Bucknell University, Lewisburg, PA 17837. *Phone:* 570-577-1101. *Fax:* 570-577-3538. *E-mail:* admissions@bucknell.edu.

■ *See page 1308 for a narrative description.*

CABRINI COLLEGE
Radnor, Pennsylvania

- **Independent Roman Catholic** comprehensive, founded 1957
- **Calendar** semesters
- **Degrees** certificates, bachelor's, and master's
- **Suburban** 112-acre campus with easy access to Philadelphia
- **Coed,** 1,715 undergraduate students, 83% full-time, 64% women, 36% men
- **Minimally difficult** entrance level, 83% of applicants were admitted

Undergraduates 1,431 full-time, 284 part-time. Students come from 20 states and territories, 33% are from out of state, 6% African American, 2% Asian American or Pacific Islander, 2% Hispanic American, 0.2% Native American, 0.3% international, 4% transferred in, 95% live on campus. *Retention:* 75% of 2002 full-time freshmen returned.

Freshmen *Admission:* 2,302 applied, 1,910 admitted, 403 enrolled. *Average high school GPA:* 3.07. *Test scores:* SAT verbal scores over 500: 47%; SAT math scores over 500: 42%; SAT verbal scores over 600: 8%; SAT math scores over 600: 8%; SAT verbal scores over 700: 1%; SAT math scores over 700: 2%.

Faculty *Total:* 222, 27% full-time, 42% with terminal degrees. *Student/faculty ratio:* 15:1.

Majors Accounting; American studies; biology/biological sciences; biology teacher education; biotechnology; business administration and management; chemistry; chemistry teacher education; clinical laboratory science/medical technology; communication/speech communication and rhetoric; computer and information sciences; early childhood education; education; elementary education; English; English/language arts teacher education; finance; fine/studio arts; French; graphic design; history; human resources management; kindergarten/preschool education; kinesiology and exercise science; liberal arts and sciences/liberal studies; management information systems; marketing/marketing management; mathematics; mathematics teacher education; philosophy; political science and government; psychology; religious studies; social studies teacher education; social work; sociology; Spanish; special education.

Academic Programs *Special study options:* academic remediation for entering students, accelerated degree program, adult/continuing education programs, advanced placement credit, cooperative education, distance learning, double majors, honors programs, independent study, internships, off-campus study, part-time degree program, services for LD students, student-designed majors, study abroad, summer session for credit. *ROTC:* Army (c). *Unusual degree programs:* 3-2 physical therapy, occupational therapy with Thomas Jefferson University.

Library Holy Spirit Library with 82,865 titles, 523 serial subscriptions, 1,164 audiovisual materials, an OPAC, a Web page.

Computers on Campus 195 computers available on campus for general student use. A campuswide network can be accessed from student residence rooms. Internet access, at least one staffed computer lab available.

Student Life *Housing options:* coed, women-only, disabled students. Campus housing is university owned. Freshman applicants given priority for college housing. *Activities and organizations:* drama/theater group, student-run newspaper, radio station, choral group, Student Government Association, student newspaper, international club, campus radio station, Council for Exceptional Children. *Campus security:* 24-hour emergency response devices and patrols, student patrols, late-night transport/escort service, controlled dormitory access, resident assistants and directors on nightly duty. *Student services:* health clinic, personal/psychological counseling.

Athletics Member NCAA. All Division III. *Intercollegiate sports:* basketball M/W, cross-country running M/W, field hockey W, golf M, lacrosse M/W, soccer M/W, softball W, tennis M/W, track and field M/W, volleyball W. *Intramural sports:* basketball M/W, football M/W, racquetball M/W, soccer M/W, softball M/W, squash M/W, swimming M/W, tennis M/W, ultimate Frisbee M/W, volleyball M/W.

Standardized Tests *Required:* SAT I or ACT (for admission).

Costs (2003–04) *Comprehensive fee:* $28,970 includes full-time tuition ($19,670), mandatory fees ($750), and room and board ($8550). Part-time tuition and fees vary according to course load. *Room and board:* Room and board charges vary according to housing facility. *Payment plan:* installment. *Waivers:* children of alumni, senior citizens, and employees or children of employees.

Financial Aid Of all full-time matriculated undergraduates who enrolled in 2003, 1,377 applied for aid, 1,059 were judged to have need, 93 had their need fully met. 203 Federal Work-Study jobs (averaging $765). In 2003, 322 non-need-based awards were made. *Average financial aid package:* $12,877. *Average need-based loan:* $5269. *Average need-based gift aid:* $5253. *Average non-need-based aid:* $4260. *Average indebtedness upon graduation:* $17,050.

Applying *Options:* common application, electronic application, early admission, deferred entrance. *Application fee:* $25. *Required:* high school transcript, minimum 2.0 GPA. *Recommended:* essay or personal statement, minimum 3.0 GPA, 3 letters of recommendation, interview. *Application deadline:* rolling (freshmen), rolling (transfers).

Admissions Contact Mr. Gary E. Johnson, Dean for Enrollment, Cabrini College, 610 King of Prussia Road, Radnor, PA 19087-3698. *Phone:* 610-902-8552. *Toll-free phone:* 800-848-1003. *Fax:* 610-902-8508. *E-mail:* admit@cabrini.edu.

■ *See page 1314 for a narrative description.*

CALIFORNIA UNIVERSITY OF PENNSYLVANIA
California, Pennsylvania

- **State-supported** comprehensive, founded 1852, part of Pennsylvania State System of Higher Education
- **Calendar** semesters
- **Degrees** associate, bachelor's, and master's
- **Small-town** 148-acre campus with easy access to Pittsburgh
- **Endowment** $328,585
- **Coed,** 5,392 undergraduate students, 87% full-time, 53% women, 47% men
- **Moderately difficult** entrance level, 75% of applicants were admitted

Cal U offers more than 100 programs. Offerings in science and technology are the University's special mission. Education and human services programs hold a long tradition of excellence. Liberal arts programs offer outstanding opportunities while providing the general education curriculum. With about 6,000 undergraduate students and a student-faculty ratio of 20:1, education is economical and personal.

Undergraduates 4,715 full-time, 677 part-time. Students come from 28 states and territories, 14 other countries, 3% are from out of state, 4% African American, 0.3% Asian American or Pacific Islander, 0.4% Hispanic American, 0.2% Native American, 0.7% international, 35% transferred in, 25% live on campus. *Retention:* 77% of 2002 full-time freshmen returned.

Freshmen *Admission:* 2,721 applied, 2,038 admitted, 996 enrolled. *Average high school GPA:* 2.95. *Test scores:* SAT verbal scores over 500: 43%; SAT math scores over 500: 36%; SAT verbal scores over 600: 8%; SAT math scores over 600: 8%; SAT verbal scores over 700: 1%; SAT math scores over 700: 1%.

Faculty *Total:* 357, 77% full-time, 52% with terminal degrees. *Student/faculty ratio:* 19:1.

California University of Pennsylvania (continued)

Majors Accounting; anthropology; art; biological and physical sciences; biology/biological sciences; business administration and management; business/commerce; chemistry; clinical/medical laboratory technology; communication/speech communication and rhetoric; computer programming; drafting and design technology; dramatic/theatre arts; economics; education; electrical, electronic and communications engineering technology; elementary education; English; environmental studies; French; geography; geology/earth science; German; gerontology; history; industrial technology; kindergarten/preschool education; liberal arts and sciences/liberal studies; mathematics; nursing (registered nurse training); occupational therapist assistant; parks, recreation and leisure facilities management; philosophy; physics; political science and government; psychology; social sciences; social work; sociology; Spanish; special education.

Academic Programs *Special study options:* academic remediation for entering students, accelerated degree program, adult/continuing education programs, advanced placement credit, cooperative education, distance learning, double majors, honors programs, internships, off-campus study, part-time degree program, services for LD students, study abroad, summer session for credit. *ROTC:* Army (b). *Unusual degree programs:* 3-2 engineering with University of Pittsburgh, Pennsylvania State University—University Park Campus.

Library Manderino Library with 437,160 titles, 881 serial subscriptions, 59,703 audiovisual materials, an OPAC, a Web page.

Computers on Campus 720 computers available on campus for general student use. A campuswide network can be accessed from student residence rooms and from off campus. Internet access, at least one staffed computer lab available.

Student Life *Housing options:* men-only, women-only. Campus housing is university owned and is provided by a third party. *Activities and organizations:* drama/theater group, student-run newspaper, radio and television station, choral group, marching band, student government, In-Res Hall Council, Graduate Student Association, Black Student Union, sports recreation, national fraternities, national sororities. *Campus security:* 24-hour emergency response devices and patrols, student patrols, late-night transport/escort service. *Student services:* health clinic, personal/psychological counseling, women's center, legal services.

Athletics Member NCAA. All Division II. *Intercollegiate sports:* basketball M(s)/W(s), cross-country running M(s)/W(s), fencing M/W, football M(s), golf M(s), rugby M/W, soccer M(s)/W, tennis W(s), track and field M(s)/W(s), volleyball W(s). *Intramural sports:* basketball M/W, cross-country running M/W, fencing M/W, football M/W, golf M/W, racquetball M/W, rugby M/W, skiing (cross-country) M/W, skiing (downhill) M/W, soccer M/W, swimming M/W, table tennis M/W, tennis M/W, track and field M/W, volleyball M/W.

Standardized Tests *Required:* SAT I (for admission). *Recommended:* SAT II: Subject Tests (for admission).

Costs (2003–04) *Tuition:* state resident $4598 full-time, $192 per credit part-time; nonresident $6948 full-time, $587 per credit part-time. Full-time tuition and fees vary according to location. Part-time tuition and fees vary according to location. *Required fees:* $1410 full-time. *Room and board:* $5378; room only: $2766. Room and board charges vary according to board plan. *Payment plan:* installment. *Waivers:* employees or children of employees.

Financial Aid *Average financial aid package:* $7025.

Applying *Options:* common application, electronic application, early admission, deferred entrance. *Application fee:* $25. *Required:* high school transcript, minimum 2.0 GPA. *Required for some:* letters of recommendation, interview. *Recommended:* essay or personal statement, minimum 3.0 GPA. *Application deadlines:* 7/30 (freshmen), 7/30 (transfers). *Notification:* continuous (freshmen), continuous (transfers).

Admissions Contact Mr. William A. Edmonds, Dean of Enrollment Management and Academic Services, California University of Pennsylvania, 250 University Avenue, California, PA 15419. *Phone:* 724-938-4404. *Fax:* 724-938-4564. *E-mail:* inquiry@cup.edu.

■ *See page 1332 for a narrative description.*

CARLOW COLLEGE
Pittsburgh, Pennsylvania

- **Independent Roman Catholic** comprehensive, founded 1929
- **Calendar** semesters
- **Degrees** bachelor's, master's, and post-master's certificates
- **Urban** 14-acre campus
- **Endowment** $3.6 million
- **Coed, primarily women,** 1,824 undergraduate students
- **Moderately difficult** entrance level

Undergraduates Students come from 12 states and territories, 4% are from out of state, 22% African American, 0.6% Asian American or Pacific Islander, 0.5% Hispanic American, 0.4% Native American, 0.9% international, 13% transferred in, 17% live on campus. *Retention:* 78% of 2002 full-time freshmen returned.

Freshmen *Average high school GPA:* 3.20. *Test scores:* SAT verbal scores over 500: 53%; SAT math scores over 500: 44%; ACT scores over 18: 88%; SAT verbal scores over 600: 16%; SAT math scores over 600: 11%; ACT scores over 24: 18%; SAT verbal scores over 700: 2%; SAT math scores over 700: 1%; ACT scores over 30: 1%.

Faculty *Total:* 229, 34% full-time. *Student/faculty ratio:* 12:1.

Majors Accounting; art; art history, criticism and conservation; art teacher education; biology/biological sciences; business/commerce; chemical engineering; chemistry; communication/speech communication and rhetoric; computer science; creative writing; design and visual communications; ecology; elementary education; English; environmental biology; health science; history; information science/studies; kindergarten/preschool education; liberal arts and sciences/liberal studies; mathematics; mathematics and computer science; nursing (registered nurse training); philosophy; psychology; social studies teacher education; social work; sociology; special education; special products marketing; technical and business writing; theology.

Academic Programs *Special study options:* academic remediation for entering students, accelerated degree program, adult/continuing education programs, advanced placement credit, cooperative education, distance learning, double majors, English as a second language, external degree program, honors programs, independent study, internships, off-campus study, part-time degree program, services for LD students, student-designed majors, summer session for credit. *ROTC:* Army (c), Navy (c), Air Force (c). *Unusual degree programs:* 3-2 engineering with Carnegie Mellon University; social work with physical therapy, occupational therapy, athletic training, physician's assistant, environmental science and management with Duquesne University.

Library Grace Library with 81,532 titles, 382 serial subscriptions, 4,631 audiovisual materials, an OPAC, a Web page.

Computers on Campus 250 computers available on campus for general student use. A campuswide network can be accessed from student residence rooms and from off campus that provide access to applications software, e-mail. Internet access, online (class) registration, at least one staffed computer lab available.

Student Life *Housing options:* women-only. Campus housing is university owned. *Activities and organizations:* drama/theater group, student-run newspaper, choral group, Commuter Student Association, Resident Student Association, Student Athletic Association, Gospel Choir "Blessed", Student Government Association. *Campus security:* 24-hour emergency response devices and patrols, late-night transport/escort service, controlled dormitory access. *Student services:* health clinic, personal/psychological counseling, women's center.

Athletics Member NAIA. *Intercollegiate sports:* basketball W(s), crew W(c), soccer W(s), softball W(s), tennis W(s), volleyball W(s).

Standardized Tests *Required:* SAT I or ACT (for admission).

Costs (2003–04) *Comprehensive fee:* $21,374 includes full-time tuition ($14,776), mandatory fees ($488), and room and board ($6110). Full-time tuition and fees vary according to course load and program. Part-time tuition and fees vary according to course load and program. *Room and board:* Room and board charges vary according to board plan. *Payment plans:* installment, deferred payment. *Waivers:* adult students and employees or children of employees.

Financial Aid Of all full-time matriculated undergraduates who enrolled in 2003, 431 Federal Work-Study jobs (averaging $776).

Applying *Options:* common application, electronic application, early admission, early action, deferred entrance. *Application fee:* $20. *Required:* high school transcript. *Required for some:* letters of recommendation. *Recommended:* minimum 3.0 GPA, interview, rank in upper two-fifths of high school class. *Application deadline:* 4/1 (freshmen), rolling (transfers). *Notification:* continuous (freshmen), 10/30 (early action), continuous (transfers).

Admissions Contact Ms. Susan Winstel, Assistant Director of Admissions, Carlow College, 3333 Fifth Avenue, Pittsburgh, PA 15213. *Phone:* 412-578-6330. *Toll-free phone:* 800-333-CARLOW. *Fax:* 412-578-6668. *E-mail:* admissions@carlow.edu.

■ *See page 1350 for a narrative description.*

CARNEGIE MELLON UNIVERSITY
Pittsburgh, Pennsylvania

- **Independent** university, founded 1900
- **Calendar** semesters
- **Degrees** bachelor's, master's, doctoral, and post-master's certificates
- **Urban** 103-acre campus
- **Coed,** 5,484 undergraduate students, 95% full-time, 40% women, 60% men
- **Very difficult** entrance level, 38% of applicants were admitted

Undergraduates 5,226 full-time, 258 part-time. Students come from 52 states and territories, 61 other countries, 76% are from out of state, 5% African American, 23% Asian American or Pacific Islander, 5% Hispanic American, 0.4% Native American, 11% international, 0.7% transferred in, 72% live on campus. *Retention:* 93% of 2001 full-time freshmen returned.

Freshmen *Admission:* 14,467 applied, 5,561 admitted, 1,341 enrolled. *Average high school GPA:* 3.60. *Test scores:* SAT verbal scores over 500: 97%; SAT math scores over 500: 100%; ACT scores over 18: 100%; SAT verbal scores over 600: 78%; SAT math scores over 600: 97%; ACT scores over 24: 96%; SAT verbal scores over 700: 30%; SAT math scores over 700: 66%; ACT scores over 30: 52%.

Faculty *Total:* 956, 81% full-time, 98% with terminal degrees. *Student/faculty ratio:* 11:1.

Majors Applied mathematics; architecture; art; biochemistry; biology/biological sciences; biomedical/medical engineering; biophysics; business administration and management; business/managerial economics; ceramic arts and ceramics; chemical engineering; chemistry; civil engineering; cognitive psychology and psycholinguistics; commercial and advertising art; computer and information sciences; computer engineering; computer science; creative writing; dramatic/theatre arts; economics; electrical, electronics and communications engineering; engineering; engineering related; English; environmental/environmental health engineering; European studies; fine/studio arts; French; German; history; humanities; industrial design; information science/studies; interdisciplinary studies; Japanese; liberal arts and sciences/liberal studies; literature; mass communication/media; materials engineering; materials science; mathematics; mechanical engineering; modern languages; music; music performance; music theory and composition; philosophy; physics; political science and government; polymer chemistry; psychology; Russian; sculpture; social sciences; Spanish; statistics; technical and business writing; western civilization.

Academic Programs *Special study options:* accelerated degree program, adult/continuing education programs, advanced placement credit, cooperative education, double majors, English as a second language, freshman honors college, honors programs, independent study, internships, off-campus study, part-time degree program, services for LD students, student-designed majors, study abroad, summer session for credit. *ROTC:* Army (b), Navy (b), Air Force (b). *Unusual degree programs:* 3-2 public management and policy.

Library Hunt Library plus 2 others with 961,507 titles, 5,714 serial subscriptions, 218,779 audiovisual materials, an OPAC, a Web page.

Computers on Campus 450 computers available on campus for general student use. A campuswide network can be accessed from student residence rooms and from off campus. Internet access, online (class) registration, at least one staffed computer lab available.

Student Life *Housing:* on-campus residence required for freshman year. *Options:* coed, men-only, women-only, disabled students. *Activities and organizations:* drama/theater group, student-run newspaper, radio station, choral group, marching band, Student Senate, Alpha Phi Omega, Tartan Club, Spirit Club, national fraternities, national sororities. *Campus security:* 24-hour emergency response devices and patrols, late-night transport/escort service, controlled dormitory access. *Student services:* health clinic, personal/psychological counseling, women's center, legal services.

Athletics Member NCAA. All Division III. *Intercollegiate sports:* badminton M(c)/W(c), baseball M(c), basketball M/W, crew M(c)/W(c), cross-country running M/W, fencing M(c)/W(c), football M, golf M, ice hockey M(c)/W(c), lacrosse M(c)/W(c), rugby M(c), soccer M/W, softball W(c), squash M(c)/W(c), swimming M/W, tennis M/W, track and field M/W, ultimate Frisbee M(c)/W(c), volleyball M(c)/W, water polo M(c)/W(c), wrestling M(c)/W(c). *Intramural sports:* badminton M/W, basketball M/W, bowling M/W, cross-country running M/W, fencing M/W, football M/W, golf M/W, racquetball M/W, soccer M/W, softball M/W, swimming M/W, table tennis M/W, tennis M/W, track and field M/W, ultimate Frisbee M/W, volleyball M/W, water polo M/W.

Standardized Tests *Required:* SAT I or ACT (for admission), SAT II: Subject Tests (for admission). *Required for some:* SAT II: Writing Test (for admission).

Costs (2003–04) *Comprehensive fee:* $37,565 includes full-time tuition ($29,190), mandatory fees ($220), and room and board ($8155). *College room only:* $4705.

Financial Aid Of all full-time matriculated undergraduates who enrolled in 2002, 3,081 applied for aid, 2,599 were judged to have need, 1,089 had their need fully met. In 2002, 626 non-need-based awards were made. *Average percent of need met:* 83%. *Average financial aid package:* $19,732. *Average need-based loan:* $5226. *Average need-based gift aid:* $13,771. *Average non-need-based aid:* $12,508. *Average indebtedness upon graduation:* $19,195.

Applying *Options:* common application, electronic application, early admission, early decision, deferred entrance. *Application fee:* $55. *Required:* essay or personal statement, high school transcript, 1 letter of recommendation. *Required for some:* portfolio, audition. *Recommended:* interview. *Application deadlines:* 1/1 (freshmen), 3/15 (transfers). *Early decision:* 11/1 (for plan 1), 11/15 (for plan 2). *Notification:* 4/15 (freshmen), 1/15 (early decision plan 1), 1/15 (early decision plan 2), 6/1 (transfers).

Admissions Contact Mr. Michael Steidel, Director of Admissions, Carnegie Mellon University, 5000 Forbes Avenue, Warner Hall, Room 101, Pittsburgh, PA 15213. *Phone:* 412-268-2082. *Fax:* 412-268-7838. *E-mail:* undergraduate-admissions@andrew.cmu.edu.

■ *See page 1352 for a narrative description.*

CEDAR CREST COLLEGE

Allentown, Pennsylvania

- **Independent** comprehensive, founded 1867, affiliated with United Church of Christ
- **Calendar** semesters
- **Degrees** associate, bachelor's, master's, and postbachelor's certificates
- **Suburban** 84-acre campus with easy access to Philadelphia
- **Endowment** $13.5 million
- **Women only,** 1,725 undergraduate students, 51% full-time
- **Moderately difficult** entrance level, 73% of applicants were admitted

For more than a decade, *U.S. News & World Report* has named Cedar Crest a top-tier regional liberal arts college. Programs most popular include conservation biology, dance, education, forensic science, nursing, and psychology. Qualified students may participate in internships, such as the FBI, CNN, and MTV as well as freshman research and honors program, cross-registration at 5 colleges, and Division III athletics.

Undergraduates 875 full-time, 850 part-time. Students come from 31 states and territories, 10 other countries, 18% are from out of state, 5% African American, 4% Asian American or Pacific Islander, 10% Hispanic American, 0.3% Native American, 0.2% international, 2% transferred in, 92% live on campus. *Retention:* 83% of 2002 full-time freshmen returned.

Freshmen *Admission:* 1,317 applied, 957 admitted, 306 enrolled. *Average high school GPA:* 3.22. *Test scores:* SAT verbal scores over 500: 75%; SAT math scores over 500: 68%; ACT scores over 18: 95%; SAT verbal scores over 600: 28%; SAT math scores over 600: 25%; ACT scores over 24: 54%; SAT verbal scores over 700: 4%; SAT math scores over 700: 1%; ACT scores over 30: 10%.

Faculty *Total:* 82, 88% full-time, 73% with terminal degrees. *Student/faculty ratio:* 11:1.

Majors Accounting; animal genetics; art; behavioral sciences; biochemistry; biological and physical sciences; biology/biological sciences; biomedical/medical engineering; biomedical sciences; biomedical technology; business administration and management; business/managerial economics; chemistry; clinical laboratory science/medical technology; communication/speech communication and rhetoric; computer and information sciences; dance; dramatic/theatre arts; education; elementary education; English; environmental biology; environmental studies; experimental psychology; fine/studio arts; foods, nutrition, and wellness; forensic science and technology; gerontology; health/health care administration; health science; history; information science/studies; international relations and affairs; legal assistant/paralegal; liberal arts and sciences/liberal studies; mathematics; middle school education; molecular biology; music; natural sciences; neuroscience; nuclear medical technology; nursing science; political science and government; pre-dentistry studies; pre-law studies; pre-medical studies; pre-veterinary studies; psychology; science teacher education; secondary education; social work; Spanish.

Academic Programs *Special study options:* academic remediation for entering students, accelerated degree program, adult/continuing education programs, advanced placement credit, distance learning, double majors, English as a second language, freshman honors college, honors programs, independent study, internships, off-campus study, part-time degree program, services for LD students, student-designed majors, study abroad, summer session for credit. *ROTC:* Army (c).

Library Cressman Library with 133,763 titles, 8,695 serial subscriptions, 16,316 audiovisual materials, an OPAC, a Web page.

Computers on Campus 227 computers available on campus for general student use. A campuswide network can be accessed from student residence rooms and from off campus that provide access to intranet. Internet access, at least one staffed computer lab available.

Student Life *Housing:* on-campus residence required through junior year. *Options:* women-only, disabled students. Freshman campus housing is guaranteed. *Activities and organizations:* drama/theater group, student-run newspaper, radio and television station, choral group, Alpha Phi Omega, Out There, athletes club, Student Activities Board, Student Government Association. *Campus security:* 24-hour emergency response devices and patrols, late-night transport/escort service, controlled dormitory access, crime prevention programs. *Student services:* health clinic, personal/psychological counseling.

Cedar Crest College (continued)

Athletics Member NCAA. All Division III. *Intercollegiate sports:* basketball W, cross-country running W, equestrian sports W(c), field hockey W, lacrosse W, soccer W, softball W, tennis W, track and field W(c), volleyball W. *Intramural sports:* badminton W, basketball W, soccer W, softball W, tennis W, volleyball W.

Standardized Tests *Required:* SAT I or ACT (for admission).

Costs (2004–05) *Comprehensive fee:* $29,495 includes full-time tuition ($21,600), mandatory fees ($300), and room and board ($7595). Full-time tuition and fees vary according to course load. Part-time tuition and fees vary according to class time. *Room and board:* Room and board charges vary according to board plan. *Payment plan:* installment. *Waivers:* children of alumni and employees or children of employees.

Financial Aid Of all full-time matriculated undergraduates who enrolled in 2003, 812 applied for aid, 761 were judged to have need, 123 had their need fully met. 101 Federal Work-Study jobs (averaging $1500). 330 state and other part-time jobs (averaging $1700). In 2003, 70 non-need-based awards were made. *Average percent of need met:* 76%. *Average financial aid package:* $15,300. *Average need-based loan:* $3806. *Average need-based gift aid:* $11,718. *Average non-need-based aid:* $12,867. *Average indebtedness upon graduation:* $21,151.

Applying *Options:* common application, electronic application, early admission, deferred entrance. *Application fee:* $30. *Required:* essay or personal statement, high school transcript. *Required for some:* 2 letters of recommendation. *Recommended:* minimum 2.0 GPA, interview. *Application deadline:* rolling (freshmen), rolling (transfers).

Admissions Contact Ms. Judith A. Neyhart, Vice President for Enrollment and Advancement, Cedar Crest College, 100 College Drive, Allentown, PA 18104-6196. *Phone:* 610-740-3780. *Toll-free phone:* 800-360-1222. *Fax:* 610-606-4647. *E-mail:* cccadmis@cedarcrest.edu.

■ *See page 1372 for a narrative description.*

CENTRAL PENNSYLVANIA COLLEGE
Summerdale, Pennsylvania

- **Proprietary** primarily 2-year, founded 1881
- **Calendar** quarters
- **Degrees** certificates, associate, and bachelor's
- **Small-town** 35-acre campus
- **Coed**
- **Noncompetitive** entrance level

Faculty *Student/faculty ratio:* 17:1.

Student Life *Campus security:* 24-hour emergency response devices and patrols.

Athletics Member NJCAA.

Costs (2004–05) *Comprehensive fee:* $17,160 includes full-time tuition ($10,440), mandatory fees ($570), and room and board ($6150). Full-time tuition and fees vary according to program. Part-time tuition: $290 per credit hour. Part-time tuition and fees vary according to course load and program. *Required fees:* $190 per term part-time. *College room only:* $4500. Room and board charges vary according to board plan and housing facility.

Financial Aid Of all full-time matriculated undergraduates who enrolled in 2001, 50 Federal Work-Study jobs (averaging $500).

Applying *Options:* electronic application. *Required:* high school transcript, interview. *Required for some:* minimum 2.0 GPA.

Admissions Contact Ms. Jennifer Verhagen, Director of Admissions, Central Pennsylvania College, Campus on College Hill and Valley Roads, Summerdale, PA 17093. *Phone:* 717-728-2213. *Toll-free phone:* 800-759-2727. *Fax:* 717-732-5254.

■ *See page 1380 for a narrative description.*

CHATHAM COLLEGE
Pittsburgh, Pennsylvania

- **Independent** comprehensive, founded 1869
- **Calendar** 4-1-4
- **Degrees** bachelor's, master's, doctoral, and postbachelor's certificates
- **Urban** 32-acre campus
- **Endowment** $51.6 million
- **Women only,** 704 undergraduate students, 58% full-time
- **Moderately difficult** entrance level, 61% of applicants were admitted

Chatham College, one of the nation's oldest women's colleges, offers a distinct undergraduate education in dynamic and beautiful Pittsburgh. Focused on preparing World Ready Women for professional careers, a Chatham education emphasizes the environment, global issues, and women's leadership. Chatham offers more than 35 undergraduate majors and seven 5-year bachelor's/master's degree programs.

Undergraduates 408 full-time, 296 part-time. Students come from 25 states and territories, 18 other countries, 21% are from out of state, 13% African American, 1% Asian American or Pacific Islander, 1% Hispanic American, 0.2% Native American, 6% international, 6% transferred in, 60% live on campus. *Retention:* 65% of 2002 full-time freshmen returned.

Freshmen *Admission:* 243 applied, 149 admitted, 78 enrolled. *Average high school GPA:* 3.24. *Test scores:* SAT verbal scores over 500: 74%; SAT math scores over 500: 41%; ACT scores over 18: 94%; SAT verbal scores over 600: 34%; SAT math scores over 600: 13%; ACT scores over 24: 50%; SAT verbal scores over 700: 3%; SAT math scores over 700: 1%.

Faculty *Total:* 75, 95% full-time, 85% with terminal degrees. *Student/faculty ratio:* 12:1.

Majors Accounting; area, ethnic, cultural, and gender studies related; art history, criticism and conservation; arts management; biochemistry; bioinformatics; biology/biological sciences; business administration and management; chemistry; chemistry teacher education; communication/speech communication and rhetoric; computer and information sciences; counseling psychology; creative writing; dramatic/theatre arts; economics; elementary education; engineering; English; English/language arts teacher education; environmental studies; fine/studio arts; French; health professions related; history; international business/trade/commerce; international/global studies; international relations and affairs; kinesiology and exercise science; landscape architecture; management information systems; marketing/marketing management; mathematics; mathematics teacher education; music; physical therapy; physics; physics teacher education; political science and government; psychology; public policy analysis; social studies teacher education; social work; Spanish; special education; women's studies.

Academic Programs *Special study options:* accelerated degree program, adult/continuing education programs, advanced placement credit, cooperative education, double majors, English as a second language, independent study, internships, off-campus study, part-time degree program, services for LD students, student-designed majors, study abroad, summer session for credit. *ROTC:* Army (c), Navy (c), Air Force (c). *Unusual degree programs:* 3-2 engineering with Carnegie Mellon University, Pennsylvania State University—University Park Campus, University of Pittsburgh; physical therapy, occupational therapy, physician assistant studies, education, counseling psychology.

Library Jennie King Mellon Library with 81,160 titles, 368 serial subscriptions, 374 audiovisual materials, an OPAC, a Web page.

Computers on Campus 265 computers available on campus for general student use. A campuswide network can be accessed from student residence rooms and from off campus that provide access to computer-aided instruction. Internet access, at least one staffed computer lab available. Computer purchase or lease plan available.

Student Life *Housing options:* women-only. Campus housing is university owned. Freshman campus housing is guaranteed. *Activities and organizations:* drama/theater group, student-run newspaper, choral group, Chatham Student Government, choir, Chatham Feminist Collective, Students of Community Service, Activities Board. *Campus security:* 24-hour emergency response devices and patrols, late-night transport/escort service, controlled dormitory access, self defense education; well lighted pathways and sidewalks. *Student services:* health clinic, personal/psychological counseling.

Athletics Member NCAA. All Division III. *Intercollegiate sports:* basketball W, crew W(c), ice hockey W, soccer W, softball W, swimming W(c), tennis W, volleyball W. *Intramural sports:* badminton W, basketball W, cross-country running W, equestrian sports W, fencing W, football W, golf W, rock climbing W, skiing (downhill) W, softball W, squash W, table tennis W, volleyball W, weight lifting W.

Standardized Tests *Required:* SAT I or ACT (for admission).

Costs (2003–04) *Comprehensive fee:* $27,266 includes full-time tuition ($20,360), mandatory fees ($192), and room and board ($6714). Full-time tuition and fees vary according to course load and degree level. Part-time tuition: $495 per credit. Part-time tuition and fees vary according to course load and degree level. *Required fees:* $48 per term part-time. *College room only:* $3514. Room and board charges vary according to board plan and housing facility. *Payment plan:* installment. *Waivers:* employees or children of employees.

Financial Aid Of all full-time matriculated undergraduates who enrolled in 2003, 379 applied for aid, 360 were judged to have need. 199 Federal Work-Study jobs (averaging $2200). *Average percent of need met:* 72%. *Average financial aid package:* $22,742. *Average need-based loan:* $4275. *Average need-based gift aid:* $7158. *Average non-need-based aid:* $5717. *Average indebtedness upon graduation:* $18,655.

Applying *Options:* common application, electronic application, early admission, deferred entrance. *Application fee:* $35. *Required:* essay or personal statement, high school transcript, minimum 2.5 GPA, 1 letter of recommendation. *Recommended:* minimum 3.0 GPA, 3 letters of recommendation, interview.

Application deadline: rolling (freshmen), rolling (transfers). *Notification:* continuous (freshmen), continuous (transfers).

Admissions Contact Mr. Alan G. McIvor, Vice President for Enrollment Management, Chatham College, Woodland Road, Pittsburgh, PA 15232. *Phone:* 412-365-1290. *Toll-free phone:* 800-837-1290. *Fax:* 412-365-1609. *E-mail:* admissions@chatham.edu.

■ *See page 1392 for a narrative description.*

CHESTNUT HILL COLLEGE
Philadelphia, Pennsylvania

- **Independent Roman Catholic** comprehensive, founded 1924
- **Calendar** semesters
- **Degrees** certificates, associate, bachelor's, master's, doctoral, post-master's, and postbachelor's certificates (profile includes figures from both traditional and accelerated (part-time) programs)
- **Suburban** 45-acre campus
- **Endowment** $4.9 million
- **Coed, primarily women,** 906 undergraduate students, 71% full-time, 81% women, 19% men
- **Moderately difficult** entrance level, 77% of applicants were admitted

Undergraduates 644 full-time, 262 part-time. Students come from 13 states and territories, 10% are from out of state, 4% transferred in, 36% live on campus. *Retention:* 61% of 2002 full-time freshmen returned.

Freshmen *Admission:* 973 applied, 751 admitted, 203 enrolled. *Average high school GPA:* 2.89. *Test scores:* SAT verbal scores over 500: 42%; SAT math scores over 500: 34%; SAT verbal scores over 600: 9%; SAT math scores over 600: 5%; SAT verbal scores over 700: 1%.

Faculty *Total:* 241, 25% full-time, 46% with terminal degrees. *Student/faculty ratio:* 12:1.

Majors Accounting; accounting and business/management; adult development and aging; biochemistry; biology/biological sciences; business administration and management; business/corporate communications; chemistry; child care and support services management; communication and journalism related; communications technologies and support services related; computer and information sciences; computer/information technology services administration related; computer science; criminal justice/law enforcement administration; early childhood education; education (multiple levels); elementary education; English; environmental studies; finance; French; health/health care administration; history; human resources management; human services; international business/trade/commerce; marketing/marketing management; mathematics and computer science; molecular biology; multi-/interdisciplinary studies related; political science and government; psychology; sociology; Spanish.

Academic Programs *Special study options:* academic remediation for entering students, adult/continuing education programs, advanced placement credit, cooperative education, double majors, English as a second language, honors programs, independent study, internships, off-campus study, part-time degree program, student-designed majors, study abroad, summer session for credit. *ROTC:* Army (c). *Unusual degree programs:* 3-2 biology, chemistry with the College of Podiatric Medicine of Temple University; biology, chemistry and medical technology with the College of Health Professions of Thomas Jefferson University; education, psychology, computer/applied technology with Chestnut Hill College.

Library Logue Library with 122,753 titles, 516 serial subscriptions, 4,804 audiovisual materials, an OPAC, a Web page.

Computers on Campus 101 computers available on campus for general student use. Internet access, at least one staffed computer lab available. Computer purchase or lease plan available.

Student Life *Housing options:* men-only, women-only. Campus housing is university owned. Freshman campus housing is guaranteed. *Activities and organizations:* drama/theater group, student-run newspaper, choral group, student government, Hispanics in Action, African American Awareness Society, Campus Ministry Community Service Group, Mosaic of Cultures Club. *Campus security:* 24-hour emergency response devices and patrols, late-night transport/escort service, controlled dormitory access. *Student services:* health clinic, personal/psychological counseling.

Athletics Member NCAA. All Division III. *Intercollegiate sports:* basketball M/W, cheerleading M(s)/W(s), golf M/W, lacrosse W, soccer M/W, softball M/W, tennis M(c)/W, volleyball W. *Intramural sports:* basketball M/W.

Standardized Tests *Required:* SAT I or ACT (for admission).

Costs (2004–05) *Comprehensive fee:* $27,845 includes full-time tuition ($19,660), mandatory fees ($685), and room and board ($7500). Full-time tuition and fees vary according to course load. *Room and board:* Room and board charges vary according to housing facility. *Payment plans:* installment, deferred payment. *Waivers:* senior citizens and employees or children of employees.

Financial Aid Of all full-time matriculated undergraduates who enrolled in 2003, 609 applied for aid, 551 were judged to have need. 214 Federal Work-Study jobs (averaging $1500). In 2003, 42 non-need-based awards were made. *Average percent of need met:* 51%. *Average financial aid package:* $16,125. *Average need-based loan:* $5500. *Average need-based gift aid:* $9205. *Average non-need-based aid:* $7225. *Average indebtedness upon graduation:* $17,125. *Financial aid deadline:* 4/15.

Applying *Options:* common application, early admission, deferred entrance. *Application fee:* $35. *Required:* essay or personal statement, high school transcript. *Required for some:* interview. *Recommended:* minimum 2.0 GPA, 1 letter of recommendation, interview. *Application deadline:* rolling (freshmen), rolling (transfers). *Notification:* continuous (transfers).

Admissions Contact Ms. Jodie King, Director of Admissions, Chestnut Hill College, 9601 Germantown Avenue, Philadelphia, PA 19118-2693. *Phone:* 215-248-7004. *Toll-free phone:* 800-248-0052. *Fax:* 215-248-7082. *E-mail:* chcapply@chc.edu.

■ *See page 1396 for a narrative description.*

CHEYNEY UNIVERSITY OF PENNSYLVANIA
Cheyney, Pennsylvania

- **State-supported** comprehensive, founded 1837, part of Pennsylvania State System of Higher Education
- **Calendar** 4-1-4
- **Degrees** bachelor's and master's
- **Suburban** 275-acre campus with easy access to Philadelphia
- **Coed,** 1,251 undergraduate students, 94% full-time, 55% women, 45% men
- **Minimally difficult** entrance level, 62% of applicants were admitted

Cheyney University of Pennsylvania, established in 1837, is America's oldest historically black educational institution. Cheyney strives to develop scholars who are not only well educated but also willing to set priorities that enable them to reach their highest potential in their personal and professional lives. Cheyney graduates are well-prepared to assume leadership roles through which they work for the greater public good.

Undergraduates 1,175 full-time, 76 part-time. Students come from 14 states and territories, 5 other countries, 16% are from out of state, 93% African American, 0.2% Asian American or Pacific Islander, 0.6% Hispanic American, 0.7% international, 4% transferred in, 66% live on campus.

Freshmen *Admission:* 2,146 applied, 1,336 admitted, 382 enrolled.

Faculty *Total:* 111, 75% full-time, 49% with terminal degrees. *Student/faculty ratio:* 13:1.

Majors Art; biological and physical sciences; biology/biological sciences; business administration and management; chemistry; clinical laboratory science/medical technology; clothing/textiles; communications technology; computer science; dramatic/theatre arts; economics; education; elementary education; English; family and consumer sciences/home economics teacher education; French; geography; hotel/motel administration; industrial technology; kindergarten/preschool education; mass communication/media; mathematics; music; parks, recreation and leisure; political science and government; psychology; secondary education; social sciences; sociology; Spanish; special education.

Academic Programs *Special study options:* academic remediation for entering students, adult/continuing education programs, cooperative education, internships, off-campus study, part-time degree program, services for LD students, summer session for credit. *ROTC:* Army (b), Air Force (c).

Library Leslie Pickney Hill Library with 85,533 titles, 1,526 serial subscriptions, 1,379 audiovisual materials, a Web page.

Computers on Campus 200 computers available on campus for general student use. A campuswide network can be accessed from student residence rooms and from off campus that provide access to various software packages. Internet access, online (class) registration, at least one staffed computer lab available.

Student Life *Housing options:* coed. Campus housing is university owned. Freshman applicants given priority for college housing. *Activities and organizations:* drama/theater group, student-run newspaper, radio station, choral group, marching band, national fraternities, national sororities. *Campus security:* 24-hour emergency response devices and patrols. *Student services:* health clinic, personal/psychological counseling, women's center.

Athletics Member NCAA. All Division II. *Intercollegiate sports:* basketball M(s)/W(s), bowling W, cross-country running M(s)/W(s), football M(s), track and field M(s)/W(s), volleyball W(s). *Intramural sports:* basketball M/W, football M.

Standardized Tests *Required:* SAT I or ACT (for admission). *Recommended:* SAT II: Subject Tests (for admission).

Costs (2003–04) *Tuition:* state resident $4598 full-time, $192 per credit part-time; nonresident $11,496 full-time, $479 per credit part-time. Full-time tuition and fees vary according to reciprocity agreements. Part-time tuition and fees vary according to reciprocity agreements. *Required fees:* $755 full-time. *Room and board:* $5383; room only: $2944. Room and board charges vary

Cheyney University of Pennsylvania (continued)
according to board plan. *Payment plan:* deferred payment. *Waivers:* senior citizens and employees or children of employees.

Financial Aid *Average percent of need met:* 87%.

Applying *Application fee:* $20. *Required:* essay or personal statement, high school transcript. *Required for some:* 3 letters of recommendation. *Recommended:* interview. *Application deadline:* rolling (freshmen), rolling (transfers). *Notification:* continuous (freshmen).

Admissions Contact Ms. Gemma Stemley, Director of Admissions, Cheyney University of Pennsylvania, 1837 University Circle, Cheyney, PA 19319. *Phone:* 610-399-2275. *Toll-free phone:* 800-CHEYNEY. *Fax:* 610-399-2099.

■ See page 1398 for a narrative description.

CLARION UNIVERSITY OF PENNSYLVANIA
Clarion, Pennsylvania

- **State-supported** comprehensive, founded 1867, part of Pennsylvania State System of Higher Education
- **Calendar** semesters
- **Degrees** certificates, diplomas, associate, bachelor's, master's, and post-master's certificates
- **Rural** 100-acre campus
- **Coed,** 5,943 undergraduate students, 89% full-time, 62% women, 38% men
- **Minimally difficult** entrance level, 78% of applicants were admitted

Undergraduates 5,277 full-time, 666 part-time. Students come from 29 states and territories, 40 other countries, 7% are from out of state, 5% African American, 0.6% Asian American or Pacific Islander, 0.7% Hispanic American, 0.2% Native American, 1% international, 6% transferred in, 34% live on campus. *Retention:* 74% of 2002 full-time freshmen returned.

Freshmen *Admission:* 3,447 applied, 2,673 admitted, 1,315 enrolled. *Average high school GPA:* 3.00. *Test scores:* SAT verbal scores over 500: 37%; SAT math scores over 500: 35%; SAT verbal scores over 600: 6%; SAT math scores over 600: 6%; SAT verbal scores over 700: 1%.

Faculty *Total:* 327, 90% full-time. *Student/faculty ratio:* 19:1.

Majors Accounting; anthropology; art; audiology and speech-language pathology; biological and physical sciences; biology/biological sciences; business administration and management; business/managerial economics; chemistry; clinical laboratory science/medical technology; communication/speech communication and rhetoric; computer and information sciences; dramatic/theatre arts; economics; education; elementary education; English; environmental studies; finance; French; geography; geology/earth science; history; humanities; information science/studies; international business/trade/commerce; kindergarten/preschool education; labor and industrial relations; legal administrative assistant/secretary; liberal arts and sciences/liberal studies; library science; management science; marketing/marketing management; mathematics; molecular biology; music management and merchandising; music performance; music teacher education; nursing (registered nurse training); occupational therapist assistant; philosophy; physics; political science and government; psychology; radiologic technology/science; reading teacher education; real estate; science teacher education; social psychology; social sciences; social studies teacher education; sociology; Spanish; special education; speech and rhetoric.

Academic Programs *Special study options:* academic remediation for entering students, accelerated degree program, adult/continuing education programs, advanced placement credit, distance learning, double majors, honors programs, internships, part-time degree program, services for LD students, study abroad, summer session for credit. *Unusual degree programs:* 3-2 engineering with University of Pittsburgh, Case Western Reserve University.

Library Carlson Library with 429,800 titles, 750 serial subscriptions, 23,444 audiovisual materials, an OPAC, a Web page.

Computers on Campus 400 computers available on campus for general student use. A campuswide network can be accessed from student residence rooms and from off campus. Internet access, online (class) registration, at least one staffed computer lab available.

Student Life *Housing options:* coed, men-only, women-only. *Activities and organizations:* drama/theater group, student-run newspaper, radio and television station, choral group, marching band, national fraternities, national sororities. *Campus security:* 24-hour emergency response devices and patrols, student patrols. *Student services:* health clinic, personal/psychological counseling, women's center.

Athletics Member NCAA. All Division II except wrestling (Division I). *Intercollegiate sports:* baseball M(s), basketball M(s)/W(s), cross-country running M(s)/W(s), football M(s), golf M(s), softball W(s), swimming M(s)/W(s), tennis W(s), track and field M(s)/W(s), volleyball W(s), wrestling M(s). *Intramural sports:* badminton M/W, basketball M/W, bowling M/W, cross-country running M/W, football M, golf M/W, racquetball M/W, soccer M/W, swimming M/W, tennis M/W, track and field M/W, volleyball M(c)/W, weight lifting M/W, wrestling M.

Standardized Tests *Required:* SAT I or ACT (for admission).

Costs (2003–04) *Tuition:* state resident $4598 full-time, $192 per credit hour part-time; nonresident $8048 full-time, $335 per credit hour part-time. *Required fees:* $1400 full-time, $37 per credit part-time, $63 per term part-time. *Room and board:* $4560; room only: $2994.

Financial Aid Of all full-time matriculated undergraduates who enrolled in 2001, 4,234 applied for aid, 3,393 were judged to have need, 1,988 had their need fully met. 300 Federal Work-Study jobs (averaging $1540). In 2001, 191 non-need-based awards were made. *Average percent of need met:* 87%. *Average financial aid package:* $6025. *Average need-based loan:* $3028. *Average need-based gift aid:* $3384. *Average non-need-based aid:* $1706. *Average indebtedness upon graduation:* $18,500.

Applying *Options:* deferred entrance. *Application fee:* $30. *Required:* high school transcript. *Required for some:* essay or personal statement, interview. *Recommended:* essay or personal statement, letters of recommendation, interview. *Application deadline:* rolling (freshmen), rolling (transfers).

Admissions Contact Ms. Sue McMillen, Interim Director of Admissions, Clarion University of Pennsylvania, 890 Wood Street, Clarion, PA 16214. *Phone:* 814-393-2306. *Toll-free phone:* 800-672-7171. *Fax:* 814-393-2030. *E-mail:* admissions@clarion.edu.

COLLEGE MISERICORDIA
Dallas, Pennsylvania

- **Independent Roman Catholic** comprehensive, founded 1924
- **Calendar** semesters
- **Degrees** bachelor's and master's
- **Small-town** 100-acre campus
- **Endowment** $8.2 million
- **Coed,** 2,360 undergraduate students, 59% full-time, 78% women, 22% men
- **Moderately difficult** entrance level, 77% of applicants were admitted

College Misericordia (CM) is highly ranked in 2 national surveys on student satisfaction. CM students report a unique blend of academics, professional preparation, and service leadership. Misericordia offers a guaranteed placement program that ensures a paid internship to graduates not employed or enrolled in graduate or professional school within 6 months of graduation.

Undergraduates 1,391 full-time, 969 part-time. Students come from 19 states and territories, 2 other countries, 17% are from out of state, 2% African American, 0.7% Asian American or Pacific Islander, 1% Hispanic American, 0.2% Native American, 0.1% international, 5% transferred in, 55% live on campus. *Retention:* 82% of 2002 full-time freshmen returned.

Freshmen *Admission:* 1,037 applied, 799 admitted, 329 enrolled. *Average high school GPA:* 3.19. *Test scores:* SAT verbal scores over 500: 57%; SAT math scores over 500: 59%; ACT scores over 18: 83%; SAT verbal scores over 600: 12%; SAT math scores over 600: 12%; ACT scores over 24: 50%; SAT verbal scores over 700: 1%; SAT math scores over 700: 1%; ACT scores over 30: 6%.

Faculty *Total:* 184, 48% full-time. *Student/faculty ratio:* 14:1.

Majors Accounting; biochemistry; biology/biological sciences; business administration and management; chemistry; clinical laboratory science/medical technology; communication/speech communication and rhetoric; computer science; elementary education; English; health science; history; information science/studies; interdisciplinary studies; kindergarten/preschool education; liberal arts and sciences/liberal studies; management information systems; marketing/marketing management; mathematics; medical radiologic technology; nursing (registered nurse training); philosophy; pre-dentistry studies; pre-law studies; pre-medical studies; pre-veterinary studies; psychology; secondary education; social work; special education; sport and fitness administration.

Academic Programs *Special study options:* academic remediation for entering students, accelerated degree program, adult/continuing education programs, advanced placement credit, cooperative education, distance learning, double majors, honors programs, independent study, internships, off-campus study, part-time degree program, services for LD students, student-designed majors, study abroad, summer session for credit. *ROTC:* Army (c), Air Force (c). *Unusual degree programs:* 3-2 occupational therapy, physical therapy, speech-language pathology.

Library Mary Kintz Bevevina Library with 90,000 titles, 782 serial subscriptions, 2,240 audiovisual materials, an OPAC, a Web page.

Computers on Campus 50 computers available on campus for general student use. A campuswide network can be accessed from student residence rooms and from off campus. Internet access, at least one staffed computer lab available.

Student Life *Housing options:* coed. *Activities and organizations:* drama/theater group, student-run newspaper, radio station, choral group, Circle K,

SOAR—Student Outdoor Adventure and Recreation, BACCHUS, Peer Advocates, Commuter Council. *Campus security:* 24-hour emergency response devices and patrols, late-night transport/escort service. *Student services:* health clinic, personal/psychological counseling, women's center.

Athletics Member NCAA. All Division III. *Intercollegiate sports:* baseball M, basketball M/W, cheerleading W, cross-country running M/W, field hockey W, golf M, lacrosse M/W, soccer M/W, softball W, swimming M/W, track and field M/W, volleyball W. *Intramural sports:* basketball M/W, cross-country running M/W, football M/W, golf M/W, lacrosse M/W, racquetball M/W, soccer M/W, softball M/W, tennis M/W, volleyball M/W, weight lifting M/W.

Standardized Tests *Required:* SAT I or ACT (for admission).

Costs (2003–04) *Comprehensive fee:* $25,470 includes full-time tuition ($17,060), mandatory fees ($910), and room and board ($7500). Part-time tuition: $395 per credit. *College room only:* $4300. Room and board charges vary according to board plan and housing facility. *Payment plans:* installment, deferred payment. *Waivers:* employees or children of employees.

Financial Aid Of all full-time matriculated undergraduates who enrolled in 2003, 1,202 applied for aid, 1,092 were judged to have need, 621 had their need fully met. 229 Federal Work-Study jobs (averaging $1100). 48 state and other part-time jobs (averaging $1100). In 2003, 110 non-need-based awards were made. *Average percent of need met:* 75%. *Average financial aid package:* $12,854. *Average need-based loan:* $2769. *Average need-based gift aid:* $5317. *Average non-need-based aid:* $5954. *Average indebtedness upon graduation:* $16,495.

Applying *Options:* common application, electronic application, early admission, deferred entrance. *Application fee:* $25. *Required:* high school transcript. *Required for some:* essay or personal statement, 2 letters of recommendation, interview. *Recommended:* interview. *Application deadline:* rolling (freshmen), rolling (transfers).

Admissions Contact Ms. Jane Dessoye, Executive Director of Admissions and Financial Aid, College Misericordia, 301 Lake Street, Dallas, PA 18612-1098. *Phone:* 570-675-4449 Ext. 6168. *Toll-free phone:* 866-262-6363 (in-state); 866-2626363 (out-of-state). *Fax:* 570-674-6232. *E-mail:* admiss@misericordia.edu.

■ *See page 1434 for a narrative description.*

THE CURTIS INSTITUTE OF MUSIC
Philadelphia, Pennsylvania

- **Independent** comprehensive, founded 1924
- **Calendar** semesters
- **Degrees** certificates, diplomas, bachelor's, and master's
- **Urban** campus
- **Coed**
- **Most difficult** entrance level

Student Life *Campus security:* 24-hour patrols.

Standardized Tests *Required:* SAT I (for placement).

Costs (2003–04) *Tuition:* $0 full-time. *Required fees:* $1550 full-time.

Financial Aid Of all full-time matriculated undergraduates who enrolled in 2003, 53 applied for aid, 53 were judged to have need, 26 had their need fully met. 54 state and other part-time jobs (averaging $1878). *Average percent of need met:* 92. *Average financial aid package:* $10,608. *Average need-based loan:* $4181. *Average need-based gift aid:* $6359. *Average indebtedness upon graduation:* $16,833. *Financial aid deadline:* 3/1.

Applying *Options:* common application, early admission. *Application fee:* $60. *Required:* essay or personal statement, high school transcript, letters of recommendation, audition.

Admissions Contact Mr. Christopher Hodges, Admissions Officer, The Curtis Institute of Music, 1726 Locust Street, Philadelphia, PA 19103-6107. *Phone:* 215-893-5262. *Fax:* 215-893-7900.

DELAWARE VALLEY COLLEGE
Doylestown, Pennsylvania

- **Independent** comprehensive, founded 1896
- **Calendar** semesters
- **Degrees** certificates, associate, bachelor's, master's, and postbachelor's certificates
- **Suburban** 600-acre campus with easy access to Philadelphia
- **Endowment** $13.2 million
- **Coed,** 1,958 undergraduate students, 74% full-time, 51% women, 49% men
- **Moderately difficult** entrance level, 82% of applicants were admitted

The distinctive DVC Employment Program gets results. All students complete 24 weeks of hands-on work in jobs related to their academic programs. This on-the-job learning expands resumes, exposes students to real-life work experience in their chosen fields, and allows employers to recognize students' skills and abilities—all before graduation.

Undergraduates 1,458 full-time, 500 part-time. Students come from 20 states and territories, 36% are from out of state, 4% African American, 0.6% Asian American or Pacific Islander, 2% Hispanic American, 0.2% Native American, 0.2% international, 4% transferred in, 63% live on campus. *Retention:* 72% of 2002 full-time freshmen returned.

Freshmen *Admission:* 1,556 applied, 1,283 admitted, 440 enrolled. *Average high school GPA:* 3.25. *Test scores:* SAT verbal scores over 500: 46%; SAT math scores over 500: 48%; ACT scores over 18: 92%; SAT verbal scores over 600: 11%; SAT math scores over 600: 9%; ACT scores over 24: 17%; SAT verbal scores over 700: 1%.

Faculty *Total:* 176, 43% full-time, 41% with terminal degrees. *Student/faculty ratio:* 15:1.

Majors Accounting; agribusiness; agronomy and crop science; animal sciences; animal sciences related; applied horticulture/horticultural business services related; biology/biological sciences; business administration and management; business/commerce; chemistry; computer and information sciences; computer and information sciences and support services related; computer programming; criminal justice/law enforcement administration; crop production; culinary arts related; dairy science; English; food science; horticultural science; management information systems; marketing/marketing management; mathematics; ornamental horticulture; secondary education; turf and turfgrass management; wildlife and wildlands science and management; zoology/animal biology.

Academic Programs *Special study options:* academic remediation for entering students, adult/continuing education programs, advanced placement credit, cooperative education, honors programs, internships, part-time degree program, services for LD students, study abroad, summer session for credit.

Library Joseph Krauskopf Memorial Library with 58,020 titles, 734 serial subscriptions, an OPAC, a Web page.

Computers on Campus 210 computers available on campus for general student use. A campuswide network can be accessed. Internet access, online (class) registration, at least one staffed computer lab available.

Student Life *Housing options:* coed. Campus housing is university owned and is provided by a third party. Freshman applicants given priority for college housing. *Activities and organizations:* drama/theater group, student-run newspaper, radio station, choral group, Block and Bridle Club, Community Service Corps, Student Government, Halloween Haunting. *Campus security:* 24-hour patrols, late-night transport/escort service, controlled dormitory access. *Student services:* health clinic, personal/psychological counseling.

Athletics Member NCAA. All Division III. *Intercollegiate sports:* baseball M, basketball M/W, cheerleading W, cross-country running M/W, equestrian sports M/W, field hockey W, football M, golf M, soccer M/W, softball W, track and field M/W, volleyball W, wrestling M. *Intramural sports:* basketball M/W, cross-country running M/W, football M, golf M, lacrosse M, racquetball M/W, soccer M, softball M/W, tennis M/W, volleyball M/W, weight lifting M.

Standardized Tests *Required:* SAT I or ACT (for admission).

Costs (2003–04) *Comprehensive fee:* $26,676 includes full-time tuition ($18,654), mandatory fees ($650), and room and board ($7372). Full-time tuition and fees vary according to program. Part-time tuition: $510 per credit. *Required fees:* $50 per term part-time. *College room only:* $3342. Room and board charges vary according to board plan. *Waivers:* employees or children of employees.

Financial Aid Of all full-time matriculated undergraduates who enrolled in 2003, 1,281 applied for aid, 1,078 were judged to have need, 405 had their need fully met. 189 Federal Work-Study jobs (averaging $932). 175 state and other part-time jobs (averaging $1828). In 2003, 276 non-need-based awards were made. *Average percent of need met:* 85%. *Average financial aid package:* $16,030. *Average need-based loan:* $3834. *Average need-based gift aid:* $11,458. *Average non-need-based aid:* $7407. *Average indebtedness upon graduation:* $17,790.

Applying *Options:* common application, electronic application, early admission, deferred entrance. *Application fee:* $35. *Required:* high school transcript, 1 letter of recommendation. *Required for some:* minimum 3.00 GPA. *Recommended:* minimum 2.75 GPA, interview. *Application deadline:* rolling (freshmen), rolling (transfers). *Notification:* continuous (freshmen), continuous (transfers).

Delaware Valley College (continued)

Admissions Contact Mr. Stephen Zenko, Director of Admissions, Delaware Valley College, 700 East Butler Avenue, Doylestown, PA 18901-2697. *Phone:* 215-489-2211 Ext. 2211. *Toll-free phone:* 800-2DELVAL. *Fax:* 215-230-2968. *E-mail:* admitme@devalcol.edu.

■ *See page 1524 for a narrative description.*

DESALES UNIVERSITY

Center Valley, Pennsylvania

- **Independent Roman Catholic** comprehensive, founded 1964
- **Calendar** semesters
- **Degrees** bachelor's, master's, post-master's, and postbachelor's certificates (also offers adult program with significant enrollment not reflected in profile)
- **Suburban** 350-acre campus with easy access to Philadelphia and New York City
- **Endowment** $23.0 million
- **Coed,** 2,167 undergraduate students, 74% full-time, 57% women, 43% men
- **Moderately difficult** entrance level, 77% of applicants were admitted

Undergraduates 1,601 full-time, 566 part-time. Students come from 10 states and territories, 29% are from out of state, 0.6% African American, 0.6% Asian American or Pacific Islander, 1% Hispanic American, 0.2% Native American, 0.2% international, 3% transferred in, 80% live on campus. *Retention:* 83% of 2002 full-time freshmen returned.

Freshmen *Admission:* 1,678 applied, 1,284 admitted, 395 enrolled. *Test scores:* SAT verbal scores over 500: 69%; SAT math scores over 500: 70%; SAT verbal scores over 600: 24%; SAT math scores over 600: 24%; SAT verbal scores over 700: 3%; SAT math scores over 700: 2%.

Faculty *Total:* 136, 65% full-time, 57% with terminal degrees. *Student/faculty ratio:* 18:1.

Majors Accounting; biology/biological sciences; business administration and management; chemistry; cinematography and film/video production; clinical laboratory science/medical technology; computer science; criminal justice/law enforcement administration; criminal justice/safety; dance; dramatic/theatre arts; e-commerce; elementary education; English; environmental science; environmental studies; finance; health/medical preparatory programs related; history; human resources management; kinesiology and exercise science; liberal arts and sciences/liberal studies; management information systems; marketing/marketing management; marketing related; mass communication/media; mathematics; nursing (registered nurse training); pharmacy administration/pharmaceutics; philosophy; political science and government; pre-dentistry studies; pre-medical studies; pre-veterinary studies; psychology; Spanish; sport and fitness administration; theology.

Academic Programs *Special study options:* accelerated degree program, adult/continuing education programs, advanced placement credit, distance learning, double majors, honors programs, independent study, internships, off-campus study, part-time degree program, services for LD students, study abroad, summer session for credit. *ROTC:* Army (c).

Library Trexler Library with 138,151 titles, 538 serial subscriptions, 5,975 audiovisual materials, an OPAC, a Web page.

Computers on Campus 200 computers available on campus for general student use. A campuswide network can be accessed from student residence rooms and from off campus. Internet access, at least one staffed computer lab available.

Student Life *Housing options:* coed, men-only, women-only. Campus housing is university owned. Freshman campus housing is guaranteed. *Activities and organizations:* drama/theater group, student-run newspaper, radio and television station, choral group, Sigma Alpha Omega, social outreach, Student Nursing Organization, Student Government Association, business club. *Campus security:* 24-hour emergency response devices and patrols, late-night transport/escort service, desk security in residence halls 24 hours per day. *Student services:* health clinic, personal/psychological counseling.

Athletics Member NCAA. All Division III. *Intercollegiate sports:* baseball M, basketball M/W, cheerleading W(c), cross-country running M/W, equestrian sports W(c), field hockey W, golf M, ice hockey M(c), lacrosse M, soccer M/W, softball W, tennis M/W, track and field M/W, volleyball M(c)/W. *Intramural sports:* badminton M/W, basketball M/W, football M/W, golf M, soccer M/W, softball M/W, volleyball M/W, weight lifting M/W.

Standardized Tests *Required:* SAT I or ACT (for admission).

Costs (2003–04) *Comprehensive fee:* $25,470 includes full-time tuition ($18,000), mandatory fees ($390), and room and board ($7080). Full-time tuition and fees vary according to class time and course load. Part-time tuition: $750 per credit. Part-time tuition and fees vary according to class time and course load. *Room and board:* Room and board charges vary according to housing facility. *Payment plans:* installment, deferred payment. *Waivers:* senior citizens and employees or children of employees.

Financial Aid Of all full-time matriculated undergraduates who enrolled in 2003, 1,183 applied for aid, 986 were judged to have need, 378 had their need fully met. 324 Federal Work-Study jobs (averaging $631). 234 state and other part-time jobs (averaging $631). In 2003, 271 non-need-based awards were made. *Average percent of need met:* 70%. *Average financial aid package:* $12,586. *Average need-based loan:* $2964. *Average need-based gift aid:* $9187. *Average non-need-based aid:* $4518. *Average indebtedness upon graduation:* $13,977.

Applying *Options:* common application, electronic application, early admission, deferred entrance. *Application fee:* $30. *Required:* high school transcript, 2 letters of recommendation. *Recommended:* essay or personal statement, interview. *Application deadlines:* 8/1 (freshmen), 8/1 (transfers). *Notification:* continuous (freshmen), continuous (transfers).

Admissions Contact Mr. Peter Rautzhan, Director of Admissions and Financial Aid, DeSales University, 2755 Station Avenue, Center Valley, PA 18034-9568. *Phone:* 610-282-1100 Ext. 1332. *Toll-free phone:* 877-4DESALES (in-state); 800-228-5114 (out-of-state). *Fax:* 610-282-2254. *E-mail:* admiss@desales.edu.

DEVRY UNIVERSITY

Chesterbrook, Pennsylvania

Admissions Contact 701 Lee Road, Suite 103, Chesterbrook, PA 19087-5612.

DEVRY UNIVERSITY

Pittsburgh, Pennsylvania

Admissions Contact FreeMarkets Center, 210 Sixth Avenue, Suite 200, Pittsburgh, PA 15222-9123. *Toll-free phone:* 866-77DEVRY.

DEVRY UNIVERSITY

Fort Washington, Pennsylvania

- **Proprietary** comprehensive, founded 2002, part of DeVry University
- **Calendar** semesters
- **Degrees** associate, bachelor's, master's, and postbachelor's certificates
- **Coed**
- **Minimally difficult** entrance level

Faculty *Student/faculty ratio:* 6:1.

Standardized Tests *Recommended:* SAT I, ACT or CPT.

Costs (2003–04) *Tuition:* $11,100 full-time, $395 per credit hour part-time. *Required fees:* $165 full-time.

Financial Aid Of all full-time matriculated undergraduates who enrolled in 2002, 286 applied for aid, 275 were judged to have need. In 2002, 13. *Average percent of need met:* 32. *Average financial aid package:* $6652. *Average need-based loan:* $3657. *Average need-based gift aid:* $4040. *Average non-need-based aid:* $8122.

Applying *Options:* electronic application, deferred entrance. *Application fee:* $50. *Required:* high school transcript, interview.

Admissions Contact Mr. Steve Cohen, Director of Admissions, DeVry University, 1140 Virginia Drive, Fort Washington, PA 19034-3204. *Toll-free phone:* 866-303-3879. *Fax:* 215-591-5745. *E-mail:* admissions@phi.devry.edu.

DICKINSON COLLEGE

Carlisle, Pennsylvania

- **Independent** 4-year, founded 1773
- **Calendar** semesters
- **Degree** bachelor's
- **Suburban** 115-acre campus with easy access to Harrisburg
- **Endowment** $154.8 million
- **Coed,** 2,276 undergraduate students, 98% full-time, 56% women, 44% men
- **Very difficult** entrance level, 52% of applicants were admitted

Undergraduates 2,241 full-time, 35 part-time. Students come from 43 states and territories, 20 other countries, 65% are from out of state, 3% African American, 3% Asian American or Pacific Islander, 2% Hispanic American, 0.4% Native American, 2% international, 0.7% transferred in, 92% live on campus. *Retention:* 90% of 2002 full-time freshmen returned.

Freshmen *Admission:* 4,633 applied, 2,394 admitted, 624 enrolled. *Test scores:* SAT verbal scores over 500: 99%; SAT math scores over 500: 98%; SAT verbal scores over 600: 73%; SAT math scores over 600: 74%; SAT verbal scores over 700: 14%; SAT math scores over 700: 18%.

Faculty *Total:* 202, 82% full-time, 88% with terminal degrees. *Student/faculty ratio:* 13:1.

Majors American studies; anthropology; archeology; Asian studies (East); biochemistry; biology/biological sciences; chemistry; classics and languages, literatures and linguistics; computer science; dance; dramatic/theatre arts; economics; engineering; English; environmental science; environmental studies; fine/studio arts; French; geology/earth science; German; history; international business/trade/commerce; international relations and affairs; Italian; Jewish/Judaic studies; mathematics; medieval and Renaissance studies; multi-/interdisciplinary studies related; music; music related; philosophy; physics; political science and government; pre-dentistry studies; pre-law studies; pre-medical studies; psychology; public policy analysis; religious studies; Russian; Russian studies; sociology; Spanish; theatre design and technology; women's studies.

Academic Programs *Special study options:* accelerated degree program, adult/continuing education programs, advanced placement credit, double majors, English as a second language, independent study, internships, off-campus study, part-time degree program, services for LD students, student-designed majors, study abroad, summer session for credit. *ROTC:* Army (b). *Unusual degree programs:* 3-2 engineering with Case Western Reserve University, University of Pennsylvania, Rensselaer Polytechnic Institute; pre-law with the The Dickinson School of Law of the Pennsylvania State University.

Library Waidner-Spahr Library plus 6 others with 305,272 titles, 6,163 serial subscriptions, 12,247 audiovisual materials, an OPAC, a Web page.

Computers on Campus 520 computers available on campus for general student use. A campuswide network can be accessed from student residence rooms and from off campus. Internet access, online (class) registration, at least one staffed computer lab available. Computer purchase or lease plan available.

Student Life *Housing:* on-campus residence required for freshman year. *Options:* coed, disabled students. Campus housing is university owned. Freshman campus housing is guaranteed. *Activities and organizations:* drama/theater group, student-run newspaper, radio station, choral group, Student Senate, College Choir, Alpha Lambda Delta, Multi-Organization Board, Alpha Phi Omega, national fraternities, national sororities. *Campus security:* 24-hour emergency response devices and patrols, student patrols, late-night transport/escort service, controlled dormitory access. *Student services:* health clinic, personal/psychological counseling, women's center.

Athletics Member NCAA. All Division III. *Intercollegiate sports:* baseball M, basketball M/W, cheerleading M(c)/W(c), cross-country running M/W, equestrian sports M(c)/W(c), fencing M(c)/W(c), field hockey W, football M, golf M/W, ice hockey M(c), lacrosse M/W, skiing (downhill) M(c)/W(c), soccer M/W, softball W, squash M(c)/W(c), swimming M/W, tennis M/W, track and field M/W, ultimate Frisbee M(c)/W(c), volleyball M(c)/W, wrestling M(c). *Intramural sports:* badminton M/W, basketball M, bowling M, field hockey W, football M, golf M/W, racquetball M/W, soccer M/W, softball M/W, squash M/W, table tennis M/W, tennis M/W, ultimate Frisbee M/W, volleyball M.

Standardized Tests *Recommended:* SAT I and SAT II or ACT (for admission).

Costs (2004–05) *Comprehensive fee:* $37,900 includes full-time tuition ($30,000), mandatory fees ($300), and room and board ($7600). Part-time tuition: $3750 per course. *Required fees:* $40 per credit part-time. *College room only:* $3920. Room and board charges vary according to housing facility. *Payment plan:* installment. *Waivers:* employees or children of employees.

Financial Aid Of all full-time matriculated undergraduates who enrolled in 2003, 1,329 applied for aid, 1,182 were judged to have need, 845 had their need fully met. 891 Federal Work-Study jobs (averaging $1562). 95 state and other part-time jobs (averaging $3353). In 2003, 263 non-need-based awards were made. *Average percent of need met:* 97%. *Average financial aid package:* $22,973. *Average need-based loan:* $4564. *Average need-based gift aid:* $18,568. *Average non-need-based aid:* $10,842. *Average indebtedness upon graduation:* $19,207. *Financial aid deadline:* 2/1.

Applying *Options:* common application, electronic application, early decision, early action, deferred entrance. *Application fee:* $50. *Required:* essay or personal statement, high school transcript, 2 letters of recommendation. *Recommended:* minimum 3.0 GPA, interview. *Application deadlines:* 2/1 (freshmen), 4/1 (transfers). *Early decision:* 11/15 (for plan 1), 1/15 (for plan 2). *Notification:* 3/31 (freshmen), 12/15 (early decision plan 1), 2/15 (early decision plan 2), 1/15 (early action), continuous (transfers).

Admissions Contact Mr. Christopher Seth Allen, Director of Admissions, Dickinson College, PO Box 1773, Carlisle, PA 17013-2896. *Phone:* 717-245-1231. *Toll-free phone:* 800-644-1773. *Fax:* 717-245-1442. *E-mail:* admit@dickinson.edu.

DREXEL UNIVERSITY
Philadelphia, Pennsylvania

- **Independent** university, founded 1891
- **Calendar** quarters
- **Degrees** certificates, associate, bachelor's, master's, doctoral, first professional, post-master's, postbachelor's, and first professional certificates
- **Urban** 42-acre campus
- **Endowment** $248.3 million
- **Coed,** 11,613 undergraduate students, 81% full-time, 40% women, 60% men
- **Moderately difficult** entrance level, 70% of applicants were admitted

Undergraduates 9,363 full-time, 2,250 part-time. Students come from 44 states and territories, 96 other countries, 40% are from out of state, 10% African American, 13% Asian American or Pacific Islander, 2% Hispanic American, 0.2% Native American, 5% international, 7% transferred in, 37% live on campus. *Retention:* 82% of 2002 full-time freshmen returned.

Freshmen *Admission:* 10,390 applied, 7,285 admitted, 2,097 enrolled. *Average high school GPA:* 3.52. *Test scores:* SAT verbal scores over 500: 90%; SAT math scores over 500: 96%; SAT verbal scores over 600: 43%; SAT math scores over 600: 61%; SAT verbal scores over 700: 7%; SAT math scores over 700: 13%.

Faculty *Total:* 1,308, 50% full-time. *Student/faculty ratio:* 10:1.

Majors Accounting; architectural engineering; architecture; area studies related; biological and physical sciences; biology/biological sciences; biomedical/medical engineering; business/commerce; business, management, and marketing related; business/managerial economics; chemical engineering; chemistry; cinematography and film/video production; civil engineering; civil engineering related; commercial and advertising art; communication and journalism related; computer engineering; computer science; culinary arts; design and applied arts related; education (specific subject areas) related; electrical, electronics and communications engineering; engineering; English language and literature related; environmental/environmental health engineering; environmental studies; fashion/apparel design; finance; general studies; health/health care administration; history; hospitality administration related; humanities; human resources management; industrial engineering; information science/studies; interior design; international business/trade/commerce; management information systems; marketing/marketing management; materials engineering; mathematics; mechanical engineering; music; nutrition sciences; photography; physics related; playwriting and screenwriting; psychology; social sciences; sociology; taxation; technical and business writing; web page, digital/multimedia and information resources design.

Academic Programs *Special study options:* academic remediation for entering students, accelerated degree program, adult/continuing education programs, advanced placement credit, cooperative education, distance learning, double majors, English as a second language, freshman honors college, honors programs, independent study, internships, part-time degree program, services for LD students, study abroad, summer session for credit. *ROTC:* Army (b), Navy (c), Air Force (c).

Library W. W. Hagerty Library with 443,597 titles, 1,461 serial subscriptions, 8,076 audiovisual materials, an OPAC, a Web page.

Computers on Campus 6500 computers available on campus for general student use. A campuswide network can be accessed from student residence rooms and from off campus that provide access to campuswide wireless network. Internet access, online (class) registration, at least one staffed computer lab available.

Student Life *Housing:* on-campus residence required for freshman year. *Options:* coed, disabled students. *Activities and organizations:* drama/theater group, student-run newspaper, radio and television station, choral group, student government, Black Student Union, Society of Hispanic Professional Engineers, Society of Minority Engineers and Scientists, Campus Activities Board, national fraternities, national sororities. *Campus security:* 24-hour emergency response devices and patrols, late-night transport/escort service, controlled dormitory access. *Student services:* health clinic, personal/psychological counseling.

Athletics Member NCAA. All Division I. *Intercollegiate sports:* baseball M(s), basketball M(s)/W(s), crew M(s)/W(s), field hockey W(s), golf M(s), lacrosse M(s)/W(s), soccer M(s)/W(s), softball W(s), swimming M(s)/W(s), tennis M(s)/W(s), volleyball W(s), wrestling M(s). *Intramural sports:* badminton M/W, basketball M/W, fencing M/W, football M, ice hockey M, riflery M/W, rugby M/W, sailing M/W, softball M, squash M/W, table tennis M/W, tennis M/W, volleyball M/W, water polo M/W.

Standardized Tests *Required:* SAT I or ACT (for admission). *Recommended:* SAT I (for admission).

Costs (2003–04) *Comprehensive fee:* $30,905 includes full-time tuition ($19,900), mandatory fees ($1405), and room and board ($9600). Full-time tuition and fees vary according to student level. *College room only:* $5700. *Waivers:* employees or children of employees.

Financial Aid Of all full-time matriculated undergraduates who enrolled in 2003, 8,349 applied for aid, 6,505 were judged to have need, 790 had their need fully met. In 2003, 1596 non-need-based awards were made. *Average percent of need met:* 46%. *Average financial aid package:* $10,266. *Average need-based loan:* $6749. *Average need-based gift aid:* $4873. *Average non-need-based aid:* $6469. *Average indebtedness upon graduation:* $22,234. *Financial aid deadline:* 2/15.

Drexel University (continued)

Applying *Options:* electronic application, deferred entrance. *Application fee:* $50. *Required:* high school transcript, minimum 2.0 GPA. *Required for some:* essay or personal statement. *Recommended:* 2 letters of recommendation, interview. *Application deadline:* 3/1 (freshmen), rolling (transfers). *Notification:* continuous (freshmen), continuous (transfers).

Admissions Contact Mr. David Eddy, Director of Undergraduate Admissions, Drexel University, 3141 Chestnut Street, Philadelphia, PA 19104-2875. *Phone:* 215-895-2400. *Toll-free phone:* 800-2-DREXEL. *Fax:* 215-895-5939. *E-mail:* enroll@drexel.edu.

■ *See page 1546 for a narrative description.*

DUQUESNE UNIVERSITY
Pittsburgh, Pennsylvania

- **Independent Roman Catholic** university, founded 1878
- **Calendar** semesters
- **Degrees** bachelor's, master's, doctoral, first professional, post-master's, and postbachelor's certificates
- **Urban** 43-acre campus
- **Endowment** $95.5 million
- **Coed,** 5,724 undergraduate students, 94% full-time, 59% women, 41% men
- **Moderately difficult** entrance level, 84% of applicants were admitted

Undergraduates 5,362 full-time, 362 part-time. Students come from 47 states and territories, 60 other countries, 19% are from out of state, 4% African American, 1% Asian American or Pacific Islander, 2% Hispanic American, 0.1% Native American, 3% international, 3% transferred in, 47% live on campus. *Retention:* 86% of 2002 full-time freshmen returned.

Freshmen *Admission:* 3,894 applied, 3,280 admitted, 1,492 enrolled. *Average high school GPA:* 3.57. *Test scores:* SAT verbal scores over 500: 79%; SAT math scores over 500: 79%; ACT scores over 18: 94%; SAT verbal scores over 600: 30%; SAT math scores over 600: 33%; ACT scores over 24: 55%; SAT verbal scores over 700: 3%; SAT math scores over 700: 3%; ACT scores over 30: 7%.

Faculty *Total:* 902, 47% full-time. *Student/faculty ratio:* 14:1.

Majors Accounting; accounting related; ancient/classical Greek; art history, criticism and conservation; athletic training; biochemistry; biology/biological sciences; biology teacher education; business administration, management and operations related; business/commerce; business, management, and marketing related; business/managerial economics; chemistry; chemistry related; chemistry teacher education; classics and languages, literatures and linguistics; communication/speech communication and rhetoric; computer science; dramatic/theatre arts; early childhood education; economics; education; education (specific subject areas) related; elementary education; English; English language and literature related; English/language arts teacher education; entrepreneurship; environmental science; finance; fine/studio arts; foreign languages and literatures; foreign language teacher education; French language teacher education; health/health care administration; health/medical preparatory programs related; history; international business/trade/commerce; international relations and affairs; investments and securities; journalism; Latin; liberal arts and sciences and humanities related; logistics and materials management; management information systems; management science; marketing/marketing management; marketing related; mathematics; mathematics teacher education; microbiology; music performance; music related; music teacher education; music therapy; nursing (registered nurse training); occupational therapy; pharmacy, pharmaceutical sciences, and administration related; philosophy; physical therapy; physician assistant; physics; political science and government; psychology; science teacher education; secondary education; social studies teacher education; sociology; Spanish; Spanish language teacher education; special education; speech-language pathology; theology; web page, digital/multimedia and information resources design.

Academic Programs *Special study options:* academic remediation for entering students, accelerated degree program, adult/continuing education programs, advanced placement credit, distance learning, double majors, English as a second language, freshman honors college, honors programs, independent study, internships, off-campus study, part-time degree program, services for LD students, student-designed majors, study abroad, summer session for credit. *ROTC:* Army (c), Navy (c), Air Force (c). *Unusual degree programs:* 3-2 engineering with Case Western Reserve University, University of Pittsburgh.

Library Gumberg Library plus 1 other with 346,718 titles, 5,862 serial subscriptions, 34,306 audiovisual materials, an OPAC, a Web page.

Computers on Campus 650 computers available on campus for general student use. A campuswide network can be accessed from student residence rooms and from off campus. Internet access, at least one staffed computer lab available.

Student Life *Housing:* on-campus residence required for freshman year. *Options:* coed, men-only, women-only, disabled students. Campus housing is university owned. Freshman applicants given priority for college housing. *Activities and organizations:* drama/theater group, student-run newspaper, radio and television station, choral group, marching band, Student Government Association, University Volunteers, Program Council, Commuter Council, Black Student Union, national fraternities, national sororities. *Campus security:* 24-hour emergency response devices and patrols, late-night transport/escort service, controlled dormitory access, 24-hour front desk personnel, 24-hour video monitors at residence hall entrances, surveillance cameras throughout the campus, card acce. *Student services:* health clinic, personal/psychological counseling.

Athletics Member NCAA. All Division I except football (Division I-AA). *Intercollegiate sports:* baseball M(s), basketball M(s)/W(s), cheerleading M(c)/W(c), crew M(c)/W(s), cross-country running M(s)/W(s), golf M(s), ice hockey M(c), lacrosse W(s), soccer M(s)/W(s), swimming M(s)/W(s), tennis M(s)/W(s), track and field M(c)/W(s), volleyball W(s), wrestling M(s). *Intramural sports:* badminton M/W, basketball M/W, bowling M/W, football M/W, racquetball M/W, skiing (cross-country) M/W, soccer M/W, softball M/W, squash M/W, table tennis M/W, tennis M/W, volleyball M/W, water polo M/W.

Standardized Tests *Required:* SAT I or ACT (for admission).

Costs (2003–04) *Comprehensive fee:* $26,907 includes full-time tuition ($17,837), mandatory fees ($1588), and room and board ($7482). Full-time tuition and fees vary according to program. Part-time tuition: $580 per credit. Part-time tuition and fees vary according to program. *Required fees:* $62 per credit part-time. *College room only:* $4082. Room and board charges vary according to board plan. *Payment plans:* installment, deferred payment.

Financial Aid Of all full-time matriculated undergraduates who enrolled in 2003, 4,160 applied for aid, 3,570 were judged to have need, 1,701 had their need fully met. 1,773 Federal Work-Study jobs (averaging $2448). In 2003, 1025 non-need-based awards were made. *Average percent of need met:* 83%. *Average financial aid package:* $15,179. *Average need-based loan:* $4478. *Average need-based gift aid:* $10,303. *Average non-need-based aid:* $8113. *Average indebtedness upon graduation:* $17,953. *Financial aid deadline:* 5/1.

Applying *Options:* common application, electronic application, early admission, early decision, early action, deferred entrance. *Application fee:* $50. *Required:* essay or personal statement, high school transcript, 2 letters of recommendation. *Recommended:* minimum 3.0 GPA, interview. *Application deadlines:* 7/1 (freshmen), 7/1 (transfers). *Early decision:* 11/1. *Notification:* continuous (freshmen), 12/15 (early decision), 1/15 (early action), continuous (transfers).

Admissions Contact Office of Admissions, Duquesne University, 600 Forbes Avenue, Pittsburgh, PA 15282-0201. *Phone:* 412-396-5000. *Toll-free phone:* 800-456-0590. *Fax:* 412-396-5644. *E-mail:* admissions@duq.edu.

EASTERN UNIVERSITY
St. Davids, Pennsylvania

- **Independent American Baptist Churches in the USA** comprehensive, founded 1952
- **Calendar** semesters
- **Degrees** associate, bachelor's, and master's
- **Small-town** 107-acre campus with easy access to Philadelphia
- **Coed,** 2,200 undergraduate students, 88% full-time, 66% women, 34% men
- **Moderately difficult** entrance level, 78% of applicants were admitted

Eastern University is a Christian university of the arts and sciences committed to the integration of faith, reason, and justice, which equip students with the knowledge and skills to make a difference in all areas of society. Eastern enrolls 3,000 students to its undergraduate, graduate, professional, and international programs. The curriculum is firmly rooted in a Christian worldview. With dramatic growth over the past decade, Eastern has increased its faculty, raised the percentage of faculty members with Ph.D. degrees to 84 percent, improved facilities, built 3 new residence halls, and raised the standards of admission. Eastern is located near Philadelphia, Pennsylvania, one of America's educational centers, and is only 2 hours from Washington, D.C. and New York City.

Undergraduates 1,946 full-time, 254 part-time. Students come from 38 states and territories, 26 other countries, 40% are from out of state, 13% African American, 2% Asian American or Pacific Islander, 5% Hispanic American, 0.3% Native American, 1% international, 3% transferred in, 47% live on campus. *Retention:* 78% of 2002 full-time freshmen returned.

Freshmen *Admission:* 1,193 applied, 929 admitted, 415 enrolled. *Average high school GPA:* 3.44. *Test scores:* SAT verbal scores over 500: 78%; SAT math scores over 500: 68%; ACT scores over 18: 78%; SAT verbal scores over 600: 30%; SAT math scores over 600: 27%; ACT scores over 24: 28%; SAT verbal scores over 700: 8%; SAT math scores over 700: 4%; ACT scores over 30: 7%.

Faculty *Total:* 343, 24% full-time. *Student/faculty ratio:* 13:1.

Majors Accounting; art history, criticism and conservation; astronomy; biblical studies; biochemistry; biology/biological sciences; chemistry; communication/speech communication and rhetoric; creative writing; elementary education;

English; English/language arts teacher education; environmental studies; finance; French; health and physical education; history; hospital and health care facilities administration; intermedia/multimedia; liberal arts and sciences/liberal studies; management information systems; management science; marketing/marketing management; mathematics; missionary studies and missiology; music; nursing (registered nurse training); philosophy; political science and government; psychology; secondary education; social work; sociology; Spanish; theology; urban studies/affairs.

Academic Programs *Special study options:* academic remediation for entering students, accelerated degree program, adult/continuing education programs, advanced placement credit, English as a second language, honors programs, independent study, internships, off-campus study, part-time degree program, student-designed majors, summer session for credit. *ROTC:* Army (c), Air Force (c).

Library Warner Library plus 1 other with 143,815 titles, 1,215 serial subscriptions, 11,673 audiovisual materials, an OPAC, a Web page.

Computers on Campus 60 computers available on campus for general student use. A campuswide network can be accessed from student residence rooms and from off campus. Internet access, at least one staffed computer lab available.

Student Life *Housing:* on-campus residence required through senior year. *Options:* coed. Campus housing is university owned and leased by the school. *Activities and organizations:* drama/theater group, student-run newspaper, radio station, choral group, Habitat for Humanity, Y.A.C.H.T. club, Angels of Harmony, Black Student League, Fellowship of Christian Athletes. *Campus security:* 24-hour emergency response devices and patrols, late-night transport/escort service, controlled dormitory access, emergency call boxes. *Student services:* health clinic, personal/psychological counseling, women's center.

Athletics Member NCAA. All Division III. *Intercollegiate sports:* baseball M, basketball M/W, field hockey W, golf M, lacrosse M/W, soccer M/W, softball W, volleyball W. *Intramural sports:* basketball M/W, soccer M/W, volleyball W.

Standardized Tests *Required:* SAT I or ACT (for admission).

Costs (2004–05) *One-time required fee:* $45. *Comprehensive fee:* $25,300 includes full-time tuition ($17,700) and room and board ($7600). Part-time tuition: $400 per credit hour. *College room only:* $4150.

Financial Aid Of all full-time matriculated undergraduates who enrolled in 2002, 1,483 applied for aid, 1,253 were judged to have need, 330 had their need fully met. 347 Federal Work-Study jobs (averaging $1050). 811 state and other part-time jobs (averaging $500). In 2002, 228 non-need-based awards were made. *Average percent of need met:* 74%. *Average financial aid package:* $11,892. *Average need-based loan:* $3505. *Average need-based gift aid:* $9959. *Average non-need-based aid:* $14,048. *Average indebtedness upon graduation:* $18,057.

Applying *Options:* electronic application, early admission, deferred entrance. *Application fee:* $25. *Required:* essay or personal statement, high school transcript, minimum 2.0 GPA, 1 letter of recommendation. *Recommended:* minimum 3.0 GPA, 3 letters of recommendation, interview. *Application deadline:* rolling (freshmen), rolling (transfers). *Notification:* continuous (freshmen), continuous (transfers).

Admissions Contact Mr. David Urban, Director of Undergraduate Admissions, Eastern University, 1300 Eagle Road, St. Davids, PA 19087-3696. *Phone:* 610-225-5005. *Toll-free phone:* 800-452-0996. *Fax:* 610-341-1723. *E-mail:* ugadm@eastern.edu.

■ *See page 1564 for a narrative description.*

EAST STROUDSBURG UNIVERSITY OF PENNSYLVANIA

East Stroudsburg, Pennsylvania

- **State-supported** comprehensive, founded 1893, part of Pennsylvania State System of Higher Education
- **Calendar** semesters
- **Degrees** associate, bachelor's, and master's
- **Small-town** 213-acre campus
- **Endowment** $7.2 million
- **Coed,** 5,121 undergraduate students, 91% full-time, 58% women, 42% men
- **Moderately difficult** entrance level, 70% of applicants were admitted

Undergraduates 4,650 full-time, 471 part-time. Students come from 21 states and territories, 23 other countries, 19% are from out of state, 4% African American, 1% Asian American or Pacific Islander, 3% Hispanic American, 0.2% Native American, 0.6% international, 7% transferred in, 44% live on campus. *Retention:* 73% of 2002 full-time freshmen returned.

Freshmen *Admission:* 4,370 applied, 3,067 admitted, 1,084 enrolled. *Average high school GPA:* 2.80. *Test scores:* SAT verbal scores over 500: 42%; SAT math scores over 500: 46%; SAT verbal scores over 600: 6%; SAT math scores over 600: 8%.

Faculty *Total:* 322, 77% full-time, 61% with terminal degrees. *Student/faculty ratio:* 19:1.

Majors Athletic training; audiology and speech-language pathology; biochemistry; biological and physical sciences; biology/biological sciences; biotechnology; business administration and management; chemistry; clinical laboratory science/medical technology; communication/speech communication and rhetoric; communications technology; computer and information sciences; computer and information systems security; dramatic/theatre arts; early childhood education; economics; elementary education; English; environmental biology; French; geography; geology/earth science; graphic design; health and physical education related; health services administration; health teacher education; history; hospitality administration; humanities; kinesiology and exercise science; liberal arts and sciences/liberal studies; marine biology and biological oceanography; mathematics; nursing (registered nurse training); parks, recreation and leisure facilities management; philosophy; physical education teaching and coaching; physical sciences; physics; political science and government; psychology; rehabilitation and therapeutic professions related; rehabilitation therapy; secondary education; social sciences; social science teacher education; sociology; Spanish; special education; visual and performing arts.

Academic Programs *Special study options:* academic remediation for entering students, adult/continuing education programs, advanced placement credit, double majors, honors programs, independent study, internships, off-campus study, part-time degree program, services for LD students, student-designed majors, study abroad, summer session for credit. *ROTC:* Army (c), Air Force (c). *Unusual degree programs:* 3-2 engineering with Pennsylvania State University—University Park Campus, University of Pittsburgh; podiatric medicine with Pennsylvania College of Podiatric Medicine.

Library Kemp Library with 449,107 titles, 1,175 serial subscriptions, 12,289 audiovisual materials, an OPAC, a Web page.

Computers on Campus 708 computers available on campus for general student use. A campuswide network can be accessed from off campus. Internet access, online (class) registration, at least one staffed computer lab available.

Student Life *Housing:* on-campus residence required for freshman year. *Options:* coed, men-only, women-only. Campus housing is university owned. Freshman campus housing is guaranteed. *Activities and organizations:* drama/theater group, student-run newspaper, radio station, choral group, Student Senate, Stage II, Council for Exceptional Children, United Campus Ministry/ESU Christian Fellowship, University Band/Vocal Performing Choirs, national fraternities, national sororities. *Campus security:* 24-hour emergency response devices and patrols, late-night transport/escort service, controlled dormitory access. *Student services:* health clinic, personal/psychological counseling, women's center.

Athletics Member NCAA. All Division II except wrestling (Division I). *Intercollegiate sports:* baseball M(s), basketball M(s)/W(s), cross-country running M(s)/W(s), field hockey W(s), football M(s), lacrosse W(s), soccer M(s)/W(s), softball W(s), swimming W(s), tennis M(s)/W(s), track and field M(s)/W(s), volleyball M(s)/W(s), wrestling M(s). *Intramural sports:* badminton M/W, basketball M/W, equestrian sports M/W, golf M/W, ice hockey M/W, lacrosse M, racquetball M/W, rugby M/W, soccer M/W, softball W, tennis M/W, track and field M/W, ultimate Frisbee M/W, volleyball M/W, water polo M/W.

Standardized Tests *Required:* SAT I or ACT (for admission).

Costs (2003–04) *Tuition:* state resident $4598 full-time, $192 per credit part-time; nonresident $11,496 full-time, $479 per credit part-time. Part-time tuition and fees vary according to course load. *Required fees:* $1381 full-time, $54 per credit part-time. *Room and board:* $4464; room only: $2868. Room and board charges vary according to board plan and housing facility. *Waivers:* senior citizens and employees or children of employees.

Financial Aid Of all full-time matriculated undergraduates who enrolled in 2002, 3,633 applied for aid, 2,581 were judged to have need, 2,037 had their need fully met. 386 Federal Work-Study jobs (averaging $1137). 779 state and other part-time jobs (averaging $1218). In 2002, 925 non-need-based awards were made. *Average percent of need met:* 89%. *Average financial aid package:* $5203. *Average need-based loan:* $3531. *Average need-based gift aid:* $3249. *Average non-need-based aid:* $6315. *Average indebtedness upon graduation:* $19,677. *Financial aid deadline:* 3/1.

Applying *Options:* electronic application. *Application fee:* $35. *Required:* high school transcript. *Recommended:* 1 letter of recommendation. *Application deadlines:* 4/1 (freshmen), 5/1 (transfers). *Notification:* continuous until 5/1 (freshmen), continuous (transfers).

East Stroudsburg University of Pennsylvania (continued)

Admissions Contact Mr. Alan T. Chesterton, Director of Admissions, East Stroudsburg University of Pennsylvania, 200 Prospect Street, East Stroudsburg, PA 18301. *Phone:* 570-422-3542. *Toll-free phone:* 877-230-5547. *Fax:* 570-422-3933. *E-mail:* undergrads@po-box.esu.edu.

EDINBORO UNIVERSITY OF PENNSYLVANIA

Edinboro, Pennsylvania

- **State-supported** comprehensive, founded 1857, part of Pennsylvania State System of Higher Education
- **Calendar** semesters
- **Degrees** associate, bachelor's, master's, post-master's, and postbachelor's certificates
- **Small-town** 585-acre campus
- **Endowment** $7.4 million
- **Coed,** 7,029 undergraduate students, 89% full-time, 58% women, 42% men
- **Moderately difficult** entrance level, 69% of applicants were admitted

Undergraduates 6,241 full-time, 788 part-time. Students come from 35 states and territories, 49 other countries, 11% are from out of state, 7% African American, 0.6% Asian American or Pacific Islander, 1% Hispanic American, 0.2% Native American, 3% international, 7% transferred in, 27% live on campus. *Retention:* 69% of 2002 full-time freshmen returned.

Freshmen *Admission:* 3,950 applied, 2,710 admitted, 1,455 enrolled. *Test scores:* SAT verbal scores over 500: 39%; SAT math scores over 500: 38%; ACT scores over 18: 67%; SAT verbal scores over 600: 8%; SAT math scores over 600: 7%; ACT scores over 24: 10%; SAT verbal scores over 700: 1%.

Faculty *Total:* 401, 91% full-time, 58% with terminal degrees. *Student/faculty ratio:* 21:1.

Majors Anthropology; art; art history, criticism and conservation; art teacher education; biochemistry; biological and physical sciences; biology/biological sciences; broadcast journalism; business administration and management; chemistry; chemistry related; clinical/medical laboratory technology; communication disorders; communication/speech communication and rhetoric; computer and information sciences; criminal justice/police science; criminal justice/safety; dramatic/theatre arts; economics; electrical, electronic and communications engineering technology; elementary education; English; environmental studies; fine/studio arts; foreign languages related; geography; geology/earth science; German; health and physical education; history; humanities; industrial technology; journalism; kindergarten/preschool education; liberal arts and sciences/liberal studies; mathematics; music; nursing (registered nurse training); nutrition sciences; operations management; philosophy; physical education teaching and coaching; physics; political science and government; psychology; social sciences; social sciences related; social studies teacher education; social work; sociology; Spanish; special education; sport and fitness administration.

Academic Programs *Special study options:* academic remediation for entering students, adult/continuing education programs, advanced placement credit, distance learning, double majors, freshman honors college, honors programs, independent study, internships, off-campus study, part-time degree program, services for LD students, student-designed majors, study abroad, summer session for credit. *ROTC:* Army (b). *Unusual degree programs:* 3-2 engineering with Pennsylvania State University—University Park Campus, University of Pittsburgh, Case Western Reserve University, Pennsylvania State University at Erie, The Behrend College; pre-pharmacy, 2+3 at Lake Erie College of Osteopathic Medicine and School of Pharmacy.

Library Baron-Forness Library plus 1 other with 478,175 titles, 1,653 serial subscriptions, 27,819 audiovisual materials, an OPAC, a Web page.

Computers on Campus 700 computers available on campus for general student use. A campuswide network can be accessed from student residence rooms and from off campus that provide access to e-mail. Internet access, online (class) registration, at least one staffed computer lab available. Computer purchase or lease plan available.

Student Life *Housing:* on-campus residence required for freshman year. *Options:* coed, men-only, women-only, disabled students. Campus housing is university owned. Freshman campus housing is guaranteed. *Activities and organizations:* drama/theater group, student-run newspaper, radio and television station, choral group, marching band, Student Government Association, AFRICA, Panhellenic Council, Gamma Sigma Sigma, health and physical education majors club, national fraternities, national sororities. *Campus security:* 24-hour emergency response devices and patrols, self-defense education. *Student services:* health clinic, personal/psychological counseling, women's center, legal services.

Athletics Member NCAA. All Division II except wrestling (Division I). *Intercollegiate sports:* basketball M(s)/W(s), cross-country running M(s)/W(s), football M(s), ice hockey M(c), soccer W(s), softball W(s), swimming M(s)/W(s), track and field M(s)/W(s), volleyball W(s), wrestling M(s). *Intramural sports:* badminton M/W, basketball M/W, football M/W, racquetball M/W, soccer M/W, softball M/W, table tennis M/W, volleyball M/W, wrestling M.

Standardized Tests *Required:* SAT I or ACT (for admission).

Costs (2003–04) *Tuition:* $192 per credit part-time; state resident $4598 full-time; nonresident $6898 full-time, $307 per credit part-time. Part-time tuition and fees vary according to course load. *Required fees:* $1166 full-time, $67 per credit part-time. *Room and board:* $5086; room only: $3120. Room and board charges vary according to board plan. *Payment plan:* installment. *Waivers:* minority students and employees or children of employees.

Financial Aid Of all full-time matriculated undergraduates who enrolled in 2002, 5,499 applied for aid, 4,544 were judged to have need, 594 had their need fully met. 652 Federal Work-Study jobs (averaging $1031). 1,083 state and other part-time jobs (averaging $1800). In 2002, 780 non-need-based awards were made. *Average percent of need met:* 81%. *Average financial aid package:* $6036. *Average need-based loan:* $4281. *Average need-based gift aid:* $1500. *Average non-need-based aid:* $2120. *Average indebtedness upon graduation:* $15,935.

Applying *Options:* electronic application, deferred entrance. *Application fee:* $25. *Required:* high school transcript. *Required for some:* interview. *Recommended:* minimum 2.0 GPA. *Application deadline:* rolling (freshmen), rolling (transfers). *Notification:* continuous (freshmen), continuous (transfers).

Admissions Contact Mr. Terrence Carlin, Assistant Vice President for Admissions, Edinboro University of Pennsylvania, Biggers House, Edinboro, PA 16444. *Phone:* 814-732-2761. *Toll-free phone:* 888-846-2676 (in-state); 800-626-2203 (out-of-state). *Fax:* 814-732-2420. *E-mail:* eup_admissions@edinboro.edu.

■ *See page 1572 for a narrative description.*

ELIZABETHTOWN COLLEGE

Elizabethtown, Pennsylvania

- **Independent** comprehensive, founded 1899, affiliated with Church of the Brethren
- **Calendar** semesters
- **Degrees** certificates, associate, bachelor's, master's, and postbachelor's certificates
- **Small-town** 185-acre campus with easy access to Baltimore and Philadelphia
- **Endowment** $34.2 million
- **Coed,** 1,975 undergraduate students, 90% full-time, 65% women, 35% men
- **Moderately difficult** entrance level, 70% of applicants were admitted

The College, founded in 1899, emphasizes the importance of a strong liberal arts background combined with preprofessional study. A dedicated faculty and a 13:1 student-faculty ratio promote mentoring relationships among students and the faculty. The 19 academic departments collectively offer 43 majors and more than 50 minors and concentrations. The campus community is made up of 1,800 students from 30 states and 40 other countries. Elizabethtown College emphasizes personal attention and experiential learning. Elizabethtown encourages all interested students to visit the campus.

Undergraduates 1,778 full-time, 197 part-time. Students come from 31 states and territories, 41 other countries, 28% are from out of state, 1% African American, 2% Asian American or Pacific Islander, 1% Hispanic American, 0.3% Native American, 4% international, 2% transferred in, 85% live on campus. *Retention:* 84% of 2002 full-time freshmen returned.

Freshmen *Admission:* 2,541 applied, 1,780 admitted, 496 enrolled. *Average high school GPA:* 3.53. *Test scores:* SAT verbal scores over 500: 77%; SAT math scores over 500: 80%; ACT scores over 18: 91%; SAT verbal scores over 600: 28%; SAT math scores over 600: 32%; ACT scores over 24: 36%; SAT verbal scores over 700: 4%; SAT math scores over 700: 4%; ACT scores over 30: 6%.

Faculty *Total:* 215, 59% full-time, 55% with terminal degrees. *Student/faculty ratio:* 12:1.

Majors Accounting; anthropology; art; biochemistry; biology/biological sciences; biotechnology; business administration and management; chemistry; communication/speech communication and rhetoric; computer engineering; computer science; criminal justice/safety; directing and theatrical production; economics; education; elementary education; engineering; engineering physics; English; environmental studies; French; German; history; industrial engineering; international business/trade/commerce; kindergarten/preschool education; mathematics; modern languages; music; music teacher education; music therapy; occupational therapy; peace studies and conflict resolution; philosophy; physics; political science and government; pre-dentistry studies; pre-law studies; pre-medical studies; pre-veterinary studies; psychology; religious studies; science teacher education; secondary education; social sciences; social work; sociology; Spanish; theatre design and technology; theatre/theatre arts management.

Academic Programs *Special study options:* adult/continuing education programs, advanced placement credit, cooperative education, double majors, English as a second language, external degree program, honors programs, independent study, internships, off-campus study, part-time degree program, study abroad, summer session for credit. *Unusual degree programs:* 3-2 engineering with Pennsylvania State University—University Park Campus; forestry with Duke University; nursing with Thomas Jefferson University; allied health programs with Thomas Jefferson University, Widener University, University of Maryland at Baltimore.

Library High Library plus 1 other with 143,302 titles, 1,090 serial subscriptions, 31,195 audiovisual materials, an OPAC, a Web page.

Computers on Campus 200 computers available on campus for general student use. A campuswide network can be accessed from student residence rooms and from off campus that provide access to e-mail, file space, personal web page. Internet access, at least one staffed computer lab available. Computer purchase or lease plan available.

Student Life *Housing:* on-campus residence required through senior year. *Options:* coed, women-only. Campus housing is university owned. Freshman campus housing is guaranteed. *Activities and organizations:* drama/theater group, student-run newspaper, radio and television station, choral group, Activities Planning Board, Student Senate, Residence Hall Association, student newspaper, Habitat for Humanity. *Campus security:* 24-hour emergency response devices and patrols, student patrols, late-night transport/escort service, self-defense workshops, crime prevention program. *Student services:* health clinic, personal/psychological counseling.

Athletics Member NCAA. All Division III. *Intercollegiate sports:* baseball M, basketball M/W, cheerleading M(c)/W(c), cross-country running M/W, field hockey W, golf M, lacrosse M/W, soccer M/W, softball W, swimming M/W, tennis M/W, track and field M/W, volleyball M(c)/W, wrestling M. *Intramural sports:* basketball M/W, racquetball M/W, soccer M/W, softball M/W, tennis M/W, volleyball M/W.

Standardized Tests *Required:* SAT I or ACT (for admission).

Costs (2003–04) *Comprehensive fee:* $28,800 includes full-time tuition ($22,500) and room and board ($6300). Part-time tuition: $575 per credit hour. Part-time tuition and fees vary according to class time, course load, and program. *College room only:* $3150. Room and board charges vary according to board plan and housing facility. *Payment plan:* installment. *Waivers:* employees or children of employees.

Financial Aid Of all full-time matriculated undergraduates who enrolled in 2003, 1,707 applied for aid, 1,558 were judged to have need, 406 had their need fully met. 842 Federal Work-Study jobs (averaging $1288). In 2003, 147 non-need-based awards were made. *Average percent of need met:* 76%. *Average financial aid package:* $15,822. *Average need-based loan:* $3875. *Average need-based gift aid:* $12,337. *Average non-need-based aid:* $13,236. *Average indebtedness upon graduation:* $19,025.

Applying *Options:* common application, electronic application, early admission, deferred entrance. *Application fee:* $30. *Required:* essay or personal statement, high school transcript, minimum 2.0 GPA, 2 letters of recommendation. *Required for some:* interview. *Recommended:* minimum 3.0 GPA, interview. *Application deadline:* rolling (freshmen), rolling (transfers).

Admissions Contact Mr. W. Kent Barnds, Dean of Admissions and Enrollment Management, Elizabethtown College, One Alpha Drive, Elizabethtown, PA 17022. *Phone:* 717-361-1400. *Fax:* 717-361-1365. *E-mail:* admissions@acad.etown.edu.

■ *See page 1576 for a narrative description.*

FRANKLIN AND MARSHALL COLLEGE

Lancaster, Pennsylvania

- **Independent** 4-year, founded 1787
- **Calendar** semesters
- **Degree** bachelor's
- **Suburban** 125-acre campus with easy access to Philadelphia
- **Endowment** $273.0 million
- **Coed,** 1,923 undergraduate students, 98% full-time, 48% women, 52% men
- **Very difficult** entrance level, 58% of applicants were admitted

Undergraduates 1,883 full-time, 40 part-time. Students come from 40 states and territories, 40 other countries, 64% are from out of state, 2% African American, 4% Asian American or Pacific Islander, 3% Hispanic American, 9% international, 0.7% transferred in, 67% live on campus. *Retention:* 90% of 2002 full-time freshmen returned.

Freshmen *Admission:* 3,616 applied, 2,085 admitted, 503 enrolled. *Test scores:* SAT verbal scores over 500: 95%; SAT math scores over 500: 97%; SAT verbal scores over 600: 64%; SAT math scores over 600: 70%; SAT verbal scores over 700: 15%; SAT math scores over 700: 21%.

Faculty *Total:* 195, 86% full-time, 90% with terminal degrees. *Student/faculty ratio:* 11:1.

Majors Accounting and finance; African studies; American studies; ancient/classical Greek; animal behavior and ethology; anthropology; art history, criticism and conservation; astronomy; astrophysics; biochemistry; biology/biological sciences; business administration and management; chemistry; classics and languages, literatures and linguistics; creative writing; dramatic/theatre arts; economics; English; environmental science; environmental studies; fine/studio arts; French; geology/earth science; German; German studies; history; Latin; mathematics; multi-/interdisciplinary studies related; music; neuroscience; philosophy; physics; political science and government; psychology; religious studies; sociology; Spanish.

Academic Programs *Special study options:* accelerated degree program, advanced placement credit, double majors, honors programs, independent study, internships, off-campus study, student-designed majors, study abroad, summer session for credit. *Unusual degree programs:* 3-2 engineering with Rensselaer Polytechnic Institute, Washington University in St. Louis, Columbia University, Case Western Reserve University, Georgia Institute of Technology; forestry with Duke University; environmental studies with Duke University.

Library Shadek-Fackenthal Library plus 1 other with 435,771 titles, 2,090 serial subscriptions, 11,649 audiovisual materials, an OPAC, a Web page.

Computers on Campus 139 computers available on campus for general student use. A campuswide network can be accessed from student residence rooms and from off campus. Internet access, online (class) registration, at least one staffed computer lab available. Computer purchase or lease plan available.

Student Life *Housing:* on-campus residence required through sophomore year. *Options:* coed, men-only, women-only, disabled students. Campus housing is university owned. Freshman campus housing is guaranteed. *Activities and organizations:* drama/theater group, student-run newspaper, radio and television station, choral group, Women's Center, Ware Institute for Community Service, College Reporter, Ben's Underground, F&M Players, national fraternities, national sororities. *Campus security:* 24-hour emergency response devices and patrols, late-night transport/escort service, controlled dormitory access, residence hall security, campus security connected to city police and fire company. *Student services:* health clinic, personal/psychological counseling, women's center.

Athletics Member NCAA. All Division III except wrestling (Division I). *Intercollegiate sports:* baseball M, basketball M/W, cheerleading M/W, crew M(c)/W(c), cross-country running M/W, equestrian sports W(c), field hockey W, football M, golf M/W, ice hockey M(c), lacrosse M/W, rugby M(c)/W(c), soccer M/W, softball W, squash M/W, swimming M/W, tennis M/W, track and field M/W, ultimate Frisbee M(c), volleyball M(c)/W, wrestling M. *Intramural sports:* archery M/W, badminton M/W, basketball M/W, bowling M/W, football M, rock climbing M/W, soccer M/W, softball M/W, squash M/W, table tennis M/W, tennis M/W, volleyball M/W, wrestling M.

Standardized Tests *Required:* SAT I and SAT II or ACT (for admission), SAT II: Writing Test (for admission).

Costs (2003–04) *Comprehensive fee:* $35,930 includes full-time tuition ($28,810), mandatory fees ($50), and room and board ($7070). Full-time tuition and fees vary according to reciprocity agreements. Part-time tuition: $3600 per course. Part-time tuition and fees vary according to course load. *College room only:* $4580. Room and board charges vary according to board plan and housing facility. *Payment plans:* installment, deferred payment. *Waivers:* employees or children of employees.

Financial Aid Of all full-time matriculated undergraduates who enrolled in 2003, 1,002 applied for aid, 877 were judged to have need, 852 had their need fully met. In 2003, 375 non-need-based awards were made. *Average percent of need met:* 97%. *Average financial aid package:* $20,915. *Average need-based loan:* $4805. *Average need-based gift aid:* $17,205. *Average non-need-based aid:* $13,067. *Average indebtedness upon graduation:* $18,370. *Financial aid deadline:* 2/1.

Applying *Options:* common application, electronic application, early admission, early decision, deferred entrance. *Application fee:* $50. *Required:* essay or personal statement, high school transcript, 2 letters of recommendation. *Recommended:* interview. *Application deadlines:* 2/1 (freshmen), 5/1 (transfers). *Early decision:* 11/15 (for plan 1), 1/15 (for plan 2). *Notification:* 4/1 (freshmen), 12/15 (early decision plan 1), 2/15 (early decision plan 2).

Admissions Contact Mr. Dennis Trotter, Vice President for Enrollment Management, Franklin and Marshall College, PO Box 3003, Lancaster, PA 17604-3003. *Phone:* 717-291-3953. *Fax:* 717-291-4389. *E-mail:* admission@fandm.edu.

GANNON UNIVERSITY

Erie, Pennsylvania

- **Independent Roman Catholic** comprehensive, founded 1925
- **Calendar** semesters plus 2 summer sessions
- **Degrees** certificates, associate, bachelor's, master's, doctoral, post-master's, and postbachelor's certificates
- **Urban** 13-acre campus with easy access to Cleveland
- **Endowment** $28.7 million
- **Coed,** 2,435 undergraduate students, 88% full-time, 58% women, 42% men
- **Moderately difficult** entrance level, 84% of applicants were admitted

Gannon University (continued)

At Gannon, students can custom-tailor their education to meet their specific personal, educational, and spiritual goals. Students explore internships, co-ops, study-abroad opportunities, service learning projects, honors courses, and campus ministry activities while developing a values-centered, liberal arts education in one of more than 70 undergraduate majors.

Undergraduates 2,145 full-time, 290 part-time. Students come from 29 states and territories, 20 other countries, 19% are from out of state, 4% African American, 1% Asian American or Pacific Islander, 0.8% Hispanic American, 0.3% Native American, 1% international, 38% live on campus. *Retention:* 80% of 2002 full-time freshmen returned.

Freshmen *Admission:* 2,227 applied, 1,872 admitted, 613 enrolled. *Average high school GPA:* 3.21. *Test scores:* SAT verbal scores over 500: 61%; SAT math scores over 500: 66%; ACT scores over 18: 87%; SAT verbal scores over 600: 17%; SAT math scores over 600: 21%; ACT scores over 24: 33%; SAT verbal scores over 700: 2%; SAT math scores over 700: 1%; ACT scores over 30: 4%.

Faculty *Total:* 285, 59% full-time, 43% with terminal degrees. *Student/faculty ratio:* 11:1.

Majors Accounting; advertising; biological and physical sciences; biology/biological sciences; biotechnology; business administration and management; business/commerce; chemistry; clinical laboratory science/medical technology; communication/speech communication and rhetoric; computer and information sciences; criminal justice/safety; dietetics; dramatic/theatre arts; electrical, electronics and communications engineering; elementary education; engineering; English literature (British and Commonwealth); environmental/environmental health engineering; finance; foreign languages and literatures; foreign language teacher education; funeral service and mortuary science; health science; history; humanities; international business/trade/commerce; kinesiology and exercise science; legal assistant/paralegal; legal studies; liberal arts and sciences/liberal studies; management information systems; marketing/marketing management; mathematics; mechanical engineering; medical radiologic technology; modern languages; nursing (registered nurse training); occupational therapy; ophthalmic/optometric services; philosophy; physician assistant; political science and government; pre-dentistry studies; pre-law studies; pre-medical studies; pre-veterinary studies; psychology; radio and television; respiratory care therapy; secondary education; social work; special education; theology.

Academic Programs *Special study options:* academic remediation for entering students, accelerated degree program, adult/continuing education programs, advanced placement credit, cooperative education, distance learning, double majors, English as a second language, external degree program, honors programs, independent study, internships, off-campus study, part-time degree program, services for LD students, study abroad, summer session for credit. *ROTC:* Army (b). *Unusual degree programs:* 3-2 engineering with University of Akron, University of Pittsburgh, University of Detroit Mercy; law with Duquesne University.

Library Nash Library plus 1 other with 257,670 titles, 9,389 serial subscriptions, 2,274 audiovisual materials, an OPAC, a Web page.

Computers on Campus 229 computers available on campus for general student use. A campuswide network can be accessed from student residence rooms and from off campus. Internet access, at least one staffed computer lab available.

Student Life *Housing:* on-campus residence required through sophomore year. *Options:* coed. Campus housing is university owned and leased by the school. *Activities and organizations:* drama/theater group, student-run newspaper, radio station, Model United Nations, Vitality Through Exercise, Gannon University Residence Union, Interfraternity Council, Panhellenic Council, national fraternities, national sororities. *Campus security:* 24-hour emergency response devices and patrols, student patrols, late-night transport/escort service, controlled dormitory access, security cameras. *Student services:* health clinic, personal/psychological counseling.

Athletics Member NCAA. All Division II. *Intercollegiate sports:* baseball M(s), basketball M(s)/W(s), cross-country running M(s)/W(s), football M, golf M(s)/W(s), lacrosse W(s), soccer M(s)/W(s), softball W(s), swimming M(s)/W(s), volleyball W(s), wrestling M(s). *Intramural sports:* badminton M/W, basketball M/W, bowling M/W, cross-country running M/W, football M, golf M/W, racquetball M/W, soccer M/W, softball M/W, swimming M/W, tennis M/W, volleyball M(c)/W, water polo M, weight lifting M, wrestling M.

Standardized Tests *Required:* SAT I or ACT (for admission).

Costs (2004–05) *Comprehensive fee:* $24,570 includes full-time tuition ($17,030), mandatory fees ($470), and room and board ($7070). Full-time tuition and fees vary according to class time and program. Part-time tuition: $530 per credit. Part-time tuition and fees vary according to class time and program. *Required fees:* $15 per credit part-time. *College room only:* $3840. Room and board charges vary according to board plan and housing facility. *Payment plans:* installment, deferred payment. *Waivers:* senior citizens and employees or children of employees.

Financial Aid Of all full-time matriculated undergraduates who enrolled in 2003, 1,988 applied for aid, 1,831 were judged to have need, 813 had their need fully met. 501 Federal Work-Study jobs (averaging $1170). 190 state and other part-time jobs (averaging $1700). In 2003, 311 non-need-based awards were made. *Average percent of need met:* 80%. *Average financial aid package:* $12,740. *Average need-based loan:* $3002. *Average need-based gift aid:* $10,140. *Average non-need-based aid:* $5940. *Average indebtedness upon graduation:* $23,710.

Applying *Options:* common application, electronic application, early admission, deferred entrance. *Application fee:* $25. *Required:* high school transcript, minimum 2.0 GPA, counselor's recommendation. *Required for some:* minimum 3.0 GPA, 3 letters of recommendation, interview. *Recommended:* essay or personal statement. *Application deadline:* rolling (freshmen), rolling (transfers).

Admissions Contact Mr. Christopher Tremblay, Director of Admissions, Gannon University, University Square, Erie, PA 16541. *Phone:* 814-871-7240. *Toll-free phone:* 800-GANNONU. *Fax:* 814-871-5803. *E-mail:* admissions@gannon.edu.

■ *See page 1660 for a narrative description.*

GENEVA COLLEGE

Beaver Falls, Pennsylvania

- **Independent** comprehensive, founded 1848, affiliated with Reformed Presbyterian Church of North America
- **Calendar** semesters
- **Degrees** associate, bachelor's, and master's
- **Small-town** 55-acre campus with easy access to Pittsburgh
- **Endowment** $25.0 million
- **Coed,** 1,817 undergraduate students, 88% full-time, 57% women, 43% men
- **Moderately difficult** entrance level, 60% of applicants were admitted

Undergraduates 1,606 full-time, 211 part-time. Students come from 37 states and territories, 27% are from out of state, 4% African American, 0.4% Asian American or Pacific Islander, 1% Hispanic American, 0.3% Native American, 1% international, 75% live on campus. *Retention:* 77% of 2002 full-time freshmen returned.

Freshmen *Admission:* 1,790 applied, 1,073 admitted. *Average high school GPA:* 3.30. *Test scores:* SAT verbal scores over 500: 72%; SAT math scores over 500: 64%; ACT scores over 18: 94%; SAT verbal scores over 600: 27%; SAT math scores over 600: 26%; ACT scores over 24: 47%; SAT verbal scores over 700: 4%; SAT math scores over 700: 4%; ACT scores over 30: 9%.

Faculty *Total:* 153, 52% full-time. *Student/faculty ratio:* 14:1.

Majors Accounting; applied mathematics; audiology and speech-language pathology; aviation/airway management; biblical studies; biology/biological sciences; business administration and management; business teacher education; chemical engineering; chemistry; communication/speech communication and rhetoric; computer science; creative writing; elementary education; engineering; English; history; human development and family studies; human services; liberal arts and sciences and humanities related; mathematics teacher education; music; music management and merchandising; music performance; music teacher education; philosophy; physics; political science and government; pre-theology/pre-ministerial studies; psychology; radio and television; radio and television broadcasting technology; secondary education; social work; sociology; Spanish; special education; speech and rhetoric.

Academic Programs *Special study options:* academic remediation for entering students, accelerated degree program, adult/continuing education programs, advanced placement credit, cooperative education, double majors, English as a second language, honors programs, independent study, internships, off-campus study, services for LD students, student-designed majors, study abroad, summer session for credit. *ROTC:* Army (c). *Unusual degree programs:* 3-2 nursing with Roberts Wesleyan College.

Library McCartney Library plus 5 others with 165,442 titles, 937 serial subscriptions, 24,393 audiovisual materials, an OPAC, a Web page.

Computers on Campus 150 computers available on campus for general student use. A campuswide network can be accessed from off campus. At least one staffed computer lab available.

Student Life *Housing:* on-campus residence required through senior year. *Options:* men-only, women-only. Campus housing is university owned. Freshman campus housing is guaranteed. *Activities and organizations:* drama/theater group, student-run newspaper, radio and television station, choral group, marching band, marching band, Genevans A Capella Choir, ministry groups, International Student Organization, discipleship. *Campus security:* 24-hour emergency response devices and patrols, late-night transport/escort service, controlled dormitory access. *Student services:* health clinic, personal/psychological counseling.

Athletics Member NAIA, NCCAA. *Intercollegiate sports:* baseball M(s), basketball M(s)/W(s), cross-country running M(s)/W(s), football M(s), soccer M(s)/W(s), softball W(s), tennis W(s), track and field M(s)/W(s), volleyball M(c)/W(s). *Intramural sports:* basketball M/W, football M, ice hockey M(c), racquetball M/W, rugby M(c)/W(c), skiing (downhill) M(c)/W(c), soccer M/W, softball M/W, volleyball M/W.

Standardized Tests *Required:* SAT I or ACT (for admission).

Costs (2004–05) *Comprehensive fee:* $23,190 includes full-time tuition ($16,030), mandatory fees ($560), and room and board ($6600). *College room only:* $3440.

Financial Aid Of all full-time matriculated undergraduates who enrolled in 2003, 1,162 applied for aid, 1,081 were judged to have need, 236 had their need fully met. In 2003, 158 non-need-based awards were made. *Average percent of need met:* 80%. *Average financial aid package:* $13,180. *Average need-based loan:* $3845. *Average need-based gift aid:* $9326. *Average non-need-based aid:* $7226. *Average indebtedness upon graduation:* $20,800.

Applying *Options:* common application, electronic application, early admission, deferred entrance. *Application fee:* $25. *Required:* essay or personal statement, high school transcript, minimum 2.0 GPA, letters of recommendation. *Required for some:* interview. *Recommended:* minimum 3.0 GPA, interview. *Application deadline:* rolling (freshmen), rolling (transfers). *Notification:* continuous (freshmen), continuous (transfers).

Admissions Contact Mr. David Layton, Associate Vice President for Enrollment Services, Geneva College, 3200 College Avenue, Beaver Falls, PA 15010-3599. *Phone:* 724-847-6500. *Toll-free phone:* 800-847-8255. *Fax:* 724-847-6776. *E-mail:* admissions@geneva.edu.

GETTYSBURG COLLEGE

Gettysburg, Pennsylvania

- **Independent** 4-year, founded 1832, affiliated with Evangelical Lutheran Church in America
- **Calendar** semesters
- **Degree** bachelor's
- **Suburban** 230-acre campus with easy access to Baltimore and Washington, DC
- **Endowment** $176.2 million
- **Coed,** 2,597 undergraduate students, 99% full-time, 52% women, 48% men
- **Most difficult** entrance level, 46% of applicants were admitted

Undergraduates 2,584 full-time, 13 part-time. Students come from 40 states and territories, 32 other countries, 72% are from out of state, 4% African American, 1% Asian American or Pacific Islander, 1% Hispanic American, 0.1% Native American, 2% international, 1% transferred in, 84% live on campus. *Retention:* 91% of 2002 full-time freshmen returned.

Freshmen *Admission:* 5,017 applied, 2,317 admitted, 695 enrolled. *Test scores:* SAT verbal scores over 500: 100%; SAT math scores over 500: 100%; SAT verbal scores over 600: 66%; SAT math scores over 600: 72%; SAT verbal scores over 700: 10%; SAT math scores over 700: 8%.

Faculty *Total:* 259, 72% full-time, 66% with terminal degrees. *Student/faculty ratio:* 11:1.

Majors Accounting; African-American/Black studies; American history; American studies; ancient/classical Greek; anthropology; area, ethnic, cultural, and gender studies related; area studies; area studies related; art; art history, criticism and conservation; Asian history; Asian studies (East); Asian studies (South); biochemistry; biological and physical sciences; biology/biological sciences; broadcast journalism; business administration and management; business administration, management and operations related; chemistry; classics and languages, literatures and linguistics; computer science; creative writing; dramatic/theatre arts; economics; education; elementary education; engineering related; English; English composition; environmental science; environmental studies; European history; fine/studio arts; French; German; health science; Hispanic-American, Puerto Rican, and Mexican-American/Chicano studies; history; interdisciplinary studies; international business/trade/commerce; international economics; international relations and affairs; Italian; Japanese; Japanese studies; journalism; Latin; Latin American studies; liberal arts and sciences/liberal studies; literature; marine biology and biological oceanography; mathematics; middle school education; modern languages; molecular biology; music; music teacher education; non-profit management; peace studies and conflict resolution; philosophy; physical education teaching and coaching; physics; political science and government; pre-dentistry studies; pre-law studies; pre-medical studies; pre-nursing studies; pre-pharmacy studies; pre-veterinary studies; psychology; religious studies; Romance languages; science teacher education; secondary education; social sciences; social sciences related; sociology; Spanish; visual and performing arts; western civilization; women's studies.

Academic Programs *Special study options:* adult/continuing education programs, advanced placement credit, double majors, independent study, internships, off-campus study, student-designed majors, study abroad. *ROTC:* Army (c). *Unusual degree programs:* 3-2 engineering with Rensselaer Polytechnic Institute, Washington University , Columbia University; forestry with Duke University; nursing with Johns Hopkins University.

Library Mussleman Library with 351,848 titles, 4,778 serial subscriptions, 21,752 audiovisual materials, an OPAC, a Web page.

Computers on Campus A campuswide network can be accessed from student residence rooms and from off campus that provide access to wireless area network. Internet access, online (class) registration, at least one staffed computer lab available.

Student Life *Housing:* on-campus residence required for freshman year. *Options:* coed, women-only. Campus housing is university owned. Freshman campus housing is guaranteed. *Activities and organizations:* drama/theater group, student-run newspaper, radio and television station, choral group, marching band, Community Service, Music, Athletics, Student Government, national fraternities, national sororities. *Campus security:* 24-hour emergency response devices and patrols, late-night transport/escort service, controlled dormitory access. *Student services:* health clinic, personal/psychological counseling, women's center.

Athletics Member NCAA. All Division III. *Intercollegiate sports:* baseball M, basketball M/W, cheerleading M/W, cross-country running M/W, field hockey W, football M, golf M/W, lacrosse M/W, soccer M/W, softball W, swimming M/W, tennis M/W, track and field M/W, volleyball W, wrestling M. *Intramural sports:* badminton M/W, basketball M/W, cross-country running M/W, equestrian sports M/W, field hockey W, football M, golf M/W, ice hockey M(c), lacrosse M/W, rugby M(c)/W(c), skiing (cross-country) M/W, skiing (downhill) M/W, soccer M/W, softball M/W, swimming M/W, tennis M/W, track and field M/W, ultimate Frisbee M(c)/W(c), volleyball M/W, wrestling M.

Standardized Tests *Required:* SAT I or ACT (for admission). *Recommended:* SAT II: Subject Tests (for admission).

Costs (2003–04) *Comprehensive fee:* $35,646 includes full-time tuition ($28,424), mandatory fees ($250), and room and board ($6972). Part-time tuition: $3150 per course. *College room only:* $3696. Room and board charges vary according to board plan and housing facility. *Payment plans:* tuition prepayment, installment. *Waivers:* employees or children of employees.

Financial Aid Of all full-time matriculated undergraduates who enrolled in 2003, 1,643 applied for aid, 1,435 were judged to have need, 1,435 had their need fully met. 588 Federal Work-Study jobs (averaging $802). 605 state and other part-time jobs (averaging $913). In 2003, 128 non-need-based awards were made. *Average percent of need met:* 100%. *Average financial aid package:* $24,317. *Average need-based loan:* $4527. *Average need-based gift aid:* $18,531. *Average non-need-based aid:* $7805. *Average indebtedness upon graduation:* $16,000. *Financial aid deadline:* 3/15.

Applying *Options:* common application, electronic application, early admission, early decision, deferred entrance. *Application fee:* $45. *Required:* essay or personal statement, high school transcript, 2 letters of recommendation. *Recommended:* minimum 3.0 GPA, interview, extracurricular activities. *Application deadline:* 2/15 (freshmen), rolling (transfers). *Early decision:* 11/15 (for plan 1), 1/15 (for plan 2). *Notification:* 4/1 (freshmen), 12/15 (early decision plan 1), 2/15 (early decision plan 2), continuous (transfers).

Admissions Contact Ms. Gail Sweezey, Director of Admissions, Gettysburg College, 300 North Washington Street, Gettysburg, PA 17325. *Phone:* 717-337-6100. *Toll-free phone:* 800-431-0803. *Fax:* 717-337-6145. *E-mail:* admiss@gettysburg.edu.

GRATZ COLLEGE

Melrose Park, Pennsylvania

- **Independent Jewish** comprehensive, founded 1895
- **Calendar** semesters
- **Degrees** certificates, bachelor's, master's, and post-master's certificates
- **Suburban** 28-acre campus with easy access to Philadelphia
- **Coed,** 16 undergraduate students, 38% full-time, 88% women, 13% men
- **Moderately difficult** entrance level, 71% of applicants were admitted

Undergraduates 6 full-time, 10 part-time. Students come from 5 states and territories, 44% are from out of state, 31% transferred in. *Retention:* 100% of 2002 full-time freshmen returned.

Freshmen *Admission:* 7 applied, 5 admitted.

Faculty *Total:* 14, 57% full-time, 100% with terminal degrees. *Student/faculty ratio:* 12:1.

Majors Jewish/Judaic studies.

Academic Programs *Special study options:* adult/continuing education programs, double majors, independent study, internships, part-time degree program, study abroad, summer session for credit.

Library Tuttleman Library with 100,000 titles, 175 serial subscriptions, 380 audiovisual materials, an OPAC.

Gratz College (continued)

Computers on Campus 2 computers available on campus for general student use. A campuswide network can be accessed from off campus.

Student Life *Housing:* college housing not available. *Activities and organizations:* choral group. *Campus security:* 24-hour patrols.

Costs (2003–04) *Tuition:* $11,000 full-time, $458 per credit part-time. *Payment plan:* installment. *Waivers:* employees or children of employees.

Financial Aid Of all full-time matriculated undergraduates who enrolled in 2002, 4 applied for aid, 4 were judged to have need. *Average percent of need met:* 86%. *Average financial aid package:* $3908. *Average need-based loan:* $3333.

Applying *Options:* electronic application, early admission, deferred entrance. *Application fee:* $50. *Required:* essay or personal statement, high school transcript, letters of recommendation. *Required for some:* interview. *Application deadline:* rolling (freshmen), rolling (transfers). *Notification:* continuous (freshmen), continuous (transfers).

Admissions Contact Ms. Adena E. Johnston, Director of Admissions, Gratz College, 7605 Old York Road, Melrose Park, PA 19027. *Phone:* 215-635-7300 Ext. 140. *Toll-free phone:* 800-475-4635 Ext. 140. *Fax:* 215-635-7320. *E-mail:* admissions@gratz.edu.

GROVE CITY COLLEGE

Grove City, Pennsylvania

- **Independent Presbyterian** 4-year, founded 1876
- **Calendar** semesters
- **Degree** bachelor's
- **Small-town** 150-acre campus with easy access to Pittsburgh
- **Coed,** 2,314 undergraduate students, 98% full-time, 50% women, 50% men
- **Most difficult** entrance level, 41% of applicants were admitted

Grove City College has won national acclaim for strong academics, Christian values, and a surprising tuition. Its humanities and social sciences emphasize classic books and great thinkers proved across the ages to be of value in the quest for knowledge; its excellent professional studies include mechanical and electrical/computer engineering programs, which are accredited by the engineering accreditation commission of the Accreditation Board for Engineering and Technology, Inc. Included in its cost of education, the Grove City College Information Technology Initiative distributes color notebook computers to every freshman.

Undergraduates 2,279 full-time, 35 part-time. Students come from 44 states and territories, 13 other countries, 47% are from out of state, 0.2% African American, 1% Asian American or Pacific Islander, 0.3% Hispanic American, 0.1% Native American, 0.8% international, 1% transferred in, 90% live on campus. *Retention:* 88% of 2002 full-time freshmen returned.

Freshmen *Admission:* 2,199 applied, 893 admitted, 567 enrolled. *Average high school GPA:* 3.73. *Test scores:* SAT verbal scores over 500: 97%; SAT math scores over 500: 97%; ACT scores over 18: 100%; SAT verbal scores over 600: 72%; SAT math scores over 600: 72%; ACT scores over 24: 88%; SAT verbal scores over 700: 18%; SAT math scores over 700: 21%; ACT scores over 30: 32%.

Faculty *Total:* 179, 70% full-time, 60% with terminal degrees. *Student/faculty ratio:* 18:1.

Majors Accounting; biochemistry; biology/biological sciences; business administration and management; business/corporate communications; business/managerial economics; chemistry; computer and information sciences; computer management; divinity/ministry; economics; electrical and electronic engineering technologies related; electrical, electronics and communications engineering; elementary education; English; entrepreneurship; finance; French; history; international business/trade/commerce; kindergarten/preschool education; literature; marketing/marketing management; mass communication/media; mathematics; mechanical engineering; mechanical engineering technologies related; modern languages; molecular biology; music; music management and merchandising; music performance; music teacher education; philosophy; physics; political science and government; pre-dentistry studies; pre-law studies; pre-medical studies; pre-veterinary studies; psychology; religious studies; science teacher education; secondary education; sociology; Spanish.

Academic Programs *Special study options:* advanced placement credit, double majors, independent study, internships, student-designed majors, study abroad, summer session for credit. *ROTC:* Army (c).

Library Henry Buhl Library with 139,000 titles, 550 serial subscriptions, an OPAC.

Computers on Campus 50 computers available on campus for general student use. A campuswide network can be accessed from student residence rooms and from off campus. Internet access, online (class) registration, at least one staffed computer lab available. Computer purchase or lease plan available.

Student Life *Housing:* on-campus residence required through senior year. *Options:* men-only, women-only. Campus housing is university owned. Freshman campus housing is guaranteed. *Activities and organizations:* drama/theater group, student-run newspaper, radio station, choral group, marching band, Salt Company, Warriors for Christ, orientation board, Orchesis, touring choir. *Campus security:* 24-hour emergency response devices and patrols, student patrols, late-night transport/escort service, controlled dormitory access, monitored women's residence hall entrances. *Student services:* health clinic, personal/psychological counseling.

Athletics Member NCAA. All Division III. *Intercollegiate sports:* baseball M, basketball M/W, cheerleading W, cross-country running M/W, football M, golf M/W, soccer M/W, softball W, swimming M/W, tennis M/W, track and field M/W, volleyball W, water polo M/W. *Intramural sports:* basketball M/W, bowling M/W, football M, golf M/W, racquetball M/W, soccer M, softball M, swimming M/W, table tennis W, tennis M/W, volleyball M/W, weight lifting M.

Standardized Tests *Required:* SAT I or ACT (for admission).

Costs (2003–04) *Comprehensive fee:* $14,378 includes full-time tuition ($9376), mandatory fees ($150), and room and board ($4852). Full-time tuition and fees vary according to course load. *Waivers:* employees or children of employees.

Financial Aid Of all full-time matriculated undergraduates who enrolled in 2003, 1,575 applied for aid, 874 were judged to have need, 73 had their need fully met. 900 state and other part-time jobs (averaging $733). In 2003, 443 non-need-based awards were made. *Average percent of need met:* 50%. *Average financial aid package:* $4385. *Average need-based gift aid:* $4672. *Average non-need-based aid:* $2572. *Average indebtedness upon graduation:* $19,986. *Financial aid deadline:* 4/15.

Applying *Options:* electronic application, early admission, early decision, deferred entrance. *Application fee:* $40. *Required:* essay or personal statement, high school transcript, 2 letters of recommendation. *Recommended:* interview. *Application deadlines:* 2/1 (freshmen), 8/15 (transfers). *Early decision:* 11/15. *Notification:* 3/15 (freshmen), 12/15 (early decision), continuous (transfers).

Admissions Contact Mr. Jeffrey C. Mincey, Director of Admissions, Grove City College, 100 Campus Drive, Grove City, PA 16127-2104. *Phone:* 724-458-2100. *Fax:* 724-458-3395. *E-mail:* admissions@gcc.edu.

■ *See page 1694 for a narrative description.*

GWYNEDD-MERCY COLLEGE

Gwynedd Valley, Pennsylvania

- **Independent Roman Catholic** comprehensive, founded 1948
- **Calendar** semesters
- **Degrees** certificates, associate, bachelor's, master's, post-master's, and postbachelor's certificates
- **Suburban** 170-acre campus with easy access to Philadelphia
- **Endowment** $6.0 million
- **Coed,** 2,177 undergraduate students, 56% full-time, 77% women, 23% men
- **Moderately difficult** entrance level, 58% of applicants were admitted

Gwynedd-Mercy combines strong academic programs with extensive opportunities for students to gain practical experience through internships, co-ops, and clinicals. With pass rates on national examinations of more than 95%, students are prepared to enter the workforce of the 21st century. The College has affiliations with more than 200 health-care organizations, businesses, and school districts.

Undergraduates 1,230 full-time, 947 part-time. Students come from 9 states and territories, 5% are from out of state, 14% African American, 3% Asian American or Pacific Islander, 2% Hispanic American, 0.1% Native American, 2% international, 8% transferred in, 22% live on campus. *Retention:* 89% of 2002 full-time freshmen returned.

Freshmen *Admission:* 1,679 applied, 972 admitted, 247 enrolled. *Test scores:* SAT verbal scores over 500: 45%; SAT math scores over 500: 42%; SAT verbal scores over 600: 7%; SAT math scores over 600: 7%; SAT verbal scores over 700: 1%.

Faculty *Total:* 265, 29% full-time, 36% with terminal degrees. *Student/faculty ratio:* 13:1.

Majors Accounting; allied health diagnostic, intervention, and treatment professions related; biological and biomedical sciences related; biology/biological sciences; business administration and management; business teacher education; cardiovascular technology; clinical laboratory science/medical technology; computer and information sciences; computer programming; education; education (K-12); elementary education; English; forensic psychology; gerontology; health information/medical records administration; health information/medical records technology; health science; health services/allied health/health sciences; history; history teacher education; hospital and health care facilities administration; liberal arts and sciences/liberal studies; mathematics; mathematics teacher education; nursing (registered nurse training); pre-law studies; psychology; public relations/image management; respiratory care therapy; science teacher education; secondary education; social work; sociology; special education.

Academic Programs *Special study options:* academic remediation for entering students, accelerated degree program, adult/continuing education programs, advanced placement credit, cooperative education, double majors, English as a second language, external degree program, freshman honors college, honors programs, independent study, internships, part-time degree program, summer session for credit.

Library Lourdes Library plus 1 other with 88,064 titles, 825 serial subscriptions, 51,443 audiovisual materials, an OPAC, a Web page.

Computers on Campus 97 computers available on campus for general student use. A campuswide network can be accessed from student residence rooms and from off campus. Internet access, at least one staffed computer lab available.

Student Life *Housing options:* coed. Campus housing is university owned. Freshman applicants given priority for college housing. *Activities and organizations:* drama/theater group, student-run newspaper, choral group, Voices of Gwynedd, Athletic Association, student government, Program Board, Peer Mentors. *Campus security:* 24-hour emergency response devices and patrols, late-night transport/escort service. *Student services:* health clinic, personal/psychological counseling.

Athletics Member NCAA. All Division III. *Intercollegiate sports:* basketball M/W, field hockey W, lacrosse W, soccer M, softball W(c), tennis M/W, volleyball W.

Standardized Tests *Required:* SAT I (for admission).

Costs (2003–04) *Comprehensive fee:* $24,000 includes full-time tuition ($16,200), mandatory fees ($500), and room and board ($7300). Full-time tuition and fees vary according to program. Part-time tuition: $320 per credit. Part-time tuition and fees vary according to program. *Required fees:* $10 per credit part-time. *Room and board:* Room and board charges vary according to board plan. *Payment plan:* installment. *Waivers:* employees or children of employees.

Financial Aid Of all full-time matriculated undergraduates who enrolled in 2003, 1,046 applied for aid, 858 were judged to have need, 632 had their need fully met. 356 Federal Work-Study jobs (averaging $1330). 10 state and other part-time jobs (averaging $2230). In 2003, 213 non-need-based awards were made. *Average percent of need met:* 82%. *Average financial aid package:* $14,523. *Average need-based loan:* $4656. *Average need-based gift aid:* $10,800. *Average non-need-based aid:* $6482. *Average indebtedness upon graduation:* $18,624.

Applying *Options:* common application, electronic application, early admission, deferred entrance. *Application fee:* $25. *Required:* high school transcript, 1 letter of recommendation. *Required for some:* interview. *Recommended:* interview. *Application deadlines:* rolling (freshmen), 8/20 (transfers). *Notification:* continuous (freshmen), continuous (transfers).

Admissions Contact Mr. Dennis Murphy, Vice President of Enrollment Management, Gwynedd-Mercy College, 1325 Sumneytown Pike, Gwynedd Valley, PA 19437-0901. *Phone:* 215-646-7300 Ext. 588. *Toll-free phone:* 800-DIAL-GMC. *E-mail:* admissions@gmc.edu.

■ *See page 1700 for a narrative description.*

HAVERFORD COLLEGE
Haverford, Pennsylvania

- **Independent** 4-year, founded 1833
- **Calendar** semesters
- **Degree** bachelor's
- **Suburban** 200-acre campus with easy access to Philadelphia
- **Endowment** $280.0 million
- **Coed,** 1,163 undergraduate students, 100% full-time, 52% women, 48% men
- **Most difficult** entrance level, 30% of applicants were admitted

Undergraduates 1,163 full-time. Students come from 50 states and territories, 83% are from out of state, 5% African American, 14% Asian American or Pacific Islander, 6% Hispanic American, 0.9% Native American, 2% international, 0.3% transferred in, 98% live on campus. *Retention:* 96% of 2002 full-time freshmen returned.

Freshmen *Admission:* 2,973 applied, 878 admitted, 313 enrolled. *Test scores:* SAT verbal scores over 500: 99%; SAT math scores over 500: 99%; SAT verbal scores over 600: 92%; SAT math scores over 600: 92%; SAT verbal scores over 700: 46%; SAT math scores over 700: 44%.

Faculty *Total:* 113, 96% full-time, 100% with terminal degrees. *Student/faculty ratio:* 8:1.

Majors African studies; anthropology; archeology; art; art history, criticism and conservation; Asian studies (East); astronomy; biochemistry; biology/biological sciences; biophysics; chemistry; classics and languages, literatures and linguistics; comparative literature; computer science; econometrics and quantitative economics; economics; education; English; French; geology/earth science; German; history; Italian; Latin; Latin American studies; mathematics; modern Greek; music; neuroscience; peace studies and conflict resolution; philosophy; physics; political science and government; pre-law studies; pre-medical studies; pre-veterinary studies; psychology; religious studies; Romance languages; Russian; sociology; Spanish; urban studies/affairs; women's studies.

Academic Programs *Special study options:* accelerated degree program, advanced placement credit, double majors, independent study, internships, off-campus study, services for LD students, student-designed majors, study abroad.

Library Magill Library plus 4 others with 395,799 titles, 3,240 serial subscriptions, 10,716 audiovisual materials, an OPAC, a Web page.

Computers on Campus 260 computers available on campus for general student use. A campuswide network can be accessed from student residence rooms and from off campus. Internet access, online (class) registration, at least one staffed computer lab available.

Student Life *Housing:* on-campus residence required for freshman year. *Options:* coed, men-only, women-only, disabled students. Campus housing is university owned. Freshman campus housing is guaranteed. *Activities and organizations:* drama/theater group, student-run newspaper, radio station, choral group, volunteer programs, student government, choral groups, multicultural groups, orientation team/residential life leaders. *Campus security:* 24-hour emergency response devices and patrols, late-night transport/escort service. *Student services:* health clinic, personal/psychological counseling, women's center.

Athletics Member NCAA. All Division III. *Intercollegiate sports:* baseball M, basketball M/W, crew M(c)/W(c), cross-country running M/W, fencing M/W, field hockey W, golf M(c)/W(c), lacrosse M/W, soccer M/W, softball W, squash M/W, tennis M/W, track and field M/W, volleyball W, wrestling M(c). *Intramural sports:* basketball M/W, cheerleading W, ice hockey M(c)/W(c), rugby M(c)/W(c), sailing M(c)/W(c), soccer M/W, softball M/W, tennis M/W, ultimate Frisbee M(c)/W(c), volleyball M/W.

Standardized Tests *Required:* SAT I or ACT (for admission), SAT II: Subject Tests (for admission), SAT II: Writing Test (for admission).

Costs (2003–04) *Comprehensive fee:* $37,900 includes full-time tuition ($28,612), mandatory fees ($268), and room and board ($9020). *College room only:* $5050. Room and board charges vary according to board plan. *Payment plan:* installment. *Waivers:* employees or children of employees.

Financial Aid Of all full-time matriculated undergraduates who enrolled in 2003, 586 applied for aid, 505 were judged to have need, 505 had their need fully met. *Average percent of need met:* 100%. *Average financial aid package:* $25,073. *Average need-based loan:* $3947. *Average need-based gift aid:* $22,203. *Average indebtedness upon graduation:* $15,362. *Financial aid deadline:* 1/31.

Applying *Options:* common application, electronic application, early admission, early decision, deferred entrance. *Application fee:* $50. *Required:* essay or personal statement, high school transcript, 2 letters of recommendation. *Recommended:* interview. *Application deadlines:* 1/15 (freshmen), 3/31 (transfers). *Early decision:* 11/15. *Notification:* 5/1 (freshmen), 12/15 (early decision), 6/1 (transfers).

Admissions Contact Ms. Delsie Z. Phillips, Director of Admission, Haverford College, 370 Lancaster Avenue, Haverford, PA 19041-1392. *Phone:* 610-896-1350. *Fax:* 610-896-1338. *E-mail:* admitme@haverford.edu.

■ *See page 1722 for a narrative description.*

HOLY FAMILY UNIVERSITY
Philadelphia, Pennsylvania

- **Independent Roman Catholic** comprehensive, founded 1954
- **Calendar** semesters
- **Degrees** certificates, associate, bachelor's, master's, and postbachelor's certificates
- **Suburban** 47-acre campus
- **Endowment** $5.2 million
- **Coed**
- **Moderately difficult** entrance level

Faculty *Student/faculty ratio:* 11:1.

Student Life *Campus security:* 24-hour emergency response devices and patrols, student patrols, late-night transport/escort service.

Athletics Member NAIA.

Standardized Tests *Required:* SAT I or ACT (for admission).

Costs (2003–04) *Tuition:* $14,990 full-time, $335 per credit hour part-time. Full-time tuition and fees vary according to course load and program. Part-time tuition and fees vary according to program. *Required fees:* $500 full-time, $60 per term part-time. *Payment plans:* installment, deferred payment.

Financial Aid Of all full-time matriculated undergraduates who enrolled in 2003, 299 Federal Work-Study jobs (averaging $1176). *Average indebtedness upon graduation:* $17,125.

Applying *Options:* common application, deferred entrance. *Application fee:* $25. *Required:* essay or personal statement, high school transcript, 1 letter of recommendation. *Recommended:* interview.

Holy Family University (continued)

Admissions Contact Ms. Lauren McDermott, Interim Director of Admissions, Holy Family University, Grant and Frankford Avenues, Philadelphia, PA 19114-2094. *Phone:* 215-637-3050. *Toll-free phone:* 800-637-1191. *Fax:* 215-281-1022. *E-mail:* undergra@hfc.edu.

IMMACULATA UNIVERSITY

Immaculata, Pennsylvania

- **Independent Roman Catholic** comprehensive, founded 1920
- **Calendar** semesters
- **Degrees** associate, bachelor's, master's, and doctoral
- **Suburban** 400-acre campus with easy access to Philadelphia
- **Endowment** $10.8 million
- **Coed,** 2,575 undergraduate students, 18% full-time, 84% women, 16% men
- **Moderately difficult** entrance level, 85% of applicants were admitted

Immaculata University is a Catholic, comprehensive liberal arts university dedicated to educating women of all faiths. Founded in 1920, Immaculata's enrollment has grown to more than 3,400. Immaculata is composed of 3 areas: the Women's College, the College of Lifelong Learning, and the College of Graduate Studies. Approximately 400 women attend the Women's College; 85% live in campus housing. A fixed tuition rate is offered to all full-time students entering the Women's College. The evening division includes graduate and undergraduate programs that are open to both men and women. The University is located 20 miles west of Philadelphia.

Undergraduates 473 full-time, 2,102 part-time. Students come from 14 states and territories, 1 other country, 17% are from out of state, 7% African American, 1% Asian American or Pacific Islander, 2% Hispanic American, 0.1% Native American, 1% international, 0.8% transferred in, 80% live on campus. *Retention:* 69% of 2002 full-time freshmen returned.

Freshmen *Admission:* 82 enrolled. *Average high school GPA:* 3.18. *Test scores:* SAT verbal scores over 500: 48%; SAT math scores over 500: 33%; SAT verbal scores over 600: 17%; SAT math scores over 600: 9%; SAT verbal scores over 700: 5%; SAT math scores over 700: 1%.

Faculty *Total:* 277, 28% full-time, 38% with terminal degrees. *Student/faculty ratio:* 10:1.

Majors Accounting; adult and continuing education; art; art teacher education; biochemistry; biology/biological sciences; biomedical sciences; business administration and management; business/managerial economics; chemistry; computer and information sciences; computer science; dietetics; economics; education; elementary education; English; family and consumer sciences/home economics teacher education; family and consumer sciences/human sciences; fashion merchandising; foods, nutrition, and wellness; French; German; history; hospitality and recreation marketing; humanities; international business/trade/commerce; international relations and affairs; Italian; kindergarten/preschool education; liberal arts and sciences/liberal studies; literature; marketing/marketing management; mathematics; modern languages; music; music teacher education; music therapy; nursing science; physics; pre-dentistry studies; pre-law studies; premedical studies; pre-veterinary studies; psychology; religious/sacred music; secondary education; social work; sociology; Spanish; special products marketing; theology; voice and opera.

Academic Programs *Special study options:* academic remediation for entering students, accelerated degree program, adult/continuing education programs, advanced placement credit, double majors, English as a second language, freshman honors college, honors programs, independent study, internships, part-time degree program, services for LD students, student-designed majors, study abroad, summer session for credit. *Unusual degree programs:* 3-2 music therapy, dietetics.

Library Gabriele Library with 1.2 million titles, 755 serial subscriptions, 1,800 audiovisual materials, an OPAC, a Web page.

Computers on Campus 215 computers available on campus for general student use. A campuswide network can be accessed from student residence rooms and from off campus. Internet access, at least one staffed computer lab available. Computer purchase or lease plan available.

Student Life *Housing options:* women-only. Campus housing is university owned. Freshman campus housing is guaranteed. *Activities and organizations:* drama/theater group, student-run newspaper, choral group, Campus Ministry, Student Association, chorale, Honor Society, Cue and Curtain. *Campus security:* 24-hour emergency response devices and patrols, late-night transport/escort service, controlled dormitory access. *Student services:* health clinic, personal/psychological counseling.

Athletics Member NCAA. All Division III. *Intercollegiate sports:* basketball W, cross-country running W, field hockey W, soccer W, softball W, tennis W, volleyball W. *Intramural sports:* archery W, badminton W, cheerleading W(c), equestrian sports W(c), fencing W, lacrosse W, swimming W.

Standardized Tests *Required:* SAT I or ACT (for admission).

Costs (2003–04) *Comprehensive fee:* $25,200 includes full-time tuition ($17,200) and room and board ($8000). Full-time tuition and fees vary according to student level. Part-time tuition and fees vary according to class time. No tuition increase for student's term of enrollment. *College room only:* $4300. Room and board charges vary according to board plan. *Payment plan:* installment. *Waivers:* senior citizens and employees or children of employees.

Financial Aid Of all full-time matriculated undergraduates who enrolled in 2002, 395 applied for aid, 316 were judged to have need, 95 had their need fully met. In 2002, 30 non-need-based awards were made. *Average percent of need met:* 47%. *Average financial aid package:* $14,800. *Average need-based loan:* $4280. *Average need-based gift aid:* $2200. *Average non-need-based aid:* $5800. *Average indebtedness upon graduation:* $17,125. *Financial aid deadline:* 4/15.

Applying *Options:* electronic application, early admission, deferred entrance. *Application fee:* $25. *Required:* high school transcript, minimum 2.0 GPA, 1 letter of recommendation. *Recommended:* essay or personal statement, minimum 3.0 GPA, interview. *Application deadline:* 8/15 (freshmen), rolling (transfers). *Notification:* 9/1 (freshmen), continuous (transfers).

Admissions Contact Ms. Sarah Fox, Assistant Director of Admission, Immaculata University, PO Box 642, Immaculata, PA 19345-0642. *Phone:* 610-647-4400 Ext. 3013. *Toll-free phone:* 877-428-6328. *Fax:* 610-640-0836. *E-mail:* admiss@immaculata.edu.

■ *See page 1762 for a narrative description.*

INDIANA UNIVERSITY OF PENNSYLVANIA

Indiana, Pennsylvania

- **State-supported** university, founded 1875, part of Pennsylvania State System of Higher Education
- **Calendar** semesters
- **Degrees** certificates, associate, bachelor's, master's, doctoral, post-master's, and postbachelor's certificates
- **Small-town** 350-acre campus with easy access to Pittsburgh
- **Endowment** $28.5 million
- **Coed,** 12,119 undergraduate students, 92% full-time, 56% women, 44% men
- **Moderately difficult** entrance level, 60% of applicants were admitted

IUP has one of the largest student internship programs in Pennsylvania. More than 50% of its students participate in experiential and cooperative education and student teaching programs prior to graduation. Many graduates are offered a selection of positions by the companies that sponsor their internships. Employers are becoming more interested in graduates who have completed a supervised experience.

Undergraduates 11,191 full-time, 928 part-time. Students come from 50 states and territories, 73 other countries, 3% are from out of state, 6% African American, 0.9% Asian American or Pacific Islander, 0.8% Hispanic American, 0.2% Native American, 2% international, 5% transferred in, 33% live on campus. *Retention:* 73% of 2002 full-time freshmen returned.

Freshmen *Admission:* 8,618 applied, 5,136 admitted, 2,761 enrolled. *Test scores:* SAT verbal scores over 500: 61%; SAT math scores over 500: 59%; SAT verbal scores over 600: 15%; SAT math scores over 600: 15%; SAT verbal scores over 700: 3%; SAT math scores over 700: 2%.

Faculty *Total:* 694, 91% full-time, 84% with terminal degrees. *Student/faculty ratio:* 19:1.

Majors Accounting; anthropology; applied mathematics; art; art teacher education; biochemistry; biological and physical sciences; biology/biological sciences; business administration and management; business teacher education; chemistry; city/urban, community and regional planning; clinical laboratory science/medical technology; communication/speech communication and rhetoric; computer and information sciences; consumer economics; criminology; dietetics; dramatic/theatre arts; economics; elementary education; English; English/language arts teacher education; environmental health; environmental studies; family and consumer sciences/home economics teacher education; fashion merchandising; finance; foods, nutrition, and wellness; French; general studies; geography; geology/earth science; German; health and physical education; history; hotel/motel administration; human development and family studies; human resources management; interior architecture; intermedia/multimedia; international business/trade/commerce; international relations and affairs; journalism; kindergarten/preschool education; management information systems; marketing/marketing management; mathematics; mathematics teacher education; music; music performance; music teacher education; nuclear medical technology; nursing (registered nurse training); occupational safety and health technology; office management; philosophy; physical education teaching and coaching; physics; political science and government; psychology; religious studies; respiratory care therapy; Russian; science teacher education; secondary education; social studies teacher education; sociology; Spanish; special education; special education (hearing impaired);

special education (orthopedic and other physical health impairments); special education (speech or language impaired); trade and industrial teacher education.

Academic Programs *Special study options:* academic remediation for entering students, accelerated degree program, adult/continuing education programs, advanced placement credit, cooperative education, distance learning, double majors, English as a second language, freshman honors college, honors programs, independent study, internships, off-campus study, part-time degree program, services for LD students, study abroad, summer session for credit. *ROTC:* Army (b). *Unusual degree programs:* 3-2 engineering with Drexel University, University of Pittsburgh; forestry with Duke University.

Library Stapleton Library with 570,735 titles, 2,626 serial subscriptions, 109,308 audiovisual materials, an OPAC, a Web page.

Computers on Campus 3500 computers available on campus for general student use. A campuswide network can be accessed from student residence rooms and from off campus. Internet access, online (class) registration, at least one staffed computer lab available. Computer purchase or lease plan available.

Student Life *Housing:* on-campus residence required for freshman year. *Options:* coed. Campus housing is university owned. Freshman campus housing is guaranteed. *Activities and organizations:* drama/theater group, student-run newspaper, radio and television station, choral group, marching band, NAACP, Interfraternity Council, Panhellenic Association, Student Congress, Alpha Phi Omega, national fraternities, national sororities. *Campus security:* 24-hour emergency response devices and patrols, late-night transport/escort service, controlled dormitory access. *Student services:* health clinic, personal/psychological counseling, women's center, legal services.

Athletics Member NCAA. All Division II. *Intercollegiate sports:* baseball M(s), basketball M(s)/W(s), cross-country running M(s)/W(s), field hockey W(s), football M(s), golf M(s), lacrosse W(s), soccer W(s), softball W(s), swimming M/W(s), tennis W(s), track and field M(s)/W(s), volleyball W(s). *Intramural sports:* archery M/W, badminton M/W, basketball M/W, bowling M/W, cheerleading W, cross-country running M(c)/W(c), equestrian sports M(c)/W(c), fencing M(c), football M/W, golf M/W, ice hockey M(c), racquetball M/W, riflery M(c)/W(c), sailing M(c)/W(c), skiing (downhill) M(c)/W(c), soccer M(c)/W(c), softball M(c)/W(c), swimming M/W, table tennis M/W, tennis M/W, track and field M/W, volleyball M/W, water polo M/W, weight lifting M/W, wrestling M.

Standardized Tests *Required:* SAT I or ACT (for admission).

Costs (2003–04) *Tuition:* state resident $4598 full-time, $192 per semester hour part-time; nonresident $11,496 full-time, $472 per semester hour part-time. Full-time tuition and fees vary according to course load, location, and reciprocity agreements. Part-time tuition and fees vary according to course load, location, and reciprocity agreements. *Required fees:* $1187 full-time, $19 per semester hour part-time, $220 per term part-time. *Room and board:* $4704; room only: $2826. Room and board charges vary according to board plan and housing facility. *Payment plans:* installment, deferred payment. *Waivers:* minority students and employees or children of employees.

Financial Aid Of all full-time matriculated undergraduates who enrolled in 2002, 9,026 applied for aid, 7,291 were judged to have need, 1,477 had their need fully met. 1,600 Federal Work-Study jobs (averaging $1267). 1,779 state and other part-time jobs (averaging $1161). In 2002, 379 non-need-based awards were made. *Average percent of need met:* 76%. *Average financial aid package:* $7067. *Average need-based loan:* $3483. *Average need-based gift aid:* $3639. *Average non-need-based aid:* $2286. *Average indebtedness upon graduation:* $17,825. *Financial aid deadline:* 4/15.

Applying *Options:* common application, electronic application, early admission, deferred entrance. *Application fee:* $30. *Required:* high school transcript. *Recommended:* letters of recommendation. *Application deadline:* rolling (freshmen), rolling (transfers). *Notification:* 9/1 (freshmen), continuous (transfers).

Admissions Contact Rhonda H. Luckey EdD, Interim Dean of Admissions, Indiana University of Pennsylvania, 1011 South Drive, Sutton Hall 214, Indiana, PA 15705. *Phone:* 724-357-2230. *Toll-free phone:* 800-442-6830. *E-mail:* admissions-inquiry@iup.edu.

■ *See page 1766 for a narrative description.*

JUNIATA COLLEGE
Huntingdon, Pennsylvania

- **Independent** 4-year, founded 1876, affiliated with Church of the Brethren
- **Calendar** semesters
- **Degree** bachelor's
- **Small-town** 110-acre campus
- **Endowment** $52.3 million
- **Coed,** 1,396 undergraduate students, 96% full-time, 56% women, 44% men
- **Moderately difficult** entrance level, 75% of applicants were admitted

Students who welcome academic challenges and are ready to discover who they are and what they are capable of should consider Juniata College. The College's traditions include excellence in academics, small classes, a close-knit community, and many surprises, like Mountain Day.

Undergraduates 1,338 full-time, 58 part-time. Students come from 32 states and territories, 21 other countries, 25% are from out of state, 1% African American, 1% Asian American or Pacific Islander, 0.8% Hispanic American, 0.2% Native American, 3% international, 2% transferred in. *Retention:* 86% of 2002 full-time freshmen returned.

Freshmen *Admission:* 1,578 applied, 1,179 admitted, 381 enrolled. *Average high school GPA:* 3.71. *Test scores:* SAT verbal scores over 500: 88%; SAT math scores over 500: 92%; SAT verbal scores over 600: 41%; SAT math scores over 600: 45%; SAT verbal scores over 700: 7%; SAT math scores over 700: 7%.

Faculty *Total:* 128, 73% full-time, 80% with terminal degrees. *Student/faculty ratio:* 13:1.

Majors Accounting; anthropology; art history, criticism and conservation; biochemistry; biological and physical sciences; biology/biological sciences; biology teacher education; botany/plant biology; business administration and management; business/commerce; cell biology and histology; chemistry; chemistry teacher education; communication and journalism related; communication/speech communication and rhetoric; computer and information sciences; criminal justice/safety; criminology; early childhood education; ecology; economics; education; education (multiple levels); education (specific subject areas) related; elementary education; engineering; engineering physics; English; English/language arts teacher education; environmental science; environmental studies; finance; fine/studio arts; foreign languages and literatures; foreign language teacher education; French; French language teacher education; geology/earth science; German; German language teacher education; health communication; health/medical preparatory programs related; history; humanities; human resources management; information resources management; information technology; interdisciplinary studies; international business/trade/commerce; international/global studies; international relations and affairs; kindergarten/preschool education; liberal arts and sciences/liberal studies; marine biology and biological oceanography; marketing/marketing management; mathematics; mathematics teacher education; medical microbiology and bacteriology; microbiology; molecular biology; museum studies; natural sciences; peace studies and conflict resolution; philosophy; philosophy and religious studies related; physical sciences; physics; physics teacher education; political science and government; pre-dentistry studies; pre-law studies; pre-medical studies; pre-pharmacy studies; pre-theology/preministerial studies; pre-veterinary studies; professional studies; psychology; public administration; religious studies; Russian; science teacher education; secondary education; social sciences; social studies teacher education; social work; sociology; Spanish; Spanish language teacher education; special education; special education (early childhood); special education related; zoology/animal biology.

Academic Programs *Special study options:* accelerated degree program, adult/continuing education programs, advanced placement credit, distance learning, double majors, English as a second language, freshman honors college, honors programs, independent study, internships, off-campus study, part-time degree program, services for LD students, student-designed majors, study abroad, summer session for credit. *Unusual degree programs:* 3-2 engineering with Pennsylvania State University—University Park Campus, Columbia University, Washington University in St. Louis, Clarkson University; nursing with Thomas Jefferson University, Johns Hopkins University, Case Western Reserve University; biotechnology; cytotechnology; diagnostic imaging; medical technology; occupational therapy, physical therapy with Thomas Jefferson University; Widener University; Allegheny University of Health Sciences.

Library Beeghly Library with 255,000 titles, 1,000 serial subscriptions, 1,500 audiovisual materials, an OPAC, a Web page.

Computers on Campus 375 computers available on campus for general student use. A campuswide network can be accessed from student residence rooms and from off campus. Internet access, online (class) registration, at least one staffed computer lab available.

Student Life *Housing:* on-campus residence required through senior year. *Options:* coed, women-only. Campus housing is university owned. Freshman campus housing is guaranteed. *Activities and organizations:* drama/theater group, student-run newspaper, radio station, choral group, student government, Activities Board, HOSA, international club, Habitat for Humanity. *Campus security:* 24-hour emergency response devices and patrols, student patrols, late-night transport/escort service, fire safety training, adopt-an-officer program, security website, weather/terror alerts, travel forecast, crime statistics. *Student services:* health clinic, personal/psychological counseling, women's center.

Athletics Member NCAA. All Division III. *Intercollegiate sports:* baseball M, basketball M/W, cross-country running M/W, equestrian sports M(c)/W(c), field hockey W, football M, golf M(c)/W(c), ice hockey M(c), lacrosse M(c), rugby M(c)/W(c), soccer M/W, softball W, swimming W, tennis M/W, track and field

Juniata College (continued)

M/W, ultimate Frisbee M(c)/W(c), volleyball M/W. *Intramural sports:* badminton M/W, basketball M/W, bowling M/W, field hockey M(c)/W(c), football M/W, gymnastics M(c)/W(c), lacrosse W(c), skiing (cross-country) M/W, skiing (downhill) M(c)/W(c), soccer M/W, volleyball M/W, water polo M(c)/W(c).

Standardized Tests *Required:* SAT I or ACT (for admission).

Costs (2004–05) *Comprehensive fee:* $31,040 includes full-time tuition ($23,720), mandatory fees ($550), and room and board ($6770). Part-time tuition: $990 per credit hour. *College room only:* $3550. *Waivers:* adult students and employees or children of employees.

Financial Aid Of all full-time matriculated undergraduates who enrolled in 2003, 1,160 applied for aid, 1,038 were judged to have need, 631 had their need fully met. 701 Federal Work-Study jobs (averaging $1135). 536 state and other part-time jobs (averaging $1365). In 2003, 276 non-need-based awards were made. *Average percent of need met:* 88%. *Average financial aid package:* $18,258. *Average need-based loan:* $3954. *Average need-based gift aid:* $14,190. *Average non-need-based aid:* $10,760. *Average indebtedness upon graduation:* $17,572.

Applying *Options:* common application, electronic application, early admission, early decision, deferred entrance. *Application fee:* $30. *Required:* essay or personal statement, high school transcript, minimum 3.0 GPA, 1 letter of recommendation. *Recommended:* interview. *Application deadlines:* 3/15 (freshmen), 6/15 (transfers). *Early decision:* 11/15. *Notification:* continuous (freshmen), 12/30 (early decision), continuous (transfers).

Admissions Contact Terry Bollman, Director of Admissions, Juniata College, 1700 Moore Street, Huntingdon, PA 16652. *Phone:* 814-641-3424. *Toll-free phone:* 877-JUNIATA. *Fax:* 814-641-3100. *E-mail:* info@juniata.edu.

■ *See page 1802 for a narrative description.*

KEYSTONE COLLEGE

La Plume, Pennsylvania

- **Independent** primarily 2-year, founded 1868
- **Calendar** semesters
- **Degrees** certificates, associate, bachelor's, and postbachelor's certificates
- **Rural** 270-acre campus
- **Endowment** $8.9 million
- **Coed,** 1,445 undergraduate students, 69% full-time, 63% women, 37% men
- **Minimally difficult** entrance level, 95% of applicants were admitted

Undergraduates 998 full-time, 447 part-time. Students come from 12 states and territories, 7 other countries, 10% are from out of state, 5% African American, 0.3% Asian American or Pacific Islander, 1% Hispanic American, 0.1% Native American, 1% international, 8% transferred in, 34% live on campus. *Retention:* 58% of 2002 full-time freshmen returned.

Freshmen *Admission:* 788 applied, 746 admitted, 468 enrolled. *Test scores:* SAT verbal scores over 500: 21%; SAT math scores over 500: 16%; ACT scores over 18: 45%; SAT verbal scores over 600: 3%; SAT math scores over 600: 2%.

Faculty *Total:* 186, 31% full-time, 21% with terminal degrees. *Student/faculty ratio:* 12:1.

Majors Accounting; accounting and business/management; accounting related; art; art teacher education; biological and physical sciences; biology/biological sciences; business administration and management; business administration, management and operations related; business/commerce; communication and journalism related; communication and media related; communication/speech communication and rhetoric; computer/information technology services administration related; computer programming; computer programming (specific applications); computer systems networking and telecommunications; criminal justice/law enforcement administration; criminal justice/safety; culinary arts; culinary arts related; data processing and data processing technology; diagnostic medical sonography and ultrasound technology; drawing; early childhood education; education; education (K-12); elementary education; environmental studies; family and community services; fine/studio arts; food preparation; forensic science and technology; forestry; forestry technology; graphic design; hotel/motel administration; human resources management; illustration; information technology; journalism; kindergarten/preschool education; landscape architecture; liberal arts and sciences and humanities related; liberal arts and sciences/liberal studies; medical radiologic technology; natural resources management; occupational therapy; painting; parks, recreation and leisure facilities management; photography; physical therapy; physician assistant; pre-medical studies; pre-nursing studies; pre-pharmacy studies; pre-veterinary studies; printmaking; public relations, advertising, and applied communication related; radio and television; radiologic technology/science; radio, television, and digital communication related; restaurant, culinary, and catering management; restaurant/food services management; sculpture; sport and fitness administration; system administration; therapeutic recreation; water, wetlands, and marine resources management; wildlife and wildlands science and management; wildlife biology.

Academic Programs *Special study options:* academic remediation for entering students, adult/continuing education programs, advanced placement credit, cooperative education, distance learning, English as a second language, external degree program, independent study, internships, part-time degree program, services for LD students, student-designed majors, summer session for credit. *ROTC:* Army (c), Air Force (c).

Library Miller Library with 65,000 titles, 309 serial subscriptions, 10,000 audiovisual materials, an OPAC, a Web page.

Computers on Campus 120 computers available on campus for general student use. A campuswide network can be accessed from student residence rooms and from off campus that provide access to wireless campus. Internet access, online (class) registration, at least one staffed computer lab available. Computer purchase or lease plan available.

Student Life *Housing options:* coed, women-only, disabled students. Campus housing is university owned. Freshman campus housing is guaranteed. *Activities and organizations:* drama/theater group, student-run newspaper, radio station, choral group, Campus Activity Board, Student Senate, Art Society, Inter-Hall Council, Commuter Council. *Campus security:* 24-hour emergency response devices and patrols, student patrols, late-night transport/escort service, controlled dormitory access. *Student services:* health clinic, personal/psychological counseling, women's center.

Athletics Member NCAA. *Intercollegiate sports:* baseball M, basketball M/W, cross-country running M/W, golf M, soccer M/W, softball W, tennis M/W, track and field M/W, volleyball W. *Intramural sports:* basketball M/W, cheerleading M(c)/W(c), equestrian sports M(c)/W(c), football M/W, lacrosse M/W, skiing (downhill) M(c)/W(c), soccer M/W, softball M/W, table tennis M/W, tennis M/W, volleyball M/W, weight lifting M/W.

Standardized Tests *Required for some:* SAT I or ACT (for admission). *Recommended:* SAT I or ACT (for admission).

Costs (2004–05) *Comprehensive fee:* $21,980 includes full-time tuition ($13,450), mandatory fees ($970), and room and board ($7560). Part-time tuition: $315 per credit. *Required fees:* $110 per term part-time. *College room only:* $3880. Room and board charges vary according to board plan and housing facility. *Payment plan:* installment. *Waivers:* senior citizens and employees or children of employees.

Financial Aid Of all full-time matriculated undergraduates who enrolled in 2001, 125 Federal Work-Study jobs (averaging $1000). 100 state and other part-time jobs (averaging $1000).

Applying *Options:* common application, electronic application, early admission, deferred entrance. *Application fee:* $25. *Required:* high school transcript. *Required for some:* interview, art portfolio. *Recommended:* essay or personal statement, minimum 2.0 GPA, 1 letter of recommendation, interview. *Application deadline:* rolling (freshmen), rolling (transfers).

Admissions Contact Ms. Sarah Keating, Director of Admissions, Keystone College, One College Green, La Plume, PA 18440-1099. *Phone:* 570-945-5141 Ext. 2403. *Toll-free phone:* 877-4COLLEGE Ext. 1. *Fax:* 570-945-7916. *E-mail:* admissions@keystone.edu.

■ *See page 1820 for a narrative description.*

KING'S COLLEGE

Wilkes-Barre, Pennsylvania

- **Independent Roman Catholic** comprehensive, founded 1946
- **Calendar** semesters
- **Degrees** certificates, associate, bachelor's, master's, and postbachelor's certificates
- **Suburban** 48-acre campus
- **Endowment** $38.4 million
- **Coed,** 2,064 undergraduate students, 86% full-time, 49% women, 51% men
- **Moderately difficult** entrance level, 81% of applicants were admitted

King's College is a Catholic liberal arts college founded more than 50 years ago by the Holy Cross Fathers and Brothers of the University of Notre Dame. There are 37 undergraduate majors in the arts and sciences and in the William G. McGowan School of Business. Graduate courses are offered in education, finance, health-care administration, and a 5-year physician assistant program. There is an innovative program of career development across the curriculum. Within 6 months of graduation, 99% of King's graduates are employed or attend graduate school. More than 85% of King's students receive financial aid.

Undergraduates 1,771 full-time, 293 part-time. Students come from 20 states and territories, 6 other countries, 24% are from out of state, 2% African American, 0.9% Asian American or Pacific Islander, 1% Hispanic American, 0.3% Native American, 0.4% international, 4% transferred in, 35% live on campus. *Retention:* 83% of 2002 full-time freshmen returned.

Freshmen *Admission:* 1,623 applied, 1,308 admitted, 450 enrolled. *Average high school GPA:* 3.30. *Test scores:* SAT verbal scores over 500: 63%; SAT math scores over 500: 65%; SAT verbal scores over 600: 17%; SAT math scores over 600: 22%; SAT verbal scores over 700: 2%; SAT math scores over 700: 2%.

Faculty *Total:* 183, 62% full-time. *Student/faculty ratio:* 14:1.

Majors Accounting; athletic training; biological and physical sciences; biology/biological sciences; business administration and management; chemistry; clinical laboratory science/medical technology; communication/speech communication and rhetoric; computer and information sciences; computer science; criminal justice/safety; dramatic/theatre arts; early childhood education; economics; elementary education; English; environmental science; environmental studies; finance; French; gerontology; health professions related; history; human resources management; international business/trade/commerce; marketing/marketing management; mathematics; neuroscience; philosophy; political science and government; pre-dentistry studies; pre-law studies; pre-medical studies; pre-pharmacy studies; pre-veterinary studies; psychology; secondary education; sociology; Spanish; special education; theology.

Academic Programs *Special study options:* accelerated degree program, adult/continuing education programs, advanced placement credit, distance learning, double majors, English as a second language, honors programs, independent study, internships, off-campus study, part-time degree program, services for LD students, student-designed majors, study abroad, summer session for credit. *ROTC:* Army (b), Air Force (b).

Library D. Leonard Corgan Library with 166,395 titles, 791 serial subscriptions, 2,478 audiovisual materials, an OPAC, a Web page.

Computers on Campus 273 computers available on campus for general student use. A campuswide network can be accessed from student residence rooms and from off campus. Internet access, at least one staffed computer lab available. Computer purchase or lease plan available.

Student Life *Housing:* on-campus residence required through sophomore year. *Options:* men-only, women-only. Campus housing is university owned. Freshman campus housing is guaranteed. *Activities and organizations:* drama/theater group, student-run newspaper, radio station, choral group, Association of Campus Events, Student Government Association, Accounting Association, international/multicultural club, biology club. *Campus security:* 24-hour emergency response devices and patrols, student patrols, late-night transport/escort service, bicycle patrols. *Student services:* health clinic, personal/psychological counseling, women's center.

Athletics Member NCAA. All Division III. *Intercollegiate sports:* baseball M, basketball M/W, cheerleading M/W, cross-country running M/W, field hockey W, football M, golf M, lacrosse M/W, soccer M/W, softball W, swimming M/W, tennis M/W, volleyball W, wrestling M. *Intramural sports:* basketball M/W, ice hockey M(c), racquetball M/W, soccer M/W, softball M/W, track and field M(c)/W(c), volleyball M.

Standardized Tests *Required:* SAT I or ACT (for admission).

Costs (2003–04) *Comprehensive fee:* $26,990 includes full-time tuition ($18,260), mandatory fees ($800), and room and board ($7930). Part-time tuition: $448 per credit hour. *College room only:* $3750. Room and board charges vary according to board plan and housing facility. *Payment plans:* installment, deferred payment. *Waivers:* senior citizens and employees or children of employees.

Financial Aid Of all full-time matriculated undergraduates who enrolled in 2003, 1,572 applied for aid, 1,386 were judged to have need, 288 had their need fully met. 360 Federal Work-Study jobs (averaging $888). 193 state and other part-time jobs (averaging $900). In 2003, 233 non-need-based awards were made. *Average percent of need met:* 76%. *Average financial aid package:* $14,394. *Average need-based loan:* $4182. *Average need-based gift aid:* $6395. *Average non-need-based aid:* $8085. *Average indebtedness upon graduation:* $20,267.

Applying *Options:* common application, electronic application, early admission, deferred entrance. *Application fee:* $30. *Required:* essay or personal statement, high school transcript. *Recommended:* 2 letters of recommendation, interview. *Application deadline:* rolling (freshmen), rolling (transfers). *Notification:* continuous (freshmen), continuous (transfers).

Admissions Contact Ms. Michelle Lawrence-Schmude, Director of Admissions, King's College, 133 North River Street, Wilkes-Barre, PA 18711-0801. *Phone:* 570-208-5858. *Toll-free phone:* 888-KINGSPA. *Fax:* 570-208-5971. *E-mail:* admissions@kings.edu.

■ *See page 1824 for a narrative description.*

KUTZTOWN UNIVERSITY OF PENNSYLVANIA
Kutztown, Pennsylvania

- **State-supported** comprehensive, founded 1866, part of Pennsylvania State System of Higher Education
- **Calendar** semesters
- **Degrees** bachelor's, master's, and postbachelor's certificates
- **Rural** 326-acre campus with easy access to Philadelphia
- **Endowment** $9.1 million
- **Coed,** 8,058 undergraduate students, 90% full-time, 60% women, 40% men
- **Moderately difficult** entrance level, 70% of applicants were admitted

Kutztown University has completed the following projects recently to enhance the quality of student life. The University dining hall has a new, modern addition. A new addition doubles the size of Rohrbach Library and provides more modern, functional, and comfortable areas and more than 500 personal computer links. All residence hall rooms are wired for Internet usage, and new multistation computer labs have been opened in buildings across the campus. A state-of-the-art science facility and a 500-bed, apartment-style residence hall also opened in fall 2003.

Undergraduates 7,242 full-time, 816 part-time. Students come from 21 states and territories, 36 other countries, 8% are from out of state, 6% African American, 0.9% Asian American or Pacific Islander, 3% Hispanic American, 0.1% Native American, 0.8% international, 8% transferred in, 35% live on campus. *Retention:* 78% of 2002 full-time freshmen returned.

Freshmen *Admission:* 7,240 applied, 5,055 admitted, 1,908 enrolled. *Average high school GPA:* 3.02. *Test scores:* SAT verbal scores over 500: 54%; SAT math scores over 500: 46%; SAT verbal scores over 600: 16%; SAT math scores over 600: 7%; SAT verbal scores over 700: 7%.

Faculty *Total:* 416, 73% full-time, 69% with terminal degrees. *Student/faculty ratio:* 20:1.

Majors Accounting; anthropology; art; art teacher education; biological and physical sciences; biology/biological sciences; business administration and management; business/managerial economics; chemistry; clinical laboratory science/medical technology; college student counseling and personnel services; commercial and advertising art; counseling psychology; counselor education/school counseling and guidance; crafts, folk art and artisanry; criminal justice/safety; digital communication and media/multimedia; dramatic/theatre arts; economics; education; educational/instructional media design; elementary education; English; environmental science; environmental studies; finance; fine/studio arts; French; general studies; geography; geology/earth science; German; history; human resources management; information technology; international business/trade/commerce; kindergarten/preschool education; liberal arts and sciences/liberal studies; library science; marketing/marketing management; mathematics; music; nursing (registered nurse training); nursing science; oceanography (chemical and physical); philosophy; physical sciences; physics; political science and government; psychology; public administration; Russian; secondary education; social sciences; social work; sociology; Spanish; special education; special education (speech or language impaired); special education (vision impaired); speech and rhetoric; telecommunications; visual and performing arts; visual and performing arts related.

Academic Programs *Special study options:* academic remediation for entering students, accelerated degree program, adult/continuing education programs, advanced placement credit, distance learning, double majors, external degree program, honors programs, independent study, internships, off-campus study, part-time degree program, services for LD students, student-designed majors, study abroad, summer session for credit. *ROTC:* Army (c), Air Force (c). *Unusual degree programs:* 3-2 engineering with Pennsylvania State Universitym—University Park Campus.

Library Rohrbach Library with 497,752 titles, 5,573 serial subscriptions, 15,981 audiovisual materials, an OPAC, a Web page.

Computers on Campus 650 computers available on campus for general student use. A campuswide network can be accessed from student residence rooms and from off campus. Internet access, online (class) registration, at least one staffed computer lab available.

Student Life *Housing options:* coed, women-only, cooperative. Campus housing is university owned and leased by the school. Freshman campus housing is guaranteed. *Activities and organizations:* drama/theater group, student-run newspaper, radio and television station, choral group, marching band, Student Government Board, Student Pennsylvania State Education Association, National Art Education Association, Greek organizations, Residence Hall Association, national fraternities, national sororities. *Campus security:* 24-hour emergency response devices and patrols, student patrols, late-night transport/escort service, secondary door electronic alarm system in residence halls, 24-hour student desk personnel at main entrance of residence halls. *Student services:* health clinic, personal/psychological counseling, women's center.

Athletics Member NCAA. All Division II. *Intercollegiate sports:* baseball M(s), basketball M(s)/W(s), cheerleading W(s), cross-country running M(s)/W(s), equestrian sports M(c)/W(c), field hockey W(s), football M(s), golf W(s), ice hockey M(c), lacrosse M(c)/W(c), riflery M(c)/W(c), rugby M(c)/W(c), skiing (downhill) M(c)/W(c), soccer M(s)/W(s), softball W(s), swimming M(s)/W(s), tennis M(s)/W(s), track and field M(s)/W(s), volleyball M(c)/W(s), wrestling M(s). *Intramural sports:* badminton M/W, basketball M/W, equestrian sports M/W, football M/W, golf M/W, ice hockey M, lacrosse M/W, riflery M/W, rugby

Kutztown University of Pennsylvania (continued)
M/W, skiing (cross-country) M/W, skiing (downhill) M/W, soccer M/W, softball M/W, tennis M/W, ultimate Frisbee M/W, volleyball M/W, weight lifting M/W.
Standardized Tests *Required:* SAT I or ACT (for admission). *Required for some:* SAT II: Subject Tests (for admission).
Costs (2003–04) *Tuition:* state resident $4598 full-time, $192 per credit part-time; nonresident $11,496 full-time, $479 per credit part-time. Part-time tuition and fees vary according to course load. *Required fees:* $1178 full-time, $52 per credit part-time. *Room and board:* $4812; room only: $3410. Room and board charges vary according to board plan. *Payment plans:* tuition prepayment, installment, deferred payment. *Waivers:* senior citizens and employees or children of employees.
Financial Aid Of all full-time matriculated undergraduates who enrolled in 2002, 5,697 applied for aid, 3,978 were judged to have need, 2,615 had their need fully met. 423 Federal Work-Study jobs (averaging $910). In 2002, 228 non-need-based awards were made. *Average percent of need met:* 68%. *Average financial aid package:* $6128. *Average need-based loan:* $3310. *Average need-based gift aid:* $3608. *Average non-need-based aid:* $1794. *Average indebtedness upon graduation:* $14,570.
Applying *Options:* electronic application, early admission, deferred entrance. *Application fee:* $35. *Required:* high school transcript, minimum 2.0 GPA. *Required for some:* audition required for music program; portfolio and/or art test required for art education, communication design, crafts, and fine arts programs. *Application deadline:* 3/1 (freshmen), rolling (transfers). *Notification:* 4/15 (freshmen), continuous (transfers).
Admissions Contact Mr. Lynold K. McGhee, Assistant provost for Research and Planning, Kutztown University of Pennsylvania, 15200 Kutztown Road, Kutztown, PA 19530-0730. *Phone:* 610-683-4060 Ext. 4053. *Toll-free phone:* 877-628-1915. *Fax:* 610-683-1375. *E-mail:* admission@kutztown.edu.

■ *See page 1828 for a narrative description.*

LAFAYETTE COLLEGE
Easton, Pennsylvania

- **Independent** 4-year, founded 1826, affiliated with Presbyterian Church (U.S.A.)
- **Calendar** semesters plus interim January program
- **Degree** bachelor's
- **Suburban** 340-acre campus with easy access to New York City and Philadelphia
- **Endowment** $565.0 million
- **Coed,** 2,285 undergraduate students, 97% full-time, 47% women, 53% men
- **Most difficult** entrance level, 36% of applicants were admitted

Undergraduates 2,214 full-time, 71 part-time. Students come from 35 states and territories, 40 other countries, 71% are from out of state, 5% African American, 2% Asian American or Pacific Islander, 3% Hispanic American, 0.3% Native American, 5% international, 0.7% transferred in, 98% live on campus. *Retention:* 94% of 2002 full-time freshmen returned.
Freshmen *Admission:* 5,835 applied, 2,122 admitted, 584 enrolled. *Average high school GPA:* 3.90. *Test scores:* SAT verbal scores over 500: 97%; SAT math scores over 500: 99%; ACT scores over 18: 100%; SAT verbal scores over 600: 64%; SAT math scores over 600: 79%; ACT scores over 24: 90%; SAT verbal scores over 700: 15%; SAT math scores over 700: 25%; ACT scores over 30: 18%.
Faculty *Total:* 224, 84% full-time, 96% with terminal degrees. *Student/faculty ratio:* 11:1.
Majors American studies; anthropology; art; art history, criticism and conservation; biochemistry; biology/biological sciences; business/managerial economics; chemical engineering; chemistry; civil engineering; computer science; economics; electrical, electronics and communications engineering; engineering; English; environmental/environmental health engineering; fine/studio arts; French; geology/earth science; German; history; international relations and affairs; mathematics; mechanical engineering; music; music history, literature, and theory; philosophy; physics; political science and government; psychology; religious studies; Russian studies; sociology; Spanish.
Academic Programs *Special study options:* academic remediation for entering students, accelerated degree program, adult/continuing education programs, advanced placement credit, honors programs, internships, off-campus study, part-time degree program, services for LD students, student-designed majors, study abroad, summer session for credit. *ROTC:* Army (c).
Library Skillman Library plus 1 other with 521,000 titles, 2,750 serial subscriptions, an OPAC, a Web page.
Computers on Campus 480 computers available on campus for general student use. A campuswide network can be accessed from student residence rooms and from off campus. Internet access, online (class) registration, at least one staffed computer lab available.
Student Life *Housing:* on-campus residence required through senior year. *Options:* coed. Campus housing is university owned. Freshman campus housing is guaranteed. *Activities and organizations:* drama/theater group, student-run newspaper, radio station, choral group, Association of Biscer Collegians, International Student Association, Activities Forum, national fraternities, national sororities. *Campus security:* 24-hour emergency response devices and patrols, student patrols, late-night transport/escort service, controlled dormitory access. *Student services:* health clinic, personal/psychological counseling, women's center.
Athletics Member NCAA. All Division I except football (Division I-AA). *Intercollegiate sports:* baseball M, basketball M/W, crew M(c)/W(c), cross-country running M/W, equestrian sports M(c)/W(c), fencing M/W, field hockey W, golf M, ice hockey M(c), lacrosse M/W, rugby M(c)/W(c), skiing (downhill) M(c)/W(c), soccer M/W, softball W, squash M(c), swimming M/W, tennis M/W, track and field M/W, volleyball W, weight lifting M(c)/W(c), wrestling M(c). *Intramural sports:* badminton M/W, baseball M, basketball M/W, bowling M/W, cross-country running M/W, fencing M/W, field hockey W, football M, golf M/W, lacrosse M/W, racquetball M/W, sailing M(c)/W(c), skiing (cross-country) M(c)/W(c), soccer M/W, softball M/W, squash M/W, swimming M/W, table tennis M/W, tennis M/W, track and field M/W, volleyball M/W, weight lifting M/W, wrestling M.
Standardized Tests *Required:* SAT I (for admission), SAT II: Subject Tests (for admission). *Recommended:* SAT II: Writing Test (for admission).
Costs (2004–05) *Comprehensive fee:* $35,746 includes full-time tuition ($27,178), mandatory fees ($150), and room and board ($8418). *College room only:* $4740.
Financial Aid Of all full-time matriculated undergraduates who enrolled in 2003, 1,375 applied for aid, 1,219 were judged to have need, 1,189 had their need fully met. 142 Federal Work-Study jobs (averaging $987). 129 state and other part-time jobs (averaging $2058). In 2003, 160 non-need-based awards were made. *Average percent of need met:* 99%. *Average financial aid package:* $22,407. *Average need-based loan:* $4437. *Average need-based gift aid:* $20,044. *Average non-need-based aid:* $12,445. *Average indebtedness upon graduation:* $17,204. *Financial aid deadline:* 3/15.
Applying *Options:* common application, electronic application, early admission, early decision, deferred entrance. *Application fee:* $60. *Required:* essay or personal statement, high school transcript, 1 letter of recommendation. *Recommended:* interview. *Application deadlines:* 1/1 (freshmen), 6/1 (transfers). *Early decision:* 12/1. *Notification:* continuous until 4/1 (freshmen), 3/15 (early decision), continuous (transfers).
Admissions Contact Ms. Carol Rowlands, Director of Admissions, Lafayette College, Easton, PA 18042-1798. *Phone:* 610-330-5100. *Fax:* 610-330-5355. *E-mail:* admissions@lafayette.edu.

■ *See page 1832 for a narrative description.*

LANCASTER BIBLE COLLEGE
Lancaster, Pennsylvania

- **Independent nondenominational** comprehensive, founded 1933
- **Calendar** semesters
- **Degrees** certificates, associate, bachelor's, master's, and postbachelor's certificates
- **Suburban** 100-acre campus with easy access to Philadelphia
- **Endowment** $3.4 million
- **Coed,** 748 undergraduate students, 76% full-time, 55% women, 45% men
- **Minimally difficult** entrance level, 51% of applicants were admitted

LBC is a nondenominational Bible college offering BS or AS degrees. Programs prepare students for Christian careers in church planting, Christian education, computer ministries, counseling, Bible education, Bible music, early childhood, elementary education, guidance counseling, health/PE, missions, pastoral studies, secretarial studies, social services, vocational technology, women's ministry, and youth ministry. Two 1-year certificate programs and graduate study are available.

Undergraduates 566 full-time, 182 part-time. Students come from 23 states and territories, 5 other countries, 25% are from out of state, 3% African American, 0.5% Asian American or Pacific Islander, 1% Hispanic American, 0.6% Native American, 0.8% international, 9% transferred in, 49% live on campus. *Retention:* 78% of 2002 full-time freshmen returned.
Freshmen *Admission:* 244 applied, 124 admitted, 124 enrolled. *Average high school GPA:* 3.22. *Test scores:* SAT verbal scores over 500: 67%; SAT math scores over 500: 62%; ACT scores over 18: 71%; SAT verbal scores over 600: 21%; SAT math scores over 600: 12%; ACT scores over 24: 19%; SAT verbal scores over 700: 1%.
Faculty *Total:* 66, 44% full-time, 41% with terminal degrees. *Student/faculty ratio:* 15:1.

Majors Administrative assistant and secretarial science; biblical studies; computer and information sciences; counselor education/school counseling and guidance; early childhood education; education; education related; elementary education; missionary studies and missiology; music teacher education; pastoral counseling and specialized ministries related; pastoral studies/counseling; physical education teaching and coaching; religious education; religious/sacred music; social work; youth ministry.

Academic Programs *Special study options:* academic remediation for entering students, adult/continuing education programs, advanced placement credit, double majors, independent study, internships, part-time degree program, services for LD students, study abroad, summer session for credit.

Library Lancaster Bible College Library with 122,993 titles, 5,539 serial subscriptions, 4,385 audiovisual materials, an OPAC.

Computers on Campus 44 computers available on campus for general student use. A campuswide network can be accessed from student residence rooms. Internet access, at least one staffed computer lab available.

Student Life *Housing:* on-campus residence required through senior year. *Options:* men-only, women-only. Campus housing is university owned. Freshman campus housing is guaranteed. *Activities and organizations:* drama/theater group, student-run newspaper, choral group, Student Government Association, Student Missionary Fellowship, International Student Fellowship, Resident Affairs Council, Student Intramural Association. *Campus security:* student patrols, late-night transport/escort service, controlled dormitory access. *Student services:* health clinic, personal/psychological counseling.

Athletics Member NCCAA. *Intercollegiate sports:* baseball M, basketball M/W, lacrosse W, soccer M/W, volleyball M/W. *Intramural sports:* basketball M/W, cheerleading M/W, football M/W, soccer M/W, softball M/W, table tennis M/W, tennis M/W, volleyball M/W.

Standardized Tests *Required:* SAT I or ACT (for admission).

Costs (2003–04) *Comprehensive fee:* $16,950 includes full-time tuition ($11,250), mandatory fees ($450), and room and board ($5250). Full-time tuition and fees vary according to course load and program. Part-time tuition: $375 per credit. Part-time tuition and fees vary according to program. *Required fees:* $15 per credit part-time. *College room only:* $2450. Room and board charges vary according to board plan. *Payment plan:* installment. *Waivers:* children of alumni, adult students, senior citizens, and employees or children of employees.

Financial Aid Of all full-time matriculated undergraduates who enrolled in 2003, 464 applied for aid, 421 were judged to have need, 43 had their need fully met. 76 Federal Work-Study jobs (averaging $1500). In 2003, 23 non-need-based awards were made. *Average percent of need met:* 66%. *Average financial aid package:* $9386. *Average need-based loan:* $3735. *Average need-based gift aid:* $6898. *Average non-need-based aid:* $3821. *Average indebtedness upon graduation:* $13,864.

Applying *Options:* early admission, deferred entrance. *Application fee:* $25. *Required:* essay or personal statement, high school transcript, minimum 2.0 GPA, 3 letters of recommendation. *Required for some:* interview. *Application deadline:* rolling (freshmen), rolling (transfers). *Notification:* continuous (freshmen), continuous (transfers).

Admissions Contact Mrs. Joanne M. Roper, Associate Vice President for Admissions, Lancaster Bible College, 901 Eden Road, Lancaster, PA 17601-5036. *Phone:* 717-560-8271. *Toll-free phone:* 866-LBC4YOU. *Fax:* 717-560-8213. *E-mail:* admissions@lbc.edu.

La Roche College
Pittsburgh, Pennsylvania

- **Independent** comprehensive, founded 1963, affiliated with Roman Catholic Church
- **Calendar** semesters plus summer term
- **Degrees** certificates, associate, bachelor's, and master's
- **Suburban** 80-acre campus
- **Endowment** $3.7 million
- **Coed,** 1,551 undergraduate students, 76% full-time, 63% women, 37% men
- **Minimally difficult** entrance level, 69% of applicants were admitted

Undergraduates 1,179 full-time, 372 part-time. Students come from 16 states and territories, 27 other countries, 8% are from out of state, 3% African American, 0.3% Asian American or Pacific Islander, 0.7% Hispanic American, 0.3% Native American, 16% international, 10% transferred in, 38% live on campus. *Retention:* 76% of 2002 full-time freshmen returned.

Freshmen *Admission:* 528 applied, 365 admitted, 175 enrolled. *Average high school GPA:* 2.86. *Test scores:* SAT verbal scores over 500: 38%; SAT math scores over 500: 49%; ACT scores over 18: 54%; SAT verbal scores over 600: 11%; SAT math scores over 600: 11%; ACT scores over 24: 16%; SAT math scores over 700: 1%.

Faculty *Total:* 204, 34% full-time, 38% with terminal degrees. *Student/faculty ratio:* 13:1.

Majors Accounting; applied mathematics; biology/biological sciences; biology teacher education; business administration and management; chemistry; chemistry teacher education; communication/speech communication and rhetoric; computer and information sciences; criminal justice/safety; dance; elementary education; English; English/language arts teacher education; finance; general studies; graphic design; history; human services; interior design; international business/trade/commerce; international relations and affairs; kindergarten/preschool education; liberal arts and sciences/liberal studies; marketing related; mathematics teacher education; medical radiologic technology; nursing science; psychology; religious education; religious studies; respiratory care therapy; sociology; Spanish language teacher education; technical and business writing.

Academic Programs *Special study options:* academic remediation for entering students, accelerated degree program, adult/continuing education programs, advanced placement credit, double majors, English as a second language, freshman honors college, honors programs, independent study, internships, part-time degree program, services for LD students, study abroad, summer session for credit. *ROTC:* Army (c), Air Force (c). *Unusual degree programs:* 3-2 engineering with University of Pittsburgh.

Library John J. Wright Library with 90,241 titles, 601 serial subscriptions, 988 audiovisual materials, an OPAC.

Computers on Campus 200 computers available on campus for general student use. A campuswide network can be accessed from student residence rooms and from off campus. Internet access, online (class) registration, at least one staffed computer lab available.

Student Life *Housing options:* coed. Campus housing is university owned and is provided by a third party. Freshman campus housing is guaranteed. *Activities and organizations:* drama/theater group, student-run newspaper, radio station, choral group, American Society of Interior Design, student government, Visions (environmental club), Helping Hands, Project Achievement. *Campus security:* 24-hour emergency response devices and patrols, student patrols, late-night transport/escort service, controlled dormitory access. *Student services:* health clinic, personal/psychological counseling.

Athletics Member NCAA. All Division III. *Intercollegiate sports:* baseball M, basketball M/W, cross-country running M/W, golf M, soccer M/W, softball W, volleyball W. *Intramural sports:* basketball M/W, football M/W, golf M/W, racquetball M/W, soccer M/W, table tennis M/W, volleyball M/W, weight lifting M/W.

Standardized Tests *Required:* SAT I or ACT (for admission).

Costs (2004–05) *Comprehensive fee:* $23,444 includes full-time tuition ($15,982), mandatory fees ($600), and room and board ($6862). Full-time tuition and fees vary according to program. Part-time tuition: $488 per credit. Part-time tuition and fees vary according to program. *Required fees:* $14 per credit part-time, $50 per term part-time. *College room only:* $4250. *Payment plan:* installment. *Waivers:* senior citizens and employees or children of employees.

Financial Aid Of all full-time matriculated undergraduates who enrolled in 2003, 780 applied for aid, 709 were judged to have need, 210 had their need fully met. In 2003, 79 non-need-based awards were made. *Average percent of need met:* 84%. *Average financial aid package:* $12,661. *Average need-based loan:* $4592. *Average need-based gift aid:* $3689. *Average non-need-based aid:* $4500. *Average indebtedness upon graduation:* $18,000. *Financial aid deadline:* 5/1.

Applying *Options:* electronic application, early admission, deferred entrance. *Application fee:* $50. *Required:* high school transcript, minimum 2.0 GPA, letters of recommendation. *Recommended:* essay or personal statement, minimum 3.0 GPA, interview. *Application deadline:* 8/23 (freshmen), rolling (transfers).

Admissions Contact Mr. Thomas Hassett, Director of Admissions, La Roche College, 9000 Babcock Boulevard. *Phone:* 412-536-1275. *Toll-free phone:* 800-838-4LRC. *Fax:* 412-536-1048. *E-mail:* admissions@laroche.edu.

■ *See page 1846 for a narrative description.*

La Salle University
Philadelphia, Pennsylvania

- **Independent Roman Catholic** comprehensive, founded 1863
- **Calendar** semesters
- **Degrees** associate, bachelor's, master's, doctoral, post-master's, and postbachelor's certificates
- **Urban** 100-acre campus
- **Endowment** $43.9 million
- **Coed,** 4,099 undergraduate students, 83% full-time, 58% women, 42% men
- **Moderately difficult** entrance level, 68% of applicants were admitted

Undergraduates 3,385 full-time, 714 part-time. Students come from 35 states and territories, 29 other countries, 37% are from out of state, 13% African American, 3% Asian American or Pacific Islander, 6% Hispanic American, 0.2% Native American, 0.9% international, 7% transferred in, 63% live on campus. *Retention:* 82% of 2002 full-time freshmen returned.

La Salle University (continued)

Freshmen *Admission:* 4,701 applied, 3,177 admitted, 866 enrolled. *Test scores:* SAT verbal scores over 500: 76%; SAT math scores over 500: 73%; SAT verbal scores over 600: 29%; SAT math scores over 600: 25%; SAT verbal scores over 700: 5%; SAT math scores over 700: 3%.

Faculty *Total:* 197. *Student/faculty ratio:* 16:1.

Majors Accounting; Air Force R.O.T.C./air science; applied mathematics; Army R.O.T.C./military science; art history, criticism and conservation; audiology and speech-language pathology; biochemistry; biology/biological sciences; broadcast journalism; business administration and management; business/managerial economics; business teacher education; chemistry; classics and languages, literatures and linguistics; computer and information sciences; computer programming; computer science; criminal justice/safety; economics; education; elementary education; English; environmental studies; film/cinema studies; finance; French; geology/earth science; German; history; human resources management; information science/studies; Italian; journalism; liberal arts and sciences/liberal studies; management information systems; marketing/marketing management; mass communication/media; mathematics; modern languages; nursing (registered nurse training); nutrition sciences; philosophy; political science and government; pre-dentistry studies; pre-medical studies; pre-veterinary studies; psychology; public administration; public relations/image management; radio and television; religious education; religious studies; Russian; Russian studies; science teacher education; secondary education; social sciences; social work; sociology; Spanish; special education.

Academic Programs *Special study options:* accelerated degree program, adult/continuing education programs, advanced placement credit, cooperative education, double majors, freshman honors college, honors programs, independent study, internships, off-campus study, part-time degree program, services for LD students, student-designed majors, study abroad, summer session for credit. *ROTC:* Army (c), Air Force (c). *Unusual degree programs:* 3-2 nursing with speech pathology; occupational therapy with Thomas Jefferson University.

Library Connelly Library with 365,000 titles, 1,700 serial subscriptions, 5,200 audiovisual materials, an OPAC, a Web page.

Computers on Campus 350 computers available on campus for general student use. A campuswide network can be accessed from student residence rooms and from off campus. Internet access, online (class) registration, at least one staffed computer lab available.

Student Life *Housing options:* coed. Campus housing is university owned and leased by the school. Freshman campus housing is guaranteed. *Activities and organizations:* drama/theater group, student-run newspaper, radio and television station, choral group, Student Government Association, Community Service Organization, La Salle Entertainment Organization, The Explorer (yearbook), The Masque (theater group), national fraternities, national sororities. *Campus security:* 24-hour emergency response devices and patrols, student patrols, late-night transport/escort service, controlled dormitory access. *Student services:* health clinic, personal/psychological counseling, women's center.

Athletics Member NCAA. All Division I except football (Division I-AA). *Intercollegiate sports:* baseball M(s), basketball M(s)/W(s), cheerleading W(c), crew M(s)/W(s), cross-country running M(s)/W(s), field hockey W(s), golf M(s)/W(s), lacrosse W(s), soccer M(s)/W(s), softball W(s), swimming M(s)/W(s), tennis M(s)/W(s), track and field M(s)/W(s), volleyball W(s). *Intramural sports:* baseball M, basketball M/W, crew M/W, field hockey W, football M/W, golf M/W, ice hockey M(c), lacrosse M(c), rock climbing M(c)/W(c), rugby M(c)/W(c), soccer M/W, softball W, swimming M/W, tennis M/W, track and field M/W, ultimate Frisbee M/W, volleyball M/W.

Standardized Tests *Required:* SAT I or ACT (for admission).

Costs (2003–04) *Comprehensive fee:* $31,730 includes full-time tuition ($22,760), mandatory fees ($200), and room and board ($8770). Full-time tuition and fees vary according to program. Part-time tuition: $740 per credit hour. Part-time tuition and fees vary according to class time and course load. *Required fees:* $100 per term part-time. *College room only:* $4420. Room and board charges vary according to board plan, housing facility, and location. *Payment plans:* installment, deferred payment. *Waivers:* employees or children of employees.

Financial Aid Of all full-time matriculated undergraduates who enrolled in 2002, 2,828 applied for aid, 2,513 were judged to have need, 546 had their need fully met. In 2002, 551 non-need-based awards were made. *Average percent of need met:* 79%. *Average financial aid package:* $15,519. *Average need-based loan:* $4251. *Average need-based gift aid:* $12,086. *Average non-need-based aid:* $9528.

Applying *Options:* common application, electronic application, early admission, early action, deferred entrance. *Application fee:* $35. *Required:* essay or personal statement, high school transcript, 1 letter of recommendation. *Recommended:* interview. *Application deadline:* 8/15 (transfers). *Notification:* continuous (freshmen), 12/15 (early action), continuous (transfers).

Admissions Contact Mr. Robert G. Voss, Dean of Admission and Financial Aid, La Salle University, 1900 West Olney Avenue, Philadelphia, PA 19141-1199. *Phone:* 215-951-1500. *Toll-free phone:* 800-328-1910. *Fax:* 215-951-1656. *E-mail:* admiss@lasalle.edu.

LEBANON VALLEY COLLEGE
Annville, Pennsylvania

- **Independent United Methodist** comprehensive, founded 1866
- **Calendar** semesters
- **Degrees** certificates, associate, bachelor's, master's, doctoral, and postbachelor's certificates (offers master of business administration degree on a part-time basis only)
- **Small-town** 275-acre campus
- **Endowment** $31.9 million
- **Coed,** 1,765 undergraduate students, 87% full-time, 58% women, 42% men
- **Moderately difficult** entrance level, 73% of applicants were admitted

Undergraduates 1,530 full-time, 235 part-time. Students come from 21 states and territories, 8 other countries, 20% are from out of state, 2% African American, 1% Asian American or Pacific Islander, 1% Hispanic American, 0.1% Native American, 0.5% international, 3% transferred in, 72% live on campus. *Retention:* 83% of 2002 full-time freshmen returned.

Freshmen *Admission:* 2,083 applied, 1,520 admitted, 429 enrolled. *Test scores:* SAT verbal scores over 500: 75%; SAT math scores over 500: 79%; SAT verbal scores over 600: 27%; SAT math scores over 600: 36%; SAT verbal scores over 700: 2%; SAT math scores over 700: 4%.

Faculty *Total:* 181, 55% full-time, 56% with terminal degrees. *Student/faculty ratio:* 13:1.

Majors Accounting; actuarial science; American studies; art history, criticism and conservation; biochemistry; biology/biological sciences; biology teacher education; business administration and management; chemistry; chemistry teacher education; clinical/medical laboratory science and allied professions related; computer science; digital communication and media/multimedia; economics; elementary education; English; English/language arts teacher education; fine/studio arts; French; French language teacher education; general studies; German; German language teacher education; health/health care administration; health professions related; health services/allied health/health sciences; history; liberal arts and sciences/liberal studies; mathematics; mathematics teacher education; multi-/interdisciplinary studies related; music management and merchandising; music performance; music related; music teacher education; philosophy; physics; physics teacher education; physiological psychology/psychobiology; political science and government; pre-law studies; pre-medical studies; pre-veterinary studies; psychology; recording arts technology; religious studies; science teacher education; secondary education; social studies teacher education; sociology; Spanish; Spanish language teacher education.

Academic Programs *Special study options:* academic remediation for entering students, adult/continuing education programs, advanced placement credit, double majors, independent study, internships, off-campus study, part-time degree program, student-designed majors, study abroad, summer session for credit. *ROTC:* Army (b). *Unusual degree programs:* 3-2 engineering with University of Pennsylvania, Case Western Reserve University, Widener University, The Pennsylvania State University; forestry with Duke University.

Library Bishop Library with 168,709 titles, 11,071 serial subscriptions, 7,205 audiovisual materials, an OPAC, a Web page.

Computers on Campus 175 computers available on campus for general student use. A campuswide network can be accessed from student residence rooms and from off campus. Internet access, online (class) registration, at least one staffed computer lab available.

Student Life *Housing:* on-campus residence required through senior year. *Options:* coed, men-only, women-only. Campus housing is university owned. Freshman campus housing is guaranteed. *Activities and organizations:* drama/theater group, student-run newspaper, radio station, choral group, marching band, LVC PSEA, Council of Christian Organization, Tae Kwon Do Club, Phi Beta Lambda, Wig and Buckle (theatrical group), national fraternities, national sororities. *Campus security:* 24-hour emergency response devices and patrols, late-night transport/escort service, controlled dormitory access, dormitory entrances locked at midnight. *Student services:* health clinic, personal/psychological counseling.

Athletics Member NCAA. All Division III. *Intercollegiate sports:* baseball M, basketball M/W, cross-country running M/W, field hockey W, football M, golf M, ice hockey M, soccer M/W, softball W, swimming M/W, tennis M/W, track and field M/W, volleyball W. *Intramural sports:* basketball M/W, football M/W, racquetball M/W, rugby M(c)/W(c), softball M/W, volleyball M(c).

Standardized Tests *Required:* SAT I or ACT (for admission). *Recommended:* SAT I (for admission).

Costs (2003–04) *Comprehensive fee:* $28,870 includes full-time tuition ($21,860), mandatory fees ($650), and room and board ($6360). Part-time tuition: $410 per credit. Part-time tuition and fees vary according to class time and degree level. *College room only:* $3110. Room and board charges vary according to board plan and housing facility. *Payment plans:* tuition prepayment, installment. *Waivers:* senior citizens and employees or children of employees.

Financial Aid Of all full-time matriculated undergraduates who enrolled in 2003, 1,326 applied for aid, 1,214 were judged to have need, 335 had their need fully met. 788 Federal Work-Study jobs (averaging $1315). In 2003, 238 non-need-based awards were made. *Average percent of need met:* 86%. *Average financial aid package:* $17,055. *Average need-based loan:* $4111. *Average need-based gift aid:* $14,062. *Average non-need-based aid:* $9062. *Average indebtedness upon graduation:* $22,027.

Applying *Options:* electronic application. *Application fee:* $30. *Required:* high school transcript. *Required for some:* essay or personal statement, audition for music majors. *Recommended:* 2 letters of recommendation, interview. *Application deadline:* rolling (freshmen). *Notification:* continuous (freshmen), continuous (transfers).

Admissions Contact William J. Brown Jr., Dean of Admission and Financial Aid, Lebanon Valley College, 101 North College Avenue, Annville, PA 17003-1400. *Phone:* 717-867-6181. *Toll-free phone:* 866-LVC-4ADM. *Fax:* 717-867-6026. *E-mail:* admission@lvc.edu.

■ *See page 1854 for a narrative description.*

LEHIGH UNIVERSITY
Bethlehem, Pennsylvania

- **Independent** university, founded 1865
- **Calendar** semesters
- **Degrees** bachelor's, master's, doctoral, and post-master's certificates
- **Suburban** 1600-acre campus with easy access to Philadelphia
- **Endowment** $705.2 million
- **Coed,** 4,679 undergraduate students, 99% full-time, 40% women, 60% men
- **Most difficult** entrance level, 40% of applicants were admitted

Located on the East coast, close to New York City and Philadelphia in Bethlehem, Pennsylvania, Lehigh is among the nation's most selective, highly ranked private research universities. Lehigh offers the broad academic programs of a large research university and the personal attention of a small college. With more than 70 majors in the liberal arts, business, education, engineering, and the sciences, students can customize their college experience through numerous academic programs and cross-disciplinary studies. Students have easy access to world-class faculty members who offer their time and attention on hands-on projects, internships, and innovative studies. With a culture that encourages diversity and involvement, it's no wonder that Lehigh is widely known as a place where students emerge as leaders in careers and life.

Undergraduates 4,625 full-time, 54 part-time. Students come from 52 states and territories, 68% are from out of state, 3% African American, 6% Asian American or Pacific Islander, 2% Hispanic American, 0.2% Native American, 3% international, 69% live on campus. *Retention:* 93% of 2002 full-time freshmen returned.

Freshmen *Admission:* 9,087 applied, 3,678 admitted, 1,125 enrolled. *Average high school GPA:* 3.75. *Test scores:* SAT verbal scores over 500: 97%; SAT math scores over 500: 99%; SAT verbal scores over 600: 71%; SAT math scores over 600: 87%; SAT verbal scores over 700: 12%; SAT math scores over 700: 35%.

Faculty *Total:* 547, 79% full-time. *Student/faculty ratio:* 10:1.

Majors Accounting; American studies; ancient/classical Greek; anthropology; architecture; astrophysics; bilingual and multilingual education; biochemistry; biological and biomedical sciences related; biological and physical sciences; biology/biological sciences; biomedical/medical engineering; business administration and management; business/commerce; business/managerial economics; chemical engineering; chemistry; chemistry related; civil engineering; classics and languages, literatures and linguistics; communication and journalism related; computer and information sciences and support services related; computer engineering; computer science; design and applied arts related; ecology; education; electrical, electronics and communications engineering; engineering mechanics; engineering physics; engineering related; environmental studies; finance; fine arts related; French; geological and earth sciences/geosciences related; German; health/medical preparatory programs related; history; humanities; industrial engineering; information science/studies; international relations and affairs; Japanese; journalism; Latin; management information systems; marketing/marketing management; materials engineering; mathematics; mechanical engineering; molecular biology; multi-/interdisciplinary studies related; music; philosophy; physical and theoretical chemistry; physics; political science and government; pre-medical studies; psychology; religious studies; Russian; Russian studies; science technologies related; social sciences; social sciences related; sociology; Spanish; statistics; urban studies/affairs; visual and performing arts.

Academic Programs *Special study options:* accelerated degree program, adult/continuing education programs, advanced placement credit, cooperative education, distance learning, double majors, English as a second language, external degree program, honors programs, independent study, internships, off-campus study, services for LD students, study abroad, summer session for credit. *ROTC:* Army (b). *Unusual degree programs:* 3-2 education.

Library E. W. Fairchild-Martindale Library plus 1 other with 1.2 million titles, 6,271 serial subscriptions, 8,415 audiovisual materials, an OPAC, a Web page.

Computers on Campus 572 computers available on campus for general student use. A campuswide network can be accessed from student residence rooms and from off campus. Internet access, online (class) registration, at least one staffed computer lab available.

Student Life *Housing options:* coed, disabled students. Campus housing is university owned. Freshman campus housing is guaranteed. *Activities and organizations:* drama/theater group, student-run newspaper, radio station, choral group, marching band, Student Senate, University Productions, Graduate Student Council, Residence Hall Association, Global Union, national fraternities, national sororities. *Campus security:* 24-hour emergency response devices and patrols, student patrols, late-night transport/escort service, controlled dormitory access. *Student services:* health clinic, personal/psychological counseling, women's center.

Athletics Member NCAA. All Division I except football (Division I-AA). *Intercollegiate sports:* baseball M(s), basketball M(s)/W, bowling M(c)/W(c), crew M(c), cross-country running M(s)/W(s), equestrian sports M(c)/W(c), field hockey W(s), football M(s)/W(c), golf M(s)/W, ice hockey M(c), lacrosse M(s)/W(s), rugby M(c), skiing (downhill) M(c)/W(c), soccer M(s)/W(s), softball W(s), squash M(c), swimming M(s)/W(s), tennis M(s)/W(s), track and field M(s)/W(s), volleyball M(c)/W(s), wrestling M(s). *Intramural sports:* badminton M/W, basketball M/W, bowling M(c)/W(c), cross-country running M/W, fencing M(c)/W(c), field hockey W(c), football M, golf M/W, gymnastics M(c)/W(c), ice hockey M(c), lacrosse M(c)/W(c), racquetball M/W, rugby W(c), skiing (cross-country) M/W, skiing (downhill) M/W, soccer M/W, softball M/W, squash M/W, swimming M/W, table tennis M/W, tennis M(c)/W(c), track and field M/W, ultimate Frisbee M/W, volleyball M/W, water polo M(c)/W(c), weight lifting M, wrestling M.

Standardized Tests *Required:* SAT I or ACT (for admission). *Recommended:* SAT II: Subject Tests (for admission).

Costs (2004–05) *Comprehensive fee:* $37,570 includes full-time tuition ($29,140), mandatory fees ($200), and room and board ($8230). Part-time tuition: $1215 per credit. *College room only:* $4700. Room and board charges vary according to board plan and student level. *Payment plan:* tuition prepayment. *Waivers:* senior citizens and employees or children of employees.

Financial Aid Of all full-time matriculated undergraduates who enrolled in 2003, 2,584 applied for aid, 2,132 were judged to have need, 1,209 had their need fully met. 1,416 Federal Work-Study jobs (averaging $1623). 247 state and other part-time jobs (averaging $2827). In 2003, 362 non-need-based awards were made. *Average percent of need met:* 99%. *Average financial aid package:* $23,533. *Average need-based loan:* $4476. *Average need-based gift aid:* $17,403. *Average non-need-based aid:* $12,536. *Average indebtedness upon graduation:* $16,774. *Financial aid deadline:* 2/1.

Applying *Options:* common application, electronic application, early admission, early decision, deferred entrance. *Application fee:* $60. *Required:* high school transcript, 1 letter of recommendation, graded writing sample. *Recommended:* essay or personal statement, interview. *Application deadlines:* 1/1 (freshmen), 4/1 (transfers). *Early decision:* 11/15 (for plan 1), 2/1 (for plan 2). *Notification:* 4/1 (freshmen), 12/15 (early decision plan 1), 2/15 (early decision plan 2), 4/15 (transfers).

Admissions Contact Mr. J. Bruce Gardiner, Interim Dean of Admissions and Financial Aid, Lehigh University, 27 Memorial Drive West, Bethlehem, PA 18015. *Phone:* 610-758-3100. *Fax:* 610-758-4361. *E-mail:* admissions@lehigh.edu.

■ *See page 1856 for a narrative description.*

LINCOLN UNIVERSITY
Lincoln University, Pennsylvania

- **State-related** comprehensive, founded 1854
- **Calendar** semesters
- **Degrees** bachelor's and master's
- **Rural** 422-acre campus with easy access to Philadelphia
- **Endowment** $15.6 million
- **Coed,** 1,530 undergraduate students, 96% full-time, 60% women, 40% men
- **Moderately difficult** entrance level, 40% of applicants were admitted

Undergraduates 1,472 full-time, 58 part-time. Students come from 25 states and territories, 33 other countries, 48% are from out of state, 91% African

Lincoln University (continued)

American, 0.2% Hispanic American, 0.1% Native American, 8% international, 2% transferred in, 97% live on campus. *Retention:* 61% of 2002 full-time freshmen returned.

Freshmen *Admission:* 3,973 applied, 1,586 admitted, 462 enrolled. *Average high school GPA:* 2.92. *Test scores:* SAT verbal scores over 500: 22%; SAT math scores over 500: 18%; SAT verbal scores over 600: 3%; SAT math scores over 600: 4%; SAT verbal scores over 700: 1%; SAT math scores over 700: 1%.

Faculty *Total:* 172, 56% full-time, 45% with terminal degrees. *Student/faculty ratio:* 18:1.

Majors Accounting; actuarial science; African-American/Black studies; African languages; anthropology; art teacher education; biology/biological sciences; business administration and management; chemistry; Chinese; communication/speech communication and rhetoric; computer and information sciences; criminal justice/safety; economics; education; elementary education; English; English/language arts teacher education; finance; foreign language teacher education; French; health and physical education; health and physical education related; history; human services; industrial and organizational psychology; international relations and affairs; Japanese; journalism; kindergarten/preschool education; mathematics; mathematics teacher education; music; music teacher education; philosophy; physical sciences; physics; physiological psychology/psychobiology; political science and government; psychology; public administration; religious studies; Russian; secondary education; social studies teacher education; sociology; Spanish; special education; therapeutic recreation.

Academic Programs *Special study options:* academic remediation for entering students, accelerated degree program, adult/continuing education programs, advanced placement credit, cooperative education, double majors, honors programs, independent study, internships, off-campus study, part-time degree program, student-designed majors, study abroad, summer session for credit. *ROTC:* Army (c), Air Force (c). *Unusual degree programs:* 3-2 engineering with Drexel University, Pennsylvania State University—University Park Campus, Lafayette College, New Jersey Institute of Technology, University of Delaware, Howard University, Rensselaer Polytechnic Institute.

Library Langston Hughes Memorial Library with 185,521 titles, 605 serial subscriptions, 2,643 audiovisual materials, an OPAC.

Computers on Campus 210 computers available on campus for general student use. A campuswide network can be accessed from student residence rooms and from off campus. Internet access, at least one staffed computer lab available. Computer purchase or lease plan available.

Student Life *Housing options:* coed, men-only, women-only. Campus housing is university owned. Freshman applicants given priority for college housing. *Activities and organizations:* drama/theater group, student-run newspaper, radio and television station, choral group, The Gospel Ensemble, Ziana Fashion Club, We R One, Panhellenic Council, Council of Independent Organizations, national fraternities, national sororities. *Campus security:* 24-hour emergency response devices and patrols, late-night transport/escort service. *Student services:* health clinic, personal/psychological counseling, women's center.

Athletics Member NCAA. All Division III. *Intercollegiate sports:* baseball M, basketball M/W, bowling M/W, cross-country running M/W, soccer M/W, tennis M/W, track and field M/W, volleyball W. *Intramural sports:* baseball M, basketball M/W, bowling M/W, cheerleading W, cross-country running M/W, football M, softball M/W, swimming M/W, tennis M/W, track and field M/W, volleyball M/W.

Standardized Tests *Required:* SAT I or ACT (for admission).

Costs (2003–04) *Tuition:* state resident $4840 full-time, $262 per credit hour part-time; nonresident $8238 full-time, $423 per credit hour part-time. Part-time tuition and fees vary according to course load. *Required fees:* $2112 full-time. *Room and board:* $6368; room only: $3462. Room and board charges vary according to board plan. *Payment plans:* installment, deferred payment. *Waivers:* employees or children of employees.

Financial Aid Of all full-time matriculated undergraduates who enrolled in 2003, 1,392 applied for aid, 1,322 were judged to have need, 1,057 had their need fully met. 490 Federal Work-Study jobs (averaging $500). In 2003, 146 non-need-based awards were made. *Average percent of need met:* 85%. *Average financial aid package:* $13,000. *Average need-based loan:* $5500. *Average need-based gift aid:* $5500. *Average non-need-based aid:* $5500. *Average indebtedness upon graduation:* $25,000.

Applying *Options:* electronic application, early admission, deferred entrance. *Application fee:* $20. *Required:* essay or personal statement, high school transcript, minimum 2.0 GPA, 2 letters of recommendation. *Recommended:* interview. *Application deadline:* rolling (freshmen), rolling (transfers). *Notification:* 2/15 (freshmen), continuous (transfers).

Admissions Contact Dr. Robert Laney Jr., Director of Admissions, Lincoln University, PO Box 179, MSC 147, Lincoln University, PA 19352-0999. *Phone:* 610-932-8300 Ext. 3206. *Toll-free phone:* 800-790-0191. *Fax:* 610-932-1209. *E-mail:* admiss@lu.lincoln.edu.

LOCK HAVEN UNIVERSITY OF PENNSYLVANIA
Lock Haven, Pennsylvania

- **State-supported** comprehensive, founded 1870, part of Pennsylvania State System of Higher Education
- **Calendar** semesters
- **Degrees** associate, bachelor's, and master's
- **Rural** 165-acre campus
- **Endowment** $5.9 million
- **Coed,** 4,696 undergraduate students, 91% full-time, 59% women, 41% men
- **Moderately difficult** entrance level, 81% of applicants were admitted

Lock Haven University (LHU) offers students a strong liberal arts education, including more than 75 degree and certification programs. University housing includes 7 residence halls and 1 University apartment complex, with a new complex opening in fall 2004. LHU provides a high-quality education that prepares students for a successful future.

Undergraduates 4,267 full-time, 429 part-time. Students come from 24 states and territories, 35 other countries, 8% are from out of state, 3% African American, 0.8% Asian American or Pacific Islander, 1% Hispanic American, 0.4% Native American, 1% international, 3% transferred in, 55% live on campus. *Retention:* 74% of 2002 full-time freshmen returned.

Freshmen *Admission:* 3,932 applied, 3,199 admitted, 1,184 enrolled. *Test scores:* SAT verbal scores over 500: 40%; SAT math scores over 500: 55%; ACT scores over 18: 73%; SAT verbal scores over 600: 6%; SAT math scores over 600: 12%; ACT scores over 24: 15%; ACT scores over 30: 1%.

Faculty *Total:* 244, 91% full-time. *Student/faculty ratio:* 19:1.

Majors Accounting; anthropology; art; athletic training; biological and physical sciences; biology/biological sciences; business administration and management; business/managerial economics; chemistry; computer and information sciences; computer science; criminal justice/law enforcement administration; curriculum and instruction; dramatic/theatre arts; economics; education; elementary education; engineering; English; French; geography; geology/earth science; German; health professions related; health science; history; humanities; international relations and affairs; journalism; kindergarten/preschool education; Latin American studies; legal assistant/paralegal; liberal arts and sciences/liberal studies; management information systems; mathematics; music; natural sciences; nursing (registered nurse training); parks, recreation and leisure; philosophy; physical education teaching and coaching; physical sciences; physics; political science and government; pre-dentistry studies; pre-medical studies; pre-veterinary studies; psychology; secondary education; social sciences; social work; sociology; Spanish; special education; special education related; speech and rhetoric.

Academic Programs *Special study options:* academic remediation for entering students, accelerated degree program, adult/continuing education programs, advanced placement credit, cooperative education, distance learning, double majors, honors programs, independent study, internships, off-campus study, part-time degree program, services for LD students, student-designed majors, study abroad, summer session for credit. *ROTC:* Army (b). *Unusual degree programs:* 3-2 engineering with Pennsylvania State University—University Park Campus; nursing with Clarion University of Pennsylvania.

Library Stevenson Library with 370,967 titles, 1,117 serial subscriptions, 8,158 audiovisual materials, an OPAC, a Web page.

Computers on Campus 270 computers available on campus for general student use. A campuswide network can be accessed from student residence rooms and from off campus. Internet access, online (class) registration, at least one staffed computer lab available.

Student Life *Housing:* on-campus residence required through sophomore year. *Options:* coed, women-only. Campus housing is university owned and is provided by a third party. Freshman applicants given priority for college housing. *Activities and organizations:* drama/theater group, student-run newspaper, radio and television station, choral group, marching band, student government, Residence Hall Association, fraternities, sororities, national fraternities, national sororities. *Campus security:* 24-hour emergency response devices and patrols. *Student services:* health clinic, personal/psychological counseling.

Athletics Member NCAA. All Division II except wrestling (Division I). *Intercollegiate sports:* baseball M(s), basketball M(s)/W(s), cross-country running M(s)/W(s), field hockey W(s), football M(s), lacrosse W(s), soccer M(s)/W(s), softball W(s), swimming W(s), track and field M(s)/W(s), volleyball W(s), wrestling M(s). *Intramural sports:* badminton M/W, basketball M/W, cross-country running M/W, fencing M/W, field hockey W, football M, golf M/W, ice hockey M, lacrosse M/W, racquetball M/W, rugby M/W, skiing (cross-country) M/W, skiing (downhill) M/W, soccer M/W, softball M/W, swimming M/W, tennis M/W, track and field M/W, ultimate Frisbee M/W, volleyball M/W, water polo M, weight lifting M/W, wrestling M.

Standardized Tests *Required:* SAT I or ACT (for admission).

Costs (2003–04) *Tuition:* state resident $4598 full-time, $192 per credit part-time; nonresident $9496 full-time, $396 per credit part-time. Full-time tuition and fees vary according to course load and location. Part-time tuition and fees vary according to course load and location. *Required fees:* $1276 full-time, $55 per credit part-time. *Room and board:* $5224; room only: $2944. Room and board charges vary according to board plan and housing facility. *Payment plans:* installment, deferred payment. *Waivers:* minority students, senior citizens, and employees or children of employees.

Financial Aid Of all full-time matriculated undergraduates who enrolled in 2001, 3,439 applied for aid, 2,670 were judged to have need, 1,298 had their need fully met. 253 Federal Work-Study jobs (averaging $1174). 951 state and other part-time jobs (averaging $711). In 2001, 308 non-need-based awards were made. *Average percent of need met:* 78%. *Average financial aid package:* $6900. *Average need-based loan:* $3767. *Average need-based gift aid:* $4500. *Average non-need-based aid:* $2300. *Average indebtedness upon graduation:* $16,472.

Applying *Options:* electronic application, deferred entrance. *Application fee:* $25. *Required for some:* essay or personal statement, high school transcript, letters of recommendation. *Recommended:* minimum 3.0 GPA. *Application deadline:* rolling (freshmen), rolling (transfers). *Notification:* continuous (freshmen), continuous (transfers).

Admissions Contact Mr. Steven Lee, Director of Admissions, Lock Haven University of Pennsylvania, Office of Admission, Akeley Hall, Lock Haven, PA 17745. *Phone:* 570-893-2027. *Toll-free phone:* 800-332-8900 (in-state); 800-233-8978 (out-of-state). *Fax:* 570-893-2201. *E-mail:* admissions@lhup.edu.

■ *See page 1878 for a narrative description.*

LYCOMING COLLEGE
Williamsport, Pennsylvania

- **Independent United Methodist** 4-year, founded 1812
- **Calendar** semesters
- **Degree** bachelor's
- **Small-town** 35-acre campus
- **Endowment** $72.4 million
- **Coed,** 1,417 undergraduate students, 97% full-time, 55% women, 45% men
- **Moderately difficult** entrance level, 80% of applicants were admitted

Undergraduates 1,379 full-time, 38 part-time. Students come from 22 states and territories, 11 other countries, 23% are from out of state, 2% African American, 0.8% Asian American or Pacific Islander, 0.6% Hispanic American, 0.3% Native American, 1% international, 3% transferred in, 83% live on campus. *Retention:* 81% of 2002 full-time freshmen returned.

Freshmen *Admission:* 1,449 applied, 1,156 admitted, 366 enrolled. *Average high school GPA:* 3.20. *Test scores:* SAT verbal scores over 500: 74%; SAT math scores over 500: 72%; SAT verbal scores over 600: 26%; SAT math scores over 600: 27%; SAT verbal scores over 700: 2%; SAT math scores over 700: 1%.

Faculty *Total:* 103, 85% full-time, 82% with terminal degrees. *Student/faculty ratio:* 13:1.

Majors Accounting; actuarial science; American studies; anthropology; archeology; art; art history, criticism and conservation; art teacher education; astronomy; biology/biological sciences; business administration and management; chemistry; clinical laboratory science/medical technology; commercial and advertising art; computer science; creative writing; criminal justice/law enforcement administration; dramatic/theatre arts; economics; education; elementary education; English; finance; fine/studio arts; French; German; history; interdisciplinary studies; international business/trade/commerce; international relations and affairs; literature; marketing/marketing management; mass communication/media; mathematics; music; music teacher education; philosophy; physics; political science and government; pre-dentistry studies; pre-law studies; pre-medical studies; preveterinary studies; psychology; religious studies; secondary education; sociology; Spanish; special education related.

Academic Programs *Special study options:* accelerated degree program, advanced placement credit, double majors, honors programs, independent study, internships, off-campus study, part-time degree program, services for LD students, student-designed majors, study abroad, summer session for credit. *ROTC:* Army (c). *Unusual degree programs:* 3-2 engineering with The Pennsylvania State University—University Park Campus; forestry with Duke University; environmental management with Duke University.

Library Snowden Library plus 1 other with 170,000 titles, 950 serial subscriptions, an OPAC, a Web page.

Computers on Campus 140 computers available on campus for general student use. A campuswide network can be accessed from student residence rooms and from off campus. Internet access, online (class) registration, at least one staffed computer lab available. Computer purchase or lease plan available.

Student Life *Housing:* on-campus residence required through senior year. *Options:* coed, women-only. Campus housing is university owned. Freshman campus housing is guaranteed. *Activities and organizations:* drama/theater group, student-run newspaper, radio and television station, choral group, radio club (WRLC), wilderness club, student newspaper, campus ministry, Habitat for Humanity, national fraternities, national sororities. *Campus security:* 24-hour emergency response devices and patrols, student patrols, late-night transport/escort service, controlled dormitory access. *Student services:* health clinic, personal/psychological counseling.

Athletics Member NCAA. All Division III. *Intercollegiate sports:* basketball M/W, cheerleading M(s)/W(s), crew M(c)/W(c), cross-country running M/W, equestrian sports M(c)/W(c), field hockey W(c), football M, golf M, lacrosse M/W, skiing (cross-country) M(c)/W(c), skiing (downhill) M(c)/W(c), soccer M/W, softball W, swimming M/W, tennis M/W, volleyball W, water polo M(c)/W(c), wrestling M. *Intramural sports:* basketball M/W, football M/W, soccer M/W, softball M/W, ultimate Frisbee M(c)/W(c), volleyball M/W.

Standardized Tests *Required:* SAT I or ACT (for admission).

Costs (2003–04) *Comprehensive fee:* $27,589 includes full-time tuition ($21,088), mandatory fees ($635), and room and board ($5866). Part-time tuition: $659 per credit. *Payment plan:* installment. *Waivers:* employees or children of employees.

Financial Aid Of all full-time matriculated undergraduates who enrolled in 2003, 1,252 applied for aid, 1,145 were judged to have need, 273 had their need fully met. 494 Federal Work-Study jobs (averaging $1138). In 2003, 160 non-need-based awards were made. *Average percent of need met:* 80%. *Average financial aid package:* $16,840. *Average need-based loan:* $4083. *Average need-based gift aid:* $13,596. *Average non-need-based aid:* $8650. *Average indebtedness upon graduation:* $15,656.

Applying *Options:* common application, electronic application, early admission, deferred entrance. *Application fee:* $35. *Required:* essay or personal statement, high school transcript, 2 letters of recommendation. *Recommended:* minimum 2.3 GPA, interview. *Application deadlines:* 4/1 (freshmen), 6/1 (transfers). *Notification:* continuous (freshmen), continuous (transfers).

Admissions Contact Mr. James Spencer, Dean of Admissions and Financial Aid, Lycoming College, 700 College Place, Williamsport, PA 17701. *Phone:* 570-321-4026. *Toll-free phone:* 800-345-3920 Ext. 4026. *Fax:* 570-321-4317. *E-mail:* admissions@lycoming.edu.

MANSFIELD UNIVERSITY OF PENNSYLVANIA
Mansfield, Pennsylvania

- **State-supported** comprehensive, founded 1857, part of Pennsylvania State System of Higher Education
- **Calendar** semesters
- **Degrees** associate, bachelor's, master's, and postbachelor's certificates
- **Small-town** 205-acre campus
- **Endowment** $7.7 million
- **Coed,** 3,168 undergraduate students, 91% full-time, 61% women, 39% men
- **Moderately difficult** entrance level, 77% of applicants were admitted

Undergraduates 2,894 full-time, 274 part-time. Students come from 14 states and territories, 13 other countries, 23% are from out of state, 5% African American, 0.7% Asian American or Pacific Islander, 0.9% Hispanic American, 0.9% Native American, 2% international, 9% transferred in, 60% live on campus. *Retention:* 72% of 2002 full-time freshmen returned.

Freshmen *Admission:* 2,348 applied, 1,801 admitted, 710 enrolled. *Average high school GPA:* 3.20. *Test scores:* SAT verbal scores over 500: 44%; SAT math scores over 500: 41%; ACT scores over 18: 66%; SAT verbal scores over 600: 10%; SAT math scores over 600: 9%; ACT scores over 24: 11%; SAT verbal scores over 700: 1%; SAT math scores over 700: 1%.

Faculty *Total:* 198, 77% full-time, 56% with terminal degrees. *Student/faculty ratio:* 18:1.

Majors Accounting; anthropology; applied art; art; art teacher education; biochemistry; biological and physical sciences; biology/biological sciences; biology teacher education; broadcast journalism; business administration and management; cartography; cell biology and histology; chemistry; chemistry teacher education; city/urban, community and regional planning; clinical laboratory science/medical technology; clinical psychology; computer and information sciences; computer science; criminal justice/law enforcement administration; dietetics; economics; education; elementary education; English; English/language arts teacher education; environmental biology; environmental studies; fishing and fisheries sciences and management; food services technology; French; French language teacher education; geography; geology/earth science; German; German language teacher education; history; human resources management; human services; information science/studies; international business/trade/commerce; international relations and affairs; journalism; kindergarten/preschool education; liberal arts and sciences/liberal studies; marketing/marketing management; mass communication/media; mathematics; mathematics teacher education; music; music

Mansfield University of Pennsylvania (continued)
management and merchandising; music performance; music teacher education; music therapy; nursing (registered nurse training); philosophy; physical sciences; physics; physics teacher education; piano and organ; political science and government; pre-law studies; pre-medical studies; psychology; public relations/image management; radio and television; radiologic technology/science; respiratory care therapy; science teacher education; secondary education; social sciences; social science teacher education; social studies teacher education; social work; sociology; Spanish; Spanish language teacher education; special education; speech and rhetoric; tourism and travel services management; voice and opera.

Academic Programs *Special study options:* academic remediation for entering students, accelerated degree program, adult/continuing education programs, advanced placement credit, distance learning, double majors, freshman honors college, honors programs, independent study, internships, off-campus study, part-time degree program, services for LD students, student-designed majors, study abroad, summer session for credit.

Library North Hall Library with 242,441 titles, 1,148 serial subscriptions, 26,831 audiovisual materials, an OPAC, a Web page.

Computers on Campus 550 computers available on campus for general student use. A campuswide network can be accessed from student residence rooms and from off campus. Internet access, at least one staffed computer lab available. Computer purchase or lease plan available.

Student Life *Housing:* on-campus residence required through senior year. *Options:* coed, women-only. Campus housing is university owned. Freshman campus housing is guaranteed. *Activities and organizations:* drama/theater group, student-run newspaper, radio station, choral group, marching band, Mansfield International Student Organization, P.R. Society, PSEA, ski club, Activities Council, national fraternities, national sororities. *Campus security:* 24-hour emergency response devices and patrols, student patrols, late-night transport/escort service, controlled dormitory access. *Student services:* health clinic, personal/psychological counseling, women's center.

Athletics Member NCAA. All Division II. *Intercollegiate sports:* baseball M(s), basketball M(s)/W(s), cross-country running M(s)/W(s), field hockey W(s), football M(s), soccer W(s), softball W(s), swimming W, track and field M(s)/W(s). *Intramural sports:* badminton M/W, basketball M/W, bowling M/W, cheerleading W, cross-country running M/W, equestrian sports M/W, football M/W, golf M/W, racquetball M/W, skiing (cross-country) M/W, skiing (downhill) M/W, soccer M/W, softball M/W, swimming M/W, tennis M/W, track and field M/W, volleyball M/W, water polo M/W, weight lifting M/W.

Standardized Tests *Required:* SAT I or ACT (for admission).

Costs (2003–04) *Tuition:* state resident $4598 full-time, $192 per credit part-time; nonresident $11,496 full-time, $479 per credit part-time. Part-time tuition and fees vary according to course load. *Required fees:* $1374 full-time, $50 per credit part-time, $350 per term part-time. *Room and board:* $5248. Room and board charges vary according to board plan. *Payment plans:* installment, deferred payment. *Waivers:* senior citizens and employees or children of employees.

Applying *Options:* electronic application, early admission, deferred entrance. *Application fee:* $25. *Required:* high school transcript. *Required for some:* interview. *Recommended:* essay or personal statement, minimum 2.5 GPA, letters of recommendation. *Application deadline:* rolling (freshmen), rolling (transfers). *Notification:* continuous (freshmen), continuous (transfers).

Admissions Contact Mr. Brian D. Barden, Director of Admissions, Mansfield University of Pennsylvania, Alumni Hall, Mansfield, PA 16933. *Phone:* 570-662-4813. *Toll-free phone:* 800-577-6826. *Fax:* 570-662-4121. *E-mail:* admissions@mansfield.edu.

MARYWOOD UNIVERSITY
Scranton, Pennsylvania

- **Independent Roman Catholic** comprehensive, founded 1915
- **Calendar** semesters
- **Degrees** certificates, associate, bachelor's, master's, doctoral, post-master's, and postbachelor's certificates
- **Suburban** 115-acre campus
- **Endowment** $22.2 million
- **Coed,** 1,751 undergraduate students, 87% full-time, 72% women, 28% men
- **Moderately difficult** entrance level, 79% of applicants were admitted

Building on its tradition of preparing students from around the world to be successful in professional life and to contribute to the welfare of others, Marywood offers over sixty undergraduate programs and nearly thirty graduate programs in the arts and sciences. Using its attractive 115-acre campus in northeastern Pennsylvania creatively, Marywood continues to expand its facilities with a new Studio Arts Center and Center for Healthy Families. Marywood is committed to a remarkable scholarship/grant program.

Undergraduates 1,530 full-time, 221 part-time. Students come from 22 states and territories, 12 other countries, 21% are from out of state, 1% African American, 1% Asian American or Pacific Islander, 2% Hispanic American, 0.2% Native American, 1% international, 8% transferred in, 34% live on campus. *Retention:* 81% of 2002 full-time freshmen returned.

Freshmen *Admission:* 1,275 applied, 1,011 admitted, 286 enrolled. *Average high school GPA:* 3.30. *Test scores:* SAT verbal scores over 500: 60%; SAT math scores over 500: 48%; ACT scores over 18: 86%; SAT verbal scores over 600: 13%; SAT math scores over 600: 11%; ACT scores over 24: 23%; SAT verbal scores over 700: 1%; SAT math scores over 700: 1%; ACT scores over 30: 5%.

Faculty *Total:* 311, 42% full-time, 35% with terminal degrees. *Student/faculty ratio:* 12:1.

Majors Accounting; advertising; applied art; arts management; art teacher education; art therapy; athletic training; audiology and speech-language pathology; aviation/airway management; biological specializations related; biology/biological sciences; biology/biotechnology laboratory technician; biology teacher education; broadcast journalism; business administration and management; clinical laboratory science/medical technology; community organization and advocacy; computer and information sciences; counseling psychology; criminal justice/law enforcement administration; criminal justice/safety; criminology; design and visual communications; developmental and child psychology; dietetics; directing and theatrical production; dramatic/theatre arts; ecology, evolution, systematics and population biology related; education related; education (specific subject areas) related; elementary education; English; English/language arts teacher education; environmental science; family and consumer sciences/home economics teacher education; family and consumer sciences/human sciences; financial planning and services; fine/studio arts; foods and nutrition related; French; French language teacher education; graphic design; health/health care administration; health professions related; health services administration; health services/allied health/health sciences; history; history teacher education; hospital and health care facilities administration; hotel/motel administration; human services; industrial and organizational psychology; interdisciplinary studies; international business/trade/commerce; legal assistant/paralegal; marketing/marketing management; mathematics; mathematics teacher education; mental health counseling; multi-/interdisciplinary studies related; music; music performance; music teacher education; music therapy; nursing (registered nurse training); parks, recreation and leisure; photography; physician assistant; pre-law studies; pre-nursing studies; psychology; public administration; public relations/image management; religious education; religious/sacred music; religious studies; science teacher education; secondary education; social sciences; social sciences related; social work; Spanish; Spanish language teacher education; special education; visual and performing arts; visual and performing arts related.

Academic Programs *Special study options:* academic remediation for entering students, accelerated degree program, adult/continuing education programs, advanced placement credit, distance learning, double majors, English as a second language, external degree program, honors programs, independent study, internships, off-campus study, part-time degree program, services for LD students, student-designed majors, study abroad, summer session for credit. *ROTC:* Army (c), Air Force (c). *Unusual degree programs:* 3-2 M.S. Physician Assistant; Master of Fine Arts.

Library Learning Resources Center plus 1 other with 220,205 titles, 913 serial subscriptions, 44,013 audiovisual materials, an OPAC, a Web page.

Computers on Campus 367 computers available on campus for general student use. A campuswide network can be accessed from student residence rooms and from off campus. Internet access, online (class) registration, at least one staffed computer lab available.

Student Life *Housing:* on-campus residence required through sophomore year. *Options:* coed, men-only, women-only, disabled students. Campus housing is university owned. Freshman campus housing is guaranteed. *Activities and organizations:* drama/theater group, student-run newspaper, radio and television station, choral group, outdoor adventure club, Psi Chi, international club, Peer Mediators, Speech and Hearing. *Campus security:* 24-hour emergency response devices and patrols, late-night transport/escort service, controlled dormitory access, apartments with deadbolts, self-defense education, lighted pathways, seminars on safety. *Student services:* health clinic, personal/psychological counseling.

Athletics Member NCAA. All Division III. *Intercollegiate sports:* baseball M, basketball M/W, cross-country running M/W, field hockey W, soccer M/W, softball W, tennis M/W, volleyball W. *Intramural sports:* badminton M/W, baseball M, basketball M/W, field hockey W, football M, golf M/W, lacrosse M(c)/W, racquetball M/W, soccer M(c)/W(c), softball M/W, swimming M/W, table tennis M/W, tennis M/W, volleyball M/W.

Standardized Tests *Required:* SAT I or ACT (for admission). *Recommended:* SAT I (for admission).

Costs (2003–04) *Comprehensive fee:* $27,609 includes full-time tuition ($18,560), mandatory fees ($915), and room and board ($8134). Part-time tuition: $580 per credit. Part-time tuition and fees vary according to course load. *Required fees:* $185 per term part-time. *College room only:* $4200. Room and board charges vary according to board plan and housing facility. *Payment plans:* installment, deferred payment. *Waivers:* senior citizens and employees or children of employees.

Financial Aid Of all full-time matriculated undergraduates who enrolled in 2003, 1,361 applied for aid, 1,274 were judged to have need, 231 had their need fully met. 643 Federal Work-Study jobs (averaging $1724). In 2003, 228 non-need-based awards were made. *Average percent of need met:* 75%. *Average financial aid package:* $14,499. *Average need-based loan:* $4185. *Average need-based gift aid:* $10,319. *Average non-need-based aid:* $6929. *Average indebtedness upon graduation:* $17,125.

Applying *Options:* common application, electronic application, early admission, deferred entrance. *Application fee:* $30. *Required:* high school transcript, 1 letter of recommendation. *Required for some:* essay or personal statement, interview. *Recommended:* essay or personal statement, interview. *Application deadline:* rolling (freshmen), rolling (transfers). *Notification:* continuous (freshmen), continuous (transfers).

Admissions Contact Mr. Robert W. Reese, Director of Admissions, Marywood University, 2300 Adams Avenue, Scranton, PA 18509-1598. *Phone:* 570-348-6234. *Toll-free phone:* 800-346-5014. *Fax:* 570-961-4763. *E-mail:* ugadm@ac.marywood.edu.

■ See page 1952 for a narrative description.

MERCYHURST COLLEGE
Erie, Pennsylvania

- **Independent Roman Catholic** comprehensive, founded 1926
- **Calendar** 4-3-3
- **Degrees** certificates, associate, bachelor's, master's, and postbachelor's certificates
- **Suburban** 88-acre campus with easy access to Buffalo
- **Endowment** $15.2 million
- **Coed,** 3,610 undergraduate students, 87% full-time, 62% women, 38% men
- **Moderately difficult** entrance level, 77% of applicants were admitted

Undergraduates 3,146 full-time, 464 part-time. Students come from 40 states and territories, 14 other countries, 45% are from out of state, 3% African American, 0.5% Asian American or Pacific Islander, 1% Hispanic American, 0.3% Native American, 3% international, 2% transferred in, 70% live on campus. *Retention:* 80% of 2002 full-time freshmen returned.

Freshmen *Admission:* 2,523 applied, 1,934 admitted, 1,020 enrolled. *Average high school GPA:* 3.41. *Test scores:* SAT verbal scores over 500: 73%; SAT math scores over 500: 72%; ACT scores over 18: 93%; SAT verbal scores over 600: 21%; SAT math scores over 600: 20%; ACT scores over 24: 34%; SAT verbal scores over 700: 2%; SAT math scores over 700: 1%; ACT scores over 30: 3%.

Faculty *Total:* 247, 60% full-time, 40% with terminal degrees. *Student/faculty ratio:* 17:1.

Majors Accounting; administrative assistant and secretarial science; advertising; anthropology; archeology; art; arts management; art teacher education; art therapy; athletic training; biochemistry; biology/biological sciences; biology teacher education; broadcast journalism; business administration and management; business, management, and marketing related; business teacher education; chemistry; chemistry teacher education; clinical laboratory science/medical technology; clothing/textiles; computer and information sciences; computer science; corrections; corrections and criminal justice related; creative writing; criminal justice/law enforcement administration; criminal justice/police science; criminal justice/safety; culinary arts; dance; dietetics; early childhood education; education; elementary education; English; English/language arts teacher education; family and consumer sciences/home economics teacher education; family and consumer sciences/human sciences; fashion merchandising; fiber, textile and weaving arts; finance; fine/studio arts; foreign languages and literatures; foreign language teacher education; forensic science and technology; French; geology/earth science; German; gerontology; health information/medical records technology; health/medical preparatory programs related; history; history related; hospitality administration; hotel/motel administration; human development and family studies; human ecology; humanities; human resources management; information science/studies; insurance; interior design; journalism; liberal arts and sciences/liberal studies; marketing/marketing management; mass communication/media; mathematics; mathematics teacher education; medical administrative assistant and medical secretary; medical transcription; multi-/interdisciplinary studies related; music; music performance; music teacher education; nursing (registered nurse training); office management; paleontology; petroleum technology; philosophy; physical therapist assistant; physical therapy; physics; political science and government; pre-dentistry studies; pre-law studies; pre-medical studies; pre-veterinary studies; psychology; public relations/image management; purchasing, procurement/acquisitions and contracts management; radio and television; religious education; religious studies; science teacher education; sculpture; secondary education; social sciences; social science teacher education; social work; sociology; Spanish; special education; sport and fitness administration; statistics; voice and opera; wind/percussion instruments.

Academic Programs *Special study options:* academic remediation for entering students, accelerated degree program, adult/continuing education programs, advanced placement credit, cooperative education, double majors, external degree program, freshman honors college, honors programs, independent study, internships, off-campus study, part-time degree program, services for LD students, student-designed majors, study abroad, summer session for credit. *ROTC:* Army (c). *Unusual degree programs:* 3-2 Law with Duquesene University.

Library Hammermill Library plus 1 other with 169,828 titles, 724 serial subscriptions, 9,557 audiovisual materials, an OPAC, a Web page.

Computers on Campus 350 computers available on campus for general student use. A campuswide network can be accessed from student residence rooms and from off campus. Internet access, at least one staffed computer lab available.

Student Life *Housing:* on-campus residence required through sophomore year. *Options:* men-only, women-only. Campus housing is university owned and leased by the school. Freshman campus housing is guaranteed. *Activities and organizations:* drama/theater group, student-run newspaper, radio and television station, choral group, student government, chorus, Admission Ambassadors, Amnesty International, The Merciad. *Campus security:* 24-hour emergency response devices and patrols, campus-wide camera system. *Student services:* health clinic, personal/psychological counseling.

Athletics Member NCAA. All Division II except men's and women's ice hockey (Division I), lacrosse (Division I). *Intercollegiate sports:* baseball M(s), basketball M(s)/W(s), crew M(s)/W(s), cross-country running M(s)/W(s), field hockey W(s), football M(s), golf M(s)/W(s), ice hockey M(s)/W(s), lacrosse M(s)/W(s), soccer M(s)/W(s), softball W(s), tennis M(s)/W(s), volleyball M(s)/W(s), water polo M(s)/W(s), wrestling M(s). *Intramural sports:* basketball M/W, football M, skiing (cross-country) M/W, skiing (downhill) M/W, tennis M/W, volleyball M/W.

Standardized Tests *Required:* SAT I or ACT (for admission).

Costs (2003–04) *Comprehensive fee:* $23,394 includes full-time tuition ($15,780), mandatory fees ($1200), and room and board ($6414). Part-time tuition: $526 per credit. Part-time tuition and fees vary according to course load and location. *Required fees:* $370 per term part-time. *College room only:* $3264. Room and board charges vary according to board plan and housing facility. *Payment plan:* installment. *Waivers:* adult students and employees or children of employees.

Financial Aid Of all full-time matriculated undergraduates who enrolled in 2003, 3,099 applied for aid, 2,450 were judged to have need, 1,960 had their need fully met. 243 Federal Work-Study jobs (averaging $1262). 1,342 state and other part-time jobs (averaging $1124). In 2003, 587 non-need-based awards were made. *Average percent of need met:* 92%. *Average financial aid package:* $12,686. *Average need-based loan:* $3554. *Average need-based gift aid:* $9050. *Average non-need-based aid:* $5010. *Average indebtedness upon graduation:* $22,125. *Financial aid deadline:* 5/1.

Applying *Options:* common application, electronic application, early admission, deferred entrance. *Application fee:* $30. *Required:* high school transcript. *Recommended:* essay or personal statement, 2 letters of recommendation, interview. *Application deadline:* rolling (freshmen), rolling (transfers). *Notification:* continuous (freshmen), continuous (transfers).

Admissions Contact Mr. Robin Engel, Director of Undergraduate Admissions, Mercyhurst College, 501 East 38th Street, Erie, PA 16546-0001. *Phone:* 814-824-2573. *Toll-free phone:* 800-825-1926 Ext. 2202. *Fax:* 814-824-2071. *E-mail:* admissions@mercyhurst.edu.

■ See page 1978 for a narrative description.

MESSIAH COLLEGE
Grantham, Pennsylvania

- **Independent interdenominational** 4-year, founded 1909
- **Calendar** semesters
- **Degree** bachelor's
- **Small-town** 400-acre campus
- **Endowment** $88.0 million
- **Coed,** 2,952 undergraduate students, 98% full-time, 63% women, 37% men
- **Moderately difficult** entrance level, 79% of applicants were admitted

Undergraduates 2,894 full-time, 58 part-time. Students come from 41 states and territories, 35 other countries, 48% are from out of state, 3% African American, 2% Asian American or Pacific Islander, 2% Hispanic American, 0.1% Native American, 3% international, 3% transferred in, 89% live on campus. *Retention:* 86% of 2002 full-time freshmen returned.

Freshmen *Admission:* 2,252 applied, 1,790 admitted, 736 enrolled. *Average high school GPA:* 3.76. *Test scores:* SAT verbal scores over 500: 93%; SAT math

Messiah College (continued)
scores over 500: 93%; ACT scores over 18: 99%; SAT verbal scores over 600: 52%; SAT math scores over 600: 48%; ACT scores over 24: 73%; SAT verbal scores over 700: 11%; SAT math scores over 700: 11%; ACT scores over 30: 23%.

Faculty *Total:* 295, 56% full-time. *Student/faculty ratio:* 13:1.

Majors Accounting; art history, criticism and conservation; art teacher education; athletic training; biblical studies; biochemistry; biology/biological sciences; biology teacher education; business administration and management; business, management, and marketing related; business/managerial economics; chemistry; chemistry teacher education; civil engineering; clinical nutrition; communication/speech communication and rhetoric; computer science; dramatic/theatre arts; early childhood education; e-commerce; economics; elementary education; engineering; English; English/language arts teacher education; entrepreneurship; environmental science; family and community services; fine/studio arts; French; French language teacher education; German; German language teacher education; history; humanities; human resources management; information science/studies; international business/trade/commerce; journalism; kinesiology and exercise science; marketing/marketing management; mathematics; mathematics teacher education; music; music teacher education; nursing (registered nurse training); parks, recreation and leisure; philosophy; physical education teaching and coaching; physics; political science and government; psychology; radio and television; religious education; religious studies; social studies teacher education; social work; sociology; Spanish; Spanish language teacher education; therapeutic recreation.

Academic Programs *Special study options:* academic remediation for entering students, accelerated degree program, adult/continuing education programs, advanced placement credit, double majors, honors programs, independent study, internships, off-campus study, part-time degree program, services for LD students, student-designed majors, study abroad, summer session for credit.

Library Murray Library with 258,097 titles, 1,327 serial subscriptions, 14,141 audiovisual materials, an OPAC, a Web page.

Computers on Campus 463 computers available on campus for general student use. A campuswide network can be accessed from student residence rooms and from off campus. Internet access, online (class) registration, at least one staffed computer lab available.

Student Life *Housing:* on-campus residence required through senior year. *Options:* coed, men-only, women-only, disabled students. Campus housing is university owned. Freshman campus housing is guaranteed. *Activities and organizations:* drama/theater group, student-run newspaper, radio station, choral group, outreach teams, student government, music ensembles, Small Group Program, outdoors club. *Campus security:* 24-hour emergency response devices and patrols, student patrols, late-night transport/escort service, controlled dormitory access, bicycle patrols, security lighting, self-defense classes, prevention/awareness programs. *Student services:* health clinic, personal/psychological counseling.

Athletics Member NCAA. All Division III. *Intercollegiate sports:* baseball M, basketball M/W, cross-country running M/W, field hockey W, golf M, lacrosse M/W, soccer M/W, softball W, tennis M/W, track and field M/W, volleyball W, wrestling M. *Intramural sports:* basketball M/W, field hockey W, racquetball M/W, soccer M/W, softball M/W, ultimate Frisbee M/W, volleyball M/W.

Standardized Tests *Required for some:* SAT I or ACT (for admission).

Costs (2003–04) *Comprehensive fee:* $25,890 includes full-time tuition ($18,880), mandatory fees ($670), and room and board ($6340). Part-time tuition: $790 per credit. *Required fees:* $28 per credit part-time. *College room only:* $3280. Room and board charges vary according to board plan, housing facility, and location. *Payment plan:* installment. *Waivers:* minority students, children of alumni, adult students, senior citizens, and employees or children of employees.

Financial Aid Of all full-time matriculated undergraduates who enrolled in 2003, 2,329 applied for aid, 2,070 were judged to have need, 348 had their need fully met. 722 Federal Work-Study jobs (averaging $1878). 640 state and other part-time jobs (averaging $2405). In 2003, 522 non-need-based awards were made. *Average percent of need met:* 65%. *Average financial aid package:* $12,798. *Average need-based loan:* $3947. *Average need-based gift aid:* $5476. *Average non-need-based aid:* $5228. *Average indebtedness upon graduation:* $23,249.

Applying *Options:* common application, electronic application, early admission, early decision, early action, deferred entrance. *Application fee:* $30. *Required:* essay or personal statement, high school transcript, 2 letters of recommendation. *Recommended:* minimum 3.0 GPA, interview. *Application deadline:* rolling (freshmen). *Early decision:* 10/15. *Notification:* continuous (freshmen), 11/1 (early decision), 12/1 (early action), continuous (transfers).

Admissions Contact Dr. William G. Strausbaugh, Dean for Enrollment Management, Messiah College, One College Avenue, PO Box 3005, Grantham, PA 17027. *Phone:* 717-691-6000. *Toll-free phone:* 800-233-4220. *Fax:* 717-796-5374. *E-mail:* admiss@messiah.edu.

■ *See page 1984 for a narrative description.*

MILLERSVILLE UNIVERSITY OF PENNSYLVANIA
Millersville, Pennsylvania

- **State-supported** comprehensive, founded 1855, part of Pennsylvania State System of Higher Education
- **Calendar** 4-1-4
- **Degrees** associate, bachelor's, master's, post-master's, and postbachelor's certificates
- **Small-town** 190-acre campus
- **Endowment** $771,550
- **Coed,** 6,820 undergraduate students, 90% full-time, 56% women, 44% men
- **Moderately difficult** entrance level, 61% of applicants were admitted

Undergraduates 6,143 full-time, 677 part-time. Students come from 23 states and territories, 4% are from out of state, 6% African American, 2% Asian American or Pacific Islander, 3% Hispanic American, 0.1% Native American, 0.4% international, 6% transferred in, 36% live on campus. *Retention:* 81% of 2002 full-time freshmen returned.

Freshmen *Admission:* 6,217 applied, 3,786 admitted, 1,353 enrolled. *Test scores:* SAT verbal scores over 500: 68%; SAT math scores over 500: 69%; SAT verbal scores over 600: 17%; SAT math scores over 600: 20%; SAT verbal scores over 700: 2%; SAT math scores over 700: 1%.

Faculty *Total:* 431, 70% full-time, 76% with terminal degrees. *Student/faculty ratio:* 18:1.

Majors Anthropology; area studies; area studies related; art; art teacher education; atmospheric sciences and meteorology; biology/biological sciences; business administration and management; chemical technology; chemistry; communication/speech communication and rhetoric; computer and information sciences; computer science; early childhood education; economics; elementary education; English; English/language arts teacher education; foreign language teacher education; French; geography; geology/earth science; German; gerontology; history; industrial production technologies related; industrial technology; liberal arts and sciences/liberal studies; mathematics; mathematics teacher education; music; music teacher education; nursing (registered nurse training); nursing science; occupational safety and health technology; oceanography (chemical and physical); philosophy; physics; political science and government; psychology; reading teacher education; science teacher education; social sciences related; social studies teacher education; social work; sociology; Spanish; special education.

Academic Programs *Special study options:* academic remediation for entering students, accelerated degree program, adult/continuing education programs, advanced placement credit, cooperative education, distance learning, double majors, honors programs, independent study, internships, off-campus study, part-time degree program, services for LD students, study abroad, summer session for credit. *ROTC:* Army (b). *Unusual degree programs:* 3-2 engineering with Pennsylvania State University—University Park Campus, University of South Carolina.

Library Helen A. Ganser Library with 499,986 titles, 5,776 serial subscriptions, 30,459 audiovisual materials, an OPAC, a Web page.

Computers on Campus 470 computers available on campus for general student use. A campuswide network can be accessed from student residence rooms and from off campus. Internet access, online (class) registration, at least one staffed computer lab available. Computer purchase or lease plan available.

Student Life *Housing:* on-campus residence required through sophomore year. *Options:* coed, women-only. Campus housing is university owned. Freshman campus housing is guaranteed. *Activities and organizations:* drama/theater group, student-run newspaper, radio and television station, choral group, marching band, Ocean Science Club, John Newman Association, United Campus Ministries, Resident Student Association, National Broadcasting Society, national fraternities, national sororities. *Campus security:* 24-hour emergency response devices and patrols, student patrols, late-night transport/escort service, controlled dormitory access, crime awareness programs, self-defense education, shuttle buses. *Student services:* health clinic, personal/psychological counseling, women's center.

Athletics Member NCAA. All Division II except wrestling (Division I). *Intercollegiate sports:* baseball M(s), basketball M(s)/W(s), cross-country running M(s)/W(s), field hockey W(s), football M(s), golf M(s), lacrosse W(s), soccer M(s)/W(s), softball W(s), swimming W(s), tennis M(s)/W(s), track and field M(s)/W(s), volleyball W(s), wrestling M(s). *Intramural sports:* archery M(c)/W(c), badminton M/W, basketball M/W, bowling M(c)/W(c), cheerleading W, fencing M(c)/W(c), golf M/W, ice hockey M(c), lacrosse M(c), racquetball M/W, rock climbing M/W, rugby M(c)/W(c), soccer M/W, softball M/W, tennis M/W, ultimate Frisbee M/W, volleyball M(c)/W, water polo M(c)/W(c).

Standardized Tests *Required:* SAT I or ACT (for admission).

Costs (2003–04) *Tuition:* state resident $4598 full-time, $192 per credit part-time; nonresident $11,496 full-time, $479 per credit part-time. Part-time tuition and fees vary according to course load. *Required fees:* $1221 full-time, $81 per credit part-time. *Room and board:* $5450; room only: $3150. Room and board charges vary according to board plan. *Payment plan:* installment. *Waivers:* senior citizens and employees or children of employees.

Financial Aid Of all full-time matriculated undergraduates who enrolled in 2002, 4,383 applied for aid, 2,910 were judged to have need, 722 had their need fully met. 429 Federal Work-Study jobs (averaging $764). 1,932 state and other part-time jobs (averaging $1108). In 2002, 1488 non-need-based awards were made. *Average percent of need met:* 90%. *Average financial aid package:* $6081. *Average need-based loan:* $3096. *Average need-based gift aid:* $3592. *Average non-need-based aid:* $4896. *Average indebtedness upon graduation:* $12,631. *Financial aid deadline:* 3/15.

Applying *Options:* common application, electronic application, early admission, deferred entrance. *Application fee:* $35. *Required:* high school transcript, minimum 2.0 GPA. *Required for some:* essay or personal statement, letters of recommendation, interview. *Recommended:* letters of recommendation. *Application deadline:* rolling (freshmen), rolling (transfers). *Notification:* continuous (freshmen), continuous (transfers).

Admissions Contact Mr. Douglas Zander, Director of Admissions, Millersville University of Pennsylvania, PO Box 1002, Millersville, PA 17551-0302. *Phone:* 717-872-3371. *Toll-free phone:* 800-MU-ADMIT. *Fax:* 717-871-2147. *E-mail:* admissions@millersville.edu.

■ *See page 1990 for a narrative description.*

MOORE COLLEGE OF ART & DESIGN
Philadelphia, Pennsylvania

- **Independent** 4-year, founded 1848
- **Calendar** semesters
- **Degrees** certificates, bachelor's, and postbachelor's certificates
- **Urban** 3-acre campus
- **Endowment** $6.8 million
- **Women only,** 501 undergraduate students, 93% full-time
- **Moderately difficult** entrance level, 46% of applicants were admitted

Moore College of Art and Design sets the standard of excellence in educating women for careers in the visual arts. Located in the museum district of Center City, Philadelphia, Moore's fully accredited BFA program offers degrees in 9 fine arts and design disciplines taught by practicing artists, designers, and scholars.

Undergraduates 464 full-time, 37 part-time. Students come from 29 states and territories, 7 other countries, 42% are from out of state, 8% African American, 7% Asian American or Pacific Islander, 3% Hispanic American, 1% international, 1% transferred in, 55% live on campus. *Retention:* 87% of 2002 full-time freshmen returned.

Freshmen *Admission:* 422 applied, 194 admitted, 88 enrolled. *Average high school GPA:* 3.08. *Test scores:* SAT verbal scores over 500: 59%; SAT math scores over 500: 35%; SAT verbal scores over 600: 18%; SAT math scores over 600: 15%; SAT verbal scores over 700: 3%.

Faculty *Total:* 108, 31% full-time, 47% with terminal degrees. *Student/faculty ratio:* 9:1.

Majors Art; art history, criticism and conservation; art teacher education; commercial and advertising art; fashion/apparel design; fiber, textile and weaving arts; fine/studio arts; interior design; sculpture.

Academic Programs *Special study options:* academic remediation for entering students, accelerated degree program, adult/continuing education programs, advanced placement credit, double majors, independent study, internships, part-time degree program, services for LD students, study abroad, summer session for credit.

Library Moore College Library plus 1 other with 40,000 titles, 124,804 audiovisual materials.

Computers on Campus 150 computers available on campus for general student use. Internet access, at least one staffed computer lab available.

Student Life *Housing options:* women-only. Freshman campus housing is guaranteed. *Activities and organizations:* student-run newspaper, Student Government Association, Into the Streets, Moore Environment Action Now, Black Student Union, Asian Student Union. *Campus security:* 24-hour patrols, late-night transport/escort service. *Student services:* health clinic, personal/psychological counseling, women's center.

Athletics *Intramural sports:* volleyball W.

Standardized Tests *Required:* SAT I or ACT (for admission).

Costs (2004–05) *Comprehensive fee:* $28,468 includes full-time tuition ($20,455) and room and board ($8013). Part-time tuition and fees vary according to course load. *College room only:* $4840. Room and board charges vary according to housing facility. *Payment plan:* installment. *Waivers:* employees or children of employees.

Financial Aid Of all full-time matriculated undergraduates who enrolled in 2003, 434 applied for aid, 408 were judged to have need, 14 had their need fully met. 110 Federal Work-Study jobs (averaging $1020). In 2003, 88 non-need-based awards were made. *Average percent of need met:* 52%. *Average financial aid package:* $12,194. *Average need-based loan:* $4487. *Average need-based gift aid:* $7627. *Average non-need-based aid:* $7619. *Average indebtedness upon graduation:* $25,000.

Applying *Options:* common application, early admission, early decision, deferred entrance. *Application fee:* $35. *Required:* high school transcript, minimum 2.5 GPA, 1 letter of recommendation, portfolio. *Required for some:* minimum 3.0 GPA. *Recommended:* essay or personal statement, interview. *Application deadline:* 8/15 (freshmen), rolling (transfers). *Early decision:* 11/15. *Notification:* continuous (freshmen), 11/30 (early decision), continuous (transfers).

Admissions Contact Ms. Wendy Elliott Pyle, Director of Admissions, Moore College of Art & Design, 20th and The Parkway, Philadelphia, PA 19103-1179. *Phone:* 215-568-4515 Ext. 1108. *Toll-free phone:* 800-523-2025. *Fax:* 215-965-8544. *E-mail:* admiss@moore.edu.

■ *See page 2026 for a narrative description.*

MORAVIAN COLLEGE
Bethlehem, Pennsylvania

- **Independent** comprehensive, founded 1742, affiliated with Moravian Church
- **Calendar** semesters
- **Degrees** bachelor's, master's, first professional, and postbachelor's certificates
- **Suburban** 65-acre campus with easy access to Philadelphia
- **Endowment** $64.1 million
- **Coed,** 1,850 undergraduate students, 83% full-time, 64% women, 36% men
- **Moderately difficult** entrance level, 68% of applicants were admitted

Undergraduates 1,533 full-time, 317 part-time. Students come from 22 states and territories, 16 other countries, 39% are from out of state, 2% African American, 2% Asian American or Pacific Islander, 3% Hispanic American, 1% international, 4% transferred in, 71% live on campus. *Retention:* 86% of 2002 full-time freshmen returned.

Freshmen *Admission:* 1,670 applied, 1,143 admitted, 380 enrolled. *Test scores:* SAT verbal scores over 500: 79%; SAT math scores over 500: 86%; SAT verbal scores over 600: 29%; SAT math scores over 600: 34%; SAT verbal scores over 700: 4%; SAT math scores over 700: 3%.

Faculty *Total:* 201, 57% full-time, 65% with terminal degrees. *Student/faculty ratio:* 11:1.

Majors Accounting; art; art history, criticism and conservation; art teacher education; biochemistry; biology/biological sciences; biology teacher education; business administration and management; chemistry; chemistry teacher education; classics and languages, literatures and linguistics; clinical laboratory science/medical technology; clinical psychology; computer science; creative writing; criminal justice/law enforcement administration; economics; education; elementary education; English; English language and literature related; experimental psychology; fine/studio arts; foreign language teacher education; French; French language teacher education; geology/earth science; German; German language teacher education; graphic design; history; history teacher education; industrial and organizational psychology; international business/trade/commerce; mathematics; mathematics teacher education; music; music performance; music teacher education; music theory and composition; natural resources management; nursing (registered nurse training); philosophy; physics; physics teacher education; political science and government; psychology; religious studies; science teacher education; secondary education; social sciences; social studies teacher education; sociology; Spanish; Spanish language teacher education; theatre literature, history and criticism.

Academic Programs *Special study options:* adult/continuing education programs, advanced placement credit, double majors, honors programs, independent study, internships, off-campus study, part-time degree program, services for LD students, student-designed majors, study abroad, summer session for credit. *ROTC:* Army (c). *Unusual degree programs:* 3-2 engineering with Washington University in St. Louis, Lehigh University; forestry with Duke University (natural resource management); allied health with Thomas Jefferson University (physical therapy and occupational therapy).

Library Reeves Library with 256,352 titles, 1,318 serial subscriptions, 1,950 audiovisual materials, an OPAC, a Web page.

Computers on Campus 170 computers available on campus for general student use. A campuswide network can be accessed from student residence rooms and from off campus. Internet access, at least one staffed computer lab available. Computer purchase or lease plan available.

Student Life *Housing:* on-campus residence required for freshman year. *Options:* coed, men-only, women-only. Campus housing is university owned. Freshman campus housing is guaranteed. *Activities and organizations:* drama/theater group, student-run newspaper, radio station, choral group, marching band,

Moravian College (continued)
Student Alumni Association, United Student Government, Moravian College Choir, Twenty-six Points (Student Ambassador Group), International Club, national fraternities, national sororities. *Campus security:* 24-hour emergency response devices and patrols, late-night transport/escort service, controlled dormitory access. *Student services:* health clinic, personal/psychological counseling.

Athletics Member NCAA. All Division III. *Intercollegiate sports:* baseball M, basketball M/W, cross-country running M/W, equestrian sports W(c), field hockey W, football M, golf M/W(c), ice hockey M(c)/W(c), lacrosse M/W, soccer M/W, softball W, tennis M/W, track and field M/W, volleyball W. *Intramural sports:* badminton M/W, basketball M/W, football M/W, racquetball M/W, skiing (downhill) M(c)/W(c), soccer M/W, softball M/W, table tennis M/W, tennis M/W, volleyball M/W.

Standardized Tests *Required:* SAT I or ACT (for admission).

Costs (2004–05) *Comprehensive fee:* $30,884 includes full-time tuition ($23,184), mandatory fees ($390), and room and board ($7310). Part-time tuition: $725 per credit. Part-time tuition and fees vary according to class time. *College room only:* $4105. Room and board charges vary according to board plan and housing facility. *Payment plan:* installment. *Waivers:* minority students, children of alumni, and employees or children of employees.

Financial Aid Of all full-time matriculated undergraduates who enrolled in 2002, 1,210 applied for aid, 1,081 were judged to have need, 222 had their need fully met. In 2002, 272 non-need-based awards were made. *Average percent of need met:* 79%. *Average financial aid package:* $15,894. *Average need-based loan:* $4112. *Average need-based gift aid:* $11,226. *Average non-need-based aid:* $10,825.

Applying *Options:* common application, electronic application, early admission, early decision, deferred entrance. *Application fee:* $40. *Required:* essay or personal statement, high school transcript, minimum 2.5 GPA. *Recommended:* interview. *Application deadlines:* 2/15 (freshmen), 3/1 (transfers). *Early decision:* 1/15. *Notification:* 3/15 (freshmen), 12/15 (early decision), continuous (transfers).

Admissions Contact Mr. James P. Mackin, Director of Admission, Moravian College, 1200 Main Street, Bethlehem, PA 18018. *Phone:* 610-861-1320. *Toll-free phone:* 800-441-3191. *Fax:* 610-625-7930. *E-mail:* admissions@moravian.edu.

■ *See page 2028 for a narrative description.*

MOUNT ALOYSIUS COLLEGE
Cresson, Pennsylvania

- **Independent Roman Catholic** comprehensive, founded 1939
- **Calendar** semesters
- **Degrees** diplomas, associate, bachelor's, master's, and postbachelor's certificates
- **Rural** 165-acre campus
- **Endowment** $7.2 million
- **Coed,** 1,447 undergraduate students, 75% full-time, 75% women, 25% men
- **Minimally difficult** entrance level, 74% of applicants were admitted

Mount Aloysius College is a small, private, Catholic college specializing in both undergraduate and graduate education. Offering more than 45 academic programs, Mount Aloysius College provides solid career-directed study within the liberal arts tradition. Boasting 150 years of academic excellence, Mount Aloysius College is committed to providing small classroom size, plenty of individual attention, and high job placement rates.

Undergraduates 1,085 full-time, 362 part-time. Students come from 18 states and territories, 3% are from out of state, 1% African American, 0.1% Asian American or Pacific Islander, 2% Hispanic American, 0.5% Native American, 11% transferred in, 25% live on campus.

Freshmen *Admission:* 760 applied, 565 admitted, 265 enrolled. *Average high school GPA:* 3.30. *Test scores:* SAT verbal scores over 500: 24%; SAT math scores over 500: 22%; ACT scores over 18: 98%; SAT verbal scores over 600: 4%; SAT math scores over 600: 4%; ACT scores over 24: 8%.

Faculty *Total:* 142, 37% full-time. *Student/faculty ratio:* 14:1.

Majors Accounting; accounting and business/management; behavioral sciences; business administration and management; child care and support services management; computer science; criminal justice/safety; criminology; English; general studies; health services/allied health/health sciences; history; humanities; information science/studies; kindergarten/preschool education; legal assistant/paralegal; liberal arts and sciences/liberal studies; medical/clinical assistant; medical office assistant; nursing (registered nurse training); nursing science; occupational therapist assistant; occupational therapy; pharmacy technician; physical therapist assistant; physical therapy; political science and government; pre-law studies; professional studies; psychology; radiologic technology/science; sign language interpretation and translation; social sciences; surgical technology.

Academic Programs *Special study options:* academic remediation for entering students, accelerated degree program, adult/continuing education programs, advanced placement credit, distance learning, honors programs, independent study, internships, part-time degree program, services for LD students, student-designed majors, summer session for credit.

Library Mount Aloysius College Library plus 1 other with 70,000 titles, 350 serial subscriptions, 2,087 audiovisual materials, an OPAC, a Web page.

Computers on Campus 175 computers available on campus for general student use. A campuswide network can be accessed from student residence rooms and from off campus. Internet access, at least one staffed computer lab available. Computer purchase or lease plan available.

Student Life *Housing options:* men-only, women-only. Campus housing is university owned. Freshman campus housing is guaranteed. *Activities and organizations:* drama/theater group, student-run newspaper, choral group, Phi Theta Kappa, Student Nursing Association, Student Government, Delta Epsilon Sigma, Residence Hall Association. *Campus security:* 24-hour emergency response devices and patrols, late-night transport/escort service, controlled dormitory access. *Student services:* health clinic, personal/psychological counseling, women's center.

Athletics Member NCAA. *Intercollegiate sports:* baseball M, basketball M/W, cross-country running M/W, golf M/W, soccer M/W, softball M/W(s), volleyball W(s). *Intramural sports:* baseball M, basketball M/W, cheerleading M/W, football M/W, skiing (cross-country) M/W, skiing (downhill) M/W, soccer M/W, softball M/W, table tennis M/W, tennis M/W, ultimate Frisbee M/W, volleyball M/W, weight lifting M/W.

Standardized Tests *Required:* SAT I or ACT (for admission).

Costs (2004–05) *Comprehensive fee:* $22,000 includes full-time tuition ($15,610), mandatory fees ($430), and room and board ($5960). Full-time tuition and fees vary according to class time, course load, and program. Part-time tuition: $450 per credit. Part-time tuition and fees vary according to class time, course load, and program. *Required fees:* $110 per term part-time. *College room only:* $2980. Room and board charges vary according to board plan. *Payment plans:* installment, deferred payment. *Waivers:* employees or children of employees.

Financial Aid Of all full-time matriculated undergraduates who enrolled in 2003, 1,138 applied for aid, 1,128 were judged to have need. 146 Federal Work-Study jobs (averaging $750). *Average percent of need met:* 83%. *Average financial aid package:* $9000. *Average need-based gift aid:* $2500. *Average indebtedness upon graduation:* $17,125.

Applying *Options:* common application, electronic application, early admission, deferred entrance. *Application fee:* $30. *Required:* high school transcript, minimum 2.5 GPA. *Required for some:* essay or personal statement, 3 letters of recommendation, interview. *Recommended:* interview. *Application deadline:* rolling (freshmen), rolling (transfers). *Notification:* continuous (freshmen), continuous (transfers).

Admissions Contact Mr. Francis Crouse, Dean of Enrollment Management, Mount Aloysius College, 7373 Admiral Peary Highway, Cresson, PA 16630. *Phone:* 814-886-6383. *Toll-free phone:* 888-823-2220. *Fax:* 814-886-6441. *E-mail:* admissions@mtaloy.edu.

■ *See page 2036 for a narrative description.*

MUHLENBERG COLLEGE
Allentown, Pennsylvania

- **Independent** 4-year, founded 1848, affiliated with Lutheran Church
- **Calendar** semesters
- **Degree** certificates and bachelor's
- **Suburban** 75-acre campus with easy access to Philadelphia
- **Endowment** $72.6 million
- **Coed,** 2,452 undergraduate students, 93% full-time, 58% women, 42% men
- **Very difficult** entrance level, 42% of applicants were admitted

"Friendly" and "challenging" are the words that students use most often to describe Muhlenberg. The educational experience is active and hands-on, with small classes, a caring environment, and easy access to faculty members. Internships, field study, study abroad, and a Washington semester supplement traditional classroom experiences. Students are taught to analyze and think critically as well as effectively express themselves in person and in writing—the most prized outcomes of a Muhlenberg education.

Undergraduates 2,290 full-time, 162 part-time. Students come from 36 states and territories, 5 other countries, 63% are from out of state, 2% African American, 2% Asian American or Pacific Islander, 3% Hispanic American, 0.2% Native American, 0.5% international, 0.2% transferred in, 90% live on campus. *Retention:* 92% of 2002 full-time freshmen returned.

Freshmen *Admission:* 4,111 applied, 1,743 admitted, 589 enrolled. *Average high school GPA:* 3.45. *Test scores:* SAT verbal scores over 500: 94%; SAT math

scores over 500: 96%; SAT verbal scores over 600: 56%; SAT math scores over 600: 60%; SAT verbal scores over 700: 8%; SAT math scores over 700: 9%.

Faculty *Total:* 273, 58% full-time. *Student/faculty ratio:* 12:1.

Majors Accounting; American studies; anthropology; art; art history, criticism and conservation; biochemistry; biology/biological sciences; business administration and management; chemistry; computer science; dance; dramatic/theatre arts; economics; elementary education; English; environmental science; fine/studio arts; French; German; history; human resources management; international economics; international relations and affairs; mathematics; music; natural sciences; philosophy; physical sciences; physics; political science and government; pre-dentistry studies; pre-law studies; pre-medical studies; pre-veterinary studies; psychology; religious studies; Russian studies; secondary education; social sciences; sociology; Spanish.

Academic Programs *Special study options:* accelerated degree program, adult/continuing education programs, advanced placement credit, distance learning, double majors, honors programs, independent study, internships, off-campus study, part-time degree program, services for LD students, student-designed majors, study abroad, summer session for credit. *ROTC:* Army (c). *Unusual degree programs:* 3-2 engineering with Columbia University, Washington University in St. Louis; forestry with Duke University.

Library Trexler Library with 270,700 titles, 1,700 serial subscriptions, 4,400 audiovisual materials, an OPAC, a Web page.

Computers on Campus 379 computers available on campus for general student use. A campuswide network can be accessed from student residence rooms and from off campus. Internet access, at least one staffed computer lab available. Computer purchase or lease plan available.

Student Life *Housing:* on-campus residence required for freshman year. *Options:* coed, women-only, disabled students. Campus housing is university owned and leased by the school. Freshman campus housing is guaranteed. *Activities and organizations:* drama/theater group, student-run newspaper, radio and television station, choral group, Theater Association, Environmental Action Team, Jefferson School Partnership, Select Choir, Habitat for Humanity, national fraternities, national sororities. *Campus security:* 24-hour emergency response devices and patrols, late-night transport/escort service, controlled dormitory access. *Student services:* health clinic, personal/psychological counseling.

Athletics Member NCAA. All Division III. *Intercollegiate sports:* baseball M, basketball M/W, cheerleading M/W, cross-country running M/W, field hockey W, football M, golf M/W, lacrosse M/W, soccer M/W, softball W, tennis M/W, track and field M/W, volleyball W, wrestling M. *Intramural sports:* basketball M/W, cross-country running M/W, football M/W, ice hockey M, racquetball M/W, rock climbing M/W, rugby M/W, soccer M/W, softball M, swimming M/W, tennis M/W, ultimate Frisbee M, volleyball M/W.

Standardized Tests *Required for some:* SAT I or ACT (for admission).

Costs (2003–04) *Comprehensive fee:* $31,700 includes full-time tuition ($24,945), mandatory fees ($215), and room and board ($6540). Part-time tuition: $2910 per course. *College room only:* $3490. Room and board charges vary according to board plan, housing facility, and location. *Payment plan:* installment. *Waivers:* senior citizens and employees or children of employees.

Financial Aid Of all full-time matriculated undergraduates who enrolled in 2003, 1,206 applied for aid, 973 were judged to have need, 895 had their need fully met. In 2003, 372 non-need-based awards were made. *Average percent of need met:* 95%. *Average financial aid package:* $16,847. *Average need-based loan:* $3894. *Average need-based gift aid:* $13,931. *Average non-need-based aid:* $9718. *Average indebtedness upon graduation:* $16,642. *Financial aid deadline:* 2/15.

Applying *Options:* common application, electronic application, early admission, early decision, deferred entrance. *Application fee:* $45. *Required:* essay or personal statement, high school transcript, 2 letters of recommendation. *Required for some:* interview. *Recommended:* interview. *Application deadlines:* 2/15 (freshmen), 6/1 (transfers). *Early decision:* 1/15. *Notification:* 4/1 (freshmen), 2/1 (early decision), continuous until 7/1 (transfers).

Admissions Contact Mr. Christopher Hooker-Haring, Dean of Admissions, Muhlenberg College, 2400 Chew Street, Allentown, PA 18104-5586. *Phone:* 484-664-3245. *Fax:* 484-664-3234. *E-mail:* adm@muhlenberg.edu.

■ *See page 2054 for a narrative description.*

NEUMANN COLLEGE
Aston, Pennsylvania

- **Independent Roman Catholic** comprehensive, founded 1965
- **Calendar** semesters
- **Degrees** certificates, associate, bachelor's, and master's
- **Suburban** 50-acre campus with easy access to Philadelphia
- **Endowment** $15.0 million
- **Coed,** 2,112 undergraduate students, 79% full-time, 66% women, 34% men
- **Moderately difficult** entrance level, 96% of applicants were admitted

Undergraduates 1,659 full-time, 453 part-time. Students come from 18 states and territories, 6 other countries, 27% are from out of state, 13% African American, 1% Asian American or Pacific Islander, 0.9% Hispanic American, 0.1% Native American, 0.4% international, 4% transferred in, 45% live on campus. *Retention:* 71% of 2002 full-time freshmen returned.

Freshmen *Admission:* 1,641 applied, 1,579 admitted, 525 enrolled. *Average high school GPA:* 3.00. *Test scores:* SAT verbal scores over 500: 18%; SAT math scores over 500: 20%; SAT verbal scores over 600: 3%; SAT math scores over 600: 3%.

Faculty *Total:* 224, 32% full-time, 34% with terminal degrees. *Student/faculty ratio:* 16:1.

Majors Accounting; athletic training/sports medicine; biology/biological sciences; business administration and management; communication/speech communication and rhetoric; computer and information sciences; criminal justice/safety; elementary education; English; environmental studies; international business/trade/commerce; kindergarten/preschool education; liberal arts and sciences/liberal studies; marketing/marketing management; nursing (registered nurse training); political science and government; psychology; sport and fitness administration.

Academic Programs *Special study options:* academic remediation for entering students, accelerated degree program, adult/continuing education programs, advanced placement credit, cooperative education, distance learning, double majors, freshman honors college, honors programs, independent study, internships, off-campus study, part-time degree program, services for LD students, student-designed majors, study abroad, summer session for credit. *ROTC:* Army (c).

Library Neumann College Library with 90,000 titles, 700 serial subscriptions, 36,562 audiovisual materials, an OPAC.

Computers on Campus 155 computers available on campus for general student use. A campuswide network can be accessed from student residence rooms and from off campus that provide access to e-mail. Internet access, at least one staffed computer lab available.

Student Life *Housing options:* coed. Campus housing is university owned. Freshman applicants given priority for college housing. *Activities and organizations:* drama/theater group, student-run newspaper, choral group, Professional Education Society, Student Nurses Association, theater ensemble, environmental club, community chorus. *Campus security:* 24-hour emergency response devices and patrols, late-night transport/escort service, controlled dormitory access. *Student services:* health clinic, personal/psychological counseling.

Athletics Member NCAA. All Division III. *Intercollegiate sports:* baseball M, basketball M/W, cheerleading W(s), field hockey W, golf M, ice hockey M/W, lacrosse M/W, soccer M/W, softball W, tennis M/W, volleyball W. *Intramural sports:* basketball M/W, lacrosse M, softball W, tennis M/W, volleyball M/W.

Standardized Tests *Required:* SAT I or ACT (for admission).

Costs (2004–05) *Comprehensive fee:* $24,930 includes full-time tuition ($16,590), mandatory fees ($600), and room and board ($7740). Part-time tuition: $380 per credit. *College room only:* $4600. *Waivers:* employees or children of employees.

Financial Aid Of all full-time matriculated undergraduates who enrolled in 2002, 1,288 applied for aid, 1,288 were judged to have need, 800 had their need fully met. 120 Federal Work-Study jobs (averaging $1200). *Average percent of need met:* 60%. *Average financial aid package:* $15,000. *Average need-based loan:* $7500. *Average need-based gift aid:* $10,000. *Average indebtedness upon graduation:* $18,000.

Applying *Options:* early admission, deferred entrance. *Application fee:* $35. *Required:* high school transcript, minimum 2.00 GPA. *Recommended:* interview. *Application deadline:* 4/1 (freshmen), rolling (transfers). *Notification:* continuous (freshmen), continuous (transfers).

Admissions Contact Ms. Renee San Giacomo, Executive Director of Admissions and Financial Aid, Neumann College, One Neumann Drive, Aston, PA 19014-1298. *Phone:* 610-558-5612. *Toll-free phone:* 800-963-8626. *Fax:* 610-558-5652. *E-mail:* neumann@neumann.edu.

■ *See page 2062 for a narrative description.*

PEIRCE COLLEGE
Philadelphia, Pennsylvania

- **Independent** 4-year, founded 1865
- **Calendar** continuous
- **Degrees** certificates, associate, bachelor's, and postbachelor's certificates
- **Urban** 1-acre campus
- **Endowment** $6.8 million
- **Coed,** 1,765 undergraduate students, 31% full-time, 71% women, 29% men
- **Minimally difficult** entrance level, 78% of applicants were admitted

Peirce College (continued)

Undergraduates 546 full-time, 1,219 part-time. Students come from 40 states and territories, 30 other countries, 19% are from out of state, 49% African American, 2% Asian American or Pacific Islander, 4% Hispanic American, 0.3% Native American, 2% international, 38% transferred in. *Retention:* 63% of 2002 full-time freshmen returned.

Freshmen *Admission:* 267 applied, 209 admitted, 209 enrolled.

Faculty *Total:* 162, 17% full-time, 23% with terminal degrees. *Student/faculty ratio:* 16:1.

Majors Accounting; accounting and business/management; accounting related; accounting technology and bookkeeping; business administration and management; business administration, management and operations related; business/commerce; computer engineering technology; computer programming (specific applications); computer technology/computer systems technology; legal administrative assistant/secretary; legal assistant/paralegal; legal professions and studies related; management information systems; marketing/marketing management; office management; pre-law studies; real estate; system, networking, and LAN/wan management.

Academic Programs *Special study options:* academic remediation for entering students, accelerated degree program, adult/continuing education programs, advanced placement credit, cooperative education, distance learning, double majors, English as a second language, external degree program, independent study, internships, off-campus study, part-time degree program, services for LD students, summer session for credit.

Library Peirce College Library with 29,844 titles, 80 serial subscriptions, 497 audiovisual materials, an OPAC, a Web page.

Computers on Campus 300 computers available on campus for general student use. A campuswide network can be accessed from off campus. Internet access, online (class) registration, at least one staffed computer lab available. Computer purchase or lease plan available.

Student Life *Housing:* college housing not available. *Campus security:* 24-hour emergency response devices and patrols, late-night transport/escort service, 24-hour security cameras.

Costs (2003–04) *Tuition:* $10,800 full-time, $360 per credit hour part-time. Full-time tuition and fees vary according to course load. Part-time tuition and fees vary according to course load. *Required fees:* $1000 full-time, $100 per course part-time. *Payment plan:* installment. *Waivers:* children of alumni and employees or children of employees.

Financial Aid Of all full-time matriculated undergraduates who enrolled in 2002, 387 applied for aid, 387 were judged to have need, 336 had their need fully met. 37 Federal Work-Study jobs (averaging $2675). In 2002, 130 non-need-based awards were made. *Average percent of need met:* 25%. *Average financial aid package:* $3500. *Average need-based loan:* $4000. *Average need-based gift aid:* $1000. *Average non-need-based aid:* $1000. *Average indebtedness upon graduation:* $13,000.

Applying *Options:* common application, electronic application. *Application fee:* $50. *Required:* high school transcript. *Application deadline:* rolling (freshmen), rolling (transfers). *Notification:* continuous (freshmen), continuous (transfers).

Admissions Contact Mr. Steve W. Bird, College Representative, Peirce College, 1420 Pine Street, Philadelphia, PA 19102. *Phone:* 215-670-9375. *Toll-free phone:* 877-670-9190 Ext. 9214. *Fax:* 215-893-4347. *E-mail:* info@peirce.edu.

PENNSYLVANIA COLLEGE OF ART & DESIGN
Lancaster, Pennsylvania

- **Independent** 4-year, founded 1982
- **Calendar** semesters
- **Degree** certificates and bachelor's
- **Urban** campus with easy access to Philadelphia and Wilmington
- **Coed**
- **Moderately difficult** entrance level

Faculty *Student/faculty ratio:* 11:1.

Student Life *Campus security:* trained evening/weekend security personnel.

Costs (2004–05) *Tuition:* $12,250 full-time, $580 per credit part-time. *Required fees:* $400 full-time, $70 per term part-time.

Applying *Options:* deferred entrance. *Application fee:* $35. *Required:* essay or personal statement, high school transcript, interview, portfolio. *Required for some:* 2 letters of recommendation. *Recommended:* minimum 2.0 GPA, 2 letters of recommendation.

Admissions Contact Ms. Wendy Sweigart, Director of Admissions, Pennsylvania College of Art & Design, PO Box 59, Lancaster, PA 17608-0059. *Phone:* 717-396-7833 Ext. 19. *Fax:* 717-396-1339. *E-mail:* admissions@pcad.edu.

PENNSYLVANIA COLLEGE OF TECHNOLOGY
Williamsport, Pennsylvania

- **State-related** primarily 2-year, founded 1965
- **Calendar** semesters
- **Degrees** associate and bachelor's
- **Small-town** 958-acre campus
- **Endowment** $650,434
- **Coed,** 6,255 undergraduate students, 83% full-time, 35% women, 65% men
- **Noncompetitive** entrance level, 51% of applicants were admitted

Pennsylvania College of Technology is Pennsylvania's premier technical college and an affiliate of The Pennsylvania State University. More than 6,000 students are enrolled in Penn College's bachelor and associate degree and certificate programs, which combine hands-on experience with theory and management education. Penn College is a special mission affiliate of Penn State, committed to applied technology education. Degrees offered represent more than 100 career fields ranging from manufacturing, design, transportation, construction, and natural resources to hospitality, health, business, and communication.

Undergraduates 5,198 full-time, 1,057 part-time. Students come from 32 states and territories, 16 other countries, 7% are from out of state, 3% African American, 1% Asian American or Pacific Islander, 0.9% Hispanic American, 0.5% Native American, 0.5% international, 8% transferred in, 19% live on campus.

Freshmen *Admission:* 5,483 applied, 2,777 admitted, 1,651 enrolled.

Faculty *Total:* 468, 60% full-time. *Student/faculty ratio:* 18:1.

Majors Accounting; accounting technology and bookkeeping; administrative assistant and secretarial science; adult health nursing; aeronautical/aerospace engineering technology; aircraft powerplant technology; allied health diagnostic, intervention, and treatment professions related; applied horticulture/horticultural business services related; architectural engineering technology; autobody/collision and repair technology; automotive engineering technology; avionics maintenance technology; baking and pastry arts; banking and financial support services; biology/biological sciences; biomedical technology; broadcast journalism; business administration and management; business administration, management and operations related; business automation/technology/data entry; cabinetmaking and millwork; cardiovascular technology; carpentry; child care and support services management; child care provision; civil engineering technology; commercial and advertising art; computer and information sciences; computer and information sciences and support services related; computer/information technology services administration related; computer programming (specific applications); computer systems analysis; computer systems networking and telecommunications; computer technology/computer systems technology; construction engineering technology; culinary arts; dental hygiene; diesel mechanics technology; dietitian assistant; drafting and design technology; drafting/design engineering technologies related; education (specific subject areas) related; electrical and electronic engineering technologies related; electrical, electronic and communications engineering technology; electrician; emergency medical technology (EMT paramedic); engineering science; engineering technologies related; environmental control technologies related; environmental engineering technology; forestry technology; general studies; graphic and printing equipment operation/production; health and medical administrative services related; health and physical education related; health information/medical records administration; health professions related; heating, air conditioning and refrigeration technology; heavy equipment maintenance technology; heavy/industrial equipment maintenance technologies related; industrial electronics technology; industrial mechanics and maintenance technology; industrial production technologies related; industrial technology; information technology; institutional food workers; instrumentation technology; laser and optical technology; legal assistant/paralegal; legal professions and studies related; legal studies; liberal arts and sciences and humanities related; liberal arts and sciences/liberal studies; machine shop technology; management information systems; manufacturing technology; masonry; mass communication/media; mechanical drafting and CAD/CADD; mechanical engineering/mechanical technology; mechanic and repair technologies related; medical administrative assistant and medical secretary; medical radiologic technology; mental and social health services and allied professions related; multi-/interdisciplinary studies related; nursing (licensed practical/vocational nurse training); nursing (registered nurse training); occupational therapist assistant; office occupations and clerical services; ornamental horticulture; physical sciences; plant nursery management; plastics engineering technology; platemaking/imaging; plumbing technology; psychiatric/mental health services technology; quality control technology; solar energy technology; survey technology; technical and business writing; tool and die technology; tourism and travel services management; turf and turfgrass management; vehicle and vehicle parts and accessories marketing; vehicle maintenance and repair technologies related; web page, digital/multimedia and information resources design; welding technology; woodworking related.

Academic Programs *Special study options:* academic remediation for entering students, advanced placement credit, cooperative education, distance learning, double majors, English as a second language, independent study, internships, off-campus study, part-time degree program, services for LD students, student-designed majors, summer session for credit. *ROTC:* Army (c).

Library Penn College Library plus 1 other with 64,462 titles, 6,985 audiovisual materials, an OPAC, a Web page.

Computers on Campus A campuswide network can be accessed from student residence rooms and from off campus. At least one staffed computer lab available.

Student Life *Housing options:* coed. Campus housing is university owned. *Activities and organizations:* student-run newspaper, radio station, Student Government Association, Resident Hall Association (RHA), Wildcats Event Board (WEB), Phi Beta Lambda, Early Educators. *Campus security:* 24-hour emergency response devices and patrols, late-night transport/escort service. *Student services:* personal/psychological counseling, women's center.

Athletics *Intercollegiate sports:* archery M/W, baseball M, basketball M/W, bowling M/W, cross-country running M/W, golf M/W, soccer M/W, softball W, tennis M/W, volleyball M/W. *Intramural sports:* archery M/W, badminton M/W, basketball M/W, bowling M/W, football M/W, golf M/W, lacrosse M/W, racquetball M/W, soccer M/W, softball M/W, table tennis M/W, tennis M/W, volleyball M/W, weight lifting M/W, wrestling M.

Standardized Tests *Required for some:* SAT I (for admission).

Costs (2003–04) *Tuition:* state resident $7860 full-time, $298 per credit part-time; nonresident $9990 full-time, $375 per credit part-time. Full-time tuition and fees vary according to course load and program. Part-time tuition and fees vary according to course load and program. *Required fees:* $1260 full-time. *Room and board:* $6186; room only: $3686. Room and board charges vary according to board plan, housing facility, and location. *Payment plan:* deferred payment. *Waivers:* employees or children of employees.

Financial Aid Of all full-time matriculated undergraduates who enrolled in 2002, 326 Federal Work-Study jobs (averaging $1339).

Applying *Options:* electronic application, early admission, deferred entrance. *Application fee:* $50. *Required:* high school transcript. *Application deadlines:* rolling (freshmen), 7/1 (out-of-state freshmen), rolling (transfers). *Early decision:* 7/1.

Admissions Contact Mr. Chester D. Schuman, Director of Admissions, Pennsylvania College of Technology, One College Avenue, DIF #119, Williamsport, PA 17701. *Phone:* 570-327-4761. *Toll-free phone:* 800-367-9222. *Fax:* 570-321-5551. *E-mail:* cschuman@pct.edu.

■ *See page 2158 for a narrative description.*

THE PENNSYLVANIA STATE UNIVERSITY ABINGTON COLLEGE

Abington, Pennsylvania

- **State-related** 4-year, founded 1950, part of Pennsylvania State University
- **Calendar** semesters
- **Degrees** associate and bachelor's
- **Small-town** 46-acre campus with easy access to Philadelphia
- **Coed,** 3,201 undergraduate students, 77% full-time, 51% women, 49% men
- **Moderately difficult** entrance level, 78% of applicants were admitted

Undergraduates 2,475 full-time, 726 part-time. 4% are from out of state, 10% African American, 12% Asian American or Pacific Islander, 5% Hispanic American, 0.2% Native American, 0.5% international, 3% transferred in. *Retention:* 75% of 2001 full-time freshmen returned.

Freshmen *Admission:* 2,813 applied, 2,206 admitted, 782 enrolled. *Average high school GPA:* 3.06. *Test scores:* SAT verbal scores over 500: 45%; SAT math scores over 500: 50%; SAT verbal scores over 600: 10%; SAT math scores over 600: 17%; SAT verbal scores over 700: 1%; SAT math scores over 700: 2%.

Faculty *Total:* 217, 51% full-time, 45% with terminal degrees. *Student/faculty ratio:* 19:1.

Majors Accounting; acting; actuarial science; adult and continuing education administration; advertising; aerospace, aeronautical and astronautical engineering; African-American/Black studies; agribusiness; agricultural and extension education; agricultural/biological engineering and bioengineering; agricultural business and management related; agricultural mechanization; agriculture; American studies; animal sciences; animal sciences related; anthropology; applied economics; archeology; architectural engineering; art; art history, criticism and conservation; art teacher education; Asian studies (East); astronomy; atmospheric sciences and meteorology; biochemistry; biological and biomedical sciences related; biological and physical sciences; biology/biological sciences; biology/biotechnology laboratory technician; biomedical/medical engineering; business/commerce; business/corporate communications; business/managerial economics; chemical engineering; chemistry; civil engineering; classics and languages, literatures and linguistics; communication and journalism related; communication disorders; communication/speech communication and rhetoric; comparative literature; computer and information sciences; computer engineering; criminal justice/law enforcement administration; criminal justice/safety; economics; electrical, electronics and communications engineering; elementary education; engineering science; English; environmental/environmental health engineering; film/cinema studies; finance; food science; forestry technology; forest sciences and biology; French; geography; geological and earth sciences/geosciences related; geology/earth science; German; graphic design; health/health care administration; history; horticultural science; hospitality administration related; human development and family studies; human nutrition; industrial engineering; information science/studies; international business/trade/commerce; international relations and affairs; Italian; Japanese; Jewish/Judaic studies; journalism; kinesiology and exercise science; labor and industrial relations; landscape architecture; landscaping and groundskeeping; Latin American studies; liberal arts and sciences/liberal studies; logistics and materials management; management information systems; management sciences and quantitative methods related; marketing/marketing management; materials science; mathematics; mechanical engineering; medical microbiology and bacteriology; medieval and Renaissance studies; mining and mineral engineering; natural resources and conservation related; natural resources/conservation; nuclear engineering; nursing (registered nurse training); organizational behavior; parks, recreation and leisure facilities management; petroleum engineering; philosophy; physics; political science and government; pre-medical studies; psychology; rehabilitation and therapeutic professions related; religious studies; Russian; secondary education; social psychology; sociology; soil science and agronomy; Spanish; special education; statistics; theatre design and technology; turf and turfgrass management; visual and performing arts; women's studies.

Academic Programs *Special study options:* academic remediation for entering students, accelerated degree program, adult/continuing education programs, advanced placement credit, cooperative education, distance learning, double majors, English as a second language, external degree program, honors programs, independent study, internships, services for LD students, student-designed majors, study abroad, summer session for credit. *ROTC:* Army (b), Air Force (c).

Library 65,866 titles, 318 serial subscriptions, 4,046 audiovisual materials.

Computers on Campus 286 computers available on campus for general student use. A campuswide network can be accessed from off campus. Internet access, online (class) registration, at least one staffed computer lab available. Computer purchase or lease plan available.

Student Life *Housing:* college housing not available. *Activities and organizations:* drama/theater group, student-run newspaper. *Campus security:* 24-hour patrols. *Student services:* personal/psychological counseling.

Athletics *Intercollegiate sports:* baseball M, basketball M/W, golf M, soccer M/W(c), softball W, tennis M/W, volleyball W. *Intramural sports:* basketball M/W, cross-country running M/W, football M, soccer M/W, softball M/W, table tennis M/W, tennis M/W, volleyball M/W, weight lifting M/W.

Standardized Tests *Required:* SAT I or ACT (for admission).

Costs (2003–04) *Tuition:* state resident $8620 full-time, $348 per credit part-time; nonresident $13,250 full-time, $552 per credit part-time. Full-time tuition and fees vary according to course level, location, program, and student level. Part-time tuition and fees vary according to course level, course load, location, program, and student level. *Required fees:* $398 full-time. *Payment plan:* deferred payment. *Waivers:* senior citizens and employees or children of employees.

Financial Aid Of all full-time matriculated undergraduates who enrolled in 2002, 1,794 applied for aid, 1,356 were judged to have need, 79 had their need fully met. 87 Federal Work-Study jobs (averaging $1122). In 2002, 102 non-need-based awards were made. *Average percent of need met:* 68%. *Average financial aid package:* $8519. *Average need-based loan:* $3267. *Average need-based gift aid:* $4590. *Average non-need-based aid:* $2459. *Average indebtedness upon graduation:* $18,200.

Applying *Options:* electronic application, early admission, deferred entrance. *Application fee:* $50. *Required:* high school transcript. *Application deadline:* rolling (freshmen), rolling (transfers). *Notification:* continuous (freshmen), continuous (transfers).

The Pennsylvania State University Abington College (continued)

Admissions Contact The Pennsylvania State University Abington College, 1600 Woodland Road, Abington, PA 19001. *Phone:* 814-865-5471. *Fax:* 215-881-7655. *E-mail:* smd15@psu.edu.

■ *See page 2160 for a narrative description.*

The Pennsylvania State University Altoona College

Altoona, Pennsylvania

■ **State-related** 4-year, founded 1939, part of Pennsylvania State University
■ **Calendar** semesters
■ **Degrees** associate and bachelor's
■ **Suburban** 106-acre campus
■ **Coed,** 3,771 undergraduate students, 92% full-time, 50% women, 50% men
■ **Moderately difficult** entrance level, 74% of applicants were admitted

Undergraduates 3,466 full-time, 305 part-time. 12% are from out of state, 5% African American, 2% Asian American or Pacific Islander, 2% Hispanic American, 0.1% Native American, 1% international, 2% transferred in, 24% live on campus. *Retention:* 87% of 2001 full-time freshmen returned.

Freshmen *Admission:* 4,664 applied, 3,448 admitted, 1,325 enrolled. *Average high school GPA:* 3.00. *Test scores:* SAT verbal scores over 500: 55%; SAT math scores over 500: 60%; SAT verbal scores over 600: 9%; SAT math scores over 600: 16%; SAT math scores over 700: 1%.

Faculty *Total:* 284, 48% full-time, 45% with terminal degrees. *Student/faculty ratio:* 19:1.

Majors Accounting; acting; actuarial science; adult and continuing education administration; advertising; aerospace, aeronautical and astronautical engineering; African-American/Black studies; agribusiness; agricultural and extension education; agricultural/biological engineering and bioengineering; agricultural business and management related; agriculture; American studies; animal sciences; animal sciences related; anthropology; applied economics; archeology; architectural engineering; art; art teacher education; Asian studies (East); astronomy; atmospheric sciences and meteorology; biochemistry; biological and biomedical sciences related; biological and physical sciences; biology/biological sciences; biology/biotechnology laboratory technician; biomedical/medical engineering; biomedical technology; business/commerce; business/managerial economics; chemical engineering; chemistry; civil engineering; classics and languages, literatures and linguistics; communication and journalism related; communication/speech communication and rhetoric; comparative literature; computer and information sciences; computer engineering; criminal justice/law enforcement administration; criminal justice/safety; economics; electrical, electronic and communications engineering technology; electrical, electronics and communications engineering; elementary education; engineering science; English; environmental/environmental health engineering; environmental studies; film/cinema studies; finance; food science; forestry technology; forest sciences and biology; French; geography; geological and earth sciences/geosciences related; geology/earth science; German; graphic design; history; horticultural science; hospitality administration related; human development and family studies; human nutrition; industrial engineering; information science/studies; international business/trade/commerce; international relations and affairs; Italian; Japanese; Jewish/Judaic studies; journalism; kinesiology and exercise science; labor and industrial relations; landscape architecture; landscaping and groundskeeping; Latin American studies; liberal arts and sciences/liberal studies; logistics and materials management; management information systems; management sciences and quantitative methods related; marketing/marketing management; materials science; mathematics; mechanical engineering; mechanical engineering/mechanical technology; medical microbiology and bacteriology; medieval and Renaissance studies; metallurgical technology; mining and mineral engineering; natural resources and conservation related; natural resources/conservation; nuclear engineering; nursing (registered nurse training); organizational behavior; parks, recreation and leisure facilities management; petroleum engineering; philosophy; physics; political science and government; pre-medical studies; psychology; rehabilitation and therapeutic professions related; religious studies; Russian; secondary education; sociology; soil science and agronomy; Spanish; special education; statistics; telecommunications technology; theatre design and technology; turf and turfgrass management; visual and performing arts; women's studies.

Academic Programs *Special study options:* academic remediation for entering students, accelerated degree program, adult/continuing education programs, advanced placement credit, cooperative education, distance learning, double majors, English as a second language, honors programs, independent study, internships, services for LD students, student-designed majors, study abroad, summer session for credit. *ROTC:* Army (b).

Library 70,851 titles, 308 serial subscriptions, 5,680 audiovisual materials.

Computers on Campus 167 computers available on campus for general student use. A campuswide network can be accessed from student residence rooms and from off campus. Internet access, online (class) registration, at least one staffed computer lab available. Computer purchase or lease plan available.

Student Life *Housing options:* coed. Campus housing is university owned. Freshman campus housing is guaranteed. *Activities and organizations:* drama/theater group, student-run newspaper, choral group, national fraternities, national sororities. *Campus security:* 24-hour emergency response devices and patrols, student patrols, late-night transport/escort service, controlled dormitory access.

Athletics Member NCAA. All Division III. *Intercollegiate sports:* baseball M, basketball M/W, cheerleading M(c)/W(c), cross-country running M/W, golf M, ice hockey M(c), soccer M/W, softball W, swimming M/W, tennis M/W, volleyball M(c)/W. *Intramural sports:* badminton M/W, baseball M/W, basketball M/W, football M/W, golf M/W, racquetball M/W, soccer M/W, softball M/W, table tennis M/W, tennis M/W, track and field M/W, volleyball M/W, weight lifting M/W.

Standardized Tests *Required:* SAT I or ACT (for admission).

Costs (2003–04) *Tuition:* state resident $8896 full-time, $371 per credit part-time; nonresident $13,716 full-time, $572 per credit part-time. Full-time tuition and fees vary according to course level, location, program, and student level. Part-time tuition and fees vary according to course level, course load, location, program, and student level. *Required fees:* $408 full-time. *Room and board:* $5940; room only: $3080. Room and board charges vary according to board plan and housing facility. *Payment plan:* deferred payment. *Waivers:* senior citizens and employees or children of employees.

Financial Aid Of all full-time matriculated undergraduates who enrolled in 2002, 2,835 applied for aid, 2,368 were judged to have need, 191 had their need fully met. 433 Federal Work-Study jobs (averaging $1490). 30 state and other part-time jobs (averaging $3728). In 2002, 105 non-need-based awards were made. *Average percent of need met:* 70%. *Average financial aid package:* $10,599. *Average need-based loan:* $3387. *Average need-based gift aid:* $4279. *Average non-need-based aid:* $3038. *Average indebtedness upon graduation:* $18,200.

Applying *Options:* electronic application, early admission, deferred entrance. *Application fee:* $50. *Required:* high school transcript. *Application deadline:* rolling (freshmen), rolling (transfers). *Notification:* continuous (freshmen), continuous (transfers).

Admissions Contact The Pennsylvania State University Altoona College, E108 E. Raymond Smith Building, Altoona, PA 16601-3760. *Phone:* 814-865-5471. *Toll-free phone:* 800-848-9843. *Fax:* 814-949-5564. *E-mail:* aaadmit@psu.edu.

The Pennsylvania State University at Erie, The Behrend College

Erie, Pennsylvania

■ **State-related** comprehensive, founded 1948, part of Pennsylvania State University
■ **Calendar** semesters
■ **Degrees** associate, bachelor's, and master's
■ **Suburban** 727-acre campus
■ **Coed,** 3,554 undergraduate students, 93% full-time, 34% women, 66% men
■ **Very difficult** entrance level, 79% of applicants were admitted

Students benefit from small classes and participate in undergraduate research as they earn an internationally recognized Penn State degree. Modern facilities include an observatory, a high-technology business park, an athletics and recreation center, a multifaith chapel, and residence halls. A new, $30-million academic center for business, engineering, and engineering technology is under construction.

Undergraduates 3,295 full-time, 259 part-time. 8% are from out of state, 3% African American, 2% Asian American or Pacific Islander, 1% Hispanic American, 0.1% Native American, 1% international, 3% transferred in, 43% live on campus. *Retention:* 86% of 2001 full-time freshmen returned.

Freshmen *Admission:* 3,045 applied, 2,411 admitted, 844 enrolled. *Average high school GPA:* 3.19. *Test scores:* SAT verbal scores over 500: 65%; SAT math scores over 500: 77%; SAT verbal scores over 600: 16%; SAT math scores over 600: 30%; SAT verbal scores over 700: 2%; SAT math scores over 700: 4%.

Faculty *Total:* 273, 72% full-time, 46% with terminal degrees. *Student/faculty ratio:* 16:1.

Majors Accounting; acting; actuarial science; adult and continuing education administration; advertising; aerospace, aeronautical and astronautical engineering; African-American/Black studies; agribusiness; agricultural and extension education; agricultural/biological engineering and bioengineering; agricultural business and management related; agricultural mechanization; agriculture; American studies; animal sciences; animal sciences related; anthropology; applied economics; archeology; architectural engineering; art; art history, criticism and conservation; art teacher education; Asian studies (East); astronomy; atmospheric sciences and meteorology; biochemistry; biological and biomedical sciences related; biological and physical sciences; biology/biological sciences; biology/biotechnology laboratory technician; biomedical/medical engineering; biomedical technology; business administration and management; business/commerce; business/managerial economics; chemical engineering; chemistry; civil engineering; classics and languages, literatures and linguistics; communication and journalism related; communication and media related; communication disorders; communication/speech communication and rhetoric; comparative literature; computer and information sciences; computer engineering; computer science; computer software engineering; criminal justice/law enforcement administration; economics; electrical, electronic and communications engineering technology; electrical, electronics and communications engineering; elementary education; engineering science; English; environmental/environmental health engineering; film/cinema studies; finance; food science; forestry technology; forest sciences and biology; French; geography; geological and earth sciences/geosciences related; geology/earth science; German; graphic design; health/health care administration; history; horticultural science; hospitality administration related; human development and family studies; human nutrition; industrial engineering; information science/studies; international business/trade/commerce; international relations and affairs; Italian; Japanese; Jewish/Judaic studies; journalism; kinesiology and exercise science; labor and industrial relations; landscape architecture; landscaping and groundskeeping; Latin American studies; liberal arts and sciences/liberal studies; logistics and materials management; management information systems; management sciences and quantitative methods related; manufacturing technology; marketing/marketing management; materials science; mathematics; mechanical engineering; mechanical engineering/mechanical technology; medical microbiology and bacteriology; medieval and Renaissance studies; metallurgical technology; mining and mineral engineering; multi-/interdisciplinary studies related; natural resources and conservation related; natural resources/conservation; nuclear engineering; nursing (registered nurse training); organizational behavior; parks, recreation and leisure facilities management; petroleum engineering; philosophy; physical sciences; physics; plastics engineering technology; political science and government; polymer/plastics engineering; pre-medical studies; psychology; rehabilitation and therapeutic professions related; religious studies; Russian; secondary education; sociology; soil science and agronomy; Spanish; special education; statistics; telecommunications technology; theatre design and technology; turf and turfgrass management; visual and performing arts; women's studies.

Academic Programs *Special study options:* academic remediation for entering students, accelerated degree program, adult/continuing education programs, advanced placement credit, cooperative education, distance learning, double majors, honors programs, independent study, internships, services for LD students, study abroad, summer session for credit. *ROTC:* Army (b).

Library 103,524 titles, 810 serial subscriptions, 3,180 audiovisual materials.

Computers on Campus 448 computers available on campus for general student use. A campuswide network can be accessed from student residence rooms and from off campus. Internet access, online (class) registration, at least one staffed computer lab available. Computer purchase or lease plan available.

Student Life *Housing options:* coed, men-only, women-only, disabled students. Campus housing is university owned. Freshman campus housing is guaranteed. *Activities and organizations:* drama/theater group, student-run newspaper, radio station, choral group, Student Government Association, national fraternities, national sororities. *Campus security:* 24-hour emergency response devices and patrols, student patrols, late-night transport/escort service, controlled dormitory access.

Athletics Member NCAA. All Division III. *Intercollegiate sports:* baseball M, basketball M/W, cheerleading M/W, cross-country running M/W, golf M/W, ice hockey M(c), lacrosse M(c), skiing (downhill) M(c)/W(c), soccer M/W, softball W, swimming M/W, tennis M/W, track and field M/W, volleyball M(c)/W, water polo M/W. *Intramural sports:* badminton M/W, basketball M/W, bowling M/W, cross-country running M/W, football M/W, golf M/W, skiing (downhill) M/W, soccer M/W, softball M/W, swimming M/W, table tennis M/W, tennis M/W, volleyball M/W.

Standardized Tests *Required:* SAT I or ACT (for admission).

Costs (2003–04) *Tuition:* state resident $8896 full-time, $371 per credit part-time; nonresident $15,466 full-time, $644 per credit part-time. Full-time tuition and fees vary according to course level, location, program, and student level. Part-time tuition and fees vary according to course level, course load, location, program, and student level. *Required fees:* $408 full-time, $68 per term part-time. *Room and board:* $5940; room only: $3080. Room and board charges vary according to board plan and housing facility. *Payment plan:* deferred payment. *Waivers:* senior citizens and employees or children of employees.

Financial Aid Of all full-time matriculated undergraduates who enrolled in 2002, 2,696 applied for aid, 2,241 were judged to have need, 232 had their need fully met. 370 Federal Work-Study jobs (averaging $1194). 47 state and other part-time jobs (averaging $3434). In 2002, 162 non-need-based awards were made. *Average percent of need met:* 73%. *Average financial aid package:* $10,916. *Average need-based loan:* $3829. *Average need-based gift aid:* $4061. *Average non-need-based aid:* $3052. *Average indebtedness upon graduation:* $18,200.

Applying *Options:* electronic application, early admission, deferred entrance. *Application fee:* $50. *Required:* high school transcript. *Application deadline:* rolling (freshmen), rolling (transfers). *Notification:* continuous (freshmen), continuous (transfers).

Admissions Contact The Pennsylvania State University at Erie, The Behrend College, 5091 Station Road, Erie, PA 16563-0105. *Phone:* 814-865-5471. *Toll-free phone:* 866-374-3378. *Fax:* 814-898-6044. *E-mail:* behrend.admissions@psu.edu.

■ *See page 2162 for a narrative description.*

THE PENNSYLVANIA STATE UNIVERSITY BEAVER CAMPUS OF THE COMMONWEALTH COLLEGE

Monaca, Pennsylvania

- **State-related** primarily 2-year, founded 1964, part of Pennsylvania State University
- **Calendar** semesters
- **Degrees** associate and bachelor's (also offers up to 2 years of most bachelor's degree programs offered at University Park campus)
- **Small-town** 91-acre campus with easy access to Pittsburgh
- **Coed,** 735 undergraduate students, 88% full-time, 35% women, 65% men
- **Moderately difficult** entrance level, 91% of applicants were admitted

Undergraduates 646 full-time, 89 part-time. 4% are from out of state, 4% African American, 2% Asian American or Pacific Islander, 2% Hispanic American, 0.5% Native American, 0.3% international, 4% transferred in, 26% live on campus. *Retention:* 71% of 2001 full-time freshmen returned.

Freshmen *Admission:* 572 applied, 523 admitted, 216 enrolled. *Average high school GPA:* 2.94. *Test scores:* SAT verbal scores over 500: 56%; SAT math scores over 500: 57%; SAT verbal scores over 600: 13%; SAT math scores over 600: 18%; SAT verbal scores over 700: 1%; SAT math scores over 700: 1%.

Faculty *Total:* 59, 61% full-time, 42% with terminal degrees. *Student/faculty ratio:* 16:1.

Majors Accounting; acting; actuarial science; adult and continuing education administration; advertising; aerospace, aeronautical and astronautical engineering; African-American/Black studies; agribusiness; agricultural and extension education; agricultural/biological engineering and bioengineering; agricultural business and management related; agricultural mechanization; agriculture; American studies; animal sciences; animal sciences related; anthropology; applied economics; archeology; architectural engineering; art; art history, criticism and conservation; art teacher education; Asian studies (East); astronomy; atmospheric sciences and meteorology; biochemistry; biological and biomedical sciences related; biological and physical sciences; biology/biological sciences; biology/biotechnology laboratory technician; biomedical/medical engineering; biomedical technology; business administration and management; business/commerce; business/managerial economics; chemical engineering; chemistry; civil engineering; classics and languages, literatures and linguistics; communication and journalism related; communication/speech communication and rhetoric; comparative literature; computer and information sciences; computer engineering; criminal justice/law enforcement administration; economics; electrical, electronic and communications engineering technology; electrical, electronics and communications engineering; elementary education; engineering science; English; environmental/environmental health engineering; film/cinema studies; finance; food science; forestry technology; forest sciences and biology; French; geography; geological and earth sciences/geosciences related; geology/earth science; German; graphic design; health/health care administration; history; horticultural science; hospitality administration related; human development and family studies; human nutrition; industrial engineering; information science/studies; international business/trade/commerce; international relations and affairs; Italian; Japanese; Jewish/Judaic studies; journalism; kinesiology and exercise science; labor and industrial relations; landscape architecture; landscaping and groundskeeping; Latin American studies; liberal arts and sciences/liberal studies; logistics and materials management; management information systems; management sciences and quantitative methods related; marketing/marketing management; materials science; mathematics; mechanical engineering; medical microbiology and bacteriology; medieval and Renaissance studies; mining and mineral engineering; natural resources and conservation related; natural resources/conservation; nuclear engineering; nursing (registered nurse training); organizational behavior; parks,

The Pennsylvania State University Beaver Campus of the Commonwealth College (continued)

recreation and leisure facilities management; petroleum engineering; philosophy; physics; political science and government; pre-medical studies; psychology; rehabilitation and therapeutic professions related; religious studies; Russian; secondary education; sociology; soil science and agronomy; Spanish; special education; statistics; telecommunications technology; theatre design and technology; turf and turfgrass management; visual and performing arts; women's studies.

Academic Programs *Special study options:* academic remediation for entering students, accelerated degree program, adult/continuing education programs, advanced placement credit, distance learning, double majors, English as a second language, honors programs, independent study, internships, services for LD students, summer session for credit.

Library 39,861 titles, 222 serial subscriptions, 6,683 audiovisual materials.

Computers on Campus 106 computers available on campus for general student use. A campuswide network can be accessed from student residence rooms and from off campus. Internet access, online (class) registration, at least one staffed computer lab available. Computer purchase or lease plan available.

Student Life *Housing options:* coed. Campus housing is university owned. Freshman campus housing is guaranteed. *Activities and organizations:* drama/theater group, student-run newspaper, radio station. *Campus security:* 24-hour patrols, controlled dormitory access.

Athletics Member NJCAA. *Intercollegiate sports:* baseball M, basketball M, golf M, softball W, volleyball W. *Intramural sports:* basketball M/W, cheerleading M(c)/W(c), cross-country running M/W, football M, golf M/W, soccer M/W, softball M/W, table tennis M/W.

Standardized Tests *Required:* SAT I or ACT (for admission).

Costs (2003–04) *Tuition:* state resident $8620 full-time, $348 per credit part-time; nonresident $13,250 full-time, $552 per credit part-time. *Required fees:* $408 full-time. *Room and board:* $5940; room only: $3080. *Waivers:* senior citizens.

Financial Aid Of all full-time matriculated undergraduates who enrolled in 2001, 38 Federal Work-Study jobs (averaging $1098).

Applying *Options:* electronic application, early admission, deferred entrance. *Application fee:* $50. *Required:* high school transcript. *Application deadline:* rolling (freshmen), rolling (transfers). *Notification:* continuous (freshmen), continuous (transfers).

Admissions Contact The Pennsylvania State University Beaver Campus of the Commonwealth College, 100 University Drive, Suite 113, Monaca, PA 15061-2799. *Phone:* 814-865-5471. *Toll-free phone:* 877-564-6778. *Fax:* 724-773-3658. *E-mail:* br-admissions@psu.edu.

The Pennsylvania State University Berks Campus of the Berks–Lehigh Valley College

Reading, Pennsylvania

- **State-related** 4-year, founded 1924, part of Pennsylvania State University
- **Calendar** semesters
- **Degrees** associate and bachelor's
- **Suburban** 240-acre campus with easy access to Philadelphia
- **Coed,** 2,394 undergraduate students, 88% full-time, 39% women, 61% men
- **Moderately difficult** entrance level, 74% of applicants were admitted

Undergraduates 2,103 full-time, 291 part-time. 8% are from out of state, 6% African American, 4% Asian American or Pacific Islander, 3% Hispanic American, 0.1% Native American, 0.5% international, 3% transferred in, 34% live on campus. *Retention:* 84% of 2001 full-time freshmen returned.

Freshmen *Admission:* 2,529 applied, 1,859 admitted, 779 enrolled. *Average high school GPA:* 2.85. *Test scores:* SAT verbal scores over 500: 52%; SAT math scores over 500: 57%; SAT verbal scores over 600: 10%; SAT math scores over 600: 16%; SAT verbal scores over 700: 1%; SAT math scores over 700: 1%.

Faculty *Total:* 180, 53% full-time, 41% with terminal degrees. *Student/faculty ratio:* 18:1.

Majors Accounting; acting; actuarial science; adult and continuing education administration; advertising; aerospace, aeronautical and astronautical engineering; African-American/Black studies; agribusiness; agricultural and extension education; agricultural/biological engineering and bioengineering; agricultural business and management related; agricultural mechanization; agriculture; American studies; animal sciences; animal sciences related; anthropology; applied economics; archeology; architectural engineering; art; art history, criticism and conservation; art teacher education; Asian studies (East); astronomy; atmospheric sciences and meteorology; biochemistry; biological and biomedical sciences related; biological and physical sciences; biology/biological sciences; biology/biotechnology laboratory technician; biomedical/medical engineering; biomedical technology; business/commerce; business/managerial economics; chemical engineering; chemistry; civil engineering; classics and languages, literatures and linguistics; communication and journalism related; communication disorders; communication/speech communication and rhetoric; comparative literature; computer and information sciences; computer engineering; criminal justice/law enforcement administration; economics; electrical, electronic and communications engineering technology; electrical, electronics and communications engineering; elementary education; engineering science; English; environmental/environmental health engineering; film/cinema studies; finance; food science; foreign languages and literatures; forestry technology; forest sciences and biology; French; geography; geological and earth sciences/geosciences related; geology/earth science; German; graphic design; health/health care administration; history; horticultural science; hospitality administration related; human development and family studies; human nutrition; industrial engineering; information science/studies; international business/trade/commerce; international relations and affairs; Italian; Japanese; Jewish/Judaic studies; journalism; kinesiology and exercise science; labor and industrial relations; landscape architecture; landscaping and groundskeeping; Latin American studies; liberal arts and sciences/liberal studies; logistics and materials management; management information systems; management sciences and quantitative methods related; marketing/marketing management; materials science; mathematics; mechanical engineering; mechanical engineering/mechanical technology; medical microbiology and bacteriology; medieval and Renaissance studies; metallurgical technology; mining and mineral engineering; natural resources and conservation related; natural resources/conservation; nuclear engineering; nursing (registered nurse training); occupational therapist assistant; organizational behavior; parks, recreation and leisure facilities management; petroleum engineering; philosophy; physics; political science and government; pre-medical studies; psychology; rehabilitation and therapeutic professions related; religious studies; Russian; secondary education; sociology; soil science and agronomy; Spanish; special education; statistics; technical and business writing; telecommunications technology; theatre design and technology; turf and turfgrass management; visual and performing arts; women's studies.

Academic Programs *Special study options:* academic remediation for entering students, accelerated degree program, adult/continuing education programs, advanced placement credit, distance learning, honors programs, independent study, internships, services for LD students, study abroad, summer session for credit.

Library 49,520 titles, 460 serial subscriptions, 2,336 audiovisual materials.

Computers on Campus 156 computers available on campus for general student use. A campuswide network can be accessed from student residence rooms and from off campus. Internet access, online (class) registration, at least one staffed computer lab available. Computer purchase or lease plan available.

Student Life *Housing options:* coed, disabled students. Campus housing is university owned. Freshman campus housing is guaranteed. *Activities and organizations:* drama/theater group, student-run newspaper, radio station, choral group. *Campus security:* 24-hour emergency response devices and patrols, controlled dormitory access.

Athletics Member NJCAA. *Intercollegiate sports:* baseball M, basketball M/W, bowling M(c)/W(c), cheerleading M/W, cross-country running M/W, golf M, ice hockey M(c)/W(c), soccer M, softball W, tennis M/W, volleyball M(c)/W. *Intramural sports:* badminton M/W, basketball M/W, football M/W, golf M/W, soccer M/W, volleyball M/W.

Standardized Tests *Required:* SAT I or ACT (for admission).

Costs (2003–04) *Tuition:* state resident $8896 full-time, $371 per credit part-time; nonresident $13,716 full-time, $572 per credit part-time. Full-time tuition and fees vary according to course level, location, program, and student level. Part-time tuition and fees vary according to course level, course load, location, program, and student level. *Required fees:* $408 full-time. *Room and board:* $6490; room only: $3630. Room and board charges vary according to board plan and housing facility. *Payment plan:* deferred payment. *Waivers:* senior citizens and employees or children of employees.

Financial Aid Of all full-time matriculated undergraduates who enrolled in 2002, 1,564 applied for aid, 1,142 were judged to have need, 97 had their need fully met. 74 Federal Work-Study jobs (averaging $1194). 29 state and other part-time jobs (averaging $2934). In 2002, 120 non-need-based awards were made. *Average percent of need met:* 69%. *Average financial aid package:* $9497. *Average need-based loan:* $3196. *Average need-based gift aid:* $4106. *Average non-need-based aid:* $4052. *Average indebtedness upon graduation:* $18,200.

Applying *Options:* electronic application, early admission, deferred entrance. *Application fee:* $50. *Required:* high school transcript. *Application deadline:* rolling (freshmen), rolling (transfers). *Notification:* continuous (freshmen), continuous (transfers).

Admissions Contact The Pennsylvania State University Berks Campus of the Berks–Lehigh Valley College, Tulpehocken Road, PO Box 7009, Reading, PA 19610-6009. *Phone:* 814-865-5471. *Fax:* 610-396-6077. *E-mail:* admissionsbk@psu.edu.

THE PENNSYLVANIA STATE UNIVERSITY DELAWARE COUNTY CAMPUS OF THE COMMONWEALTH COLLEGE

Media, Pennsylvania

- **State-related** primarily 2-year, founded 1966, part of Pennsylvania State University
- **Calendar** semesters
- **Degrees** associate and bachelor's (also offers up to 2 years of most bachelor's degree programs offered at University Park campus)
- **Small-town** 87-acre campus with easy access to Philadelphia
- **Coed,** 1,733 undergraduate students, 83% full-time, 44% women, 56% men
- **Moderately difficult** entrance level, 78% of applicants were admitted

Undergraduates 1,439 full-time, 294 part-time. 4% are from out of state, 13% African American, 9% Asian American or Pacific Islander, 2% Hispanic American, 0.1% Native American, 0.7% international, 3% transferred in. *Retention:* 72% of 2001 full-time freshmen returned.

Freshmen *Admission:* 1,573 applied, 1,221 admitted, 465 enrolled. *Average high school GPA:* 2.87. *Test scores:* SAT verbal scores over 500: 31%; SAT math scores over 500: 37%; SAT verbal scores over 600: 7%; SAT math scores over 600: 10%; SAT verbal scores over 700: 1%; SAT math scores over 700: 2%.

Faculty *Total:* 132, 52% full-time, 42% with terminal degrees. *Student/faculty ratio:* 17:1.

Majors Accounting; acting; actuarial science; adult and continuing education administration; advertising; aerospace, aeronautical and astronautical engineering; African-American/Black studies; agribusiness; agricultural and extension education; agricultural/biological engineering and bioengineering; agricultural business and management related; agricultural mechanization; agriculture; American studies; animal sciences; animal sciences related; anthropology; applied economics; archeology; architectural engineering; art; art history, criticism and conservation; art teacher education; Asian studies (East); astronomy; atmospheric sciences and meteorology; biochemistry; biological and biomedical sciences related; biological and physical sciences; biology/biological sciences; biology/biotechnology laboratory technician; biomedical/medical engineering; business administration and management; business/commerce; business/managerial economics; chemical engineering; chemistry; civil engineering; classics and languages, literatures and linguistics; communication and journalism related; communication disorders; communication/speech communication and rhetoric; comparative literature; computer and information sciences; computer engineering; criminal justice/law enforcement administration; economics; electrical, electronics and communications engineering; elementary education; engineering science; English; environmental/environmental health engineering; film/cinema studies; finance; food science; forestry technology; forest sciences and biology; French; geography; geological and earth sciences/geosciences related; geology/earth science; German; graphic design; health/health care administration; history; horticultural science; hospitality administration related; human development and family studies; human nutrition; industrial engineering; information science/studies; international business/trade/commerce; international relations and affairs; Italian; Japanese; Jewish/Judaic studies; journalism; kinesiology and exercise science; labor and industrial relations; landscape architecture; landscaping and groundskeeping; Latin American studies; liberal arts and sciences/liberal studies; logistics and materials management; management information systems; management sciences and quantitative methods related; marketing/marketing management; materials science; mathematics; mechanical engineering; medical microbiology and bacteriology; medieval and Renaissance studies; mining and mineral engineering; natural resources and conservation related; natural resources/conservation; nuclear engineering; nursing (registered nurse training); organizational behavior; parks, recreation and leisure facilities management; petroleum engineering; philosophy; physics; political science and government; pre-medical studies; psychology; rehabilitation and therapeutic professions related; religious studies; Russian; secondary education; sociology; soil science and agronomy; Spanish; special education; statistics; theatre design and technology; turf and turfgrass management; visual and performing arts; women's studies.

Academic Programs *Special study options:* academic remediation for entering students, accelerated degree program, adult/continuing education programs, advanced placement credit, distance learning, double majors, English as a second language, honors programs, independent study, internships, services for LD students, student-designed majors, study abroad, summer session for credit. *ROTC:* Army (c).

Library 59,930 titles, 457 serial subscriptions, 3,987 audiovisual materials.

Computers on Campus 180 computers available on campus for general student use. A campuswide network can be accessed from off campus. Internet access, online (class) registration, at least one staffed computer lab available. Computer purchase or lease plan available.

Student Life *Housing:* college housing not available. *Activities and organizations:* drama/theater group, student-run newspaper. *Campus security:* late-night transport/escort service, part-time trained security personnel.

Athletics Member NJCAA. *Intercollegiate sports:* baseball M, basketball M/W, lacrosse M(c)/W(c), soccer M/W, tennis M/W, volleyball W. *Intramural sports:* basketball M/W, cheerleading M(c)/W(c), golf M/W, ice hockey M(c)/W(c), lacrosse M/W, soccer M/W, softball W(c), tennis M/W, volleyball M(c)/W.

Standardized Tests *Required:* SAT I or ACT (for admission).

Costs (2003–04) *Tuition:* state resident $8620 full-time, $348 per credit part-time; nonresident $13,250 full-time, $552 per credit part-time. *Required fees:* $398 full-time.

Financial Aid Of all full-time matriculated undergraduates who enrolled in 2001, 28 Federal Work-Study jobs (averaging $615).

Applying *Options:* electronic application, early admission, deferred entrance. *Application fee:* $50. *Application deadline:* rolling (freshmen), rolling (transfers). *Notification:* continuous (freshmen), continuous (transfers).

Admissions Contact The Pennsylvania State University Delaware County Campus of the Commonwealth College, 25 Yearsley Mill Road, Media, PA 19063-5596. *Phone:* 814-865-5471. *Fax:* 610-892-1357. *E-mail:* admissions-delco@psu.edu.

THE PENNSYLVANIA STATE UNIVERSITY DUBOIS CAMPUS OF THE COMMONWEALTH COLLEGE

DuBois, Pennsylvania

- **State-related** primarily 2-year, founded 1935, part of Pennsylvania State University
- **Calendar** semesters
- **Degrees** associate and bachelor's (also offers up to 2 years of most bachelor's degree programs offered at University Park campus)
- **Small-town** 20-acre campus
- **Coed,** 919 undergraduate students, 75% full-time, 51% women, 49% men
- **Moderately difficult** entrance level, 92% of applicants were admitted

Undergraduates 688 full-time, 231 part-time. 1% are from out of state, 0.8% African American, 0.9% Asian American or Pacific Islander, 0.4% Hispanic American, 0.3% Native American, 3% transferred in. *Retention:* 75% of 2001 full-time freshmen returned.

Freshmen *Admission:* 417 applied, 385 admitted, 216 enrolled. *Average high school GPA:* 2.87. *Test scores:* SAT verbal scores over 500: 48%; SAT math scores over 500: 50%; SAT verbal scores over 600: 9%; SAT math scores over 600: 12%.

Faculty *Total:* 90, 52% full-time, 39% with terminal degrees. *Student/faculty ratio:* 13:1.

Majors Accounting; acting; actuarial science; adult and continuing education administration; advertising; aerospace, aeronautical and astronautical engineering; African-American/Black studies; agribusiness; agricultural and extension education; agricultural/biological engineering and bioengineering; agricultural business and management related; agricultural mechanization; agriculture; American studies; animal sciences; animal sciences related; anthropology; applied economics; archeology; architectural engineering; art; art history, criticism and conservation; art teacher education; Asian studies (East); astronomy; atmospheric sciences and meteorology; biochemistry; biological and biomedical sciences related; biological and physical sciences; biology/biological sciences; biology/biotechnology laboratory technician; biomedical/medical engineering; biomedical technology; business administration and management; business/commerce; business/managerial economics; chemical engineering; chemistry; civil engineering; classics and languages, literatures and linguistics; clinical/medical laboratory technology; communication and journalism related; communication disorders; communication/speech communication and rhetoric; comparative literature; computer and information sciences; computer engineering; criminal justice/law enforcement administration; economics; electrical, electronic and communications engineering technology; electrical, electronics and communications engineering; elementary education; engineering science; English; environmental/environmental health engineering; film/cinema studies; finance; food science; forestry technology; forest sciences and biology; French; geography; geological and earth sciences/geosciences related; geology/earth science; German; graphic design; health/health care administration; history; horticultural science; hospitality administration related; human development and family studies; human nutrition; industrial engineering; information science/studies; international business/trade/commerce; international relations and affairs; Italian; Japanese; Jewish/Judaic studies; journalism; kinesiology and exercise science; labor and industrial relations; landscape architecture; landscaping and groundskeeping; Latin American studies; liberal arts and sciences/liberal studies; logistics and materials management; management information systems; management sciences and quantitative

The Pennsylvania State University DuBois Campus of the Commonwealth College (continued)

methods related; marketing/marketing management; materials science; mathematics; mechanical engineering; mechanical engineering/mechanical technology; medical microbiology and bacteriology; medieval and Renaissance studies; metallurgical technology; mining and mineral engineering; natural resources and conservation related; natural resources/conservation; nuclear engineering; nursing (registered nurse training); occupational therapist assistant; organizational behavior; parks, recreation and leisure facilities management; petroleum engineering; philosophy; physical therapist assistant; physics; political science and government; pre-medical studies; psychology; rehabilitation and therapeutic professions related; religious studies; Russian; secondary education; sociology; soil science and agronomy; Spanish; special education; statistics; telecommunications technology; theatre design and technology; turf and turfgrass management; visual and performing arts; wildlife and wildlands science and management; women's studies.

Academic Programs *Special study options:* academic remediation for entering students, accelerated degree program, adult/continuing education programs, advanced placement credit, distance learning, double majors, honors programs, independent study, internships, services for LD students, student-designed majors, summer session for credit.

Library 43,710 titles, 224 serial subscriptions, 1,091 audiovisual materials.

Computers on Campus 126 computers available on campus for general student use. A campuswide network can be accessed from off campus. Internet access, online (class) registration, at least one staffed computer lab available. Computer purchase or lease plan available.

Student Life *Housing:* college housing not available. *Activities and organizations:* student-run newspaper, choral group.

Athletics Member NJCAA. *Intercollegiate sports:* basketball M, cross-country running M/W, golf M/W, volleyball W. *Intramural sports:* basketball M/W, football M, soccer M/W, table tennis M/W, volleyball M/W.

Standardized Tests *Required:* SAT I or ACT (for admission).

Costs (2003–04) *Tuition:* state resident $8620 full-time, $348 per credit part-time; nonresident $13,250 full-time, $552 per credit part-time. *Required fees:* $388 full-time.

Financial Aid Of all full-time matriculated undergraduates who enrolled in 2001, 79 Federal Work-Study jobs (averaging $1252).

Applying *Options:* electronic application, early admission, deferred entrance. *Application fee:* $50. *Required:* high school transcript. *Application deadline:* rolling (freshmen), rolling (transfers). *Notification:* continuous (freshmen), continuous (transfers).

Admissions Contact The Pennsylvania State University DuBois Campus of the Commonwealth College, 101 Hiller Building, College Place, DuBois, PA 15801-3199. *Phone:* 814-865-5471. *Toll-free phone:* 800-346-7627. *Fax:* 814-375-4784. *E-mail:* ds-admissions@psu.edu.

THE PENNSYLVANIA STATE UNIVERSITY FAYETTE CAMPUS OF THE COMMONWEALTH COLLEGE

Uniontown, Pennsylvania

- **State-related** primarily 2-year, founded 1934, part of Pennsylvania State University
- **Calendar** semesters
- **Degrees** associate and bachelor's (also offers up to 2 years of most bachelor's degree programs offered at University Park campus)
- **Small-town** 92-acre campus
- **Coed,** 1,156 undergraduate students, 75% full-time, 62% women, 38% men
- **Moderately difficult** entrance level, 87% of applicants were admitted

Undergraduates 869 full-time, 287 part-time. 1% are from out of state, 5% African American, 0.8% Asian American or Pacific Islander, 0.5% Hispanic American, 4% transferred in. *Retention:* 67% of 2001 full-time freshmen returned.

Freshmen *Admission:* 398 applied, 347 admitted, 212 enrolled. *Average high school GPA:* 2.87. *Test scores:* SAT verbal scores over 500: 33%; SAT math scores over 500: 39%; SAT verbal scores over 600: 2%; SAT math scores over 600: 5%; SAT verbal scores over 700: 2%; SAT math scores over 700: 1%.

Faculty *Total:* 88, 60% full-time, 39% with terminal degrees. *Student/faculty ratio:* 15:1.

Majors Accounting; acting; actuarial science; adult and continuing education administration; advertising; aerospace, aeronautical and astronautical engineering; African-American/Black studies; agribusiness; agricultural and extension education; agricultural/biological engineering and bioengineering; agricultural business and management related; agricultural mechanization; agriculture; American studies; animal sciences; animal sciences related; anthropology; applied economics; archeology; architectural engineering; architectural engineering technology; art; art history, criticism and conservation; art teacher education; Asian studies (East); astronomy; atmospheric sciences and meteorology; biochemistry; biological and biomedical sciences related; biological and physical sciences; biology/biological sciences; biology/biotechnology laboratory technician; biomedical/medical engineering; biomedical technology; business administration and management; business/commerce; business/managerial economics; chemical engineering; chemistry; civil engineering; classics and languages, literatures and linguistics; communication and journalism related; communication disorders; communication/speech communication and rhetoric; comparative literature; computer and information sciences; computer engineering; criminal justice/law enforcement administration; criminal justice/safety; economics; electrical, electronic and communications engineering technology; electrical, electronics and communications engineering; elementary education; engineering science; English; environmental/environmental health engineering; film/cinema studies; finance; food science; forestry technology; forest sciences and biology; French; geography; geological and earth sciences/geosciences related; geology/earth science; German; graphic design; health/health care administration; history; horticultural science; hospitality administration related; human development and family studies; human nutrition; industrial engineering; information science/studies; international business/trade/commerce; international relations and affairs; Italian; Japanese; Jewish/Judaic studies; journalism; kinesiology and exercise science; labor and industrial relations; landscape architecture; landscaping and groundskeeping; Latin American studies; liberal arts and sciences/liberal studies; logistics and materials management; management information systems; management sciences and quantitative methods related; manufacturing engineering; marketing/marketing management; materials science; mathematics; mechanical engineering; medical microbiology and bacteriology; medieval and Renaissance studies; metallurgical technology; mining and mineral engineering; natural resources and conservation related; natural resources/conservation; nuclear engineering; nursing (registered nurse training); organizational behavior; parks, recreation and leisure facilities management; petroleum engineering; philosophy; physics; political science and government; pre-medical studies; psychology; rehabilitation and therapeutic professions related; religious studies; Russian; secondary education; sociology; soil science and agronomy; Spanish; special education; statistics; telecommunications technology; theatre design and technology; turf and turfgrass management; visual and performing arts; women's studies.

Academic Programs *Special study options:* academic remediation for entering students, accelerated degree program, adult/continuing education programs, advanced placement credit, distance learning, double majors, honors programs, independent study, internships, services for LD students, student-designed majors, summer session for credit.

Library 54,610 titles, 187 serial subscriptions, 6,721 audiovisual materials.

Computers on Campus 103 computers available on campus for general student use. A campuswide network can be accessed from off campus. Internet access, online (class) registration, at least one staffed computer lab available. Computer purchase or lease plan available.

Student Life *Housing:* college housing not available. *Activities and organizations:* drama/theater group, student-run newspaper. *Campus security:* student patrols, 8-hour patrols by trained security personnel.

Athletics Member NJCAA. *Intercollegiate sports:* baseball M, basketball M, softball W, volleyball W. *Intramural sports:* badminton M/W, basketball M/W, cheerleading M(c)/W(c), equestrian sports M(c)/W(c), football M/W, golf M(c)/W(c), softball M/W, tennis M/W, volleyball M/W, weight lifting M/W.

Standardized Tests *Required:* SAT I or ACT (for admission).

Costs (2003–04) *Tuition:* state resident $8620 full-time, $348 per credit part-time; nonresident $13,250 full-time, $552 per credit part-time. *Required fees:* $388 full-time.

Financial Aid Of all full-time matriculated undergraduates who enrolled in 2001, 63 Federal Work-Study jobs (averaging $1017).

Applying *Options:* electronic application, early admission, deferred entrance. *Application fee:* $50. *Required:* high school transcript. *Application deadline:* rolling (freshmen), rolling (transfers). *Notification:* continuous (freshmen), continuous (transfers).

Admissions Contact The Pennsylvania State University Fayette Campus of the Commonwealth College, PO Box 519, Route 119 North, 108 Williams Building, Uniontown, PA 15401-0519. *Phone:* 814-865-5471. *Toll-free phone:* 877-568-4130. *Fax:* 724-430-4175. *E-mail:* feadm@psu.edu.

THE PENNSYLVANIA STATE UNIVERSITY HARRISBURG CAMPUS OF THE CAPITAL COLLEGE

Middletown, Pennsylvania

- **State-related** comprehensive, founded 1966, part of Pennsylvania State University
- **Calendar** semesters
- **Degrees** associate, bachelor's, master's, doctoral, and postbachelor's certificates
- **Small-town** 218-acre campus
- **Coed,** 1,746 undergraduate students, 72% full-time, 46% women, 54% men
- **Moderately difficult** entrance level, 43% of applicants were admitted

Penn State Harrisburg, Capital College, is an undergraduate college and graduate school of The Pennsylvania State University, one of the largest and most widely recognized institutions in the nation. At the undergraduate level, the College offers two associate and twenty-seven baccalaureate degrees, as well as the first two years of study leading to more than 160 undergraduate majors available throughout the Penn State system. The College features all the resources of a major research university in a smaller setting in the capital region of the state. For more information, students can visit the Web site at http://www.hbg.psu.edu and can apply online.

Undergraduates 1,256 full-time, 490 part-time. 4% are from out of state, 5% African American, 5% Asian American or Pacific Islander, 2% Hispanic American, 0.1% Native American, 0.7% international, 13% transferred in, 17% live on campus. *Retention:* 89% of 2001 full-time freshmen returned.

Freshmen *Admission:* 268 applied, 116 admitted, 57 enrolled. *Average high school GPA:* 3.01. *Test scores:* SAT verbal scores over 500: 51%; SAT math scores over 500: 81%; SAT verbal scores over 600: 13%; SAT math scores over 600: 34%; SAT math scores over 700: 4%.

Faculty *Total:* 258, 62% full-time, 63% with terminal degrees. *Student/faculty ratio:* 11:1.

Majors American studies; applied mathematics; business administration and management; business/commerce; communication/speech communication and rhetoric; computer and information sciences; criminal justice/safety; electrical, electronics and communications engineering; elementary education; English; English/language arts teacher education; environmental/environmental health engineering; finance; health/health care administration; humanities; information science/studies; international business/trade/commerce; liberal arts and sciences/liberal studies; management information systems; marketing/marketing management; mechanical engineering; nursing (registered nurse training); organizational behavior; psychology; public policy analysis; social studies teacher education; sociology; structural engineering.

Academic Programs *Special study options:* academic remediation for entering students, accelerated degree program, adult/continuing education programs, advanced placement credit, cooperative education, distance learning, double majors, honors programs, independent study, internships, part-time degree program, services for LD students, study abroad, summer session for credit. *ROTC:* Army (b).

Library 285,171 titles, 1,903 serial subscriptions, 5,144 audiovisual materials.

Computers on Campus 132 computers available on campus for general student use. A campuswide network can be accessed from student residence rooms and from off campus. Internet access, online (class) registration, at least one staffed computer lab available. Computer purchase or lease plan available.

Student Life *Housing options:* Campus housing is university owned. Freshman campus housing is guaranteed. *Activities and organizations:* drama/theater group, student-run newspaper, radio station, choral group. *Campus security:* 24-hour patrols, student patrols, late-night transport/escort service.

Athletics *Intercollegiate sports:* volleyball M(c)/W(c). *Intramural sports:* basketball M/W, bowling M/W, football M, racquetball M/W, skiing (downhill) M(c)/W(c), softball M/W, table tennis M/W, volleyball M/W.

Standardized Tests *Required:* SAT I or ACT (for admission).

Costs (2003–04) *Tuition:* state resident $8896 full-time, $371 per credit part-time; nonresident $15,466 full-time, $644 per credit part-time. Full-time tuition and fees vary according to course level, location, program, and student level. Part-time tuition and fees vary according to course level, course load, location, program, and student level. *Required fees:* $388 full-time, $65 per term part-time. *Room and board:* $7290; room only: $4430. Room and board charges vary according to board plan and housing facility. *Payment plan:* deferred payment. *Waivers:* senior citizens and employees or children of employees.

Financial Aid Of all full-time matriculated undergraduates who enrolled in 2002, 840 applied for aid, 706 were judged to have need, 89 had their need fully met. 58 Federal Work-Study jobs (averaging $1341). 4 state and other part-time jobs (averaging $2700). In 2002, 46 non-need-based awards were made. *Average percent of need met:* 75%. *Average financial aid package:* $11,610. *Average need-based loan:* $4755. *Average need-based gift aid:* $4270. *Average non-need-based aid:* $3859. *Average indebtedness upon graduation:* $18,200.

Applying *Options:* electronic application, early admission, deferred entrance. *Application fee:* $50. *Required:* high school transcript. *Application deadline:* rolling (freshmen), rolling (transfers). *Notification:* continuous (freshmen), continuous (transfers).

Admissions Contact The Pennsylvania State University Harrisburg Campus of the Capital College, Swatapa Building, 777 West Harrisburg Pike, Middletown, PA 17057-4898. *Phone:* 814-865-5471. *Toll-free phone:* 800-222-2056. *Fax:* 717-948-6325. *E-mail:* hbgadmit@psu.edu.

THE PENNSYLVANIA STATE UNIVERSITY HAZLETON CAMPUS OF THE COMMONWEALTH COLLEGE

Hazleton, Pennsylvania

- **State-related** primarily 2-year, founded 1934, part of Pennsylvania State University
- **Calendar** semesters
- **Degrees** associate and bachelor's (also offers up to 2 years of most bachelor's degree programs offered at University Park campus)
- **Small-town** 98-acre campus
- **Coed,** 1,214 undergraduate students, 94% full-time, 40% women, 60% men
- **Moderately difficult** entrance level, 91% of applicants were admitted

Undergraduates 1,141 full-time, 73 part-time. 21% are from out of state, 6% African American, 4% Asian American or Pacific Islander, 4% Hispanic American, 0.2% Native American, 0.3% international, 2% transferred in, 37% live on campus. *Retention:* 80% of 2001 full-time freshmen returned.

Freshmen *Admission:* 1,243 applied, 1,125 admitted, 506 enrolled. *Average high school GPA:* 2.87. *Test scores:* SAT verbal scores over 500: 47%; SAT math scores over 500: 49%; SAT verbal scores over 600: 9%; SAT math scores over 600: 15%; SAT math scores over 700: 1%.

Faculty *Total:* 96, 60% full-time, 42% with terminal degrees. *Student/faculty ratio:* 17:1.

Majors Accounting; acting; actuarial science; adult and continuing education administration; advertising; aerospace, aeronautical and astronautical engineering; African-American/Black studies; agribusiness; agricultural and extension education; agricultural/biological engineering and bioengineering; agricultural business and management related; agricultural mechanization; agriculture; American studies; animal sciences; animal sciences related; anthropology; applied economics; archeology; architectural engineering; art; art history, criticism and conservation; art teacher education; Asian studies (East); astronomy; atmospheric sciences and meteorology; biochemistry; biological and biomedical sciences related; biological and physical sciences; biology/biological sciences; biology/biotechnology laboratory technician; biomedical/medical engineering; biomedical technology; business administration and management; business/commerce; business/managerial economics; chemical engineering; chemistry; civil engineering; classics and languages, literatures and linguistics; clinical/medical laboratory technology; communication and journalism related; communication disorders; communication/speech communication and rhetoric; comparative literature; computer and information sciences; computer engineering; criminal justice/law enforcement administration; economics; electrical, electronic and communications engineering technology; electrical, electronics and communications engineering; elementary education; engineering science; English; environmental/environmental health engineering; film/cinema studies; finance; food science; forestry technology; forest sciences and biology; French; geography; geological and earth sciences/geosciences related; geology/earth science; German; graphic design; health/health care administration; history; horticultural science; hospitality administration related; human development and family studies; human nutrition; industrial engineering; information science/studies; international business/trade/commerce; international relations and affairs; Italian; Japanese; Jewish/Judaic studies; journalism; kinesiology and exercise science; labor and industrial relations; landscape architecture; landscaping and groundskeeping; Latin American studies; liberal arts and sciences/liberal studies; logistics and materials management; management information systems; management sciences and quantitative methods related; manufacturing engineering; marketing/marketing management; materials science; mathematics; mechanical engineering; mechanical engineering/mechanical technology; medical microbiology and bacteriology; medieval and Renaissance studies; metallurgical technology; mining and mineral engineering; natural resources and conservation related; natural resources/conservation; nuclear engineering; nursing (registered nurse training); organizational behavior; parks, recreation and leisure facilities management; petroleum engineering; philosophy; physical therapist assistant; physics; political science and government; premedical studies; psychology; rehabilitation and therapeutic professions related;

The Pennsylvania State University Hazleton Campus of the Commonwealth College (continued)

religious studies; Russian; secondary education; sociology; soil science and agronomy; Spanish; special education; statistics; telecommunications technology; theatre design and technology; turf and turfgrass management; visual and performing arts; women's studies.

Academic Programs *Special study options:* academic remediation for entering students, accelerated degree program, adult/continuing education programs, advanced placement credit, distance learning, double majors, honors programs, independent study, internships, services for LD students, summer session for credit. *ROTC:* Army (b).

Library 83,266 titles, 996 serial subscriptions, 6,771 audiovisual materials.

Computers on Campus 131 computers available on campus for general student use. A campuswide network can be accessed from student residence rooms and from off campus. Internet access, online (class) registration, at least one staffed computer lab available. Computer purchase or lease plan available.

Student Life *Housing options:* coed. Campus housing is university owned. Freshman campus housing is guaranteed. *Activities and organizations:* drama/theater group, student-run newspaper, radio station, choral group. *Campus security:* 24-hour patrols, late-night transport/escort service, controlled dormitory access.

Athletics Member NJCAA. *Intercollegiate sports:* baseball M, basketball M/W, cheerleading M/W, soccer M, softball W, tennis M/W, volleyball M(c)/W. *Intramural sports:* basketball M/W, skiing (downhill) M(c)/W(c), soccer M/W, volleyball M/W.

Standardized Tests *Required:* SAT I or ACT (for admission).

Costs (2003–04) *Tuition:* state resident $8620 full-time, $348 per credit part-time; nonresident $13,250 full-time, $552 per credit part-time. *Required fees:* $398 full-time. *Room and board:* $5940; room only: $3080.

Financial Aid Of all full-time matriculated undergraduates who enrolled in 2001, 111 Federal Work-Study jobs (averaging $1151).

Applying *Options:* electronic application, early admission, deferred entrance. *Application fee:* $50. *Required:* high school transcript. *Application deadline:* rolling (freshmen), rolling (transfers). *Notification:* continuous (freshmen), continuous (transfers).

Admissions Contact The Pennsylvania State University Hazleton Campus of the Commonwealth College, 110 Administration Building, 76 University Drive, Hazleton, PA 18202. *Phone:* 814-865-5471. *Toll-free phone:* 800-279-8495. *Fax:* 570-450-3182. *E-mail:* admissions-hn@psu.edu.

The Pennsylvania State University, Lehigh Valley Campus of the Berks-Lehigh Valley College

Fogelsville, Pennsylvania

- **State-related** 4-year, founded 1912, part of Pennsylvania State University
- **Calendar** semesters
- **Degrees** associate and bachelor's
- **Small-town** 42-acre campus
- **Coed,** 720 undergraduate students, 79% full-time, 36% women, 64% men
- **Moderately difficult** entrance level, 82% of applicants were admitted

Undergraduates 569 full-time, 151 part-time. 3% are from out of state, 2% African American, 7% Asian American or Pacific Islander, 6% Hispanic American, 0.6% international, 7% transferred in. *Retention:* 82% of 2001 full-time freshmen returned.

Freshmen *Admission:* 809 applied, 666 admitted, 193 enrolled. *Average high school GPA:* 2.85. *Test scores:* SAT verbal scores over 500: 51%; SAT math scores over 500: 53%; SAT verbal scores over 600: 7%; SAT math scores over 600: 21%; SAT verbal scores over 700: 1%; SAT math scores over 700: 2%.

Faculty *Total:* 74, 41% full-time, 39% with terminal degrees. *Student/faculty ratio:* 14:1.

Majors Accounting; acting; actuarial science; adult and continuing education administration; advertising; aerospace, aeronautical and astronautical engineering; African-American/Black studies; agribusiness; agricultural and extension education; agricultural/biological engineering and bioengineering; agricultural business and management related; agricultural mechanization; agriculture; American studies; animal sciences; animal sciences related; anthropology; applied economics; archeology; architectural engineering; art; art history, criticism and conservation; art teacher education; Asian studies (East); astronomy; atmospheric sciences and meteorology; biochemistry; biological and biomedical sciences related; biological and physical sciences; biology/biological sciences; biology/biotechnology laboratory technician; biomedical/medical engineering; business/commerce; business/managerial economics; chemical engineering; chemistry; civil engineering; classics and languages, literatures and linguistics; communication and journalism related; communication disorders; communication/speech communication and rhetoric; comparative literature; computer and information sciences; computer engineering; criminal justice/law enforcement administration; economics; electrical, electronics and communications engineering; elementary education; engineering science; English; environmental/environmental health engineering; film/cinema studies; finance; food science; foreign languages and literatures; forestry technology; forest sciences and biology; French; geography; geological and earth sciences/geosciences related; geology/earth science; German; graphic design; health/health care administration; history; horticultural science; hospitality administration related; human development and family studies; human nutrition; industrial engineering; information science/studies; international business/trade/commerce; international relations and affairs; Italian; Japanese; Jewish/Judaic studies; journalism; kinesiology and exercise science; labor and industrial relations; landscape architecture; landscaping and groundskeeping; Latin American studies; liberal arts and sciences/liberal studies; logistics and materials management; management information systems; management sciences and quantitative methods related; marketing/marketing management; materials science; mathematics; mechanical engineering; medical microbiology and bacteriology; medieval and Renaissance studies; mining and mineral engineering; natural resources and conservation related; natural resources/conservation; nuclear engineering; nursing (registered nurse training); organizational behavior; parks, recreation and leisure facilities management; petroleum engineering; philosophy; physics; political science and government; pre-medical studies; psychology; rehabilitation and therapeutic professions related; religious studies; Russian; secondary education; sociology; soil science and agronomy; Spanish; special education; statistics; technical and business writing; theatre design and technology; turf and turfgrass management; visual and performing arts; women's studies.

Academic Programs *Special study options:* academic remediation for entering students, accelerated degree program, adult/continuing education programs, advanced placement credit, distance learning, honors programs, independent study, internships, services for LD students, study abroad, summer session for credit.

Library 36,641 titles, 152 serial subscriptions, 6,579 audiovisual materials.

Computers on Campus 62 computers available on campus for general student use. A campuswide network can be accessed from off campus. Internet access, online (class) registration, at least one staffed computer lab available. Computer purchase or lease plan available.

Student Life *Housing:* college housing not available. *Activities and organizations:* drama/theater group.

Athletics Member NJCAA. *Intercollegiate sports:* baseball M, basketball M/W, bowling M(c)/W(c), cheerleading M/W, cross-country running M/W, football M(c), golf M(c)/W(c), ice hockey M(c)/W(c), skiing (downhill) M(c)/W(c), soccer M(c)/W, tennis M/W, volleyball M(c)/W. *Intramural sports:* badminton M/W, basketball M/W, football M/W, golf M/W, soccer M/W, volleyball M/W.

Standardized Tests *Required:* SAT I or ACT (for admission).

Costs (2003–04) *Tuition:* state resident $8620 full-time, $348 per credit part-time; nonresident $13,250 full-time, $552 per credit part-time. Full-time tuition and fees vary according to course level, location, program, and student level. Part-time tuition and fees vary according to course level, course load, location, program, and student level. *Required fees:* $408 full-time. *Payment plan:* deferred payment. *Waivers:* senior citizens and employees or children of employees.

Financial Aid Of all full-time matriculated undergraduates who enrolled in 2002, 408 applied for aid, 313 were judged to have need, 36 had their need fully met. 36 Federal Work-Study jobs (averaging $992). In 2002, 32 non-need-based awards were made. *Average percent of need met:* 71%. *Average financial aid package:* $8411. *Average need-based loan:* $3176. *Average need-based gift aid:* $3929. *Average non-need-based aid:* $2314. *Average indebtedness upon graduation:* $18,200.

Applying *Options:* electronic application, early admission, deferred entrance. *Application fee:* $50. *Required:* high school transcript. *Application deadline:* rolling (freshmen), rolling (transfers). *Notification:* continuous (freshmen), continuous (transfers).

Admissions Contact The Pennsylvania State University, Lehigh Valley Campus of the Berks-Lehigh Valley College, 8380 Mohr Lane, Academic Building, Fogelsville, PA 18051-9999. *Phone:* 814-865-5471. *Fax:* 610-285-5220. *E-mail:* admission-lv@psu.edu.

THE PENNSYLVANIA STATE UNIVERSITY MCKEESPORT CAMPUS OF THE COMMONWEALTH COLLEGE

McKeesport, Pennsylvania

- **State-related** primarily 2-year, founded 1947, part of Pennsylvania State University
- **Calendar** semesters
- **Degrees** associate and bachelor's (also offers up to 2 years of most bachelor's degree programs offered at University Park campus)
- **Small-town** 40-acre campus with easy access to Pittsburgh
- **Coed,** 826 undergraduate students, 91% full-time, 38% women, 62% men
- **Moderately difficult** entrance level, 88% of applicants were admitted

Undergraduates 749 full-time, 77 part-time. 8% are from out of state, 14% African American, 3% Asian American or Pacific Islander, 0.9% Hispanic American, 0.3% international, 3% transferred in, 16% live on campus. *Retention:* 79% of 2001 full-time freshmen returned.

Freshmen *Admission:* 578 applied, 510 admitted, 245 enrolled. *Average high school GPA:* 2.92. *Test scores:* SAT verbal scores over 500: 45%; SAT math scores over 500: 47%; SAT verbal scores over 600: 9%; SAT math scores over 600: 15%; SAT verbal scores over 700: 1%; SAT math scores over 700: 3%.

Faculty *Total:* 75, 52% full-time, 40% with terminal degrees. *Student/faculty ratio:* 15:1.

Majors Accounting; acting; actuarial science; adult and continuing education administration; advertising; aerospace, aeronautical and astronautical engineering; African-American/Black studies; agribusiness; agricultural and extension education; agricultural/biological engineering and bioengineering; agricultural business and management related; agricultural mechanization; agriculture; American studies; animal sciences; animal sciences related; anthropology; applied economics; archeology; architectural engineering; art; art history, criticism and conservation; art teacher education; Asian studies (East); astronomy; atmospheric sciences and meteorology; biochemistry; biological and biomedical sciences related; biological and physical sciences; biology/biological sciences; biology/biotechnology laboratory technician; biomedical/medical engineering; business administration and management; business/commerce; business/managerial economics; chemical engineering; chemistry; civil engineering; classics and languages, literatures and linguistics; communication and journalism related; communication disorders; communication/speech communication and rhetoric; comparative literature; computer and information sciences; computer engineering; criminal justice/law enforcement administration; economics; electrical, electronics and communications engineering; elementary education; engineering science; English; environmental/environmental health engineering; film/cinema studies; finance; food science; forestry technology; forest sciences and biology; French; geography; geological and earth sciences/geosciences related; geology/earth science; German; graphic design; health/health care administration; history; horticultural science; hospitality administration related; human development and family studies; human nutrition; industrial engineering; information science/studies; international business/trade/commerce; international relations and affairs; Italian; Japanese; Jewish/Judaic studies; journalism; kinesiology and exercise science; labor and industrial relations; landscape architecture; landscaping and groundskeeping; Latin American studies; liberal arts and sciences/liberal studies; logistics and materials management; management information systems; management sciences and quantitative methods related; marketing/marketing management; materials science; mathematics; mechanical engineering; medical microbiology and bacteriology; medieval and Renaissance studies; mining and mineral engineering; natural resources and conservation related; natural resources/conservation; nuclear engineering; nursing (registered nurse training); organizational behavior; parks, recreation and leisure facilities management; petroleum engineering; philosophy; physics; political science and government; pre-medical studies; psychology; rehabilitation and therapeutic professions related; religious studies; Russian; secondary education; sociology; soil science and agronomy; Spanish; special education; statistics; theatre design and technology; turf and turfgrass management; visual and performing arts; women's studies.

Academic Programs *Special study options:* academic remediation for entering students, accelerated degree program, adult/continuing education programs, advanced placement credit, distance learning, double majors, honors programs, independent study, internships, services for LD students, summer session for credit. *ROTC:* Army (c), Air Force (c).

Library 40,851 titles, 300 serial subscriptions, 2,783 audiovisual materials.

Computers on Campus 167 computers available on campus for general student use. A campuswide network can be accessed from student residence rooms and from off campus. Internet access, online (class) registration, at least one staffed computer lab available. Computer purchase or lease plan available.

Student Life *Housing options:* coed. Campus housing is university owned. Freshman campus housing is guaranteed. *Activities and organizations:* drama/theater group, student-run newspaper, radio station. *Campus security:* 24-hour patrols, controlled dormitory access.

Athletics Member NJCAA. *Intercollegiate sports:* baseball M, basketball M, softball W, volleyball W. *Intramural sports:* basketball M/W, cheerleading M(c)/W(c), football M/W, ice hockey M(c), racquetball M/W, skiing (cross-country) M(c)/W(c), skiing (downhill) M(c)/W(c), soccer M(c)/W(c), softball M/W, tennis M/W, volleyball M/W.

Standardized Tests *Required:* SAT I or ACT (for admission).

Costs (2003–04) *Tuition:* state resident $8620 full-time, $348 per credit part-time; nonresident $13,250 full-time, $552 per credit part-time. *Required fees:* $388 full-time. *Room and board:* $5940; room only: $3080.

Financial Aid Of all full-time matriculated undergraduates who enrolled in 2001, 63 Federal Work-Study jobs (averaging $1017).

Applying *Options:* electronic application, early admission, deferred entrance. *Application fee:* $50. *Required:* high school transcript. *Application deadline:* rolling (freshmen), rolling (transfers). *Notification:* continuous (freshmen), continuous (transfers).

Admissions Contact The Pennsylvania State University McKeesport Campus of the Commonwealth College, 101 Frable Building, 4000 University Drive, McKeesport, PA 15132-7698. *Phone:* 814-865-5471. *Fax:* 412-9056. *E-mail:* psumk@psu.edu.

THE PENNSYLVANIA STATE UNIVERSITY MONT ALTO CAMPUS OF THE COMMONWEALTH COLLEGE

Mont Alto, Pennsylvania

- **State-related** primarily 2-year, founded 1929, part of Pennsylvania State University
- **Calendar** semesters
- **Degrees** associate and bachelor's (also offers up to 2 years of most bachelor's degree programs offered at University Park campus)
- **Small-town** 64-acre campus
- **Coed,** 1,098 undergraduate students, 69% full-time, 56% women, 44% men
- **Moderately difficult** entrance level, 87% of applicants were admitted

Undergraduates 757 full-time, 341 part-time. 14% are from out of state, 8% African American, 3% Asian American or Pacific Islander, 2% Hispanic American, 0.2% Native American, 0.3% international, 5% transferred in, 34% live on campus. *Retention:* 78% of 2001 full-time freshmen returned.

Freshmen *Admission:* 700 applied, 606 admitted, 339 enrolled. *Average high school GPA:* 2.84. *Test scores:* SAT verbal scores over 500: 46%; SAT math scores over 500: 48%; SAT verbal scores over 600: 11%; SAT math scores over 600: 15%; SAT verbal scores over 700: 1%; SAT math scores over 700: 1%.

Faculty *Total:* 96, 57% full-time, 31% with terminal degrees. *Student/faculty ratio:* 13:1.

Majors Accounting; acting; actuarial science; adult and continuing education administration; advertising; aerospace, aeronautical and astronautical engineering; African-American/Black studies; agribusiness; agricultural and extension education; agricultural/biological engineering and bioengineering; agricultural business and management related; agricultural mechanization; agriculture; American studies; animal sciences; animal sciences related; anthropology; applied economics; archeology; architectural engineering; art; art history, criticism and conservation; art teacher education; Asian studies (East); astronomy; atmospheric sciences and meteorology; biochemistry; biological and biomedical sciences related; biological and physical sciences; biology/biological sciences; biology/biotechnology laboratory technician; biomedical/medical engineering; business administration and management; business/commerce; business/managerial economics; chemical engineering; chemistry; civil engineering; classics and languages, literatures and linguistics; communication and journalism related; communication disorders; communication/speech communication and rhetoric; comparative literature; computer and information sciences; computer engineering; criminal justice/law enforcement administration; economics; electrical, electronics and communications engineering; elementary education; engineering science; English; environmental/environmental health engineering; film/cinema studies; finance; food science; forestry technology; forest sciences and biology; French; geography; geological and earth sciences/geosciences related; geology/earth science; German; graphic design; health/health care administration; history; horticultural science; hospitality administration related; human development and

The Pennsylvania State University Mont Alto Campus of the Commonwealth College (continued)

family studies; human nutrition; industrial engineering; information science/studies; international business/trade/commerce; international relations and affairs; Italian; Japanese; Jewish/Judaic studies; journalism; kinesiology and exercise science; labor and industrial relations; landscape architecture; landscaping and groundskeeping; Latin American studies; liberal arts and sciences/liberal studies; logistics and materials management; management information systems; management sciences and quantitative methods related; marketing/marketing management; materials science; mathematics; mechanical engineering; medical microbiology and bacteriology; medieval and Renaissance studies; mining and mineral engineering; natural resources and conservation related; natural resources/conservation; nuclear engineering; nursing (registered nurse training); occupational therapist assistant; occupational therapy; organizational behavior; parks, recreation and leisure facilities management; petroleum engineering; philosophy; physical therapist assistant; physics; political science and government; pre-medical studies; psychology; rehabilitation and therapeutic professions related; religious studies; Russian; secondary education; sociology; soil science and agronomy; Spanish; special education; statistics; theatre design and technology; turf and turfgrass management; visual and performing arts; women's studies.

Academic Programs *Special study options:* academic remediation for entering students, accelerated degree program, adult/continuing education programs, advanced placement credit, distance learning, double majors, honors programs, independent study, internships, services for LD students, summer session for credit. *ROTC:* Army (c).

Library 38,962 titles, 273 serial subscriptions, 1,418 audiovisual materials.

Computers on Campus 182 computers available on campus for general student use. A campuswide network can be accessed from student residence rooms and from off campus. Internet access, online (class) registration, at least one staffed computer lab available. Computer purchase or lease plan available.

Student Life *Housing options:* coed. Campus housing is university owned. Freshman campus housing is guaranteed. *Activities and organizations:* student-run radio station. *Campus security:* 24-hour patrols, controlled dormitory access.

Athletics Member NJCAA. *Intercollegiate sports:* basketball M/W, cheerleading M/W, cross-country running M/W, golf M/W, soccer M/W, softball W, tennis M/W, volleyball W. *Intramural sports:* badminton M/W, basketball M/W, cheerleading M(c)/W(c), racquetball M/W, soccer M/W, softball W, volleyball M/W.

Standardized Tests *Required:* SAT I or ACT (for admission).

Costs (2003–04) *Tuition:* state resident $8620 full-time, $348 per credit part-time; nonresident $13,250 full-time, $552 per credit part-time. *Required fees:* $398 full-time. *Room and board:* $5940; room only: $3080.

Financial Aid Of all full-time matriculated undergraduates who enrolled in 2001, 89 Federal Work-Study jobs (averaging $844).

Applying *Options:* electronic application, early admission, deferred entrance. *Application fee:* $50. *Required:* high school transcript. *Application deadline:* rolling (freshmen), rolling (transfers). *Notification:* continuous (freshmen), continuous (transfers).

Admissions Contact The Pennsylvania State University Mont Alto Campus of the Commonwealth College, 1 Campus Drive, Mont Alto, PA 17237-9703. *Phone:* 814-865-5471. *Toll-free phone:* 800-392-6173. *Fax:* 717-749-6132. *E-mail:* psuma@psu.edu.

THE PENNSYLVANIA STATE UNIVERSITY NEW KENSINGTON CAMPUS OF THE COMMONWEALTH COLLEGE

New Kensington, Pennsylvania

- **State-related** primarily 2-year, founded 1958, part of Pennsylvania State University
- **Calendar** semesters
- **Degrees** associate and bachelor's (also offers up to 2 years of most bachelor's degree programs offered at University Park campus)
- **Small-town** 71-acre campus with easy access to Pittsburgh
- **Coed,** 1,082 undergraduate students, 73% full-time, 43% women, 57% men
- **Moderately difficult** entrance level, 88% of applicants were admitted

Undergraduates 788 full-time, 294 part-time. 1% are from out of state, 2% African American, 0.6% Asian American or Pacific Islander, 0.7% Hispanic American, 4% transferred in. *Retention:* 77% of 2001 full-time freshmen returned.

Freshmen *Admission:* 463 applied, 409 admitted, 224 enrolled. *Average high school GPA:* 2.98. *Test scores:* SAT verbal scores over 500: 51%; SAT math scores over 500: 54%; SAT verbal scores over 600: 9%; SAT math scores over 600: 14%; SAT verbal scores over 700: 1%.

Faculty *Total:* 103, 42% full-time, 38% with terminal degrees. *Student/faculty ratio:* 14:1.

Majors Accounting; acting; actuarial science; adult and continuing education administration; advertising; aerospace, aeronautical and astronautical engineering; African-American/Black studies; agribusiness; agricultural and extension education; agricultural/biological engineering and bioengineering; agricultural business and management related; agricultural mechanization; agriculture; American studies; animal sciences; animal sciences related; anthropology; applied economics; archeology; architectural engineering; art; art history, criticism and conservation; art teacher education; Asian studies (East); astronomy; atmospheric sciences and meteorology; biochemistry; biological and biomedical sciences related; biological and physical sciences; biology/biological sciences; biology/biotechnology laboratory technician; biomedical/medical engineering; biomedical technology; business administration and management; business/commerce; business/managerial economics; chemical engineering; chemistry; civil engineering; classics and languages, literatures and linguistics; communication and journalism related; communication disorders; communication/speech communication and rhetoric; comparative literature; computer and information sciences; computer engineering; computer engineering technology; criminal justice/law enforcement administration; economics; electrical, electronic and communications engineering technology; electrical, electronics and communications engineering; elementary education; engineering science; English; environmental/environmental health engineering; film/cinema studies; finance; food science; forestry technology; forest sciences and biology; French; geography; geological and earth sciences/geosciences related; geology/earth science; German; graphic design; health/health care administration; history; horticultural science; hospitality administration related; human development and family studies; human nutrition; industrial engineering; information science/studies; international business/trade/commerce; international relations and affairs; Italian; Japanese; Jewish/Judaic studies; journalism; kinesiology and exercise science; labor and industrial relations; landscape architecture; landscaping and groundskeeping; Latin American studies; liberal arts and sciences/liberal studies; logistics and materials management; management information systems; management sciences and quantitative methods related; marketing/marketing management; materials science; mathematics; mechanical engineering; mechanical engineering/mechanical technology; medical microbiology and bacteriology; medical radiologic technology; medieval and Renaissance studies; metallurgical technology; mining and mineral engineering; natural resources and conservation related; natural resources/conservation; nuclear engineering; nursing (registered nurse training); organizational behavior; parks, recreation and leisure facilities management; petroleum engineering; philosophy; physics; political science and government; pre-medical studies; psychology; rehabilitation and therapeutic professions related; religious studies; Russian; secondary education; sociology; soil science and agronomy; Spanish; special education; statistics; telecommunications technology; theatre design and technology; turf and turfgrass management; visual and performing arts; women's studies.

Academic Programs *Special study options:* academic remediation for entering students, accelerated degree program, adult/continuing education programs, advanced placement credit, distance learning, double majors, honors programs, independent study, internships, services for LD students, summer session for credit.

Library 28,897 titles, 404 serial subscriptions, 4,294 audiovisual materials.

Computers on Campus 264 computers available on campus for general student use. A campuswide network can be accessed from off campus. Internet access, online (class) registration, at least one staffed computer lab available. Computer purchase or lease plan available.

Student Life *Housing:* college housing not available. *Activities and organizations:* drama/theater group, student-run newspaper, choral group. *Campus security:* part-time trained security personnel.

Athletics Member NJCAA. *Intercollegiate sports:* baseball M, basketball M/W, cheerleading M/W, golf M/W, softball W, volleyball W. *Intramural sports:* badminton M/W, basketball M/W, bowling M/W, cheerleading M(c)/W(c), football M/W, ice hockey M(c)/W(c), racquetball M/W, skiing (downhill) M(c)/W(c), soccer M/W, softball W, volleyball M/W.

Standardized Tests *Required:* SAT I or ACT (for admission).

Costs (2003–04) *Tuition:* state resident $8620 full-time, $348 per credit part-time; nonresident $13,250 full-time, $552 per credit part-time. *Required fees:* $408 full-time.

Financial Aid Of all full-time matriculated undergraduates who enrolled in 2001, 44 Federal Work-Study jobs (averaging $1297).

Applying *Options:* electronic application, early admission, deferred entrance. *Application fee:* $50. *Required:* high school transcript. *Application deadline:* rolling (freshmen), rolling (transfers). *Notification:* continuous (freshmen), continuous (transfers).

Admissions Contact The Pennsylvania State University New Kensington Campus of the Commonwealth College, 3550 7th Street Road, Route 780, New Kensington, PA 15068. *Phone:* 814-865-5471. *Toll-free phone:* 888-968-7297. *Fax:* 724-334-6111. *E-mail:* nkadmissions@psu.edu.

THE PENNSYLVANIA STATE UNIVERSITY SCHUYLKILL CAMPUS OF THE CAPITAL COLLEGE

Schuylkill Haven, Pennsylvania

- **State-related** 4-year, founded 1934, part of Pennsylvania State University
- **Calendar** semesters
- **Degrees** associate and bachelor's (bachelor's degree programs completed at the Harrisburg campus)
- **Small-town** 42-acre campus
- **Coed,** 977 undergraduate students, 83% full-time, 58% women, 42% men
- **Moderately difficult** entrance level, 87% of applicants were admitted

Undergraduates 811 full-time, 166 part-time. 15% are from out of state, 16% African American, 4% Asian American or Pacific Islander, 3% Hispanic American, 0.2% Native American, 0.2% international, 2% transferred in, 26% live on campus. *Retention:* 81% of 2001 full-time freshmen returned.

Freshmen *Admission:* 713 applied, 621 admitted, 297 enrolled. *Average high school GPA:* 2.75. *Test scores:* SAT verbal scores over 500: 35%; SAT math scores over 500: 38%; SAT verbal scores over 600: 9%; SAT math scores over 600: 13%.

Faculty *Total:* 87, 59% full-time, 51% with terminal degrees. *Student/faculty ratio:* 14:1.

Majors Accounting; acting; actuarial science; adult and continuing education administration; advertising; aerospace, aeronautical and astronautical engineering; African-American/Black studies; agribusiness; agricultural and extension education; agricultural/biological engineering and bioengineering; agricultural business and management related; agricultural mechanization; agriculture; American studies; animal sciences; animal sciences related; anthropology; applied economics; archeology; architectural engineering; art; art history, criticism and conservation; art teacher education; Asian studies (East); astronomy; atmospheric sciences and meteorology; biochemistry; biological and biomedical sciences related; biological and physical sciences; biology/biological sciences; biology/biotechnology laboratory technician; biomedical/medical engineering; biomedical technology; business/commerce; business/managerial economics; chemical engineering; chemistry; civil engineering; classics and languages, literatures and linguistics; clinical/medical laboratory technology; communication and journalism related; communication disorders; communication/speech communication and rhetoric; comparative literature; computer and information sciences; computer engineering; criminal justice/law enforcement administration; criminal justice/safety; economics; electrical, electronic and communications engineering technology; electrical, electronics and communications engineering; elementary education; engineering science; English; environmental/environmental health engineering; film/cinema studies; finance; food science; forestry technology; forest sciences and biology; French; geography; geological and earth sciences/geosciences related; geology/earth science; German; graphic design; health/health care administration; history; horticultural science; hospitality administration related; human development and family studies; human nutrition; industrial engineering; information science/studies; international business/trade/commerce; international relations and affairs; Italian; Japanese; Jewish/Judaic studies; journalism; kinesiology and exercise science; labor and industrial relations; landscape architecture; landscaping and groundskeeping; Latin American studies; liberal arts and sciences/liberal studies; logistics and materials management; management information systems; management sciences and quantitative methods related; marketing/marketing management; materials science; mathematics; mechanical engineering; medical microbiology and bacteriology; medical radiologic technology; medieval and Renaissance studies; metallurgical technology; mining and mineral engineering; natural resources and conservation related; natural resources/conservation; nuclear engineering; nursing (registered nurse training); organizational behavior; parks, recreation and leisure facilities management; petroleum engineering; philosophy; physics; political science and government; pre-medical studies; psychology; rehabilitation and therapeutic professions related; religious studies; Russian; secondary education; sociology; soil science and agronomy; Spanish; special education; statistics; telecommunications technology; theatre design and technology; turf and turfgrass management; visual and performing arts; women's studies.

Academic Programs *Special study options:* academic remediation for entering students, accelerated degree program, adult/continuing education programs, advanced placement credit, cooperative education, distance learning, double majors, independent study, internships, services for LD students, study abroad, summer session for credit.

Library 39,289 titles, 518 serial subscriptions, 930 audiovisual materials.

Computers on Campus 146 computers available on campus for general student use. A campuswide network can be accessed from student residence rooms and from off campus. Internet access, online (class) registration, at least one staffed computer lab available. Computer purchase or lease plan available.

Student Life *Housing options:* Campus housing is provided by a third party. Freshman campus housing is guaranteed. *Activities and organizations:* drama/theater group, student-run newspaper, choral group. *Campus security:* 24-hour patrols, controlled dormitory access.

Athletics Member NJCAA. *Intercollegiate sports:* basketball M, cross-country running M/W, golf M, soccer M, softball W, volleyball W. *Intramural sports:* basketball M/W, football M, soccer M/W, softball M/W, table tennis M/W, volleyball M/W.

Standardized Tests *Required:* SAT I or ACT (for admission).

Costs (2003–04) *Tuition:* state resident $8620 full-time, $348 per credit part-time; nonresident $13,250 full-time, $552 per credit part-time. Full-time tuition and fees vary according to course level, location, program, and student level. Part-time tuition and fees vary according to course level, course load, location, program, and student level. *Required fees:* $388 full-time. *Room only:* $3882. Room and board charges vary according to board plan and housing facility. *Payment plan:* deferred payment. *Waivers:* senior citizens and employees or children of employees.

Financial Aid Of all full-time matriculated undergraduates who enrolled in 2002, 762 applied for aid, 678 were judged to have need, 46 had their need fully met. 99 Federal Work-Study jobs (averaging $936). 6 state and other part-time jobs (averaging $3097). In 2002, 25 non-need-based awards were made. *Average percent of need met:* 71%. *Average financial aid package:* $10,375. *Average need-based loan:* $3200. *Average need-based gift aid:* $4578. *Average non-need-based aid:* $2873. *Average indebtedness upon graduation:* $18,200.

Applying *Options:* electronic application, early admission, deferred entrance. *Application fee:* $50. *Required:* high school transcript. *Application deadline:* rolling (freshmen), rolling (transfers). *Notification:* continuous (freshmen), continuous (transfers).

Admissions Contact The Pennsylvania State University Schuylkill Campus of the Capital College, 200 University Drive, A102 Administration Building, Schuylkill Haven, PA 17972-2208. *Phone:* 814-865-5471. *Fax:* 570-385-3672. *E-mail:* sl-admissions@psu.edu.

THE PENNSYLVANIA STATE UNIVERSITY SHENANGO CAMPUS OF THE COMMONWEALTH COLLEGE

Sharon, Pennsylvania

- **State-related** primarily 2-year, founded 1965, part of Pennsylvania State University
- **Calendar** semesters
- **Degrees** associate and bachelor's (also offers up to 2 years of most bachelor's degree programs offered at University Park campus)
- **Small-town** 14-acre campus
- **Coed,** 904 undergraduate students, 58% full-time, 62% women, 38% men
- **Moderately difficult** entrance level, 86% of applicants were admitted

Undergraduates 520 full-time, 384 part-time. 11% are from out of state, 4% African American, 0.7% Asian American or Pacific Islander, 1% Hispanic American, 0.1% Native American, 4% transferred in. *Retention:* 74% of 2001 full-time freshmen returned.

Freshmen *Admission:* 256 applied, 220 admitted, 141 enrolled. *Average high school GPA:* 2.87. *Test scores:* SAT verbal scores over 500: 36%; SAT math scores over 500: 44%; SAT verbal scores over 600: 5%; SAT math scores over 600: 5%.

Faculty *Total:* 82, 35% full-time, 30% with terminal degrees. *Student/faculty ratio:* 14:1.

Majors Accounting; acting; actuarial science; adult and continuing education administration; advertising; aerospace, aeronautical and astronautical engineering; African-American/Black studies; agribusiness; agricultural and extension education; agricultural/biological engineering and bioengineering; agricultural business and management related; agricultural mechanization; agriculture; American studies; animal sciences; animal sciences related; anthropology; applied economics; archeology; architectural engineering; art; art history, criticism and conservation; art teacher education; Asian studies (East); astronomy; atmospheric sciences and meteorology; biochemistry; biological and biomedical sciences related; biological and physical sciences; biology/biological sciences; biology/biotechnology laboratory technician; biomedical/medical engineering; biomedical technology; business administration and management; business/commerce; business/managerial economics; chemical engineering; chemistry; civil engineering; classics and languages, literatures and linguistics; communication and journalism related; communication disorders; communication/speech communication and rhetoric; comparative literature; computer and information sciences; computer engineering; criminal justice/law enforcement administration; economics; electrical, electronics and communications engineering; elementary education; engineering science; English; environmental/environmental health engi-

The Pennsylvania State University Shenango Campus of the Commonwealth College (continued)

neering; film/cinema studies; finance; food science; forestry technology; forest sciences and biology; French; geography; geological and earth sciences/geosciences related; geology/earth science; German; graphic design; health/health care administration; history; horticultural science; hospitality administration related; human development and family studies; human nutrition; industrial engineering; information science/studies; international business/trade/commerce; international relations and affairs; Italian; Japanese; Jewish/Judaic studies; journalism; kinesiology and exercise science; labor and industrial relations; landscape architecture; landscaping and groundskeeping; Latin American studies; liberal arts and sciences/liberal studies; logistics and materials management; management information systems; management sciences and quantitative methods related; marketing/marketing management; materials science; mathematics; mechanical engineering; mechanical engineering/mechanical technology; medical microbiology and bacteriology; medieval and Renaissance studies; metallurgical technology; mining and mineral engineering; natural resources and conservation related; natural resources/conservation; nuclear engineering; nursing (registered nurse training); organizational behavior; parks, recreation and leisure facilities management; petroleum engineering; philosophy; physical therapist assistant; physics; political science and government; pre-medical studies; psychology; rehabilitation and therapeutic professions related; religious studies; Russian; secondary education; sociology; soil science and agronomy; Spanish; special education; statistics; telecommunications technology; theatre design and technology; turf and turfgrass management; visual and performing arts; women's studies.

Academic Programs *Special study options:* academic remediation for entering students, accelerated degree program, adult/continuing education programs, advanced placement credit, distance learning, double majors, honors programs, independent study, internships, services for LD students, study abroad, summer session for credit.

Library 25,273 titles, 346 serial subscriptions, 2,064 audiovisual materials.

Computers on Campus 102 computers available on campus for general student use. A campuswide network can be accessed from off campus. Internet access, online (class) registration, at least one staffed computer lab available. Computer purchase or lease plan available.

Student Life *Housing:* college housing not available. *Campus security:* part-time trained security personnel.

Athletics *Intramural sports:* basketball M(c)/W, bowling M/W, football M(c), golf M/W, softball M/W, tennis M/W, volleyball M/W.

Standardized Tests *Required:* SAT I or ACT (for admission).

Costs (2003–04) *Tuition:* state resident $8620 full-time, $348 per credit part-time; nonresident $13,250 full-time, $552 per credit part-time. *Required fees:* $398 full-time.

Financial Aid Of all full-time matriculated undergraduates who enrolled in 2001, 24 Federal Work-Study jobs (averaging $1166).

Applying *Options:* electronic application, early admission, deferred entrance. *Application fee:* $50. *Required:* high school transcript. *Application deadline:* rolling (freshmen), rolling (transfers). *Notification:* continuous (freshmen), continuous (transfers).

Admissions Contact The Pennsylvania State University Shenango Campus of the Commonwealth College, 147 Shenango Avenue, Sharon, PA 16146-1597. *Phone:* 814-865-5471. *Fax:* 724-983-2820. *E-mail:* psushenango@psu.edu.

The Pennsylvania State University University Park Campus

State College, Pennsylvania

- **State-related** university, founded 1855, part of Pennsylvania State University
- **Calendar** semesters
- **Degrees** certificates, associate, bachelor's, master's, doctoral, and postbachelor's certificates
- **Small-town** 6388-acre campus
- **Coed,** 35,002 undergraduate students, 96% full-time, 47% women, 53% men
- **Very difficult** entrance level, 55% of applicants were admitted

Undergraduates 33,462 full-time, 1,540 part-time. Students come from 54 states and territories, 25% are from out of state, 4% African American, 6% Asian American or Pacific Islander, 3% Hispanic American, 0.1% Native American, 2% international, 1% transferred in, 37% live on campus. *Retention:* 91% of 2002 full-time freshmen returned.

Freshmen *Admission:* 31,264 applied, 17,174 admitted, 6,048 enrolled. *Average high school GPA:* 3.54. *Test scores:* SAT verbal scores over 500: 88%; SAT math scores over 500: 93%; SAT verbal scores over 600: 44%; SAT math scores over 600: 62%; SAT verbal scores over 700: 8%; SAT math scores over 700: 15%.

Faculty *Total:* 2,516, 87% full-time, 71% with terminal degrees. *Student/faculty ratio:* 17:1.

Majors Accounting; acting; actuarial science; adult and continuing education administration; advertising; aerospace, aeronautical and astronautical engineering; African-American/Black studies; agribusiness; agricultural and extension education; agricultural/biological engineering and bioengineering; agricultural business and management related; agricultural mechanization; agriculture; American studies; animal sciences; animal sciences related; anthropology; applied economics; archeology; architectural engineering; architecture; art; art history, criticism and conservation; art teacher education; Asian studies (East); astronomy; atmospheric sciences and meteorology; biochemistry; biological and biomedical sciences related; biological and physical sciences; biology/biological sciences; biology/biotechnology laboratory technician; biomedical/medical engineering; business/commerce; business/managerial economics; chemical engineering; chemistry; civil engineering; classics and languages, literatures and linguistics; communication and journalism related; communication disorders; communication/speech communication and rhetoric; comparative literature; computer and information sciences; computer engineering; criminal justice/law enforcement administration; cultural studies; dietitian assistant; economics; electrical, electronics and communications engineering; elementary education; engineering science; English; environmental/environmental health engineering; film/cinema studies; finance; food science; forestry technology; forest sciences and biology; French; geography; geological and earth sciences/geosciences related; geology/earth science; German; graphic design; health/health care administration; history; horticultural science; hospitality administration related; human development and family studies; human nutrition; industrial engineering; information science/studies; international business/trade/commerce; international relations and affairs; Italian; Japanese; Jewish/Judaic studies; journalism; kinesiology and exercise science; labor and industrial relations; landscape architecture; landscaping and groundskeeping; Latin American studies; liberal arts and sciences/liberal studies; logistics and materials management; management information systems; management sciences and quantitative methods related; marketing/marketing management; materials science; mathematics; mechanical engineering; medical microbiology and bacteriology; medieval and Renaissance studies; mining and mineral engineering; music; music performance; music teacher education; natural resources and conservation related; natural resources/conservation; nuclear engineering; nursing (registered nurse training); organizational behavior; parks, recreation and leisure facilities management; petroleum engineering; philosophy; physics; political science and government; pre-medical studies; psychology; rehabilitation and therapeutic professions related; religious studies; Russian; secondary education; sociology; soil science and agronomy; Spanish; special education; statistics; telecommunications; theatre design and technology; turf and turfgrass management; visual and performing arts; women's studies.

Academic Programs *Special study options:* academic remediation for entering students, accelerated degree program, adult/continuing education programs, advanced placement credit, cooperative education, distance learning, double majors, English as a second language, external degree program, freshman honors college, honors programs, independent study, internships, part-time degree program, services for LD students, student-designed majors, study abroad, summer session for credit. *ROTC:* Army (b), Navy (b), Air Force (b). *Unusual degree programs:* 3-2 nursing with Lincoln University (PA); earth science, mineral science.

Library Pattee Library plus 7 others with 3.1 million titles, 36,856 serial subscriptions, 146,254 audiovisual materials, an OPAC, a Web page.

Computers on Campus 3589 computers available on campus for general student use. A campuswide network can be accessed from student residence rooms and from off campus. Internet access, online (class) registration, at least one staffed computer lab available.

Student Life *Housing:* on-campus residence required for freshman year. *Options:* coed, men-only, women-only, disabled students. Campus housing is university owned. Freshman campus housing is guaranteed. *Activities and organizations:* drama/theater group, student-run newspaper, radio and television station, choral group, marching band, national fraternities, national sororities. *Campus security:* 24-hour emergency response devices and patrols, student patrols, late-night transport/escort service, controlled dormitory access. *Student services:* health clinic, personal/psychological counseling, women's center, legal services.

Athletics Member NCAA. All Division I except football (Division I-A). *Intercollegiate sports:* baseball M(s), basketball M(s)/W(s), bowling M(c), cheerleading M(s)/W(s), cross-country running M(s)/W(s), equestrian sports M(c)/W(c), fencing M(s)/W(s), field hockey W(s), golf M(s)/W(s), gymnastics M(s)/W(s), ice hockey M(c)/W(c), lacrosse M(s)/W(s), rugby M(c)/W(c), skiing (downhill) M(c)/W(c), soccer M(s)/W(s), softball W, swimming M(s)/W(s), table tennis M(c), tennis M(s)/W(s), track and field M(s)/W(s), volleyball M(s)/W(s), water polo M(c)/W(c), weight lifting M(c)/W(c), wrestling M(s). *Intramural sports:* archery M(c)/W(c), badminton M/W, basketball M/W, bowling M/W, crew M(c)/W(c), cross-country running M/W, fencing M(c)/W(c), field hockey W, football M, golf M/W, gymnastics M(c)/W(c), lacrosse M(c)/W(c), racquetball M/W, riflery M(c)/W(c), rock climbing W(c), sailing M(c)/W(c), soccer M/W, softball M/W, squash M/W, tennis M/W, track and field M/W, ultimate Frisbee M(c)/W(c), volleyball M/W, wrestling M.

Standardized Tests *Required:* SAT I or ACT (for admission).

Costs (2003–04) *Tuition:* state resident $9296 full-time, $387 per credit part-time; nonresident $18,918 full-time, $788 per credit part-time. *Required fees:* $410 full-time, $68 per term part-time. *Room and board:* $5940; room only: $3080.

Financial Aid Of all full-time matriculated undergraduates who enrolled in 2002, 22,031 applied for aid, 16,428 were judged to have need, 2,058 had their need fully met. 2,024 Federal Work-Study jobs (averaging $1284). 306 state and other part-time jobs (averaging $2752). In 2002, 3678 non-need-based awards were made. *Average percent of need met:* 72%. *Average financial aid package:* $11,831. *Average need-based loan:* $4240. *Average need-based gift aid:* $4349. *Average non-need-based aid:* $3633. *Average indebtedness upon graduation:* $18,200.

Applying *Options:* electronic application, early admission, deferred entrance. *Application fee:* $50. *Required:* high school transcript, minimum 2.0 GPA. *Required for some:* 1 letter of recommendation, interview. *Recommended:* essay or personal statement. *Application deadline:* rolling (freshmen). *Notification:* continuous (freshmen), continuous (transfers).

Admissions Contact Undergraduate Admissions Office, The Pennsylvania State University University Park Campus, 201 Shields Building, Box 3000, University Park, PA 16804-3000. *Phone:* 814-865-5471. *Fax:* 814-863-7590. *E-mail:* admissions@psu.edu.

The Pennsylvania State University Wilkes-Barre Campus of the Commonwealth College

Lehman, Pennsylvania

- **State-related** primarily 2-year, founded 1916, part of Pennsylvania State University
- **Calendar** semesters
- **Degrees** associate and bachelor's (also offers up to 2 years of most bachelor's degree programs offered at University Park campus)
- **Rural** 156-acre campus
- **Coed,** 782 undergraduate students, 75% full-time, 31% women, 69% men
- **Moderately difficult** entrance level, 83% of applicants were admitted

Undergraduates 586 full-time, 196 part-time. 3% are from out of state, 0.5% African American, 2% Asian American or Pacific Islander, 0.5% Hispanic American, 0.2% Native American, 3% transferred in. *Retention:* 79% of 2001 full-time freshmen returned.

Freshmen *Admission:* 524 applied, 434 admitted, 190 enrolled. *Average high school GPA:* 2.98. *Test scores:* SAT verbal scores over 500: 53%; SAT math scores over 500: 54%; SAT verbal scores over 600: 11%; SAT math scores over 600: 17%; SAT verbal scores over 700: 1%; SAT math scores over 700: 2%.

Faculty *Total:* 78, 53% full-time, 33% with terminal degrees. *Student/faculty ratio:* 13:1.

Majors Accounting; acting; actuarial science; adult and continuing education administration; advertising; aerospace, aeronautical and astronautical engineering; African-American/Black studies; agribusiness; agricultural and extension education; agricultural/biological engineering and bioengineering; agricultural business and management related; agricultural mechanization; agriculture; American studies; animal sciences; animal sciences related; anthropology; applied economics; archeology; architectural engineering; art; art history, criticism and conservation; art teacher education; Asian studies (East); astronomy; atmospheric sciences and meteorology; biochemistry; biological and biomedical sciences related; biological and physical sciences; biology/biological sciences; biology/biotechnology laboratory technician; biomedical/medical engineering; business administration and management; business/commerce; business/managerial economics; chemical engineering; chemistry; civil engineering; classics and languages, literatures and linguistics; communication and journalism related; communication disorders; communication/speech communication and rhetoric; comparative literature; computer and information sciences; computer engineering; criminal justice/law enforcement administration; economics; electrical, electronic and communications engineering technology; electrical, electronics and communications engineering; elementary education; engineering science; English; environmental/environmental health engineering; film/cinema studies; finance; food science; forestry technology; forest sciences and biology; French; geography; geological and earth sciences/geosciences related; geology/earth science; German; graphic design; health/health care administration; history; horticultural science; hospitality administration related; human development and family studies; human nutrition; industrial engineering; information science/studies; international business/trade/commerce; international relations and affairs; Italian; Japanese; Jewish/Judaic studies; journalism; kinesiology and exercise science; labor and industrial relations; landscape architecture; landscaping and groundskeeping; Latin American studies; liberal arts and sciences/liberal studies; logistics and materials management; management information systems; management sciences and quantitative methods related; manufacturing engineering; marketing/marketing management; materials science; mathematics; mechanical engineering; medical microbiology and bacteriology; medieval and Renaissance studies; metallurgical technology; mining and mineral engineering; natural resources and conservation related; natural resources/conservation; nuclear engineering; nursing (registered nurse training); organizational behavior; parks, recreation and leisure facilities management; petroleum engineering; philosophy; physics; political science and government; pre-medical studies; psychology; rehabilitation and therapeutic professions related; religious studies; Russian; secondary education; sociology; soil science and agronomy; Spanish; special education; statistics; survey technology; telecommunications technology; theatre design and technology; turf and turfgrass management; visual and performing arts; women's studies.

Academic Programs *Special study options:* academic remediation for entering students, accelerated degree program, adult/continuing education programs, advanced placement credit, distance learning, double majors, honors programs, independent study, internships, services for LD students, summer session for credit. *ROTC:* Air Force (c).

Library 35,697 titles, 199 serial subscriptions, 394 audiovisual materials.

Computers on Campus 137 computers available on campus for general student use. A campuswide network can be accessed from off campus. Internet access, online (class) registration, at least one staffed computer lab available. Computer purchase or lease plan available.

Student Life *Housing:* college housing not available. *Activities and organizations:* student-run newspaper, radio station. *Campus security:* part-time trained security personnel.

Athletics Member NJCAA. *Intercollegiate sports:* baseball M, basketball M, cross-country running M/W, golf M/W, soccer M/W, volleyball W. *Intramural sports:* basketball M/W, bowling M(c)/W(c), cheerleading M(c)/W(c), football M, racquetball M/W, softball W, volleyball M(c)/W.

Standardized Tests *Required:* SAT I or ACT (for admission).

Costs (2003–04) *Tuition:* state resident $8620 full-time, $348 per credit part-time; nonresident $13,250 full-time, $552 per credit part-time. *Required fees:* $408 full-time.

Financial Aid Of all full-time matriculated undergraduates who enrolled in 2001, 22 Federal Work-Study jobs (averaging $971).

Applying *Options:* electronic application, early admission, deferred entrance. *Application fee:* $50. *Required:* high school transcript. *Application deadline:* rolling (freshmen), rolling (transfers). *Notification:* continuous (freshmen), continuous (transfers).

Admissions Contact The Pennsylvania State University Wilkes-Barre Campus of the Commonwealth College, PO Box PSU, Lehman, PA 18627-0217. *Phone:* 814-865-5471. *Toll-free phone:* 800-966-6613. *Fax:* 570-675-9113. *E-mail:* wbadmissions@psu.edu.

The Pennsylvania State University Worthington Scranton Campus of the Commonwealth College

Dunmore, Pennsylvania

- **State-related** primarily 2-year, founded 1923, part of Pennsylvania State University
- **Calendar** semesters
- **Degrees** associate and bachelor's (also offers up to 2 years of most bachelor's degree programs offered at University Park campus)
- **Small-town** 43-acre campus
- **Coed,** 1,338 undergraduate students, 76% full-time, 50% women, 50% men
- **Moderately difficult** entrance level, 80% of applicants were admitted

Undergraduates 1,018 full-time, 320 part-time. 1% are from out of state, 1% African American, 1% Asian American or Pacific Islander, 1% Hispanic American, 0.1% Native American, 0.1% international, 5% transferred in. *Retention:* 77% of 2001 full-time freshmen returned.

Freshmen *Admission:* 681 applied, 543 admitted, 254 enrolled. *Average high school GPA:* 2.83. *Test scores:* SAT verbal scores over 500: 43%; SAT math scores over 500: 41%; SAT verbal scores over 600: 8%; SAT math scores over 600: 10%.

Faculty *Total:* 116, 59% full-time, 36% with terminal degrees. *Student/faculty ratio:* 14:1.

Majors Accounting; acting; actuarial science; adult and continuing education administration; advertising; aerospace, aeronautical and astronautical engineering; African-American/Black studies; agribusiness; agricultural and extension education; agricultural/biological engineering and bioengineering; agricultural

The Pennsylvania State University Worthington Scranton Campus of the Commonwealth College (continued)

business and management related; agricultural mechanization; agriculture; American studies; animal sciences; animal sciences related; anthropology; applied economics; archeology; architectural engineering; architectural engineering technology; art; art history, criticism and conservation; art teacher education; Asian studies (East); astronomy; atmospheric sciences and meteorology; biochemistry; biological and biomedical sciences related; biological and physical sciences; biology/biological sciences; biology/biotechnology laboratory technician; biomedical/medical engineering; business administration and management; business/commerce; business/managerial economics; chemical engineering; chemistry; civil engineering, classics and languages, literatures and linguistics; communication and journalism related; communication disorders; communication/speech communication and rhetoric; comparative literature; computer and information sciences; computer engineering; criminal justice/law enforcement administration; economics; electrical, electronics and communications engineering; elementary education; engineering science; English; environmental/environmental health engineering; film/cinema studies; finance; food science; forestry technology; forest sciences and biology; French; geography; geological and earth sciences/geosciences related; geology/earth science; German; graphic design; health/health care administration; history; horticultural science; hospitality administration related; human development and family studies; human nutrition; industrial engineering; information science/studies; international business/trade/commerce; international relations and affairs; Italian; Japanese; Jewish/Judaic studies; journalism; kinesiology and exercise science; labor and industrial relations; landscape architecture; landscaping and groundskeeping; Latin American studies; liberal arts and sciences/liberal studies; logistics and materials management; management information systems; management sciences and quantitative methods related; marketing/marketing management; materials science; mathematics; mechanical engineering; medical microbiology and bacteriology; medieval and Renaissance studies; mining and mineral engineering; natural resources and conservation related; natural resources/conservation; nuclear engineering; nursing (registered nurse training); occupational therapist assistant; organizational behavior; parks, recreation and leisure facilities management; petroleum engineering; philosophy; physics; political science and government; pre-medical studies; psychology; rehabilitation and therapeutic professions related; religious studies; Russian; secondary education; sociology; soil science and agronomy; Spanish; special education; statistics; theatre design and technology; turf and turfgrass management; visual and performing arts; women's studies.

Academic Programs *Special study options:* academic remediation for entering students, accelerated degree program, adult/continuing education programs, advanced placement credit, distance learning, double majors, honors programs, independent study, internships, services for LD students, summer session for credit. *ROTC:* Army (c), Air Force (c).

Library 53,572 titles, 102 serial subscriptions, 3,048 audiovisual materials.

Computers on Campus 104 computers available on campus for general student use. A campuswide network can be accessed from off campus. Internet access, online (class) registration, at least one staffed computer lab available. Computer purchase or lease plan available.

Student Life *Housing:* college housing not available. *Activities and organizations:* drama/theater group, student-run newspaper. *Campus security:* part-time trained security personnel.

Athletics Member NJCAA. *Intercollegiate sports:* baseball M, basketball M/W, cheerleading M/W, cross-country running M/W, soccer M, softball W, volleyball W. *Intramural sports:* basketball M/W, bowling M(c)/W(c), skiing (downhill) M(c)/W(c), soccer M/W, softball M/W, volleyball M/W(c), weight lifting M(c)/W(c).

Standardized Tests *Required:* SAT I or ACT (for admission).

Costs (2003–04) *Tuition:* state resident $8620 full-time, $348 per credit part-time; nonresident $13,250 full-time, $552 per credit part-time. *Required fees:* $388 full-time.

Financial Aid Of all full-time matriculated undergraduates who enrolled in 2001, 24 Federal Work-Study jobs (averaging $957).

Applying *Options:* electronic application, early admission, deferred entrance. *Application fee:* $50. *Required:* high school transcript. *Application deadline:* rolling (freshmen), rolling (transfers). *Notification:* continuous (freshmen), continuous (transfers).

Admissions Contact The Pennsylvania State University Worthington Scranton Campus of the Commonwealth College, 120 Ridge View Drive, Dunmore, PA 18512-1699. *Phone:* 814-865-5471. *Fax:* 570-963-2524. *E-mail:* wsadmissions@psu.edu.

■ *See page 2164 for a narrative description.*

THE PENNSYLVANIA STATE UNIVERSITY YORK CAMPUS OF THE COMMONWEALTH COLLEGE

York, Pennsylvania

- **State-related** primarily 2-year, founded 1926, part of Pennsylvania State University
- **Calendar** semesters
- **Degrees** associate and bachelor's (also offers up to 2 years of most bachelor's degree programs offered at University Park campus)
- **Suburban** 53-acre campus
- **Coed,** 1,730 undergraduate students, 58% full-time, 44% women, 56% men
- **Moderately difficult** entrance level, 85% of applicants were admitted

Undergraduates 1,000 full-time, 730 part-time. 2% are from out of state, 4% African American, 6% Asian American or Pacific Islander, 2% Hispanic American, 0.4% Native American, 0.1% international, 2% transferred in. *Retention:* 74% of 2001 full-time freshmen returned.

Freshmen *Admission:* 979 applied, 835 admitted, 347 enrolled. *Average high school GPA:* 2.81. *Test scores:* SAT verbal scores over 500: 52%; SAT math scores over 500: 56%; SAT verbal scores over 600: 16%; SAT math scores over 600: 19%; SAT verbal scores over 700: 1%.

Faculty *Total:* 127, 49% full-time, 39% with terminal degrees. *Student/faculty ratio:* 16:1.

Majors Accounting; acting; actuarial science; adult and continuing education administration; advertising; aerospace, aeronautical and astronautical engineering; African-American/Black studies; agribusiness; agricultural and extension education; agricultural/biological engineering and bioengineering; agricultural business and management related; agricultural mechanization; agriculture; American studies; animal sciences; animal sciences related; anthropology; applied economics; archeology; architectural engineering; art; art history, criticism and conservation; art teacher education; Asian studies (East); astronomy; atmospheric sciences and meteorology; biochemistry; biological and biomedical sciences related; biological and physical sciences; biology/biological sciences; biology/biotechnology laboratory technician; biomedical/medical engineering; biomedical technology; business/commerce; business/managerial economics; chemical engineering; chemistry; civil engineering; classics and languages, literatures and linguistics; communication and journalism related; communication disorders; communication/speech communication and rhetoric; comparative literature; computer and information sciences; computer engineering; criminal justice/law enforcement administration; economics; electrical, electronic and communications engineering technology; electrical, electronics and communications engineering; elementary education; engineering science; English; environmental/environmental health engineering; film/cinema studies; finance; food science; forestry technology; forest sciences and biology; French; geography; geological and earth sciences/geosciences related; geology/earth science; German; graphic design; health/health care administration; history; horticultural science; hospitality administration related; human development and family studies; human nutrition; industrial engineering; industrial technology; information science/studies; international business/trade/commerce; international relations and affairs; Italian; Japanese; Jewish/Judaic studies; journalism; kinesiology and exercise science; labor and industrial relations; landscape architecture; landscaping and groundskeeping; Latin American studies; liberal arts and sciences/liberal studies; logistics and materials management; management information systems; management sciences and quantitative methods related; manufacturing engineering; marketing/marketing management; materials science; mathematics; mechanical engineering; mechanical engineering/mechanical technology; medical microbiology and bacteriology; medieval and Renaissance studies; metallurgical technology; mining and mineral engineering; natural resources and conservation related; natural resources/conservation; nuclear engineering; nursing (registered nurse training); organizational behavior; parks, recreation and leisure facilities management; petroleum engineering; philosophy; physics; political science and government; pre-medical studies; psychology; rehabilitation and therapeutic professions related; religious studies; Russian; secondary education; sociology; soil science and agronomy; Spanish; special education; statistics; telecommunications technology; theatre design and technology; turf and turfgrass management; visual and performing arts; women's studies.

Academic Programs *Special study options:* academic remediation for entering students, accelerated degree program, adult/continuing education programs, advanced placement credit, distance learning, double majors, English as a second language, honors programs, independent study, internships, services for LD students, student-designed majors, study abroad, summer session for credit.

Library 49,996 titles, 243 serial subscriptions, 3,567 audiovisual materials.

Computers on Campus 155 computers available on campus for general student use. A campuswide network can be accessed from off campus. Internet access, online (class) registration, at least one staffed computer lab available. Computer purchase or lease plan available.

Student Life *Housing:* college housing not available. *Activities and organizations:* student-run newspaper. *Campus security:* part-time trained security personnel.

Athletics Member NJCAA. *Intercollegiate sports:* basketball M/W, cross-country running M/W, soccer M, tennis M/W, volleyball W. *Intramural sports:* badminton M/W, basketball M/W, cheerleading M(c)/W(c), football M, soccer M/W, softball M/W, tennis M/W, ultimate Frisbee M/W, volleyball M/W.

Standardized Tests *Required:* SAT I or ACT (for admission).

Costs (2003–04) *Tuition:* state resident $8620 full-time, $348 per credit part-time; nonresident $13,250 full-time, $552 per credit part-time. *Required fees:* $388 full-time.

Financial Aid Of all full-time matriculated undergraduates who enrolled in 2001, 37 Federal Work-Study jobs (averaging $772).

Applying *Options:* electronic application, early admission, deferred entrance. *Application fee:* $50. *Required:* high school transcript. *Application deadline:* rolling (freshmen), rolling (transfers). *Notification:* continuous (freshmen), continuous (transfers).

Admissions Contact The Pennsylvania State University York Campus of the Commonwealth College, 1031 Edgecomb Avenue, York, PA 17403-3398. *Phone:* 814-865-5471. *Toll-free phone:* 800-778-6227. *Fax:* 717-771-4005. *E-mail:* ykadmission@psu.edu.

PHILADELPHIA BIBLICAL UNIVERSITY

Langhorne, Pennsylvania

- **Independent nondenominational** comprehensive, founded 1913
- **Calendar** semesters
- **Degrees** certificates, bachelor's, master's, and first professional
- **Suburban** 105-acre campus with easy access to Philadelphia
- **Endowment** $4.5 million
- **Coed,** 1,045 undergraduate students, 88% full-time, 54% women, 46% men
- **Moderately difficult** entrance level, 76% of applicants were admitted

Undergraduates 918 full-time, 127 part-time. Students come from 41 states and territories, 49% are from out of state, 10% African American, 2% Asian American or Pacific Islander, 2% Hispanic American, 0.1% Native American, 2% international, 9% transferred in, 52% live on campus. *Retention:* 77% of 2002 full-time freshmen returned.

Freshmen *Admission:* 412 applied, 313 admitted, 187 enrolled. *Average high school GPA:* 3.24. *Test scores:* SAT verbal scores over 500: 72%; SAT math scores over 500: 60%; ACT scores over 18: 92%; SAT verbal scores over 600: 27%; SAT math scores over 600: 19%; ACT scores over 24: 31%; SAT verbal scores over 700: 4%; SAT math scores over 700: 1%; ACT scores over 30: 15%.

Faculty *Total:* 144, 47% full-time, 44% with terminal degrees. *Student/faculty ratio:* 14:1.

Majors Biblical studies; business administration and management; elementary education; English/language arts teacher education; kindergarten/preschool education; mathematics teacher education; music; physical education teaching and coaching; religious studies; social studies teacher education; social work.

Academic Programs *Special study options:* academic remediation for entering students, accelerated degree program, adult/continuing education programs, advanced placement credit, double majors, honors programs, independent study, internships, off-campus study, part-time degree program, services for LD students, study abroad, summer session for credit. *ROTC:* Air Force (c).

Library Masland Learning Resource Center with 96,988 titles, 733 serial subscriptions, 13,740 audiovisual materials, an OPAC.

Computers on Campus 90 computers available on campus for general student use. A campuswide network can be accessed from student residence rooms and from off campus. Internet access, at least one staffed computer lab available.

Student Life *Housing:* on-campus residence required through senior year. *Options:* men-only, women-only, disabled students. Freshman campus housing is guaranteed. *Activities and organizations:* drama/theater group, student-run newspaper, choral group, Student Theological Society, Student Missionary Fellowship, Cultural Awareness Association, University Social Committee, Student Senate. *Campus security:* 24-hour emergency response devices and patrols, student patrols, late-night transport/escort service, controlled dormitory access. *Student services:* health clinic, personal/psychological counseling.

Athletics Member NCAA, NCCAA. All NCAA Division III. *Intercollegiate sports:* baseball M, basketball M/W, field hockey W, golf M, soccer M/W, softball W, tennis M/W, volleyball M/W. *Intramural sports:* basketball M/W, soccer M/W, table tennis M/W, tennis M/W, volleyball M/W.

Standardized Tests *Required for some:* SAT I or ACT (for admission).

Costs (2004–05) *Comprehensive fee:* $19,350 includes full-time tuition ($13,190), mandatory fees ($305), and room and board ($5855). Full-time tuition and fees vary according to course load, location, and program. Part-time tuition: $397 per credit. Part-time tuition and fees vary according to course load, location, and program. *College room only:* $2930. Room and board charges vary according to board plan, housing facility, and location. *Payment plan:* installment. *Waivers:* children of alumni and employees or children of employees.

Financial Aid Of all full-time matriculated undergraduates who enrolled in 2003, 819 applied for aid, 749 were judged to have need, 112 had their need fully met. 106 Federal Work-Study jobs (averaging $1270). In 2003, 166 non-need-based awards were made. *Average percent of need met:* 63%. *Average financial aid package:* $8842. *Average need-based loan:* $3370. *Average need-based gift aid:* $6985. *Average non-need-based aid:* $6224. *Average indebtedness upon graduation:* $13,000.

Applying *Options:* electronic application, early admission, deferred entrance. *Application fee:* $25. *Required:* essay or personal statement, high school transcript, 1 letter of recommendation. *Required for some:* minimum 2.0 GPA, interview. *Recommended:* minimum 3.0 GPA, interview. *Application deadline:* rolling (freshmen), rolling (transfers). *Notification:* continuous (freshmen), continuous (transfers).

Admissions Contact Ms. Lisa Fuller, Director of Undergraduate Admissions, Philadelphia Biblical University, 200 Manor Avenue, Langhorne, PA 19047. *Phone:* 215-702-4550. *Toll-free phone:* 800-366-0049. *Fax:* 215-702-4248. *E-mail:* admissions@pbu.edu.

■ *See page 2170 for a narrative description.*

PHILADELPHIA UNIVERSITY

Philadelphia, Pennsylvania

- **Independent** comprehensive, founded 1884
- **Calendar** semesters
- **Degrees** certificates, associate, bachelor's, and master's
- **Suburban** 100-acre campus
- **Endowment** $17.4 million
- **Coed,** 2,603 undergraduate students, 87% full-time, 68% women, 32% men
- **Moderately difficult** entrance level, 70% of applicants were admitted

Undergraduates 2,257 full-time, 346 part-time. Students come from 42 states and territories, 30 other countries, 42% are from out of state, 10% African American, 4% Asian American or Pacific Islander, 3% Hispanic American, 0.1% Native American, 3% international, 4% transferred in, 53% live on campus. *Retention:* 71% of 2002 full-time freshmen returned.

Freshmen *Admission:* 3,461 applied, 2,420 admitted, 624 enrolled. *Average high school GPA:* 3.33. *Test scores:* SAT verbal scores over 500: 70%; SAT math scores over 500: 72%; SAT verbal scores over 600: 19%; SAT math scores over 600: 21%; SAT verbal scores over 700: 1%; SAT math scores over 700: 1%.

Faculty *Total:* 406, 27% full-time. *Student/faculty ratio:* 13:1.

Majors Accounting; apparel and accessories marketing; architecture; biochemistry; biology/biological sciences; biopsychology; business administration and management; chemistry; clothing/textiles; commercial and advertising art; computer and information sciences; computer science; conservation biology; e-commerce; environmental biology; fashion/apparel design; fashion merchandising; fiber, textile and weaving arts; finance; graphic design; industrial design; information science/studies; interior architecture; interior design; international business/trade/commerce; landscape architecture; management information systems; marketing/marketing management; physician assistant; pre-medical studies; psychology; textile sciences and engineering.

Academic Programs *Special study options:* academic remediation for entering students, accelerated degree program, adult/continuing education programs, advanced placement credit, cooperative education, English as a second language, freshman honors college, honors programs, independent study, internships, off-campus study, part-time degree program, services for LD students, study abroad, summer session for credit.

Library Paul J. Gutman Library plus 1 other with 124,525 titles, 2,150 serial subscriptions, 36,844 audiovisual materials, an OPAC, a Web page.

Computers on Campus 400 computers available on campus for general student use. A campuswide network can be accessed from student residence rooms and from off campus that provide access to on-line registration for advanced workshops and seminars. Internet access, at least one staffed computer lab available.

Student Life *Housing options:* coed, women-only. Campus housing is university owned and leased by the school. Freshman campus housing is guaranteed. *Activities and organizations:* drama/theater group, student-run newspaper, choral group, Gemini Theatre, Black Student Union, Cornerstone, Phila'cappella, Global Friends, national fraternities, national sororities. *Campus security:* 24-hour emergency response devices and patrols, late-night transport/escort service, controlled dormitory access. *Student services:* health clinic, personal/psychological counseling.

Philadelphia University (continued)

Athletics Member NCAA. All Division II except soccer (Division I). *Intercollegiate sports:* baseball M(s), basketball M(s)/W(s), field hockey W(s), golf M(s), lacrosse W(s), soccer M(s)/W(s), softball W(s), tennis M(s)/W(s), volleyball W(s). *Intramural sports:* basketball M/W, cross-country running M/W, football M, skiing (downhill) M(c)/W(c), soccer M/W, softball M/W, swimming M/W, table tennis M/W, tennis M/W, volleyball M/W, weight lifting M/W.

Standardized Tests *Required:* SAT I or ACT (for admission).

Costs (2003–04) *Comprehensive fee:* $27,392 includes full-time tuition ($19,962), mandatory fees ($60), and room and board ($7370). Full-time tuition and fees vary according to program. Part-time tuition and fees vary according to class time and program. *College room only:* $3630. Room and board charges vary according to board plan and housing facility. *Payment plans:* installment, deferred payment. *Waivers:* employees or children of employees.

Financial Aid Of all full-time matriculated undergraduates who enrolled in 2003, 1,835 applied for aid, 1,599 were judged to have need, 187 had their need fully met. 850 Federal Work-Study jobs (averaging $2000). In 2003, 528 non-need-based awards were made. *Average percent of need met:* 73%. *Average financial aid package:* $14,577. *Average need-based loan:* $4269. *Average need-based gift aid:* $9274. *Average non-need-based aid:* $4016. *Financial aid deadline:* 4/15.

Applying *Options:* common application, electronic application, deferred entrance. *Application fee:* $35. *Required:* high school transcript. *Recommended:* essay or personal statement, 2 letters of recommendation, interview. *Application deadline:* rolling (freshmen), rolling (transfers).

Admissions Contact Ms. Christine Greb, Director of Admissions, Philadelphia University, School House Lane and Henry Avenue, Philadelphia, PA 19144-5497. *Phone:* 215-951-2800. *Fax:* 215-951-2907. *E-mail:* admissions@philau.edu.

■ *See page 2172 for a narrative description.*

POINT PARK UNIVERSITY
Pittsburgh, Pennsylvania

- **Independent** comprehensive, founded 1960
- **Calendar** semesters
- **Degrees** certificates, associate, bachelor's, master's, post-master's, and postbachelor's certificates
- **Urban** campus
- **Endowment** $6.9 million
- **Coed,** 2,827 undergraduate students, 73% full-time, 58% women, 42% men
- **Moderately difficult** entrance level, 81% of applicants were admitted

Point Park University offers students the opportunity to attend small, intimate classes in a facility located in the midst of vibrant downtown Pittsburgh. Recognized for providing a liberal arts education with career preparation, Point Park's location gives students access to important internships that provide valuable professional-level experience to complement classroom activities.

Undergraduates 2,061 full-time, 766 part-time. Students come from 40 states and territories, 27 other countries, 16% are from out of state, 13% African American, 0.6% Asian American or Pacific Islander, 0.9% Hispanic American, 0.4% Native American, 1% international, 15% transferred in, 21% live on campus. *Retention:* 72% of 2002 full-time freshmen returned.

Freshmen *Admission:* 1,715 applied, 1,391 admitted, 439 enrolled. *Average high school GPA:* 3.26. *Test scores:* SAT verbal scores over 500: 66%; SAT math scores over 500: 53%; ACT scores over 18: 91%; SAT verbal scores over 600: 18%; SAT math scores over 600: 12%; ACT scores over 24: 29%; SAT verbal scores over 700: 1%; SAT math scores over 700: 1%; ACT scores over 30: 3%.

Faculty *Total:* 343, 24% full-time, 35% with terminal degrees. *Student/faculty ratio:* 14:1.

Majors Accounting; advertising; arts management; behavioral sciences; biology/biological sciences; biology/biotechnology laboratory technician; biology teacher education; biotechnology; broadcast journalism; business administration and management; business administration, management and operations related; business/corporate communications; cinematography and film/video production; civil engineering technology; communication and media related; computer/information technology services administration related; criminal justice/law enforcement administration; criminal justice/safety; dance; design and applied arts related; drama and dance teacher education; dramatic/theatre arts; early childhood education; education; education (specific subject areas) related; electrical, electronic and communications engineering technology; elementary education; English; English/language arts teacher education; environmental science; funeral service and mortuary science; general studies; health/health care administration; history; human resources management; information technology; journalism; legal studies; mass communication/media; mathematics teacher education; mechanical engineering/mechanical technology; photography; photojournalism; political science and government; psychology; public administration; public relations/image management; radio and television; respiratory care therapy; secondary education; social sciences; social science teacher education.

Academic Programs *Special study options:* academic remediation for entering students, accelerated degree program, adult/continuing education programs, advanced placement credit, distance learning, double majors, English as a second language, honors programs, independent study, internships, off-campus study, part-time degree program, services for LD students, student-designed majors, summer session for credit. *ROTC:* Army (c), Air Force (c).

Library The Library Center with 163,197 titles, 765 serial subscriptions, 5,595 audiovisual materials, an OPAC.

Computers on Campus 183 computers available on campus for general student use. A campuswide network can be accessed from student residence rooms and from off campus. Internet access, at least one staffed computer lab available.

Student Life *Housing options:* coed. Campus housing is university owned. Freshman campus housing is guaranteed. *Activities and organizations:* drama/theater group, student-run newspaper, radio and television station, Black Student Union, student radio station, Dance Club, Alpha Phi Omega, College Students in Broadcasting. *Campus security:* 24-hour emergency response devices and patrols, late-night transport/escort service, 24-hour security desk, video security. *Student services:* health clinic, personal/psychological counseling.

Athletics Member NAIA. *Intercollegiate sports:* baseball M(s), basketball M(s)/W(s), cross-country running M(s)/W(s), soccer M(s), softball W(s), volleyball W(s). *Intramural sports:* basketball M, football M, golf M, tennis M/W, volleyball M/W, weight lifting M/W.

Standardized Tests *Required:* SAT I or ACT (for admission).

Costs (2003–04) *Comprehensive fee:* $21,840 includes full-time tuition ($14,720), mandatory fees ($460), and room and board ($6660). Full-time tuition and fees vary according to program. Part-time tuition: $397 per credit. Part-time tuition and fees vary according to program. *Required fees:* $10 per credit part-time. *College room only:* $3140. Room and board charges vary according to board plan. *Payment plans:* installment, deferred payment. *Waivers:* children of alumni and employees or children of employees.

Financial Aid Of all full-time matriculated undergraduates who enrolled in 2003, 1,614 applied for aid, 1,467 were judged to have need, 332 had their need fully met. 210 Federal Work-Study jobs (averaging $2086). 237 state and other part-time jobs (averaging $1966). In 2003, 434 non-need-based awards were made. *Average percent of need met:* 72%. *Average financial aid package:* $12,285. *Average need-based loan:* $4772. *Average need-based gift aid:* $6841. *Average non-need-based aid:* $6706. *Average indebtedness upon graduation:* $9835.

Applying *Options:* common application, electronic application, early admission, deferred entrance. *Application fee:* $40. *Required:* high school transcript. *Required for some:* 2 letters of recommendation, interview, audition. *Recommended:* essay or personal statement, minimum 2.0 GPA. *Application deadline:* rolling (freshmen), rolling (transfers).

Admissions Contact Mr. Rob Sheinkopf, Dean, Full-Time Admissions, Point Park University, 201 Wood Street, Pittsburgh, PA 15222. *Phone:* 412-392-3430. *Toll-free phone:* 800-321-0129. *Fax:* 412-391-1980. *E-mail:* enroll@ppc.edu.

■ *See page 2182 for a narrative description.*

THE RESTAURANT SCHOOL AT WALNUT HILL COLLEGE
Philadelphia, Pennsylvania

- **Proprietary** primarily 2-year, founded 1974
- **Calendar** semesters
- **Degrees** associate and bachelor's
- **Urban** 2-acre campus
- **Coed**

Faculty *Student/faculty ratio:* 25:1.

Standardized Tests *Recommended:* SAT I or ACT (for admission).

Costs (2004–05) *Tuition:* $12,100 full-time.

Applying *Options:* common application, early admission, early decision, deferred entrance. *Application fee:* $50. *Required:* essay or personal statement, high school transcript, 2 letters of recommendation, interview. *Required for some:* entrance exam. *Recommended:* minimum 2.0 GPA.

Admissions Contact Mr. Karl D. Becker, Director of Admissions, The Restaurant School at Walnut Hill College, 4207 Walnut Street, Philadelphia, PA 19104. *Phone:* 215-222-4200 Ext. 3011. *Toll-free phone:* 877-925-6884 Ext. 3011. *Fax:* 215-222-4219. *E-mail:* info@walnuthillcollege.edu.

■ *See page 2226 for a narrative description.*

ROBERT MORRIS UNIVERSITY

Moon Township, Pennsylvania

- **Independent** comprehensive, founded 1921
- **Calendar** semesters
- **Degrees** certificates, bachelor's, master's, doctoral, and postbachelor's certificates
- **Suburban** 230-acre campus with easy access to Pittsburgh
- **Endowment** $13.3 million
- **Coed,** 3,735 undergraduate students, 74% full-time, 48% women, 52% men
- **Moderately difficult** entrance level, 91% of applicants were admitted

Robert Morris University, founded in 1921, is a private, four-year institution with an enrollment of approximately 5,000 undergraduate and graduate students. The University offers more than 30 undergraduate degree programs and 14 master's and doctoral degree programs and has the second lowest tuition among private universities in Pennsylvania. An estimated 22,000 alumni live and work in Western Pennsylvania.

Undergraduates 2,750 full-time, 985 part-time. Students come from 27 states and territories, 20 other countries, 8% are from out of state, 9% African American, 0.7% Asian American or Pacific Islander, 1% Hispanic American, 0.2% Native American, 2% international, 12% transferred in, 37% live on campus. *Retention:* 74% of 2002 full-time freshmen returned.

Freshmen *Admission:* 1,816 applied, 1,645 admitted, 557 enrolled. *Average high school GPA:* 3.09. *Test scores:* SAT verbal scores over 500: 48%; SAT math scores over 500: 54%; ACT scores over 18: 89%; SAT verbal scores over 600: 8%; SAT math scores over 600: 16%; ACT scores over 24: 10%; SAT math scores over 700: 1%.

Faculty *Total:* 342, 36% full-time, 45% with terminal degrees. *Student/faculty ratio:* 16:1.

Majors Accounting; actuarial science; applied mathematics; aviation/airway management; business administration and management; business/managerial economics; business teacher education; communication/speech communication and rhetoric; computer engineering; design and visual communications; economics; elementary education; engineering; engineering/industrial management; English; finance; health and medical administrative services related; health/health care administration; hospitality administration; human resources management; industrial engineering; information science/studies; logistics and materials management; management information systems; marketing/marketing management; mass communication/media; multi-/interdisciplinary studies related; nursing (registered nurse training); operations management; organizational behavior; social sciences; sport and fitness administration; tourism and travel services management.

Academic Programs *Special study options:* academic remediation for entering students, accelerated degree program, adult/continuing education programs, advanced placement credit, cooperative education, distance learning, double majors, honors programs, independent study, internships, off-campus study, part-time degree program, services for LD students, study abroad, summer session for credit. *ROTC:* Army (c), Air Force (c).

Library Robert Morris University Library with 187,897 titles, 740 serial subscriptions, 2,994 audiovisual materials, an OPAC.

Computers on Campus 300 computers available on campus for general student use. A campuswide network can be accessed from student residence rooms and from off campus. Internet access, online (class) registration, at least one staffed computer lab available.

Student Life *Housing options:* coed, men-only, women-only, disabled students. Campus housing is university owned. Freshman applicants given priority for college housing. *Activities and organizations:* drama/theater group, student-run newspaper, television station, marching band, Student Government Association, Residence Hall Association, Interfraternity Council/Panhellenic Council, R-MOVE, National Society of Collegiate Scholars, national fraternities, national sororities. *Campus security:* 24-hour emergency response devices and patrols, late-night transport/escort service, controlled dormitory access. *Student services:* health clinic, personal/psychological counseling.

Athletics Member NCAA. All Division I except football (Division I-AA). *Intercollegiate sports:* baseball M(c), basketball M(s)/W(s), cheerleading M/W, crew W(s), cross-country running M(s)/W(s), field hockey W(s), golf M(s)/W(s), ice hockey M(s), lacrosse M(s)/W(s), rugby M, soccer M(s)/W(s), softball W(s), tennis M(s)/W(s), track and field M(s)/W(s), volleyball W(s). *Intramural sports:* basketball M/W, bowling M(c)/W(c), crew M(c), football M/W, ice hockey M(c), rugby M(c), softball M/W, table tennis M/W, volleyball W.

Standardized Tests *Required:* SAT I or ACT (for admission).

Costs (2003–04) *Comprehensive fee:* $20,438 includes full-time tuition ($13,484) and room and board ($6954). Full-time tuition and fees vary according to course load and student level. Part-time tuition: $405 per credit. Part-time tuition and fees vary according to course load. *College room only:* $4138. Room and board charges vary according to board plan and housing facility. *Payment plans:* installment, deferred payment. *Waivers:* employees or children of employees.

Financial Aid Of all full-time matriculated undergraduates who enrolled in 2003, 2,273 applied for aid, 2,029 were judged to have need, 427 had their need fully met. In 2003, 403 non-need-based awards were made. *Average percent of need met:* 70%. *Average financial aid package:* $11,526. *Average need-based loan:* $4977. *Average need-based gift aid:* $6462. *Average non-need-based aid:* $7366.

Applying *Options:* common application, electronic application, deferred entrance. *Application fee:* $30. *Required:* high school transcript, minimum 2.5 GPA. *Required for some:* interview. *Recommended:* minimum 3.0 GPA, letters of recommendation, interview. *Application deadlines:* 7/1 (freshmen), 7/1 (transfers). *Notification:* continuous (freshmen), continuous (transfers).

Admissions Contact Mr. J. Donald Williams, Assistant Dean of Enrollment Services, Robert Morris University, Enrollment Services Department, 6001 University Boulevard, Moon Township, PA 15108-1189. *Phone:* 412-262-8206. *Toll-free phone:* 800-762-0097. *Fax:* 412-299-2425. *E-mail:* enrollmentoffice@rmu.edu.

■ *See page 2244 for a narrative description.*

ROSEMONT COLLEGE

Rosemont, Pennsylvania

- **Independent Roman Catholic** comprehensive, founded 1921
- **Calendar** semesters
- **Degrees** certificates, bachelor's, master's, and postbachelor's certificates
- **Suburban** 56-acre campus with easy access to Philadelphia
- **Endowment** $7.8 million
- **Women only,** 697 undergraduate students, 60% full-time
- **Moderately difficult** entrance level, 70% of applicants were admitted

Founded in 1921 as a women's college in the Catholic tradition, Rosemont College has been ranked by *U.S. News & World Report* for consecutive years.

Undergraduates 421 full-time, 276 part-time. Students come from 15 states and territories, 10 other countries, 31% are from out of state, 23% African American, 6% Asian American or Pacific Islander, 5% Hispanic American, 2% international, 4% transferred in, 68% live on campus. *Retention:* 92% of 2002 full-time freshmen returned.

Freshmen *Admission:* 337 applied, 235 admitted, 97 enrolled. *Average high school GPA:* 3.60. *Test scores:* SAT verbal scores over 500: 76%; SAT math scores over 500: 61%; ACT scores over 18: 100%; SAT verbal scores over 600: 37%; SAT math scores over 600: 24%; SAT verbal scores over 700: 10%; SAT math scores over 700: 8%.

Faculty *Total:* 157, 20% full-time, 87% with terminal degrees. *Student/faculty ratio:* 8:1.

Majors Accounting; art history, criticism and conservation; biochemistry; biology/biological sciences; business administration and management; chemistry; communication/speech communication and rhetoric; economics; English; fine/studio arts; French; German; history; humanities; Italian; mathematics; philosophy; political science and government; psychology; religious studies; social sciences; sociology; Spanish; women's studies.

Academic Programs *Special study options:* accelerated degree program, adult/continuing education programs, advanced placement credit, double majors, English as a second language, honors programs, independent study, internships, off-campus study, part-time degree program, services for LD students, student-designed majors, study abroad, summer session for credit. *ROTC:* Army (c). *Unusual degree programs:* 3-2 engineering with Villanova University; nursing with Villanova University; counseling psychology, dentistry.

Library Kistler Library with 158,000 titles, 557 serial subscriptions, 2,700 audiovisual materials, an OPAC, a Web page.

Computers on Campus 90 computers available on campus for general student use. A campuswide network can be accessed from student residence rooms and from off campus. Internet access, at least one staffed computer lab available.

Student Life *Housing:* on-campus residence required through junior year. *Options:* women-only. Campus housing is university owned. Freshman campus housing is guaranteed. *Activities and organizations:* drama/theater group, student-run newspaper, choral group, marching band, student government, Triad, Jest and Gesture, Best Buddies, political science club. *Campus security:* 24-hour emergency response devices and patrols, late-night transport/escort service, controlled dormitory access. *Student services:* health clinic, personal/psychological counseling, women's center, legal services.

Athletics Member NCAA. All Division III. *Intercollegiate sports:* basketball W, field hockey W, softball W, tennis W, volleyball W. *Intramural sports:* rock climbing M/W, ultimate Frisbee M/W.

Rosemont College (continued)

Standardized Tests *Required:* SAT I or ACT (for admission).

Costs (2004–05) *Comprehensive fee:* $27,870 includes full-time tuition ($18,500), mandatory fees ($970), and room and board ($8400). *Room and board:* Room and board charges vary according to housing facility. *Payment plan:* installment. *Waivers:* senior citizens and employees or children of employees.

Financial Aid Of all full-time matriculated undergraduates who enrolled in 2003, 244 applied for aid, 207 were judged to have need. 111 Federal Work-Study jobs (averaging $2000). 41 state and other part-time jobs (averaging $1000). In 2003, 21 non-need-based awards were made. *Average financial aid package:* $15,975. *Average need-based loan:* $5500. *Average need-based gift aid:* $9178. *Average non-need-based aid:* $9500. *Average indebtedness upon graduation:* $16,500.

Applying *Options:* common application, electronic application, early admission, deferred entrance. *Application fee:* $35. *Required:* essay or personal statement, high school transcript, 2 letters of recommendation. *Recommended:* minimum 3.0 GPA, interview. *Application deadline:* rolling (freshmen), rolling (transfers). *Notification:* continuous until 8/1 (freshmen), continuous until 8/1 (transfers).

Admissions Contact Ms. Rennie H. Andrews, Dean of Admissions, Rosemont College, 1400 Montgomery Avenue, Rosemont, PA 19010. *Phone:* 610-527-0200 Ext. 2952. *Toll-free phone:* 800-331-0708. *Fax:* 610-520-4399. *E-mail:* admissions@rosemont.edu.

■ *See page 2260 for a narrative description.*

ST. CHARLES BORROMEO SEMINARY, OVERBROOK

Wynnewood, Pennsylvania

- **Independent Roman Catholic** comprehensive, founded 1832
- **Calendar** semesters
- **Degrees** certificates, bachelor's, master's, and first professional (also offers co-ed part-time programs)
- **Suburban** 77-acre campus with easy access to Philadelphia
- **Men only,** 278 undergraduate students, 31% full-time
- **Moderately difficult** entrance level, 100% of applicants were admitted

Undergraduates 85 full-time, 193 part-time. Students come from 9 states and territories, 1 other country, 36% are from out of state, 5% Asian American or Pacific Islander, 6% Hispanic American, 2% international, 6% transferred in. *Retention:* 75% of 2002 full-time freshmen returned.

Freshmen *Admission:* 15 applied, 15 admitted, 15 enrolled. *Test scores:* SAT verbal scores over 500: 54%; SAT math scores over 500: 62%; SAT verbal scores over 600: 46%; SAT math scores over 600: 31%; SAT math scores over 700: 8%.

Faculty *Total:* 39, 44% full-time, 44% with terminal degrees. *Student/faculty ratio:* 8:1.

Majors Philosophy.

Academic Programs *Special study options:* academic remediation for entering students, accelerated degree program, adult/continuing education programs, advanced placement credit, English as a second language, independent study, summer session for credit.

Library Ryan Memorial Library with 130,485 titles, 564 serial subscriptions, 8,838 audiovisual materials, a Web page.

Computers on Campus 48 computers available on campus for general student use. Internet access, at least one staffed computer lab available.

Student Life *Housing:* on-campus residence required through senior year. *Options:* men-only. Campus housing is university owned. Freshman campus housing is guaranteed. *Activities and organizations:* drama/theater group, student-run newspaper, choral group, Seminarians for Life, student council. *Campus security:* 24-hour emergency response devices and patrols. *Student services:* health clinic, personal/psychological counseling.

Athletics *Intramural sports:* basketball M, soccer M, volleyball M.

Standardized Tests *Recommended:* SAT I or ACT (for admission).

Costs (2003–04) *Comprehensive fee:* $16,160 includes full-time tuition ($9600) and room and board ($6560). Part-time tuition: $110 per credit. *Payment plan:* installment.

Applying *Options:* deferred entrance. *Required:* essay or personal statement, high school transcript, 3 letters of recommendation, interview, sponsorship by diocese or religious community. *Application deadlines:* 7/15 (freshmen), 7/15 (transfers). *Notification:* continuous (freshmen).

Admissions Contact Rev. Joseph G. Prior, Chief Academic Officer, St. Charles Borromeo Seminary, Overbrook, 100 East Wynnewood Road, Wynnewood, PA 19096. *Phone:* 610-785-6271 Ext. 271. *E-mail:* cao@adphila.org.

SAINT FRANCIS UNIVERSITY

Loretto, Pennsylvania

- **Independent Roman Catholic** comprehensive, founded 1847
- **Calendar** semesters
- **Degrees** certificates, associate, bachelor's, and master's
- **Rural** 600-acre campus
- **Endowment** $13.8 million
- **Coed,** 1,401 undergraduate students, 83% full-time, 60% women, 40% men
- **Moderately difficult** entrance level, 87% of applicants were admitted

Saint Francis University continues to be at the forefront of technology. Each first-year student receives a laptop computer as part of the cost of attendance. Students benefit from a totally wireless campus, a Web-based curriculum guide to enhance their learning experiences, and "smart" technology classrooms.

Undergraduates 1,157 full-time, 244 part-time. Students come from 29 states and territories, 23% are from out of state, 6% African American, 0.3% Asian American or Pacific Islander, 0.8% Hispanic American, 0.2% Native American, 0.6% international, 8% transferred in, 83% live on campus. *Retention:* 70% of 2002 full-time freshmen returned.

Freshmen *Admission:* 1,280 applied, 1,116 admitted, 335 enrolled. *Average high school GPA:* 3.39. *Test scores:* SAT verbal scores over 500: 59%; SAT math scores over 500: 60%; ACT scores over 18: 93%; SAT verbal scores over 600: 12%; SAT math scores over 600: 18%; ACT scores over 24: 47%; SAT verbal scores over 700: 1%; SAT math scores over 700: 3%.

Faculty *Total:* 117, 74% full-time, 58% with terminal degrees. *Student/faculty ratio:* 11:1.

Majors Accounting; accounting and finance; American studies; anthropology; biology/biological sciences; biology teacher education; business administration and management; chemistry; chemistry teacher education; clinical laboratory science/medical technology; computer programming; computer science; criminal justice/law enforcement administration; criminology; culinary arts; data processing and data processing technology; drafting and design technology; economics; education; elementary education; emergency medical technology (EMT paramedic); engineering; English; English/language arts teacher education; environmental science; environmental studies; finance; fine arts related; foreign language teacher education; forensic science and technology; French; French language teacher education; history; history teacher education; human resources management; international business/trade/commerce; international relations and affairs; journalism; labor and industrial relations; literature; management information systems; marine biology and biological oceanography; marketing/marketing management; mass communication/media; mathematics; mathematics and computer science; mathematics teacher education; modern languages; nursing (registered nurse training); occupational therapy; pastoral studies/counseling; philosophy; physical therapy; physician assistant; political science and government; pre-dentistry studies; pre-law studies; pre-medical studies; pre-veterinary studies; psychology; public administration; public relations/image management; real estate; religious studies; science teacher education; secondary education; social studies teacher education; social work; sociology; Spanish; special education.

Academic Programs *Special study options:* academic remediation for entering students, accelerated degree program, adult/continuing education programs, advanced placement credit, distance learning, double majors, freshman honors college, honors programs, internships, off-campus study, part-time degree program, student-designed majors, study abroad, summer session for credit. *ROTC:* Army (c). *Unusual degree programs:* 3-2 engineering with Pennsylvania State University—University Park Campus, University of Pittsburgh, Clarkson University; forestry with Duke University.

Library Pasquerella Library with 121,940 titles, 5,386 serial subscriptions, 2,899 audiovisual materials, an OPAC, a Web page.

Computers on Campus 60 computers available on campus for general student use. A campuswide network can be accessed from student residence rooms. At least one staffed computer lab available.

Student Life *Housing:* on-campus residence required through junior year. *Options:* men-only, women-only. Campus housing is university owned. Freshman campus housing is guaranteed. *Activities and organizations:* drama/theater group, student-run newspaper, radio and television station, choral group, Student Activities Organization, New Theatre, Student Government Association, national fraternities, national sororities. *Campus security:* 24-hour emergency response devices and patrols, late-night transport/escort service, controlled dormitory access. *Student services:* health clinic, personal/psychological counseling.

Athletics Member NCAA. All Division I except football (Division I-AA). *Intercollegiate sports:* basketball M(s)/W(s), cross-country running M(s)/W(s), field hockey W(s), golf M(s)/W(s), lacrosse W(s), soccer M(s)/W(s), softball W(s), swimming M(s)/W(s), tennis M(s)/W(s), track and field M(s)/W(s), volleyball M(s)/W(s). *Intramural sports:* basketball M/W, bowling M/W, cross-country running M/W, football M, golf M/W, lacrosse W, racquetball M/W, skiing (cross-country) M/W, skiing (downhill) M/W, soccer M/W, softball W, swimming M/W, table tennis M/W, tennis M/W, track and field M/W, ultimate Frisbee M/W, volleyball M/W, weight lifting M/W.

Standardized Tests *Required:* SAT I or ACT (for admission).

Costs (2003–04) *Comprehensive fee:* $26,688 includes full-time tuition ($18,292), mandatory fees ($1050), and room and board ($7346). Part-time tuition: $572 per hour. Part-time tuition and fees vary according to course load. *College room only:* $3564. Room and board charges vary according to board plan, housing facility, and location. *Payment plans:* installment, deferred payment. *Waivers:* children of alumni and employees or children of employees.

Financial Aid Of all full-time matriculated undergraduates who enrolled in 2003, 1,027 applied for aid, 941 were judged to have need, 305 had their need fully met. 724 Federal Work-Study jobs (averaging $1000). 30 state and other part-time jobs (averaging $991). In 2003, 138 non-need-based awards were made. *Average percent of need met:* 82%. *Average financial aid package:* $17,128. *Average need-based loan:* $4531. *Average need-based gift aid:* $12,421. *Average non-need-based aid:* $9562. *Average indebtedness upon graduation:* $14,100.

Applying *Options:* electronic application, deferred entrance. *Application fee:* $30. *Required:* high school transcript, 1 letter of recommendation. *Required for some:* 3 letters of recommendation, interview. *Recommended:* essay or personal statement, interview. *Application deadline:* rolling (freshmen), rolling (transfers). *Notification:* continuous (transfers).

Admissions Contact Mr. Evan E. Lipp, Dean for Enrollment Management, Saint Francis University, PO Box 600, Loretto, PA 15940-0600. *Phone:* 814-472-3100. *Toll-free phone:* 800-342-5732. *Fax:* 814-472-3335. *E-mail:* admission@sfcpa.edu.

■ *See page 2282 for a narrative description.*

SAINT JOSEPH'S UNIVERSITY

Philadelphia, Pennsylvania

- **Independent Roman Catholic (Jesuit)** comprehensive, founded 1851
- **Calendar** semesters
- **Degrees** certificates, bachelor's, master's, doctoral, post-master's, and postbachelor's certificates
- **Suburban** 65-acre campus
- **Endowment** $75.3 million
- **Coed,** 4,656 undergraduate students, 82% full-time, 53% women, 47% men
- **Very difficult** entrance level, 48% of applicants were admitted

Founded by the Society of Jesus in 1851, Saint Joseph's University advances the professional and personal ambitions of men and women by providing a demanding and supportive experience. One of only 137 schools with a Phi Beta Kappa chapter and AACSB-International accreditation, Saint Joseph's is home to 3,900 full-time undergraduates and 3,400 graduate, part-time, and doctoral students.

Undergraduates 3,819 full-time, 837 part-time. Students come from 35 states and territories, 29 other countries, 44% are from out of state, 7% African American, 3% Asian American or Pacific Islander, 2% Hispanic American, 0.1% Native American, 1% international, 2% transferred in, 53% live on campus. *Retention:* 88% of 2002 full-time freshmen returned.

Freshmen *Admission:* 7,765 applied, 3,753 admitted, 998 enrolled. *Average high school GPA:* 3.41. *Test scores:* SAT verbal scores over 500: 86%; SAT math scores over 500: 88%; SAT verbal scores over 600: 33%; SAT math scores over 600: 40%; SAT verbal scores over 700: 5%; SAT math scores over 700: 6%.

Faculty *Total:* 514, 49% full-time. *Student/faculty ratio:* 15:1.

Majors Accounting; biochemistry; biology/biological sciences; business administration and management; chemistry; communication/speech communication and rhetoric; computer and information sciences; computer science; criminal justice/law enforcement administration; criminology; economics; education; elementary education; English; environmental science; finance; French; French studies; German; health/health care administration; health professions related; history; hospital and health care facilities administration; human services; information science/studies; interdisciplinary studies; international relations and affairs; legal professions and studies related; liberal arts and sciences/liberal studies; management information systems; management science; marketing/marketing management; marketing related; mathematics; philosophy; physics; political science and government; psychology; public administration; purchasing, procurement/acquisitions and contracts management; religious studies; secondary education; social sciences; sociology; Spanish; special education related; theology; visual and performing arts.

Academic Programs *Special study options:* academic remediation for entering students, adult/continuing education programs, advanced placement credit, cooperative education, double majors, English as a second language, honors programs, independent study, internships, off-campus study, part-time degree program, services for LD students, student-designed majors, study abroad, summer session for credit. *ROTC:* Army (c), Air Force (b).

Library Francis A. Drexel Library plus 1 other with 347,877 titles, 3,949 audiovisual materials, an OPAC, a Web page.

Computers on Campus 180 computers available on campus for general student use. A campuswide network can be accessed from student residence rooms and from off campus. Internet access, online (class) registration, at least one staffed computer lab available. Computer purchase or lease plan available.

Student Life *Housing:* on-campus residence required through sophomore year. *Options:* coed, men-only, women-only, disabled students. Campus housing is university owned and leased by the school. Freshman campus housing is guaranteed. *Activities and organizations:* drama/theater group, student-run newspaper, radio station, choral group, University Student Senate, Student Union Board, Cap and Bells Dramatic Arts Society, Hand-in-Hand, Up 'til Dawn, national fraternities, national sororities. *Campus security:* 24-hour emergency response devices and patrols, late-night transport/escort service, controlled dormitory access, 24-hour shuttle/escort service, bicycle patrols. *Student services:* health clinic, personal/psychological counseling.

Athletics Member NCAA. All Division I. *Intercollegiate sports:* baseball M(s), basketball M(s)/W(s), crew M(s)(c)/W(s)(c), cross-country running M(s)/W(s), field hockey W(s), golf M(s), lacrosse M(s)/W(s), soccer M(s)/W(s), softball W(s), tennis M(s)/W(s), track and field M(s)/W(s). *Intramural sports:* basketball M/W, field hockey W(c), golf M, ice hockey M(c), racquetball M/W, rugby M(c)/W(c), tennis M/W.

Standardized Tests *Required:* SAT I or ACT (for admission). *Recommended:* SAT II: Subject Tests (for admission).

Costs (2003–04) *Comprehensive fee:* $33,630 includes full-time tuition ($24,095), mandatory fees ($135), and room and board ($9400). Full-time tuition and fees vary according to program. Part-time tuition: $375 per credit. *College room only:* $5950. Room and board charges vary according to housing facility. *Payment plans:* installment, deferred payment. *Waivers:* employees or children of employees.

Financial Aid Of all full-time matriculated undergraduates who enrolled in 2002, 2,620 applied for aid, 2,175 were judged to have need, 891 had their need fully met. 350 Federal Work-Study jobs (averaging $949). In 2002, 737 non-need-based awards were made. *Average percent of need met:* 80%. *Average financial aid package:* $11,862. *Average need-based loan:* $4890. *Average need-based gift aid:* $7590. *Average non-need-based aid:* $6580. *Average indebtedness upon graduation:* $15,734.

Applying *Options:* common application, electronic application, deferred entrance. *Application fee:* $45. *Required:* essay or personal statement, high school transcript, 1 letter of recommendation. *Recommended:* minimum 3.0 GPA. *Application deadline:* 3/1 (transfers). *Notification:* 10/1 (freshmen), continuous until 5/1 (transfers).

Admissions Contact Ms. Susan Kassab, Director of Admissions, Saint Joseph's University, 5600 City Avenue, Philadelphia, PA 19131-1395. *Phone:* 610-660-1300. *Toll-free phone:* 888-BEAHAWK. *Fax:* 610-660-1314. *E-mail:* admit@sju.edu.

■ *See page 2300 for a narrative description.*

SAINT VINCENT COLLEGE

Latrobe, Pennsylvania

- **Independent Roman Catholic** comprehensive, founded 1846
- **Calendar** semesters
- **Degrees** certificates, bachelor's, master's, and postbachelor's certificates
- **Suburban** 200-acre campus with easy access to Pittsburgh
- **Endowment** $33.8 million
- **Coed,** 1,440 undergraduate students, 88% full-time, 50% women, 50% men
- **Moderately difficult** entrance level, 75% of applicants were admitted

Undergraduates 1,265 full-time, 175 part-time. Students come from 26 states and territories, 20 other countries, 15% are from out of state, 2% African American, 1% Asian American or Pacific Islander, 0.9% Hispanic American, 0.4% Native American, 2% international, 4% transferred in, 78% live on campus. *Retention:* 87% of 2002 full-time freshmen returned.

Freshmen *Admission:* 1,327 applied, 989 admitted, 361 enrolled. *Average high school GPA:* 3.53. *Test scores:* SAT verbal scores over 500: 73%; SAT math scores over 500: 69%; ACT scores over 18: 92%; SAT verbal scores over 600: 22%; SAT math scores over 600: 26%; ACT scores over 24: 38%; SAT verbal scores over 700: 3%; SAT math scores over 700: 3%; ACT scores over 30: 3%.

Faculty *Total:* 138, 59% full-time, 61% with terminal degrees. *Student/faculty ratio:* 13:1.

Majors Accounting; anthropology; art history, criticism and conservation; art teacher education; biochemistry; biology/biological sciences; business administration and management; business, management, and marketing related; business

Saint Vincent College (continued)
teacher education; chemistry; communication/speech communication and rhetoric; computer and information sciences; dramatic/theatre arts; economics; engineering; English; environmental science; environmental studies; finance; fine/studio arts; French; history; international business/trade/commerce; liberal arts and sciences/liberal studies; marketing/marketing management; mathematics; music; music performance; music teacher education; occupational therapy; pharmacy; philosophy; physical therapy; physician assistant; physics; physics teacher education; political science and government; psychology; public policy analysis; religious education; sociology; Spanish; theology.

Academic Programs *Special study options:* accelerated degree program, adult/continuing education programs, advanced placement credit, cooperative education, honors programs, independent study, internships, off-campus study, part-time degree program, study abroad, summer session for credit. *ROTC:* Air Force (c). *Unusual degree programs:* 3-2 engineering with University of Pittsburgh, Pennsylvania State University, Boston University, The Catholic University of America; physician assistant, physical therapy, occupational therapy with Duquesne University.

Library Saint Vincent College Library with 268,324 titles, 791 serial subscriptions, 3,966 audiovisual materials, an OPAC.

Computers on Campus 192 computers available on campus for general student use. A campuswide network can be accessed from student residence rooms and from off campus. Internet access, at least one staffed computer lab available.

Student Life *Housing options:* coed. Campus housing is university owned. Freshman applicants given priority for college housing. *Activities and organizations:* drama/theater group, student-run newspaper, radio and television station, choral group, The Company (Student Theatre Group), Dreamkeepers Society (Student Multicultural Organization), Student Orientation Program, student government, Alpha Lambda Delta (Academic Honor Society). *Campus security:* 24-hour emergency response devices and patrols, late-night transport/escort service, controlled dormitory access, limited access to residence halls on weekends. *Student services:* health clinic, personal/psychological counseling.

Athletics Member NAIA. *Intercollegiate sports:* baseball M(s), basketball M(s)/W(s), cheerleading M(s)/W(s), cross-country running M(s)/W(s), golf M(s)/W(s), lacrosse M(s)/W(s), soccer M(s)/W(s), softball W(s), tennis M(s)/W(s), ultimate Frisbee M(c)/W(c), volleyball W(s). *Intramural sports:* basketball M/W, equestrian sports W(c), fencing M/W, football M/W, ice hockey M(c), rock climbing M/W, softball M/W, table tennis M/W, ultimate Frisbee M/W, volleyball M/W.

Standardized Tests *Required:* SAT I or ACT (for admission).

Costs (2003–04) *Comprehensive fee:* $25,530 includes full-time tuition ($19,000), mandatory fees ($470), and room and board ($6060). Part-time tuition: $594 per credit hour. *Required fees:* $45 per term part-time. *College room only:* $3080. Room and board charges vary according to student level. *Payment plan:* installment. *Waivers:* senior citizens and employees or children of employees.

Financial Aid Of all full-time matriculated undergraduates who enrolled in 2002, 1,108 applied for aid, 909 were judged to have need, 252 had their need fully met. 146 Federal Work-Study jobs (averaging $1875). In 2002, 199 non-need-based awards were made. *Average percent of need met:* 86%. *Average financial aid package:* $14,796. *Average need-based loan:* $4101. *Average need-based gift aid:* $10,150. *Average non-need-based aid:* $5799. *Financial aid deadline:* 5/1.

Applying *Options:* early admission, deferred entrance. *Application fee:* $25. *Required:* essay or personal statement, high school transcript, minimum 2.5 GPA. *Required for some:* interview. *Recommended:* minimum 3.2 GPA, 3 letters of recommendation, interview. *Application deadlines:* 5/1 (freshmen), 7/1 (transfers). *Notification:* continuous (freshmen), continuous (transfers).

Admissions Contact Mr. David A. Collins, Assistant Vice President of Admission and Financial Aid, Saint Vincent College, 300 Fraser Purchase Road, Latrobe, PA 15650. *Phone:* 724-532-5089. *Toll-free phone:* 800-782-5549. *Fax:* 724-532-5069. *E-mail:* admission@stvincent.edu.

■ *See page 2332 for a narrative description.*

SETON HILL UNIVERSITY
Greensburg, Pennsylvania

- **Independent Roman Catholic** comprehensive, founded 1883
- **Calendar** semesters
- **Degrees** certificates, bachelor's, master's, post-master's, and postbachelor's certificates
- **Small-town** 200-acre campus with easy access to Pittsburgh
- **Endowment** $7.6 million
- **Coed,** 1,292 undergraduate students, 74% full-time, 74% women, 26% men
- **Moderately difficult** entrance level, 84% of applicants were admitted

Seton Hill University offers 30 undergraduate majors, including physician assistant studies, dietetics, and teacher training, and master's degrees in education, art therapy, business administration, writing, marriage and family therapy, and technologies enhanced learning.

Undergraduates 951 full-time, 341 part-time. Students come from 26 states and territories, 17 other countries, 17% are from out of state, 6% African American, 2% Asian American or Pacific Islander, 1% Hispanic American, 0.3% Native American, 2% international, 12% transferred in, 65% live on campus. *Retention:* 79% of 2002 full-time freshmen returned.

Freshmen *Admission:* 945 applied, 798 admitted, 231 enrolled. *Average high school GPA:* 3.19.

Faculty *Total:* 140, 43% full-time, 49% with terminal degrees. *Student/faculty ratio:* 13:1.

Majors Accounting; acting; actuarial science; art history, criticism and conservation; arts management; art teacher education; art therapy; biochemistry; biology/biological sciences; biology teacher education; business administration and management; business/managerial economics; ceramic arts and ceramics; chemistry; chemistry teacher education; child care and support services management; child development; clinical laboratory science/medical technology; commercial and advertising art; communication/speech communication and rhetoric; community health services counseling; community psychology; computer science; creative writing; dietetics; dramatic/theatre arts; dramatic/theatre arts and stagecraft related; drawing; economics; educational/instructional media design; elementary education; engineering; English; English/language arts teacher education; entrepreneurship; family and consumer sciences/home economics teacher education; family and consumer sciences/human sciences; finance; fine/studio arts; foreign language teacher education; general studies; history; hospitality administration; human resources management; human services; international business/trade/commerce; international relations and affairs; journalism; kindergarten/preschool education; management information systems; marketing/marketing management; marriage and family therapy/counseling; mathematics; mathematics related; mathematics teacher education; metal and jewelry arts; music; music performance; music teacher education; music theory and composition; nursing (registered nurse training); painting; physician assistant; physics; piano and organ; political science and government; pre-dentistry studies; pre-law studies; pre-medical studies; pre-veterinary studies; printmaking; psychology; religious/sacred music; religious studies; sales, distribution and marketing; sculpture; social studies teacher education; social work; sociology; Spanish; Spanish language teacher education; special education; theatre design and technology; theatre/theatre arts management; violin, viola, guitar and other stringed instruments; voice and opera; wind/percussion instruments.

Academic Programs *Special study options:* academic remediation for entering students, accelerated degree program, adult/continuing education programs, advanced placement credit, distance learning, double majors, English as a second language, honors programs, independent study, internships, off-campus study, part-time degree program, student-designed majors, study abroad, summer session for credit. *ROTC:* Army (c). *Unusual degree programs:* 3-2 engineering with University of Pittsburgh, Pennsylvania State University—University Park Campus, Georgia Institute of Technology; nursing with Catholic University of America.

Library Reeves Memorial Library with 80,370 titles, 361 serial subscriptions, 6,185 audiovisual materials, an OPAC, a Web page.

Computers on Campus 251 computers available on campus for general student use. A campuswide network can be accessed from student residence rooms and from off campus that provide access to e-mail. Internet access, online (class) registration, at least one staffed computer lab available.

Student Life *Housing options:* coed, men-only, women-only. Campus housing is university owned. Freshman campus housing is guaranteed. *Activities and organizations:* drama/theater group, student-run newspaper, television station, choral group, Intercultural Student Organization, Biology/Environmental Club, Association of Black Collegians, Chemistry Club, Pennsylvania Student Education Association. *Campus security:* 24-hour emergency response devices and patrols, late-night transport/escort service, controlled dormitory access, student personnel at entrances during evening hours, 15-hour overnight patrols by trained police officers. *Student services:* health clinic, personal/psychological counseling.

Athletics Member NAIA. *Intercollegiate sports:* baseball M(s), basketball M(s)/W(s), cross-country running M(s)/W(s), equestrian sports M(s)/W(s), field hockey W(s), golf M(s)/W(s), lacrosse M(s)/W(s), soccer M(s)/W(s), softball W(s), tennis M(s)/W(s), volleyball W(s). *Intramural sports:* basketball W, cheerleading M/W, skiing (cross-country) M(c)/W(c), skiing (downhill) M(c)/W(c).

Standardized Tests *Recommended:* SAT I or ACT (for admission).

Costs (2003–04) *Comprehensive fee:* $24,930 includes full-time tuition ($18,930) and room and board ($6000). Part-time tuition: $500 per credit. Part-time tuition and fees vary according to course load. *Required fees:* $50 per term part-time. *Room and board:* Room and board charges vary according to board plan. *Payment plans:* installment, deferred payment. *Waivers:* employees or children of employees.

Financial Aid Of all full-time matriculated undergraduates who enrolled in 2003, 791 applied for aid, 765 were judged to have need, 145 had their need fully met. 180 Federal Work-Study jobs (averaging $1236). 250 state and other part-time jobs (averaging $1200). In 2003, 20 non-need-based awards were made. *Average percent of need met:* 75%. *Average financial aid package:* $14,658. *Average need-based loan:* $3449. *Average need-based gift aid:* $11,000. *Average non-need-based aid:* $7667. *Average indebtedness upon graduation:* $17,014.

Applying *Options:* common application, electronic application, early admission, deferred entrance. *Application fee:* $30. *Required:* high school transcript, minimum 2.0 GPA, portfolio for art program, audition for music and theater programs, separate application process required for physician assistant program. *Recommended:* essay or personal statement, letters of recommendation, interview. *Application deadline:* 8/15 (freshmen), rolling (transfers). *Notification:* continuous (freshmen), continuous (transfers).

Admissions Contact Ms. Mary Kay Cooper, Director of Admissions, Seton Hill University, Seton Hill Drive, Greensburg, PA 15601. *Phone:* 724-838-4255. *Toll-free phone:* 800-826-6234. *Fax:* 724-830-1294. *E-mail:* admit@setonhill.edu.

■ *See page 2370 for a narrative description.*

SHIPPENSBURG UNIVERSITY OF PENNSYLVANIA

Shippensburg, Pennsylvania

- **State-supported** comprehensive, founded 1871, part of Pennsylvania State System of Higher Education
- **Calendar** semesters
- **Degrees** certificates, bachelor's, master's, and post-master's certificates
- **Rural** 200-acre campus
- **Endowment** $16.4 million
- **Coed,** 6,567 undergraduate students, 96% full-time, 53% women, 47% men
- **Moderately difficult** entrance level, 67% of applicants were admitted

Recognized for its academic excellence, Shippensburg University has a national reputation for providing students with opportunities for student-faculty research, volunteer community service projects, and internships. The talented, dedicated faculty offers a personalized education. Recent renovations of several academic buildings further complement the academic quality.

Undergraduates 6,294 full-time, 273 part-time. Students come from 23 states and territories, 24 other countries, 5% are from out of state, 4% African American, 1% Asian American or Pacific Islander, 1% Hispanic American, 0.2% Native American, 0.4% international, 5% transferred in, 41% live on campus. *Retention:* 79% of 2002 full-time freshmen returned.

Freshmen *Admission:* 5,863 applied, 3,916 admitted, 1,493 enrolled. *Average high school GPA:* 3.20. *Test scores:* SAT verbal scores over 500: 64%; SAT math scores over 500: 68%; SAT verbal scores over 600: 16%; SAT math scores over 600: 18%; SAT verbal scores over 700: 1%; SAT math scores over 700: 2%.

Faculty *Total:* 365, 84% full-time, 80% with terminal degrees. *Student/faculty ratio:* 21:1.

Majors Accounting; art; biology/biological sciences; business administration and management; business/commerce; chemistry; computer and information sciences; computer systems analysis; criminal justice/safety; economics; elementary education; English; environmental studies; finance; French; geography; geology/earth science; history; journalism; management science; marketing/marketing management; mathematics; multi-/interdisciplinary studies related; physics; political science and government; psychology; public administration; social work; sociology; Spanish; speech and rhetoric.

Academic Programs *Special study options:* academic remediation for entering students, accelerated degree program, advanced placement credit, cooperative education, double majors, honors programs, independent study, internships, off-campus study, part-time degree program, services for LD students, study abroad, summer session for credit. *ROTC:* Army (b). *Unusual degree programs:* 3-2 engineering with Pennsylvania State University—University Park and Harrisburg Campus, University of Maryland College Park.

Library Ezra Lehman Memorial Library plus 1 other with 449,590 titles, 1,757 serial subscriptions, 76,583 audiovisual materials, an OPAC, a Web page.

Computers on Campus 527 computers available on campus for general student use. A campuswide network can be accessed from student residence rooms and from off campus that provide access to personal web pages. Internet access, at least one staffed computer lab available.

Student Life *Housing:* on-campus residence required for freshman year. *Options:* coed, men-only, women-only. Campus housing is university owned and leased by the school. Freshman campus housing is guaranteed. *Activities and organizations:* drama/theater group, student-run newspaper, radio and television station, choral group, marching band, band, Christian Fellowship, Residence Hall Association, United Campus Ministry, African-American Organization, national fraternities, national sororities. *Campus security:* 24-hour emergency response devices and patrols, student patrols, late-night transport/escort service, controlled dormitory access, surveillance cameras in certain parking lots and buildings, foot, vehicular and bicycle patrols by security officers. *Student services:* health clinic, personal/psychological counseling, women's center.

Athletics Member NCAA. All Division II. *Intercollegiate sports:* baseball M(s), basketball M(s)/W(s), cross-country running M(s)/W(s), field hockey W(s), football M(s), lacrosse W(s), soccer M(s)/W(s), softball W(s), swimming M(s)/W(s), tennis W(s), track and field M(s)/W(s), volleyball W(s), wrestling M(s). *Intramural sports:* basketball M/W, bowling M/W, cross-country running M/W, football M, ice hockey M(c)/W(c), lacrosse M(c), racquetball M/W, rugby M(c)/W(c), soccer M/W, softball M/W, swimming M/W, table tennis M/W, tennis M(c), volleyball M/W, water polo M(c)/W(c), wrestling M.

Standardized Tests *Required:* SAT I or ACT (for admission).

Costs (2003–04) *Tuition:* state resident $4598 full-time, $192 per credit hour part-time; nonresident $11,546 full-time, $492 per credit hour part-time. *Required fees:* $1148 full-time, $19 per credit hour part-time, $127 per term part-time. *Room and board:* $5080; room only: $3086. Room and board charges vary according to board plan and housing facility. *Payment plan:* installment. *Waivers:* senior citizens and employees or children of employees.

Financial Aid Of all full-time matriculated undergraduates who enrolled in 2003, 4,564 applied for aid, 3,279 were judged to have need, 784 had their need fully met. 356 Federal Work-Study jobs (averaging $1748). 275 state and other part-time jobs (averaging $1922). In 2003, 1683 non-need-based awards were made. *Average percent of need met:* 72%. *Average financial aid package:* $5980. *Average need-based loan:* $3352. *Average need-based gift aid:* $3596. *Average non-need-based aid:* $727. *Average indebtedness upon graduation:* $15,464.

Applying *Options:* common application, electronic application, early admission, deferred entrance. *Application fee:* $30. *Required:* high school transcript. *Required for some:* essay or personal statement. *Recommended:* letters of recommendation, class rank. *Application deadline:* rolling (freshmen), rolling (transfers). *Notification:* continuous (freshmen), continuous (transfers).

Admissions Contact Mr. Joseph Cretella, Dean of Undergraduate and Graduate Admissions, Shippensburg University of Pennsylvania, 1871 Old Main Drive, Shippensburg, PA 17257-2299. *Phone:* 717-477-1231. *Toll-free phone:* 800-822-8028. *Fax:* 717-477-4016. *E-mail:* admiss@ship.edu.

■ *See page 2380 for a narrative description.*

SLIPPERY ROCK UNIVERSITY OF PENNSYLVANIA

Slippery Rock, Pennsylvania

- **State-supported** comprehensive, founded 1889, part of Pennsylvania State System of Higher Education
- **Calendar** semesters
- **Degrees** bachelor's, master's, doctoral, and postbachelor's certificates
- **Rural** 600-acre campus with easy access to Pittsburgh
- **Endowment** $10.9 million
- **Coed,** 7,054 undergraduate students, 91% full-time, 56% women, 44% men
- **Moderately difficult** entrance level, 81% of applicants were admitted

A Slippery Rock University "Rock Solid Education" is an intellectually challenging and fun living and learning experience at a comprehensive, medium-sized university for a reasonable price. A "Rock Solid Education" is a student's once-in-a-lifetime opportunity to lay the foundation for the future. Slippery Rock University of Pennsylvania is a rolling campus of more than 600 acres located in a college town in western Pennsylvania just north of Pittsburgh. Nestled among scenic forests and lakes, it is no wonder so many visitors comment on the natural beauty of the area. The mix of modern and stately architecture blends a sense of tradition with the latest technologies for an outstanding living and learning experience.

Undergraduates 6,415 full-time, 639 part-time. Students come from 29 states and territories, 47 other countries, 4% are from out of state, 4% African American, 0.6% Asian American or Pacific Islander, 0.7% Hispanic American, 0.4% Native American, 2% international, 8% transferred in, 38% live on campus. *Retention:* 78% of 2002 full-time freshmen returned.

Freshmen *Admission:* 4,310 applied, 3,481 admitted, 1,491 enrolled. *Average high school GPA:* 3.17. *Test scores:* SAT verbal scores over 500: 48%; SAT math scores over 500: 47%; ACT scores over 18: 83%; SAT verbal scores over 600: 8%; SAT math scores over 600: 9%; ACT scores over 24: 20%; SAT verbal scores over 700: 1%; SAT math scores over 700: 1%; ACT scores over 30: 1%.

Faculty *Total:* 388, 90% full-time, 75% with terminal degrees. *Student/faculty ratio:* 20:1.

Majors Anthropology; art; athletic training; biology/biological sciences; business administration and management; chemistry; clinical/medical laboratory

Slippery Rock University of Pennsylvania (continued)
technology; clinical/medical social work; communication/speech communication and rhetoric; computer and information sciences; cytotechnology; dance; dramatic/theatre arts; economics; elementary education; English; environmental science; environmental studies; French; geography; geology/earth science; health and physical education; history; information technology; mathematics; modern languages; music; music performance; music therapy; natural resources/conservation; nursing (registered nurse training); occupational safety and health technology; parks, recreation and leisure facilities management; philosophy; physics; political science and government; psychology; public health; science, technology and society; social work; sociology; Spanish; special education.

Academic Programs *Special study options:* academic remediation for entering students, accelerated degree program, adult/continuing education programs, advanced placement credit, distance learning, double majors, honors programs, independent study, internships, off-campus study, part-time degree program, services for LD students, study abroad, summer session for credit. *ROTC:* Army (b). *Unusual degree programs:* 3-2 engineering with Pennsylvania State University, University Park Campus.

Library Bailey Library with 774,723 titles, 14,101 serial subscriptions, 86,686 audiovisual materials, an OPAC, a Web page.

Computers on Campus 940 computers available on campus for general student use. A campuswide network can be accessed from student residence rooms and from off campus. Internet access, online (class) registration, at least one staffed computer lab available. Computer purchase or lease plan available.

Student Life *Housing:* on-campus residence required for freshman year. *Options:* coed, women-only, disabled students. Campus housing is university owned. Freshman campus housing is guaranteed. *Activities and organizations:* drama/theater group, student-run newspaper, radio station, choral group, marching band, Association of Residence Hall Students, University Program Board, Student Union for Minority Affairs, Fraternity and Sorority Life, Student Government Association, national fraternities, national sororities. *Campus security:* 24-hour emergency response devices and patrols, late-night transport/escort service, controlled dormitory access. *Student services:* health clinic, personal/psychological counseling, women's center, legal services.

Athletics Member NCAA. All Division II except wrestling (Division I). *Intercollegiate sports:* baseball M(s), basketball M(s)/W(s), cheerleading M/W, cross-country running M(s)/W(s), field hockey W(s), football M(s), golf M(s)/W(s), soccer M(s)/W(s), softball W(s), swimming M(s)/W(s), tennis M/W(s), track and field M(s)/W(s), volleyball W(s), water polo M(s)/W(s), wrestling M(s). *Intramural sports:* badminton M/W, basketball M/W, cross-country running M/W, equestrian sports W(c), football M/W, golf M/W, ice hockey M(c)/W(c), lacrosse M(c)/W(c), racquetball M/W, rugby M(c)/W(c), soccer M/W, softball M/W, swimming M/W, tennis M/W, track and field M/W, ultimate Frisbee M/W, volleyball M(c)/W, water polo M/W, weight lifting M/W, wrestling M/W.

Standardized Tests *Required:* SAT I or ACT (for admission).

Costs (2003–04) *Tuition:* state resident $4598 full-time, $192 per credit part-time; nonresident $11,496 full-time, $479 per credit part-time. Full-time tuition and fees vary according to course load. Part-time tuition and fees vary according to course load. *Required fees:* $1203 full-time, $48 per credit part-time, $25 per term part-time. *Room and board:* $4542; room only: $2438. Room and board charges vary according to board plan, housing facility, and location. *Payment plan:* installment. *Waivers:* minority students, senior citizens, and employees or children of employees.

Financial Aid Of all full-time matriculated undergraduates who enrolled in 2003, 5,593 applied for aid, 3,944 were judged to have need, 2,751 had their need fully met. In 2003, 1377 non-need-based awards were made. *Average percent of need met:* 85%. *Average financial aid package:* $6402. *Average need-based loan:* $2964. *Average need-based gift aid:* $2767. *Average non-need-based aid:* $4471. *Average indebtedness upon graduation:* $19,195.

Applying *Options:* electronic application, early admission, deferred entrance. *Application fee:* $25. *Required:* high school transcript, standardized test scores. *Application deadline:* 6/1 (freshmen). *Notification:* continuous (freshmen), continuous (transfers).

Admissions Contact Mr. James Barrett, Director of Undergraduate Admissions, Slippery Rock University of Pennsylvania, 1 Morrow Way, 146 North Hall, Slippery Rock, PA 16057. *Phone:* 724-738-2015 Ext. 4984. *Toll-free phone:* 800-SRU-9111. *Fax:* 724-738-2913. *E-mail:* asktherock@sru.edu.

■ *See page 2396 for a narrative description.*

SUSQUEHANNA UNIVERSITY
Selinsgrove, Pennsylvania

- **Independent** 4-year, founded 1858, affiliated with Evangelical Lutheran Church in America
- **Calendar** semesters
- **Degrees** bachelor's (also offers associate degree through evening program to local students)
- **Suburban** 220-acre campus with easy access to Harrisburg
- **Endowment** $81.3 million
- **Coed,** 2,009 undergraduate students, 96% full-time, 57% women, 43% men
- **Moderately difficult** entrance level, 70% of applicants were admitted

Undergraduates 1,919 full-time, 90 part-time. Students come from 24 states and territories, 11 other countries, 40% are from out of state, 2% African American, 2% Asian American or Pacific Islander, 2% Hispanic American, 0.3% Native American, 0.6% international, 2% transferred in, 80% live on campus. *Retention:* 88% of 2002 full-time freshmen returned.

Freshmen *Admission:* 2,373 applied, 1,660 admitted, 499 enrolled. *Test scores:* SAT verbal scores over 500: 89%; SAT math scores over 500: 90%; SAT verbal scores over 600: 33%; SAT math scores over 600: 42%; SAT verbal scores over 700: 3%; SAT math scores over 700: 3%.

Faculty *Total:* 186, 63% full-time, 67% with terminal degrees. *Student/faculty ratio:* 13:1.

Majors Accounting; art; art history, criticism and conservation; biochemistry; biology/biological sciences; broadcast journalism; business administration and management; business/managerial economics; chemistry; communication/speech communication and rhetoric; computer science; creative writing; dramatic/theatre arts; ecology; economics; elementary education; English; finance; French; geology/earth science; German; graphic design; history; human resources management; information science/studies; international relations and affairs; journalism; kindergarten/preschool education; marketing/marketing management; mass communication/media; mathematics; music; music teacher education; philosophy; physics; piano and organ; political science and government; pre-dentistry studies; pre-law studies; pre-medical studies; pre-veterinary studies; psychology; public relations/image management; radio and television; religious/sacred music; religious studies; secondary education; sociology; Spanish; speech and rhetoric; violin, viola, guitar and other stringed instruments; voice and opera; wind/percussion instruments.

Academic Programs *Special study options:* accelerated degree program, adult/continuing education programs, advanced placement credit, double majors, honors programs, independent study, internships, off-campus study, part-time degree program, student-designed majors, study abroad, summer session for credit. *ROTC:* Army (c). *Unusual degree programs:* 3-2 engineering with Pennsylvania State University—University Park Campus; forestry with Duke University; environmental management with Duke University, allied health programs with Thomas Jefferson University, dentistry with Temple University.

Library Blough-Weis Library with 279,149 titles, 11,078 serial subscriptions, 21,052 audiovisual materials, an OPAC, a Web page.

Computers on Campus 295 computers available on campus for general student use. A campuswide network can be accessed from student residence rooms and from off campus that provide access to e-mail, class listings and assignments, online voting booth. Internet access, at least one staffed computer lab available.

Student Life *Housing:* on-campus residence required through junior year. *Options:* coed. Campus housing is university owned. Freshman campus housing is guaranteed. *Activities and organizations:* drama/theater group, student-run newspaper, radio station, choral group, Student Government Association, community service organizations, music performance groups, theater performance groups, intramurals and outdoor recreation, national fraternities, national sororities. *Campus security:* 24-hour patrols, late-night transport/escort service, controlled dormitory access. *Student services:* health clinic, personal/psychological counseling, women's center.

Athletics Member NCAA. All Division III. *Intercollegiate sports:* baseball M, basketball M/W, cheerleading M(c)/W(c), crew M(c)/W(c), cross-country running M/W, equestrian sports M(c)/W(c), field hockey W, football M, golf M, lacrosse M/W, rugby M(c)/W(c), soccer M/W, softball W, swimming M/W, tennis M/W, track and field M/W, volleyball M(c)/W. *Intramural sports:* basketball M/W, football M/W, soccer M/W, softball M/W, tennis M/W, ultimate Frisbee M, volleyball M/W.

Standardized Tests *Required for some:* SAT I or ACT (for admission). *Recommended:* SAT II: Subject Tests (for admission), SAT II: Writing Test (for admission).

Costs (2003–04) *Comprehensive fee:* $29,990 includes full-time tuition ($23,170), mandatory fees ($310), and room and board ($6510). Part-time tuition: $740 per semester hour. *College room only:* $3440. *Payment plans:* tuition prepayment, installment, deferred payment. *Waivers:* employees or children of employees.

Financial Aid Of all full-time matriculated undergraduates who enrolled in 2003, 1,415 applied for aid, 1,229 were judged to have need, 285 had their need fully met. 910 Federal Work-Study jobs (averaging $1517). 65 state and other part-time jobs (averaging $3600). In 2003, 454 non-need-based awards were made. *Average percent of need met:* 82%. *Average financial aid package:*

$17,158. *Average need-based loan:* $3703. *Average need-based gift aid:* $13,319. *Average non-need-based aid:* $8143. *Average indebtedness upon graduation:* $16,756. *Financial aid deadline:* 5/1.

Applying *Options:* common application, electronic application, early admission, early decision, deferred entrance. *Application fee:* $35. *Required:* essay or personal statement, high school transcript, minimum 2.5 GPA, 1 letter of recommendation. *Required for some:* writing portfolio, auditions for music programs. *Recommended:* minimum 3.0 GPA, interview. *Application deadlines:* 3/1 (freshmen), 7/1 (transfers). *Early decision:* 11/15 (for plan 1), 1/1 (for plan 2). *Notification:* 4/15 (freshmen), 12/1 (early decision plan 1), 1/15 (early decision plan 2), 8/15 (transfers).

Admissions Contact Mr. Chris Markle, Director of Admissions, Susquehanna University, 514 University Avenue, Selinsgrove, PA 17870-1040. *Phone:* 570-372-4260. *Toll-free phone:* 800-326-9672. *Fax:* 570-372-2722. *E-mail:* suadmiss@susqu.edu.

■ *See page 2474 for a narrative description.*

SWARTHMORE COLLEGE
Swarthmore, Pennsylvania

- **Independent** 4-year, founded 1864
- **Calendar** semesters
- **Degree** bachelor's
- **Suburban** 357-acre campus with easy access to Philadelphia
- **Endowment** $930.4 million
- **Coed**, 1,500 undergraduate students, 99% full-time, 53% women, 47% men
- **Most difficult** entrance level, 24% of applicants were admitted

Consistently ranked among the top 3 small liberal arts colleges, Swarthmore is a coeducational institution located 11 miles southwest of Philadelphia. It has a student-faculty ratio of 8:1, an engineering department, and need-blind admission. The student body includes more than 30% students of color and 8% international students.

Undergraduates 1,487 full-time, 13 part-time. Students come from 53 states and territories, 42 other countries, 84% are from out of state, 7% African American, 16% Asian American or Pacific Islander, 8% Hispanic American, 0.9% Native American, 5% international, 0.3% transferred in, 93% live on campus. *Retention:* 97% of 2002 full-time freshmen returned.

Freshmen *Admission:* 3,908 applied, 920 admitted, 368 enrolled. *Test scores:* SAT verbal scores over 500: 100%; SAT math scores over 500: 100%; SAT verbal scores over 600: 93%; SAT math scores over 600: 92%; SAT verbal scores over 700: 67%; SAT math scores over 700: 65%.

Faculty *Total:* 203, 83% full-time, 95% with terminal degrees. *Student/faculty ratio:* 8:1.

Majors Ancient/classical Greek; area studies related; art history, criticism and conservation; Asian studies; astronomy; astrophysics; biochemistry; biological and biomedical sciences related; biology/biological sciences; chemical physics; chemistry; Chinese; classics and languages, literatures and linguistics; comparative literature; computer and information sciences; dance; dramatic/theatre arts; economics; education related; engineering; English; fine/studio arts; French; German; German studies; history; Latin; linguistics; mathematics; mathematics and computer science; medieval and Renaissance studies; music; philosophy; physics; physiological psychology/psychobiology; political science and government; psychology; religious studies; Russian; social sciences related; Spanish; visual and performing arts related.

Academic Programs *Special study options:* advanced placement credit, double majors, honors programs, independent study, internships, off-campus study, services for LD students, student-designed majors, study abroad. *ROTC:* Army (c), Air Force (c).

Library McCabe Library plus 3 others with 567,875 titles, 4,949 serial subscriptions, 19,751 audiovisual materials, an OPAC, a Web page.

Computers on Campus 168 computers available on campus for general student use. A campuswide network can be accessed from student residence rooms and from off campus. Internet access, online (class) registration, at least one staffed computer lab available. Computer purchase or lease plan available.

Student Life *Housing:* on-campus residence required for freshman year. *Options:* coed, men-only, women-only. Campus housing is university owned. Freshman campus housing is guaranteed. *Activities and organizations:* drama/theater group, student-run newspaper, radio station, choral group, community service and activist groups, club sports and intramurals, music/acapella groups, social/cultural clubs, political and debate, national fraternities. *Campus security:* 24-hour emergency response devices and patrols, student patrols, late-night transport/escort service. *Student services:* health clinic, personal/psychological counseling, women's center.

Athletics Member NCAA. All Division III. *Intercollegiate sports:* badminton M(c)/W, baseball M, basketball M/W, cheerleading M(c)/W(c), cross-country running M/W, field hockey W, golf M, ice hockey M(c)/W(c), lacrosse M/W, rock climbing W(c), rugby M(c)/W(c), soccer M/W, softball W, squash M(c)/W(c), swimming M/W, tennis M/W, track and field M/W, ultimate Frisbee M(c)/W(c), volleyball M(c)/W. *Intramural sports:* basketball M/W, football M/W, soccer M/W, softball M/W, tennis M/W, volleyball M/W.

Standardized Tests *Required:* SAT I and SAT II or ACT (for admission). *Required for some:* SAT II Subject Tests in mathematics.

Costs (2003–04) *Comprehensive fee:* $37,716 includes full-time tuition ($28,500), mandatory fees ($302), and room and board ($8914). *College room only:* $4572. Room and board charges vary according to board plan. *Payment plan:* installment. *Waivers:* employees or children of employees.

Financial Aid Of all full-time matriculated undergraduates who enrolled in 2003, 806 applied for aid, 719 were judged to have need, 719 had their need fully met. 596 Federal Work-Study jobs (averaging $1519). In 2003, 10 non-need-based awards were made. *Average percent of need met:* 100%. *Average financial aid package:* $26,088. *Average need-based loan:* $3141. *Average need-based gift aid:* $22,251. *Average non-need-based aid:* $28,500. *Average indebtedness upon graduation:* $13,533.

Applying *Options:* common application, electronic application, early admission, early decision, deferred entrance. *Application fee:* $60. *Required:* essay or personal statement, high school transcript, 2 letters of recommendation. *Recommended:* interview. *Application deadlines:* 1/1 (freshmen), 4/1 (transfers). *Early decision:* 11/15 (for plan 1), 1/1 (for plan 2). *Notification:* 4/1 (freshmen), 12/15 (early decision plan 1), 2/1 (early decision plan 2), 5/30 (transfers).

Admissions Contact Office of Admissions, Swarthmore College, Swarthmore, PA 19081. *Phone:* 610-328-8300. *Toll-free phone:* 800-667-3110. *Fax:* 610-328-8580. *E-mail:* admissions@swarthmore.edu.

■ *See page 2476 for a narrative description.*

TALMUDICAL YESHIVA OF PHILADELPHIA
Philadelphia, Pennsylvania

- **Independent Jewish** 4-year, founded 1953
- **Calendar** trimesters
- **Degrees** bachelor's (also offers some graduate courses)
- **Urban** 3-acre campus
- **Men only**
- **Moderately difficult** entrance level

Faculty *Student/faculty ratio:* 23:1.

Student Life *Campus security:* controlled dormitory access, night security patrol.

Costs (2003–04) *Tuition:* $5500 full-time.

Financial Aid Of all full-time matriculated undergraduates who enrolled in 1998, 71 applied for aid, 71 were judged to have need, 71 had their need fully met. 28 Federal Work-Study jobs (averaging $1000). *Average percent of need met:* 100. *Average financial aid package:* $4870.

Applying *Options:* common application, early admission, deferred entrance. *Required:* high school transcript, 1 letter of recommendation, interview, oral examination.

Admissions Contact Rabbi Shmuel Kamenetsky, Co-Dean, Talmudical Yeshiva of Philadelphia, 6063 Drexel Road, Philadelphia, PA 19131-1296. *Phone:* 215-473-1212.

TEMPLE UNIVERSITY
Philadelphia, Pennsylvania

- **State-related** university, founded 1884
- **Calendar** semesters
- **Degrees** associate, bachelor's, master's, doctoral, first professional, post-master's, and first professional certificates
- **Urban** 110-acre campus
- **Endowment** $158.1 million
- **Coed**
- **Moderately difficult** entrance level

Temple University is a major teaching and research university with a faculty of men and women who are nationally and internationally recognized in their fields. Taking full advantage of its location in Philadelphia, Temple actively promotes programs that help students bridge the worlds of academia and work.

Faculty *Student/faculty ratio:* 18:1.

Student Life *Campus security:* 24-hour emergency response devices and patrols, late-night transport/escort service, controlled dormitory access.

Athletics Member NCAA. All Division I except football (Division I-A).

Temple University (continued)

Standardized Tests *Required:* SAT I or ACT (for admission).

Costs (2003–04) *Tuition:* state resident $8134 full-time, $315 per credit hour part-time; nonresident $14,894 full-time, $530 per credit hour part-time. Full-time tuition and fees vary according to course load, location, program, and reciprocity agreements. Part-time tuition and fees vary according to course load, location, program, and reciprocity agreements. *Required fees:* $460 full-time. *Room and board:* $7276; room only: $4668. Room and board charges vary according to board plan and housing facility.

Financial Aid Of all full-time matriculated undergraduates who enrolled in 2002, 16,094 applied for aid, 12,629 were judged to have need, 4,180 had their need fully met. In 2002, 3453. *Average percent of need met:* 87. *Average financial aid package:* $11,416. *Average need-based loan:* $3394. *Average need-based gift aid:* $4310. *Average non-need-based aid:* $3130. *Average indebtedness upon graduation:* $22,041.

Applying *Options:* electronic application, early admission, deferred entrance. *Application fee:* $35. *Required:* high school transcript, minimum 2.0 GPA. *Required for some:* letters of recommendation, interview, portfolio, audition. *Recommended:* essay or personal statement.

Admissions Contact Dr. Timm Rinehart, Acting Director of Admissions, Temple University, 1801 North Broad Street, Philadelphia, PA 19122-6096. *Phone:* 215-204-8556. *Toll-free phone:* 888-340-2222. *Fax:* 215-204-5694. *E-mail:* tuadm@vm.temple.edu.

■ *See page 2488 for a narrative description.*

THIEL COLLEGE

Greenville, Pennsylvania

- **Independent** 4-year, founded 1866, affiliated with Evangelical Lutheran Church in America
- **Calendar** semesters
- **Degrees** associate and bachelor's
- **Rural** 135-acre campus with easy access to Cleveland and Pittsburgh
- **Endowment** $17.1 million
- **Coed,** 1,261 undergraduate students, 94% full-time, 47% women, 53% men
- **Moderately difficult** entrance level, 76% of applicants were admitted

Undergraduates 1,183 full-time, 78 part-time. Students come from 16 states and territories, 14 other countries, 27% are from out of state, 9% African American, 0.6% Asian American or Pacific Islander, 0.7% Hispanic American, 0.2% Native American, 4% international, 5% transferred in, 78% live on campus. *Retention:* 64% of 2002 full-time freshmen returned.

Freshmen *Admission:* 1,557 applied, 1,182 admitted, 349 enrolled. *Average high school GPA:* 3.00. *Test scores:* SAT verbal scores over 500: 45%; SAT math scores over 500: 42%; ACT scores over 18: 73%; SAT verbal scores over 600: 10%; SAT math scores over 600: 7%; ACT scores over 24: 17%; SAT verbal scores over 700: 1%; SAT math scores over 700: 1%.

Faculty *Total:* 114, 46% full-time, 43% with terminal degrees. *Student/faculty ratio:* 16:1.

Majors Accounting; actuarial science; art; audiology and speech-language pathology; biology/biological sciences; business administration and management; chemical engineering; chemistry; clinical laboratory science/medical technology; communication/speech communication and rhetoric; computer science; criminal justice/safety; cytotechnology; elementary education; engineering physics; English; environmental studies; funeral service and mortuary science; history; information science/studies; international business/trade/commerce; liberal arts and sciences/liberal studies; management information systems; mathematics; philosophy; physics; political science and government; pre-dentistry studies; pre-law studies; pre-medical studies; pre-veterinary studies; psychology; religious education; religious studies; secondary education; sociology; Spanish.

Academic Programs *Special study options:* academic remediation for entering students, adult/continuing education programs, advanced placement credit, cooperative education, double majors, English as a second language, freshman honors college, honors programs, internships, off-campus study, part-time degree program, services for LD students, study abroad, summer session for credit. *Unusual degree programs:* 3-2 engineering with Case Western Reserve University, Point Park College, University of Pittsburgh; forestry with Duke University.

Library Langenheim Library with 131,176 titles, 532 serial subscriptions, 6,463 audiovisual materials, an OPAC, a Web page.

Computers on Campus 220 computers available on campus for general student use. A campuswide network can be accessed from student residence rooms. Internet access, at least one staffed computer lab available.

Student Life *Housing options:* coed. Campus housing is university owned and leased by the school. Freshman campus housing is guaranteed. *Activities and organizations:* drama/theater group, student-run newspaper, radio and television station, choral group, Thiel Players Theatre Group, Greek organizations, student government, Thiel Choir, national fraternities, national sororities. *Campus security:* 24-hour emergency response devices and patrols, student patrols, late-night transport/escort service, controlled dormitory access. *Student services:* health clinic, personal/psychological counseling, women's center.

Athletics Member NCAA. All Division III. *Intercollegiate sports:* baseball M, basketball M/W, cross-country running M/W, football M, golf M/W, lacrosse M/W, soccer M/W, softball W, tennis M/W, track and field M/W, volleyball W, wrestling M. *Intramural sports:* badminton M/W, basketball M/W, football M, soccer M, softball M/W, volleyball M/W.

Standardized Tests *Required:* SAT I or ACT (for admission).

Costs (2003–04) *Comprehensive fee:* $20,970 includes full-time tuition ($13,500), mandatory fees ($886), and room and board ($6584). Part-time tuition and fees vary according to course load. *College room only:* $3396. Room and board charges vary according to board plan and housing facility. *Payment plan:* installment. *Waivers:* senior citizens and employees or children of employees.

Financial Aid Of all full-time matriculated undergraduates who enrolled in 2003, 1,132 applied for aid, 1,020 were judged to have need, 171 had their need fully met. 154 Federal Work-Study jobs (averaging $1013). 416 state and other part-time jobs (averaging $1014). In 2003, 163 non-need-based awards were made. *Average percent of need met:* 81%. *Average financial aid package:* $13,200. *Average need-based loan:* $3648. *Average need-based gift aid:* $8920. *Average non-need-based aid:* $3845. *Average indebtedness upon graduation:* $19,394.

Applying *Options:* common application, electronic application, early action, deferred entrance. *Application fee:* $25. *Required:* high school transcript, minimum 2.0 GPA. *Required for some:* essay or personal statement, letters of recommendation, interview. *Recommended:* essay or personal statement, letters of recommendation, interview. *Application deadlines:* 8/15 (freshmen), 8/15 (transfers). *Notification:* continuous (freshmen), 1/6 (early action), 9/15 (transfers).

Admissions Contact Mr. Jeff Baylor, Vice President Enrollment Management, Thiel College, 75 College Avenue, Greenville, PA 16125. *Phone:* 724-589-2176. *Toll-free phone:* 800-248-4435. *Fax:* 724-589-2013. *E-mail:* admissions@thiel.edu.

■ *See page 2502 for a narrative description.*

THOMAS JEFFERSON UNIVERSITY

Philadelphia, Pennsylvania

- **Independent** upper-level, founded 1824
- **Calendar** semesters
- **Degrees** bachelor's, master's, and postbachelor's certificates
- **Urban** 13-acre campus
- **Endowment** $15.2 million
- **Coed,** 798 undergraduate students, 57% full-time, 84% women, 16% men
- **Moderately difficult** entrance level, 31% of applicants were admitted

Jefferson is one of the oldest and largest academic health centers in the US. Students benefit from clinical affiliations in more than 1,700 sites and faculty members who are active practitioners in their fields. The University is composed of a medical school, graduate school, and Jefferson College of Health Professions and shares its campus with a 620-bed hospital.

Undergraduates 457 full-time, 341 part-time. Students come from 16 states and territories, 37% are from out of state, 13% African American, 5% Asian American or Pacific Islander, 3% Hispanic American, 0.5% Native American, 1% international, 41% transferred in, 30% live on campus.

Faculty *Total:* 221, 21% full-time, 35% with terminal degrees. *Student/faculty ratio:* 8:1.

Majors Biotechnology; cardiovascular technology; clinical laboratory science/medical technology; cytotechnology; industrial radiologic technology; nursing (registered nurse training); occupational therapy; physical therapy.

Academic Programs *Special study options:* adult/continuing education programs, advanced placement credit, part-time degree program, services for LD students, study abroad. *ROTC:* Air Force (c).

Library Scott Memorial Library plus 1 other with 170,000 titles, 2,290 serial subscriptions, a Web page.

Computers on Campus 100 computers available on campus for general student use. A campuswide network can be accessed from off campus. At least one staffed computer lab available.

Student Life *Housing options:* coed. Campus housing is university owned and is provided by a third party. Freshman campus housing is guaranteed. *Activities and organizations:* choral group, Commons Board, student government, choir, Admission Ambassadors, Student Nurses Association of Pennsylvania. *Campus security:* 24-hour emergency response devices and patrols, late-night transport/escort service, controlled dormitory access. *Student services:* health clinic, personal/psychological counseling.

Athletics *Intercollegiate sports:* rugby M(c). *Intramural sports:* basketball M/W, fencing M(c)/W(c), racquetball M(c)/W(c), soccer M(c)/W(c), softball M/W, swimming M/W, tennis W, volleyball M/W, water polo M(c)/W(c).

Standardized Tests *Recommended:* SAT I or ACT (for admission).

Costs (2003–04) *Comprehensive fee:* $27,648 includes full-time tuition ($19,824), mandatory fees ($1155), and room and board ($6669). Full-time tuition and fees vary according to course level. Part-time tuition and fees vary according to course level. *College room only:* $2754. Room and board charges vary according to housing facility. *Payment plan:* installment. *Waivers:* employees or children of employees.

Financial Aid Of all full-time matriculated undergraduates who enrolled in 2001, 338 applied for aid, 322 were judged to have need, 15 had their need fully met. 114 Federal Work-Study jobs (averaging $1476). In 2001, 6 non-need-based awards were made. *Average need-based loan:* $10,479. *Average non-need-based aid:* $5000. *Average indebtedness upon graduation:* $26,460.

Applying *Options:* deferred entrance. *Application fee:* $45. *Application deadline:* rolling (transfers). *Notification:* continuous (transfers).

Admissions Contact Assistant Director of Admissions, Thomas Jefferson University, Edison Building, Suite 1610, 130 South Ninth Street, Philadelphia, PA 19107. *Phone:* 215-503-8890. *Toll-free phone:* 877-533-3247. *Fax:* 215-503-7241. *E-mail:* chpadmissions@mail.tju.edu.

■ *See page 2506 for a narrative description.*

UNIVERSITY OF PENNSYLVANIA
Philadelphia, Pennsylvania

- **Independent** university, founded 1740
- **Calendar** semesters plus 2 5-week summer sessions
- **Degrees** associate, bachelor's, master's, doctoral, first professional, post-master's, postbachelor's, and first professional certificates (also offers evening program with significant enrollment not reflected in profile)
- **Urban** 269-acre campus
- **Endowment** $3.5 billion
- **Coed,** 9,836 undergraduate students, 96% full-time, 50% women, 50% men
- **Most difficult** entrance level, 20% of applicants were admitted

Undergraduates 9,448 full-time, 388 part-time. Students come from 54 states and territories, 109 other countries, 81% are from out of state, 6% African American, 16% Asian American or Pacific Islander, 5% Hispanic American, 0.3% Native American, 12% international, 2% transferred in, 63% live on campus. *Retention:* 97% of 2002 full-time freshmen returned.

Freshmen *Admission:* 18,831 applied, 3,837 admitted, 2,419 enrolled. *Average high school GPA:* 3.84. *Test scores:* SAT verbal scores over 500: 100%; SAT math scores over 500: 100%; ACT scores over 18: 100%; SAT verbal scores over 600: 93%; SAT math scores over 600: 96%; ACT scores over 24: 97%; SAT verbal scores over 700: 51%; SAT math scores over 700: 65%; ACT scores over 30: 63%.

Faculty *Total:* 1,879, 74% full-time, 100% with terminal degrees. *Student/faculty ratio:* 6:1.

Majors Accounting; actuarial science; African-American/Black studies; African studies; American studies; anthropology; architecture; art history, criticism and conservation; Asian studies (East); Asian studies (South); biochemistry; bioinformatics; biology/biological sciences; biomedical/medical engineering; biomedical sciences; biophysics; business administration and management; business administration, management and operations related; chemical engineering; chemistry; civil engineering; classics and languages, literatures and linguistics; cognitive science; communication/speech communication and rhetoric; community health services counseling; comparative literature; computer engineering; computer graphics; computer systems networking and telecommunications; dramatic/theatre arts; e-commerce; economics; electrical, electronics and communications engineering; elementary education; engineering related; English; English language and literature related; environmental design/architecture; environmental/environmental health engineering; environmental studies; finance; fine/studio arts; French; geology/earth science; German; health/health care administration; health professions related; history; history and philosophy of science and technology; human resources management; insurance; international business/trade/commerce; international/global studies; international relations and affairs; Italian; Jewish/Judaic studies; Latin American studies; legal professions and studies related; liberal arts and sciences/liberal studies; linguistics; management information systems; management sciences and quantitative methods related; marketing/marketing management; materials engineering; materials science; mathematics; mechanical engineering; music; natural sciences; neuroscience; nursing (registered nurse training); nursing related; operations management; philosophy; philosophy related; physics; political science and government; psychology; public policy analysis; real estate; religious studies; Romance languages related; Russian; sales, distribution and marketing; sociology; Spanish; statistics; systems engineering; transportation management; urban studies/affairs; visual and performing arts; women's studies.

Academic Programs *Special study options:* academic remediation for entering students, accelerated degree program, adult/continuing education programs, advanced placement credit, distance learning, double majors, English as a second language, honors programs, independent study, internships, off-campus study, part-time degree program, services for LD students, student-designed majors, study abroad, summer session for credit. *ROTC:* Army (c), Navy (b), Air Force (c). *Unusual degree programs:* 3-2 education.

Library Van Pelt-Dietrich Library plus 13 others with 5.2 million titles, 40,840 serial subscriptions, an OPAC, a Web page.

Computers on Campus 1575 computers available on campus for general student use. A campuswide network can be accessed from student residence rooms and from off campus. Internet access, online (class) registration, at least one staffed computer lab available.

Student Life *Housing options:* coed, disabled students. Campus housing is university owned. Freshman campus housing is guaranteed. *Activities and organizations:* drama/theater group, student-run newspaper, radio and television station, choral group, marching band, Interfraternity Council, Kite and Key Society, Social Planning and Events Committee, Hillel at Penn, Sports Club Council, national fraternities, national sororities. *Campus security:* 24-hour emergency response devices and patrols, student patrols, late-night transport/escort service, controlled dormitory access. *Student services:* health clinic, personal/psychological counseling, women's center.

Athletics Member NCAA. All Division I except football (Division I-AA). *Intercollegiate sports:* baseball M, basketball M/W, crew M/W, cross-country running M/W, fencing M/W, field hockey W, golf M/W, gymnastics W, lacrosse M/W, soccer M/W, softball W, squash M/W, swimming M/W, tennis M/W, track and field M/W, volleyball W, wrestling M. *Intramural sports:* badminton M/W, baseball M(c), basketball M/W, cheerleading M/W, equestrian sports M(c)/W(c), football M/W, golf M/W, gymnastics M(c), ice hockey M(c)/W(c), lacrosse M/W, rock climbing M/W, rugby M(c)/W(c), sailing M(c)/W(c), skiing (downhill) M(c)/W(c), soccer M/W, softball M/W, squash M/W, swimming M/W, table tennis M/W, tennis M/W, track and field M/W, ultimate Frisbee M(c)/W(c), volleyball M/W, water polo M(c)/W(c).

Standardized Tests *Required:* SAT I and SAT II or ACT (for admission), SAT II: Writing Test (for admission).

Costs (2003–04) *Comprehensive fee:* $37,960 includes full-time tuition ($26,282), mandatory fees ($3036), and room and board ($8642). Part-time tuition: $3357 per course. Part-time tuition and fees vary according to course load. *Required fees:* $354 per course part-time. *College room only:* $5130. Room and board charges vary according to board plan and housing facility. *Payment plans:* tuition prepayment, installment. *Waivers:* employees or children of employees.

Financial Aid Of all full-time matriculated undergraduates who enrolled in 2002, 4,939 applied for aid, 4,202 were judged to have need, 4,202 had their need fully met. 3,776 Federal Work-Study jobs (averaging $3529). *Average percent of need met:* 100%. *Average financial aid package:* $25,155. *Average need-based loan:* $4250. *Average need-based gift aid:* $19,934. *Average indebtedness upon graduation:* $19,579.

Applying *Options:* electronic application, early admission, early decision, deferred entrance. *Application fee:* $70. *Required:* essay or personal statement, high school transcript, 2 letters of recommendation. *Application deadlines:* 1/1 (freshmen), 3/15 (transfers). *Early decision:* 11/1. *Notification:* 4/1 (freshmen), 12/15 (early decision), continuous (transfers).

Admissions Contact Mr. Willis J. Stetson Jr., Dean of Admissions, University of Pennsylvania, 1 College Hall, Levy Park, Philadelphia, PA 19104. *Phone:* 215-898-7507.

UNIVERSITY OF PHOENIX–PHILADELPHIA CAMPUS
Wayne, Pennsylvania

- **Proprietary** comprehensive, founded 1999
- **Calendar** continuous
- **Degrees** certificates, associate, bachelor's, master's, doctoral, post-master's, and postbachelor's certificates (courses conducted at 121 campuses and learning centers in 25 states)
- **Urban** campus
- **Coed,** 628 undergraduate students, 100% full-time, 61% women, 39% men
- **Noncompetitive** entrance level

Undergraduates 628 full-time. 28% African American, 0.8% Asian American or Pacific Islander, 3% Hispanic American, 0.5% Native American, 12% international.

Freshmen *Admission:* 40 enrolled.

Faculty *Total:* 80, 6% full-time, 13% with terminal degrees. *Student/faculty ratio:* 10:1.

University of Phoenix–Philadelphia Campus (continued)

Majors Business administration and management; information technology; management science; marketing/marketing management.

Academic Programs *Special study options:* accelerated degree program, adult/continuing education programs, advanced placement credit, distance learning, external degree program, independent study.

Library University Library with 27.1 million titles, 11,648 serial subscriptions, an OPAC, a Web page.

Computers on Campus A campuswide network can be accessed from off campus. Internet access, at least one staffed computer lab available.

Student Life *Housing:* college housing not available.

Costs (2003–04) *Tuition:* $11,400 full-time, $380 per credit part-time. *Waivers:* employees or children of employees.

Financial Aid *Average financial aid package:* $1333.

Applying *Options:* deferred entrance. *Application fee:* $85. *Required:* 1 letter of recommendation, 2 years of work experience, 23 years of age. *Required for some:* high school transcript. *Application deadline:* rolling (freshmen), rolling (transfers).

Admissions Contact Ms. Beth Barilla, Director of Admissions, University of Phoenix–Philadelphia Campus, 4615 East Elwood Street, Mail Stop AA-K101, Phoenix, AZ 85040-1958. *Phone:* 480-317-6000. *Toll-free phone:* 800-228-7240. *Fax:* 480-594-1758. *E-mail:* beth.barilla@phoenix.edu.

UNIVERSITY OF PHOENIX–PITTSBURGH CAMPUS

Pittsburgh, Pennsylvania

- **Proprietary** comprehensive, founded 2001
- **Calendar** continuous
- **Degrees** certificates, associate, bachelor's, master's, doctoral, post-master's, and postbachelor's certificates (courses conducted at 121 campuses and learning centers in 25 states)
- **Urban** campus
- **Coed,** 175 undergraduate students, 100% full-time, 54% women, 46% men
- **Noncompetitive** entrance level

Undergraduates 175 full-time. 10% African American, 0.6% Hispanic American.

Freshmen *Admission:* 14 enrolled.

Faculty *Total:* 35, 11% full-time, 20% with terminal degrees. *Student/faculty ratio:* 4:1.

Majors Business administration and management; corrections and criminal justice related; information technology; management information systems; management science; marketing/marketing management.

Academic Programs *Special study options:* accelerated degree program, adult/continuing education programs, cooperative education, external degree program, independent study.

Library University Library with 27.1 million titles, 11,648 serial subscriptions, an OPAC, a Web page.

Computers on Campus A campuswide network can be accessed from off campus. Internet access, at least one staffed computer lab available.

Student Life *Housing:* college housing not available.

Costs (2003–04) *Tuition:* $11,400 full-time, $380 per credit part-time. *Waivers:* employees or children of employees.

Financial Aid *Average financial aid package:* $1434.

Applying *Options:* deferred entrance. *Application fee:* $85. *Required:* 1 letter of recommendation, 2 years of work experience, 23 years of age. *Required for some:* high school transcript. *Application deadline:* rolling (freshmen), rolling (transfers).

Admissions Contact Ms. Beth Barilla, Director of Admissions, University of Phoenix–Pittsburgh Campus, 4615 East Elwood Street, Mail Stop AA-K101, Phoenix, AZ 85040-1958. *Phone:* 480-317-6000. *Toll-free phone:* 800-228-7240. *Fax:* 480-594-1758. *E-mail:* beth.barilla@phoenix.edu.

UNIVERSITY OF PITTSBURGH

Pittsburgh, Pennsylvania

- **State-related** university, founded 1787, part of Commonwealth System of Higher Education
- **Calendar** semesters plus summer term
- **Degrees** certificates, bachelor's, master's, doctoral, first professional, post-master's, and postbachelor's certificates
- **Urban** 132-acre campus
- **Endowment** $1.1 billion
- **Coed,** 17,413 undergraduate students, 87% full-time, 52% women, 48% men
- **Moderately difficult** entrance level, 48% of applicants were admitted

Undergraduates 15,141 full-time, 2,272 part-time. Students come from 53 states and territories, 14% are from out of state, 9% African American, 4% Asian American or Pacific Islander, 1% Hispanic American, 0.2% Native American, 0.8% international, 3% transferred in, 41% live on campus. *Retention:* 88% of 2001 full-time freshmen returned.

Freshmen *Admission:* 17,494 applied, 8,413 admitted, 2,964 enrolled. *Test scores:* SAT verbal scores over 500: 93%; SAT math scores over 500: 94%; SAT verbal scores over 600: 51%; SAT math scores over 600: 61%; SAT verbal scores over 700: 11%; SAT math scores over 700: 13%.

Faculty *Total:* 1,914, 75% full-time. *Student/faculty ratio:* 17:1.

Majors Accounting; African-American/Black studies; anthropology; applied mathematics; art history, criticism and conservation; audiology and speech-language pathology; biological and physical sciences; biology/biological sciences; biomedical/medical engineering; business/commerce; chemical engineering; chemistry; child development; Chinese; civil engineering; classics and languages, literatures and linguistics; clinical laboratory science/medical technology; communication/speech communication and rhetoric; computer and information sciences and support services related; computer engineering; computer science; corrections; creative writing; dental hygiene; dietetics; dramatic/theatre arts; ecology; economics; educational psychology; electrical, electronics and communications engineering; engineering; engineering physics; English; English literature (British and Commonwealth); ethnic, cultural minority, and gender studies related; film/cinema studies; finance; fine/studio arts; French; geological and earth sciences/geosciences related; geology/earth science; German; health information/medical records administration; health professions related; history; history and philosophy of science and technology; humanities; industrial engineering; information science/studies; interdisciplinary studies; Italian; Japanese; legal studies; liberal arts and sciences/liberal studies; linguistics; marketing/marketing management; materials engineering; mathematics; mathematics and statistics related; mechanical engineering; medical microbiology and bacteriology; metallurgical engineering; molecular biology; music; neuroscience; nursing (registered nurse training); occupational therapy; pharmacy; philosophy; physical education teaching and coaching; physical sciences; physics; political science and government; psychology; public administration; rehabilitation and therapeutic professions related; religious studies; Russian; Slavic languages; social sciences; social work; sociology; Spanish; speech and rhetoric; statistics; urban studies/affairs.

Academic Programs *Special study options:* academic remediation for entering students, adult/continuing education programs, advanced placement credit, cooperative education, distance learning, double majors, English as a second language, external degree program, freshman honors college, honors programs, independent study, internships, off-campus study, part-time degree program, services for LD students, student-designed majors, study abroad, summer session for credit. *ROTC:* Army (b), Navy (c), Air Force (b). *Unusual degree programs:* 3-2 statistics.

Library Hillman Library plus 26 others with 3.6 million titles, 22,058 serial subscriptions, 926,142 audiovisual materials, an OPAC, a Web page.

Computers on Campus 600 computers available on campus for general student use. A campuswide network can be accessed from student residence rooms and from off campus that provide access to online class listings. Internet access, at least one staffed computer lab available.

Student Life *Housing options:* coed, women-only. Campus housing is university owned. Freshman campus housing is guaranteed. *Activities and organizations:* drama/theater group, student-run newspaper, radio and television station, choral group, marching band, Pitt Program Council, Quo Vadis, Black Action Society, crew team, Blue and Gold Society, national fraternities, national sororities. *Campus security:* 24-hour emergency response devices and patrols, late-night transport/escort service, controlled dormitory access, on-call van transportation. *Student services:* health clinic, personal/psychological counseling, women's center.

Athletics Member NCAA. All Division I except football (Division I-A). *Intercollegiate sports:* baseball M(s), basketball M(s)/W(s), cross-country running M(s)/W(s), gymnastics W(s), soccer M(s)/W(s), softball W(s), swimming M(s)/W(s), tennis W(s), track and field M(s)/W(s), volleyball W(s), wrestling M(s). *Intramural sports:* badminton M/W, basketball M/W, bowling M(c)/W(c), crew M(c)/W(c), equestrian sports M(c)/W(c), football M, ice hockey M(c)/W(c), lacrosse M(c)/W(c), racquetball M/W, skiing (downhill) M(c)/W(c), soccer M/W, softball M/W, squash M/W, swimming M/W, table tennis M(c)/W(c), ultimate Frisbee M(c)/W(c), volleyball M/W, water polo M(c)/W(c), weight lifting M(c)/W(c), wrestling M.

Standardized Tests *Required:* SAT I or ACT (for admission). *Recommended:* SAT I (for admission).

Costs (2003–04) *Tuition:* state resident $8614 full-time, $296 per credit part-time; nonresident $17,926 full-time, $610 per credit part-time. Full-time tuition and fees vary according to degree level and program. Part-time tuition and fees vary according to degree level and program. *Required fees:* $660 full-time, $158 per term part-time. *Room and board:* $6800; room only: $4050. Room and board charges vary according to board plan and housing facility. *Payment plans:* installment, deferred payment. *Waivers:* employees or children of employees.

Financial Aid Of all full-time matriculated undergraduates who enrolled in 2003, 10,559 applied for aid, 8,674 were judged to have need, 3,498 had their need fully met. 1,643 Federal Work-Study jobs (averaging $1722). In 2003, 1882 non-need-based awards were made. *Average percent of need met:* 77%. *Average financial aid package:* $10,003. *Average need-based loan:* $4641. *Average need-based gift aid:* $5183. *Average non-need-based aid:* $7188. *Average indebtedness upon graduation:* $20,154.

Applying *Options:* common application, early admission, deferred entrance. *Application fee:* $35. *Required:* high school transcript. *Recommended:* essay or personal statement, letters of recommendation, interview. *Application deadline:* rolling (freshmen), rolling (transfers). *Notification:* continuous (freshmen), continuous (transfers).

Admissions Contact Dr. Betsy A. Porter, Director of Office of Admissions and Financial Aid, University of Pittsburgh, 4227 Fifth Avenue, First Floor, Alumni Hall, Pittsburgh, PA 15213. *Phone:* 412-624-7488. *Fax:* 412-648-8815. *E-mail:* oafa@pitt.edu.

UNIVERSITY OF PITTSBURGH AT BRADFORD

Bradford, Pennsylvania

- **State-related** 4-year, founded 1963, part of University of Pittsburgh System
- **Calendar** semesters
- **Degrees** associate and bachelor's
- **Small-town** 170-acre campus with easy access to Buffalo
- **Endowment** $11.0 million
- **Coed,** 1,417 undergraduate students, 73% full-time, 60% women, 40% men
- **Minimally difficult** entrance level, 82% of applicants were admitted

Undergraduates 1,033 full-time, 384 part-time. Students come from 20 states and territories, 3 other countries, 14% are from out of state, 2% African American, 1% Asian American or Pacific Islander, 0.7% Hispanic American, 0.6% Native American, 0.2% international, 7% transferred in, 45% live on campus. *Retention:* 68% of 2002 full-time freshmen returned.

Freshmen *Admission:* 677 applied, 555 admitted, 315 enrolled. *Average high school GPA:* 3.13. *Test scores:* SAT verbal scores over 500: 52%; SAT math scores over 500: 54%; SAT verbal scores over 600: 15%; SAT math scores over 600: 14%; SAT verbal scores over 700: 2%; SAT math scores over 700: 2%.

Faculty *Total:* 121, 56% full-time, 44% with terminal degrees. *Student/faculty ratio:* 14:1.

Majors American studies; applied mathematics; athletic training; biology/biological sciences; business administration and management; chemistry; computer science; creative writing; criminal justice/law enforcement administration; economics; English; environmental studies; geology/earth science; history; information science/studies; liberal arts and sciences/liberal studies; mass communication/media; nursing (registered nurse training); physical sciences; political science and government; psychology; public relations/image management; radiologic technology/science; social sciences; social sciences related; sociology; sport and fitness administration.

Academic Programs *Special study options:* academic remediation for entering students, accelerated degree program, adult/continuing education programs, advanced placement credit, distance learning, double majors, independent study, internships, off-campus study, part-time degree program, services for LD students, summer session for credit. *ROTC:* Army (c).

Library T. Edward and Tullah Hanley Library with 83,104 titles, 440 serial subscriptions, 3,277 audiovisual materials, an OPAC, a Web page.

Computers on Campus 90 computers available on campus for general student use. A campuswide network can be accessed from student residence rooms and from off campus. Internet access, at least one staffed computer lab available.

Student Life *Housing:* on-campus residence required through sophomore year. *Options:* coed, disabled students. Campus housing is university owned. Freshman campus housing is guaranteed. *Activities and organizations:* drama/theater group, student-run newspaper, radio station, choral group, Student Government Association, Student Activities Board, The Source (student newspaper), Alpha Phi Omega (national service fraternity), WDRQ (student radio station). *Campus security:* 24-hour emergency response devices and patrols, late-night transport/escort service. *Student services:* health clinic, personal/psychological counseling.

Athletics Member NCAA. All Division III. *Intercollegiate sports:* baseball M, basketball M/W, cross-country running M/W, golf M/W, soccer M/W, softball W, volleyball W. *Intramural sports:* basketball M/W, bowling M/W, cheerleading W(c), equestrian sports M/W, football M/W, golf M/W, rock climbing M/W, rugby M(c)/W(c), skiing (cross-country) M/W, soccer M/W, softball M/W, table tennis M/W, tennis M/W, ultimate Frisbee M/W, volleyball M/W, water polo M/W.

Standardized Tests *Required:* SAT I or ACT (for admission).

Costs (2003–04) *Tuition:* state resident $8614 full-time, $296 per credit part-time; nonresident $17,926 full-time, $610 per credit part-time. Full-time tuition and fees vary according to course load and program. Part-time tuition and fees vary according to course load and program. *Required fees:* $650 full-time, $95 per term part-time. *Room and board:* $6030; room only: $3340. Room and board charges vary according to board plan and housing facility. *Payment plan:* installment. *Waivers:* employees or children of employees.

Financial Aid Of all full-time matriculated undergraduates who enrolled in 2003, 959 applied for aid, 810 were judged to have need. 200 Federal Work-Study jobs (averaging $1400). 10 state and other part-time jobs (averaging $1400). *Average indebtedness upon graduation:* $17,502.

Applying *Options:* common application, deferred entrance. *Application fee:* $35. *Required:* high school transcript, minimum 2.0 GPA. *Required for some:* minimum 3.0 GPA. *Recommended:* essay or personal statement, letters of recommendation, interview. *Application deadline:* rolling (freshmen), rolling (transfers). *Notification:* continuous (transfers).

Admissions Contact Janet Shade. Administrative Secretary, University of Pittsburgh at Bradford, 300 Campus Drive, Bradford, PA 16701. *Phone:* 814-362-7555. *Toll-free phone:* 800-872-1787. *Fax:* 814-362-7578. *E-mail:* admissions@upb.pitt.edu.

■ *See page 2682 for a narrative description.*

UNIVERSITY OF PITTSBURGH AT GREENSBURG

Greensburg, Pennsylvania

- **State-related** 4-year, founded 1963, part of University of Pittsburgh System
- **Calendar** semesters
- **Degree** bachelor's
- **Small-town** 219-acre campus with easy access to Pittsburgh
- **Endowment** $523,014
- **Coed,** 1,918 undergraduate students, 89% full-time, 52% women, 48% men
- **Moderately difficult** entrance level, 89% of applicants were admitted

Undergraduates 1,711 full-time, 207 part-time. Students come from 10 states and territories, 1 other country, 1% are from out of state, 2% African American, 1% Asian American or Pacific Islander, 0.6% Hispanic American, 0.3% Native American, 0.1% international, 6% transferred in, 35% live on campus. *Retention:* 75% of 2002 full-time freshmen returned.

Freshmen *Admission:* 4,381 applied, 3,895 admitted, 525 enrolled. *Average high school GPA:* 3.20. *Test scores:* SAT verbal scores over 500: 68%; SAT math scores over 500: 71%; ACT scores over 18: 89%; SAT verbal scores over 600: 15%; SAT math scores over 600: 16%; ACT scores over 24: 22%; SAT verbal scores over 700: 1%; SAT math scores over 700: 1%; ACT scores over 30: 2%.

Faculty *Total:* 131, 60% full-time, 60% with terminal degrees. *Student/faculty ratio:* 20:1.

Majors Accounting; American studies; anthropology; applied mathematics; biology/biological sciences; business administration and management; computer and information sciences; creative writing; criminal justice/law enforcement administration; criminal justice/police science; education; English; environmental biology; humanities; journalism; literature; mass communication/media; natural sciences; political science and government; pre-law studies; psychology; social sciences.

Academic Programs *Special study options:* academic remediation for entering students, accelerated degree program, adult/continuing education programs, advanced placement credit, distance learning, double majors, independent study, internships, off-campus study, part-time degree program, services for LD students, student-designed majors, study abroad, summer session for credit. *ROTC:* Army (c), Air Force (c).

Library Millstein Library with 75,000 titles, 418 serial subscriptions, an OPAC, a Web page.

Computers on Campus 400 computers available on campus for general student use. A campuswide network can be accessed from student residence rooms and from off campus. Internet access, at least one staffed computer lab available.

Student Life *Housing options:* coed. Campus housing is university owned. *Activities and organizations:* drama/theater group, student-run newspaper, choral group, Student Government Association, Circle K, Freshmen Honor Society-Phi Eta Sigma, Senior Honor Society-Phi Kappa Phi, Student Activities Board. *Campus security:* 24-hour emergency response devices and patrols, late-night transport/escort service, controlled dormitory access. *Student services:* health clinic, personal/psychological counseling.

Athletics Member NCAA. All Division III. *Intercollegiate sports:* baseball M, basketball M/W, cross-country running M/W, golf M/W, soccer M/W, softball W, tennis M/W, volleyball W. *Intramural sports:* baseball M, basketball M/W, bowling M/W, football M/W, golf M/W, racquetball M/W, skiing (cross-country)

University of Pittsburgh at Greensburg (continued)
M/W, skiing (downhill) M/W, soccer M/W, softball M/W, table tennis M/W, tennis M/W, volleyball M/W, weight lifting M/W.

Standardized Tests *Required:* SAT I or ACT (for admission).

Costs (2003–04) *Tuition:* state resident $8614 full-time, $296 per credit part-time; nonresident $17,926 full-time, $610 per credit part-time. Full-time tuition and fees vary according to course load. Part-time tuition and fees vary according to course load. *Required fees:* $600 full-time, $110 per term part-time. *Room and board:* $6770; room only: $3870. Room and board charges vary according to board plan and housing facility. *Payment plans:* installment, deferred payment. *Waivers:* senior citizens and employees or children of employees.

Financial Aid Of all full-time matriculated undergraduates who enrolled in 2002, 1,487 applied for aid, 1,338 were judged to have need, 125 had their need fully met. 163 Federal Work-Study jobs (averaging $2063). In 2002, 36 non-need-based awards were made. *Average percent of need met:* 70%. *Average financial aid package:* $10,815. *Average need-based loan:* $5500. *Average need-based gift aid:* $6315. *Average non-need-based aid:* $2500. *Average indebtedness upon graduation:* $17,125.

Applying *Options:* common application, electronic application, early admission, deferred entrance. *Application fee:* $35. *Required:* high school transcript, minimum 2.5 GPA. *Required for some:* letters of recommendation. *Recommended:* essay or personal statement, interview. *Application deadlines:* 8/1 (freshmen), 8/1 (transfers). *Notification:* continuous (freshmen), continuous (transfers).

Admissions Contact Mrs. Brandi S. Darr, Director of Admissions and Financial Aid, University of Pittsburgh at Greensburg, 1150 Mount Pleasant Road, Greensburg, PA 15601-5860. *Phone:* 724-836-9880. *Fax:* 724-836-7160. *E-mail:* upgadmit@pitt.edu.

■ *See page 2684 for a narrative description.*

UNIVERSITY OF PITTSBURGH AT JOHNSTOWN
Johnstown, Pennsylvania

- **State-related** 4-year, founded 1927, part of University of Pittsburgh System
- **Calendar** semesters
- **Degrees** certificates, associate, and bachelor's
- **Suburban** 650-acre campus with easy access to Pittsburgh
- **Coed,** 3,146 undergraduate students, 90% full-time, 52% women, 48% men
- **Moderately difficult** entrance level, 84% of applicants were admitted

Undergraduates 2,822 full-time, 324 part-time. Students come from 11 states and territories, 1% are from out of state, 1% African American, 1% Asian American or Pacific Islander, 0.4% Hispanic American, 0.1% Native American, 3% transferred in, 66% live on campus. *Retention:* 77% of 2002 full-time freshmen returned.

Freshmen *Admission:* 2,955 applied, 2,479 admitted, 881 enrolled. *Average high school GPA:* 3.20. *Test scores:* SAT verbal scores over 500: 57%; SAT math scores over 500: 63%; ACT scores over 18: 90%; SAT verbal scores over 600: 8%; SAT math scores over 600: 14%; ACT scores over 24: 13%; SAT verbal scores over 700: 1%; SAT math scores over 700: 1%; ACT scores over 30: 1%.

Faculty *Student/faculty ratio:* 20:1.

Majors Accounting; American studies; biology/biological sciences; biology teacher education; biopsychology; business administration and management; business/managerial economics; chemistry; chemistry teacher education; civil engineering technology; computer science; creative writing; dramatic/theatre arts; ecology; economics; education; electrical, electronic and communications engineering technology; elementary education; emergency medical technology (EMT paramedic); engineering technology; English; English/language arts teacher education; environmental biology; environmental studies; finance; geography; geology/earth science; history; history teacher education; humanities; journalism; literature; mass communication/media; mathematics; mathematics teacher education; mechanical engineering/mechanical technology; natural sciences; political science and government; pre-dentistry studies; pre-law studies; pre-medical studies; pre-veterinary studies; psychology; respiratory care therapy; science teacher education; secondary education; social sciences; social studies teacher education; sociology; surgical technology.

Academic Programs *Special study options:* accelerated degree program, adult/continuing education programs, advanced placement credit, cooperative education, distance learning, double majors, independent study, internships, off-campus study, part-time degree program, services for LD students, student-designed majors, study abroad, summer session for credit.

Library Owen Library with 145,507 titles, 450 serial subscriptions, 711 audiovisual materials, an OPAC, a Web page.

Computers on Campus 150 computers available on campus for general student use. A campuswide network can be accessed from student residence rooms and from off campus. Internet access, at least one staffed computer lab available. Computer purchase or lease plan available.

Student Life *Housing options:* coed. Campus housing is university owned. Freshman campus housing is guaranteed. *Activities and organizations:* drama/theater group, student-run newspaper, radio and television station, choral group, student radio station, Student Senate, Programming Board, dance ensemble, Greek organizations, national fraternities, national sororities. *Campus security:* 24-hour patrols, late-night transport/escort service. *Student services:* health clinic, personal/psychological counseling.

Athletics Member NCAA. All Division II. *Intercollegiate sports:* baseball M, basketball M(s)/W(s), cheerleading W, cross-country running W, soccer M, track and field W, volleyball W, wrestling M(s). *Intramural sports:* archery M(c)/W(c), basketball M/W, cross-country running M/W, football M/W, ice hockey M(c), rugby M(c)/W(c), sailing M(c)/W(c), skiing (cross-country) M/W, skiing (downhill) M(c)/W(c), soccer M/W(c), softball M/W, table tennis M/W, ultimate Frisbee M(c)/W(c), volleyball M/W.

Standardized Tests *Required:* SAT I or ACT (for admission).

Costs (2003–04) *Tuition:* $296 per credit part-time; state resident $8614 full-time, $296 per credit part-time; nonresident $17,926 full-time, $610 per credit part-time. Full-time tuition and fees vary according to program. Part-time tuition and fees vary according to program. *Required fees:* $642 full-time, $77 per term part-time. *Room and board:* $5760; room only: $3480. Room and board charges vary according to board plan and housing facility. *Payment plan:* installment. *Waivers:* employees or children of employees.

Financial Aid Of all full-time matriculated undergraduates who enrolled in 2003, 2,632 applied for aid, 2,141 were judged to have need, 322 had their need fully met. 359 Federal Work-Study jobs (averaging $1643). 323 state and other part-time jobs (averaging $918). In 2003, 57 non-need-based awards were made. *Average percent of need met:* 56%. *Average financial aid package:* $7406. *Average need-based loan:* $3618. *Average need-based gift aid:* $4065. *Average non-need-based aid:* $2806. *Average indebtedness upon graduation:* $17,952.

Applying *Options:* electronic application, early admission, deferred entrance. *Application fee:* $35. *Required:* high school transcript, minimum 2.0 GPA, SAT I or ACT. *Required for some:* interview. *Recommended:* essay or personal statement, 3 letters of recommendation. *Application deadline:* rolling (freshmen), rolling (transfers). *Notification:* continuous (freshmen), continuous (transfers).

Admissions Contact Mr. James F. Gyure, Director of Admissions, University of Pittsburgh at Johnstown, 157 Blackington Hall, 450 Schoolhouse Road, Johnstown, PA 15904-2990. *Phone:* 814-269-7050. *Toll-free phone:* 800-765-4875. *Fax:* 814-269-7044. *E-mail:* upjadmit@pitt.edu.

■ *See page 2686 for a narrative description.*

THE UNIVERSITY OF SCRANTON
Scranton, Pennsylvania

- **Independent Roman Catholic (Jesuit)** comprehensive, founded 1888
- **Calendar** 4-1-4
- **Degrees** certificates, associate, bachelor's, master's, doctoral, post-master's, and postbachelor's certificates
- **Urban** 50-acre campus
- **Endowment** $78.7 million
- **Coed,** 4,073 undergraduate students, 93% full-time, 57% women, 43% men
- **Moderately difficult** entrance level, 75% of applicants were admitted

Undergraduates 3,773 full-time, 300 part-time. Students come from 30 states and territories, 12 other countries, 49% are from out of state, 1% African American, 2% Asian American or Pacific Islander, 3% Hispanic American, 0.1% Native American, 0.5% international, 3% transferred in, 50% live on campus. *Retention:* 89% of 2002 full-time freshmen returned.

Freshmen *Admission:* 5,669 applied, 4,270 admitted, 980 enrolled. *Average high school GPA:* 3.35. *Test scores:* SAT verbal scores over 500: 80%; SAT math scores over 500: 85%; SAT verbal scores over 600: 27%; SAT math scores over 600: 32%; SAT verbal scores over 700: 3%; SAT math scores over 700: 4%.

Faculty *Total:* 396, 62% full-time, 59% with terminal degrees. *Student/faculty ratio:* 13:1.

Majors Accounting; ancient/classical Greek; biology/biological sciences; biomathematics and bioinformatics related; biophysics; business administration and management; business administration, management and operations related; chemistry; chemistry related; clinical laboratory science/medical technology; communication/speech communication and rhetoric; communications technologies and support services related; computer and information sciences and support services related; computer engineering; computer science; criminal justice/safety; dramatic/theatre arts; early childhood education; economics; electrical, electronics and communications engineering; elementary education; English; entrepreneurship; finance; foreign languages and literatures; French; German; gerontology; health/health care administration; history; human resources management; human services;

information science/studies; international business/trade/commerce; international relations and affairs; Italian; kindergarten/preschool education; kinesiology and exercise science; Latin; management science; marketing/marketing management; mathematics; mathematics and statistics related; neuroscience; nursing (registered nurse training); operations management; philosophy; physics; political science and government; psychology; religious studies; secondary education; sociology; Spanish; special education.

Academic Programs *Special study options:* academic remediation for entering students, adult/continuing education programs, advanced placement credit, distance learning, double majors, external degree program, freshman honors college, honors programs, independent study, internships, off-campus study, part-time degree program, services for LD students, student-designed majors, study abroad, summer session for credit. *ROTC:* Army (b), Air Force (c). *Unusual degree programs:* 3-2 engineering with University of Detroit Mercy, Widener University.

Library Harry and Jeanette Weinberg Memorial Library plus 1 other with 443,144 titles, 1,750 serial subscriptions, 13,075 audiovisual materials, an OPAC, a Web page.

Computers on Campus 837 computers available on campus for general student use. A campuswide network can be accessed from student residence rooms and from off campus. Internet access, online (class) registration, at least one staffed computer lab available.

Student Life *Housing:* on-campus residence required through sophomore year. *Options:* coed, men-only, women-only, disabled students. Campus housing is university owned. Freshman campus housing is guaranteed. *Activities and organizations:* drama/theater group, student-run newspaper, radio and television station, choral group, Service-Oriented Students Club, United Colors, retreat program, biology/pre-medicine club, pre-law society. *Campus security:* 24-hour emergency response devices and patrols, student patrols, late-night transport/escort service, controlled dormitory access. *Student services:* health clinic, personal/psychological counseling, women's center.

Athletics Member NCAA. All Division III. *Intercollegiate sports:* baseball M, basketball M/W, bowling M(c)/W(c), crew M(c)/W(c), cross-country running M/W, equestrian sports M(c)/W(c), field hockey W, golf M, ice hockey M, lacrosse M/W(c), rugby M(c)/W(c), skiing (downhill) M(c)/W(c), soccer M/W, softball W, swimming M/W, tennis M/W, track and field M(c)/W(c), volleyball M(c)/W, wrestling M. *Intramural sports:* badminton M/W, baseball M, basketball M/W, bowling M/W, cross-country running M/W, football M, golf M/W, racquetball M/W, soccer M/W, softball M/W, swimming M/W, table tennis M/W, tennis M/W, ultimate Frisbee M/W, volleyball M/W, water polo M/W, weight lifting M/W, wrestling M.

Standardized Tests *Required:* SAT I or ACT (for admission).

Costs (2003–04) *Comprehensive fee:* $30,743 includes full-time tuition ($21,208), mandatory fees ($200), and room and board ($9335). Full-time tuition and fees vary according to degree level, program, and student level. Part-time tuition: $590 per credit. Part-time tuition and fees vary according to degree level and student level. *College room only:* $5532. Room and board charges vary according to board plan and housing facility. *Payment plan:* installment. *Waivers:* senior citizens and employees or children of employees.

Financial Aid Of all full-time matriculated undergraduates who enrolled in 2003, 2,910 applied for aid, 2,539 were judged to have need, 354 had their need fully met. 969 Federal Work-Study jobs (averaging $1800). 237 state and other part-time jobs (averaging $1500). In 2003, 200 non-need-based awards were made. *Average percent of need met:* 72%. *Average financial aid package:* $14,666. *Average need-based loan:* $4073. *Average need-based gift aid:* $10,625. *Average non-need-based aid:* $8085. *Average indebtedness upon graduation:* $15,800.

Applying *Options:* common application, electronic application, early admission, early action, deferred entrance. *Application fee:* $40. *Required:* high school transcript. *Required for some:* 2 letters of recommendation, interview. *Recommended:* essay or personal statement. *Application deadline:* 3/1 (freshmen). *Notification:* continuous until 5/1 (freshmen), 12/15 (early action).

Admissions Contact Mr. Joseph Roback, Director of Admissions, The University of Scranton, Scranton, PA 18510-4622. *Phone:* 570-941-7540. *Toll-free phone:* 888-SCRANTON. *Fax:* 570-941-4370. *E-mail:* admissions@uofs.edu.

■ *See page 2706 for a narrative description.*

THE UNIVERSITY OF THE ARTS

Philadelphia, Pennsylvania

- **Independent** comprehensive, founded 1870
- **Calendar** semesters
- **Degrees** certificates, diplomas, bachelor's, master's, and postbachelor's certificates
- **Urban** 18-acre campus
- **Endowment** $15.9 million
- **Coed,** 1,968 undergraduate students, 97% full-time, 56% women, 44% men
- **Moderately difficult** entrance level, 51% of applicants were admitted

The University of the Arts (UArts) is the nation's first and only university dedicated solely to the visual, performing, and communication arts. Its 2,100 students are enrolled in undergraduate and graduate programs on its campus located in the heart of Philadelphia's Avenue of the Arts. Its history as a leader in educating creative individuals spans more than 125 years.

Undergraduates 1,911 full-time, 57 part-time. Students come from 42 states and territories, 38 other countries, 61% are from out of state, 9% African American, 3% Asian American or Pacific Islander, 4% Hispanic American, 0.2% Native American, 2% international, 7% transferred in, 36% live on campus. *Retention:* 82% of 2002 full-time freshmen returned.

Freshmen *Admission:* 1,951 applied, 987 admitted, 475 enrolled. *Average high school GPA:* 2.87. *Test scores:* SAT verbal scores over 500: 64%; SAT math scores over 500: 54%; ACT scores over 18: 81%; SAT verbal scores over 600: 22%; SAT math scores over 600: 13%; ACT scores over 24: 33%; SAT verbal scores over 700: 3%; SAT math scores over 700: 1%; ACT scores over 30: 4%.

Faculty *Total:* 434, 26% full-time, 29% with terminal degrees. *Student/faculty ratio:* 9:1.

Majors Acting; cinematography and film/video production; communication and journalism related; communication and media related; communication/speech communication and rhetoric; crafts, folk art and artisanry; dance; digital communication and media/multimedia; drama and dance teacher education; dramatic/theatre arts; dramatic/theatre arts and stagecraft related; film/video and photographic arts related; graphic design; illustration; industrial design; music performance; music theory and composition; painting; photography; printmaking; sculpture; theatre design and technology; visual and performing arts related.

Academic Programs *Special study options:* academic remediation for entering students, adult/continuing education programs, advanced placement credit, double majors, English as a second language, independent study, internships, off-campus study, part-time degree program, services for LD students, study abroad.

Library Albert M. Greenfield Library plus 2 others with 123,175 titles, 538 serial subscriptions, 321,710 audiovisual materials, an OPAC, a Web page.

Computers on Campus 475 computers available on campus for general student use. A campuswide network can be accessed from student residence rooms. Internet access, at least one staffed computer lab available. Computer purchase or lease plan available.

Student Life *Housing options:* coed. Campus housing is university owned. Freshman campus housing is guaranteed. *Activities and organizations:* drama/theater group, choral group, African-American Student Union, Gaming Society, Outreach, Multimedia Artist Society, Student Council. *Campus security:* 24-hour emergency response devices and patrols, late-night transport/escort service, crime prevention workshops and seminars. *Student services:* health clinic, personal/psychological counseling.

Standardized Tests *Required:* SAT I or ACT (for admission).

Costs (2004–05) *Tuition:* $22,060 full-time, $954 per credit part-time. Part-time tuition and fees vary according to course load. *Required fees:* $850 full-time. *Room only:* $5800. Room and board charges vary according to housing facility. *Waivers:* children of alumni and employees or children of employees.

Financial Aid In 2002, 561 non-need-based awards were made. *Average percent of need met:* 65%. *Average financial aid package:* $16,500. *Average indebtedness upon graduation:* $17,000.

Applying *Options:* common application, electronic application, early admission, deferred entrance. *Application fee:* $50. *Required:* essay or personal statement, high school transcript, minimum 2.0 GPA, 1 letter of recommendation, portfolio or audition. *Required for some:* interview. *Recommended:* interview. *Application deadline:* rolling (freshmen), rolling (transfers). *Notification:* continuous (freshmen), continuous (transfers).

Admissions Contact Ms. Barbara Elliott, Director of Admissions, The University of the Arts, 320 South Broad Street, Philadelphia, PA 19102-4944. *Phone:* 215-717-6030. *Toll-free phone:* 800-616-ARTS. *Fax:* 215-717-6045. *E-mail:* admissions@uarts.edu.

■ *See page 2720 for a narrative description.*

UNIVERSITY OF THE SCIENCES IN PHILADELPHIA

Philadelphia, Pennsylvania

- **Independent** university, founded 1821
- **Calendar** semesters
- **Degrees** bachelor's, master's, doctoral, and first professional
- **Urban** 35-acre campus
- **Endowment** $77.4 million
- **Coed,** 2,323 undergraduate students, 95% full-time, 67% women, 33% men
- **Moderately difficult** entrance level, 68% of applicants were admitted

University of the Sciences in Philadelphia (continued)

The University of the Sciences in Philadelphia, formerly known as the Philadelphia College of Pharmacy and Science, is a private university of more than 2,300 students. USP offers 20 majors in 3 colleges: Philadelphia College of Pharmacy, College of Health Sciences, and Misher College of Arts and Sciences. All students are admitted directly into their major of choice for the entire program length and are not required to reapply for admission at a later date. Prospective students should contact the Admission Office at 888-996-8747 (toll-free).

Undergraduates 2,216 full-time, 107 part-time. Students come from 30 states and territories, 16 other countries, 48% are from out of state, 6% African American, 34% Asian American or Pacific Islander, 2% Hispanic American, 0.3% Native American, 2% international, 5% transferred in, 29% live on campus. *Retention:* 87% of 2002 full-time freshmen returned.

Freshmen *Admission:* 2,966 applied, 2,029 admitted, 532 enrolled. *Average high school GPA:* 3.40. *Test scores:* SAT verbal scores over 500: 73%; SAT math scores over 500: 91%; SAT verbal scores over 600: 20%; SAT math scores over 600: 39%; SAT verbal scores over 700: 1%; SAT math scores over 700: 5%.

Faculty *Total:* 241, 57% full-time. *Student/faculty ratio:* 14:1.

Majors Biochemistry; bioinformatics; biology/biological sciences; chemistry; clinical laboratory science/medical technology; computer science; environmental science; health/medical psychology; health services/allied health/health sciences; marketing/marketing management; medical pharmacology and pharmaceutical sciences; medicinal and pharmaceutical chemistry; microbiology; pharmacology and toxicology; pharmacy, pharmaceutical sciences, and administration related; psychology.

Academic Programs *Special study options:* academic remediation for entering students, adult/continuing education programs, advanced placement credit, cooperative education, distance learning, double majors, English as a second language, honors programs, internships, off-campus study, part-time degree program, services for LD students, summer session for credit. *ROTC:* Army (c), Air Force (c).

Library Joseph W. England Library with 84,848 titles, 6,500 serial subscriptions, 5,965 audiovisual materials, an OPAC, a Web page.

Computers on Campus 105 computers available on campus for general student use. A campuswide network can be accessed from student residence rooms and from off campus. Internet access, at least one staffed computer lab available.

Student Life *Housing:* on-campus residence required through sophomore year. *Options:* coed. Campus housing is university owned. Freshman campus housing is guaranteed. *Activities and organizations:* drama/theater group, student-run newspaper, choral group, student government, Bharat, Academy of Students of Pharmacy, Student Physical Therapy Association, Asian Student Association, national fraternities, national sororities. *Campus security:* 24-hour emergency response devices and patrols, late-night transport/escort service, controlled dormitory access. *Student services:* health clinic, personal/psychological counseling.

Athletics Member NCAA, NAIA. All NCAA Division II. *Intercollegiate sports:* baseball M(s), basketball M(s)/W(s), cross-country running M/W, golf M/W, riflery M/W, softball W(s), tennis M/W, volleyball W(s). *Intramural sports:* archery M/W, basketball M/W, bowling M/W, riflery M/W, softball M/W, table tennis M/W, ultimate Frisbee M(c)/W(c), volleyball M/W.

Standardized Tests *Required:* SAT I or ACT (for admission). *Recommended:* SAT I (for admission).

Costs (2003–04) *Comprehensive fee:* $29,310 includes full-time tuition ($19,934), mandatory fees ($1024), and room and board ($8352). Full-time tuition and fees vary according to degree level and program. Part-time tuition: $831 per credit. Part-time tuition and fees vary according to course load and degree level. *Required fees:* $32 per credit part-time. *College room only:* $5134. Room and board charges vary according to board plan. *Payment plans:* tuition prepayment, installment. *Waivers:* employees or children of employees.

Applying *Options:* electronic application, deferred entrance. *Application fee:* $45. *Required:* high school transcript. *Recommended:* minimum 3.0 GPA. *Application deadline:* rolling (freshmen), rolling (transfers). *Notification:* continuous (freshmen), continuous (transfers).

Admissions Contact Mr. Louis L. Hegyes, Director of Admission, University of the Sciences in Philadelphia, 600 South 43rd Street, Philadelphia, PA 19104-4495. *Phone:* 215-596-8810. *Toll-free phone:* 888-996-8747. *Fax:* 215-596-8821. *E-mail:* admit@usip.edu.

■ *See page 2728 for a narrative description.*

URSINUS COLLEGE
Collegeville, Pennsylvania

- **Independent** 4-year, founded 1869
- **Calendar** semesters
- **Degree** bachelor's
- **Suburban** 168-acre campus with easy access to Philadelphia
- **Endowment** $84.2 million
- **Coed,** 1,485 undergraduate students, 99% full-time, 54% women, 46% men
- **Very difficult** entrance level, 74% of applicants were admitted

Ursinus College, founded in 1869, is selective and coeducational and offers a high-quality liberal arts curriculum that prepares students for professional and graduate schools. Ursinus, known for its excellent placement of graduates in advanced schools of medicine, science, law, education, and business, provides each incoming freshman with a laptop computer. Ursinus holds a distinguished campus chapter of Phi Beta Kappa.

Undergraduates 1,468 full-time, 17 part-time. Students come from 28 states and territories, 14 other countries, 37% are from out of state, 8% African American, 4% Asian American or Pacific Islander, 3% Hispanic American, 0.3% Native American, 1% international, 0.3% transferred in, 91% live on campus. *Retention:* 88% of 2002 full-time freshmen returned.

Freshmen *Admission:* 1,775 applied, 1,322 admitted, 454 enrolled. *Average high school GPA:* 3.50. *Test scores:* SAT verbal scores over 500: 93%; SAT math scores over 500: 91%; SAT verbal scores over 600: 52%; SAT math scores over 600: 57%; SAT verbal scores over 700: 12%; SAT math scores over 700: 12%.

Faculty *Total:* 158, 70% full-time, 73% with terminal degrees. *Student/faculty ratio:* 11:1.

Majors American studies; anthropology; art; Asian studies (East); biological and physical sciences; biology/biological sciences; business administration and management; chemistry; civil engineering; classics; classics and languages, literatures and linguistics; computer science; economics; electrical, electronics and communications engineering; English; environmental studies; fine arts related; French; German; health and physical education; history; international relations and affairs; mass communication/media; mathematics; mechanical engineering; metallurgical engineering; multi-/interdisciplinary studies related; neuroscience; philosophy; philosophy and religious studies related; physics; political science and government; psychology; social sciences related; sociology; Spanish.

Academic Programs *Special study options:* adult/continuing education programs, advanced placement credit, double majors, English as a second language, honors programs, independent study, internships, off-campus study, part-time degree program, student-designed majors, study abroad. *Unusual degree programs:* 3-2 engineering with University of Pennsylvania, Georgia Institute of Technology, University of Southern California.

Library Myrin Library plus 2 others with 200,000 titles, 900 serial subscriptions, 17,500 audiovisual materials, an OPAC, a Web page.

Computers on Campus 350 computers available on campus for general student use. A campuswide network can be accessed from student residence rooms and from off campus that provide access to laptop computers. Internet access, at least one staffed computer lab available.

Student Life *Housing options:* coed, men-only, women-only. Campus housing is university owned. Freshman campus housing is guaranteed. *Activities and organizations:* drama/theater group, student-run newspaper, radio and television station, choral group, Environmental Action Committee, Habitat for Humanity, Campus Activities Board, Christian Fellowship, Multicultural Student Union, national fraternities, national sororities. *Campus security:* 24-hour emergency response devices and patrols, late-night transport/escort service, student EMT Corps for first aid/emergency first response. *Student services:* health clinic, personal/psychological counseling.

Athletics Member NCAA. All Division III. *Intercollegiate sports:* baseball M, basketball M/W, cross-country running M/W, field hockey W, football M, golf M/W, gymnastics W, lacrosse M/W, rugby M(c)/W(c), soccer M/W, softball W, swimming M/W, tennis M/W, track and field M/W, volleyball W, wrestling M. *Intramural sports:* basketball M/W, cheerleading W, cross-country running W, fencing M/W, field hockey W, football M/W, lacrosse M, racquetball M/W, rugby M/W, sailing M/W, skiing (cross-country) M/W, skiing (downhill) M/W, softball M/W, squash M/W, swimming M/W, tennis M/W, ultimate Frisbee M/W, volleyball M/W, water polo M/W, weight lifting M/W.

Standardized Tests *Required for some:* SAT I or ACT (for admission). *Recommended:* SAT II: Subject Tests (for admission).

Costs (2003–04) *Comprehensive fee:* $34,400 includes full-time tuition ($27,500) and room and board ($6900). *Payment plan:* installment. *Waivers:* senior citizens and employees or children of employees.

Financial Aid Of all full-time matriculated undergraduates who enrolled in 2003, 1,412 applied for aid, 1,367 were judged to have need, 746 had their need fully met. 637 Federal Work-Study jobs (averaging $1540). In 2003, 118 non-need-based awards were made. *Average percent of need met:* 90%. *Average financial aid package:* $22,129. *Average need-based loan:* $5155. *Average need-based gift aid:* $15,874. *Average non-need-based aid:* $11,500. *Average indebtedness upon graduation:* $18,000.

Applying *Options:* common application, electronic application, early admission, early decision, deferred entrance. *Application fee:* $45. *Required:* essay or personal statement, high school transcript, 2 letters of recommendation, a graded paper. *Recommended:* interview. *Application deadlines:* 2/15 (freshmen), 8/1 (transfers). *Early decision:* 1/15. *Notification:* 4/1 (freshmen), 2/1 (early decision), 9/1 (transfers).

Admissions Contact Mr. Paul M. Cramer, Director of Admissions, Ursinus College, Box 1000, Main Street, Collegeville, PA 19426. *Phone:* 610-409-3200. *Fax:* 610-409-3662. *E-mail:* admissions@ursinus.edu.

■ See page 2746 for a narrative description.

VALLEY FORGE CHRISTIAN COLLEGE
Phoenixville, Pennsylvania

- **Independent Assemblies of God** 4-year, founded 1938
- **Calendar** semesters
- **Degrees** certificates, associate, and bachelor's
- **Small-town** 77-acre campus with easy access to Philadelphia
- **Endowment** $548,572
- **Coed**
- **Minimally difficult** entrance level

Faculty *Student/faculty ratio:* 19:1.

Student Life *Campus security:* late-night transport/escort service, 16-hour patrols by trained security personnel.

Athletics Member NCCAA.

Standardized Tests *Required:* SAT I or ACT (for admission).

Costs (2003–04) *Comprehensive fee:* $14,430 includes full-time tuition ($8720), mandatory fees ($850), and room and board ($4860). Part-time tuition: $337 per credit. *College room only:* $2200.

Financial Aid Of all full-time matriculated undergraduates who enrolled in 2003, 758 applied for aid, 688 were judged to have need, 77 had their need fully met. 64 Federal Work-Study jobs (averaging $1240). In 2003, 137. *Average percent of need met:* 58. *Average financial aid package:* $7305. *Average need-based loan:* $3391. *Average need-based gift aid:* $4349. *Average non-need-based aid:* $5981. *Average indebtedness upon graduation:* $24,423.

Applying *Options:* common application, electronic application, early admission, deferred entrance. *Application fee:* $25. *Required:* high school transcript, 2 letters of recommendation. *Required for some:* interview. *Recommended:* essay or personal statement.

Admissions Contact Rev. William Chenco, Director of Admissions, Valley Forge Christian College, 1401 Charlestown Road, Phoenixville, PA 19460. *Phone:* 610-935-0450 Ext. 1430. *Toll-free phone:* 800-432-8322. *Fax:* 610-935-9353. *E-mail:* admissions@vfcc.edu.

VILLANOVA UNIVERSITY
Villanova, Pennsylvania

- **Independent Roman Catholic** comprehensive, founded 1842
- **Calendar** semesters
- **Degrees** certificates, associate, bachelor's, master's, doctoral, and first professional
- **Suburban** 254-acre campus with easy access to Philadelphia
- **Endowment** $176.5 million
- **Coed,** 7,267 undergraduate students, 90% full-time, 51% women, 49% men
- **Very difficult** entrance level, 53% of applicants were admitted

Undergraduates 6,570 full-time, 697 part-time. Students come from 49 states and territories, 28 other countries, 66% are from out of state, 3% African American, 5% Asian American or Pacific Islander, 5% Hispanic American, 0.2% Native American, 2% international, 1% transferred in, 65% live on campus. *Retention:* 94% of 2002 full-time freshmen returned.

Freshmen *Admission:* 10,896 applied, 5,781 admitted, 1,566 enrolled. *Average high school GPA:* 3.63. *Test scores:* SAT verbal scores over 500: 96%; SAT math scores over 500: 97%; SAT verbal scores over 600: 61%; SAT math scores over 600: 77%; SAT verbal scores over 700: 10%; SAT math scores over 700: 17%.

Faculty *Total:* 973, 56% full-time, 76% with terminal degrees. *Student/faculty ratio:* 13:1.

Majors Accounting; art history, criticism and conservation; astronomy; astrophysics; biology/biological sciences; business administration and management; business/managerial economics; chemical engineering; chemistry; civil engineering; classics and languages, literatures and linguistics; computer engineering; computer science; criminal justice/law enforcement administration; economics; education; electrical, electronics and communications engineering; elementary education; English; finance; French; geography; German; history; human services; information science/studies; international business/trade/commerce; Italian; liberal arts and sciences/liberal studies; management information systems; marketing/marketing management; mass communication/media; mathematics; mechanical engineering; natural sciences; nursing (registered nurse training); philosophy; physics; political science and government; psychology; religious studies; secondary education; sociology; Spanish.

Academic Programs *Special study options:* accelerated degree program, adult/continuing education programs, advanced placement credit, distance learning, double majors, English as a second language, honors programs, independent study, internships, off-campus study, part-time degree program, services for LD students, study abroad, summer session for credit. *ROTC:* Army (c), Navy (b), Air Force (c). *Unusual degree programs:* 3-2 allied health programs with Thomas Jefferson University, MCP Hannemann, University of Pennsylvania, Philadelphia College of Optometry.

Library Falvey Library plus 2 others with 1.0 million titles, 5,338 serial subscriptions, 8,000 audiovisual materials, an OPAC, a Web page.

Computers on Campus 800 computers available on campus for general student use. A campuswide network can be accessed from student residence rooms and from off campus. Internet access, online (class) registration, at least one staffed computer lab available.

Student Life *Housing options:* coed, men-only, women-only, disabled students. Campus housing is university owned. Freshman campus housing is guaranteed. *Activities and organizations:* drama/theater group, student-run newspaper, radio and television station, choral group, marching band, Blue Key Society, orientation counselor program, Special Olympics, campus activities team, national fraternities, national sororities. *Campus security:* 24-hour emergency response devices and patrols, student patrols, late-night transport/escort service, controlled dormitory access. *Student services:* health clinic, personal/psychological counseling, legal services.

Athletics Member NCAA. All Division I except football (Division I-A). *Intercollegiate sports:* baseball M(s), basketball M(s)/W(s), cheerleading M/W, crew M(c)/W(s), cross-country running M(s)/W(s), field hockey W(s), golf M, ice hockey M(c), lacrosse M/W, rugby M(c), sailing M(c)/W(c), skiing (downhill) M(c)/W(c), soccer M(s)/W(s), softball W(s), swimming M/W(s), tennis M/W, track and field M(s)/W(s), volleyball M(c)/W(s), water polo M(c)/W, weight lifting M(c)/W(c). *Intramural sports:* basketball M/W, football M/W, soccer M/W, softball M/W, tennis M/W, track and field M/W, ultimate Frisbee M/W, volleyball M/W.

Standardized Tests *Required:* SAT I or ACT (for admission).

Costs (2003–04) *Comprehensive fee:* $35,050 includes full-time tuition ($25,673), mandatory fees ($550), and room and board ($8827). Full-time tuition and fees vary according to program and student level. Part-time tuition: $535. Part-time tuition and fees vary according to class time and program. *Required fees:* $275 per term part-time. *College room only:* $4667. Room and board charges vary according to board plan and housing facility. *Payment plan:* installment. *Waivers:* senior citizens and employees or children of employees.

Financial Aid Of all full-time matriculated undergraduates who enrolled in 2003, 3,749 applied for aid, 3,088 were judged to have need, 432 had their need fully met. 1,220 Federal Work-Study jobs (averaging $1933). In 2003, 315 non-need-based awards were made. *Average percent of need met:* 76%. *Average financial aid package:* $18,217. *Average need-based loan:* $4778. *Average need-based gift aid:* $11,669. *Average non-need-based aid:* $10,338. *Average indebtedness upon graduation:* $30,178.

Applying *Options:* electronic application, early admission, early action, deferred entrance. *Application fee:* $60. *Required:* essay or personal statement, high school transcript, activities resume. *Application deadlines:* 1/7 (freshmen), 7/15 (transfers). *Notification:* 4/1 (freshmen), 12/20 (early action), continuous (transfers).

Admissions Contact Mr. Michael M. Gaynor, Director of University Admission, Villanova University, 800 Lancaster Avenue, Villanova, PA 19085-1672. *Phone:* 610-519-4000. *Toll-free phone:* 610-519-4000. *Fax:* 610-519-6450. *E-mail:* gotovu@villanova.edu.

■ See page 2762 for a narrative description.

WASHINGTON & JEFFERSON COLLEGE
Washington, Pennsylvania

- **Independent** 4-year, founded 1781
- **Calendar** 4-1-4
- **Degrees** associate and bachelor's
- **Small-town** 51-acre campus with easy access to Pittsburgh
- **Endowment** $72.1 million
- **Coed,** 1,233 undergraduate students, 99% full-time, 48% women, 52% men
- **Very difficult** entrance level, 40% of applicants were admitted

Now in its 3rd century, Washington & Jefferson College continues to be one of America's premier liberal arts colleges. High-quality academic programs and a student-centered approach characterize a W&J education. Programs in prehealth and prelaw are nationally recognized, with medical and law school acceptance rates being among the highest in the country.

Washington & Jefferson College (continued)

Undergraduates 1,219 full-time, 14 part-time. Students come from 28 states and territories, 4 other countries, 20% are from out of state, 2% African American, 1% Asian American or Pacific Islander, 1% Hispanic American, 0.2% Native American, 0.2% international, 2% transferred in, 82% live on campus. *Retention:* 84% of 2002 full-time freshmen returned.

Freshmen *Admission:* 3,135 applied, 1,260 admitted, 347 enrolled. *Average high school GPA:* 3.13. *Test scores:* SAT verbal scores over 500: 84%; SAT math scores over 500: 87%; ACT scores over 18: 99%; SAT verbal scores over 600: 32%; SAT math scores over 600: 40%; ACT scores over 24: 53%; SAT verbal scores over 700: 4%; SAT math scores over 700: 6%; ACT scores over 30: 8%.

Faculty *Total:* 119, 80% full-time, 73% with terminal degrees. *Student/faculty ratio:* 12:1.

Majors Accounting; art; art teacher education; biochemistry; biology/biological sciences; business administration and management; chemistry; chemistry related; child development; dramatic/theatre arts; economics; English; French; German; history; information technology; international business/trade/commerce; mathematics; music; philosophy; physics; political science and government; psychology; sociology; Spanish.

Academic Programs *Special study options:* academic remediation for entering students, accelerated degree program, advanced placement credit, double majors, honors programs, independent study, internships, part-time degree program, services for LD students, student-designed majors, study abroad, summer session for credit. *ROTC:* Army (c), Air Force (c). *Unusual degree programs:* 3-2 engineering with Case Western Reserve University, Washington University in St. Louis.

Library U. Grant Miller Library with 184,858 titles, 8,124 serial subscriptions, 4,112 audiovisual materials, an OPAC, a Web page.

Computers on Campus 237 computers available on campus for general student use. A campuswide network can be accessed from student residence rooms and from off campus. Internet access, at least one staffed computer lab available. Computer purchase or lease plan available.

Student Life *Housing:* on-campus residence required through senior year. *Options:* coed, men-only, women-only, disabled students. Campus housing is university owned. Freshman campus housing is guaranteed. *Activities and organizations:* drama/theater group, student-run newspaper, radio station, choral group, student government, Saturday Nite Life, George and Tom's, Pre-health Society, Pre-legal Society, national fraternities, national sororities. *Campus security:* 24-hour emergency response devices and patrols, late-night transport/escort service, controlled dormitory access. *Student services:* health clinic, personal/psychological counseling.

Athletics Member NCAA. All Division III. *Intercollegiate sports:* baseball M, basketball M/W, cross-country running M/W, field hockey W, football M, golf M/W, ice hockey M(c), lacrosse M, soccer M/W, softball W, swimming M/W, tennis M/W, track and field M/W, volleyball W, water polo M/W, wrestling M. *Intramural sports:* basketball M/W, bowling M/W, cross-country running M/W, football M/W, golf M/W, ice hockey M, racquetball M/W, soccer M/W, softball W, swimming M/W, table tennis M/W, tennis M/W, track and field M/W, ultimate Frisbee M/W, volleyball M/W, wrestling M.

Standardized Tests *Required:* SAT I or ACT (for admission).

Costs (2003–04) *Comprehensive fee:* $29,570 includes full-time tuition ($22,860), mandatory fees ($400), and room and board ($6310). Part-time tuition: $714 per credit hour. *College room only:* $3440. Room and board charges vary according to board plan and housing facility. *Payment plans:* installment, deferred payment. *Waivers:* employees or children of employees.

Financial Aid Of all full-time matriculated undergraduates who enrolled in 2003, 1,009 applied for aid, 922 were judged to have need, 160 had their need fully met. 438 Federal Work-Study jobs (averaging $1500). 195 state and other part-time jobs (averaging $1200). In 2003, 220 non-need-based awards were made. *Average percent of need met:* 72%. *Average financial aid package:* $15,658. *Average need-based loan:* $3875. *Average need-based gift aid:* $9984. *Average non-need-based aid:* $8025. *Average indebtedness upon graduation:* $16,384.

Applying *Options:* common application, electronic application, early admission, early decision, early action, deferred entrance. *Application fee:* $25. *Required:* essay or personal statement, high school transcript. *Recommended:* 1 letter of recommendation, interview. *Application deadline:* 3/1 (freshmen), rolling (transfers). *Early decision:* 12/1. *Notification:* 4/1 (freshmen), 12/15 (early decision), 2/15 (early action).

Admissions Contact Mr. Alton E. Newell, Dean of Enrollment, Washington & Jefferson College, 60 South Lincoln Street, Washington, PA 15301. *Phone:* 724-223-6025. *Toll-free phone:* 888-WANDJAY. *Fax:* 724-223-6534. *E-mail:* admission@washjeff.edu.

■ *See page 2786 for a narrative description.*

WAYNESBURG COLLEGE

Waynesburg, Pennsylvania

- ■ **Independent** comprehensive, founded 1849, affiliated with Presbyterian Church (U.S.A.)
- ■ **Calendar** semesters
- ■ **Degrees** associate, bachelor's, and master's
- ■ **Small-town** 30-acre campus with easy access to Pittsburgh
- ■ **Endowment** $27.7 million
- ■ **Coed,** 1,530 undergraduate students, 83% full-time, 58% women, 42% men
- ■ **Moderately difficult** entrance level, 78% of applicants were admitted

Undergraduates 1,272 full-time, 258 part-time. Students come from 18 states and territories, 4 other countries, 18% are from out of state, 3% African American, 0.1% Asian American or Pacific Islander, 0.3% Hispanic American, 0.6% international, 3% transferred in, 55% live on campus. *Retention:* 68% of 2002 full-time freshmen returned.

Freshmen *Admission:* 1,467 applied, 1,147 admitted, 330 enrolled. *Average high school GPA:* 3.18.

Faculty *Total:* 122, 52% full-time, 29% with terminal degrees. *Student/faculty ratio:* 13:1.

Majors Accounting; advertising; art; arts management; athletic training; biology/biological sciences; biology teacher education; business administration and management; chemistry; chemistry teacher education; commercial and advertising art; communication/speech communication and rhetoric; computer and information sciences; computer science; creative writing; criminal justice/law enforcement administration; elementary education; engineering related; English; English/language arts teacher education; environmental studies; finance; forensic science and technology; graphic design; health/health care administration; history; international business/trade/commerce; journalism; kinesiology and exercise science; liberal arts and sciences/liberal studies; marine biology and biological oceanography; marketing/marketing management; mathematics; mathematics teacher education; nursing (registered nurse training); political science and government; pre-dentistry studies; pre-engineering; pre-law studies; pre-medical studies; pre-theology/pre-ministerial studies; pre-veterinary studies; psychology; public administration; radio and television; science teacher education; secondary education; social sciences; social studies teacher education; sociology; special education.

Academic Programs *Special study options:* academic remediation for entering students, accelerated degree program, adult/continuing education programs, advanced placement credit, distance learning, double majors, honors programs, independent study, internships, study abroad. *ROTC:* Army (c). *Unusual degree programs:* 3-2 engineering with Case Western Reserve University, Washington University in St. Louis, Pennsylvania State University—University Park Campus.

Library Waynesburg College Library with 100,000 titles, 492 serial subscriptions, an OPAC, a Web page.

Computers on Campus 150 computers available on campus for general student use. A campuswide network can be accessed from student residence rooms and from off campus. Internet access, at least one staffed computer lab available.

Student Life *Housing:* on-campus residence required through junior year. *Options:* men-only, women-only. Campus housing is university owned. Freshman campus housing is guaranteed. *Activities and organizations:* drama/theater group, student-run newspaper, radio and television station, choral group, marching band, Student Senate, Student Activities Board (SAB), Student Nurses Association, Christian Fellowship. *Campus security:* 24-hour emergency response devices and patrols, late-night transport/escort service, controlled dormitory access. *Student services:* health clinic, personal/psychological counseling.

Athletics Member NCAA. All Division III. *Intercollegiate sports:* baseball M, basketball M/W, cheerleading M/W, cross-country running M/W, football M, golf M/W, soccer M/W, softball W, tennis M/W, track and field M/W, volleyball W, wrestling M. *Intramural sports:* basketball M/W, bowling M/W, football M/W, racquetball M/W, softball M/W, table tennis M/W, volleyball M/W.

Standardized Tests *Required:* SAT I or ACT (for admission).

Costs (2003–04) *Comprehensive fee:* $19,370 includes full-time tuition ($13,520), mandatory fees ($330), and room and board ($5520). Full-time tuition and fees vary according to class time. Part-time tuition: $565 per credit. Part-time tuition and fees vary according to class time, course load, and location. *Required fees:* $14 per credit part-time. *College room only:* $2820. Room and board charges vary according to board plan. *Waivers:* employees or children of employees.

Financial Aid Of all full-time matriculated undergraduates who enrolled in 2003, 1,269 applied for aid, 1,180 were judged to have need, 419 had their need fully met. 300 Federal Work-Study jobs (averaging $650). In 2003, 42 non-need-based awards were made. *Average percent of need met:* 83%. *Average financial aid package:* $11,120. *Average need-based loan:* $4150. *Average need-based gift aid:* $7748. *Average non-need-based aid:* $4175. *Average indebtedness upon graduation:* $19,000.

Applying *Options:* common application, early admission. *Application fee:* $20. *Required:* high school transcript, minimum 2.0 GPA. *Required for some:* essay or personal statement, letters of recommendation. *Recommended:* minimum 3.0 GPA, interview. *Application deadline:* rolling (freshmen), rolling (transfers). *Notification:* continuous (freshmen), continuous (transfers).

Admissions Contact Ms. Robin L. King, Dean of Admissions, Waynesburg College, 51 West College Street, Waynesburg, PA 15070. *Phone:* 724-852-3333. *Toll-free phone:* 800-225-7393. *Fax:* 724-627-8124. *E-mail:* admissions@waynesburg.edu.

■ *See page 2790 for a narrative description.*

WEST CHESTER UNIVERSITY OF PENNSYLVANIA

West Chester, Pennsylvania

- **State-supported** comprehensive, founded 1871, part of Pennsylvania State System of Higher Education
- **Calendar** semesters
- **Degrees** bachelor's and master's
- **Suburban** 547-acre campus with easy access to Philadelphia
- **Endowment** $9.5 million
- **Coed,** 10,562 undergraduate students, 87% full-time, 61% women, 39% men
- **Moderately difficult** entrance level, 46% of applicants were admitted

Undergraduates 9,241 full-time, 1,321 part-time. Students come from 32 states and territories, 11% are from out of state, 8% African American, 2% Asian American or Pacific Islander, 2% Hispanic American, 0.3% Native American, 0.5% international, 9% transferred in, 35% live on campus. *Retention:* 83% of 2002 full-time freshmen returned.

Freshmen *Admission:* 10,207 applied, 4,720 admitted, 1,729 enrolled. *Average high school GPA:* 3.27. *Test scores:* SAT verbal scores over 500: 71%; SAT math scores over 500: 70%; SAT verbal scores over 600: 15%; SAT math scores over 600: 16%; SAT verbal scores over 700: 1%; SAT math scores over 700: 1%.

Faculty *Total:* 762, 74% full-time, 71% with terminal degrees. *Student/faculty ratio:* 17:1.

Majors Accounting; American studies; anthropology; art; athletic training; audiology and speech-language pathology; biochemistry; biology/biological sciences; biology teacher education; business administration and management; business/managerial economics; chemistry; chemistry teacher education; city/urban, community and regional planning; clinical nutrition; communication/speech communication and rhetoric; comparative literature; computer and information sciences; criminal justice/safety; dietetics; dramatic/theatre arts; ecology; elementary education; English; English/language arts teacher education; environmental health; environmental studies; finance; fine/studio arts; foreign language teacher education; French; French language teacher education; geography; geology/earth science; German; health and physical education; health/health care administration; health teacher education; history; history teacher education; international relations and affairs; kinesiology and exercise science; Latin; liberal arts and sciences/liberal studies; mathematics; mathematics teacher education; molecular biology; music; music history, literature, and theory; music performance; music teacher education; music theory and composition; nursing (registered nurse training); philosophy; physical education teaching and coaching; physics; physics teacher education; piano and organ; political science and government; pre-medical studies; psychology; public health; public health education and promotion; public health related; Russian; sales, distribution and marketing; science teacher education; social studies teacher education; social work; sociology; Spanish; Spanish language teacher education; special education; speech and rhetoric; voice and opera; women's studies.

Academic Programs *Special study options:* academic remediation for entering students, adult/continuing education programs, advanced placement credit, distance learning, double majors, English as a second language, honors programs, independent study, internships, off-campus study, part-time degree program, services for LD students, student-designed majors, study abroad, summer session for credit. *ROTC:* Army (c), Air Force (c).

Library Francis Harvey Green Library plus 1 other with 524,976 titles, 2,800 serial subscriptions, an OPAC, a Web page.

Computers on Campus 700 computers available on campus for general student use. A campuswide network can be accessed from student residence rooms and from off campus. Internet access, online (class) registration, at least one staffed computer lab available.

Student Life *Housing options:* coed, women-only, disabled students. Campus housing is university owned. Freshman applicants given priority for college housing. *Activities and organizations:* drama/theater group, student-run newspaper, radio station, choral group, marching band, Off Campus and Commuter Association, Residence Hall Association, Student Government Association, Inter-Greek Council, Sports Club Council, national fraternities, national sororities. *Campus security:* 24-hour emergency response devices and patrols, late-night transport/escort service. *Student services:* health clinic, personal/psychological counseling, women's center, legal services.

Athletics Member NCAA. All Division II except field hockey (Division I). *Intercollegiate sports:* baseball M(s), basketball M(s)/W(s), cross-country running M(s)/W(s), equestrian sports M(c)/W(c), field hockey W(s), football M(s), golf M(s), gymnastics W(s), ice hockey M(c)/W(c), lacrosse M/W(s), rugby M(c)/W(c), soccer M(s)/W(s), softball W(s), swimming M(s)/W(s), tennis M(s)/W(s), track and field M(s)/W(s), volleyball W(s), water polo M(c)/W(c). *Intramural sports:* badminton M/W, basketball M/W, cheerleading W, cross-country running M, fencing M/W, football M/W, soccer M/W, softball M/W, tennis M/W, volleyball M/W.

Standardized Tests *Required:* SAT I or ACT (for admission).

Costs (2003–04) *Tuition:* state resident $4598 full-time, $192 per credit part-time; nonresident $11,496 full-time, $479 per credit part-time. Full-time tuition and fees vary according to course load. Part-time tuition and fees vary according to course load. *Required fees:* $44 per credit part-time. *Room and board:* $5642; room only: $4960. Room and board charges vary according to board plan and housing facility. *Payment plan:* installment.

Financial Aid *Average indebtedness upon graduation:* $17,500.

Applying *Options:* early admission, deferred entrance. *Application fee:* $35. *Required:* essay or personal statement, high school transcript. *Required for some:* letters of recommendation, interview. *Recommended:* minimum 3.0 GPA. *Application deadline:* rolling (freshmen), rolling (transfers). *Notification:* continuous (freshmen), continuous (transfers).

Admissions Contact Ms. Marsha Haug, Director of Admissions, West Chester University of Pennsylvania, Messikomer Hall, Rosedale Avenue, West Chester, PA 19383. *Phone:* 610-436-3411. *Toll-free phone:* 877-315-2165. *Fax:* 610-436-2907. *E-mail:* ugadmiss@wcupa.edu.

■ *See page 2806 for a narrative description.*

WESTMINSTER COLLEGE

New Wilmington, Pennsylvania

- **Independent** comprehensive, founded 1852, affiliated with Presbyterian Church (U.S.A.)
- **Calendar** semesters
- **Degrees** bachelor's and master's
- **Small-town** 350-acre campus with easy access to Pittsburgh
- **Endowment** $85.0 million
- **Coed,** 1,425 undergraduate students, 96% full-time, 61% women, 39% men
- **Moderately difficult** entrance level, 77% of applicants were admitted

Westminster College, an independent, coeducational liberal arts college affiliated with the Presbyterian Church (USA), was founded in 1852. Westminster's liberal arts foundation thrives in a caring environment supported by an integrative curriculum featuring state-of-the-art technology and opportunities for involvement to prepare students for a diverse world while choosing from more than 40 different majors.

Undergraduates 1,374 full-time, 51 part-time. Students come from 22 states and territories, 3 other countries, 22% are from out of state, 1% African American, 0.4% Asian American or Pacific Islander, 0.6% Hispanic American, 2% transferred in. *Retention:* 83% of 2002 full-time freshmen returned.

Freshmen *Admission:* 1,244 applied, 953 admitted, 339 enrolled. *Average high school GPA:* 3.39. *Test scores:* SAT verbal scores over 500: 73%; SAT math scores over 500: 72%; ACT scores over 18: 91%; SAT verbal scores over 600: 28%; SAT math scores over 600: 29%; ACT scores over 24: 49%; SAT verbal scores over 700: 2%; SAT math scores over 700: 3%; ACT scores over 30: 10%.

Faculty *Total:* 147, 66% full-time, 63% with terminal degrees. *Student/faculty ratio:* 12:1.

Majors Accounting; art; behavioral sciences; biology/biological sciences; biology/biotechnology laboratory technician; broadcast journalism; business administration and management; chemistry; classics and languages, literatures and linguistics; computer science; creative writing; criminal justice/law enforcement administration; dramatic/theatre arts; economics; education; elementary education; English; environmental studies; French; German; history; information science/studies; interdisciplinary studies; international business/trade/commerce; international economics; international relations and affairs; labor and industrial relations; Latin; mass communication/media; mathematics; modern languages; molecular biology; music; music teacher education; philosophy; physics; physiological psychology/psychobiology; political science and government; pre-dentistry studies; pre-law studies; pre-medical studies; pre-veterinary studies; psychology; public relations/image management; radio and television; religious education; religious/sacred music; religious studies; sociology; Spanish; telecommunications; voice and opera.

Westminster College (continued)

Academic Programs *Special study options:* adult/continuing education programs, advanced placement credit, double majors, honors programs, independent study, internships, off-campus study, part-time degree program, student-designed majors, study abroad, summer session for credit. *ROTC:* Army (c). *Unusual degree programs:* 3-2 engineering with Pennsylvania State University—University Park Campus, Washington University in St. Louis, Case Western Reserve University.

Library McGill Memorial Library plus 1 other with 283,070 titles, 848 serial subscriptions, 14,251 audiovisual materials, an OPAC, a Web page.

Computers on Campus 158 computers available on campus for general student use. A campuswide network can be accessed from student residence rooms and from off campus. Internet access, at least one staffed computer lab available.

Student Life *Housing:* on-campus residence required through junior year. *Options:* men-only, women-only. Freshman campus housing is guaranteed. *Activities and organizations:* drama/theater group, student-run newspaper, radio station, choral group, marching band, student government, Greek life, Habitat for Humanity, established service teams, national fraternities, national sororities. *Campus security:* 24-hour patrols, late-night transport/escort service. *Student services:* health clinic, personal/psychological counseling.

Athletics Member NCAA. All Division III. *Intercollegiate sports:* baseball M, basketball M/W, cross-country running M/W, equestrian sports M(c)/W(c), football M(s), golf M/W, soccer M/W, softball W, swimming M/W, tennis M/W, track and field M/W, volleyball W. *Intramural sports:* archery M/W, badminton M/W, basketball M/W, cross-country running M/W, football M, golf M/W, racquetball M/W, skiing (cross-country) M/W, skiing (downhill) M/W, softball M, swimming M/W, tennis M/W, track and field W, volleyball W, weight lifting M/W.

Standardized Tests *Required:* SAT I or ACT (for admission).

Costs (2004–05) *Comprehensive fee:* $27,830 includes full-time tuition ($20,530), mandatory fees ($940), and room and board ($6360). Part-time tuition: $645 per hour. *Required fees:* $10 per hour part-time. *College room only:* $3360. Room and board charges vary according to board plan. *Payment plan:* installment.

Financial Aid Of all full-time matriculated undergraduates who enrolled in 2003, 1,177 applied for aid, 1,081 were judged to have need, 401 had their need fully met. 356 Federal Work-Study jobs (averaging $1587). 239 state and other part-time jobs (averaging $1638). In 2003, 237 non-need-based awards were made. *Average percent of need met:* 90%. *Average financial aid package:* $17,237. *Average need-based loan:* $3972. *Average need-based gift aid:* $7719. *Average non-need-based aid:* $7990. *Average indebtedness upon graduation:* $16,353.

Applying *Options:* common application, deferred entrance. *Application fee:* $35. *Required:* essay or personal statement, high school transcript, minimum 2.0 GPA, 2 letters of recommendation. *Recommended:* minimum 3.0 GPA, interview. *Application deadline:* 5/1 (freshmen), rolling (transfers). *Notification:* continuous (freshmen), continuous (transfers).

Admissions Contact Mr. Doug Swartz, Director of Admissions, Westminster College, 319 South Market Street, New Wilmington, PA 16172-0001. *Phone:* 724-946-7100. *Toll-free phone:* 800-942-8033. *Fax:* 724-946-7171. *E-mail:* swartzdl@westminster.edu.

■ *See page 2824 for a narrative description.*

WIDENER UNIVERSITY

Chester, Pennsylvania

- **Independent** comprehensive, founded 1821
- **Calendar** semesters
- **Degrees** bachelor's, master's, doctoral, and first professional
- **Suburban** 110-acre campus with easy access to Philadelphia
- **Endowment** $33.0 million
- **Coed,** 2,400 undergraduate students, 94% full-time, 46% women, 54% men
- **Moderately difficult** entrance level, 74% of applicants were admitted

Located just 12 miles from historic and culturally rich Philadelphia, Widener University provides a unique combination of liberal arts and professional education, along with opportunities for civic engagement. Through dynamic teaching, active scholarship, personal attention, and experiential learning, Widener offers its students the support they need to succeed.

Undergraduates 2,266 full-time, 134 part-time. Students come from 33 states and territories, 35 other countries, 45% are from out of state, 9% African American, 3% Asian American or Pacific Islander, 2% Hispanic American, 0.3% Native American, 2% international, 5% transferred in, 60% live on campus. *Retention:* 85% of 2002 full-time freshmen returned.

Freshmen *Admission:* 3,008 applied, 2,229 admitted, 715 enrolled. *Average high school GPA:* 3.25. *Test scores:* SAT verbal scores over 500: 46%; SAT math scores over 500: 53%; SAT verbal scores over 600: 10%; SAT math scores over 600: 15%; SAT verbal scores over 700: 1%; SAT math scores over 700: 2%.

Faculty *Total:* 398, 56% full-time. *Student/faculty ratio:* 12:1.

Majors Accounting; advertising; anthropology; behavioral sciences; biochemistry; biology/biological sciences; biology teacher education; business administration and management; business administration, management and operations related; business/managerial economics; chemical engineering; chemistry; chemistry teacher education; civil engineering; computer and information sciences; computer science; criminal justice/law enforcement administration; early childhood education; economics; educational/instructional media design; electrical, electronics and communications engineering; elementary education; engineering; engineering/industrial management; English; English/language arts teacher education; environmental studies; financial planning and services; fine arts related; foreign languages and literatures; French; French language teacher education; health services/allied health/health sciences; history; history teacher education; hospitality administration related; hotel/motel administration; humanities; human resources management and services related; industrial radiologic technology; information science/studies; international business/trade/commerce; international relations and affairs; kindergarten/preschool education; legal assistant/paralegal; management information systems and services related; marketing/marketing management; mass communication/media; mathematics; mathematics teacher education; mechanical engineering; modern languages; nursing (registered nurse training); operations management; physics; political science and government; pre-dentistry studies; pre-medical studies; pre-veterinary studies; psychology; psychology teacher education; science teacher education; social sciences; social studies teacher education; social work; sociology; Spanish; Spanish language teacher education; special education; sport and fitness administration.

Academic Programs *Special study options:* academic remediation for entering students, accelerated degree program, adult/continuing education programs, advanced placement credit, cooperative education, distance learning, double majors, English as a second language, honors programs, independent study, internships, off-campus study, part-time degree program, services for LD students, student-designed majors, study abroad, summer session for credit. *ROTC:* Army (b), Air Force (c). *Unusual degree programs:* 3-2 physical therapy.

Library Wolfgram Memorial Library with 241,088 titles, 2,250 serial subscriptions, 12,663 audiovisual materials, an OPAC, a Web page.

Computers on Campus 310 computers available on campus for general student use. A campuswide network can be accessed from student residence rooms and from off campus. Internet access, at least one staffed computer lab available. Computer purchase or lease plan available.

Student Life *Housing:* on-campus residence required through sophomore year. *Options:* coed, men-only, women-only. Campus housing is university owned. Freshman campus housing is guaranteed. *Activities and organizations:* drama/theater group, student-run newspaper, radio and television station, choral group, WDNR Radio, Black Student Union, volunteer services, rugby club, Theatre Widener, national fraternities, national sororities. *Campus security:* 24-hour emergency response devices and patrols, late-night transport/escort service, controlled dormitory access, "blue light" emergency phones located throughout campus. *Student services:* health clinic, personal/psychological counseling.

Athletics Member NCAA. All Division III. *Intercollegiate sports:* baseball M, basketball M/W, cheerleading W, cross-country running M/W, field hockey W, football M, golf M, lacrosse M/W, soccer M/W, softball W, swimming M/W, tennis M/W, track and field M/W, volleyball W. *Intramural sports:* basketball M/W, cross-country running M/W, ice hockey M(c), riflery M(c)/W(c), rugby M(c)/W(c), skiing (downhill) M(c)/W(c), soccer M, softball W, tennis M/W, volleyball M(c), water polo M(c).

Standardized Tests *Required:* SAT I or ACT (for admission). *Recommended:* SAT II: Subject Tests (for admission), SAT II: Subject Tests (for placement).

Costs (2003–04) *Comprehensive fee:* $30,295 includes full-time tuition ($21,400), mandatory fees ($100), and room and board ($8795). Full-time tuition and fees vary according to program. Part-time tuition: $713 per credit. *College room only:* $4095. Room and board charges vary according to board plan and housing facility. *Payment plan:* installment. *Waivers:* senior citizens and employees or children of employees.

Financial Aid Of all full-time matriculated undergraduates who enrolled in 2003, 1,714 applied for aid, 1,674 were judged to have need, 502 had their need fully met. In 2003, 276 non-need-based awards were made. *Average percent of need met:* 91%. *Average financial aid package:* $18,668. *Average need-based loan:* $5781. *Average need-based gift aid:* $11,379. *Average non-need-based aid:* $8117. *Average indebtedness upon graduation:* $18,465.

Applying *Options:* common application, electronic application, early admission, early action, deferred entrance. *Application fee:* $35. *Required:* essay or personal statement, high school transcript, letters of recommendation, interview. *Required for some:* minimum 2.5 GPA. *Recommended:* minimum 3.0 GPA. *Application deadline:* rolling (freshmen), rolling (transfers). *Notification:* continuous (freshmen), 12/15 (early action), continuous (transfers).

Admissions Contact Mr. Michael Hendricks, Dean of Admissions, Widener University, One University Place, Chester, PA 19013. *Phone:* 610-499-4126. *Toll-free phone:* 888-WIDENER. *Fax:* 610-499-4676. *E-mail:* admissions.office@widener.edu.

■ *See page 2846 for a narrative description.*

WILKES UNIVERSITY
Wilkes-Barre, Pennsylvania

- **Independent** comprehensive, founded 1933
- **Calendar** semesters
- **Degrees** bachelor's, master's, and first professional
- **Urban** 25-acre campus
- **Endowment** $26.7 million
- **Coed,** 2,055 undergraduate students, 87% full-time, 50% women, 50% men
- **Moderately difficult** entrance level, 81% of applicants were admitted

A comprehensive private university of intimate size, Wilkes University offers high-quality academic programs in business, engineering, sciences, and liberal arts; preprofessional programs in dentistry, medicine, optometry, and law; and a 6-year Doctor of Pharmacy degree. Students have unparalleled access to faculty members and research opportunities, and 99% gain employment or attend graduate/professional school within 6 months of graduation.

Undergraduates 1,785 full-time, 270 part-time. Students come from 22 states and territories, 14% are from out of state, 2% African American, 2% Asian American or Pacific Islander, 1% Hispanic American, 0.3% Native American, 0.2% international, 7% transferred in, 41% live on campus. *Retention:* 79% of 2002 full-time freshmen returned.

Freshmen *Admission:* 2,332 applied, 1,878 admitted, 523 enrolled. *Test scores:* SAT verbal scores over 500: 68%; SAT math scores over 500: 71%; SAT verbal scores over 600: 24%; SAT math scores over 600: 31%; SAT verbal scores over 700: 3%; SAT math scores over 700: 6%.

Faculty *Total:* 104. *Student/faculty ratio:* 15:1.

Majors Accounting; biochemistry; biology/biological sciences; business administration and management; chemistry; clinical laboratory science/medical technology; communication/speech communication and rhetoric; computer and information sciences; criminal justice/safety; dramatic/theatre arts; e-commerce; education; electrical, electronics and communications engineering; elementary education; engineering; engineering/industrial management; English; environmental/environmental health engineering; French; geology/earth science; history; information science/studies; international relations and affairs; liberal arts and sciences/liberal studies; mathematics; mechanical engineering; multi-/interdisciplinary studies related; music performance; music teacher education; nursing (registered nurse training); philosophy; political science and government; psychology; sociology; Spanish.

Academic Programs *Special study options:* academic remediation for entering students, accelerated degree program, adult/continuing education programs, advanced placement credit, cooperative education, distance learning, double majors, honors programs, independent study, internships, part-time degree program, student-designed majors, study abroad, summer session for credit. *ROTC:* Army (c), Air Force (b).

Library Eugene S. Farley Library with 236,942 titles, 848 serial subscriptions, 159 audiovisual materials, an OPAC.

Computers on Campus 700 computers available on campus for general student use. A campuswide network can be accessed from student residence rooms and from off campus. Internet access, online (class) registration, at least one staffed computer lab available.

Student Life *Housing:* on-campus residence required through sophomore year. *Options:* coed, men-only, women-only. Campus housing is university owned. *Activities and organizations:* drama/theater group, student-run newspaper, radio and television station, choral group. *Campus security:* 24-hour emergency response devices and patrols, late-night transport/escort service, controlled dormitory access. *Student services:* health clinic, personal/psychological counseling.

Athletics Member NCAA. All Division III. *Intercollegiate sports:* baseball M, basketball M/W, cheerleading W(c), field hockey W, football M, golf M, lacrosse W, soccer M/W, softball W, tennis M/W, volleyball W, wrestling M. *Intramural sports:* basketball M/W, football M, rock climbing M(c)/W(c), ultimate Frisbee M/W, volleyball M/W, weight lifting M/W.

Standardized Tests *Required:* SAT I or ACT (for admission).

Costs (2003–04) *Comprehensive fee:* $28,060 includes full-time tuition ($18,680), mandatory fees ($950), and room and board ($8430). Part-time tuition: $520 per credit. *Required fees:* $20 per credit part-time. *College room only:* $5080. Room and board charges vary according to board plan and housing facility. *Payment plans:* installment, deferred payment. *Waivers:* employees or children of employees.

Financial Aid Of all full-time matriculated undergraduates who enrolled in 2003, 1,778 applied for aid, 1,636 were judged to have need, 456 had their need fully met. 990 Federal Work-Study jobs (averaging $1584). 144 state and other part-time jobs (averaging $1907). In 2003, 193 non-need-based awards were made. *Average percent of need met:* 83%. *Average financial aid package:* $15,863. *Average need-based loan:* $4008. *Average need-based gift aid:* $11,152. *Average non-need-based aid:* $7916. *Average indebtedness upon graduation:* $19,467.

Applying *Options:* electronic application, early admission, deferred entrance. *Application fee:* $35. *Required:* high school transcript. *Required for some:* letters of recommendation. *Recommended:* interview. *Application deadline:* rolling (freshmen), rolling (transfers). *Notification:* continuous until 8/30 (freshmen), continuous until 8/30 (transfers).

Admissions Contact Mr. Michael Frantz, Dean, Enrollment, Wilkes University, PO Box 111, Wilkes-Barre, PA 18766. *Phone:* 570-408-4400. *Toll-free phone:* 800-945-5378 Ext. 4400. *Fax:* 570-408-4904. *E-mail:* admissions@wilkes.edu.

■ *See page 2850 for a narrative description.*

WILSON COLLEGE
Chambersburg, Pennsylvania

- **Independent** 4-year, founded 1869, affiliated with Presbyterian Church (U.S.A.)
- **Calendar** 4-1-4
- **Degrees** associate and bachelor's
- **Small-town** 300-acre campus
- **Endowment** $30.3 million
- **Women only,** 791 undergraduate students, 50% full-time
- **Moderately difficult** entrance level, 68% of applicants were admitted

For more than 130 years, Wilson has been educating women in a rich tradition of liberal arts. The College offers rigorous and timely courses of study grounded in the liberal arts and sciences, engaging students in intercultural and environmental studies and a wide range of majors in promising professional fields.

Undergraduates 396 full-time, 395 part-time. Students come from 20 states and territories, 12 other countries, 23% are from out of state, 4% African American, 0.5% Asian American or Pacific Islander, 2% Hispanic American, 6% international, 3% transferred in, 32% live on campus. *Retention:* 74% of 2002 full-time freshmen returned.

Freshmen *Admission:* 88 enrolled. *Average high school GPA:* 3.4. *Test scores:* SAT verbal scores over 500: 42%; SAT math scores over 500: 53%; ACT scores over 18: 91%; SAT verbal scores over 600: 10%; SAT math scores over 600: 20%; ACT scores over 24: 36%; SAT verbal scores over 700: 1%; SAT math scores over 700: 3%; ACT scores over 30: 9%.

Faculty *Total:* 90, 41% full-time, 53% with terminal degrees. *Student/faculty ratio:* 9:1.

Majors Accounting; art; behavioral sciences; biology/biological sciences; business administration and management; chemistry; early childhood education; elementary education; English; environmental studies; equestrian studies; French; international relations and affairs; kinesiology and exercise science; liberal arts and sciences/liberal studies; management information systems; marketing/marketing management; mass communication/media; mathematics; philosophy and religious studies related; physiological psychology/psychobiology; rehabilitation and therapeutic professions related; social sciences; Spanish; veterinary/animal health technology.

Academic Programs *Special study options:* academic remediation for entering students, adult/continuing education programs, advanced placement credit, cooperative education, double majors, English as a second language, external degree program, independent study, internships, off-campus study, part-time degree program, services for LD students, student-designed majors, study abroad, summer session for credit. *ROTC:* Army (c).

Library Stewart Library with 172,205 titles, 312 serial subscriptions, 1,664 audiovisual materials, an OPAC, a Web page.

Computers on Campus 80 computers available on campus for general student use. A campuswide network can be accessed from student residence rooms and from off campus. Internet access, online (class) registration, at least one staffed computer lab available.

Student Life *Housing:* on-campus residence required through junior year. *Options:* women-only. Campus housing is university owned. Freshman campus housing is guaranteed. *Activities and organizations:* drama/theater group, student-run newspaper, radio station, choral group, Muhibbah Club, Orchesis Club, student newspaper, student government, Black Student Union. *Campus security:* 24-hour emergency response devices and patrols, late-night transport/escort service, controlled dormitory access. *Student services:* health clinic, personal/psychological counseling, women's center.

Wilson College (continued)

Athletics Member NCAA. All Division III. *Intercollegiate sports:* basketball W, equestrian sports W, field hockey W, gymnastics W, soccer W, softball W, tennis W, volleyball W. *Intramural sports:* archery W, badminton W, bowling W, equestrian sports W, gymnastics W, volleyball W.

Standardized Tests *Required:* SAT I or ACT (for admission).

Costs (2003–04) *Comprehensive fee:* $23,912 includes full-time tuition ($16,466), mandatory fees ($450), and room and board ($6996). Part-time tuition: $1647 per course. *Required fees:* $25 per course part-time, $15 per course part-time. *College room only:* $3604. Room and board charges vary according to board plan. *Payment plan:* installment. *Waivers:* children of alumni and employees or children of employees.

Financial Aid Of all full-time matriculated undergraduates who enrolled in 2003, 250 applied for aid, 224 were judged to have need, 40 had their need fully met. 49 Federal Work-Study jobs (averaging $1340). 97 state and other part-time jobs (averaging $1340). In 2003, 74 non-need-based awards were made. *Average percent of need met:* 83%. *Average financial aid package:* $16,002. *Average need-based loan:* $3797. *Average need-based gift aid:* $12,357. *Average non-need-based aid:* $14,243. *Average indebtedness upon graduation:* $21,925.

Applying *Options:* common application, electronic application, early admission, deferred entrance. *Application fee:* $30. *Required:* essay or personal statement, high school transcript, letters of recommendation. *Recommended:* minimum 2.7 GPA, interview. *Application deadline:* rolling (freshmen), rolling (transfers). *Notification:* continuous (freshmen), continuous (transfers).

Admissions Contact Deborah Arthur, Admissions Administrator, Wilson College, 1015 Philadelphia Avenue, Chambersburg, PA 17201. *Phone:* 717-262-2002. *Toll-free phone:* 800-421-8402. *Fax:* 717-262-2546. *E-mail:* admissions@wilson.edu.

■ *See page 2866 for a narrative description.*

YESHIVA BETH MOSHE

Scranton, Pennsylvania

Admissions Contact Rabbi I. Bressler, Dean, Yeshiva Beth Moshe, 930 Hickory Street, PO Box 1141, Scranton, PA 18505-2124. *Phone:* 717-346-1747.

YORK COLLEGE OF PENNSYLVANIA

York, Pennsylvania

- **Independent** comprehensive, founded 1787
- **Calendar** semesters
- **Degrees** certificates, associate, bachelor's, and master's
- **Suburban** 118-acre campus with easy access to Baltimore
- **Endowment** $47.0 million
- **Coed,** 5,281 undergraduate students, 80% full-time, 60% women, 40% men
- **Moderately difficult** entrance level, 74% of applicants were admitted

Undergraduates 4,227 full-time, 1,054 part-time. Students come from 36 states and territories, 35 other countries, 45% are from out of state, 1% African American, 1% Asian American or Pacific Islander, 1% Hispanic American, 0.1% Native American, 1% international, 5% transferred in, 45% live on campus. *Retention:* 83% of 2002 full-time freshmen returned.

Freshmen *Admission:* 4,141 applied, 3,070 admitted, 1,024 enrolled. *Average high school GPA:* 3.00. *Test scores:* SAT verbal scores over 500: 83%; SAT math scores over 500: 83%; SAT verbal scores over 600: 28%; SAT math scores over 600: 23%; SAT verbal scores over 700: 4%; SAT math scores over 700: 2%.

Faculty *Total:* 404, 35% full-time, 38% with terminal degrees. *Student/faculty ratio:* 15:1.

Majors Accounting; behavioral sciences; biology/biological sciences; business administration and management; business, management, and marketing related; business/managerial economics; chemistry; clinical laboratory science/medical technology; commercial and advertising art; computer and information sciences; computer and information sciences and support services related; computer programming; computer science; corrections; criminal justice/police science; economics; education related; elementary education; engineering; engineering/industrial management; English; English/language arts teacher education; finance; fine arts related; health/health care administration; history; international business/trade/commerce; international relations and affairs; liberal arts and sciences/liberal studies; marketing/marketing management; mass communication/media; mathematics; mathematics teacher education; mechanical engineering; modern languages; music; music teacher education; nuclear medical technology; nursing (registered nurse training); parks, recreation and leisure; philosophy; physical sciences; physics; political science and government; pre-dentistry studies; pre-law studies; pre-medical studies; pre-veterinary studies; psychology; public administration; public relations/image management; radio and television; respiratory care therapy; safety/security technology; science teacher education; secondary education; security and loss prevention; social science teacher education; social studies teacher education; sociology; Spanish; special education related; speech and rhetoric; sport and fitness administration; technical and business writing; urban studies/affairs.

Academic Programs *Special study options:* academic remediation for entering students, accelerated degree program, adult/continuing education programs, advanced placement credit, internships, part-time degree program, student-designed majors, study abroad, summer session for credit.

Library Schmidt Library plus 1 other with 300,000 titles, 1,400 serial subscriptions, 11,000 audiovisual materials, an OPAC, a Web page.

Computers on Campus 250 computers available on campus for general student use. A campuswide network can be accessed from student residence rooms and from off campus. Internet access, online (class) registration, at least one staffed computer lab available.

Student Life *Housing:* on-campus residence required through sophomore year. *Options:* coed, women-only. Freshman campus housing is guaranteed. *Activities and organizations:* drama/theater group, student-run newspaper, radio station, choral group, Student Senate, Theater Company, ski and outdoor club, marketing club, Student Education Association, national fraternities, national sororities. *Campus security:* 24-hour emergency response devices and patrols, late-night transport/escort service. *Student services:* health clinic, personal/psychological counseling.

Athletics Member NCAA. All Division III. *Intercollegiate sports:* baseball M, basketball M/W, cheerleading W, cross-country running M/W, field hockey W, golf M, ice hockey M(c), lacrosse M/W, soccer M/W, softball W, swimming M/W, tennis M/W, track and field M/W, volleyball M(c)/W, wrestling M. *Intramural sports:* badminton M/W, basketball M/W, football M/W, lacrosse M(c)/W(c), rugby M(c)/W(c), skiing (downhill) M(c)/W(c), soccer M/W, softball M/W, swimming M/W, table tennis M, tennis M/W, track and field M/W, volleyball M/W, water polo M/W, weight lifting M(c)/W(c), wrestling M.

Standardized Tests *Required:* SAT I or ACT (for admission).

Costs (2003–04) *Comprehensive fee:* $14,500 includes full-time tuition ($8000), mandatory fees ($550), and room and board ($5950). Full-time tuition and fees vary according to course load and program. Part-time tuition: $243 per credit hour. Part-time tuition and fees vary according to course load and program. *Required fees:* $122 per term part-time. *College room only:* $3250. Room and board charges vary according to housing facility. *Payment plan:* installment. *Waivers:* employees or children of employees.

Financial Aid Of all full-time matriculated undergraduates who enrolled in 2003, 3,144 applied for aid, 2,137 were judged to have need, 543 had their need fully met. 264 Federal Work-Study jobs (averaging $1397). 86 state and other part-time jobs (averaging $876). In 2003, 326 non-need-based awards were made. *Average percent of need met:* 73%. *Average financial aid package:* $6717. *Average need-based loan:* $3666. *Average need-based gift aid:* $3727. *Average non-need-based aid:* $2794. *Average indebtedness upon graduation:* $15,913.

Applying *Options:* common application, electronic application, early admission, deferred entrance. *Application fee:* $30. *Required:* essay or personal statement, high school transcript. *Required for some:* interview. *Recommended:* 1 letter of recommendation. *Application deadline:* 8/1 (freshmen), rolling (transfers). *Notification:* continuous (freshmen), continuous (transfers).

Admissions Contact Mrs. Nancy L. Spataro, Director of Admissions, York College of Pennsylvania, York, PA 17405-7199. *Phone:* 717-849-1600. *Toll-free phone:* 800-455-8018. *Fax:* 717-849-1607. *E-mail:* admissions@ycp.edu.

RHODE ISLAND

BROWN UNIVERSITY

Providence, Rhode Island

- **Independent** university, founded 1764
- **Calendar** semesters
- **Degrees** bachelor's, master's, doctoral, and first professional
- **Urban** 140-acre campus with easy access to Boston
- **Coed,** 5,906 undergraduate students, 96% full-time, 55% women, 45% men
- **Most difficult** entrance level, 16% of applicants were admitted

Undergraduates 5,660 full-time, 246 part-time. Students come from 52 states and territories, 72 other countries, 96% are from out of state, 6% African American, 13% Asian American or Pacific Islander, 7% Hispanic American, 0.5% Native American, 6% international, 2% transferred in, 85% live on campus. *Retention:* 97% of 2002 full-time freshmen returned.

Freshmen *Admission:* 15,157 applied, 2,442 admitted, 1,393 enrolled. *Test scores:* SAT verbal scores over 500: 98%; SAT math scores over 500: 99%; ACT scores over 18: 100%; SAT verbal scores over 600: 87%; SAT math scores over

600: 91%; ACT scores over 24: 91%; SAT verbal scores over 700: 51%; SAT math scores over 700: 55%; ACT scores over 30: 50%.

Faculty *Total:* 789, 98% full-time, 98% with terminal degrees. *Student/faculty ratio:* 8:1.

Majors African-American/Black studies; American studies; anthropology; applied mathematics; archeology; architectural history and criticism; art; art history, criticism and conservation; Asian studies (East); Asian studies (South); behavioral sciences; biochemistry; biology/biological sciences; biomedical/medical engineering; biomedical sciences; biophysics; chemical engineering; chemistry; civil engineering; classics and languages, literatures and linguistics; cognitive psychology and psycholinguistics; comparative literature; computer engineering; computer science; creative writing; development economics and international development; dramatic/theatre arts; economics; education; electrical, electronics and communications engineering; engineering; engineering physics; English; environmental science; environmental studies; film/cinema studies; fine/studio arts; French; French studies; geochemistry; geology/earth science; geophysics and seismology; German; German studies; Hispanic-American, Puerto Rican, and Mexican-American/Chicano studies; history; international relations and affairs; Italian; Italian studies; Jewish/Judaic studies; Latin American studies; linguistics; literature; marine biology and biological oceanography; materials engineering; mathematics; mathematics and computer science; mechanical engineering; medieval and Renaissance studies; molecular biology; music; musicology and ethnomusicology; music related; Near and Middle Eastern studies; neuroscience; organizational behavior; philosophy; physics; political science and government; psychology; religious studies; Russian studies; sociology; Spanish; urban studies/affairs; visual and performing arts; women's studies.

Academic Programs *Special study options:* accelerated degree program, adult/continuing education programs, advanced placement credit, double majors, honors programs, independent study, internships, off-campus study, part-time degree program, services for LD students, student-designed majors, study abroad, summer session for credit. *ROTC:* Army (c).

Library John D. Rockefeller Library plus 5 others with 3.0 million titles, 17,000 serial subscriptions, an OPAC, a Web page.

Computers on Campus 400 computers available on campus for general student use. A campuswide network can be accessed from student residence rooms and from off campus. Internet access, online (class) registration, at least one staffed computer lab available. Computer purchase or lease plan available.

Student Life *Housing:* on-campus residence required through junior year. *Options:* coed, women-only, cooperative. Campus housing is university owned. Freshman campus housing is guaranteed. *Activities and organizations:* drama/theater group, student-run newspaper, radio and television station, choral group, marching band, Community Outreach, Bruin Club, Undergraduate Council of Students, orchestra and chorus, Daily Herald, national fraternities, national sororities. *Campus security:* 24-hour emergency response devices and patrols, late-night transport/escort service, controlled dormitory access. *Student services:* health clinic, personal/psychological counseling, women's center, legal services.

Athletics Member NCAA. All Division I except football (Division I-AA). *Intercollegiate sports:* baseball M, basketball M/W, crew M/W, cross-country running M/W, equestrian sports W, fencing M/W, field hockey W, golf M/W, gymnastics W, ice hockey M/W, lacrosse M/W, rugby M(c)/W(c), sailing M(c)/W(c), skiing (downhill) M(c)/W, soccer M/W, softball W, squash M/W, swimming M/W, tennis M/W, track and field M/W, volleyball M(c)/W, water polo M/W, wrestling M. *Intramural sports:* badminton M(c)/W(c), basketball M/W, cheerleading M/W, fencing M/W, field hockey W, football M, ice hockey M/W, lacrosse M/W, racquetball M/W, rock climbing M(c)/W(c), rugby M/W, skiing (downhill) M/W, soccer M/W, softball M/W, squash M/W, swimming M/W, table tennis M(c)/W(c), tennis M/W, ultimate Frisbee M(c)/W(c), volleyball M/W, water polo M/W.

Standardized Tests *Required:* SAT I and SAT II or ACT (for admission).

Costs (2003–04) *Comprehensive fee:* $37,942 includes full-time tuition ($29,200), mandatory fees ($646), and room and board ($8096). Part-time tuition: $3650 per course. *College room only:* $5030. Room and board charges vary according to board plan. *Payment plans:* tuition prepayment, installment. *Waivers:* employees or children of employees.

Financial Aid Of all full-time matriculated undergraduates who enrolled in 2003, 2,833 applied for aid, 2,473 were judged to have need, 2,433 had their need fully met. 1,372 Federal Work-Study jobs (averaging $1960). 71 state and other part-time jobs (averaging $2018). *Average percent of need met:* 100%. *Average financial aid package:* $24,402. *Average need-based loan:* $4642. *Average need-based gift aid:* $19,877. *Average indebtedness upon graduation:* $16,040. *Financial aid deadline:* 2/1.

Applying *Options:* electronic application, early admission, early decision, deferred entrance. *Application fee:* $70. *Required:* essay or personal statement, high school transcript, 2 letters of recommendation. *Required for some:* 3 letters of recommendation. *Application deadlines:* 1/1 (freshmen), 3/1 (transfers). *Early decision:* 11/1. *Notification:* 4/1 (freshmen), 12/15 (early decision), 5/25 (transfers).

Admissions Contact Mr. Michael Goldberger, Director of Admission, Brown University, Box 1876, Providence, RI 02912. *Phone:* 401-863-2378. *Fax:* 401-863-9300. *E-mail:* admission_undergraduate@brown.edu.

■ *See page 1302 for a narrative description.*

BRYANT COLLEGE
Smithfield, Rhode Island

- **Independent** comprehensive, founded 1863
- **Calendar** semesters
- **Degrees** bachelor's, master's, and post-master's certificates
- **Suburban** 392-acre campus with easy access to Boston and Providence
- **Endowment** $116.9 million
- **Coed,** 2,976 undergraduate students, 92% full-time, 41% women, 59% men
- **Moderately difficult** entrance level, 59% of applicants were admitted

Undergraduates 2,729 full-time, 247 part-time. Students come from 31 states and territories, 33 other countries, 75% are from out of state, 3% African American, 2% Asian American or Pacific Islander, 3% Hispanic American, 0.2% Native American, 2% international, 5% transferred in, 77% live on campus. *Retention:* 79% of 2002 full-time freshmen returned.

Freshmen *Admission:* 3,910 applied, 2,320 admitted, 778 enrolled. *Average high school GPA:* 3.19. *Test scores:* SAT verbal scores over 500: 74%; SAT math scores over 500: 86%; ACT scores over 18: 100%; SAT verbal scores over 600: 15%; SAT math scores over 600: 30%; ACT scores over 24: 50%; SAT verbal scores over 700: 1%; SAT math scores over 700: 3%.

Faculty *Total:* 228, 59% full-time, 66% with terminal degrees. *Student/faculty ratio:* 16:1.

Majors Accounting; accounting technology and bookkeeping; actuarial science; business administration and management; communication/speech communication and rhetoric; computer and information sciences; economics; English; finance; finance and financial management services related; history; information technology; international relations and affairs; marketing/marketing management; psychology.

Academic Programs *Special study options:* academic remediation for entering students, adult/continuing education programs, advanced placement credit, double majors, English as a second language, honors programs, independent study, internships, part-time degree program, services for LD students, study abroad, summer session for credit. *ROTC:* Army (b).

Library Douglas and Judith Krupp Library with 4.1 million titles, 1,000 serial subscriptions, 908 audiovisual materials, an OPAC, a Web page.

Computers on Campus 486 computers available on campus for general student use. A campuswide network can be accessed from student residence rooms and from off campus that provide access to e-mail, on-line library, wireless network, student web hosts. Internet access, online (class) registration, at least one staffed computer lab available.

Student Life *Housing options:* coed, women-only, disabled students. Campus housing is university owned. Freshman campus housing is guaranteed. *Activities and organizations:* drama/theater group, student-run newspaper, radio station, choral group, Bryant Outdoor Activities Club, Student Programming Board, Rhythm and Pride Dance Team, radio station, Bryant Players (drama club), national fraternities, national sororities. *Campus security:* 24-hour emergency response devices and patrols, late-night transport/escort service, controlled dormitory access, bicycle patrols, video cameras, lighted pathways/sidewalks, monitored one point of access/egress. *Student services:* health clinic, personal/psychological counseling, women's center.

Athletics Member NCAA. All Division II. *Intercollegiate sports:* baseball M, basketball M(s)/W(s), bowling M(c)/W(c), cheerleading W(c), cross-country running M/W, field hockey W, football M, golf M/W, ice hockey M(c), lacrosse M/W, racquetball M(c)/W(c), rugby M(c)/W(c), soccer M/W, softball W, squash M(c)/W(c), tennis M/W, track and field M/W, ultimate Frisbee M(c)/W(c), volleyball W, wrestling M(c). *Intramural sports:* basketball M/W, field hockey W, football M, rock climbing M/W, soccer M/W, softball M/W, volleyball M/W.

Standardized Tests *Required:* SAT I or ACT (for admission).

Costs (2004–05) *Comprehensive fee:* $32,554 includes full-time tuition ($23,580) and room and board ($8974). Full-time tuition and fees vary according to course load and program. Part-time tuition: $849 per course. Part-time tuition and fees vary according to course load and program. *College room only:* $5148. Room and board charges vary according to board plan and housing facility. *Payment plan:* installment. *Waivers:* employees or children of employees.

Financial Aid Of all full-time matriculated undergraduates who enrolled in 2003, 2,014 applied for aid, 1,767 were judged to have need, 230 had their need fully met. 286 Federal Work-Study jobs (averaging $1120). 1,011 state and other

Bryant College (continued)

part-time jobs (averaging $1494). *Average percent of need met:* 73%. *Average financial aid package:* $14,521. *Average need-based loan:* $4713. *Average need-based gift aid:* $6654. *Average non-need-based aid:* $7247. *Average indebtedness upon graduation:* $22,909.

Applying *Options:* common application, electronic application, early admission, early decision, early action, deferred entrance. *Application fee:* $50. *Required:* essay or personal statement, high school transcript, 1 letter of recommendation, senior year first-quarter grades. *Recommended:* minimum 3.0 GPA, interview. *Application deadlines:* 2/15 (freshmen), 8/15 (transfers). *Early decision:* 11/15. *Notification:* 3/15 (freshmen), 12/15 (early decision), 1/15 (early action), continuous (transfers).

Admissions Contact Ms. Cynthia Bonn, Director of Admission, Bryant College, 1150 Douglas Pike, Smithfield, RI 02917. *Phone:* 401-232-6100. *Toll-free phone:* 800-622-7001. *Fax:* 401-232-6741. *E-mail:* admission@bryant.edu.

■ *See page 1304 for a narrative description.*

JOHNSON & WALES UNIVERSITY

Providence, Rhode Island

- **Independent** comprehensive, founded 1914
- **Calendar** quarters
- **Degrees** certificates, diplomas, associate, bachelor's, master's, and doctoral (branch locations: Charleston, SC; Denver, CO; North Miami, FL; Norfolk, VA; Gothenberg, Sweden)
- **Urban** 47-acre campus with easy access to Boston
- **Endowment** $161.5 million
- **Coed,** 9,220 undergraduate students, 90% full-time, 52% women, 48% men
- **Minimally difficult** entrance level, 85% of applicants were admitted

Undergraduates 8,261 full-time, 959 part-time. Students come from 50 states and territories, 88 other countries, 11% African American, 3% Asian American or Pacific Islander, 6% Hispanic American, 0.1% Native American, 4% international, 4% transferred in.

Freshmen *Admission:* 11,174 applied, 9,548 admitted, 2,388 enrolled. *Average high school GPA:* 2.80. *Test scores:* SAT verbal scores over 500: 37%; SAT math scores over 500: 37%; SAT verbal scores over 600: 6%; SAT math scores over 600: 7%.

Faculty *Total:* 644, 69% full-time. *Student/faculty ratio:* 31:1.

Majors Accounting; administrative assistant and secretarial science; advertising; baking and pastry arts; business administration and management; computer and information sciences; computer engineering; computer engineering technology; computer programming; computer science; consumer merchandising/retailing management; court reporting; criminal justice/law enforcement administration; culinary arts; electrical, electronic and communications engineering technology; electrical, electronics and communications engineering; electrical/electronics drafting and CAD/CADD; equestrian studies; farm and ranch management; fashion merchandising; finance; food services technology; foodservice systems administration; health/health care administration; hospitality administration; hospitality and recreation marketing; hotel/motel administration; information science/studies; interdisciplinary studies; international business/trade/commerce; legal administrative assistant/secretary; legal assistant/paralegal; marketing/marketing management; mass communication/media; mechanical engineering; mechanical engineering/mechanical technology; parks, recreation and leisure; parks, recreation and leisure facilities management; public relations/image management; restaurant, culinary, and catering management; retailing; sales, distribution and marketing; special products marketing; structural engineering; therapeutic recreation; tourism and travel services management; tourism/travel marketing.

Academic Programs *Special study options:* academic remediation for entering students, accelerated degree program, adult/continuing education programs, advanced placement credit, cooperative education, double majors, English as a second language, freshman honors college, honors programs, independent study, internships, part-time degree program, services for LD students, study abroad, summer session for credit.

Library Johnson & Wales University Library plus 2 others with 85,523 titles, 1,921 serial subscriptions, 531 audiovisual materials, an OPAC, a Web page.

Computers on Campus 340 computers available on campus for general student use. A campuswide network can be accessed from student residence rooms and from off campus. Internet access, at least one staffed computer lab available.

Student Life *Housing:* on-campus residence required for freshman year. *Options:* coed. Freshman campus housing is guaranteed. *Activities and organizations:* drama/theater group, student-run newspaper, choral group, Delta Epsilon Chi, Vocational Industrial Clubs of America, Phi Beta Lambda, FHA/HERO, FFA, national fraternities, national sororities. *Campus security:* 24-hour emergency response devices and patrols, student patrols, late-night transport/escort service. *Student services:* health clinic, personal/psychological counseling, women's center.

Athletics Member NCAA. All Division III. *Intercollegiate sports:* baseball M(c), basketball M/W, cheerleading M/W, cross-country running M/W, equestrian sports M(c)/W(c), golf M/W, ice hockey M(c), soccer M/W, tennis M/W, volleyball M/W. *Intramural sports:* basketball M/W, bowling M(c)/W(c), football M/W, golf M(c)/W(c), gymnastics M(c), skiing (downhill) M(c)/W(c), tennis M(c)/W(c), volleyball M/W.

Standardized Tests *Required for some:* SAT I or ACT (for admission). *Recommended:* SAT I or ACT (for admission).

Costs (2004–05) *Comprehensive fee:* $24,645 includes full-time tuition ($16,650), mandatory fees ($810), and room and board ($7185). Full-time tuition and fees vary according to location and program. Part-time tuition: $308 per quarter hour. No tuition increase for student's term of enrollment. *Room and board:* Room and board charges vary according to housing facility and location. *Payment plan:* installment. *Waivers:* employees or children of employees.

Financial Aid Of all full-time matriculated undergraduates who enrolled in 2003, 6,934 applied for aid, 6,088 were judged to have need, 4,175 had their need fully met. In 2003, 393 non-need-based awards were made. *Average percent of need met:* 69%. *Average financial aid package:* $11,459. *Average need-based loan:* $5250. *Average need-based gift aid:* $4065. *Average non-need-based aid:* $3239. *Average indebtedness upon graduation:* $20,268.

Applying *Options:* common application, early admission, deferred entrance. *Required:* high school transcript. *Required for some:* minimum 3.0 GPA, 1 letter of recommendation. *Recommended:* minimum 2.0 GPA, interview. *Application deadline:* rolling (freshmen), rolling (transfers). *Notification:* continuous (freshmen), continuous (transfers).

Admissions Contact Ms. Maureen Dumas, Dean of Admissions, Johnson & Wales University, 8 Abbott Park Place, Providence, RI 02903-3703. *Phone:* 401-598-2310. *Toll-free phone:* 800-598-1000 (in-state); 800-342-5598 (out-of-state). *Fax:* 401-598-2948. *E-mail:* pvd.admissions@jwu.edu.

■ *See page 1794 for a narrative description.*

NEW ENGLAND INSTITUTE OF TECHNOLOGY

Warwick, Rhode Island

- **Independent** primarily 2-year, founded 1940
- **Calendar** quarters
- **Degrees** associate and bachelor's
- **Suburban** 10-acre campus with easy access to Boston
- **Coed**
- **Noncompetitive** entrance level

Student Life *Campus security:* security personnel during open hours.

Costs (2003–04) *Tuition:* $12,750 full-time. *Required fees:* $1280 full-time.

Financial Aid Of all full-time matriculated undergraduates who enrolled in 2001, 250 Federal Work-Study jobs (averaging $2290).

Applying *Options:* early admission, deferred entrance. *Application fee:* $25. *Required:* high school transcript, interview.

Admissions Contact Mr. Michael Kwiatkowski, Director of Admissions, New England Institute of Technology, 2500 Post Road, Warwick, RI 02886-2266. *Phone:* 401-739-5000. *E-mail:* neit@ids.net.

PROVIDENCE COLLEGE

Providence, Rhode Island

- **Independent Roman Catholic** comprehensive, founded 1917
- **Calendar** semesters
- **Degrees** certificates, associate, bachelor's, and master's
- **Suburban** 105-acre campus with easy access to Boston
- **Endowment** $95.4 million
- **Coed,** 4,342 undergraduate students, 86% full-time, 58% women, 42% men
- **Very difficult** entrance level, 53% of applicants were admitted

Providence College is the only liberal arts college in the US that was founded and administered by the Dominican Friars, a Catholic teaching order whose heritage spans nearly 800 years. The College is not only concerned with the rigors of intellectual life but also recognizes the importance of students' experiences outside the classroom, including service to others. Scholarship, service, and the exuberant PC spirit—these are the qualities that shape the character of Providence College.

Undergraduates 3,714 full-time, 628 part-time. Students come from 38 states and territories, 16 other countries, 80% are from out of state, 2% African American, 2% Asian American or Pacific Islander, 2% Hispanic American, 0.1%

Native American, 0.9% international, 2% transferred in, 75% live on campus. *Retention:* 91% of 2002 full-time freshmen returned.

Freshmen *Admission:* 7,397 applied, 3,906 admitted, 975 enrolled. *Average high school GPA:* 3.44. *Test scores:* SAT verbal scores over 500: 93%; SAT math scores over 500: 95%; ACT scores over 18: 100%; SAT verbal scores over 600: 53%; SAT math scores over 600: 58%; ACT scores over 24: 75%; SAT verbal scores over 700: 8%; SAT math scores over 700: 8%; ACT scores over 30: 15%.

Faculty *Total:* 337, 78% full-time, 68% with terminal degrees. *Student/faculty ratio:* 13:1.

Majors Accounting; American studies; art history, criticism and conservation; biology/biological sciences; business administration and management; business/managerial economics; chemistry; community organization and advocacy; computer science; economics; English; finance; fine/studio arts; fire science; French; health/health care administration; history; humanities; Italian; labor and industrial relations; liberal arts and sciences/liberal studies; marketing/marketing management; mathematics; music; pastoral studies/counseling; philosophy; political science and government; psychology; secondary education; social sciences; social work; sociology; Spanish; special education; systems science and theory; theology; visual and performing arts.

Academic Programs *Special study options:* adult/continuing education programs, advanced placement credit, cooperative education, double majors, honors programs, independent study, internships, part-time degree program, services for LD students, student-designed majors, study abroad, summer session for credit. *ROTC:* Army (b). *Unusual degree programs:* 3-2 engineering with Columbia University, Washington University in St. Louis.

Library Phillips Memorial Library with 397,630 titles, 1,759 serial subscriptions, 278 audiovisual materials, an OPAC, a Web page.

Computers on Campus 160 computers available on campus for general student use. A campuswide network can be accessed from student residence rooms and from off campus. Internet access, online (class) registration, at least one staffed computer lab available.

Student Life *Housing:* on-campus residence required through sophomore year. *Options:* coed, men-only, women-only, disabled students. Campus housing is university owned. Freshman campus housing is guaranteed. *Activities and organizations:* drama/theater group, student-run newspaper, radio and television station, choral group, Board of Programmers, Student Congress, student newspaper, Big Brothers/Big Sisters, Pastoral Council. *Campus security:* 24-hour emergency response devices and patrols, student patrols, late-night transport/escort service, controlled dormitory access. *Student services:* health clinic, personal/psychological counseling, legal services.

Athletics Member NCAA. All Division I. *Intercollegiate sports:* basketball M(s)/W(s), cross-country running M(s)/W(s), field hockey W(s), ice hockey M(s)/W(s), lacrosse M, racquetball M(c)/W(c), rugby M(c)/W(c), soccer M(s)/W(s), softball W(s), swimming M/W, tennis W(s), track and field M(s)/W(s), volleyball W(s). *Intramural sports:* basketball M/W, cross-country running M/W, field hockey W, football M/W, ice hockey M/W, sailing M(c)/W(c), skiing (cross-country) M(c)/W(c), skiing (downhill) M(c)/W(c), soccer M/W, softball M/W, tennis M/W, ultimate Frisbee M/W, volleyball M/W.

Standardized Tests *Required:* SAT I or ACT (for admission). *Recommended:* SAT II: Subject Tests (for admission), SAT II: Writing Test (for admission).

Costs (2003–04) *Comprehensive fee:* $30,604 includes full-time tuition ($21,665), mandatory fees ($439), and room and board ($8500). Part-time tuition: $207 per credit. *College room only:* $4350. Room and board charges vary according to board plan and housing facility. *Payment plan:* installment. *Waivers:* minority students, senior citizens, and employees or children of employees.

Financial Aid Of all full-time matriculated undergraduates who enrolled in 2003, 2,429 applied for aid, 1,846 were judged to have need, 358 had their need fully met. 700 Federal Work-Study jobs (averaging $1800). 600 state and other part-time jobs (averaging $1800). In 2003, 350 non-need-based awards were made. *Average percent of need met:* 85%. *Average financial aid package:* $14,600. *Average need-based loan:* $4833. *Average need-based gift aid:* $8900. *Average non-need-based aid:* $10,500. *Average indebtedness upon graduation:* $22,500. *Financial aid deadline:* 2/1.

Applying *Options:* common application, electronic application, early admission, early action, deferred entrance. *Application fee:* $55. *Required:* essay or personal statement, high school transcript, 2 letters of recommendation. *Application deadlines:* 1/15 (freshmen), 4/15 (transfers). *Notification:* 4/1 (freshmen), 1/1 (early action), 5/30 (transfers).

Admissions Contact Mr. Christopher Lydon, Dean of Enrollment Management, Providence College, River Avenue and Eaton Street, Providence, RI 02918. *Phone:* 401-865-2535. *Toll-free phone:* 800-721-6444. *Fax:* 401-865-2826. *E-mail:* pcadmiss@providence.edu.

■ *See page 2198 for a narrative description.*

RHODE ISLAND COLLEGE

Providence, Rhode Island

- **State-supported** comprehensive, founded 1854
- **Calendar** semesters
- **Degrees** bachelor's, master's, doctoral, and post-master's certificates
- **Suburban** 180-acre campus with easy access to Boston
- **Coed,** 7,305 undergraduate students, 68% full-time, 67% women, 33% men
- **Moderately difficult** entrance level, 73% of applicants were admitted

Undergraduates 4,968 full-time, 2,337 part-time. Students come from 10 states and territories, 8% are from out of state, 4% African American, 2% Asian American or Pacific Islander, 5% Hispanic American, 0.4% Native American, 0.5% international, 8% transferred in, 14% live on campus. *Retention:* 77% of 2002 full-time freshmen returned.

Freshmen *Admission:* 3,088 applied, 2,257 admitted, 1,043 enrolled. *Test scores:* SAT verbal scores over 500: 44%; SAT math scores over 500: 43%; SAT verbal scores over 600: 10%; SAT math scores over 600: 10%; SAT verbal scores over 700: 1%.

Faculty *Total:* 628, 48% full-time. *Student/faculty ratio:* 16:1.

Majors Accounting; African-American/Black studies; anthropology; Army R.O.T.C./military science; art; art history, criticism and conservation; art teacher education; behavioral sciences; biological and physical sciences; biology/biological sciences; business administration and management; chemistry; clinical laboratory science/medical technology; computer science; criminal justice/safety; dance; dramatic/theatre arts; economics; education; elementary education; English; film/cinema studies; finance; fine/studio arts; French; geography; health/medical preparatory programs related; health teacher education; history; industrial arts; industrial technology; information science/studies; kindergarten/preschool education; labor and industrial relations; liberal arts and sciences/liberal studies; management information systems; marketing/marketing management; mass communication/media; mathematics; middle school education; music; music teacher education; nursing (registered nurse training); philosophy; physical education teaching and coaching; physical sciences; physics; political science and government; pre-dentistry studies; pre-law studies; pre-medical studies; pre-veterinary studies; psychology; public administration; science teacher education; secondary education; social sciences; social work; sociology; Spanish; special education; speech and rhetoric.

Academic Programs *Special study options:* academic remediation for entering students, adult/continuing education programs, advanced placement credit, double majors, freshman honors college, honors programs, independent study, internships, off-campus study, part-time degree program, services for LD students, student-designed majors, study abroad, summer session for credit. *ROTC:* Army (c). *Unusual degree programs:* 3-2 engineering with University of Rhode Island; occupational therapy with Washington University in St. Louis.

Library Adams Library with 368,891 titles, 1,766 serial subscriptions, 3,982 audiovisual materials, an OPAC, a Web page.

Computers on Campus 350 computers available on campus for general student use. A campuswide network can be accessed from off campus. At least one staffed computer lab available.

Student Life *Housing options:* coed, women-only, disabled students. *Activities and organizations:* drama/theater group, student-run newspaper, radio and television station, choral group, student government, newspaper, campus radio station (WXIN), OASPA (Organization of African Students and Professionals in the Americas), Asian Student Association. *Campus security:* 24-hour patrols, late-night transport/escort service. *Student services:* health clinic, personal/psychological counseling, women's center.

Athletics Member NCAA. All Division III. *Intercollegiate sports:* baseball M, basketball M/W, cross-country running M/W, gymnastics W, soccer M/W, softball W, tennis M/W, track and field M/W, volleyball W, wrestling M. *Intramural sports:* basketball M/W, football M, golf M, tennis M/W, volleyball M/W.

Standardized Tests *Required:* SAT I (for admission).

Costs (2004–05) *Tuition:* state resident $3530 full-time; nonresident $10,170 full-time. Part-time tuition and fees vary according to course load. *Required fees:* $740 full-time. *Room and board:* $6550; room only: $3500. Room and board charges vary according to board plan and housing facility. *Payment plan:* installment. *Waivers:* senior citizens and employees or children of employees.

Applying *Options:* common application, early admission, deferred entrance. *Application fee:* $25. *Required:* essay or personal statement, high school transcript, letters of recommendation. *Required for some:* interview. *Application deadlines:* 5/1 (freshmen), 6/1 (transfers). *Notification:* continuous (freshmen), continuous (transfers).

Admissions Contact Dr. Holly L. Shadoian, Director of Admissions, Rhode Island College, 600 Mount Pleasant Avenue, Providence, RI 02908-1924. *Phone:* 401-456-8234. *Toll-free phone:* 800-669-5760. *Fax:* 401-456-8817. *E-mail:* admissions@ric.edu.

Rhode Island School of Design
Providence, Rhode Island

- **Independent** comprehensive, founded 1877
- **Calendar** 4-1-4
- **Degrees** bachelor's, master's, and first professional
- **Urban** 13-acre campus with easy access to Boston
- **Endowment** $205.7 million
- **Coed,** 1,920 undergraduate students, 100% full-time, 65% women, 35% men
- **Very difficult** entrance level, 35% of applicants were admitted

Undergraduates 1,920 full-time. Students come from 51 states and territories, 53 other countries, 94% are from out of state, 2% African American, 13% Asian American or Pacific Islander, 5% Hispanic American, 0.5% Native American, 12% international, 6% transferred in, 40% live on campus. *Retention:* 96% of 2002 full-time freshmen returned.

Freshmen *Admission:* 2,420 applied, 835 admitted, 391 enrolled. *Average high school GPA:* 3.30.

Faculty *Total:* 502, 29% full-time. *Student/faculty ratio:* 11:1.

Majors Architecture; ceramic arts and ceramics; fashion/apparel design; fiber, textile and weaving arts; film/cinema studies; fine arts related; furniture design and manufacturing; graphic design; illustration; industrial design; interior architecture; interior design; metal and jewelry arts; painting; photography; printmaking; sculpture.

Academic Programs *Special study options:* academic remediation for entering students, adult/continuing education programs, advanced placement credit, English as a second language, independent study, internships, off-campus study, study abroad.

Library RISD Library plus 1 other with 100,961 titles, 419 serial subscriptions, 680,663 audiovisual materials, an OPAC.

Computers on Campus 300 computers available on campus for general student use. A campuswide network can be accessed from student residence rooms and from off campus. Internet access, at least one staffed computer lab available. Computer purchase or lease plan available.

Student Life *Housing:* on-campus residence required for freshman year. *Options:* coed. Campus housing is university owned. Freshman campus housing is guaranteed. *Activities and organizations:* drama/theater group, student-run newspaper, athletic clubs, industrial design club, Korean Students Association, Lesbian/Gay/Bisexual Alliance. *Campus security:* 24-hour emergency response devices and patrols, late-night transport/escort service, controlled dormitory access. *Student services:* health clinic, personal/psychological counseling, legal services.

Athletics *Intramural sports:* baseball M/W, basketball M/W, bowling M(c)/W(c), ice hockey M/W, sailing M(c)/W(c), skiing (downhill) M(c)/W(c), soccer M/W, softball M/W, table tennis M/W, volleyball M/W, weight lifting M/W.

Standardized Tests *Required:* SAT I or ACT (for admission).

Costs (2003–04) *Comprehensive fee:* $34,035 includes full-time tuition ($26,200), mandatory fees ($465), and room and board ($7370). *College room only:* $4040. Room and board charges vary according to board plan and housing facility. *Payment plan:* installment. *Waivers:* employees or children of employees.

Financial Aid Of all full-time matriculated undergraduates who enrolled in 2003, 1,140 applied for aid, 919 were judged to have need, 87 had their need fully met. 469 Federal Work-Study jobs (averaging $1364). 350 state and other part-time jobs (averaging $1400). In 2003, 35 non-need-based awards were made. *Average percent of need met:* 69%. *Average financial aid package:* $15,300. *Average need-based loan:* $5600. *Average need-based gift aid:* $9200. *Average indebtedness upon graduation:* $21,700.

Applying *Options:* early admission, early action, deferred entrance. *Application fee:* $50. *Required:* essay or personal statement, high school transcript, portfolio, drawing assignments. *Recommended:* 3 letters of recommendation. *Application deadlines:* 2/15 (freshmen), 3/31 (transfers). *Notification:* 4/2 (freshmen), 1/25 (early action), 4/30 (transfers).

Admissions Contact Mr. Edward Newhall, Director of Admissions, Rhode Island School of Design, 2 College Street, Providence, RI 02905-2791. *Phone:* 401-454-6300. *Toll-free phone:* 800-364-RISD. *Fax:* 401-454-6309. *E-mail:* admissions@risd.edu.

Roger Williams University
Bristol, Rhode Island

- **Independent** comprehensive, founded 1956
- **Calendar** semesters
- **Degrees** certificates, associate, bachelor's, master's, and first professional
- **Small-town** 140-acre campus with easy access to Boston
- **Endowment** $45.2 million
- **Coed,** 4,110 undergraduate students, 82% full-time, 50% women, 50% men
- **Moderately difficult** entrance level, 80% of applicants were admitted

Roger Williams University (RWU) is a leading liberal arts university located in historic Bristol, Rhode Island. The modern, secure campus is situated on 140 breathtaking, waterfront acres. Accredited by the New England Association of Schools and Colleges, RWU draws 3,400 full-time undergraduates, who each benefit from attentive, mentoring faculty members.

Undergraduates 3,388 full-time, 722 part-time. Students come from 42 states and territories, 38 other countries, 87% are from out of state, 1% African American, 1% Asian American or Pacific Islander, 2% Hispanic American, 0.2% Native American, 2% international, 2% transferred in, 81% live on campus. *Retention:* 72% of 2002 full-time freshmen returned.

Freshmen *Admission:* 5,438 applied, 4,326 admitted, 959 enrolled. *Average high school GPA:* 3.04. *Test scores:* SAT verbal scores over 500: 66%; SAT math scores over 500: 70%; SAT verbal scores over 600: 18%; SAT math scores over 600: 22%; SAT verbal scores over 700: 2%; SAT math scores over 700: 2%.

Faculty *Total:* 435, 37% full-time, 46% with terminal degrees. *Student/faculty ratio:* 14:1.

Majors Accounting; American studies; anthropology; architecture; art; art history, criticism and conservation; biology/biological sciences; business administration and management; chemistry; chemistry related; communication and media related; computer science; construction management; creative writing; criminal justice/law enforcement administration; dance; dramatic/theatre arts; elementary education; English; environmental/environmental health engineering; environmental science; finance; financial planning and services; foreign languages and literatures; health/health care administration; historic preservation and conservation; history; international business/trade/commerce; legal assistant/paralegal; legal professions and studies related; liberal arts and sciences/liberal studies; management information systems; manufacturing technology; marine biology and biological oceanography; marketing/marketing management; mathematics; multi-/interdisciplinary studies related; philosophy; political science and government; pre-dentistry studies; pre-medical studies; pre-veterinary studies; psychology; public administration; secondary education; social sciences; sociology; visual and performing arts.

Academic Programs *Special study options:* adult/continuing education programs, advanced placement credit, cooperative education, distance learning, double majors, English as a second language, external degree program, freshman honors college, honors programs, independent study, internships, part-time degree program, services for LD students, student-designed majors, study abroad, summer session for credit. *ROTC:* Army (b).

Library Roger Williams University Library plus 2 others with 168,460 titles, 1,225 serial subscriptions, 60,694 audiovisual materials, an OPAC, a Web page.

Computers on Campus 500 computers available on campus for general student use. A campuswide network can be accessed from student residence rooms and from off campus that provide access to telephone registration. Internet access, at least one staffed computer lab available. Computer purchase or lease plan available.

Student Life *Housing:* on-campus residence required through sophomore year. *Options:* coed, disabled students. Campus housing is university owned and leased by the school. Freshman campus housing is guaranteed. *Activities and organizations:* drama/theater group, student-run newspaper, radio station, choral group, Entertainment Network, Student Senate, American Institute of Architects, John Jay Society, residence hall councils. *Campus security:* 24-hour emergency response devices and patrols, student patrols, late-night transport/escort service, controlled dormitory access. *Student services:* health clinic, personal/psychological counseling, women's center.

Athletics Member NCAA. All Division III. *Intercollegiate sports:* baseball M, basketball M/W, crew M(c)/W(c), cross-country running M/W, equestrian sports M/W, golf M/W, lacrosse M, rugby M(c), sailing M/W, soccer M/W, softball W, tennis M/W, track and field M(c)/W(c), volleyball M/W, wrestling M. *Intramural sports:* basketball M/W, field hockey M/W, football M/W, golf M/W, lacrosse M, soccer M/W, softball M/W, tennis M/W, volleyball M/W.

Standardized Tests *Required:* SAT I or ACT (for admission).

Costs (2003–04) *Comprehensive fee:* $30,296 includes full-time tuition ($19,920), mandatory fees ($920), and room and board ($9456). Full-time tuition and fees vary according to class time, course load, and program. Part-time tuition: $870 per credit hour. Part-time tuition and fees vary according to class time. *College room only:* $4860. Room and board charges vary according to board plan and housing facility. *Payment plans:* installment, deferred payment. *Waivers:* employees or children of employees.

Financial Aid Of all full-time matriculated undergraduates who enrolled in 2003, 2,763 applied for aid, 2,359 were judged to have need, 1,113 had their need fully met. 434 Federal Work-Study jobs (averaging $1783). 598 state and other part-time jobs (averaging $1714). In 2003, 270 non-need-based awards were made. *Average percent of need met:* 83%. *Average financial aid package:*

$14,260. *Average need-based loan:* $4187. *Average need-based gift aid:* $8067. *Average non-need-based aid:* $5865. *Average indebtedness upon graduation:* $17,125. *Financial aid deadline:* 2/1.

Applying *Options:* common application, electronic application, early decision, deferred entrance. *Application fee:* $50. *Required:* essay or personal statement, high school transcript, minimum 2.0 GPA, letters of recommendation. *Recommended:* 2.0 letters of recommendation, interview. *Application deadline:* rolling (freshmen), rolling (transfers). *Early decision:* 12/1. *Notification:* continuous (freshmen), 12/15 (early decision), continuous (transfers).

Admissions Contact Ms. Michelle L. Beauregard, Associate Director of Freshman Admission, Roger Williams University, 1 Old Ferry Road, Bristol, RI 02809. *Phone:* 401-254-3500. *Toll-free phone:* 800-458-7144. *Fax:* 401-254-3557. *E-mail:* admit@rwu.edu.

■ *See page 2254 for a narrative description.*

SALVE REGINA UNIVERSITY
Newport, Rhode Island

- **Independent Roman Catholic** comprehensive, founded 1934
- **Calendar** semesters
- **Degrees** certificates, associate, bachelor's, master's, doctoral, post-master's, and postbachelor's certificates
- **Suburban** 70-acre campus with easy access to Boston and Providence
- **Endowment** $26.3 million
- **Coed,** 2,026 undergraduate students, 95% full-time, 69% women, 31% men
- **Moderately difficult** entrance level, 56% of applicants were admitted

Undergraduates 1,927 full-time, 99 part-time. Students come from 33 states and territories, 14 other countries, 82% are from out of state, 1% African American, 1% Asian American or Pacific Islander, 2% Hispanic American, 0.5% Native American, 1% international, 3% transferred in, 60% live on campus. *Retention:* 80% of 2002 full-time freshmen returned.

Freshmen *Admission:* 4,131 applied, 2,294 admitted, 571 enrolled. *Average high school GPA:* 3.20. *Test scores:* SAT verbal scores over 500: 76%; SAT math scores over 500: 71%; ACT scores over 18: 96%; SAT verbal scores over 600: 16%; SAT math scores over 600: 15%; ACT scores over 24: 26%; SAT verbal scores over 700: 1%; ACT scores over 30: 1%.

Faculty *Total:* 277, 38% full-time. *Student/faculty ratio:* 13:1.

Majors Accounting; American studies; anthropology; art history, criticism and conservation; biology/biological sciences; biology teacher education; business administration and management; chemistry; clinical laboratory science/medical technology; communications technology; criminal justice/law enforcement administration; cytotechnology; drama and dance teacher education; dramatic/theatre arts; early childhood education; economics; elementary education; English; English/language arts teacher education; fine/studio arts; French; French language teacher education; historic preservation and conservation; history; history teacher education; information science/studies; liberal arts and sciences/liberal studies; mathematics; mathematics teacher education; music; music teacher education; nursing (registered nurse training); philosophy; political science and government; psychology; religious studies; secondary education; social work; sociology; Spanish; Spanish language teacher education; special education.

Academic Programs *Special study options:* accelerated degree program, adult/continuing education programs, advanced placement credit, distance learning, double majors, English as a second language, freshman honors college, honors programs, independent study, internships, part-time degree program, services for LD students, study abroad, summer session for credit. *ROTC:* Army (c).

Library McKillop Library with 139,161 titles, 1,041 serial subscriptions, 19,420 audiovisual materials, an OPAC, a Web page.

Computers on Campus 163 computers available on campus for general student use. A campuswide network can be accessed from student residence rooms and from off campus. Internet access, at least one staffed computer lab available.

Student Life *Housing:* on-campus residence required through sophomore year. *Options:* coed, men-only, women-only, disabled students. Campus housing is university owned and leased by the school. Freshman applicants given priority for college housing. *Activities and organizations:* drama/theater group, student-run newspaper, radio station, choral group, Orpheus Musical Society, Student Government Association, Student Outdoor Adventures, Student Nurse Organization, Stagefright Theatre Company. *Campus security:* 24-hour emergency response devices and patrols, late-night transport/escort service, controlled dormitory access. *Student services:* health clinic, personal/psychological counseling.

Athletics Member NCAA. All Division III. *Intercollegiate sports:* baseball M, basketball M/W, cross-country running W, equestrian sports M(c)/W(c), field hockey W, football M, golf M(c)/W, ice hockey M/W, lacrosse M/W, rugby M(c), sailing M/W, soccer M/W, softball W, tennis W, track and field W, volleyball W. *Intramural sports:* baseball M, basketball M/W, cheerleading W, field hockey W, football M/W, golf M/W, soccer M/W, softball M/W, tennis M/W, track and field W, volleyball M/W, weight lifting M/W.

Standardized Tests *Required:* SAT I or ACT (for admission).

Costs (2003–04) *Comprehensive fee:* $29,210 includes full-time tuition ($20,100), mandatory fees ($410), and room and board ($8700). Part-time tuition: $670 per credit. Part-time tuition and fees vary according to course load. *Required fees:* $40 per term part-time. *Room and board:* Room and board charges vary according to board plan. *Payment plan:* installment. *Waivers:* employees or children of employees.

Financial Aid Of all full-time matriculated undergraduates who enrolled in 2003, 1,461 applied for aid, 1,289 were judged to have need. 377 Federal Work-Study jobs (averaging $944). 227 state and other part-time jobs (averaging $1295). In 2003, 267 non-need-based awards were made. *Average percent of need met:* 73%. *Average financial aid package:* $15,618. *Average need-based loan:* $5079. *Average need-based gift aid:* $10,505. *Average non-need-based aid:* $9688. *Average indebtedness upon graduation:* $19,840.

Applying *Options:* common application, electronic application, early action, deferred entrance. *Application fee:* $40. *Required:* essay or personal statement, high school transcript, 2 letters of recommendation. *Required for some:* interview. *Recommended:* minimum 2.5 GPA. *Application deadline:* 3/1 (freshmen), rolling (transfers). *Notification:* continuous (freshmen), 12/15 (early action), continuous (transfers).

Admissions Contact Ms. Colleen Emerson, Director of Admissions, Salve Regina University, 100 Ochre Point Avenue, Newport, RI 02840-4192. *Phone:* 401-341-2109. *Toll-free phone:* 888-GO SALVE. *Fax:* 401-848-2823. *E-mail:* sruadmis@salve.edu.

■ *See page 2340 for a narrative description.*

UNIVERSITY OF RHODE ISLAND
Kingston, Rhode Island

- **State-supported** university, founded 1892, part of Rhode Island State System of Higher Education
- **Calendar** semesters
- **Degrees** bachelor's, master's, doctoral, first professional, and postbachelor's certificates
- **Small-town** 1200-acre campus
- **Endowment** $39.6 million
- **Coed,** 11,298 undergraduate students, 83% full-time, 57% women, 43% men
- **Moderately difficult** entrance level, 70% of applicants were admitted

Undergraduates 9,429 full-time, 1,869 part-time. Students come from 38 states and territories, 47 other countries, 39% are from out of state, 4% African American, 3% Asian American or Pacific Islander, 4% Hispanic American, 0.4% Native American, 0.3% international, 5% transferred in, 41% live on campus. *Retention:* 81% of 2002 full-time freshmen returned.

Freshmen *Admission:* 12,963 applied, 9,074 admitted, 2,590 enrolled. *Test scores:* SAT verbal scores over 500: 79%; SAT math scores over 500: 84%; SAT verbal scores over 600: 25%; SAT math scores over 600: 32%; SAT verbal scores over 700: 3%; SAT math scores over 700: 4%.

Faculty *Total:* 693, 94% full-time, 89% with terminal degrees. *Student/faculty ratio:* 19:1.

Majors Accounting; animal sciences; anthropology; apparel and accessories marketing; apparel and textiles; applied economics; art; art history, criticism and conservation; biology/biological sciences; biomedical/medical engineering; business administration and management; chemical engineering; chemistry; civil engineering; classics and languages, literatures and linguistics; clinical laboratory science/medical technology; communication disorders; communication/speech communication and rhetoric; comparative literature; computer and information sciences; computer engineering; consumer economics; dental hygiene; dietetics; econometrics and quantitative economics; economics; electrical, electronics and communications engineering; elementary education; English; environmental studies; finance; fishing and fisheries sciences and management; foods, nutrition, and wellness; French; geology/earth science; German; health/health care administration; history; human development and family studies; human services; industrial engineering; interdisciplinary studies; international business/trade/commerce; Italian; journalism; landscape architecture; Latin American studies; liberal arts and sciences/liberal studies; management information systems; marine biology and biological oceanography; marketing/marketing management; mathematics; mechanical engineering; medical microbiology and bacteriology; music; music performance; music teacher education; music theory and composition; natural resources/conservation; natural resources management and policy; nursing (registered nurse training); ocean engineering; pharmacy; philosophy; physical education teaching and coaching; physics; political science and government; psychology; public policy analysis; secondary education; sociology; Spanish; turf and turfgrass management; wildlife and wildlands science and management; women's studies; zoology/animal biology.

University of Rhode Island (continued)

Academic Programs *Special study options:* academic remediation for entering students, accelerated degree program, adult/continuing education programs, advanced placement credit, cooperative education, distance learning, double majors, honors programs, independent study, internships, off-campus study, part-time degree program, services for LD students, student-designed majors, study abroad, summer session for credit. *ROTC:* Army (b). *Unusual degree programs:* 3-2 physical therapy, speech pathology, audiology.

Library University Library plus 1 other with 1.2 million titles, 7,926 serial subscriptions, 11,671 audiovisual materials, an OPAC, a Web page.

Computers on Campus 552 computers available on campus for general student use. A campuswide network can be accessed from off campus. At least one staffed computer lab available.

Student Life *Housing options:* coed, women-only, disabled students. *Activities and organizations:* drama/theater group, student-run newspaper, radio and television station, choral group, marching band, Student Entertainment Committee, student radio station, intramural sport clubs, Student Alumni Association, student newspaper, national fraternities, national sororities. *Campus security:* 24-hour emergency response devices and patrols, student patrols, late-night transport/escort service, controlled dormitory access. *Student services:* health clinic, personal/psychological counseling, women's center.

Athletics Member NCAA. All Division I except football (Division I-AA). *Intercollegiate sports:* baseball M(s), basketball M(s)/W(s), crew M(c)/W, cross-country running M(s)/W(s), equestrian sports M(c)/W(c), fencing M(c)/W(c), field hockey W(s), golf M(s), gymnastics W(s), ice hockey M(c), lacrosse M(c)/W(c), rugby M(c)/W(c), sailing M(c)/W(c), skiing (downhill) M(c)/W(c), soccer M(s)/W(s), softball W(s), swimming M(s)/W(s), tennis M/W(s), track and field M(s)/W(s), volleyball M(c)/W(s), water polo M(c). *Intramural sports:* badminton M/W, basketball M/W, football M/W, golf M/W, soccer M/W, softball M/W, swimming M/W, tennis M/W, volleyball M/W, water polo M/W.

Standardized Tests *Required:* SAT I or ACT (for admission).

Costs (2003–04) *Tuition:* state resident $4136 full-time, $172 per credit part-time; nonresident $14,268 full-time, $595 per credit part-time. Full-time tuition and fees vary according to reciprocity agreements. Part-time tuition and fees vary according to reciprocity agreements. *Required fees:* $2066 full-time. *Room and board:* $7518; room only: $4256. Room and board charges vary according to board plan and housing facility. *Payment plan:* installment. *Waivers:* minority students, senior citizens, and employees or children of employees.

Financial Aid Of all full-time matriculated undergraduates who enrolled in 2003, 7,709 applied for aid, 6,495 were judged to have need, 2,904 had their need fully met. In 2003, 350 non-need-based awards were made. *Average percent of need met:* 56%. *Average financial aid package:* $9430. *Average need-based loan:* $4862. *Average need-based gift aid:* $5501. *Average non-need-based aid:* $4543. *Average indebtedness upon graduation:* $14,000.

Applying *Options:* electronic application, early admission, early action. *Application fee:* $40. *Required:* high school transcript. *Required for some:* minimum 3.0 GPA. *Recommended:* minimum 3.0 GPA, letters of recommendation, interview. *Application deadlines:* 2/1 (freshmen), 5/1 (transfers). *Notification:* continuous (freshmen), 1/15 (early action), continuous (transfers).

Admissions Contact Ms. Catherine Zeiser, Assistant Dean of Admissions, University of Rhode Island, 8 Ranger Road, Suite 1, Kingston, RI 02881-2020. *Phone:* 401-874-7100. *Fax:* 401-874-5523. *E-mail:* uriadmit@etal.uri.edu.

■ *See page 2692 for a narrative description.*

ZION BIBLE INSTITUTE
Barrington, Rhode Island

Admissions Contact 27 Middle Highway, Barrington, RI 02806. *Toll-free phone:* 800-356-4014.

SOUTH CAROLINA

ALLEN UNIVERSITY
Columbia, South Carolina

- **Independent African Methodist Episcopal** 4-year, founded 1870
- **Calendar** semesters
- **Degree** bachelor's
- **Suburban** campus
- **Coed,** 565 undergraduate students, 98% full-time, 38% women, 62% men
- **Minimally difficult** entrance level, 61% of applicants were admitted

Undergraduates 552 full-time, 13 part-time. Students come from 14 states and territories, 1 other country, 9% are from out of state, 97% African American, 3% international, 12% transferred in, 80% live on campus. *Retention:* 41% of 2002 full-time freshmen returned.

Freshmen *Admission:* 784 applied, 479 admitted, 145 enrolled. *Average high school GPA:* 2.50.

Faculty *Total:* 39, 64% full-time, 41% with terminal degrees. *Student/faculty ratio:* 10:1.

Majors Biology/biological sciences; business administration and management; chemistry; education; elementary education; English; humanities; mathematics; music; religious studies; social sciences.

Academic Programs *Special study options:* academic remediation for entering students, adult/continuing education programs, cooperative education, honors programs, independent study, internships, part-time degree program, study abroad, summer session for credit. *ROTC:* Army (c).

Library J. S. Flipper Library with 50,000 titles, 175 serial subscriptions.

Computers on Campus 130 computers available on campus for general student use. A campuswide network can be accessed. Internet access, online (class) registration, at least one staffed computer lab available.

Student Life *Housing options:* men-only, women-only. Campus housing is university owned and leased by the school. Freshman campus housing is guaranteed. *Activities and organizations:* student-run newspaper, choral group, International Students Club, Social Science Club, Gospel Choir, national fraternities, national sororities. *Campus security:* 24-hour patrols. *Student services:* health clinic, personal/psychological counseling.

Athletics Member NAIA. *Intercollegiate sports:* basketball M(s)/W(s), football M(c), volleyball W. *Intramural sports:* basketball M/W, cheerleading M(c)/W(c).

Standardized Tests *Required:* SAT I or ACT (for admission).

Costs (2003–04) *Comprehensive fee:* $9913 includes full-time tuition ($7218), mandatory fees ($590), and room and board ($2105). Part-time tuition: $301 per credit.

Financial Aid Of all full-time matriculated undergraduates who enrolled in 2003, 552 applied for aid, 442 were judged to have need, 54 had their need fully met. 160 Federal Work-Study jobs (averaging $1000). In 2003, 3 non-need-based awards were made. *Average percent of need met:* 74%. *Average financial aid package:* $8081. *Average need-based loan:* $4833. *Average need-based gift aid:* $2213. *Average non-need-based aid:* $3609. *Average indebtedness upon graduation:* $13,037.

Applying *Options:* common application. *Application fee:* $20. *Required:* essay or personal statement, high school transcript, 3 letters of recommendation. *Application deadline:* 7/31 (freshmen).

Admissions Contact Ms. Constants Adams, Admissions Representative, Allen University, 1530 Harden Street, Columbia, SC 29204-1085. *Phone:* 803-376-5735. *Toll-free phone:* 877-625-5368. *Fax:* 803-376-5731. *E-mail:* admissions@allenuniversity.edu.

ANDERSON COLLEGE
Anderson, South Carolina

- **Independent Baptist** 4-year, founded 1911
- **Calendar** semesters
- **Degree** bachelor's
- **Suburban** 44-acre campus
- **Endowment** $15.8 million
- **Coed,** 1,664 undergraduate students, 75% full-time, 63% women, 37% men
- **Moderately difficult** entrance level, 79% of applicants were admitted

Undergraduates 1,250 full-time, 414 part-time. Students come from 27 states and territories, 11 other countries, 12% are from out of state, 12% African American, 0.4% Asian American or Pacific Islander, 1% Hispanic American, 0.3% Native American, 1% international, 6% transferred in, 49% live on campus. *Retention:* 65% of 2002 full-time freshmen returned.

Freshmen *Admission:* 822 applied, 647 admitted, 344 enrolled. *Average high school GPA:* 3.55. *Test scores:* SAT verbal scores over 500: 51%; SAT math scores over 500: 57%; ACT scores over 18: 80%; SAT verbal scores over 600: 11%; SAT math scores over 600: 14%; ACT scores over 24: 20%; SAT verbal scores over 700: 1%; SAT math scores over 700: 1%.

Faculty *Total:* 122, 52% full-time, 45% with terminal degrees. *Student/faculty ratio:* 14:1.

Majors Accounting; art; art teacher education; biology/biological sciences; biology teacher education; business administration and management; commercial and advertising art; creative writing; cytotechnology; dramatic/theatre arts; drawing; education; elementary education; English; English/language arts teacher education; finance; fine/studio arts; history; history teacher education; human resources management; human services; interior design; journalism; kindergarten/preschool education; liberal arts and sciences/liberal studies; management information systems and services related; marketing/marketing management; mass communication/media; mathematics; mathematics teacher education; music; music teacher education; physical education teaching and coaching; psychology; religious studies; secondary education; Spanish; Spanish language teacher education; special education; speech and rhetoric; sport and fitness administration.

Academic Programs *Special study options:* academic remediation for entering students, adult/continuing education programs, advanced placement credit, freshman honors college, honors programs, independent study, internships, part-time degree program, services for LD students, study abroad, summer session for credit. *ROTC:* Army (c), Air Force (c).

Library Olin D. Johnston Library with 65,602 titles, 355 serial subscriptions, 4,591 audiovisual materials, an OPAC, a Web page.

Computers on Campus 100 computers available on campus for general student use. A campuswide network can be accessed from student residence rooms and from off campus. Internet access, at least one staffed computer lab available.

Student Life *Housing:* on-campus residence required through sophomore year. *Options:* men-only, women-only. Campus housing is university owned. *Activities and organizations:* drama/theater group, student-run newspaper, choral group, Baptist Campus Ministries, Fellowship of Christian Athletes, Student Government Association, Gamma Beta Phi, Student Alumni Council. *Campus security:* 24-hour emergency response devices and patrols, late-night transport/escort service, controlled dormitory access. *Student services:* health clinic, personal/psychological counseling.

Athletics Member NCAA. All Division II. *Intercollegiate sports:* baseball M(s), basketball M(s)/W(s), cheerleading W(s), cross-country running M(s)/W(s), equestrian sports M/W, golf M(s)/W(s), soccer M(s)/W(s), softball W(s), tennis M(s)/W(s), track and field M(s)/W(s), volleyball W(s), wrestling M(s). *Intramural sports:* basketball M/W, football M/W, racquetball M/W, softball M/W, tennis M/W, volleyball M/W, weight lifting M.

Standardized Tests *Required:* SAT I or ACT (for admission).

Costs (2004–05) *Comprehensive fee:* $19,990 includes full-time tuition ($13,190), mandatory fees ($1035), and room and board ($5765). Part-time tuition: $370 per credit hour. Part-time tuition and fees vary according to program. *College room only:* $2910. Room and board charges vary according to board plan and housing facility. *Payment plan:* installment. *Waivers:* adult students, senior citizens, and employees or children of employees.

Financial Aid Of all full-time matriculated undergraduates who enrolled in 2003, 1,165 applied for aid, 1,051 were judged to have need, 363 had their need fully met. 270 Federal Work-Study jobs (averaging $1760). 146 state and other part-time jobs (averaging $1505). In 2003, 76 non-need-based awards were made. *Average percent of need met:* 79%. *Average financial aid package:* $13,694. *Average need-based loan:* $4242. *Average need-based gift aid:* $6760. *Average non-need-based aid:* $5333. *Average indebtedness upon graduation:* $14,874. *Financial aid deadline:* 7/30.

Applying *Options:* common application, electronic application, early admission, deferred entrance. *Application fee:* $40. *Required:* high school transcript. *Required for some:* essay or personal statement, 2 letters of recommendation, interview. *Recommended:* minimum 2.5 GPA. *Application deadlines:* 7/1 (freshmen), 8/1 (transfers). *Notification:* continuous (freshmen), continuous (transfers).

Admissions Contact Ms. Pam Bryant, Director of Admissions, Anderson College, 316 Boulevard, Anderson, SC 29621. *Phone:* 864-231-5607. *Toll-free phone:* 800-542-3594. *Fax:* 864-231-3033. *E-mail:* admissions@ac.edu.

■ *See page 1172 for a narrative description.*

BENEDICT COLLEGE

Columbia, South Carolina

- **Independent Baptist** 4-year, founded 1870
- **Calendar** semesters
- **Degree** bachelor's
- **Urban** 20-acre campus
- **Endowment** $17.0 million
- **Coed**
- **Minimally difficult** entrance level

Faculty *Student/faculty ratio:* 19:1.

Student Life *Campus security:* 24-hour emergency response devices and patrols.

Athletics Member NCAA.

Standardized Tests *Recommended:* SAT I or ACT (for placement).

Costs (2003–04) *Comprehensive fee:* $17,020 includes full-time tuition ($10,498), mandatory fees ($1088), and room and board ($5434). Part-time tuition: $351 per credit hour. *Required fees:* $41 per credit hour part-time.

Financial Aid *Average percent of need met:* 100.

Applying *Options:* common application, early admission, deferred entrance. *Application fee:* $25. *Required:* high school transcript.

Admissions Contact Mr. Gary Knight, Interim Vice President, Institutional Effectiveness, Benedict College, PO Box 98, Columbia, SC 29204. *Phone:* 803-253-5275. *Toll-free phone:* 800-868-6598. *Fax:* 803-253-5167.

CHARLESTON SOUTHERN UNIVERSITY

Charleston, South Carolina

- **Independent Baptist** comprehensive, founded 1964
- **Calendar** 4-4-1
- **Degrees** associate, bachelor's, and master's
- **Suburban** 500-acre campus
- **Endowment** $10.6 million
- **Coed,** 2,676 undergraduate students, 79% full-time, 62% women, 38% men
- **Moderately difficult** entrance level, 80% of applicants were admitted

Located in one of the Southeast's most beautiful regions, Charleston Southern University (CSU) is a fully accredited, private university in South Carolina. CSU's enrollment has grown to almost 3,000 students and offers both a traditional liberal arts curriculum and a comprehensive professional program. CSU encourages interested students to schedule a campus visit.

Undergraduates 2,116 full-time, 560 part-time. Students come from 45 states and territories, 22 other countries, 17% are from out of state, 28% African American, 3% Asian American or Pacific Islander, 0.7% Hispanic American, 2% international, 8% transferred in, 46% live on campus. *Retention:* 70% of 2002 full-time freshmen returned.

Freshmen *Admission:* 2,111 applied, 1,688 admitted, 440 enrolled. *Average high school GPA:* 3.20. *Test scores:* SAT verbal scores over 500: 47%; SAT math scores over 500: 44%; ACT scores over 18: 67%; SAT verbal scores over 600: 9%; SAT math scores over 600: 12%; ACT scores over 24: 13%; SAT verbal scores over 700: 1%; SAT math scores over 700: 1%.

Faculty *Total:* 176, 61% full-time, 45% with terminal degrees. *Student/faculty ratio:* 19:1.

Majors Accounting; American history; applied mathematics; athletic training; biochemistry; biological and biomedical sciences related; biological and physical sciences; biology/biological sciences; biology teacher education; business administration and management; business administration, management and operations related; business/managerial economics; chemistry; computer programming; computer science; criminal justice/law enforcement administration; criminal justice/safety; dramatic/theatre arts and stagecraft related; early childhood education; economics; education; educational leadership and administration; education (K-12); elementary and middle school administration/principalship; elementary education; engineering related; engineering technology; English; English/language arts teacher education; environmental studies; European history; finance; health/medical preparatory programs related; history; history teacher education; humanities; kindergarten/preschool education; liberal arts and sciences/liberal studies; management information systems; marketing/marketing management; mathematics; mathematics teacher education; music; music performance; music teacher education; music therapy; natural resources management and policy; natural sciences; nursing (registered nurse training); pastoral studies/counseling; physical education teaching and coaching; physical sciences related; political science and government; pre-dentistry studies; pre-engineering; pre-law studies; pre-medical studies; pre-pharmacy studies; psychology; religious/sacred music; religious studies; science teacher education; science technologies related; secondary education; secondary school administration/principalship; social sciences; social studies teacher education; sociology; Spanish; Spanish language teacher education; speech and rhetoric; voice and opera; youth ministry.

Academic Programs *Special study options:* academic remediation for entering students, accelerated degree program, advanced placement credit, double majors, honors programs, internships, off-campus study, part-time degree program, services for LD students, summer session for credit. *ROTC:* Air Force (b). *Unusual degree programs:* 3-2 engineering with University of South Carolina.

Library L. Mendel Rivers Library with 163,738 titles, 831 serial subscriptions, 7,745 audiovisual materials, an OPAC.

Computers on Campus 190 computers available on campus for general student use. A campuswide network can be accessed. Internet access, online (class) registration, at least one staffed computer lab available.

Student Life *Housing:* on-campus residence required through sophomore year. *Options:* men-only, women-only. Campus housing is university owned. Freshman applicants given priority for college housing. *Activities and organizations:* drama/theater group, student-run newspaper, choral group, marching band, student government, Baptist Student Union, Fellowship of Christian Athletics. *Campus security:* 24-hour emergency response devices and patrols, late-night transport/escort service. *Student services:* personal/psychological counseling.

Athletics Member NCAA. All Division I except football (Division I-AA). *Intercollegiate sports:* baseball M(s), basketball M(s)/W(s), cheerleading M/W, cross-country running M(s)/W(s), golf M(s)/W(s), soccer W(s), softball W(s),

Charleston Southern University (continued)
tennis M(s)/W(s), track and field M(s)/W(s), volleyball W(s). *Intramural sports:* basketball M/W, football M/W, soccer M/W, softball M/W, volleyball M/W.

Standardized Tests *Required:* SAT I or ACT (for admission).

Costs (2003–04) *Comprehensive fee:* $20,000 includes full-time tuition ($14,426), mandatory fees ($30), and room and board ($5544). Part-time tuition: $233 per credit. Part-time tuition and fees vary according to course load. *Room and board:* Room and board charges vary according to housing facility. *Waivers:* employees or children of employees.

Financial Aid Of all full-time matriculated undergraduates who enrolled in 2001, 1,301 applied for aid, 1,155 were judged to have need, 255 had their need fully met. 614 Federal Work-Study jobs (averaging $1406). In 2001, 222 non-need-based awards were made. *Average percent of need met:* 72%. *Average financial aid package:* $10,613. *Average need-based loan:* $3554. *Average need-based gift aid:* $7405. *Average non-need-based aid:* $7529. *Average indebtedness upon graduation:* $14,500.

Applying *Application fee:* $30. *Required:* high school transcript, minimum 2.0 GPA. *Required for some:* essay or personal statement, 1 letter of recommendation, interview. *Application deadline:* rolling (freshmen), rolling (transfers). *Notification:* continuous (freshmen), continuous (transfers).

Admissions Contact Ms. Cheryl Burton, Director of Enrollment Management, Charleston Southern University, PO Box 118087, 9200 University Boulevard, Charleston, SC 19423-8087. *Phone:* 843-863-7050. *Toll-free phone:* 800-947-7474. *E-mail:* enroll@csuniv.edu.

■ *See page 1390 for a narrative description.*

THE CITADEL, THE MILITARY COLLEGE OF SOUTH CAROLINA

Charleston, South Carolina

- **State-supported** comprehensive, founded 1842
- **Calendar** semesters
- **Degrees** bachelor's, master's, and post-master's certificates
- **Urban** 130-acre campus
- **Endowment** $35.7 million
- **Coed, primarily men,** 2,150 undergraduate students, 95% full-time, 8% women, 92% men
- **Moderately difficult** entrance level, 31% of applicants were admitted

The Citadel, a comprehensive military college, prepares students for leadership through a challenging curriculum of 20 majors. Graduates participate in all walks of life, from graduate study to private sector and military careers. New barracks and a first-class campuswide computer network are recent features. The college actively seeks qualified students regardless of gender or ethnicity.

Undergraduates 2,037 full-time, 113 part-time. Students come from 49 states and territories, 27 other countries, 55% are from out of state, 8% African American, 3% Asian American or Pacific Islander, 4% Hispanic American, 0.2% Native American, 2% international, 3% transferred in, 100% live on campus. *Retention:* 78% of 2002 full-time freshmen returned.

Freshmen *Admission:* 1,919 applied, 588 admitted, 553 enrolled. *Average high school GPA:* 3.31. *Test scores:* SAT verbal scores over 500: 77%; SAT math scores over 500: 80%; ACT scores over 18: 94%; SAT verbal scores over 600: 26%; SAT math scores over 600: 30%; ACT scores over 24: 43%; SAT verbal scores over 700: 3%; SAT math scores over 700: 3%; ACT scores over 30: 3%.

Faculty *Total:* 221, 67% full-time, 80% with terminal degrees. *Student/faculty ratio:* 15:1.

Majors Biology/biological sciences; biology teacher education; business administration and management; chemistry; civil engineering; computer science; criminal justice/law enforcement administration; electrical, electronics and communications engineering; English; English/language arts teacher education; French; German; history; history teacher education; mathematics; mathematics teacher education; physical education teaching and coaching; physics; political science and government; psychology; science teacher education; social studies teacher education; Spanish.

Academic Programs *Special study options:* adult/continuing education programs, advanced placement credit, double majors, English as a second language, honors programs, independent study, internships, off-campus study, part-time degree program, services for LD students, study abroad, summer session for credit. *ROTC:* Army (b), Navy (b), Air Force (b).

Library Daniel Library with 234,282 titles, 1,336 serial subscriptions, 4,507 audiovisual materials, an OPAC, a Web page.

Computers on Campus 350 computers available on campus for general student use. A campuswide network can be accessed from student residence rooms and from off campus. Internet access, online (class) registration, at least one staffed computer lab available.

Student Life *Housing:* on-campus residence required through senior year. *Options:* coed. Campus housing is university owned. Freshman campus housing is guaranteed. *Activities and organizations:* drama/theater group, student-run newspaper, choral group, marching band. *Campus security:* 24-hour patrols, student patrols, late-night transport/escort service. *Student services:* health clinic, personal/psychological counseling.

Athletics Member NCAA. All Division I except football (Division I-AA). *Intercollegiate sports:* baseball M(s), basketball M(s), crew M(c)/W(c), cross-country running M(s)/W(s), golf M(s)/W(s), ice hockey M(c)/W(c), lacrosse M(c)/W(c), riflery M(c)/W(c), rugby M(c)/W(c), sailing M(c)/W(c), soccer M(s)/W(s), tennis M(s), track and field M(s)/W(s), volleyball M(c)/W(s), weight lifting M(c)/W(c), wrestling M(s). *Intramural sports:* badminton M/W, basketball M/W, football M/W, racquetball M/W, softball M/W, swimming M/W, table tennis M/W, tennis M/W, track and field M/W, volleyball M/W, water polo M/W, weight lifting M/W, wrestling M/W.

Standardized Tests *Required:* SAT I or ACT (for admission).

Costs (2003–04) *Tuition:* state resident $4999 full-time, $173 per credit hour part-time; nonresident $13,410 full-time, $348 per credit hour part-time. *Required fees:* $898 full-time, $15 per term part-time. *Room and board:* $4778. *Payment plan:* installment. *Waivers:* senior citizens.

Financial Aid Of all full-time matriculated undergraduates who enrolled in 2002, 1,440 applied for aid, 1,116 were judged to have need, 192 had their need fully met. 19 Federal Work-Study jobs (averaging $863). In 2002, 172 non-need-based awards were made. *Average percent of need met:* 78%. *Average financial aid package:* $7992. *Average need-based loan:* $5000. *Average need-based gift aid:* $4980. *Average non-need-based aid:* $7438. *Average indebtedness upon graduation:* $14,396.

Applying *Options:* electronic application. *Application fee:* $35. *Required:* high school transcript, minimum 2.0 GPA. *Recommended:* interview. *Application deadline:* rolling (freshmen), rolling (transfers). *Notification:* 4/15 (freshmen), 4/15 (transfers).

Admissions Contact Lt. Col. John Powell, Director of Admissions, The Citadel, The Military College of South Carolina, 171 Moultrie Street, Charleston, SC 29409. *Phone:* 843-953-5230. *Toll-free phone:* 800-868-1842. *Fax:* 843-953-7036. *E-mail:* admissions@citadel.edu.

■ *See page 1402 for a narrative description.*

CLAFLIN UNIVERSITY

Orangeburg, South Carolina

- **Independent United Methodist** 4-year, founded 1869
- **Calendar** semesters
- **Degree** bachelor's
- **Small-town** 32-acre campus with easy access to Columbia
- **Endowment** $12.0 million
- **Coed**
- **Minimally difficult** entrance level

Faculty *Student/faculty ratio:* 14:1.

Student Life *Campus security:* 24-hour emergency response devices and patrols, student patrols.

Athletics Member NAIA.

Standardized Tests *Required:* SAT I or ACT (for admission). *Recommended:* SAT II: Subject Tests (for admission).

Costs (2003–04) *Comprehensive fee:* $14,838 includes full-time tuition ($7970), mandatory fees ($1684), and room and board ($5184). Part-time tuition: $332. *Required fees:* $63 per credit hour part-time. *College room only:* $2348.

Financial Aid In 2002, 300. *Average percent of need met:* 70. *Average financial aid package:* $9000. *Average indebtedness upon graduation:* $16,100.

Applying *Options:* common application, deferred entrance. *Application fee:* $20. *Required:* essay or personal statement, high school transcript, minimum 2.00 GPA, interview. *Recommended:* letters of recommendation.

Admissions Contact Mr. Michael Zeigler, Director of Admissions, Claflin University, 400 Magnolia Street, Orangeburg, SC 29115. *Phone:* 803-535-5340. *Toll-free phone:* 800-922-1276. *Fax:* 803-535-5387. *E-mail:* zeiglerm@claf1.claflin.edu.

CLEMSON UNIVERSITY

Clemson, South Carolina

- **State-supported** university, founded 1889
- **Calendar** semesters
- **Degrees** bachelor's, master's, and doctoral
- **Small-town** 1400-acre campus
- **Endowment** $213.4 million

■ **Coed,** 13,813 undergraduate students, 93% full-time, 45% women, 55% men
■ **Moderately difficult** entrance level, 52% of applicants were admitted

Undergraduates 12,857 full-time, 956 part-time. Students come from 52 states and territories, 58 other countries, 29% are from out of state, 7% African American, 2% Asian American or Pacific Islander, 0.9% Hispanic American, 0.2% Native American, 0.5% international, 6% transferred in, 49% live on campus. *Retention:* 89% of 2002 full-time freshmen returned.

Freshmen *Admission:* 11,315 applied, 5,864 admitted, 2,753 enrolled. *Average high school GPA:* 3.88. *Test scores:* SAT verbal scores over 500: 91%; SAT math scores over 500: 95%; ACT scores over 18: 99%; SAT verbal scores over 600: 47%; SAT math scores over 600: 63%; ACT scores over 24: 79%; SAT verbal scores over 700: 7%; SAT math scores over 700: 13%; ACT scores over 30: 20%.

Faculty *Total:* 1,107, 86% full-time, 82% with terminal degrees. *Student/faculty ratio:* 15:1.

Majors Accounting; agricultural/biological engineering and bioengineering; agricultural business and management; agricultural economics; agricultural teacher education; animal genetics; animal sciences; aquaculture; architecture; art; biochemistry; biology/biological sciences; biomedical/medical engineering; business administration and management; business, management, and marketing related; ceramic sciences and engineering; chemical engineering; chemistry; chemistry related; civil engineering; clinical laboratory science/medical technology; communication and journalism related; computer and information sciences; computer engineering; computer programming; counselor education/school counseling and guidance; economics; electrical, electronics and communications engineering; elementary education; engineering mechanics; English; entomology; environmental/environmental health engineering; finance; food science; foreign languages and literatures; foreign languages related; forest/forest resources management; geology/earth science; health professions related; history; horticultural science; industrial design; industrial engineering; information science/studies; kindergarten/preschool education; landscape architecture; marketing/marketing management; materials engineering; mathematics; mathematics teacher education; mechanical engineering; microbiology; middle school education; nursing (registered nurse training); operations management; parks, recreation and leisure facilities management; philosophy; physics; plant pathology/phytopathology; political science and government; polymer chemistry; premedical studies; pre-pharmacy studies; pre-veterinary studies; psychology; reading teacher education; science teacher education; science technologies related; secondary education; sociology; special education; speech and rhetoric; technology/industrial arts teacher education; trade and industrial teacher education; visual and performing arts related.

Academic Programs *Special study options:* academic remediation for entering students, accelerated degree program, advanced placement credit, cooperative education, distance learning, double majors, honors programs, internships, part-time degree program, services for LD students, study abroad, summer session for credit. *ROTC:* Army (b), Air Force (b).

Library Robert Muldrow Cooper Library plus 1 other with 1.6 million titles, 5,978 serial subscriptions, 94,641 audiovisual materials, an OPAC, a Web page.

Computers on Campus 1000 computers available on campus for general student use. A campuswide network can be accessed from student residence rooms and from off campus that provide access to wireless network. Internet access, online (class) registration, at least one staffed computer lab available.

Student Life *Housing:* on-campus residence required for freshman year. *Options:* coed, men-only, women-only. Campus housing is university owned. Freshman campus housing is guaranteed. *Activities and organizations:* drama/theater group, student-run newspaper, radio and television station, choral group, marching band, student government, Fellowship of Christian Athletes, Tiger Band, national fraternities, national sororities. *Campus security:* 24-hour emergency response devices and patrols, late-night transport/escort service, controlled dormitory access. *Student services:* health clinic, personal/psychological counseling, legal services.

Athletics Member NCAA. All Division I except football (Division I-A). *Intercollegiate sports:* baseball M, basketball M(s)/W(s), bowling M(c)/W(c), cheerleading M/W, crew M(c)/W(s), cross-country running M(s)/W(s), equestrian sports M(c)/W(c), fencing M(c)/W(c), field hockey M(c)/W(c), golf M(s), ice hockey M(c)/W(c), lacrosse M(c)/W(c), riflery M(c)/W(c), rugby M(c)/W(c), sailing M(c)/W(c), soccer M(s)/W(s), softball W(c), swimming M(s)/W(s), tennis M(s)/W(s), track and field M(s)/W(s), ultimate Frisbee M(c)/W(c), volleyball M(c)/W(s), weight lifting M(c)/W(c), wrestling M(c). *Intramural sports:* basketball M/W, golf M/W, racquetball M/W, soccer M/W, softball M/W, swimming M(c)/W(c), table tennis M/W, tennis M(c)/W(c), volleyball M/W, water polo M/W.

Standardized Tests *Required:* SAT I or ACT (for admission).

Costs (2003–04) *Tuition:* state resident $6934 full-time, $288 per hour part-time; nonresident $14,532 full-time, $600 per hour part-time. *Required fees:* $5 per term part-time. *Room and board:* $5038; room only: $2894. Room and board charges vary according to board plan and housing facility. *Payment plan:* installment.

Financial Aid Of all full-time matriculated undergraduates who enrolled in 2003, 6,695 applied for aid, 5,093 were judged to have need, 1,447 had their need fully met. 811 Federal Work-Study jobs (averaging $2445). 3,137 state and other part-time jobs (averaging $2549). In 2003, 4184 non-need-based awards were made. *Average percent of need met:* 69%. *Average financial aid package:* $8669. *Average need-based loan:* $4126. *Average need-based gift aid:* $3301. *Average non-need-based aid:* $6598. *Average indebtedness upon graduation:* $15,125.

Applying *Options:* electronic application, early action. *Application fee:* $40. *Required:* high school transcript. *Recommended:* essay or personal statement, letters of recommendation. *Application deadlines:* 5/1 (freshmen), 8/1 (transfers). *Notification:* continuous (freshmen), 2/15 (early action), continuous (transfers).

Admissions Contact Mr. Timothy R. Galbreath, Assistant Director of Admissions, Clemson University, 105 Sikes Hall, PO Box 345124, Clemson, SC 29634. *Phone:* 864-656-2287. *Fax:* 864-656-2464. *E-mail:* cuadmissions@clemson.edu.

■ *See page 1416 for a narrative description.*

COASTAL CAROLINA UNIVERSITY

Conway, South Carolina

■ **State-supported** comprehensive, founded 1954
■ **Calendar** semesters
■ **Degrees** bachelor's, master's, and postbachelor's certificates
■ **Suburban** 244-acre campus
■ **Endowment** $11.6 million
■ **Coed,** 5,610 undergraduate students, 88% full-time, 52% women, 48% men
■ **Moderately difficult** entrance level, 71% of applicants were admitted

Undergraduates 4,961 full-time, 649 part-time. Students come from 50 states and territories, 44 other countries, 44% are from out of state, 11% African American, 0.8% Asian American or Pacific Islander, 1% Hispanic American, 0.4% Native American, 3% international, 10% transferred in, 32% live on campus. *Retention:* 73% of 2002 full-time freshmen returned.

Freshmen *Admission:* 4,527 applied, 3,208 admitted, 1,272 enrolled. *Average high school GPA:* 3.27. *Test scores:* SAT verbal scores over 500: 56%; SAT math scores over 500: 68%; ACT scores over 18: 100%; SAT verbal scores over 600: 12%; SAT math scores over 600: 18%; ACT scores over 24: 23%; SAT verbal scores over 700: 1%; SAT math scores over 700: 1%; ACT scores over 30: 1%.

Faculty *Total:* 398, 52% full-time, 53% with terminal degrees. *Student/faculty ratio:* 19:1.

Majors Accounting; applied mathematics; biology/biological sciences; business administration and management; chemistry; computer and information sciences; dramatic/theatre arts; dramatic/theatre arts and stagecraft related; early childhood education; elementary education; English; finance; fine/studio arts; history; liberal arts and sciences/liberal studies; marine biology and biological oceanography; marketing/marketing management; middle school education; music; philosophy; physical education teaching and coaching; political science and government; psychology; public health education and promotion; secondary education; sociology; Spanish; special education.

Academic Programs *Special study options:* accelerated degree program, adult/continuing education programs, advanced placement credit, cooperative education, distance learning, double majors, honors programs, independent study, internships, part-time degree program, student-designed majors, study abroad, summer session for credit. *Unusual degree programs:* 3-2 engineering with Clemson University.

Library Kimbel Library with 201,805 titles, 958 serial subscriptions, 12,465 audiovisual materials, an OPAC, a Web page.

Computers on Campus 550 computers available on campus for general student use. A campuswide network can be accessed from student residence rooms and from off campus that provide access to on-line grades. Internet access, online (class) registration, at least one staffed computer lab available.

Student Life *Housing options:* coed, disabled students. Campus housing is university owned. *Activities and organizations:* drama/theater group, student-run newspaper, choral group, marching band, Student Government Association, Coastal Productions Board, STAR (Students Taking Active Responsibility), FCA (Fellowship of Christian Athletes), Diversity of Programming, national fraternities, national sororities. *Campus security:* 24-hour emergency response devices and patrols, late-night transport/escort service. *Student services:* health clinic, personal/psychological counseling, women's center.

Athletics Member NCAA. All Division I. *Intercollegiate sports:* baseball M(s), basketball M(s)/W(s), cheerleading M(c)/W(c), cross-country running M(s)/W(s), football M(s), golf M(s)/W(s), soccer M(s)/W(s), softball W(s), tennis M(s)/W(s), track and field M(s)/W(s), volleyball W(s). *Intramural sports:* badminton M/W, basketball M/W, bowling M/W, football M/W, golf M/W, lacrosse

Coastal Carolina University (continued)
M/W, racquetball M/W, rugby M, soccer M/W, softball M/W, swimming M/W, table tennis M/W, tennis M/W, track and field M/W, volleyball M/W, water polo M/W, weight lifting M/W.

Standardized Tests *Required:* SAT I or ACT (for admission).

Costs (2003–04) *Tuition:* state resident $5190 full-time, $215 per credit hour part-time; nonresident $12,870 full-time, $540 per credit hour part-time. Full-time tuition and fees vary according to course load. Part-time tuition and fees vary according to course load. *Required fees:* $80 full-time. *Room and board:* $5770; room only: $3700. Room and board charges vary according to board plan. *Payment plans:* installment, deferred payment. *Waivers:* senior citizens and employees or children of employees.

Financial Aid Of all full-time matriculated undergraduates who enrolled in 2002, 3,247 applied for aid, 2,803 were judged to have need, 1,175 had their need fully met. 197 Federal Work-Study jobs (averaging $1292). In 2002, 1032 non-need-based awards were made. *Average percent of need met:* 64%. *Average financial aid package:* $7163. *Average need-based loan:* $6508. *Average need-based gift aid:* $3165. *Average non-need-based aid:* $5594. *Average indebtedness upon graduation:* $19,323.

Applying *Options:* common application, electronic application, deferred entrance. *Application fee:* $45. *Required:* high school transcript, minimum 2.0 GPA. *Recommended:* essay or personal statement, 1 letter of recommendation, interview. *Application deadlines:* 8/15 (freshmen), 8/15 (transfers). *Notification:* continuous until 9/15 (freshmen), continuous until 8/15 (transfers).

Admissions Contact Dr. Judy Vogt, Associate Vice President, Enrollment Services, Coastal Carolina University, PO Box 261954, Kingston Hall, Room 119, Conway, SC 29528. *Phone:* 843-349-2037. *Toll-free phone:* 800-277-7000. *Fax:* 843-349-2127. *E-mail:* admissions@coastal.edu.

COKER COLLEGE
Hartsville, South Carolina

- **Independent** 4-year, founded 1908
- **Calendar** semesters
- **Degrees** bachelor's (also offers evening program with significant enrollment not reflected in profile)
- **Small-town** 30-acre campus with easy access to Charlotte
- **Coed,** 482 undergraduate students, 98% full-time, 58% women, 42% men
- **Moderately difficult** entrance level, 95% of applicants were admitted

Undergraduates 473 full-time, 9 part-time. Students come from 28 states and territories, 6 other countries, 19% are from out of state, 26% African American, 0.2% Asian American or Pacific Islander, 2% Hispanic American, 0.4% Native American, 2% international, 9% transferred in, 70% live on campus. *Retention:* 69% of 2002 full-time freshmen returned.

Freshmen *Admission:* 654 applied, 619 admitted, 148 enrolled. *Average high school GPA:* 3.18. *Test scores:* SAT verbal scores over 500: 47%; SAT math scores over 500: 52%; ACT scores over 18: 67%; SAT verbal scores over 600: 11%; SAT math scores over 600: 11%; ACT scores over 24: 19%; SAT math scores over 700: 1%.

Faculty *Total:* 64, 83% full-time, 72% with terminal degrees. *Student/faculty ratio:* 8:1.

Majors Accounting; acting; art; art teacher education; biology/biological sciences; biology teacher education; business administration and management; chemistry; chemistry teacher education; clinical laboratory science/medical technology; computer science; corrections; counseling psychology; criminal justice/law enforcement administration; criminology; dance; dramatic/theatre arts; dramatic/theatre arts and stagecraft related; early childhood education; education; elementary education; English; English/language arts teacher education; finance; fine/studio arts; French; graphic design; health and physical education; health and physical education related; history; history teacher education; international business/trade/commerce; kinesiology and exercise science; management information systems; marketing/marketing management; mass communication/media; mathematics; mathematics teacher education; music; music management and merchandising; music teacher education; operations management; parks, recreation, and leisure related; philosophy and religious studies related; photography; physical education teaching and coaching; piano and organ; political science and government; psychology; social work; sociology; Spanish; special education; sport and fitness administration; theatre design and technology; therapeutic recreation; voice and opera.

Academic Programs *Special study options:* academic remediation for entering students, adult/continuing education programs, advanced placement credit, cooperative education, double majors, English as a second language, honors programs, independent study, internships, part-time degree program, student-designed majors, study abroad, summer session for credit.

Library James Lide Coker III Memorial Library plus 1 other with 78,706 titles, 575 serial subscriptions, 5,741 audiovisual materials, an OPAC, a Web page.

Computers on Campus 40 computers available on campus for general student use. A campuswide network can be accessed from student residence rooms and from off campus. Internet access, at least one staffed computer lab available.

Student Life *Housing:* on-campus residence required through junior year. *Options:* coed, men-only, women-only. Campus housing is university owned. Freshman campus housing is guaranteed. *Activities and organizations:* drama/theater group, student-run newspaper, choral group, Coker College Union, student government, Pan-African American Sisterhood Association, Sigma Alpha Chi, Commissioners. *Campus security:* 24-hour patrols, late-night transport/escort service, controlled dormitory access. *Student services:* health clinic, personal/psychological counseling.

Athletics Member NCAA. All Division II. *Intercollegiate sports:* baseball M(s), basketball M(s)/W(s), cheerleading M(s)/W(s), cross-country running M(s)/W(s), golf M(s), soccer M(s)/W(s), softball W(s), tennis M(s)/W(s), volleyball W(s). *Intramural sports:* basketball M/W, bowling M/W, crew W, cross-country running M/W, football M/W, racquetball M/W, soccer M/W, softball M/W, swimming M/W, table tennis M/W, tennis M/W, track and field M/W, volleyball M/W, weight lifting M/W.

Standardized Tests *Required:* SAT I or ACT (for admission).

Costs (2003–04) *Comprehensive fee:* $21,491 includes full-time tuition ($15,840), mandatory fees ($325), and room and board ($5326). Full-time tuition and fees vary according to course load and location. Part-time tuition: $660 per semester hour. Part-time tuition and fees vary according to location. *Required fees:* $3 per semester hour part-time. *College room only:* $2846. Room and board charges vary according to housing facility. *Payment plan:* installment. *Waivers:* employees or children of employees.

Financial Aid Of all full-time matriculated undergraduates who enrolled in 2003, 434 applied for aid, 398 were judged to have need, 158 had their need fully met. 157 Federal Work-Study jobs (averaging $1078). In 2003, 75 non-need-based awards were made. *Average percent of need met:* 97%. *Average financial aid package:* $16,531. *Average need-based loan:* $3775. *Average need-based gift aid:* $5885. *Average non-need-based aid:* $5269. *Average indebtedness upon graduation:* $17,093. *Financial aid deadline:* 6/1.

Applying *Options:* common application, electronic application, deferred entrance. *Application fee:* $15. *Required:* high school transcript. *Required for some:* essay or personal statement, minimum 2.2 GPA. *Recommended:* minimum 2.2 GPA. *Application deadline:* rolling (freshmen), rolling (transfers). *Notification:* continuous until 8/1 (freshmen), continuous until 8/1 (transfers).

Admissions Contact Ms. Perry Kirven, Director of Admissions, Coker College, 300 East College Avenue, Hartsville, SC 29550. *Phone:* 843-383-8050. *Toll-free phone:* 800-950-1908. *Fax:* 843-383-8056. *E-mail:* admissions@coker.edu.

COLLEGE OF CHARLESTON
Charleston, South Carolina

- **State-supported** comprehensive, founded 1770
- **Calendar** semesters
- **Degrees** bachelor's and master's (also offers graduate degree programs through University of Charleston, South Carolina)
- **Urban** 52-acre campus
- **Endowment** $32.1 million
- **Coed,** 9,824 undergraduate students, 91% full-time, 63% women, 37% men
- **Moderately difficult** entrance level, 60% of applicants were admitted

Undergraduates 8,921 full-time, 903 part-time. Students come from 52 states and territories, 76 other countries, 33% are from out of state, 8% African American, 1% Asian American or Pacific Islander, 1% Hispanic American, 0.3% Native American, 2% international, 5% transferred in, 26% live on campus. *Retention:* 84% of 2002 full-time freshmen returned.

Freshmen *Admission:* 7,606 applied, 4,560 admitted, 1,874 enrolled. *Average high school GPA:* 3.67. *Test scores:* SAT verbal scores over 500: 97%; SAT math scores over 500: 97%; ACT scores over 18: 99%; SAT verbal scores over 600: 56%; SAT math scores over 600: 53%; ACT scores over 24: 52%; SAT verbal scores over 700: 8%; SAT math scores over 700: 6%; ACT scores over 30: 2%.

Faculty *Total:* 853, 57% full-time, 63% with terminal degrees. *Student/faculty ratio:* 14:1.

Majors Accounting; anthropology; art history, criticism and conservation; arts management; biochemistry; biology/biological sciences; business administration and management; chemistry; classics and languages, literatures and linguistics; communication/speech communication and rhetoric; computer and information sciences; dramatic/theatre arts; early childhood education; economics; elementary education; English; fine/studio arts; French; geology/earth science; German; historic preservation and conservation; history; information science/studies; international business/trade/commerce; marine biology and biological oceanography; mathematics; middle school education; music; philosophy; physical education teaching and coaching; physics; political science and government; pre-dentistry studies; pre-medical studies; psychology; religious studies; secondary education; sociology; Spanish; special education; urban studies/affairs.

Academic Programs *Special study options:* accelerated degree program, adult/continuing education programs, advanced placement credit, cooperative education, double majors, English as a second language, honors programs, independent study, internships, off-campus study, part-time degree program, services for LD students, study abroad, summer session for credit. *ROTC:* Air Force (c). *Unusual degree programs:* 3-2 engineering with Case Western Reserve University, Clemson University, Georgia Institute of Technology, University of South Carolina; biometry with Medical University of South Carolina, marine engineering with University of Michigan.

Library Robert Scott Small Library plus 1 other with 476,108 titles, 3,723 serial subscriptions, 5,024 audiovisual materials, an OPAC, a Web page.

Computers on Campus 300 computers available on campus for general student use. A campuswide network can be accessed from student residence rooms and from off campus. Internet access, online (class) registration, at least one staffed computer lab available. Computer purchase or lease plan available.

Student Life *Housing options:* coed, men-only, women-only, disabled students. Campus housing is university owned. Freshman campus housing is guaranteed. *Activities and organizations:* drama/theater group, student-run newspaper, radio station, choral group, Student Government Association, Cougar Productions, intramural basketball, Black Student Union, Inter-Fraternity Council/Panhellenic Council, national fraternities, national sororities. *Campus security:* 24-hour emergency response devices and patrols, student patrols, late-night transport/escort service. *Student services:* health clinic, personal/psychological counseling, women's center, legal services.

Athletics Member NCAA. All Division I. *Intercollegiate sports:* baseball M(s), basketball M(s)/W(s), cross-country running M(s)/W(s), equestrian sports W, golf M(s)/W(s), sailing M/W, soccer M(s)/W(s), softball W(s), swimming M(s)/W(s), tennis M(s)/W(s), volleyball W(s). *Intramural sports:* badminton M/W, basketball M/W, crew M/W, equestrian sports W, fencing M/W, football M/W, racquetball M/W, rugby W, soccer M/W, softball M/W, tennis M/W, volleyball M/W, weight lifting M/W.

Standardized Tests *Required:* SAT I or ACT (for admission).

Costs (2003–04) *Tuition:* state resident $5770 full-time, $240 per semester hour part-time; nonresident $13,032 full-time, $553 per semester hour part-time. Part-time tuition and fees vary according to course load. *Required fees:* $15 per term part-time. *Room and board:* $6117; room only: $4057. Room and board charges vary according to board plan and housing facility. *Payment plan:* installment. *Waivers:* senior citizens.

Financial Aid Of all full-time matriculated undergraduates who enrolled in 2003, 4,517 applied for aid, 3,428 were judged to have need, 846 had their need fully met. In 2003, 721 non-need-based awards were made. *Average percent of need met:* 63%. *Average financial aid package:* $8696. *Average need-based loan:* $3500. *Average need-based gift aid:* $2854. *Average non-need-based aid:* $10,338. *Average indebtedness upon graduation:* $16,626.

Applying *Options:* common application, electronic application, early admission, early action, deferred entrance. *Application fee:* $45. *Required:* essay or personal statement, high school transcript, letters of recommendation. *Recommended:* interview. *Application deadlines:* 4/1 (freshmen), 4/1 (out-of-state freshmen), 4/1 (transfers). *Notification:* 5/15 (freshmen), 6/15 (out-of-state freshmen), 2/1 (early action), continuous (transfers).

Admissions Contact Mr. Donald Burkard, Dean of Admissions, College of Charleston, 66 George Street, Charleston, SC 29424-0001. *Phone:* 843-953-5670. *Toll-free phone:* 843-953-5670. *Fax:* 843-953-6322. *E-mail:* admissions@cofc.edu.

COLUMBIA COLLEGE
Columbia, South Carolina

- **Independent United Methodist** comprehensive, founded 1854
- **Calendar** semesters
- **Degrees** bachelor's and master's
- **Suburban** 33-acre campus
- **Endowment** $16.6 million
- **Women only,** 1,187 undergraduate students, 78% full-time
- **Moderately difficult** entrance level, 86% of applicants were admitted

Undergraduates 923 full-time, 264 part-time. Students come from 14 states and territories, 15 other countries, 4% are from out of state, 49% African American, 0.9% Asian American or Pacific Islander, 2% Hispanic American, 0.3% Native American, 0.7% international, 11% transferred in, 58% live on campus. *Retention:* 63% of 2002 full-time freshmen returned.

Freshmen *Admission:* 960 applied, 824 admitted, 180 enrolled. *Average high school GPA:* 3.20. *Test scores:* SAT verbal scores over 500: 39%; SAT math scores over 500: 35%; SAT verbal scores over 600: 8%; SAT math scores over 600: 5%; SAT math scores over 700: 1%.

Faculty *Total:* 146, 63% full-time, 57% with terminal degrees. *Student/faculty ratio:* 12:1.

Majors Accounting; applied art; biology/biological sciences; business administration and management; chemistry; communication and journalism related; communication/speech communication and rhetoric; computer and information sciences and support services related; dance; drama and dance teacher education; elementary education; English; English language and literature related; fine/studio arts; French; history; human development and family studies related; journalism; journalism related; kindergarten/preschool education; liberal arts and sciences/liberal studies; mathematics; multi-/interdisciplinary studies related; music; music performance; music teacher education; piano and organ; political science and government; psychology; public administration and social service professions related; public relations/image management; religious education; religious/sacred music; religious studies; social sciences; social studies teacher education; social work; Spanish; special education; speech-language pathology; voice and opera.

Academic Programs *Special study options:* academic remediation for entering students, accelerated degree program, adult/continuing education programs, advanced placement credit, distance learning, double majors, freshman honors college, honors programs, independent study, internships, part-time degree program, student-designed majors, study abroad, summer session for credit. *ROTC:* Army (c).

Library Edens Library with 140,909 titles, 513 serial subscriptions, 18,144 audiovisual materials, an OPAC, a Web page.

Computers on Campus 182 computers available on campus for general student use. A campuswide network can be accessed from student residence rooms and from off campus that provide access to e-mail. Internet access, online (class) registration, at least one staffed computer lab available.

Student Life *Housing:* on-campus residence required through sophomore year. *Options:* women-only. Campus housing is university owned. Freshman campus housing is guaranteed. *Activities and organizations:* drama/theater group, student-run newspaper, choral group, Student Government Association, African-American Student Association, Columbia College Activities Board, Heavenly Creations Gospel Choir, Student Christian Association. *Campus security:* 24-hour emergency response devices and patrols, late-night transport/escort service, controlled dormitory access. *Student services:* health clinic, personal/psychological counseling, women's center.

Athletics Member NAIA. *Intercollegiate sports:* cross-country running W(s), soccer W(s), tennis W(s), volleyball W(s). *Intramural sports:* basketball W, crew W.

Standardized Tests *Required:* SAT I or ACT (for admission).

Costs (2003–04) *Comprehensive fee:* $22,525 includes full-time tuition ($16,930), mandatory fees ($350), and room and board ($5245). Part-time tuition: $454 per credit. Part-time tuition and fees vary according to course load. *College room only:* $2830. Room and board charges vary according to board plan. *Payment plan:* installment. *Waivers:* employees or children of employees.

Financial Aid Of all full-time matriculated undergraduates who enrolled in 2003, 811 applied for aid, 802 were judged to have need, 547 had their need fully met. 200 Federal Work-Study jobs (averaging $1000). In 2003, 51 non-need-based awards were made. *Average percent of need met:* 92%. *Average financial aid package:* $18,516. *Average need-based loan:* $4427. *Average need-based gift aid:* $6167. *Average non-need-based aid:* $6458.

Applying *Options:* common application, electronic application, early admission, deferred entrance. *Application fee:* $25. *Required:* high school transcript, 1 letter of recommendation. *Required for some:* interview. *Recommended:* minimum 3.0 GPA. *Application deadline:* rolling (freshmen), rolling (transfers). *Notification:* continuous (freshmen), continuous (transfers).

Admissions Contact Ms. Julie King, Director of Admissions, Columbia College, 1301 Columbia College Drive, Columbia, SC 29203. *Phone:* 803-786-3871. *Toll-free phone:* 800-277-1301. *Fax:* 803-786-3674. *E-mail:* admissions@colacoll.edu.

COLUMBIA INTERNATIONAL UNIVERSITY
Columbia, South Carolina

- **Independent nondenominational** comprehensive, founded 1923
- **Calendar** semesters
- **Degrees** certificates, associate, bachelor's, master's, doctoral, first professional, and postbachelor's certificates
- **Suburban** 450-acre campus
- **Endowment** $6.4 million
- **Coed,** 622 undergraduate students, 91% full-time, 59% women, 41% men

Columbia International University (continued)
■ **Minimally difficult** entrance level, 87% of applicants were admitted

Undergraduates 566 full-time, 56 part-time. Students come from 39 states and territories, 15 other countries, 6% are from out of state, 2% African American, 1% Asian American or Pacific Islander, 1% Hispanic American, 0.3% Native American, 3% international, 10% transferred in, 59% live on campus. *Retention:* 75% of 2002 full-time freshmen returned.

Freshmen *Admission:* 200 applied, 173 admitted, 108 enrolled. *Average high school GPA:* 3.54. *Test scores:* SAT verbal scores over 500: 69%; SAT math scores over 500: 53%; ACT scores over 18: 94%; SAT verbal scores over 600: 25%; SAT math scores over 600: 19%; ACT scores over 24: 39%; SAT verbal scores over 700: 5%; SAT math scores over 700: 3%; ACT scores over 30: 3%.

Faculty *Total:* 43, 56% full-time, 42% with terminal degrees. *Student/faculty ratio:* 18:1.

Majors Ancient Near Eastern and biblical languages; biblical studies; communication/speech communication and rhetoric; education (multiple levels); general studies; humanities; intercultural/multicultural and diversity studies; music; Near and Middle Eastern studies; nursing (registered nurse training); pastoral studies/counseling; pre-theology/pre-ministerial studies; psychology; religious education; religious/sacred music; youth ministry.

Academic Programs *Special study options:* academic remediation for entering students, accelerated degree program, advanced placement credit, cooperative education, distance learning, double majors, independent study, internships, off-campus study, part-time degree program, study abroad, summer session for credit.

Library G. Allen Fleece Library with 99,052 titles, 425 serial subscriptions, 6,781 audiovisual materials, an OPAC.

Computers on Campus 42 computers available on campus for general student use. A campuswide network can be accessed. Internet access, online (class) registration, at least one staffed computer lab available.

Student Life *Housing options:* men-only, women-only, disabled students. Campus housing is university owned. Freshman campus housing is guaranteed. *Activities and organizations:* drama/theater group, student-run newspaper, radio station, choral group, Student Union, Student Senate, Student Missions Connection. *Campus security:* 24-hour emergency response devices and patrols, late-night transport/escort service. *Student services:* health clinic, personal/psychological counseling.

Athletics *Intercollegiate sports:* cheerleading M(s)/W(s). *Intramural sports:* basketball M/W, football M/W, soccer M/W, softball M/W, table tennis M/W, tennis M/W, ultimate Frisbee M/W, volleyball M/W.

Standardized Tests *Required:* SAT I or ACT (for admission).

Costs (2004–05) *Comprehensive fee:* $18,225 includes full-time tuition ($12,400), mandatory fees ($445), and room and board ($5380). Full-time tuition and fees vary according to course load. Part-time tuition: $511 per semester hour. Part-time tuition and fees vary according to course load. *College room only:* $2430. Room and board charges vary according to board plan. *Payment plan:* installment. *Waivers:* employees or children of employees.

Financial Aid Of all full-time matriculated undergraduates who enrolled in 2002, 527 applied for aid, 469 were judged to have need, 43 had their need fully met. 330 Federal Work-Study jobs (averaging $2671). In 2002, 24 non-need-based awards were made. *Average percent of need met:* 66%. *Average financial aid package:* $4074. *Average need-based loan:* $3618. *Average need-based gift aid:* $3635. *Average non-need-based aid:* $3610. *Average indebtedness upon graduation:* $12,050. *Financial aid deadline:* 3/15.

Applying *Options:* common application, electronic application, deferred entrance. *Application fee:* $35. *Required:* essay or personal statement, minimum 2.0 GPA, 4 letters of recommendation. *Required for some:* high school transcript, interview. *Application deadline:* rolling (freshmen). *Notification:* continuous (transfers).

Admissions Contact Columbia International University, PO Box 3122, Columbia, SC 29230-3122. *Phone:* 803-754-4100 Ext. 3024. *Toll-free phone:* 800-777-2227 Ext. 3024. *Fax:* 803-786-4041. *E-mail:* yesciu@ciu.edu.

CONVERSE COLLEGE
Spartanburg, South Carolina

- **Independent** comprehensive, founded 1889
- **Calendar** 4-2-4
- **Degrees** bachelor's, master's, and post-master's certificates
- **Urban** 70-acre campus
- **Endowment** $33.4 million
- **Women only,** 701 undergraduate students, 84% full-time
- **Moderately difficult** entrance level, 69% of applicants were admitted

Undergraduates 591 full-time, 110 part-time. Students come from 25 states and territories, 6 other countries, 25% are from out of state, 10% African American, 0.3% Asian American or Pacific Islander, 1% Hispanic American, 0.6% Native American, 2% international, 3% transferred in, 90% live on campus. *Retention:* 69% of 2002 full-time freshmen returned.

Freshmen *Admission:* 508 applied, 349 admitted, 179 enrolled. *Average high school GPA:* 3.60. *Test scores:* SAT verbal scores over 500: 80%; SAT math scores over 500: 72%; ACT scores over 18: 91%; SAT verbal scores over 600: 33%; SAT math scores over 600: 27%; ACT scores over 24: 48%; SAT verbal scores over 700: 6%; SAT math scores over 700: 4%; ACT scores over 30: 7%.

Faculty *Total:* 87, 83% full-time, 78% with terminal degrees. *Student/faculty ratio:* 14:1.

Majors Accounting; applied art; art; art history, criticism and conservation; art teacher education; art therapy; biochemistry; biology/biological sciences; business administration and management; chemistry; computer science; dramatic/theatre arts; economics; education; elementary education; English; fine/studio arts; French; history; interior design; international business/trade/commerce; kindergarten/preschool education; marketing/marketing management; mathematics; modern languages; music; music history, literature, and theory; music teacher education; piano and organ; political science and government; pre-dentistry studies; pre-law studies; pre-medical studies; pre-veterinary studies; psychology; religious studies; secondary education; sign language interpretation and translation; sociology; Spanish; special education; violin, viola, guitar and other stringed instruments; voice and opera.

Academic Programs *Special study options:* accelerated degree program, adult/continuing education programs, advanced placement credit, distance learning, double majors, English as a second language, honors programs, independent study, internships, off-campus study, part-time degree program, study abroad, summer session for credit. *ROTC:* Army (c).

Library Mickel Library with 129,411 titles, 1,467 serial subscriptions, 30,132 audiovisual materials, an OPAC, a Web page.

Computers on Campus 65 computers available on campus for general student use. A campuswide network can be accessed from student residence rooms and from off campus. Internet access, at least one staffed computer lab available.

Student Life *Housing:* on-campus residence required through senior year. *Options:* women-only. Campus housing is university owned. Freshman campus housing is guaranteed. *Activities and organizations:* drama/theater group, student-run newspaper, choral group, student government, student volunteer services, Student Christian Organization, Student Activities Committee, Athletic Association. *Campus security:* 24-hour emergency response devices and patrols, late-night transport/escort service, controlled dormitory access. *Student services:* health clinic, personal/psychological counseling, women's center.

Athletics Member NCAA. All Division II. *Intercollegiate sports:* basketball W(s), cheerleading W, cross-country running W(s), soccer W(s), tennis W(s), volleyball W(s). *Intramural sports:* archery W, basketball W, bowling W, equestrian sports W, fencing W, field hockey W, gymnastics W, soccer W, softball W, swimming W, tennis W, volleyball W, weight lifting W.

Standardized Tests *Required:* SAT I or ACT (for admission).

Costs (2003–04) *Comprehensive fee:* $24,710 includes full-time tuition ($18,915) and room and board ($5795). Full-time tuition and fees vary according to program. Part-time tuition and fees vary according to program. *Payment plan:* installment. *Waivers:* adult students, senior citizens, and employees or children of employees.

Financial Aid Of all full-time matriculated undergraduates who enrolled in 2003, 459 applied for aid, 416 were judged to have need, 169 had their need fully met. 151 Federal Work-Study jobs (averaging $1498). 60 state and other part-time jobs (averaging $1000). In 2003, 153 non-need-based awards were made. *Average percent of need met:* 88%. *Average financial aid package:* $16,521. *Average need-based loan:* $4120. *Average need-based gift aid:* $13,836. *Average non-need-based aid:* $16,158. *Average indebtedness upon graduation:* $18,036.

Applying *Options:* electronic application, early admission, early decision, early action, deferred entrance. *Application fee:* $35. *Required:* essay or personal statement, high school transcript, minimum 2.00 GPA. *Required for some:* 1 letter of recommendation. *Recommended:* minimum 2.50 GPA, interview. *Application deadlines:* 8/1 (freshmen), 7/1 (transfers). *Early decision:* 11/15. *Notification:* continuous until 8/15 (freshmen), 1/1 (early decision), 7/1 (early action), continuous until 8/15 (transfers).

Admissions Contact Director of Undergraduate Admissions, Converse College, 580 East Main Street, Spartanburg, SC 29302. *Phone:* 864-596-9040 Ext. 9746. *Toll-free phone:* 800-766-1125. *Fax:* 864-596-9225. *E-mail:* admissions@converse.edu.

■ *See page 1492 for a narrative description.*

ERSKINE COLLEGE
Due West, South Carolina

- **Independent** 4-year, founded 1839, affiliated with Associate Reformed Presbyterian Church

- **Calendar** 4-1-4
- **Degrees** bachelor's, master's, doctoral, and first professional
- **Rural** 85-acre campus
- **Endowment** $39.1 million
- **Coed,** 589 undergraduate students, 98% full-time, 58% women, 42% men
- **Moderately difficult** entrance level, 70% of applicants were admitted

Undergraduates 578 full-time, 11 part-time. Students come from 20 states and territories, 10 other countries, 26% are from out of state, 6% African American, 0.5% Asian American or Pacific Islander, 0.7% Hispanic American, 0.2% Native American, 2% international, 2% transferred in, 92% live on campus. *Retention:* 68% of 2002 full-time freshmen returned.

Freshmen *Admission:* 806 applied, 567 admitted, 176 enrolled. *Average high school GPA:* 3.59. *Test scores:* SAT verbal scores over 500: 77%; SAT math scores over 500: 79%; ACT scores over 18: 98%; SAT verbal scores over 600: 32%; SAT math scores over 600: 33%; ACT scores over 24: 61%; SAT verbal scores over 700: 10%; SAT math scores over 700: 6%; ACT scores over 30: 10%.

Faculty *Total:* 68, 56% full-time, 69% with terminal degrees. *Student/faculty ratio:* 12:1.

Majors American studies; art; athletic training; behavioral sciences; biblical studies; biological and physical sciences; biology/biological sciences; business administration and management; chemistry; clinical laboratory science/medical technology; elementary education; English; French; health science; history; kindergarten/preschool education; mathematics; music; music teacher education; natural sciences; philosophy; physical education teaching and coaching; physics; psychology; religious education; religious/sacred music; religious studies; social studies teacher education; Spanish; special education; sport and fitness administration.

Academic Programs *Special study options:* advanced placement credit, double majors, independent study, internships, off-campus study, part-time degree program, study abroad, summer session for credit. *Unusual degree programs:* 3-2 engineering with Clemson University, University of Tennessee, Knoxville; allied health programs with Medical University of South Carolina.

Library McCain Library with 352,292 titles, 683 serial subscriptions, 1,582 audiovisual materials, an OPAC, a Web page.

Computers on Campus 65 computers available on campus for general student use. A campuswide network can be accessed from student residence rooms and from off campus. Internet access, at least one staffed computer lab available. Computer purchase or lease plan available.

Student Life *Housing:* on-campus residence required through senior year. *Options:* men-only, women-only. Campus housing is university owned. Freshman campus housing is guaranteed. *Activities and organizations:* drama/theater group, student-run newspaper, radio station, choral group, literary societies, religious organizations, Student Government Organization, publications, honor societies. *Campus security:* 24-hour patrols, late-night transport/escort service, controlled dormitory access. *Student services:* health clinic, personal/psychological counseling.

Athletics Member NCAA. All Division II. *Intercollegiate sports:* baseball M(s), basketball M(s)/W(s), cross-country running M(s)/W(s), equestrian sports M(c)/W(c), soccer M(s)/W(s), softball W(s), tennis M(s)/W(s). *Intramural sports:* basketball M/W, football M/W, racquetball M/W, soccer M/W, softball M/W, tennis M/W, volleyball M/W.

Standardized Tests *Required:* SAT I or ACT (for admission). *Required for some:* SAT II: Subject Tests (for admission).

Costs (2003–04) *Comprehensive fee:* $23,166 includes full-time tuition ($16,312), mandatory fees ($1055), and room and board ($5799). Part-time tuition: $255 per semester hour. *Room and board:* Room and board charges vary according to board plan and housing facility. *Payment plan:* installment. *Waivers:* children of alumni and employees or children of employees.

Financial Aid Of all full-time matriculated undergraduates who enrolled in 2003, 550 applied for aid, 452 were judged to have need, 138 had their need fully met. 140 Federal Work-Study jobs (averaging $950). 60 state and other part-time jobs (averaging $950). In 2003, 103 non-need-based awards were made. *Average percent of need met:* 84%. *Average financial aid package:* $16,500. *Average need-based loan:* $3250. *Average need-based gift aid:* $8456. *Average non-need-based aid:* $8550. *Average indebtedness upon graduation:* $10,000.

Applying *Options:* electronic application. *Application fee:* $15. *Required:* high school transcript, 1 letter of recommendation. *Required for some:* essay or personal statement, interview. *Recommended:* interview. *Application deadline:* rolling (freshmen), rolling (transfers). *Notification:* continuous (freshmen), continuous (transfers).

Admissions Contact Mr. Bart Walker, Director of Admissions, Erskine College, PO Box 176, Due West, SC 29639. *Phone:* 864-379-8830. *Toll-free phone:* 800-241-8721. *Fax:* 864-379-8759. *E-mail:* admissions@erskine.edu.

FRANCIS MARION UNIVERSITY
Florence, South Carolina

- **State-supported** comprehensive, founded 1970
- **Calendar** semesters
- **Degrees** bachelor's and master's
- **Rural** 309-acre campus
- **Endowment** $200,000
- **Coed,** 3,097 undergraduate students, 93% full-time, 61% women, 39% men
- **Moderately difficult** entrance level, 76% of applicants were admitted

Undergraduates 2,869 full-time, 228 part-time. Students come from 31 states and territories, 29 other countries, 5% are from out of state, 35% African American, 1% Asian American or Pacific Islander, 0.6% Hispanic American, 0.5% Native American, 2% international, 7% transferred in, 38% live on campus. *Retention:* 65% of 2002 full-time freshmen returned.

Freshmen *Admission:* 2,057 applied, 1,565 admitted, 764 enrolled. *Average high school GPA:* 3.32. *Test scores:* SAT verbal scores over 500: 35%; SAT math scores over 500: 40%; ACT scores over 18: 68%; SAT verbal scores over 600: 6%; SAT math scores over 600: 7%; ACT scores over 24: 7%; SAT verbal scores over 700: 1%; SAT math scores over 700: 1%.

Faculty *Total:* 214, 78% full-time, 71% with terminal degrees. *Student/faculty ratio:* 15:1.

Majors Accounting; art; art teacher education; biology/biological sciences; business administration and management; chemistry; computer and information sciences; dramatic/theatre arts; early childhood education; economics; elementary education; English; finance; foreign languages and literatures; French; geography; history; international relations and affairs; liberal arts and sciences/liberal studies; management information systems; marketing/marketing management; mass communication/media; mathematics; physics; political science and government; pre-law studies; psychology; sociology; Spanish.

Academic Programs *Special study options:* accelerated degree program, adult/continuing education programs, advanced placement credit, cooperative education, double majors, honors programs, independent study, internships, off-campus study, part-time degree program, services for LD students, study abroad, summer session for credit. *ROTC:* Army (b). *Unusual degree programs:* 3-2 engineering with Clemson University; forestry with Clemson University.

Library James A. Rogers Library plus 1 other with 315,613 titles, 1,653 serial subscriptions, an OPAC, a Web page.

Computers on Campus 409 computers available on campus for general student use. A campuswide network can be accessed from student residence rooms and from off campus that provide access to blackboard. Internet access, online (class) registration, at least one staffed computer lab available.

Student Life *Housing options:* coed, men-only, women-only. Campus housing is university owned. Freshman applicants given priority for college housing. *Activities and organizations:* drama/theater group, student-run newspaper, choral group, Baptist Campus Ministries, education club, University Ambassadors, psychology club, Campus Outreach, national fraternities, national sororities. *Campus security:* 24-hour emergency response devices and patrols, late-night transport/escort service, controlled dormitory access. *Student services:* health clinic, personal/psychological counseling.

Athletics Member NCAA. All Division II. *Intercollegiate sports:* baseball M(s), basketball M(s)/W(s), cheerleading M/W, cross-country running M(s)/W(s), golf M(s), soccer M(s)/W(s), softball W(s), tennis M(s)/W(s), track and field M/W, volleyball W(s). *Intramural sports:* basketball M/W, bowling M/W, football M/W, golf M/W, racquetball M/W, soccer M, softball M/W, table tennis M/W, tennis M/W, track and field M/W, ultimate Frisbee M/W, volleyball M/W, water polo M/W.

Standardized Tests *Required:* SAT I or ACT (for admission).

Costs (2003–04) *Tuition:* state resident $4947 full-time, $247 per credit hour part-time; nonresident $9894 full-time, $495 per credit hour part-time. Part-time tuition and fees vary according to course load. *Required fees:* $135 full-time, $2 per credit hour part-time. *Room and board:* $4282; room only: $2092. Room and board charges vary according to board plan and housing facility. *Payment plan:* installment. *Waivers:* senior citizens and employees or children of employees.

Financial Aid Of all full-time matriculated undergraduates who enrolled in 2002, 2,057 applied for aid, 1,269 were judged to have need. 128 Federal Work-Study jobs (averaging $1335). *Average indebtedness upon graduation:* $22,311.

Applying *Options:* common application, electronic application, early admission, deferred entrance. *Application fee:* $30. *Required:* high school transcript. *Application deadline:* rolling (freshmen), rolling (transfers). *Notification:* continuous (freshmen).

Francis Marion University (continued)

Admissions Contact Ms. Drucilla S. Russell, Director of Admissions, Francis Marion University, PO Box 100547, Florence, SC 29501-0547. *Phone:* 843-661-1231. *Toll-free phone:* 800-368-7551. *Fax:* 843-661-4635. *E-mail:* admission@fmarion.edu.

■ See page 1648 for a narrative description.

FURMAN UNIVERSITY
Greenville, South Carolina

- **Independent** comprehensive, founded 1826
- **Calendar** 3-2-3
- **Degrees** bachelor's, master's, and postbachelor's certificates
- **Suburban** 750-acre campus
- **Endowment** $231.5 million
- **Coed,** 2,814 undergraduate students, 96% full-time, 57% women, 43% men
- **Very difficult** entrance level, 60% of applicants were admitted

Undergraduates 2,695 full-time, 119 part-time. Students come from 45 states and territories, 27 other countries, 70% are from out of state, 6% African American, 2% Asian American or Pacific Islander, 1% Hispanic American, 0.1% Native American, 1% international, 1% transferred in, 95% live on campus. *Retention:* 90% of 2002 full-time freshmen returned.

Freshmen *Admission:* 3,773 applied, 2,259 admitted, 687 enrolled. *Average high school GPA:* 3.80. *Test scores:* SAT verbal scores over 500: 97%; SAT math scores over 500: 98%; ACT scores over 18: 99%; SAT verbal scores over 600: 75%; SAT math scores over 600: 75%; ACT scores over 24: 90%; SAT verbal scores over 700: 23%; SAT math scores over 700: 19%; ACT scores over 30: 32%.

Faculty *Total:* 253, 85% full-time, 86% with terminal degrees. *Student/faculty ratio:* 12:1.

Majors Accounting; art; art history, criticism and conservation; Asian studies; biochemistry; biology/biological sciences; business administration and management; chemistry; communication/speech communication and rhetoric; computer science; dramatic/theatre arts; economics; education; elementary education; English; environmental studies; fine/studio arts; French; geology/earth science; German; history; kindergarten/preschool education; kinesiology and exercise science; Latin; mathematics; modern Greek; music; music teacher education; philosophy; physics; piano and organ; political science and government; pre-dentistry studies; pre-law studies; pre-medical studies; pre-veterinary studies; psychology; religious/sacred music; religious studies; secondary education; sociology; Spanish; special education; urban studies/affairs; voice and opera.

Academic Programs *Special study options:* accelerated degree program, adult/continuing education programs, advanced placement credit, double majors, independent study, internships, part-time degree program, services for LD students, student-designed majors, study abroad, summer session for credit. *ROTC:* Army (b). *Unusual degree programs:* 3-2 engineering with Georgia Institute of Technology, Clemson University, Auburn University, North Carolina State University, Washington University in St. Louis; forestry with Duke University.

Library James Buchanan Duke Library plus 2 others with 453,211 titles, 2,052 serial subscriptions, 5,644 audiovisual materials, an OPAC, a Web page.

Computers on Campus 340 computers available on campus for general student use. A campuswide network can be accessed from student residence rooms and from off campus. Internet access, online (class) registration, at least one staffed computer lab available.

Student Life *Housing:* on-campus residence required through senior year. *Options:* coed, men-only, women-only. Campus housing is university owned. Freshman campus housing is guaranteed. *Activities and organizations:* drama/theater group, student-run newspaper, radio and television station, choral group, marching band, Collegiate Educational Service Corps, Fellowship of Christian Athletes, Baptist Student Union, Student Activities Board, Furman Singers, national fraternities, national sororities. *Campus security:* 24-hour emergency response devices and patrols, student patrols, late-night transport/escort service, controlled dormitory access. *Student services:* health clinic, personal/psychological counseling.

Athletics Member NCAA. All Division I except football (Division I-AA). *Intercollegiate sports:* baseball M(s), basketball M(s)/W(s), cheerleading M/W, crew M(c)/W(c), cross-country running M(s)/W(s), fencing M(c)/W(c), golf M(s)/W(s), ice hockey M(c), lacrosse M(c), rugby M(c)/W(c), soccer M(s)/W(s), softball W(s), swimming M(c)/W(c), tennis M(s)/W(s), track and field M(s)/W(s), volleyball M(c)/W(s), weight lifting M(c)/W(c). *Intramural sports:* basketball M/W, bowling M/W, cross-country running M/W, football M/W, golf M/W, racquetball M/W, rock climbing M/W, soccer M/W, softball M/W, swimming M/W, tennis M/W, track and field M/W, ultimate Frisbee M/W, volleyball M/W.

Standardized Tests *Required:* SAT I or ACT (for admission). *Required for some:* SAT II: Subject Tests (for admission), SAT II: Writing Test (for admission).

Costs (2003–04) *Comprehensive fee:* $28,680 includes full-time tuition ($22,288), mandatory fees ($424), and room and board ($5968). Part-time tuition: $697 per credit hour. Part-time tuition and fees vary according to course load. *College room only:* $3288. Room and board charges vary according to board plan and housing facility. *Payment plan:* installment. *Waivers:* employees or children of employees.

Financial Aid Of all full-time matriculated undergraduates who enrolled in 2003, 1,434 applied for aid, 1,146 were judged to have need, 498 had their need fully met. 516 Federal Work-Study jobs (averaging $1449). In 2003, 651 non-need-based awards were made. *Average percent of need met:* 87%. *Average financial aid package:* $19,647. *Average need-based loan:* $2934. *Average need-based gift aid:* $16,061. *Average non-need-based aid:* $10,875. *Average indebtedness upon graduation:* $19,170. *Financial aid deadline:* 1/15.

Applying *Options:* common application, electronic application, early admission, early decision. *Application fee:* $40. *Required:* essay or personal statement, high school transcript. *Recommended:* minimum 3.0 GPA, 2 letters of recommendation. *Application deadlines:* 1/15 (freshmen), 6/1 (transfers). *Early decision:* 11/15. *Notification:* 3/15 (freshmen), 12/1 (early decision), 6/15 (transfers).

Admissions Contact Mr. David R. O'Cain, Director of Admissions, Furman University, 3300 Poinsett Highway, Greenville, SC 29613. *Phone:* 864-294-2034. *Fax:* 864-294-3127. *E-mail:* admissions@furman.edu.

ITT TECHNICAL INSTITUTE
Greenville, South Carolina

- **Proprietary** primarily 2-year, founded 1992, part of ITT Educational Services, Inc.
- **Calendar** quarters
- **Degrees** associate and bachelor's
- **Coed**
- **Minimally difficult** entrance level

Standardized Tests *Required:* Wonderlic aptitude test (for admission).

Costs (2003–04) *Tuition:* $347 per credit hour part-time.

Financial Aid Of all full-time matriculated undergraduates who enrolled in 2001, 3 Federal Work-Study jobs.

Applying *Options:* deferred entrance. *Application fee:* $100. *Required:* high school transcript, interview. *Recommended:* letters of recommendation.

Admissions Contact Ms. Pamela Carpenter, Director of Recruitment, ITT Technical Institute, One Marcus Drive, Building 4, Suite 402, Greenville, SC 29615. *Phone:* 864-288-0777. *Toll-free phone:* 800-932-4488. *Fax:* 864-297-0930.

LANDER UNIVERSITY
Greenwood, South Carolina

- **State-supported** comprehensive, founded 1872, part of South Carolina Commission on Higher Education
- **Calendar** semesters plus 3 summer sessions
- **Degrees** certificates, bachelor's, and master's
- **Small-town** 100-acre campus
- **Coed,** 2,634 undergraduate students, 87% full-time, 65% women, 35% men
- **Moderately difficult** entrance level, 81% of applicants were admitted

Undergraduates 2,281 full-time, 353 part-time. Students come from 29 states and territories, 19 other countries, 4% are from out of state, 21% African American, 0.5% Asian American or Pacific Islander, 1% Hispanic American, 0.1% Native American, 2% international, 9% transferred in, 37% live on campus. *Retention:* 64% of 2002 full-time freshmen returned.

Freshmen *Admission:* 1,668 applied, 1,351 admitted, 547 enrolled. *Average high school GPA:* 3.53. *Test scores:* SAT verbal scores over 500: 45%; SAT math scores over 500: 50%; ACT scores over 18: 81%; SAT verbal scores over 600: 8%; SAT math scores over 600: 10%; ACT scores over 24: 17%.

Faculty *Total:* 208, 67% full-time, 56% with terminal degrees. *Student/faculty ratio:* 15:1.

Majors Art; athletic training; biology/biological sciences; business administration and management; chemistry; computer and information sciences; early childhood education; elementary education; English; environmental science; history; interdisciplinary studies; kinesiology and exercise science; liberal arts and sciences/liberal studies; mathematics; music; nursing (registered nurse training); physical education teaching and coaching; political science and government; psychology; secondary education; sociology; Spanish; special education.

Academic Programs *Special study options:* academic remediation for entering students, accelerated degree program, adult/continuing education programs, advanced placement credit, cooperative education, distance learning, double majors, honors programs, independent study, internships, off-campus study, part-time degree program, services for LD students, student-designed majors, study abroad, summer session for credit. *ROTC:* Army (b). *Unusual degree programs:* 3-2 engineering with Clemson University.

Library Jackson Library with 170,091 titles, 692 serial subscriptions, 2,170 audiovisual materials, an OPAC, a Web page.

Computers on Campus 125 computers available on campus for general student use. A campuswide network can be accessed from student residence rooms and from off campus. Internet access, online (class) registration, at least one staffed computer lab available.

Student Life *Housing options:* coed, women-only. Campus housing is university owned and leased by the school. Freshman applicants given priority for college housing. *Activities and organizations:* drama/theater group, student-run newspaper, choral group, Students Promoting Intelligent Choices and Experiences (S.P.I.C.E.), Lander Association of Biological Science, national fraternities, national sororities. *Campus security:* 24-hour emergency response devices and patrols, late-night transport/escort service, controlled dormitory access. *Student services:* health clinic, personal/psychological counseling.

Athletics Member NCAA. All Division II. *Intercollegiate sports:* baseball M(s), basketball M(s)/W(s), cross-country running W(s), soccer M(s)/W(s), softball W(s), tennis M(s), volleyball W(s). *Intramural sports:* basketball M/W, bowling M/W, equestrian sports M/W, football M/W, golf M/W, soccer M/W, softball M/W, ultimate Frisbee M/W, volleyball M/W.

Standardized Tests *Required:* SAT I or ACT (for admission).

Costs (2003–04) *Tuition:* state resident $5400 full-time, $225 per semester hour part-time; nonresident $11,050 full-time, $462 per semester hour part-time. Full-time tuition and fees vary according to degree level. Part-time tuition and fees vary according to degree level. *Required fees:* $150 full-time. *Room and board:* $4946; room only: $3016. Room and board charges vary according to board plan and housing facility. *Payment plan:* installment. *Waivers:* senior citizens.

Financial Aid Of all full-time matriculated undergraduates who enrolled in 2002, 1,548 applied for aid, 929 were judged to have need, 481 had their need fully met. 189 Federal Work-Study jobs (averaging $1529). 348 state and other part-time jobs (averaging $2021). In 2002, 419 non-need-based awards were made. *Average percent of need met:* 68%. *Average financial aid package:* $5105. *Average need-based loan:* $3870. *Average need-based gift aid:* $1903. *Average non-need-based aid:* $3417. *Average indebtedness upon graduation:* $16,450.

Applying *Options:* common application, electronic application, early admission, deferred entrance. *Application fee:* $35. *Required:* high school transcript, 1 letter of recommendation. *Recommended:* interview. *Application deadline:* 8/1 (freshmen), rolling (transfers). *Notification:* continuous (freshmen), continuous (transfers).

Admissions Contact Mr. Jeffrey A. Constant, Assistant Director of Admissions, Lander University, Greenwood, SC 29649. *Phone:* 864-388-8307. *Toll-free phone:* 888-452-6337. *Fax:* 864-388-8125. *E-mail:* admissions@lander.edu.

■ See page 1844 for a narrative description.

LIMESTONE COLLEGE

Gaffney, South Carolina

- **Independent** 4-year, founded 1845
- **Calendar** semesters
- **Degrees** associate and bachelor's
- **Suburban** 115-acre campus with easy access to Charlotte
- **Endowment** $7.5 million
- **Coed,** 552 undergraduate students, 97% full-time, 48% women, 52% men
- **Minimally difficult** entrance level, 19% of applicants were admitted

Founded in 1845, Limestone is a private, coeducational liberal arts college that maintains a small student body and a well-qualified faculty, creating an atmosphere that assures intellectual, social, ethical, and physical development of students. With a student-faculty ratio of 12:1, Limestone provides the individual attention often lacking in larger institutions.

Undergraduates 537 full-time, 15 part-time. Students come from 22 states and territories, 39% are from out of state, 20% African American, 0.7% Asian American or Pacific Islander, 1% Hispanic American, 0.2% Native American, 0.9% international, 9% transferred in, 46% live on campus. *Retention:* 63% of 2002 full-time freshmen returned.

Freshmen *Admission:* 758 applied, 145 admitted, 136 enrolled. *Average high school GPA:* 2.90. *Test scores:* SAT verbal scores over 500: 36%; SAT math scores over 500: 38%; ACT scores over 18: 62%; SAT verbal scores over 600: 4%; SAT math scores over 600: 9%; ACT scores over 24: 14%.

Faculty *Total:* 61, 79% full-time, 57% with terminal degrees. *Student/faculty ratio:* 11:1.

Majors Accounting; art teacher education; athletic training; biology/biological sciences; biology teacher education; business administration and management; business/commerce; business/managerial economics; chemistry; computer programming; computer science; corrections; corrections and criminal justice related; criminal justice/safety; dramatic/theatre arts; education; elementary education; English; English/language arts teacher education; fine/studio arts; graphic design; health and physical education related; history; human resources development; information science/studies; jazz/jazz studies; liberal arts and sciences/liberal studies; marketing/marketing management; marriage and family therapy/counseling; mathematics; mathematics teacher education; music; music teacher education; physical education teaching and coaching; pre-dentistry studies; pre-law studies; pre-medical studies; pre-nursing studies; pre-pharmacy studies; pre-veterinary studies; psychology; social studies teacher education; social work; sport and fitness administration; web/multimedia management and webmaster.

Academic Programs *Special study options:* academic remediation for entering students, accelerated degree program, adult/continuing education programs, advanced placement credit, distance learning, double majors, honors programs, independent study, internships, part-time degree program, services for LD students, student-designed majors, summer session for credit. *ROTC:* Army (c).

Library A. J. Eastwood Library with 95,155 titles, 292 serial subscriptions, 2,049 audiovisual materials, an OPAC, a Web page.

Computers on Campus 63 computers available on campus for general student use. A campuswide network can be accessed from student residence rooms and from off campus that provide access to online (class) registration for internet classes only. Internet access, at least one staffed computer lab available.

Student Life *Housing:* on-campus residence required through junior year. *Options:* men-only, women-only. Campus housing is university owned. Freshman applicants given priority for college housing. *Activities and organizations:* drama/theater group, choral group, Fellowship of Christian Athletes, Student Government Association, Gospel Choir, KDK, Student Ambassadors. *Campus security:* 24-hour emergency response devices and patrols, late-night transport/escort service, controlled dormitory access. *Student services:* health clinic, personal/psychological counseling.

Athletics Member NCAA. All Division II. *Intercollegiate sports:* baseball M(s), basketball M(s)/W(s), cross-country running M(s)/W(s), golf M(s)/W(s), lacrosse M(s)/W(s), soccer M(s)/W(s), softball W(s), swimming W(s), tennis M(s)/W(s), volleyball W(s), wrestling M(s). *Intramural sports:* bowling M/W, cheerleading M/W, tennis M/W, ultimate Frisbee M/W.

Standardized Tests *Required:* SAT I or ACT (for admission).

Costs (2004–05) *Comprehensive fee:* $18,600 includes full-time tuition ($13,200) and room and board ($5400). Full-time tuition and fees vary according to course load and program. Part-time tuition: $550 per credit hour. Part-time tuition and fees vary according to program. *Payment plan:* installment. *Waivers:* employees or children of employees.

Financial Aid Of all full-time matriculated undergraduates who enrolled in 2002, 509 applied for aid, 435 were judged to have need, 94 had their need fully met. 74 Federal Work-Study jobs (averaging $2194). 47 state and other part-time jobs (averaging $1018). In 2002, 79 non-need-based awards were made. *Average percent of need met:* 65%. *Average financial aid package:* $9074. *Average need-based loan:* $3329. *Average need-based gift aid:* $6435. *Average non-need-based aid:* $8060. *Average indebtedness upon graduation:* $8612.

Applying *Options:* common application, electronic application. *Application fee:* $25. *Required:* high school transcript, minimum 2.0 GPA. *Recommended:* 2 letters of recommendation, interview. *Application deadline:* rolling (freshmen), rolling (transfers). *Notification:* continuous (freshmen), continuous (transfers).

Admissions Contact Ms. Debbie Borders, Admissions Office Manager, Limestone College, 1115 College Drive, Gaffney, SC 29340-3799. *Phone:* 864-488-4554. *Toll-free phone:* 800-795-7151 Ext. 554. *Fax:* 864-487-8706. *E-mail:* cphenicie@limestone.edu.

■ See page 1870 for a narrative description.

MEDICAL UNIVERSITY OF SOUTH CAROLINA

Charleston, South Carolina

- **State-supported** upper-level, founded 1824
- **Calendar** semesters
- **Degrees** bachelor's, master's, doctoral, first professional, and postbachelor's certificates
- **Urban** 61-acre campus
- **Endowment** $68.4 million
- **Coed,** 321 undergraduate students, 72% full-time, 82% women, 18% men
- **Very difficult** entrance level

Undergraduates 232 full-time, 89 part-time. Students come from 19 states and territories, 10% are from out of state, 16% African American, 2% Asian American or Pacific Islander, 0.3% Hispanic American, 0.9% Native American.

Faculty *Total:* 1,264, 87% full-time, 86% with terminal degrees. *Student/faculty ratio:* 12:1.

Medical University of South Carolina (continued)

Majors Health services administration; nursing (registered nurse training); perfusion technology.

Academic Programs *Special study options:* advanced placement credit, distance learning, independent study, internships, off-campus study, part-time degree program.

Library Medical University of South Carolina Library plus 1 other with 225,061 titles, 3,746 serial subscriptions, 1,570 audiovisual materials, an OPAC, a Web page.

Computers on Campus 200 computers available on campus for general student use. A campuswide network can be accessed from off campus. Internet access, at least one staffed computer lab available.

Student Life *Housing:* college housing not available. *Activities and organizations:* MUSC Student Government Association, Multicultural Group Advisory Board, Public Health Interest Group, International Association, Crisis Ministries. *Campus security:* 24-hour emergency response devices and patrols, late-night transport/escort service. *Student services:* health clinic, personal/psychological counseling.

Athletics *Intramural sports:* basketball M/W, softball M/W, volleyball M/W.

Costs (2003–04) *Tuition:* state resident $7608 full-time, $661 per credit hour part-time; nonresident $21,040 full-time, $1846 per credit hour part-time. Full-time tuition and fees vary according to program. Part-time tuition and fees vary according to program. Tuition state resident $7354 nursing full-time, $7860 health professions full-time; nonresident $20,138 nursing, $21942 health professions. *Required fees:* $674 full-time, $906 per term part-time. *Payment plan:* installment. *Waivers:* senior citizens and employees or children of employees.

Financial Aid Of all full-time matriculated undergraduates who enrolled in 2002, 216 applied for aid, 190 were judged to have need, 5 had their need fully met. *Average percent of need met:* 42%. *Average financial aid package:* $6863. *Average need-based loan:* $5759. *Average need-based gift aid:* $3661. *Average indebtedness upon graduation:* $25,454.

Applying *Options:* electronic application, deferred entrance. *Application fee:* $80. *Application deadline:* 8/25 (transfers).

Admissions Contact Mr. George W. Ohlandt, Director of Admissions, Medical University of South Carolina, PO Box 250203, Charleston, SC 29425. *Phone:* 843-792-3813. *Fax:* 843-792-6615. *E-mail:* oes-web@musc.edu.

MORRIS COLLEGE
Sumter, South Carolina

- **Independent** 4-year, founded 1908, affiliated with Baptist Educational and Missionary Convention of South Carolina
- **Calendar** semesters
- **Degree** bachelor's
- **Small-town** 34-acre campus
- **Endowment** $4.2 million
- **Coed,** 1,007 undergraduate students, 98% full-time, 62% women, 38% men
- **Minimally difficult** entrance level, 94% of applicants were admitted

Undergraduates 988 full-time, 19 part-time. Students come from 23 states and territories, 13% are from out of state, 100% African American, 2% transferred in, 72% live on campus. *Retention:* 57% of 2002 full-time freshmen returned.

Freshmen *Admission:* 1,778 applied, 1,677 admitted, 276 enrolled. *Average high school GPA:* 2.56.

Faculty *Total:* 63, 76% full-time, 59% with terminal degrees. *Student/faculty ratio:* 19:1.

Majors Biology/biological sciences; biology teacher education; broadcast journalism; business administration and management; business administration, management and operations related; community health services counseling; criminal justice/law enforcement administration; early childhood education; elementary education; English; English/language arts teacher education; entrepreneurship; history; journalism; liberal arts and sciences/liberal studies; mathematics; mathematics teacher education; parks, recreation and leisure; political science and government; religious education; social studies teacher education; sociology; theology.

Academic Programs *Special study options:* academic remediation for entering students, accelerated degree program, adult/continuing education programs, advanced placement credit, cooperative education, double majors, honors programs, internships, summer session for credit. *ROTC:* Army (b).

Library Richardson-Johnson Learning Resources Center with 101,296 titles, 395 serial subscriptions, 3,734 audiovisual materials, an OPAC.

Computers on Campus 202 computers available on campus for general student use. A campuswide network can be accessed from student residence rooms. Internet access, at least one staffed computer lab available.

Student Life *Housing options:* men-only, women-only. Campus housing is university owned. Freshman applicants given priority for college housing. *Activities and organizations:* drama/theater group, student-run newspaper, radio station, choral group, Student Government Association, New Emphasis on Nontraditional Students, Block "M" club, Students of South Carolina Educational Association, Baptist Student Union, national fraternities, national sororities. *Campus security:* 24-hour patrols, controlled dormitory access. *Student services:* health clinic, personal/psychological counseling.

Athletics Member NAIA. *Intercollegiate sports:* baseball M(s), basketball M(s)/W(s), cross-country running M(s)/W(s), golf M(s), softball W(s), tennis M(s)/W(s), track and field M(s)/W(s), volleyball W(s). *Intramural sports:* basketball M/W, football M/W, golf M/W, softball M/W, table tennis M/W, tennis M/W, volleyball M/W.

Standardized Tests *Required for some:* SAT I or ACT (for admission).

Costs (2003–04) *Comprehensive fee:* $10,974 includes full-time tuition ($7190), mandatory fees ($220), and room and board ($3564). Part-time tuition: $300 per credit hour. *Required fees:* $75 per term part-time. *Payment plan:* installment.

Financial Aid Of all full-time matriculated undergraduates who enrolled in 2003, 988 applied for aid, 980 were judged to have need, 45 had their need fully met. 400 Federal Work-Study jobs (averaging $1500). *Average percent of need met:* 83%. *Average financial aid package:* $11,000. *Average need-based loan:* $3500. *Average need-based gift aid:* $1500. *Average indebtedness upon graduation:* $15,000.

Applying *Options:* deferred entrance. *Application fee:* $10. *Required:* high school transcript, minimum 2.0 GPA, medical examination. *Application deadline:* rolling (freshmen), rolling (transfers).

Admissions Contact Ms. Deborah Calhoun, Director of Admissions and Records, Morris College, 100 West College Street, Sumter, SC 29150-3599. *Phone:* 803-934-3225. *Toll-free phone:* 866-853-1345. *Fax:* 803-773-8241.

NEWBERRY COLLEGE
Newberry, South Carolina

- **Independent Evangelical Lutheran** 4-year, founded 1856
- **Calendar** semesters
- **Degree** bachelor's
- **Small-town** 60-acre campus
- **Endowment** $14.0 million
- **Coed,** 744 undergraduate students, 96% full-time, 43% women, 57% men
- **Moderately difficult** entrance level, 70% of applicants were admitted

Newberry College has the only bachelor's-level veterinary technology program in the southeastern US, an innovative general honors program, a communications program with a television studio and a radio studio, a major in sports management, a professional writing and editing minor, exceptional teacher education and music programs, a beautiful campus, small classes, strong athletic programs, and a familial environment.

Undergraduates 714 full-time, 30 part-time. Students come from 26 states and territories, 6 other countries, 12% are from out of state, 26% African American, 0.3% Asian American or Pacific Islander, 0.8% Hispanic American, 0.3% Native American, 1% international, 8% transferred in, 78% live on campus. *Retention:* 66% of 2002 full-time freshmen returned.

Freshmen *Admission:* 1,057 applied, 744 admitted, 206 enrolled. *Average high school GPA:* 3.10. *Test scores:* SAT verbal scores over 500: 40%; SAT math scores over 500: 45%; ACT scores over 18: 60%; SAT verbal scores over 600: 6%; SAT math scores over 600: 10%; ACT scores over 24: 12%; SAT verbal scores over 700: 1%; SAT math scores over 700: 1%; ACT scores over 30: 1%.

Faculty *Total:* 67, 69% full-time, 49% with terminal degrees. *Student/faculty ratio:* 12:1.

Majors Art; athletic training; biology/biological sciences; business administration and management; chemistry; computer science; dramatic/theatre arts; education; elementary education; English; French; German; history; kindergarten/preschool education; mass communication/media; mathematics; music; music teacher education; philosophy; physical education teaching and coaching; piano and organ; political science and government; pre-dentistry studies; pre-law studies; pre-medical studies; pre-veterinary studies; psychology; religious/sacred music; religious studies; secondary education; sociology; Spanish; special education; speech and rhetoric; veterinary technology; voice and opera.

Academic Programs *Special study options:* adult/continuing education programs, advanced placement credit, cooperative education, double majors, honors programs, independent study, internships, part-time degree program, student-designed majors, study abroad, summer session for credit. *ROTC:* Army (c). *Unusual degree programs:* 3-2 engineering with Clemson University; forestry with Duke University.

Library Wessels Library with 77,460 titles, 399 serial subscriptions, 1,369 audiovisual materials, an OPAC, a Web page.

Computers on Campus 81 computers available on campus for general student use. A campuswide network can be accessed from student residence rooms and from off campus. Internet access, at least one staffed computer lab available.

Student Life *Housing:* on-campus residence required through junior year. *Options:* coed, men-only, women-only. Campus housing is university owned. Freshman campus housing is guaranteed. *Activities and organizations:* drama/theater group, student-run newspaper, radio and television station, choral group, marching band, Fellowship of Christian Athletes (FCA), Metoka Galeda (gospel choir and service group), Lutheran Student Movement (LSM), Baptist Student Union (BSU), Students Organized for Community Service (SOCS), national fraternities, national sororities. *Campus security:* 24-hour patrols. *Student services:* health clinic, personal/psychological counseling.

Athletics Member NCAA. All Division II. *Intercollegiate sports:* baseball M(s), basketball M(s)/W(s), cross-country running M(s)/W(s), football M(s), golf M(s)/W(s), soccer M(s)/W(s), softball W(s), tennis M(s)/W(s), volleyball W(s). *Intramural sports:* basketball M/W, football M.

Standardized Tests *Required:* SAT I or ACT (for admission).

Costs (2003–04) *Comprehensive fee:* $22,871 includes full-time tuition ($16,640), mandatory fees ($611), and room and board ($5620). Part-time tuition: $300 per credit hour. *College room only:* $2620. Room and board charges vary according to board plan and housing facility. *Payment plan:* installment. *Waivers:* employees or children of employees.

Financial Aid Of all full-time matriculated undergraduates who enrolled in 2002, 658 applied for aid, 591 were judged to have need, 188 had their need fully met. 52 Federal Work-Study jobs (averaging $804). 45 state and other part-time jobs (averaging $518). In 2002, 104 non-need-based awards were made. *Average percent of need met:* 79%. *Average financial aid package:* $13,886. *Average need-based loan:* $3866. *Average need-based gift aid:* $10,899. *Average non-need-based aid:* $11,851. *Average indebtedness upon graduation:* $13,477.

Applying *Options:* common application, electronic application, early admission, deferred entrance. *Application fee:* $30. *Required:* high school transcript, minimum 2.0 GPA. *Required for some:* essay or personal statement. *Recommended:* 2 letters of recommendation, interview. *Application deadline:* rolling (freshmen), rolling (transfers). *Notification:* continuous (freshmen), continuous (transfers).

Admissions Contact Mimi Meyer, Director of Admissions, Newberry College, 2100 College Street, Holland Hall, Newberry, SC 29108. *Phone:* 803-321-5127 Ext. 5127. *Toll-free phone:* 800-845-4955 Ext. 5127. *Fax:* 803-321-5138. *E-mail:* admissions@newberry.edu.

■ *See page 2064 for a narrative description.*

NORTH GREENVILLE COLLEGE
Tigerville, South Carolina

- **Independent Southern Baptist** 4-year, founded 1892
- **Calendar** semesters
- **Degrees** associate and bachelor's
- **Rural** 500-acre campus with easy access to Greenville
- **Endowment** $8.9 million
- **Coed,** 1,615 undergraduate students, 93% full-time, 49% women, 51% men
- **Minimally difficult** entrance level, 95% of applicants were admitted

Undergraduates 1,498 full-time, 117 part-time. Students come from 28 states and territories, 19 other countries, 19% are from out of state, 10% African American, 0.4% Asian American or Pacific Islander, 0.4% Hispanic American, 0.2% Native American, 2% international, 7% transferred in, 67% live on campus.

Freshmen *Admission:* 769 applied, 731 admitted, 408 enrolled. *Average high school GPA:* 3.80. *Test scores:* SAT verbal scores over 500: 61%; SAT math scores over 500: 62%; ACT scores over 18: 89%; SAT verbal scores over 600: 21%; SAT math scores over 600: 18%; ACT scores over 24: 30%; SAT verbal scores over 700: 2%; SAT math scores over 700: 1%; ACT scores over 30: 1%.

Faculty *Total:* 131, 53% full-time. *Student/faculty ratio:* 17:1.

Majors Accounting and business/management; ancient Near Eastern and biblical languages; art; biblical studies; biology/biological sciences; business administration and management; business/managerial economics; dramatic/theatre arts; elementary education; English; humanities; interdisciplinary studies; journalism; kindergarten/preschool education; liberal arts and sciences/liberal studies; mass communication/media; multi-/interdisciplinary studies related; music; music history, literature, and theory; music teacher education; pastoral studies/counseling; piano and organ; psychology; religious education; religious/sacred music; religious studies; sport and fitness administration; theatre/theatre arts management; theology; voice and opera.

Academic Programs *Special study options:* academic remediation for entering students, accelerated degree program, advanced placement credit, double majors, English as a second language, external degree program, freshman honors college, honors programs, independent study, internships, part-time degree program, services for LD students, student-designed majors, summer session for credit. *ROTC:* Army (c).

Library Hester Memorial Library with 47,000 titles, 536 serial subscriptions, 4,170 audiovisual materials, an OPAC, a Web page.

Computers on Campus 71 computers available on campus for general student use. A campuswide network can be accessed from student residence rooms and from off campus. Internet access, at least one staffed computer lab available.

Student Life *Housing:* on-campus residence required through sophomore year. *Options:* men-only, women-only. Campus housing is university owned. Freshman campus housing is guaranteed. *Activities and organizations:* drama/theater group, student-run newspaper, radio station, choral group, Baptist Student Union, Fellowship of Christians in Service, Fellowship of Christian Athletes, Black Student Fellowship, education club. *Campus security:* 24-hour emergency response devices and patrols, controlled dormitory access. *Student services:* health clinic, personal/psychological counseling.

Athletics Member NCCAA. *Intercollegiate sports:* baseball M(s), basketball M(s)/W(s), cheerleading M(s)/W(s), cross-country running M(s)/W(s), football M(s), golf M(s), soccer M(s)/W(s), softball W(s), tennis M(s)/W(s), volleyball W(s). *Intramural sports:* basketball M/W, bowling M/W, football M, golf M/W, skiing (downhill) M/W, softball M/W, table tennis M/W, tennis M/W, volleyball W, weight lifting M/W.

Standardized Tests *Required:* SAT I or ACT (for admission). *Required for some:* CPT. *Recommended:* CPT.

Costs (2003–04) *Comprehensive fee:* $14,580 includes full-time tuition ($9100), mandatory fees ($200), and room and board ($5280). Part-time tuition and fees vary according to course load. *Payment plan:* installment. *Waivers:* employees or children of employees.

Financial Aid Of all full-time matriculated undergraduates who enrolled in 2003, 173 Federal Work-Study jobs (averaging $1000). 76 state and other part-time jobs (averaging $1000). *Average indebtedness upon graduation:* $10,000.

Applying *Options:* electronic application, early admission, deferred entrance. *Application fee:* $25. *Required:* high school transcript. *Required for some:* interview. *Recommended:* minimum 2.0 GPA. *Application deadlines:* 8/18 (freshmen), 8/21 (transfers). *Notification:* continuous (freshmen), continuous until 8/21 (transfers).

Admissions Contact Mr. Buddy Freeman, Executive Director of Admissions, North Greenville College, PO Box 1872, Tigerville, SC 29688. *Phone:* 864-977-7052. *Toll-free phone:* 800-468-6642 Ext. 7001. *Fax:* 864-977-7177. *E-mail:* bfreeman@ngc.edu.

PRESBYTERIAN COLLEGE
Clinton, South Carolina

- **Independent** 4-year, founded 1880, affiliated with Presbyterian Church (U.S.A.)
- **Calendar** semesters
- **Degree** bachelor's
- **Small-town** 215-acre campus with easy access to Greenville—Spartanburg
- **Endowment** $72.2 million
- **Coed,** 1,175 undergraduate students
- **Very difficult** entrance level, 78% of applicants were admitted

Undergraduates Students come from 28 states and territories, 10 other countries, 39% are from out of state, 5% African American, 0.9% Asian American or Pacific Islander, 1% Hispanic American, 90% live on campus. *Retention:* 85% of 2002 full-time freshmen returned.

Freshmen *Admission:* 1,103 applied, 865 admitted. *Average high school GPA:* 3.39. *Test scores:* SAT verbal scores over 500: 86%; SAT math scores over 500: 84%; ACT scores over 18: 97%; SAT verbal scores over 600: 36%; SAT math scores over 600: 38%; ACT scores over 24: 49%; SAT verbal scores over 700: 5%; SAT math scores over 700: 4%; ACT scores over 30: 5%.

Faculty *Total:* 111, 71% full-time, 74% with terminal degrees. *Student/faculty ratio:* 13:1.

Majors Accounting; art; biology/biological sciences; business administration and management; chemistry; computer science; dramatic/theatre arts; economics; education; elementary education; English; French; German; history; kindergarten/preschool education; mathematics; modern languages; music; music teacher education; philosophy; physics; political science and government; pre-dentistry studies; pre-law studies; pre-medical studies; pre-veterinary studies; psychology; religious studies; social sciences; sociology; Spanish; special education.

Academic Programs *Special study options:* advanced placement credit, double majors, freshman honors college, honors programs, independent study, internships, off-campus study, part-time degree program, services for LD students, study abroad, summer session for credit. *ROTC:* Army (b). *Unusual degree programs:* 3-2 engineering with Auburn University, Clemson University, Mercer University, Vanderbilt University; forestry with Duke University.

Library James H. Thomason Library with 149,273 titles, 797 serial subscriptions, 7,204 audiovisual materials, an OPAC, a Web page.

Presbyterian College (continued)

Computers on Campus 130 computers available on campus for general student use. A campuswide network can be accessed from student residence rooms and from off campus. Internet access, online (class) registration, at least one staffed computer lab available.

Student Life *Housing:* on-campus residence required through senior year. *Options:* coed, men-only, women-only, disabled students. Campus housing is university owned. *Activities and organizations:* drama/theater group, student-run newspaper, radio station, choral group, student volunteer services, intramurals, Student Union Board, Fellowship of Christian Athletes, national fraternities, national sororities. *Campus security:* 24-hour emergency response devices and patrols, late-night transport/escort service, controlled dormitory access. *Student services:* health clinic, personal/psychological counseling.

Athletics Member NCAA. All Division II. *Intercollegiate sports:* baseball M(s), basketball M(s)/W(s), cross-country running M(s)/W(s), football M(s), golf M(s), riflery M/W, soccer M(s)/W(s), softball W(s), tennis M(s)/W(s), volleyball W(s). *Intramural sports:* basketball M/W, cross-country running M/W, football M/W, golf M/W, racquetball M/W, soccer M/W, softball M/W, swimming M/W, table tennis M/W, tennis M/W, volleyball M/W.

Standardized Tests *Required:* SAT I or ACT (for admission).

Costs (2003–04) *Comprehensive fee:* $25,921 includes full-time tuition ($18,360), mandatory fees ($1750), and room and board ($5811). Full-time tuition and fees vary according to program. Part-time tuition: $765 per semester hour. Part-time tuition and fees vary according to program. *College room only:* $2816. Room and board charges vary according to board plan and housing facility. *Payment plan:* installment. *Waivers:* senior citizens and employees or children of employees.

Financial Aid Of all full-time matriculated undergraduates who enrolled in 2003, 823 applied for aid, 707 were judged to have need, 227 had their need fully met. 206 Federal Work-Study jobs (averaging $910). 200 state and other part-time jobs (averaging $750). In 2003, 408 non-need-based awards were made. *Average percent of need met:* 83%. *Average financial aid package:* $19,217. *Average need-based loan:* $3800. *Average need-based gift aid:* $16,206. *Average non-need-based aid:* $10,178. *Average indebtedness upon graduation:* $14,018.

Applying *Options:* electronic application, early action, deferred entrance. *Application fee:* $30. *Required:* essay or personal statement, high school transcript, 1 letter of recommendation. *Recommended:* interview. *Application deadlines:* 4/1 (freshmen), 7/1 (transfers). *Notification:* continuous until 6/1 (freshmen), 1/31 (early action).

Admissions Contact Mr. Richard Dana Paul, Vice President of Enrollment and Dean of Admissions, Presbyterian College, South Broad Street, Clinton, SC 29325. *Phone:* 864-833-8229. *Toll-free phone:* 800-476-7272. *Fax:* 864-833-8481. *E-mail:* rdpaul@presby.edu.

■ *See page 2192 for a narrative description.*

SOUTH CAROLINA STATE UNIVERSITY
Orangeburg, South Carolina

- **State-supported** comprehensive, founded 1896, part of South Carolina Commission on Higher Education
- **Calendar** semesters
- **Degrees** bachelor's, master's, doctoral, post-master's, and postbachelor's certificates
- **Small-town** 160-acre campus
- **Endowment** $651,061
- **Coed,** 3,585 undergraduate students, 90% full-time, 58% women, 42% men
- **Minimally difficult** entrance level, 80% of applicants were admitted

Undergraduates 3,225 full-time, 360 part-time. Students come from 36 states and territories, 26 other countries, 20% are from out of state, 97% African American, 0.2% Asian American or Pacific Islander, 0.2% Hispanic American, 0.1% Native American, 0.1% international, 5% transferred in, 53% live on campus. *Retention:* 76% of 2002 full-time freshmen returned.

Freshmen *Admission:* 2,558 applied, 2,045 admitted, 810 enrolled. *Average high school GPA:* 2.91. *Test scores:* SAT verbal scores over 500: 17%; SAT math scores over 500: 23%; ACT scores over 18: 30%; SAT verbal scores over 600: 4%; SAT math scores over 600: 6%; ACT scores over 24: 2%; SAT verbal scores over 700: 1%; SAT math scores over 700: 1%.

Faculty *Total:* 220, 86% full-time, 76% with terminal degrees. *Student/faculty ratio:* 18:1.

Majors Accounting; administrative assistant and secretarial science; agricultural business and management; art teacher education; audiology and speech-language pathology; biology/biological sciences; business administration and management; business/managerial economics; business teacher education; chemistry; civil engineering technology; computer science; criminal justice/law enforcement administration; dramatic/theatre arts; economics; education; electrical, electronic and communications engineering technology; elementary education; English; family and consumer sciences/home economics teacher education; family and consumer sciences/human sciences; fashion merchandising; foods, nutrition, and wellness; French; health teacher education; history; industrial arts; industrial technology; kindergarten/preschool education; marketing/marketing management; mathematics; mechanical engineering/mechanical technology; music management and merchandising; music teacher education; nuclear engineering; nursing (registered nurse training); physical education teaching and coaching; physics; political science and government; pre-dentistry studies; pre-law studies; pre-medical studies; pre-veterinary studies; psychology; social work; sociology; Spanish; special education; trade and industrial teacher education.

Academic Programs *Special study options:* academic remediation for entering students, adult/continuing education programs, advanced placement credit, cooperative education, distance learning, honors programs, independent study, internships, off-campus study, part-time degree program, study abroad, summer session for credit. *ROTC:* Army (b), Air Force (c).

Library Miller F. Whittaker Library plus 1 other with 273,264 titles, 1,346 serial subscriptions, a Web page.

Computers on Campus 300 computers available on campus for general student use. A campuswide network can be accessed. Internet access, at least one staffed computer lab available.

Student Life *Housing options:* men-only, women-only. Campus housing is university owned. Freshman applicants given priority for college housing. *Activities and organizations:* drama/theater group, student-run newspaper, choral group, marching band, student government, Student Union Board, NAACP, national fraternities, national sororities. *Campus security:* 24-hour emergency response devices and patrols, late-night transport/escort service, controlled dormitory access. *Student services:* health clinic, personal/psychological counseling.

Athletics Member NCAA. All Division I except football (Division I-AA). *Intercollegiate sports:* basketball M(s)/W(s), cross-country running M(s)/W(s), golf M(s), softball W(s), tennis M(s)/W(s), track and field M(s)/W(s), volleyball W(s).

Standardized Tests *Required:* SAT I or ACT (for admission). *Recommended:* SAT II: Subject Tests (for admission).

Costs (2003–04) *Tuition:* state resident $5570 full-time; nonresident $10,850 full-time. *Required fees:* $185 full-time. *Room and board:* $4672; room only: $2826. Room and board charges vary according to board plan and housing facility. *Payment plan:* deferred payment. *Waivers:* senior citizens and employees or children of employees.

Financial Aid *Average percent of need met:* 56%. *Average indebtedness upon graduation:* $17,000.

Applying *Options:* common application, deferred entrance. *Application fee:* $25. *Required:* high school transcript, minimum 2.0 GPA. *Application deadlines:* 7/31 (freshmen), 7/31 (transfers). *Notification:* continuous (freshmen), continuous (transfers).

Admissions Contact Ms. Lillian Adderson, Director of Admissions, South Carolina State University, 300 College Street Northeast, Orangeburg, SC 29117-0001. *Phone:* 803-536-8408. *Toll-free phone:* 800-260-5956. *Fax:* 803-536-8990. *E-mail:* admissions@scsu.edu.

SOUTHERN METHODIST COLLEGE
Orangeburg, South Carolina

- **Independent religious** 4-year, founded 1956
- **Degrees** certificates, associate, and bachelor's
- **Coed**
- **Moderately difficult** entrance level

Faculty *Student/faculty ratio:* 8:1.

Standardized Tests *Recommended:* SAT I (for admission), ACT (for admission).

Costs (2003–04) *Comprehensive fee:* $9000 includes full-time tuition ($4200), mandatory fees ($600), and room and board ($4200).

Applying *Options:* early admission. *Application fee:* $25. *Required:* essay or personal statement, high school transcript, 3 letters of recommendation, interview, health certificate.

Admissions Contact Mr. Glenn Blank, Director of Admissions, Southern Methodist College, PO Box 1027, 541 Broughton Street, Orangeburg, SC 29116-1027. *Phone:* 803-534-7826.

SOUTHERN WESLEYAN UNIVERSITY
Central, South Carolina

- **Independent** comprehensive, founded 1906, affiliated with Wesleyan Church
- **Calendar** semesters

- **Degrees** associate, bachelor's, and master's
- **Small-town** 230-acre campus
- **Endowment** $2.2 million
- **Coed,** 1,965 undergraduate students, 93% full-time, 64% women, 36% men
- **Minimally difficult** entrance level, 68% of applicants were admitted

Undergraduates 1,819 full-time, 146 part-time. Students come from 24 states and territories, 5 other countries, 14% are from out of state, 32% African American, 0.4% Asian American or Pacific Islander, 1% Hispanic American, 0.7% Native American, 0.7% international, 3% transferred in, 14% live on campus. *Retention:* 70% of 2002 full-time freshmen returned.

Freshmen *Admission:* 516 applied, 350 admitted, 129 enrolled. *Average high school GPA:* 3.60. *Test scores:* SAT verbal scores over 500: 57%; SAT math scores over 500: 57%; ACT scores over 18: 60%; SAT verbal scores over 600: 19%; SAT math scores over 600: 18%; ACT scores over 24: 20%; SAT verbal scores over 700: 3%; SAT math scores over 700: 2%.

Faculty *Total:* 236, 20% full-time, 48% with terminal degrees. *Student/faculty ratio:* 15:1.

Majors Accounting; biology/biological sciences; business administration and management; business/commerce; chemistry; clinical laboratory science/medical technology; computer and information sciences; divinity/ministry; education; elementary education; English; health and physical education; history; human resources management; kindergarten/preschool education; mathematics; mathematics teacher education; music; music teacher education; parks, recreation and leisure; parks, recreation, and leisure related; physical education teaching and coaching; pre-medical studies; psychology; religious/sacred music; religious studies; science teacher education; social sciences; special education; special education (emotionally disturbed); special education (mentally retarded); special education (specific learning disabilities); sport and fitness administration; theology.

Academic Programs *Special study options:* academic remediation for entering students, accelerated degree program, adult/continuing education programs, advanced placement credit, cooperative education, double majors, freshman honors college, honors programs, independent study, internships, off-campus study, part-time degree program, services for LD students, student-designed majors, study abroad, summer session for credit. *ROTC:* Army (c), Air Force (c). *Unusual degree programs:* 3-2 cytotechnology with Medical University of South Carolina.

Library Rickman Library with 84,340 titles, 520 serial subscriptions, 3,291 audiovisual materials, an OPAC.

Computers on Campus 78 computers available on campus for general student use. A campuswide network can be accessed from student residence rooms and from off campus. Internet access, at least one staffed computer lab available.

Student Life *Housing:* on-campus residence required through senior year. *Options:* coed, men-only, women-only. Campus housing is university owned. Freshman campus housing is guaranteed. *Activities and organizations:* drama/theater group, choral group, Student Government Association, Student Missions Fellowship, Ministry Teams, Music Club, Council for Exceptional Children. *Campus security:* 24-hour emergency response devices, late night security patrols. *Student services:* health clinic, personal/psychological counseling.

Athletics Member NAIA, NCCAA. *Intercollegiate sports:* baseball M(s), basketball M(s)/W(s), cheerleading M(s)/W(s), cross-country running M(s)/W(s), golf M(s), soccer M(s)/W(s), softball W(s), volleyball W(s). *Intramural sports:* basketball M/W, football M/W, softball M/W, table tennis M/W, tennis M/W, ultimate Frisbee M/W, volleyball M/W.

Standardized Tests *Required:* SAT I or ACT (for admission).

Costs (2004–05) *Comprehensive fee:* $19,035 includes full-time tuition ($13,650), mandatory fees ($450), and room and board ($4935). Full-time tuition and fees vary according to course load, degree level, and program. Part-time tuition: $460 per credit hour. Part-time tuition and fees vary according to course load and degree level. *Required fees:* $162 per term part-time. *Room and board:* Room and board charges vary according to board plan and housing facility. *Payment plan:* installment. *Waivers:* senior citizens and employees or children of employees.

Financial Aid Of all full-time matriculated undergraduates who enrolled in 2003, 1,262 applied for aid, 1,070 were judged to have need, 167 had their need fully met. 137 Federal Work-Study jobs (averaging $1150). 60 state and other part-time jobs (averaging $1150). In 2003, 233 non-need-based awards were made. *Average percent of need met:* 58%. *Average financial aid package:* $7554. *Average need-based loan:* $3352. *Average need-based gift aid:* $5489. *Average non-need-based aid:* $5838. *Average indebtedness upon graduation:* $19,416.

Applying *Options:* early admission, deferred entrance. *Application fee:* $25. *Required:* high school transcript, minimum 2.0 GPA, 2 letters of recommendation, lifestyle statement. *Required for some:* interview. *Application deadlines:* 8/11 (freshmen), 8/10 (transfers). *Notification:* continuous (freshmen), continuous (transfers).

Admissions Contact Mr. Chad Peters, Director of Admissions, Southern Wesleyan University, PO Box 1020, 907 Wesleyan Drive, Central, SC 29630-1020. *Phone:* 864-644-5550 Ext. 5558. *Toll-free phone:* 800-289-1292 Ext. 5550. *Fax:* 864-644-5972. *E-mail:* admissions@swu.edu.

SOUTH UNIVERSITY

Columbia, South Carolina

- **Proprietary** primarily 2-year, founded 1935
- **Calendar** quarters
- **Degrees** certificates, associate, and bachelor's
- **Urban** 2-acre campus
- **Coed**
- **Minimally difficult** entrance level

Faculty *Student/faculty ratio:* 15:1.

Student Life *Campus security:* 24-hour emergency response devices.

Standardized Tests *Required:* SAT I or ACT (for admission).

Costs (2003–04) *Tuition:* $9285 full-time, $2695 per term part-time. Part-time tuition and fees vary according to course load. *Required fees:* $1200 full-time.

Applying *Options:* deferred entrance. *Application fee:* $25. *Required:* high school transcript, interview, admissions test.

Admissions Contact South University, 3810 Main Street, Columbia, SC 29203-6443. *Phone:* 803-799-9082. *Toll-free phone:* 866-629-3031. *Fax:* 803-799-9038.

■ *See page 2426 for a narrative description.*

UNIVERSITY OF SOUTH CAROLINA

Columbia, South Carolina

- **State-supported** university, founded 1801, part of University of South Carolina System
- **Calendar** semesters
- **Degrees** associate, bachelor's, master's, doctoral, first professional, post-master's, and postbachelor's certificates
- **Urban** 315-acre campus
- **Endowment** $312.5 million
- **Coed,** 17,133 undergraduate students, 87% full-time, 55% women, 45% men
- **Moderately difficult** entrance level, 64% of applicants were admitted

Undergraduates 14,884 full-time, 2,249 part-time. Students come from 54 states and territories, 72 other countries, 12% are from out of state, 15% African American, 3% Asian American or Pacific Islander, 2% Hispanic American, 0.3% Native American, 1% international, 7% transferred in, 46% live on campus. *Retention:* 84% of 2002 full-time freshmen returned.

Freshmen *Admission:* 12,817 applied, 8,260 admitted, 3,491 enrolled. *Average high school GPA:* 3.77. *Test scores:* SAT verbal scores over 500: 82%; SAT math scores over 500: 85%; ACT scores over 18: 99%; SAT verbal scores over 600: 35%; SAT math scores over 600: 39%; ACT scores over 24: 57%; SAT verbal scores over 700: 7%; SAT math scores over 700: 7%; ACT scores over 30: 11%.

Faculty *Total:* 1,461, 75% full-time, 76% with terminal degrees. *Student/faculty ratio:* 17:1.

Majors Accounting; advertising; African-American/Black studies; anthropology; art history, criticism and conservation; art teacher education; biology/biological sciences; broadcast journalism; business administration and management; business/managerial economics; chemical engineering; chemistry; civil engineering; classics and languages, literatures and linguistics; computer and information sciences; computer engineering; criminal justice/law enforcement administration; dramatic/theatre arts; economics; electrical, electronics and communications engineering; English; European studies; experimental psychology; finance; fine/studio arts; French; general retailing/wholesaling; geography; geology/earth science; geophysics and seismology; German; history; hospitality administration; insurance; international relations and affairs; Italian; journalism; kinesiology and exercise science; Latin American studies; liberal arts and sciences/liberal studies; management science; marine biology and biological oceanography; marketing/marketing management; mathematics; mechanical engineering; music; music teacher education; nursing (registered nurse training); office management; philosophy; physical education teaching and coaching; physics; political science and government; public relations/image management; real estate; religious studies; sociology; Spanish; sport and fitness administration; statistics; women's studies.

Academic Programs *Special study options:* accelerated degree program, adult/continuing education programs, advanced placement credit, cooperative education, distance learning, double majors, English as a second language, external degree program, freshman honors college, honors programs, independent study, internships, part-time degree program, services for LD students, student-designed majors, study abroad, summer session for credit. *ROTC:* Army (b), Air Force (b).

University of South Carolina (continued)

Library Thomas Cooper Library plus 7 others with 3.3 million titles, 21,836 serial subscriptions, 45,930 audiovisual materials, an OPAC, a Web page.

Computers on Campus 11000 computers available on campus for general student use. A campuswide network can be accessed from student residence rooms and from off campus. Internet access, online (class) registration, at least one staffed computer lab available.

Student Life *Housing:* on-campus residence required for freshman year. *Options:* coed, men-only, women-only, disabled students. Campus housing is university owned. Freshman campus housing is guaranteed. *Activities and organizations:* drama/theater group, student-run newspaper, radio station, choral group, marching band, Fellowship of Christian Athletes, Association of African-American Students, Baptist Student Union, Garnet Circle/Student Alumni, Fraternity Council, national fraternities, national sororities. *Campus security:* 24-hour emergency response devices and patrols, student patrols, late-night transport/escort service, controlled dormitory access, Division of Law Enforcement and Safety. *Student services:* health clinic, personal/psychological counseling, women's center.

Athletics Member NCAA. All Division I except football (Division I-A). *Intercollegiate sports:* baseball M(s), basketball M(s)/W(s), cross-country running W(s), equestrian sports W(s), golf M(s)/W(s), soccer M(s)/W(s), softball W(s), swimming M(s)/W(s), tennis M(s)/W(s), track and field M(s)/W(s), volleyball W(s). *Intramural sports:* badminton M/W, basketball M/W, bowling M/W, football M/W, golf M/W, racquetball M/W, soccer M/W, softball M/W, swimming M/W, table tennis M/W, tennis M/W, track and field M/W, volleyball M/W, weight lifting M(c)/W(c), wrestling M(c).

Standardized Tests *Required:* SAT I or ACT (for admission).

Costs (2003–04) *Tuition:* state resident $5548 full-time, $260 per credit hour part-time; nonresident $14,886 full-time, $677 per credit hour part-time. Full-time tuition and fees vary according to program and reciprocity agreements. *Required fees:* $200 full-time, $9 per credit hour part-time. *Room and board:* $5327; room only: $3040. Room and board charges vary according to board plan, housing facility, and location. *Payment plans:* installment, deferred payment. *Waivers:* senior citizens and employees or children of employees.

Financial Aid Of all full-time matriculated undergraduates who enrolled in 2002, 8,084 applied for aid, 6,189 were judged to have need, 1,903 had their need fully met. 948 Federal Work-Study jobs (averaging $1980). In 2002, 5970 non-need-based awards were made. *Average percent of need met:* 91%. *Average financial aid package:* $9371. *Average need-based loan:* $3962. *Average need-based gift aid:* $3060. *Average non-need-based aid:* $4037. *Average indebtedness upon graduation:* $16,105.

Applying *Options:* electronic application. *Application fee:* $40. *Required:* high school transcript, minimum 2.0 GPA. *Application deadlines:* 12/1 (freshmen), 6/1 (transfers). *Notification:* continuous until 10/1 (freshmen), continuous until 10/1 (transfers).

Admissions Contact Ms. Terry L. Davis, Director of Undergraduate Admissions, University of South Carolina, Columbia, SC 29208. *Phone:* 803-777-7700. *Toll-free phone:* 800-868-5872. *Fax:* 803-777-0101. *E-mail:* admissions-ugrad@sc.edu.

■ See page 2708 for a narrative description.

UNIVERSITY OF SOUTH CAROLINA AIKEN

Aiken, South Carolina

- **State-supported** comprehensive, founded 1961, part of University of South Carolina System
- **Calendar** semesters
- **Degrees** associate, bachelor's, and master's
- **Suburban** 453-acre campus with easy access to Columbia
- **Endowment** $10.3 million
- **Coed,** 3,247 undergraduate students, 72% full-time, 68% women, 32% men
- **Minimally difficult** entrance level, 68% of applicants were admitted

Undergraduates 2,329 full-time, 918 part-time. Students come from 37 states and territories, 23 other countries, 12% are from out of state, 23% African American, 0.9% Asian American or Pacific Islander, 1% Hispanic American, 0.4% Native American, 2% international, 10% transferred in, 12% live on campus. *Retention:* 68% of 2002 full-time freshmen returned.

Freshmen *Admission:* 1,336 applied, 907 admitted, 564 enrolled. *Average high school GPA:* 3.41. *Test scores:* SAT verbal scores over 500: 46%; SAT math scores over 500: 52%; ACT scores over 18: 74%; SAT verbal scores over 600: 10%; SAT math scores over 600: 12%; ACT scores over 24: 12%; SAT verbal scores over 700: 1%; SAT math scores over 700: 1%.

Faculty *Total:* 232, 61% full-time. *Student/faculty ratio:* 16:1.

Majors Applied mathematics; biology/biological sciences; business administration and management; chemistry; communication/speech communication and rhetoric; early childhood education; elementary education; English; fine/studio arts; history; kindergarten/preschool education; kinesiology and exercise science; liberal arts and sciences/liberal studies; nursing (registered nurse training); political science and government; psychology; secondary education; sociology; special education.

Academic Programs *Special study options:* accelerated degree program, adult/continuing education programs, advanced placement credit, cooperative education, double majors, English as a second language, honors programs, independent study, internships, off-campus study, part-time degree program, services for LD students, student-designed majors, study abroad, summer session for credit.

Library Gregg-Graniteville Library with 138,077 titles, 853 serial subscriptions, an OPAC, a Web page.

Computers on Campus 350 computers available on campus for general student use. A campuswide network can be accessed from student residence rooms that provide access to student email. Internet access, online (class) registration, at least one staffed computer lab available.

Student Life *Housing options:* coed. Campus housing is university owned. *Activities and organizations:* drama/theater group, student-run newspaper, choral group, student government, Pacesetters, Student Alumni Ambassadors, African-American Student Alliance, Pacer Union Board, national fraternities, national sororities. *Campus security:* 24-hour emergency response devices and patrols, late-night transport/escort service. *Student services:* health clinic, personal/psychological counseling.

Athletics Member NCAA. All Division II. *Intercollegiate sports:* baseball M(s), basketball M(s)/W(s), cheerleading M(s)/W(s), cross-country running W(s), golf M(s), soccer M(s)/W(s), softball W(s), tennis M(s)/W(s), volleyball W(s). *Intramural sports:* basketball M/W, football M/W, softball M/W, table tennis M/W, tennis M/W, weight lifting M.

Standardized Tests *Required:* SAT I or ACT (for admission).

Costs (2003–04) *Tuition:* state resident $4926 full-time, $215 per semester hour part-time; nonresident $10,066 full-time, $443 per semester hour part-time. Part-time tuition and fees vary according to course load. *Required fees:* $158 full-time, $5 per semester hour part-time. *Room and board:* $4400; room only: $2750. Room and board charges vary according to board plan. *Waivers:* senior citizens and employees or children of employees.

Applying *Options:* electronic application, early admission, deferred entrance. *Application fee:* $35. *Required:* high school transcript. *Application deadline:* 8/1 (freshmen), rolling (transfers). *Notification:* continuous (freshmen), continuous (transfers).

Admissions Contact Mr. Andrew Hendrix, Director of Admissions, University of South Carolina Aiken, 471 University Parkway, Aiken, SC 29801-6309. *Phone:* 803-648-6851 Ext. 3366. *Toll-free phone:* 888-WOW-USCA. *Fax:* 803-641-3727. *E-mail:* admit@usca.edu.

UNIVERSITY OF SOUTH CAROLINA BEAUFORT

Beaufort, South Carolina

- **State-supported** 4-year, founded 1959, part of University of South Carolina System
- **Calendar** semesters
- **Degrees** associate (offers courses for bachelor's degrees awarded by other University of South Carolina system schools)
- **Small-town** 5-acre campus
- **Coed**
- **Noncompetitive** entrance level

Faculty *Student/faculty ratio:* 17:1.

Student Life *Campus security:* 24-hour emergency response devices, evening security service.

Standardized Tests *Required:* SAT I or ACT (for admission).

Costs (2003–04) *Tuition:* state resident $4208 full-time, $167 per hour part-time; nonresident $10,112 full-time, $413 per hour part-time. *Required fees:* $8 per hour part-time.

Financial Aid Of all full-time matriculated undergraduates who enrolled in 2001, 30 Federal Work-Study jobs (averaging $3000).

Applying *Options:* electronic application, deferred entrance. *Application fee:* $40. *Required:* high school transcript. *Recommended:* minimum 2.0 GPA.

Admissions Contact Ms. Anita Folsom, Director of Admissions, University of South Carolina Beaufort, 801 Carteret Street, Beaufort, SC 29902. *Phone:* 843-521-4101 Ext. 4101. *Fax:* 843-521-4194. *E-mail:* tmfolsom@gwm.sc.edu.

University of South Carolina Spartanburg
Spartanburg, South Carolina

- **State-supported** comprehensive, founded 1967, part of University of South Carolina System
- **Calendar** semesters
- **Degrees** associate, bachelor's, and master's
- **Urban** 300-acre campus with easy access to Charlotte
- **Endowment** $2.2 million
- **Coed,** 4,397 undergraduate students, 78% full-time, 65% women, 35% men
- **Moderately difficult** entrance level, 49% of applicants were admitted

Undergraduates 3,445 full-time, 952 part-time. Students come from 34 states and territories, 33 other countries, 5% are from out of state, 26% African American, 3% Asian American or Pacific Islander, 2% Hispanic American, 0.3% Native American, 2% international, 14% transferred in, 10% live on campus. *Retention:* 63% of 2002 full-time freshmen returned.

Freshmen *Admission:* 1,904 applied, 938 admitted, 701 enrolled. *Average high school GPA:* 3.46. *Test scores:* SAT verbal scores over 500: 45%; SAT math scores over 500: 47%; ACT scores over 18: 96%; SAT verbal scores over 600: 10%; SAT math scores over 600: 9%; ACT scores over 24: 14%; SAT verbal scores over 700: 1%; SAT math scores over 700: 1%.

Faculty *Total:* 340, 53% full-time. *Student/faculty ratio:* 17:1.

Majors Biology/biological sciences; business administration and management; chemistry; communication/speech communication and rhetoric; computer and information sciences; criminal justice/law enforcement administration; elementary education; English; French; history; interdisciplinary studies; kindergarten/preschool education; mathematics; nursing (registered nurse training); physical education teaching and coaching; political science and government; psychology; secondary education; sociology; Spanish.

Academic Programs *Special study options:* academic remediation for entering students, accelerated degree program, adult/continuing education programs, advanced placement credit, cooperative education, distance learning, double majors, independent study, internships, off-campus study, part-time degree program, services for LD students, student-designed majors, study abroad, summer session for credit. *ROTC:* Army (c).

Library University of South Carolina Spartanburg Library with 156,558 titles, 3,151 serial subscriptions, 11,119 audiovisual materials, an OPAC, a Web page.

Computers on Campus 254 computers available on campus for general student use. A campuswide network can be accessed from student residence rooms and from off campus. Internet access, online (class) registration, at least one staffed computer lab available.

Student Life *Housing options:* coed. Campus housing is university owned. *Activities and organizations:* drama/theater group, student-run newspaper, choral group, African-American Association, Campus Activity Board, Student Nurses Association, Student Government Association, Association for the Education of Young Children, national fraternities, national sororities. *Campus security:* 24-hour emergency response devices and patrols, late-night transport/escort service, campus security cameras. *Student services:* health clinic, personal/psychological counseling, women's center.

Athletics Member NCAA. All Division II. *Intercollegiate sports:* baseball M(s), basketball M(s)/W(s), cross-country running M(s)/W(s), soccer M(s)/W(s), softball W(s), tennis M(s)/W(s), volleyball W(s). *Intramural sports:* basketball M/W, football M/W, golf M/W, soccer M/W, softball M/W, table tennis M/W, tennis M/W, track and field M/W, volleyball M/W.

Standardized Tests *Required:* SAT I or ACT (for admission).

Costs (2003–04) *Tuition:* state resident $5310 full-time, $233 per hour part-time; nonresident $10,936 full-time, $481 per hour part-time. Part-time tuition and fees vary according to course load. *Required fees:* $276 full-time, $15 per hour part-time, $25 per term part-time. *Room and board:* $4310; room only: $2900. Room and board charges vary according to board plan. *Payment plan:* deferred payment.

Financial Aid Of all full-time matriculated undergraduates who enrolled in 2002, 2,415 applied for aid, 1,959 were judged to have need, 248 had their need fully met. 110 Federal Work-Study jobs (averaging $1399). 255 state and other part-time jobs (averaging $1198). In 2002, 125 non-need-based awards were made. *Average percent of need met:* 20%. *Average financial aid package:* $6148. *Average need-based loan:* $3352. *Average need-based gift aid:* $3298. *Average non-need-based aid:* $4203. *Average indebtedness upon graduation:* $15,779.

Applying *Options:* electronic application, deferred entrance. *Application fee:* $35. *Required:* minimum 2.0 GPA. *Notification:* continuous (freshmen), continuous (transfers).

Admissions Contact Ms. Donette Stewart, Director of Admissions, University of South Carolina Spartanburg, 800 University Way, Spartanburg, SC 29303. *Phone:* 864-503-5280. *Toll-free phone:* 800-277-8727. *Fax:* 864-503-5727. *E-mail:* dstawart@uscs.edu.

Voorhees College
Denmark, South Carolina

- **Independent Episcopal** 4-year, founded 1897
- **Calendar** semesters
- **Degree** bachelor's
- **Rural** 350-acre campus
- **Endowment** $5.0 million
- **Coed,** 847 undergraduate students, 95% full-time, 65% women, 35% men
- **Moderately difficult** entrance level, 41% of applicants were admitted

Founded in 1897, Voorhees was the first historically black institution in South Carolina to achieve full accreditation by the Southern Association of Colleges and Schools. It is a small liberal arts college with a family-like atmosphere and a caring faculty, 70 percent of which hold doctorate degrees.

Undergraduates 807 full-time, 40 part-time. Students come from 18 states and territories, 5 other countries, 95% African American, 4% international, 5% transferred in, 85% live on campus. *Retention:* 58% of 2002 full-time freshmen returned.

Freshmen *Admission:* 2,624 applied, 1,066 admitted, 156 enrolled. *Average high school GPA:* 2.00. *Test scores:* SAT verbal scores over 500: 16%; SAT math scores over 500: 13%.

Faculty *Total:* 64, 58% full-time, 36% with terminal degrees. *Student/faculty ratio:* 20:1.

Majors Accounting; biology/biological sciences; business administration and management; chemistry; computer science; criminal justice/law enforcement administration; education; elementary education; English; kindergarten/preschool education; kinesiology and exercise science; mathematics; physical education teaching and coaching; political science and government; sociology; therapeutic recreation.

Academic Programs *Special study options:* academic remediation for entering students, adult/continuing education programs, advanced placement credit, cooperative education, double majors, honors programs, internships, part-time degree program, summer session for credit. *ROTC:* Army (c).

Library Wright-Potts Library with 107,260 titles, 408 serial subscriptions, 1,172 audiovisual materials, an OPAC, a Web page.

Computers on Campus 300 computers available on campus for general student use. A campuswide network can be accessed from student residence rooms and from off campus. Internet access, at least one staffed computer lab available.

Student Life *Housing:* on-campus residence required through sophomore year. *Options:* Campus housing is university owned. Freshman campus housing is guaranteed. *Activities and organizations:* drama/theater group, student-run newspaper, choral group, White Rose, Elizabeth Evelyn Wright Culture Club, Panhellenic Council, national fraternities, national sororities. *Campus security:* 24-hour emergency response devices and patrols, student patrols, late-night transport/escort service. *Student services:* health clinic, personal/psychological counseling.

Athletics Member NAIA. *Intercollegiate sports:* baseball M(s), basketball M(s)/W(s), cross-country running M(s)/W(s), softball W(s), track and field M(s)/W(s), volleyball W(s). *Intramural sports:* basketball M/W, table tennis M/W, volleyball M/W.

Standardized Tests *Required:* SAT I or ACT (for admission).

Costs (2004–05) *Comprehensive fee:* $11,848 includes full-time tuition ($7106), mandatory fees ($170), and room and board ($4572). Part-time tuition: $242 per credit hour. *College room only:* $1904.

Financial Aid Of all full-time matriculated undergraduates who enrolled in 2003, 823 applied for aid, 805 were judged to have need, 55 had their need fully met. 263 Federal Work-Study jobs (averaging $2000). 1 state and other part-time job (averaging $1334). In 2003, 34 non-need-based awards were made. *Average percent of need met:* 55%. *Average financial aid package:* $7947. *Average need-based loan:* $2965. *Average need-based gift aid:* $5188. *Average non-need-based aid:* $8089. *Average indebtedness upon graduation:* $13,283.

Applying *Options:* common application, electronic application, deferred entrance. *Application fee:* $25. *Required:* high school transcript, minimum 2.0 GPA. *Required for some:* high school transcript, interview. *Application deadline:* rolling (freshmen), rolling (transfers).

Admissions Contact Mr. Benjamin O. Watson, Assistant Director, Admission and Recruitment, Voorhees College, Halmi Hall, PO Box 678, Denmark, SC 29042. *Phone:* 803-703-7124. *Toll-free phone:* 800-446-6250. *Fax:* 803-793-1117. *E-mail:* bwatson@voorhees.edu.

■ *See page 2772 for a narrative description.*

WINTHROP UNIVERSITY

Rock Hill, South Carolina

- **State-supported** comprehensive, founded 1886, part of South Carolina Commission on Higher Education
- **Calendar** semesters
- **Degrees** bachelor's and master's
- **Suburban** 418-acre campus with easy access to Charlotte
- **Endowment** $693,815
- **Coed,** 5,161 undergraduate students, 89% full-time, 70% women, 30% men
- **Moderately difficult** entrance level, 66% of applicants were admitted

Undergraduates 4,597 full-time, 564 part-time. Students come from 41 states and territories, 30 other countries, 12% are from out of state, 27% African American, 1% Asian American or Pacific Islander, 1% Hispanic American, 0.4% Native American, 2% international, 3% transferred in, 48% live on campus. *Retention:* 78% of 2002 full-time freshmen returned.

Freshmen *Admission:* 3,965 applied, 2,632 admitted, 1,074 enrolled. *Average high school GPA:* 3.63. *Test scores:* SAT verbal scores over 500: 67%; SAT math scores over 500: 67%; ACT scores over 18: 96%; SAT verbal scores over 600: 22%; SAT math scores over 600: 19%; ACT scores over 24: 30%; SAT verbal scores over 700: 3%; SAT math scores over 700: 2%; ACT scores over 30: 2%.

Faculty *Total:* 486, 54% full-time, 53% with terminal degrees. *Student/faculty ratio:* 16:1.

Majors Art; art history, criticism and conservation; biology/biological sciences; business administration and management; business teacher education; chemistry; clinical laboratory science/medical technology; communication disorders; computer science; dance; dramatic/theatre arts; elementary education; English; family and consumer sciences/home economics teacher education; foods, nutrition, and wellness; history; kindergarten/preschool education; mass communication/media; mathematics; modern languages; music; music teacher education; philosophy; physical education teaching and coaching; political science and government; psychology; religious studies; social work; sociology; special education; sport and fitness administration; technical and business writing.

Academic Programs *Special study options:* adult/continuing education programs, advanced placement credit, cooperative education, distance learning, double majors, honors programs, independent study, internships, off-campus study, part-time degree program, services for LD students, study abroad, summer session for credit.

Library Dacus Library with 424,681 titles, 1,856 serial subscriptions, 2,555 audiovisual materials, an OPAC, a Web page.

Computers on Campus 250 computers available on campus for general student use. A campuswide network can be accessed from student residence rooms and from off campus. Internet access, at least one staffed computer lab available.

Student Life *Housing options:* coed, men-only, women-only. Campus housing is university owned. Freshman campus housing is guaranteed. *Activities and organizations:* drama/theater group, student-run newspaper, radio station, choral group, Ebonites, Greek organizations, campus ministries, student government association, Dinkins Student Union, national fraternities, national sororities. *Campus security:* 24-hour emergency response devices and patrols, late-night transport/escort service. *Student services:* health clinic, personal/psychological counseling.

Athletics Member NCAA. All Division I. *Intercollegiate sports:* baseball M(s), basketball M(s)/W(s), cheerleading M(c)/W(c), cross-country running M(s)/W(s), fencing M(c)/W(c), golf M(s)/W(s), lacrosse M(c)/W(c), rugby M(c), soccer M(s), softball W(s), tennis M(s)/W(s), track and field M(s)/W(s), volleyball W(s). *Intramural sports:* badminton M/W, basketball M/W, cross-country running M/W, equestrian sports M(c)/W(c), football M/W, golf M/W, racquetball M/W, soccer M/W, softball M/W, swimming M/W, table tennis M/W, tennis M/W, ultimate Frisbee M/W, volleyball M/W, water polo M/W, weight lifting M/W.

Standardized Tests *Required:* SAT I or ACT (for admission).

Costs (2003–04) *Tuition:* state resident $6652 full-time, $277 per semester hour part-time; nonresident $12,258 full-time, $511 per semester hour part-time. *Required fees:* $20 full-time, $10 per term part-time. *Room and board:* $4630; room only: $2770.

Financial Aid Of all full-time matriculated undergraduates who enrolled in 2003, 3,473 applied for aid, 2,779 were judged to have need, 626 had their need fully met. 250 Federal Work-Study jobs (averaging $800). In 2003, 565 non-need-based awards were made. *Average percent of need met:* 68%. *Average financial aid package:* $7917. *Average need-based loan:* $4740. *Average need-based gift aid:* $4783. *Average non-need-based aid:* $5070. *Average indebtedness upon graduation:* $17,482.

Applying *Options:* deferred entrance. *Application fee:* $40. *Required:* high school transcript, 1 letter of recommendation. *Recommended:* essay or personal statement. *Application deadline:* 5/1 (freshmen). *Notification:* continuous (freshmen), continuous (transfers).

Admissions Contact Ms. Deborah Barber, Director of Admissions, Winthrop University, Stewart House, Rock Hill, SC 29733. *Phone:* 803-323-2191. *Toll-free phone:* 800-763-0230. *Fax:* 803-323-2137. *E-mail:* admissions@winthrop.edu.

■ See page 2870 for a narrative description.

WOFFORD COLLEGE

Spartanburg, South Carolina

- **Independent** 4-year, founded 1854, affiliated with United Methodist Church
- **Calendar** 4-1-4
- **Degree** bachelor's
- **Urban** 140-acre campus with easy access to Charlotte
- **Endowment** $101.4 million
- **Coed,** 1,132 undergraduate students, 99% full-time, 51% women, 49% men
- **Very difficult** entrance level, 80% of applicants were admitted

Undergraduates 1,119 full-time, 13 part-time. Students come from 31 states and territories, 6 other countries, 35% are from out of state, 8% African American, 2% Asian American or Pacific Islander, 1% Hispanic American, 0.1% Native American, 0.5% international, 2% transferred in, 88% live on campus. *Retention:* 93% of 2002 full-time freshmen returned.

Freshmen *Admission:* 1,317 applied, 1,053 admitted, 330 enrolled. *Test scores:* SAT verbal scores over 500: 93%; SAT math scores over 500: 98%; ACT scores over 18: 100%; SAT verbal scores over 600: 62%; SAT math scores over 600: 68%; ACT scores over 24: 64%; SAT verbal scores over 700: 13%; SAT math scores over 700: 17%; ACT scores over 30: 5%.

Faculty *Total:* 110, 75% full-time, 83% with terminal degrees. *Student/faculty ratio:* 12:1.

Majors Accounting; art history, criticism and conservation; biology/biological sciences; business/managerial economics; chemistry; computer science; creative writing; dramatic/theatre arts; economics; English; finance; French; German; history; humanities; international business/trade/commerce; international relations and affairs; mathematics; neuroscience; philosophy; physics; political science and government; pre-dentistry studies; pre-law studies; pre-medical studies; pre-veterinary studies; psychology; religious studies; sociology; Spanish.

Academic Programs *Special study options:* accelerated degree program, advanced placement credit, double majors, independent study, internships, off-campus study, part-time degree program, student-designed majors, study abroad, summer session for credit. *ROTC:* Army (b). *Unusual degree programs:* 3-2 engineering with Clemson University, Columbia University.

Library Sandor Teszler Library with 209,084 titles, 551 serial subscriptions, 3,602 audiovisual materials, an OPAC.

Computers on Campus 43 computers available on campus for general student use. A campuswide network can be accessed from student residence rooms and from off campus. Internet access, at least one staffed computer lab available.

Student Life *Housing:* on-campus residence required through senior year. *Options:* coed, men-only, women-only. Campus housing is university owned. Freshman applicants given priority for college housing. *Activities and organizations:* drama/theater group, student-run newspaper, choral group, performing arts groups, Twin Towers student volunteers, Fellowship of Christian Athletes, national fraternities, national sororities. *Campus security:* 24-hour emergency response devices and patrols, late-night transport/escort service, controlled dormitory access. *Student services:* health clinic, personal/psychological counseling.

Athletics Member NCAA. All Division I except football (Division I-AA). *Intercollegiate sports:* baseball M(s), basketball M(s)/W(s), cross-country running M(s)/W(s), fencing M(c)/W(c), golf M(s)/W(s), riflery M/W, soccer M(s)/W(s), tennis M(s)/W(s), track and field M(s)/W(s), volleyball W(s). *Intramural sports:* basketball M/W, bowling M/W, football M/W, racquetball M/W, soccer M/W, softball M/W, tennis M/W, volleyball M/W, weight lifting M/W.

Standardized Tests *Required:* SAT I or ACT (for admission). *Recommended:* SAT II: Writing Test (for admission).

Costs (2003–04) *Comprehensive fee:* $26,710 includes full-time tuition ($19,815), mandatory fees ($795), and room and board ($6100). Part-time tuition: $740 per hour. *College room only:* $3280. *Payment plan:* installment. *Waivers:* employees or children of employees.

Financial Aid Of all full-time matriculated undergraduates who enrolled in 2003, 720 applied for aid, 590 were judged to have need, 294 had their need fully met. In 2003, 236 non-need-based awards were made. *Average percent of need met:* 88%. *Average financial aid package:* $20,014. *Average need-based loan:* $3890. *Average need-based gift aid:* $14,581. *Average non-need-based aid:* $8268. *Average indebtedness upon graduation:* $12,281.

Applying *Options:* common application, electronic application, early admission, early decision, deferred entrance. *Application fee:* $40. *Required:* essay or personal statement, high school transcript. *Recommended:* 2 letters of recommendation, interview. *Application deadline:* 2/1 (freshmen), rolling (transfers). *Early decision:* 11/15. *Notification:* 3/15 (freshmen), 12/1 (early decision), continuous (transfers).

Admissions Contact Mr. Brand Stille, Director of Admissions, Wofford College, 429 North Church Street, Spartanburg, SC 29303-3663. *Phone:* 864-597-4130. *Fax:* 864-597-4147. *E-mail:* admissions@wofford.edu.

SOUTH DAKOTA

AUGUSTANA COLLEGE

Sioux Falls, South Dakota

- **Independent** comprehensive, founded 1860, affiliated with Evangelical Lutheran Church in America
- **Calendar** 4-1-4
- **Degrees** bachelor's and master's
- **Urban** 100-acre campus
- **Endowment** $26.0 million
- **Coed,** 1,810 undergraduate students, 93% full-time, 63% women, 37% men
- **Moderately difficult** entrance level, 79% of applicants were admitted

Undergraduates 1,686 full-time, 124 part-time. Students come from 35 states and territories, 12 other countries, 55% are from out of state, 0.8% African American, 0.7% Asian American or Pacific Islander, 0.5% Hispanic American, 0.3% Native American, 2% international, 5% transferred in, 68% live on campus. *Retention:* 76% of 2001 full-time freshmen returned.

Freshmen *Admission:* 1,692 applied, 1,338 admitted, 438 enrolled. *Average high school GPA:* 3.60. *Test scores:* SAT verbal scores over 500: 88%; SAT math scores over 500: 88%; ACT scores over 18: 100%; SAT verbal scores over 600: 57%; SAT math scores over 600: 46%; ACT scores over 24: 70%; SAT verbal scores over 700: 19%; SAT math scores over 700: 15%; ACT scores over 30: 18%.

Faculty *Total:* 166, 64% full-time, 60% with terminal degrees. *Student/faculty ratio:* 13:1.

Majors Accounting; art; art teacher education; athletic training; audiology and speech-language pathology; biology/biological sciences; business administration and management; business/corporate communications; chemistry; clinical laboratory science/medical technology; communication/speech communication and rhetoric; computer science; dramatic/theatre arts; economics; education (K-12); elementary education; engineering physics; English; foreign languages and literatures; French; German; health/health care administration; history; international relations and affairs; journalism; kinesiology and exercise science; liberal arts and sciences/liberal studies; management information systems; mathematics; music; music teacher education; nursing (registered nurse training); philosophy; physical education teaching and coaching; physics; political science and government; pre-dentistry studies; pre-law studies; pre-medical studies; pre-veterinary studies; psychology; religious studies; secondary education; social studies teacher education; social work; sociology; Spanish; special education; special education (hearing impaired); speech/theater education; sport and fitness administration.

Academic Programs *Special study options:* academic remediation for entering students, accelerated degree program, adult/continuing education programs, advanced placement credit, cooperative education, double majors, honors programs, independent study, internships, off-campus study, part-time degree program, services for LD students, student-designed majors, study abroad, summer session for credit. *Unusual degree programs:* 3-2 engineering with Columbia University, Washington University in St. Louis, South Dakota State University, University of Minnesota; occupational therapy with Washington University in St. Louis.

Library Mikkelsen Library plus 1 other with 268,645 titles, 1,418 serial subscriptions, 7,280 audiovisual materials, an OPAC, a Web page.

Computers on Campus 360 computers available on campus for general student use. A campuswide network can be accessed from student residence rooms and from off campus. Internet access, online (class) registration, at least one staffed computer lab available.

Student Life *Housing:* on-campus residence required through sophomore year. *Options:* coed. Campus housing is university owned. Freshman campus housing is guaranteed. *Activities and organizations:* drama/theater group, student-run newspaper, radio station, choral group, Fellowship of Christian Athletes, Circle K, Student Council for Exceptional Children, Habitat for Humanity, Spanish Club. *Campus security:* 24-hour emergency response devices and patrols, late-night transport/escort service, controlled dormitory access. *Student services:* health clinic, personal/psychological counseling, legal services.

Athletics Member NCAA. All Division II. *Intercollegiate sports:* baseball M(s), basketball M(s)/W(s), cheerleading W, cross-country running M(s)/W(s), football M(s), golf M/W, soccer W(s), softball W(s), tennis M/W, track and field M(s)/W(s), volleyball W(s), wrestling M(s). *Intramural sports:* basketball M/W, bowling M/W, cross-country running M/W, football M, golf M/W, racquetball M/W, soccer M/W, softball M/W, swimming M/W, tennis M/W, volleyball M/W.

Standardized Tests *Required:* SAT I or ACT (for admission).

Costs (2003–04) *Comprehensive fee:* $21,998 includes full-time tuition ($16,766), mandatory fees ($206), and room and board ($5026). Part-time tuition: $247 per credit. Part-time tuition and fees vary according to course load. No tuition increase for student's term of enrollment. *College room only:* $2600. Room and board charges vary according to board plan and housing facility. *Payment plan:* installment. *Waivers:* adult students, senior citizens, and employees or children of employees.

Financial Aid Of all full-time matriculated undergraduates who enrolled in 2003, 1,384 applied for aid, 1,174 were judged to have need, 223 had their need fully met. 446 Federal Work-Study jobs (averaging $1292). In 2003, 476 non-need-based awards were made. *Average percent of need met:* 87%. *Average financial aid package:* $14,299. *Average need-based loan:* $4759. *Average need-based gift aid:* $9932. *Average non-need-based aid:* $6695. *Average indebtedness upon graduation:* $18,315.

Applying *Options:* common application, deferred entrance. *Required:* high school transcript, minimum 2.5 GPA, 1 letter of recommendation, minimum ACT score of 20. *Required for some:* essay or personal statement. *Recommended:* interview. *Application deadline:* 8/1 (freshmen), rolling (transfers). *Notification:* continuous (freshmen).

Admissions Contact Mr. Robert Preloger, Vice President for Enrollment, Augustana College, 2001 South Summit Avenue, Sioux Falls, SD 57197. *Phone:* 605-274-5516 Ext. 5504. *Toll-free phone:* 800-727-2844 Ext. 5516 (in-state); 800-727-2844 (out-of-state). *Fax:* 605-274-5518. *E-mail:* info@augie.edu.

BLACK HILLS STATE UNIVERSITY

Spearfish, South Dakota

- **State-supported** comprehensive, founded 1883, part of South Dakota University System
- **Calendar** semesters
- **Degrees** associate, bachelor's, master's, post-master's, and postbachelor's certificates
- **Small-town** 123-acre campus
- **Endowment** $7.5 million
- **Coed,** 3,671 undergraduate students, 73% full-time, 64% women, 36% men
- **Minimally difficult** entrance level, 99% of applicants were admitted

BHSU is a coeducational, 4-year undergraduate institution with an enrollment of 4,060 students. Students looking for a small but growing public university located in one of the most scenic parts of the US should consider Black Hills State. BHSU's liberal arts philosophy and state-of-the-art technology provide the tools necessary for success.

Undergraduates 2,679 full-time, 992 part-time. Students come from 33 states and territories, 6 other countries, 19% are from out of state, 0.8% African American, 0.8% Asian American or Pacific Islander, 2% Hispanic American, 3% Native American, 0.2% international, 13% transferred in, 20% live on campus. *Retention:* 56% of 2002 full-time freshmen returned.

Freshmen *Admission:* 1,299 applied, 1,288 admitted, 707 enrolled. *Average high school GPA:* 3.08. *Test scores:* ACT scores over 18: 83%; ACT scores over 24: 21%; ACT scores over 30: 1%.

Faculty *Total:* 194, 57% full-time. *Student/faculty ratio:* 23:1.

Majors Accounting; administrative assistant and secretarial science; American Indian/Native American studies; art; biology/biological sciences; business administration and management; business teacher education; chemistry; commercial and advertising art; computer and information sciences; computer programming; computer science; drafting and design technology; elementary education; English; environmental studies; general studies; health and physical education; health/health care administration; history; hospital and health care facilities administration; human resources management; human services; industrial technology; kindergarten/preschool education; marketing/marketing management; mass communication/media; mathematics; mathematics teacher education; middle school education; music; music performance; parks, recreation and leisure; physical sciences; political science and government; psychology; sales, distribution and marketing; science teacher education; secondary education; social sciences; sociology; Spanish; special education; speech and rhetoric; sport and fitness administration; tourism and travel services management; voice and opera.

Academic Programs *Special study options:* academic remediation for entering students, accelerated degree program, advanced placement credit, cooperative education, distance learning, double majors, independent study, internships, off-campus study, part-time degree program, services for LD students, summer session for credit. *ROTC:* Army (b).

Library E. Y. Berry Library-Learning Center with 209,738 titles, 4,481 serial subscriptions, 23,901 audiovisual materials, an OPAC.

Black Hills State University (continued)

Computers on Campus 220 computers available on campus for general student use. A campuswide network can be accessed from student residence rooms and from off campus. Internet access available.

Student Life *Housing:* on-campus residence required through sophomore year. *Options:* coed, men-only, women-only, disabled students. Campus housing is university owned. *Activities and organizations:* drama/theater group, student-run newspaper, radio station, choral group, Student Activities Committee, student government, national fraternities, national sororities. *Campus security:* 24-hour patrols, late-night transport/escort service, controlled dormitory access. *Student services:* health clinic, personal/psychological counseling.

Athletics Member NAIA. *Intercollegiate sports:* basketball M(s)/W(s), cross-country running M(s)/W(s), football M(s), track and field M(s)/W(s), volleyball W(s). *Intramural sports:* archery M/W, badminton M/W, basketball M/W, bowling M/W, football M, golf M/W, racquetball M/W, skiing (cross-country) M/W, skiing (downhill) M/W, soccer M/W, softball M/W, tennis M/W, volleyball M/W, weight lifting M/W.

Standardized Tests *Required:* SAT I or ACT (for admission).

Costs (2003–04) *Tuition:* state resident $2308 full-time, $142 per credit part-time; nonresident $7333 full-time, $299 per credit part-time. Full-time tuition and fees vary according to course load and reciprocity agreements. Part-time tuition and fees vary according to course load and reciprocity agreements. *Required fees:* $3196 full-time. *Room and board:* $3196; room only: $1716. Room and board charges vary according to board plan and housing facility. *Waivers:* senior citizens and employees or children of employees.

Financial Aid Of all full-time matriculated undergraduates who enrolled in 2002, 289 Federal Work-Study jobs (averaging $1321). 459 state and other part-time jobs (averaging $1638). *Average financial aid package:* $4638. *Average indebtedness upon graduation:* $20,174.

Applying *Options:* electronic application. *Application fee:* $20. *Required:* high school transcript, minimum 2.0 high school GPA in core curriculum. *Application deadline:* 7/1 (freshmen), rolling (transfers).

Admissions Contact Mr. Steve Ochsner, Dean of Admissions, Black Hills State University, University Street Box 9502, Spearfish, SD 57799-9502. *Phone:* 605-642-6343. *Toll-free phone:* 800-255-2478. *E-mail:* admissions@bhsu.edu.

COLORADO TECHNICAL UNIVERSITY SIOUX FALLS CAMPUS

Sioux Falls, South Dakota

- **Proprietary** comprehensive, founded 1965, part of Colorado Technical University—Main Campus Colorado Springs, CO
- **Calendar** quarters
- **Degrees** certificates, associate, bachelor's, and master's
- **Urban** 3-acre campus
- **Coed,** 912 undergraduate students, 48% full-time, 59% women, 41% men
- **Minimally difficult** entrance level

Undergraduates 441 full-time, 471 part-time. Students come from 3 states and territories, 5% are from out of state, 2% African American, 1% Asian American or Pacific Islander, 0.5% Hispanic American, 1% Native American, 12% transferred in.

Freshmen *Admission:* 209 enrolled.

Faculty *Total:* 61, 15% full-time, 13% with terminal degrees. *Student/faculty ratio:* 18:1.

Majors Accounting; business administration and management; computer science; criminal justice/safety; finance; human resources management; information science/studies; management information systems; marketing/marketing management; medical/clinical assistant; sales, distribution and marketing.

Academic Programs *Special study options:* accelerated degree program, adult/continuing education programs, cooperative education, distance learning, double majors, internships, part-time degree program, summer session for credit. *ROTC:* Army (c).

Library Resource Center with 5,787 titles, 25 serial subscriptions, 280 audiovisual materials, an OPAC, a Web page.

Computers on Campus 55 computers available on campus for general student use. A campuswide network can be accessed from off campus. Internet access, at least one staffed computer lab available. Computer purchase or lease plan available.

Student Life *Housing:* college housing not available. *Activities and organizations:* Phi Beta Lambda, AITP, CJ Honor Society, SHRM Student Chapter.

Athletics *Intramural sports:* cheerleading W.

Standardized Tests *Recommended:* ACT (for admission).

Costs (2003–04) *Tuition:* $9450 full-time, $195 per credit hour part-time. Full-time tuition and fees vary according to course load. Part-time tuition and fees vary according to course load. *Required fees:* $513 full-time, $50 per term part-time. *Payment plans:* installment, deferred payment. *Waivers:* employees or children of employees.

Financial Aid Of all full-time matriculated undergraduates who enrolled in 2000, 280 applied for aid, 280 were judged to have need. *Average percent of need met:* 45%. *Average financial aid package:* $3500. *Average need-based loan:* $4648. *Average need-based gift aid:* $3300.

Applying *Options:* early admission, deferred entrance. *Application fee:* $50. *Required:* high school transcript, interview. *Application deadline:* rolling (freshmen), rolling (transfers). *Notification:* continuous (freshmen), continuous (transfers).

Admissions Contact Elizabeth Carlson, Regional High School Representative, Colorado Technical University Sioux Falls Campus, 3901 West 59th Street, Sioux Falls, SD 57108. *Phone:* 605-361-0200 Ext. 152. *Fax:* 605-361-5954. *E-mail:* callen@sf.coloradotech.edu.

DAKOTA STATE UNIVERSITY

Madison, South Dakota

- **State-supported** comprehensive, founded 1881
- **Calendar** semesters
- **Degrees** certificates, associate, bachelor's, and master's
- **Rural** 40-acre campus with easy access to Sioux Falls
- **Endowment** $4.1 million
- **Coed,** 2,098 undergraduate students, 60% full-time, 53% women, 47% men
- **Minimally difficult** entrance level, 93% of applicants were admitted

Undergraduates 1,251 full-time, 847 part-time. Students come from 12 states and territories, 6 other countries, 17% are from out of state, 0.9% African American, 0.5% Asian American or Pacific Islander, 0.5% Hispanic American, 1% Native American, 0.7% international, 7% transferred in, 34% live on campus. *Retention:* 71% of 2002 full-time freshmen returned.

Freshmen *Admission:* 525 applied, 487 admitted, 320 enrolled. *Average high school GPA:* 3.08. *Test scores:* ACT scores over 18: 83%; ACT scores over 24: 22%; ACT scores over 30: 1%.

Faculty *Total:* 98, 74% full-time, 48% with terminal degrees. *Student/faculty ratio:* 24:1.

Majors Accounting; administrative assistant and secretarial science; arts management; art teacher education; biology/biological sciences; business administration and management; business teacher education; chemistry; clinical/medical laboratory technology; computer and information systems security; computer graphics; computer programming; computer science; education; elementary education; English; finance; health information/medical records administration; information science/studies; kinesiology and exercise science; liberal arts and sciences/liberal studies; marketing/marketing management; mathematics; music teacher education; physical education teaching and coaching; physics; pre-dentistry studies; pre-law studies; pre-medical studies; pre-veterinary studies; respiratory care therapy; secondary education; special education; trade and industrial teacher education; web page, digital/multimedia and information resources design.

Academic Programs *Special study options:* academic remediation for entering students, adult/continuing education programs, advanced placement credit, cooperative education, distance learning, double majors, English as a second language, external degree program, honors programs, independent study, internships, off-campus study, part-time degree program, services for LD students, study abroad, summer session for credit. *ROTC:* Air Force (c).

Library Karl E. Mundt Library plus 1 other with 98,156 titles, 350 serial subscriptions, 2,435 audiovisual materials, an OPAC, a Web page.

Computers on Campus 417 computers available on campus for general student use. A campuswide network can be accessed from student residence rooms and from off campus. Internet access, online (class) registration, at least one staffed computer lab available. Computer purchase or lease plan available.

Student Life *Housing:* on-campus residence required through sophomore year. *Options:* coed, men-only, women-only, disabled students. Campus housing is university owned and leased by the school. Freshman campus housing is guaranteed. *Activities and organizations:* drama/theater group, student-run newspaper, choral group, marching band, business club, band, computer club. *Campus security:* controlled dormitory access, night watchman. *Student services:* health clinic, personal/psychological counseling.

Athletics Member NAIA. *Intercollegiate sports:* baseball M, basketball M(s)/W(s), cheerleading M/W, cross-country running M(s)/W(s), football M(s), golf M/W, softball W, track and field M(s)/W(s), volleyball W(s). *Intramural sports:* archery M/W, badminton M/W, basketball M/W, bowling M/W, softball M/W, tennis M/W, ultimate Frisbee M/W, volleyball M/W, weight lifting M/W.

Standardized Tests *Required:* ACT (for admission).

Costs (2003–04) *Tuition:* state resident $4378 full-time, $134 per credit hour part-time; nonresident $9090 full-time, $276 per credit hour part-time. *Room and board:* $3089. *Payment plans:* installment, deferred payment.

Financial Aid Of all full-time matriculated undergraduates who enrolled in 2002, 1,131 applied for aid, 882 were judged to have need. 156 Federal Work-Study jobs (averaging $1960). 180 state and other part-time jobs (averaging $1427). In 2002, 228 non-need-based awards were made. *Average financial aid package:* $5593. *Average non-need-based aid:* $4932. *Average indebtedness upon graduation:* $18,430.

Applying *Options:* electronic application, early admission. *Application fee:* $20. *Required:* high school transcript, rank in upper two-thirds of high school class. *Application deadline:* rolling (freshmen), rolling (transfers). *Notification:* continuous (freshmen), continuous (transfers).

Admissions Contact Ms. Katy O'Hara, Admissions Secretary, Dakota State University, 820 North Washington, Madison, SD 57042-1799. *Phone:* 605-256-5139. *Toll-free phone:* 888-DSU-9988. *Fax:* 605-256-5316. *E-mail:* yourfuture@dsu.edu.

DAKOTA WESLEYAN UNIVERSITY

Mitchell, South Dakota

- **Independent United Methodist** comprehensive, founded 1885
- **Calendar** semesters
- **Degrees** associate, bachelor's, and master's
- **Small-town** 50-acre campus
- **Endowment** $17.1 million
- **Coed,** 738 undergraduate students, 90% full-time, 58% women, 42% men
- **Moderately difficult** entrance level, 77% of applicants were admitted

Undergraduates 665 full-time, 73 part-time. Students come from 29 states and territories, 28% are from out of state, 6% African American, 0.9% Asian American or Pacific Islander, 2% Hispanic American, 2% Native American, 0.9% international, 12% transferred in, 43% live on campus. *Retention:* 62% of 2002 full-time freshmen returned.

Freshmen *Admission:* 543 applied, 418 admitted, 162 enrolled. *Average high school GPA:* 2.94. *Test scores:* ACT scores over 18: 83%; ACT scores over 24: 19%; ACT scores over 30: 1%.

Faculty *Total:* 70, 60% full-time, 39% with terminal degrees. *Student/faculty ratio:* 17:1.

Majors Accounting; adult and continuing education; art; art teacher education; athletic training; behavioral sciences; biology/biological sciences; biology teacher education; business administration and management; business teacher education; computer software and media applications related; criminal justice/law enforcement administration; dramatic/theatre arts; education; education (multiple levels); elementary education; English; English/language arts teacher education; finance; history; history teacher education; human services; liberal arts and sciences/liberal studies; marketing/marketing management; mathematics; mathematics teacher education; middle school education; music; music teacher education; nursing (registered nurse training); philosophy; physical education teaching and coaching; psychology; religious studies; science teacher education; secondary education; social studies teacher education; sociology; Spanish; special education; theology.

Academic Programs *Special study options:* academic remediation for entering students, adult/continuing education programs, advanced placement credit, distance learning, double majors, English as a second language, honors programs, independent study, internships, part-time degree program, services for LD students, student-designed majors, study abroad, summer session for credit.

Library Layne Library with 61,000 titles, 404 serial subscriptions, 7,600 audiovisual materials, an OPAC, a Web page.

Computers on Campus 100 computers available on campus for general student use. A campuswide network can be accessed from student residence rooms and from off campus. Internet access, at least one staffed computer lab available.

Student Life *Housing:* on-campus residence required through sophomore year. *Options:* coed, men-only, women-only. Campus housing is university owned and leased by the school. Freshman campus housing is guaranteed. *Activities and organizations:* drama/theater group, student-run newspaper, choral group, DWU Future Teachers Organization, Student Nurses Association, culture club, human services club, Student Ministry Council. *Campus security:* 24-hour emergency response devices, student patrols, late-night transport/escort service, controlled dormitory access, campus patrol from 2am to 6am by special request only. *Student services:* health clinic, personal/psychological counseling.

Athletics Member NAIA. *Intercollegiate sports:* baseball M(s), basketball M(s)/W(s), cheerleading M(s)/W(s), cross-country running M(s)/W(s), football M(s), golf M(s)/W(s), softball W(s), track and field M(s)/W(s), volleyball W(s), wrestling M(s). *Intramural sports:* basketball M/W, softball M/W, volleyball M/W, weight lifting M/W.

Standardized Tests *Required:* SAT I or ACT (for admission).

Costs (2004–05) *Comprehensive fee:* $18,820 includes full-time tuition ($14,158), mandatory fees ($400), and room and board ($4262). Full-time tuition and fees vary according to program. Part-time tuition: $280 per credit. Part-time tuition and fees vary according to course load and program. *Required fees:* $15 per credit part-time. *College room only:* $1802. Room and board charges vary according to board plan and student level. *Payment plan:* installment. *Waivers:* children of alumni, senior citizens, and employees or children of employees.

Financial Aid Of all full-time matriculated undergraduates who enrolled in 2003, 661 applied for aid, 656 were judged to have need, 102 had their need fully met. 80 Federal Work-Study jobs (averaging $1307). 134 state and other part-time jobs (averaging $1307). In 2003, 5 non-need-based awards were made. *Average percent of need met:* 71%. *Average financial aid package:* $11,061. *Average need-based loan:* $4778. *Average need-based gift aid:* $3869. *Average non-need-based aid:* $5241. *Average indebtedness upon graduation:* $13,925.

Applying *Options:* electronic application. *Application fee:* $25. *Required:* high school transcript. *Recommended:* minimum 2.0 GPA. *Application deadlines:* 8/25 (freshmen), 8/25 (transfers). *Notification:* continuous (freshmen), continuous (transfers).

Admissions Contact Ms. Laura Miller, Director of Admissions Operations and Outreach Programming, Dakota Wesleyan University, 1200 West University Avenue, Mitchell, SD 57301-4398. *Phone:* 605-995-2650 Ext. 2651. *Toll-free phone:* 800-333-8506. *Fax:* 605-995-2699. *E-mail:* admissions@dwu.edu.

MOUNT MARTY COLLEGE

Yankton, South Dakota

- **Independent Roman Catholic** comprehensive, founded 1936
- **Calendar** semesters
- **Degrees** certificates, associate, bachelor's, master's, and postbachelor's certificates
- **Small-town** 80-acre campus
- **Endowment** $7.5 million
- **Coed,** 1,095 undergraduate students, 67% full-time, 69% women, 31% men
- **Moderately difficult** entrance level, 80% of applicants were admitted

Undergraduates 730 full-time, 365 part-time. Students come from 18 states and territories, 3 other countries, 22% are from out of state, 2% African American, 0.2% Asian American or Pacific Islander, 2% Hispanic American, 1% Native American, 0.7% international, 9% transferred in. *Retention:* 69% of 2002 full-time freshmen returned.

Freshmen *Admission:* 439 applied, 352 admitted, 184 enrolled. *Average high school GPA:* 3.20. *Test scores:* ACT scores over 18: 90%; ACT scores over 24: 28%; SAT verbal scores over 700: 17%; ACT scores over 30: 2%.

Faculty *Total:* 107, 39% full-time, 30% with terminal degrees. *Student/faculty ratio:* 13:1.

Majors Accounting; athletic training; behavioral sciences; biology/biological sciences; business administration and management; chemistry; chemistry teacher education; clinical laboratory science/medical technology; computer science; criminal justice/safety; education; elementary education; English; English/language arts teacher education; foods, nutrition, and wellness; general studies; history; history teacher education; liberal arts and sciences/liberal studies; mathematics; mathematics teacher education; medical radiologic technology; music; music teacher education; nursing (registered nurse training); parks, recreation and leisure facilities management; physical education teaching and coaching; religious studies; secondary education; special education.

Academic Programs *Special study options:* academic remediation for entering students, accelerated degree program, adult/continuing education programs, advanced placement credit, cooperative education, double majors, honors programs, independent study, internships, off-campus study, part-time degree program, services for LD students, student-designed majors, summer session for credit. *ROTC:* Army (c).

Library Mount Marty College Library with 79,167 titles, 439 serial subscriptions, 8,537 audiovisual materials, an OPAC, a Web page.

Computers on Campus 21 computers available on campus for general student use. A campuswide network can be accessed from student residence rooms and from off campus. Internet access, at least one staffed computer lab available. Computer purchase or lease plan available.

Student Life *Housing:* on-campus residence required through senior year. *Options:* coed. Freshman campus housing is guaranteed. *Activities and organizations:* drama/theater group, student-run newspaper, radio station, choral group, campus ministry, Student Government Association, nursing club, education club, theater club or SIFE (Students in Free Enterprise). *Campus security:* 24-hour emergency response devices and patrols, controlled dormitory access. *Student services:* health clinic, personal/psychological counseling.

Athletics Member NAIA. *Intercollegiate sports:* baseball M(s), basketball M(s)/W(s), cross-country running M(s)/W(s), golf M(s)/W(s), soccer M(s),

Mount Marty College (continued)
softball W(s), track and field M(s)/W(s), volleyball W(s). *Intramural sports:* basketball M/W, cheerleading W, soccer M, softball W, tennis M/W, volleyball M/W.

Standardized Tests *Required:* ACT (for admission).

Costs (2003–04) *Comprehensive fee:* $18,856 includes full-time tuition ($12,506), mandatory fees ($1680), and room and board ($4670). Full-time tuition and fees vary according to location. Part-time tuition: $205 per credit. Part-time tuition and fees vary according to location. *Waivers:* employees or children of employees.

Financial Aid Of all full-time matriculated undergraduates who enrolled in 2003, 478 applied for aid, 448 were judged to have need, 88 had their need fully met. 231 Federal Work-Study jobs (averaging $1000). 72 state and other part-time jobs (averaging $1000). In 2003, 60 non-need-based awards were made. *Average percent of need met:* 75%. *Average financial aid package:* $12,417. *Average need-based loan:* $4468. *Average need-based gift aid:* $7863. *Average non-need-based aid:* $5764. *Average indebtedness upon graduation:* $21,492.

Applying *Options:* electronic application, early admission, deferred entrance. *Application fee:* $35. *Required:* high school transcript, minimum 2.0 GPA. *Required for some:* letters of recommendation. *Recommended:* interview. *Application deadline:* rolling (freshmen), rolling (transfers). *Notification:* continuous (freshmen), continuous (transfers).

Admissions Contact Ms. Brandi Tschumper, Vice President for Enrollment Management, Mount Marty College, 1105 West 8th Street, Yankton, SD 57078. *Phone:* 605-668-1545. *Toll-free phone:* 800-658-4552. *Fax:* 605-668-1607. *E-mail:* mmcadmit@mtmc.edu.

■ *See page 2042 for a narrative description.*

NATIONAL AMERICAN UNIVERSITY

Rapid City, South Dakota

- **Proprietary** comprehensive, founded 1941, part of National College
- **Calendar** quarters
- **Degrees** certificates, diplomas, associate, bachelor's, and master's
- **Urban** 8-acre campus
- **Endowment** $30,000
- **Coed,** 714 undergraduate students, 46% full-time, 48% women, 52% men
- **Noncompetitive** entrance level

Undergraduates 330 full-time, 384 part-time. Students come from 25 states and territories, 21% are from out of state, 3% African American, 5% Asian American or Pacific Islander, 3% Hispanic American, 3% Native American, 0.7% international, 21% live on campus.

Freshmen *Admission:* 166 enrolled.

Faculty *Student/faculty ratio:* 15:1.

Majors Accounting; athletic training; business administration and management; computer engineering technology; computer management; computer programming; equestrian studies; information science/studies; legal assistant/paralegal; liberal arts and sciences/liberal studies; management information systems; sport and fitness administration; veterinary technology.

Academic Programs *Special study options:* academic remediation for entering students, accelerated degree program, adult/continuing education programs, advanced placement credit, cooperative education, distance learning, English as a second language, external degree program, independent study, internships, part-time degree program, services for LD students, summer session for credit. *ROTC:* Army (c).

Library Jefferson Library with 31,018 titles, 268 serial subscriptions, a Web page.

Computers on Campus 50 computers available on campus for general student use. A campuswide network can be accessed. Internet access, at least one staffed computer lab available.

Student Life *Housing:* on-campus residence required through sophomore year. *Options:* coed. Freshman campus housing is guaranteed. *Activities and organizations:* Student Senate, Phi Beta Lambda, Dormitory Council, Student Association of Legal Assistants, President's Advisory Council. *Campus security:* part-time security personnel. *Student services:* personal/psychological counseling.

Athletics Member NAIA. *Intercollegiate sports:* equestrian sports M(s)/W(s), volleyball W(s). *Intramural sports:* basketball M/W, bowling M/W, skiing (cross-country) M/W, skiing (downhill) M(c)/W(c), softball M/W, volleyball W.

Standardized Tests *Recommended:* ACT (for admission).

Costs (2003–04) *Comprehensive fee:* $13,710 includes full-time tuition ($9675), mandatory fees ($315), and room and board ($3720). *College room only:* $1725. Room and board charges vary according to board plan. *Payment plan:* installment. *Waivers:* employees or children of employees.

Applying *Options:* common application, electronic application, early admission, deferred entrance. *Application fee:* $25. *Required:* high school transcript. *Recommended:* interview. *Application deadline:* rolling (freshmen), rolling (transfers). *Notification:* continuous (freshmen), continuous (transfers).

Admissions Contact Mr. Tom Shea, Vice President of Enrollment Management, National American University, 321 Kansas City Street, Rapid City, SD 57701. *Phone:* 605-394-4902. *Toll-free phone:* 800-843-8892. *Fax:* 605-394-4871.

■ *See page 2058 for a narrative description.*

NATIONAL AMERICAN UNIVERSITY–SIOUX FALLS BRANCH

Sioux Falls, South Dakota

- **Proprietary** 4-year, founded 1941, part of National College
- **Calendar** quarters
- **Degrees** certificates, diplomas, associate, bachelor's, and master's
- **Urban** campus
- **Coed, primarily women,** 350 undergraduate students
- **Noncompetitive** entrance level, 100% of applicants were admitted

Undergraduates Students come from 5 states and territories, 0.6% African American, 0.6% Native American. *Retention:* 70% of 2002 full-time freshmen returned.

Freshmen *Admission:* 9 applied, 9 admitted.

Faculty *Total:* 35.

Majors Accounting; business administration and management; computer programming; computer programming (vendor/product certification); customer service support/call center/teleservice operation; information science/studies; information technology; legal assistant/paralegal; management information systems; massage therapy; medical/clinical assistant; web page, digital/multimedia and information resources design.

Academic Programs *Special study options:* academic remediation for entering students, accelerated degree program, adult/continuing education programs, advanced placement credit, cooperative education, distance learning, double majors, English as a second language, internships, part-time degree program, summer session for credit.

Library 1,580 titles, 57 serial subscriptions, a Web page.

Computers on Campus 60 computers available on campus for general student use. A campuswide network can be accessed. Internet access, at least one staffed computer lab available.

Student Life *Housing:* college housing not available. *Campus security:* 24-hour emergency response devices.

Costs (2004–05) *Tuition:* $7740 full-time, $215 per credit part-time.

Applying *Options:* common application, electronic application, deferred entrance. *Application fee:* $25. *Required:* high school transcript, interview. *Application deadline:* rolling (freshmen), rolling (transfers). *Notification:* continuous (freshmen), continuous (transfers).

Admissions Contact Ms. Lisa Houtsma, Director of Admissions, National American University–Sioux Falls Branch, 2801 South Kiwanis Avenue, Suite 100, Sioux Falls, SD 57105. *Phone:* 605-334-5430. *Toll-free phone:* 800-358-5430. *Fax:* 605-334-1575. *E-mail:* lhautsma@national.edu.

NORTHERN STATE UNIVERSITY

Aberdeen, South Dakota

- **State-supported** comprehensive, founded 1901, part of South Dakota Board of Regents
- **Calendar** semesters
- **Degrees** certificates, diplomas, associate, bachelor's, master's, and postbachelor's certificates
- **Small-town** 52-acre campus
- **Endowment** $7.7 million
- **Coed,** 2,842 undergraduate students, 57% full-time, 59% women, 41% men
- **Minimally difficult** entrance level, 92% of applicants were admitted

Northern State University offers the personalized academic atmosphere of a private college at a public school price. Northern has 45 nationally accredited majors in business, education, fine arts, and arts and sciences. Cutting-edge technology, with superior access, numerous social opportunities, and an almost perfect placement rate are some of the benefits that Northern's 3,200 students enjoy. Telephone: 800-NSU-5330 (toll-free).

Undergraduates 1,625 full-time, 1,217 part-time. Students come from 29 states and territories, 16 other countries, 15% are from out of state, 6% transferred in. *Retention:* 69% of 2002 full-time freshmen returned.

Freshmen *Admission:* 902 applied, 833 admitted, 434 enrolled. *Average high school GPA:* 3.28. *Test scores:* ACT scores over 18: 81%; ACT scores over 24: 25%; ACT scores over 30: 3%.

Faculty *Total:* 111, 100% full-time, 73% with terminal degrees. *Student/faculty ratio:* 20:1.

Majors Accounting; administrative assistant and secretarial science; art; art teacher education; audiology and speech-language pathology; biological and physical sciences; biology/biological sciences; business administration and management; business/managerial economics; business teacher education; chemistry; clinical laboratory science/medical technology; clinical/medical laboratory technology; commercial and advertising art; community organization and advocacy; criminal justice/police science; data processing and data processing technology; drafting and design technology; dramatic/theatre arts; economics; education; electrical, electronic and communications engineering technology; elementary education; English; environmental studies; finance; French; German; health teacher education; history; industrial arts; international business/trade/commerce; liberal arts and sciences/liberal studies; management information systems; marketing/marketing management; mathematics; music; music teacher education; physical education teaching and coaching; political science and government; pre-dentistry studies; pre-engineering; pre-law studies; pre-medical studies; psychology; public administration; secondary education; social work; sociology; Spanish; special education; speech and rhetoric; voice and opera.

Academic Programs *Special study options:* academic remediation for entering students, accelerated degree program, adult/continuing education programs, advanced placement credit, cooperative education, distance learning, English as a second language, honors programs, internships, off-campus study, part-time degree program, services for LD students, student-designed majors, study abroad, summer session for credit.

Library Beulah Williams Library with 187,961 titles, 880 serial subscriptions, an OPAC, a Web page.

Computers on Campus 900 computers available on campus for general student use. A campuswide network can be accessed from student residence rooms and from off campus. Internet access, online (class) registration, at least one staffed computer lab available.

Student Life *Housing:* on-campus residence required through sophomore year. *Options:* coed. Campus housing is university owned. *Activities and organizations:* drama/theater group, student-run newspaper, choral group, marching band, Student Ambassadors, Choices, honor society, Native American Student Association. *Campus security:* 24-hour emergency response devices, controlled dormitory access, evening patrols. *Student services:* health clinic, personal/psychological counseling.

Athletics Member NCAA. All Division II. *Intercollegiate sports:* baseball M, basketball M(s)/W(s), cross-country running M(s)/W(s), football M(s), golf M/W(s), soccer W(s), softball W(s), tennis M/W(s), track and field M(s)/W(s), volleyball W(s), wrestling M(s). *Intramural sports:* archery M/W, badminton M/W, basketball M/W, cross-country running M/W, football M, golf M/W, ice hockey M(c), racquetball M/W, softball M/W, swimming M/W, table tennis M/W, tennis M/W, track and field M/W, volleyball M/W, weight lifting M/W, wrestling M.

Standardized Tests *Required:* SAT I or ACT (for admission).

Costs (2003–04) *Tuition:* state resident $2163 full-time, $72 per credit hour part-time; nonresident $6875 full-time, $229 per credit hour part-time. Full-time tuition and fees vary according to course level, course load, and reciprocity agreements. Part-time tuition and fees vary according to course level, course load, and reciprocity agreements. *Required fees:* $2045 full-time, $68 per credit hour part-time. *Room and board:* $3306; room only: $1478. Room and board charges vary according to board plan. *Payment plan:* installment.

Financial Aid Of all full-time matriculated undergraduates who enrolled in 2002, 1,383 applied for aid, 1,105 were judged to have need, 1,087 had their need fully met. 395 Federal Work-Study jobs (averaging $1635). 379 state and other part-time jobs (averaging $1303). In 2002, 90 non-need-based awards were made. *Average financial aid package:* $5041. *Average need-based loan:* $3062. *Average need-based gift aid:* $2544. *Average non-need-based aid:* $1246. *Average indebtedness upon graduation:* $18,129.

Applying *Options:* common application, early admission, deferred entrance. *Application fee:* $15. *Required:* high school transcript, minimum X GPA. *Required for some:* letters of recommendation. *Application deadlines:* 9/1 (freshmen), 9/1 (transfers). *Notification:* continuous (freshmen), continuous (transfers).

Admissions Contact Ms. Sara Hanson, Interim Director of Admissions-Campus, Northern State University, 1200 South Jay Street, Aberdeen, SD 57401. *Phone:* 605-626-2544. *Toll-free phone:* 800-678-5330. *Fax:* 605-626-2587. *E-mail:* admissions1@northern.edu.

OGLALA LAKOTA COLLEGE
Kyle, South Dakota

Admissions Contact Miss Billi K. Hornbeck, Registrar, Oglala Lakota College, 490 Piya Wiconi Road, Kyle, SD 57752-0490. *Phone:* 605-455-2321 Ext. 236.

PRESENTATION COLLEGE
Aberdeen, South Dakota

- **Independent Roman Catholic** 4-year, founded 1951
- **Calendar** semesters
- **Degrees** certificates, associate, and bachelor's
- **Small-town** 100-acre campus
- **Endowment** $11.0 million
- **Coed,** 618 undergraduate students, 70% full-time, 88% women, 12% men
- **Noncompetitive** entrance level

Undergraduates 435 full-time, 183 part-time. Students come from 1 other state, 1 other country, 24% are from out of state, 2% African American, 0.5% Asian American or Pacific Islander, 1% Hispanic American, 10% Native American, 0.7% international, 17% transferred in, 15% live on campus. *Retention:* 74% of 2002 full-time freshmen returned.

Freshmen *Admission:* 163 applied, 162 enrolled. *Average high school GPA:* 2.88. *Test scores:* ACT scores over 18: 72%; ACT scores over 24: 11%.

Faculty *Total:* 68, 43% full-time, 10% with terminal degrees. *Student/faculty ratio:* 12:1.

Majors Biology/biological sciences; business administration and management; clinical/medical laboratory technology; communication/speech communication and rhetoric; English; health/health care administration; liberal arts and sciences/liberal studies; medical/clinical assistant; medical radiologic technology; nursing (registered nurse training); religious studies; social work; surgical technology.

Academic Programs *Special study options:* academic remediation for entering students, accelerated degree program, adult/continuing education programs, advanced placement credit, cooperative education, distance learning, double majors, external degree program, internships, part-time degree program, summer session for credit.

Library Presentation College Library plus 1 other with 40,000 titles, 430 serial subscriptions, 2,900 audiovisual materials, an OPAC.

Computers on Campus 30 computers available on campus for general student use. A campuswide network can be accessed from student residence rooms. Internet access, at least one staffed computer lab available.

Student Life *Housing:* on-campus residence required for freshman year. *Options:* coed. Campus housing is university owned. Freshman campus housing is guaranteed. *Activities and organizations:* choral group, Wellness, National Student Nursing Association, Social Work Organization. *Campus security:* 24-hour emergency response devices and patrols, late-night transport/escort service, controlled dormitory access. *Student services:* personal/psychological counseling.

Athletics Member NAIA, NSCAA. *Intercollegiate sports:* baseball M, basketball M/W, cheerleading W, cross-country running M/W, golf M/W, soccer M/W, softball W, volleyball W. *Intramural sports:* football M, table tennis M/W, tennis M/W.

Standardized Tests *Required:* ACT ASSET (for admission). *Required for some:* ACT (for admission). *Recommended:* ACT (for admission).

Costs (2003–04) *Comprehensive fee:* $14,200 includes full-time tuition ($10,050) and room and board ($4150). Full-time tuition and fees vary according to course load, location, and program. Part-time tuition: $354 per credit. Part-time tuition and fees vary according to course load, location, and program. *College room only:* $3400. Room and board charges vary according to board plan, housing facility, and student level. *Payment plan:* installment. *Waivers:* senior citizens and employees or children of employees.

Financial Aid Of all full-time matriculated undergraduates who enrolled in 2002, 315 applied for aid, 301 were judged to have need, 144 had their need fully met. 48 Federal Work-Study jobs (averaging $1500). 23 state and other part-time jobs (averaging $1500). In 2002, 32 non-need-based awards were made. *Average percent of need met:* 60%. *Average financial aid package:* $6845. *Average need-based loan:* $3670. *Average need-based gift aid:* $3182. *Average non-need-based aid:* $2392. *Average indebtedness upon graduation:* $23,460. *Financial aid deadline:* 4/1.

Presentation College (continued)

Applying *Options:* electronic application. *Required:* high school transcript. *Required for some:* 2 letters of recommendation. *Recommended:* minimum 2.0 GPA. *Application deadline:* rolling (freshmen), rolling (transfers). *Notification:* continuous (transfers).

Admissions Contact Ms. Jo Ellen Lindner, Director of Admissions, Presentation College, 1500 North Main Street, Aberdeen, SD 57401. *Phone:* 605-229-8493 Ext. 492. *Toll-free phone:* 800-437-6060. *E-mail:* admit@presentation.edu.

SINTE GLESKA UNIVERSITY
Rosebud, South Dakota

Admissions Contact Mr. Jack Herman, Registrar and Director of Admissions, Sinte Gleska University, PO Box 490, Rosebud, SD 57570-0490. *Phone:* 605-747-2263 Ext. 224. *Fax:* 605-747-2098.

SI TANKA HURON UNIVERSITY
Huron, South Dakota

- **Proprietary** 4-year, founded 1883
- **Calendar** quarters
- **Degrees** associate and bachelor's
- **Small-town** 15-acre campus
- **Coed**
- **Minimally difficult** entrance level

Faculty *Student/faculty ratio:* 12:1.

Student Life *Campus security:* 24-hour emergency response devices, student patrols, controlled dormitory access.

Athletics Member NAIA.

Standardized Tests *Recommended:* SAT I or ACT (for admission).

Financial Aid Of all full-time matriculated undergraduates who enrolled in 2001, 406 applied for aid, 385 were judged to have need, 306 had their need fully met. *Average percent of need met:* 75. *Average financial aid package:* $5250. *Average need-based loan:* $1260. *Average need-based gift aid:* $3848. *Average indebtedness upon graduation:* $12,000.

Applying *Options:* common application, early admission, deferred entrance. *Application fee:* $35. *Required:* high school transcript, minimum 2.0 GPA, applicants for athletic scholarship programs must meet approved ACT requirement. *Recommended:* interview.

Admissions Contact Mr. Tyler Fisher, Director of Admissions, Si Tanka Huron University, 333 9th Street Southwest, Huron, SD 57350. *Phone:* 605-352-8721 Ext. 41. *Toll-free phone:* 800-710-7159. *Fax:* 605-352-7421. *E-mail:* admissions@huron.edu.

SOUTH DAKOTA SCHOOL OF MINES AND TECHNOLOGY
Rapid City, South Dakota

- **State-supported** university, founded 1885, part of South Dakota State University System
- **Calendar** semesters
- **Degrees** associate, bachelor's, master's, and doctoral
- **Suburban** 120-acre campus
- **Endowment** $21.9 million
- **Coed,** 2,112 undergraduate students, 82% full-time, 31% women, 69% men
- **Moderately difficult** entrance level, 94% of applicants were admitted

Undergraduates 1,722 full-time, 390 part-time. Students come from 34 states and territories, 8 other countries, 27% are from out of state, 0.7% African American, 1% Asian American or Pacific Islander, 1% Hispanic American, 3% Native American, 0.8% international, 6% transferred in, 28% live on campus. *Retention:* 73% of 2002 full-time freshmen returned.

Freshmen *Admission:* 811 applied, 762 admitted, 420 enrolled. *Average high school GPA:* 3.32. *Test scores:* SAT verbal scores over 500: 71%; SAT math scores over 500: 85%; ACT scores over 18: 94%; SAT verbal scores over 600: 30%; SAT math scores over 600: 46%; ACT scores over 24: 56%; SAT verbal scores over 700: 7%; SAT math scores over 700: 8%; ACT scores over 30: 10%.

Faculty *Total:* 133, 78% full-time, 78% with terminal degrees. *Student/faculty ratio:* 18:1.

Majors Chemical engineering; chemistry; civil engineering; computer engineering; computer science; electrical, electronics and communications engineering; environmental/environmental health engineering; general studies; geological/geophysical engineering; geology/earth science; industrial engineering; interdisciplinary studies; mathematics; mechanical engineering; metallurgical engineering; mining and mineral engineering; physics.

Academic Programs *Special study options:* academic remediation for entering students, adult/continuing education programs, advanced placement credit, cooperative education, distance learning, double majors, English as a second language, independent study, internships, part-time degree program, services for LD students, study abroad, summer session for credit. *ROTC:* Army (b).

Library Devereaux Library with 219,961 titles, 496 serial subscriptions, 1,610 audiovisual materials, an OPAC, a Web page.

Computers on Campus 210 computers available on campus for general student use. A campuswide network can be accessed from student residence rooms and from off campus. Internet access, online (class) registration, at least one staffed computer lab available.

Student Life *Housing:* on-campus residence required through sophomore year. *Options:* coed, men-only, women-only. Campus housing is university owned and leased by the school. Freshman campus housing is guaranteed. *Activities and organizations:* drama/theater group, student-run newspaper, radio station, choral group, TONITE (Techs Outrageous New Initiative for Total Entertainment), SADD (Students Against Drunk Driving), ASCE (American Society of Civil Engineers), ASME (American Society of Mechanical Engineers), ski club, national fraternities, national sororities. *Campus security:* 24-hour emergency response devices and patrols, student patrols, late-night transport/escort service, controlled dormitory access. *Student services:* health clinic, personal/psychological counseling.

Athletics Member NAIA. *Intercollegiate sports:* basketball M(s)/W(s), cross-country running M(s)/W(s), football M(s), golf M/W, tennis M, track and field M(s)/W(s), volleyball W(s). *Intramural sports:* basketball M/W, bowling M/W, football M/W, racquetball M/W, skiing (cross-country) M/W, soccer M/W, softball M/W, squash M/W, swimming M/W, tennis M/W, track and field M/W, volleyball M/W, weight lifting M/W.

Standardized Tests *Required:* SAT I or ACT (for admission). *Required for some:* ACT (for placement).

Costs (2003–04) *Tuition:* state resident $2163 full-time, $72 per credit hour part-time; nonresident $6875 full-time, $229 per credit hour part-time. Full-time tuition and fees vary according to course load, program, and reciprocity agreements. Part-time tuition and fees vary according to course load, program, and reciprocity agreements. *Required fees:* $2130 full-time, $71 per credit hour part-time. *Room and board:* $3561; room only: $1625. Room and board charges vary according to board plan and housing facility. *Payment plan:* installment. *Waivers:* senior citizens.

Financial Aid Of all full-time matriculated undergraduates who enrolled in 2003, 1,504 applied for aid, 894 were judged to have need, 269 had their need fully met. In 2003, 245 non-need-based awards were made. *Average percent of need met:* 76%. *Average financial aid package:* $6048. *Average need-based loan:* $3199. *Average need-based gift aid:* $3175. *Average non-need-based aid:* $2439. *Average indebtedness upon graduation:* $12,975.

Applying *Options:* electronic application. *Application fee:* $20. *Required:* high school transcript. *Recommended:* minimum 2.6 GPA. *Application deadline:* rolling (freshmen), rolling (transfers). *Notification:* continuous (freshmen), continuous (transfers).

Admissions Contact Mr. Joseph Mueller, Director of Admissions, South Dakota School of Mines and Technology, 501 East Saint Joseph, Rapid City, SD 57701-3995. *Phone:* 605-394-2414 Ext. 1266. *Toll-free phone:* 800-544-8162 Ext. 2414. *Fax:* 605-394-1268. *E-mail:* admissions@sdsmt.edu.

SOUTH DAKOTA STATE UNIVERSITY
Brookings, South Dakota

- **State-supported** university, founded 1881
- **Calendar** semesters
- **Degrees** associate, bachelor's, master's, doctoral, and first professional
- **Small-town** 272-acre campus
- **Endowment** $55.1 million
- **Coed,** 9,284 undergraduate students, 80% full-time, 53% women, 47% men
- **Moderately difficult** entrance level, 96% of applicants were admitted

SDSU is a 4-year, comprehensive university ranked in the past by *U.S. News & World Report* as the most efficient university in the Midwest and a best-value university. SDSU offers the largest selection of academic programs within the state. Majors are available in agriculture and biological sciences, arts and science, education, engineering, family and consumer sciences, general studies, nursing, and pharmacy.

Undergraduates 7,408 full-time, 1,876 part-time. Students come from 39 states and territories, 19 other countries, 26% are from out of state, 0.6% African American, 0.7% Asian American or Pacific Islander, 0.5% Hispanic American, 1% Native American, 0.2% international, 8% transferred in, 33% live on campus. *Retention:* 75% of 2002 full-time freshmen returned.

Freshmen *Admission:* 3,748 applied, 3,586 admitted, 2,073 enrolled. *Average high school GPA:* 3.28. *Test scores:* ACT scores over 18: 92%; ACT scores over 24: 39%; ACT scores over 30: 3%.

Faculty *Total:* 638, 79% full-time, 60% with terminal degrees. *Student/faculty ratio:* 18:1.

Majors Agribusiness; agricultural/biological engineering and bioengineering; agricultural economics; agricultural mechanization; agricultural teacher education; agriculture; agronomy and crop science; animal sciences; applied horticulture; art; art teacher education; athletic training; biochemistry; biology/biological sciences; chemistry; child development; civil engineering; clinical laboratory science/medical technology; computer and information sciences; computer graphics; computer software engineering; computer teacher education; construction engineering technology; consumer services and advocacy; dairy science; dietetics; dramatic/theatre arts; economics; education; electrical, electronic and communications engineering technology; electrical, electronics and communications engineering; engineering/industrial management; engineering physics; English; environmental/environmental health engineering; family and consumer sciences/ home economics teacher education; fashion merchandising; fish/game management; food science; foods, nutrition, and wellness; French; geography; German; health and physical education; history; hotel/motel administration; human development and family studies; industrial safety technology; industrial technology; information science/studies; interior design; journalism; kindergarten/preschool education; landscaping and groundskeeping; mass communication/media; mathematics; mechanical engineering; medical microbiology and bacteriology; music; music management and merchandising; music teacher education; nursing (registered nurse training); parks, recreation and leisure; parks, recreation and leisure facilities management; pharmacy; physical education teaching and coaching; physics; political science and government; pre-dentistry studies; pre-law studies; pre-medical studies; pre-veterinary studies; psychology; range science and management; secondary education; sociology; Spanish; speech and rhetoric; visual and performing arts; wildlife and wildlands science and management.

Academic Programs *Special study options:* academic remediation for entering students, accelerated degree program, adult/continuing education programs, advanced placement credit, cooperative education, distance learning, double majors, English as a second language, freshman honors college, honors programs, independent study, internships, off-campus study, part-time degree program, services for LD students, study abroad, summer session for credit. *ROTC:* Army (b), Air Force (b).

Library H. M. Briggs Library with 555,523 titles, 6,023 serial subscriptions, 2,504 audiovisual materials, an OPAC, a Web page.

Computers on Campus 278 computers available on campus for general student use. A campuswide network can be accessed from student residence rooms and from off campus. Internet access, at least one staffed computer lab available.

Student Life *Housing:* on-campus residence required through sophomore year. *Options:* coed. Campus housing is university owned. Freshman campus housing is guaranteed. *Activities and organizations:* drama/theater group, student-run newspaper, radio station, choral group, marching band, Student Association, University Programming Council, Block and Bridle club, national fraternities, national sororities. *Campus security:* 24-hour emergency response devices and patrols, student patrols, late-night transport/escort service. *Student services:* health clinic, personal/psychological counseling, women's center, legal services.

Athletics Member NCAA. All Division I. *Intercollegiate sports:* baseball M(s), basketball M(s)/W(s), cross-country running M(s)/W(s), football M(s), golf M/W, soccer W(s), softball W(s), swimming M(s)/W(s), tennis M/W, track and field M(s)/W(s), volleyball W(s), wrestling M(s). *Intramural sports:* archery M(c)/ W(c), badminton M/W, baseball M, basketball M/W, fencing M(c)/W(c), football M/W, golf M/W, ice hockey M(c)/W, racquetball M/W, riflery M(c)/W(c), rugby M(c)/W(c), soccer M(c), softball M/W, swimming M/W, table tennis M/W, tennis M/W, track and field M/W, volleyball M/W, water polo M(c)/W(c), weight lifting M(c)/W(c), wrestling M.

Standardized Tests *Required:* ACT (for admission).

Costs (2003–04) *Tuition:* state resident $2308 full-time, $72 per credit part-time; nonresident $7332 full-time, $229 per credit part-time. Full-time tuition and fees vary according to course load and program. Part-time tuition and fees vary according to course load and program. *Required fees:* $2228 full-time, $70 per credit part-time. *Room and board:* $3586; room only: $1862. Room and board charges vary according to board plan and housing facility. *Payment plans:* installment, deferred payment. *Waivers:* children of alumni, senior citizens, and employees or children of employees.

Financial Aid Of all full-time matriculated undergraduates who enrolled in 2003, 6,258 applied for aid, 5,787 were judged to have need, 4,472 had their need fully met. 690 Federal Work-Study jobs (averaging $1046). 2,126 state and other part-time jobs (averaging $1339). In 2003, 866 non-need-based awards were made. *Average percent of need met:* 85%. *Average financial aid package:* $7126. *Average need-based loan:* $4310. *Average need-based gift aid:* $3015. *Average non-need-based aid:* $910. *Average indebtedness upon graduation:* $16,660.

Applying *Options:* electronic application, deferred entrance. *Application fee:* $20. *Required:* high school transcript, minimum 2.6 GPA, minimum ACT score of 18. *Application deadline:* rolling (freshmen), rolling (transfers). *Notification:* continuous (transfers).

Admissions Contact Ms. Michelle Kuebler, Assistant Director of Admissions, South Dakota State University, PO Box 2201, Brookings, SD 57007. *Phone:* 605-688-4121. *Toll-free phone:* 800-952-3541. *Fax:* 605-688-6891. *E-mail:* sdsu_admissions@sdstate.edu.

UNIVERSITY OF SIOUX FALLS

Sioux Falls, South Dakota

- **Independent American Baptist Churches in the USA** comprehensive, founded 1883
- **Calendar** 4-1-4
- **Degrees** associate, bachelor's, master's, and doctoral
- **Suburban** 22-acre campus
- **Endowment** $7.2 million
- **Coed,** 1,260 undergraduate students, 82% full-time, 56% women, 44% men
- **Moderately difficult** entrance level, 95% of applicants were admitted

Undergraduates 1,031 full-time, 229 part-time. Students come from 20 states and territories, 3 other countries, 34% are from out of state, 2% African American, 0.5% Asian American or Pacific Islander, 0.9% Hispanic American, 0.4% Native American, 0.8% international, 11% transferred in, 28% live on campus. *Retention:* 68% of 2002 full-time freshmen returned.

Freshmen *Admission:* 774 applied, 732 admitted, 236 enrolled. *Average high school GPA:* 3.30. *Test scores:* ACT scores over 18: 79%; ACT scores over 24: 31%; ACT scores over 30: 1%.

Faculty *Total:* 128, 41% full-time, 29% with terminal degrees. *Student/faculty ratio:* 17:1.

Majors Accounting; administrative assistant and secretarial science; applied art; applied mathematics; art teacher education; behavioral sciences; biology/ biological sciences; business administration and management; chemistry; clinical laboratory science/medical technology; commercial and advertising art; computer science; developmental and child psychology; dramatic/theatre arts; economics; education; elementary education; English; health teacher education; history; humanities; industrial radiologic technology; information science/studies; interdisciplinary studies; kindergarten/preschool education; kinesiology and exercise science; liberal arts and sciences/liberal studies; management information systems; marketing/marketing management; mass communication/media; mathematics; middle school education; music; music management and merchandising; music teacher education; pastoral studies/counseling; philosophy; physical education teaching and coaching; piano and organ; political science and government; pre-dentistry studies; pre-engineering; pre-law studies; pre-medical studies; pre-veterinary studies; psychology; public relations/image management; radio and television; religious studies; science teacher education; secondary education; social sciences; social work; sociology; speech and rhetoric; voice and opera; wind/percussion instruments.

Academic Programs *Special study options:* academic remediation for entering students, accelerated degree program, adult/continuing education programs, advanced placement credit, cooperative education, distance learning, double majors, external degree program, honors programs, independent study, internships, off-campus study, part-time degree program, services for LD students, student-designed majors, study abroad, summer session for credit. *Unusual degree programs:* 3-2 engineering with South Dakota State University, Washington University (St. Louis); religious studies with North American Baptist Seminary.

Library Norman B. Mears Library with 57,750 titles, 382 serial subscriptions, 4,480 audiovisual materials, an OPAC, a Web page.

Computers on Campus 142 computers available on campus for general student use. A campuswide network can be accessed from student residence rooms and from off campus. Internet access, at least one staffed computer lab available.

Student Life *Housing:* on-campus residence required through sophomore year. *Options:* coed, men-only, women-only. Campus housing is university owned and leased by the school. Freshman applicants given priority for college housing. *Activities and organizations:* drama/theater group, student-run newspaper, radio and television station, choral group, Fellowship of Christian Athletes, Campus Ministry Outreach. *Campus security:* late-night transport/escort service, controlled dormitory access. *Student services:* health clinic, personal/psychological counseling, women's center.

Athletics Member NAIA. *Intercollegiate sports:* baseball M(s), basketball M(s)/W(s), cheerleading W(s), cross-country running M(s)/W(s), football M(s), golf M(s)/W(s), soccer M(s)/W(s), softball W(s), tennis M(s)/W(s), track and field M(s)/W(s), volleyball W(s). *Intramural sports:* basketball M/W, football M/W, table tennis M/W, ultimate Frisbee M/W, volleyball M/W.

University of Sioux Falls (continued)

Standardized Tests *Required:* SAT I and SAT II or ACT (for admission).

Costs (2004–05) *Comprehensive fee:* $19,100 includes full-time tuition ($14,900) and room and board ($4200). Part-time tuition: $240 per semester hour. *College room only:* $1830. Room and board charges vary according to board plan and housing facility.

Applying *Options:* electronic application, early admission, deferred entrance. *Application fee:* $25. *Required:* high school transcript. *Required for some:* 2 letters of recommendation, interview. *Recommended:* essay or personal statement, minimum 2.0 GPA. *Application deadline:* rolling (freshmen), rolling (transfers). *Notification:* continuous (freshmen), continuous (transfers).

Admissions Contact Ms. Patti Klinkhammer, Office Manager, University of Sioux Falls, 1101 West 22nd Street, Sioux Falls, SD 57105. *Phone:* 605-331-6600 Ext. 6700. *Toll-free phone:* 800-888-1047. *Fax:* 605-331-6615. *E-mail:* admissions@usiouxfalls.edu.

THE UNIVERSITY OF SOUTH DAKOTA

Vermillion, South Dakota

- **State-supported** university, founded 1862
- **Calendar** semesters
- **Degrees** associate, bachelor's, master's, doctoral, first professional, post-master's, and postbachelor's certificates
- **Small-town** 216-acre campus
- **Endowment** $63.4 million
- **Coed,** 5,851 undergraduate students, 70% full-time, 61% women, 39% men
- **Moderately difficult** entrance level, 83% of applicants were admitted

Undergraduates 4,102 full-time, 1,749 part-time. Students come from 34 states and territories, 23 other countries, 23% are from out of state, 0.8% African American, 0.6% Asian American or Pacific Islander, 1% Hispanic American, 2% Native American, 2% international, 12% transferred in, 36% live on campus. *Retention:* 69% of 2002 full-time freshmen returned.

Freshmen *Admission:* 2,570 applied, 2,134 admitted, 1,078 enrolled. *Average high school GPA:* 3.20. *Test scores:* SAT verbal scores over 500: 86%; SAT math scores over 500: 80%; ACT scores over 18: 92%; SAT verbal scores over 600: 43%; SAT math scores over 600: 33%; ACT scores over 24: 41%; SAT verbal scores over 700: 6%; SAT math scores over 700: 6%; ACT scores over 30: 4%.

Faculty *Total:* 297, 97% full-time, 77% with terminal degrees. *Student/faculty ratio:* 15:1.

Majors Accounting; American Indian/Native American studies; anthropology; art; art teacher education; biology/biological sciences; biology teacher education; business administration and management; business/managerial economics; chemistry; classics and languages, literatures and linguistics; communication disorders; computer and information sciences; criminal justice/law enforcement administration; curriculum and instruction; dental hygiene; drama and dance teacher education; dramatic/theatre arts; economics; education; elementary education; English; English/language arts teacher education; finance; foreign language teacher education; French; French language teacher education; general studies; geology/earth science; German; German language teacher education; health teacher education; history; history teacher education; hospital and health care facilities administration; liberal arts and sciences/liberal studies; marketing/marketing management; mass communication/media; mathematics; mathematics teacher education; middle school education; music; music teacher education; nursing (registered nurse training); parks, recreation and leisure; philosophy; physical education teaching and coaching; physics; physics teacher education; political science and government; psychology; science teacher education; secondary education; social science teacher education; social work; sociology; Spanish; Spanish language teacher education; special education; speech teacher education; substance abuse/addiction counseling.

Academic Programs *Special study options:* advanced placement credit, distance learning, double majors, English as a second language, honors programs, independent study, internships, off-campus study, part-time degree program, services for LD students, study abroad, summer session for credit. *ROTC:* Army (b). *Unusual degree programs:* 3-2 accounting.

Library I. D. Weeks Library plus 2 others with 335,757 titles, 2,852 serial subscriptions, 30,885 audiovisual materials, an OPAC.

Computers on Campus 750 computers available on campus for general student use. A campuswide network can be accessed from student residence rooms and from off campus. Internet access, at least one staffed computer lab available.

Student Life *Housing:* on-campus residence required through sophomore year. *Options:* coed, men-only, women-only. Campus housing is university owned. Freshman campus housing is guaranteed. *Activities and organizations:* drama/theater group, student-run newspaper, radio station, choral group, marching band, Program Council, Residence Hall Association, Interfraternity/Panhellenic Council, Student Ambassadors, Delta Sigma Pi, national fraternities, national sororities. *Campus security:* 24-hour emergency response devices and patrols, student patrols, late-night transport/escort service, controlled dormitory access. *Student services:* health clinic, personal/psychological counseling, legal services.

Athletics Member NCAA. All Division II. *Intercollegiate sports:* baseball M(s), basketball M(s)/W(s), cross-country running M(s)/W(s), football M(s), softball W(s), swimming M(s)/W, tennis M(s)/W(s), track and field M(s)/W(s), volleyball W(s). *Intramural sports:* badminton M/W, basketball M(c)/W(c), bowling M/W, cross-country running M/W, fencing M(c)/W(c), football M(c)/W(c), golf M/W, ice hockey M(c), racquetball M(c)/W(c), riflery M/W, rugby M(c), soccer M(c)/W(c), softball M(c)/W(c), swimming M/W, table tennis M/W, tennis M/W, track and field M/W, volleyball M/W, water polo M/W.

Standardized Tests *Required:* SAT I or ACT (for admission).

Costs (2003–04) *Tuition:* state resident $2163 full-time, $72 per credit hour part-time; nonresident $6875 full-time, $229 per credit hour part-time. Full-time tuition and fees vary according to course load and reciprocity agreements. Part-time tuition and fees vary according to course load and reciprocity agreements. *Required fees:* $2042 full-time, $68 per credit hour part-time. *Room and board:* $3504; room only: $1777. Room and board charges vary according to board plan and housing facility. *Payment plan:* deferred payment. *Waivers:* senior citizens and employees or children of employees.

Financial Aid Of all full-time matriculated undergraduates who enrolled in 2003, 3,172 applied for aid, 2,549 were judged to have need, 1,631 had their need fully met. In 2003, 932 non-need-based awards were made. *Average percent of need met:* 81%. *Average financial aid package:* $5644. *Average need-based loan:* $3184. *Average need-based gift aid:* $2939. *Average non-need-based aid:* $5415. *Average indebtedness upon graduation:* $18,810.

Applying *Options:* electronic application, early admission, deferred entrance. *Application fee:* $20. *Required:* high school transcript. *Required for some:* letters of recommendation. *Recommended:* minimum 2.6 GPA. *Application deadline:* 9/4 (freshmen), rolling (transfers). *Notification:* continuous (freshmen), continuous (transfers).

Admissions Contact Ms. Paula Tacke, Director of Admissions, The University of South Dakota, 414 East Clark Street, Vermillion, SD 57069. *Phone:* 605-677-5434. *Toll-free phone:* 877-269-6837. *Fax:* 605-677-6753. *E-mail:* admiss@usd.edu.

TENNESSEE

AMERICAN BAPTIST COLLEGE OF AMERICAN BAPTIST THEOLOGICAL SEMINARY

Nashville, Tennessee

- **Independent Baptist** 4-year, founded 1924
- **Calendar** semesters
- **Degrees** associate and bachelor's
- **Urban** 52-acre campus
- **Endowment** $1.5 million
- **Coed,** 140 undergraduate students, 66% full-time, 28% women, 72% men
- **Noncompetitive** entrance level, 83% of applicants were admitted

Undergraduates 92 full-time, 48 part-time. Students come from 12 states and territories, 3 other countries, 25% are from out of state, 9% transferred in, 20% live on campus. *Retention:* 85% of 2002 full-time freshmen returned.

Freshmen *Admission:* 46 applied, 38 admitted, 30 enrolled. *Average high school GPA:* 2.70.

Faculty *Total:* 16, 6% full-time, 75% with terminal degrees. *Student/faculty ratio:* 17:1.

Majors Biblical studies; theology.

Academic Programs *Special study options:* academic remediation for entering students, adult/continuing education programs, advanced placement credit, double majors, off-campus study, part-time degree program, summer session for credit. *Unusual degree programs:* 3-2 Bible Theology.

Library T. L. Holcolm Library with 34,899 titles, 142 serial subscriptions, 87 audiovisual materials.

Computers on Campus 20 computers available on campus for general student use. A campuswide network can be accessed from off campus. Internet access, at least one staffed computer lab available.

Student Life *Housing options:* coed, men-only, women-only. Campus housing is university owned. *Activities and organizations:* choral group, Student Government Association, Vespers Service, national fraternities. *Campus security:* student patrols, security patrols from 10 p.m. to 7 a.m.

Athletics *Intramural sports:* basketball M, football M, golf M.

Costs (2004–05) *Tuition:* $3003 full-time, $143 per credit hour part-time. Full-time tuition and fees vary according to course load. Part-time tuition and fees vary according to course load. *Required fees:* $140 full-time, $140 per year part-time. *Room only:* $1600. Room and board charges vary according to housing facility. *Payment plan:* deferred payment.

Financial Aid Of all full-time matriculated undergraduates who enrolled in 2002, 42 applied for aid, 42 were judged to have need. *Average percent of need met:* 20%. *Average financial aid package:* $2025. *Financial aid deadline:* 7/23.

Applying *Options:* common application, deferred entrance. *Application fee:* $20. *Required:* essay or personal statement, high school transcript, minimum 2.0 GPA, 3 letters of recommendation, interview. *Application deadlines:* 7/12 (freshmen), 7/12 (transfers). *Notification:* 8/15 (freshmen), 8/15 (transfers).

Admissions Contact Ms. Marcella Lockhart, Executive Assistant for Administration, American Baptist College of American Baptist Theological Seminary, 1800 Baptist World Center Drive, Nashville, TN 37207. *Phone:* 615-256-1463 Ext. 2227. *Fax:* 615-226-7855.

AQUINAS COLLEGE

Nashville, Tennessee

- **Independent Roman Catholic** 4-year, founded 1961
- **Calendar** semesters
- **Degrees** diplomas, associate, and bachelor's
- **Urban** 92-acre campus
- **Endowment** $2.3 million
- **Coed**
- **Moderately difficult** entrance level

Faculty *Student/faculty ratio:* 19:1.

Student Life *Campus security:* 24-hour emergency response devices, patrols by security after class hours.

Standardized Tests *Required:* SAT I or ACT (for admission).

Costs (2003–04) *Tuition:* $9720 full-time, $385 per credit hour part-time. Full-time tuition and fees vary according to program. Part-time tuition and fees vary according to program. *Required fees:* $330 full-time, $180 per term part-time.

Financial Aid Of all full-time matriculated undergraduates who enrolled in 2003, 154 applied for aid, 123 were judged to have need, 84 had their need fully met. 52 Federal Work-Study jobs (averaging $1200). *Average percent of need met:* 76. *Average financial aid package:* $7050. *Average need-based loan:* $3150. *Average need-based gift aid:* $2550. *Average indebtedness upon graduation:* $8500.

Applying *Options:* common application, electronic application, deferred entrance. *Application fee:* $10. *Required:* high school transcript, minimum 2.0 GPA, interview.

Admissions Contact Mr. Neil J. Devine, Director of Career Planning and Admission, Aquinas College, 4210 Harding Road, Nashville, TN 37205-2005. *Phone:* 615-297-7545 Ext. 426. *Fax:* 615-297-7970.

AUSTIN PEAY STATE UNIVERSITY

Clarksville, Tennessee

- **State-supported** comprehensive, founded 1927, part of Tennessee Board of Regents
- **Calendar** semesters
- **Degrees** associate, bachelor's, master's, and post-master's certificates
- **Suburban** 200-acre campus with easy access to Nashville
- **Endowment** $2.8 million
- **Coed,** 7,188 undergraduate students, 73% full-time, 63% women, 37% men
- **Moderately difficult** entrance level, 94% of applicants were admitted

Undergraduates 5,258 full-time, 1,930 part-time. Students come from 36 states and territories, 7% are from out of state, 19% African American, 3% Asian American or Pacific Islander, 5% Hispanic American, 0.8% Native American, 0.3% international, 11% transferred in, 15% live on campus. *Retention:* 65% of 2002 full-time freshmen returned.

Freshmen *Admission:* 2,207 applied, 2,064 admitted, 1,191 enrolled. *Average high school GPA:* 2.96. *Test scores:* SAT verbal scores over 500: 38%; SAT math scores over 500: 30%; ACT scores over 18: 63%; SAT verbal scores over 600: 11%; SAT math scores over 600: 7%; ACT scores over 24: 17%; SAT verbal scores over 700: 1%; ACT scores over 30: 1%.

Faculty *Total:* 453, 58% full-time, 60% with terminal degrees. *Student/faculty ratio:* 18:1.

Majors Agriculture; art; biology/biological sciences; business administration and management; business automation/technology/data entry; business/commerce; chemistry; clinical laboratory science/medical technology; computer and information sciences; engineering technology; English; foreign languages and literatures; general studies; geography; geology/earth science; health and physical education; health teacher education; history; industrial arts; interdisciplinary studies; mass communication/media; mathematics; music; non-profit management; nursing (registered nurse training); philosophy; physics; political science and government; psychology; radiologic technology/science; social work; sociology; Spanish; special education.

Academic Programs *Special study options:* academic remediation for entering students, adult/continuing education programs, advanced placement credit, distance learning, double majors, English as a second language, honors programs, independent study, internships, part-time degree program, services for LD students, study abroad, summer session for credit. *ROTC:* Army (b).

Library Felix G. Woodward Library with 355,372 titles, 1,754 serial subscriptions, 6,786 audiovisual materials, an OPAC, a Web page.

Computers on Campus 600 computers available on campus for general student use. A campuswide network can be accessed from student residence rooms and from off campus. Internet access, online (class) registration, at least one staffed computer lab available.

Student Life *Housing:* on-campus residence required for freshman year. *Options:* coed, men-only, women-only, disabled students. Campus housing is university owned. Freshman campus housing is guaranteed. *Activities and organizations:* drama/theater group, student-run newspaper, radio and television station, choral group, marching band, national fraternities, national sororities. *Campus security:* 24-hour patrols, late-night transport/escort service, controlled dormitory access. *Student services:* health clinic, personal/psychological counseling.

Athletics Member NCAA. All Division I except football (Division I-AA). *Intercollegiate sports:* baseball M(s), basketball M(s)/W(s), cheerleading M(s)/W(s), cross-country running M(s)/W(s), golf M(s), riflery W(s), softball W(s), tennis M(s)/W(s), track and field W(s), volleyball W(s). *Intramural sports:* basketball M/W, football M/W, golf M, gymnastics M/W, racquetball M/W, riflery W, soccer M, swimming M/W, tennis M/W, track and field M, volleyball M/W.

Standardized Tests *Required for some:* SAT I or ACT (for admission).

Costs (2003–04) *Tuition:* state resident $3132 full-time, $137 per credit hour part-time; nonresident $11,064 full-time, $481 per credit hour part-time. Full-time tuition and fees vary according to location. Part-time tuition and fees vary according to location. *Required fees:* $872 full-time, $41 per credit hour part-time, $4 per term part-time. *Room and board:* $4096; room only: $2450. Room and board charges vary according to board plan and housing facility. *Payment plans:* installment, deferred payment. *Waivers:* senior citizens and employees or children of employees.

Financial Aid Of all full-time matriculated undergraduates who enrolled in 2002, 3,360 applied for aid, 2,418 were judged to have need, 1,510 had their need fully met. 242 Federal Work-Study jobs (averaging $1900). 385 state and other part-time jobs (averaging $1300). In 2002, 540 non-need-based awards were made. *Average percent of need met:* 74%. *Average financial aid package:* $3882. *Average need-based loan:* $3267. *Average need-based gift aid:* $2726. *Average non-need-based aid:* $2318. *Average indebtedness upon graduation:* $17,086.

Applying *Options:* early admission, deferred entrance. *Application fee:* $15. *Required:* high school transcript, 2.75 high school GPA, minimum ACT composite score of 19. *Application deadline:* 9/3 (freshmen), rolling (transfers). *Notification:* continuous (freshmen), continuous (transfers).

Admissions Contact Mr. Scott McDonald, Director of Admissions, Austin Peay State University, PO Box 4548, Clarksville, TN 37044-4548. *Phone:* 931-221-7661. *Toll-free phone:* 800-844-2778. *Fax:* 931-221-6168. *E-mail:* admissions@apsu01.apsu.edu.

BAPTIST COLLEGE OF HEALTH SCIENCES

Memphis, Tennessee

- **Independent Southern Baptist** 4-year, founded 1994
- **Calendar** semesters
- **Degree** certificates and bachelor's
- **Urban** campus
- **Coed, primarily women,** 823 undergraduate students

Undergraduates Students come from 9 states and territories, 34% African American, 3% Asian American or Pacific Islander, 0.7% Hispanic American, 12% live on campus.

Freshmen *Admission:* 260 applied.

Faculty *Total:* 77, 64% full-time.

Majors Diagnostic medical sonography and ultrasound technology; health/health care administration; health services/allied health/health sciences; medical radiologic technology; nuclear medical technology; nursing (registered nurse training); radiologic technology/science; respiratory care therapy.

Academic Programs *Special study options:* advanced placement credit, cooperative education.

Baptist College of Health Sciences (continued)

Computers on Campus A campuswide network can be accessed from student residence rooms. Internet access available.

Student Life *Housing options:* Campus housing is university owned. *Activities and organizations:* student-run newspaper, Student Govenment Association, Student Nursing Association, Allied Health Organization. *Campus security:* 24-hour emergency response devices, late-night transport/escort service, controlled dormitory access, 16 to 20-hour trained security personnel.

Standardized Tests *Required:* ACT (for admission).

Costs (2003–04) *Tuition:* $150 per credit hour part-time. Full-time tuition and fees vary according to course load. Part-time tuition and fees vary according to course load. No tuition increase for student's term of enrollment. *Required fees:* $10 per credit hour part-time. *Room only:* $2400.

Applying *Options:* common application, early admission. *Application fee:* $25. *Required:* high school transcript, minimum 2.75 GPA, 3 letters of recommendation. *Required for some:* essay or personal statement, interview. *Application deadlines:* 6/1 (freshmen), 6/1 (transfers).

Admissions Contact Ms. Cynthia Davis, Manager of Admissions/Retention, Baptist College of Health Sciences, 1003 Monroe Avenue, Memphis, TN 38104. *Phone:* 901-572-2465. *Toll-free phone:* 866-575-2247. *Fax:* 901-572-2461.

BELMONT UNIVERSITY

Nashville, Tennessee

- **Independent Baptist** comprehensive, founded 1951
- **Calendar** semesters
- **Degrees** bachelor's, master's, doctoral, and postbachelor's certificates
- **Urban** 34-acre campus
- **Endowment** $35.6 million
- **Coed,** 2,989 undergraduate students, 89% full-time, 61% women, 39% men
- **Moderately difficult** entrance level, 75% of applicants were admitted

Undergraduates 2,649 full-time, 340 part-time. Students come from 49 states and territories, 23 other countries, 51% are from out of state, 4% African American, 1% Asian American or Pacific Islander, 2% Hispanic American, 0.5% Native American, 2% international, 14% transferred in, 57% live on campus. *Retention:* 77% of 2002 full-time freshmen returned.

Freshmen *Admission:* 1,607 applied, 1,207 admitted, 603 enrolled. *Average high school GPA:* 3.43. *Test scores:* SAT verbal scores over 500: 86%; SAT math scores over 500: 83%; ACT scores over 18: 100%; SAT verbal scores over 600: 34%; SAT math scores over 600: 37%; ACT scores over 24: 63%; SAT verbal scores over 700: 2%; SAT math scores over 700: 6%; ACT scores over 30: 10%.

Faculty *Total:* 421, 47% full-time, 32% with terminal degrees. *Student/faculty ratio:* 11:1.

Majors Accounting; administrative assistant and secretarial science; advertising; ancient Near Eastern and biblical languages; applied mathematics; art; art teacher education; behavioral sciences; biblical studies; bilingual and multilingual education; biochemistry; biological and physical sciences; biology/biological sciences; broadcast journalism; business administration and management; business/managerial economics; business teacher education; chemistry; clinical laboratory science/medical technology; computer management; computer programming; computer science; consumer merchandising/retailing management; counselor education/school counseling and guidance; developmental and child psychology; divinity/ministry; dramatic/theatre arts; economics; education; education (K-12); elementary education; engineering science; English; finance; fine/studio arts; health and physical education; health/health care administration; health teacher education; history; hospitality administration; hotel/motel administration; information science/studies; international business/trade/commerce; journalism; kindergarten/preschool education; marketing/marketing management; mass communication/media; mathematics; modern Greek; music; music history, literature, and theory; music management and merchandising; music teacher education; nursing (registered nurse training); parks, recreation and leisure; pastoral studies/counseling; pharmacology; philosophy; physical education teaching and coaching; physics; piano and organ; political science and government; psychology; radio and television; reading teacher education; religious/sacred music; social work; sociology; Spanish; special education; speech and rhetoric; voice and opera; western civilization.

Academic Programs *Special study options:* accelerated degree program, adult/continuing education programs, advanced placement credit, cooperative education, distance learning, double majors, honors programs, independent study, internships, part-time degree program, student-designed majors, study abroad, summer session for credit. *ROTC:* Army (c). *Unusual degree programs:* 3-2 engineering with Auburn University, Georgia Institute of Technology, University of Tennessee.

Library Lila D. Bunch Library with 184,835 titles, 1,311 serial subscriptions, 26,289 audiovisual materials, an OPAC, a Web page.

Computers on Campus 350 computers available on campus for general student use. A campuswide network can be accessed from student residence rooms and from off campus that provide access to individual student information via BANNER web. Internet access, online (class) registration, at least one staffed computer lab available.

Student Life *Housing:* on-campus residence required through sophomore year. *Options:* men-only, women-only. Campus housing is university owned. Freshman applicants given priority for college housing. *Activities and organizations:* drama/theater group, student-run newspaper, radio and television station, choral group, marching band, national fraternities, national sororities. *Campus security:* 24-hour emergency response devices and patrols, late-night transport/escort service, controlled dormitory access, bicycle patrol. *Student services:* health clinic, personal/psychological counseling.

Athletics Member NCAA. All Division I. *Intercollegiate sports:* baseball M(s), basketball M(s)/W(s), cheerleading M(s)/W(s), cross-country running M(s)/W(s), golf M(s)/W(s), soccer M(s)/W(s), softball W(s), tennis M(s)/W(s), track and field M(s)/W(s), ultimate Frisbee M(c)/W(c), volleyball W(s). *Intramural sports:* basketball M/W, bowling M/W, football M, golf M, racquetball M/W, rock climbing M/W, table tennis M/W, tennis M/W, ultimate Frisbee M/W, volleyball M/W.

Standardized Tests *Required:* SAT I or ACT (for admission).

Costs (2003–04) *Comprehensive fee:* $21,986 includes full-time tuition ($15,164), mandatory fees ($790), and room and board ($6032). Full-time tuition and fees vary according to class time and course load. Part-time tuition: $546 per credit hour. Part-time tuition and fees vary according to course load. *Required fees:* $265 per term part-time. *College room only:* $2850. Room and board charges vary according to board plan, housing facility, and location. *Payment plans:* installment, deferred payment. *Waivers:* senior citizens and employees or children of employees.

Financial Aid Of all full-time matriculated undergraduates who enrolled in 2002, 1,977 applied for aid, 1,237 were judged to have need, 261 had their need fully met. 260 Federal Work-Study jobs (averaging $1200). In 2002, 532 non-need-based awards were made. *Average percent of need met:* 34%. *Average financial aid package:* $2796. *Average need-based loan:* $3435. *Average need-based gift aid:* $2161. *Average non-need-based aid:* $4792. *Average indebtedness upon graduation:* $15,954.

Applying *Options:* common application, early admission, deferred entrance. *Application fee:* $35. *Required:* essay or personal statement, high school transcript, minimum 3.0 GPA, letters of recommendation, resume of activities. *Required for some:* interview. *Application deadlines:* 5/1 (freshmen), 5/1 (transfers). *Notification:* continuous (freshmen), continuous (transfers).

Admissions Contact Dr. Kathryn Baugher, Dean of Enrollment Services, Belmont University, 1900 Belmont Boulevard, Nashville, TN 37212-3757. *Phone:* 615-460-6785. *Toll-free phone:* 800-56E-NROL. *Fax:* 615-460-5434. *E-mail:* buadmission@mail.belmont.edu.

■ *See page 1230 for a narrative description.*

BETHEL COLLEGE

McKenzie, Tennessee

- **Independent Cumberland Presbyterian** comprehensive, founded 1842
- **Calendar** semesters
- **Degrees** bachelor's, master's, and first professional
- **Small-town** 100-acre campus
- **Endowment** $6.6 million
- **Coed,** 1,149 undergraduate students, 83% full-time, 56% women, 44% men
- **Minimally difficult** entrance level, 54% of applicants were admitted

Undergraduates 954 full-time, 195 part-time. Students come from 14 states and territories, 11 other countries, 12% are from out of state, 22% African American, 0.1% Asian American or Pacific Islander, 1% Hispanic American, 0.3% Native American, 2% international, 5% transferred in, 50% live on campus. *Retention:* 51% of 2002 full-time freshmen returned.

Freshmen *Admission:* 492 applied, 264 admitted, 132 enrolled. *Average high school GPA:* 2.85. *Test scores:* SAT verbal scores over 500: 27%; SAT math scores over 500: 54%; ACT scores over 18: 67%; ACT scores over 24: 15%; ACT scores over 30: 1%.

Faculty *Total:* 45, 78% full-time, 47% with terminal degrees. *Student/faculty ratio:* 14:1.

Majors Accounting; biology/biological sciences; biology teacher education; business administration and management; chemistry; dramatic/theatre arts; education; education (K-12); elementary education; English; English/language arts teacher education; health and physical education; history; history teacher education; human services; interdisciplinary studies; liberal arts and sciences/liberal studies; mathematics; physical education teaching and coaching; physician assistant; pre-dentistry studies; pre-medical studies; psychology; special education.

Academic Programs *Special study options:* academic remediation for entering students, accelerated degree program, adult/continuing education programs, advanced placement credit, double majors, internships, off-campus study, part-time degree program, services for LD students, student-designed majors, summer session for credit. *Unusual degree programs:* 3-2 engineering with Tennessee Technological University, The University of Memphis; religion with Memphis Theological Seminary.

Library Burroughs Learning Center with 73,288 titles, 254 serial subscriptions.

Computers on Campus 35 computers available on campus for general student use. A campuswide network can be accessed from student residence rooms that provide access to each traditional student receives a lap-top computer. Internet access, at least one staffed computer lab available. Computer purchase or lease plan available.

Student Life *Housing:* on-campus residence required through sophomore year. *Options:* coed, men-only, women-only, disabled students. Campus housing is university owned. Freshman campus housing is guaranteed. *Activities and organizations:* drama/theater group, choral group, FCA, SETA (Education), Black Student Union, honor club. *Campus security:* night patrols by trained security personnel. *Student services:* personal/psychological counseling.

Athletics Member NAIA. *Intercollegiate sports:* baseball M(s), basketball M(s)/W(s), cheerleading M(s)/W(s), cross-country running M(s)/W(s), football M(s), golf M(s)/W(s), soccer M(s)/W(s), softball W(s), tennis M(s)/W(s), track and field M(s)/W(s), volleyball W(s). *Intramural sports:* basketball M/W, football M, golf M/W, soccer M/W, softball M/W, table tennis M/W, tennis M/W, volleyball M/W, weight lifting M/W.

Standardized Tests *Required:* SAT I or ACT (for admission).

Costs (2003–04) *Comprehensive fee:* $14,710 includes full-time tuition ($9360), mandatory fees ($270), and room and board ($5080). Part-time tuition and fees vary according to course load. *Payment plan:* installment. *Waivers:* employees or children of employees.

Financial Aid Of all full-time matriculated undergraduates who enrolled in 2002, 536 applied for aid, 383 were judged to have need, 299 had their need fully met. In 2002, 54 non-need-based awards were made. *Average percent of need met:* 79%. *Average financial aid package:* $9023. *Average need-based loan:* $2959. *Average need-based gift aid:* $3133. *Average non-need-based aid:* $3921. *Average indebtedness upon graduation:* $12,160.

Applying *Options:* early admission, deferred entrance. *Application fee:* $30. *Required:* high school transcript, minimum 2.25 GPA. *Required for some:* essay or personal statement, 1 letter of recommendation, interview. *Application deadline:* rolling (freshmen), rolling (transfers). *Notification:* continuous (freshmen), continuous (transfers).

Admissions Contact Mrs. Tina Hodges, Director of Admissions and Marketing, Bethel College, 325 Cherry Avenue, McKenzie, TN 38201. *Phone:* 731-352-4030. *Fax:* 731-352-4069. *E-mail:* admissions@bethel-college.edu.

BRYAN COLLEGE
Dayton, Tennessee

- **Independent interdenominational** 4-year, founded 1930
- **Calendar** semesters
- **Degrees** associate and bachelor's
- **Small-town** 100-acre campus
- **Endowment** $2.0 million
- **Coed,** 557 undergraduate students
- **Moderately difficult** entrance level, 35% of applicants were admitted

Bryan College is a 4-year, interdenominational, Christian liberal arts college. High-quality academics, spiritual atmosphere, and close interpersonal relationships highlight the reasons students choose Bryan College. Bryan's unique Biblical Worldview approach to education equips students to see the world through the lens of Scripture. As a result, students are better able to understand and interpret the world around them through a biblical worldview. Visits to the Bryan campus are encouraged.

Undergraduates Students come from 33 states and territories, 7 other countries, 74% live on campus. *Retention:* 77% of 2002 full-time freshmen returned.

Freshmen *Admission:* 539 applied, 186 admitted. *Average high school GPA:* 3.48. *Test scores:* SAT verbal scores over 500: 76%; SAT math scores over 500: 68%; ACT scores over 18: 87%; SAT verbal scores over 600: 31%; SAT math scores over 600: 23%; ACT scores over 24: 49%; SAT verbal scores over 700: 11%; SAT math scores over 700: 6%; ACT scores over 30: 7%.

Faculty *Total:* 70, 50% full-time, 53% with terminal degrees. *Student/faculty ratio:* 14:1.

Majors Biblical studies; biology/biological sciences; business administration and management; computer science; education; elementary education; English; history; kindergarten/preschool education; liberal arts and sciences/liberal studies; literature; mass communication/media; mathematics; middle school education; music; music management and merchandising; music teacher education; physical education teaching and coaching; piano and organ; pre-medical studies; psychology; religious education; religious/sacred music; science teacher education; secondary education; voice and opera; wind/percussion instruments.

Academic Programs *Special study options:* academic remediation for entering students, adult/continuing education programs, advanced placement credit, double majors, honors programs, independent study, internships, part-time degree program, study abroad, summer session for credit. *Unusual degree programs:* 3-2 nursing with Vanderbilt University.

Library Ironside Memorial Library with 98,413 titles, 4,212 serial subscriptions, 1,396 audiovisual materials, an OPAC, a Web page.

Computers on Campus 74 computers available on campus for general student use. A campuswide network can be accessed from student residence rooms. Internet access, at least one staffed computer lab available.

Student Life *Housing:* on-campus residence required through senior year. *Options:* men-only, women-only. Campus housing is university owned. Freshman campus housing is guaranteed. *Activities and organizations:* drama/theater group, student-run newspaper, choral group, Practical Christian Involvement, Student Government Association, Fellowship of Christian Athletes, Hilltop Players, chorale. *Campus security:* student patrols, late-night transport/escort service, controlled dormitory access, police patrols. *Student services:* personal/psychological counseling.

Athletics Member NAIA, NCCAA. *Intercollegiate sports:* baseball M(s), basketball M(s)/W(s), soccer M(s)/W(s), tennis M(s)/W(s), volleyball W(s). *Intramural sports:* basketball M/W, football M/W, golf M, soccer M/W, softball M/W, table tennis M/W, tennis M/W, volleyball M/W.

Standardized Tests *Required:* ACT (for admission).

Costs (2003–04) *Comprehensive fee:* $17,900 includes full-time tuition ($13,500) and room and board ($4400). Part-time tuition: $500 per credit hour. *Payment plan:* installment. *Waivers:* children of alumni and employees or children of employees.

Financial Aid Of all full-time matriculated undergraduates who enrolled in 2002, 464 applied for aid, 413 were judged to have need, 69 had their need fully met. 229 Federal Work-Study jobs (averaging $829). In 2002, 144 non-need-based awards were made. *Average percent of need met:* 69%. *Average financial aid package:* $10,035. *Average need-based loan:* $3497. *Average need-based gift aid:* $3586. *Average non-need-based aid:* $4417. *Average indebtedness upon graduation:* $14,069.

Applying *Options:* electronic application, early admission, deferred entrance. *Application fee:* $30. *Required:* essay or personal statement, high school transcript, minimum 2.0 GPA, 3 letters of recommendation. *Required for some:* interview. *Application deadline:* rolling (freshmen), rolling (transfers).

Admissions Contact Mr. Mark A. Cruver, Director of Admissions and Enrollment Management, Bryan College, PO Box 7000, Dayton, TN 37321-7000. *Phone:* 423-775-2041 Ext. 207. *Toll-free phone:* 800-277-9522. *Fax:* 423-775-7199. *E-mail:* admiss@bryan.edu.

CARSON-NEWMAN COLLEGE
Jefferson City, Tennessee

- **Independent Southern Baptist** comprehensive, founded 1851
- **Calendar** semesters
- **Degrees** associate, bachelor's, and master's
- **Small-town** 90-acre campus with easy access to Knoxville
- **Endowment** $30.1 million
- **Coed,** 1,942 undergraduate students, 92% full-time, 55% women, 45% men
- **Moderately difficult** entrance level, 88% of applicants were admitted

Undergraduates 1,785 full-time, 157 part-time. Students come from 37 states and territories, 21 other countries, 32% are from out of state, 8% African American, 0.3% Asian American or Pacific Islander, 0.6% Hispanic American, 0.2% Native American, 4% international, 9% transferred in, 51% live on campus. *Retention:* 74% of 2002 full-time freshmen returned.

Freshmen *Admission:* 1,124 applied, 992 admitted, 367 enrolled. *Average high school GPA:* 3.28. *Test scores:* ACT scores over 18: 90%; ACT scores over 24: 35%; ACT scores over 30: 5%.

Faculty *Total:* 199, 64% full-time, 34% with terminal degrees. *Student/faculty ratio:* 13:1.

Majors Accounting; ancient Near Eastern and biblical languages; art; art teacher education; athletic training; biblical studies; biology/biological sciences; broadcast journalism; business administration and management; business/managerial economics; business teacher education; chemistry; child development; clinical laboratory science/medical technology; commercial and advertising art; computer science; consumer services and advocacy; creative writing; developmental and child psychology; dietetics; divinity/ministry; dramatic/theatre arts; drawing; economics; education; elementary education; English; family and consumer

Carson-Newman College (continued)
economics related; family and consumer sciences/home economics teacher education; family and consumer sciences/human sciences; fashion merchandising; film/cinema studies; foods, nutrition, and wellness; French; history; hospital and health care facilities administration; human services; information science/studies; interdisciplinary studies; interior design; international economics; journalism; kindergarten/preschool education; kinesiology and exercise science; liberal arts and sciences/liberal studies; literature; management information systems; marketing/marketing management; mass communication/media; mathematics; music; music teacher education; music theory and composition; nursing (registered nurse training); parks, recreation and leisure; philosophy; photography; physical education teaching and coaching; piano and organ; political science and government; psychology; religious studies; secondary education; sociology; Spanish; special education; speech and rhetoric; voice and opera.

Academic Programs *Special study options:* academic remediation for entering students, accelerated degree program, adult/continuing education programs, advanced placement credit, English as a second language, honors programs, internships, off-campus study, part-time degree program, services for LD students, student-designed majors, study abroad, summer session for credit. *ROTC:* Army (b), Air Force (c). *Unusual degree programs:* 3-2 engineering with Georgia Institute of Technology, University of Tennessee, Tennessee Technological University; pharmacy with Campbell University, Mercer University, University of Georgia.

Library Stephens-Burnett Library plus 1 other with 218,371 titles, 3,966 serial subscriptions, 14,713 audiovisual materials, an OPAC, a Web page.

Computers on Campus 200 computers available on campus for general student use. A campuswide network can be accessed from student residence rooms and from off campus. Internet access, at least one staffed computer lab available.

Student Life *Housing:* on-campus residence required through junior year. *Options:* men-only, women-only. Freshman campus housing is guaranteed. *Activities and organizations:* drama/theater group, student-run newspaper, choral group, marching band, Baptist Student Union, Fellowship of Christian Athletes, Student Government Association, Student Ambassadors Association, Columbians, national fraternities, national sororities. *Campus security:* 24-hour emergency response devices and patrols, late-night transport/escort service, controlled dormitory access. *Student services:* health clinic, personal/psychological counseling.

Athletics Member NCAA. All Division II. *Intercollegiate sports:* baseball M(s), basketball M(s)/W(s), cheerleading W, cross-country running M(s)/W(s), football M(s), golf M(s), soccer M(s)/W(s), softball W(s), tennis M(s)/W(s), track and field M(s)/W(s), volleyball W(s), wrestling M(s). *Intramural sports:* badminton M/W, baseball M/W, basketball M/W, football M/W, golf M/W, racquetball M/W, skiing (downhill) M/W, soccer M/W, softball M/W, table tennis M/W, tennis M/W, volleyball M/W.

Standardized Tests *Required:* SAT I or ACT (for admission).

Costs (2004–05) *Comprehensive fee:* $19,350 includes full-time tuition ($13,700), mandatory fees ($720), and room and board ($4930). Full-time tuition and fees vary according to class time. Part-time tuition: $565 per semester hour. Part-time tuition and fees vary according to class time. *Required fees:* $220 per term part-time. *College room only:* $1850. Room and board charges vary according to board plan. *Payment plan:* installment. *Waivers:* senior citizens and employees or children of employees.

Financial Aid Of all full-time matriculated undergraduates who enrolled in 2003, 1,476 applied for aid, 1,305 were judged to have need, 185 had their need fully met. 399 Federal Work-Study jobs (averaging $1725). 296 state and other part-time jobs (averaging $1587). In 2003, 373 non-need-based awards were made. *Average percent of need met:* 72%. *Average financial aid package:* $12,525. *Average need-based loan:* $3752. *Average need-based gift aid:* $8095. *Average non-need-based aid:* $4585. *Average indebtedness upon graduation:* $11,957.

Applying *Options:* electronic application, deferred entrance. *Application fee:* $25. *Required:* high school transcript, minimum 2.25 GPA, medical history. *Required for some:* essay or personal statement, letters of recommendation, interview. *Recommended:* interview. *Application deadlines:* 8/1 (freshmen), 8/1 (transfers). *Notification:* continuous (freshmen), continuous (transfers).

Admissions Contact Mrs. Sheryl M. Gray, Director of Undergraduate Admissions, Carson-Newman College, PO Box 72025, Jefferson City, TN 37760. *Phone:* 865-471-3223. *Toll-free phone:* 800-678-9061. *Fax:* 865-471-3502. *E-mail:* cnadmiss@cn.edu.

■ *See page 1358 for a narrative description.*

CHRISTIAN BROTHERS UNIVERSITY
Memphis, Tennessee

- **Independent Roman Catholic** comprehensive, founded 1871
- **Calendar** semesters
- **Degrees** bachelor's and master's
- **Urban** 70-acre campus
- **Endowment** $21.3 million
- **Coed,** 1,582 undergraduate students, 76% full-time, 57% women, 43% men
- **Moderately difficult** entrance level, 85% of applicants were admitted

Undergraduates 1,203 full-time, 379 part-time. Students come from 33 states and territories, 26 other countries, 15% are from out of state, 35% African American, 5% Asian American or Pacific Islander, 2% Hispanic American, 0.1% Native American, 2% international, 10% transferred in, 31% live on campus. *Retention:* 84% of 2002 full-time freshmen returned.

Freshmen *Admission:* 879 applied, 749 admitted, 281 enrolled. *Average high school GPA:* 3.38. *Test scores:* SAT verbal scores over 500: 70%; SAT math scores over 500: 71%; ACT scores over 18: 96%; SAT verbal scores over 600: 24%; SAT math scores over 600: 30%; ACT scores over 24: 41%; SAT verbal scores over 700: 3%; SAT math scores over 700: 4%; ACT scores over 30: 6%.

Faculty *Total:* 243, 43% full-time, 60% with terminal degrees. *Student/faculty ratio:* 12:1.

Majors Accounting; biology/biological sciences; biology teacher education; business administration and management; business/commerce; business/managerial economics; chemical engineering; chemistry; chemistry teacher education; civil engineering; computer engineering; computer science; economics; education; educational psychology; electrical, electronics and communications engineering; elementary education; engineering physics; English; English/language arts teacher education; environmental/environmental health engineering; finance; history; history teacher education; management information systems; marketing/marketing management; mathematics; mathematics teacher education; mechanical engineering; natural sciences; physics; physics teacher education; pre-dentistry studies; pre-law studies; pre-medical studies; pre-pharmacy studies; pre-theology/pre-ministerial studies; psychology; religious studies; technical and business writing.

Academic Programs *Special study options:* accelerated degree program, advanced placement credit, double majors, honors programs, internships, off-campus study, part-time degree program, study abroad, summer session for credit. *ROTC:* Army (c), Navy (c), Air Force (c).

Library Plough Memorial Library and Media Center with 92,000 titles, 520 serial subscriptions, 1,100 audiovisual materials, an OPAC, a Web page.

Computers on Campus 300 computers available on campus for general student use. A campuswide network can be accessed from student residence rooms and from off campus that provide access to online class listings, e-mail, course assignments. Internet access, online (class) registration, at least one staffed computer lab available.

Student Life *Housing:* on-campus residence required for freshman year. *Options:* coed. Campus housing is university owned. Freshman applicants given priority for college housing. *Activities and organizations:* drama/theater group, student-run newspaper, choral group, Black Student Association, BACCHUS Alcohol Awareness Group, Intercultural Club, College Republicans, Beta Beta Beta, national fraternities, national sororities. *Campus security:* 24-hour emergency response devices and patrols, student patrols, late-night transport/escort service, controlled dormitory access. *Student services:* health clinic, personal/psychological counseling.

Athletics Member NCAA. All Division II except men's and women's cheerleading (Division I). *Intercollegiate sports:* baseball M(s), basketball M(s)/W(s), cheerleading M/W, cross-country running M/W, golf M, soccer M(s)/W(s), softball W(s), tennis M/W, volleyball W(s). *Intramural sports:* basketball M/W, bowling M/W, cross-country running M/W, football M/W, golf M, racquetball M/W, rock climbing M/W, soccer M/W, softball M/W, swimming M/W, table tennis M/W, ultimate Frisbee M/W, volleyball M/W.

Standardized Tests *Required:* SAT I or ACT (for admission).

Costs (2003–04) *Comprehensive fee:* $22,290 includes full-time tuition ($16,740), mandatory fees ($450), and room and board ($5100). Part-time tuition: $525 per credit hour. Part-time tuition and fees vary according to class time. *College room only:* $2300. Room and board charges vary according to board plan and housing facility. *Payment plans:* installment, deferred payment. *Waivers:* children of alumni and employees or children of employees.

Financial Aid Of all full-time matriculated undergraduates who enrolled in 2003, 884 applied for aid, 746 were judged to have need, 122 had their need fully met. 289 Federal Work-Study jobs (averaging $1050). 313 state and other part-time jobs (averaging $1000). In 2003, 368 non-need-based awards were made. *Average percent of need met:* 72%. *Average financial aid package:* $13,146. *Average need-based loan:* $4043. *Average need-based gift aid:* $5604. *Average non-need-based aid:* $4043. *Average indebtedness upon graduation:* $17,200.

Applying *Options:* common application, electronic application, early admission, deferred entrance. *Application fee:* $25. *Required:* essay or personal statement, high school transcript, minimum 2.5 GPA. *Required for some:* letters of recommendation. *Recommended:* interview. *Application deadlines:* 3/1 (freshmen), 8/23 (transfers). *Notification:* 8/1 (freshmen), continuous (transfers).

Admissions Contact Ms. Tracey Dysart, Dean of Admissions, Christian Brothers University, 650 East Parkway South, Memphis, TN 38104. *Phone:* 901-321-3205. *Toll-free phone:* 800-288-7576. *Fax:* 901-321-3202. *E-mail:* admissions@cbu.edu.

CRICHTON COLLEGE
Memphis, Tennessee

- **Independent** 4-year, founded 1941
- **Calendar** semesters
- **Degrees** certificates, bachelor's, and postbachelor's certificates
- **Urban** 7-acre campus
- **Endowment** $398,150
- **Coed,** 1,032 undergraduate students, 71% full-time, 59% women, 41% men
- **Moderately difficult** entrance level, 79% of applicants were admitted

Undergraduates 737 full-time, 295 part-time. Students come from 15 states and territories, 4 other countries, 15% are from out of state, 47% African American, 0.4% Asian American or Pacific Islander, 0.6% Hispanic American, 0.4% Native American, 1% international, 86% transferred in, 5% live on campus. *Retention:* 45% of 2002 full-time freshmen returned.

Freshmen *Admission:* 196 applied, 155 admitted, 149 enrolled. *Average high school GPA:* 3.28. *Test scores:* SAT verbal scores over 500: 100%; SAT math scores over 500: 100%; ACT scores over 18: 89%; ACT scores over 24: 43%; ACT scores over 30: 2%.

Faculty *Total:* 115, 26% full-time, 30% with terminal degrees. *Student/faculty ratio:* 15:1.

Majors Biblical studies; biology/biological sciences; biology teacher education; business administration and management; chemistry; chemistry teacher education; clinical psychology; counseling psychology; elementary education; English; English/language arts teacher education; history; human resources management; liberal arts and sciences/liberal studies; management information systems and services related; non-profit management; pre-law studies; pre-nursing studies; psychology; school psychology; secondary education; youth ministry.

Academic Programs *Special study options:* academic remediation for entering students, accelerated degree program, adult/continuing education programs, advanced placement credit, cooperative education, distance learning, double majors, honors programs, independent study, internships, off-campus study, part-time degree program, student-designed majors, study abroad, summer session for credit.

Library J.W. and Dorothy Bell Library plus 1 other with 46,777 titles, 3,655 serial subscriptions, 1,079 audiovisual materials, an OPAC.

Computers on Campus 48 computers available on campus for general student use. A campuswide network can be accessed from off campus. Internet access, at least one staffed computer lab available.

Student Life *Housing options:* men-only, women-only. Campus housing is leased by the school. Freshman campus housing is guaranteed. *Activities and organizations:* drama/theater group, choral group, Student Government Association, orientation staff, Presidential Ambassadors, American Humanics, Alpha Sigma Lambda. *Campus security:* 24-hour patrols, controlled dormitory access, security alarms in campus apartments. *Student services:* personal/psychological counseling.

Athletics Member NCCAA. *Intercollegiate sports:* baseball M(s), basketball M(s). *Intramural sports:* football M/W, softball M/W, volleyball M/W.

Standardized Tests *Required:* SAT I or ACT (for admission).

Costs (2003–04) *One-time required fee:* $5. *Tuition:* $11,400 full-time, $475 per credit hour part-time. Full-time tuition and fees vary according to course load and program. Part-time tuition and fees vary according to program. *Required fees:* $215 full-time, $125 per year part-time. *Room only:* $3600. *Waivers:* minority students, children of alumni, adult students, and employees or children of employees.

Financial Aid Of all full-time matriculated undergraduates who enrolled in 2002, 304 applied for aid, 246 were judged to have need, 16 had their need fully met. 38 Federal Work-Study jobs (averaging $1839). In 2002, 34 non-need-based awards were made. *Average percent of need met:* 53%. *Average financial aid package:* $8381. *Average need-based loan:* $4031. *Average need-based gift aid:* $5240. *Average non-need-based aid:* $6173. *Average indebtedness upon graduation:* $22,514.

Applying *Options:* electronic application, deferred entrance. *Application fee:* $25. *Required:* essay or personal statement, high school transcript, minimum 2.0 GPA, 2 letters of recommendation, minimum ACT score of 18. *Recommended:* interview. *Application deadlines:* rolling (freshmen), 8/15 (transfers). *Notification:* continuous (freshmen), continuous (transfers).

Admissions Contact Mr. David Wilson, Director of Admissions, Crichton College, 255 North Highland, Memphis, TN 38111-1375. *Phone:* 901-320-9797 Ext. 1041. *Toll-free phone:* 800-960-9777. *Fax:* 901-320-9709. *E-mail:* info@crichton.edu.

CUMBERLAND UNIVERSITY
Lebanon, Tennessee

- **Independent** comprehensive, founded 1842
- **Calendar** semesters
- **Degrees** associate, bachelor's, and master's
- **Small-town** 44-acre campus with easy access to Nashville
- **Endowment** $6.3 million
- **Coed,** 921 undergraduate students, 84% full-time, 57% women, 43% men
- **Moderately difficult** entrance level, 66% of applicants were admitted

Undergraduates 778 full-time, 143 part-time. Students come from 25 states and territories, 14% are from out of state, 15% African American, 2% Asian American or Pacific Islander, 2% Hispanic American, 0.4% Native American, 8% transferred in, 43% live on campus. *Retention:* 69% of 2002 full-time freshmen returned.

Freshmen *Admission:* 532 applied, 353 admitted, 210 enrolled. *Average high school GPA:* 3.03. *Test scores:* SAT verbal scores over 500: 40%; SAT math scores over 500: 35%; ACT scores over 18: 69%; SAT verbal scores over 600: 10%; SAT math scores over 600: 10%; ACT scores over 24: 16%.

Faculty *Total:* 123, 64% full-time, 54% with terminal degrees. *Student/faculty ratio:* 13:1.

Majors Accounting; American studies; athletic training; biology/biological sciences; biology teacher education; business/commerce; criminal justice/law enforcement administration; dramatic/theatre arts; education; elementary education; English; fine/studio arts; geography teacher education; health/medical preparatory programs related; history; history teacher education; liberal arts and sciences/liberal studies; mathematics; mathematics teacher education; music; music teacher education; nursing (registered nurse training); parks, recreation and leisure; physical education teaching and coaching; political science and government; pre-dentistry studies; pre-law studies; pre-medical studies; pre-pharmacy studies; pre-veterinary studies; psychology; psychology teacher education; secondary education; social sciences; sociology; special education; visual and performing arts related.

Academic Programs *Special study options:* academic remediation for entering students, accelerated degree program, adult/continuing education programs, advanced placement credit, cooperative education, double majors, freshman honors college, honors programs, internships, part-time degree program, services for LD students, summer session for credit. *ROTC:* Army (b).

Library Doris and Harry Vise Library with 50,000 titles, 130 serial subscriptions, 250 audiovisual materials, an OPAC, a Web page.

Computers on Campus 150 computers available on campus for general student use. A campuswide network can be accessed from student residence rooms and from off campus. Internet access, at least one staffed computer lab available.

Student Life *Housing:* on-campus residence required for freshman year. *Options:* men-only, women-only, disabled students. Campus housing is university owned. *Activities and organizations:* drama/theater group, student-run newspaper, radio station, choral group, marching band, African-American Student Association, Baptist Collegiate Ministry, Law and Government Club, Student Government Association, Student Nurses' Association, national fraternities, national sororities. *Campus security:* 24-hour patrols. *Student services:* personal/psychological counseling.

Athletics Member NAIA. *Intercollegiate sports:* baseball M(s), basketball M(s)/W(s), cheerleading M(s)/W(s), cross-country running M(s)/W(s), football M(s), golf M(s)/W(s), soccer M(s)/W(s), softball W(s), tennis M(s)/W(s), volleyball W(s), wrestling M(s). *Intramural sports:* basketball M/W, bowling M/W, softball W, table tennis M/W, volleyball M/W.

Standardized Tests *Required:* SAT I or ACT (for admission).

Costs (2003–04) *Comprehensive fee:* $16,710 includes full-time tuition ($12,130), mandatory fees ($100), and room and board ($4480). Full-time tuition and fees vary according to course load. Part-time tuition: $506 per semester hour. *Room and board:* Room and board charges vary according to board plan and housing facility. *Payment plans:* installment, deferred payment. *Waivers:* employees or children of employees.

Financial Aid In 2002, 253 non-need-based awards were made. *Average percent of need met:* 65%. *Average financial aid package:* $10,192.

Applying *Options:* deferred entrance. *Application fee:* $25. *Required:* high school transcript. *Required for some:* 3 letters of recommendation. *Recommended:* minimum 2.0 GPA. *Application deadline:* rolling (freshmen). *Notification:* continuous (freshmen), continuous (transfers).

Admissions Contact Dr. James Dressler, Vice President of Student Affairs and Dean of Students, Cumberland University, One Cumberland Square, Lebanon, TN 37087. *Phone:* 615-444-2562 Ext. 1226. *Toll-free phone:* 800-467-0562. *Fax:* 615-444-2569. *E-mail:* admissions@cumberland.edu.

EAST TENNESSEE STATE UNIVERSITY

Johnson City, Tennessee

- **State-supported** university, founded 1911, part of State University and Community College System of Tennessee, Tennessee Board of Regents
- **Calendar** semesters
- **Degrees** associate, bachelor's, master's, doctoral, first professional, post-master's, and postbachelor's certificates
- **Small-town** 366-acre campus
- **Endowment** $41.8 million
- **Coed**
- **Moderately difficult** entrance level

East Tennessee State University serves 12,000 students in the beautiful mountain and lake region of northeast Tennessee. Programs are offered in arts and sciences, business, medicine, education, applied science and technology, public and allied health, and nursing. Extensive graduate study includes a master's in physical therapy. An astronomy observatory and a $28-million library recently opened. Unique programs include bluegrass music, Appalachian studies, storytelling, and computer animation.

Faculty *Student/faculty ratio:* 17:1.

Student Life *Campus security:* 24-hour emergency response devices and patrols, student patrols, late-night transport/escort service, controlled dormitory access.

Athletics Member NCAA. All Division I except football (Division I-AA).

Standardized Tests *Required:* SAT I or ACT (for admission).

Costs (2003–04) *Tuition:* state resident $3132 full-time, $137 per semester hour part-time; nonresident $11,064 full-time, $481 per semester hour part-time. Full-time tuition and fees vary according to course load and program. *Required fees:* $707 full-time, $49 per semester hour part-time. *Room and board:* $4658; room only: $2000. Room and board charges vary according to board plan and housing facility. *Payment plans:* tuition prepayment, installment, deferred payment.

Financial Aid Of all full-time matriculated undergraduates who enrolled in 2003, 5,701 applied for aid, 3,956 were judged to have need, 1,736 had their need fully met. 751 Federal Work-Study jobs (averaging $1183). 426 state and other part-time jobs (averaging $916). In 2003, 1198. *Average percent of need met:* 81. *Average financial aid package:* $4585. *Average need-based loan:* $3268. *Average need-based gift aid:* $2999. *Average non-need-based aid:* $2777. *Average indebtedness upon graduation:* $18,425.

Applying *Options:* electronic application, early admission. *Application fee:* $15. *Required:* high school transcript, minimum 2.3 GPA, minimum high school GPA of 2.3 or minimum ACT score of 19.

Admissions Contact Mr. Mike Pitts, Director of Admissions, East Tennessee State University, Box 70731, Johnson City, TN 37614-0731. *Phone:* 423-439-4213. *Toll-free phone:* 800-462-3878. *Fax:* 423-439-4630. *E-mail:* go2etsu@mail.etsu.edu.

FISK UNIVERSITY

Nashville, Tennessee

- **Independent** comprehensive, founded 1866, affiliated with United Church of Christ
- **Calendar** semesters
- **Degrees** bachelor's, master's, and postbachelor's certificates
- **Urban** 40-acre campus
- **Endowment** $12.0 million
- **Coed**
- **Moderately difficult** entrance level

Faculty *Student/faculty ratio:* 13:1.

Student Life *Campus security:* 24-hour patrols, late-night transport/escort service.

Athletics Member NCAA. All Division III.

Standardized Tests *Required:* SAT I or ACT (for admission).

Costs (2003–04) *Comprehensive fee:* $17,005 includes full-time tuition ($10,900), mandatory fees ($335), and room and board ($5770). Full-time tuition and fees vary according to course load and degree level. Part-time tuition and fees vary according to course load and degree level. *College room only:* $3350. Room and board charges vary according to board plan.

Financial Aid Of all full-time matriculated undergraduates who enrolled in 2003, 783 applied for aid, 776 were judged to have need, 44 had their need fully met. 167 Federal Work-Study jobs (averaging $1323). In 2003, 23. *Average percent of need met:* 55. *Average financial aid package:* $13,650. *Average need-based loan:* $3750. *Average need-based gift aid:* $3700. *Average non-need-based aid:* $8200. *Average indebtedness upon graduation:* $20,000. *Financial aid deadline:* 6/1.

Applying *Options:* electronic application. *Application fee:* $50. *Required:* essay or personal statement, high school transcript, minimum 2.5 GPA, 2 letters of recommendation.

Admissions Contact Director of Admissions, Fisk University, 1000 17th Avenue North, Nashville, TN 37208-3051. *Phone:* 615-329-8666. *Toll-free phone:* 800-443-FISK. *Fax:* 615-329-8774. *E-mail:* admit@fisk.edu.

FOUNTAINHEAD COLLEGE OF TECHNOLOGY

Knoxville, Tennessee

- **Proprietary** primarily 2-year, founded 1947
- **Calendar** quarters
- **Degrees** associate and bachelor's
- **Suburban** 1-acre campus
- **Coed**
- **Noncompetitive** entrance level

Student Life *Campus security:* 24-hour emergency response devices.

Applying *Application fee:* $100. *Recommended:* high school transcript.

Admissions Contact Ms. Casey Rackley, Director of Administration, Fountainhead College of Technology, 3203 Tazewell Pike, Knoxville, TN 37918-2530. *Phone:* 865-688-9422. *Toll-free phone:* 888-218-7335.

FREED-HARDEMAN UNIVERSITY

Henderson, Tennessee

- **Independent** comprehensive, founded 1869, affiliated with Church of Christ
- **Calendar** semesters
- **Degrees** bachelor's, master's, and postbachelor's certificates
- **Small-town** 96-acre campus
- **Endowment** $20.7 million
- **Coed,** 1,447 undergraduate students, 95% full-time, 53% women, 47% men
- **Moderately difficult** entrance level, 99% of applicants were admitted

Undergraduates 1,378 full-time, 69 part-time. Students come from 36 states and territories, 17 other countries, 50% are from out of state, 4% African American, 0.6% Asian American or Pacific Islander, 0.6% Hispanic American, 0.5% Native American, 2% international, 6% transferred in, 78% live on campus. *Retention:* 74% of 2002 full-time freshmen returned.

Freshmen *Admission:* 663 applied, 658 admitted, 375 enrolled. *Average high school GPA:* 3.38. *Test scores:* ACT scores over 18: 93%; ACT scores over 24: 40%; ACT scores over 30: 8%.

Faculty *Total:* 117, 83% full-time, 74% with terminal degrees. *Student/faculty ratio:* 16:1.

Majors Accounting; agricultural business and management; apparel and textiles; art; art teacher education; behavioral sciences; biblical studies; biochemistry; biological and physical sciences; biology/biological sciences; biology teacher education; biophysics; business administration and management; business/managerial economics; chemistry; child development; commercial and advertising art; computer and information sciences; computer science; dramatic/theatre arts; education; elementary education; English; English/language arts teacher education; family and consumer sciences/human sciences; fashion merchandising; finance; health and physical education; health services administration; health teacher education; history; humanities; human resources management; information science/studies; interdisciplinary studies; liberal arts and sciences/liberal studies; marketing/marketing management; mathematics; mathematics teacher education; missionary studies and missiology; music; music teacher education; philosophy; physical education teaching and coaching; physical sciences; psychology; public relations/image management; radio and television; science teacher education; secondary education; social sciences; social work; special education.

Academic Programs *Special study options:* academic remediation for entering students, accelerated degree program, advanced placement credit, cooperative education, double majors, honors programs, independent study, internships, off-campus study, part-time degree program, services for LD students, student-designed majors, study abroad, summer session for credit. *Unusual degree programs:* 3-2 engineering with Tennessee Technological University, Auburn University, Vanderbilt University, University of Tennessee, Oklahoma Christian University, The University of Memphis.

Library Loden-Daniel Library with 154,689 titles, 1,715 serial subscriptions, 42,735 audiovisual materials, an OPAC, a Web page.

Computers on Campus 250 computers available on campus for general student use. A campuswide network can be accessed from student residence rooms and from off campus. Internet access, at least one staffed computer lab available. Computer purchase or lease plan available.

Student Life *Housing:* on-campus residence required through senior year. *Options:* men-only, women-only. Campus housing is university owned. Freshman campus housing is guaranteed. *Activities and organizations:* drama/theater group, student-run newspaper, radio and television station, choral group, Student Alumni Association, University Program Council, University Student Ambassadors, Evangelism Forum. *Campus security:* 24-hour emergency response devices and patrols, late-night transport/escort service, controlled dormitory access. *Student services:* health clinic, personal/psychological counseling.

Athletics Member NAIA. *Intercollegiate sports:* baseball M(s), basketball M(s)/W(s), cheerleading M/W(s), cross-country running M(s)/W(s), golf M(s)/W(s), soccer M(s)/W(s), softball W(s), tennis M(s)/W(s), volleyball W(s). *Intramural sports:* basketball M/W, football M/W, racquetball M/W, softball M/W, table tennis M/W, tennis M/W, volleyball M/W.

Standardized Tests *Required:* SAT I or ACT (for admission).

Costs (2003–04) *Comprehensive fee:* $16,366 includes full-time tuition ($9300), mandatory fees ($1746), and room and board ($5320). Full-time tuition and fees vary according to course load and degree level. Part-time tuition: $310 per semester hour. Part-time tuition and fees vary according to course load and degree level. *Required fees:* $65 per semester hour part-time. *College room only:* $2960. Room and board charges vary according to board plan and housing facility. *Payment plans:* tuition prepayment, installment. *Waivers:* senior citizens and employees or children of employees.

Financial Aid Of all full-time matriculated undergraduates who enrolled in 2003, 1,008 applied for aid, 882 were judged to have need, 100 had their need fully met. In 2003, 251 non-need-based awards were made. *Average percent of need met:* 59%. *Average financial aid package:* $9025. *Average need-based loan:* $3689. *Average need-based gift aid:* $5761. *Average non-need-based aid:* $10,088. *Average indebtedness upon graduation:* $22,135.

Applying *Options:* early admission, deferred entrance. *Required:* high school transcript, minimum 2.25 GPA. *Required for some:* interview. *Recommended:* essay or personal statement, letters of recommendation. *Application deadline:* rolling (freshmen), rolling (transfers). *Notification:* continuous until 9/1 (freshmen), continuous until 9/1 (transfers).

Admissions Contact Mr. Jim Brown, Director of Admissions, Freed-Hardeman University, 158 East Main Street, Henderson, TN 38340. *Phone:* 731-989-6651. *Toll-free phone:* 800-630-3480. *Fax:* 731-989-6047. *E-mail:* admissions@fhu.edu.

FREE WILL BAPTIST BIBLE COLLEGE
Nashville, Tennessee

- **Independent Free Will Baptist** 4-year, founded 1942
- **Calendar** semesters
- **Degrees** associate and bachelor's
- **Suburban** 10-acre campus
- **Coed**
- **Noncompetitive** entrance level

Faculty *Student/faculty ratio:* 9:1.

Student Life *Campus security:* 24-hour emergency response devices, student patrols, late-night transport/escort service, controlled dormitory access.

Athletics Member NCCAA.

Standardized Tests *Required:* ACT (for admission).

Costs (2003–04) *Comprehensive fee:* $11,316 includes full-time tuition ($6450), mandatory fees ($516), and room and board ($4350). Part-time tuition and fees vary according to course load. *Room and board:* Room and board charges vary according to board plan.

Financial Aid Of all full-time matriculated undergraduates who enrolled in 2002, 18 Federal Work-Study jobs (averaging $1564). 80 state and other part-time jobs (averaging $1794). *Average indebtedness upon graduation:* $14,509.

Applying *Options:* early admission, deferred entrance. *Application fee:* $30. *Required:* essay or personal statement, high school transcript, 3 letters of recommendation, medical history.

Admissions Contact Mr. Frederick Burch, Registrar, Free Will Baptist Bible College, 3606 West End Avenue, Nashville, TN 37205. *Phone:* 615-383-1340 Ext. 5233. *Toll-free phone:* 800-763-9222. *Fax:* 615-269-6028.

ITT TECHNICAL INSTITUTE
Knoxville, Tennessee

- **Proprietary** primarily 2-year, founded 1988, part of ITT Educational Services, Inc.
- **Calendar** quarters
- **Degrees** associate and bachelor's
- **Suburban** 5-acre campus
- **Coed**
- **Minimally difficult** entrance level

Standardized Tests *Required:* Wonderlic aptitude test (for admission).

Costs (2003–04) *Tuition:* $347 per credit hour part-time.

Applying *Options:* deferred entrance. *Application fee:* $100. *Required:* high school transcript, interview. *Recommended:* letters of recommendation.

Admissions Contact Mr. Mike Burke, Director of Recruitment, ITT Technical Institute, 10208 Technology Drive, Knoxville, TN 37932. *Phone:* 865-671-2800. *Toll-free phone:* 800-671-2801. *Fax:* 865-671-2811.

ITT TECHNICAL INSTITUTE
Memphis, Tennessee

- **Proprietary** primarily 2-year, founded 1994, part of ITT Educational Services, Inc.
- **Calendar** quarters
- **Degrees** associate and bachelor's
- **Suburban** 1-acre campus
- **Coed**
- **Minimally difficult** entrance level

Standardized Tests *Required:* Wonderlic aptitude test (for admission).

Costs (2003–04) *Tuition:* $347 per credit hour part-time.

Applying *Options:* deferred entrance. *Application fee:* $100. *Required:* high school transcript, interview. *Recommended:* letters of recommendation.

Admissions Contact Mr. James R. Mills, Director of Recruitment, ITT Technical Institute, 1255 Lynnfield Road, Suite 192, Memphis, TN 38119. *Phone:* 901-762-0556. *Fax:* 901-762-0566.

ITT TECHNICAL INSTITUTE
Nashville, Tennessee

- **Proprietary** primarily 2-year, founded 1984, part of ITT Educational Services, Inc.
- **Calendar** quarters
- **Degrees** associate and bachelor's
- **Urban** 21-acre campus
- **Coed**
- **Minimally difficult** entrance level

Standardized Tests *Required:* Wonderlic aptitude test (for admission).

Costs (2003–04) *Tuition:* $347 per credit hour part-time.

Applying *Options:* deferred entrance. *Application fee:* $100. *Required:* high school transcript, interview. *Recommended:* letters of recommendation.

Admissions Contact Mr. Ronald Binkley, Director of Recruitment, ITT Technical Institute, 441 Donnelson Pike, Nashville, TN 37214. *Phone:* 615-889-8700. *Toll-free phone:* 800-331-8386. *Fax:* 615-872-7209.

JOHNSON BIBLE COLLEGE
Knoxville, Tennessee

- **Independent** comprehensive, founded 1893, affiliated with Christian Churches and Churches of Christ
- **Calendar** semesters
- **Degrees** certificates, associate, bachelor's, and master's
- **Rural** 75-acre campus
- **Coed,** 737 undergraduate students, 97% full-time, 50% women, 50% men
- **Minimally difficult** entrance level, 98% of applicants were admitted

Undergraduates 718 full-time, 19 part-time. Students come from 34 states and territories, 11 other countries, 77% are from out of state, 3% African American, 0.8% Asian American or Pacific Islander, 1% Hispanic American, 0.1% Native American, 2% international, 7% transferred in, 88% live on campus. *Retention:* 68% of 2002 full-time freshmen returned.

Freshmen *Admission:* 175 applied, 171 admitted, 171 enrolled. *Average high school GPA:* 3.29. *Test scores:* SAT verbal scores over 500: 71%; SAT math scores over 500: 60%; ACT scores over 18: 90%; SAT verbal scores over 600: 21%; SAT math scores over 600: 19%; ACT scores over 24: 41%; SAT verbal scores over 700: 1%; SAT math scores over 700: 5%; ACT scores over 30: 5%.

Faculty *Total:* 51, 51% full-time, 45% with terminal degrees. *Student/faculty ratio:* 19:1.

Majors Biblical studies; elementary education; kindergarten/preschool education; middle school education; religious/sacred music; teacher assistant/aide.

Academic Programs *Special study options:* academic remediation for entering students, accelerated degree program, adult/continuing education programs, advanced placement credit, cooperative education, distance learning, double

Johnson Bible College (continued)
majors, English as a second language, honors programs, independent study, internships, part-time degree program, services for LD students, summer session for credit.

Library Glass Memorial Library plus 1 other with 101,086 titles, 402 serial subscriptions, 12,334 audiovisual materials, an OPAC, a Web page.

Computers on Campus 34 computers available on campus for general student use. A campuswide network can be accessed from student residence rooms and from off campus. Internet access, at least one staffed computer lab available.

Student Life *Housing:* on-campus residence required through senior year. *Options:* men-only, women-only. Campus housing is university owned. *Activities and organizations:* student-run radio station, choral group, Quest, Timothy Club, International Harvesters. *Campus security:* 24-hour emergency response devices, student patrols, controlled dormitory access. *Student services:* health clinic, personal/psychological counseling.

Athletics Member NCCAA. *Intercollegiate sports:* baseball M, basketball M/W, cheerleading M/W, soccer M/W, volleyball W. *Intramural sports:* basketball M, tennis M/W, ultimate Frisbee M/W, volleyball M/W.

Standardized Tests *Required:* SAT I or ACT (for admission). *Required for some:* ACT (for admission).

Costs (2004–05) *Comprehensive fee:* $10,050 includes full-time tuition ($5520), mandatory fees ($640), and room and board ($3890). Part-time tuition: $230 per semester hour. Part-time tuition and fees vary according to course load. *Required fees:* $20 per semester hour part-time. *Room and board:* Room and board charges vary according to board plan and housing facility. *Payment plan:* installment. *Waivers:* employees or children of employees.

Financial Aid Of all full-time matriculated undergraduates who enrolled in 2003, 696 applied for aid, 680 were judged to have need. 91 Federal Work-Study jobs (averaging $637). *Average percent of need met:* 39%. *Average financial aid package:* $2924. *Average need-based loan:* $1611. *Average need-based gift aid:* $1485. *Average indebtedness upon graduation:* $10,108.

Applying *Options:* deferred entrance. *Application fee:* $35. *Required:* essay or personal statement, high school transcript, 3 letters of recommendation. *Required for some:* interview. *Application deadlines:* 8/1 (freshmen), 8/1 (transfers). *Notification:* continuous (freshmen), continuous (transfers).

Admissions Contact Mr. Tim Wingfield, Director of Admissions, Johnson Bible College, 7900 Johnson Drive, Knoxville, TN 37998. *Phone:* 865-251-2346. *Toll-free phone:* 800-827-2122. *Fax:* 423-251-2336. *E-mail:* twingfield@jbc.edu.

KING COLLEGE
Bristol, Tennessee

- **Independent** comprehensive, founded 1867, affiliated with Presbyterian Church (U.S.A.)
- **Calendar** semesters
- **Degrees** bachelor's and master's
- **Suburban** 135-acre campus
- **Endowment** $25.0 million
- **Coed,** 687 undergraduate students, 85% full-time, 62% women, 38% men
- **Moderately difficult** entrance level, 87% of applicants were admitted

Undergraduates 583 full-time, 104 part-time. 42% are from out of state, 1% African American, 0.4% Asian American or Pacific Islander, 1% Hispanic American, 0.3% Native American, 2% international, 8% transferred in, 46% live on campus. *Retention:* 77% of 2002 full-time freshmen returned.

Freshmen *Admission:* 627 applied, 545 admitted, 98 enrolled. *Average high school GPA:* 3.50. *Test scores:* SAT verbal scores over 500: 76%; SAT math scores over 500: 67%; ACT scores over 18: 96%; SAT verbal scores over 600: 45%; SAT math scores over 600: 34%; ACT scores over 24: 61%; SAT verbal scores over 700: 7%; SAT math scores over 700: 10%; ACT scores over 30: 7%.

Faculty *Total:* 87, 63% full-time. *Student/faculty ratio:* 11:1.

Majors Accounting; American studies; behavioral sciences; biblical studies; biochemistry; biological and physical sciences; biological specializations related; biology/biological sciences; biology teacher education; biophysics; business administration and management; chemistry; chemistry teacher education; clinical laboratory science/medical technology; communication/speech communication and rhetoric; creative writing; economics; education; elementary education; English; English/language arts teacher education; fine/studio arts; French; French language teacher education; health professions related; history; history teacher education; information science/studies; international business/trade/commerce; kindergarten/preschool education; mathematics; mathematics and computer science; mathematics teacher education; middle school education; modern languages; music; nursing (registered nurse training); physics; physics teacher education; political science and government; pre-law studies; pre-medical studies; pre-pharmacy studies; pre-veterinary studies; psychology; religious studies; secondary education; Spanish; Spanish language teacher education; speech/theater education.

Academic Programs *Special study options:* accelerated degree program, advanced placement credit, double majors, English as a second language, honors programs, independent study, internships, off-campus study, part-time degree program, study abroad, summer session for credit. *ROTC:* Army (c). *Unusual degree programs:* 3-2 engineering with University of Tennessee, Vanderbilt University.

Library E. W. King Library with 80,888 titles, 1,539 serial subscriptions, 5,074 audiovisual materials, an OPAC, a Web page.

Computers on Campus 80 computers available on campus for general student use. A campuswide network can be accessed from student residence rooms and from off campus. Internet access, at least one staffed computer lab available. Computer purchase or lease plan available.

Student Life *Housing:* on-campus residence required for freshman year. *Options:* men-only, women-only, disabled students. Campus housing is university owned. Freshman campus housing is guaranteed. *Activities and organizations:* drama/theater group, student-run newspaper, choral group, Student Government Association, Campus Life Committee, World Christian Fellowship, Fellowship of Christian Athletes, drama club. *Campus security:* late-night transport/escort service. *Student services:* personal/psychological counseling.

Athletics Member NAIA. *Intercollegiate sports:* baseball M(s), basketball M(s)/W(s), golf M(s), soccer M(s)/W(s), tennis M(s)/W(s), volleyball W(s). *Intramural sports:* badminton M/W, basketball M/W, cross-country running M(c)/W(c), soccer M/W, softball M/W, table tennis M/W, tennis M/W, volleyball M/W, weight lifting M.

Standardized Tests *Required:* SAT I or ACT (for admission).

Costs (2004–05) *Comprehensive fee:* $22,500 includes full-time tuition ($15,986), mandatory fees ($1054), and room and board ($5460). Part-time tuition and fees vary according to course load and program. *College room only:* $2700. *Payment plans:* tuition prepayment, installment. *Waivers:* employees or children of employees.

Financial Aid Of all full-time matriculated undergraduates who enrolled in 2003, 427 applied for aid, 402 were judged to have need, 69 had their need fully met. 52 Federal Work-Study jobs (averaging $1134). In 2003, 104 non-need-based awards were made. *Average percent of need met:* 74%. *Average financial aid package:* $14,354. *Average need-based loan:* $4355. *Average need-based gift aid:* $10,866. *Average non-need-based aid:* $6881. *Average indebtedness upon graduation:* $12,859.

Applying *Options:* common application, electronic application, early admission, deferred entrance. *Application fee:* $20. *Required:* essay or personal statement, high school transcript, minimum 2.4 GPA, minimum ACT score of 20 or SAT score of 1000. *Recommended:* interview. *Application deadline:* rolling (freshmen), rolling (transfers). *Notification:* continuous (freshmen), continuous (transfers).

Admissions Contact Mr. Darren Parker, Director of Recruitment, King College, 1350 King College Road, Bristol, TN 37620-2699. *Phone:* 423-652-4861. *Toll-free phone:* 800-362-0014. *Fax:* 423-652-4727. *E-mail:* admissions@king.edu.

■ *See page 1822 for a narrative description.*

LAMBUTH UNIVERSITY
Jackson, Tennessee

- **Independent United Methodist** 4-year, founded 1843
- **Calendar** semesters
- **Degree** bachelor's
- **Urban** 50-acre campus with easy access to Memphis
- **Endowment** $6.4 million
- **Coed,** 836 undergraduate students, 93% full-time, 52% women, 48% men
- **Moderately difficult** entrance level, 65% of applicants were admitted

Undergraduates 777 full-time, 59 part-time. Students come from 25 states and territories, 7 other countries, 20% are from out of state, 17% African American, 0.4% Asian American or Pacific Islander, 2% Hispanic American, 0.4% Native American, 2% international, 12% transferred in, 62% live on campus. *Retention:* 60% of 2002 full-time freshmen returned.

Freshmen *Admission:* 881 applied, 575 admitted, 181 enrolled. *Average high school GPA:* 3.20. *Test scores:* SAT verbal scores over 500: 70%; SAT math scores over 500: 70%; ACT scores over 18: 94%; SAT verbal scores over 600: 31%; SAT math scores over 600: 28%; ACT scores over 24: 37%; SAT verbal scores over 700: 6%; SAT math scores over 700: 6%; ACT scores over 30: 6%.

Faculty *Total:* 93, 57% full-time, 47% with terminal degrees. *Student/faculty ratio:* 13:1.

Majors Accounting; art; art history, criticism and conservation; art teacher education; athletic training; audiology and speech-language pathology; biology/biological sciences; biology teacher education; business administration and management; business teacher education; chemistry; chemistry teacher education; computer and information sciences; criminal justice/law enforcement administration; design and visual communications; dramatic/theatre arts; education; education (K-12); elementary education; English; English/language arts teacher education; environmental science; environmental studies; family and consumer sciences/human sciences; fashion merchandising; fine/studio arts; foods, nutrition, and wellness; foreign languages and literatures; French; German; health and physical education related; history; history teacher education; interior design; international relations and affairs; liberal arts and sciences and humanities related; marketing/marketing management; mass communication/media; mathematics; mathematics teacher education; middle school education; modern languages; multi-/interdisciplinary studies related; music; music performance; music teacher education; parks, recreation, and leisure related; philosophy and religious studies related; physical education teaching and coaching; political science and government; pre-dentistry studies; pre-law studies; pre-medical studies; pre-nursing studies; pre-pharmacy studies; pre-theology/pre-ministerial studies; pre-veterinary studies; psychology; public relations, advertising, and applied communication related; religious/sacred music; religious studies; secondary education; sociology; Spanish; special education; special education (hearing impaired); sport and fitness administration; visual and performing arts.

Academic Programs *Special study options:* academic remediation for entering students, accelerated degree program, adult/continuing education programs, advanced placement credit, double majors, English as a second language, honors programs, independent study, internships, off-campus study, part-time degree program, services for LD students, student-designed majors, study abroad, summer session for credit.

Library Luther L. Gobbel Library with 177,792 titles, 56,927 serial subscriptions, 1,044 audiovisual materials, an OPAC, a Web page.

Computers on Campus 100 computers available on campus for general student use. A campuswide network can be accessed from student residence rooms and from off campus. Internet access, at least one staffed computer lab available.

Student Life *Housing:* on-campus residence required through senior year. *Options:* coed, men-only, women-only. Campus housing is university owned. Freshman campus housing is guaranteed. *Activities and organizations:* drama/theater group, student-run newspaper, choral group, student government, Student Activities Committee, Black Student Union, Religious Life Council, International Students Organization, national fraternities, national sororities. *Campus security:* 24-hour emergency response devices and patrols, late-night transport/escort service, controlled dormitory access. *Student services:* health clinic, personal/psychological counseling.

Athletics Member NAIA. *Intercollegiate sports:* baseball M(s), basketball M(s)/W(s), cheerleading M(s)/W(s), cross-country running M(s)/W(s), football M(s), golf M(s), soccer M(s)/W(s), softball W(s), swimming M(s)/W(s), tennis M(s)/W(s), volleyball W(s). *Intramural sports:* basketball M/W, football M/W, softball M/W.

Standardized Tests *Required:* SAT I or ACT (for admission).

Costs (2003–04) *Comprehensive fee:* $16,768 includes full-time tuition ($11,290), mandatory fees ($300), and room and board ($5178). Part-time tuition: $447 per credit hour. Part-time tuition and fees vary according to class time and course load. *Required fees:* $150 per term part-time. *College room only:* $2364. Room and board charges vary according to board plan and housing facility. *Payment plans:* installment, deferred payment. *Waivers:* adult students, senior citizens, and employees or children of employees.

Financial Aid Of all full-time matriculated undergraduates who enrolled in 2003, 740 applied for aid, 533 were judged to have need, 106 had their need fully met. 143 Federal Work-Study jobs (averaging $1033). 45 state and other part-time jobs (averaging $1277). In 2003, 170 non-need-based awards were made. *Average percent of need met:* 63%. *Average financial aid package:* $9704. *Average need-based loan:* $4519. *Average need-based gift aid:* $9125. *Average non-need-based aid:* $5563. *Average indebtedness upon graduation:* $15,000.

Applying *Options:* common application, electronic application, early admission, deferred entrance. *Application fee:* $25. *Required:* essay or personal statement, high school transcript, minimum 2.0 GPA. *Required for some:* 3 letters of recommendation. *Recommended:* interview. *Application deadline:* rolling (freshmen), rolling (transfers). *Notification:* continuous (freshmen), continuous (transfers).

Admissions Contact Ms. Andrea Shumate, Associate Director of Admissions, Lambuth University, 705 Lambuth Boulevard, Jackson, TN 38301. *Phone:* 731-425-3324. *Toll-free phone:* 800-526-2884. *Fax:* 731-425-3496. *E-mail:* admit@lambuth.edu.

■ *See page 1842 for a narrative description.*

LANE COLLEGE
Jackson, Tennessee

- **Independent** 4-year, founded 1882, affiliated with Christian Methodist Episcopal Church
- **Calendar** semesters
- **Degree** bachelor's
- **Suburban** 25-acre campus with easy access to Memphis
- **Endowment** $2.2 million
- **Coed,** 952 undergraduate students, 99% full-time, 52% women, 48% men
- **Minimally difficult** entrance level, 28% of applicants were admitted

Undergraduates 938 full-time, 14 part-time. Students come from 30 states and territories, 42% are from out of state, 99% African American, 0.2% Asian American or Pacific Islander, 0.5% Hispanic American, 11% transferred in, 64% live on campus. *Retention:* 74% of 2002 full-time freshmen returned.

Freshmen *Admission:* 2,636 applied, 733 admitted, 296 enrolled. *Average high school GPA:* 2.80. *Test scores:* ACT scores over 18: 25%; ACT scores over 24: 2%.

Faculty *Total:* 50, 100% full-time, 60% with terminal degrees. *Student/faculty ratio:* 19:1.

Majors Biology/biological sciences; business administration and management; chemistry; communication and media related; computer and information sciences; criminal justice/safety; English; French; history; interdisciplinary studies; mathematics; multi-/interdisciplinary studies related; music; physical education teaching and coaching; physics; religious studies; sociology.

Academic Programs *Special study options:* academic remediation for entering students, accelerated degree program, advanced placement credit, cooperative education, double majors, honors programs, independent study, internships, off-campus study, part-time degree program, study abroad, summer session for credit.

Library Chambers-McClure Resource Center with 129,953 titles, 187 serial subscriptions, 720 audiovisual materials, an OPAC, a Web page.

Computers on Campus 475 computers available on campus for general student use. A campuswide network can be accessed from student residence rooms and from off campus that provide access to online admissions and advising. Internet access, at least one staffed computer lab available.

Student Life *Housing options:* men-only, women-only. Campus housing is university owned. Freshman applicants given priority for college housing. *Activities and organizations:* drama/theater group, student-run newspaper, choral group, marching band, Student Government Association, Pre-Law Club, Student Christian Association, Drama Club, national fraternities, national sororities. *Campus security:* 24-hour emergency response devices and patrols, surveillance cameras, lighted parking areas. *Student services:* health clinic, personal/psychological counseling.

Athletics Member NCAA. All Division II. *Intercollegiate sports:* baseball M, basketball M(s)/W(s), cheerleading M(c)/W(c), cross-country running M/W, football M(s), golf M, tennis M/W, track and field M/W, volleyball W. *Intramural sports:* basketball M/W, softball W, swimming M/W, table tennis M/W, track and field M/W, volleyball M/W.

Standardized Tests *Required:* SAT I or ACT (for admission).

Costs (2003–04) *Comprehensive fee:* $11,178 includes full-time tuition ($6262), mandatory fees ($550), and room and board ($4366). Part-time tuition: $292 per semester hour. *Payment plans:* installment, deferred payment. *Waivers:* employees or children of employees.

Financial Aid Of all full-time matriculated undergraduates who enrolled in 2003, 924 applied for aid, 897 were judged to have need, 238 had their need fully met. 378 Federal Work-Study jobs (averaging $781). *Average percent of need met:* 79%. *Average financial aid package:* $8052. *Average need-based loan:* $2850. *Average need-based gift aid:* $4792. *Average indebtedness upon graduation:* $19,681.

Applying *Options:* common application, electronic application, early admission, early decision. *Required:* high school transcript, minimum 2.0 GPA, 2 letters of recommendation. *Application deadline:* rolling (freshmen), rolling (transfers). *Early decision:* 1/15. *Notification:* continuous (freshmen), continuous (transfers).

Admissions Contact Ms. E. Brown, Director of Admissions, Lane College, 545 Lane Avenue, Bray Administration Building 2nd Floor, Jackson, TN 38301-4598. *Phone:* 901-426-7532. *Toll-free phone:* 800-960-7533. *Fax:* 731-426-7559. *E-mail:* admissions@lanecollege.edu.

LEE UNIVERSITY
Cleveland, Tennessee

- **Independent** comprehensive, founded 1918, affiliated with Church of God
- **Calendar** semesters
- **Degrees** bachelor's and master's
- **Small-town** 115-acre campus
- **Coed**
- **Minimally difficult** entrance level

Faculty *Student/faculty ratio:* 17:1.

Lee University (continued)

Student Life *Campus security:* 24-hour emergency response devices and patrols, late-night transport/escort service.

Athletics Member NAIA, NCCAA.

Standardized Tests *Required:* SAT I or ACT (for admission). *Recommended:* ACT (for admission).

Costs (2004–05) *Comprehensive fee:* $13,635 includes full-time tuition ($8950), mandatory fees ($125), and room and board ($4560). Full-time tuition and fees vary according to program. Part-time tuition: $373 per credit hour. Part-time tuition and fees vary according to program. *Required fees:* $25 per term part-time. *College room only:* $2350. Room and board charges vary according to board plan and housing facility.

Financial Aid Of all full-time matriculated undergraduates who enrolled in 2003, 2,278 applied for aid, 2,033 were judged to have need, 273 had their need fully met. In 2003, 691. *Average percent of need met:* 56. *Average financial aid package:* $7539. *Average need-based loan:* $4098. *Average need-based gift aid:* $4993. *Average non-need-based aid:* $6142. *Average indebtedness upon graduation:* $21,616.

Applying *Options:* common application, electronic application, early admission, deferred entrance. *Application fee:* $25. *Required:* high school transcript, minimum 2.0 GPA, MMR immunization record. *Required for some:* 1 letter of recommendation. *Recommended:* 3 letters of recommendation.

Admissions Contact Admissions Coordinator, Lee University, PO Box 3450, Cleveland, TN 37320-3450. *Phone:* 423-614-8500. *Toll-free phone:* 800-533-9930. *Fax:* 423-614-8533. *E-mail:* admissions@leeuniversity.edu.

LeMoyne-Owen College
Memphis, Tennessee

Admissions Contact Mr. Lonnie Morris, Director of Admissions/Recruitment, LeMoyne-Owen College, 807 Walker Avenue, Memphis, TN 38126. *Phone:* 901-942-7302. *Toll-free phone:* 800-737-7778. *E-mail:* admission@loc.edu.

Lincoln Memorial University
Harrogate, Tennessee

- **Independent** comprehensive, founded 1897
- **Calendar** semesters
- **Degrees** associate, bachelor's, master's, and post-master's certificates
- **Small-town** 1000-acre campus
- **Endowment** $26.2 million
- **Coed,** 1,117 undergraduate students, 77% full-time, 73% women, 27% men
- **Moderately difficult** entrance level, 85% of applicants were admitted

Undergraduates 862 full-time, 255 part-time. Students come from 30 states and territories, 15 other countries, 33% are from out of state, 3% African American, 0.4% Asian American or Pacific Islander, 0.2% Hispanic American, 0.2% Native American, 4% international, 12% transferred in, 32% live on campus. *Retention:* 54% of 2002 full-time freshmen returned.

Freshmen *Admission:* 577 applied, 488 admitted, 279 enrolled. *Average high school GPA:* 3.40. *Test scores:* ACT scores over 18: 91%; ACT scores over 24: 42%; ACT scores over 30: 3%.

Faculty *Total:* 152, 57% full-time, 53% with terminal degrees. *Student/faculty ratio:* 9:1.

Majors Accounting; art; art teacher education; athletic training; biology/biological sciences; biology teacher education; business administration and management; business/managerial economics; business teacher education; chemistry; chemistry teacher education; clinical laboratory science/medical technology; computer and information sciences; criminal justice/law enforcement administration; economics; education; elementary education; English; environmental studies; finance; fish/game management; health and physical education; health teacher education; history; history teacher education; humanities; kindergarten/preschool education; kinesiology and exercise science; liberal arts and sciences/liberal studies; marketing/marketing management; mass communication/media; mathematics; mathematics teacher education; nursing (registered nurse training); physical education teaching and coaching; pre-law studies; pre-medical studies; pre-veterinary studies; psychology; science teacher education; secondary education; social science teacher education; social work; veterinary sciences; veterinary technology; wildlife and wildlands science and management.

Academic Programs *Special study options:* accelerated degree program, adult/continuing education programs, advanced placement credit, double majors, English as a second language, honors programs, independent study, part-time degree program, student-designed majors, summer session for credit.

Library Carnegie Library with 145,537 titles, 251 serial subscriptions, 3,369 audiovisual materials, an OPAC, a Web page.

Computers on Campus 150 computers available on campus for general student use. A campuswide network can be accessed from student residence rooms. Internet access, at least one staffed computer lab available.

Student Life *Housing options:* coed, men-only, women-only. Campus housing is university owned. *Activities and organizations:* drama/theater group, student-run newspaper, radio and television station, choral group, Baptist Student Association, Wesleyan Association, Student Nurses Association, Student National Education Association, Student Alumni Association. *Campus security:* 24-hour emergency response devices and patrols. *Student services:* personal/psychological counseling.

Athletics Member NCAA. All Division II. *Intercollegiate sports:* baseball M(s), basketball M(s)/W(s), cross-country running M(s)/W(s), golf M(s)/W, soccer M(s)/W(s), softball W(s), tennis M(s)/W(s), volleyball W(s). *Intramural sports:* basketball M/W, football M, golf M/W, soccer M/W, softball M/W, tennis M/W, ultimate Frisbee M(c)/W(c), volleyball M/W.

Standardized Tests *Required:* SAT I or ACT (for admission).

Costs (2004–05) *Comprehensive fee:* $17,510 includes full-time tuition ($12,600) and room and board ($4910). Part-time tuition: $525 per semester hour. *College room only:* $2250. Room and board charges vary according to board plan and housing facility. *Payment plans:* installment, deferred payment. *Waivers:* senior citizens and employees or children of employees.

Financial Aid Of all full-time matriculated undergraduates who enrolled in 2002, 841 applied for aid, 563 were judged to have need, 493 had their need fully met. 146 Federal Work-Study jobs (averaging $1600). In 2002, 137 non-need-based awards were made. *Average percent of need met:* 90%. *Average financial aid package:* $9800. *Average need-based loan:* $3000. *Average need-based gift aid:* $5620. *Average non-need-based aid:* $5725. *Average indebtedness upon graduation:* $11,500.

Applying *Options:* common application. *Application fee:* $25. *Required:* high school transcript, minimum 2.3 GPA. *Required for some:* essay or personal statement. *Recommended:* interview. *Application deadline:* rolling (freshmen), rolling (transfers).

Admissions Contact Mr. Conrad Daniels, Dean of Admissions and Recruitment, Lincoln Memorial University, 6965 Cumberland Gap Parkway, Harrogate, TN 37752-1901. *Phone:* 423-869-6280. *Toll-free phone:* 800-325-0900. *Fax:* 423-869-6250. *E-mail:* admissions@lmunet.edu.

■ *See page 1872 for a narrative description.*

Lipscomb University
Nashville, Tennessee

- **Independent** comprehensive, founded 1891, affiliated with Church of Christ
- **Calendar** semesters
- **Degrees** bachelor's, master's, and first professional
- **Urban** 65-acre campus
- **Endowment** $46.3 million
- **Coed,** 2,433 undergraduate students, 90% full-time, 56% women, 44% men
- **Moderately difficult** entrance level, 73% of applicants were admitted

Undergraduates 2,191 full-time, 242 part-time. Students come from 46 states and territories, 38% are from out of state, 5% African American, 0.1% Asian American or Pacific Islander, 1% Hispanic American, 0.2% Native American, 0.9% international, 5% transferred in, 49% live on campus. *Retention:* 78% of 2002 full-time freshmen returned.

Freshmen *Admission:* 2,344 applied, 1,700 admitted, 596 enrolled. *Average high school GPA:* 3.35. *Test scores:* SAT verbal scores over 500: 76%; SAT math scores over 500: 70%; ACT scores over 18: 93%; SAT verbal scores over 600: 30%; SAT math scores over 600: 28%; ACT scores over 24: 48%; SAT verbal scores over 700: 7%; SAT math scores over 700: 7%; ACT scores over 30: 10%.

Faculty *Total:* 215, 54% full-time, 60% with terminal degrees. *Student/faculty ratio:* 16:1.

Majors Accounting; American government and politics; American studies; ancient Near Eastern and biblical languages; art; athletic training; biblical studies; biochemistry; biology/biological sciences; biology teacher education; business administration and management; business/managerial economics; chemistry; commercial and advertising art; computer science; dietetics; divinity/ministry; education; elementary education; engineering; engineering science; English; environmental studies; family and consumer economics related; family and consumer sciences/human sciences; fashion merchandising; finance; fine/studio arts; French; French language teacher education; German; health teacher education; history; information science/studies; kinesiology and exercise science; liberal arts and sciences/liberal studies; marketing/marketing management; mass communication/media; mathematics; middle school education; music; music teacher education; nursing (registered nurse training); philosophy; physical education teaching and coaching; physics; piano and organ; political science and government; pre-dentistry studies; pre-law studies; pre-medical studies; pre-veterinary studies; psychology; public administration; public relations/image management; secondary education; social work; Spanish; special products marketing; speech and rhetoric; theology; urban studies/affairs; violin, viola, guitar and other stringed instruments; voice and opera; wind/percussion instruments.

Academic Programs *Special study options:* academic remediation for entering students, accelerated degree program, adult/continuing education programs, advanced placement credit, distance learning, double majors, honors programs, independent study, internships, part-time degree program, services for LD students, study abroad, summer session for credit. *ROTC:* Army (c), Air Force (c). *Unusual degree programs:* 3-2 engineering with Auburn University, Vanderbilt University, Tennessee Technical University, University of Tennessee; nursing with Vanderbilt University, Belmont University.

Library Beaman Library plus 1 other with 199,400 titles, 886 serial subscriptions, 724 audiovisual materials, an OPAC.

Computers on Campus 232 computers available on campus for general student use. A campuswide network can be accessed from student residence rooms and from off campus. Internet access, online (class) registration, at least one staffed computer lab available.

Student Life *Housing:* on-campus residence required through senior year. *Options:* men-only, women-only. Campus housing is university owned. Freshman applicants given priority for college housing. *Activities and organizations:* drama/theater group, student-run newspaper, radio station, choral group, social clubs, Sigma Pi Beta, Circle K, business fraternities, intramural program. *Campus security:* 24-hour emergency response devices and patrols, late-night transport/escort service, controlled dormitory access. *Student services:* health clinic, personal/psychological counseling.

Athletics Member NCAA. All Division I. *Intercollegiate sports:* baseball M(s), basketball M(s)/W(s), cross-country running M(s)/W(s), golf M(s)/W(s), soccer M(s)/W(s), softball W(s), tennis M(s)/W(s), volleyball W(s). *Intramural sports:* basketball M/W, football M/W, racquetball M/W, soccer M/W, softball M/W, table tennis M/W, tennis M/W, volleyball M/W.

Standardized Tests *Required:* SAT I or ACT (for admission).

Costs (2004–05) *Comprehensive fee:* $19,037 includes full-time tuition ($13,022), mandatory fees ($425), and room and board ($5590). Full-time tuition and fees vary according to degree level and location. Part-time tuition and fees vary according to class time, degree level, and location. *Room and board:* Room and board charges vary according to board plan, housing facility, and location. *Payment plan:* installment. *Waivers:* minority students and employees or children of employees.

Financial Aid Of all full-time matriculated undergraduates who enrolled in 2002, 1,300 applied for aid, 1,139 were judged to have need. 48 Federal Work-Study jobs (averaging $1545). In 2002, 987 non-need-based awards were made. *Average financial aid package:* $8454. *Average need-based gift aid:* $2921. *Average non-need-based aid:* $4714.

Applying *Options:* electronic application, early admission, early action. *Application fee:* $50. *Required:* high school transcript, minimum 2.25 GPA, 2 letters of recommendation. *Recommended:* essay or personal statement, interview. *Application deadline:* rolling (freshmen), rolling (transfers). *Notification:* continuous (freshmen), 12/15 (early action), continuous (transfers).

Admissions Contact Mr. Phillip Doncan, Director of Admissions, Lipscomb University, 3901 Granny White Pike, Nashville, TN 37204-3951. *Phone:* 615-269-1000. *Toll-free phone:* 877-582-4766. *Fax:* 615-269-1804. *E-mail:* admissions@lipscomb.edu.

Martin Methodist College

Pulaski, Tennessee

- **Independent United Methodist** 4-year, founded 1870
- **Calendar** semesters
- **Degree** diplomas and bachelor's
- **Small-town** 6-acre campus with easy access to Nashville
- **Endowment** $6.6 million
- **Coed**
- **Minimally difficult** entrance level

Faculty *Student/faculty ratio:* 17:1.

Student Life *Campus security:* controlled dormitory access.

Athletics Member NAIA.

Standardized Tests *Required:* SAT I or ACT (for admission).

Costs (2003–04) *Comprehensive fee:* $17,000 includes full-time tuition ($12,800), mandatory fees ($200), and room and board ($4000). Full-time tuition and fees vary according to class time. Part-time tuition and fees vary according to class time. *Room and board:* Room and board charges vary according to housing facility.

Financial Aid Of all full-time matriculated undergraduates who enrolled in 2001, 502 applied for aid, 354 were judged to have need, 253 had their need fully met. 55 Federal Work-Study jobs (averaging $767). 35 state and other part-time jobs (averaging $979). In 2001, 87. *Average percent of need met:* 82. *Average financial aid package:* $5625. *Average need-based loan:* $3032. *Average need-based gift aid:* $3840. *Average non-need-based aid:* $2320. *Average indebtedness upon graduation:* $9120.

Applying *Options:* common application, early admission, deferred entrance. *Application fee:* $25. *Required:* high school transcript, minimum 2.0 GPA. *Recommended:* essay or personal statement, interview.

Admissions Contact Tony Booker, Director of Admissions, Martin Methodist College, 433 West Madison Street, Pulaski, TN 38478-2716. *Phone:* 931-363-9804. *Toll-free phone:* 800-467-1273. *Fax:* 931-363-9818. *E-mail:* admissions@martinmethodist.edu.

Maryville College

Maryville, Tennessee

- **Independent Presbyterian** 4-year, founded 1819
- **Calendar** 4-1-4
- **Degree** bachelor's
- **Suburban** 350-acre campus with easy access to Knoxville
- **Endowment** $23.2 million
- **Coed,** 1,052 undergraduate students, 98% full-time, 56% women, 44% men
- **Moderately difficult** entrance level, 81% of applicants were admitted

Undergraduates 1,026 full-time, 26 part-time. Students come from 29 states and territories, 19 other countries, 21% are from out of state, 6% African American, 0.8% Asian American or Pacific Islander, 1% Hispanic American, 0.4% Native American, 4% international, 5% transferred in, 68% live on campus. *Retention:* 70% of 2002 full-time freshmen returned.

Freshmen *Admission:* 1,378 applied, 1,112 admitted, 292 enrolled. *Average high school GPA:* 3.56. *Test scores:* SAT verbal scores over 500: 72%; SAT math scores over 500: 69%; ACT scores over 18: 98%; SAT verbal scores over 600: 39%; SAT math scores over 600: 40%; ACT scores over 24: 55%; SAT verbal scores over 700: 4%; SAT math scores over 700: 7%; ACT scores over 30: 8%.

Faculty *Total:* 103, 68% full-time, 71% with terminal degrees. *Student/faculty ratio:* 12:1.

Majors American Sign Language (ASL); art teacher education; atomic/molecular physics; biochemistry; biology/biological sciences; biology teacher education; business administration and management; chemistry; chemistry teacher education; computer and information sciences related; computer science; developmental and child psychology; dramatic/theatre arts; economics; education; engineering; English; English as a second/foreign language (teaching); English/language arts teacher education; environmental studies; fine/studio arts; health and physical education; health teacher education; history; history teacher education; international business/trade/commerce; international relations and affairs; mathematics; mathematics and computer science; mathematics teacher education; multi-/interdisciplinary studies related; music performance; music teacher education; nursing (registered nurse training); parks, recreation and leisure; physical education teaching and coaching; physics teacher education; piano and organ; political science and government; psychology; religious studies; sign language interpretation and translation; social studies teacher education; sociology; Spanish; Spanish language teacher education; technical and business writing; voice and opera; wind/percussion instruments.

Academic Programs *Special study options:* adult/continuing education programs, advanced placement credit, double majors, English as a second language, honors programs, independent study, internships, off-campus study, part-time degree program, services for LD students, student-designed majors, study abroad, summer session for credit. *Unusual degree programs:* 3-2 engineering with Vanderbilt University, Washington University in St. Louis, Auburn University, Tennessee Technological University; nursing with Vanderbilt University.

Library Lamar Memorial Library plus 1 other with 103,912 titles, 16,000 serial subscriptions, 703 audiovisual materials, an OPAC, a Web page.

Computers on Campus 79 computers available on campus for general student use. A campuswide network can be accessed from student residence rooms and from off campus. Internet access, at least one staffed computer lab available.

Student Life *Housing:* on-campus residence required through senior year. *Options:* coed, men-only, women-only, disabled students. Campus housing is university owned. Freshman campus housing is guaranteed. *Activities and organizations:* drama/theater group, student-run newspaper, radio station, choral group, Voices of Praise, student government, Student Programming Board, equestrian club, peer mentors. *Campus security:* 24-hour emergency response devices and patrols, late-night transport/escort service, controlled dormitory access. *Student services:* health clinic, personal/psychological counseling.

Athletics Member NCAA. All Division III. *Intercollegiate sports:* baseball M, basketball M/W, cheerleading M/W, cross-country running M/W, equestrian sports M/W, football M, soccer M/W, softball W, tennis M/W, volleyball W,

Maryville College (continued)

wrestling M. *Intramural sports:* badminton M/W, baseball M, basketball M/W, bowling M/W, football M/W, golf M/W, racquetball M/W, rock climbing M/W, soccer M/W, softball M/W, swimming M/W, table tennis M/W, tennis M/W, track and field M/W, ultimate Frisbee M/W, volleyball M/W, water polo M/W, weight lifting M/W.

Standardized Tests *Required:* SAT I or ACT (for admission).

Costs (2004–05) *Comprehensive fee:* $27,565 includes full-time tuition ($20,465), mandatory fees ($600), and room and board ($6500). Full-time tuition and fees vary according to course load. Part-time tuition: $853 per hour. Part-time tuition and fees vary according to course load. *Required fees:* $12 per hour part-time. *College room only:* $3200. Room and board charges vary according to board plan, housing facility, and location. *Payment plan:* installment. *Waivers:* employees or children of employees.

Financial Aid Of all full-time matriculated undergraduates who enrolled in 2003, 1,025 applied for aid, 811 were judged to have need, 404 had their need fully met. 412 Federal Work-Study jobs (averaging $1537). 145 state and other part-time jobs (averaging $1417). In 2003, 214 non-need-based awards were made. *Average percent of need met:* 92%. *Average financial aid package:* $19,013. *Average need-based loan:* $3301. *Average need-based gift aid:* $12,475. *Average non-need-based aid:* $11,668.

Applying *Options:* common application, electronic application, early admission, early decision, early action, deferred entrance. *Application fee:* $25. *Required:* high school transcript, minimum 2.5 GPA. *Required for some:* essay or personal statement, letters of recommendation, interview. *Recommended:* minimum 3.0 GPA. *Application deadline:* 3/1 (freshmen), rolling (transfers). *Early decision:* 11/15. *Notification:* 4/1 (freshmen), 12/1 (early decision), 10/1 (early action), 8/15 (transfers).

Admissions Contact Ms. Linda L. Moore, Administrative Assistant of Admissions, Maryville College, 502 East Lamar Alexander Parkway, Maryville, TN 37804-5907. *Phone:* 865-981-8092. *Toll-free phone:* 800-597-2687. *Fax:* 865-981-8005. *E-mail:* admissions@maryvillecollege.edu.

■ *See page 1948 for a narrative description.*

MEMPHIS COLLEGE OF ART

Memphis, Tennessee

- **Independent** comprehensive, founded 1936
- **Calendar** semesters
- **Degrees** bachelor's and master's
- **Urban** 200-acre campus
- **Endowment** $5.3 million
- **Coed,** 300 undergraduate students, 91% full-time, 52% women, 48% men
- **Moderately difficult** entrance level, 76% of applicants were admitted

Since 1938, Memphis College of Art has been a small, distinctive community of artists. Students of diverse backgrounds work together in the shared pursuit of a challenging professional education in the visual arts. The College is situated in 340-acre Overton Park in midtown Memphis. Students have access to excellent equipment—from looms and presses to the latest in computer technology. Degrees are offered in both fine arts and commercial arts.

Undergraduates 272 full-time, 28 part-time. Students come from 28 states and territories, 11 other countries, 53% are from out of state, 14% African American, 2% Asian American or Pacific Islander, 2% Hispanic American, 0.7% Native American, 5% international, 12% transferred in, 11% live on campus. *Retention:* 68% of 2002 full-time freshmen returned.

Freshmen *Admission:* 207 applied, 158 admitted, 60 enrolled. *Average high school GPA:* 2.91. *Test scores:* ACT scores over 18: 75%; ACT scores over 24: 23%; ACT scores over 30: 2%.

Faculty *Total:* 41, 41% full-time, 41% with terminal degrees. *Student/faculty ratio:* 11:1.

Majors Advertising; applied art; art; ceramic arts and ceramics; commercial and advertising art; commercial photography; computer graphics; design and visual communications; drawing; fiber, textile and weaving arts; fine arts related; fine/studio arts; graphic communications; graphic design; illustration; intermedia/multimedia; metal and jewelry arts; painting; photography; printmaking; sculpture; wood science and wood products/pulp and paper technology.

Academic Programs *Special study options:* adult/continuing education programs, advanced placement credit, double majors, independent study, internships, off-campus study, part-time degree program, summer session for credit.

Library G. Pillow Lewis Library plus 1 other with 14,500 titles, 102 serial subscriptions.

Computers on Campus 40 computers available on campus for general student use. Internet access, at least one staffed computer lab available.

Student Life *Housing:* on-campus residence required for freshman year. *Options:* coed. Campus housing is university owned. Freshman campus housing is guaranteed. *Activities and organizations:* student-run newspaper, student government. *Campus security:* late-night transport/escort service, late night security patrols by trained personnel. *Student services:* personal/psychological counseling.

Standardized Tests *Required:* SAT I or ACT (for admission).

Costs (2004–05) *Comprehensive fee:* $23,260 includes full-time tuition ($15,800), mandatory fees ($60), and room and board ($7400). Part-time tuition: $670 per credit hour. Part-time tuition and fees vary according to course load. *College room only:* $5400. Room and board charges vary according to housing facility. *Payment plans:* installment, deferred payment. *Waivers:* employees or children of employees.

Financial Aid Of all full-time matriculated undergraduates who enrolled in 2002, 250 applied for aid, 225 were judged to have need, 180 had their need fully met. 121 Federal Work-Study jobs (averaging $1000). 172 state and other part-time jobs (averaging $1000). In 2002, 14 non-need-based awards were made. *Average percent of need met:* 90%. *Average financial aid package:* $7000. *Average need-based loan:* $5500. *Average need-based gift aid:* $3000. *Average non-need-based aid:* $5500. *Average indebtedness upon graduation:* $20,000.

Applying *Options:* common application, electronic application, early admission, deferred entrance. *Application fee:* $25. *Required:* high school transcript, portfolio. *Recommended:* essay or personal statement, interview. *Application deadline:* rolling (freshmen), rolling (transfers). *Notification:* continuous (freshmen), continuous (transfers).

Admissions Contact Ms. Annette Moore, Director of Admission, Memphis College of Art, 1930 Poplar Avenue, Memphis, TN 38104. *Phone:* 901-272-5153. *Toll-free phone:* 800-727-1088. *Fax:* 901-272-5158. *E-mail:* info@mca.edu.

MIDDLE TENNESSEE STATE UNIVERSITY

Murfreesboro, Tennessee

- **State-supported** university, founded 1911, part of Tennessee Board of Regents
- **Calendar** semesters
- **Degrees** certificates, associate, bachelor's, master's, doctoral, post-master's, and postbachelor's certificates
- **Urban** 500-acre campus with easy access to Nashville
- **Endowment** $870,747
- **Coed,** 19,754 undergraduate students, 84% full-time, 53% women, 47% men
- **Moderately difficult** entrance level, 75% of applicants were admitted

Undergraduates 16,679 full-time, 3,075 part-time. Students come from 47 states and territories, 8% are from out of state, 12% African American, 2% Asian American or Pacific Islander, 2% Hispanic American, 0.4% Native American, 10% transferred in, 20% live on campus. *Retention:* 68% of 2002 full-time freshmen returned.

Freshmen *Admission:* 7,206 applied, 5,398 admitted, 3,037 enrolled. *Test scores:* ACT scores over 18: 92%; ACT scores over 24: 32%; ACT scores over 30: 3%.

Faculty *Total:* 1,007, 73% full-time. *Student/faculty ratio:* 24:1.

Majors Accounting; aeronautics/aviation/aerospace science and technology; agribusiness; animal sciences; anthropology; apparel and textiles; art; art teacher education; athletic training; biological and physical sciences; biology/biological sciences; business administration and management; business/managerial economics; business teacher education; chemistry; computer science; criminal justice/law enforcement administration; criminal justice/police science; dramatic/theatre arts; economics; engineering/industrial management; engineering technology; English; environmental engineering technology; family resource management; finance; foods, nutrition, and wellness; foreign languages and literatures; geology/earth science; health and physical education; health teacher education; history; industrial and organizational psychology; industrial technology; interdisciplinary studies; interior design; international relations and affairs; kindergarten/preschool education; liberal arts and sciences/liberal studies; management information systems; marketing/marketing management; mass communication/media; mathematics; multi-/interdisciplinary studies related; music; music management and merchandising; nursing (registered nurse training); office management; parks, recreation and leisure facilities management; philosophy; physics; plant sciences; political science and government; psychology; public relations/image management; sales and marketing/marketing and distribution teacher education; sales, distribution and marketing; social work; sociology; special education; technology/industrial arts teacher education.

Academic Programs *Special study options:* academic remediation for entering students, accelerated degree program, adult/continuing education programs, advanced placement credit, cooperative education, distance learning, double majors, English as a second language, freshman honors college, honors programs, independent study, internships, off-campus study, part-time degree program, services for LD students, student-designed majors, study abroad, summer session for credit. *ROTC:* Army (b), Air Force (c). *Unusual degree programs:* 3-2 engineering with University of Tennessee, Knoxville; Georgia Institute of Technology; Tennessee Technological University; The University of Memphis; Tennessee State University; Vanderbilt University.

Library James E. Walker Library with 687,649 titles, 3,611 serial subscriptions, an OPAC, a Web page.

Computers on Campus 2300 computers available on campus for general student use. A campuswide network can be accessed from student residence rooms and from off campus. Internet access, online (class) registration, at least one staffed computer lab available.

Student Life *Housing options:* men-only, women-only. Campus housing is university owned. *Activities and organizations:* drama/theater group, student-run newspaper, radio station, choral group, marching band, African-American Student Association, Student Tennessee Education Association, Gamma Beta Phi, Golden Key National Honor Society, Inter-Fraternity Council, national fraternities, national sororities. *Campus security:* 24-hour emergency response devices and patrols, student patrols, late-night transport/escort service, controlled dormitory access. *Student services:* health clinic, personal/psychological counseling, women's center, legal services.

Athletics Member NCAA. All Division I except football (Division I-A). *Intercollegiate sports:* baseball M(s), basketball M(s)/W(s), cheerleading M(s)/W(s), cross-country running M(s)/W(s), equestrian sports M/W, golf M(s), soccer W(s), softball W(s), tennis M(s)/W(s), track and field M(s)/W(s), volleyball W(s). *Intramural sports:* basketball M/W, bowling M(c)/W(c), fencing M(c)/W(c), field hockey M(c)/W(c), football M, lacrosse M(c)/W(c), racquetball M(c)/W(c), riflery M, rugby M(c)/W(c), soccer M(c)/W, softball M/W, swimming M/W, tennis M/W, ultimate Frisbee M(c)/W(c), volleyball M(c)/W(c), wrestling M(c)/W(c).

Standardized Tests *Required:* SAT I or ACT (for admission).

Costs (2003–04) *Tuition:* state resident $3132 full-time, $137 per semester hour part-time; nonresident $11,064 full-time, $481 per semester hour part-time. Part-time tuition and fees vary according to course load. *Required fees:* $778 full-time. *Room and board:* $4624; room only: $2386. Room and board charges vary according to board plan and housing facility. *Payment plan:* deferred payment. *Waivers:* senior citizens and employees or children of employees.

Financial Aid Of all full-time matriculated undergraduates who enrolled in 2003, 11,604 applied for aid, 7,748 were judged to have need, 4,402 had their need fully met. 479 Federal Work-Study jobs (averaging $2353). In 2003, 1945 non-need-based awards were made. *Average percent of need met:* 78%. *Average financial aid package:* $4840. *Average need-based loan:* $4582. *Average need-based gift aid:* $2633. *Average non-need-based aid:* $2300. *Average indebtedness upon graduation:* $18,347.

Applying *Options:* electronic application, early admission, deferred entrance. *Application fee:* $15. *Required:* high school transcript, minimum 3.0 GPA. *Required for some:* essay or personal statement. *Application deadlines:* 7/1 (freshmen), 7/1 (transfers). *Notification:* continuous (freshmen), continuous (transfers).

Admissions Contact Ms. Lynn Palmer, Director of Admissions, Middle Tennessee State University, 1301 East Main Street, MTSU-CAB 208, Murfreesboro, TN 37132. *Phone:* 615-898-2111. *Toll-free phone:* 800-331-MTSU (in-state); 800-433-MTSU (out-of-state). *Fax:* 615-898-5478. *E-mail:* admissions@mtsu.edu.

MILLIGAN COLLEGE

Milligan College, Tennessee

- **Independent Christian** comprehensive, founded 1866
- **Calendar** semesters
- **Degrees** bachelor's and master's
- **Suburban** 145-acre campus
- **Endowment** $7.3 million
- **Coed,** 733 undergraduate students, 97% full-time, 61% women, 39% men
- **Moderately difficult** entrance level, 76% of applicants were admitted

Undergraduates 711 full-time, 22 part-time. Students come from 35 states and territories, 8 other countries, 56% are from out of state, 1% African American, 0.4% Asian American or Pacific Islander, 0.4% Hispanic American, 0.1% Native American, 2% international, 6% transferred in, 70% live on campus. *Retention:* 83% of 2002 full-time freshmen returned.

Freshmen *Admission:* 613 applied, 466 admitted, 179 enrolled. *Average high school GPA:* 3.58. *Test scores:* SAT verbal scores over 500: 81%; SAT math scores over 500: 75%; ACT scores over 18: 98%; SAT verbal scores over 600: 31%; SAT math scores over 600: 26%; ACT scores over 24: 54%; SAT verbal scores over 700: 4%; SAT math scores over 700: 4%; ACT scores over 30: 9%.

Faculty *Total:* 94, 70% full-time, 59% with terminal degrees. *Student/faculty ratio:* 11:1.

Majors Accounting; biblical studies; biology/biological sciences; business administration and management; chemistry; communication and media related; computer and information sciences; computer science; early childhood education; education; English; English language and literature related; fine/studio arts; health and physical education; health science; history; humanities; mathematics; music; music related; music teacher education; nursing (registered nurse training); pastoral studies/counseling; psychology; public administration and social service professions related; sociology.

Academic Programs *Special study options:* academic remediation for entering students, adult/continuing education programs, advanced placement credit, cooperative education, double majors, independent study, internships, off-campus study, part-time degree program, study abroad, summer session for credit. *ROTC:* Army (c).

Library P. H. Welshimer Memorial Library with 125,504 titles, 6,332 serial subscriptions, 3,335 audiovisual materials, an OPAC, a Web page.

Computers on Campus 119 computers available on campus for general student use. A campuswide network can be accessed from student residence rooms and from off campus. Internet access, at least one staffed computer lab available. Computer purchase or lease plan available.

Student Life *Housing:* on-campus residence required through senior year. *Options:* men-only, women-only. Campus housing is university owned. Freshman campus housing is guaranteed. *Activities and organizations:* drama/theater group, student-run newspaper, radio station, choral group, Social Affairs Committee, Buffalo Ramblers, Concert Council, Volunteer Milligan, Students for Life. *Campus security:* 24-hour patrols, late-night transport/escort service. *Student services:* health clinic, personal/psychological counseling.

Athletics Member NAIA. *Intercollegiate sports:* baseball M(s), basketball M(s)/W(s), cross-country running M(s)/W(s), golf M(s), soccer M(s)/W(s), softball W(s), tennis M(s)/W(s), volleyball W(s). *Intramural sports:* basketball M/W, cheerleading M(c)/W(c), football M/W, rock climbing M(c)/W(c), softball M/W, swimming M/W, table tennis M/W, tennis M/W, ultimate Frisbee M(c)/W(c), volleyball M/W, weight lifting M/W.

Standardized Tests *Required:* SAT I or ACT (for admission).

Costs (2003–04) *Comprehensive fee:* $19,860 includes full-time tuition ($14,750), mandatory fees ($510), and room and board ($4600). *College room only:* $2250. Room and board charges vary according to board plan and housing facility. *Payment plan:* installment. *Waivers:* employees or children of employees.

Financial Aid Of all full-time matriculated undergraduates who enrolled in 2002, 696 applied for aid, 596 were judged to have need, 160 had their need fully met. 133 Federal Work-Study jobs (averaging $1062). 163 state and other part-time jobs (averaging $890). In 2002, 69 non-need-based awards were made. *Average percent of need met:* 79%. *Average financial aid package:* $13,184. *Average need-based loan:* $2752. *Average need-based gift aid:* $1108. *Average non-need-based aid:* $4823. *Average indebtedness upon graduation:* $17,712.

Applying *Options:* electronic application, deferred entrance. *Application fee:* $30. *Required:* essay or personal statement, high school transcript, minimum 2.0 GPA, 2 letters of recommendation. *Required for some:* interview. *Recommended:* minimum 3.0 GPA. *Application deadline:* 8/1 (freshmen), rolling (transfers). *Notification:* continuous (freshmen), continuous (transfers).

Admissions Contact Mr. David Mee, Vice President for Enrollment Management, Milligan College, PO Box 210, Milligan College, TN 37682. *Phone:* 423-461-8730. *Toll-free phone:* 800-262-8337. *Fax:* 423-461-8982. *E-mail:* admissions@milligan.edu.

■ *See page 1992 for a narrative description.*

O'MORE COLLEGE OF DESIGN

Franklin, Tennessee

- **Independent** 4-year, founded 1970
- **Calendar** semesters
- **Degree** bachelor's
- **Small-town** 6-acre campus with easy access to Nashville
- **Coed, primarily women,** 127 undergraduate students, 71% full-time, 85% women, 15% men
- **Moderately difficult** entrance level, 72% of applicants were admitted

Undergraduates 90 full-time, 37 part-time. Students come from 18 states and territories, 5 other countries, 0.1% are from out of state, 27% transferred in, 30% live on campus. *Retention:* 85% of 2002 full-time freshmen returned.

Freshmen *Admission:* 90 applied, 65 admitted, 17 enrolled. *Average high school GPA:* 3.43.

Faculty *Total:* 54, 13% full-time, 35% with terminal degrees. *Student/faculty ratio:* 3:1.

Majors Commercial and advertising art; fashion/apparel design; fashion merchandising; interior design.

O'More College of Design (continued)

Academic Programs *Special study options:* academic remediation for entering students, adult/continuing education programs, advanced placement credit, cooperative education, double majors, independent study, internships, part-time degree program, summer session for credit.

Library Fleming-Farrar Hall with 4,000 titles, 60 serial subscriptions.

Computers on Campus 20 computers available on campus for general student use. Internet access, at least one staffed computer lab available.

Student Life *Housing:* college housing not available. *Options:* cooperative. *Campus security:* 24-hour emergency response devices.

Standardized Tests *Required:* SAT I or ACT (for admission).

Costs (2003–04) *Tuition:* $10,440 full-time. Full-time tuition and fees vary according to course load, program, and reciprocity agreements. Part-time tuition and fees vary according to course load, program, and reciprocity agreements. *Required fees:* $350 full-time. *Payment plan:* installment.

Applying *Options:* deferred entrance. *Application fee:* $40. *Required:* high school transcript, minimum 2.1 GPA. *Required for some:* essay or personal statement, interview, portfolio. *Application deadlines:* 8/1 (freshmen), 8/1 (transfers). *Notification:* continuous until 8/1 (freshmen), continuous (transfers).

Admissions Contact Mr. Chris Lee, Director of Enrollment Management, O'More College of Design, 423 South Margin Street, Franklin, TN 37064-2816. *Phone:* 615-794-4254 Ext. 32. *Fax:* 615-790-1662.

REMINGTON COLLEGE–MEMPHIS CAMPUS

Memphis, Tennessee

Admissions Contact Dr. Lori May, Campus President, Remington College–Memphis Campus, 2731 Nonconnah Boulevard, Memphis, TN 38132-2131. *Phone:* 901-291-4225.

RHODES COLLEGE

Memphis, Tennessee

- **Independent Presbyterian** comprehensive, founded 1848
- **Calendar** semesters
- **Degrees** bachelor's and master's (master's degree in accounting only)
- **Suburban** 100-acre campus
- **Endowment** $190.6 million
- **Coed,** 1,551 undergraduate students, 98% full-time, 58% women, 42% men
- **Very difficult** entrance level, 72% of applicants were admitted

Undergraduates 1,520 full-time, 31 part-time. Students come from 43 states and territories, 71% are from out of state, 4% African American, 3% Asian American or Pacific Islander, 1% Hispanic American, 0.3% Native American, 0.6% international, 0.9% transferred in, 76% live on campus. *Retention:* 83% of 2002 full-time freshmen returned.

Freshmen *Admission:* 2,326 applied, 1,686 admitted, 457 enrolled. *Average high school GPA:* 3.45. *Test scores:* SAT verbal scores over 500: 99%; SAT math scores over 500: 99%; ACT scores over 18: 100%; SAT verbal scores over 600: 75%; SAT math scores over 600: 68%; ACT scores over 24: 93%; SAT verbal scores over 700: 22%; SAT math scores over 700: 16%; ACT scores over 30: 29%.

Faculty *Total:* 173, 76% full-time, 87% with terminal degrees. *Student/faculty ratio:* 11:1.

Majors Anthropology; art; art history, criticism and conservation; biochemistry; biology/biological sciences; business administration and management; chemistry; classics and languages, literatures and linguistics; computer science; dramatic/theatre arts; economics; English; fine/studio arts; French; German; history; interdisciplinary studies; international business/trade/commerce; international economics; international relations and affairs; Latin; mathematics; modern Greek; music; philosophy; physics; political science and government; psychology; religious studies; Russian studies; sociology; Spanish; urban studies/affairs.

Academic Programs *Special study options:* accelerated degree program, advanced placement credit, double majors, honors programs, independent study, internships, off-campus study, part-time degree program, services for LD students, student-designed majors, study abroad. *ROTC:* Army (c), Air Force (c). *Unusual degree programs:* 3-2 engineering with Washington University in St. Louis.

Library Burrow Library plus 3 others with 270,761 titles, 1,179 serial subscriptions, 10,299 audiovisual materials, an OPAC, a Web page.

Computers on Campus 220 computers available on campus for general student use. A campuswide network can be accessed from student residence rooms and from off campus. At least one staffed computer lab available.

Student Life *Housing:* on-campus residence required through sophomore year. *Options:* coed, men-only, women-only. Campus housing is university owned. Freshman campus housing is guaranteed. *Activities and organizations:* drama/theater group, student-run newspaper, choral group, Kinney Volunteer Program, Habitat for Humanity, Adopt A Friend, Foster, national fraternities, national sororities. *Campus security:* 24-hour emergency response devices and patrols, student patrols, late-night transport/escort service, 24-hour monitored security cameras in parking areas, fenced campus with monitored access at night. *Student services:* health clinic, personal/psychological counseling.

Athletics Member NCAA. All Division III. *Intercollegiate sports:* baseball M, basketball M/W, cheerleading W(c), cross-country running M/W, field hockey W, football M, golf M/W, lacrosse M(c)/W(c), rugby M(c), soccer M/W, softball W, swimming M/W, tennis M/W, track and field M/W, volleyball W. *Intramural sports:* basketball M/W, football M/W, racquetball M/W, soccer M/W, softball M/W, squash M, volleyball M/W.

Standardized Tests *Required:* SAT I or ACT (for admission).

Costs (2004–05) *Comprehensive fee:* $30,916 includes full-time tuition ($23,968), mandatory fees ($310), and room and board ($6638). Part-time tuition: $999 per credit hour. *Room and board:* Room and board charges vary according to board plan. *Payment plan:* installment. *Waivers:* employees or children of employees.

Financial Aid Of all full-time matriculated undergraduates who enrolled in 2002, 715 applied for aid, 568 were judged to have need, 203 had their need fully met. 204 Federal Work-Study jobs (averaging $1501). 263 state and other part-time jobs (averaging $1340). In 2002, 484 non-need-based awards were made. *Average percent of need met:* 84%. *Average financial aid package:* $16,054. *Average need-based loan:* $4413. *Average need-based gift aid:* $11,181. *Average non-need-based aid:* $8784. *Average indebtedness upon graduation:* $15,100.

Applying *Options:* common application, electronic application, early admission, early decision, deferred entrance. *Application fee:* $45. *Required:* essay or personal statement, high school transcript, 2 letters of recommendation. *Recommended:* interview. *Application deadlines:* 2/1 (freshmen), 2/1 (transfers). *Early decision:* 11/1 (for plan 1), 1/1 (for plan 2). *Notification:* 4/1 (freshmen), 12/1 (early decision plan 1), 2/1 (early decision plan 2), 4/1 (transfers).

Admissions Contact Mr. David J. Wottle, Dean of Admissions and Financial Aid, Rhodes College, 2000 North Parkway, Memphis, TN 38112. *Phone:* 901-843-3700. *Toll-free phone:* 800-844-5969. *Fax:* 901-843-3631. *E-mail:* adminfo@rhodes.edu.

■ See page 2228 for a narrative description.

SOUTH COLLEGE

Knoxville, Tennessee

- **Proprietary** primarily 2-year, founded 1882
- **Calendar** quarters
- **Degrees** certificates, diplomas, associate, and bachelor's
- **Urban** 2-acre campus
- **Coed, primarily women**
- **Moderately difficult** entrance level

Faculty *Student/faculty ratio:* 12:1.

Student Life *Campus security:* evening and morning security patrols.

Standardized Tests *Recommended:* SAT I, ACT, or CPT.

Applying *Options:* common application, early admission, deferred entrance. *Application fee:* $40. *Required:* high school transcript, interview.

Admissions Contact Mr. Kevin Spath, Director of Admissions, South College, 720 North Fifth Avenue, Knoxville, TN 37917. *Phone:* 865-524-3043 Ext. 7419. *Fax:* 865-637-0127.

SOUTHERN ADVENTIST UNIVERSITY

Collegedale, Tennessee

- **Independent Seventh-day Adventist** comprehensive, founded 1892
- **Calendar** semesters
- **Degrees** certificates, associate, bachelor's, and master's
- **Small-town** 1000-acre campus with easy access to Chattanooga
- **Endowment** $20.1 million
- **Coed,** 2,249 undergraduate students, 80% full-time, 55% women, 45% men
- **Moderately difficult** entrance level, 76% of applicants were admitted

Undergraduates 1,796 full-time, 453 part-time. Students come from 48 states and territories, 55 other countries, 70% are from out of state, 8% African American, 5% Asian American or Pacific Islander, 11% Hispanic American, 0.4% Native American, 5% international, 10% transferred in, 65% live on campus. *Retention:* 77% of 2002 full-time freshmen returned.

Freshmen *Admission:* 1,252 applied, 951 admitted, 458 enrolled. *Average high school GPA:* 3.30. *Test scores:* ACT scores over 18: 90%; ACT scores over 24: 40%; ACT scores over 30: 8%.

Faculty *Total:* 193, 64% full-time. *Student/faculty ratio:* 16:1.

Majors Accounting; actuarial science; art; automobile/automotive mechanics technology; biochemistry; biology/biological sciences; broadcast journalism; business administration and management; chemistry; cinematography and film/video production; clinical laboratory science/medical technology; computer graphics; computer science; dental hygiene; elementary education; engineering; English; English/language arts teacher education; family systems; foods, nutrition, and wellness; foreign languages and literatures; general studies; health/health care administration; history; international business/trade/commerce; journalism; kindergarten/preschool education; kinesiology and exercise science; management information systems; management science; marketing/marketing management; mass communication/media; mathematics; medical radiologic technology; music; music performance; music teacher education; music theory and composition; non-profit management; nursing (registered nurse training); nursing science; occupational therapy; physical education teaching and coaching; physical therapy; physician assistant; physics; psychology; public relations/image management; radio and television broadcasting technology; religious education; religious studies; respiratory care therapy; social work; speech-language pathology; sport and fitness administration; theology.

Academic Programs *Special study options:* advanced placement credit, double majors, English as a second language, honors programs, independent study, internships, part-time degree program, services for LD students, study abroad, summer session for credit.

Library McKee Library with 144,846 titles, 14,458 serial subscriptions, 5,045 audiovisual materials, an OPAC, a Web page.

Computers on Campus 200 computers available on campus for general student use. A campuswide network can be accessed from student residence rooms and from off campus. Internet access, at least one staffed computer lab available.

Student Life *Housing:* on-campus residence required through senior year. *Options:* men-only, women-only. Campus housing is university owned. Freshman campus housing is guaranteed. *Activities and organizations:* drama/theater group, student-run newspaper, radio and television station, choral group, Student Association, Black Christian Union, Campus Ministries. *Campus security:* 24-hour patrols, late-night transport/escort service, controlled dormitory access. *Student services:* health clinic, personal/psychological counseling.

Athletics *Intramural sports:* badminton M/W, basketball M/W, gymnastics M/W, racquetball M/W, soccer M/W, softball M/W, table tennis M/W, tennis M/W, volleyball M/W.

Standardized Tests *Required:* SAT I or ACT (for admission).

Costs (2004–05) *Comprehensive fee:* $17,800 includes full-time tuition ($12,990), mandatory fees ($420), and room and board ($4390). Part-time tuition: $550 per semester hour. Part-time tuition and fees vary according to course load. *Required fees:* $210 per term part-time. *College room only:* $2390. Room and board charges vary according to housing facility. *Payment plans:* tuition prepayment, installment, deferred payment. *Waivers:* adult students, senior citizens, and employees or children of employees.

Financial Aid Of all full-time matriculated undergraduates who enrolled in 2003, 1,534 applied for aid, 968 were judged to have need, 137 had their need fully met. In 2003, 560 non-need-based awards were made. *Average percent of need met:* 64%. *Average financial aid package:* $9121. *Average need-based loan:* $4128. *Average need-based gift aid:* $3889. *Average non-need-based aid:* $2853. *Average indebtedness upon graduation:* $14,900.

Applying *Options:* early admission, deferred entrance. *Application fee:* $25. *Required:* high school transcript, minimum 2.0 GPA, 2 letters of recommendation. *Required for some:* essay or personal statement. *Recommended:* interview. *Application deadline:* rolling (freshmen), rolling (transfers). *Notification:* continuous (freshmen), continuous (transfers).

Admissions Contact Mr. Marc Grundy, Director of Admissions and Recruitment, Southern Adventist University, PO Box 370, Collegedale, TN 37315-0370. *Phone:* 423-238-2843. *Toll-free phone:* 800-768-8437. *Fax:* 423-238-3005. *E-mail:* admissions@southern.edu.

TENNESSEE STATE UNIVERSITY
Nashville, Tennessee

- **State-supported** comprehensive, founded 1912, part of Tennessee Board of Regents
- **Calendar** semesters
- **Degrees** associate, bachelor's, master's, and doctoral
- **Urban** 450-acre campus
- **Coed,** 7,118 undergraduate students, 84% full-time, 63% women, 37% men
- **Minimally difficult** entrance level, 35% of applicants were admitted

Undergraduates 5,949 full-time, 1,169 part-time. Students come from 45 states and territories, 42% are from out of state, 81% African American, 1% Asian American or Pacific Islander, 0.6% Hispanic American, 0.1% Native American, 1% international, 6% transferred in, 39% live on campus. *Retention:* 74% of 2002 full-time freshmen returned.

Freshmen *Admission:* 7,850 applied, 2,711 admitted, 1,188 enrolled. *Average high school GPA:* 2.90.

Faculty *Total:* 578, 70% full-time. *Student/faculty ratio:* 17:1.

Majors Accounting; administrative assistant and secretarial science; adult and continuing education; African studies; agriculture; animal sciences; architectural engineering; art; audiology and speech-language pathology; biology/biological sciences; business administration and management; business/managerial economics; business teacher education; chemistry; civil engineering; clinical laboratory science/medical technology; clinical psychology; computer science; consumer services and advocacy; criminal justice/law enforcement administration; dental hygiene; education; educational leadership and administration; electrical, electronics and communications engineering; elementary education; engineering; English; family and consumer economics related; food services technology; French; health/health care administration; health information/medical records administration; health teacher education; history; humanities; industrial arts; industrial engineering; industrial technology; kindergarten/preschool education; liberal arts and sciences/liberal studies; mass communication/media; mathematics; mechanical engineering; music; nursing (registered nurse training); parks, recreation and leisure; physical education teaching and coaching; physical therapy; physics; political science and government; psychology; public administration; reading teacher education; respiratory care therapy; social work; sociology; Spanish; special education; transportation technology.

Academic Programs *Special study options:* academic remediation for entering students, accelerated degree program, adult/continuing education programs, cooperative education, external degree program, freshman honors college, honors programs, independent study, internships, off-campus study, part-time degree program, services for LD students, summer session for credit. *ROTC:* Army (c), Navy (c), Air Force (b).

Library Martha M. Brown/Lois H. Daniel Library plus 1 other with 580,650 titles, 23,668 audiovisual materials, an OPAC, a Web page.

Computers on Campus 320 computers available on campus for general student use. A campuswide network can be accessed from student residence rooms and from off campus. At least one staffed computer lab available.

Student Life *Housing options:* coed, men-only, women-only. Campus housing is university owned. Freshman applicants given priority for college housing. *Activities and organizations:* drama/theater group, student-run newspaper, radio station, choral group, marching band, SADD, Pre Alumni Council, Baptist Student Union, T. E. Poag Players, national fraternities, national sororities. *Campus security:* 24-hour patrols, controlled dormitory access. *Student services:* health clinic, personal/psychological counseling, women's center.

Athletics Member NCAA. All Division I except football (Division I-AA). *Intercollegiate sports:* basketball M(s)/W(s), cross-country running M(s)/W(s), golf M(s), softball W, tennis M(s)/W(s), track and field M(s)/W(s), volleyball W. *Intramural sports:* baseball M, basketball M/W, cheerleading M/W, football M, softball W, track and field M/W, volleyball M/W.

Standardized Tests *Required:* SAT I or ACT (for admission).

Costs (2003–04) *Tuition:* state resident $3818 full-time; nonresident $11,750 full-time. Full-time tuition and fees vary according to course load and program. Part-time tuition and fees vary according to course load. *Room and board:* $4270; room only: $2460. Room and board charges vary according to board plan. *Waivers:* senior citizens.

Financial Aid Of all full-time matriculated undergraduates who enrolled in 2003, 5,171 applied for aid, 4,368 were judged to have need, 533 had their need fully met. In 2003, 383 non-need-based awards were made. *Average percent of need met:* 81%. *Average financial aid package:* $3687. *Average need-based loan:* $2170. *Average need-based gift aid:* $1208. *Average non-need-based aid:* $6004. *Average indebtedness upon graduation:* $22,723.

Applying *Options:* electronic application. *Application fee:* $15. *Required:* high school transcript. *Required for some:* 3 letters of recommendation. *Application deadlines:* 8/1 (freshmen), 8/1 (transfers). *Notification:* continuous until 8/15 (freshmen), continuous until 8/15 (transfers).

Admissions Contact Ms. Vernella Smith, Admissions Coordinator, Tennessee State University, 3500 John A Merritt Boulevard, Nashville, TN 37209-1561. *Phone:* 615-963-5104. *Fax:* 615-963-5108. *E-mail:* jcade@tnstate.edu.

■ *See page 2490 for a narrative description.*

TENNESSEE TECHNOLOGICAL UNIVERSITY
Cookeville, Tennessee

- **State-supported** university, founded 1915, part of Tennessee Board of Regents
- **Calendar** semesters

Tennessee Technological University (continued)
- **Degrees** bachelor's, master's, doctoral, and postbachelor's certificates
- **Small-town** 235-acre campus
- **Endowment** $32.0 million
- **Coed,** 7,273 undergraduate students, 88% full-time, 45% women, 55% men
- **Moderately difficult** entrance level, 81% of applicants were admitted

Undergraduates 6,416 full-time, 857 part-time. Students come from 43 states and territories, 54 other countries, 5% are from out of state, 4% African American, 1% Asian American or Pacific Islander, 0.9% Hispanic American, 0.3% Native American, 0.6% international, 8% transferred in, 25% live on campus. *Retention:* 72% of 2002 full-time freshmen returned.

Freshmen *Admission:* 3,182 applied, 2,570 admitted, 1,388 enrolled. *Average high school GPA:* 3.22. *Test scores:* SAT verbal scores over 500: 76%; SAT math scores over 500: 78%; ACT scores over 18: 94%; SAT verbal scores over 600: 36%; SAT math scores over 600: 40%; ACT scores over 24: 45%; SAT verbal scores over 700: 6%; SAT math scores over 700: 6%; ACT scores over 30: 8%.

Faculty *Total:* 509, 71% full-time, 68% with terminal degrees. *Student/faculty ratio:* 19:1.

Majors Accounting; agricultural/biological engineering and bioengineering; agricultural business and management; agricultural teacher education; agronomy and crop science; animal sciences; art; art teacher education; biochemistry; biology/biological sciences; business administration and management; chemical engineering; chemistry; child development; civil engineering; clothing/textiles; computer engineering; computer science; dietetics; economics; education; electrical, electronics and communications engineering; elementary education; English; family and consumer sciences/home economics teacher education; family and consumer sciences/human sciences; fashion merchandising; finance; foods, nutrition, and wellness; French; geology/earth science; German; health teacher education; history; horticultural science; industrial engineering; industrial technology; information science/studies; international business/trade/commerce; journalism; kindergarten/preschool education; labor and industrial relations; landscaping and groundskeeping; marketing/marketing management; mathematics; mechanical engineering; music; music teacher education; nursing (registered nurse training); operations management; physical education teaching and coaching; physics; political science and government; pre-dentistry studies; pre-law studies; premedical studies; pre-veterinary studies; psychology; secondary education; social work; sociology; Spanish; special education; technical and business writing; turf and turfgrass management; web page, digital/multimedia and information resources design; wildlife and wildlands science and management.

Academic Programs *Special study options:* academic remediation for entering students, accelerated degree program, adult/continuing education programs, advanced placement credit, cooperative education, distance learning, double majors, English as a second language, honors programs, independent study, internships, off-campus study, part-time degree program, services for LD students, study abroad, summer session for credit. *ROTC:* Army (b), Air Force (c).

Library Angelo and Jennette Volpe Library and Media Center with 624,952 titles, 3,843 serial subscriptions, 18,138 audiovisual materials, an OPAC, a Web page.

Computers on Campus 600 computers available on campus for general student use. A campuswide network can be accessed from student residence rooms and from off campus. Internet access, online (class) registration, at least one staffed computer lab available.

Student Life *Housing:* on-campus residence required through sophomore year. *Options:* coed, men-only, women-only. Campus housing is university owned. Freshman campus housing is guaranteed. *Activities and organizations:* drama/theater group, student-run newspaper, radio station, choral group, marching band, Baptist Collegiate Center, Fellowship of Christian Athletes, University Christian Student Center, Inter-Fraternity Council, Residence Hall Association, national fraternities, national sororities. *Campus security:* 24-hour emergency response devices and patrols, late-night transport/escort service, student safety organization, lighted pathways. *Student services:* health clinic, personal/psychological counseling, women's center.

Athletics Member NCAA. All Division I except football (Division I-AA). *Intercollegiate sports:* baseball M(s), basketball M(s)/W(s), cheerleading M(s)/W(s), cross-country running M(s)/W(s), golf M(s)/W(s), riflery M(s)/W(s), soccer W(s), softball W(s), tennis M(s)/W(s), track and field W(s), volleyball W(s). *Intramural sports:* basketball M/W, fencing M(c)/W(c), football M/W, golf M/W, racquetball M/W, rugby M(c)/W(c), soccer M/W, softball M/W, tennis M/W, ultimate Frisbee M/W, volleyball M/W, wrestling M.

Standardized Tests *Required:* SAT I or ACT (for admission). *Recommended:* ACT (for admission).

Costs (2003–04) *Tuition:* state resident $3778 full-time, $137 per hour part-time; nonresident $11,710 full-time, $481 per hour part-time. Part-time tuition and fees vary according to course load. *Required fees:* $41 per hour part-time. *Room and board:* $5092; room only: $2300. Room and board charges vary according to board plan and housing facility. *Waivers:* employees or children of employees.

Financial Aid Of all full-time matriculated undergraduates who enrolled in 2003, 4,695 applied for aid, 2,733 were judged to have need, 642 had their need fully met. 577 Federal Work-Study jobs (averaging $1350). In 2003, 1153 non-need-based awards were made. *Average percent of need met:* 77%. *Average financial aid package:* $3691. *Average need-based loan:* $3164. *Average need-based gift aid:* $2642. *Average non-need-based aid:* $2553. *Average indebtedness upon graduation:* $13,359.

Applying *Options:* electronic application, early admission, deferred entrance. *Application fee:* $15. *Required:* high school transcript, 2.35 high school GPA or ACT composite score of 19. *Recommended:* interview. *Application deadline:* rolling (freshmen), rolling (transfers). *Notification:* continuous (freshmen), continuous (transfers).

Admissions Contact Mr. Robert L. Hodum, Assistant Director of Admissions, Tennessee Technological University, TTU Box 5006, Cookeville, TN 38505. *Phone:* 931-372-3888 Ext. 3636. *Toll-free phone:* 800-255-8881. *Fax:* 931-372-6250. *E-mail:* admissions@tntech.edu.

■ *See page 2492 for a narrative description.*

TENNESSEE TEMPLE UNIVERSITY
Chattanooga, Tennessee

- **Independent Baptist** comprehensive, founded 1946
- **Calendar** semesters
- **Degrees** diplomas, associate, bachelor's, and master's
- **Urban** 55-acre campus
- **Endowment** $600,000
- **Coed**
- **Minimally difficult** entrance level

Faculty *Student/faculty ratio:* 15:1.

Student Life *Campus security:* 24-hour emergency response devices and patrols, late-night transport/escort service.

Athletics Member NCCAA.

Standardized Tests *Required:* SAT I or ACT (for placement).

Costs (2003–04) *Comprehensive fee:* $12,130 includes full-time tuition ($5780), mandatory fees ($950), and room and board ($5400). Part-time tuition: $185 per semester hour. *Required fees:* $200 per term part-time. *Room and board:* Room and board charges vary according to board plan.

Financial Aid Of all full-time matriculated undergraduates who enrolled in 2003, 54 Federal Work-Study jobs (averaging $1724). 36 state and other part-time jobs (averaging $1682). *Financial aid deadline:* 5/15.

Applying *Options:* electronic application, deferred entrance. *Application fee:* $30. *Required:* high school transcript, minimum 2.0 GPA, 3 letters of recommendation, interview. *Required for some:* essay or personal statement.

Admissions Contact Mr. Mark Mathews, Director of Enrollment Services, Tennessee Temple University, 1815 Union Avenue, Chattanooga, TN 37404-3587. *Phone:* 423-493-4371. *Toll-free phone:* 800-553-4050. *Fax:* 423-492-4308. *E-mail:* ttuinfo@tntemple.edu.

TENNESSEE WESLEYAN COLLEGE
Athens, Tennessee

- **Independent United Methodist** 4-year, founded 1857
- **Calendar** semesters
- **Degrees** bachelor's (all information includes both main and branch campuses)
- **Small-town** 40-acre campus with easy access to Knoxville and Chattanooga
- **Endowment** $7.5 million
- **Coed,** 793 undergraduate students, 81% full-time, 68% women, 32% men
- **Moderately difficult** entrance level, 83% of applicants were admitted

Undergraduates 646 full-time, 147 part-time. Students come from 19 states and territories, 18 other countries, 8% are from out of state, 3% African American, 0.1% Asian American or Pacific Islander, 1% Hispanic American, 0.3% Native American, 5% international, 19% transferred in, 33% live on campus. *Retention:* 58% of 2002 full-time freshmen returned.

Freshmen *Admission:* 452 applied, 376 admitted, 106 enrolled. *Average high school GPA:* 3.21. *Test scores:* ACT scores over 18: 92%; ACT scores over 24: 28%; ACT scores over 30: 2%.

Faculty *Total:* 100, 52% full-time, 46% with terminal degrees. *Student/faculty ratio:* 10:1.

Majors Accounting; athletic training; behavioral sciences; biology/biological sciences; biology teacher education; business administration and management;

chemistry; chemistry teacher education; education; education (K-12); elementary education; English; English/language arts teacher education; finance; health and physical education; health science; history; history teacher education; human resources management; human services; interdisciplinary studies; kinesiology and exercise science; mathematics; mathematics teacher education; music; music teacher education; nursing (registered nurse training); ophthalmic and optometric support services and allied professions related; parks, recreation and leisure; physical education teaching and coaching; pre-dentistry studies; pre-law studies; pre-medical studies; pre-pharmacy studies; pre-theology/pre-ministerial studies; pre-veterinary studies; psychology; religious studies; secondary education; sport and fitness administration.

Academic Programs *Special study options:* academic remediation for entering students, accelerated degree program, adult/continuing education programs, advanced placement credit, cooperative education, double majors, English as a second language, freshman honors college, honors programs, independent study, internships, off-campus study, part-time degree program, student-designed majors, study abroad, summer session for credit.

Library Merner-Pfeifer Library with 79,328 titles, 408 serial subscriptions, 3,610 audiovisual materials, an OPAC, a Web page.

Computers on Campus 92 computers available on campus for general student use. A campuswide network can be accessed from student residence rooms. Internet access, at least one staffed computer lab available.

Student Life *Housing:* on-campus residence required through senior year. *Options:* men-only, women-only. Campus housing is university owned and leased by the school. Freshman campus housing is guaranteed. *Activities and organizations:* drama/theater group, student-run newspaper, choral group, Wesleyan Christian Fellowship, Circle K, Baptist Student Union, Student Government Association, choir, national sororities. *Campus security:* controlled dormitory access, night patrols by trained security personnel. *Student services:* health clinic, personal/psychological counseling.

Athletics Member NAIA. *Intercollegiate sports:* baseball M(s), basketball M(s)/W(s), cheerleading M(s)/W(s), cross-country running M(s)/W(s), golf M(s), soccer M(s)/W(s), softball W(s), tennis M(s)/W(s), volleyball W(s). *Intramural sports:* basketball M/W, table tennis M/W, tennis M/W, volleyball M/W.

Standardized Tests *Required:* SAT I or ACT (for admission).

Costs (2004–05) *Comprehensive fee:* $17,190 includes full-time tuition ($12,000), mandatory fees ($340), and room and board ($4850). Part-time tuition: $335 per semester hour. Part-time tuition and fees vary according to class time and location. *Required fees:* $35 per semester hour part-time. *Room and board:* Room and board charges vary according to housing facility. *Payment plans:* installment, deferred payment. *Waivers:* employees or children of employees.

Financial Aid Of all full-time matriculated undergraduates who enrolled in 2002, 529 applied for aid, 456 were judged to have need, 95 had their need fully met. 103 Federal Work-Study jobs (averaging $678). 39 state and other part-time jobs (averaging $837). In 2002, 113 non-need-based awards were made. *Average percent of need met:* 76%. *Average financial aid package:* $9251. *Average need-based loan:* $3430. *Average need-based gift aid:* $6812. *Average non-need-based aid:* $5524. *Average indebtedness upon graduation:* $10,870. *Financial aid deadline:* 5/1.

Applying *Options:* electronic application, early admission, deferred entrance. *Application fee:* $25. *Required:* high school transcript, minimum 2.0 GPA, 1 letter of recommendation. *Required for some:* interview. *Recommended:* essay or personal statement. *Application deadline:* rolling (freshmen), rolling (transfers). *Notification:* continuous (freshmen), continuous (transfers).

Admissions Contact Mrs. Ruthie Cawood, Director of Admission, Tennessee Wesleyan College, PO Box 40, Athens, TN 37371-0040. *Phone:* 423-746-5287. *Toll-free phone:* 800-PICK-TWC. *Fax:* 423-745-9335.

TREVECCA NAZARENE UNIVERSITY
Nashville, Tennessee

- **Independent Nazarene** comprehensive, founded 1901
- **Calendar** semesters
- **Degrees** associate, bachelor's, master's, doctoral, and post-master's certificates
- **Urban** 65-acre campus
- **Endowment** $11.3 million
- **Coed,** 1,232 undergraduate students, 77% full-time, 59% women, 41% men
- **Moderately difficult** entrance level, 67% of applicants were admitted

Undergraduates 948 full-time, 284 part-time. Students come from 37 states and territories, 12 other countries, 49% are from out of state, 7% African American, 0.7% Asian American or Pacific Islander, 1% Hispanic American, 0.2% Native American, 2% international, 4% transferred in, 56% live on campus. *Retention:* 68% of 2002 full-time freshmen returned.

Freshmen *Admission:* 680 applied, 454 admitted, 224 enrolled. *Average high school GPA:* 3.19. *Test scores:* ACT scores over 18: 86%; ACT scores over 24: 32%; ACT scores over 30: 7%.

Faculty *Total:* 184, 42% full-time, 49% with terminal degrees. *Student/faculty ratio:* 16:1.

Majors Accounting; behavioral sciences; biological and physical sciences; biology/biological sciences; biology teacher education; broadcast journalism; business administration and management; chemistry; chemistry teacher education; child development; clinical laboratory science/medical technology; communication/speech communication and rhetoric; dramatic/theatre arts; education (K-12); English; English/language arts teacher education; general studies; history; history teacher education; information science/studies; kinesiology and exercise science; marketing/marketing management; mass communication/media; mathematics; mathematics teacher education; music; music management and merchandising; music teacher education; physical education teaching and coaching; physics; psychology; radio and television broadcasting technology; religious/sacred music; religious studies; secondary education; social sciences.

Academic Programs *Special study options:* academic remediation for entering students, adult/continuing education programs, advanced placement credit, double majors, internships, part-time degree program, services for LD students, summer session for credit. *ROTC:* Army (c).

Library Mackey Library with 100,231 titles, 507 serial subscriptions, 3,060 audiovisual materials, an OPAC, a Web page.

Computers on Campus 200 computers available on campus for general student use. A campuswide network can be accessed from student residence rooms and from off campus. Internet access, at least one staffed computer lab available.

Student Life *Housing:* on-campus residence required through junior year. *Options:* men-only, women-only. Campus housing is university owned. *Activities and organizations:* drama/theater group, student-run newspaper, radio station, choral group. *Campus security:* 24-hour patrols, student patrols, late-night transport/escort service. *Student services:* health clinic, personal/psychological counseling.

Athletics Member NAIA. *Intercollegiate sports:* baseball M(s), basketball M(s)/W(s), golf M(s)/W(s), soccer M(s)/W(s), softball W(s), volleyball W(s). *Intramural sports:* badminton M/W, basketball M/W, football M/W, golf M/W, racquetball M/W, softball M/W, table tennis M/W, track and field M/W, volleyball M/W.

Standardized Tests *Required:* SAT I or ACT (for admission).

Costs (2004–05) *Comprehensive fee:* $18,660 includes full-time tuition ($12,792) and room and board ($5868). Full-time tuition and fees vary according to course load. Part-time tuition: $492 per semester hour. Part-time tuition and fees vary according to course load. *College room only:* $2648. Room and board charges vary according to board plan. *Payment plan:* installment. *Waivers:* senior citizens and employees or children of employees.

Financial Aid Of all full-time matriculated undergraduates who enrolled in 2003, 520 applied for aid, 440 were judged to have need, 380 had their need fully met. In 2003, 110 non-need-based awards were made. *Average percent of need met:* 45%. *Average financial aid package:* $10,450. *Average need-based loan:* $4430. *Average need-based gift aid:* $4320. *Average non-need-based aid:* $3150. *Average indebtedness upon graduation:* $15,060.

Applying *Options:* early admission, deferred entrance. *Application fee:* $25. *Required:* high school transcript, minimum 2.5 GPA, medical history and immunization records. *Recommended:* letters of recommendation. *Application deadline:* 7/1 (freshmen), rolling (transfers). *Notification:* continuous (freshmen), continuous (transfers).

Admissions Contact Ms. Patricia D. Cook, Director of Admissions, Trevecca Nazarene University, 333 Murfreesboro Road, Nashville, TN 37210-2834. *Phone:* 615-248-1320. *Toll-free phone:* 888-210-4TNU. *Fax:* 615-248-7406. *E-mail:* admissions_und@trevecca.edu.

■ See page 2520 for a narrative description.

TUSCULUM COLLEGE
Greeneville, Tennessee

- **Independent Presbyterian** comprehensive, founded 1794
- **Calendar** semesters
- **Degrees** bachelor's and master's
- **Small-town** 140-acre campus
- **Endowment** $12.8 million
- **Coed,** 1,914 undergraduate students, 99% full-time, 53% women, 47% men
- **Moderately difficult** entrance level, 76% of applicants were admitted

Imagine an education that goes far beyond the 4 walls of a classroom. Tusculum believes that to actually learn something, students need to experience it. With the focused calendar (1 course at a time for 3 weeks), students have hands-on experiences that allow them to travel to such places as Costa Rica, England, Mexico, Scotland, and Spain.

Tusculum College (continued)

Undergraduates 1,899 full-time, 15 part-time. Students come from 36 states and territories, 18 other countries, 19% are from out of state, 12% African American, 0.4% Asian American or Pacific Islander, 2% Hispanic American, 0.3% Native American, 3% international, 10% transferred in, 23% live on campus. *Retention:* 68% of 2002 full-time freshmen returned.

Freshmen *Admission:* 1,381 applied, 1,050 admitted, 303 enrolled. *Average high school GPA:* 2.89. *Test scores:* SAT verbal scores over 500: 39%; SAT math scores over 500: 43%; ACT scores over 18: 76%; SAT verbal scores over 600: 8%; SAT math scores over 600: 12%; ACT scores over 24: 23%; SAT verbal scores over 700: 1%; SAT math scores over 700: 1%; ACT scores over 30: 2%.

Faculty *Total:* 207, 37% full-time. *Student/faculty ratio:* 15:1.

Majors Accounting; art; art teacher education; athletic training; biology/biological sciences; business administration and management; clinical laboratory science/medical technology; computer science; education; elementary education; English; environmental studies; history; information science/studies; kindergarten/preschool education; mathematics; middle school education; museum studies; physical education teaching and coaching; pre-law studies; pre-medical studies; pre-veterinary studies; psychology; secondary education; special education; sport and fitness administration; telecommunications.

Academic Programs *Special study options:* academic remediation for entering students, adult/continuing education programs, advanced placement credit, double majors, English as a second language, independent study, internships, part-time degree program, student-designed majors, study abroad, summer session for credit.

Library Albert Columbus Tate Library plus 2 others with 49,905 titles, 1,000 serial subscriptions, 832 audiovisual materials, an OPAC, a Web page.

Computers on Campus 102 computers available on campus for general student use. A campuswide network can be accessed from student residence rooms and from off campus. Internet access, at least one staffed computer lab available.

Student Life *Housing:* on-campus residence required through senior year. *Options:* coed, men-only, women-only. Campus housing is university owned. Freshman campus housing is guaranteed. *Activities and organizations:* drama/theater group, student-run newspaper, radio station, choral group, Pioneer Newspaper, Bonwondi, Campus Activities Board, Fellowship of Christian Athletes, "Tusculana" (yearbook). *Campus security:* 24-hour emergency response devices and patrols, student patrols, late-night transport/escort service, controlled dormitory access, trained security personnel on duty. *Student services:* health clinic, personal/psychological counseling, women's center.

Athletics Member NCAA. All Division II. *Intercollegiate sports:* baseball M(s), basketball M(s)/W(s), cheerleading W(s), cross-country running M(s)/W(s), football M(s), golf M/W, soccer M(s)/W(s), softball W(s), tennis M(s)/W(s), volleyball W(s). *Intramural sports:* baseball M, basketball M/W, football M, softball M, tennis M/W, volleyball M/W.

Standardized Tests *Required:* SAT I or ACT (for admission).

Costs (2003–04) *Comprehensive fee:* $20,290 includes full-time tuition ($14,110), mandatory fees ($300), and room and board ($5880). Full-time tuition and fees vary according to degree level, program, and reciprocity agreements. Part-time tuition: $650 per credit hour. Part-time tuition and fees vary according to degree level, program, and reciprocity agreements. *Room and board:* Room and board charges vary according to housing facility. *Payment plan:* installment. *Waivers:* employees or children of employees.

Financial Aid Of all full-time matriculated undergraduates who enrolled in 2002, 1,410 applied for aid, 1,070 were judged to have need, 220 had their need fully met. 221 Federal Work-Study jobs (averaging $1074). 266 state and other part-time jobs (averaging $776). In 2002, 239 non-need-based awards were made. *Average percent of need met:* 67%. *Average financial aid package:* $9213. *Average need-based loan:* $3402. *Average need-based gift aid:* $1415. *Average non-need-based aid:* $5452. *Average indebtedness upon graduation:* $14,633.

Applying *Options:* early admission, deferred entrance. *Required:* essay or personal statement, high school transcript, minimum 2.0 GPA, letters of recommendation. *Recommended:* interview. *Application deadline:* rolling (freshmen), rolling (transfers).

Admissions Contact Mr. George Wolf, Director of Admissions, Tusculum College, PO Box 5047, Greeneville, TN 37743-9997. *Phone:* 423-636-7300 Ext. 611. *Toll-free phone:* 800-729-0256. *Fax:* 423-638-7166. *E-mail:* admissions@tusculum.edu.

■ *See page 2538 for a narrative description.*

UNION UNIVERSITY

Jackson, Tennessee

- **Independent Southern Baptist** comprehensive, founded 1823
- **Calendar** 4-1-4
- **Degrees** diplomas, associate, bachelor's, master's, doctoral, and post-master's certificates
- **Small-town** 290-acre campus with easy access to Memphis
- **Endowment** $23.6 million
- **Coed,** 2,022 undergraduate students, 80% full-time, 61% women, 39% men
- **Moderately difficult** entrance level, 61% of applicants were admitted

Undergraduates 1,620 full-time, 402 part-time. Students come from 43 states and territories, 36 other countries, 32% are from out of state, 8% African American, 0.7% Asian American or Pacific Islander, 0.6% Hispanic American, 0.1% Native American, 2% international, 10% transferred in, 59% live on campus. *Retention:* 67% of 2002 full-time freshmen returned.

Freshmen *Admission:* 1,461 applied, 893 admitted, 450 enrolled. *Average high school GPA:* 3.54. *Test scores:* SAT verbal scores over 500: 75%; SAT math scores over 500: 84%; ACT scores over 18: 97%; SAT verbal scores over 600: 33%; SAT math scores over 600: 36%; ACT scores over 24: 54%; SAT verbal scores over 700: 9%; SAT math scores over 700: 16%; ACT scores over 30: 14%.

Faculty *Total:* 227, 64% full-time, 64% with terminal degrees. *Student/faculty ratio:* 12:1.

Majors Accounting; advertising; ancient Near Eastern and biblical languages; art; art teacher education; athletic training; biblical studies; biological and physical sciences; biology/biological sciences; broadcast journalism; business administration and management; business/managerial economics; business teacher education; chemistry; clinical laboratory science/medical technology; computer science; dramatic/theatre arts; economics; education; elementary education; English; English as a second/foreign language (teaching); family and community services; finance; foreign languages and literatures; French; history; information science/studies; journalism; kindergarten/preschool education; kinesiology and exercise science; marketing/marketing management; mass communication/media; mathematics; music; music management and merchandising; music performance; music teacher education; nursing (registered nurse training); parks, recreation and leisure facilities management; philosophy; philosophy and religious studies related; physical education teaching and coaching; physics; piano and organ; political science and government; pre-dentistry studies; pre-law studies; pre-medical studies; pre-pharmacy studies; psychology; public relations/image management; radio and television; religious/sacred music; religious studies; science teacher education; secondary education; social work; sociology; Spanish; special education; speech and rhetoric; sport and fitness administration; theology; theology and religious vocations related; voice and opera.

Academic Programs *Special study options:* accelerated degree program, adult/continuing education programs, advanced placement credit, cooperative education, distance learning, double majors, English as a second language, honors programs, independent study, internships, off-campus study, part-time degree program, services for LD students, study abroad, summer session for credit.

Library Emma Waters Summar Library plus 1 other with 135,877 titles, 4,655 serial subscriptions, 11,526 audiovisual materials, an OPAC, a Web page.

Computers on Campus 236 computers available on campus for general student use. A campuswide network can be accessed from student residence rooms and from off campus. Internet access, at least one staffed computer lab available.

Student Life *Housing:* on-campus residence required through junior year. *Options:* men-only, women-only, disabled students. Campus housing is university owned. Freshman applicants given priority for college housing. *Activities and organizations:* drama/theater group, student-run newspaper, choral group, campus ministries, Student Government Association, Student Activities Council, SIFE, national fraternities, national sororities. *Campus security:* 24-hour emergency response devices and patrols, student patrols, late-night transport/escort service. *Student services:* health clinic, personal/psychological counseling.

Athletics Member NAIA, NCCAA. *Intercollegiate sports:* baseball M(s), basketball M(s)/W(s), cheerleading W(s), cross-country running M/W(s), soccer M(s), softball W(s), track and field M/W, volleyball W(s). *Intramural sports:* basketball M/W, bowling M/W, cross-country running M/W, football M/W, golf M/W, racquetball M/W, soccer W, softball M/W, swimming M/W, table tennis M/W, track and field M/W, ultimate Frisbee M/W, volleyball M/W.

Standardized Tests *Required:* SAT I or ACT (for admission).

Costs (2004–05) *Comprehensive fee:* $20,320 includes full-time tuition ($14,850), mandatory fees ($500), and room and board ($4970). Full-time tuition and fees vary according to class time, course load, location, and program. Part-time tuition: $495. *College room only:* $2990. Room and board charges vary according to board plan and location. *Payment plans:* tuition prepayment, installment, deferred payment. *Waivers:* employees or children of employees.

Financial Aid Of all full-time matriculated undergraduates who enrolled in 2003, 1,414 applied for aid, 869 were judged to have need. 127 Federal Work-Study jobs (averaging $985). 111 state and other part-time jobs (averaging $1440). *Average financial aid package:* $10,492. *Average need-based loan:* $3782. *Average need-based gift aid:* $3719. *Average non-need-based aid:* $4884. *Average indebtedness upon graduation:* $15,328.

Applying *Options:* common application, electronic application, early admission, early action, deferred entrance. *Application fee:* $25. *Required:* high school transcript, minimum 2.5 GPA. *Required for some:* letters of recommendation.

Recommended: essay or personal statement, interview. *Application deadline:* rolling (freshmen), rolling (transfers). *Notification:* continuous until 8/15 (freshmen), 12/20 (early action), continuous until 8/15 (transfers).

Admissions Contact Mr. Robbie Graves, Director of Enrollment Services, Union University, 1050 Union University Drive, Jackson, TN 38305-3697. *Phone:* 731-661-5008. *Toll-free phone:* 800-33-UNION. *Fax:* 731-661-5017. *E-mail:* info@uu.edu.

■ See page 2546 for a narrative description.

THE UNIVERSITY OF MEMPHIS
Memphis, Tennessee

- **State-supported** university, founded 1912, part of Tennessee Board of Regents
- **Calendar** semesters
- **Degrees** certificates, diplomas, bachelor's, master's, doctoral, first professional, post-master's, postbachelor's, and first professional certificates
- **Urban** 1100-acre campus
- **Endowment** $171.8 million
- **Coed,** 15,209 undergraduate students, 74% full-time, 60% women, 40% men
- **Moderately difficult** entrance level, 73% of applicants were admitted

Undergraduates 11,256 full-time, 3,953 part-time. Students come from 43 states and territories, 81 other countries, 5% are from out of state, 35% African American, 2% Asian American or Pacific Islander, 1% Hispanic American, 0.3% Native American, 2% international, 13% live on campus. *Retention:* 72% of 2002 full-time freshmen returned.

Freshmen *Admission:* 4,764 applied, 3,471 admitted. *Average high school GPA:* 3.04. *Test scores:* SAT verbal scores over 500: 67%; SAT math scores over 500: 65%; ACT scores over 18: 79%; SAT verbal scores over 600: 27%; SAT math scores over 600: 26%; ACT scores over 24: 32%; SAT verbal scores over 700: 4%; SAT math scores over 700: 5%; ACT scores over 30: 2%.

Faculty *Total:* 1,435, 63% full-time, 45% with terminal degrees. *Student/faculty ratio:* 14:1.

Majors Accounting; African-American/Black studies; anthropology; architecture; art; art history, criticism and conservation; biochemistry/biophysics and molecular biology; biology/biological sciences; business/managerial economics; chemistry; civil engineering; communication/speech communication and rhetoric; computer engineering; computer engineering technology; computer science; consumer merchandising/retailing management; criminal justice/law enforcement administration; criminology; dramatic/theatre arts; economics; education (multiple levels); electrical, electronic and communications engineering technology; electrical, electronics and communications engineering; English; finance; foreign languages and literatures; general studies; geography; geology/earth science; history; hospitality administration; human development and family studies; insurance; interdisciplinary studies; international business/trade/commerce; international relations and affairs; journalism; kinesiology and exercise science; legal assistant/paralegal; liberal arts and sciences/liberal studies; management information systems; management science; manufacturing technology; marketing/marketing management; mathematics; mechanical engineering; microbiology; molecular biology; multi-/interdisciplinary studies related; music; music management and merchandising; nursing (registered nurse training); philosophy; physical education teaching and coaching; physics; political science and government; professional studies; psychology; real estate; sales, distribution and marketing; social work; sociology; special education; sport and fitness administration; systems engineering.

Academic Programs *Special study options:* academic remediation for entering students, accelerated degree program, adult/continuing education programs, advanced placement credit, cooperative education, distance learning, double majors, English as a second language, external degree program, honors programs, independent study, internships, part-time degree program, services for LD students, student-designed majors, study abroad, summer session for credit. *ROTC:* Army (b), Navy (b), Air Force (b).

Library McWherter Library plus 6 others with 1.1 million titles, 10,578 serial subscriptions, 32,212 audiovisual materials, an OPAC, a Web page.

Computers on Campus 2000 computers available on campus for general student use. A campuswide network can be accessed from off campus. Internet access, online (class) registration, at least one staffed computer lab available.

Student Life *Housing options:* coed, men-only, women-only, disabled students. Campus housing is university owned. *Activities and organizations:* drama/theater group, student-run newspaper, radio station, choral group, marching band, national fraternities, national sororities. *Campus security:* 24-hour emergency response devices and patrols, student patrols, late-night transport/escort service. *Student services:* health clinic, personal/psychological counseling, women's center, legal services.

Athletics Member NCAA. All Division I except football (Division I-A). *Intercollegiate sports:* baseball M(s), basketball M(s)/W(s), cross-country running M(s)/W(s), golf M(s)/W(s), racquetball M(c)/W(c), riflery M(s)/W(s), soccer M(s)/W(s), swimming M(c)/W(c), tennis M(s)/W(s), track and field M(s)/W(s), volleyball W(s). *Intramural sports:* archery M/W, badminton M/W, basketball M/W, bowling M/W, fencing M, golf M/W, rugby M/W, soccer M, softball M/W, swimming M/W, table tennis M/W, tennis M/W, track and field M/W, volleyball M/W.

Standardized Tests *Required:* SAT I or ACT (for admission).

Costs (2003–04) *Tuition:* state resident $3502 full-time, $199 per credit hour part-time; nonresident $11,656 full-time, $539 per credit hour part-time. Part-time tuition and fees vary according to course load. *Required fees:* $732 full-time. *Room and board:* $4690; room only: $2700. Room and board charges vary according to housing facility. *Payment plan:* installment. *Waivers:* senior citizens and employees or children of employees.

Financial Aid Of all full-time matriculated undergraduates who enrolled in 2002, 6,630 applied for aid, 6,388 were judged to have need, 1,066 had their need fully met. 287 Federal Work-Study jobs (averaging $2122). In 2002, 416 non-need-based awards were made. *Average percent of need met:* 76%. *Average financial aid package:* $3816. *Average need-based loan:* $3598. *Average need-based gift aid:* $3361. *Average non-need-based aid:* $2963. *Average indebtedness upon graduation:* $20,491.

Applying *Options:* early admission. *Application fee:* $15. *Required:* high school transcript. *Required for some:* minimum 2.0 GPA, 2 letters of recommendation, interview. *Application deadlines:* 8/1 (freshmen), 8/1 (transfers). *Notification:* continuous (freshmen), continuous (transfers).

Admissions Contact Mr. David Wallace, Director of Admissions, The University of Memphis, Memphis, TN 38152. *Phone:* 901-678-2101. *Fax:* 901-678-3053. *E-mail:* dwallace@memphis.edu.

■ See page 2650 for a narrative description.

UNIVERSITY OF PHOENIX–NASHVILLE CAMPUS
Nashville, Tennessee

Admissions Contact 616 Marriott Drive, Suite 150, Nashville, TN 37214.

THE UNIVERSITY OF TENNESSEE
Knoxville, Tennessee

- **State-supported** university, founded 1794, part of University of Tennessee System
- **Calendar** semesters
- **Degrees** bachelor's, master's, doctoral, first professional, post-master's, postbachelor's, and first professional certificates
- **Urban** 533-acre campus
- **Coed,** 19,224 undergraduate students, 91% full-time, 51% women, 49% men
- **Moderately difficult** entrance level, 71% of applicants were admitted

Undergraduates 17,513 full-time, 1,711 part-time. Students come from 50 states and territories, 101 other countries, 14% are from out of state, 7% African American, 2% Asian American or Pacific Islander, 1% Hispanic American, 0.3% Native American, 1% international, 6% transferred in, 37% live on campus. *Retention:* 78% of 2002 full-time freshmen returned.

Freshmen *Admission:* 9,514 applied, 6,790 admitted, 3,579 enrolled. *Average high school GPA:* 3.40. *Test scores:* SAT verbal scores over 500: 76%; SAT math scores over 500: 78%; ACT scores over 18: 99%; SAT verbal scores over 600: 32%; SAT math scores over 600: 33%; ACT scores over 24: 52%; SAT verbal scores over 700: 6%; SAT math scores over 700: 5%; ACT scores over 30: 10%.

Faculty *Total:* 1,534, 94% full-time, 83% with terminal degrees. *Student/faculty ratio:* 15:1.

Majors Accounting; advertising; aerospace, aeronautical and astronautical engineering; agricultural/biological engineering and bioengineering; agricultural business and management related; agricultural economics; agricultural teacher education; animal sciences; anthropology; architecture; area, ethnic, cultural, and gender studies related; art history, criticism and conservation; art teacher education; audiology and hearing sciences; biochemistry; biology/biological sciences; botany/plant biology; business administration and management; business/commerce; business/managerial economics; business teacher education; chemical engineering; chemistry; civil engineering; classics and languages, literatures and linguistics; clinical laboratory science/medical technology; commercial and advertising art; computer engineering; computer science; consumer economics; cultural studies; dramatic/theatre arts; ecology; economics; electrical, electronics and communications engineering; engineering physics; engineering science; English; family and consumer sciences/home economics teacher education; family systems; finance; fine/studio arts; food science; foods, nutrition, and wellness; forestry; French; geography; geology/earth science; German; health teacher education; history; hotel/motel administration; human development and family

The University of Tennessee (continued)

studies; industrial engineering; interior design; Italian; journalism; kinesiology and exercise science; logistics and materials management; marketing/marketing management; materials engineering; mathematics; mechanical engineering; medical microbiology and bacteriology; multi-/interdisciplinary studies related; music; music teacher education; nuclear engineering; nursing (registered nurse training); ornamental horticulture; parks, recreation and leisure facilities management; philosophy; physics; plant protection and integrated pest management; plant sciences; political science and government; psychology; public administration; radio and television; religious studies; Russian; social work; sociology; Spanish; special education; speech and rhetoric; speech-language pathology; sport and fitness administration; statistics; technical teacher education; wildlife and wildlands science and management; zoology/animal biology.

Academic Programs *Special study options:* accelerated degree program, adult/continuing education programs, advanced placement credit, cooperative education, distance learning, double majors, English as a second language, honors programs, independent study, internships, off-campus study, part-time degree program, services for LD students, student-designed majors, study abroad, summer session for credit. *ROTC:* Army (b), Air Force (b).

Library John C. Hodges Library plus 6 others with 24.4 million titles, 17,628 serial subscriptions, 175,541 audiovisual materials, an OPAC, a Web page.

Computers on Campus 1500 computers available on campus for general student use. A campuswide network can be accessed from student residence rooms and from off campus. Internet access, online (class) registration, at least one staffed computer lab available. Computer purchase or lease plan available.

Student Life *Housing:* on-campus residence required for freshman year. *Options:* coed. Campus housing is university owned and leased by the school. Freshman campus housing is guaranteed. *Activities and organizations:* drama/theater group, student-run newspaper, radio station, choral group, marching band, Central Program Council, religious organizations, Volunteer Outreach for Leadership and Service, Student Government Association, dance marathon, national fraternities, national sororities. *Campus security:* 24-hour emergency response devices and patrols, late-night transport/escort service. *Student services:* health clinic, personal/psychological counseling, women's center, legal services.

Athletics Member NCAA. All Division I except football (Division I-A). *Intercollegiate sports:* baseball M(s), basketball M(s)/W(s), cheerleading M(s)/W(s), crew W(s), cross-country running M(s)/W(s), golf M(s)/W(s), soccer W(s), softball W(s), swimming M(s)/W(s), tennis M(s)/W(s), track and field M(s)/W(s), volleyball W(s). *Intramural sports:* badminton M/W, basketball M/W, bowling M/W, crew M(c)/W(c), cross-country running M/W, equestrian sports M(c)/W(c), fencing M(c)/W(c), field hockey M/W, football M/W, golf M/W, gymnastics M(c)/W(c), ice hockey M(c)/W(c), lacrosse M(c)/W(c), racquetball M/W, riflery M(c)/W(c), rugby M(c)/W(c), sailing M(c)/W(c), skiing (downhill) M(c)/W(c), soccer M/W, softball M/W, swimming M/W, table tennis M/W, tennis M/W, track and field M/W, volleyball M(c)/W, water polo M/W, weight lifting M(c)/W(c).

Standardized Tests *Required:* SAT I or ACT (for admission).

Costs (2003–04) *Tuition:* state resident $4950 full-time, $187 per semester hour part-time; nonresident $13,532 full-time, $569 per semester hour part-time. Full-time tuition and fees vary according to location and program. Part-time tuition and fees vary according to location and program. *Room and board:* $5110; room only: $2490. Room and board charges vary according to board plan and housing facility. *Payment plan:* installment. *Waivers:* senior citizens and employees or children of employees.

Financial Aid Of all full-time matriculated undergraduates who enrolled in 2003, 9,261 applied for aid, 6,651 were judged to have need, 1,268 had their need fully met. In 2003, 126 non-need-based awards were made. *Average percent of need met:* 64%. *Average financial aid package:* $6954. *Average need-based loan:* $3523. *Average need-based gift aid:* $5115. *Average non-need-based aid:* $8931. *Average indebtedness upon graduation:* $21,713.

Applying *Options:* electronic application, early admission, early action, deferred entrance. *Application fee:* $25. *Required:* essay or personal statement, high school transcript, minimum 2.0 GPA, specific high school units. *Application deadlines:* 2/1 (freshmen), 6/1 (transfers). *Notification:* continuous (freshmen), 1/15 (early action), continuous (transfers).

Admissions Contact Mr. Marshall Rose, Acting Director of Admissions, The University of Tennessee, 320 Student services Building, Knoxville, TN 37996-0230. *Phone:* 865-974-2184. *Toll-free phone:* 800-221-8657. *Fax:* 865-974-6341. *E-mail:* admissions@tennessee.edu.

THE UNIVERSITY OF TENNESSEE AT CHATTANOOGA

Chattanooga, Tennessee

- **State-supported** comprehensive, founded 1886, part of University of Tennessee System
- **Calendar** semesters
- **Degrees** bachelor's, master's, first professional, post-master's, and postbachelor's certificates
- **Urban** 117-acre campus with easy access to Atlanta
- **Endowment** $101.2 million
- **Coed,** 7,197 undergraduate students, 83% full-time, 58% women, 42% men
- **Moderately difficult** entrance level, 52% of applicants were admitted

UTC is a comprehensive, state-supported, coeducational institution. With an enrollment of almost 8,600 students, UTC offers a diverse educational and extracurricular experience. UTC offers more than 70 undergraduate and 35 master's programs within four distinct schools and colleges. Located in scenic downtown Chattanooga, students can learn, work, and play within walking distance of premiere apartment-style residence hall facilities. Merit scholarships and need-based aid are available.

Undergraduates 5,970 full-time, 1,227 part-time. Students come from 41 states and territories, 49 other countries, 8% are from out of state, 21% African American, 2% Asian American or Pacific Islander, 0.9% Hispanic American, 0.3% Native American, 1% international, 9% transferred in, 29% live on campus. *Retention:* 70% of 2002 full-time freshmen returned.

Freshmen *Admission:* 3,156 applied, 1,638 admitted, 1,410 enrolled. *Average high school GPA:* 3.20. *Test scores:* ACT scores over 18: 83%; ACT scores over 24: 31%; ACT scores over 30: 3%.

Faculty *Total:* 607, 57% full-time, 55% with terminal degrees. *Student/faculty ratio:* 16:1.

Majors Applied mathematics; art; art teacher education; biology/biological sciences; business administration and management; chemistry; clinical laboratory science/medical technology; computer science; criminal justice/law enforcement administration; criminal justice/police science; dramatic/theatre arts; economics; engineering; engineering/industrial management; English; environmental studies; fine/studio arts; French; geology/earth science; history; human ecology; humanities; human services; kinesiology and exercise science; Latin; legal assistant/paralegal; mass communication/media; mathematics; middle school education; modern Greek; music; nursing (registered nurse training); parks, recreation and leisure; philosophy and religious studies related; physical therapy; physics; political science and government; psychology; science teacher education; secondary education; social work; sociology; Spanish; special education.

Academic Programs *Special study options:* academic remediation for entering students, adult/continuing education programs, advanced placement credit, cooperative education, distance learning, double majors, English as a second language, honors programs, independent study, internships, off-campus study, part-time degree program, services for LD students, study abroad, summer session for credit. *Unusual degree programs:* 3-2 engineering with Georgia Institute of Technology, University of Tennessee, Knoxville.

Library Lupton Library with 491,179 titles, 2,488 serial subscriptions, 17,567 audiovisual materials, an OPAC, a Web page.

Computers on Campus 300 computers available on campus for general student use. A campuswide network can be accessed from student residence rooms and from off campus. Internet access, online (class) registration, at least one staffed computer lab available.

Student Life *Housing options:* coed. *Activities and organizations:* drama/theater group, student-run newspaper, radio station, choral group, marching band, Student Government Association, Black Student Association, Association for Campus Entertainment, International Student Association, Baptist Student Union, national fraternities, national sororities. *Campus security:* 24-hour emergency response devices and patrols, late-night transport/escort service. *Student services:* health clinic, personal/psychological counseling.

Athletics Member NCAA. All Division I except football (Division I-AA). *Intercollegiate sports:* basketball M(s)/W(s), crew M/W, cross-country running M(s)/W(s), golf M(s)/W, soccer M(s)/W(s), softball W(s), tennis M(s)/W(s), track and field M/W, volleyball W(s), wrestling M(s). *Intramural sports:* badminton M/W, basketball M/W, bowling M/W, cross-country running M/W, fencing M, football M, golf M, racquetball M/W, swimming M/W, tennis M/W, volleyball W, weight lifting M, wrestling M.

Standardized Tests *Required:* SAT I or ACT (for admission).

Costs (2003–04) *Tuition:* state resident $3852 full-time, $211 per hour part-time; nonresident $11,504 full-time, $530 per hour part-time. *Room only:* $3000. Room and board charges vary according to housing facility. *Payment plan:* deferred payment. *Waivers:* senior citizens and employees or children of employees.

Financial Aid Of all full-time matriculated undergraduates who enrolled in 2003, 4,215 applied for aid, 3,580 were judged to have need, 426 had their need fully met. 217 Federal Work-Study jobs (averaging $1612). 400 state and other part-time jobs (averaging $1875). In 2003, 840 non-need-based awards were made. *Average percent of need met:* 78%. *Average financial aid package:* $8200. *Average need-based loan:* $4525. *Average need-based gift aid:* $3500. *Average non-need-based aid:* $3800. *Average indebtedness upon graduation:* $14,675.

Applying *Options:* deferred entrance. *Application fee:* $25. *Required:* high school transcript, 1 letter of recommendation. *Recommended:* essay or personal statement. *Notification:* continuous (freshmen), continuous (transfers).

Admissions Contact Mr. Yancy Freeman, Director of Student Recruitment, The University of Tennessee at Chattanooga, 131 Hooper Hall, Chattanooga, TN 37403. *Phone:* 423-755-4597. *Toll-free phone:* 800-UTC-MOCS. *Fax:* 423-425-4157. *E-mail:* yancy-freeman@utc.edu.

THE UNIVERSITY OF TENNESSEE AT MARTIN

Martin, Tennessee

- **State-supported** comprehensive, founded 1900, part of University of Tennessee System
- **Calendar** semesters
- **Degrees** bachelor's and master's
- **Small-town** 250-acre campus
- **Endowment** $21.0 million
- **Coed,** 5,404 undergraduate students, 84% full-time, 58% women, 42% men
- **Moderately difficult** entrance level, 51% of applicants were admitted

Undergraduates 4,524 full-time, 880 part-time. Students come from 20 states and territories, 28 other countries, 5% are from out of state, 16% African American, 0.6% Asian American or Pacific Islander, 0.7% Hispanic American, 0.4% Native American, 3% international, 7% transferred in, 40% live on campus. *Retention:* 71% of 2002 full-time freshmen returned.

Freshmen *Admission:* 2,627 applied, 1,341 admitted, 1,000 enrolled. *Average high school GPA:* 3.28. *Test scores:* ACT scores over 18: 89%; ACT scores over 24: 30%; ACT scores over 30: 2%.

Faculty *Total:* 402, 60% full-time, 45% with terminal degrees. *Student/faculty ratio:* 17:1.

Majors Accounting; agricultural business and management; agricultural teacher education; agriculture; agronomy and crop science; animal/livestock husbandry and production; animal sciences; art teacher education; athletic training; biology/biological sciences; biology teacher education; broadcast journalism; business administration and management; business/managerial economics; business teacher education; chemistry; chemistry teacher education; child development; commercial and advertising art; computer science; criminal justice/law enforcement administration; dietetics; economics; education (K-12); elementary education; engineering; English; English/language arts teacher education; environmental studies; family and consumer sciences/home economics teacher education; family and consumer sciences/human sciences; fashion merchandising; finance; French; French language teacher education; geography; geology/earth science; German language teacher education; health and physical education; history; history teacher education; interdisciplinary studies; interior design; international business/trade/commerce; international relations and affairs; journalism; kindergarten/preschool education; landscaping and groundskeeping; management information systems; marketing/marketing management; mathematics; mathematics teacher education; music; music teacher education; nursing (registered nurse training); parks, recreation and leisure facilities management; philosophy; piano and organ; political science and government; pre-dentistry studies; pre-medical studies; pre-pharmacy studies; pre-veterinary studies; professional studies; psychology; public administration; public relations/image management; science teacher education; social work; sociology; soil conservation; Spanish; Spanish language teacher education; special education; sport and fitness administration; violin, viola, guitar and other stringed instruments; visual and performing arts; voice and opera; wildlife and wildlands science and management; wind/percussion instruments.

Academic Programs *Special study options:* academic remediation for entering students, accelerated degree program, adult/continuing education programs, advanced placement credit, cooperative education, distance learning, double majors, English as a second language, honors programs, independent study, internships, off-campus study, part-time degree program, services for LD students, student-designed majors, study abroad, summer session for credit. *ROTC:* Army (b).

Library Paul Meek Library plus 1 other with 372,008 titles, 1,607 serial subscriptions, 11,669 audiovisual materials, an OPAC, a Web page.

Computers on Campus 185 computers available on campus for general student use. A campuswide network can be accessed from student residence rooms and from off campus. At least one staffed computer lab available.

Student Life *Housing:* on-campus residence required through sophomore year. *Options:* coed, men-only, women-only, disabled students. Campus housing is university owned. Freshman campus housing is guaranteed. *Activities and organizations:* drama/theater group, student-run newspaper, radio and television station, choral group, marching band, Student Government Association, Greek organizations, religious affiliated groups, Student Activities Council, Black Student Association (BSA), national fraternities, national sororities. *Campus security:* 24-hour emergency response devices and patrols, student patrols, late-night transport/escort service, controlled dormitory access. *Student services:* health clinic, personal/psychological counseling.

Athletics Member NCAA. All Division I except football (Division I-AA). *Intercollegiate sports:* baseball M(s), basketball M(s)/W(s), cheerleading M/W, cross-country running W(s), golf M(s), riflery M(s)/W(s), soccer W(s), softball W(s), tennis M(s)/W(s), track and field M(s)/W(s), volleyball W(s). *Intramural sports:* basketball M/W, cross-country running M/W, equestrian sports W, football M/W, golf M/W, racquetball M/W, soccer M/W, softball M/W, swimming M/W, tennis M/W, track and field M/W, volleyball M/W.

Standardized Tests *Required:* SAT I or ACT (for admission).

Costs (2003–04) *Tuition:* state resident $3846 full-time; nonresident $11,496 full-time. *Room and board:* $3800; room only: $1910. Room and board charges vary according to board plan and housing facility. *Payment plan:* deferred payment. *Waivers:* senior citizens and employees or children of employees.

Financial Aid Of all full-time matriculated undergraduates who enrolled in 2003, 4,080 applied for aid, 2,574 were judged to have need, 491 had their need fully met. 270 Federal Work-Study jobs (averaging $2122). In 2003, 992 non-need-based awards were made. *Average percent of need met:* 73%. *Average financial aid package:* $7154. *Average need-based loan:* $3527. *Average need-based gift aid:* $3793. *Average non-need-based aid:* $2880. *Average indebtedness upon graduation:* $12,920.

Applying *Options:* common application, electronic application, deferred entrance. *Application fee:* $25. *Required:* high school transcript, minimum 2.25 GPA. *Application deadline:* rolling (freshmen), rolling (transfers). *Notification:* continuous until 8/1 (freshmen), continuous until 8/1 (transfers).

Admissions Contact Director of Admission, The University of Tennessee at Martin, 200 Hall-Moody Administration Building, Martin, TN 38238. *Phone:* 731-587-7032. *Toll-free phone:* 800-829-8861. *Fax:* 731-587-7029. *E-mail:* jrayburn@utm.edu.

THE UNIVERSITY OF TENNESSEE HEALTH SCIENCE CENTER

Memphis, Tennessee

Admissions Contact Ms. June Peoples, Director of Admissions, The University of Tennessee Health Science Center, 800 Madison Avenue, Memphis, TN 38163-0002. *Phone:* 901-448-5560. *Fax:* 901-448-7585. *E-mail:* jpeoples@utmem1.utmem.edu.

UNIVERSITY OF THE SOUTH

Sewanee, Tennessee

- **Independent Episcopal** comprehensive, founded 1857
- **Calendar** semesters
- **Degrees** certificates, bachelor's, master's, doctoral, first professional, post-master's, postbachelor's, and first professional certificates
- **Small-town** 10,000-acre campus
- **Endowment** $232.9 million
- **Coed,** 1,374 undergraduate students, 99% full-time, 54% women, 46% men
- **Very difficult** entrance level, 72% of applicants were admitted

Undergraduates 1,356 full-time, 18 part-time. Students come from 76 states and territories, 76% are from out of state, 4% African American, 1% Asian American or Pacific Islander, 2% Hispanic American, 0.2% Native American, 1% international, 1% transferred in, 92% live on campus. *Retention:* 84% of 2002 full-time freshmen returned.

Freshmen *Admission:* 1,825 applied, 1,316 admitted, 427 enrolled. *Average high school GPA:* 3.41. *Test scores:* SAT verbal scores over 500: 97%; SAT math scores over 500: 96%; ACT scores over 18: 99%; SAT verbal scores over 600: 63%; SAT math scores over 600: 64%; ACT scores over 24: 83%; SAT verbal scores over 700: 16%; SAT math scores over 700: 10%; ACT scores over 30: 23%.

Faculty *Total:* 172, 77% full-time, 87% with terminal degrees. *Student/faculty ratio:* 10:1.

Majors American studies; anthropology; applied art; art; art history, criticism and conservation; Asian studies; biology/biological sciences; chemistry; classics and languages, literatures and linguistics; comparative literature; computer science; dramatic/theatre arts; drawing; economics; English; environmental studies; European studies; fine/studio arts; forestry; French; geology/earth science; German; history; international relations and affairs; Latin; literature; mathematics; medieval and Renaissance studies; modern Greek; music; music history, literature, and theory; natural resources management and policy; philosophy; physics; political science and government; psychology; religious studies; Russian; Russian studies; social sciences; Spanish.

University of the South (continued)

Academic Programs *Special study options:* advanced placement credit, double majors, independent study, internships, services for LD students, student-designed majors, study abroad, summer session for credit. *Unusual degree programs:* 3-2 engineering with Georgia Institute of Technology, Washington University in St. Louis, Vanderbilt University, Rensselaer Polytechnic Institute, Columbia University; forestry with Duke University, Yale University.

Library Jessie Ball duPont Library with 648,459 titles, 3,444 serial subscriptions, 72,964 audiovisual materials, an OPAC, a Web page.

Computers on Campus 92 computers available on campus for general student use. A campuswide network can be accessed from student residence rooms and from off campus. At least one staffed computer lab available.

Student Life *Housing:* on-campus residence required through senior year. *Options:* coed, men-only, women-only, disabled students. *Activities and organizations:* drama/theater group, student-run newspaper, radio station, choral group, Sewanee Outing Program, Community Service Council, Student Activities Programming Board, student radio station, BACCHUS (alcohol and drug education), national fraternities. *Campus security:* 24-hour emergency response devices and patrols, late-night transport/escort service, security lighting. *Student services:* health clinic, personal/psychological counseling, women's center, legal services.

Athletics Member NCAA. All Division III. *Intercollegiate sports:* baseball M, basketball M/W, crew M(c)/W(c), cross-country running M/W, equestrian sports M(c)/W(c), fencing M(c)/W(c), field hockey W, football M, golf M/W, lacrosse M(c)/W(c), rugby M(c), soccer M/W, softball W(c), swimming M/W, tennis M/W, track and field M/W, ultimate Frisbee M(c)/W(c), volleyball W. *Intramural sports:* basketball M/W, cross-country running M/W, football M, golf M/W, racquetball M/W, soccer M/W, softball M/W, swimming M/W, table tennis M/W, tennis M/W, track and field M/W, ultimate Frisbee M/W, volleyball M/W.

Standardized Tests *Required:* SAT I or ACT (for admission). *Recommended:* SAT II: Subject Tests (for admission).

Costs (2003–04) *Comprehensive fee:* $30,855 includes full-time tuition ($23,930), mandatory fees ($205), and room and board ($6720). *College room only:* $3440. *Payment plans:* installment, deferred payment. *Waivers:* employees or children of employees.

Financial Aid Of all full-time matriculated undergraduates who enrolled in 2003, 644 applied for aid, 607 were judged to have need, 607 had their need fully met. 366 Federal Work-Study jobs (averaging $1128). 149 state and other part-time jobs (averaging $1325). In 2003, 171 non-need-based awards were made. *Average percent of need met:* 100%. *Average financial aid package:* $19,633. *Average need-based loan:* $3496. *Average need-based gift aid:* $16,520. *Average non-need-based aid:* $12,155. *Average indebtedness upon graduation:* $14,441.

Applying *Options:* common application, electronic application, early admission, early decision, deferred entrance. *Application fee:* $45. *Required:* essay or personal statement, high school transcript, 2 letters of recommendation. *Recommended:* interview. *Application deadlines:* 2/1 (freshmen), 4/1 (transfers). *Early decision:* 11/15. *Notification:* 4/1 (freshmen), 12/15 (early decision), continuous (transfers).

Admissions Contact Mr. David Lesesne, Dean of Admission, University of the South, 735 University Avenue, Sewanee, TN 37383-1000. *Phone:* 931-598-1238. *Toll-free phone:* 800-522-2234. *Fax:* 931-598-3248. *E-mail:* collegeadmission@sewanee.edu.

VANDERBILT UNIVERSITY
Nashville, Tennessee

- **Independent** university, founded 1873
- **Calendar** semesters
- **Degrees** bachelor's, master's, doctoral, and first professional
- **Urban** 330-acre campus
- **Endowment** $1.4 billion
- **Coed,** 6,283 undergraduate students, 99% full-time, 52% women, 48% men
- **Very difficult** entrance level, 40% of applicants were admitted

Undergraduates 6,231 full-time, 52 part-time. Students come from 54 states and territories, 36 other countries, 7% African American, 6% Asian American or Pacific Islander, 4% Hispanic American, 0.2% Native American, 2% international, 0.8% transferred in, 84% live on campus. *Retention:* 94% of 2002 full-time freshmen returned.

Freshmen *Admission:* 10,960 applied, 4,405 admitted, 1,546 enrolled. *Test scores:* SAT verbal scores over 500: 98%; SAT math scores over 500: 99%; ACT scores over 18: 100%; SAT verbal scores over 600: 84%; SAT math scores over 600: 89%; ACT scores over 24: 95%; SAT verbal scores over 700: 31%; SAT math scores over 700: 39%; ACT scores over 30: 56%.

Faculty *Total:* 713. *Student/faculty ratio:* 9:1.

Majors African-American/Black studies; African studies; American studies; anthropology; art; Asian studies (East); astronomy; biology/biological sciences; biomedical/medical engineering; chemical engineering; chemistry; civil engineering; classics and languages, literatures and linguistics; cognitive psychology and psycholinguistics; computer engineering; computer science; dramatic/theatre arts; ecology; economics; education; electrical, electronics and communications engineering; elementary education; engineering; engineering science; English; European studies; French; geology/earth science; German; history; human development and family studies; human resources management; interdisciplinary studies; kindergarten/preschool education; Latin American studies; mass communication/media; mathematics; mechanical engineering; molecular biology; music; philosophy; physics; piano and organ; political science and government; Portuguese; psychology; religious studies; Russian; secondary education; sociology; Spanish; special education; urban studies/affairs; violin, viola, guitar and other stringed instruments; voice and opera; wind/percussion instruments.

Academic Programs *Special study options:* accelerated degree program, advanced placement credit, cooperative education, distance learning, double majors, English as a second language, honors programs, independent study, internships, off-campus study, services for LD students, student-designed majors, study abroad, summer session for credit. *ROTC:* Army (b), Navy (b), Air Force (c).

Library Jean and Alexander Heard Library plus 7 others with 1.8 million titles, 26,885 serial subscriptions, 153,450 audiovisual materials.

Computers on Campus 400 computers available on campus for general student use. A campuswide network can be accessed from student residence rooms and from off campus that provide access to productivity and educational software. At least one staffed computer lab available.

Student Life *Housing:* on-campus residence required through senior year. *Options:* coed, men-only, women-only, disabled students. *Activities and organizations:* drama/theater group, student-run newspaper, radio station, choral group, marching band, national fraternities, national sororities. *Campus security:* 24-hour emergency response devices and patrols, student patrols, late-night transport/escort service, controlled dormitory access. *Student services:* health clinic, personal/psychological counseling, women's center.

Athletics Member NCAA. All Division I except football (Division I-A). *Intercollegiate sports:* baseball M(s), basketball M(s)/W(s), crew M(c)/W(c), cross-country running M(s)/W(s), equestrian sports M(c)/W(c), fencing M(c)/W(c), field hockey M(c)/W(c), golf M(s)/W(s), ice hockey M(c)/W(c), lacrosse M(c)/W(s), rugby M(c)/W(c), sailing M(c)/W(c), soccer M(s)/W(s), squash M(c)/W(c), tennis M(s)/W(s), track and field M(c)/W(s), volleyball M(c)/W(c), water polo M(c)/W(c), wrestling M(c)/W(c). *Intramural sports:* badminton M/W, baseball M, basketball M/W, bowling M/W, football M/W, golf M/W, racquetball M/W, soccer M/W, softball M/W, squash M/W, swimming M/W, table tennis M/W, tennis M/W, volleyball M/W, water polo M/W, weight lifting M/W.

Standardized Tests *Required:* SAT I or ACT (for admission). *Recommended:* SAT II: Subject Tests (for admission), SAT II: Writing Test (for admission).

Costs (2003–04) *Comprehensive fee:* $37,897 includes full-time tuition ($27,720), mandatory fees ($720), and room and board ($9457). Part-time tuition: $1155 per credit hour. Part-time tuition and fees vary according to course load. *College room only:* $6182. Room and board charges vary according to board plan and housing facility. *Payment plans:* tuition prepayment, installment, deferred payment. *Waivers:* employees or children of employees.

Financial Aid Of all full-time matriculated undergraduates who enrolled in 2003, 2,573 applied for aid, 2,385 were judged to have need, 2,095 had their need fully met. In 2003, 983 non-need-based awards were made. *Average percent of need met:* 98%. *Average financial aid package:* $28,906. *Average need-based loan:* $4939. *Average need-based gift aid:* $20,555. *Average non-need-based aid:* $15,141. *Average indebtedness upon graduation:* $23,334.

Applying *Options:* common application, electronic application, early admission, early decision, deferred entrance. *Application fee:* $50. *Required:* essay or personal statement, high school transcript, 2 letters of recommendation. *Application deadlines:* 1/2 (freshmen), 3/1 (transfers). *Early decision:* 11/1 (for plan 1), 1/2 (for plan 2). *Notification:* 4/1 (freshmen), 12/15 (early decision plan 1), 2/15 (early decision plan 2), 4/15 (transfers).

Admissions Contact Mr. Bill Shain, Dean of Undergraduate Admissions, Vanderbilt University, 2305 West End Avenue, Nashville, TN 37203. *Phone:* 615-322-2561. *Toll-free phone:* 800-288-0432. *Fax:* 615-343-7765. *E-mail:* admissions@vanderbilt.edu.

■ *See page 2752 for a narrative description.*

WATKINS COLLEGE OF ART AND DESIGN
Nashville, Tennessee

- **Independent** 4-year, founded 1885
- **Calendar** semesters
- **Degrees** associate, bachelor's, and postbachelor's certificates
- **Urban** 13-acre campus

- **Coed,** 384 undergraduate students, 46% full-time, 64% women, 36% men
- **Moderately difficult** entrance level, 77% of applicants were admitted

Undergraduates 178 full-time, 206 part-time. Students come from 12 states and territories, 4 other countries, 38% are from out of state, 7% African American, 1% Asian American or Pacific Islander, 2% Hispanic American, 0.5% Native American, 1% international, 20% transferred in. *Retention:* 68% of 2002 full-time freshmen returned.

Freshmen *Admission:* 87 applied, 67 admitted, 43 enrolled. *Average high school GPA:* 2.95.

Faculty *Total:* 43, 35% full-time, 65% with terminal degrees.

Majors Cinematography and film/video production; film/cinema studies; film/video and photographic arts related; fine/studio arts; graphic communications; graphic design; interior architecture; interior design; photography.

Academic Programs *Special study options:* cooperative education, double majors, internships, summer session for credit.

Library The George B. Allen Library with 5,000 titles, 42 serial subscriptions.

Computers on Campus 10 computers available on campus for general student use. Internet access, at least one staffed computer lab available. Computer purchase or lease plan available.

Student Life *Housing:* college housing not available. *Activities and organizations:* student-run newspaper. *Campus security:* 24-hour patrols. *Student services:* personal/psychological counseling.

Standardized Tests *Required:* SAT I or ACT (for admission).

Costs (2004–05) *Tuition:* $10,040 full-time, $437 per hour part-time. Full-time tuition and fees vary according to course load and program. Part-time tuition and fees vary according to course load and program. *Required fees:* $432 full-time, $48 per hour part-time. *Payment plan:* deferred payment. *Waivers:* employees or children of employees.

Financial Aid Of all full-time matriculated undergraduates who enrolled in 2003, 98 applied for aid, 96 were judged to have need. 15 Federal Work-Study jobs (averaging $1500). 15 state and other part-time jobs (averaging $1500). *Average percent of need met:* 60%. *Average financial aid package:* $9000. *Average need-based loan:* $4000. *Average need-based gift aid:* $1500. *Average indebtedness upon graduation:* $18,000.

Applying *Options:* early action, deferred entrance. *Application fee:* $35. *Required:* essay or personal statement, high school transcript, minimum 2.5 GPA, letters of recommendation. *Required for some:* interview, statement of good standing from prior institution(s), portfolio and home exercises. *Recommended:* interview. *Application deadlines:* 4/1 (freshmen), 4/1 (transfers). *Notification:* 4/30 (freshmen), 4/1 (early action), 4/30 (transfers).

Admissions Contact Mr. Ted Gray, Director of Admissions, Watkins College of Art and Design, 2298 Metro Center Boulevard, Nashville, TN 37228. *Phone:* 615-383-4848. *Fax:* 615-383-4849. *E-mail:* tgray@watkins.edu.

WILLIAMSON CHRISTIAN COLLEGE

Franklin, Tennessee

- **Independent interdenominational** 4-year, founded 1997
- **Calendar** semesters
- **Degrees** associate and bachelor's
- **Suburban** 1-acre campus with easy access to Nashville
- **Endowment** $11,155
- **Coed,** 67 undergraduate students, 84% full-time, 55% women, 45% men
- **Noncompetitive** entrance level, 59% of applicants were admitted

Undergraduates 56 full-time, 11 part-time. Students come from 2 states and territories, 0.1% are from out of state, 3% African American, 1% Hispanic American, 88% transferred in.

Freshmen *Admission:* 22 applied, 13 admitted, 5 enrolled.

Faculty *Total:* 19, 21% full-time, 53% with terminal degrees. *Student/faculty ratio:* 10:1.

Majors Biblical studies; business administration and management; pre-theology/pre-ministerial studies; theological and ministerial studies related; theology and religious vocations related.

Academic Programs *Special study options:* accelerated degree program, adult/continuing education programs, distance learning, double majors, external degree program, independent study, internships, part-time degree program.

Library John W. Neth, Jr. Library.

Computers on Campus 8 computers available on campus for general student use. Internet access, online (class) registration available.

Student Life *Housing:* college housing not available. *Student services:* health clinic, personal/psychological counseling.

Costs (2004–05) *Tuition:* $7350 full-time, $260 per credit part-time. Part-time tuition and fees vary according to course load. No tuition increase for student's term of enrollment. *Required fees:* $50 full-time, $15 per course part-time. *Payment plans:* installment, deferred payment. *Waivers:* employees or children of employees.

Financial Aid Of all full-time matriculated undergraduates who enrolled in 2003, 11 applied for aid, 10 were judged to have need, 1 had their need fully met. 2 Federal Work-Study jobs (averaging $2000). *Average percent of need met:* 50%. *Average financial aid package:* $4858. *Average need-based gift aid:* $2556.

Applying *Options:* early admission. *Application fee:* $25. *Required:* high school transcript, interview. *Application deadlines:* 9/1 (freshmen), 9/1 (transfers). *Notification:* continuous until 10/1 (freshmen), continuous until 10/1 (transfers).

Admissions Contact Mr. Steven T. Smith, Registrar/Director or Admissions, Williamson Christian College, 200 Seaboard Lane, Franklin, TN 37067. *Phone:* 615-771-7821. *Fax:* 615-771-7810. *E-mail:* info@williamsoncc.edu.

TEXAS

ABILENE CHRISTIAN UNIVERSITY

Abilene, Texas

- **Independent** comprehensive, founded 1906, affiliated with Church of Christ
- **Calendar** semesters
- **Degrees** certificates, associate, bachelor's, master's, doctoral, first professional, and postbachelor's certificates
- **Urban** 208-acre campus
- **Endowment** $137.7 million
- **Coed,** 4,111 undergraduate students, 94% full-time, 56% women, 44% men
- **Moderately difficult** entrance level, 53% of applicants were admitted

Undergraduates 3,877 full-time, 234 part-time. Students come from 47 states and territories, 40 other countries, 18% are from out of state, 5% transferred in, 41% live on campus. *Retention:* 74% of 2002 full-time freshmen returned.

Freshmen *Admission:* 4,011 applied, 2,117 admitted, 949 enrolled. *Average high school GPA:* 3.60. *Test scores:* SAT verbal scores over 500: 71%; SAT math scores over 500: 72%; ACT scores over 18: 95%; SAT verbal scores over 600: 27%; SAT math scores over 600: 30%; ACT scores over 24: 48%; SAT verbal scores over 700: 5%; SAT math scores over 700: 5%; ACT scores over 30: 8%.

Faculty *Total:* 330, 69% full-time, 53% with terminal degrees. *Student/faculty ratio:* 16:1.

Majors Accounting; agribusiness; animal sciences; architecture related; area studies; art; art teacher education; biblical studies; biochemistry; biology/biological sciences; biology teacher education; business administration and management; chemistry; clinical laboratory science/medical technology; clinical/medical laboratory science and allied professions related; commercial and advertising art; communication and journalism related; computer hardware engineering; computer science; dietetics; digital communication and media/multimedia; dramatic/theatre arts; elementary education; engineering; engineering physics; engineering science; English; English/language arts teacher education; environmental science; family and consumer sciences/human sciences; finance; fine arts related; fine/studio arts; health and physical education; history; history teacher education; human development and family studies; industrial and organizational psychology; interdisciplinary studies; interior design; international/global studies; journalism; liberal arts and sciences/liberal studies; marketing/marketing management; mathematics; mathematics teacher education; medical laboratory technology; middle school education; missionary studies and missiology; multi-/interdisciplinary studies related; music; music teacher education; nursing (registered nurse training); ophthalmic laboratory technology; pastoral studies/counseling; physical education teaching and coaching; physics; piano and organ; political science and government; pre-dentistry studies; pre-law studies; pre-medical studies; pre-pharmacy studies; pre-veterinary studies; psychology; reading teacher education; science teacher education; secondary education; social sciences related; social studies teacher education; social work; sociology; Spanish; Spanish language teacher education; special education; speech and rhetoric; speech-language pathology; sport and fitness administration; theology and religious vocations related; voice and opera.

Academic Programs *Special study options:* academic remediation for entering students, adult/continuing education programs, advanced placement credit, distance learning, double majors, English as a second language, external degree program, honors programs, independent study, internships, off-campus study, part-time degree program, services for LD students, student-designed majors, study abroad, summer session for credit. *Unusual degree programs:* 3-2 engineering with The University of Texas at Dallas, The University of Texas at Arlington.

Library Brown Library with 481,689 titles, 2,439 serial subscriptions, 62,224 audiovisual materials, an OPAC, a Web page.

Computers on Campus 700 computers available on campus for general student use. A campuswide network can be accessed from student residence rooms and from off campus. Internet access, online (class) registration, at least one staffed computer lab available.

Abilene Christian University (continued)

Student Life *Housing:* on-campus residence required through sophomore year. *Options:* men-only, women-only. Campus housing is university owned. Freshman campus housing is guaranteed. *Activities and organizations:* drama/theater group, student-run newspaper, radio and television station, choral group, marching band, Student Association, Alpha Phi Omega, "W" Club, Spring Break Campaign, Student Alumni Association. *Campus security:* 24-hour emergency response devices and patrols, late-night transport/escort service. *Student services:* health clinic, personal/psychological counseling.

Athletics Member NCAA. All Division II. *Intercollegiate sports:* baseball M(s), basketball M(s)/W(s), cheerleading M(c)/W(c), cross-country running M(s)/W(s), football M(s), golf M(s), soccer M(c)/W(c), softball W(s), tennis M(s)/W(s), track and field M(s)/W(s), volleyball W(s). *Intramural sports:* badminton M/W, basketball M/W, bowling M/W, cross-country running M/W, football M/W, racquetball M/W, rock climbing M(c)/W(c), soccer M/W, softball M/W, table tennis M/W, tennis M/W, track and field M/W, ultimate Frisbee M/W, volleyball M/W, water polo M.

Standardized Tests *Required:* SAT I or ACT (for admission).

Costs (2003–04) *Comprehensive fee:* $18,370 includes full-time tuition ($12,750), mandatory fees ($540), and room and board ($5080). Full-time tuition and fees vary according to course load. Part-time tuition: $425 per semester hour. Part-time tuition and fees vary according to course load. *Required fees:* $17 per semester hour part-time, $5 per term part-time. *College room only:* $2160. Room and board charges vary according to board plan and housing facility. *Payment plans:* tuition prepayment, installment. *Waivers:* employees or children of employees.

Financial Aid Of all full-time matriculated undergraduates who enrolled in 2002, 3,866 applied for aid, 2,320 were judged to have need, 1,143 had their need fully met. 440 Federal Work-Study jobs (averaging $1454). In 2002, 1075 non-need-based awards were made. *Average percent of need met:* 77%. *Average financial aid package:* $10,210. *Average need-based loan:* $3815. *Average need-based gift aid:* $7196. *Average non-need-based aid:* $4697. *Average indebtedness upon graduation:* $25,845.

Applying *Options:* common application, electronic application. *Application fee:* $25. *Required:* high school transcript, 2 letters of recommendation. *Recommended:* minimum 2.0 GPA, interview. *Application deadline:* 8/1 (freshmen), rolling (transfers). *Notification:* continuous until 9/1 (freshmen), continuous until 9/1 (transfers).

Admissions Contact Mr. Robert Heil, Director of Admissions and Enrollment, Abilene Christian University, Zellner Hall Room 2006A, ACU Box 29000, Abilene, TX 79699-9000. *Phone:* 325-674-2765. *Toll-free phone:* 800-460-6228. *Fax:* 915-674-2130. *E-mail:* info@admissions.acu.edu.

■ *See page 1126 for a narrative description.*

AMBERTON UNIVERSITY
Garland, Texas

- **Independent nondenominational** upper-level, founded 1971
- **Calendar** 4 10-week terms
- **Degrees** bachelor's and master's
- **Suburban** 5-acre campus with easy access to Dallas–Fort Worth
- **Endowment** $5.0 million
- **Coed,** 633 undergraduate students, 20% full-time, 67% women, 33% men
- **Minimally difficult** entrance level

Undergraduates 126 full-time, 507 part-time. Students come from 1 other state, 0.1% are from out of state, 31% African American, 1% Asian American or Pacific Islander, 6% Hispanic American, 1% Native American.

Faculty *Total:* 39, 36% full-time, 82% with terminal degrees. *Student/faculty ratio:* 25:1.

Majors Accounting; business administration and management; computer and information sciences; counselor education/school counseling and guidance; human development and family studies; human resources management; interdisciplinary studies; management information systems; marketing/marketing management.

Academic Programs *Special study options:* adult/continuing education programs, external degree program, internships, part-time degree program, student-designed majors, summer session for credit.

Library Library Resource Center plus 1 other with 21,000 titles, 120 serial subscriptions, an OPAC, a Web page.

Computers on Campus 30 computers available on campus for general student use. Internet access, at least one staffed computer lab available.

Student Life *Housing:* college housing not available. *Campus security:* 24-hour emergency response devices and patrols.

Costs (2003–04) *Tuition:* $6000 full-time, $200 per hour part-time. *Payment plan:* installment.

Applying *Options:* common application, deferred entrance. *Application deadline:* rolling (transfers). *Notification:* continuous (transfers).

Admissions Contact Dr. Algia Allen, Vice President for Academic Services, Amberton University, 1700 Eastgate Drive, Garland, TX 75041-5595. *Phone:* 972-279-6511 Ext. 135. *E-mail:* advisor@amberton.edu.

AMERICAN INTERCONTINENTAL UNIVERSITY
Houston, Texas

Admissions Contact 9999 Richmond Avenue, Houston, TX 77042.

ANGELO STATE UNIVERSITY
San Angelo, Texas

- **State-supported** comprehensive, founded 1928, part of Texas State University System
- **Calendar** semesters
- **Degrees** certificates, associate, bachelor's, and master's
- **Urban** 268-acre campus
- **Endowment** $73.4 million
- **Coed,** 5,618 undergraduate students, 81% full-time, 56% women, 44% men
- **Moderately difficult** entrance level, 99% of applicants were admitted

Undergraduates 4,577 full-time, 1,041 part-time. Students come from 40 states and territories, 22 other countries, 2% are from out of state, 6% African American, 1% Asian American or Pacific Islander, 22% Hispanic American, 0.4% Native American, 1% international, 7% transferred in, 25% live on campus. *Retention:* 69% of 2002 full-time freshmen returned.

Freshmen *Admission:* 2,146 applied, 2,126 admitted, 1,148 enrolled. *Test scores:* SAT verbal scores over 500: 42%; SAT math scores over 500: 43%; ACT scores over 18: 74%; SAT verbal scores over 600: 11%; SAT math scores over 600: 11%; ACT scores over 24: 18%; SAT verbal scores over 700: 1%; SAT math scores over 700: 1%; ACT scores over 30: 1%.

Faculty *Total:* 314, 75% full-time, 58% with terminal degrees. *Student/faculty ratio:* 21:1.

Majors Accounting; animal sciences; art; athletic training; biochemistry; biological and physical sciences; biology/biological sciences; business administration and management; chemistry; clinical laboratory science/medical technology; communication/speech communication and rhetoric; computer and information sciences; criminal justice/safety; dramatic/theatre arts; English; finance; fine/studio arts; French; general studies; German; health and physical education; history; humanities; interdisciplinary studies; journalism; liberal arts and sciences/liberal studies; management information systems; marketing/marketing management; mathematics; multi-/interdisciplinary studies related; music; nursing (registered nurse training); physics; physics related; political science and government; psychology; real estate; social sciences; sociology; Spanish; visual and performing arts.

Academic Programs *Special study options:* academic remediation for entering students, accelerated degree program, adult/continuing education programs, advanced placement credit, distance learning, double majors, independent study, internships, off-campus study, part-time degree program, services for LD students, study abroad, summer session for credit. *ROTC:* Air Force (b). *Unusual degree programs:* 3-2 engineering with University of Texas at El Paso, Texas A&M University; agriculture education with Texas A&M University.

Library Porter Henderson Library plus 1 other with 470,245 titles, 1,712 serial subscriptions, 29,794 audiovisual materials, an OPAC, a Web page.

Computers on Campus 500 computers available on campus for general student use. A campuswide network can be accessed from student residence rooms and from off campus. Internet access, online (class) registration, at least one staffed computer lab available.

Student Life *Housing:* on-campus residence required through sophomore year. *Options:* coed, men-only, women-only, disabled students. Campus housing is university owned. *Activities and organizations:* drama/theater group, student-run newspaper, radio and television station, choral group, marching band, Block and Bridle Club, Baptist Student Union, Delta Sigma Pi, Air Force ROTC, Association of Mexican-American Students, national fraternities, national sororities. *Campus security:* 24-hour emergency response devices and patrols, student patrols, late-night transport/escort service, controlled dormitory access. *Student services:* health clinic, personal/psychological counseling.

Athletics Member NCAA, NAIA. All NCAA Division II. *Intercollegiate sports:* baseball M(s), basketball M(s)/W(s), cross-country running M(s)/W(s), football M(s), rugby M(c), soccer W(s), softball W(s), track and field M(s)/W(s), volleyball W(s). *Intramural sports:* archery M/W, badminton M/W, basketball M/W, bowling M/W, football M/W, golf M/W, racquetball M/W, rugby M, soccer M/W, softball M/W, swimming M/W, table tennis M/W, tennis M/W, ultimate Frisbee M/W, volleyball M/W, weight lifting M/W.

Standardized Tests *Required:* SAT I or ACT (for admission).
Costs (2003–04) *Tuition:* state resident $2064 full-time, $86 per credit part-time; nonresident $7728 full-time, $322 per credit part-time. Full-time tuition and fees vary according to course load. Part-time tuition and fees vary according to course load. *Required fees:* $866 full-time, $32 per credit part-time, $91 per term part-time. *Room and board:* $4646; room only: $3024. Room and board charges vary according to board plan and housing facility. *Payment plan:* installment.
Financial Aid Of all full-time matriculated undergraduates who enrolled in 2002, 4,320 applied for aid, 3,268 were judged to have need, 2,540 had their need fully met. 148 Federal Work-Study jobs (averaging $1687). 16 state and other part-time jobs (averaging $1145). In 2002, 255 non-need-based awards were made. *Average percent of need met:* 64%. *Average financial aid package:* $4204. *Average need-based loan:* $2540. *Average need-based gift aid:* $1659. *Average non-need-based aid:* $1866. *Average indebtedness upon graduation:* $14,711.
Applying *Options:* common application, electronic application, early admission, deferred entrance. *Application fee:* $20. *Required:* high school transcript. *Application deadlines:* 8/1 (freshmen), 8/1 (transfers). *Notification:* continuous (freshmen), continuous (transfers).
Admissions Contact Director of Admissions, Angelo State University, ASU Station #11014, Administration and Journalism Building, San Angelo, TX 76909-1014. *Phone:* 325-942-2185 Ext. 231. *Toll-free phone:* 800-946-8627. *Fax:* 325-942-2078. *E-mail:* admissions@angelo.edu.

■ *See page 1174 for a narrative description.*

ARGOSY UNIVERSITY/DALLAS
Dallas, Texas

- **Proprietary** upper-level, founded 2002, part of Argosy University System
- **Calendar** semesters
- **Degrees** bachelor's, master's, and doctoral
- **Urban** campus
- **Coed,** 18 undergraduate students, 61% full-time, 72% women, 28% men

Undergraduates 11 full-time, 7 part-time. Students come from 1 other state, 53% African American, 56% transferred in.
Faculty *Total:* 8, 100% full-time, 100% with terminal degrees. *Student/faculty ratio:* 17:1.
Majors Psychology.
Academic Programs *Special study options:* accelerated degree program, adult/continuing education programs, distance learning, part-time degree program, summer session for credit.
Computers on Campus Internet access, online (class) registration, at least one staffed computer lab available.
Student Life *Housing:* college housing not available. *Campus security:* late-night transport/escort service.
Costs (2004–05) *Tuition:* $9120 full-time, $375 per semester hour part-time. *Payment plan:* installment.
Financial Aid Of all full-time matriculated undergraduates who enrolled in 2003, 1 Federal Work-Study job (averaging $805).
Applying *Options:* common application, electronic application, early admission, deferred entrance. *Application fee:* $50. *Application deadline:* rolling (transfers). *Notification:* continuous (transfers).
Admissions Contact Ms. Kara Smith, Associate Director of Admissions, Argosy University/Dallas, 8950 North Central Expressway, Suite 315, Dallas, TX 75231. *Phone:* 214-890-9900 Ext. 2208. *Toll-free phone:* 866-954-9900. *E-mail:* dallasadmissions@argosyu.edu.

ARLINGTON BAPTIST COLLEGE
Arlington, Texas

- **Independent Baptist** 4-year, founded 1939
- **Calendar** semesters
- **Degree** certificates, diplomas, and bachelor's
- **Urban** 32-acre campus with easy access to Dallas–Fort Worth
- **Endowment** $19,511
- **Coed,** 178 undergraduate students, 87% full-time, 40% women, 60% men
- **Noncompetitive** entrance level, 100% of applicants were admitted

Undergraduates 154 full-time, 24 part-time. Students come from 13 states and territories, 8 other countries, 19% are from out of state, 1% African American, 0.6% Asian American or Pacific Islander, 4% Hispanic American, 0.6% Native American, 8% international, 33% transferred in, 49% live on campus. *Retention:* 64% of 2002 full-time freshmen returned.
Freshmen *Admission:* 63 applied, 63 admitted, 39 enrolled. *Average high school GPA:* 3.01.
Faculty *Total:* 14, 36% full-time, 7% with terminal degrees. *Student/faculty ratio:* 17:1.
Majors Biblical studies; early childhood education; education; elementary education; English/language arts teacher education; middle school education; music; music teacher education; religious studies; theology and religious vocations related.
Academic Programs *Special study options:* academic remediation for entering students, advanced placement credit, distance learning, double majors, independent study, internships, part-time degree program, summer session for credit.
Library Dr. Earl K. Oldham Library with 28,715 titles, 156 serial subscriptions, 812 audiovisual materials.
Computers on Campus 21 computers available on campus for general student use. A campuswide network can be accessed. Internet access, at least one staffed computer lab available.
Student Life *Housing:* on-campus residence required through senior year. *Options:* men-only, women-only. Campus housing is university owned. Freshman campus housing is guaranteed. *Activities and organizations:* student-run newspaper, choral group, Preachers Fellowship. Student Missionary Association, L.I.F.T., International Students Association, 4-12 Group. *Campus security:* student patrols, controlled dormitory access, night security guards. *Student services:* personal/psychological counseling.
Athletics Member NCCAA. *Intercollegiate sports:* baseball M, basketball M/W, cheerleading W, volleyball W. *Intramural sports:* baseball M, basketball M/W, volleyball W.
Standardized Tests *Recommended:* SAT I and SAT II or ACT (for placement).
Costs (2003–04) *Comprehensive fee:* $8490 includes full-time tuition ($4350), mandatory fees ($540), and room and board ($3600). Part-time tuition: $145 per semester hour. *Required fees:* $270 per term part-time. *Payment plan:* installment. *Waivers:* employees or children of employees.
Financial Aid Of all full-time matriculated undergraduates who enrolled in 2002, 172 applied for aid, 172 were judged to have need, 140 had their need fully met. *Average financial aid package:* $5081. *Average indebtedness upon graduation:* $8750.
Applying *Options:* early admission, deferred entrance. *Application fee:* $15. *Required:* essay or personal statement, high school transcript, 1 letter of recommendation, pastoral recommendation, medical examination. *Required for some:* interview. *Application deadline:* rolling (freshmen), rolling (transfers). *Notification:* continuous (freshmen), continuous (transfers).
Admissions Contact Ms. Janie Hall, Registrar/Admissions, Arlington Baptist College, 3001 West Division, Arlington, TX 76012-3425. *Phone:* 817-461-8741 Ext. 105. *Fax:* 817-274-1138. *E-mail:* jhall@abconline.org.

THE ART INSTITUTE OF HOUSTON
Houston, Texas

- **Proprietary** primarily 2-year, founded 1978, part of The Art Institutes International
- **Calendar** quarters
- **Degrees** diplomas, associate, and bachelor's
- **Urban** campus
- **Coed**
- **Moderately difficult** entrance level

Faculty *Student/faculty ratio:* 18:1.
Student Life *Campus security:* 24-hour emergency response devices.
Standardized Tests *Recommended:* SAT I or ACT (for admission).
Costs (2003–04) *Tuition:* $15,525 full-time, $345 per credit part-time. Full-time tuition and fees vary according to course load. No tuition increase for student's term of enrollment. *Room only:* $4185. Room and board charges vary according to housing facility. *Payment plans:* tuition prepayment, installment.
Applying *Options:* common application, electronic application. *Application fee:* $50. *Required:* essay or personal statement, high school transcript, letters of recommendation, interview. *Required for some:* minimum 2.5 GPA, portfolio. *Recommended:* minimum 2.0 GPA.
Admissions Contact Mr. Aaron McCardell, Director of Admissions, The Art Institute of Houston, 1900 Yorktown Street, Houston, TX 77056-4115. *Phone:* 713-623-2040 Ext. 3612. *Toll-free phone:* 800-275-4244. *Fax:* 713-966-2797. *E-mail:* aihadm@aih.aii.edu.

AUSTIN COLLEGE
Sherman, Texas

- **Independent Presbyterian** comprehensive, founded 1849
- **Calendar** 4-1-4

Austin College (continued)
- **Degrees** bachelor's and master's
- **Suburban** 60-acre campus with easy access to Dallas–Fort Worth
- **Endowment** $86.0 million
- **Coed,** 1,294 undergraduate students, 99% full-time, 56% women, 44% men
- **Very difficult** entrance level, 72% of applicants were admitted

Undergraduates 1,278 full-time, 16 part-time. Students come from 30 states and territories, 25 other countries, 10% are from out of state, 4% African American, 10% Asian American or Pacific Islander, 7% Hispanic American, 1% Native American, 2% international, 4% transferred in, 74% live on campus. *Retention:* 86% of 2002 full-time freshmen returned.

Freshmen *Admission:* 1,328 applied, 960 admitted, 338 enrolled. *Average high school GPA:* 3.39. *Test scores:* SAT verbal scores over 500: 94%; SAT math scores over 500: 93%; ACT scores over 18: 98%; SAT verbal scores over 600: 62%; SAT math scores over 600: 63%; ACT scores over 24: 69%; SAT verbal scores over 700: 15%; SAT math scores over 700: 10%; ACT scores over 30: 14%.

Faculty *Total:* 122, 75% full-time, 90% with terminal degrees. *Student/faculty ratio:* 13:1.

Majors American studies; art; biology/biological sciences; business administration and management; chemistry; classics and classical languages related; classics and languages, literatures and linguistics; communication/speech communication and rhetoric; computer science; economics; English; French; German; history; international economics; international relations and affairs; Latin; Latin American studies; mathematics; multi-/interdisciplinary studies related; music; philosophy; physical education teaching and coaching; physics; political science and government; psychology; religious studies; sociology; Spanish.

Academic Programs *Special study options:* adult/continuing education programs, advanced placement credit, double majors, honors programs, independent study, internships, off-campus study, part-time degree program, student-designed majors, study abroad, summer session for credit. *Unusual degree programs:* 3-2 engineering with University of Texas at Dallas; Texas A&M University; Washington University in St. Louis; Columbia University, The Fu Foundation School of Engineering and Applied Science.

Library Abell Library with 195,328 titles, 1,008 serial subscriptions, 7,418 audiovisual materials, an OPAC, a Web page.

Computers on Campus 165 computers available on campus for general student use. A campuswide network can be accessed from student residence rooms and from off campus. Internet access, at least one staffed computer lab available.

Student Life *Housing:* on-campus residence required through junior year. *Options:* coed, men-only, women-only, disabled students. Campus housing is university owned. Freshman campus housing is guaranteed. *Activities and organizations:* drama/theater group, student-run newspaper, choral group, Fellowship of Christian Athletes, Campus Activity Board, Indian Cultural Association, Student Development Board, international relations club. *Campus security:* 24-hour emergency response devices and patrols, late-night transport/escort service, controlled dormitory access. *Student services:* health clinic, personal/psychological counseling.

Athletics Member NCAA. All Division III. *Intercollegiate sports:* baseball M, basketball M/W, cheerleading M/W, cross-country running M/W, football M, golf M, soccer M/W, swimming M/W, tennis M/W, volleyball W. *Intramural sports:* basketball M/W, bowling M/W, football M/W, lacrosse M(c), racquetball M/W, soccer M/W, softball M/W, table tennis M/W, tennis M/W, ultimate Frisbee M/W, volleyball M/W.

Standardized Tests *Required:* SAT I or ACT (for admission).

Costs (2004–05) *Comprehensive fee:* $26,254 includes full-time tuition ($18,980), mandatory fees ($185), and room and board ($7089). Part-time tuition: $2750 per course. *College room only:* $3255. Room and board charges vary according to board plan. *Payment plan:* installment. *Waivers:* employees or children of employees.

Financial Aid Of all full-time matriculated undergraduates who enrolled in 2003, 935 applied for aid, 763 were judged to have need, 529 had their need fully met. In 2003, 455 non-need-based awards were made. *Average percent of need met:* 96%. *Average financial aid package:* $17,454. *Average need-based loan:* $4856. *Average need-based gift aid:* $11,753. *Average non-need-based aid:* $8473. *Average indebtedness upon graduation:* $22,085.

Applying *Options:* common application, electronic application, early admission, early decision, early action, deferred entrance. *Application fee:* $35. *Required:* essay or personal statement, high school transcript, 2 letters of recommendation. *Required for some:* interview. *Recommended:* minimum 3.0 GPA, interview. *Application deadlines:* 8/15 (freshmen), 8/15 (transfers). *Early decision:* 12/1. *Notification:* 1/10 (early decision), 3/1 (early action).

Admissions Contact Ms. Nan Davis, Vice President for Institutional Enrollment, Austin College, 900 North Grand Avenue, Suite 6N, Sherman, TX 75090-4400. *Phone:* 903-813-3000. *Toll-free phone:* 800-442-5363. *Fax:* 903-813-3198. *E-mail:* admission@austincollege.edu.

■ *See page 1200 for a narrative description.*

AUSTIN GRADUATE SCHOOL OF THEOLOGY
Austin, Texas

- **Independent** upper-level, founded 1917, affiliated with Church of Christ
- **Calendar** semesters
- **Degrees** bachelor's and master's
- **Urban** campus
- **Endowment** $4.0 million
- **Coed,** 30 undergraduate students, 10% full-time, 40% women, 60% men
- **Minimally difficult** entrance level

Undergraduates 3 full-time, 27 part-time. Students come from 2 states and territories, 3% are from out of state, 37% African American, 3% Hispanic American, 40% transferred in.

Faculty *Total:* 8, 63% full-time, 88% with terminal degrees. *Student/faculty ratio:* 7:1.

Majors Biblical studies.

Academic Programs *Special study options:* adult/continuing education programs, advanced placement credit, part-time degree program, summer session for credit.

Library Austin Graduate School Library plus 1 other with 25,000 titles, 95 serial subscriptions, an OPAC, a Web page.

Computers on Campus 8 computers available on campus for general student use. A campuswide network can be accessed from off campus. Internet access, at least one staffed computer lab available.

Student Life *Housing:* college housing not available. *Activities and organizations:* student-run newspaper, student government. *Campus security:* 24-hour emergency response devices.

Standardized Tests *Required for some:* SAT I or ACT (for admission).

Costs (2003–04) *Tuition:* $4200 full-time, $525 per course part-time. Full-time tuition and fees vary according to course load. Part-time tuition and fees vary according to course load. *Payment plan:* installment. *Waivers:* employees or children of employees.

Financial Aid Of all full-time matriculated undergraduates who enrolled in 2002, 9 applied for aid, 7 were judged to have need. 1 Federal Work-Study job (averaging $330). In 2002, 2 non-need-based awards were made. *Average need-based loan:* $2854. *Average need-based gift aid:* $2395. *Average non-need-based aid:* $788. *Average indebtedness upon graduation:* $10,373.

Applying *Application deadline:* rolling (freshmen), rolling (transfers).

Admissions Contact Ms. Beverly Martin, Registrar, Austin Graduate School of Theology, 1909 University Avenue, Austin, TX 78705. *Phone:* 512-476-2772 Ext. 200. *Toll-free phone:* 866-AUS-GRAD. *Fax:* 512-476-3919. *E-mail:* registrar@austingrad.edu.

BAPTIST MISSIONARY ASSOCIATION THEOLOGICAL SEMINARY
Jacksonville, Texas

- **Independent Baptist** comprehensive, founded 1955
- **Calendar** semesters
- **Degrees** associate, bachelor's, master's, and first professional
- **Small-town** 17-acre campus
- **Endowment** $613,239
- **Coed, primarily men**
- **Noncompetitive** entrance level

Faculty *Student/faculty ratio:* 10:1.

Costs (2003–04) *Tuition:* $2250 full-time, $75 per credit hour part-time. *Required fees:* $80 full-time, $40 per term part-time. *Room only:* $1800.

Financial Aid Of all full-time matriculated undergraduates who enrolled in 2001, 2 applied for aid, 2 were judged to have need. *Average percent of need met:* 50. *Average financial aid package:* $1098.

Applying *Application fee:* $20. *Required:* 3 letters of recommendation, interview.

Admissions Contact Dr. Philip Attebery, Dean and Registrar, Baptist Missionary Association Theological Seminary, 1530 East Pine Street, Jacksonville, TX 75766-5407. *Phone:* 903-586-2501 Ext. 229. *Fax:* 903-586-0378. *E-mail:* bmatsem@fbmats.edu.

BAPTIST UNIVERSITY OF THE AMERICAS
San Antonio, Texas

Admissions Contact 8019 South Pan Am Expressway, San Antonio, TX 78224-2701. *Toll-free phone:* 800-721-1396.

BAYLOR UNIVERSITY
Waco, Texas

- **Independent Baptist** university, founded 1845
- **Calendar** semesters
- **Degrees** bachelor's, master's, doctoral, first professional, and post-master's certificates
- **Urban** 432-acre campus with easy access to Dallas–Fort Worth
- **Endowment** $556.8 million
- **Coed,** 11,712 undergraduate students, 96% full-time, 58% women, 42% men
- **Moderately difficult** entrance level, 82% of applicants were admitted

Undergraduates 11,260 full-time, 452 part-time. Students come from 50 states and territories, 90 other countries, 15% are from out of state, 6% African American, 5% Asian American or Pacific Islander, 8% Hispanic American, 0.6% Native American, 1% international, 4% transferred in, 32% live on campus. *Retention:* 84% of 2002 full-time freshmen returned.

Freshmen *Admission:* 8,931 applied, 7,341 admitted, 2,678 enrolled. *Test scores:* SAT verbal scores over 500: 88%; SAT math scores over 500: 92%; ACT scores over 18: 100%; SAT verbal scores over 600: 43%; SAT math scores over 600: 51%; ACT scores over 24: 56%; SAT verbal scores over 700: 9%; SAT math scores over 700: 10%; ACT scores over 30: 6%.

Faculty *Total:* 921, 84% full-time. *Student/faculty ratio:* 16:1.

Majors Accounting; acting; airline pilot and flight crew; American studies; ancient/classical Greek; ancient Near Eastern and biblical languages; anthropology; applied mathematics; archeology; architecture; art; art history, criticism and conservation; art teacher education; Asian studies; athletic training; biochemistry; bioinformatics; biology/biological sciences; biology teacher education; business administration and management; business/commerce; business, management, and marketing related; business/managerial economics; business statistics; business teacher education; chemistry; chemistry teacher education; classics and languages, literatures and linguistics; clinical laboratory science/medical technology; communication disorders; communication/speech communication and rhetoric; computer science; computer teacher education; drama and dance teacher education; dramatic/theatre arts; economics; education; education (specific subject areas) related; electrical, electronics and communications engineering; elementary education; engineering; English; English composition; English/language arts teacher education; entrepreneurship; environmental studies; family and consumer sciences/human sciences; fashion/apparel design; fashion merchandising; finance; financial planning and services; fine/studio arts; foreign language teacher education; forensic science and technology; forestry; French; French language teacher education; geological and earth sciences/geosciences related; geology/earth science; geophysics and seismology; German; German language teacher education; health and physical education; health/medical preparatory programs related; health occupations teacher education; health teacher education; history; history teacher education; human development and family studies; humanities; human nutrition; human resources management; insurance; interior design; international business/trade/commerce; international relations and affairs; journalism; kindergarten/preschool education; Latin; Latin American studies; Latin teacher education; linguistics; management information systems; marketing/marketing management; mathematics; mathematics teacher education; mechanical engineering; multi-/interdisciplinary studies related; museum studies; music; music history, literature, and theory; music pedagogy; music performance; music teacher education; music theory and composition; neuroscience; nursing (registered nurse training); operations management; philosophy; physical education teaching and coaching; physics; physics teacher education; political science and government; pre-dentistry studies; pre-law studies; pre-medical studies; pre-nursing studies; psychology; public administration; radio and television; reading teacher education; real estate; religious/sacred music; religious studies; Russian; sales, distribution and marketing; science teacher education; secondary education; Slavic studies; social science teacher education; social studies teacher education; social work; sociology; Spanish; Spanish language teacher education; special education; special education (speech or language impaired); speech teacher education; sport and fitness administration; theatre design and technology; urban studies/affairs.

Academic Programs *Special study options:* accelerated degree program, advanced placement credit, double majors, honors programs, internships, part-time degree program, services for LD students, student-designed majors, study abroad, summer session for credit. *ROTC:* Air Force (b). *Unusual degree programs:* 3-2 forestry with Duke University; architecture with Washington University in St. Louis, medical technology and biology, medicine, dentistry, optometry.

Library Moody Memorial Library plus 8 others with 2.3 million titles, 8,429 serial subscriptions, 73,228 audiovisual materials, an OPAC, a Web page.

Computers on Campus 1500 computers available on campus for general student use. A campuswide network can be accessed from student residence rooms and from off campus. Internet access, online (class) registration, at least one staffed computer lab available. Computer purchase or lease plan available.

Student Life *Housing:* on-campus residence required for freshman year. *Options:* men-only, women-only, disabled students. Campus housing is university owned. Freshman campus housing is guaranteed. *Activities and organizations:* drama/theater group, student-run newspaper, radio and television station, choral group, marching band, Alpha Phi Omega, College Republicans, Gamma Beta Phi, student government, national fraternities, national sororities. *Campus security:* 24-hour emergency response devices and patrols, late-night transport/escort service, controlled dormitory access, bicycle patrols. *Student services:* health clinic, personal/psychological counseling, legal services.

Athletics Member NCAA. All Division I except football (Division I-A). *Intercollegiate sports:* badminton M(c)/W(c), baseball M(s), basketball M(s)/W(s), crew M(c)/W(c), cross-country running M(s)/W(s), fencing M(c)/W(c), golf M(s)/W(s), ice hockey M(c), lacrosse M(c)/W(c), rugby M(c)/W(c), sailing M(c)/W(c), soccer M(c)/W(s), softball W(s), tennis M(s)/W(s), track and field M(s)/W(s), volleyball M(c)/W(s), water polo M(c)/W(c). *Intramural sports:* basketball M/W, bowling M/W, football M/W, golf M/W, racquetball M/W, soccer M/W, softball M/W, swimming M/W, table tennis M/W, tennis M/W, track and field M/W, volleyball M/W, weight lifting M/W.

Standardized Tests *Required:* SAT I or ACT (for admission).

Costs (2003–04) *Comprehensive fee:* $23,864 includes full-time tuition ($16,750), mandatory fees ($1680), and room and board ($5434). Part-time tuition: $698 per semester hour. No tuition increase for student's term of enrollment. *Required fees:* $52 per semester hour part-time. *College room only:* $2728. Room and board charges vary according to board plan and housing facility. *Payment plan:* installment. *Waivers:* employees or children of employees.

Financial Aid Of all full-time matriculated undergraduates who enrolled in 2003, 6,595 applied for aid, 5,166 were judged to have need, 952 had their need fully met. 2,948 Federal Work-Study jobs (averaging $2519). In 2003, 3106 non-need-based awards were made. *Average percent of need met:* 66%. *Average financial aid package:* $12,282. *Average need-based loan:* $2429. *Average need-based gift aid:* $7954. *Average non-need-based aid:* $5419.

Applying *Options:* electronic application, early admission. *Application fee:* $35. *Required:* essay or personal statement, high school transcript. *Recommended:* interview. *Application deadline:* rolling (freshmen), rolling (transfers). *Notification:* continuous (freshmen), continuous (transfers).

Admissions Contact Mr. James Steen, Director of Admission Services, Baylor University, PO Box 97056, Waco, TX 76798-7056. *Phone:* 254-710-3435. *Toll-free phone:* 800-BAYLOR U. *Fax:* 254-710-3436. *E-mail:* admissions_office@baylor.edu.

■ *See page 1220 for a narrative description.*

COLLEGE OF BIBLICAL STUDIES–HOUSTON
Houston, Texas

- **Independent nondenominational** 4-year, founded 1979
- **Calendar** semesters
- **Degrees** certificates, associate, and bachelor's
- **Urban** 10-acre campus
- **Endowment** $22,686
- **Coed,** 1,472 undergraduate students, 24% full-time, 45% women, 55% men
- **Noncompetitive** entrance level

Undergraduates 348 full-time, 1,124 part-time. Students come from 1 other state, 0.1% are from out of state, 56% African American, 3% Asian American or Pacific Islander, 21% Hispanic American, 0.2% Native American, 5% transferred in.

Freshmen *Admission:* 17 enrolled.

Faculty *Total:* 46, 22% full-time, 26% with terminal degrees. *Student/faculty ratio:* 33:1.

Majors Biblical studies; Christian studies; divinity/ministry.

Academic Programs *Special study options:* academic remediation for entering students, accelerated degree program, adult/continuing education programs, double majors, independent study, part-time degree program.

College of Biblical Studies–Houston (continued)

Library College of Biblical Studies Library with 33,661 titles, 194 serial subscriptions, 515 audiovisual materials.

Computers on Campus 18 computers available on campus for general student use. Internet access, online (class) registration, at least one staffed computer lab available.

Student Life *Housing:* college housing not available. *Activities and organizations:* Student Development Committee. *Campus security:* hourly patrols by trained security guards and police. *Student services:* personal/psychological counseling.

Standardized Tests *Recommended:* SAT I and SAT II or ACT (for admission), SAT II: Writing Test (for admission), TAAS. TASP.

Costs (2004–05) *Tuition:* $4000 full-time, $86 per credit part-time. Full-time tuition and fees vary according to program. Part-time tuition and fees vary according to program. *Required fees:* $50 full-time, $20 per term part-time. *Payment plans:* installment, deferred payment. *Waivers:* employees or children of employees.

Applying *Application fee:* $50. *Required:* essay or personal statement, high school transcript. *Required for some:* interview. *Application deadline:* rolling (freshmen), rolling (transfers).

Admissions Contact Mr. Daniel Lopez, Registrar, College of Biblical Studies–Houston, 6000 Dale Carnegie Drive, Houston, TX 77036. *Phone:* 832-252-4638. *E-mail:* cbs@cbshouston.edu.

■ *See page 1436 for a narrative description.*

THE COLLEGE OF SAINT THOMAS MORE

Fort Worth, Texas

- **Independent** 4-year, founded 1981, affiliated with Roman Catholic Church
- **Calendar** semesters
- **Degrees** associate and bachelor's
- **Urban** 1-acre campus with easy access to Dallas
- **Coed**
- **Moderately difficult** entrance level

Faculty *Student/faculty ratio:* 4:1.

Student Life *Campus security:* 24-hour patrols, student patrols, late-night transport/escort service.

Standardized Tests *Required:* SAT I or ACT (for admission).

Costs (2003–04) *Tuition:* $12,000 full-time, $1200 per course part-time. *Room only:* $2300.

Financial Aid Of all full-time matriculated undergraduates who enrolled in 2001, 6 state and other part-time jobs (averaging $500).

Applying *Options:* early admission, deferred entrance. *Application fee:* $35. *Required:* essay or personal statement, high school transcript, minimum 2.0 GPA, 1 letter of recommendation. *Recommended:* interview.

Admissions Contact Mrs. Bethany Konlande, Assistant to the Provost, The College of Saint Thomas More, 3020 Lubbock Avenue, Fort Worth, TX 76109-2323. *Phone:* 817-923-8459. *Toll-free phone:* 800-583-6489. *Fax:* 817-924-3206. *E-mail:* more-info@cstm.edu.

CONCORDIA UNIVERSITY AT AUSTIN

Austin, Texas

- **Independent** comprehensive, founded 1926, affiliated with Lutheran Church–Missouri Synod, part of Concordia University System
- **Calendar** semesters
- **Degrees** certificates, diplomas, associate, bachelor's, master's, and postbachelor's certificates
- **Urban** 20-acre campus with easy access to San Antonio
- **Coed,** 1,031 undergraduate students, 69% full-time, 56% women, 44% men
- **Moderately difficult** entrance level, 76% of applicants were admitted

Undergraduates 708 full-time, 323 part-time. Students come from 21 states and territories, 7% are from out of state, 8% African American, 2% Asian American or Pacific Islander, 13% Hispanic American, 0.6% Native American, 0.8% international, 10% transferred in, 32% live on campus. *Retention:* 56% of 2002 full-time freshmen returned.

Freshmen *Admission:* 523 applied, 396 admitted, 170 enrolled. *Average high school GPA:* 3.14. *Test scores:* SAT verbal scores over 500: 47%; SAT math scores over 500: 53%; ACT scores over 18: 81%; SAT verbal scores over 600: 7%; SAT math scores over 600: 14%; ACT scores over 24: 30%; SAT verbal scores over 700: 1%; SAT math scores over 700: 2%; ACT scores over 30: 5%.

Faculty *Total:* 85, 39% full-time, 46% with terminal degrees. *Student/faculty ratio:* 19:1.

Majors Biology/biological sciences; business administration and management; business/commerce; computer science; criminal justice/law enforcement administration; elementary education; English; environmental studies; general studies; history; human resources development; kinesiology and exercise science; liberal arts and sciences/liberal studies; mass communication/media; mathematics; middle school education; religious education; religious/sacred music; religious studies; secondary education; social sciences related.

Academic Programs *Special study options:* academic remediation for entering students, accelerated degree program, adult/continuing education programs, advanced placement credit, distance learning, double majors, external degree program, honors programs, independent study, internships, part-time degree program, services for LD students, study abroad, summer session for credit. *ROTC:* Army (c), Air Force (c).

Library Founders Library with 50,756 titles, 814 serial subscriptions, 3,859 audiovisual materials, an OPAC, a Web page.

Computers on Campus 40 computers available on campus for general student use. Internet access, at least one staffed computer lab available.

Student Life *Housing:* on-campus residence required for freshman year. *Options:* coed, men-only, women-only, disabled students. Campus housing is university owned. *Activities and organizations:* drama/theater group, choral group, student government, Education Club, Lutheran Student Fellowship, Students Active for the Environment, Accounting Club. *Campus security:* 24-hour emergency response devices, student patrols, late-night transport/escort service, controlled dormitory access. *Student services:* personal/psychological counseling.

Athletics Member NCAA. All Division III. *Intercollegiate sports:* baseball M, basketball M/W, cross-country running M/W, golf M/W, soccer M/W, softball W, tennis M/W, volleyball W. *Intramural sports:* badminton M/W, basketball M/W, football M/W, golf M/W, racquetball M/W, softball M/W, table tennis M/W, tennis M/W, volleyball M/W.

Standardized Tests *Required:* SAT I or ACT (for admission).

Costs (2003–04) *Comprehensive fee:* $20,560 includes full-time tuition ($14,300), mandatory fees ($110), and room and board ($6150). Full-time tuition and fees vary according to course load and location. Part-time tuition and fees vary according to location. *College room only:* $3590. Room and board charges vary according to board plan. *Waivers:* employees or children of employees.

Financial Aid Of all full-time matriculated undergraduates who enrolled in 2002, 586 applied for aid, 472 were judged to have need, 464 had their need fully met. 83 Federal Work-Study jobs (averaging $1120). In 2002, 60 non-need-based awards were made. *Average percent of need met:* 83%. *Average financial aid package:* $11,423. *Average need-based loan:* $3440. *Average need-based gift aid:* $9652. *Average non-need-based aid:* $5565. *Average indebtedness upon graduation:* $29,449. *Financial aid deadline:* 7/1.

Applying *Options:* early admission, deferred entrance. *Application fee:* $25. *Required:* high school transcript, minimum 2.5 GPA. *Required for some:* letters of recommendation, interview. *Application deadline:* rolling (freshmen), rolling (transfers). *Notification:* continuous (freshmen), continuous (transfers).

Admissions Contact Kristi Kirk, Director of Enrollment Services, Concordia University at Austin, 3400 Interstate 35 North, Austin, TX 78705-2799. *Phone:* 512-486-2000 Ext. 1156. *Toll-free phone:* 800-285-4252. *Fax:* 512-459-8517. *E-mail:* ctxadmis@crf.cuis.edu.

THE CRISWELL COLLEGE

Dallas, Texas

Admissions Contact Mr. W. Danny Blair, Vice President for Enrollment and Academic Services, The Criswell College, 4010 Gaston Avenue, Dallas, TX 75246-1537. *Phone:* 214-818-1305. *Toll-free phone:* 800-899-0012. *Fax:* 214-818-1310.

DALLAS BAPTIST UNIVERSITY

Dallas, Texas

- **Independent** comprehensive, founded 1965, affiliated with Baptist General Convention of Texas
- **Calendar** 4-1-4
- **Degrees** associate, bachelor's, master's, and postbachelor's certificates
- **Urban** 293-acre campus
- **Endowment** $18.4 million
- **Coed,** 3,444 undergraduate students, 55% full-time, 60% women, 40% men
- **Moderately difficult** entrance level, 68% of applicants were admitted

Undergraduates 1,892 full-time, 1,552 part-time. Students come from 40 states and territories, 45 other countries, 5% are from out of state, 20% African American, 2% Asian American or Pacific Islander, 9% Hispanic American, 2%

Native American, 6% international, 8% transferred in, 32% live on campus. *Retention:* 69% of 2002 full-time freshmen returned.

Freshmen *Admission:* 740 applied, 505 admitted, 298 enrolled. *Average high school GPA:* 3.54. *Test scores:* SAT verbal scores over 500: 75%; SAT math scores over 500: 75%; ACT scores over 18: 97%; SAT verbal scores over 600: 26%; SAT math scores over 600: 24%; ACT scores over 24: 36%; SAT verbal scores over 700: 3%; SAT math scores over 700: 3%; ACT scores over 30: 6%.

Faculty *Total:* 379, 24% full-time, 41% with terminal degrees. *Student/faculty ratio:* 18:1.

Majors Accounting; art; biblical studies; biology/biological sciences; business administration and management; business/managerial economics; communication/speech communication and rhetoric; computer and information sciences; computer science; criminal justice/law enforcement administration; education; elementary education; English; finance; general studies; health/health care administration; history; interdisciplinary studies; kindergarten/preschool education; liberal arts and sciences/liberal studies; management information systems; marketing/marketing management; mathematics; multi-/interdisciplinary studies related; music; music teacher education; music theory and composition; pastoral studies/counseling; philosophy; physical education teaching and coaching; piano and organ; political science and government; psychology; religious education; religious/sacred music; science teacher education; secondary education; sociology; voice and opera.

Academic Programs *Special study options:* adult/continuing education programs, advanced placement credit, distance learning, double majors, English as a second language, independent study, internships, off-campus study, part-time degree program, services for LD students, study abroad, summer session for credit. *ROTC:* Army (c), Air Force (c).

Library Vance Memorial Library with 221,742 titles, 626 serial subscriptions, 6,378 audiovisual materials, an OPAC, a Web page.

Computers on Campus 182 computers available on campus for general student use. A campuswide network can be accessed from student residence rooms and from off campus. Internet access, online (class) registration, at least one staffed computer lab available.

Student Life *Housing:* on-campus residence required through senior year. *Options:* men-only, women-only. Campus housing is university owned. Freshman applicants given priority for college housing. *Activities and organizations:* drama/theater group, choral group, Student Activities Board, Baptist Student Ministry, Student Government Association, Student Education Association, International Student Organization. *Campus security:* 24-hour emergency response devices and patrols, late-night transport/escort service, controlled dormitory access. *Student services:* health clinic, personal/psychological counseling.

Athletics Member NCAA, NCCAA. All NCAA Division II. *Intercollegiate sports:* baseball M(s), cross-country running M/W(s), golf M, soccer M/W(s), tennis M/W(s), track and field M/W(s), volleyball M/W(s). *Intramural sports:* basketball M/W, football M/W, golf M/W, softball M/W, table tennis M/W, tennis M/W, volleyball M/W.

Standardized Tests *Required:* SAT I or ACT (for admission).

Costs (2003–04) *Comprehensive fee:* $15,300 includes full-time tuition ($11,010) and room and board ($4290). Part-time tuition: $367 per credit hour. *College room only:* $1790. Room and board charges vary according to board plan and housing facility. *Payment plan:* installment. *Waivers:* employees or children of employees.

Financial Aid Of all full-time matriculated undergraduates who enrolled in 2003, 1,646 applied for aid, 1,195 were judged to have need, 490 had their need fully met. 123 Federal Work-Study jobs (averaging $2301). 39 state and other part-time jobs (averaging $733). In 2003, 347 non-need-based awards were made. *Average percent of need met:* 73%. *Average financial aid package:* $9192. *Average need-based loan:* $3242. *Average need-based gift aid:* $2467. *Average non-need-based aid:* $8310. *Average indebtedness upon graduation:* $12,276.

Applying *Options:* common application, electronic application. *Application fee:* $25. *Required:* essay or personal statement, high school transcript, rank in upper 50% of high school class or 2.5 high school GPA, minimum ACT score of 21, combined SAT score of 1,000. *Recommended:* minimum 2.5 GPA, letters of recommendation, interview. *Application deadline:* rolling (freshmen), rolling (transfers). *Notification:* continuous (freshmen), continuous (transfers).

Admissions Contact Ms. Anita Douris, Director of Undergraduate Admissions, Dallas Baptist University, 3000 Mountain Creek Parkway, Dallas, TX 75211-9299. *Phone:* 214-333-5360. *Toll-free phone:* 800-460-1328. *Fax:* 214-333-5447. *E-mail:* admiss@dbu.edu.

DALLAS CHRISTIAN COLLEGE
Dallas, Texas

- **Independent** 4-year, founded 1950, affiliated with Christian Churches and Churches of Christ
- **Calendar** semesters
- **Degree** diplomas and bachelor's
- **Urban** 22-acre campus with easy access to Fort Worth
- **Endowment** $117,260
- **Coed,** 336 undergraduate students, 65% full-time, 42% women, 58% men
- **Minimally difficult** entrance level, 22% of applicants were admitted

Undergraduates 219 full-time, 117 part-time. Students come from 19 states and territories, 2 other countries, 15% are from out of state, 19% African American, 0.3% Asian American or Pacific Islander, 9% Hispanic American, 0.9% Native American, 18% transferred in, 36% live on campus. *Retention:* 69% of 2002 full-time freshmen returned.

Freshmen *Admission:* 212 applied, 47 admitted, 47 enrolled. *Average high school GPA:* 2.83. *Test scores:* SAT verbal scores over 500: 57%; SAT math scores over 500: 50%; ACT scores over 18: 87%; SAT verbal scores over 600: 7%; SAT math scores over 600: 7%; ACT scores over 24: 20%.

Faculty *Total:* 41, 12% full-time, 24% with terminal degrees. *Student/faculty ratio:* 14:1.

Majors Biblical studies; business administration and management; education.

Academic Programs *Special study options:* academic remediation for entering students, accelerated degree program, adult/continuing education programs, advanced placement credit, distance learning, double majors, independent study, internships, part-time degree program, summer session for credit.

Library C. C. Crawford Memorial Library plus 1 other with 26,893 titles, 3,151 serial subscriptions, 1,701 audiovisual materials, an OPAC, a Web page.

Computers on Campus 16 computers available on campus for general student use. A campuswide network can be accessed. Internet access, at least one staffed computer lab available.

Student Life *Housing:* on-campus residence required through senior year. *Options:* men-only, women-only. Campus housing is university owned. Freshman campus housing is guaranteed. *Activities and organizations:* choral group. *Campus security:* controlled dormitory access. *Student services:* personal/psychological counseling.

Athletics Member NCCAA. *Intercollegiate sports:* basketball M/W, soccer M, volleyball W. *Intramural sports:* volleyball M/W.

Standardized Tests *Required:* SAT I or ACT (for admission).

Costs (2003–04) *Comprehensive fee:* $11,200 includes full-time tuition ($6300), mandatory fees ($500), and room and board ($4400). *Payment plan:* installment. *Waivers:* employees or children of employees.

Financial Aid Of all full-time matriculated undergraduates who enrolled in 2003, 201 applied for aid, 148 were judged to have need. 28 Federal Work-Study jobs (averaging $2000). *Average percent of need met:* 38%. *Average financial aid package:* $6067. *Average need-based loan:* $2497. *Average need-based gift aid:* $1156. *Average non-need-based aid:* $555. *Average indebtedness upon graduation:* $8760.

Applying *Options:* deferred entrance. *Application fee:* $30. *Required:* high school transcript, 2 letters of recommendation. *Required for some:* essay or personal statement, interview. *Application deadline:* rolling (freshmen), rolling (transfers).

Admissions Contact Mr. Marty McKee, Director of Admissions, Dallas Christian College, 2700 Christian Parkway, Dallas, TX 75234-7299. *Phone:* 972-241-3371 Ext. 153. *Fax:* 972-241-8021. *E-mail:* dcc@dallas.edu.

■ See page 1512 for a narrative description.

DEVRY UNIVERSITY
Houston, Texas

Admissions Contact 2000 West Loop South, Suite 150, Houston, TX 77027.3513.

DEVRY UNIVERSITY
Plano, Texas

Admissions Contact Plano Corporate Center II, 2301 West Plano Parkway, Suite 101, Plano, TX 75075-8435.

DEVRY UNIVERSITY
Irving, Texas

- **Proprietary** comprehensive, founded 1969, part of DeVry University
- **Calendar** semesters
- **Degrees** associate, bachelor's, master's, and postbachelor's certificates
- **Suburban** 13-acre campus with easy access to Dallas
- **Coed**

DeVry University (continued)
■ **Minimally difficult** entrance level

Student Life *Campus security:* 24-hour emergency response devices, student patrols, late-night transport/escort service, lighted pathways/sidewalks.
Standardized Tests *Recommended:* SAT I, ACT or CPT.
Costs (2003–04) *Tuition:* $9960 full-time, $355 per credit hour part-time. Full-time tuition and fees vary according to course load. Part-time tuition and fees vary according to course load. *Required fees:* $165 full-time. *Payment plans:* installment, deferred payment.
Financial Aid Of all full-time matriculated undergraduates who enrolled in 2002, 1,511 applied for aid, 1,418 were judged to have need, 32 had their need fully met. In 2002, 177. *Average percent of need met:* 43. *Average financial aid package:* $8767. *Average need-based loan:* $6064. *Average need-based gift aid:* $4189. *Average non-need-based aid:* $11,101.
Applying *Options:* electronic application, deferred entrance. *Application fee:* $50. *Required:* high school transcript, interview.
Admissions Contact Ms. Vicki Carroll, New Student Coordinator, DeVry University, 4800 Regent Boulevard, Irving, TX 75063-2439. *Phone:* 972-929-5777. *Toll-free phone:* 800-633-3879. *Fax:* 972-929-2860. *E-mail:* cwilliams@mail.dal.devry.edu.

EAST TEXAS BAPTIST UNIVERSITY
Marshall, Texas

■ **Independent Baptist** 4-year, founded 1912
■ **Calendar** 4-4-1
■ **Degrees** associate and bachelor's
■ **Small-town** 200-acre campus
■ **Endowment** $43.9 million
■ **Coed,** 1,354 undergraduate students, 88% full-time, 51% women, 49% men
■ **Moderately difficult** entrance level, 55% of applicants were admitted

Undergraduates 1,195 full-time, 159 part-time. Students come from 26 states and territories, 16 other countries, 10% are from out of state, 13% African American, 0.3% Asian American or Pacific Islander, 4% Hispanic American, 0.7% Native American, 1% international, 9% transferred in, 70% live on campus. *Retention:* 63% of 2002 full-time freshmen returned.
Freshmen *Admission:* 742 applied, 407 admitted, 248 enrolled. *Test scores:* ACT scores over 18: 83%; ACT scores over 24: 24%; ACT scores over 30: 2%.
Faculty *Total:* 107, 67% full-time, 58% with terminal degrees. *Student/faculty ratio:* 15:1.
Majors Accounting; athletic training; biblical studies; biology/biological sciences; biology teacher education; business administration and management; business/commerce; chemistry; chemistry teacher education; clinical laboratory science/medical technology; computer and information sciences; drama and dance teacher education; dramatic/theatre arts; education; elementary education; English; English/language arts teacher education; health and physical education; history; history teacher education; industrial and organizational psychology; liberal arts and sciences/liberal studies; marketing/marketing management; mathematics; mathematics teacher education; missionary studies and missiology; music; music teacher education; nursing (registered nurse training); nursing related; pastoral studies/counseling; physical education teaching and coaching; piano and organ; psychology; religious education; religious/sacred music; religious studies; social studies teacher education; sociology; Spanish; Spanish language teacher education; speech and rhetoric; speech teacher education; voice and opera; youth ministry.
Academic Programs *Special study options:* academic remediation for entering students, accelerated degree program, adult/continuing education programs, advanced placement credit, double majors, English as a second language, external degree program, honors programs, independent study, internships, off-campus study, part-time degree program, study abroad, summer session for credit.
Library Mamye Jarrett Library with 116,895 titles, 668 serial subscriptions, an OPAC.
Computers on Campus 203 computers available on campus for general student use. A campuswide network can be accessed from student residence rooms and from off campus. Internet access, online (class) registration, at least one staffed computer lab available.
Student Life *Housing:* on-campus residence required through senior year. *Options:* men-only, women-only, disabled students. Campus housing is university owned. Freshman campus housing is guaranteed. *Activities and organizations:* drama/theater group, student-run newspaper, choral group, marching band, Baptist Student Ministry, Residence Hall Councils, Student Government Association, REACT, Student Foundation Association, national fraternities, national sororities. *Campus security:* 24-hour emergency response devices, controlled dormitory access. *Student services:* personal/psychological counseling.
Athletics Member NCAA. All Division III. *Intercollegiate sports:* baseball M, basketball M/W, cross-country running M/W, football M, soccer M/W, softball W, volleyball W. *Intramural sports:* basketball M/W, football M, racquetball M/W, soccer M/W, softball M/W, table tennis M/W, volleyball M/W.
Standardized Tests *Required:* ACT (for admission).
Costs (2003–04) *Comprehensive fee:* $13,914 includes full-time tuition ($9450), mandatory fees ($840), and room and board ($3624). Part-time tuition: $315 per semester hour. *Required fees:* $35 per semester hour part-time. *College room only:* $1470. Room and board charges vary according to board plan and housing facility. *Payment plan:* installment. *Waivers:* employees or children of employees.
Financial Aid Of all full-time matriculated undergraduates who enrolled in 2003, 987 applied for aid, 927 were judged to have need, 239 had their need fully met. 92 Federal Work-Study jobs (averaging $1530). 268 state and other part-time jobs (averaging $1678). In 2003, 208 non-need-based awards were made. *Average percent of need met:* 87%. *Average financial aid package:* $9293. *Average need-based loan:* $4481. *Average need-based gift aid:* $5297. *Average non-need-based aid:* $3372. *Average indebtedness upon graduation:* $9982.
Applying *Options:* common application, electronic application, deferred entrance. *Application fee:* $25. *Required:* essay or personal statement, high school transcript, minimum 2.0 GPA. *Required for some:* interview. *Application deadline:* 8/15 (freshmen), rolling (transfers). *Notification:* continuous (freshmen), continuous (transfers).
Admissions Contact Mr. Vince Blankenship, Dean of Admissions and Marketing, East Texas Baptist University, 1209 North Grove, Marshall, TX 75670-1498. *Phone:* 903-923-2000. *Toll-free phone:* 800-804-ETBU. *Fax:* 903-923-2001. *E-mail:* admissions@etbu.edu.

HARDIN-SIMMONS UNIVERSITY
Abilene, Texas

■ **Independent Baptist** comprehensive, founded 1891
■ **Calendar** semesters
■ **Degrees** bachelor's, master's, doctoral, and first professional
■ **Urban** 120-acre campus
■ **Endowment** $72.1 million
■ **Coed,** 1,954 undergraduate students, 87% full-time, 54% women, 46% men
■ **Moderately difficult** entrance level, 53% of applicants were admitted

Undergraduates 1,707 full-time, 247 part-time. Students come from 28 states and territories, 5% are from out of state, 5% African American, 0.7% Asian American or Pacific Islander, 8% Hispanic American, 0.6% Native American, 0.1% international, 8% transferred in, 55% live on campus. *Retention:* 69% of 2002 full-time freshmen returned.
Freshmen *Admission:* 1,202 applied, 643 admitted, 444 enrolled. *Test scores:* SAT verbal scores over 500: 61%; SAT math scores over 500: 64%; ACT scores over 18: 86%; SAT verbal scores over 600: 17%; SAT math scores over 600: 19%; ACT scores over 24: 27%; SAT verbal scores over 700: 1%; SAT math scores over 700: 2%; ACT scores over 30: 5%.
Faculty *Total:* 183, 70% full-time, 62% with terminal degrees. *Student/faculty ratio:* 14:1.
Majors Accounting; agricultural business and management; agronomy and crop science; animal sciences; art teacher education; audiology and speech-language pathology; biblical studies; biochemistry/biophysics and molecular biology; biology/biological sciences; biology teacher education; broadcast journalism; business administration and management; business teacher education; chemistry; chemistry teacher education; clinical laboratory science/medical technology; communication/speech communication and rhetoric; computer programming; computer teacher education; corrections; criminal justice/police science; divinity/ministry; drama and dance teacher education; dramatic/theatre arts; economics; education; elementary education; English; English/language arts teacher education; environmental science; finance; fine/studio arts; French language teacher education; geology/earth science; German language teacher education; health and physical education; history; history teacher education; interdisciplinary studies; international business/trade/commerce; kinesiology and exercise science; management science; marketing/marketing management; mathematics; mathematics teacher education; middle school education; music history, literature, and theory; music management and merchandising; music performance; music teacher education; music theory and composition; nursing (registered nurse training); pastoral studies/counseling; philosophy; physical education teaching and coaching; physics teacher education; piano and organ; political science and government; predentistry studies; pre-law studies; pre-medical studies; psychology; psychology teacher education; public relations/image management; radio and television; religious/sacred music; science teacher education; secondary education; social science teacher education; social studies teacher education; social work; sociology; Spanish; Spanish language teacher education; speech and rhetoric; theology; violin, viola, guitar and other stringed instruments; voice and opera; wind/percussion instruments; youth ministry.

Academic Programs *Special study options:* academic remediation for entering students, accelerated degree program, adult/continuing education programs, advanced placement credit, double majors, independent study, internships, off-campus study, part-time degree program, services for LD students, study abroad, summer session for credit. *Unusual degree programs:* 3-2 biology, physical therapy.

Library Richardson Library plus 1 other with 223,275 titles, 920 serial subscriptions, 16,390 audiovisual materials, an OPAC, a Web page.

Computers on Campus 250 computers available on campus for general student use. A campuswide network can be accessed from student residence rooms and from off campus. Internet access, at least one staffed computer lab available.

Student Life *Housing:* on-campus residence required through sophomore year. *Options:* men-only, women-only. Campus housing is university owned. Freshman campus housing is guaranteed. *Activities and organizations:* drama/theater group, student-run newspaper, choral group, marching band, Baptist Student Union, Student Foundation, Student Congress, Fellowship Christian Athletes, national fraternities. *Campus security:* 24-hour patrols, controlled dormitory access. *Student services:* health clinic, personal/psychological counseling.

Athletics Member NCAA. All Division III. *Intercollegiate sports:* baseball M, basketball M/W, cheerleading M(c)/W(c), football M, golf M/W, soccer M/W, softball W, tennis M/W, volleyball W. *Intramural sports:* badminton M/W, basketball M/W, bowling M/W, cross-country running M(c)/W(c), football M/W, golf M/W, racquetball M/W, soccer M/W, softball M/W, table tennis M(c)/W(c), tennis M/W, ultimate Frisbee M(c)/W(c), volleyball M/W.

Standardized Tests *Required:* SAT I or ACT (for admission).

Costs (2004–05) *Comprehensive fee:* $17,298 includes full-time tuition ($12,600), mandatory fees ($776), and room and board ($3922). Full-time tuition and fees vary according to program. Part-time tuition: $420 per credit. Part-time tuition and fees vary according to course load and program. No tuition increase for student's term of enrollment. *Required fees:* $96 per term part-time. *College room only:* $1953. Room and board charges vary according to board plan and housing facility. *Payment plans:* tuition prepayment, installment, deferred payment. *Waivers:* employees or children of employees.

Financial Aid Of all full-time matriculated undergraduates who enrolled in 2003, 1,569 applied for aid, 1,092 were judged to have need, 218 had their need fully met. 191 Federal Work-Study jobs (averaging $1554). 381 state and other part-time jobs (averaging $1199). In 2003, 140 non-need-based awards were made. *Average percent of need met:* 66%. *Average financial aid package:* $11,521. *Average need-based loan:* $3913. *Average need-based gift aid:* $4733. *Average non-need-based aid:* $3111. *Average indebtedness upon graduation:* $26,729.

Applying *Options:* electronic application, early admission, deferred entrance. *Application fee:* $50. *Required:* high school transcript, minimum 2.0 GPA. *Application deadline:* rolling (freshmen), rolling (transfers). *Notification:* continuous (freshmen), continuous (transfers).

Admissions Contact Mr. Forrest McMillan, Director of Recruiting, Hardin-Simmons University, Box 16050, Abilene, TX 79698-6050. *Phone:* 325-670-1207. *Toll-free phone:* 800-568-2692. *Fax:* 325-671-2115. *E-mail:* enroll@hsutx.edu.

HOUSTON BAPTIST UNIVERSITY

Houston, Texas

- **Independent Baptist** comprehensive, founded 1960
- **Calendar** quarters
- **Degrees** associate, bachelor's, and master's
- **Urban** 100-acre campus
- **Endowment** $60.7 million
- **Coed,** 1,866 undergraduate students, 87% full-time, 69% women, 31% men
- **Moderately difficult** entrance level, 62% of applicants were admitted

Undergraduates 1,629 full-time, 237 part-time. Students come from 19 states and territories, 24 other countries, 2% are from out of state, 18% African American, 14% Asian American or Pacific Islander, 15% Hispanic American, 0.3% Native American, 6% international, 12% transferred in, 36% live on campus. *Retention:* 74% of 2002 full-time freshmen returned.

Freshmen *Admission:* 896 applied, 559 admitted, 280 enrolled. *Test scores:* SAT verbal scores over 500: 69%; SAT math scores over 500: 68%; ACT scores over 18: 90%; SAT verbal scores over 600: 23%; SAT math scores over 600: 27%; ACT scores over 24: 24%; SAT verbal scores over 700: 3%; SAT math scores over 700: 4%; ACT scores over 30: 3%.

Faculty *Total:* 189, 62% full-time, 61% with terminal degrees. *Student/faculty ratio:* 14:1.

Majors Accounting; art teacher education; biblical studies; bilingual and multilingual education; biology/biological sciences; biology teacher education; business administration and management; business/commerce; business/managerial economics; chemistry; child development; Christian studies; communication and media related; communication/speech communication and rhetoric; computer and information sciences; computer science; counselor education/school counseling and guidance; developmental and child psychology; early childhood education; economics; education; elementary education; engineering science; English; English/language arts teacher education; entrepreneurship; finance; fine/studio arts; foreign languages related; French; health and physical education; history; information science/studies; interdisciplinary studies; kindergarten/preschool education; kinesiology and exercise science; liberal arts and sciences/liberal studies; marketing/marketing management; mass communication/media; mathematics; mathematics teacher education; middle school education; molecular biology; music; music performance; music teacher education; music theory and composition; nursing (registered nurse training); physical education teaching and coaching; physics; political science and government; pre-law studies; psychology; religious/sacred music; religious studies; Romance languages related; science teacher education; secondary education; social studies teacher education; sociology; Spanish; special education; speech and rhetoric.

Academic Programs *Special study options:* academic remediation for entering students, adult/continuing education programs, advanced placement credit, double majors, English as a second language, honors programs, independent study, internships, part-time degree program, study abroad, summer session for credit. *ROTC:* Army (c). *Unusual degree programs:* 3-2 engineering with University of Houston, Baylor University.

Library Moody Library with 161,035 titles, 26,447 serial subscriptions, 9,328 audiovisual materials, an OPAC, a Web page.

Computers on Campus 93 computers available on campus for general student use. A campuswide network can be accessed from off campus. Internet access, at least one staffed computer lab available.

Student Life *Housing:* on-campus residence required for freshman year. *Options:* men-only, women-only, disabled students. Campus housing is university owned. Freshman campus housing is guaranteed. *Activities and organizations:* student-run newspaper, choral group, Alpha Epsilon Delta, Alpha Phi Omega, Association of Student Educators, Alpha Kappa Psi, Phi Mu, national fraternities, national sororities. *Campus security:* 24-hour emergency response devices and patrols, late-night transport/escort service. *Student services:* health clinic, personal/psychological counseling.

Athletics Member NAIA. *Intercollegiate sports:* baseball M(s), basketball M(s)/W(s), cheerleading M(s)/W(s), softball W(s), volleyball W(s). *Intramural sports:* badminton M/W, basketball M/W, bowling M/W, football M/W, golf M/W, soccer M/W, softball M/W, table tennis M/W, tennis M/W, ultimate Frisbee M(c)/W(c), volleyball M/W.

Standardized Tests *Required:* SAT I (for admission), ACT (for admission).

Costs (2003–04) *Comprehensive fee:* $16,860 includes full-time tuition ($11,100), mandatory fees ($1080), and room and board ($4680). Full-time tuition and fees vary according to course load and student level. Part-time tuition and fees vary according to course load and student level. *Room and board:* Room and board charges vary according to board plan. *Payment plan:* installment. *Waivers:* senior citizens and employees or children of employees.

Financial Aid Of all full-time matriculated undergraduates who enrolled in 2003, 1,112 applied for aid, 1,106 were judged to have need, 380 had their need fully met. In 2003, 56 non-need-based awards were made. *Average percent of need met:* 66%. *Average financial aid package:* $16,000. *Average need-based loan:* $3663. *Average indebtedness upon graduation:* $16,324. *Financial aid deadline:* 4/15.

Applying *Options:* early admission, deferred entrance. *Application fee:* $25. *Required:* essay or personal statement, high school transcript, 2 letters of recommendation. *Recommended:* interview. *Application deadline:* rolling (freshmen), rolling (transfers). *Notification:* continuous (freshmen), continuous (transfers).

Admissions Contact Mr. David Melton, Director of Admissions, Houston Baptist University, 7502 Fondren Road, Houston, TX 77074-3298. *Phone:* 281-649-3211 Ext. 3208. *Toll-free phone:* 800-696-3210. *Fax:* 281-649-3217. *E-mail:* unadm@hbu.edu.

■ *See page 1748 for a narrative description.*

HOWARD PAYNE UNIVERSITY

Brownwood, Texas

- **Independent** 4-year, founded 1889, affiliated with Baptist General Convention of Texas
- **Calendar** semesters
- **Degrees** certificates, associate, and bachelor's
- **Small-town** 30-acre campus
- **Endowment** $33.7 million
- **Coed,** 1,385 undergraduate students, 78% full-time, 49% women, 51% men
- **Minimally difficult** entrance level, 79% of applicants were admitted

Howard Payne University (continued)

Undergraduates 1,081 full-time, 304 part-time. Students come from 16 states and territories, 8 other countries, 2% are from out of state, 8% African American, 1% Asian American or Pacific Islander, 15% Hispanic American, 0.4% Native American, 0.8% international, 5% transferred in, 48% live on campus. *Retention:* 58% of 2002 full-time freshmen returned.

Freshmen *Admission:* 904 applied, 717 admitted, 345 enrolled. *Average high school GPA:* 3.10. *Test scores:* SAT verbal scores over 500: 51%; SAT math scores over 500: 53%; ACT scores over 18: 71%; SAT verbal scores over 600: 19%; SAT math scores over 600: 15%; ACT scores over 24: 22%; SAT verbal scores over 700: 2%; SAT math scores over 700: 1%; ACT scores over 30: 1%.

Faculty *Total:* 125, 57% full-time, 51% with terminal degrees. *Student/faculty ratio:* 13:1.

Majors Accounting; American studies; ancient Near Eastern and biblical languages; applied art; art; art teacher education; athletic training; behavioral sciences; biblical studies; biology/biological sciences; biology teacher education; business administration and management; business/commerce; business teacher education; chemistry; communication/speech communication and rhetoric; computer science; drama and dance teacher education; dramatic/theatre arts; education; education (multiple levels); elementary education; English; English as a second/foreign language (teaching); English/language arts teacher education; European studies; finance; fine/studio arts; general studies; health and physical education; health/health care administration; health professions related; health science; history; history teacher education; information science/studies; kindergarten/preschool education; kinesiology and exercise science; legal assistant/paralegal; liberal arts and sciences and humanities related; liberal arts and sciences/liberal studies; marketing/marketing management; mathematics; mathematics teacher education; modern languages; music; music performance; music teacher education; parks, recreation and leisure; philosophy; physical education teaching and coaching; piano and organ; political science and government; pre-law studies; pre-medical studies; psychology; public relations/image management; religious education; religious/sacred music; religious studies; science teacher education; secondary education; social sciences; social science teacher education; social studies teacher education; social work; sociology; Spanish; Spanish language teacher education; speech and rhetoric; speech teacher education; sport and fitness administration; telecommunications; theology; violin, viola, guitar and other stringed instruments; voice and opera; wind/percussion instruments.

Academic Programs *Special study options:* academic remediation for entering students, adult/continuing education programs, advanced placement credit, double majors, English as a second language, honors programs, independent study, internships, part-time degree program, services for LD students, study abroad, summer session for credit.

Library Walker Memorial Library with 78,825 titles, 1,017 serial subscriptions, an OPAC, a Web page.

Computers on Campus 220 computers available on campus for general student use. A campuswide network can be accessed from student residence rooms and from off campus. Internet access, at least one staffed computer lab available.

Student Life *Housing:* on-campus residence required through junior year. *Options:* men-only, women-only. Campus housing is university owned. Freshman campus housing is guaranteed. *Activities and organizations:* drama/theater group, student-run newspaper, radio and television station, choral group, marching band, Baptist Student Ministry, Zeta Zeta Zeta, Delta Chi Ro, Student Foundation, Iota Chi Alpha. *Campus security:* 24-hour emergency response devices, controlled dormitory access, 12-hour patrols by trained security personnel. *Student services:* health clinic, personal/psychological counseling.

Athletics Member NCAA. All Division III. *Intercollegiate sports:* baseball M, basketball M/W, cross-country running M/W, football M, golf M/W, soccer M(c), softball W, tennis M/W, track and field M/W, volleyball W. *Intramural sports:* basketball M/W, football M/W, softball M/W, tennis M/W, volleyball M/W.

Standardized Tests *Required:* SAT I or ACT (for admission).

Costs (2003–04) *Comprehensive fee:* $15,176 includes full-time tuition ($10,300), mandatory fees ($850), and room and board ($4026). Part-time tuition: $300 per credit hour. Part-time tuition and fees vary according to course load. No tuition increase for student's term of enrollment. *College room only:* $1660. Room and board charges vary according to board plan, gender, and housing facility. *Payment plans:* installment, deferred payment. *Waivers:* senior citizens and employees or children of employees.

Financial Aid Of all full-time matriculated undergraduates who enrolled in 2003, 954 applied for aid, 825 were judged to have need, 44 had their need fully met. 118 Federal Work-Study jobs (averaging $2000). 9 state and other part-time jobs (averaging $2000). In 2003, 181 non-need-based awards were made. *Average percent of need met:* 82%. *Average financial aid package:* $10,464. *Average need-based loan:* $3516. *Average need-based gift aid:* $6761. *Average non-need-based aid:* $4331. *Average indebtedness upon graduation:* $17,735.

Applying *Options:* common application, early admission. *Application fee:* $25. *Required:* high school transcript, minimum 3.0 GPA. *Required for some:* letters of recommendation, interview. *Application deadline:* 8/1 (freshmen), rolling (transfers).

Admissions Contact Ms. Cheryl Mangrum, Coordinator of Admission Services, Howard Payne University, HPU Station Box 828, 1000 Fisk Avenue, Brownwood, TX 76801. *Phone:* 325-649-8027. *Toll-free phone:* 800-880-4478. *Fax:* 325-649-8901. *E-mail:* enroll@hputx.edu.

HUSTON-TILLOTSON COLLEGE

Austin, Texas

- **Independent interdenominational** 4-year, founded 1875
- **Calendar** semesters
- **Degrees** bachelor's and postbachelor's certificates
- **Urban** 23-acre campus
- **Endowment** $6.6 million
- **Coed,** 583 undergraduate students, 94% full-time, 54% women, 46% men
- **Moderately difficult** entrance level, 98% of applicants were admitted

Undergraduates 550 full-time, 33 part-time. Students come from 13 states and territories, 13 other countries, 7% are from out of state, 78% African American, 1% Asian American or Pacific Islander, 10% Hispanic American, 5% international, 10% transferred in, 42% live on campus. *Retention:* 45% of 2002 full-time freshmen returned.

Freshmen *Admission:* 332 applied, 325 admitted, 175 enrolled. *Average high school GPA:* 2.70. *Test scores:* SAT verbal scores over 500: 16%; SAT math scores over 500: 15%; ACT scores over 18: 27%; SAT verbal scores over 600: 1%; SAT math scores over 600: 1%; ACT scores over 24: 5%.

Faculty *Total:* 64, 61% full-time, 50% with terminal degrees. *Student/faculty ratio:* 11:1.

Majors Accounting; American government and politics; biology/biological sciences; business administration and management; chemistry; computer science; education; elementary education; English; mathematics; music; physical education teaching and coaching; political science and government; pre-medical studies; psychology; secondary education; social studies teacher education; sociology.

Academic Programs *Special study options:* academic remediation for entering students, accelerated degree program, advanced placement credit, cooperative education, double majors, English as a second language, internships, part-time degree program, services for LD students, summer session for credit. *ROTC:* Army (c), Navy (c). *Unusual degree programs:* 3-2 engineering with Prairie View A&M University.

Library Downs–Jones Library with 88,455 titles, 330 serial subscriptions, 8,753 audiovisual materials.

Computers on Campus 400 computers available on campus for general student use. A campuswide network can be accessed. Internet access, at least one staffed computer lab available.

Student Life *Housing options:* men-only, women-only. Campus housing is university owned. Freshman campus housing is guaranteed. *Activities and organizations:* choral group, Student Government Association, Campus Pals, national fraternities, national sororities. *Campus security:* 24-hour patrols. *Student services:* health clinic, personal/psychological counseling, women's center.

Athletics Member NAIA. *Intercollegiate sports:* baseball M, basketball M/W, cross-country running W, soccer M, track and field M/W, volleyball W. *Intramural sports:* basketball M/W, football M, volleyball M/W.

Standardized Tests *Required:* SAT I and SAT II or ACT (for admission).

Costs (2003–04) *Comprehensive fee:* $13,486 includes full-time tuition ($6824), mandatory fees ($1286), and room and board ($5376). Full-time tuition and fees vary according to program. Part-time tuition and fees vary according to course load. *College room only:* $3000. Room and board charges vary according to board plan and housing facility. *Payment plan:* installment. *Waivers:* employees or children of employees.

Financial Aid Of all full-time matriculated undergraduates who enrolled in 2002, 581 applied for aid, 558 were judged to have need, 96 had their need fully met. 96 Federal Work-Study jobs (averaging $1247). 3 state and other part-time jobs (averaging $1662). *Average financial aid package:* $8471. *Average need-based loan:* $3245. *Average need-based gift aid:* $8293.

Applying *Options:* common application. *Application fee:* $25. *Required:* essay or personal statement, high school transcript, minimum 2.0 GPA. *Required for some:* interview. *Application deadlines:* 3/1 (freshmen), 3/1 (transfers).

Admissions Contact Ms. Brontë D. Jones, Admission and Financial Aid Services, Huston-Tillotson College, 900 Chicon Street, Austin, TX 78702. *Phone:* 512-505-3027. *Fax:* 512-505-3192. *E-mail:* taglenn@htc.edu.

JARVIS CHRISTIAN COLLEGE
Hawkins, Texas

- **Independent** 4-year, founded 1912, affiliated with Christian Church (Disciples of Christ)
- **Calendar** semesters
- **Degree** bachelor's
- **Rural** 465-acre campus
- **Endowment** $14.0 million
- **Coed,** 654 undergraduate students, 100% full-time, 60% women, 40% men
- **Minimally difficult** entrance level, 50% of applicants were admitted

Undergraduates 654 full-time. Students come from 15 states and territories, 92% are from out of state, 96% African American, 1% Hispanic American, 0.9% international, 5% transferred in, 85% live on campus. *Retention:* 50% of 2002 full-time freshmen returned.

Freshmen *Admission:* 594 applied, 298 admitted, 132 enrolled. *Average high school GPA:* 2.70. *Test scores:* SAT math scores over 500: 1%; ACT scores over 18: 1%; SAT math scores over 600: 1%.

Faculty *Total:* 44, 89% full-time, 48% with terminal degrees. *Student/faculty ratio:* 14:1.

Majors Accounting; biology/biological sciences; business administration and management; business teacher education; chemistry; computer science; economics; elementary education; English; health and physical education; history; kindergarten/preschool education; marketing/marketing management; mathematics; music; music teacher education; physical education teaching and coaching; physics; reading teacher education; religious studies; secondary education; sociology; special education.

Academic Programs *Special study options:* academic remediation for entering students, advanced placement credit, cooperative education, distance learning, honors programs, internships, off-campus study, part-time degree program. *Unusual degree programs:* 3-2 engineering with University of Texas at Arlington; nursing with University of Texas at Tyler.

Library Olin Library with 74,002 titles, 495 serial subscriptions.

Computers on Campus 75 computers available on campus for general student use. At least one staffed computer lab available.

Student Life *Housing:* on-campus residence required through senior year. *Options:* men-only, women-only. Campus housing is university owned. *Activities and organizations:* drama/theater group, student-run newspaper, choral group, Student Government Association, SIFE, Student Ministers' Association, SNEA, Residence Hall Councils, national fraternities, national sororities. *Campus security:* 24-hour patrols. *Student services:* health clinic, personal/psychological counseling.

Athletics Member NAIA. *Intercollegiate sports:* baseball M, basketball M/W, cheerleading W, softball W, track and field M/W, volleyball W. *Intramural sports:* baseball M, basketball M/W, football M, golf M, softball M/W, swimming M/W, table tennis M/W, tennis M/W, volleyball M/W.

Standardized Tests *Required:* SAT I or ACT (for admission). *Recommended:* ACT (for admission).

Costs (2003–04) *Comprehensive fee:* $9815 includes full-time tuition ($5980), mandatory fees ($350), and room and board ($3485). Full-time tuition and fees vary according to program. Part-time tuition: $199 per hour. Part-time tuition and fees vary according to program. No tuition increase for student's term of enrollment. *Required fees:* $175 per term part-time. *College room only:* $1610. *Payment plans:* installment, deferred payment.

Financial Aid In 2002, 17 non-need-based awards were made. *Average percent of need met:* 85%. *Average financial aid package:* $9635.

Applying *Options:* common application, early admission, deferred entrance. *Application fee:* $25. *Required:* high school transcript. *Recommended:* minimum 2.0 GPA. *Application deadline:* 8/1 (freshmen), rolling (transfers).

Admissions Contact Vicki Jackson, Admissions Counselor, Jarvis Christian College, PO Box 1470, Hawkins, TX 75765-9989. *Phone:* 903-769-5433. *Toll-free phone:* 800-292-9517. *Fax:* 903-769-4842.

LAMAR UNIVERSITY
Beaumont, Texas

- **State-supported** university, founded 1923, part of Texas State University System
- **Calendar** semesters
- **Degrees** associate, bachelor's, master's, and doctoral
- **Suburban** 200-acre campus with easy access to Houston
- **Coed,** 9,184 undergraduate students, 68% full-time, 60% women, 40% men
- **Minimally difficult** entrance level, 68% of applicants were admitted

Undergraduates 6,252 full-time, 2,932 part-time. Students come from 27 states and territories, 22% African American, 3% Asian American or Pacific Islander, 5% Hispanic American, 0.6% Native American, 0.7% international, 7% transferred in. *Retention:* 69% of 2002 full-time freshmen returned.

Freshmen *Admission:* 4,147 applied, 2,834 admitted, 1,411 enrolled. *Average high school GPA:* 3.0. *Test scores:* SAT verbal scores over 500: 39%; SAT math scores over 500: 37%; ACT scores over 18: 59%; SAT verbal scores over 600: 9%; SAT math scores over 600: 9%; ACT scores over 24: 13%; SAT verbal scores over 700: 1%; SAT math scores over 700: 2%; ACT scores over 30: 1%.

Faculty *Total:* 491, 73% full-time, 54% with terminal degrees. *Student/faculty ratio:* 20:1.

Majors Accounting; administrative assistant and secretarial science; applied art; applied mathematics; art; artificial intelligence and robotics; art teacher education; audiology and speech-language pathology; automobile/automotive mechanics technology; biology/biological sciences; broadcast journalism; business administration and management; business machine repair; chemical engineering; chemistry; child development; civil engineering; clinical laboratory science/medical technology; clinical psychology; commercial and advertising art; computer programming; computer science; corrections; cosmetology; counselor education/school counseling and guidance; criminal justice/law enforcement administration; criminal justice/police science; dance; data processing and data processing technology; dental hygiene; dietetics; drafting and design technology; dramatic/theatre arts; economics; education; educational leadership and administration; electrical, electronic and communications engineering technology; electrical, electronics and communications engineering; elementary education; energy management and systems technology; engineering science; English; environmental studies; family and consumer sciences/home economics teacher education; family and consumer sciences/human sciences; fashion/apparel design; fashion merchandising; finance; fine/studio arts; fire science; food science; French; geology/earth science; health science; health teacher education; heating, air conditioning, ventilation and refrigeration maintenance technology; history; industrial engineering; industrial radiologic technology; industrial technology; information science/studies; interdisciplinary studies; interior design; jazz/jazz studies; journalism; kindergarten/preschool education; legal administrative assistant/secretary; liberal arts and sciences/liberal studies; machine tool technology; marine technology; marketing/marketing management; mass communication/media; mathematics; mechanical engineering; medical administrative assistant and medical secretary; music; music teacher education; nursing (licensed practical/vocational nurse training); nursing (registered nurse training); occupational safety and health technology; oceanography (chemical and physical); physical education teaching and coaching; physics; piano and organ; political science and government; pre-dentistry studies; psychology; radio and television; real estate; respiratory care therapy; safety/security technology; secondary education; social work; sociology; Spanish; special education; special products marketing; speech therapy; teacher assistant/aide; violin, viola, guitar and other stringed instruments; voice and opera; welding technology.

Academic Programs *Special study options:* academic remediation for entering students, accelerated degree program, adult/continuing education programs, advanced placement credit, cooperative education, English as a second language, honors programs, internships, off-campus study, part-time degree program, services for LD students, student-designed majors, study abroad, summer session for credit.

Library Mary and John Gray Library with 600,000 titles, 2,900 serial subscriptions, an OPAC, a Web page.

Computers on Campus 120 computers available on campus for general student use. A campuswide network can be accessed from student residence rooms and from off campus. At least one staffed computer lab available.

Student Life *Housing options:* coed. *Activities and organizations:* drama/theater group, student-run newspaper, choral group, national fraternities, national sororities. *Campus security:* 24-hour emergency response devices and patrols, student patrols, late-night transport/escort service. *Student services:* health clinic, personal/psychological counseling.

Athletics Member NCAA. All Division I except football (Division I-AA). *Intercollegiate sports:* baseball M(s), basketball M(s)/W(s), cheerleading M/W, cross-country running M(s)/W(s), golf M(s)/W(s), tennis M(s)/W(s), track and field M(s)/W(s), volleyball W(s). *Intramural sports:* basketball M/W, cross-country running M/W, football M, golf M/W, gymnastics W, racquetball M/W, rugby M/W, sailing M/W, soccer M/W, swimming M/W, tennis M/W, track and field M/W, volleyball M/W, weight lifting M/W.

Standardized Tests *Required:* SAT I or ACT (for admission). *Required for some:* SAT II: Subject Tests (for admission).

Costs (2003–04) *Tuition:* state resident $2520 full-time; nonresident $10,530 full-time. Part-time tuition and fees vary according to course load. *Required fees:* $740 full-time. *Room and board:* $5760; room only: $3960. Room and board charges vary according to board plan and housing facility. *Payment plan:* installment.

Financial Aid Of all full-time matriculated undergraduates who enrolled in 2003, 4,415 applied for aid, 2,964 were judged to have need, 189 had their need

Lamar University (continued)
fully met. 94 Federal Work-Study jobs (averaging $3000). 21 state and other part-time jobs (averaging $3000). In 2003, 1500 non-need-based awards were made. *Average percent of need met:* 15%. *Average financial aid package:* $1215. *Average non-need-based aid:* $1300. *Average indebtedness upon graduation:* $7020.

Applying *Options:* electronic application, early admission. *Required:* high school transcript. *Required for some:* essay or personal statement. *Application deadlines:* 8/1 (freshmen), 8/1 (transfers). *Notification:* continuous (freshmen).

Admissions Contact Ms. Melissa Chesser, Director of Recruitment, Lamar University, PO Box 10009, Beaumont, TX 77710. *Phone:* 409-880-8888. *Fax:* 409-880-8463. *E-mail:* admissions@hal.lamar.edu.

LeTourneau University

Longview, Texas

- **Independent nondenominational** comprehensive, founded 1946
- **Calendar** semesters
- **Degrees** associate, bachelor's, and master's
- **Suburban** 162-acre campus
- **Coed,** 3,175 undergraduate students, 40% full-time, 53% women, 47% men
- 80% of applicants were admitted

Undergraduates 1,284 full-time, 1,891 part-time. 50% are from out of state, 19% African American, 2% Asian American or Pacific Islander, 7% Hispanic American, 0.5% Native American, 1% international, 3% transferred in, 72% live on campus. *Retention:* 66% of 2002 full-time freshmen returned.

Freshmen *Admission:* 849 applied, 680 admitted, 340 enrolled. *Average high school GPA:* 3.52. *Test scores:* SAT verbal scores over 500: 81%; SAT math scores over 500: 85%; ACT scores over 18: 98%; SAT verbal scores over 600: 48%; SAT math scores over 600: 46%; ACT scores over 24: 62%; SAT verbal scores over 700: 13%; SAT math scores over 700: 12%; ACT scores over 30: 15%.

Faculty *Total:* 260, 25% full-time, 48% with terminal degrees. *Student/faculty ratio:* 16:1.

Majors Accounting; airframe mechanics and aircraft maintenance technology; airline pilot and flight crew; avionics maintenance technology; biblical studies; biology/biological sciences; biomedical/medical engineering; business administration and management; chemistry; computer engineering; computer engineering technology; computer science; drafting and design technology; electrical, electronic and communications engineering technology; electrical, electronics and communications engineering; elementary education; engineering; engineering technology; English; finance; history; information science/studies; interdisciplinary studies; international business/trade/commerce; management information systems; marketing/marketing management; mathematics; mechanical engineering; mechanical engineering/mechanical technology; missionary studies and missiology; natural sciences; physical education teaching and coaching; predentistry studies; pre-law studies; pre-medical studies; pre-veterinary studies; psychology; religious studies; secondary education; sport and fitness administration; welding technology.

Academic Programs *Special study options:* cooperative education, distance learning, double majors, honors programs, independent study, internships, study abroad.

Library Margaret Estes Resource Center with 84,779 titles, 383 serial subscriptions, 3,144 audiovisual materials.

Student Life *Housing:* on-campus residence required through junior year. *Options:* men-only, women-only, disabled students. Campus housing is university owned. *Activities and organizations:* drama/theater group, student-run newspaper, choral group, student ministries, Themelios, Student Foundation, Student Senate, roller hockey club. *Campus security:* 24-hour emergency response devices and patrols, late-night transport/escort service, controlled dormitory access. *Student services:* health clinic, personal/psychological counseling.

Athletics *Intercollegiate sports:* cheerleading M/W. *Intramural sports:* ultimate Frisbee M(c)/W(c).

Standardized Tests *Required:* SAT I or ACT (for admission).

Costs (2004–05) *Comprehensive fee:* $21,080 includes full-time tuition ($14,850), mandatory fees ($180), and room and board ($6050). Part-time tuition: $270 per hour. Part-time tuition and fees vary according to course load. *Room and board:* Room and board charges vary according to board plan. *Payment plan:* installment. *Waivers:* employees or children of employees.

Financial Aid Of all full-time matriculated undergraduates who enrolled in 2002, 1,126 applied for aid, 924 were judged to have need, 217 had their need fully met. In 2002, 110 non-need-based awards were made. *Average percent of need met:* 76%. *Average financial aid package:* $12,190. *Average need-based loan:* $4476. *Average need-based gift aid:* $5665. *Average non-need-based aid:* $2830. *Average indebtedness upon graduation:* $20,055.

Applying *Options:* deferred entrance. *Application fee:* $25. *Application deadlines:* 8/1 (freshmen), 8/1 (transfers). *Notification:* continuous (freshmen), continuous (transfers).

Admissions Contact Mr. James Townsend, Director of Admissions, LeTourneau University, PO Box 7001, 2100 South Mobberly Avenue, Longview, TX 75607-7001. *Phone:* 903-233-3400. *Toll-free phone:* 800-759-8811. *Fax:* 903-233-3411. *E-mail:* admissions@letu.edu.

Lubbock Christian University

Lubbock, Texas

- **Independent** comprehensive, founded 1957, affiliated with Church of Christ
- **Calendar** semesters
- **Degrees** associate, bachelor's, and master's
- **Suburban** 120-acre campus
- **Endowment** $3.5 million
- **Coed,** 1,759 undergraduate students, 77% full-time, 58% women, 42% men
- **Moderately difficult** entrance level, 72% of applicants were admitted

Undergraduates 1,346 full-time, 413 part-time. Students come from 29 states and territories, 12 other countries, 10% are from out of state, 6% African American, 0.4% Asian American or Pacific Islander, 14% Hispanic American, 0.5% Native American, 0.6% international, 16% transferred in, 29% live on campus. *Retention:* 63% of 2002 full-time freshmen returned.

Freshmen *Admission:* 807 applied, 579 admitted, 298 enrolled. *Average high school GPA:* 3.36. *Test scores:* SAT verbal scores over 500: 57%; SAT math scores over 500: 50%; ACT scores over 18: 82%; SAT verbal scores over 600: 16%; SAT math scores over 600: 11%; ACT scores over 24: 28%; SAT verbal scores over 700: 1%; ACT scores over 30: 3%.

Faculty *Total:* 134, 54% full-time, 47% with terminal degrees. *Student/faculty ratio:* 17:1.

Majors Accounting; agricultural business and management; agriculture; ancient Near Eastern and biblical languages; animal sciences; applied art; art teacher education; biblical studies; biology/biological sciences; business administration and management; chemistry; clinical laboratory science/medical technology; computer and information sciences; computer science; criminal justice/safety; design and visual communications; early childhood education; education; elementary education; engineering; environmental science; family and community services; finance; health and physical education; humanities; kinesiology and exercise science; marketing/marketing management; mass communication/media; mathematics; middle school education; missionary studies and missiology; music; music teacher education; nursing related; physical education teaching and coaching; plant protection and integrated pest management; plant sciences; pre-law studies; psychology; secondary education; social work; special education; sport and fitness administration; theology and religious vocations related; youth ministry.

Academic Programs *Special study options:* academic remediation for entering students, accelerated degree program, adult/continuing education programs, advanced placement credit, distance learning, double majors, honors programs, internships, part-time degree program, services for LD students, student-designed majors, study abroad, summer session for credit. *ROTC:* Army (c), Air Force (c). *Unusual degree programs:* 3-2 engineering with Texas Tech University.

Library University Library with 108,000 titles, 556 serial subscriptions.

Computers on Campus 159 computers available on campus for general student use. A campuswide network can be accessed from student residence rooms and from off campus that provide access to e-mail. Internet access, online (class) registration, at least one staffed computer lab available.

Student Life *Housing:* on-campus residence required through sophomore year. *Options:* men-only, women-only, disabled students. Campus housing is university owned. Freshman campus housing is guaranteed. *Activities and organizations:* drama/theater group, student-run newspaper, choral group. *Campus security:* 24-hour patrols. *Student services:* health clinic, personal/psychological counseling.

Athletics Member NAIA. *Intercollegiate sports:* baseball M(s), basketball M(s)/W(s), cheerleading M/W, soccer M, track and field M/W, volleyball W(s). *Intramural sports:* badminton M/W, basketball M/W, bowling M/W, cross-country running M/W, football M/W, golf M/W, racquetball M/W, soccer M/W, softball M/W, table tennis M/W, tennis M/W, track and field M/W, volleyball M/W.

Standardized Tests *Required:* SAT I or ACT (for admission).

Costs (2003–04) *Comprehensive fee:* $15,832 includes full-time tuition ($10,662), mandatory fees ($790), and room and board ($4380). Full-time tuition and fees vary according to program. Part-time tuition: $288 per credit hour. Part-time tuition and fees vary according to course load and program. *Required fees:* $220 per term part-time. *College room only:* $2460. Room and board charges vary according to board plan and housing facility. *Payment plan:* installment. *Waivers:* employees or children of employees.

Financial Aid Of all full-time matriculated undergraduates who enrolled in 2003, 1,020 applied for aid, 919 were judged to have need, 61 had their need fully met. 897 Federal Work-Study jobs (averaging $2000). 113 state and other part-time jobs (averaging $262). In 2003, 164 non-need-based awards were made. *Average percent of need met:* 74%. *Average financial aid package:* $11,286. *Average need-based loan:* $3597. *Average need-based gift aid:* $7396. *Average non-need-based aid:* $9617. *Average indebtedness upon graduation:* $17,189.

Applying *Options:* common application, electronic application. *Application fee:* $20. *Required:* high school transcript. *Application deadline:* 8/1 (freshmen), rolling (transfers). *Notification:* continuous (freshmen), continuous (transfers).

Admissions Contact Mr. Mondy Brewer, Director of Admissions, Lubbock Christian University, 5601 19th Street, Lubbock, TX 79407. *Phone:* 806-720-7803. *Toll-free phone:* 800-933-7601. *Fax:* 806-720-7162. *E-mail:* admissions@lcu.edu.

McMurry University

Abilene, Texas

- **Independent United Methodist** 4-year, founded 1923
- **Calendar** semesters plus May term
- **Degree** bachelor's
- **Urban** 41-acre campus
- **Endowment** $39.6 million
- **Coed,** 1,376 undergraduate students, 84% full-time, 49% women, 51% men
- **Moderately difficult** entrance level, 61% of applicants were admitted

Undergraduates 1,162 full-time, 214 part-time. Students come from 16 states and territories, 7 other countries, 4% are from out of state, 8% African American, 0.7% Asian American or Pacific Islander, 12% Hispanic American, 1% Native American, 0.5% international, 11% transferred in, 50% live on campus. *Retention:* 60% of 2002 full-time freshmen returned.

Freshmen *Admission:* 908 applied, 556 admitted, 258 enrolled. *Average high school GPA:* 3.32. *Test scores:* SAT verbal scores over 500: 36%; SAT math scores over 500: 45%; ACT scores over 18: 73%; SAT verbal scores over 600: 9%; SAT math scores over 600: 11%; ACT scores over 24: 16%; SAT verbal scores over 700: 1%; SAT math scores over 700: 2%.

Faculty *Total:* 119, 66% full-time, 52% with terminal degrees. *Student/faculty ratio:* 14:1.

Majors Accounting; art; art teacher education; athletic training; biochemistry; biological and physical sciences; biology/biological sciences; business administration and management; business/commerce; business/managerial economics; ceramic arts and ceramics; chemistry; communication/speech communication and rhetoric; computer and information sciences; computer software and media applications related; creative writing; dramatic/theatre arts; elementary education; English; environmental science; finance; French; German; graphic design; history; information science/studies; management information systems; marketing/marketing management; mathematics; mathematics and computer science; middle school education; music performance; music teacher education; nursing (registered nurse training); painting; philosophy; physical education teaching and coaching; physics; piano and organ; political science and government; psychology; religious/sacred music; religious studies; secondary education; sociology; Spanish; speech and rhetoric; voice and opera.

Academic Programs *Special study options:* academic remediation for entering students, accelerated degree program, advanced placement credit, double majors, honors programs, independent study, internships, part-time degree program, services for LD students, study abroad, summer session for credit. *Unusual degree programs:* 3-2 engineering with Texas Tech University, Texas A&M University.

Library Jay-Rollins Library with 115,704 titles, 698 serial subscriptions, 9,341 audiovisual materials, an OPAC, a Web page.

Computers on Campus 165 computers available on campus for general student use. A campuswide network can be accessed from student residence rooms that provide access to blackboard. Internet access, at least one staffed computer lab available.

Student Life *Housing:* on-campus residence required through junior year. *Options:* men-only, women-only. Campus housing is university owned. Freshman campus housing is guaranteed. *Activities and organizations:* drama/theater group, student-run newspaper, choral group, marching band, Alpha Phi Omega, McMurry Christian Ministries, Indian Insight Service Club, Campus Activity Board, Servant Leadership Mentors. *Campus security:* 24-hour emergency response devices and patrols, late-night transport/escort service, controlled dormitory access. *Student services:* health clinic, personal/psychological counseling.

Athletics Member NCAA. All Division III. *Intercollegiate sports:* baseball M, basketball M/W, cross-country running M/W, football M, golf M/W, soccer M/W, swimming M/W, tennis M/W, track and field M/W, volleyball W. *Intramural sports:* basketball M/W, football M/W, soccer M/W, softball M/W, volleyball M/W.

Standardized Tests *Required:* SAT I or ACT (for admission).

Costs (2003–04) *Comprehensive fee:* $18,026 includes full-time tuition ($12,930), mandatory fees ($50), and room and board ($5046). Full-time tuition and fees vary according to course load. Part-time tuition: $405 per semester hour. Part-time tuition and fees vary according to course load. *College room only:* $2350. Room and board charges vary according to board plan and housing facility. *Payment plan:* installment. *Waivers:* employees or children of employees.

Financial Aid Of all full-time matriculated undergraduates who enrolled in 2003, 1,036 applied for aid, 926 were judged to have need, 211 had their need fully met. 243 Federal Work-Study jobs (averaging $1277). 112 state and other part-time jobs (averaging $1224). In 2003, 129 non-need-based awards were made. *Average percent of need met:* 78%. *Average financial aid package:* $12,932. *Average need-based loan:* $3917. *Average need-based gift aid:* $6002. *Average non-need-based aid:* $5421. *Average indebtedness upon graduation:* $15,125.

Applying *Options:* common application, electronic application, deferred entrance. *Application fee:* $20. *Required:* high school transcript, minimum 2.0 GPA. *Required for some:* essay or personal statement, 3 letters of recommendation. *Application deadlines:* 8/15 (freshmen), 8/15 (transfers). *Notification:* continuous (freshmen), continuous (transfers).

Admissions Contact Ms. Amy Weyant, Director of Admissions, McMurry University, Box 947, Abilene, TX 79697. *Phone:* 325-793-4705. *Toll-free phone:* 800-477-0077. *Fax:* 325-793-4718. *E-mail:* admissions@mcm.edu.

■ *See page 1966 for a narrative description.*

Midwestern State University

Wichita Falls, Texas

- **State-supported** comprehensive, founded 1922
- **Calendar** semesters
- **Degrees** associate, bachelor's, and master's
- **Urban** 172-acre campus
- **Endowment** $5.4 million
- **Coed,** 5,645 undergraduate students, 70% full-time, 57% women, 43% men
- **Minimally difficult** entrance level, 65% of applicants were admitted

Undergraduates 3,930 full-time, 1,715 part-time. Students come from 46 states and territories, 34 other countries. 5% are from out of state, 10% African American, 3% Asian American or Pacific Islander, 9% Hispanic American, 1% Native American, 5% international, 13% transferred in, 15% live on campus. *Retention:* 67% of 2002 full-time freshmen returned.

Freshmen *Admission:* 2,294 applied, 1,496 admitted, 702 enrolled. *Average high school GPA:* 3.1. *Test scores:* SAT verbal scores over 500: 41%; SAT math scores over 500: 39%; ACT scores over 18: 69%; SAT verbal scores over 600: 11%; SAT math scores over 600: 7%; ACT scores over 24: 10%; SAT verbal scores over 700: 1%; ACT scores over 30: 1%.

Faculty *Total:* 307, 65% full-time, 52% with terminal degrees. *Student/faculty ratio:* 21:1.

Majors Accounting; applied art; art; biology/biological sciences; business administration and management; business/commerce; chemistry; clinical laboratory science/medical technology; computer engineering; computer science; criminal justice/law enforcement administration; dental hygiene; dramatic/theatre arts; early childhood education; economics; engineering technology; English; environmental science; finance; geology/earth science; health and physical education related; history; humanities; information science/studies; interdisciplinary studies; international business/trade/commerce; international/global studies; kinesiology and exercise science; management information systems and services related; manufacturing technology; marketing/marketing management; mass communication/media; mathematics; multi-/interdisciplinary studies related; music; nursing (registered nurse training); physics; political science and government; psychology; radiologic technology/science; respiratory care therapy; social sciences related; social work; sociology; Spanish.

Academic Programs *Special study options:* academic remediation for entering students, accelerated degree program, adult/continuing education programs, advanced placement credit, distance learning, English as a second language, honors programs, internships, part-time degree program, services for LD students, study abroad, summer session for credit. *ROTC:* Air Force (c).

Library Moffett Library with 366,350 titles, 1,100 serial subscriptions, an OPAC, a Web page.

Computers on Campus 425 computers available on campus for general student use. A campuswide network can be accessed from student residence rooms and from off campus. Internet access, online (class) registration, at least one staffed computer lab available.

Student Life *Housing:* on-campus residence required through sophomore year. *Options:* coed. Campus housing is university owned and leased by the school. Freshman applicants given priority for college housing. *Activities and organiza-*

Midwestern State University (continued)

tions: drama/theater group, student-run newspaper, television station, choral group, marching band, honor societies, Greek organizations, political groups, national fraternities, national sororities. *Campus security:* 24-hour emergency response devices and patrols, controlled dormitory access. *Student services:* health clinic, personal/psychological counseling, legal services.

Athletics Member NCAA. All Division II. *Intercollegiate sports:* basketball M(s)/W(s), cheerleading M(s)(c)/W(s)(c), fencing M(c)/W(c), football M(s), soccer M(s)/W(s), softball W(s), tennis M(s)/W(s), volleyball W(s). *Intramural sports:* archery M/W, badminton M/W, basketball M/W, bowling M/W, football M/W, golf M/W, rugby M(c), soccer M/W, softball M/W, table tennis M/W, tennis M/W, volleyball M/W, weight lifting M/W.

Standardized Tests *Required:* SAT I or ACT (for admission).

Costs (2004–05) *Tuition:* state resident $1380 full-time; nonresident $8460 full-time. Part-time tuition and fees vary according to course load. *Required fees:* $2270 full-time. *Room and board:* $4630; room only: $2260. Room and board charges vary according to board plan and housing facility. *Payment plan:* installment. *Waivers:* senior citizens and employees or children of employees.

Financial Aid Of all full-time matriculated undergraduates who enrolled in 2003, 56 Federal Work-Study jobs (averaging $1200). 15 state and other part-time jobs (averaging $897). In 2003, 639 non-need-based awards were made. *Average percent of need met:* 60%. *Average financial aid package:* $4035. *Average need-based loan:* $4715. *Average need-based gift aid:* $3937. *Average non-need-based aid:* $3932. *Average indebtedness upon graduation:* $11,046.

Applying *Options:* common application, early admission, deferred entrance. *Required:* high school transcript. *Application deadlines:* 8/7 (freshmen), 8/7 (transfers). *Notification:* continuous until 8/31 (freshmen), continuous (transfers).

Admissions Contact Ms. Barbara Merkle, Director of Admissions, Midwestern State University, Wichita Falls, TX 76308. *Phone:* 940-397-4334. *Toll-free phone:* 800-842-1922. *Fax:* 940-397-4672. *E-mail:* admissions@mwsu.edu.

NORTHWOOD UNIVERSITY, TEXAS CAMPUS

Cedar Hill, Texas

- **Independent** 4-year, founded 1966
- **Calendar** quarters
- **Degrees** associate and bachelor's
- **Small-town** 360-acre campus with easy access to Dallas
- **Endowment** $54.4 million
- **Coed,** 1,117 undergraduate students, 78% full-time, 59% women, 41% men
- **Moderately difficult** entrance level, 59% of applicants were admitted

Undergraduates 874 full-time, 243 part-time. Students come from 17 states and territories, 8 other countries, 5% are from out of state, 20% African American, 2% Asian American or Pacific Islander, 28% Hispanic American, 0.2% Native American, 5% international, 4% transferred in, 27% live on campus. *Retention:* 61% of 2002 full-time freshmen returned.

Freshmen *Admission:* 864 applied, 508 admitted, 188 enrolled. *Average high school GPA:* 3.24. *Test scores:* SAT verbal scores over 500: 27%; SAT math scores over 500: 31%; ACT scores over 18: 66%; SAT verbal scores over 600: 2%; SAT math scores over 600: 5%; ACT scores over 24: 3%; SAT math scores over 700: 1%.

Faculty *Total:* 33, 70% full-time, 15% with terminal degrees. *Student/faculty ratio:* 25:1.

Majors Accounting; advertising; banking and financial support services; business administration and management; computer and information sciences; entrepreneurship; fashion merchandising; hotel/motel administration; international business/trade/commerce; management information systems; marketing/marketing management; sport and fitness administration; vehicle and vehicle parts and accessories marketing.

Academic Programs *Special study options:* academic remediation for entering students, accelerated degree program, adult/continuing education programs, advanced placement credit, distance learning, double majors, external degree program, honors programs, independent study, internships, off-campus study, part-time degree program, study abroad, summer session for credit.

Library Hach Library with 9,793 titles, 161 serial subscriptions, 350 audiovisual materials, an OPAC.

Computers on Campus 30 computers available on campus for general student use. A campuswide network can be accessed from student residence rooms and from off campus. Internet access, at least one staffed computer lab available.

Student Life *Housing:* on-campus residence required for freshman year. *Options:* men-only, women-only. Campus housing is university owned. Freshman campus housing is guaranteed. *Activities and organizations:* Association of Entertainment and Sports Management, In-Line Hockey Club, Alpha Nu Omega Sorority, Alpha Omega Fraternity, Delta Epsilon Chi. *Campus security:* 24-hour emergency response devices and patrols, student patrols. *Student services:* health clinic, personal/psychological counseling.

Athletics Member NAIA. *Intercollegiate sports:* baseball M(s), cross-country running M(s)/W(s), golf M(s)/W(s), soccer M(s)/W(s), softball W(s), track and field M(s)/W(s). *Intramural sports:* basketball M/W, volleyball M/W.

Standardized Tests *Required:* SAT I or ACT (for admission).

Costs (2003–04) *Comprehensive fee:* $19,905 includes full-time tuition ($13,485), mandatory fees ($510), and room and board ($5910). Part-time tuition: $281 per credit. *College room only:* $3120. Room and board charges vary according to board plan and location. *Payment plan:* installment. *Waivers:* children of alumni and employees or children of employees.

Financial Aid Of all full-time matriculated undergraduates who enrolled in 2003, 525 applied for aid, 460 were judged to have need, 62 had their need fully met. 58 Federal Work-Study jobs (averaging $2065). In 2003, 140 non-need-based awards were made. *Average percent of need met:* 71%. *Average financial aid package:* $11,654. *Average need-based loan:* $3483. *Average need-based gift aid:* $4686. *Average non-need-based aid:* $4512. *Average indebtedness upon graduation:* $19,085.

Applying *Options:* common application, electronic application, early admission, deferred entrance. *Application fee:* $25. *Required:* essay or personal statement, high school transcript. *Recommended:* minimum 2.0 GPA, 1 letter of recommendation, interview. *Application deadline:* rolling (freshmen), rolling (transfers). *Notification:* continuous (freshmen), continuous (transfers).

Admissions Contact Mr. James R. Hickerson, Director of Admissions, Northwood University, Texas Campus, 1114 West FM 1382, Cedar Hill, TX 75104. *Phone:* 972-293-5400. *Toll-free phone:* 800-927-9663. *Fax:* 972-291-3824. *E-mail:* txadmit@northwood.edu.

OUR LADY OF THE LAKE UNIVERSITY OF SAN ANTONIO

San Antonio, Texas

- **Independent Roman Catholic** comprehensive, founded 1895
- **Calendar** semesters plus 2 summer sessions
- **Degrees** bachelor's, master's, and doctoral
- **Urban** 75-acre campus
- **Endowment** $25.9 million
- **Coed,** 2,114 undergraduate students, 63% full-time, 77% women, 23% men
- **Moderately difficult** entrance level, 65% of applicants were admitted

Undergraduates 1,325 full-time, 789 part-time. Students come from 28 states and territories, 17 other countries, 1% are from out of state, 7% African American, 2% Asian American or Pacific Islander, 66% Hispanic American, 0.5% international, 6% transferred in, 29% live on campus. *Retention:* 90% of 2002 full-time freshmen returned.

Freshmen *Admission:* 1,858 applied, 1,216 admitted, 330 enrolled. *Average high school GPA:* 3.37. *Test scores:* SAT verbal scores over 500: 42%; SAT math scores over 500: 40%; ACT scores over 18: 85%; SAT verbal scores over 600: 8%; SAT math scores over 600: 7%; ACT scores over 24: 20%; ACT scores over 30: 1%.

Faculty *Total:* 310, 60% full-time. *Student/faculty ratio:* 9:1.

Majors Accounting; American studies; art; audiology and speech-language pathology; biology/biological sciences; business administration and management; chemistry; communication/speech communication and rhetoric; computer systems networking and telecommunications; dramatic/theatre arts; English; family and community services; fashion merchandising; fine arts related; Hispanic-American, Puerto Rican, and Mexican-American/Chicano studies; history; human resources management; kindergarten/preschool education; liberal arts and sciences/liberal studies; marketing/marketing management; mathematics; natural sciences; philosophy; political science and government; psychology; religious studies; social sciences; social work; sociology; Spanish; special education.

Academic Programs *Special study options:* academic remediation for entering students, adult/continuing education programs, advanced placement credit, double majors, English as a second language, internships, off-campus study, part-time degree program, services for LD students, summer session for credit. *ROTC:* Army (c), Air Force (c). *Unusual degree programs:* 3-2 engineering with Texas Tech University, Washington University in St. Louis.

Library Saint Florence Library plus 2 others with 141,126 titles, 38,807 serial subscriptions, 6,774 audiovisual materials, an OPAC, a Web page.

Computers on Campus 200 computers available on campus for general student use. A campuswide network can be accessed from off campus. At least one staffed computer lab available.

Student Life *Housing options:* coed, men-only, women-only, disabled students. *Activities and organizations:* drama/theater group, student-run newspaper, television station, choral group. *Campus security:* 24-hour emergency response devices and patrols, late-night transport/escort service, controlled dormitory access. *Student services:* health clinic, personal/psychological counseling, women's center.

Athletics *Intramural sports:* basketball M/W, football M/W, golf M/W, racquetball M/W, soccer M/W, softball M/W, swimming M/W, tennis M/W, track and field M/W, volleyball M/W.
Standardized Tests *Required:* SAT I or ACT (for admission).
Costs (2004–05) *Comprehensive fee:* $21,588 includes full-time tuition ($15,932), mandatory fees ($426), and room and board ($5230). Part-time tuition: $517 per credit hour. *Required fees:* $12 per credit hour part-time, $48 per semester part-time. *College room only:* $3072. Room and board charges vary according to board plan and housing facility. *Payment plan:* installment. *Waivers:* employees or children of employees.
Financial Aid Of all full-time matriculated undergraduates who enrolled in 2003, 1,236 applied for aid, 1,183 were judged to have need, 173 had their need fully met. 312 Federal Work-Study jobs (averaging $1437). 64 state and other part-time jobs (averaging $1508). In 2003, 65 non-need-based awards were made. *Average percent of need met:* 87%. *Average financial aid package:* $12,944. *Average need-based loan:* $3857. *Average need-based gift aid:* $3032. *Average non-need-based aid:* $7256. *Average indebtedness upon graduation:* $17,650.
Applying *Options:* common application, deferred entrance. *Application fee:* $25. *Required:* high school transcript. *Required for some:* interview. *Application deadline:* rolling (freshmen), rolling (transfers). *Notification:* continuous (freshmen), continuous (transfers).
Admissions Contact Mr. Michael Boatner, Acting Director of Admissions, Our Lady of the Lake University of San Antonio, 411 Southwest 24th Street, San Antonio, TX 78207-4689. *Phone:* 210-434-6711 Ext. 314. *Toll-free phone:* 800-436-6558. *Fax:* 210-431-4036. *E-mail:* admission@lake.ollusa.edu.

■ *See page 2142 for a narrative description.*

PAUL QUINN COLLEGE
Dallas, Texas

- **Independent African Methodist Episcopal** 4-year, founded 1872
- **Calendar** semesters
- **Degree** bachelor's
- **Suburban** 132-acre campus
- **Endowment** $1.5 million
- **Coed**
- **Moderately difficult** entrance level

Faculty *Student/faculty ratio:* 22:1.
Student Life *Campus security:* 24-hour patrols.
Athletics Member NAIA, NSCAA.
Standardized Tests *Required:* SAT I or ACT (for placement).
Costs (2003–04) *Comprehensive fee:* $8780 includes full-time tuition ($4080), mandatory fees ($900), and room and board ($3800). *College room only:* $1400.
Financial Aid Of all full-time matriculated undergraduates who enrolled in 2002, 642 applied for aid, 611 were judged to have need, 597 had their need fully met. 88 Federal Work-Study jobs (averaging $1500). In 2002, 27. *Average percent of need met:* 98. *Average financial aid package:* $8752. *Average need-based loan:* $1800. *Average need-based gift aid:* $4050. *Average non-need-based aid:* $6900. *Average indebtedness upon graduation:* $4000.
Applying *Options:* electronic application. *Application fee:* $15. *Required:* high school transcript, minimum 2.0 GPA. *Required for some:* letters of recommendation, interview.
Admissions Contact Ms. Nena Taylor-Richey, Director of Admissions and Recruitment, Paul Quinn College, 3837 Simpson-Stuart Road, Dallas, TX 75241-4331. *Phone:* 214-302-3575. *Toll-free phone:* 800-237-2648. *Fax:* 214-302-3520.

PRAIRIE VIEW A&M UNIVERSITY
Prairie View, Texas

- **State-supported** comprehensive, founded 1878, part of Texas A&M University System
- **Calendar** semesters
- **Degrees** bachelor's, master's, and doctoral
- **Small-town** 1440-acre campus with easy access to Houston
- **Coed,** 6,042 undergraduate students, 89% full-time, 56% women, 44% men
- **Moderately difficult** entrance level, 98% of applicants were admitted

Prairie View A&M University is the second-oldest public institution of higher education in Texas, originating in the Texas Constitution of 1876. The University opened in 1878 as the Agricultural and Mechanical College of Texas for Colored Youth, with 8 students and 2 faculty members. Today, the University enrolls more than 7,600 students and offers undergraduate and graduate degrees. Its most prominent programs are in accounting, computer science, criminal justice, education, engineering, nursing, and premedicine. Major academic units include the School of Architecture, the College of Agriculture and Human Sciences, the College of Arts and Sciences, the College of Business, the College of Education, the College of Engineering, The School of Juvenile Justice, the College of Nursing, and the Graduate School. The University is fully accredited by the Southern Association of Colleges and Schools and has specialized accreditation in several areas, including computer science, education, engineering, nursing, nutrition, and social work.

Undergraduates 5,397 full-time, 645 part-time. Students come from 44 states and territories, 44 other countries, 6% are from out of state, 92% African American, 0.6% Asian American or Pacific Islander, 2% Hispanic American, 0.1% Native American, 1% international, 4% transferred in. *Retention:* 67% of 2002 full-time freshmen returned.
Freshmen *Admission:* 2,767 applied, 2,710 admitted, 1,459 enrolled. *Average high school GPA:* 2.84.
Faculty *Total:* 387, 83% full-time. *Student/faculty ratio:* 20:1.
Majors Accounting; agricultural teacher education; agriculture; architecture; biology/biological sciences; business administration and management; chemical engineering; chemistry; civil engineering; clinical laboratory science/medical technology; community health services counseling; computer science; computer technology/computer systems technology; criminal justice/safety; drafting and design technology; dramatic/theatre arts; electrical, electronic and communications engineering technology; electrical, electronics and communications engineering; engineering technology; English; family and community services; finance; foods, nutrition, and wellness; history; industrial technology; interdisciplinary studies; marketing/marketing management; mathematics; mechanical engineering; music; nursing (registered nurse training); physics; piano and organ; political science and government; psychology; social work; sociology; Spanish; trade and industrial teacher education; voice and opera; wind/percussion instruments.
Academic Programs *Special study options:* academic remediation for entering students, accelerated degree program, advanced placement credit, cooperative education, distance learning, double majors, English as a second language, honors programs, independent study, internships, part-time degree program, summer session for credit. *ROTC:* Army (b), Navy (b).
Library John B. Coleman Library with an OPAC, a Web page.
Computers on Campus 504 computers available on campus for general student use. A campuswide network can be accessed from student residence rooms that provide access to e-mail. At least one staffed computer lab available.
Student Life *Housing:* on-campus residence required for freshman year. *Options:* coed, men-only, women-only. Campus housing is provided by a third party. *Activities and organizations:* drama/theater group, student-run newspaper, radio station, choral group, marching band, National Society of Black Engineers, National Association of Black Accountants, National Organization of Black Chemists and Chemical Engineers, Toastmasters International, Baptist Student Movement, national fraternities, national sororities. *Campus security:* 24-hour emergency response devices and patrols. *Student services:* health clinic, personal/psychological counseling.
Athletics Member NCAA. All Division I except football (Division I-AA). *Intercollegiate sports:* baseball M(s), basketball M(s)/W(s), cross-country running M(s)/W(s), golf M(s)/W(s), soccer W(s), softball W(s), tennis M(s)/W(s), track and field M(s)/W(s), volleyball W(s). *Intramural sports:* baseball M, basketball M/W, bowling W, cross-country running M/W, equestrian sports M/W, golf M/W, soccer W, softball W, tennis M/W, track and field M/W, volleyball M/W.
Standardized Tests *Required:* SAT I or ACT (for admission).
Costs (2003–04) *Tuition:* state resident $1380 full-time, $46 per credit hour part-time; nonresident $8460 full-time, $282 per credit hour part-time. Full-time tuition and fees vary according to course load and degree level. Part-time tuition and fees vary according to course load and degree level. *Required fees:* $2212 full-time. *Room and board:* $5826; room only: $3536. Room and board charges vary according to board plan and housing facility. *Payment plans:* installment, deferred payment. *Waivers:* senior citizens.
Financial Aid Of all full-time matriculated undergraduates who enrolled in 2002, 4,622 applied for aid, 4,311 were judged to have need. 732 Federal Work-Study jobs (averaging $1934). 328 state and other part-time jobs (averaging $1146). In 2002, 271 non-need-based awards were made. *Average percent of need met:* 75%. *Average financial aid package:* $6920. *Average need-based loan:* $4000. *Average need-based gift aid:* $3300. *Average non-need-based aid:* $1400. *Average indebtedness upon graduation:* $11,000.
Applying *Options:* deferred entrance. *Application fee:* $25. *Required:* high school transcript, minimum 2.5 GPA, letters of recommendation. *Application deadline:* 7/1 (freshmen). *Notification:* continuous (freshmen), continuous (transfers).
Admissions Contact Ms. Mary Gooch, Director of Admissions, Prairie View A&M University, PO Box 3089, Prairie View, TX 77446-0188. *Phone:* 936-857-2626. *Fax:* 936-857-2699. *E-mail:* mary_gooch@pvamu.edu.

■ *See page 2188 for a narrative description.*

RICE UNIVERSITY
Houston, Texas

- **Independent** university, founded 1912
- **Calendar** semesters
- **Degrees** bachelor's, master's, and doctoral
- **Urban** 300-acre campus
- **Endowment** $2.9 billion
- **Coed,** 2,921 undergraduate students, 98% full-time, 48% women, 52% men
- **Most difficult** entrance level, 24% of applicants were admitted

Undergraduates 2,849 full-time, 72 part-time. Students come from 53 states and territories, 37 other countries, 48% are from out of state, 6% African American, 15% Asian American or Pacific Islander, 11% Hispanic American, 0.5% Native American, 3% international, 2% transferred in, 71% live on campus. *Retention:* 96% of 2002 full-time freshmen returned.

Freshmen *Admission:* 7,501 applied, 1,821 admitted, 715 enrolled. *Test scores:* SAT verbal scores over 500: 98%; SAT math scores over 500: 99%; ACT scores over 18: 100%; SAT verbal scores over 600: 91%; SAT math scores over 600: 93%; ACT scores over 24: 94%; SAT verbal scores over 700: 57%; SAT math scores over 700: 64%; ACT scores over 30: 66%.

Faculty *Total:* 802, 66% full-time, 91% with terminal degrees. *Student/faculty ratio:* 5:1.

Majors Ancient/classical Greek; anthropology; applied mathematics; architecture; art; art history, criticism and conservation; Asian studies; astronomy; astrophysics; biochemistry; biology/biological sciences; biomedical/medical engineering; business administration and management; chemical engineering; chemistry; civil engineering; classics and languages, literatures and linguistics; computer and information sciences; computer engineering; ecology; economics; electrical, electronics and communications engineering; English; environmental/environmental health engineering; evolutionary biology; fine/studio arts; French; geology/earth science; geophysics and seismology; German; history; kinesiology and exercise science; Latin; Latin American studies; linguistics; materials engineering; materials science; mathematics; mechanical engineering; multi-/interdisciplinary studies related; music; music history, literature, and theory; music performance; music theory and composition; neuroscience; philosophy; physical and theoretical chemistry; physics; political science and government; psychology; public policy analysis; religious studies; Russian; Russian studies; sociology; Spanish; statistics; visual and performing arts related; women's studies.

Academic Programs *Special study options:* accelerated degree program, advanced placement credit, double majors, honors programs, independent study, internships, off-campus study, services for LD students, student-designed majors, study abroad, summer session for credit. *ROTC:* Army (c), Navy (b). *Unusual degree programs:* 3-2 five year joint degree BSE/MSE in Engineering; five year joint degree BSE/MBA in Engineering and Business.

Library Fondren Library with 2.1 million titles, 28,000 serial subscriptions, 51,000 audiovisual materials, an OPAC, a Web page.

Computers on Campus 600 computers available on campus for general student use. A campuswide network can be accessed from student residence rooms and from off campus. Internet access, at least one staffed computer lab available.

Student Life *Housing options:* coed. Campus housing is university owned. Freshman campus housing is guaranteed. *Activities and organizations:* drama/theater group, student-run newspaper, radio and television station, choral group, marching band, drama club, volunteer program, intramural sports, college government, Marching Owl Band. *Campus security:* 24-hour emergency response devices and patrols, late-night transport/escort service, controlled dormitory access. *Student services:* health clinic, personal/psychological counseling, women's center.

Athletics Member NCAA. All Division I except football (Division I-A). *Intercollegiate sports:* badminton M(c)/W(c), baseball M(s), basketball M(s)/W(s), cheerleading M(c)/W(c), crew M(c)/W(c), cross-country running M(s)/W(s), fencing M(c)/W(c), field hockey W(c), golf M(s), lacrosse M(c)/W(c), rugby M(c)/W(c), sailing M(c)/W(c), soccer M(c)/W(s), swimming W(s), tennis M(s)/W(s), track and field M(s)/W(s), ultimate Frisbee M(c)/W(c), volleyball M(c)/W(s), water polo M(c)/W(c), wrestling M(c). *Intramural sports:* badminton M/W, basketball M/W, football M/W, racquetball M/W, soccer M/W, softball M/W, squash M, swimming M/W, table tennis M/W, tennis M/W, track and field M/W, volleyball M/W.

Standardized Tests *Required:* SAT I or ACT (for admission), SAT II: Subject Tests (for admission), SAT II: Writing Test (for admission).

Costs (2003–04) *Comprehensive fee:* $27,550 includes full-time tuition ($18,850), mandatory fees ($820), and room and board ($7880). Full-time tuition and fees vary according to student level. *College room only:* $4800. Room and board charges vary according to board plan. *Payment plan:* installment. *Waivers:* employees or children of employees.

Financial Aid Of all full-time matriculated undergraduates who enrolled in 2003, 2,172 applied for aid, 1,058 were judged to have need, 1,058 had their need fully met. In 2003, 532 non-need-based awards were made. *Average percent of need met:* 100%. *Average financial aid package:* $12,903. *Average need-based loan:* $3103. *Average need-based gift aid:* $10,461. *Average non-need-based aid:* $3101. *Average indebtedness upon graduation:* $12,942.

Applying *Options:* common application, electronic application, early admission, early decision, early action, deferred entrance. *Application fee:* $40. *Required:* essay or personal statement, high school transcript, 2 letters of recommendation, portfolio required for architecture students; audition required for music students. *Recommended:* interview. *Application deadlines:* 1/10 (freshmen), 3/15 (transfers). *Early decision:* 11/1. *Notification:* 4/1 (freshmen), 12/15 (early decision), 2/10 (early action), 6/1 (transfers).

Admissions Contact Ms. Julie M. Browning, Dean for Undergraduate Enrollment, Rice University, Office of Admission, PO Box 1892, MS 17, Houston, TX 77251-1892. *Phone:* 713-348-RICE. *Toll-free phone:* 800-527-OWLS.

■ *See page 2230 for a narrative description.*

ST. EDWARD'S UNIVERSITY
Austin, Texas

- **Independent Roman Catholic** comprehensive, founded 1885
- **Calendar** semesters
- **Degrees** bachelor's, master's, and postbachelor's certificates
- **Urban** 160-acre campus
- **Endowment** $37.2 million
- **Coed,** 3,531 undergraduate students, 70% full-time, 57% women, 43% men
- **Moderately difficult** entrance level, 70% of applicants were admitted

Undergraduates 2,466 full-time, 1,065 part-time. Students come from 33 states and territories, 33 other countries, 4% are from out of state, 5% African American, 3% Asian American or Pacific Islander, 30% Hispanic American, 0.7% Native American, 3% international, 7% transferred in, 39% live on campus. *Retention:* 79% of 2002 full-time freshmen returned.

Freshmen *Admission:* 2,005 applied, 1,396 admitted, 563 enrolled. *Test scores:* SAT verbal scores over 500: 77%; SAT math scores over 500: 73%; ACT scores over 18: 96%; SAT verbal scores over 600: 28%; SAT math scores over 600: 27%; ACT scores over 24: 45%; SAT verbal scores over 700: 3%; SAT math scores over 700: 1%; ACT scores over 30: 5%.

Faculty *Total:* 389, 36% full-time, 53% with terminal degrees. *Student/faculty ratio:* 15:1.

Majors Accounting; accounting technology and bookkeeping; art; art teacher education; biochemistry; bioinformatics; biology/biological sciences; biology teacher education; business administration and management; chemistry; communication and media related; computer and information sciences; computer science; criminal justice/safety; drama and dance teacher education; dramatic/theatre arts; economics; education (specific subject areas) related; English; English composition; entrepreneurship; finance; forensic science and technology; graphic design; history; history teacher education; international business/trade/commerce; international relations and affairs; kinesiology and exercise science; Latin American studies; liberal arts and sciences/liberal studies; marketing/marketing management; mathematics; multi-/interdisciplinary studies related; parks, recreation, and leisure related; philosophy; photography; physical education teaching and coaching; political science and government; psychology; religious education; social studies teacher education; social work; sociology; Spanish; Spanish language teacher education; theology and religious vocations related.

Academic Programs *Special study options:* academic remediation for entering students, adult/continuing education programs, advanced placement credit, double majors, honors programs, internships, part-time degree program, services for LD students, study abroad, summer session for credit. *ROTC:* Army (c), Air Force (c).

Library Scarborough-Phillips Library with 150,478 titles, 977 serial subscriptions, 2,251 audiovisual materials, an OPAC, a Web page.

Computers on Campus 498 computers available on campus for general student use. A campuswide network can be accessed from student residence rooms and from off campus. Internet access, online (class) registration, at least one staffed computer lab available.

Student Life *Housing:* on-campus residence required for freshman year. *Options:* coed, men-only, women-only. Campus housing is university owned. Freshman campus housing is guaranteed. *Activities and organizations:* drama/theater group, student-run newspaper, choral group, Student Government Association, University Programming Board, SEUTV, Alpha Phi Omega, Emerging Leaders. *Campus security:* 24-hour emergency response devices and patrols, late-night transport/escort service, controlled dormitory access, self-defense educations, informal discussions, pamphlets, posters, films, lighted pathways and sidewalks. *Student services:* health clinic, personal/psychological counseling.

Athletics Member NCAA. All Division II. *Intercollegiate sports:* baseball M(s), basketball M(s)/W(s), golf M(s)/W(s), soccer M(s)/W(s), softball W(s), tennis

M(s)/W(s), volleyball W(s). *Intramural sports:* basketball M/W, football M/W, lacrosse M(c), racquetball M/W, soccer M/W, softball M/W, tennis M/W, volleyball M/W.

Standardized Tests *Required:* SAT I or ACT (for admission).

Costs (2003–04) *Comprehensive fee:* $20,728 includes full-time tuition ($14,710) and room and board ($6018). Part-time tuition: $490 per credit hour. *Room and board:* Room and board charges vary according to board plan and housing facility. *Payment plans:* installment, deferred payment. *Waivers:* employees or children of employees.

Financial Aid Of all full-time matriculated undergraduates who enrolled in 2003, 1,810 applied for aid, 1,486 were judged to have need, 210 had their need fully met. 240 Federal Work-Study jobs (averaging $1915). 50 state and other part-time jobs (averaging $1800). In 2003, 82 non-need-based awards were made. *Average percent of need met:* 69%. *Average financial aid package:* $11,577. *Average need-based loan:* $4221. *Average need-based gift aid:* $7793. *Average non-need-based aid:* $4770. *Average indebtedness upon graduation:* $22,331. *Financial aid deadline:* 4/15.

Applying *Options:* common application, electronic application, deferred entrance. *Application fee:* $45. *Required:* essay or personal statement, high school transcript. *Recommended:* 2 letters of recommendation, interview. *Application deadlines:* 6/1 (freshmen), 7/1 (transfers). *Notification:* continuous (freshmen), continuous (transfers).

Admissions Contact Ms. Tracy Manier, Director of Admission, St. Edward's University, 3001 South Congress Avenue, Austin, TX 78704. *Phone:* 512-448-8602. *Toll-free phone:* 800-555-0164. *Fax:* 512-464-8877. *E-mail:* seu.admit@admin.stedwards.edu.

■ *See page 2280 for a narrative description.*

ST. MARY'S UNIVERSITY OF SAN ANTONIO

San Antonio, Texas

- **Independent Roman Catholic** comprehensive, founded 1852
- **Calendar** semesters
- **Degrees** bachelor's, master's, doctoral, and first professional
- **Urban** 135-acre campus
- **Endowment** $84.1 million
- **Coed,** 2,582 undergraduate students, 92% full-time, 59% women, 41% men
- **Moderately difficult** entrance level, 81% of applicants were admitted

Undergraduates 2,370 full-time, 212 part-time. Students come from 33 states and territories, 37 other countries, 4% are from out of state, 3% African American, 2% Asian American or Pacific Islander, 69% Hispanic American, 0.2% Native American, 4% international, 5% transferred in, 41% live on campus. *Retention:* 80% of 2002 full-time freshmen returned.

Freshmen *Admission:* 1,464 applied, 1,189 admitted, 472 enrolled. *Average high school GPA:* 3.53. *Test scores:* SAT verbal scores over 500: 69%; SAT math scores over 500: 72%; ACT scores over 18: 92%; SAT verbal scores over 600: 22%; SAT math scores over 600: 20%; ACT scores over 24: 28%; SAT verbal scores over 700: 1%; SAT math scores over 700: 3%; ACT scores over 30: 1%.

Faculty *Total:* 328, 58% full-time, 72% with terminal degrees. *Student/faculty ratio:* 13:1.

Majors Accounting; art teacher education; biochemistry; biology/biological sciences; business administration and management; business teacher education; chemistry; communication/speech communication and rhetoric; computer engineering; computer management; computer science; criminal justice/law enforcement administration; criminology; economics; education; electrical, electronics and communications engineering; engineering; engineering science; English; finance; French; geology/earth science; health and physical education; history; human resources management; industrial engineering; information science/studies; international business/trade/commerce; kinesiology and exercise science; marketing/marketing management; mass communication/media; mathematics; music; philosophy; physics; political science and government; pre-dentistry studies; psychology; reading teacher education; sales, distribution and marketing; social studies teacher education; sociology; Spanish; speech and rhetoric; statistics; theology.

Academic Programs *Special study options:* academic remediation for entering students, adult/continuing education programs, advanced placement credit, cooperative education, distance learning, double majors, English as a second language, honors programs, independent study, internships, off-campus study, part-time degree program, study abroad, summer session for credit. *ROTC:* Army (b).

Library Academic Library plus 1 other with 481,137 titles, 1,126 serial subscriptions, 3,104 audiovisual materials, an OPAC, a Web page.

Computers on Campus 100 computers available on campus for general student use. A campuswide network can be accessed from student residence rooms and from off campus. At least one staffed computer lab available.

Student Life *Housing:* on-campus residence required for freshman year. *Options:* coed, men-only, women-only, disabled students. Campus housing is university owned. Freshman applicants given priority for college housing. *Activities and organizations:* drama/theater group, student-run newspaper, choral group, Beta Beta Beta Biology Society, Emerging Leaders, Student Government Association, Mexican Student Organization, Delta Zeta, national fraternities, national sororities. *Campus security:* 24-hour emergency response devices and patrols, late-night transport/escort service, controlled dormitory access. *Student services:* health clinic, personal/psychological counseling.

Athletics Member NCAA, NAIA. All NCAA Division II. *Intercollegiate sports:* baseball M(s), basketball M(s)/W(s), golf M(s), rugby M(c), soccer M(s)/W(s), softball W, tennis M(s)/W(s), volleyball W(s). *Intramural sports:* badminton M/W, basketball M/W, bowling M/W, cross-country running M/W, football M/W, softball M/W, table tennis M/W, tennis M/W, volleyball M/W, water polo M/W.

Standardized Tests *Required:* SAT I or ACT (for admission).

Costs (2004–05) *Comprehensive fee:* $24,254 includes full-time tuition ($17,256), mandatory fees ($500), and room and board ($6498). Full-time tuition and fees vary according to course load. Part-time tuition: $517 per credit hour. Part-time tuition and fees vary according to course load. *Required fees:* $250 per term part-time. *College room only:* $3802. Room and board charges vary according to board plan, housing facility, and student level. *Payment plan:* installment. *Waivers:* employees or children of employees.

Financial Aid Of all full-time matriculated undergraduates who enrolled in 2003, 1,872 applied for aid, 1,709 were judged to have need, 390 had their need fully met. 561 Federal Work-Study jobs (averaging $2147). 171 state and other part-time jobs (averaging $1915). In 2003, 168 non-need-based awards were made. *Average percent of need met:* 69%. *Average financial aid package:* $13,454. *Average need-based loan:* $4488. *Average need-based gift aid:* $7492. *Average non-need-based aid:* $8897. *Average indebtedness upon graduation:* $23,406.

Applying *Options:* common application, early admission, deferred entrance. *Application fee:* $30. *Required:* essay or personal statement, high school transcript. *Required for some:* letters of recommendation. *Recommended:* interview. *Application deadline:* rolling (freshmen), rolling (transfers). *Notification:* continuous (freshmen), continuous (transfers).

Admissions Contact Mr. Richard Castillo, Director of Admissions, St. Mary's University of San Antonio, 1 Camino Santa Maria, San Antonio, TX 78228-8503. *Phone:* 210-436-3126. *Toll-free phone:* 800-FOR-STMU. *Fax:* 210-431-6742. *E-mail:* uadm@stmarytx.edu.

■ *See page 2320 for a narrative description.*

SAM HOUSTON STATE UNIVERSITY

Huntsville, Texas

- **State-supported** university, founded 1879, part of The Texas State University System
- **Calendar** semesters
- **Degrees** bachelor's, master's, and doctoral
- **Small-town** 1256-acre campus with easy access to Houston
- **Endowment** $69.4 million
- **Coed,** 11,504 undergraduate students, 85% full-time, 58% women, 42% men
- **Moderately difficult** entrance level, 76% of applicants were admitted

Undergraduates 9,739 full-time, 1,765 part-time. Students come from 37 states and territories, 33 other countries, 2% are from out of state, 15% African American, 0.9% Asian American or Pacific Islander, 9% Hispanic American, 0.6% Native American, 0.8% international, 13% transferred in, 23% live on campus. *Retention:* 64% of 2002 full-time freshmen returned.

Freshmen *Admission:* 5,182 applied, 3,915 admitted, 1,810 enrolled. *Test scores:* SAT verbal scores over 500: 55%; SAT math scores over 500: 55%; ACT scores over 18: 85%; SAT verbal scores over 600: 13%; SAT math scores over 600: 11%; ACT scores over 24: 18%; SAT verbal scores over 700: 1%; SAT math scores over 700: 1%.

Faculty *Total:* 541, 72% full-time, 72% with terminal degrees. *Student/faculty ratio:* 22:1.

Majors Accounting; advertising; agribusiness; agricultural business and management; agricultural mechanization; agricultural teacher education; agriculture; animal sciences; art; art teacher education; biological and physical sciences; biology/biological sciences; business administration and management; business/commerce; business/managerial economics; business teacher education; chemistry; clinical laboratory science/medical technology; clinical psychology; commercial and advertising art; community health services counseling; computer and information sciences; conducting; construction engineering technology; construction management; corrections; corrections and criminal justice related; counseling psychology; counselor education/school counseling and guidance; criminal justice/

Sam Houston State University (continued)
law enforcement administration; criminal justice/police science; criminal justice/safety; curriculum and instruction; dance; digital communication and media/multimedia; drafting and design technology; dramatic/theatre arts; education; electrical, electronic and communications engineering technology; English; English/language arts teacher education; environmental studies; family and consumer sciences/home economics teacher education; family and consumer sciences/human sciences; fashion merchandising; finance; fine/studio arts; foods, nutrition, and wellness; foreign language teacher education; forensic psychology; forensic science and technology; French; geography; geology/earth science; German; health and physical education related; health teacher education; history; horticultural science; human resources management; industrial technology; interior design; international business/trade/commerce; journalism; kinesiology and exercise science; marketing/marketing management; mathematics; mathematics teacher education; multi-/interdisciplinary studies related; music; music performance; music teacher education; music therapy; operations management; painting; philosophy; photography; physical education teaching and coaching; physician assistant; physics; political science and government; pre-dentistry studies; pre-law studies; pre-medical studies; pre-nursing studies; pre-pharmacy studies; psychology; public relations/image management; radio and television; reading teacher education; respiratory care therapy; sociology; Spanish; speech and rhetoric; statistics; technology/industrial arts teacher education.

Academic Programs *Special study options:* academic remediation for entering students, accelerated degree program, adult/continuing education programs, advanced placement credit, cooperative education, distance learning, double majors, English as a second language, honors programs, independent study, internships, part-time degree program, services for LD students, summer session for credit. *ROTC:* Army (b). *Unusual degree programs:* 3-2 engineering with Texas A&M University.

Library Newton Gresham Library with 1.8 million titles, 3,263 serial subscriptions, 19,716 audiovisual materials, an OPAC.

Computers on Campus 455 computers available on campus for general student use. A campuswide network can be accessed from student residence rooms and from off campus. Internet access, online (class) registration, at least one staffed computer lab available.

Student Life *Housing:* on-campus residence required for freshman year. *Options:* coed. Campus housing is university owned and is provided by a third party. Freshman campus housing is guaranteed. *Activities and organizations:* drama/theater group, student-run newspaper, radio and television station, choral group, marching band, Residence Hall Association, Inter-Fraternal Council, Pan-Hellenic Council, NAACP, Baptist Student Ministry, national fraternities, national sororities. *Campus security:* 24-hour emergency response devices and patrols, student patrols, late-night transport/escort service. *Student services:* health clinic, personal/psychological counseling, legal services.

Athletics Member NCAA. All Division I except football (Division I-AA). *Intercollegiate sports:* baseball M(s), basketball M(s)/W(s), cross-country running M/W, equestrian sports M/W, golf M(s), lacrosse M(c), riflery M(c)/W(c), rugby M(c), soccer M(c), tennis M(s)/W(s), track and field M(s)/W(s), volleyball W(s). *Intramural sports:* basketball M/W, bowling M/W, football M, gymnastics W(c), racquetball M/W, soccer M/W, softball M/W, swimming M/W, tennis M/W, volleyball M/W, water polo M/W.

Standardized Tests *Required:* SAT I or ACT (for admission).

Costs (2003–04) *Tuition:* state resident $2550 full-time, $85 per semester hour part-time; nonresident $9630 full-time, $321 per semester hour part-time. Full-time tuition and fees vary according to course load. Part-time tuition and fees vary according to course load. *Required fees:* $1102 full-time, $522 per term part-time. *Room and board:* $4160; room only: $2112. Room and board charges vary according to board plan and housing facility. *Payment plan:* installment.

Financial Aid Of all full-time matriculated undergraduates who enrolled in 2003, 5,873 applied for aid, 4,184 were judged to have need. In 2003, 704 non-need-based awards were made. *Average financial aid package:* $5637. *Average need-based loan:* $3467. *Average need-based gift aid:* $3507. *Average non-need-based aid:* $1626. *Average indebtedness upon graduation:* $14,047. *Financial aid deadline:* 5/31.

Applying *Options:* common application, early admission. *Application fee:* $35. *Required:* high school transcript, minimum 2.0 GPA. *Application deadline:* 8/1 (freshmen), rolling (transfers). *Notification:* continuous (freshmen), continuous (transfers).

Admissions Contact Ms. Joey Chandler, Director of Admissions and Recruitment, Sam Houston State University, PO Box 2418, Huntsville, TX 77341. *Phone:* 936-294-1828. *Fax:* 936-294-3758.

SCHREINER UNIVERSITY
Kerrville, Texas

- **Independent Presbyterian** comprehensive, founded 1923
- **Calendar** semesters
- **Degrees** certificates, associate, bachelor's, master's, and postbachelor's certificates
- **Small-town** 175-acre campus with easy access to San Antonio and Austin
- **Endowment** $33.9 million
- **Coed,** 732 undergraduate students, 90% full-time, 58% women, 42% men
- **Moderately difficult** entrance level, 63% of applicants were admitted

Undergraduates 662 full-time, 70 part-time. 2% are from out of state, 2% African American, 0.8% Asian American or Pacific Islander, 16% Hispanic American, 1% Native American, 1% international, 13% transferred in, 49% live on campus. *Retention:* 63% of 2002 full-time freshmen returned.

Freshmen *Admission:* 570 applied, 359 admitted, 173 enrolled. *Average high school GPA:* 3.48. *Test scores:* SAT verbal scores over 500: 45%; SAT math scores over 500: 48%; ACT scores over 18: 74%; SAT verbal scores over 600: 17%; SAT math scores over 600: 9%; ACT scores over 24: 17%; SAT verbal scores over 700: 3%; ACT scores over 30: 2%.

Faculty *Total:* 67, 73% full-time, 54% with terminal degrees. *Student/faculty ratio:* 13:1.

Majors Accounting; biochemistry; biology/biological sciences; business/commerce; chemistry; dramatic/theatre arts; early childhood education; education; education (specific subject areas) related; elementary education; engineering; English; English/language arts teacher education; graphic design; history; history teacher education; humanities; kinesiology and exercise science; legal studies; liberal arts and sciences/liberal studies; literature; management information systems; mathematics; mathematics teacher education; music; physical education teaching and coaching; political science and government; pre-dentistry studies; pre-engineering; pre-law studies; pre-medical studies; psychology; religious studies.

Academic Programs *Special study options:* academic remediation for entering students, accelerated degree program, advanced placement credit, cooperative education, distance learning, double majors, English as a second language, freshman honors college, honors programs, independent study, internships, part-time degree program, services for LD students, student-designed majors, study abroad, summer session for credit. *Unusual degree programs:* 3-2 engineering with University of Texas at Austin, Texas A&M University.

Library W. M. Logan Library with 69,873 titles, 225 serial subscriptions, 477 audiovisual materials, an OPAC, a Web page.

Computers on Campus 106 computers available on campus for general student use. A campuswide network can be accessed from student residence rooms and from off campus. Internet access, at least one staffed computer lab available.

Student Life *Housing:* on-campus residence required through junior year. *Options:* coed, men-only, disabled students. Campus housing is university owned. Freshman campus housing is guaranteed. *Activities and organizations:* drama/theater group, student-run newspaper, choral group, Student Senate, Back on Campus Again (non-traditional student organization), Campus Ministry, international club, Best Buddies, national fraternities, national sororities. *Campus security:* 24-hour emergency response devices and patrols, late-night transport/escort service. *Student services:* health clinic, personal/psychological counseling.

Athletics Member NCAA. All Division III. *Intercollegiate sports:* baseball M, basketball M/W, cheerleading W, golf M/W, soccer M/W, softball W, tennis M/W, volleyball W. *Intramural sports:* basketball M/W, cross-country running M(c)/W(c), football M/W, golf M/W, racquetball M/W, rock climbing M/W, skiing (downhill) M/W, soccer M/W, table tennis M/W, tennis M/W, ultimate Frisbee M/W, volleyball M/W.

Standardized Tests *Required:* SAT I or ACT (for admission).

Costs (2003–04) *Comprehensive fee:* $20,440 includes full-time tuition ($13,240), mandatory fees ($400), and room and board ($6800). Part-time tuition: $565 per credit. *College room only:* $3500. Room and board charges vary according to board plan and housing facility. *Payment plan:* installment. *Waivers:* employees or children of employees.

Financial Aid Of all full-time matriculated undergraduates who enrolled in 2003, 527 applied for aid, 479 were judged to have need, 68 had their need fully met. 110 Federal Work-Study jobs (averaging $897). 170 state and other part-time jobs (averaging $638). In 2003, 91 non-need-based awards were made. *Average percent of need met:* 71%. *Average financial aid package:* $12,423. *Average need-based loan:* $3036. *Average need-based gift aid:* $9666. *Average non-need-based aid:* $8421. *Average indebtedness upon graduation:* $19,208. *Financial aid deadline:* 8/1.

Applying *Options:* common application, deferred entrance. *Application fee:* $25. *Required:* high school transcript. *Required for some:* essay or personal statement, 1 letter of recommendation. *Recommended:* essay or personal statement, minimum 2.0 GPA, interview. *Application deadlines:* 8/1 (freshmen), 8/1 (transfers). *Notification:* continuous (freshmen), continuous (transfers).

Admissions Contact Ms. Peg Layton, Dean of Admission and Financial Aid, Schreiner University, 2100 Memorial Boulevard, Kerrville, TX 78028. *Phone:* 830-792-7277. *Toll-free phone:* 800-343-4919. *Fax:* 830-792-7226. *E-mail:* admissions@schreiner.edu.

SOUTHERN METHODIST UNIVERSITY
Dallas, Texas

- **Independent** university, founded 1911, affiliated with United Methodist Church
- **Calendar** semesters
- **Degrees** bachelor's, master's, doctoral, first professional, and postbachelor's certificates
- **Suburban** 165-acre campus
- **Endowment** $807.6 million
- **Coed,** 6,299 undergraduate students, 94% full-time, 55% women, 45% men
- **Moderately difficult** entrance level, 65% of applicants were admitted

Undergraduates 5,918 full-time, 381 part-time. Students come from 45 states and territories, 105 other countries, 36% are from out of state, 6% African American, 6% Asian American or Pacific Islander, 9% Hispanic American, 0.7% Native American, 5% international, 5% transferred in, 45% live on campus. *Retention:* 87% of 2002 full-time freshmen returned.

Freshmen *Admission:* 6,293 applied, 4,076 admitted, 1,383 enrolled. *Average high school GPA:* 3.47. *Test scores:* SAT verbal scores over 500: 92%; SAT math scores over 500: 94%; ACT scores over 18: 99%; SAT verbal scores over 600: 48%; SAT math scores over 600: 57%; ACT scores over 24: 82%; SAT verbal scores over 700: 8%; SAT math scores over 700: 11%; ACT scores over 30: 15%.

Faculty *Total:* 887, 64% full-time. *Student/faculty ratio:* 11:1.

Majors Accounting; advertising; African-American/Black studies; anthropology; applied economics; art history, criticism and conservation; biochemistry; biology/biological sciences; broadcast journalism; business administration and management; chemistry; computer engineering; computer science; creative writing; dance; dramatic/theatre arts; econometrics and quantitative economics; economics; electrical, electronics and communications engineering; English; environmental/environmental health engineering; environmental studies; European studies; film/cinema studies; finance; fine/studio arts; foreign languages and literatures; French; geology/earth science; geophysics and seismology; German; Hispanic-American, Puerto Rican, and Mexican-American/Chicano studies; history; humanities; international relations and affairs; journalism; Latin American studies; management information systems; management science; marketing/marketing management; mathematics; mechanical engineering; medieval and Renaissance studies; music; music performance; music teacher education; music theory and composition; music therapy; organizational behavior; philosophy; physics; piano and organ; political science and government; psychology; public policy analysis; public relations/image management; radio and television; real estate; religious studies; Russian; Russian studies; social sciences; sociology; Spanish; statistics.

Academic Programs *Special study options:* academic remediation for entering students, accelerated degree program, adult/continuing education programs, advanced placement credit, distance learning, double majors, English as a second language, honors programs, independent study, internships, part-time degree program, services for LD students, student-designed majors, study abroad, summer session for credit. *ROTC:* Army (b), Air Force (c).

Library Central University Library plus 7 others with 2.6 million titles, 11,727 serial subscriptions, 39,444 audiovisual materials, an OPAC, a Web page.

Computers on Campus 409 computers available on campus for general student use. A campuswide network can be accessed from student residence rooms and from off campus. At least one staffed computer lab available.

Student Life *Housing:* on-campus residence required for freshman year. *Options:* coed, disabled students. *Activities and organizations:* drama/theater group, student-run newspaper, radio station, choral group, marching band, Program Council, Student Senate, Student Foundation, Residence Hall Association, United Methodist Campus Ministries, national fraternities, national sororities. *Campus security:* 24-hour emergency response devices and patrols, late-night transport/escort service, controlled dormitory access. *Student services:* health clinic, personal/psychological counseling, women's center.

Athletics Member NCAA. All Division I except football (Division I-A). *Intercollegiate sports:* baseball M(c), basketball M(s)/W(s), crew M(c)/W(s), cross-country running M(s)/W(s), fencing M(c)/W(c), golf M(s)/W(s), ice hockey M(c), lacrosse M(c)/W(c), rugby M(c), sailing M(c)/W(c), soccer M(s)/W(s), swimming M(s)/W(s), tennis M(s)/W(s), track and field M(s)/W(s), volleyball M(c)/W(s), wrestling M(c). *Intramural sports:* badminton M/W, basketball M/W, bowling M/W, football M/W, golf M/W, racquetball M/W, soccer M/W, softball M/W, swimming M/W, tennis M/W, track and field M/W, volleyball M/W, weight lifting M/W.

Standardized Tests *Required:* SAT I or ACT (for admission). *Required for some:* SAT II: Subject Tests (for admission).

Costs (2004–05) *Comprehensive fee:* $34,210 includes full-time tuition ($22,496), mandatory fees ($2862), and room and board ($8852). Part-time tuition and fees vary according to class time and course load. *Room and board:* Room and board charges vary according to board plan and housing facility. *Payment plan:* installment. *Waivers:* employees or children of employees.

Financial Aid Of all full-time matriculated undergraduates who enrolled in 2003, 2,688 applied for aid, 2,274 were judged to have need, 1,011 had their need fully met. In 2003, 1695 non-need-based awards were made. *Average percent of need met:* 93%. *Average financial aid package:* $22,358. *Average need-based loan:* $3581. *Average need-based gift aid:* $13,542. *Average non-need-based aid:* $5780. *Average indebtedness upon graduation:* $20,079.

Applying *Options:* common application, early admission, early action, deferred entrance. *Application fee:* $50. *Required:* essay or personal statement, high school transcript, 1 letter of recommendation. *Application deadlines:* 1/15 (freshmen), 7/1 (transfers). *Notification:* continuous (freshmen), 12/31 (early action), continuous (transfers).

Admissions Contact Mr. Ron W. Moss, Director of Admission and Enrollment Management, Southern Methodist University, PO Box 750181, Dallas, TX 75275-0181. *Phone:* 214-768-2058. *Toll-free phone:* 800-323-0672. *Fax:* 214-768-0103. *E-mail:* enrol_serv@mail.smu.edu.

■ *See page 2410 for a narrative description.*

SOUTHWESTERN ADVENTIST UNIVERSITY
Keene, Texas

Admissions Contact Mrs. Sylvia Peterson, Admissions Counselor, Southwestern Adventist University, PO Box 567, Keene, TX 76059. *Phone:* 817-645-3921 Ext. 294. *Toll-free phone:* 800-433-2240. *Fax:* 817-556-4744. *E-mail:* sylviap@swau.edu.

SOUTHWESTERN ASSEMBLIES OF GOD UNIVERSITY
Waxahachie, Texas

- **Independent** comprehensive, founded 1927, affiliated with Assemblies of God
- **Calendar** semesters
- **Degrees** associate, bachelor's, and master's
- **Small-town** 70-acre campus with easy access to Dallas
- **Endowment** $853,777
- **Coed**
- **Noncompetitive** entrance level

Faculty *Student/faculty ratio:* 20:1.

Student Life *Campus security:* student patrols, late-night transport/escort service.

Athletics Member NAIA, NCCAA.

Standardized Tests *Required:* SAT I or ACT (for admission).

Costs (2003–04) *Comprehensive fee:* $12,900 includes full-time tuition ($7800), mandatory fees ($630), and room and board ($4470). *College room only:* $3000.

Financial Aid Of all full-time matriculated undergraduates who enrolled in 2000, 1,116 applied for aid, 1,002 were judged to have need, 110 had their need fully met. 178 Federal Work-Study jobs, 7 state and other part-time jobs (averaging $890). In 2000, 316. *Average percent of need met:* 64. *Average financial aid package:* $6728. *Average need-based loan:* $3177. *Average need-based gift aid:* $3511. *Average indebtedness upon graduation:* $13,938. *Financial aid deadline:* 7/1.

Applying *Options:* early admission, deferred entrance. *Application fee:* $35. *Required:* essay or personal statement, high school transcript, 2 letters of recommendation, medical history, evidence of approved Christian character.

Admissions Contact Mr. Pat Thompson, Admissions Counselor, Southwestern Assemblies of God University, 1200 Sycamore Street, Waxahachie, TX 75165-2397. *Phone:* 972-937-4010. *Toll-free phone:* 888-937-7248. *Fax:* 972-923-0006. *E-mail:* info@sagu.edu.

SOUTHWESTERN CHRISTIAN COLLEGE
Terrell, Texas

- **Independent** 4-year, founded 1949, affiliated with Church of Christ
- **Calendar** semesters
- **Degrees** associate and bachelor's
- **Small-town** 25-acre campus with easy access to Dallas–Fort Worth
- **Coed**
- **Noncompetitive** entrance level

Student Life *Campus security:* 24-hour patrols.

Athletics Member NJCAA.

Standardized Tests *Recommended:* SAT I or ACT (for placement).

Costs (2003–04) *Comprehensive fee:* $8624 includes full-time tuition ($4350), mandatory fees ($984), and room and board ($3290). *College room only:* $1450.

Applying *Options:* common application, early admission, deferred entrance. *Application fee:* $10. *Required:* high school transcript, 1 letter of recommendation.

Admissions Contact Admissions Department, Southwestern Christian College, Box 10, 200 Bowser Street, Terrell, TX 75160. *Phone:* 214-524-3341.

SOUTHWESTERN UNIVERSITY
Georgetown, Texas

- **Independent Methodist** 4-year, founded 1840
- **Calendar** semesters
- **Degree** bachelor's
- **Suburban** 700-acre campus with easy access to Austin
- **Endowment** $265.4 million
- **Coed**, 1,265 undergraduate students, 98% full-time, 58% women, 42% men
- **Very difficult** entrance level, 63% of applicants were admitted

Undergraduates 1,237 full-time, 28 part-time. Students come from 33 states and territories, 9% are from out of state, 3% African American, 3% Asian American or Pacific Islander, 14% Hispanic American, 0.6% Native American, 3% transferred in, 82% live on campus. *Retention:* 86% of 2002 full-time freshmen returned.

Freshmen *Admission:* 1,765 applied, 1,115 admitted, 343 enrolled. *Average high school GPA:* 3.5. *Test scores:* SAT verbal scores over 500: 96%; SAT math scores over 500: 96%; ACT scores over 18: 99%; SAT verbal scores over 600: 64%; SAT math scores over 600: 64%; ACT scores over 24: 76%; SAT verbal scores over 700: 17%; SAT math scores over 700: 12%; ACT scores over 30: 19%.

Faculty *Total:* 165, 69% full-time, 75% with terminal degrees. *Student/faculty ratio:* 10:1.

Majors Accounting; American studies; animal sciences; art; art history, criticism and conservation; art teacher education; biology/biological sciences; business administration and management; chemistry; computer science; dramatic/theatre arts; economics; English; experimental psychology; fine/studio arts; French; German; history; international relations and affairs; literature; mass communication/media; mathematics; modern languages; music; music history, literature, and theory; music teacher education; philosophy; physical education teaching and coaching; physics; piano and organ; political science and government; psychology; religious/sacred music; religious studies; social sciences; sociology; Spanish; women's studies.

Academic Programs *Special study options:* accelerated degree program, advanced placement credit, double majors, freshman honors college, honors programs, independent study, internships, off-campus study, part-time degree program, student-designed majors, study abroad, summer session for credit. *Unusual degree programs:* 3-2 engineering with Washington University in St. Louis, Arizona State University, Texas A&M University.

Library A. Frank Smith Jr. Library Center with 312,982 titles, 1,469 serial subscriptions, 11,396 audiovisual materials, an OPAC, a Web page.

Computers on Campus 223 computers available on campus for general student use. A campuswide network can be accessed from student residence rooms and from off campus that provide access to course schedule, course catalog. Internet access, at least one staffed computer lab available.

Student Life *Housing:* on-campus residence required for freshman year. *Options:* coed, men-only, women-only. Campus housing is university owned. Freshman campus housing is guaranteed. *Activities and organizations:* drama/theater group, student-run newspaper, television station, choral group, Alpha Phi Omega, international club, Latinos Unidos, national fraternities, national sororities. *Campus security:* 24-hour emergency response devices and patrols, student patrols, late-night transport/escort service, controlled dormitory access. *Student services:* health clinic, personal/psychological counseling, women's center.

Athletics Member NCAA. All Division III. *Intercollegiate sports:* baseball M, basketball M/W, cross-country running M/W, golf M/W, soccer M/W, swimming M/W, tennis M/W, volleyball W. *Intramural sports:* basketball M/W, bowling M/W, cheerleading M/W, football M, golf M/W, racquetball M/W, rock climbing M(c)/W(c), soccer M/W, softball M, swimming M/W, table tennis M, tennis M/W, ultimate Frisbee M(c)/W(c), volleyball W.

Standardized Tests *Required:* SAT I or ACT (for admission).

Costs (2003–04) *Comprehensive fee:* $25,410 includes full-time tuition ($18,870) and room and board ($6540). Part-time tuition: $790 per semester hour. *College room only:* $3240. Room and board charges vary according to board plan, housing facility, and student level. *Payment plans:* installment, deferred payment. *Waivers:* employees or children of employees.

Financial Aid Of all full-time matriculated undergraduates who enrolled in 2003, 776 applied for aid, 630 were judged to have need, 630 had their need fully met. 185 Federal Work-Study jobs (averaging $1788). 267 state and other part-time jobs (averaging $1863). In 2003, 312 non-need-based awards were made. *Average percent of need met:* 98%. *Average financial aid package:* $15,038. *Average need-based loan:* $4216. *Average need-based gift aid:* $10,534. *Average non-need-based aid:* $6591. *Average indebtedness upon graduation:* $17,505. *Financial aid deadline:* 3/1.

Applying *Options:* common application, electronic application, early admission, early decision, deferred entrance. *Application fee:* $40. *Required:* essay or personal statement, high school transcript, 1 letter of recommendation. *Required for some:* interview. *Recommended:* interview. *Application deadlines:* 2/15 (freshmen), 4/1 (transfers). *Early decision:* 11/1. *Notification:* 3/31 (freshmen), 12/1 (early decision), continuous (transfers).

Admissions Contact Mr. John W. Lind, Vice President for Enrollment Management, Southwestern University, 1001 East University Avenue, Georgetown, TX 78626. *Phone:* 512-863-1200. *Toll-free phone:* 800-252-3166. *Fax:* 512-863-9601. *E-mail:* admission@southwestern.edu.

STEPHEN F. AUSTIN STATE UNIVERSITY
Nacogdoches, Texas

- **State-supported** comprehensive, founded 1923
- **Calendar** semesters
- **Degrees** bachelor's, master's, and doctoral
- **Small-town** 400-acre campus
- **Coed**
- **Moderately difficult** entrance level

Faculty *Student/faculty ratio:* 19:1.

Student Life *Campus security:* 24-hour emergency response devices and patrols, student patrols, late-night transport/escort service, controlled dormitory access.

Athletics Member NCAA. All Division I except football (Division I-AA).

Standardized Tests *Required:* SAT I or ACT (for admission).

Costs (2003–04) *Tuition:* state resident $2639 full-time; nonresident $8307 full-time. *Room and board:* $4766.

Financial Aid Of all full-time matriculated undergraduates who enrolled in 2002, 5,024 applied for aid, 3,776 were judged to have need, 854 had their need fully met. 534 Federal Work-Study jobs (averaging $1398). 47 state and other part-time jobs (averaging $1128). In 2002, 305. *Average percent of need met:* 82. *Average financial aid package:* $4219. *Average need-based loan:* $1907. *Average need-based gift aid:* $1896. *Average non-need-based aid:* $1989. *Average indebtedness upon graduation:* $11,070. *Financial aid deadline:* 4/15.

Applying *Options:* common application. *Application fee:* $25. *Required:* high school transcript.

Admissions Contact Ms. Beth Smith, Assistant Director of Admissions, Stephen F. Austin State University, PO Box 13051, SFA Station, Nacogdoches, TX 75962. *Phone:* 936-468-2504. *Toll-free phone:* 800-731-2902. *Fax:* 936-468-3849. *E-mail:* admissions@sfasu.edu.

SUL ROSS STATE UNIVERSITY
Alpine, Texas

- **State-supported** comprehensive, founded 1920, part of Texas State University System
- **Calendar** semesters
- **Degrees** certificates, associate, bachelor's, and master's
- **Small-town** 640-acre campus
- **Endowment** $5.9 million
- **Coed**
- **Noncompetitive** entrance level

Faculty *Student/faculty ratio:* 13:1.

Student Life *Campus security:* 24-hour patrols, late-night transport/escort service.

Athletics Member NCAA. All Division III.

Standardized Tests *Required:* SAT I or ACT (for admission).

Costs (2003–04) *Tuition:* state resident $2280 full-time; nonresident $8580 full-time. *Required fees:* $1122 full-time. *Room and board:* $3850; room only: $1700.

Applying *Options:* deferred entrance. *Application fee:* $25. *Required:* high school transcript. *Recommended:* interview.

Admissions Contact Dr. Nadine Jenkins, Vice President for Enrollment Management and Student services, Sul Ross State University, Box C-2, Alpine, TX 79832. *Phone:* 915-837-8050. *Toll-free phone:* 888-722-7778. *Fax:* 915-837-8431. *E-mail:* rcullins@sulross.edu.

TARLETON STATE UNIVERSITY

Stephenville, Texas

- **State-supported** comprehensive, founded 1899, part of Texas A&M University System
- **Calendar** semesters
- **Degrees** bachelor's, master's, and doctoral
- **Small-town** 125-acre campus with easy access to Fort Worth
- **Endowment** $5.4 million
- **Coed,** 7,429 undergraduate students, 77% full-time, 56% women, 44% men
- **Moderately difficult** entrance level, 90% of applicants were admitted

Undergraduates 5,726 full-time, 1,703 part-time. Students come from 49 states and territories, 26 other countries, 3% are from out of state, 8% African American, 0.7% Asian American or Pacific Islander, 7% Hispanic American, 1% Native American, 0.5% international, 13% transferred in, 19% live on campus. *Retention:* 61% of 2002 full-time freshmen returned.

Freshmen *Admission:* 3,181 applied, 2,867 admitted, 1,313 enrolled. *Test scores:* SAT verbal scores over 500: 39%; SAT math scores over 500: 40%; ACT scores over 18: 73%; SAT verbal scores over 600: 7%; SAT math scores over 600: 6%; ACT scores over 24: 12%; SAT verbal scores over 700: 1%; SAT math scores over 700: 1%; ACT scores over 30: 1%.

Faculty *Total:* 471, 61% full-time, 46% with terminal degrees. *Student/faculty ratio:* 18:1.

Majors Accounting; agricultural and domestic animals services related; agricultural economics; agricultural production related; agricultural teacher education; agriculture and agriculture operations related; animal/livestock husbandry and production; art; aviation/airway management; biology/biological sciences; business administration and management; business/commerce; chemistry; clinical laboratory science/medical technology; computer and information sciences; counselor education/school counseling and guidance; criminal justice/safety; curriculum and instruction; dramatic/theatre arts; economics; education; educational leadership and administration; education (multiple levels); engineering physics; English; English as a second/foreign language (teaching); family and consumer sciences/human sciences; farm and ranch management; finance; geology/earth science; history; human nutrition; human resources management; hydrology and water resources science; industrial arts; industrial production technologies related; interdisciplinary studies; international agriculture; international business/trade/commerce; kinesiology and exercise science; liberal arts and sciences/liberal studies; management information systems; manufacturing technology; mathematics; multi-/interdisciplinary studies related; music; music teacher education; nursing (registered nurse training); office management; ornamental horticulture; physical education teaching and coaching; physical therapy; physics; political science and government; pre-dentistry studies; pre-medical studies; pre-pharmacy studies; pre-veterinary studies; psychology; range science and management; science teacher education; secondary education; social work; sociology; Spanish; speech and rhetoric; technical and business writing; zoology/animal biology.

Academic Programs *Special study options:* academic remediation for entering students, accelerated degree program, adult/continuing education programs, advanced placement credit, cooperative education, distance learning, double majors, honors programs, internships, off-campus study, part-time degree program, services for LD students, study abroad, summer session for credit. *ROTC:* Army (b).

Library Dick Smith Library plus 1 other with 293,149 titles, 3,000 serial subscriptions, 7,954 audiovisual materials, an OPAC, a Web page.

Computers on Campus 600 computers available on campus for general student use. A campuswide network can be accessed from student residence rooms and from off campus. Internet access, online (class) registration, at least one staffed computer lab available.

Student Life *Housing:* on-campus residence required through sophomore year. *Options:* coed, men-only, women-only. Campus housing is university owned. Freshman campus housing is guaranteed. *Activities and organizations:* drama/theater group, student-run newspaper, radio station, choral group, marching band, Student Government Association, Student Programming Association, Plowboys Association, Student Organizational Forum, Tarleton Association of Student Leaders, national fraternities, national sororities. *Campus security:* 24-hour emergency response devices and patrols, student patrols, late-night transport/escort service, controlled dormitory access. *Student services:* health clinic, personal/psychological counseling, legal services.

Athletics Member NCAA. All Division II. *Intercollegiate sports:* baseball M(s), basketball M(s)/W(s), cross-country running M/W, football M(s), golf W, softball W(s), tennis W, track and field M(s)/W(s), volleyball W(s). *Intramural sports:* archery M/W, basketball M/W, football M/W, golf M/W, racquetball M/W, soccer M/W, softball M/W, table tennis M/W, tennis M/W, volleyball M/W.

Standardized Tests *Required:* SAT I or ACT (for admission).

Costs (2003–04) *Tuition:* state resident $2670 full-time; nonresident $9750 full-time. Full-time tuition and fees vary according to course load. Part-time tuition and fees vary according to course load. *Required fees:* $835 full-time. *Room and board:* $4804. Room and board charges vary according to board plan and housing facility. *Payment plan:* installment. *Waivers:* senior citizens and employees or children of employees.

Financial Aid Of all full-time matriculated undergraduates who enrolled in 2003, 3,426 applied for aid, 2,702 were judged to have need, 2,269 had their need fully met. 73 Federal Work-Study jobs, 10 state and other part-time jobs (averaging $3300). *Average percent of need met:* 61%. *Average financial aid package:* $6323. *Average need-based loan:* $3258. *Average need-based gift aid:* $2461. *Average indebtedness upon graduation:* $15,522.

Applying *Options:* electronic application, early admission, deferred entrance. *Application fee:* $25. *Required:* high school transcript. *Required for some:* interview. *Application deadline:* 4/28 (freshmen).

Admissions Contact Ms. Denise Groves, Director of Undergraduate Admissions, Tarleton State University, Box T-0030, Tarleton Station, Stephenville, TX 76402. *Phone:* 254-968-9125. *Toll-free phone:* 800-687-8236. *Fax:* 254-968-9951. *E-mail:* uadm@tarleton.edu.

TEXAS A&M INTERNATIONAL UNIVERSITY

Laredo, Texas

- **State-supported** comprehensive, founded 1969, part of Texas A&M University System
- **Calendar** semesters
- **Degrees** bachelor's, master's, and doctoral
- **Urban** 300-acre campus
- **Endowment** $4.4 million
- **Coed,** 3,116 undergraduate students, 67% full-time, 64% women, 36% men
- **Moderately difficult** entrance level, 52% of applicants were admitted

Undergraduates 2,084 full-time, 1,032 part-time. Students come from 30 states and territories, 9 other countries, 1% are from out of state, 0.4% African American, 0.5% Asian American or Pacific Islander, 92% Hispanic American, 0.1% Native American, 4% international, 8% transferred in. *Retention:* 65% of 2002 full-time freshmen returned.

Freshmen *Admission:* 1,494 applied, 780 admitted, 497 enrolled. *Average high school GPA:* 3.00. *Test scores:* SAT verbal scores over 500: 24%; SAT math scores over 500: 27%; ACT scores over 18: 52%; SAT verbal scores over 600: 4%; SAT math scores over 600: 4%; ACT scores over 24: 4%; SAT verbal scores over 700: 1%; SAT math scores over 700: 1%.

Faculty *Total:* 252, 60% full-time, 55% with terminal degrees. *Student/faculty ratio:* 13:1.

Majors Accounting; bilingual and multilingual education; biology/biological sciences; biology teacher education; business administration and management; business/managerial economics; chemistry; communication/speech communication and rhetoric; criminal justice/safety; English; English/language arts teacher education; finance; health and physical education; history; history teacher education; information science/studies; kindergarten/preschool education; marketing/marketing management; mathematics; mathematics teacher education; nursing (registered nurse training); perioperative/operating room and surgical nursing; physical education teaching and coaching; physical sciences; political science and government; psychology; reading teacher education; science teacher education; social sciences; social studies teacher education; sociology; Spanish; Spanish language teacher education; special education.

Academic Programs *Special study options:* academic remediation for entering students, advanced placement credit, English as a second language, honors programs, internships, part-time degree program, services for LD students, study abroad, summer session for credit.

Library Sue and Radcliff Killam Library with 166,951 titles, 8,492 serial subscriptions, 1,040 audiovisual materials, an OPAC, a Web page.

Computers on Campus 200 computers available on campus for general student use. A campuswide network can be accessed from off campus. At least one staffed computer lab available.

Texas A&M International University (continued)

Student Life *Housing options:* Campus housing is provided by a third party. Freshman applicants given priority for college housing. *Activities and organizations:* student-run newspaper, choral group, TAMIU Ambassadors, Electronic Commerce Association, Rainbow Education Association of Laredo, Student Finance Society, psychology club. *Campus security:* 24-hour emergency response devices and patrols. *Student services:* health clinic, personal/psychological counseling.

Athletics Member NAIA. *Intercollegiate sports:* basketball M/W, golf M/W, soccer M/W, volleyball W.

Standardized Tests *Required:* SAT I or ACT (for admission).

Costs (2004–05) *Tuition:* state resident $2820 full-time, $90 per credit part-time; nonresident $10,560 full-time, $352 per credit part-time. *Required fees:* $1013 full-time, $35 per credit part-time, $53 per term part-time. *Room and board:* $5240; room only: $3400.

Financial Aid Of all full-time matriculated undergraduates who enrolled in 2002, 1,910 applied for aid, 1,758 were judged to have need, 467 had their need fully met. 89 Federal Work-Study jobs (averaging $1492). 7 state and other part-time jobs (averaging $1365). In 2002, 78 non-need-based awards were made. *Average percent of need met:* 84%. *Average financial aid package:* $7593. *Average need-based loan:* $3168. *Average need-based gift aid:* $5221. *Average non-need-based aid:* $3257. *Average indebtedness upon graduation:* $9872.

Applying *Options:* common application, electronic application, early admission, deferred entrance. *Required:* high school transcript. *Application deadlines:* 7/1 (freshmen), 7/1 (transfers). *Notification:* 7/15 (freshmen), 7/15 (transfers).

Admissions Contact Ms. Veronica Gonzalez, Director of Enrollment Management and School Relations, Texas A&M International University, 5201 University Boulevard, Laredo, TX 78041-1900. *Phone:* 956-326-2270. *Toll-free phone:* 888-489-2648. *Fax:* 956-326-2199. *E-mail:* enroll@tamiu.edu.

TEXAS A&M UNIVERSITY
College Station, Texas

- **State-supported** university, founded 1876, part of Texas A&M University System
- **Calendar** semesters
- **Degrees** bachelor's, master's, doctoral, first professional, and postbachelor's certificates
- **Suburban** 5200-acre campus with easy access to Houston
- **Endowment** $3.8 billion
- **Coed,** 36,066 undergraduate students, 91% full-time, 49% women, 51% men
- **Moderately difficult** entrance level, 67% of applicants were admitted

Undergraduates 32,818 full-time, 3,248 part-time. Students come from 52 states and territories, 111 other countries, 3% are from out of state, 2% African American, 3% Asian American or Pacific Islander, 9% Hispanic American, 0.5% Native American, 1% international, 5% transferred in, 27% live on campus. *Retention:* 89% of 2002 full-time freshmen returned.

Freshmen *Admission:* 17,250 applied, 11,639 admitted, 6,726 enrolled. *Test scores:* SAT verbal scores over 500: 83%; SAT math scores over 500: 92%; ACT scores over 18: 98%; SAT verbal scores over 600: 43%; SAT math scores over 600: 58%; ACT scores over 24: 67%; SAT verbal scores over 700: 8%; SAT math scores over 700: 17%; ACT scores over 30: 18%.

Faculty *Total:* 2,276, 84% full-time, 85% with terminal degrees. *Student/faculty ratio:* 21:1.

Majors Accounting; aerospace, aeronautical and astronautical engineering; agribusiness; agricultural and food products processing; agricultural animal breeding; agricultural/biological engineering and bioengineering; agricultural business and management; agricultural economics; agricultural/farm supplies retailing and wholesaling; agricultural production; agriculture; agronomy and crop science; American studies; animal/livestock husbandry and production; animal sciences; anthropology; applied horticulture; applied mathematics; aquaculture; architecture; atmospheric sciences and meteorology; biochemistry; biology/biological sciences; biomedical/medical engineering; biomedical sciences; botany/plant biology; business administration and management; cartography; cell and molecular biology; chemical engineering; chemistry; civil engineering; community health services counseling; computer engineering; computer science; construction engineering technology; curriculum and instruction; dairy science; digital communication and media/multimedia; dramatic/theatre arts; ecology; economics; electrical, electronic and communications engineering technology; electrical, electronics and communications engineering; engineering technology; English; entomology; environmental design/architecture; environmental science; environmental studies; farm and ranch management; finance; fishing and fisheries sciences and management; food science; foods, nutrition, and wellness; forest/forest resources management; forestry; French; geography; geological and earth sciences/geosciences related; geology/earth science; geophysics and seismology; German; health and physical education; history; horticultural science; industrial engineering; interdisciplinary studies; international/global studies; journalism; landscape architecture; management science; manufacturing technology; marketing/marketing management; mathematics; mechanical engineering; mechanical engineering/mechanical technology; microbiology; molecular genetics; multi-/interdisciplinary studies related; museum studies; music; natural resources/conservation; nuclear engineering; ocean engineering; ornamental horticulture; parks, recreation and leisure; parks, recreation and leisure facilities management; petroleum engineering; philosophy; physics; plant protection and integrated pest management; political science and government; poultry science; pre-veterinary studies; psychology; public relations, advertising, and applied communication related; range science and management; Russian; sales, distribution and marketing; sociology; Spanish; speech and rhetoric; tourism and travel services management; urban forestry; wildlife and wildlands science and management; zoology/animal biology.

Academic Programs *Special study options:* academic remediation for entering students, accelerated degree program, advanced placement credit, cooperative education, distance learning, double majors, English as a second language, honors programs, independent study, internships, off-campus study, part-time degree program, services for LD students, study abroad, summer session for credit. *ROTC:* Army (b), Navy (b), Air Force (b).

Library Sterling C. Evans Library plus 4 others with 4.4 million titles, 30,459 serial subscriptions, 318,876 audiovisual materials, an OPAC, a Web page.

Computers on Campus 1500 computers available on campus for general student use. A campuswide network can be accessed from student residence rooms and from off campus. Internet access, online (class) registration, at least one staffed computer lab available.

Student Life *Housing options:* coed, men-only, women-only, disabled students. Campus housing is university owned. *Activities and organizations:* drama/theater group, student-run newspaper, radio and television station, choral group, marching band, Memorial Student Center, Corps of Cadets, Greek organizations, Fish Camp, student government, national fraternities, national sororities. *Campus security:* 24-hour emergency response devices and patrols, late-night transport/escort service, controlled dormitory access, student escorts. *Student services:* health clinic, personal/psychological counseling, women's center, legal services.

Athletics Member NCAA. All Division I except football (Division I-A). *Intercollegiate sports:* archery W(s), baseball M(s), basketball M(s)/W(s), cross-country running M(s)/W(s), equestrian sports W(s), golf M(s)/W(s), soccer W(s), softball W(s), swimming M(s)/W(s), tennis M(s)/W(s), track and field M(s)/W(s), volleyball W(s). *Intramural sports:* archery M/W, badminton M/W, basketball M/W, bowling M/W, cross-country running M/W, fencing M(c)/W(c), field hockey M(c)/W(c), football M/W, golf M/W, gymnastics M(c)/W(c), lacrosse M(c)/W(c), racquetball M(c)/W(c), riflery M/W, rugby M(c)/W(c), sailing M(c)/W(c), soccer M/W, softball M/W, squash M/W, swimming M/W, table tennis M/W, tennis M/W, track and field M/W, ultimate Frisbee M(c)/W(c), volleyball M/W, water polo M/W, weight lifting M(c)/W(c), wrestling M(c).

Standardized Tests *Required:* SAT I or ACT (for admission).

Costs (2003–04) *Tuition:* state resident $2895 full-time, $97 per semester hour part-time; nonresident $9975 full-time, $333 per semester hour part-time. Full-time tuition and fees vary according to course load, location, and program. *Required fees:* $2156 full-time. *Room and board:* $6030; room only: $3192. Room and board charges vary according to board plan and housing facility. *Payment plan:* installment.

Financial Aid Of all full-time matriculated undergraduates who enrolled in 2002, 16,022 applied for aid, 10,327 were judged to have need, 4,608 had their need fully met. 700 Federal Work-Study jobs (averaging $2324). 4,500 state and other part-time jobs (averaging $2599). In 2002, 2188 non-need-based awards were made. *Average percent of need met:* 82%. *Average financial aid package:* $6664. *Average need-based loan:* $3315. *Average need-based gift aid:* $4842. *Average non-need-based aid:* $2943. *Average indebtedness upon graduation:* $15,670.

Applying *Options:* electronic application. *Application fee:* $50. *Required:* essay or personal statement, high school transcript. *Application deadlines:* 2/1 (freshmen), 3/15 (transfers). *Notification:* continuous (freshmen), continuous (transfers).

Admissions Contact Dr. Frank Ashley, Director of Admissions, Texas A&M University, 217 John J. Koldus Building, College Station, TX 77843-1265. *Phone:* 979-845-3741. *Fax:* 979-845-8737. *E-mail:* admissions@tamu.edu.

TEXAS A&M UNIVERSITY AT GALVESTON
Galveston, Texas

- **State-supported** comprehensive, founded 1962, part of Texas A&M University System
- **Calendar** semesters
- **Degrees** bachelor's and master's

■ **Suburban** 122-acre campus with easy access to Houston
■ **Endowment** $1.5 million
■ **Coed,** 1,585 undergraduate students, 93% full-time, 46% women, 54% men
■ **Moderately difficult** entrance level, 95% of applicants were admitted

Undergraduates 1,469 full-time, 116 part-time. Students come from 50 states and territories, 8 other countries, 20% are from out of state, 3% African American, 2% Asian American or Pacific Islander, 9% Hispanic American, 0.5% Native American, 0.8% international, 18% transferred in, 54% live on campus. *Retention:* 71% of 2002 full-time freshmen returned.

Freshmen *Admission:* 1,035 applied, 984 admitted, 414 enrolled. *Test scores:* SAT verbal scores over 500: 76%; SAT math scores over 500: 80%; ACT scores over 18: 96%; SAT verbal scores over 600: 22%; SAT math scores over 600: 29%; ACT scores over 24: 48%; SAT verbal scores over 700: 3%; SAT math scores over 700: 3%; ACT scores over 30: 3%.

Faculty *Total:* 154, 38% full-time, 46% with terminal degrees. *Student/faculty ratio:* 14:1.

Majors Biological and physical sciences; business administration and management; fish/game management; marine biology and biological oceanography; marine science/merchant marine officer; maritime science; multi-/interdisciplinary studies related; natural resources/conservation; naval architecture and marine engineering; ocean engineering; oceanography (chemical and physical); transportation technology.

Academic Programs *Special study options:* academic remediation for entering students, accelerated degree program, advanced placement credit, cooperative education, double majors, English as a second language, independent study, internships, part-time degree program, study abroad, summer session for credit. *ROTC:* Navy (b).

Library Jack K. Williams Library with 61,436 titles, an OPAC, a Web page.

Computers on Campus 122 computers available on campus for general student use. A campuswide network can be accessed from student residence rooms and from off campus that provide access to grades, degree plan progress, billing statement. Internet access, online (class) registration, at least one staffed computer lab available.

Student Life *Housing:* on-campus residence required through sophomore year. *Options:* coed, men-only, women-only, disabled students. Campus housing is university owned. Freshman applicants given priority for college housing. *Activities and organizations:* drama/theater group, student-run newspaper, choral group, sail club, caving club, dive club, rowing club, Rifle Drill Team. *Campus security:* 24-hour emergency response devices and patrols. *Student services:* health clinic, personal/psychological counseling.

Athletics *Intercollegiate sports:* crew M/W, lacrosse M, sailing M/W. *Intramural sports:* basketball M/W, bowling M/W, football M/W, racquetball M/W, soccer M/W, softball M/W, swimming M/W, tennis M/W, volleyball M/W, water polo M/W.

Standardized Tests *Required:* SAT I or ACT (for admission), TASP (for admission). *Recommended:* SAT II: Subject Tests (for admission), SAT II: Writing Test (for admission).

Costs (2003–04) *Tuition:* state resident $2760 full-time, $46 per credit hour part-time; nonresident $9840 full-time, $282 per credit hour part-time. Full-time tuition and fees vary according to course load. Part-time tuition and fees vary according to course load and program. *Required fees:* $938 full-time, $439 per term part-time. *Room and board:* $4870; room only: $1958. Room and board charges vary according to board plan and housing facility. *Payment plan:* installment.

Financial Aid Of all full-time matriculated undergraduates who enrolled in 2003, 805 applied for aid, 699 were judged to have need, 252 had their need fully met. In 2003, 84 non-need-based awards were made. *Average percent of need met:* 37%. *Average financial aid package:* $9281. *Average need-based loan:* $2656. *Average need-based gift aid:* $4201. *Average non-need-based aid:* $4969. *Average indebtedness upon graduation:* $9870.

Applying *Options:* electronic application, early admission, deferred entrance. *Application fee:* $35. *Required:* essay or personal statement, high school transcript. *Required for some:* interview. *Recommended:* essay or personal statement, letters of recommendation, community involvement. *Application deadline:* rolling (freshmen), rolling (transfers). *Notification:* continuous (freshmen), continuous (transfers).

Admissions Contact Ms. Sarah Wilson, Assistant Director of Admissions and Records, Texas A&M University at Galveston, PO Box 1675, Galveston, TX 77553-1675. *Phone:* 409-740-4448. *Toll-free phone:* 87—SEAAGGIE. *Fax:* 409-740-4731. *E-mail:* seaaggie@tamug.edu.

TEXAS A&M UNIVERSITY–COMMERCE
Commerce, Texas

■ **State-supported** university, founded 1889, part of Texas A&M University System
■ **Calendar** semesters
■ **Degrees** bachelor's, master's, and doctoral
■ **Small-town** 140-acre campus with easy access to Dallas–Fort Worth
■ **Endowment** $8.6 million
■ **Coed,** 5,066 undergraduate students
■ **Moderately difficult** entrance level, 56% of applicants were admitted

Undergraduates Students come from 27 states and territories, 31 other countries, 3% are from out of state, 18% African American, 1% Asian American or Pacific Islander, 6% Hispanic American, 1% Native American, 1% international, 24% live on campus. *Retention:* 66% of 2002 full-time freshmen returned.

Freshmen *Admission:* 1,910 applied, 1,075 admitted. *Average high school GPA:* 3.35. *Test scores:* ACT scores over 18: 48%; ACT scores over 24: 13%.

Faculty *Total:* 488, 58% full-time. *Student/faculty ratio:* 17:1.

Majors Accounting; administrative assistant and secretarial science; advertising; agricultural economics; agricultural teacher education; agriculture; agronomy and crop science; animal sciences; anthropology; art; art history, criticism and conservation; art teacher education; biology/biological sciences; business administration and management; business teacher education; chemistry; commercial and advertising art; computer science; construction engineering; counselor education/school counseling and guidance; criminal justice/law enforcement administration; criminal justice/police science; dramatic/theatre arts; drawing; economics; education; elementary education; English; finance; French; geography; geology/earth science; graphic and printing equipment operation/production; health teacher education; history; human resources management; industrial arts; industrial engineering; information science/studies; interdisciplinary studies; journalism; kindergarten/preschool education; labor and industrial relations; legal administrative assistant/secretary; liberal arts and sciences/liberal studies; management information systems; marketing/marketing management; mathematics; music; music teacher education; photography; physical education teaching and coaching; physics; piano and organ; political science and government; psychology; radio and television; reading teacher education; sculpture; secondary education; social sciences; social work; sociology; Spanish; special education; trade and industrial teacher education; voice and opera.

Academic Programs *Special study options:* academic remediation for entering students, adult/continuing education programs, advanced placement credit, cooperative education, distance learning, double majors, honors programs, independent study, internships, off-campus study, part-time degree program, services for LD students, study abroad, summer session for credit. *Unusual degree programs:* 3-2 engineering with Texas A&M University.

Library Gee Library with 1.1 million titles, 1,711 serial subscriptions, 49,849 audiovisual materials, an OPAC, a Web page.

Computers on Campus 405 computers available on campus for general student use. A campuswide network can be accessed from student residence rooms and from off campus. Internet access, online (class) registration, at least one staffed computer lab available.

Student Life *Housing:* on-campus residence required for freshman year. *Options:* coed, men-only, women-only, disabled students. Campus housing is university owned. Freshman campus housing is guaranteed. *Activities and organizations:* drama/theater group, student-run newspaper, radio and television station, choral group, marching band, national fraternities, national sororities. *Campus security:* 24-hour emergency response devices and patrols, controlled dormitory access. *Student services:* health clinic, personal/psychological counseling, legal services.

Athletics Member NCAA. All Division II. *Intercollegiate sports:* basketball M(s)/W(s), cheerleading M(s)/W(s), cross-country running M(s)/W(s), football M(s), golf M(s)/W(s), soccer W(s), track and field M(s)/W(s), volleyball W(s). *Intramural sports:* badminton M/W, basketball M/W, cross-country running M/W, football M/W, racquetball M/W, soccer M, softball M/W, table tennis M/W, tennis M/W, track and field M/W, volleyball M/W.

Standardized Tests *Required:* SAT I or ACT (for admission).

Costs (2003–04) *Tuition:* state resident $3624 full-time; nonresident $10,704 full-time. Full-time tuition and fees vary according to course load. Part-time tuition and fees vary according to course load. *Required fees:* $954 full-time. *Room and board:* $5004; room only: $2610. Room and board charges vary according to board plan and housing facility. *Payment plan:* installment. *Waivers:* senior citizens.

Financial Aid Of all full-time matriculated undergraduates who enrolled in 2002, 2,446 applied for aid, 2,014 were judged to have need, 529 had their need fully met. 171 Federal Work-Study jobs (averaging $1723). In 2002, 547 non-need-based awards were made. *Average percent of need met:* 76%. *Average financial aid package:* $6741. *Average need-based loan:* $2953. *Average need-based gift aid:* $4785. *Average non-need-based aid:* $1559. *Average indebtedness upon graduation:* $16,888.

Texas A&M University–Commerce (continued)

Applying *Options:* common application, electronic application, early admission. *Application fee:* $25. *Required:* high school transcript. *Application deadline:* 8/9 (freshmen), rolling (transfers). *Notification:* continuous (freshmen), continuous (transfers).

Admissions Contact Mr. Randy McDonald, Director of Admissions, Texas A&M University–Commerce, PO Box 3011, Commerce, TX 75429. *Phone:* 903-886-5103. *Toll-free phone:* 800-331-3878. *Fax:* 903-886-5888. *E-mail:* admissions@tamu-commerce.edu.

TEXAS A&M UNIVERSITY–CORPUS CHRISTI

Corpus Christi, Texas

- **State-supported** comprehensive, founded 1947, part of Texas A&M University System
- **Calendar** semesters
- **Degrees** bachelor's, master's, and doctoral
- **Suburban** 240-acre campus
- **Endowment** $2.3 million
- **Coed,** 6,330 undergraduate students, 76% full-time, 60% women, 40% men
- **Moderately difficult** entrance level, 84% of applicants were admitted

Undergraduates 4,819 full-time, 1,511 part-time. Students come from 37 states and territories, 23 other countries, 2% are from out of state, 2% African American, 2% Asian American or Pacific Islander, 37% Hispanic American, 0.6% Native American, 0.7% international, 21% transferred in, 16% live on campus. *Retention:* 64% of 2002 full-time freshmen returned.

Freshmen *Admission:* 2,841 applied, 2,379 admitted, 1,170 enrolled. *Test scores:* SAT verbal scores over 500: 51%; SAT math scores over 500: 52%; ACT scores over 18: 80%; SAT verbal scores over 600: 12%; SAT math scores over 600: 11%; ACT scores over 24: 20%; SAT verbal scores over 700: 1%; SAT math scores over 700: 1%; ACT scores over 30: 1%.

Faculty *Total:* 386, 68% full-time, 62% with terminal degrees. *Student/faculty ratio:* 20:1.

Majors Accounting; art; biology/biological sciences; business administration and management; cartography; chemistry; clinical laboratory science/medical technology; communication/speech communication and rhetoric; computer science; criminal justice/law enforcement administration; engineering technology; English; environmental studies; finance; fine/studio arts; geology/earth science; health science; history; information science/studies; interdisciplinary studies; marketing/marketing management; mathematics; music; nursing (registered nurse training); physical education teaching and coaching; political science and government; psychology; sociology; Spanish; survey technology; trade and industrial teacher education.

Academic Programs *Special study options:* academic remediation for entering students, advanced placement credit, cooperative education, distance learning, double majors, independent study, internships, off-campus study, part-time degree program, services for LD students, summer session for credit. *ROTC:* Army (b).

Library Mary and Jeff Bell Library with 731,586 titles, 1,901 serial subscriptions, 6,012 audiovisual materials, an OPAC, a Web page.

Computers on Campus 500 computers available on campus for general student use. A campuswide network can be accessed from student residence rooms and from off campus. Internet access, online (class) registration, at least one staffed computer lab available.

Student Life *Housing options:* coed, men-only, women-only. Campus housing is provided by a third party. *Activities and organizations:* drama/theater group, student-run newspaper, choral group, marching band, Student Accounting Society, Student Art Association, science clubs, national fraternities, national sororities. *Campus security:* 24-hour emergency response devices and patrols, late-night transport/escort service, security gate access with card after 10 p.m. *Student services:* health clinic, personal/psychological counseling, women's center.

Athletics Member NCAA. *Intercollegiate sports:* baseball M(s), basketball M(s)/W(s), golf W, softball W, tennis M/W, track and field M/W, volleyball W. *Intramural sports:* baseball M, basketball M/W, cross-country running M/W, golf W, racquetball M/W, softball W, tennis M/W, track and field M/W, volleyball W.

Standardized Tests *Required:* SAT I or ACT (for admission).

Costs (2003–04) *Tuition:* state resident $2760 full-time; nonresident $9840 full-time. Full-time tuition and fees vary according to course load. Part-time tuition and fees vary according to course load. No tuition increase for student's term of enrollment. *Required fees:* $1073 full-time. *Room and board:* $7688; room only: $5088. Room and board charges vary according to housing facility. *Payment plans:* installment, deferred payment. *Waivers:* employees or children of employees.

Financial Aid Of all full-time matriculated undergraduates who enrolled in 2002, 3,205 applied for aid, 2,637 were judged to have need, 218 had their need fully met. 6 state and other part-time jobs (averaging $2400). In 2002, 510 non-need-based awards were made. *Average percent of need met:* 69%. *Average financial aid package:* $6202. *Average need-based loan:* $3644. *Average need-based gift aid:* $3659. *Average non-need-based aid:* $4281. *Average indebtedness upon graduation:* $16,886.

Applying *Application fee:* $20. *Required:* high school transcript, minimum 2.0 GPA. *Application deadline:* 7/1 (freshmen). *Notification:* continuous (transfers).

Admissions Contact Ms. Margaret Dechant, Director of Admissions, Texas A&M University–Corpus Christi, 6300 Ocean Drive, Corpus Christi, TX 78412-5503. *Phone:* 361-825-2414. *Toll-free phone:* 800-482-6822. *Fax:* 361-825-5887. *E-mail:* judith.perales@mail.tamucc.edu.

TEXAS A&M UNIVERSITY–KINGSVILLE

Kingsville, Texas

- **State-supported** university, founded 1925, part of Texas A&M University System
- **Calendar** semesters
- **Degrees** bachelor's, master's, doctoral, and postbachelor's certificates
- **Small-town** 255-acre campus
- **Coed,** 5,546 undergraduate students, 73% full-time, 51% women, 49% men
- **Moderately difficult** entrance level, 99% of applicants were admitted

Undergraduates 4,067 full-time, 1,479 part-time. Students come from 37 states and territories, 58 other countries, 2% are from out of state, 5% African American, 0.7% Asian American or Pacific Islander, 66% Hispanic American, 0.3% Native American, 1% international, 8% transferred in, 30% live on campus. *Retention:* 55% of 2002 full-time freshmen returned.

Freshmen *Admission:* 2,105 applied, 2,092 admitted, 844 enrolled. *Average high school GPA:* 3.36. *Test scores:* SAT verbal scores over 500: 30%; SAT math scores over 500: 38%; ACT scores over 18: 54%; SAT verbal scores over 600: 8%; SAT math scores over 600: 12%; ACT scores over 24: 10%; SAT verbal scores over 700: 1%; SAT math scores over 700: 1%; ACT scores over 30: 1%.

Faculty *Total:* 412, 67% full-time, 58% with terminal degrees. *Student/faculty ratio:* 15:1.

Majors Accounting; agricultural business and management; agricultural teacher education; agriculture; agronomy and crop science; animal sciences; anthropology; art; bilingual and multilingual education; biology/biological sciences; business administration and management; business/managerial economics; chemical engineering; chemistry; child development; civil engineering; computer science; criminology; dietetics; dramatic/theatre arts; economics; education; electrical, electronics and communications engineering; elementary education; English; environmental/environmental health engineering; family and consumer sciences/home economics teacher education; family and consumer sciences/human sciences; fashion merchandising; finance; fish/game management; food science; foods, nutrition, and wellness; geography; geology/earth science; health teacher education; history; horticultural science; hotel/motel administration; human services; industrial engineering; industrial technology; information science/studies; interior design; international business/trade/commerce; journalism; kindergarten/preschool education; marketing/marketing management; mass communication/media; mathematics; mechanical engineering; music; music teacher education; petroleum engineering; physical education teaching and coaching; physics; political science and government; pre-dentistry studies; pre-law studies; pre-medical studies; pre-veterinary studies; psychology; public administration; range science and management; real estate; secondary education; social work; sociology; Spanish; speech and rhetoric; speech therapy; wildlife and wildlands science and management.

Academic Programs *Special study options:* academic remediation for entering students, accelerated degree program, adult/continuing education programs, advanced placement credit, cooperative education, distance learning, double majors, English as a second language, honors programs, internships, part-time degree program, services for LD students, study abroad, summer session for credit. *ROTC:* Army (b).

Library James C. Jernigan Library with 358,466 titles, 2,304 serial subscriptions, 3,224 audiovisual materials, an OPAC.

Computers on Campus 600 computers available on campus for general student use. A campuswide network can be accessed from student residence rooms and from off campus. At least one staffed computer lab available.

Student Life *Housing:* on-campus residence required through sophomore year. *Options:* coed, men-only, women-only. *Activities and organizations:* drama/theater group, student-run newspaper, radio and television station, choral group, marching band, Aggie Club, rodeo club, educational association, child development club, resident's hall club, national fraternities, national sororities. *Campus security:* 24-hour emergency response devices and patrols, late-night transport/escort service. *Student services:* health clinic, personal/psychological counseling, women's center.

Athletics Member NCAA, NAIA. All NCAA Division II. *Intercollegiate sports:* baseball M(s), basketball M(s)/W(s), cross-country running M(s)/W(s), equestrian sports M/W, football M(s), riflery M/W, softball W(s), tennis M(s)/W(s), track and field M(s)/W(s), volleyball W(s). *Intramural sports:* badminton M/W, basketball M/W, bowling M/W, fencing M/W, football M/W, golf M/W, racquetball M/W, soccer M/W, swimming M/W, tennis M/W, volleyball W, weight lifting M/W.

Standardized Tests *Required for some:* SAT I or ACT (for admission).

Costs (2003–04) *Tuition:* state resident $1380 full-time; nonresident $8460 full-time. *Required fees:* $2466 full-time. *Room and board:* $3966; room only: $2166.

Financial Aid Of all full-time matriculated undergraduates who enrolled in 2002, 4,121 applied for aid, 4,009 were judged to have need, 2,764 had their need fully met. *Average percent of need met:* 89%. *Average financial aid package:* $6500. *Average need-based loan:* $3875. *Average need-based gift aid:* $6500. *Average indebtedness upon graduation:* $2867.

Applying *Options:* common application, early admission, deferred entrance. *Application fee:* $15. *Required:* high school transcript. *Required for some:* interview. *Recommended:* minimum 2.0 GPA. *Application deadline:* rolling (freshmen), rolling (transfers). *Notification:* continuous (freshmen), continuous (transfers).

Admissions Contact Ms. Maggie Williams, Director of Admissions, Texas A&M University–Kingsville, Campus Box 105, Kingsville, TX 78363. *Phone:* 361-593-2811. *Toll-free phone:* 800-687-6000. *Fax:* 361-593-2195.

TEXAS A&M UNIVERSITY SYSTEM HEALTH SCIENCE CENTER

College Station, Texas

- **State-supported** upper-level, founded 1999, part of Texas A&M University System Health Science Center
- **Calendar** semesters
- **Degrees** bachelor's, master's, doctoral, first professional, post-master's, and first professional certificates
- **Urban** campus
- **Coed,** 56 undergraduate students, 100% full-time, 100% women

Undergraduates 56 full-time. Students come from 4 states and territories, 3% are from out of state, 4% African American, 5% Asian American or Pacific Islander, 14% Hispanic American, 4% Native American, 54% transferred in.

Faculty *Total:* 255, 54% full-time.

Majors Dental hygiene.

Academic Programs *Special study options:* services for LD students.

Library Baylor Hospital.

Student Life *Housing:* college housing not available. *Campus security:* 24-hour emergency response devices and patrols, late-night transport/escort service, electronically operated building access. *Student services:* health clinic, personal/psychological counseling.

Costs (2003–04) *Tuition:* $46 per semester hour part-time; nonresident $282 per semester hour part-time. *Payment plan:* installment.

Applying *Application fee:* $35. *Application deadline:* rolling (transfers).

Admissions Contact Dr. Jack L. Long, Director of Admissions and Records, Texas A&M University System Health Science Center, PO Box 660677, 3302 Gaston Avenue, Dallas, TX 75266-0677. *Phone:* 214-828-8230. *Fax:* 214-874-4567.

TEXAS A&M UNIVERSITY–TEXARKANA

Texarkana, Texas

- **State-supported** upper-level, founded 1971, part of Texas A&M University System
- **Calendar** semesters
- **Degrees** bachelor's and master's
- **Small-town** 1-acre campus
- **Endowment** $273,967
- **Coed,** 954 undergraduate students, 42% full-time, 72% women, 28% men
- **Noncompetitive** entrance level

Undergraduates 396 full-time, 558 part-time. Students come from 4 states and territories, 28% are from out of state, 13% African American, 0.1% Asian American or Pacific Islander, 3% Hispanic American, 1% Native American.

Faculty *Total:* 98, 63% with terminal degrees. *Student/faculty ratio:* 15:1.

Majors Accounting; biology/biological sciences; business administration and management; business/commerce; criminal justice/safety; English; finance; general studies; history; human resources management; interdisciplinary studies; international business/trade/commerce; management information systems; marketing/marketing management; mass communication/media; mathematics; multi-/interdisciplinary studies related; nursing (registered nurse training); psychology.

Academic Programs *Special study options:* advanced placement credit, distance learning, independent study, internships, part-time degree program, services for LD students, student-designed majors, summer session for credit.

Library John F. Moss Library plus 1 other with 125,115 titles, 396 serial subscriptions, 3,720 audiovisual materials, an OPAC, a Web page.

Computers on Campus 133 computers available on campus for general student use. A campuswide network can be accessed from off campus. Internet access, online (class) registration, at least one staffed computer lab available.

Student Life *Housing:* college housing not available. *Activities and organizations:* student-run newspaper, education club, psychology club, science club, Multicultural Association, reading club. *Campus security:* 24-hour patrols, late-night transport/escort service.

Standardized Tests *Required:* THEA (for admission).

Costs (2003–04) *Tuition:* state resident $1728 full-time, $72 per credit hour part-time; nonresident $7392 full-time, $308 per credit hour part-time. Full-time tuition and fees vary according to course level, course load, and degree level. Part-time tuition and fees vary according to course level, course load, and degree level. *Required fees:* $372 full-time, $15 per credit hour part-time, $6 per term part-time. *Payment plan:* installment. *Waivers:* senior citizens.

Financial Aid Of all full-time matriculated undergraduates who enrolled in 2002, 231 applied for aid. 15 Federal Work-Study jobs (averaging $791).

Applying *Options:* common application, electronic application. *Application deadline:* rolling (transfers). *Notification:* continuous (transfers).

Admissions Contact Mrs. Patricia E. Black, Director of Admissions and Registrar, Texas A&M University–Texarkana, PO Box 5518, Texarkana, TX 75505-5518. *Phone:* 903-223-3068. *Fax:* 903-223-3140. *E-mail:* admissions@tamut.edu.

TEXAS CHIROPRACTIC COLLEGE

Pasadena, Texas

- **Independent** upper-level, founded 1908
- **Calendar** trimesters
- **Degrees** incidental bachelor's and first professional
- **Suburban** 18-acre campus with easy access to Houston
- **Coed,** 53 undergraduate students
- **Moderately difficult** entrance level, 75% of applicants were admitted

Undergraduates Students come from 7 other countries.

Faculty *Total:* 47, 98% with terminal degrees. *Student/faculty ratio:* 13:1.

Majors Biology/biological sciences; public health related.

Academic Programs *Special study options:* internships, off-campus study.

Library Mae Hilty Memorial Library with 10,500 titles, 160 serial subscriptions.

Student Life *Housing:* college housing not available. *Student services:* health clinic, personal/psychological counseling.

Athletics *Intramural sports:* basketball M, swimming M/W, table tennis M/W, volleyball M/W.

Costs (2004–05) *Comprehensive fee:* $17,565.

Financial Aid Of all full-time matriculated undergraduates who enrolled in 2003, 7 applied for aid, 7 were judged to have need.

Applying *Options:* deferred entrance. *Application fee:* $50. *Application deadline:* rolling (transfers). *Notification:* continuous (transfers).

Admissions Contact Dr. Sandra Hughes, Director of Admissions, Texas Chiropractic College, 5912 Spencer Highway, Pasadena, TX 77505-1699. *Phone:* 281-998-6017. *Toll-free phone:* 800-468-6839. *Fax:* 281-487-1280. *E-mail:* shughes@txchiro.edu.

TEXAS CHRISTIAN UNIVERSITY

Fort Worth, Texas

- **Independent** university, founded 1873, affiliated with Christian Church (Disciples of Christ)
- **Calendar** semesters
- **Degrees** certificates, bachelor's, master's, doctoral, first professional, postbachelor's, and first professional certificates
- **Suburban** 260-acre campus
- **Endowment** $744.9 million
- **Coed,** 6,933 undergraduate students, 92% full-time, 59% women, 41% men
- **Moderately difficult** entrance level, 65% of applicants were admitted

TCU's mission—to educate individuals to think and act as ethical leaders and responsible citizens in the global community—influences every area of this person-centered private university. From leadership development to one of the

Texas Christian University (continued)

top study-abroad programs in the nation, TCU graduates earn more than degrees that will improve their lives. They learn to change their world.

Undergraduates 6,391 full-time, 542 part-time. Students come from 50 states and territories, 75 other countries, 22% are from out of state, 5% African American, 2% Asian American or Pacific Islander, 6% Hispanic American, 0.5% Native American, 4% international, 6% transferred in, 48% live on campus. *Retention:* 81% of 2002 full-time freshmen returned.

Freshmen *Admission:* 7,654 applied, 4,971 admitted, 1,596 enrolled.

Faculty *Total:* 703, 60% full-time, 70% with terminal degrees. *Student/faculty ratio:* 15:1.

Majors Accounting; advertising; anthropology; art history, criticism and conservation; art teacher education; astronomy and astrophysics related; ballet; bilingual and multilingual education; biochemistry; biology/biological sciences; broadcast journalism; chemistry; communication/speech communication and rhetoric; computer and information sciences; computer and information sciences related; counselor education/school counseling and guidance; criminal justice/safety; dietetics; dietetics and clinical nutrition services related; dramatic/theatre arts; early childhood education; e-commerce; economics; educational leadership and administration; elementary education; engineering; English; English/language arts teacher education; environmental science; fashion merchandising; finance; fine/studio arts; French; general studies; geology/earth science; health and physical education; health and physical education related; health science; history; interior design; international business/trade/commerce; international economics; international finance; international marketing; international relations and affairs; journalism; Latin American studies; liberal arts and sciences/liberal studies; management science; marketing/marketing management; mass communication/media; mathematics; mathematics teacher education; military studies; movement therapy and movement education; music; music performance; music teacher education; music theory and composition; neuroscience; nursing (registered nurse training); painting; philosophy; photography; physical education teaching and coaching; physics; piano and organ; political science and government; printmaking; psychology; radio and television; real estate; religious studies; science teacher education; sculpture; secondary education; social studies teacher education; social work; sociology; Spanish; special education; special education (gifted and talented); special education (hearing impaired); speech-language pathology; technical teacher education; theatre literature, history and criticism.

Academic Programs *Special study options:* adult/continuing education programs, advanced placement credit, distance learning, double majors, English as a second language, honors programs, independent study, internships, part-time degree program, services for LD students, study abroad, summer session for credit. *ROTC:* Army (b), Air Force (b). *Unusual degree programs:* 3-2 education, economics.

Library Mary Couts Burnett Library with 1.3 million titles, 4,629 serial subscriptions, 57,562 audiovisual materials, an OPAC, a Web page.

Computers on Campus 4225 computers available on campus for general student use. A campuswide network can be accessed from student residence rooms and from off campus. Internet access, online (class) registration, at least one staffed computer lab available. Computer purchase or lease plan available.

Student Life *Housing:* on-campus residence required for freshman year. *Options:* coed, men-only, women-only. Campus housing is university owned. Freshman campus housing is guaranteed. *Activities and organizations:* drama/theater group, student-run newspaper, radio and television station, choral group, marching band, national fraternities, national sororities. *Campus security:* 24-hour emergency response devices and patrols, student patrols, late-night transport/escort service, controlled dormitory access, emergency call boxes, video camera surveillance in parking lots. *Student services:* health clinic, personal/psychological counseling, women's center, legal services.

Athletics Member NCAA. All Division I. *Intercollegiate sports:* baseball M(s), basketball M(s)/W(s), cross-country running M(s)/W(s), football M(s), golf M(s)/W(s), riflery W(s), soccer M/W(s), swimming M(s)/W(s), tennis M(s)/W(s), track and field M(s)/W(s), volleyball W(s). *Intramural sports:* basketball M/W, bowling M/W, lacrosse M/W, racquetball M/W, rugby M/W, soccer M/W, softball M/W, table tennis M/W, tennis M/W, ultimate Frisbee M/W, volleyball M/W, weight lifting M/W.

Standardized Tests *Required:* SAT I or ACT (for admission).

Costs (2003–04) *Comprehensive fee:* $23,410 includes full-time tuition ($17,590), mandatory fees ($40), and room and board ($5780). *College room only:* $3780. Room and board charges vary according to board plan and housing facility. *Payment plan:* installment. *Waivers:* employees or children of employees.

Financial Aid Of all full-time matriculated undergraduates who enrolled in 2003, 3,541 applied for aid, 2,778 were judged to have need, 1,131 had their need fully met. 1,180 Federal Work-Study jobs (averaging $2220). 21 state and other part-time jobs (averaging $2216). In 2003, 1295 non-need-based awards were made. *Average percent of need met:* 94%. *Average financial aid package:* $12,614. *Average need-based loan:* $4970. *Average need-based gift aid:* $8877. *Average non-need-based aid:* $7979.

Applying *Options:* common application, electronic application, early action, deferred entrance. *Application fee:* $40. *Required:* essay or personal statement, high school transcript, minimum 2.0 GPA, 2 letters of recommendation. *Recommended:* minimum 3.0 GPA, interview. *Application deadlines:* 2/15 (freshmen), 4/15 (transfers). *Notification:* 4/1 (freshmen), 1/1 (early action), continuous (transfers).

Admissions Contact Mr. Tom Oliver, Director of Freshman Admissions, Texas Christian University, TCU Box 297013, Fort Worth, TX 76129-0002. *Phone:* 817-257-7490. *Toll-free phone:* 800-828-3764. *Fax:* 817-257-7268. *E-mail:* frogmail@tcu.edu.

■ *See page 2494 for a narrative description.*

TEXAS COLLEGE
Tyler, Texas

- **Independent** 4-year, founded 1894, affiliated with Christian Methodist Episcopal Church
- **Calendar** semesters
- **Degree** certificates and bachelor's
- **Coed**
- **Noncompetitive** entrance level

Faculty *Student/faculty ratio:* 10:1.

Athletics Member NAIA.

Standardized Tests *Recommended:* SAT I and SAT II or ACT (for admission).

Costs (2003–04) *Comprehensive fee:* $12,410 includes full-time tuition ($7680) and room and board ($4730).

Financial Aid Of all full-time matriculated undergraduates who enrolled in 2002, 671 applied for aid, 616 were judged to have need, 550 had their need fully met. 210 Federal Work-Study jobs (averaging $1200). 5 state and other part-time jobs (averaging $1200). *Average percent of need met:* 75. *Average financial aid package:* $3500. *Average need-based loan:* $2500. *Average need-based gift aid:* $1000. *Average indebtedness upon graduation:* $2000.

Applying *Options:* common application. *Application fee:* $15. *Required:* high school transcript.

Admissions Contact Ms. Teresa Galinda, Enrollment Services Clerk, Texas College, PO Box 4500, 2404 North Grand Avenue, Tyler, TX 75702. *Phone:* 903-593-8311 Ext. 2297. *Toll-free phone:* 800-306-6299. *Fax:* 903-596-0001. *E-mail:* admissions@texascollege.edu.

TEXAS LUTHERAN UNIVERSITY
Seguin, Texas

- **Independent** 4-year, founded 1891, affiliated with Evangelical Lutheran Church
- **Calendar** semesters
- **Degrees** bachelor's and postbachelor's certificates
- **Suburban** 196-acre campus with easy access to San Antonio
- **Endowment** $30.0 million
- **Coed,** 1,410 undergraduate students, 92% full-time, 55% women, 45% men
- **Moderately difficult** entrance level, 78% of applicants were admitted

The high-quality education that Texas Lutheran University (TLU) provides has been recognized repeatedly in *U.S. News & World Report's* survey of America's best colleges and universities. The magazine also recognized TLU as one of the best values for the money among its peers in the Western United States. This recognition affirms the high-quality education offered at Texas Lutheran.

Undergraduates 1,296 full-time, 114 part-time. Students come from 23 states and territories, 12 other countries, 4% are from out of state, 7% African American, 1% Asian American or Pacific Islander, 17% Hispanic American, 0.4% Native American, 2% international, 6% transferred in, 70% live on campus. *Retention:* 74% of 2002 full-time freshmen returned.

Freshmen *Admission:* 1,065 applied, 831 admitted, 377 enrolled. *Average high school GPA:* 3.33. *Test scores:* SAT verbal scores over 500: 62%; SAT math scores over 500: 67%; ACT scores over 18: 89%; SAT verbal scores over 600: 17%; SAT math scores over 600: 25%; ACT scores over 24: 32%; SAT verbal scores over 700: 3%; SAT math scores over 700: 2%; ACT scores over 30: 5%.

Faculty *Total:* 118, 57% full-time, 58% with terminal degrees. *Student/faculty ratio:* 15:1.

Majors Accounting; art; art teacher education; athletic training; biology/biological sciences; business administration and management; chemistry; communication/speech communication and rhetoric; computer science; dramatic/theatre arts;

economics; education; education (multiple levels); elementary education; English; finance; health and physical education related; history; history teacher education; information science/studies; international relations and affairs; kinesiology and exercise science; mathematics; mathematics teacher education; middle school education; molecular biology; music; music teacher education; philosophy; physical education teaching and coaching; physics; political science and government; pre-dentistry studies; pre-law studies; pre-medical studies; pre-veterinary studies; psychology; social studies teacher education; sociology; Spanish; sport and fitness administration; theology.

Academic Programs *Special study options:* adult/continuing education programs, advanced placement credit, double majors, honors programs, independent study, internships, part-time degree program, services for LD students, study abroad, summer session for credit. *ROTC:* Army (c), Air Force (c). *Unusual degree programs:* 3-2 engineering with Texas A&M University, Texas Tech University, Texas State University.

Library Blumberg Memorial Library with 159,307 titles, 619 serial subscriptions, 4,968 audiovisual materials, an OPAC, a Web page.

Computers on Campus 48 computers available on campus for general student use. A campuswide network can be accessed from student residence rooms and from off campus. Internet access, at least one staffed computer lab available.

Student Life *Housing:* on-campus residence required through senior year. *Options:* coed, men-only, women-only. Campus housing is university owned. Freshman campus housing is guaranteed. *Activities and organizations:* drama/theater group, student-run newspaper, choral group, Campus Ministry, Mexican American Student Association, Student Government Association. *Campus security:* 24-hour emergency response devices and patrols, late-night transport/escort service, controlled dormitory access. *Student services:* health clinic, personal/psychological counseling, women's center.

Athletics Member NCAA. All Division III. *Intercollegiate sports:* baseball M, basketball M/W, cross-country running W, football M, golf M/W, soccer M/W, softball W, tennis M/W, track and field W, volleyball W. *Intramural sports:* basketball M/W, bowling M/W, football M, racquetball M/W, softball M/W, tennis M/W, volleyball M/W.

Standardized Tests *Required:* SAT I or ACT (for admission).

Costs (2003–04) *Comprehensive fee:* $20,370 includes full-time tuition ($15,470), mandatory fees ($120), and room and board ($4780). Full-time tuition and fees vary according to course load. Part-time tuition: $515 per credit hour. Part-time tuition and fees vary according to course load. *Required fees:* $60 per term part-time. *College room only:* $2230. Room and board charges vary according to board plan, housing facility, and location. *Payment plan:* installment. *Waivers:* children of alumni and employees or children of employees.

Financial Aid Of all full-time matriculated undergraduates who enrolled in 2001, 1,239 applied for aid, 850 were judged to have need, 774 had their need fully met. 304 Federal Work-Study jobs (averaging $960). In 2001, 392 non-need-based awards were made. *Average percent of need met:* 91%. *Average financial aid package:* $13,991. *Average need-based loan:* $5051. *Average non-need-based aid:* $5823. *Average indebtedness upon graduation:* $21,500.

Applying *Options:* common application, electronic application, deferred entrance. *Application fee:* $25. *Required:* essay or personal statement, high school transcript, letters of recommendation. *Required for some:* minimum 2.0 GPA, 2 letters of recommendation. *Recommended:* interview. *Application deadline:* rolling (freshmen), rolling (transfers). *Notification:* continuous until 8/1 (freshmen), continuous until 8/1 (transfers).

Admissions Contact Mr. E. Norman Jones, Vice President for Enrollment Services, Texas Lutheran University, 1000 West Court Street, Seguin, TX 78155-5999. *Phone:* 830-372-8050. *Toll-free phone:* 800-771-8521. *Fax:* 830-372-8096. *E-mail:* admissions@tlu.edu.

■ See page 2496 for a narrative description.

TEXAS SOUTHERN UNIVERSITY
Houston, Texas

- **State-supported** university, founded 1947, part of Texas Higher Education Coordinating Board
- **Calendar** semesters
- **Degrees** bachelor's, master's, doctoral, and first professional
- **Urban** 147-acre campus
- **Endowment** $11.4 million
- **Coed,** 8,920 undergraduate students, 88% full-time, 57% women, 43% men
- **Noncompetitive** entrance level, 44% of applicants were admitted

Undergraduates 7,816 full-time, 1,104 part-time. Students come from 38 states and territories, 42 other countries, 8% are from out of state, 91% African American, 2% Asian American or Pacific Islander, 3% Hispanic American, 0.1% Native American, 4% international, 13% transferred in, 4% live on campus. *Retention:* 65% of 2002 full-time freshmen returned.

Freshmen *Admission:* 5,574 applied, 2,448 admitted, 2,448 enrolled. *Average high school GPA:* 2.59. *Test scores:* SAT verbal scores over 500: 86%; SAT math scores over 500: 100%; ACT scores over 18: 32%; SAT math scores over 600: 14%; ACT scores over 24: 3%.

Faculty *Total:* 511, 64% full-time, 45% with terminal degrees. *Student/faculty ratio:* 25:1.

Majors Accounting; African-American/Black studies; air traffic control; architectural engineering technology; art; art teacher education; aviation/airway management; banking and financial support services; bilingual and multilingual education; biological and physical sciences; biology/biological sciences; biomedical technology; business administration and management; business teacher education; chemistry; child development; civil engineering technology; clinical laboratory science/medical technology; clothing/textiles; communication/speech communication and rhetoric; computer and information sciences; computer engineering technology; computer programming; computer science; construction engineering technology; counselor education/school counseling and guidance; criminal justice/law enforcement administration; curriculum and instruction; dietetics; drafting and design technology; dramatic/theatre arts; economics; education; educational leadership and administration; education related; electrical, electronic and communications engineering technology; elementary education; engineering technology; English; environmental engineering technology; environmental health; environmental science; family and consumer sciences/human sciences; fashion/apparel design; fashion merchandising; finance; fine/studio arts; foods, nutrition, and wellness; foreign languages and literatures; French; general studies; German; health and physical education; health/health care administration; health information/medical records administration; health science; health teacher education; history; industrial technology; insurance; interdisciplinary studies; jazz/jazz studies; journalism; journalism related; kindergarten/preschool education; liberal arts and sciences/liberal studies; marketing/marketing management; mass communication/media; mathematics; multi-/interdisciplinary studies related; music; music teacher education; nursing (registered nurse training); occupational safety and health technology; office management; operations management; pharmacy; photography; physical education teaching and coaching; physical therapy; physics; piano and organ; political science and government; pre-dentistry studies; pre-medical studies; pre-pharmacy studies; psychology; public administration; radio and television; radio, television, and digital communication related; reading teacher education; respiratory care therapy; science, technology and society; secondary education; social and philosophical foundations of education; social work; sociology; Spanish; special education; speech and rhetoric; speech therapy; technology/industrial arts teacher education; telecommunications; visual and performing arts; voice and opera; wind/percussion instruments.

Academic Programs *Special study options:* academic remediation for entering students, accelerated degree program, adult/continuing education programs, cooperative education, distance learning, English as a second language, honors programs, internships, part-time degree program, services for LD students, summer session for credit. *ROTC:* Army (c), Navy (c).

Library Robert J. Terry Library plus 2 others with 266,888 titles, 1,715 serial subscriptions, 4,016 audiovisual materials, an OPAC.

Computers on Campus 410 computers available on campus for general student use. A campuswide network can be accessed. Internet access, online (class) registration, at least one staffed computer lab available.

Student Life *Housing:* on-campus residence required for freshman year. *Options:* men-only, women-only. Campus housing is university owned, leased by the school and is provided by a third party. Freshman campus housing is guaranteed. *Activities and organizations:* drama/theater group, student-run newspaper, radio station, choral group, marching band, Debate Team, University Program Council, Student Government Association, Band, national fraternities, national sororities. *Campus security:* 24-hour emergency response devices and patrols, student patrols, late-night transport/escort service. *Student services:* health clinic, personal/psychological counseling, legal services.

Athletics Member NCAA. All Division I except football (Division I-AA). *Intercollegiate sports:* baseball M(s), basketball M(s)/W(s), bowling W(s), cross-country running M(s)/W(s), golf M(s), soccer M/W(s), softball W(s), tennis M(s)/W(s), track and field M(s)/W(s), volleyball M/W(s). *Intramural sports:* softball M/W, swimming M/W, volleyball M/W.

Standardized Tests *Required:* SAT I (for admission), ACT (for admission), SAT I or ACT (for placement).

Costs (2003–04) *Tuition:* $46 per hour part-time; state resident $1104 full-time, $46 per hour part-time; nonresident $6768 full-time, $282 per hour part-time. Full-time tuition and fees vary according to course load and program. Part-time tuition and fees vary according to course load and program. *Required fees:* $1992 full-time, $83 per credit hour part-time. *Room and board:* $5824. Room and board charges vary according to board plan. *Payment plan:* installment. *Waivers:* minority students and senior citizens.

Texas Southern University (continued)

Financial Aid Of all full-time matriculated undergraduates who enrolled in 2003, 7,047 applied for aid, 5,708 were judged to have need, 1,600 had their need fully met. 225 Federal Work-Study jobs (averaging $4000). 29 state and other part-time jobs (averaging $4000). *Average percent of need met:* 48%. *Average financial aid package:* $14,065. *Average need-based loan:* $6625. *Average need-based gift aid:* $9050. *Average indebtedness upon graduation:* $25,310.

Applying *Options:* common application, electronic application. *Application fee:* $40. *Required:* high school transcript. *Application deadlines:* 8/10 (freshmen), 8/13 (transfers). *Notification:* continuous until 8/28 (freshmen), continuous until 8/28 (transfers).

Admissions Contact Mrs. Joyce Waddell, Director of Admissions, Texas Southern University, 3100 Cleburne Street, Houston, TX 77004-4598. *Phone:* 713-313-7472.

TEXAS STATE UNIVERSITY-SAN MARCOS

San Marcos, Texas

- **State-supported** university, founded 1899, part of Texas State University System
- **Calendar** semesters
- **Degrees** bachelor's, master's, doctoral, and postbachelor's certificates
- **Suburban** 423-acre campus with easy access to San Antonio and Austin
- **Endowment** $18.5 million
- **Coed,** 21,974 undergraduate students, 80% full-time, 55% women, 45% men
- **Moderately difficult** entrance level, 56% of applicants were admitted

Undergraduates 17,679 full-time, 4,295 part-time. Students come from 45 states and territories, 53 other countries, 2% are from out of state, 5% African American, 2% Asian American or Pacific Islander, 19% Hispanic American, 0.7% Native American, 1% international, 12% transferred in, 23% live on campus. *Retention:* 77% of 2002 full-time freshmen returned.

Freshmen *Admission:* 11,483 applied, 6,435 admitted, 2,874 enrolled. *Test scores:* SAT verbal scores over 500: 74%; SAT math scores over 500: 77%; ACT scores over 18: 96%; SAT verbal scores over 600: 20%; SAT math scores over 600: 22%; ACT scores over 24: 35%; SAT verbal scores over 700: 1%; SAT math scores over 700: 1%; ACT scores over 30: 1%.

Faculty *Total:* 1,098, 64% full-time, 59% with terminal degrees. *Student/faculty ratio:* 26:1.

Majors Accounting; advertising; agribusiness; agriculture; American studies; animal sciences; anthropology; applied mathematics; aquatic biology/limnology; art; Asian studies; athletic training; audiology and speech-language pathology; biochemistry; biology/biological sciences; botany/plant biology; business administration and management; business/managerial economics; cartography; chemistry; city/urban, community and regional planning; clinical laboratory science/medical technology; commercial and advertising art; community health services counseling; computer and information sciences; conservation biology; construction engineering technology; corrections; criminal justice/police science; criminal justice/safety; dance; data processing and data processing technology; desktop publishing and digital imaging design; dramatic/theatre arts; economics; engineering technology; English; environmental science; European studies; family and consumer sciences/human sciences; fashion merchandising; finance; fine/studio arts; foods, nutrition, and wellness; French; geography; German; health and physical education; health/health care administration; health information/medical records administration; health services/allied health/health sciences; history; hospital and health care facilities administration; human development and family studies; industrial technology; interior architecture; international/global studies; international relations and affairs; jazz/jazz studies; journalism; management information systems; manufacturing engineering; manufacturing technology; marine biology and biological oceanography; marketing/marketing management; mass communication/media; mathematics; medical radiologic technology; microbiology; multi-/interdisciplinary studies related; music; music performance; Near and Middle Eastern studies; parks, recreation and leisure facilities management; philosophy; physics; political science and government; psychology; public administration; public relations/image management; radio and television; recording arts technology; respiratory care therapy; Russian studies; social work; sociology; Spanish; speech and rhetoric; sport and fitness administration; water, wetlands, and marine resources management; wildlife and wildlands science and management; zoology/animal biology.

Academic Programs *Special study options:* academic remediation for entering students, accelerated degree program, adult/continuing education programs, advanced placement credit, distance learning, double majors, English as a second language, honors programs, independent study, internships, off-campus study, part-time degree program, services for LD students, study abroad, summer session for credit. *ROTC:* Army (b), Air Force (b). *Unusual degree programs:* 3-2 engineering with University of Texas at Austin, Texas A&M University, Texas Tech University, University of Texas at San Antonio; dentistry with University of Texas Health Science Center at San Antonio.

Library Alkek Library with 710,223 titles, 6,252 serial subscriptions, 276,299 audiovisual materials, an OPAC, a Web page.

Computers on Campus 750 computers available on campus for general student use. A campuswide network can be accessed from student residence rooms and from off campus. Internet access, at least one staffed computer lab available. Computer purchase or lease plan available.

Student Life *Housing:* on-campus residence required through sophomore year. *Options:* coed, men-only, women-only. Campus housing is university owned. Freshman campus housing is guaranteed. *Activities and organizations:* drama/theater group, student-run newspaper, radio station, choral group, marching band, Non-traditional Students Association (NTSO), Panhellenic Council (PC), Student Association for Campus Activities (SACA), Association Student Government (ASG), Interfraternity Council (IFC), national fraternities, national sororities. *Campus security:* 24-hour emergency response devices and patrols, late-night transport/escort service, controlled dormitory access. *Student services:* health clinic, personal/psychological counseling, legal services.

Athletics Member NCAA. All Division I except football (Division I-AA). *Intercollegiate sports:* baseball M(s), basketball M(s)/W(s), cheerleading M/W, cross-country running M(s)/W(s), fencing M(c)/W(c), golf M(s)/W(s), gymnastics M(c)/W(c), ice hockey M(c), lacrosse M(c)/W(c), racquetball M(c)/W(c), rugby M(c), soccer M(c)/W(s), softball M(c)/W(s)(c), tennis M(c)/W(s), track and field M(s)/W(s), ultimate Frisbee M(c)/W(c), volleyball M(c)/W(s), weight lifting M(c)/W(c). *Intramural sports:* basketball M/W, bowling M/W, cross-country running M/W, football M/W, golf M/W, racquetball M/W, soccer M/W, softball M/W, tennis M/W, ultimate Frisbee M, volleyball M/W.

Standardized Tests *Required:* SAT I or ACT (for admission).

Costs (2003–04) *Tuition:* state resident $2760 full-time, $92 per semester hour part-time; nonresident $9840 full-time, $328 per semester hour part-time. Full-time tuition and fees vary according to course load. Part-time tuition and fees vary according to course load. *Required fees:* $1250 full-time, $31 per semester hour part-time, $235 per term part-time. *Room and board:* $5310; room only: $3224. Room and board charges vary according to board plan and housing facility. *Payment plan:* installment. *Waivers:* employees or children of employees.

Financial Aid Of all full-time matriculated undergraduates who enrolled in 2003, 10,682 applied for aid, 8,086 were judged to have need, 1,310 had their need fully met. 719 Federal Work-Study jobs (averaging $2017). 130 state and other part-time jobs (averaging $780). In 2003, 2073 non-need-based awards were made. *Average percent of need met:* 71%. *Average financial aid package:* $8752. *Average need-based loan:* $5142. *Average need-based gift aid:* $3919. *Average non-need-based aid:* $7026. *Average indebtedness upon graduation:* $15,055.

Applying *Options:* electronic application, early admission, deferred entrance. *Application fee:* $40. *Required:* essay or personal statement, high school transcript. *Required for some:* interview. *Application deadlines:* 6/1 (freshmen), 7/1 (transfers). *Notification:* continuous (freshmen), continuous (transfers).

Admissions Contact Mrs. Christie Kangas, Director of Admissions, Texas State University-San Marcos, Admissions and Visitors Center, San Marcos, TX 78666-5709. *Phone:* 512-245-2364 Ext. 2803. *Fax:* 512-245-8044. *E-mail:* admissions@txstate.edu.

TEXAS TECH UNIVERSITY

Lubbock, Texas

- **State-supported** university, founded 1923, part of Texas Tech University System
- **Calendar** semesters
- **Degrees** bachelor's, master's, doctoral, and first professional
- **Urban** 1839-acre campus
- **Endowment** $343.8 million
- **Coed,** 23,595 undergraduate students, 89% full-time, 45% women, 55% men
- **Moderately difficult** entrance level, 67% of applicants were admitted

Undergraduates 21,030 full-time, 2,565 part-time. Students come from 50 states and territories, 113 other countries, 5% are from out of state, 3% African American, 2% Asian American or Pacific Islander, 11% Hispanic American, 0.6% Native American, 0.9% international, 9% transferred in, 25% live on campus. *Retention:* 82% of 2002 full-time freshmen returned.

Freshmen *Admission:* 13,755 applied, 9,257 admitted, 4,445 enrolled. *Test scores:* SAT verbal scores over 500: 78%; SAT math scores over 500: 86%; ACT scores over 18: 99%; SAT verbal scores over 600: 26%; SAT math scores over 600: 37%; ACT scores over 24: 50%; SAT verbal scores over 700: 3%; SAT math scores over 700: 5%; ACT scores over 30: 6%.

Faculty *Total:* 1,070, 91% full-time, 89% with terminal degrees. *Student/faculty ratio:* 21:1.

Majors Accounting; acting; advertising; agricultural business and management; agricultural economics; agricultural production; agriculture; agronomy and crop science; animal/livestock husbandry and production; animal sciences; anthropology; apparel and textiles; applied horticulture; architectural engineering technology; architecture; art; art history, criticism and conservation; audiology and hearing sciences; biochemistry; biological and physical sciences; biology/biological sciences; business administration and management; business administration, management and operations related; business/commerce; cell and molecular biology; cell biology and histology; chemical engineering; chemistry; child development; civil engineering; classics and languages, literatures and linguistics; commercial and advertising art; community health services counseling; computer and information sciences; computer engineering; dance; dietetics; dramatic/theatre arts; economics; electrical, electronic and communications engineering technology; electrical, electronics and communications engineering; engineering; engineering physics; engineering technology; English; environmental/environmental health engineering; family and consumer sciences/human sciences; family systems; fashion/apparel design; fashion merchandising; finance; fine/studio arts; fishing and fisheries sciences and management; food science; foods, nutrition, and wellness; French; general studies; geography; geology/earth science; geophysics and seismology; German; graphic design; health and physical education; health services/allied health/health sciences; history; horticultural science; hotel/motel administration; human development and family studies; industrial engineering; interdisciplinary studies; interior architecture; international business/trade/commerce; journalism; kinesiology and exercise science; landscape architecture; Latin American studies; liberal arts and sciences/liberal studies; management information systems; marketing/marketing management; mathematics; mechanical engineering; mechanical engineering/mechanical technology; medical microbiology and bacteriology; molecular biology; multi-/interdisciplinary studies related; music; music performance; music theory and composition; natural resources/conservation; parks, recreation and leisure; petroleum engineering; philosophy; photojournalism; physics; plant protection and integrated pest management; political science and government; psychology; public relations/image management; radio and television; radio and television broadcasting technology; range science and management; Russian studies; social work; sociology; Spanish; speech and rhetoric; textile sciences and engineering; theatre design and technology; wildlife and wildlands science and management; work and family studies; zoology/animal biology.

Academic Programs *Special study options:* academic remediation for entering students, accelerated degree program, adult/continuing education programs, advanced placement credit, cooperative education, distance learning, double majors, English as a second language, external degree program, freshman honors college, honors programs, independent study, internships, off-campus study, services for LD students, student-designed majors, study abroad, summer session for credit. *ROTC:* Army (b), Air Force (b). *Unusual degree programs:* 3-2 architecture.

Library Texas Tech Library plus 3 others with 2.2 million titles, 18,082 serial subscriptions, 82,191 audiovisual materials, an OPAC, a Web page.

Computers on Campus 3000 computers available on campus for general student use. A campuswide network can be accessed from student residence rooms and from off campus that provide access to online degree plans, accounts, transcripts, schedules. Internet access, online (class) registration, at least one staffed computer lab available. Computer purchase or lease plan available.

Student Life *Housing:* on-campus residence required for freshman year. *Options:* coed, men-only, women-only, disabled students. Campus housing is university owned. Freshman campus housing is guaranteed. *Activities and organizations:* drama/theater group, student-run newspaper, radio and television station, choral group, marching band, national fraternities, national sororities. *Campus security:* 24-hour emergency response devices and patrols, late-night transport/escort service, controlled dormitory access. *Student services:* health clinic, personal/psychological counseling, legal services.

Athletics Member NCAA. All Division I except football (Division I-A). *Intercollegiate sports:* baseball M(s), basketball M(s)/W(s), cross-country running M(s)/W(s), golf M(s)/W(s), soccer W(s), softball W(s), tennis M(s)/W(s), track and field M(s)/W(s), volleyball W(s). *Intramural sports:* archery M, badminton M/W, basketball M/W, bowling M/W, cross-country running M/W, equestrian sports M, football M, golf M/W, gymnastics W, racquetball M/W, soccer M/W, softball W, table tennis M/W, tennis M/W, track and field M/W, volleyball M/W, water polo M/W.

Standardized Tests *Required:* SAT I or ACT (for admission).

Costs (2003–04) *Tuition:* state resident $2760 full-time, $92 per credit hour part-time; nonresident $9840 full-time, $328 per credit hour part-time. Full-time tuition and fees vary according to course load, program, and reciprocity agreements. Part-time tuition and fees vary according to course load, program, and reciprocity agreements. *Required fees:* $1985 full-time. *Room and board:* $6023; room only: $3308. Room and board charges vary according to board plan and housing facility. *Payment plans:* tuition prepayment, installment. *Waivers:* adult students, senior citizens, and employees or children of employees.

Financial Aid Of all full-time matriculated undergraduates who enrolled in 2002, 12,320 applied for aid, 8,060 were judged to have need. 587 Federal Work-Study jobs (averaging $1432). In 2002, 5460 non-need-based awards were made. *Average financial aid package:* $6421. *Average need-based loan:* $3505. *Average need-based gift aid:* $3458. *Average non-need-based aid:* $2194. *Average indebtedness upon graduation:* $15,780.

Applying *Options:* electronic application, early admission, deferred entrance. *Application fee:* $50. *Required:* high school transcript, minimum 2.0 GPA. *Required for some:* essay or personal statement. *Application deadline:* rolling (freshmen), rolling (transfers). *Notification:* continuous (freshmen), continuous (transfers).

Admissions Contact Ms. Marlene Hernandez, Associate Director, Admissions and School Relations, Texas Tech University, Box 45005, Lubbock, TX 79409-5005. *Phone:* 806-742-1480. *Fax:* 806-742-0980. *E-mail:* admissions@ttu.edu.

■ *See page 2498 for a narrative description.*

TEXAS WESLEYAN UNIVERSITY
Fort Worth, Texas

- **Independent United Methodist** comprehensive, founded 1890
- **Calendar** semesters
- **Degrees** bachelor's, master's, and first professional
- **Urban** 74-acre campus
- **Endowment** $37.1 million
- **Coed,** 1,506 undergraduate students, 69% full-time, 62% women, 38% men
- **Moderately difficult** entrance level, 43% of applicants were admitted

Undergraduates 1,045 full-time, 461 part-time. Students come from 20 states and territories, 4% are from out of state, 20% African American, 2% Asian American or Pacific Islander, 20% Hispanic American, 0.6% Native American, 2% international, 13% transferred in. 10% live on campus. *Retention:* 67% of 2002 full-time freshmen returned.

Freshmen *Admission:* 411 applied, 175 admitted, 175 enrolled. *Test scores:* SAT verbal scores over 500: 40%; SAT math scores over 500: 38%; ACT scores over 18: 68%; SAT verbal scores over 600: 8%; SAT math scores over 600: 10%; ACT scores over 24: 11%; SAT verbal scores over 700: 1%; SAT math scores over 700: 1%.

Faculty *Total:* 266, 52% full-time, 42% with terminal degrees. *Student/faculty ratio:* 15:1.

Majors Accounting; advertising; art; art teacher education; athletic training; behavioral sciences; bilingual and multilingual education; biochemistry; biological and biomedical sciences related; biology/biological sciences; biology teacher education; business administration and management; business, management, and marketing related; business/managerial economics; business teacher education; chemistry; chemistry related; computer and information sciences; counseling psychology; criminal justice/safety; drama and dance teacher education; dramatic/theatre arts; economics; education; elementary education; engineering related; English; English as a second/foreign language (teaching); English/language arts teacher education; foreign language teacher education; health and physical education; history; history teacher education; humanities; industrial and organizational psychology; international business/trade/commerce; international relations and affairs; journalism; legal professions and studies related; management information systems; marketing/marketing management; mass communication/media; mathematics; mathematics teacher education; multi-/interdisciplinary studies related; music; music teacher education; physical education teaching and coaching; political science and government; pre-dentistry studies; pre-law studies; pre-medical studies; psychology; radio and television; reading teacher education; religious education; religious studies; school psychology; science teacher education; social sciences; social studies teacher education; sociology; Spanish; speech and rhetoric; speech teacher education; sport and fitness administration; technology/industrial arts teacher education; visual and performing arts; voice and opera; wind/percussion instruments.

Academic Programs *Special study options:* academic remediation for entering students, adult/continuing education programs, advanced placement credit, distance learning, English as a second language, internships, part-time degree program, services for LD students, study abroad, summer session for credit. *ROTC:* Army (c), Air Force (c). *Unusual degree programs:* 3-2 engineering with Case Western Reserve University, Southern Methodist University, University of Texas at Arlington, Vanderbilt University, Washington University in St. Louis.

Library Eunice and James L. West Library plus 1 other with 192,044 titles, 632 serial subscriptions, 5,302 audiovisual materials, an OPAC.

Computers on Campus 65 computers available on campus for general student use. A campuswide network can be accessed. Internet access, at least one staffed computer lab available.

Student Life *Housing options:* coed, men-only, women-only. Campus housing is university owned. *Activities and organizations:* drama/theater group, student-run newspaper, choral group, national fraternities, national sororities. *Campus security:* 24-hour emergency response devices and patrols, student patrols,

Texas Wesleyan University (continued)
late-night transport/escort service, controlled dormitory access. *Student services:* health clinic, personal/psychological counseling.

Athletics Member NAIA. *Intercollegiate sports:* baseball M, basketball M/W, cheerleading M/W, golf M(s), soccer M/W, softball W, table tennis M, volleyball W. *Intramural sports:* badminton M/W, basketball M/W, bowling M/W, field hockey M/W, football M, golf M, racquetball M/W, rock climbing M(c)/W(c), soccer M/W, swimming M/W, table tennis M/W, track and field M, ultimate Frisbee M/W, volleyball W.

Standardized Tests *Required:* SAT I or ACT (for admission).

Costs (2003–04) *Comprehensive fee:* $17,202 includes full-time tuition ($10,950), mandatory fees ($1010), and room and board ($5242). Full-time tuition and fees vary according to program. Part-time tuition: $365 per credit. Part-time tuition and fees vary according to program. *Required fees:* $40 per credit part-time. *College room only:* $1680. Room and board charges vary according to board plan and student level. *Payment plans:* installment, deferred payment. *Waivers:* employees or children of employees.

Applying *Options:* common application, deferred entrance. *Application fee:* $25. *Required:* essay or personal statement, high school transcript, minimum 2.5 GPA. *Required for some:* interview. *Application deadline:* rolling (freshmen), rolling (transfers). *Notification:* continuous (freshmen), continuous (transfers).

Admissions Contact Ms. Andrea Canales, Director, Admissions, Texas Wesleyan University, 1201 Wesleyan Street, Fort Worth, TX 76105-1536. *Phone:* 817-531-4422. *Toll-free phone:* 800-580-8980. *Fax:* 817-531-7515. *E-mail:* freshman@txwesleyan.edu.

TEXAS WOMAN'S UNIVERSITY
Denton, Texas

- **State-supported** university, founded 1901
- **Calendar** semesters
- **Degrees** bachelor's, master's, doctoral, and post-master's certificates
- **Suburban** 270-acre campus with easy access to Dallas–Fort Worth
- **Endowment** $7.7 million
- **Coed, primarily women,** 5,344 undergraduate students, 72% full-time, 95% women, 5% men
- **Minimally difficult** entrance level, 72% of applicants were admitted

TWU offers more than 100 bachelor's, master's, and doctoral degree programs to approximately 9,700 students. A teaching and research institution, TWU emphasizes the health sciences, education, and the liberal arts. TWU offers a university experience focusing on the priorities and potential of all students. TWU welcomes women and men and traditional and nontraditional students to its campuses in Denton, Dallas, and Houston.

Undergraduates 3,830 full-time, 1,514 part-time. Students come from 24 states and territories, 44 other countries, 1% are from out of state, 22% African American, 4% Asian American or Pacific Islander, 11% Hispanic American, 0.9% Native American, 3% international, 16% transferred in, 19% live on campus. *Retention:* 75% of 2002 full-time freshmen returned.

Freshmen *Admission:* 1,964 applied, 1,413 admitted, 616 enrolled. *Average high school GPA:* 3.36. *Test scores:* SAT verbal scores over 500: 75%; SAT math scores over 500: 75%; ACT scores over 18: 75%.

Faculty *Total:* 592, 66% full-time. *Student/faculty ratio:* 13:1.

Majors Accounting; administrative assistant and secretarial science; art; audiology and speech-language pathology; biology/biological sciences; business administration and management; chemistry; child development; clinical laboratory science/medical technology; community health liaison; computer and information sciences; criminal justice/safety; dance; dental hygiene; dramatic/theatre arts; elementary education; English; family and consumer sciences/human sciences; fashion/apparel design; fashion merchandising; foods, nutrition, and wellness; history; human development and family studies; institutional food workers; interdisciplinary studies; journalism; kinesiology and exercise science; legal assistant/paralegal; library science; marketing/marketing management; mathematics; music; music therapy; nursing (registered nurse training); nutritional sciences; nutrition science; occupational therapy; political science and government; psychology; public administration and social service professions related; reading teacher education; science teacher education; social work; sociology; special education; speech-language pathology.

Academic Programs *Special study options:* academic remediation for entering students, accelerated degree program, adult/continuing education programs, advanced placement credit, cooperative education, distance learning, double majors, honors programs, independent study, internships, off-campus study, part-time degree program, services for LD students, summer session for credit. *Unusual degree programs:* 3-2 engineering with The University of Texas at Dallas; physical therapy, human biology, kinesiology, nursing.

Library Blagg-Huey Library with 531,718 titles, 2,537 serial subscriptions, 86,628 audiovisual materials, an OPAC, a Web page.

Computers on Campus 400 computers available on campus for general student use. A campuswide network can be accessed from student residence rooms and from off campus. Internet access, at least one staffed computer lab available.

Student Life *Housing:* on-campus residence required for freshman year. *Options:* coed, women-only. Campus housing is university owned. Freshman applicants given priority for college housing. *Activities and organizations:* drama/theater group, student-run newspaper, choral group, Campus Activities Board, Helping Hands, Gandsys, Trailblazers, Delta Phi Delta, national sororities. *Campus security:* 24-hour emergency response devices and patrols, late-night transport/escort service, controlled dormitory access. *Student services:* health clinic, personal/psychological counseling.

Athletics Member NCAA. All Division II. *Intercollegiate sports:* basketball W(s), cheerleading M(c)/W(c), gymnastics W(s), soccer W(s), softball W(s), volleyball W(s). *Intramural sports:* badminton M(c)/W(c), basketball M(c)/W(c), bowling M(c)/W(c), cheerleading M/W, football M(c)/W(c), golf M(c)/W(c), soccer M(c)/W(c), softball M(c)/W(c), tennis M(c), volleyball M(c)/W(c).

Standardized Tests *Required:* SAT I or ACT (for admission).

Costs (2003–04) *Tuition:* state resident $2208 full-time, $92 per semester hour part-time; nonresident $7872 full-time, $328 per semester hour part-time. Full-time tuition and fees vary according to course load, degree level, location, program, and reciprocity agreements. Part-time tuition and fees vary according to course load, degree level, location, program, and reciprocity agreements. *Required fees:* $756 full-time, $154 per semester hour part-time. *Room and board:* $4780; room only: $2420. Room and board charges vary according to board plan and housing facility. *Payment plan:* installment.

Financial Aid Of all full-time matriculated undergraduates who enrolled in 2003, 2,787 applied for aid, 2,249 were judged to have need, 1,805 had their need fully met. 131 Federal Work-Study jobs (averaging $1702). 481 state and other part-time jobs (averaging $3144). In 2003, 174 non-need-based awards were made. *Average percent of need met:* 98%. *Average financial aid package:* $10,412. *Average need-based loan:* $3720. *Average need-based gift aid:* $3934. *Average non-need-based aid:* $2100. *Average indebtedness upon graduation:* $14,173.

Applying *Options:* electronic application, early admission, deferred entrance. *Application fee:* $30. *Required:* high school transcript, minimum 2.0 GPA. *Application deadlines:* 7/15 (freshmen), 7/15 (transfers). *Notification:* continuous until 8/15 (freshmen), continuous until 8/15 (transfers).

Admissions Contact Ms. Teresa Mauk, Director of Admissions, Texas Woman's University, PO Box 425589, Denton, TX 76204-5589. *Phone:* 940-898-3040. *Toll-free phone:* 888-948-9984. *Fax:* 940-898-3081. *E-mail:* admissions@twu.edu.

■ *See page 2500 for a narrative description.*

TRINITY UNIVERSITY
San Antonio, Texas

- **Independent** comprehensive, founded 1869, affiliated with Presbyterian Church
- **Calendar** semesters
- **Degrees** bachelor's and master's
- **Urban** 113-acre campus
- **Endowment** $599.3 million
- **Coed,** 2,407 undergraduate students, 99% full-time, 52% women, 48% men
- **Very difficult** entrance level, 64% of applicants were admitted

Undergraduates 2,371 full-time, 36 part-time. Students come from 51 states and territories, 18 other countries, 2% African American, 6% Asian American or Pacific Islander, 11% Hispanic American, 0.5% Native American, 1% international, 1% transferred in, 77% live on campus. *Retention:* 86% of 2002 full-time freshmen returned.

Freshmen *Admission:* 3,675 applied, 2,360 admitted, 633 enrolled. *Average high school GPA:* 3.50. *Test scores:* SAT verbal scores over 500: 99%; SAT math scores over 500: 100%; ACT scores over 18: 100%; SAT verbal scores over 600: 79%; SAT math scores over 600: 84%; ACT scores over 24: 99%; SAT verbal scores over 700: 21%; SAT math scores over 700: 22%; ACT scores over 30: 40%.

Faculty *Total:* 295, 77% full-time. *Student/faculty ratio:* 10:1.

Majors Accounting; acting; anthropology; art; art history, criticism and conservation; Asian studies; biochemistry; biology/biological sciences; business administration and management; chemistry; Chinese; classics and languages, literatures and linguistics; communication/speech communication and rhetoric; computer and information sciences; dramatic/theatre arts; economics; engineering science; English; European studies; finance; French; geology/earth science; German; history; humanities; international business/trade/commerce; Latin American studies; management science; marketing/marketing management; mathematics; music; music performance; music theory and composition; philosophy; physics; political science and government; pre-dentistry studies; pre-law studies; pre-medical studies; pre-veterinary studies; psychology; religious studies; Russian; sociology; Spanish; speech and rhetoric; theatre design and technology; urban studies/affairs; voice and opera.

Academic Programs *Special study options:* accelerated degree program, advanced placement credit, double majors, honors programs, independent study, internships, part-time degree program, services for LD students, study abroad, summer session for credit. *ROTC:* Air Force (c).

Library Elizabeth Huth Coates Library with 898,527 titles, 2,311 serial subscriptions, 24,742 audiovisual materials, an OPAC, a Web page.

Computers on Campus 100 computers available on campus for general student use. A campuswide network can be accessed from student residence rooms and from off campus. Internet access, at least one staffed computer lab available.

Student Life *Housing:* on-campus residence required through junior year. *Options:* coed. Campus housing is university owned. *Activities and organizations:* drama/theater group, student-run newspaper, radio and television station, choral group, Voluntary Action Center, Alpha Phi Omega, Association of Student Representatives, Activities Council, Multicultural Network. *Campus security:* 24-hour emergency response devices and patrols, late-night transport/escort service, controlled dormitory access. *Student services:* health clinic, personal/psychological counseling.

Athletics Member NCAA. All Division III. *Intercollegiate sports:* baseball M, basketball M/W, cross-country running M/W, football M, golf M/W, lacrosse M(c)/W(c), riflery M(c)/W(c), soccer M/W, softball W, swimming M/W, tennis M/W, track and field M/W, volleyball M(c)/W. *Intramural sports:* basketball M/W, cross-country running M/W, football M/W, golf M, racquetball M/W, soccer M/W, softball M/W, swimming M/W, table tennis M/W, tennis M/W, track and field M/W, volleyball M/W, water polo M/W, wrestling M.

Standardized Tests *Recommended:* SAT I or ACT (for admission).

Costs (2003–04) *Comprehensive fee:* $26,466 includes full-time tuition ($18,402), mandatory fees ($774), and room and board ($7290). Part-time tuition: $767 per semester hour. *College room only:* $4590. Room and board charges vary according to board plan. *Payment plans:* tuition prepayment, installment. *Waivers:* employees or children of employees.

Financial Aid Of all full-time matriculated undergraduates who enrolled in 2003, 1,276 applied for aid, 990 were judged to have need, 616 had their need fully met. 10 state and other part-time jobs (averaging $1435). In 2003, 871 non-need-based awards were made. *Average percent of need met:* 86%. *Average financial aid package:* $15,486. *Average need-based loan:* $4215. *Average need-based gift aid:* $10,905. *Average non-need-based aid:* $6358. *Financial aid deadline:* 4/1.

Applying *Options:* common application, electronic application, early decision, deferred entrance. *Required:* essay or personal statement, high school transcript, 2 letters of recommendation. *Recommended:* interview. *Application deadlines:* 2/1 (freshmen), 3/1 (transfers). *Early decision:* 11/1. *Notification:* 4/1 (freshmen), 12/15 (early decision), 2/1 (early action), 4/1 (transfers).

Admissions Contact Mr. Christopher Ellertson, Dean of Admissions and Financial Aid, Trinity University, One Trinity Place, San Antonio, TX 78212-7200. *Phone:* 210-999-7207. *Toll-free phone:* 800-TRINITY. *Fax:* 210-999-8164. *E-mail:* admissions@trinity.edu.

■ *See page 2528 for a narrative description.*

UNIVERSITY OF DALLAS
Irving, Texas

- **Independent Roman Catholic** university, founded 1955
- **Calendar** semesters
- **Degrees** certificates, bachelor's, master's, and doctoral
- **Suburban** 750-acre campus with easy access to Dallas–Fort Worth
- **Endowment** $38.1 million
- **Coed,** 1,250 undergraduate students, 90% full-time, 56% women, 44% men
- **Moderately difficult** entrance level, 89% of applicants were admitted

Undergraduates 1,119 full-time, 131 part-time. Students come from 46 states and territories, 19 other countries, 37% are from out of state, 2% African American, 7% Asian American or Pacific Islander, 15% Hispanic American, 0.3% Native American, 2% international, 5% transferred in, 62% live on campus. *Retention:* 73% of 2002 full-time freshmen returned.

Freshmen *Admission:* 1,080 applied, 956 admitted, 299 enrolled. *Test scores:* SAT verbal scores over 500: 89%; SAT math scores over 500: 85%; ACT scores over 18: 99%; SAT verbal scores over 600: 53%; SAT math scores over 600: 47%; ACT scores over 24: 69%; SAT verbal scores over 700: 18%; SAT math scores over 700: 7%; ACT scores over 30: 15%.

Faculty *Total:* 215, 58% full-time, 67% with terminal degrees. *Student/faculty ratio:* 12:1.

Majors Art; art history, criticism and conservation; art teacher education; biochemistry; biology/biological sciences; ceramic arts and ceramics; chemistry; classics and languages, literatures and linguistics; computer science; dramatic/theatre arts; economics; economics related; education; elementary education; English; fine/studio arts; French; German; history; mathematics; painting; philosophy; physics; political science and government; pre-dentistry studies; pre-law studies; pre-medical studies; pre-theology/pre-ministerial studies; printmaking; psychology; sculpture; secondary education; Spanish; theology.

Academic Programs *Special study options:* academic remediation for entering students, accelerated degree program, advanced placement credit, double majors, English as a second language, independent study, internships, off-campus study, part-time degree program, services for LD students, student-designed majors, study abroad, summer session for credit. *ROTC:* Army (c), Air Force (c).

Library William A. Blakley Library with 232,472 titles, 767 serial subscriptions, 1,922 audiovisual materials, an OPAC, a Web page.

Computers on Campus 105 computers available on campus for general student use. A campuswide network can be accessed from student residence rooms and from off campus. Internet access, online (class) registration, at least one staffed computer lab available. Computer purchase or lease plan available.

Student Life *Housing:* on-campus residence required through junior year. *Options:* coed, men-only, women-only. Campus housing is university owned. Freshman campus housing is guaranteed. *Activities and organizations:* drama/theater group, student-run newspaper, radio station, choral group, SPUD (Programming Board), Residence Hall Association, student government, Best Buddies, Alpha Phi Omega. *Campus security:* 24-hour emergency response devices and patrols, late-night transport/escort service, controlled dormitory access. *Student services:* health clinic, personal/psychological counseling.

Athletics Member NCAA. All Division III. *Intercollegiate sports:* baseball M, basketball M/W, cheerleading M(c)/W(c), cross-country running M/W, golf M/W, lacrosse W, soccer M/W, softball W, tennis M/W, track and field M/W, volleyball W. *Intramural sports:* basketball M/W, equestrian sports M(c)/W(c), football M/W, rugby M(c), sailing M(c)/W(c), soccer M/W, softball M/W, tennis M/W, ultimate Frisbee M(c)/W(c), volleyball M/W.

Standardized Tests *Required:* SAT I or ACT (for admission).

Costs (2004–05) *Comprehensive fee:* $25,898 includes full-time tuition ($18,582), mandatory fees ($580), and room and board ($6736). Part-time tuition: $780 per credit. *Required fees:* $530 per year part-time. *College room only:* $3200. Room and board charges vary according to board plan and housing facility. *Payment plan:* installment. *Waivers:* employees or children of employees.

Financial Aid Of all full-time matriculated undergraduates who enrolled in 2002, 1,123 applied for aid, 768 were judged to have need, 164 had their need fully met. In 2002, 326 non-need-based awards were made. *Average percent of need met:* 78%. *Average financial aid package:* $14,144. *Average need-based loan:* $5049. *Average need-based gift aid:* $11,108. *Average non-need-based aid:* $9352. *Average indebtedness upon graduation:* $20,836.

Applying *Options:* common application, electronic application, early admission, early action, deferred entrance. *Application fee:* $50. *Required:* essay or personal statement, high school transcript, 1 letter of recommendation. *Required for some:* interview. *Recommended:* interview. *Application deadlines:* 8/1 (freshmen), 7/1 (transfers). *Notification:* continuous (freshmen), 1/15 (early action), continuous (transfers).

Admissions Contact Sr. Mary Brian Poole SSND, Assistant Dean of Admission, University of Dallas, 1845 East Northgate Drive, Irving, TX 75062-4799. *Phone:* 972-721-5266. *Toll-free phone:* 800-628-6999. *Fax:* 972-721-5017. *E-mail:* ugadmis@mailadmin.udallas.edu.

■ *See page 2594 for a narrative description.*

UNIVERSITY OF HOUSTON
Houston, Texas

- **State-supported** university, founded 1927, part of University of Houston System
- **Calendar** semesters
- **Degrees** bachelor's, master's, doctoral, and first professional
- **Urban** 550-acre campus
- **Endowment** $189.6 million
- **Coed,** 27,048 undergraduate students, 71% full-time, 52% women, 48% men
- **Moderately difficult** entrance level, 78% of applicants were admitted

Undergraduates 19,112 full-time, 7,936 part-time. Students come from 52 states and territories, 130 other countries, 2% are from out of state, 15% African American, 21% Asian American or Pacific Islander, 21% Hispanic American, 0.3% Native American, 5% international, 10% transferred in, 10% live on campus. *Retention:* 79% of 2002 full-time freshmen returned.

Freshmen *Admission:* 8,177 applied, 6,380 admitted, 3,325 enrolled. *Average high school GPA:* 3.00. *Test scores:* SAT verbal scores over 500: 57%; SAT math scores over 500: 67%; ACT scores over 18: 86%; SAT verbal scores over 600: 18%; SAT math scores over 600: 26%; ACT scores over 24: 25%; SAT verbal scores over 700: 3%; SAT math scores over 700: 4%; ACT scores over 30: 3%.

University of Houston (continued)

Faculty *Total:* 1,513, 71% full-time, 73% with terminal degrees. *Student/faculty ratio:* 22:1.

Majors Accounting; anthropology; applied mathematics; architecture; architecture related; art; art history, criticism and conservation; audiology and speech-language pathology; bilingual and multilingual education; biochemistry; biology/biological sciences; biomedical/medical engineering; business administration and management; business/corporate communications; business family and consumer sciences/human sciences; business statistics; chemical engineering; chemistry; civil engineering; civil engineering technology; classics and languages, literatures and linguistics; clinical laboratory science/medical technology; communication disorders; communication/speech communication and rhetoric; community health services counseling; computer and information sciences; computer engineering; computer engineering technology; computer systems analysis; construction engineering technology; creative writing; drafting and design technology; dramatic/theatre arts; economics; education; electrical, electronics and communications engineering; electromechanical technology; English; environmental design/architecture; environmental studies; European studies (Western); family and consumer sciences/human sciences; finance; fine/studio arts; foods, nutrition, and wellness; French; geology/earth science; geophysics and seismology; German; German studies; graphic communications; health and physical education; history; hotel/motel administration; human development and family studies; human nutrition; industrial engineering; industrial technology; information science/studies; information technology; interdisciplinary studies; interior architecture; interior design; Italian; journalism; kinesiology and exercise science; Latin; management information systems; marketing/marketing management; mass communication/media; mathematics; mechanical engineering; music; music performance; music theory and composition; operations management; organizational behavior; organizational communication; painting; pharmacy; philosophy; photography; physics; political science and government; pre-dentistry studies; pre-law studies; pre-medical studies; pre-veterinary studies; printmaking; psychology; public relations/image management; Russian studies; sales, distribution and marketing; sculpture; sociology; Spanish; Spanish and Iberian studies; speech and rhetoric; statistics.

Academic Programs *Special study options:* academic remediation for entering students, accelerated degree program, adult/continuing education programs, advanced placement credit, cooperative education, distance learning, double majors, English as a second language, freshman honors college, honors programs, independent study, internships, off-campus study, part-time degree program, services for LD students, study abroad, summer session for credit. *ROTC:* Army (b), Navy (c).

Library M.D. Anderson Library plus 5 others with 2.1 million titles, 20,276 serial subscriptions, 8,834 audiovisual materials, an OPAC, a Web page.

Computers on Campus 825 computers available on campus for general student use. A campuswide network can be accessed from student residence rooms and from off campus. Internet access, online (class) registration, at least one staffed computer lab available.

Student Life *Housing options:* coed. Campus housing is university owned. *Activities and organizations:* drama/theater group, student-run newspaper, radio and television station, choral group, marching band, Council of Ethnic Organizations, Greek life, Frontier Fiesta Association, intramural sports, Golden Key National Honor Society, national fraternities, national sororities. *Campus security:* 24-hour emergency response devices and patrols, student patrols, late-night transport/escort service, controlled dormitory access, vehicle assistance. *Student services:* health clinic, personal/psychological counseling, women's center, legal services.

Athletics Member NCAA. All Division I except football (Division I-A). *Intercollegiate sports:* baseball M(s), basketball M(s)/W(s), cheerleading M/W, cross-country running M(s)/W(s), golf M(s), soccer W(s), softball W(s), swimming W(s), tennis W(s), track and field M(s)/W(s), volleyball W(s). *Intramural sports:* badminton M/W, baseball M, basketball M/W, bowling M(c)/W(c), cheerleading M/W, cross-country running M/W, football M/W, golf M/W, lacrosse M, racquetball M/W, rock climbing M/W, rugby M, soccer M(c), swimming M/W, table tennis M/W, tennis M/W, track and field M/W, ultimate Frisbee M/W, volleyball M/W, water polo M/W, weight lifting M.

Standardized Tests *Required:* SAT I or ACT (for admission). *Recommended:* SAT II: Subject Tests (for admission).

Costs (2003–04) *Tuition:* state resident $1380 full-time, $46 per credit part-time; nonresident $8460 full-time, $282 per credit part-time. Full-time tuition and fees vary according to course level, course load, degree level, location, program, reciprocity agreements, and student level. Part-time tuition and fees vary according to course level, course load, degree level, location, program, reciprocity agreements, and student level. *Required fees:* $2568 full-time. *Room and board:* $5870; room only: $3290. Room and board charges vary according to board plan and housing facility. *Payment plan:* installment.

Financial Aid Of all full-time matriculated undergraduates who enrolled in 2002, 16,800 applied for aid, 10,500 were judged to have need, 680 had their need fully met. In 2002, 3150 non-need-based awards were made. *Average percent of need met:* 80%. *Average financial aid package:* $11,340. *Average need-based loan:* $5300. *Average need-based gift aid:* $6200. *Average non-need-based aid:* $2730. *Average indebtedness upon graduation:* $12,988.

Applying *Options:* common application, electronic application, early admission, deferred entrance. *Application fee:* $40. *Required:* high school transcript, minimum 2.0 GPA. *Recommended:* letters of recommendation. *Application deadlines:* 4/1 (freshmen), 4/1 (transfers). *Notification:* continuous (freshmen), continuous (transfers).

Admissions Contact Mr. Jeff Fuller, Admissions, University of Houston, Room 122, Ezekiel Cullen Building, Houston, TX 77204-2023. *Phone:* 713-743-9620. *Fax:* 713-743-9633. *E-mail:* admissions@uh.edu.

■ *See page 2616 for a narrative description.*

UNIVERSITY OF HOUSTON–CLEAR LAKE
Houston, Texas

- **State-supported** upper-level, founded 1971, part of University of Houston System
- **Calendar** semesters
- **Degrees** bachelor's and master's
- **Suburban** 487-acre campus
- **Endowment** $7.8 million
- **Coed,** 3,926 undergraduate students, 50% full-time, 66% women, 34% men
- **Minimally difficult** entrance level, 99% of applicants were admitted

Undergraduates 1,972 full-time, 1,954 part-time. Students come from 16 states and territories, 84 other countries, 1% are from out of state, 7% African American, 6% Asian American or Pacific Islander, 16% Hispanic American, 0.4% Native American, 3% international, 94% transferred in, 3% live on campus.

Faculty *Total:* 444, 48% full-time. *Student/faculty ratio:* 16:1.

Majors Accounting; anthropology; art; behavioral sciences; biology/biological sciences; business administration and management; business administration, management and operations related; business/commerce; chemistry; clinical psychology; communication/speech communication and rhetoric; computer and information sciences; computer engineering; computer science; computer software engineering; computer systems networking and telecommunications; counselor education/school counseling and guidance; curriculum and instruction; early childhood education; educational/instructional media design; educational leadership and administration; English; environmental science; finance; geography; health and physical education; health/health care administration; history; humanities; human resources development; information science/studies; intercultural/multicultural and diversity studies; legal assistant/paralegal; library science; management information systems; marketing/marketing management; marriage and family therapy/counseling; mathematics; multi-/interdisciplinary studies related; parks, recreation and leisure facilities management; physical sciences; political science and government; psychology; public administration; reading teacher education; school psychology; social work; sociology; statistics; systems engineering.

Academic Programs *Special study options:* accelerated degree program, cooperative education, distance learning, double majors, English as a second language, independent study, internships, part-time degree program, services for LD students, student-designed majors, summer session for credit.

Library Neumann Library with 650,000 titles, 984 serial subscriptions, 795 audiovisual materials, an OPAC.

Computers on Campus 383 computers available on campus for general student use. A campuswide network can be accessed from off campus. Internet access, online (class) registration, at least one staffed computer lab available.

Student Life *Housing options:* Campus housing is provided by a third party. *Activities and organizations:* student-run newspaper, Beta Alpha Psi, The Indian Student Association, The Management Association, Texas Student Education Association, Accounting Association. *Campus security:* 24-hour emergency response devices and patrols, late-night transport/escort service. *Student services:* health clinic, personal/psychological counseling, women's center.

Athletics *Intramural sports:* football M(c)/W(c), golf M(c)/W(c), rugby M(c), soccer M(c)/W(c), softball M(c)/W(c), tennis M(c)/W(c), volleyball M(c)/W(c).

Costs (2003–04) *Tuition:* state resident $1104 full-time, $120 per credit hour part-time; nonresident $6768 full-time, $282 per credit hour part-time. *Required fees:* $1535 full-time. *Payment plan:* installment.

Financial Aid Of all full-time matriculated undergraduates who enrolled in 2003, 756 applied for aid, 642 were judged to have need, 89 had their need fully met. 58 Federal Work-Study jobs, 5 state and other part-time jobs. In 2003, 350 non-need-based awards were made. *Average percent of need met:* 53%. *Average* *financial aid package:* $5435. *Average need-based loan:* $4397. *Average need-based gift aid:* $2760. *Average non-need-based aid:* $2064. *Average indebtedness upon graduation:* $10,728.

Applying *Options:* common application, electronic application, deferred entrance. *Application fee:* $35. *Application deadline:* rolling (transfers). *Notification:* continuous (transfers).

Admissions Contact Ms. Rose Sklar, Director of Admissions and Registrar, University of Houston–Clear Lake, 2700 Bay Area Boulevard, Box 13, Houston, TX 77058-1098. *Phone:* 281-283-2533. *Fax:* 281-283-2530. *E-mail:* admissions@cl.uh.edu.

UNIVERSITY OF HOUSTON–DOWNTOWN

Houston, Texas

- **State-supported** comprehensive, founded 1974, part of University of Houston System
- **Calendar** semesters
- **Degrees** bachelor's and master's
- **Urban** 20-acre campus
- **Endowment** $8.3 million
- **Coed**
- **Noncompetitive** entrance level

Faculty *Student/faculty ratio:* 19:1.

Student Life *Campus security:* 24-hour emergency response devices and patrols, late-night transport/escort service.

Costs (2003–04) *Tuition:* state resident $3164 full-time; nonresident $10,244 full-time.

Financial Aid Of all full-time matriculated undergraduates who enrolled in 2002, 2,284 applied for aid, 2,105 were judged to have need, 296 had their need fully met. 120 Federal Work-Study jobs (averaging $2500). 8 state and other part-time jobs (averaging $2196). In 2002, 389. *Average percent of need met:* 58. *Average financial aid package:* $4393. *Average need-based loan:* $2416. *Average need-based gift aid:* $3813. *Average non-need-based aid:* $3357.

Applying *Options:* common application, deferred entrance. *Application fee:* $10. *Required:* high school transcript.

Admissions Contact Ms. Penny Cureton, Executive Director of Enrollment Management, University of Houston–Downtown, One Main Street, Houston, TX 77002. *Phone:* 713-221-8522. *Fax:* 713-221-8157. *E-mail:* uhdadmit@dt.uh.edu.

UNIVERSITY OF HOUSTON–VICTORIA

Victoria, Texas

- **State-supported** upper-level, founded 1973, part of University of Houston System
- **Calendar** semesters
- **Degrees** bachelor's and master's
- **Small-town** 20-acre campus
- **Endowment** $4.3 million
- **Coed,** 1,139 undergraduate students, 35% full-time, 72% women, 28% men
- **Minimally difficult** entrance level

Undergraduates 403 full-time, 736 part-time. Students come from 1 other state, 0.1% are from out of state, 8% African American, 4% Asian American or Pacific Islander, 21% Hispanic American, 0.4% Native American, 0.9% international, 25% transferred in.

Faculty *Total:* 115, 60% full-time, 77% with terminal degrees. *Student/faculty ratio:* 16:1.

Majors Accounting; biology/biological sciences; business administration and management; computer science; education; history; humanities; marketing/marketing management; mathematics; social sciences.

Academic Programs *Special study options:* adult/continuing education programs, distance learning, double majors, external degree program, independent study, internships, off-campus study, part-time degree program, services for LD students, study abroad, summer session for credit.

Library VC/UHV Library plus 1 other with 227,800 titles, 10,652 serial subscriptions, 7,553 audiovisual materials, an OPAC, a Web page.

Computers on Campus 150 computers available on campus for general student use. A campuswide network can be accessed from off campus. Internet access, online (class) registration, at least one staffed computer lab available.

Student Life *Housing:* college housing not available. *Activities and organizations:* student-run newspaper, Texas Student Education Association. *Campus security:* 24-hour emergency response devices and patrols.

Costs (2003–04) *Tuition:* state resident $2760 full-time, $92 per semester hour part-time; nonresident $9840 full-time, $328 per semester hour part-time. Full-time tuition and fees vary according to course load. Part-time tuition and fees vary according to course load. *Required fees:* $300 full-time, $15 per semester hour part-time. *Payment plan:* installment. *Waivers:* senior citizens.

Financial Aid Of all full-time matriculated undergraduates who enrolled in 2002, 234 applied for aid, 209 were judged to have need, 6 had their need fully met. 17 Federal Work-Study jobs (averaging $2949). 2 state and other part-time jobs (averaging $1708). In 2002, 46 non-need-based awards were made. *Average percent of need met:* 58%. *Average financial aid package:* $6725. *Average need-based loan:* $4280. *Average need-based gift aid:* $3806. *Average non-need-based aid:* $3627. *Average indebtedness upon graduation:* $17,000.

Applying *Application deadline:* rolling (freshmen), rolling (transfers). *Notification:* continuous (transfers).

Admissions Contact Mr. Richard Phillips, Director of Enrollment Management, University of Houston–Victoria, 3007 North Ben Wilson, Victoria, TX 77901-4450. *Phone:* 361-570-4110. *Toll-free phone:* 877-940-4848. *Fax:* 361-570-4114. *E-mail:* urbanom@uhv.edu.

UNIVERSITY OF MARY HARDIN-BAYLOR

Belton, Texas

- **Independent Southern Baptist** comprehensive, founded 1845
- **Calendar** semesters
- **Degrees** bachelor's and master's
- **Small-town** 100-acre campus with easy access to Austin
- **Endowment** $38.7 million
- **Coed,** 2,479 undergraduate students, 88% full-time, 65% women, 35% men
- **Moderately difficult** entrance level, 76% of applicants were admitted

Undergraduates 2,174 full-time, 305 part-time. Students come from 24 states and territories, 13 other countries, 3% are from out of state, 11% African American, 2% Asian American or Pacific Islander, 10% Hispanic American, 0.3% Native American, 0.8% international, 11% transferred in, 48% live on campus. *Retention:* 63% of 2002 full-time freshmen returned.

Freshmen *Admission:* 1,173 applied, 890 admitted, 508 enrolled. *Test scores:* SAT verbal scores over 500: 59%; SAT math scores over 500: 61%; ACT scores over 18: 97%; SAT verbal scores over 600: 16%; SAT math scores over 600: 18%; ACT scores over 24: 35%; SAT verbal scores over 700: 2%; SAT math scores over 700: 2%; ACT scores over 30: 4%.

Faculty *Total:* 201, 63% full-time, 55% with terminal degrees. *Student/faculty ratio:* 16:1.

Majors Accounting; American native/native American education; art; art teacher education; athletic training; behavioral sciences; biology/biological sciences; business administration and management; business/commerce; business teacher education; chemistry; clinical laboratory science/medical technology; commercial and advertising art; communication/speech communication and rhetoric; computer and information sciences; computer graphics; computer science; criminal justice/law enforcement administration; data processing and data processing technology; dramatic/theatre arts; economics; education; elementary education; English; finance; fine/studio arts; general studies; history; information science/studies; kindergarten/preschool education; management information systems; marketing/marketing management; mass communication/media; mathematics; middle school education; music performance; music teacher education; nursing (registered nurse training); parks, recreation and leisure; physical education teaching and coaching; political science and government; pre-dentistry studies; pre-law studies; pre-medical studies; pre-pharmacy studies; pre-veterinary studies; psychology; reading teacher education; religious/sacred music; religious studies; secondary education; social work; sociology; Spanish; special education; speech and rhetoric.

Academic Programs *Special study options:* academic remediation for entering students, accelerated degree program, adult/continuing education programs, advanced placement credit, distance learning, double majors, English as a second language, honors programs, independent study, internships, part-time degree program, services for LD students, summer session for credit. *ROTC:* Air Force (c).

Library Townsend Memorial Library with 192,526 titles, 1,631 serial subscriptions, 5,484 audiovisual materials, an OPAC, a Web page.

Computers on Campus 262 computers available on campus for general student use. A campuswide network can be accessed from student residence rooms. Internet access, at least one staffed computer lab available. Computer purchase or lease plan available.

Student Life *Housing:* on-campus residence required through junior year. *Options:* men-only, women-only, disabled students. Campus housing is university owned. Freshman applicants given priority for college housing. *Activities and organizations:* drama/theater group, student-run newspaper, choral group, marching band, Baptist Student Ministry, Student Government Association, Residence Hall Association, Campus Activities Board, Crusaders for Christ. *Campus security:* 24-hour emergency response devices and patrols, late-night transport/escort

University of Mary Hardin-Baylor (continued)
service, controlled dormitory access, campus police force, lighted pathways and sidewalks. *Student services:* health clinic, personal/psychological counseling.

Athletics Member NCAA. All Division III. *Intercollegiate sports:* baseball M, basketball M/W, football M, golf M/W, soccer M/W, softball W, tennis M/W, volleyball W. *Intramural sports:* basketball M/W, bowling M/W, football M/W, softball M/W, table tennis M/W, tennis M/W, ultimate Frisbee M/W, volleyball M/W.

Standardized Tests *Required:* SAT I or ACT (for admission).

Costs (2003–04) *Comprehensive fee:* $15,540 includes full-time tuition ($10,650), mandatory fees ($890), and room and board ($4000). Part-time tuition: $355 per semester hour. *Required fees:* $28 per semester hour part-time, $25 per term part-time. *Room and board:* Room and board charges vary according to housing facility. *Payment plans:* tuition prepayment, installment. *Waivers:* employees or children of employees.

Financial Aid Of all full-time matriculated undergraduates who enrolled in 2003, 1,862 applied for aid, 1,491 were judged to have need, 183 had their need fully met. 241 Federal Work-Study jobs (averaging $2300). 195 state and other part-time jobs (averaging $2300). In 2003, 445 non-need-based awards were made. *Average percent of need met:* 75%. *Average financial aid package:* $11,228. *Average need-based loan:* $4516. *Average need-based gift aid:* $4922. *Average non-need-based aid:* $3141. *Average indebtedness upon graduation:* $13,437.

Applying *Options:* common application, electronic application, early admission, deferred entrance. *Application fee:* $35. *Required:* high school transcript. *Required for some:* interview. *Application deadline:* rolling (freshmen), rolling (transfers). *Notification:* continuous (freshmen), continuous (transfers).

Admissions Contact University of Mary Hardin-Baylor, UMHB Station Box 8004, 900 College Street, Belton, TX 76513-2599. *Phone:* 254-295-4520. *Toll-free phone:* 800-727-8642. *Fax:* 254-295-5049. *E-mail:* admission@umhb.edu.

UNIVERSITY OF NORTH TEXAS

Denton, Texas

- **State-supported** university, founded 1890
- **Calendar** semesters
- **Degrees** bachelor's, master's, doctoral, and postbachelor's certificates
- **Suburban** 744-acre campus with easy access to Dallas–Fort Worth
- **Endowment** $11.1 million
- **Coed,** 23,862 undergraduate students, 78% full-time, 55% women, 45% men
- **Moderately difficult** entrance level, 68% of applicants were admitted

Undergraduates 18,654 full-time, 5,208 part-time. Students come from 53 states and territories, 137 other countries, 3% are from out of state, 11% African American, 5% Asian American or Pacific Islander, 10% Hispanic American, 0.8% Native American, 3% international, 13% transferred in, 15% live on campus. *Retention:* 75% of 2002 full-time freshmen returned.

Freshmen *Admission:* 10,335 applied, 7,046 admitted, 3,618 enrolled. *Test scores:* SAT verbal scores over 500: 72%; SAT math scores over 500: 69%; ACT scores over 18: 94%; SAT verbal scores over 600: 29%; SAT math scores over 600: 27%; ACT scores over 24: 39%; SAT verbal scores over 700: 4%; SAT math scores over 700: 5%; ACT scores over 30: 4%.

Faculty *Total:* 1,573, 58% full-time. *Student/faculty ratio:* 18:1.

Majors Accounting; advertising; anthropology; art; art history, criticism and conservation; audiology and speech-language pathology; banking and financial support services; behavioral sciences; biochemistry; biology/biological sciences; broadcast journalism; business/commerce; business/managerial economics; ceramic arts and ceramics; chemistry; child guidance; city/urban, community and regional planning; civil engineering technology; clinical laboratory science/medical technology; communication/speech communication and rhetoric; computer and information sciences; computer engineering; computer teacher education; construction engineering technology; criminal justice/safety; cytotechnology; dance; dramatic/theatre arts; drawing; economics; electrical, electronic and communications engineering technology; engineering technology; English; English composition; English language and literature related; family living/parenthood; fashion/apparel design; fashion merchandising; fiber, textile and weaving arts; finance; financial planning and services; French; general studies; geography; geology/earth science; German; gerontology; health and physical education; history; hospitality administration; human development and family studies; information science/studies; insurance; interdisciplinary studies; international/global studies; jazz/jazz studies; journalism; kinesiology and exercise science; landscape architecture; library science; logistics and materials management; management information systems; marketing/marketing management; mathematics; mechanical engineering/mechanical technology; metal and jewelry arts; multi-/interdisciplinary studies related; music; music history, literature, and theory; music performance; music teacher education; music theory and composition; nuclear/nuclear power technology; operations management; organizational behavior; painting; parks, recreation and leisure facilities management; philosophy; photography; photojournalism; physics; physics related; piano and organ; political science and government; printmaking; psychology; public administration; public health education and promotion; public relations/image management; radio and television; real estate; rehabilitation and therapeutic professions related; rehabilitation therapy; sales, distribution and marketing; sculpture; social sciences; social sciences related; social work; sociology; Spanish; violin, viola, guitar and other stringed instruments; voice and opera; wind/percussion instruments.

Academic Programs *Special study options:* academic remediation for entering students, accelerated degree program, advanced placement credit, cooperative education, distance learning, double majors, English as a second language, external degree program, freshman honors college, honors programs, internships, part-time degree program, services for LD students, study abroad, summer session for credit. *ROTC:* Army (c), Navy (b).

Library Willis Library plus 4 others with 2.0 million titles, 12,243 serial subscriptions, 16,007 audiovisual materials, an OPAC, a Web page.

Computers on Campus 2006 computers available on campus for general student use. A campuswide network can be accessed from student residence rooms and from off campus. At least one staffed computer lab available.

Student Life *Housing:* on-campus residence required for freshman year. *Options:* coed, women-only, disabled students. Freshman applicants given priority for college housing. *Activities and organizations:* drama/theater group, student-run newspaper, radio and television station, choral group, marching band, Student Government Association, Residence Hall Association, Interfraternity Council, Coalition of Black Student Organizations, Panhellenic, national fraternities, national sororities. *Campus security:* 24-hour emergency response devices and patrols, late-night transport/escort service, controlled dormitory access. *Student services:* health clinic, personal/psychological counseling, women's center, legal services.

Athletics Member NCAA. All Division I. *Intercollegiate sports:* baseball M(c), basketball M(s)/W(s), bowling M(c)/W(c), cheerleading M/W, cross-country running M(s)/W(s), fencing M(c)/W(c), football M(s), golf M(s)/W(s), ice hockey M(c), lacrosse M(c)/W(c), rugby M(c), sailing M(c)/W(c), soccer W, softball W, swimming M(c)/W(c), tennis M(c)/W(s), track and field M(s)/W(s), ultimate Frisbee M(c)/W(c), volleyball W(s). *Intramural sports:* basketball M/W, bowling M/W, field hockey M/W, football M/W, golf M/W, racquetball M/W, soccer M/W, softball M/W, table tennis M/W, tennis M/W, track and field M/W, volleyball M/W, water polo M/W, weight lifting M(c)/W(c).

Standardized Tests *Required:* SAT I or ACT (for admission).

Costs (2003–04) *Tuition:* state resident $2292 full-time, $99 per credit part-time; nonresident $7958 full-time, $335 per credit part-time. Full-time tuition and fees vary according to course load and location. Part-time tuition and fees vary according to course load and location. *Required fees:* $1490 full-time, $496 per term part-time. *Room and board:* $4885; room only: $2726. Room and board charges vary according to board plan. *Payment plan:* installment. *Waivers:* senior citizens and employees or children of employees.

Financial Aid Of all full-time matriculated undergraduates who enrolled in 2003, 11,236 applied for aid, 8,099 were judged to have need, 1,495 had their need fully met. In 2003, 2085 non-need-based awards were made. *Average percent of need met:* 66%. *Average financial aid package:* $6179. *Average need-based loan:* $3433. *Average need-based gift aid:* $3626. *Average non-need-based aid:* $2555. *Average indebtedness upon graduation:* $15,466.

Applying *Options:* common application, electronic application, early admission, deferred entrance. *Application fee:* $40. *Required:* high school transcript. *Required for some:* essay or personal statement, 3 letters of recommendation, interview. *Application deadlines:* 6/15 (freshmen), 6/15 (transfers). *Notification:* continuous (freshmen), continuous (transfers).

Admissions Contact Ms. Janet Trepka, Coordinator or New Student Mentoring Programs and Vice President of Student Development, University of North Texas, Box 311277, Denton, TX 76203-9988. *Phone:* 940-565-3190. *Toll-free phone:* 800-868-8211. *Fax:* 940-565-2408. *E-mail:* undergrad@unt.edu.

UNIVERSITY OF PHOENIX–DALLAS CAMPUS

Dallas, Texas

- **Proprietary** comprehensive, founded 2001
- **Calendar** continuous
- **Degrees** certificates, associate, bachelor's, master's, doctoral, post-master's, and postbachelor's certificates (courses conducted at 121 campuses and learning centers in 25 states)
- **Urban** campus
- **Coed,** 1,327 undergraduate students, 100% full-time, 59% women, 41% men
- **Noncompetitive** entrance level

Undergraduates 1,327 full-time. 19% African American, 1% Asian American or Pacific Islander, 7% Hispanic American, 0.2% Native American, 24% international.

Freshmen *Admission:* 93 enrolled.

Faculty *Total:* 70, 6% full-time, 39% with terminal degrees. *Student/faculty ratio:* 11:1.

Majors Accounting; business administration and management; management information systems; management science; marketing/marketing management.

Academic Programs *Special study options:* accelerated degree program, advanced placement credit, distance learning, independent study.

Library 27.1 million titles, 11,648 serial subscriptions, an OPAC, a Web page.

Computers on Campus A campuswide network can be accessed from off campus. At least one staffed computer lab available.

Student Life *Housing:* college housing not available.

Costs (2003–04) *Tuition:* $9360 full-time, $312 per credit part-time. *Waivers:* employees or children of employees.

Financial Aid *Average financial aid package:* $1246.

Applying *Application fee:* $100. *Required:* 1 letter of recommendation, 2 years of work experience, 23 years of age. *Required for some:* high school transcript. *Application deadline:* rolling (freshmen), rolling (transfers).

Admissions Contact Ms. Beth Barilla, Director of Admissions, University of Phoenix–Dallas Campus, 4615 East Elwood Street, Mail Stop AA-K101, Phoenix, AZ 85040-1958. *Phone:* 480-317-6000. *Toll-free phone:* 800-228-7240. *Fax:* 480-594-1758. *E-mail:* beth.barilla@phoenix.edu.

UNIVERSITY OF PHOENIX–HOUSTON CAMPUS

Houston, Texas

- **Proprietary** comprehensive, founded 2001
- **Calendar** continuous
- **Degrees** certificates, associate, bachelor's, master's, doctoral, post-master's, and postbachelor's certificates (courses conducted at 121 campuses and learning centers in 25 states)
- **Urban** campus
- **Coed,** 1,940 undergraduate students, 100% full-time, 64% women, 36% men
- **Noncompetitive** entrance level

Undergraduates 1,940 full-time. 17% African American, 1% Asian American or Pacific Islander, 8% Hispanic American, 0.2% Native American, 41% international.

Freshmen *Admission:* 116 enrolled.

Faculty *Total:* 141, 3% full-time, 28% with terminal degrees. *Student/faculty ratio:* 12:1.

Majors Accounting; business administration and management; e-commerce; management information systems; management science; marketing/marketing management.

Academic Programs *Special study options:* accelerated degree program, adult/continuing education programs, advanced placement credit, distance learning, external degree program, independent study.

Library University Library with 27.1 million titles, 11,648 serial subscriptions, an OPAC, a Web page.

Computers on Campus A campuswide network can be accessed from off campus. Internet access, at least one staffed computer lab available.

Student Life *Housing:* college housing not available.

Costs (2003–04) *Tuition:* $9360 full-time, $312 per credit part-time. *Waivers:* employees or children of employees.

Financial Aid *Average financial aid package:* $1409.

Applying *Options:* deferred entrance. *Application fee:* $100. *Required:* 1 letter of recommendation, 2 years of work experience, 23 years of age. *Required for some:* high school transcript. *Application deadline:* rolling (freshmen), rolling (transfers).

Admissions Contact Ms. Beth Barilla, Director of Admissions, University of Phoenix–Houston Campus, 4615 East Elwood Street, Mail Stop AA-K101, Phoenix, AZ 85040-1958. *Phone:* 480-317-6000. *Toll-free phone:* 800-228-7240. *Fax:* 480-594-1758. *E-mail:* beth.barilla@phoenix.edu.

UNIVERSITY OF ST. THOMAS

Houston, Texas

- **Independent Roman Catholic** comprehensive, founded 1947
- **Calendar** semesters
- **Degrees** diplomas, bachelor's, master's, doctoral, and first professional
- **Urban** 21-acre campus
- **Endowment** $37.0 million
- **Coed,** 1,907 undergraduate students, 73% full-time, 65% women, 35% men
- **Moderately difficult** entrance level, 89% of applicants were admitted

Undergraduates 1,383 full-time, 524 part-time. Students come from 27 states and territories, 32 other countries, 3% are from out of state, 6% African American, 14% Asian American or Pacific Islander, 27% Hispanic American, 0.7% Native American, 3% international, 10% transferred in, 13% live on campus. *Retention:* 68% of 2002 full-time freshmen returned.

Freshmen *Admission:* 808 applied, 718 admitted, 302 enrolled. *Average high school GPA:* 3.54. *Test scores:* SAT verbal scores over 500: 83%; SAT math scores over 500: 86%; ACT scores over 18: 98%; SAT verbal scores over 600: 39%; SAT math scores over 600: 38%; ACT scores over 24: 56%; SAT verbal scores over 700: 6%; SAT math scores over 700: 5%; ACT scores over 30: 7%.

Faculty *Total:* 271, 42% full-time, 72% with terminal degrees. *Student/faculty ratio:* 14:1.

Majors Accounting; biology/biological sciences; business administration and management; chemistry; communication/speech communication and rhetoric; dramatic/theatre arts; economics; education; elementary education; English; environmental studies; finance; fine/studio arts; French; general studies; history; international relations and affairs; liberal arts and sciences/liberal studies; management information systems; marketing related; mathematics; music; music teacher education; pastoral studies/counseling; philosophy; political science and government; pre-dentistry studies; pre-law studies; pre-medical studies; pre-pharmacy studies; pre-veterinary studies; psychology; secondary education; Spanish; theology; theology and religious vocations related.

Academic Programs *Special study options:* academic remediation for entering students, accelerated degree program, adult/continuing education programs, advanced placement credit, cooperative education, double majors, English as a second language, honors programs, independent study, internships, off-campus study, part-time degree program, services for LD students, study abroad, summer session for credit. *ROTC:* Army (c). *Unusual degree programs:* 3-2 engineering with University of Notre Dame, University of Houston, Texas A&M University.

Library Doherty Library plus 1 other with 206,410 titles, 10,000 serial subscriptions, 1,125 audiovisual materials, an OPAC, a Web page.

Computers on Campus 153 computers available on campus for general student use. A campuswide network can be accessed from student residence rooms and from off campus. Internet access, at least one staffed computer lab available.

Student Life *Housing options:* coed. Campus housing is university owned. Freshman applicants given priority for college housing. *Activities and organizations:* drama/theater group, student-run newspaper, choral group. *Campus security:* 24-hour emergency response devices and patrols, late-night transport/escort service, controlled dormitory access. *Student services:* health clinic, personal/psychological counseling.

Athletics *Intramural sports:* baseball M(c), basketball M/W(c), cheerleading W, fencing M(c)/W(c), golf M/W, racquetball M/W, rugby M, soccer M(c)/W(c), table tennis M/W, tennis M/W, ultimate Frisbee M(c)/W(c), volleyball M/W(c).

Standardized Tests *Required:* SAT I or ACT (for admission).

Costs (2003–04) *Comprehensive fee:* $21,952 includes full-time tuition ($15,000), mandatory fees ($112), and room and board ($6840). Full-time tuition and fees vary according to course load and degree level. Part-time tuition: $500 per credit hour. Part-time tuition and fees vary according to course load and degree level. *Required fees:* $30 per term part-time. *College room only:* $3700. Room and board charges vary according to board plan and housing facility. *Payment plans:* installment, deferred payment. *Waivers:* senior citizens and employees or children of employees.

Financial Aid Of all full-time matriculated undergraduates who enrolled in 2003, 895 applied for aid, 798 were judged to have need, 126 had their need fully met. 37 Federal Work-Study jobs (averaging $2753). 2 state and other part-time jobs (averaging $3000). In 2003, 263 non-need-based awards were made. *Average percent of need met:* 68%. *Average financial aid package:* $10,983. *Average need-based loan:* $3712. *Average need-based gift aid:* $7775. *Average non-need-based aid:* $6795. *Average indebtedness upon graduation:* $20,393.

Applying *Options:* common application, electronic application, deferred entrance. *Application fee:* $35. *Required:* essay or personal statement, high school transcript, minimum 2.25 GPA. *Application deadline:* rolling (freshmen). *Notification:* continuous (freshmen), continuous (transfers).

Admissions Contact Mr. Eduardo Prieto, Dean of Admissions, University of St. Thomas, 3800 Montrose Boulevard, Houston, TX 77006-4696. *Phone:* 713-525-3500. *Toll-free phone:* 800-856-8565. *Fax:* 713-525-3558. *E-mail:* admissions@stthom.edu.

THE UNIVERSITY OF TEXAS AT ARLINGTON

Arlington, Texas

- **State-supported** university, founded 1895, part of University of Texas System

The University of Texas at Arlington (continued)
- **Calendar** semesters
- **Degrees** bachelor's, master's, doctoral, post-master's, and postbachelor's certificates
- **Urban** 395-acre campus with easy access to Dallas–Fort Worth
- **Endowment** $33.2 million
- **Coed,** 18,870 undergraduate students, 71% full-time, 53% women, 47% men
- **Moderately difficult** entrance level, 77% of applicants were admitted

Undergraduates 13,486 full-time, 5,384 part-time. Students come from 44 states and territories, 126 other countries, 2% are from out of state, 14% African American, 11% Asian American or Pacific Islander, 13% Hispanic American, 0.8% Native American, 5% international, 16% transferred in, 13% live on campus. *Retention:* 70% of 2002 full-time freshmen returned.

Freshmen *Admission:* 5,092 applied, 3,928 admitted, 1,986 enrolled. *Test scores:* SAT verbal scores over 500: 65%; SAT math scores over 500: 71%; ACT scores over 18: 91%; SAT verbal scores over 600: 19%; SAT math scores over 600: 25%; ACT scores over 24: 29%; SAT verbal scores over 700: 2%; SAT math scores over 700: 3%; ACT scores over 30: 2%.

Faculty *Total:* 1,034, 72% full-time. *Student/faculty ratio:* 26:1.

Majors Accounting; advertising; aerospace, aeronautical and astronautical engineering; anthropology; architecture; art; art history, criticism and conservation; athletic training; banking and financial support services; biochemistry; biology/biological sciences; business administration and management; business/managerial economics; chemistry; child development; civil engineering; classics and languages, literatures and linguistics; clinical laboratory science/medical technology; computer and information sciences; computer engineering; computer science; computer software engineering; criminal justice/safety; digital communication and media/multimedia; dramatic/theatre arts; economics; electrical, electronics and communications engineering; English; fine/studio arts; foreign languages and literatures; French; geology/earth science; German; health and physical education; history; industrial engineering; interdisciplinary studies; interior architecture; international business/trade/commerce; journalism; management information systems; marketing/marketing management; mathematics; mechanical engineering; microbiology; multi-/interdisciplinary studies related; music; nursing (registered nurse training); philosophy; physics; political science and government; psychology; public relations/image management; radio and television; real estate; Russian; social work; sociology; Spanish; speech and rhetoric.

Academic Programs *Special study options:* academic remediation for entering students, adult/continuing education programs, advanced placement credit, cooperative education, distance learning, double majors, English as a second language, freshman honors college, honors programs, independent study, internships, part-time degree program, services for LD students, student-designed majors, study abroad, summer session for credit. *ROTC:* Army (b), Air Force (c).

Library Central Library plus 2 others with 1.1 million titles, 3,977 serial subscriptions, 5,240 audiovisual materials, an OPAC, a Web page.

Computers on Campus 1000 computers available on campus for general student use. A campuswide network can be accessed from student residence rooms and from off campus. Internet access, online (class) registration, at least one staffed computer lab available.

Student Life *Housing options:* coed, men-only, women-only. Campus housing is university owned and leased by the school. *Activities and organizations:* drama/theater group, student-run newspaper, radio station, choral group, marching band, Medical/Dental Preparatory Association, Institute of Electronic and Electrical Engineers, Tai Wanese Students Association, Accounting Society, Upsilon Pi Epsilon, national fraternities, national sororities. *Campus security:* 24-hour emergency response devices and patrols, late-night transport/escort service, controlled dormitory access, remote emergency telephones, bicycle patrols, crime prevention program, student shuttle service from 7:30 a.m. to 4:30 p.m. *Student services:* health clinic, personal/psychological counseling, legal services.

Athletics Member NCAA. All Division I. *Intercollegiate sports:* baseball M(s), basketball M(s)/W(s), cross-country running M(s)/W(s), golf M(s), softball W(s), tennis M(s)/W(s), track and field M(s)/W(s), volleyball W(s). *Intramural sports:* badminton M/W, basketball M/W, bowling M/W, football M/W, golf M/W, racquetball M/W, soccer M/W, softball M/W, table tennis M/W, tennis M/W, ultimate Frisbee M/W, volleyball M/W, weight lifting M/W.

Standardized Tests *Required:* SAT I or ACT (for admission).

Costs (2003–04) *Tuition:* state resident $2760 full-time, $92 per hour part-time; nonresident $9840 full-time, $328 per hour part-time. Full-time tuition and fees vary according to course load. Part-time tuition and fees vary according to course load. *Required fees:* $1663 full-time, $54 per hour part-time, $99 per term part-time. *Room and board:* $4829; room only: $2643. Room and board charges vary according to board plan and housing facility. *Payment plan:* installment. *Waivers:* employees or children of employees.

Financial Aid Of all full-time matriculated undergraduates who enrolled in 2003, 8,204 applied for aid, 6,287 were judged to have need, 1,213 had their need fully met. 1,659 Federal Work-Study jobs (averaging $1991). In 2003, 1582 non-need-based awards were made. *Average percent of need met:* 80%. *Average financial aid package:* $8014. *Average need-based loan:* $4975. *Average need-based gift aid:* $4381. *Average non-need-based aid:* $2114. *Average indebtedness upon graduation:* $12,934.

Applying *Options:* early admission, deferred entrance. *Application fee:* $35. *Required:* high school transcript, class rank. *Application deadline:* 6/1 (freshmen), rolling (transfers). *Notification:* continuous (freshmen), continuous (transfers).

Admissions Contact Dr. Hans Gatterdam, Director of Admissions, The University of Texas at Arlington, PO Box 19111, 701 South Nedderman Drive, Room 110, Davis Hall, Arlington, TX 76019-0088. *Phone:* 817-272-6287. *Fax:* 817-272-3435. *E-mail:* admissions@uta.edu.

THE UNIVERSITY OF TEXAS AT AUSTIN
Austin, Texas

- **State-supported** university, founded 1883, part of University of Texas System
- **Calendar** semesters
- **Degrees** bachelor's, master's, doctoral, and first professional
- **Urban** 350-acre campus with easy access to San Antonio
- **Endowment** $1.6 billion
- **Coed,** 38,383 undergraduate students, 90% full-time, 51% women, 49% men
- **Very difficult** entrance level, 47% of applicants were admitted

Undergraduates 34,601 full-time, 3,782 part-time. Students come from 53 states and territories, 94 other countries, 5% are from out of state, 4% African American, 17% Asian American or Pacific Islander, 14% Hispanic American, 0.4% Native American, 3% international, 4% transferred in, 18% live on campus. *Retention:* 92% of 2002 full-time freshmen returned.

Freshmen *Admission:* 24,519 applied, 11,504 admitted, 6,544 enrolled. *Test scores:* SAT verbal scores over 500: 88%; SAT math scores over 500: 92%; ACT scores over 18: 96%; SAT verbal scores over 600: 55%; SAT math scores over 600: 67%; ACT scores over 24: 72%; SAT verbal scores over 700: 15%; SAT math scores over 700: 24%; ACT scores over 30: 19%.

Faculty *Total:* 2,646, 92% full-time, 89% with terminal degrees. *Student/faculty ratio:* 19:1.

Majors Accounting; advertising; aerospace, aeronautical and astronautical engineering; American studies; ancient/classical Greek; ancient studies; anthropology; apparel and textiles; Arabic; archeology; architectural engineering; architecture; art; art history, criticism and conservation; Asian studies; astronomy; athletic training; biochemistry; biology/biological sciences; biomedical/medical engineering; botany/plant biology; business administration and management; business administration, management and operations related; business/commerce; chemical engineering; chemistry; civil engineering; classics and languages, literatures and linguistics; clinical laboratory science/medical technology; communication disorders; communication/speech communication and rhetoric; computer and information sciences; Czech; dance; design and visual communications; dramatic/theatre arts; East Asian languages; ecology; economics; electrical, electronics and communications engineering; English; ethnic, cultural minority, and gender studies related; family and consumer sciences/human sciences; finance; fine/studio arts; foods, nutrition, and wellness; foreign languages and literatures; French; geography; geological and earth sciences/geosciences related; geology/earth science; geophysics and seismology; German; health and physical education; health services/allied health/health sciences; Hebrew; history; human development and family studies; humanities; hydrology and water resources science; interior design; Iranian/Persian languages; Islamic studies; Italian; Jewish/Judaic studies; journalism; Latin; Latin American studies; liberal arts and sciences/liberal studies; linguistics; management information systems; marketing/marketing management; mathematics; mechanical engineering; microbiology; molecular biology; multi-/interdisciplinary studies related; music; music history, literature, and theory; music performance; music theory and composition; Near and Middle Eastern studies; nursing (registered nurse training); petroleum engineering; philosophy; physics; political science and government; Portuguese; psychology; public relations/image management; radio and television; religious studies; Russian; Russian studies; Scandinavian languages; Semitic languages; social work; sociology; Spanish; sport and fitness administration; Turkish; urban studies/affairs; visual and performing arts; zoology/animal biology.

Academic Programs *Special study options:* academic remediation for entering students, accelerated degree program, adult/continuing education programs, advanced placement credit, cooperative education, distance learning, double majors, English as a second language, honors programs, independent study, internships, part-time degree program, services for LD students, student-designed majors, study abroad, summer session for credit. *ROTC:* Army (b), Navy (b), Air Force (b). *Unusual degree programs:* 3-2 architecture.

Library Perry-Castañeda Library plus 16 others with 4.3 million titles, 49,771 serial subscriptions, 622,610 audiovisual materials, an OPAC, a Web page.

Computers on Campus 4000 computers available on campus for general student use. A campuswide network can be accessed from student residence rooms and from off campus that provide access to e-mail. Internet access, at least one staffed computer lab available.

Student Life *Housing options:* coed, men-only, women-only. Campus housing is university owned. Freshman applicants given priority for college housing. *Activities and organizations:* drama/theater group, student-run newspaper, radio and television station, choral group, marching band, Alpha Phi Omega, Student Events Center, Texas Exes-Student Chapter, Longhorn Band Student Organization, Student Volunteer Board, national fraternities, national sororities. *Campus security:* 24-hour emergency response devices and patrols, student patrols, late-night transport/escort service, controlled dormitory access. *Student services:* health clinic, personal/psychological counseling, legal services.

Athletics Member NCAA. All Division I except football (Division I-A). *Intercollegiate sports:* baseball M(s), basketball M(s)/W(s), cheerleading M/W, crew W(s), cross-country running M(s)/W(s), golf M(s)/W(s), soccer W(s), softball W(s), swimming M(s)/W(s), tennis M(s)/W(s), track and field M(s)/W(s), volleyball W(s). *Intramural sports:* archery M(c)/W(c), badminton M/W, baseball M(c), basketball M/W, bowling M/W, crew M(c)/W(c), equestrian sports M(c)/W(c), fencing M(c)/W(c), field hockey M(c)/W(c), football M/W, golf M/W, gymnastics M(c)/W(c), ice hockey M(c), lacrosse M(c)/W(c), racquetball M/W, rugby M(c), sailing M(c)/W(c), soccer M/W, softball M/W, squash M/W, swimming M/W, table tennis M/W, tennis M/W, track and field M/W, ultimate Frisbee M/W, volleyball M/W, water polo M(c)/W(c), weight lifting M/W.

Standardized Tests *Required:* SAT I or ACT (for admission).

Costs (2003–04) *Tuition:* state resident $3120 full-time; nonresident $10,240 full-time. Full-time tuition and fees vary according to course load and program. Part-time tuition and fees vary according to course load and program. *Required fees:* $1428 full-time. *Room and board:* $6082; room only: $3499. Room and board charges vary according to board plan and housing facility. *Payment plans:* tuition prepayment, installment. *Waivers:* senior citizens and employees or children of employees.

Financial Aid Of all full-time matriculated undergraduates who enrolled in 2003, 22,700 applied for aid, 17,300 were judged to have need, 14,900 had their need fully met. In 2003, 8750 non-need-based awards were made. *Average percent of need met:* 94%. *Average financial aid package:* $8750. *Average need-based loan:* $4530. *Average need-based gift aid:* $5450. *Average non-need-based aid:* $4560. *Average indebtedness upon graduation:* $16,500.

Applying *Options:* common application, electronic application, deferred entrance. *Application fee:* $50. *Required:* high school transcript. *Required for some:* essay or personal statement. *Application deadlines:* 2/1 (freshmen), 3/1 (transfers). *Notification:* continuous (freshmen), continuous (transfers).

Admissions Contact Freshman Admissions Center, The University of Texas at Austin, PO Box 8058, Austin, TX 78713-8058. *Phone:* 512-475-7440. *Fax:* 512-475-7475.

THE UNIVERSITY OF TEXAS AT BROWNSVILLE

Brownsville, Texas

- **State-supported** upper-level, founded 1973, part of University of Texas System
- **Calendar** semesters
- **Degrees** bachelor's and master's
- **Urban** 380-acre campus
- **Coed,** 6,167 undergraduate students, 48% full-time, 63% women, 37% men
- **Noncompetitive** entrance level, 100% of applicants were admitted

Undergraduates 2,989 full-time, 3,178 part-time. Students come from 6 states and territories, 11 other countries, 0.2% are from out of state, 6% transferred in.

Freshmen *Admission:* 2,044 applied, 2,044 admitted.

Faculty *Total:* 553, 51% full-time, 27% with terminal degrees. *Student/faculty ratio:* 18:1.

Majors Accounting; applied art; art; bilingual and multilingual education; biology/biological sciences; business administration and management; chemistry; computer and information sciences; corrections; criminal justice/law enforcement administration; criminal justice/police science; criminal justice/safety; electrical, electronic and communications engineering technology; engineering physics; English; finance; health and physical education; health services/allied health/health sciences; history; industrial technology; information science/studies; kindergarten/preschool education; kinesiology and exercise science; liberal arts and sciences/liberal studies; manufacturing technology; marketing/marketing management; mathematics; mechanical engineering/mechanical technology; multi-/interdisciplinary studies related; music; nursing (registered nurse training); office occupations and clerical services; physics; political science and government; psychology; sociology; Spanish; special education.

Academic Programs *Special study options:* academic remediation for entering students, advanced placement credit, cooperative education, distance learning, double majors, English as a second language, independent study, internships, part-time degree program, summer session for credit.

Library Arnulfo L. Oliveira Library with 174,660 titles, 4,447 serial subscriptions, 1,000 audiovisual materials, an OPAC, a Web page.

Computers on Campus 650 computers available on campus for general student use. A campuswide network can be accessed from off campus. Internet access, online (class) registration available. Computer purchase or lease plan available.

Student Life *Housing options:* Campus housing is university owned. *Activities and organizations:* student-run newspaper, choral group, Student Activities Programming Board, criminal justice club, Gorgas Science Club, Club Cultural Latinoamericano. *Campus security:* 24-hour emergency response devices and patrols. *Student services:* health clinic, personal/psychological counseling.

Athletics Member NJCAA. *Intercollegiate sports:* baseball M(s), golf M(s)/W(s), volleyball W(s). *Intramural sports:* badminton W.

Standardized Tests *Required:* TASP (for placement).

Costs (2003–04) *Tuition:* state resident $1920 full-time; nonresident $7536 full-time. *Required fees:* $513 full-time. *Room and board:* $6276; room only: $2580. *Payment plan:* installment. *Waivers:* employees or children of employees.

Financial Aid Of all full-time matriculated undergraduates who enrolled in 2003, 3,973 applied for aid, 3,736 were judged to have need. In 2003, 79 non-need-based awards were made. *Average percent of need met:* 16%. *Average financial aid package:* $3040. *Average need-based loan:* $1770. *Average need-based gift aid:* $2263. *Average non-need-based aid:* $2096.

Applying *Options:* common application, early admission. *Application deadlines:* 7/10 (freshmen), 8/1 (transfers). *Notification:* continuous (transfers).

Admissions Contact Carlo Tamayo, New Student Relations Coordinator, The University of Texas at Brownsville, 80 Fort Brown, Brownsville, TX 78520-4991. *Phone:* 956-544-8860. *Toll-free phone:* 800-850-0160. *Fax:* 956-983-7810. *E-mail:* cata01@utb.edu.

THE UNIVERSITY OF TEXAS AT DALLAS

Richardson, Texas

- **State-supported** university, founded 1969, part of University of Texas System
- **Calendar** semesters
- **Degrees** bachelor's, master's, and doctoral
- **Suburban** 455-acre campus with easy access to Dallas
- **Endowment** $181.8 million
- **Coed,** 8,688 undergraduate students, 69% full-time, 49% women, 51% men
- **Very difficult** entrance level, 50% of applicants were admitted

Undergraduates 5,998 full-time, 2,690 part-time. Students come from 46 states and territories, 129 other countries, 2% are from out of state, 7% African American, 20% Asian American or Pacific Islander, 10% Hispanic American, 0.7% Native American, 5% international, 17% transferred in, 40% live on campus. *Retention:* 84% of 2002 full-time freshmen returned.

Freshmen *Admission:* 5,048 applied, 2,501 admitted, 1,060 enrolled. *Average high school GPA:* 3.44. *Test scores:* SAT verbal scores over 500: 90%; SAT math scores over 500: 97%; ACT scores over 18: 99%; SAT verbal scores over 600: 55%; SAT math scores over 600: 66%; ACT scores over 24: 74%; SAT verbal scores over 700: 14%; SAT math scores over 700: 21%; ACT scores over 30: 22%.

Faculty *Total:* 626, 66% full-time, 98% with terminal degrees. *Student/faculty ratio:* 20:1.

Majors Accounting; American studies; applied mathematics; audiology and speech-language pathology; biochemistry; biology/biological sciences; business/commerce; chemistry; cognitive psychology and psycholinguistics; computer and information sciences; computer engineering; computer science; criminology; economics; electrical, electronics and communications engineering; ethnic, cultural minority, and gender studies related; geography; geology/earth science; history; humanities; interdisciplinary studies; international business/trade/commerce; literature; management information systems; marketing/marketing management; mathematics; molecular biology; neuroscience; organizational behavior; physics; political science and government; psychology; public administration; sociology; statistics; visual and performing arts.

Academic Programs *Special study options:* academic remediation for entering students, accelerated degree program, adult/continuing education programs, advanced placement credit, cooperative education, distance learning, double majors, freshman honors college, honors programs, independent study, internships, part-time degree program, services for LD students, student-designed

The University of Texas at Dallas (continued)

majors, study abroad, summer session for credit. *ROTC:* Army (c), Air Force (c). *Unusual degree programs:* 3-2 engineering with Abilene Christian University, Austin College, Paul Quinn College, Texas Woman's University.

Library Eugene McDermott Library plus 2 others with 754,491 titles, 3,078 serial subscriptions, 5,080 audiovisual materials, an OPAC, a Web page.

Computers on Campus 630 computers available on campus for general student use. A campuswide network can be accessed from student residence rooms and from off campus. Internet access, online (class) registration, at least one staffed computer lab available.

Student Life *Housing options:* coed. Campus housing is university owned and is provided by a third party. Freshman applicants given priority for college housing. *Activities and organizations:* drama/theater group, student-run newspaper, radio station, Student Government Association, Golden Key National Honor Society, Muslim Students Association, Indian Student Association, Friendship Association of Chinese Students and Scholars, national fraternities, national sororities. *Campus security:* 24-hour emergency response devices and patrols, late-night transport/escort service. *Student services:* health clinic, personal/psychological counseling, women's center, legal services.

Athletics Member NCAA. All Division III. *Intercollegiate sports:* baseball M, basketball M/W, cross-country running M/W, golf M/W, soccer M/W, softball W, tennis M/W. *Intramural sports:* badminton M/W, basketball M/W, cheerleading M/W, cross-country running M/W, football M/W, golf M/W, ice hockey M, lacrosse M, racquetball M/W, rugby M, soccer M/W, softball M/W, squash M/W, table tennis M/W, tennis M/W, ultimate Frisbee M/W, volleyball M/W, weight lifting M/W.

Standardized Tests *Required:* SAT I or ACT (for admission). *Required for some:* TASP. *Recommended:* SAT II: Writing Test (for admission).

Costs (2003–04) *Tuition:* state resident $1380 full-time, $46 per credit part-time; nonresident $8460 full-time, $282 per credit part-time. Full-time tuition and fees vary according to course load, degree level, program, and student level. Part-time tuition and fees vary according to course load, degree level, program, and student level. *Required fees:* $4113 full-time, $143 per credit part-time, $167 per term part-time. *Room and board:* $6122. Room and board charges vary according to board plan and housing facility. *Payment plan:* installment. *Waivers:* senior citizens.

Financial Aid Of all full-time matriculated undergraduates who enrolled in 2003, 3,339 applied for aid, 2,642 were judged to have need, 194 had their need fully met. 2 Federal Work-Study jobs (averaging $2730). In 2003, 225 non-need-based awards were made. *Average percent of need met:* 67%. *Average financial aid package:* $7909. *Average need-based loan:* $3926. *Average need-based gift aid:* $3134. *Average non-need-based aid:* $4250. *Average indebtedness upon graduation:* $12,605.

Applying *Options:* electronic application, deferred entrance. *Application fee:* $50. *Required:* essay or personal statement, high school transcript. *Required for some:* interview. *Recommended:* 3 letters of recommendation. *Application deadline:* 7/1 (freshmen). *Notification:* continuous (freshmen), continuous (transfers).

Admissions Contact Mr. Barry Samsula, Director of Enrollment Services, The University of Texas at Dallas, PO Box 830688 Mail Station MC11, Richardson, TX 75083-0688. *Phone:* 972-883-2270. *Toll-free phone:* 800-889-2443. *Fax:* 972-883-2599. *E-mail:* admissions-status@utdallas.edu.

■ *See page 2718 for a narrative description.*

THE UNIVERSITY OF TEXAS AT EL PASO
El Paso, Texas

- **State-supported** university, founded 1913
- **Calendar** semesters
- **Degrees** bachelor's, master's, and doctoral
- **Urban** 360-acre campus
- **Coed**
- **Minimally difficult** entrance level

Faculty *Student/faculty ratio:* 21:1.

Student Life *Campus security:* 24-hour emergency response devices and patrols, late-night transport/escort service.

Athletics Member NCAA. All Division I except football (Division I-A).

Standardized Tests *Required for some:* SAT I or ACT (for admission), PAA.

Costs (2003–04) *Tuition:* state resident $2208 full-time; nonresident $7872 full-time. Full-time tuition and fees vary according to reciprocity agreements. Part-time tuition and fees vary according to course load and reciprocity agreements. *Required fees:* $756 full-time. *Room only:* $2835. Room and board charges vary according to housing facility.

Financial Aid Of all full-time matriculated undergraduates who enrolled in 2002, 7,537 applied for aid, 5,944 were judged to have need, 1,687 had their need fully met. 848 Federal Work-Study jobs (averaging $2122). 58 state and other part-time jobs (averaging $952). In 2002, 668. *Average percent of need met:* 78. *Average financial aid package:* $9044. *Average need-based loan:* $4964. *Average need-based gift aid:* $4516. *Average non-need-based aid:* $1874. *Average indebtedness upon graduation:* $7704.

Applying *Options:* deferred entrance. *Required:* high school transcript.

Admissions Contact Ms. Diana Guerrero, Director of Admissions, The University of Texas at El Paso, 500 West University Avenue, El Paso, TX 79968-0510. *Phone:* 915-747-5588. *Toll-free phone:* 877-746-4636. *Fax:* 915-747-8893. *E-mail:* futureminer@utep.edu.

THE UNIVERSITY OF TEXAS AT SAN ANTONIO
San Antonio, Texas

- **State-supported** university, founded 1969, part of University of Texas System
- **Calendar** semesters
- **Degrees** bachelor's, master's, and doctoral
- **Suburban** 600-acre campus with easy access to San Antonio, Texas
- **Coed**
- **Moderately difficult** entrance level

Faculty *Student/faculty ratio:* 26:1.

Student Life *Campus security:* 24-hour emergency response devices and patrols.

Athletics Member NCAA. All Division I.

Standardized Tests *Required:* SAT I or ACT (for admission).

Costs (2003–04) *Tuition:* state resident $2760 full-time, $92 per credit hour part-time; nonresident $9840 full-time, $328 per credit hour part-time. *Required fees:* $1559 full-time. *Room and board:* $7898; room only: $3339.

Applying *Options:* common application, electronic application. *Application fee:* $30. *Required:* high school transcript.

Admissions Contact The University of Texas at San Antonio, 6900 North Loop 1604 West, San Antonio, TX 78249-0617. *Phone:* 210-458-4530. *Toll-free phone:* 800-669-0919. *Fax:* 210-458-2001. *E-mail:* prospects@utsa.edu.

THE UNIVERSITY OF TEXAS AT TYLER
Tyler, Texas

- **State-supported** comprehensive, founded 1971, part of University of Texas System
- **Calendar** semesters
- **Degrees** bachelor's and master's
- **Urban** 200-acre campus
- **Endowment** $39.2 million
- **Coed,** 3,597 undergraduate students, 74% full-time, 62% women, 38% men
- 82% of applicants were admitted

Undergraduates 2,670 full-time, 927 part-time. Students come from 27 states and territories, 48 other countries, 2% are from out of state, 9% African American, 1% Asian American or Pacific Islander, 5% Hispanic American, 0.5% Native American, 2% international, 69% transferred in, 8% live on campus. *Retention:* 56% of 2002 full-time freshmen returned.

Freshmen *Admission:* 1,182 applied, 967 admitted, 434 enrolled. *Test scores:* SAT verbal scores over 500: 61%; SAT math scores over 500: 61%; ACT scores over 18: 95%; SAT verbal scores over 600: 21%; SAT math scores over 600: 16%; ACT scores over 24: 38%; SAT verbal scores over 700: 2%; SAT math scores over 700: 2%; ACT scores over 30: 4%.

Faculty *Total:* 265, 67% full-time, 63% with terminal degrees. *Student/faculty ratio:* 17:1.

Majors Accounting; art; biology/biological sciences; business administration and management; business/managerial economics; chemistry; clinical laboratory science/medical technology; computer and information sciences; criminal justice/safety; dramatic/theatre arts; electrical, electronics and communications engineering; engineering technology; English; finance; foreign languages and literatures; health and physical education; history; industrial technology; interdisciplinary studies; journalism; liberal arts and sciences/liberal studies; marketing/marketing management; mathematics; mechanical engineering; multi-/interdisciplinary studies related; music; nursing (registered nurse training); occupational safety and health technology; political science and government; psychology; sociology; Spanish; speech and rhetoric.

Academic Programs *Special study options:* adult/continuing education programs, advanced placement credit, cooperative education, distance learning, double majors, English as a second language, honors programs, independent study, internships, part-time degree program, services for LD students, student-designed majors, study abroad, summer session for credit.

Library Robert Muntz Library with 136,402 titles, 1,546 serial subscriptions, 10,864 audiovisual materials, an OPAC, a Web page.

Computers on Campus 125 computers available on campus for general student use. A campuswide network can be accessed from student residence rooms and from off campus. Internet access, online (class) registration, at least one staffed computer lab available.

Student Life *Housing options:* coed. Campus housing is university owned and is provided by a third party. Freshman applicants given priority for college housing. *Activities and organizations:* drama/theater group, student-run newspaper, choral group, Student Government Association, Pre-Med/Pre-Dental, American Chemistry Society, Press Club, Latin Club. *Campus security:* 24-hour emergency response devices and patrols, late-night transport/escort service, controlled dormitory access. *Student services:* personal/psychological counseling.

Athletics Member NCAA, NSCAA. All NCAA Division III. *Intercollegiate sports:* basketball M/W, cheerleading M/W, cross-country running M/W, golf M/W, soccer M/W, tennis M/W, volleyball W. *Intramural sports:* basketball M/W, bowling M/W, football M/W, golf M/W, racquetball M/W, soccer M/W, softball M/W, table tennis M/W, volleyball W.

Standardized Tests *Required:* SAT I or ACT (for admission).

Costs (2003–04) *Tuition:* state resident $2280 full-time, $95 per semester hour part-time; nonresident $7944 full-time, $331 per semester hour part-time. Full-time tuition and fees vary according to course load. *Required fees:* $664 full-time, $28 per semester hour part-time. *Room only:* $3240. Room and board charges vary according to housing facility. *Payment plan:* installment. *Waivers:* employees or children of employees.

Financial Aid Of all full-time matriculated undergraduates who enrolled in 2003, 1,734 applied for aid, 1,411 were judged to have need, 445 had their need fully met. 69 Federal Work-Study jobs (averaging $1724). 49 state and other part-time jobs (averaging $1681). In 2003, 674 non-need-based awards were made. *Average percent of need met:* 80%. *Average financial aid package:* $6714. *Average need-based loan:* $3494. *Average need-based gift aid:* $3456. *Average non-need-based aid:* $1699. *Average indebtedness upon graduation:* $13,904.

Applying *Options:* common application, electronic application, deferred entrance. *Required:* high school transcript. *Notification:* continuous (freshmen), continuous (transfers).

Admissions Contact Mr. Jim Hutto, Dean of Enrollment Management, The University of Texas at Tyler, 3900 University Boulevard, Tyler, TX 75799-0001. *Phone:* 903-566-7195. *Toll-free phone:* 800-UTTYLER. *Fax:* 903-566-7068. *E-mail:* admissions@uttyler.edu.

The University of Texas Health Science Center at Houston

Houston, Texas

- **State-supported** upper-level, founded 1972, part of University of Texas System
- **Calendar** semesters
- **Degrees** certificates, bachelor's, master's, doctoral, first professional, and post-master's certificates
- **Urban** campus
- **Endowment** $76.4 million
- **Coed,** 347 undergraduate students, 91% full-time, 87% women, 13% men
- **Moderately difficult** entrance level

Undergraduates 315 full-time, 32 part-time. 10% African American, 13% Asian American or Pacific Islander, 16% Hispanic American, 0.3% Native American, 0.6% international.

Majors Dental hygiene; nursing (registered nurse training).

Academic Programs *Special study options:* accelerated degree program, distance learning, double majors, independent study, internships, part-time degree program. *ROTC:* Army (c).

Library Houston Academy of Medicine-Texas Medical Center Library plus 3 others with 344,015 titles, 5,019 serial subscriptions, an OPAC, a Web page.

Computers on Campus A campuswide network can be accessed from off campus. Internet access, online (class) registration, at least one staffed computer lab available.

Student Life *Activities and organizations:* student-run newspaper. *Campus security:* 24-hour emergency response devices and patrols, late-night transport/escort service, controlled access to all buildings. *Student services:* health clinic, personal/psychological counseling.

Costs (2004–05) *Tuition:* state resident $4140 full-time, $92 per hour part-time; nonresident $14,760 full-time, $328 per hour part-time. Part-time tuition and fees vary according to course load. *Required fees:* $696 full-time. *Payment plan:* installment.

Financial Aid Of all full-time matriculated undergraduates who enrolled in 2003, 293 applied for aid, 198 were judged to have need. *Average percent of need met:* 95%. *Average financial aid package:* $15,050. *Average need-based loan:* $5724. *Average need-based gift aid:* $5495. *Average indebtedness upon graduation:* $16,474.

Applying *Options:* electronic application. *Application fee:* $30. *Application deadline:* 12/31 (transfers).

Admissions Contact Mr. Robert L. Jenkins, Associate Registrar, The University of Texas Health Science Center at Houston, 7000 Fannin, PO Box 20036, Houston, TX 77225-0036. *Phone:* 713-500-3361. *Fax:* 713-500-3356. *E-mail:* registrar@uth.tmc.edu.

The University of Texas Health Science Center at San Antonio

San Antonio, Texas

- **State-supported** upper-level, founded 1976, part of University of Texas System
- **Calendar** semesters
- **Degrees** certificates, bachelor's, master's, doctoral, and first professional
- **Suburban** 100-acre campus
- **Coed**
- **Moderately difficult** entrance level

Undergraduates Students come from 41 states and territories, 6 other countries.

Faculty *Total:* 1,372. *Student/faculty ratio:* 2:1.

Majors Clinical laboratory science/medical technology; dental hygiene; nursing (registered nurse training); occupational therapy; physician assistant; respiratory care therapy.

Academic Programs *Special study options:* academic remediation for entering students, adult/continuing education programs, part-time degree program, summer session for credit. *ROTC:* Army (c), Air Force (c).

Library Dolph Briso Library with 192,576 titles, 2,501 serial subscriptions.

Computers on Campus 1000 computers available on campus for general student use. A campuswide network can be accessed from off campus. Internet access available.

Student Life *Housing:* college housing not available. *Campus security:* 24-hour emergency response devices and patrols, late-night transport/escort service. *Student services:* health clinic, personal/psychological counseling.

Athletics *Intramural sports:* basketball M/W, softball M/W, tennis M/W, volleyball M/W.

Standardized Tests *Required for some:* SAT I or ACT (for admission), TASP.

Costs (2003–04) *Tuition:* state resident $1380 full-time, $46 per semester hour part-time; nonresident $8460 full-time, $282 per semester hour part-time. *Required fees:* $1727 full-time, $40 per semester hour part-time.

Financial Aid In 2002, 30 non-need-based awards were made. *Average percent of need met:* 30%. *Average financial aid package:* $14,000. *Average indebtedness upon graduation:* $14,536.

Applying *Application fee:* $50.

Admissions Contact Mr. James B. Peak, Associate Registrar, The University of Texas Health Science Center at San Antonio, 7703 Floyd Curl Drive, San Antonio, TX 78229-3900. *Phone:* 210-567-2629.

The University of Texas Medical Branch

Galveston, Texas

- **State-supported** upper-level, founded 1891, part of University of Texas System
- **Calendar** semesters (early semester)
- **Degrees** bachelor's, master's, doctoral, and first professional
- **Small-town** 85-acre campus with easy access to Houston
- **Coed,** 521 undergraduate students, 51% full-time, 84% women, 16% men
- **Very difficult** entrance level

Undergraduates 267 full-time, 254 part-time. Students come from 3 states and territories, 7 other countries, 1% are from out of state, 13% African American, 7% Asian American or Pacific Islander, 18% Hispanic American, 2% Native American, 2% international, 39% transferred in.

Majors Clinical laboratory science/medical technology; nursing (registered nurse training); occupational therapy; respiratory care therapy.

Academic Programs *Special study options:* advanced placement credit, distance learning, independent study, internships, part-time degree program, services for LD students, summer session for credit.

The University of Texas Medical Branch (continued)

Library Moody Medical Library with 248,370 titles, 1,980 serial subscriptions, 960 audiovisual materials, an OPAC, a Web page.

Computers on Campus 200 computers available on campus for general student use. A campuswide network can be accessed from student residence rooms and from off campus. Internet access, online (class) registration, at least one staffed computer lab available.

Student Life *Housing options:* coed. Campus housing is university owned. *Activities and organizations:* student-run newspaper, Texas Medical Association, American Medical Student Association, American Medical Women's Association, Texas Association Latin American Medical Students, National Medical Student Association, national fraternities. *Campus security:* 24-hour emergency response devices and patrols, late-night transport/escort service. *Student services:* health clinic, personal/psychological counseling, legal services.

Athletics *Intramural sports:* basketball M/W, football M/W, soccer M/W, softball M/W, volleyball M/W.

Costs (2003–04) *Tuition:* state resident $46 per credit hour part-time; nonresident $282 per credit hour part-time. Full-time tuition and fees vary according to course load and program. Part-time tuition and fees vary according to course load and program. *Room and board:* Room and board charges vary according to housing facility. *Payment plan:* installment.

Financial Aid Of all full-time matriculated undergraduates who enrolled in 2002, 27 Federal Work-Study jobs.

Applying *Options:* electronic application. *Application fee:* $25. *Notification:* continuous (transfers).

Admissions Contact Ms. Vicki L. Brewer, Registrar, The University of Texas Medical Branch, 301 University Boulevard, Galveston, TX 77555-1305. *Phone:* 409-772-1215. *Fax:* 409-772-5056. *E-mail:* student.admissions@utmb.edu.

THE UNIVERSITY OF TEXAS OF THE PERMIAN BASIN

Odessa, Texas

- **State-supported** comprehensive, founded 1969, part of University of Texas System
- **Calendar** semesters
- **Degrees** bachelor's and master's
- **Urban** 600-acre campus
- **Coed**
- **Moderately difficult** entrance level

Faculty *Student/faculty ratio:* 18:1.

Student Life *Campus security:* 24-hour patrols, late-night transport/escort service.

Athletics Member NAIA.

Standardized Tests *Required:* SAT I or ACT (for admission).

Costs (2003–04) *Tuition:* state resident $2580 full-time, $86 per credit hour part-time; nonresident $9660 full-time, $322 per credit hour part-time. *Required fees:* $1320 full-time, $44 per credit hour part-time. *Room and board:* $4176; room only: $2526.

Financial Aid Of all full-time matriculated undergraduates who enrolled in 2002, 1,247 applied for aid, 1,007 were judged to have need, 284 had their need fully met. 94 Federal Work-Study jobs (averaging $924). 11 state and other part-time jobs (averaging $561). In 2002, 178. *Average percent of need met:* 88. *Average financial aid package:* $6865. *Average need-based loan:* $3581. *Average need-based gift aid:* $7016. *Average non-need-based aid:* $3799. *Average indebtedness upon graduation:* $15,424.

Applying *Options:* electronic application, deferred entrance. *Required:* high school transcript. *Required for some:* letters of recommendation, interview.

Admissions Contact Ms. Vicki Gomez, Assistant Vice President for Enrollment Management, Director of Admissions, The University of Texas of the Permian Basin, 4901 East University, Odessa, TX 79762-0001. *Phone:* 915-552-2605. *Toll-free phone:* 866-552-UTPB. *Fax:* 915-552-3605. *E-mail:* admissions@utpb.edu.

THE UNIVERSITY OF TEXAS–PAN AMERICAN

Edinburg, Texas

- **State-supported** comprehensive, founded 1927, part of University of Texas System
- **Calendar** semesters
- **Degrees** bachelor's, master's, doctoral, post-master's, and postbachelor's certificates
- **Small-town** 238-acre campus with easy access to McAllen-Edinburg-Mission MSA
- **Endowment** $35.5 million
- **Coed,** 13,868 undergraduate students, 70% full-time, 58% women, 42% men
- **Noncompetitive** entrance level, 64% of applicants were admitted

Undergraduates 9,733 full-time, 4,135 part-time. Students come from 35 states and territories, 10 other countries, 0.5% are from out of state, 0.3% African American, 1% Asian American or Pacific Islander, 88% Hispanic American, 0.1% Native American, 2% international, 6% transferred in. *Retention:* 66% of 2002 full-time freshmen returned.

Freshmen *Admission:* 6,622 applied, 4,257 admitted, 2,420 enrolled. *Test scores:* SAT verbal scores over 500: 32%; SAT math scores over 500: 36%; ACT scores over 18: 50%; SAT verbal scores over 600: 7%; SAT math scores over 600: 9%; ACT scores over 24: 10%; SAT verbal scores over 700: 1%; SAT math scores over 700: 1%; ACT scores over 30: 1%.

Faculty *Total:* 713, 67% full-time. *Student/faculty ratio:* 23:1.

Majors Accounting; American studies; anthropology; art; audiology and speech-language pathology; biology/biological sciences; business administration and management; chemistry; clinical laboratory science/medical technology; commercial and advertising art; communication/speech communication and rhetoric; computer science; corrections; criminal justice/law enforcement administration; criminal justice/police science; dietetics; dramatic/theatre arts; economics; electrical, electronics and communications engineering; elementary education; engineering; English; finance; fine/studio arts; general studies; health and physical education; Hispanic-American, Puerto Rican, and Mexican-American/Chicano studies; history; human services; interdisciplinary studies; international business/trade/commerce; journalism; management information systems; manufacturing engineering; marketing/marketing management; mass communication/media; mathematics; mechanical engineering; multi-/interdisciplinary studies related; music; nursing (registered nurse training); occupational therapy; philosophy; physics; political science and government; pre-dentistry studies; pre-medical studies; pre-pharmacy studies; psychology; rehabilitation and therapeutic professions related; rehabilitation therapy; science teacher education; social sciences; social work; sociology; Spanish; speech and rhetoric; speech therapy.

Academic Programs *Special study options:* academic remediation for entering students, adult/continuing education programs, cooperative education, distance learning, double majors, honors programs, independent study, internships, part-time degree program, services for LD students, study abroad, summer session for credit. *ROTC:* Army (b).

Library University Library with 505,641 titles, 8,135 serial subscriptions, 25,862 audiovisual materials.

Computers on Campus 500 computers available on campus for general student use. A campuswide network can be accessed from off campus. Internet access, online (class) registration, at least one staffed computer lab available.

Student Life *Housing options:* men-only, women-only. Campus housing is university owned. *Activities and organizations:* drama/theater group, student-run newspaper, television station, choral group, Accounting Society, American Marketing Association, Pre-Medical/Bio Medical Society, Association of Texas Professional Educators, Financial Management Association, national fraternities, national sororities. *Campus security:* 24-hour emergency response devices and patrols, late-night transport/escort service. *Student services:* health clinic, personal/psychological counseling.

Athletics Member NCAA. All Division I. *Intercollegiate sports:* baseball M(s), basketball M(s)/W(s), cross-country running M(s)/W(s), golf M(s)/W(s), tennis M(s)/W(s), track and field M(s)/W(s), volleyball W(s). *Intramural sports:* basketball M/W, bowling M/W, cheerleading M/W, football M/W, racquetball M/W, soccer M/W, softball M/W, tennis M/W, volleyball M/W.

Standardized Tests *Required:* SAT I or ACT (for admission).

Costs (2003–04) *Tuition:* state resident $3456 full-time, $72 per semester hour part-time; nonresident $11,232 full-time, $299 per semester hour part-time. Full-time tuition and fees vary according to reciprocity agreements. Part-time tuition and fees vary according to reciprocity agreements. *Required fees:* $619 full-time, $285 per term part-time. *Room and board:* $3488; room only: $2406. Room and board charges vary according to housing facility.

Financial Aid Of all full-time matriculated undergraduates who enrolled in 2002, 6,160 applied for aid, 5,922 were judged to have need, 362 had their need fully met. 841 Federal Work-Study jobs (averaging $2065). 53 state and other part-time jobs (averaging $1166). In 2002, 373 non-need-based awards were made. *Average percent of need met:* 75%. *Average financial aid package:* $7241. *Average need-based loan:* $3389. *Average need-based gift aid:* $7278. *Average non-need-based aid:* $3775. *Average indebtedness upon graduation:* $12,175.

Applying *Options:* common application, electronic application, early admission. *Required:* high school transcript, minimum 2.0 GPA. *Required for some:* letters of recommendation, interview. *Application deadlines:* 8/10 (freshmen), 8/10 (transfers). *Notification:* continuous (freshmen), continuous (transfers).

Admissions Contact Mr. David Zuniga, Director of Admissions, The University of Texas–Pan American, Office of Admissions and Records, 1201 West University Drive, Edinburg, TX 78541. *Phone:* 956-381-2201. *Fax:* 956-381-2212. *E-mail:* admissions@panam.edu.

THE UNIVERSITY OF TEXAS SOUTHWESTERN MEDICAL CENTER AT DALLAS
Dallas, Texas

- **State-supported** upper-level, founded 1943, part of University of Texas System
- **Calendar** trimesters
- **Degrees** bachelor's, master's, doctoral, first professional, and postbachelor's certificates
- **Urban** 98-acre campus
- **Endowment** $586.0 million
- **Coed,** 146 undergraduate students, 67% full-time, 74% women, 26% men
- **Moderately difficult** entrance level

Undergraduates 98 full-time, 48 part-time. Students come from 5 states and territories, 8% are from out of state, 9% African American, 10% Asian American or Pacific Islander, 18% Hispanic American, 1% Native American, 2% international, 28% transferred in.

Faculty *Total:* 111, 61% full-time, 51% with terminal degrees. *Student/faculty ratio:* 3:1.

Majors Clinical laboratory science/medical technology; dietetics; health/health care administration; hospital and health care facilities administration; orthotics/prosthetics; rehabilitation and therapeutic professions related.

Academic Programs *Special study options:* advanced placement credit, independent study, internships, part-time degree program.

Library University of Texas Southwestern Library with 257,782 titles, 2,865 serial subscriptions, an OPAC, a Web page.

Computers on Campus 150 computers available on campus for general student use. A campuswide network can be accessed from off campus. Internet access, at least one staffed computer lab available.

Student Life *Housing:* college housing not available. *Campus security:* 24-hour patrols, late-night transport/escort service. *Student services:* health clinic.

Athletics *Intramural sports:* basketball M/W, football M, golf M/W, soccer M/W, tennis M/W, volleyball M/W, weight lifting M/W.

Costs (2004–05) *Tuition:* state resident $2820 full-time, $48 per credit hour part-time; nonresident $11,880 full-time, $350 per credit hour part-time. Full-time tuition and fees vary according to course load. Part-time tuition and fees vary according to course load. *Payment plan:* installment.

Financial Aid Of all full-time matriculated undergraduates who enrolled in 2002, 201 applied for aid, 201 were judged to have need. 4 Federal Work-Study jobs (averaging $1750).

Applying *Options:* electronic application. *Application fee:* $10. *Application deadline:* rolling (transfers). *Notification:* continuous (transfers).

Admissions Contact Dr. Scott Wright, Director of Admissions, The University of Texas Southwestern Medical Center at Dallas, 5323 Harry Hines Boulevard, Dallas, TX 75390-9096. *Phone:* 214-648-5617. *Fax:* 214-648-3289. *E-mail:* admissions@utsouthwestern.edu.

UNIVERSITY OF THE INCARNATE WORD
San Antonio, Texas

- **Independent Roman Catholic** comprehensive, founded 1881
- **Calendar** semesters
- **Degrees** associate, bachelor's, master's, and doctoral
- **Urban** 200-acre campus
- **Endowment** $25.3 million
- **Coed,** 3,665 undergraduate students, 58% full-time, 67% women, 33% men
- **Moderately difficult** entrance level, 87% of applicants were admitted

Undergraduates 2,112 full-time, 1,553 part-time. Students come from 27 states and territories, 20 other countries, 2% are from out of state, 6% African American, 2% Asian American or Pacific Islander, 54% Hispanic American, 0.5% Native American, 6% international, 15% transferred in, 18% live on campus. *Retention:* 66% of 2002 full-time freshmen returned.

Freshmen *Admission:* 1,422 applied, 1,234 admitted, 406 enrolled. *Average high school GPA:* 3.74. *Test scores:* SAT verbal scores over 500: 48%; SAT math scores over 500: 41%; ACT scores over 18: 75%; SAT verbal scores over 600: 14%; SAT math scores over 600: 12%; ACT scores over 24: 23%; SAT verbal scores over 700: 2%; SAT math scores over 700: 1%; ACT scores over 30: 1%.

Faculty *Total:* 379, 36% full-time. *Student/faculty ratio:* 14:1.

Majors Accounting; adult and continuing education; American Indian/Native American studies; area, ethnic, cultural, and gender studies related; art; art teacher education; athletic training; biology/biological sciences; business administration and management; business/commerce; chemistry; chemistry related; clinical laboratory science/medical technology; commercial and advertising art; communication/speech communication and rhetoric; computer management; developmental and child psychology; dramatic/theatre arts; education; elementary education; engineering related; English; environmental studies; fashion/apparel design; fashion merchandising; finance; foods, nutrition, and wellness; history; housing and human environments; interdisciplinary studies; interior design; international business/trade/commerce; kindergarten/preschool education; liberal arts and sciences/liberal studies; management information systems; management science; marketing/marketing management; mass communication/media; mathematics; music; music management and merchandising; music teacher education; music therapy; nuclear medical technology; nursing (registered nurse training); organizational behavior; philosophy; physical education teaching and coaching; political science and government; pre-dentistry studies; pre-law studies; pre-medical studies; psychology; reading teacher education; religious studies; secondary education; sociology; Spanish; special education; speech and rhetoric; sport and fitness administration.

Academic Programs *Special study options:* academic remediation for entering students, accelerated degree program, adult/continuing education programs, advanced placement credit, double majors, English as a second language, external degree program, independent study, internships, off-campus study, part-time degree program, services for LD students, study abroad, summer session for credit. *ROTC:* Army (c), Air Force (c).

Library J.E. and L.E. Mabee Library plus 1 other with 225,852 titles, 577 serial subscriptions, 36,845 audiovisual materials, an OPAC, a Web page.

Computers on Campus 200 computers available on campus for general student use. A campuswide network can be accessed from student residence rooms and from off campus. Internet access, online (class) registration, at least one staffed computer lab available. Computer purchase or lease plan available.

Student Life *Housing options:* coed, men-only, women-only. Campus housing is university owned. Freshman applicants given priority for college housing. *Activities and organizations:* drama/theater group, student-run newspaper, choral group, Alpha Phi Omega, business club, Red Alert Dance Team, Cheerleading, Black Student Association, national fraternities, national sororities. *Campus security:* 24-hour emergency response devices and patrols, late-night transport/escort service, controlled dormitory access. *Student services:* health clinic, personal/psychological counseling.

Athletics Member NCAA, NAIA. All NCAA Division II. *Intercollegiate sports:* baseball M(s), basketball M(s)/W(s), cheerleading M/W, cross-country running M(s)/W(s), golf M(s)/W(s), soccer M(s)/W(s), softball W(s), tennis M(s)/W(s), volleyball W(s). *Intramural sports:* archery M/W, badminton M/W, basketball M/W, bowling M/W, cheerleading M/W, cross-country running M/W, football M/W, golf M/W, racquetball M/W, soccer M/W, swimming M/W, table tennis M/W, tennis M/W, track and field M/W, volleyball M/W.

Standardized Tests *Required:* SAT I or ACT (for admission).

Costs (2004–05) *One-time required fee:* $30. *Comprehensive fee:* $21,772 includes full-time tuition ($15,600), mandatory fees ($482), and room and board ($5690). Part-time tuition and fees vary according to course load. *College room only:* $3590. Room and board charges vary according to board plan. *Payment plan:* installment. *Waivers:* employees or children of employees.

Financial Aid Of all full-time matriculated undergraduates who enrolled in 2003, 2,109 applied for aid, 1,726 were judged to have need, 445 had their need fully met. 440 Federal Work-Study jobs (averaging $1739). 26 state and other part-time jobs (averaging $1859). In 2003, 317 non-need-based awards were made. *Average percent of need met:* 76%. *Average financial aid package:* $13,246. *Average need-based loan:* $4072. *Average need-based gift aid:* $6181. *Average non-need-based aid:* $4303. *Average indebtedness upon graduation:* $24,998.

Applying *Options:* electronic application, early admission, deferred entrance. *Application fee:* $20. *Required:* high school transcript. *Required for some:* essay or personal statement, interview. *Recommended:* minimum 2.0 GPA, 1 letter of recommendation, interview. *Application deadline:* rolling (freshmen), rolling (transfers).

University of the Incarnate Word (continued)

Admissions Contact Ms. Andrea Cyterski, Director of Admissions, University of the Incarnate Word, Box 285, San Antonio, TX 78209-6397. *Phone:* 210-829-6005. *Toll-free phone:* 800-749-WORD. *Fax:* 210-829-3921. *E-mail:* admis@universe.uiwtx.edu.

■ *See page 2724 for a narrative description.*

WAYLAND BAPTIST UNIVERSITY
Plainview, Texas

- **Independent Baptist** comprehensive, founded 1908
- **Calendar** semesters
- **Degrees** associate, bachelor's, and master's (branch locations: Anchorage, AK; Amarillo, TX; Luke Airforce Base, AZ; Glorieta, NM; Aiea, HI; Lubbock, TX; San Antonio, TX; Wichita Falls, TX)
- **Small-town** 80-acre campus
- **Endowment** $41.7 million
- **Coed,** 998 undergraduate students, 81% full-time, 59% women, 41% men
- **Minimally difficult** entrance level, 98% of applicants were admitted

Undergraduates 813 full-time, 185 part-time. Students come from 13 states and territories, 10 other countries, 13% are from out of state, 3% African American, 0.5% Asian American or Pacific Islander, 16% Hispanic American, 0.5% Native American, 2% international, 7% transferred in, 56% live on campus. *Retention:* 70% of 2002 full-time freshmen returned.

Freshmen *Admission:* 303 applied, 296 admitted, 215 enrolled. *Average high school GPA:* 3.83. *Test scores:* SAT verbal scores over 500: 55%; SAT math scores over 500: 59%; ACT scores over 18: 67%; SAT verbal scores over 600: 18%; SAT math scores over 600: 17%; ACT scores over 24: 29%; SAT verbal scores over 700: 4%; SAT math scores over 700: 1%; ACT scores over 30: 1%.

Faculty *Total:* 77, 84% full-time. *Student/faculty ratio:* 13:1.

Majors Art; biological and biomedical sciences related; biology/biological sciences; business administration and management; chemistry; Christian studies; criminal justice/safety; divinity/ministry; dramatic/theatre arts; education related; elementary education; English; history; mass communication/media; mathematics; music; music teacher education; physical education teaching and coaching; physical sciences; political science and government; psychology; religious education; religious/sacred music; social sciences; social sciences related; Spanish; theology and religious vocations related; trade and industrial teacher education.

Academic Programs *Special study options:* academic remediation for entering students, accelerated degree program, adult/continuing education programs, advanced placement credit, distance learning, double majors, external degree program, honors programs, internships, part-time degree program, summer session for credit. *ROTC:* Army (c), Air Force (c). *Unusual degree programs:* 3-2 engineering with Texas Tech University.

Library J.E. and L.E. Mabee Learning Resource Center with 107,285 titles, 541 serial subscriptions, 10,937 audiovisual materials, an OPAC, a Web page.

Computers on Campus 123 computers available on campus for general student use. A campuswide network can be accessed from student residence rooms and from off campus. Internet access, at least one staffed computer lab available.

Student Life *Housing:* on-campus residence required through junior year. *Options:* men-only, women-only. Campus housing is university owned. Freshman campus housing is guaranteed. *Activities and organizations:* drama/theater group, student-run newspaper, radio and television station, choral group, marching band, student government, national fraternities, national sororities. *Campus security:* 24-hour emergency response devices and patrols, security lighting. *Student services:* health clinic, personal/psychological counseling.

Athletics Member NAIA. *Intercollegiate sports:* baseball M(s), basketball M(s)/W(s), cheerleading M(s)/W(s), cross-country running M(s)/W(s), golf M(s), soccer W, track and field M(s)/W(s), volleyball W(s). *Intramural sports:* basketball M/W, football M/W, golf M/W, rock climbing M(c)/W(c), softball M/W, ultimate Frisbee M/W, volleyball M/W.

Standardized Tests *Required:* SAT I or ACT (for admission). *Recommended:* ACT (for admission).

Costs (2003–04) *Comprehensive fee:* $11,854 includes full-time tuition ($8100), mandatory fees ($400), and room and board ($3354). Part-time tuition: $270 per credit hour. Part-time tuition and fees vary according to course load. *Required fees:* $50 per term part-time. *College room only:* $1276. Room and board charges vary according to board plan and housing facility. *Payment plan:* installment. *Waivers:* employees or children of employees.

Financial Aid Of all full-time matriculated undergraduates who enrolled in 2003, 643 applied for aid, 571 were judged to have need, 129 had their need fully met. 139 Federal Work-Study jobs (averaging $2057). 336 state and other part-time jobs (averaging $1103). In 2003, 120 non-need-based awards were made. *Average percent of need met:* 76%. *Average financial aid package:* $8436. *Average need-based loan:* $2772. *Average need-based gift aid:* $6213. *Average non-need-based aid:* $8315.

Applying *Application fee:* $35. *Required:* high school transcript. *Recommended:* interview. *Application deadline:* 8/1 (freshmen), rolling (transfers). *Notification:* continuous (freshmen), continuous (transfers).

Admissions Contact Mr. Shawn Thomas, Director of Student Admissions, Wayland Baptist University, 1900 West 7th Street, CMB #712, Plainview, TX 79072. *Phone:* 806-291-3500. *Toll-free phone:* 800-588-1928. *E-mail:* admityou@wbu.edu.

WEST TEXAS A&M UNIVERSITY
Canyon, Texas

- **State-supported** comprehensive, founded 1909, part of Texas A&M University System
- **Calendar** semesters
- **Degrees** bachelor's, master's, and doctoral
- **Small-town** 128-acre campus
- **Endowment** $11.9 million
- **Coed,** 5,583 undergraduate students, 78% full-time, 56% women, 44% men
- **Moderately difficult** entrance level, 71% of applicants were admitted

Undergraduates 4,331 full-time, 1,252 part-time. Students come from 32 states and territories, 30 other countries, 8% are from out of state, 3% African American, 1% Asian American or Pacific Islander, 14% Hispanic American, 0.8% Native American, 2% international, 14% transferred in, 29% live on campus. *Retention:* 66% of 2002 full-time freshmen returned.

Freshmen *Admission:* 1,899 applied, 1,341 admitted, 799 enrolled. *Average high school GPA:* 3.80. *Test scores:* SAT verbal scores over 500: 48%; SAT math scores over 500: 50%; ACT scores over 18: 79%; SAT verbal scores over 600: 13%; SAT math scores over 600: 12%; ACT scores over 24: 19%; SAT verbal scores over 700: 1%; SAT math scores over 700: 2%; ACT scores over 30: 1%.

Faculty *Total:* 294, 77% full-time, 61% with terminal degrees. *Student/faculty ratio:* 24:1.

Majors Accounting; advertising; agribusiness; agricultural business and management; agriculture; agronomy and crop science; animal sciences; art; biology/biological sciences; biotechnology; broadcast journalism; business administration and management; business/commerce; business/managerial economics; chemistry; clinical laboratory science/medical technology; commercial and advertising art; communication disorders; computer and information sciences; criminal justice/law enforcement administration; dance; dramatic/theatre arts; economics; English; environmental science; equestrian studies; finance; fine/studio arts; general studies; geography; geology/earth science; health and physical education; history; industrial technology; interdisciplinary studies; journalism; management information systems; marketing/marketing management; mass communication/media; mathematics; mechanical engineering; multi-/interdisciplinary studies related; music; music performance; music theory and composition; music therapy; nursing (registered nurse training); physics; plant protection and integrated pest management; political science and government; pre-law studies; psychology; public administration; social sciences; social work; sociology; Spanish; speech and rhetoric; wildlife and wildlands science and management.

Academic Programs *Special study options:* academic remediation for entering students, adult/continuing education programs, advanced placement credit, cooperative education, distance learning, double majors, English as a second language, honors programs, independent study, internships, part-time degree program, services for LD students, student-designed majors, summer session for credit. *Unusual degree programs:* 3-2 engineering with Texas Tech University, Texas A&M University; accounting.

Library Cornette Library with 1.1 million titles, 5,464 serial subscriptions, 1,572 audiovisual materials, an OPAC, a Web page.

Computers on Campus 1200 computers available on campus for general student use. A campuswide network can be accessed from student residence rooms and from off campus. Internet access, online (class) registration, at least one staffed computer lab available.

Student Life *Housing:* on-campus residence required through sophomore year. *Options:* coed, men-only, women-only, disabled students. Campus housing is university owned. Freshman campus housing is guaranteed. *Activities and organizations:* drama/theater group, student-run newspaper, radio station, choral group, marching band, Residence Hall Association, Greek system, Student Organizations' Roundtable, student government, Students in Free Enterprise, national fraternities, national sororities. *Campus security:* 24-hour emergency response devices and patrols, late-night transport/escort service, controlled dormitory access. *Student services:* health clinic, personal/psychological counseling.

Athletics Member NCAA. All Division II. *Intercollegiate sports:* baseball M(s), basketball M(s)/W(s), bowling M(s)(c)/W(s)(c), cross-country running M(s)/

W(s), equestrian sports M(c)/W(s), football M(s), golf M(s)/W(s), soccer M(s)/W(s), volleyball W(s). *Intramural sports:* badminton M/W, basketball M/W, bowling M/W, football M/W, golf M/W, racquetball M/W, soccer M/W, softball M/W, swimming M/W, table tennis M/W, tennis M/W, volleyball M/W, wrestling M.

Standardized Tests *Required:* SAT I or ACT (for admission).

Costs (2003–04) *One-time required fee:* $10. *Tuition:* state resident $2445 full-time, $82 per hour part-time; nonresident $9525 full-time, $318 per hour part-time. Full-time tuition and fees vary according to course load. *Required fees:* $782 full-time, $24 per hour part-time, $103 per term part-time. *Room and board:* $4342; room only: $1930. Room and board charges vary according to board plan and housing facility. *Payment plan:* installment.

Financial Aid Of all full-time matriculated undergraduates who enrolled in 2002, 3,253 applied for aid, 2,614 were judged to have need, 2,561 had their need fully met. 136 Federal Work-Study jobs (averaging $1874). 39 state and other part-time jobs (averaging $570). In 2002, 546 non-need-based awards were made. *Average percent of need met:* 69%. *Average financial aid package:* $5800. *Average need-based loan:* $3544. *Average need-based gift aid:* $3592. *Average non-need-based aid:* $4190.

Applying *Options:* common application, electronic application. *Application fee:* $25. *Required:* high school transcript, class rank. *Application deadline:* rolling (freshmen), rolling (transfers). *Notification:* continuous (freshmen), continuous (transfers).

Admissions Contact Ms. Lila Vars, Director of Admissions, West Texas A&M University, WT Box 60907, Canyon, TX 79016-0001. *Phone:* 806-651-2020. *Toll-free phone:* 800-99-WTAMU. *Fax:* 806-651-5285. *E-mail:* lvars@mail.wtamu.edu.

WILEY COLLEGE
Marshall, Texas

- **Independent** 4-year, founded 1873, affiliated with United Methodist Church
- **Calendar** semesters
- **Degrees** associate and bachelor's
- **Small-town** 58-acre campus
- **Endowment** $5.1 million
- **Coed**
- **Minimally difficult** entrance level

Faculty *Student/faculty ratio:* 8:1.

Standardized Tests *Recommended:* SAT I or ACT (for admission).

Costs (2003–04) *Comprehensive fee:* $10,468 includes full-time tuition ($5282), mandatory fees ($1094), and room and board ($4092). *College room only:* $1966.

Financial Aid In 2002, 45. *Average percent of need met:* 65. *Average financial aid package:* $8500.

Applying *Options:* early admission, deferred entrance. *Application fee:* $10. *Required:* high school transcript, 1 letter of recommendation.

Admissions Contact Ms. Lalita Estes, Director of Admissions, Wiley College, 711 Wiley Avenue, Marshall, TX 75670. *Phone:* 903-927-3356. *Toll-free phone:* 800-658-6889. *E-mail:* vvalentine@wileyc.edu.

UTAH

BRIGHAM YOUNG UNIVERSITY
Provo, Utah

- **Independent** university, founded 1875, affiliated with The Church of Jesus Christ of Latter-day Saints, part of Church Education System (CES) of The Church of Jesus Christ of Latter-day Saints
- **Calendar** 4-4-2-2
- **Degrees** bachelor's, master's, doctoral, and first professional
- **Suburban** 557-acre campus with easy access to Salt Lake City
- **Coed,** 29,932 undergraduate students, 89% full-time, 49% women, 51% men
- **Moderately difficult** entrance level, 78% of applicants were admitted

Undergraduates 26,586 full-time, 3,346 part-time. Students come from 54 states and territories, 119 other countries, 72% are from out of state, 0.4% African American, 3% Asian American or Pacific Islander, 3% Hispanic American, 0.7% Native American, 3% international, 3% transferred in, 20% live on campus. *Retention:* 93% of 2002 full-time freshmen returned.

Freshmen *Admission:* 9,300 applied, 7,227 admitted, 5,331 enrolled. *Average high school GPA:* 3.71. *Test scores:* SAT verbal scores over 500: 91%; SAT math scores over 500: 94%; ACT scores over 18: 100%; SAT verbal scores over 600: 54%; SAT math scores over 600: 60%; ACT scores over 24: 83%; SAT verbal scores over 700: 14%; SAT math scores over 700: 17%; ACT scores over 30: 22%.

Faculty *Total:* 1,741, 73% full-time. *Student/faculty ratio:* 21:1.

Majors Accounting; accounting related; acting; advertising; agribusiness; agricultural business and management; agricultural economics; American studies; ancient/classical Greek; animation, interactive technology, video graphics and special effects; anthropology; applied economics; art; art history, criticism and conservation; art teacher education; Asian studies; astronomy; athletic training; ballet; biochemistry; bioinformatics; biological and physical sciences; biology/biological sciences; biomedical sciences; biophysics; biostatistics; biotechnology; botany/plant biology; broadcast journalism; business administration and management; business family and consumer sciences/human sciences; business statistics; cartography; ceramic arts and ceramics; chemical engineering; chemistry; chemistry teacher education; child care and support services management; child care provision; child development; Chinese; cinematography and film/video production; civil engineering; classics and languages, literatures and linguistics; clinical laboratory science/medical technology; communication and journalism related; comparative literature; computer engineering; computer science; conservation biology; crafts, folk art and artisanry; dance; dance related; design and visual communications; dietetics; directing and theatrical production; drama and dance teacher education; dramatic/theatre arts; dramatic/theatre arts and stagecraft related; drawing; early childhood education; ecology, evolution, systematics and population biology related; economics; education related; education (specific levels and methods) related; education (specific subject areas) related; electrical, electronics and communications engineering; elementary education; engineering technology; English; English as a second/foreign language (teaching); English composition; English/language arts teacher education; entrepreneurship; environmental science; European studies (Central and Eastern); family and consumer economics related; family and consumer sciences/human sciences; family and consumer sciences/human sciences business services related; family resource management; family systems; film/cinema studies; film/video and photographic arts related; financial planning and services; fine/studio arts; food science; food technology and processing; foreign language teacher education; French; French language teacher education; geography; geography related; geological and earth sciences/geosciences related; geology/earth science; German; German language teacher education; graphic design; health and physical education; health and physical education related; Hebrew; history; history teacher education; home furnishings and equipment installation; human development and family studies; humanities; human resources development; human resources management; illustration; industrial design; information technology; interior design; international finance; international marketing; international relations and affairs; Italian; Japanese; jazz/jazz studies; journalism; kinesiology and exercise science; Korean; language interpretation and translation; Latin; Latin American studies; Latin teacher education; liberal arts and sciences and humanities related; liberal arts and sciences/liberal studies; linguistic and comparative language studies related; linguistics; logistics and materials management; management information systems; manufacturing engineering; marketing/marketing management; mass communication/media; mathematics; mathematics teacher education; mechanical engineering; merchandising, sales, and marketing operations related (general); microbiology; molecular biology; music; music history, literature, and theory; music pedagogy; music performance; music related; music teacher education; music theory and composition; neuroscience; Norwegian; nursing (registered nurse training); nutrition sciences; organizational communication; painting; parks, recreation and leisure; parks, recreation, and leisure related; philosophy; photography; physical education teaching and coaching; physics; physics related; physics teacher education; physiology; piano and organ; plant genetics; playwriting and screenwriting; political science and government; Portuguese; pre-nursing studies; printmaking; psychology; psychology teacher education; public policy analysis; public relations, advertising, and applied communication related; radio, television, and digital communication related; range science and management; retailing; Russian; science teacher education; sculpture; social psychology; social science teacher education; social work; sociology; soil sciences related; Spanish; Spanish language teacher education; special education; speech and rhetoric; speech teacher education; statistics; statistics related; Swedish; technology/industrial arts teacher education; theatre design and technology; therapeutic recreation; veterinary/animal health technology; violin, viola, guitar and other stringed instruments; visual and performing arts related; voice and opera; wildlife and wildlands science and management; work and family studies; zoology/animal biology.

Academic Programs *Special study options:* academic remediation for entering students, accelerated degree program, adult/continuing education programs, advanced placement credit, cooperative education, distance learning, double majors, English as a second language, external degree program, freshman honors college, honors programs, independent study, internships, off-campus study, part-time degree program, services for LD students, study abroad, summer session for credit. *ROTC:* Army (b), Air Force (b).

Library Harold B. Lee Library plus 2 others with 2.5 million titles, 619,493 serial subscriptions, 56,353 audiovisual materials, an OPAC, a Web page.

Brigham Young University (continued)

Computers on Campus 2000 computers available on campus for general student use. A campuswide network can be accessed from student residence rooms and from off campus that provide access to intranet. Internet access, online (class) registration, at least one staffed computer lab available.

Student Life *Housing options:* men-only, women-only. Campus housing is university owned. *Activities and organizations:* drama/theater group, student-run newspaper, radio and television station, choral group, marching band. *Campus security:* 24-hour emergency response devices and patrols, late-night transport/escort service, controlled dormitory access. *Student services:* health clinic, personal/psychological counseling, women's center, legal services.

Athletics Member NCAA. All Division I except football (Division I-A). *Intercollegiate sports:* baseball M(s), basketball M(s)/W(s), cheerleading M(s)/W(s), cross-country running M(s)/W(s), golf M(s)/W(s), gymnastics W(s), lacrosse M(c), racquetball M(c)/W(c), rugby M(c), soccer M(c)/W(s), softball W(s), swimming M(s)/W(s), tennis M(s)/W(s), track and field M(s)/W(s), volleyball M(s)/W(s). *Intramural sports:* badminton M/W, basketball M/W, field hockey M, football M/W, golf M/W, racquetball M/W, soccer M/W, softball M/W, table tennis M/W, tennis M/W, ultimate Frisbee M/W, volleyball M/W, water polo M/W.

Standardized Tests *Required:* ACT (for admission).

Costs (2003–04) *Comprehensive fee:* $8504 includes full-time tuition ($3150) and room and board ($5354). Full-time tuition and fees vary according to reciprocity agreements. Part-time tuition: $161 per credit hour. Part-time tuition and fees vary according to course load and reciprocity agreements. *Room and board:* Room and board charges vary according to board plan and housing facility. *Waivers:* employees or children of employees.

Financial Aid Of all full-time matriculated undergraduates who enrolled in 2001, 21,099 applied for aid, 11,652 were judged to have need, 8 had their need fully met. 234 state and other part-time jobs (averaging $636). In 2001, 7071 non-need-based awards were made. *Average percent of need met:* 40%. *Average financial aid package:* $3853. *Average need-based loan:* $1811. *Average need-based gift aid:* $2042. *Average non-need-based aid:* $3140. *Average indebtedness upon graduation:* $11,000.

Applying *Options:* electronic application, early admission, deferred entrance. *Application fee:* $25. *Required:* essay or personal statement, high school transcript, 1 letter of recommendation, interview. *Application deadlines:* 2/15 (freshmen), 3/15 (transfers). *Notification:* continuous (freshmen), continuous (transfers).

Admissions Contact Mr. Tom Gourley, Dean of Admissions and Records, Brigham Young University, A-153 Abraham Smoot Building, Provo, UT 84602. *Phone:* 801-422-2507. *Fax:* 801-422-0005. *E-mail:* admissions@byu.edu.

DIXIE STATE COLLEGE OF UTAH

St. George, Utah

- **State-supported** primarily 2-year, founded 1911, part of Utah System of Higher Education
- **Calendar** semesters
- **Degrees** certificates, diplomas, associate, and bachelor's
- **Small-town** 60-acre campus
- **Endowment** $9.9 million
- **Coed**
- **Noncompetitive** entrance level

Faculty *Student/faculty ratio:* 34:1.

Student Life *Campus security:* 24-hour emergency response devices and patrols.

Athletics Member NJCAA.

Standardized Tests *Required:* CPT or ACT COMPASS (if not submitting SAT I or ACT) (for placement). *Recommended:* SAT I or ACT (for placement).

Costs (2003–04) *Tuition:* state resident $1416 full-time; nonresident $6192 full-time. Full-time tuition and fees vary according to course level. Part-time tuition and fees vary according to course level and course load. *Required fees:* $362 full-time. *Room and board:* $3262.

Financial Aid Of all full-time matriculated undergraduates who enrolled in 2001, 100 Federal Work-Study jobs (averaging $2700). 20 state and other part-time jobs (averaging $2700).

Applying *Options:* electronic application, early admission, deferred entrance. *Application fee:* $25. *Required:* high school transcript.

Admissions Contact Ms. Darla Rollins, Admissions Coordinator, Dixie State College of Utah, 225 South 700 East, St. George, UT 84770-3876. *Phone:* 435-652-7702. *Toll-free phone:* 888-GO2DIXIE. *Fax:* 435-656-4005. *E-mail:* rollins@dixie.edu.

ITT TECHNICAL INSTITUTE

Murray, Utah

- **Proprietary** primarily 2-year, founded 1984, part of ITT Educational Services, Inc.
- **Calendar** quarters
- **Degrees** associate and bachelor's
- **Suburban** 3-acre campus with easy access to Salt Lake City
- **Coed**
- **Minimally difficult** entrance level

Standardized Tests *Required:* Wonderlic aptitude test (for admission).

Costs (2003–04) *Tuition:* $347 per credit hour part-time.

Applying *Options:* deferred entrance. *Application fee:* $100. *Required:* high school transcript, interview. *Recommended:* letters of recommendation.

Admissions Contact Ms. JoAnn Meron, Director of Recruitment, ITT Technical Institute, 920 West LeVoy Drive, Murray, UT 84123. *Phone:* 801-263-3313. *Toll-free phone:* 800-365-2136. *Fax:* 801-263-3497.

NORTHFACE UNIVERSITY

Salt Lake City, Utah

- **Proprietary** comprehensive, founded 2002
- **Calendar** quarters
- **Degrees** bachelor's and master's
- **Suburban** campus
- **Coed,** 100 undergraduate students
- 25% of applicants were admitted

Undergraduates 10% African American, 10% Asian American or Pacific Islander, 10% Hispanic American, 2% international. *Retention:* 96% of 2002 full-time freshmen returned.

Freshmen *Admission:* 400 applied, 100 admitted. *Average high school GPA:* 3.10.

Faculty *Total:* 17. *Student/faculty ratio:* 11:1.

Majors Computer and information sciences; computer and information sciences related; computer programming; computer programming related; computer programming (specific applications); computer programming (vendor/product certification); computer science; computer software and media applications related; data modeling/warehousing and database administration; information technology; web page, digital/multimedia and information resources design.

Student Life *Housing options:* coed. Campus housing is leased by the school and is provided by a third party. Freshman campus housing is guaranteed. *Student services:* health clinic, personal/psychological counseling.

Costs (2003–04) *One-time required fee:* $75. *Comprehensive fee:* $32,445 includes full-time tuition ($25,700), mandatory fees ($1120), and room and board ($5625). Part-time tuition: $59,500 per degree program.

Applying *Application fee:* $125.

Admissions Contact Mr. Jamie Wyse, Senior Vice President, Strategic Development, Northface University, 2755 East Cottonwood Parkway, Suite 600, Salt Lake City, UT 84121. *Phone:* 801-438-1107.

SOUTHERN UTAH UNIVERSITY

Cedar City, Utah

- **State-supported** comprehensive, founded 1897, part of Utah System of Higher Education
- **Calendar** semesters
- **Degrees** certificates, diplomas, associate, bachelor's, and master's
- **Small-town** 113-acre campus
- **Endowment** $5.1 million
- **Coed,** 5,840 undergraduate students, 74% full-time, 55% women, 45% men
- **Moderately difficult** entrance level, 78% of applicants were admitted

Undergraduates 4,302 full-time, 1,538 part-time. Students come from 40 states and territories, 14 other countries, 15% are from out of state, 0.7% African American, 1% Asian American or Pacific Islander, 2% Hispanic American, 0.9% Native American, 1% international, 8% transferred in, 6% live on campus. *Retention:* 51% of 2002 full-time freshmen returned.

Freshmen *Admission:* 1,355 applied, 1,054 admitted, 725 enrolled. *Average high school GPA:* 3.41. *Test scores:* SAT verbal scores over 500: 57%; SAT math scores over 500: 62%; ACT scores over 18: 81%; SAT verbal scores over 600: 13%; SAT math scores over 600: 19%; ACT scores over 24: 25%; ACT scores over 30: 2%.

Faculty *Total:* 252, 83% full-time, 58% with terminal degrees. *Student/faculty ratio:* 22:1.

Majors Accounting; agriculture; art; art teacher education; automobile/automotive mechanics technology; biology/biological sciences; botany/plant biology; business administration and management; business teacher education; carpentry; chemistry; child development; computer science; construction engineering technology; criminal justice/law enforcement administration; dance; drafting and design technology; dramatic/theatre arts; economics; education; electrical, electronic and communications engineering technology; elementary education; English; family and community services; family and consumer sciences/home economics teacher education; family and consumer sciences/human sciences; French; geology/earth science; German; history; industrial arts; information science/studies; interior design; mass communication/media; mathematics; music; music teacher education; physical education teaching and coaching; physical sciences; political science and government; pre-engineering; psychology; secondary education; social sciences; sociology; Spanish; special education; speech and rhetoric; zoology/animal biology.

Academic Programs *Special study options:* academic remediation for entering students, adult/continuing education programs, advanced placement credit, cooperative education, distance learning, double majors, English as a second language, honors programs, independent study, internships, part-time degree program, services for LD students, summer session for credit. *ROTC:* Army (b).

Library Southern Utah University Library with 180,424 titles, 6,165 serial subscriptions, 13,352 audiovisual materials, an OPAC, a Web page.

Computers on Campus 300 computers available on campus for general student use. A campuswide network can be accessed from student residence rooms and from off campus. At least one staffed computer lab available.

Student Life *Housing options:* coed, men-only, women-only, disabled students. *Activities and organizations:* drama/theater group, student-run newspaper, radio and television station, choral group, marching band, outdoor club, intertribal club, Latter Day Saints Student Association, ski club, Residence Halls Association, national fraternities, national sororities. *Campus security:* 24-hour emergency response devices, student patrols, late-night transport/escort service, controlled dormitory access. *Student services:* health clinic, personal/psychological counseling, women's center.

Athletics Member NCAA. All Division I except football (Division I-AA). *Intercollegiate sports:* baseball M(s), basketball M(s)/W(s), cross-country running M/W, golf M(s), gymnastics W(s), softball W(s), tennis W(s), track and field M(s)/W(s). *Intramural sports:* basketball M/W, football M, golf M/W, soccer M/W, tennis M/W, track and field M/W, volleyball M/W.

Standardized Tests *Required:* SAT I or ACT (for admission). *Recommended:* ACT (for admission).

Costs (2003–04) *Tuition:* state resident $2332 full-time, $117 per credit hour part-time; nonresident $7696 full-time, $385 per credit hour part-time. Part-time tuition and fees vary according to course load. *Required fees:* $462 full-time. *Room and board:* $5400; room only: $2400. Room and board charges vary according to board plan and housing facility. *Waivers:* employees or children of employees.

Financial Aid Of all full-time matriculated undergraduates who enrolled in 2002, 2,440 applied for aid, 2,276 were judged to have need, 762 had their need fully met. In 2002, 662 non-need-based awards were made. *Average percent of need met:* 80%. *Average financial aid package:* $3418. *Average need-based loan:* $3326. *Average need-based gift aid:* $2870. *Average non-need-based aid:* $3202. *Average indebtedness upon graduation:* $11,119.

Applying *Options:* electronic application, early admission, deferred entrance. *Application fee:* $25. *Required:* high school transcript, minimum 2.0 GPA. *Application deadline:* rolling (transfers). *Notification:* continuous (freshmen), continuous (transfers).

Admissions Contact Mr. Dale S. Orton, Director of Admissions, Southern Utah University, 351 West Center Street, Cedar City, UT 84720. *Phone:* 801-586-7740. *Fax:* 435-865-8223. *E-mail:* adminfo@suu.edu.

STEVENS-HENAGER COLLEGE
Ogden, Utah

- **Proprietary** primarily 2-year, founded 1891, part of CollegeAmerica, Inc.
- **Calendar** quarters
- **Degrees** associate and bachelor's
- **Urban** 1-acre campus with easy access to Salt Lake City
- **Coed**
- **Noncompetitive** entrance level

Faculty *Student/faculty ratio:* 17:1.

Standardized Tests *Required:* Wonderlic aptitude test (for admission). *Recommended:* SAT I or ACT (for admission).

Applying *Options:* common application, early admission, deferred entrance. *Application fee:* $25. *Required:* high school transcript.

Admissions Contact Admissions Office, Stevens-Henager College, PO Box 9428, Ogden, UT 84409. *Phone:* 801-394-7791. *Toll-free phone:* 800-371-7791.

UNIVERSITY OF PHOENIX–UTAH CAMPUS
Salt Lake City, Utah

- **Proprietary** comprehensive, founded 1984
- **Calendar** continuous
- **Degrees** certificates, associate, bachelor's, master's, doctoral, post-master's, and postbachelor's certificates (courses conducted at 121 campuses and learning centers in 25 states)
- **Urban** campus
- **Coed,** 1,432 undergraduate students, 100% full-time, 41% women, 59% men
- **Noncompetitive** entrance level

Undergraduates 1,432 full-time. 0.5% African American, 1% Asian American or Pacific Islander, 3% Hispanic American, 0.1% Native American, 2% international.

Freshmen *Admission:* 45 enrolled.

Faculty *Total:* 629, 1% full-time, 26% with terminal degrees. *Student/faculty ratio:* 8:1.

Majors Accounting; business administration and management; computer and information sciences; corrections and criminal justice related; finance; management information systems; management science; marketing/marketing management; nursing (registered nurse training); public administration and social service professions related.

Academic Programs *Special study options:* accelerated degree program, adult/continuing education programs, advanced placement credit, distance learning, external degree program, independent study.

Library University Library with 27.1 million titles, 11,648 serial subscriptions, an OPAC, a Web page.

Computers on Campus A campuswide network can be accessed from off campus. Internet access, at least one staffed computer lab available.

Student Life *Housing:* college housing not available.

Costs (2003–04) *Tuition:* $9120 full-time, $304 per credit part-time. *Waivers:* employees or children of employees.

Financial Aid *Average financial aid package:* $1492.

Applying *Options:* deferred entrance. *Application fee:* $85. *Required:* 1 letter of recommendation, 2 years of work experience, 23 years of age. *Required for some:* high school transcript. *Application deadline:* rolling (freshmen), rolling (transfers).

Admissions Contact Ms. Beth Barilla, Director of Admissions, University of Phoenix–Utah Campus, 4615 East Elwood Street, Mail Stop AA-K101, Phoenix, AZ 85040-1958. *Phone:* 480-317-6000. *Toll-free phone:* 800-224-2844. *Fax:* 480-594-1758. *E-mail:* beth.barilla@phoenix.edu.

UNIVERSITY OF UTAH
Salt Lake City, Utah

- **State-supported** university, founded 1850, part of Utah System of Higher Education
- **Calendar** semesters
- **Degrees** certificates, bachelor's, master's, doctoral, first professional, post-master's, and postbachelor's certificates
- **Urban** 1500-acre campus
- **Endowment** $295.9 million
- **Coed,** 22,421 undergraduate students, 68% full-time, 45% women, 55% men
- **Moderately difficult** entrance level, 86% of applicants were admitted

Undergraduates 15,242 full-time, 7,179 part-time. Students come from 55 states and territories, 106 other countries, 7% are from out of state, 0.6% African American, 4% Asian American or Pacific Islander, 4% Hispanic American, 0.7% Native American, 3% international, 10% transferred in, 11% live on campus. *Retention:* 79% of 2002 full-time freshmen returned.

Freshmen *Admission:* 5,842 applied, 5,036 admitted, 2,653 enrolled. *Average high school GPA:* 3.48. *Test scores:* ACT scores over 18: 93%; ACT scores over 24: 48%; ACT scores over 30: 8%.

Faculty *Total:* 1,246, 89% full-time, 85% with terminal degrees. *Student/faculty ratio:* 16:1.

Majors Accounting; anthropology; Arabic; architecture; architecture related; art; art history, criticism and conservation; Asian studies; atmospheric sciences and meteorology; audiology and speech-language pathology; ballet; behavioral sciences; biology/biological sciences; biology teacher education; biomedical/medical engineering; biomedical sciences; broadcast journalism; business administration and management; business/commerce; business, management, and marketing related; cell biology and histology; chemical engineering; chemistry;

University of Utah (continued)

child development; Chinese; civil engineering; classics and languages, literatures and linguistics; clinical laboratory science/medical technology; clinical/medical laboratory technology; communication/speech communication and rhetoric; computer engineering; computer science; dance; developmental and child psychology; drama and dance teacher education; dramatic/theatre arts; economics; education; electrical, electronics and communications engineering; elementary education; engineering; English; environmental/environmental health engineering; environmental health; environmental studies; family and community services; family and consumer economics related; family and consumer sciences/home economics teacher education; family and consumer sciences/human sciences; family resource management; film/cinema studies; finance; food science; foreign languages and literatures; French; French language teacher education; geography; geological and earth sciences/geosciences related; geological/geophysical engineering; geology/earth science; geophysics and seismology; German; German language teacher education; health and physical education; health professions related; health services/allied health/health sciences; health teacher education; history; history teacher education; human development and family studies; humanities; international/global studies; Japanese; journalism; kindergarten/preschool education; kinesiology and exercise science; liberal arts and sciences and humanities related; liberal arts and sciences/liberal studies; linguistics; management information systems; marketing/marketing management; marketing related; mass communication/media; materials engineering; materials science; mathematics; mathematics teacher education; mechanical engineering; metallurgical engineering; meteorology; mining and mineral engineering; modern Greek; music; music teacher education; Near and Middle Eastern studies; nursing (registered nurse training); occupational therapy; parks, recreation and leisure; parks, recreation and leisure facilities management; pharmacy; pharmacy, pharmaceutical sciences, and administration related; philosophy; physical education teaching and coaching; physical sciences; physical sciences related; physical therapy; physics; physics teacher education; political science and government; pre-pharmacy studies; psychology; public relations/image management; radio and television; Russian; science teacher education; secondary education; social sciences; social sciences related; social science teacher education; social studies teacher education; social work; sociology; Spanish; Spanish language teacher education; special education; speech and rhetoric; urban studies/affairs; visual and performing arts; women's studies.

Academic Programs *Special study options:* academic remediation for entering students, accelerated degree program, adult/continuing education programs, advanced placement credit, cooperative education, distance learning, double majors, English as a second language, honors programs, independent study, internships, off-campus study, part-time degree program, services for LD students, student-designed majors, study abroad, summer session for credit. *ROTC:* Army (b), Navy (b), Air Force (b). *Unusual degree programs:* 3-2 physical therapy, occupational therapy.

Library Marriott Library plus 3 others with 3.0 million titles, 33,517 serial subscriptions, 62,356 audiovisual materials, an OPAC, a Web page.

Computers on Campus 5000 computers available on campus for general student use. A campuswide network can be accessed from student residence rooms and from off campus that provide access to online classes. Internet access, online (class) registration, at least one staffed computer lab available.

Student Life *Housing options:* coed. Campus housing is university owned. *Activities and organizations:* drama/theater group, student-run newspaper, radio and television station, choral group, marching band, Bennion Center, Latter-Day Saints Student Association, Newman Center, Greek System, Center for Ethnic Student Affairs, national fraternities, national sororities. *Campus security:* 24-hour emergency response devices and patrols, student patrols, late-night transport/escort service, controlled dormitory access. *Student services:* health clinic, personal/psychological counseling, women's center, legal services.

Athletics Member NCAA. All Division I except football (Division I-A). *Intercollegiate sports:* baseball M(s), basketball M(s)/W(s), bowling M(c)/W(c), cheerleading M(s)/W(s), cross-country running M(s)/W(s), golf M(s), gymnastics W(s), ice hockey M(c), racquetball M(c)/W(c), rugby M(c), skiing (cross-country) M(s)/W(s), skiing (downhill) M(s)/W(s), soccer M(c)/W(s), softball W, swimming M(s)/W(s), table tennis M(c)/W(c), tennis M(s)/W(s), track and field M(s)/W(s), volleyball W(s). *Intramural sports:* badminton M/W, basketball M/W, bowling M/W, cross-country running M/W, football M/W, golf M/W, racquetball M/W, archery M/W, rugby M/W, skiing (cross-country) M/W, skiing (downhill) M/W, soccer M/W, softball M/W, squash M/W, swimming M/W, table tennis M/W, tennis M/W, track and field M/W, volleyball M/W, water polo M/W, weight lifting M/W, wrestling M.

Standardized Tests *Required:* SAT I or ACT (for admission). *Recommended:* ACT (for admission).

Costs (2003–04) *Tuition:* state resident $3058 full-time, $86 per credit part-time; nonresident $10,704 full-time, $295 per credit part-time. Full-time tuition and fees vary according to course level, course load, degree level, and program. Part-time tuition and fees vary according to course level, course load, degree level, and program. *Required fees:* $589 full-time, $295 per term part-time. *Room and board:* $5036; room only: $2472. Room and board charges vary according to board plan and housing facility. *Payment plan:* installment. *Waivers:* senior citizens and employees or children of employees.

Financial Aid Of all full-time matriculated undergraduates who enrolled in 2003, 8,454 applied for aid, 5,904 were judged to have need, 831 had their need fully met. In 2003, 362 non-need-based awards were made. *Average percent of need met:* 59%. *Average financial aid package:* $7286. *Average need-based loan:* $4759. *Average need-based gift aid:* $4075. *Average non-need-based aid:* $3127. *Average indebtedness upon graduation:* $12,400.

Applying *Options:* common application, electronic application, early admission, deferred entrance. *Application fee:* $35. *Required:* high school transcript, minimum 2.0 GPA. *Recommended:* minimum 3.0 GPA. *Application deadlines:* 4/1 (freshmen), 4/1 (transfers).

Admissions Contact Ms. Suzanne Espinoza, Director of High School Services, University of Utah, 250 South Student services Building, 201 South, 460 E Room 205, Salt Lake City, UT 84112. *Phone:* 801-581-8761. *Toll-free phone:* 800-444-8638. *Fax:* 801-585-7864. *E-mail:* admissions@sa.utah.edu.

UTAH COLLEGE OF MIDWIFERY
Orem, Utah

- **Independent** comprehensive, founded 1980
- **Calendar** semesters
- **Degrees** certificates, diplomas, bachelor's, and master's
- **Urban** campus
- **Women only,** 66 undergraduate students
- 100% of applicants were admitted

Undergraduates 66 part-time. *Retention:* 93% of 2002 full-time freshmen returned.

Freshmen *Admission:* 32 applied, 32 admitted.

Faculty *Total:* 8, 88% with terminal degrees. *Student/faculty ratio:* 1:1.

Majors Direct entry midwifery.

Costs (2004–05) *Tuition:* $115 per credit part-time. *Required fees:* $100 per year part-time.

Admissions Contact Ms. Jodie Fisher, President, Utah College of Midwifery, 282 North State Street, Orem, UT 84057. *Phone:* 801-764-9068. *Toll-free phone:* 888-489-1238.

UTAH STATE UNIVERSITY
Logan, Utah

- **State-supported** university, founded 1888, part of Utah System of Higher Education
- **Calendar** semesters
- **Degrees** certificates, associate, bachelor's, master's, and doctoral
- **Urban** 456-acre campus
- **Endowment** $74.4 million
- **Coed,** 13,958 undergraduate students, 84% full-time, 49% women, 51% men
- **Moderately difficult** entrance level, 94% of applicants were admitted

Undergraduates 11,772 full-time, 2,186 part-time. Students come from 52 states and territories, 49 other countries, 29% are from out of state, 0.6% African American, 1% Asian American or Pacific Islander, 2% Hispanic American, 0.5% Native American, 3% international, 8% transferred in. *Retention:* 69% of 2001 full-time freshmen returned.

Freshmen *Admission:* 5,165 applied, 4,851 admitted, 2,548 enrolled. *Average high school GPA:* 3.56. *Test scores:* SAT verbal scores over 500: 72%; SAT math scores over 500: 75%; ACT scores over 18: 95%; SAT verbal scores over 600: 31%; SAT math scores over 600: 39%; ACT scores over 24: 50%; SAT verbal scores over 700: 7%; SAT math scores over 700: 8%; ACT scores over 30: 8%.

Faculty *Total:* 737, 96% full-time, 82% with terminal degrees. *Student/faculty ratio:* 19:1.

Majors Accounting; administrative assistant and secretarial science; aeronautical/aerospace engineering technology; aerospace, aeronautical and astronautical engineering; agricultural/biological engineering and bioengineering; agricultural business and management; agricultural business and management related; agricultural economics; agricultural teacher education; agriculture; agronomy and crop science; airframe mechanics and aircraft maintenance technology; American studies; animal physiology; animal sciences; anthropology; area studies related; art; Asian studies; audiology and speech-language pathology; biological specializations related; biology/biological sciences; biology teacher education; botany/plant biology; business administration and management; business/commerce; business teacher education; chemistry; chemistry teacher education; civil engineering; clinical laboratory science/medical technology; computer and information sciences; computer and information sciences and support services related; computer engineering; computer engineering technology; curriculum and instruction; dairy science; dance; drafting and design technology; dramatic/theatre arts; ecology; economics; education (multiple levels); education (specific subject areas) related; electrical, electronics and communications engineering; elementary education; English; entomology; environmental/environmental health engineering; family and consumer economics related; family and consumer sciences/home economics teacher education; fashion merchandising; finance; foods and nutrition related; forestry; forestry related; French; general studies; geography; geology/earth science; German; health teacher education; history; horticultural science; housing and human environments; human development and family studies; human development and family studies related; human resources management; industrial production technologies related; information science/studies; interior design; international agriculture; journalism; kindergarten/preschool education; landscape architecture; liberal arts and sciences/liberal studies; marketing/marketing management; mathematics; mathematics teacher education; mechanical engineering; medical microbiology and bacteriology; multi-/interdisciplinary studies related; music; music teacher education; music therapy; natural resources and conservation related; occupational safety and health technology; operations management; ornamental horticulture; parks, recreation and leisure; parks, recreation, and leisure related; philosophy; physical education teaching and coaching; physics; physics teacher education; plant sciences; plant sciences related; political science and government; pre-dentistry studies; pre-law studies; pre-medical studies; pre-veterinary studies; psychology; public health related; range science and management; sales and marketing/marketing and distribution teacher education; science teacher education; secondary education; social studies teacher education; social work; sociology; soil science and agronomy; Spanish; special education; speech and rhetoric; statistics; technical teacher education; technology/industrial arts teacher education; tool and die technology; wildlife and wildlands science and management; zoology/animal biology.

Academic Programs *Special study options:* academic remediation for entering students, accelerated degree program, adult/continuing education programs, advanced placement credit, cooperative education, distance learning, double majors, English as a second language, freshman honors college, honors programs, independent study, internships, off-campus study, part-time degree program, services for LD students, student-designed majors, study abroad, summer session for credit. *ROTC:* Army (b), Air Force (b).

Library Merrill Library plus 4 others with 1.5 million titles, 13,971 serial subscriptions, 17,008 audiovisual materials, an OPAC, a Web page.

Computers on Campus 850 computers available on campus for general student use. A campuswide network can be accessed from student residence rooms and from off campus. Internet access, online (class) registration, at least one staffed computer lab available.

Student Life *Housing options:* coed, men-only, women-only, disabled students. Campus housing is university owned. *Activities and organizations:* drama/theater group, student-run newspaper, choral group, marching band, Latter-Day Saints Student Association, Greek organizations, multicultural clubs, volunteer groups, college councils, national fraternities, national sororities. *Campus security:* 24-hour emergency response devices and patrols, student patrols, late-night transport/escort service, video monitors in pedestrian tunnels. *Student services:* health clinic, personal/psychological counseling, women's center, legal services.

Athletics Member NCAA. All Division I except football (Division I-A). *Intercollegiate sports:* baseball M(c), basketball M(s)/W(s), cheerleading M(s)/W(s), cross-country running M(s)/W(s), equestrian sports M(c)/W(c), golf M(s), gymnastics W(s), ice hockey M(c), rugby M(c)/W(c), soccer M(c)/W(s), softball W(s), tennis M(s)/W(s), track and field M(s)/W(s), volleyball M(c)/W(s). *Intramural sports:* badminton M/W, basketball M/W, cross-country running M/W, fencing M(c)/W(c), football M/W, golf M/W, ice hockey W(c), lacrosse M(c), racquetball M(c)/W(c), skiing (cross-country) M(c)/W(c), skiing (downhill) M(c)/W(c), soccer M/W, softball M/W, squash M/W, swimming M/W, table tennis M/W, tennis M/W, ultimate Frisbee M(c)/W(c), volleyball M/W, water polo M(c)/W(c).

Standardized Tests *Required:* SAT I or ACT (for admission). *Recommended:* ACT (for admission).

Costs (2003–04) *Tuition:* state resident $2615 full-time; nonresident $8420 full-time. Full-time tuition and fees vary according to course load and student level. Part-time tuition and fees vary according to course load and student level. *Required fees:* $526 full-time. *Room and board:* $3930; room only: $1550. Room and board charges vary according to board plan and housing facility. *Payment plan:* deferred payment. *Waivers:* minority students, children of alumni, adult students, senior citizens, and employees or children of employees.

Financial Aid Of all full-time matriculated undergraduates who enrolled in 2002, 7,538 applied for aid, 6,753 were judged to have need, 857 had their need fully met. 508 Federal Work-Study jobs (averaging $3097). 129 state and other part-time jobs (averaging $5041). In 2002, 1437 non-need-based awards were made. *Average percent of need met:* 59%. *Average financial aid package:* $5000. *Average need-based loan:* $3800. *Average need-based gift aid:* $3025. *Average non-need-based aid:* $2550. *Average indebtedness upon graduation:* $11,500.

Applying *Options:* electronic application, early admission, deferred entrance. *Application fee:* $35. *Required:* high school transcript. *Recommended:* minimum 2.75 GPA. *Application deadline:* rolling (freshmen), rolling (transfers). *Notification:* continuous (freshmen), continuous (transfers).

Admissions Contact Dr. Eric Olsen, Director, Recruitment and Enrollment Services, Utah State University, 0160 Old Main Hill, Logan, UT 84322-0160. *Phone:* 435-797-1129. *Toll-free phone:* 800-488-8108. *Fax:* 435-797-3708. *E-mail:* admit@cc.usu.edu.

UTAH VALLEY STATE COLLEGE
Orem, Utah

- **State-supported** primarily 2-year, founded 1941, part of Utah System of Higher Education
- **Calendar** semesters
- **Degrees** certificates, diplomas, associate, and bachelor's
- **Suburban** 200-acre campus with easy access to Salt Lake City
- **Endowment** $5.1 million
- **Coed**
- **Noncompetitive** entrance level

Faculty *Student/faculty ratio:* 19:1.

Student Life *Campus security:* 24-hour patrols.

Athletics Member NCAA. All Division I.

Standardized Tests *Required:* SAT I, ACT, or in-house tests (for placement).

Costs (2004–05) *Tuition:* state resident $2788 full-time; nonresident $8718 full-time. Full-time tuition and fees vary according to course level. Part-time tuition and fees vary according to course level. *Payment plans:* installment, deferred payment.

Applying *Options:* electronic application, deferred entrance. *Application fee:* $30. *Recommended:* high school transcript.

Admissions Contact Mrs. Liz Childs, Director of Admissions, Utah Valley State College, 800 West University Parkway, Orem, UT 84058-5999. *Phone:* 801-863-8460. *Fax:* 801-225-4677. *E-mail:* info@uvsc.edu.

WEBER STATE UNIVERSITY
Ogden, Utah

- **State-supported** comprehensive, founded 1889, part of Utah System of Higher Education
- **Calendar** semesters
- **Degrees** certificates, associate, bachelor's, master's, and postbachelor's certificates
- **Urban** 526-acre campus with easy access to Salt Lake City
- **Endowment** $23.8 million
- **Coed,** 18,452 undergraduate students, 60% full-time, 51% women, 49% men
- **Noncompetitive** entrance level, 100% of applicants were admitted

Undergraduates 11,015 full-time, 7,437 part-time. Students come from 50 states and territories, 39 other countries, 7% are from out of state, 0.9% African American, 2% Asian American or Pacific Islander, 3% Hispanic American, 0.7% Native American, 0.9% international, 10% transferred in, 3% live on campus. *Retention:* 70% of 2002 full-time freshmen returned.

Freshmen *Admission:* 5,893 applied, 5,893 admitted, 2,878 enrolled. *Average high school GPA:* 3.22. *Test scores:* SAT verbal scores over 500: 55%; SAT math scores over 500: 52%; ACT scores over 18: 80%; SAT verbal scores over 600: 16%; SAT math scores over 600: 18%; ACT scores over 24: 29%; SAT verbal scores over 700: 3%; SAT math scores over 700: 2%; ACT scores over 30: 2%.

Faculty *Total:* 802, 57% full-time, 53% with terminal degrees. *Student/faculty ratio:* 22:1.

Majors Accounting; administrative assistant and secretarial science; aerospace, aeronautical and astronautical engineering; Air Force R.O.T.C./air science; applied mathematics; archeology; art; art teacher education; athletic training; autobody/collision and repair technology; automobile/automotive mechanics technology; automotive engineering technology; bilingual and multilingual education; biology/biotechnology laboratory technician; biology teacher education; botany/plant biology; business administration and management; business/managerial economics; business teacher education; chemical technology; chemistry; chemistry teacher education; child care and support services management; child development; clinical laboratory science/medical technology; clinical/medical laboratory technology; commercial and advertising art; computer and information sciences; computer engineering technology; computer science; computer systems networking and telecommunications; corrections; criminal justice/police science; criminal justice/safety; dance; dental hygiene; design and visual communications; diag-

Weber State University (continued)
nostic medical sonography and ultrasound technology; diesel mechanics technology; drafting and design technology; drama and dance teacher education; dramatic/theatre arts; economics; electrical, electronic and communications engineering technology; elementary education; emergency medical technology (EMT paramedic); English; English/language arts teacher education; family systems; fashion merchandising; finance; French; French language teacher education; geography; geology/earth science; German; German language teacher education; gerontology; health and physical education; health/health care administration; health information/medical records technology; history; history teacher education; human resources management; industrial arts; industrial technology; information science/studies; interior design; journalism; kindergarten/preschool education; kinesiology and exercise science; liberal arts and sciences/liberal studies; logistics and materials management; machine tool technology; management information systems; marketing/marketing management; mathematics; mechanical engineering/mechanical technology; medical microbiology and bacteriology; medical radiologic technology; music; music performance; music teacher education; nuclear medical technology; nursing (registered nurse training); office management; photography; physical education teaching and coaching; physics; physics teacher education; piano and organ; political science and government; psychology; public relations/image management; radio and television; respiratory care therapy; science teacher education; secondary education; social science teacher education; social studies teacher education; social work; sociology; Spanish; Spanish language teacher education; technical and business writing; zoology/animal biology.

Academic Programs *Special study options:* academic remediation for entering students, accelerated degree program, adult/continuing education programs, advanced placement credit, cooperative education, distance learning, double majors, English as a second language, external degree program, freshman honors college, honors programs, independent study, internships, off-campus study, part-time degree program, services for LD students, student-designed majors, study abroad, summer session for credit. *ROTC:* Army (b), Navy (b), Air Force (b).

Library Stewart Library plus 1 other with 686,681 titles, 2,331 serial subscriptions, 17,499 audiovisual materials, an OPAC, a Web page.

Computers on Campus 558 computers available on campus for general student use. A campuswide network can be accessed from student residence rooms and from off campus that provide access to online grades. Internet access, online (class) registration, at least one staffed computer lab available. Computer purchase or lease plan available.

Student Life *Housing options:* men-only, women-only, disabled students. Campus housing is university owned and is provided by a third party. *Activities and organizations:* drama/theater group, student-run newspaper, radio and television station, choral group, marching band, LDSSA, mountaineering club, rodeo club, Beta Alpha Psi, student nurses, national fraternities, national sororities. *Campus security:* 24-hour emergency response devices and patrols, student patrols, late-night transport/escort service, controlled dormitory access. *Student services:* health clinic, personal/psychological counseling, women's center, legal services.

Athletics Member NCAA. All Division I except football (Division I-AA). *Intercollegiate sports:* baseball M(c), basketball M(s)/W(s), bowling M(c)/W(c), cheerleading M(s)/W(s), cross-country running M(s)/W(s), fencing M(c)/W(c), golf M(s)/W(s), ice hockey M(c), lacrosse M(c)/W(c), racquetball M(c)/W(c), rugby M(c)/W(c), skiing (downhill) M(c)/W(c), soccer M(c)/W(s), softball W(c), swimming M(c)/W(c), tennis M(s)/W(s), track and field M(s)/W(s), volleyball W(s), water polo M(c)/W(c). *Intramural sports:* baseball M/W, basketball M/W, bowling M/W, cross-country running M/W, football M/W, golf M/W, racquetball M/W, soccer M/W, softball M/W, tennis M/W, volleyball M/W.

Standardized Tests *Required:* SAT I or ACT (for placement).

Costs (2003–04) *Tuition:* state resident $2632 full-time; nonresident $7958 full-time. Part-time tuition and fees vary according to course load. *Required fees:* $502 full-time. *Room and board:* $5313; room only: $2223. Room and board charges vary according to board plan and housing facility. *Payment plans:* installment, deferred payment. *Waivers:* senior citizens and employees or children of employees.

Financial Aid Of all full-time matriculated undergraduates who enrolled in 2001, 8,410 applied for aid, 7,401 were judged to have need, 5,462 had their need fully met. In 2001, 2470 non-need-based awards were made. *Average percent of need met:* 87%. *Average financial aid package:* $5300. *Average need-based loan:* $2620. *Average need-based gift aid:* $3750. *Average non-need-based aid:* $1420. *Average indebtedness upon graduation:* $10,500.

Applying *Options:* electronic application, early admission, deferred entrance. *Application fee:* $30. *Required:* high school transcript. *Application deadline:* 8/22 (freshmen), rolling (transfers). *Notification:* continuous (freshmen), continuous (transfers).

Admissions Contact John Allred, Admissions Advisor, Weber State University, 1137 University Circle, 3750 Harrison Boulevard, Ogden, UT 84408-1137. *Phone:* 801-626-6050. *Toll-free phone:* 800-634-6568 (in-state); 800-848-7770 (out-of-state). *Fax:* 801-626-6744. *E-mail:* admissions@weber.edu.

WESTERN GOVERNORS UNIVERSITY
Salt Lake City, Utah

- **Independent** comprehensive, founded 1998
- **Calendar** continuous
- **Degrees** certificates, diplomas, associate, bachelor's, master's, post-master's, and postbachelor's certificates
- **Coed**

Faculty *Student/faculty ratio:* 46:1.

Costs (2003–04) *Tuition:* $4780 full-time. *Required fees:* $50 full-time.

Financial Aid Of all full-time matriculated undergraduates who enrolled in 2002, 195 applied for aid, 120 were judged to have need, 120 had their need fully met. *Average percent of need met:* 100. *Average financial aid package:* $2719. *Average need-based loan:* $1215. *Average need-based gift aid:* $2180.

Applying *Options:* electronic application. *Application fee:* $100. *Required for some:* high school transcript.

Admissions Contact Ms. Wendy Gregory, Admissions Manager, Western Governors University, 2040 East Murray Holladay Road, Suite 106, Salt Lake City, UT 84117. *Phone:* 801-274-3280 Ext. 315. *Toll-free phone:* 877-435-7948. *Fax:* 801-274-3305. *E-mail:* info@wgu.edu.

WESTMINSTER COLLEGE
Salt Lake City, Utah

- **Independent** comprehensive, founded 1875
- **Calendar** 4-4-1
- **Degrees** bachelor's, master's, and postbachelor's certificates
- **Suburban** 27-acre campus
- **Endowment** $43.0 million
- **Coed,** 2,017 undergraduate students, 89% full-time, 58% women, 42% men
- **Moderately difficult** entrance level, 82% of applicants were admitted

Undergraduates 1,788 full-time, 229 part-time. Students come from 34 states and territories, 28 other countries, 8% are from out of state, 0.4% African American, 3% Asian American or Pacific Islander, 4% Hispanic American, 0.8% Native American, 2% international, 14% transferred in, 24% live on campus. *Retention:* 77% of 2002 full-time freshmen returned.

Freshmen *Admission:* 865 applied, 713 admitted, 374 enrolled. *Average high school GPA:* 3.48. *Test scores:* ACT scores over 18: 93%; ACT scores over 24: 47%; ACT scores over 30: 9%.

Faculty *Total:* 253, 47% full-time, 52% with terminal degrees. *Student/faculty ratio:* 11:1.

Majors Accounting; airline pilot and flight crew; art; aviation/airway management; biology/biological sciences; biology teacher education; business administration and management; business/commerce; business/managerial economics; chemistry; communication/speech communication and rhetoric; computer science; elementary education; English; finance; history; human resources management; international business/trade/commerce; kindergarten/preschool education; management information systems and services related; marketing/marketing management; mathematics; nursing (registered nurse training); philosophy; physics; political science and government; psychology; social sciences; social science teacher education; sociology; special education.

Academic Programs *Special study options:* academic remediation for entering students, accelerated degree program, advanced placement credit, cooperative education, English as a second language, honors programs, independent study, internships, part-time degree program, services for LD students, student-designed majors, summer session for credit. *ROTC:* Army (c), Navy (c), Air Force (c). *Unusual degree programs:* 3-2 engineering with University of Southern California, Washington University in St. Louis.

Library Giovale Library plus 1 other with 119,212 titles, 437 serial subscriptions, 6,165 audiovisual materials, an OPAC, a Web page.

Computers on Campus 409 computers available on campus for general student use. A campuswide network can be accessed from student residence rooms. Internet access, online (class) registration, at least one staffed computer lab available.

Student Life *Housing:* on-campus residence required for freshman year. *Options:* coed. Campus housing is university owned. Freshman campus housing is guaranteed. *Activities and organizations:* drama/theater group, student-run newspaper, choral group, outdoor club, Pre-Med Society, English club, Theatre Society, Students Educators Association. *Campus security:* 24-hour emergency response devices and patrols, student patrols, late-night transport/escort service, controlled dormitory access. *Student services:* personal/psychological counseling.

Athletics Member NAIA. *Intercollegiate sports:* basketball M/W, cheerleading M/W, golf M/W, soccer M, volleyball W. *Intramural sports:* basketball M/W, cross-country running M/W, football M/W, rock climbing M(c)/W(c), skiing (cross-country) M/W, soccer M/W, table tennis M/W, tennis M/W, ultimate Frisbee M/W, volleyball M/W, weight lifting M/W.

Standardized Tests *Required:* SAT I or ACT (for admission).

Costs (2003–04) *Comprehensive fee:* $22,294 includes full-time tuition ($16,704), mandatory fees ($290), and room and board ($5300). Full-time tuition and fees vary according to course load. Part-time tuition: $696. *Required fees:* $50 per term part-time. *Room and board:* Room and board charges vary according to board plan. *Payment plans:* installment, deferred payment. *Waivers:* employees or children of employees.

Financial Aid Of all full-time matriculated undergraduates who enrolled in 2003, 1,404 applied for aid, 1,246 were judged to have need, 572 had their need fully met. 321 Federal Work-Study jobs (averaging $2200). In 2003, 451 non-need-based awards were made. *Average percent of need met:* 89%. *Average financial aid package:* $14,130. *Average need-based loan:* $3921. *Average need-based gift aid:* $9761. *Average non-need-based aid:* $7385. *Average indebtedness upon graduation:* $15,600.

Applying *Options:* common application, electronic application, early admission, deferred entrance. *Application fee:* $30. *Required:* high school transcript, minimum 2.5 GPA. *Recommended:* essay or personal statement, minimum 3.0 GPA, 1 letter of recommendation, interview. *Application deadline:* rolling (freshmen), rolling (transfers). *Notification:* continuous (freshmen), continuous (transfers).

Admissions Contact Ms. Mary Hyland, Director of Admissions, Westminster College, 1840 South 1300 East, Salt Lake City, UT 84105-3697. *Phone:* 801-832-2200. *Toll-free phone:* 800-748-4753. *Fax:* 801-832-3101. *E-mail:* admispub@westminstercollege.edu.

■ See page 2826 for a narrative description.

VERMONT

BENNINGTON COLLEGE

Bennington, Vermont

- **Independent** comprehensive, founded 1932
- **Calendar** semesters plus winter work term in January and February
- **Degrees** bachelor's, master's, and postbachelor's certificates
- **Small-town** 550-acre campus with easy access to Albany
- **Endowment** $9.6 million
- **Coed,** 642 undergraduate students, 99% full-time, 67% women, 33% men
- **Very difficult** entrance level, 68% of applicants were admitted

Bennington regards education as an aesthetic and ethical, no less than intellectual, process. It seeks to liberate and nurture the individuality, the creative intelligence, and the ethical and visual sensibility of its students, to the end that their richly varied natural endowments will be directed toward self-fulfillment and toward constructive social purposes.

Undergraduates 635 full-time, 7 part-time. Students come from 45 states and territories, 18 other countries, 95% are from out of state, 1% African American, 1% Asian American or Pacific Islander, 3% Hispanic American, 0.3% Native American, 6% international, 3% transferred in, 95% live on campus. *Retention:* 80% of 2002 full-time freshmen returned.

Freshmen *Admission:* 773 applied, 526 admitted, 172 enrolled. *Average high school GPA:* 3.48. *Test scores:* SAT verbal scores over 500: 95%; SAT math scores over 500: 84%; ACT scores over 18: 97%; SAT verbal scores over 600: 76%; SAT math scores over 600: 45%; ACT scores over 24: 80%; SAT verbal scores over 700: 29%; SAT math scores over 700: 6%; ACT scores over 30: 30%.

Faculty *Total:* 87, 74% full-time, 59% with terminal degrees. *Student/faculty ratio:* 9:1.

Majors Anthropology; architecture; art; biochemistry; biological and physical sciences; biology/biological sciences; ceramic arts and ceramics; chemistry; Chinese; comparative literature; computer science; creative writing; dance; design and applied arts related; developmental and child psychology; dramatic/theatre arts; drawing; ecology; English; environmental biology; environmental studies; European studies; film/cinema studies; fine/studio arts; French; German; history; history of philosophy; humanities; interdisciplinary studies; international relations and affairs; Italian studies; Japanese; jazz/jazz studies; kindergarten/preschool education; liberal arts and sciences/liberal studies; literature; mathematics; modern languages; music; music history, literature, and theory; natural sciences; philosophy; photography; physics; pre-medical studies; pre-veterinary studies; printmaking; psychology; sculpture; social sciences; sociology; Spanish; violin, viola, guitar and other stringed instruments; visual and performing arts; voice and opera.

Academic Programs *Special study options:* accelerated degree program, cooperative education, distance learning, double majors, English as a second language, independent study, internships, off-campus study, part-time degree program, services for LD students, student-designed majors, study abroad. *Unusual degree programs:* 3-2 education.

Library Crossett Library plus 2 others with 128,413 titles, 250 serial subscriptions, 40,219 audiovisual materials, an OPAC, a Web page.

Computers on Campus 61 computers available on campus for general student use. A campuswide network can be accessed from student residence rooms and from off campus. Internet access, at least one staffed computer lab available.

Student Life *Housing:* on-campus residence required through senior year. *Options:* coed, cooperative. Campus housing is university owned. Freshman campus housing is guaranteed. *Activities and organizations:* drama/theater group, student-run newspaper, radio station, choral group, Literary Magazine, Amnesty International, Campus Activities Board, film society, student newspaper. *Campus security:* 24-hour emergency response devices and patrols, late-night transport/escort service. *Student services:* health clinic, personal/psychological counseling.

Athletics *Intercollegiate sports:* baseball M/W, basketball M/W, soccer M(c)/W(c), softball M(c)/W(c). *Intramural sports:* archery M/W, badminton M/W, baseball M/W, basketball M/W, skiing (cross-country) M/W, skiing (downhill) M/W, soccer M/W, softball M(c)/W(c), table tennis M/W, tennis M/W, ultimate Frisbee M/W, volleyball M/W, weight lifting M/W.

Standardized Tests *Required:* SAT I or ACT (for admission).

Costs (2003–04) *Comprehensive fee:* $35,910 includes full-time tuition ($28,030), mandatory fees ($740), and room and board ($7140). Part-time tuition: $900 per credit. *College room only:* $3820. *Payment plan:* installment. *Waivers:* employees or children of employees.

Financial Aid Of all full-time matriculated undergraduates who enrolled in 2003, 418 applied for aid, 378 were judged to have need, 21 had their need fully met. 330 Federal Work-Study jobs (averaging $1500). 50 state and other part-time jobs (averaging $1500). In 2003, 79 non-need-based awards were made. *Average percent of need met:* 75%. *Average financial aid package:* $21,821. *Average need-based loan:* $3780. *Average need-based gift aid:* $17,520. *Average non-need-based aid:* $4589. *Average indebtedness upon graduation:* $17,558.

Applying *Options:* common application, early admission, early decision, deferred entrance. *Application fee:* $50. *Required:* essay or personal statement, high school transcript, 2 letters of recommendation, interview. *Application deadlines:* 1/1 (freshmen), 6/1 (transfers). *Early decision:* 11/15. *Notification:* 4/1 (freshmen), 12/1 (early decision), 7/1 (transfers).

Admissions Contact Mr. Ben Jones, Dean of Admissions and Financial Aid, Bennington College, One College Drive, Bennington, VT 05201. *Phone:* 802-440-4312. *Toll-free phone:* 800-833-6845. *Fax:* 802-440-4320. *E-mail:* admissions@bennington.edu.

■ See page 1238 for a narrative description.

BURLINGTON COLLEGE

Burlington, Vermont

- **Independent** 4-year, founded 1972
- **Calendar** semesters
- **Degrees** certificates, associate, and bachelor's
- **Urban** 1-acre campus
- **Endowment** $76,000
- **Coed,** 241 undergraduate students, 49% full-time, 57% women, 43% men
- **Noncompetitive** entrance level, 72% of applicants were admitted

Burlington College is a small, progressive liberal arts college offering personalized services to self-motivated students of all ages. Programs are offered in cinema studies and film production, fine arts, humanities, human services, inter-American culture and development, legal and justice studies, paralegal studies, psychology, transpersonal psychology, and writing and literature. Upper-level distance learning is available.

Undergraduates 117 full-time, 124 part-time. Students come from 23 states and territories, 1 other country, 45% are from out of state, 23% transferred in, 6% live on campus. *Retention:* 60% of 2002 full-time freshmen returned.

Freshmen *Admission:* 46 applied, 33 admitted, 17 enrolled.

Faculty *Total:* 68. *Student/faculty ratio:* 8:1.

Majors Animation, interactive technology, video graphics and special effects; art; cinematography and film/video production; city/urban, community and regional planning; film/cinema studies; humanities; human services; interdisciplinary studies; land use planning and management; Latin American studies; legal assistant/paralegal; legal studies; liberal arts and sciences/liberal studies; literature; natural resources management; photographic and film/video technology; psychology; psychology related; women's studies.

Academic Programs *Special study options:* academic remediation for entering students, accelerated degree program, adult/continuing education programs, coop-

Burlington College (continued)
erative education, distance learning, double majors, external degree program, independent study, internships, off-campus study, part-time degree program, services for LD students, student-designed majors, study abroad, summer session for credit.

Library Burlington College Library with 5,700 titles, 80 serial subscriptions, 1,050 audiovisual materials, an OPAC, a Web page.

Computers on Campus 21 computers available on campus for general student use. A campuswide network can be accessed. Internet access, at least one staffed computer lab available.

Student Life *Housing options:* coed, cooperative. Campus housing is university owned and leased by the school. Freshman applicants given priority for college housing. *Activities and organizations:* student-run newspaper, Student Association. *Campus security:* 24-hour emergency response devices. *Student services:* personal/psychological counseling.

Costs (2003–04) *Tuition:* $13,120 full-time, $435 per credit hour part-time. Full-time tuition and fees vary according to course load. Part-time tuition and fees vary according to course load. *Room only:* $5750. Room and board charges vary according to gender and housing facility. *Payment plan:* installment. *Waivers:* employees or children of employees.

Financial Aid Of all full-time matriculated undergraduates who enrolled in 2003, 99 applied for aid, 94 were judged to have need, 3 had their need fully met. 39 Federal Work-Study jobs (averaging $1345). *Average percent of need met:* 53%. *Average financial aid package:* $9500. *Average need-based loan:* $4522. *Average need-based gift aid:* $5145. *Average indebtedness upon graduation:* $10,229.

Applying *Options:* common application, electronic application, deferred entrance. *Application fee:* $35. *Required:* essay or personal statement, high school transcript, 2 letters of recommendation, interview. *Application deadlines:* 8/1 (freshmen), 8/1 (transfers). *Notification:* continuous (freshmen), continuous (transfers).

Admissions Contact Ms. Christa Henderson, Admissions Coordinator, Burlington College, 95 North Avenue, Burlington, VT 05401-2998. *Phone:* 802-862-9616 Ext. 124. *Toll-free phone:* 800-862-9616. *Fax:* 802-660-4331. *E-mail:* admissions@burlcol.edu.

CASTLETON STATE COLLEGE

Castleton, Vermont

- **State-supported** comprehensive, founded 1787, part of Vermont State Colleges System
- **Calendar** semesters
- **Degrees** associate, bachelor's, master's, and post-master's certificates
- **Rural** 160-acre campus
- **Endowment** $3.9 million
- **Coed,** 1,699 undergraduate students, 88% full-time, 59% women, 41% men
- **Moderately difficult** entrance level, 79% of applicants were admitted

Located in a historic Vermont village close to skiing, Castleton is small enough to be a community where individuals matter yet large enough to offer 30 academic programs, 17 intercollegiate sports, and more than 40 clubs and student organizations. Castleton stresses community service and internships and provides exceptional programs for first-year students.

Undergraduates 1,488 full-time, 211 part-time. Students come from 29 states and territories, 30% are from out of state, 0.4% African American, 0.8% Asian American or Pacific Islander, 0.9% Hispanic American, 0.6% Native American, 0.1% international, 11% transferred in, 41% live on campus. *Retention:* 70% of 2002 full-time freshmen returned.

Freshmen *Admission:* 1,434 applied, 1,139 admitted, 410 enrolled. *Average high school GPA:* 3.32. *Test scores:* SAT verbal scores over 500: 41%; SAT math scores over 500: 40%; ACT scores over 18: 45%; SAT verbal scores over 600: 9%; SAT math scores over 600: 9%; ACT scores over 24: 15%; SAT math scores over 700: 1%.

Faculty *Total:* 182, 46% full-time, 62% with terminal degrees. *Student/faculty ratio:* 13:1.

Majors Accounting; American literature; art; athletic training; biological and physical sciences; biology/biological sciences; business administration and management; business/commerce; chemistry; computer and information sciences; computer programming; criminal justice/law enforcement administration; criminology; developmental and child psychology; dramatic/theatre arts; environmental studies; finance; general studies; geology/earth science; health and physical education; health science; history; journalism; kinesiology and exercise science; literature; marketing/marketing management; mathematics; mathematics teacher education; music; music teacher education; natural sciences; nursing (registered nurse training); physical education teaching and coaching; psychology; public relations/image management; radio and television; science teacher education; social sciences; social studies teacher education; social work; sociology; Spanish.

Academic Programs *Special study options:* academic remediation for entering students, advanced placement credit, cooperative education, double majors, honors programs, independent study, internships, off-campus study, part-time degree program, services for LD students, student-designed majors, study abroad, summer session for credit. *ROTC:* Army (b). *Unusual degree programs:* 3-2 business administration with Clarkson University; engineering with Clarkson University.

Library Calvin Coolidge Library with 157,075 titles, 938 serial subscriptions, 2,922 audiovisual materials, an OPAC, a Web page.

Computers on Campus 225 computers available on campus for general student use. A campuswide network can be accessed from student residence rooms. Internet access, at least one staffed computer lab available. Computer purchase or lease plan available.

Student Life *Housing:* on-campus residence required for freshman year. *Options:* coed. Campus housing is university owned. Freshman campus housing is guaranteed. *Activities and organizations:* drama/theater group, student-run newspaper, radio station, choral group, student radio station, community service, women's issues, rugby, snowboarding. *Campus security:* 24-hour emergency response devices and patrols, student patrols, late-night transport/escort service, controlled dormitory access. *Student services:* health clinic, personal/psychological counseling.

Athletics Member NCAA. All Division III. *Intercollegiate sports:* baseball M, basketball M/W, cheerleading M(c)/W(c), cross-country running M/W, field hockey W, ice hockey M/W, lacrosse M/W, rugby M(c)/W(c), skiing (downhill) M(c)/W(c), soccer M/W, softball W, tennis M/W, volleyball M(c)/W(c). *Intramural sports:* basketball M/W, equestrian sports M/W, football M/W, golf M/W, racquetball M/W, soccer M/W, softball M/W, swimming M/W, table tennis M/W, tennis M/W, volleyball M/W, water polo M/W, weight lifting M/W.

Standardized Tests *Required:* SAT I or ACT (for admission).

Costs (2003–04) *One-time required fee:* $160. *Tuition:* state resident $5646 full-time, $244 per credit part-time; nonresident $12,200 full-time, $518 per credit part-time. Part-time tuition and fees vary according to course load. *Required fees:* $320 full-time. *Room and board:* $6014; room only: $3518. Room and board charges vary according to board plan. *Payment plan:* installment. *Waivers:* senior citizens and employees or children of employees.

Financial Aid Of all full-time matriculated undergraduates who enrolled in 2002, 360 Federal Work-Study jobs (averaging $1000).

Applying *Options:* common application, electronic application, deferred entrance. *Application fee:* $30. *Required:* essay or personal statement, high school transcript, minimum 2.5 GPA, letters of recommendation. *Recommended:* interview. *Application deadline:* rolling (freshmen), rolling (transfers). *Notification:* continuous (freshmen), continuous (transfers).

Admissions Contact Castleton State College, Seminary Street, Castleton, VT 05735. *Phone:* 802-468-1213. *Toll-free phone:* 800-639-8521. *Fax:* 802-468-1476. *E-mail:* info@castleton.edu.

■ *See page 1364 for a narrative description.*

CHAMPLAIN COLLEGE

Burlington, Vermont

- **Independent** comprehensive, founded 1878
- **Calendar** semesters
- **Degrees** certificates, associate, bachelor's, master's, and postbachelor's certificates (baccalaureate programs are part of the 2+2 curriculum)
- **Suburban** 21-acre campus with easy access to Montreal, Canada
- **Endowment** $4.7 million
- **Coed,** 2,528 undergraduate students, 66% full-time, 52% women, 48% men
- **Moderately difficult** entrance level, 63% of applicants were admitted

Since 1878, Champlain has delivered challenging professional majors in a liberal arts campus setting. Built-in internship opportunities, an "upside-down" curriculum format, and nationally recognized career-planning services contribute to employment success upon graduation. Burlington, a great college town, has a lively music and arts environment, world-class skiing, and outdoor recreation nearby.

Undergraduates 1,668 full-time, 860 part-time. Students come from 28 states and territories, 26 other countries, 44% are from out of state, 0.7% African American, 2% Asian American or Pacific Islander, 1% Hispanic American, 1% Native American, 1% international, 8% transferred in, 41% live on campus. *Retention:* 82% of 2002 full-time freshmen returned.

Freshmen *Admission:* 1,436 applied, 907 admitted, 362 enrolled. *Average high school GPA:* 2.90. *Test scores:* SAT verbal scores over 500: 58%; SAT math scores over 500: 59%; ACT scores over 18: 81%; SAT verbal scores over 600: 10%; SAT math scores over 600: 13%; ACT scores over 24: 15%; SAT verbal scores over 700: 1%; SAT math scores over 700: 1%.

Faculty *Total:* 215, 26% full-time, 22% with terminal degrees. *Student/faculty ratio:* 17:1.

Majors Accounting; animation, interactive technology, video graphics and special effects; business administration and management; business/commerce; commercial and advertising art; communication and journalism related; communication and media related; computer and information sciences; computer and information systems security; computer graphics; computer/information technology services administration related; computer management; computer software and media applications related; computer software engineering; computer systems networking and telecommunications; creative writing; criminal justice/law enforcement administration; criminal justice/safety; design and visual communications; digital communication and media/multimedia; early childhood education; e-commerce; elementary education; forensic science and technology; graphic design; hospitality administration; hospitality administration related; hospitality and recreation marketing; hotel/motel administration; human services; information science/studies; intermedia/multimedia; international business/trade/commerce; journalism related; kindergarten/preschool education; legal assistant/paralegal; liberal arts and sciences/liberal studies; marketing/marketing management; mass communication/media; middle school education; pre-law studies; professional studies; public relations, advertising, and applied communication related; public relations/image management; radiologic technology/science; sales, distribution and marketing; secondary education; social work; system administration; system, networking, and LAN/wan management; technical and business writing; telecommunications; tourism and travel services management; tourism and travel services marketing; tourism promotion; web/multimedia management and webmaster; web page, digital/multimedia and information resources design.

Academic Programs *Special study options:* advanced placement credit, cooperative education, distance learning, double majors, freshman honors college, honors programs, internships, off-campus study, part-time degree program, services for LD students, study abroad, summer session for credit. *ROTC:* Army (c).

Library Miller Information Commons with 60,000 titles, 270 audiovisual materials, an OPAC, a Web page.

Computers on Campus 260 computers available on campus for general student use. A campuswide network can be accessed from student residence rooms and from off campus that provide access to wireless laptops available. Internet access, online (class) registration, at least one staffed computer lab available.

Student Life *Housing options:* coed, women-only. Campus housing is university owned. Freshman campus housing is guaranteed. *Activities and organizations:* drama/theater group, student-run newspaper, choral group, Diversity Champlain, international club, community service organization, theater group (Champlain Players), outing club/skiing snowboarding club. *Campus security:* 24-hour emergency response devices and patrols, late-night transport/escort service, controlled dormitory access. *Student services:* health clinic, personal/psychological counseling.

Athletics *Intramural sports:* basketball M/W, bowling M/W, cheerleading W(c), cross-country running M/W, golf M/W, ice hockey M/W, lacrosse M, sailing M/W, skiing (cross-country) M/W, skiing (downhill) M/W, soccer M/W, ultimate Frisbee M/W, volleyball M/W.

Standardized Tests *Required:* SAT I or ACT (for admission). *Required for some:* SAT II: Subject Tests (for admission).

Costs (2003–04) *Comprehensive fee:* $22,030 includes full-time tuition ($12,925), mandatory fees ($150), and room and board ($8955). Full-time tuition and fees vary according to course load. Part-time tuition: $380 per credit hour. Part-time tuition and fees vary according to course load. *Required fees:* $150 per year part-time. *College room only:* $5405. Room and board charges vary according to board plan and housing facility. *Payment plan:* installment. *Waivers:* senior citizens and employees or children of employees.

Financial Aid Of all full-time matriculated undergraduates who enrolled in 2003, 1,180 applied for aid, 984 were judged to have need, 160 had their need fully met. 346 Federal Work-Study jobs (averaging $2100). In 2003, 244 non-need-based awards were made. *Average percent of need met:* 65%. *Average financial aid package:* $8751. *Average need-based loan:* $4322. *Average need-based gift aid:* $5211. *Average non-need-based aid:* $11,070.

Applying *Options:* common application, electronic application, deferred entrance. *Application fee:* $40. *Required:* essay or personal statement, high school transcript. *Recommended:* minimum 2.0 GPA, 1 letter of recommendation, interview. *Application deadline:* rolling (freshmen), rolling (transfers). *Notification:* continuous (freshmen), continuous (transfers).

Admissions Contact Ms. Josephine H. Churchill, Director of Admissions, Champlain College, 163 South Willard Street, Burlington, VT 05401. *Phone:* 802-860-2727. *Toll-free phone:* 800-570-5858. *Fax:* 802-860-2767. *E-mail:* admission@champlain.edu.

■ *See page 1386 for a narrative description.*

COLLEGE OF ST. JOSEPH

Rutland, Vermont

- **Independent Roman Catholic** comprehensive, founded 1950
- **Calendar** semesters
- **Degrees** certificates, associate, bachelor's, master's, and postbachelor's certificates
- **Small-town** 90-acre campus
- **Endowment** $1.7 million
- **Coed,** 309 undergraduate students, 68% full-time, 61% women, 39% men
- **Minimally difficult** entrance level, 81% of applicants were admitted

Undergraduates 209 full-time, 100 part-time. Students come from 12 states and territories, 2 other countries, 37% are from out of state, 7% transferred in, 31% live on campus. *Retention:* 60% of 2002 full-time freshmen returned.

Freshmen *Admission:* 141 applied, 114 admitted, 39 enrolled. *Average high school GPA:* 2.6. *Test scores:* SAT verbal scores over 500: 35%; SAT math scores over 500: 27%; SAT verbal scores over 600: 4%; SAT math scores over 600: 6%.

Faculty *Total:* 64, 19% full-time, 34% with terminal degrees. *Student/faculty ratio:* 11:1.

Majors Accounting; American studies; business administration and management; communication/speech communication and rhetoric; education; elementary education; English; finance; history; human services; information science/studies; journalism; kindergarten/preschool education; liberal arts and sciences/liberal studies; parks, recreation and leisure facilities management; political science and government; pre-law studies; psychology; secondary education; special education.

Academic Programs *Special study options:* academic remediation for entering students, accelerated degree program, adult/continuing education programs, advanced placement credit, double majors, English as a second language, internships, part-time degree program, services for LD students, study abroad, summer session for credit.

Library St. Joseph Library plus 1 other with 50,000 titles, 3,000 serial subscriptions, 5,500 audiovisual materials, an OPAC.

Computers on Campus 30 computers available on campus for general student use. A campuswide network can be accessed from student residence rooms and from off campus. Internet access, at least one staffed computer lab available. Computer purchase or lease plan available.

Student Life *Housing:* on-campus residence required through sophomore year. *Options:* men-only, women-only. Campus housing is university owned. Freshman campus housing is guaranteed. *Activities and organizations:* drama/theater group, student-run newspaper, choral group, human services club, campus ministry club, Psi Chi, Ambassadors, chorus. *Campus security:* 24-hour emergency response devices. *Student services:* personal/psychological counseling.

Athletics Member NAIA. *Intercollegiate sports:* basketball M/W, soccer M/W, softball W. *Intramural sports:* baseball M, basketball M/W, bowling M/W, racquetball M/W, skiing (downhill) M/W, soccer M/W, softball M/W, tennis M/W, volleyball M/W.

Standardized Tests *Required:* SAT I or ACT (for admission).

Costs (2003–04) *Comprehensive fee:* $19,100 includes full-time tuition ($12,500), mandatory fees ($200), and room and board ($6400). Full-time tuition and fees vary according to program. Part-time tuition: $220 per credit. Part-time tuition and fees vary according to program. *Required fees:* $45 per term part-time. *College room only:* $3100. Room and board charges vary according to housing facility. *Payment plan:* installment. *Waivers:* senior citizens and employees or children of employees.

Financial Aid Of all full-time matriculated undergraduates who enrolled in 2003, 174 applied for aid, 164 were judged to have need, 34 had their need fully met. 53 Federal Work-Study jobs (averaging $900). 53 state and other part-time jobs (averaging $1000). In 2003, 9 non-need-based awards were made. *Average percent of need met:* 74%. *Average financial aid package:* $10,432. *Average need-based loan:* $4515. *Average need-based gift aid:* $6430. *Average non-need-based aid:* $3160. *Average indebtedness upon graduation:* $15,048.

Applying *Options:* early admission, deferred entrance. *Application fee:* $25. *Required:* essay or personal statement, high school transcript, minimum 2.0 GPA,

College of St. Joseph (continued)
2 letters of recommendation. *Recommended:* interview. *Application deadline:* rolling (freshmen), rolling (transfers). *Notification:* continuous (freshmen), continuous (transfers).

Admissions Contact Pat Ryan, Director of Admissions and Marketing, College of St. Joseph, 71 Clement Road, VT 05701. *Phone:* 802-773-5900 Ext. 3206. *Toll-free phone:* 877-270-9998. *Fax:* 802-773-5900 Ext. 4. *E-mail:* admissions@csj.edu.

GODDARD COLLEGE
Plainfield, Vermont

- **Independent** comprehensive, founded 1938
- **Calendar** semesters
- **Degrees** bachelor's and master's
- **Rural** 250-acre campus
- **Endowment** $600,000
- **Coed,** 182 undergraduate students, 100% full-time, 68% women, 32% men
- **Moderately difficult** entrance level

Undergraduates 182 full-time. Students come from 32 states and territories, 1 other country, 82% are from out of state, 3% African American, 2% Asian American or Pacific Islander, 2% Hispanic American, 2% Native American, 0.5% international, 24% transferred in. *Retention:* 68% of 2002 full-time freshmen returned.

Freshmen *Admission:* 11 enrolled.

Faculty *Total:* 72, 3% full-time, 94% with terminal degrees. *Student/faculty ratio:* 11:1.

Majors Botany/plant biology; foods, nutrition, and wellness; interdisciplinary studies; liberal arts and sciences and humanities related; nutrition sciences; reproductive biology.

Academic Programs *Special study options:* adult/continuing education programs, advanced placement credit, cooperative education, distance learning, double majors, external degree program, independent study, internships, off-campus study, services for LD students, student-designed majors.

Library Eliot Pratt Center with 70,000 titles, 280 serial subscriptions, 175 audiovisual materials, a Web page.

Computers on Campus 27 computers available on campus for general student use. A campuswide network can be accessed from student residence rooms and from off campus. Internet access, at least one staffed computer lab available.

Student Life *Housing:* college housing not available. *Activities and organizations:* drama/theater group, student-run newspaper, radio station. *Campus security:* 24-hour patrols, patrols by trained security personnel 9 p.m. to 6 a.m. *Student services:* personal/psychological counseling.

Standardized Tests *Recommended:* SAT I and SAT II or ACT (for admission).

Costs (2004–05) *Tuition:* $8550 full-time.

Financial Aid Of all full-time matriculated undergraduates who enrolled in 2002, 157 applied for aid, 151 were judged to have need, 6 had their need fully met. In 2002, 9 non-need-based awards were made. *Average percent of need met:* 40%. *Average financial aid package:* $6302. *Average need-based loan:* $4101. *Average need-based gift aid:* $2997. *Average non-need-based aid:* $5244. *Average indebtedness upon graduation:* $15,921.

Applying *Options:* electronic application, deferred entrance. *Application fee:* $40. *Required:* essay or personal statement, high school transcript, 2 letters of recommendation, interview. *Application deadline:* rolling (freshmen), rolling (transfers). *Notification:* continuous (freshmen), continuous (transfers).

Admissions Contact Admissions Counselor, Goddard College, 123 Pitkin Road, Plainfield, VT 05667-9432. *Phone:* 802-454-8311 Ext. 322. *Toll-free phone:* 800-468-4888 Ext. 307. *Fax:* 802-454-1029. *E-mail:* admissions@earth.goddard.edu.

GREEN MOUNTAIN COLLEGE
Poultney, Vermont

- **Independent** 4-year, founded 1834, affiliated with United Methodist Church
- **Calendar** semesters
- **Degree** bachelor's
- **Small-town** 155-acre campus
- **Endowment** $1.7 million
- **Coed**
- **Moderately difficult** entrance level

Faculty *Student/faculty ratio:* 14:1.

Student Life *Campus security:* 24-hour emergency response devices and patrols, student patrols, late-night transport/escort service, controlled dormitory access.

Athletics Member NCAA. All Division II.

Standardized Tests *Required:* SAT I or ACT (for admission).

Costs (2003–04) *Comprehensive fee:* $26,590 includes full-time tuition ($19,670), mandatory fees ($620), and room and board ($6300). Full-time tuition and fees vary according to course load. Part-time tuition: $655 per credit. Part-time tuition and fees vary according to course load. *Required fees:* $220 per term part-time. *Room and board:* Room and board charges vary according to board plan.

Financial Aid Of all full-time matriculated undergraduates who enrolled in 2003, 508 applied for aid, 392 were judged to have need, 73 had their need fully met. 111 Federal Work-Study jobs (averaging $1300). 202 state and other part-time jobs (averaging $1300). In 2003, 48. *Average percent of need met:* 68. *Average financial aid package:* $11,780. *Average need-based loan:* $3850. *Average need-based gift aid:* $7930. *Average non-need-based aid:* $9268. *Average indebtedness upon graduation:* $19,638.

Applying *Options:* common application, electronic application, deferred entrance. *Application fee:* $30. *Required:* high school transcript, 2 letters of recommendation. *Recommended:* minimum 2.4 GPA, interview.

Admissions Contact Ms. Noka Garrapy, Assistant Dean of Admissions, Green Mountain College, One College Circle, Poultney, VT 05764. *Phone:* 802-287-8000 Ext. 8305. *Toll-free phone:* 800-776-6675. *Fax:* 802-287-8099. *E-mail:* admiss@greenmtn.edu.

JOHNSON STATE COLLEGE
Johnson, Vermont

- **State-supported** comprehensive, founded 1828, part of Vermont State Colleges System
- **Calendar** semesters
- **Degrees** certificates, associate, bachelor's, and master's
- **Rural** 350-acre campus with easy access to Montreal
- **Endowment** $581,961
- **Coed,** 1,532 undergraduate students, 73% full-time, 60% women, 40% men
- **Moderately difficult** entrance level, 87% of applicants were admitted

Undergraduates 1,111 full-time, 421 part-time. Students come from 22 states and territories, 4 other countries, 27% are from out of state, 0.9% African American, 0.5% Asian American or Pacific Islander, 1% Hispanic American, 1% Native American, 0.3% international, 12% transferred in, 57% live on campus. *Retention:* 63% of 2002 full-time freshmen returned.

Freshmen *Admission:* 1,076 applied, 934 admitted, 277 enrolled. *Average high school GPA:* 2.50. *Test scores:* SAT verbal scores over 500: 45%; SAT math scores over 500: 36%; SAT verbal scores over 600: 11%; SAT math scores over 600: 6%; SAT verbal scores over 700: 1%.

Faculty *Total:* 203, 27% full-time. *Student/faculty ratio:* 16:1.

Majors Accounting; acting; anthropology; art; art teacher education; athletic training; biology/biological sciences; biology teacher education; business administration and management; business/commerce; creative writing; dance; drama and dance teacher education; dramatic/theatre arts; education; elementary education; English; English/language arts teacher education; environmental education; environmental studies; fine/studio arts; general studies; health and physical education; health science; history; history teacher education; hospitality administration; humanities; information science/studies; jazz/jazz studies; journalism; kinesiology and exercise science; liberal arts and sciences/liberal studies; literature; management information systems; marketing/marketing management; mathematics; mathematics teacher education; middle school education; music; music management and merchandising; music performance; music teacher education; natural resources management and policy; parks, recreation and leisure; physical education teaching and coaching; political science and government; pre-medical studies; psychology; secondary education; social science teacher education; social studies teacher education; sociology; sport and fitness administration; theatre design and technology; tourism and travel services management; visual and performing arts.

Academic Programs *Special study options:* accelerated degree program, advanced placement credit, cooperative education, distance learning, double majors, English as a second language, external degree program, honors programs, independent study, internships, off-campus study, part-time degree program, services for LD students, summer session for credit. *ROTC:* Army (c).

Library Library and Learning Center with 100,053 titles, 522 serial subscriptions, 7,200 audiovisual materials, an OPAC.

Computers on Campus 131 computers available on campus for general student use. A campuswide network can be accessed from student residence rooms and from off campus. Internet access, at least one staffed computer lab available.

Student Life *Housing:* on-campus residence required through sophomore year. *Options:* coed. Campus housing is university owned. *Activities and organizations:* drama/theater group, student-run newspaper, radio station, choral group,

SERVE (Break Away, Habitat for Humanity), outing club, snowboarding, Earth Action Club, Gay Straight Alliance. *Campus security:* 24-hour emergency response devices and patrols, student patrols, late-night transport/escort service, controlled dormitory access. *Student services:* health clinic, personal/psychological counseling.

Athletics Member NCAA. All Division III. *Intercollegiate sports:* basketball M/W, cross-country running M/W, lacrosse M, soccer M/W, softball W, tennis M/W. *Intramural sports:* badminton M/W, basketball M/W, cross-country running M/W, golf M(c)/W(c), ice hockey M(c)/W(c), lacrosse M, racquetball M/W, rugby M(c)/W(c), soccer M/W, softball M/W, swimming M(c)/W(c), table tennis M/W, tennis M/W, volleyball M/W, water polo M/W, weight lifting M/W.

Standardized Tests *Required:* SAT I and SAT II or ACT (for admission).

Costs (2003–04) *Tuition:* state resident $5646 full-time, $237 per credit part-time; nonresident $12,200 full-time, $511 per credit part-time. Part-time tuition and fees vary according to course load. *Required fees:* $230 full-time, $40 per term part-time. *Room and board:* $6013; room only: $3517. Room and board charges vary according to board plan and housing facility. *Payment plans:* installment, deferred payment. *Waivers:* senior citizens and employees or children of employees.

Financial Aid *Average percent of need met:* 80%. *Average financial aid package:* $7835. *Average indebtedness upon graduation:* $16,910.

Applying *Options:* electronic application, deferred entrance. *Application fee:* $30. *Required:* essay or personal statement, high school transcript, minimum 2.0 GPA, 1 letter of recommendation. *Recommended:* minimum 2.5 GPA, interview. *Application deadline:* rolling (freshmen), rolling (transfers). *Notification:* continuous (freshmen), continuous (transfers).

Admissions Contact Mr. Drew Farrell, Associate Director of Admissions, Johnson State College, 337 College Hill, Johnson, VT 05656-9405. *Phone:* 802-635-1219. *Toll-free phone:* 800-635-2356. *Fax:* 802-635-1230. *E-mail:* jscapply@badger.jsc.vsc.edu.

■ *See page 1798 for a narrative description.*

LYNDON STATE COLLEGE
Lyndonville, Vermont

- **State-supported** comprehensive, founded 1911, part of Vermont State Colleges System
- **Calendar** semesters
- **Degrees** associate, bachelor's, and master's
- **Rural** 175-acre campus
- **Coed,** 1,384 undergraduate students, 81% full-time, 55% women, 45% men
- **Moderately difficult** entrance level, 94% of applicants were admitted

Undergraduates 1,124 full-time, 260 part-time. Students come from 28 states and territories, 40% are from out of state, 0.2% African American, 0.3% Asian American or Pacific Islander, 0.7% Hispanic American, 0.4% Native American, 0.2% international, 6% transferred in, 50% live on campus. *Retention:* 66% of 2002 full-time freshmen returned.

Freshmen *Admission:* 941 applied, 881 admitted, 368 enrolled. *Average high school GPA:* 2.5. *Test scores:* SAT verbal scores over 500: 42%; SAT math scores over 500: 39%; SAT verbal scores over 600: 8%; SAT math scores over 600: 7%.

Faculty *Total:* 141, 40% full-time, 48% with terminal degrees. *Student/faculty ratio:* 17:1.

Majors Accounting; athletic training; atmospheric sciences and meteorology; biological and physical sciences; business administration and management; commercial and advertising art; communication/speech communication and rhetoric; computer and information sciences; computer science; elementary education; English; English/language arts teacher education; entrepreneurship; health and physical education; journalism; liberal arts and sciences/liberal studies; mathematics; mathematics teacher education; parks, recreation and leisure; parks, recreation and leisure facilities management; physical education teaching and coaching; physical sciences; psychology; radio and television; radio and television broadcasting technology; reading teacher education; science teacher education; social sciences; social science teacher education; special education; sport and fitness administration.

Academic Programs *Special study options:* academic remediation for entering students, accelerated degree program, adult/continuing education programs, advanced placement credit, cooperative education, double majors, honors programs, independent study, internships, part-time degree program, services for LD students, student-designed majors, study abroad, summer session for credit. *ROTC:* Air Force (c).

Library Samuel Read Hall Library with 101,872 titles, 16,468 serial subscriptions, 4,883 audiovisual materials, an OPAC, a Web page.

Computers on Campus 125 computers available on campus for general student use. A campuswide network can be accessed from student residence rooms and from off campus. Internet access, at least one staffed computer lab available. Computer purchase or lease plan available.

Student Life *Housing:* on-campus residence required through sophomore year. *Options:* coed, women-only, disabled students. Campus housing is university owned and leased by the school. Freshman applicants given priority for college housing. *Activities and organizations:* drama/theater group, student-run newspaper, radio station, choral group, American Meteorological Society, ASSIST (A Society of Students in Service Together), Student Senate, Campus Activities Board, outing club. *Campus security:* 24-hour emergency response devices, student patrols, late-night transport/escort service, controlled dormitory access. *Student services:* health clinic, personal/psychological counseling.

Athletics Member NAIA. *Intercollegiate sports:* baseball M, basketball M/W, cross-country running M/W, soccer M/W, softball W, tennis M/W. *Intramural sports:* badminton M/W, basketball M/W, bowling M/W, cross-country running M/W, field hockey M/W, football M/W, golf M/W, ice hockey M/W, racquetball M/W, rugby M/W, skiing (cross-country) M/W, skiing (downhill) M/W, softball M/W, squash M/W, swimming M/W, table tennis M/W, tennis M/W, track and field M/W, volleyball M/W, water polo M/W, weight lifting M/W.

Standardized Tests *Required:* SAT I or ACT (for admission).

Costs (2003–04) *Tuition:* state resident $5646 full-time, $237 per credit hour part-time; nonresident $12,200 full-time, $511 per credit hour part-time. Full-time tuition and fees vary according to course load. Part-time tuition and fees vary according to course load. *Required fees:* $160 full-time. *Room and board:* $6014; room only: $3518. Room and board charges vary according to board plan. *Payment plan:* installment. *Waivers:* employees or children of employees.

Applying *Options:* common application, electronic application, early admission, deferred entrance. *Application fee:* $32. *Required:* high school transcript, minimum 2.0 GPA, 1 letter of recommendation. *Required for some:* minimum 3.0 GPA. *Recommended:* essay or personal statement, minimum 3.0 GPA, interview. *Application deadline:* rolling (freshmen), rolling (transfers). *Notification:* continuous (freshmen), continuous (transfers).

Admissions Contact Ms. Michelle McCaffrey, Assistant Dean of Admissions, Lyndon State College, 1001 College Road, PO Box 919, Lyndonville, VT 05851. *Phone:* 802-626-6413. *Toll-free phone:* 800-225-1998. *Fax:* 802-626-6335. *E-mail:* admissions@lyndonstate.edu.

■ *See page 1906 for a narrative description.*

MARLBORO COLLEGE
Marlboro, Vermont

- **Independent** comprehensive, founded 1946
- **Calendar** semesters
- **Degrees** bachelor's and master's
- **Rural** 350-acre campus
- **Endowment** $15.4 million
- **Coed,** 331 undergraduate students, 98% full-time, 60% women, 40% men
- **Moderately difficult** entrance level, 82% of applicants were admitted

Undergraduates 323 full-time, 8 part-time. Students come from 36 states and territories, 89% are from out of state, 0.6% African American, 2% Asian American or Pacific Islander, 2% Hispanic American, 0.6% Native American, 0.9% international, 6% transferred in, 74% live on campus. *Retention:* 77% of 2002 full-time freshmen returned.

Freshmen *Admission:* 261 applied, 214 admitted, 81 enrolled. *Average high school GPA:* 3.34. *Test scores:* SAT verbal scores over 500: 96%; SAT math scores over 500: 86%; ACT scores over 18: 100%; SAT verbal scores over 600: 70%; SAT math scores over 600: 45%; ACT scores over 24: 100%; SAT verbal scores over 700: 23%; SAT math scores over 700: 10%; ACT scores over 30: 69%.

Faculty *Total:* 53, 70% full-time, 74% with terminal degrees. *Student/faculty ratio:* 8:1.

Majors African studies; American studies; anthropology; applied mathematics; art; art history, criticism and conservation; Asian studies; Asian studies (East); astronomy; astrophysics; behavioral sciences; biblical studies; biochemistry; biology/biological sciences; botany/plant biology; cell biology and histology; ceramic arts and ceramics; chemistry; classics and languages, literatures and linguistics; comparative literature; computer science; creative writing; cultural studies; dance; developmental and child psychology; dramatic/theatre arts; drawing; ecology; economics; English; environmental biology; environmental studies; European studies; European studies (Central and Eastern); experimental psychology; film/cinema studies; fine/studio arts; folklore; French; German; history; history of philosophy; humanities; interdisciplinary studies; international economics; international relations and affairs; Italian; Latin; Latin American studies; linguistics; literature; mathematics; medieval and Renaissance studies; modern Greek; modern languages; molecular biology; music; music history, literature, and theory; natural resources/conservation; natural sciences; philosophy; photography; physics; political science and government; Portuguese; pre-law studies;

Marlboro College (continued)
pre-medical studies; pre-veterinary studies; psychology; religious studies; Romance languages; Russian studies; sculpture; social sciences; sociology; Spanish; women's studies.

Academic Programs *Special study options:* accelerated degree program, advanced placement credit, double majors, independent study, internships, off-campus study, part-time degree program, services for LD students, student-designed majors, study abroad.

Library Rice Memorial Library with 54,289 titles, 250 serial subscriptions, 746 audiovisual materials, an OPAC, a Web page.

Computers on Campus 42 computers available on campus for general student use. A campuswide network can be accessed from student residence rooms and from off campus. Internet access, at least one staffed computer lab available.

Student Life *Housing:* on-campus residence required for freshman year. *Options:* coed, women-only, cooperative. Campus housing is university owned. *Activities and organizations:* drama/theater group, student-run newspaper, choral group, theater club, outdoor program, fencing club, Gay/Lesbian/Bisexual Alliance, women's chorus. *Campus security:* 24-hour emergency response devices. *Student services:* health clinic, personal/psychological counseling.

Athletics *Intercollegiate sports:* skiing (downhill) M/W, soccer M/W. *Intramural sports:* basketball M/W, fencing M/W, ice hockey M/W, skiing (cross-country) M/W, skiing (downhill) M/W, soccer M/W, softball M/W, table tennis M/W, volleyball M/W, weight lifting M/W.

Standardized Tests *Required:* SAT I or ACT (for admission). *Recommended:* SAT II: Subject Tests (for admission).

Costs (2004–05) *Comprehensive fee:* $33,540 includes full-time tuition ($24,930), mandatory fees ($810), and room and board ($7800). Part-time tuition: $832 per credit. *College room only:* $4175. *Payment plan:* installment. *Waivers:* senior citizens and employees or children of employees.

Financial Aid Of all full-time matriculated undergraduates who enrolled in 2000, 240 applied for aid, 213 were judged to have need, 114 had their need fully met. 189 Federal Work-Study jobs (averaging $1647). 3 state and other part-time jobs (averaging $1930). In 2000, 3 non-need-based awards were made. *Average percent of need met:* 94%. *Average financial aid package:* $15,091. *Average need-based loan:* $3754. *Average need-based gift aid:* $9346. *Average non-need-based aid:* $1416. *Average indebtedness upon graduation:* $18,212.

Applying *Options:* common application, electronic application, early admission, early decision, early action, deferred entrance. *Application fee:* $50. *Required:* essay or personal statement, high school transcript, 2 letters of recommendation, interview, graded expository essay. *Recommended:* minimum 3.0 GPA. *Application deadlines:* 3/1 (freshmen), 4/1 (transfers). *Early decision:* 11/15. *Notification:* 4/1 (freshmen), 12/15 (early decision), 2/1 (early action), 4/15 (transfers).

Admissions Contact Ms. Julie E. Richardson, Vice President, Enrollment and Financial Aid, Marlboro College, PO Box A, South Road, Marlboro, VT 05344-0300. *Phone:* 802-258-9261. *Toll-free phone:* 800-343-0049. *Fax:* 802-451-7555. *E-mail:* admissions@marlboro.edu.

■ *See page 1932 for a narrative description.*

MIDDLEBURY COLLEGE
Middlebury, Vermont

- **Independent** comprehensive, founded 1800
- **Calendar** 4-1-4
- **Degrees** bachelor's, master's, and doctoral
- **Small-town** 350-acre campus
- **Coed,** 2,424 undergraduate students, 99% full-time, 53% women, 47% men
- **Most difficult** entrance level, 23% of applicants were admitted

Undergraduates 2,399 full-time, 25 part-time. Students come from 52 states and territories, 70 other countries, 86% are from out of state, 3% African American, 7% Asian American or Pacific Islander, 5% Hispanic American, 0.9% Native American, 8% international, 0.2% transferred in, 94% live on campus.

Freshmen *Admission:* 5,468 applied, 1,273 admitted, 580 enrolled. *Test scores:* SAT verbal scores over 500: 99%; SAT math scores over 500: 99%; ACT scores over 18: 100%; SAT verbal scores over 600: 97%; SAT math scores over 600: 95%; ACT scores over 24: 96%; SAT verbal scores over 700: 69%; SAT math scores over 700: 61%; ACT scores over 30: 62%.

Faculty *Total:* 237, 92% full-time, 93% with terminal degrees. *Student/faculty ratio:* 11:1.

Majors American literature; American studies; Arabic; art history, criticism and conservation; Asian studies (East); biochemistry; biology/biological sciences; chemistry; Chinese; cinematography and film/video production; classics and languages, literatures and linguistics; computer science; dance; dramatic/theatre arts; economics; education; English; environmental studies; European studies; European studies (Central and Eastern); fine/studio arts; French; geography; geology/earth science; German; history; international relations and affairs; Italian; Japanese; Latin American studies; liberal arts and sciences/liberal studies; literature; mathematics; modern languages; molecular biology; music; neuroscience; philosophy; physics; political science and government; pre-law studies; psychology; religious studies; Russian; Russian studies; sociology; Spanish; women's studies.

Academic Programs *Special study options:* accelerated degree program, advanced placement credit, double majors, honors programs, independent study, internships, off-campus study, services for LD students, student-designed majors, study abroad, summer session for credit. *ROTC:* Army (c). *Unusual degree programs:* 3-2 business administration with University of Chicago; New York University; Rutgers, The State University of New Jersey, Graduate School of Management; University of Rochester; Columbia University; Boston University; Dartmouth College; engineering with Columbia University, Rensselaer Polytechnic Institute, University of Rochester; forestry with Duke University; nursing with Columbia University.

Library Egbert Starr Library plus 3 others with 950,000 titles, 2,694 serial subscriptions, 31,059 audiovisual materials, an OPAC, a Web page.

Computers on Campus 225 computers available on campus for general student use. A campuswide network can be accessed from student residence rooms and from off campus that provide access to computer help-line, e-mail, personal web pages, file servers. Internet access, online (class) registration, at least one staffed computer lab available. Computer purchase or lease plan available.

Student Life *Housing:* on-campus residence required through junior year. *Options:* coed, disabled students. Campus housing is university owned. Freshman campus housing is guaranteed. *Activities and organizations:* drama/theater group, student-run newspaper, radio station, choral group, Volunteer Service Organization, International Students Organization, mountain club, Activities Board, WRMC radio. *Campus security:* 24-hour patrols, student patrols, late-night transport/escort service, controlled dormitory access. *Student services:* health clinic, personal/psychological counseling, women's center.

Athletics Member NCAA. All Division III except men's and women's skiing (cross-country) (Division I), men's and women's skiing (downhill) (Division I). *Intercollegiate sports:* baseball M, basketball M/W, cheerleading M/W, cross-country running M/W, field hockey W, football M, golf M/W, ice hockey M/W, lacrosse M/W, skiing (cross-country) M/W, skiing (downhill) M/W, soccer M/W, softball W, squash W, swimming M/W, tennis M/W, track and field M/W, volleyball W. *Intramural sports:* badminton M/W, basketball M/W, crew M(c)/W(c), cross-country running M/W, equestrian sports M(c)/W(c), football M/W, golf M/W, ice hockey M/W, rock climbing M(c)/W(c), rugby M(c)/W(c), sailing M(c)/W(c), skiing (downhill) M/W, soccer M/W, softball M/W, squash M/W, swimming M/W, table tennis M/W, tennis M/W, ultimate Frisbee M(c)/W(c), volleyball M/W, water polo M(c)/W(c).

Standardized Tests *Required:* ACT or 3 SAT II Subject Tests (including SAT II: Writing Test and 1 quantitative SAT II Test), or 3 Advanced Placement Tests (including AP English and 1 quantitative AP Test), or 3 I.B. Subsidiary Tests (including I.B. Languages and 1 quantitative I.B. Test) (for admission).

Costs (2003–04) *Comprehensive fee:* $38,100. *Payment plan:* tuition prepayment. *Waivers:* employees or children of employees.

Financial Aid Of all full-time matriculated undergraduates who enrolled in 2002, 980 applied for aid, 825 were judged to have need, 825 had their need fully met. 503 Federal Work-Study jobs (averaging $1529). 114 state and other part-time jobs (averaging $1601). *Average percent of need met:* 100%. *Average financial aid package:* $26,979. *Average need-based loan:* $4595. *Average need-based gift aid:* $21,244. *Average indebtedness upon graduation:* $21,751.

Applying *Options:* common application, electronic application, early admission, early decision, deferred entrance. *Application fee:* $55. *Required:* essay or personal statement, high school transcript, 3 letters of recommendation. *Recommended:* interview. *Application deadlines:* 1/1 (freshmen), 3/1 (transfers). *Early decision:* 11/15 (for plan 1), 12/15 (for plan 2). *Notification:* 4/1 (freshmen), 12/15 (early decision plan 1), 2/15 (early decision plan 2), 4/15 (transfers).

Admissions Contact Mr. John Hanson, Director of Admissions, Middlebury College, Emma Willard House, Middlebury, VT 05753-6002. *Phone:* 802-443-3000. *Fax:* 802-443-2056. *E-mail:* admissions@middlebury.edu.

NEW ENGLAND CULINARY INSTITUTE
Montpelier, Vermont

- **Proprietary** primarily 2-year, founded 1980
- **Calendar** quarters
- **Degrees** certificates, associate, and bachelor's
- **Small-town** campus
- **Endowment** $291,550
- **Coed**
- **Moderately difficult** entrance level

Faculty *Student/faculty ratio:* 6:1.

Student Life *Campus security:* 24-hour emergency response devices, student patrols, Mod patrols in the evening.
Standardized Tests *Recommended:* SAT I (for placement).
Costs (2003–04) *Comprehensive fee:* $26,365 includes full-time tuition ($20,450), mandatory fees ($390), and room and board ($5525). Full-time tuition and fees vary according to program. *College room only:* $3500.
Financial Aid Of all full-time matriculated undergraduates who enrolled in 2001, 320 Federal Work-Study jobs (averaging $1000).
Applying *Options:* common application, electronic application, early admission, deferred entrance. *Required:* essay or personal statement, high school transcript, 1 letter of recommendation, interview. *Required for some:* minimum TOEFL scores for foreign students.
Admissions Contact Ms. Dawn Hayward, Director of Admissions, New England Culinary Institute, 250 Main Street, Montpelier, VT 05602. *Phone:* 877-223-6324 Ext. 3211. *Toll-free phone:* 877-223-6324. *Fax:* 802-225-3280. *E-mail:* info@neci.edu.

NORWICH UNIVERSITY

Northfield, Vermont

- **Independent** comprehensive, founded 1819
- **Calendar** semesters
- **Degrees** bachelor's and master's
- **Small-town** 1125-acre campus with easy access to Burlington
- **Endowment** $110.9 million
- **Coed**
- **Moderately difficult** entrance level

Faculty *Student/faculty ratio:* 14:1.
Student Life *Campus security:* 24-hour emergency response devices and patrols, late-night transport/escort service.
Athletics Member NCAA. All Division III.
Standardized Tests *Required:* SAT I or ACT (for admission). *Recommended:* SAT II: Subject Tests (for admission).
Costs (2003–04) *One-time required fee:* $1120. *Comprehensive fee:* $24,932 includes full-time tuition ($17,630), mandatory fees ($580), and room and board ($6722). Part-time tuition and fees vary according to course load. *Room and board:* Room and board charges vary according to board plan and location.
Applying *Options:* electronic application, early admission, early decision, deferred entrance. *Application fee:* $35. *Required:* high school transcript. *Required for some:* essay or personal statement, portfolio. *Recommended:* essay or personal statement, minimum 2.0 GPA, 2 letters of recommendation, interview.
Admissions Contact Ms. Karen McGrath, Dean of Enrollment Management, Norwich University, 27 I.D. White Avenue, Northfield, VT 05663. *Phone:* 802-485-2013. *Toll-free phone:* 800-468-6679. *Fax:* 802-485-2032. *E-mail:* nuadm@norwich.edu.

■ *See page 2110 for a narrative description.*

SAINT MICHAEL'S COLLEGE

Colchester, Vermont

- **Independent Roman Catholic** comprehensive, founded 1904
- **Calendar** semesters
- **Degrees** bachelor's, master's, post-master's, and postbachelor's certificates
- **Small-town** 440-acre campus with easy access to Montreal
- **Endowment** $48.8 million
- **Coed,** 1,991 undergraduate students, 96% full-time, 54% women, 46% men
- **Moderately difficult** entrance level, 67% of applicants were admitted

Undergraduates 1,914 full-time, 77 part-time. Students come from 28 states and territories, 20 other countries, 75% are from out of state, 1% African American, 1% Asian American or Pacific Islander, 1% Hispanic American, 0.1% Native American, 3% international, 3% transferred in, 88% live on campus. *Retention:* 90% of 2002 full-time freshmen returned.
Freshmen *Admission:* 2,777 applied, 1,872 admitted, 512 enrolled. *Test scores:* SAT verbal scores over 500: 82%; SAT math scores over 500: 83%; SAT verbal scores over 600: 30%; SAT math scores over 600: 30%; SAT verbal scores over 700: 3%; SAT math scores over 700: 2%.
Faculty *Total:* 200, 72% full-time, 72% with terminal degrees. *Student/faculty ratio:* 12:1.
Majors Accounting; American studies; art; art teacher education; biochemistry; biology/biological sciences; business administration and management; chemistry; classics and languages, literatures and linguistics; computer science; dramatic/theatre arts; economics; education; elementary education; English; environmental science; French; history; information science/studies; journalism; mathematics; modern languages; music; philosophy; physical sciences; physics; political science and government; pre-dentistry studies; pre-law studies; pre-medical studies; pre-veterinary studies; psychology; religious studies; secondary education; sociology; Spanish.
Academic Programs *Special study options:* advanced placement credit, double majors, English as a second language, honors programs, independent study, internships, off-campus study, part-time degree program, student-designed majors, study abroad, summer session for credit. *ROTC:* Army (c), Air Force (c). *Unusual degree programs:* 3-2 engineering with University of Vermont, Clarkson University.
Library Durick Library with 141,000 titles, 1,726 serial subscriptions, 7,525 audiovisual materials, an OPAC, a Web page.
Computers on Campus 233 computers available on campus for general student use. A campuswide network can be accessed from student residence rooms and from off campus. Internet access, online (class) registration, at least one staffed computer lab available.
Student Life *Housing:* on-campus residence required through senior year. *Options:* coed, men-only, women-only, cooperative, disabled students. Campus housing is university owned. Freshman campus housing is guaranteed. *Activities and organizations:* drama/theater group, student-run newspaper, radio station, choral group, Student Association, Mobilization of Volunteer Efforts (MOVE), student radio station, wilderness program, student newspaper. *Campus security:* 24-hour emergency response devices and patrols, student patrols, late-night transport/escort service, bicycle patrols. *Student services:* health clinic, personal/psychological counseling, women's center.
Athletics Member NCAA. All Division II. *Intercollegiate sports:* baseball M, basketball M(s)/W(s), cheerleading M(c)/W(c), cross-country running M/W, field hockey W, golf M, ice hockey M/W, lacrosse M/W, rugby M(c)/W(c), skiing (cross-country) M/W, skiing (downhill) M/W, soccer M/W, softball W, swimming M/W, tennis M/W, volleyball W. *Intramural sports:* badminton M/W, basketball M/W, racquetball M/W, skiing (cross-country) M/W, skiing (downhill) M/W, soccer M/W, softball M/W, squash M/W, swimming M/W, table tennis M/W, tennis M/W, track and field M(c)/W(c), volleyball M/W, water polo M/W.
Standardized Tests *Required:* SAT I or ACT (for admission). *Recommended:* SAT II: Subject Tests (for placement).
Costs (2003–04) *Comprehensive fee:* $30,100 includes full-time tuition ($22,220), mandatory fees ($200), and room and board ($7680). Part-time tuition: $740 per semester hour. *College room only:* $4775. Room and board charges vary according to board plan and housing facility. *Payment plan:* installment. *Waivers:* employees or children of employees.
Financial Aid Of all full-time matriculated undergraduates who enrolled in 2003, 1,404 applied for aid, 1,217 were judged to have need, 310 had their need fully met. 150 Federal Work-Study jobs (averaging $2000). In 2003, 284 non-need-based awards were made. *Average percent of need met:* 86%. *Average financial aid package:* $17,529. *Average need-based loan:* $4805. *Average need-based gift aid:* $12,743. *Average non-need-based aid:* $6784. *Average indebtedness upon graduation:* $20,233.
Applying *Options:* common application, electronic application, early action, deferred entrance. *Application fee:* $45. *Required:* essay or personal statement, high school transcript. *Recommended:* minimum 3.0 GPA, letters of recommendation, interview. *Application deadlines:* 2/1 (freshmen), 2/1 (transfers). *Notification:* 4/1 (freshmen), 1/1 (early action), 4/1 (transfers).
Admissions Contact Ms. Jacqueline Murphy, Director of Admission, Saint Michael's College, One Winooski Park, Colchester, VT 05439. *Phone:* 802-654-3000. *Toll-free phone:* 800-762-8000. *Fax:* 802-654-2906. *E-mail:* admission@smcvt.edu.

■ *See page 2322 for a narrative description.*

SOUTHERN VERMONT COLLEGE

Bennington, Vermont

- **Independent** 4-year, founded 1926
- **Calendar** semesters
- **Degrees** associate and bachelor's
- **Small-town** 371-acre campus with easy access to Albany
- **Endowment** $1.2 million
- **Coed,** 464 undergraduate students, 73% full-time, 64% women, 36% men
- **Minimally difficult** entrance level, 71% of applicants were admitted

Undergraduates 341 full-time, 123 part-time. Students come from 22 states and territories, 6 other countries, 66% are from out of state, 5% African American, 0.6% Asian American or Pacific Islander, 3% Hispanic American, 1% international, 50% live on campus. *Retention:* 54% of 2002 full-time freshmen returned.
Freshmen *Admission:* 373 applied, 264 admitted. *Average high school GPA:* 2.63. *Test scores:* SAT verbal scores over 500: 36%; SAT math scores over 500: 19%; ACT scores over 18: 76%; SAT verbal scores over 600: 8%; SAT math scores over 600: 4%; ACT scores over 24: 15%.

Southern Vermont College (continued)

Faculty *Total:* 45, 47% full-time, 13% with terminal degrees. *Student/faculty ratio:* 11:1.

Majors Business administration and management; child development; communication/speech communication and rhetoric; creative writing; criminal justice/law enforcement administration; English; environmental studies; human services; liberal arts and sciences/liberal studies; literature; mass communication/media; nursing (registered nurse training); pre-law studies; psychology.

Academic Programs *Special study options:* academic remediation for entering students, accelerated degree program, adult/continuing education programs, advanced placement credit, cooperative education, distance learning, double majors, external degree program, honors programs, independent study, internships, part-time degree program, services for LD students, student-designed majors, study abroad, summer session for credit.

Library Southern Vermont College Library with 26,000 titles, 250 serial subscriptions, 500 audiovisual materials, a Web page.

Computers on Campus 35 computers available on campus for general student use. A campuswide network can be accessed from student residence rooms and from off campus. Internet access, at least one staffed computer lab available.

Student Life *Housing:* on-campus residence required for freshman year. *Options:* coed. Campus housing is university owned. Freshman campus housing is guaranteed. *Activities and organizations:* drama/theater group, student-run newspaper, radio station, Student Government Association, Men's and Women's Rugby Club, Community Action Club, Mountaineer Cheerleaders, Madhatters Club (drama). *Campus security:* 24-hour patrols, late-night transport/escort service, controlled dormitory access. *Student services:* health clinic, personal/psychological counseling.

Athletics Member NCAA. All Division III. *Intercollegiate sports:* baseball M, basketball M/W, cross-country running M/W, soccer M/W, softball W, track and field M/W, volleyball W. *Intramural sports:* baseball M/W, basketball M/W, cheerleading W(c), football M/W, golf M/W, lacrosse M(c), rugby M(c)/W(c), skiing (cross-country) M(c)/W(c), skiing (downhill) M(c)/W(c), soccer M/W, softball M/W, tennis M/W, volleyball M/W.

Standardized Tests *Required:* SAT I or ACT (for admission).

Costs (2003–04) *Comprehensive fee:* $18,226 includes full-time tuition ($11,996) and room and board ($6230). Part-time tuition: $295 per credit. Part-time tuition and fees vary according to course load. *College room only:* $2900. *Payment plan:* installment. *Waivers:* senior citizens and employees or children of employees.

Financial Aid Of all full-time matriculated undergraduates who enrolled in 2003, 294 applied for aid, 270 were judged to have need, 44 had their need fully met. 146 Federal Work-Study jobs (averaging $1250). In 2003, 8 non-need-based awards were made. *Average percent of need met:* 79%. *Average financial aid package:* $12,111. *Average need-based loan:* $3773. *Average need-based gift aid:* $8999. *Average non-need-based aid:* $2800. *Average indebtedness upon graduation:* $11,585.

Applying *Options:* common application, electronic application, early admission, deferred entrance. *Application fee:* $30. *Required:* essay or personal statement, high school transcript, 2 letters of recommendation. *Required for some:* interview. *Recommended:* minimum 2.0 GPA, interview. *Application deadline:* rolling (freshmen), rolling (transfers). *Notification:* continuous (freshmen), continuous (transfers).

Admissions Contact Ms. Elizabeth Gatti, Director of Admissions, Southern Vermont College, 982 Mansion Drive, Bennington, VT 05201. *Phone:* 802-447-6304. *Toll-free phone:* 800-378-2782. *Fax:* 802-447-4695. *E-mail:* admis@svc.edu.

■ *See page 2416 for a narrative description.*

STERLING COLLEGE
Craftsbury Common, Vermont

- **Independent** 4-year, founded 1958
- **Calendar** semesters
- **Degrees** associate and bachelor's
- **Rural** 150-acre campus
- **Endowment** $687,306
- **Coed,** 102 undergraduate students, 93% full-time, 44% women, 56% men
- **Moderately difficult** entrance level, 95% of applicants were admitted

Undergraduates 95 full-time, 7 part-time. Students come from 21 states and territories, 80% are from out of state, 1% African American, 2% Hispanic American, 17% transferred in, 74% live on campus. *Retention:* 46% of 2002 full-time freshmen returned.

Freshmen *Admission:* 62 applied, 59 admitted, 22 enrolled. *Average high school GPA:* 2.90. *Test scores:* SAT verbal scores over 500: 80%; SAT math scores over 500: 70%; ACT scores over 18: 100%; SAT verbal scores over 600: 50%; SAT math scores over 600: 40%; ACT scores over 24: 100%.

Faculty *Total:* 26, 35% full-time, 27% with terminal degrees. *Student/faculty ratio:* 7:1.

Majors Agricultural and domestic animals services related; agricultural and horticultural plant breeding; agricultural animal breeding; agricultural business and management; agricultural business and management related; agricultural communication/journalism; agricultural production related; agricultural public services related; agricultural teacher education; agriculture; agriculture and agriculture operations related; agronomy and crop science; animal health; animal/livestock husbandry and production; animal nutrition; animal sciences; animal sciences related; animal training; applied horticulture; area, ethnic, cultural, and gender studies related; biological and physical sciences; Canadian studies; conservation biology; crop production; cultural resource management and policy analysis; curriculum and instruction; dairy husbandry and production; dairy science; ecology; ecology, evolution, systematics and population biology related; educational, instructional, and curriculum supervision; educational leadership and administration; education related; energy management and systems technology; environmental biology; environmental design/architecture; environmental engineering technology; environmental studies; equestrian studies; ethnic, cultural minority, and gender studies related; farm and ranch management; fishing and fisheries sciences and management; forest/forest resources management; forest resources production and management; forestry; forestry related; forest sciences and biology; greenhouse management; horse husbandry/equine science and management; horticultural science; human ecology; intercultural/multicultural and diversity studies; international agriculture; international and comparative education; international/global studies; land use planning and management; liberal arts and sciences/liberal studies; livestock management; multi-/interdisciplinary studies related; natural resources and conservation related; natural resources/conservation; natural resources/conservation related; natural resources management; natural resources management and policy; natural sciences; parks, recreation and leisure; parks, recreation and leisure facilities management; plant protection and integrated pest management; plant sciences; plant sciences related; poultry science; range science and management; Scandinavian studies; science teacher education; social and philosophical foundations of education; soil science and agronomy; soil sciences related; solar energy technology; special education (administration); systems science and theory; Waldorf/Steiner teacher education; water, wetlands, and marine resources management; wildlife and wildlands science and management; wildlife biology; wood science and wood products/pulp and paper technology.

Academic Programs *Special study options:* honors programs, independent study, internships, off-campus study, part-time degree program, services for LD students, student-designed majors, study abroad, summer session for credit.

Library Brown Library plus 1 other with 8,990 titles, 85 serial subscriptions, 370 audiovisual materials, an OPAC.

Computers on Campus 15 computers available on campus for general student use. A campuswide network can be accessed. Internet access, at least one staffed computer lab available.

Student Life *Housing:* on-campus residence required for freshman year. *Options:* coed, men-only, women-only. Campus housing is university owned. Freshman campus housing is guaranteed. *Activities and organizations:* outing club, Timbersports Team, Student Life, art club. *Campus security:* student patrols. *Student services:* health clinic, personal/psychological counseling.

Athletics *Intramural sports:* baseball M/W, basketball M/W, rock climbing M/W, skiing (cross-country) M/W, skiing (downhill) M/W, soccer M/W, softball M/W, table tennis M/W, ultimate Frisbee M/W, volleyball M/W.

Standardized Tests *Recommended:* SAT I or ACT (for admission).

Costs (2003–04) *Comprehensive fee:* $21,114 includes full-time tuition ($15,080), mandatory fees ($250), and room and board ($5784). Full-time tuition and fees vary according to course load, program, and student level. Part-time tuition: $425 per credit. Part-time tuition and fees vary according to course load, program, and student level. *College room only:* $2400. Room and board charges vary according to board plan and student level. *Payment plan:* installment. *Waivers:* employees or children of employees.

Financial Aid Of all full-time matriculated undergraduates who enrolled in 2003, 106 applied for aid, 66 were judged to have need, 9 had their need fully met. 36 Federal Work-Study jobs (averaging $431). 94 state and other part-time jobs (averaging $1464). In 2003, 7 non-need-based awards were made. *Average percent of need met:* 78%. *Average financial aid package:* $14,334. *Average need-based loan:* $3517. *Average need-based gift aid:* $4975. *Average non-need-based aid:* $2050. *Average indebtedness upon graduation:* $14,665.

Applying *Options:* common application, electronic application, early admission, deferred entrance. *Application fee:* $35. *Required:* essay or personal statement, high school transcript, 3 letters of recommendation, interview. *Recommended:* minimum 2.0 GPA. *Application deadline:* rolling (freshmen), rolling (transfers). *Notification:* continuous until 8/30 (freshmen), continuous (transfers).

Admissions Contact John Zaber, Director of Admissions, Sterling College, PO Box 72, Craftsbury Common, VT 05827. *Phone:* 802-586-7711 Ext. 135. *Toll-free phone:* 800-648-3591 Ext. 1. *Fax:* 802-586-2596. *E-mail:* admissions@sterlingcollege.edu.

■ *See page 2460 for a narrative description.*

UNIVERSITY OF VERMONT
Burlington, Vermont

- **State-supported** university, founded 1791
- **Calendar** semesters
- **Degrees** certificates, associate, bachelor's, master's, doctoral, first professional, post-master's, and postbachelor's certificates
- **Suburban** 425-acre campus
- **Endowment** $194.8 million
- **Coed,** 9,234 undergraduate students, 84% full-time, 57% women, 43% men
- **Moderately difficult** entrance level, 75% of applicants were admitted

Undergraduates 7,768 full-time, 1,466 part-time. Students come from 51 states and territories, 30 other countries, 62% are from out of state, 1% African American, 2% Asian American or Pacific Islander, 2% Hispanic American, 0.2% Native American, 0.8% international, 5% transferred in, 51% live on campus. *Retention:* 84% of 2002 full-time freshmen returned.

Freshmen *Admission:* 10,456 applied, 7,792 admitted, 1,923 enrolled. *Test scores:* SAT verbal scores over 500: 87%; SAT math scores over 500: 87%; ACT scores over 18: 97%; SAT verbal scores over 600: 38%; SAT math scores over 600: 42%; ACT scores over 24: 61%; SAT verbal scores over 700: 4%; SAT math scores over 700: 4%; ACT scores over 30: 6%.

Faculty *Total:* 678, 79% full-time, 76% with terminal degrees. *Student/faculty ratio:* 15:1.

Majors Agricultural business and management; agricultural economics; agriculture; ancient/classical Greek; animal sciences; anthropology; applied horticulture; applied horticulture/horticultural business services related; art history, criticism and conservation; art teacher education; Asian studies; athletic training; audiology and speech-language pathology; biochemistry; biology/biological sciences; biology/biotechnology laboratory technician; botany/plant biology; business administration and management; Canadian studies; chemistry; civil engineering; classics and languages, literatures and linguistics; clinical laboratory science/medical technology; clinical/medical laboratory assistant; communication disorders; computer and information sciences; computer science; dairy husbandry and production; dietetics; dramatic/theatre arts; early childhood education; economics; education; electrical, electronics and communications engineering; elementary education; engineering/industrial management; English; English/language arts teacher education; environmental/environmental health engineering; environmental science; environmental studies; equestrian studies; European studies; European studies (Central and Eastern); family and consumer economics related; family and consumer sciences/human sciences; fine/studio arts; fish/game management; foods, nutrition, and wellness; foreign language teacher education; forestry; French; geography; geology/earth science; German; history; human development and family studies; information science/studies; interdisciplinary studies; Italian studies; kindergarten/preschool education; Latin; Latin American studies; mathematics; mathematics teacher education; mechanical engineering; medical microbiology and bacteriology; medical radiologic technology; middle school education; molecular genetics; music; music history, literature, and theory; music performance; music teacher education; natural resources/conservation; natural resources management and policy; nuclear and industrial radiologic technologies related; nursing (registered nurse training); nutrition sciences; parks, recreation and leisure; parks, recreation and leisure facilities management; philosophy; physical education teaching and coaching; physics; plant sciences; plant sciences related; political science and government; pre-law studies; premedical studies; pre-veterinary studies; psychology; religious studies; Russian; Russian studies; science teacher education; secondary education; social science teacher education; social work; sociology; soil science and agronomy; Spanish; statistics; wildlife biology; women's studies; zoology/animal biology.

Academic Programs *Special study options:* advanced placement credit, cooperative education, distance learning, double majors, English as a second language, honors programs, independent study, internships, off-campus study, part-time degree program, services for LD students, student-designed majors, study abroad, summer session for credit. *ROTC:* Army (b). *Unusual degree programs:* 3-2 computer science.

Library Bailey-Howe Library plus 3 others with 2.4 million titles, 20,216 serial subscriptions, 36,531 audiovisual materials, an OPAC, a Web page.

Computers on Campus 685 computers available on campus for general student use. A campuswide network can be accessed from student residence rooms and from off campus that provide access to e-mail, web pages, on-line course support. Internet access, online (class) registration, at least one staffed computer lab available. Computer purchase or lease plan available.

Student Life *Housing:* on-campus residence required through sophomore year. *Options:* coed, cooperative. Campus housing is university owned. Freshman campus housing is guaranteed. *Activities and organizations:* drama/theater group, student-run newspaper, radio and television station, choral group, Volunteers in Action, outing club, club sports, national fraternities, national sororities. *Campus security:* 24-hour emergency response devices and patrols, late-night transport/escort service, controlled dormitory access. *Student services:* health clinic, personal/psychological counseling, women's center, legal services.

Athletics Member NCAA. All Division I. *Intercollegiate sports:* baseball M(s), basketball M(s)/W(s), crew M(c)/W(c), cross-country running M(s)/W(s), equestrian sports M(c)/W(c), field hockey W(s), gymnastics M(c)/W(c), ice hockey M(s)/W(s), lacrosse M(s)/W(s), rugby M(c)/W(c), sailing M(c)/W(c), skiing (cross-country) M(s)/W(s), skiing (downhill) M(s)/W(s), soccer M(s)/W(s), softball W(s), swimming W(s), track and field M(s)/W(s), volleyball M(c)/W(c), water polo M(c)/W(c). *Intramural sports:* basketball M/W, ice hockey M/W, lacrosse M/W, racquetball M/W, soccer M/W, softball M/W, tennis M/W, volleyball M/W, water polo M/W.

Standardized Tests *Required:* SAT I or ACT (for admission).

Costs (2003–04) *Tuition:* state resident $8696 full-time, $362 per credit part-time; nonresident $21,748 full-time, $906 per credit part-time. Part-time tuition and fees vary according to course load. *Required fees:* $940 full-time. *Room and board:* $6680; room only: $4464. Room and board charges vary according to board plan. *Payment plans:* installment, deferred payment. *Waivers:* senior citizens and employees or children of employees.

Financial Aid Of all full-time matriculated undergraduates who enrolled in 2002, 4,647 applied for aid, 3,927 were judged to have need, 3,491 had their need fully met. 2,142 Federal Work-Study jobs (averaging $2017). In 2002, 823 non-need-based awards were made. *Average percent of need met:* 90%. *Average financial aid package:* $10,781. *Average need-based loan:* $5201. *Average need-based gift aid:* $10,129. *Average non-need-based aid:* $2307. *Average indebtedness upon graduation:* $23,161.

Applying *Options:* common application, electronic application, early decision, early action, deferred entrance. *Application fee:* $45. *Required:* essay or personal statement, high school transcript, 1 letter of recommendation. *Recommended:* 2 letters of recommendation. *Application deadlines:* 1/15 (freshmen), 4/1 (transfers). *Early decision:* 11/1. *Notification:* 3/31 (freshmen), 12/15 (early decision), 12/15 (early action), continuous until 6/15 (transfers).

Admissions Contact Mr. Donald M. Honeman, Director of Admissions, University of Vermont, Office of Admissions, 194 South Prospect Street, Burlington, VT 05401-3596. *Phone:* 802-656-3370. *Fax:* 802-656-8611. *E-mail:* admissions@uvm.edu.

■ *See page 2736 for a narrative description.*

VERMONT TECHNICAL COLLEGE
Randolph Center, Vermont

- **State-supported** 4-year, founded 1866, part of Vermont State Colleges System
- **Calendar** semesters
- **Degrees** certificates, associate, and bachelor's
- **Rural** 544-acre campus
- **Endowment** $3.8 million
- **Coed,** 1,218 undergraduate students, 73% full-time, 33% women, 67% men
- **Minimally difficult** entrance level, 61% of applicants were admitted

Undergraduates 889 full-time, 329 part-time. Students come from 14 states and territories, 17% are from out of state, 0.6% African American, 2% Asian American or Pacific Islander, 0.7% Hispanic American, 0.9% Native American, 16% transferred in, 66% live on campus. *Retention:* 59% of 2002 full-time freshmen returned.

Freshmen *Admission:* 750 applied, 456 admitted, 234 enrolled. *Average high school GPA:* 3.00. *Test scores:* SAT verbal scores over 500: 49%; SAT math scores over 500: 54%; SAT verbal scores over 600: 14%; SAT math scores over 600: 14%; SAT verbal scores over 700: 1%; SAT math scores over 700: 1%.

Faculty *Total:* 106, 65% full-time, 54% with terminal degrees. *Student/faculty ratio:* 9:1.

Majors Administrative assistant and secretarial science; agribusiness; architectural engineering technology; automotive engineering technology; biomedical/medical engineering; biotechnology; business administration and management; civil engineering technology; computer engineering technology; computer systems networking and telecommunications; construction engineering technology; dairy science; dental hygiene; electrical, electronic and communications engineering technology; electromechanical technology; engineering technology; environmental engineering technology; horticultural science; landscaping and groundskeeping; mechanical engineering/mechanical technology; nursing (licensed practical/vocational nurse training); nursing (registered nurse training); ornamen-

Vermont Technical College (continued)

tal horticulture; pharmacy, pharmaceutical sciences, and administration related; respiratory care therapy; telecommunications; veterinary technology.

Academic Programs *Special study options:* academic remediation for entering students, accelerated degree program, advanced placement credit, cooperative education, distance learning, double majors, English as a second language, honors programs, independent study, internships, part-time degree program, services for LD students, summer session for credit. *ROTC:* Army (c).

Library Hartness Library with 58,801 titles, 1,156 serial subscriptions, 2,045 audiovisual materials, an OPAC, a Web page.

Computers on Campus 300 computers available on campus for general student use. A campuswide network can be accessed from student residence rooms and from off campus. Internet access, online (class) registration, at least one staffed computer lab available.

Student Life *Housing:* on-campus residence required through senior year. *Options:* coed, men-only, women-only. Campus housing is university owned. Freshman campus housing is guaranteed. *Activities and organizations:* drama/theater group, student-run radio station, ASVTC (student government), Hockey Club, student radio station, American Institute of Architecture Students, Golf Club. *Campus security:* 24-hour emergency response devices and patrols, late-night transport/escort service, controlled dormitory access. *Student services:* health clinic, personal/psychological counseling, women's center.

Athletics Member NSCAA. *Intercollegiate sports:* baseball M, basketball M/W, ice hockey M(c)/W(c), soccer M/W, softball W, volleyball M/W. *Intramural sports:* basketball M/W, bowling M(c)/W(c), cross-country running M/W, fencing M(c)/W(c), football M/W, golf M(c)/W(c), racquetball M/W, riflery M(c)/W(c), skiing (cross-country) M(c)/W(c), skiing (downhill) M(c)/W(c), soccer M/W, softball M/W, squash M/W, swimming M/W, table tennis M/W, tennis M/W, volleyball M/W, water polo M/W, weight lifting M(c)/W(c).

Standardized Tests *Required for some:* SAT I (for admission), SAT I or ACT (for admission), nursing examination. *Recommended:* SAT I or ACT (for admission).

Costs (2003–04) *Tuition:* state resident $6844 full-time; nonresident $12,876 full-time. Full-time tuition and fees vary according to course load and program. Part-time tuition and fees vary according to program. *Room and board:* $6014; room only: $3518. Room and board charges vary according to board plan. *Payment plans:* installment, deferred payment. *Waivers:* employees or children of employees.

Financial Aid Of all full-time matriculated undergraduates who enrolled in 2002, 866 applied for aid, 753 were judged to have need, 144 had their need fully met. 213 Federal Work-Study jobs (averaging $850). In 2002, 41 non-need-based awards were made. *Average percent of need met:* 73%. *Average financial aid package:* $7031. *Average need-based loan:* $2681. *Average need-based gift aid:* $4654. *Average non-need-based aid:* $2300. *Average indebtedness upon graduation:* $11,000.

Applying *Options:* common application, electronic application. *Application fee:* $32. *Required:* high school transcript. *Required for some:* essay or personal statement, letters of recommendation, interview. *Recommended:* minimum 3.0 GPA, letters of recommendation, interview. *Application deadline:* rolling (freshmen), rolling (transfers). *Notification:* continuous until 9/1 (freshmen), continuous until 9/1 (transfers).

Admissions Contact Ms. Rosemary W. Distel, Director of Admissions, Vermont Technical College, PO Box 500, Randolph Center, VT 05061. *Phone:* 802-728-1245. *Toll-free phone:* 800-442-VTC1. *Fax:* 802-728-1390. *E-mail:* admissions@vtc.edu.

■ *See page 2758 for a narrative description.*

WOODBURY COLLEGE
Montpelier, Vermont

- **Independent** primarily 2-year, founded 1975
- **Calendar** trimesters
- **Degrees** certificates, associate, and bachelor's
- **Small-town** 8-acre campus
- **Endowment** $71,024
- **Coed**
- **Noncompetitive** entrance level

Faculty *Student/faculty ratio:* 12:1.

Costs (2003–04) *Tuition:* $13,500 full-time. *Required fees:* $150 full-time.

Applying *Options:* electronic application. *Application fee:* $30. *Required:* essay or personal statement, interview. *Required for some:* high school transcript.

Admissions Contact Ms. Kathleen Moore, Admissions Director, Woodbury College, 660 Elm Street, Montpelier, VT 05602. *Phone:* 802-229-0516. *Toll-free phone:* 800-639-6039. *Fax:* 802-229-2141. *E-mail:* admiss@woodbury-college.edu.

VIRGINIA

ARGOSY UNIVERSITY/WASHINGTON D.C.
Arlington, Virginia

- **Proprietary** upper-level, founded 1994, part of Argosy Education Group
- **Calendar** semesters
- **Degrees** bachelor's, master's, and doctoral
- **Urban** campus with easy access to Washington D.C.
- **Coed,** 13 undergraduate students, 100% full-time, 62% women, 38% men

Undergraduates 13 full-time. 15% African American, 8% Asian American or Pacific Islander, 8% Hispanic American.

Faculty *Total:* 21, 100% full-time, 100% with terminal degrees. *Student/faculty ratio:* 7:1.

Majors Psychology.

Student Life *Housing:* college housing not available. *Activities and organizations:* Student Government Association.

Costs (2003–04) *Tuition:* $360 part-time. *Required fees:* $100 per year part-time. *Payment plan:* installment.

Applying *Application fee:* $50. *Notification:* continuous (transfers).

Admissions Contact Argosy University/Washington D.C., 1550 Wilson Boulevard, Suite 600, Arlington, VA 22209. *Phone:* 703-526-5818. *Toll-free phone:* 866-703-2777 Ext. 5833. *Fax:* 703-243-8973. *E-mail:* dcadmissions@argosyu.edu.

THE ART INSTITUTE OF WASHINGTON
Arlington, Virginia

- **Proprietary** 4-year, founded 2000, part of The Art Institutes International
- **Calendar** quarters
- **Degrees** associate and bachelor's
- **Urban** campus
- **Coed**

Faculty *Total:* 64, 39% full-time. *Student/faculty ratio:* 20:1.

Majors Advertising; commercial and advertising art; computer graphics; culinary arts; design and visual communications; digital communication and media/multimedia; interior design; intermedia/multimedia; web page, digital/multimedia and information resources design.

Costs (2004–05) *Tuition:* $16,560 full-time. *Room only:* $7704.

Applying *Options:* electronic application. *Application fee:* $50. *Required:* essay or personal statement, high school transcript, interview. *Application deadline:* rolling (freshmen). *Notification:* continuous (freshmen).

Admissions Contact Mr. Larry McHugh, Director of Admissions, The Art Institute of Washington, 1820 North Fort Myer Drive, Arlington, VA 22209. *Phone:* 703-358-9550 Ext. 6580. *Toll-free phone:* 877-303-3771.

AVERETT UNIVERSITY
Danville, Virginia

- **Independent** comprehensive, founded 1859, affiliated with Baptist General Association of Virginia
- **Calendar** semesters
- **Degrees** associate, bachelor's, and master's
- **Small-town** 19-acre campus with easy access to Greensboro and Raleigh
- **Endowment** $18.4 million
- **Coed,** 2,087 undergraduate students, 61% full-time, 58% women, 42% men
- **Moderately difficult** entrance level, 89% of applicants were admitted

Undergraduates 1,265 full-time, 822 part-time. Students come from 30 states and territories, 22 other countries, 13% are from out of state, 33% African American, 1% Asian American or Pacific Islander, 2% Hispanic American, 0.5% Native American, 2% international, 10% transferred in, 54% live on campus. *Retention:* 67% of 2002 full-time freshmen returned.

Freshmen *Admission:* 778 applied, 694 admitted, 230 enrolled. *Average high school GPA:* 3.00. *Test scores:* SAT verbal scores over 500: 39%; SAT math scores over 500: 34%; ACT scores over 18: 59%; SAT verbal scores over 600: 10%; SAT math scores over 600: 7%; ACT scores over 24: 9%; SAT verbal scores over 700: 1%; ACT scores over 30: 2%.

Faculty *Total:* 252, 26% full-time, 48% with terminal degrees. *Student/faculty ratio:* 14:1.

Majors Accounting; airline pilot and flight crew; air transportation related; applied mathematics related; art; art teacher education; athletic training; aviation/airway management; avionics maintenance technology; biological and physical sciences; biology/biological sciences; biology teacher education; business administration and management; business administration, management and operations related; business/commerce; chemistry; chemistry teacher education; clinical laboratory science/medical technology; clinical psychology; cognitive psychology and psycholinguistics; corrections and criminal justice related; criminal justice/law enforcement administration; dramatic/theatre arts; ecology; e-commerce; education (multiple levels); education (specific subject areas) related; English; English/language arts teacher education; environmental science; equestrian studies; finance; general studies; health and physical education; health and physical education related; health teacher education; history; industrial and organizational psychology; information science/studies; journalism; journalism related; liberal arts and sciences/liberal studies; management science; marketing/marketing management; mathematics; mathematics and computer science; mathematics teacher education; medical radiologic technology; music; music performance; physical education teaching and coaching; physiological psychology/psychobiology; political science and government; pre-medical studies; psychology; psychology related; religious education; religious/sacred music; religious studies; social sciences; social studies teacher education; sociology; sport and fitness administration; theatre literature, history and criticism; transportation and materials moving related.

Academic Programs *Special study options:* academic remediation for entering students, accelerated degree program, adult/continuing education programs, advanced placement credit, double majors, honors programs, independent study, internships, off-campus study, part-time degree program, services for LD students, student-designed majors, study abroad, summer session for credit. *Unusual degree programs:* 3-2 education.

Library Mary B. Blount Library with 130,519 titles, 512 serial subscriptions, 84 audiovisual materials, an OPAC, a Web page.

Computers on Campus 100 computers available on campus for general student use. A campuswide network can be accessed. Internet access, at least one staffed computer lab available.

Student Life *Housing:* on-campus residence required through junior year. *Options:* men-only, women-only. Campus housing is university owned. Freshman campus housing is guaranteed. *Activities and organizations:* drama/theater group, student-run newspaper, choral group, Student Government Association, Baptist Student Union, Phi Sigma Sigma, Pi Kappa Phi, Averett Gospel Choir, national fraternities, national sororities. *Campus security:* 24-hour emergency response devices and patrols, late-night transport/escort service, controlled dormitory access. *Student services:* personal/psychological counseling.

Athletics Member NCAA. All Division III. *Intercollegiate sports:* baseball M, basketball M/W, cross-country running M/W, equestrian sports M/W, football M, golf M, lacrosse W, soccer M/W, softball W, tennis M/W, volleyball W. *Intramural sports:* basketball M/W, cheerleading M/W, equestrian sports M/W, football M/W, golf M/W, racquetball M/W, soccer M/W, softball M/W, table tennis M/W, tennis M/W, volleyball M/W.

Standardized Tests *Required:* SAT I or ACT (for admission).

Costs (2003–04) *Comprehensive fee:* $23,620 includes full-time tuition ($16,600), mandatory fees ($1000), and room and board ($6020). Full-time tuition and fees vary according to location and program. Part-time tuition: $280 per credit. Part-time tuition and fees vary according to course load, location, and program. *College room only:* $4460. Room and board charges vary according to board plan and housing facility. *Payment plan:* installment. *Waivers:* senior citizens and employees or children of employees.

Financial Aid Of all full-time matriculated undergraduates who enrolled in 2002, 1,131 applied for aid, 1,054 were judged to have need, 163 had their need fully met. 156 Federal Work-Study jobs (averaging $883). In 2002, 186 non-need-based awards were made. *Average percent of need met:* 60%. *Average financial aid package:* $9601. *Average need-based loan:* $3799. *Average need-based gift aid:* $7267. *Average non-need-based aid:* $8979. *Average indebtedness upon graduation:* $18,507.

Applying *Options:* common application, electronic application, early admission, deferred entrance. *Required:* essay or personal statement, high school transcript, minimum 2.0 GPA, 1 letter of recommendation. *Recommended:* interview. *Application deadline:* 9/1 (freshmen), rolling (transfers). *Notification:* continuous until 9/1 (freshmen), continuous until 9/1 (transfers).

Admissions Contact Dr. Vicki Richmond, Dean of Admissions, Averett University, English Hall, Danville, VA 24541. *Phone:* 434-791-7301. *Toll-free phone:* 800-AVERETT. *Fax:* 434-797-2784. *E-mail:* admit@averett.edu.

BLUEFIELD COLLEGE

Bluefield, Virginia

- **Independent Southern Baptist** 4-year, founded 1922
- **Calendar** semesters
- **Degree** bachelor's
- **Small-town** 85-acre campus
- **Endowment** $3.3 million
- **Coed,** 731 undergraduate students, 90% full-time, 53% women, 47% men
- **Moderately difficult** entrance level, 67% of applicants were admitted

Undergraduates 661 full-time, 70 part-time. Students come from 14 states and territories, 3 other countries, 21% are from out of state, 18% African American, 3% Asian American or Pacific Islander, 0.4% Native American, 0.4% international, 17% transferred in, 17% live on campus. *Retention:* 58% of 2002 full-time freshmen returned.

Freshmen *Admission:* 415 applied, 278 admitted, 88 enrolled. *Average high school GPA:* 3.00. *Test scores:* SAT verbal scores over 500: 31%; SAT math scores over 500: 31%; ACT scores over 18: 75%; SAT verbal scores over 600: 7%; SAT math scores over 600: 7%; ACT scores over 24: 9%; SAT verbal scores over 700: 2%; ACT scores over 30: 2%.

Faculty *Total:* 113, 27% full-time, 47% with terminal degrees. *Student/faculty ratio:* 15:1.

Majors Accounting; art; athletic training; biblical studies; biology/biological sciences; biology teacher education; business administration and management; business teacher education; chemistry; chemistry teacher education; computer science; criminal justice/law enforcement administration; divinity/ministry; dramatic/theatre arts; education; elementary education; English; English/language arts teacher education; health teacher education; history; history teacher education; human resources management; interdisciplinary studies; kindergarten/preschool education; kinesiology and exercise science; liberal arts and sciences/liberal studies; mass communication/media; mathematics; mathematics teacher education; middle school education; music; music teacher education; philosophy; physical education teaching and coaching; psychology; religious/sacred music; religious studies; science teacher education; secondary education; social sciences; social studies teacher education; sociology; theology.

Academic Programs *Special study options:* academic remediation for entering students, accelerated degree program, adult/continuing education programs, advanced placement credit, double majors, external degree program, freshman honors college, honors programs, internships, part-time degree program, services for LD students, student-designed majors, study abroad, summer session for credit.

Library Easley Library with 72,000 titles, 94,210 serial subscriptions, 1,745 audiovisual materials, an OPAC, a Web page.

Computers on Campus 100 computers available on campus for general student use. A campuswide network can be accessed from student residence rooms that provide access to blackboard, COWL, career assessment tests, library database. Internet access, at least one staffed computer lab available.

Student Life *Housing:* on-campus residence required through junior year. *Options:* coed, men-only, women-only. Campus housing is university owned. Freshman applicants given priority for college housing. *Activities and organizations:* drama/theater group, student-run newspaper, radio station, choral group, Baptist Student Union, Fellowship of Christian Athletes, Student Union Board, Student Government Association, Bluefield Singers. *Campus security:* controlled dormitory access, night security patrols. *Student services:* health clinic, personal/psychological counseling.

Athletics Member NAIA. *Intercollegiate sports:* baseball M(s), basketball M(s)/W(s), golf M(s), soccer M(s)/W(s), softball W(s), tennis M(s)/W(s), volleyball W(s). *Intramural sports:* badminton M/W, baseball M, basketball M/W, football M, softball M/W, table tennis M/W, tennis M/W, volleyball M/W.

Standardized Tests *Required:* SAT I or ACT (for admission).

Costs (2003–04) *Comprehensive fee:* $15,575 includes full-time tuition ($9715), mandatory fees ($450), and room and board ($5410). Full-time tuition and fees vary according to program. Part-time tuition: $320 per hour. *Required fees:* $220 per year part-time. *College room only:* $2090. Room and board charges vary according to board plan and housing facility. *Payment plan:* installment. *Waivers:* senior citizens and employees or children of employees.

Financial Aid Of all full-time matriculated undergraduates who enrolled in 2003, 606 applied for aid, 543 were judged to have need, 128 had their need fully met. 98 Federal Work-Study jobs (averaging $800). In 2003, 137 non-need-based awards were made. *Average percent of need met:* 68%. *Average financial aid package:* $8957. *Average need-based loan:* $4430. *Average need-based gift aid:* $5403. *Average non-need-based aid:* $6464. *Average indebtedness upon graduation:* $12,177.

Applying *Options:* electronic application, deferred entrance. *Application fee:* $20. *Required:* high school transcript, minimum 2.0 GPA. *Required for some:* letters of recommendation, interview. *Recommended:* interview. *Application deadline:* rolling (freshmen), rolling (transfers). *Notification:* continuous (freshmen), continuous (transfers).

Admissions Contact Office of Admissions, Bluefield College, 3000 College Drive, Bluefield, VA 24605-1799. *Phone:* 276-326-4214. *Toll-free phone:* 800-872-0175. *Fax:* 276-326-4288. *E-mail:* admissions@mail.bluefield.edu.

Bridgewater College
Bridgewater, Virginia

- **Independent** 4-year, founded 1880, affiliated with Church of the Brethren
- **Calendar** 4-1-4
- **Degree** bachelor's
- **Small-town** 190-acre campus
- **Endowment** $43.9 million
- **Coed,** 1,403 undergraduate students, 98% full-time, 55% women, 45% men
- **Moderately difficult** entrance level, 88% of applicants were admitted

Bridgewater College offers academic majors that are enhanced by a balanced liberal arts and sciences program. The liberal arts curriculum for first-year students focuses on effective writing, oral communication, quantitative reasoning, and critical thinking. In the College's award-winning Personal Development Portfolio program, each student is paired with a faculty mentor who aids the student's development in citizenship, ethical and spiritual growth, intellectual discovery, and wellness. The program culminates in a senior portfolio, documenting achievement in these areas and supplementing the academic transcript. Excellent facilities include a $12-million center for science, computer science, and mathematics; the 34,000-square-foot Funkhouser Center for Health and Wellness; and residence halls that are fully wired for Internet, phone, and cable television access.

Undergraduates 1,376 full-time, 27 part-time. Students come from 21 states and territories, 9 other countries, 22% are from out of state, 8% African American, 1% Asian American or Pacific Islander, 1% Hispanic American, 0.5% Native American, 0.7% international, 6% transferred in, 76% live on campus. *Retention:* 74% of 2002 full-time freshmen returned.

Freshmen *Admission:* 1,388 applied, 1,221 admitted, 391 enrolled. *Average high school GPA:* 3.30. *Test scores:* SAT verbal scores over 500: 53%; SAT math scores over 500: 55%; ACT scores over 18: 77%; SAT verbal scores over 600: 14%; SAT math scores over 600: 15%; ACT scores over 24: 18%; SAT verbal scores over 700: 2%; SAT math scores over 700: 1%.

Faculty *Total:* 121, 73% full-time, 66% with terminal degrees. *Student/faculty ratio:* 14:1.

Majors Accounting; American history; athletic training; biology/biological sciences; biology teacher education; business administration and management; chemistry; chemistry teacher education; clinical laboratory science/medical technology; computer science; computer teacher education; cultural studies; driver and safety teacher education; economics; English; English as a second/foreign language (teaching); English/language arts teacher education; environmental science; ethnic, cultural minority, and gender studies related; family and consumer sciences/home economics teacher education; family and consumer sciences/human sciences; fashion merchandising; finance; fine/studio arts; foods, nutrition, and wellness; French; French language teacher education; health and physical education; history; history related; history teacher education; interior design; international business/trade/commerce; international relations and affairs; kinesiology and exercise science; liberal arts and sciences/liberal studies; management information systems; marketing/marketing management; mass communication/media; mathematics; mathematics teacher education; music history, literature, and theory; music teacher education; organizational behavior; philosophy and religious studies related; physics; physics related; physics teacher education; political science and government; psychology; public relations/image management; secondary education; social science teacher education; sociology; Spanish; Spanish language teacher education; special education; visual and performing arts related.

Academic Programs *Special study options:* adult/continuing education programs, advanced placement credit, double majors, honors programs, independent study, internships, part-time degree program, study abroad, summer session for credit. *Unusual degree programs:* 3-2 engineering with George Washington University; forestry with Duke University; physical therapy with George Washington University.

Library Alexander Mack Memorial Library with 132,739 titles, 659 serial subscriptions, 8,793 audiovisual materials, an OPAC, a Web page.

Computers on Campus 149 computers available on campus for general student use. A campuswide network can be accessed from student residence rooms and from off campus that provide access to on-line course and grade information. Internet access, at least one staffed computer lab available. Computer purchase or lease plan available.

Student Life *Housing:* on-campus residence required through senior year. *Options:* men-only, women-only, disabled students. Campus housing is university owned. Freshman campus housing is guaranteed. *Activities and organizations:* drama/theater group, student-run newspaper, radio station, choral group, Eagle Productions, pep band, Oratorio Choir, Baptist Student Union, Brethren Student Fellowship. *Campus security:* 24-hour emergency response devices and patrols, controlled dormitory access. *Student services:* health clinic, personal/psychological counseling.

Athletics Member NCAA. All Division III. *Intercollegiate sports:* baseball M, basketball M/W, cross-country running M/W, equestrian sports M/W, field hockey W, football M, golf M, lacrosse W, soccer M/W, softball W, tennis M/W, track and field M/W, volleyball W. *Intramural sports:* badminton M/W, basketball M/W, bowling M/W, cheerleading M(c)/W(c), football M/W, golf M/W, racquetball M/W, soccer M/W, softball M/W, table tennis M/W, tennis M/W, ultimate Frisbee M(c)/W(c), volleyball M/W.

Standardized Tests *Required:* SAT I or ACT (for admission). *Recommended:* SAT I (for admission).

Costs (2004–05) *Comprehensive fee:* $26,470 includes full-time tuition ($17,990) and room and board ($8480). Part-time tuition: $590 per credit hour. *Required fees:* $30 per term part-time. *College room only:* $4245. Room and board charges vary according to board plan and housing facility. *Payment plan:* installment. *Waivers:* minority students, senior citizens, and employees or children of employees.

Financial Aid Of all full-time matriculated undergraduates who enrolled in 2003, 1,124 applied for aid, 984 were judged to have need, 271 had their need fully met. 455 Federal Work-Study jobs (averaging $1051). 99 state and other part-time jobs (averaging $671). In 2003, 327 non-need-based awards were made. *Average percent of need met:* 83%. *Average financial aid package:* $16,169. *Average need-based loan:* $4628. *Average need-based gift aid:* $12,092. *Average non-need-based aid:* $7633. *Average indebtedness upon graduation:* $20,099.

Applying *Options:* common application, electronic application, deferred entrance. *Application fee:* $30. *Required:* essay or personal statement, high school transcript, minimum 2.0 GPA, 2 letters of recommendation. *Required for some:* interview. *Recommended:* minimum 3.0 GPA, interview. *Application deadline:* rolling (freshmen), rolling (transfers). *Notification:* continuous (transfers).

Admissions Contact Ms. Linda F. Stout, Director of Enrollment Operations, Bridgewater College, 402 East College Street, Bridgewater, VA 22812-1599. *Phone:* 540-828-5375. *Toll-free phone:* 800-759-8328. *Fax:* 540-828-5481. *E-mail:* admissions@bridgewater.edu.

■ See page 1294 for a narrative description.

Bryant and Stratton College, Virginia Beach
Virginia Beach, Virginia

- **Proprietary** primarily 2-year, founded 1952, part of Bryant and Stratton Business Institute, Inc.
- **Calendar** semesters
- **Degrees** associate and bachelor's
- **Suburban** campus
- **Coed, primarily women**
- **Minimally difficult** entrance level

Faculty *Student/faculty ratio:* 10:1.

Student Life *Campus security:* late-night transport/escort service.

Standardized Tests *Required:* CPAt (for admission).

Costs (2003–04) *One-time required fee:* $100. *Tuition:* $9900 full-time, $330 per credit hour part-time. Full-time tuition and fees vary according to class time and course load. *Required fees:* $200 full-time, $100 per term part-time.

Financial Aid Of all full-time matriculated undergraduates who enrolled in 2001, 30 Federal Work-Study jobs (averaging $5000).

Applying *Options:* common application, electronic application. *Application fee:* $25. *Required:* interview. *Required for some:* high school transcript.

Admissions Contact Mr. Greg Smith, Director of Admissions, Bryant and Stratton College, Virginia Beach, 301 Centre Pointe Drive, Virginia Beach, VA 23462-4417. *Phone:* 757-499-7900.

Christendom College
Front Royal, Virginia

- **Independent Roman Catholic** comprehensive, founded 1977
- **Calendar** semesters
- **Degrees** associate, bachelor's, and master's
- **Rural** 100-acre campus with easy access to Washington, DC
- **Endowment** $3.1 million
- **Coed,** 366 undergraduate students, 99% full-time, 57% women, 43% men
- **Very difficult** entrance level, 80% of applicants were admitted

Undergraduates 363 full-time, 3 part-time. Students come from 41 states and territories, 2 other countries, 78% are from out of state, 0.3% African American, 2% Asian American or Pacific Islander, 4% Hispanic American, 3% international, 4% transferred in, 95% live on campus. *Retention:* 84% of 2002 full-time freshmen returned.

Freshmen *Admission:* 227 applied, 182 admitted, 98 enrolled. *Average high school GPA:* 3.54. *Test scores:* SAT verbal scores over 500: 100%; SAT math scores over 500: 91%; SAT verbal scores over 600: 80%; SAT math scores over 600: 41%; SAT verbal scores over 700: 33%; SAT math scores over 700: 12%.

Faculty *Total:* 33, 70% full-time, 73% with terminal degrees. *Student/faculty ratio:* 12:1.

Majors Classics and languages, literatures and linguistics; French; history; liberal arts and sciences/liberal studies; literature; philosophy; political science and government; theology.

Academic Programs *Special study options:* academic remediation for entering students, accelerated degree program, advanced placement credit, cooperative education, double majors, independent study, internships, services for LD students, study abroad, summer session for credit.

Library O'Reilly Memorial Library with 64,265 titles, 249 serial subscriptions, 1,302 audiovisual materials, an OPAC.

Computers on Campus 24 computers available on campus for general student use. Internet access, at least one staffed computer lab available.

Student Life *Housing:* on-campus residence required through senior year. *Options:* men-only, women-only. Campus housing is university owned. Freshman campus housing is guaranteed. *Activities and organizations:* drama/theater group, student-run newspaper, choral group, drama, choir, Shield of Roses, Legion of Mary, debate. *Campus security:* 24-hour emergency response devices, late-night transport/escort service, night patrols by trained security personnel. *Student services:* health clinic, personal/psychological counseling.

Athletics Member NCCAA. *Intramural sports:* basketball M/W, fencing M/W, football M/W, golf M/W, racquetball M/W, soccer M/W, softball M/W, table tennis M/W, tennis M/W, volleyball M/W.

Standardized Tests *Required:* SAT I or ACT (for admission).

Costs (2003–04) *Comprehensive fee:* $18,410 includes full-time tuition ($12,970), mandatory fees ($450), and room and board ($4990). Part-time tuition: $605 per hour. *Required fees:* $450 per year part-time. *Payment plans:* tuition prepayment, installment. *Waivers:* employees or children of employees.

Financial Aid Of all full-time matriculated undergraduates who enrolled in 2003, 248 applied for aid, 196 were judged to have need, 196 had their need fully met. 125 state and other part-time jobs (averaging $1810). In 2003, 50 non-need-based awards were made. *Average percent of need met:* 90%. *Average financial aid package:* $9730. *Average need-based loan:* $3855. *Average need-based gift aid:* $4180. *Average non-need-based aid:* $3800. *Average indebtedness upon graduation:* $10,050.

Applying *Options:* common application, electronic application, early admission, early action. *Application fee:* $25. *Required:* essay or personal statement, high school transcript, 2 letters of recommendation. *Recommended:* minimum 3.0 GPA, interview. *Application deadlines:* 3/1 (freshmen), 3/1 (transfers). *Notification:* 4/1 (freshmen), 12/15 (early action), continuous until 4/1 (transfers).

Admissions Contact Mr. Paul Heisler, Director of Admissions, Christendom College, 134 Christendom Drive, Front Royal, VA 22630-5103. *Phone:* 540-636-2900 Ext. 290. *Toll-free phone:* 800-877-5456 Ext. 290. *Fax:* 540-636-1655. *E-mail:* admissions@christendom.edu.

CHRISTOPHER NEWPORT UNIVERSITY

Newport News, Virginia

- **State-supported** comprehensive, founded 1960
- **Calendar** semesters
- **Degrees** bachelor's and master's
- **Suburban** 175-acre campus with easy access to Norfolk
- **Endowment** $2.5 million
- **Coed,** 4,680 undergraduate students, 87% full-time, 56% women, 44% men
- **Moderately difficult** entrance level, 58% of applicants were admitted

Undergraduates 4,080 full-time, 600 part-time. Students come from 28 states and territories, 10 other countries, 3% are from out of state, 10% African American, 3% Asian American or Pacific Islander, 2% Hispanic American, 0.4% Native American, 0.3% international, 5% transferred in, 30% live on campus. *Retention:* 64% of 2002 full-time freshmen returned.

Freshmen *Admission:* 4,794 applied, 2,787 admitted, 1,210 enrolled. *Average high school GPA:* 3.30. *Test scores:* SAT verbal scores over 500: 91%; SAT math scores over 500: 88%; ACT scores over 18: 97%; SAT verbal scores over 600: 33%; SAT math scores over 600: 30%; ACT scores over 24: 32%; SAT verbal scores over 700: 4%; SAT math scores over 700: 3%.

Faculty *Total:* 311, 58% full-time. *Student/faculty ratio:* 19:1.

Majors Accounting; art; biology/biological sciences; business administration and management; business/managerial economics; communication/speech communication and rhetoric; computer and information sciences; computer engineering; computer science; developmental and child psychology; dramatic/theatre arts; economics; education; English; environmental studies; finance; French; German; history; horticultural science; information science/studies; interdisciplinary studies; international business/trade/commerce; international relations and affairs; legal studies; literature; marketing/marketing management; mathematics; middle school education; music; music history, literature, and theory; music theory and composition; philosophy; physics; political science and government; pre-law studies; psychology; public administration; religious studies; social work; sociology; Spanish; visual and performing arts.

Academic Programs *Special study options:* academic remediation for entering students, accelerated degree program, adult/continuing education programs, advanced placement credit, cooperative education, distance learning, double majors, honors programs, independent study, internships, off-campus study, part-time degree program, services for LD students, student-designed majors, study abroad, summer session for credit. *ROTC:* Army (b). *Unusual degree programs:* 3-2 engineering with Old Dominion University; forestry with Duke University; environmental management with Duke University.

Library Captain John Smith Library with 328,319 titles, 1,695 serial subscriptions, 10,238 audiovisual materials, an OPAC, a Web page.

Computers on Campus 1000 computers available on campus for general student use. A campuswide network can be accessed from student residence rooms and from off campus. Internet access, at least one staffed computer lab available.

Student Life *Housing:* on-campus residence required for freshman year. *Options:* coed. *Activities and organizations:* drama/theater group, student-run newspaper, radio station, choral group, Student Virginia Education Association, Student Government Association, national fraternities, national sororities. *Campus security:* 24-hour emergency response devices and patrols, late-night transport/escort service, controlled dormitory access, campus police. *Student services:* health clinic, personal/psychological counseling.

Athletics Member NCAA. All Division III. *Intercollegiate sports:* baseball M, basketball M/W, cross-country running M/W, equestrian sports M(c)/W(c), field hockey W, football M, golf M, lacrosse M(c)/W(c), rugby M(c), sailing M/W, soccer M/W, softball W, tennis M/W, track and field M/W, volleyball W. *Intramural sports:* badminton M/W, basketball M/W, bowling M/W, cross-country running M/W, football M/W, golf M/W, softball M/W, table tennis M/W, tennis M/W, volleyball M/W, weight lifting M/W.

Standardized Tests *Required:* SAT I or ACT (for admission).

Costs (2003–04) *Tuition:* state resident $4600 full-time, $191 per credit part-time; nonresident $12,300 full-time, $512 per credit part-time. Full-time tuition and fees vary according to course load. Part-time tuition and fees vary according to course load. *Room and board:* $6700; room only: $4400. Room and board charges vary according to housing facility. *Payment plan:* installment. *Waivers:* senior citizens and employees or children of employees.

Financial Aid Of all full-time matriculated undergraduates who enrolled in 2003, 2,868 applied for aid, 1,979 were judged to have need, 95 had their need fully met. 185 Federal Work-Study jobs (averaging $907). 776 state and other part-time jobs (averaging $1755). In 2003, 354 non-need-based awards were made. *Average percent of need met:* 54%. *Average financial aid package:* $3951. *Average need-based loan:* $2823. *Average need-based gift aid:* $2770. *Average non-need-based aid:* $1451. *Average indebtedness upon graduation:* $8035.

Applying *Options:* common application, electronic application, early admission, early action, deferred entrance. *Application fee:* $35. *Required:* high school transcript, minimum 3.0 GPA. *Required for some:* essay or personal statement, 3 letters of recommendation, interview. *Application deadlines:* 3/1 (freshmen), 6/1 (transfers). *Notification:* continuous (freshmen).

Admissions Contact Ms. Rebecca Ducknuall, Assistant Director of Admissions, Christopher Newport University, 1 University Place, Newport News, VA 23606-2998. *Phone:* 757-594-7205. *Toll-free phone:* 800-333-4268. *Fax:* 757-594-7333. *E-mail:* admit@cnu.edu.

■ *See page 1400 for a narrative description.*

THE COLLEGE OF WILLIAM AND MARY

Williamsburg, Virginia

- **State-supported** university, founded 1693
- **Calendar** semesters
- **Degrees** bachelor's, master's, doctoral, first professional, and post-master's certificates
- **Small-town** 1200-acre campus with easy access to Richmond
- **Endowment** $357.0 million
- **Coed,** 5,748 undergraduate students, 99% full-time, 56% women, 44% men
- **Very difficult** entrance level, 34% of applicants were admitted

Undergraduates 5,666 full-time, 82 part-time. Students come from 50 states and territories, 52 other countries, 35% are from out of state, 6% African American, 7% Asian American or Pacific Islander, 3% Hispanic American, 0.5% Native American, 2% international, 3% transferred in, 75% live on campus. *Retention:* 94% of 2002 full-time freshmen returned.

The College of William and Mary (continued)

Freshmen *Admission:* 10,161 applied, 3,488 admitted, 1,326 enrolled. *Average high school GPA:* 4.00. *Test scores:* SAT verbal scores over 500: 99%; SAT math scores over 500: 100%; ACT scores over 18: 100%; SAT verbal scores over 600: 88%; SAT math scores over 600: 86%; ACT scores over 24: 89%; SAT verbal scores over 700: 43%; SAT math scores over 700: 35%; ACT scores over 30: 78%.

Faculty *Total:* 729, 77% full-time, 83% with terminal degrees. *Student/faculty ratio:* 12:1.

Majors African-American/Black studies; American studies; anthropology; art; art history, criticism and conservation; Asian studies (East); biology/biological sciences; biopsychology; business administration and management; chemistry; classics and languages, literatures and linguistics; computer and information sciences; cultural studies; dramatic/theatre arts; economics; English; environmental studies; European studies; French; geology/earth science; German; history; interdisciplinary studies; international relations and affairs; Latin; Latin American studies; linguistics; mathematics; medieval and Renaissance studies; modern Greek; modern languages; multi-/interdisciplinary studies related; music; philosophy; physical education teaching and coaching; physics; political science and government; psychology; public policy analysis; religious studies; Russian studies; sociology; Spanish; women's studies.

Academic Programs *Special study options:* accelerated degree program, advanced placement credit, double majors, honors programs, independent study, services for LD students, student-designed majors, study abroad, summer session for credit. *ROTC:* Army (b). *Unusual degree programs:* 3-2 engineering with Columbia University, Washington University in St. Louis, Rensselaer Polytechnic Institute, Case Western Reserve University, University of Virginia; forestry with Duke University.

Library Swem Library plus 9 others with 2.0 million titles, 11,688 serial subscriptions, 29,316 audiovisual materials, an OPAC, a Web page.

Computers on Campus 225 computers available on campus for general student use. A campuswide network can be accessed from student residence rooms and from off campus. Internet access, online (class) registration, at least one staffed computer lab available.

Student Life *Housing:* on-campus residence required for freshman year. *Options:* coed, women-only. Campus housing is university owned and leased by the school. Freshman campus housing is guaranteed. *Activities and organizations:* drama/theater group, student-run newspaper, radio and television station, choral group, Alpha Phi Omega, College Partnership for Kids, student assembly, Flat Hat (student newspaper), Resident Housing Association, national fraternities, national sororities. *Campus security:* 24-hour emergency response devices and patrols, student patrols, late-night transport/escort service, controlled dormitory access. *Student services:* health clinic, personal/psychological counseling, legal services.

Athletics Member NCAA. All Division I except football (Division I-AA). *Intercollegiate sports:* baseball M(s), basketball M(s)/W(s), cross-country running M(s)/W(s), field hockey W(s), golf M/W, gymnastics M(s)/W(s), lacrosse W(s), soccer M(s)/W(s), swimming M(s)/W, tennis M(s)/W(s), track and field M(s)/W(s), volleyball W(s). *Intramural sports:* badminton M(c)/W(c), baseball M(c), basketball M/W, bowling M/W, crew M(c)/W(c), cross-country running M(c)/W(c), equestrian sports M(c)/W(c), fencing M(c)/W(c), field hockey W(c), football M/W, golf M/W, gymnastics M(c)/W(c), ice hockey M(c), lacrosse M(c)/W(c), racquetball M(c)/W(c), rock climbing M/W, rugby M(c)/W(c), sailing M(c)/W(c), soccer M(c)/W(c), softball M(c)/W, swimming M(c)/W(c), table tennis M/W, tennis M(c)/W(c), ultimate Frisbee M/W, volleyball M(c)/W(c), weight lifting M(c)/W(c), wrestling M.

Standardized Tests *Required:* SAT I or ACT (for admission). *Recommended:* SAT II: Subject Tests (for admission), SAT II: Writing Test (for admission).

Costs (2003–04) *Tuition:* state resident $3760 full-time, $162 per credit part-time; nonresident $18,460 full-time, $646 per credit part-time. Full-time tuition and fees vary according to program. Part-time tuition and fees vary according to program. *Required fees:* $2670 full-time. *Room and board:* $5794; room only: $3428. Room and board charges vary according to board plan and housing facility. *Payment plan:* installment. *Waivers:* senior citizens and employees or children of employees.

Financial Aid Of all full-time matriculated undergraduates who enrolled in 2002, 2,309 applied for aid, 1,485 were judged to have need, 282 had their need fully met. 46 Federal Work-Study jobs (averaging $1078). In 2002, 952 non-need-based awards were made. *Average percent of need met:* 80%. *Average financial aid package:* $8664. *Average need-based loan:* $3197. *Average need-based gift aid:* $6963. *Average non-need-based aid:* $7173. *Average indebtedness upon graduation:* $19,952. *Financial aid deadline:* 3/15.

Applying *Options:* common application, electronic application, early admission, early decision, deferred entrance. *Application fee:* $60. *Required:* essay or personal statement, high school transcript. *Recommended:* 1 letter of recommendation. *Application deadlines:* 1/5 (freshmen), 2/15 (transfers). *Early decision:* 11/1. *Notification:* 4/1 (freshmen), 12/1 (early decision), 4/15 (transfers).

Admissions Contact Ms. Karen R. Cottrell, Associate Provost for Enrollment, The College of William and Mary, PO Box 8795, Williamsburg, VA 23187-8795. *Phone:* 757-221-4223. *Fax:* 757-221-1242. *E-mail:* admiss@wm.edu.

DEVRY UNIVERSITY
McLean, Virginia

Admissions Contact 1751 Pinnacle Drive, Suite 250, McLean, VA 22102-3832.

DEVRY UNIVERSITY
Arlington, Virginia

- **Proprietary** comprehensive, founded 2001, part of DeVry University
- **Calendar** semesters
- **Degrees** associate, bachelor's, master's, and postbachelor's certificates
- **Coed**
- **Minimally difficult** entrance level

Standardized Tests *Recommended:* SAT I, ACT or CPT.

Costs (2003–04) *Tuition:* $11,100 full-time, $395 per credit hour part-time. Full-time tuition and fees vary according to course load. Part-time tuition and fees vary according to course load. *Required fees:* $165 full-time. *Payment plans:* installment, deferred payment.

Financial Aid Of all full-time matriculated undergraduates who enrolled in 2002, 350 applied for aid, 325 were judged to have need, 4 had their need fully met. In 2002, 46. *Average percent of need met:* 31. *Average financial aid package:* $6344. *Average need-based loan:* $4422. *Average need-based gift aid:* $3585. *Average non-need-based aid:* $8612.

Applying *Options:* electronic application, deferred entrance. *Application fee:* $50. *Required:* high school transcript, interview.

Admissions Contact Mr. Todd Marshburn, Director of Enrollment Services, DeVry University, 2450 Crystal Drive, 2341 Jefferson Davis Highway, Arlington, VA 22202-3843. *Phone:* 866-338-7932. *Toll-free phone:* 866-338-7932. *Fax:* 703-414-4040. *E-mail:* admissions@devry.edu.

EASTERN MENNONITE UNIVERSITY
Harrisonburg, Virginia

- **Independent Mennonite** comprehensive, founded 1917
- **Calendar** semesters
- **Degrees** certificates, associate, bachelor's, master's, first professional, and postbachelor's certificates
- **Small-town** 93-acre campus
- **Endowment** $13.7 million
- **Coed,** 965 undergraduate students, 96% full-time, 60% women, 40% men
- **Moderately difficult** entrance level, 82% of applicants were admitted

International education is a special mission of Eastern Mennonite University. The University's distinctive Global Village curriculum builds an outstanding liberal arts education on a foundation of Christian values and cross-cultural understanding. Every student engages in cross-cultural study in locations such as Latin America, Eastern and Western Europe, the Middle East, Asia, Africa, and an American Indian reservation.

Undergraduates 931 full-time, 34 part-time. Students come from 35 states and territories, 21 other countries, 56% are from out of state, 5% African American, 2% Asian American or Pacific Islander, 1% Hispanic American, 0.1% Native American, 5% international, 8% transferred in, 66% live on campus. *Retention:* 75% of 2002 full-time freshmen returned.

Freshmen *Admission:* 605 applied, 498 admitted, 196 enrolled. *Average high school GPA:* 3.40. *Test scores:* SAT verbal scores over 500: 68%; SAT math scores over 500: 59%; ACT scores over 18: 85%; SAT verbal scores over 600: 32%; SAT math scores over 600: 32%; ACT scores over 24: 49%; SAT verbal scores over 700: 5%; SAT math scores over 700: 13%; ACT scores over 30: 9%.

Faculty *Total:* 154, 70% full-time, 62% with terminal degrees. *Student/faculty ratio:* 9:1.

Majors Accounting; art; art teacher education; biblical studies; biochemistry; biology/biological sciences; biology teacher education; business administration and management; chemistry; chemistry teacher education; clinical laboratory science/medical technology; communication/speech communication and rhetoric; computer science; computer systems analysis; development economics and international development; dramatic/theatre arts; economics; elementary education; English; English/language arts teacher education; environmental science; French; French language teacher education; general studies; German; German language teacher education; health teacher education; history; international agriculture; international business/trade/commerce; kindergarten/preschool education; liberal arts and sciences/liberal studies; mathematics; mathematics teacher education; middle school education; multi-/interdisciplinary studies related; music; music teacher education; nursing (registered nurse training); peace studies and conflict resolution; philosophy and religious studies related; physical education teaching and coaching; pre-dentistry studies; pre-medical studies; pre-veterinary studies; psychology; secondary education; social sciences; social science teacher education; social work; sociology; Spanish; Spanish language teacher education; special education (emotionally disturbed); special education (mentally retarded); special education (specific learning disabilities); sport and fitness administration; theology.

Academic Programs *Special study options:* academic remediation for entering students, adult/continuing education programs, advanced placement credit, distance learning, double majors, English as a second language, honors programs, independent study, internships, off-campus study, part-time degree program, services for LD students, study abroad, summer session for credit. *Unusual degree programs:* 3-2 engineering with Pennsylvania State University—University Park Campus; appropriate technology with Drexel University.

Library Sadie Hartzler Library with 156,268 titles, 1,287 serial subscriptions, 3,002 audiovisual materials, an OPAC, a Web page.

Computers on Campus 110 computers available on campus for general student use. A campuswide network can be accessed from student residence rooms and from off campus. Internet access available.

Student Life *Housing:* on-campus residence required through junior year. *Options:* coed, men-only, women-only, disabled students. Campus housing is university owned. Freshman campus housing is guaranteed. *Activities and organizations:* drama/theater group, student-run newspaper, radio station, choral group, YPCA, Students in Free Enterprise, Student Government Association, Student Education Association, International Student Organization. *Campus security:* 24-hour emergency response devices, controlled dormitory access, night watchman. *Student services:* health clinic, personal/psychological counseling.

Athletics Member NCAA. All Division III. *Intercollegiate sports:* baseball M, basketball M/W, cross-country running M/W, soccer M/W, softball W, tennis M/W, track and field M/W, volleyball M/W. *Intramural sports:* basketball M/W, rock climbing M/W, soccer M/W, softball M/W, table tennis M/W, tennis M/W, volleyball M/W.

Standardized Tests *Required:* SAT I or ACT (for admission).

Costs (2003–04) *Comprehensive fee:* $22,990 includes full-time tuition ($17,304), mandatory fees ($46), and room and board ($5640). Full-time tuition and fees vary according to course load and program. Part-time tuition: $726 per credit hour. Part-time tuition and fees vary according to course load and program. *College room only:* $2900. Room and board charges vary according to board plan, housing facility, and student level. *Payment plans:* tuition prepayment, installment. *Waivers:* employees or children of employees.

Financial Aid Of all full-time matriculated undergraduates who enrolled in 2002, 921 applied for aid, 639 were judged to have need, 94 had their need fully met. 326 Federal Work-Study jobs (averaging $1787). In 2002, 280 non-need-based awards were made. *Average percent of need met:* 85%. *Average financial aid package:* $13,140. *Average need-based loan:* $4912. *Average need-based gift aid:* $7600. *Average non-need-based aid:* $6012. *Average indebtedness upon graduation:* $19,300.

Applying *Options:* common application, electronic application, early admission, deferred entrance. *Application fee:* $25. *Required:* high school transcript, minimum 2.2 GPA, 1 letter of recommendation, statement of commitment. *Recommended:* interview. *Application deadlines:* 8/1 (freshmen), 8/1 (transfers). *Notification:* continuous (freshmen), continuous (transfers).

Admissions Contact Mr. Lawrence W. Miller, Director of Admissions, Eastern Mennonite University, 1200 Park Road, Harrisonburg, VA 22802-2462. *Phone:* 540-432-4118. *Toll-free phone:* 800-368-2665. *Fax:* 540-432-4444. *E-mail:* admiss@emu.edu.

■ *See page 1556 for a narrative description.*

EMORY & HENRY COLLEGE
Emory, Virginia

- **Independent United Methodist** comprehensive, founded 1836
- **Calendar** semesters
- **Degrees** bachelor's and master's
- **Rural** 331-acre campus
- **Endowment** $59.2 million
- **Coed,** 886 undergraduate students, 97% full-time, 51% women, 49% men
- **Moderately difficult** entrance level, 81% of applicants were admitted

Emory & Henry continues to build on a long-standing tradition of excellence. The College recently completed the construction of a 70,000-square-foot academic center, which provides high-tech science laboratories and modern classroom space. Emory & Henry also has joined with Barter Theater, the state theater of Virginia, to integrate college-level studies in theater with professional stage experience. Founded in 1836, Emory & Henry offers small classes, a wide range of academic programs, professors who have been honored nationally, and a variety of student life activities in one of the nation's most beautiful settings.

Undergraduates 856 full-time, 30 part-time. Students come from 25 states and territories, 2 other countries, 33% are from out of state, 4% African American, 1% Asian American or Pacific Islander, 0.8% Hispanic American, 0.3% Native American, 0.2% international, 5% transferred in, 68% live on campus. *Retention:* 70% of 2002 full-time freshmen returned.

Freshmen *Admission:* 916 applied, 746 admitted, 224 enrolled. *Average high school GPA:* 3.3. *Test scores:* SAT verbal scores over 500: 65%; SAT math scores over 500: 64%; ACT scores over 18: 89%; SAT verbal scores over 600: 29%; SAT math scores over 600: 21%; ACT scores over 24: 35%; SAT verbal scores over 700: 2%; SAT math scores over 700: 3%; ACT scores over 30: 4%.

Faculty *Total:* 88, 78% full-time, 64% with terminal degrees. *Student/faculty ratio:* 14:1.

Majors Accounting; applied mathematics; art; Asian studies (East); biology/biological sciences; business administration and management; chemistry; clinical laboratory science/medical technology; community organization and advocacy; computer science; creative writing; dramatic/theatre arts; economics; English; environmental studies; European studies; French; geography; health and physical education; history; interdisciplinary studies; international relations and affairs; mass communication/media; mathematics; music; Near and Middle Eastern studies; philosophy; physics; political science and government; pre-dentistry studies; pre-law studies; pre-medical studies; pre-veterinary studies; psychology; religious studies; sociology; Spanish.

Academic Programs *Special study options:* advanced placement credit, double majors, English as a second language, honors programs, independent study, internships, off-campus study, services for LD students, student-designed majors, study abroad, summer session for credit. *Unusual degree programs:* 3-2 engineering with University of Virginia, University of Tennessee, Tennessee Technical Institute; forestry with Duke University.

Library Kelly Library with 176,450 titles, 5,129 serial subscriptions, 6,169 audiovisual materials, an OPAC, a Web page.

Computers on Campus 121 computers available on campus for general student use. A campuswide network can be accessed from student residence rooms and from off campus. Internet access, at least one staffed computer lab available.

Student Life *Housing:* on-campus residence required through senior year. *Options:* men-only, women-only. Campus housing is university owned. Freshman campus housing is guaranteed. *Activities and organizations:* drama/theater group, student-run newspaper, radio station, choral group, Alpha Phi Omega, Student Virginia Education Association, student radio station, Campus Christian Fellowship, Greek organizations. *Campus security:* 24-hour emergency response devices and patrols, late-night transport/escort service. *Student services:* health clinic, personal/psychological counseling, women's center.

Athletics Member NCAA. All Division III. *Intercollegiate sports:* baseball M, basketball M/W, cross-country running M/W, football M, golf M, soccer M/W, softball W, tennis M/W, volleyball W. *Intramural sports:* basketball M/W, football M/W, golf M/W, racquetball M/W, skiing (cross-country) M(c)/W(c), skiing (downhill) M(c), soccer M/W, softball M/W, table tennis M/W, tennis M/W, volleyball M/W, water polo M/W, weight lifting M/W.

Standardized Tests *Required:* SAT I or ACT (for admission).

Costs (2003–04) *Comprehensive fee:* $21,950 includes full-time tuition ($15,700), mandatory fees ($200), and room and board ($6050). Full-time tuition and fees vary according to course load. Part-time tuition: $655 per semester hour. Part-time tuition and fees vary according to course load. *Required fees:* $10 per semester hour part-time. *College room only:* $2930. Room and board charges vary according to board plan. *Payment plan:* installment. *Waivers:* employees or children of employees.

Financial Aid Of all full-time matriculated undergraduates who enrolled in 2003, 787 applied for aid, 653 were judged to have need, 184 had their need fully met. 123 Federal Work-Study jobs (averaging $1428). In 2003, 218 non-need-based awards were made. *Average percent of need met:* 83%. *Average financial aid package:* $12,706. *Average need-based loan:* $3564. *Average need-based gift aid:* $9830. *Average non-need-based aid:* $6601. *Average indebtedness upon graduation:* $14,466. *Financial aid deadline:* 8/1.

Applying *Options:* common application, electronic application, early admission, early decision, deferred entrance. *Application fee:* $30. *Required:* essay or personal statement, high school transcript. *Required for some:* 2 letters of recommendation. *Recommended:* interview. *Application deadline:* rolling (freshmen), rolling (transfers). *Early decision:* 11/1. *Notification:* continuous (freshmen), 12/15 (early decision), continuous (transfers).

Emory & Henry College (continued)

Admissions Contact Ms. Liz Daniels, Director of Admissions and Financial Aid, Emory & Henry College, 30479 Armbrister Drive, PO Box 10, Emory, VA 24327. *Phone:* 276-944-6133. *Toll-free phone:* 800-848-5493. *Fax:* 276-944-6935. *E-mail:* ehadmiss@ehc.edu.

■ *See page 1594 for a narrative description.*

FERRUM COLLEGE

Ferrum, Virginia

- **Independent United Methodist** 4-year, founded 1913
- **Calendar** semesters
- **Degree** bachelor's
- **Rural** 720-acre campus
- **Endowment** $32.7 million
- **Coed,** 954 undergraduate students, 100% full-time, 43% women, 57% men
- **Minimally difficult** entrance level, 74% of applicants were admitted

Undergraduates 954 full-time. Students come from 21 states and territories, 5 other countries, 15% are from out of state, 18% African American, 0.6% Asian American or Pacific Islander, 1% Hispanic American, 0.2% Native American, 0.8% international, 7% transferred in, 81% live on campus. *Retention:* 54% of 2002 full-time freshmen returned.

Freshmen *Admission:* 1,126 applied, 829 admitted, 304 enrolled. *Average high school GPA:* 2.74. *Test scores:* SAT verbal scores over 500: 27%; SAT math scores over 500: 24%; SAT verbal scores over 600: 5%; SAT math scores over 600: 4%.

Faculty *Total:* 83, 82% full-time, 54% with terminal degrees. *Student/faculty ratio:* 14:1.

Majors Accounting; agriculture; applied horticulture; art; athletic training; biology/biological sciences; business administration and management; chemistry; clinical laboratory science/medical technology; computer science; criminal justice/safety; dramatic/theatre arts; education; English; environmental studies; finance; fine/studio arts; general studies; history; information science/studies; international relations and affairs; liberal arts and sciences/liberal studies; mathematics; parks, recreation and leisure; philosophy; physical education teaching and coaching; political science and government; psychology; religious studies; Russian; social sciences; social work; Spanish.

Academic Programs *Special study options:* adult/continuing education programs, advanced placement credit, cooperative education, distance learning, double majors, independent study, internships, part-time degree program, services for LD students, student-designed majors, study abroad, summer session for credit.

Library Stanley Library with 7,739 serial subscriptions, 1,610 audiovisual materials, an OPAC, a Web page.

Computers on Campus 470 computers available on campus for general student use. A campuswide network can be accessed from student residence rooms and from off campus. Internet access, at least one staffed computer lab available.

Student Life *Housing:* on-campus residence required through senior year. *Options:* coed, women-only. Campus housing is university owned. Freshman campus housing is guaranteed. *Activities and organizations:* drama/theater group, student-run newspaper, radio station, choral group, Student Government Association, agriculture club, BACCHUS, Panther Productions, African American Student Association, Students in Free Enterprise. *Campus security:* 24-hour emergency response devices and patrols, student patrols, late-night transport/escort service, controlled dormitory access. *Student services:* health clinic.

Athletics Member NCAA. All Division III. *Intercollegiate sports:* baseball M, basketball M/W, cheerleading M/W, cross-country running M/W, equestrian sports M/W, football M, golf M, lacrosse W, soccer M/W, softball W, tennis M/W, volleyball W. *Intramural sports:* basketball M/W, bowling M/W, football M/W, golf M, racquetball M/W, soccer M/W, softball M/W, swimming M/W, table tennis M/W, tennis M/W, ultimate Frisbee M/W, volleyball M/W.

Standardized Tests *Required:* SAT I or ACT (for admission).

Costs (2004–05) *Comprehensive fee:* $22,540 includes full-time tuition ($16,840) and room and board ($5700). Part-time tuition: $340 per hour. *Payment plan:* installment. *Waivers:* senior citizens and employees or children of employees.

Financial Aid Of all full-time matriculated undergraduates who enrolled in 2003, 910 applied for aid, 804 were judged to have need. 493 Federal Work-Study jobs (averaging $1992). 190 state and other part-time jobs (averaging $1817). In 2003, 105 non-need-based awards were made. *Average percent of need met:* 53%. *Average financial aid package:* $11,370. *Average need-based loan:* $2931. *Average need-based gift aid:* $9035. *Average non-need-based aid:* $4000. *Average indebtedness upon graduation:* $15,900.

Applying *Options:* common application, electronic application, early admission, deferred entrance. *Application fee:* $25. *Required:* high school transcript. *Required for some:* interview. *Recommended:* essay or personal statement, minimum 2.0 GPA, 2 letters of recommendation, interview. *Application deadline:* rolling (freshmen), rolling (transfers). *Notification:* continuous (freshmen), continuous (transfers).

Admissions Contact Ms. Gilda Q. Woods, Director of Admissions, Ferrum College, Spilman-Daniel House, PO Box 1000, Ferrum, VA 24088-9001. *Phone:* 540-365-4290. *Toll-free phone:* 800-868-9797. *Fax:* 540-365-4266. *E-mail:* admissions@ferrum.edu.

■ *See page 1618 for a narrative description.*

GEORGE MASON UNIVERSITY

Fairfax, Virginia

- **State-supported** university, founded 1957
- **Calendar** semesters
- **Degrees** bachelor's, master's, doctoral, first professional, and postbachelor's certificates
- **Suburban** 677-acre campus with easy access to Washington, DC
- **Endowment** $29.7 million
- **Coed,** 17,102 undergraduate students, 75% full-time, 55% women, 45% men
- **Moderately difficult** entrance level, 66% of applicants were admitted

Undergraduates 12,796 full-time, 4,306 part-time. Students come from 52 states and territories, 129 other countries, 10% are from out of state, 8% African American, 17% Asian American or Pacific Islander, 8% Hispanic American, 0.4% Native American, 4% international, 13% transferred in, 21% live on campus. *Retention:* 82% of 2002 full-time freshmen returned.

Freshmen *Admission:* 9,768 applied, 6,460 admitted, 2,251 enrolled. *Average high school GPA:* 3.32. *Test scores:* SAT verbal scores over 500: 75%; SAT math scores over 500: 80%; ACT scores over 18: 91%; SAT verbal scores over 600: 27%; SAT math scores over 600: 31%; ACT scores over 24: 34%; SAT verbal scores over 700: 3%; SAT math scores over 700: 4%; ACT scores over 30: 4%.

Faculty *Total:* 1,855, 52% full-time, 51% with terminal degrees. *Student/faculty ratio:* 16:1.

Majors Accounting; anthropology; art; art history, criticism and conservation; biology/biological sciences; business administration and management; business, management, and marketing related; chemistry; civil engineering related; clinical laboratory science/medical technology; computer and information sciences; computer engineering; criminal justice/police science; dance; dramatic/theatre arts; economics; electrical, electronics and communications engineering; English; finance; fine/studio arts; foreign languages and literatures; geography; geology/earth science; health professions related; health teacher education; history; interdisciplinary studies; international relations and affairs; liberal arts and sciences/liberal studies; marketing/marketing management; mathematics; music performance; nursing (registered nurse training); philosophy; physical education teaching and coaching; physics; political science and government; psychology; public administration; religious studies; Russian studies; social work; sociology; solid state and low-temperature physics; speech and rhetoric; systems engineering; visual and performing arts.

Academic Programs *Special study options:* accelerated degree program, adult/continuing education programs, advanced placement credit, cooperative education, distance learning, double majors, English as a second language, external degree program, honors programs, independent study, internships, off-campus study, part-time degree program, services for LD students, student-designed majors, study abroad, summer session for credit. *ROTC:* Army (b), Air Force (c).

Library Fenwick Library plus 1 other with 1.5 million titles, 27,708 serial subscriptions, 27,344 audiovisual materials, an OPAC, a Web page.

Computers on Campus 1500 computers available on campus for general student use. A campuswide network can be accessed from student residence rooms and from off campus that provide access to telephone registration. Internet access, at least one staffed computer lab available.

Student Life *Housing options:* coed, men-only, women-only, disabled students. Campus housing is university owned and leased by the school. Freshman campus housing is guaranteed. *Activities and organizations:* drama/theater group, student-run newspaper, radio and television station, choral group, intramurals, Greek life, student government, club sports, volunteer and community service, national fraternities, national sororities. *Campus security:* 24-hour emergency response devices and patrols, student patrols, late-night transport/escort service, controlled dormitory access. *Student services:* health clinic, personal/psychological counseling, women's center.

Athletics Member NCAA. All Division I. *Intercollegiate sports:* baseball M(s), basketball M(s)/W(s), cheerleading M/W, cross-country running M(s)/W(s), golf M(s), lacrosse W(s), soccer M(s)/W(s), softball W(s), swimming M(s)/W(s), tennis M(s)/W(s), track and field M(s)/W(s), volleyball M(s)/W(s), wrestling M(s). *Intramural sports:* archery M, basketball M/W, crew M/W, cross-country running M/W, field hockey W, football M, ice hockey M, lacrosse M, racquetball

M/W, rugby M/W, soccer M/W, tennis M/W, track and field M/W, ultimate Frisbee M/W, volleyball M/W, water polo M/W.

Standardized Tests *Required:* SAT I or ACT (for admission). *Recommended:* SAT II: Subject Tests (for admission).

Costs (2003–04) *Tuition:* state resident $3630 full-time, $213 per credit part-time; nonresident $13,470 full-time, $623 per credit part-time. Full-time tuition and fees vary according to course load. Part-time tuition and fees vary according to course load. *Required fees:* $1482 full-time. *Room and board:* $6040; room only: $3640. Room and board charges vary according to board plan and housing facility. *Payment plans:* tuition prepayment, installment, deferred payment. *Waivers:* senior citizens and employees or children of employees.

Financial Aid Of all full-time matriculated undergraduates who enrolled in 2003, 9,257 applied for aid, 6,351 were judged to have need, 2,866 had their need fully met. 438 Federal Work-Study jobs (averaging $2327). In 2003, 1840 non-need-based awards were made. *Average percent of need met:* 63%. *Average financial aid package:* $6917. *Average need-based loan:* $3628. *Average need-based gift aid:* $4266. *Average non-need-based aid:* $6815. *Average indebtedness upon graduation:* $14,215.

Applying *Options:* common application, electronic application, early admission, deferred entrance. *Application fee:* $40. *Required:* essay or personal statement, high school transcript, minimum 2.0 GPA, interview. *Recommended:* minimum 3.0 GPA, letters of recommendation. *Application deadlines:* 1/15 (freshmen), 3/15 (transfers). *Notification:* 4/1 (freshmen), 4/1 (transfers).

Admissions Contact Mr. Eddie Tallent, Director of Admissions, George Mason University, 4400 University Drive, MSN 3A4, Fairfax, VA 22030-4444. *Phone:* 703-993-2398. *Fax:* 703-993-2392. *E-mail:* admissions@gmu.edu.

HAMPDEN-SYDNEY COLLEGE

Hampden-Sydney, Virginia

- **Independent** 4-year, founded 1776, affiliated with Presbyterian Church (U.S.A.)
- **Calendar** semesters
- **Degree** bachelor's
- **Rural** 660-acre campus with easy access to Richmond
- **Endowment** $87.6 million
- **Men only,** 1,039 undergraduate students, 99% full-time
- **Moderately difficult** entrance level, 71% of applicants were admitted

Undergraduates 1,033 full-time, 6 part-time. Students come from 36 states and territories, 9 other countries, 36% are from out of state, 4% African American, 1% Asian American or Pacific Islander, 1% Hispanic American, 0.5% Native American, 2% international, 2% transferred in, 95% live on campus. *Retention:* 74% of 2002 full-time freshmen returned.

Freshmen *Admission:* 306 enrolled. *Average high school GPA:* 3.1. *Test scores:* SAT verbal scores over 500: 80%; SAT math scores over 500: 85%; ACT scores over 18: 87%; SAT verbal scores over 600: 34%; SAT math scores over 600: 35%; ACT scores over 24: 41%; SAT verbal scores over 700: 7%; SAT math scores over 700: 3%; ACT scores over 30: 7%.

Faculty *Total:* 106, 82% full-time, 73% with terminal degrees. *Student/faculty ratio:* 11:1.

Majors Ancient/classical Greek; applied mathematics; biochemistry; biology/biological sciences; biophysics; business/managerial economics; chemistry; classics and languages, literatures and linguistics; computer science; econometrics and quantitative economics; economics; English; fine/studio arts; French; German; history; humanities; international relations and affairs; Latin; mathematics; mathematics and computer science; philosophy; physics; physics related; political science and government; psychology; religious studies; Spanish.

Academic Programs *Special study options:* academic remediation for entering students, accelerated degree program, advanced placement credit, double majors, honors programs, independent study, internships, off-campus study, study abroad, summer session for credit. *ROTC:* Army (c). *Unusual degree programs:* 3-2 engineering with University of Virginia.

Library Eggleston Library with 219,221 titles, 948 serial subscriptions, an OPAC, a Web page.

Computers on Campus 140 computers available on campus for general student use. A campuswide network can be accessed from student residence rooms and from off campus. At least one staffed computer lab available.

Student Life *Housing:* on-campus residence required through senior year. *Options:* men-only. Campus housing is university owned. Freshman campus housing is guaranteed. *Activities and organizations:* drama/theater group, student-run newspaper, radio station, choral group, Republican Society, Pre-Health Society, Outsiders Club, Tiger Athletic Club, Pre-Law Society, national fraternities. *Campus security:* 24-hour emergency response devices and patrols. *Student services:* health clinic, personal/psychological counseling.

Athletics Member NCAA. All Division III. *Intercollegiate sports:* baseball M, basketball M, crew M(c), cross-country running M, fencing M(c), football M, golf M, lacrosse M, riflery M(c), rugby M(c), soccer M, tennis M, ultimate Frisbee M(c). *Intramural sports:* basketball M, football M, soccer M, softball M, volleyball M.

Standardized Tests *Required:* SAT I or ACT (for admission). *Recommended:* SAT II: Subject Tests (for admission), SAT II: Writing Test (for admission).

Costs (2003–04) *Comprehensive fee:* $28,407 includes full-time tuition ($20,446), mandatory fees ($941), and room and board ($7020). Part-time tuition: $665 per credit hour. *College room only:* $2968. Room and board charges vary according to board plan and housing facility. *Payment plan:* installment. *Waivers:* employees or children of employees.

Financial Aid Of all full-time matriculated undergraduates who enrolled in 2003, 954 applied for aid, 539 were judged to have need, 171 had their need fully met. 257 Federal Work-Study jobs (averaging $1262). In 2003, 436 non-need-based awards were made. *Average percent of need met:* 84%. *Average financial aid package:* $15,761. *Average need-based loan:* $3801. *Average need-based gift aid:* $12,389. *Average non-need-based aid:* $14,307. *Average indebtedness upon graduation:* $15,571.

Applying *Options:* common application, electronic application, early admission, early decision, early action. *Application fee:* $30. *Required:* essay or personal statement, high school transcript, minimum 2.0 GPA, 2 letters of recommendation. *Recommended:* minimum 3.0 GPA, interview. *Application deadlines:* 3/1 (freshmen), 7/1 (transfers). *Early decision:* 11/15. *Notification:* continuous until 4/15 (freshmen), 12/15 (early decision), 2/15 (early action).

Admissions Contact Ms. Anita H. Garland, Dean of Admissions, Hampden-Sydney College, PO Box 667, Hampden-Sydney, VA 23943-0667. *Phone:* 434-223-6120. *Toll-free phone:* 800-755-0733. *Fax:* 434-223-6346. *E-mail:* hsapp@hsc.edu.

■ *See page 1704 for a narrative description.*

HAMPTON UNIVERSITY

Hampton, Virginia

- **Independent** university, founded 1868
- **Calendar** semesters
- **Degrees** certificates, associate, bachelor's, master's, doctoral, and first professional
- **Urban** 210-acre campus with easy access to Norfolk
- **Endowment** $165.3 million
- **Coed,** 4,979 undergraduate students, 90% full-time, 61% women, 39% men
- **Moderately difficult** entrance level, 62% of applicants were admitted

Undergraduates 4,486 full-time, 493 part-time. Students come from 37 states and territories, 69% are from out of state, 96% African American, 0.1% Asian American or Pacific Islander, 0.5% Hispanic American, 0.2% Native American, 0.5% international, 2% transferred in, 59% live on campus. *Retention:* 85% of 2002 full-time freshmen returned.

Freshmen *Admission:* 5,696 applied, 3,505 admitted, 1,050 enrolled. *Average high school GPA:* 3.00. *Test scores:* SAT verbal scores over 500: 66%; SAT math scores over 500: 53%; ACT scores over 18: 64%; SAT verbal scores over 600: 19%; SAT math scores over 600: 7%; ACT scores over 24: 4%; SAT verbal scores over 700: 1%; SAT math scores over 700: 1%; ACT scores over 30: 1%.

Faculty *Total:* 400, 71% full-time, 59% with terminal degrees. *Student/faculty ratio:* 16:1.

Majors Accounting; advertising; air traffic control; architecture; Army R.O.T.C./military science; art; art teacher education; audiology and speech-language pathology; aviation/airway management; avionics maintenance technology; biology/biological sciences; broadcast journalism; business administration and management; business teacher education; ceramic arts and ceramics; chemical engineering; chemistry; child development; commercial and advertising art; computer science; construction engineering technology; construction management; criminal justice/law enforcement administration; developmental and child psychology; dramatic/theatre arts; drawing; economics; education; electrical, electronic and communications engineering technology; electrical, electronics and communications engineering; elementary education; English; environmental studies; family and consumer sciences/home economics teacher education; fashion/apparel design; fashion merchandising; finance; fire science; general studies; health teacher education; history; hotel/motel administration; information science/studies; interior design; jazz/jazz studies; journalism; kindergarten/preschool education; legal assistant/paralegal; marine biology and biological oceanography; marine science/merchant marine officer; marketing/marketing management; mass communication/media; mathematics; middle school education; modern languages; molecular biology; music; music related; music teacher education; Navy/Marine Corps R.O.T.C./naval science; nursing (registered nurse training); photography; physical education teaching and coaching; physical sciences; physical therapy; physics; political science and government; pre-dentistry studies; pre-law studies; pre-medical studies; pre-veterinary studies; psychology; public

Hampton University (continued)
relations/image management; religious studies; sales, distribution and marketing; secondary education; social sciences; social work; sociology; special education; speech therapy; sport and fitness administration; therapeutic recreation.

Academic Programs *Special study options:* academic remediation for entering students, accelerated degree program, adult/continuing education programs, advanced placement credit, cooperative education, distance learning, double majors, honors programs, independent study, internships, off-campus study, part-time degree program, services for LD students, study abroad, summer session for credit. *ROTC:* Army (b), Navy (b).

Library William R. and Norma B. Harvey Library plus 3 others with 336,092 titles, 1,414 serial subscriptions, 1,649 audiovisual materials, an OPAC, a Web page.

Computers on Campus 1300 computers available on campus for general student use. A campuswide network can be accessed from student residence rooms and from off campus. Internet access, online (class) registration, at least one staffed computer lab available. Computer purchase or lease plan available.

Student Life *Housing options:* coed, men-only, women-only. Campus housing is university owned. Freshman applicants given priority for college housing. *Activities and organizations:* drama/theater group, student-run newspaper, radio station, choral group, marching band, student government, student leaders, Student Union Board, student recruitment team, resident assistants, national fraternities, national sororities. *Campus security:* 24-hour emergency response devices and patrols, controlled dormitory access, emergency call boxes. *Student services:* health clinic, personal/psychological counseling, women's center.

Athletics Member NCAA. All Division I. *Intercollegiate sports:* basketball M(s)/W(s), bowling W(s), cross-country running M(s)/W(s), football M(s), golf M(s)/W(s), sailing M(s)/W(s), softball W(s), tennis M(s)/W(s), track and field M(s)/W(s), volleyball W(s). *Intramural sports:* basketball M/W, bowling W, football M, sailing M/W, soccer M/W, softball M/W, volleyball W.

Standardized Tests *Required:* SAT I or ACT (for admission).

Costs (2003–04) *Comprehensive fee:* $18,982 includes full-time tuition ($12,864) and room and board ($6118). Part-time tuition: $290 per credit. *Room and board:* Room and board charges vary according to housing facility. *Payment plan:* deferred payment.

Financial Aid Of all full-time matriculated undergraduates who enrolled in 2003, 3,043 applied for aid, 3,021 were judged to have need, 49 had their need fully met. 362 Federal Work-Study jobs (averaging $1703). In 2003, 88 non-need-based awards were made. *Average percent of need met:* 27%. *Average financial aid package:* $2660. *Average need-based loan:* $2445. *Average need-based gift aid:* $1852. *Average non-need-based aid:* $1686. *Average indebtedness upon graduation:* $5433. *Financial aid deadline:* 3/1.

Applying *Options:* common application, electronic application, early admission, deferred entrance. *Application fee:* $25. *Required:* essay or personal statement, high school transcript, minimum 2.0 GPA, 1 letter of recommendation. *Application deadlines:* 3/1 (freshmen), 3/1 (transfers). *Notification:* continuous until 7/31 (freshmen), continuous until 7/31 (transfers).

Admissions Contact Ms. Angela Boyd, Director of Admissions, Hampton University, Hampton, VA 23668. *Phone:* 757-727-5328. *Toll-free phone:* 800-624-3328. *Fax:* 757-727-5095. *E-mail:* admit@hamptonu.edu.

■ *See page 1708 for a narrative description.*

HOLLINS UNIVERSITY
Roanoke, Virginia

- **Independent** comprehensive, founded 1842
- **Calendar** 4-1-4
- **Degrees** bachelor's, master's, and post-master's certificates
- **Suburban** 475-acre campus
- **Endowment** $85.1 million
- **Women only,** 812 undergraduate students, 97% full-time
- **Moderately difficult** entrance level, 86% of applicants were admitted

Undergraduates 784 full-time, 28 part-time. Students come from 47 states and territories, 10 other countries, 50% are from out of state, 7% African American, 1% Asian American or Pacific Islander, 3% Hispanic American, 0.9% Native American, 3% international, 3% transferred in, 91% live on campus. *Retention:* 71% of 2002 full-time freshmen returned.

Freshmen *Admission:* 202 enrolled. *Average high school GPA:* 3.38. *Test scores:* SAT verbal scores over 500: 89%; SAT math scores over 500: 77%; ACT scores over 18: 93%; SAT verbal scores over 600: 53%; SAT math scores over 600: 26%; ACT scores over 24: 53%; SAT verbal scores over 700: 12%; SAT math scores over 700: 2%; ACT scores over 30: 6%.

Faculty *Total:* 107, 69% full-time, 82% with terminal degrees. *Student/faculty ratio:* 9:1.

Majors Art history, criticism and conservation; biology/biological sciences; business/commerce; chemistry; classics and languages, literatures and linguistics; communication/speech communication and rhetoric; computer science; creative writing; dance; dramatic/theatre arts; economics; English; fine/studio arts; French; German; history; information science/studies; interdisciplinary studies; international relations and affairs; liberal arts and sciences/liberal studies; mathematics; music; philosophy; physics; political science and government; psychology; religious studies; sociology; Spanish; women's studies.

Academic Programs *Special study options:* accelerated degree program, adult/continuing education programs, advanced placement credit, double majors, independent study, internships, off-campus study, part-time degree program, student-designed majors, study abroad. *Unusual degree programs:* 3-2 engineering with Virginia Polytechnic Institute and State University, Washington University in St. Louis.

Library Wyndham Robertson Library plus 1 other with 163,896 titles, 12,749 serial subscriptions, 3,867 audiovisual materials, an OPAC, a Web page.

Computers on Campus 100 computers available on campus for general student use. A campuswide network can be accessed from student residence rooms and from off campus that provide access to applications software. Internet access, at least one staffed computer lab available.

Student Life *Housing:* on-campus residence required through senior year. *Options:* women-only. Campus housing is university owned. Freshman campus housing is guaranteed. *Activities and organizations:* drama/theater group, student-run newspaper, choral group, Student Government Association, SHARE (volunteer group), Religious Life Association, Student Athletic Association, campus political organizations. *Campus security:* 24-hour emergency response devices and patrols, late-night transport/escort service, controlled dormitory access, emergency call boxes. *Student services:* health clinic, personal/psychological counseling, women's center.

Athletics Member NCAA. All Division III. *Intercollegiate sports:* basketball W, cross-country running W, equestrian sports W, fencing W(c), field hockey W, golf W, lacrosse W, soccer W, swimming W, tennis W, volleyball W.

Standardized Tests *Required:* SAT I or ACT (for admission). *Recommended:* SAT II: Subject Tests (for admission).

Costs (2003–04) *Comprehensive fee:* $27,965 includes full-time tuition ($20,200), mandatory fees ($475), and room and board ($7290). Part-time tuition: $631 per credit. *Required fees:* $188 per year part-time. *College room only:* $4374. *Payment plan:* installment.

Financial Aid Of all full-time matriculated undergraduates who enrolled in 2003, 745 applied for aid, 505 were judged to have need, 106 had their need fully met. 281 Federal Work-Study jobs (averaging $2020). 77 state and other part-time jobs (averaging $1553). In 2003, 235 non-need-based awards were made. *Average percent of need met:* 79%. *Average financial aid package:* $17,513. *Average need-based loan:* $4630. *Average need-based gift aid:* $12,402. *Average non-need-based aid:* $7558. *Average indebtedness upon graduation:* $18,167. *Financial aid deadline:* 2/15.

Applying *Options:* common application, electronic application, early decision, deferred entrance. *Application fee:* $35. *Required:* essay or personal statement, high school transcript, 1 letter of recommendation. *Recommended:* interview. *Application deadlines:* 2/15 (freshmen), 6/1 (transfers). *Early decision:* 12/1. *Notification:* continuous (freshmen), 12/15 (early decision), continuous (transfers).

Admissions Contact Ms. Celia McCormick, Dean of Admissions, Hollins University, PO Box 9707, Roanoke, VA 24020-1707. *Phone:* 540-362-6401. *Toll-free phone:* 800-456-9595. *Fax:* 540-362-6218. *E-mail:* huadm@hollins.edu.

■ *See page 1742 for a narrative description.*

ITT TECHNICAL INSTITUTE
Norfolk, Virginia

- **Proprietary** primarily 2-year, founded 1988, part of ITT Educational Services, Inc.
- **Calendar** quarters
- **Degrees** associate and bachelor's
- **Suburban** 2-acre campus
- **Coed**
- **Minimally difficult** entrance level

Standardized Tests *Required:* Wonderlic aptitude test (for admission).

Costs (2003–04) *Tuition:* $347 per credit hour part-time.

Financial Aid Of all full-time matriculated undergraduates who enrolled in 2001, 3 Federal Work-Study jobs (averaging $5000).

Applying *Options:* deferred entrance. *Application fee:* $100. *Required:* high school transcript, interview. *Recommended:* letters of recommendation.

Admissions Contact Mr. Jack Keesee, Director of Recruitment, ITT Technical Institute, 863 Glenrock Road, Norfolk, VA 23502. *Phone:* 757-466-1260. *Toll-free phone:* 888-253-8324. *Fax:* 757-466-7630.

ITT TECHNICAL INSTITUTE
Richmond, Virginia

- **Proprietary** primarily 2-year, part of ITT Educational Services, Inc.
- **Calendar** quarters
- **Degrees** associate and bachelor's
- **Coed**
- **Minimally difficult** entrance level

Standardized Tests *Required:* Wonderlic aptitude test (for admission).

Costs (2003–04) *Tuition:* $347 per credit hour part-time.

Applying *Options:* deferred entrance. *Application fee:* $100. *Required:* high school transcript, interview. *Recommended:* letters of recommendation.

Admissions Contact Mr. Marc Wright, Director of Recruitment, ITT Technical Institute, 300 Gateway Centre Parkway, Richmond, VA 23235. *Phone:* 804-330-4992. *Toll-free phone:* 888-330-4888. *Fax:* 804-330-4993.

JAMES MADISON UNIVERSITY
Harrisonburg, Virginia

- **State-supported** comprehensive, founded 1908
- **Calendar** semesters
- **Degrees** bachelor's, master's, doctoral, and post-master's certificates (also offers specialist in education degree)
- **Small-town** 605-acre campus
- **Endowment** $23.8 million
- **Coed,** 14,991 undergraduate students, 96% full-time, 60% women, 40% men
- **Very difficult** entrance level, 62% of applicants were admitted

Undergraduates 14,354 full-time, 637 part-time. Students come from 49 states and territories, 48 other countries, 30% are from out of state, 3% African American, 5% Asian American or Pacific Islander, 2% Hispanic American, 0.2% Native American, 0.9% international, 4% transferred in, 40% live on campus. *Retention:* 92% of 2002 full-time freshmen returned.

Freshmen *Admission:* 15,056 applied, 9,404 admitted, 3,388 enrolled. *Test scores:* SAT verbal scores over 500: 89%; SAT math scores over 500: 89%; SAT verbal scores over 600: 35%; SAT math scores over 600: 39%; SAT verbal scores over 700: 3%; SAT math scores over 700: 3%.

Faculty *Total:* 996, 72% full-time, 67% with terminal degrees. *Student/faculty ratio:* 17:1.

Majors Accounting; anthropology; art; art history, criticism and conservation; biology/biological sciences; business administration and management; business/managerial economics; business teacher education; chemistry; communication/speech communication and rhetoric; community health services counseling; computer and information sciences; dramatic/theatre arts; economics; English; finance; foods, nutrition, and wellness; foreign languages and literatures; geography; geology/earth science; health and physical education; history; hospitality administration; information science/studies; international business/trade/commerce; international relations and affairs; liberal arts and sciences/liberal studies; marketing/marketing management; mathematics; music performance; nursing (registered nurse training); philosophy and religious studies related; physics; political science and government; psychology; public administration; science, technology and society; social sciences; social work; sociology; speech-language pathology; technical and business writing.

Academic Programs *Special study options:* accelerated degree program, adult/continuing education programs, advanced placement credit, distance learning, double majors, freshman honors college, honors programs, independent study, internships, part-time degree program, services for LD students, study abroad, summer session for credit. *ROTC:* Army (b), Air Force (c).

Library Carrier Library plus 2 others with 744,041 titles, 3,367 serial subscriptions, 31,424 audiovisual materials, an OPAC, a Web page.

Computers on Campus 600 computers available on campus for general student use. A campuswide network can be accessed from student residence rooms and from off campus. Internet access, online (class) registration, at least one staffed computer lab available. Computer purchase or lease plan available.

Student Life *Housing:* on-campus residence required for freshman year. *Options:* coed. Campus housing is university owned and leased by the school. *Activities and organizations:* drama/theater group, student-run newspaper, radio station, choral group, marching band, Student Ambassadors, sports clubs, Greek organizations, service organizations, special interest groups, national fraternities, national sororities. *Campus security:* 24-hour emergency response devices and patrols, student patrols, late-night transport/escort service, controlled dormitory access, lighted pathways. *Student services:* health clinic, personal/psychological counseling.

Athletics Member NCAA. All Division I except football (Division I-AA). *Intercollegiate sports:* archery M/W, baseball M(s), basketball M(s)/W(s), cross-country running M(s)/W(s), fencing W, field hockey W(s), golf M/W, gymnastics M/W, lacrosse W(s), soccer M(s)/W(s), softball W(s), swimming M/W, tennis M/W, track and field M(s)/W(s), volleyball W(s), wrestling M. *Intramural sports:* badminton M/W, baseball M(c), basketball M/W, bowling M/W, cheerleading W(c), cross-country running M(c)/W(c), equestrian sports M(c)/W(c), fencing M(c)/W(c), field hockey M(c)/W(c), football M/W, golf M/W, gymnastics M(c)/W(c), lacrosse M(c)/W(c), racquetball M/W, rugby M(c)/W(c), skiing (downhill) M(c)/W(c), soccer M/W, softball M/W, swimming M(c)/W(c), table tennis M/W, tennis M/W, ultimate Frisbee M/W, volleyball M/W.

Standardized Tests *Required:* SAT I or ACT (for admission).

Costs (2003–04) *Tuition:* state resident $5058 full-time; nonresident $13,280 full-time. Part-time tuition and fees vary according to course load. *Room and board:* $5966; room only: $3088. Room and board charges vary according to board plan and housing facility. *Payment plan:* installment. *Waivers:* senior citizens and employees or children of employees.

Financial Aid Of all full-time matriculated undergraduates who enrolled in 2003, 10,875 applied for aid, 6,716 were judged to have need, 2,116 had their need fully met. 1,728 Federal Work-Study jobs (averaging $1638). In 2003, 287 non-need-based awards were made. *Average percent of need met:* 52%. *Average financial aid package:* $6102. *Average need-based loan:* $3676. *Average need-based gift aid:* $4380. *Average non-need-based aid:* $1602. *Average indebtedness upon graduation:* $11,639.

Applying *Options:* electronic application, early action, deferred entrance. *Application fee:* $40. *Required:* essay or personal statement, high school transcript. *Recommended:* minimum 3.0 GPA. *Application deadlines:* 1/15 (freshmen), 3/1 (transfers). *Notification:* 4/1 (freshmen), 1/15 (early action), 4/15 (transfers).

Admissions Contact Ms. Laika K. Tamny, Associate Director of Admissions, James Madison University, Office of Admission, Sonner Hall MSC 0101, Harrisonburg, VA 22807. *Phone:* 540-568-5681. *Fax:* 540-568-3332. *E-mail:* gotojmu@jmu.edu.

JEFFERSON COLLEGE OF HEALTH SCIENCES
Roanoke, Virginia

- **Independent** 4-year, founded 1982
- **Calendar** semesters
- **Degrees** certificates, associate, and bachelor's
- **Urban** 1-acre campus
- **Endowment** $3.8 million
- **Coed**
- **Moderately difficult** entrance level

Faculty *Student/faculty ratio:* 11:1.

Student Life *Campus security:* 24-hour emergency response devices and patrols, late-night transport/escort service, controlled dormitory access.

Standardized Tests *Required for some:* SAT I or ACT (for admission), ACT ASSET. *Recommended:* SAT I (for admission).

Costs (2003–04) *Tuition:* $5640 full-time, $235 per credit hour part-time. Full-time tuition and fees vary according to course level, course load, degree level, and program. Part-time tuition and fees vary according to course level, course load, degree level, and program. *Required fees:* $150 full-time. *Room only:* $2000.

Financial Aid Of all full-time matriculated undergraduates who enrolled in 2001, 195 applied for aid, 182 were judged to have need, 9 had their need fully met. In 2001, 33. *Average percent of need met:* 58. *Average financial aid package:* $8457. *Average need-based loan:* $5397. *Average need-based gift aid:* $4275. *Average non-need-based aid:* $5787. *Average indebtedness upon graduation:* $4112.

Applying *Options:* early decision. *Application fee:* $50. *Required:* essay or personal statement, high school transcript, minimum 2.0 GPA. *Required for some:* letters of recommendation, interview, volunteer experience.

Admissions Contact Ms. Connie Cook, Admissions Representative, Jefferson College of Health Sciences, PO Box 13186, Roanoke, VA 24031-3186. *Phone:* 540-985-8563. *Toll-free phone:* 888-985-8483. *Fax:* 540-985-9773. *E-mail:* jmckeon@chs.edu.

LIBERTY UNIVERSITY
Lynchburg, Virginia

- **Independent nondenominational** comprehensive, founded 1971
- **Calendar** semesters
- **Degrees** certificates, associate, bachelor's, master's, doctoral, first professional, and post-master's certificates (also offers external degree program with significant enrollment not reflected in profile)
- **Suburban** 230-acre campus
- **Endowment** $3.3 million

Liberty University (continued)

■ **Coed,** 7,613 undergraduate students, 85% full-time, 52% women, 48% men
■ **Minimally difficult** entrance level, 96% of applicants were admitted

Undergraduates 6,487 full-time, 1,126 part-time. Students come from 52 states and territories, 72 other countries, 60% are from out of state, 11% African American, 2% Asian American or Pacific Islander, 3% Hispanic American, 0.6% Native American, 3% international, 13% transferred in, 53% live on campus. *Retention:* 70% of 2002 full-time freshmen returned.

Freshmen *Admission:* 4,055 applied, 3,883 admitted, 1,897 enrolled. *Average high school GPA:* 3.10. *Test scores:* SAT verbal scores over 500: 56%; SAT math scores over 500: 46%; ACT scores over 18: 79%; SAT verbal scores over 600: 18%; SAT math scores over 600: 13%; ACT scores over 24: 29%; SAT verbal scores over 700: 3%; SAT math scores over 700: 1%; ACT scores over 30: 3%.

Faculty *Total:* 339, 64% full-time, 51% with terminal degrees. *Student/faculty ratio:* 25:1.

Majors Accounting; adult development and aging; advertising; athletic training; biblical studies; biology/biological sciences; biology teacher education; broadcast journalism; business administration and management; business/commerce; business teacher education; clinical psychology; communication/speech communication and rhetoric; computer and information sciences; computer teacher education; counseling psychology; criminal justice/law enforcement administration; developmental and child psychology; divinity/ministry; economics; educational leadership and administration; education (multiple levels); elementary education; English; English as a second/foreign language (teaching); English/language arts teacher education; family and community services; family and consumer sciences/home economics teacher education; family and consumer sciences/human sciences; fashion merchandising; finance; general studies; graphic design; health and physical education; health services/allied health/health sciences; health teacher education; history; history teacher education; interdisciplinary studies; international business/trade/commerce; journalism; journalism related; kinesiology and exercise science; management information systems; marketing/marketing management; mathematics; mathematics teacher education; missionary studies and missiology; multi-/interdisciplinary studies related; music; music teacher education; nursing (registered nurse training); pastoral studies/counseling; philosophy; physical education teaching and coaching; political science and government; political science and government related; pre-theology/pre-ministerial studies; psychology; public relations/image management; radio and television broadcasting technology; religious/sacred music; religious studies; science teacher education; secondary education; social sciences; social sciences related; social science teacher education; Spanish; Spanish language teacher education; special education; sport and fitness administration; youth ministry.

Academic Programs *Special study options:* academic remediation for entering students, accelerated degree program, advanced placement credit, distance learning, double majors, English as a second language, external degree program, honors programs, independent study, internships, part-time degree program, services for LD students, student-designed majors, summer session for credit. *ROTC:* Army (b), Air Force (c).

Library A. Pierre Guillermin Integrated Learning Resource Center plus 1 other with 192,985 titles, 9,072 serial subscriptions, 5,027 audiovisual materials, an OPAC, a Web page.

Computers on Campus 250 computers available on campus for general student use. A campuswide network can be accessed from student residence rooms and from off campus. Internet access, online (class) registration, at least one staffed computer lab available.

Student Life *Housing:* on-campus residence required through junior year. *Options:* men-only, women-only, disabled students. Campus housing is university owned and leased by the school. Freshman campus housing is guaranteed. *Activities and organizations:* drama/theater group, student-run newspaper, radio station, choral group, marching band, College Republicans, Youthquest, Circle K. *Campus security:* 24-hour patrols, late-night transport/escort service, 24-hour emergency dispatch. *Student services:* health clinic, personal/psychological counseling.

Athletics Member NCAA. All Division I except football (Division I-AA). *Intercollegiate sports:* baseball M(s), basketball M(s)/W(s), cheerleading M(s)/W(s), cross-country running M(s)/W(s), field hockey W(c), golf M(s), ice hockey M(c), lacrosse M(c), soccer M(s)/W(s), softball W(s), tennis M(s)/W(s), track and field M(s)/W(s), volleyball W(s). *Intramural sports:* basketball M/W, football M/W, soccer M/W, softball M/W, tennis M/W, volleyball M/W.

Standardized Tests *Required:* SAT I or ACT (for admission). *Required for some:* ACT (for admission).

Costs (2004–05) *Comprehensive fee:* $18,550 includes full-time tuition ($12,600), mandatory fees ($550), and room and board ($5400). Full-time tuition and fees vary according to course load. Part-time tuition: $420 per semester hour. Part-time tuition and fees vary according to course load. *Required fees:* $275 per term part-time. *Room and board:* Room and board charges vary according to housing facility. *Payment plan:* installment. *Waivers:* employees or children of employees.

Financial Aid Of all full-time matriculated undergraduates who enrolled in 2003, 6,288 applied for aid, 4,998 were judged to have need, 613 had their need fully met. 1,046 Federal Work-Study jobs (averaging $2000). In 2003, 880 non-need-based awards were made. *Average percent of need met:* 66%. *Average financial aid package:* $9689. *Average need-based loan:* $3267. *Average need-based gift aid:* $4736. *Average non-need-based aid:* $5199. *Average indebtedness upon graduation:* $15,085.

Applying *Options:* electronic application, early admission, deferred entrance. *Application fee:* $35. *Required:* essay or personal statement, high school transcript. *Required for some:* 1 letter of recommendation, interview. *Recommended:* minimum 2.0 GPA, 1 letter of recommendation. *Application deadline:* 6/30 (freshmen). *Notification:* continuous until 8/15 (freshmen), continuous (transfers).

Admissions Contact Mr. David Hart, Director of Admissions, Liberty University, 1971 University Boulevard, Lynchburg, VA 24502. *Phone:* 434-582-2866. *Toll-free phone:* 800-543-5317. *Fax:* 800-542-2311. *E-mail:* admissions@liberty.edu.

■ *See page 1868 for a narrative description.*

LIFE BIBLE COLLEGE EAST
Christiansburg, Virginia

Admissions Contact 900 Life Drive, Christiansburg, VA 24073.

LONGWOOD UNIVERSITY
Farmville, Virginia

■ **State-supported** comprehensive, founded 1839, part of The State Council of Higher Education for Virginia (SCHEV)
■ **Calendar** semesters
■ **Degrees** bachelor's and master's
■ **Small-town** 160-acre campus with easy access to Richmond
■ **Endowment** $26.5 million
■ **Coed,** 3,685 undergraduate students, 97% full-time, 66% women, 34% men
■ **Moderately difficult** entrance level, 70% of applicants were admitted

Undergraduates 3,565 full-time, 120 part-time. Students come from 25 states and territories, 11 other countries, 10% are from out of state, 8% African American, 1% Asian American or Pacific Islander, 2% Hispanic American, 0.3% Native American, 0.5% international, 6% transferred in, 77% live on campus. *Retention:* 80% of 2002 full-time freshmen returned.

Freshmen *Admission:* 3,472 applied, 2,441 admitted, 880 enrolled. *Average high school GPA:* 3.30. *Test scores:* SAT verbal scores over 500: 79%; SAT math scores over 500: 75%; SAT verbal scores over 600: 19%; SAT math scores over 600: 15%; SAT verbal scores over 700: 1%; SAT math scores over 700: 1%.

Faculty *Total:* 228, 79% full-time, 66% with terminal degrees. *Student/faculty ratio:* 20:1.

Majors Accounting; anthropology; applied mathematics; Army R.O.T.C./military science; art; art history, criticism and conservation; art teacher education; athletic training; biology/biological sciences; biophysics; business administration and management; business/managerial economics; chemistry; clinical laboratory science/medical technology; clinical/medical laboratory technology; commercial and advertising art; communication disorders; communication/speech communication and rhetoric; community health services counseling; computer science; criminal justice/law enforcement administration; developmental and child psychology; dramatic/theatre arts; drawing; economics; education; elementary education; English; environmental studies; experimental psychology; finance; fine/studio arts; French; geography; geology/earth science; German; health science; health teacher education; history; interior design; international economics; international relations and affairs; journalism; kindergarten/preschool education; kinesiology and exercise science; liberal arts and sciences/liberal studies; library science; management information systems; marketing/marketing management; mathematics; modern languages; music; music teacher education; natural sciences; physical education teaching and coaching; physics; political science and government; pre-dentistry studies; pre-law studies; pre-medical studies; pre-pharmacy studies; pre-veterinary studies; printmaking; psychology; reading teacher education; science teacher education; sculpture; secondary education; social work; sociology; Spanish; special education; sport and fitness administration; therapeutic recreation.

Academic Programs *Special study options:* academic remediation for entering students, accelerated degree program, adult/continuing education programs, advanced placement credit, distance learning, double majors, English as a second language, honors programs, independent study, internships, off-campus study, part-time degree program, services for LD students, study abroad, summer session for credit. *ROTC:* Army (b). *Unusual degree programs:* 3-2 engineering with University of Virginia, Old Dominion University, University of Tennessee, Virginia Polytechnic Institute and University, Christopher Newport University.

Library Longwood Library with 242,056 titles, 2,505 serial subscriptions, 31,587 audiovisual materials, an OPAC, a Web page.

Computers on Campus 270 computers available on campus for general student use. A campuswide network can be accessed from student residence rooms and from off campus. Internet access, online (class) registration, at least one staffed computer lab available. Computer purchase or lease plan available.

Student Life *Housing:* on-campus residence required through junior year. *Options:* coed, women-only, disabled students. Campus housing is university owned. Freshman campus housing is guaranteed. *Activities and organizations:* drama/theater group, student-run newspaper, radio station, choral group, Student Government Association, Alpha Phi Omega, Intervarsity Christian, Longwood Ambassadors, Wellness Advocates, national fraternities, national sororities. *Campus security:* 24-hour emergency response devices and patrols, late-night transport/escort service, controlled dormitory access, security lighting. *Student services:* health clinic, personal/psychological counseling.

Athletics Member NCAA. All Division II. *Intercollegiate sports:* baseball M(s), basketball M(s)/W(s), cross-country running M(s)/W(s), equestrian sports M(c)/W(c), field hockey W(s), golf M(s)/W(s), lacrosse W(s), rugby M(c)/W(c), soccer M(s)/W(s), softball W(s), swimming M(c)/W(c), tennis M(s)/W(s), track and field M(c)/W(c), volleyball M(c)/W(c), wrestling M(c). *Intramural sports:* badminton M/W, basketball W, bowling M/W, cheerleading M/W, football M/W, golf M/W, racquetball M/W, soccer M/W, softball M/W, table tennis M/W, tennis M/W, ultimate Frisbee M/W, volleyball M/W.

Standardized Tests *Required:* SAT I or ACT (for admission).

Costs (2003–04) *Tuition:* state resident $3046 full-time, $127 per credit hour part-time; nonresident $8972 full-time, $374 per credit hour part-time. *Required fees:* $2831 full-time, $110 per credit hour part-time. *Room and board:* $5298; room only: $3114. Room and board charges vary according to board plan. *Payment plan:* installment. *Waivers:* senior citizens and employees or children of employees.

Financial Aid Of all full-time matriculated undergraduates who enrolled in 2002, 2,297 applied for aid, 1,557 were judged to have need, 524 had their need fully met. 404 Federal Work-Study jobs (averaging $1782). 405 state and other part-time jobs (averaging $766). In 2002, 788 non-need-based awards were made. *Average percent of need met:* 78%. *Average financial aid package:* $7200. *Average need-based loan:* $4011. *Average need-based gift aid:* $3855. *Average non-need-based aid:* $4746. *Average indebtedness upon graduation:* $14,495.

Applying *Options:* common application, electronic application, early admission, early action, deferred entrance. *Application fee:* $40. *Required:* essay or personal statement, high school transcript. *Required for some:* letters of recommendation, interview. *Recommended:* minimum 2.7 GPA. *Application deadlines:* 3/1 (freshmen), 6/1 (transfers). *Notification:* continuous until 6/1 (freshmen), 1/1 (early action), continuous until 8/1 (transfers).

Admissions Contact Mr. Robert J. Chonko, Director of Admissions, Longwood University, 201 High Street, Farmville, VA 23909. *Phone:* 434-395-2060. *Toll-free phone:* 800-281-4677. *Fax:* 434-395-2332. *E-mail:* admit@longwood.edu.

LYNCHBURG COLLEGE

Lynchburg, Virginia

- **Independent** comprehensive, founded 1903, affiliated with Christian Church (Disciples of Christ)
- **Calendar** semesters
- **Degrees** bachelor's and master's
- **Suburban** 214-acre campus
- **Endowment** $55.4 million
- **Coed,** 1,777 undergraduate students, 93% full-time, 60% women, 40% men
- **Moderately difficult** entrance level, 76% of applicants were admitted

Undergraduates 1,653 full-time, 124 part-time. Students come from 39 states and territories, 14 other countries, 44% are from out of state, 7% African American, 1% Asian American or Pacific Islander, 3% Hispanic American, 0.4% Native American, 0.9% international, 83% live on campus. *Retention:* 68% of 2002 full-time freshmen returned.

Freshmen *Admission:* 3,119 applied, 2,380 admitted, 589 enrolled. *Average high school GPA:* 3.00. *Test scores:* SAT verbal scores over 500: 56%; SAT math scores over 500: 58%; ACT scores over 18: 80%; SAT verbal scores over 600: 14%; SAT math scores over 600: 15%; ACT scores over 24: 16%; SAT verbal scores over 700: 1%; SAT math scores over 700: 1%; ACT scores over 30: 1%.

Faculty *Total:* 170, 73% full-time, 71% with terminal degrees. *Student/faculty ratio:* 13:1.

Majors Accounting; art; athletic training; biological and biomedical sciences related; biology/biological sciences; business administration and management; chemistry; communication/speech communication and rhetoric; computer science; creative writing; dramatic/theatre arts; economics; education; elementary education; English; environmental studies; French; health teacher education; history; international relations and affairs; journalism; kindergarten/preschool education; kinesiology and exercise science; marketing/marketing management; mass communication/media; mathematics; music; music performance; music theory and composition; nursing (registered nurse training); organizational communication; philosophy; physical education teaching and coaching; physics; political science and government; pre-dentistry studies; pre-law studies; pre-medical studies; pre-veterinary studies; psychology; religious studies; secondary education; sociology; Spanish; special education; speech and rhetoric; sport and fitness administration.

Academic Programs *Special study options:* accelerated degree program, adult/continuing education programs, advanced placement credit, double majors, honors programs, internships, off-campus study, part-time degree program, services for LD students, summer session for credit. *Unusual degree programs:* 3-2 engineering with Old Dominion University, University of Virginia.

Library Knight-Capron Library with 287,601 titles, 636 serial subscriptions, 9,360 audiovisual materials, an OPAC, a Web page.

Computers on Campus 217 computers available on campus for general student use. A campuswide network can be accessed from student residence rooms. Internet access, at least one staffed computer lab available.

Student Life *Housing:* on-campus residence required through junior year. *Options:* coed. Campus housing is university owned. Freshman campus housing is guaranteed. *Activities and organizations:* drama/theater group, student-run newspaper, choral group, Association of Commuter Students, Omicron Delta Kappa, Ski and Snowboarding Club, Kappa Delta, Baptist Student Union, national fraternities, national sororities. *Campus security:* 24-hour emergency response devices and patrols, late-night transport/escort service, controlled dormitory access. *Student services:* health clinic, personal/psychological counseling.

Athletics Member NCAA. All Division III. *Intercollegiate sports:* baseball M, basketball M/W, cheerleading M/W, cross-country running M/W, equestrian sports M/W, field hockey W, golf M, lacrosse M/W, soccer M/W, softball W, tennis M/W, track and field M/W, volleyball W. *Intramural sports:* badminton M/W, baseball M, basketball M/W, bowling M/W, equestrian sports M/W, football M, golf M, racquetball M/W, rugby M/W, soccer M/W, softball W, tennis M/W, track and field M/W, volleyball M/W.

Standardized Tests *Required:* SAT I or ACT (for admission).

Costs (2003–04) *Comprehensive fee:* $26,315 includes full-time tuition ($21,270), mandatory fees ($245), and room and board ($4800). Part-time tuition: $310 per credit hour. Part-time tuition and fees vary according to course load. *College room only:* $2800. Room and board charges vary according to board plan. *Payment plan:* installment. *Waivers:* adult students, senior citizens, and employees or children of employees.

Financial Aid Of all full-time matriculated undergraduates who enrolled in 2003, 1,235 applied for aid, 1,047 were judged to have need, 357 had their need fully met. 479 Federal Work-Study jobs (averaging $1064). In 2003, 596 non-need-based awards were made. *Average percent of need met:* 84%. *Average financial aid package:* $15,969. *Average need-based loan:* $4441. *Average need-based gift aid:* $11,958. *Average non-need-based aid:* $7856. *Average indebtedness upon graduation:* $17,727.

Applying *Options:* early admission, early decision, deferred entrance. *Application fee:* $30. *Required:* high school transcript. *Recommended:* essay or personal statement, 2 letters of recommendation, interview. *Application deadline:* rolling (freshmen), rolling (transfers). *Early decision:* 11/15. *Notification:* continuous (freshmen), 12/15 (early decision), continuous (transfers).

Admissions Contact Ms. Sharon Walters-Bower, Director of Admissions, Lynchburg College, 1501 Lakeside Drive, Lynchburg, VA 24501-3199. *Phone:* 434-544-8300. *Toll-free phone:* 800-426-8101. *Fax:* 434-544-8653. *E-mail:* admissions@lynchburg.edu.

■ *See page 1904 for a narrative description.*

MARY BALDWIN COLLEGE

Staunton, Virginia

- **Independent** comprehensive, founded 1842
- **Calendar** 4-4-1
- **Degrees** certificates, bachelor's, and master's
- **Small-town** 54-acre campus
- **Endowment** $33.1 million
- **Coed,** 1,565 undergraduate students, 70% full-time, 94% women, 6% men
- **Moderately difficult** entrance level, 76% of applicants were admitted

Undergraduates 1,100 full-time, 465 part-time. Students come from 39 states and territories, 7 other countries, 25% are from out of state, 18% African American, 2% Asian American or Pacific Islander, 3% Hispanic American, 0.4%

Mary Baldwin College (continued)
Native American, 1% international, 2% transferred in, 82% live on campus. *Retention:* 65% of 2002 full-time freshmen returned.

Freshmen *Admission:* 1,443 applied, 1,094 admitted, 278 enrolled. *Average high school GPA:* 3.25. *Test scores:* SAT verbal scores over 500: 71%; SAT math scores over 500: 55%; ACT scores over 18: 87%; SAT verbal scores over 600: 30%; SAT math scores over 600: 12%; ACT scores over 24: 43%; SAT verbal scores over 700: 5%; SAT math scores over 700: 5%; ACT scores over 30: 3%.

Faculty *Total:* 133, 57% full-time, 53% with terminal degrees. *Student/faculty ratio:* 11:1.

Majors Applied mathematics; art; arts management; Asian studies; biochemistry; biology/biological sciences; business administration and management; chemistry; clinical laboratory science/medical technology; communication and journalism related; communication/speech communication and rhetoric; computer and information sciences; dramatic/theatre arts; economics; English; French; German; health/health care administration; history; international relations and affairs; mathematics; multi-/interdisciplinary studies related; music; philosophy; physics; political science and government; psychology; religious studies; social work; sociology; Spanish.

Academic Programs *Special study options:* academic remediation for entering students, accelerated degree program, adult/continuing education programs, advanced placement credit, distance learning, double majors, English as a second language, external degree program, freshman honors college, honors programs, independent study, internships, off-campus study, part-time degree program, services for LD students, student-designed majors, study abroad. *ROTC:* Army (b), Navy (c), Air Force (c). *Unusual degree programs:* 3-2 engineering with University of Virginia; nursing with Vanderbilt University.

Library Grafton Library with 168,900 titles, 8,000 serial subscriptions, 9,250 audiovisual materials, an OPAC, a Web page.

Computers on Campus 220 computers available on campus for general student use. A campuswide network can be accessed from student residence rooms and from off campus. Internet access, online (class) registration, at least one staffed computer lab available.

Student Life *Housing:* on-campus residence required through senior year. *Options:* women-only. Campus housing is university owned. Freshman campus housing is guaranteed. *Activities and organizations:* drama/theater group, student-run newspaper, radio station, choral group, marching band, Student Senate, Baldwin Program Board, President's Society, Black Student Alliance, Stars. *Campus security:* 24-hour emergency response devices and patrols, late-night transport/escort service, controlled dormitory access. *Student services:* health clinic, personal/psychological counseling.

Athletics Member NCAA. All Division III. *Intercollegiate sports:* basketball W, cross-country running W(c), field hockey W(c), soccer W, softball W, swimming W, tennis W, volleyball W.

Standardized Tests *Required:* SAT I or ACT (for admission).

Costs (2003–04) *Comprehensive fee:* $24,939 includes full-time tuition ($19,234), mandatory fees ($180), and room and board ($5525). Full-time tuition and fees vary according to degree level and program. Part-time tuition: $325 per credit hour. Part-time tuition and fees vary according to degree level. *College room only:* $3525. Room and board charges vary according to housing facility. *Payment plan:* installment. *Waivers:* employees or children of employees.

Financial Aid Of all full-time matriculated undergraduates who enrolled in 2002, 928 applied for aid, 837 were judged to have need, 124 had their need fully met. 393 Federal Work-Study jobs (averaging $1691). 72 state and other part-time jobs (averaging $1397). In 2002, 195 non-need-based awards were made. *Average percent of need met:* 91%. *Average financial aid package:* $20,028. *Average need-based loan:* $4159. *Average need-based gift aid:* $10,228. *Average non-need-based aid:* $11,835. *Average indebtedness upon graduation:* $19,752. *Financial aid deadline:* 5/15.

Applying *Options:* common application, electronic application, early admission, early decision, deferred entrance. *Application fee:* $25. *Required:* high school transcript, minimum 2.0 GPA, 1 letter of recommendation. *Recommended:* interview. *Application deadline:* rolling (freshmen), rolling (transfers). *Early decision:* 11/15. *Notification:* continuous (freshmen), 12/1 (early decision), continuous (transfers).

Admissions Contact Ms. Brandy Tricia Caleb, Director, Freshmen Services, Mary Baldwin College, Frederick and New Streets, Staunton, VA 24401. *Phone:* 540-887-7221. *Toll-free phone:* 800-468-2262. *Fax:* 540-887-7292. *E-mail:* admit@mbc.edu.

MARYMOUNT UNIVERSITY
Arlington, Virginia

- **Independent** comprehensive, founded 1950, affiliated with Roman Catholic Church
- **Calendar** semesters plus 2 summer terms
- **Degrees** certificates, associate, bachelor's, master's, post-master's, and postbachelor's certificates
- **Suburban** 21-acre campus with easy access to Washington, DC
- **Endowment** $19.0 million
- **Coed,** 2,179 undergraduate students, 79% full-time, 75% women, 25% men
- **Moderately difficult** entrance level, 81% of applicants were admitted

Marymount is a comprehensive, coeducational Catholic university where students come first. It's a learning community where each student is known and valued, and where faculty members are committed to students' success. The University serves approximately 2,200 undergraduates and 1,600 graduate students. Located in Arlington, Virginia, Marymount University is just minutes from the resources of Washington, DC.

Undergraduates 1,725 full-time, 454 part-time. Students come from 43 states and territories, 61 other countries, 42% are from out of state, 17% African American, 7% Asian American or Pacific Islander, 10% Hispanic American, 0.2% Native American, 9% international, 15% transferred in, 31% live on campus. *Retention:* 69% of 2002 full-time freshmen returned.

Freshmen *Admission:* 1,665 applied, 1,349 admitted, 386 enrolled. *Average high school GPA:* 3.00. *Test scores:* SAT verbal scores over 500: 56%; SAT math scores over 500: 48%; ACT scores over 18: 62%; SAT verbal scores over 600: 14%; SAT math scores over 600: 10%; ACT scores over 24: 15%; SAT verbal scores over 700: 2%; SAT math scores over 700: 2%; ACT scores over 30: 3%.

Faculty *Total:* 378, 34% full-time, 53% with terminal degrees. *Student/faculty ratio:* 13:1.

Majors Accounting; biology/biological sciences; business administration and management; business administration, management and operations related; cell and molecular biology; communication/speech communication and rhetoric; computer and information sciences; computer science; criminal justice/safety; criminology; economics; economics related; educational psychology; English; environmental science; fashion/apparel design; fashion merchandising; finance; fine/studio arts; graphic design; history; human resources management; industrial and organizational psychology; interior design; international business/trade/commerce; legal assistant/paralegal; liberal arts and sciences/liberal studies; management science; marketing/marketing management; mathematics; mental and social health services and allied professions related; nursing (registered nurse training); philosophy; political science and government; psychology; religious studies; social psychology; sociology; special education; sport and fitness administration.

Academic Programs *Special study options:* academic remediation for entering students, advanced placement credit, double majors, English as a second language, independent study, internships, off-campus study, part-time degree program, services for LD students, student-designed majors, study abroad, summer session for credit. *ROTC:* Army (c).

Library Emerson C. Reinsch Library plus 1 other with 187,097 titles, 1,048 serial subscriptions, 908 audiovisual materials, an OPAC.

Computers on Campus 177 computers available on campus for general student use. A campuswide network can be accessed from off campus that provide access to on-line registration for graduate students and seniors. Internet access, at least one staffed computer lab available. Computer purchase or lease plan available.

Student Life *Housing:* on-campus residence required through sophomore year. *Options:* coed, men-only, women-only. Campus housing is university owned. Freshman applicants given priority for college housing. *Activities and organizations:* drama/theater group, student-run newspaper, choral group, American Society of Interior Design, Student Nurses Association, fashion club, international club, One 2 One (drama club). *Campus security:* 24-hour emergency response devices and patrols, late-night transport/escort service, controlled dormitory access. *Student services:* health clinic, personal/psychological counseling.

Athletics Member NCAA. All Division III. *Intercollegiate sports:* basketball M/W, cross-country running M/W, golf M, lacrosse M/W, soccer M/W, swimming M/W, volleyball W. *Intramural sports:* basketball M/W, cheerleading W, football M/W, golf M, soccer M/W, softball M/W, swimming M/W, volleyball M/W.

Standardized Tests *Required:* SAT I or ACT (for admission).

Costs (2003–04) *Comprehensive fee:* $23,668 includes full-time tuition ($16,300), mandatory fees ($138), and room and board ($7230). Part-time tuition: $528 per credit hour. *Required fees:* $6 per credit hour part-time. *Payment plans:* installment, deferred payment. *Waivers:* senior citizens and employees or children of employees.

Financial Aid Of all full-time matriculated undergraduates who enrolled in 2003, 1,457 applied for aid, 989 were judged to have need, 202 had their need fully met. 284 Federal Work-Study jobs (averaging $1800). In 2003, 298 non-need-based awards were made. *Average percent of need met:* 75%. *Average financial* *aid package:* $13,256. *Average need-based loan:* $3865. *Average need-based gift aid:* $6461. *Average non-need-based aid:* $6870. *Average indebtedness upon graduation:* $21,366.

Applying *Options:* common application, electronic application, early admission, deferred entrance. *Application fee:* $35. *Required:* high school transcript, minimum 2.0 GPA, 1 letter of recommendation. *Recommended:* essay or personal statement, interview. *Application deadline:* rolling (freshmen), rolling (transfers). *Notification:* 10/15 (freshmen), continuous (transfers).

Admissions Contact Mr. Mike Canfield, Associate Director of Undergraduate Admissions, Marymount University, 2807 North Glebe Road, Arlington, VA 22207-4299. *Phone:* 703-284-1500. *Toll-free phone:* 800-548-7638. *Fax:* 703-522-0349. *E-mail:* admissions@marymount.edu.

■ *See page 1946 for a narrative description.*

MARY WASHINGTON COLLEGE

Fredericksburg, Virginia

- **State-supported** comprehensive, founded 1908
- **Calendar** semesters
- **Degrees** bachelor's, master's, and postbachelor's certificates
- **Small-town** 176-acre campus with easy access to Richmond and Washington, DC
- **Endowment** $25.3 million
- **Coed,** 4,220 undergraduate students, 85% full-time, 67% women, 33% men
- **Very difficult** entrance level, 60% of applicants were admitted

Undergraduates 3,573 full-time, 647 part-time. Students come from 44 states and territories, 15 other countries, 35% are from out of state, 4% African American, 5% Asian American or Pacific Islander, 3% Hispanic American, 0.4% Native American, 0.5% international, 4% transferred in, 70% live on campus. *Retention:* 85% of 2002 full-time freshmen returned.

Freshmen *Admission:* 4,472 applied, 2,676 admitted, 869 enrolled. *Average high school GPA:* 3.63. *Test scores:* SAT verbal scores over 500: 96%; SAT math scores over 500: 96%; SAT verbal scores over 600: 63%; SAT math scores over 600: 57%; SAT verbal scores over 700: 11%; SAT math scores over 700: 8%.

Faculty *Total:* 331, 62% full-time. *Student/faculty ratio:* 17:1.

Majors American studies; art; art history, criticism and conservation; biology/biological sciences; business administration and management; chemistry; classics and languages, literatures and linguistics; computer science; dramatic/theatre arts; economics; elementary education; English; environmental studies; fine/studio arts; French; geography; geology/earth science; German; historic preservation and conservation; history; interdisciplinary studies; international relations and affairs; Latin; liberal arts and sciences/liberal studies; mathematics; modern languages; music; music teacher education; philosophy; physics; political science and government; pre-dentistry studies; pre-law studies; pre-medical studies; pre-veterinary studies; psychology; religious studies; secondary education; sociology; Spanish.

Academic Programs *Special study options:* accelerated degree program, adult/continuing education programs, advanced placement credit, cooperative education, double majors, independent study, internships, part-time degree program, services for LD students, student-designed majors, study abroad, summer session for credit.

Library Simpson Library with 355,478 titles, 2,419 serial subscriptions, 1,079 audiovisual materials, an OPAC, a Web page.

Computers on Campus 244 computers available on campus for general student use. A campuswide network can be accessed from student residence rooms and from off campus. Internet access, online (class) registration, at least one staffed computer lab available.

Student Life *Housing options:* coed, men-only, women-only. Campus housing is university owned. Freshman campus housing is guaranteed. *Activities and organizations:* drama/theater group, student-run newspaper, radio station, choral group, Community Outreach, debate team, Washington Guides, Trek Club, entertainment committee. *Campus security:* 24-hour emergency response devices and patrols, student patrols, late-night transport/escort service, controlled dormitory access, self-defense and safety classes. *Student services:* health clinic, personal/psychological counseling, women's center.

Athletics Member NCAA. All Division III. *Intercollegiate sports:* baseball M, basketball M/W, cheerleading M(c)/W(c), crew M/W, cross-country running M/W, equestrian sports M/W, field hockey W, lacrosse M/W, rugby M(c)/W(c), soccer M/W, softball W, swimming M/W, tennis M/W, track and field M/W, volleyball M(c)/W. *Intramural sports:* baseball M/W, basketball M/W, fencing M/W, football M/W, golf M/W, ice hockey M(c), soccer M/W, softball M/W, table tennis M/W, tennis M/W, ultimate Frisbee M/W, volleyball M/W, water polo M/W.

Standardized Tests *Required:* SAT I or ACT (for admission). *Recommended:* SAT II: Subject Tests (for admission).

Costs (2003–04) *Tuition:* state resident $2344 full-time, $164 per semester hour part-time; nonresident $10,092 full-time, $486 per semester hour part-time. Part-time tuition and fees vary according to course load. *Required fees:* $2080 full-time. *Room and board:* $5478; room only: $3160. Room and board charges vary according to board plan and housing facility. *Payment plan:* installment. *Waivers:* senior citizens.

Financial Aid Of all full-time matriculated undergraduates who enrolled in 2003, 2,501 applied for aid, 1,589 were judged to have need, 89 had their need fully met. 45 Federal Work-Study jobs (averaging $1600). 751 state and other part-time jobs (averaging $1480). In 2003, 415 non-need-based awards were made. *Average percent of need met:* 56%. *Average financial aid package:* $5300. *Average need-based loan:* $4000. *Average need-based gift aid:* $3200. *Average non-need-based aid:* $1180. *Average indebtedness upon graduation:* $12,665.

Applying *Options:* common application, electronic application, deferred entrance. *Application fee:* $35. *Required:* essay or personal statement, high school transcript. *Application deadlines:* 2/1 (freshmen), 3/1 (transfers). *Notification:* 4/1 (freshmen), 5/1 (transfers).

Admissions Contact Dr. Martin A. Wilder, Vice President for Enrollment, Mary Washington College, 1301 College Avenue, Fredericksburg, VA 22401-5358. *Phone:* 540-654-2000. *Toll-free phone:* 800-468-5614. *Fax:* 540-654-1857. *E-mail:* admit@mwc.edu.

NATIONAL COLLEGE OF BUSINESS & TECHNOLOGY

Salem, Virginia

Admissions Contact Ms. Bunnie Hancock, Admissions Representative, National College of Business & Technology, PO Box 6400, Roanoke, VA 24017. *Phone:* 540-986-1800. *Toll-free phone:* 800-664-1886. *Fax:* 540-986-1344. *E-mail:* market@educorp.edu.

NORFOLK STATE UNIVERSITY

Norfolk, Virginia

- **State-supported** comprehensive, founded 1935, part of State Council of Higher Education for Virginia
- **Calendar** semesters
- **Degrees** certificates, associate, bachelor's, master's, and doctoral
- **Urban** 134-acre campus
- **Endowment** $4.8 million
- **Coed,** 6,039 undergraduate students, 79% full-time, 63% women, 37% men
- **Moderately difficult** entrance level, 71% of applicants were admitted

Undergraduates 4,777 full-time, 1,262 part-time. Students come from 43 states and territories, 38 other countries, 28% are from out of state, 90% African American, 0.8% Asian American or Pacific Islander, 2% Hispanic American, 0.3% Native American, 0.7% international, 8% transferred in, 32% live on campus. *Retention:* 70% of 2002 full-time freshmen returned.

Freshmen *Admission:* 4,627 applied, 3,297 admitted, 1,154 enrolled. *Average high school GPA:* 2.61. *Test scores:* SAT verbal scores over 500: 21%; SAT math scores over 500: 19%; ACT scores over 18: 56%; SAT verbal scores over 600: 3%; SAT math scores over 600: 3%; ACT scores over 24: 6%.

Faculty *Total:* 446, 67% full-time, 42% with terminal degrees. *Student/faculty ratio:* 17:1.

Majors Accounting; architectural engineering technology; art; biology/biological sciences; business/commerce; business teacher education; chemistry; clinical laboratory science/medical technology; communication and journalism related; computer and information sciences; computer engineering technology; construction engineering technology; drafting and design technology; electrical, electronic and communications engineering technology; electrical, electronics and communications engineering; English; family and consumer sciences/human sciences related; health/health care administration; health information/medical records administration; history; journalism; kindergarten/preschool education; kinesiology and exercise science; mathematics; multi-/interdisciplinary studies related; music; nursing (registered nurse training); office management; physics; political science and government; psychology; social work; sociology; trade and industrial teacher education.

Academic Programs *Special study options:* accelerated degree program, adult/continuing education programs, advanced placement credit, cooperative education, distance learning, double majors, freshman honors college, honors programs, independent study, internships, off-campus study, part-time degree program, services for LD students, student-designed majors, study abroad, summer session for credit. *ROTC:* Army (b), Navy (b).

Library Lymon Beecher Brooks Library with 378,323 titles, 124,460 serial subscriptions, an OPAC, a Web page.

Norfolk State University (continued)

Computers on Campus 512 computers available on campus for general student use. A campuswide network can be accessed. Internet access, online (class) registration, at least one staffed computer lab available. Computer purchase or lease plan available.

Student Life *Housing options:* men-only, women-only. Campus housing is university owned. Freshman applicants given priority for college housing. *Activities and organizations:* drama/theater group, student-run newspaper, radio and television station, choral group, marching band, Alpha Kappa Alpha, Alpha Phi Alpha, Kappa Alpha Psi, Omega Phi Psi, Sigma Gamma Rho, national fraternities, national sororities. *Campus security:* 24-hour emergency response devices and patrols, late-night transport/escort service, controlled dormitory access, campus call boxes. *Student services:* health clinic, personal/psychological counseling.

Athletics Member NCAA. All Division I except football (Division I-AA). *Intercollegiate sports:* baseball M(s), basketball M(s)/W(s), bowling W(s), cheerleading M/W, cross-country running M(s)/W(s), softball W(s), tennis M(s)/W(s), track and field M(s)/W(s), volleyball W(s). *Intramural sports:* basketball M/W, bowling M/W, football M, soccer M, softball M/W, swimming M/W, tennis M/W, volleyball M/W.

Standardized Tests *Required:* SAT I or ACT (for admission).

Costs (2003–04) *Tuition:* state resident $1920 full-time, $58 per credit hour part-time; nonresident $11,340 full-time, $370 per credit hour part-time. Full-time tuition and fees vary according to course load. Part-time tuition and fees vary according to course load. *Required fees:* $1920 full-time, $62 per credit hour part-time. *Room and board:* $5882; room only: $3718. Room and board charges vary according to board plan. *Payment plans:* installment, deferred payment. *Waivers:* senior citizens and employees or children of employees.

Financial Aid Of all full-time matriculated undergraduates who enrolled in 2003, 4,240 applied for aid, 3,769 were judged to have need, 369 had their need fully met. 404 Federal Work-Study jobs (averaging $1891). 135 state and other part-time jobs (averaging $1778). In 2003, 433 non-need-based awards were made. *Average percent of need met:* 87%. *Average financial aid package:* $8146. *Average need-based loan:* $3295. *Average need-based gift aid:* $5086. *Average non-need-based aid:* $4984. *Average indebtedness upon graduation:* $15,467. *Financial aid deadline:* 8/15.

Applying *Options:* electronic application, deferred entrance. *Application fee:* $25. *Required:* high school transcript, minimum 2.3 GPA, 2.0 letters of recommendation, minimum SAT score of 800 or ACT score of 17. *Application deadlines:* 7/15 (freshmen), 7/15 (transfers).

Admissions Contact Ms. Michelle Marable, Director of Admissions, Norfolk State University, 700 Park Avenue, Norfolk, VA 23504. *Phone:* 757-823-8396. *Fax:* 757-823-2078. *E-mail:* admissions@nsu.edu.

OLD DOMINION UNIVERSITY
Norfolk, Virginia

- **State-supported** university, founded 1930
- **Calendar** semesters
- **Degrees** bachelor's, master's, doctoral, and post-master's certificates
- **Urban** 188-acre campus with easy access to Virginia Beach
- **Endowment** $108.0 million
- **Coed,** 14,209 undergraduate students, 69% full-time, 58% women, 42% men
- 82% of applicants were admitted

Undergraduates 9,757 full-time, 4,452 part-time. Students come from 37 states and territories, 79 other countries, 7% are from out of state, 23% African American, 6% Asian American or Pacific Islander, 3% Hispanic American, 0.7% Native American, 3% international, 11% transferred in, 24% live on campus. *Retention:* 77% of 2002 full-time freshmen returned.

Freshmen *Admission:* 5,425 applied, 4,444 admitted, 2,047 enrolled. *Average high school GPA:* 3.18. *Test scores:* SAT verbal scores over 500: 62%; SAT math scores over 500: 60%; ACT scores over 18: 69%; SAT verbal scores over 600: 17%; SAT math scores over 600: 18%; ACT scores over 24: 8%; SAT verbal scores over 700: 2%; SAT math scores over 700: 2%; ACT scores over 30: 1%.

Faculty *Total:* 896, 65% full-time, 53% with terminal degrees. *Student/faculty ratio:* 17:1.

Majors Accounting; acting; anthropology; art; art history, criticism and conservation; art teacher education; audiology and speech-language pathology; biochemistry; biology/biological sciences; biology teacher education; business administration and management; business/managerial economics; chemistry; chemistry teacher education; civil engineering; civil engineering technology; clinical laboratory science/medical technology; communication and journalism related; computer and information sciences; computer engineering; computer engineering technologies related; criminology; cytotechnology; dance; dental hygiene; drama and dance teacher education; dramatic/theatre arts; economics; electrical and electronic engineering technologies related; electrical, electronics and communications engineering; engineering technologies related; English; English/language arts teacher education; environmental/environmental health engineering; environmental health; finance; fine/studio arts; foreign languages and literatures; foreign language teacher education; French; French language teacher education; geography; geography teacher education; geology/earth science; German; German language teacher education; graphic design; health services/allied health/health sciences; history; history teacher education; international business/trade/commerce; international relations and affairs; kinesiology and exercise science; management information systems; marine biology and biological oceanography; marketing/marketing management; mathematics; mathematics teacher education; mechanical engineering; mechanical engineering technologies related; mental and social health services and allied professions related; multi-/interdisciplinary studies related; music; music performance; music teacher education; nuclear engineering technology; nuclear medical technology; nursing (registered nurse training); oceanography (chemical and physical); ophthalmic technology; parks, recreation and leisure facilities management; philosophy; physical education teaching and coaching; physics; physics teacher education; political science and government; psychology; sales and marketing/marketing and distribution teacher education; sociology; Spanish; Spanish language teacher education; speech and rhetoric; sport and fitness administration; technology/industrial arts teacher education; women's studies.

Academic Programs *Special study options:* accelerated degree program, adult/continuing education programs, advanced placement credit, cooperative education, distance learning, double majors, English as a second language, freshman honors college, honors programs, independent study, internships, off-campus study, part-time degree program, services for LD students, student-designed majors, study abroad, summer session for credit. *ROTC:* Army (b), Navy (b). *Unusual degree programs:* 3-2 International Studies, Dental Hygiene, Communications/Humanities English, English/Applied Linguistics, History, Interdisciplinary Studies/Humanities, Health Science/Community Health, Biology, Chemistry, Geology, Oceanography, History, Women's Studies/Humanities.

Library Douglas and Patricia Perry Library plus 3 others with 985,801 titles, 10,579 serial subscriptions, 40,628 audiovisual materials, an OPAC, a Web page.

Computers on Campus 800 computers available on campus for general student use. A campuswide network can be accessed from student residence rooms and from off campus that provide access to on-line courses. Internet access, online (class) registration, at least one staffed computer lab available.

Student Life *Housing options:* coed. Campus housing is university owned, leased by the school and is provided by a third party. *Activities and organizations:* drama/theater group, student-run newspaper, radio station, choral group, Black Student Alliance, Council of International Student Organizations, Student Activities Council, Fraternities and Sororities, Filipino American Student Association, national fraternities, national sororities. *Campus security:* 24-hour emergency response devices and patrols, late-night transport/escort service, controlled dormitory access. *Student services:* health clinic, personal/psychological counseling, women's center.

Athletics Member NCAA. All Division I. *Intercollegiate sports:* baseball M(s), basketball M(s)/W(s), cheerleading M(s)/W(s), crew M(c)/W(c), fencing M(c)/W(c), field hockey M(c)/W(s)(c), golf M(s)/W, lacrosse M(c)/W(s), rugby M(c)/W(c), sailing M/W, soccer M(s)(c)/W(s), softball W(c), swimming M(s)/W(s), tennis M(s)/W(s), volleyball M(c)/W(c), wrestling M(s). *Intramural sports:* badminton M/W, basketball M/W, bowling M/W, cross-country running M/W, golf M/W, sailing M, soccer M/W, softball M/W, swimming M/W, table tennis M/W, tennis M/W, ultimate Frisbee M/W, volleyball M/W, water polo M/W, wrestling M/W.

Standardized Tests *Required:* SAT I or ACT (for admission).

Costs (2003–04) *Tuition:* state resident $4770 full-time, $98 per credit hour part-time; nonresident $13,920 full-time, $400 per credit hour part-time. Full-time tuition and fees vary according to course level and course load. Part-time tuition and fees vary according to course level and course load. *Required fees:* $158 full-time, $61 per term part-time, $31 per term part-time. *Room and board:* $5513; room only: $3704. Room and board charges vary according to board plan and housing facility. *Payment plans:* installment, deferred payment. *Waivers:* senior citizens and employees or children of employees.

Financial Aid Of all full-time matriculated undergraduates who enrolled in 2002, 7,316 applied for aid, 5,024 were judged to have need, 1,782 had their need fully met. In 2002, 719 non-need-based awards were made. *Average percent of need met:* 71%. *Average financial aid package:* $6916. *Average need-based loan:* $3686. *Average need-based gift aid:* $4155. *Average non-need-based aid:* $3037. *Average indebtedness upon graduation:* $16,500. *Financial aid deadline:* 3/15.

Applying *Options:* common application, electronic application, early admission, early action, deferred entrance. *Application fee:* $40. *Required:* essay or personal statement, high school transcript, minimum 2.5 GPA, 1 letter of recommendation. *Required for some:* interview. *Application deadlines:* 3/15 (freshmen), 5/1 (transfers). *Notification:* continuous (freshmen), 1/15 (early action), continuous (transfers).

Admissions Contact Ms. Alice McAdory, Director of Admissions, Old Dominion University, 108 Rollins Hall, Norfolk, VA 23529-0050. *Phone:* 757-683-3648. *Toll-free phone:* 800-348-7926. *Fax:* 757-683-3255. *E-mail:* admit@odu.edu.

■ *See page 2132 for a narrative description.*

PATRICK HENRY COLLEGE
Purcellville, Virginia

- **Independent nondenominational** 4-year, founded 1999
- **Calendar** semesters
- **Degree** bachelor's
- **Small-town** 106-acre campus with easy access to Washington, DC
- **Coed,** 260 undergraduate students, 91% full-time, 53% women, 47% men
- 86% of applicants were admitted

Undergraduates 237 full-time, 23 part-time. Students come from 43 states and territories, 87% are from out of state, 2% Asian American or Pacific Islander, 0.8% Hispanic American, 0.4% transferred in, 94% live on campus. *Retention:* 68% of 2002 full-time freshmen returned.

Freshmen *Admission:* 136 applied, 117 admitted, 72 enrolled. *Average high school GPA:* 3.70. *Test scores:* SAT verbal scores over 500: 100%; SAT math scores over 500: 95%; ACT scores over 18: 100%; SAT verbal scores over 600: 89%; SAT math scores over 600: 66%; ACT scores over 24: 90%; SAT verbal scores over 700: 45%; SAT math scores over 700: 22%; ACT scores over 30: 37%.

Faculty *Total:* 23, 57% full-time, 78% with terminal degrees. *Student/faculty ratio:* 19:1.

Majors American government and politics; creative writing; education; English language and literature related; history; international relations and affairs; journalism.

Student Life *Housing:* on-campus residence required through senior year. *Options:* men-only, women-only. Campus housing is university owned, leased by the school and is provided by a third party. Freshman campus housing is guaranteed. *Activities and organizations:* drama/theater group, student-run newspaper, choral group, Student Government, Intramural Athletics, Debate, Intercollegiate Soccer, Drama Troupe. *Campus security:* 24-hour emergency response devices, student patrols, late-night transport/escort service, controlled dormitory access, after hours patrols by trained security personnel. *Student services:* personal/psychological counseling.

Athletics *Intercollegiate sports:* cheerleading M(s)/W(s), soccer M/W. *Intramural sports:* basketball M, soccer M/W, softball M/W, ultimate Frisbee M/W.

Standardized Tests *Required:* SAT I or ACT (for admission).

Costs (2004–05) *One-time required fee:* $200. *Comprehensive fee:* $19,925 includes full-time tuition ($14,320), mandatory fees ($325), and room and board ($5280). Part-time tuition: $450 per credit. *Payment plans:* installment, deferred payment. *Waivers:* employees or children of employees.

Applying *Application fee:* $50. *Required:* essay or personal statement, high school transcript, 3 letters of recommendation, interview. *Application deadline:* 4/1 (freshmen). *Notification:* 5/1 (freshmen), continuous (transfers).

Admissions Contact Mr. Robert E. Beavin, Director of Admissions, Patrick Henry College, PO Box 1776, One Patrick Henry Circle, Purcellville, VA 20134. *Phone:* 540-338-1776. *Fax:* 540-338-9808. *E-mail:* admissions@phc.edu.

RADFORD UNIVERSITY
Radford, Virginia

- **State-supported** comprehensive, founded 1910
- **Calendar** semesters
- **Degrees** bachelor's, master's, and post-master's certificates
- **Small-town** 177-acre campus
- **Endowment** $28.3 million
- **Coed,** 8,167 undergraduate students, 95% full-time, 59% women, 41% men
- **Moderately difficult** entrance level, 74% of applicants were admitted

Undergraduates 7,719 full-time, 448 part-time. Students come from 43 states and territories, 68 other countries, 9% are from out of state, 6% African American, 2% Asian American or Pacific Islander, 2% Hispanic American, 0.2% Native American, 1% international, 9% transferred in, 40% live on campus. *Retention:* 78% of 2002 full-time freshmen returned.

Freshmen *Admission:* 6,379 applied, 4,709 admitted, 1,806 enrolled. *Average high school GPA:* 3.08. *Test scores:* SAT verbal scores over 500: 51%; SAT math scores over 500: 49%; ACT scores over 18: 83%; SAT verbal scores over 600: 12%; SAT math scores over 600: 10%; SAT verbal scores over 700: 1%; SAT math scores over 700: 1%.

Faculty *Total:* 522, 65% full-time. *Student/faculty ratio:* 21:1.

Majors Accounting; anthropology; art; athletic training; biology/biological sciences; business administration and management; chemistry; clinical laboratory science/medical technology; communication disorders sciences and services related; communication/speech communication and rhetoric; computer science; counselor education/school counseling and guidance; criminal justice/law enforcement administration; dance; dramatic/theatre arts; economics; English; finance; food/nutrition; foreign languages and literatures; geography; geology/earth science; health and physical education; history; information science/studies; interdisciplinary studies; interior design; intermedia/multimedia; kinesiology and exercise science; marketing/marketing management; mathematics; music; nursing (registered nurse training); office management; parks, recreation and leisure; philosophy and religious studies related; physical education teaching and coaching; physical sciences; political science and government; psychology; social sciences; social work; sociology.

Academic Programs *Special study options:* accelerated degree program, adult/continuing education programs, advanced placement credit, distance learning, double majors, English as a second language, honors programs, independent study, internships, off-campus study, part-time degree program, services for LD students, student-designed majors, study abroad, summer session for credit. *ROTC:* Army (b), Navy (c).

Library McConnell Library with 527,789 titles, 14,914 audiovisual materials, an OPAC, a Web page.

Computers on Campus 460 computers available on campus for general student use. A campuswide network can be accessed from student residence rooms and from off campus. Internet access, at least one staffed computer lab available.

Student Life *Housing:* on-campus residence required for freshman year. *Options:* coed, men-only, women-only, disabled students. Campus housing is university owned and leased by the school. *Activities and organizations:* drama/theater group, student-run newspaper, radio and television station, choral group, Student Government Association, Student Education Association, international club, ski club, Student Life Committee, national fraternities, national sororities. *Campus security:* 24-hour emergency response devices and patrols, student patrols, late-night transport/escort service, controlled dormitory access. *Student services:* health clinic, personal/psychological counseling.

Athletics Member NCAA. All Division I. *Intercollegiate sports:* baseball M(s), basketball M(s)/W(s), cross-country running M(s)/W(s), field hockey W(s), golf M(s)/W(s), soccer M(s)/W(s), softball W(s), swimming W(s), tennis M(s)/W(s), track and field M(s)/W(s), volleyball W(s). *Intramural sports:* basketball M/W, bowling M/W, cross-country running M/W, equestrian sports W(c), football M/W, ice hockey M(c), racquetball M/W, rock climbing M/W, rugby M(c)/W(c), skiing (downhill) M(c)/W(c), soccer M/W, softball M/W, tennis M/W, ultimate Frisbee M(c), volleyball M/W, weight lifting M/W, wrestling M/W.

Standardized Tests *Required:* SAT I or ACT (for admission).

Costs (2003–04) *Tuition:* state resident $4140 full-time; nonresident $11,202 full-time. *Room and board:* $5660; room only: $3034. Room and board charges vary according to board plan and housing facility. *Payment plan:* installment. *Waivers:* employees or children of employees.

Financial Aid Of all full-time matriculated undergraduates who enrolled in 2003, 4,725 applied for aid, 3,229 were judged to have need, 2,375 had their need fully met. 429 Federal Work-Study jobs (averaging $1391). 594 state and other part-time jobs (averaging $1398). In 2003, 1719 non-need-based awards were made. *Average percent of need met:* 77%. *Average financial aid package:* $7789. *Average need-based loan:* $3312. *Average need-based gift aid:* $3739. *Average non-need-based aid:* $5684. *Average indebtedness upon graduation:* $14,906.

Applying *Options:* common application, electronic application. *Application fee:* $35. *Required:* high school transcript. *Required for some:* essay or personal statement. *Recommended:* 1 letter of recommendation, interview. *Application deadlines:* 4/1 (freshmen), 6/1 (transfers). *Notification:* continuous until 6/1 (freshmen), continuous (transfers).

Admissions Contact Mr. David Kraus, Director of Admissions, Radford University, PO Box 6903, RU Station, Radford, VA 24142. *Phone:* 540-831-5371. *Toll-free phone:* 800-890-4265. *Fax:* 540-831-5038. *E-mail:* ruadmiss@radford.edu.

■ *See page 2210 for a narrative description.*

RANDOLPH-MACON COLLEGE
Ashland, Virginia

- **Independent United Methodist** 4-year, founded 1830
- **Calendar** 4-1-4
- **Degree** bachelor's
- **Suburban** 110-acre campus with easy access to Richmond
- **Endowment** $81.2 million
- **Coed,** 1,118 undergraduate students, 97% full-time, 52% women, 48% men
- **Moderately difficult** entrance level, 77% of applicants were admitted

Undergraduates 1,083 full-time, 35 part-time. Students come from 30 states and territories, 34% are from out of state, 5% African American, 1% Asian

Randolph-Macon College (continued)
American or Pacific Islander, 1% Hispanic American, 1% international, 3% transferred in, 84% live on campus. *Retention:* 77% of 2002 full-time freshmen returned.

Freshmen *Admission:* 1,661 applied, 1,285 admitted, 326 enrolled. *Average high school GPA:* 3.30. *Test scores:* SAT verbal scores over 500: 82%; SAT math scores over 500: 74%; SAT verbal scores over 600: 30%; SAT math scores over 600: 27%; SAT verbal scores over 700: 3%; SAT math scores over 700: 1%.

Faculty *Total:* 134, 65% full-time, 78% with terminal degrees. *Student/faculty ratio:* 11:1.

Majors Accounting; ancient/classical Greek; art history, criticism and conservation; arts management; biology/biological sciences; business/managerial economics; chemistry; classics and languages, literatures and linguistics; computer science; dramatic/theatre arts; economics; English; environmental studies; fine/studio arts; French; German; history; international/global studies; international relations and affairs; Latin; mathematics; music; philosophy; physics; political science and government; psychology; religious studies; sociology; Spanish; women's studies.

Academic Programs *Special study options:* academic remediation for entering students, accelerated degree program, advanced placement credit, double majors, honors programs, independent study, internships, off-campus study, part-time degree program, services for LD students, study abroad, summer session for credit. *ROTC:* Army (c). *Unusual degree programs:* 3-2 engineering with Columbia University, University of Virginia; forestry with Duke University; accounting with Commonwealth University.

Library McGraw-Page Library with 152,257 titles, 1,006 serial subscriptions, 5,184 audiovisual materials, an OPAC, a Web page.

Computers on Campus 330 computers available on campus for general student use. A campuswide network can be accessed from student residence rooms and from off campus. Internet access, at least one staffed computer lab available. Computer purchase or lease plan available.

Student Life *Housing:* on-campus residence required through junior year. *Options:* coed, men-only, women-only, disabled students. Campus housing is university owned. Freshman campus housing is guaranteed. *Activities and organizations:* drama/theater group, student-run newspaper, radio and television station, choral group, Macon Outdoors Club, Campus Activities Board/Student Government Association, Drama Guild, intramural sports, Student Honors Association, national fraternities, national sororities. *Campus security:* 24-hour emergency response devices and patrols, late-night transport/escort service, controlled dormitory access. *Student services:* health clinic, personal/psychological counseling, women's center.

Athletics Member NCAA. All Division III. *Intercollegiate sports:* baseball M, basketball M/W, field hockey W, football M, golf M, lacrosse M/W, soccer M/W, softball W, swimming M/W, tennis M/W, volleyball W. *Intramural sports:* basketball M/W, cheerleading W, football M/W, lacrosse M/W, racquetball M/W, soccer M/W, softball M/W, table tennis M/W, ultimate Frisbee M/W, volleyball M/W.

Standardized Tests *Required:* SAT I or ACT (for admission). *Recommended:* SAT II: Subject Tests (for admission), SAT II: Writing Test (for admission).

Costs (2003–04) *Comprehensive fee:* $27,190 includes full-time tuition ($20,550), mandatory fees ($610), and room and board ($6030). Part-time tuition: $250 per credit hour. *College room only:* $3160. Room and board charges vary according to board plan and housing facility. *Payment plans:* installment, deferred payment. *Waivers:* employees or children of employees.

Financial Aid Of all full-time matriculated undergraduates who enrolled in 2003, 738 applied for aid, 618 were judged to have need, 139 had their need fully met. 360 Federal Work-Study jobs (averaging $1609). In 2003, 400 non-need-based awards were made. *Average percent of need met:* 84%. *Average financial aid package:* $15,701. *Average need-based loan:* $4902. *Average need-based gift aid:* $11,040. *Average non-need-based aid:* $11,012. *Average indebtedness upon graduation:* $17,066.

Applying *Options:* common application, electronic application, early admission, early decision, deferred entrance. *Application fee:* $30. *Required:* essay or personal statement, high school transcript, minimum 2.0 GPA, 1 letter of recommendation. *Recommended:* interview. *Application deadlines:* 3/1 (freshmen), 3/1 (transfers). *Early decision:* 11/15. *Notification:* 4/1 (freshmen), 12/1 (early decision), 4/1 (transfers).

Admissions Contact Mr. John C. Conkright, Dean of Admissions and Financial Aid, Randolph-Macon College, PO Box 5005, Ashland, VA 23005-5505. *Phone:* 804-752-7305. *Toll-free phone:* 800-888-1762. *Fax:* 804-752-4707. *E-mail:* admissions@rmc.edu.

■ *See page 2214 for a narrative description.*

RANDOLPH-MACON WOMAN'S COLLEGE
Lynchburg, Virginia

- **Independent Methodist** 4-year, founded 1891
- **Calendar** semesters
- **Degree** bachelor's
- **Suburban** 100-acre campus
- **Endowment** $107.6 million
- **Women only,** 737 undergraduate students, 96% full-time
- **Moderately difficult** entrance level, 86% of applicants were admitted

Undergraduates 706 full-time, 31 part-time. Students come from 45 states and territories, 46 other countries, 58% are from out of state, 8% African American, 3% Asian American or Pacific Islander, 3% Hispanic American, 0.3% Native American, 10% international, 4% transferred in, 90% live on campus. *Retention:* 79% of 2002 full-time freshmen returned.

Freshmen *Admission:* 177 enrolled. *Average high school GPA:* 3.4. *Test scores:* SAT verbal scores over 500: 92%; SAT math scores over 500: 79%; ACT scores over 18: 98%; SAT verbal scores over 600: 54%; SAT math scores over 600: 32%; ACT scores over 24: 65%; SAT verbal scores over 700: 14%; SAT math scores over 700: 4%; ACT scores over 30: 13%.

Faculty *Total:* 93, 81% full-time, 78% with terminal degrees. *Student/faculty ratio:* 9:1.

Majors American studies; ancient/classical Greek; art; art history, criticism and conservation; biology/biological sciences; chemistry; classics and languages, literatures and linguistics; communication/speech communication and rhetoric; creative writing; dance; dramatic/theatre arts; economics; elementary education; engineering physics; English; environmental studies; fine/studio arts; French; German; health professions related; history; international relations and affairs; Latin; liberal arts and sciences/liberal studies; mathematics; museum studies; music history, literature, and theory; music performance; music theory and composition; philosophy; physics; political science and government; psychology; religious studies; Russian studies; sociology; Spanish.

Academic Programs *Special study options:* accelerated degree program, adult/continuing education programs, advanced placement credit, double majors, honors programs, independent study, internships, off-campus study, part-time degree program, services for LD students, student-designed majors, study abroad. *Unusual degree programs:* 3-2 nursing with Johns Hopkins University.

Library Lipscomb Library with 197,332 titles, 618 serial subscriptions, 3,600 audiovisual materials, an OPAC, a Web page.

Computers on Campus 154 computers available on campus for general student use. A campuswide network can be accessed from student residence rooms and from off campus. Internet access, online (class) registration, at least one staffed computer lab available. Computer purchase or lease plan available.

Student Life *Housing:* on-campus residence required through senior year. *Options:* women-only. Campus housing is university owned. Freshman campus housing is guaranteed. *Activities and organizations:* drama/theater group, student-run newspaper, radio station, choral group, Pan World Club, Macon Activities Council, Model United Nations, BIONIC (Believe It or Not, I Care volunteer organization), Black Woman's Alliance. *Campus security:* 24-hour emergency response devices and patrols, late-night transport/escort service. *Student services:* health clinic, personal/psychological counseling.

Athletics Member NCAA. All Division III. *Intercollegiate sports:* basketball W, equestrian sports W, field hockey W, soccer W, softball W, swimming W, tennis W, volleyball W. *Intramural sports:* basketball W, softball W, table tennis W, ultimate Frisbee W.

Standardized Tests *Required:* SAT I or ACT (for admission).

Costs (2003–04) *Comprehensive fee:* $28,430 includes full-time tuition ($20,150), mandatory fees ($380), and room and board ($7900). Part-time tuition: $840 per semester hour. Part-time tuition and fees vary according to course load. *Required fees:* $45 per term part-time. *Payment plan:* installment. *Waivers:* adult students and employees or children of employees.

Financial Aid Of all full-time matriculated undergraduates who enrolled in 2003, 505 applied for aid, 454 were judged to have need, 173 had their need fully met. 100 Federal Work-Study jobs (averaging $1860). 408 state and other part-time jobs (averaging $1600). In 2003, 229 non-need-based awards were made. *Average percent of need met:* 89%. *Average financial aid package:* $19,958. *Average need-based loan:* $4281. *Average need-based gift aid:* $14,203. *Average non-need-based aid:* $15,351. *Average indebtedness upon graduation:* $21,992.

Applying *Options:* common application, electronic application, early admission, early decision, deferred entrance. *Application fee:* $35. *Required:* essay or personal statement, high school transcript, 2 letters of recommendation. *Recom-*

mended: interview. *Application deadlines:* 3/1 (freshmen), 6/1 (transfers). *Early decision:* 11/15. *Notification:* continuous (freshmen), 12/15 (early decision), continuous (transfers).

Admissions Contact Pat LeDonne, Director of Admissions, Randolph-Macon Woman's College, 2500 Rivermont Avenue, Lynchburg, VA 24503-1526. *Phone:* 434-947-8100. *Toll-free phone:* 800-745-7692. *Fax:* 434-947-8996. *E-mail:* admissions@rmwc.edu.

■ *See page 2216 for a narrative description.*

ROANOKE COLLEGE

Salem, Virginia

- **Independent** 4-year, founded 1842, affiliated with Evangelical Lutheran Church in America
- **Calendar** semesters
- **Degree** bachelor's
- **Suburban** 68-acre campus
- **Endowment** $85.0 million
- **Coed,** 1,899 undergraduate students, 93% full-time, 58% women, 42% men
- **Moderately difficult** entrance level, 77% of applicants were admitted

Undergraduates 1,773 full-time, 126 part-time. Students come from 40 states and territories, 40% are from out of state, 3% African American, 1% Asian American or Pacific Islander, 2% Hispanic American, 0.6% Native American, 1% international, 4% transferred in, 57% live on campus. *Retention:* 79% of 2002 full-time freshmen returned.

Freshmen *Admission:* 2,827 applied, 2,164 admitted, 519 enrolled. *Average high school GPA:* 3.20. *Test scores:* SAT verbal scores over 500: 78%; SAT math scores over 500: 78%; SAT verbal scores over 600: 30%; SAT math scores over 600: 26%; SAT verbal scores over 700: 4%; SAT math scores over 700: 3%.

Faculty *Total:* 166, 73% full-time, 72% with terminal degrees. *Student/faculty ratio:* 14:1.

Majors Art; athletic training; biochemistry; biology/biological sciences; business administration and management; chemistry; clinical laboratory science/medical technology; computer science; criminal justice/safety; dramatic/theatre arts; economics; English; environmental science; French; health and physical education; history; information science/studies; international relations and affairs; mathematics; music; natural resources management and policy; philosophy; philosophy and religious studies related; physics; political science and government; psychology; religious studies; sociology; Spanish; theology.

Academic Programs *Special study options:* accelerated degree program, adult/continuing education programs, advanced placement credit, double majors, English as a second language, honors programs, independent study, internships, off-campus study, part-time degree program, services for LD students, study abroad, summer session for credit. *Unusual degree programs:* 3-2 engineering with Washington University in St. Louis, Virginia Polytechnic Institute and State University.

Library Fintel Library plus 1 other with 134,035 titles, 719 serial subscriptions, 7,635 audiovisual materials, an OPAC, a Web page.

Computers on Campus 170 computers available on campus for general student use. A campuswide network can be accessed from student residence rooms and from off campus. Internet access, at least one staffed computer lab available.

Student Life *Housing options:* coed, men-only, women-only. Campus housing is university owned and leased by the school. Freshman campus housing is guaranteed. *Activities and organizations:* drama/theater group, student-run newspaper, radio station, choral group, Outdoor Adventures, Habitat for Humanity, Honors Association, Campus Activities Board, InterVarsity Christian Fellowship, national fraternities, national sororities. *Campus security:* 24-hour emergency response devices and patrols, late-night transport/escort service, controlled dormitory access. *Student services:* health clinic, personal/psychological counseling.

Athletics Member NCAA. All Division III. *Intercollegiate sports:* baseball M, basketball M/W, cross-country running M/W, field hockey W, golf M/W(c), ice hockey M(c), lacrosse M/W, soccer M/W, softball W, tennis M/W, track and field M/W, volleyball M(c)/W. *Intramural sports:* badminton M/W, basketball M/W, cheerleading M/W, field hockey W, football M/W, ice hockey M, lacrosse M, racquetball M/W, soccer M/W, softball M/W, table tennis M/W, tennis M/W, volleyball M/W, water polo M/W.

Standardized Tests *Required:* SAT I or ACT (for admission).

Costs (2003–04) *Comprehensive fee:* $27,393 includes full-time tuition ($20,335), mandatory fees ($530), and room and board ($6528). Part-time tuition: $965 per course. *College room only:* $3168. *Payment plan:* installment. *Waivers:* senior citizens and employees or children of employees.

Financial Aid Of all full-time matriculated undergraduates who enrolled in 2003, 1,248 applied for aid, 1,245 were judged to have need, 369 had their need fully met. 620 Federal Work-Study jobs (averaging $1409). In 2003, 438 non-need-based awards were made. *Average percent of need met:* 91%. *Average financial aid package:* $17,852. *Average need-based loan:* $4464. *Average need-based gift aid:* $13,649. *Average non-need-based aid:* $9396. *Average indebtedness upon graduation:* $17,679.

Applying *Options:* common application, electronic application, early admission, early decision, early action, deferred entrance. *Application fee:* $30. *Required:* high school transcript. *Recommended:* essay or personal statement, 3 letters of recommendation, interview. *Application deadlines:* 3/1 (freshmen), 8/1 (transfers). *Early decision:* 11/15. *Notification:* 4/1 (freshmen), 11/30 (early decision), 10/15 (early action), 8/15 (transfers).

Admissions Contact Mr. Michael C. Maxey, Vice President of Admissions, Roanoke College, 221 College Lane, Salem, VA 24153. *Phone:* 540-375-2270. *Toll-free phone:* 800-388-2276. *Fax:* 540-375-2267. *E-mail:* admissions@roanoke.edu.

SAINT PAUL'S COLLEGE

Lawrenceville, Virginia

Admissions Contact Mrs. Rosemary Lewis, Vice President for Student Affairs, Saint Paul's College, 115 College Drive, Lawrenceville, VA 23868. *Phone:* 804-848-6493. *Toll-free phone:* 800-678-7071.

SHENANDOAH UNIVERSITY

Winchester, Virginia

- **Independent United Methodist** comprehensive, founded 1875
- **Calendar** semesters
- **Degrees** certificates, associate, bachelor's, master's, doctoral, first professional, post-master's, and postbachelor's certificates
- **Small-town** 100-acre campus with easy access to Baltimore and Washington, DC
- **Endowment** $37.1 million
- **Coed,** 1,415 undergraduate students, 94% full-time, 58% women, 42% men
- **Moderately difficult** entrance level, 73% of applicants were admitted

Undergraduates 1,327 full-time, 88 part-time. Students come from 37 states and territories, 24 other countries, 35% are from out of state, 6% African American, 1% Asian American or Pacific Islander, 1% Hispanic American, 0.2% Native American, 5% international, 13% transferred in, 54% live on campus. *Retention:* 69% of 2002 full-time freshmen returned.

Freshmen *Admission:* 1,319 applied, 961 admitted, 329 enrolled. *Average high school GPA:* 3.08. *Test scores:* SAT verbal scores over 500: 55%; SAT math scores over 500: 51%; ACT scores over 18: 80%; SAT verbal scores over 600: 17%; SAT math scores over 600: 15%; SAT verbal scores over 700: 2%; SAT math scores over 700: 1%.

Faculty *Total:* 320, 55% full-time, 58% with terminal degrees. *Student/faculty ratio:* 9:1.

Majors Acting; American studies; arts management; biology/biological sciences; business administration and management; chemistry; communication/speech communication and rhetoric; criminal justice/law enforcement administration; dance; dramatic/theatre arts; dramatic/theatre arts and stagecraft related; educational psychology; English; environmental studies; history; liberal arts and sciences/liberal studies; mathematics; music; music performance; music related; music teacher education; music theory and composition; music therapy; nursing (registered nurse training); physical education teaching and coaching; piano and organ; psychology; public administration; religious studies; respiratory care therapy; sociology; Spanish; theatre design and technology; visual and performing arts.

Academic Programs *Special study options:* accelerated degree program, adult/continuing education programs, advanced placement credit, distance learning, double majors, English as a second language, independent study, internships, off-campus study, part-time degree program, services for LD students, study abroad, summer session for credit.

Library Alson H. Smith Jr. Library plus 1 other with 123,628 titles, 11,000 serial subscriptions, 17,823 audiovisual materials, an OPAC, a Web page.

Computers on Campus 170 computers available on campus for general student use. A campuswide network can be accessed from student residence rooms and from off campus that provide access to online grades and student account information. Internet access, online (class) registration, at least one staffed computer lab available. Computer purchase or lease plan available.

Student Life *Housing:* on-campus residence required through senior year. *Options:* coed, disabled students. Campus housing is university owned. Freshman campus housing is guaranteed. *Activities and organizations:* drama/theater group, student-run newspaper, radio and television station, choral group, Harambee Singers, Alpha Psi Omega, Phi Mu Alpha, Student Government Association, Inter-Varsity Student Council. *Campus security:* 24-hour emergency response devices and patrols, late-night transport/escort service, controlled dormitory

Shenandoah University (continued)
access, side door alarms, guard gate house, bike patrols. *Student services:* health clinic, personal/psychological counseling.

Athletics Member NCAA. All Division III. *Intercollegiate sports:* baseball M, basketball M/W, cross-country running M/W, field hockey W, football M, golf M, lacrosse M/W, soccer M/W, softball W, tennis M/W, volleyball W. *Intramural sports:* basketball M/W, cheerleading M/W, volleyball M.

Standardized Tests *Required:* SAT I or ACT (for admission).

Costs (2003–04) *Comprehensive fee:* $25,190 includes full-time tuition ($18,310), mandatory fees ($80), and room and board ($6800). Full-time tuition and fees vary according to course load. Part-time tuition: $560 per credit hour. Part-time tuition and fees vary according to course load. *Room and board:* Room and board charges vary according to board plan. *Payment plan:* deferred payment. *Waivers:* employees or children of employees.

Financial Aid Of all full-time matriculated undergraduates who enrolled in 2003, 860 applied for aid, 860 were judged to have need, 255 had their need fully met. 373 Federal Work-Study jobs (averaging $1480). 244 state and other part-time jobs (averaging $1471). In 2003, 149 non-need-based awards were made. *Average percent of need met:* 84%. *Average financial aid package:* $12,712. *Average need-based loan:* $4671. *Average need-based gift aid:* $6655. *Average non-need-based aid:* $3589. *Average indebtedness upon graduation:* $18,588.

Applying *Options:* common application, electronic application, deferred entrance. *Application fee:* $30. *Required:* high school transcript. *Required for some:* essay or personal statement, interview, audition. *Recommended:* minimum 2.0 GPA. *Application deadline:* rolling (freshmen). *Notification:* continuous (transfers).

Admissions Contact Mr. David Anthony, Dean of Admissions, Shenandoah University, 1460 University Drive, Winchester, VA 22601-5195. *Phone:* 540-665-4581. *Toll-free phone:* 800-432-2266. *Fax:* 540-665-4627. *E-mail:* admit@su.edu.

■ *See page 2376 for a narrative description.*

SOUTHERN VIRGINIA UNIVERSITY
Buena Vista, Virginia

- **Independent Latter-day Saints** 4-year, founded 1867
- **Calendar** semesters
- **Degree** bachelor's
- **Small-town** 155-acre campus
- **Endowment** $600,000
- **Coed,** 579 undergraduate students, 84% full-time, 53% women, 47% men
- 52% of applicants were admitted

Undergraduates 488 full-time, 91 part-time. Students come from 12 other countries, 75% are from out of state, 8% transferred in, 85% live on campus.

Freshmen *Admission:* 1,394 applied, 730 admitted, 271 enrolled. *Average high school GPA:* 3.20.

Faculty *Total:* 60. *Student/faculty ratio:* 12:1.

Majors Art; biology/biological sciences; business administration and management; dramatic/theatre arts; English; family and consumer sciences/human sciences related; health and physical education; history; liberal arts and sciences/liberal studies; music; parks, recreation and leisure facilities management; philosophy; Spanish; web page, digital/multimedia and information resources design.

Academic Programs *Special study options:* cooperative education, summer session for credit. *ROTC:* Army (c).

Library Von Canon Library with 107,630 titles, 37,000 serial subscriptions, 4,350 audiovisual materials, an OPAC.

Computers on Campus A campuswide network can be accessed from student residence rooms and from off campus. Internet access, online (class) registration, at least one staffed computer lab available.

Student Life *Housing:* on-campus residence required through sophomore year. *Options:* men-only, women-only. Campus housing is university owned. Freshman applicants given priority for college housing. *Activities and organizations:* drama/theater group, choral group, student association, LDS Institute of Religion. *Campus security:* 24-hour emergency response devices and patrols. *Student services:* health clinic, personal/psychological counseling.

Athletics Member NAIA. *Intercollegiate sports:* baseball M, basketball M/W, cheerleading W, cross-country running M/W, football M, lacrosse M, soccer M/W, softball W, track and field M/W, volleyball W, wrestling M.

Standardized Tests *Required:* SAT I or ACT (for admission).

Costs (2004–05) *Comprehensive fee:* $19,940 includes full-time tuition ($14,640) and room and board ($5300). Part-time tuition: $475 per credit hour. *Payment plan:* installment. *Waivers:* employees or children of employees.

Financial Aid Of all full-time matriculated undergraduates who enrolled in 2003, 411 applied for aid, 374 were judged to have need, 90 had their need fully met. 64 Federal Work-Study jobs (averaging $1000). 140 state and other part-time jobs (averaging $1000). In 2003, 169 non-need-based awards were made. *Average percent of need met:* 87%. *Average financial aid package:* $9377. *Average need-based loan:* $3632. *Average need-based gift aid:* $7896. *Average non-need-based aid:* $5000. *Average indebtedness upon graduation:* $7531.

Applying *Options:* common application. *Application fee:* $35. *Required:* high school transcript, ecclesiastical endorsement. *Recommended:* minimum 2.5 GPA. *Application deadline:* 7/31 (freshmen).

Admissions Contact Mr. Tony Caputo, Dean of Admissions, Southern Virginia University, One University Hill Drive, Buena Vista, VA 24416. *Phone:* 540-261-2756. *Toll-free phone:* 800-229-8420. *E-mail:* admissions@southernvirginia.edu.

■ *See page 2418 for a narrative description.*

STRATFORD UNIVERSITY
Falls Church, Virginia

- **Proprietary** comprehensive, founded 1976
- **Calendar** quarters
- **Degrees** diplomas, associate, bachelor's, and master's
- **Suburban** campus
- **Coed,** 606 undergraduate students, 93% full-time, 41% women, 59% men
- **Minimally difficult** entrance level

Undergraduates 566 full-time, 40 part-time. Students come from 9 states and territories, 36% are from out of state, 46% African American, 7% Asian American or Pacific Islander, 8% Hispanic American, 0.2% Native American, 3% international, 5% transferred in.

Freshmen *Admission:* 109 enrolled. *Average high school GPA:* 2.50.

Faculty *Total:* 48, 35% full-time, 10% with terminal degrees. *Student/faculty ratio:* 20:1.

Majors Business administration and management; computer programming; computer programming related; computer systems networking and telecommunications; culinary arts; hotel/motel administration.

Academic Programs *Special study options:* accelerated degree program, advanced placement credit, cooperative education, internships.

Library Stratford University Library with 1,800 titles, 75 serial subscriptions, 283 audiovisual materials.

Computers on Campus 7 computers available on campus for general student use. A campuswide network can be accessed. Internet access, online (class) registration, at least one staffed computer lab available.

Student Life *Housing:* college housing not available. *Campus security:* 24-hour emergency response devices.

Standardized Tests *Required:* CPAt (for admission). *Recommended:* SAT I (for admission).

Costs (2003–04) *Tuition:* $16,500 full-time, $275 per credit part-time. Full-time tuition and fees vary according to program. *Payment plans:* tuition prepayment, installment, deferred payment. *Waivers:* employees or children of employees.

Applying *Options:* common application, electronic application, early decision. *Application fee:* $100. *Required:* high school transcript, minimum 2.0 GPA, interview. *Application deadlines:* 7/30 (freshmen), 7/30 (transfers). *Early decision:* 4/29. *Notification:* continuous until 8/6 (freshmen), 6/15 (early decision), continuous until 8/6 (transfers).

Admissions Contact Ms. Denise Baxter, Director of High School Program, Stratford University, 7777 Leesburg Pike, Falls Church, VA 22043. *Phone:* 703-821-8570. *Toll-free phone:* 800-444-0804. *Fax:* 703-734-5339. *E-mail:* dbaxter@stratford.edu.

■ *See page 2470 for a narrative description.*

SWEET BRIAR COLLEGE
Sweet Briar, Virginia

- **Independent** 4-year, founded 1901
- **Calendar** semesters
- **Degree** bachelor's
- **Rural** 3250-acre campus
- **Endowment** $86.6 million
- **Women only,** 709 undergraduate students, 93% full-time
- **Moderately difficult** entrance level, 88% of applicants were admitted

Undergraduates 662 full-time, 47 part-time. Students come from 44 states and territories, 51% are from out of state, 3% African American, 2% Asian American or Pacific Islander, 2% Hispanic American, 1% Native American, 3% international, 3% transferred in, 90% live on campus. *Retention:* 79% of 2002 full-time freshmen returned.

Freshmen *Admission:* 133 enrolled. *Average high school GPA:* 3.39. *Test scores:* SAT verbal scores over 500: 80%; SAT math scores over 500: 69%; ACT scores over 18: 94%; SAT verbal scores over 600: 36%; SAT math scores over 600: 20%; ACT scores over 24: 56%; SAT verbal scores over 700: 10%; SAT math scores over 700: 2%; ACT scores over 30: 9%.

Faculty *Total:* 102, 71% full-time, 78% with terminal degrees. *Student/faculty ratio:* 7:1.

Majors Anthropology; art history, criticism and conservation; biochemistry, biophysics and molecular biology related; biology/biological sciences; business/commerce; business, management, and marketing related; chemistry; classics and languages, literatures and linguistics; communication/speech communication and rhetoric; computer science; creative writing; dance; dramatic/theatre arts; economics; engineering science; English; environmental science; environmental studies; fine/studio arts; foreign languages and literatures; French; German; history; international relations and affairs; Italian; liberal arts and sciences/liberal studies; mathematics; music; philosophy; physics; political science and government; psychology; religious studies; sociology; Spanish; theoretical and mathematical physics.

Academic Programs *Special study options:* accelerated degree program, adult/continuing education programs, advanced placement credit, double majors, honors programs, independent study, internships, off-campus study, part-time degree program, services for LD students, student-designed majors, study abroad, summer session for credit. *Unusual degree programs:* 3-2 engineering with Virginia Polytechnic Institute and State University, University of Virginia, Columbia University, Washington University in St. Louis.

Library Mary Helen Cochran Library plus 3 others with 177,110 titles, 996 serial subscriptions, 6,816 audiovisual materials, an OPAC, a Web page.

Computers on Campus 117 computers available on campus for general student use. A campuswide network can be accessed from student residence rooms and from off campus. Internet access, at least one staffed computer lab available.

Student Life *Housing:* on-campus residence required through senior year. *Options:* women-only. Campus housing is university owned. Freshman campus housing is guaranteed. *Activities and organizations:* drama/theater group, student-run newspaper, radio and television station, choral group, WNRS radio station, American Chemical Society, cheerleaders, Sweet Tones, Student Government Association/Campus Events Organization. *Campus security:* 24-hour emergency response devices and patrols, late-night transport/escort service, controlled dormitory access, front gate security. *Student services:* health clinic, personal/psychological counseling.

Athletics Member NCAA. All Division III. *Intercollegiate sports:* equestrian sports W(c), fencing W(c), field hockey W, lacrosse W, soccer W, softball W(c), swimming W, tennis W, volleyball W.

Standardized Tests *Required:* SAT I or ACT (for admission). *Recommended:* SAT II: Subject Tests (for admission).

Costs (2004–05) *Comprehensive fee:* $29,600 includes full-time tuition ($20,880), mandatory fees ($200), and room and board ($8520). Full-time tuition and fees vary according to program. Part-time tuition: $695 per credit hour. Part-time tuition and fees vary according to program. *Payment plan:* installment. *Waivers:* adult students, senior citizens, and employees or children of employees.

Financial Aid Of all full-time matriculated undergraduates who enrolled in 2001, 372 applied for aid, 299 were judged to have need, 160 had their need fully met. 67 Federal Work-Study jobs (averaging $929). In 2001, 267 non-need-based awards were made. *Average percent of need met:* 92%. *Average financial aid package:* $16,690. *Average need-based loan:* $3088. *Average need-based gift aid:* $13,088. *Average indebtedness upon graduation:* $18,718.

Applying *Options:* common application, electronic application, early admission, early decision, deferred entrance. *Application fee:* $25. *Required:* essay or personal statement, high school transcript, 2 letters of recommendation. *Required for some:* interview, portfolio with courses taken, list of texts covered, essay about homeschooling, campus visit, interview for homeschooled applicants. *Application deadlines:* 2/1 (freshmen), 7/1 (transfers). *Early decision:* 12/1. *Notification:* continuous until 4/1 (freshmen), 12/15 (early decision), 8/1 (transfers).

Admissions Contact Mr. Ken Huus, Director of Admissions, Sweet Briar College, PO Box B, Sweet Briar, VA 24595. *Phone:* 434-381-6142. *Toll-free phone:* 800-381-6142. *Fax:* 434-381-6152. *E-mail:* admissions@sbc.edu.

■ *See page 2478 for a narrative description.*

University of Management and Technology

Arlington, Virginia

Admissions Contact Dr. C. Eric Kirkland, Vice President, University of Management and Technology, 1901 North Fort Meyers Drive, Suite 700, Arlington, VA 22209. *Phone:* 703-516-0035. *Toll-free phone:* 800-924-4885. *E-mail:* admissions@umtweb.edu.

University of Richmond

Richmond, Virginia

- **Independent** comprehensive, founded 1830
- **Calendar** semesters
- **Degrees** certificates, diplomas, associate, bachelor's, master's, first professional, and postbachelor's certificates
- **Suburban** 350-acre campus
- **Endowment** $996.7 million
- **Coed,** 2,926 undergraduate students, 98% full-time, 51% women, 49% men
- **Very difficult** entrance level, 42% of applicants were admitted

Undergraduates 2,873 full-time, 53 part-time. Students come from 48 states and territories, 75 other countries, 84% are from out of state, 5% African American, 4% Asian American or Pacific Islander, 2% Hispanic American, 0.1% Native American, 4% international, 1% transferred in, 92% live on campus. *Retention:* 92% of 2002 full-time freshmen returned.

Freshmen *Admission:* 6,079 applied, 2,560 admitted, 835 enrolled. *Average high school GPA:* 3.53. *Test scores:* SAT verbal scores over 500: 96%; SAT math scores over 500: 98%; ACT scores over 18: 99%; SAT verbal scores over 600: 80%; SAT math scores over 600: 87%; ACT scores over 24: 92%; SAT verbal scores over 700: 21%; SAT math scores over 700: 28%; ACT scores over 30: 33%.

Faculty *Total:* 366, 79% full-time, 84% with terminal degrees. *Student/faculty ratio:* 9:1.

Majors Accounting; American studies; art; art history, criticism and conservation; art teacher education; biology/biological sciences; business administration and management; business/managerial economics; chemistry; classics and languages, literatures and linguistics; computer science; criminal justice/law enforcement administration; dramatic/theatre arts; economics; education; elementary education; English; environmental studies; European studies; European studies (Central and Eastern); finance; fine/studio arts; French; German; health teacher education; history; human resources management; interdisciplinary studies; international business/trade/commerce; international economics; international relations and affairs; journalism; Latin; Latin American studies; legal administrative assistant/secretary; management information systems; marketing/marketing management; mathematics; middle school education; modern Greek; molecular biology; music; music history, literature, and theory; philosophy; physical education teaching and coaching; physics; political science and government; psychology; religious studies; secondary education; sociology; Spanish; speech and rhetoric; urban studies/affairs; women's studies.

Academic Programs *Special study options:* accelerated degree program, adult/continuing education programs, advanced placement credit, cooperative education, distance learning, double majors, English as a second language, honors programs, independent study, internships, off-campus study, part-time degree program, services for LD students, student-designed majors, study abroad, summer session for credit. *ROTC:* Army (b). *Unusual degree programs:* 3-2 engineering with Columbia University, George Washington University, University of Virginia, Virginia Commonwealth University, Virginia Polytechnic Institute and State University.

Library Boatwright Memorial Library plus 4 others with 1.0 million titles, 703,111 serial subscriptions, 15,892 audiovisual materials, an OPAC, a Web page.

Computers on Campus 500 computers available on campus for general student use. A campuswide network can be accessed from student residence rooms and from off campus. Internet access, online (class) registration, at least one staffed computer lab available.

Student Life *Housing options:* coed, men-only, women-only, disabled students. Campus housing is university owned. Freshman applicants given priority for college housing. *Activities and organizations:* drama/theater group, student-run newspaper, radio station, choral group, Volunteer Action Council, Student Government Association, Campus Activities Board, Multicultural Student Union, intramurals, national fraternities, national sororities. *Campus security:* 24-hour emergency response devices and patrols, late-night transport/escort service, controlled dormitory access, campus police. *Student services:* health clinic, personal/psychological counseling, women's center.

Athletics Member NCAA. All Division I except football (Division I-AA). *Intercollegiate sports:* baseball M(s), basketball M(s)/W(s), cheerleading M/W, crew M(c)/W(c), cross-country running M/W(s), equestrian sports W(c), fencing M(c)/W(c), field hockey W(s), golf M/W(s), ice hockey M(c), lacrosse M(c)/W(s), rugby M(c)/W(c), soccer M(s)/W(s), swimming M(c)/W(s), tennis M/W(s), track and field M/W, ultimate Frisbee M(c)/W(c), volleyball M(c)/W(c), water polo M(c)/W(c), wrestling M(c). *Intramural sports:* archery M/W, badminton M/W, baseball M(c), basketball M/W, field hockey W(c), football M/W, golf M/W, lacrosse W(c), racquetball M/W, soccer M(c)/W(c), softball M/W, squash M/W, swimming M/W, table tennis M/W, tennis M/W, volleyball M/W, water polo M, wrestling M.

Standardized Tests *Required:* SAT I and SAT II or ACT (for admission), SAT II: Writing Test (for admission), SAT II Subject Test in math (for admission).

University of Richmond (continued)

Costs (2003–04) *Comprehensive fee:* $30,100 includes full-time tuition ($24,940) and room and board ($5160). Full-time tuition and fees vary according to course load and student level. Part-time tuition: $1170 per semester hour. *College room only:* $2810. Room and board charges vary according to board plan and housing facility. *Payment plans:* installment, deferred payment.

Financial Aid Of all full-time matriculated undergraduates who enrolled in 2003, 1,375 applied for aid, 948 were judged to have need, 386 had their need fully met. 270 Federal Work-Study jobs (averaging $1300). In 2003, 397 non-need-based awards were made. *Average percent of need met:* 96%. *Average financial aid package:* $19,220. *Average need-based loan:* $3505. *Average need-based gift aid:* $15,685. *Average non-need-based aid:* $12,929. *Average indebtedness upon graduation:* $16,370. *Financial aid deadline:* 2/25.

Applying *Options:* common application, electronic application, early admission, early decision, deferred entrance. *Application fee:* $40. *Required:* essay or personal statement, high school transcript, minimum 2.0 GPA, 1 letter of recommendation, signed character statement. *Application deadlines:* 1/15 (freshmen), 2/15 (transfers). *Early decision:* 11/15 (for plan 1), 1/15 (for plan 2). *Notification:* 4/1 (freshmen), 12/15 (early decision plan 1), 2/15 (early decision plan 2), 4/15 (transfers).

Admissions Contact Ms. Pamela Spence, Dean of Admission, University of Richmond, 28 Westhampton Way, University of Richmond, VA 23173. *Phone:* 804-289-8640. *Toll-free phone:* 800-700-1662. *Fax:* 804-287-6003. *E-mail:* admissions@richmond.edu.

UNIVERSITY OF VIRGINIA
Charlottesville, Virginia

- **State-supported** university, founded 1819
- **Calendar** semesters
- **Degrees** bachelor's, master's, doctoral, first professional, and post-master's certificates
- **Suburban** 1160-acre campus with easy access to Richmond
- **Endowment** $1.8 billion
- **Coed,** 13,829 undergraduate students, 94% full-time, 53% women, 47% men
- **Most difficult** entrance level, 39% of applicants were admitted

Undergraduates 13,050 full-time, 779 part-time. Students come from 52 states and territories, 110 other countries, 28% are from out of state, 9% African American, 11% Asian American or Pacific Islander, 3% Hispanic American, 0.3% Native American, 4% international, 4% transferred in, 45% live on campus. *Retention:* 97% of 2002 full-time freshmen returned.

Freshmen *Admission:* 14,627 applied, 5,775 admitted, 3,101 enrolled. *Average high school GPA:* 4.00. *Test scores:* SAT verbal scores over 500: 98%; SAT math scores over 500: 97%; ACT scores over 18: 98%; SAT verbal scores over 600: 80%; SAT math scores over 600: 84%; ACT scores over 24: 85%; SAT verbal scores over 700: 32%; SAT math scores over 700: 39%; ACT scores over 30: 43%.

Faculty *Total:* 1,292, 88% full-time, 87% with terminal degrees. *Student/faculty ratio:* 16:1.

Majors Aerospace, aeronautical and astronautical engineering; African-American/Black studies; anthropology; applied mathematics; architectural history and criticism; architecture; area studies related; art; astronomy; audiology and speech-language pathology; biology/biological sciences; biomedical/medical engineering; business/commerce; chemical engineering; chemistry; city/urban, community and regional planning; civil engineering; classics and languages, literatures and linguistics; comparative literature; computer and information sciences; computer engineering; cultural studies; dramatic/theatre arts; economics; electrical, electronics and communications engineering; engineering; English; environmental science; French; German; history; international relations and affairs; Italian; liberal arts and sciences/liberal studies; mathematics; mechanical engineering; multi-/interdisciplinary studies related; music; nursing (registered nurse training); philosophy; physical education teaching and coaching; physics; political science and government; psychology; religious studies; Slavic languages; sociology; Spanish; systems engineering.

Academic Programs *Special study options:* accelerated degree program, adult/continuing education programs, advanced placement credit, cooperative education, double majors, honors programs, independent study, internships, part-time degree program, services for LD students, student-designed majors, study abroad, summer session for credit. *ROTC:* Army (b), Navy (b), Air Force (b).

Library Alderman Library plus 14 others with 3.4 million titles, 55,843 serial subscriptions, 84,035 audiovisual materials, an OPAC, a Web page.

Computers on Campus 1645 computers available on campus for general student use. A campuswide network can be accessed from student residence rooms and from off campus. Internet access, online (class) registration, at least one staffed computer lab available. Computer purchase or lease plan available.

Student Life *Housing:* on-campus residence required for freshman year. *Options:* coed. Campus housing is university owned. Freshman campus housing is guaranteed. *Activities and organizations:* drama/theater group, student-run newspaper, radio and television station, choral group, marching band, Madison House, student government, University guides, University Union, The Cavalier Daily, national fraternities, national sororities. *Campus security:* 24-hour emergency response devices and patrols, late-night transport/escort service, controlled dormitory access. *Student services:* health clinic, personal/psychological counseling, women's center, legal services.

Athletics Member NCAA. All Division I except football (Division I-A). *Intercollegiate sports:* baseball M(s), basketball M(s)/W(s), crew W(s), cross-country running M(s)/W(s), field hockey W(s), golf M(s)/W(s), ice hockey M(c)/W(c), lacrosse M(s)/W(s), soccer M(s)/W(s), softball W(s), swimming M(s)/W(s), tennis M(s)/W(s), track and field M(s)/W(s), ultimate Frisbee M(c)/W(c), volleyball M(c)/W(s), wrestling M(s). *Intramural sports:* archery M/W, badminton M/W, basketball M/W, bowling M/W, cheerleading M/W, crew M(c)/W, cross-country running M/W, equestrian sports M/W, fencing M(c)/W(c), field hockey W, football M/W, golf M/W, gymnastics M(c)/W(c), lacrosse M/W, racquetball M(c)/W(c), riflery M(c)/W(c), rock climbing M/W, rugby M(c)/W(c), sailing M(c)/W(c), skiing (cross-country) M/W, skiing (downhill) M(c)/W(c), soccer M(c)/W(c), softball M/W, squash M(c)/W(c), swimming M/W, tennis M/W(c), track and field M/W, ultimate Frisbee M(c)/W(c), volleyball M(c)/W(c), water polo M(c)/W(c), weight lifting M(c)/W(c), wrestling M.

Standardized Tests *Required:* SAT I or ACT (for admission), SAT II: Subject Tests (for admission), SAT II: Writing Test (for admission), SAT II Math and one other subject test (for admission).

Costs (2003–04) *Tuition:* state resident $4584 full-time; nonresident $20,554 full-time. Full-time tuition and fees vary according to program. *Required fees:* $1565 full-time. *Room and board:* $5591; room only: $2711. Room and board charges vary according to board plan and housing facility. *Payment plan:* installment. *Waivers:* senior citizens and employees or children of employees.

Financial Aid Of all full-time matriculated undergraduates who enrolled in 2003, 4,827 applied for aid, 3,077 were judged to have need, 1,703 had their need fully met. 580 Federal Work-Study jobs (averaging $1447). In 2003, 2243 non-need-based awards were made. *Average percent of need met:* 92%. *Average financial aid package:* $12,408. *Average need-based loan:* $4368. *Average need-based gift aid:* $9564. *Average non-need-based aid:* $5667. *Average indebtedness upon graduation:* $13,522.

Applying *Options:* electronic application, early decision, deferred entrance. *Application fee:* $40. *Required:* essay or personal statement, high school transcript, 1 letter of recommendation. *Application deadlines:* 1/2 (freshmen), 3/1 (transfers). *Early decision:* 11/1. *Notification:* 4/1 (freshmen), 12/1 (early decision), 4/15 (transfers).

Admissions Contact Mr. John A. Blackburn, Dean of Admission, University of Virginia, PO Box 400160, Charlottesville, VA 22904-4160. *Phone:* 434-982-3200. *Fax:* 434-924-3587. *E-mail:* undergradadmission@virginia.edu.

THE UNIVERSITY OF VIRGINIA'S COLLEGE AT WISE
Wise, Virginia

- **State-supported** 4-year, founded 1954, part of University of Virginia
- **Calendar** semesters
- **Degrees** bachelor's and postbachelor's certificates
- **Small-town** 396-acre campus
- **Endowment** $20.6 million
- **Coed,** 1,703 undergraduate students, 80% full-time, 56% women, 44% men
- **Moderately difficult** entrance level, 78% of applicants were admitted

Undergraduates 1,363 full-time, 340 part-time. Students come from 9 states and territories, 9 other countries, 6% are from out of state, 5% African American, 1% Asian American or Pacific Islander, 1% Hispanic American, 0.4% Native American, 0.9% international, 8% transferred in, 30% live on campus. *Retention:* 73% of 2002 full-time freshmen returned.

Freshmen *Admission:* 987 applied, 766 admitted, 349 enrolled. *Average high school GPA:* 3.30. *Test scores:* SAT verbal scores over 500: 48%; SAT math scores over 500: 49%; ACT scores over 18: 74%; SAT verbal scores over 600: 13%; SAT math scores over 600: 10%; ACT scores over 24: 11%; SAT verbal scores over 700: 2%; SAT math scores over 700: 1%.

Faculty *Total:* 124, 61% full-time, 52% with terminal degrees. *Student/faculty ratio:* 18:1.

Majors Accounting; art; biology/biological sciences; business administration and management; chemistry; clinical laboratory science/medical technology; communication/speech communication and rhetoric; computer and information sciences; criminal justice/safety; dramatic/theatre arts; economics; English; environmental studies; family practice nursing/nurse practitioner; foreign languages and literatures; French; history; interdisciplinary studies; liberal arts and sciences/liberal studies; mathematics; political science and government; psychology; sociology; Spanish.

Academic Programs *Special study options:* academic remediation for entering students, accelerated degree program, adult/continuing education programs, advanced placement credit, cooperative education, distance learning, double majors, honors programs, independent study, internships, part-time degree program, services for LD students, student-designed majors, study abroad, summer session for credit.

Library Wyllie Library with 95,861 titles, 1,029 serial subscriptions, 11,582 audiovisual materials, an OPAC, a Web page.

Computers on Campus 130 computers available on campus for general student use. A campuswide network can be accessed from student residence rooms and from off campus. Internet access, at least one staffed computer lab available.

Student Life *Housing options:* coed, men-only, women-only. Campus housing is university owned. *Activities and organizations:* drama/theater group, student-run newspaper, radio and television station, choral group, student government, Student Activities Board, Inter-Greek Council, Multi-Cultural Association, Residence Hall Association, national fraternities, national sororities. *Campus security:* 24-hour emergency response devices and patrols, student patrols, late-night transport/escort service, self-defense, informal discussions, pamphlets/posters/films, and crime prevention office. *Student services:* health clinic, personal/psychological counseling.

Athletics Member NAIA. *Intercollegiate sports:* baseball M(s), basketball M(s)/W(s), cross-country running M(s)/W(s), football M(s), golf M/W, softball W(s), tennis M(s)/W(s), track and field M/W, volleyball W(s). *Intramural sports:* badminton M/W, basketball M/W, football M/W, golf M/W, racquetball M/W, soccer M/W, softball M/W, table tennis M/W, tennis M/W, ultimate Frisbee M/W, volleyball M/W, water polo M/W.

Standardized Tests *Required:* SAT I or ACT (for admission).

Costs (2003–04) *Tuition:* state resident $2630 full-time, $108 per semester hour part-time; nonresident $11,518 full-time, $475 per semester hour part-time. Part-time tuition and fees vary according to course load. *Required fees:* $1901 full-time, $34 per semester hour part-time, $25 per term part-time. *Room and board:* $5586; room only: $3104. Room and board charges vary according to board plan and housing facility. *Payment plans:* installment, deferred payment. *Waivers:* senior citizens.

Financial Aid Of all full-time matriculated undergraduates who enrolled in 2003, 1,193 applied for aid, 919 were judged to have need, 873 had their need fully met. 196 Federal Work-Study jobs (averaging $1147). In 2003, 235 non-need-based awards were made. *Average percent of need met:* 95%. *Average financial aid package:* $5197. *Average need-based loan:* $2656. *Average need-based gift aid:* $3413. *Average non-need-based aid:* $1507. *Average indebtedness upon graduation:* $6560.

Applying *Options:* early admission, early action. *Application fee:* $25. *Required:* high school transcript, minimum 2.3 GPA. *Required for some:* interview. *Recommended:* 2 letters of recommendation. *Application deadlines:* 8/1 (freshmen), 8/15 (transfers). *Notification:* continuous until 8/20 (freshmen), 2/15 (early action), continuous until 8/20 (transfers).

Admissions Contact Mr. Russell Necessary, Vice Chancellor for Enrollment Management, The University of Virginia's College at Wise, 1 College Avenue, Wise, VA 24293. *Phone:* 276-328-0322. *Toll-free phone:* 888-282-9324. *Fax:* 276-328-0251. *E-mail:* admissions@uvawise.edu.

VIRGINIA COMMONWEALTH UNIVERSITY
Richmond, Virginia

- **State-supported** university, founded 1838
- **Calendar** semesters
- **Degrees** bachelor's, master's, doctoral, first professional, post-master's, and postbachelor's certificates
- **Urban** 126-acre campus
- **Endowment** $227.6 million
- **Coed,** 18,312 undergraduate students, 76% full-time, 58% women, 42% men
- **Moderately difficult** entrance level, 74% of applicants were admitted

Virginia Commonwealth University (VCU) is noted for excellent programs in the arts, business, education, engineering, humanities, life sciences, mass communications, pre-health sciences, and social work and for its diverse student body and faculty. Honors and guaranteed admission programs, cooperative education and internship programs, undergraduate research, and study abroad opportunities are also offered.

Undergraduates 13,991 full-time, 4,321 part-time. Students come from 47 states and territories, 73 other countries, 7% are from out of state, 21% African American, 9% Asian American or Pacific Islander, 3% Hispanic American, 0.7% Native American, 1% international, 9% transferred in, 22% live on campus. *Retention:* 79% of 2002 full-time freshmen returned.

Freshmen *Admission:* 9,435 applied, 6,993 admitted, 3,326 enrolled. *Average high school GPA:* 3.18. *Test scores:* SAT verbal scores over 500: 68%; SAT math scores over 500: 62%; ACT scores over 18: 87%; SAT verbal scores over 600: 24%; SAT math scores over 600: 21%; ACT scores over 24: 21%; SAT verbal scores over 700: 3%; SAT math scores over 700: 3%; ACT scores over 30: 2%.

Faculty *Total:* 1,991, 55% full-time. *Student/faculty ratio:* 14:1.

Majors Accounting; African-American/Black studies; area studies related; art history, criticism and conservation; art teacher education; biological and physical sciences; biology/biological sciences; biomedical/medical engineering; business administration and management; business/managerial economics; chemical engineering; chemistry; clinical laboratory science/medical technology; computer and information sciences; computer engineering; crafts, folk art and artisanry; criminal justice/law enforcement administration; dance; dental hygiene; design and visual communications; dramatic/theatre arts; electrical, electronics and communications engineering; English; fashion/apparel design; finance and financial management services related; foreign languages and literatures; forensic science and technology; general studies; health teacher education; history; information science/studies; interior design; marketing/marketing management; mass communication/media; mathematics; mechanical engineering; music performance; nursing (registered nurse training); painting; parks, recreation and leisure facilities management; philosophy; photography; physics; political science and government; psychology; radiologic technology/science; religious studies; sculpture; social work; sociology; urban studies/affairs.

Academic Programs *Special study options:* academic remediation for entering students, accelerated degree program, adult/continuing education programs, advanced placement credit, cooperative education, distance learning, double majors, English as a second language, honors programs, independent study, internships, off-campus study, part-time degree program, services for LD students, student-designed majors, study abroad, summer session for credit. *ROTC:* Army (b).

Library James Branch Cabell and Tompkins-McCaw Library with 1.7 million titles, 13,886 serial subscriptions, 44,434 audiovisual materials, an OPAC, a Web page.

Computers on Campus 1000 computers available on campus for general student use. A campuswide network can be accessed from student residence rooms and from off campus. At least one staffed computer lab available.

Student Life *Housing options:* coed, men-only, women-only, disabled students. Campus housing is university owned. *Activities and organizations:* drama/theater group, student-run newspaper, radio station, choral group, Student Government Organization, Activities Programming Board, Muslim Student Association, Black Caucus, Greek Council, national fraternities, national sororities. *Campus security:* 24-hour emergency response devices and patrols, student patrols, late-night transport/escort service, controlled dormitory access, security personnel in residence halls. *Student services:* health clinic, personal/psychological counseling.

Athletics Member NCAA. All Division I. *Intercollegiate sports:* baseball M(s), basketball M(s)/W(s), cross-country running M(s)/W(s), field hockey W(s), golf M(s), rugby M(c)/W(c), soccer M(s)/W(s), tennis M(s)/W(s), track and field M(s)/W(s), volleyball W(s), weight lifting M(c)/W(c). *Intramural sports:* badminton M/W, basketball M/W, cross-country running M(c), fencing M(c)/W(c), football M, ice hockey M(c), racquetball M/W, soccer M/W, softball M/W, table tennis M/W, tennis M(c)/W(c), volleyball M/W, water polo M/W.

Standardized Tests *Required:* SAT I or ACT (for admission).

Costs (2003–04) *Tuition:* state resident $3600 full-time, $150 per credit part-time; nonresident $15,904 full-time, $663 per credit part-time. *Required fees:* $1269 full-time, $46 per credit part-time. *Room and board:* $6723; room only: $3873. Room and board charges vary according to board plan. *Waivers:* senior citizens.

Financial Aid Of all full-time matriculated undergraduates who enrolled in 2002, 9,699 applied for aid, 6,984 were judged to have need, 589 had their need fully met. 887 Federal Work-Study jobs (averaging $1675). In 2002, 596 non-need-based awards were made. *Average percent of need met:* 54%. *Average financial aid package:* $6932. *Average need-based loan:* $3687. *Average need-based gift aid:* $3389. *Average non-need-based aid:* $3946. *Average indebtedness upon graduation:* $19,370.

Applying *Options:* common application, electronic application, early admission, early decision, deferred entrance. *Application fee:* $30. *Required:* high school transcript. *Required for some:* minimum 3.0 GPA, 2 letters of recommendation, interview. *Recommended:* essay or personal statement, minimum 2.5 GPA. *Application deadlines:* 2/1 (freshmen), 8/1 (transfers). *Early decision:* 11/1. *Notification:* continuous until 4/1 (freshmen), 12/1 (early decision), continuous (transfers).

Admissions Contact Counseling Staff, Virginia Commonwealth University, 821 West Franklin Street, Box 842526, Richmond, VA 23284-2526. *Phone:* 804-828-1222. *Toll-free phone:* 800-841-3638. *Fax:* 804-828-1899. *E-mail:* vcuinfo@vcu.edu.

■ *See page 2764 for a narrative description.*

Virginia Intermont College

Bristol, Virginia

- **Independent** 4-year, founded 1884, affiliated with Baptist Church
- **Calendar** semesters
- **Degrees** associate and bachelor's
- **Small-town** 13-acre campus
- **Endowment** $4.2 million
- **Coed,** 1,147 undergraduate students, 86% full-time, 73% women, 27% men
- **Minimally difficult** entrance level, 65% of applicants were admitted

Students from all over the world who are looking for a solid liberal arts background with a variety of academic majors come to Virginia Intermont. They appreciate the individualized instruction and challenging academic atmosphere. Specialized areas, such as photography and digital imaging, equine studies, paralegal studies, and culinary arts are invaluable additions to the educational background and practical experience that Virginia Intermont College has to offer.

Undergraduates 991 full-time, 156 part-time. Students come from 37 states and territories, 29 other countries, 46% are from out of state, 6% African American, 0.2% Asian American or Pacific Islander, 1% Hispanic American, 0.8% Native American, 5% international, 10% transferred in, 63% live on campus. *Retention:* 58% of 2002 full-time freshmen returned.

Freshmen *Admission:* 831 applied, 542 admitted, 191 enrolled. *Average high school GPA:* 3.13. *Test scores:* SAT verbal scores over 500: 40%; SAT math scores over 500: 39%; ACT scores over 18: 67%; SAT verbal scores over 600: 12%; SAT math scores over 600: 11%; ACT scores over 24: 17%; SAT verbal scores over 700: 1%; SAT math scores over 700: 1%; ACT scores over 30: 1%.

Faculty *Total:* 152, 30% full-time, 44% with terminal degrees. *Student/faculty ratio:* 15:1.

Majors Art; art teacher education; biology/biological sciences; biology teacher education; business administration and management; commercial and advertising art; communication and journalism related; computer and information sciences; criminal justice/law enforcement administration; culinary arts; dance; dramatic/theatre arts; education; elementary education; English; English/language arts teacher education; environmental studies; equestrian studies; food preparation; general studies; health and physical education; history; interdisciplinary studies; international business/trade/commerce; legal assistant/paralegal; legal studies; liberal arts and sciences and humanities related; liberal arts and sciences/liberal studies; marketing/marketing management; photography; physical education teaching and coaching; political science and government; pre-law studies; pre-medical studies; pre-veterinary studies; psychology; public administration; religious studies; restaurant, culinary, and catering management; secondary education; social studies teacher education; social work; sport and fitness administration.

Academic Programs *Special study options:* academic remediation for entering students, adult/continuing education programs, advanced placement credit, double majors, independent study, internships, off-campus study, part-time degree program, services for LD students, study abroad, summer session for credit.

Library J. F. Hicks Library with 60,000 titles, 310 serial subscriptions, 5,750 audiovisual materials, an OPAC, a Web page.

Computers on Campus 80 computers available on campus for general student use. A campuswide network can be accessed from student residence rooms and from off campus. Internet access, at least one staffed computer lab available.

Student Life *Housing:* on-campus residence required through junior year. *Options:* coed, men-only, women-only. Campus housing is university owned. Freshman campus housing is guaranteed. *Activities and organizations:* drama/theater group, choral group, Student Government Association, Student Activities Committee, Christian Student Union, equestrian club, Business Organization for Student Success. *Campus security:* 24-hour patrols, late-night transport/escort service. *Student services:* health clinic, personal/psychological counseling, women's center.

Athletics Member NAIA. *Intercollegiate sports:* baseball M(s), basketball M(s)/W(s), cross-country running M(s)/W(s), equestrian sports M(s)/W(s), golf M(s), soccer M(s)/W(s), softball W(s), tennis M(s)/W(s), track and field M(s)/W(s), volleyball W(s). *Intramural sports:* basketball M/W, bowling M/W, football M/W, golf M/W, skiing (downhill) M/W, softball M/W, swimming M/W, table tennis M/W, tennis M/W, volleyball M/W, weight lifting M/W.

Standardized Tests *Required:* SAT I or ACT (for admission).

Costs (2003–04) *Comprehensive fee:* $19,800 includes full-time tuition ($13,900), mandatory fees ($500), and room and board ($5400). Part-time tuition: $180 per credit. Part-time tuition and fees vary according to course load. *Required fees:* $30 per credit part-time. *College room only:* $2600. *Payment plan:* installment. *Waivers:* senior citizens and employees or children of employees.

Financial Aid Of all full-time matriculated undergraduates who enrolled in 2003, 826 applied for aid, 776 were judged to have need, 75 had their need fully met. 272 Federal Work-Study jobs (averaging $681). In 2003, 87 non-need-based awards were made. *Average percent of need met:* 10%. *Average financial aid package:* $10,935. *Average need-based loan:* $4192. *Average need-based gift aid:* $3014. *Average non-need-based aid:* $4690. *Average indebtedness upon graduation:* $12,131.

Applying *Options:* common application, electronic application, early admission, deferred entrance. *Application fee:* $15. *Required:* high school transcript, minimum 2.0 GPA. *Required for some:* essay or personal statement. *Recommended:* interview. *Application deadline:* rolling (freshmen), rolling (transfers). *Notification:* continuous (freshmen), continuous (transfers).

Admissions Contact Mr. Everett Honaker, Vice President for Admissions and Financial Aid, Virginia Intermont College, 1013 Moore Street, Campus Box D-460, Bristol, VA 24201. *Phone:* 540-645-7857. *Toll-free phone:* 800-451-1842. *Fax:* 540-466-7855. *E-mail:* viadmit@vic.edu.

■ *See page 2766 for a narrative description.*

Virginia Military Institute

Lexington, Virginia

- **State-supported** 4-year, founded 1839
- **Calendar** semesters
- **Degree** bachelor's
- **Small-town** 134-acre campus
- **Endowment** $281.4 million
- **Coed, primarily men,** 1,333 undergraduate students, 100% full-time, 6% women, 94% men
- **Moderately difficult** entrance level, 51% of applicants were admitted

Undergraduates 1,333 full-time. Students come from 45 states and territories, 17 other countries, 48% are from out of state, 6% African American, 3% Asian American or Pacific Islander, 3% Hispanic American, 0.5% Native American, 3% international, 2% transferred in, 100% live on campus. *Retention:* 87% of 2002 full-time freshmen returned.

Freshmen *Admission:* 1,609 applied, 813 admitted, 338 enrolled. *Average high school GPA:* 3.35. *Test scores:* SAT verbal scores over 500: 87%; SAT math scores over 500: 88%; ACT scores over 18: 100%; SAT verbal scores over 600: 33%; SAT math scores over 600: 37%; ACT scores over 24: 58%; SAT verbal scores over 700: 6%; SAT math scores over 700: 3%; ACT scores over 30: 3%.

Faculty *Total:* 148, 68% full-time, 77% with terminal degrees. *Student/faculty ratio:* 12:1.

Majors Biology/biological sciences; chemistry; civil engineering; computer science; economics; electrical, electronics and communications engineering; English; history; international relations and affairs; mathematics; mechanical engineering; modern languages; physics; psychology.

Academic Programs *Special study options:* accelerated degree program, advanced placement credit, double majors, honors programs, independent study, internships, services for LD students, study abroad, summer session for credit. *ROTC:* Army (b), Navy (b), Air Force (b).

Library Preston Library plus 1 other with 162,053 titles, 785 serial subscriptions, 4,896 audiovisual materials, an OPAC, a Web page.

Computers on Campus 200 computers available on campus for general student use. A campuswide network can be accessed from student residence rooms and from off campus. Internet access, at least one staffed computer lab available.

Student Life *Housing:* on-campus residence required through senior year. *Activities and organizations:* drama/theater group, student-run newspaper, choral group, marching band, Newman Club, Officers Christian Fellowship, strength & fitness, Promaji, Pre-law Society. *Campus security:* 24-hour emergency response devices and patrols, student patrols. *Student services:* health clinic, personal/psychological counseling.

Athletics Member NCAA. All Division I except football (Division I-AA). *Intercollegiate sports:* baseball M(s), basketball M(s), cross-country running M(s)/W(s), fencing M(c)/W(c), golf M(s), ice hockey M(c), lacrosse M(s), racquetball M(c)/W(c), riflery M(s)/W(s), rugby M(c)/W(c), soccer M(s), swimming M(s)/W, tennis M(s), track and field M(s)/W(s), volleyball M(c)/W(c), water polo M(c)/W(c), weight lifting M(c)/W(c), wrestling M(s). *Intramural sports:* basketball M/W, football M/W, soccer M/W, softball M/W.

Standardized Tests *Required:* SAT I or ACT (for admission).

Costs (2003–04) *Tuition:* state resident $3856 full-time; nonresident $16,568 full-time. *Required fees:* $2325 full-time. *Room and board:* $5266. *Payment plan:* installment.

Financial Aid Of all full-time matriculated undergraduates who enrolled in 2002, 687 applied for aid, 547 were judged to have need, 229 had their need fully met. 40 Federal Work-Study jobs (averaging $825). In 2002, 289 non-need-based awards were made. *Average percent of need met:* 88%. *Average financial aid package:* $12,681. *Average need-based loan:* $3660. *Average need-based gift aid:* $10,906. *Average non-need-based aid:* $6121. *Average indebtedness upon graduation:* $15,533.

Applying *Options:* electronic application, early admission, early decision. *Application fee:* $35. *Required:* high school transcript. *Recommended:* essay or personal statement, 2 letters of recommendation, interview. *Application deadlines:* 3/1 (freshmen), 3/1 (transfers). *Early decision:* 11/15. *Notification:* continuous (freshmen), 12/15 (early decision), continuous (transfers).

Admissions Contact Lt. Col. Tom Mortenson, Associate Director of Admissions, Virginia Military Institute, 309 Letcher Avenue, Lexington, VA 24450. *Phone:* 540-464-7211. *Toll-free phone:* 800-767-4207. *Fax:* 540-464-7746. *E-mail:* admissions@vmi.edu.

■ *See page 2768 for a narrative description.*

VIRGINIA POLYTECHNIC INSTITUTE AND STATE UNIVERSITY

Blacksburg, Virginia

- **State-supported** university, founded 1872
- **Calendar** semesters
- **Degrees** associate, bachelor's, master's, doctoral, and first professional
- **Small-town** 2600-acre campus
- **Coed,** 21,343 undergraduate students, 97% full-time, 41% women, 59% men
- **Moderately difficult** entrance level, 69% of applicants were admitted

Undergraduates 20,727 full-time, 616 part-time. Students come from 52 states and territories, 104 other countries, 27% are from out of state, 6% African American, 7% Asian American or Pacific Islander, 2% Hispanic American, 0.3% Native American, 3% international, 3% transferred in, 44% live on campus. *Retention:* 90% of 2002 full-time freshmen returned.

Freshmen *Admission:* 18,028 applied, 12,387 admitted, 5,874 enrolled. *Average high school GPA:* 3.6. *Test scores:* SAT verbal scores over 500: 88%; SAT math scores over 500: 91%; SAT verbal scores over 600: 39%; SAT math scores over 600: 52%; SAT verbal scores over 700: 5%; SAT math scores over 700: 11%.

Faculty *Total:* 1,463, 86% full-time. *Student/faculty ratio:* 16:1.

Majors Accounting; aerospace, aeronautical and astronautical engineering; agricultural economics; agricultural mechanization; agricultural teacher education; agronomy and crop science; animal sciences; architecture; art; biochemistry; biology/biological sciences; business administration and management; business/commerce; business teacher education; chemical engineering; chemistry; civil engineering; clothing/textiles; communication/speech communication and rhetoric; computer engineering; computer science; construction engineering technology; consumer/homemaking education; dairy science; dietetics; dramatic/theatre arts; economics; electrical, electronics and communications engineering; engineering; engineering science; English; environmental studies; finance; food science; foods, nutrition, and wellness; forestry; French; geography; geology/earth science; German; health teacher education; history; horticultural science; human resources management; human services; industrial design; industrial engineering; information science/studies; interdisciplinary studies; international relations and affairs; kindergarten/preschool education; landscape architecture; management information systems; marketing/marketing management; materials engineering; mathematics; mechanical engineering; mining and mineral engineering; music; ocean engineering; philosophy; physics; political science and government; poultry science; psychology; sales and marketing/marketing and distribution teacher education; sociology; Spanish; statistics; technology/industrial arts teacher education; tourism and travel services management; trade and industrial teacher education; urban studies/affairs.

Academic Programs *Special study options:* accelerated degree program, adult/continuing education programs, advanced placement credit, cooperative education, distance learning, double majors, English as a second language, honors programs, independent study, internships, part-time degree program, services for LD students, study abroad, summer session for credit. *ROTC:* Army (b), Navy (b), Air Force (b).

Library Newman Library plus 4 others with 2.1 million titles, 17,562 serial subscriptions, 19,206 audiovisual materials, an OPAC, a Web page.

Computers on Campus 8000 computers available on campus for general student use. A campuswide network can be accessed from student residence rooms and from off campus. Internet access, online (class) registration, at least one staffed computer lab available. Computer purchase or lease plan available.

Student Life *Housing:* on-campus residence required for freshman year. *Options:* coed, men-only, women-only. Campus housing is university owned. Freshman campus housing is guaranteed. *Activities and organizations:* drama/theater group, student-run newspaper, radio and television station, choral group, marching band, Virginia Tech Union, Student Government Association, international student organizations, national fraternities, national sororities. *Campus security:* 24-hour emergency response devices and patrols, student patrols, late-night transport/escort service, controlled dormitory access. *Student services:* health clinic, personal/psychological counseling, women's center, legal services.

Athletics Member NCAA. All Division I except football (Division I-A). *Intercollegiate sports:* baseball M(s), basketball M(s)/W(s), bowling M(c)/W(c), crew M(c)/W(c), cross-country running M(s)/W(s), equestrian sports M(c)/W(c), fencing M(c)/W(c), field hockey M(c)/W(c), golf M(s), gymnastics M(c)/W(c), ice hockey M(c)/W(c), lacrosse M(c)/W(s), rugby M(c)/W(c), skiing (downhill) M(c)/W(c), soccer M(s)/W(s), softball W, swimming M(s)/W(s), tennis M(s)/W(s), track and field M(s)/W(s), ultimate Frisbee M/W, volleyball M(c)/W(s), water polo M(c)/W(c), weight lifting M(c)/W(c), wrestling M(s). *Intramural sports:* badminton M/W, basketball M/W, cross-country running M/W, football M/W, golf M/W, ice hockey M/W, racquetball M/W, riflery M/W, skiing (downhill) M/W, soccer M/W, softball W, squash M/W, swimming M/W, table tennis M/W, tennis M/W, track and field M/W, ultimate Frisbee M/W, volleyball M/W, wrestling M.

Standardized Tests *Required:* SAT I or ACT (for admission).

Costs (2004–05) *Tuition:* state resident $4190 full-time, $175 per credit hour part-time; nonresident $14,074 full-time, $587 per credit hour part-time. *Required fees:* $905 full-time, $121 per term part-time. *Room and board:* $4146; room only: $2064. Room and board charges vary according to board plan and location. *Payment plan:* installment.

Financial Aid Of all full-time matriculated undergraduates who enrolled in 2002, 12,966 applied for aid, 8,489 were judged to have need, 2,192 had their need fully met. 1,274 Federal Work-Study jobs (averaging $1295). 3,925 state and other part-time jobs (averaging $1419). In 2002, 1218 non-need-based awards were made. *Average percent of need met:* 74%. *Average financial aid package:* $7104. *Average need-based loan:* $3679. *Average need-based gift aid:* $3586. *Average non-need-based aid:* $1500. *Average indebtedness upon graduation:* $16,229.

Applying *Options:* electronic application, early admission, early decision, deferred entrance. *Application fee:* $40. *Required:* high school transcript, minimum 2.0 GPA. *Recommended:* minimum 3.3 GPA. *Application deadlines:* 1/15 (freshmen), 3/1 (transfers). *Early decision:* 11/1. *Notification:* 4/1 (freshmen), 12/15 (early decision), 5/15 (transfers).

Admissions Contact Ms. Mildred Johnson, Associate Director for Freshmen Admissions, Virginia Polytechnic Institute and State University, 201 Burruss Hall, Blacksburg, VA 24061. *Phone:* 540-231-6267. *Fax:* 540-231-3242. *E-mail:* vtadmiss@vt.edu.

VIRGINIA STATE UNIVERSITY

Petersburg, Virginia

- **State-supported** comprehensive, founded 1882, part of State Council of Higher Education for Virginia
- **Calendar** semesters
- **Degrees** bachelor's, master's, doctoral, and post-master's certificates
- **Suburban** 236-acre campus with easy access to Richmond
- **Endowment** $7.8 million
- **Coed,** 4,033 undergraduate students, 92% full-time, 57% women, 43% men
- **Minimally difficult** entrance level, 66% of applicants were admitted

Undergraduates 3,707 full-time, 326 part-time. Students come from 35 states and territories, 35% are from out of state, 97% African American, 0.2% Asian American or Pacific Islander, 0.7% Hispanic American, 0.2% Native American, 3% transferred in, 52% live on campus. *Retention:* 71% of 2002 full-time freshmen returned.

Freshmen *Admission:* 3,675 applied, 2,442 admitted, 964 enrolled. *Average high school GPA:* 2.70. *Test scores:* SAT verbal scores over 500: 11%; SAT math scores over 500: 8%; ACT scores over 18: 16%; SAT verbal scores over 600: 1%; ACT scores over 24: 3%.

Faculty *Total:* 285, 73% full-time. *Student/faculty ratio:* 18:1.

Majors Accounting; agriculture; biology/biological sciences; business administration and management; business/managerial economics; business teacher education; chemistry; computer engineering; computer science; criminal justice/safety; engineering technologies related; engineering technology; English; family and consumer economics related; history; hospitality administration; interdisciplinary studies; liberal arts and sciences/liberal studies; management information systems; manufacturing engineering; marketing/marketing management; mass communication/media; mathematics; multi-/interdisciplinary studies related; music performance; physical education teaching and coaching; physics; political science and government; psychology; public administration; social work; sociology; trade and industrial teacher education; visual and performing arts.

Academic Programs *Special study options:* adult/continuing education programs, advanced placement credit, cooperative education, double majors, honors programs, independent study, internships, part-time degree program, services for LD students, student-designed majors, summer session for credit. *ROTC:* Army (b). *Unusual degree programs:* 3-2 engineering with Old Dominion University.

Library Johnston Memorial Library with 282,353 titles, 1,150 serial subscriptions, an OPAC, a Web page.

Virginia State University (continued)

Computers on Campus 491 computers available on campus for general student use. A campuswide network can be accessed from student residence rooms and from off campus. Internet access, online (class) registration, at least one staffed computer lab available.

Student Life *Housing:* on-campus residence required for freshman year. *Options:* coed, men-only, women-only. Campus housing is university owned. Freshman applicants given priority for college housing. *Activities and organizations:* drama/theater group, student-run newspaper, choral group, marching band, NAACP, Betterment of Brothers/Sisters, Student Government Association, dormitory cabinets, pre-alumni associations, national fraternities, national sororities. *Campus security:* 24-hour emergency response devices and patrols, late-night transport/escort service. *Student services:* health clinic, personal/psychological counseling.

Athletics Member NCAA. All Division II. *Intercollegiate sports:* baseball M(s), basketball M(s)/W(s), bowling W(s), cheerleading M/W, cross-country running M(s)/W(s), football M(s), golf M(s)/W(s), softball W(s), tennis M(s)/W(s), track and field M(s)/W(s), volleyball W(s). *Intramural sports:* basketball M/W, football M, tennis M/W, track and field M/W, volleyball W.

Standardized Tests *Required:* SAT I or ACT (for admission).

Costs (2003–04) *Tuition:* state resident $1888 full-time, $105 per credit part-time; nonresident $8748 full-time, $405 per credit part-time. *Required fees:* $2642 full-time, $34 per credit part-time. *Room and board:* $6008; room only: $3464. *Payment plan:* deferred payment.

Financial Aid Of all full-time matriculated undergraduates who enrolled in 2003, 3,548 applied for aid, 3,264 were judged to have need. 340 Federal Work-Study jobs (averaging $1600). 225 state and other part-time jobs (averaging $2220). In 2003, 201 non-need-based awards were made. *Average percent of need met:* 75%. *Average financial aid package:* $8225. *Average need-based loan:* $4905. *Average need-based gift aid:* $4150. *Average non-need-based aid:* $5000. *Average indebtedness upon graduation:* $19,200. *Financial aid deadline:* 5/1.

Applying *Options:* common application, electronic application. *Application fee:* $25. *Required:* high school transcript, minimum 2.2 GPA, 2 letters of recommendation. *Application deadlines:* 5/1 (freshmen), 5/1 (transfers). *Notification:* continuous (freshmen), continuous (transfers).

Admissions Contact Mrs. Irene Logan, Director of Admissions, Virginia State University, PO Box 9018, Petersburg, VA 23806-2096. *Phone:* 804-524-5902. *Toll-free phone:* 800-871-7611. *E-mail:* ilogan@vsu.edu.

■ *See page 2770 for a narrative description.*

VIRGINIA UNION UNIVERSITY
Richmond, Virginia

- **Independent Baptist** comprehensive, founded 1865
- **Calendar** semesters
- **Degrees** bachelor's, master's, doctoral, and first professional
- **Urban** 72-acre campus
- **Coed,** 1,286 undergraduate students, 97% full-time, 57% women, 43% men
- **Moderately difficult** entrance level, 61% of applicants were admitted

Undergraduates 1,243 full-time, 43 part-time. Students come from 21 states and territories, 97% African American, 0.2% Asian American or Pacific Islander, 0.5% Hispanic American, 0.8% international. *Retention:* 69% of 2002 full-time freshmen returned.

Freshmen *Admission:* 3,251 applied, 1,981 admitted, 491 enrolled. *Average high school GPA:* 2.61.

Faculty *Total:* 140, 60% full-time, 29% with terminal degrees. *Student/faculty ratio:* 15:1.

Majors Accounting; biology/biological sciences; business administration and management; business teacher education; chemistry; criminology; drama therapy; elementary education; English; history; jazz/jazz studies; journalism; kindergarten/preschool education; management information systems; marketing/marketing management; mathematics; music; political science and government; psychology; social work; sociology; special education.

Academic Programs *Special study options:* academic remediation for entering students, adult/continuing education programs, advanced placement credit, cooperative education, English as a second language, honors programs, internships, off-campus study, summer session for credit. *ROTC:* Army (c). *Unusual degree programs:* 3-2 engineering with Howard University, University of Michigan (Ann Arbor), University of Iowa, Virginia Commonwealth University.

Library L. Douglas Wilder Learning Resource Center and Library with 147,611 titles, 311 serial subscriptions, an OPAC.

Computers on Campus 128 computers available on campus for general student use. Internet access, at least one staffed computer lab available.

Student Life *Housing options:* coed. Campus housing is university owned and leased by the school. *Activities and organizations:* drama/theater group, student-run newspaper, choral group, marching band, national fraternities, national sororities. *Campus security:* 24-hour emergency response devices and patrols, controlled dormitory access. *Student services:* health clinic, personal/psychological counseling.

Athletics Member NCAA. All Division II. *Intercollegiate sports:* basketball M(s)/W(s), cross-country running M(s)/W(s), football M(s), golf M(s), softball W(s), tennis M(s), track and field M(s)/W(s), volleyball W(s). *Intramural sports:* basketball M, softball W.

Standardized Tests *Required:* SAT I or ACT (for placement).

Costs (2004–05) *Comprehensive fee:* $17,625 includes full-time tuition ($10,900), mandatory fees ($1305), and room and board ($5420). Part-time tuition: $440 per credit hour. *Required fees:* $385 per term part-time. *College room only:* $2755.

Financial Aid Of all full-time matriculated undergraduates who enrolled in 2002, 1,184 applied for aid, 1,082 were judged to have need, 396 had their need fully met. 343 Federal Work-Study jobs (averaging $1605). In 2002, 67 non-need-based awards were made. *Average percent of need met:* 77%. *Average financial aid package:* $7075. *Average need-based loan:* $3233. *Average need-based gift aid:* $3784. *Average non-need-based aid:* $9122. *Average indebtedness upon graduation:* $11,787.

Applying *Options:* common application, early admission, deferred entrance. *Application fee:* $15. *Required:* high school transcript. *Recommended:* essay or personal statement, 3 letters of recommendation. *Application deadline:* rolling (freshmen), rolling (transfers). *Notification:* continuous (freshmen), continuous (transfers).

Admissions Contact Mr. Gil Powell, Director of Admissions, Virginia Union University, 1500 North Lombardy Street, Richmond, VA 23220-1170. *Phone:* 804-257-5881. *Toll-free phone:* 800-368-3227.

VIRGINIA UNIVERSITY OF LYNCHBURG
Lynchburg, Virginia

Admissions Contact 2058 Garfield Avenue, Lynchburg, VA 24501-6417.

VIRGINIA WESLEYAN COLLEGE
Norfolk, Virginia

- **Independent United Methodist** 4-year, founded 1961
- **Calendar** 4-1-4
- **Degree** bachelor's
- **Urban** 300-acre campus with easy access to Norfolk/Virginia Beach
- **Endowment** $32.0 million
- **Coed,** 1,429 undergraduate students
- **Moderately difficult** entrance level, 80% of applicants were admitted

Undergraduates Students come from 33 states and territories, 9 other countries, 22% are from out of state, 13% African American, 2% Asian American or Pacific Islander, 4% Hispanic American, 0.8% Native American, 0.7% international, 40% live on campus. *Retention:* 66% of 2002 full-time freshmen returned.

Freshmen *Admission:* 1,147 applied, 920 admitted. *Average high school GPA:* 3.00. *Test scores:* SAT verbal scores over 500: 46%; SAT math scores over 500: 45%; ACT scores over 18: 68%; SAT verbal scores over 600: 9%; SAT math scores over 600: 9%; ACT scores over 24: 18%; SAT verbal scores over 700: 1%; SAT math scores over 700: 1%.

Faculty *Total:* 123, 63% full-time, 53% with terminal degrees. *Student/faculty ratio:* 13:1.

Majors American studies; art; art teacher education; biology/biological sciences; business administration and management; chemistry; communication/speech communication and rhetoric; computer science; criminology; dramatic/theatre arts; education (K-12); elementary education; English; environmental studies; foreign languages and literatures; foreign language teacher education; French; geology/earth science; German; history; humanities; human services; interdisciplinary studies; international relations and affairs; liberal arts and sciences/liberal studies; mathematics; middle school education; music; natural sciences; parks, recreation and leisure; philosophy; political science and government; pre-dentistry studies; pre-law studies; pre-medical studies; pre-veterinary studies; psychology; religious studies; secondary education; social sciences; sociology; Spanish; theatre literature, history and criticism.

Academic Programs *Special study options:* academic remediation for entering students, adult/continuing education programs, advanced placement credit, double majors, freshman honors college, honors programs, independent study, internships, off-campus study, part-time degree program, services for LD students, student-designed majors, study abroad, summer session for credit. *ROTC:* Army (c).

Library H. C. Hofheimer II Library with 130,352 titles, 617 serial subscriptions, 3,521 audiovisual materials, an OPAC, a Web page.

Computers on Campus 100 computers available on campus for general student use. A campuswide network can be accessed from student residence rooms that provide access to network programs, Web pages, on-line grades. Internet access, at least one staffed computer lab available.

Student Life *Housing:* on-campus residence required through senior year. *Options:* coed. Campus housing is university owned and leased by the school. Freshman campus housing is guaranteed. *Activities and organizations:* drama/theater group, student-run newspaper, radio station, choral group, student government, student radio station, student newspaper, Black Student Union, Leadership Council, national fraternities, national sororities. *Campus security:* 24-hour emergency response devices and patrols, late-night transport/escort service, controlled dormitory access, well-lit pathways. *Student services:* health clinic, personal/psychological counseling, women's center.

Athletics Member NCAA. All Division III. *Intercollegiate sports:* baseball M, basketball M/W, cheerleading M/W, cross-country running M/W, field hockey W, golf M, lacrosse M/W, soccer M/W, softball W, tennis M/W, volleyball W. *Intramural sports:* basketball M/W, football M/W, soccer M/W, softball M/W, table tennis M/W, volleyball M/W.

Standardized Tests *Required:* SAT I or ACT (for admission).

Costs (2003–04) *Comprehensive fee:* $25,350 includes full-time tuition ($19,200) and room and board ($6150). Full-time tuition and fees vary according to class time. Part-time tuition: $800 per semester hour. Part-time tuition and fees vary according to class time and course load. *Room and board:* Room and board charges vary according to board plan and housing facility. *Payment plans:* installment, deferred payment. *Waivers:* senior citizens and employees or children of employees.

Financial Aid Of all full-time matriculated undergraduates who enrolled in 2002, 1,135 applied for aid, 988 were judged to have need, 110 had their need fully met. 157 Federal Work-Study jobs. In 2002, 142 non-need-based awards were made. *Average percent of need met:* 70%. *Average financial aid package:* $13,105. *Average need-based loan:* $4206. *Average need-based gift aid:* $3404. *Average non-need-based aid:* $4766. *Average indebtedness upon graduation:* $15,408.

Applying *Options:* common application, electronic application, early admission, deferred entrance. *Application fee:* $40. *Required:* essay or personal statement, high school transcript, minimum 2.0 GPA. *Recommended:* minimum 2.5 GPA, interview. *Application deadline:* rolling (freshmen), rolling (transfers). *Notification:* continuous (freshmen), continuous (transfers).

Admissions Contact Mr. Richard T. Hinshaw, Vice President for Enrollment Management, Dean of Admissions, Virginia Wesleyan College, 1584 Wesleyan Drive, Norfolk, VA 23502-5599. *Phone:* 757-455-3208. *Toll-free phone:* 800-737-8684. *Fax:* 757-461-5238. *E-mail:* admissions@vwc.edu.

WASHINGTON AND LEE UNIVERSITY
Lexington, Virginia

- **Independent** comprehensive, founded 1749
- **Calendar** 4-4-2
- **Degrees** bachelor's, master's, and first professional
- **Small-town** 322-acre campus
- **Endowment** $416.9 million
- **Coed,** 1,740 undergraduate students, 100% full-time, 48% women, 52% men
- **Most difficult** entrance level, 31% of applicants were admitted

Undergraduates 1,738 full-time, 2 part-time. Students come from 47 states and territories, 37 other countries, 85% are from out of state, 4% African American, 2% Asian American or Pacific Islander, 0.9% Hispanic American, 0.1% Native American, 4% international, 0.1% transferred in, 63% live on campus. *Retention:* 95% of 2001 full-time freshmen returned.

Freshmen *Admission:* 3,185 applied, 996 admitted, 453 enrolled. *Test scores:* SAT verbal scores over 500: 100%; SAT math scores over 500: 100%; ACT scores over 18: 100%; SAT verbal scores over 600: 92%; SAT math scores over 600: 96%; ACT scores over 24: 100%; SAT verbal scores over 700: 44%; SAT math scores over 700: 46%; ACT scores over 30: 47%.

Faculty *Total:* 203, 100% full-time, 90% with terminal degrees. *Student/faculty ratio:* 11:1.

Majors Accounting; anthropology; archeology; art history, criticism and conservation; Asian studies (East); biochemistry; biology/biological sciences; business administration and management; chemical engineering; chemistry; classics; computer science; dramatic/theatre arts; economics; engineering physics; English; fine/studio arts; foreign languages and literatures; French; geological and earth sciences/geosciences related; geology/earth science; German; history; interdisciplinary studies; journalism; mathematics; medieval and Renaissance studies; multi-/interdisciplinary studies related; music; neuroscience; philosophy; physics; political science and government; psychology; public policy analysis; religious studies; Russian studies; sociology; Spanish.

Academic Programs *Special study options:* accelerated degree program, advanced placement credit, double majors, honors programs, independent study, internships, off-campus study, services for LD students, student-designed majors, study abroad. *ROTC:* Army (c). *Unusual degree programs:* 3-2 forestry with Duke University.

Library James G. Leyburn Library plus 4 others with 1.0 million titles, 7,811 serial subscriptions, 13,104 audiovisual materials, an OPAC, a Web page.

Computers on Campus 291 computers available on campus for general student use. A campuswide network can be accessed from student residence rooms and from off campus that provide access to e-mail. Internet access, online (class) registration, at least one staffed computer lab available. Computer purchase or lease plan available.

Student Life *Housing:* on-campus residence required through sophomore year. *Options:* coed, men-only, women-only. Campus housing is university owned. Freshman campus housing is guaranteed. *Activities and organizations:* drama/theater group, student-run newspaper, radio and television station, choral group, outing club, Student Activities Board, Nabors Service League, Mock Convention, College Republicans, national fraternities, national sororities. *Campus security:* 24-hour emergency response devices and patrols, late-night transport/escort service, controlled dormitory access. *Student services:* health clinic, personal/psychological counseling, women's center.

Athletics Member NCAA. All Division III. *Intercollegiate sports:* baseball M, basketball M/W, cross-country running M/W, equestrian sports M/W, fencing M(c)/W(c), field hockey W, football M, golf M, ice hockey M(c)/W(c), lacrosse M(s)/W(s), racquetball M(c)/W(c), rugby M(c)/W(c), skiing (cross-country) M(c)/W(c), soccer M/W, softball W(c), squash M(c)/W(c), swimming M/W, tennis M/W, track and field M/W, volleyball M(c)/W, water polo M(c)/W(c), wrestling M. *Intramural sports:* badminton M, basketball M/W, bowling M/W, cross-country running M/W, football M, golf M/W, skiing (downhill) M(c)/W(c), softball M, swimming M/W, table tennis M, tennis M, ultimate Frisbee M, volleyball M/W, wrestling M.

Standardized Tests *Required:* SAT I or ACT (for admission), 3 unrelated SAT II Subject Tests (including SAT II: Writing Test) (for admission).

Costs (2003–04) *Comprehensive fee:* $29,663 includes full-time tuition ($22,900), mandatory fees ($395), and room and board ($6368). *College room only:* $2698. Room and board charges vary according to housing facility and student level. *Waivers:* employees or children of employees.

Financial Aid Of all full-time matriculated undergraduates who enrolled in 2003, 614 applied for aid, 510 were judged to have need, 491 had their need fully met. 128 Federal Work-Study jobs (averaging $1463). 264 state and other part-time jobs (averaging $1416). In 2003, 387 non-need-based awards were made. *Average percent of need met:* 99%. *Average financial aid package:* $21,045. *Average need-based loan:* $4334. *Average need-based gift aid:* $17,829. *Average non-need-based aid:* $8661. *Average indebtedness upon graduation:* $14,592.

Applying *Options:* common application, electronic application, early decision, deferred entrance. *Application fee:* $40. *Required:* essay or personal statement, high school transcript, 3 letters of recommendation. *Recommended:* interview. *Application deadlines:* 1/15 (freshmen), 4/1 (transfers). *Early decision:* 12/1. *Notification:* 4/1 (freshmen), 12/22 (early decision), continuous (transfers).

Admissions Contact Mr. William M. Hartog, Dean of Admissions and Financial Aid, Washington and Lee University, Lexington, VA 24450-0303. *Phone:* 540-458-8710. *Fax:* 540-458-8062. *E-mail:* admissions@wlu.edu.

WORLD COLLEGE
Virginia Beach, Virginia

- **Proprietary** 4-year, founded 1992
- **Calendar** semesters
- **Degrees** bachelor's (offers only external degree programs)
- **Suburban** campus
- **Coed,** 329 undergraduate students
- **Noncompetitive** entrance level

Undergraduates Students come from 50 states and territories, 25 other countries.

Faculty *Total:* 4, 75% full-time.

Majors Electrical, electronic and communications engineering technology.

Academic Programs *Special study options:* academic remediation for entering students, accelerated degree program, adult/continuing education programs, distance learning, external degree program, part-time degree program.

Student Life *Housing:* college housing not available.

Costs (2003–04) *Tuition:* $2468 full-time, $3290 per term part-time.

Applying *Options:* common application, early admission. *Required:* high school transcript. *Application deadline:* rolling (freshmen). *Notification:* continuous (freshmen).

World College (continued)

Admissions Contact Mr. Michael Smith, Director of Operations and Registrar, World College, 5193 Shore Drive, Suite 105, Virginia Beach, VA 23455. *Phone:* 757-464-4600. *Toll-free phone:* 800-696-7532. *Fax:* 757-464-3687. *E-mail:* instruct@cie-wc.edu.

WASHINGTON

ANTIOCH UNIVERSITY SEATTLE
Seattle, Washington

- **Independent** upper-level, founded 1975, part of Antioch University
- **Calendar** quarters
- **Degrees** certificates, bachelor's, master's, and doctoral
- **Urban** campus with easy access to Seattle
- **Coed,** 209 undergraduate students
- **Noncompetitive** entrance level

Undergraduates Students come from 3 states and territories, 2 other countries, 1% are from out of state, 8% African American, 3% Asian American or Pacific Islander, 3% Hispanic American, 4% Native American, 1% international.

Faculty *Total:* 19, 42% full-time, 58% with terminal degrees. *Student/faculty ratio:* 10:1.

Majors Liberal arts and sciences/liberal studies.

Academic Programs *Special study options:* academic remediation for entering students, accelerated degree program, adult/continuing education programs, advanced placement credit, external degree program, part-time degree program, student-designed majors, study abroad, summer session for credit.

Library Antioch Seattle Library with 4,750 titles, 85 serial subscriptions, an OPAC, a Web page.

Computers on Campus 8 computers available on campus for general student use. A campuswide network can be accessed from off campus. Internet access, at least one staffed computer lab available.

Student Life *Housing:* college housing not available. *Activities and organizations:* student-run newspaper.

Costs (2004–05) *Tuition:* $18,480 full-time, $385 per credit part-time. Full-time tuition and fees vary according to course load. Part-time tuition and fees vary according to course load and program. *Required fees:* $180 full-time, $25 per term part-time. *Payment plan:* installment. *Waivers:* employees or children of employees.

Financial Aid Of all full-time matriculated undergraduates who enrolled in 2002, 201 applied for aid, 201 were judged to have need, 150 had their need fully met. *Average percent of need met:* 75%. *Average financial aid package:* $6681. *Average need-based loan:* $5500. *Average indebtedness upon graduation:* $15,999.

Applying *Options:* electronic application, deferred entrance. *Application fee:* $50. *Application deadline:* 9/15 (transfers). *Notification:* continuous until 10/1 (transfers).

Admissions Contact Ms. Vickie Lopez, Admissions Associate, Antioch University Seattle, 2326 Sixth Avenue, Seattle, WA 98121-1814. *Phone:* 206-441-5352 Ext. 5205. *E-mail:* admissions@antiochsea.edu.

ARGOSY UNIVERSITY/SEATTLE
Seattle, Washington

- **Proprietary** upper-level, founded 1995
- **Calendar** semesters
- **Degrees** bachelor's, master's, and doctoral
- **Urban** campus with easy access to Seattle
- **Coed,** 23 undergraduate students, 100% full-time, 87% women, 13% men
- 100% of applicants were admitted

Undergraduates 23 full-time. Students come from 23 states and territories, 4% are from out of state, 13% African American, 4% Asian American or Pacific Islander, 9% Hispanic American.

Faculty *Total:* 5, 20% full-time, 100% with terminal degrees.

Majors Business/commerce; psychology.

Student Life *Housing:* college housing not available.

Costs (2003–04) *Tuition:* $360 per credit hour part-time. Full-time tuition and fees vary according to course load. Part-time tuition and fees vary according to course load. *Required fees:* $30 per term part-time. *Payment plan:* installment.

Financial Aid Of all full-time matriculated undergraduates who enrolled in 2003, 11 applied for aid, 11 were judged to have need. 1 Federal Work-Study job (averaging $452). *Average financial aid package:* $4734. *Average need-based loan:* $3318. *Average need-based gift aid:* $1572.

Applying *Notification:* continuous (transfers).

Admissions Contact Ms. Heather Simpson, Director of Admissions, Argosy University/Seattle, 1019 Eighth Avenue North, Seattle, WA 98109. *Phone:* 206-283-4500 Ext. 206. *Toll-free phone:* 866-283-2777. *Fax:* 206-283-5777. *E-mail:* seattleadmissions@argosyu.edu.

THE ART INSTITUTE OF SEATTLE
Seattle, Washington

- **Proprietary** primarily 2-year, founded 1982, part of Art Institutes International
- **Calendar** quarters
- **Degrees** diplomas, associate, and bachelor's
- **Urban** campus
- **Endowment** $1950
- **Coed**
- **Moderately difficult** entrance level

Faculty *Student/faculty ratio:* 19:1.

Student Life *Campus security:* 24-hour emergency response devices and patrols, controlled dormitory access, patrols by trained security personnel for 17 hours.

Standardized Tests *Recommended:* SAT I or ACT (for admission).

Costs (2004–05) *Tuition:* $15,750 full-time, $350 per credit part-time. *Room only:* $8355.

Financial Aid Of all full-time matriculated undergraduates who enrolled in 2001, 18 Federal Work-Study jobs (averaging $1795).

Applying *Options:* electronic application, deferred entrance. *Application fee:* $50. *Required:* essay or personal statement, high school transcript, interview. *Recommended:* 3 letters of recommendation.

Admissions Contact Ms. Laine Morgan, Director of Admissions, The Art Institute of Seattle, 2323 Elliott Avenue, Seattle, WA 98121-1622. *Phone:* 800-275-2471. *Toll-free phone:* 800-275-2471. *Fax:* 206-269-0275. *E-mail:* adm@ais.edu.

BASTYR UNIVERSITY
Kenmore, Washington

- **Independent** upper-level, founded 1978
- **Calendar** quarters
- **Degrees** bachelor's, master's, first professional, post-master's, postbachelor's, and first professional certificates
- **Suburban** 50-acre campus with easy access to Seattle
- **Coed,** 224 undergraduate students, 81% full-time, 81% women, 19% men
- 82% of applicants were admitted

Undergraduates 181 full-time, 43 part-time. Students come from 20 states and territories, 5 other countries, 5% Asian American or Pacific Islander, 3% Hispanic American, 0.9% Native American, 6% international, 55% transferred in, 6% live on campus.

Faculty *Total:* 130, 38% full-time, 100% with terminal degrees. *Student/faculty ratio:* 15:1.

Majors Dietetics; foods, nutrition, and wellness; health science; herbalism; kinesiology and exercise science; psychology.

Academic Programs *Special study options:* cooperative education, double majors, independent study, internships, part-time degree program, summer session for credit.

Library Bastyr University Library with 12,000 titles, 250 serial subscriptions, 4,800 audiovisual materials, an OPAC, a Web page.

Computers on Campus 16 computers available on campus for general student use. A campuswide network can be accessed from student residence rooms and from off campus. Internet access, at least one staffed computer lab available.

Student Life *Housing options:* coed. Campus housing is university owned. *Activities and organizations:* student-run newspaper, Parent Resource Center, nature club, Spirituality in Focus, Environmental Action Team, Toastmasters. *Campus security:* student patrols, late-night transport/escort service. *Student services:* health clinic, personal/psychological counseling.

Athletics *Intramural sports:* basketball M, soccer M/W, ultimate Frisbee M/W, volleyball M/W.

Costs (2003–04) *Tuition:* $11,600 full-time, $252 per credit part-time. Full-time tuition and fees vary according to course load and program. Part-time tuition and fees vary according to course load and program. *Required fees:* $918 full-time. *Room only:* $4420. Room and board charges vary according to board plan and housing facility. *Waivers:* employees or children of employees.

Financial Aid Of all full-time matriculated undergraduates who enrolled in 2003, 210 applied for aid, 190 were judged to have need. 49 Federal Work-Study jobs (averaging $3066). 44 state and other part-time jobs (averaging $2648). *Average percent of need met:* 50%. *Average financial aid package:* $15,650. *Average need-based loan:* $5500. *Average need-based gift aid:* $4350. *Average indebtedness upon graduation:* $21,000.

Applying *Options:* deferred entrance. *Application fee:* $60. *Application deadline:* 3/15 (transfers). *Notification:* continuous until 9/1 (transfers).

Admissions Contact Mr. Richard Dent, Director of Student Enrollment, Bastyr University, 14500 Juanita Drive NE, Kenmore, WA 98028-4966. *Phone:* 425-602-3080. *Fax:* 425-602-3090. *E-mail:* admiss@bastyr.edu.

■ *See page 1218 for a narrative description.*

CENTRAL WASHINGTON UNIVERSITY

Ellensburg, Washington

- **State-supported** comprehensive, founded 1891
- **Calendar** quarters
- **Degrees** bachelor's, master's, and postbachelor's certificates
- **Small-town** 380-acre campus
- **Endowment** $8.6 million
- **Coed,** 9,296 undergraduate students, 88% full-time, 52% women, 48% men
- **Moderately difficult** entrance level, 84% of applicants were admitted

Undergraduates 8,187 full-time, 1,109 part-time. Students come from 29 states and territories, 40 other countries, 2% are from out of state, 2% African American, 5% Asian American or Pacific Islander, 5% Hispanic American, 2% Native American, 1% international, 13% transferred in, 33% live on campus. *Retention:* 76% of 2002 full-time freshmen returned.

Freshmen *Admission:* 3,905 applied, 3,261 admitted, 1,336 enrolled. *Average high school GPA:* 3.19. *Test scores:* SAT verbal scores over 500: 47%; SAT math scores over 500: 49%; ACT scores over 18: 79%; SAT verbal scores over 600: 13%; SAT math scores over 600: 12%; ACT scores over 24: 21%; SAT verbal scores over 700: 1%; SAT math scores over 700: 1%; ACT scores over 30: 2%.

Faculty *Total:* 494, 68% full-time, 71% with terminal degrees. *Student/faculty ratio:* 23:1.

Majors Accounting; aeronautics/aviation/aerospace science and technology; anthropology; art; art teacher education; Asian studies; biology/biological sciences; biology teacher education; business administration and management; business teacher education; chemistry; chemistry teacher education; community health services counseling; computer and information sciences; criminal justice/law enforcement administration; drama and dance teacher education; dramatic/theatre arts; early childhood education; economics; electrical, electronic and communications engineering technology; elementary education; emergency medical technology (EMT paramedic); English; English/language arts teacher education; family and consumer sciences/human sciences; fashion merchandising; foods, nutrition, and wellness; foreign languages and literatures; French language teacher education; geography; geology/earth science; German language teacher education; gerontology; health teacher education; history; history teacher education; industrial technology; journalism; kindergarten/preschool education; kinesiology and exercise science; mass communication/media; mathematics; mathematics teacher education; mechanical engineering/mechanical technology; music; music management and merchandising; music teacher education; music theory and composition; natural resources management; occupational safety and health technology; office management; operations management; parks, recreation and leisure; philosophy; physical education teaching and coaching; physics; piano and organ; political science and government; psychology; public policy analysis; public relations/image management; radio and television; religious studies; science teacher education; social science teacher education; sociology; Spanish language teacher education; special education; sport and fitness administration; technology/industrial arts teacher education; trade and industrial teacher education; voice and opera.

Academic Programs *Special study options:* academic remediation for entering students, adult/continuing education programs, advanced placement credit, cooperative education, distance learning, double majors, English as a second language, honors programs, independent study, internships, off-campus study, part-time degree program, services for LD students, student-designed majors, study abroad, summer session for credit. *ROTC:* Army (b), Air Force (b). *Unusual degree programs:* 3-2 engineering with University of Washington, Washington State University.

Library Central Washington University Library with 434,424 titles, 1,469 serial subscriptions, 9,230 audiovisual materials, an OPAC, a Web page.

Computers on Campus 712 computers available on campus for general student use. A campuswide network can be accessed from student residence rooms and from off campus. Internet access, at least one staffed computer lab available.

Student Life *Housing:* on-campus residence required for freshman year. *Options:* coed, women-only, disabled students. Campus housing is university owned. Freshman campus housing is guaranteed. *Activities and organizations:* drama/theater group, student-run newspaper, radio station, choral group, marching band, international business club, marketing club, Associated Students of CWU. *Campus security:* 24-hour emergency response devices and patrols, late-night transport/escort service, controlled dormitory access. *Student services:* health clinic, personal/psychological counseling.

Athletics Member NCAA. All Division II. *Intercollegiate sports:* baseball M(s), basketball M(s)/W(s), bowling M(c)/W(c), cheerleading M/W, cross-country running M(s)/W(s), fencing M(c)/W(c), football M(s), golf M(c)/W(c), ice hockey M(c)/W(c), rugby M(c)/W(c), soccer M(c)/W(s), softball W(s), swimming M(s)/W(s), track and field M(s)/W(s), volleyball W(s), water polo M(c)/W(c), wrestling M(s). *Intramural sports:* badminton M/W, basketball M/W, football M/W, golf M/W, racquetball M/W, soccer M/W, softball M/W, tennis M/W, ultimate Frisbee M/W, volleyball M/W.

Standardized Tests *Required:* SAT I or ACT (for admission).

Costs (2003–04) *Tuition:* state resident $3654 full-time, $122 per credit part-time; nonresident $11,430 full-time, $381 per credit part-time. Full-time tuition and fees vary according to location. Part-time tuition and fees vary according to course load and location. *Required fees:* $369 full-time. *Room and board:* $5745; room only: $3000. Room and board charges vary according to board plan and housing facility. *Waivers:* senior citizens and employees or children of employees.

Financial Aid Of all full-time matriculated undergraduates who enrolled in 2002, 5,057 applied for aid, 3,618 were judged to have need, 698 had their need fully met. 242 Federal Work-Study jobs (averaging $2027). 234 state and other part-time jobs (averaging $2484). In 2002, 2286 non-need-based awards were made. *Average percent of need met:* 83%. *Average financial aid package:* $4567. *Average need-based loan:* $3998. *Average need-based gift aid:* $5098. *Average non-need-based aid:* $4186. *Average indebtedness upon graduation:* $16,382.

Applying *Options:* electronic application. *Application fee:* $35. *Required:* high school transcript, minimum 2.0 GPA. *Required for some:* essay or personal statement, letters of recommendation, interview. *Application deadline:* 5/1 (freshmen), rolling (transfers). *Notification:* continuous (freshmen), continuous (transfers).

Admissions Contact Mr. Mike Reilly, Director of Admissions, Central Washington University, 400 East University Way, Ellensburg, WA 98926-7463. *Phone:* 509-963-1211. *Toll-free phone:* 866-298-4968. *Fax:* 509-963-3022. *E-mail:* cwuadmis@cwu.edu.

CITY UNIVERSITY

Bellevue, Washington

- **Independent** comprehensive, founded 1973
- **Calendar** quarters
- **Degrees** certificates, diplomas, associate, bachelor's, master's, and postbachelor's certificates
- **Suburban** campus with easy access to Seattle
- **Endowment** $195,000
- **Coed,** 2,877 undergraduate students, 10% full-time, 45% women, 55% men
- **Noncompetitive** entrance level, 100% of applicants were admitted

Undergraduates 297 full-time, 2,580 part-time. Students come from 47 states and territories, 33 other countries, 35% are from out of state, 6% African American, 9% Asian American or Pacific Islander, 3% Hispanic American, 1% Native American, 5% international, 73% transferred in.

Freshmen *Admission:* 1,460 applied, 1,460 admitted.

Faculty *Total:* 1,095, 5% full-time, 98% with terminal degrees. *Student/faculty ratio:* 18:1.

Majors Accounting; business administration and management; clinical/medical laboratory technology; computer and information sciences and support services related; computer programming; elementary education; general studies; international business/trade/commerce; journalism related; mass communication/media; psychology; special education.

Academic Programs *Special study options:* accelerated degree program, adult/continuing education programs, advanced placement credit, distance learning, double majors, English as a second language, external degree program, honors programs, independent study, internships, part-time degree program, services for LD students, summer session for credit.

Library City University Library with 32,329 titles, 1,518 serial subscriptions, 5,184 audiovisual materials, an OPAC, a Web page.

Computers on Campus 145 computers available on campus for general student use. A campuswide network can be accessed from off campus. Internet access, at least one staffed computer lab available.

Student Life *Housing:* college housing not available. *Campus security:* 24-hour emergency response devices.

City University (continued)

Costs (2003–04) *Tuition:* $7960 full-time, $199 per credit hour part-time. *Required fees:* $100 full-time.

Financial Aid Of all full-time matriculated undergraduates who enrolled in 2002, 651 applied for aid, 586 were judged to have need. In 2002, 9 non-need-based awards were made. *Average percent of need met:* 20%. *Average financial aid package:* $4690. *Average need-based loan:* $4191. *Average need-based gift aid:* $2118. *Average non-need-based aid:* $4132. *Average indebtedness upon graduation:* $18,540.

Applying *Options:* common application, electronic application, deferred entrance. *Application fee:* $80. *Recommended:* high school transcript. *Application deadline:* rolling (freshmen), rolling (transfers). *Notification:* continuous (freshmen).

Admissions Contact Mr. Kent Gibson, Executive Vice President, Admissions and Administration, City University, 11900 NE First Street, Bellevue, WA 98005. *Phone:* 800-426-5596 Ext. 4661. *Toll-free phone:* 888-42-CITYU. *Fax:* 425-709-7699. *E-mail:* info@cityu.edu.

■ *See page 1406 for a narrative description.*

CORNISH COLLEGE OF THE ARTS
Seattle, Washington

- **Independent** 4-year, founded 1914
- **Calendar** semesters
- **Degree** certificates and bachelor's
- **Urban** 4-acre campus
- **Endowment** $636,870
- **Coed,** 696 undergraduate students, 97% full-time, 64% women, 36% men
- **Moderately difficult** entrance level, 81% of applicants were admitted

Undergraduates 672 full-time, 24 part-time. Students come from 27 states and territories, 14 other countries, 40% are from out of state, 4% African American, 6% Asian American or Pacific Islander, 4% Hispanic American, 1% Native American, 3% international, 5% transferred in.

Freshmen *Admission:* 602 applied, 488 admitted, 128 enrolled. *Average high school GPA:* 3.03.

Faculty *Total:* 135, 39% full-time, 35% with terminal degrees. *Student/faculty ratio:* 12:1.

Majors Acting; art; dance; directing and theatrical production; dramatic/theatre arts; fine/studio arts; graphic design; illustration; interior design; jazz/jazz studies; music; piano and organ; theatre design and technology; violin, viola, guitar and other stringed instruments; voice and opera.

Academic Programs *Special study options:* academic remediation for entering students, advanced placement credit, independent study, internships, services for LD students, study abroad, summer session for credit.

Library Cornish College of the Arts Library plus 2 others with 12,000 titles, 3,000 serial subscriptions, an OPAC.

Computers on Campus 20 computers available on campus for general student use. A campuswide network can be accessed from off campus. Internet access, at least one staffed computer lab available.

Student Life *Housing:* college housing not available. *Activities and organizations:* drama/theater group, student-run newspaper, choral group, Birds and Whistles (Arts Magazine), film society, Black Student Alliance, Student Leadership Council, Sports/Intramural Club. *Campus security:* 24-hour emergency response devices and patrols, late-night transport/escort service. *Student services:* personal/psychological counseling.

Standardized Tests *Recommended:* SAT I or ACT (for admission).

Costs (2003–04) *Tuition:* $18,300 full-time, $775 per credit part-time. Part-time tuition and fees vary according to program. *Required fees:* $300 full-time. *Payment plan:* installment. *Waivers:* employees or children of employees.

Financial Aid Of all full-time matriculated undergraduates who enrolled in 2001, 573 applied for aid, 485 were judged to have need, 24 had their need fully met. In 2001, 40 non-need-based awards were made. *Average percent of need met:* 51%. *Average financial aid package:* $10,240. *Average need-based loan:* $4005. *Average need-based gift aid:* $5265. *Average indebtedness upon graduation:* $23,000.

Applying *Options:* electronic application, deferred entrance. *Application fee:* $35. *Required:* essay or personal statement, high school transcript, minimum 2.0 GPA, portfolio or audition. *Required for some:* 2 letters of recommendation. *Recommended:* 2 letters of recommendation, interview. *Application deadlines:* 8/15 (freshmen), 8/15 (transfers). *Notification:* continuous (freshmen), continuous (transfers).

Admissions Contact Ms. Sharron Starling, Associate Director of Admissions, Cornish College of the Arts, 1000 Lenora Street, Seattle, WA 98121. *Phone:* 206-726-5017. *Toll-free phone:* 800-726-ARTS. *Fax:* 206-720-1011. *E-mail:* admissions@cornish.edu.

CROWN COLLEGE
Tacoma, Washington

- **Proprietary** primarily 2-year, founded 1969
- **Calendar** continuous
- **Degrees** associate and bachelor's (bachelor's degree in public administration only)
- **Urban** campus with easy access to Seattle
- **Coed**
- 95% of applicants were admitted

Faculty *Student/faculty ratio:* 20:1.

Student Life *Campus security:* 24-hour emergency response devices.

Applying *Options:* common application, electronic application. *Application fee:* $135. *Required:* high school transcript, interview. *Required for some:* essay or personal statement.

Admissions Contact Ms. Sheila Millineaux, Admissions Director, Crown College, 8739 South Hosmer, Tacoma, WA 98444. *Phone:* 253-531-3123. *Toll-free phone:* 800-755-9525 (in-state); 888-689-3688 (out-of-state). *Fax:* 253-531-3521. *E-mail:* admissions@crowncollege.edu.

DEVRY UNIVERSITY
Bellevue, Washington

Admissions Contact 500 108th Avenue NE, Suite 320, Bellevue, WA 98004-5519.

DEVRY UNIVERSITY
Federal Way, Washington

- **Proprietary** comprehensive, founded 2001, part of DeVry University
- **Calendar** semesters
- **Degrees** associate, bachelor's, and postbachelor's certificates
- **Suburban** 12-acre campus
- **Coed**
- **Minimally difficult** entrance level

Student Life *Campus security:* 24-hour emergency response devices and patrols, lighted pathways, emergency response team.

Standardized Tests *Recommended:* SAT I, ACT or CPT.

Costs (2003–04) *Tuition:* $11,100 full-time, $395 per credit hour part-time. Full-time tuition and fees vary according to course load. Part-time tuition and fees vary according to course load. *Required fees:* $165 full-time. *Payment plans:* installment, deferred payment.

Financial Aid Of all full-time matriculated undergraduates who enrolled in 2002, 684 applied for aid, 657 were judged to have need, 15 had their need fully met. In 2002, 40. *Average percent of need met:* 33. *Average financial aid package:* $7190. *Average need-based loan:* $5153. *Average need-based gift aid:* $3856. *Average non-need-based aid:* $11,520.

Applying *Options:* electronic application, deferred entrance. *Application fee:* $50. *Required:* high school transcript, interview.

Admissions Contact Ms. Latanya Kibby, Assistant New Student Coordinator, DeVry University, 3600 South 344th Way, Federal Way, WA 98001-9558. *Phone:* 253-943-2800. *Toll-free phone:* 877-923-3879. *Fax:* 253-943-3291. *E-mail:* admissions@sea.devry.edu.

EASTERN WASHINGTON UNIVERSITY
Cheney, Washington

- **State-supported** comprehensive, founded 1882
- **Calendar** quarters
- **Degrees** bachelor's, master's, and doctoral
- **Small-town** 335-acre campus
- **Endowment** $4.5 million
- **Coed,** 9,067 undergraduate students, 85% full-time, 58% women, 42% men
- **Moderately difficult** entrance level, 81% of applicants were admitted

Undergraduates 7,679 full-time, 1,388 part-time. 9% are from out of state, 2% African American, 3% Asian American or Pacific Islander, 5% Hispanic American, 2% Native American, 1% international, 12% transferred in, 21% live on campus. *Retention:* 82% of 2002 full-time freshmen returned.

Freshmen *Admission:* 3,585 applied, 2,913 admitted, 1,393 enrolled. *Average high school GPA:* 3.29. *Test scores:* SAT verbal scores over 500: 50%; SAT math scores over 500: 51%; ACT scores over 18: 81%; SAT verbal scores over 600: 16%; SAT math scores over 600: 16%; ACT scores over 24: 25%; SAT verbal scores over 700: 1%; SAT math scores over 700: 1%; ACT scores over 30: 2%.

Faculty *Total:* 505, 73% full-time, 72% with terminal degrees. *Student/faculty ratio:* 23:1.

Majors Accounting; anthropology; art history, criticism and conservation; art teacher education; athletic training; audiology and speech-language pathology; biochemistry; biological and physical sciences; biology/biological sciences; biotechnology; business administration and management; business/managerial economics; business teacher education; chemistry; chemistry teacher education; child care and support services management; child development; city/urban, community and regional planning; communication and journalism related; communication disorders; communication/speech communication and rhetoric; computer and information sciences; computer engineering technology; computer software and media applications related; computer teacher education; construction engineering technology; corrections; creative writing; criminal justice/law enforcement administration; dental hygiene; developmental and child psychology; digital communication and media/multimedia; drafting/design engineering technologies related; drama and dance teacher education; dramatic/theatre arts; early childhood education; economics; education related; education (specific subject areas) related; electrical, electronic and communications engineering technology; elementary education; engineering technology; English; English as a second/foreign language (teaching); English/language arts teacher education; environmental biology; environmental science; finance; fine/studio arts; French; French language teacher education; geography; geology/earth science; German language teacher education; health and physical education; health/health care administration; health teacher education; history; humanities; human resources management; interdisciplinary studies; international relations and affairs; journalism; journalism related; kinesiology and exercise science; liberal arts and sciences/liberal studies; literature; management information systems; manufacturing technology; marketing/marketing management; mathematics; mathematics related; mathematics teacher education; mechanical engineering/mechanical technology; music; music performance; music teacher education; music theory and composition; natural sciences; nursing (registered nurse training); occupational therapy; organizational communication; parks, recreation and leisure; parks, recreation and leisure facilities management; philosophy; physical education teaching and coaching; physical sciences; physical therapy; physics; physics teacher education; piano and organ; political science and government; pre-dentistry studies; pre-law studies; premedical studies; pre-veterinary studies; psychology; public administration; reading teacher education; school librarian/school library media; science teacher education; social studies teacher education; social work; sociology; Spanish; Spanish language teacher education; special education; special education (early childhood); speech therapy; statistics; therapeutic recreation; voice and opera.

Academic Programs *Special study options:* advanced placement credit, cooperative education, distance learning, double majors, English as a second language, honors programs, independent study, internships, off-campus study, part-time degree program, services for LD students, student-designed majors, study abroad, summer session for credit. *ROTC:* Army (b).

Library John F. Kennedy Library plus 1 other with 852,186 titles, 6,429 serial subscriptions, 31,832 audiovisual materials, an OPAC, a Web page.

Computers on Campus 226 computers available on campus for general student use. A campuswide network can be accessed from student residence rooms and from off campus that provide access to e-mail. Internet access, online (class) registration, at least one staffed computer lab available. Computer purchase or lease plan available.

Student Life *Housing options:* coed, men-only, women-only, disabled students. Campus housing is university owned. *Activities and organizations:* drama/theater group, student-run newspaper, radio and television station, choral group, marching band, International Student Association, cultural heritage groups, Eagle Ambassadors, business/honor fraternities, religious organizations, national fraternities, national sororities. *Campus security:* 24-hour emergency response devices and patrols, student patrols, late-night transport/escort service, controlled dormitory access, emergency call boxes. *Student services:* health clinic, personal/psychological counseling, women's center.

Athletics Member NCAA. All Division I except football (Division I-AA). *Intercollegiate sports:* badminton M(c), baseball M(c), basketball M(s)/W(s), cross-country running M(s)/W(s), golf M(s)/W(s), ice hockey M(c), soccer W(s), tennis M(s)/W(s), track and field M(s)/W(s), volleyball W(s). *Intramural sports:* baseball M/W, basketball M/W, bowling M/W, cross-country running M/W, football M/W, golf M/W, racquetball M/W, rugby W(c), soccer M/W, softball M/W, tennis M/W, track and field M/W, volleyball M/W, wrestling M(c).

Standardized Tests *Required:* SAT I or ACT (for admission).

Costs (2003–04) *Tuition:* state resident $3582 full-time, $119 per credit part-time; nonresident $12,438 full-time, $415 per credit part-time. Part-time tuition and fees vary according to course load. *Required fees:* $230 full-time. *Room and board:* $5200. Room and board charges vary according to board plan and housing facility. *Payment plan:* installment. *Waivers:* employees or children of employees.

Financial Aid Of all full-time matriculated undergraduates who enrolled in 2002, 5,224 applied for aid, 4,376 were judged to have need, 624 had their need fully met. 365 Federal Work-Study jobs (averaging $2034). 497 state and other part-time jobs (averaging $2422). In 2002, 154 non-need-based awards were made. *Average percent of need met:* 40%. *Average financial aid package:* $15,444. *Average need-based loan:* $3654. *Average need-based gift aid:* $4676. *Average non-need-based aid:* $3309. *Average indebtedness upon graduation:* $17,357.

Applying *Options:* common application, electronic application, early admission, deferred entrance. *Application fee:* $35. *Required:* high school transcript, minimum 2.0 GPA. *Required for some:* essay or personal statement, letters of recommendation, interview. *Recommended:* minimum 3.0 GPA. *Application deadline:* rolling (freshmen), rolling (transfers). *Notification:* continuous (freshmen), continuous (transfers).

Admissions Contact Ms. Michelle Whittingham, Director of Admissions, Eastern Washington University, 526 Fifth Street, SUT 101, Cheney, WA 99004-2447. *Phone:* 509-359-6582. *Fax:* 509-359-6692. *E-mail:* admissions@mail.ewu.edu.

■ *See page 1566 for a narrative description.*

THE EVERGREEN STATE COLLEGE
Olympia, Washington

- **State-supported** comprehensive, founded 1967
- **Calendar** quarters
- **Degrees** bachelor's and master's
- **Small-town** 1000-acre campus with easy access to Seattle
- **Endowment** $2.4 million
- **Coed,** 4,103 undergraduate students, 86% full-time, 56% women, 44% men
- **Moderately difficult** entrance level, 93% of applicants were admitted

Undergraduates 3,546 full-time, 557 part-time. Students come from 54 states and territories, 15 other countries, 23% are from out of state, 5% African American, 4% Asian American or Pacific Islander, 4% Hispanic American, 4% Native American, 0.2% international, 21% transferred in, 21% live on campus. *Retention:* 75% of 2002 full-time freshmen returned.

Freshmen *Admission:* 1,521 applied, 1,422 admitted, 460 enrolled. *Average high school GPA:* 3.15. *Test scores:* SAT verbal scores over 500: 88%; SAT math scores over 500: 73%; ACT scores over 18: 96%; SAT verbal scores over 600: 52%; SAT math scores over 600: 29%; ACT scores over 24: 55%; SAT verbal scores over 700: 12%; SAT math scores over 700: 4%; ACT scores over 30: 9%.

Faculty *Total:* 219, 72% full-time, 74% with terminal degrees. *Student/faculty ratio:* 21:1.

Majors American Indian/Native American studies; area, ethnic, cultural, and gender studies related; art; biological and physical sciences; biology/biological sciences; business administration and management; cinematography and film/video production; classics and languages, literatures and linguistics; computer and information sciences; cultural studies; dramatic/theatre arts; environmental studies; fine/studio arts; humanities; intermedia/multimedia; international/global studies; liberal arts and sciences/liberal studies; multi-/interdisciplinary studies related; natural sciences; physical sciences; political science and government; social sciences; visual and performing arts.

Academic Programs *Special study options:* accelerated degree program, advanced placement credit, cooperative education, distance learning, double majors, independent study, internships, off-campus study, part-time degree program, services for LD students, student-designed majors, study abroad, summer session for credit.

Library Daniel J. Evans Library with 473,386 titles, 7,682 serial subscriptions, 90,396 audiovisual materials, an OPAC, a Web page.

Computers on Campus 300 computers available on campus for general student use. A campuswide network can be accessed from student residence rooms and from off campus. Internet access, online (class) registration, at least one staffed computer lab available.

Student Life *Housing options:* coed. Campus housing is university owned. Freshman campus housing is guaranteed. *Activities and organizations:* drama/theater group, student-run newspaper, radio and television station, choral group, Environmental Resource Center, Women's Resource Center, Evergreen Queer Alliance, Evergreen Political Information Center. *Campus security:* 24-hour emergency response devices and patrols, student patrols, late-night transport/escort service, controlled dormitory access. *Student services:* health clinic, personal/psychological counseling, women's center.

Athletics Member NAIA. *Intercollegiate sports:* basketball M(s)/W(s), cross-country running M(s)/W(s), soccer M(s)/W(s), volleyball W(s). *Intramural sports:* badminton M/W, basketball M/W, soccer M/W, softball M/W, table tennis M/W, tennis M/W, ultimate Frisbee M/W, volleyball M/W, water polo M/W.

Standardized Tests *Required:* SAT I or ACT (for admission).

The Evergreen State College (continued)

Costs (2003–04) *Tuition:* state resident $3651 full-time, $122 per quarter hour part-time; nonresident $13,332 full-time, $444 per quarter hour part-time. Full-time tuition and fees vary according to course load and degree level. Part-time tuition and fees vary according to course load and degree level. *Required fees:* $153 full-time, $1 per credit hour part-time, $39 per term part-time. *Room and board:* $5772; room only: $3582. Room and board charges vary according to board plan and housing facility. *Payment plan:* installment. *Waivers:* employees or children of employees.

Financial Aid Of all full-time matriculated undergraduates who enrolled in 2002, 2,684 applied for aid, 2,044 were judged to have need, 663 had their need fully met. 193 Federal Work-Study jobs (averaging $1934). 162 state and other part-time jobs (averaging $2155). In 2002, 22 non-need-based awards were made. *Average percent of need met:* 79%. *Average financial aid package:* $10,006. *Average need-based loan:* $3984. *Average need-based gift aid:* $5406. *Average non-need-based aid:* $3862. *Average indebtedness upon graduation:* $13,000.

Applying *Options:* electronic application, early admission. *Application fee:* $36. *Required:* high school transcript, minimum 2.0 GPA. *Required for some:* interview. *Recommended:* essay or personal statement. *Application deadlines:* 3/1 (freshmen), 3/1 (transfers). *Notification:* 4/1 (freshmen), 4/1 (transfers).

Admissions Contact Mr. Doug P. Scrima, Director of Admissions, The Evergreen State College, 2700 Evergreen Parkway NW, Olympia, WA 98505. *Phone:* 360-867-6170. *Fax:* 360-867-6576. *E-mail:* admissions@evergreen.edu.

■ *See page 1602 for a narrative description.*

GONZAGA UNIVERSITY
Spokane, Washington

- **Independent Roman Catholic** comprehensive, founded 1887
- **Calendar** semesters
- **Degrees** bachelor's, master's, doctoral, first professional, and post-master's certificates
- **Urban** 94-acre campus
- **Endowment** $95.0 million
- **Coed,** 3,981 undergraduate students, 95% full-time, 55% women, 45% men
- **Moderately difficult** entrance level, 77% of applicants were admitted

Gonzaga's nationally dominant debate team, exceptional medical school acceptance rate, and CPA examination pass rates exemplify its commitment to academic excellence. A 37,000-square-foot addition to Hughes Hall Life Sciences Building is expected to add new laboratories and the Inland Northwest Natural Resources Research Center. The Martin Athletic Center's face-lift includes a 13,000-square-foot modern fitness center.

Undergraduates 3,766 full-time, 215 part-time. Students come from 44 states and territories, 33 other countries, 48% are from out of state, 1% African American, 5% Asian American or Pacific Islander, 3% Hispanic American, 1% Native American, 1% international, 5% transferred in, 51% live on campus. *Retention:* 90% of 2002 full-time freshmen returned.

Freshmen *Admission:* 3,713 applied, 2,846 admitted, 908 enrolled. *Average high school GPA:* 3.66. *Test scores:* SAT verbal scores over 500: 89%; SAT math scores over 500: 89%; ACT scores over 18: 99%; SAT verbal scores over 600: 48%; SAT math scores over 600: 50%; ACT scores over 24: 81%; SAT verbal scores over 700: 9%; SAT math scores over 700: 9%; ACT scores over 30: 20%.

Faculty *Total:* 532, 57% full-time. *Student/faculty ratio:* 12:1.

Majors Accounting; art; Asian studies; biochemistry; biology/biological sciences; broadcast journalism; business administration and management; business/managerial economics; chemistry; civil engineering; computer engineering; computer science; criminal justice/law enforcement administration; dramatic/theatre arts; economics; electrical, electronics and communications engineering; elementary education; engineering; English; finance; French; German; history; information science/studies; international business/trade/commerce; international relations and affairs; Italian; journalism; kinesiology and exercise science; liberal arts and sciences/liberal studies; literature; marketing/marketing management; mass communication/media; mathematics; mechanical engineering; music; music teacher education; nursing (registered nurse training); philosophy; physical education teaching and coaching; physics; political science and government; psychology; public relations/image management; religious studies; secondary education; sociology; Spanish; special education; speech and rhetoric; sport and fitness administration.

Academic Programs *Special study options:* adult/continuing education programs, advanced placement credit, distance learning, double majors, English as a second language, honors programs, independent study, internships, off-campus study, part-time degree program, services for LD students, student-designed majors, study abroad, summer session for credit. *ROTC:* Army (b).

Library Ralph E. and Helen Higgins Foley Center plus 1 other with 228,622 titles, 1,435 serial subscriptions, 2,617 audiovisual materials, an OPAC, a Web page.

Computers on Campus 350 computers available on campus for general student use. A campuswide network can be accessed from student residence rooms and from off campus. Internet access, online (class) registration, at least one staffed computer lab available. Computer purchase or lease plan available.

Student Life *Housing:* on-campus residence required through sophomore year. *Options:* coed, men-only, women-only. Campus housing is university owned and leased by the school. Freshman campus housing is guaranteed. *Activities and organizations:* drama/theater group, student-run newspaper, radio and television station, choral group, Student Body Association, Search, Circle K, Encore, Knights and Setons. *Campus security:* 24-hour emergency response devices and patrols, late-night transport/escort service, controlled dormitory access. *Student services:* health clinic, personal/psychological counseling.

Athletics Member NCAA. All Division I except men's and women's cheerleading (Division III). *Intercollegiate sports:* baseball M(s), basketball M(s)/W(s), cheerleading M/W, crew M(c)/W(c), cross-country running M/W, golf M/W, skiing (cross-country) M(c)/W(c), skiing (downhill) M(c)/W(c), soccer M(s)/W(s), tennis M(s)/W(s), track and field M/W, volleyball W(s). *Intramural sports:* basketball M(c)/W(c), football M(c)/W(c), racquetball M(c)/W(c), softball M(c)/W(c), ultimate Frisbee M(c)/W(c), volleyball M(c)/W(c).

Standardized Tests *Required:* SAT I or ACT (for admission).

Costs (2003–04) *Comprehensive fee:* $26,695 includes full-time tuition ($20,510), mandatory fees ($225), and room and board ($5960). Part-time tuition: $595 per credit. *Required fees:* $25 per term part-time. *College room only:* $3110. Room and board charges vary according to board plan and housing facility. *Payment plan:* installment. *Waivers:* employees or children of employees.

Financial Aid Of all full-time matriculated undergraduates who enrolled in 2002, 2,744 applied for aid, 2,483 were judged to have need, 699 had their need fully met. 391 Federal Work-Study jobs (averaging $2874). 430 state and other part-time jobs (averaging $4307). In 2002, 1012 non-need-based awards were made. *Average percent of need met:* 83%. *Average financial aid package:* $13,271. *Average need-based loan:* $5165. *Average need-based gift aid:* $10,710. *Average non-need-based aid:* $6420. *Average indebtedness upon graduation:* $21,469.

Applying *Options:* common application, electronic application, early admission, early action, deferred entrance. *Application fee:* $40. *Required:* essay or personal statement, high school transcript, minimum 3.0 GPA, 1 letter of recommendation. *Recommended:* interview. *Application deadlines:* 2/1 (freshmen), 7/1 (transfers). *Notification:* 3/15 (freshmen), 1/15 (early action), continuous (transfers).

Admissions Contact Ms. Julie McCulloh, Dean of Admission, Gonzaga University, 502 East Boone Avenue, Spokane, WA 99258-0102. *Phone:* 509-323-6591. *Toll-free phone:* 800-322-2584 Ext. 6572. *Fax:* 509-323-5780. *E-mail:* admissions@gonzaga.edu.

■ *See page 1672 for a narrative description.*

HENRY COGSWELL COLLEGE
Everett, Washington

- **Independent** 4-year, founded 1979
- **Calendar** trimesters
- **Degree** bachelor's
- **Urban** 1-acre campus with easy access to Seattle
- **Endowment** $161,758
- **Coed,** 230 undergraduate students, 77% full-time, 25% women, 75% men
- **Noncompetitive** entrance level, 83% of applicants were admitted

Undergraduates 178 full-time, 52 part-time. Students come from 3 states and territories, 0.9% African American, 10% Asian American or Pacific Islander, 1% Hispanic American, 0.9% Native American, 3% international, 11% transferred in. *Retention:* 85% of 2002 full-time freshmen returned.

Freshmen *Admission:* 60 applied, 50 admitted, 27 enrolled. *Average high school GPA:* 3.21. *Test scores:* SAT verbal scores over 500: 86%; SAT math scores over 500: 73%; SAT verbal scores over 600: 27%; SAT math scores over 600: 32%; SAT verbal scores over 700: 9%; SAT math scores over 700: 5%.

Faculty *Total:* 31, 26% full-time, 32% with terminal degrees. *Student/faculty ratio:* 12:1.

Majors Business administration and management; computer science; design and visual communications; electrical, electronics and communications engineering; mechanical engineering.

Academic Programs *Special study options:* academic remediation for entering students, accelerated degree program, adult/continuing education programs, advanced placement credit, cooperative education, double majors, independent study, part-time degree program, summer session for credit.

Library Robert W. Phinney Library with 9,423 titles, 60 serial subscriptions, 53 audiovisual materials, an OPAC.

Computers on Campus 100 computers available on campus for general student use. A campuswide network can be accessed from off campus. Internet access, at least one staffed computer lab available.

Student Life *Housing:* college housing not available. *Activities and organizations:* Leadership Council, IEEE, ASME, ACM, Sigma Iota Epsilon. *Campus security:* controlled dormitory access.

Standardized Tests *Required:* SAT I or ACT (for admission). *Recommended:* SAT I (for admission).

Costs (2004–05) *One-time required fee:* $75. *Tuition:* $15,840 full-time, $660 per credit part-time. Full-time tuition and fees vary according to course load. No tuition increase for student's term of enrollment. *Payment plans:* installment, deferred payment. *Waivers:* employees or children of employees.

Financial Aid Of all full-time matriculated undergraduates who enrolled in 2003, 127 applied for aid, 99 were judged to have need. 9 Federal Work-Study jobs (averaging $903). 9 state and other part-time jobs (averaging $684). In 2003, 8 non-need-based awards were made. *Average financial aid package:* $5584. *Average need-based loan:* $3642. *Average need-based gift aid:* $4690. *Average non-need-based aid:* $3053. *Average indebtedness upon graduation:* $23,650.

Applying *Options:* common application, electronic application, deferred entrance. *Application fee:* $50. *Required:* essay or personal statement, high school transcript. *Required for some:* 3 letters of recommendation, portfolio. *Recommended:* interview. *Application deadline:* rolling (freshmen), rolling (transfers). *Notification:* continuous (freshmen), continuous (transfers).

Admissions Contact Mr. Paul Wells, Director of Admissions, Henry Cogswell College, 3002 Colby Avenue, Everett, WA 98201. *Phone:* 425-258-3351 Ext. 116. *Toll-free phone:* 866-411-HCC1. *Fax:* 425-257-0405. *E-mail:* information@henrycogswell.edu.

HERITAGE COLLEGE
Toppenish, Washington

Admissions Contact Mr. Norberto T. Espindola, Director of Admissions and Recruitment, Heritage College, 3240 Fort Road, Toppenish, WA 98948-9599. *Phone:* 509-865-8500 Ext. 2002. *Toll-free phone:* 509-865-8508. *Fax:* 509-865-4469. *E-mail:* espindola_b@heritage.edu.

ITT TECHNICAL INSTITUTE
Bothell, Washington

- **Proprietary** primarily 2-year, founded 1993, part of ITT Educational Services, Inc.
- **Calendar** quarters
- **Degrees** associate and bachelor's
- **Coed**
- **Minimally difficult** entrance level

Standardized Tests *Required:* Wonderlic aptitude test (for admission).

Costs (2003–04) *Tuition:* $347 per credit hour part-time.

Applying *Options:* deferred entrance. *Application fee:* $100. *Required:* high school transcript, interview. *Recommended:* letters of recommendation.

Admissions Contact Mr. Jon L. Scherrer, Director of Recruitment, ITT Technical Institute, 2525 223rd Street SE, Bothell, WA 98021. *Phone:* 425-485-0303. *Toll-free phone:* 800-272-3791. *Fax:* 425-485-3438.

ITT TECHNICAL INSTITUTE
Seattle, Washington

- **Proprietary** primarily 2-year, founded 1932, part of ITT Educational Services, Inc.
- **Calendar** quarters
- **Degrees** associate and bachelor's
- **Urban** campus
- **Coed**
- **Minimally difficult** entrance level

Standardized Tests *Required:* Wonderlic aptitude test (for admission).

Costs (2003–04) *Tuition:* $347 per credit hour part-time.

Applying *Options:* deferred entrance. *Application fee:* $100. *Required:* high school transcript, interview. *Recommended:* letters of recommendation.

Admissions Contact Mr. Rocco Liace, Director of Recruitment, ITT Technical Institute, 12720 Gateway Drive, Suite 100, Seattle, WA 98168. *Phone:* 206-244-3300. *Toll-free phone:* 800-422-2029. *Fax:* 206-246-7635.

ITT TECHNICAL INSTITUTE
Spokane, Washington

- **Proprietary** primarily 2-year, founded 1985, part of ITT Educational Services, Inc.
- **Calendar** quarters
- **Degrees** associate and bachelor's
- **Suburban** 3-acre campus
- **Coed**
- **Minimally difficult** entrance level

Standardized Tests *Required:* Wonderlic aptitude test (for admission).

Costs (2003–04) *Tuition:* $347 per credit hour part-time.

Financial Aid Of all full-time matriculated undergraduates who enrolled in 2001, 9 Federal Work-Study jobs (averaging $4000).

Applying *Options:* deferred entrance. *Application fee:* $100. *Required:* high school transcript, interview. *Recommended:* letters of recommendation.

Admissions Contact Mr. Gregory L. Alexander, Director of Recruitment, ITT Technical Institute, North 1050 Argonne Road, Spokane, WA 99212. *Phone:* 509-926-2900. *Toll-free phone:* 800-777-8324. *Fax:* 509-926-2908.

NORTHWEST COLLEGE
Kirkland, Washington

- **Independent** comprehensive, founded 1934, affiliated with Assemblies of God
- **Calendar** semesters
- **Degrees** certificates, diplomas, associate, bachelor's, and master's
- **Suburban** 56-acre campus with easy access to Seattle
- **Coed**
- **Moderately difficult** entrance level

Faculty *Student/faculty ratio:* 15:1.

Student Life *Campus security:* 24-hour emergency response devices and patrols, late-night transport/escort service, controlled dormitory access.

Athletics Member NAIA, NCCAA.

Standardized Tests *Required:* SAT I or ACT (for admission).

Costs (2004–05) *Comprehensive fee:* $21,210 includes full-time tuition ($14,200), mandatory fees ($560), and room and board ($6450). Part-time tuition: $595 per credit. Part-time tuition and fees vary according to course load.

Financial Aid Of all full-time matriculated undergraduates who enrolled in 2003, 775 applied for aid, 682 were judged to have need, 150 had their need fully met. 80 Federal Work-Study jobs (averaging $2200). 32 state and other part-time jobs (averaging $3102). In 2003, 145. *Average percent of need met:* 57. *Average financial aid package:* $10,592. *Average need-based loan:* $3768. *Average need-based gift aid:* $6853. *Average non-need-based aid:* $9059. *Average indebtedness upon graduation:* $20,015.

Applying *Options:* common application, early decision, deferred entrance. *Application fee:* $30. *Required:* essay or personal statement, high school transcript, minimum 2.3 GPA, 2 letters of recommendation. *Required for some:* interview.

Admissions Contact Ms. Rose-Mary K. Smith, Director of Admissions, Northwest College, PO Box 579, Kirkland, WA 98083-0579. *Phone:* 425-889-5598. *Toll-free phone:* 800-669-3781. *Fax:* 425-889-5224. *E-mail:* admissions@ncag.edu.

NORTHWEST COLLEGE OF ART
Poulsbo, Washington

- **Proprietary** 4-year, founded 1982
- **Calendar** semesters
- **Degree** bachelor's
- **Small-town** 26-acre campus with easy access to Seattle
- **Coed,** 134 undergraduate students
- **Moderately difficult** entrance level

Majors Art; commercial and advertising art.

Academic Programs *Special study options:* double majors, internships, summer session for credit.

Library Northwest College of Art Library.

Computers on Campus 28 computers available on campus for general student use. Internet access, at least one staffed computer lab available.

Student Life *Housing:* college housing not available.

Costs (2004–05) *Tuition:* $13,500 full-time, $585 per credit part-time. Part-time tuition and fees vary according to course load. No tuition increase for

Northwest College of Art (continued)
student's term of enrollment. *Required fees:* $100 full-time. *Payment plan:* installment. *Waivers:* employees or children of employees.

Financial Aid *Financial aid deadline:* 5/1.

Applying *Options:* deferred entrance. *Application fee:* $50. *Required:* essay or personal statement, high school transcript, minimum 2.0 GPA, 3 letters of recommendation, interview, portfolio. *Application deadlines:* 6/1 (freshmen), 6/1 (transfers). *Notification:* continuous (freshmen), continuous (transfers).

Admissions Contact Mr. Craig Freeman, President, Northwest College of Art, 16464 State Highway 305, Poulsbo, WA 98370. *Phone:* 360-779-9993. *Toll-free phone:* 800-769-ARTS. *Fax:* 360-779-9933. *E-mail:* kperigard@nca.edu.

PACIFIC LUTHERAN UNIVERSITY
Tacoma, Washington

- **Independent** comprehensive, founded 1890, affiliated with Evangelical Lutheran Church in America
- **Calendar** 4-1-4
- **Degrees** bachelor's, master's, post-master's, and postbachelor's certificates
- **Suburban** 126-acre campus with easy access to Seattle
- **Endowment** $41.5 million
- **Coed,** 3,185 undergraduate students, 92% full-time, 63% women, 37% men
- **Moderately difficult** entrance level, 80% of applicants were admitted

Success is measured differently for every student at PLU. It springs from academic challenge in a community where everyone has high expectations for one another. It's developed when every member of the PLU community supports each other in meeting challenges and helps students define success in a way that best fits their goals and abilities.

Undergraduates 2,922 full-time, 263 part-time. Students come from 42 states and territories, 23 other countries, 26% are from out of state, 2% African American, 5% Asian American or Pacific Islander, 2% Hispanic American, 0.7% Native American, 5% international, 9% transferred in, 50% live on campus. *Retention:* 83% of 2002 full-time freshmen returned.

Freshmen *Admission:* 1,973 applied, 1,575 admitted, 694 enrolled. *Average high school GPA:* 3.62. *Test scores:* SAT verbal scores over 500: 77%; SAT math scores over 500: 76%; ACT scores over 18: 94%; SAT verbal scores over 600: 38%; SAT math scores over 600: 35%; ACT scores over 24: 61%; SAT verbal scores over 700: 8%; SAT math scores over 700: 3%; ACT scores over 30: 13%.

Faculty *Total:* 304, 77% full-time, 74% with terminal degrees. *Student/faculty ratio:* 13:1.

Majors Accounting; anthropology; art; art history, criticism and conservation; art teacher education; biochemistry; biology/biological sciences; broadcast journalism; business administration and management; chemistry; Chinese; classics and languages, literatures and linguistics; computer engineering; computer science; dramatic/theatre arts; economics; education; electrical, electronics and communications engineering; elementary education; engineering physics; engineering science; English; environmental studies; finance; fine/studio arts; French; geology/earth science; German; history; international business/trade/commerce; international relations and affairs; journalism; kindergarten/preschool education; literature; management information systems; marketing/marketing management; mass communication/media; mathematics; modern languages; music; music teacher education; nursing (registered nurse training); philosophy; physical education teaching and coaching; physics; piano and organ; political science and government; psychology; radio and television; reading teacher education; religious/sacred music; religious studies; Scandinavian languages; science teacher education; secondary education; social work; sociology; Spanish; special education; therapeutic recreation; voice and opera; women's studies.

Academic Programs *Special study options:* accelerated degree program, adult/continuing education programs, advanced placement credit, cooperative education, double majors, English as a second language, honors programs, independent study, internships, part-time degree program, services for LD students, student-designed majors, study abroad, summer session for credit. *ROTC:* Army (b). *Unusual degree programs:* 3-2 engineering with Columbia University, Washington University in St. Louis.

Library Mortvedt Library with 367,628 titles, 1,949 serial subscriptions, 13,965 audiovisual materials, an OPAC, a Web page.

Computers on Campus 200 computers available on campus for general student use. A campuswide network can be accessed from student residence rooms and from off campus. Internet access, online (class) registration, at least one staffed computer lab available. Computer purchase or lease plan available.

Student Life *Housing:* on-campus residence required through sophomore year. *Options:* coed, women-only. Campus housing is university owned. Freshman campus housing is guaranteed. *Activities and organizations:* drama/theater group, student-run newspaper, radio and television station, choral group, Rejoice, Circle K, adult students club, Residence Hall Government, Inter-Varsity Fellowship. *Campus security:* 24-hour emergency response devices and patrols, student patrols, late-night transport/escort service. *Student services:* health clinic, personal/psychological counseling, women's center.

Athletics Member NCAA. All Division III. *Intercollegiate sports:* baseball M, basketball M/W, cheerleading M/W, crew M/W, cross-country running M/W, football M, golf M/W, lacrosse M(c)/W(c), rugby M(c), skiing (cross-country) M(c)/W(c), skiing (downhill) M(c)/W(c), soccer M/W, softball W, swimming M/W, tennis M/W, track and field M/W, ultimate Frisbee M(c)/W(c), volleyball M(c)/W. *Intramural sports:* badminton M/W, basketball M/W, bowling M/W, cross-country running M/W, football M/W, golf M/W, racquetball M/W, rock climbing M/W, soccer M/W, softball M/W, squash M/W, swimming M/W, table tennis M/W, tennis M/W, track and field M/W, volleyball M/W.

Standardized Tests *Required:* SAT I or ACT (for admission).

Costs (2003–04) *Comprehensive fee:* $25,715 includes full-time tuition ($19,610) and room and board ($6105). Full-time tuition and fees vary according to course load. Part-time tuition: $612 per semester hour. Part-time tuition and fees vary according to course load. *College room only:* $3000. Room and board charges vary according to board plan and housing facility. *Payment plan:* installment. *Waivers:* senior citizens and employees or children of employees.

Financial Aid Of all full-time matriculated undergraduates who enrolled in 2003, 2,452 applied for aid, 2,087 were judged to have need, 585 had their need fully met. 685 Federal Work-Study jobs (averaging $1228). 1,390 state and other part-time jobs (averaging $1923). In 2003, 497 non-need-based awards were made. *Average percent of need met:* 88%. *Average financial aid package:* $17,229. *Average need-based loan:* $6802. *Average need-based gift aid:* $7135. *Average non-need-based aid:* $6135. *Average indebtedness upon graduation:* $22,190.

Applying *Options:* common application, early admission, deferred entrance. *Application fee:* $35. *Required:* essay or personal statement, high school transcript, minimum 2.5 GPA, 1 letter of recommendation. *Required for some:* interview. *Application deadline:* rolling (freshmen), rolling (transfers). *Notification:* continuous (freshmen), continuous (transfers).

Admissions Contact Office of Admissions, Pacific Lutheran University, Tacoma, WA 98447. *Phone:* 253-535-7151. *Toll-free phone:* 800-274-6758. *Fax:* 253-536-5136. *E-mail:* admissions@plu.edu.

PUGET SOUND CHRISTIAN COLLEGE
Mountlake Terrace, Washington

Admissions Contact Mr. Ben Maxson, Admissions Counselor, Puget Sound Christian College, 7011 226th Place, SW, Mountlake Terrace, WA 98043. *Phone:* 425-775-8686 Ext. 506. *Toll-free phone:* 888-775-8699. *Fax:* 425-775-8688. *E-mail:* admissions@pscc.edu.

SAINT MARTIN'S COLLEGE
Lacey, Washington

- **Independent Roman Catholic** comprehensive, founded 1895
- **Calendar** semesters
- **Degrees** bachelor's and master's
- **Suburban** 300-acre campus with easy access to Tacoma
- **Endowment** $8.4 million
- **Coed,** 1,246 undergraduate students, 66% full-time, 56% women, 44% men
- **Moderately difficult** entrance level, 76% of applicants were admitted

Undergraduates 817 full-time, 429 part-time. Students come from 19 states and territories, 13 other countries, 7% are from out of state, 8% African American, 9% Asian American or Pacific Islander, 5% Hispanic American, 2% Native American, 4% international, 10% transferred in, 25% live on campus. *Retention:* 73% of 2002 full-time freshmen returned.

Freshmen *Admission:* 462 applied, 352 admitted, 145 enrolled. *Average high school GPA:* 3.30. *Test scores:* SAT verbal scores over 500: 53%; SAT math scores over 500: 48%; ACT scores over 18: 65%; SAT verbal scores over 600: 15%; SAT math scores over 600: 18%; ACT scores over 24: 21%; SAT verbal scores over 700: 2%; SAT math scores over 700: 2%; ACT scores over 30: 4%.

Faculty *Total:* 72, 79% full-time, 74% with terminal degrees. *Student/faculty ratio:* 14:1.

Majors Accounting; biology/biological sciences; business administration and management; chemistry; civil engineering; community organization and advocacy; computer science; criminal justice/law enforcement administration; dramatic/theatre arts; economics; education; elementary education; English; finance; history; humanities; information science/studies; management information systems; marketing/marketing management; mathematics; mechanical engineering; political science and government; pre-dentistry studies; pre-law studies; premedical studies; pre-pharmacy studies; pre-veterinary studies; psychology; religious studies; secondary education; special education.

Academic Programs *Special study options:* academic remediation for entering students, accelerated degree program, adult/continuing education programs, advanced placement credit, cooperative education, double majors, English as a second language, independent study, internships, off-campus study, part-time degree program, services for LD students, study abroad, summer session for credit. *ROTC:* Army (c).

Library Saint Martin's College Library with 84,220 titles, 852 serial subscriptions, 1,239 audiovisual materials, an OPAC, a Web page.

Computers on Campus 110 computers available on campus for general student use. A campuswide network can be accessed from student residence rooms and from off campus. Internet access, at least one staffed computer lab available.

Student Life *Housing:* on-campus residence required through sophomore year. *Options:* coed. Campus housing is university owned. Freshman campus housing is guaranteed. *Activities and organizations:* drama/theater group, student-run newspaper, choral group, Mexico Service Club, education club, Campus Ministry, SWE, Soccer Club. *Campus security:* 24-hour emergency response devices and patrols, late-night transport/escort service, night patrols by security personnel. *Student services:* personal/psychological counseling.

Athletics Member NCAA. All Division II. *Intercollegiate sports:* baseball M(s), basketball M(s)/W(s), cross-country running M(s)/W(s), golf M(s)/W(s), softball W(s), track and field M(s)/W(s), volleyball W(s). *Intramural sports:* basketball M/W, soccer M/W, softball W, tennis M/W, volleyball M/W.

Standardized Tests *Required:* SAT I or ACT (for admission).

Costs (2004–05) *One-time required fee:* $130. *Comprehensive fee:* $24,670 includes full-time tuition ($18,660), mandatory fees ($290), and room and board ($5720). Part-time tuition: $622 per credit. Part-time tuition and fees vary according to course load. *Required fees:* $130 per term part-time. *College room only:* $2420. *Payment plan:* installment. *Waivers:* employees or children of employees.

Financial Aid Of all full-time matriculated undergraduates who enrolled in 2003, 768 applied for aid, 679 were judged to have need, 240 had their need fully met. 210 Federal Work-Study jobs (averaging $1875). 389 state and other part-time jobs (averaging $1893). In 2003, 117 non-need-based awards were made. *Average percent of need met:* 80%. *Average financial aid package:* $14,451. *Average need-based loan:* $4160. *Average need-based gift aid:* $9895. *Average non-need-based aid:* $10,336. *Average indebtedness upon graduation:* $18,898.

Applying *Options:* common application, electronic application. *Application fee:* $35. *Required:* essay or personal statement, high school transcript, minimum 2.5 GPA, 1 letter of recommendation. *Required for some:* interview. *Application deadline:* 8/1 (transfers). *Notification:* continuous until 8/15 (freshmen), continuous until 8/15 (transfers).

Admissions Contact Mr. Todd Abbott, Director of Admission, Saint Martin's College, 5300 Pacific Avenue, SE, Lacey, WA 98503. *Phone:* 360-438-4590. *Toll-free phone:* 800-368-8803. *Fax:* 360-412-6189. *E-mail:* admissions@stmartin.edu.

■ *See page 2310 for a narrative description.*

SEATTLE PACIFIC UNIVERSITY

Seattle, Washington

- **Independent Free Methodist** comprehensive, founded 1891
- **Calendar** quarters
- **Degrees** certificates, bachelor's, master's, doctoral, and post-master's certificates
- **Urban** 35-acre campus
- **Endowment** $24.0 million
- **Coed,** 2,859 undergraduate students, 92% full-time, 67% women, 33% men
- **Moderately difficult** entrance level, 92% of applicants were admitted

As part of its vision to engage the culture through the sciences, Seattle Pacific University opened a new science building in Fall 2003. Within the $24-million facility, students focus on undergraduate research in order to develop into scientifically literate citizens, pursue careers in science, and become influential science teachers in public and private school settings.

Undergraduates 2,619 full-time, 240 part-time. Students come from 39 states and territories, 34 other countries, 37% are from out of state, 2% African American, 6% Asian American or Pacific Islander, 2% Hispanic American, 0.8% Native American, 1% international, 8% transferred in, 61% live on campus. *Retention:* 79% of 2002 full-time freshmen returned.

Freshmen *Admission:* 1,778 applied, 1,635 admitted, 683 enrolled. *Average high school GPA:* 3.65. *Test scores:* SAT verbal scores over 500: 84%; SAT math scores over 500: 80%; ACT scores over 18: 99%; SAT verbal scores over 600: 42%; SAT math scores over 600: 40%; ACT scores over 24: 63%; SAT verbal scores over 700: 9%; SAT math scores over 700: 5%; ACT scores over 30: 11%.

Faculty *Total:* 283, 60% full-time. *Student/faculty ratio:* 15:1.

Majors Accounting; apparel and textiles; art; art teacher education; biochemistry; biology/biological sciences; biology teacher education; business administration and management; chemistry; classics and languages, literatures and linguistics; communication/speech communication and rhetoric; computer/information technology services administration related; computer science; computer systems analysis; dramatic/theatre arts; economics; electrical, electronics and communications engineering; engineering science; English; English/language arts teacher education; European studies; family and consumer economics related; family and consumer sciences/home economics teacher education; foods, nutrition, and wellness; French; general studies; German; history; kinesiology and exercise science; Latin; Latin American studies; liberal arts and sciences/liberal studies; mathematics; mathematics and statistics related; mathematics teacher education; music; music teacher education; nursing (registered nurse training); philosophy; physical education teaching and coaching; physics; political science and government; pre-dentistry studies; pre-law studies; pre-medical studies; psychology; religious education; Russian; science teacher education; social science teacher education; sociology; Spanish; special education; theology.

Academic Programs *Special study options:* academic remediation for entering students, adult/continuing education programs, advanced placement credit, cooperative education, distance learning, double majors, English as a second language, external degree program, honors programs, independent study, internships, off-campus study, part-time degree program, services for LD students, student-designed majors, study abroad, summer session for credit. *ROTC:* Army (c), Navy (c), Air Force (c).

Library Seattle Pacific University Library with 169,527 titles, 1,336 serial subscriptions, 3,002 audiovisual materials, an OPAC, a Web page.

Computers on Campus 150 computers available on campus for general student use. A campuswide network can be accessed from student residence rooms and from off campus. Internet access, online (class) registration, at least one staffed computer lab available.

Student Life *Housing:* on-campus residence required through senior year. *Options:* coed, women-only. Campus housing is university owned. Freshman campus housing is guaranteed. *Activities and organizations:* drama/theater group, student-run newspaper, radio station, choral group, Centurions, Falconettes, forensics, Amnesty International, University Players. *Campus security:* 24-hour emergency response devices and patrols, student patrols, late-night transport/escort service, closed-circuit TV monitors. *Student services:* health clinic, personal/psychological counseling.

Athletics Member NCAA. All Division II. *Intercollegiate sports:* basketball M(s)/W(s), cheerleading M(s)/W(s), crew M/W, cross-country running M(s)/W(s), gymnastics W(s), soccer M(s)/W, track and field M(s)/W(s), ultimate Frisbee M(c)/W(c), volleyball W(s). *Intramural sports:* badminton M/W, basketball M/W, bowling M/W, cross-country running M/W, football M/W, golf M/W, rock climbing W(c), skiing (cross-country) M(c)/W(c), skiing (downhill) M(c)/W(c), soccer M/W(c), softball M/W, swimming M/W, table tennis M/W, tennis M/W, track and field M/W, volleyball M(c)/W(c), weight lifting M/W, wrestling M.

Standardized Tests *Required:* SAT I or ACT (for admission). *Recommended:* SAT I (for admission).

Costs (2003–04) *Comprehensive fee:* $26,175 includes full-time tuition ($18,822), mandatory fees ($336), and room and board ($7017). Part-time tuition: $523 per credit. Part-time tuition and fees vary according to course load. *College room only:* $3762. Room and board charges vary according to board plan and housing facility. *Payment plan:* installment. *Waivers:* senior citizens and employees or children of employees.

Financial Aid Of all full-time matriculated undergraduates who enrolled in 2002, 1,953 applied for aid, 1,649 were judged to have need, 306 had their need fully met. 380 Federal Work-Study jobs (averaging $1417). 400 state and other part-time jobs (averaging $1997). In 2002, 732 non-need-based awards were made. *Average percent of need met:* 80%. *Average financial aid package:* $16,249. *Average need-based loan:* $5566. *Average need-based gift aid:* $12,206. *Average non-need-based aid:* $8832. *Average indebtedness upon graduation:* $19,714.

Applying *Options:* common application, electronic application, early admission, early action, deferred entrance. *Application fee:* $45. *Required:* essay or personal statement, high school transcript, minimum 2.5 GPA, 2 letters of recommendation. *Application deadlines:* 6/1 (freshmen), 8/1 (transfers). *Notification:* continuous (freshmen), 2/15 (early action), continuous (transfers).

Admissions Contact Mrs. Jennifer Feddern Kenney, Director of Admissions, Seattle Pacific University, 3307 Third Avenue West, Seattle, WA 98119-1997. *Phone:* 206-281-2517. *Toll-free phone:* 800-366-3344. *Fax:* 206-281-2544. *E-mail:* admissions@spu.edu.

■ *See page 2364 for a narrative description.*

SEATTLE UNIVERSITY
Seattle, Washington

- **Independent Roman Catholic** comprehensive, founded 1891
- **Calendar** quarters
- **Degrees** certificates, bachelor's, master's, doctoral, first professional, post-master's, and postbachelor's certificates
- **Urban** 46-acre campus
- **Endowment** $124.3 million
- **Coed,** 3,765 undergraduate students, 92% full-time, 62% women, 38% men
- **Moderately difficult** entrance level, 78% of applicants were admitted

Undergraduates 3,482 full-time, 283 part-time. Students come from 49 states and territories, 75 other countries, 35% are from out of state, 5% African American, 21% Asian American or Pacific Islander, 7% Hispanic American, 1% Native American, 10% international, 10% transferred in, 38% live on campus. *Retention:* 84% of 2002 full-time freshmen returned.

Freshmen *Admission:* 2,985 applied, 2,321 admitted, 665 enrolled. *Average high school GPA:* 3.52. *Test scores:* SAT verbal scores over 500: 83%; SAT math scores over 500: 79%; ACT scores over 18: 100%; SAT verbal scores over 600: 38%; SAT math scores over 600: 35%; ACT scores over 24: 66%; SAT verbal scores over 700: 6%; SAT math scores over 700: 4%; ACT scores over 30: 17%.

Faculty *Total:* 522, 66% full-time, 77% with terminal degrees. *Student/faculty ratio:* 14:1.

Majors Accounting; applied mathematics; art; art history, criticism and conservation; Asian studies (East); biochemistry; biological and physical sciences; biology/biological sciences; business administration and management; business/managerial economics; chemistry; civil engineering; clinical laboratory science/medical technology; computer science; creative writing; criminal justice/law enforcement administration; diagnostic medical sonography and ultrasound technology; dramatic/theatre arts; economics; electrical, electronics and communications engineering; English; environmental/environmental health engineering; environmental studies; European studies (Western); finance; fine/studio arts; forensic science and technology; French; German; history; humanities; industrial engineering; insurance; international business/trade/commerce; international economics; international relations and affairs; journalism; liberal arts and sciences/liberal studies; management information systems; marketing/marketing management; mass communication/media; mathematics; mechanical engineering; nursing (registered nurse training); operations management; philosophy; photography; physics; political science and government; psychology; public administration; public relations/image management; religious studies; social work; sociology; Spanish.

Academic Programs *Special study options:* accelerated degree program, adult/continuing education programs, advanced placement credit, double majors, English as a second language, freshman honors college, honors programs, independent study, internships, off-campus study, part-time degree program, services for LD students, student-designed majors, study abroad, summer session for credit. *ROTC:* Army (b), Air Force (c).

Library Lemieux Library plus 1 other with 141,478 titles, 2,701 serial subscriptions, 5,649 audiovisual materials, an OPAC, a Web page.

Computers on Campus 401 computers available on campus for general student use. A campuswide network can be accessed from student residence rooms and from off campus. Internet access, online (class) registration, at least one staffed computer lab available.

Student Life *Housing:* on-campus residence required through sophomore year. *Options:* coed, disabled students. Campus housing is university owned. Freshman campus housing is guaranteed. *Activities and organizations:* drama/theater group, student-run newspaper, radio station, choral group, student government, Volunteer Center, Hawaiian club, international student club. *Campus security:* 24-hour emergency response devices and patrols, late-night transport/escort service, controlled dormitory access, bicycle patrols. *Student services:* health clinic, personal/psychological counseling, women's center.

Athletics Member NCAA, NAIA. All NCAA Division II. *Intercollegiate sports:* archery M(c)/W(c), baseball M(c)/W(c), basketball M(s)/W(s), cheerleading M(c)/W(c), crew M(c)/W(c), cross-country running M(s)/W(s), golf M(c)/W(c), riflery M(c)/W(c), skiing (downhill) M(c)/W(c), soccer M(s)/W(s), softball W(s), swimming M(s)/W(s), track and field M(s)/W(s), volleyball M(c)/W, water polo M(c)/W(c). *Intramural sports:* basketball M/W, field hockey M/W, football M/W, soccer M/W, softball M/W, tennis M/W, ultimate Frisbee M/W, volleyball M/W.

Standardized Tests *Required:* SAT I or ACT (for admission).

Costs (2003–04) *Comprehensive fee:* $26,928 includes full-time tuition ($20,070) and room and board ($6858). Full-time tuition and fees vary according to course load. Part-time tuition: $446 per credit hour. Part-time tuition and fees vary according to course load. *College room only:* $4473. Room and board charges vary according to board plan. *Waivers:* employees or children of employees.

Financial Aid Of all full-time matriculated undergraduates who enrolled in 2003, 2,716 applied for aid, 2,301 were judged to have need, 1,316 had their need fully met. 704 Federal Work-Study jobs (averaging $3899). 830 state and other part-time jobs (averaging $5119). In 2003, 243 non-need-based awards were made. *Average percent of need met:* 87%. *Average financial aid package:* $19,380. *Average need-based loan:* $4590. *Average need-based gift aid:* $9058. *Average non-need-based aid:* $1282. *Average indebtedness upon graduation:* $26,096.

Applying *Options:* common application, electronic application, early admission, deferred entrance. *Application fee:* $45. *Required:* essay or personal statement, high school transcript, minimum 2.5 GPA, 2 letters of recommendation. *Application deadlines:* 7/1 (freshmen), 8/1 (transfers). *Notification:* continuous (freshmen), continuous (transfers).

Admissions Contact Mr. Michael K. McKeon, Dean of Admissions, Seattle University, 900 Broadway, Seattle, WA 98122-4340. *Phone:* 206-296-2000. *Toll-free phone:* 800-542-0833 (in-state); 800-426-7123 (out-of-state). *Fax:* 206-296-5656. *E-mail:* admissions@seattleu.edu.

■ *See page 2366 for a narrative description.*

TRINITY LUTHERAN COLLEGE
Issaquah, Washington

- **Independent Lutheran** 4-year, founded 1944
- **Calendar** quarters
- **Degrees** associate, bachelor's, and postbachelor's certificates
- **Suburban** 46-acre campus with easy access to Seattle
- **Endowment** $1.2 million
- **Coed**
- **Minimally difficult** entrance level

Faculty *Student/faculty ratio:* 9:1.

Student Life *Campus security:* 24-hour emergency response devices, student patrols, controlled dormitory access.

Standardized Tests *Required:* SAT I or ACT (for admission).

Costs (2003–04) *Comprehensive fee:* $15,990 includes full-time tuition ($10,170), mandatory fees ($200), and room and board ($5620).

Financial Aid Of all full-time matriculated undergraduates who enrolled in 2002, 43 Federal Work-Study jobs (averaging $584).

Applying *Options:* early admission, deferred entrance. *Application fee:* $30. *Required:* high school transcript, minimum 2.0 GPA, 2 letters of recommendation. *Required for some:* interview.

Admissions Contact Ms. Sigrid Olsen, Director of Admission, Trinity Lutheran College, 4221 228th Avenue, SE, Issaquah, WA 98029-9299. *Phone:* 425-961-5516. *Toll-free phone:* 800-843-5659. *Fax:* 425-392-0404. *E-mail:* admission@tlc.edu.

UNIVERSITY OF PHOENIX–SPOKANE CAMPUS
Spokane, Washington

Admissions Contact Rock Point Corporate Center, 1330 North Washington Street, Suite 2460, Spokane, WA 99201.

UNIVERSITY OF PHOENIX–WASHINGTON CAMPUS
Seattle, Washington

- **Proprietary** comprehensive, founded 1997
- **Calendar** continuous
- **Degrees** certificates, associate, bachelor's, master's, doctoral, post-master's, and postbachelor's certificates (courses conducted at 121 campuses and learning centers in 25 states)
- **Coed,** 1,012 undergraduate students, 100% full-time, 57% women, 43% men
- **Noncompetitive** entrance level

Undergraduates 1,012 full-time. 9% African American, 7% Asian American or Pacific Islander, 3% Hispanic American, 1% Native American, 2% international.

Freshmen *Admission:* 33 enrolled.

Faculty *Total:* 232, 2% full-time, 22% with terminal degrees. *Student/faculty ratio:* 8:1.

Majors Accounting; business administration and management; computer and information sciences; computer programming; criminal justice/law enforcement administration; health/health care administration; management information systems; management science; marketing/marketing management; public administration and social service professions related.

Academic Programs *Special study options:* accelerated degree program, adult/continuing education programs, advanced placement credit, distance learning, external degree program, independent study.

Library University Library with 27.1 million titles, 11,648 serial subscriptions, an OPAC, a Web page.

Computers on Campus A campuswide network can be accessed from off campus. Internet access, at least one staffed computer lab available.

Student Life *Housing:* college housing not available.

Athletics *Intramural sports:* cheerleading M/W.

Costs (2003–04) *Tuition:* $9900 full-time, $330 per credit part-time. *Waivers:* employees or children of employees.

Financial Aid *Average financial aid package:* $1285.

Applying *Options:* deferred entrance. *Application fee:* $100. *Required:* minimum 1 GPA, 2 years of work experience, 23 years of age. *Required for some:* high school transcript. *Application deadline:* rolling (freshmen), rolling (transfers).

Admissions Contact Ms. Beth Barilla, Director of Admissions, University of Phoenix–Washington Campus, 4615 East Elwood Street, Mail Stop AA-K101, Phoenix, AZ 85040-1958. *Phone:* 480-317-6000. *Toll-free phone:* 800-228-7240. *Fax:* 480-894-1758. *E-mail:* beth.barilla@pheonix.edu.

UNIVERSITY OF PUGET SOUND
Tacoma, Washington

- **Independent** comprehensive, founded 1888
- **Calendar** semesters
- **Degrees** bachelor's, master's, first professional, and post-master's certificates
- **Suburban** 97-acre campus with easy access to Seattle
- **Endowment** $167.6 million
- **Coed,** 2,516 undergraduate students, 98% full-time, 59% women, 41% men
- **Very difficult** entrance level, 71% of applicants were admitted

Undergraduates 2,461 full-time, 55 part-time. Students come from 46 states and territories, 14 other countries, 71% are from out of state, 2% African American, 9% Asian American or Pacific Islander, 3% Hispanic American, 1% Native American, 0.9% international, 3% transferred in, 62% live on campus. *Retention:* 85% of 2002 full-time freshmen returned.

Freshmen *Admission:* 4,237 applied, 3,022 admitted, 641 enrolled. *Average high school GPA:* 3.53. *Test scores:* SAT verbal scores over 500: 96%; SAT math scores over 500: 95%; ACT scores over 18: 99%; SAT verbal scores over 600: 66%; SAT math scores over 600: 60%; ACT scores over 24: 81%; SAT verbal scores over 700: 19%; SAT math scores over 700: 14%; ACT scores over 30: 17%.

Faculty *Total:* 259, 83% full-time, 77% with terminal degrees. *Student/faculty ratio:* 11:1.

Majors Art; Asian studies; biology/biological sciences; business/commerce; chemistry; classics and languages, literatures and linguistics; communication/speech communication and rhetoric; computer programming (specific applications); computer science; creative writing; dramatic/theatre arts; economics; English; French; geology/earth science; German; history; interdisciplinary studies; international business/trade/commerce; international economics; international relations and affairs; kinesiology and exercise science; mathematics; music; music management and merchandising; music performance; music teacher education; natural sciences; philosophy; physics; political science and government; pre-dentistry studies; pre-law studies; pre-medical studies; pre-veterinary studies; psychology; religious studies; science, technology and society; sociology; Spanish.

Academic Programs *Special study options:* advanced placement credit, cooperative education, double majors, honors programs, independent study, internships, part-time degree program, student-designed majors, study abroad, summer session for credit. *ROTC:* Army (c). *Unusual degree programs:* 3-2 engineering with Washington University in St. Louis, Columbia University, Duke University, Boston University, University of Southern California.

Library Collins Memorial Library with 343,787 titles, 5,609 serial subscriptions, 17,328 audiovisual materials, an OPAC, a Web page.

Computers on Campus 304 computers available on campus for general student use. A campuswide network can be accessed from student residence rooms and from off campus that provide access to financial aid, admission, student employment. Internet access, at least one staffed computer lab available.

Student Life *Housing options:* coed, women-only, disabled students. Campus housing is university owned. Freshman applicants given priority for college housing. *Activities and organizations:* drama/theater group, student-run newspaper, radio station, choral group, Hui-O-Hawaii, Repertory Dance Group, Film and Theatre Society, outdoor programs, Lighthouse, national fraternities, national sororities. *Campus security:* 24-hour emergency response devices and patrols, student patrols, late-night transport/escort service, controlled dormitory access, 24-hour locked residence hall entrances. *Student services:* health clinic, personal/psychological counseling, legal services.

Athletics Member NCAA. All Division III. *Intercollegiate sports:* baseball M, basketball M/W, cheerleading M/W, crew M/W, cross-country running M/W, football M, golf M/W, lacrosse M(c)/W, rugby M(c)/W(c), skiing (downhill) M/W, soccer M/W, softball W, swimming M/W, tennis M/W, track and field M/W, volleyball W. *Intramural sports:* badminton M/W, basketball M/W, bowling M/W, football M/W, golf M/W, racquetball M/W, soccer M/W, softball M/W, tennis M/W, track and field M/W, ultimate Frisbee M/W, volleyball M/W.

Standardized Tests *Required:* SAT I or ACT (for admission).

Costs (2003–04) *Comprehensive fee:* $31,760 includes full-time tuition ($25,190), mandatory fees ($170), and room and board ($6400). *College room only:* $3500. Room and board charges vary according to board plan and housing facility. *Payment plans:* installment, deferred payment. *Waivers:* employees or children of employees.

Financial Aid Of all full-time matriculated undergraduates who enrolled in 2003, 1,636 applied for aid, 1,461 were judged to have need, 332 had their need fully met. 699 Federal Work-Study jobs (averaging $2500). 766 state and other part-time jobs (averaging $2500). In 2003, 627 non-need-based awards were made. *Average percent of need met:* 83%. *Average financial aid package:* $19,217. *Average need-based loan:* $5825. *Average need-based gift aid:* $13,011. *Average non-need-based aid:* $6766. *Average indebtedness upon graduation:* $23,782. *Financial aid deadline:* 2/1.

Applying *Options:* common application, electronic application, early admission, early decision, deferred entrance. *Application fee:* $40. *Required:* essay or personal statement, high school transcript, 2 letters of recommendation. *Recommended:* minimum 3.0 GPA, interview. *Application deadlines:* 5/1 (freshmen), 7/1 (transfers). *Early decision:* 11/15 (for plan 1), 12/15 (for plan 2). *Notification:* continuous until 5/1 (freshmen), 12/15 (early decision plan 1), 1/15 (early decision plan 2), continuous (transfers).

Admissions Contact Dr. George H. Mills Jr., Vice President for Enrollment, University of Puget Sound, 1500 North Warner Street, Tacoma, WA 98416-1062. *Phone:* 253-879-3211. *Toll-free phone:* 800-396-7191. *Fax:* 253-879-3993. *E-mail:* admission@ups.edu.

■ *See page 2688 for a narrative description.*

UNIVERSITY OF WASHINGTON
Seattle, Washington

- **State-supported** university, founded 1861
- **Calendar** quarters
- **Degrees** bachelor's, master's, doctoral, and first professional
- **Urban** 703-acre campus
- **Endowment** $963.0 million
- **Coed,** 28,362 undergraduate students, 83% full-time, 52% women, 48% men
- **Moderately difficult** entrance level, 68% of applicants were admitted

Undergraduates 23,552 full-time, 4,810 part-time. Students come from 52 states and territories, 59 other countries, 13% are from out of state, 3% African American, 24% Asian American or Pacific Islander, 3% Hispanic American, 1% Native American, 3% international, 6% transferred in, 17% live on campus. *Retention:* 91% of 2002 full-time freshmen returned.

Freshmen *Admission:* 15,950 applied, 10,884 admitted, 4,771 enrolled. *Average high school GPA:* 3.67. *Test scores:* SAT verbal scores over 500: 83%; SAT math scores over 500: 91%; ACT scores over 18: 96%; SAT verbal scores over 600: 44%; SAT math scores over 600: 58%; ACT scores over 24: 68%; SAT verbal scores over 700: 10%; SAT math scores over 700: 15%; ACT scores over 30: 16%.

Faculty *Total:* 3,383, 82% full-time, 93% with terminal degrees. *Student/faculty ratio:* 11:1.

Majors Accounting; aerospace, aeronautical and astronautical engineering; African-American/Black studies; Air Force R.O.T.C./air science; American Indian/Native American studies; ancient/classical Greek; anthropology; applied mathematics; architecture; Army R.O.T.C./military science; art; art history, criticism and conservation; Asian studies; Asian studies (East); Asian studies (South); Asian studies (Southeast); astronomy; atmospheric sciences and meteorology; audiology and speech-language pathology; bilingual and multilingual education; biochemistry; biology/biological sciences; biology teacher education; biostatistics; botany/plant biology; business administration and management; business/commerce; Canadian studies; cell biology and histology; ceramic arts and ceramics; ceramic sciences and engineering; chemical engineering; chemistry; Chinese; city/urban, community and regional planning; civil engineering; classics and languages, literatures and linguistics; clinical laboratory science/medical technology; commercial and advertising art; communication/speech communication and rhetoric; comparative literature; computer and information sciences; computer engineering; computer science; construction management; creative writing; criminal justice/law enforcement administration; cultural studies; dance; data processing and data processing technology; dental hygiene; dramatic/theatre arts; economics; education; education (multiple levels); electrical, electronics and

University of Washington (continued)
communications engineering; elementary education; engineering; English; English as a second/foreign language (teaching); environmental health; environmental studies; European studies; fiber, textile and weaving arts; fishing and fisheries sciences and management; forest engineering; forest/forest resources management; forestry; forest sciences and biology; French; general studies; geography; geology/earth science; geophysics and seismology; German; Hispanic-American, Puerto Rican, and Mexican-American/Chicano studies; history; history and philosophy of science and technology; humanities; industrial design; industrial engineering; information science/studies; interdisciplinary studies; interior architecture; international business/trade/commerce; international relations and affairs; Italian; Japanese; Jewish/Judaic studies; landscape architecture; Latin; Latin American studies; liberal arts and sciences/liberal studies; linguistics; management information systems; management science; materials engineering; maternal/child health and neonatal nursing; mathematics; mechanical engineering; medical microbiology and bacteriology; metal and jewelry arts; metallurgical engineering; molecular biology; music; musical instrument fabrication and repair; music history, literature, and theory; musicology and ethnomusicology; music performance; music teacher education; music theory and composition; natural resources management and policy; Navy/Marine Corps R.O.T.C./naval science; Near and Middle Eastern studies; nursing (registered nurse training); occupational therapy; oceanography (chemical and physical); orthotics/prosthetics; painting; pharmacy; philosophy; photography; physical therapy; physician assistant; physics; piano and organ; political science and government; printmaking; psychology; public administration; public health; public health/community nursing; religious studies; Romance languages; Russian; Russian studies; Scandinavian languages; Scandinavian studies; science teacher education; sculpture; secondary education; Slavic languages; social sciences; social work; sociology; Spanish; speech and rhetoric; statistics; technical and business writing; violin, viola, guitar and other stringed instruments; voice and opera; wildlife and wildlands science and management; women's studies; wood science and wood products/pulp and paper technology; zoology/animal biology.

Academic Programs *Special study options:* academic remediation for entering students, accelerated degree program, adult/continuing education programs, advanced placement credit, cooperative education, distance learning, double majors, English as a second language, external degree program, honors programs, independent study, internships, part-time degree program, services for LD students, student-designed majors, study abroad, summer session for credit. *ROTC:* Army (b), Navy (b), Air Force (b).

Library Suzzallo/Allen Library plus 21 others with 5.8 million titles, 50,245 serial subscriptions, 1.4 million audiovisual materials, a Web page.

Computers on Campus 285 computers available on campus for general student use. A campuswide network can be accessed from student residence rooms and from off campus. Internet access, online (class) registration, at least one staffed computer lab available.

Student Life *Housing options:* coed, disabled students. Campus housing is university owned and leased by the school. *Activities and organizations:* drama/theater group, student-run newspaper, radio and television station, choral group, marching band, national fraternities, national sororities. *Campus security:* 24-hour emergency response devices and patrols, late-night transport/escort service, controlled dormitory access. *Student services:* health clinic, personal/psychological counseling, women's center, legal services.

Athletics Member NCAA. All Division I except football (Division I-A). *Intercollegiate sports:* baseball M(s), basketball M(s)/W(s), crew M(s)/W(s), cross-country running M(s)/W(s), golf M(s)/W(s), gymnastics W(s), soccer M(s)/W, softball W(s), swimming M(s)/W(s), tennis M(s)/W(s), track and field M(s)/W(s), volleyball W(s), wrestling M(c). *Intramural sports:* archery M(c)/W(c), badminton M/W, basketball M/W, bowling M/W, crew M(c)/W(c), fencing M(c)/W(c), field hockey M(c)/W(c), football M/W, golf M/W, gymnastics M(c)/W(c), ice hockey M(c), lacrosse M(c)/W(c), racquetball M(c)/W(c), rugby M(c), sailing M(c)/W(c), skiing (cross-country) M(c)/W(c), skiing (downhill) M(c)/W(c), soccer M(c)/W(c), squash M(c)/W(c), swimming M/W, table tennis M/W, tennis M/W, track and field M/W, volleyball M/W, water polo M(c)/W(c), wrestling M.

Standardized Tests *Required:* SAT I or ACT (for admission).

Costs (2003–04) *Tuition:* state resident $4968 full-time; nonresident $16,124 full-time. *Room and board:* $6726.

Financial Aid Of all full-time matriculated undergraduates who enrolled in 2002, 16,443 applied for aid, 12,100 were judged to have need, 5,685 had their need fully met. 1,026 Federal Work-Study jobs (averaging $2500). 211 state and other part-time jobs (averaging $2929). In 2002, 2728 non-need-based awards were made. *Average percent of need met:* 88%. *Average financial aid package:* $10,043. *Average need-based loan:* $4600. *Average need-based gift aid:* $5772. *Average non-need-based aid:* $2774. *Average indebtedness upon graduation:* $14,760.

Applying *Options:* electronic application, early admission. *Application fee:* $37. *Required:* essay or personal statement, high school transcript, minimum 2.0 GPA. *Application deadlines:* 1/15 (freshmen), 2/15 (transfers). *Notification:* continuous until 4/15 (freshmen), continuous (transfers).

Admissions Contact Mr. Wilbur W. Washburn IV, Assistant Vice President for Enrollment Services, University of Washington, Box 355852, Seattle, WA 98195-5852. *Phone:* 206-543-9686.

WALLA WALLA COLLEGE

College Place, Washington

- **Independent Seventh-day Adventist** comprehensive, founded 1892
- **Calendar** quarters
- **Degrees** associate, bachelor's, and master's
- **Small-town** 77-acre campus
- **Endowment** $9.0 million
- **Coed,** 1,667 undergraduate students, 92% full-time, 48% women, 52% men
- **Moderately difficult** entrance level, 55% of applicants were admitted

Undergraduates 1,528 full-time, 139 part-time. Students come from 45 states and territories, 61% are from out of state, 2% African American, 6% Asian American or Pacific Islander, 6% Hispanic American, 0.3% Native American, 0.2% international, 10% transferred in, 58% live on campus. *Retention:* 100% of 2002 full-time freshmen returned.

Freshmen *Admission:* 631 applied, 348 admitted, 326 enrolled. *Average high school GPA:* 3.27.

Faculty *Total:* 201, 60% full-time, 43% with terminal degrees. *Student/faculty ratio:* 13:1.

Majors Accounting; ancient Near Eastern and biblical languages; art; art teacher education; automobile/automotive mechanics technology; avionics maintenance technology; biology/biological sciences; biomedical/medical engineering; biomedical technology; biophysics; business administration and management; business teacher education; chemistry; civil engineering; clinical laboratory science/medical technology; commercial and advertising art; computer programming; computer science; economics; education (K-12); electrical, electronics and communications engineering; electromechanical technology; elementary education; engineering; engineering technology; English; environmental studies; French; German; health and physical education; health science; history; humanities; industrial arts; journalism; kinesiology and exercise science; management information systems; marketing/marketing management; mass communication/media; mathematics; mechanical engineering; modern languages; music; music teacher education; nursing (registered nurse training); philosophy; physical education teaching and coaching; physics; piano and organ; pre-dentistry studies; pre-law studies; pre-medical studies; pre-veterinary studies; psychology; public health education and promotion; public relations/image management; radio and television; religious studies; social work; sociology; Spanish; speech and rhetoric; theology; voice and opera.

Academic Programs *Special study options:* academic remediation for entering students, advanced placement credit, cooperative education, double majors, English as a second language, freshman honors college, honors programs, independent study, internships, part-time degree program, services for LD students, study abroad, summer session for credit.

Library Peterson Memorial Library plus 3 others with 128,747 titles, 1,317 serial subscriptions, 3,483 audiovisual materials, an OPAC, a Web page.

Computers on Campus 108 computers available on campus for general student use. A campuswide network can be accessed from student residence rooms and from off campus. Internet access, online (class) registration, at least one staffed computer lab available.

Student Life *Housing:* on-campus residence required through junior year. *Options:* men-only, women-only. Freshman campus housing is guaranteed. *Activities and organizations:* drama/theater group, student-run newspaper, radio station, choral group, Associated Students of Walla Walla College (ASWWC), Village Singles' Club, Aleph Gimel Ain (women's club), Amnesty International, Omicron Pi Sigma (men's club). *Campus security:* 24-hour emergency response devices and patrols, student patrols, late-night transport/escort service, controlled dormitory access. *Student services:* health clinic, personal/psychological counseling.

Athletics Member NCCAA. *Intercollegiate sports:* basketball M/W, golf M, ice hockey M, soccer M, softball W, volleyball M/W. *Intramural sports:* basketball M/W, football M/W, gymnastics M/W, ice hockey M, racquetball M/W, softball M/W, table tennis M/W, tennis M/W, volleyball M/W.

Standardized Tests *Required:* SAT I or ACT (for admission). *Recommended:* ACT (for admission).

Costs (2003–04) *Comprehensive fee:* $20,880 includes full-time tuition ($16,860), mandatory fees ($165), and room and board ($3855). Full-time tuition and fees vary according to course load, degree level, and location. Part-time tuition: $442 per credit. *College room only:* $2280. Room and board charges vary according to housing facility and location. *Payment plan:* installment. *Waivers:* senior citizens and employees or children of employees.

Financial Aid Of all full-time matriculated undergraduates who enrolled in 2002, 1,296 applied for aid, 1,026 were judged to have need, 172 had their need fully met. 723 Federal Work-Study jobs (averaging $2313). 75 state and other part-time jobs (averaging $2822). In 2002, 275 non-need-based awards were made. *Average percent of need met:* 81%. *Average financial aid package:* $14,161. *Average need-based loan:* $4659. *Average need-based gift aid:* $5834. *Average non-need-based aid:* $5492. *Average indebtedness upon graduation:* $21,273.

Applying *Options:* common application, electronic application, deferred entrance. *Application fee:* $30. *Required:* high school transcript, minimum 2.0 GPA, 3 letters of recommendation. *Application deadline:* rolling (freshmen), rolling (transfers). *Notification:* continuous (freshmen), continuous (transfers).

Admissions Contact Mr. Dallas Weis, Director of Admissions, Walla Walla College, 204 South College Avenue, College Place, WA 99324. *Phone:* 509-527-2327. *Toll-free phone:* 800-541-8900. *Fax:* 509-527-2397. *E-mail:* info@wwc.edu.

WASHINGTON STATE UNIVERSITY

Pullman, Washington

- **State-supported** university, founded 1890
- **Calendar** semesters
- **Degrees** bachelor's, master's, doctoral, first professional, and postbachelor's certificates
- **Rural** 620-acre campus
- **Endowment** $495.6 million
- **Coed,** 18,746 undergraduate students, 84% full-time, 53% women, 47% men
- **Moderately difficult** entrance level, 78% of applicants were admitted

Undergraduates 15,826 full-time, 2,920 part-time. Students come from 55 states and territories, 77 other countries, 2% are from out of state, 3% African American, 5% Asian American or Pacific Islander, 4% Hispanic American, 1% Native American, 3% international, 13% transferred in, 49% live on campus. *Retention:* 84% of 2002 full-time freshmen returned.

Freshmen *Admission:* 9,182 applied, 7,206 admitted, 3,043 enrolled. *Average high school GPA:* 3.44. *Test scores:* SAT verbal scores over 500: 66%; SAT math scores over 500: 70%; SAT verbal scores over 600: 21%; SAT math scores over 600: 25%; SAT verbal scores over 700: 2%; SAT math scores over 700: 3%.

Faculty *Total:* 1,289, 83% full-time, 82% with terminal degrees. *Student/faculty ratio:* 18:1.

Majors Accounting; accounting technology and bookkeeping; adult development and aging; advertising; agricultural/biological engineering and bioengineering; agricultural business and management; agricultural communication/journalism; agricultural economics; agricultural mechanization; agricultural production; agricultural teacher education; agriculture; agriculture and agriculture operations related; agronomy and crop science; American studies; animal genetics; animal sciences; anthropology; apparel and textiles; applied mathematics; architecture; art history, criticism and conservation; Asian studies; athletic training; audiology and speech-language pathology; biochemistry; biochemistry, biophysics and molecular biology related; biological and biomedical sciences related; biological and physical sciences; biology/biological sciences; biophysics; biotechnology; botany/plant biology; broadcast journalism; business administration and management; business/commerce; business/managerial economics; chemical engineering; chemistry; civil engineering; classics and languages, literatures and linguistics; communication and media related; communication/speech communication and rhetoric; computer engineering; computer science; computer software engineering; construction engineering technology; criminal justice/law enforcement administration; crop production; dramatic/theatre arts; ecology; economics; electrical, electronics and communications engineering; elementary education; engineering/industrial management; engineering science; English; entomology; entrepreneurship; environmental/environmental health engineering; environmental science; ethnic, cultural minority, and gender studies related; finance; fine/studio arts; food science; foods, nutrition, and wellness; foreign languages and literatures; forestry; French; genetics related; geology/earth science; German; health and physical education; health and physical education related; history; horticultural science; hospitality administration; human development and family studies; humanities; human nutrition; human resources management; industrial engineering; insurance; interior architecture; international business/trade/commerce; Japanese; kinesiology and exercise science; landscape architecture; land use planning and management; legal professions and studies related; liberal arts and sciences and humanities related; liberal arts and sciences/liberal studies; linguistics; management information systems; management information systems and services related; management science; marketing/marketing management; materials engineering; materials science; mathematics; mathematics and computer science; mechanical engineering; microbiology; music; music performance; music teacher education; music theory and composition; natural resources/conservation; neuroscience; nursing (registered nurse training); nutrition sciences; operations management; parks, recreation, and leisure related; pharmacology and toxicology; philosophy; physical sciences; physics; plant pathology/phytopathology; plant physiology; plant sciences; plant sciences related; political science and government; pre-dentistry studies; pre-law studies; pre-medical studies; psychology; public administration; public relations/image management; range science and management; real estate; religious studies; restaurant, culinary, and catering management; Russian; Russian studies; Scandinavian languages; secondary education; social sciences; social work; sociology; soil science and agronomy; Spanish; special education; sport and fitness administration; statistics; veterinary sciences; wildlife and wildlands science and management; wildlife biology; women's studies; zoology/animal biology.

Academic Programs *Special study options:* academic remediation for entering students, adult/continuing education programs, advanced placement credit, cooperative education, distance learning, double majors, English as a second language, external degree program, honors programs, internships, off-campus study, part-time degree program, services for LD students, study abroad, summer session for credit. *ROTC:* Army (b), Navy (b), Air Force (b).

Library Holland Library plus 5 others with 2.0 million titles, 31,237 serial subscriptions, 316,707 audiovisual materials, an OPAC, a Web page.

Computers on Campus 10000 computers available on campus for general student use. A campuswide network can be accessed from student residence rooms and from off campus. Internet access, online (class) registration, at least one staffed computer lab available.

Student Life *Housing:* on-campus residence required for freshman year. *Options:* coed, men-only, women-only. Campus housing is university owned. Freshman applicants given priority for college housing. *Activities and organizations:* drama/theater group, student-run newspaper, radio and television station, choral group, marching band, Sigma Iota Hospitality Association, Student Alumni Connection, K-House, Fellowship for Student Athletes, Black Woman's Caucus, national fraternities, national sororities. *Campus security:* 24-hour emergency response devices and patrols, student patrols, late-night transport/escort service, controlled dormitory access. *Student services:* health clinic, personal/psychological counseling, women's center, legal services.

Athletics Member NCAA, NAIA. All NCAA Division I except football (Division I-A). *Intercollegiate sports:* baseball M(s), basketball M(s)/W(s), bowling M(c)/W(c), crew M(c)/W(s), cross-country running M(s)/W(s), equestrian sports M(c)/W(c), golf M(s)/W(s), ice hockey M(c)/W(c), lacrosse M(c)/W(c), rugby M(c)/W(c), skiing (cross-country) M(c)/W(c), skiing (downhill) M(c)/W(c), soccer M(c)/W(s), softball W(c), swimming W(s), tennis W(s), track and field M(s)/W(s), volleyball M(c)/W(s), water polo M(c). *Intramural sports:* badminton M/W, basketball M/W, bowling M/W, cheerleading M/W, cross-country running M/W, fencing M(c)/W(c), football M/W, golf M/W, racquetball M/W, soccer M/W, softball M/W, table tennis M/W, tennis M/W, track and field M/W, volleyball M/W, wrestling M.

Standardized Tests *Required:* SAT I or ACT (for admission).

Costs (2003–04) *Tuition:* state resident $4435 full-time; nonresident $12,537 full-time. Part-time tuition and fees vary according to course load. *Required fees:* $775 full-time. *Room and board:* $6054; room only: $3010. Room and board charges vary according to board plan and housing facility. *Payment plans:* tuition prepayment, installment. *Waivers:* children of alumni and employees or children of employees.

Financial Aid Of all full-time matriculated undergraduates who enrolled in 2002, 11,926 applied for aid, 7,967 were judged to have need, 3,655 had their need fully met. 875 Federal Work-Study jobs (averaging $2000). 1,269 state and other part-time jobs (averaging $2000). In 2002, 1994 non-need-based awards were made. *Average percent of need met:* 95%. *Average financial aid package:* $11,511. *Average need-based loan:* $4653. *Average need-based gift aid:* $5188. *Average non-need-based aid:* $3034. *Average indebtedness upon graduation:* $19,788.

Applying *Options:* electronic application, early admission. *Application fee:* $37. *Required:* essay or personal statement, high school transcript, minimum 2.0 GPA. *Required for some:* 3 letters of recommendation. *Notification:* continuous until 12/1 (freshmen), 12/1 (transfers).

Admissions Contact Ms. Wendy Peterson, Director of Admissions, Washington State University, Lighty 370, Pullman, WA 99164-1067. *Phone:* 509-335-5586. *Toll-free phone:* 888-468-6978. *Fax:* 509-335-7468. *E-mail:* admiss2@wsu.edu.

WESTERN WASHINGTON UNIVERSITY

Bellingham, Washington

- **State-supported** comprehensive, founded 1893
- **Calendar** quarters
- **Degrees** bachelor's, master's, and postbachelor's certificates

Western Washington University (continued)

- **Small-town** 223-acre campus with easy access to Seattle and Vancouver
- **Endowment** $4.3 million
- **Coed,** 12,477 undergraduate students, 92% full-time, 57% women, 43% men
- **Moderately difficult** entrance level, 76% of applicants were admitted

Western Washington University is an innovative public university considered to be among the best in the Pacific Northwest. Western is recognized for excellence in undergraduate education, an increasingly diverse and multicultural learning environment, and a strong sense of community. Primary reasons for attending Western are academic quality, location, size, job placement, and cost.

Undergraduates 11,451 full-time, 1,026 part-time. Students come from 47 states and territories, 35 other countries, 7% are from out of state, 2% African American, 7% Asian American or Pacific Islander, 3% Hispanic American, 2% Native American, 0.4% international, 8% transferred in, 30% live on campus. *Retention:* 84% of 2002 full-time freshmen returned.

Freshmen *Admission:* 7,652 applied, 5,843 admitted, 2,214 enrolled. *Average high school GPA:* 3.52. *Test scores:* SAT verbal scores over 500: 79%; SAT math scores over 500: 81%; ACT scores over 18: 97%; SAT verbal scores over 600: 35%; SAT math scores over 600: 31%; ACT scores over 24: 52%; SAT verbal scores over 700: 5%; SAT math scores over 700: 3%; ACT scores over 30: 7%.

Faculty *Total:* 618, 73% full-time, 74% with terminal degrees. *Student/faculty ratio:* 20:1.

Majors Accounting; accounting and computer science; American studies; anthropology; archeology; art; art history, criticism and conservation; art teacher education; Asian studies; Asian studies (East); athletic training; audiology and speech-language pathology; automotive engineering technology; biochemistry; biological and physical sciences; biology/biological sciences; broadcast journalism; business administration and management; business/managerial economics; Canadian studies; cell and molecular biology; cell biology and histology; ceramic arts and ceramics; chemistry; chemistry teacher education; city/urban, community and regional planning; classics and languages, literatures and linguistics; commercial and advertising art; communication/speech communication and rhetoric; community health services counseling; comparative literature; computer management; computer programming; computer science; counselor education/school counseling and guidance; creative writing; cultural studies; design and visual communications; developmental and child psychology; dramatic/theatre arts; drawing; ecology; economics; education; educational leadership and administration; education (multiple levels); electrical, electronic and communications engineering technology; elementary education; engineering related; engineering technology; English; environmental biology; environmental education; environmental science; environmental studies; fiber, textile and weaving arts; finance; fine/studio arts; French; general studies; geography; geology/earth science; geophysics and seismology; German; graphic design; health teacher education; history; humanities; human resources management; human services; industrial design; industrial technology; interdisciplinary studies; intermedia/multimedia; international business/trade/commerce; jazz/jazz studies; journalism; kindergarten/preschool education; kinesiology and exercise science; Latin American studies; liberal arts and sciences/liberal studies; linguistics; literature; management information systems; manufacturing technology; marine biology and biological oceanography; marketing/marketing management; mass communication/media; mathematics; molecular biology; music; music history, literature, and theory; music teacher education; natural resources management and policy; operations management; painting; parks, recreation and leisure; philosophy; physical education teaching and coaching; physics; plastics engineering technology; political science and government; pre-law studies; printmaking; psychology; public health education and promotion; science teacher education; sculpture; secondary education; sociology; Spanish; special education; visual and performing arts; western civilization; women's studies.

Academic Programs *Special study options:* accelerated degree program, adult/continuing education programs, advanced placement credit, cooperative education, distance learning, double majors, English as a second language, honors programs, independent study, internships, off-campus study, services for LD students, student-designed majors, study abroad, summer session for credit.

Library Wilson Library plus 3 others with 1.3 million titles, 4,834 serial subscriptions, 26,095 audiovisual materials, an OPAC, a Web page.

Computers on Campus 1567 computers available on campus for general student use. A campuswide network can be accessed from student residence rooms and from off campus. Internet access, online (class) registration, at least one staffed computer lab available.

Student Life *Housing options:* coed. Campus housing is university owned. Freshman campus housing is guaranteed. *Activities and organizations:* drama/theater group, student-run newspaper, radio and television station, choral group, intramurals, Residence Hall Association, Associated Students, Outdoor Center, Ethnic Student Center. *Campus security:* 24-hour emergency response devices and patrols, student patrols, late-night transport/escort service, controlled dormitory access. *Student services:* health clinic, personal/psychological counseling, women's center, legal services.

Athletics Member NCAA. All Division II. *Intercollegiate sports:* basketball M(s)/W(s), cheerleading M/W, crew M(s)/W(s), cross-country running M(s)/W(s), football M(s), golf M(s)/W(s), soccer M(s)/W(s), softball W(s), track and field M(s)/W(s), volleyball W(s). *Intramural sports:* badminton M/W, baseball M, basketball M/W, ice hockey M, lacrosse M/W, racquetball M/W, rugby M/W, sailing M/W, skiing (downhill) M/W, soccer M/W, softball M/W, swimming M/W, table tennis M/W, tennis M/W, volleyball M/W, water polo M/W, wrestling M.

Standardized Tests *Required:* SAT I or ACT (for admission), TOEFL for international applicants (for admission).

Costs (2003–04) *Tuition:* state resident $3639 full-time, $121 per credit part-time; nonresident $12,411 full-time, $414 per credit part-time. Full-time tuition and fees vary according to location. Part-time tuition and fees vary according to location. *Required fees:* $543 full-time, $181 per year part-time. *Room and board:* $5945; room only: $3902. Room and board charges vary according to board plan and housing facility. *Payment plan:* installment. *Waivers:* employees or children of employees.

Financial Aid Of all full-time matriculated undergraduates who enrolled in 2003, 6,894 applied for aid, 4,885 were judged to have need, 1,514 had their need fully met. 246 Federal Work-Study jobs (averaging $2887). 316 state and other part-time jobs (averaging $3276). In 2003, 179 non-need-based awards were made. *Average percent of need met:* 86%. *Average financial aid package:* $8258. *Average need-based loan:* $4052. *Average need-based gift aid:* $5027. *Average non-need-based aid:* $3359. *Average indebtedness upon graduation:* $14,616.

Applying *Options:* common application, electronic application. *Application fee:* $37. *Required:* high school transcript, minimum 2.5 GPA. *Recommended:* essay or personal statement. *Application deadlines:* 3/1 (freshmen), 4/1 (transfers). *Notification:* continuous until 4/15 (freshmen), continuous until 6/1 (transfers).

Admissions Contact Ms. Karen Copetas, Director of Admissions, Western Washington University, 516 High Street, Bellingham, WA 98225-9009. *Phone:* 360-650-3440. *Fax:* 360-650-7369. *E-mail:* admit@wwu.edu.

WHITMAN COLLEGE

Walla Walla, Washington

- **Independent** 4-year, founded 1859
- **Calendar** semesters
- **Degree** bachelor's
- **Small-town** 117-acre campus
- **Endowment** $250.3 million
- **Coed,** 1,454 undergraduate students, 97% full-time, 56% women, 44% men
- **Very difficult** entrance level, 56% of applicants were admitted

Whitman College, one of the nation's leading liberal arts colleges, develops its students' capacities to analyze, interpret, criticize, communicate, and engage. Strong residential life and active cocurricular programs encourage personal and social development. A Whitman education is intended to foster intellectual vitality, confidence, leadership, and the flexibility to succeed in a changing technological, multicultural world. Whitman's location in Walla Walla, Washington, offers an ideal setting for a rigorous education, an active campus life, and a strong sense of community in the beautiful Pacific Northwest.

Undergraduates 1,415 full-time, 39 part-time. Students come from 27 states and territories, 24 other countries, 51% are from out of state, 2% African American, 8% Asian American or Pacific Islander, 3% Hispanic American, 0.8% Native American, 2% international, 2% transferred in, 59% live on campus. *Retention:* 95% of 2002 full-time freshmen returned.

Freshmen *Admission:* 2,143 applied, 1,196 admitted, 362 enrolled. *Average high school GPA:* 3.76. *Test scores:* SAT verbal scores over 500: 98%; SAT math scores over 500: 99%; ACT scores over 18: 100%; SAT verbal scores over 600: 85%; SAT math scores over 600: 82%; ACT scores over 24: 88%; SAT verbal scores over 700: 40%; SAT math scores over 700: 28%; ACT scores over 30: 45%.

Faculty *Total:* 185, 63% full-time, 82% with terminal degrees. *Student/faculty ratio:* 10:1.

Majors Anthropology; art; art history, criticism and conservation; Asian studies; astronomy; biochemistry; biology/biological sciences; biophysics; chemistry; classics and languages, literatures and linguistics; dramatic/theatre arts; economics; English; environmental studies; film/cinema studies; French; geology/earth science; German; history; mathematics; molecular biology; music; philosophy; physics; political science and government; psychology; religious studies; sociology; Spanish.

Academic Programs *Special study options:* advanced placement credit, double majors, honors programs, independent study, internships, off-campus study, services for LD students, student-designed majors, study abroad. *Unusual degree programs:* 3-2 engineering with California Institute of Technology, Columbia

University, Duke University, University of Washington, Washington University in St. Louis; forestry with Duke University; international studies with Monterey Institute of International Studies, oceanography with University of Washington, teacher education with Bank Street College of Education, law with Columbia University.

Library Penrose Library plus 1 other with 350,699 titles, 2,175 serial subscriptions, 4,500 audiovisual materials, an OPAC, a Web page.

Computers on Campus 250 computers available on campus for general student use. A campuswide network can be accessed from student residence rooms and from off campus that provide access to course registration information. Internet access, at least one staffed computer lab available.

Student Life *Housing:* on-campus residence required through sophomore year. *Options:* coed, women-only. Campus housing is university owned. Freshman campus housing is guaranteed. *Activities and organizations:* drama/theater group, student-run newspaper, radio station, choral group, Associated Students, outdoor program, Center for Community Service, national fraternities, national sororities. *Campus security:* 24-hour emergency response devices and patrols, student patrols, late-night transport/escort service, controlled dormitory access. *Student services:* health clinic, personal/psychological counseling, women's center.

Athletics Member NCAA. All Division III. *Intercollegiate sports:* baseball M, basketball M/W, cheerleading M/W, cross-country running M/W, golf M/W, ice hockey M(c), lacrosse M(c)/W(c), rugby M(c)/W(c), skiing (cross-country) M/W, skiing (downhill) M/W, soccer M(s)/W(s), softball M(c)/W(c), swimming M/W, tennis M/W, track and field M(c)/W(c), ultimate Frisbee M(c)/W(c), volleyball M(s)(c)/W(s). *Intramural sports:* basketball M/W, football M/W, soccer M/W, softball M/W, tennis M/W, ultimate Frisbee M/W, volleyball M/W.

Standardized Tests *Required:* SAT I or ACT (for admission). *Recommended:* SAT II: Writing Test (for admission).

Costs (2003–04) *Comprehensive fee:* $32,526 includes full-time tuition ($25,400), mandatory fees ($226), and room and board ($6900). *College room only:* $3170. Room and board charges vary according to board plan and housing facility. *Payment plan:* deferred payment. *Waivers:* employees or children of employees.

Financial Aid Of all full-time matriculated undergraduates who enrolled in 2003, 733 applied for aid, 595 were judged to have need, 325 had their need fully met. 483 Federal Work-Study jobs (averaging $1989). 220 state and other part-time jobs (averaging $1529). In 2003, 96 non-need-based awards were made. *Average percent of need met:* 89%. *Average financial aid package:* $17,750. *Average need-based loan:* $3625. *Average need-based gift aid:* $12,775. *Average non-need-based aid:* $7450. *Average indebtedness upon graduation:* $15,075.

Applying *Options:* common application, electronic application, early decision, deferred entrance. *Application fee:* $45. *Required:* essay or personal statement, high school transcript, 1 letter of recommendation. *Recommended:* interview. *Application deadlines:* 1/15 (freshmen), 1/15 (transfers). *Early decision:* 11/15 (for plan 1), 1/1 (for plan 2). *Notification:* 4/1 (freshmen), 12/15 (early decision plan 1), 1/23 (early decision plan 2), 4/1 (transfers).

Admissions Contact Mr. Tony Cabasco, Acting Dean of Admission and Financial Aid, Whitman College, 345 Boyer Avenue, Walla Walla, WA 99362-2083. *Phone:* 509-527-5176. *Toll-free phone:* 877-462-9448. *Fax:* 509-527-4967. *E-mail:* admission@whitman.edu.

■ *See page 2842 for a narrative description.*

WHITWORTH COLLEGE

Spokane, Washington

- **Independent Presbyterian** comprehensive, founded 1890
- **Calendar** 4-1-4
- **Degrees** bachelor's and master's
- **Suburban** 200-acre campus
- **Endowment** $54.0 million
- **Coed,** 2,071 undergraduate students, 94% full-time, 59% women, 41% men
- **Very difficult** entrance level, 75% of applicants were admitted

Undergraduates 1,950 full-time, 121 part-time. Students come from 31 states and territories, 25 other countries, 38% are from out of state, 2% African American, 5% Asian American or Pacific Islander, 2% Hispanic American, 1% Native American, 3% international, 65% live on campus. *Retention:* 87% of 2002 full-time freshmen returned.

Freshmen *Admission:* 1,890 applied, 1,413 admitted. *Average high school GPA:* 3.59. *Test scores:* SAT verbal scores over 500: 86%; SAT math scores over 500: 88%; SAT verbal scores over 600: 40%; SAT math scores over 600: 40%; SAT verbal scores over 700: 7%; SAT math scores over 700: 5%.

Faculty *Student/faculty ratio:* 13:1.

Majors Accounting; American studies; art; art history, criticism and conservation; arts management; art teacher education; athletic training; biology/biological sciences; business administration and management; chemistry; computer science; dramatic/theatre arts; economics; elementary education; English; fine/studio arts; French; history; international business/trade/commerce; international relations and affairs; journalism; mass communication/media; mathematics; music; music teacher education; nursing (registered nurse training); peace studies and conflict resolution; philosophy; physical education teaching and coaching; physics; piano and organ; political science and government; pre-dentistry studies; pre-law studies; pre-medical studies; pre-veterinary studies; psychology; religious studies; secondary education; sociology; Spanish; special education; speech and rhetoric; voice and opera.

Academic Programs *Special study options:* adult/continuing education programs, advanced placement credit, cooperative education, double majors, English as a second language, independent study, internships, off-campus study, part-time degree program, services for LD students, student-designed majors, study abroad, summer session for credit. *ROTC:* Army (c). *Unusual degree programs:* 3-2 engineering with Seattle Pacific University, University of Southern California, Washington University in St. Louis, Columbia University; nursing with Intercollegiate Center for Nursing.

Library Harriet Cheney Cowles Library plus 2 others with 17,982 titles, 773 serial subscriptions, an OPAC, a Web page.

Computers on Campus 200 computers available on campus for general student use. A campuswide network can be accessed from student residence rooms and from off campus. Internet access, online (class) registration, at least one staffed computer lab available. Computer purchase or lease plan available.

Student Life *Housing:* on-campus residence required through sophomore year. *Options:* coed. Campus housing is university owned. Freshman campus housing is guaranteed. *Activities and organizations:* drama/theater group, student-run newspaper, radio station, choral group, International Club, Young Life, En Christo, Hawaiian club, Intramural Sports. *Campus security:* 24-hour emergency response devices and patrols, late-night transport/escort service. *Student services:* health clinic, personal/psychological counseling.

Athletics Member NCAA. All Division III. *Intercollegiate sports:* baseball M, basketball M/W, cross-country running M/W, football M, golf M/W, soccer M/W, swimming M/W, tennis M/W, track and field M/W, volleyball W. *Intramural sports:* basketball M/W, football M/W, skiing (downhill) M/W, soccer M/W, ultimate Frisbee M/W, volleyball M/W, water polo M/W.

Standardized Tests *Required:* SAT I or ACT (for admission).

Costs (2003–04) *Comprehensive fee:* $26,428 includes full-time tuition ($19,810), mandatory fees ($268), and room and board ($6350). Part-time tuition and fees vary according to class time. *Room and board:* Room and board charges vary according to board plan and housing facility. *Payment plan:* installment. *Waivers:* employees or children of employees.

Financial Aid Of all full-time matriculated undergraduates who enrolled in 2003, 1,834 applied for aid, 1,396 were judged to have need, 268 had their need fully met. 520 Federal Work-Study jobs (averaging $2090). 396 state and other part-time jobs (averaging $2510). In 2003, 388 non-need-based awards were made. *Average percent of need met:* 84%. *Average financial aid package:* $17,443. *Average need-based loan:* $4559. *Average need-based gift aid:* $11,552. *Average non-need-based aid:* $6947. *Average indebtedness upon graduation:* $17,000.

Applying *Options:* common application, electronic application, early admission, early action, deferred entrance. *Required:* essay or personal statement, high school transcript, letters of recommendation. *Required for some:* interview. *Application deadlines:* 3/1 (freshmen), 8/1 (transfers). *Notification:* 12/20 (early action).

Admissions Contact Ms. Marianne Hansen, Director of Admission, Whitworth College, 300 West, Hawthorne Road, Spokane, WA 99251. *Phone:* 800-533-4668. *Toll-free phone:* 800-533-4668. *Fax:* 509-777-3758. *E-mail:* admission@whitworth.edu.

■ *See page 2844 for a narrative description.*

WEST VIRGINIA

ALDERSON-BROADDUS COLLEGE

Philippi, West Virginia

- **Independent** comprehensive, founded 1871, affiliated with American Baptist Churches in the U.S.A.
- **Calendar** semesters
- **Degrees** certificates, associate, bachelor's, and master's
- **Rural** 170-acre campus
- **Endowment** $12.0 million
- **Coed,** 674 undergraduate students, 90% full-time, 70% women, 30% men
- **Moderately difficult** entrance level, 64% of applicants were admitted

Alderson-Broaddus College (continued)

Undergraduates 605 full-time, 69 part-time. Students come from 26 states and territories, 5 other countries, 25% are from out of state, 2% African American, 1% Asian American or Pacific Islander, 0.8% Hispanic American, 0.5% Native American, 1% international, 8% transferred in. *Retention:* 67% of 2002 full-time freshmen returned.

Freshmen *Admission:* 864 applied, 551 admitted, 129 enrolled. *Average high school GPA:* 3.34. *Test scores:* SAT verbal scores over 500: 42%; SAT math scores over 500: 63%; ACT scores over 18: 74%; SAT verbal scores over 600: 9%; SAT math scores over 600: 13%; ACT scores over 24: 17%; SAT math scores over 700: 2%.

Faculty *Total:* 87, 64% full-time, 31% with terminal degrees. *Student/faculty ratio:* 12:1.

Majors Accounting; applied mathematics; athletic training; biology/biological sciences; broadcast journalism; business administration and management; chemistry; clinical laboratory science/medical technology; computer and information sciences; computer science; creative writing; cytotechnology; dramatic/theatre arts; education; elementary education; environmental studies; finance; history; industrial radiologic technology; liberal arts and sciences/liberal studies; literature; management information systems; marketing/marketing management; mass communication/media; mathematics; music; music teacher education; natural sciences; nursing (registered nurse training); parks, recreation and leisure; physical education teaching and coaching; physician assistant; political science and government; pre-dentistry studies; pre-law studies; pre-medical studies; preveterinary studies; psychology; religious/sacred music; religious studies; science teacher education; secondary education; sociology; special education; speech and rhetoric; technical and business writing; therapeutic recreation.

Academic Programs *Special study options:* academic remediation for entering students, advanced placement credit, double majors, honors programs, independent study, internships, off-campus study, part-time degree program, student-designed majors, study abroad, summer session for credit. *ROTC:* Army (c).

Library Pickett Library with 82,685 titles, 270 serial subscriptions, an OPAC, a Web page.

Computers on Campus 92 computers available on campus for general student use. A campuswide network can be accessed from student residence rooms and from off campus. Internet access, at least one staffed computer lab available.

Student Life *Housing:* on-campus residence required through senior year. *Options:* coed, women-only. Campus housing is university owned. *Activities and organizations:* drama/theater group, student-run newspaper, radio and television station, choral group, Baptist Campus Ministry, Collegiate 4-H, American Academy of Physician Assistants, S.L.I.C.E. (Students Learning in Community Education), Association of Women Students. *Campus security:* 24-hour patrols, late-night transport/escort service, controlled dormitory access. *Student services:* health clinic, personal/psychological counseling.

Athletics Member NCAA. All Division II. *Intercollegiate sports:* baseball M(s), basketball M(s)/W(s), cross-country running M(s)/W(s), soccer M(s), softball W(s), volleyball W(s). *Intramural sports:* archery M/W, badminton M/W, baseball M, basketball M/W, bowling M/W, football M, golf M, racquetball M/W, soccer M/W, softball W, swimming M/W, table tennis M/W, tennis M/W, volleyball M/W, water polo M/W, weight lifting M/W.

Standardized Tests *Required:* SAT I or ACT (for admission).

Costs (2004–05) *Comprehensive fee:* $22,650 includes full-time tuition ($16,950), mandatory fees ($166), and room and board ($5534). Part-time tuition: $564 per credit hour. *Required fees:* $42 per semester part-time. *Payment plan:* installment. *Waivers:* employees or children of employees.

Financial Aid Of all full-time matriculated undergraduates who enrolled in 2002, 625 applied for aid, 551 were judged to have need, 106 had their need fully met. 294 Federal Work-Study jobs (averaging $1400). 107 state and other part-time jobs (averaging $1400). In 2002, 27 non-need-based awards were made. *Average percent of need met:* 77%. *Average financial aid package:* $15,369. *Average need-based loan:* $4461. *Average need-based gift aid:* $4371. *Average non-need-based aid:* $12,263. *Average indebtedness upon graduation:* $19,750.

Applying *Options:* electronic application, deferred entrance. *Application fee:* $10. *Required:* high school transcript, minimum 2.0 GPA. *Required for some:* 3 letters of recommendation, interview. *Application deadline:* rolling (freshmen), rolling (transfers). *Notification:* continuous until 8/31 (freshmen), continuous until 8/31 (transfers).

Admissions Contact Ms. Kimberly N. Klaus, Associate Director of Admissions, Alderson-Broaddus College, PO Box 2003, Philippi, WV 26416. *Phone:* 304-457-1700 Ext. 6255. *Toll-free phone:* 800-263-1549. *Fax:* 304-457-6239. *E-mail:* admissions@ab.edu.

■ *See page 1148 for a narrative description.*

AMERICAN PUBLIC UNIVERSITY SYSTEM

Charles Town, West Virginia

- **Proprietary** comprehensive, founded 1991
- **Calendar** trimesters
- **Degrees** certificates, associate, bachelor's, and master's (profile includes American Public University, American Military University and American Community College)
- **Coed**
- **Noncompetitive** entrance level

Undergraduates Students come from 52 states and territories, 23 other countries, 90% are from out of state. *Retention:* 68% of 2002 full-time freshmen returned.

Freshmen *Average high school GPA:* 2.50.

Faculty *Total:* 342, 7% full-time, 49% with terminal degrees. *Student/faculty ratio:* 11:1.

Majors African studies; American studies; Army R.O.T.C./military science; Asian studies; business administration and management; business and personal/financial services marketing; computer science; criminal justice/safety; English language and literature related; environmental studies; general studies; history; information technology; Latin American studies; management science; philosophy related; psychology; public administration; sport and fitness administration; work and family studies.

Academic Programs *Special study options:* adult/continuing education programs, distance learning, external degree program, independent study, part-time degree program.

Student Life *Housing:* college housing not available.

Costs (2003–04) *One-time required fee:* $75. *Tuition:* $9000 full-time, $750 per course part-time. Full-time tuition and fees vary according to course load. *Payment plan:* installment.

Applying *Options:* electronic application, deferred entrance. *Required:* high school transcript. *Application deadline:* rolling (freshmen), rolling (transfers).

Admissions Contact Ms. Lyn Geer, Associate Vice President Student services, American Public University System, 322-C West Washington Street, Charles Town, WV 25414. *Phone:* 703-330-5398. *Toll-free phone:* 877-468-6268. *E-mail:* admissions@amunet.edu.

APPALACHIAN BIBLE COLLEGE

Bradley, West Virginia

- **Independent nondenominational** 4-year, founded 1950
- **Calendar** semesters
- **Degrees** certificates, associate, and bachelor's
- **Small-town** 110-acre campus
- **Endowment** $242,376
- **Coed,** 322 undergraduate students, 74% full-time, 55% women, 45% men
- **Minimally difficult** entrance level, 76% of applicants were admitted

Undergraduates 238 full-time, 84 part-time. Students come from 31 states and territories, 8 other countries, 0.8% African American, 1% Asian American or Pacific Islander, 3% international, 11% transferred in.

Freshmen *Admission:* 145 applied, 110 admitted, 54 enrolled.

Faculty *Total:* 15, 67% full-time, 33% with terminal degrees. *Student/faculty ratio:* 17:1.

Majors Biblical studies; theology.

Academic Programs *Special study options:* academic remediation for entering students, adult/continuing education programs, advanced placement credit, honors programs, independent study, internships, part-time degree program, summer session for credit.

Library John Van Puffien Library with 44,944 titles, 347 serial subscriptions, 4,268 audiovisual materials, an OPAC.

Computers on Campus 7 computers available on campus for general student use. A campuswide network can be accessed from off campus. Internet access, at least one staffed computer lab available.

Student Life *Housing:* on-campus residence required through senior year. *Options:* men-only, women-only. Campus housing is university owned. Freshman applicants given priority for college housing. *Activities and organizations:* drama/theater group, choral group, Campus Missionary Fellowship. *Campus security:* 24-hour emergency response devices, patrols by trained security personnel. *Student services:* health clinic, personal/psychological counseling.

Athletics Member NCCAA. *Intercollegiate sports:* basketball M/W, soccer M, volleyball W. *Intramural sports:* table tennis M/W, tennis M/W.

Standardized Tests *Required:* SAT I or ACT (for admission).

Costs (2004–05) *Comprehensive fee:* $12,240 includes full-time tuition ($6816), mandatory fees ($1224), and room and board ($4200). Part-time tuition: $284 per credit hour. *Required fees:* $31 per credit hour part-time. *Payment plan:* installment. *Waivers:* employees or children of employees.

Financial Aid Of all full-time matriculated undergraduates who enrolled in 2003, 258 applied for aid, 258 were judged to have need. 31 Federal Work-Study jobs (averaging $714). *Average percent of need met:* 90%. *Average financial aid package:* $3625. *Average need-based loan:* $4000. *Average need-based gift aid:* $3625. *Average indebtedness upon graduation:* $18,500. *Financial aid deadline:* 6/30.

Applying *Application fee:* $10. *Required:* essay or personal statement, high school transcript, 3 letters of recommendation. *Recommended:* minimum 2.5 GPA, interview. *Application deadline:* rolling (freshmen), rolling (transfers).

Admissions Contact Miss Karen Nelson, Admissions Counselor, Appalachian Bible College, PO Box ABC, Bradley, WV 25818. *Phone:* 800-678-9ABC Ext. 3213. *Toll-free phone:* 800-678-9ABC Ext. 3213. *Fax:* 304-877-5082. *E-mail:* admissions@abc.edu.

BETHANY COLLEGE

Bethany, West Virginia

- **Independent** 4-year, founded 1840, affiliated with Christian Church (Disciples of Christ)
- **Calendar** 4-1-4
- **Degree** bachelor's
- **Rural** 1600-acre campus with easy access to Pittsburgh
- **Endowment** $46.2 million
- **Coed,** 900 undergraduate students, 98% full-time, 51% women, 49% men
- **Moderately difficult** entrance level, 73% of applicants were admitted

Undergraduates 882 full-time, 18 part-time. Students come from 26 states and territories, 20 other countries, 73% are from out of state, 2% African American, 0.7% Asian American or Pacific Islander, 0.8% Hispanic American, 0.1% Native American, 2% international, 6% transferred in, 88% live on campus. *Retention:* 84% of 2002 full-time freshmen returned.

Freshmen *Admission:* 957 applied, 703 admitted, 271 enrolled. *Average high school GPA:* 3.40. *Test scores:* SAT verbal scores over 500: 53%; SAT math scores over 500: 50%; ACT scores over 18: 86%; SAT verbal scores over 600: 14%; SAT math scores over 600: 14%; ACT scores over 24: 33%; SAT verbal scores over 700: 1%; SAT math scores over 700: 1%; ACT scores over 30: 3%.

Faculty *Total:* 89, 69% full-time, 48% with terminal degrees. *Student/faculty ratio:* 13:1.

Majors Accounting; art; biology/biological sciences; business/managerial economics; chemistry; communication/speech communication and rhetoric; computer science; dramatic/theatre arts; economics; education; English; environmental studies; fine/studio arts; French; German; history; horse husbandry/equine science and management; interdisciplinary studies; international relations and affairs; mathematics; music; philosophy; physical education teaching and coaching; physics; political science and government; pre-dentistry studies; pre-law studies; pre-medical studies; pre-veterinary studies; psychology; religious studies; social work; Spanish; sport and fitness administration.

Academic Programs *Special study options:* academic remediation for entering students, advanced placement credit, double majors, English as a second language, independent study, internships, off-campus study, services for LD students, student-designed majors, study abroad. *Unusual degree programs:* 3-2 engineering with Columbia University, Washington University in St. Louis, Case Western Reserve University.

Library T. W. Phillips Memorial Library with 130,696 titles, 785 serial subscriptions, 3,101 audiovisual materials, an OPAC, a Web page.

Computers on Campus 136 computers available on campus for general student use. A campuswide network can be accessed from student residence rooms and from off campus. Internet access, at least one staffed computer lab available. Computer purchase or lease plan available.

Student Life *Housing:* on-campus residence required through senior year. *Options:* coed, men-only, women-only, disabled students. Campus housing is university owned. Freshman campus housing is guaranteed. *Activities and organizations:* drama/theater group, student-run newspaper, radio and television station, choral group, Student Board of Governors, outdoor club, Model United Nations, Public Relations Society, International Student Association, national fraternities, national sororities. *Campus security:* 24-hour emergency response devices and patrols, late-night transport/escort service. *Student services:* health clinic, personal/psychological counseling.

Athletics Member NCAA. All Division III. *Intercollegiate sports:* baseball M, basketball M/W, cheerleading M(c)/W(c), cross-country running M/W, football M, ice hockey M(c), lacrosse M(c)/W(c), rugby M(c), soccer M/W, softball W, swimming M/W, tennis M/W, track and field M/W, volleyball W, weight lifting M(c). *Intramural sports:* basketball M/W, football M/W, racquetball M/W, rock climbing M(c)/W(c), soccer M/W, softball M/W, swimming M/W, table tennis M/W, tennis M/W, ultimate Frisbee M(c)/W(c), volleyball M/W, weight lifting M/W.

Standardized Tests *Required:* SAT I or ACT (for admission).

Costs (2003–04) *Comprehensive fee:* $19,835 includes full-time tuition ($12,760), mandatory fees ($775), and room and board ($6300). Part-time tuition: $455 per credit. *Required fees:* $387 per term part-time. *College room only:* $3200. Room and board charges vary according to housing facility. *Payment plan:* installment. *Waivers:* children of alumni and employees or children of employees.

Financial Aid Of all full-time matriculated undergraduates who enrolled in 2003, 858 applied for aid, 802 were judged to have need, 428 had their need fully met. 310 state and other part-time jobs (averaging $290). In 2003, 68 non-need-based awards were made. *Average percent of need met:* 88%. *Average financial aid package:* $16,500. *Average need-based loan:* $4100. *Average indebtedness upon graduation:* $18,500.

Applying *Options:* common application, electronic application, deferred entrance. *Application fee:* $25. *Required:* essay or personal statement, high school transcript, minimum 2.0 GPA, 1 letter of recommendation, documentation of student involvement. *Required for some:* interview. *Recommended:* interview. *Application deadline:* 8/15 (freshmen), rolling (transfers). *Notification:* continuous until 8/15 (freshmen), continuous until 8/15 (transfers).

Admissions Contact Ms. Penny Cunningham, Dean of Admission, Bethany College, Office of Admission, Bethany, WV 26032. *Phone:* 304-829-7591. *Toll-free phone:* 800-922-7611. *Fax:* 304-829-7142. *E-mail:* admission@bethanywv.edu.

■ *See page 1254 for a narrative description.*

BLUEFIELD STATE COLLEGE

Bluefield, West Virginia

- **State-supported** 4-year, founded 1895, part of Higher Education Policy Commission System
- **Calendar** semesters
- **Degrees** certificates, associate, and bachelor's
- **Small-town** 45-acre campus
- **Endowment** $7.3 million
- **Coed,** 3,511 undergraduate students, 68% full-time, 63% women, 37% men
- **Noncompetitive** entrance level, 97% of applicants were admitted

Undergraduates 2,383 full-time, 1,128 part-time. Students come from 11 states and territories, 14 other countries, 5% are from out of state, 9% African American, 0.3% Asian American or Pacific Islander, 0.4% Hispanic American, 0.4% Native American, 0.9% international, 15% transferred in. *Retention:* 53% of 2002 full-time freshmen returned.

Freshmen *Admission:* 1,359 applied, 1,315 admitted, 664 enrolled. *Average high school GPA:* 3.15. *Test scores:* SAT verbal scores over 500: 28%; SAT math scores over 500: 33%; ACT scores over 18: 65%; SAT math scores over 600: 3%; ACT scores over 24: 8%.

Faculty *Total:* 296, 32% full-time, 19% with terminal degrees. *Student/faculty ratio:* 17:1.

Majors Accounting; administrative assistant and secretarial science; architectural engineering technology; biological and physical sciences; business administration and management; business/commerce; civil engineering technology; communications technology; computer and information sciences; corrections; criminal justice/police science; criminal justice/safety; electrical, electronic and communications engineering technology; elementary education; general studies; hotel/motel administration; humanities; interdisciplinary studies; legal assistant/paralegal; liberal arts and sciences/liberal studies; marketing/marketing management; mechanical engineering/mechanical technology; medical/clinical assistant; medical radiologic technology; mining technology; nursing (registered nurse training); psychology; social sciences.

Academic Programs *Special study options:* academic remediation for entering students, adult/continuing education programs, advanced placement credit, distance learning, double majors, external degree program, honors programs, internships, part-time degree program, student-designed majors, summer session for credit.

Library Hardway Library with 84,857 titles, 2,453 serial subscriptions, 341 audiovisual materials, an OPAC, a Web page.

Computers on Campus 358 computers available on campus for general student use. A campuswide network can be accessed from off campus. Internet access, at least one staffed computer lab available.

Student Life *Housing:* college housing not available. *Activities and organizations:* student-run newspaper, choral group, Phi Eta Sigma, Student Nurses Association, Student Government Association, Minorities on the Move, national

Bluefield State College (continued)
fraternities, national sororities. *Campus security:* 24-hour emergency response devices and patrols, student patrols. *Student services:* health clinic, personal/psychological counseling.

Athletics Member NCAA. All Division II. *Intercollegiate sports:* baseball M(s), basketball M(s)/W(s), cheerleading W, cross-country running M(s)/W(s), golf M(s), softball W(s), tennis M(s)/W(s). *Intramural sports:* badminton M/W, basketball M/W, football M, soccer M, swimming M/W, table tennis M/W, volleyball M/W, water polo M/W.

Standardized Tests *Recommended:* SAT I or ACT (for admission).

Costs (2003–04) *Tuition:* state resident $2806 full-time, $117 per credit part-time; nonresident $6894 full-time, $289 per credit part-time. Full-time tuition and fees vary according to degree level, program, and reciprocity agreements. Part-time tuition and fees vary according to course load, program, and reciprocity agreements. *Payment plan:* deferred payment. *Waivers:* senior citizens.

Financial Aid Of all full-time matriculated undergraduates who enrolled in 2003, 1,600 applied for aid, 900 were judged to have need, 160 had their need fully met. 114 Federal Work-Study jobs (averaging $1005). 150 state and other part-time jobs (averaging $1650). In 2003, 315 non-need-based awards were made. *Average percent of need met:* 70%. *Average financial aid package:* $5000. *Average need-based loan:* $3000. *Average need-based gift aid:* $3060. *Average non-need-based aid:* $1400. *Average indebtedness upon graduation:* $9000.

Applying *Options:* common application, electronic application, deferred entrance. *Required:* high school transcript, minimum 2.0 GPA. *Application deadline:* rolling (freshmen), rolling (transfers). *Notification:* continuous (freshmen).

Admissions Contact Mr. Kenneth Mandeville, Director of Student Recruitment, Bluefield State College, 219 Rock Street, Bluefield, WV 24701-2198. *Phone:* 304-327-4067. *Toll-free phone:* 800-344-8892 Ext. 4065 (in-state); 800-654-7798 Ext. 4065 (out-of-state). *Fax:* 304-325-7747. *E-mail:* bscadmit@bluefield.wvnet.edu.

CONCORD COLLEGE
Athens, West Virginia

- **State-supported** 4-year, founded 1872, part of State College System of West Virginia
- **Calendar** semesters
- **Degrees** associate, bachelor's, and master's
- **Rural** 100-acre campus
- **Endowment** $15.8 million
- **Coed,** 2,933 undergraduate students
- **Minimally difficult** entrance level, 63% of applicants were admitted

Undergraduates Students come from 27 states and territories, 14 other countries, 15% are from out of state, 5% African American, 1% Asian American or Pacific Islander, 0.4% Hispanic American, 0.1% Native American, 39% live on campus. *Retention:* 64% of 2002 full-time freshmen returned.

Freshmen *Admission:* 2,121 applied, 1,334 admitted. *Average high school GPA:* 3.24. *Test scores:* SAT verbal scores over 500: 50%; SAT math scores over 500: 48%; ACT scores over 18: 78%; SAT verbal scores over 600: 17%; SAT math scores over 600: 19%; ACT scores over 24: 25%; SAT verbal scores over 700: 1%; SAT math scores over 700: 3%; ACT scores over 30: 2%.

Faculty *Total:* 189, 52% full-time, 37% with terminal degrees. *Student/faculty ratio:* 21:1.

Majors Accounting; art teacher education; biology/biological sciences; business administration and management; business teacher education; ceramic arts and ceramics; chemistry; clinical laboratory science/medical technology; commercial and advertising art; computer science; education; elementary education; English; geography; health teacher education; history; hospitality administration; hotel/motel administration; information science/studies; kindergarten/preschool education; library science; mass communication/media; mathematics; music teacher education; parks, recreation and leisure facilities management; physical education teaching and coaching; political science and government; pre-medical studies; pre-veterinary studies; psychology; secondary education; social work; sociology; special education; special products marketing; tourism and travel services management.

Academic Programs *Special study options:* academic remediation for entering students, accelerated degree program, advanced placement credit, distance learning, double majors, English as a second language, external degree program, honors programs, independent study, internships, off-campus study, part-time degree program, services for LD students, student-designed majors, study abroad, summer session for credit.

Library J. Frank Marsh Library with 150,151 titles, 227 serial subscriptions, 4,060 audiovisual materials, an OPAC, a Web page.

Computers on Campus 250 computers available on campus for general student use. A campuswide network can be accessed from student residence rooms and from off campus. Internet access, at least one staffed computer lab available.

Student Life *Housing:* on-campus residence required through senior year. *Options:* coed, men-only, women-only. Campus housing is university owned. Freshman campus housing is guaranteed. *Activities and organizations:* drama/theater group, student-run newspaper, radio and television station, choral group, Student Union Board, student government, student-run publications, Greek organizations, music groups, national fraternities, national sororities. *Campus security:* 24-hour emergency response devices and patrols, student patrols, late-night transport/escort service, controlled dormitory access. *Student services:* health clinic.

Athletics Member NCAA, NAIA. All NCAA Division II. *Intercollegiate sports:* baseball M(s), basketball M(s)/W(s), cheerleading M(s)/W(s), cross-country running M(s)/W(s), football M(s), golf M(s), soccer W(s), softball W, tennis M(s)/W(s), track and field M(s)/W(s), volleyball W(s). *Intramural sports:* archery M/W, badminton M/W, basketball M/W, bowling M/W, football M, golf M/W, lacrosse M, racquetball M/W, skiing (downhill) M/W, soccer M/W, swimming M/W, tennis M/W, track and field M/W, volleyball M/W, water polo M/W, weight lifting M/W, wrestling M.

Standardized Tests *Required:* SAT I or ACT (for admission). *Recommended:* ACT (for admission).

Costs (2003–04) *Tuition:* state resident $3198 full-time, $133 per credit hour part-time; nonresident $7278 full-time, $303 per credit hour part-time. Full-time tuition and fees vary according to course load. Part-time tuition and fees vary according to course load. *Room and board:* $4938; room only: $2284. *Payment plan:* installment. *Waivers:* adult students, senior citizens, and employees or children of employees.

Financial Aid Of all full-time matriculated undergraduates who enrolled in 2002, 2,158 applied for aid, 1,491 were judged to have need, 566 had their need fully met. 188 Federal Work-Study jobs (averaging $1690). 245 state and other part-time jobs (averaging $1659). In 2002, 424 non-need-based awards were made. *Average percent of need met:* 79%. *Average financial aid package:* $6321. *Average need-based loan:* $2043. *Average need-based gift aid:* $2916. *Average non-need-based aid:* $3568. *Average indebtedness upon graduation:* $12,052.

Applying *Options:* common application, electronic application, early admission, early decision. *Required:* high school transcript, minimum 2.0 GPA. *Required for some:* essay or personal statement, interview. *Recommended:* interview. *Application deadlines:* rolling (freshmen), 1/15 (out-of-state freshmen), rolling (transfers). *Notification:* continuous (freshmen), 3/1 (out-of-state freshmen), continuous (transfers).

Admissions Contact Mr. Michael Curry, Vice President of Admissions and Financial Aid, Concord College, 1000 Vermillion Street, Athens, WV 24712. *Phone:* 304-384-5248. *Toll-free phone:* 888-384-5249. *Fax:* 304-384-9044. *E-mail:* admissions@concord.edu.

■ *See page 1484 for a narrative description.*

DAVIS & ELKINS COLLEGE
Elkins, West Virginia

- **Independent Presbyterian** 4-year, founded 1904
- **Calendar** 4-1-4
- **Degrees** associate and bachelor's
- **Small-town** 170-acre campus
- **Endowment** $17.6 million
- **Coed,** 624 undergraduate students, 91% full-time, 60% women, 40% men
- **Minimally difficult** entrance level, 70% of applicants were admitted

Undergraduates 569 full-time, 55 part-time. Students come from 20 states and territories, 45% are from out of state, 3% African American, 3% Asian American or Pacific Islander, 2% Hispanic American, 0.6% Native American, 0.2% international, 11% transferred in, 44% live on campus. *Retention:* 73% of 2002 full-time freshmen returned.

Freshmen *Admission:* 691 applied, 484 admitted, 116 enrolled. *Average high school GPA:* 3.07. *Test scores:* SAT verbal scores over 500: 43%; SAT math scores over 500: 37%; ACT scores over 18: 68%; SAT verbal scores over 600: 13%; SAT math scores over 600: 12%; ACT scores over 24: 16%; SAT verbal scores over 700: 3%; ACT scores over 30: 1%.

Faculty *Total:* 47, 100% full-time. *Student/faculty ratio:* 12:1.

Majors Accounting; accounting and business/management; art teacher education; biological and biomedical sciences related; biology/biological sciences; business administration and management; business teacher education; chemistry; communication/speech communication and rhetoric; computer science; computer typography and composition equipment operation; creative writing; drama and dance teacher education; dramatic/theatre arts; economics; education; elementary education; English; environmental control technologies related; forestry related; French; history; hospitality administration; information science/studies; international business/trade/commerce; international marketing; kinesiology and exercise science; literature; management information systems; management information systems and services related; marketing/marketing management; mathematics; mathematics teacher education; music; music teacher education; natural sciences; nursing (registered nurse training); painting; parks, recreation and leisure; physical education teaching and coaching; political science and government; predentistry studies; pre-law studies; pre-medical studies; pre-veterinary studies; psychology; religious education; religious studies; secondary education; sociology; Spanish; sport and fitness administration; tourism and travel services management.

Academic Programs *Special study options:* accelerated degree program, adult/continuing education programs, advanced placement credit, cooperative education, double majors, English as a second language, external degree program, honors programs, independent study, internships, part-time degree program, services for LD students, student-designed majors, study abroad, summer session for credit. *Unusual degree programs:* 3-2 forestry with Duke University, State University of New York College of Environmental Science and Forestry.

Library Booth Library with 12,540 audiovisual materials, an OPAC, a Web page.

Computers on Campus 101 computers available on campus for general student use. A campuswide network can be accessed from student residence rooms and from off campus. Internet access, at least one staffed computer lab available. Computer purchase or lease plan available.

Student Life *Housing:* on-campus residence required through senior year. *Options:* coed, men-only, women-only, disabled students. Campus housing is university owned. Freshman campus housing is guaranteed. *Activities and organizations:* drama/theater group, student-run newspaper, radio station, choral group, Beta Alpha Beta, campus radio station, Student Nurses Association, Student Education Association, International Student Organization, national fraternities, national sororities. *Campus security:* late-night transport/escort service, controlled dormitory access, late night security personnel. *Student services:* health clinic, personal/psychological counseling.

Athletics Member NCAA. All Division II except field hockey (Division I). *Intercollegiate sports:* baseball M(s), basketball M(s)/W(s), cross-country running M(s)/W(s), field hockey W(s), golf M(s), skiing (downhill) M(s)/W(s), soccer M(s)/W(s), softball W(s), tennis M(s)/W(s), volleyball W(s). *Intramural sports:* basketball M/W, football M/W, lacrosse M(c)/W, skiing (cross-country) M/W, skiing (downhill) M/W, soccer M/W, softball M/W, swimming M/W, tennis M/W, track and field M/W, volleyball M/W(c), water polo M/W.

Standardized Tests *Required:* SAT I or ACT (for admission).

Costs (2004–05) *Comprehensive fee:* $20,594 includes full-time tuition ($14,248), mandatory fees ($420), and room and board ($5926). Part-time tuition and fees vary according to course load. *Payment plan:* installment. *Waivers:* employees or children of employees.

Financial Aid Of all full-time matriculated undergraduates who enrolled in 2002, 556 applied for aid, 431 were judged to have need, 74 had their need fully met. 184 Federal Work-Study jobs (averaging $941). 27 state and other part-time jobs (averaging $1010). In 2002, 42 non-need-based awards were made. *Average percent of need met:* 78%. *Average financial aid package:* $12,259. *Average need-based loan:* $3025. *Average need-based gift aid:* $4726. *Average non-need-based aid:* $11,821. *Average indebtedness upon graduation:* $8789.

Applying *Options:* common application, electronic application, early admission, deferred entrance. *Application fee:* $35. *Required:* high school transcript, minimum 2.0 GPA. *Required for some:* essay or personal statement, 2 letters of recommendation. *Recommended:* interview. *Application deadline:* rolling (freshmen), rolling (transfers). *Notification:* continuous (freshmen), continuous (transfers).

Admissions Contact Ms. Reneé Heckel, Director of Admissions, Davis & Elkins College, 100 Campus Drive, Elkins, WV 26241. *Phone:* 304-637-1328. *Toll-free phone:* 800-624-3157 Ext. 1328. *Fax:* 304-637-1800. *E-mail:* admis@davisandelkins.edu.

■ *See page 1520 for a narrative description.*

FAIRMONT STATE COLLEGE
Fairmont, West Virginia

- **State-supported** comprehensive, founded 1865, part of State College System of West Virginia
- **Calendar** semesters
- **Degrees** certificates, associate, bachelor's, and master's
- **Small-town** 80-acre campus
- **Endowment** $6.4 million
- **Coed,** 6,813 undergraduate students, 70% full-time, 56% women, 44% men
- **Minimally difficult** entrance level, 97% of applicants were admitted

Undergraduates 4,741 full-time, 2,072 part-time. Students come from 22 states and territories, 23 other countries, 6% are from out of state, 4% African American, 0.4% Asian American or Pacific Islander, 0.6% Hispanic American, 0.4% Native American, 1% international, 4% transferred in, 6% live on campus. *Retention:* 63% of 2002 full-time freshmen returned.

Freshmen *Admission:* 2,057 applied, 1,986 admitted, 1,254 enrolled. *Average high school GPA:* 2.60. *Test scores:* ACT scores over 18: 60%; ACT scores over 24: 11%; ACT scores over 30: 1%.

Faculty *Total:* 517, 54% full-time, 24% with terminal degrees. *Student/faculty ratio:* 17:1.

Majors Accounting; administrative assistant and secretarial science; art teacher education; aviation/airway management; avionics maintenance technology; biology/biological sciences; business administration and management; business teacher education; chemistry; child development; civil engineering technology; clinical/medical laboratory technology; commercial and advertising art; community organization and advocacy; computer science; construction engineering technology; consumer merchandising/retailing management; criminal justice/police science; drafting and design technology; dramatic/theatre arts; economics; education; electrical, electronic and communications engineering technology; elementary education; engineering technology; English; family and consumer economics related; family and consumer sciences/home economics teacher education; family and consumer sciences/human sciences; fashion merchandising; finance; French; graphic and printing equipment operation/production; health information/medical records administration; health science; history; human services; industrial arts; industrial technology; information science/studies; institutional food workers; interior design; liberal arts and sciences/liberal studies; mathematics; mechanical engineering/mechanical technology; music teacher education; nursing (registered nurse training); occupational safety and health technology; physical education teaching and coaching; physical therapy; political science and government; psychology; real estate; science teacher education; secondary education; sign language interpretation and translation; sociology; special education; speech and rhetoric; veterinary technology.

Academic Programs *Special study options:* academic remediation for entering students, accelerated degree program, adult/continuing education programs, advanced placement credit, double majors, English as a second language, honors programs, internships, part-time degree program, services for LD students, summer session for credit. *ROTC:* Army (b).

Library Musick Library with 276,722 titles, 883 serial subscriptions, 2,066 audiovisual materials, an OPAC, a Web page.

Computers on Campus 1300 computers available on campus for general student use. A campuswide network can be accessed from off campus. Internet access, at least one staffed computer lab available.

Student Life *Housing options:* coed, men-only, women-only. *Activities and organizations:* drama/theater group, student-run newspaper, choral group, marching band, Alpha Phi Omega, Circle K, Society for Non-traditional Students, criminal justice club, Honors Association, national fraternities, national sororities. *Campus security:* 24-hour emergency response devices and patrols, student patrols, controlled dormitory access. *Student services:* health clinic, personal/psychological counseling, legal services.

Athletics Member NCAA. All Division II. *Intercollegiate sports:* baseball M, basketball M(s)/W(s), cross-country running M/W, football M(s), golf M(s)/W, softball W, swimming M(s)/W(s), tennis M(s)/W(s), volleyball W. *Intramural sports:* archery M/W, basketball M/W, bowling M/W, cross-country running M/W, football M, golf M/W, swimming M/W, table tennis M/W, tennis M/W, volleyball M/W, wrestling M.

Standardized Tests *Required:* SAT I or ACT (for admission).

Costs (2003–04) *Tuition:* state resident $3130 full-time; nonresident $7038 full-time. Full-time tuition and fees vary according to program. Part-time tuition and fees vary according to program. *Room and board:* $5080; room only: $2410. Room and board charges vary according to board plan. *Payment plan:* installment. *Waivers:* senior citizens and employees or children of employees.

Financial Aid Of all full-time matriculated undergraduates who enrolled in 2002, 2,999 applied for aid, 2,579 were judged to have need, 280 had their need fully met. 384 Federal Work-Study jobs (averaging $952). 400 state and other part-time jobs (averaging $1167). In 2002, 512 non-need-based awards were made. *Average percent of need met:* 66%. *Average financial aid package:* $4972. *Average need-based loan:* $2507. *Average need-based gift aid:* $3552. *Average non-need-based aid:* $3331. *Average indebtedness upon graduation:* $16,292.

Applying *Options:* common application, electronic application, early admission. *Required:* high school transcript. *Recommended:* minimum 2.0 GPA. *Application deadlines:* 6/15 (freshmen), 6/15 (transfers).

Fairmont State College (continued)

Admissions Contact Mr. Douglas Dobbins, Executive Director of Enrollment Services, Fairmont State College, 1201 Locust Avenue, Fairmont, WV 26554. *Phone:* 304-367-4000. *Toll-free phone:* 800-641-5678. *Fax:* 304-367-4789. *E-mail:* fscinfo@mail.fscwv.edu.

■ See page 1608 for a narrative description.

GLENVILLE STATE COLLEGE
Glenville, West Virginia

- **State-supported** 4-year, founded 1872, part of West Virginia Higher Education Policy Commission
- **Calendar** semesters
- **Degrees** associate and bachelor's
- **Rural** 331-acre campus
- **Endowment** $4.3 million
- **Coed,** 1,377 undergraduate students, 88% full-time, 54% women, 46% men
- **Noncompetitive** entrance level, 100% of applicants were admitted

Undergraduates 1,208 full-time, 169 part-time. Students come from 19 states and territories, 9% are from out of state, 6% African American, 1% Asian American or Pacific Islander, 0.7% Hispanic American, 0.1% Native American, 9% transferred in, 30% live on campus.

Freshmen *Admission:* 777 applied, 777 admitted, 313 enrolled. *Average high school GPA:* 2.97. *Test scores:* SAT verbal scores over 500: 30%; SAT math scores over 500: 29%; ACT scores over 18: 66%; SAT verbal scores over 600: 9%; SAT math scores over 600: 6%; ACT scores over 24: 13%; SAT verbal scores over 700: 2%; SAT math scores over 700: 1%.

Faculty *Total:* 96, 52% full-time, 24% with terminal degrees. *Student/faculty ratio:* 19:1.

Majors Accounting; behavioral sciences; biology/biological sciences; biology teacher education; business administration and management; business/commerce; business teacher education; chemistry; chemistry teacher education; computer science; criminal justice/law enforcement administration; education; elementary education; English; English/language arts teacher education; forestry technology; history; information science/studies; kindergarten/preschool education; liberal arts and sciences/liberal studies; marketing/marketing management; mathematics teacher education; multi-/interdisciplinary studies related; music teacher education; nursing (registered nurse training); physical education teaching and coaching; science teacher education; secondary education; social studies teacher education; special education; survey technology.

Academic Programs *Special study options:* academic remediation for entering students, accelerated degree program, adult/continuing education programs, advanced placement credit, cooperative education, distance learning, double majors, English as a second language, honors programs, internships, part-time degree program, services for LD students, student-designed majors, summer session for credit. *ROTC:* Army (b).

Library Robert F. Kidd Library with an OPAC, a Web page.

Computers on Campus 232 computers available on campus for general student use. A campuswide network can be accessed from student residence rooms and from off campus. Internet access, at least one staffed computer lab available.

Student Life *Housing:* on-campus residence required through sophomore year. *Options:* coed, men-only, women-only, disabled students. Campus housing is university owned. Freshman campus housing is guaranteed. *Activities and organizations:* drama/theater group, choral group, marching band, Student Government Association, Percussion Ensemble, Band, Choir, Fellowship of Christian Athletes, national fraternities. *Campus security:* 24-hour emergency response devices, student patrols, late-night transport/escort service, controlled dormitory access. *Student services:* health clinic, personal/psychological counseling.

Athletics Member NCAA, CIS. All NCAA Division II. *Intercollegiate sports:* basketball M(s)/W(s), cheerleading M/W, cross-country running M(s)/W(s), football M(s), golf M(s)/W(s), softball W(s), track and field M(s)/W(s), volleyball W(s). *Intramural sports:* basketball M/W, softball M/W, swimming M/W, tennis M/W, volleyball M/W.

Standardized Tests *Required:* SAT I or ACT (for admission).

Costs (2003–04) *Tuition:* state resident $2952 full-time, $123 per credit hour part-time; nonresident $7306 full-time, $305 per credit hour part-time. *Room and board:* $4860; room only: $2400. Room and board charges vary according to housing facility. *Payment plan:* installment. *Waivers:* senior citizens.

Financial Aid Of all full-time matriculated undergraduates who enrolled in 2003, 1,051 applied for aid, 936 were judged to have need, 257 had their need fully met. 130 Federal Work-Study jobs (averaging $1100). 250 state and other part-time jobs (averaging $936). In 2003, 99 non-need-based awards were made. *Average percent of need met:* 81%. *Average financial aid package:* $7554. *Average need-based loan:* $3493. *Average need-based gift aid:* $4026. *Average non-need-based aid:* $2845. *Average indebtedness upon graduation:* $1958.

Applying *Options:* common application, electronic application, deferred entrance. *Application fee:* $10. *Required:* high school transcript, minimum 2.0 GPA, completion of college-preparatory program. *Application deadline:* rolling (freshmen), rolling (transfers). *Notification:* continuous (freshmen), continuous (transfers).

Admissions Contact Ms. Brenda McCartney, Associate Registrar, Glenville State College, 200 High Street, Glenville, WV 26351-1200. *Phone:* 304-462-7361 Ext. 7123. *Toll-free phone:* 800-924-2010. *Fax:* 304-462-8619. *E-mail:* visitor@glenville.edu.

MARSHALL UNIVERSITY
Huntington, West Virginia

- **State-supported** university, founded 1837, part of University System of West Virginia
- **Calendar** semesters
- **Degrees** certificates, associate, bachelor's, master's, doctoral, first professional, and post-master's certificates
- **Urban** 70-acre campus
- **Endowment** $47.4 million
- **Coed,** 9,958 undergraduate students, 85% full-time, 56% women, 44% men
- **Minimally difficult** entrance level, 88% of applicants were admitted

Undergraduates 8,434 full-time, 1,524 part-time. Students come from 44 states and territories, 37 other countries, 17% are from out of state, 5% African American, 0.9% Asian American or Pacific Islander, 0.8% Hispanic American, 0.3% Native American, 1% international, 5% transferred in, 20% live on campus. *Retention:* 75% of 2002 full-time freshmen returned.

Freshmen *Admission:* 2,578 applied, 2,274 admitted, 1,938 enrolled. *Average high school GPA:* 3.32. *Test scores:* SAT verbal scores over 500: 49%; SAT math scores over 500: 50%; ACT scores over 18: 92%; SAT verbal scores over 600: 15%; SAT math scores over 600: 18%; ACT scores over 24: 32%; SAT verbal scores over 700: 3%; SAT math scores over 700: 1%; ACT scores over 30: 4%.

Faculty *Total:* 721, 63% full-time, 54% with terminal degrees. *Student/faculty ratio:* 20:1.

Majors Accounting; adult and continuing education administration; art; biology/biological sciences; business administration and management; business/managerial economics; chemistry; clinical laboratory science/medical technology; clinical/medical laboratory technology; communication disorders; computer and information sciences; computer engineering technology; counselor education/school counseling and guidance; criminal justice/safety; cytotechnology; dietetics; economics; elementary education; English; environmental science; family and consumer sciences/human sciences; finance; foreign languages and literatures; general studies; geography; geology/earth science; history; humanities; international relations and affairs; journalism; marketing/marketing management; mathematics; multi-/interdisciplinary studies related; nursing (registered nurse training); occupational safety and health technology; parks, recreation and leisure facilities management; physical education teaching and coaching; physics; political science and government; psychology; secondary education; social work; sociology; speech and rhetoric; speech-language pathology; systems science and theory.

Academic Programs *Special study options:* academic remediation for entering students, accelerated degree program, adult/continuing education programs, advanced placement credit, cooperative education, distance learning, double majors, English as a second language, honors programs, independent study, internships, off-campus study, part-time degree program, services for LD students, study abroad, summer session for credit. *ROTC:* Army (b). *Unusual degree programs:* 3-2 forestry with Duke University.

Library John Deaver Drinko Library plus 2 others with 42,394 titles, 2,189 serial subscriptions, 24,412 audiovisual materials, an OPAC, a Web page.

Computers on Campus 1090 computers available on campus for general student use. A campuswide network can be accessed from student residence rooms and from off campus. Internet access, online (class) registration, at least one staffed computer lab available.

Student Life *Housing:* on-campus residence required through sophomore year. *Options:* coed, men-only, women-only, disabled students. Campus housing is university owned. Freshman campus housing is guaranteed. *Activities and organizations:* drama/theater group, student-run newspaper, radio and television station, choral group, marching band, Campus Crusade for Christ, Gamma Beta Phi, The International Students' Organization, Newman Association, Phi Alpha Theta, national fraternities, national sororities. *Campus security:* 24-hour emergency response devices and patrols, student patrols, late-night transport/escort service, controlled dormitory access. *Student services:* health clinic, personal/psychological counseling, women's center, legal services.

Athletics Member NCAA. All Division I except football (Division I-A). *Intercollegiate sports:* baseball M(s), basketball M(s)/W(s), cheerleading M/W, golf M(s)/W(s), lacrosse M(c)/W(c), rugby M(c)/W(c), soccer M(s)/W(s), softball

W(s), swimming W(s), tennis W(s), track and field M(s)/W(s), volleyball W(s). *Intramural sports:* baseball M, basketball M/W, football M, golf M/W, soccer M/W, softball M/W, swimming M/W, track and field M/W, volleyball M/W, wrestling M/W.

Standardized Tests *Required:* SAT I or ACT (for admission).

Costs (2003–04) *Tuition:* state resident $2746 full-time, $115 per semester hour part-time; nonresident $8430 full-time, $351 per semester hour part-time. Full-time tuition and fees vary according to program and reciprocity agreements. Part-time tuition and fees vary according to program and reciprocity agreements. *Required fees:* $514 full-time, $22 per semester hour part-time. *Room and board:* $5856. Room and board charges vary according to board plan and housing facility. *Payment plans:* installment, deferred payment. *Waivers:* employees or children of employees.

Financial Aid Of all full-time matriculated undergraduates who enrolled in 2003, 6,524 applied for aid, 4,921 were judged to have need, 1,825 had their need fully met. 331 Federal Work-Study jobs (averaging $1661). 57 state and other part-time jobs (averaging $5835). In 2003, 1389 non-need-based awards were made. *Average percent of need met:* 63%. *Average financial aid package:* $6555. *Average need-based loan:* $4498. *Average need-based gift aid:* $3932. *Average non-need-based aid:* $4129. *Average indebtedness upon graduation:* $15,230.

Applying *Options:* common application, electronic application, early admission, deferred entrance. *Application fee:* $25. *Required:* high school transcript, minimum 2.0 GPA. *Application deadline:* rolling (freshmen), rolling (transfers). *Notification:* continuous (freshmen), continuous (transfers).

Admissions Contact Mr. Craig S. Grooms, Admissions Director, Marshall University, 1 John Marshall Drive, Huntington, WV 25755. *Phone:* 304-696-3160. *Toll-free phone:* 800-642-3499. *Fax:* 304-696-3135. *E-mail:* admissions@marshall.edu.

■ See page 1934 for a narrative description.

MOUNTAIN STATE UNIVERSITY
Beckley, West Virginia

- **Independent** comprehensive, founded 1933
- **Calendar** semesters
- **Degrees** certificates, associate, bachelor's, and master's
- **Small-town** 7-acre campus
- **Endowment** $7.4 million
- **Coed,** 3,644 undergraduate students, 76% full-time, 66% women, 34% men
- **Noncompetitive** entrance level, 96% of applicants were admitted

Undergraduates 2,758 full-time, 886 part-time. Students come from 43 states and territories, 42 other countries, 15% are from out of state, 7% African American, 0.6% Asian American or Pacific Islander, 1% Hispanic American, 1% Native American, 3% international, 19% transferred in, 5% live on campus. *Retention:* 55% of 2002 full-time freshmen returned.

Freshmen *Admission:* 1,448 applied, 1,394 admitted, 1,282 enrolled. *Average high school GPA:* 2.80. *Test scores:* SAT verbal scores over 500: 40%; SAT math scores over 500: 40%; ACT scores over 18: 54%; SAT verbal scores over 600: 10%; SAT math scores over 600: 20%; ACT scores over 24: 6%; ACT scores over 30: 1%.

Faculty *Total:* 236, 33% full-time, 13% with terminal degrees. *Student/faculty ratio:* 21:1.

Majors Accounting; administrative assistant and secretarial science; aviation/airway management; avionics maintenance technology; banking and financial support services; behavioral sciences; business administration and management; business administration, management and operations related; computer and information sciences and support services related; computer science; criminal justice/law enforcement administration; criminal justice/police science; criminal justice/safety; diagnostic medical sonography and ultrasound technology; education; elementary education; emergency medical technology (EMT paramedic); engineering; environmental studies; fire science; forensic science and technology; health/health care administration; health professions related; hospitality administration related; human resources management and services related; information science/studies; interdisciplinary studies; legal administrative assistant/secretary; legal assistant/paralegal; legal studies; liberal arts and sciences/liberal studies; medical/clinical assistant; multi-/interdisciplinary studies related; nursing (registered nurse training); occupational therapist assistant; physical therapist assistant; physician assistant; radio and television broadcasting technology; radiologic technology/science; respiratory care therapy; secondary education; social work; surgical technology; tourism and travel services management.

Academic Programs *Special study options:* academic remediation for entering students, accelerated degree program, adult/continuing education programs, advanced placement credit, cooperative education, distance learning, double majors, English as a second language, external degree program, independent study, internships, part-time degree program, student-designed majors, summer session for credit.

Library Mountain State University Library with 90,929 titles, 2,300 serial subscriptions, 5,269 audiovisual materials, an OPAC.

Computers on Campus 90 computers available on campus for general student use. A campuswide network can be accessed from off campus. Internet access, at least one staffed computer lab available.

Student Life *Housing:* on-campus residence required through sophomore year. *Options:* coed. Campus housing is provided by a third party. Freshman campus housing is guaranteed. *Activities and organizations:* drama/theater group, Student Christian Organization, astronomy club, creative writing group, Gay, Lesbian, and Bisexual Student Support Group, Student Government Association. *Campus security:* 24-hour emergency response devices, late-night transport/escort service, controlled dormitory access, night patrols by security.

Athletics Member NAIA. *Intercollegiate sports:* basketball M(s), softball W(s), volleyball W. *Intramural sports:* basketball M/W, racquetball M/W, soccer M, swimming M/W, table tennis M, tennis M/W, volleyball M/W.

Standardized Tests *Required for some:* SAT I or ACT (for admission).

Costs (2003–04) *Comprehensive fee:* $11,472 includes full-time tuition ($4950), mandatory fees ($1350), and room and board ($5172). Full-time tuition and fees vary according to program. Part-time tuition and fees vary according to program. *College room only:* $2672. Room and board charges vary according to board plan. *Payment plan:* installment. *Waivers:* senior citizens and employees or children of employees.

Financial Aid Of all full-time matriculated undergraduates who enrolled in 2002, 3,000 applied for aid, 2,358 were judged to have need, 14 had their need fully met. 198 Federal Work-Study jobs (averaging $4000). In 2002, 107 non-need-based awards were made. *Average percent of need met:* 68%. *Average financial aid package:* $5565. *Average need-based loan:* $3556. *Average need-based gift aid:* $3600. *Average non-need-based aid:* $2325. *Average indebtedness upon graduation:* $9500.

Applying *Options:* common application, electronic application, early admission, deferred entrance. *Application fee:* $25. *Required:* high school transcript. *Application deadline:* rolling (freshmen), rolling (transfers).

Admissions Contact Ms. Darlene Brown, Administrative Assistant for Enrollment Management, Mountain State University, PO Box 9003, Beckley, WV 25802-9003. *Phone:* 304-253-7351 Ext. 1433. *Toll-free phone:* 800-766-6067 Ext. 1433. *Fax:* 304-253-5072. *E-mail:* gomsu@mountainstate.edu.

■ See page 2034 for a narrative description.

OHIO VALLEY COLLEGE
Vienna, West Virginia

- **Independent** 4-year, founded 1960, affiliated with Church of Christ
- **Calendar** semesters
- **Degrees** associate and bachelor's
- **Small-town** 299-acre campus
- **Endowment** $931,240
- **Coed,** 515 undergraduate students, 96% full-time, 50% women, 50% men
- **Minimally difficult** entrance level, 47% of applicants were admitted

Undergraduates 495 full-time, 20 part-time. Students come from 26 states and territories, 12 other countries, 53% are from out of state, 5% African American, 0.6% Asian American or Pacific Islander, 0.6% Hispanic American, 0.6% Native American, 6% international, 9% transferred in, 60% live on campus. *Retention:* 72% of 2002 full-time freshmen returned.

Freshmen *Admission:* 445 applied, 210 admitted, 103 enrolled. *Average high school GPA:* 2.96. *Test scores:* SAT verbal scores over 500: 55%; SAT math scores over 500: 42%; ACT scores over 18: 72%; SAT verbal scores over 600: 7%; SAT math scores over 600: 12%; ACT scores over 24: 20%; SAT math scores over 700: 5%; ACT scores over 30: 1%.

Faculty *Total:* 59, 44% full-time, 24% with terminal degrees. *Student/faculty ratio:* 15:1.

Majors Accounting; biblical studies; business administration and management; education; education (multiple levels); elementary education; English/language arts teacher education; human resources management; liberal arts and sciences/liberal studies; marketing/marketing management; mathematics teacher education; physical education teaching and coaching; professional studies; psychology; religious studies; science teacher education; science technologies related; secondary education; social studies teacher education.

Academic Programs *Special study options:* academic remediation for entering students, adult/continuing education programs, advanced placement credit, double majors, English as a second language, external degree program, honors programs, internships, part-time degree program, study abroad, summer session for credit. *ROTC:* Air Force (c).

Library Icy Belle Library with 34,000 titles, 455 serial subscriptions, 6,303 audiovisual materials, an OPAC.

Ohio Valley College (continued)

Computers on Campus 34 computers available on campus for general student use. A campuswide network can be accessed from student residence rooms that provide access to e-mail. Internet access, at least one staffed computer lab available.

Student Life *Housing:* on-campus residence required through sophomore year. *Options:* men-only, women-only. Campus housing is university owned. Freshman campus housing is guaranteed. *Activities and organizations:* drama/theater group, student-run newspaper, choral group, Mission Club, Women for Christ, SIFE, Ambassadors, Black Student Union. *Campus security:* 24-hour emergency response devices, late-night transport/escort service. *Student services:* health clinic, personal/psychological counseling.

Athletics Member NCAA. All Division II. *Intercollegiate sports:* baseball M(s), basketball M(s)/W(s), cheerleading W(s), cross-country running M(s)/W(s), golf M(s), soccer M(s)/W(s), softball W(s), volleyball W(s). *Intramural sports:* basketball M/W, bowling M/W, football M/W, golf M/W, soccer M/W, softball M/W, table tennis M/W, volleyball M/W.

Standardized Tests *Required:* SAT I or ACT (for admission).

Costs (2004–05) *Comprehensive fee:* $17,392 includes full-time tuition ($10,740), mandatory fees ($1272), and room and board ($5380). Full-time tuition and fees vary according to course load. Part-time tuition: $392 per credit hour. Part-time tuition and fees vary according to course load. *Required fees:* $55 per credit hour part-time. *College room only:* $2930. Room and board charges vary according to board plan. *Payment plan:* installment. *Waivers:* senior citizens and employees or children of employees.

Financial Aid Of all full-time matriculated undergraduates who enrolled in 2002, 398 applied for aid, 358 were judged to have need, 110 had their need fully met. 181 Federal Work-Study jobs (averaging $800). 102 state and other part-time jobs (averaging $800). In 2002, 74 non-need-based awards were made. *Average percent of need met:* 89%. *Average financial aid package:* $9223. *Average need-based loan:* $3644. *Average need-based gift aid:* $3616. *Average non-need-based aid:* $2895. *Average indebtedness upon graduation:* $16,717.

Applying *Options:* common application, electronic application, early admission, early action, deferred entrance. *Application fee:* $20. *Required:* high school transcript. *Required for some:* essay or personal statement, interview. *Recommended:* letters of recommendation. *Application deadline:* 8/15 (freshmen), rolling (transfers). *Notification:* continuous (freshmen), 10/1 (early action), continuous (transfers).

Admissions Contact Ms. Sharon Woomer, Admissions Office Manager, Ohio Valley College, 1 Campus View Drive, Vienna, WV 26105. *Phone:* 304-865-6200. *Toll-free phone:* 877-446-8668 Ext. 6200. *Fax:* 304-865-6001. *E-mail:* admissions@ovc.edu.

SALEM INTERNATIONAL UNIVERSITY

Salem, West Virginia

- **Independent** comprehensive, founded 1888
- **Calendar** modular
- **Degrees** associate, bachelor's, and master's
- **Rural** 300-acre campus
- **Coed**
- **Minimally difficult** entrance level

Faculty *Student/faculty ratio:* 14:1.

Student Life *Campus security:* 24-hour emergency response devices and patrols, late-night transport/escort service, controlled dormitory access.

Athletics Member NCAA. All Division II.

Standardized Tests *Required:* SAT I or ACT (for admission).

Costs (2003–04) *Comprehensive fee:* $19,790 includes full-time tuition ($14,695), mandatory fees ($310), and room and board ($4785). *College room only:* $1845.

Financial Aid Of all full-time matriculated undergraduates who enrolled in 2003, 240 applied for aid, 218 were judged to have need, 122 had their need fully met. 187 Federal Work-Study jobs (averaging $2121). 9 state and other part-time jobs. In 2003, 50. *Average percent of need met:* 92. *Average financial aid package:* $15,950. *Average need-based loan:* $4582. *Average need-based gift aid:* $5289. *Average non-need-based aid:* $11,058. *Average indebtedness upon graduation:* $15,994.

Applying *Options:* electronic application, deferred entrance. *Application fee:* $25. *Required:* high school transcript, minimum 2.00 GPA. *Required for some:* interview. *Recommended:* essay or personal statement, interview.

Admissions Contact Director of Admissions, Salem International University, PO Box 500, Salem, WV 26426-0500. *Phone:* 304-782-5336 Ext. 336. *Toll-free phone:* 800-283-4562. *E-mail:* admiss_new@salemiu.edu.

SHEPHERD UNIVERSITY

Shepherdstown, West Virginia

- **State-supported comprehensive, founded 1871, part of West Virginia Higher Education Policy Commission**
- **Calendar semesters**
- **Degrees associate, bachelor's, and master's**
- **Small-town 320-acre campus with easy access to Washington, DC**
- **Endowment $17.6 million**
- **Coed, 4,804 undergraduate students, 65% full-time, 60% women, 40% men**
- **Moderately difficult entrance level, 89% of applicants were admitted**

Shepherd University, a public liberal arts institution, has a long-standing reputation for providing high-quality education at a reasonable cost. Recently, the University was number 12 on *Money* magazine's list of the 25 public schools providing the best buys in education, marking the 5th time Shepherd has been named to one of *Money*'s best buys in education lists.

Undergraduates 3,132 full-time, 1,672 part-time. Students come from 31 states and territories, 28 other countries, 33% are from out of state, 5% African American, 1% Asian American or Pacific Islander, 2% Hispanic American, 0.7% Native American, 1% international, 8% transferred in, 25% live on campus. *Retention:* 69% of 2002 full-time freshmen returned.

Freshmen *Admission:* 1,061 applied, 948 admitted, 845 enrolled. *Average high school GPA:* 2.98. *Test scores:* SAT verbal scores over 500: 57%; SAT math scores over 500: 54%; ACT scores over 18: 78%; SAT verbal scores over 600: 13%; SAT math scores over 600: 9%; ACT scores over 24: 21%; ACT scores over 30: 1%.

Majors Accounting; art; biology/biological sciences; business administration and management; chemistry; communication/speech communication and rhetoric; computer and information sciences; criminal justice/safety; culinary arts related; design and visual communications; economics; electrical, electronic and communications engineering technology; electromechanical technology; elementary education; emergency medical technology (EMT paramedic); engineering technologies related; English; environmental studies; family and consumer sciences/human sciences; fashion merchandising; general studies; history; information science/studies; legal assistant/paralegal; mathematics; multi-/interdisciplinary studies related; music; nursing (registered nurse training); occupational safety and health technology; parks, recreation and leisure; political science and government; psychology; secondary education; social work; sociology.

Academic Programs *Special study options:* academic remediation for entering students, accelerated degree program, adult/continuing education programs, advanced placement credit, cooperative education, distance learning, double majors, English as a second language, honors programs, internships, part-time degree program, services for LD students, summer session for credit.

Library Ruth Scarborough Library with 183,197 titles, 918 serial subscriptions, 11,393 audiovisual materials, an OPAC, a Web page.

Computers on Campus 350 computers available on campus for general student use. A campuswide network can be accessed from student residence rooms and from off campus that provide access to personal web pages. Internet access, online (class) registration, at least one staffed computer lab available.

Student Life *Housing:* on-campus residence required through senior year. *Options:* coed. Campus housing is university owned. Freshman applicants given priority for college housing. *Activities and organizations:* drama/theater group, student-run newspaper, radio station, choral group, marching band, Student Government Association, Program Board, Student Community Services, United Brothers, Common Ground, national fraternities, national sororities. *Campus security:* 24-hour emergency response devices and patrols, late-night transport/escort service, controlled dormitory access. *Student services:* health clinic, personal/psychological counseling.

Athletics Member NCAA. All Division II. *Intercollegiate sports:* baseball M(s), basketball M(s)/W(s), cross-country running M/W, football M(s), golf M, soccer M(s)/W(s), softball W(s), tennis M/W, volleyball W(s). *Intramural sports:* basketball M/W, bowling M/W, football M/W, racquetball M/W, soccer M/W, softball M/W, swimming M/W, tennis M/W, ultimate Frisbee M/W, volleyball M/W, weight lifting M/W, wrestling M/W.

Standardized Tests *Required:* SAT I or ACT (for admission).

Costs (2003–04) *Tuition:* state resident $3270 full-time; nonresident $8030 full-time. Full-time tuition and fees vary according to degree level, location, program, and reciprocity agreements. Part-time tuition and fees vary according to degree level, location, and program. *Room and board:* $5338. Room and board charges vary according to board plan and housing facility. *Payment plan:* installment. *Waivers:* minority students and senior citizens.

Financial Aid Of all full-time matriculated undergraduates who enrolled in 2003, 2,468 applied for aid, 1,562 were judged to have need, 364 had their need fully met. 183 Federal Work-Study jobs (averaging $1500). 325 state and other part-time jobs (averaging $3000). In 2003, 394 non-need-based awards were made. *Average percent of need met:* 76%. *Average financial aid package:* $7442. *Average need-based loan:* $3424. *Average need-based gift aid:* $3411. *Average non-need-based aid:* $6119. *Average indebtedness upon graduation:* $13,981.

Applying *Options:* early admission, early action, deferred entrance. *Application fee:* $35. *Required:* high school transcript, minimum 2.5 GPA. *Recommended:* essay or personal statement, minimum 3.0 GPA, 3 letters of recommendation, interview. *Application deadlines:* 2/1 (freshmen), 3/15 (transfers). *Notification:* continuous until 6/15 (freshmen), 12/15 (early action), continuous until 6/15 (transfers).

Admissions Contact Mr. Karl L. Wolf, Director of Admissions, Shepherd University, PO Box 3210, Shepherdstown, WV 25443-3210. *Phone:* 304-876-5212. *Toll-free phone:* 800-344-5231. *Fax:* 304-876-5165. *E-mail:* admoff@shepherd.edu.

■ *See page 2378 for a narrative description.*

UNIVERSITY OF CHARLESTON
Charleston, West Virginia

- **Independent** comprehensive, founded 1888
- **Calendar** semesters
- **Degrees** associate, bachelor's, and master's
- **Urban** 40-acre campus
- **Endowment** $24.3 million
- **Coed,** 981 undergraduate students, 85% full-time, 63% women, 37% men
- **Moderately difficult** entrance level, 63% of applicants were admitted

Undergraduates 837 full-time, 144 part-time. Students come from 40 states and territories, 24 other countries, 30% are from out of state, 7% African American, 0.1% Asian American or Pacific Islander, 1% Hispanic American, 0.3% Native American, 4% international, 17% transferred in, 29% live on campus. *Retention:* 67% of 2002 full-time freshmen returned.

Freshmen *Admission:* 1,160 applied, 725 admitted, 205 enrolled. *Average high school GPA:* 3.33. *Test scores:* SAT verbal scores over 500: 43%; SAT math scores over 500: 54%; ACT scores over 18: 94%; SAT verbal scores over 600: 10%; SAT math scores over 600: 7%; ACT scores over 24: 23%.

Faculty *Total:* 99, 62% full-time. *Student/faculty ratio:* 13:1.

Majors Accounting; art; athletic training; biology/biological sciences; biology teacher education; business administration and management; business administration, management and operations related; chemistry; computer and information sciences; creative writing; education; elementary education; English; environmental biology; environmental science; finance; financial planning and services; general studies; health teacher education; history; information science/studies; interior design; marketing/marketing management; mass communication/media; music; music management and merchandising; music teacher education; nursing (registered nurse training); political science and government; psychology; radiologic technology/science; science teacher education; social studies teacher education; voice and opera.

Academic Programs *Special study options:* academic remediation for entering students, accelerated degree program, adult/continuing education programs, advanced placement credit, distance learning, double majors, independent study, internships, part-time degree program, student-designed majors, study abroad, summer session for credit. *ROTC:* Army (b).

Library Schoenbaum Library with 111,264 titles, 2,011 serial subscriptions, 2,505 audiovisual materials, an OPAC, a Web page.

Computers on Campus 200 computers available on campus for general student use. A campuswide network can be accessed from student residence rooms and from off campus that provide access to campus cruiser. Internet access, at least one staffed computer lab available.

Student Life *Housing:* on-campus residence required through sophomore year. *Options:* coed. Campus housing is university owned. Freshman campus housing is guaranteed. *Activities and organizations:* drama/theater group, student-run newspaper, choral group, Student Activities Board, American Society of Interior Designers, Student Government Association, Capitol Association of Nursing Students, International Student Organization, national fraternities. *Campus security:* 24-hour emergency response devices and patrols, student patrols, late-night transport/escort service, controlled dormitory access, radio connection to city police and ambulance. *Student services:* personal/psychological counseling.

Athletics Member NCAA. All Division II. *Intercollegiate sports:* baseball M(s), basketball M(s)/W(s), cheerleading W(s), crew M(s)/W(s), cross-country running M(s)/W(s), football M(s), golf M(s), soccer M(s)/W(s), softball W(s), swimming M(s)/W(s), tennis M(s)/W(s), track and field M(s)/W(s), volleyball W(s). *Intramural sports:* basketball M/W, bowling M/W, football M/W, tennis M/W, volleyball M/W, water polo M/W.

Standardized Tests *Required:* SAT I or ACT (for admission).

Costs (2004–05) *Comprehensive fee:* $26,600 includes full-time tuition ($19,400) and room and board ($7200). Part-time tuition and fees vary according to course load and program. No tuition increase for student's term of enrollment. *Room and board:* Room and board charges vary according to board plan and housing facility. *Payment plan:* installment. *Waivers:* senior citizens and employees or children of employees.

Financial Aid Of all full-time matriculated undergraduates who enrolled in 2003, 682 applied for aid, 577 were judged to have need, 518 had their need fully met. In 2003, 160 non-need-based awards were made. *Average percent of need met:* 84%. *Average financial aid package:* $15,245. *Average need-based loan:* $4832. *Average need-based gift aid:* $4875. *Average non-need-based aid:* $4715. *Average indebtedness upon graduation:* $19,250.

Applying *Options:* electronic application, early admission, deferred entrance. *Application fee:* $25. *Required:* high school transcript, minimum 2.25 GPA, minimum scores ACT 19; SAT 900. *Required for some:* interview. *Recommended:* essay or personal statement, letters of recommendation. *Application deadline:* rolling (freshmen), rolling (out-of-state freshmen), rolling (transfers). *Notification:* continuous (freshmen), continuous (out-of-state freshmen), continuous (transfers).

Admissions Contact University of Charleston, 2300 MacCorkle Avenue, SE, Charleston, WV 25304. *Phone:* 304-357-4750. *Toll-free phone:* 800-995-GOUC. *Fax:* 304-357-4781. *E-mail:* admissions@ucwv.edu.

■ *See page 2582 for a narrative description.*

WEST LIBERTY STATE COLLEGE
West Liberty, West Virginia

- **State-supported** 4-year, founded 1837, part of West Virginia Higher Education Policy Commission
- **Calendar** semesters
- **Degrees** associate and bachelor's
- **Rural** 290-acre campus with easy access to Pittsburgh
- **Endowment** $5.0 million
- **Coed,** 2,491 undergraduate students, 87% full-time, 55% women, 45% men
- **Minimally difficult** entrance level, 86% of applicants were admitted

Undergraduates 2,162 full-time, 329 part-time. Students come from 24 states and territories, 9 other countries, 27% are from out of state, 3% African American, 0.2% Asian American or Pacific Islander, 1% Hispanic American, 0.2% Native American, 0.5% international, 10% transferred in, 45% live on campus. *Retention:* 72% of 2002 full-time freshmen returned.

Freshmen *Admission:* 1,309 applied, 1,120 admitted, 463 enrolled. *Average high school GPA:* 3.01. *Test scores:* SAT verbal scores over 500: 22%; SAT math scores over 500: 18%; ACT scores over 18: 64%; SAT verbal scores over 600: 10%; SAT math scores over 600: 4%; ACT scores over 24: 11%.

Faculty *Total:* 158, 68% full-time, 34% with terminal degrees. *Student/faculty ratio:* 23:1.

Majors Accounting; art teacher education; banking and financial support services; biology/biological sciences; business administration and management; business/managerial economics; chemistry; clinical laboratory science/medical technology; commercial and advertising art; criminal justice/law enforcement administration; dental hygiene; education; elementary education; English; health science; health teacher education; history; information science/studies; interdisciplinary studies; kindergarten/preschool education; kinesiology and exercise science; marketing/marketing management; mass communication/media; mathematics; music teacher education; nursing (registered nurse training); physical education teaching and coaching; political science and government; pre-dentistry studies; pre-law studies; pre-medical studies; psychology; secondary education; social sciences; sociology.

Academic Programs *Special study options:* academic remediation for entering students, accelerated degree program, adult/continuing education programs, advanced placement credit, double majors, external degree program, honors programs, independent study, internships, off-campus study, part-time degree program, student-designed majors, summer session for credit.

Library Paul N. Elbin Library plus 1 other with 194,715 titles, 485 serial subscriptions, an OPAC, a Web page.

Computers on Campus 300 computers available on campus for general student use. A campuswide network can be accessed from student residence rooms and from off campus. Internet access, at least one staffed computer lab available.

Student Life *Housing options:* coed, men-only, women-only, disabled students. Campus housing is university owned. *Activities and organizations:* drama/theater group, student-run newspaper, radio and television station, choral group, marching band, Delta Sigma Pi, Student Senate, drama club, Students in Free Enterprise, Chi Omega Sorority, national fraternities, national sororities. *Campus security:* 24-hour emergency response devices and patrols, late-night transport/escort service. *Student services:* health clinic, personal/psychological counseling.

Athletics Member NCAA. All Division II. *Intercollegiate sports:* baseball M(s), basketball M(s)/W(s), cross-country running M(s)/W(s), football M(s), golf

West Liberty State College (continued)
M(s)/W(s), softball W(s), tennis M(s)/W(s), track and field M(s)/W(s), volleyball W(s), wrestling M(s). *Intramural sports:* basketball M/W, golf M/W, racquetball M/W, softball M/W, table tennis M/W, tennis M/W, volleyball M/W.

Standardized Tests *Required:* SAT I or ACT (for admission).

Costs (2003–04) *Tuition:* state resident $3138 full-time, $131 per semester hour part-time; nonresident $7790 full-time, $325 per semester hour part-time. *Room and board:* $4730; room only: $2750. Room and board charges vary according to board plan and housing facility. *Payment plans:* installment, deferred payment. *Waivers:* senior citizens and employees or children of employees.

Financial Aid Of all full-time matriculated undergraduates who enrolled in 2003, 1,747 applied for aid, 1,295 were judged to have need, 460 had their need fully met. In 2003, 237 non-need-based awards were made. *Average percent of need met:* 77%. *Average financial aid package:* $5025. *Average need-based loan:* $3940. *Average need-based gift aid:* $3649. *Average non-need-based aid:* $2464. *Average indebtedness upon graduation:* $13,800.

Applying *Options:* electronic application. *Required:* high school transcript, minimum 2.0 GPA. *Recommended:* interview. *Notification:* continuous (freshmen), continuous (transfers).

Admissions Contact Ms. Stephanie North, Admissions Counselor, West Liberty State College, PO Box 295, West Liberty, WV 26074. *Phone:* 304-336-8078. *Toll-free phone:* 800-732-6204 Ext. 8076. *Fax:* 304-336-8403. *E-mail:* wladmsn1@whsc.edu.

West Virginia State College
Institute, West Virginia

- **State-supported** comprehensive, founded 1891, part of State College System of West Virginia
- **Calendar** semesters
- **Degrees** certificates, diplomas, associate, bachelor's, and master's
- **Suburban** 90-acre campus
- **Coed,** 4,992 undergraduate students, 64% full-time, 60% women, 40% men
- **Minimally difficult** entrance level

Undergraduates 3,211 full-time, 1,781 part-time. Students come from 34 states and territories, 3% are from out of state, 15% African American, 1% Asian American or Pacific Islander, 0.5% Hispanic American, 0.4% Native American, 6% transferred in, 7% live on campus.

Freshmen *Admission:* 732 enrolled. *Average high school GPA:* 2.84.

Faculty *Total:* 282, 53% full-time, 33% with terminal degrees. *Student/faculty ratio:* 23:1.

Majors Accounting; administrative assistant and secretarial science; advertising; applied mathematics; architectural engineering technology; art; art teacher education; biology/biological sciences; biotechnology; business administration and management; business teacher education; chemical engineering; chemistry; communication/speech communication and rhetoric; computer programming; computer science; criminal justice/law enforcement administration; drafting and design technology; economics; education; electrical, electronic and communications engineering technology; elementary education; English; fashion merchandising; finance; gerontology; health teacher education; history; hotel/motel administration; kindergarten/preschool education; liberal arts and sciences/liberal studies; marketing/marketing management; mathematics; medical/clinical assistant; music teacher education; nuclear medical technology; parks, recreation and leisure; physical education teaching and coaching; political science and government; pre-dentistry studies; pre-engineering; pre-medical studies; pre-veterinary studies; psychology; science teacher education; secondary education; social work; sociology; therapeutic recreation.

Academic Programs *Special study options:* academic remediation for entering students, accelerated degree program, adult/continuing education programs, advanced placement credit, cooperative education, external degree program, internships, part-time degree program, services for LD students, summer session for credit. *ROTC:* Army (b).

Library Drain-Jordan Library with 194,706 titles, 1,678 serial subscriptions, 3,290 audiovisual materials, an OPAC.

Computers on Campus A campuswide network can be accessed from student residence rooms and from off campus. At least one staffed computer lab available.

Student Life *Housing:* on-campus residence required for freshman year. *Options:* men-only, women-only. *Activities and organizations:* student-run newspaper, choral group, marching band, national fraternities, national sororities. *Campus security:* 24-hour emergency response devices and patrols, late-night transport/escort service. *Student services:* health clinic, personal/psychological counseling.

Athletics Member NCAA. All Division II. *Intercollegiate sports:* baseball M, basketball M(s)/W(s), cross-country running M/W, football M(s), golf M(s), softball W(s), tennis M/W, track and field M/W, volleyball W. *Intramural sports:* basketball M/W, bowling M/W, football M, golf M.

Standardized Tests *Required:* SAT I or ACT (for placement).

Costs (2003–04) *Tuition:* state resident $2754 full-time, $115 per credit hour part-time; nonresident $6334 full-time, $265 per credit hour part-time. Full-time tuition and fees vary according to program. Part-time tuition and fees vary according to course load and program. *Required fees:* $60 full-time. *Room and board:* $4400; room only: $2100. *Payment plans:* tuition prepayment, installment.

Financial Aid *Financial aid deadline:* 6/15.

Applying *Options:* common application, early admission. *Required:* high school transcript. *Application deadlines:* 8/11 (freshmen), 8/11 (transfers). *Notification:* continuous (freshmen), continuous (transfers).

Admissions Contact Mr. Jason Meeks, Associate Director of Admissions, West Virginia State College, Campus Box 197, PO Box 1000, Ferrell Hall, Room 106, Institute, WV 25112-1000. *Phone:* 304-766-3032. *Toll-free phone:* 800-987-2112. *Fax:* 304-766-4158. *E-mail:* meeksjd@wvsc.edu.

West Virginia University
Morgantown, West Virginia

- **State-supported** university, founded 1867, part of West Virginia Higher Education System
- **Calendar** semesters
- **Degrees** bachelor's, master's, doctoral, and first professional
- **Small-town** 913-acre campus with easy access to Pittsburgh
- **Endowment** $305.0 million
- **Coed,** 17,517 undergraduate students, 94% full-time, 47% women, 53% men
- **Moderately difficult** entrance level, 92% of applicants were admitted

Undergraduates 16,543 full-time, 974 part-time. Students come from 53 states and territories, 59 other countries, 39% are from out of state, 4% African American, 2% Asian American or Pacific Islander, 1% Hispanic American, 0.4% Native American, 2% international, 7% transferred in, 28% live on campus. *Retention:* 78% of 2002 full-time freshmen returned.

Freshmen *Admission:* 10,049 applied, 9,281 admitted, 4,415 enrolled. *Average high school GPA:* 3.22. *Test scores:* SAT verbal scores over 500: 63%; SAT math scores over 500: 68%; ACT scores over 18: 95%; SAT verbal scores over 600: 15%; SAT math scores over 600: 21%; ACT scores over 24: 40%; SAT verbal scores over 700: 1%; SAT math scores over 700: 2%; ACT scores over 30: 5%.

Faculty *Total:* 1,061, 73% full-time, 66% with terminal degrees. *Student/faculty ratio:* 21:1.

Majors Accounting; advertising; aerospace, aeronautical and astronautical engineering; agricultural economics; agricultural teacher education; animal sciences; anthropology; art; audiology and speech-language pathology; biology/biological sciences; business administration and management; business/managerial economics; chemical engineering; chemistry; civil engineering; clinical laboratory science/medical technology; communication and journalism related; computer and information sciences related; computer engineering; computer science; criminalistics and criminal science; dental hygiene; dramatic/theatre arts; economics; electrical, electronics and communications engineering; elementary education; English; environmental studies; exercise physiology; family and consumer sciences/human sciences; finance; fish/game management; foreign languages and literatures; forensic science and technology; forest/forest resources management; forestry; general studies; geography; geology/earth science; health and physical education; history; industrial engineering; interdisciplinary studies; international relations and affairs; journalism; kinesiology and exercise science; landscape architecture; liberal arts and sciences/liberal studies; marketing/marketing management; mass communication/media; mathematics; mechanical engineering; mining and mineral engineering; music; natural resources management and policy; nursing (registered nurse training); occupational therapy; parks, recreation and leisure; parks, recreation and leisure facilities management; petroleum engineering; pharmacy; philosophy; physical education teaching and coaching; physical therapy; physics; plant sciences related; political science and government; psychology; secondary education; social work; sociology; sport and fitness administration; visual and performing arts; visual and performing arts related; wildlife and wildlands science and management; wood science and wood products/pulp and paper technology.

Academic Programs *Special study options:* academic remediation for entering students, accelerated degree program, adult/continuing education programs, advanced placement credit, distance learning, double majors, English as a second language, external degree program, honors programs, independent study, internships, off-campus study, part-time degree program, services for LD students, student-designed majors, study abroad, summer session for credit. *ROTC:* Army (b), Air Force (b). *Unusual degree programs:* 3-2 education, business foreign language, occupational therapy, physical therapy, social work.

Library Wise Library plus 9 others with 1.7 million titles, 11,114 serial subscriptions, 45,126 audiovisual materials, an OPAC, a Web page.

Computers on Campus 1600 computers available on campus for general student use. A campuswide network can be accessed from student residence rooms

and from off campus. Internet access, online (class) registration, at least one staffed computer lab available. Computer purchase or lease plan available.

Student Life *Housing:* on-campus residence required for freshman year. *Options:* coed, men-only, women-only, disabled students. Campus housing is university owned and leased by the school. Freshman campus housing is guaranteed. *Activities and organizations:* drama/theater group, student-run newspaper, radio station, choral group, marching band, Residential Hall Association, Gamma Beta Phi, Alpha Beta Phi, national fraternities, national sororities. *Campus security:* 24-hour emergency response devices and patrols, student patrols, late-night transport/escort service. *Student services:* health clinic, personal/psychological counseling, women's center, legal services.

Athletics Member NCAA. All Division I except football (Division I-A). *Intercollegiate sports:* baseball M(s), basketball M(s)/W(s), cheerleading M(s)/W(s), crew W(s), cross-country running W(s), gymnastics W(s), soccer M(s)/W(s), swimming M(s)/W(s), tennis W(s), track and field W(s), volleyball W(s), wrestling M(s). *Intramural sports:* archery M(c)/W(c), badminton M(c)/W(c), basketball M/W, bowling M/W, crew M(c)/W(c), equestrian sports M(c)/W(c), fencing M(c)/W(c), football M, golf M/W, ice hockey M(c), lacrosse M(c), racquetball M/W, riflery M/W, rugby M(c)/W(c), skiing (cross-country) M(c)/W(c), skiing (downhill) M(c)/W(c), soccer M/W, softball M/W, swimming M/W, tennis M/W, track and field M/W, ultimate Frisbee M(c)/W(c), volleyball M/W, wrestling M.

Standardized Tests *Required:* SAT I or ACT (for admission).

Costs (2003–04) *Tuition:* state resident $3548 full-time, $150 per credit hour part-time; nonresident $10,768 full-time, $451 per credit hour part-time. Full-time tuition and fees vary according to location, program, and reciprocity agreements. Part-time tuition and fees vary according to course load, location, program, and reciprocity agreements. *Room and board:* $5822; room only: $3074. Room and board charges vary according to board plan, housing facility, and location. *Payment plans:* installment, deferred payment. *Waivers:* senior citizens and employees or children of employees.

Financial Aid Of all full-time matriculated undergraduates who enrolled in 2003, 12,028 applied for aid, 8,520 were judged to have need, 2,080 had their need fully met. 1,575 Federal Work-Study jobs (averaging $1003). 1,161 state and other part-time jobs (averaging $941). In 2003, 5979 non-need-based awards were made. *Average percent of need met:* 88%. *Average financial aid package:* $8015. *Average need-based loan:* $4106. *Average need-based gift aid:* $3327. *Average non-need-based aid:* $3324. *Average indebtedness upon graduation:* $20,145. *Financial aid deadline:* 3/1.

Applying *Options:* common application, electronic application, early admission, deferred entrance. *Application fee:* $25. *Required:* high school transcript, minimum 2.0 GPA. *Required for some:* essay or personal statement, minimum 2.25 GPA. *Application deadlines:* 8/1 (freshmen), 8/1 (transfers). *Notification:* continuous (transfers).

Admissions Contact Ms. Kim Guynn, Admissions Supervisor, West Virginia University, Box 6009, Morgantown, WV 26506-6009. *Phone:* 304-293-2124 Ext. 1560. *Toll-free phone:* 800-344-9881. *Fax:* 304-293-3080. *E-mail:* go2wvu@mail.wvu.edu.

WEST VIRGINIA UNIVERSITY AT PARKERSBURG

Parkersburg, West Virginia

- **State-supported** primarily 2-year, founded 1961
- **Calendar** semesters
- **Degrees** certificates, associate, and bachelor's
- **Small-town** 140-acre campus
- **Coed**
- **Noncompetitive** entrance level

Faculty *Student/faculty ratio:* 17:1.

Standardized Tests *Required:* ACT (for placement).

Costs (2003–04) *Tuition:* state resident $1620 full-time; nonresident $5604 full-time. Full-time tuition and fees vary according to degree level. Part-time tuition and fees vary according to degree level.

Applying *Options:* common application, electronic application, early admission, deferred entrance. *Required for some:* high school transcript.

Admissions Contact Ms. Violet Mosser, Senior Admissions Counselor, West Virginia University at Parkersburg, 300 Campus Drive, Parkersburg, WV 26101. *Phone:* 304-424-8223 Ext. 223. *Toll-free phone:* 800-WVA-WVUP. *Fax:* 304-424-8332.

WEST VIRGINIA UNIVERSITY INSTITUTE OF TECHNOLOGY

Montgomery, West Virginia

- **State-supported** comprehensive, founded 1895, part of University System of West Virginia
- **Calendar** semesters
- **Degrees** certificates, associate, bachelor's, and master's
- **Small-town** 200-acre campus with easy access to Charleston
- **Endowment** $5.2 million
- **Coed**
- **Noncompetitive** entrance level

Tech's home is in scenic, wild-and-wonderful West Virginia, with opportunities for snow skiing and white-water rafting nearby. Tech offers more than 35 majors, including engineering, engineering technologies, business, computer science, social sciences, nursing, dental hygiene, health service administration, and printing. In addition, Tech offers an optional 5-year program in cooperative education and a practicum experience in social science. The low student-faculty ratio (16:1) ensures a personalized education for Tech students.

Faculty *Student/faculty ratio:* 16:1.

Student Life *Campus security:* 24-hour emergency response devices and patrols, late-night transport/escort service.

Athletics Member NCAA. All Division II.

Standardized Tests *Required:* SAT I or ACT (for admission).

Costs (2003–04) *Tuition:* state resident $3488 full-time; nonresident $8371 full-time. Full-time tuition and fees vary according to location and program. Part-time tuition and fees vary according to location and program. *Room and board:* $4832; room only: $2259. Room and board charges vary according to board plan. *Payment plans:* installment, deferred payment.

Financial Aid Of all full-time matriculated undergraduates who enrolled in 2002, 1,375 applied for aid, 941 were judged to have need, 129 had their need fully met. 282 Federal Work-Study jobs (averaging $1010). In 2002, 160. *Average percent of need met:* 90. *Average financial aid package:* $6536. *Average need-based loan:* $3290. *Average need-based gift aid:* $3158. *Average non-need-based aid:* $2806. *Average indebtedness upon graduation:* $13,421.

Applying *Options:* common application, electronic application, early admission. *Required:* high school transcript. *Required for some:* minimum 2.0 GPA.

Admissions Contact Ms. Lisa Graham, Director of Admissions, West Virginia University Institute of Technology, Box 10, Old Main, Montgomery, WV 25136. *Phone:* 304-442-3167. *Toll-free phone:* 888-554-8324. *Fax:* 304-442-3097. *E-mail:* admissions@wvutech.edu.

■ *See page 2830 for a narrative description.*

WEST VIRGINIA WESLEYAN COLLEGE

Buckhannon, West Virginia

- **Independent** comprehensive, founded 1890, affiliated with United Methodist Church
- **Calendar** semesters
- **Degrees** bachelor's and master's
- **Small-town** 80-acre campus
- **Endowment** $34.3 million
- **Coed,** 1,589 undergraduate students, 98% full-time, 55% women, 45% men
- **Moderately difficult** entrance level, 79% of applicants were admitted

West Virginia Wesleyan's new programs of study include criminal justice, musical theater, and human services. The Bachelor of Fine Arts degree has also been added in musical theater, theater performance, and technical theater. In addition, Wesleyan offers a five-year undergraduate/Master of Business Administration program in accounting, business, economics, finance, international business, management, and marketing.

Undergraduates 1,553 full-time, 36 part-time. Students come from 26 other countries, 48% are from out of state, 5% African American, 1% Asian American or Pacific Islander, 1% Hispanic American, 0.1% Native American, 3% international, 29% transferred in, 80% live on campus. *Retention:* 74% of 2002 full-time freshmen returned.

Freshmen *Admission:* 1,461 applied, 1,155 admitted, 464 enrolled. *Average high school GPA:* 3.27. *Test scores:* SAT verbal scores over 500: 63%; SAT math scores over 500: 60%; ACT scores over 18: 93%; SAT verbal scores over 600: 21%; SAT math scores over 600: 17%; ACT scores over 24: 45%; SAT verbal scores over 700: 2%; SAT math scores over 700: 2%; ACT scores over 30: 5%.

Faculty *Total:* 150, 58% full-time. *Student/faculty ratio:* 15:1.

West Virginia Wesleyan College (continued)

Majors Accounting; art; art history, criticism and conservation; art teacher education; athletic training; biology/biological sciences; business administration and management; business/managerial economics; ceramic arts and ceramics; chemistry; commercial and advertising art; communication/speech communication and rhetoric; computer and information sciences; computer science; creative writing; criminal justice/law enforcement administration; dramatic/theatre arts; drawing; economics; education; education (K-12); elementary education; engineering mechanics; engineering physics; English; English/language arts teacher education; environmental science; finance; fine/studio arts; health and physical education; health teacher education; history; information science/studies; international relations and affairs; kindergarten/preschool education; literature; marketing/marketing management; mathematics; mathematics teacher education; middle school education; music; music teacher education; nursing (registered nurse training); painting; philosophy; philosophy and religious studies related; physical education teaching and coaching; physics; political science and government; pre-dentistry studies; pre-law studies; pre-medical studies; pre-pharmacy studies; pre-veterinary studies; psychology; public relations/image management; religious education; religious studies; secondary education; sociology; special education; special education (specific learning disabilities); speech and rhetoric; sport and fitness administration.

Academic Programs *Special study options:* academic remediation for entering students, adult/continuing education programs, advanced placement credit, double majors, English as a second language, honors programs, independent study, internships, off-campus study, part-time degree program, services for LD students, student-designed majors, study abroad, summer session for credit.

Library A. M. Pfeiffer Library with 91,061 titles, 2,462 serial subscriptions, 7,605 audiovisual materials, an OPAC, a Web page.

Computers on Campus A campuswide network can be accessed from student residence rooms and from off campus that provide access to laptop computer provided to all full time students. Internet access, at least one staffed computer lab available.

Student Life *Housing:* on-campus residence required through senior year. *Options:* coed, men-only, women-only, disabled students. Campus housing is university owned. Freshman campus housing is guaranteed. *Activities and organizations:* drama/theater group, student-run newspaper, radio station, choral group, Campus Activities Board, environmental club, American Marketing Club, Wesleyan Ambassadors, national fraternities, national sororities. *Campus security:* 24-hour emergency response devices and patrols, student patrols, late-night transport/escort service, controlled dormitory access. *Student services:* health clinic, personal/psychological counseling.

Athletics Member NCAA. All Division II. *Intercollegiate sports:* baseball M, basketball M(s)/W(s), cheerleading M/W, cross-country running M(s)/W(s), football M(s), golf M(s), lacrosse M(c)/W(c), soccer M(s)/W(s), softball W(s), swimming M(s)/W(s), tennis M(s)/W(s), track and field M(s)/W(s), volleyball W(s). *Intramural sports:* basketball M/W, bowling M/W, football M/W, golf M/W, racquetball M/W, soccer M/W, softball M/W, table tennis M/W, volleyball M/W, water polo M/W.

Standardized Tests *Required:* SAT I or ACT (for admission). *Required for some:* SAT II: Subject Tests (for admission).

Costs (2004–05) *Comprehensive fee:* $25,650 includes full-time tuition ($19,450), mandatory fees ($1000), and room and board ($5200). *Waivers:* employees or children of employees.

Financial Aid Of all full-time matriculated undergraduates who enrolled in 2003, 1,295 applied for aid, 1,157 were judged to have need, 514 had their need fully met. 675 state and other part-time jobs. In 2003, 319 non-need-based awards were made. *Average percent of need met:* 91%. *Average financial aid package:* $18,927. *Average need-based loan:* $2959. *Average need-based gift aid:* $15,165. *Average non-need-based aid:* $9631.

Applying *Options:* common application, electronic application, early decision, deferred entrance. *Application fee:* $25. *Required:* high school transcript. *Recommended:* essay or personal statement, letters of recommendation, interview. *Application deadlines:* 8/1 (freshmen), 8/1 (transfers). *Early decision:* 12/1. *Notification:* continuous (freshmen), 1/31 (early decision), continuous (transfers).

Admissions Contact Mr. Robert N. Skinner II, Director of Admission, West Virginia Wesleyan College, 59 College Avenue, Buckhannon, WV 26201. *Phone:* 304-473-8510. *Toll-free phone:* 800-722-9933. *Fax:* 304-473-8108. *E-mail:* admissions@wvwc.edu.

■ *See page 2832 for a narrative description.*

WHEELING JESUIT UNIVERSITY
Wheeling, West Virginia

- **Independent Roman Catholic (Jesuit)** comprehensive, founded 1954
- **Calendar** semesters
- **Degrees** bachelor's, master's, and doctoral
- **Suburban** 65-acre campus with easy access to Pittsburgh, PA
- **Endowment** $14.4 million
- **Coed,** 1,251 undergraduate students, 84% full-time, 61% women, 39% men
- **Moderately difficult** entrance level, 77% of applicants were admitted

***U.S. News & World Report* has ranked the University for 7 consecutive years as one of the top in the south and as the best private university in the state. The campus is home to the National Technology Transfer Center, the Center for Educational Technologies, a Challenger Learning Center, the Appalachian Institute, a new $1.5-million soccer/track and field complex, and a 100,000 square-foot recreation center.**

Undergraduates 1,045 full-time, 206 part-time. Students come from 31 states and territories, 22 other countries, 59% are from out of state, 2% African American, 1% Asian American or Pacific Islander, 1% Hispanic American, 0.1% Native American, 2% international, 7% transferred in, 78% live on campus. *Retention:* 72% of 2002 full-time freshmen returned.

Freshmen *Admission:* 1,188 applied, 919 admitted, 247 enrolled. *Average high school GPA:* 3.40. *Test scores:* SAT verbal scores over 500: 71%; SAT math scores over 500: 66%; ACT scores over 18: 70%; SAT verbal scores over 600: 37%; SAT math scores over 600: 26%; ACT scores over 24: 42%; SAT verbal scores over 700: 10%; SAT math scores over 700: 9%; ACT scores over 30: 8%.

Faculty *Total:* 86, 98% full-time, 83% with terminal degrees. *Student/faculty ratio:* 13:1.

Majors Accounting; biology/biological sciences; biology teacher education; business administration and management; chemistry; chemistry teacher education; communication and journalism related; computer programming; computer science; criminal justice/law enforcement administration; digital communication and media/multimedia; education; elementary education; English; English/language arts teacher education; environmental studies; foreign language teacher education; French; French language teacher education; health/health care administration; history; history teacher education; international business/trade/commerce; international relations and affairs; journalism; liberal arts and sciences/liberal studies; management science; marketing/marketing management; mathematics; mathematics teacher education; middle school education; nuclear medical technology; nursing administration; nursing (registered nurse training); philosophy; physical therapy; physics; physics teacher education; political science and government; pre-dentistry studies; pre-law studies; pre-medical studies; pre-veterinary studies; psychology; public relations/image management; religious studies; respiratory care therapy; science teacher education; secondary education; social studies teacher education; Spanish; Spanish language teacher education; special education (specific learning disabilities); theology.

Academic Programs *Special study options:* academic remediation for entering students, adult/continuing education programs, advanced placement credit, cooperative education, English as a second language, external degree program, honors programs, internships, off-campus study, part-time degree program, student-designed majors, summer session for credit. *Unusual degree programs:* 3-2 engineering with Case Western Reserve University.

Library Bishop Hodges Library plus 1 other with 155,953 titles, 487 serial subscriptions, an OPAC, a Web page.

Computers on Campus 125 computers available on campus for general student use. A campuswide network can be accessed from student residence rooms and from off campus. Internet access, at least one staffed computer lab available.

Student Life *Housing:* on-campus residence required through senior year. *Options:* coed, men-only, women-only, disabled students. Campus housing is university owned. Freshman campus housing is guaranteed. *Activities and organizations:* drama/theater group, student-run newspaper, television station, choral group, Student Government, Student Senate, Campus Activity Board, Inter Hall Council, Campus Ministry. *Campus security:* 24-hour emergency response devices and patrols, student patrols, late-night transport/escort service, controlled dormitory access. *Student services:* health clinic, personal/psychological counseling, women's center.

Athletics Member NCAA. All Division II. *Intercollegiate sports:* basketball M/W, cheerleading M/W, cross-country running M/W, golf M/W, lacrosse M, soccer M/W, softball W, swimming M/W, track and field M/W, volleyball W. *Intramural sports:* basketball M/W, football M, ice hockey M(c), softball W, tennis M/W, ultimate Frisbee M/W, volleyball W.

Standardized Tests *Required:* SAT I or ACT (for admission).

Costs (2004–05) *One-time required fee:* $140. *Comprehensive fee:* $26,645 includes full-time tuition ($19,900), mandatory fees ($440), and room and board ($6305). Part-time tuition: $515 per term. *Required fees:* $465 per term part-time. *College room only:* $2925. Room and board charges vary according to board plan and housing facility. *Payment plan:* installment. *Waivers:* adult students and employees or children of employees.

Financial Aid Of all full-time matriculated undergraduates who enrolled in 2003, 933 applied for aid, 806 were judged to have need, 335 had their need fully

met. 379 Federal Work-Study jobs (averaging $1407). 165 state and other part-time jobs (averaging $1888). In 2003, 218 non-need-based awards were made. *Average percent of need met:* 91%. *Average financial aid package:* $16,062. *Average need-based loan:* $4361. *Average need-based gift aid:* $4852. *Average non-need-based aid:* $5250. *Average indebtedness upon graduation:* $11,440.

Applying *Options:* common application, electronic application, early admission, deferred entrance. *Application fee:* $25. *Required:* high school transcript. *Required for some:* interview. *Recommended:* essay or personal statement, minimum 2.5 GPA, 2 letters of recommendation, interview. *Application deadline:* rolling (freshmen), rolling (transfers). *Notification:* continuous (freshmen), continuous (out-of-state freshmen), continuous (transfers).

Admissions Contact Ms. Carol Descak, Acting Director of Admission, Wheeling Jesuit University, 316 Washington Avenue, Wheeling, WV 26003. *Phone:* 800-624-6992 Ext. 2359. *Toll-free phone:* 800-624-6992 Ext. 2359. *Fax:* 304-243-2397. *E-mail:* admiss@wju.edu.

■ *See page 2838 for a narrative description.*

WISCONSIN

ALVERNO COLLEGE
Milwaukee, Wisconsin

- **Independent Roman Catholic** comprehensive, founded 1887
- **Calendar** semesters
- **Degrees** certificates, associate, bachelor's, and master's (also offers weekend program with significant enrollment not reflected in profile)
- **Suburban** 46-acre campus
- **Endowment** $17.9 million
- **Women only,** 1,951 undergraduate students, 62% full-time
- **Moderately difficult** entrance level, 56% of applicants were admitted

Undergraduates 1,201 full-time, 750 part-time. Students come from 8 states and territories, 9 other countries, 3% are from out of state, 23% African American, 4% Asian American or Pacific Islander, 9% Hispanic American, 1% Native American, 0.9% international, 10% transferred in, 13% live on campus. *Retention:* 75% of 2002 full-time freshmen returned.

Freshmen *Admission:* 279 enrolled.

Faculty *Total:* 205, 51% full-time, 46% with terminal degrees. *Student/faculty ratio:* 14:1.

Majors Art; art teacher education; art therapy; biology/biological sciences; business administration and management; business administration, management and operations related; chemistry; communication/speech communication and rhetoric; communications technologies and support services related; community organization and advocacy; computer and information sciences; computer science; education; elementary education; English; English/language arts teacher education; environmental studies; general studies; history; international business/trade/commerce; international/global studies; international relations and affairs; liberal arts and sciences/liberal studies; marketing/marketing management; mathematics; mathematics teacher education; middle school education; molecular biology; music; music related; music teacher education; music therapy; nursing (registered nurse training); nursing related; philosophy; political science and government; psychology; religious studies; science teacher education; social sciences; social science teacher education; social studies teacher education; teacher assistant/aide.

Academic Programs *Special study options:* academic remediation for entering students, adult/continuing education programs, advanced placement credit, double majors, internships, part-time degree program, services for LD students, study abroad, summer session for credit. *ROTC:* Army (c), Air Force (c).

Library Library Media Center with 92,076 titles, 1,001 serial subscriptions, 34,795 audiovisual materials, an OPAC, a Web page.

Computers on Campus 250 computers available on campus for general student use. A campuswide network can be accessed from student residence rooms and from off campus that provide access to email. Internet access, at least one staffed computer lab available.

Student Life *Housing:* on-campus residence required for freshman year. *Options:* women-only. *Activities and organizations:* drama/theater group, student-run newspaper, choral group, Student Nurses Association, Women in Communication, Pi Sigma Epsilon, Students in Free Enterprise, Alverno Student Educators Organization. *Campus security:* 24-hour emergency response devices and patrols, late-night transport/escort service, controlled dormitory access, well-lit parking lots and pathways, emergency first-aid and CPR, crisis intervention team and plan in place. *Student services:* health clinic.

Athletics Member NCAA. All Division III. *Intercollegiate sports:* basketball W, cross-country running W, soccer W, softball W, volleyball W. *Intramural sports:* basketball W, cross-country running W, soccer W, volleyball W.

Standardized Tests *Required:* SAT I or ACT (for admission). *Recommended:* ACT (for admission).

Costs (2003–04) *Comprehensive fee:* $18,898 includes full-time tuition ($13,488), mandatory fees ($150), and room and board ($5260). Full-time tuition and fees vary according to class time and program. Part-time tuition: $562 per credit hour. Part-time tuition and fees vary according to class time and program. *Required fees:* $75 per term part-time. *Room and board:* Room and board charges vary according to board plan. *Payment plans:* installment, deferred payment. *Waivers:* employees or children of employees.

Financial Aid Of all full-time matriculated undergraduates who enrolled in 2002, 259 Federal Work-Study jobs (averaging $1915).

Applying *Options:* common application, electronic application, deferred entrance. *Application fee:* $20. *Required:* essay or personal statement, high school transcript. *Required for some:* letters of recommendation. *Recommended:* interview. *Application deadline:* rolling (freshmen), rolling (transfers). *Notification:* continuous (freshmen), continuous (transfers).

Admissions Contact Ms. Mary Kay Farrell, Director of Admissions, Alverno College, 3400 South 43 Street, PO Box 343922, Milwaukee, WI 53234-3922. *Phone:* 414-382-6113. *Toll-free phone:* 800-933-3401. *Fax:* 414-382-6354. *E-mail:* admissions@alverno.edu.

■ *See page 1160 for a narrative description.*

BELLIN COLLEGE OF NURSING
Green Bay, Wisconsin

- **Independent** 4-year, founded 1909
- **Calendar** semesters
- **Degree** bachelor's
- **Urban** campus
- **Endowment** $7.0 million
- **Coed, primarily women,** 206 undergraduate students, 83% full-time, 95% women, 5% men
- **Moderately difficult** entrance level, 84% of applicants were admitted

Undergraduates 170 full-time, 36 part-time. Students come from 2 states and territories, 0.1% are from out of state, 2% Asian American or Pacific Islander, 0.5% Hispanic American, 0.5% Native American, 18% transferred in. *Retention:* 90% of 2002 full-time freshmen returned.

Freshmen *Admission:* 80 applied, 67 admitted, 36 enrolled. *Average high school GPA:* 3.23. *Test scores:* ACT scores over 18: 100%; ACT scores over 24: 28%; ACT scores over 30: 3%.

Faculty *Total:* 18, 89% full-time, 17% with terminal degrees. *Student/faculty ratio:* 10:1.

Majors Nursing (registered nurse training).

Academic Programs *Special study options:* accelerated degree program, advanced placement credit, independent study, off-campus study, summer session for credit. *ROTC:* Army (c).

Library Meredith B. and John M. Rose Library with 7,000 titles, 225 serial subscriptions, 600 audiovisual materials.

Computers on Campus 18 computers available on campus for general student use. A campuswide network can be accessed. Internet access, at least one staffed computer lab available.

Student Life *Housing:* college housing not available. *Activities and organizations:* Student Senate, Student Nurses Association. *Campus security:* 24-hour patrols, late-night transport/escort service, electronically operated building access after hours. *Student services:* health clinic, personal/psychological counseling.

Standardized Tests *Required:* ACT (for admission).

Costs (2003–04) *Tuition:* $12,672 full-time, $610 per credit hour part-time. Full-time tuition and fees vary according to student level. *Required fees:* $279 full-time, $279 per year part-time. *Payment plan:* installment.

Financial Aid Of all full-time matriculated undergraduates who enrolled in 2003, 106 applied for aid, 100 were judged to have need, 17 had their need fully met. 7 Federal Work-Study jobs (averaging $1400). In 2003, 3 non-need-based awards were made. *Average percent of need met:* 89%. *Average financial aid package:* $12,996. *Average need-based loan:* $4723. *Average need-based gift aid:* $5075. *Average non-need-based aid:* $1813. *Average indebtedness upon graduation:* $22,206.

Applying *Options:* electronic application. *Application fee:* $20. *Required:* high school transcript, 3 letters of recommendation, interview. *Recommended:* minimum 3.0 GPA. *Application deadline:* rolling (freshmen), rolling (transfers). *Notification:* continuous (freshmen), continuous (transfers).

Bellin College of Nursing (continued)

Admissions Contact Dr. Penny Croghan, Admissions Director, Bellin College of Nursing, 725 South Webster Avenue, Green Bay, WI 54301. *Phone:* 920-433-5803. *Toll-free phone:* 800-236-8707. *Fax:* 920-433-7416. *E-mail:* admissio@bcon.edu.

BELOIT COLLEGE
Beloit, Wisconsin

- **Independent** 4-year, founded 1846
- **Calendar** semesters
- **Degree** bachelor's
- **Small-town** 65-acre campus with easy access to Chicago and Milwaukee
- **Endowment** $82.9 million
- **Coed,** 1,332 undergraduate students, 92% full-time, 61% women, 39% men
- **Very difficult** entrance level, 69% of applicants were admitted

Beloit College is an independent, residential liberal arts and sciences college where students and faculty are engaged in a community that values experiential learning, interdisciplinary thought, and global understanding. Beloit attracts students from nearly every state and more than 40 countries who are interested in combining a rigorous academic program with internships, research, service, and a global perspective.

Undergraduates 1,226 full-time, 106 part-time. Students come from 47 states and territories, 40 other countries, 82% are from out of state, 3% African American, 3% Asian American or Pacific Islander, 3% Hispanic American, 0.3% Native American, 6% international, 2% transferred in, 93% live on campus. *Retention:* 91% of 2002 full-time freshmen returned.

Freshmen *Admission:* 1,901 applied, 1,321 admitted, 346 enrolled. *Average high school GPA:* 3.51. *Test scores:* SAT verbal scores over 500: 95%; SAT math scores over 500: 91%; ACT scores over 18: 100%; SAT verbal scores over 600: 70%; SAT math scores over 600: 53%; ACT scores over 24: 87%; SAT verbal scores over 700: 22%; SAT math scores over 700: 11%; ACT scores over 30: 27%.

Faculty *Total:* 126, 82% full-time, 93% with terminal degrees. *Student/faculty ratio:* 11:1.

Majors Anthropology; art history, criticism and conservation; art teacher education; Asian studies; biochemistry; biology/biological sciences; business administration and management; business/managerial economics; cell biology and histology; chemistry; classics and languages, literatures and linguistics; comparative literature; computer science; creative writing; dramatic/theatre arts; economics; education; elementary education; engineering; English; environmental biology; environmental studies; European studies; fine/studio arts; French; geology/earth science; German; history; interdisciplinary studies; international relations and affairs; Latin American studies; literature; mass communication/media; mathematics; modern languages; molecular biology; museum studies; music; music teacher education; philosophy; physics; political science and government; pre-dentistry studies; pre-law studies; pre-medical studies; psychology; religious studies; Romance languages; Russian; Russian studies; science teacher education; secondary education; sociobiology; sociology; Spanish; women's studies.

Academic Programs *Special study options:* adult/continuing education programs, advanced placement credit, double majors, English as a second language, independent study, internships, off-campus study, services for LD students, student-designed majors, study abroad, summer session for credit. *Unusual degree programs:* 3-2 engineering with University of Illinois at Urbana-Champaign, University of Michigan, Rensselaer Polytechnic Institute, Georgia Institute of Technology; forestry with Duke University; medical technology with Rush University.

Library Morse Library and Black Information Center with 183,736 titles, 946 serial subscriptions, 7,285 audiovisual materials, an OPAC, a Web page.

Computers on Campus 152 computers available on campus for general student use. A campuswide network can be accessed from student residence rooms and from off campus. Internet access, at least one staffed computer lab available.

Student Life *Housing:* on-campus residence required through junior year. *Options:* coed, men-only, women-only, cooperative. Campus housing is university owned. Freshman campus housing is guaranteed. *Activities and organizations:* drama/theater group, student-run newspaper, radio and television station, choral group, Science Fiction and Fantasy Association, Black Student's Union, international club, Alliance, Ballroom Dancing, national fraternities. *Campus security:* 24-hour emergency response devices and patrols, late-night transport/escort service, controlled dormitory access. *Student services:* health clinic, personal/psychological counseling, women's center.

Athletics Member NCAA. All Division III. *Intercollegiate sports:* baseball M, basketball M/W, crew M(c)/W(c), cross-country running M/W, fencing M(c)/W(c), football M, golf M/W, ice hockey M(c)/W(c), lacrosse M(c)/W(c), soccer M/W, softball W, swimming M/W, tennis M/W, track and field M/W, volleyball W. *Intramural sports:* badminton M/W, basketball M/W, bowling M/W, football M, racquetball M/W, sailing M/W, soccer M/W, tennis M/W, ultimate Frisbee M/W, volleyball M/W, water polo M/W.

Standardized Tests *Required:* SAT I or ACT (for admission).

Costs (2003–04) *Comprehensive fee:* $29,864 includes full-time tuition ($24,166), mandatory fees ($220), and room and board ($5478). *College room only:* $2672. Room and board charges vary according to board plan. *Payment plan:* installment. *Waivers:* employees or children of employees.

Financial Aid Of all full-time matriculated undergraduates who enrolled in 2003, 979 applied for aid, 900 were judged to have need, 900 had their need fully met. 524 Federal Work-Study jobs (averaging $1399). 498 state and other part-time jobs (averaging $1155). In 2003, 186 non-need-based awards were made. *Average percent of need met:* 100%. *Average financial aid package:* $18,635. *Average need-based loan:* $3344. *Average need-based gift aid:* $14,026. *Average non-need-based aid:* $8372. *Average indebtedness upon graduation:* $18,783.

Applying *Options:* common application, electronic application, early admission, early action, deferred entrance. *Application fee:* $30. *Required:* essay or personal statement, high school transcript, 1 letter of recommendation. *Required for some:* interview. *Recommended:* interview. *Application deadline:* 1/15 (freshmen), rolling (transfers). *Notification:* 4/1 (freshmen), 1/15 (early action), continuous (transfers).

Admissions Contact Mr. James S. Zielinski, Director of Admissions, Beloit College, 700 College Street, Beloit, WI 53511-5596. *Phone:* 608-363-2500. *Toll-free phone:* 800-9-BELOIT. *Fax:* 608-363-2075. *E-mail:* admiss@beloit.edu.

■ *See page 1232 for a narrative description.*

BRYANT AND STRATTON COLLEGE
Milwaukee, Wisconsin

- **Proprietary** primarily 2-year, founded 1863, part of Bryant and Stratton Business Institute, Inc.
- **Calendar** semesters
- **Degrees** associate and bachelor's
- **Urban** 2-acre campus
- **Coed**
- **Minimally difficult** entrance level

Faculty *Student/faculty ratio:* 14:1.

Student Life *Campus security:* 24-hour emergency response devices and patrols.

Standardized Tests *Required:* TABE (for admission). *Recommended:* SAT I or ACT (for admission).

Costs (2003–04) *One-time required fee:* $25. *Tuition:* $10,200 full-time, $340 per credit hour part-time. Full-time tuition and fees vary according to class time and course load. Part-time tuition and fees vary according to class time and course load. *Required fees:* $200 full-time, $100 per term part-time.

Applying *Application fee:* $25. *Required:* high school transcript. *Required for some:* letters of recommendation, interview. *Recommended:* minimum 2.0 GPA.

Admissions Contact Ms. Kathryn Cotey, Director of Admissions, Bryant and Stratton College, 310 West Wisconsin Avenue, Milwaukee, WI 53203-2214. *Phone:* 414-276-5200.

CARDINAL STRITCH UNIVERSITY
Milwaukee, Wisconsin

- **Independent Roman Catholic** comprehensive, founded 1937
- **Calendar** semesters
- **Degrees** certificates, associate, bachelor's, master's, doctoral, and postbachelor's certificates
- **Suburban** 40-acre campus
- **Endowment** $17.7 million
- **Coed,** 3,251 undergraduate students, 90% full-time, 68% women, 32% men
- **Moderately difficult** entrance level, 93% of applicants were admitted

Cardinal Stritch University is a Catholic, coeducational institution rooted in the liberal arts. The University provides all of the resources associated with a large university yet offers the benefits of personal attention and 1-on-1 instruction associated with a smaller institution. Graduate and undergraduate programs, offered in traditional and nontraditional formats, range from business and education to religious studies and art.

Undergraduates 2,936 full-time, 315 part-time. Students come from 16 states and territories, 27 other countries, 18% African American, 2% Asian American or Pacific Islander, 4% Hispanic American, 0.8% Native American, 2% international, 5% transferred in, 5% live on campus. *Retention:* 73% of 2002 full-time freshmen returned.

Freshmen *Admission:* 617 applied, 572 admitted, 241 enrolled. *Average high school GPA:* 2.97. *Test scores:* SAT verbal scores over 500: 50%; SAT math scores over 500: 60%; ACT scores over 18: 92%; SAT verbal scores over 600: 30%; ACT scores over 24: 38%; ACT scores over 30: 9%.

Faculty *Total:* 880, 12% full-time. *Student/faculty ratio:* 18:1.

Majors Accounting; art; art teacher education; biology/biological sciences; business administration and management; business/managerial economics; chemistry; commercial and advertising art; communication/speech communication and rhetoric; computer science; creative writing; divinity/ministry; dramatic/theatre arts; education; elementary education; English; fine/studio arts; French; history; interdisciplinary studies; international business/trade/commerce; kindergarten/preschool education; liberal arts and sciences/liberal studies; mathematics; mathematics and computer science; music; nursing (registered nurse training); political science and government; pre-dentistry studies; pre-law studies; pre-medical studies; pre-veterinary studies; psychology; public relations/image management; religious education; religious studies; science teacher education; secondary education; social sciences; sociology; Spanish; special education.

Academic Programs *Special study options:* academic remediation for entering students, accelerated degree program, adult/continuing education programs, advanced placement credit, cooperative education, distance learning, double majors, English as a second language, external degree program, honors programs, independent study, internships, off-campus study, part-time degree program, services for LD students, student-designed majors, summer session for credit.

Library Cardinal Stritch University Library with 124,897 titles, 667 serial subscriptions, 6,250 audiovisual materials, an OPAC, a Web page.

Computers on Campus 236 computers available on campus for general student use. A campuswide network can be accessed from student residence rooms and from off campus. Internet access, at least one staffed computer lab available.

Student Life *Housing options:* coed. *Activities and organizations:* drama/theater group, student-run newspaper, radio station, choral group, Residence Hall Association, Student Government Association, Student Activities Board. *Campus security:* 24-hour emergency response devices and patrols, late-night transport/escort service. *Student services:* health clinic, personal/psychological counseling.

Athletics Member NAIA. *Intercollegiate sports:* baseball M, basketball M/W, cross-country running M/W, soccer M/W, softball W, volleyball M/W. *Intramural sports:* basketball M/W, volleyball M/W.

Standardized Tests *Required:* SAT I or ACT (for admission). *Recommended:* ACT (for admission).

Costs (2003–04) *Comprehensive fee:* $19,700 includes full-time tuition ($14,240), mandatory fees ($300), and room and board ($5160). Full-time tuition and fees vary according to program. Part-time tuition: $445 per credit. Part-time tuition and fees vary according to course load and program. *Required fees:* $100 per term part-time. *Room and board:* Room and board charges vary according to board plan. *Payment plan:* installment. *Waivers:* employees or children of employees.

Financial Aid Of all full-time matriculated undergraduates who enrolled in 2002, 2,176 applied for aid, 2,037 were judged to have need, 188 had their need fully met. In 2002, 234 non-need-based awards were made. *Average percent of need met:* 43%. *Average financial aid package:* $7843. *Average need-based loan:* $3575. *Average need-based gift aid:* $5634. *Average non-need-based aid:* $9402.

Applying *Options:* common application, electronic application, deferred entrance. *Application fee:* $25. *Required:* essay or personal statement, high school transcript, minimum 2.0 GPA. *Required for some:* letters of recommendation. *Recommended:* interview. *Application deadline:* rolling (freshmen), rolling (transfers).

Admissions Contact Mr. David Wegener, Director of Admissions, Cardinal Stritch University, 6801 North Yates Road, Milwaukee, WI 53217-3985. *Phone:* 414-410-4040. *Toll-free phone:* 800-347-8822 Ext. 4040. *Fax:* 414-410-4058. *E-mail:* admityou@stritch.edu.

■ *See page 1346 for a narrative description.*

CARROLL COLLEGE
Waukesha, Wisconsin

- **Independent Presbyterian** comprehensive, founded 1846
- **Calendar** semesters
- **Degrees** bachelor's and master's
- **Suburban** 52-acre campus with easy access to Milwaukee
- **Endowment** $28.8 million
- **Coed,** 2,699 undergraduate students, 76% full-time, 67% women, 33% men
- **Moderately difficult** entrance level, 78% of applicants were admitted

Carroll College gives its students the support they need to learn and grow—small classes and individual attention provide a quality educational experience at Wisconsin's oldest college. Students are encouraged to explore the world around them by studying in other countries or participating in internships. An Honors Program is available to academically talented students.

Undergraduates 2,062 full-time, 637 part-time. Students come from 28 states and territories, 27 other countries, 23% are from out of state, 2% African American, 1% Asian American or Pacific Islander, 2% Hispanic American, 0.3% Native American, 2% international, 6% transferred in, 58% live on campus. *Retention:* 76% of 2002 full-time freshmen returned.

Freshmen *Admission:* 2,064 applied, 1,607 admitted, 513 enrolled. *Average high school GPA:* 3.34. *Test scores:* ACT scores over 18: 92%; ACT scores over 24: 42%; ACT scores over 30: 3%.

Faculty *Total:* 243, 40% full-time, 37% with terminal degrees. *Student/faculty ratio:* 16:1.

Majors Accounting; actuarial science; animal behavior and ethology; applied mathematics related; art; art teacher education; athletic training; biochemistry; biology/biological sciences; biology teacher education; business administration and management; chemistry; chemistry teacher education; clinical laboratory science/medical technology; commercial and advertising art; communication/speech communication and rhetoric; computer and information sciences; computer science; computer software engineering; creative writing; criminal justice/law enforcement administration; drama and dance teacher education; dramatic/theatre arts; early childhood education; education; elementary education; English; English/language arts teacher education; environmental science; finance; fine/studio arts; foreign language teacher education; forensic science and technology; French language teacher education; geography; geography teacher education; German language teacher education; graphic communications; health and physical education; health teacher education; history; history teacher education; information science/studies; international relations and affairs; journalism; kindergarten/preschool education; kinesiology and exercise science; management information systems and services related; marketing/marketing management; mathematics; mathematics teacher education; middle school education; music; music teacher education; natural resources/conservation; nursing (registered nurse training); organizational behavior; organizational communication; photography; physical education teaching and coaching; physics teacher education; political science and government; pre-dentistry studies; pre-medical studies; pre-pharmacy studies; pre-veterinary studies; printing management; psychology; psychology teacher education; public relations, advertising, and applied communication related; religious studies; science teacher education; secondary education; social science teacher education; social studies teacher education; sociology; Spanish; Spanish language teacher education; system, networking, and LAN/wan management.

Academic Programs *Special study options:* academic remediation for entering students, adult/continuing education programs, advanced placement credit, distance learning, double majors, honors programs, independent study, internships, part-time degree program, services for LD students, student-designed majors, study abroad, summer session for credit. *ROTC:* Air Force (c).

Library Todd Wehr Memorial Library with 200,000 titles, 520 serial subscriptions, 362 audiovisual materials, an OPAC, a Web page.

Computers on Campus 250 computers available on campus for general student use. A campuswide network can be accessed from student residence rooms and from off campus. Internet access, at least one staffed computer lab available.

Student Life *Housing:* on-campus residence required through sophomore year. *Options:* coed, women-only. Campus housing is university owned. Freshman campus housing is guaranteed. *Activities and organizations:* drama/theater group, student-run newspaper, radio station, choral group, College Activities Board, Student Senate, Black Student Union, Carroll College Christian Fellowship, Residence Hall Association, national sororities. *Campus security:* 24-hour emergency response devices and patrols, student patrols, late-night transport/escort service, controlled dormitory access. *Student services:* health clinic, personal/psychological counseling.

Athletics Member NCAA. All Division III. *Intercollegiate sports:* baseball M, basketball M/W, cross-country running M/W, football M, golf M/W, soccer M/W, softball W, swimming M/W, tennis M/W, track and field M/W, volleyball W. *Intramural sports:* badminton M/W, basketball M/W, football M/W, soccer M/W, softball M/W, table tennis M/W, volleyball M/W, water polo M/W.

Standardized Tests *Required:* SAT I and SAT II or ACT (for admission).

Costs (2004–05) *Comprehensive fee:* $23,770 includes full-time tuition ($17,800), mandatory fees ($370), and room and board ($5600). Full-time tuition and fees vary according to program. Part-time tuition: $220 per credit. Part-time tuition and fees vary according to course load and program. *College room only:* $3030. Room and board charges vary according to board plan and housing facility. *Payment plan:* installment. *Waivers:* employees or children of employees.

Financial Aid Of all full-time matriculated undergraduates who enrolled in 2002, 1,989 applied for aid, 1,492 were judged to have need, 1,194 had their need fully met. 469 Federal Work-Study jobs (averaging $1659). 696 state and other part-time jobs (averaging $1591). In 2002, 436 non-need-based awards were made. *Average percent of need met:* 100%. *Average financial aid package:*

Carroll College (continued)
$12,999. *Average need-based loan:* $3699. *Average need-based gift aid:* $9966. *Average non-need-based aid:* $6544. *Average indebtedness upon graduation:* $15,195.
Applying *Options:* common application, electronic application, early admission, deferred entrance. *Required:* high school transcript, minimum 2.0 GPA, 1 letter of recommendation. *Required for some:* essay or personal statement. *Recommended:* interview. *Application deadline:* rolling (freshmen), rolling (transfers). *Notification:* continuous until 8/20 (freshmen), continuous until 8/20 (transfers).
Admissions Contact Mr. James V. Wiseman III, Vice President of Enrollment, Carroll College, 100 North East Avenue, Waukesha, WI 53186-5593. *Phone:* 262-524-7221. *Toll-free phone:* 800-CARROLL. *Fax:* 262-524-7139. *E-mail:* cc.info@ccadmin.cc.edu.

■ *See page 1354 for a narrative description.*

CARTHAGE COLLEGE
Kenosha, Wisconsin

- **Independent** comprehensive, founded 1847, affiliated with Evangelical Lutheran Church in America
- **Calendar** 4-1-4
- **Degrees** bachelor's and master's
- **Suburban** 72-acre campus with easy access to Chicago and Milwaukee
- **Endowment** $31.8 million
- **Coed,** 2,508 undergraduate students, 78% full-time, 58% women, 42% men
- **Moderately difficult** entrance level, 73% of applicants were admitted

Undergraduates 1,956 full-time, 552 part-time. Students come from 25 states and territories, 12 other countries, 54% are from out of state, 5% African American, 1% Asian American or Pacific Islander, 4% Hispanic American, 0.4% Native American, 0.7% international, 3% transferred in, 68% live on campus. *Retention:* 74% of 2002 full-time freshmen returned.
Freshmen *Admission:* 3,346 applied, 2,449 admitted, 582 enrolled. *Average high school GPA:* 3.23. *Test scores:* SAT verbal scores over 500: 77%; SAT math scores over 500: 77%; ACT scores over 18: 95%; SAT verbal scores over 600: 37%; SAT math scores over 600: 54%; ACT scores over 24: 51%; SAT verbal scores over 700: 2%; SAT math scores over 700: 10%; ACT scores over 30: 9%.
Faculty *Total:* 170, 64% full-time, 61% with terminal degrees. *Student/faculty ratio:* 17:1.
Majors Accounting; applied art; athletic training; biology/biological sciences; business administration and management; chemistry; classics and languages, literatures and linguistics; commercial and advertising art; computer science; criminal justice/law enforcement administration; dramatic/theatre arts; economics; education; elementary education; engineering; English; environmental studies; fine/studio arts; French; geography; German; history; international economics; marketing research; mathematics; middle school education; modern languages; music; music teacher education; natural sciences; neuroscience; occupational therapy; parks, recreation and leisure; philosophy; physical education teaching and coaching; physics; political science and government; pre-dentistry studies; pre-law studies; pre-medical studies; pre-veterinary studies; psychology; religious studies; science teacher education; secondary education; social sciences; social work; sociology; Spanish; special education; speech and rhetoric.
Academic Programs *Special study options:* accelerated degree program, adult/continuing education programs, advanced placement credit, cooperative education, double majors, honors programs, independent study, internships, off-campus study, part-time degree program, services for LD students, student-designed majors, study abroad, summer session for credit. *ROTC:* Army (c), Air Force (c). *Unusual degree programs:* 3-2 engineering with Case Western Reserve University, University of Wisconsin-Madison, University of Minnesota; occupational therapy with Washington University in St. Louis.
Library Hedberg Library with 128,551 titles, 425 serial subscriptions, 4,361 audiovisual materials, an OPAC, a Web page.
Computers on Campus 200 computers available on campus for general student use. A campuswide network can be accessed from student residence rooms and from off campus. Internet access, at least one staffed computer lab available. Computer purchase or lease plan available.
Student Life *Housing:* on-campus residence required through senior year. *Options:* coed, men-only, women-only, disabled students. Campus housing is university owned and leased by the school. Freshman campus housing is guaranteed. *Activities and organizations:* drama/theater group, student-run newspaper, radio station, choral group, Residence Life Council, Alpha Lambda Delta, Circle K, Inter-Varsity Christian Fellowship, Pals-n-Partners, national fraternities, national sororities. *Campus security:* 24-hour emergency response devices and patrols, student patrols, late-night transport/escort service, controlled dormitory access. *Student services:* health clinic, personal/psychological counseling.
Athletics Member NCAA. All Division III. *Intercollegiate sports:* baseball M, basketball M/W, cross-country running M/W, football M, golf M/W, ice hockey M(c), soccer M/W, softball W, swimming M/W, tennis M/W, track and field M/W, volleyball W. *Intramural sports:* badminton M/W, basketball M/W, bowling M/W, cheerleading M/W, football M/W, golf M/W, racquetball M/W, skiing (downhill) M/W, soccer M/W, softball M/W, table tennis M/W, tennis M/W, volleyball M/W, weight lifting M/W.
Standardized Tests *Required:* SAT I or ACT (for admission).
Costs (2004–05) *Comprehensive fee:* $27,500 includes full-time tuition ($21,250) and room and board ($6250). Full-time tuition and fees vary according to reciprocity agreements. Part-time tuition: $315 per credit hour. Part-time tuition and fees vary according to class time and course load. *Room and board:* Room and board charges vary according to board plan. *Payment plan:* installment. *Waivers:* employees or children of employees.
Financial Aid Of all full-time matriculated undergraduates who enrolled in 2002, 1,713 applied for aid, 1,482 were judged to have need, 75 had their need fully met. In 2002, 213 non-need-based awards were made. *Average percent of need met:* 39%. *Average financial aid package:* $8222. *Average need-based loan:* $4043. *Average need-based gift aid:* $4262. *Average non-need-based aid:* $7185. *Average indebtedness upon graduation:* $17,100.
Applying *Options:* electronic application, early action, deferred entrance. *Application fee:* $25. *Required:* high school transcript, minimum 2.0 GPA. *Required for some:* essay or personal statement, 2 letters of recommendation. *Recommended:* essay or personal statement, minimum 3.0 GPA, interview. *Application deadline:* rolling (freshmen), rolling (transfers). *Notification:* continuous (freshmen), 7/15 (early action), continuous (transfers).
Admissions Contact Carthage College, 2001 Alford Park Drive, Kenosha, WI 53140-1994. *Phone:* 262-551-5850. *Toll-free phone:* 800-351-4058. *Fax:* 262-551-5762. *E-mail:* admissions@carthage.edu.

■ *See page 1360 for a narrative description.*

COLUMBIA COLLEGE OF NURSING
Milwaukee, Wisconsin

- **Independent** 4-year, founded 1901
- **Calendar** semesters
- **Degrees** bachelor's (nursing degree is awarded in conjunction with Mount Mary College)
- **Urban** campus
- **Endowment** $1.2 million
- **Coed, primarily women,** 190 undergraduate students, 92% full-time, 97% women, 3% men
- **Moderately difficult** entrance level

Undergraduates 174 full-time, 16 part-time. 13% are from out of state, 7% African American, 1% Asian American or Pacific Islander, 1% Hispanic American, 24% transferred in, 7% live on campus. *Retention:* 63% of 2002 full-time freshmen returned.
Freshmen *Admission:* 185 enrolled. *Test scores:* ACT scores over 18: 96%; ACT scores over 24: 34%.
Faculty *Total:* 18, 61% full-time, 28% with terminal degrees. *Student/faculty ratio:* 15:1.
Majors Nursing (registered nurse training).
Academic Programs *Special study options:* advanced placement credit, double majors, honors programs, independent study, off-campus study, part-time degree program, summer session for credit.
Library Ellen Bacon Library plus 1 other with 9,060 titles, 253 serial subscriptions, 508 audiovisual materials, an OPAC.
Computers on Campus 18 computers available on campus for general student use. A campuswide network can be accessed. Internet access, at least one staffed computer lab available.
Student Life *Housing:* on-campus residence required through sophomore year. *Options:* coed. *Activities and organizations:* Student Senate, Student Nurses Association. *Campus security:* 24-hour emergency response devices and patrols, student patrols, late-night transport/escort service, controlled dormitory access. *Student services:* health clinic, personal/psychological counseling.
Standardized Tests *Required:* SAT I or ACT (for admission).
Costs (2004–05) *Comprehensive fee:* $19,770 includes full-time tuition ($15,100), mandatory fees ($670), and room and board ($4000). Part-time tuition: $420 per credit hour. Part-time tuition and fees vary according to program. *Required fees:* $500 per term part-time. *College room only:* $3000. Room and board charges vary according to board plan, housing facility, location, and student level. *Payment plan:* installment. *Waivers:* employees or children of employees.
Financial Aid Of all full-time matriculated undergraduates who enrolled in 2000, 1,782 applied for aid, 1,336 were judged to have need, 1,336 had their need

fully met. In 2000, 426 non-need-based awards were made. *Average percent of need met:* 100%. *Average financial aid package:* $13,219. *Average need-based loan:* $3186. *Average need-based gift aid:* $9050. *Average non-need-based aid:* $7051. *Average indebtedness upon graduation:* $16,000.

Applying *Options:* common application. *Application fee:* $25. *Required:* high school transcript. *Required for some:* essay or personal statement. *Recommended:* essay or personal statement, 1 letter of recommendation, interview. *Application deadline:* 8/1 (freshmen), rolling (transfers).

Admissions Contact Ms. Amy Dobson, Dean of Admissions, Columbia College of Nursing, 2900 North Menomonee River Parkway, Milwaukee, WI 53222-4597. *Phone:* 414-256-1219. *Toll-free phone:* 800-321-6265. *Fax:* 414-256-0180. *E-mail:* admiss@mtmary.edu.

CONCORDIA UNIVERSITY WISCONSIN
Mequon, Wisconsin

- **Independent** comprehensive, founded 1881, affiliated with Lutheran Church–Missouri Synod
- **Calendar** 4-1-4
- **Degrees** certificates, associate, bachelor's, master's, and doctoral
- **Suburban** 155-acre campus with easy access to Milwaukee
- **Endowment** $31.8 million
- **Coed,** 3,990 undergraduate students, 54% full-time, 63% women, 37% men
- **Moderately difficult** entrance level, 80% of applicants were admitted

Undergraduates 2,142 full-time, 1,848 part-time. Students come from 35 states and territories, 21 other countries, 37% are from out of state, 11% African American, 0.7% Asian American or Pacific Islander, 2% Hispanic American, 0.7% Native American, 0.6% international, 3% transferred in, 71% live on campus. *Retention:* 78% of 2002 full-time freshmen returned.

Freshmen *Admission:* 1,276 applied, 1,024 admitted, 362 enrolled. *Average high school GPA:* 3.2. *Test scores:* ACT scores over 18: 93%; ACT scores over 24: 39%; ACT scores over 30: 6%.

Faculty *Total:* 191, 49% full-time, 40% with terminal degrees. *Student/faculty ratio:* 11:1.

Majors Accounting; ancient Near Eastern and biblical languages; art; art teacher education; athletic training; biology/biological sciences; business administration and management; business teacher education; commercial and advertising art; computer science; criminal justice/law enforcement administration; economics; education; education (multiple levels); elementary education; English; English as a second/foreign language (teaching); exercise physiology; general studies; German; German language teacher education; graphic design; health and physical education; health and physical education related; health/health care administration; Hebrew; history; history teacher education; humanities; industrial radiologic technology; interior design; kindergarten/preschool education; legal assistant/paralegal; liberal arts and sciences/liberal studies; marketing/marketing management; mass communication/media; mathematics; medical office assistant; middle school education; missionary studies and missiology; modern Greek; music; music teacher education; nursing (registered nurse training); occupational therapy; pastoral studies/counseling; physical education teaching and coaching; physical therapy; pre-dentistry studies; pre-law studies; pre-medical studies; pre-nursing studies; psychology; religious studies; science teacher education; secondary education; social work; Spanish; Spanish language teacher education; sport and fitness administration; theology; youth ministry.

Academic Programs *Special study options:* academic remediation for entering students, accelerated degree program, adult/continuing education programs, advanced placement credit, distance learning, double majors, English as a second language, honors programs, independent study, internships, off-campus study, part-time degree program, services for LD students, student-designed majors, study abroad, summer session for credit.

Library Rinker Memorial Library with 110,929 titles, 1,411 serial subscriptions, 4,645 audiovisual materials, an OPAC.

Computers on Campus 100 computers available on campus for general student use. A campuswide network can be accessed from student residence rooms and from off campus. Internet access, at least one staffed computer lab available.

Student Life *Housing options:* men-only, women-only. Campus housing is university owned. Freshman applicants given priority for college housing. *Activities and organizations:* drama/theater group, student-run newspaper, radio station, choral group, Fellowship of Christian Athletes, Kammerchor, Youth Ministry, band. *Campus security:* student patrols, controlled dormitory access. *Student services:* health clinic, personal/psychological counseling.

Athletics Member NCAA. All Division III. *Intercollegiate sports:* baseball M, basketball M/W, cross-country running M/W, football M, golf M/W, soccer M/W, softball W, tennis M/W, track and field M/W, volleyball W, wrestling M. *Intramural sports:* basketball M/W, softball M/W, volleyball M/W.

Standardized Tests *Required:* SAT I or ACT (for admission).

Costs (2003–04) *Comprehensive fee:* $21,365 includes full-time tuition ($15,515), mandatory fees ($60), and room and board ($5790). Part-time tuition: $645 per credit hour. Part-time tuition and fees vary according to class time and program. No tuition increase for student's term of enrollment. *Room and board:* Room and board charges vary according to board plan. *Payment plans:* installment, deferred payment. *Waivers:* employees or children of employees.

Financial Aid Of all full-time matriculated undergraduates who enrolled in 2002, 1,306 applied for aid, 1,306 were judged to have need, 391 had their need fully met. 80 Federal Work-Study jobs (averaging $1600). 80 state and other part-time jobs (averaging $400). *Average percent of need met:* 80%. *Average financial aid package:* $14,124. *Average need-based loan:* $3500. *Average need-based gift aid:* $11,000. *Average non-need-based aid:* $5200. *Average indebtedness upon graduation:* $17,600.

Applying *Options:* deferred entrance. *Application fee:* $35. *Required:* high school transcript, minimum 2.0 GPA. *Required for some:* essay or personal statement, minimum 3.0 GPA, 3 letters of recommendation. *Recommended:* interview. *Application deadlines:* 8/15 (freshmen), 8/15 (transfers). *Notification:* continuous until 8/15 (freshmen), continuous until 8/15 (transfers).

Admissions Contact Mr. Ken Gaschk, Director of Admissions, Concordia University Wisconsin, 12800 North Lake Shore Drive, Mequon, WI 53097. *Phone:* 262-243-4305 Ext. 4305. *Toll-free phone:* 888-628-9472. *Fax:* 262-243-4351. *E-mail:* admissions@cuw.edu.

DEVRY UNIVERSITY
Waukesha, Wisconsin

Admissions Contact 20935 Swenson Drive, Suite 450, Waukesha, WI 53186-4047.

DEVRY UNIVERSITY
Milwaukee, Wisconsin

Admissions Contact 100 East Wisconsin Avenue, Suite 2550, Milwaukee, WI 53202-4107. *Fax:* 414-278-0137. *E-mail:* ejohnson@keller.edu.

EDGEWOOD COLLEGE
Madison, Wisconsin

- **Independent Roman Catholic** comprehensive, founded 1927
- **Calendar** 4-1-4
- **Degrees** associate, bachelor's, and master's
- **Urban** 55-acre campus
- **Endowment** $5.0 million
- **Coed,** 1,909 undergraduate students, 76% full-time, 73% women, 27% men
- **Moderately difficult** entrance level, 80% of applicants were admitted

Undergraduates 1,448 full-time, 461 part-time. Students come from 16 states and territories, 22 other countries, 8% are from out of state, 2% African American, 2% Asian American or Pacific Islander, 1% Hispanic American, 0.4% Native American, 2% international, 12% transferred in, 20% live on campus. *Retention:* 73% of 2002 full-time freshmen returned.

Freshmen *Admission:* 1,060 applied, 852 admitted, 314 enrolled. *Average high school GPA:* 3.26. *Test scores:* SAT verbal scores over 500: 60%; SAT math scores over 500: 80%; ACT scores over 18: 91%; SAT verbal scores over 600: 20%; SAT math scores over 600: 20%; ACT scores over 24: 31%; ACT scores over 30: 4%.

Faculty *Total:* 235, 39% full-time, 48% with terminal degrees. *Student/faculty ratio:* 13:1.

Majors Accounting; art; art teacher education; art therapy; biology/biological sciences; business administration and management; chemistry; clinical laboratory science/medical technology; commercial and advertising art; criminal justice/law enforcement administration; cytotechnology; developmental and child psychology; dramatic/theatre arts; economics; education; elementary education; English; French; history; information science/studies; international relations and affairs; kindergarten/preschool education; liberal arts and sciences/liberal studies; mass communication/media; mathematics; music; natural sciences; nursing (registered nurse training); political science and government; pre-dentistry studies; pre-engineering; pre-law studies; pre-medical studies; pre-veterinary studies; psychology; public administration; public policy analysis; religious studies; social sciences; sociology; Spanish.

Academic Programs *Special study options:* academic remediation for entering students, adult/continuing education programs, advanced placement credit, independent study, off-campus study, part-time degree program, services for LD students, summer session for credit. *Unusual degree programs:* 3-2 engineering with University of Wisconsin–Madison.

Edgewood College (continued)

Library Oscar Rennebohm Library with 90,253 titles, 447 serial subscriptions, 4,359 audiovisual materials, an OPAC, a Web page.

Computers on Campus 140 computers available on campus for general student use. A campuswide network can be accessed from student residence rooms and from off campus. Internet access, online (class) registration, at least one staffed computer lab available. Computer purchase or lease plan available.

Student Life *Housing options:* coed, women-only, disabled students. Campus housing is university owned. Freshman applicants given priority for college housing. *Activities and organizations:* drama/theater group, student-run newspaper, choral group, Student Government Association, Student Programming Board, Resident Life Association, Chalk Talk, Student Nurses Association. *Campus security:* 24-hour emergency response devices and patrols, student patrols, late-night transport/escort service, controlled dormitory access. *Student services:* health clinic, personal/psychological counseling.

Athletics Member NCAA. All Division III. *Intercollegiate sports:* baseball M, basketball M/W, cross-country running M/W, golf M/W, soccer M/W, softball W, tennis M/W, volleyball W. *Intramural sports:* basketball M/W, bowling M/W, golf M/W, soccer M/W, softball M/W, table tennis M/W, volleyball M/W, weight lifting M/W.

Standardized Tests *Required:* SAT I or ACT (for admission).

Costs (2003–04) *Comprehensive fee:* $20,450 includes full-time tuition ($15,100) and room and board ($5350). Full-time tuition and fees vary according to program. Part-time tuition: $457 per credit. Part-time tuition and fees vary according to course load and program. *College room only:* $2708. Room and board charges vary according to housing facility and location. *Waivers:* employees or children of employees.

Financial Aid Of all full-time matriculated undergraduates who enrolled in 2002, 1,068 applied for aid, 931 were judged to have need, 134 had their need fully met. 347 Federal Work-Study jobs (averaging $1441). 795 state and other part-time jobs (averaging $1884). In 2002, 245 non-need-based awards were made. *Average percent of need met:* 75%. *Average financial aid package:* $10,888. *Average non-need-based aid:* $8015. *Average indebtedness upon graduation:* $19,551.

Applying *Options:* deferred entrance. *Application fee:* $25. *Required:* high school transcript, minimum 2.5 GPA. *Required for some:* essay or personal statement, 2 letters of recommendation, interview. *Application deadline:* rolling (freshmen), rolling (transfers). *Notification:* continuous (freshmen), continuous (transfers).

Admissions Contact Mr. Jim Krystofiak, Associate Director of Admissions, Edgewood College, 1000 Edgewood College Drive, Madison, WI 53711-1997. *Phone:* 608-663-2265. *Toll-free phone:* 800-444-4861 Ext. 2294. *Fax:* 608-663-3291. *E-mail:* admissions@edgewood.edu.

■ *See page 1570 for a narrative description.*

HERZING COLLEGE
Madison, Wisconsin

- **Proprietary** primarily 2-year, founded 1948, part of Herzing Institutes, Inc.
- **Calendar** semesters
- **Degrees** diplomas, associate, and bachelor's
- **Suburban** campus with easy access to Milwaukee
- **Coed, primarily men**
- **Moderately difficult** entrance level

Faculty *Student/faculty ratio:* 13:1.

Student Life *Campus security:* 24-hour emergency response devices.

Costs (2003–04) *Tuition:* $10,000 full-time. Full-time tuition and fees vary according to course level and program. Part-time tuition and fees vary according to course level and program. *Required fees:* $100 full-time.

Financial Aid *Financial aid deadline:* 6/30.

Applying *Options:* common application, electronic application, early admission. *Required:* high school transcript, interview.

Admissions Contact Ms. Renee Herzing, Admissions Director, Herzing College, 5218 East Terrace Drive, Madison, WI 53718. *Phone:* 608-249-6611. *Toll-free phone:* 800-582-1227. *E-mail:* mailbag@msn.herzing.edu.

ITT TECHNICAL INSTITUTE
Green Bay, Wisconsin

- **Proprietary** primarily 2-year, founded 2000, part of ITT Educational Services, Inc.
- **Calendar** quarters
- **Degrees** associate and bachelor's
- **Coed**
- **Minimally difficult** entrance level

Standardized Tests *Required:* (for admission).

Costs (2003–04) *Tuition:* $347 per credit hour part-time.

Applying *Options:* deferred entrance. *Application fee:* $100. *Required:* high school transcript, interview. *Recommended:* letters of recommendation.

Admissions Contact Mr. Raymond Sweetman, ITT Technical Institute, 470 Security Boulevard, Green Bay, WI 54313. *Phone:* 920-662-9000. *Fax:* 920-662-9384.

ITT TECHNICAL INSTITUTE
Greenfield, Wisconsin

- **Proprietary** primarily 2-year, founded 1968, part of ITT Educational Services, Inc.
- **Calendar** quarters
- **Degrees** associate and bachelor's
- **Suburban** campus with easy access to Milwaukee
- **Coed**
- **Minimally difficult** entrance level

Standardized Tests *Required:* Wonderlic aptitude test (for admission).

Costs (2003–04) *Tuition:* $347 per credit hour part-time.

Applying *Options:* deferred entrance. *Application fee:* $100. *Required:* high school transcript, interview. *Recommended:* letters of recommendation.

Admissions Contact Mr. Al Hedin, Director of Recruitment, ITT Technical Institute, 6300 West Layton Avenue, Greenfield, WI 53220. *Phone:* 414-282-9494. *Fax:* 414-282-9698.

LAKELAND COLLEGE
Sheboygan, Wisconsin

- **Independent** comprehensive, founded 1862, affiliated with United Church of Christ
- **Calendar** 4-4-1
- **Degrees** bachelor's and master's
- **Rural** 240-acre campus with easy access to Milwaukee
- **Endowment** $8.2 million
- **Coed,** 3,399 undergraduate students, 40% full-time, 61% women, 39% men
- **Minimally difficult** entrance level, 68% of applicants were admitted

Undergraduates 1,346 full-time, 2,053 part-time. Students come from 42 states and territories, 40 other countries, 9% are from out of state, 6% African American, 3% Asian American or Pacific Islander, 2% Hispanic American, 0.7% Native American, 5% international, 11% transferred in, 60% live on campus. *Retention:* 73% of 2002 full-time freshmen returned.

Freshmen *Admission:* 584 applied, 399 admitted, 155 enrolled. *Average high school GPA:* 2.82. *Test scores:* ACT scores over 18: 66%; ACT scores over 24: 15%; ACT scores over 30: 1%.

Faculty *Total:* 65, 74% full-time, 55% with terminal degrees. *Student/faculty ratio:* 19:1.

Majors Accounting; art; biochemistry; biology/biological sciences; business administration and management; business teacher education; chemistry; computer science; criminal justice/safety; elementary education; English; English composition; German; history; international business/trade/commerce; kindergarten/preschool education; marketing/marketing management; mathematics; middle school education; music; music teacher education; non-profit management; psychology; religious studies; resort management; science teacher education; secondary education; sociology; Spanish.

Academic Programs *Special study options:* academic remediation for entering students, adult/continuing education programs, advanced placement credit, distance learning, English as a second language, honors programs, independent study, internships, off-campus study, part-time degree program, services for LD students, study abroad, summer session for credit. *Unusual degree programs:* 3-2 engineering with University of Wisconsin–Madison; nursing with Bellin College of Nursing.

Library Esch Memorial Library with 64,970 titles, 317 serial subscriptions, 647 audiovisual materials, a Web page.

Computers on Campus 100 computers available on campus for general student use. A campuswide network can be accessed from student residence rooms and from off campus. Internet access, at least one staffed computer lab available. Computer purchase or lease plan available.

Student Life *Housing:* on-campus residence required through senior year. *Options:* coed, men-only, women-only. Campus housing is university owned. Freshman campus housing is guaranteed. *Activities and organizations:* drama/theater group, student-run newspaper, choral group, Lakeland College Campus

Activities Board, Student Association, Black Student Union, Mortar Board, Global Students Association. *Campus security:* 24-hour emergency response devices, student patrols, late-night transport/escort service, controlled dormitory access. *Student services:* health clinic, personal/psychological counseling.

Athletics Member NCAA. All Division III. *Intercollegiate sports:* baseball M, basketball M/W, cross-country running M/W, football M, golf M/W, soccer M/W, softball W, tennis M/W, volleyball M(c)/W, wrestling M.

Standardized Tests *Required:* SAT I or ACT (for admission).

Costs (2004–05) *Comprehensive fee:* $20,555 includes full-time tuition ($14,265), mandatory fees ($635), and room and board ($5655). Full-time tuition and fees vary according to location. Part-time tuition: $1585 per course. Part-time tuition and fees vary according to class time and location. *College room only:* $2655. Room and board charges vary according to board plan and housing facility. *Payment plan:* installment. *Waivers:* employees or children of employees.

Financial Aid Of all full-time matriculated undergraduates who enrolled in 2002, 910 applied for aid, 804 were judged to have need, 258 had their need fully met. 250 Federal Work-Study jobs (averaging $1400). 38 state and other part-time jobs (averaging $1200). In 2002, 246 non-need-based awards were made. *Average percent of need met:* 83%. *Average financial aid package:* $9976. *Average need-based loan:* $3572. *Average need-based gift aid:* $7234. *Average non-need-based aid:* $6595. *Average indebtedness upon graduation:* $16,560. *Financial aid deadline:* 7/1.

Applying *Options:* common application, electronic application, deferred entrance. *Application fee:* $20. *Required:* essay or personal statement, high school transcript, minimum 2.0 GPA. *Required for some:* interview. *Recommended:* letters of recommendation. *Application deadline:* 9/1 (freshmen). *Notification:* continuous until 9/1 (freshmen), continuous (transfers).

Admissions Contact Lakeland College, PO Box 359, Nash Visitors Center, Sheboygan, WI 53082-0359. *Phone:* 920-565-1588. *Toll-free phone:* 800-242-3347. *Fax:* 920-565-1206. *E-mail:* admissions@lakeland.edu.

LAWRENCE UNIVERSITY

Appleton, Wisconsin

- **Independent** 4-year, founded 1847
- **Calendar** trimesters
- **Degree** bachelor's
- **Small-town** 84-acre campus
- **Endowment** $164.4 million
- **Coed,** 1,407 undergraduate students, 95% full-time, 53% women, 47% men
- **Very difficult** entrance level, 58% of applicants were admitted

Lawrence is committed to development of intellect and talent, acquisition of knowledge and understanding, and cultivation of judgment and values. Research opportunities and independent study with faculty members, an academic honor code, a conservatory of music, a freshman seminar that focuses on developing communication and analysis skills, and weekend retreats to the college's 425-acre estate on Lake Michigan are among the programs that contribute to "the Lawrence Difference."

Undergraduates 1,342 full-time, 65 part-time. Students come from 49 states and territories, 51 other countries, 58% are from out of state, 2% African American, 2% Asian American or Pacific Islander, 3% Hispanic American, 0.2% Native American, 11% international, 2% transferred in, 98% live on campus.

Freshmen *Admission:* 2,044 applied, 1,192 admitted, 356 enrolled. *Average high school GPA:* 3.67. *Test scores:* SAT verbal scores over 500: 93%; SAT math scores over 500: 96%; ACT scores over 18: 99%; SAT verbal scores over 600: 63%; SAT math scores over 600: 62%; ACT scores over 24: 84%; SAT verbal scores over 700: 19%; SAT math scores over 700: 18%; ACT scores over 30: 30%.

Faculty *Total:* 166, 78% full-time, 79% with terminal degrees. *Student/faculty ratio:* 11:1.

Majors Ancient/classical Greek; anthropology; archeology; art history, criticism and conservation; art teacher education; Asian studies (East); biochemistry; biology/biological sciences; chemistry; Chinese; classics and classical languages related; classics and languages, literatures and linguistics; cognitive psychology and psycholinguistics; cognitive science; computer science; dramatic/theatre arts; ecology; economics; English; environmental studies; ethnic, cultural minority, and gender studies related; fine/studio arts; French; geology/earth science; German; history; international economics; international relations and affairs; Japanese; Latin; linguistics; mathematics; mathematics and computer science; music; music pedagogy; music performance; music teacher education; music theory and composition; neuroscience; philosophy; physics; piano and organ; political science and government; pre-dentistry studies; pre-law studies; pre-medical studies; pre-veterinary studies; psychology; religious studies; Russian; Russian studies; secondary education; Slavic studies; social psychology; Spanish; violin, viola, guitar and other stringed instruments; voice and opera; wind/percussion instruments.

Academic Programs *Special study options:* advanced placement credit, double majors, independent study, internships, off-campus study, services for LD students, student-designed majors, study abroad. *Unusual degree programs:* 3-2 engineering with Rensselaer Polytechnic Institute, University of Michigan, Washington University in St. Louis, Columbia University; forestry with Duke University; nursing with Rush University; medical technology with Rush University, occupational therapy with Washington University.

Library Seeley G. Mudd Library with 376,814 titles, 1,586 serial subscriptions, 21,086 audiovisual materials, an OPAC, a Web page.

Computers on Campus 160 computers available on campus for general student use. A campuswide network can be accessed from student residence rooms. At least one staffed computer lab available.

Student Life *Housing:* on-campus residence required through senior year. *Options:* coed, women-only, cooperative. Campus housing is university owned. Freshman campus housing is guaranteed. *Activities and organizations:* drama/theater group, student-run newspaper, radio station, choral group, Lawrence Swing Dancers, Lawrence International, Outdoor Recreation Club, Lawrence Christian Fellowship, Lambda Sigma, national fraternities, national sororities. *Campus security:* 24-hour emergency response devices, student patrols, late-night transport/escort service, controlled dormitory access, evening patrols by trained security personnel. *Student services:* health clinic, personal/psychological counseling.

Athletics Member NCAA. All Division III. *Intercollegiate sports:* baseball M, basketball M/W, crew M(c)/W(c), cross-country running M/W, fencing M/W, football M, golf M, ice hockey M/W(c), lacrosse M(c)/W(c), rugby W(c), soccer M/W, softball W, swimming M/W, tennis M/W, track and field M/W, ultimate Frisbee M(c)/W(c), volleyball M(c)/W, wrestling M. *Intramural sports:* badminton M/W, basketball M/W, bowling M/W, cheerleading W, cross-country running M/W, equestrian sports M(c)/W(c), fencing M/W, football M/W, golf M/W, racquetball M/W, sailing M/W, skiing (cross-country) M/W, skiing (downhill) M/W, squash M/W, swimming M/W, table tennis M/W, tennis M/W, track and field M/W, volleyball M/W, weight lifting M/W, wrestling M.

Standardized Tests *Required:* SAT I or ACT (for admission).

Costs (2003–04) *Comprehensive fee:* $30,741 includes full-time tuition ($24,900), mandatory fees ($189), and room and board ($5652). *Room and board:* Room and board charges vary according to board plan. *Payment plan:* installment. *Waivers:* employees or children of employees.

Financial Aid Of all full-time matriculated undergraduates who enrolled in 2003, 940 applied for aid, 811 were judged to have need, 811 had their need fully met. 682 Federal Work-Study jobs (averaging $2076). 194 state and other part-time jobs (averaging $2507). In 2003, 419 non-need-based awards were made. *Average percent of need met:* 100%. *Average financial aid package:* $21,596. *Average need-based loan:* $4888. *Average need-based gift aid:* $15,380. *Average non-need-based aid:* $9662. *Average indebtedness upon graduation:* $17,366.

Applying *Options:* common application, electronic application, early admission, early decision, early action, deferred entrance. *Application fee:* $30. *Required:* essay or personal statement, high school transcript, 2 letters of recommendation, audition for music program. *Recommended:* minimum 3.0 GPA, interview. *Application deadline:* 1/15 (freshmen), rolling (transfers). *Early decision:* 11/15. *Notification:* 4/1 (freshmen), 12/1 (early decision), 1/15 (early action), continuous (transfers).

Admissions Contact Lawrence University, PO Box 599, Appleton, WI 54912-0599. *Phone:* 920-832-6500. *Toll-free phone:* 800-227-0982. *Fax:* 920-832-6782. *E-mail:* excel@lawrence.edu.

■ *See page 1852 for a narrative description.*

MARANATHA BAPTIST BIBLE COLLEGE

Watertown, Wisconsin

- **Independent Baptist** comprehensive, founded 1968
- **Calendar** semesters
- **Degrees** certificates, associate, bachelor's, and master's
- **Small-town** 60-acre campus with easy access to Milwaukee
- **Endowment** $151,276
- **Coed**
- **Noncompetitive** entrance level

Faculty *Student/faculty ratio:* 16:1.

Student Life *Campus security:* student patrols, late-night transport/escort service, controlled dormitory access.

Athletics Member NCAA, NCCAA. All NCAA Division III.

Standardized Tests *Recommended:* ACT (for admission).

Costs (2003–04) *Comprehensive fee:* $12,300 includes full-time tuition ($7040), mandatory fees ($740), and room and board ($4520). Part-time tuition: $220 per semester hour.

Maranatha Baptist Bible College (continued)

Financial Aid Of all full-time matriculated undergraduates who enrolled in 2002, 628 applied for aid, 573 were judged to have need, 35 had their need fully met. 290 state and other part-time jobs (averaging $2811). In 2002, 20. *Average percent of need met:* 32. *Average financial aid package:* $2868. *Average need-based loan:* $3317. *Average need-based gift aid:* $923. *Average non-need-based aid:* $796. *Average indebtedness upon graduation:* $13,076.

Applying *Options:* common application, early admission, deferred entrance. *Application fee:* $40. *Required:* essay or personal statement, high school transcript, 3 letters of recommendation.

Admissions Contact Mr. James H. Harrison, Director of Admissions, Maranatha Baptist Bible College, 745 West Main Street, Watertown, WI 53094. *Phone:* 920-206-2327. *Toll-free phone:* 800-622-2947. *Fax:* 920-261-9109. *E-mail:* admissions@mbbc.edu.

MARIAN COLLEGE OF FOND DU LAC

Fond du Lac, Wisconsin

- **Independent Roman Catholic** comprehensive, founded 1936
- **Calendar** semesters
- **Degrees** bachelor's and master's
- **Small-town** 77-acre campus with easy access to Milwaukee
- **Endowment** $6.5 million
- **Coed,** 1,856 undergraduate students, 66% full-time, 70% women, 30% men
- **Moderately difficult** entrance level, 77% of applicants were admitted

Marian College distinguishes itself from other institutions with extensive clinical, internship, and cooperative education experiences. More than 95% of students gain valuable applied experiences in their chosen field of study. As a result of these experiences, students develop the knowledge and skills necessary to be competent and marketable in their chosen fields. Marian students enjoy the benefits of a truly personal education and make their home away from home in unique housing options, including residence halls, town houses, and courtyard suites.

Undergraduates 1,217 full-time, 639 part-time. Students come from 17 states and territories, 8 other countries, 6% are from out of state, 5% African American, 0.6% Asian American or Pacific Islander, 1% Hispanic American, 0.9% Native American, 2% international, 12% transferred in, 34% live on campus. *Retention:* 68% of 2002 full-time freshmen returned.

Freshmen *Admission:* 884 applied, 684 admitted, 251 enrolled. *Average high school GPA:* 2.96. *Test scores:* ACT scores over 18: 76%; ACT scores over 24: 17%; ACT scores over 30: 1%.

Faculty *Total:* 151, 50% full-time, 35% with terminal degrees. *Student/faculty ratio:* 15:1.

Majors Accounting; art teacher education; art therapy; biological and physical sciences; biology/biological sciences; biology teacher education; business administration and management; business/managerial economics; chemistry; chemistry teacher education; clinical laboratory science/medical technology; communication/speech communication and rhetoric; criminal justice/law enforcement administration; cytotechnology; education; elementary education; English; English/language arts teacher education; finance; fine/studio arts; foreign languages and literatures; history; history teacher education; information technology; international relations and affairs; kindergarten/preschool education; liberal arts and sciences/liberal studies; marketing/marketing management; mathematics; mathematics teacher education; medical radiologic technology; middle school education; music; music management and merchandising; music teacher education; nursing (registered nurse training); political science and government; pre-dentistry studies; pre-law studies; pre-medical studies; pre-veterinary studies; psychology; science teacher education; secondary education; social sciences; social work; sociology; Spanish; Spanish language teacher education; sport and fitness administration.

Academic Programs *Special study options:* academic remediation for entering students, accelerated degree program, adult/continuing education programs, advanced placement credit, cooperative education, distance learning, double majors, external degree program, honors programs, independent study, internships, part-time degree program, services for LD students, student-designed majors, study abroad, summer session for credit. *ROTC:* Army (b).

Library Cardinal Meyer Library with 91,708 titles, 698 serial subscriptions, 397 audiovisual materials, an OPAC, a Web page.

Computers on Campus 200 computers available on campus for general student use. A campuswide network can be accessed from student residence rooms. Internet access, online (class) registration, at least one staffed computer lab available.

Student Life *Housing options:* coed. Campus housing is university owned. Freshman campus housing is guaranteed. *Activities and organizations:* drama/theater group, student-run newspaper, choral group, Student Senate, Student Nurses Association, Student Education Association, arts and humanities club, Music Performance Organization, national fraternities, national sororities. *Campus security:* 24-hour emergency response devices and patrols, student patrols, late-night transport/escort service, controlled dormitory access. *Student services:* health clinic, personal/psychological counseling.

Athletics Member NCAA. All Division III. *Intercollegiate sports:* baseball M, basketball M/W, golf M/W, ice hockey M, soccer M/W, softball W, tennis M/W, volleyball W. *Intramural sports:* basketball M/W, bowling M/W, football M, skiing (downhill) M/W, tennis M/W, volleyball M/W.

Standardized Tests *Required:* SAT I or ACT (for admission).

Costs (2003–04) *Comprehensive fee:* $19,625 includes full-time tuition ($14,700), mandatory fees ($325), and room and board ($4600). Part-time tuition: $270 per credit. Part-time tuition and fees vary according to class time, course load, and program. *College room only:* $2600. Room and board charges vary according to board plan and housing facility. *Payment plan:* installment. *Waivers:* senior citizens and employees or children of employees.

Financial Aid Of all full-time matriculated undergraduates who enrolled in 2003, 1,123 applied for aid, 959 were judged to have need, 342 had their need fully met. 518 Federal Work-Study jobs (averaging $1900). 250 state and other part-time jobs (averaging $1000). In 2003, 144 non-need-based awards were made. *Average percent of need met:* 91%. *Average financial aid package:* $13,560. *Average need-based loan:* $4115. *Average need-based gift aid:* $5220. *Average non-need-based aid:* $4299. *Average indebtedness upon graduation:* $20,000.

Applying *Options:* common application, electronic application, deferred entrance. *Application fee:* $20. *Required:* high school transcript. *Required for some:* interview. *Recommended:* minimum 2.0 GPA, letters of recommendation. *Application deadline:* rolling (freshmen), rolling (transfers). *Notification:* continuous until 8/15 (freshmen), continuous until 8/15 (transfers).

Admissions Contact Stacey L. Akey, Dean of Admissions, Marian College of Fond du Lac, 45 South National Avenue, Fond du Lac, WI 54935. *Phone:* 920-923-7652. *Toll-free phone:* 800-2-MARIAN Ext. 7652. *Fax:* 920-923-8755. *E-mail:* admit@mariancollege.edu.

■ *See page 1926 for a narrative description.*

MARQUETTE UNIVERSITY

Milwaukee, Wisconsin

- **Independent Roman Catholic (Jesuit)** university, founded 1881
- **Calendar** semesters
- **Degrees** associate, bachelor's, master's, doctoral, first professional, post-master's, and postbachelor's certificates
- **Urban** 80-acre campus
- **Endowment** $203.4 million
- **Coed,** 7,775 undergraduate students, 93% full-time, 55% women, 45% men
- **Moderately difficult** entrance level, 83% of applicants were admitted

Undergraduates 7,242 full-time, 533 part-time. Students come from 54 states and territories, 80 other countries, 58% are from out of state, 5% African American, 4% Asian American or Pacific Islander, 4% Hispanic American, 0.3% Native American, 2% international, 3% transferred in, 50% live on campus. *Retention:* 89% of 2002 full-time freshmen returned.

Freshmen *Admission:* 8,232 applied, 6,817 admitted, 1,889 enrolled. *Test scores:* SAT verbal scores over 500: 86%; SAT math scores over 500: 84%; ACT scores over 18: 95%; SAT verbal scores over 600: 42%; SAT math scores over 600: 49%; ACT scores over 24: 65%; SAT verbal scores over 700: 7%; SAT math scores over 700: 9%; ACT scores over 30: 14%.

Faculty *Total:* 1,018, 57% full-time, 67% with terminal degrees. *Student/faculty ratio:* 15:1.

Majors Accounting; advertising; African-American/Black studies; anthropology; athletic training; audiology and speech-language pathology; biochemistry; biology/biological sciences; biomedical/medical engineering; biomedical sciences; broadcast journalism; business administration and management; business/managerial economics; chemistry; civil engineering; classics and languages, literatures and linguistics; clinical/medical laboratory technology; communication and journalism related; communication/speech communication and rhetoric; computational mathematics; computer engineering; computer science; creative writing; criminology; dental hygiene; dramatic/theatre arts; economics; education; education (specific subject areas) related; electrical, electronics and communications engineering; elementary education; engineering; engineering related; English; English/language arts teacher education; environmental/environmental health engineering; finance; foreign languages related; foreign language teacher education; French; German; history; history of philosophy; history related; human resources management; industrial engineering; information science/studies; intercultural/multicultural and diversity studies; interdisciplinary studies; international business/trade/commerce; international/global studies; international relations and affairs; journalism; kinesiology and exercise science; management information systems; marketing/marketing management; mass communication/media; mathematics; mathematics teacher education; mechanical engineering; middle school education; molecular biology; multi-/interdisciplinary studies related; nursing (registered nurse training); philosophy; physical therapy; physician assistant; physics; political science and government; pre-dentistry studies; pre-law studies; pre-medical studies; psychology; public relations/image management; religious studies; science teacher education; secondary education; social science teacher education; social studies teacher education; social work; sociology; Spanish; speech and rhetoric; statistics; women's studies.

Academic Programs *Special study options:* adult/continuing education programs, advanced placement credit, cooperative education, double majors, English as a second language, honors programs, internships, off-campus study, part-time degree program, services for LD students, study abroad, summer session for credit. *ROTC:* Army (b), Navy (b), Air Force (b).

Library Memorial Library plus 2 others with 1.1 million titles, 5,894 serial subscriptions, 9,332 audiovisual materials, an OPAC, a Web page.

Computers on Campus 1003 computers available on campus for general student use. A campuswide network can be accessed from student residence rooms and from off campus. Internet access, at least one staffed computer lab available. Computer purchase or lease plan available.

Student Life *Housing:* on-campus residence required through sophomore year. *Options:* coed, men-only, women-only, disabled students. Campus housing is university owned. *Activities and organizations:* drama/theater group, student-run newspaper, radio and television station, choral group, student government, club sports, community service organizations, band/jazz/orchestra, Residence Hall Association, national fraternities, national sororities. *Campus security:* 24-hour emergency response devices and patrols, student patrols, late-night transport/escort service, 24-hour desk attendants in residence halls. *Student services:* health clinic, personal/psychological counseling.

Athletics Member NCAA. All Division I. *Intercollegiate sports:* baseball M(c), basketball M(s)/W(s), cheerleading M/W, crew M(c)/W(c), cross-country running M(s)/W(s), fencing M(c)/W(c), football M(c), golf M(s), lacrosse M(c), rugby M(c)/W(c), skiing (downhill) M(c)/W(c), soccer M(s)/W(s), softball W(c), swimming M(c)/W(c), tennis M(s)/W(s), track and field M(s)/W(s), volleyball M(c)/W(s). *Intramural sports:* badminton M/W, basketball M/W, football W, golf M/W, racquetball M/W, rock climbing M/W, soccer M/W, softball M/W, squash M/W, tennis M/W, track and field M/W, ultimate Frisbee M/W, volleyball M/W, water polo M/W, weight lifting M/W.

Standardized Tests *Required:* SAT I or ACT (for admission).

Costs (2003–04) *Comprehensive fee:* $27,710 includes full-time tuition ($20,350), mandatory fees ($360), and room and board ($7000). Full-time tuition and fees vary according to course load, program, and reciprocity agreements. Part-time tuition: $600 per credit. Part-time tuition and fees vary according to program. *College room only:* $4550. Room and board charges vary according to board plan, housing facility, and location. *Payment plan:* installment. *Waivers:* adult students, senior citizens, and employees or children of employees.

Financial Aid Of all full-time matriculated undergraduates who enrolled in 2003, 5,184 applied for aid, 4,345 were judged to have need, 2,088 had their need fully met. 300 Federal Work-Study jobs (averaging $2500). In 2003, 1498 non-need-based awards were made. *Average percent of need met:* 86%. *Average financial aid package:* $16,853. *Average need-based loan:* $5591. *Average need-based gift aid:* $10,774. *Average non-need-based aid:* $6674. *Average indebtedness upon graduation:* $22,924.

Applying *Options:* common application, electronic application, early admission, deferred entrance. *Application fee:* $30. *Required:* essay or personal statement, high school transcript, minimum 2.5 GPA, 1 letter of recommendation. *Recommended:* minimum 3.4 GPA. *Application deadline:* rolling (freshmen), rolling (transfers). *Notification:* continuous (freshmen), continuous (transfers).

Admissions Contact Mr. Robert Blust, Dean of Undergraduate Admissions, Marquette University, PO Box 1881, Milwaukee, WI 53201-1881. *Phone:* 414-288-7004. *Toll-free phone:* 800-222-6544. *Fax:* 414-288-3764. *E-mail:* admissions@marquette.edu.

MILWAUKEE INSTITUTE OF ART AND DESIGN

Milwaukee, Wisconsin

- **Independent** 4-year, founded 1974
- **Calendar** semesters
- **Degree** bachelor's
- **Urban** campus
- **Endowment** $1.8 million
- **Coed,** 629 undergraduate students, 92% full-time, 54% women, 46% men
- **Moderately difficult** entrance level, 83% of applicants were admitted

Undergraduates 578 full-time, 51 part-time. Students come from 16 states and territories, 5 other countries, 28% are from out of state, 3% African American, 3% Asian American or Pacific Islander, 7% Hispanic American, 0.8% Native American, 2% international, 7% transferred in, 22% live on campus. *Retention:* 54% of 2002 full-time freshmen returned.

Freshmen *Admission:* 360 applied, 298 admitted, 161 enrolled. *Average high school GPA:* 3.06. *Test scores:* ACT scores over 18: 80%; ACT scores over 24: 38%; ACT scores over 30: 2%.

Faculty *Total:* 93, 35% full-time. *Student/faculty ratio:* 12:1.

Majors Art; commercial and advertising art; drawing; industrial design; interior design; painting; photography; printmaking; sculpture.

Academic Programs *Special study options:* academic remediation for entering students, adult/continuing education programs, advanced placement credit, cooperative education, double majors, independent study, internships, off-campus study, services for LD students, study abroad, summer session for credit.

Library 23,000 titles, 84 serial subscriptions, 360 audiovisual materials, an OPAC, a Web page.

Computers on Campus 110 computers available on campus for general student use. A campuswide network can be accessed. Internet access, at least one staffed computer lab available.

Student Life *Housing:* on-campus residence required for freshman year. *Options:* coed. Campus housing is university owned. Freshman applicants given priority for college housing. *Activities and organizations:* drama/theater group, student government, Student Gallery Committee, Student Activities Committee, Minority Student Organization, community service. *Campus security:* 24-hour emergency response devices, late-night transport/escort service. *Student services:* health clinic, personal/psychological counseling.

Standardized Tests *Recommended:* SAT I or ACT (for placement).

Costs (2003–04) *Comprehensive fee:* $26,701 includes full-time tuition ($19,900), mandatory fees ($130), and room and board ($6671). Part-time tuition and fees vary according to course load. *Room and board:* Room and board charges vary according to board plan. *Payment plan:* deferred payment. *Waivers:* employees or children of employees.

Financial Aid Of all full-time matriculated undergraduates who enrolled in 2002, 476 applied for aid, 454 were judged to have need, 119 had their need fully met. In 2002, 65 non-need-based awards were made. *Average percent of need met:* 76%. *Average financial aid package:* $16,857. *Average need-based loan:* $7756. *Average need-based gift aid:* $8890. *Average non-need-based aid:* $7344. *Average indebtedness upon graduation:* $19,328. *Financial aid deadline:* 3/1.

Applying *Options:* common application, electronic application, deferred entrance. *Application fee:* $25. *Required:* essay or personal statement, high school transcript, interview, portfolio. *Required for some:* letters of recommendation. *Recommended:* minimum 2.0 GPA. *Application deadline:* rolling (freshmen), rolling (transfers).

Admissions Contact Mr. Mark Fetherston, Director of Admissions, Milwaukee Institute of Art and Design, 273 East Erie Street, Milwaukee, WI 53202. *Phone:* 414-847-3259. *Toll-free phone:* 888-749-MIAD. *Fax:* 414-291-8077. *E-mail:* admissions@miad.edu.

MILWAUKEE SCHOOL OF ENGINEERING

Milwaukee, Wisconsin

- **Independent** comprehensive, founded 1903
- **Calendar** quarters
- **Degrees** bachelor's and master's
- **Urban** 15-acre campus
- **Endowment** $42.1 million
- **Coed, primarily men,** 2,101 undergraduate students, 84% full-time, 17% women, 83% men
- **Moderately difficult** entrance level, 65% of applicants were admitted

Undergraduates 1,762 full-time, 339 part-time. Students come from 31 states and territories, 24 other countries, 31% are from out of state, 3% African American, 3% Asian American or Pacific Islander, 2% Hispanic American, 0.3% Native American, 2% international, 7% transferred in, 52% live on campus. *Retention:* 74% of 2002 full-time freshmen returned.

Freshmen *Admission:* 1,809 applied, 1,177 admitted, 439 enrolled. *Average high school GPA:* 3.48. *Test scores:* SAT verbal scores over 500: 89%; SAT math scores over 500: 93%; ACT scores over 18: 99%; SAT verbal scores over 600: 43%; SAT math scores over 600: 61%; ACT scores over 24: 75%; SAT verbal scores over 700: 9%; SAT math scores over 700: 16%; ACT scores over 30: 15%.

Faculty *Total:* 294, 43% full-time, 38% with terminal degrees. *Student/faculty ratio:* 11:1.

Majors Architectural engineering; biomedical/medical engineering; business administration and management; business/commerce; communication and journalism related; computer engineering; computer software engineering; construction management; electrical, electronic and communications engineering technology; electrical, electronics and communications engineering; industrial

Milwaukee School of Engineering (continued)
engineering; international business/trade/commerce; management information systems; mechanical engineering; mechanical engineering/mechanical technology; nursing (registered nurse training).

Academic Programs *Special study options:* academic remediation for entering students, accelerated degree program, adult/continuing education programs, advanced placement credit, distance learning, double majors, independent study, internships, part-time degree program, services for LD students, study abroad, summer session for credit. *ROTC:* Army (c), Navy (c), Air Force (c).

Library Walter Schroeder Library with 56,044 titles, 416 serial subscriptions, 852 audiovisual materials, an OPAC, a Web page.

Computers on Campus 105 computers available on campus for general student use. A campuswide network can be accessed from student residence rooms and from off campus that provide access to e-mail. Internet access, at least one staffed computer lab available. Computer purchase or lease plan available.

Student Life *Housing:* on-campus residence required through sophomore year. *Options:* coed, disabled students. Campus housing is university owned. Freshman campus housing is guaranteed. *Activities and organizations:* drama/theater group, student-run newspaper, radio station, Architectural Engineering and Construction Management Societies, Student Athletic Advisory Committee, Greek Council, MAGE, Student Government, national fraternities, national sororities. *Campus security:* 24-hour emergency response devices and patrols, late-night transport/escort service, controlled dormitory access. *Student services:* health clinic, personal/psychological counseling.

Athletics Member NCAA. All Division III. *Intercollegiate sports:* baseball M, basketball M/W, cross-country running M/W, golf M/W, ice hockey M, soccer M/W, softball W, tennis M/W, track and field M/W, volleyball M/W, wrestling M. *Intramural sports:* basketball M/W, bowling M(c)/W(c), football M/W, soccer M/W, softball M/W, ultimate Frisbee M/W, volleyball M/W.

Standardized Tests *Required:* SAT I or ACT (for admission).

Costs (2003–04) *Comprehensive fee:* $28,479 includes full-time tuition ($23,034) and room and board ($5445). Full-time tuition and fees vary according to student level. Part-time tuition: $402 per quarter hour. Part-time tuition and fees vary according to course load. *College room only:* $3500. Room and board charges vary according to board plan and housing facility. *Payment plan:* installment. *Waivers:* employees or children of employees.

Financial Aid Of all full-time matriculated undergraduates who enrolled in 2002, 1,625 applied for aid, 1,501 were judged to have need, 168 had their need fully met. In 2002, 327 non-need-based awards were made. *Average percent of need met:* 62%. *Average financial aid package:* $13,375. *Average need-based loan:* $3347. *Average need-based gift aid:* $10,538. *Average non-need-based aid:* $6201. *Average indebtedness upon graduation:* $32,567.

Applying *Options:* common application, electronic application, deferred entrance. *Application fee:* $25. *Required:* high school transcript, minimum 2.5 GPA. *Required for some:* essay or personal statement, interview. *Application deadline:* rolling (freshmen), rolling (transfers). *Notification:* continuous (freshmen), continuous (transfers).

Admissions Contact Mr. Paul Borens, Director, Admission, Milwaukee School of Engineering, 1025 North Broadway, Milwaukee, WI 53202-3109. *Phone:* 414-277-6765. *Toll-free phone:* 800-332-6763. *Fax:* 414-277-7475. *E-mail:* explore@msoe.edu.

■ *See page 1996 for a narrative description.*

MOUNT MARY COLLEGE
Milwaukee, Wisconsin

- **Independent Roman Catholic** comprehensive, founded 1913
- **Calendar** semesters
- **Degrees** bachelor's, master's, and postbachelor's certificates
- **Urban** 80-acre campus
- **Endowment** $10.4 million
- **Women only,** 1,371 undergraduate students, 52% full-time
- **Moderately difficult** entrance level, 78% of applicants were admitted

Undergraduates 708 full-time, 663 part-time. Students come from 7 states and territories, 6 other countries, 3% are from out of state, 17% African American, 4% Asian American or Pacific Islander, 4% Hispanic American, 0.9% Native American, 0.5% international, 15% transferred in, 11% live on campus. *Retention:* 68% of 2002 full-time freshmen returned.

Freshmen *Admission:* 108 enrolled. *Average high school GPA:* 3.05. *Test scores:* SAT verbal scores over 500: 100%; SAT math scores over 500: 50%; ACT scores over 18: 74%; SAT verbal scores over 600: 50%; ACT scores over 24: 23%; ACT scores over 30: 1%.

Faculty *Total:* 192, 35% full-time, 39% with terminal degrees. *Student/faculty ratio:* 14:1.

Majors Accounting; art; art teacher education; art therapy; behavioral sciences; bilingual and multilingual education; biology/biological sciences; biology teacher education; business administration and management; business teacher education; chemistry; commercial and advertising art; communication/speech communication and rhetoric; computer science; corrections and criminal justice related; dietetics; education; elementary education; English; English/language arts teacher education; fashion/apparel design; fashion merchandising; French; history; interior design; international relations and affairs; kindergarten/preschool education; marketing/marketing management; mathematics; mathematics teacher education; music; music teacher education; nursing (registered nurse training); occupational therapy; philosophy; pre-dentistry studies; pre-law studies; pre-medical studies; pre-veterinary studies; psychology; public relations/image management; religious education; religious studies; secondary education; social work; Spanish; technical and business writing.

Academic Programs *Special study options:* academic remediation for entering students, accelerated degree program, adult/continuing education programs, advanced placement credit, double majors, honors programs, independent study, internships, part-time degree program, services for LD students, student-designed majors, study abroad, summer session for credit. *ROTC:* Army (c). *Unusual degree programs:* 3-2 dentistry with Marquette University.

Library Haggerty Library with 113,006 titles, 500 serial subscriptions, 9,832 audiovisual materials, an OPAC, a Web page.

Computers on Campus 150 computers available on campus for general student use. A campuswide network can be accessed from student residence rooms and from off campus. Internet access, at least one staffed computer lab available.

Student Life *Housing options:* women-only. Campus housing is university owned. Freshman campus housing is guaranteed. *Activities and organizations:* drama/theater group, student-run newspaper, choral group, Department Affiliated Clubs, Campus Ministry, Student Athletics, Student Government. *Campus security:* 24-hour patrols, late-night transport/escort service, controlled dormitory access. *Student services:* health clinic, personal/psychological counseling, women's center.

Athletics *Intercollegiate sports:* basketball W, cheerleading M/W, soccer W, softball W, tennis W, volleyball W. *Intramural sports:* basketball W, bowling W, golf W, skiing (cross-country) W, soccer W, swimming W, tennis W, track and field W, volleyball W.

Standardized Tests *Required:* SAT I or ACT (for admission).

Costs (2003–04) *Comprehensive fee:* $20,370 includes full-time tuition ($15,100), mandatory fees ($170), and room and board ($5100). Part-time tuition: $440 per credit. Part-time tuition and fees vary according to course load. *Required fees:* $43 per term part-time. *Room and board:* Room and board charges vary according to board plan. *Payment plan:* installment. *Waivers:* senior citizens and employees or children of employees.

Financial Aid Of all full-time matriculated undergraduates who enrolled in 2003, 494 applied for aid, 441 were judged to have need, 90 had their need fully met. 267 Federal Work-Study jobs (averaging $1500). 73 state and other part-time jobs (averaging $1200). In 2003, 131 non-need-based awards were made. *Average percent of need met:* 71%. *Average financial aid package:* $11,347. *Average need-based loan:* $4194. *Average need-based gift aid:* $6983. *Average non-need-based aid:* $6037. *Average indebtedness upon graduation:* $20,715.

Applying *Options:* common application, electronic application, deferred entrance. *Application fee:* $25. *Required:* high school transcript, minimum 2.5 GPA. *Required for some:* essay or personal statement, 2 letters of recommendation. *Recommended:* interview. *Application deadline:* rolling (freshmen), rolling (transfers). *Notification:* continuous (freshmen), continuous (transfers).

Admissions Contact Ms. Amy Dobson, Director of Enrollment, Mount Mary College, 2900 North Menomonee River Parkway, Milwaukee, WI 53222-4597. *Phone:* 414-258-4810 Ext. 360. *Fax:* 414-256-1205. *E-mail:* admiss@mtmary.edu.

■ *See page 2044 for a narrative description.*

NORTHLAND COLLEGE
Ashland, Wisconsin

- **Independent** 4-year, founded 1892, affiliated with United Church of Christ
- **Calendar** 4-4-1
- **Degree** bachelor's
- **Small-town** 130-acre campus
- **Endowment** $15.4 million
- **Coed,** 750 undergraduate students, 95% full-time, 54% women, 46% men
- **Moderately difficult** entrance level, 73% of applicants were admitted

Undergraduates 711 full-time, 39 part-time. Students come from 43 states and territories, 11 other countries, 65% are from out of state, 1% African American, 0.5% Asian American or Pacific Islander, 2% Hispanic American, 2% Native American, 3% international, 9% transferred in, 60% live on campus. *Retention:* 94% of 2002 full-time freshmen returned.

Freshmen *Admission:* 875 applied, 640 admitted, 115 enrolled. *Average high school GPA:* 3.50. *Test scores:* SAT verbal scores over 500: 79%; SAT math scores over 500: 78%; ACT scores over 18: 95%; SAT verbal scores over 600: 25%; SAT math scores over 600: 20%; ACT scores over 24: 50%; SAT verbal scores over 700: 5%; SAT math scores over 700: 5%; ACT scores over 30: 10%.

Faculty *Total:* 80, 54% full-time, 58% with terminal degrees. *Student/faculty ratio:* 13:1.

Majors American Indian/Native American studies; applied mathematics; art; art teacher education; atmospheric sciences and meteorology; biological and physical sciences; biology/biological sciences; business administration and management; business/managerial economics; chemistry; creative writing; ecology; economics; education; elementary education; English; environmental biology; environmental education; environmental studies; fine/studio arts; fish/game management; forestry; geology/earth science; history; hydrology and water resources science; information science/studies; interdisciplinary studies; land use planning and management; mathematics; middle school education; music; music teacher education; natural resources/conservation; natural resources management and policy; natural sciences; parks, recreation and leisure; parks, recreation and leisure facilities management; peace studies and conflict resolution; philosophy; predentistry studies; pre-law studies; pre-medical studies; pre-veterinary studies; psychology; religious studies; science teacher education; secondary education; social sciences; sociology; therapeutic recreation; veterinary sciences; wildlife and wildlands science and management; wildlife biology; zoology/animal biology.

Academic Programs *Special study options:* accelerated degree program, adult/continuing education programs, advanced placement credit, cooperative education, distance learning, double majors, honors programs, independent study, internships, off-campus study, part-time degree program, services for LD students, student-designed majors, study abroad, summer session for credit. *Unusual degree programs:* 3-2 engineering with Michigan Technological University, Washington University in St. Louis; forestry with Michigan Technological University.

Library Dexter Library with 75,000 titles, 260 serial subscriptions, an OPAC.

Computers on Campus 120 computers available on campus for general student use. A campuswide network can be accessed from student residence rooms and from off campus. Internet access, at least one staffed computer lab available.

Student Life *Housing:* on-campus residence required through sophomore year. *Options:* coed, men-only, women-only. Campus housing is university owned. Freshman campus housing is guaranteed. *Activities and organizations:* drama/theater group, student-run newspaper, radio station, choral group, Psi Chi, the National Honor Society in Psychology, Northland College Student Association, Native American Student Association, Northland Greens, "N" Club. *Campus security:* 24-hour emergency response devices, controlled dormitory access. *Student services:* health clinic, personal/psychological counseling, women's center.

Athletics Member NCAA, NAIA. All NCAA Division III. *Intercollegiate sports:* baseball M, basketball M/W, cross-country running M/W, ice hockey M, soccer M/W, softball W, volleyball W. *Intramural sports:* archery M/W, badminton M/W, basketball M/W, cross-country running M/W, football M/W, golf M/W, ice hockey M/W, lacrosse M, racquetball M/W, rugby M(c)/W(c), skiing (cross-country) M(c)/W(c), skiing (downhill) M(c)/W(c), soccer M/W, softball M/W, swimming M/W, table tennis M/W, tennis M/W, volleyball M/W, water polo M/W, weight lifting M/W.

Standardized Tests *Required:* SAT I or ACT (for admission).

Costs (2004–05) *Comprehensive fee:* $24,105 includes full-time tuition ($18,135), mandatory fees ($580), and room and board ($5390). Part-time tuition: $330 per credit. Part-time tuition and fees vary according to course load. *College room only:* $2170. Room and board charges vary according to board plan and housing facility. *Payment plan:* installment. *Waivers:* employees or children of employees.

Financial Aid Of all full-time matriculated undergraduates who enrolled in 2003, 669 applied for aid, 618 were judged to have need, 104 had their need fully met. 322 Federal Work-Study jobs (averaging $1375). 291 state and other part-time jobs (averaging $1547). In 2003, 51 non-need-based awards were made. *Average percent of need met:* 79%. *Average financial aid package:* $14,321. *Average need-based loan:* $3708. *Average need-based gift aid:* $8937. *Average non-need-based aid:* $7832. *Average indebtedness upon graduation:* $18,622.

Applying *Options:* common application, electronic application, early admission, deferred entrance. *Required:* essay or personal statement, high school transcript, 1 letter of recommendation. *Recommended:* minimum 2.0 GPA, interview. *Application deadlines:* 8/1 (freshmen), 8/1 (transfers). *Notification:* continuous (freshmen), continuous (transfers).

Admissions Contact Mr. Eric Peterson, Director of Admission, Northland College, 1411 Ellis Avenue, Ashland, WI 54806. *Phone:* 715-682-1224. *Toll-free phone:* 800-753-1840 (in-state); 800-753-1040 (out-of-state). *Fax:* 715-682-1258. *E-mail:* admit@northland.edu.

RIPON COLLEGE
Ripon, Wisconsin

- **Independent** 4-year, founded 1851
- **Calendar** semesters
- **Degree** bachelor's
- **Small-town** 250-acre campus with easy access to Milwaukee
- **Endowment** $33.9 million
- **Coed,** 998 undergraduate students, 98% full-time, 52% women, 48% men
- **Moderately difficult** entrance level, 84% of applicants were admitted

Undergraduates 978 full-time, 20 part-time. Students come from 33 states and territories, 14 other countries, 31% are from out of state, 2% African American, 2% Asian American or Pacific Islander, 4% Hispanic American, 0.7% Native American, 2% international, 2% transferred in, 90% live on campus. *Retention:* 84% of 2002 full-time freshmen returned.

Freshmen *Admission:* 959 applied, 809 admitted, 259 enrolled. *Average high school GPA:* 3.45. *Test scores:* SAT verbal scores over 500: 81%; SAT math scores over 500: 76%; ACT scores over 18: 97%; SAT verbal scores over 600: 51%; SAT math scores over 600: 46%; ACT scores over 24: 56%; SAT verbal scores over 700: 14%; SAT math scores over 700: 25%; ACT scores over 30: 11%.

Faculty *Total:* 75, 67% full-time, 80% with terminal degrees. *Student/faculty ratio:* 15:1.

Majors Anthropology; art; biochemistry; biology/biological sciences; business administration and management; chemistry; communication/speech communication and rhetoric; computer science; dramatic/theatre arts; early childhood education; economics; education; elementary education; English; environmental studies; French; German; history; interdisciplinary studies; Latin American studies; mathematics; music; music teacher education; philosophy; physical education teaching and coaching; physical sciences; physiological psychology/psychobiology; political science and government; pre-dentistry studies; pre-law studies; pre-medical studies; pre-veterinary studies; psychology; religious studies; Romance languages; secondary education; sociology; Spanish.

Academic Programs *Special study options:* accelerated degree program, advanced placement credit, double majors, internships, off-campus study, part-time degree program, services for LD students, student-designed majors, study abroad. *ROTC:* Army (b). *Unusual degree programs:* 3-2 engineering with Rensselaer Polytechnic Institute, Washington University in St. Louis, University of Wisconsin-Madison; forestry with Duke University; nursing with Rush University; environmental studies with Duke University.

Library Lane Library with 169,523 titles, 985 serial subscriptions, 662 audiovisual materials, an OPAC, a Web page.

Computers on Campus 150 computers available on campus for general student use. A campuswide network can be accessed from student residence rooms and from off campus. Internet access, at least one staffed computer lab available.

Student Life *Housing:* on-campus residence required through senior year. *Options:* coed, men-only, women-only. Campus housing is university owned. Freshman campus housing is guaranteed. *Activities and organizations:* drama/theater group, student-run newspaper, radio station, choral group, Environmental Group, Student Senate, Community Service Coalition, SMAC (Student Media and Activities Committee), national fraternities, national sororities. *Campus security:* 24-hour emergency response devices and patrols, student patrols, late-night transport/escort service, controlled dormitory access. *Student services:* health clinic, personal/psychological counseling.

Athletics Member NCAA. All Division III. *Intercollegiate sports:* baseball M, basketball M/W, cheerleading W, cross-country running M/W, football M, golf M/W, ice hockey M(c)/W(c), rugby M(c), soccer M/W, softball W, swimming M/W, tennis M/W, track and field M/W, volleyball W, wrestling M(c)/W(c). *Intramural sports:* basketball M/W, bowling M/W, fencing M/W, football M/W, golf M/W, racquetball M/W, soccer M/W, softball M/W, table tennis M/W, tennis M/W, ultimate Frisbee M/W, volleyball M/W, water polo M(c)/W(c).

Standardized Tests *Required:* SAT I or ACT (for admission).

Costs (2004–05) *Comprehensive fee:* $26,090 includes full-time tuition ($20,490), mandatory fees ($240), and room and board ($5360). Part-time tuition: $825 per credit. No tuition increase for student's term of enrollment. *College room only:* $2530. *Payment plan:* installment. *Waivers:* children of alumni and employees or children of employees.

Financial Aid Of all full-time matriculated undergraduates who enrolled in 2003, 874 applied for aid, 726 were judged to have need, 273 had their need fully met. 210 Federal Work-Study jobs (averaging $1313). 397 state and other part-time jobs (averaging $1634). In 2003, 206 non-need-based awards were made. *Average percent of need met:* 98%. *Average financial aid package:* $17,108. *Average need-based loan:* $4117. *Average need-based gift aid:* $13,810. *Average non-need-based aid:* $14,071. *Average indebtedness upon graduation:* $17,028.

Ripon College (continued)

Applying *Options:* common application, electronic application, deferred entrance. *Application fee:* $30. *Required:* high school transcript, minimum 2.0 GPA, 1 letter of recommendation. *Recommended:* essay or personal statement, interview. *Application deadline:* rolling (freshmen), rolling (transfers). *Notification:* continuous (freshmen), continuous (transfers).

Admissions Contact Mr. Scott J. Goplin, Vice President and Dean of Admission and Financial Aid, Ripon College, 300 Seward Street, PO Box 248, Ripon, WI 54971. *Phone:* 920-748-8185. *Toll-free phone:* 800-947-4766. *Fax:* 920-748-8335. *E-mail:* adminfo@ripon.edu.

■ *See page 2238 for a narrative description.*

ST. NORBERT COLLEGE

De Pere, Wisconsin

- **Independent Roman Catholic** comprehensive, founded 1898
- **Calendar** semesters
- **Degrees** bachelor's and master's
- **Suburban** 92-acre campus
- **Endowment** $42.3 million
- **Coed,** 2,086 undergraduate students, 96% full-time, 57% women, 43% men
- **Moderately difficult** entrance level, 86% of applicants were admitted

To firmly address the concerns associated with financing a private school education, St. Norbert College offers a 4-year graduation guarantee. This guarantee reflects the strengths of the College's advisement program, the flexibility and integrity of the curriculum, and the St. Norbert commitment to making private education affordable. The College also guarantees campus employment to all first-year students, regardless of need.

Undergraduates 2,006 full-time, 80 part-time. Students come from 26 states and territories, 15 other countries, 29% are from out of state, 0.8% African American, 1% Asian American or Pacific Islander, 2% Hispanic American, 0.8% Native American, 2% international, 2% transferred in, 76% live on campus. *Retention:* 85% of 2002 full-time freshmen returned.

Freshmen *Admission:* 1,658 applied, 1,432 admitted, 529 enrolled. *Average high school GPA:* 3.43. *Test scores:* ACT scores over 18: 100%; ACT scores over 24: 54%; ACT scores over 30: 9%.

Faculty *Total:* 164, 74% full-time, 73% with terminal degrees. *Student/faculty ratio:* 15:1.

Majors Accounting; art; biological and physical sciences; biology/biological sciences; business/commerce; chemistry; commercial and advertising art; communication/speech communication and rhetoric; computer programming (specific applications); economics; education (K-12); elementary education; English; French; geology/earth science; German; history; humanities; interdisciplinary studies; international business/trade/commerce; international relations and affairs; management information systems; mathematics; mathematics and computer science; music; music teacher education; philosophy; physics; political science and government; pre-dentistry studies; pre-law studies; pre-medical studies; pre-veterinary studies; psychology; religious studies; sociology; Spanish.

Academic Programs *Special study options:* academic remediation for entering students, advanced placement credit, cooperative education, distance learning, double majors, English as a second language, honors programs, independent study, internships, off-campus study, part-time degree program, services for LD students, student-designed majors, study abroad, summer session for credit. *ROTC:* Army (c).

Library Todd Wehr Library with 115,553 titles, 690 serial subscriptions, 7,625 audiovisual materials, an OPAC, a Web page.

Computers on Campus 202 computers available on campus for general student use. A campuswide network can be accessed from student residence rooms and from off campus. Internet access, online (class) registration, at least one staffed computer lab available. Computer purchase or lease plan available.

Student Life *Housing:* on-campus residence required through senior year. *Options:* coed, women-only, disabled students. Campus housing is university owned. Freshman campus housing is guaranteed. *Activities and organizations:* drama/theater group, student-run newspaper, radio and television station, choral group, Yes! Your Entertainment Service, Student Government Association, Residence Hall Association, social organizations, academic organizations, national fraternities, national sororities. *Campus security:* 24-hour emergency response devices and patrols, student patrols, late-night transport/escort service, controlled dormitory access, crime prevention programs. *Student services:* health clinic, personal/psychological counseling, women's center.

Athletics Member NCAA. All Division III. *Intercollegiate sports:* baseball M, basketball M/W, cheerleading M/W, cross-country running M/W, football M, golf M/W, ice hockey M, soccer M/W, softball W, swimming W, tennis M/W, track and field M/W, ultimate Frisbee M(c)/W(c), volleyball W. *Intramural sports:* basketball M/W, crew M(c)/W(c), football M/W, rock climbing M/W, rugby M(c)/W(c), soccer M/W, softball M/W, ultimate Frisbee M/W, volleyball M/W.

Standardized Tests *Required:* SAT I or ACT (for admission).

Costs (2004–05) *Comprehensive fee:* $27,490 includes full-time tuition ($21,210), mandatory fees ($300), and room and board ($5980). Full-time tuition and fees vary according to course load. Part-time tuition: $2651 per course. Part-time tuition and fees vary according to course load. *College room only:* $3160. Room and board charges vary according to board plan, housing facility, and student level. *Payment plans:* installment, deferred payment. *Waivers:* employees or children of employees.

Financial Aid Of all full-time matriculated undergraduates who enrolled in 2003, 1,498 applied for aid, 1,305 were judged to have need, 471 had their need fully met. 387 Federal Work-Study jobs (averaging $1096). 785 state and other part-time jobs (averaging $1458). In 2003, 593 non-need-based awards were made. *Average percent of need met:* 89%. *Average financial aid package:* $15,507. *Average need-based loan:* $4562. *Average need-based gift aid:* $10,899. *Average non-need-based aid:* $9259. *Average indebtedness upon graduation:* $16,854.

Applying *Options:* common application, electronic application, early decision, deferred entrance. *Application fee:* $25. *Required:* essay or personal statement, high school transcript, 1 letter of recommendation. *Recommended:* interview. *Application deadline:* rolling (freshmen), rolling (transfers). *Early decision:* 12/1. *Notification:* continuous (freshmen), 12/15 (early decision), continuous (transfers).

Admissions Contact Mr. Daniel L. Meyer, Dean of Admission and Enrollment Management, St. Norbert College, 100 Grant Street, De Pere, WI 54115-2099. *Phone:* 920-403-3005. *Toll-free phone:* 800-236-4878. *Fax:* 920-403-4072. *E-mail:* admit@snc.edu.

■ *See page 2324 for a narrative description.*

SILVER LAKE COLLEGE

Manitowoc, Wisconsin

- **Independent Roman Catholic** comprehensive, founded 1869
- **Calendar** semesters
- **Degrees** certificates, associate, bachelor's, master's, and postbachelor's certificates
- **Rural** 30-acre campus with easy access to Milwaukee
- **Endowment** $4.7 million
- **Coed,** 780 undergraduate students, 32% full-time, 68% women, 32% men
- **Minimally difficult** entrance level, 77% of applicants were admitted

In a recent survey of Silver Lake College (SLC) graduates, 99 percent of those responding said that they are very satisfied or satisfied with their education. For information about the College's outstanding programs of study, students should contact the admissions office at 800-236-4SLC Ext. 175 (toll-free) or visit the College's Web site at http://www.sl.edu.

Undergraduates 246 full-time, 534 part-time. Students come from 3 states and territories, 2% are from out of state, 0.4% African American, 1% Asian American or Pacific Islander, 0.8% Hispanic American, 5% Native American, 12% transferred in, 3% live on campus. *Retention:* 66% of 2002 full-time freshmen returned.

Freshmen *Admission:* 84 applied, 65 admitted, 27 enrolled. *Average high school GPA:* 2.96. *Test scores:* ACT scores over 18: 50%; ACT scores over 24: 18%.

Faculty *Total:* 162, 27% full-time, 26% with terminal degrees. *Student/faculty ratio:* 8:1.

Majors Accounting; art; art teacher education; biology/biological sciences; business administration and management; commercial and advertising art; computer and information sciences; elementary education; English; general studies; history; human resources management; information science/studies; interdisciplinary studies; kindergarten/preschool education; mathematics; music; music teacher education; psychology; social sciences; special education (mentally retarded); special education (specific learning disabilities); theology; web page, digital/multimedia and information resources design.

Academic Programs *Special study options:* academic remediation for entering students, accelerated degree program, adult/continuing education programs, advanced placement credit, cooperative education, distance learning, double majors, English as a second language, independent study, internships, part-time degree program, student-designed majors, summer session for credit.

Library The Erma M. and Theodore M. Zigmunt Library with 60,466 titles, 296 serial subscriptions, 11,458 audiovisual materials, an OPAC.

Computers on Campus 50 computers available on campus for general student use. A campuswide network can be accessed from off campus. Internet access, at least one staffed computer lab available.

Student Life *Housing:* on-campus residence required through sophomore year. *Options:* men-only, women-only. Campus housing is leased by the school.

Freshman campus housing is guaranteed. *Activities and organizations:* student-run newspaper, choral group, Campus Ministry projects, Education related clubs. *Campus security:* 24-hour emergency response devices. *Student services:* personal/psychological counseling.

Athletics *Intercollegiate sports:* basketball W, cheerleading M/W. *Intramural sports:* rock climbing M/W, table tennis M/W, ultimate Frisbee M/W, volleyball M/W.

Standardized Tests *Required:* SAT I or ACT (for admission).

Costs (2003–04) *Tuition:* $14,350 full-time, $360 per credit part-time. Full-time tuition and fees vary according to location and program. Part-time tuition and fees vary according to course load, location, and program. *Room only:* $4100. Room and board charges vary according to board plan. *Waivers:* children of alumni, senior citizens, and employees or children of employees.

Financial Aid Of all full-time matriculated undergraduates who enrolled in 2002, 172 applied for aid, 154 were judged to have need, 21 had their need fully met. 65 Federal Work-Study jobs (averaging $1305). In 2002, 6 non-need-based awards were made. *Average percent of need met:* 70%. *Average financial aid package:* $11,276. *Average need-based loan:* $3911. *Average need-based gift aid:* $7909. *Average non-need-based aid:* $10,043. *Average indebtedness upon graduation:* $16,575.

Applying *Options:* electronic application, early admission, deferred entrance. *Application fee:* $35. *Required:* high school transcript, minimum 2.0 GPA. *Required for some:* interview, audition. *Application deadlines:* 8/31 (freshmen), 8/31 (transfers). *Notification:* continuous (freshmen), continuous (transfers).

Admissions Contact Ms. Janis Algozine, Vice President, Dean of Students, Silver Lake College, 2406 South Alverno Road, Manitowoc, WI. *Phone:* 920-684-5955 Ext. 175. *Toll-free phone:* 800-236-4752 Ext. 175. *Fax:* 920-684-7082. *E-mail:* admslc@silver.sl.edu.

University of Phoenix–Wisconsin Campus

Brookfield, Wisconsin

- **Proprietary** comprehensive, founded 2001
- **Calendar** continuous
- **Degrees** certificates, associate, bachelor's, master's, doctoral, post-master's, and postbachelor's certificates (courses conducted at 121 campuses and learning centers in 25 states)
- **Urban** campus
- **Coed,** 502 undergraduate students, 100% full-time, 59% women, 41% men
- **Noncompetitive** entrance level

Undergraduates 502 full-time. 11% African American, 1% Asian American or Pacific Islander, 4% Hispanic American, 0.2% Native American, 3% international.

Freshmen *Admission:* 41 enrolled.

Faculty *Total:* 56, 7% full-time, 16% with terminal degrees. *Student/faculty ratio:* 7:1.

Majors Accounting; business administration and management; computer and information sciences; management science; marketing/marketing management.

Academic Programs *Special study options:* accelerated degree program, adult/continuing education programs, advanced placement credit, distance learning, external degree program, independent study.

Library 27.1 million titles, 11,648 serial subscriptions, an OPAC, a Web page.

Computers on Campus A campuswide network can be accessed from off campus. Internet access, at least one staffed computer lab available.

Student Life *Housing:* college housing not available.

Costs (2003–04) *Tuition:* $9600 full-time, $320 per credit part-time. *Waivers:* employees or children of employees.

Financial Aid *Average financial aid package:* $1301.

Applying *Options:* deferred entrance. *Required:* 1 letter of recommendation, 2 years of work experience, 23 years of age. *Required for some:* high school transcript. *Application deadline:* rolling (freshmen), rolling (transfers).

Admissions Contact Ms. Beth Barilla, Director of Admissions, University of Phoenix–Wisconsin Campus, 4615 East Elwood Street, Mail Stop AA-K101, Phoenix, AZ 85040-1958. *Phone:* 480-317-6000. *Toll-free phone:* 800-228-7240. *E-mail:* beth.barilla@phoenix.edu.

University of Wisconsin–Eau Claire

Eau Claire, Wisconsin

- **State-supported** comprehensive, founded 1916, part of University of Wisconsin System
- **Calendar** semesters
- **Degrees** associate, bachelor's, master's, post-master's, and postbachelor's certificates
- **Urban** 333-acre campus
- **Endowment** $21.6 million
- **Coed,** 10,059 undergraduate students, 92% full-time, 60% women, 40% men
- **Moderately difficult** entrance level, 60% of applicants were admitted

Undergraduates 9,230 full-time, 829 part-time. Students come from 26 states and territories, 43 other countries, 22% are from out of state, 0.5% African American, 3% Asian American or Pacific Islander, 1% Hispanic American, 0.6% Native American, 1% international, 5% transferred in, 37% live on campus. *Retention:* 81% of 2002 full-time freshmen returned.

Freshmen *Admission:* 7,055 applied, 4,258 admitted, 1,879 enrolled. *Test scores:* SAT verbal scores over 500: 81%; SAT math scores over 500: 84%; ACT scores over 18: 100%; SAT verbal scores over 600: 51%; SAT math scores over 600: 46%; ACT scores over 24: 61%; SAT verbal scores over 700: 13%; SAT math scores over 700: 8%; ACT scores over 30: 6%.

Faculty *Total:* 479, 85% full-time, 78% with terminal degrees. *Student/faculty ratio:* 22:1.

Majors Accounting; American Indian/Native American studies; art; athletic training; biomedical sciences; business administration and management; chemistry; chemistry related; communication disorders; communication/speech communication and rhetoric; computer and information sciences; criminal justice/safety; dramatic/theatre arts; economics; education (specific subject areas) related; elementary education; English; environmental health; finance; French; geography; geology/earth science; Germanic languages; health/health care administration; history; information resources management; journalism; kinesiology and exercise science; Latin American studies; liberal arts and sciences/liberal studies; marketing/marketing management; mass communication/media; mathematics; molecular biology; music; music therapy; nursing (registered nurse training); philosophy; physics; political science and government; psychology; religious studies; science teacher education; social studies teacher education; social work; sociology; Spanish; special education.

Academic Programs *Special study options:* academic remediation for entering students, adult/continuing education programs, advanced placement credit, cooperative education, distance learning, double majors, English as a second language, honors programs, independent study, internships, off-campus study, part-time degree program, services for LD students, study abroad, summer session for credit.

Library William D. McIntyre Library plus 1 other with 605,639 titles, 2,570 serial subscriptions, 14,545 audiovisual materials, an OPAC, a Web page.

Computers on Campus 925 computers available on campus for general student use. A campuswide network can be accessed from student residence rooms and from off campus. Internet access, online (class) registration, at least one staffed computer lab available.

Student Life *Housing:* on-campus residence required for freshman year. *Options:* coed, men-only, women-only. Campus housing is university owned. Freshman campus housing is guaranteed. *Activities and organizations:* drama/theater group, student-run newspaper, radio and television station, choral group, marching band, American Marketing Association, Beta Upsilon Sigma, International Greek Association, Student Information Management Society, Hobnailers, national fraternities, national sororities. *Campus security:* 24-hour emergency response devices and patrols, late-night transport/escort service, controlled dormitory access. *Student services:* health clinic, personal/psychological counseling, legal services.

Athletics Member NCAA. All Division III. *Intercollegiate sports:* basketball M/W, cross-country running M/W, football M, golf M/W, gymnastics W, ice hockey M/W, soccer W, softball W, swimming M/W, tennis M/W, track and field M/W, volleyball W, wrestling M. *Intramural sports:* badminton M/W, baseball M, basketball M/W, bowling M/W, football M/W, golf M/W, ice hockey M/W, racquetball M/W, rugby M/W, skiing (cross-country) M/W, skiing (downhill) M/W, soccer M/W, softball M/W, swimming M/W, table tennis M/W, tennis M/W, volleyball M/W, water polo M, weight lifting M/W.

Standardized Tests *Required:* SAT I or ACT (for admission).

Costs (2003–04) *Tuition:* state resident $4313 full-time, $180 per credit part-time; nonresident $14,360 full-time, $598 per credit part-time. Full-time tuition and fees vary according to reciprocity agreements. Part-time tuition and fees vary according to reciprocity agreements. *Room and board:* $4150; room only: $2410. Room and board charges vary according to board plan. *Payment plan:* installment. *Waivers:* minority students and senior citizens.

Financial Aid Of all full-time matriculated undergraduates who enrolled in 2002, 5,998 applied for aid, 3,852 were judged to have need, 2,912 had their need fully met. 1,605 Federal Work-Study jobs (averaging $1716). 2,302 state and other part-time jobs (averaging $1217). In 2002, 343 non-need-based awards were made. *Average percent of need met:* 95%. *Average financial aid package:* $6083. *Average need-based loan:* $3452. *Average need-based gift aid:* $3887. *Average non-need-based aid:* $1314. *Average indebtedness upon graduation:* $15,061.

University of Wisconsin–Eau Claire (continued)

Applying *Options:* electronic application, early admission. *Application fee:* $35. *Required:* high school transcript, rank in upper 50% of high school class. *Application deadlines:* rolling (freshmen), 7/1 (transfers). *Notification:* continuous (freshmen), continuous (transfers).

Admissions Contact Ms. Kristina Anderson, Interim Executive Director of Enrollment Management and Director of Admissions, University of Wisconsin–Eau Claire, PO Box 4004, Eau Claire, WI 54702-4004. *Phone:* 715-836-5415. *Fax:* 715-836-2409. *E-mail:* admissions@uwec.edu.

UNIVERSITY OF WISCONSIN–GREEN BAY

Green Bay, Wisconsin

- **State-supported** comprehensive, founded 1968, part of University of Wisconsin System
- **Calendar** semesters
- **Degrees** associate, bachelor's, master's, and postbachelor's certificates
- **Suburban** 700-acre campus
- **Endowment** $7.7 million
- **Coed,** 5,256 undergraduate students, 83% full-time, 66% women, 34% men
- **Moderately difficult** entrance level, 78% of applicants were admitted

Undergraduates 4,374 full-time, 882 part-time. Students come from 30 states and territories, 28 other countries, 4% are from out of state, 0.7% African American, 2% Asian American or Pacific Islander, 0.7% Hispanic American, 1% Native American, 0.9% international, 9% transferred in, 30% live on campus. *Retention:* 83% of 2002 full-time freshmen returned.

Freshmen *Admission:* 2,979 applied, 2,322 admitted, 964 enrolled. *Average high school GPA:* 3.35. *Test scores:* ACT scores over 18: 96%; ACT scores over 24: 38%; ACT scores over 30: 3%.

Faculty *Total:* 274, 61% full-time. *Student/faculty ratio:* 23:1.

Majors Accounting; art; biology/biological sciences; biomedical sciences; business administration and management; chemistry; communication and journalism related; computer science; developmental and child psychology; dramatic/theatre arts; economics; elementary education; English; environmental science; environmental studies; French; general studies; geology/earth science; Germanic languages; history; humanities; information science/studies; interdisciplinary studies; management information systems; mathematics; music; music related; nursing science; nutrition sciences; philosophy; political science and government; pre-dentistry studies; psychology; social work; Spanish; urban studies/affairs.

Academic Programs *Special study options:* academic remediation for entering students, accelerated degree program, adult/continuing education programs, advanced placement credit, cooperative education, distance learning, double majors, English as a second language, external degree program, independent study, internships, off-campus study, part-time degree program, services for LD students, student-designed majors, study abroad, summer session for credit. *ROTC:* Army (b). *Unusual degree programs:* 3-2 engineering with University of Wisconsin-Milwaukee.

Library Cofrin Library with 333,482 titles, 5,512 serial subscriptions, 45,396 audiovisual materials, an OPAC, a Web page.

Computers on Campus 550 computers available on campus for general student use. A campuswide network can be accessed from student residence rooms and from off campus that provide access to on-line degree progress. Internet access, online (class) registration, at least one staffed computer lab available.

Student Life *Housing options:* coed. Campus housing is university owned. Freshman applicants given priority for college housing. *Activities and organizations:* drama/theater group, student-run newspaper, radio station, choral group, marching band, Good Times, Psych and Human Development Club, Ambassadors, Residence Hall Apartment Association, Student Government Association, national fraternities, national sororities. *Campus security:* 24-hour emergency response devices and patrols, late-night transport/escort service, controlled dormitory access. *Student services:* health clinic, personal/psychological counseling.

Athletics Member NCAA. All Division I. *Intercollegiate sports:* basketball M(s)/W(s), cross-country running M(s)/W(s), skiing (cross-country) M(s)/W(s), soccer M(s)/W(s), softball W(s), swimming M(s)/W(s), tennis M(s)/W(s), volleyball W(s). *Intramural sports:* basketball M/W, bowling M/W, cheerleading M/W, football M/W, golf M/W, racquetball M/W, sailing M/W, skiing (cross-country) M/W, soccer M/W, softball M/W, swimming M/W, tennis M/W, ultimate Frisbee M/W, volleyball M/W, weight lifting M/W.

Standardized Tests *Required:* SAT I or ACT (for admission).

Costs (2003–04) *Tuition:* state resident $3500 full-time, $149 per credit part-time; nonresident $13,547 full-time, $564 per credit part-time. Full-time tuition and fees vary according to reciprocity agreements. Part-time tuition and fees vary according to reciprocity agreements. *Required fees:* $1154 full-time, $38 per credit part-time. *Room and board:* $4500; room only: $2500. Room and board charges vary according to board plan and housing facility. *Payment plan:* installment. *Waivers:* senior citizens.

Financial Aid Of all full-time matriculated undergraduates who enrolled in 2003, 3,285 applied for aid, 2,469 were judged to have need, 1,099 had their need fully met. In 2003, 64 non-need-based awards were made. *Average percent of need met:* 80%. *Average financial aid package:* $6831. *Average need-based loan:* $3544. *Average need-based gift aid:* $3970. *Average non-need-based aid:* $2103.

Applying *Options:* electronic application, deferred entrance. *Application fee:* $35. *Required:* essay or personal statement, high school transcript, minimum ACT score of 17. *Required for some:* letters of recommendation, interview. *Recommended:* minimum 2.25 GPA. *Notification:* continuous until 8/15 (freshmen), continuous until 8/15 (transfers).

Admissions Contact Ms. Pam Harvey-Jacobs, Director of Admissions, University of Wisconsin–Green Bay, 2420 Nicolet Drive, Green Bay, WI 54311-7001. *Phone:* 920-465-2111. *Toll-free phone:* 888-367-8942. *Fax:* 920-465-5754. *E-mail:* admissions@uwgb.edu.

■ *See page 2742 for a narrative description.*

UNIVERSITY OF WISCONSIN–LA CROSSE

La Crosse, Wisconsin

- **State-supported** comprehensive, founded 1909, part of University of Wisconsin System
- **Calendar** semesters
- **Degrees** associate, bachelor's, and master's
- **Suburban** 121-acre campus
- **Endowment** $10.9 million
- **Coed,** 8,100 undergraduate students, 93% full-time, 60% women, 40% men
- **Moderately difficult** entrance level, 53% of applicants were admitted

Undergraduates 7,548 full-time, 552 part-time. Students come from 33 states and territories, 43 other countries, 18% are from out of state, 0.9% African American, 3% Asian American or Pacific Islander, 2% Hispanic American, 0.7% Native American, 1% international, 4% transferred in, 32% live on campus. *Retention:* 85% of 2002 full-time freshmen returned.

Freshmen *Admission:* 6,376 applied, 3,357 admitted, 1,509 enrolled. *Test scores:* SAT verbal scores over 500: 88%; SAT math scores over 500: 94%; ACT scores over 18: 100%; SAT verbal scores over 600: 45%; SAT math scores over 600: 61%; ACT scores over 24: 66%; SAT verbal scores over 700: 6%; SAT math scores over 700: 9%; ACT scores over 30: 5%.

Faculty *Total:* 410, 80% full-time, 70% with terminal degrees. *Student/faculty ratio:* 22:1.

Majors Accounting; archeology; art; art teacher education; athletic training; biology/biological sciences; business administration and management; chemistry; clinical laboratory science/medical technology; communication/speech communication and rhetoric; computer science; dramatic/theatre arts; economics; education; elementary education; English; finance; French; geography; German; health teacher education; history; international business/trade/commerce; kindergarten/preschool education; kinesiology and exercise science; liberal arts and sciences/liberal studies; management information systems; marketing/marketing management; mathematics; medical microbiology and bacteriology; music; music teacher education; nuclear medical technology; occupational therapy; parks, recreation and leisure facilities management; philosophy; physical education teaching and coaching; physician assistant; physics; political science and government; psychology; public administration; public health education and promotion; science teacher education; secondary education; social studies teacher education; sociology; Spanish; speech and rhetoric; sport and fitness administration; therapeutic recreation.

Academic Programs *Special study options:* academic remediation for entering students, adult/continuing education programs, advanced placement credit, distance learning, double majors, English as a second language, freshman honors college, honors programs, internships, off-campus study, part-time degree program, services for LD students, study abroad, summer session for credit. *ROTC:* Army (b). *Unusual degree programs:* 3-2 engineering with University of Wisconsin-Madison, University of Wisconsin-Milwaukee.

Library Murphy Library with 660,159 titles, 1,603 serial subscriptions, 1,648 audiovisual materials, an OPAC, a Web page.

Computers on Campus 600 computers available on campus for general student use. A campuswide network can be accessed from student residence rooms and from off campus. Internet access, at least one staffed computer lab available.

Student Life *Housing:* on-campus residence required for freshman year. *Options:* coed, women-only. Campus housing is university owned. Freshman applicants given priority for college housing. *Activities and organizations:* drama/theater group, student-run newspaper, radio station, choral group, marching band, Greek Organization Council, sports and activities club, Residential Hall Council, national fraternities, national sororities. *Campus security:* 24-hour emergency response devices and patrols, late-night transport/escort service, controlled dormitory access. *Student services:* health clinic, personal/psychological counseling, women's center, legal services.

Athletics Member NCAA. All Division III. *Intercollegiate sports:* baseball M, basketball M/W, cross-country running M/W, football M, gymnastics W, soccer W, softball W, swimming M/W, tennis M/W, track and field M/W, volleyball W, wrestling M. *Intramural sports:* basketball M/W, bowling M/W, football M/W, golf M/W, lacrosse M, racquetball M/W, rugby M/W, sailing M/W, skiing (downhill) M/W, soccer M, softball M/W, tennis M/W, volleyball M/W, weight lifting M/W.

Standardized Tests *Required:* SAT I or ACT (for admission). *Recommended:* ACT (for admission).

Costs (2003–04) *Tuition:* $182 per credit part-time; state resident $4741 full-time, $198 per credit part-time; nonresident $14,404 full-time, $600 per credit part-time. Full-time tuition and fees vary according to program and reciprocity agreements. Part-time tuition and fees vary according to course load, program, and reciprocity agreements. *Room and board:* $4050; room only: $2200. *Payment plan:* installment. *Waivers:* minority students.

Financial Aid Of all full-time matriculated undergraduates who enrolled in 2002, 5,487 applied for aid, 4,389 were judged to have need, 3,816 had their need fully met. 581 Federal Work-Study jobs (averaging $1056). 1,049 state and other part-time jobs (averaging $2461). In 2002, 399 non-need-based awards were made. *Average percent of need met:* 82%. *Average financial aid package:* $5499. *Average need-based loan:* $3284. *Average need-based gift aid:* $1836. *Average non-need-based aid:* $701. *Average indebtedness upon graduation:* $13,613.

Applying *Options:* electronic application, early admission, deferred entrance. *Application fee:* $35. *Required:* high school transcript. *Required for some:* interview. *Recommended:* essay or personal statement. *Application deadline:* rolling (freshmen), rolling (transfers). *Notification:* continuous (freshmen), continuous (transfers).

Admissions Contact Mr. Tim Lewis, Director of Admissions, University of Wisconsin–La Crosse, 1725 State Street, LaCrosse, WI 54601. *Phone:* 608-785-8939. *Fax:* 608-785-8940. *E-mail:* admissions@uwlax.edu.

UNIVERSITY OF WISCONSIN–MADISON

Madison, Wisconsin

- **State-supported** university, founded 1848, part of University of Wisconsin System
- **Calendar** semesters
- **Degrees** bachelor's, master's, doctoral, first professional, post-master's, and postbachelor's certificates
- **Urban** 1050-acre campus with easy access to Milwaukee
- **Endowment** $767.6 million
- **Coed,** 28,583 undergraduate students
- **Very difficult** entrance level, 61% of applicants were admitted

Undergraduates Students come from 54 states and territories, 131 other countries, 38% are from out of state. *Retention:* 96% of 2002 full-time freshmen returned.

Freshmen *Admission:* 21,335 applied, 12,931 admitted. *Average high school GPA:* 3.88. *Test scores:* SAT verbal scores over 500: 97%; SAT math scores over 500: 98%; ACT scores over 18: 100%; SAT verbal scores over 600: 71%; SAT math scores over 600: 79%; ACT scores over 24: 87%; SAT verbal scores over 700: 26%; SAT math scores over 700: 25%; ACT scores over 30: 39%.

Faculty *Total:* 2,225, 100% full-time, 100% with terminal degrees. *Student/faculty ratio:* 14:1.

Majors Accounting; actuarial science; advertising; African-American/Black studies; African languages; African studies; agricultural/biological engineering and bioengineering; agricultural business and management; agricultural economics; agricultural teacher education; agriculture; agronomy and crop science; American studies; animal genetics; animal sciences; anthropology; applied art; applied mathematics; art; art history, criticism and conservation; art teacher education; Asian studies; Asian studies (Southeast); astronomy; biochemistry; biology/biological sciences; biomedical/medical engineering; botany/plant biology; broadcast journalism; business administration and management; cartography; cell biology and histology; chemical engineering; chemistry; child development; Chinese; civil engineering; classics and languages, literatures and linguistics; clinical laboratory science/medical technology; clothing/textiles; comparative literature; computer engineering; computer science; construction management; consumer services and advocacy; dairy science; developmental and child psychology; dietetics; dramatic/theatre arts; economics; electrical, electronics and communications engineering; elementary education; engineering; engineering mechanics; engineering physics; English; entomology; environmental/environmental health engineering; experimental psychology; family and consumer economics related; family and consumer sciences/home economics teacher education; family and consumer sciences/human sciences; farm and ranch management; fashion merchandising; finance; food science; foods, nutrition, and wellness; forestry; French; geography; geology/earth science; geophysics and seismology; German; Hebrew; Hispanic-American, Puerto Rican, and Mexican-American/Chicano studies; history; history and philosophy of science and technology; horticultural science; hydrology and water resources science; industrial engineering; insurance; interior design; international relations and affairs; Italian; Japanese; journalism; kindergarten/preschool education; labor and industrial relations; landscape architecture; Latin; Latin American studies; linguistics; mass communication/media; mathematics; mechanical engineering; medical microbiology and bacteriology; metallurgical engineering; mining and mineral engineering; modern Greek; molecular biology; music; music teacher education; natural resources management and policy; nuclear engineering; nursing (registered nurse training); occupational therapy; parks, recreation and leisure; pharmacology; pharmacy; philosophy; physical education teaching and coaching; physician assistant; physics; political science and government; Portuguese; poultry science; psychology; public relations/image management; radio and television; real estate; Russian; Scandinavian languages; science teacher education; secondary education; Slavic languages; social sciences; social work; sociology; Spanish; special education; speech therapy; statistics; survey technology; toxicology; urban studies/affairs; wildlife and wildlands science and management; women's studies; zoology/animal biology.

Academic Programs *Special study options:* adult/continuing education programs, advanced placement credit, cooperative education, distance learning, double majors, English as a second language, freshman honors college, honors programs, independent study, internships, part-time degree program, services for LD students, student-designed majors, study abroad, summer session for credit. *ROTC:* Army (b).

Library Memorial Library plus 40 others with 6.1 million titles, 66,000 serial subscriptions, an OPAC, a Web page.

Computers on Campus 2800 computers available on campus for general student use. A campuswide network can be accessed from student residence rooms and from off campus. Internet access, at least one staffed computer lab available.

Student Life *Housing options:* coed, men-only, women-only, cooperative, disabled students. Campus housing is university owned and is provided by a third party. Freshman applicants given priority for college housing. *Activities and organizations:* drama/theater group, student-run newspaper, radio station, choral group, marching band, national fraternities, national sororities. *Campus security:* 24-hour emergency response devices and patrols, late-night transport/escort service, controlled dormitory access, free cab rides throughout the city. *Student services:* health clinic, personal/psychological counseling, women's center, legal services.

Athletics Member NCAA. All Division I except football (Division I-A). *Intercollegiate sports:* basketball M(s)/W(s), cheerleading M/W, crew M(s)/W(s), cross-country running M(s)/W(s), golf M(s)/W(s), ice hockey M(s)/W(s), lacrosse W(s), rugby M(c), sailing M(c)/W(c), soccer M(s)/W(s), softball W(s), swimming M(s)/W(s), tennis M(s)/W(s), track and field M(s)/W(s), volleyball W(s), wrestling M(s). *Intramural sports:* archery M/W, badminton M/W, basketball M/W, bowling M/W, crew M/W, equestrian sports M/W, fencing M/W, football M, golf M/W, gymnastics M/W, ice hockey M/W, lacrosse M/W, racquetball M/W, riflery M/W, rock climbing M/W, rugby M/W, sailing M/W, skiing (cross-country) M/W, skiing (downhill) M/W, soccer M/W, softball M/W, squash M/W, swimming M/W, table tennis M/W, tennis M/W, track and field M/W, ultimate Frisbee M/W, volleyball M/W, water polo M/W, wrestling M.

Standardized Tests *Required:* SAT I or ACT (for admission). *Required for some:* SAT II: Subject Tests (for admission). *Recommended:* SAT II: Subject Tests (for admission).

Costs (2003–04) *Tuition:* state resident $5140 full-time; nonresident $19,150 full-time. *Room and board:* $6130.

Financial Aid Of all full-time matriculated undergraduates who enrolled in 2003, 13,734 applied for aid, 8,656 were judged to have need, 2,770 had their need fully met. In 2003, 3665 non-need-based awards were made. *Average financial aid package:* $10,305. *Average need-based loan:* $4328. *Average need-based gift aid:* $5675. *Average non-need-based aid:* $2648. *Average indebtedness upon graduation:* $16,395.

Applying *Options:* electronic application, early admission, deferred entrance. *Application fee:* $35. *Required:* essay or personal statement, high school transcript. *Recommended:* interview. *Application deadlines:* 2/1 (freshmen), 2/1 (transfers). *Notification:* continuous (freshmen), continuous (transfers).

Admissions Contact Mr. Keith White, Associate Director of Admission, University of Wisconsin–Madison, 716 Langdon Street, Madison, WI 53706-1481. *Phone:* 608-262-3961. *Fax:* 608-262-7706. *E-mail:* on.wisconsin@admissions.wisc.edu.

UNIVERSITY OF WISCONSIN–MILWAUKEE

Milwaukee, Wisconsin

- **State-supported** university, founded 1956, part of University of Wisconsin System

University of Wisconsin–Milwaukee (continued)

- **Calendar** semesters
- **Degrees** certificates, bachelor's, master's, doctoral, post-master's, and postbachelor's certificates
- **Urban** 90-acre campus
- **Coed,** 21,052 undergraduate students, 80% full-time, 55% women, 45% men
- **Moderately difficult** entrance level, 79% of applicants were admitted

Undergraduates 16,816 full-time, 4,236 part-time. Students come from 53 states and territories, 1% are from out of state, 7% African American, 5% Asian American or Pacific Islander, 4% Hispanic American, 0.7% Native American, 0.7% international, 7% transferred in, 13% live on campus. *Retention:* 72% of 2002 full-time freshmen returned.

Freshmen *Admission:* 9,918 applied, 7,881 admitted, 3,855 enrolled. *Average high school GPA:* 3.10. *Test scores:* SAT verbal scores over 500: 60%; SAT math scores over 500: 71%; ACT scores over 18: 90%; SAT verbal scores over 600: 19%; SAT math scores over 600: 23%; ACT scores over 24: 34%; SAT math scores over 700: 1%; ACT scores over 30: 2%.

Majors Accounting; African-American/Black studies; American Indian/Native American studies; anthropology; applied mathematics; architecture; art; art history, criticism and conservation; art teacher education; atmospheric sciences and meteorology; audiology and speech-language pathology; bilingual and multilingual education; biochemistry; biology/biological sciences; broadcast journalism; business administration and management; ceramic arts and ceramics; chemistry; civil engineering; classics and languages, literatures and linguistics; clinical laboratory science/medical technology; comparative literature; computer science; criminal justice/law enforcement administration; criminal justice/police science; cultural studies; dance; dramatic/theatre arts; ecology; economics; education; electrical, electronics and communications engineering; elementary education; engineering; English; fiber, textile and weaving arts; film/cinema studies; finance; fine/studio arts; forestry; French; geography; geology/earth science; German; health/health care administration; health information/medical records administration; health science; Hebrew; history; human resources management; industrial engineering; interdisciplinary studies; international relations and affairs; Italian; journalism; kindergarten/preschool education; labor and industrial relations; Latin; Latin American studies; linguistics; literature; management information systems; marketing/marketing management; mass communication/media; materials engineering; mathematics; mechanical engineering; metal and jewelry arts; modern Greek; music; music history, literature, and theory; music teacher education; music therapy; natural resources/conservation; nursing (registered nurse training); occupational therapy; parks, recreation and leisure; peace studies and conflict resolution; philosophy; physical therapy; physics; political science and government; pre-dentistry studies; pre-law studies; pre-medical studies; psychology; real estate; religious studies; Russian; Russian studies; sculpture; secondary education; Slavic languages; social work; sociology; Spanish; special education; statistics; therapeutic recreation; urban studies/affairs; violin, viola, guitar and other stringed instruments; voice and opera; wind/percussion instruments; women's studies; zoology/animal biology.

Academic Programs *Special study options:* academic remediation for entering students, accelerated degree program, adult/continuing education programs, advanced placement credit, cooperative education, distance learning, double majors, English as a second language, honors programs, independent study, internships, off-campus study, part-time degree program, services for LD students, student-designed majors, study abroad, summer session for credit.

Library Golda Meir Library with 1.4 million titles, 8,240 serial subscriptions, 37,376 audiovisual materials, an OPAC, a Web page.

Computers on Campus 310 computers available on campus for general student use. A campuswide network can be accessed from off campus. At least one staffed computer lab available.

Student Life *Housing options:* coed. *Activities and organizations:* drama/theater group, student-run newspaper, radio station, choral group, marching band, national fraternities, national sororities. *Campus security:* 24-hour emergency response devices, late-night transport/escort service. *Student services:* health clinic, personal/psychological counseling, women's center, legal services.

Athletics Member NCAA. All Division I. *Intercollegiate sports:* baseball M, basketball M(s)/W(s), cross-country running M(s)/W(s), soccer M(s)/W(s), swimming M(s)/W(s), tennis M(s)/W(s), track and field M(s)/W(s), volleyball M/W(s). *Intramural sports:* badminton M/W, basketball M/W, bowling M(c)/W(c), fencing M(c)/W(c), field hockey M/W, football M, golf M/W, racquetball M/W, riflery M(c)/W(c), rugby M(c)/W(c), sailing M(c)/W(c), skiing (downhill) M(c)/W(c), soccer M/W, swimming M/W, tennis M/W, volleyball M/W, water polo M/W, weight lifting M/W, wrestling M.

Standardized Tests *Required:* SAT I or ACT (for admission), ACT for state residents (for admission). *Recommended:* SAT I (for admission).

Costs (2003–04) *Tuition:* state resident $4439 full-time, $185 per credit part-time; nonresident $17,190 full-time, $716 per credit part-time. Full-time tuition and fees vary according to location, program, and reciprocity agreements. Part-time tuition and fees vary according to course load, location, program, and reciprocity agreements. *Required fees:* $668 full-time. *Room and board:* $4320; room only: $2540. Room and board charges vary according to board plan. *Payment plan:* installment.

Financial Aid Of all full-time matriculated undergraduates who enrolled in 2002, 13,507 applied for aid, 9,027 were judged to have need, 3,811 had their need fully met. In 2002, 324 non-need-based awards were made. *Average percent of need met:* 69%. *Average financial aid package:* $7300. *Average need-based loan:* $3443. *Average need-based gift aid:* $4337. *Average non-need-based aid:* $1771. *Average indebtedness upon graduation:* $20,925.

Applying *Options:* deferred entrance. *Application fee:* $35. *Required:* high school transcript. *Application deadline:* 8/1 (freshmen), rolling (transfers). *Notification:* continuous (freshmen), continuous (transfers).

Admissions Contact Ms. Jan Ford, Director, Recruitment and Outreach, University of Wisconsin–Milwaukee, PO Box 749, Milwaukee, WI 53201. *Phone:* 414-229-4397. *Fax:* 414-229-6940. *E-mail:* uwmlook@uwm.edu.

UNIVERSITY OF WISCONSIN–OSHKOSH

Oshkosh, Wisconsin

- **State-supported** comprehensive, founded 1871, part of University of Wisconsin System
- **Calendar** semesters
- **Degrees** associate, bachelor's, and master's
- **Suburban** 192-acre campus with easy access to Milwaukee
- **Endowment** $350,000
- **Coed,** 9,804 undergraduate students, 86% full-time, 60% women, 40% men
- **Moderately difficult** entrance level, 47% of applicants were admitted

Undergraduates 8,440 full-time, 1,364 part-time. Students come from 30 states and territories, 32 other countries, 2% are from out of state, 1% African American, 2% Asian American or Pacific Islander, 1% Hispanic American, 0.7% Native American, 0.7% international, 8% transferred in, 34% live on campus. *Retention:* 76% of 2002 full-time freshmen returned.

Freshmen *Admission:* 5,395 applied, 2,553 admitted, 1,780 enrolled. *Average high school GPA:* 3.10. *Test scores:* ACT scores over 18: 96%; ACT scores over 24: 30%; ACT scores over 30: 3%.

Faculty *Total:* 575, 73% full-time, 99% with terminal degrees. *Student/faculty ratio:* 20:1.

Majors Accounting; anthropology; art; art teacher education; audiology and speech-language pathology; biology/biological sciences; broadcast journalism; business administration and management; chemistry; clinical laboratory science/medical technology; computer science; criminal justice/law enforcement administration; dramatic/theatre arts; economics; education; elementary education; English; English as a second/foreign language (teaching); finance; fine/studio arts; French; geography; geology/earth science; German; history; human services; international relations and affairs; journalism; kindergarten/preschool education; liberal arts and sciences/liberal studies; management information systems; marketing/marketing management; mass communication/media; mathematics; medical microbiology and bacteriology; music; music teacher education; music therapy; nursing (registered nurse training); philosophy; physical education teaching and coaching; physics; political science and government; pre-dentistry studies; pre-law studies; pre-medical studies; pre-veterinary studies; psychology; radio and television; religious studies; secondary education; social work; sociology; Spanish; special education; urban studies/affairs.

Academic Programs *Special study options:* academic remediation for entering students, accelerated degree program, adult/continuing education programs, advanced placement credit, cooperative education, distance learning, double majors, English as a second language, honors programs, independent study, internships, part-time degree program, services for LD students, student-designed majors, study abroad, summer session for credit. *ROTC:* Army (b).

Library Forrest R. Polk Library with 446,774 titles, 5,219 serial subscriptions, 9,102 audiovisual materials, an OPAC, a Web page.

Computers on Campus 475 computers available on campus for general student use. A campuswide network can be accessed from student residence rooms and from off campus. Internet access, online (class) registration, at least one staffed computer lab available.

Student Life *Housing:* on-campus residence required through sophomore year. *Options:* coed, women-only. Freshman campus housing is guaranteed. *Activities and organizations:* drama/theater group, student-run newspaper, radio station, choral group, USRH, Model UN, Pi Sigma Epsilon, Panhellenic, Human Services Organization, national fraternities, national sororities. *Campus security:* 24-hour emergency response devices and patrols, student patrols, late-night transport/escort service, controlled dormitory access. *Student services:* health clinic, personal/psychological counseling, women's center, legal services.

Athletics Member NCAA. All Division III. *Intercollegiate sports:* baseball M, basketball M/W, cross-country running M/W, football M, golf W, gymnastics W, riflery M/W, soccer M/W, softball W, swimming M/W, tennis M/W, track and field M/W, volleyball W, wrestling M. *Intramural sports:* basketball M/W, bowling M(c)/W(c), cross-country running M/W, football M/W, golf M/W, gymnastics M(c), ice hockey M(c), lacrosse M(c)/W(c), racquetball M/W, skiing (downhill) M/W, soccer M/W, softball M/W, tennis M/W, volleyball M(c)/W, wrestling M.

Standardized Tests *Required:* SAT I or ACT for nonresidents, ACT for state residents (for admission).

Costs (2004–05) *Tuition:* state resident $4044 full-time, $168 per credit hour part-time; nonresident $14,320 full-time, $587 per credit hour part-time. *Room and board:* $4100; room only: $2278.

Financial Aid Of all full-time matriculated undergraduates who enrolled in 2002, 5,501 applied for aid, 3,026 were judged to have need, 1,504 had their need fully met. In 2002, 56 non-need-based awards were made. *Average percent of need met:* 55%. *Average financial aid package:* $5000. *Average need-based loan:* $3500. *Average need-based gift aid:* $2000. *Average non-need-based aid:* $2511. *Average indebtedness upon graduation:* $15,000.

Applying *Options:* electronic application, deferred entrance. *Application fee:* $35. *Required:* high school transcript, rank in upper 50% of high school class or ACT composite score of 23 or above. *Recommended:* essay or personal statement. *Application deadlines:* 8/1 (freshmen), 8/1 (transfers). *Notification:* continuous (freshmen), continuous (transfers).

Admissions Contact Mr. Richard Hillman, Associate Director of Admissions, University of Wisconsin–Oshkosh, Oshkosh, WI 54901-8602. *Phone:* 920-424-0202. *E-mail:* oshadmuw@uwosh.edu.

UNIVERSITY OF WISCONSIN–PARKSIDE
Kenosha, Wisconsin

- **State-supported** comprehensive, founded 1968, part of University of Wisconsin System
- **Calendar** semesters
- **Degrees** certificates, bachelor's, and master's
- **Suburban** 700-acre campus with easy access to Chicago and Milwaukee
- **Endowment** $837,167
- **Coed,** 4,939 undergraduate students, 71% full-time, 57% women, 43% men
- **Moderately difficult** entrance level, 60% of applicants were admitted

Undergraduates 3,512 full-time, 1,427 part-time. Students come from 24 states and territories, 27 other countries, 8% are from out of state, 9% African American, 3% Asian American or Pacific Islander, 7% Hispanic American, 0.5% Native American, 2% international, 10% transferred in, 16% live on campus. *Retention:* 67% of 2002 full-time freshmen returned.

Freshmen *Admission:* 2,096 applied, 1,262 admitted, 975 enrolled. *Test scores:* ACT scores over 18: 82%; ACT scores over 24: 25%; ACT scores over 30: 1%.

Faculty *Total:* 282, 62% full-time, 54% with terminal degrees. *Student/faculty ratio:* 19:1.

Majors Accounting; art; biological and biomedical sciences related; business administration and management; chemistry; communication/speech communication and rhetoric; computer science; creative writing; criminal justice/law enforcement administration; dramatic/theatre arts; economics; English; finance; French; geography; geology/earth science; German; history; humanities; interdisciplinary studies; international relations and affairs; mathematics; molecular biology; music; nursing (registered nurse training); philosophy; physics; political science and government; pre-dentistry studies; pre-law studies; pre-medical studies; pre-pharmacy studies; pre-veterinary studies; psychology; sociology; Spanish; sport and fitness administration.

Academic Programs *Special study options:* academic remediation for entering students, accelerated degree program, advanced placement credit, distance learning, double majors, English as a second language, external degree program, independent study, internships, off-campus study, part-time degree program, services for LD students, summer session for credit. *ROTC:* Army (c). *Unusual degree programs:* 3-2 molecular biology.

Library Library-Learning Center with 400,000 titles, 1,590 serial subscriptions, 21,220 audiovisual materials, an OPAC, a Web page.

Computers on Campus 228 computers available on campus for general student use. A campuswide network can be accessed from student residence rooms and from off campus. Internet access, online (class) registration, at least one staffed computer lab available.

Student Life *Housing options:* coed, disabled students. Campus housing is university owned. *Activities and organizations:* drama/theater group, student-run newspaper, radio station, choral group, Black Student Union, Latinos Unidos, Parkside Student Government Association, Asian American Club, Parkside Adult Student Alliance, national fraternities, national sororities. *Campus security:* 24-hour emergency response devices and patrols, late-night transport/escort service, controlled dormitory access. *Student services:* health clinic, personal/psychological counseling, women's center.

Athletics Member NCAA, NAIA. All NCAA Division II. *Intercollegiate sports:* baseball M(s), basketball M(s)/W(s), cross-country running M(s)/W(s), golf M(s), soccer M(s)/W(s), softball W(s), track and field M(s)/W(s), volleyball W(s), wrestling M(s). *Intramural sports:* badminton M/W, basketball M/W, bowling M(c)/W(c), cheerleading M/W, football M/W, racquetball M/W, rugby M(c), soccer M/W, softball M/W, swimming M/W, table tennis M/W, tennis M/W, volleyball M/W.

Standardized Tests *Required for some:* SAT I or ACT (for admission).

Costs (2004–05) *One-time required fee:* $87. *Tuition:* state resident $3532 full-time, $180 per credit hour part-time; nonresident $13,578 full-time, $598 per credit hour part-time. Full-time tuition and fees vary according to course load and reciprocity agreements. Part-time tuition and fees vary according to course load. *Room and board:* $5056; room only: $3156. Room and board charges vary according to board plan and housing facility. *Payment plan:* installment. *Waivers:* senior citizens.

Financial Aid Of all full-time matriculated undergraduates who enrolled in 2003, 2,597 applied for aid, 1,721 were judged to have need, 679 had their need fully met. In 2003, 125 non-need-based awards were made. *Average percent of need met:* 78%. *Average financial aid package:* $5953. *Average need-based loan:* $3405. *Average need-based gift aid:* $4098. *Average non-need-based aid:* $2105. *Average indebtedness upon graduation:* $12,500.

Applying *Options:* electronic application, deferred entrance. *Application fee:* $35. *Required:* high school transcript, minimum of 17 high school units distributed as specified in the UW-Parkside catalog. *Application deadlines:* 8/1 (freshmen), 8/1 (transfers). *Notification:* continuous (freshmen), continuous (transfers).

Admissions Contact Mr. Matthew Jensen, Director of Admissions, University of Wisconsin–Parkside, PO Box 2000, 900 Wood Road, Kenosha, WI 53141-2000. *Phone:* 262-595-2757. *Toll-free phone:* 877-633-3897. *Fax:* 262-595-2008. *E-mail:* matthew.jensen@uwp.edu.

UNIVERSITY OF WISCONSIN–PLATTEVILLE
Platteville, Wisconsin

- **State-supported** comprehensive, founded 1866, part of University of Wisconsin System
- **Calendar** semesters
- **Degrees** certificates, diplomas, associate, bachelor's, and master's
- **Small-town** 380-acre campus
- **Endowment** $3.0 million
- **Coed,** 5,541 undergraduate students, 91% full-time, 39% women, 61% men
- **Moderately difficult** entrance level, 80% of applicants were admitted

Undergraduates 5,015 full-time, 526 part-time. Students come from 34 states and territories, 11% are from out of state, 0.8% African American, 1% Asian American or Pacific Islander, 0.6% Hispanic American, 0.2% Native American, 0.6% international, 6% transferred in, 55% live on campus.

Freshmen *Admission:* 2,789 applied, 2,229 admitted, 1,103 enrolled. *Test scores:* ACT scores over 18: 92%; ACT scores over 24: 35%; ACT scores over 30: 4%.

Faculty *Total:* 306, 76% full-time, 67% with terminal degrees. *Student/faculty ratio:* 19:1.

Majors Accounting; agricultural business and management; agronomy and crop science; animal sciences; art; biological and physical sciences; biology/biological sciences; broadcast journalism; business administration and management; business/managerial economics; cartography; civil engineering; commercial and advertising art; computer science; construction management; criminal justice/law enforcement administration; economics; education; electrical, electronics and communications engineering; elementary education; English; French; geography; geology/earth science; German; history; industrial arts; industrial design; industrial engineering; industrial technology; international relations and affairs; kindergarten/preschool education; land use planning and management; liberal arts and sciences/liberal studies; mass communication/media; mathematics; mechanical engineering; middle school education; music; philosophy; political science and government; psychology; science teacher education; secondary education; social sciences; Spanish; speech and rhetoric; telecommunications.

Academic Programs *Special study options:* academic remediation for entering students, adult/continuing education programs, advanced placement credit, cooperative education, distance learning, double majors, external degree program, honors programs, independent study, internships, off-campus study, part-time degree program, services for LD students, student-designed majors, study abroad, summer session for credit.

Library Karrmann Library with 321,456 titles, 1,280 serial subscriptions, 13,879 audiovisual materials, an OPAC, a Web page.

Computers on Campus 250 computers available on campus for general student use. A campuswide network can be accessed from student residence rooms and from off campus. Internet access, at least one staffed computer lab available.

University of Wisconsin–Platteville (continued)

Student Life *Housing:* on-campus residence required through sophomore year. *Options:* coed, men-only, women-only. *Activities and organizations:* drama/theater group, student-run newspaper, radio and television station, choral group, marching band, national fraternities, national sororities. *Campus security:* 24-hour emergency response devices and patrols, student patrols, late-night transport/escort service. *Student services:* health clinic, personal/psychological counseling, women's center.

Athletics Member NCAA. All Division III. *Intercollegiate sports:* baseball M, basketball M/W, cross-country running M/W, football M, golf M, ice hockey M(c), rugby M(c), soccer M/W, softball W, track and field M/W, volleyball M(c)/W, wrestling M. *Intramural sports:* badminton M/W, basketball M/W, bowling M/W, football M, golf M, racquetball M/W, soccer M/W, softball M/W, table tennis M/W, tennis M/W, volleyball M/W, water polo M/W.

Standardized Tests *Required:* SAT I or ACT (for admission). *Recommended:* ACT (for admission).

Costs (2003–04) *Tuition:* $146 per credit part-time; state resident $3500 full-time; nonresident $13,546 full-time, $564 per credit part-time. No tuition increase for student's term of enrollment. *Required fees:* $754 full-time. *Room and board:* $4196; room only: $2120. *Payment plan:* installment.

Financial Aid Of all full-time matriculated undergraduates who enrolled in 2002, 3,289 applied for aid, 2,468 were judged to have need. 382 Federal Work-Study jobs (averaging $1392). In 2002, 652 non-need-based awards were made. *Average financial aid package:* $6161. *Average need-based loan:* $3499. *Average need-based gift aid:* $3599. *Average non-need-based aid:* $1427. *Average indebtedness upon graduation:* $15,785.

Applying *Options:* electronic application. *Application fee:* $35. *Required:* high school transcript. *Required for some:* letters of recommendation. *Application deadline:* rolling (freshmen), rolling (transfers). *Notification:* continuous (transfers).

Admissions Contact Dr. Richard Schumacher, Dean of Admissions and Enrollment Management, University of Wisconsin–Platteville, 1 University Plaza, Platteville, WI 53818-3099. *Phone:* 608-342-1125. *Toll-free phone:* 800-362-5515. *Fax:* 608-342-1122. *E-mail:* admissions@uwplatt.edu.

UNIVERSITY OF WISCONSIN–RIVER FALLS

River Falls, Wisconsin

- **State-supported** comprehensive, founded 1874, part of University of Wisconsin System
- **Calendar** semesters
- **Degrees** certificates, bachelor's, master's, and post-master's certificates
- **Suburban** 225-acre campus with easy access to Minneapolis–St. Paul
- **Coed,** 5,413 undergraduate students, 93% full-time, 61% women, 39% men
- **Moderately difficult** entrance level, 76% of applicants were admitted

Undergraduates 5,019 full-time, 394 part-time. Students come from 26 states and territories, 12 other countries, 48% are from out of state, 1% African American, 3% Asian American or Pacific Islander, 1% Hispanic American, 0.5% Native American, 0.9% international, 7% transferred in, 38% live on campus. *Retention:* 75% of 2002 full-time freshmen returned.

Freshmen *Admission:* 2,786 applied, 2,108 admitted, 1,227 enrolled. *Average high school GPA:* 3.34. *Test scores:* ACT scores over 18: 93%; ACT scores over 24: 35%; ACT scores over 30: 3%.

Faculty *Total:* 337, 69% full-time. *Student/faculty ratio:* 20:1.

Majors Accounting; agricultural/biological engineering and bioengineering; agricultural business and management; agricultural teacher education; agriculture; agronomy and crop science; animal sciences; art; art teacher education; biochemistry; biology/biological sciences; biology teacher education; biotechnology; broadcast journalism; business administration and management; chemistry; chemistry teacher education; communication disorders; computer and information sciences; computer science; computer teacher education; dairy science; dramatic/theatre arts; economics; education; elementary education; engineering technology; English; English as a second/foreign language (teaching); English/language arts teacher education; environmental studies; equestrian studies; finance; food science; French; French language teacher education; geography; geology/earth science; German; German language teacher education; history; history teacher education; horticultural science; information science/studies; journalism; land use planning and management; liberal arts and sciences/liberal studies; management information systems; marketing/marketing management; mathematics; mathematics teacher education; music; music teacher education; natural resources/conservation; natural sciences; physical education teaching and coaching; physical sciences; physics; physics teacher education; political science and government; pre-dentistry studies; pre-law studies; pre-medical studies; pre-pharmacy studies; pre-veterinary studies; psychology; public relations/image management; radio and television; science teacher education; secondary education; social sciences; social science teacher education; social studies teacher education; social work; sociology; soil science and agronomy; Spanish; Spanish language teacher education; speech and rhetoric; speech therapy.

Academic Programs *Special study options:* academic remediation for entering students, accelerated degree program, adult/continuing education programs, advanced placement credit, cooperative education, distance learning, double majors, external degree program, honors programs, independent study, internships, off-campus study, part-time degree program, services for LD students, student-designed majors, study abroad, summer session for credit. *Unusual degree programs:* 3-2 engineering with University of Wisconsin, Madison and University of Minnesota, Twin Cities.

Library Chalmer Davee Library with 448,088 titles, 1,660 serial subscriptions, 7,500 audiovisual materials, an OPAC, a Web page.

Computers on Campus 387 computers available on campus for general student use. A campuswide network can be accessed from student residence rooms and from off campus. Internet access, online (class) registration, at least one staffed computer lab available.

Student Life *Housing:* on-campus residence required through sophomore year. *Options:* coed, women-only. Campus housing is university owned. *Activities and organizations:* drama/theater group, student-run newspaper, radio and television station, choral group, Bushwackers (high adventure club), Habitat for Humanity, Agricultural Education Society, dairy club, rodeo club, national fraternities, national sororities. *Campus security:* 24-hour emergency response devices and patrols, student patrols, late-night transport/escort service, controlled dormitory access. *Student services:* health clinic, personal/psychological counseling, women's center.

Athletics Member NCAA. All Division III. *Intercollegiate sports:* basketball M/W, cross-country running M/W, equestrian sports M(c)/W(c), football M, ice hockey M/W, rugby M(c)/W(c), soccer M(c)/W, softball W, swimming M/W, tennis W, track and field M(c)/W, volleyball M(c)/W, weight lifting M(c)/W(c). *Intramural sports:* badminton M/W, basketball M/W, football M/W, golf M/W, softball M/W, tennis M/W, volleyball M/W.

Standardized Tests *Required:* ACT (for admission).

Costs (2003–04) *Tuition:* state resident $4450 full-time; nonresident $14,496 full-time. Full-time tuition and fees vary according to course load and reciprocity agreements. Part-time tuition and fees vary according to course load and reciprocity agreements. *Room and board:* $3968; room only: $2248. Room and board charges vary according to board plan. *Payment plan:* installment.

Financial Aid Of all full-time matriculated undergraduates who enrolled in 1999, 3,631 applied for aid, 2,727 were judged to have need, 1,240 had their need fully met. *Average percent of need met:* 77%. *Average financial aid package:* $4429. *Average need-based loan:* $2353. *Average need-based gift aid:* $1652. *Average non-need-based aid:* $3738. *Average indebtedness upon graduation:* $12,500.

Applying *Options:* common application, electronic application, deferred entrance. *Application fee:* $35. *Required:* high school transcript. *Recommended:* rank in upper 40% of high school class. *Application deadline:* rolling (freshmen), rolling (transfers). *Notification:* continuous (freshmen), continuous (transfers).

Admissions Contact Mr. Alan Tuchtenhagen, Director of Admissions, University of Wisconsin–River Falls, 410 South Third Street, 112 South Hall, River Falls, WI 54022-5001. *Phone:* 715-425-3500. *Fax:* 715-425-0676. *E-mail:* admit@uwrf.edu.

UNIVERSITY OF WISCONSIN–STEVENS POINT

Stevens Point, Wisconsin

- **State-supported** comprehensive, founded 1894, part of University of Wisconsin System
- **Calendar** semesters
- **Degrees** associate, bachelor's, and master's
- **Small-town** 335-acre campus
- **Endowment** $11.0 million
- **Coed,** 8,503 undergraduate students, 91% full-time, 56% women, 44% men
- **Moderately difficult** entrance level, 75% of applicants were admitted

Undergraduates 7,739 full-time, 764 part-time. Students come from 29 states and territories, 27 other countries, 6% are from out of state, 0.8% African American, 2% Asian American or Pacific Islander, 1% Hispanic American, 0.8% Native American, 2% international, 7% transferred in, 36% live on campus. *Retention:* 77% of 2002 full-time freshmen returned.

Freshmen *Admission:* 4,621 applied, 3,484 admitted, 1,506 enrolled. *Average high school GPA:* 3.40. *Test scores:* SAT verbal scores over 500: 92%; SAT math scores over 500: 84%; ACT scores over 18: 96%; SAT verbal scores over 600: 36%; SAT math scores over 600: 60%; ACT scores over 24: 38%; SAT verbal scores over 700: 12%; SAT math scores over 700: 4%; ACT scores over 30: 3%.

Faculty *Total:* 424, 85% full-time, 79% with terminal degrees. *Student/faculty ratio:* 20:1.

Majors Accounting; actuarial science; art; arts management; athletic training; audiology and speech-language pathology; biology/biological sciences; business administration and management; chemistry; clinical laboratory science/medical technology; commercial and advertising art; communication/speech communication and rhetoric; computer and information sciences; dance; dietetics; dramatic/theatre arts; economics; education; elementary education; English; family and consumer economics related; family and consumer sciences/home economics teacher education; fine/studio arts; forestry; French; general studies; geography; German; health and physical education; history; hydrology and water resources science; interior design; international relations and affairs; kindergarten/preschool education; liberal arts and sciences/liberal studies; mathematics; music; music teacher education; natural resources/conservation; natural resources management and policy; natural sciences; philosophy; physical education teaching and coaching; physics; political science and government; polymer chemistry; psychology; public administration; secondary education; social sciences; sociology; soil conservation; Spanish; web page, digital/multimedia and information resources design; wildlife and wildlands science and management; wood science and wood products/pulp and paper technology.

Academic Programs *Special study options:* academic remediation for entering students, accelerated degree program, adult/continuing education programs, advanced placement credit, cooperative education, distance learning, double majors, English as a second language, independent study, internships, off-campus study, part-time degree program, services for LD students, student-designed majors, study abroad, summer session for credit. *ROTC:* Army (b).

Library Learning Resources Center with 978,112 titles, 8,470 serial subscriptions, 32,916 audiovisual materials, an OPAC, a Web page.

Computers on Campus 800 computers available on campus for general student use. A campuswide network can be accessed from student residence rooms and from off campus. Internet access, at least one staffed computer lab available.

Student Life *Housing:* on-campus residence required through sophomore year. *Options:* coed, men-only, women-only. Campus housing is university owned. *Activities and organizations:* drama/theater group, student-run newspaper, radio and television station, choral group, national fraternities, national sororities. *Campus security:* 24-hour emergency response devices and patrols, student patrols, late-night transport/escort service, controlled dormitory access. *Student services:* health clinic, personal/psychological counseling, women's center.

Athletics Member NCAA. All Division III. *Intercollegiate sports:* baseball M, basketball M/W, cross-country running M/W, football M, golf W, ice hockey M/W, soccer W, softball W, swimming M/W, tennis W, track and field M/W, volleyball W, wrestling M. *Intramural sports:* badminton M/W, basketball M/W, football M/W, golf M/W, ice hockey M/W, racquetball M/W, soccer M/W, softball M/W, table tennis M/W, tennis M/W, volleyball M/W, wrestling M/W.

Standardized Tests *Required:* SAT I or ACT (for admission).

Costs (2003–04) *Tuition:* state resident $3500 full-time, $146 per credit part-time; nonresident $13,547 full-time, $564 per credit part-time. Full-time tuition and fees vary according to course load and reciprocity agreements. Part-time tuition and fees vary according to course load and reciprocity agreements. *Required fees:* $648 full-time, $58 per credit part-time. *Room and board:* $3964; room only: $2324. *Payment plan:* installment.

Financial Aid Of all full-time matriculated undergraduates who enrolled in 2002, 6,847 applied for aid, 3,784 were judged to have need, 2,707 had their need fully met. 1,232 Federal Work-Study jobs (averaging $1683). In 2002, 501 non-need-based awards were made. *Average percent of need met:* 90%. *Average financial aid package:* $6047. *Average need-based loan:* $3675. *Average need-based gift aid:* $4085. *Average non-need-based aid:* $1563. *Average indebtedness upon graduation:* $13,504.

Applying *Options:* electronic application, deferred entrance. *Application fee:* $50. *Required:* high school transcript. *Recommended:* campus visit. *Application deadline:* rolling (freshmen), rolling (transfers). *Notification:* continuous (freshmen), continuous (transfers).

Admissions Contact Ms. Catherine Glennon, Director of Admissions, University of Wisconsin–Stevens Point, 2100 Main Street, Stevens Point, WI 54481. *Phone:* 715-346-2441. *Fax:* 715-346-3296. *E-mail:* admiss@uwsp.edu.

UNIVERSITY OF WISCONSIN–STOUT

Menomonie, Wisconsin

- **State-supported** comprehensive, founded 1891, part of University of Wisconsin System
- **Calendar** 4-1-4
- **Degrees** certificates, bachelor's, master's, and post-master's certificates
- **Small-town** 120-acre campus with easy access to Minneapolis–St. Paul
- **Endowment** $465,500
- **Coed,** 7,101 undergraduate students, 90% full-time, 49% women, 51% men
- **Moderately difficult** entrance level, 66% of applicants were admitted

Undergraduates 6,392 full-time, 709 part-time. Students come from 26 states and territories, 29% are from out of state, 1% African American, 2% Asian American or Pacific Islander, 0.7% Hispanic American, 0.3% Native American, 0.4% international, 7% transferred in, 35% live on campus. *Retention:* 72% of 2002 full-time freshmen returned.

Freshmen *Admission:* 3,876 applied, 2,576 admitted, 1,275 enrolled. *Average high school GPA:* 3.23. *Test scores:* SAT verbal scores over 500: 67%; SAT math scores over 500: 72%; ACT scores over 18: 89%; SAT verbal scores over 600: 14%; SAT math scores over 600: 19%; ACT scores over 24: 25%; ACT scores over 30: 1%.

Faculty *Total:* 389, 75% full-time, 63% with terminal degrees. *Student/faculty ratio:* 19:1.

Majors Apparel and textiles; applied mathematics; art teacher education; business administration and management; computer systems networking and telecommunications; construction engineering technology; customer service management; design and applied arts related; dietetics; early childhood education; engineering/industrial management; engineering technology; family and consumer sciences/home economics teacher education; foods and nutrition related; foodservice systems administration; hospitality administration; human development and family studies; industrial production technologies related; manufacturing engineering; operations management; printing management; psychology; sales and marketing/marketing and distribution teacher education; sales, distribution and marketing; science technologies related; technical and business writing; technical teacher education; technology/industrial arts teacher education; vocational rehabilitation counseling.

Academic Programs *Special study options:* academic remediation for entering students, accelerated degree program, adult/continuing education programs, advanced placement credit, cooperative education, distance learning, double majors, external degree program, honors programs, independent study, internships, off-campus study, part-time degree program, services for LD students, study abroad, summer session for credit.

Library Library Learning Center with 229,986 titles, 1,784 serial subscriptions, 16,142 audiovisual materials, an OPAC, a Web page.

Computers on Campus 590 computers available on campus for general student use. A campuswide network can be accessed from student residence rooms and from off campus. Internet access, online (class) registration, at least one staffed computer lab available. Computer purchase or lease plan available.

Student Life *Housing:* on-campus residence required through sophomore year. *Options:* coed. Campus housing is university owned. Freshman campus housing is guaranteed. *Activities and organizations:* drama/theater group, student-run newspaper, radio station, choral group, marching band, Hotel/Motel Management Association, Inter-Greek Council, DECA-District Educational Clubs of America, Recreation Commission, OASIS, national fraternities, national sororities. *Campus security:* 24-hour patrols, student patrols, controlled dormitory access. *Student services:* health clinic, personal/psychological counseling, legal services.

Athletics Member NCAA. All Division III. *Intercollegiate sports:* baseball M, basketball M/W, cheerleading W, cross-country running M/W, football M, gymnastics W, ice hockey M/W(c), soccer M(c)/W, softball W, tennis W, track and field M/W, volleyball M(c)/W. *Intramural sports:* baseball M, basketball M/W, bowling M(c)/W(c), football M/W, golf M/W, ice hockey M/W, racquetball M/W, rugby M(c)/W(c), skiing (cross-country) M(c)/W(c), skiing (downhill) M(c)/W(c), softball M/W, ultimate Frisbee M/W, volleyball M/W.

Standardized Tests *Required:* SAT I or ACT (for admission). *Recommended:* ACT (for admission).

Costs (2003–04) *Tuition:* state resident $5024 full-time; nonresident $15,360 full-time. Full-time tuition and fees vary according to reciprocity agreements. Part-time tuition and fees vary according to reciprocity agreements. *Required fees:* $656 full-time. *Room and board:* $4038; room only: $2292. Room and board charges vary according to board plan. *Payment plan:* installment.

Financial Aid Of all full-time matriculated undergraduates who enrolled in 2003, 4,598 applied for aid, 3,215 were judged to have need, 1,978 had their need fully met. 1,271 Federal Work-Study jobs (averaging $1445). In 2003, 393 non-need-based awards were made. *Average percent of need met:* 91%. *Average financial aid package:* $6746. *Average need-based loan:* $3978. *Average need-based gift aid:* $4204. *Average non-need-based aid:* $1749. *Average indebtedness upon graduation:* $16,746.

Applying *Options:* electronic application. *Application fee:* $35. *Required:* high school transcript. *Required for some:* minimum 2.75 GPA. *Application deadline:* rolling (freshmen), rolling (transfers). *Notification:* continuous (freshmen), continuous (transfers).

Admissions Contact Ms. Cynthia Jenkins, Director of Admissions, University of Wisconsin–Stout, Admissions UW-Stout, Bowman Hall, Menomonie, WI 54751. *Phone:* 715-232-2639. *Toll-free phone:* 800-HI-STOUT. *Fax:* 715-232-1667. *E-mail:* admissions@uwstout.edu.

UNIVERSITY OF WISCONSIN–SUPERIOR
Superior, Wisconsin

- **State-supported** comprehensive, founded 1893, part of University of Wisconsin System
- **Calendar** semesters
- **Degrees** certificates, diplomas, associate, bachelor's, master's, first professional, and postbachelor's certificates
- **Small-town** 230-acre campus
- **Endowment** $7.5 million
- **Coed,** 2,530 undergraduate students, 77% full-time, 59% women, 41% men
- **Moderately difficult** entrance level, 77% of applicants were admitted

Undergraduates 1,947 full-time, 583 part-time. Students come from 17 states and territories, 32 other countries, 40% are from out of state, 0.9% African American, 0.8% Asian American or Pacific Islander, 0.3% Hispanic American, 2% Native American, 6% international, 13% transferred in, 21% live on campus. *Retention:* 69% of 2002 full-time freshmen returned.

Freshmen *Admission:* 869 applied, 673 admitted, 352 enrolled. *Test scores:* SAT verbal scores over 500: 50%; SAT math scores over 500: 67%; ACT scores over 18: 92%; SAT math scores over 600: 33%; ACT scores over 24: 33%; ACT scores over 30: 2%.

Faculty *Total:* 198, 57% full-time, 52% with terminal degrees. *Student/faculty ratio:* 17:1.

Majors Accounting; administrative assistant and secretarial science; art history, criticism and conservation; art teacher education; art therapy; biological and physical sciences; biology/biological sciences; biology teacher education; broadcast journalism; business administration and management; business/managerial economics; business teacher education; cell biology and histology; chemistry; chemistry teacher education; communication/speech communication and rhetoric; computer and information sciences; computer science; counselor education/school counseling and guidance; criminal justice/police science; criminal justice/safety; dramatic/theatre arts; economics; education; educational/instructional media design; educational leadership and administration; education (K-12); elementary education; English; English/language arts teacher education; fine/studio arts; history; history teacher education; information science/studies; journalism; legal assistant/paralegal; legal studies; liberal arts and sciences/liberal studies; marine biology and biological oceanography; marketing/marketing management; mass communication/media; mathematics; mathematics teacher education; molecular biology; music; music teacher education; physical education teaching and coaching; physical sciences; political science and government; pre-law studies; psychology; radio and television; reading teacher education; sales, distribution and marketing; science teacher education; social psychology; social sciences; social science teacher education; social studies teacher education; social work; sociology; special education; speech and rhetoric.

Academic Programs *Special study options:* academic remediation for entering students, adult/continuing education programs, advanced placement credit, cooperative education, distance learning, double majors, English as a second language, external degree program, freshman honors college, honors programs, independent study, internships, off-campus study, part-time degree program, services for LD students, student-designed majors, study abroad, summer session for credit. *ROTC:* Air Force (c). *Unusual degree programs:* 3-2 engineering with Michigan Technological University, University of Wisconsin-Madison; forestry with Michigan Technological University.

Library Jim Dan Hill Library with 467,700 titles, 753 serial subscriptions, 5,467 audiovisual materials, an OPAC, a Web page.

Computers on Campus 161 computers available on campus for general student use. A campuswide network can be accessed from student residence rooms and from off campus. Internet access, online (class) registration, at least one staffed computer lab available. Computer purchase or lease plan available.

Student Life *Housing:* on-campus residence required for freshman year. *Options:* coed, men-only, women-only, disabled students. Campus housing is university owned. Freshman campus housing is guaranteed. *Activities and organizations:* drama/theater group, student-run newspaper, radio and television station, choral group, Student Senate, Student Activities Board, Residence Hall Association, Intervarsity Christian Fellowship. *Campus security:* 24-hour emergency response devices and patrols, student patrols, late-night transport/escort service, controlled dormitory access. *Student services:* health clinic, personal/psychological counseling, women's center.

Athletics Member NCAA. All Division III. *Intercollegiate sports:* baseball M, basketball M/W, cheerleading M/W, cross-country running M/W, golf W, ice hockey M/W, soccer M/W, softball W, track and field M/W, volleyball W. *Intramural sports:* badminton M/W, baseball M/W, basketball M/W, bowling M/W, cross-country running M/W, golf M/W, ice hockey M, racquetball M/W, riflery M/W, skiing (cross-country) M/W, skiing (downhill) M/W, softball M/W, table tennis M/W, tennis M/W, volleyball M/W.

Standardized Tests *Required:* SAT I or ACT (for admission). *Recommended:* ACT (for admission).

Costs (2003–04) *Tuition:* state resident $4276 full-time; nonresident $14,322 full-time. Full-time tuition and fees vary according to course load and reciprocity agreements. Part-time tuition and fees vary according to course load and reciprocity agreements. *Room and board:* $4246; room only: $2406. Room and board charges vary according to housing facility. *Payment plan:* installment. *Waivers:* minority students and senior citizens.

Financial Aid Of all full-time matriculated undergraduates who enrolled in 2003, 1,366 applied for aid, 1,090 were judged to have need, 633 had their need fully met. 260 Federal Work-Study jobs (averaging $1320). In 2003, 46 non-need-based awards were made. *Average financial aid package:* $8274. *Average need-based loan:* $3966. *Average need-based gift aid:* $4260. *Average non-need-based aid:* $1263. *Average indebtedness upon graduation:* $11,564.

Applying *Options:* electronic application, early admission, deferred entrance. *Application fee:* $35. *Required:* high school transcript. *Required for some:* minimum 2.6 GPA, letters of recommendation. *Recommended:* interview. *Application deadline:* 4/1 (freshmen), rolling (transfers). *Notification:* continuous (freshmen), continuous (transfers).

Admissions Contact Lee Parker, Admissions Advisor, University of Wisconsin–Superior, Belknap and Catlin, PO Box 2000, Superior, WI 54880-4500. *Phone:* 715-394-8217. *Toll-free phone:* 715-394-8230. *Fax:* 715-394-8407. *E-mail:* admissions@uwsuper.edu.

UNIVERSITY OF WISCONSIN–WHITEWATER
Whitewater, Wisconsin

- **State-supported** comprehensive, founded 1868, part of University of Wisconsin System
- **Calendar** semesters
- **Degrees** associate, bachelor's, and master's
- **Small-town** 385-acre campus with easy access to Milwaukee
- **Endowment** $6.6 million
- **Coed,** 9,429 undergraduate students, 92% full-time, 53% women, 47% men
- **Moderately difficult** entrance level, 68% of applicants were admitted

Undergraduates 8,633 full-time, 796 part-time. Students come from 29 states and territories, 37 other countries, 4% are from out of state, 4% African American, 2% Asian American or Pacific Islander, 2% Hispanic American, 0.4% Native American, 0.8% international, 6% transferred in, 40% live on campus. *Retention:* 78% of 2002 full-time freshmen returned.

Freshmen *Admission:* 5,639 applied, 3,821 admitted, 1,832 enrolled. *Test scores:* ACT scores over 18: 89%; ACT scores over 24: 32%; ACT scores over 30: 1%.

Faculty *Total:* 506, 74% full-time, 65% with terminal degrees. *Student/faculty ratio:* 20:1.

Majors Accounting; art; art history, criticism and conservation; art teacher education; biological and physical sciences; biology/biological sciences; business administration and management; business/commerce; business/managerial economics; business teacher education; chemistry; chemistry related; communication/speech communication and rhetoric; computer and information sciences; dramatic/theatre arts; early childhood education; education; elementary education; English; environmental engineering technology; finance; French; geography; German; history; human resources management; information technology; international/global studies; international relations and affairs; journalism; liberal arts and sciences and humanities related; liberal arts and sciences/liberal studies; management information systems; marketing/marketing management; mathematics; music; music teacher education; occupational safety and health technology; operations management; physical education teaching and coaching; physics; political science and government; psychology; public administration; public policy analysis; science teacher education; secondary education; social sciences; social work; sociology; Spanish; special education; speech and rhetoric; speech-language pathology; women's studies.

Academic Programs *Special study options:* academic remediation for entering students, accelerated degree program, adult/continuing education programs, advanced placement credit, cooperative education, distance learning, double majors, external degree program, honors programs, independent study, internships, part-time degree program, services for LD students, student-designed majors, study abroad, summer session for credit. *ROTC:* Army (b), Air Force (b).

Library Andersen Library with 647,029 titles, 3,358 serial subscriptions, 15,974 audiovisual materials, an OPAC, a Web page.

Computers on Campus 700 computers available on campus for general student use. A campuswide network can be accessed from student residence rooms and from off campus. At least one staffed computer lab available.

Student Life *Housing:* on-campus residence required through sophomore year. *Options:* coed. Campus housing is university owned. Freshman campus housing is guaranteed. *Activities and organizations:* drama/theater group, student-run newspaper, radio and television station, choral group, marching band, Finance Association, American Marketing Association, Black Student Union, Golden Key, Wisconsin Education Association, national fraternities, national sororities. *Campus security:* 24-hour emergency response devices, late-night transport/escort service. *Student services:* health clinic, personal/psychological counseling, women's center, legal services.

Athletics Member NCAA. All Division III. *Intercollegiate sports:* baseball M, basketball M/W, bowling M(c)/W(s)(c), cheerleading M(c)/W(c), cross-country running M/W, football M, golf W, gymnastics W, ice hockey M(c)/W(c), lacrosse M(c), rugby M(c)/W(c), soccer M/W, softball W, swimming M/W, tennis M/W, track and field M/W, volleyball M(c)/W, weight lifting M(c), wrestling M/W(c). *Intramural sports:* badminton M/W, basketball M/W, football M, golf M/W, racquetball M/W, soccer M/W, softball M/W, table tennis M/W, tennis M/W, volleyball M/W, water polo M/W.

Standardized Tests *Required for some:* SAT I or ACT (for admission). *Recommended:* SAT I or ACT (for admission).

Costs (2003–04) *Tuition:* state resident $4278 full-time, $178 per credit part-time; nonresident $14,324 full-time, $597 per credit part-time. *Required fees:* $656 full-time. *Room and board:* $3742; room only: $2232. Room and board charges vary according to board plan.

Financial Aid Of all full-time matriculated undergraduates who enrolled in 2003, 5,710 applied for aid, 4,042 were judged to have need, 1,992 had their need fully met. 600 Federal Work-Study jobs (averaging $1160). 2,000 state and other part-time jobs (averaging $1550). In 2003, 903 non-need-based awards were made. *Average percent of need met:* 75%. *Average financial aid package:* $5970. *Average need-based loan:* $3829. *Average need-based gift aid:* $3790. *Average non-need-based aid:* $1595.

Applying *Options:* early admission, deferred entrance. *Application fee:* $35. *Required:* high school transcript. *Required for some:* letters of recommendation. *Application deadline:* rolling (freshmen), rolling (transfers). *Notification:* continuous (transfers).

Admissions Contact Dr. Tori A. Erickson, Executive Director of Admissions, University of Wisconsin–Whitewater, 800 West Main Street, Whitewater, WI 53190-1790. *Phone:* 262-472-1440 Ext. 1512. *Fax:* 262-472-1515. *E-mail:* uwwadmit@uww.edu.

VITERBO UNIVERSITY

La Crosse, Wisconsin

- **Independent Roman Catholic** comprehensive, founded 1890
- **Calendar** semesters
- **Degrees** bachelor's and master's
- **Suburban** 72-acre campus
- **Endowment** $11.6 million
- **Coed,** 1,862 undergraduate students, 81% full-time, 75% women, 25% men
- **Moderately difficult** entrance level, 88% of applicants were admitted

Established in 1890, Viterbo University, located in La Crosse, Wisconsin, is western Wisconsin's premier private university. Viterbo offers undergraduate and graduate degrees through 5 undergraduate schools and the School of Extended Learning, which allows students to select from 38 majors and 27 minors. Viterbo's nursing, fine arts, and education programs have earned outstanding reputations for exceptional quality. Some 2,100 students are formally enrolled with a student-faculty ratio of 16:1. More than 95% of all Viterbo graduates have been placed. A total of 70% of the students are men; 30% are women. Named a character-building college by the prestigious Templeton Foundation, Viterbo is housed on 21 acres in a residential area and has recently opened a new $11-million science center.

Undergraduates 1,503 full-time, 359 part-time. Students come from 22 states and territories, 11 other countries, 19% are from out of state, 1% African American, 2% Asian American or Pacific Islander, 1% Hispanic American, 0.4% Native American, 0.9% international, 13% transferred in, 37% live on campus. *Retention:* 66% of 2002 full-time freshmen returned.

Freshmen *Admission:* 1,293 applied, 1,136 admitted, 356 enrolled. *Average high school GPA:* 3.24. *Test scores:* ACT scores over 18: 93%; ACT scores over 24: 31%; ACT scores over 30: 4%.

Faculty *Total:* 169, 59% full-time, 49% with terminal degrees. *Student/faculty ratio:* 13:1.

Majors Accounting; art; arts management; art teacher education; biochemistry; biology/biological sciences; biology teacher education; business administration and management; business administration, management and operations related; business teacher education; chemistry; chemistry teacher education; computer and information sciences; computer teacher education; criminal justice/safety; design and visual communications; dietetics; drama and dance teacher education; dramatic/theatre arts; elementary education; English; English language and literature related; English/language arts teacher education; fine/studio arts; graphic design; liberal arts and sciences/liberal studies; management information systems; marketing/marketing management; mathematics; mathematics teacher education; multi-/interdisciplinary studies related; music; music pedagogy; music performance; music teacher education; nursing (registered nurse training); pre-theology/pre-ministerial studies; psychology; religious education; religious studies; restaurant/food services management; science teacher education; social sciences; social studies teacher education; social work; sociology; Spanish; Spanish language teacher education; technology/industrial arts teacher education; visual and performing arts.

Academic Programs *Special study options:* academic remediation for entering students, accelerated degree program, adult/continuing education programs, advanced placement credit, cooperative education, distance learning, double majors, independent study, internships, off-campus study, part-time degree program, student-designed majors, study abroad, summer session for credit. *ROTC:* Army (c).

Library Todd Wehr Memorial Library with 1.1 million titles, 3,541 serial subscriptions, 6,181 audiovisual materials, an OPAC, a Web page.

Computers on Campus 215 computers available on campus for general student use. A campuswide network can be accessed from student residence rooms and from off campus that provide access to e-mail; blackboard courses. Internet access, at least one staffed computer lab available.

Student Life *Housing:* on-campus residence required through sophomore year. *Options:* coed. Campus housing is university owned. Freshman campus housing is guaranteed. *Activities and organizations:* drama/theater group, student-run newspaper, choral group, Viterbo Student Nurses Association, Viterbo Education Students Club, Connect—AODA peer counselors, campus ministry—volunteer services and service trips, Sigma Pi Delta. *Campus security:* 24-hour emergency response devices, late-night transport/escort service, controlled dormitory access, security officers on campus 5:00 p.m. to 7:00 a.m, lighted pathways, emergency evacuation plan, self-defense education programs. *Student services:* health clinic, personal/psychological counseling.

Athletics Member NAIA. *Intercollegiate sports:* baseball M(s), basketball M(s)/W(s), soccer M(s)/W(s), softball W(s), volleyball W(s). *Intramural sports:* badminton M/W, basketball M/W, bowling M/W, cross-country running M/W, golf M/W, racquetball M/W, skiing (cross-country) M/W, skiing (downhill) M/W, soccer M/W, softball M/W, swimming M/W, table tennis M/W, tennis M/W, ultimate Frisbee M/W, volleyball M/W.

Standardized Tests *Required:* ACT (for admission).

Costs (2004–05) *Comprehensive fee:* $21,210 includes full-time tuition ($15,570), mandatory fees ($420), and room and board ($5220). Part-time tuition: $455 per credit. Part-time tuition and fees vary according to course load. *Required fees:* $120 per semester part-time. *College room only:* $2250. Room and board charges vary according to board plan and housing facility. *Payment plan:* installment. *Waivers:* senior citizens and employees or children of employees.

Financial Aid Of all full-time matriculated undergraduates who enrolled in 2003, 1,311 applied for aid, 1,208 were judged to have need, 309 had their need fully met. 387 Federal Work-Study jobs (averaging $1680). 19 state and other part-time jobs (averaging $1615). In 2003, 223 non-need-based awards were made. *Average percent of need met:* 71%. *Average financial aid package:* $13,534. *Average need-based loan:* $4317. *Average need-based gift aid:* $8859. *Average non-need-based aid:* $5629. *Average indebtedness upon graduation:* $16,619.

Applying *Options:* common application. *Application fee:* $25. *Required:* high school transcript, minimum 2.0 GPA. *Required for some:* essay or personal statement, 1 letter of recommendation, interview, audition for theater and music; portfolio for art. *Application deadline:* rolling (freshmen), rolling (transfers). *Notification:* continuous until 8/15 (freshmen), continuous until 8/15 (transfers).

Admissions Contact Admission Counselor, Viterbo University, 900 Viterbo Drive, LaCrosse, WI 54601. *Phone:* 608-796-3010 Ext. 3010. *Toll-free phone:* 800-VITERBO Ext. 3010. *Fax:* 608-796-3020. *E-mail:* admission@viterbo.edu.

WISCONSIN LUTHERAN COLLEGE

Milwaukee, Wisconsin

- **Independent** 4-year, founded 1973, affiliated with Wisconsin Evangelical Lutheran Synod
- **Calendar** semesters
- **Degree** bachelor's
- **Suburban** 21-acre campus
- **Endowment** $10.3 million
- **Coed,** 706 undergraduate students, 95% full-time, 60% women, 40% men
- **Moderately difficult** entrance level, 84% of applicants were admitted

Undergraduates 672 full-time, 34 part-time. Students come from 28 states and territories, 6 other countries, 19% are from out of state, 1% African American,

Wisconsin Lutheran College (continued)

0.6% Asian American or Pacific Islander, 1% Hispanic American, 1% international, 3% transferred in, 78% live on campus. *Retention:* 80% of 2002 full-time freshmen returned.

Freshmen *Admission:* 531 applied, 444 admitted, 207 enrolled. *Average high school GPA:* 3.48. *Test scores:* ACT scores over 18: 99%; ACT scores over 24: 59%; ACT scores over 30: 5%.

Faculty *Total:* 88, 53% full-time, 40% with terminal degrees. *Student/faculty ratio:* 11:1.

Majors Art; biochemistry; biology/biological sciences; business/managerial economics; chemistry; communication and journalism related; communication/speech communication and rhetoric; dramatic/theatre arts; elementary education; English; history; interdisciplinary studies; mathematics; multi-/interdisciplinary studies related; music; political science and government; psychology; social sciences; Spanish; theology.

Academic Programs *Special study options:* advanced placement credit, double majors, independent study, internships, part-time degree program, services for LD students, student-designed majors, study abroad, summer session for credit. *ROTC:* Army (c), Navy (c), Air Force (c).

Library Marvin M. Schwan Library with 71,731 titles, 614 serial subscriptions, 4,409 audiovisual materials, an OPAC, a Web page.

Computers on Campus 200 computers available on campus for general student use. A campuswide network can be accessed from student residence rooms and from off campus. Internet access, at least one staffed computer lab available.

Student Life *Housing:* on-campus residence required through senior year. *Options:* men-only, women-only. Campus housing is university owned. Freshman campus housing is guaranteed. *Activities and organizations:* drama/theater group, student-run newspaper, choral group. *Campus security:* 24-hour emergency response devices and patrols, late-night transport/escort service, controlled dormitory access, closed-circuit TV monitors. *Student services:* health clinic, personal/psychological counseling.

Athletics Member NCAA. All Division III. *Intercollegiate sports:* baseball M, basketball M/W, cross-country running M/W, football M, golf M/W, soccer M/W, softball W, tennis W, track and field M/W, volleyball M(c)/W. *Intramural sports:* basketball M/W, cheerleading W(c), football M/W, softball M/W, volleyball M/W.

Standardized Tests *Required:* SAT I or ACT (for admission).

Costs (2003–04) *Comprehensive fee:* $21,175 includes full-time tuition ($15,720), mandatory fees ($130), and room and board ($5325). Part-time tuition: $480 per credit. *Required fees:* $50 per year part-time. *College room only:* $2775. Room and board charges vary according to board plan and housing facility. *Payment plan:* installment. *Waivers:* employees or children of employees.

Financial Aid Of all full-time matriculated undergraduates who enrolled in 2003, 539 applied for aid, 502 were judged to have need, 153 had their need fully met. 250 Federal Work-Study jobs (averaging $1624). 23 state and other part-time jobs (averaging $4904). In 2003, 149 non-need-based awards were made. *Average percent of need met:* 86%. *Average financial aid package:* $13,342. *Average need-based loan:* $3447. *Average need-based gift aid:* $9403. *Average non-need-based aid:* $9161. *Average indebtedness upon graduation:* $13,707.

Applying *Options:* common application, electronic application. *Application fee:* $20. *Required:* high school transcript, minimum 2.70 GPA, 1 letter of recommendation, minimum ACT score of 21. *Required for some:* interview. *Notification:* continuous (freshmen), continuous (transfers).

Admissions Contact Mr. Craig Swiontek, Director of Admissions, Wisconsin Lutheran College, 8800 West Bluemound Road, Milwaukee, WI 53226-9942. *Phone:* 414-443-8811. *Toll-free phone:* 888-WIS LUTH. *Fax:* 414-443-8514. *E-mail:* admissions@wlc.edu.

WYOMING

UNIVERSITY OF WYOMING
Laramie, Wyoming

- **State-supported** university, founded 1886
- **Calendar** semesters
- **Degrees** certificates, bachelor's, master's, doctoral, first professional, and post-master's certificates
- **Small-town** 785-acre campus
- **Endowment** $143.9 million
- **Coed,** 9,385 undergraduate students, 81% full-time, 53% women, 47% men
- **Moderately difficult** entrance level, 95% of applicants were admitted

Undergraduates 7,605 full-time, 1,780 part-time. Students come from 52 states and territories, 48 other countries, 27% are from out of state, 1% African American, 1% Asian American or Pacific Islander, 4% Hispanic American, 1% Native American, 1% international, 12% transferred in, 23% live on campus. *Retention:* 75% of 2002 full-time freshmen returned.

Freshmen *Admission:* 2,948 applied, 2,796 admitted, 1,416 enrolled. *Average high school GPA:* 3.41. *Test scores:* SAT verbal scores over 500: 65%; SAT math scores over 500: 71%; ACT scores over 18: 93%; SAT verbal scores over 600: 24%; SAT math scores over 600: 30%; ACT scores over 24: 45%; SAT verbal scores over 700: 3%; SAT math scores over 700: 5%; ACT scores over 30: 6%.

Faculty *Total:* 655, 95% full-time, 86% with terminal degrees. *Student/faculty ratio:* 16:1.

Majors Accounting; agribusiness; agricultural communication/journalism; agricultural teacher education; agriculture and agriculture operations related; American studies; animal sciences related; anthropology; applied mathematics related; architectural engineering; art; astronomy and astrophysics related; audiology and speech-language pathology; biology/biological sciences; botany/plant biology; business administration and management; business/managerial economics; chemical engineering; chemistry; civil engineering; communication/speech communication and rhetoric; computer engineering; computer science; criminal justice/safety; dental hygiene; dramatic/theatre arts; electrical, electronics and communications engineering; elementary education; English; environmental studies; family and consumer sciences/human sciences; finance; French; geography; geological and earth sciences/geosciences related; geology/earth science; German; health services/allied health/health sciences; health teacher education; history; humanities; international relations and affairs; journalism; kinesiology and exercise science; management information systems; management science; marketing/marketing management; mathematics; mechanical engineering; microbiology; molecular biology; multi-/interdisciplinary studies related; music; music performance; music teacher education; music theory and composition; natural resources/conservation; nursing (registered nurse training); parks, recreation and leisure facilities management; philosophy; physical education teaching and coaching; physics; political science and government; psychology; range science and management; Russian; secondary education; social sciences; social work; sociology; Spanish; special education; special education related; statistics; technology/industrial arts teacher education; trade and industrial teacher education; women's studies; zoology/animal biology.

Academic Programs *Special study options:* accelerated degree program, advanced placement credit, distance learning, double majors, external degree program, honors programs, independent study, internships, off-campus study, part-time degree program, services for LD students, student-designed majors, study abroad, summer session for credit. *ROTC:* Army (b), Air Force (b).

Library William Robertson Coe Library plus 6 others with 1.3 million titles, 13,256 serial subscriptions, 4,161 audiovisual materials, an OPAC, a Web page.

Computers on Campus 1300 computers available on campus for general student use. A campuswide network can be accessed from student residence rooms and from off campus. Internet access, online (class) registration, at least one staffed computer lab available. Computer purchase or lease plan available.

Student Life *Housing:* on-campus residence required for freshman year. *Options:* coed, men-only, disabled students. Campus housing is university owned. Freshman campus housing is guaranteed. *Activities and organizations:* drama/theater group, student-run newspaper, radio and television station, choral group, marching band, Golden Key, SPURS, Fellowship of Christian Athletes, MECHA, national fraternities, national sororities. *Campus security:* 24-hour emergency response devices and patrols, student patrols, late-night transport/escort service, controlled dormitory access. *Student services:* health clinic, personal/psychological counseling, women's center, legal services.

Athletics Member NCAA. All Division I except football (Division I-A). *Intercollegiate sports:* badminton M(c)/W(c), baseball M(c), basketball M(s)/W(s), cheerleading M(s)/W(s), cross-country running M(s)/W(s), fencing M(c)/W(c), golf M(s)/W(s), ice hockey M(c)/W(c), riflery M(c)/W(c), rugby M(c)/W(c), skiing (downhill) M(c)/W(c), soccer M(c)/W(s), swimming M(s)/W(s), tennis W(s), track and field M(s)/W(s), volleyball M(c)/W(s), wrestling M(s). *Intramural sports:* archery M/W, badminton M/W, baseball M, basketball M/W, bowling M/W, cross-country running M/W, fencing M/W, football M/W, golf M/W, racquetball M/W, rock climbing M/W, skiing (downhill) M/W, soccer M/W, softball M/W, table tennis M/W, tennis M/W, ultimate Frisbee M/W, volleyball M/W, water polo M/W, weight lifting M/W, wrestling M/W.

Standardized Tests *Required for some:* SAT I or ACT (for admission).

Costs (2003–04) *Tuition:* state resident $2520 full-time, $84 per credit hour part-time; nonresident $8370 full-time, $279 per credit hour part-time. Full-time tuition and fees vary according to course load, program, and reciprocity agreements. Part-time tuition and fees vary according to course load, program, and reciprocity agreements. *Required fees:* $570 full-time, $134 per term part-time. *Room and board:* $5546; room only: $2372. Room and board charges vary according to board plan and housing facility. *Payment plans:* installment, deferred payment. *Waivers:* children of alumni, senior citizens, and employees or children of employees.

Financial Aid Of all full-time matriculated undergraduates who enrolled in 2002, 4,871 applied for aid, 3,647 were judged to have need, 2,498 had their need fully met. 516 Federal Work-Study jobs (averaging $1175). In 2002, 2971 non-need-based awards were made. *Average percent of need met:* 75%. *Average financial aid package:* $8944. *Average need-based loan:* $5474. *Average need-based gift aid:* $4030. *Average non-need-based aid:* $3421. *Average indebtedness upon graduation:* $15,250.
Applying *Options:* electronic application, deferred entrance. *Application fee:* $30. *Required:* high school transcript, minimum 2.75 GPA. *Required for some:* minimum 3.0 GPA. *Recommended:* interview. *Application deadlines:* 8/10 (freshmen), 8/10 (transfers). *Notification:* continuous (freshmen), continuous (transfers).
Admissions Contact Ms. Sara Axelson, Associate Vice President Enrollment and Director of Admissions, University of Wyoming, Box 3435, Laramie, WY 82071. *Phone:* 307-766-5160. *Toll-free phone:* 800-342-5996. *Fax:* 307-766-4042. *E-mail:* why-wyo@uwyo.edu.

■ *See page 2744 for a narrative description.*

GUAM

PACIFIC ISLANDS BIBLE COLLEGE
Mangilao, Guam

Admissions Contact Karin Schulz, Admissions Office, Pacific Islands Bible College, PO Box 22619, Guam Main Facility, GU 96921-2619. *Phone:* 671-734-1812.

UNIVERSITY OF GUAM
Mangilao, Guam

Admissions Contact Ms. Katherine King-Nwosisi, Director of Admissions and Records, University of Guam, UOG Station, Mangilao, GU 96923. *Phone:* 671-735-2213. *E-mail:* admrecs@uog.edu.

NORTHERN MARIANA ISLANDS

NORTHERN MARIANAS COLLEGE
Saipan, Northern Mariana Islands

- **Territory-supported** primarily 2-year, founded 1981
- **Calendar** semesters
- **Degrees** certificates, diplomas, associate, and bachelor's
- **Rural** 14-acre campus
- **Coed**
- **Noncompetitive** entrance level

Student Life *Campus security:* patrols by trained security personnel.
Costs (2003–04) *Tuition:* territory resident $1560 full-time, $65 per credit part-time; nonresident $2340 full-time, $130 per credit part-time. Full-time tuition and fees vary according to course level. Part-time tuition and fees vary according to course level. *Required fees:* $210 full-time, $2 per credit part-time, $25 per term part-time.
Applying *Options:* early admission, deferred entrance. *Application fee:* $25. *Required:* high school transcript.
Admissions Contact Ms. Joyce Taro, Admission Specialist, Northern Marianas College, PO Box 501250, Saipan, MP 96950-1250. *Phone:* 670-234-3690 Ext. 1528. *Fax:* 670-235-4967. *E-mail:* joycet@nmcnet.edu.

PUERTO RICO

AMERICAN UNIVERSITY OF PUERTO RICO
Bayamón, Puerto Rico

- **Independent** 4-year, founded 1963
- **Calendar** semesters
- **Degrees** certificates, diplomas, associate, and bachelor's
- **Urban** 21-acre campus with easy access to San Juan
- **Coed,** 4,060 undergraduate students, 100% full-time, 59% women, 41% men
- **Noncompetitive** entrance level, 100% of applicants were admitted

Undergraduates 4,060 full-time. Students come from 1 other state, 100% Hispanic American.
Freshmen *Admission:* 583 applied, 583 admitted.
Faculty *Total:* 221, 46% full-time.
Majors Accounting; administrative assistant and secretarial science; business administration and management; education; elementary education; liberal arts and sciences/liberal studies; physical education teaching and coaching; purchasing, procurement/acquisitions and contracts management; special education.
Academic Programs *Special study options:* adult/continuing education programs, advanced placement credit, cooperative education, freshman honors college, honors programs, internships, part-time degree program, services for LD students, summer session for credit. *ROTC:* Army (c).
Library Loida Figueroa Meacado with 91,835 titles, 231 serial subscriptions, 2,091 audiovisual materials.
Computers on Campus 85 computers available on campus for general student use. At least one staffed computer lab available.
Student Life *Housing:* college housing not available. *Activities and organizations:* drama/theater group. *Campus security:* 24-hour patrols. *Student services:* health clinic.
Athletics *Intercollegiate sports:* basketball M, cross-country running M/W, swimming M/W, tennis M/W, track and field M/W, volleyball M/W. *Intramural sports:* basketball M, softball M/W, table tennis M/W, volleyball M/W.
Standardized Tests *Required:* SAT I (for placement), CEEB (for placement).
Costs (2004–05) *Tuition:* $3480 full-time, $1740 per term part-time. *Required fees:* $320 full-time, $160 per term part-time.
Financial Aid *Financial aid deadline:* 5/30.
Applying *Options:* deferred entrance. *Application fee:* $25. *Required:* high school transcript. *Application deadlines:* 8/1 (freshmen), 7/1 (transfers). *Notification:* continuous (freshmen), continuous until 8/31 (transfers).
Admissions Contact Ms. Margarita Cruz, Director of Admissions, American University of Puerto Rico, PO Box 2037, Bayamón, PR 00960-2037. *Phone:* 787-740-6410. *Fax:* 787-785-7377.

ATLANTIC COLLEGE
Guaynabo, Puerto Rico

Admissions Contact Zaida Perez, Admission's Officer, Atlantic College, PO Box 3918, Colton Street No. 9, Guaynabo, PR 00970. *Phone:* 787-720-1022 Ext. 13. *Fax:* 787-720-1092. *E-mail:* atlancol@coqui.net.

BAYAMÓN CENTRAL UNIVERSITY
Bayamón, Puerto Rico

- **Independent Roman Catholic** comprehensive, founded 1970
- **Calendar** semesters for undergraduate programs, trimesters for graduate programs
- **Degrees** certificates, associate, bachelor's, and master's
- **Suburban** 55-acre campus with easy access to San Juan
- **Endowment** $7.3 million
- **Coed**
- **Moderately difficult** entrance level

Faculty *Student/faculty ratio:* 23:1.
Student Life *Campus security:* 24-hour patrols.
Standardized Tests *Required:* College Examination Entrance Board Test (for admission).
Costs (2003–04) *Tuition:* $3420 full-time, $115 per credit part-time. *Required fees:* $320 full-time, $160 per term part-time.
Applying *Options:* common application. *Application fee:* $15. *Required:* high school transcript, medical history. *Required for some:* letters of recommendation, interview. *Recommended:* minimum 2.0 GPA.
Admissions Contact Sra. Christine M. Hernandez, Director of Admissions, Bayamón Central University, PO Box 1725, Bayamón, PR 00960-1725. *Phone:* 787-786-3030 Ext. 2102. *Fax:* 787-740-2200. *E-mail:* chernandez@ucb.edu.pr.

CARIBBEAN UNIVERSITY
Bayamón, Puerto Rico

Admissions Contact Mr. Hector Gracia, Director of Admissions, Caribbean University, Box 493, Bayamón, PR 00960-0493. *Phone:* 787-780-0070 Ext. 226.

CARLOS ALBIZU UNIVERSITY
San Juan, Puerto Rico

Admissions Contact PO Box 9023711, San Juan, PR 00902-3711.

COLEGIO BIBLICO PENTECOSTAL
St. Just, Puerto Rico

Admissions Contact Ms. Gladys Santiago, Registrar, Colegio Biblico Pentecostal, PO Box 901, St. Just, PR 00978-0901. *Phone:* 787-761-0640.

COLEGIO PENTECOSTAL MIZPA
Río Piedras, Puerto Rico

Admissions Contact Km. 0 Hm. 2, Bo. Caimito, Apartado 20966, Río Piedras, PR 00928-0966.

COLUMBIA COLLEGE
Caguas, Puerto Rico

- **Proprietary** 4-year, founded 1966
- **Calendar** semesters
- **Degrees** certificates, associate, bachelor's, and master's
- **Rural** 6-acre campus with easy access to San Juan
- **Coed,** 845 undergraduate students, 42% full-time, 66% women, 34% men
- **Noncompetitive** entrance level, 60% of applicants were admitted

Undergraduates 355 full-time, 490 part-time. 100% Hispanic American.
Freshmen *Admission:* 378 applied, 225 admitted, 65 enrolled. *Average high school GPA:* 2.00.
Faculty *Total:* 67, 25% full-time, 7% with terminal degrees. *Student/faculty ratio:* 18:1.
Majors Administrative assistant and secretarial science; business administration and management; business/commerce; electrical, electronic and communications engineering technology; management information systems; nursing (registered nurse training); nursing science.
Academic Programs *Special study options:* accelerated degree program, adult/continuing education programs, external degree program, independent study, part-time degree program.
Library Efrain Sola Bezares Library with 10,200 titles, 164 serial subscriptions, an OPAC.
Computers on Campus 55 computers available on campus for general student use. Internet access, at least one staffed computer lab available.
Student Life *Housing:* college housing not available. *Campus security:* 24-hour patrols. *Student services:* personal/psychological counseling.
Costs (2003–04) *Tuition:* $3380 full-time, $130 per unit part-time. *Required fees:* $300 full-time, $100 per term part-time.
Applying *Options:* common application. *Application fee:* $50. *Required:* high school transcript. *Recommended:* essay or personal statement. *Application deadline:* rolling (freshmen).
Admissions Contact Ms. Ana Rosa Burgos, Admission Director, Columbia College, PO Box 8517, Caguas, PR 00726. *Phone:* 787-743-4041 Ext. 234. *Toll-free phone:* 800-981-4877 Ext. 239. *Fax:* 787-744-7031. *E-mail:* arburgos@columbiaco.edu.

CONSERVATORY OF MUSIC OF PUERTO RICO
San Juan, Puerto Rico

- **Commonwealth-supported** 4-year, founded 1959
- **Calendar** semesters
- **Degree** bachelor's
- **Urban** 6-acre campus
- **Endowment** $465,949
- **Coed**
- **Moderately difficult** entrance level

Faculty *Student/faculty ratio:* 4:1.
Student Life *Campus security:* 24-hour patrols.
Standardized Tests *Required:* SAT I (for admission), SAT II: Subject Tests (for admission).
Costs (2003–04) *Tuition:* $60 per credit part-time. *Required fees:* $170 full-time, $85 per term part-time.
Financial Aid Of all full-time matriculated undergraduates who enrolled in 2000, 130 applied for aid, 130 were judged to have need. *Average percent of need met:* 62. *Average need-based gift aid:* $4951. *Average indebtedness upon graduation:* $5500.
Applying *Options:* common application, early admission. *Application fee:* $25. *Required:* high school transcript, minimum 2.0 GPA, interview, audition, music and theory examinations. *Required for some:* essay or personal statement, minimum 2.50 GPA.
Admissions Contact Ms. Sandra Rodriquez, Marketing and Recruitment Officer, Conservatory of Music of Puerto Rico, 350 Calle Rafael Lamar, San Juian, PR 00718. *Phone:* 787-751-6180 Ext. 285. *Fax:* 787-758-8268. *E-mail:* srodriquez@cmpr.gobierno.pr.

ELECTRONIC DATA PROCESSING COLLEGE OF PUERTO RICO
San Juan, Puerto Rico

Admissions Contact Mrs. Elsie Zayas, Admissions Director, Electronic Data Processing College of Puerto Rico, 555 Munoz Rivera Avenue, San Juan, PR 00919-2303. *Phone:* 787-765-3560 Ext. 138.

ESCUELA DE ARTES PLASTICAS DE PUERTO RICO
San Juan, Puerto Rico

- **Commonwealth-supported** 4-year, founded 1966
- **Calendar** semesters
- **Degree** bachelor's
- **Urban** campus
- **Endowment** $323,000
- **Coed,** 501 undergraduate students, 58% full-time, 41% women, 59% men
- **Moderately difficult** entrance level, 55% of applicants were admitted

Undergraduates 290 full-time, 211 part-time. Students come from 1 other state, 100% Hispanic American, 19% transferred in. *Retention:* 81% of 2002 full-time freshmen returned.
Freshmen *Admission:* 157 applied, 86 admitted, 86 enrolled. *Average high school GPA:* 2.80. *Test scores:* SAT verbal scores over 500: 34%; SAT math scores over 500: 41%; SAT verbal scores over 600: 4%; SAT math scores over 600: 14%; SAT math scores over 700: 1%.
Faculty *Total:* 48, 44% full-time, 4% with terminal degrees. *Student/faculty ratio:* 9:1.
Majors Art teacher education; commercial and advertising art; industrial design; painting; printmaking; sculpture.
Academic Programs *Special study options:* cooperative education, off-campus study, services for LD students, summer session for credit.
Library Francisco Oller Library with 24,582 titles, 111 serial subscriptions, 34,082 audiovisual materials, an OPAC.
Computers on Campus 36 computers available on campus for general student use. Internet access, at least one staffed computer lab available.
Student Life *Housing:* college housing not available. *Activities and organizations:* student government. *Campus security:* 24-hour patrols, security cameras.
Standardized Tests *Required:* SAT I (for placement).
Costs (2003–04) *Tuition:* area resident $1996 full-time, $55 per credit part-time. Full-time tuition and fees vary according to course load and program. Part-time tuition and fees vary according to course load and program. *Required fees:* $116 full-time, $116 per year part-time. *Room and board:* Room and board charges vary according to housing facility. *Payment plan:* deferred payment. *Waivers:* employees or children of employees.
Financial Aid Of all full-time matriculated undergraduates who enrolled in 2000, 256 applied for aid, 256 were judged to have need. 10 Federal Work-Study jobs (averaging $1800). *Average percent of need met:* 82%.
Applying *Options:* common application. *Application fee:* $20. *Required:* essay or personal statement, high school transcript, minimum 2.0 GPA, interview, portfolio. *Application deadlines:* 4/1 (freshmen), 5/1 (transfers). *Notification:* 5/1 (freshmen), 7/1 (transfers).
Admissions Contact Ms. Brenda Rodríguez, Admission Assistant, Escuela de Artes Plasticas de Puerto Rico, PO Box 9021112, San Juan, PR 00902-1112. *Phone:* 787-725-8120 Ext. 250. *Fax:* 787-725-8111. *E-mail:* eap@coqui.net.

INTER AMERICAN UNIVERSITY OF PUERTO RICO, AGUADILLA CAMPUS
Aguadilla, Puerto Rico

- **Independent** 4-year, founded 1957, part of Inter American University of Puerto Rico
- **Calendar** semesters
- **Degrees** certificates, associate, and bachelor's
- **Small-town** 50-acre campus
- **Endowment** $667,103
- **Coed,** 4,197 undergraduate students, 85% full-time, 58% women, 42% men

■ **Moderately difficult** entrance level

Undergraduates 3,581 full-time, 616 part-time. Students come from 1 other state, 100% Hispanic American, 0.3% transferred in.
Freshmen *Admission:* 930 enrolled. *Average high school GPA:* 2.34.
Faculty *Total:* 254, 30% full-time. *Student/faculty ratio:* 19:1.
Majors Accounting; administrative assistant and secretarial science; biology/biological sciences; biology teacher education; business administration and management; computer hardware technology; computer science; criminal justice/safety; early childhood education; electrical, electronic and communications engineering technology; elementary education; English as a second/foreign language (teaching); hotel/motel administration; kindergarten/preschool education; management information systems; marketing/marketing management; microbiology; nursing related; parks, recreation and leisure facilities management; social psychology; Spanish language teacher education.
Academic Programs *Special study options:* academic remediation for entering students, adult/continuing education programs, advanced placement credit, cooperative education, distance learning, double majors, external degree program, honors programs, independent study, internships, part-time degree program, services for LD students, summer session for credit. *ROTC:* Army (b).
Library Access Information Center with 56,037 titles, 461 serial subscriptions, 24,434 audiovisual materials, an OPAC, a Web page.
Computers on Campus 292 computers available on campus for general student use. A campuswide network can be accessed from off campus. Internet access, online (class) registration, at least one staffed computer lab available.
Student Life *Housing:* college housing not available. *Activities and organizations:* drama/theater group, student-run newspaper, radio station, choral group, Criminal Justice Association, Secretarial Sciences Association, Future Teachers Association, Psychosocial Human Services Association, IPDAS (Drugs, Alcohol and Aids Prevention Institute). *Campus security:* 24-hour emergency response devices and patrols. *Student services:* health clinic, personal/psychological counseling.
Athletics *Intercollegiate sports:* baseball M(s), basketball M(s)/W(s), cheerleading M/W, cross-country running M(s)/W(s), soccer M(s), softball M(s)/W(s), table tennis M(s)/W(s), tennis M(s)/W(s), track and field M(s)/W(s), volleyball M(s)/W(s), weight lifting M(s)/W(s). *Intramural sports:* basketball M/W, cross-country running M/W, softball M/W, table tennis M/W, tennis M/W, track and field M/W, volleyball M/W, weight lifting M/W.
Standardized Tests *Required:* PAA (for admission). *Required for some:* SAT I (for admission).
Costs (2004–05) *Tuition:* $3240 full-time, $135 per credit hour part-time. Full-time tuition and fees vary according to course load. Part-time tuition and fees vary according to course load. *Required fees:* $364 full-time, $144 per term part-time. *Payment plan:* deferred payment. *Waivers:* employees or children of employees.
Applying *Options:* common application, electronic application, early admission. *Required:* high school transcript, minimum 2.00 GPA. *Application deadline:* rolling (freshmen), rolling (transfers).
Admissions Contact Ms. Doris Pe'rez, Director of Admissions, Inter American University of Puerto Rico, Aguadilla Campus, PO Box 20,000, Road 459 Interstate 463, Aguadilla, PR 00605. *Phone:* 787-891-0925 Ext. 2101. *Fax:* 787-882-3020.

Inter American University of Puerto Rico, Arecibo Campus
Arecibo, Puerto Rico

Admissions Contact Ms. Provi Montalvo, Admission Director, Inter American University of Puerto Rico, Arecibo Campus, PO Box 4050, Arecibo, PR 00614-4050. *Phone:* 787-878-5475 Ext. 2268.

Inter American University of Puerto Rico, Barranquitas Campus
Barranquitas, Puerto Rico

■ **Independent** 4-year, founded 1957, part of Inter American University of Puerto Rico
■ **Calendar** semesters
■ **Degrees** associate, bachelor's, and postbachelor's certificates
■ **Small-town** campus with easy access to San Juan
■ **Endowment** $3.0 million
■ **Coed,** 2,271 undergraduate students, 77% full-time, 66% women, 34% men
■ **Moderately difficult** entrance level, 100% of applicants were admitted

Undergraduates 1,757 full-time, 514 part-time. Students come from 1 other state, 100% Hispanic American. *Retention:* 76% of 2002 full-time freshmen returned.
Freshmen *Admission:* 550 applied, 550 admitted.
Faculty *Total:* 105, 33% full-time.
Majors Accounting; administrative assistant and secretarial science; biology/biological sciences; business administration and management; computer and information sciences; computer programming related; computer science; criminal justice/law enforcement administration; education; elementary and middle school administration/principalship; elementary education; floriculture/floristry management; microbiology; nursing (registered nurse training); plant nursery management; radiation biology; secondary education; special education (multiply disabled).
Academic Programs *Special study options:* academic remediation for entering students, adult/continuing education programs, advanced placement credit, English as a second language, part-time degree program, study abroad, summer session for credit. *ROTC:* Army (c).
Library Luis Muñoz Marín with 32,863 titles, 224 serial subscriptions, an OPAC, a Web page.
Computers on Campus 365 computers available on campus for general student use. A campuswide network can be accessed from student residence rooms. Internet access, online (class) registration, at least one staffed computer lab available.
Student Life *Campus security:* 24-hour patrols.
Athletics *Intercollegiate sports:* basketball M/W, cross-country running M/W, softball M/W, table tennis M/W, tennis M/W, track and field M/W, volleyball M/W, weight lifting M. *Intramural sports:* basketball M/W, cross-country running M/W, softball M, table tennis M/W, track and field M/W, volleyball M/W.
Standardized Tests *Required:* SAT I or ACT (for admission).
Costs (2003–04) *Tuition:* $3200 full-time, $130 per credit part-time. *Required fees:* $800 full-time, $150 per term part-time.
Financial Aid Of all full-time matriculated undergraduates who enrolled in 2000, 1,350 applied for aid, 1,350 were judged to have need. 466 Federal Work-Study jobs.
Applying *Options:* common application, deferred entrance. *Required:* high school transcript, interview. *Application deadlines:* 5/15 (freshmen), 5/15 (transfers).
Admissions Contact Ms. Carmen L. Ortiz, Admission Director, Inter American University of Puerto Rico, Barranquitas Campus, Box 517, Barranquitas, PR 00794. *Phone:* 787-857-3600 Ext. 2011. *Fax:* 787-857-2244. *E-mail:* clortiz@inter.edu.

Inter American University of Puerto Rico, Bayamón Campus
Bayamón, Puerto Rico

■ **Independent** 4-year, founded 1912, part of Inter American University of Puerto Rico
■ **Calendar** semesters
■ **Degrees** certificates, associate, bachelor's, and master's
■ **Urban** 51-acre campus with easy access to San Juan
■ **Endowment** $2.0 million
■ **Coed,** 5,264 undergraduate students, 83% full-time, 45% women, 55% men
■ 65% of applicants were admitted

Undergraduates 4,387 full-time, 877 part-time. 0.1% are from out of state, 100% Hispanic American, 3% transferred in. *Retention:* 59% of 2002 full-time freshmen returned.
Freshmen *Admission:* 2,502 applied, 1,635 admitted, 1,053 enrolled. *Average high school GPA:* 2.65.
Faculty *Total:* 283, 34% full-time, 13% with terminal degrees. *Student/faculty ratio:* 28:1.
Majors Accounting; administrative assistant and secretarial science; aeronautics/aviation/aerospace science and technology; aerospace, aeronautical and astronautical engineering; airline pilot and flight crew; air traffic control; applied mathematics; aviation/airway management; biochemistry; biological and biomedical sciences related; biology/biological sciences; business administration and management; business automation/technology/data entry; business, management, and marketing related; business/managerial economics; chemical technology; chemistry; communication/speech communication and rhetoric; communications technology; computer and information sciences and support services related; computer installation and repair technology; computer programming; computer science; computer systems analysis; electrical, electronic and communications engineering technology; electrical, electronics and communications engineering; engineering; entrepreneurship; environmental biology; environmental control technologies related; executive assistant/executive secretary; finance; forensic

Inter American University of Puerto Rico, Bayamón Campus (continued)
science and technology; human resources management; industrial engineering; management information systems; management science; marketing/marketing management; marketing research; mass communication/media; mathematics; mechanical engineering; medical microbiology and bacteriology; pre-medical studies; telecommunications.

Academic Programs *Special study options:* academic remediation for entering students, accelerated degree program, adult/continuing education programs, cooperative education, double majors, English as a second language, external degree program, honors programs, independent study, internships, part-time degree program, services for LD students, summer session for credit. *ROTC:* Army (c).

Library Centro de Acceso a la Informacion with 54,601 titles, 1,228 serial subscriptions, 1,782 audiovisual materials, an OPAC.

Computers on Campus 400 computers available on campus for general student use. A campuswide network can be accessed from off campus. Internet access, at least one staffed computer lab available.

Student Life *Housing:* college housing not available. *Activities and organizations:* student-run newspaper, choral group, Associacion de Estudiantes de Administracion de Empresas, Estudiantes Unidos por la Ciencia, Associacion Estudiantes de Aviacion, Consejo de Estudiante, Asociacion Estudiantes de Ingenieria. *Campus security:* 24-hour patrols. *Student services:* health clinic, personal/psychological counseling.

Athletics *Intercollegiate sports:* baseball M(s), basketball M(s)/W(s), cross-country running M(s)/W(s), softball M(s)/W(s), swimming M(s)/W(s), table tennis M(s)/W(s), track and field M(s)/W(s), volleyball M(s)/W(s), weight lifting M(s). *Intramural sports:* basketball M/W, cross-country running M/W, softball M/W, swimming M/W, table tennis M/W, tennis M/W, track and field M/W, volleyball M/W, weight lifting M.

Standardized Tests *Required:* CEEB (for admission). *Required for some:* SAT I (for admission).

Costs (2004–05) *Tuition:* $3522 full-time, $130 per credit part-time. *Payment plan:* deferred payment. *Waivers:* employees or children of employees.

Applying *Options:* common application. *Required:* high school transcript, minimum 2.0 GPA, 2.50 GPA for engineering programs. *Recommended:* interview. *Application deadline:* rolling (freshmen), rolling (transfers). *Notification:* continuous (freshmen), continuous (transfers).

Admissions Contact Mr. Carlos Alicia, Director of Admissions, Inter American University of Puerto Rico, Bayamón Campus, 500 Road 830, Bayamon, PR 00957. *Phone:* 787-279-1912 Ext. 2017. *Fax:* 787-279-2205. *E-mail:* calicea@bc.inter.edu.

INTER AMERICAN UNIVERSITY OF PUERTO RICO, FAJARDO CAMPUS

Fajardo, Puerto Rico

- **Independent** 4-year, founded 1965, part of Inter American University of Puerto Rico
- **Calendar** semesters
- **Degrees** associate and bachelor's
- **Small-town** 11-acre campus with easy access to San Juan
- **Coed,** 1,710 undergraduate students
- **Moderately difficult** entrance level, 37% of applicants were admitted

Undergraduates *Retention:* 65% of 2002 full-time freshmen returned.

Freshmen *Admission:* 1,373 applied, 507 admitted. *Average high school GPA:* 2.0.

Faculty *Total:* 118, 34% full-time, 8% with terminal degrees.

Majors Accounting; administrative assistant and secretarial science; art teacher education; aviation/airway management; avionics maintenance technology; biology/biological sciences; business administration and management; business teacher education; clinical laboratory science/medical technology; computer science; criminal justice/law enforcement administration; criminal justice/police science; economics; education; electrical, electronics and communications engineering; elementary education; English as a second/foreign language (teaching); history; hotel/motel administration; marketing/marketing management; music; nursing (registered nurse training); physical education teaching and coaching; social work; sociology; special education; tourism and travel services management.

Academic Programs *Special study options:* academic remediation for entering students, adult/continuing education programs, advanced placement credit, English as a second language, freshman honors college, honors programs, off-campus study, part-time degree program, summer session for credit.

Library Antonio S. Belaval Library with 39,951 titles, 686 serial subscriptions, a Web page.

Computers on Campus 90 computers available on campus for general student use. At least one staffed computer lab available.

Student Life *Housing:* college housing not available. *Activities and organizations:* Future Teachers Association, Criminal Justice Student Association, Student Counseling Association, Practical Teaching Association. *Campus security:* 24-hour patrols. *Student services:* personal/psychological counseling.

Athletics *Intramural sports:* basketball M/W, track and field M/W, volleyball M/W.

Standardized Tests *Required:* SAT I (for admission), PAA (for admission).

Costs (2004–05) *Comprehensive fee:* $3296 includes full-time tuition ($3120) and mandatory fees ($176).

Applying *Options:* early admission, deferred entrance. *Required:* high school transcript, minimum 2.0 GPA. *Required for some:* letters of recommendation. *Application deadline:* rolling (freshmen), rolling (transfers). *Notification:* 5/1 (freshmen).

Admissions Contact Ms. Jackeline Melèndez, Secretary III, Inter American University of Puerto Rico, Fajardo Campus, Call Box 70003, Fajaido, PR 00738-7003. *Phone:* 787-863-2390 Ext. 2210. *E-mail:* adcaraba@inter.edu.

INTER AMERICAN UNIVERSITY OF PUERTO RICO, GUAYAMA CAMPUS

Guayama, Puerto Rico

- **Independent** 4-year, founded 1958, part of Inter American University of Puerto Rico
- **Calendar** semesters
- **Degrees** certificates, associate, and bachelor's
- **Small-town** 50-acre campus
- **Coed**
- **Moderately difficult** entrance level

Standardized Tests *Required:* SAT I (for admission), PAA (for admission).

Costs (2003–04) *Tuition:* $1682 full-time. Full-time tuition and fees vary according to location and program. Part-time tuition and fees vary according to location and program. No tuition increase for student's term of enrollment. *Payment plans:* tuition prepayment, deferred payment.

Financial Aid Of all full-time matriculated undergraduates who enrolled in 2002, 1,722 applied for aid, 1,662 were judged to have need, 3 had their need fully met. 307 Federal Work-Study jobs (averaging $1000). In 2002, 37. *Average percent of need met:* 3. *Average financial aid package:* $2341. *Average need-based loan:* $8. *Average need-based gift aid:* $1693. *Average non-need-based aid:* $227.

Applying *Options:* common application. *Required:* high school transcript, minimum 2.00 GPA. *Required for some:* essay or personal statement, interview.

Admissions Contact Mrs. Laura E. Ferrer, Director of Admissions, Inter American University of Puerto Rico, Guayama Campus, Interamerican University of Puerto Rico, Guayoma Campus, Call Box 10004 Attention: Laura Ferrer, Guayama, PR 00785. *Phone:* 787-864-2222 Ext. 220. *Toll-free phone:* 787-864-2222 Ext. 2243. *Fax:* 787-866-4986.

INTER AMERICAN UNIVERSITY OF PUERTO RICO, METROPOLITAN CAMPUS

San Juan, Puerto Rico

Admissions Contact Ms. Ida G. Betancourt, Official Admission, Inter American University of Puerto Rico, Metropolitan Campus, Metropolitan Campus—Admission Office, PO Box 191293, San Juan, PR 00919-1293. *Phone:* 787-250-1912 Ext. 2100. *Fax:* 787-764-6963.

INTER AMERICAN UNIVERSITY OF PUERTO RICO, PONCE CAMPUS

Mercedita, Puerto Rico

- **Independent** comprehensive, founded 1962, part of Inter American University of Puerto Rico
- **Calendar** semesters
- **Degrees** associate, bachelor's, and master's
- **Urban** 50-acre campus with easy access to San Juan
- **Coed,** 5,134 undergraduate students, 84% full-time, 62% women, 38% men
- **Moderately difficult** entrance level, 26% of applicants were admitted

Undergraduates 4,294 full-time, 840 part-time. Students come from 1 other state, 100% Hispanic American, 0.7% transferred in.

Freshmen *Admission:* 5,053 applied, 1,301 admitted, 1,079 enrolled. *Average high school GPA:* 2.68.

Faculty *Total:* 242, 33% full-time, 21% with terminal degrees. *Student/faculty ratio:* 34:1.

Majors Accounting; administrative assistant and secretarial science; biology/biological sciences; business administration and management; communication and journalism related; computer science; criminal justice/law enforcement administration; criminal justice/police science; education; elementary education; environmental science; finance; hotel/motel administration; human resources management; information science/studies; international business/trade/commerce; journalism; kindergarten/preschool education; marketing/marketing management; nursing (registered nurse training); secondary education; special education; tourism and travel services management.

Academic Programs *Special study options:* academic remediation for entering students, adult/continuing education programs, cooperative education, distance learning, English as a second language, honors programs, independent study, internships, off-campus study, part-time degree program, services for LD students, study abroad, summer session for credit.

Library Centro de Acceso a la Informacion plus 1 other with 64,981 titles, 355 serial subscriptions, 2,623 audiovisual materials, an OPAC, a Web page.

Computers on Campus 252 computers available on campus for general student use. A campuswide network can be accessed from off campus. Internet access, online (class) registration, at least one staffed computer lab available.

Student Life *Housing:* college housing not available. *Activities and organizations:* drama/theater group, choral group, marching band, IKARUS "Drama Association", American Marketing Associations, ABACUS, ECOS, Cheer-Leaders. *Campus security:* 24-hour patrols. *Student services:* health clinic, personal/psychological counseling.

Athletics *Intercollegiate sports:* baseball M(s)/W, cross-country running M/W, softball M(s)/W, table tennis M/W, track and field M(s)/W(s), volleyball M/W, weight lifting M(s)/W. *Intramural sports:* basketball M/W, table tennis M/W, weight lifting M.

Standardized Tests *Required:* CEEB (for admission). *Required for some:* SAT I (for admission).

Costs (2004–05) *Tuition:* $3886 full-time, $135 per credit part-time. Full-time tuition and fees vary according to class time, course load, degree level, and program. Part-time tuition and fees vary according to class time, course load, degree level, and program. *Required fees:* $376 full-time, $300 per term part-time. *Payment plan:* deferred payment. *Waivers:* employees or children of employees.

Applying *Options:* common application, deferred entrance. *Required:* high school transcript, minimum 2.00 GPA. *Application deadlines:* 8/1 (freshmen), 5/15 (transfers).

Admissions Contact Mr. Franco Diaz, Admissions Officer, Inter American University of Puerto Rico, Ponce Campus, Ponce Campus, 104 Turpo Industrial Park Road #1, Mercedita, PR 00715-1602. *Phone:* 787-284-1912 Ext. 2025. *Fax:* 787-841-0103. *E-mail:* fldiaz@ponce.inter.edu.

INTER AMERICAN UNIVERSITY OF PUERTO RICO, SAN GERMÁN CAMPUS

San Germán, Puerto Rico

- **Independent** university, founded 1912, part of Inter American University of Puerto Rico
- **Calendar** semesters
- **Degrees** certificates, associate, bachelor's, master's, doctoral, and postbachelor's certificates
- **Small-town** 260-acre campus
- **Coed,** 5,158 undergraduate students
- **Moderately difficult** entrance level, 95% of applicants were admitted

Undergraduates Students come from 15 states and territories, 1% are from out of state, 10% live on campus.

Freshmen *Admission:* 1,735 applied, 1,647 admitted.

Faculty *Total:* 311, 41% full-time, 24% with terminal degrees. *Student/faculty ratio:* 26:1.

Majors Accounting; administrative assistant and secretarial science; applied art; applied mathematics; art; art history, criticism and conservation; art teacher education; behavioral sciences; biology/biological sciences; biomedical sciences; business administration and management; business/managerial economics; ceramic arts and ceramics; chemistry; clinical laboratory science/medical technology; computer programming; computer science; drawing; economics; education; electrical, electronic and communications engineering technology; elementary education; English; English as a second/foreign language (teaching); environmental studies; finance; health information/medical records administration; health science; human resources management; industrial radiologic technology; information science/studies; kindergarten/preschool education; linguistics; literature; marketing/marketing management; marketing related; mathematics; medical microbiology and bacteriology; music; music teacher education; natural sciences; nursing (registered nurse training); photography; physical education teaching and coaching; piano and organ; political science and government; psychology; public administration; science teacher education; sculpture; secondary education; social sciences; sociology; Spanish; violin, viola, guitar and other stringed instruments; voice and opera; wind/percussion instruments.

Academic Programs *Special study options:* academic remediation for entering students, accelerated degree program, adult/continuing education programs, advanced placement credit, cooperative education, distance learning, double majors, English as a second language, external degree program, honors programs, independent study, internships, off-campus study, part-time degree program, services for LD students, summer session for credit. *ROTC:* Army (c), Navy (c), Air Force (c).

Library Juan Cancio Ortiz Library with 151,506 titles, 3,790 serial subscriptions, 3,357 audiovisual materials, an OPAC, a Web page.

Computers on Campus 1600 computers available on campus for general student use. A campuswide network can be accessed. Internet access, online (class) registration, at least one staffed computer lab available.

Student Life *Housing options:* men-only, women-only. Campus housing is university owned. *Activities and organizations:* drama/theater group, student-run newspaper, choral group, Future Teachers Association, PolyNature, Association for Computer Machinery, International Association of Administrative Professionals, Biology Honor Society, national fraternities, national sororities. *Campus security:* 24-hour emergency response devices and patrols. *Student services:* personal/psychological counseling.

Athletics *Intercollegiate sports:* baseball M(s), basketball M(s)/W(s), cross-country running M(s)/W(s), soccer M(s), softball M/W, swimming M/W, table tennis M(s)/W(s), tennis M(s)/W(s), track and field M(s)/W(s), volleyball M(s)/W(s), weight lifting M(s). *Intramural sports:* badminton M/W, basketball M/W, cross-country running M/W, softball M/W, table tennis M/W, tennis M/W, track and field M/W, volleyball M/W.

Standardized Tests *Required:* CEEB (for admission).

Costs (2004–05) *Comprehensive fee:* $6866 includes full-time tuition ($4050), mandatory fees ($416), and room and board ($2400). Part-time tuition: $135 per credit hour. *Required fees:* $208 per term part-time. *College room only:* $900. Room and board charges vary according to board plan and housing facility. *Payment plan:* deferred payment. *Waivers:* employees or children of employees.

Financial Aid Of all full-time matriculated undergraduates who enrolled in 1998, 3,992 applied for aid, 3,535 were judged to have need, 46 had their need fully met. *Average percent of need met:* 36%. *Average financial aid package:* $1592.

Applying *Options:* early admission. *Required:* high school transcript, medical history. *Required for some:* 1 letter of recommendation, interview. *Recommended:* essay or personal statement, minimum 2.50 GPA. *Application deadlines:* 5/13 (freshmen), 5/15 (transfers). *Notification:* continuous (freshmen), continuous (transfers).

Admissions Contact Mrs. Mildred Camacho, Director of Admissions, Inter American University of Puerto Rico, San Germán Campus, PO Box 5100, San Germán, PR 00683-5008. *Phone:* 787-264-1912 Ext. 7283. *Fax:* 787-892-6350. *E-mail:* milcama@sg.inter.edu.

POLYTECHNIC UNIVERSITY OF PUERTO RICO

Hato Rey, Puerto Rico

- **Independent** comprehensive, founded 1966
- **Calendar** trimesters
- **Degrees** bachelor's and master's
- **Urban** 10-acre campus with easy access to San Juan
- **Endowment** $12.9 million
- **Coed,** 5,071 undergraduate students, 52% full-time, 23% women, 77% men
- **Minimally difficult** entrance level, 92% of applicants were admitted

Undergraduates 2,650 full-time, 2,421 part-time. Students come from 1 other state, 0.1% are from out of state, 100% Hispanic American, 8% transferred in. *Retention:* 70% of 2002 full-time freshmen returned.

Freshmen *Admission:* 970 applied, 895 admitted, 655 enrolled. *Average high school GPA:* 3.00.

Faculty *Total:* 404, 54% full-time, 14% with terminal degrees. *Student/faculty ratio:* 14:1.

Majors Accounting; architecture; business administration and management; chemical engineering; civil engineering; computer engineering; electrical, electronics and communications engineering; environmental/environmental health engineering; finance; industrial engineering; marketing/marketing management; mechanical engineering; survey technology.

Academic Programs *Special study options:* academic remediation for entering students, English as a second language, part-time degree program, student-designed majors, summer session for credit. *ROTC:* Army (c).

Polytechnic University of Puerto Rico (continued)

Library Main Library plus 1 other with 81,899 titles, 2,025 serial subscriptions, 1,728 audiovisual materials, an OPAC, a Web page.

Computers on Campus 375 computers available on campus for general student use. A campuswide network can be accessed from student residence rooms and from off campus. At least one staffed computer lab available.

Student Life *Activities and organizations:* drama/theater group, choral group, Society of Women Engineers, American Civil Engineering—Student Chapter, Society of Hispanic Professional Engineers, Society of Automotive Engineers, Capitulo Estuadiantil Ingenieros Electricos. *Campus security:* 24-hour patrols. *Student services:* health clinic, personal/psychological counseling.

Athletics *Intercollegiate sports:* basketball M/W, cross-country running M/W, soccer M, softball M/W, table tennis M/W, tennis M/W, track and field M/W, volleyball M/W. *Intramural sports:* basketball M, cross-country running M/W, soccer M/W, table tennis M/W, tennis M/W, volleyball M/W.

Standardized Tests *Required for some:* SAT I (for admission).

Costs (2003–04) *Tuition:* $5040 full-time, $130 per credit part-time. Full-time tuition and fees vary according to program. Part-time tuition and fees vary according to program. *Required fees:* $330 full-time, $110 per term part-time. *Payment plan:* deferred payment. *Waivers:* employees or children of employees.

Financial Aid *Financial aid deadline:* 5/15.

Applying *Options:* early admission, deferred entrance. *Application fee:* $30. *Required:* high school transcript. *Application deadline:* 8/15 (freshmen).

Admissions Contact Ms. Teresa Cardona, Director of Admissions, Polytechnic University of Puerto Rico, PO Box 192017, San Juan, PR 00919-2017. *Phone:* 787-754-8000 Ext. 240. *E-mail:* rbelvis@pupr.edu.

Pontifical Catholic University of Puerto Rico

Ponce, Puerto Rico

- **Independent Roman Catholic** university, founded 1948
- **Calendar** semesters
- **Degrees** associate, bachelor's, master's, doctoral, and first professional (branch locations: Arecibo, Guayana, Mayagüez)
- **Urban** 120-acre campus with easy access to San Juan
- **Endowment** $14.4 million
- **Coed,** 5,688 undergraduate students, 89% full-time, 65% women, 35% men
- **Moderately difficult** entrance level, 89% of applicants were admitted

Undergraduates 5,050 full-time, 638 part-time. Students come from 1 other state, 0.1% are from out of state, 100% Hispanic American, 3% transferred in, 4% live on campus.

Freshmen *Admission:* 1,530 applied, 1,365 admitted, 1,137 enrolled. *Average high school GPA:* 2.75. *Test scores:* SAT verbal scores over 500: 30%; SAT math scores over 500: 31%; SAT verbal scores over 600: 7%; SAT math scores over 600: 9%; SAT math scores over 700: 1%.

Faculty *Total:* 234, 100% full-time. *Student/faculty ratio:* 33:1.

Majors Accounting; administrative assistant and secretarial science; art; art teacher education; biological and physical sciences; biology/biological sciences; biology teacher education; business administration and management; business teacher education; chemistry; clinical laboratory science/medical technology; computer management; computer programming; computer science; computer teacher education; criminal justice/law enforcement administration; criminology; economics; education; elementary education; English; English/language arts teacher education; environmental studies; family and consumer sciences/home economics teacher education; family and consumer sciences/human sciences; fashion/apparel design; finance; French; gerontology; health teacher education; Hispanic-American, Puerto Rican, and Mexican-American/Chicano studies; history; history teacher education; human resources management; international business/trade/commerce; kindergarten/preschool education; liberal arts and sciences/liberal studies; marketing/marketing management; mass communication/media; mathematics; mathematics teacher education; music; music teacher education; nursing (registered nurse training); philosophy; physical education teaching and coaching; physics; political science and government; pre-law studies; premedical studies; psychology; public administration; public relations/image management; publishing; radio and television; science teacher education; secondary education; social studies teacher education; social work; sociology; Spanish; special education; theology; tourism and travel services management; tourism/travel marketing; veterinary sciences.

Academic Programs *Special study options:* academic remediation for entering students, adult/continuing education programs, advanced placement credit, cooperative education, double majors, English as a second language, honors programs, independent study, off-campus study, part-time degree program, services for LD students, summer session for credit. *ROTC:* Army (c). *Unusual degree programs:* 3-2 engineering with Case Western Reserve University; pharmacy with Massachusetts College of Pharmacy and Allied Health Sciences.

Library Encarnacion Valdes Library plus 1 other with 58,185 serial subscriptions, an OPAC, a Web page.

Computers on Campus 419 computers available on campus for general student use. A campuswide network can be accessed from off campus. Internet access, at least one staffed computer lab available.

Student Life *Housing options:* men-only, women-only. Campus housing is university owned. *Activities and organizations:* drama/theater group, student-run newspaper, radio and television station, choral group, Accounting Students Club, Foreign Students Club, Christ Heralds, national fraternities, national sororities. *Campus security:* 24-hour emergency response devices and patrols. *Student services:* health clinic, personal/psychological counseling.

Athletics Member NAIA. *Intercollegiate sports:* basketball M/W, cross-country running M/W, swimming M/W, table tennis M/W, tennis M/W, track and field M(s)/W(s), volleyball M/W, water polo M, weight lifting M, wrestling M. *Intramural sports:* baseball M, basketball M/W, cross-country running M/W, swimming M/W, table tennis M/W, tennis M/W, track and field M/W, volleyball M/W, weight lifting M, wrestling M.

Standardized Tests *Required:* SAT I (for admission).

Costs (2003–04) *Comprehensive fee:* $7458 includes full-time tuition ($4160), mandatory fees ($458), and room and board ($2840). Full-time tuition and fees vary according to course load. Part-time tuition: $130 per credit. Part-time tuition and fees vary according to course load. *College room only:* $800. *Payment plan:* deferred payment. *Waivers:* employees or children of employees.

Financial Aid Of all full-time matriculated undergraduates who enrolled in 2003, 6,225 applied for aid, 6,140 were judged to have need, 85 had their need fully met. 1,100 Federal Work-Study jobs (averaging $750). *Average percent of need met:* 71%. *Average need-based loan:* $3108. *Average need-based gift aid:* $3961. *Average indebtedness upon graduation:* $3500.

Applying *Options:* early admission, deferred entrance. *Application fee:* $15. *Required:* high school transcript, minimum 2.0 GPA. *Required for some:* essay or personal statement, minimum 3.0 GPA, 1 letter of recommendation, interview. *Application deadlines:* 3/15 (freshmen), 3/15 (transfers). *Notification:* continuous (freshmen), continuous (transfers).

Admissions Contact Sra. Ana O. Bonilla, Director of Admissions, Pontifical Catholic University of Puerto Rico, 2250 Avenida Las Americas, Ponce, PR 00717-0777. *Phone:* 787-841-2000 Ext. 1004. *Toll-free phone:* 800-981-5040. *Fax:* 787-840-4295. *E-mail:* admissions@pucpr.edu.

Universidad Adventista de las Antillas

Mayagüez, Puerto Rico

- **Independent Seventh-day Adventist** comprehensive, founded 1957
- **Calendar** semesters
- **Degrees** associate, bachelor's, and master's
- **Rural** 284-acre campus
- **Endowment** $10,000
- **Coed,** 821 undergraduate students, 91% full-time, 59% women, 41% men
- **Minimally difficult** entrance level, 84% of applicants were admitted

Undergraduates 745 full-time, 76 part-time. Students come from 11 states and territories, 20 other countries, 25% are from out of state, 0.7% African American, 96% Hispanic American, 3% international, 6% transferred in, 27% live on campus. *Retention:* 72% of 2002 full-time freshmen returned.

Freshmen *Admission:* 509 applied, 429 admitted, 188 enrolled. *Average high school GPA:* 2.83.

Faculty *Total:* 61, 69% full-time, 20% with terminal degrees. *Student/faculty ratio:* 13:1.

Majors Administrative assistant and secretarial science; biblical studies; biology/biological sciences; biology teacher education; business administration and management; chemistry; computer science; elementary education; health information/medical records administration; history; history teacher education; mathematics teacher education; medical administrative assistant and medical secretary; music; music teacher education; nursing (registered nurse training); pastoral studies/counseling; religious education; respiratory care therapy; secondary education; social studies teacher education; Spanish; Spanish language teacher education; theology.

Academic Programs *Special study options:* academic remediation for entering students, adult/continuing education programs, advanced placement credit, cooperative education, double majors, English as a second language, internships, part-time degree program, services for LD students, summer session for credit. *Unusual degree programs:* 3-2 engineering with Walla Walla College; nursing with Loma Linda University.

Library Biblioteca Dennis Soto plus 1 other with 86,465 titles, 452 serial subscriptions, 325 audiovisual materials, an OPAC, a Web page.

Computers on Campus 62 computers available on campus for general student use. Internet access, at least one staffed computer lab available.
Student Life *Housing:* on-campus residence required for freshman year. *Options:* coed, men-only, women-only. Freshman applicants given priority for college housing. *Activities and organizations:* student-run newspaper, choral group, Score Group, gymnastic club, student council, Group Life. *Campus security:* 24-hour emergency response devices and patrols, student patrols, controlled dormitory access. *Student services:* health clinic, personal/psychological counseling.
Athletics *Intercollegiate sports:* softball M. *Intramural sports:* basketball M/W, gymnastics M/W, soccer M, softball M, swimming M/W, tennis M/W, volleyball M/W.
Standardized Tests *Recommended:* SAT I or ACT (for admission), PAA.
Costs (2003–04) *Comprehensive fee:* $7890 includes full-time tuition ($4470), mandatory fees ($870), and room and board ($2550). Full-time tuition and fees vary according to course load. Part-time tuition: $120 per credit. Part-time tuition and fees vary according to course load. *Required fees:* $225 per term part-time. *College room only:* $750. Room and board charges vary according to board plan. *Payment plans:* tuition prepayment, installment, deferred payment. *Waivers:* employees or children of employees.
Financial Aid Of all full-time matriculated undergraduates who enrolled in 2002, 723 applied for aid, 723 were judged to have need. *Average percent of need met:* 70%. *Average need-based loan:* $2500. *Average need-based gift aid:* $6624. *Average indebtedness upon graduation:* $3500.
Applying *Options:* common application, early admission. *Application fee:* $20. *Required:* high school transcript, minimum 2.0 GPA, letters of recommendation. *Required for some:* interview.
Admissions Contact Universidad Adventista de las Antillas, Oficina de Admisiones, PO Box 118, Mayaguez, PR 00681-0118. *Phone:* 787-834-9595 Ext. 2208. *Fax:* 787-834-9597. *E-mail:* admissions@uaa.edu.

UNIVERSIDAD DEL ESTE
Carolina, Puerto Rico

Admissions Contact Carmen Rodríguez, Associate Director, Universidad del Este, PO Box 2010, Carolina, PR 00984-2010. *Phone:* 787-257-7373 Ext. 3300.

UNIVERSIDAD DEL TURABO
Turabo, Puerto Rico

Admissions Contact Sr. Jesús Torres, Director of Admissions, Universidad del Turabo, PO Box 3030, Turabo, PR 00778-3030. *Phone:* 787-743-7979 Ext. 201.

UNIVERSIDAD METROPOLITANA
Río Piedras, Puerto Rico

Admissions Contact Ms. Carmen Rosado, Director of Admissions, Universidad Metropolitana, Call Box 21150, Río Piedras, PR 00928-1150. *Phone:* 787-766-1717 Ext. 540. *Toll-free phone:* 800-747-8362. *E-mail:* um_frivera@suagm1.suagm.edu.

UNIVERSITY OF PHOENIX–PUERTO RICO CAMPUS
Guaynabo, Puerto Rico

- **Proprietary** comprehensive, founded 1995
- **Calendar** continuous
- **Degrees** certificates, associate, bachelor's, master's, doctoral, post-master's, and postbachelor's certificates (courses conducted at 121 campuses and learning centers in 25 states)
- **Urban** campus
- **Coed,** 406 undergraduate students, 100% full-time, 51% women, 49% men
- **Noncompetitive** entrance level

Undergraduates 406 full-time. 0.7% African American, 61% Hispanic American, 2% international.
Freshmen *Admission:* 31 enrolled.
Faculty *Total:* 115, 5% full-time, 51% with terminal degrees. *Student/faculty ratio:* 15:1.
Majors Accounting; business administration and management; management information systems; marketing/marketing management.
Academic Programs *Special study options:* accelerated degree program, adult/continuing education programs, advanced placement credit, distance learning, external degree program, independent study.
Library University Library with 27.1 million titles, 11,648 serial subscriptions, an OPAC, a Web page.
Computers on Campus A campuswide network can be accessed from off campus. Internet access, at least one staffed computer lab available.
Student Life *Housing:* college housing not available.
Costs (2003–04) *Tuition:* $5160 full-time, $172 per credit part-time. *Waivers:* employees or children of employees.
Financial Aid *Average financial aid package:* $2396.
Applying *Options:* deferred entrance. *Application fee:* $85. *Required:* 1 letter of recommendation, 2 years of work experience, 23 years of age. *Required for some:* high school transcript. *Application deadline:* rolling (freshmen), rolling (transfers).
Admissions Contact Ms. Beth Barilla, Director of Admissions, University of Phoenix–Puerto Rico Campus, 4615 East Elwood Street, Mail Stop AA-K101, Phoenix, AZ 85040-1958. *Phone:* 480-317-6000. *Toll-free phone:* 800-228-7240. *Fax:* 480-594-1758. *E-mail:* beth.barilla@phoenix.edu.

UNIVERSITY OF PUERTO RICO, AGUADILLA UNIVERSITY COLLEGE
Aguadilla, Puerto Rico

Admissions Contact Ms. Melba Serrano Lugo, Admissions Officer, University of Puerto Rico, Aguadilla University College, Admission Office, PO Box 250160, Aguadilla, PR 00604-0160. *Phone:* 787-890-2681 Ext. 280. *E-mail:* m_serrano@upr.clue.edu.

UNIVERSITY OF PUERTO RICO AT ARECIBO
Arecibo, Puerto Rico

- **Commonwealth-supported** 4-year, founded 1967, part of University of Puerto Rico System
- **Calendar** semesters
- **Degrees** associate and bachelor's
- **Urban** 44-acre campus with easy access to San Juan
- **Coed**
- **Very difficult** entrance level

Faculty *Student/faculty ratio:* 17:1.
Student Life *Campus security:* 24-hour emergency response devices and patrols.
Standardized Tests *Required:* SAT II: Subject Tests (for admission), PAA or SAT I, CEEB (for admission), SAT II: Subject Tests (for placement).
Financial Aid Of all full-time matriculated undergraduates who enrolled in 1999, 274 Federal Work-Study jobs (averaging $1100). *Financial aid deadline:* 6/2.
Applying *Required:* high school transcript.
Admissions Contact Mrs. Delma Barrios, Director of Admissions, University of Puerto Rico at Arecibo, PO Box 4010, Arecibo, PR 00614-4010. *Phone:* 787-878-2830 Ext. 3023.

UNIVERSITY OF PUERTO RICO AT BAYAMÓN
Bayamón, Puerto Rico

Admissions Contact Ms. Vivian Rivera, Officer of Admission, University of Puerto Rico at Bayamón, 170 Carretera 174 Parque Industrial Minillas, Bayamón, PR 00959-1919. *Phone:* 787-786-2885 Ext. 2425. *E-mail:* e_velez@cutb.upr.clu.edu.

UNIVERSITY OF PUERTO RICO AT CAROLINA
Carolina, Puerto Rico

Admissions Contact Mrs. Ivonne Calderon, Admissions Officer, University of Puerto Rico at Carolina, PO Box 4800, Carolina, PR 00984-4800. *Phone:* 787-257-0000 Ext. 3347.

UNIVERSITY OF PUERTO RICO AT HUMACAO
Humacao, Puerto Rico

- **Commonwealth-supported** 4-year, founded 1962, part of University of Puerto Rico System

University of Puerto Rico at Humacao (continued)
- **Calendar** semesters
- **Degrees** associate and bachelor's
- **Suburban** 62-acre campus with easy access to San Juan
- **Coed**
- **Moderately difficult** entrance level

Faculty *Student/faculty ratio:* 15:1.
Student Life *Campus security:* 24-hour patrols, 24-hour gate security.
Standardized Tests *Required:* CEEB for Puerto Rican applicants, PAA and 3 achievement tests (for admission). *Required for some:* SAT I (for admission), SAT II: Subject Tests (for admission).
Costs (2003–04) *Tuition:* commonwealth resident $1020 full-time. *Required fees:* $70 full-time.
Financial Aid Of all full-time matriculated undergraduates who enrolled in 2001, 3,515 applied for aid, 2,883 were judged to have need, 7 had their need fully met. 278 Federal Work-Study jobs (averaging $1318). *Average percent of need met:* 50. *Average financial aid package:* $3929. *Average need-based loan:* $3295. *Average need-based gift aid:* $3664. *Average indebtedness upon graduation:* $2749. *Financial aid deadline:* 6/30.
Applying *Options:* deferred entrance. *Application fee:* $15. *Required:* high school transcript, minimum 2.0 GPA.
Admissions Contact Mrs. Inara Ferrer, Director of Admissions, University of Puerto Rico at Humacao, CUH Station 100 Road 908, Humacao, PR 00791-4300. *Phone:* 787-850-9301. *Fax:* 787-850-9428. *E-mail:* i_ferrer@cuhac.upr.clu.edu.

University of Puerto Rico at Ponce
Ponce, Puerto Rico

- **Commonwealth-supported** 4-year, founded 1970, part of University of Puerto Rico System
- **Calendar** semesters
- **Degrees** associate and bachelor's
- **Urban** 86-acre campus with easy access to San Juan
- **Coed**
- **Moderately difficult** entrance level

Faculty *Student/faculty ratio:* 19:1.
Student Life *Campus security:* 24-hour patrols.
Standardized Tests *Required:* SAT I (for admission), PAA (for admission).
Financial Aid Of all full-time matriculated undergraduates who enrolled in 1998, 3,461 applied for aid, 3,133 were judged to have need. *Average percent of need met:* 40. *Financial aid deadline:* 6/30.
Applying *Options:* common application, early admission, early decision. *Application fee:* $15. *Required:* high school transcript.
Admissions Contact Mr. William Rodriguez Mercado, Admissions Officer, University of Puerto Rico at Ponce, PO Box 7186, Ponce, PR 00732-7186. *Phone:* 787-844-8181 Ext. 2530. *Fax:* 787-842-3875.

University of Puerto Rico at Utuado
Utuado, Puerto Rico

- **Commonwealth-supported** 4-year, founded 1979, part of University of Puerto Rico System
- **Calendar** semesters
- **Degrees** associate and bachelor's
- **Small-town** 180-acre campus with easy access to San Juan
- **Coed**
- **Moderately difficult** entrance level

Faculty *Student/faculty ratio:* 17:1.
Student Life *Campus security:* 24-hour emergency response devices and patrols.
Standardized Tests *Required:* SAT I and SAT II or ACT (for admission), PAA (for admission).
Financial Aid Of all full-time matriculated undergraduates who enrolled in 2001, 143 Federal Work-Study jobs. *Financial aid deadline:* 6/15.
Applying *Options:* common application, electronic application, early admission, deferred entrance. *Application fee:* $15.
Admissions Contact Mrs. Maria V. Robles Serrano, Admissions Officer, University of Puerto Rico at Utuado, PO Box 2500, Utuado, PR 00641-2500. *Phone:* 787-894-2828 Ext. 2240. *Fax:* 787-894-2877.

University of Puerto Rico, Cayey University College
Cayey, Puerto Rico

- **Commonwealth-supported** 4-year, founded 1967, part of University of Puerto Rico System
- **Calendar** semesters
- **Degrees** associate and bachelor's
- **Urban** 177-acre campus with easy access to San Juan
- **Coed,** 3,987 undergraduate students, 90% full-time, 72% women, 28% men
- **Very difficult** entrance level, 22% of applicants were admitted

Undergraduates 3,595 full-time, 392 part-time. Students come from 1 other state, 100% Hispanic American, 2% transferred in. *Retention:* 89% of 2002 full-time freshmen returned.
Freshmen *Admission:* 4,084 applied, 891 admitted, 814 enrolled. *Average high school GPA:* 3.46.
Faculty *Total:* 219, 82% full-time, 46% with terminal degrees. *Student/faculty ratio:* 18:1.
Majors Accounting; administrative assistant and secretarial science; Army R.O.T.C./military science; biology/biological sciences; biology teacher education; business administration and management; chemistry; chemistry teacher education; economics; elementary education; English; English as a second/foreign language (teaching); English/language arts teacher education; history; history teacher education; humanities; mathematics; mathematics teacher education; mental health/rehabilitation; natural sciences; office management; physical education teaching and coaching; physics teacher education; psychology; psychology related; science teacher education; secondary education; social sciences; social science teacher education; social studies teacher education; sociology; Spanish; Spanish and Iberian studies; Spanish language teacher education.
Academic Programs *Special study options:* academic remediation for entering students, accelerated degree program, advanced placement credit, honors programs, off-campus study, part-time degree program, study abroad, summer session for credit. *ROTC:* Army (b).
Library Victor M. Pons Library with 109,776 titles, 2,013 serial subscriptions, 2,286 audiovisual materials, an OPAC, a Web page.
Computers on Campus 265 computers available on campus for general student use. A campuswide network can be accessed from off campus. Internet access, online (class) registration, at least one staffed computer lab available.
Student Life *Housing:* college housing not available. *Activities and organizations:* drama/theater group, choral group, Business Administration Circle, Christian University Association, national fraternities, national sororities. *Campus security:* 24-hour emergency response devices and patrols, late-night transport/escort service. *Student services:* health clinic, personal/psychological counseling, women's center.
Athletics Member NCAA. *Intercollegiate sports:* basketball M(s)/W(s), cross-country running M(s)/W(s), soccer M(s), softball M(s)/W(s), swimming M(s), table tennis M(s), tennis M(s)/W(s), track and field M(s)/W(s), volleyball M(s)/W(s), weight lifting M, wrestling M. *Intramural sports:* basketball M/W, cross-country running M/W, soccer M/W, softball M/W, swimming M/W, tennis M/W, track and field M/W, volleyball M/W, weight lifting M, wrestling M.
Standardized Tests *Required:* CEEB (for admission). *Required for some:* SAT I (for admission).
Costs (2004–05) *Tuition:* area resident $1020 full-time, $30 per credit part-time. Full-time tuition and fees vary according to degree level and program. *Required fees:* $225 full-time, $225 per year part-time. *Waivers:* employees or children of employees.
Financial Aid Of all full-time matriculated undergraduates who enrolled in 2000, 2,866 applied for aid, 2,819 were judged to have need. 281 Federal Work-Study jobs. *Average financial aid package:* $4200. *Average need-based loan:* $3000. *Average need-based gift aid:* $3300.
Applying *Options:* common application, early admission. *Application fee:* $15. *Required:* high school transcript, minimum 2.0 GPA. *Application deadlines:* 12/1 (freshmen), 2/15 (transfers). *Notification:* continuous until 5/5 (freshmen).

Admissions Contact Mr. Wilfredo Lopez, Admissions Officer, University of Puerto Rico, Cayey University College, Avenue Antonio R. Barcelo, Cayey, PR 00736. *Phone:* 787-738-2161 Ext. 2208. *Fax:* 787-738-5633.

UNIVERSITY OF PUERTO RICO, MAYAGÜEZ CAMPUS

Mayagüez, Puerto Rico

Admissions Contact Ms. Norma Torres, Director, Admissions Office, University of Puerto Rico, Mayagüez Campus, PO Box 9021, Mayaguez, PR 00681-9021. *Phone:* 787-265-3811. *Fax:* 787-834-5265. *E-mail:* norma_t@dediego.uprm.edu.

UNIVERSITY OF PUERTO RICO, MEDICAL SCIENCES CAMPUS

San Juan, Puerto Rico

- **Commonwealth-supported** upper-level, founded 1950, part of University of Puerto Rico System
- **Calendar** semesters
- **Degrees** certificates, associate, bachelor's, master's, doctoral, first professional, postbachelor's, and first professional certificates (bachelor's degree is upper-level)
- **Urban** 11-acre campus
- **Coed, primarily women**
- **Moderately difficult** entrance level

Student Life *Campus security:* 24-hour emergency response devices.

Standardized Tests *Required:* SAT I (for placement). *Required for some:* PCAT, MCAT, DAT, ASPHAT, GRE, PAEG.

Financial Aid Of all full-time matriculated undergraduates who enrolled in 2001, 785 applied for aid, 763 were judged to have need, 451 had their need fully met. 76 Federal Work-Study jobs (averaging $618). *Average percent of need met:* 68. *Average financial aid package:* $4535. *Average need-based loan:* $3794. *Average need-based gift aid:* $3504. *Average indebtedness upon graduation:* $4500. *Financial aid deadline:* 5/15.

Applying *Application fee:* $15.

Admissions Contact Mrs. Rosa Vèlez, Acting Director of Admission Office, University of Puerto Rico, Medical Sciences Campus, PO Box 365067, San Juan, PR 00936-5067. *Phone:* 787-758-2525 Ext. 5211. *E-mail:* rvelez@rcm.upr.edu.

UNIVERSITY OF PUERTO RICO, RÍO PIEDRAS

San Juan, Puerto Rico

- **Commonwealth-supported** university, founded 1903, part of University of Puerto Rico System
- **Calendar** semesters
- **Degrees** bachelor's, master's, doctoral, first professional, post-master's, and postbachelor's certificates
- **Urban** 281-acre campus
- **Coed**
- **Very difficult** entrance level

Faculty *Student/faculty ratio:* 22:1.

Student Life *Campus security:* 24-hour emergency response devices, late-night transport/escort service.

Athletics Member NCAA, NAIA. All NCAA Division II.

Standardized Tests *Required:* SAT I (for admission), SAT II: Subject Tests (for admission), CEEB (for admission).

Costs (2003–04) *Tuition:* commonwealth resident $790 full-time; nonresident $2470 full-time. *Required fees:* $593 full-time. *Room and board:* $4940.

Applying *Options:* common application, electronic application. *Application fee:* $15. *Required:* high school transcript, minimum 2.0 GPA. *Required for some:* interview.

Admissions Contact Mrs. Cruz B. Valentìn, Director of Admissions, University of Puerto Rico, Río Piedras, PO Box 21907, San Juan, PR 00931-1907. *Phone:* 787-764-0000 Ext. 5666. *Fax:* 787-764-3680.

UNIVERSITY OF THE SACRED HEART

San Juan, Puerto Rico

- **Independent Roman Catholic** comprehensive, founded 1935
- **Calendar** semesters
- **Degrees** certificates, associate, bachelor's, master's, and postbachelor's certificates
- **Urban** 33-acre campus
- **Endowment** $16.0 million
- **Coed,** 4,560 undergraduate students, 71% full-time, 65% women, 35% men
- **Moderately difficult** entrance level, 74% of applicants were admitted

Undergraduates 3,248 full-time, 1,312 part-time. Students come from 1 other state, 2% are from out of state, 100% Hispanic American, 4% transferred in. *Retention:* 77% of 2002 full-time freshmen returned.

Freshmen *Admission:* 2,321 applied, 1,706 admitted, 722 enrolled. *Average high school GPA:* 2.89.

Faculty *Total:* 338, 39% full-time, 24% with terminal degrees. *Student/faculty ratio:* 18:1.

Majors Accounting; administrative assistant and secretarial science; advertising; bilingual and multilingual education; biology/biological sciences; business administration and management; chemistry; clinical laboratory science/medical technology; communication/speech communication and rhetoric; computer science; criminal justice/safety; dramatic/theatre arts; education; elementary education; foreign languages related; humanities; information science/studies; interdisciplinary studies; journalism; kinesiology and exercise science; literature; marketing/marketing management; mass communication/media; nursing (registered nurse training); office management; psychology; secondary education; social sciences; social work; telecommunications; telecommunications technology; tourism and travel services management; tourism/travel marketing; visual and performing arts.

Academic Programs *Special study options:* academic remediation for entering students, accelerated degree program, adult/continuing education programs, advanced placement credit, cooperative education, honors programs, internships, part-time degree program, services for LD students, study abroad, summer session for credit.

Library Maria Teresa Guevara Library plus 1 other with 1,525 serial subscriptions, 67,048 audiovisual materials, an OPAC, a Web page.

Computers on Campus 500 computers available on campus for general student use. A campuswide network can be accessed from off campus. At least one staffed computer lab available.

Student Life *Housing options:* men-only, women-only. Campus housing is university owned. *Activities and organizations:* drama/theater group, student-run newspaper, television station, choral group, La Red (personal development center), Student Council, Judo Club, Athletic Association. *Campus security:* 24-hour patrols. *Student services:* health clinic, personal/psychological counseling.

Athletics *Intercollegiate sports:* basketball M(s)/W(s), cross-country running M(s)/W(s), swimming M(s)/W(s), tennis M(s)/W(s), track and field M(s)/W(s), volleyball M(s)/W(s), weight lifting M(s)/W(s). *Intramural sports:* basketball M/W, cross-country running M/W, softball M/W, table tennis M/W, tennis M/W, volleyball M/W, weight lifting M/W.

Standardized Tests *Required:* PAA, CEEB (for admission).

Costs (2003–04) *Tuition:* $4350 full-time, $145 per credit part-time. *Required fees:* $440 full-time, $225 per term part-time. *Room only:* $1900.

Applying *Options:* common application, early admission. *Application fee:* $15. *Required:* high school transcript, minimum 2.5 GPA, 1 letter of recommendation. *Application deadlines:* 6/30 (freshmen), 6/30 (transfers).

Admissions Contact Mr. Luis Heviquez, Director of Admissions, University of the Sacred Heart, PO Box 12383, San Juan, PR 00914-0383. *Phone:* 787-728-1515 Ext. 3237. *E-mail:* registro@sagrado.edu.

VIRGIN ISLANDS

UNIVERSITY OF THE VIRGIN ISLANDS

Charlotte Amalie, Virgin Islands

- **Territory-supported** comprehensive, founded 1962
- **Calendar** semesters
- **Degrees** associate, bachelor's, and master's
- **Small-town** 175-acre campus
- **Endowment** $6.3 million
- **Coed,** 2,683 undergraduate students
- **Minimally difficult** entrance level

Undergraduates Students come from 29 states and territories, 10 other countries, 3% are from out of state, 60% African American, 1% Asian American or Pacific Islander, 4% Hispanic American, 0.2% Native American, 8% international. *Retention:* 65% of 2002 full-time freshmen returned.

University of the Virgin Islands (continued)

Freshmen *Average high school GPA:* 2.10. *Test scores:* SAT verbal scores over 500: 23%; SAT math scores over 500: 20%; SAT verbal scores over 600: 3%; SAT math scores over 600: 5%; SAT math scores over 700: 1%.

Faculty *Total:* 264, 41% full-time, 32% with terminal degrees. *Student/faculty ratio:* 9:1.

Majors Accounting; administrative assistant and secretarial science; biology/biological sciences; business administration and management; chemistry; computer science; criminal justice/police science; data processing and data processing technology; dramatic/theatre arts; elementary education; English; hotel/motel administration; humanities; marine biology and biological oceanography; mathematics; music teacher education; nursing (registered nurse training); physics; psychology; social sciences; social work; speech and rhetoric; trade and industrial teacher education.

Academic Programs *Special study options:* academic remediation for entering students, adult/continuing education programs, advanced placement credit, distance learning, external degree program, independent study, internships, off-campus study, part-time degree program, summer session for credit.

Library Ralph M. Paiewonsky Library with 106,361 titles, 136,790 serial subscriptions, an OPAC, a Web page.

Computers on Campus 100 computers available on campus for general student use. A campuswide network can be accessed from off campus. At least one staffed computer lab available.

Student Life *Housing options:* men-only, women-only. Campus housing is university owned. *Activities and organizations:* drama/theater group, student-run newspaper, choral group, The Squad, Predators, Golden Key Honor Society, National Student Exchange club, St. Kitts and Nevis, national fraternities, national sororities. *Campus security:* 24-hour patrols. *Student services:* health clinic, personal/psychological counseling.

Athletics *Intercollegiate sports:* basketball M/W, cross-country running M/W, tennis M/W, volleyball M/W. *Intramural sports:* basketball M/W, tennis M/W, volleyball M/W.

Standardized Tests *Required:* SAT I or ACT (for admission).

Costs (2004–05) *Tuition:* territory resident $2730 full-time, $91 per credit hour part-time; nonresident $8190 full-time, $273 per credit hour part-time. Full-time tuition and fees vary according to course load, degree level, and program. Part-time tuition and fees vary according to course load, degree level, and program. *Required fees:* $256 full-time. *Room only:* $2000. Room and board charges vary according to board plan and housing facility. *Waivers:* senior citizens and employees or children of employees.

Financial Aid Of all full-time matriculated undergraduates who enrolled in 2002, 1,139 applied for aid, 1,017 were judged to have need, 26 had their need fully met. 90 Federal Work-Study jobs (averaging $3000). 50 state and other part-time jobs (averaging $3500). *Average percent of need met:* 45%. *Average financial aid package:* $4000. *Average need-based loan:* $2500. *Average need-based gift aid:* $2000. *Average indebtedness upon graduation:* $3500.

Applying *Options:* early admission, deferred entrance. *Application fee:* $20. *Required:* essay or personal statement, high school transcript, 2 letters of recommendation. *Application deadlines:* 4/30 (freshmen), 4/30 (transfers). *Notification:* continuous (freshmen), 6/15 (transfers).

Admissions Contact Ms. Carolyn Cook, Director of Admissions & New Student services, University of the Virgin Islands, No. 2 John Brewers Bay, St. Thomas, VI 00802. *Phone:* 340-693-1224. *Fax:* 340-693-1155. *E-mail:* admissions@uvi.edu.

■ *See page 2730 for a narrative description.*

CANADA

ACADIA UNIVERSITY
Wolfville, Nova Scotia, Canada

- **Province-supported** comprehensive, founded 1838
- **Calendar** Canadian standard year
- **Degrees** bachelor's and master's
- **Small-town** 250-acre campus
- **Endowment** $26.0 million
- **Coed,** 4,035 undergraduate students, 97% full-time, 55% women, 45% men
- **Moderately difficult** entrance level, 40% of applicants were admitted

Undergraduates 3,894 full-time, 141 part-time. Students come from 12 provinces and territories, 70 other countries, 42% are from out of state, 9% transferred in, 40% live on campus. *Retention:* 84% of 2002 full-time freshmen returned.

Freshmen *Admission:* 3,103 applied, 1,253 admitted, 1,229 enrolled.

Faculty *Total:* 308, 65% full-time. *Student/faculty ratio:* 17:1.

Majors Biology/biological sciences; business administration and management; Canadian studies; chemistry; classics and languages, literatures and linguistics; computer science; dietetics; dramatic/theatre arts; economics; education; elementary education; English; environmental studies; food science; foods, nutrition, and wellness; French; geology/earth science; history; kinesiology and exercise science; Latin; mathematics; music; music teacher education; philosophy; physics; piano and organ; political science and government; pre-dentistry studies; pre-law studies; pre-medical studies; pre-veterinary studies; psychology; secondary education; sociology; violin, viola, guitar and other stringed instruments; voice and opera; wind/percussion instruments.

Academic Programs *Special study options:* academic remediation for entering students, advanced placement credit, cooperative education, distance learning, double majors, English as a second language, honors programs, internships, off-campus study, part-time degree program, study abroad, summer session for credit.

Library Vaughan Memorial Library with 846,073 titles, 11,268 serial subscriptions, 4,419 audiovisual materials, an OPAC, a Web page.

Computers on Campus 3700 computers available on campus for general student use. A campuswide network can be accessed from student residence rooms and from off campus that provide access to online course and grade information. Internet access, online (class) registration, at least one staffed computer lab available.

Student Life *Housing options:* coed, men-only, women-only. Campus housing is university owned. *Activities and organizations:* drama/theater group, student-run newspaper, radio station, choral group, marching band, Acadia recreation club, Acadia ski club, Education Society, Computer science club, Caricom. *Campus security:* 24-hour emergency response devices and patrols, student patrols, late-night transport/escort service, controlled dormitory access. *Student services:* health clinic, personal/psychological counseling, women's center, legal services.

Athletics Member CIS. *Intercollegiate sports:* baseball M(c), basketball M/W, bowling M(c), cheerleading M(c), cross-country running M/W, football M, ice hockey M/W, rugby M(c)/W(c), soccer M/W, track and field M/W, volleyball W. *Intramural sports:* badminton M/W, baseball M/W, basketball M/W, bowling M/W, cheerleading M/W, cross-country running M/W, field hockey M/W, ice hockey M/W, racquetball M/W, rugby M/W, skiing (cross-country) M/W, skiing (downhill) M/W, soccer M/W, softball M/W, squash M/W, swimming M/W, table tennis M/W, tennis M/W, track and field M/W, ultimate Frisbee M/W, volleyball M/W, water polo M/W, wrestling M.

Standardized Tests *Required:* SAT I (for admission). *Required for some:* SAT II: Subject Tests (for admission).

Costs (2003–04) *Tuition:* nonresident $7012 Canadian dollars full-time, $1358 Canadian dollars per course part-time; International tuition $12,480 Canadian dollars full-time. *Required fees:* $158 Canadian dollars full-time, $5 Canadian dollars per course part-time. *Room and board:* $5781 Canadian dollars; room only: $3042 Canadian dollars. Room and board charges vary according to board plan and housing facility. *Payment plan:* installment. *Waivers:* senior citizens and employees or children of employees.

Applying *Options:* electronic application, deferred entrance. *Application fee:* $25 Canadian dollars. *Required:* high school transcript, minimum 2.5 GPA. *Required for some:* essay or personal statement, letters of recommendation, interview. *Application deadlines:* 7/1 (freshmen), 5/31 (out-of-state freshmen), 7/1 (transfers). *Notification:* continuous (freshmen), continuous (transfers).

Admissions Contact Ms. Anne Scott, Manager of Admissions, Acadia University, Wolfville, NS B4P 2R6, Canada. *Phone:* 902-585-1222. *Fax:* 902-585-1081. *E-mail:* admissions@acadiau.ca.

ALBERTA COLLEGE OF ART & DESIGN
Calgary, Alberta, Canada

- **Province-supported** 4-year, founded 1926
- **Calendar** semesters
- **Degree** bachelor's
- **Urban** 1-acre campus
- **Coed,** 1,044 undergraduate students
- **Moderately difficult** entrance level, 52% of applicants were admitted

Undergraduates Students come from 7 provinces and territories, 11 other countries. *Retention:* 92% of 2002 full-time freshmen returned.

Freshmen *Admission:* 580 applied, 300 admitted.

Faculty *Total:* 107, 36% full-time. *Student/faculty ratio:* 11:1.

Majors Art; ceramic arts and ceramics; commercial and advertising art; computer graphics; design and visual communications; drawing; fiber, textile and weaving arts; fine/studio arts; graphic design; illustration; intermedia/multimedia; metal and jewelry arts; painting; photography; printmaking; sculpture.

Academic Programs *Special study options:* academic remediation for entering students, adult/continuing education programs, advanced placement credit, external degree program, independent study, internships, part-time degree program, services for LD students, study abroad, summer session for credit.

Library Luke Lindoe Library with 25,000 titles, 66 serial subscriptions, an OPAC, a Web page.

Computers on Campus 65 computers available on campus for general student use. A campuswide network can be accessed. Internet access, at least one staffed computer lab available.

Student Life *Housing:* college housing not available. *Campus security:* 24-hour emergency response devices and patrols, late-night transport/escort service, controlled dormitory access. *Student services:* health clinic, personal/psychological counseling.

Athletics *Intercollegiate sports:* basketball M(s)/W(s), ice hockey M/W, soccer M(s)/W(s), volleyball M(s)/W(s). *Intramural sports:* basketball M/W, ice hockey M/W, soccer M/W, volleyball M/W.

Costs (2003–04) *Tuition:* province resident $4005 Canadian dollars full-time, $452 Canadian dollars per credit part-time; International tuition $9165 Canadian dollars full-time. Room and board is available at the Southern Alberta Institute of Technology (SAIT). *Required fees:* $465 Canadian dollars full-time.

Applying *Options:* early admission, early decision, early action. *Application fee:* $50 Canadian dollars. *Required:* essay or personal statement, high school transcript, portfolio of artwork. *Recommended:* minimum 2.0 GPA. *Application deadlines:* 4/1 (freshmen), 4/1 (transfers). *Notification:* 6/15 (freshmen), 4/30 (early action), 6/15 (transfers).

Admissions Contact Ms. Joy Borman, Associate Director of Admissions, Alberta College of Art & Design, 1407-14 Avenue NW, Calgary, AB T2N 4R3, Canada. *Phone:* 403-284-7689. *Toll-free phone:* 800-251-8290. *Fax:* 403-284-7644. *E-mail:* admissions@acad.ca.

ALLIANCE UNIVERSITY COLLEGE

Calgary, Alberta, Canada

- **Independent** comprehensive, founded 1941, affiliated with The Christian and Missionary Alliance
- **Calendar** semesters
- **Degrees** certificates, diplomas, and bachelor's (graduate and professional degrees are offered by Canadian Theological Seminary)
- **Urban** 16-acre campus
- **Endowment** $1.2 million
- **Coed**
- **Noncompetitive** entrance level

Student Life *Campus security:* 24-hour emergency response devices, controlled dormitory access.

Costs (2003–04) *Tuition:* $6600 Canadian dollars full-time, $220 Canadian dollars per credit part-time. *Required fees:* $200 Canadian dollars full-time, $100 Canadian dollars per term part-time. *Room only:* $3180 Canadian dollars.

Applying *Options:* common application, electronic application, early admission, deferred entrance. *Application fee:* $50 Canadian dollars. *Required:* essay or personal statement, high school transcript, 2 letters of recommendation. *Required for some:* interview. *Recommended:* medical history.

Admissions Contact Admissions Officer, Alliance University College, 630, 833-4th Avenue SW, Calgary, AB T2P 3T5, Canada. *Toll-free phone:* 800-461-1222. *Fax:* 403-471-2566. *E-mail:* enrolment@auc-nuc.ca.

ATHABASCA UNIVERSITY

Athabasca, Alberta, Canada

- **Province-supported** comprehensive, founded 1970
- **Calendar** continuous
- **Degrees** certificates, diplomas, bachelor's, and master's (offers only external degree programs)
- **Small-town** 480-acre campus
- **Endowment** $1.1 million
- **Coed,** 26,235 undergraduate students, 66% women, 34% men
- **Noncompetitive** entrance level

Undergraduates 26,235 part-time. Students come from 13 provinces and territories, 70 other countries, 50% are from out of state.

Freshmen *Admission:* 4,542 enrolled.

Faculty *Total:* 496, 50% full-time.

Majors Accounting; anthropology; applied art; biological and physical sciences; business administration and management; Canadian studies; communication and media related; computer and information sciences; criminal justice/police science; English; French; general studies; history; human resources management; information science/studies; labor and industrial relations; liberal arts and sciences/liberal studies; marketing/marketing management; nursing (registered nurse training); organizational behavior; political science and government; psychology; public administration; sociology; women's studies.

Academic Programs *Special study options:* academic remediation for entering students, accelerated degree program, adult/continuing education programs, advanced placement credit, cooperative education, distance learning, English as a second language, external degree program, off-campus study, part-time degree program, services for LD students, student-designed majors, study abroad, summer session for credit.

Library Athabasca University Library plus 1 other with 130,000 titles, 7,000 serial subscriptions, 3,345 audiovisual materials, an OPAC, a Web page.

Computers on Campus 28 computers available on campus for general student use. A campuswide network can be accessed from off campus that provide access to computing services help desk. Internet access, online (class) registration, at least one staffed computer lab available.

Student Life *Housing:* college housing not available. *Activities and organizations:* student-run newspaper. *Campus security:* 24-hour emergency response devices.

Costs (2003–04) *Tuition:* $541 Canadian dollars per course part-time; province resident $5410 Canadian dollars full-time, $596 Canadian dollars per course part-time; nonresident $5960 Canadian dollars full-time, $791 Canadian dollars per course part-time; International tuition $7910 Canadian dollars full-time.

Applying *Options:* common application, electronic application. *Application fee:* $60 Canadian dollars. *Required:* high school transcript. *Application deadline:* rolling (freshmen), rolling (transfers). *Notification:* continuous (freshmen), continuous (transfers).

Admissions Contact Ms. Teresa Wylie, Assistant Registrar, Admissions, Athabasca University, 1 University Drive, Athabasca, AB T9S 3A3. *Phone:* 780-675-6377. *Toll-free phone:* 800-788-9041. *Fax:* 780-675-6437. *E-mail:* inquire@athabascau.ca.

ATLANTIC BAPTIST UNIVERSITY

Moncton, New Brunswick, Canada

- **Independent Baptist** 4-year, founded 1949
- **Calendar** semesters
- **Degrees** certificates, bachelor's, and postbachelor's certificates
- **Urban** 220-acre campus
- **Endowment** $1.5 million
- **Coed,** 677 undergraduate students, 89% full-time, 70% women, 30% men
- **Minimally difficult** entrance level

Undergraduates 603 full-time, 74 part-time. Students come from 12 provinces and territories, 5 other countries, 25% are from out of state, 2% international, 7% transferred in, 22% live on campus. *Retention:* 77% of 2002 full-time freshmen returned.

Freshmen *Admission:* 272 enrolled.

Faculty *Total:* 43, 49% full-time, 100% with terminal degrees. *Student/faculty ratio:* 23:1.

Majors Biblical studies; biology/biological sciences; business administration and management; education; education (K-12); English; history; interdisciplinary studies; mass communication/media; psychology; religious studies; sociology.

Academic Programs *Special study options:* accelerated degree program, cooperative education, double majors, honors programs, internships, part-time degree program, study abroad, summer session for credit. *Unusual degree programs:* 3-2 education.

Library George A. Rawlyk Library with 57,000 titles, 185 serial subscriptions, 350 audiovisual materials, an OPAC.

Computers on Campus 35 computers available on campus for general student use. A campuswide network can be accessed from student residence rooms. At least one staffed computer lab available.

Student Life *Housing options:* men-only, women-only, disabled students. Campus housing is university owned. *Activities and organizations:* drama/theater group, student-run newspaper, choral group, Student Association, drama, intramurals, debate team, choir. *Campus security:* 24-hour emergency response devices, student patrols, controlled dormitory access.

Athletics *Intercollegiate sports:* basketball M/W, soccer M/W. *Intramural sports:* badminton M/W, basketball M/W, cross-country running M/W, football M/W, golf M/W, ice hockey M, skiing (downhill) M/W, soccer M/W, softball M/W, swimming M/W, table tennis M/W, volleyball M/W, weight lifting M/W.

Costs (2003–04) *Comprehensive fee:* $10,266 Canadian dollars includes full-time tuition ($4990 Canadian dollars), mandatory fees ($596 Canadian dollars), and room and board ($4680 Canadian dollars). Full-time tuition and fees

Atlantic Baptist University (continued)
vary according to program. Part-time tuition: $535 Canadian dollars per course. *College room only:* $2080 Canadian dollars. Room and board charges vary according to board plan. *Payment plan:* installment. *Waivers:* senior citizens and employees or children of employees.

Financial Aid *Financial aid deadline:* 5/15.

Applying *Options:* common application, deferred entrance. *Application fee:* $35 Canadian dollars. *Required:* essay or personal statement, high school transcript, minimum 2.60 GPA, 3 letters of recommendation. *Required for some:* interview. *Application deadline:* rolling (freshmen), rolling (transfers). *Notification:* continuous until 9/15 (freshmen), continuous until 9/15 (transfers).

Admissions Contact Atlantic Baptist University, Box 6004, Moncton, NB E1C 9L7, Canada. *Phone:* 506-858-8970 Ext. 106. *Toll-free phone:* 888-YOU-N-ABU. *Fax:* 506-858-9694. *E-mail:* admissions@abu.nb.ca.

AUGUSTANA UNIVERSITY COLLEGE
Camrose, Alberta, Canada

- **Province-supported** 4-year
- **Calendar** semesters
- **Degree** bachelor's
- **Small-town** campus
- **Endowment** $2.0 million
- **Coed**
- **Moderately difficult** entrance level

Faculty *Student/faculty ratio:* 15:1.

Standardized Tests *Required for some:* SAT I and SAT II or ACT (for admission), SAT II: Subject Tests (for admission), SAT II: Writing Test (for admission).

Costs (2003–04) *Comprehensive fee:* $10,326 includes full-time tuition ($5620), mandatory fees ($130), and room and board ($4576). Part-time tuition: $258 per credit. International tuition: $7684 full-time. *College room only:* $1830.

Financial Aid *Financial aid deadline:* 7/15.

Applying *Options:* electronic application, early admission, early decision, early action, deferred entrance. *Application fee:* $30 Canadian dollars. *Required:* high school transcript, minimum 2.0 GPA.

Admissions Contact Mr. Tim Hanson, Director of Admissions, Augustana University College, 4901-46 Ave, Camrose, AB T4V 2R3. *Phone:* 780-649-1135 Ext. 1135. *Toll-free phone:* 800-661-8714. *E-mail:* admissions@augustana.ab.ca.

BETHANY BIBLE COLLEGE
Sussex, New Brunswick, Canada

- **Independent** 4-year, founded 1945, affiliated with Wesleyan Church
- **Calendar** semesters
- **Degree** bachelor's
- **Small-town** 55-acre campus
- **Endowment** $94,150
- **Coed,** 271 undergraduate students, 94% full-time, 51% women, 49% men
- **Moderately difficult** entrance level

Undergraduates 255 full-time, 16 part-time. Students come from 5 provinces and territories, 21% are from out of state, 1% African American, 0.7% Hispanic American, 1% Native American, 3% transferred in, 77% live on campus. *Retention:* 74% of 2003 full-time freshmen returned.

Freshmen *Admission:* 45 enrolled. *Test scores:* SAT verbal scores over 500: 54%; SAT math scores over 500: 27%; ACT scores over 18: 83%; SAT verbal scores over 600: 9%; ACT scores over 24: 17%.

Faculty *Total:* 22, 55% full-time, 18% with terminal degrees. *Student/faculty ratio:* 18:1.

Majors Biblical studies; divinity/ministry; elementary education; music; religious education; religious studies.

Academic Programs *Special study options:* academic remediation for entering students, double majors, independent study, internships, part-time degree program, summer session for credit.

Library Rogers Memorial Library with 27,319 titles, 124 serial subscriptions, 347 audiovisual materials, an OPAC.

Computers on Campus 23 computers available on campus for general student use. Internet access, at least one staffed computer lab available.

Student Life *Housing:* on-campus residence required through senior year. *Options:* Campus housing is university owned. *Activities and organizations:* drama/theater group, choral group, Ministerial Association, Athletic Association, Student Mission Fellowship, Social Committee, Drama Club. *Campus security:* controlled dormitory access. *Student services:* personal/psychological counseling.

Athletics *Intercollegiate sports:* basketball M/W, ice hockey M, soccer M/W, softball M/W, volleyball W. *Intramural sports:* basketball M/W, table tennis M/W, volleyball M/W.

Standardized Tests *Required for some:* SAT I or ACT (for admission).

Costs (2003–04) *Comprehensive fee:* $9836 Canadian dollars includes full-time tuition ($5536 Canadian dollars) and room and board ($4300 Canadian dollars). Part-time tuition: $173 Canadian dollars per credit hour. *College room only:* $2000 Canadian dollars.

Financial Aid *Financial aid deadline:* 10/15.

Applying *Options:* common application, electronic application. *Application fee:* $20 Canadian dollars. *Required:* high school transcript, 2 letters of recommendation. *Recommended:* interview. *Application deadline:* rolling (freshmen), rolling (transfers).

Admissions Contact Mr. D. Scott Rhyno, Executive Director of Admissions, Bethany Bible College, 26 Western Street, Sussex, NB E4E 1E6, Canada. *Phone:* 506-432-4422. *Toll-free phone:* 888-432-4422. *Fax:* 506-432-4425. *E-mail:* steppej@bethany-ca.edu.

BETHANY COLLEGE
Hepburn, Saskatchewan, Canada

- **Independent** 4-year, founded 1927, affiliated with Mennonite Brethren Church
- **Calendar** semesters
- **Degrees** certificates, diplomas, associate, and bachelor's
- **Small-town** 13-acre campus
- **Coed,** 162 undergraduate students, 97% full-time, 48% women, 52% men
- 86% of applicants were admitted

Undergraduates 157 full-time, 5 part-time. Students come from 5 provinces and territories, 1 other country, 88% live on campus. *Retention:* 43% of 2002 full-time freshmen returned.

Freshmen *Admission:* 80 applied, 69 admitted, 69 enrolled.

Faculty *Total:* 15. *Student/faculty ratio:* 11:1.

Majors Biblical studies; missionary studies and missiology; music performance; pastoral studies/counseling; theology and religious vocations related.

Student Life *Housing:* on-campus residence required through junior year. *Options:* men-only, women-only. Campus housing is university owned. Freshman campus housing is guaranteed. *Activities and organizations:* drama/theater group, student-run newspaper, choral group, concert choir, art club, photography club, campus recreation. *Campus security:* controlled dormitory access. *Student services:* health clinic, personal/psychological counseling.

Athletics *Intercollegiate sports:* basketball M/W, ice hockey M, soccer M/W, volleyball M/W. *Intramural sports:* badminton M/W, football M, ice hockey M, soccer M/W, table tennis M/W, ultimate Frisbee M/W, volleyball M/W.

Costs (2004–05) *Comprehensive fee:* $8650 Canadian dollars includes full-time tuition ($4760 Canadian dollars) and room and board ($3890 Canadian dollars). Full-time tuition and fees vary according to course load and student level. Part-time tuition: $140 Canadian dollars per credit. Part-time tuition and fees vary according to course load and student level. *Waivers:* employees or children of employees.

Applying *Application fee:* $55 Canadian dollars. *Required:* essay or personal statement, high school transcript, letters of recommendation.

Admissions Contact Mr. Dave Carey, Admissions Director, Bethany College, Box 160, Hepburn, SK S0K IZ0, Canada. *Phone:* 306-947-2175. *Toll-free phone:* 866-772-2175. *E-mail:* info@bethany.sk.ca.

BISHOP'S UNIVERSITY
Lennoxville, Quebec, Canada

- **Province-supported** comprehensive, founded 1843
- **Calendar** Canadian standard year
- **Degrees** certificates, bachelor's, and master's
- **Small-town** 500-acre campus
- **Endowment** $25.0 million
- **Coed,** 2,658 undergraduate students, 81% full-time, 57% women, 43% men
- **Moderately difficult** entrance level, 80% of applicants were admitted

Undergraduates 2,163 full-time, 495 part-time. Students come from 12 provinces and territories, 37 other countries, 46% are from out of state, 2% transferred in, 31% live on campus. *Retention:* 82% of 2002 full-time freshmen returned.

Freshmen *Admission:* 2,406 applied, 1,923 admitted, 827 enrolled. *Test scores:* SAT verbal scores over 500: 94%; SAT math scores over 500: 100%; SAT verbal scores over 600: 34%; SAT math scores over 600: 60%; SAT verbal scores over 700: 7%; SAT math scores over 700: 7%.

Faculty *Total:* 165, 72% full-time, 59% with terminal degrees. *Student/faculty ratio:* 14:1.
Majors Accounting; art; arts management; art teacher education; biochemistry; biological and physical sciences; biology/biological sciences; biology teacher education; business administration and management; business/managerial economics; Canadian studies; chemistry; chemistry teacher education; classics and languages, literatures and linguistics; computer and information sciences; computer programming; computer science; computer teacher education; drama and dance teacher education; dramatic/theatre arts; economics; education; elementary education; English; English/language arts teacher education; finance; fine/studio arts; French; French as a second/foreign language (teaching); French language teacher education; geography; geography teacher education; German; gerontology; history; history teacher education; humanities; human resources management; international business/trade/commerce; Italian; liberal arts and sciences/liberal studies; literature; management information systems; marketing/marketing management; mathematics; mathematics teacher education; modern languages; music; music teacher education; natural sciences; neuroscience; philosophy; physics; physics teacher education; political science and government; psychology; religious studies; science teacher education; secondary education; social sciences; sociology; Spanish; Spanish language teacher education; women's studies.
Academic Programs *Special study options:* academic remediation for entering students, accelerated degree program, adult/continuing education programs, advanced placement credit, cooperative education, double majors, English as a second language, honors programs, independent study, internships, off-campus study, part-time degree program, services for LD students, student-designed majors, study abroad, summer session for credit. *Unusual degree programs:* 3-2 engineering with Universitè de Sherbrooke.
Library John Bassett Memorial Library plus 1 other with 458,882 titles, 5,662 serial subscriptions, 23,440 audiovisual materials, an OPAC, a Web page.
Computers on Campus 200 computers available on campus for general student use. A campuswide network can be accessed from student residence rooms and from off campus. Internet access, online (class) registration, at least one staffed computer lab available. Computer purchase or lease plan available.
Student Life *Housing options:* coed, women-only, disabled students. Campus housing is university owned. Freshman campus housing is guaranteed. *Activities and organizations:* drama/theater group, student-run newspaper, radio station, choral group, Big Buddies, The Campus, psychology club, Student Patrol, Inter-Varsity Christian Fellowship, national fraternities, national sororities. *Campus security:* 24-hour emergency response devices and patrols, student patrols, late-night transport/escort service, controlled dormitory access. *Student services:* health clinic, personal/psychological counseling, women's center.
Athletics Member CIS. *Intercollegiate sports:* basketball M/W, field hockey W(c), football M, golf M, ice hockey W(c), lacrosse M(c)/W(c), rugby M/W, skiing (downhill) M/W, soccer W, volleyball W(c). *Intramural sports:* badminton M/W, basketball M/W, cross-country running M/W, equestrian sports M(c)/W(c), football M, golf M/W, ice hockey M/W, riflery M(c)/W(c), soccer M/W, softball M/W, squash M/W, swimming M/W, table tennis M/W, tennis M/W, ultimate Frisbee M/W, volleyball M/W, water polo M/W, weight lifting M/W.
Standardized Tests *Required:* SAT I or ACT (for admission). *Recommended:* SAT II: Subject Tests (for admission).
Costs (2003–04) *Tuition:* $56 Canadian dollars per credit part-time; province resident $1668 Canadian dollars full-time, $139 Canadian dollars per credit part-time; nonresident $4173 Canadian dollars full-time, $351 Canadian dollars per credit part-time; International tuition $10,518 Canadian dollars full-time. Full-time tuition and fees vary according to course load. Part-time tuition and fees vary according to course load. *Required fees:* $763 Canadian dollars full-time, $25 Canadian dollars per credit part-time, $381 Canadian dollars per term part-time. *Room and board:* $5740 Canadian dollars; room only: $3460 Canadian dollars. Room and board charges vary according to board plan and housing facility. *Waivers:* employees or children of employees.
Applying *Application fee:* $55 Canadian dollars. *Required:* high school transcript, minimum 3.0 GPA, birth certificate, copy of student visa. *Required for some:* 1 letter of recommendation. *Application deadlines:* 3/1 (freshmen), 3/1 (transfers). *Notification:* continuous until 8/31 (freshmen), continuous until 8/31 (transfers).
Admissions Contact Mr. Hans Rouleau, Coordinator of Liaison, Bishop's University, Lennoxville, QC J1M 1Z7, Canada. *Phone:* 819-822-9600 Ext. 2217. *Toll-free phone:* 800-567-2792 Ext. 2681. *Fax:* 819-822-9661. *E-mail:* liaison@ubishops.ca.

BRANDON UNIVERSITY
Brandon, Manitoba, Canada

- **Province-supported** comprehensive, founded 1899
- **Calendar** Canadian standard year
- **Degrees** certificates, bachelor's, and master's
- **Small-town** 30-acre campus
- **Endowment** $14.0 million
- **Coed**
- **Noncompetitive** entrance level

Faculty *Student/faculty ratio:* 11:1.
Student Life *Campus security:* 24-hour emergency response devices, controlled dormitory access, night residence hall security personnel.
Athletics Member CIS.
Costs (2003–04) *Tuition:* nonresident $2861 Canadian dollars full-time; International tuition $5136 Canadian dollars full-time. *Room and board:* $5800 Canadian dollars; room only: $3360 Canadian dollars.
Applying *Options:* common application, electronic application, deferred entrance. *Application fee:* $35 Canadian dollars. *Required:* high school transcript. *Required for some:* letters of recommendation, criminal and child abuse registry checks.
Admissions Contact Ms. Faye Douglas, Director of Admissions, Brandon University, 270 18th Street, Brandon, MB R7A 6A9, Canada. *Phone:* 204-727-7352. *Toll-free phone:* 800-644-7644. *Fax:* 204-728-3221. *E-mail:* douglas@brandonu.ca.

BRIERCREST BIBLE COLLEGE
Caronport, Saskatchewan, Canada

- **Independent interdenominational** 4-year, founded 1935, part of Briercrest Family of Schools
- **Calendar** semesters
- **Degrees** certificates, diplomas, associate, and bachelor's
- **Rural** 300-acre campus
- **Endowment** $800,212
- **Coed,** 788 undergraduate students, 84% full-time, 50% women, 50% men
- **Noncompetitive** entrance level, 63% of applicants were admitted

Undergraduates 664 full-time, 124 part-time. Students come from 10 provinces and territories, 5 other countries, 76% are from out of state, 75% live on campus. *Retention:* 69% of 2002 full-time freshmen returned.
Freshmen *Admission:* 585 applied, 371 admitted.
Faculty *Total:* 49, 59% full-time, 45% with terminal degrees. *Student/faculty ratio:* 21:1.
Majors Accounting; biblical studies; business administration and management; child development; cultural studies; divinity/ministry; missionary studies and missiology; music; pastoral studies/counseling; religious/sacred music; religious studies; theology.
Academic Programs *Special study options:* academic remediation for entering students, accelerated degree program, adult/continuing education programs, distance learning, double majors, external degree program, independent study, internships, off-campus study, part-time degree program, summer session for credit.
Library Archibald Library with 71,280 titles, 375 serial subscriptions, 3,327 audiovisual materials, an OPAC, a Web page.
Computers on Campus 30 computers available on campus for general student use. A campuswide network can be accessed from off campus. Internet access, online (class) registration, at least one staffed computer lab available.
Student Life *Housing:* on-campus residence required through senior year. *Options:* men-only, women-only. Campus housing is university owned. Freshman campus housing is guaranteed. *Activities and organizations:* drama/theater group, student-run radio station, choral group, Student Missions Fellowship, Student Families Association, yearbook committee, Weekend Activities Committee. *Campus security:* 24-hour patrols. *Student services:* health clinic, personal/psychological counseling, legal services.
Athletics *Intercollegiate sports:* basketball M/W, ice hockey M, soccer M/W, volleyball M/W. *Intramural sports:* badminton M/W, basketball M/W, football M/W, golf M/W, ice hockey M/W, lacrosse M/W, soccer M/W, softball M/W, table tennis M/W, tennis M/W, volleyball M/W, weight lifting M/W.
Costs (2004–05) *Comprehensive fee:* $11,024 Canadian dollars includes full-time tuition ($6624 Canadian dollars) and room and board ($4400 Canadian dollars). Part-time tuition: $207 Canadian dollars per credit. *College room only:* $2640 Canadian dollars. Room and board charges vary according to housing facility. *Payment plan:* installment. *Waivers:* senior citizens and employees or children of employees.
Applying *Options:* common application, electronic application, early admission, deferred entrance. *Application fee:* $35 Canadian dollars. *Required:* essay or personal statement, high school transcript, 2 letters of recommendation. *Required for some:* interview. *Application deadlines:* 8/15 (freshmen), 8/15 (transfers). *Notification:* continuous until 9/1 (freshmen), continuous until 9/1 (transfers).

Briercrest Bible College (continued)

Admissions Contact Mr. Mike Benallick, Director of Enrollment Management, Briercrest Bible College, 510 College Drive, Caronport, SK S0H 0S0, Canada. *Phone:* 306-756-3200 Ext. 257. *Toll-free phone:* 800-667-5199. *E-mail:* enrollment@briercrest.ca.

British Columbia Institute of Technology

Burnaby, British Columbia, Canada

- **Province-supported** 4-year, founded 1964
- **Calendar** quarters
- **Degree** certificates, diplomas, and bachelor's
- **Urban** 103-acre campus with easy access to Vancouver
- **Endowment** $7.8 million
- **Coed,** 22,942 undergraduate students, 32% full-time, 42% women, 58% men
- 35% of applicants were admitted

Undergraduates 7,369 full-time, 15,573 part-time. 0.1% are from out of state, 5% live on campus.

Freshmen *Admission:* 7,212 applied, 2,532 admitted.

Faculty *Total:* 1,236, 52% full-time.

Majors Accounting; accounting technology and bookkeeping; administrative assistant and secretarial science; aeronautical/aerospace engineering technology; aircraft powerplant technology; airframe mechanics and aircraft maintenance technology; allied health diagnostic, intervention, and treatment professions related; architectural drafting and CAD/CADD; architectural engineering technology; autobody/collision and repair technology; automobile/automotive mechanics technology; avionics maintenance technology; biology/biotechnology laboratory technician; biotechnology; business administration and management; cabinetmaking and millwork; cardiovascular technology; carpentry; chemical technology; civil drafting and CAD/CADD; civil engineering technology; clinical/medical laboratory technology; commercial and advertising art; computer science; computer systems analysis; construction engineering technology; construction management; construction trades related; critical care nursing; data processing and data processing technology; diesel mechanics technology; drafting and design technology; electrical and power transmission installation; electrical, electronic and communications engineering technology; engineering related; entrepreneurship; environmental engineering technology; environmental/environmental health engineering; environmental health; finance; finance and financial management services related; financial planning and services; fire protection and safety technology; forensic science and technology; forest/forest resources management; forestry technology; health and medical administrative services related; health/health care administration; health professions related; heating, air conditioning, ventilation and refrigeration maintenance technology; heavy equipment maintenance technology; human resources management; industrial mechanics and maintenance technology; industrial technology; information science/studies; interior design; international business/trade/commerce; machine tool technology; management science; marketing/marketing management; mechanical drafting and CAD/CADD; mechanical engineering/mechanical technology; medical administrative assistant and medical secretary; medical laboratory technology; medical radiologic technology; mining technology; naval architecture and marine engineering; nuclear medical technology; nursing administration; nursing (registered nurse training); nursing related; occupational and environmental health nursing; occupational health and industrial hygiene; operations management; pediatric nursing; perioperative/operating room and surgical nursing; petroleum technology; pipefitting and sprinkler fitting; plastics engineering technology; precision systems maintenance and repair technologies related; radio and television broadcasting technology; real estate; robotics technology; science technologies related; sheet metal technology; small engine mechanics and repair technology; survey technology; taxation; tourism and travel services management; trade and industrial teacher education; transportation and highway engineering; vehicle maintenance and repair technologies related; welding technology; wildlife and wildlands science and management.

Student Life *Housing options:* coed, men-only, women-only, disabled students. Campus housing is university owned. Freshman applicants given priority for college housing. *Activities and organizations:* student-run newspaper, radio station. *Campus security:* 24-hour emergency response devices and patrols, student patrols, late-night transport/escort service. *Student services:* health clinic, personal/psychological counseling.

Athletics *Intramural sports:* archery M(c)/W(c), basketball M/W, crew M(c)/W(c), football M/W, ice hockey M/W, rugby M(c)/W(c), soccer M/W, softball M/W, volleyball M/W.

Costs (2003–04) *Tuition:* province resident $2664 full-time; International tuition $8211 full-time. Full-time tuition and fees vary according to class time, course load, degree level, location, and program. Part-time tuition and fees vary according to class time, course load, degree level, location, and program. No tuition increase for student's term of enrollment. *Required fees:* $112 full-time. *Room only:* $3445. *Payment plan:* deferred payment.

Applying *Application fee:* $43.

Admissions Contact Ms. Anna Dosen, Supervisor of Admissions, British Columbia Institute of Technology, 3700 Willingdon Avenue, Burnaby, BC V5G 3H2, Canada. *Phone:* 604-432-8576. *Fax:* 604-431-6917.

Brock University

St. Catharines, Ontario, Canada

- **Province-supported** university, founded 1964
- **Calendar** Canadian standard year
- **Degrees** certificates, bachelor's, master's, and doctoral
- **Urban** 540-acre campus with easy access to Toronto
- **Coed, primarily women,** 13,300 undergraduate students
- **Moderately difficult** entrance level, 16% of applicants were admitted

Undergraduates Students come from 8 provinces and territories, 66 other countries, 16% live on campus.

Freshmen *Admission:* 27,557 applied, 4,309 admitted. *Average high school GPA:* 3.00.

Faculty *Total:* 435, 100% full-time. *Student/faculty ratio:* 23:1.

Majors Accounting; adult and continuing education; ancient/classical Greek; applied mathematics; archeology; art; biochemistry; biological and physical sciences; biology/biological sciences; biomedical sciences; biotechnology; business administration and management; business/commerce; business/corporate communications; business/managerial economics; Canadian studies; chemistry; classics and languages, literatures and linguistics; communication disorders; communication/speech communication and rhetoric; computer engineering technology; computer programming; computer science; computer software engineering; dramatic/theatre arts; drawing; economics; education; elementary education; English; English as a second/foreign language (teaching); environmental studies; European studies; film/cinema studies; finance; fine/studio arts; French; French studies; geography; geology/earth science; German; German studies; health/health care administration; health science; history; humanities; human resources management; information science/studies; interdisciplinary studies; international business/trade/commerce; international economics; Italian; Italian studies; kinesiology and exercise science; labor and industrial relations; liberal arts and sciences/liberal studies; linguistics; literature; marketing/marketing management; mass communication/media; mathematics; mathematics teacher education; movement therapy and movement education; music; music teacher education; neuroscience; nursing science; parks, recreation and leisure; philosophy; physical education teaching and coaching; physical sciences; physics; political science and government; psychology; public administration; public health; Russian studies; sales, distribution and marketing; science teacher education; secondary education; social sciences; sociology; Spanish; sport and fitness administration; statistics; tourism and travel services management; women's studies.

Academic Programs *Special study options:* academic remediation for entering students, accelerated degree program, adult/continuing education programs, advanced placement credit, cooperative education, double majors, English as a second language, honors programs, internships, part-time degree program, services for LD students, student-designed majors, study abroad, summer session for credit.

Library James A. Gibson Library plus 1 other with 1.6 million titles, 7,043 serial subscriptions, 24,498 audiovisual materials, an OPAC, a Web page.

Computers on Campus 379 computers available on campus for general student use. A campuswide network can be accessed from student residence rooms and from off campus. Internet access, online (class) registration, at least one staffed computer lab available.

Student Life *Housing options:* coed. Campus housing is university owned and leased by the school. Freshman applicants given priority for college housing. *Activities and organizations:* drama/theater group, student-run newspaper, radio station, choral group, International Students Association, Brock University Student Association, Business Administration Association, Brock Christian Fellowship, Ace Brock. *Campus security:* 24-hour emergency response devices and patrols, student patrols, late-night transport/escort service, controlled dormitory access. *Student services:* health clinic, personal/psychological counseling, women's center.

Athletics Member CIS. *Intercollegiate sports:* badminton M/W, baseball M, basketball M/W, cheerleading M/W, crew M/W, cross-country running M/W, fencing M/W, field hockey W(c), golf M, ice hockey M/W, lacrosse M(c)/W, rugby M/W, soccer M/W, squash M, swimming M/W, tennis M, volleyball M/W, wrestling M/W. *Intramural sports:* badminton M/W, basketball M/W, bowling M/W, cross-country running M/W, fencing M/W, field hockey M/W, football M/W, golf M/W, gymnastics M/W, ice hockey M/W, racquetball M/W, sailing

M/W, skiing (cross-country) M/W, skiing (downhill) M/W, soccer M/W, softball M/W, squash M/W, swimming M/W, tennis M/W, volleyball M/W, water polo M/W, weight lifting M/W.

Standardized Tests *Recommended:* SAT I and SAT II or ACT (for admission).

Costs (2004–05) *Tuition:* nonresident $4611 Canadian dollars full-time; International tuition $10,363 Canadian dollars full-time. Full-time tuition and fees vary according to course load. Part-time tuition and fees vary according to course load. *Room and board:* $6695 Canadian dollars; room only: $3470 Canadian dollars. Room and board charges vary according to board plan and housing facility. *Payment plan:* installment. *Waivers:* employees or children of employees.

Financial Aid Of all full-time matriculated undergraduates who enrolled in 2001, 80 state and other part-time jobs.

Applying *Options:* common application, electronic application. *Application fee:* $95 Canadian dollars. *Required:* high school transcript, minimum 3.0 GPA. *Required for some:* essay or personal statement, interview, audition, portfolio. *Application deadline:* 6/1 (transfers). *Notification:* continuous (freshmen), continuous (transfers).

Admissions Contact Ms. Jeanette Davis, Undergraduate Admissions Officer, Brock University, 500 Glenridge Avenue, St. Catharines, ON L2S 3A1, Canada. *Phone:* 905-688-5550 Ext. 3434. *E-mail:* mlea@spartan.ac.brockv.ca.

■ *See page 1298 for a narrative description.*

CANADIAN MENNONITE UNIVERSITY
Winnipeg, Manitoba, Canada

- **Independent Mennonite** comprehensive, founded 1943
- **Calendar** semesters
- **Degree** certificates, diplomas, and bachelor's
- **Urban** 44-acre campus
- **Coed,** 407 undergraduate students, 81% full-time, 54% women, 46% men
- **Moderately difficult** entrance level, 75% of applicants were admitted

Undergraduates 331 full-time, 76 part-time. Students come from 6 provinces and territories, 8 other countries, 50% are from out of state, 1% African American, 0.9% Asian American or Pacific Islander, 0.2% Hispanic American, 3% international, 4% transferred in, 30% live on campus. *Retention:* 70% of 2002 full-time freshmen returned.

Freshmen *Admission:* 238 applied, 178 admitted, 165 enrolled.

Faculty *Total:* 28, 79% with terminal degrees. *Student/faculty ratio:* 7:1.

Majors Biblical studies; biology/biological sciences; computer science; conducting; development economics and international development; divinity/ministry; economics; English; geography; history; international relations and affairs; mathematics; microbiology; missionary studies and missiology; music; music history, literature, and theory; musicology and ethnomusicology; music performance; music theory and composition; music therapy; pastoral studies/counseling; peace studies and conflict resolution; philosophy; piano and organ; political science and government; pre-nursing studies; psychology; religious education; religious studies; theology; voice and opera; youth ministry.

Academic Programs *Special study options:* adult/continuing education programs, double majors, internships, off-campus study, part-time degree program, services for LD students, study abroad.

Library Canadian Mennonite University Library with 40,000 titles, 125 serial subscriptions, an OPAC.

Computers on Campus 5 computers available on campus for general student use. A campuswide network can be accessed from student residence rooms and from off campus. Internet access, at least one staffed computer lab available.

Student Life *Housing options:* coed. Campus housing is university owned. Freshman applicants given priority for college housing. *Activities and organizations:* drama/theater group, student-run newspaper, choral group, Oratorio Choir, Fellowship Groups, Christian Emphasis Committee, Peace and Social Concerns, Witness and Service Committee. *Campus security:* student patrols, late-night transport/escort service, controlled dormitory access, combination door locks to sections of the campus. *Student services:* personal/psychological counseling.

Athletics *Intercollegiate sports:* basketball M/W, ice hockey M/W, soccer M/W, volleyball M/W. *Intramural sports:* badminton M/W, basketball M/W, ice hockey M/W, table tennis M/W, volleyball M/W.

Costs (2003–04) *Comprehensive fee:* $8528 Canadian dollars includes full-time tuition ($3930 Canadian dollars), mandatory fees ($290 Canadian dollars), and room and board ($4308 Canadian dollars). International tuition: $6900 Canadian dollars full-time. *College room only:* $1990 Canadian dollars. Room and board charges vary according to board plan and housing facility. *Payment plan:* installment. *Waivers:* employees or children of employees.

Financial Aid *Financial aid deadline:* 9/30.

Applying *Options:* common application, deferred entrance. *Application fee:* $35 Canadian dollars. *Required:* high school transcript, minimum 2.0 GPA, letters of recommendation. *Required for some:* essay or personal statement. *Application deadlines:* 9/4 (freshmen), 8/31 (transfers). *Notification:* continuous (freshmen), continuous until 8/31 (transfers).

Admissions Contact Mr. Abe Bergen, Director of Enrollment Services, Canadian Mennonite University, 500 Shaftesbury Boulevard, Winnipeg, MB R3P 2N2, Canada. *Phone:* 204-487-3300 Ext. 652. *Toll-free phone:* 877-231-4570. *Fax:* 204-487-3858. *E-mail:* cu@cmu.ca.

CARLETON UNIVERSITY
Ottawa, Ontario, Canada

- **Province-supported** university, founded 1942
- **Calendar** Canadian standard year
- **Degrees** diplomas, bachelor's, master's, and doctoral
- **Urban** 152-acre campus
- **Endowment** $101.3 million
- **Coed,** 19,682 undergraduate students, 80% full-time, 50% women, 50% men
- **Moderately difficult** entrance level, 71% of applicants were admitted

Undergraduates 15,683 full-time, 3,999 part-time. Students come from 13 provinces and territories, 139 other countries, 11% are from out of state, 3% transferred in, 15% live on campus. *Retention:* 87% of 2002 full-time freshmen returned.

Freshmen *Admission:* 28,220 applied, 20,080 admitted, 4,998 enrolled.

Faculty *Total:* 716, 97% full-time, 82% with terminal degrees. *Student/faculty ratio:* 26:1.

Majors Accounting; aerospace, aeronautical and astronautical engineering; African studies; anthropology; applied mathematics; architecture; art history, criticism and conservation; Asian studies; Asian studies (East); biochemistry; biological and physical sciences; biology/biological sciences; biology/biotechnology laboratory technician; botany/plant biology; business administration and management; Canadian studies; chemistry; child development; city/urban, community and regional planning; civil engineering; classics and languages, literatures and linguistics; cognitive psychology and psycholinguistics; comparative literature; computer engineering; computer programming; computer science; computer software and media applications related; criminal justice/law enforcement administration; criminal justice/police science; criminology; dramatic/theatre arts; ecology; economics; electrical, electronics and communications engineering; engineering; English; English as a second/foreign language (teaching); environmental/environmental health engineering; environmental studies; European studies; European studies (Central and Eastern); film/cinema studies; finance; French; geography; geology/earth science; German; history; humanities; human resources management; industrial design; information science/studies; interdisciplinary studies; international business/trade/commerce; international relations and affairs; Italian; journalism; labor and industrial relations; Latin; Latin American studies; linguistics; management information systems; marketing/marketing management; mass communication/media; mathematics; mechanical engineering; medieval and Renaissance studies; modern Greek; modern languages; music; Near and Middle Eastern studies; operations research; philosophy; physics; political science and government; pre-law studies; psychology; public administration; religious studies; Russian; Russian studies; social work; sociology; Spanish; statistics; systems engineering; urban studies/affairs; women's studies.

Academic Programs *Special study options:* academic remediation for entering students, accelerated degree program, adult/continuing education programs, cooperative education, distance learning, double majors, English as a second language, honors programs, internships, off-campus study, part-time degree program, services for LD students, student-designed majors, study abroad, summer session for credit.

Library MacOdrum Library with 10,174 serial subscriptions, 19,994 audiovisual materials, an OPAC, a Web page.

Computers on Campus 504 computers available on campus for general student use. A campuswide network can be accessed from student residence rooms and from off campus. Internet access, at least one staffed computer lab available.

Student Life *Housing options:* coed, men-only, women-only, disabled students. Campus housing is university owned. Freshman applicants given priority for college housing. *Activities and organizations:* drama/theater group, student-run newspaper, radio station, choral group. *Campus security:* 24-hour emergency response devices and patrols, student patrols, late-night transport/escort service, controlled dormitory access. *Student services:* health clinic, personal/psychological counseling, women's center.

Athletics Member CIS. *Intercollegiate sports:* basketball M(s)/W(s), crew M/W, fencing M(s)/W(s), field hockey W(s), football M, golf M, ice hockey M(c)/W(c), lacrosse M(c), rugby M(s)/W(c), skiing (cross-country) M(s)/W(s), soccer M(s)/W(s), swimming M/W, volleyball W(c), water polo M(s)/W(s). *Intramural sports:* badminton M/W, baseball W, basketball M/W, football M/W,

Carleton University (continued)
golf M/W, ice hockey M, skiing (downhill) M/W, soccer M/W, softball M/W, squash M/W, swimming M/W, tennis M/W, volleyball M/W, water polo M/W.

Standardized Tests *Required for some:* SAT I and SAT II or ACT (for admission). *Recommended:* SAT I (for admission).

Costs (2003–04) *Tuition:* area resident $4670 full-time, $889 per credit part-time; nonresident $2361 per credit part-time; International tuition $11,430 full-time. Full-time tuition and fees vary according to course load, program, and reciprocity agreements. Part-time tuition and fees vary according to course load, program, and reciprocity agreements. *Required fees:* $518 full-time. *Room and board:* $6649; room only: $4875. Room and board charges vary according to board plan and housing facility. *Payment plans:* installment, deferred payment. *Waivers:* senior citizens and employees or children of employees.

Applying *Options:* common application, deferred entrance. *Application fee:* $85 Canadian dollars. *Required:* high school transcript, minimum 3.0 GPA. *Required for some:* essay or personal statement, minimum 3.4 GPA, letters of recommendation, interview. *Application deadlines:* 6/1 (freshmen), 4/1 (out-of-state freshmen), 6/1 (transfers). *Notification:* continuous (freshmen), continuous (out-of-state freshmen), continuous (transfers).

Admissions Contact Ms. Jean Mullan, Director, Undergraduate Recruitment Office, Carleton University, 1125 Colonel By Drive, Ottawa, ON K1S 5B6, Canada. *Phone:* 613-520-3663. *Toll-free phone:* 888-354-4414. *Fax:* 613-520-3847. *E-mail:* liaison@admissions.carleton.ca.

CENTRAL PENTECOSTAL COLLEGE

Saskatoon, Saskatchewan, Canada

- **Independent** 4-year, founded 1930, affiliated with Pentecostal Assemblies of Canada
- **Calendar** semesters
- **Degree** certificates, diplomas, and bachelor's
- **Urban** 5-acre campus
- **Coed,** 94 undergraduate students, 77% full-time, 50% women, 50% men
- **Minimally difficult** entrance level, 83% of applicants were admitted

Undergraduates 72 full-time, 22 part-time. Students come from 5 provinces and territories, 36% are from out of state, 2% Asian American or Pacific Islander, 5% Native American, 1% transferred in, 40% live on campus. *Retention:* 86% of 2002 full-time freshmen returned.

Freshmen *Admission:* 46 applied, 38 admitted, 22 enrolled.

Faculty *Total:* 12, 25% full-time, 83% with terminal degrees. *Student/faculty ratio:* 14:1.

Majors Biblical studies; Christian studies; missionary studies and missiology; pastoral counseling and specialized ministries related; pastoral studies/counseling; religious/sacred music; theological and ministerial studies related; theology; theology and religious vocations related; youth ministry.

Academic Programs *Special study options:* academic remediation for entering students, distance learning, independent study, internships, part-time degree program, student-designed majors, study abroad.

Library A. C. Schindel Library with 18,016 titles, 60 serial subscriptions, 323 audiovisual materials, an OPAC, a Web page.

Computers on Campus 21 computers available on campus for general student use. A campuswide network can be accessed from student residence rooms and from off campus. Internet access, at least one staffed computer lab available. Computer purchase or lease plan available.

Student Life *Housing:* on-campus residence required through sophomore year. *Options:* Campus housing is university owned. Freshman campus housing is guaranteed. *Activities and organizations:* drama/theater group, student-run newspaper, choral group. *Campus security:* 24-hour emergency response devices, late-night transport/escort service. *Student services:* personal/psychological counseling.

Athletics *Intramural sports:* basketball M/W, ice hockey M, soccer M/W, volleyball M/W.

Costs (2004–05) *Comprehensive fee:* $9532 Canadian dollars includes full-time tuition ($5167 Canadian dollars), mandatory fees ($465 Canadian dollars), and room and board ($3900 Canadian dollars). Part-time tuition: $147 Canadian dollars per credit hour. *Required fees:* $12 Canadian dollars per credit hour part-time. *Room and board:* Room and board charges vary according to housing facility. *Payment plans:* installment, deferred payment. *Waivers:* senior citizens and employees or children of employees.

Applying *Options:* common application, electronic application, deferred entrance. *Application fee:* $30 Canadian dollars. *Required:* essay or personal statement, high school transcript, 3 letters of recommendation. *Required for some:* interview. *Application deadline:* 8/15 (freshmen).

Admissions Contact Angie Hume, Registrar, Central Pentecostal College, 1303 Jackson Avenue, Saskatoon, SK S7H 2M9, Canada. *Phone:* 306-374-6655. *Fax:* 306-373-6968. *E-mail:* admissions@cpc-paoc.edu.

COLLÈGE DOMINICAIN DE PHILOSOPHIE ET DE THÉOLOGIE

Ottawa, Ontario, Canada

- **Independent Roman Catholic** comprehensive, founded 1909
- **Calendar** semesters
- **Degrees** certificates, bachelor's, master's, and doctoral
- **Urban** campus
- **Coed**
- **Noncompetitive** entrance level

Student Life *Campus security:* late-night transport/escort service.

Costs (2003–04) *Comprehensive fee:* $7900 Canadian dollars includes full-time tuition ($2900 Canadian dollars) and room and board ($5000 Canadian dollars). Part-time tuition: $120 Canadian dollars per credit. Part-time tuition and fees vary according to course load. International tuition: $6900 Canadian dollars full-time.

Applying *Options:* common application, electronic application. *Application fee:* $25 Canadian dollars. *Required:* high school transcript. *Recommended:* interview.

Admissions Contact Fr. Maxime Allard OP, Registrar, Collège Dominicain de Philosophie et de Théologie, 96 Empress Avenue, Ottawa, ON, Canada. *Phone:* 613-233-5696. *Fax:* 613-233-6064. *E-mail:* registraire@collegedominicain.ca.

COLLEGE OF EMMANUEL AND ST. CHAD

Saskatoon, Saskatchewan, Canada

- **Independent Episcopal** comprehensive, founded 1879
- **Calendar** Canadian standard year
- **Degrees** bachelor's and master's
- **Urban** campus
- **Endowment** $2.9 million
- **Coed,** 8 undergraduate students, 50% women, 50% men
- **Noncompetitive** entrance level

Undergraduates 8 part-time. Students come from 4 provinces and territories, 4% are from out of state. *Retention:* 100% of 2002 full-time freshmen returned.

Freshmen *Admission:* 8 admitted.

Faculty *Total:* 4, 100% full-time, 100% with terminal degrees. *Student/faculty ratio:* 7:1.

Majors Theology.

Academic Programs *Special study options:* academic remediation for entering students, adult/continuing education programs, cooperative education, distance learning, internships, off-campus study, part-time degree program, services for LD students, summer session for credit.

Library H. E. Sellers Library plus 11 others with 15,000 titles, 93 serial subscriptions.

Computers on Campus 1 computer available on campus for general student use. .

Student Life *Campus security:* 24-hour emergency response devices and patrols, late-night transport/escort service.

Costs (2003–04) *Comprehensive fee:* $9470 Canadian dollars includes full-time tuition ($4300 Canadian dollars), mandatory fees ($170 Canadian dollars), and room and board ($5000 Canadian dollars). Full-time tuition and fees vary according to course level and course load. Part-time tuition: $430 Canadian dollars per course. Part-time tuition and fees vary according to course level and course load. *College room only:* $1700 Canadian dollars.

Applying *Application fee:* $50 Canadian dollars. *Required:* essay or personal statement, high school transcript, 3 letters of recommendation, interview. *Application deadline:* 6/30 (freshmen). *Notification:* 8/1 (freshmen).

Admissions Contact Ms. Colleen Walker, Registrar, College of Emmanuel and St. Chad, 1337 College Drive, Saskatoon, SK S7N0W6, Canada. *Phone:* 306-975-1558. *E-mail:* colleen.walker@usadk.ca.

COLLÈGE UNIVERSITAIRE DE SAINT-BONIFACE

Saint-Boniface, Manitoba, Canada

Admissions Contact Collège universitaire de Saint-Boniface, 200 avenue de la Cathèdrale, Saint-Boniface, MB R2H 0H7, Canada.

COLUMBIA BIBLE COLLEGE
Abbotsford, British Columbia, Canada

- **Independent Mennonite Brethren** 4-year, founded 1936
- **Calendar** semesters
- **Degree** certificates, diplomas, and bachelor's
- **Urban** 9-acre campus with easy access to Vancouver
- **Coed**
- **Noncompetitive** entrance level

Faculty *Student/faculty ratio:* 18:1.
Student Life *Campus security:* late-night transport/escort service, night watchman 11 p.m. to 6 a.m.
Costs (2003–04) *Comprehensive fee:* $10,320 includes full-time tuition ($5520), mandatory fees ($400), and room and board ($4400). Part-time tuition: $184 per credit hour. *Required fees:* $17 per credit hour part-time.
Applying *Application fee:* $50. *Required:* essay or personal statement, high school transcript, letters of recommendation. *Required for some:* interview.
Admissions Contact Ms. Esther Martens, Academic Assistant, Columbia Bible College, 2940 Clearbrook Road, Abbotsford, BC V2T 2Z8. *Phone:* 604-853-3358 Ext. 306. *Toll-free phone:* 800-283-0881. *Fax:* 604-853-3063. *E-mail:* ron.penner@columbiabc.edu.

CONCORDIA UNIVERSITY
Montréal, Quebec, Canada

- **Province-supported** university, founded 1974
- **Calendar** trimesters
- **Degrees** certificates, diplomas, bachelor's, master's, doctoral, post-master's, and postbachelor's certificates
- **Urban** 110-acre campus
- **Endowment** $35.3 million
- **Coed,** 25,906 undergraduate students, 65% full-time, 51% women, 49% men
- **Moderately difficult** entrance level, 62% of applicants were admitted

Undergraduates 16,806 full-time, 9,100 part-time. Students come from 10 provinces and territories, 125 other countries, 1% live on campus. *Retention:* 76% of 2002 full-time freshmen returned.
Freshmen *Admission:* 17,233 applied, 10,708 admitted. *Average high school GPA:* 2.76.
Faculty *Total:* 1,463, 53% full-time, 100% with terminal degrees. *Student/faculty ratio:* 30:1.
Majors Accounting; acting; actuarial science; anthropology; applied mathematics; art; art history, criticism and conservation; art teacher education; art therapy; Asian studies (South); athletic training; behavioral sciences; biochemistry; biology/biological sciences; business administration and management; business/managerial economics; cell biology and histology; ceramic arts and ceramics; chemistry; cinematography and film/video production; civil engineering; classics and languages, literatures and linguistics; commercial and advertising art; communication/speech communication and rhetoric; computer engineering; computer science; creative writing; cultural studies; dance; developmental and child psychology; drama and dance teacher education; dramatic/theatre arts; drawing; ecology; economics; electrical, electronics and communications engineering; elementary education; English; English as a second/foreign language (teaching); entrepreneurship; environmental biology; environmental/environmental health engineering; environmental studies; fiber, textile and weaving arts; film/cinema studies; finance; fine/studio arts; French; geography; German; history; human resources management; industrial engineering; interdisciplinary studies; international business/trade/commerce; Italian; jazz/jazz studies; journalism; kindergarten/preschool education; kinesiology and exercise science; language interpretation and translation; linguistics; literature; management information systems; marketing/marketing management; marketing research; mass communication/media; mathematics; mechanical engineering; modern languages; molecular biology; music; music performance; neuroscience; painting; parks, recreation and leisure; philosophy; photography; physics; playwriting and screenwriting; political science and government; printmaking; psychology; public administration; public policy analysis; religious studies; sculpture; social sciences; sociology; Spanish; statistics; theatre design and technology; theology; therapeutic recreation; urban studies/affairs; western civilization; women's studies.
Academic Programs *Special study options:* academic remediation for entering students, accelerated degree program, adult/continuing education programs, advanced placement credit, cooperative education, double majors, English as a second language, external degree program, honors programs, independent study, internships, off-campus study, part-time degree program, services for LD students, student-designed majors, study abroad, summer session for credit.
Library Webster Library plus 2 others with 3.0 million titles, 5,900 serial subscriptions, an OPAC, a Web page.
Computers on Campus 350 computers available on campus for general student use. A campuswide network can be accessed from student residence rooms and from off campus that provide access to specialized software applications. Internet access, online (class) registration, at least one staffed computer lab available.
Student Life *Housing options:* coed. Campus housing is university owned. *Activities and organizations:* drama/theater group, student-run newspaper, radio and television station, choral group, ethnic clubs, student media, departmental clubs, national fraternities, national sororities. *Campus security:* 24-hour emergency response devices and patrols, student patrols, late-night transport/escort service, controlled dormitory access. *Student services:* health clinic, personal/psychological counseling, women's center, legal services.
Athletics Member CIS. *Intercollegiate sports:* basketball M/W, football M, ice hockey M/W, rugby M/W, soccer M/W, wrestling M/W. *Intramural sports:* badminton M/W, basketball M/W, cross-country running M/W, football M/W, ice hockey M/W, lacrosse M/W, soccer M/W, softball M/W, squash M/W, swimming M/W, volleyball M/W, weight lifting M/W.
Costs (2004–05) *Tuition:* province resident $1668 Canadian dollars full-time, $56 Canadian dollars per credit part-time; nonresident $4013 Canadian dollars full-time, $129 Canadian dollars per credit part-time; International tuition $12,000 Canadian dollars full-time. Full-time tuition and fees vary according to program. Part-time tuition and fees vary according to program. *Required fees:* $931 Canadian dollars full-time, $30 Canadian dollars per credit part-time. *Room and board:* $6664 Canadian dollars. Room and board charges vary according to housing facility. *Payment plan:* installment. *Waivers:* senior citizens and employees or children of employees.
Financial Aid *Financial aid deadline:* 3/31.
Applying *Options:* common application, electronic application. *Application fee:* $50 Canadian dollars. *Required:* high school transcript, minimum 2.76 GPA. *Required for some:* essay or personal statement, 2 letters of recommendation, interview. *Application deadlines:* 3/1 (freshmen), 3/1 (transfers). *Notification:* continuous until 9/1 (freshmen), continuous until 9/1 (transfers).
Admissions Contact Ms. Assunta Fargnoli, Assistant Registrar, Concordia University, Admissions Application Center, PO Box 2900, Montréal, QC H3G 2S2, Canada. *Phone:* 514-848-2424 Ext. 2628. *Fax:* 514-848-8621. *E-mail:* admreg@alcor.concordia.ca.

CONCORDIA UNIVERSITY COLLEGE OF ALBERTA
Edmonton, Alberta, Canada

- **Independent Lutheran** 4-year, founded 1921
- **Calendar** semesters
- **Degrees** certificates, diplomas, bachelor's, and postbachelor's certificates
- **Urban** 15-acre campus
- **Coed,** 1,717 undergraduate students
- **Moderately difficult** entrance level, 38% of applicants were admitted

Undergraduates Students come from 7 provinces and territories, 15 other countries, 3% live on campus.
Freshmen *Admission:* 1,790 applied, 682 admitted.
Faculty *Total:* 149, 40% full-time. *Student/faculty ratio:* 18:1.
Majors Biology/biological sciences; business administration and management; Canadian studies; chemistry; education; elementary education; English; environmental biology; environmental health; environmental science; environmental studies; foreign languages and literatures; French; French studies; history; human resources management and services related; mathematics; music; non-profit management; philosophy; political science and government; pre-theology/pre-ministerial studies; psychology; public health related; religious education; religious studies; social sciences; sociology; theology and religious vocations related; visual and performing arts.
Academic Programs *Special study options:* advanced placement credit, double majors, external degree program, honors programs, independent study, internships, part-time degree program, services for LD students, study abroad.
Library Arnold Guebert Memorial Library plus 1 other with 75,200 titles, 5,234 serial subscriptions, an OPAC, a Web page.
Computers on Campus 250 computers available on campus for general student use. A campuswide network can be accessed from student residence rooms and from off campus. Internet access, at least one staffed computer lab available.
Student Life *Housing options:* men-only, women-only. Campus housing is university owned. *Activities and organizations:* drama/theater group, student-run newspaper, choral group, orchestra, community chorus, Toastmasters. *Campus security:* 24-hour patrols, late-night transport/escort service. *Student services:* personal/psychological counseling.

Concordia University College of Alberta (continued)

Athletics *Intercollegiate sports:* badminton M(s)/W(s), basketball M(s)/W(s), cross-country running M(s)/W(s), golf M(s)/W(s), ice hockey M(s), soccer M(s)/W(s), swimming M(s)/W(s). *Intramural sports:* skiing (cross-country) M/W, volleyball M/W.

Costs (2004–05) *Comprehensive fee:* $10,154 includes full-time tuition ($5540), mandatory fees ($328), and room and board ($4286). Full-time tuition and fees vary according to class time, course load, and program. Part-time tuition: $692 per course. Part-time tuition and fees vary according to class time, course load, and program. International tuition: $8040 full-time. *College room only:* $2336. Room and board charges vary according to board plan. *Payment plans:* installment, deferred payment. *Waivers:* employees or children of employees.

Applying *Options:* common application, electronic application, early admission, early decision. *Required:* high school transcript, minimum 2.0 GPA. *Required for some:* essay or personal statement, 2 letters of recommendation, interview. *Application deadline:* 6/30 (freshmen). *Notification:* 9/5 (freshmen).

Admissions Contact Mr. Tony Norrad, Dean of Admissions and Financial Aid, Concordia University College of Alberta, 7128 Ada Boulevard, Edmonton, AB T5B 4E4, Canada. *Phone:* 780-479-9224. *Fax:* 780-474-1933. *E-mail:* admits@concordia.ab.ca.

DALHOUSIE UNIVERSITY
Halifax, Nova Scotia, Canada

- **Province-supported** university, founded 1818
- **Calendar** semesters
- **Degrees** diplomas, bachelor's, master's, doctoral, first professional, and postbachelor's certificates
- **Urban** 80-acre campus
- **Endowment** $230.3 million
- **Coed,** 10,640 undergraduate students, 88% full-time, 57% women, 43% men
- **Moderately difficult** entrance level, 85% of applicants were admitted

Undergraduates 9,326 full-time, 1,314 part-time. Students come from 13 provinces and territories, 84 other countries, 14% live on campus. *Retention:* 82% of 2002 full-time freshmen returned.

Freshmen *Admission:* 7,663 applied, 6,510 admitted. *Test scores:* SAT verbal scores over 500: 83%; SAT math scores over 500: 80%; SAT verbal scores over 600: 36%; SAT math scores over 600: 39%; SAT verbal scores over 700: 4%; SAT math scores over 700: 4%.

Faculty *Total:* 1,516. *Student/faculty ratio:* 12:1.

Majors Accounting; acting; advanced/graduate dentistry and oral sciences related; agricultural/biological engineering and bioengineering; anthropology; architecture; atmospheric sciences and meteorology; biochemistry; biology/biological sciences; biomedical/medical engineering; business administration and management; business/commerce; Canadian studies; chemical engineering; chemistry; city/urban, community and regional planning; civil engineering; classics and languages, literatures and linguistics; communication and journalism related; computer engineering; computer/information technology services administration related; computer science; dental hygiene; development economics and international development; diagnostic medical sonography and ultrasound technology; dramatic/theatre arts; dramatic/theatre arts and stagecraft related; economics; engineering; English; entrepreneurship; environmental design/architecture; environmental science; environmental studies; finance; food science; French; geology/earth science; German; health and physical education; health information/medical records administration; health science; health services/allied health/health sciences; health teacher education; history; history and philosophy of science and technology; industrial engineering; international business/trade/commerce; international relations and affairs; kinesiology and exercise science; linguistics; literature; management science; marine biology and biological oceanography; marketing/marketing management; mathematics; mechanical engineering; medical microbiology and bacteriology; metallurgical engineering; microbiological sciences and immunology related; mining and mineral engineering; multi-/interdisciplinary studies related; music; music history, literature, and theory; music performance; music theory and composition; neuroscience; non-profit management; nuclear medical technology; nursing (registered nurse training); occupational therapy; oceanography (chemical and physical); parks, recreation and leisure; pharmacy; pharmacy, pharmaceutical sciences, and administration related; philosophy; physical therapy; physics; political science and government; pre-dentistry studies; pre-law studies; pre-medical studies; pre-pharmacy studies; pre-veterinary studies; psychology; public health education and promotion; radiologic technology/science; religious studies; respiratory care therapy; respiratory therapy technician; Russian; Russian studies; science, technology and society; small business administration; social work; sociology; Spanish; statistics; theatre literature, history and criticism; therapeutic recreation; women's studies.

Academic Programs *Special study options:* academic remediation for entering students, adult/continuing education programs, advanced placement credit, cooperative education, distance learning, double majors, English as a second language, honors programs, off-campus study, part-time degree program, services for LD students, study abroad, summer session for credit.

Library The Killam Memorial Library plus 4 others with 1.7 million titles, 8,306 serial subscriptions, 6,001 audiovisual materials, an OPAC, a Web page.

Computers on Campus 710 computers available on campus for general student use. A campuswide network can be accessed from student residence rooms and from off campus. Internet access, at least one staffed computer lab available.

Student Life *Housing options:* coed, men-only, women-only, disabled students. Freshman applicants given priority for college housing. *Activities and organizations:* drama/theater group, student-run newspaper, radio station, choral group, International Students Association, Arts Society, Science Society, Commerce Society, Dalhousie Outdoors Club, national fraternities, national sororities. *Campus security:* 24-hour emergency response devices and patrols, student patrols, late-night transport/escort service, controlled dormitory access. *Student services:* health clinic, personal/psychological counseling, women's center, legal services.

Athletics Member CIS. *Intercollegiate sports:* basketball M/W, cross-country running M/W, field hockey W(c), ice hockey M/W, soccer M/W, swimming M/W, track and field M/W, volleyball M/W. *Intramural sports:* badminton M(c)/W(c), baseball M(c), basketball M/W, crew M(c)/W(c), cross-country running M/W, fencing M(c)/W(c), field hockey W, football M/W, golf M/W, gymnastics M/W, ice hockey M, lacrosse M, racquetball M/W, rugby M(c)/W(c), sailing M(c)/W(c), skiing (cross-country) M/W, skiing (downhill) M/W, soccer M/W, softball M/W, squash M(c)/W(c), swimming M(c)/W(c), tennis M/W, track and field M/W, ultimate Frisbee M/W, volleyball M/W, water polo M/W, weight lifting M/W, wrestling M(c)/W(c).

Standardized Tests *Required:* SAT I (for admission).

Costs (2003–04) *Comprehensive fee:* $12,664 Canadian dollars includes full-time tuition ($5860 Canadian dollars) and room and board ($6804 Canadian dollars). Full-time tuition and fees vary according to course load. Part-time tuition and fees vary according to course load. International tuition: $10,360 Canadian dollars full-time. *Room and board:* Room and board charges vary according to board plan and housing facility. *Waivers:* minority students, senior citizens, and employees or children of employees.

Applying *Options:* electronic application, early decision, deferred entrance. *Application fee:* $45 Canadian dollars. *Required:* high school transcript, minimum 3.0 GPA. *Required for some:* essay or personal statement, 1 letter of recommendation, interview, minimum 1100 comprehensive score on SAT I for U.S. applicants. *Application deadlines:* 6/1 (freshmen), 6/1 (transfers). *Early decision:* 3/15. *Notification:* continuous (freshmen), continuous (transfers).

Admissions Contact Ms. Susan Tanner, Associate Registrar of Admissions, Dalhousie University, Office of the Registrar, Halifax, NS B3H 4H6. *Phone:* 902-494-2148. *Fax:* 902-494-1630. *E-mail:* admissions@dal.ca.

EMMANUEL BIBLE COLLEGE
Kitchener, Ontario, Canada

Admissions Contact Mrs. Ruth Scott, Recruitment Officer, Emmanuel Bible College, 100 Fergus Avenue, Kitchener, ON N2A 2H2, Canada. *Phone:* 519-894-8900 Ext. 30.

HEC MONTREAL
Montréal, Quebec, Canada

- **Province-supported** comprehensive, founded 1910, part of Université de Montréal
- **Calendar** trimesters
- **Degrees** certificates, bachelor's, master's, doctoral, and postbachelor's certificates
- **Urban** 9-acre campus
- **Coed,** 9,077 undergraduate students, 54% full-time, 49% women, 51% men
- **Moderately difficult** entrance level, 44% of applicants were admitted

Undergraduates 4,917 full-time, 4,160 part-time. Students come from 3 provinces and territories, 39 other countries, 0.6% are from out of state. *Retention:* 90% of 2002 full-time freshmen returned.

Freshmen *Admission:* 2,472 applied, 1,100 admitted, 880 enrolled.

Faculty *Total:* 593, 35% full-time, 25% with terminal degrees. *Student/faculty ratio:* 23:1.

Majors Accounting; applied economics; business administration and management; business/commerce; business/managerial economics; business statistics; computer management; computer systems analysis; consumer merchandising/retailing management; entrepreneurship; finance; human resources management; information science/studies; international business/trade/commerce; international economics; international finance; management information systems; management science; marketing/marketing management; sales, distribution and marketing.

Academic Programs *Special study options:* academic remediation for entering students, adult/continuing education programs, English as a second language, honors programs, independent study, off-campus study, part-time degree program, student-designed majors, study abroad, summer session for credit.
Library Myriam et J.-Robert Ouimet Library plus 1 other with 345,143 titles, 5,557 serial subscriptions, 2,313 audiovisual materials, an OPAC, a Web page.
Computers on Campus 250 computers available on campus for general student use. A campuswide network can be accessed from off campus. Internet access, online (class) registration, at least one staffed computer lab available.
Student Life *Housing options:* Campus housing is provided by a third party. *Activities and organizations:* student-run newspaper, radio station. *Campus security:* 24-hour emergency response devices and patrols. *Student services:* health clinic, personal/psychological counseling, legal services.
Athletics *Intramural sports:* ultimate Frisbee M/W.
Costs (2003–04) *Tuition:* province resident $1668 Canadian dollars full-time, $56 Canadian dollars per credit part-time; nonresident $4173 Canadian dollars full-time, $139 Canadian dollars per credit part-time; International tuition $10,518 Canadian dollars full-time. Full-time tuition and fees vary according to program. Part-time tuition and fees vary according to program. Nonresident alien program tuitions range from $9468.30 to $10,518.30. *Required fees:* $521 Canadian dollars full-time, $16 Canadian dollars per credit part-time. *Room only:* $3793 Canadian dollars. Room and board charges vary according to housing facility. *Waivers:* employees or children of employees.
Applying *Options:* common application, deferred entrance. *Application fee:* $60 Canadian dollars. *Required:* high school transcript. *Required for some:* cote de rendement collégial. *Application deadlines:* 3/1 (freshmen), 3/1 (out-of-state freshmen), 3/1 (transfers). *Notification:* 3/30 (freshmen), 5/31 (out-of-state freshmen), 3/15 (transfers).
Admissions Contact Ms. Lyne Héroux, Administrative Director of Bachelor Program, HEC Montreal, 3000 chemin de la Côte-Sainte-Catherine, Montréal, QC H3T 2A7. *Phone:* 514-340-6139. *Fax:* 514-340-5640. *E-mail:* registraire.info@hec.ca.

HERITAGE BAPTIST COLLEGE AND HERITAGE THEOLOGICAL SEMINARY
Cambridge, Ontario, Canada

Admissions Contact Mr. Alan Wiseman, Registrar/Director of Admissions, Heritage Baptist College and Heritage Theological Seminary, 175 Holiday Inn Drive, Cambridge, ON N3C 3T2, Canada. *Phone:* 519-651-2869 Ext. 227. *Fax:* 519-651-2870. *E-mail:* admissions@heritage-theo.edu.

THE KING'S UNIVERSITY COLLEGE
Edmonton, Alberta, Canada

- **Independent interdenominational** 4-year, founded 1979
- **Calendar** Canadian standard year
- **Degree** bachelor's
- **Suburban** 20-acre campus
- **Endowment** $662,431
- **Coed,** 666 undergraduate students, 95% full-time, 61% women, 39% men
- **Moderately difficult** entrance level, 83% of applicants were admitted

Undergraduates 630 full-time, 36 part-time. Students come from 7 provinces and territories, 30 other countries, 26% are from out of state, 11% transferred in, 20% live on campus. *Retention:* 71% of 2002 full-time freshmen returned.
Freshmen *Admission:* 534 applied, 444 admitted, 144 enrolled. *Average high school GPA:* 3.30.
Faculty *Total:* 110, 35% full-time, 42% with terminal degrees. *Student/faculty ratio:* 10:1.
Majors Biology/biological sciences; business administration and management; chemistry; computer science; elementary education; English; environmental studies; history; music; philosophy; psychology; social sciences; sociology; theology.
Academic Programs *Special study options:* adult/continuing education programs, advanced placement credit, double majors, English as a second language, independent study, internships, off-campus study, services for LD students, study abroad. *Unusual degree programs:* 3-2 Bachelor of Education (After Degree) in Elementary Education.
Library Simona Maaskant with 71,257 titles, 3,305 serial subscriptions, 4,536 audiovisual materials, an OPAC, a Web page.
Computers on Campus 37 computers available on campus for general student use. A campuswide network can be accessed. Internet access, at least one staffed computer lab available.
Student Life *Housing options:* coed, women-only. Campus housing is university owned. Freshman applicants given priority for college housing. *Activities and organizations:* drama/theater group, student-run newspaper, choral group, Action and Awareness, The King's Players (drama club), chamber and concert choirs, King's Science Society, hockey club. *Campus security:* 24-hour emergency response devices, student patrols, controlled dormitory access. *Student services:* personal/psychological counseling.
Athletics *Intercollegiate sports:* basketball M(s)/W(s), soccer M(s)/W(s), volleyball M(s)/W(s). *Intramural sports:* basketball M/W, ice hockey M, volleyball M/W.
Standardized Tests *Recommended:* SAT I and SAT II or ACT (for admission).
Costs (2004–05) *Comprehensive fee:* $12,934 Canadian dollars includes full-time tuition ($6696 Canadian dollars), mandatory fees ($305 Canadian dollars), and room and board ($5933 Canadian dollars). Full-time tuition and fees vary according to course load and program. Part-time tuition: $216 Canadian dollars per credit. Part-time tuition and fees vary according to course load and program. International tuition: $8196 Canadian dollars full-time. *Required fees:* $76 Canadian dollars per term part-time. *College room only:* $2850 Canadian dollars. Room and board charges vary according to board plan and housing facility. *Waivers:* employees or children of employees.
Financial Aid Of all full-time matriculated undergraduates who enrolled in 2001, 105 state and other part-time jobs. *Financial aid deadline:* 3/31.
Applying *Options:* electronic application. *Application fee:* $50 Canadian dollars. *Required:* high school transcript, minimum 2.0 GPA, 1 letter of recommendation. *Required for some:* essay or personal statement, interview. *Application deadline:* rolling (freshmen), rolling (transfers). *Notification:* 8/15 (freshmen), 8/15 (transfers).
Admissions Contact Mr. Glenn J. Keeler, Registrar/Director of Admissions, The King's University College, 9125-50 Street, Edmonton, AB T6B 2H3. *Phone:* 780-465-3500 Ext. 8035. *Toll-free phone:* 800-661-8582. *Fax:* 780-465-3534. *E-mail:* admissions@kingsu.ca.

KWANTLEN UNIVERSITY COLLEGE
Surrey, British Columbia, Canada

- **Province-supported** 4-year
- **Calendar** semesters
- **Degrees** certificates, diplomas, associate, and bachelor's (profile includes information from Langley, Richmond, Newton and Surrey campuses)
- **Urban** campus with easy access to Vancouver
- **Endowment** $4.6 million
- **Coed,** 13,600 undergraduate students, 71% full-time, 55% women, 45% men
- 92% of applicants were admitted

Undergraduates 9,600 full-time, 4,000 part-time. Students come from 41 other countries, 21% transferred in. *Retention:* 90% of 2002 full-time freshmen returned.
Freshmen *Admission:* 12,000 applied, 11,000 admitted, 11,500 enrolled.
Faculty *Total:* 672. *Student/faculty ratio:* 35:1.
Majors Accounting; anthropology; community psychology; criminology; English; English composition; entrepreneurship; fashion/apparel design; geography; geological and earth sciences/geosciences related; graphic design; history; information technology; interior design; journalism; music; music theory and composition; nursing (registered nurse training); philosophy; piano and organ; political science and government; psychology; social psychology; social sciences; sociology; violin, viola, guitar and other stringed instruments; voice and opera.
Academic Programs *Special study options:* academic remediation for entering students, accelerated degree program, adult/continuing education programs, advanced placement credit, cooperative education, distance learning, double majors, English as a second language, independent study, internships, part-time degree program, services for LD students, study abroad, summer session for credit.
Library Kwantlen University College Library—Surrey Campus plus 2 others with an OPAC, a Web page.
Computers on Campus 100 computers available on campus for general student use. A campuswide network can be accessed from off campus. Internet access, online (class) registration, at least one staffed computer lab available.
Student Life *Housing:* college housing not available. *Activities and organizations:* student-run newspaper, choral group, academic clubs, Rowing Club, Cultural Diversity Club, Buddy Language Club. *Campus security:* 24-hour emergency response devices and patrols. *Student services:* health clinic, personal/psychological counseling, women's center.
Athletics *Intercollegiate sports:* baseball M/W, basketball M/W, golf M/W, soccer M/W. *Intramural sports:* badminton M/W, basketball M/W, soccer M/W, volleyball M/W.

Kwantlen University College (continued)

Costs (2003–04) *Tuition:* province resident $3030 Canadian dollars full-time, $101 Canadian dollars per credit part-time; International tuition $10,200 Canadian dollars full-time. *Required fees:* $349 Canadian dollars full-time. *Waivers:* senior citizens.

Applying *Options:* electronic application, early admission. *Application fee:* $40 Canadian dollars. *Required:* high school transcript. *Required for some:* essay or personal statement, minimum 2.0 GPA, interview, portfolio, external testing, certain levels of certification (i.e.—first aid). *Recommended:* high school transcript. *Application deadlines:* 6/30 (freshmen), 6/30 (transfers). *Notification:* continuous until 6/30 (freshmen).

Admissions Contact Ms. Jody Gordon, Registrar, Kwantlen University College, 12666—72nd Avenue, Surrey, BC V3W 2M8, Canada. *Phone:* 604-599-2018. *Toll-free phone:* 604-599-2100. *Fax:* 604-599-2068. *E-mail:* admissio@kwantlen.ca.

LAKEHEAD UNIVERSITY
Thunder Bay, Ontario, Canada

- **Province-supported** comprehensive, founded 1965
- **Calendar** Canadian standard year
- **Degrees** diplomas, bachelor's, master's, and doctoral
- **Suburban** 345-acre campus
- **Coed,** 6,874 undergraduate students, 81% full-time, 58% women, 42% men
- **Moderately difficult** entrance level, 68% of applicants were admitted

Undergraduates 5,552 full-time, 1,322 part-time. Students come from 13 provinces and territories, 52 other countries, 6% are from out of state, 22% live on campus.

Freshmen *Admission:* 7,037 applied, 4,750 admitted. *Average high school GPA:* 3.06.

Faculty *Total:* 547, 46% full-time. *Student/faculty ratio:* 19:1.

Majors Accounting; anthropology; art; athletic training; biological and physical sciences; biology/biological sciences; business administration and management; chemical engineering; chemistry; civil engineering; civil engineering technology; clinical psychology; computer engineering; computer science; economics; education; electrical, electronic and communications engineering technology; electrical, electronics and communications engineering; elementary education; engineering; English; environmental biology; environmental studies; finance; forestry; French; geography; geology/earth science; gerontology; history; human resources management; hydrology and water resources science; information science/studies; labor and industrial relations; liberal arts and sciences/liberal studies; management information systems; marketing/marketing management; mathematics; mechanical engineering; mechanical engineering/mechanical technology; music; natural sciences; nursing (registered nurse training); parks, recreation and leisure; philosophy; physical education teaching and coaching; physics; plant sciences; political science and government; psychology; science teacher education; secondary education; social work; sociology; women's studies.

Academic Programs *Special study options:* accelerated degree program, adult/continuing education programs, advanced placement credit, cooperative education, distance learning, double majors, English as a second language, honors programs, independent study, part-time degree program, services for LD students, student-designed majors, summer session for credit.

Library Chancellor Norman M. Paterson Library plus 1 other with 719,253 titles, 2,100 serial subscriptions, 260 audiovisual materials, an OPAC, a Web page.

Computers on Campus 700 computers available on campus for general student use. A campuswide network can be accessed from student residence rooms and from off campus. Internet access, online (class) registration, at least one staffed computer lab available.

Student Life *Housing options:* coed. Campus housing is university owned. Freshman campus housing is guaranteed. *Activities and organizations:* drama/theater group, student-run newspaper, radio station, Outdoor Recreation Students Association, Engineering Students Society, Business Association, ECHO/LUFROG, Educational Students Association. *Campus security:* 24-hour emergency response devices and patrols, student patrols, late-night transport/escort service, controlled dormitory access. *Student services:* health clinic, personal/psychological counseling, women's center.

Athletics Member CIS. *Intercollegiate sports:* basketball M/W, cheerleading W, crew M/W, cross-country running M/W, ice hockey M, rugby M/W, skiing (cross-country) M/W, soccer M(c)/W(c), track and field M/W, volleyball M(c)/W, weight lifting M, wrestling M/W. *Intramural sports:* badminton M/W, baseball M/W, basketball M/W, bowling M/W, ice hockey M/W, soccer M/W, volleyball M/W.

Costs (2003–04) *Tuition:* nonresident $4140 Canadian dollars full-time, $900 Canadian dollars per course part-time; International tuition $9000 Canadian dollars full-time. Full-time tuition and fees vary according to program. Part-time tuition and fees vary according to program. *Required fees:* $433 Canadian dollars full-time, $65 Canadian dollars per course part-time. *Room and board:* $6222 Canadian dollars. Room and board charges vary according to housing facility. *Payment plans:* installment, deferred payment. *Waivers:* senior citizens and employees or children of employees.

Financial Aid *Financial aid deadline:* 6/30.

Applying *Options:* common application, early admission. *Application fee:* $85 Canadian dollars. *Required for some:* essay or personal statement, 3 letters of recommendation. *Recommended:* high school transcript. *Application deadline:* rolling (freshmen), rolling (transfers). *Notification:* continuous until 9/18 (freshmen), continuous (transfers).

Admissions Contact Ms. Sarena Knapik, Director, Admissions and Recruitment, Lakehead University, 955 Oliver Road, Thunder Bay, ON P7B 5E1, Canada. *Phone:* 807-343-8500. *Toll-free phone:* 800-465-3959. *Fax:* 807-343-8156. *E-mail:* admissions@lakeheadu.ca.

LAURENTIAN UNIVERSITY
Sudbury, Ontario, Canada

- **Province-supported** comprehensive, founded 1960
- **Calendar** Canadian standard year
- **Degrees** certificates, diplomas, bachelor's, master's, and doctoral
- **Suburban** 700-acre campus
- **Endowment** $9.0 million
- **Coed,** 7,275 undergraduate students
- **Minimally difficult** entrance level

Undergraduates Students come from 6 provinces and territories, 38 other countries.

Freshmen *Admission:* 10,402 applied.

Faculty *Total:* 295.

Majors Adult and continuing education; American Indian/Native American studies; anthropology; astronomy; behavioral sciences; biochemistry; biology/biological sciences; biophysics; business administration and management; chemistry; classics and languages, literatures and linguistics; computer science; dramatic/theatre arts; economics; education; English; film/cinema studies; folklore; French; geography; geological/geophysical engineering; geology/earth science; history; Italian; kinesiology and exercise science; language interpretation and translation; legal studies; liberal arts and sciences/liberal studies; mathematics; metallurgical engineering; mining and mineral engineering; modern languages; music; nursing (registered nurse training); philosophy; physical education teaching and coaching; physics; political science and government; psychology; public health education and promotion; religious studies; social work; sociology; Spanish; sport and fitness administration; women's studies.

Academic Programs *Special study options:* academic remediation for entering students, accelerated degree program, adult/continuing education programs, cooperative education, external degree program, honors programs, off-campus study, part-time degree program, services for LD students, summer session for credit.

Library J. N. Desmarais Library plus 3 others with 696,838 titles, a Web page.

Computers on Campus 125 computers available on campus for general student use. Internet access, at least one staffed computer lab available.

Student Life *Housing options:* coed. *Activities and organizations:* drama/theater group, student-run newspaper, radio station, Students General Association, Association des Etudiants Francophone, Association of Laurentian Part-time Students. *Campus security:* 24-hour emergency response devices and patrols, late-night transport/escort service. *Student services:* health clinic, personal/psychological counseling.

Athletics Member CIS. *Intercollegiate sports:* basketball M/W, cross-country running M/W, field hockey W, ice hockey M/W, skiing (cross-country) M/W, skiing (downhill) M/W, soccer M, swimming M/W, track and field M/W, volleyball M. *Intramural sports:* basketball M/W, cross-country running M/W, football M/W, golf M/W, gymnastics M/W, ice hockey M/W, skiing (cross-country) M/W, skiing (downhill) M/W, swimming M/W, tennis M/W, volleyball M/W.

Costs (2003–04) *Comprehensive fee:* $8706 Canadian dollars includes full-time tuition ($4184 Canadian dollars), mandatory fees ($337 Canadian dollars), and room and board ($4185 Canadian dollars). Part-time tuition: $836 Canadian dollars per course. International tuition: $10,087 Canadian dollars full-time. *Required fees:* $25 Canadian dollars per term part-time. *College room only:* $2660 Canadian dollars.

Financial Aid Of all full-time matriculated undergraduates who enrolled in 2001, 180 state and other part-time jobs (averaging $1700).

Applying *Options:* common application, early admission. *Application fee:* $50 Canadian dollars. *Required:* high school transcript. *Required for some:* essay or personal statement, 2 letters of recommendation, interview. *Application deadlines:* 2/1 (freshmen), 2/1 (out-of-state freshmen), rolling (transfers).

Admissions Contact Mr. Ron Smith, Registrar, Laurentian University, Ramsey Lake Road, Sudbury, ON P3E 2C6, Canada. *Phone:* 705-675-1151 Ext. 3919. *Fax:* 705-675-4891. *E-mail:* admissions@nickel.laurentian.ca.

MALASPINA UNIVERSITY-COLLEGE
Nanaimo, British Columbia, Canada

■ **Province-supported** comprehensive, founded 1969
■ **Calendar** semesters
■ **Degrees** certificates, diplomas, associate, bachelor's, master's, and postbachelor's certificates
■ 110-acre campus
■ **Coed**

Undergraduates Students come from 52 other countries.
Faculty *Total:* 1,074.
Majors Anthropology; biology/biological sciences; business/commerce; child care and support services management; computer and information sciences; creative writing; education; fishing and fisheries sciences and management; history; liberal arts and sciences/liberal studies; nursing related; psychology; sociology; tourism and travel services management.
Costs (2003–04) *Tuition:* area resident $3060 Canadian dollars full-time, $102 Canadian dollars per credit hour part-time. *Required fees:* $117 Canadian dollars full-time.
Applying *Application fee:* $30 Canadian dollars.
Admissions Contact Mr. Fred Jarklin, Admissions Manager, Malaspina University-College, 900 Fifth Street, Nanaimo, BC V9R 5S5, Canada. *Phone:* 250-740-6356 Ext. 6356.

MASTER'S COLLEGE AND SEMINARY
Toronto, Ontario, Canada

■ **Independent Pentecostal** 4-year, founded 1939
■ **Calendar** semesters
■ **Degree** certificates, diplomas, and bachelor's
■ **Urban** campus
■ **Coed,** 504 undergraduate students
■ **Noncompetitive** entrance level, 80% of applicants were admitted

Undergraduates Students come from 8 provinces and territories, 5 other countries. *Retention:* 52% of 2002 full-time freshmen returned.
Freshmen *Admission:* 96 applied, 77 admitted.
Faculty *Total:* 50, 12% full-time, 14% with terminal degrees. *Student/faculty ratio:* 15:1.
Majors Biblical studies; divinity/ministry; missionary studies and missiology; religious education; theology; theology and religious vocations related; youth ministry.
Academic Programs *Special study options:* academic remediation for entering students, accelerated degree program, distance learning, independent study, internships, off-campus study, part-time degree program, services for LD students, study abroad, summer session for credit. *Unusual degree programs:* 3-2 theology.
Library 44,531 titles, 284 serial subscriptions, 2,564 audiovisual materials, an OPAC.
Computers on Campus 10 computers available on campus for general student use. A campuswide network can be accessed from off campus that provide access to e-mail. Internet access, at least one staffed computer lab available.
Student Life *Housing:* college housing not available.
Athletics *Intercollegiate sports:* basketball W, volleyball W.
Costs (2003–04) *Tuition:* $5536 Canadian dollars full-time, $173 Canadian dollars per credit hour part-time. *Payment plan:* installment. *Waivers:* employees or children of employees.
Applying *Options:* deferred entrance. *Application fee:* $75 Canadian dollars. *Required:* essay or personal statement, high school transcript, 3 letters of recommendation, Christian commitment. *Required for some:* interview. *Recommended:* minimum 2.0 GPA. *Application deadlines:* 8/31 (freshmen), 8/31 (transfers).
Admissions Contact Ms. Flora Anthony, Recruitment, Master's College and Seminary, 3080 Yonge Street, Suite 3040, Toronto, ON M4N 3N1, Canada. *Phone:* 416-482-2224 Ext. 243. *Toll-free phone:* 800-295-6368. *E-mail:* fanthony@mcs.edu.

MCGILL UNIVERSITY
Montréal, Quebec, Canada

■ **Province-supported** university, founded 1821
■ **Calendar** semesters
■ **Degrees** certificates, diplomas, bachelor's, master's, doctoral, first professional, and postbachelor's certificates
■ **Urban** 80-acre campus
■ **Endowment** $472.2 million
■ **Coed,** 21,827 undergraduate students, 78% full-time, 60% women, 40% men
■ **Very difficult** entrance level, 48% of applicants were admitted

Undergraduates 17,049 full-time, 4,778 part-time. Students come from 12 provinces and territories, 133 other countries, 29% are from out of state, 3% transferred in, 10% live on campus.
Freshmen *Admission:* 20,635 applied, 9,959 admitted, 4,493 enrolled. *Average high school GPA:* 3.50.
Faculty *Total:* 2,232, 69% full-time, 95% with terminal degrees. *Student/faculty ratio:* 12:1.
Majors Accounting; African studies; agribusiness; agricultural/biological engineering and bioengineering; agricultural business and management; agricultural economics; animal genetics; animal physiology; animal sciences; animal sciences related; anthropology; applied mathematics; architecture; area studies related; art history, criticism and conservation; Asian studies (East); atmospheric sciences and meteorology; biochemistry; biology/biological sciences; biology teacher education; botany/plant biology; botany/plant biology related; business administration and management; business/managerial economics; business teacher education; Canadian studies; chemical engineering; chemistry; chemistry related; chemistry teacher education; classics and languages, literatures and linguistics; computer and information sciences; computer and information sciences related; computer engineering; computer science; dietetics; dramatic/theatre arts; ecology; economics; education; electrical, electronics and communications engineering; elementary education; engineering related; English; English as a second/foreign language (teaching); English language and literature related; English/language arts teacher education; entrepreneurship; environmental biology; environmental studies; European studies (Central and Eastern); finance; food science; foods, nutrition, and wellness; foreign languages and literatures; French; French language teacher education; geography; geology/earth science; geophysics and seismology; German; history; history teacher education; humanities; human resources management; information science/studies; international agriculture; international business/trade/commerce; Italian; jazz/jazz studies; Jewish/Judaic studies; kinesiology and exercise science; labor and industrial relations; Latin American studies; linguistics; management science; marine biology and biological oceanography; marketing research; mathematics; mathematics and computer science; mathematics teacher education; mechanical engineering; medical microbiology and bacteriology; metallurgical engineering; mining and mineral engineering; molecular biology; music; music history, literature, and theory; music performance; music related; music teacher education; music theory and composition; natural resources/conservation; natural resources management; natural resources management and policy; Near and Middle Eastern studies; nursing (registered nurse training); nutrition sciences; occupational therapy; organizational behavior; philosophy; philosophy and religious studies related; physical education teaching and coaching; physical therapy; physics; physics teacher education; physiological psychology/psychobiology; piano and organ; plant sciences; political science and government; psychology; religious education; religious studies; Russian; Russian studies; sales, distribution and marketing; science teacher education; secondary education; social science teacher education; social studies teacher education; social work; sociology; soil science and agronomy; Spanish; special education; statistics; urban studies/affairs; voice and opera; wildlife and wildlands science and management; wildlife biology; women's studies; zoology/animal biology; zoology/animal biology related.
Academic Programs *Special study options:* adult/continuing education programs, advanced placement credit, double majors, English as a second language, honors programs, internships, off-campus study, part-time degree program, services for LD students, student-designed majors, study abroad, summer session for credit.
Library Humanities and Social Sciences Library plus 16 others with 4.0 million titles, 22,513 serial subscriptions, 571,768 audiovisual materials, an OPAC, a Web page.
Computers on Campus 1500 computers available on campus for general student use. A campuswide network can be accessed from student residence rooms and from off campus. Internet access, online (class) registration, at least one staffed computer lab available.
Student Life *Housing options:* coed, women-only, cooperative. Campus housing is university owned. Freshman campus housing is guaranteed. *Activities and organizations:* drama/theater group, student-run newspaper, radio station, choral group, Debating Union, UNSAM (Model United Nations), Sexual Assault Centre, Walksafe, Queer McGill, national fraternities, national sororities. *Campus security:* 24-hour emergency response devices and patrols, student patrols, late-night transport/escort service, controlled dormitory access. *Student services:* health clinic, personal/psychological counseling, women's center, legal services.

McGill University (continued)

Athletics Member CIS. *Intercollegiate sports:* badminton M/W, baseball M, basketball M/W, cheerleading W, crew M/W, cross-country running M/W, fencing M/W, field hockey W, football M, golf M/W, ice hockey M/W, lacrosse M/W, rugby M/W, sailing M/W, skiing (cross-country) M/W, skiing (downhill) M/W, soccer M/W, squash M/W, swimming M/W, tennis M/W, track and field M/W, ultimate Frisbee M/W, volleyball M/W, wrestling M/W. *Intramural sports:* badminton M/W, basketball M/W, football M/W, ice hockey M/W, soccer M/W, squash M/W, table tennis M/W, tennis M/W, volleyball M/W.

Standardized Tests *Required:* SAT I and SAT II or ACT (for admission).

Costs (2004–05) *Tuition:* province resident $1668 Canadian dollars full-time; nonresident $4173 Canadian dollars full-time; International tuition $10,260 Canadian dollars full-time. Full-time tuition and fees vary according to course load and program. Part-time tuition and fees vary according to course load and program. *Required fees:* $1200 Canadian dollars full-time. *Room and board:* $8000 Canadian dollars; room only: $5000 Canadian dollars. Room and board charges vary according to board plan, gender, housing facility, and location. *Payment plan:* installment. *Waivers:* senior citizens and employees or children of employees.

Financial Aid Of all full-time matriculated undergraduates who enrolled in 2001, 578 state and other part-time jobs (averaging $1014).

Applying *Options:* electronic application, deferred entrance. *Application fee:* $60. *Required:* high school transcript, minimum 3.3 GPA. *Required for some:* letters of recommendation, audition for music program, portfolio for architecture program. *Application deadlines:* 1/15 (freshmen), 1/15 (transfers). *Notification:* continuous (freshmen), continuous (transfers).

Admissions Contact Ms. Kim Bartlett, Director of Admissions, McGill University, 845 Sherbrooke Street West, Montreal, QC H3A 2T5, Canada. *Phone:* 514-398-4462. *Fax:* 514-398-4193. *E-mail:* admissions@mcgill.ca.

■ *See page 1964 for a narrative description.*

McMaster University
Hamilton, Ontario, Canada

- **Province-supported** university, founded 1887
- **Calendar** Canadian standard year
- **Degrees** certificates, bachelor's, master's, doctoral, and first professional
- **Suburban** 300-acre campus with easy access to Toronto
- **Coed**
- **Very difficult** entrance level

Student Life *Campus security:* 24-hour emergency response devices and patrols, student patrols, late-night transport/escort service, controlled dormitory access.

Athletics Member CIS.

Costs (2003–04) *Tuition:* area resident $4814 full-time; International tuition $13,130 full-time. *Room and board:* $6260; room only: $3585.

Applying *Options:* early action. *Application fee:* $95 Canadian dollars. *Required:* high school transcript. *Required for some:* essay or personal statement, interview.

Admissions Contact Mrs. Lynn Giordano, Associate Registrar, Admissions, McMaster University, 1280 Main Street West, Hamilton, ON L8S 4M2, Canada. *Phone:* 905-525-9140 Ext. 24034. *Fax:* 905-527-1105. *E-mail:* macadmit@mcmaster.ca.

Memorial University of Newfoundland
St. John's, Newfoundland and Labrador, Canada

- **Province-supported** university, founded 1925
- **Calendar** trimesters
- **Degrees** diplomas, bachelor's, master's, doctoral, and postbachelor's certificates
- **Urban** 220-acre campus
- **Coed,** 15,207 undergraduate students
- **Moderately difficult** entrance level, 76% of applicants were admitted

Undergraduates Students come from 12 provinces and territories, 5% are from out of state, 10% live on campus. *Retention:* 82% of 2002 full-time freshmen returned.

Freshmen *Admission:* 3,578 applied, 2,721 admitted.

Faculty *Total:* 1,123, 98% full-time. *Student/faculty ratio:* 15:1.

Majors Accounting; acting; adult and continuing education; anthropology; applied mathematics; archeology; area studies; art; art history, criticism and conservation; athletic training; biochemistry; biological and physical sciences; biology/biological sciences; business administration and management; Canadian studies; cartography; cell biology and histology; chemical engineering; chemistry; civil engineering; classics and languages, literatures and linguistics; computer programming; computer science; counselor education/school counseling and guidance; criminal justice/police science; criminology; dietetics; dramatic/theatre arts; drawing; ecology; economics; education; electrical, electronics and communications engineering; elementary education; engineering; English; entomology; environmental biology; environmental studies; finance; folklore; food science; foods, nutrition, and wellness; forest sciences and biology; French; geography; geological/geophysical engineering; geology/earth science; geophysics and seismology; German; history; humanities; industrial engineering; information science/studies; kinesiology and exercise science; labor and industrial relations; Latin; linguistics; literature; marine biology and biological oceanography; marine science/merchant marine officer; marketing/marketing management; mathematics; mechanical engineering; medical microbiology and bacteriology; medieval and Renaissance studies; middle school education; modern Greek; music; music history, literature, and theory; music teacher education; music theory and composition; naval architecture and marine engineering; neuroscience; nursing (registered nurse training); ocean engineering; oceanography (chemical and physical); organizational behavior; painting; parks, recreation and leisure; pharmacy; philosophy; photography; physical education teaching and coaching; physics; piano and organ; political science and government; pre-medical studies; printmaking; psychology; religious studies; Russian; science teacher education; sculpture; secondary education; social sciences; social work; sociology; Spanish; special education; statistics; theatre design and technology; theatre literature, history and criticism; trade and industrial teacher education; violin, viola, guitar and other stringed instruments; voice and opera; wind/percussion instruments; women's studies; zoology/animal biology.

Academic Programs *Special study options:* academic remediation for entering students, accelerated degree program, adult/continuing education programs, advanced placement credit, cooperative education, distance learning, double majors, English as a second language, honors programs, internships, off-campus study, part-time degree program, services for LD students, study abroad, summer session for credit. *Unusual degree programs:* 3-2 forestry with University of New Brunswick; pharmacy, music.

Library Queen Elizabeth II Library plus 2 others with 1.2 million titles, 17,000 serial subscriptions, an OPAC, a Web page.

Computers on Campus 800 computers available on campus for general student use. A campuswide network can be accessed from student residence rooms and from off campus. Internet access, at least one staffed computer lab available.

Student Life *Housing options:* coed, men-only, women-only, disabled students. *Activities and organizations:* drama/theater group, student-run newspaper, radio station, choral group, International Student Center, Students Older Than Average, Memorial's Organization for the Disabled, Biology Society, Student Parents at MUN. *Campus security:* 24-hour emergency response devices and patrols, student patrols, late-night transport/escort service. *Student services:* health clinic, personal/psychological counseling, women's center, legal services.

Athletics Member CIS. *Intercollegiate sports:* basketball M/W, cross-country running M/W, soccer M/W, swimming M/W, volleyball M/W, wrestling M/W. *Intramural sports:* badminton M/W, basketball M/W, cross-country running M/W, soccer M/W, softball M/W, squash M/W, swimming M/W, table tennis M/W, tennis M/W, volleyball M/W, water polo M/W, weight lifting M(c).

Costs (2003–04) *Tuition:* nonresident $2550 Canadian dollars full-time, $85 Canadian dollars per credit hour part-time; International tuition $8800 Canadian dollars full-time. *Required fees:* $442 Canadian dollars full-time, $9 Canadian dollars per term part-time. *Room and board:* $4282 Canadian dollars; room only: $1482 Canadian dollars. Room and board charges vary according to board plan, housing facility, and location. *Waivers:* employees or children of employees.

Applying *Options:* electronic application. *Application fee:* $80 Canadian dollars. *Required:* high school transcript. *Required for some:* essay or personal statement, 2 letters of recommendation, interview, audition, portfolio. *Application deadlines:* rolling (freshmen), 3/1 (out-of-state freshmen), 3/1 (transfers). *Notification:* continuous (freshmen), continuous (out-of-state freshmen), continuous (transfers).

Admissions Contact Ms. Phyllis McCann, Admissions Manager, Memorial University of Newfoundland, Elizabeth Avenue, St. John's, NL A1C 5S7, Canada. *Phone:* 709-737-3705. *E-mail:* sturecru@morgan.ucs.mun.ca.

■ *See page 1970 for a narrative description.*

Mount Allison University
Sackville, New Brunswick, Canada

- **Province-supported** comprehensive, founded 1839
- **Calendar** Canadian standard year
- **Degrees** bachelor's and master's
- **Small-town** 50-acre campus
- **Endowment** $65.0 million
- **Coed,** 2,509 undergraduate students, 88% full-time, 61% women, 39% men

■ **Moderately difficult** entrance level

Undergraduates 2,208 full-time, 301 part-time. Students come from 13 provinces and territories, 46 other countries, 65% are from out of state, 4% transferred in, 50% live on campus. *Retention:* 90% of 2002 full-time freshmen returned.

Freshmen *Admission:* 1,083 applied, 634 enrolled. *Average high school GPA:* 3.80.

Faculty *Total:* 165, 75% full-time. *Student/faculty ratio:* 18:1.

Majors Accounting; American studies; ancient/classical Greek; anthropology; applied mathematics; art history, criticism and conservation; biochemistry; biological and physical sciences; biology/biological sciences; biopsychology; business administration and management; business/commerce; business/managerial economics; Canadian studies; chemistry; classics and languages, literatures and linguistics; computer science; dramatic/theatre arts; drawing; economics; English; environmental studies; fine/studio arts; French; geography; geology/earth science; German; history; humanities; interdisciplinary studies; international business/trade/commerce; international relations and affairs; Latin; liberal arts and sciences/liberal studies; literature; mathematics; mathematics and computer science; medieval and Renaissance studies; modern languages; music; music history, literature, and theory; music performance; natural sciences; philosophy; photography; physics; physiological psychology/psychobiology; piano and organ; political science and government; pre-dentistry studies; pre-law studies; pre-medical studies; pre-pharmacy studies; pre-theology/pre-ministerial studies; pre-veterinary studies; printmaking; psychology; religious studies; Romance languages; sculpture; sociology; Spanish; violin, viola, guitar and other stringed instruments; voice and opera; wind/percussion instruments.

Academic Programs *Special study options:* academic remediation for entering students, adult/continuing education programs, advanced placement credit, distance learning, double majors, honors programs, independent study, internships, off-campus study, part-time degree program, services for LD students, student-designed majors, study abroad, summer session for credit.

Library Ralph Pickard Bell Library plus 3 others with 400,000 titles, 1,700 serial subscriptions, an OPAC, a Web page.

Computers on Campus 100 computers available on campus for general student use. A campuswide network can be accessed from student residence rooms and from off campus. Internet access, at least one staffed computer lab available.

Student Life *Housing options:* coed. Campus housing is university owned. Freshman campus housing is guaranteed. *Activities and organizations:* drama/theater group, student-run newspaper, radio station, choral group, Commerce Society, Windsor Theatre, President's Leadership Development Certificate, Leadership Mount Allison, Garnet and Gold Society. *Campus security:* 24-hour emergency response devices, late-night transport/escort service. *Student services:* health clinic, personal/psychological counseling.

Athletics Member CIS. *Intercollegiate sports:* badminton M/W, baseball M/W, basketball M/W, football M, ice hockey W, rugby M/W, soccer M/W, swimming M/W. *Intramural sports:* badminton M/W, baseball M/W, basketball M/W, football M/W, golf M/W, ice hockey M/W, rugby M/W, skiing (cross-country) M/W, skiing (downhill) M/W, soccer M/W, softball M/W, tennis M/W, track and field M/W, ultimate Frisbee M/W, volleyball M/W, weight lifting M/W.

Standardized Tests *Required for some:* SAT I and SAT II or ACT (for admission), SAT II: Writing Test (for admission). *Recommended:* SAT I or ACT (for admission), SAT II: Subject Tests (for admission).

Costs (2003–04) *Tuition:* $536 Canadian dollars per course part-time; province resident $5360 Canadian dollars full-time; nonresident $1072 Canadian dollars per course part-time; International tuition $10,720 Canadian dollars full-time. Full-time tuition and fees vary according to course load. Part-time tuition and fees vary according to course load. *Required fees:* $187 Canadian dollars full-time. *Room and board:* $6250 Canadian dollars; room only: $3230 Canadian dollars. Room and board charges vary according to board plan. *Waivers:* senior citizens and employees or children of employees.

Applying *Options:* electronic application, deferred entrance. *Application fee:* $50 Canadian dollars. *Required:* high school transcript, minimum 3.0 GPA. *Required for some:* essay or personal statement, interview. *Recommended:* 2 letters of recommendation. *Application deadline:* rolling (freshmen), rolling (transfers). *Notification:* continuous (freshmen), continuous (transfers).

Admissions Contact Admissions Counselor, Mount Allison University, 65 York Street, Sackville, NB E4L 1E4, Canada. *Phone:* 506-364-2110. *E-mail:* admissions@mta.ca.

MOUNT SAINT VINCENT UNIVERSITY

Halifax, Nova Scotia, Canada

■ **Province-supported** comprehensive, founded 1873
■ **Calendar** Canadian standard year
■ **Degrees** certificates, diplomas, bachelor's, master's, first professional, and postbachelor's certificates
■ **Suburban** 40-acre campus
■ **Endowment** $16.2 million
■ **Coed, primarily women,** 3,526 undergraduate students
■ **Moderately difficult** entrance level, 72% of applicants were admitted

Undergraduates Students come from 13 provinces and territories, 41 other countries, 15% are from out of state, 6% live on campus. *Retention:* 70% of 2002 full-time freshmen returned.

Freshmen *Admission:* 2,511 applied, 1,804 admitted. *Average high school GPA:* 3.50.

Faculty *Total:* 267, 54% full-time. *Student/faculty ratio:* 15:1.

Majors Accounting; adult development and aging; anthropology; applied mathematics; art teacher education; biological and physical sciences; biology/biological sciences; business administration and management; chemistry; child development; computer and information sciences; computer systems analysis; developmental and child psychology; dietetics; economics; education; elementary education; English; family and consumer economics related; fine/studio arts; foods, nutrition, and wellness; French; German; gerontology; history; hospitality administration; hotel/motel administration; human ecology; humanities; information science/studies; interdisciplinary studies; kindergarten/preschool education; liberal arts and sciences/liberal studies; linguistics; literature; management information systems; marketing/marketing management; marketing research; mathematics; mathematics and computer science; modern languages; nutrition sciences; peace studies and conflict resolution; philosophy; political science and government; psychology; public relations/image management; reading teacher education; religious studies; secondary education; social sciences; sociology; Spanish; special products marketing; statistics; tourism and travel services management; tourism/travel marketing; women's studies.

Academic Programs *Special study options:* academic remediation for entering students, accelerated degree program, adult/continuing education programs, advanced placement credit, cooperative education, distance learning, double majors, English as a second language, external degree program, honors programs, independent study, internships, off-campus study, part-time degree program, services for LD students, student-designed majors, study abroad, summer session for credit.

Library E. Margaret Fulton Communications Centre Library plus 3 others with 207,140 titles, 3,570 serial subscriptions, 1,243 audiovisual materials, an OPAC, a Web page.

Computers on Campus 150 computers available on campus for general student use. A campuswide network can be accessed from student residence rooms. Internet access, online (class) registration, at least one staffed computer lab available.

Student Life *Housing options:* coed, men-only, women-only. Campus housing is university owned. Freshman applicants given priority for college housing. *Activities and organizations:* student-run newspaper, choral group, Business Society, Residence Society, Science Society, History Society, Queer/Straight Alliance. *Campus security:* 24-hour emergency response devices and patrols, late-night transport/escort service, controlled dormitory access. *Student services:* health clinic, personal/psychological counseling, women's center.

Athletics *Intercollegiate sports:* badminton M/W, basketball M/W, cheerleading M/W, soccer M/W, volleyball W. *Intramural sports:* badminton M/W, basketball M/W, soccer M/W, volleyball M/W.

Standardized Tests *Required for some:* SAT I and SAT II or ACT (for admission).

Costs (2003–04) *Tuition:* nonresident $4850 Canadian dollars full-time; International tuition $8970 Canadian dollars full-time. Full-time tuition and fees vary according to class time, course load, degree level, and program. Part-time tuition and fees vary according to class time, course load, degree level, and program. *Required fees:* $247 Canadian dollars full-time. *Room and board:* $5960 Canadian dollars; room only: $3920 Canadian dollars. Room and board charges vary according to board plan and housing facility. *Payment plan:* installment. *Waivers:* senior citizens and employees or children of employees.

Financial Aid *Financial aid deadline:* 1/3.

Applying *Options:* common application, electronic application, deferred entrance. *Application fee:* $30 Canadian dollars. *Required:* high school transcript, minimum 2.0 GPA. *Required for some:* essay or personal statement, minimum 3.0 GPA, 2 letters of recommendation, interview. *Application deadlines:* 3/12 (freshmen), 5/30 (out-of-state freshmen), 8/14 (transfers). *Notification:* continuous until 9/1 (freshmen), 6/1 (out-of-state freshmen), continuous until 9/1 (transfers).

Admissions Contact Ms. Tara Wigglesworth-Hines, Assistant Registrar/Admissions, Mount Saint Vincent University, 166 Bedford Highway, Halifax, NS B3M2J6, Canada. *Phone:* 902-457-6117. *Fax:* 902-457-6498. *E-mail:* admissions@msvu.ca.

NER ISRAEL YESHIVA COLLEGE OF TORONTO
Thornhill, Ontario, Canada

Admissions Contact Rabbi Y. Kravetz, Director of Admissions, Ner Israel Yeshiva College of Toronto, 8950 Bathurst Street, Thornhill, ON L4J 8A7, Canada. *Phone:* 905-731-1224.

NIPISSING UNIVERSITY
North Bay, Ontario, Canada

- **Province-supported** comprehensive, founded 1992
- **Calendar** semesters
- **Degrees** bachelor's, master's, and postbachelor's certificates
- **Small-town** 290-hectare campus
- **Endowment** $4.4 million
- **Coed,** 2,829 undergraduate students, 78% full-time, 71% women, 29% men
- **Minimally difficult** entrance level, 17% of applicants were admitted

Undergraduates 2,201 full-time, 628 part-time. Students come from 23 other countries, 3% transferred in, 22% live on campus.

Freshmen *Admission:* 6,474 applied, 1,111 admitted, 1,111 enrolled.

Faculty *Total:* 194, 67% full-time, 46% with terminal degrees. *Student/faculty ratio:* 18:1.

Majors Biology/biological sciences; business administration and management; business and personal/financial services marketing; classics and languages, literatures and linguistics; computer science; economics; education; English; environmental biology; environmental studies; geography; history; liberal arts and sciences/liberal studies; mathematics; nursing (registered nurse training); philosophy; psychology; sociology; women's studies.

Academic Programs *Special study options:* academic remediation for entering students, distance learning, double majors, external degree program, honors programs, independent study, off-campus study, part-time degree program, services for LD students, study abroad, summer session for credit.

Library Education Centre Library with 180,397 titles, 5,680 serial subscriptions, 2,689 audiovisual materials, an OPAC, a Web page.

Computers on Campus 163 computers available on campus for general student use. A campuswide network can be accessed from student residence rooms and from off campus. Internet access, online (class) registration, at least one staffed computer lab available. Computer purchase or lease plan available.

Student Life *Housing options:* coed, disabled students. Campus housing is university owned. Freshman campus housing is guaranteed. *Activities and organizations:* drama/theater group, student-run newspaper, BACCHUS, NUSAC (Nipissing University Student Athletic Counsel), Business Society, drama club Students on Stage, Literacy Club Frontier College. *Campus security:* 24-hour emergency response devices and patrols, student patrols, late-night transport/escort service, controlled dormitory access. *Student services:* health clinic, personal/psychological counseling, women's center.

Athletics Member CIS. *Intercollegiate sports:* soccer M/W, volleyball M/W. *Intramural sports:* badminton M/W, baseball M/W, basketball M/W, ice hockey M/W, soccer M/W, softball M/W, volleyball M/W.

Costs (2003–04) *Tuition:* nonresident $3950 Canadian dollars full-time, $790 Canadian dollars per course part-time; International tuition $8500 Canadian dollars full-time. Full-time tuition and fees vary according to course load and program. Part-time tuition and fees vary according to course load, location, and program. *Required fees:* $748 Canadian dollars full-time, $81 Canadian dollars per course part-time. *Room only:* $3630 Canadian dollars. Room and board charges vary according to housing facility and location. *Payment plan:* installment. *Waivers:* employees or children of employees.

Applying *Options:* early admission. *Application fee:* $40 Canadian dollars. *Required:* high school transcript. *Application deadlines:* 6/1 (freshmen), 6/1 (transfers). *Notification:* continuous until 6/1 (freshmen), continuous until 6/1 (transfers).

Admissions Contact Ms. Heather Brown, Assistant Registrar-Liaison, Nipissing University, 100 College Drive. *Phone:* 705-474-3461 Ext. 4518. *Fax:* 705-495-1772. *E-mail:* liaison@nipissingu.ca.

NORTHWEST BIBLE COLLEGE
Edmonton, Alberta, Canada

- **Independent** 4-year, founded 1946, affiliated with Pentecostal Assemblies of Canada
- **Calendar** semesters
- **Degree** certificates, diplomas, and bachelor's
- **Urban** 1-hectare campus
- **Coed**
- 99% of applicants were admitted

Faculty *Student/faculty ratio:* 12:1.

Costs (2003–04) *Tuition:* $4620 full-time. Full-time tuition and fees vary according to course load and program. Part-time tuition and fees vary according to course load and program. *Required fees:* $445 full-time.

Applying *Options:* common application. *Application fee:* $50 Canadian dollars. *Required:* essay or personal statement, high school transcript, letters of recommendation.

Admissions Contact Ingrid Thompson, Registrar, Northwest Bible College, 11617-106 Avenue, Edmonton, AB T5H 0S1, Canada. *Phone:* 780-452-0808. *Toll-free phone:* 866-222-0808. *E-mail:* info@nwbc.ab.ca.

NOVA SCOTIA AGRICULTURAL COLLEGE
Truro, Nova Scotia, Canada

- **Province-supported** comprehensive, founded 1905
- **Calendar** semesters
- **Degrees** diplomas, bachelor's, and master's
- **Small-town** 408-acre campus with easy access to Halifax
- **Coed,** 667 undergraduate students
- **Minimally difficult** entrance level, 65% of applicants were admitted

Undergraduates Students come from 14 provinces and territories, 25% are from out of state. *Retention:* 85% of 2002 full-time freshmen returned.

Freshmen *Admission:* 500 applied, 325 admitted.

Faculty *Total:* 74, 81% full-time, 73% with terminal degrees. *Student/faculty ratio:* 9:1.

Majors Agricultural business and management; agricultural economics; agricultural mechanization; agriculture; animal sciences; applied horticulture; engineering; environmental studies; plant sciences; pre-veterinary studies.

Academic Programs *Special study options:* academic remediation for entering students, adult/continuing education programs, advanced placement credit, cooperative education, internships, off-campus study, part-time degree program.

Library MacRae Library with 23,000 titles, 800 serial subscriptions.

Computers on Campus 110 computers available on campus for general student use. A campuswide network can be accessed. Internet access, at least one staffed computer lab available.

Student Life *Housing options:* coed. *Activities and organizations:* student-run newspaper. *Campus security:* 24-hour patrols, student patrols. *Student services:* health clinic, personal/psychological counseling.

Athletics *Intercollegiate sports:* badminton M/W, basketball M/W, soccer M/W, volleyball M/W. *Intramural sports:* badminton M/W, basketball M/W, ice hockey M, racquetball M/W, rugby M/W, skiing (cross-country) M/W, skiing (downhill) M/W, soccer M/W, softball M/W, squash M/W, volleyball M/W.

Standardized Tests *Required:* SAT I and SAT II or ACT (for admission).

Costs (2004–05) *Room and board:* $5430.

Applying *Options:* common application. *Application fee:* $25 Canadian dollars. *Required:* high school transcript. *Required for some:* interview. *Application deadline:* 8/1 (freshmen).

Admissions Contact Ms. Elizabeth Johnson, Admissions Officer, Nova Scotia Agricultural College, PO Box 550, Truro, NS B2N 5E3, Canada. *Phone:* 902-893-8212. *E-mail:* reg_info@nsac.ns.ca.

NOVA SCOTIA COLLEGE OF ART AND DESIGN
Halifax, Nova Scotia, Canada

- **Province-supported** comprehensive, founded 1887
- **Calendar** semesters
- **Degrees** bachelor's and master's
- **Urban** 1-acre campus
- **Endowment** $1.1 million
- **Coed,** 930 undergraduate students, 80% full-time, 71% women, 29% men
- **Very difficult** entrance level, 60% of applicants were admitted

Undergraduates 743 full-time, 187 part-time. Students come from 11 provinces and territories, 21 other countries, 12% transferred in.

Freshmen *Admission:* 222 applied, 134 admitted, 111 enrolled.

Faculty *Total:* 81, 52% full-time, 47% with terminal degrees. *Student/faculty ratio:* 17:1.

Majors Art; art history, criticism and conservation; ceramic arts and ceramics; commercial and advertising art; crafts, folk art and artisanry; design and applied arts related; design and visual communications; drawing; fiber, textile and weaving arts; film/cinema studies; fine/studio arts; graphic design; metal and jewelry arts; painting; photography; printmaking; sculpture.

Academic Programs *Special study options:* cooperative education, distance learning, double majors, external degree program, honors programs, independent study, internships, off-campus study, part-time degree program, services for LD students, student-designed majors, study abroad, summer session for credit.

Library Nova Scotia College of Art and Design Library with 32,000 titles, 235 serial subscriptions, 120,000 audiovisual materials, an OPAC.

Computers on Campus 60 computers available on campus for general student use. Internet access, at least one staffed computer lab available.

Student Life *Housing:* college housing not available. *Campus security:* evening patrols by trained security personnel. *Student services:* personal/psychological counseling.

Costs (2003–04) *Tuition:* $204 Canadian dollars per credit part-time; province resident $204 Canadian dollars per credit part-time; nonresident $3834 Canadian dollars full-time, $450 Canadian dollars per credit part-time; International tuition $8327 Canadian dollars full-time. Full-time tuition and fees vary according to course load. Part-time tuition and fees vary according to course load. *Room and board:* $4829 Canadian dollars; room only: $3253 Canadian dollars. *Payment plan:* deferred payment. *Waivers:* senior citizens and employees or children of employees.

Applying *Options:* deferred entrance. *Application fee:* $35. *Required:* essay or personal statement, high school transcript, portfolio. *Required for some:* 2 letters of recommendation, interview. *Recommended:* minimum 3.0 GPA. *Application deadlines:* 5/15 (freshmen), 4/1 (transfers). *Notification:* continuous until 6/30 (freshmen), continuous until 6/30 (transfers).

Admissions Contact Mr. Terry Bailey, Coordinator of Admissions, Off Campus and Recruitment, Nova Scotia College of Art and Design, 5163 Duke Street, Halifax, NS B3J 3J6, Canada. *Phone:* 902-494-8129. *Fax:* 902-425-2987. *E-mail:* admiss@nscad.ns.ca.

OKANAGAN UNIVERSITY COLLEGE
Kelowna, British Columbia, Canada

- **Province-supported** 4-year, part of British Columbia Provincial Government Institution
- **Calendar** semesters
- **Degrees** certificates, diplomas, associate, and bachelor's
- **Urban** 26-acre campus
- **Endowment** $5.3 million
- **Coed,** 7,767 undergraduate students, 70% full-time, 60% women, 40% men
- 38% of applicants were admitted

Undergraduates 5,458 full-time, 2,309 part-time. Students come from 9 provinces and territories, 27 other countries, 10% are from out of state, 3% Native American, 2% international, 13% transferred in. *Retention:* 55% of 2002 full-time freshmen returned.

Freshmen *Admission:* 3,195 applied, 1,218 admitted, 1,083 enrolled.

Faculty *Total:* 400, 94% full-time, 48% with terminal degrees. *Student/faculty ratio:* 15:1.

Majors Adult health nursing; animal physiology; anthropology; biological specializations related; biology/biological sciences; business administration and management; cell biology and histology; chemistry; chemistry related; ecology; economics; education; English; fine arts related; general studies; history; international relations and affairs; liberal arts and sciences/liberal studies; mathematics; philosophy; physics; political science and government; psychology; social work; sociology.

Academic Programs *Special study options:* academic remediation for entering students, adult/continuing education programs, advanced placement credit, cooperative education, distance learning, double majors, English as a second language, honors programs, independent study, part-time degree program, services for LD students, study abroad, summer session for credit.

Library OUC Library with 295,800 titles, 1,585 serial subscriptions, an OPAC, a Web page.

Computers on Campus 250 computers available on campus for general student use. A campuswide network can be accessed. Internet access, online (class) registration, at least one staffed computer lab available.

Student Life *Housing options:* coed, disabled students. Campus housing is university owned. *Activities and organizations:* student-run newspaper, choral group. *Campus security:* 24-hour emergency response devices and patrols, controlled dormitory access. *Student services:* health clinic, personal/psychological counseling, women's center.

Athletics Member NCAA. *Intercollegiate sports:* basketball M/W, soccer M/W, volleyball M/W. *Intramural sports:* badminton M/W, basketball M/W, bowling M/W, crew M/W, football M/W, ice hockey M/W, rugby M/W, sailing M/W, skiing (downhill) M/W, soccer M/W, softball M/W, swimming M/W, table tennis M/W, tennis M/W, volleyball M/W, weight lifting M/W.

Costs (2003–04) *Tuition:* area resident $2405 full-time; International tuition $5727 full-time. Full-time tuition and fees vary according to course load and program. Part-time tuition and fees vary according to course load and program. *Required fees:* $335 full-time. *Room and board:* $3147; room only: $1959. Room and board charges vary according to board plan and housing facility. *Payment plan:* deferred payment. *Waivers:* senior citizens and employees or children of employees.

Applying *Options:* common application, electronic application. *Application fee:* $20 Canadian dollars. *Required for some:* essay or personal statement, high school transcript, minimum 2.0 GPA, interview. *Application deadline:* rolling (freshmen), rolling (transfers). *Notification:* continuous (freshmen), continuous (transfers).

Admissions Contact Ms. Lynn Grahame, Manager of Admissions, Okanagan University College, 1000 K. L. O. Road, Kelowna, BC V1Y 4X8, Canada. *Phone:* 250-862-5417 Ext. 4213. *Toll-free phone:* 877-755-2266. *Fax:* 250-862-5466.

OPEN LEARNING AGENCY
Burnaby, British Columbia, Canada

Admissions Contact Mr. Robert Ruff, Registrar, Open Learning Agency, 4355 Mathissi Place, Burnaby, BC V5G 4S8, Canada. *Phone:* 604-431-3000 Ext. 3055. *Toll-free phone:* 800-663-9711. *Fax:* 604-431-3344. *E-mail:* student@ola.bc.ca.

PRAIRIE BIBLE COLLEGE
Three Hills, Alberta, Canada

- **Independent interdenominational** 4-year, founded 1922
- **Calendar** semesters
- **Degree** certificates, diplomas, and bachelor's
- **Small-town** 130-acre campus with easy access to Calgary
- **Coed,** 457 undergraduate students, 81% full-time, 40% women, 60% men
- **Minimally difficult** entrance level

Undergraduates 371 full-time, 86 part-time. Students come from 7 other countries, 78% live on campus. *Retention:* 43% of 2002 full-time freshmen returned.

Freshmen *Admission:* 216 admitted, 179 enrolled.

Faculty *Total:* 42, 74% full-time, 26% with terminal degrees. *Student/faculty ratio:* 12:1.

Majors Ancient Near Eastern and biblical languages; biblical studies; dramatic/theatre arts; education; international relations and affairs; missionary studies and missiology; music; musicology and ethnomusicology; pastoral counseling and specialized ministries related; pastoral studies/counseling; pre-theology/pre-ministerial studies; religious education; theological and ministerial studies related; theology; theology and religious vocations related; youth ministry.

Academic Programs *Special study options:* accelerated degree program, adult/continuing education programs, advanced placement credit, English as a second language, internships, part-time degree program, study abroad.

Library T. S. Rendall Library with 60,745 titles, 458 serial subscriptions.

Computers on Campus 30 computers available on campus for general student use. Internet access, at least one staffed computer lab available.

Student Life *Housing:* on-campus residence required for freshman year. *Options:* men-only, women-only. Campus housing is university owned. Freshman campus housing is guaranteed. *Activities and organizations:* drama/theater group, student-run newspaper, radio station, choral group, WIN, SMF, student government, Off-Campus. *Campus security:* 24-hour emergency response devices and patrols, late-night transport/escort service, controlled dormitory access. *Student services:* health clinic, personal/psychological counseling.

Athletics Member CIS. *Intercollegiate sports:* basketball M/W, cross-country running M/W, volleyball M/W. *Intramural sports:* badminton M/W, basketball M/W, football M, ice hockey M, soccer M, volleyball M/W.

Costs (2004–05) *Comprehensive fee:* $9816 Canadian dollars includes full-time tuition ($6240 Canadian dollars), mandatory fees ($176 Canadian dollars), and room and board ($3400 Canadian dollars). Full-time tuition and fees vary according to course load. Part-time tuition: $195 Canadian dollars per credit. Part-time tuition and fees vary according to course load. *Required fees:* $6 Canadian dollars per credit part-time. *Room and board:* Room and board charges vary according to location. *Payment plan:* deferred payment. *Waivers:* senior citizens.

Applying *Options:* common application, electronic application. *Required:* essay or personal statement, high school transcript, 2 letters of recommendation. *Required for some:* minimum 3.0 GPA. *Recommended:* minimum 2.0 GPA. *Application deadlines:* 8/15 (freshmen), 8/15 (transfers). *Early decision:* 3/1.

Admissions Contact Mr. Kevin Kirk, Vice President Marketing and Enrollment Management, Prairie Bible College, 319 Sixth Avenue North, PO Box 4000,

Prairie Bible College (continued)
Three Hills, AB T0M 2N0, Canada. *Phone:* 403-443-5511 Ext. 3007. *Toll-free phone:* 800-661-2425. *Fax:* 403-443-5540. *E-mail:* admissions@prairie.edu.

PROVIDENCE COLLEGE AND THEOLOGICAL SEMINARY

Otterburne, Manitoba, Canada

- **Independent interdenominational** comprehensive, founded 1925
- **Calendar** semesters
- **Degrees** bachelor's, master's, and doctoral
- **Rural** 100-acre campus with easy access to Winnipeg
- **Endowment** $715,028
- **Coed,** 452 undergraduate students, 84% full-time, 53% women, 47% men
- **Noncompetitive** entrance level

Undergraduates 381 full-time, 71 part-time. Students come from 16 provinces and territories, 17 other countries, 30% are from out of state, 60% live on campus. *Retention:* 70% of 2002 full-time freshmen returned.

Faculty *Total:* 50, 36% full-time, 64% with terminal degrees. *Student/faculty ratio:* 19:1.

Majors Airline pilot and flight crew; biblical studies; business administration and management; communication and media related; divinity/ministry; dramatic/theatre arts; education; English as a second/foreign language (teaching); history; humanities; liberal arts and sciences/liberal studies; missionary studies and missiology; music; parks, recreation, and leisure related; pastoral studies/counseling; religious education; religious studies; social sciences; theology; youth ministry.

Academic Programs *Special study options:* academic remediation for entering students, accelerated degree program, distance learning, double majors, English as a second language, freshman honors college, independent study, internships, part-time degree program.

Library 47,756 titles, 635 serial subscriptions.

Computers on Campus 14 computers available on campus for general student use. A campuswide network can be accessed from off campus. Internet access, at least one staffed computer lab available.

Student Life *Housing:* on-campus residence required for freshman year. *Options:* men-only, women-only. Campus housing is university owned. Freshman campus housing is guaranteed. *Activities and organizations:* drama/theater group, student-run newspaper, choral group. *Campus security:* student patrols, controlled dormitory access. *Student services:* health clinic, personal/psychological counseling.

Athletics Member NCCAA. *Intercollegiate sports:* badminton M/W, basketball M/W, ice hockey M, soccer M/W, table tennis M/W, volleyball M/W. *Intramural sports:* badminton M/W, basketball M/W, cross-country running M/W, football M, golf M, ice hockey W, skiing (cross-country) M/W, soccer M/W, table tennis M/W, tennis M/W, volleyball M/W, weight lifting M/W.

Costs (2004–05) *Comprehensive fee:* $9850 includes full-time tuition ($5400), mandatory fees ($450), and room and board ($4000). Part-time tuition: $192 per credit hour. *Required fees:* $18 per credit hour part-time. *Room and board:* Room and board charges vary according to board plan. *Payment plan:* installment. *Waivers:* children of alumni, senior citizens, and employees or children of employees.

Applying *Options:* deferred entrance. *Application fee:* $35 Canadian dollars. *Required:* high school transcript, 4 letters of recommendation. *Application deadline:* rolling (freshmen), rolling (transfers).

Admissions Contact Ms. Joy Lise, Director of Environment Management, Providence College and Theological Seminary, General Delivery, Otterburne, MB R0A 1G0, Canada. *Phone:* 204-433-7488 Ext. 247. *Toll-free phone:* 800-668-7768. *Fax:* 204-433-7158. *E-mail:* info@prov.ca.

QUEEN'S UNIVERSITY AT KINGSTON

Kingston, Ontario, Canada

- **Province-supported** university, founded 1841
- **Calendar** Canadian standard year
- **Degrees** bachelor's, master's, doctoral, and first professional
- **Urban** 160-acre campus
- **Endowment** $273.6 million
- **Coed,** 15,190 undergraduate students
- **Most difficult** entrance level, 38% of applicants were admitted

Undergraduates Students come from 13 provinces and territories, 76 other countries, 11% are from out of state, 25% live on campus.

Freshmen *Admission:* 31,844 applied, 11,972 admitted. *Average high school GPA:* 3.50. *Test scores:* SAT verbal scores over 500: 81%; SAT math scores over 500: 90%; SAT verbal scores over 600: 49%; SAT math scores over 600: 66%; SAT verbal scores over 700: 15%; SAT math scores over 700: 25%.

Faculty *Total:* 984. *Student/faculty ratio:* 13:1.

Majors Art history, criticism and conservation; artificial intelligence and robotics; art teacher education; astrophysics; atomic/molecular physics; biochemistry; biology/biological sciences; business administration and management; Canadian studies; chemical engineering; chemistry; civil engineering; classics and languages, literatures and linguistics; cognitive psychology and psycholinguistics; computer and information sciences; computer and information sciences related; computer engineering; computer engineering related; computer hardware engineering; computer science; computer software engineering; dramatic/theatre arts; economics; education; electrical, electronics and communications engineering; elementary education; engineering; engineering physics; engineering science; English; environmental science; environmental studies; film/cinema studies; fine/studio arts; French; geography; geological/geophysical engineering; geology/earth science; German; health and physical education; health science; health teacher education; Hispanic-American, Puerto Rican, and Mexican-American/Chicano studies; history; interdisciplinary studies; Italian; Jewish/Judaic studies; Latin; Latin American studies; linguistics; mathematics; mechanical engineering; medieval and Renaissance studies; mining and mineral engineering; modern Greek; music; music teacher education; nursing (registered nurse training); philosophy; physical education teaching and coaching; physics; political science and government; psychology; religious studies; science teacher education; secondary education; sociology; Spanish; statistics; violin, viola, guitar and other stringed instruments; women's studies.

Academic Programs *Special study options:* accelerated degree program, adult/continuing education programs, cooperative education, distance learning, double majors, English as a second language, honors programs, internships, part-time degree program, services for LD students, student-designed majors, study abroad, summer session for credit.

Library Joseph S. Stauffer Library with 3.5 million titles, 16,109 serial subscriptions, an OPAC, a Web page.

Computers on Campus 455 computers available on campus for general student use. A campuswide network can be accessed from student residence rooms and from off campus that provide access to e-mail. Internet access, online (class) registration, at least one staffed computer lab available.

Student Life *Housing options:* coed, men-only, women-only, cooperative, disabled students. Campus housing is university owned. Freshman campus housing is guaranteed. *Activities and organizations:* drama/theater group, student-run newspaper, radio station, choral group, marching band, Arts and Sciences Undergraduate Society, Alma Mater Society, Engineering Society, Commerce Society, Dance Club. *Campus security:* 24-hour emergency response devices and patrols, student patrols, late-night transport/escort service, controlled dormitory access. *Student services:* health clinic, personal/psychological counseling, women's center, legal services.

Athletics Member CIS. *Intercollegiate sports:* baseball M(c), basketball M/W, cheerleading M(c)/W(c), crew M/W, cross-country running M/W, fencing M/W, field hockey W, football M, golf M, gymnastics M(c)/W(c), ice hockey M/W, lacrosse M(c)/W, rugby M/W, sailing M(c)/W(c), skiing (cross-country) M/W, skiing (downhill) M(c)/W(c), soccer M/W, squash M/W, swimming M/W, table tennis M(c)/W(c), tennis M/W, track and field M/W, volleyball M/W, water polo M/W, wrestling M/W. *Intramural sports:* archery M(c)/W(c), badminton M/W, basketball M/W, cheerleading M(c)/W(c), crew M(c)/W(c), equestrian sports M(c)/W(c), fencing M(c)/W(c), football M, golf M, ice hockey M/W, rugby M/W, skiing (cross-country) M(c)/W(c), soccer M/W, softball M/W, squash M/W, swimming M/W, tennis M/W, ultimate Frisbee M(c)/W(c), volleyball M/W, water polo M/W.

Standardized Tests *Required:* SAT I or ACT (for admission). *Required for some:* SAT II: Subject Tests (for admission).

Costs (2003–04) *Tuition:* nonresident $4193 Canadian dollars full-time, $838 Canadian dollars per credit part-time; International tuition $13,980 Canadian dollars full-time. Full-time tuition and fees vary according to program. *Required fees:* $739 Canadian dollars full-time. *Room and board:* $7966 Canadian dollars; room only: $4466 Canadian dollars. Room and board charges vary according to board plan, housing facility, location, and student level.

Financial Aid Of all full-time matriculated undergraduates who enrolled in 2001, 478 state and other part-time jobs (averaging $1046).

Applying *Options:* common application, deferred entrance. *Application fee:* $90 Canadian dollars. *Required:* essay or personal statement, high school transcript, minimum 2.3 GPA. *Required for some:* 1 letter of recommendation. *Application deadlines:* 2/20 (freshmen), 5/15 (transfers). *Notification:* 5/28 (freshmen), 6/15 (transfers).

Admissions Contact Mr. Nicholas Snider, Manager of Student Recruitment, Queen's University at Kingston, Richardson Hall, Kingston, ON K7L 3N6, Canada. *Phone:* 613-533-2217. *Fax:* 613-533-6810. *E-mail:* admissn@post.queensu.ca.

■ *See page 2204 for a narrative description.*

REDEEMER UNIVERSITY COLLEGE
Ancaster, Ontario, Canada

- **Independent interdenominational** 4-year, founded 1980
- **Calendar** semesters
- **Degree** certificates and bachelor's
- **Small-town** 78-acre campus with easy access to Toronto
- **Endowment** $507,705
- **Coed,** 770 undergraduate students, 90% full-time, 63% women, 37% men
- **Moderately difficult** entrance level, 82% of applicants were admitted

Undergraduates 695 full-time, 75 part-time. Students come from 14 provinces and territories, 7 other countries, 60% live on campus.

Freshmen *Admission:* 431 applied, 352 admitted. *Average high school GPA:* 3.3. *Test scores:* ACT scores over 18: 100%; ACT scores over 24: 64%.

Faculty *Total:* 60, 58% full-time, 57% with terminal degrees. *Student/faculty ratio:* 17:1.

Majors Accounting; art; biblical studies; biological and physical sciences; biology/biological sciences; business administration and management; computer science; dramatic/theatre arts; education; education (K-12); elementary education; English; French; health and physical education; history; humanities; human resources management; kinesiology and exercise science; liberal arts and sciences/liberal studies; mathematics; music; natural sciences; parks, recreation and leisure; philosophy; political science and government; pre-dentistry studies; pre-law studies; pre-medical studies; pre-theology/pre-ministerial studies; pre-veterinary studies; psychology; religious studies; social work; sociology; theology.

Academic Programs *Special study options:* academic remediation for entering students, cooperative education, double majors, English as a second language, honors programs, independent study, internships, off-campus study, part-time degree program, services for LD students, study abroad, summer session for credit. *Unusual degree programs:* 3-2 chemistry with University of Guelph.

Library Redeemer College Library with 93,500 titles, 419 serial subscriptions, an OPAC, a Web page.

Computers on Campus 35 computers available on campus for general student use. A campuswide network can be accessed from off campus. Internet access, at least one staffed computer lab available.

Student Life *Housing:* on-campus residence required through sophomore year. *Options:* men-only, women-only. *Activities and organizations:* drama/theater group, student-run newspaper, choral group, Church in the Box, mission trips, bible study groups, choir, intramurals. *Campus security:* 24-hour emergency response devices, student patrols, late-night transport/escort service, controlled dormitory access, path lighting. *Student services:* health clinic, personal/psychological counseling.

Athletics *Intercollegiate sports:* basketball M/W, golf M/W, soccer M/W, volleyball M/W. *Intramural sports:* badminton M/W, basketball M/W, bowling M/W, football M/W, ice hockey M, racquetball M/W, skiing (cross-country) M/W, skiing (downhill) M/W, soccer M/W, softball M/W, squash M/W, table tennis M/W, tennis M/W, volleyball M/W, weight lifting M/W.

Standardized Tests *Required for some:* SAT I or ACT (for admission).

Costs (2004–05) *Comprehensive fee:* $16,015 Canadian dollars includes full-time tuition ($10,606 Canadian dollars), mandatory fees ($393 Canadian dollars), and room and board ($5016 Canadian dollars). Part-time tuition: $1061 Canadian dollars per course. *Required fees:* $39 Canadian dollars per course part-time. *Room and board:* Room and board charges vary according to housing facility. *Payment plans:* installment, deferred payment. *Waivers:* minority students, senior citizens, and employees or children of employees.

Applying *Options:* deferred entrance. *Application fee:* $35 Canadian dollars. *Required:* essay or personal statement, high school transcript, minimum 2.0 GPA, 2 letters of recommendation, pastoral reference. *Required for some:* interview. *Application deadlines:* 5/31 (freshmen), 5/31 (transfers). *Notification:* continuous (freshmen), continuous (transfers).

Admissions Contact Office of Admissions, Redeemer University College, 777 Garner Road East, Ancaster, ON L9K 1J4, Canada. *Phone:* 905-648-2131 Ext. 4280. *Toll-free phone:* 800-263-6467 Ext. 4280. *Fax:* 905-648-2134. *E-mail:* adm@redeemer.on.ca.

ROCKY MOUNTAIN COLLEGE
Calgary, Alberta, Canada

- **Independent** 4-year, founded 1992, affiliated with Missionary Church
- **Calendar** semesters
- **Degree** certificates, diplomas, and bachelor's
- **Suburban** 1-acre campus
- **Endowment** $343,200
- **Coed,** 342 undergraduate students
- **Noncompetitive** entrance level, 96% of applicants were admitted

Undergraduates Students come from 8 provinces and territories, 13 other countries, 20% live on campus.

Freshmen *Admission:* 169 applied, 163 admitted.

Faculty *Total:* 27, 52% full-time, 22% with terminal degrees. *Student/faculty ratio:* 20:1.

Majors Biblical studies; counseling psychology; education; missionary studies and missiology; music; pastoral studies/counseling; religious education; social sciences; theology; youth ministry.

Academic Programs *Special study options:* academic remediation for entering students, adult/continuing education programs, advanced placement credit, internships, part-time degree program, summer session for credit.

Library Main Library plus 1 other with 25,280 titles, 135 serial subscriptions.

Computers on Campus 5 computers available on campus for general student use. At least one staffed computer lab available.

Student Life *Housing options:* coed. Campus housing is university owned. *Activities and organizations:* drama/theater group, choral group, missions fellowship. *Campus security:* 24-hour emergency response devices. *Student services:* personal/psychological counseling.

Athletics *Intercollegiate sports:* basketball M/W, ice hockey M, soccer M, volleyball M/W. *Intramural sports:* basketball M/W, volleyball M/W.

Costs (2004–05) *Tuition:* $6600 Canadian dollars full-time, $220 Canadian dollars per credit hour part-time. *Required fees:* $272 Canadian dollars full-time, $5 Canadian dollars per credit hour part-time. *Room only:* $2850 Canadian dollars.

Applying *Options:* deferred entrance. *Application fee:* $50 Canadian dollars. *Required:* essay or personal statement, high school transcript, 2 letters of recommendation. *Required for some:* interview. *Application deadline:* rolling (freshmen), rolling (transfers).

Admissions Contact Ms. Dayna Chu, Student Enrollment Advisor, Rocky Mountain College, 4039 Brentwood Drive NW, Calgary, AB T2L 1L1. *Phone:* 403-284-5100 Ext. 222. *E-mail:* admissions@rockymountaincollege.ca.

ROYAL MILITARY COLLEGE OF CANADA
Kingston, Ontario, Canada

Admissions Contact Mr. J. Ross McKenzie, Assistant Registrar (Liaison), Royal Military College of Canada, PO Box 17000, Station Forces, Kingston, ON K7K 7B4, Canada. *Phone:* 613-541-6000 Ext. 6652. *Fax:* 613-542-3565. *E-mail:* registrar@rmc.ca.

ROYAL ROADS UNIVERSITY
Victoria, British Columbia, Canada

- **Province-supported** upper-level, founded 1996
- **Calendar** continuous
- **Degrees** certificates, diplomas, bachelor's, and master's
- **Suburban** 125-acre campus
- **Endowment** $2.0 million
- **Coed**
- **Moderately difficult** entrance level

Faculty *Student/faculty ratio:* 23:1.

Student Life *Campus security:* 24-hour emergency response devices and patrols, late-night transport/escort service, controlled dormitory access.

Costs (2003–04) *Tuition:* nonresident $5625 full-time, $188 per credit part-time; International tuition $11,250 full-time. No tuition increase for student's term of enrollment. *Required fees:* $360 full-time, $180 per year part-time. *Payment plans:* tuition prepayment, installment.

Applying *Options:* common application, electronic application. *Application fee:* $50 Canadian dollars.

Admissions Contact Ms. Ann Nightingale, Registrar and Director, Learner Services, Royal Roads University, Office of Learner Services and Registrar, 2005 Sooke Road, Victoria, BC V9B 5Y2, Canada. *Phone:* 250-391-2552. *Toll-free phone:* 800-788-8028. *E-mail:* rruregistrar@royalroads.ca.

RYERSON UNIVERSITY
Toronto, Ontario, Canada

- **Province-supported** comprehensive, founded 1948
- **Calendar** Canadian standard year or semesters depending on program
- **Degrees** certificates, diplomas, bachelor's, and master's
- **Urban** 20-acre campus
- **Endowment** $18.0 million
- **Coed,** 24,041 undergraduate students, 48% full-time, 56% women, 44% men
- **Moderately difficult** entrance level

Undergraduates 11,634 full-time, 12,407 part-time. Students come from 68 other countries, 6% live on campus.

Freshmen *Admission:* 4,068 enrolled.

Faculty *Total:* 794, 66% full-time.

Majors Accounting; acting; administrative assistant and secretarial science; aerospace, aeronautical and astronautical engineering; architecture; biology/biological sciences; broadcast journalism; business administration and management; business/managerial economics; chemical engineering; chemistry; child development; city/urban, community and regional planning; civil engineering; commercial and advertising art; computer engineering related; computer science; computer systems networking and telecommunications; consumer merchandising/retailing management; criminal justice/law enforcement administration; dance; drama and dance teacher education; dramatic/theatre arts; economics; electrical, electronics and communications engineering; environmental health; family and consumer economics related; fashion/apparel design; fashion merchandising; film/cinema studies; finance; foods, nutrition, and wellness; geography; health/health care administration; hospitality administration; hotel/motel administration; human resources management; industrial engineering; information science/studies; information technology; interior design; international business/trade/commerce; international economics; international finance; journalism; kindergarten/preschool education; landscape architecture; marketing/marketing management; mechanical engineering; nursing administration; nursing midwifery; nursing (registered nurse training); occupational health and industrial hygiene; photographic and film/video technology; photography; public administration; public health; public health/community nursing; radio and television; sales, distribution and marketing; social work; theatre design and technology; tourism and travel services management; urban studies/affairs; web page, digital/multimedia and information resources design.

Academic Programs *Special study options:* academic remediation for entering students, adult/continuing education programs, advanced placement credit, cooperative education, distance learning, double majors, English as a second language, honors programs, internships, off-campus study, part-time degree program, services for LD students, study abroad, summer session for credit.

Library Ryerson Library with 606,603 titles, 25,675 serial subscriptions, 16,244 audiovisual materials, an OPAC, a Web page.

Computers on Campus 1400 computers available on campus for general student use. A campuswide network can be accessed from student residence rooms and from off campus. Internet access, at least one staffed computer lab available. Computer purchase or lease plan available.

Student Life *Housing options:* coed. Campus housing is university owned. Freshman applicants given priority for college housing. *Activities and organizations:* drama/theater group, student-run newspaper, radio station, choral group. *Campus security:* 24-hour emergency response devices and patrols, late-night transport/escort service, controlled dormitory access. *Student services:* health clinic, personal/psychological counseling, women's center.

Athletics Member CIS. *Intercollegiate sports:* badminton M/W, basketball M/W, cheerleading W, fencing M/W, ice hockey M, soccer M/W, squash M/W, swimming M/W, volleyball M/W. *Intramural sports:* badminton M/W, basketball M/W, ice hockey M, soccer M/W, softball M/W, squash M/W, volleyball M/W, water polo M/W, weight lifting M/W.

Costs (2003–04) *Tuition:* province resident $4261 Canadian dollars full-time; International tuition $12,240 Canadian dollars full-time. *Room and board:* $6945 Canadian dollars.

Financial Aid *Financial aid deadline:* 1/15.

Applying *Options:* electronic application. *Application fee:* $95 Canadian dollars. *Required:* high school transcript. *Required for some:* essay or personal statement, letters of recommendation, interview, portfolio, audition, entrance examination. *Application deadline:* 3/1 (transfers). *Notification:* continuous (freshmen), continuous (transfers).

Admissions Contact Office of Admissions, Ryerson University, 350 Victoria Street, Toronto, ON M5B 2K3, Canada. *Phone:* 416-979-5036. *Fax:* 416-979-5221. *E-mail:* inquire@ryerson.ca.

ST. FRANCIS XAVIER UNIVERSITY
Antigonish, Nova Scotia, Canada

- **Independent Roman Catholic** comprehensive, founded 1853
- **Calendar** Canadian standard year
- **Degrees** diplomas, bachelor's, and master's
- **Small-town** 100-acre campus
- **Endowment** $34.9 million
- **Coed,** 4,495 undergraduate students, 85% full-time, 62% women, 38% men
- **Moderately difficult** entrance level, 42% of applicants were admitted

Undergraduates 3,838 full-time, 657 part-time. Students come from 12 provinces and territories, 25 other countries, 41% are from out of state, 43% live on campus. *Retention:* 88% of 2002 full-time freshmen returned.

Freshmen *Admission:* 2,281 applied, 958 admitted.

Faculty *Total:* 265, 84% full-time, 66% with terminal degrees. *Student/faculty ratio:* 16:1.

Majors Accounting; anthropology; biological and physical sciences; biology/biological sciences; business administration and management; Canadian studies; chemistry; classics and languages, literatures and linguistics; computer and information sciences; cultural studies; economics; education; elementary education; English; environmental studies; foods, nutrition, and wellness; French; geology/earth science; history; hydrology and water resources science; information science/studies; jazz/jazz studies; kinesiology and exercise science; liberal arts and sciences/liberal studies; management information systems; mathematics; modern languages; music; nursing (registered nurse training); nursing science; philosophy; physical education teaching and coaching; physical sciences; physics; political science and government; pre-dentistry studies; pre-law studies; pre-medical studies; pre-veterinary studies; psychology; religious studies; secondary education; sociology; women's studies.

Academic Programs *Special study options:* academic remediation for entering students, accelerated degree program, adult/continuing education programs, advanced placement credit, cooperative education, distance learning, double majors, English as a second language, honors programs, independent study, internships, off-campus study, part-time degree program, services for LD students, student-designed majors, study abroad, summer session for credit.

Library Angus L. MacDonald Library plus 1 other with 632,575 titles, 3,282 serial subscriptions, 6,598 audiovisual materials, an OPAC, a Web page.

Computers on Campus 350 computers available on campus for general student use. A campuswide network can be accessed from student residence rooms and from off campus. Internet access, online (class) registration, at least one staffed computer lab available.

Student Life *Housing options:* coed, men-only, women-only, disabled students. Campus housing is university owned. Freshman campus housing is guaranteed. *Activities and organizations:* drama/theater group, student-run newspaper, radio station, choral group, X-Project, Walkhome Program, orientation committee, Exekoi Tutoring, Off-Campus Society. *Campus security:* 24-hour emergency response devices and patrols, student patrols, late-night transport/escort service, controlled dormitory access. *Student services:* health clinic, personal/psychological counseling.

Athletics Member CIS. *Intercollegiate sports:* basketball M/W, cross-country running M/W, football M, ice hockey M/W, rugby M/W, soccer M, tennis M/W, volleyball W. *Intramural sports:* badminton M/W, basketball M/W, cross-country running M/W, football M/W, golf M/W, ice hockey M/W, racquetball M/W, rugby M/W, soccer M/W, softball M/W, squash M/W, swimming M/W, table tennis M/W, tennis M/W, track and field M/W, ultimate Frisbee M/W, volleyball M/W, water polo M/W, weight lifting M/W.

Standardized Tests *Required for some:* SAT I or ACT (for admission), SAT II: Writing Test (for admission). *Recommended:* SAT I or ACT (for admission), SAT II: Subject Tests (for admission), SAT II: Writing Test (for admission).

Costs (2003–04) *Comprehensive fee:* $11,878 Canadian dollars includes full-time tuition ($5310 Canadian dollars), mandatory fees ($573 Canadian dollars), and room and board ($5995 Canadian dollars). Full-time tuition and fees vary according to course load. Part-time tuition and fees vary according to course load. International tuition: $3900 Canadian dollars full-time. *Room and board:* Room and board charges vary according to board plan and housing facility. *Waivers:* senior citizens and employees or children of employees.

Applying *Options:* common application, early decision. *Application fee:* $40 Canadian dollars. *Required:* high school transcript. *Application deadline:* rolling (freshmen), rolling (transfers). *Notification:* continuous until 8/15 (freshmen), continuous until 8/15 (transfers).

Admissions Contact Ms. Janice Lukeman, Admissions Officer, St. Francis Xavier University, PO Box 5000, Antigonish, NS B2G 2W5, Canada. *Phone:* 902-867-2219. *Toll-free phone:* 877-867-7839 (in-state); 877-867-STFX (out-of-state). *Fax:* 902-867-2329. *E-mail:* admit@stfx.ca.

■ *See page 2284 for a narrative description.*

SAINT MARY'S UNIVERSITY
Halifax, Nova Scotia, Canada

- **Province-supported** comprehensive, founded 1802
- **Calendar** semesters
- **Degrees** certificates, diplomas, bachelor's, master's, and doctoral
- **Urban** 30-acre campus
- **Coed**
- **Moderately difficult** entrance level

Faculty *Student/faculty ratio:* 24:1.
Student Life *Campus security:* 24-hour emergency response devices and patrols, student patrols, late-night transport/escort service, controlled dormitory access, electronic surveillance of labs and key areas.
Athletics Member CIS.
Costs (2003–04) *Tuition:* nonresident $4965 Canadian dollars full-time; International tuition $9890 Canadian dollars full-time. *Required fees:* $232 Canadian dollars full-time. *Room and board:* $6435 Canadian dollars.
Applying *Options:* early action. *Application fee:* $35 Canadian dollars. *Required:* high school transcript, minimum 2.0 GPA. *Required for some:* interview.
Admissions Contact Mr. Greg Ferguson, Director of Admissions, Saint Mary's University, Halifax, NS B3H 3C3, Canada. *Phone:* 902-420-5415. *Fax:* 902-496-8100. *E-mail:* jim.dunn@stmarys.ca.

SAINT PAUL UNIVERSITY
Ottawa, Ontario, Canada

- **Province-supported** university, founded 1848
- **Calendar** Canadian standard year
- **Degrees** bachelor's, master's, and doctoral
- **Urban** 4-acre campus
- **Coed**
- **Moderately difficult** entrance level

Standardized Tests *Recommended:* SAT I (for admission).
Costs (2003–04) *Tuition:* nonresident $3300 full-time; International tuition $7460 full-time. *Required fees:* $49 full-time.
Applying *Options:* common application, deferred entrance. *Application fee:* $35 Canadian dollars. *Required:* high school transcript.
Admissions Contact Claudette Dubé-Socqué, Registrar, Saint Paul University, 223 Main, Ottowa. *Phone:* 613-236-1393 Ext. 2238. *Fax:* 613-782-3014.

ST. THOMAS UNIVERSITY
Fredericton, New Brunswick, Canada

- **Independent Roman Catholic** 4-year, founded 1910
- **Calendar** Canadian standard year
- **Degrees** bachelor's and postbachelor's certificates
- **Small-town** 16-acre campus
- **Endowment** $18.9 million
- **Coed,** 3,028 undergraduate students, 91% full-time, 67% women, 33% men
- **Moderately difficult** entrance level, 57% of applicants were admitted

Undergraduates 2,754 full-time, 274 part-time. Students come from 9 provinces and territories, 26 other countries, 25% are from out of state, 14% transferred in, 28% live on campus.
Freshmen *Admission:* 2,758 applied, 1,580 admitted, 976 enrolled.
Faculty *Total:* 180, 61% full-time. *Student/faculty ratio:* 25:1.
Majors Adult development and aging; American Indian/Native American studies; anthropology; criminology; economics; education; English; French; gerontology; history; journalism; mathematics; philosophy; political science and government; psychology; religious studies; Russian; social work; sociology; Spanish.
Academic Programs *Special study options:* academic remediation for entering students, accelerated degree program, cooperative education, distance learning, double majors, English as a second language, honors programs, independent study, internships, off-campus study, part-time degree program, services for LD students, student-designed majors, summer session for credit. *Unusual degree programs:* 3-2 education.
Library Harriet Irving Library plus 2 others with 1.2 million titles, 10,137 serial subscriptions, 4,166 audiovisual materials, an OPAC, a Web page.
Computers on Campus 78 computers available on campus for general student use. A campuswide network can be accessed from off campus. Internet access, at least one staffed computer lab available.
Student Life *Housing options:* Campus housing is university owned. Freshman campus housing is guaranteed. *Activities and organizations:* drama/theater group, student-run newspaper, radio station, choral group, Theatre St. Thomas, St. Thomas Student Union, Political Science Society, Economics Society, Student Help Centre. *Campus security:* 24-hour emergency response devices and patrols, late-night transport/escort service, controlled dormitory access. *Student services:* health clinic, personal/psychological counseling.
Athletics Member CIS. *Intercollegiate sports:* basketball M/W, ice hockey M(s)/W(s), rugby M/W, soccer M/W, volleyball M/W. *Intramural sports:* badminton M/W, basketball M/W, cheerleading M/W, cross-country running M/W, fencing M/W, football M, ice hockey M/W, racquetball M/W, skiing (cross-country) M/W, soccer M/W, softball M/W, squash M/W, swimming M/W, table tennis M/W, tennis M/W, track and field M/W, volleyball M/W, water polo M/W.
Standardized Tests *Required for some:* SAT I (for admission), SAT II: Subject Tests (for admission), SAT II: Writing Test (for admission).
Costs (2003–04) *Comprehensive fee:* $9309 includes full-time tuition ($3695), mandatory fees ($114), and room and board ($5500). Full-time tuition and fees vary according to course load, degree level, and program. Part-time tuition and fees vary according to course load. International tuition: $7390 full-time. *College room only:* $2700. Room and board charges vary according to board plan and location. *Payment plans:* installment, deferred payment. *Waivers:* senior citizens and employees or children of employees.
Applying *Options:* electronic application, early action, deferred entrance. *Application fee:* $25 Canadian dollars. *Required:* high school transcript, minimum 2.5 GPA. *Required for some:* essay or personal statement, letters of recommendation, interview. *Recommended:* minimum 3.0 GPA. *Application deadlines:* 7/31 (freshmen), 7/31 (transfers). *Notification:* continuous until 8/31 (freshmen), 5/15 (early action), continuous until 8/31 (transfers).
Admissions Contact Ms. Kathryn Monti, Director of Admissions, St. Thomas University, Admissions and Welcome Building, Fredericton, NB E3B 5G3. *Phone:* 506-452-0603. *Fax:* 506-452-0617. *E-mail:* admissions@stu.ca.

SIMON FRASER UNIVERSITY
Burnaby, British Columbia, Canada

- **Province-supported** university, founded 1965
- **Calendar** trimesters
- **Degrees** certificates, diplomas, bachelor's, master's, doctoral, post-master's, and postbachelor's certificates
- **Suburban** campus with easy access to Vancouver
- **Endowment** $108.1 million
- **Coed,** 18,188 undergraduate students, 54% full-time, 56% women, 44% men
- **Moderately difficult** entrance level

Undergraduates 9,808 full-time, 8,380 part-time. Students come from 11 provinces and territories, 78 other countries, 7% are from out of state, 5% transferred in, 4% live on campus. *Retention:* 83% of 2002 full-time freshmen returned.
Freshmen *Admission:* 5,538 admitted, 2,692 enrolled. *Average high school GPA:* 3.20.
Faculty *Total:* 663, 1% full-time. *Student/faculty ratio:* 23:1.
Majors Actuarial science; applied mathematics; archeology; art; biochemistry; biological and physical sciences; biology/biological sciences; business administration and management; Canadian studies; chemical physics; chemistry; clinical psychology; cognitive science; communication/speech communication and rhetoric; computer science; criminology; dance; dramatic/theatre arts; economics; education; engineering science; English; environmental science; film/cinema studies; French; general studies; geography; geology/earth science; history; humanities; kinesiology and exercise science; liberal arts and sciences/liberal studies; linguistics; management information systems; management science; mathematics; molecular biochemistry; molecular biology; music; philosophy; physics; political science and government; psychology; social sciences related; sociology; statistics; visual and performing arts related; women's studies.
Academic Programs *Special study options:* adult/continuing education programs, advanced placement credit, cooperative education, distance learning, double majors, honors programs, independent study, off-campus study, part-time degree program, student-designed majors, study abroad, summer session for credit.
Library W. A. C. Bennett Library with 1.3 million titles, 16,331 serial subscriptions, 142,922 audiovisual materials, an OPAC, a Web page.
Computers on Campus 900 computers available on campus for general student use. A campuswide network can be accessed from off campus. Internet access, online (class) registration, at least one staffed computer lab available.
Student Life *Housing options:* coed, women-only, disabled students. Campus housing is university owned. Freshman campus housing is guaranteed. *Activities and organizations:* drama/theater group, student-run newspaper, radio station, The Peak Newspaper, orientation leaders, crisis line, Women's Centre, Simon Fraser Public Interest Research Group. *Campus security:* 24-hour emergency

Simon Fraser University (continued)
response devices and patrols, student patrols, late-night transport/escort service, controlled dormitory access, safe-walk stations, 24-hour safe study area. *Student services:* health clinic, personal/psychological counseling, women's center, legal services.

Athletics Member NAIA. *Intercollegiate sports:* basketball M(s)/W(s), cross-country running M(s)/W(s), field hockey W, football M(s), golf M(s), gymnastics M, soccer M(s)/W(s), softball W(s), swimming M(s)/W(s), track and field M(s)/W(s), volleyball W(s), wrestling M(s). *Intramural sports:* archery M(c)/W(c), badminton M(c)/W(c), basketball M/W, cheerleading M(c)/W(c), crew M(c)/W(c), fencing M(c)/W(c), field hockey W(c), football M/W, golf W(c), gymnastics W(c), ice hockey W(c), lacrosse M(c), rugby M(c)/W(c), soccer M/W, softball M/W, squash M(c)/W(c), table tennis M(c)/W(c), tennis M/W, ultimate Frisbee M(c)/W(c), volleyball M(c)/W(c), water polo M(c)/W(c).

Standardized Tests *Required:* SAT I or ACT (for admission).

Costs (2003–04) *Tuition:* province resident $95 Canadian dollars per credit hour part-time; nonresident $3711 Canadian dollars full-time, $285 Canadian dollars per credit hour part-time; International tuition $13,713 Canadian dollars full-time. Full-time tuition and fees vary according to course level, degree level, and program. Part-time tuition and fees vary according to course level, degree level, and program. *Required fees:* $279 Canadian dollars full-time. *Room only:* $5984 Canadian dollars. Room and board charges vary according to housing facility. *Waivers:* employees or children of employees.

Financial Aid Of all full-time matriculated undergraduates who enrolled in 2001, 363 state and other part-time jobs (averaging $907). *Financial aid deadline:* 11/15.

Applying *Options:* electronic application, early admission. *Application fee:* $35 Canadian dollars. *Required:* high school transcript, minimum 3.2 GPA. *Required for some:* essay or personal statement, letters of recommendation, interview. *Application deadline:* 4/30 (freshmen), rolling (transfers). *Notification:* 6/30 (freshmen), continuous (transfers).

Admissions Contact Mr. Nick Heath, Director of Admissions, Simon Fraser University, 8888 University Drive, Burnaby, BC V5A 1S6, Canada. *Phone:* 604-291-3224. *Fax:* 604-291-4969. *E-mail:* undergraduate-admissions@sfu.ca.

SOUTHERN ALBERTA INSTITUTE OF TECHNOLOGY

Calgary, Alberta, Canada

- **Province-supported** 4-year, founded 1916
- **Calendar** trimesters
- **Degrees** certificates, diplomas, associate, and bachelor's
- **Coed**

Majors Accounting; accounting and finance; aeronautical/aerospace engineering technology; architectural engineering technology; architectural technology; artificial intelligence and robotics; automobile/automotive mechanics technology; avionics maintenance technology; broadcast journalism; business administration and management; business administration, management and operations related; CAD/CADD drafting/design technology; cartography; chemical technology; civil drafting and CAD/CADD; civil engineering technology; clinical/medical laboratory technology; computer engineering technologies related; computer graphics; computer/information technology services administration related; computer software and media applications related; computer systems networking and telecommunications; diagnostic medical sonography and ultrasound technology; electrical and electronic engineering technologies related; electromechanical and instrumentation and maintenance technologies related; emergency care attendant (EMT ambulance); engineering-related technologies; environmental engineering technology; finance; health information/medical records administration; hotel/motel administration; industrial technology; information technology; legal administrative assistant/secretary; library assistant; management information systems; marketing related; mechanical engineering/mechanical technology; medical radiologic technology; nuclear medical technology; petroleum technology; photojournalism; printing management; radio and television; radio, television, and digital communication related; telecommunications technology; tourism and travel services management; transportation and materials moving related; welding technology.

Student Life *Housing options:* Campus housing is university owned.

Applying *Application fee:* $25 Canadian dollars. *Application deadline:* 2/28 (freshmen).

Admissions Contact Ms. Jennifer Bennett, Team Leader, Learner Records, Southern Alberta Institute of Technology, 1301-16 Avenue, NW, Calgary, AB T2N 3W2, Canada. *Phone:* 403-284-7248. *Toll-free phone:* 877-284-SAIT. *Fax:* 403-284-7112. *E-mail:* advising@sait.ca.

STEINBACH BIBLE COLLEGE

Steinbach, Manitoba, Canada

- **Independent Mennonite** 4-year, founded 1936
- **Calendar** semesters
- **Degree** certificates, diplomas, and bachelor's
- **Small-town** 16-acre campus with easy access to Winnipeg
- **Coed,** 118 undergraduate students, 69% full-time, 47% women, 53% men
- **Minimally difficult** entrance level, 83% of applicants were admitted

Undergraduates 82 full-time, 36 part-time.

Freshmen *Admission:* 54 applied, 45 admitted.

Faculty *Total:* 13, 46% full-time, 31% with terminal degrees. *Student/faculty ratio:* 10:1.

Majors Biblical studies; music; religious studies.

Computers on Campus 24 computers available on campus for general student use.

Costs (2004–05) *Comprehensive fee:* $8476 includes full-time tuition ($4480) and room and board ($3996). Part-time tuition: $140 per credit hour. *Required fees:* $97 per year part-time.

Admissions Contact Dr. Terry Hiebert, Registrar, Steinbach Bible College, 50 PTH 12 North, Steinbach, MB RSG 1T4, Canada. *Phone:* 204-326-6451 Ext. 230. *E-mail:* info@sbcollege.mb.ca.

SUMMIT PACIFIC COLLEGE

Abbotsford, British Columbia, Canada

Admissions Contact Ms. Melody Deeley, Registrar, Summit Pacific College, Box 1700, Abbotsford, BC V2S 7E7, Canada. *Phone:* 604-853-7491. *Toll-free phone:* 800-976-8388.

TAYLOR UNIVERSITY COLLEGE AND SEMINARY

Edmonton, Alberta, Canada

Admissions Contact Mrs. Dawn Cunningham Hall, Admissions Counselor, Taylor University College and Seminary, 11525 Twenty-third Avenue, AB T6J 4T3, Canada. *Phone:* 780-431-5200 Ext. 231. *Toll-free phone:* 800-567-4988. *Fax:* 780-436-9416. *E-mail:* nabc@nabcebs.ab.ca.

TÉLÉ-UNIVERSITÉ

Québec, Quebec, Canada

Admissions Contact Ms. Louise Bertrand, Registraire, Télé-université, 455, rue de l'Église, C.P. 4800, succ. Terminus, Québec, QC G1K 9H5, Canada. *Phone:* 418-657-2262 Ext. 5307. *Toll-free phone:* 888-843-4333. *E-mail:* info@teluq.uquebec.ca.

TRENT UNIVERSITY

Peterborough, Ontario, Canada

- **Province-supported** university, founded 1963
- **Calendar** Canadian standard year
- **Degrees** diplomas, bachelor's, master's, and doctoral
- **Suburban** 1400-acre campus with easy access to Toronto
- **Endowment** $19.5 million
- **Coed,** 7,119 undergraduate students, 82% full-time, 67% women, 33% men
- **Moderately difficult** entrance level

Undergraduates 5,850 full-time, 1,269 part-time. Students come from 21 provinces and territories, 106 other countries. *Retention:* 84% of 2003 full-time freshmen returned.

Freshmen *Admission:* 2,333 enrolled. *Average high school GPA:* 3.06.

Faculty *Total:* 357, 71% full-time, 81% with terminal degrees. *Student/faculty ratio:* 20:1.

Majors American Indian/Native American studies; anthropology; applied mathematics; biochemistry; biological and physical sciences; biology/biological sciences; business administration and management; Canadian studies; chemistry; classics and languages, literatures and linguistics; computer science; economics; education; elementary education; English; environmental studies; French; geography; German; Hispanic-American, Puerto Rican, and Mexican-American/Chicano studies; history; humanities; interdisciplinary studies; international relations and affairs; Latin; liberal arts and sciences/liberal studies; literature; mathematics; modern Greek; modern languages; natural sciences; nursing (registered nurse training); philosophy; physical sciences; physics; political science and government; psychology; secondary education; social sciences; sociology; Spanish; women's studies.

Academic Programs *Special study options:* academic remediation for entering students, accelerated degree program, adult/continuing education programs, advanced placement credit, double majors, honors programs, off-campus study, part-time degree program, services for LD students, student-designed majors, study abroad, summer session for credit.

Library Thomas J. Bata Library plus 2 others with 579,557 titles, 2,312 serial subscriptions, an OPAC, a Web page.

Computers on Campus 250 computers available on campus for general student use. A campuswide network can be accessed from student residence rooms and from off campus. Internet access, at least one staffed computer lab available.

Student Life *Housing options:* coed, women-only. *Activities and organizations:* drama/theater group, student-run newspaper, radio station, choral group, Trent Radio, Trent International Program, Trent Central Student Association, Arthur (student newspaper), Excalibur (yearbook). *Campus security:* 24-hour emergency response devices and patrols, student patrols, late-night transport/escort service. *Student services:* health clinic, personal/psychological counseling, women's center.

Athletics Member CIS. *Intercollegiate sports:* basketball M(c)/W(c), crew M/W, cross-country running M/W, fencing M/W, field hockey W, golf M/W, rugby M/W, skiing (cross-country) M/W, soccer M/W, squash M/W, swimming M/W, volleyball M(c)/W(c). *Intramural sports:* badminton M/W, basketball M/W, cross-country running M/W, football M/W, ice hockey M/W, soccer M/W, softball M/W, squash M/W, swimming M/W, tennis M/W, track and field M/W, volleyball M/W, water polo M/W.

Standardized Tests *Required for some:* SAT I or ACT (for admission).

Costs (2003–04) *Tuition:* area resident $4184 full-time, $837 per course part-time; International tuition $10,936 full-time. Part-time tuition and fees vary according to course load. *Required fees:* $579 full-time, $83 per course part-time. *Room and board:* $6620. Room and board charges vary according to board plan and housing facility. *Payment plan:* installment. *Waivers:* senior citizens and employees or children of employees.

Applying *Options:* deferred entrance. *Application fee:* $95 Canadian dollars. *Required:* high school transcript, minimum 2.8 GPA. *Required for some:* essay or personal statement, letters of recommendation, interview. *Application deadlines:* 6/1 (freshmen), 6/1 (transfers).

Admissions Contact Mrs. Carol Murray, Admissions Officer, Trent University, Office of the Registrar, Peterborough, ON K9J 7B8, Canada. *Phone:* 705-748-1215. *Fax:* 705-748-1629. *E-mail:* leaders@trentu.ca.

■ *See page 2518 for a narrative description.*

TRINITY WESTERN UNIVERSITY

Langley, British Columbia, Canada

- **Independent** comprehensive, founded 1962, affiliated with Evangelical Free Church of America
- **Calendar** semesters
- **Degrees** certificates, bachelor's, master's, and doctoral
- **Suburban** 150-acre campus with easy access to Vancouver
- **Endowment** $4.5 million
- **Coed,** 2,950 undergraduate students
- **Moderately difficult** entrance level, 77% of applicants were admitted

Undergraduates Students come from 10 provinces and territories, 29 other countries, 33% are from out of state, 40% live on campus. *Retention:* 79% of 2002 full-time freshmen returned.

Freshmen *Admission:* 1,759 applied, 1,346 admitted. *Average high school GPA:* 3.27.

Faculty *Total:* 138, 56% full-time, 61% with terminal degrees. *Student/faculty ratio:* 18:1.

Majors Airline pilot and flight crew; applied mathematics; biblical studies; biological and physical sciences; biology/biological sciences; business administration and management; chemistry; communication/speech communication and rhetoric; computer science; divinity/ministry; dramatic/theatre arts; education; elementary education; English; environmental biology; environmental science; environmental studies; general studies; geography; health and physical education; history; humanities; human services; international relations and affairs; liberal arts and sciences/liberal studies; linguistics; mathematics; mathematics and computer science; missionary studies and missiology; music; natural sciences; nursing (registered nurse training); philosophy; physical education teaching and coaching; political science and government; pre-dentistry studies; pre-law studies; pre-medical studies; pre-veterinary studies; psychology; religious studies; secondary education; social sciences; visual and performing arts.

Academic Programs *Special study options:* advanced placement credit, cooperative education, distance learning, double majors, English as a second language, honors programs, independent study, internships, off-campus study, part-time degree program, study abroad, summer session for credit.

Library Norma Marion Alloway Library with 190,565 titles, 11,000 serial subscriptions, 2,974 audiovisual materials, an OPAC, a Web page.

Computers on Campus 50 computers available on campus for general student use. A campuswide network can be accessed from student residence rooms and from off campus. Internet access, at least one staffed computer lab available.

Student Life *Housing:* on-campus residence required through sophomore year. *Options:* coed, men-only, women-only, disabled students. Campus housing is university owned. Freshman applicants given priority for college housing. *Activities and organizations:* drama/theater group, student-run newspaper, choral group, Campus Ministries, choir, student newspaper, discipleship program. *Campus security:* 24-hour emergency response devices and patrols, late-night transport/escort service, controlled dormitory access. *Student services:* health clinic, personal/psychological counseling.

Athletics Member CIS. *Intercollegiate sports:* basketball M(s)/W(s), soccer M(s)/W(s), volleyball M(s)/W(s). *Intramural sports:* badminton M/W, basketball M/W, ice hockey M, soccer M/W, softball M/W, table tennis M/W, tennis M/W, volleyball M/W.

Standardized Tests *Required for some:* SAT I or ACT (for admission).

Costs (2004–05) *Comprehensive fee:* $21,100 Canadian dollars includes full-time tuition ($13,500 Canadian dollars), mandatory fees ($200 Canadian dollars), and room and board ($7400 Canadian dollars). Full-time tuition and fees vary according to course level and program. *Part-time tuition:* $450 Canadian dollars per semester hour. Part-time tuition and fees vary according to course level and program. *Required fees:* $50 Canadian dollars per term part-time. *Room and board:* Room and board charges vary according to board plan, housing facility, and student level. *Payment plan:* installment. *Waivers:* employees or children of employees.

Applying *Options:* common application, electronic application, deferred entrance. *Application fee:* $35. *Required:* essay or personal statement, high school transcript, minimum 2.5 GPA, 2 letters of recommendation, community standards document. *Required for some:* interview. *Application deadlines:* 6/15 (freshmen), 6/15 (transfers). *Notification:* continuous (freshmen), continuous (transfers).

Admissions Contact Mr. Jeff Suderman, Executive Director of Admissions, Trinity Western University, 7600 Glover Road, Langley, BC V2Y 1Y1, Canada. *Phone:* 604-888-7511 Ext. 3004. *Toll-free phone:* 888-468-6898. *Fax:* 604-513-2064. *E-mail:* admissions@twu.ca.

TYNDALE UNIVERSITY COLLEGE & SEMINARY

Toronto, Ontario, Canada

- **Independent interdenominational** comprehensive, founded 1894
- **Calendar** semesters
- **Degrees** bachelor's, master's, and first professional
- **Urban** 10-acre campus
- **Endowment** $2.0 million
- **Coed,** 503 undergraduate students, 72% full-time, 46% women, 54% men
- **Moderately difficult** entrance level, 60% of applicants were admitted

Undergraduates 363 full-time, 140 part-time. Students come from 7 provinces and territories, 12 other countries, 30% live on campus. *Retention:* 49% of 2002 full-time freshmen returned.

Freshmen *Admission:* 357 applied, 215 admitted, 198 enrolled.

Faculty *Total:* 48, 48% full-time, 92% with terminal degrees. *Student/faculty ratio:* 10:1.

Majors Biblical studies; business/commerce; divinity/ministry; English; history; hospitality and recreation marketing; human services; liberal arts and sciences/liberal studies; parks, recreation and leisure; pastoral studies/counseling; philosophy; psychology; religious education.

Academic Programs *Special study options:* academic remediation for entering students, accelerated degree program, adult/continuing education programs, honors programs, off-campus study, part-time degree program, summer session for credit.

Library J. William Horsey Library with 65,013 titles, 410 serial subscriptions, an OPAC.

Computers on Campus 10 computers available on campus for general student use. A campuswide network can be accessed. Internet access, at least one staffed computer lab available.

Student Life *Housing options:* coed. Campus housing is university owned. Freshman applicants given priority for college housing. *Activities and organizations:* drama/theater group, student-run newspaper, choral group, choir, student government, Urban Ministry Team, """Steadfast" drama team. *Campus security:*

Tyndale University College & Seminary (continued)
student patrols, late-night transport/escort service, controlled dormitory access. *Student services:* personal/psychological counseling.

Athletics *Intercollegiate sports:* basketball M/W, ice hockey M, volleyball M/W. *Intramural sports:* badminton M(c)/W(c), basketball M(c), football M, golf M, skiing (cross-country) M(c)/W(c), skiing (downhill) M(c)/W(c), soccer M(c)/W(c), softball M/W, swimming M(c)/W(c), volleyball W, weight lifting M(c)/W(c).

Costs (2004–05) *Comprehensive fee:* $12,200 Canadian dollars includes full-time tuition ($8100 Canadian dollars) and room and board ($4100 Canadian dollars). Full-time tuition and fees vary according to course load. Part-time tuition: $265 Canadian dollars per credit hour. Part-time tuition and fees vary according to course load. *Required fees:* $25 Canadian dollars per credit hour part-time. *Payment plan:* installment. *Waivers:* employees or children of employees.

Applying *Options:* deferred entrance. *Application fee:* $50 Canadian dollars. *Required:* essay or personal statement, high school transcript, 2 letters of recommendation, all post-secondary transcripts. *Required for some:* interview. *Application deadlines:* 8/15 (freshmen), 8/15 (transfers). *Notification:* 9/19 (freshmen), 9/19 (transfers).

Admissions Contact Ms. Kathleen Steadman, Assistant Registrar, Tyndale University College & Seminary, 25 Ballyconnor Court, Toronto, ON M2M 4B3, Canada. *Phone:* 416-226-6620 Ext. 6738. *Toll-free phone:* 800-663-6052. *E-mail:* enroll@tyndale.ca.

Université de Moncton
Moncton, New Brunswick, Canada

Admissions Contact Miss Nicole Savois, Chief Admission Officer, Université de Moncton, Moncton, NB E1A 3E9, Canada. *Phone:* 506-858-4115. *Toll-free phone:* 800-363-8336. *Fax:* 506-858-4544. *E-mail:* registrariat@umoncton.ca.

Université de Montréal
Montréal, Quebec, Canada

- **Independent** university, founded 1920
- **Calendar** trimesters
- **Degrees** certificates, bachelor's, master's, and doctoral
- **Urban** 150-acre campus
- **Coed,** 40,128 undergraduate students, 66% full-time, 61% women, 39% men
- **Moderately difficult** entrance level

Undergraduates 26,574 full-time, 13,554 part-time. *Retention:* 83% of 2002 full-time freshmen returned.

Majors Actuarial science; anthropology; applied mathematics; archeology; architecture; art; art history, criticism and conservation; Asian studies (East); audiology and speech-language pathology; biblical studies; biochemistry; biology/biological sciences; biomedical sciences; chemical engineering; chemistry; classics and languages, literatures and linguistics; computer science; criminology; developmental and child psychology; ecology; economics; education; elementary education; English; film/cinema studies; foods, nutrition, and wellness; French; geography; geology/earth science; German; Hispanic-American, Puerto Rican, and Mexican-American/Chicano studies; history; human resources management; industrial design; interdisciplinary studies; jazz/jazz studies; kindergarten/preschool education; labor and industrial relations; landscape architecture; legal studies; linguistics; literature; mass communication/media; mathematics; medical microbiology and bacteriology; modern languages; music; nursing (registered nurse training); occupational therapy; operations research; ophthalmic/optometric services; pharmacy; philosophy; physical education teaching and coaching; physical therapy; physics; political science and government; pre-dentistry studies; pre-medical studies; psychology; rehabilitation therapy; religious studies; secondary education; social sciences; social work; sociology; Spanish; special education; statistics; theology; urban studies/affairs; veterinary sciences.

Academic Programs *Special study options:* accelerated degree program, adult/continuing education programs, distance learning, English as a second language, internships, off-campus study, part-time degree program, summer session for credit.

Library Main Library plus 18 others with 15,300 serial subscriptions, 164,079 audiovisual materials, an OPAC, a Web page.

Computers on Campus 600 computers available on campus for general student use. A campuswide network can be accessed from student residence rooms and from off campus. Internet access, at least one staffed computer lab available.

Student Life *Housing options:* coed. *Activities and organizations:* drama/theater group, student-run newspaper, radio station, choral group, Federation des Associations Etudiantes du Campus. *Campus security:* 24-hour emergency response devices and patrols, student patrols, late-night transport/escort service, controlled dormitory access, cameras, alarm systems, crime prevention programs. *Student services:* health clinic, personal/psychological counseling, legal services.

Athletics Member CIS. *Intercollegiate sports:* badminton M/W, skiing (downhill) M/W, soccer M/W, swimming M/W, volleyball M/W. *Intramural sports:* archery M/W, badminton M/W, basketball M/W, fencing M/W, golf M/W, gymnastics M/W, ice hockey M/W, racquetball M/W, soccer M/W, squash M/W, swimming M/W, table tennis M/W, tennis M/W, volleyball M/W, water polo M/W.

Financial Aid Of all full-time matriculated undergraduates who enrolled in 2001, 400 state and other part-time jobs. *Financial aid deadline:* 3/1.

Applying *Options:* common application. *Application fee:* $30 Canadian dollars. *Required:* Diploma of Collegiate Studies (and transcript) or equivalent. *Required for some:* interview. *Application deadlines:* 3/1 (freshmen), 3/1 (transfers). *Notification:* 5/15 (freshmen), 5/15 (transfers).

Admissions Contact Mr. Fernand Boucher, Registrar, Université de Montréal, Case postale 6205, Succursale Centre-ville, 2332 boul. Èdouard-Gontprtit, Montréal, QC H3C 3T5, Canada. *Phone:* 514-343-7076. *Fax:* 514-343-2097. *E-mail:* fernand.boucher@umontreal.ca.

Université de Sherbrooke
Sherbrooke, Quebec, Canada

- **Independent** university, founded 1954
- **Calendar** Canadian standard year
- **Degrees** certificates, diplomas, bachelor's, master's, doctoral, and first professional
- **Urban** 800-acre campus with easy access to Montreal
- **Coed,** 13,108 undergraduate students, 71% full-time, 55% women, 45% men
- **Moderately difficult** entrance level, 73% of applicants were admitted

Undergraduates 9,301 full-time, 3,807 part-time. Students come from 3 provinces and territories, 62 other countries.

Freshmen *Admission:* 7,820 applied, 5,713 admitted, 2,308 enrolled.

Faculty *Total:* 2,837, 36% full-time.

Majors Accounting; adult and continuing education; applied mathematics; athletic training; biochemistry; biology/biological sciences; biology/biotechnology laboratory technician; biotechnology; business administration and management; chemical engineering; chemistry; civil engineering; communication and journalism related; communication and media related; computer and information sciences; computer and information sciences related; computer engineering; computer management; computer programming; computer science; counselor education/school counseling and guidance; digital communication and media/multimedia; ecology; economics; education; electrical, electronics and communications engineering; elementary education; engineering; English; finance; French; geography; geophysics and seismology; history; information science/studies; information technology; interdisciplinary studies; kindergarten/preschool education; kinesiology and exercise science; kinesiotherapy; legal studies; liberal arts and sciences/liberal studies; management information systems; marketing/marketing management; mass communication/media; mathematics; mechanical engineering; medical microbiology and bacteriology; music; nursing (registered nurse training); operations research; philosophy; physical education teaching and coaching; physics; pre-medical studies; psychology; secondary education; social work; special education; theology.

Academic Programs *Special study options:* accelerated degree program, adult/continuing education programs, cooperative education, English as a second language, internships, off-campus study, part-time degree program, services for LD students, student-designed majors, study abroad, summer session for credit.

Library Bibliothéque Generale plus 3 others with 1.2 million titles, 5,937 serial subscriptions, an OPAC, a Web page.

Computers on Campus 300 computers available on campus for general student use. A campuswide network can be accessed from student residence rooms and from off campus. Internet access, at least one staffed computer lab available.

Student Life *Housing options:* coed. *Activities and organizations:* drama/theater group, student-run newspaper, radio station. *Campus security:* 24-hour emergency response devices and patrols. *Student services:* health clinic, personal/psychological counseling, legal services.

Athletics Member CIS. *Intercollegiate sports:* badminton M/W, cross-country running M(s)/W(s), football M(s), skiing (cross-country) M/W, soccer M(s)/W(s), swimming M(s)/W(s), track and field M(s)/W(s), volleyball M(s)/W(s). *Intramural sports:* badminton M/W, basketball M/W, cheerleading M/W, cross-country running M/W, ice hockey M, racquetball M/W, skiing (cross-country) M/W, skiing (downhill) M/W, soccer M/W, softball M/W, squash M/W, swimming M/W, tennis M/W, track and field M/W, ultimate Frisbee M/W, volleyball M/W.

Costs (2003–04) *Comprehensive fee:* $8159 Canadian dollars includes full-time tuition ($4173 Canadian dollars), mandatory fees ($226 Canadian dollars), and room and board ($3760 Canadian dollars). International tuition: $10,764

Canadian dollars full-time. *College room only:* $2000 Canadian dollars. Room and board charges vary according to board plan, housing facility, and student level.

Financial Aid Of all full-time matriculated undergraduates who enrolled in 2001, 332 state and other part-time jobs. *Financial aid deadline:* 3/31.

Applying *Options:* electronic application, early admission. *Application fee:* $30 Canadian dollars. *Required:* high school transcript. *Required for some:* letters of recommendation, interview. *Application deadline:* 3/1 (freshmen). *Notification:* continuous until 5/15 (freshmen).

Admissions Contact Ms. Lisa Bedard, Admissions Officer, Université de Sherbrooke, 2500, Boulevard de l'Université, Sherbrooke, QC J1K 2R1, Canada. *Phone:* 819-821-7687. *Toll-free phone:* 800-267-UDES. *E-mail:* information@usherbrooke.ca.

Université du Québec à Chicoutimi

Chicoutimi, Quebec, Canada

Admissions Contact Mr. Claudio Zoccastello, Admissions Officer, Université du Québec à Chicoutimi, 555, boulevard de L'Université, Chicoutimi, QC G7H 2B1, Canada. *Phone:* 418-545-5005. *E-mail:* czoccast@uqac.uquebec.ca.

Université du Québec à Montréal

Montréal, Quebec, Canada

Admissions Contact Ms. Lucille Boisselle-Roy, Admissions Officer, Université du Québec à Montréal, CP 8888, Succursale Centre-ville, Montréal, QC H2L 4S8, Canada. *Phone:* 514-987-3132. *Fax:* 514-987-7728. *E-mail:* admission@uqam.ca.

Université du Québec à Rimouski

Rimouski, Quebec, Canada

Admissions Contact Mr. Conrad Lavoie, Admissions Officer, Université du Québec à Rimouski, 300, Allee des Ursulines, CP 3300, Rimouski, QC G5L 3A1, Canada. *Phone:* 418-724-1433. *E-mail:* raymond_cote@uqar.uquebec.ca.

Université du Québec à Trois-Rivières

Trois-Rivières, Quebec, Canada

- **Province-supported** university, founded 1969, part of Université du Québec
- **Calendar** trimesters
- **Degrees** certificates, bachelor's, master's, and doctoral
- **Urban** campus with easy access to Montreal
- **Endowment** $3.3 million
- **Coed**
- **Noncompetitive** entrance level

Student Life *Campus security:* 24-hour emergency response devices and patrols, late-night transport/escort service, controlled dormitory access.

Athletics Member CIS.

Applying *Application fee:* $30 Canadian dollars. *Required:* Diploma of Collegiate Studies (and transcript) or equivalent. *Required for some:* interview.

Admissions Contact Mrs. Suzanne Camirand, Admissions Officer, Université du Québec à Trois-Rivières, Bureau du registraire, Service des admissions, 3350 Boulevard Des Forges, Trois Rivieres, QC G9A 5H7, Canada. *Phone:* 819-376-5045. *Toll-free phone:* 800-365-0922. *Fax:* 819-376-5210. *E-mail:* registraire@uqtr.uquebec.ca.

Université du Québec, École de Technologie Supérieure

Montréal, Quebec, Canada

- **Province-supported** comprehensive, founded 1974, part of Université du Québec
- **Calendar** trimesters
- **Degrees** bachelor's, master's, and doctoral
- **Urban** campus
- **Coed, primarily men**
- **Noncompetitive** entrance level

Costs (2003–04) *Tuition:* province resident $2787 Canadian dollars full-time; International tuition $17,700 Canadian dollars full-time. *Room and board:* $9000 Canadian dollars; room only: $5400 Canadian dollars.

Applying *Application fee:* $30 Canadian dollars. *Required:* Diploma of Collegiate Studies (and transcript) or equivalent.

Admissions Contact Mme. Francine Gamache, Registraire, Université du Québec, École de Technologie Supérieure, 1100, rue Notre Dame Ouest, Montréal, QC H3C 1K3, Canada. *Phone:* 514-396-8885. *E-mail:* admission@ets.mtl.ca.

Université du Québec en Abitibi-Témiscamingue

Rouyn-Noranda, Quebec, Canada

Admissions Contact Mrs. Monique Fay, Admissions Officer, Université du Québec en Abitibi-Témiscamingue, 445 boulevard de l'Université, Rouyn-Noranda, QC J9X 5E4, Canada. *Phone:* 819-762-0971. *Fax:* 819-797-4727. *E-mail:* micheline.chevalier@uqat.uquebec.ca.

Université du Québec en Outaouais

Gatineau, Quebec, Canada

- **Province-supported** comprehensive, founded 1981, part of Université du Québec
- **Calendar** trimesters
- **Degrees** certificates, bachelor's, master's, and doctoral
- **Small-town** campus with easy access to Ottawa
- **Coed**
- **Noncompetitive** entrance level

Undergraduates Students come from 42 other countries. *Retention:* 90% of 2002 full-time freshmen returned.

Majors Accounting; art; business administration and management; computer engineering; computer science; design and visual communications; education; elementary education; fine/studio arts; human resources management and services related; international business/trade/commerce; kindergarten/preschool education; labor and industrial relations; language interpretation and translation; management information systems; nursing (registered nurse training); psychology; secondary education; social sciences; social work; sociology; special education.

Academic Programs *Special study options:* accelerated degree program, adult/continuing education programs, internships, off-campus study, part-time degree program, services for LD students, study abroad, summer session for credit.

Library Brault Library plus 2 others with 169,289 titles, 4,458 serial subscriptions, an OPAC, a Web page.

Computers on Campus 120 computers available on campus for general student use. A campuswide network can be accessed from off campus. Internet access, at least one staffed computer lab available. Computer purchase or lease plan available.

Student Life *Housing:* on-campus residence required through senior year. *Options:* coed. Campus housing is university owned. *Activities and organizations:* student-run newspaper, AGE, AIESEC, AEME, REMAA. *Campus security:* 24-hour emergency response devices and patrols, late-night transport/escort service. *Student services:* health clinic.

Athletics *Intramural sports:* badminton M/W, baseball M/W, basketball M/W, ice hockey M, skiing (downhill) M/W, soccer M/W, swimming M/W, table tennis M/W, tennis M/W, volleyball M/W, water polo M/W.

Costs (2003–04) *Tuition:* International tuition $11,739 Canadian dollars full-time. *Required fees:* $1867 Canadian dollars full-time. *Room only:* $375 Canadian dollars.

Applying *Required:* high school transcript, Diploma of Collegiate Studies (and transcript) or equivalent. *Required for some:* interview. *Application deadline:* 3/1 (freshmen). *Notification:* 5/15 (freshmen).

Admissions Contact Ms. Line Blais, Admissions Officer, Université du Québec en Outaouais, CP 1250, Station Hull, 101, rue Saint-Jean-Bosco, bureau B-0150, Gatineau, QC J8X 3X7, Canada. *Phone:* 819-595-3900 Ext. 1841. *Fax:* 819-773-1835. *E-mail:* line.blais@uqo.ca.

Université Laval

Québec, Quebec, Canada

- **Independent** university, founded 1852
- **Calendar** trimesters
- **Degrees** certificates, diplomas, associate, bachelor's, master's, doctoral, first professional, postbachelor's, and first professional certificates
- **Urban** 465-acre campus with easy access to Quebec City
- **Endowment** $503.8 million
- **Coed,** 26,419 undergraduate students, 66% full-time, 59% women, 41% men
- **Minimally difficult** entrance level, 64% of applicants were admitted

Université Laval (continued)

Undergraduates 17,481 full-time, 8,938 part-time. Students come from 7 provinces and territories, 86 other countries, 2% are from out of state, 3% transferred in, 7% live on campus. *Retention:* 77% of 2002 full-time freshmen returned.

Freshmen *Admission:* 21,290 applied, 13,700 admitted, 4,150 enrolled.

Faculty *Total:* 1,453, 98% full-time, 88% with terminal degrees. *Student/faculty ratio:* 15:1.

Majors Actuarial science; agricultural economics; agronomy and crop science; anthropology; archeology; architecture; art history, criticism and conservation; art teacher education; biochemistry; biology/biological sciences; business administration and management; chemical engineering; chemistry; civil engineering; classics and classical languages related; commercial and advertising art; computer engineering; computer science; computer software engineering; consumer services and advocacy; counselor education/school counseling and guidance; dramatic/theatre arts; econometrics and quantitative economics; economics; electrical, electronics and communications engineering; elementary education; engineering physics; engineering related; English; English as a second/foreign language (teaching); environmental/environmental health engineering; environmental studies; fine/studio arts; folklore; food science; foods, nutrition, and wellness; forest/forest resources management; forestry related; French; French as a second/foreign language (teaching); French language teacher education; geography; geography teacher education; geological/geophysical engineering; geology/earth science; history; history teacher education; insurance; interdisciplinary studies; jazz/jazz studies; kindergarten/preschool education; kinesiology and exercise science; labor and industrial relations; language interpretation and translation; legal studies; linguistics; literature; mass communication/media; mathematics; mathematics and computer science; mathematics teacher education; mechanical engineering; medical microbiology and bacteriology; metallurgical engineering; mining and mineral engineering; modern languages; multi-/interdisciplinary studies related; music; music teacher education; nursing (registered nurse training); nutrition sciences; occupational therapy; pharmacy; pharmacy, pharmaceutical sciences, and administration related; philosophy; physical education teaching and coaching; physical therapy; physics; political science and government; pre-dentistry studies; pre-law studies; pre-medical studies; pre-pharmacy studies; psychology; rabbinical studies; science teacher education; secondary education; social work; sociology; Spanish; statistics; survey technology; technical teacher education; theology; urban forestry; wood science and wood products/pulp and paper technology.

Academic Programs *Special study options:* academic remediation for entering students, accelerated degree program, adult/continuing education programs, cooperative education, distance learning, English as a second language, honors programs, internships, off-campus study, part-time degree program, services for LD students, student-designed majors, study abroad, summer session for credit.

Library Bibliothèque Générale plus 1 other with 2.8 million titles, 13,928 serial subscriptions, 20,094 audiovisual materials, an OPAC, a Web page.

Computers on Campus 2200 computers available on campus for general student use. A campuswide network can be accessed from student residence rooms and from off campus. Internet access, online (class) registration, at least one staffed computer lab available. Computer purchase or lease plan available.

Student Life *Housing options:* coed, men-only, women-only, disabled students. Campus housing is university owned. *Activities and organizations:* drama/theater group, student-run newspaper, radio station, choral group, drama club, Improvisation Ligue, Création Littéraire, Chorale de L'université Laval, Amnistie Internationale, national fraternities. *Campus security:* 24-hour emergency response devices and patrols, student patrols, late-night transport/escort service, controlled dormitory access, video cameras in most buildings, underground walkways. *Student services:* health clinic, personal/psychological counseling.

Athletics Member CIS. *Intercollegiate sports:* badminton M(s)/W(s), baseball M(s), basketball M(s)/W(s), cross-country running M(s)/W(s), football M(s), golf M(s)/W, gymnastics M(s)/W(s), skiing (downhill) M(s)/W(s), soccer M(s)/W(s), swimming M(s)/W(s), track and field M(s)/W(s), volleyball M(s)/W(s). *Intramural sports:* badminton M/W, baseball M, basketball M/W, cross-country running M/W, fencing M/W, field hockey M/W, football M, golf M/W, gymnastics M/W, ice hockey M/W, racquetball M/W, skiing (cross-country) M/W, skiing (downhill) M/W, soccer M/W, softball M/W, squash M/W, swimming M/W, tennis M/W, track and field M/W, volleyball M/W, water polo M/W, weight lifting M/W.

Costs (2004–05) *Tuition:* province resident $2016 Canadian dollars full-time, $69 Canadian dollars per credit part-time; nonresident $4521 Canadian dollars full-time, $152 Canadian dollars per credit part-time; International tuition $10,866 Canadian dollars full-time. Full-time tuition and fees vary according to program and reciprocity agreements. Part-time tuition and fees vary according to program. *Required fees:* $905 Canadian dollars full-time. *Room and board:* $9000 Canadian dollars; room only: $2664 Canadian dollars. *Waivers:* employees or children of employees.

Applying *Options:* common application, electronic application. *Application fee:* $30 Canadian dollars. *Required:* high school transcript, general knowledge of French language. *Required for some:* essay or personal statement, interview. *Application deadlines:* 3/1 (freshmen), 5/1 (transfers).

Admissions Contact Mrs. Sylvie Brillon, Director of Information and Promotion Office, Université Laval, Bureau Du Secrètaire Gènèral, Pavilion J.C. Bonenfant, Quèbec, QC G1K 7P4, Canada. *Phone:* 877-785-2825. *Toll-free phone:* 877-785-2825. *Fax:* 418-656-5216. *E-mail:* marie-josee.dufour@sg.ulaval.ca.

■ *See page 2556 for a narrative description.*

UNIVERSITÉ SAINTE-ANNE
Church Point, Nova Scotia, Canada

Admissions Contact Mrs. Blanche Thériault, Admissions Officer, Université Sainte-Anne, Church Point, NS B0W 1M0. *Phone:* 902-769-2114 Ext. 116. *Fax:* 902-769-2930. *E-mail:* admission@ustanne.ednet.ns.ca.

UNIVERSITY COLLEGE OF CAPE BRETON
Sydney, Nova Scotia, Canada

Admissions Contact Ms. Cheryl Livingstone, Admissions Officer, University College of Cape Breton, PO Box 5300, Sydney, NS B1P 6L2, Canada. *Phone:* 902-563-1166. *Toll-free phone:* 888-959-9995. *Fax:* 902-563-1371. *E-mail:* admissions@uccb.ns.ca.

UNIVERSITY COLLEGE OF THE CARIBOO
Kamloops, British Columbia, Canada

- **Province-supported** 4-year, founded 1970
- **Calendar** semesters
- **Degrees** certificates, diplomas, associate, bachelor's, master's, and postbachelor's certificates
- **Small-town** 100-acre campus
- **Endowment** $6.7 million
- **Coed,** 4,886 undergraduate students, 77% full-time, 61% women, 39% men
- 54% of applicants were admitted

Undergraduates 3,776 full-time, 1,110 part-time. Students come from 10 provinces and territories, 48 other countries, 7% are from out of state, 9% live on campus.

Freshmen *Admission:* 2,450 applied, 1,320 admitted.

Faculty *Total:* 590, 75% full-time. *Student/faculty ratio:* 13:1.

Majors Accounting; anesthesiologist assistant; animal/livestock husbandry and production; animal sciences; biochemistry; biology/biological sciences; business administration and management; business/commerce; Canadian studies; cardiovascular technology; carpentry; cell and molecular biology; cell biology and histology; chemistry; child care and support services management; communications systems installation and repair technology; computer and information sciences; computer engineering related; computer graphics; computer installation and repair technology; computer programming; computer science; computer systems analysis; computer technology/computer systems technology; desktop publishing and digital imaging design; drafting and design technology; dramatic/theatre arts; dramatic/theatre arts and stagecraft related; early childhood education; ecology; economics; electrical, electronics and communications engineering; electrical/electronics equipment installation and repair; electrician; elementary education; engineering; English; environmental biology; executive assistant/executive secretary; finance; fine/studio arts; geography; graphic design; health services/allied health/health sciences; history; hospitality administration; hospitality administration related; hospitality and recreation marketing; hotel/motel administration; human resources management; human resources management and services related; industrial electronics technology; journalism; manufacturing technology; marketing/marketing management; mathematics; molecular biology; natural resources/conservation; nursing (licensed practical/vocational nurse training); nursing (registered nurse training); nursing science; office management; perfusion technology; physics; pipefitting and sprinkler fitting; plumbing technology; political science and government; pre-dentistry studies; pre-medical studies; pre-pharmacy studies; pre-veterinary studies; psychology; public relations, advertising, and applied communication related; resort management; respiratory care therapy; respiratory therapy technician; sales, distribution and marketing; social sciences; social work; sociology; sport and fitness administration; system administration; system, networking, and LAN/wan management; tourism promotion; tourism/travel marketing; veterinary/animal health technology; visual and performing arts; visual and performing arts related; web page, digital/multimedia and information resources design; zoology/animal biology related.

Academic Programs *Special study options:* adult/continuing education programs, advanced placement credit, cooperative education, distance learning, double majors, English as a second language, honors programs, independent study, internships, off-campus study, part-time degree program, services for LD students, study abroad, summer session for credit.

Library University College of the Cariboo Library with 223,300 titles, 920 serial subscriptions, 10,300 audiovisual materials, an OPAC, a Web page.

Computers on Campus 300 computers available on campus for general student use. A campuswide network can be accessed from student residence rooms and from off campus that provide access to Web CT. Internet access, online (class) registration, at least one staffed computer lab available.

Student Life *Housing:* college housing not available. *Options:* coed. Campus housing is provided by a third party. *Activities and organizations:* student-run newspaper, radio station, choral group. *Campus security:* 24-hour emergency response devices and patrols, student patrols, late-night transport/escort service. *Student services:* health clinic, personal/psychological counseling.

Athletics Member CIS. *Intercollegiate sports:* badminton M(s)/W(s), baseball M, basketball M(s)/W(s), soccer M(s)/W(s), volleyball M(s)/W(s). *Intramural sports:* crew M/W, cross-country running M/W, football M, ice hockey M, racquetball M/W, rugby M, skiing (cross-country) M/W, skiing (downhill) M/W, softball M/W, squash M/W, swimming M/W, table tennis M/W, track and field M/W.

Costs (2003–04) *Tuition:* province resident $104 Canadian dollars per credit part-time; nonresident $3120 Canadian dollars full-time, $104 Canadian dollars per credit part-time; International tuition $10,500 Canadian dollars full-time. *Required fees:* $500 Canadian dollars full-time, $12 Canadian dollars per credit part-time. *Room only:* $2600 Canadian dollars. *Payment plan:* installment.

Applying *Options:* electronic application. *Application fee:* $25 Canadian dollars. *Required:* high school transcript. *Required for some:* letters of recommendation, interview. *Application deadlines:* 3/1 (freshmen), 3/1 (transfers). *Notification:* continuous until 3/1 (freshmen).

Admissions Contact Mr. Josh Keller, Director, Public Relations and Student Recruitment, University College of the Cariboo, PO Box 3010, 900 McGill Road, Kamloops, BC V2C 5N3, Canada. *Phone:* 250-828-5008. *Toll-free phone:* 250-828-5071. *Fax:* 250-828-5159. *E-mail:* jkeller@cariboo.bc.ca.

UNIVERSITY COLLEGE OF THE FRASER VALLEY

Abbotsford, British Columbia, Canada

- **Province-supported** 4-year, founded 1974, part of B.C. provincial education
- **Calendar** semesters
- **Degrees** certificates, diplomas, associate, and bachelor's
- **Urban** campus with easy access to Vancouver
- **Endowment** $1.1 million
- **Coed,** 5,987 undergraduate students, 39% full-time, 60% women, 40% men

Undergraduates 2,331 full-time, 3,656 part-time.

Faculty *Total:* 322, 83% full-time, 15% with terminal degrees. *Student/faculty ratio:* 13:1.

Majors Adult and continuing education; adult and continuing education administration; anthropology; aviation/airway management; biology/biological sciences; business administration and management; chemistry; child care and support services management; computer and information sciences; computer systems analysis; criminal justice/safety; dramatic/theatre arts; English; geography; history; interdisciplinary studies; Latin American studies; mass communication/media; mathematics; nursing (registered nurse training); physical education teaching and coaching; physics; psychology; social work; sociology; statistics.

Academic Programs *Special study options:* academic remediation for entering students, adult/continuing education programs, advanced placement credit, cooperative education, distance learning, double majors, English as a second language, independent study, internships, part-time degree program, services for LD students, summer session for credit.

Library Peter Jones Library plus 3 others with an OPAC, a Web page.

Computers on Campus 850 computers available on campus for general student use. Internet access, at least one staffed computer lab available.

Student Life *Housing:* college housing not available. *Activities and organizations:* drama/theater group, student-run newspaper. *Campus security:* late-night transport/escort service. *Student services:* personal/psychological counseling.

Athletics *Intercollegiate sports:* basketball M(s)/W(s), soccer M(s)/W(s). *Intramural sports:* badminton M/W, basketball M/W, cross-country running M(c)/W(c), soccer M/W, volleyball M/W, wrestling M(c)/W(c).

Costs (2003–04) *Tuition:* nonresident $3000 full-time; International tuition $8850 full-time. *Required fees:* $354 full-time.

Applying *Options:* common application, electronic application, deferred entrance. *Application fee:* $45 Canadian dollars. *Required for some:* essay or personal statement, high school transcript, minimum 2.5 GPA, 2 letters of recommendation, interview. *Application deadlines:* 1/31 (freshmen), 2/28 (transfers). *Notification:* continuous until 9/1 (freshmen), 9/1 (transfers).

Admissions Contact Ms. Robin Smith, Admissions Coordinator, University College of the Fraser Valley, 33844 King Road, Abbotsford, BC V2S 7M8, Canada. *Phone:* -853-7441 Ext. 4242. *E-mail:* reginfo@ucfv.bc.ca.

UNIVERSITY OF ALBERTA

Edmonton, Alberta, Canada

- **Province-supported** university, founded 1906
- **Calendar** Canadian standard year
- **Degrees** certificates, diplomas, bachelor's, master's, doctoral, and first professional
- **Urban** 154-acre campus
- **Endowment** $540.0 million
- **Coed,** 31,818 undergraduate students, 83% full-time, 57% women, 43% men
- **Moderately difficult** entrance level, 40% of applicants were admitted

Undergraduates 26,443 full-time, 5,375 part-time. Students come from 13 provinces and territories, 110 other countries, 14% are from out of state, 7% transferred in, 15% live on campus.

Freshmen *Admission:* 14,700 applied, 5,924 admitted, 5,924 enrolled. *Average high school GPA:* 3.60.

Faculty *Total:* 1,506. *Student/faculty ratio:* 14:1.

Majors Accounting; adult and continuing education; agricultural business and management; agricultural economics; agriculture; agronomy and crop science; American Indian/Native American studies; animal genetics; animal physiology; animal sciences; anthropology; applied mathematics; Arabic; art; art history, criticism and conservation; art teacher education; Asian studies (East); athletic training; atmospheric sciences and meteorology; bilingual and multilingual education; biochemistry; bioinformatics; biological and physical sciences; biology/biological sciences; biology/biotechnology laboratory technician; botany/plant biology; business administration and management; business teacher education; Canadian studies; cartography; cell biology and histology; chemical engineering; chemistry; child development; Chinese; civil engineering; classics and languages, literatures and linguistics; clinical/medical laboratory technology; clinical psychology; clothing/textiles; comparative literature; computer engineering; computer science; construction engineering; criminal justice/law enforcement administration; criminology; dairy science; dance; dental hygiene; developmental and child psychology; dramatic/theatre arts; drawing; economics; education; electrical, electronics and communications engineering; elementary education; engineering; engineering physics; English; English as a second/foreign language (teaching); entomology; entrepreneurial and small business related; environmental biology; environmental/environmental health engineering; environmental science; environmental studies; European studies (Central and Eastern); experimental psychology; family and consumer economics related; family and consumer sciences/home economics teacher education; family and consumer sciences/human sciences; farm and ranch management; film/cinema studies; finance; fine/studio arts; folklore; food science; foods, nutrition, and wellness; forest/forest resources management; forestry; French; geography; geology/earth science; geophysics and seismology; German; Hebrew; history; human ecology; humanities; human resources management; immunology; industrial arts; industrial design; information science/studies; international business/trade/commerce; international relations and affairs; Italian; Japanese; kindergarten/preschool education; kinesiology and exercise science; labor and industrial relations; land use planning and management; Latin; Latin American studies; legal studies; liberal arts and sciences/liberal studies; linguistics; literature; management information systems; marketing/marketing management; mathematics; mechanical engineering; medical microbiology and bacteriology; metallurgical engineering; mining and mineral engineering; modern Greek; modern languages; molecular biology; music; music history, literature, and theory; music teacher education; natural resources/conservation; natural resources management and policy; nursing (registered nurse training); occupational therapy; paleontology; parks, recreation and leisure; parks, recreation and leisure facilities management; petroleum engineering; pharmacology; pharmacy; philosophy; physical education teaching and coaching; physical sciences; physical therapy; physics; physiology; piano and organ; political science and government; pre-dentistry studies; pre-law studies; pre-medical studies; pre-veterinary studies; printmaking; psychology; range science and management; reading teacher education; religious studies; Romance languages; Russian; Russian studies; Scandinavian languages; science teacher education; sculpture; secondary education; Slavic languages; sociology; Spanish; special education; special products marketing; sport and fitness administration; statistics; theatre design and technology; trade and industrial teacher education; urban studies/affairs; violin, viola, guitar and other stringed instruments; voice and opera; wildlife and wildlands science and management; wind/percussion instruments; women's studies; zoology/animal biology.

University of Alberta (continued)

Academic Programs *Special study options:* academic remediation for entering students, adult/continuing education programs, advanced placement credit, cooperative education, distance learning, double majors, English as a second language, honors programs, internships, off-campus study, part-time degree program, services for LD students, study abroad, summer session for credit. *Unusual degree programs:* 3-2 education.

Library Cameron Library plus 10 others with 9.7 million titles, an OPAC, a Web page.

Computers on Campus 721 computers available on campus for general student use. A campuswide network can be accessed from student residence rooms and from off campus that provide access to e-mail. Internet access, online (class) registration, at least one staffed computer lab available. Computer purchase or lease plan available.

Student Life *Housing:* on-campus residence required through senior year. *Options:* coed, disabled students. Campus housing is university owned. Freshman applicants given priority for college housing. *Activities and organizations:* drama/theater group, student-run newspaper, radio station, choral group, national fraternities, national sororities. *Campus security:* 24-hour emergency response devices, student patrols, late-night transport/escort service. *Student services:* health clinic, personal/psychological counseling, women's center, legal services.

Athletics Member CIS. *Intercollegiate sports:* basketball M(s)/W(s), cross-country running M/W, field hockey M(s)/W(s), football M(s), gymnastics M(s)/W(s), ice hockey M(s)/W(s), rugby W, soccer M(s)/W(s), swimming M(s)/W(s), track and field M/W, volleyball M(s)/W(s), wrestling M(s)/W. *Intramural sports:* archery M(c)/W(c), badminton M(c)/W(c), basketball M/W, bowling M(c)/W(c), crew M(c)/W(c), cross-country running M/W, fencing M(c)/W(c), field hockey W, football M, golf M/W, gymnastics M/W, ice hockey M/W, lacrosse M(c)/W(c), racquetball M/W, rock climbing M/W, rugby M(c)/W(c), skiing (cross-country) M(c)/W(c), skiing (downhill) M(c)/W(c), soccer M/W, squash M/W, swimming M/W, table tennis M/W, tennis M/W, track and field M(c)/W(c), volleyball M/W, water polo M/W, weight lifting M(c)/W(c), wrestling M/W.

Standardized Tests *Recommended:* SAT I (for admission), SAT II: Subject Tests (for admission).

Costs (2004–05) *Tuition:* province resident $454 Canadian dollars per course part-time; nonresident $4537 Canadian dollars full-time, $1167 Canadian dollars per course part-time; International tuition $11,665 Canadian dollars full-time. Full-time tuition and fees vary according to course load and program. Part-time tuition and fees vary according to course load and program. *Required fees:* $494 Canadian dollars full-time, $134 Canadian dollars per term part-time. *Room and board:* $3915 Canadian dollars. Room and board charges vary according to board plan and housing facility. *Payment plan:* installment.

Applying *Options:* electronic application, deferred entrance. *Application fee:* $60 Canadian dollars. *Required:* high school transcript. *Required for some:* essay or personal statement, letters of recommendation, interview. *Recommended:* minimum 2.0 GPA. *Application deadlines:* 5/1 (freshmen), 5/1 (transfers). *Notification:* continuous until 9/1 (freshmen), continuous until 9/1 (transfers).

Admissions Contact Ms. Carole Byrne, Associate Registrar/Director of Admissions, University of Alberta, 201 Administration Building, Edmonton, AB T6G 2M7, Canada. *Phone:* 780-492-3113. *Fax:* 780-492-7172. *E-mail:* registrar@ualberta.ca.

THE UNIVERSITY OF BRITISH COLUMBIA

Vancouver, British Columbia, Canada

- **Province-supported** university, founded 1915
- **Calendar** Canadian standard year
- **Degrees** certificates, diplomas, bachelor's, master's, doctoral, first professional, and postbachelor's certificates
- **Urban** 1000-acre campus
- **Endowment** $592,292
- **Coed,** 29,538 undergraduate students, 69% full-time, 56% women, 44% men
- **Very difficult** entrance level, 50% of applicants were admitted

Undergraduates 20,447 full-time, 9,091 part-time. Students come from 31 provinces and territories, 127 other countries, 10% are from out of state, 23% live on campus. *Retention:* 91% of 2002 full-time freshmen returned.

Freshmen *Admission:* 21,552 applied, 10,741 admitted, 5,122 enrolled.

Faculty *Total:* 1,970. *Student/faculty ratio:* 15:1.

Majors Accounting; agricultural and food products processing; agricultural economics; agriculture; animal genetics; animal/livestock husbandry and production; animal sciences; anthropology; applied mathematics; aquaculture; archeology; art history, criticism and conservation; art teacher education; Asian studies; Asian studies (South); astronomy; atmospheric sciences and meteorology; biochemistry; biochemistry/biophysics and molecular biology; biology/biological sciences; biomedical/medical engineering; biophysics; biotechnology; business administration and management; business/commerce; business teacher education; Canadian government and politics; Canadian studies; cell biology and histology; chemical engineering; chemistry; Chinese; civil engineering; classics and languages, literatures and linguistics; clinical/medical laboratory technology; clinical psychology; cognitive science; computer engineering; computer science; counselor education/school counseling and guidance; creative writing; cultural studies; dental hygiene; developmental and child psychology; dietetics; dramatic/theatre arts; economics; education; educational leadership and administration; electrical, electronics and communications engineering; elementary education; engineering physics; engineering technologies related; English; English as a second/foreign language (teaching); environmental biology; environmental engineering technology; environmental studies; European studies; European studies (Central and Eastern); experimental psychology; family and consumer sciences/home economics teacher education; family and consumer sciences/human sciences; film/cinema studies; finance; fine/studio arts; fish/game management; foods and nutrition related; food science; food science and technology related; foods, nutrition, and wellness; forest/forest resources management; forestry; forestry technology; French; geography; geological/geophysical engineering; geology/earth science; geophysics and seismology; German; history; horticultural science; human nutrition; human resources management and services related; industrial arts; interdisciplinary studies; international business/trade/commerce; international relations and affairs; Italian; Japanese; kindergarten/preschool education; kinesiology and exercise science; labor and industrial relations; landscape architecture; Latin; Latin American studies; liberal arts and sciences/liberal studies; linguistics; management information systems; marine biology and biological oceanography; marketing/marketing management; materials engineering; mathematics; mechanical engineering; mechanical engineering/mechanical technology; medical microbiology and bacteriology; metallurgical engineering; mining and mineral engineering; music; music history, literature, and theory; music teacher education; music theory and composition; natural resources and conservation related; natural resources/conservation; natural resources management; natural resources management and policy; nursing (registered nurse training); occupational therapy; oceanography (chemical and physical); parks, recreation and leisure facilities management; pharmacology; pharmacy; philosophy; physical therapy; physics; physiology; piano and organ; political science and government; pre-dentistry studies; pre-law studies; pre-medical studies; pre-veterinary studies; psychology; reading teacher education; real estate; rehabilitation therapy; religious studies; Romance languages; Russian; Russian studies; science teacher education; secondary education; Slavic languages; social sciences; social work; sociology; soil science and agronomy; South Asian languages; Spanish; special education; speech therapy; statistics; theatre/theatre arts management; transportation technology; urban studies/affairs; violin, viola, guitar and other stringed instruments; visual and performing arts; voice and opera; wildlife and wildlands science and management; women's studies; wood science and wood products/pulp and paper technology; zoology/animal biology.

Academic Programs *Special study options:* academic remediation for entering students, adult/continuing education programs, advanced placement credit, cooperative education, distance learning, double majors, English as a second language, external degree program, freshman honors college, honors programs, internships, off-campus study, part-time degree program, services for LD students, student-designed majors, study abroad, summer session for credit. *ROTC:* Army (c), Air Force (c).

Library Walter C. Koerner Library plus 9 others with 4.0 million titles, 26,016 serial subscriptions, an OPAC, a Web page.

Computers on Campus 1100 computers available on campus for general student use. A campuswide network can be accessed from student residence rooms and from off campus that provide access to campus-wide wireless network. Internet access, online (class) registration, at least one staffed computer lab available.

Student Life *Housing options:* coed, men-only, women-only, disabled students. Campus housing is university owned. Freshman applicants given priority for college housing. *Activities and organizations:* drama/theater group, student-run newspaper, radio station, choral group, ski and board club, dance club, AIESEC Club, UBC Film Society, Varsity Outdoors Club, national fraternities, national sororities. *Campus security:* 24-hour emergency response devices and patrols, student patrols, late-night transport/escort service, 24-hour desk attendants in residence halls. *Student services:* health clinic, personal/psychological counseling, women's center, legal services.

Athletics Member NAIA, CIS. *Intercollegiate sports:* baseball M(s), basketball M(s)/W(s), cheerleading M(c)/W(c), crew M(s)/W(s), cross-country running M(s)/W(s), fencing W(c), field hockey M/W(s), football M(s), golf M(s)/W(s), ice hockey M(s)/W(s), rugby M(s)/W(s), skiing (cross-country) M(s)/W(s), skiing (downhill) M(s)/W(s), soccer M(s)/W(s), swimming M(s)/W(s), track and field M(s)/W(s), ultimate Frisbee M(c), volleyball M(s)/W(s), water polo M(c)/W(c). *Intramural sports:* badminton M/W, basketball M/W, cross-country running

M/W, football M/W, ice hockey M/W, racquetball M/W, soccer M/W, softball M/W, squash M/W, swimming M/W, table tennis M/W, tennis M/W, ultimate Frisbee M/W, volleyball M/W.

Standardized Tests *Recommended:* SAT I or ACT (for admission).

Costs (2003–04) *Tuition:* province resident $3459 Canadian dollars full-time, $115 Canadian dollars per credit part-time; nonresident $542 Canadian dollars per credit part-time; International tuition $16,260 Canadian dollars full-time. Full-time tuition and fees vary according to course load. Part-time tuition and fees vary according to course load. *Required fees:* $605 Canadian dollars full-time. *Room and board:* $6000 Canadian dollars. Room and board charges vary according to board plan and housing facility. *Payment plan:* installment. *Waivers:* senior citizens and employees or children of employees.

Financial Aid Of all full-time matriculated undergraduates who enrolled in 2001, 825 state and other part-time jobs (averaging $3000). *Financial aid deadline:* 9/15.

Applying *Options:* electronic application, early admission. *Application fee:* $100 Canadian dollars. *Required:* high school transcript, minimum 2.6 GPA. *Required for some:* essay or personal statement, letters of recommendation. *Application deadlines:* 2/28 (freshmen), 2/28 (transfers). *Notification:* continuous until 8/31 (freshmen), continuous until 8/31 (transfers).

Admissions Contact International Student Recruitment and Reception, The University of British Columbia, 1874 East Mall, Vancouver, BC V6T 1Z1, Canada. *Phone:* 604-822-8999. *Toll-free phone:* 877-292-1422. *Fax:* 604-822-9888. *E-mail:* international.reception@ubc.ca.

■ *See page 2578 for a narrative description.*

UNIVERSITY OF CALGARY

Calgary, Alberta, Canada

- **Province-supported** university, founded 1945
- **Calendar** semesters
- **Degrees** diplomas, bachelor's, master's, doctoral, and postbachelor's certificates
- **Urban** 213-hectare campus
- **Coed,** 23,952 undergraduate students, 84% full-time, 56% women, 44% men
- **Moderately difficult** entrance level, 66% of applicants were admitted

Undergraduates 20,139 full-time, 3,813 part-time. Students come from 12 provinces and territories, 73 other countries.

Freshmen *Admission:* 6,650 applied, 4,397 admitted.

Faculty *Total:* 2,356, 65% full-time. *Student/faculty ratio:* 13:1.

Majors Accounting; actuarial science; American Indian/Native American studies; anthropology; applied mathematics; archeology; art; art history, criticism and conservation; art teacher education; Asian studies (East); astrophysics; biochemistry; biology/biological sciences; biomedical science; botany/plant biology; business administration and management; Canadian studies; cell biology and histology; chemical engineering; chemistry; civil engineering; classics and languages, literatures and linguistics; communication/speech communication and rhetoric; computer engineering; computer science; dance; drama and dance teacher education; dramatic/theatre arts; ecology; economics; education; electrical, electronics and communications engineering; elementary education; English; environmental studies; finance; French; general studies; geography; geological/geophysical engineering; geology/earth science; geophysics and seismology; German; history; hotel/motel administration; humanities; industrial engineering; insurance; international relations and affairs; kinesiology and exercise science; Latin American studies; legal studies; liberal arts and sciences/liberal studies; linguistics; management information systems; marketing/marketing management; mathematics; mechanical engineering; medieval and Renaissance studies; molecular biology; music; nursing (registered nurse training); parks, recreation and leisure; philosophy; physics; political science and government; psychology; religious studies; Russian; secondary education; social work; sociology; Spanish; statistics; tourism and travel services management; urban studies/affairs; women's studies; zoology/animal biology.

Academic Programs *Special study options:* adult/continuing education programs, advanced placement credit, cooperative education, distance learning, double majors, English as a second language, honors programs, internships, part-time degree program, services for LD students, study abroad, summer session for credit.

Library MacKimmie Library plus 4 others with 2.4 million titles, 18,000 serial subscriptions, 146,131 audiovisual materials, an OPAC, a Web page.

Computers on Campus 800 computers available on campus for general student use. A campuswide network can be accessed from student residence rooms and from off campus. Internet access, online (class) registration, at least one staffed computer lab available.

Student Life *Housing options:* coed, disabled students. Campus housing is university owned. Freshman applicants given priority for college housing. *Activities and organizations:* student-run newspaper, radio and television station, choral group. *Campus security:* 24-hour emergency response devices and patrols, late-night transport/escort service, controlled dormitory access. *Student services:* health clinic, personal/psychological counseling, legal services.

Athletics Member CIS. *Intercollegiate sports:* basketball M(s)/W(s), cross-country running M(s)/W(s), field hockey W(s), football M(s), golf M/W, ice hockey M(s)/W(s), soccer M(s)/W(s), swimming M(s)/W(s), tennis M(s)/W(s), track and field M(s)/W(s), volleyball M(s)/W(s), wrestling M(s)/W(s). *Intramural sports:* badminton M(c)/W(c), basketball M/W, fencing M(c)/W(c), field hockey M(c)/W(c), football M, gymnastics M(c)/W(c), ice hockey M/W, rugby M(c)/W(c), soccer M/W, softball M/W, squash M(c)/W(c), swimming M(c)/W(c), table tennis M(c)/W(c), ultimate Frisbee M/W, volleyball M/W.

Standardized Tests *Required for some:* SAT I (for admission), SAT II: Subject Tests (for admission), SAT II: Writing Test (for admission).

Costs (2004–05) *Tuition:* area resident $4590 Canadian dollars full-time; International tuition $9180 Canadian dollars full-time. *Required fees:* $549 Canadian dollars full-time. *Room and board:* $3590 Canadian dollars; room only: $2670 Canadian dollars.

Financial Aid *Financial aid deadline:* 6/15.

Applying *Options:* electronic application, early admission. *Application fee:* $65 Canadian dollars. *Required:* high school transcript. *Application deadline:* 3/1 (freshmen). *Notification:* continuous (freshmen).

Admissions Contact Director of Enrollment Services, University of Calgary, Office of Admissions, Calgary, AB T2N 1N4, Canada. *Phone:* 403-220-6645. *Fax:* 403-220-0762. *E-mail:* applinfo@ucalgary.ca.

UNIVERSITY OF GUELPH

Guelph, Ontario, Canada

- **Province-supported** university, founded 1964
- **Calendar** trimesters
- **Degrees** certificates, diplomas, bachelor's, master's, doctoral, and first professional
- **Urban** 817-acre campus with easy access to Toronto
- **Coed,** 16,188 undergraduate students, 84% full-time, 61% women, 39% men
- **Moderately difficult** entrance level, 59% of applicants were admitted

Undergraduates 13,566 full-time, 2,622 part-time. Students come from 12 provinces and territories, 85 other countries, 38% live on campus. *Retention:* 94% of 2002 full-time freshmen returned.

Freshmen *Admission:* 31,272 applied, 18,520 admitted.

Faculty *Total:* 950, 80% full-time. *Student/faculty ratio:* 22:1.

Majors Adult development and aging; agricultural/biological engineering and bioengineering; agricultural business and management; agricultural economics; agriculture; agriculture and agriculture operations related; agronomy and crop science; animal sciences; anthropology; applied economics; applied mathematics; art history, criticism and conservation; atomic/molecular physics; biochemistry; biological and physical sciences; biology/biological sciences; biomedical/medical engineering; biomedical sciences; biophysics; biotechnology; botany/plant biology; business/managerial economics; chemical engineering; chemistry; child development; classical, ancient Mediterranean and Near Eastern studies and archaeology; classics and languages, literatures and linguistics; computer and information sciences; computer engineering technology; computer science; criminal justice/law enforcement administration; development economics and international development; dietetics; dramatic/theatre arts; ecology; econometrics and quantitative economics; economics; English; environmental biology; environmental engineering technology; environmental/environmental health engineering; environmental studies; environmental toxicology; European studies; fine/studio arts; food science; French; geography; geology/earth science; gerontology; history; horticultural science; hotel/motel administration; human development and family studies; human nutrition; human resources management; information science/studies; kinesiology and exercise science; landscape architecture; marine biology and biological oceanography; marketing/marketing management; mathematics; medical microbiology and bacteriology; microbiology; molecular biology; molecular genetics; music; natural resources management and policy; non-profit management; nutrition sciences; philosophy; physical sciences; physics; political science and government; psychology; real estate; sociology; Spanish; statistics; theoretical and mathematical physics; tourism and travel services management; toxicology; veterinary sciences; water resources engineering; wildlife biology; women's studies; zoology/animal biology.

Academic Programs *Special study options:* academic remediation for entering students, accelerated degree program, adult/continuing education programs, advanced placement credit, cooperative education, distance learning, double majors, freshman honors college, honors programs, independent study, part-time degree program, services for LD students, student-designed majors, study abroad, summer session for credit.

University of Guelph (continued)

Library McLaughlin Library plus 1 other with 2.1 million titles, 7,294 serial subscriptions, 16,437 audiovisual materials, an OPAC, a Web page.

Computers on Campus 1200 computers available on campus for general student use. A campuswide network can be accessed from student residence rooms and from off campus. Internet access, online (class) registration, at least one staffed computer lab available.

Student Life *Housing options:* coed, men-only, women-only, cooperative. Campus housing is university owned. Freshman campus housing is guaranteed. *Activities and organizations:* drama/theater group, student-run newspaper, radio station, choral group. *Campus security:* 24-hour emergency response devices and patrols, late-night transport/escort service, video camera surveillance in parking lots, alarms in women's locker room. *Student services:* health clinic, personal/psychological counseling, women's center, legal services.

Athletics Member CIS. *Intercollegiate sports:* baseball M, basketball M/W, crew M/W, cross-country running M/W, field hockey W, football M, golf M, ice hockey M/W, lacrosse M/W, rugby M/W, skiing (cross-country) M/W, soccer M/W, swimming M/W, track and field M/W, volleyball M/W, wrestling M/W. *Intramural sports:* archery M(c)/W(c), badminton M(c)/W(c), baseball M(c), basketball M/W, cheerleading M/W, fencing M(c)/W(c), football M/W, ice hockey M/W, lacrosse M(c)/W(c), skiing (cross-country) M(c)/W(c), soccer M/W, softball M/W, squash M(c)/W(c), tennis M(c)/W(c), ultimate Frisbee M(c)/W(c), volleyball M/W, water polo M/W.

Standardized Tests *Required:* SAT I or ACT (for admission).

Costs (2003–04) *Tuition:* province resident $4184 Canadian dollars full-time; nonresident $418 Canadian dollars per course part-time; International tuition $9356 Canadian dollars full-time. Full-time tuition and fees vary according to program. Part-time tuition and fees vary according to course load. *Required fees:* $988 Canadian dollars full-time, $16 Canadian dollars per course part-time, $326 Canadian dollars per term part-time. *Room and board:* $6675 Canadian dollars; room only: $3475 Canadian dollars. Room and board charges vary according to board plan and housing facility. *Waivers:* senior citizens and employees or children of employees.

Applying *Options:* early admission. *Application fee:* $85 Canadian dollars. *Required:* high school transcript, minimum 3.0 GPA. *Required for some:* essay or personal statement, letters of recommendation. *Application deadlines:* 3/1 (freshmen), 5/1 (transfers). *Notification:* 4/20 (freshmen), continuous until 8/1 (transfers).

Admissions Contact Mr. Hugh Clark, Admissions Coordinator, University of Guelph, L-3 University Centre, Guelph, ON N1G 2W1, Canada. *Phone:* 519-824-4120 Ext. 56066. *E-mail:* usinfo@registrar.uoguelph.ca.

■ See page 2610 for a narrative description.

UNIVERSITY OF KING'S COLLEGE

Halifax, Nova Scotia, Canada

- **Province-supported** 4-year, founded 1789
- **Calendar** Canadian standard year
- **Degree** bachelor's
- **Urban** 4-acre campus
- **Endowment** $18.0 million
- **Coed,** 1,050 undergraduate students, 98% full-time, 60% women, 40% men
- **Moderately difficult** entrance level, 73% of applicants were admitted

Undergraduates 1,030 full-time, 20 part-time. Students come from 11 provinces and territories, 10 other countries, 54% are from out of state, 2% transferred in, 26% live on campus. *Retention:* 65% of 2002 full-time freshmen returned.

Freshmen *Admission:* 1,171 applied, 849 admitted, 304 enrolled. *Average high school GPA:* 3.50.

Faculty *Total:* 43, 100% full-time, 65% with terminal degrees.

Majors Anthropology; biochemistry; biology/biological sciences; chemistry; classics and languages, literatures and linguistics; computer science; development economics and international development; dramatic/theatre arts; economics; English; French; geology/earth science; German; history; journalism; linguistics; marine biology and biological oceanography; mathematics; medical microbiology and bacteriology; multi-/interdisciplinary studies related; music; neuroscience; philosophy; physics; political science and government; psychology; religious studies; Russian; science, technology and society; sociology; Spanish; statistics; western civilization; women's studies.

Academic Programs *Special study options:* accelerated degree program, advanced placement credit, cooperative education, double majors, honors programs, independent study, internships, off-campus study, part-time degree program, services for LD students, student-designed majors, study abroad, summer session for credit.

Library University of King's College Library with 80,000 titles, 192 serial subscriptions, 74 audiovisual materials, an OPAC.

Computers on Campus 51 computers available on campus for general student use. A campuswide network can be accessed from student residence rooms and from off campus. Internet access, at least one staffed computer lab available. Computer purchase or lease plan available.

Student Life *Housing options:* coed, men-only, women-only. Campus housing is university owned. Freshman applicants given priority for college housing. *Activities and organizations:* drama/theater group, student-run newspaper, radio station, choral group, King's Theatrical Society, student newspaper, King's College Dance Collective, St. Andrew's Missionary Society, King's Independent Film-Makers Society. *Campus security:* student patrols, late-night transport/escort service. *Student services:* health clinic, personal/psychological counseling, women's center, legal services.

Athletics *Intercollegiate sports:* badminton M/W, basketball M/W, cheerleading M(s)/W(s), rugby M/W, soccer M/W, volleyball M/W. *Intramural sports:* badminton M/W, basketball M/W, field hockey M/W, soccer M/W, softball M/W, tennis M/W, ultimate Frisbee M/W, volleyball M/W, water polo M/W.

Standardized Tests *Required for some:* SAT I (for admission).

Costs (2003–04) *Tuition:* province resident $5220 Canadian dollars full-time, $174 Canadian dollars per credit hour part-time; nonresident $5220 Canadian dollars full-time; International tuition $9720 Canadian dollars full-time. Full-time tuition and fees vary according to course load and program. Part-time tuition and fees vary according to course load and program. *Required fees:* $763 Canadian dollars full-time, $601 Canadian dollars per term part-time. *Room and board:* $6829 Canadian dollars. Room and board charges vary according to housing facility. *Payment plan:* installment. *Waivers:* senior citizens and employees or children of employees.

Applying *Required:* high school transcript, minimum 3.0 GPA. *Required for some:* essay or personal statement, letters of recommendation, writing sample. *Application deadlines:* 3/1 (freshmen), 6/1 (transfers). *Notification:* 4/15 (freshmen), continuous (transfers).

Admissions Contact Karl Turner, Admissions Officer, University of King's College, Registrar's Office, Halifax, NS B3H 2A1, Canada. *Phone:* 902-422-1271 Ext. 193. *Fax:* 902-425-8183. *E-mail:* admissions@ukings.ns.ca.

THE UNIVERSITY OF LETHBRIDGE

Lethbridge, Alberta, Canada

- **Province-supported** comprehensive, founded 1967
- **Calendar** semesters
- **Degrees** certificates, diplomas, bachelor's, master's, and doctoral
- **Urban** 576-acre campus
- **Endowment** $11.4 million
- **Coed,** 7,094 undergraduate students, 90% full-time, 57% women, 43% men
- **Moderately difficult** entrance level, 53% of applicants were admitted

Undergraduates 6,392 full-time, 702 part-time. Students come from 12 provinces and territories, 56 other countries, 20% are from out of state, 10% live on campus. *Retention:* 73% of 2002 full-time freshmen returned.

Freshmen *Admission:* 2,374 applied, 1,264 admitted. *Average high school GPA:* 3.30.

Faculty *Total:* 336, 71% with terminal degrees. *Student/faculty ratio:* 22:1.

Majors Accounting; agricultural business and management; agriculture; American Indian/Native American studies; American native/native American education; American Native/Native American languages; anthropology; art; art teacher education; biochemistry; biological and physical sciences; biology/biological sciences; biotechnology; business administration and management; business teacher education; Canadian studies; chemistry; computer and information sciences related; computer science; counseling psychology; digital communication and media/multimedia; drama and dance teacher education; dramatic/theatre arts; economics; education; educational leadership and administration; education (K-12); English; environmental science; finance; foreign language teacher education; French; geography; German; health teacher education; history; humanities; human resources management; international business/trade/commerce; kinesiology and exercise science; management information systems; marketing/marketing management; mathematics; mathematics teacher education; modern languages; music; music teacher education; neuroscience; nursing (registered nurse training); parks, recreation and leisure; philosophy; physical education teaching and coaching; physics; political science and government; psychology; public administration; religious studies; science teacher education; social sciences; social studies teacher education; sociology; special education; substance abuse/addiction counseling; technology/industrial arts teacher education; theatre design and technology; urban studies/affairs.

Academic Programs *Special study options:* academic remediation for entering students, accelerated degree program, cooperative education, distance learning, double majors, English as a second language, independent study, internships, off-campus study, part-time degree program, student-designed majors, study abroad, summer session for credit. *Unusual degree programs:* 3-2 education.

Library The University of Lethbridge Library with 511,183 titles, 1,897 serial subscriptions, 4,106 audiovisual materials, an OPAC, a Web page.

Computers on Campus 550 computers available on campus for general student use. A campuswide network can be accessed from student residence rooms and from off campus. Internet access, online (class) registration, at least one staffed computer lab available. Computer purchase or lease plan available.

Student Life *Housing options:* coed. Campus housing is university owned. *Activities and organizations:* drama/theater group, student-run newspaper, radio station, choral group, Management Students Society, Inter-Varsity Christian Fellowship, Organization of Residence Students, The University of Lethbridge Geography Club, Education Undergraduate Society. *Campus security:* 24-hour emergency response devices and patrols, student patrols, late-night transport/escort service, controlled dormitory access, video camera monitored entrances, hallways. *Student services:* health clinic, personal/psychological counseling, women's center.

Athletics Member CIS. *Intercollegiate sports:* basketball M(s)/W(s), cross-country running M(s)/W(s), ice hockey M(s)/W(s), soccer M(s)/W(s), swimming M(s)/W(s), track and field M(s)/W(s), volleyball W. *Intramural sports:* badminton M/W, basketball M/W, fencing M(c)/W(c), football M/W, golf M/W, gymnastics M/W, ice hockey M/W, racquetball M/W, rugby M(c)/W(c), skiing (cross-country) M/W, skiing (downhill) M/W, soccer M/W, softball M/W, squash M/W, tennis M(c)/W(c), volleyball M/W, water polo M/W, weight lifting M/W.

Standardized Tests *Required for some:* SAT I and SAT II or ACT (for admission), SAT II: Writing Test (for admission).

Costs (2003–04) *Tuition:* nonresident $3730 Canadian dollars full-time, $373 Canadian dollars per course part-time; International tuition $7460 Canadian dollars full-time. Full-time tuition and fees vary according to course load. Part-time tuition and fees vary according to course load. *Required fees:* $846 Canadian dollars full-time, $102 Canadian dollars per course part-time. *Room and board:* $5638 Canadian dollars; room only: $3296 Canadian dollars. Room and board charges vary according to board plan and housing facility. *Waivers:* employees or children of employees.

Applying *Options:* common application, electronic application, early admission, early decision, deferred entrance. *Application fee:* $60 Canadian dollars. *Required:* high school transcript, minimum 2.0 GPA. *Required for some:* minimum 3.0 GPA, letters of recommendation, interview. *Application deadlines:* 8/25 (freshmen), 8/26 (transfers). *Early decision:* 4/1. *Notification:* continuous (freshmen), 4/22 (early decision), continuous (transfers).

Admissions Contact Mr. Peter Haney, Assistant Registrar, The University of Lethbridge, 4401 University Drive, AB. *Phone:* 403-382-7134. *Toll-free phone:* 403-320-5700. *Fax:* 403-329-5159. *E-mail:* inquiries@uleth.ca.

UNIVERSITY OF MANITOBA

Winnipeg, Manitoba, Canada

- **Province-supported** university, founded 1877
- **Calendar** 8-month academic year plus 6-week summer session
- **Degrees** bachelor's, master's, and doctoral
- **Suburban** 685-acre campus
- **Coed,** 23,032 undergraduate students, 73% full-time, 57% women, 43% men
- **Moderately difficult** entrance level, 73% of applicants were admitted

Undergraduates 16,885 full-time, 6,147 part-time.

Freshmen *Admission:* 11,184 applied, 8,190 admitted, 7,966 enrolled.

Faculty *Total:* 1,141.

Majors Accounting; actuarial science; agricultural/biological engineering and bioengineering; agricultural economics; agriculture; agronomy and crop science; animal genetics; animal sciences; anthropology; applied mathematics; architecture; art; art history, criticism and conservation; Asian studies (South); astronomy; biology/biological sciences; botany/plant biology; business administration and management; business/managerial economics; Canadian studies; chemistry; child development; civil engineering; classics and languages, literatures and linguistics; clothing/textiles; computer engineering; computer science; dental hygiene; dramatic/theatre arts; ecology; economics; education; electrical, electronics and communications engineering; elementary education; engineering science; English; entomology; environmental design/architecture; environmental studies; family and consumer sciences/human sciences; film/cinema studies; finance; food science; foods, nutrition, and wellness; French; geography; geological/geophysical engineering; geology/earth science; German; history; human ecology; industrial engineering; interior design; Jewish/Judaic studies; kindergarten/preschool education; labor and industrial relations; Latin; mathematics; mechanical engineering; medical microbiology and bacteriology; medieval and Renaissance studies; modern Greek; music; nursing (registered nurse training); occupational therapy; pharmacy; philosophy; physical education teaching and coaching; physical therapy; physics; political science and government; pre-dentistry studies; pre-law studies; pre-medical studies; pre-veterinary studies; psychology; public administration; rehabilitation therapy; religious studies; Russian; Russian studies; science teacher education; secondary education; Slavic languages; social work; sociology; Spanish; statistics; women's studies; zoology/animal biology.

Academic Programs *Special study options:* academic remediation for entering students, adult/continuing education programs, external degree program, honors programs, internships, off-campus study, part-time degree program, summer session for credit. *ROTC:* Army (b), Air Force (b).

Library Elizabeth Dafoe Library plus 12 others with 1.6 million titles, 12,800 serial subscriptions.

Computers on Campus A campuswide network can be accessed from student residence rooms and from off campus.

Student Life *Housing options:* coed. *Activities and organizations:* drama/theater group, student-run newspaper, national fraternities. *Campus security:* 24-hour emergency response devices, student patrols, late-night transport/escort service. *Student services:* health clinic, personal/psychological counseling, women's center.

Athletics Member CIS. *Intercollegiate sports:* basketball M/W, cross-country running M/W, field hockey M/W, football M/W, gymnastics M/W, ice hockey M/W, swimming M/W, track and field M/W, volleyball M/W. *Intramural sports:* basketball M/W, cross-country running M/W, fencing M/W, field hockey M/W, football M/W, golf M/W, gymnastics M/W, ice hockey M/W, lacrosse M/W, skiing (cross-country) M/W, skiing (downhill) M/W, soccer M/W, squash M/W, swimming M/W, tennis M/W, track and field M/W, volleyball M/W, wrestling M/W.

Costs (2003–04) *Tuition:* nonresident $3000 Canadian dollars full-time. Full-time tuition and fees vary according to program. *Required fees:* $165 Canadian dollars full-time. *Room and board:* $4925 Canadian dollars.

Financial Aid Of all full-time matriculated undergraduates who enrolled in 2001, 50 state and other part-time jobs (averaging $980).

Applying *Application fee:* $35 Canadian dollars. *Required:* high school transcript. *Application deadlines:* 7/1 (freshmen), 7/1 (transfers). *Notification:* continuous (freshmen), continuous until 8/1 (transfers).

Admissions Contact Mr. Peter Dueck, Director of Enrollment Services, University of Manitoba, Winnipeg, MB R3T 2N2, Canada. *Phone:* 204-474-6382.

UNIVERSITY OF NEW BRUNSWICK FREDERICTON

Fredericton, New Brunswick, Canada

- **Province-supported** university, founded 1785
- **Calendar** Canadian standard year
- **Degrees** bachelor's, master's, and doctoral
- **Urban** 7100-acre campus
- **Coed,** 11,199 undergraduate students, 86% full-time, 54% women, 46% men
- **Moderately difficult** entrance level, 76% of applicants were admitted

Undergraduates 9,585 full-time, 1,614 part-time. Students come from 12 provinces and territories, 65 other countries, 20% live on campus.

Freshmen *Admission:* 2,858 applied, 2,185 admitted.

Faculty *Total:* 645, 78% full-time. *Student/faculty ratio:* 15:1.

Majors Accounting; adult and continuing education; animal physiology; anthropology; applied mathematics; art teacher education; biochemistry; biological and physical sciences; biology/biological sciences; biophysics; botany/plant biology; business administration and management; business/managerial economics; business teacher education; Canadian studies; chemical engineering; chemistry; civil engineering; classics and languages, literatures and linguistics; clinical psychology; comparative literature; computer engineering; computer science; construction engineering; counselor education/school counseling and guidance; data processing and data processing technology; developmental and child psychology; dramatic/theatre arts; ecology; economics; education; electrical, electronics and communications engineering; elementary education; engineering; English; English as a second/foreign language (teaching); entomology; family and consumer sciences/home economics teacher education; finance; fire science; fish/game management; forest engineering; forestry; French; geochemistry; geological/geophysical engineering; geology/earth science; geophysics and seismology; German; health teacher education; history; human resources management; information science/studies; international business/trade/commerce; international relations and affairs; kindergarten/preschool education; kinesiology and exercise science; Latin; legal studies; liberal arts and sciences/liberal studies; linguistics; literature; marketing/marketing management; mathematics; mechanical engineering; medical microbiology and bacteriology; modern Greek; modern languages; molecular biology; music teacher education; nursing (registered nurse training); operations research; parks, recreation and leisure; philosophy; physical education teaching and coaching; physics; physiological psychology/psychobiology; political science and government; pre-dentistry studies; pre-law studies; pre-medical studies; pre-veterinary studies; psychology; Romance languages; Russian; sci-

University of New Brunswick Fredericton (continued)
ence teacher education; secondary education; sociology; Spanish; special education; statistics; survey technology; wildlife and wildlands science and management; wildlife biology; zoology/animal biology.

Academic Programs *Special study options:* accelerated degree program, adult/continuing education programs, advanced placement credit, cooperative education, distance learning, double majors, English as a second language, external degree program, honors programs, independent study, internships, off-campus study, part-time degree program, student-designed majors, study abroad, summer session for credit.

Library Harriet Irving Library plus 3 others with 1.1 million titles, 4,817 serial subscriptions, 65,000 audiovisual materials, an OPAC, a Web page.

Computers on Campus 750 computers available on campus for general student use. A campuswide network can be accessed from student residence rooms and from off campus. Internet access, online (class) registration, at least one staffed computer lab available.

Student Life *Housing options:* coed, men-only, women-only. Campus housing is university owned. Freshman campus housing is guaranteed. *Activities and organizations:* drama/theater group, student-run newspaper, radio station, choral group. *Campus security:* late-night transport/escort service. *Student services:* health clinic, personal/psychological counseling, women's center.

Athletics Member CIS. *Intercollegiate sports:* basketball M/W, cross-country running M/W, field hockey W, ice hockey M/W, soccer M/W, swimming M/W, volleyball M/W, wrestling M/W. *Intramural sports:* badminton M/W, baseball M/W, basketball M/W, cheerleading M/W, crew M/W, fencing M/W, ice hockey M/W, rock climbing M/W, rugby M/W, soccer M/W, swimming M/W, volleyball M/W.

Standardized Tests *Required for some:* SAT I (for admission).

Costs (2003–04) *Comprehensive fee:* $11,025 includes full-time tuition ($4510), mandatory fees ($450), and room and board ($6065). Part-time tuition: $466 per course.

Financial Aid Of all full-time matriculated undergraduates who enrolled in 2001, 106 state and other part-time jobs (averaging $1700). *Financial aid deadline:* 5/15.

Applying *Options:* early admission, deferred entrance. *Application fee:* $35 Canadian dollars. *Required:* high school transcript. *Required for some:* essay or personal statement, 1 letter of recommendation, interview. *Application deadlines:* 3/31 (freshmen), 3/31 (transfers). *Notification:* continuous until 8/31 (freshmen), continuous until 8/31 (transfers).

Admissions Contact Ms. Shirley Carroll, Assistant Registrar/Admissions, University of New Brunswick Fredericton, PO Box 4400, Sir Howard Douglas Hall, Fredericton, NB E3B 5A3, Canada. *Phone:* 506-453-4865. *Fax:* 506-453-5016. *E-mail:* chooseunb@unb.ca.

University of New Brunswick Saint John

Saint John, New Brunswick, Canada

- **Province-supported** comprehensive, founded 1964
- **Calendar** Canadian standard year
- **Degrees** certificates, diplomas, bachelor's, master's, doctoral, and postbachelor's certificates
- **Urban** 250-acre campus
- **Coed**
- **Moderately difficult** entrance level

Faculty *Student/faculty ratio:* 10:1.

Student Life *Campus security:* 24-hour emergency response devices and patrols, student patrols, late-night transport/escort service, controlled dormitory access.

Standardized Tests *Required:* SAT I (for admission).

Costs (2003–04) *Tuition:* province resident $4510 full-time; International tuition $9602 full-time. *Required fees:* $175 full-time. *Room and board:* $5064.

Financial Aid Of all full-time matriculated undergraduates who enrolled in 2001, 140 state and other part-time jobs (averaging $500).

Applying *Options:* electronic application, early admission, deferred entrance. *Application fee:* $35 Canadian dollars. *Required:* high school transcript. *Required for some:* letters of recommendation.

Admissions Contact Ms. Sue Ellis Loparco, Admissions Officer, University of New Brunswick Saint John, PO Box 5050, Tucker Park Road, Saint John, NB E2L 4L5. *Phone:* 506-648-5674. *Toll-free phone:* 800-743-4333 (in-state); 800-743-5691 (out-of-state). *Fax:* 506-648-5691. *E-mail:* apply@unbsj.ca.

University of Northern British Columbia

Prince George, British Columbia, Canada

- **Province-supported** university
- **Degrees** certificates, diplomas, bachelor's, master's, doctoral, first professional, and postbachelor's certificates
- **Coed,** 3,281 undergraduate students, 66% full-time, 58% women, 42% men
- 59% of applicants were admitted

Undergraduates 2,166 full-time, 1,115 part-time. *Retention:* 67% of 2002 full-time freshmen returned.

Freshmen *Admission:* 2,031 applied, 1,192 admitted, 430 enrolled. *Average high school GPA:* 3.22.

Faculty *Total:* 335, 49% full-time, 59% with terminal degrees. *Student/faculty ratio:* 11:1.

Student Life *Housing options:* Campus housing is university owned.

Costs (2004–05) *Tuition:* area resident $2931 full-time, $122 per credit hour part-time; International tuition $8059 full-time. *Required fees:* $5 per credit hour part-time, $114 per semester part-time. *Room only:* $3391.

Admissions Contact Mr. Grant Kerr, Assistant Registrar-Admissions, University of Northern British Columbia, 3333 University Way, Prince George, BC V2N 4Z9, Canada. *Phone:* 250-960-6347. *Fax:* 800-871-8747.

University of Ottawa

Ottawa, Ontario, Canada

- **Province-supported** university, founded 1848
- **Calendar** semesters
- **Degrees** certificates, bachelor's, master's, doctoral, first professional, and postbachelor's certificates
- **Urban** 70-acre campus
- **Endowment** $57.2 million
- **Coed,** 26,265 undergraduate students, 80% full-time, 60% women, 40% men
- **Moderately difficult** entrance level, 68% of applicants were admitted

Undergraduates 20,970 full-time, 5,295 part-time. Students come from 13 provinces and territories, 163 other countries, 17% are from out of state. *Retention:* 89% of 2002 full-time freshmen returned.

Freshmen *Admission:* 27,031 applied, 18,504 admitted. *Average high school GPA:* 3.27.

Faculty *Total:* 987.

Majors Accounting; animal physiology; applied art; applied mathematics; art; arts management; behavioral sciences; bilingual and multilingual education; biochemistry; biological and physical sciences; biology/biological sciences; biology/biotechnology laboratory technician; biomedical sciences; business administration and management; business/managerial economics; Canadian studies; chemical engineering; chemistry; civil engineering; classics and languages, literatures and linguistics; communication and media related; computer and information sciences; computer engineering; computer science; criminal justice/law enforcement administration; criminology; developmental and child psychology; dietetics; dramatic/theatre arts; economics; education; electrical, electronics and communications engineering; elementary education; engineering; engineering/industrial management; engineering science; English; English as a second/foreign language (teaching); environmental science; environmental studies; finance; fine/studio arts; foods, nutrition, and wellness; French; geography; geology/earth science; geophysics and seismology; German; history; humanities; human resources management; information science/studies; interdisciplinary studies; international business/trade/commerce; international relations and affairs; Italian; journalism; kindergarten/preschool education; Latin; liberal arts and sciences/liberal studies; linguistics; literature; management information systems; marketing/marketing management; mass communication/media; mathematics; mechanical engineering; medical microbiology and bacteriology; medieval and Renaissance studies; modern languages; music; music history, literature, and theory; music teacher education; natural sciences; nursing (registered nurse training); occupational therapy; parks, recreation and leisure; pastoral studies/counseling; philosophy; photography; physical education teaching and coaching; physical sciences; physical therapy; physics; political science and government; pre-law studies; premedical studies; psychology; public administration; public policy analysis; rehabilitation therapy; religious studies; Russian; secondary education; Slavic languages; Slavic studies; social sciences; sociology; Spanish; special education; statistics; systems science and theory; theology; voice and opera; women's studies.

Academic Programs *Special study options:* academic remediation for entering students, accelerated degree program, adult/continuing education programs, advanced placement credit, cooperative education, distance learning, double majors, English as a second language, external degree program, honors programs, internships, off-campus study, part-time degree program, services for LD students, student-designed majors, study abroad, summer session for credit. *Unusual degree programs:* 3-2 law.

Library Morisset Library plus 3 others with 2.6 million titles, 9,183 serial subscriptions, an OPAC, a Web page.

Computers on Campus 1500 computers available on campus for general student use. A campuswide network can be accessed from student residence rooms and from off campus. Internet access, online (class) registration, at least one staffed computer lab available. Computer purchase or lease plan available.

Student Life *Housing options:* coed. Campus housing is university owned. Freshman applicants given priority for college housing. *Activities and organizations:* drama/theater group, student-run newspaper, radio station, choral group, Student Federation of the University of Ottawa (SFUO). *Campus security:* 24-hour emergency response devices and patrols, student patrols, late-night transport/escort service, controlled dormitory access. *Student services:* health clinic, personal/psychological counseling, women's center, legal services.

Athletics Member CIS. *Intercollegiate sports:* basketball M/W, cross-country running M/W, fencing M/W, football M, ice hockey M/W, rugby W, soccer W, swimming M/W, track and field M/W, volleyball W. *Intramural sports:* basketball M/W, football M, ice hockey M/W, soccer M/W, ultimate Frisbee M/W, volleyball M/W.

Costs (2003–04) *Tuition:* nonresident $4163 Canadian dollars full-time; International tuition $11,500 Canadian dollars full-time. Full-time tuition and fees vary according to program. Part-time tuition and fees vary according to program. *Required fees:* $413 Canadian dollars full-time. *Room and board:* $5509 Canadian dollars; room only: $3259 Canadian dollars. Room and board charges vary according to board plan and housing facility. *Waivers:* employees or children of employees.

Financial Aid Of all full-time matriculated undergraduates who enrolled in 2001, 749 state and other part-time jobs (averaging $3000). *Financial aid deadline:* 1/31.

Applying *Options:* electronic application, early admission. *Application fee:* $85 Canadian dollars. *Required:* high school transcript. *Required for some:* interview. *Application deadline:* 6/30 (freshmen). *Notification:* continuous until 8/30 (freshmen).

Admissions Contact Ms. Michéle Dextras, Manager, Admissions, University of Ottawa, 550 Cumberland Street, PO Box 450, Station A, Ottawa, ON K1N 6N5, Canada. *Phone:* 613-562-5800 Ext. 1593. *E-mail:* admissio@uottawa.ca.

UNIVERSITY OF PHOENIX–VANCOUVER CAMPUS

Burnaby, British Columbia, Canada

- **Proprietary** comprehensive, founded 1998
- **Calendar** continuous
- **Degrees** certificates, associate, bachelor's, master's, doctoral, post-master's, and postbachelor's certificates (courses conducted at 121 campuses and learning centers in 25 states)
- **Urban** campus
- **Coed,** 125 undergraduate students, 100% full-time, 56% women, 44% men
- **Noncompetitive** entrance level

Undergraduates 125 full-time. 14% Asian American or Pacific Islander, 0.8% Hispanic American.

Faculty *Total:* 21, 10% with terminal degrees. *Student/faculty ratio:* 6:1.

Majors Computer and information sciences; corrections and criminal justice related; health/health care administration; management information systems.

Academic Programs *Special study options:* accelerated degree program, adult/continuing education programs, advanced placement credit, distance learning, external degree program, independent study.

Library University Library with 27.1 million titles, 11,648 serial subscriptions, an OPAC, a Web page.

Computers on Campus A campuswide network can be accessed from off campus. Internet access, at least one staffed computer lab available.

Student Life *Housing:* college housing not available.

Costs (2003–04) *Tuition:* $11,250 full-time, $375 per credit part-time. *Waivers:* employees or children of employees.

Applying *Options:* deferred entrance. *Application fee:* $85. *Required:* 2 years of work experience, 23 years of age. *Required for some:* high school transcript. *Application deadline:* rolling (freshmen), rolling (transfers).

Admissions Contact Ms. Beth Barilla, Director of Admissions, University of Phoenix–Vancouver Campus, 4615 East Elwood Street, Mail Stop AA-K101, Phoenix, AZ 85040-1958. *Phone:* 480-317-6000. *Fax:* 480-594-1758. *E-mail:* beth.barilla@phoenix.edu.

UNIVERSITY OF PRINCE EDWARD ISLAND

Charlottetown, Prince Edward Island, Canada

- **Province-supported** comprehensive, founded 1834
- **Calendar** Canadian standard year
- **Degrees** certificates, diplomas, bachelor's, master's, doctoral, and first professional
- **Small-town** 130-acre campus
- **Coed,** 3,362 undergraduate students, 85% full-time, 63% women, 37% men
- **Moderately difficult** entrance level, 89% of applicants were admitted

Undergraduates 2,845 full-time, 517 part-time. Students come from 12 provinces and territories, 28 other countries, 14% live on campus. *Retention:* 69% of 2002 full-time freshmen returned.

Freshmen *Admission:* 2,143 applied, 1,903 admitted.

Faculty *Total:* 208. *Student/faculty ratio:* 16:1.

Majors Anthropology; biology/biological sciences; business administration and management; Canadian studies; chemistry; computer science; economics; education; elementary education; English; family and consumer economics related; foods, nutrition, and wellness; French; German; history; hospitality administration; mathematics; medical radiologic technology; music; music teacher education; nursing (registered nurse training); philosophy; physics; political science and government; pre-dentistry studies; pre-medical studies; pre-veterinary studies; psychology; religious studies; secondary education; sociology; Spanish.

Academic Programs *Special study options:* distance learning, double majors, English as a second language, honors programs, part-time degree program, summer session for credit.

Library Robertson Library with 394,000 titles, 1,700 serial subscriptions, an OPAC, a Web page.

Computers on Campus 120 computers available on campus for general student use. A campuswide network can be accessed from student residence rooms and from off campus. Internet access, at least one staffed computer lab available.

Student Life *Housing options:* coed. Campus housing is university owned. *Activities and organizations:* drama/theater group, student-run newspaper, choral group, Business Society, biology club, Music Society, intramurals, Theatre Society. *Campus security:* 24-hour emergency response devices and patrols, late-night transport/escort service, controlled dormitory access, late night residence hall security personnel. *Student services:* health clinic, personal/psychological counseling, women's center.

Athletics Member CIS. *Intercollegiate sports:* basketball M/W, field hockey W, ice hockey M/W, rugby M/W, soccer M/W, volleyball W. *Intramural sports:* badminton M/W, basketball M/W, fencing M(c)/W(c), ice hockey M, racquetball M(c)/W(c), rugby M(c)/W(c), skiing (cross-country) M(c)/W(c), skiing (downhill) M(c)/W(c), soccer M, squash M(c)/W(c), tennis M(c)/W(c), volleyball M/W, weight lifting M(c)/W(c).

Costs (2003–04) *Tuition:* province resident $2918 Canadian dollars full-time; International tuition $5332 Canadian dollars full-time. *Required fees:* $318 Canadian dollars full-time. *Room and board:* $4231 Canadian dollars; room only: $2230 Canadian dollars.

Applying *Options:* common application, early admission. *Application fee:* $35 Canadian dollars. *Required:* high school transcript, minimum 2.0 GPA. *Required for some:* 3 letters of recommendation. *Application deadlines:* 8/15 (freshmen), 4/1 (out-of-state freshmen), 8/15 (transfers). *Notification:* continuous until 8/31 (freshmen), continuous until 6/30 (out-of-state freshmen), continuous until 8/31 (transfers).

Admissions Contact Mr. Paul Cantelo, Liaison Officer, University of Prince Edward Island, Registrar's Office, Charlottetown, PE C1A 4D3, Canada. *Phone:* 902-628-4353. *Fax:* 902-566-0795. *E-mail:* registrar@upei.ca.

UNIVERSITY OF REGINA

Regina, Saskatchewan, Canada

- **Province-supported** university, founded 1974
- **Calendar** semesters
- **Degrees** certificates, diplomas, bachelor's, master's, and doctoral
- **Urban** 930-hectare campus
- **Endowment** $11.3 million
- **Coed,** 11,387 undergraduate students, 63% full-time, 61% women, 39% men
- **Minimally difficult** entrance level, 84% of applicants were admitted

University of Regina (continued)

Undergraduates 7,230 full-time, 4,157 part-time. Students come from 11 provinces and territories, 75 other countries, 42% are from out of state, 6% transferred in. *Retention:* 76% of 2002 full-time freshmen returned.

Freshmen *Admission:* 1,511 applied, 1,267 admitted, 1,010 enrolled. *Average high school GPA:* 3.24.

Faculty *Total:* 441, 95% full-time, 74% with terminal degrees. *Student/faculty ratio:* 22:1.

Majors Accounting; acting; actuarial science; adult and continuing education; American history; American Indian/Native American studies; American native/native American education; American Native/Native American languages; anthropology; art; art history, criticism and conservation; art teacher education; Asian history; bilingual and multilingual education; biochemistry; biological and physical sciences; biology/biological sciences; biology teacher education; business administration and management; business teacher education; Canadian history; Canadian studies; ceramic arts and ceramics; chemical technology; chemistry; chemistry teacher education; Chinese; cinematography and film/video production; classics and languages, literatures and linguistics; computer science; computer software engineering; criminal justice/law enforcement administration; criminal justice/police science; criminal justice/safety; dramatic/theatre arts; dramatic/theatre arts and stagecraft related; drawing; early childhood education; economics; education; educational psychology; electrical, electronic and communications engineering technology; electrical, electronics and communications engineering; elementary education; engineering; English; English/language arts teacher education; environmental biology; environmental/environmental health engineering; environmental studies; ethnic, cultural minority, and gender studies related; European history; film/cinema studies; finance; fine arts related; French; French language teacher education; geography; geology/earth science; German; health teacher education; history; history of philosophy; history related; humanities; industrial engineering; intermedia/multimedia; Japanese; journalism; kindergarten/preschool education; kinesiology and exercise science; kinesiotherapy; liberal arts and sciences/liberal studies; linguistics; marketing/marketing management; mathematics; mathematics and computer science; mathematics and statistics related; mathematics teacher education; middle school education; music; music history, literature, and theory; musicology and ethnomusicology; music performance; music teacher education; music theory and composition; painting; petroleum engineering; philosophy; physical education teaching and coaching; physics; physics related; physics teacher education; political science and government; pre-dentistry studies; pre-law studies; pre-medical studies; pre-pharmacy studies; pre-veterinary studies; printmaking; psychology; public administration; religious studies; religious studies related; science teacher education; sculpture; secondary education; social sciences; social studies teacher education; social work; sociology; Spanish; sport and fitness administration; statistics; systems engineering; technology/industrial arts teacher education; theatre design and technology; trade and industrial teacher education; visual and performing arts; women's studies.

Academic Programs *Special study options:* academic remediation for entering students, adult/continuing education programs, advanced placement credit, cooperative education, English as a second language, honors programs, internships, off-campus study, part-time degree program, services for LD students, student-designed majors, summer session for credit.

Library Dr. John Archer Library plus 6 others with 2.3 million titles.

Computers on Campus 150 computers available on campus for general student use. A campuswide network can be accessed from student residence rooms and from off campus. Internet access, at least one staffed computer lab available.

Student Life *Housing options:* coed. Campus housing is university owned. *Activities and organizations:* drama/theater group, student-run newspaper, television station, choral group, Administration Students' Society, Education Students' Society, Engineering Students Society, Chinese Students and Scholars Association, Luther Student Association. *Campus security:* 24-hour emergency response devices and patrols, student patrols, late-night transport/escort service, controlled dormitory access. *Student services:* health clinic, personal/psychological counseling, women's center.

Athletics Member CIS. *Intercollegiate sports:* basketball M(s)/W(s), cross-country running M(s)/W(s), football M(s), ice hockey M(s)/W(s), soccer W(s), swimming M(s)/W(s), track and field M(s)/W(s), volleyball M(s)/W(s), wrestling M(s)/W(s). *Intramural sports:* badminton M/W, basketball M/W, cheerleading M/W, football M, ice hockey M/W, soccer M/W, softball M/W, tennis M/W, ultimate Frisbee M/W, volleyball M/W, water polo M/W.

Standardized Tests *Required for some:* SAT I or ACT (for admission).

Costs (2003–04) *Tuition:* province resident $130 per credit hour part-time; nonresident $3890 full-time, $260 per credit hour part-time; International tuition $7780 full-time. Full-time tuition and fees vary according to course load and program. Part-time tuition and fees vary according to course load and program. *Required fees:* $307 full-time, $90 per term part-time. *Room only:* $3100. Room and board charges vary according to housing facility. *Waivers:* senior citizens.

Applying *Options:* early admission, early action, deferred entrance. *Application fee:* $60 Canadian dollars. *Required:* high school transcript, minimum 2.3 GPA. *Required for some:* essay or personal statement, letters of recommendation, interview. *Application deadlines:* 7/1 (freshmen), 7/1 (transfers). *Early decision:* 7/1.

Admissions Contact Mr. Clarence Gray, Assistant Registrar/Admissions and Awards, University of Regina, AH 213, Regina, SK 5450A2. *Phone:* 306-585-4591. *Toll-free phone:* 306-585-4591 (in-state); 306-585-5165 (out-of-state). *Fax:* 306-337-2525. *E-mail:* admissions.office@uregina.ca.

UNIVERSITY OF SASKATCHEWAN

Saskatoon, Saskatchewan, Canada

- **Province-supported** university, founded 1907
- **Calendar** Canadian standard year
- **Degrees** certificates, diplomas, bachelor's, master's, doctoral, and first professional
- **Urban** 363-acre campus
- **Coed,** 15,893 undergraduate students
- **Moderately difficult** entrance level, 85% of applicants were admitted

Undergraduates Students come from 13 provinces and territories, 75 other countries.

Freshmen *Admission:* 6,689 applied, 5,659 admitted. *Average high school GPA:* 3.7.

Faculty *Total:* 983.

Majors Accounting; agribusiness; agricultural/biological engineering and bioengineering; agricultural economics; agriculture; agronomy and crop science; American Indian/Native American studies; American studies; anatomy; animal physiology; animal sciences; anthropology; archeology; art history, criticism and conservation; astronomy; biochemistry; bioinformatics; biology/biological sciences; biotechnology; business/commerce; business/managerial economics; chemical engineering; chemistry; civil engineering; classics and languages, literatures and linguistics; computer science; dramatic/theatre arts; economics; education; electrical, electronics and communications engineering; elementary education; engineering; engineering physics; English; English as a second/foreign language (teaching); environmental studies; family and consumer sciences/home economics teacher education; finance; fine/studio arts; food science; French; geography; geological/geophysical engineering; geology/earth science; geophysics and seismology; German; health/health care administration; Hebrew; history; horticultural science; human resources management; information science/studies; international relations and affairs; kinesiology and exercise science; land use planning and management; Latin; linguistics; marketing/marketing management; mathematics; mechanical engineering; medical microbiology and bacteriology; microbiology; modern Greek; music; music teacher education; nursing administration; nursing (registered nurse training); nutrition sciences; operations management; parks, recreation and leisure; pharmacy; philosophy; physical education teaching and coaching; physical therapy; physics; physiology; plant sciences; political science and government; pre-dentistry studies; pre-law studies; pre-medical studies; pre-pharmacy studies; pre-veterinary studies; psychology; public administration; range science and management; religious studies; Russian; secondary education; Slavic languages; sociology; soil science and agronomy; Spanish; sport and fitness administration; statistics; technical teacher education; theoretical and mathematical physics; toxicology; trade and industrial teacher education; Ukrainian; urban studies/affairs; women's studies.

Academic Programs *Special study options:* academic remediation for entering students, accelerated degree program, adult/continuing education programs, advanced placement credit, cooperative education, distance learning, double majors, English as a second language, honors programs, independent study, internships, off-campus study, part-time degree program, services for LD students, study abroad, summer session for credit.

Library University of Saskatchewan Main Library plus 7 others with 1.8 million titles, 16,900 serial subscriptions, an OPAC, a Web page.

Computers on Campus 900 computers available on campus for general student use. A campuswide network can be accessed from off campus. Internet access, at least one staffed computer lab available.

Student Life *Housing options:* coed, men-only, women-only. Campus housing is university owned. *Activities and organizations:* drama/theater group, student-run newspaper, choral group, ballroom dancing club, ski club, AIESEC. *Campus security:* 24-hour emergency response devices and patrols, late-night transport/escort service. *Student services:* health clinic, personal/psychological counseling, women's center.

Athletics Member CIS. *Intercollegiate sports:* basketball M/W, cheerleading M(s)/W(s), cross-country running M/W, football M, ice hockey M/W, soccer M/W, track and field M/W, volleyball M/W, wrestling M/W(c). *Intramural sports:* badminton M/W, baseball M/W, basketball M/W, crew M(c)/W(c), cross-country running M/W, football M/W, ice hockey M/W, soccer M/W, softball M/W, swimming M/W, tennis M/W, volleyball M/W.

Costs (2003–04) *Tuition:* area resident $5364 Canadian dollars full-time, $165 Canadian dollars per credit part-time; International tuition $12,605 Canadian dollars full-time. Full-time tuition and fees vary according to program. Part-time tuition and fees vary according to program. *Required fees:* $389 Canadian dollars full-time, $106 Canadian dollars per term part-time. *Room and board:* $5313 Canadian dollars; room only: $2061 Canadian dollars. *Payment plan:* installment.

Financial Aid *Financial aid deadline:* 4/1.

Applying *Options:* electronic application, early admission, early action. *Application fee:* $75 Canadian dollars. *Required:* high school transcript. *Required for some:* essay or personal statement, interview. *Application deadlines:* 5/15 (freshmen), 5/15 (transfers). *Notification:* continuous (freshmen), continuous (transfers).

Admissions Contact Director of Admissions, University of Saskatchewan, Recruitment and Admissions, 105 Administration Place, Saskatoon, SK S7N 5A2. *Phone:* 306-966-6718. *Fax:* 306-966-2115. *E-mail:* admissions@usask.ca.

University of Toronto

Toronto, Ontario, Canada

- **Province-supported** university, founded 1827
- **Calendar** Canadian standard year
- **Degrees** certificates, diplomas, bachelor's, master's, doctoral, and first professional
- **Urban** 714-hectare campus
- **Endowment** $1.2 billion
- **Coed,** 40,341 undergraduate students, 78% full-time, 56% women, 44% men
- **Very difficult** entrance level, 59% of applicants were admitted

Undergraduates 31,539 full-time, 8,802 part-time. Students come from 12 provinces and territories, 126 other countries, 3% are from out of state. *Retention:* 94% of 2002 full-time freshmen returned.

Freshmen *Admission:* 75,382 applied, 44,852 admitted, 13,027 enrolled.

Faculty *Total:* 3,084, 89% full-time. *Student/faculty ratio:* 15:1.

Majors Actuarial science; aerospace, aeronautical and astronautical engineering; African studies; American Indian/Native American studies; American studies; anatomy; ancient Near Eastern and biblical languages; animal genetics; animal physiology; anthropology; applied mathematics; Arabic; archeology; architecture; art; art history, criticism and conservation; arts management; Asian studies; Asian studies (East); Asian studies (South); astronomy; biochemistry; biological and physical sciences; biology/biological sciences; biomedical/medical engineering; biophysics; botany/plant biology; business administration and management; Canadian studies; chemical engineering; chemistry; Chinese; civil engineering; classics and languages, literatures and linguistics; computer engineering; computer science; criminal justice/police science; cultural studies; dramatic/theatre arts; ecology; economics; education; electrical, electronics and communications engineering; engineering; engineering science; English; environmental studies; European studies; European studies (Central and Eastern); film/cinema studies; finance; fine/studio arts; foods, nutrition, and wellness; forestry; French; geography; geology/earth science; geophysics and seismology; German; health teacher education; Hebrew; history; history and philosophy of science and technology; history of philosophy; humanities; industrial engineering; international relations and affairs; Islamic studies; Italian; Japanese; Jewish/Judaic studies; labor and industrial relations; Latin; Latin American studies; linguistics; literature; mass communication/media; materials engineering; materials science; mathematics; mechanical engineering; medical microbiology and bacteriology; medieval and Renaissance studies; metallurgical engineering; modern Greek; modern languages; molecular biology; music; music history, literature, and theory; music teacher education; Near and Middle Eastern studies; neuroscience; nuclear engineering; nursing (registered nurse training); paleontology; petroleum engineering; pharmacology; pharmacy; philosophy; physical education teaching and coaching; physical sciences related; physics; political science and government; Portuguese; psychology; public administration; religious studies; Romance languages; Russian; Russian studies; Slavic languages; sociology; Spanish; statistics; theology; toxicology; urban studies/affairs; women's studies; wood science and wood products/pulp and paper technology; zoology/animal biology.

Academic Programs *Special study options:* adult/continuing education programs, cooperative education, double majors, English as a second language, off-campus study, part-time degree program, services for LD students, study abroad, summer session for credit.

Library Robart's Library plus 43 others with 10.3 million titles, 53,547 serial subscriptions, 1.2 million audiovisual materials, an OPAC, a Web page.

Computers on Campus 2000 computers available on campus for general student use. A campuswide network can be accessed from student residence rooms and from off campus. Internet access, at least one staffed computer lab available.

Student Life *Housing options:* coed. Campus housing is university owned and leased by the school. Freshman campus housing is guaranteed. *Activities and organizations:* drama/theater group, student-run newspaper, radio station, choral group, national fraternities, national sororities. *Campus security:* 24-hour emergency response devices and patrols, student patrols, late-night transport/escort service. *Student services:* health clinic, personal/psychological counseling, women's center, legal services.

Athletics Member CIS. *Intercollegiate sports:* archery M/W, badminton M/W, basketball M/W, crew M, cross-country running M/W, fencing M/W, field hockey W, football M, golf M, gymnastics M/W, ice hockey M/W, rugby M, skiing (cross-country) M/W, skiing (downhill) M/W, soccer M/W, squash M/W, swimming M/W, tennis M/W, track and field M/W, volleyball M/W, wrestling M. *Intramural sports:* archery M/W, badminton M/W, basketball M/W, crew M, fencing M/W, field hockey W, football M/W, gymnastics M/W, ice hockey M/W, lacrosse M/W, racquetball M, rugby M, skiing (downhill) M/W, soccer M/W, squash M/W, swimming M/W, tennis M/W, track and field M/W, volleyball M/W, water polo M/W.

Standardized Tests *Required for some:* SAT I (for admission), SAT II: Subject Tests (for admission).

Costs (2003–04) *Tuition:* nonresident $3160 full-time; International tuition $8102 full-time. Full-time tuition and fees vary according to program. *Required fees:* $800 full-time. *Room and board:* $6000; room only: $3400. Room and board charges vary according to board plan, housing facility, and location. *Payment plan:* installment. *Waivers:* senior citizens and employees or children of employees.

Applying *Options:* deferred entrance. *Application fee:* $43 Canadian dollars. *Required:* high school transcript. *Required for some:* interview. *Application deadlines:* 3/1 (freshmen), 7/1 (transfers). *Notification:* continuous (freshmen), continuous (transfers).

Admissions Contact Admissions and Awards, University of Toronto, Toronto, ON M5S 1A1, Canada. *Phone:* 416-978-2190. *Fax:* 416-978-7022. *E-mail:* ask@adm.utoronto.ca.

University of Victoria

Victoria, British Columbia, Canada

- **Province-supported** university, founded 1963
- **Calendar** Canadian standard year
- **Degrees** certificates, diplomas, bachelor's, master's, doctoral, and first professional
- **Suburban** 380-acre campus with easy access to Vancouver
- **Coed,** 16,090 undergraduate students, 64% full-time, 60% women, 40% men
- **Moderately difficult** entrance level, 58% of applicants were admitted

Undergraduates 10,316 full-time, 5,774 part-time. Students come from 11 provinces and territories, 71 other countries, 13% are from out of state, 8% transferred in, 12% live on campus.

Freshmen *Admission:* 8,082 applied, 4,677 admitted, 2,127 enrolled. *Average high school GPA:* 3.69.

Faculty *Total:* 655, 94% full-time. *Student/faculty ratio:* 28:1.

Majors Ancient/classical Greek; anthropology; art history, criticism and conservation; art teacher education; Asian studies; astronomy; atmospheric sciences and meteorology; biochemistry; biology/biological sciences; botany/plant biology; business/commerce; chemistry; child development; Chinese; classics and languages, literatures and linguistics; computer engineering; computer science; computer software engineering; creative writing; dramatic/theatre arts; ecology; economics; education; electrical, electronics and communications engineering; elementary education; English; English as a second/foreign language (teaching); environmental studies; European studies (Central and Eastern); fine/studio arts; French; French studies; geography; geology/earth science; geophysics and seismology; German; German studies; health and physical education related; health/health care administration; history; hotel/motel administration; international business/trade/commerce; Italian; Italian studies; Japanese; kindergarten/preschool education; kinesiology and exercise science; Latin; liberal arts and sciences/liberal studies; linguistics; literature; marine biology and biological oceanography; mathematics; mechanical engineering; medical microbiology and bacteriology; medieval and Renaissance studies; modern languages; music; music history, literature, and theory; music teacher education; music theory and composition; nursing (registered nurse training); nursing science; oceanography (chemical and physical); Pacific area/Pacific rim studies; philosophy; physical education teaching and coaching; physics; piano and organ; political science and government; pre-dentistry studies; pre-law studies; pre-medical studies; pre-veterinary studies; psychology; public administration; Romance languages; Russian; Russian studies; secondary education; Slavic languages; social work; sociology; Spanish; special education; sport and fitness administration; statistics; technical and business writing; voice and opera; women's studies; zoology/animal biology.

University of Victoria (continued)

Academic Programs *Special study options:* academic remediation for entering students, adult/continuing education programs, advanced placement credit, cooperative education, distance learning, double majors, English as a second language, honors programs, independent study, internships, off-campus study, part-time degree program, services for LD students, study abroad, summer session for credit.

Library McPherson Library plus 4 others with 1.6 million titles, 12,000 serial subscriptions, an OPAC, a Web page.

Computers on Campus 400 computers available on campus for general student use. A campuswide network can be accessed from student residence rooms and from off campus. Internet access, at least one staffed computer lab available.

Student Life *Housing options:* coed. Campus housing is university owned. Freshman campus housing is guaranteed. *Activities and organizations:* drama/theater group, student-run newspaper, radio station, choral group. *Campus security:* 24-hour emergency response devices and patrols, student patrols, late-night transport/escort service. *Student services:* health clinic, personal/psychological counseling, women's center, legal services.

Athletics Member CIS. *Intercollegiate sports:* basketball M/W, crew M/W, cross-country running M/W, field hockey W, golf M/W, rugby M/W, soccer M/W, swimming M/W, track and field M/W, volleyball M/W. *Intramural sports:* badminton M/W, baseball W, basketball M/W, cross-country running M/W, fencing M/W, field hockey M/W, football M/W, golf M/W, ice hockey M/W, racquetball M/W, rugby M/W, sailing M/W, skiing (downhill) M/W, soccer M/W, softball M/W, squash M/W, swimming M/W, table tennis M/W, tennis M/W, ultimate Frisbee M/W, volleyball M/W, water polo M/W, weight lifting M/W.

Costs (2004–05) *Tuition:* province resident $3634 Canadian dollars full-time; nonresident $3634 Canadian dollars full-time; International tuition $10,902 Canadian dollars full-time. *Required fees:* $345 Canadian dollars full-time. *Room and board:* $4980 Canadian dollars; room only: $3360 Canadian dollars. Room and board charges vary according to board plan and housing facility. *Payment plan:* installment. *Waivers:* senior citizens.

Applying *Options:* electronic application, early admission, early action, deferred entrance. *Application fee:* $100 Canadian dollars. *Required:* high school transcript, minimum 2.5 GPA. *Required for some:* essay or personal statement, minimum 3.0 GPA, interview, audition, portfolio. *Application deadlines:* 4/30 (freshmen), 4/30 (transfers). *Notification:* continuous (freshmen), 5/1 (early action), continuous (transfers).

Admissions Contact Mr. Bruno Rocca, Admission Services Office, University of Victoria, PO Box 3025, Victoria, BC V8W 3P2. *Phone:* 250-721-8121 Ext. 8109. *Fax:* 250-721-6225. *E-mail:* admit@uvic.ca.

UNIVERSITY OF WATERLOO
Waterloo, Ontario, Canada

- **Province-supported** university, founded 1957
- **Calendar** trimesters
- **Degrees** certificates, diplomas, bachelor's, master's, doctoral, and first professional
- **Suburban** 900-acre campus with easy access to Toronto
- **Coed,** 22,240 undergraduate students, 90% full-time, 48% women, 52% men
- **Moderately difficult** entrance level, 52% of applicants were admitted

Undergraduates 20,046 full-time, 2,194 part-time. Students come from 12 provinces and territories, 103 other countries, 29% live on campus.

Freshmen *Admission:* 39,360 applied, 20,500 admitted. *Average high school GPA:* 3.50.

Faculty *Total:* 1,436, 55% full-time. *Student/faculty ratio:* 16:1.

Majors Accounting; accounting and finance; actuarial science; anthropology; applied economics; applied mathematics; applied mathematics related; architecture; art history, criticism and conservation; arts management; atmospheric sciences and meteorology; atomic/molecular physics; biochemistry; biochemistry/biophysics and molecular biology; biochemistry, biophysics and molecular biology related; bioinformatics; biological and physical sciences; biology/biological sciences; biology teacher education; biotechnology; business administration and management; business administration, management and operations related; Canadian studies; chemical engineering; chemical physics; chemistry; chemistry teacher education; city/urban, community and regional planning; civil engineering; classics and languages, literatures and linguistics; communication/speech communication and rhetoric; computational mathematics; computer engineering; computer science; computer software engineering; cultural resource management and policy analysis; digital communication and media/multimedia; dramatic/theatre arts; ecology; economics; education related; electrical, electronics and communications engineering; engineering related; English; environmental/environmental health engineering; environmental science; environmental studies; film/cinema studies; fine/studio arts; French; French language teacher education; French studies; geochemistry; geography; geological/geophysical engineering; geology/earth science; geophysics and seismology; German; health/medical preparatory programs related; health science; history; human development and family studies; human resources management; interdisciplinary studies; international business/trade/commerce; international/global studies; international relations and affairs; kinesiology and exercise science; liberal arts and sciences/liberal studies; mathematics; mathematics and computer science; mathematics related; mathematics teacher education; mechanical engineering; medical informatics; medieval and Renaissance studies; multi-/interdisciplinary studies related; music; operations research; ophthalmic/optometric services; parks, recreation and leisure; parks, recreation and leisure facilities management; parks, recreation, and leisure related; philosophy; physics; physics teacher education; planetary astronomy and science; political science and government; psychology; rehabilitation and therapeutic professions related; religious studies; respiratory care therapy; Russian; Russian studies; Slavic studies; social sciences related; social work; sociology; Spanish; speech and rhetoric; statistics; systems engineering; therapeutic recreation; women's studies.

Academic Programs *Special study options:* academic remediation for entering students, accelerated degree program, adult/continuing education programs, cooperative education, distance learning, double majors, external degree program, honors programs, independent study, internships, off-campus study, part-time degree program, services for LD students, student-designed majors, study abroad, summer session for credit.

Library Dana Porter Library plus 7 others with 3.0 million titles, an OPAC, a Web page.

Computers on Campus 6000 computers available on campus for general student use. A campuswide network can be accessed from student residence rooms and from off campus that provide access to e-mail. Internet access, online (class) registration, at least one staffed computer lab available. Computer purchase or lease plan available.

Student Life *Housing options:* coed, men-only, women-only. Campus housing is university owned. Freshman campus housing is guaranteed. *Activities and organizations:* drama/theater group, student-run newspaper, radio station, choral group, marching band, national fraternities, national sororities. *Campus security:* 24-hour emergency response devices and patrols, student patrols, late-night transport/escort service. *Student services:* health clinic, personal/psychological counseling, women's center, legal services.

Athletics Member CIS. *Intercollegiate sports:* badminton M/W, baseball M, basketball M/W, cheerleading M/W, cross-country running M/W, field hockey W, football M, golf M, ice hockey M/W, rugby M/W, skiing (cross-country) M/W, soccer M/W, squash M, swimming M/W, tennis M/W, track and field M/W, volleyball M/W. *Intramural sports:* archery M(c)/W(c), badminton M(c)/W(c), basketball M/W, crew M(c)/W(c), fencing M(c)/W(c), golf M(c)/W(c), ice hockey M/W, rock climbing M/W, skiing (cross-country) M(c)/W(c), skiing (downhill) M(c)/W(c), soccer M(c)/W(c), squash M(c)/W(c), swimming M/W, table tennis M(c)/W(c), tennis M/W, ultimate Frisbee M(c)/W(c), volleyball M/W, water polo M/W, weight lifting M/W.

Standardized Tests *Required for some:* SAT I or ACT (for admission), SAT II: Subject Tests (for admission).

Costs (2003–04) *Tuition:* nonresident $4194 Canadian dollars full-time, $470 Canadian dollars per course part-time; International tuition $15,326 Canadian dollars full-time. Full-time tuition and fees vary according to program. Part-time tuition and fees vary according to course load and program. *Required fees:* $491 Canadian dollars full-time. *Room and board:* $6500 Canadian dollars; room only: $4058 Canadian dollars. Room and board charges vary according to board plan, housing facility, and location.

Financial Aid Of all full-time matriculated undergraduates who enrolled in 2001, 500 state and other part-time jobs (averaging $1000).

Applying *Options:* electronic application, early admission. *Application fee:* $95 Canadian dollars. *Required:* high school transcript. *Required for some:* essay or personal statement, minimum 3.0 GPA, letters of recommendation, interview. *Application deadline:* 3/31 (freshmen). *Notification:* continuous until 7/30 (freshmen), continuous until 7/30 (transfers).

Admissions Contact Mr. P. Burroughs, Director of Admissions, University of Waterloo, 200 University Avenue West, Waterloo, ON N2L 3G1, Canada. *Phone:* 519-888-4567 Ext. 3777. *Fax:* 519-746-8088.

THE UNIVERSITY OF WESTERN ONTARIO
London, Ontario, Canada

- **Province-supported** university, founded 1878
- **Calendar** Canadian standard year
- **Degrees** certificates, diplomas, bachelor's, master's, doctoral, and first professional
- **Suburban** 420-acre campus
- **Coed,** 25,378 undergraduate students, 89% full-time, 59% women, 41% men

■ **Very difficult** entrance level, 47% of applicants were admitted

Undergraduates 22,524 full-time, 2,854 part-time. Students come from 12 provinces and territories, 13% live on campus. *Retention:* 93% of 2002 full-time freshmen returned.

Freshmen *Admission:* 43,845 applied, 20,534 admitted.

Faculty *Total:* 1,206, 100% full-time. *Student/faculty ratio:* 18:1.

Majors Actuarial science; ancient/classical Greek; animal genetics; animal physiology; anthropology; applied mathematics; art; art history, criticism and conservation; art teacher education; astronomy; biochemistry; biological and physical sciences; biology/biological sciences; biophysics; business administration and management; business teacher education; cell biology and histology; chemical engineering; chemistry; city/urban, community and regional planning; civil engineering; classics and languages, literatures and linguistics; clothing/textiles; comparative literature; computer and information sciences; computer science; computer software engineering; dietetics; ecology; economics; education; electrical, electronics and communications engineering; elementary education; engineering science; English; English/language arts teacher education; environmental/environmental health engineering; environmental studies; ethnic, cultural minority, and gender studies related; family and consumer sciences/human sciences; film/cinema studies; fine/studio arts; foods, nutrition, and wellness; French; geography; geology/earth science; geophysics and seismology; German; health science; history; information science/studies; journalism related; kindergarten/preschool education; kinesiology and exercise science; Latin; linguistics; mass communication/media; materials engineering; mathematics; mathematics teacher education; mechanical engineering; medical microbiology and bacteriology; middle school education; music; music history, literature, and theory; music teacher education; natural resources management and policy; nursing administration; nursing (registered nurse training); occupational therapy; pharmacology; philosophy; physical education teaching and coaching; physical therapy; physics; piano and organ; planetary astronomy and science; plant sciences; political science and government; psychology; public administration; religious studies; Russian; secondary education; social work; sociology; Spanish; special education; statistics; toxicology; urban studies/affairs; violin, viola, guitar and other stringed instruments; voice and opera; western civilization; wind/percussion instruments; women's studies; zoology/animal biology.

Academic Programs *Special study options:* academic remediation for entering students, adult/continuing education programs, cooperative education, distance learning, double majors, honors programs, internships, off-campus study, part-time degree program, services for LD students, student-designed majors, study abroad, summer session for credit.

Library The University of Western Ontario Library System plus 7 others with 2.5 million titles, 21,900 serial subscriptions, 939,229 audiovisual materials, an OPAC.

Computers on Campus 100 computers available on campus for general student use. A campuswide network can be accessed from student residence rooms and from off campus. Internet access, online (class) registration, at least one staffed computer lab available.

Student Life *Housing options:* coed. Campus housing is university owned. *Activities and organizations:* drama/theater group, student-run newspaper, radio station, choral group, marching band. *Campus security:* 24-hour emergency response devices and patrols, student patrols, late-night transport/escort service. *Student services:* health clinic, personal/psychological counseling, women's center, legal services.

Athletics Member CIS. *Intercollegiate sports:* badminton M/W, baseball M, basketball M/W, cheerleading M/W, crew M/W, cross-country running M/W, fencing M/W, field hockey W, football M, golf M/W, ice hockey M/W, lacrosse W, rugby M/W, skiing (cross-country) M/W, soccer M/W, squash M/W, swimming M/W, tennis M/W, track and field M/W, volleyball M/W, water polo M, wrestling M/W. *Intramural sports:* badminton M/W, basketball M/W, equestrian sports M(c)/W(c), fencing M(c)/W(c), football M/W, ice hockey M/W, racquetball M/W, riflery M(c)/W(c), rugby W, skiing (cross-country) M(c)/W(c), skiing (downhill) M(c)/W(c), soccer M/W, softball M/W, squash M(c)/W(c), swimming M(c)/W(c), table tennis M(c)/W(c), tennis M/W, volleyball M/W, water polo M/W.

Standardized Tests *Required for some:* SAT I (for admission).

Costs (2003–04) *Tuition:* nonresident $4140 Canadian dollars full-time, $1315 Canadian dollars per course part-time; International tuition $11,750 Canadian dollars full-time. Full-time tuition and fees vary according to program. *Required fees:* $827 Canadian dollars full-time. *Room and board:* $6145 Canadian dollars; room only: $4085 Canadian dollars. Room and board charges vary according to board plan and housing facility. *Payment plans:* installment, deferred payment.

Financial Aid Of all full-time matriculated undergraduates who enrolled in 2001, 1,600 state and other part-time jobs (averaging $1600).

Applying *Options:* deferred entrance. *Application fee:* $95 Canadian dollars. *Required:* high school transcript, minimum 3.0 GPA. *Application deadlines:* 6/1 (freshmen), 5/15 (out-of-state freshmen), 6/1 (transfers).

Admissions Contact Ms. Lori Gribbon, Manager, Admissions, The University of Western Ontario, London, ON N6A 5B8, Canada. *Phone:* 519-661-2116. *Fax:* 519-661-3710. *E-mail:* reg-admissions@uwo.ca.

UNIVERSITY OF WINDSOR
Windsor, Ontario, Canada

■ **Province-supported** university, founded 1857
■ **Calendar** semesters
■ **Degrees** certificates, bachelor's, master's, doctoral, and postbachelor's certificates
■ **Urban** 125-acre campus with easy access to Detroit
■ **Endowment** $26.0 million
■ **Coed,** 13,688 undergraduate students, 76% full-time, 54% women, 46% men
■ **Moderately difficult** entrance level, 67% of applicants were admitted

Undergraduates 10,451 full-time, 3,237 part-time. Students come from 21 provinces and territories, 88 other countries, 5% transferred in, 13% live on campus. *Retention:* 83% of 2002 full-time freshmen returned.

Freshmen *Admission:* 21,521 applied, 14,420 admitted, 4,123 enrolled.

Faculty *Total:* 709, 72% full-time, 69% with terminal degrees. *Student/faculty ratio:* 22:1.

Majors Accounting; accounting and finance; acting; anthropology; applied mathematics; art; art history, criticism and conservation; artificial intelligence and robotics; arts management; art teacher education; athletic training; biochemical technology; biochemistry; bioinformatics; biological and physical sciences; biology/biological sciences; biology teacher education; biophysics; biopsychology; biotechnology; broadcast journalism; business administration and management; business/commerce; business/managerial economics; chemistry; chemistry teacher education; city/urban, community and regional planning; civil engineering; classics and languages, literatures and linguistics; clinical child psychology; clinical psychology; communication/speech communication and rhetoric; communications technologies and support services related; comparative literature; computer and information sciences; computer and information sciences related; computer engineering; computer programming (specific applications); computer science; computer software and media applications related; computer systems networking and telecommunications; counselor education/school counseling and guidance; creative writing; criminal justice/safety; criminology; developmental and child psychology; development economics and international development; drama and dance teacher education; dramatic/theatre arts; drawing; economics; education; educational leadership and administration; education (K-12); electrical, electronics and communications engineering; elementary education; engineering; engineering mechanics; English; English/language arts teacher education; environmental biology; environmental/environmental health engineering; environmental science; environmental studies; family and consumer economics related; family practice nursing/nurse practitioner; film/cinema studies; finance; fine/studio arts; foreign language teacher education; forensic science and technology; French; French as a second/foreign language (teaching); French language teacher education; French studies; general studies; geography teacher education; geology/earth science; German; German language teacher education; German studies; health and physical education; health teacher education; Hispanic-American, Puerto Rican, and Mexican-American/Chicano studies; history; history teacher education; humanities; human resources management; industrial engineering; information science/studies; information technology; intermedia/multimedia; international relations and affairs; Italian; Italian studies; Japanese; journalism; kindergarten/preschool education; kinesiology and exercise science; labor and industrial relations; labor studies; Latin; legal studies; linguistics; literature; management information systems; management science; marketing/marketing management; marketing research; mass communication/media; materials engineering; mathematics; mathematics and computer science; mathematics teacher education; mechanical engineering; medical laboratory technology; medical microbiology and bacteriology; modern Greek; modern languages; music; music history, literature, and theory; music performance; music teacher education; music theory and composition; music therapy; natural resources management and policy; neuroscience; nursing administration; nursing (registered nurse training); organizational communication; painting; parks, recreation and leisure; philosophy; physical education teaching and coaching; physics; physics teacher education; political science and government; pre-dentistry studies; pre-law studies; pre-medical studies; pre-pharmacy studies; printmaking; psychology; public administration; radio and television; Romance languages; Russian; science teacher education; science, technology and society; sculpture; secondary education; Slavic languages; social sciences; social work; sociology; Spanish; special education; speech/theater education; sport and fitness administration; statistics; visual and performing arts; women's studies.

Academic Programs *Special study options:* academic remediation for entering students, accelerated degree program, adult/continuing education programs, advanced placement credit, cooperative education, distance learning, double

University of Windsor (continued)
majors, external degree program, honors programs, internships, off-campus study, part-time degree program, services for LD students, student-designed majors, study abroad, summer session for credit. *Unusual degree programs:* 3-2 business administration with business for university graduates; social work with social work for university graduates.
Library Leddy Library plus 2 others with 2.7 million titles, 10,720 serial subscriptions, 3,774 audiovisual materials, an OPAC, a Web page.
Computers on Campus 925 computers available on campus for general student use. A campuswide network can be accessed from student residence rooms and from off campus that provide access to online transcripts, degree audits, grades. Internet access, online (class) registration, at least one staffed computer lab available. Computer purchase or lease plan available.
Student Life *Housing options:* coed, men-only, women-only, disabled students. Campus housing is university owned. Freshman campus housing is guaranteed. *Activities and organizations:* drama/theater group, student-run newspaper, radio station, choral group, University of Windsor Student Alliance, Environmental Awareness Association, Social Science Society, Commerce Society, Science Society. *Campus security:* 24-hour emergency response devices and patrols, student patrols, late-night transport/escort service, controlled dormitory access. *Student services:* health clinic, personal/psychological counseling, women's center, legal services.
Athletics Member CIS. *Intercollegiate sports:* basketball M/W, cross-country running M/W, football M, golf M, ice hockey M/W, rugby M/W, soccer M/W, track and field M/W, volleyball M/W. *Intramural sports:* badminton M/W, baseball M/W, basketball M/W, bowling M/W, football M/W, golf M/W, ice hockey M/W, rugby M/W, soccer M/W, softball M/W, swimming M/W, table tennis M/W, tennis M/W, track and field M/W, volleyball M/W, water polo M/W, weight lifting M/W.
Standardized Tests *Required for some:* SAT I (for admission), SAT I and SAT II or ACT (for admission).
Costs (2003–04) *Tuition:* area resident $4084 Canadian dollars full-time; nonresident $408 Canadian dollars per course part-time; International tuition $9750 Canadian dollars full-time. Full-time tuition and fees vary according to program. Part-time tuition and fees vary according to program. $4700-$6000 for out-of-province Canadian students; $11,000-$14,000 for international students. *Required fees:* $645 Canadian dollars full-time, $10 Canadian dollars per course part-time, $51 Canadian dollars per term part-time. *Room and board:* $7000 Canadian dollars; room only: $3649 Canadian dollars. Room and board charges vary according to board plan and housing facility. *Waivers:* senior citizens and employees or children of employees.
Financial Aid *Financial aid deadline:* 6/15.
Applying *Options:* common application, electronic application, early admission. *Application fee:* $30 Canadian dollars. *Required:* high school transcript, minimum 2.7 GPA. *Required for some:* essay or personal statement, minimum 3.3 GPA, 1 letter of recommendation, interview. *Application deadlines:* rolling (freshmen), 7/1 (out-of-state freshmen), rolling (transfers).
Admissions Contact Ms. Charlene Yates, Assistant Registrar, University of Windsor, Office of the Registrar, 401 Sunset Avenue, Windsor, ON N9B 3P4, Canada. *Phone:* 519-253-3000 Ext. 3332. *Toll-free phone:* 800-864-2860. *Fax:* 519-971-3653. *E-mail:* registr@uwindsor.ca.

THE UNIVERSITY OF WINNIPEG
Winnipeg, Manitoba, Canada

Admissions Contact Ms. Nancy Latocki, Director, Student services, Admissions/Records, The University of Winnipeg, 515 Portage Avenue, Winnipeg, MB R3B 2E9, Canada. *Phone:* 204-786-9740. *E-mail:* admissions@uwinnipeg.ca.

WESTERN CHRISTIAN COLLEGE
Dauphin, Manitoba, Canada

Admissions Contact Western Christian College, 220 Whitmore Avenue West, Box 5000, Dauphin, MB R7N 2V5, Canada.

WILFRID LAURIER UNIVERSITY
Waterloo, Ontario, Canada

Admissions Contact Ms. Gail Forsyth, Manager of Admissions, Wilfrid Laurier University, 75 University Avenue West, Waterloo, ON N2L 3C5, Canada. *Phone:* 519-884-0710 Ext. 6099. *Fax:* 519-884-8826. *E-mail:* admissions@mach1.wlu.ca.

WILLIAM AND CATHERINE BOOTH COLLEGE
Winnipeg, Manitoba, Canada

Admissions Contact Ms. Mary Ann Austin, Registrar, William and Catherine Booth College, 447 Webb Place, Winnipeg, MB R3B 2P2, Canada. *Phone:* 204-947-6701. *Toll-free phone:* 800-781-6044.

YORK UNIVERSITY
Toronto, Ontario, Canada

- **Province-supported** university, founded 1959
- **Calendar** semesters
- **Degrees** certificates, bachelor's, master's, doctoral, first professional, post-master's, and postbachelor's certificates
- **Urban** 650-acre campus
- **Endowment** $145.2 million
- **Coed,** 42,021 undergraduate students, 83% full-time, 62% women, 38% men
- **Moderately difficult** entrance level, 22% of applicants were admitted

Undergraduates 35,029 full-time, 6,992 part-time. Students come from 174 other countries, 3% are from out of state, 6% live on campus.
Freshmen *Admission:* 39,225 applied, 8,769 admitted. *Average high school GPA:* 3.10.
Faculty *Total:* 3,164, 100% with terminal degrees. *Student/faculty ratio:* 23:1.
Majors Accounting; acting; actuarial science; aeronautics/aviation/aerospace science and technology; aerospace, aeronautical and astronautical engineering; African studies; ancient Near Eastern and biblical languages; anthropology; applied art; applied mathematics; art; art history, criticism and conservation; art teacher education; Asian studies; Asian studies (East); astronomy; atmospheric sciences and meteorology; behavioral sciences; bilingual and multilingual education; biological and physical sciences; biology/biological sciences; biology teacher education; biotechnology; business administration and management; business/commerce; business/managerial economics; business statistics; Canadian studies; chemistry; chemistry teacher education; cinematography and film/video production; classics and languages, literatures and linguistics; commercial and advertising art; communication/speech communication and rhetoric; computer and information sciences; computer engineering; computer hardware engineering; computer programming; computer science; computer software engineering; creative writing; cultural studies; curriculum and instruction; dance; design and visual communications; development economics and international development; drama and dance teacher education; dramatic/theatre arts; drawing; ecology; economics; education; education (K-12); elementary education; engineering; engineering physics; English; English as a second/foreign language (teaching); English/language arts teacher education; environmental biology; environmental design/architecture; environmental education; environmental science; environmental studies; European studies; film/cinema studies; finance; fine/studio arts; French; French studies; geography; geology/earth science; geotechnical engineering; German; German studies; gerontology; health and physical education; health science; health services/allied health/health sciences; Hebrew; Hispanic-American, Puerto Rican, and Mexican-American/Chicano studies; history; history teacher education; hospital and health care facilities administration; humanities; human resources management; information technology; interdisciplinary studies; international business/trade/commerce; international finance; international marketing; international relations and affairs; Italian; Italian studies; Japanese; jazz/jazz studies; Jewish/Judaic studies; kindergarten/preschool education; labor and industrial relations; language interpretation and translation; Latin; Latin American studies; legal studies; liberal arts and sciences/liberal studies; linguistics; literature; management information systems; management science; marketing/marketing management; marketing research; mass communication/media; mathematics; mathematics and computer science; mathematics teacher education; middle school education; modern Greek; modern languages; molecular biology; music; music history, literature, and theory; musicology and ethnomusicology; music performance; music teacher education; music theory and composition; natural sciences; nursing (registered nurse training); nursing science; operations research; organizational behavior; painting; philosophy; photography; physical education teaching and coaching; physical sciences; physics; physics teacher education; piano and organ; playwriting and screenwriting; political science and government; pre-dentistry studies; pre-law studies; pre-medical studies; pre-pharmacy studies; pre-veterinary studies; printmaking; psychology; public administration; public health; public policy analysis; rehabilitation therapy; religious studies; Romance languages; Russian; Russian studies; sales, distribution and marketing; science teacher education; science, technology and society; sculpture; secondary education; sign language interpretation and translation; social sciences; social science teacher education; social studies teacher education; social work; sociology; Spanish; Spanish and Iberian studies; special education; speech/theater education; sport and fitness administration; statistics; technical and business

writing; theatre design and technology; urban studies/affairs; visual and performing arts; voice and opera; women's studies.

Academic Programs *Special study options:* academic remediation for entering students, accelerated degree program, adult/continuing education programs, advanced placement credit, distance learning, double majors, English as a second language, honors programs, independent study, internships, off-campus study, part-time degree program, services for LD students, student-designed majors, study abroad, summer session for credit. *Unusual degree programs:* 3-2 education.

Library Scott Library plus 4 others with 6.1 million titles, 540,000 serial subscriptions, an OPAC, a Web page.

Computers on Campus 1900 computers available on campus for general student use. A campuswide network can be accessed from student residence rooms and from off campus. Internet access, online (class) registration, at least one staffed computer lab available.

Student Life *Housing options:* coed, disabled students. Campus housing is university owned. Freshman applicants given priority for college housing. *Activities and organizations:* drama/theater group, student-run newspaper, radio station, choral group, college student councils, York Federation of Students, Jewish Student Association, First Nations and Aboriginal Student Association, international and exchange students club. *Campus security:* 24-hour emergency response devices and patrols, student patrols, late-night transport/escort service, controlled dormitory access. *Student services:* health clinic, personal/psychological counseling, women's center, legal services.

Athletics Member CIS. *Intercollegiate sports:* badminton M/W, basketball M/W, cross-country running M/W, fencing M/W, field hockey W, football M, golf M, ice hockey M/W, lacrosse W, rugby M/W, soccer M/W, swimming M/W, tennis M/W, track and field M/W, volleyball M/W, water polo M/W. *Intramural sports:* badminton M/W, baseball M/W, basketball M/W, bowling M/W, cross-country running M/W, football M/W, golf M/W, ice hockey M/W, soccer M/W, softball M/W, squash M/W, swimming M/W, table tennis M/W, tennis M/W, volleyball M/W, water polo M/W.

Standardized Tests *Required:* SAT I or ACT (for admission).

Costs (2003–04) *Tuition:* nonresident $4824 Canadian dollars full-time, $1164 Canadian dollars per course part-time; International tuition $11,474 Canadian dollars full-time. Full-time tuition and fees vary according to degree level and program. Part-time tuition and fees vary according to program. *Room and board:* $5323 Canadian dollars; room only: $3323 Canadian dollars. Room and board charges vary according to board plan and housing facility. *Payment plan:* installment.

Applying *Options:* electronic application, early admission, early action, deferred entrance. *Application fee:* $90 Canadian dollars. *Required:* high school transcript, minimum 3.0 GPA, audition/evaluation for fine arts program, supplemental applications for business and environmental studies. *Required for some:* essay or personal statement, 1 letter of recommendation, interview. *Application deadlines:* 2/1 (freshmen), 2/1 (transfers). *Notification:* 6/1 (early action).

Admissions Contact Ms. Amber Burkett, International Recruitment Officer, York University, 4700 Keele Street, Toronto, ON M3J 1P3, Canada. *Phone:* 416-736-5000 Ext. 60595. *Fax:* 416-650-8195. *E-mail:* intlenq@yorku.ca.

■ *See page 2886 for a narrative description.*

INTERNATIONAL

BULGARIA

AMERICAN UNIVERSITY IN BULGARIA

Blagoevgrad, Bulgaria

- **Independent** comprehensive, founded 1991
- **Calendar** semesters
- **Degrees** bachelor's and master's
- **Small-town** campus with easy access to Sofia
- **Endowment** $2.1 million
- **Coed,** 783 undergraduate students, 100% full-time, 58% women, 42% men
- 56% of applicants were admitted

Undergraduates 783 full-time. Students come from 24 other countries, 38% are from out of state, 0.8% transferred in, 91% live on campus. *Retention:* 84% of 2002 full-time freshmen returned.

Freshmen *Admission:* 678 applied, 377 admitted, 233 enrolled. *Test scores:* SAT verbal scores over 500: 70%; SAT math scores over 500: 97%; SAT verbal scores over 600: 24%; SAT math scores over 600: 67%; SAT verbal scores over 700: 2%; SAT math scores over 700: 20%.

Faculty *Total:* 67, 61% full-time, 64% with terminal degrees. *Student/faculty ratio:* 16:1.

Majors American studies; business administration and management; business/managerial economics; computer and information sciences; English; European studies; European studies (Central and Eastern); history; international relations and affairs; journalism; mathematics; political science and government.

Student Life *Housing:* on-campus residence required through senior year. *Options:* cooperative, disabled students. Campus housing is university owned. Freshman campus housing is guaranteed. *Activities and organizations:* drama/theater group, student-run newspaper, radio station, choral group, AEGEE, Basketball club, Cinema club, Shooting club, Aerobics. *Campus security:* 24-hour emergency response devices and patrols. *Student services:* health clinic, personal/psychological counseling, women's center.

Athletics *Intramural sports:* basketball M(c)/W(c), gymnastics M(c)/W(c), soccer M(c)/W(c).

Standardized Tests *Required:* SAT I (for admission).

Costs (2003–04) *Comprehensive fee:* $13,900 includes full-time tuition ($12,050), mandatory fees ($425), and room and board ($1425). No tuition increase for student's term of enrollment. *College room only:* $825. *Payment plan:* deferred payment. *Waivers:* employees or children of employees.

Applying *Application fee:* $25. *Required:* minimum 3.00 GPA, 3 letters of recommendation. *Application deadlines:* 6/1 (freshmen), 6/1 (transfers).

Admissions Contact Yordanka Melnikliyska, Director of Admissions, American University in Bulgaria, Blagoevgrad 2700, Bulgaria. *Phone:* 359-73 888 218.

CAYMAN ISLANDS

INTERNATIONAL COLLEGE OF THE CAYMAN ISLANDS

Newlands, Cayman Islands

- **Independent** comprehensive, founded 1970
- **Calendar** quarters
- **Degrees** associate, bachelor's, and master's
- **Rural** 3-acre campus
- **Coed**
- **Moderately difficult** entrance level

Faculty *Student/faculty ratio:* 15:1.

Student Life *Campus security:* 24-hour emergency response devices.

Standardized Tests *Required:* SAT I or ACT (for admission).

Costs (2003–04) *Tuition:* $469 per course part-time.

Financial Aid *Financial aid deadline:* 8/15.

Applying *Options:* common application, deferred entrance. *Application fee:* $38. *Required:* essay or personal statement, high school transcript, minimum 2.0 GPA, 2 letters of recommendation, rank in upper 50% of high school class. *Required for some:* interview.

Admissions Contact Ms. Dianne Levy, Admissions Representative, International College of the Cayman Islands, PO Box 136, Savannah Post Office, Newlands, Grand Cayman, Cayman Islands. *Phone:* 345-947-1100 Ext. 301. *Fax:* 345-947-1210. *E-mail:* icci@candw.ky.

■ *See page 1770 for a narrative description.*

CHINA

CHRIST'S COLLEGE

Taipei, China

Admissions Contact 51 Tzu Chiang Road, Tanshui 251 Tapei, Taiwan, China.

EGYPT

THE AMERICAN UNIVERSITY IN CAIRO

Cairo, Egypt

- **Independent** comprehensive, founded 1919
- **Calendar** semesters
- **Degrees** certificates, diplomas, bachelor's, and master's (majority of students are Egyptians; enrollment open to all nationalities)

The American University in Cairo (continued)
- **Urban** 26-acre campus
- **Endowment** $352.8 million
- **Coed,** 4,258 undergraduate students, 89% full-time, 53% women, 47% men
- **Very difficult** entrance level, 57% of applicants were admitted

Undergraduates 3,773 full-time, 485 part-time. Students come from 59 other countries, 0.1% transferred in, 6% live on campus. *Retention:* 95% of 2002 full-time freshmen returned.
Freshmen *Admission:* 1,532 applied, 872 admitted, 543 enrolled. *Average high school GPA:* 3.37. *Test scores:* SAT verbal scores over 500: 37%; SAT math scores over 500: 77%; SAT verbal scores over 600: 6%; SAT math scores over 600: 22%; SAT math scores over 700: 2%.
Faculty *Total:* 522, 55% full-time. *Student/faculty ratio:* 13:1.
Majors Accounting; anthropology; archeology; area studies; art; biology/biological sciences; business administration and management; chemistry; comparative literature; computer science; construction engineering; dramatic/theatre arts; economics; electrical, electronics and communications engineering; English; history; journalism; mass communication/media; mathematics; mechanical engineering; Near and Middle Eastern studies; philosophy; physics; political science and government; psychology; sociology.
Academic Programs *Special study options:* academic remediation for entering students, adult/continuing education programs, advanced placement credit, double majors, independent study, off-campus study, part-time degree program, study abroad, summer session for credit.
Library American University in Cairo Library plus 2 others with 377,790 titles, 1,780 serial subscriptions, an OPAC, a Web page.
Computers on Campus 500 computers available on campus for general student use. A campuswide network can be accessed from student residence rooms and from off campus. Internet access, online (class) registration, at least one staffed computer lab available.
Student Life *Housing options:* men-only, women-only. Campus housing is university owned. Freshman applicants given priority for college housing. *Activities and organizations:* drama/theater group, student-run newspaper, radio station, choral group, student government, choral groups/folklore dancing groups, community service groups, Model UN and Model Arab League Clubs, intramural sports. *Campus security:* 24-hour emergency response devices and patrols, controlled dormitory access. *Student services:* health clinic, personal/psychological counseling.
Athletics *Intercollegiate sports:* badminton M/W, basketball M/W, crew M/W, fencing M/W, gymnastics M/W, soccer M/W, squash M/W, swimming M/W, table tennis M/W, tennis M/W, track and field M/W, volleyball M/W, water polo M, wrestling M. *Intramural sports:* basketball M/W, soccer M/W, squash M/W, table tennis M/W, tennis M/W, volleyball M/W, weight lifting M.
Standardized Tests *Required for some:* SAT I or ACT (for admission).
Costs (2003–04) *Tuition:* $12,400 full-time, $517 per credit part-time. *Required fees:* $110 full-time, $60 per term part-time. *Room only:* $2800.
Applying *Options:* electronic application, early decision. *Application fee:* $50. *Required:* essay or personal statement, high school transcript, minimum 2.00 GPA. *Application deadlines:* 6/15 (freshmen), 6/15 (transfers). *Early decision:* 3/1.
Admissions Contact Randa Kamel, Associate Director of Admissions, The American University in Cairo, The Office of Student Affairs, 420 Fifth Avenue, 3rd Floor, New York, NY 10018-2728. *Phone:* 202-357-5199. *Fax:* 212-730-1600. *E-mail:* davidson@aucnyu.edu.

FRANCE

THE AMERICAN UNIVERSITY OF PARIS
Paris, France

- **Independent** 4-year, founded 1962
- **Calendar** semesters
- **Degree** bachelor's
- **Urban** campus
- **Endowment** $1.7 million
- **Coed**
- **Moderately difficult** entrance level

Faculty *Student/faculty ratio:* 12:1.
Student Life *Campus security:* 24-hour emergency response devices.
Standardized Tests *Required for some:* SAT I or ACT (for admission).
Costs (2003–04) *Tuition:* $10,210 full-time. Full-time tuition and fees vary according to course load. Part-time tuition and fees vary according to course load. *Required fees:* $490 full-time.
Applying *Options:* electronic application, deferred entrance. *Application fee:* $55. *Required:* essay or personal statement, high school transcript, 2 letters of recommendation. *Recommended:* minimum 3.0 GPA, interview.
Admissions Contact Ms. Candace McLaughlin, The American University of Paris, US Office, 820 South Monaco Parkway #304, Denver, CO 80224. *Phone:* 303-355-1946. *E-mail:* usoffice@aup.edu.

SCHILLER INTERNATIONAL UNIVERSITY
Paris, France

- **Independent** comprehensive, founded 1967, part of Schiller International University
- **Calendar** semesters
- **Degrees** associate, bachelor's, and master's
- **Urban** campus
- **Coed,** 65 undergraduate students, 92% full-time, 49% women, 51% men
- **Noncompetitive** entrance level

Schiller International University (SIU) is an independent American university with campuses in England, France, Germany, Spain, Switzerland, and the United States. In addition, students can transfer without loss of credit. English is the language of instruction at all campuses. SIU offers undergraduate and graduate students an American education in an international setting.

Undergraduates 60 full-time, 5 part-time.
Freshmen *Admission:* 2 enrolled.
Faculty *Total:* 24, 8% full-time, 46% with terminal degrees.
Majors Business administration and management; interdisciplinary studies; international business/trade/commerce; international relations and affairs; liberal arts and sciences/liberal studies.
Academic Programs *Special study options:* accelerated degree program, adult/continuing education programs, advanced placement credit, English as a second language, internships, part-time degree program, student-designed majors, study abroad, summer session for credit.
Library 3,797 titles, 41 serial subscriptions.
Computers on Campus 11 computers available on campus for general student use. At least one staffed computer lab available.
Student Life *Housing:* college housing not available. *Activities and organizations:* student-run newspaper, student government, student newspaper, yearbook staff. *Student services:* personal/psychological counseling.
Athletics *Intramural sports:* soccer M/W.
Costs (2003–04) *Tuition:* 15,000 euros full-time. *Required fees:* 300 euros full-time, 150 euros per term part-time.
Financial Aid *Financial aid deadline:* 6/1.
Applying *Options:* common application, deferred entrance. *Application fee:* $35. *Required:* essay or personal statement, high school transcript. *Recommended:* minimum 2.0 GPA. *Application deadline:* rolling (freshmen), rolling (transfers).
Admissions Contact Ms. Kamala Dontamsetti, Associate Director of Admissions, Schiller International University, 32 Boulevard de Vaugirard, 75015 Paris, France. *Phone:* 727-736-5082 Ext. 240.

■ See page 2354 for a narrative description.

GERMANY

SCHILLER INTERNATIONAL UNIVERSITY
Heidelberg, Germany

- **Independent** comprehensive, founded 1969, part of Schiller International University
- **Calendar** semesters
- **Degrees** associate, bachelor's, and master's
- **Urban** campus with easy access to Frankfurt
- **Coed,** 163 undergraduate students, 93% full-time, 45% women, 55% men
- **Noncompetitive** entrance level

Schiller International University (SIU) is an independent American university with campuses in England, France, Germany, Spain, Switzerland, and the United States. In addition, students can transfer without loss of credit. English is the language of instruction at all campuses. SIU offers undergraduate and graduate students an American education in an international setting.

Undergraduates 152 full-time, 11 part-time. Students come from 130 other countries.
Freshmen *Admission:* 43 enrolled.

Faculty *Total:* 22, 41% full-time.
Majors Economics; interdisciplinary studies; international business/trade/commerce; international relations and affairs; liberal arts and sciences/liberal studies.
Academic Programs *Special study options:* accelerated degree program, adult/continuing education programs, advanced placement credit, English as a second language, part-time degree program, student-designed majors, study abroad, summer session for credit.
Library 8,000 titles, 94 serial subscriptions.
Computers on Campus 16 computers available on campus for general student use. At least one staffed computer lab available.
Student Life *Housing options:* coed. Campus housing is university owned. *Activities and organizations:* student-run newspaper, student government, yearbook staff. *Campus security:* 24-hour emergency response devices. *Student services:* personal/psychological counseling.
Athletics *Intramural sports:* basketball M/W, soccer M/W, swimming M/W, table tennis M/W, volleyball M/W.
Costs (2003–04) *Tuition:* 13,600 euros full-time, 363 euros per credit part-time. *Required fees:* 450 euros full-time, 150 euros per term part-time. *Room only:* 3000 euros.
Financial Aid *Financial aid deadline:* 6/1.
Applying *Options:* common application, deferred entrance. *Application fee:* $35. *Required:* essay or personal statement, high school transcript. *Recommended:* minimum 2.0 GPA. *Application deadline:* rolling (freshmen), rolling (transfers).
Admissions Contact Ms. Kamala Dontamasetti, Associate Director of Admissions, Schiller International University, Bergstrasse 106, 69121 Heidelberg, Germany. *Phone:* 727-736-5082 Ext. 240. *E-mail:* siu_hd@compuserve.com.

■ *See page 2354 for a narrative description.*

GREECE

AMERICAN COLLEGE OF THESSALONIKI
Thessaloniki, Greece

- **Independent** comprehensive
- **Calendar** semesters
- **Degrees** certificates, bachelor's, and master's
- **Suburban** 40-acre campus
- **Coed,** 520 undergraduate students, 63% full-time, 54% women, 46% men
- **Minimally difficult** entrance level

Undergraduates 328 full-time, 192 part-time. Students come from 28 other countries, 1% transferred in, 1% live on campus. *Retention:* 90% of 2002 full-time freshmen returned.
Freshmen *Admission:* 108 applied, 64 enrolled. *Average high school GPA:* 2.50.
Faculty *Total:* 69, 35% full-time, 28% with terminal degrees. *Student/faculty ratio:* 10:1.
Majors Balkans studies; business administration and management; computer science; English; finance; history; hospitality administration; international business/trade/commerce; international relations and affairs; management information systems; management science; marketing/marketing management.
Academic Programs *Special study options:* academic remediation for entering students, advanced placement credit, double majors, English as a second language, independent study, internships, part-time degree program, study abroad, summer session for credit.
Library Bissell Library plus 1 other with 14,000 titles, 5,000 serial subscriptions, 530 audiovisual materials, an OPAC, a Web page.
Computers on Campus 180 computers available on campus for general student use. A campuswide network can be accessed. Internet access, at least one staffed computer lab available.
Student Life *Housing options:* Campus housing is university owned and leased by the school. *Activities and organizations:* drama/theater group, student-run newspaper, radio station, choral group, Field Trip Club, History and International Relations Society, International Student Society, Marketing Society, radio station. *Campus security:* 24-hour patrols. *Student services:* personal/psychological counseling.
Athletics *Intercollegiate sports:* basketball M/W, soccer M, volleyball M/W. *Intramural sports:* basketball M, soccer M, volleyball M/W.
Standardized Tests *Required for some:* English Proficiency Test.
Costs (2003–04) *Tuition:* 6150 euros full-time, 205 euros per credit hour part-time; International tuition 6600 euros full-time. Full-time tuition and fees vary according to program. Part-time tuition and fees vary according to program. *Required fees:* 50 euros full-time, 50 euros per term part-time. *Room only:* 3400 euros.
Applying *Options:* common application, deferred entrance. *Application fee:* 70 euros. *Required:* high school transcript, proficiency in English. *Required for some:* essay or personal statement, interview. *Recommended:* minimum 2.0 GPA. *Application deadlines:* 7/4 (freshmen), 9/1 (transfers). *Notification:* 9/10 (freshmen), 9/10 (transfers).
Admissions Contact Ms. Roula Lebetli, Admissions Officer, American College of Thessaloniki, PO Box 21021, Pylea, Thessaloniki 55510, Greece. *Phone:* -30-2310-398239. *Fax:* 30-2310-301076. *E-mail:* rleb@ac.anatolia.edu.gr.

THE COLLEGE OF SOUTHEASTERN EUROPE, THE AMERICAN UNIVERSITY OF ATHENS
Athens, Greece

- **Independent** comprehensive, founded 1982
- **Calendar** semesters
- **Degrees** bachelor's and master's
- **Urban** campus
- **Endowment** $6.7 million
- **Coed,** 454 undergraduate students, 87% full-time, 39% women, 61% men
- **Moderately difficult** entrance level, 80% of applicants were admitted

Undergraduates 394 full-time, 60 part-time. Students come from 38 other countries, 17% Asian American or Pacific Islander, 17% transferred in. *Retention:* 84% of 2002 full-time freshmen returned.
Freshmen *Admission:* 165 applied, 132 admitted, 132 enrolled. *Average high school GPA:* 2.80.
Faculty *Total:* 53, 77% full-time, 49% with terminal degrees. *Student/faculty ratio:* 9:1.
Majors Accounting; advertising; archeology; architectural engineering; art history, criticism and conservation; biochemistry; biology/biological sciences; business administration and management; business/commerce; business/managerial economics; chemistry; civil engineering; computer and information sciences; computer graphics; computer science; computer systems networking and telecommunications; electrical, electronics and communications engineering; engineering science; English; English literature (British and Commonwealth); environmental design/architecture; fashion/apparel design; finance; foreign languages and literatures; graphic design; history; hospitality administration; hotel/motel administration; human resources management; industrial engineering; international business/trade/commerce; journalism; legal studies; management science; management sciences and quantitative methods related; marketing/marketing management; mathematics; mechanical engineering; molecular biology; philosophy; physics; political science and government; public relations/image management; sociology; structural engineering; tourism and travel services management; western civilization.
Academic Programs *Special study options:* accelerated degree program, adult/continuing education programs, cooperative education, double majors, English as a second language, independent study, internships, part-time degree program, study abroad, summer session for credit.
Library The College of Southeastern Europe Library with 42,000 titles, 250 serial subscriptions, 51 audiovisual materials, an OPAC.
Computers on Campus 48 computers available on campus for general student use. A campuswide network can be accessed from off campus. Internet access, at least one staffed computer lab available. Computer purchase or lease plan available.
Student Life *Housing options:* Campus housing is leased by the school. Freshman campus housing is guaranteed. *Activities and organizations:* drama/theater group, student-run newspaper, Poetry and Literature Society, journalism association, drama club, political science association, Parliamentary Debating Society. *Campus security:* 24-hour emergency response devices and patrols, closed-circuit TV. *Student services:* personal/psychological counseling.
Athletics *Intramural sports:* basketball M, sailing M, skiing (downhill) M/W, soccer M, swimming M/W, table tennis M/W, volleyball M/W, water polo M/W.
Costs (2003–04) *Comprehensive fee:* $13,030 includes full-time tuition ($5450), mandatory fees ($300), and room and board ($7280). *College room only:* $3360.
Financial Aid Of all full-time matriculated undergraduates who enrolled in 2001, 15 state and other part-time jobs (averaging $1125).
Applying *Options:* common application. *Application fee:* 100 euros. *Required:* essay or personal statement, high school transcript, 2 letters of recommendation, interview. *Application deadline:* 8/15 (freshmen). *Notification:* continuous (transfers).
Admissions Contact Ms. Thalia Poulos, Director of Admissions, The College of Southeastern Europe, The American University of Athens, 17 Patriarchou

The College of Southeastern Europe, The American University of Athens (continued)
Ieremiou Street, Athens 11475, Greece. *Phone:* 301-725-9301. *Fax:* 30-210-725-9304. *E-mail:* admissions@southeastern.edu.gr.

■ *See page 1456 for a narrative description.*

DEREE COLLEGE
Aghia Paraskevi, Greece

- **Independent** 4-year, founded 1875
- **Calendar** 4-1-4
- **Degrees** associate and bachelor's
- **Urban** 60-acre campus
- **Coed**
- **Moderately difficult** entrance level

Faculty *Student/faculty ratio:* 21:1.
Student Life *Campus security:* 24-hour emergency response devices and patrols.
Standardized Tests *Required for some:* SAT I and SAT II or ACT (for admission).
Costs (2003–04) *One-time required fee:* $339. *Tuition:* $3297 full-time. *Required fees:* $671 full-time.
Financial Aid Of all full-time matriculated undergraduates who enrolled in 2001, 132 state and other part-time jobs (averaging $778). *Financial aid deadline:* 1/15.
Applying *Options:* deferred entrance. *Required:* high school transcript, minimum 2.0 GPA, 1 letter of recommendation, interview. *Required for some:* essay or personal statement. *Recommended:* medical certificate.
Admissions Contact Mr. Nick Jiavaras, Director of Enrollment Management, Deree College, 6 Gravias Street, Aghia Paraskevi 153-42, Athens, Greece. *Phone:* 301-210-600-9800 Ext. 1322. *Fax:* 301-801-600-9811. *E-mail:* dereeadm@hol.gr.

IRELAND

INSTITUTE OF PUBLIC ADMINISTRATION
Dublin, Ireland

- **Proprietary** comprehensive, founded 1957
- **Degrees** certificates, diplomas, bachelor's, master's, doctoral, and postbachelor's certificates
- **Coed**
- 100% of applicants were admitted

Faculty *Student/faculty ratio:* 22:1.
Student Life *Campus security:* 24-hour emergency response devices.
Costs (2003–04) *Tuition:* 2200 Irish punt full-time.
Admissions Contact Dr. Denis O'Brien, Registrar, Institute of Public Administration, 57-61 Lansdowne Road, Dublin 4, Ireland. *Phone:* 353-1-240-3600. *Fax:* 353-01269-8644.

ITALY

THE AMERICAN UNIVERSITY OF ROME
Rome, Italy

- **Independent** 4-year, founded 1969
- **Calendar** semesters
- **Degrees** associate and bachelor's
- **Urban** 1-acre campus
- **Endowment** $3.0 million
- **Coed,** 450 undergraduate students, 100% full-time, 64% women, 36% men
- **Moderately difficult** entrance level, 46% of applicants were admitted

Undergraduates 450 full-time. Students come from 13 states and territories, 30 other countries, 8% transferred in, 57% live on campus. *Retention:* 52% of 2002 full-time freshmen returned.
Freshmen *Admission:* 351 applied, 160 admitted, 66 enrolled. *Average high school GPA:* 2.70.
Faculty *Total:* 63, 13% full-time, 32% with terminal degrees. *Student/faculty ratio:* 13:1.
Majors Business administration and management; communication/speech communication and rhetoric; interdisciplinary studies; international business/trade/commerce; international relations and affairs; Italian; liberal arts and sciences/liberal studies.
Academic Programs *Special study options:* academic remediation for entering students, advanced placement credit, distance learning, double majors, English as a second language, independent study, internships, part-time degree program, student-designed majors, summer session for credit.
Library American University of Rome Library with 5,500 titles, 25 serial subscriptions.
Computers on Campus 65 computers available on campus for general student use. A campuswide network can be accessed. Internet access, at least one staffed computer lab available.
Student Life *Housing options:* men-only, women-only. Campus housing is provided by a third party. Freshman applicants given priority for college housing. *Activities and organizations:* drama/theater group, student-run newspaper. *Campus security:* 24-hour emergency response devices, security guards during opening hours and 24-hour surveillance cameras. *Student services:* personal/psychological counseling.
Athletics *Intercollegiate sports:* soccer M. *Intramural sports:* soccer W.
Standardized Tests *Required for some:* SAT I (for admission), ACT (for admission), SAT I or ACT (for admission).
Costs (2004–05) *Tuition:* $11,030 full-time. Part-time tuition and fees vary according to course load. *Required fees:* $315 full-time. *Room only:* $7150. Room and board charges vary according to housing facility. *Payment plan:* installment. *Waivers:* employees or children of employees.
Applying *Options:* common application, deferred entrance. *Application fee:* $55. *Required:* essay or personal statement, high school transcript, minimum 2.5 GPA, letters of recommendation. *Required for some:* interview. *Recommended:* minimum 2.5 GPA. *Application deadline:* 5/15 (freshmen). *Notification:* continuous (freshmen).
Admissions Contact Ms. Mara Nisdeo, Assistant Director for Admissions, The American University of Rome, Via Pietro Roselli 4, Rome 00153, Italy. *Phone:* 39-06-58330919 Ext. 206. *Toll-free phone:* 888-791-8327. *Fax:* 202-296-9577. *E-mail:* aurinfo@aur.edu.

■ *See page 1170 for a narrative description.*

JOHN CABOT UNIVERSITY
Rome, Italy

- **Independent** 4-year, founded 1972
- **Calendar** semesters
- **Degrees** associate and bachelor's
- **Urban** campus
- **Coed,** 516 undergraduate students, 100% full-time, 54% women, 46% men
- **Moderately difficult** entrance level, 88% of applicants were admitted

Located in Rome, Italy, John Cabot University is an accredited independent institution offering an American university education with a distinctive international character. John Cabot students come from more than 50 countries. The average class size is 30–35 students, and there are more than 50 dedicated faculty members. Scholarships and FAFSA loans are available.

Undergraduates 516 full-time. Students come from 50 other countries. *Retention:* 87% of 2002 full-time freshmen returned.
Freshmen *Admission:* 110 applied, 97 admitted, 53 enrolled. *Average high school GPA:* 3.0.
Faculty *Total:* 60, 18% full-time, 43% with terminal degrees. *Student/faculty ratio:* 12:1.
Majors Art history, criticism and conservation; business administration and management; humanities; international relations and affairs; Italian studies; literature; political science and government.
Academic Programs *Special study options:* advanced placement credit, cooperative education, double majors, English as a second language, freshman honors college, honors programs, independent study, internships, part-time degree program, study abroad, summer session for credit.
Library Frohring Library with 18,000 titles, 35,000 serial subscriptions, 50 audiovisual materials, an OPAC, a Web page.
Computers on Campus 40 computers available on campus for general student use. A campuswide network can be accessed. Internet access, at least one staffed computer lab available.
Student Life *Housing options:* Campus housing is leased by the school. Freshman campus housing is guaranteed. *Activities and organizations:* drama/theater group, student-run newspaper. *Campus security:* 24-hour emergency response devices. *Student services:* personal/psychological counseling.
Athletics *Intramural sports:* soccer M/W.

Standardized Tests *Required for some:* SAT I or ACT (for admission).
Costs (2003–04) *Tuition:* $12,500 full-time, $580 per credit part-time. *Required fees:* $450 full-time. *Room only:* $7750.
Applying *Options:* common application, electronic application, deferred entrance. *Application fee:* $50. *Required:* essay or personal statement, high school transcript, 2 letters of recommendation. *Recommended:* minimum 2.69 GPA, interview. *Application deadlines:* 7/15 (freshmen), 7/15 (transfers). *Notification:* continuous until 8/1 (freshmen), continuous until 8/1 (transfers).
Admissions Contact Dr. Francesca R. Gleason, Director of Admissions, John Cabot University, Via della Lungara 233, Roma 00165, Italy. *Phone:* 39-06 6819121. *Toll-free phone:* 866-227-0112. *Fax:* 39-06 6833738. *E-mail:* admissions@johncabot.edu.

■ *See page 1784 for a narrative description.*

KENYA

UNITED STATES INTERNATIONAL UNIVERSITY
Nairobi, Kenya

- **Independent** comprehensive, founded 1977, part of Alliant International University
- **Calendar** trimesters
- **Degrees** bachelor's and master's
- **Urban** 120-acre campus
- **Endowment** $10,000
- **Coed,** 2,248 undergraduate students, 88% full-time, 53% women, 47% men
- **Moderately difficult** entrance level, 56% of applicants were admitted

Undergraduates 1,979 full-time, 269 part-time. Students come from 45 other countries, 2% transferred in, 11% live on campus. *Retention:* 84% of 2002 full-time freshmen returned.
Freshmen *Admission:* 564 applied, 315 admitted, 260 enrolled. *Average high school GPA:* 2.75.
Faculty *Total:* 163, 31% full-time, 40% with terminal degrees. *Student/faculty ratio:* 30:1.
Majors Business administration and management; hotel/motel administration; information technology; international business/trade/commerce; international relations and affairs; journalism; psychology; tourism and travel services management.
Academic Programs *Special study options:* academic remediation for entering students, accelerated degree program, adult/continuing education programs, advanced placement credit, internships, part-time degree program, study abroad, summer session for credit.
Library Lillian K. Beam Library with 50,000 titles, 200 serial subscriptions.
Computers on Campus 30 computers available on campus for general student use. Internet access, at least one staffed computer lab available.
Student Life *Housing options:* coed, men-only, women-only. Campus housing is university owned and is provided by a third party. Freshman applicants given priority for college housing. *Activities and organizations:* drama/theater group, student-run newspaper, choral group, AISEC, Peer Counseling, CHATS, Rotaract, Information Technology Club. *Campus security:* 24-hour patrols. *Student services:* health clinic, personal/psychological counseling.
Athletics *Intercollegiate sports:* basketball M(s)/W(s), field hockey M(s)/W(s), rugby M(s)/W(s), soccer M(s)/W(s), swimming M(s)/W(s). *Intramural sports:* basketball M/W, field hockey M/W, rugby M, soccer M/W, swimming M/W.
Standardized Tests *Required for some:* SAT I or ACT (for admission).
Costs (2003–04) *Comprehensive fee:* $6855 includes full-time tuition ($3690), mandatory fees ($333), and room and board ($2832). Full-time tuition and fees vary according to course load. Part-time tuition: $103 per unit. Part-time tuition and fees vary according to course load. *Required fees:* $111 per term part-time. *College room only:* $1590. Room and board charges vary according to board plan. *Payment plan:* installment. *Waivers:* employees or children of employees.
Applying *Options:* common application, deferred entrance. *Application fee:* $50. *Required:* high school transcript, minimum 2.0 GPA. *Required for some:* essay or personal statement, letters of recommendation, interview. *Recommended:* minimum 2.5 GPA. *Application deadlines:* 7/15 (freshmen), 7/15 (transfers). *Notification:* 8/1 (freshmen), 8/1 (transfers).
Admissions Contact United States International University, PO Box 14634, Thika Road, Kasarani, Nairobi 00800, Kenya. *Phone:* 254-020-3606563. *Fax:* 254-2-3606100. *E-mail:* admission@usiu.ac.ke.

LEBANON

AMERICAN UNIVERSITY OF BEIRUT
Beirut, Lebanon

Admissions Contact American University of Beirut, PO Box 11-236, Beirut 1107 2020, Lebanon.

LEBANESE AMERICAN UNIVERSITY
Beirut, Lebanon

Admissions Contact Leila Saleeby Dapher, Director of Admissions, Lebanese American University, PO Box 13-5053, Beirut, Lebanon. *Phone:* 961-1 786456 Ext. 1129.

MEXICO

ALLIANT INTERNATIONAL UNIVERSITY–MÉXICO CITY
Mexico City, Mexico

- **Independent** comprehensive, founded 1970, part of Alliant International University
- **Calendar** semesters
- **Degrees** bachelor's and master's
- **Urban** campus
- **Coed,** 53 undergraduate students, 57% full-time, 43% women, 57% men
- **Moderately difficult** entrance level, 38% of applicants were admitted

Undergraduates 30 full-time, 23 part-time. Students come from 3 states and territories, 14 other countries, 17% Hispanic American, 64% international, 19% transferred in. *Retention:* 100% of 2002 full-time freshmen returned.
Freshmen *Admission:* 42 applied, 16 admitted, 5 enrolled. *Average high school GPA:* 3.2.
Faculty *Total:* 24, 33% full-time, 54% with terminal degrees. *Student/faculty ratio:* 12:1.
Majors Business administration and management; international business/trade/commerce; international relations and affairs; Latin American studies; liberal arts and sciences/liberal studies; management information systems; psychology; tourism and travel services management.
Academic Programs *Special study options:* accelerated degree program, advanced placement credit, English as a second language, internships, study abroad, summer session for credit.
Library Campus Library with 12,000 titles.
Computers on Campus 15 computers available on campus for general student use. Internet access, at least one staffed computer lab available.
Student Life *Housing:* college housing not available. *Activities and organizations:* student-run newspaper, International Business Club, German Club, Student Council.
Standardized Tests *Required:* SAT I or ACT (for admission).
Costs (2003–04) *Tuition:* 62,400 Mexican pesos full-time, 2600 Mexican pesos per unit part-time. Full-time tuition and fees vary according to course load. Part-time tuition and fees vary according to course load. *Required fees:* 1800 Mexican pesos full-time, 900 Mexican pesos per term part-time. *Payment plan:* installment.
Applying *Options:* common application, deferred entrance. *Application fee:* 500 Mexican pesos. *Required:* essay or personal statement, high school transcript, minimum 2.0 GPA, 1 letter of recommendation. *Required for some:* interview. *Recommended:* minimum 3.0 GPA. *Application deadline:* rolling (freshmen), rolling (transfers).
Admissions Contact Hernan Bucheli, Director, Enrollment Management, Alliant International University–México City, 10455 Pomerado Road, San Diego, CA 92131-1799. *Phone:* 619-635-4777. *Fax:* 619-635-4739. *E-mail:* info@usiumexico.edu.

INSTITUTO TECNOLÓGICO Y DE ESTUDIOS SUPERIORES DE MONTERREY, CAMPUS CENTRAL DE VERACRUZ
Córdoba, Mexico

Admissions Contact Ing. Luis Pablo Villareal, Registrar, Instituto Tecnológico y de Estudios Superiores de Monterrey, Campus Central de Veracruz, Avenida

Instituto Tecnológico y de Estudios Superiores de Monterrey, Campus Central de Veracruz (continued)
Eugenio Garza Sada 1, Apartado Postal 314, 94500 Córdoba, Veracruz, Mexico. *Phone:* -27-13-23-40 Ext. 123. *Fax:* 83-58-19-54.

Instituto Tecnológico y de Estudios Superiores de Monterrey, Campus Chiapas

Tuxtla Gutiérrez, Mexico

Admissions Contact Lic. Luis Enrique Cancino, Registrar, Instituto Tecnológico y de Estudios Superiores de Monterrey, Campus Chiapas, Carretera a Tapanatepec Km 149&746, Apartado Postal 312, 29000 Tuxtla Gutiérrez, Chiapas, Mexico. *Phone:* -96-15-1723. *Fax:* 83-58-19-54.

Instituto Tecnológico y de Estudios Superiores de Monterrey, Campus Chihuahua

Chihuahua, Mexico

Admissions Contact Ing. Juan Manuel Fernandez, Registrar, Instituto Tecnológico y de Estudios Superiores de Monterrey, Campus Chihuahua, Colegio Militar 4700, Colonia Nombre de Dios, Apartado Postal 728, 31300 Chihuahua, Chihuahua, Mexico. *Phone:* -14-17-48-58 Ext. 117. *Fax:* 83-58-19-54.

Instituto Tecnológico y de Estudios Superiores de Monterrey, Campus Ciudad de México

Ciudad de Mexico, Mexico

Admissions Contact Admissions Office, Instituto Tecnológico y de Estudios Superiores de Monterrey, Campus Ciudad de México, Calle del Puente #222 esquina con Periférico, 14380 Colonia Huipulco, Tlalpan, MDF, Mexico. *Phone:* 5-673-6488. *Fax:* 83-58-19-54.

Instituto Tecnológico y de Estudios Superiores de Monterrey, Campus Ciudad Juárez

Ciudad Juárez, Mexico

Admissions Contact Lic. Alberto Trejo, Registrar, Instituto Tecnológico y de Estudios Superiores de Monterrey, Campus Ciudad Juárez, Boulevard Tomas Fernandez y Avenida A J Bermudez, Apartado Postal 3105-J, 32320 Ciudad Juárez, Chihuahua, Mexico. *Phone:* -16-17-88-07 Ext. 113. *Fax:* 83-58-19-54.

Instituto Tecnológico y de Estudios Superiores de Monterrey, Campus Ciudad Obregón

Ciudad Obregón, Mexico

Admissions Contact Lic. Judith Almeida, Registrar, Instituto Tecnológico y de Estudios Superiores de Monterrey, Campus Ciudad Obregón, Dr Norman E Borlaug Km 14, Apartado Postal 662, 85000 Ciudad Obregón, Sonora, Mexico. *Phone:* -64-15-03-12. *Fax:* 83-58-19-54.

Instituto Tecnológico y de Estudios Superiores de Monterrey, Campus Colima

Colima, Mexico

Admissions Contact Lic. Manuel Perez Rivera, Registrar, Instituto Tecnológico y de Estudios Superiores de Monterrey, Campus Colima, Prolongacion Ignacio Sandoval s/n, Fraccionamiento Jardines de Vista Hermosa, Apartado Postal 190, 28010 Colima, Colima, Mexico. *Phone:* -33-12-53-39. *Fax:* 83-58-19-54.

Instituto Tecnológico y de Estudios Superiores de Monterrey, Campus Cuernavaca

Temixco, Mexico

Admissions Contact Lic. Miguel Angel Machua S., Registrar, Instituto Tecnológico y de Estudios Superiores de Monterrey, Campus Cuernavaca, Paseo de la Reforma 182-A, Colonia Lomas de Cuernavaca, 62000 Temixco, Morelos, Mexico. *Phone:* -73 18-49-57. *Fax:* 83-58-19-54.

Instituto Tecnológico y de Estudios Superiores de Monterrey, Campus Estado de México

Estado de Mexico, Mexico

Admissions Contact Prof. Jose de Jesus Molina, Registrar, Instituto Tecnológico y de Estudios Superiores de Monterrey, Campus Estado de México, Carretera Lago de Guadalupe Km. 3.5, Atizapan de Zaragoza, Estado de Mexico 52926, Mexico. *Phone:* -5-873-3600. *Fax:* 83-58-19-54.

Instituto Tecnológico y de Estudios Superiores de Monterrey, Campus Guadalajara

Zapopan, Mexico

Admissions Contact Ms. Janet Martell Sotomayor, Registration Director, Instituto Tecnológico y de Estudios Superiores de Monterrey, Campus Guadalajara, Avenida General Ramón Corona 2514, 44100 Zapopan, Jalisco, Mexico. *Phone:* -3-669-3006.

Instituto Tecnológico y de Estudios Superiores de Monterrey, Campus Hidalgo

Pachuca, Mexico

Admissions Contact Lic. Lizbet Melo, Registrar, Instituto Tecnológico y de Estudios Superiores de Monterrey, Campus Hidalgo, Apartado Postal 237. *Phone:* -714-25-00 Ext. 128. *Fax:* 83-58-19-54. *E-mail:* lizmelo@campus.hgo.itesm.mx.

Instituto Tecnológico y de Estudios Superiores de Monterrey, Campus Irapuato

Irapuato, Mexico

Admissions Contact Ing. Marcela Beltrán, Registrar, Instituto Tecnológico y de Estudios Superiores de Monterrey, Campus Irapuato, Paseo Mirador del Valle No. 445, Col. Villas de Irapuato, Apartado Postal 568, 36660 Irapuato, Guanajuato, Mexico. *Phone:* -46-230342. *Fax:* 83-58-19-54.

Instituto Tecnológico y de Estudios Superiores de Monterrey, Campus Laguna

Torreón, Mexico

Admissions Contact Ing. Aroldo Camargo Soto, Registrar, Instituto Tecnológico y de Estudios Superiores de Monterrey, Campus Laguna, Paseo del Tecnologico s/n Ampliacion La Rosita, Apartado Postal 506, 27250 Torreón, Coahuila, Mexico. *Phone:* -17-20-66-61 Ext. 23. *Fax:* 83-58-19-54.

Instituto Tecnológico y de Estudios Superiores de Monterrey, Campus León

León, Mexico

Admissions Contact Lic. Eddie Villegas, Registrar, Instituto Tecnológico y de Estudios Superiores de Monterrey, Campus León, Apdo. Postal No. 872, Leon 37120, Mexico. *Phone:* -47-17-10-00 Ext. 131. *Fax:* 83-58-19-54.

INSTITUTO TECNOLÓGICO Y DE ESTUDIOS SUPERIORES DE MONTERREY, CAMPUS MAZATLÁN

Mazatlán, Mexico

Admissions Contact Ing. Martin Ley Urias, Registrar, Instituto Tecnológico y de Estudios Superiores de Monterrey, Campus Mazatlán, Carretera Mazatlan-Higueras, Km 3, Camino al Conchi, Apartado Postal 799, 82000 Mazatlán, Sinaloa, Mexico. *Phone:* -69-80-1143. *Fax:* 83-58-19-54.

INSTITUTO TECNOLÓGICO Y DE ESTUDIOS SUPERIORES DE MONTERREY, CAMPUS MONTERREY

Monterrey, Mexico

- **Independent** university, founded 1943, part of Sistema Instituto Tecnológico y de Estudios Superiores de Monterrey
- **Calendar** semesters
- **Degrees** certificates, bachelor's, master's, and doctoral
- **Urban** 86-acre campus
- **Coed**
- **Very difficult** entrance level

Student Life *Campus security:* 24-hour patrols, late-night transport/escort service.

Standardized Tests *Required:* SAT I (for admission).

Costs (2003–04) *Tuition:* $9445 full-time. *Required fees:* $650 full-time. *Room only:* $5316.

Applying *Options:* deferred entrance. *Application fee:* $100. *Required:* high school transcript. *Recommended:* essay or personal statement.

Admissions Contact Lic. Carlos Ordoñez, International Student Advisor, Instituto Tecnológico y de Estudios Superiores de Monterrey, Campus Monterrey, Avenida Eugenio Garza Sada 2501 Sur Colonia Tecnnologico, Sucursal de Correos J, 64849 Monterrey, Nuevo León, Mexico. *Phone:* -52 81 8328 4065. *Fax:* 83-58-19-54.

INSTITUTO TECNOLÓGICO Y DE ESTUDIOS SUPERIORES DE MONTERREY, CAMPUS QUERÉTARO

Santiago de Querétaro, Mexico

Admissions Contact Lic. Marco Vinicio Lopez, Registrar, Instituto Tecnológico y de Estudios Superiores de Monterrey, Campus Querétaro, Avenida Epigmenio Gonzalez #500, Fracc. San Pablo, Queretaro 76130, Mexico. *Phone:* -42-17-38-25 Ext. 156. *Fax:* 83-58-19-54.

INSTITUTO TECNOLÓGICO Y DE ESTUDIOS SUPERIORES DE MONTERREY, CAMPUS SALTILLO

Saltillo, Mexico

Admissions Contact Lic. Esteban Ramos, Registrar, Instituto Tecnológico y de Estudios Superiores de Monterrey, Campus Saltillo, Prolongacion Juan de la Barrera 1241 Ote, Apartado Postal 539, 25270 Saltillo, Coahuila, Mexico. *Phone:* -84-15-06-90 Ext. 12. *Fax:* 83-58-19-54.

INSTITUTO TECNOLÓGICO Y DE ESTUDIOS SUPERIORES DE MONTERREY, CAMPUS SAN LUIS POTOSÍ

San Luis Potosí, Mexico

Admissions Contact Ing. Consuelo Gonzalez, Registrar, Instituto Tecnológico y de Estudios Superiores de Monterrey, Campus San Luis Potosí, Avenida Robles 600, Colonia Jacarandas, Apartado Postal 1473 Suc E, 78140 San Luis Potosí, SLP, Mexico. *Phone:* 48-13-3441 Ext. 14. *Fax:* 83-58-19-54.

INSTITUTO TECNOLÓGICO Y DE ESTUDIOS SUPERIORES DE MONTERREY, CAMPUS SINALOA

Culiacán, Mexico

Admissions Contact Lic. Hugo Guerrero, Registrar, Instituto Tecnológico y de Estudios Superiores de Monterrey, Campus Sinaloa, Boulevard Culiacán 3773, Apartado Postal 69-F, 80800 Culiacán, Sinaloa, Mexico. *Phone:* -67-14-03-69. *Fax:* 83-58-19-54.

INSTITUTO TECNOLÓGICO Y DE ESTUDIOS SUPERIORES DE MONTERREY, CAMPUS SONORA NORTE

Hermosillo, Mexico

Admissions Contact Ing. Victor Eduardo Perez Orozco, Library and Admissions/Registration Director, Instituto Tecnológico y de Estudios Superiores de Monterrey, Campus Sonora Norte, Carretera Hermosillo-Nogales Km 9, Apartado Postal 216, 83000 Hermosillo, Sonora, Mexico. *Phone:* -62-15-52-05 Ext. 131. *Fax:* 83-58-19-54.

INSTITUTO TECNOLÓGICO Y DE ESTUDIOS SUPERIORES DE MONTERREY, CAMPUS TAMPICO

Altimira, Mexico

Admissions Contact Ing. Javier Ponce, Registrar, Instituto Tecnológico y de Estudios Superiores de Monterrey, Campus Tampico, Apdo. Postal 7, Conedor Industrial, Canekra Tampico-Mark, Altamira 89600, Mexico. *Phone:* 126-4-19-79.

INSTITUTO TECNOLÓGICO Y DE ESTUDIOS SUPERIORES DE MONTERREY, CAMPUS TOLUCA

Toluca, Mexico

Admissions Contact Ing. Victor M. Martinez Orta, Registrar, Instituto Tecnológico y de Estudios Superiores de Monterrey, Campus Toluca, Ex-hacienda La Pila, 100 metros al norte de San Antonio Buenavista, 50252 Toluca, Estado de Mexico, Mexico. *Phone:* -72-74-11-92. *Fax:* 83-58-19-54.

INSTITUTO TECNOLÓGICO Y DE ESTUDIOS SUPERIORES DE MONTERREY, CAMPUS ZACATECAS

Zacatecas, Mexico

Admissions Contact Lic. Ma. de Lourdes Zorrilla, Business Affairs Director and Registrar, Instituto Tecnológico y de Estudios Superiores de Monterrey, Campus Zacatecas, Calzada Pedro Coronel #16, Frente al Club Bernades, Municipio de Guadalupe, 98000 Zacatecas, Zacatecas, Mexico. *Phone:* 49-23-00-40.

UNIVERSIDAD DE LAS AMERICAS, A.C.

Mexico City, Mexico

Admissions Contact Calle de Puebla 223, Col. Roma, Mexico City 06700, Mexico.

UNIVERSIDAD DE LAS AMÉRICAS–PUEBLA

Puebla, Mexico

Admissions Contact Lic. Jorge A. Varela Olivares, Chief of Admissions, Universidad de las Américas–Puebla, Cholula Apartado 359, 72820 Cholula, Mexico. *Phone:* 22-29-20-17 Ext. 4015. *Fax:* 22-29-20-18. *E-mail:* jvarela@udlapvms.pue.udlap.mx.

Universidad de Monterrey
San Pedro Garza Garcia, Mexico

Admissions Contact Av. Ignacio Morones Prieto 4500 Pte, San Pedro Garza García, NL CP 66238, Mexico. *Toll-free phone:* 800-849-4757.

MONACO

The International University of Monaco
Monte Carlo, Monaco

Admissions Contact Dr. Gisele Dudognon, Director, Undergraduate Admissions, The International University of Monaco, 2, Avenue Prince Hereditaire Albert, Stade Louis II, Entree B, Monte Carlo 98000, Monaco. *Phone:* 377-97986 986.

NICARAGUA

Ave Maria College of the Americas
San Marcos, Nicaragua

Admissions Contact Mr. Patrick Clark, Director of Admissions, Ave Maria College of the Americas, San Marcos, Carazo, Nicaragua. *Phone:* 43-22314-138.

NIGERIA

The Nigerian Baptist Theological Seminary
Ogbomoso, Nigeria

Admissions Contact Mr. Daniel F. Oroniran, Registrar, The Nigerian Baptist Theological Seminary, PO Box 30, Ogbomoso, Oyo, Nigeria. *Phone:* -038-710011.

SPAIN

Saint Louis University, Madrid Campus
Madrid, Spain

- **Independent Roman Catholic (Jesuit)** comprehensive
- **Calendar** semesters
- **Degrees** bachelor's and master's
- **Urban** 1-acre campus
- **Coed,** 492 undergraduate students, 100% full-time, 60% women, 40% men
- 80% of applicants were admitted

Undergraduates 492 full-time. Students come from 34 states and territories, 65 other countries, 1% transferred in, 45% live on campus.

Freshmen *Admission:* 353 applied, 284 admitted, 147 enrolled. *Average high school GPA:* 3.21. *Test scores:* SAT verbal scores over 500: 79%; SAT math scores over 500: 92%; ACT scores over 18: 100%; SAT verbal scores over 600: 43%; SAT math scores over 600: 26%; ACT scores over 24: 87%; SAT verbal scores over 700: 3%; SAT math scores over 700: 3%; ACT scores over 30: 13%.

Faculty *Total:* 80, 25% full-time. *Student/faculty ratio:* 8:1.

Student Life *Housing:* on-campus residence required for freshman year. *Options:* men-only, women-only. Campus housing is university owned. Freshman campus housing is guaranteed. *Activities and organizations:* drama/theater group, student-run newspaper, choral group, Sierra Club, Latin Dance Club, Yearbook, Theatre, Choir. *Campus security:* 24-hour patrols. *Student services:* health clinic, personal/psychological counseling.

Athletics *Intramural sports:* basketball M/W, soccer M/W, volleyball M/W.

Standardized Tests *Required:* SAT I or ACT (for admission). *Required for some:* SAT II: Writing Test (for admission).

Costs (2003–04) *Tuition:* $14,810 full-time, $625 per credit part-time. *Required fees:* $300 full-time. *Room only:* Room and board charges vary according to housing facility. *Payment plan:* installment. *Waivers:* children of alumni and employees or children of employees.

Applying *Required:* essay or personal statement, high school transcript. *Required for some:* interview. *Recommended:* 2 letters of recommendation. *Application deadlines:* 5/30 (freshmen), 6/30 (transfers). *Notification:* 6/15 (freshmen), continuous (transfers).

Admissions Contact Ms. Phyllis Chaney, Director, Saint Louis University, Madrid Campus, Avda. del Valle 34, 28003 Madrid, Spain. *Phone:* 34-91-554-5858. *Fax:* 34-91-554-6202. *E-mail:* madrid@madrid.sluiberica.slu.edu.

■ *See page 2308 for a narrative description.*

Schiller International University
Madrid, Spain

- **Independent** comprehensive, founded 1967, part of Schiller International University
- **Calendar** semesters
- **Degrees** associate, bachelor's, and master's
- **Urban** campus
- **Coed,** 139 undergraduate students, 94% full-time, 55% women, 45% men
- **Noncompetitive** entrance level

Schiller International University (SIU) is an independent American university with campuses in England, France, Germany, Spain, Switzerland, and the United States. In addition, students can transfer without loss of credit. English is the language of instruction at all campuses. SIU offers undergraduate and graduate students an American education in an international setting.

Undergraduates 131 full-time, 8 part-time.

Freshmen *Admission:* 30 enrolled.

Faculty *Total:* 30, 7% full-time.

Majors Business administration and management; hotel/motel administration; interdisciplinary studies; international business/trade/commerce; international relations and affairs; liberal arts and sciences/liberal studies; marketing/marketing management; pre-medical studies; pre-veterinary studies.

Academic Programs *Special study options:* accelerated degree program, adult/continuing education programs, advanced placement credit, English as a second language, internships, part-time degree program, student-designed majors, study abroad, summer session for credit.

Library 4,216 titles, 58 serial subscriptions.

Computers on Campus 8 computers available on campus for general student use. At least one staffed computer lab available.

Student Life *Housing:* college housing not available. *Activities and organizations:* student government. *Student services:* personal/psychological counseling.

Athletics *Intramural sports:* soccer M/W, volleyball M/W.

Costs (2003–04) *Tuition:* 20,000 euros full-time, 363 euros per credit part-time. *Required fees:* 400 euros full-time.

Financial Aid Of all full-time matriculated undergraduates who enrolled in 2001, 3 Federal Work-Study jobs (averaging $4880). *Financial aid deadline:* 4/15.

Applying *Options:* common application, deferred entrance. *Application fee:* $50. *Required:* essay or personal statement, high school transcript. *Recommended:* minimum 2.0 GPA. *Application deadline:* rolling (freshmen), rolling (transfers).

Admissions Contact Ms. Kamala Dontamsetti, Associate Director of Admissions, Schiller International University, San Bernardo 97-99, Edif. Colomina, 28015 Madrid, Spain. *Phone:* 727-736-5082 Ext. 240.

■ *See page 2354 for a narrative description.*

SWITZERLAND

Ecole Hôtelière de Lausanne
Lausanne, Switzerland

- **Independent** 4-year, founded 1893
- **Degree** bachelor's
- 5-acre campus
- **Coed**
- **Moderately difficult** entrance level

Faculty *Student/faculty ratio:* 15:1.

Costs (2003–04) *Comprehensive fee:* 54,000 Swiss francs includes full-time tuition (31,000 Swiss francs), mandatory fees (5000 Swiss francs), and room and board (18,000 Swiss francs). *College room only:* 11,500 Swiss francs.

Applying *Application fee:* 300 Swiss francs.

Admissions Contact Ms. Margaret Boule, Head of Admissions, Ecole Hôtelière de Lausanne, Le Chalet-a-Gobet, 1000 Lausanne 25, Switzerland. *Phone:* 41-21 785 1111 Ext. 1345.

FRANKLIN COLLEGE SWITZERLAND
Sorengo, Switzerland

- **Independent** 4-year, founded 1969
- **Calendar** semesters
- **Degrees** certificates, associate, and bachelor's
- **Suburban** 5-acre campus with easy access to Milan
- **Endowment** $217,912
- **Coed,** 312 undergraduate students, 97% full-time, 60% women, 40% men
- **Moderately difficult** entrance level, 83% of applicants were admitted

Franklin College is a 4-year, coeducational, residential American liberal arts college located in southern Switzerland and specializing in international studies. Students from more than 50 countries attend. Semester and year-abroad students are welcome. Summer sessions are offered May–July. Every semester, students take faculty-led academic travel trips to destinations worldwide.

Undergraduates 303 full-time, 9 part-time. Students come from 30 states and territories, 57 other countries, 100% are from out of state, 6% transferred in, 75% live on campus. *Retention:* 67% of 2002 full-time freshmen returned.

Freshmen *Admission:* 315 applied, 262 admitted, 97 enrolled. *Average high school GPA:* 2.98. *Test scores:* SAT verbal scores over 500: 96%; SAT math scores over 500: 85%; ACT scores over 18: 100%; SAT verbal scores over 600: 58%; SAT math scores over 600: 29%; ACT scores over 24: 79%; SAT verbal scores over 700: 11%; ACT scores over 30: 7%.

Faculty *Total:* 45, 40% full-time, 38% with terminal degrees. *Student/faculty ratio:* 10:1.

Majors Art history, criticism and conservation; communication and media related; European studies; history; international business/trade/commerce; international economics; international finance; international relations and affairs; liberal arts and sciences/liberal studies; literature; modern languages; Romance languages.

Academic Programs *Special study options:* accelerated degree program, advanced placement credit, double majors, English as a second language, honors programs, independent study, internships, part-time degree program, study abroad, summer session for credit.

Library David R. Grace Library with 32,755 titles, 177 serial subscriptions, 1,526 audiovisual materials, an OPAC, a Web page.

Computers on Campus 38 computers available on campus for general student use. A campuswide network can be accessed from off campus. Internet access, at least one staffed computer lab available. Computer purchase or lease plan available.

Student Life *Housing:* on-campus residence required through sophomore year. *Options:* coed, women-only. Campus housing is university owned and leased by the school. Freshman campus housing is guaranteed. *Activities and organizations:* drama/theater group, student-run newspaper, radio station, Student Union, newspaper, Literary Society, Drama Society, photography club. *Campus security:* controlled dormitory access, late night patrols by trained security personnel. *Student services:* health clinic, personal/psychological counseling.

Athletics *Intramural sports:* badminton M(c)/W(c), basketball M(c)/W(c), crew M(c)/W(c), equestrian sports W(c), ice hockey M(c)/W(c), rock climbing M/W, sailing M(c)/W(c), skiing (cross-country) M(c)/W(c), skiing (downhill) M(c)/W(c), soccer M(c)/W(c), swimming M(c)/W(c), tennis M(c)/W(c), volleyball M(c)/W(c), weight lifting M(c)/W(c).

Standardized Tests *Required:* SAT I or ACT (for admission). *Recommended:* SAT II: Subject Tests (for admission), SAT II: Writing Test (for admission).

Costs (2003–04) *Comprehensive fee:* $33,800 includes full-time tuition ($24,600), mandatory fees ($1200), and room and board ($8000). Part-time tuition: $2120 per course. *Required fees:* $147 per course part-time. *College room only:* $6000. Room and board charges vary according to housing facility. *Payment plan:* deferred payment.

Applying *Options:* common application, early admission, early decision, early action, deferred entrance. *Application fee:* $50. *Required:* essay or personal statement, high school transcript, minimum 2.0 GPA, 3 letters of recommendation. *Recommended:* interview. *Application deadlines:* 3/15 (freshmen), 6/15 (transfers). *Early decision:* 12/1. *Notification:* continuous (freshmen), 1/1 (early decision), 1/15 (early action), continuous (transfers).

Admissions Contact Ms. Karen Ballard, Director of Admissions, Franklin College Switzerland, 91-31 Queens Boulevard, Suite 411, Elmhurst, NY 11373. *Phone:* 212-772-2090. *E-mail:* info@fc.edu.

■ *See page 1652 for a narrative description.*

GLION INSTITUTE OF HIGHER EDUCATION
Glion-sur-Montreux, Switzerland

Admissions Contact Route de Glion 111, 1823 Glion-sur-Montreux, Switzerland.

INTERNATIONAL UNIVERSITY IN GENEVA
Geneva, Switzerland

- **Private** comprehensive
- **Calendar** trimesters
- **Degrees** bachelor's and master's
- **Urban** campus
- **Coed,** 185 undergraduate students
- **Moderately difficult** entrance level, 61% of applicants were admitted

Undergraduates Students come from 8 states and territories, 43 other countries, 0.1% are from out of state, 2% African American, 6% Asian American or Pacific Islander, 10% Hispanic American, 18% international.

Freshmen *Admission:* 122 applied, 74 admitted. *Average high school GPA:* 2.40.

Faculty *Total:* 31, 32% full-time, 68% with terminal degrees. *Student/faculty ratio:* 12:1.

Majors Business administration and management; international relations and affairs; mass communication/media.

Academic Programs *Special study options:* academic remediation for entering students, accelerated degree program, adult/continuing education programs, advanced placement credit, double majors, English as a second language, honors programs, off-campus study, study abroad, summer session for credit.

Library 6,000 titles, 500 serial subscriptions.

Computers on Campus 60 computers available on campus for general student use. A campuswide network can be accessed from off campus. Internet access, at least one staffed computer lab available. Computer purchase or lease plan available.

Student Life *Housing:* college housing not available. *Options:* Campus housing is provided by a third party.

Costs (2003–04) *Tuition:* 22,200 Swiss francs full-time, 690 Swiss francs per credit part-time. No tuition increase for student's term of enrollment. *Payment plan:* installment. *Waivers:* employees or children of employees.

Applying *Options:* common application, electronic application, deferred entrance. *Application fee:* 150 Swiss francs. *Required:* essay or personal statement, high school transcript, minimum 2.3 GPA, 2 letters of recommendation. *Required for some:* TOEFL. *Application deadline:* rolling (freshmen), rolling (transfers). *Notification:* continuous (freshmen), continuous (transfers).

Admissions Contact Mrs. Martha Negaard-Muller, Admissions Offices, International University in Geneva, International University in Geneva, ICC, Rte. de Pre-Bois 20, Geneva 1215, Switzerland. *Phone:* 41-227107110. *Fax:* 41-22710-7111. *E-mail:* info@iun.ch.

■ *See page 1772 for a narrative description.*

LES ROCHES, SWISS HOTEL ASSOCIATION, SCHOOL OF HOTEL MANAGEMENT
Bluche, Switzerland

Admissions Contact LES ROCHES, Swiss Hotel Association, School of Hotel Management, CH 3975 Bluche, Switzerland.

SCHILLER INTERNATIONAL UNIVERSITY, AMERICAN COLLEGE OF SWITZERLAND
Leysin, Switzerland

- **Independent** comprehensive, founded 1963, part of Schiller International University
- **Calendar** semesters
- **Degrees** associate, bachelor's, and master's
- **Small-town** 15-acre campus with easy access to Geneva
- **Coed,** 66 undergraduate students, 98% full-time, 50% women, 50% men
- **Minimally difficult** entrance level

Schiller International University, American College of Switzerland (continued)

Schiller International University (SIU) is an independent American university with campuses in England, France, Germany, Spain, Switzerland, and the United States. In addition, students can transfer without loss of credit. English is the language of instruction at all campuses. SIU offers undergraduate and graduate students an American education in an international setting.

Undergraduates 65 full-time, 1 part-time. Students come from 7 states and territories, 25 other countries, 21% transferred in, 90% live on campus. *Retention:* 75% of 2002 full-time freshmen returned.

Freshmen *Admission:* 10 enrolled.

Faculty *Total:* 15, 33% full-time.

Majors Business administration and management; economics; hotel/motel administration; interdisciplinary studies; international business/trade/commerce; international economics; international relations and affairs; liberal arts and sciences/liberal studies; tourism and travel services management.

Academic Programs *Special study options:* academic remediation for entering students, accelerated degree program, advanced placement credit, English as a second language, internships, part-time degree program, student-designed majors, study abroad, summer session for credit.

Library 48,355 titles, 200 serial subscriptions.

Computers on Campus 17 computers available on campus for general student use. Internet access, at least one staffed computer lab available.

Student Life *Housing:* on-campus residence required through sophomore year. *Options:* coed. Campus housing is university owned. *Campus security:* 24-hour patrols. *Student services:* health clinic, personal/psychological counseling.

Athletics *Intramural sports:* badminton M/W, basketball M/W, equestrian sports M/W, skiing (cross-country) M/W, skiing (downhill) M/W, soccer M/W, squash M/W, swimming M/W, table tennis M/W, tennis M/W, volleyball M/W.

Costs (2003–04) *Comprehensive fee:* 28,300 Swiss francs includes full-time tuition (15,200 Swiss francs), mandatory fees (600 Swiss francs), and room and board (12,500 Swiss francs). Part-time tuition: 820 Swiss francs per credit. *Required fees:* 300 Swiss francs per term part-time.

Applying *Options:* common application, deferred entrance. *Application fee:* $50. *Required:* essay or personal statement, high school transcript, minimum 2.0 GPA, 1 letter of recommendation. *Application deadline:* rolling (freshmen), rolling (transfers).

Admissions Contact United States Admissions Representative (ACS), Schiller International University, American College of Switzerland, 453 Edgewater Drive, Dunedin, FL 34698. *Phone:* -813-736-5082. *Toll-free phone:* 800-336-4133. *Fax:* 813-734-0359.

■ *See page 2354 for a narrative description.*

UNITED ARAB EMIRATES

THE AMERICAN UNIVERSITY IN DUBAI

Dubai, United Arab Emirates

- **Proprietary** comprehensive
- **Calendar** quarters
- **Degrees** associate, bachelor's, and master's
- **Urban** campus
- **Coed,** 1,493 undergraduate students, 75% full-time, 48% women, 52% men
- 56% of applicants were admitted

Undergraduates 1,120 full-time, 373 part-time. Students come from 69 other countries, 3% transferred in, 15% live on campus. *Retention:* 76% of 2002 full-time freshmen returned.

Freshmen *Admission:* 565 applied, 316 admitted, 295 enrolled.

Faculty *Total:* 57, 32% full-time, 65% with terminal degrees. *Student/faculty ratio:* 25:1.

Majors Business administration and management; design and visual communications; engineering; information science/studies; interior design.

Academic Programs *Special study options:* accelerated degree program, advanced placement credit, double majors, English as a second language, honors programs, independent study, internships, part-time degree program, services for LD students, study abroad, summer session for credit.

Library University Library with 236,000 titles, 160 serial subscriptions, 75 audiovisual materials, an OPAC, a Web page.

Computers on Campus 270 computers available on campus for general student use. A campuswide network can be accessed from student residence rooms and from off campus. Internet access, at least one staffed computer lab available. Computer purchase or lease plan available.

Student Life *Housing:* on-campus residence required through senior year. *Options:* men-only, women-only. Campus housing is university owned. Freshman campus housing is guaranteed. *Activities and organizations:* drama/theater group, student-run newspaper, Student Government Association, community service club, drama club, music club, debate club. *Campus security:* 24-hour patrols. *Student services:* health clinic, personal/psychological counseling.

Athletics *Intercollegiate sports:* basketball M(s)/W(s), soccer M(s)/W(s), table tennis M/W, tennis M(s)/W(s), volleyball M(s)/W(s). *Intramural sports:* basketball M/W, bowling M/W, rugby M, soccer M/W, squash M/W, swimming M/W, table tennis M/W, tennis M/W, volleyball M/W, weight lifting M/W.

Standardized Tests *Required for some:* SAT I (for admission). *Recommended:* SAT I (for admission).

Costs (2003–04) *Tuition:* $11,035 full-time, $259 per credit part-time. *Room only:* $3840. *Waivers:* employees or children of employees.

Applying *Options:* common application, early admission. *Application fee:* 50 United Arab Emirates dirhams. *Required:* high school transcript, minimum 2.0 GPA, 2 letters of recommendation, interview. *Recommended:* essay or personal statement. *Application deadline:* 10/3 (freshmen).

Admissions Contact Ms. Sarah McConnell, Admissions Coordinator, The American University in Dubai, PO Box 28282, Dubai. *Phone:* (4)-3999000 Ext. 172. *Fax:* 971-4-3998899. *E-mail:* info@aud.edu, admissions@aud.edu.

AMERICAN UNIVERSITY OF SHARJAH

Sharjah, United Arab Emirates

Admissions Contact PO Box 26666, Sharjah, United Arab Emirates.

UNITED KINGDOM

AMERICAN INTERCONTINENTAL UNIVERSITY-LONDON

London, United Kingdom

- **Proprietary** comprehensive, founded 1970, part of Career Education Corporation
- **Calendar** 3 10-week terms plus 2 8-week summer terms
- **Degrees** associate, bachelor's, and master's
- **Urban** campus
- **Coed,** 674 undergraduate students, 100% full-time, 53% women, 47% men
- **Noncompetitive** entrance level, 79% of applicants were admitted

Undergraduates 674 full-time. Students come from 89 other countries, 26% transferred in, 40% live on campus.

Freshmen *Admission:* 877 applied, 694 admitted, 232 enrolled.

Faculty *Total:* 94, 19% full-time, 46% with terminal degrees. *Student/faculty ratio:* 8:1.

Majors Business administration and management; cinematography and film/video production; computer management; fashion/apparel design; fashion merchandising; information technology; interior design; international marketing; management information systems; marketing/marketing management; photography.

Academic Programs *Special study options:* academic remediation for entering students, accelerated degree program, double majors, English as a second language, independent study, internships, part-time degree program, study abroad, summer session for credit.

Library Niklaus Weibel Library plus 1 other with 26,000 titles, 350 serial subscriptions, 15,000 audiovisual materials, an OPAC.

Computers on Campus 120 computers available on campus for general student use. A campuswide network can be accessed from off campus. Internet access, at least one staffed computer lab available.

Student Life *Housing options:* coed. Campus housing is leased by the school and is provided by a third party. Freshman applicants given priority for college housing. *Activities and organizations:* drama/theater group, student-run newspaper, Student Government Association, Drama Group, International Interior Designers Association. *Campus security:* 24-hour emergency response devices, controlled dormitory access. *Student services:* personal/psychological counseling.

Athletics *Intramural sports:* badminton M/W, baseball M/W, basketball M/W, rugby M/W, soccer M/W, softball M/W, table tennis M/W.

Costs (2003–04) *Tuition:* 11,460 British pounds full-time. Full-time tuition and fees vary according to course load and location. Part-time tuition and fees vary according to course load and location. *Room only:* 5910 British pounds. *Payment plan:* installment.
Applying *Options:* common application, electronic application, early admission, deferred entrance. *Application fee:* 35 British pounds. *Required:* essay or personal statement, high school transcript, 2 letters of recommendation, interview. *Application deadline:* rolling (freshmen), rolling (transfers). *Notification:* continuous (freshmen), continuous (transfers).
Admissions Contact Mr. Jonathan Besser, Director of Admissions and Marketing, American InterContinental University-London, 110 Marylebone High Street, London W1M 3DB, United Kingdom. *Phone:* -44 (0) 207 467-5642. *Fax:* +44 (0) 207 467-5641. *E-mail:* admissions@aiulondon.ac.uk.

HURON UNIVERSITY USA IN LONDON

London, United Kingdom

- **Independent** comprehensive, founded 1975
- **Calendar** semesters
- **Degrees** certificates, diplomas, associate, bachelor's, and master's
- **Urban** 1-acre campus
- **Coed,** 200 undergraduate students, 100% full-time, 51% women, 49% men
- **Moderately difficult** entrance level, 63% of applicants were admitted

Undergraduates 200 full-time. Students come from 6 states and territories, 61 other countries, 8% transferred in, 70% live on campus. *Retention:* 95% of 2002 full-time freshmen returned.
Freshmen *Admission:* 80 applied, 50 admitted, 27 enrolled. *Average high school GPA:* 3.00.
Faculty *Total:* 45, 44% full-time, 100% with terminal degrees. *Student/faculty ratio:* 8:1.
Majors American literature; art; art history, criticism and conservation; artificial intelligence and robotics; business administration and management; communication/speech communication and rhetoric; computer and information sciences; computer and information sciences and support services related; computer and information sciences related; computer and information systems security; computer graphics; computer/information technology services administration related; computer programming; computer programming related; computer programming (specific applications); computer programming (vendor/product certification); computer science; computer software and media applications related; computer systems analysis; computer systems networking and telecommunications; creative writing; data entry/microcomputer applications; data entry/microcomputer applications related; data modeling/warehousing and database administration; data processing and data processing technology; English; English composition; English literature (British and Commonwealth); general studies; humanities; information science/studies; information technology; international relations and affairs; liberal arts and sciences and humanities related; liberal arts and sciences/liberal studies; mathematics; statistics; system administration; system, networking, and LAN/wan management; web/multimedia management and webmaster; web page, digital/multimedia and information resources design; word processing.
Academic Programs *Special study options:* academic remediation for entering students, accelerated degree program, advanced placement credit, cooperative education, double majors, English as a second language, honors programs, independent study, internships, off-campus study, part-time degree program, student-designed majors, study abroad, summer session for credit.
Library Huron University Resource Center with 5,000 titles, 63 serial subscriptions, 150 audiovisual materials.
Computers on Campus 28 computers available on campus for general student use. A campuswide network can be accessed from student residence rooms and from off campus. Internet access, at least one staffed computer lab available. Computer purchase or lease plan available.
Student Life *Housing options:* coed. Campus housing is leased by the school. Freshman campus housing is guaranteed. *Activities and organizations:* drama/theater group, student-run newspaper. *Campus security:* 24-hour emergency response devices, controlled dormitory access. *Student services:* health clinic, personal/psychological counseling.
Standardized Tests *Required for some:* SAT I or ACT (for admission).
Costs (2004–05) *Tuition:* $15,000 full-time. Full-time tuition and fees vary according to course level. *Room only:* $6000. *Payment plans:* tuition prepayment, installment.
Applying *Options:* electronic application. *Application fee:* $50. *Required:* essay or personal statement, high school transcript, minimum 2.0 GPA, 2 letters of recommendation. *Required for some:* interview. *Recommended:* minimum 2.5 GPA. *Application deadline:* 7/1 (freshmen). *Notification:* 7/15 (freshmen).
Admissions Contact Mr. Rob Atkinson, Director of Admissions, Huron University USA in London, 46/47 Russell Square, Bloomsbury, London WC1B 4JP, United Kingdom. *Phone:* 207-636-5667. *Fax:* 44-636-5662. *E-mail:* admissions@huron.ac.uk.

RICHMOND, THE AMERICAN INTERNATIONAL UNIVERSITY IN LONDON

Richmond, United Kingdom

- **Independent** comprehensive, founded 1972
- **Calendar** semesters
- **Degrees** associate, bachelor's, master's, and postbachelor's certificates
- **Urban** 5-acre campus with easy access to London
- **Coed,** 982 undergraduate students, 100% full-time, 55% women, 45% men
- **Moderately difficult** entrance level, 52% of applicants were admitted

Undergraduates 982 full-time. Students come from 40 states and territories, 104 other countries. *Retention:* 73% of 2002 full-time freshmen returned.
Freshmen *Admission:* 1,641 applied, 857 admitted, 236 enrolled. *Average high school GPA:* 3.15. *Test scores:* SAT verbal scores over 500: 80%; SAT math scores over 500: 85%; ACT scores over 18: 100%; SAT verbal scores over 600: 20%; SAT math scores over 600: 5%; ACT scores over 24: 60%; ACT scores over 30: 10%.
Faculty *Total:* 106, 39% full-time, 44% with terminal degrees. *Student/faculty ratio:* 12:1.
Majors Anthropology; art; business administration and management; computer engineering; computer programming; computer science; economics; English; European studies; fine/studio arts; history; information science/studies; international business/trade/commerce; international relations and affairs; liberal arts and sciences/liberal studies; mass communication/media; mathematics; political science and government; pre-engineering; psychology; social sciences; sociology; systems engineering.
Academic Programs *Special study options:* academic remediation for entering students, advanced placement credit, English as a second language, honors programs, independent study, internships, study abroad, summer session for credit.
Library Taylor Library plus 2 others with 70,000 titles, 300 serial subscriptions, 737 audiovisual materials, an OPAC, a Web page.
Computers on Campus 420 computers available on campus for general student use. A campuswide network can be accessed from off campus. Internet access, online (class) registration, at least one staffed computer lab available.
Student Life *Housing options:* coed. Campus housing is university owned and leased by the school. Freshman campus housing is guaranteed. *Activities and organizations:* drama/theater group, student-run newspaper, radio station, international club, computer club, ethnic clubs, Debate Society, sports clubs. *Campus security:* 24-hour patrols. *Student services:* health clinic, personal/psychological counseling.
Athletics *Intercollegiate sports:* basketball M, rugby M, soccer M/W, table tennis M, volleyball M/W. *Intramural sports:* basketball M/W, crew M/W, cross-country running M/W, equestrian sports M/W, rugby M/W, soccer M/W, squash M/W, swimming M/W, table tennis M/W, tennis M/W, volleyball M/W.
Standardized Tests *Required:* SAT I or ACT (for admission).
Costs (2004–05) *Comprehensive fee:* $28,000 includes full-time tuition ($18,400) and room and board ($9600). Part-time tuition: $670 per credit. *Payment plan:* installment. *Waivers:* employees or children of employees.
Applying *Options:* common application, electronic application, deferred entrance. *Application fee:* $50. *Required:* essay or personal statement, high school transcript, minimum 2.5 GPA, 1 letter of recommendation. *Application deadline:* 8/1 (freshmen). *Notification:* continuous until 8/15 (freshmen), continuous (transfers).
Admissions Contact Mr. Brian E. Davis, Director of United States Admissions, Richmond, The American International University in London, 343 Congress Street, Suite 3100, Boston, MA 02210-1214. *Phone:* 617-450-5617. *Fax:* 617-450-5601. *E-mail:* us_admissions@richmond.ac.uk.

■ *See page 2234 for a narrative description.*

SCHILLER INTERNATIONAL UNIVERSITY

London, United Kingdom

- **Independent** comprehensive, founded 1970, part of Schiller International University
- **Calendar** semesters
- **Degrees** associate, bachelor's, and master's
- **Urban** campus
- **Coed,** 283 undergraduate students

Schiller International University (continued)
■ **Noncompetitive** entrance level

Schiller International University (SIU) is an independent American university with campuses in England, France, Germany, Spain, Switzerland, and the United States. In addition, students can transfer without loss of credit. English is the language of instruction at all campuses. SIU offers undergraduate and graduate students an American education in an international setting.

Undergraduates Students come from 60 other countries.

Majors Economics; hotel/motel administration; interdisciplinary studies; international business/trade/commerce; international relations and affairs; liberal arts and sciences/liberal studies; pre-medical studies; pre-veterinary studies; psychology.

Academic Programs *Special study options:* accelerated degree program, adult/continuing education programs, advanced placement credit, double majors, English as a second language, independent study, internships, part-time degree program, student-designed majors, study abroad, summer session for credit.

Library 21,603 titles, 143 serial subscriptions.

Computers on Campus 39 computers available on campus for general student use. At least one staffed computer lab available.

Student Life *Housing options:* coed. *Activities and organizations:* student-run newspaper, student government, campus newspaper, yearbook staff. *Campus security:* 24-hour patrols. *Student services:* personal/psychological counseling.

Athletics *Intramural sports:* archery M/W, baseball M/W, rugby M, soccer M/W, volleyball M/W.

Costs (2003–04) *Comprehensive fee:* $21,380 includes full-time tuition ($14,400), mandatory fees ($480), and room and board ($6500).

Financial Aid Of all full-time matriculated undergraduates who enrolled in 2001, 2 Federal Work-Study jobs (averaging $4330).

Applying *Options:* common application, deferred entrance. *Application fee:* $50. *Required:* essay or personal statement, high school transcript. *Recommended:* minimum 2.0 GPA. *Application deadline:* rolling (freshmen), rolling (transfers).

Admissions Contact Ms. Susan Russeff, Associate Director of Admissions, Schiller International University, 453 Edgewater Drive, Dunedin, FL 34698. *Phone:* 727-736-5082 Ext. 239. *Toll-free phone:* 800-336-4133 Ext. 234. *Fax:* 727-734-0359. *E-mail:* admissions@schiller.edu.

■ *See page 2354 for a narrative description.*

In-Depth Descriptions of Four-Year Colleges

ABILENE CHRISTIAN UNIVERSITY

ABILENE, TEXAS

The University

Abilene Christian University (ACU) offers an exceptional education in a distinctive Christian environment at an affordable price. ACU believes strongly in the dignity and worth of the individual and in academic integrity, achieving success, and enjoying life. Christian education at ACU integrates faith and hands-on learning, represented in every facet of campus life.

Founded in 1906, ACU is an independent comprehensive university with an enrollment of approximately 4,700 students and is one of the largest private universities in the Southwest. The school is affiliated with the Churches of Christ and is governed by its own Board of Trustees.

The University offers more than fifty bachelor's programs, twenty-five master's programs, and one doctoral program. Work completed at ACU is accepted by all colleges and universities in the United States. The University is accredited by the Commission on Colleges of the Southern Association of Colleges and Schools, and the College of Business Administration is accredited by the Association of Collegiate Business Schools and Programs (ACBSP).

As a teaching institution, ACU emphasizes a dynamic personal relationship between professors and their students. Qualified faculty members, not graduate assistants, teach undergraduate students, and when professors do research, undergraduates work with them. Each year, some of the nation's top companies come to campus to interview because they hold ACU graduates in high regard for their blend of creativity, technical skills, thorough training, and moral integrity. ACU students have an acceptance rate of more than 80 percent to medical and other professional schools, well above the national average. The *Optimist,* the ACU student newspaper, has been rated All-American every year since 1975.

ACU supports an environment of honesty, Christian care, and relationships that start even before classes begin. Each fall during Welcome Week, upperclass students help freshmen adjust to the social side of college life through diverse activities, including heart-to-heart discussions and possibly the world's largest game of Twister. The student body is enriched by people from fifty states and about sixty countries. More than 175 international students are enrolled at ACU.

The University is a member of the National Collegiate Athletic Association (NCAA) and the Lone Star Conference. ACU competes in NCAA Division II athletics, including men's baseball, football, and golf; women's softball and volleyball; and basketball, cross-country, tennis, and outdoor and indoor track and field for both men and women. The University also offers an intramural sports program for its students, and the ACU soccer club competes against other college and university soccer clubs.

Active campus organizations, including men's and women's social clubs, offer students a variety of interests and opportunities for involvement. Movie nights, devotionals, big-name concerts, intercollegiate sports, and student music and theatre productions ensure that students can find great entertainment without leaving campus. There is also a medical clinic on campus.

Location

Abilene, Texas, has the reputation of being a friendly city and was named an All-America City. It is located 180 miles west of Dallas and has a population of about 110,000. Its climate is relatively warm, although it occasionally snows during the winter. Residents of Abilene are served by shopping malls, major restaurant chains, specialty shops, two hospitals, and a regional airport. The city is second only to Houston in cultural events per capita in Texas, and it has one of the lowest crime rates in the state.

Majors and Degrees

The Bachelor of Arts degree is awarded in art, art for all-level teacher certification, art history, art/marketing, biblical text, biochemistry, biology, chemistry, Christian ministry, communication sciences and disorders, computer science, English, graphic design/advertising, history, human communication, international studies, mathematics, missions, music, political science, sociology, Spanish, theater, and youth and family ministry.

The Bachelor of Science degree is available in agricultural business; animal science; biochemistry; biology; broadcast journalism; chemistry; Christian ministry; computer science; criminal justice; electronic media; engineering physics; environmental science; exercise science; food, nutrition, and dietetics; human development and family studies; industrial psychology; integrated marketing communication; interior design; journalism; mathematics; medical technology; microelectronics; missions; photojournalism; physics; predentistry; pre-engineering; premedicine; preoptometry; pre–veterinary medicine; psychology; range and agronomy; religious journalism; social work; sociology; and youth and family ministry. Also, the Bachelor of Science degree is offered in elementary and secondary education, with specialization in numerous areas. A Bachelor of Science in Nursing degree is also available.

The Bachelor of Business Administration degree is offered in accounting, financial management, management, and marketing. The Bachelor of Fine Arts degree is available in art and theater, and the Bachelor of Music degree (with teacher certification) is offered in instrumental, piano, and vocal (all levels).

The Bachelor of Applied Studies offers adults the opportunity to combine previous college experience, on-the-job training, and courses at ACU to complete their degrees. Areas of emphasis include biblical and related sciences, business, communication, family studies, general business, human services, liberal arts, psychology, sociology, and teacher preparation.

The preprofessional programs offered by ACU are of special interest. In general, students attend ACU for one to four years and then transfer to a professional school to complete their degree. During the past decade, more than 80 percent of ACU graduates who applied to medical and dental schools were accepted, putting ACU among the top preprofessional schools in the state.

Academic Program

A minimum of 128 semester hours is required for most baccalaureate degrees, with 30 of these hours in a major and a total of 33 hours in upper-division work. All degrees require 15 hours of Bible studies, and most require courses in communication/speech, English, exercise science, fine arts, mathematics, science, and social and behavioral science.

ACU serves a broad spectrum of students. To help challenge the exceptionally bright student, CLEP and a comprehensive honors program are available. For the underprepared, developmental programs are offered by a well-equipped learning center. The University also offers various enriching seminars and lectures by internationally known guests such as Linda Chavez, Max Lucado, James Dobson, Marilyn Quayle, George W. Bush, William Bennett, John Wooden, and Ray Bradbury.

Off-Campus Programs

In the Study Abroad program, students may study in countries such as China, England, Mexico, and Uruguay. All courses completed during this cultural and educational experience are counted toward the student's degree.

Academic Facilities

Resources of the Abilene Christian University library include books, microforms, audiovisual materials, government documents, and periodicals that total more than 1.7 million items. Online research and access to a local library consortium greatly expand student access to worldwide resources. The Learning Enhancement Center (LEC) offers free tutoring at all levels, numerous audiovisual materials, and a thirty-workstation Macintosh computer lab. More than 700 computers across campus are available to students during days and evenings.

Exercise science and athletic activities are centered in the huge exercise science complex, which contains several gymnasiums, training rooms, racquetball courts, an Olympic-size swimming pool, a coliseum, and a state-of-the-art fitness center for student athletes. The Teague Special Events Center is used for a variety of special events that occur in both the ACU and Abilene communities. The four-story science facility contains laboratories, an outstanding collection of experimental equipment, an observatory, and computer labs. A three-story communications complex houses art studios and classrooms, newspaper and yearbook workshops, a low-power VHF TV station that broadcasts on a local station and on cable, and an FM National Public Radio station.

In addition to 100-acre and 400-acre farms, the University has access to 2,500 acres of land for observation, research, and study projects. Students enrolled in agriculture, environment, biology, and ecology courses are able to study basic and applied science in an integrated setting.

Classrooms in the Mabee Business Building and Biblical Studies Building are equipped with the latest in audiovisual and computer equipment. Business students work in a lab equipped with state-of-the-art Apple Power Macs and Pentium processors. The newest academic building is Williams Performing Arts Center, which houses the music and theater departments, and offices.

Costs

The typical expenses for 2003–04 for two semesters include tuition and fees (30 semester hours), $13,290; room, $2160; board, $2920; and books, $800 for a total of $19,170. Personal expenses vary according to an individual's needs. All fees are subject to change.

Financial Aid

Eighty-eight percent of ACU students are assisted through loans, grants, scholarships, and/or employment. In 2002–03, more than $50 million in financial aid was awarded to ACU students. The number of students employed on campus was more than 1,300. Academic scholarships are awarded according to scores on standardized tests such as the SAT I and ACT examinations, class rank, and leadership activities. Full tuition scholarships are offered to National Merit Finalists. All financial aid forms may be obtained through the ACU Student Financial Services Office. It is suggested, and even required for some financial aid programs, that applicants for aid complete a need analysis form, preferably the Free Application for Federal Student Aid (FAFSA).

Faculty

ACU has a faculty of outstanding teachers, scholars, and specialists. Seventy-four percent of full-time faculty members hold a doctorate or the highest degree in their field. There are 229 full-time and 80 part-time faculty members committed to educating the whole student, academically, socially, and spiritually. A student-teacher ratio of 17:1 allows students ready access to their teachers for counseling on careers, academics, and personal issues.

Student Government

Abilene Christian University has an active, progressive Students' Association, of which every full-time student is a member. Officers of the association and the Student Senate carry out various social and community service programs. The Student Foundation promotes awareness of the purposes of ACU and maintains communication among the administration, students, and alumni.

Admission Requirements

To qualify for admission, a student must have graduated from high school and must submit information concerning SAT I or ACT scores, high school class rank, and reference letters. Generally, transfer students are required to have a 2.0 grade point average or better. Abilene Christian University does not discriminate on the basis of race, color, age, or national or ethnic origin in its admissions, employment opportunities, educational programs, or activities that it sponsors.

Application and Information

Prospective students should write or call the admissions office for application forms and financial aid information, indicating their academic and social areas of interest. Applicants should submit the necessary forms with a nonrefundable $25 processing fee ($45 for international applicants) and have their academic records (SAT I or ACT scores, transcript, and class rank) sent to the University. Residence hall room reservations, accompanied by a $100 deposit, should be made early to ensure choice of a dorm. Students are encouraged to visit the campus at any time.

Office of Admissions
Abilene Christian University
ACU Station, Box 29000
Abilene, Texas 79699-9000
Telephone: 915-674-2650
800-460-6228 (toll-free)
E-mail: info@admissions.acu.edu
World Wide Web: http://www.acu.edu

ACU's Biblical Studies Building features a magnificent chapel, a huge amphitheater, and the latest in instructional technology.

ACADEMY OF ART UNIVERSITY

SAN FRANCISCO, CALIFORNIA

The University

In 1929, Academy of Art University founder Richard S. Stephens, who was the advertising creative director of *Sunset* magazine, acted on his belief that "aspiring artists and designers, given proper instruction, hard work, and dedication, can learn the skills needed to become successful professionals." His new school of advertising art consisted of 46 students meeting in one room on San Francisco's Kearny Street. The instructors, who were professional artists, brought real-world problems, situations, solutions, and practical experience to the students. Thus was born the school's philosophy by the founder: Hire today's best practicing professionals to teach the art and design professionals of tomorrow. At that time, advertising consisted primarily of illustrations, photos, and copy. Consequently, it became necessary to teach beginning students the fundamentals of drawing, painting, color, light, and photography as well as layout and typography.

When Richard A. Stephens succeeded his father as president in 1951, the Foundations Department was added, ensuring all students comprehended the basic principles of traditional art and design. Illustration soon expanded to include fine arts (drawing, painting, sculpture, and printmaking), and advertising design spawned the Graphic Design Department. Fashion (design, textiles, and merchandising) and Interior Design Departments were also added. In 1966, the Academy officially became a college, and in a decade, the Master of Fine Arts degree was offered. Five more buildings were purchased, and by 1992, there were more than 2,500 students. The leadership of the Academy was then turned over to the third generation, Elisa Stephens, granddaughter of the school's founder. She quickly determined that the school's small Computer Arts Department had enormous potential to prepare students for multimedia careers when allied with such companies as Silicon Graphics, Pixar, Adobe, and Walt Disney Productions. It is now the fastest-growing department at the Academy.

Today, Academy of Art University is the largest private art and design school in the nation and has an enrollment of more than 7,000 students from nearly every country in the world. More than one third of the student body is made up of international students. The Academy has more than twenty facilities that house classrooms, studios, galleries, and dormitories. The students, who are admitted through an open enrollment policy, aspire to earn either an A.A., a B.F.A., or a certificate in one of twelve design majors. The school maintains a fleet of buses to connect the different points of the campus, all of which are located within the city limits of San Francisco, one of the world's most vibrant and beautiful cities. The faculty, which is 80 percent part-time and made up of working art and design professionals, is recruited from all across the nation and is drawn to the creative and intellectual center that is the Bay Area. Extensive senior-year internship programs allow students to gain valuable experience and develop strong portfolios in their chosen field before graduation.

Academy of Art University offers an M.F.A. program in architecture.

Location

The city of San Francisco is one of the great cultural centers of the world; a melting pot of diversity, ethnicity, and creativity that has spawned major museums and galleries, world-class opera and theaters, dance companies, film production and recording studios, technological innovation, performing artists ranging from classical to popular music, and numerous other cultural opportunities. The city's status as a tourist mecca located on the Pacific Rim ensures that one encounters people from all corners of the world. The climate is moderate and offers kaleidoscopic blends of sunshine and fog nine months of the year. The Northpoint campus is located at world-famous Pier 39; one can view Alcatraz Island from classroom windows. Four other buildings are two blocks from historic Union Square in the commercial heart of the city. Three other buildings are located near the Financial District. The city offers myriad locations for field trips and studio visits. World-renowned artists display their creations in the Academy's four nonprofit art galleries, which are open to the public. The University is an urban institution that both draws upon and contributes to the cultural wealth of the community in which it resides.

Majors and Degrees

The University offers A.A. and B.F.A. degrees and certificates in the following majors: advertising (account planning, art direction, copywriting, and television commercials), animation/visual effects (storyboard art, background painting/layout design, game design, visual development, 3-D modeling, character development, and VFX/compositing), computer arts/new media (computer graphics, new media, Web design, and digital imaging), fashion (fashion design, fashion illustration, knitwear, merchandising, and textiles), fine art (ceramics, metal arts, painting/drawing, printmaking, and sculpture), graphic design (corporate and brand identity, Web site design, motion graphics, multimedia, package design, print and collateral), illustration (cartooning, children's books, editorial, feature film animation, and 2-D animation), industrial design (product, transportation, furniture, and toy design), interior architecture and design (commercial, residential, and furniture design), motion pictures and television (acting, advertising/director–camera, cinematography, directing, editing, producing, production design, screenwriting, and special effects), and photography (advertising, documentary, digital photography, fashion, fine art, photo illustration, and photojournalism).

Academic Programs

A total of 132 credit units are required to earn a Bachelor of Fine Arts degree, consisting of 18 units of foundations courses, 60 units in the major, 12 units of art electives, and 42 units of liberal arts/art history courses. First-year students must complete six foundations courses before the end of the year. Fundamental courses are related specifically to students' majors in preparation to begin intense focus courses in his or her field by the sophomore year. All major courses of study are structured so the student builds upon skills learned the previous semester and advances to the next level of technical or creative proficiency. Some related major courses may be taken concurrently. Each course is worth 3 credits. Liberal arts courses teach practical applications for forging a professional career in art and design. International students who come from countries where English is not the primary language may take additional ESL classes, as determined by English language proficiency testing. Students are advised to meet with departmental directors at least once during the academic year to have their progress assessed. Portfolios are reviewed before the junior year to determine whether or not a student has progressed sufficiently to continue study at the Academy.

Academic Facilities

The Academy's facilities reflect its commitment to training students for careers in art and design; not only do students have access to some of the most advanced facilities in the nation, but the Academy continually invests in new equipment to ensure that it remains on the cutting edge of technology. By learning on industry-standard equipment, students gain valuable professional techniques that make them highly employable.

The Academy's eight-story Digital Arts Center offers students from the Computer Arts, Animation/Visual Effects, Motion Pictures and Television, Advertising, and Fashion Departments access to an incredible array of technology. The center has more than 800 computer workstations, including approximately 100 Silicon Graphics workstations, 300 Adobe Premier workstations, and more than 200 autoCAD workstations. Students also have the use of fourteen Avid digital editing suites, seven multitrack sound editing studios, one dedicated blue screen studio, and various other video equipment, including Bosch Telecine equipment.

The Photography Department occupies its own building and shares half of another Academy building with the fine arts, painting, and printmaking departments. Photography students can utilize a wide range of equipment, including full-length shooting studios; Hasselblad, Mamyia, Canon, and Sinar cameras; Broncolor, Norman, and Speedotron strobe systems; seven black-and-white darkrooms; a color lab facility with fifteen single-print stations; and the latest technology, including eight MAC G4 computers, for digital imaging and output. In addition, the Academy's modern, professional studio is one of the largest of any photography school in the nation and is ideal for shooting automobiles, motorcycles, and large sets.

The Academy's Fine Art Sculpture Center is a 58,000-square-foot facility that houses state-of-the-art studios for figure, ceramic, neon/illumination, bronze, metal fabrication, and mold-making sculpture. Students also have use of an off-site bronze-casting facility. When students graduate from the Academy, they have the opportunity to exhibit in one of four nonprofit galleries in the heart of downtown San Francisco's premier gallery district. These street-level facilities are an excellent way for students to promote and sell their work and to gain networking experience.

The Library houses more than 30,000 books and magazines, as well as 375 CD-ROM titles, 150,000 slides, and 2,000 videos. Computers with Internet access are available to students as well as an online catalog, color scanners, and color and black-and-white copiers. Workshops and electronic study guides are also available. The Academy Resource Center offers all students free learning support services that include study hall, tutoring, mentoring, midpoint review and study skills workshops, a writing lab, a state-of-the-art multimedia language lab, an English for Art Program, and a Conversation Partner Program.

Costs

Tuition is $550 per credit unit for undergraduates. Full-time students carry either 12 or 15 units per semester. There is a nonrefundable $140 registration fee—$100 is applicable toward tuition. Lab fees run from $25 to $400 per semester, depending on the class. Tuition and fees are subject to change at any time. Art supplies can run from $250 to $500 per semester, depending on the major. The Academy has most of the expensive technical equipment available for students to borrow or use in a lab.

The Academy of Art University operates more than ten campus housing facilities within the city. Several housing options are offered, and costs vary from $6600 to $10,000 per academic year (fall and spring semesters). For further information, students may contact the Academy Housing Office directly at 415-263-7727 or via e-mail at housing@academyart.edu.

Financial Aid

The Academy offers financial aid packages consisting of grants, loans, and work-study to eligible students with a demonstrated need. Low-interest loans are available to all eligible students, regardless of need. As financial aid programs, procedures, and eligibility requirements change frequently, applicants should contact the Financial Aid Office for current requirements at the address or phone number listed below.

Faculty

The Academy averages nearly 500 faculty members each semester, most of whom are full-time art and design professionals and part-time teachers. The student-teacher ratio for undergraduate classes averages 15:1.

Student Government

Although there is no formal student government, each department has between 2 and 3 student representatives who meet with the president as needed throughout the semester to discuss any student issues.

Admission Requirements

Applicants for the B.F.A. program must have a high school diploma or GED equivalent. There is no portfolio requirement for the A.A. and B.F.A. programs. International students take a written and speech test to determine which ESL classes may have to be completed. Most ESL classes can be taken in conjunction with art and design classes. All foundations classes offer specialized ESL sections with instructors trained for language assistance. The application fee is $100 for undergraduates. A $500 tuition deposit applies to international applicants.

Application and Information

Students may apply to enter the Academy at the beginning of the spring, fall, or summer semesters. Information in this profile is subject to change. Students should contact the Academy of Art University for current information or visit its Web site, which is listed below.

For further information and a catalog, students may contact:

Prospective Student Services
Academy of Art University
79 New Montgomery Street
San Francisco, California 94105
Telephone: 415-274-2222
800-544-ARTS (2787) (toll-free)
Fax: 415-263-4130
World Wide Web: http://academyart.edu

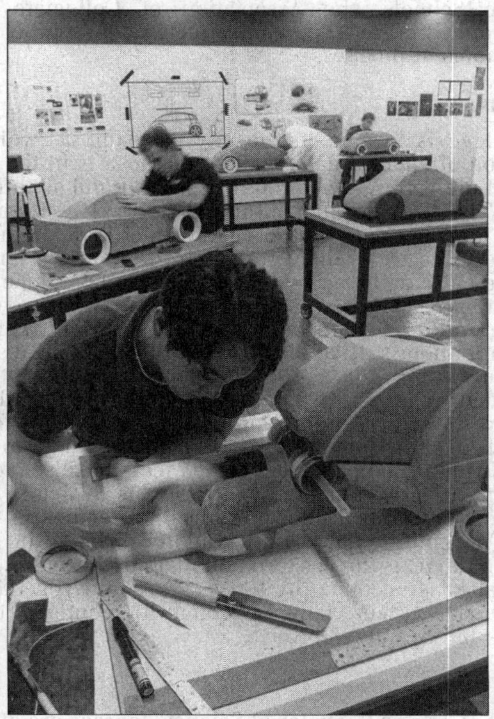

The city of San Francisco is a dynamic setting for campus life at the Academy.

ADAMS STATE COLLEGE

ALAMOSA, COLORADO

The College

Adams State College is dedicated to offering a high-quality education with a personal touch. The academic and social atmosphere of the campus allows each student to feel at home. The College has excellent physical facilities. Attractive academic buildings are complemented by a complete and comfortable College Center. The student body is composed of individuals from various ethnic and racial backgrounds. The fall 2003 enrollment was 2,668, including 677 graduate students. Forty percent of the undergraduate students are men. The dignity of each person as an individual is paramount, and equal consideration is extended to all. The close working relationship between students and the members of the faculty and administration is indicative of the importance of the individual at Adams State. At the graduate level, Adams State offers programs leading to the Master of Arts degree in elementary education, guidance and counseling, secondary education, special education/moderate needs (level one), art, and physical education.

Adams State College is accredited by the North Central Association of Colleges and Schools, the National Council for Accreditation of Teacher Education, the Council for Accreditation of Counseling and Related Educational Programs, and the National Association of Schools of Music. The College is an institutional member of the American Council on Education and the American Association of Colleges for Teacher Education. It is approved by the American Association of University Women. Adams State is also a member of the North Central Conference on Summer Schools, the Midwestern Association of Graduate Schools, the Association of Collegiate Business Schools and Programs, and the American Assembly of Collegiate Schools of Business.

Location

The College is located in the city of Alamosa, which has a population of approximately 9,000. Alamosa is in the center of the San Luis Valley, about 220 miles south and slightly west of Denver. The city is located at the junction of U.S. Highways 160 and 285 on the route of the Old Navajo Trail. Both bus and airline services are available to and from Alamosa. The College is located close to the art centers at Taos and Santa Fe and near excellent recreational opportunities for hiking, mountain climbing, rafting, fishing, and hunting. The Wolf Creek ski area is within an hour's drive of the campus. The San Luis Valley is almost level and is larger than the state of Connecticut. It is surrounded by ranges of mountains that rise more than 6,500 feet above the elevation of Alamosa, which is 7,500 feet above sea level. In the beautiful Sangre de Cristo range to the east, majestic Mount Blanca towers 14,363 feet above sea level. This mountain is nearly equaled in height and is rivaled in beauty by the rugged Crestone Peak and Crestone needles in the same range. The Continental Divide, winding through the San Juan mountain range, is the western boundary of the valley. The floor of the valley is occupied by fertile grain and vegetable farms and extensive grazing lands. Through the center of the valley flows the Rio Grande del Norte.

Majors and Degrees

Bachelor of Arts or Bachelor of Science degrees are awarded in art (emphasis in art education, art history, ceramics, design, drawing, fiber, metalsmithing, painting, photography, printmaking, or sculpture), biology (emphasis required in molecular cell biology, organismal, science education, or wildlife), business administration (emphasis required in accounting, advertising, business education, economics, finance, general business, management, management information systems, marketing, pre–international business, or small business), chemistry (emphasis in allied health, biochemistry, chemical physics, or science education), elementary education licensure, English (emphasis required in communications: print/radio, liberal arts, or secondary teacher licensure), exercise physiology and leisure science (emphasis in coaching, sport and exercise management, or teacher licensure), geology (emphasis in secondary education), history/government (emphasis in history, government, or social studies education), mathematics (emphasis in computer science or math education), music (emphasis in music education, K–12, or performance), psychology, selected studies (emphasis in liberal arts), sociology (emphasis in criminology, general sociology, and social welfare), Spanish (emphasis in foreign language for secondary teacher licensure), and speech/theater (emphasis in secondary teacher licensure–English education). Associate of Arts degree programs are also available. Preprofessional studies are offered in architectural engineering, dentistry, engineering, law, medicine, nursing, optometry, osteopathy, pharmacy, physical therapy, and veterinary medicine.

Academic Programs

The academic year is divided into fall and spring semesters. Normally, the baccalaureate degree is earned in eight semesters, while the Associate of Arts degree is earned in four. The associate degree is conferred upon completion of an approved curriculum with a total of 60 hours of academic credit and, in some A.A. programs, 2 additional hours of credit in physical education activities. The Bachelor of Arts or Bachelor of Science degree is conferred upon completion of an approved curriculum with a total of 120 hours of academic credit plus 2 to 4 semester hours of credit in physical education activities. A minimum cumulative scholastic average of 2.0 must be earned in all courses taken at Adams State College for the A.A., B.S., and B.A. degrees in all areas except teacher education, for which a minimum cumulative grade point average of 2.75 must be earned in all work attempted. All requirements of the general education courses and the major must be satisfied. Students transferring from a two-year college must earn at least 60 additional semester hours to graduate from Adams State College with a bachelor's degree. Opportunities are available for independent study, special-topics courses, and discussion groups on current issues.

Off-Campus Programs

A number of low-cost tours to nearby points of historical, archaeological, and ethnological interest are arranged by the College, usually in the spring and summer months.

Academic Facilities

The library, which serves as a government depository, has 142,624 books, 38,226 bound periodicals, 297,484 government documents, 706,547 ERIC microfiche, and 15,250 other nonbook items.

A state-of-the-art science and mathematics building opened in 1998. An art building opened in fall 2000, and a theater building opened in fall 2001.

Costs

For the 2004–05 academic year, the approximate comprehensive cost of tuition, fees, room, and board for residence hall students who are Colorado residents is $8600. For nonresident students, the approximate cost is $14,200. Married student housing units, with utilities furnished, are available at about $375 per month.

Financial Aid

Opportunities for financial aid are provided through scholarships, grants, loan funds, and part-time employment. Entering freshmen may gain consideration for all types of financial aid by completing the Free Application for Federal Student Aid (FAFSA) and submitting it by March 1 of the year of expected fall enrollment. Scholarships (entitled National Scholarships) are available for nonresidents of Colorado who reside in Adams State residence halls. The value of each of these scholarships is one half the cost of nonresident tuition for one year (approximately $3300). To be eligible for one of these scholarships, an entering freshman must have ranked in the top third of his or her high school graduating class or ranked in the top third on the ACT or SAT I (national norms for ACT composite or SAT I combined scores). Transfer students may qualify for the scholarship if they have maintained a GPA of 2.5 or higher for 12 or more semester hours of academic credit.

Faculty

Adams State College has 101 full-time faculty members. Of these, 90 hold a doctorate and 11, a master's degree. Faculty members have received degrees from more than 100 colleges and universities. In addition to carrying out their teaching assignments, faculty members serve as counselors and advisers and as members of many committees.

Student Government

Each student at Adams State College becomes a member of the Associated Students and Faculty organization upon registration. The organization was founded to promote cooperation between students and faculty members of the College. The general social life, social programs, and other student activities are directed by this organization. Elected officers and representatives of the student body and elected faculty members form the Associated Students and Faculty Senate, which regulates matters pertaining to student life.

Admission Requirements

Applicants to a bachelor's degree program should meet the following criteria: a class rank in the upper two thirds of their high school graduating class or a grade point average of at least 2.0 and a composite ACT score of at least 21 or a combined SAT I score of at least 970. Students ranking in the lower third of their high school graduating class and who have less than a 2.0 average may be considered for admission to the A.A. degree program under the condition that they may be required to register for remedial classes. Upon successful completion of at least one semester of academic work at Adams State College with a minimum 2.0 grade point average, an A.A. student may transfer to the baccalaureate degree program. Prospective transfer students must have at least a C (2.0) average to be unconditionally accepted for admission to Adams State College. Those not meeting this criterion are considered individually. In the case of repeated courses, honor points for grade point averages are compiled on the basis of performance in the repeat.

Application and Information

Applications for admission to Adams State should be completed well in advance of the beginning of the semester to which admission is sought. Applications received less than thirty days prior to the beginning of a semester may cause a delay in registration. Freshman applicants must submit the application for undergraduate admission to Colorado collegiate institutions, which is available from most Colorado high school counselors or from the Adams State College Admissions Office. The freshman applicant should submit this completed application along with a nonrefundable $20 application fee and have his or her high school mail a copy of the high school transcript directly to the Admissions Office at Adams State. The student should also submit ACT or SAT I scores to the Admissions Office. Transfer applicants must also submit the application for undergraduate admission to Colorado collegiate institutions and a nonrefundable $20 application fee. In addition, the student must request that all colleges previously attended forward transcripts to support the student's request for admission. If the student has completed fewer than 12 semester hours of credit, he or she must also submit an official high school transcript and ACT or SAT I scores. Application forms, financial aid forms, and other information are mailed upon request. Inquiries should be made to:

Admissions Office
Adams State College
Alamosa, Colorado 81102
Telephone: 719-587-7712
800-824-6494 (toll-free)
Fax: 719-587-7522
E-mail: ascadmit@adams.edu
World Wide Web: http://www.adams.edu

The Rex Activity Center on the campus of Adams State College.

ADELPHI UNIVERSITY

GARDEN CITY, NEW YORK

The University

Adelphi University, founded in 1896, was Long Island's first private institution of higher learning. Adelphi is chartered by the Board of Regents of the University of the State of New York. It is fully accredited by the Middle States Association of Colleges and Schools and by the New York State Education Department, the National League for Nursing Accrediting Commission, the Commission on Collegiate Nursing Education, the American Psychological Association, the American Speech-Language and Hearing Association, and the Council on Social Work Education. It is a member of the College Board and the Association of American Colleges/Universities.

A nonsectarian, independent university, Adelphi welcomes men and women of all backgrounds who display intellectual inquisitiveness, academic commitment, and a desire for achievement and purpose in life. The University enrolls approximately 8,000 students, including 4,157 graduate students. Forty states and fifty countries are represented in its diverse student body. The campus is located on 75 landscaped acres in Garden City, New York, 20 miles east of New York City and easily accessible by public transportation. The University also has three off-campus centers: the Manhattan Center in the Tribeca section of Manhattan, the Hauppauge Center on Long Island, and the Hudson Valley Site in Poughkeepsie, New York.

Adelphi University is composed of eight schools: the College of Arts and Sciences, the Honors College, the School of Business, the School of Education, the School of Nursing, the School of Social Work, the Gordon F. Derner Institute of Advanced Psychological Studies, and University College.

The Graduate School of Arts and Sciences offers programs leading to the M.A. and M.S. degrees. The Graduate School of Business offers the M.S. in accounting and in finance, the M.B.A., and the M.B.A./CPA programs. Graduate degrees in the School of Social Work are the M.S.W. and D.S.W., and the School of Nursing offers the M.S. degree. The School of Education offers a variety of programs leading to the M.A., M.S., and D.A. degrees. The Derner Institute of Advanced Psychological Studies offers an M.A. in general psychology, the Ph.D., and postdoctoral programs. Certificate programs are offered in many of these graduate areas. Joint-degree programs are offered in computer science, dentistry, engineering, environmental studies, law, optometry, and physical therapy.

Six University residence halls accommodate more than 1,000 students. The Residential Life staff at Adelphi is committed to bringing education to the residence halls. A lecture and discussion series brings faculty members together with students to examine events of the day and issues related to the classroom. In addition, about 200 seminars, workshops, and events are offered each year. Faculty and guest lecturers lead discussions on such topics as American politics, ethnic diversity, legal affairs, job interviewing, sexual conduct, and AIDS.

Opportunities for enhancing life beyond the classroom abound at Adelphi. Students participate in intramural and intercollegiate athletics (including nationally ranked men's and women's soccer, women's softball, and men's baseball, basketball, and lacrosse), drama productions, community-service groups, and clubs. The University gymnasium houses a swimming pool; basketball, racquetball, and squash courts; weight-training and exercise rooms; and dance studios. Other physical education facilities include tennis courts, a large indoor running track, and separate fields for baseball, lacrosse, soccer, and softball. In addition, a vast array of activities such as movies, exhibits, cabarets, symposia, and field trips are scheduled every semester.

The Adelphi student newspapers (*Delphian* and *Afrika Unbound*), the yearbook (*Oracle*), and *Ascent*, the student literary magazine, welcome writers and photographers.

In the Ruth S. Harley University Center—the central meeting place on campus—Adelphi students browse in the recently renovated bookstore, refresh themselves and relax in one of the center's lounges (commuter students have a special lounge equipped with lockers), and enjoy a vast array of activities including movies, comedy shows, lectures, dance parties, and musical events. Cultural trips are also offered. The University Center also houses Adelphi's seventy student organizations.

Location

Adelphi's main campus is located in the picturesque and architecturally distinctive suburban community of Garden City, New York, a village of stately homes, historic buildings, and parks. The cultural and commercial resources of New York City and the recreation and entertainment of Long Island are only a short distance away by public or private transit.

Majors and Degrees

Studies leading to the degrees of Bachelor of Arts, Bachelor of Fine Arts, Bachelor of Science, Bachelor of Business Administration, and Bachelor of Science in education are offered at Adelphi University.

Majors offered lead to the B.A. in anthropology, art, art education, biology, chemistry, communication disorders, communications, dance, economics, English, environmental studies, fine arts, history, international studies, Latin American studies, mathematics, philosophy, physical education, physics, political science, psychology, sociology, and speech arts/communicative disorders.

The B.S. is offered in art, biochemistry, biology, chemistry, computer science, criminal justice administration, finance, management and communication, mathematics, music, nursing, and physical education. The B.B.A. is conferred in accounting and management. The B.F.A. is granted in theater. The B.S.W. is granted in social work.

Combined graduate and undergraduate programs are offered in business, education, nursing, physics, and social work.

In education, five-year combined bachelor's/master's degree programs are offered in adolescence education and childhood education. Students who wish to obtain certification in secondary education major in art, English, foreign languages (French and Spanish), mathematics, music, physical education, the sciences (biology, chemistry, and physics), or social studies (anthropology, economics, history, political science, and sociology).

Adelphi also offers a seven-year optometry program leading to the B.S. and O.D. degrees in cooperation with the State University of New York's College of Optometry, a seven-year dental program leading to the B.S. and D.M.D. degrees in cooperation with the Tufts University School of Dental Medicine, a six-year law program leading to either the B.A. or B.S. and the J.D. degrees in cooperation with New York Law School, a seven-year physical therapy program leading to the B.S. and D.P.T. degrees in cooperation with New York Medical College, a five- or six-year environmental studies program leading to either the B.A./B.S. or B.A./M.S. degrees in cooperation with Columbia University, a five-year computer science program leading to the B.A. or B.S. degree and the M.S. degree in cooperation with Polytechnic University, and a five-year engineering program leading to both the B.A. and B.S. degrees in cooperation with Columbia University, Polytechnic University, Rensselaer Polytechnic Institute, and Stevens Institute of Technology.

The ABLE (Adult Baccalaureate Learning Experience) program, housed in the School of Business, offers a B.A. in humanistic studies, fine arts, and the social sciences and B.S. degree programs in management and communications and in criminal justice.

Academic Program

The goal of the academic program at Adelphi is to provide higher education that cultivates the intellect and prepares students for the future. Consistent with the University's approach to liberal learning, students take part in the University's general education distribution requirements.

A minimum of 120 credits is required for a baccalaureate degree, with a specified number in the chosen major. Double majors and various minors may be elected. Seniors of superior academic ability may be admitted to graduate courses in their major field.

Off-Campus Programs

Adelphi University offers study-abroad programs in Europe, Asia, Latin America, and Africa. Qualified Adelphi students may also apply for admission to overseas programs sponsored by other accredited universities.

Academic Facilities

The University libraries are composed of the Swirbul Library, the Science Library, and the libraries at the Manhattan and Huntington centers. These libraries contain 464,489 volumes and 789,694 items in microformat, plus 44,538 audiovisual items, 1,625 periodical subscriptions, and 494 electronic subscriptions. The University libraries are fully automated. Total holdings are accessible through ALICAT (the Adelphi Libraries Catalog Online). As an enhancement of the traditional reference services, computerized information retrieval services are available for accessing some 300 extensive national databases.

The Swirbul Library is also the center of information technology on campus. Its amenities include a battery of personal computers that are fully networked for student use, a faculty development lab, and a technology infrastructure that reaches into every classroom and every part of the curriculum to provide Web-based learning and other applications of communication and information media.

The University recently completed the $1.7-million renovation of the Olmsted Theatre, including a new storage area for props and scenery, a new lobby, a concession stand and box office, handicapped accessibility, and an additional 90 seats bringing the new seating capacity to 314.

Costs

The 2003–04 tuition and for full-time undergraduates was $17,800. Additional charges included room (double occupancy) costs ranging from $6000 to $7000 and board costs ranging from $2200 to $3200.

Financial Aid

The Office of Student Financial Services administers federal and New York State programs that provide funds to assist students in pursuing their academic goals. In addition to grants based on need, Adelphi annually offers almost 1,000 of its own scholarships based on merit, talent, and extracurricular excellence. Seventy-seven percent of Adelphi freshmen receive scholarships or need-based grants. The average financial aid package award for a full-time freshman is approximately $13,500.

Faculty

At Adelphi, the quality of education is entrusted to its distinguished faculty members, who are noted for their serious commitment to students, as well as for their research and professional contributions. Here, professors, not graduate assistants, teach undergraduate courses, and students do not encounter large, impersonal lecture halls.

Student Government

The Student Government Association is the elected student group that represents the opinions of the full-time undergraduate body to the administration and other groups. The Student Government Association hosts speakers, sponsors awareness days, and serves as a voice for student concerns and interests.

Admission Requirements

Recommended admission qualifications include graduation from a four-year public or private high school or equivalent credentials, 4 years of English, 3 years of science, 3 years of mathematics, 2–3 years of a foreign language or languages, and 4 additional units chosen from the fields mentioned or from history and social studies. Official test results from the SAT I or ACT are required.

Personal interviews and campus tours are strongly recommended for all applicants. Arrangements can be made by contacting the Office of Admissions.

Application and Information

The following admission credentials should be submitted by applicants: a completed application for admission, the $35 application fee, an official high school transcript or graduate equivalency diploma, official results of the SAT I or ACT, and letters of recommendation. Transfer students must submit official transcripts from all colleges previously attended.

Adelphi accepts applications on a rolling basis, with admission twice each year for the semesters beginning in September and January. Freshman filing dates are December 1 for early action, March 1 for regular admission to the fall semester (applications received later are reviewed on a rolling basis), and November 1 for regular admission for the spring semester (applications received later are reviewed on a rolling basis). The nonbinding early-action plan is available only for the September term. An early-action decision means that applicants who submit their applications by December 1 receive an admissions decision by December 31 and that they are considered for scholarships and financial aid.

For more information, students should contact:

University Admissions
Adelphi University
Garden City, New York 11530
Telephone: 800-ADELPHI (toll-free)
E-mail: admissions@adelphi.edu
World Wide Web: http://www.adelphi.edu

ADRIAN COLLEGE

ADRIAN, MICHIGAN

The College

Adrian College, chartered in 1859, is a private liberal arts college affiliated with the United Methodist Church. Recognized for providing high-quality education by the *College Board Review* and *U.S. News & World Report,* Adrian is characterized by teaching excellence and individual treatment of students. The College's mission is to maintain a learning environment that stimulates individual growth and academic excellence. To fulfill this mission, the College is committed to fostering creativity, encouraging ethical values and the pursuit of truth, and helping students develop the necessary skills to lead satisfying lives and careers within a global society.

In fall 2003, Adrian College enrolled 1,028 students (455 men and 573 women) of whom 986 were full-time. Approximately 98 percent of the student body is of traditional college age. Currently, students come from sixteen states, but most come from the surrounding Midwest states of Michigan, Ohio, and Indiana. The international student population represents China, India, Ireland, Japan, Kenya, South Africa, Vietnam, and Zambia.

Adrian College students enjoy a lifestyle that combines residential life with academic challenges and social opportunities. Nearly all of Adrian's students live on campus in one of nine residence halls that provide unique living and learning environments for residents. With more than sixty-five organizations to choose from, students can apply their talents, interests, and skills in extracurricular activities ranging from academic honoraries and religious, cultural, and social organizations to intercollegiate and intramural athletic teams. Adrian College is a member of the NCAA Division III and the Michigan Intercollegiate Athletics Association. The Merillat Sport and Fitness Center is an 80,000-square-foot multisport forum that includes basketball, volleyball, and tennis courts surrounded by a 1/10-mile indoor track as well as two racquetball courts, an athletic training room, a weight-training and conditioning room, classrooms, a physiology laboratory, and a dance studio. The performance gymnasium, which seats 1,300 people, is host to numerous intercollegiate basketball and volleyball matches.

Location

Adrian College is located in Adrian, Michigan, the county seat of Lenawee County in the southeastern part of the state. Adrian is a city of approximately 22,000 people, situated in the center of an agricultural, industrial, and recreational area. State and U.S. highways and nearby expressways provide convenient access to the metropolitan areas of Detroit, Toledo, Chicago, Indianapolis, Cleveland, and Pittsburgh. Both the Detroit and Toledo airports are within an hour's drive of the College.

Majors and Degrees

Adrian College is authorized by its Board of Trustees to grant the following degrees: Associate of Arts, Bachelor of Science, Bachelor of Arts, Bachelor of Fine Arts, Bachelor of Music, Bachelor of Music Education, and Bachelor of Business Administration. Majors include accountancy; art; arts management; biology; business administration (management or marketing); chemistry; communication arts and sciences; criminal justice; earth science; economics; English (journalism, literature, or writing); environmental science; environmental studies; exercise science; French; German; health, physical education, and recreation; history; human services; interior design; international business; international studies; mathematics; music; musical theatre; philosophy/religion; physics; political science; psychology; religion; sociology; Spanish; teacher education; and theatre. Students may also choose to design their own major, in consultation with the appropriate department chairpersons, or even major in two or more areas of study. Professional certification areas include elementary and secondary education. Preprofessional programs are offered in architecture, art therapy, dentistry, engineering, law, medicine, optometry, pharmacy, physical therapy, podiatry, seminary, and veterinary studies.

Academic Program

Distribution requirements are designed to emphasize liberal education through a broad understanding of the liberal arts and have been established in several liberal arts areas (arts, humanities, social sciences, natural and physical sciences, and cross-cultural perspective) and in basic skill areas that indicate education proficiency (communication, linguistics, and physical development). All students must complete at least one course in religion or philosophy and at least one 4-hour laboratory science course. Students must also declare their major during their sophomore year. Successful completion of a minimum of 124 semester hours, with at least 30 hours at the most advanced level, is needed to obtain a baccalaureate degree. Up to 60 semester hours may be earned through nontraditional credit programs such as CLEP, PEP, LLE, Advanced Placement, and others. An honors program is open to highly motivated students of proven ability. Successful completion of the honors program is noted on the student's transcript and diploma.

Adrian maintains a two-semester calendar. The first semester runs from late August to mid-December; the second semester from early January to the end of April. A May term and summer session are offered for students who wish to intensify or accelerate their studies.

Off-Campus Programs

Participation in approved off-campus and cooperative programs can help students earn academic credit. Adrian offers a variety of ways to visit and study other cultures through established formal arrangements, as well as gain professional experience via cooperative arrangements with a variety of off-campus sites. Formal arrangements for study abroad are available in Australia, Austria, Britain, China, Denmark, France, Germany, Hong Kong, Iceland, Italy, Japan, Mexico, the Netherlands, Russia, and Spain, although students may arrange opportunities to study in other countries. Opportunities for domestic study and living experience are available through the Appalachian Semester, the Philadelphia Urban Semester, American University's Washington Semester, and programs offered by the Urban Life Center in Chicago and the Washington Center.

Career internships, available in all academic disciplines, provide all students with opportunities to test their career interests and develop job-related skills through College-approved work experiences. Students may earn up to 12 semester hours working for domestic or international employers.

Academic Facilities

Shipman Library includes a complete line of academic library services. The collection numbers more than 82,000 volumes, plus substantial holdings of microforms, art prints, sound recordings, and subscriptions to more than 750 periodicals. The College completed a $6-million library expansion and renovation project in summer 2000.

Computer terminals and printers for student use are located in Jones Hall, Mahan Hall, North Hall, Peele Hall, The Student Center, and Shipman Library. Access to IBM and IBM-compatible personal computers, printers, scanners, and Internet services is available to students at no charge. Many classrooms and all residence hall rooms are networked for Internet access.

General chemistry and biology laboratories equipped with sophisticated chemical and biochemical instrumentation are provided by the College. Labs for psychology, language study, physics, acoustical studies, and tissue culture provide students with access to a variety of research opportunities. Special facilities include art studios, music practice rooms, greenhouses, and a planetarium.

Downs Hall, the only remaining building from Adrian College's original campus, houses the Stubnitz Gallery of Art and the Downs Studio Theater, a 199-seat facility with a thrust-style stage, where most student theater productions take place. Dawson Auditorium, with its traditional proscenium stage, is used for College musical and theatrical productions, Adrian Symphony concerts, and guest artist appearances.

Costs

Full-time tuition for 2003–04 was $16,470, and room and board were $5380. The required activity fee of $100 covered the cost of student participation in a variety of campuswide social activities and attendance at Adrian College sports events. The average cost of books and supplies was about $400 per year. No additional costs for laboratory or computer use are assessed.

Financial Aid

Adrian College strives to make a high-quality private liberal arts education affordable to its students through various forms of financial assistance. Approximately 85 percent of the student body receives some form of financial aid through scholarships, grants, loans, and campus employment. The College also participates in all applicable Michigan aid programs, as well as the Federal Work-Study, Federal Pell Grant, and Federal Supplemental Educational Opportunity Grant (FSEOG) programs. The Federal Perkins Loan, Federal Stafford Student Loan, TERI Supplemental Loan, and Federal Parent Loan (PLUS) programs are also available. A number of part-time positions are available for those who wish to work on campus while earning applicable financial assistance. For those with a demonstrated record of high academic ability, merit-based scholarship assistance is available.

To be considered for any financial assistance, a student must complete the Free Application for Federal Student Aid (FAFSA) form, which is used to conduct a need analysis for the student. The FAFSA may be obtained from most high school counselors or directly from the Adrian College Office of Financial Aid.

Faculty

Teaching with a personal approach is a top priority at Adrian College. Classes at Adrian are not conducted by teaching assistants. Instead, classes are taught by dedicated faculty members—most of whom hold the terminal degree in their field. With a student-faculty ratio of 13:1 and an average class size of 14, students are assured of a high-quality education that unites challenge and opportunity within a framework of personal and institutional support.

Student Government

Adrian College Student Government is the student organization charged with representing student views on matters of institutional policy and operation at all levels of College organization. As a student organization, it also provides students with a common forum where their individual ideas may be heard, debated, and perhaps adopted. Appropriations and other major decisions are made in full-senate sessions. Other work is carried out through the Cooperative Activities Board or through the College governance system. Any student who wishes to run for student-elected office may do so.

Admission Requirements

Adrian College enrolls qualified students regardless of age, disability, ethnicity, gender, physical characteristics, race, religion, or sexual orientation. Applicants should present at least 15 units of secondary school preparation, including 4 units of English, 3 units of mathematics, 3 units in sciences, 2 units in social sciences, and 2 units in foreign language.

Students applying for freshman admission must also perform satisfactorily on either the ACT Assessment or the SAT I and must request that their scores be sent directly to Adrian College. The average high school GPA of entering Adrian College students who have taken college-preparatory courses during their four years of high school is 3.2. The mean ACT Assessment composite score is 22. Transfer students must be eligible to return immediately to the last attended college and must have an above-average cumulative GPA. Prospective transfer students must request an official transcript from each college attended to be sent directly to the Office of Admissions at Adrian College. Nontraditional students must complete a different application for admission but are evaluated on the same basis as traditional freshmen. A GED equivalency certificate may be substituted for a full high school transcript.

Students from other countries are always welcome at Adrian College and are encouraged to apply. International applicants must file an international application for admission and must submit complete secondary school records, transcripts of any university credit, and TOEFL test scores demonstrating sufficient fluency in English to participate in the regular instructional program of the College. A minimum TOEFL score of 500 is required for admission. A full program of services for international students includes English as a second language (ESL) classes for further assistance in English, housing and food service, and pick-up service from the airport. International students are eligible for grants that cover the cost of room and board for the academic year.

Application and Information

A nonrefundable fee of $20 must be submitted with an application for admission. Application can be made anytime following the completion of the junior year of high school. Students are usually notified of the admissions decision within two weeks after the application file is complete. Campus visits are strongly encouraged but not required.

For more information about Adrian College or to schedule a campus visit, students should contact:

Office of Admissions
Adrian College
110 South Madison Street
Adrian, Michigan 49221-2575

Telephone: 517-265-5161 Ext. 4326
800-877-2246 (toll-free)
E-mail: admissions@adrian.edu
World Wide Web: http://www.adrian.edu

AGNES SCOTT COLLEGE

ATLANTA, GEORGIA

The College

For more than a century, minds have sparked minds at Agnes Scott College, a highly selective, independent, national liberal arts college for women, located in metropolitan Atlanta. Agnes Scott College educates women to think deeply, live honorably, and engage the intellectual and social challenges of their times. Founded in 1889 by Presbyterians, Agnes Scott College is a diverse and growing residential community of scholars, with one of the largest endowments per student of any college or university in the United States. In offering the world for women, Agnes Scott's curriculum encourages students to become fluent across disciplines, continents, and centuries.

Agnes Scott was the first accredited college or university in Georgia, and the College's Phi Beta Kappa chapter is the second oldest in the state. Agnes Scott's tradition of academic excellence continues today with a student body numbering 945. Students come from thirty-nine states, the District of Columbia, the U.S. Virgin Islands, and twenty-nine countries, and 90 percent of traditional-age students live on campus in residence halls and apartments. More than 30 percent represent diverse ethnic or cultural backgrounds.

Students may pursue special interests in the arts (music, dance, and theater); with clubs for international cultures, politics, cultural awareness, religious affiliations, and foreign languages; and through student publications, sports, and volunteer community service. Social Council plans dances, mixers, and parties with neighboring colleges. Traditional annual highlights are Black Cat (the culmination of first-year student orientation), Senior Investiture, and Sophomore Family Weekend. The College sponsors a variety of events, from lectures by noted authorities to concerts by world-famous artists; each spring, the Writers' Festival brings well-known authors and poets to the campus for readings and informal meetings with students.

The College is a member of the NCAA Division III and sponsors seven varsity sports: basketball, cross-country, soccer, softball, swimming, tennis, and volleyball. Club and intramural sports are also available. The Woodruff Physical Activities Building features an eight-lane swimming pool, a large weight and aerobic exercise room, a gymnasium, and an athletic training room. The Gellerstedt track is an all-weather, six-lane running track circling varsity soccer's game field.

Location

The 100-acre wooded campus is located in metropolitan Atlanta and the historic residential community of Decatur. Six miles away is downtown Atlanta, accessible by a rapid-transit rail station two blocks from campus. An international city, Atlanta offers a multitude of opportunities for personal contact with most of the world's cultures and for study, through internships and volunteer work, with art, business, educational, and political organizations. Atlanta is the cultural center of the South, with entertainment and cultural events and facilities ranging from rock concerts to performances by the Atlanta Symphony Orchestra, from local theater to touring Broadway shows, and from recreational parks to major-league sports.

Majors and Degrees

Agnes Scott College confers the Bachelor of Arts degree with majors in art history, astrophysics, biochemistry and molecular biology, biology, chemistry, classical languages and literatures, classical civilization, economics, economics and business, English, English literature–creative writing, French, German studies, history, international relations, mathematics, mathematics-economics, mathematics-physics, music, philosophy, physics, political science, psychology, religion and social justice, religious studies, sociology and anthropology, Spanish, studio art, theater, and women's studies. Students may design their own interdisciplinary majors. Through a dual-degree program, a student may combine three years of liberal arts studies at Agnes Scott with two years of specialized engineering studies at Georgia Tech, receiving a bachelor's degree from each institution. Also available is a 3-4 Master of Architecture program offered with Washington University in St. Louis, resulting in a bachelor's degree from Agnes Scott and a master's degree from Washington University.

Academic Program

Agnes Scott's curriculum is designed to help students gain an understanding of the humanities and fine arts, natural sciences and mathematics, and social sciences, with particular competence in one or two disciplines. The graduation requirement of 130 semester hours includes specific standards in English composition, physical education, and foreign language. The Language Across the Curriculum Program links foreign languages with other disciplines. Students prepare for world citizenship through a curriculum with international perspectives. In the last ten years, Agnes Scott has had 5 Fulbright Scholars, 6 Goldwater Scholars, 1 Gates Millenium Scholar, 1 Gillman International Scholar, and 1 Pickering Fellow.

The Atlanta Semester in Women, Leadership, and Social Program Change provides an opportunity for Agnes Scott students to combine internships with independent research projects, interdisciplinary academic course work, and a weekly speakers' forum. The Preparatory Program for Business is designed to facilitate a student's entry into the business world. The state-approved teacher education program leads to the Georgia professional certificate, which is recognized and accepted by most states. The Woodruff Scholars Program provides women beyond traditional college age with the opportunity to complete the Bachelor of Arts degree.

Off-Campus Programs

Study abroad enriches classroom learning experiences and expands world views. Agnes Scott offers two faculty-led programs—Global Awareness and Global Connections. Recent destinations have included China, Cuba, France, Ghana, Greece, India, Ireland, Japan, Jordan, and Mexico. Agnes Scott has a scholarly exchange agreement with Japan's Kinjo Gakuin University and is the only women's college admitted to the International Student Exchange Program (ISEP), which provides study-abroad opportunities with more than 123 institutions in thirty-three countries.

With opportunities to cross-register at member institutions of the Atlanta Regional Consortium for Higher Education (ARCHE), Agnes Scott students enjoy the advantages of a small-college environment while benefiting from a variety of programs at neighboring schools, including Emory University, Spelman College, and Georgia Institute of Technology. ARCHE shares courses of instruction, library services, and visiting scholars. Air

Force and Navy ROTC programs are available through cross-registration. An exchange program with Mills College in Oakland, California, enables students to study for a semester or year in the San Francisco Bay area. Students may participate in the Washington Semester program, coordinated by American University, or the PLEN Public Policy Semester, both in Washington, D.C.

Academic Facilities

A $120-million building program to enhance academic and student life facilities is complete. A new $36.5-million Science Center and tennis courts have recently opened. The Alston Campus Center, which includes meeting rooms, a 24-hour-access Cyber Café, and a computer lab, opened during the 2000–01 academic year. Other enhancements include a renovated and expanded Evans Dining Hall, with a marketplace servery, and a new 500-car parking and public safety facility, both of which have opened within the last three to five years.

The new Science Center has laboratories and computer facilities for experimentation and research in biology, chemistry, physics, and psychology. These include a nuclear magnetic resonance (NMR) machine/lab; high-end computers for scientific computing, teaching, and research; walk-in controlled environment rooms; a neurophysiology laboratory; and animal physiology workstations. Bradley Observatory has undergone extensive renovation and addition. The new Delafield Planetarium has a computer-controlled Zeiss projector, one of only ten in the United States, as well as its 3-inch Beck telescope, one of the largest in the Southeast.

McCain Library has been completely renovated and doubled in size, with access to the Internet available at every seat. The library contains 215,138 volumes, 17,828 audiovisual items, and 32,257 microforms and receives 1,118 periodicals. It also provides a home for the Center for Speaking and Writing. The library holds several noteworthy collections of rare books and manuscripts, including one of the leading Robert Frost collections and the papers of alumna Catherine Marshall. Agnes Scott's reciprocal library service gives students direct access to the libraries of eighteen other institutions in the Atlanta-Athens area. Extensive electronic resources are available through the GALILEO project of the University System of Georgia.

Personal computers are available to students in the technology commons, Cyber Café, Academic Computing Center, Center for Writing and Speaking, Science Resource Center, Macintosh lab, and residence halls. An interactive learning center, multimedia classrooms, and a computer network with one port per student in residence hall rooms are part of Agnes Scott's commitment to keeping pace with current technologies.

The Dana Fine Arts Building houses the departments of theater and art; its facilities include a thrust-stage theater, two floors of balcony art studios, pottery and sculpture studios with kilns, and a darkroom. The Dalton Gallery exhibits the College's permanent and traveling collections and student and faculty member exhibitions. Presser Hall contains soundproof recording studios and practice rooms for music students. Gaines Chapel, with a 3,000-pipe Austin organ, has a large stage for dance, music, and theatrical performances. Maclean Auditorium, which houses a Schlicker organ, is used for chamber music concerts and student recitals.

Costs

Tuition for 2003–04 was $20,310. Residence costs, including room, board, and health services, were $7760, and the student activity fee was $160. Personal expenses, including books and supplies, are estimated at $1600.

Financial Aid

Agnes Scott admits most students without regard to financial need, and the College makes every effort to meet the need of qualified students whose resources are insufficient to meet expenses. More than 60 percent of students receive need-based financial assistance through grants, loans, and campus employment. Outstanding first-year students are offered renewable merit-based Honor Scholarships, and music scholarships are available for new students intending to major in music. Community Service and Leadership Awards, Middle Income Assistance Awards, and Transfer Scholarships are also offered.

Faculty

A 10:1 student-faculty ratio allows for small classes with lively participation and individual attention. One hundred percent of Agnes Scott's tenure-track faculty members hold the highest degree in their field. Senior faculty members teach first-year students as well as upperclass students. Every student is assigned a faculty adviser to assist in course selection and academic counseling.

Student Government

Agnes Scott is a self-governing community, and each student is a member of the Student Government Association. A strong honor system places responsibility for integrity, honesty, and judgment in self-government on the individual and allows unproctored tests and self-scheduled final examinations. Regulations governing student life are made by the students with approval of the Judicial Review Committee, on which the Student Government Association, Student Senate, Honor Court, and Judicial Board presidents serve as voting members. Policies are formulated with the goal of maintaining an individual's maximum freedom within the framework of community responsibility.

Admission Requirements

Agnes Scott admits, without regard to race, color, creed, national or ethnic origin, or physical handicap, students whose academic and personal qualities give promise of success. Transfer and international students are welcome. Each applicant's school record, SAT I or ACT scores, recommendations, and essay are reviewed carefully, and interviews are recommended but not required. Arrangements for an interview at the College, a campus tour with a student guide, and visits to classes may be made through the Office of Admission.

Application and Information

An application for admission and supporting credentials should be filed with the Office of Admission by the following dates: November 15 for early decision, with notification by December 15; January 15 for scholarship candidates; March 1 for regular decision; and November 1 for the spring semester.

Dean of Admission
Agnes Scott College
141 East College Avenue
Decatur, Georgia 30030-3797
Telephone: 404-471-6285
800-868-8602 (toll-free)
Fax: 404-471-6414
E-mail: admission@agnesscott.edu
World Wide Web: http://www.agnesscott.edu

ALABAMA STATE UNIVERSITY

MONTGOMERY, ALABAMA

The University

Founded in 1867 to make the dream of a college education a reality for thousands of Alabamians, Alabama State University (ASU) is America's oldest publicly assisted liberal arts institution for African Americans. Today, ASU has a record enrollment of approximately 6,025 students from thirty-seven states and nine countries. The University has more than 5,000 undergraduate students. Almost one third of the students are non-Alabamians, and 12 percent are minorities. ASU is the college of choice for a diverse student body who are able to choose from more than fifty bachelor's, master's, and educational specialist's degree programs and who go on to become preeminent surgeons, chemists, historians, lawyers, politicians, philosophers, musicians, engineers, filmmakers, business leaders, and educators.

Alabama State University offers a full array of NCAA intercollegiate sports throughout the year. Men's sports include baseball, basketball, football, golf, tennis, and track. Women's sports include basketball, bowling, golf, softball, tennis, track, and volleyball.

ASU is divided into six major divisions. These areas include the College of Health Sciences, the College of Arts and Sciences, the College of Business Administration, the College of Education, the School of Music, and University College. The College of Arts and Sciences is the University's largest college. Theater arts is directed by the nationally acclaimed actress Dr. Tommie "Tonea" Stewart; the biomedical research program serves future leaders in the health professions, and Department of Mathematics faculty members captured national recognition for having solved a 23-year-old math mystery. College of Business Administration graduates are climbing corporate ladders in Fortune 500 companies, as well as becoming thriving entrepreneurs. The College of Education is one of the nation's leading producers of African-American teachers. The School of Music's education students are in great demand for band- and choral-directing positions upon graduation. Interested students may become involved in one of many band and choral ensembles, including the Marching Hornets, University Choir, Wind Ensemble, Chamber Singers, and Jazz Band. University College serves as the point of entry for all ASU students. Students are aided in making the transition to college and are taught survival skills for college life.

Doctoral degrees in environmental biology and education are under development.

Location

Montgomery, the state's capital, has a metropolitan population of more than 320,000. Centrally located in the state and on the Alabama River, Montgomery is 2½ hours from Atlanta, Georgia; 1½ hours from Birmingham, Alabama; less than 3 hours from the beaches of Alabama and northwest Florida's Gulf Coast; and 4 hours from the scenic mountains of Tennessee and the Carolinas. The climate is moderate year-round. Among Montgomery's historic sites are the Civil Rights Memorial, Dexter Avenue King Memorial Baptist Church, the first pulpit of Dr. Martin Luther King Jr., and the First White House of the Confederacy.

The city offers diverse entertainment, shopping, dining, living, and social venues. Area highlights include the Alabama Shakespeare Festival, the Montgomery Museum of Fine Arts, and Jasmine Hill Gardens.

Majors and Degrees

The bachelor's degree programs are offered in accounting, art, art education, banking and finance, biology, business economics, business education, business management and administration, chemistry, computer information systems, computer science, criminal justice, early childhood education, elementary education, English, French, graphic arts, health education, health information management, history, marine biology, marketing and purchasing, mathematics/engineering, music education, music performance, occupational therapy, parks and recreation management, physical education, physics, political science and government, print journalism, psychology, public relations, radio/television, secondary education, social work, sociology, Spanish, special education, speech, and theater arts. The University offers a dual-degree program in mathematics/engineering in cooperation with Auburn University and the University of Alabama at Birmingham.

The list of studies in career fields includes bachelor's degree programs in health information management and occupational therapy and a graduate program in physical therapy. Students who seek a challenging career should also check into the division of aerospace studies, which awards numerous scholarships each year to cadets who are serious about becoming Air Force officers.

Academic Programs

As a liberal arts institution, the University seeks to provide students with a broad-based education that prepares them to be well-rounded and productive members of society. The academic year consists of two semesters—fall semester and spring semester—and one summer term. Each of the two semesters lasts sixteen weeks. The fall semester generally begins in late August and ends in mid-December; the spring semester begins in early January and ends in early May.

The number of semester hours required for graduation varies with each program of study; however, a minimum of 120 semester hours is required for graduation. All ASU students must fulfill the required number of semester hours in a major as well as the core curriculum. Students are required to have a minimum grade point average of 2.2 (on a 4.0 scale) to be eligible for graduation.

The University's W. E. B. DuBois Honors Program offers a two-track interdisciplinary program with emphasis in the areas of humanities and math/science.

Students may gain advanced placement and college credit by participating in the Advanced Placement (AP) Program and the College-Level Examination Program (CLEP).

Off-Campus Programs

Alabama State University has five off-campus sites for students enrolled in graduate programs. In addition, the University has cross-enrollment agreements with two local universities, Auburn University at Montgomery and Troy State University Montgomery. These agreements allow students to take classes that may not be offered at ASU. Students who wish to study at other institutions for one academic year may also participate in the National Student Exchange Program.

Academic Facilities

ASU has a beautiful campus, with rolling lawns and flower gardens punctuated by an eclectic mix of Georgian-style, red-brick classroom buildings. The campus has architecturally contemporary structures, such as the state-of-the-art, 7,400-seat academic and sports facility known as the Joe L. Reed Acadome.

ASU reaches beyond the traditional university setting with several unique programs. WVAS-FM 90.7, the 80,000-watt, University-operated public radio station, is a real-world training ground for future broadcast journalists; the Zelia Stephens Early Childhood Center offers classroom instruction and student training; the Distance Learning Center allows students to take classes at off-campus locations; the Business and Technology Center functions as a small-business incubator; and the Center for Leadership and Public Policy grooms students for leadership positions.

The Levi Watkins Learning Center, a five-story brick structure, houses more than 267,000 volumes. The University is also the home of the National Center for the Study of Civil Rights and African-American Culture. Programs in health information management and occupational therapy and a graduate program in physical therapy are housed in the new, three-story, 80,000-square-foot John L. Buskey Health Sciences Center.

Costs

Tuition and fees for 2003–04 were $3600 for Alabama residents and $7200 for out-of-state students. Students who reside on campus pay an average of $3600 for room and board. All students are required to pay a $200 housing deposit. Students should estimate their personal expenses for books, supplies, automobile registration, and other items to be $1200.

Financial Aid

More than 90 percent of the ASU students receive some form of financial assistance. The University awards more than 200 scholarships annually. Academic, diversity, athletic, music, band, choir, and theater scholarships are available. To apply for financial aid, students should complete the Free Application for Federal Student Aid (FAFSA). Students who are interested in academic or diversity scholarships should contact the Office of Admissions and Recruitment.

Faculty

Alabama State has a dynamic and diverse faculty. The student-faculty ratio is 20:1. This ratio allows for a great amount of faculty-student interaction. Sixty percent of the full-time faculty members have earned a doctorate or terminal degree.

Student Government

The Student Government Association (SGA) is a particularly rewarding aspect of student life at Alabama State University. Each student, upon enrollment at ASU, becomes a member of the SGA. The student body, through elected officials, has the opportunity to share in policymaking and the overall governance of the students, the general welfare, and student concerns at ASU. The SGA is the primary channel through which students can participate in decision making productively and effectively.

Admission Requirements

Alabama State University believes that the broadest academic experience in high school is the best preparation for admission to the University. In considering the academic record of an applicant, attention is given to the subjects studied and the grades received. The applicant's high school record should include 4 units in English, 3 in mathematics, 2 in social science, 2 in natural science, and 1 in a foreign language. High school graduates must have at least a 2.0 grade point average to be admitted. Transfer students must be eligible for readmission to the institution last attended. Transfer applicants must have a cumulative grade point average of at least 2.2 to be admitted to the University.

Application and Information

To be considered for admission, a student must submit an application for admission, an official transcript, and ACT or SAT scores. The University has rolling admission. Students are notified within approximately three to four weeks after the application is complete. Students are encouraged to visit the campus; scheduled campus tours are available. Students should contact the Office of Admissions and Recruitment for details. The University also sponsors two campus visitation days for prospective students and their parents to learn more about ASU and its offerings.

Students may obtain more information about ASU and apply for admission online at the Web address below. Students should contact:

Office of Admissions and Recruitment
Alabama State University
915 South Jackson Street
Montgomery, Alabama 36104
Telephone: 334-229-4291
800-253-5037 (toll-free)
World Wide Web: http://www.alasu.edu

A view of the campus of Alabama State University.

ALASKA PACIFIC UNIVERSITY

ANCHORAGE, ALASKA

The University

Alaska Pacific University (APU) believes that how a student learns is as important as what a student learns. Alaska Pacific University employs an active model of learning that transcends the traditional classroom and the conventional format of lecture and examination. APU students—through projects, self-directed study, collaborative study, internships, research, field study, and study abroad—are prepared for leadership and self-direction in their careers, professions, or graduate school. All undergraduate students are involved in internships and project-based learning from the first year forward, a process that culminates in each student's senior project. Upon graduation, every APU student has not only learned, but also has demonstrated the ability to apply what has been learned in the real world.

APU's 284 undergraduate students currently represent thirty-four states and three countries. Minority students make up a growing portion of APU's undergraduate enrollment, which is strengthened by close working relationships between native Alaskan communities and the University. Small classes; lively interaction among students, faculty members, and staff members; and personal academic advising are special benefits of the Alaska Pacific experience. There are 102 men and 182 women currently enrolled in undergraduate programs at APU. APU is proud of its 10:1 student-faculty ratio, and that 99 percent of classes consist of less than 20 students. Class size is kept deliberately small to maintain Alaska Pacific's commitment to individualized learning and the freedom necessary for its students to create an expressive and meaningful relationship with their academic interests.

All freshmen are required to live on campus during their first year. APU's residence halls are centrally located, offering breathtaking views of the Chugach mountains and convenient access to the dining facility, sports center, and classes. The residence halls offer 1-, 2-, and 3-bedroom suites, while upperclassmen and graduate students have the opportunity to live in alternative housing on campus.

Alaska Pacific University has a world-class Nordic ski team that trains in Alaska and competes in national and international events. The Nordic ski team has a summer Nordic ski facility on Eagle Glacier, where the American Olympic Team trains, along with other world-class skiers. Downhill skiers and snowboarders take advantage of two major ski resorts, each within an hour's drive of the campus, offering some of the most challenging, exciting, and varied ski conditions in the world.

Alaska Pacific students are encouraged to take a high degree of initiative in organizing and participating in campus activities. Extracurricular activities range from intramural club sports such as ice-skating, snowshoe softball, volleyball, Nordic skiing, and basketball to participation in the various student government–sponsored activities such as the student newspaper and yearbook. APU offers a wide variety of programs for all ability levels, including the use of a new indoor climbing wall, kayaking, ice climbing, and weekend camping and hiking trips. Students are also encouraged to take advantage of the extensive collection of recreational equipment offered through the Moseley Sports Center, including, but not limited to, backpacks, tents, sleeping bags, kayaks, canoes, skis, and snowshoes.

Graduate programs include the Master of Arts in Teaching (M.A.T., K–8), Master of Business Administration (M.B.A.), M.B.A. in telecommunications management, M.B.A. in global financial management, Master of Arts, Master of Science in Counseling Psychology, and the Master of Science in Environmental Science.

Location

Alaska Pacific University is located on a 170-acre campus in suburban Anchorage. It is unquestionably one of the most beautiful campuses in the United States. Expansive lawns, woods, and University Lake frame nearly 3 miles of campus trails that lead bikers, hikers, in-line skaters, skiers, and runners into an extensive regional trail system that stretches from the ocean waters of Cook Inlet throughout the city and into the mountains to the east. The campus is a world unto itself, with no through roads or traffic; it has an atmosphere appropriate to the dynamic, student-centered, personal style of education for which APU is known.

Anchorage is an outdoor enthusiast's dream. In spring and summer, opportunities for fishing, hiking, mountain climbing, biking, sea kayaking, and camping abound. Winter sports activities include downhill and cross-country skiing, hockey, broomball, and sled-dog racing.

Anchorage's resident population has a strong interest in arts and entertainment. Cultural facilities and organizations in the Anchorage community include the Anchorage Museum of History and Art, the Alaskan Center for the Performing Arts, the Anchorage Symphony Orchestra, the Anchorage Concert Association, and the Anchorage Opera. APU's Grant Hall Theatre is the scene of a variety of student-sponsored and local productions, concerts, and lectures. With a population of 263,000, Anchorage offers a multitude of malls, cafés, clubs, and restaurants.

Majors and Degrees

Alaska Pacific University offers the Bachelor of Arts degree with majors in business administration, counseling and psychological studies, education (with K–8 certification), environmental science, environmental policy and planning, liberal studies, marine biology, and outdoor studies.

Academic Programs

Alaska Pacific University's undergraduate curriculum is designed to integrate a comprehensive background in the liberal arts and in-depth study in their major, a chosen career discipline. APU structures its classes around its active, hands-on learning philosophy. The curriculum emphasizes personal growth through student-centered, experiential education using Alaska, the Arctic, the Pacific Rim, and study abroad as active laboratories for learning.

APU focuses on developing student leadership skills for active service to society by encouraging openness to positive change, innovation, and individual initiative. Central to the philosophy of education at APU is the block-and-session academic calendar. In addition to two traditional sessions, three times per year students may take a block class—a one-month intensive course allowing students to focus entirely on a specific subject. Block courses enable students and faculty members to travel together to different parts of Alaska and the world and also to pursue internships and self-directed studies. Block courses regularly travel to such locations as rural Alaska, Russia, England, Italy, Costa Rica, Mexico, and the Pacific Rim.

Academic Facilities

The Consortium Library serves University students and faculty members. It is operated through an agreement between APU and the University of Alaska, Anchorage. Centrally located, the library contains more than 384,000 bound volumes, including original government documents, sheet music, nonprint media, and a special Alaskana collection. The Academic Support Center located in Atwood Center has forty-two computers no more than 1½ years old and offers Internet access and e-mail accounts for all APU students. The Atwood Center also contains an excellent climbing wall, exercise room, ski team facilities, bookstore, art center, and photo lab along with the cafeteria and two residence halls; Grant Hall houses the community theater, coffee shop, art gallery, numerous faculty offices, and classrooms; the Carr-Gottstein Building features seminar and conference rooms, lecture halls, a computer lab, and an art exhibition area.

Costs

Undergraduate tuition for 2003–04 was $17,200 for all students. Room and board charges were $6000 per year. The year's activity fees for full-time students were $110, and books and miscellaneous supplies were estimated at $1000. Incoming freshmen are guaranteed no tuition increases for up to five years; transfer students receive the same guarantee, prorated.

Financial Aid

The primary purpose of student financial assistance at Alaska Pacific University is to provide financial resources to students who would otherwise be unable to pursue their educational goals. Most assistance is available on the basis of demonstrated need, although some funds are specifically allocated for the recognition of academic excellence and special talents. While the primary responsibility for financing their education rests with the student and his or her family, APU supplements their efforts with aid in the form of grants, loans, work opportunities, and scholarships. In order to be considered for assistance, students are required to submit the Free Application for Federal Student Aid (FAFSA). APU's federal school code is #001061. Funds are also available for international students.

Faculty

Alaska Pacific University is a teaching university, not a research university. Members of the full-time faculty are selected for their teaching abilities and are encouraged to involve their students in their research and professional activities. Sixty-six percent hold terminal degrees in their fields, and many are in demand as consultants in areas such as international business, environmental quality, telecommunications, and multicultural education. The University's faculty-student ratio of 1:10 allows frequent and meaningful faculty-student interaction, resulting in a learning environment of the highest quality.

Student Government

The Associated Students of Alaska Pacific University (ASAPU) is the student-elected governance responsible for campus leadership. ASAPU initiates and sponsors many student activities, including student orientation events, student banquets, sports events, cultural activities, special awards, and student assemblies. All campus clubs and organizations work through ASAPU for formal recognition and funding. Student representatives sit on most major University committees and task forces.

Admission Requirements

In admitting students, Alaska Pacific University considers grade point average, SAT or ACT scores, essays, letters of recommendation, and extracurricular activities. In general, APU recognizes that some students may flourish for the first time within APU's distinctive approach to education. APU welcomes diversity, uniqueness, and personal integrity. To apply, a candidate for freshman admission must submit an application for admission, two letters of recommendation, a personal essay, official high school transcripts, SAT or ACT scores, and a $25 application fee. Transfer applicants must submit an application for admission, transcripts from all colleges or universities they have attended, a personal essay, and a $25 application fee. International students must meet all of the above requirements, as well as submit evidence of financial support and obtain a minimum of 550 on the pen-and-paper TOEFL or 213 on the computerized version.

Application and Information

Applications for fall should be received by February 1. Thereafter, admission decisions are made on a rolling basis; however, competition for a space in each class intensifies following each application deadline.

All inquiries and application material should be directed to:

Office of Admission
Alaska Pacific University
4101 University Drive
Anchorage, Alaska 99508-4672
Telephone: 907-564-8248
800-252-7528 (toll-free)
E-mail: admissions@alaskapacific.edu
World Wide Web: http://www.alaskapacific.edu

Students gathered at the entrance to APU's campus.

ALBERTUS MAGNUS COLLEGE

NEW HAVEN, CONNECTICUT

The College

Founded in 1925 by the Dominican Sisters of St. Mary of the Springs, Albertus Magnus College educates men and women to become leaders in all walks of life. The College is committed to providing a liberal arts education rooted in the Dominican tradition of scholarship. Professors at Albertus strive to help their students develop in all areas; as much attention is paid to the nurturing of a student's aesthetic, physical, and moral capacities as to his or her intellectual capabilities. In 1992, the College began offering its first graduate-level course of study through the Master of Arts in Liberal Studies program. More recently, the College has expanded its offerings to include graduate-level programs that include the Master of Liberal Studies program, the Master of Science in Management program, the Master of Arts in Art Therapy program, and the Master of Business Administration program.

The 2,200 students who attend Albertus find their academic home in one of the three major programs of the College. The traditional undergraduate program numbers just under 500 students, who live and learn on the beautiful 50-acre campus in the Prospect Hill neighborhood of New Haven. These students come from various parts of the United States (largely the New England area), Europe, Africa, Asia, and South and Central America. About 70 percent of the students live on campus in student dormitories that are renovated mansions from the early 1900s. The housing program fosters a strong sense of community spirit, and students often plan workshops, parties, and other social and learning events in their residence halls.

The Campus Center is a hub of student activities such as comedy shows, live music, contests, and other unique functions. There are dozens of on-campus organizations. They include the intramural athletic association, a Future Business Leaders of America chapter, and numerous journalistic and creative writing options, such as *Breakwater* (literary magazine), *Prospect* (yearbook), and *Silverhorn* (newspaper). The Multicultural Student Union, a student organization composed of members of minority groups, provides compelling, diverse points of view.

The College has recently introduced Arts in Action, which offers students an opportunity to participate in the performing arts. Students may also share in the excitement of live drama through the College's professionally managed ACT 2 Theatre, providing a number of artistic, academic, and recreational possibilities. In addition, students are encouraged to become part of the New Haven community through extracurricular and volunteer activities.

The Cosgrove, Marcus, Messer Athletic Center houses an Olympic-size pool, a Jacuzzi, three racquetball courts, a weight and cardio room, a dance studio, and a gymnasium. In addition to this facility, there are soccer and softball fields, an outdoor track, and several tennis courts. Albertus fields intercollegiate athletic teams in baseball, basketball, cross-country, soccer, swimming, and tennis for men and basketball, cross-country, soccer, softball, swimming, tennis, and volleyball for women. Albertus's teams compete in NCAA Division III/Great Northeast Athletic Conference (GNAC) and the Eastern College Athletic Conference (ECAC).

Location

New Haven is a college town, and many activities are planned for the benefit of the students from all seven area colleges and universities. Lectures and musical performances presented by renowned figures as well as a variety of sports events draw large audiences. The city has some of the finest theaters in the country, including the Long Wharf and Shubert theaters. There are many fantastic art collections, museums, and movie theaters. Large shopping facilities, excellent restaurants, and several recreational areas are only a short distance from the Albertus Magnus College campus.

Majors and Degrees

Albertus Magnus College confers the Bachelor of Arts, Bachelor of Science, Bachelor of Fine Arts, and Associate of Arts degrees. The areas of study include accounting, art (history and studio), art therapy, biology, biology-chemistry, business administration, chemistry, child development and community psychology, classical languages and literature, communications, criminal justice, drama, economics, English, finance, foreign language, general studies, graphic design, history, humanities, human services, industrial and organizational psychology, international business, management information systems, mathematics, performance arts theater, philosophy/religion, physical sciences, political science, predentistry, prelaw, premedicine, preoptometry, pre–veterinary studies, psychology, social gerontology, social science, social work, sociology, teacher preparation (4–12), urban studies, and visual and performing arts.

Academic Programs

The B.A. and B.S. degrees require 120 credits for graduation, the B.F.A. requires 129 credits, and the A.A. requires 60 credits. Within these credit hours, students take core courses to fulfill broad distributional requirements and courses for the major. Students may relate academic study to work experience through a system of academically credited internships. The College's Office of Career Services helps graduating students prepare for career direction and job placement. The Academic Development Center provides personal instruction to students who need extra help with their school work. The center also caters to those students with learning disabilities. Students who show strong academic potential may pursue a course of study through the College's honors program. Through the College's system of internships for juniors and seniors, Albertus students have become increasingly involved in New Haven community life and gain valuable, practical, professional training. Often, internships lead to permanent positions with local companies and corporations.

Off-Campus Programs

Cross-registration is available with the University of New Haven and Quinnipiac College. Students may take internships for college credit at various Yale University facilities or at area industries, psychological institutes, hospitals, law firms, banks, laboratories, and public and private agencies. Through a study-abroad program, students may also spend a semester or a year abroad.

Academic Facilities

Rosary Hall, the original College building, now houses a library collection of 110,000 volumes, 600 periodicals, 4,400 pieces of microfilm, and full access to the Internet, which includes Lexis-Nexis, EBSCOhost, and PsycINFO. The interlibrary loan program has national access to materials at academic and public libraries across the country. The Media Center has equipment that students may use to produce new materials as well as review older materials. Interlibrary services with the University of New Haven and Quinnipiac College are also available. Walsh Hall Science Building provides the most modern scientific equipment available for students majoring in biological and physical sciences. Aquinas Hall, the main academic building, houses the academic computer labs, which are equipped with personal computers, digital scanners, laser printers, and full Internet access. Every classroom in Aquinas Hall is laptop compatible.

Costs

The costs for the 2003–04 school year were $16,160 for tuition, $7300 for room and board (nineteen meals per week), and $500 for student fees. Expenses for books, travel, and personal supplies vary.

Financial Aid

Albertus Magnus College offers a variety of merit-based scholarships to students who have achieved high academic standing in high school or in their two-year college programs. The College offers the Mohun Scholarships, which award $5000 per year toward tuition, to students who attended Catholic high schools. In addition, all students may compete for the Presidential Scholarships, which award a one-third tuition reduction annually. The Valedictorian/Salutatorian Scholarships award full tuition annually. Students from the New Haven area public schools may compete for the New Haven Area Scholarships, which award up to 75 percent tuition reduction annually. Transfer students of superior academic ability are eligible for a $3500 transfer scholarship. Interested students should contact the Office of Admission for the specifics of these and other scholarship awards.

Approximately 85 percent of the College's students receive financial aid in some form. The College requires that students file the Albertus Magnus College financial aid application form and the Free Application for Federal Student Aid (FAFSA) to be considered for Albertus scholarships and grants, Federal Perkins Loans, Federal Supplemental Educational Opportunity Grants, and Federal Work-Study awards. There is no specific deadline to apply for financial aid, which is awarded on a rolling basis; however, it is recommended that applicants file for aid by February 15 for priority consideration.

Faculty

Faculty members at Albertus come from leading universities of the United States and abroad and are one of the College's greatest assets. Ninety percent of the 75 full- and part-time faculty members hold a Ph.D. or the equivalent. Their primary concern is teaching, although the work of many faculty members has been published. Students find faculty members accessible for academic or personal counseling and for campus sports and activities.

Student Government

Through the Student Government Association (SGA), Albertus students have the primary responsibility for governing their own residential and social life. All full-time matriculated students are members of the SGA and, through its committees and officers, manage student government and social affairs and participate in the campus judicial system. Students serve on faculty committees, the Academic Policy Committee, and the Library Committee.

Admission Requirements

Albertus Magnus College welcomes applications from students of all ages, nationalities, and ethnic, cultural, racial, and religious groups. Applicants may be admitted as freshmen or as transfer, provisional, or special students.

In evaluating freshman candidates, the Office of Admission considers a student's application, counselor recommendation, high school transcript, extracurricular activities, and scores on the SAT I or ACT. Emphasis is placed on the student's record of performance rather than on the results of standardized tests. Sixteen high school units in academic subjects are required for entrance.

Transfer students are welcome at the College. They must submit high school and college records (if necessary) for evaluation in addition to the application and the recommendation.

Interviews are recommended for freshman and transfer applicants.

More information is available on the University's Web site (listed below).

Application and Information

The College accepts students for entrance on a rolling admission basis. Students may also apply online at the Web site below. As soon as all of a candidate's admission material has been received, his or her application is considered, and notification is made as soon as a decision has been reached.

Application forms, recommendation forms, and information may be obtained by contacting:

Office of Admission
Albertus Magnus College
700 Prospect Street
New Haven, Connecticut 06511-1189
Telephone: 203-773-8501
800-578-9160 (toll-free)
Fax: 203-773-5248
E-mail: admissions@albertus.edu
World Wide Web: http://www.albertus.edu

Beautiful Rosary Hall.

ALBION COLLEGE

ALBION, MICHIGAN

The College

Albion College offers the powerful combination of a traditional liberal arts curriculum coupled with a strong professional focus. "Liberal Arts At Work" aptly characterizes Albion's commitment to preparing students for admission into top graduate schools and their first career assignments in medicine, law, teaching, business, the arts, and many other areas. All students have an opportunity to enhance their education through value-added programming in one or more academic institutes, including the Gerald R. Ford Institute for Public Service, the Carl A. Gerstacker Liberal Arts Program in Professional Management, the Pre-Med/Allied Health Institute, the Honors Institute, the Fritz Shurmur Education Institute, and the Institute for the Study of the Environment.

Albion is a national leader for the percentage of students involved in undergraduate research. It is ranked seventh in *Yahoo! Internet Life*'s Most Wired Colleges in the U.S.A., and first among colleges and universities in Michigan. In addition, 52 percent of Albion's alumni regularly support the College, the highest percentage among schools in Michigan and among the top twenty in the nation. Albion is among the top eighty-five private, liberal arts colleges for the number of alumni who are corporate executives, including top executives and CEOs of *Newsweek*, the Lahey Clinic (MA), PricewaterhouseCoopers, Dow Corning, the NCAA, Avon, and the Financial Accounting Standards Board (FASB). Albion's 2003 graduate school placement was 100 percent for law, 96 percent for dental, and 94 percent for medical schools, including Harvard, Michigan, Columbia, Northwestern, Notre Dame, Vanderbilt, and Wisconsin.

Albion's 2003 fall enrollment was 1,743 students. Approximately 87 percent of Albion's students are from Michigan; the rest come from twenty-eight states and nineteen countries. Albion is a residential college and campus life is important for every student. Campus lecturers and other recent performers and speakers include James Earl Jones, Salman Rushdie, Kurt Vonnegut, Duke University basketball coach Mike Krzyzewski, Gloria Steinem, Three Doors Down, Shawn Colvin, and various federal and state legislators. The Kellogg Center, completed in 1996, provides space for concerts and dances, meeting rooms and offices for student organizations, the College bookstore, and a snack bar. The more than 100 student organizations include clubs in academic departments, student publications, a campus radio station, religious fellowship groups, the Black Student Alliance, intercollegiate and intramural athletics, and national fraternities and sororities.

Ninety-six percent of students live on campus. Residence halls, located within walking distance of other campus buildings, are coed, with separate sections for men and women. A comprehensive student services program includes a career development office that assists students in exploring career options and arranges on-campus interviews with employers and graduate schools. More than 40 percent of Albion graduates go directly to graduate or professional school each year; virtually everyone seeking immediate employment has found a position within six months of graduation. Within five years of graduation, more than 75 percent of Albion alumni have enrolled for graduate work.

Location

A 1½-hour drive west of Detroit and a 3-hour drive east of Chicago, the College is located on I-94 in the small city of Albion (population 10,000). Eight other colleges and universities, including Michigan State and the University of Michigan, are located within an hour's drive. The 225-acre main campus is a few blocks from the downtown business section. Students and faculty members are very involved in community activities and regional volunteer efforts and internships.

Majors and Degrees

Albion College awards the Bachelor of Arts and Bachelor of Fine Arts degrees. Majors include American studies, anthropology and sociology, art, art history, athletic training, biology, chemistry, computer science, earth sciences, economics and management, English, French, geological sciences, German, history, human services, international studies, mathematics, music, philosophy, physical education, physics, political science, psychology, public policy, religious studies, Spanish, and speech communication and theater. Individually designed majors, created with faculty approval, are also offered. Students may be certified in secondary education and for grades K–12 in art, music, and physical education.

Preprofessional programs include business management, dentistry, law, medicine, and the ministry. Combined three-year preprofessional programs, involving three years of study at Albion and additional work at other institutions, are available in engineering, health services and nursing, natural resources management, and public policy. Students in these programs are awarded the bachelor's degree from Albion after completing one additional year of study at the participating institutions.

Academic Programs

Albion expects its students to gain a broad knowledge in the arts and sciences while also developing an area of specialization. To graduate with the Bachelor of Arts degree, students must complete 32 units (128 semester hours); to earn the Bachelor of Fine Arts degree, art majors must complete 34 units (136 semester hours). All students must pass a writing examination.

To introduce students to important areas of knowledge, Albion has a core curriculum requirement for study in the natural sciences and mathematics, the social sciences, the humanities, interdisciplinary studies, and the fine arts, together with additional studies in environmental science, ethnic studies, neuroscience, and prelaw. The core curriculum and the requirements for a major total about one half to two thirds of a student's program at Albion. The remainder can be used for electives, to complete a second major, or for a six- to eight-course sequence in business management, computer science, human services, mass communication, public service, or women's studies. Independent study and on-the-job internships for academic credit are also available. College credit can be obtained through Advanced Placement exams, College-Level Examination Program (CLEP) tests, or Albion departmental exams.

Off-Campus Programs

Albion College, together with other leading educational institutions, offers off-campus study in Australia, China, Costa Rica, the Dominican Republic, France, Germany, Great Britain, India, Ireland, Israel, Italy, Japan, Mexico, New Zealand, Russia, Spain, and several African countries. Semester-long programs are available in the United States through the Washington (D.C.) Center for Learning Alternatives, the New York City Arts Program, the Philadelphia Center, the Chicago Urban Life Center, the Newberry Library Program in the Humanities (Chicago), and the Oak Ridge National Laboratory (Tennessee). All arrangements are supervised by the Director of Off-Campus Programs.

Academic Facilities

Olin Hall, the $4.5-million home of the biology and psychology departments, features excellent laboratory equipment, including scanning and transmission electron microscopes. In the Stockwell/Mudd Libraries, researchers are helped by an online catalog of the College's book and periodical collections and by access to national databases in many different academic areas.

Other prominent campus facilities include the Herrick Center for Speech and Theatre; the 144-acre Whitehouse Nature Center, used for both science instruction and recreation; and the Nancy G. Held Equestrian Center, featuring indoor and outdoor arenas, boarding in College stables, and 340 acres of pasture and trails. The Dow Recreation and Wellness Center offers a 1/9-mile indoor track, canoe and kayak livery, multipurpose court space, indoor tennis courts, a swimming pool, weight-training facilities for physical education courses, intramural sports, individual conditioning, and wellness programs.

Albion students also have access to Digital Equipment Corporation VAX 4000-200 computers and to the Internet through PCs located throughout the campus and in individual rooms. More than 500 microcomputers are available for various research activities. Albion is a leader in Michigan for wireless networking across campus, digital imaging and digital video editing capabilities, and satellite downlink services and is a member of the Internet2 group, the fastest computing and transmission system in the nation, restricted to use by the higher education and nonprofit community.

Costs

Projected costs for the 2004–05 academic year are $22,650 for tuition, $6536 for room and board, and a $268 student activity fee. Laboratory fees and music lessons are additional, as are personal expenses and travel. Costs are the same for both in-state and out-of-state students.

Financial Aid

Every student admitted to Albion College receives financial assistance if need is determined from the Free Application for Federal Student Aid (FAFSA). Families should file the FAFSA as soon as possible after January 1 so that the College receives the analysis from the federal government by February 15. For each student, Albion builds a financial aid package using federal grants and loans and College aid funds. Many Michigan residents are eligible for state scholarships and grants of more than $2000 that are reserved for people attending private colleges and universities in the state. More than 50 percent of Albion students also have jobs on campus. Students must apply for admission and be accepted before a financial aid package is prepared. Students with strong academic records are also eligible for academic scholarships. These range from a few thousand dollars to full tuition. The scholarship application deadline is February 1. Students with special talent in art, music, and theater may qualify for scholarships in these areas of up to $5000.

Faculty

Ninety-two percent of Albion's faculty members hold the doctorate or terminal degree in their field. There are 121 full-time faculty members. Courses and laboratories are taught by regular faculty members and not by graduate teaching assistants. The average class size is 19. First- and second-year courses have average enrollments of 24 students, with the exception of special First Year Experience courses, which limit enrollment to 16 students. Upper-level courses average 15 students.

Albion's faculty members are dedicated to teaching at a liberal arts college. Faculty members know their students personally and are available outside class hours for discussion and counseling. They are also active scholars and researchers, as shown by the grants that they receive from the National Science Foundation, the National Endowment for the Humanities, and many other sources.

Student Government

An elected Student Senate oversees the operation of campus organizations and disburses student activity fee funds to these groups. The Board of Trustees invites Student Senate members to sit on its committees for academic and student affairs, institutional advancement, and buildings and grounds. Student representatives also sit on the faculty's Educational Policies Committee, which reviews the College curriculum.

Admission Requirements

Albion is a selective national liberal arts college, and admission is mainly based on the applicant's academic record in high school with special attention to the college-preparatory courses completed. Standard test scores from either the ACT or SAT are also an important factor, as are personal qualifications and accomplishments outside the classroom. The College seeks a diverse enrollment without regard to race, religion, or national origin. In 2004, entering freshmen have an average GPA of 3.6, with an average ACT score of 26 and SAT score of 1160. Prospective freshmen can take either the SAT I or ACT. The new College Board–sponsored SAT Essay is not required, but is accepted as part of the total application package and can be used in place of the College's own essay if desired. These exams are not required of transfer students who have earned at least a semester of college credit. Candidates for admission are expected to be graduates of an accredited high school or preparatory school and have at least 15 acceptable credit units. Applicants should have a strong background in English, mathematics, and the laboratory and social sciences. Home-schooled applicants are reviewed on an individual basis and need to complete either the SAT I or ACT. International applicants are welcome and must have a minimum TOEFL score of 550 and submit a Declaration of Finances form to show adequate financial resources. An interview may be required. Arrangements for a personal campus visit should be made in advance in writing, by phone, or by e-mail.

Application and Information

Applications for admission are accepted at any time, but most students apply after September 1 of their senior year in high school. Before a decision is made, applicants must submit an application form and $20 application fee (there is no fee for Web applications), high school transcripts, test score results, and recommendations. Students should submit all materials by April 1. Albion is also a member of the Common Application and accepts applications completed on its Web site. Students who wish to receive an admission decision before Albion's regular decision candidates may apply under the early action program. Applications need to be completed by December 1, and notification of an admission decision is mailed prior to January 1. Students do not have to make a final commitment to Albion until May 1, when the $300 enrollment deposit is required to reserve a place in the class. (The deposit may be refunded if the admissions office receives a written request before May 1.) Students who apply after December 1 are considered for regular decision. Notification of an admission decision is made on a regular basis beginning February 1. All applicants are encouraged to submit their application for admission prior to March 1, as students who apply after this date are considered for admission on a space-available basis. For further information, students should contact:

Albion College
611 East Porter Street
Albion, Michigan 49224
Telephone: 800-858-6770 (toll-free)
Fax: 517-629-0569
E-mail: admissions@albion.edu
World Wide Web: http://www.albion.edu

Robinson Hall.

ALBRIGHT COLLEGE

READING, PENNSYLVANIA

The College

Success in the twenty-first century requires innovative thinkers, creative problem solvers, and skilled communicators. Albright offers its students unique opportunities to develop these skills and create academic paths specially tailored to their goals and interests.

The Albright community is just that—a real community. With 1,550 students coming from twenty-six states and twenty other countries, Albright students learn to interact with people from a wide array of social, ethnic, cultural, and economic backgrounds. Students and educators work together to explore ideas, collaborate on projects, conduct research, and share extracurricular interests.

More than eighty clubs and organizations enhance the life of the College, including performing arts groups, religious organizations, student government, volunteer service organizations, student publications, and political action groups. In addition, approximately 25 percent of Albright students belong to one of Albright's nationally affiliated fraternities and sororities.

Intercollegiate, intramural, and club sports are a major part of the extracurricular life at Albright. Two thirds of all students participate in some form of athletics. At the intercollegiate level, Albright is a member of the Middle Atlantic Conference, one of the strongest conferences in the NCAA's Division III.

Location

The College is located on a 118-acre suburban campus in Reading, Pennsylvania, a city of 80,000 in a metropolitan area of 250,000. Albright's location provides the perfect balance between the excitement of the city of Reading (with its numerous cultural opportunities, active nightlife, and renowned outlet stores) and the recreational and sporting opportunities of southeastern Pennsylvania.

Things to do in and around Reading include shopping the "Outlet Capital of the World," the Reading Phillies, Dorney Park and Wildwater Kingdom, the Reading Comedy Outlet, the Sovereign Fine Arts Center, Appalachian Trail, the Reading Royals hockey team, and Maplegrove Raceway.

Albright is an hour from Philadelphia and the Pocono Mountains ski resorts, 2 hours from Baltimore, and 3 hours from New York and Washington, D.C.

Majors and Degrees

Albright offers the Bachelor of Arts (B.A.) or Bachelor of Science (B.S.) in the following majors: accounting, American civilization, art, biochemistry, biology (biotechnology and general biology), business administration (economics, finance, international business, management, and marketing), chemistry (environmental chemistry and general chemistry), child and family studies, communications, computer science, crime and justice, digital media, economics, education (art, early childhood, elementary, secondary, and special), English, environmental science, environmental studies, fashion merchandising and design, French, history, information systems, Latin American studies, mathematics, music (music business, music history, and music performance), optics, philosophy, physics, political science, psychobiology, psychology (general psychology and human resources), religious studies, sociology (anthropology, criminology, family studies, and general sociology), Spanish, theater, and women's studies.

Preprofessional programs are available in dentistry, law, medicine, and veterinary medicine.

Academic Program

Albright offers fifty programs of study, including excellent preprofessional programs, a strong honors program, and special programs/minors in film/video, Holocaust studies, marine science, and music business.

Students may choose to focus on a single field of study or combine two or three to create an individualized major. Nearly half of Albright students graduate with combined, interdisciplinary, or multiple majors. Last year, students created more than 200 different combinations of majors.

Off-Campus Programs

Off-campus study options for Albright students include study abroad (e.g., Tel Aviv University in Israel, University of Guadalajara in Mexico, American University in France, Studio Art Centers International in Italy, and the American Soviet Theatre Initiative in Russia), domestic programs (e.g., the Washington, D.C., Center; the National Theatre Institute in Connecticut; Duke University's Marine Science Lab in Beaufort, North Carolina, and Bermuda Station for Research; and Humpback Whale Migration Research in Hawaii), and internships (e.g., the Internal Revenue Service [accounting], Bayer Corporation [chemistry], Caron Foundation [psychology], Reading Hospital and Medical Center [premed], and Macy's [fashion merchandising]).

Academic Facilities

Albright students and faculty members have access to outstanding teaching and research facilities. The College has state-of-the-art labs in digital media, optical physics, and foreign languages. The Merner-Pfeiffer Hall of Science is home to two nuclear magnetic resonance spectrometers (each worth $500,000 and one reserved exclusively for student use), scanning and transmission electron microscopes, molecular genetics, and microcomputer facilities.

Costs

The comprehensive cost for the 2004–05 academic year is $32,090. This includes $24,030 for tuition, $7410 for room and board, and $550 for fees.

Financial Aid

Albright offers numerous merit scholarships and awards in addition to generous need-based financial aid awards. The College has pledged to help families make Albright affordable.

Albright believes that high school students who have excelled academically and demonstrated leadership skills add to the quality of life at the College. For this reason, Albright offers a variety of renewable scholarships, ranging in value from $20,000 to full tuition for four years.

In addition, the College gives a variety of renewable awards, ranging from $2000 to $12,000 ($500 to $3000 per year). Often, recipients of scholarships also earn one or more awards that go to members of the National Honor Society, students with special talent (art, music, theater, and journalism), class valedictorians and salutatorians, National Merit Finalists and Semifinalists, outstanding students of color, HOBY alumni, and Eagle Scouts and Girl Scout Gold Award winners.

Financial aid is awarded on the basis of demonstrated family financial need. Students who receive scholarships are also eligible for financial aid; in fact, most scholarship and award recipients also receive need-based financial aid. Students applying for financial aid must submit the Free Application for Federal Student Aid (FAFSA) no later than March 1.

Faculty

The College has 95 distinguished full-time faculty members, and they are legendary for being available to students and for keeping their doors open. Albright's 12:1 student-faculty ratio means that classes are small and interactive.

In addition, students may perform research side by side with Albright's faculty members, after which they may present their findings at national and international symposiums.

Admission Requirements

Albright looks for students who will thrive in a close-knit, academically challenging, and active community of learners. Admission is primarily based on a student's academic preparation and extracurricular activities. Applicants must submit an application, high school transcript, counselor and teacher recommendations, and SAT I or ACT scores. Freshman applications should be received by March 1. Albright welcomes transfer and international student applicants.

Application and Information

An application and information may be obtained by contacting the College by mail, telephone, or e-mail.

Admission Office
Albright College
13th and Bern Streets
P.O. Box 15234
Reading, Pennsylvania 19612-5234
Telephone: 610-921-7512
800-252-1856 (toll-free)
E-mail: albright@alb.edu
World Wide Web: http://www.albright.edu

Albright values each student's unique qualities.

ALDERSON–BROADDUS COLLEGE

PHILIPPI, WEST VIRGINIA

The College

Located on a mountaintop overlooking the Tygart River valley in Philippi, West Virginia, Alderson-Broaddus College is a four-year, coeducational, independent liberal arts college with a history of educational excellence and innovation. Affiliated with the American Baptist Churches, U.S.A., the College has been preparing men and women for leadership for more than 130 years. Today, more than 750 men and women from thirty-eight states and eight countries study at Alderson-Broaddus, preparing for the future with quality programs in a variety of fields.

Alderson-Broaddus emphasizes an innovative approach to quality liberal arts education. For example, the College pioneered the first undergraduate physician assistant program in the nation. With a state-of-the-art computer network in advance of most universities, the College also makes extensive computer resources available to all students and programs of study. Close student-faculty relationships and an average class size of 15 encourage involvement. Hands-on experience begins in the freshman year in all fields—from nursing to broadcasting, education to political science, biology to music. Alderson-Broaddus is accredited by the North Central Association of Colleges and Schools. The baccalaureate program in nursing is accredited by the National League for Nursing. The master's program for physician assistants is accredited by the Commission on Accreditation of Allied Health Programs (CAAHEP). The teacher education programs are accredited by the National Council for Accreditation of Teacher Education (NCATE).

More than fifty student organizations and hundreds of activities provide opportunities for recreation, personal development, and service. The A-B Battlers have a championship tradition in intercollegiate athletics that includes baseball, basketball, cross-country, and soccer for men, and basketball, cross-country, softball, and volleyball for women. A wide range of intramural sports involves most of the student body. The attractions of West Virginia's unspoiled state and national parks are nearby.

The wooded 170-acre campus offers outstanding facilities, including modern academic facilities, a 7,200-watt FM radio station, an on-campus cafe, an art gallery, a bookstore, a post office, student lounges, and a sports coliseum with a pool, two gyms, a racquetball court, and a fitness center.

The College provides varied, comfortable residential options and a flexible, high-quality meal plan. There are excellent medical facilities on campus and in the surrounding area.

In addition to undergraduate degrees in various programs, Alderson-Broaddus also offers the M.S. degree for physician assistants.

Location

Located in the historic town of Philippi, West Virginia, Alderson-Broaddus enjoys a safe and secure environment and the friendly atmosphere of a college town but has easy access to wider resources. Clarksburg is 25 minutes away; Morgantown and West Virginia University, 1 hour; and Pittsburgh and Charleston, 2 hours. Alderson-Broaddus is 17 miles from I-79's Exit 115 and is accessible by nearby bus and airline service.

Majors and Degrees

The College offers programs leading to the B.A. and B.S. degrees in accounting, applied mathematics, applied music, athletic training, biology, business administration, Christian studies, church music, communications, computer science, cytotechnology, digital arts, elementary education, environmental science—biology track and chemistry track, family studies, finance, history, literature, management information systems, marketing, mass communications, medical science/physician assistant studies, medical technology, music education, musical arts, nursing, political science, professional writing and editing, psychology, radiography, recreation leadership, recreation leadership—therapeutic recreation track, secondary education, special education/elementary, speech, and theater. Associate degrees may be obtained in business, general studies, and natural sciences.

Alderson-Broaddus also offers a diversified major in liberal arts for students who prefer not to specialize at the undergraduate level.

Preprofessional courses are available in such areas as dentistry, law, medicine, the ministry, and physical therapy.

Academic Programs

The academic year consists of two 15-week semesters. Students generally take 15 to 18 semester hours each semester. In addition, the College offers a 10-week summer term.

Completion of 128 hours of study is required for graduation. Most of the degree requirements are fulfilled through on-campus study, but some majors require off-campus field work and internships for which credit is awarded. With the help of their academic advisers, students select courses to fulfill requirements for liberal studies and a major. Students may choose elective minors in such areas as business, computer science, education, recreation, and technical writing. An honors program offers academically talented students opportunities for independent scholarship and research.

Off-Campus Programs

In years when there is sufficient student demand, the College offers an International Studies program. Also, with the proper clearance, Alderson-Broaddus students may enroll in any one of a number of overseas experiences administered by other cooperating institutions or agencies.

Certain majors require specific field or clinical internship experiences; other majors make such internships optional. Students may elect to do independent or guided, individualized study for credit in a pre-approved subject area while off campus.

Academic Facilities

The College offers modern, well-equipped facilities to support academic programs, including labs with up-to-date advanced instrumentation, a television and radio broadcast studio with public access channeling and a 7,200-watt FM station, a campuswide computer network with individual accounts for all students, a 725-seat theater, and separate facilities for the natural sciences, nursing and allied health, the humanities, the social sciences, education, athletics, and administration. The library houses more than 107,000 volumes and subscribes to more than 800 periodicals. The Hazel Ruby McQuain Research Center provides computerized, international access to current information in many fields. Wilcox Chapel is a meaningful addition to the religious life on campus and also houses the music department, which has been named a Clay-Yamaha School of Music Excellence.

Costs

The cost of attending Alderson-Broaddus is low compared with that of most private colleges in the East. Room, board, tuition, and fees for 2003–04 were $22,406. Costs are subject to change, and the Admissions Office can provide up-to-date information.

Financial Aid

Alderson-Broaddus College has an excellent program of financial aid that includes merit, performance, and need-based grants and scholarships, loans, and college work-study. Applicants requesting financial aid are required to submit the Free Application for Federal Student Aid (FAFSA). Nearly 99 percent of all students receive some form of financial assistance.

Faculty

Alderson-Broaddus has a faculty of approximately 60 full-time members, 45 percent of whom hold terminal degrees in their fields. The student-faculty ratio is 13:1.

Student Government

A number of avenues are provided for student participation in decision making at Alderson-Broaddus. The Student Government Association consists of student officials elected by the entire student body. Students also serve on the President's Staff and in other groups responsible for determining College policy.

Admission Requirements

Alderson-Broaddus College admits qualified students of any race, color, or national or ethnic origin. There are no geographic or other quotas, although certain programs are limited to specific numbers of enrollees.

Applicants to the nursing and physician assistant programs are expected to have strong college-preparatory backgrounds with above-average grades in science, particularly in biology and chemistry. Other programs are more flexible.

Applicants are required to submit ACT or SAT I scores for admission purposes. Consequently, it is advisable to take these tests prior to enrollment, but students may take the test on campus during new-student orientation. Advanced Placement (AP) and College-Level Examination Program (CLEP) scores are accepted as additional indicators of an applicant's ability. Advanced standing may be awarded for satisfactory scores on AP or CLEP tests.

Applicants are encouraged to visit the campus and have a personal interview. Applicants to the physician assistant program are required to have a personal interview.

Alderson-Broaddus welcomes transfers from other colleges. Transfer students must submit high school and college transcripts for evaluation in addition to ACT or SAT I results. Credit is granted for all courses successfully completed at another accredited institution if the student has maintained at least a 2.0 cumulative GPA and the course work is applicable to the College's curriculum. Students with 29 or more transferable semester credit hours may not be required to submit ACT or SAT I results.

Application and Information

General admission to the College is on a rolling basis. Students seeking freshman admission must submit a completed application form, a $10 nonrefundable application fee, results of the ACT or SAT I, and official copies of secondary school transcripts. In addition to these materials, transfer students must submit a transfer clearance form, provided by Alderson-Broaddus College, and official transcripts from all colleges attended. Separate application requirements apply to the physician assistant program. Specific information and applicable deadlines are forwarded with application materials.

When requesting information, applicants should specify a major interest area or note that they are undecided. For additional information, students should contact:

Admissions Office
Alderson-Broaddus College
P.O. Box 2003
Philippi, West Virginia 26416
Telephone: 800-263-1549 (toll-free)
E-mail: admissions@ab.edu
World Wide Web: http://www.admissions.ab.edu/

Students outside of Withers-Brandon Hall on the Alderson-Broaddus campus.

ALFRED UNIVERSITY

ALFRED, NEW YORK

The University

Alfred University (AU) is a residential institution of 2,500 undergraduate and graduate students, located 70 miles south of Rochester, between the Finger Lakes region and the Allegheny Mountains in western New York State. AU comprises four colleges and schools: the Colleges of Business and Liberal Arts and Sciences and the Schools of Art and Design and Engineering, which includes biomedical materials engineering science, ceramic engineering, electrical engineering, glass science engineering, materials science and engineering, and mechanical engineering. AU is noted for its superior academic quality, outstanding faculty, and commitment to student development. Alfred University is regarded as the world leader in the field of ceramic engineering. The state of New York has identified Alfred University as one of its ten centers for advanced technology research.

One distinctive characteristic of Alfred University is the diversity of its student body. With men and women nearly equal in number, the University's 2,000 undergraduates include representatives from more than forty U.S. states and territories as well as from twenty different nations. Those from the United States come from rural, urban, and suburban neighborhoods, as well as public, parochial, and private secondary schools.

Alfred University has a strong commitment to student development through residential life. Students are required to live on campus their first two years, and about 75 percent of all students reside on campus. Housing options include traditional residence halls, suites, and on-campus apartments. Alternative options such as off-campus special interest housing are also available for upperclass students.

Alfred University students come from many social, cultural, and economic backgrounds, which are reflected in various campus organizations such as Hillel, Women's Issues Coalition (WIC), and the African, Latino, Asian, Native American (ALANA) Club. Students participate in and support AU athletic events, which are held on Merrill Field or in the McLane Center. The University schedules a variety of nationally acclaimed performers who attract students and area residents alike. Students participate in more than 100 campus clubs and organizations, including the American Ceramic Society, Forest People, Jazz Ensemble, Karate Club, and Ski Club.

The following graduate degrees are offered: Master of Arts and Doctor of Psychology in school psychology; Master of Business Administration; Master of Professional Studies in community services administration; Master of Science in Education, with concentrations in twelve different areas; Master of Science in electrical and mechanical engineering; Master of Fine Arts in ceramics, electronic integrated arts, glass, and sculpture; Master of Science in ceramic engineering, glass science, and materials science and engineering; and Doctor of Philosophy in ceramics and glass science.

Location

The village of Alfred is a classic college community. Local businesses cater to student and faculty needs, and the cities of Hornell and Wellsville, within 12 miles of the campus, offer additional restaurants, theaters, and recreational facilities.

Majors and Degrees

The bachelor's degree is offered in a variety of majors. Double majors, interdisciplinary majors, and dual degrees are available for students as well. There are also more than forty minors, ranging from astronomy to women's studies.

The College of Business offers the B.S. in accounting and business administration with career emphases in business economics, entrepreneurial studies, family business, finance, international business, management, management information systems, and marketing. The College of Business is accredited by the AACSB International–The Association to Advance Collegiate Schools of Business.

The College of Liberal Arts and Sciences offers the B.A. in athletic training, biology, chemistry, communication studies, comparative cultures, computer science, criminal justice studies, economics, elementary education, English, environmental studies, fine arts, general science, geology, gerontology, global studies, history, mathematics, modern languages (French, German, and Spanish), performing arts, philosophy, physics, political science, psychology, public administration, and sociology. Preprofessional programs are available in dentistry, law, medicine, and veterinary medicine. The Track II option permits the student, in cooperation with a team of faculty advisers, to design an individual academic program tailored to meet his or her needs.

The School of Engineering offers the B.S. in biomedical materials engineering science, ceramic engineering, electrical engineering, glass science engineering, materials science and engineering, and mechanical engineering.

The School of Art and Design confers the B.F.A. in art education, ceramics, electronic arts, glass, graphic design, painting, photography, printmaking, sculpture, video, and wood design.

Academic Programs

All academic programs require courses in the liberal arts and sciences; however, specific graduation requirements differ for each college and school within the University. All candidates are required to satisfy a physical education requirement through courses or proficiency examinations. To encourage students with strong ability and initiative, the University recognizes the Advanced Placement and International Baccalaureate programs. In addition, the University offers its own challenge examination program for currently enrolled students. The University Honors Program is open to all majors and requires an additional essay application for admission to the program. Army ROTC is also available.

Off-Campus Programs

A significant number of Alfred University students study abroad each year, in countries such as France, Germany, Great Britain, and Switzerland, through University programs or programs maintained by other universities. Additional off-campus programs include the Washington Semester with American University and the United Nations Semester with Drew University. Students also participate in numerous cooperative education and internship experiences.

Academic Facilities

Herrick Memorial Library and Scholes Library of Ceramics house 330,000 volumes, 60,000 government documents, 154,000 slides, and 1,000 journal subscriptions. Students have access to an additional 3,000 journals through Internet workstations. Several campus buildings are devoted to engineering and contain some of the most complete laboratory facilities in the world, including a radioisotope lab, petrographic and metallographic labs, five electron microscopes, and a glass drawing tower. The Science Center features a genetic engineering laboratory and the Stull Observatory, considered one of the finest teaching facilities in the country, which houses seven principle telescopes.

Harder Hall is an impressive fine arts facility that features studio space for all media, the most extensive kiln facility in the nation (thirty-eight indoor and outdoor kilns), two galleries, and Holmes auditorium. The Miller Performing Arts Center houses a flexible theater with state-of-the-art sound and lighting equipment, individual and group rehearsal rooms, and acting and dance studios.

The campus is fully wired with switched 100-Mbps Ethernet network access in every residence hall room, classroom, and office. The student-computer ratio is 6:1, with a wide range of computer access options, including open computer labs in residence halls, libraries, and academic buildings and a laptop-lending program. Connection to the Internet is through a T-1 line, and all Internet services (including e-mail) are provided at no additional charge. The Helpdesk facility provides service-oriented support for technology needs.

Costs

The tuition in the Colleges of Business and Liberal Arts and Sciences is $19,250 for entering freshmen. Tuition for mechanical and electrical engineering is $15,600, and tuition for the School of Art and Design and the other four engineering degree programs is $11,326 for in-state students and $15,600 for out-of-state students.

Financial Aid

During the 2003–04 academic year, University-funded aid sources provided more than $19 million to undergraduate students. For most programs, 95 percent of freshmen received some form of financial assistance. Aid administered by the University usually consists of a combination of scholarships or grants, loans, and part-time work. Students may be eligible for financial assistance under the Federal Pell Grant, Federal Supplemental Educational Opportunity Grant, Federal Perkins Loan, and Federal Work-Study programs. New York State residents may be eligible for aid under the Tuition Assistance Program. The University sponsors National Merit Scholarships; departmental talent awards; Presidential, Southern Tier, and transfer scholarships; and the Johnathan Allen Award for Leadership.

Faculty

There are 186 full-time faculty members; 93 percent of the teaching faculty members hold the doctorate or highest degree in their field. While the faculty members are actively involved in research or other scholarly activities, the education at Alfred University is classroom oriented. The average class size is 18, and the faculty-student ratio is 1:12. Courses are taught by faculty members, not teaching assistants. All faculty members serve as academic advisers and are accessible and responsive to students.

Student Government

The Student Senate has elected officials, receives an annual appropriation, and disburses funds to other campus organizations to finance their activities. It also elects student representatives to various University and college committees and sponsors a leadership seminar.

Admission Requirements

Candidates for admission are required to complete a college-preparatory program of 16 academic units or provide evidence of an equivalent education. The 16 units should include 4 in English, 3–4 in social studies and history, 2–3 in mathematics, and 2–3 in laboratory science. The remaining units are usually completed in a foreign language or in any of the aforementioned fields. Specific requirements of the colleges within the University vary. Admissions criteria include secondary school record, cumulative average, class rank, recommendations from guidance counselors or teachers, and SAT I or ACT scores. The SAT II: Writing Test is recommended for placement purposes. Personal accomplishments and extracurricular activities are also reviewed before a final decision is made regarding each candidate. An on-campus interview is highly recommended.

The Opportunity Programs at AU enable students whose economic and educational circumstances have placed limitations on their opportunities to further their education.

Application and Information

Candidates must submit a completed Alfred University application form or the Common Application form, SAT I or ACT results, a letter of recommendation, and a $40 application fee. Students who visit campus receive an application fee waiver certificate that may be used on that day or at a later time. They must also have their high school guidance office submit an official transcript. Applicants to the School of Art and Design must submit a portfolio of their work, typically fifteen to twenty slides. The application and portfolio deadline under the early decision plan is December 1, with notification by December 15. The application and portfolio deadline for regular admission is February 1, with notification by mid-March. Transfer applicants should file an application by August 1 for September admission or December 1 for January admission. The School of Art and Design has different application and portfolio deadlines for transfer students, dependent upon the student's previous course work in art. Students should contact the Office of Admissions for further information regarding these deadlines.

Applications and inquiries should be addressed to:

Scott C. Hooker
Director of Admissions
Alumni Hall
Alfred University
Saxon Drive
Alfred, New York 14802

Telephone: 607-871-2115
800-541-9229 (toll-free)
Fax: 607-871-2198
E-mail: admwww@alfred.edu
World Wide Web: http://www.alfred.edu

ALLEGHENY COLLEGE

MEADVILLE, PENNSYLVANIA

The College

Founded on America's western frontier in 1815, Allegheny is a classical, selective college of the liberal arts and sciences. Although highly regarded as a preprofessional school, its impact on students goes well beyond career preparation. Allegheny not only develops in its students such essential skills as writing, critical thinking, and problem solving, it also fosters a capacity for lifelong learning, the ability to manage everyday affairs, responsible citizenship, social skills, and values. While nonsectarian in outlook and practice, Allegheny has been affiliated with the United Methodist Church since 1833.

Allegheny's nearly 2,000 students come from thirty-three states and twenty-five other countries. About 7 percent are members of minority groups and three fourths reside on campus. On-campus residence is required of first-year students and sophomores and juniors and is optional for seniors, but it is guaranteed for all four years for all who seek it. Faculty members describe Allegheny students as active and hardworking. Approximately 65 percent come from the highest fifth of their high school class, 1 in 3 was a leader of a student organization, and 70 percent were active in volunteer service groups. Regardless of their particular academic program, Allegheny students are strongly encouraged to participate in education-enriching activities outside the classroom. Choosing from more than 100 clubs, committees, and organizations in drama, dance, vocal and instrumental music, publications, radio, religious life, politics, social service, professional and multicultural interest areas, and the governance of student life, students explore and develop their own unique combination of interests. Intramural athletics involve three fourths of the students, and the varsity program is one of the best in NCAA Division III.

Location

Located in Meadville, Pennsylvania (city population 14,000; county population 90,000), in the picturesque rolling foothills of the Allegheny Mountains, Allegheny's students take advantage of the enormous variety of recreational opportunities in the area. The students also use the shopping centers, entertainment venues, and restaurants in the city, and most are actively involved in volunteer work with organizations such as Habitat for Humanity.

Students also enjoy the many advantages of Pittsburgh and Cleveland, both 90 miles from Meadville. These and other cities are easily accessible by several interstate highways, and Meadville is served by bus.

Majors and Degrees

Departmental majors leading to Bachelor of Arts or Bachelor of Science degrees are offered in applied computing, art (studio or history), art and technology, biochemistry, biology, chemistry, communication arts, computer science, economics, English, environmental geology, environmental science, environmental studies, French, geology, German, history, international studies, mathematics, music, neuroscience, philosophy, physics, political science, psychology, religious studies, Spanish, theater, and women's studies. Preprofessional programs are offered in dentistry, law, medicine, and veterinary medicine.

The independent study option allows students to pursue an interest not included in the formal College curriculum. Through this option, each student designs a course program, with the agreement of a faculty adviser, to be completed on or off campus.

The College offers cooperative 3-2 liberal arts/professional programs in engineering with Case Western Reserve University, Columbia University, Duke University, the University of Pittsburgh, and Washington University. There is a 3-1 program with the University of Rochester that leads to a bachelor's degree from Allegheny and certification in medical technology, while a 3-4 program in nursing leads to a doctorate from Case Western Reserve. It has a 4-2 program in physical therapy and physician assistant studies with Chatham College. The College has an exclusive agreement with Teachers College Columbia University, for guaranteed interviews for students seeking admission to its competitive graduate programs in teacher education. Allegheny also has a guaranteed graduate admissions agreement with the University of Pittsburgh School of Education.

Academic Programs

Allegheny has as its first concern intellectual growth. The curriculum and graduation requirements are designed to provide educational depth as well as intellectual breadth, allowing students to combine their varied interests and talents. It is not unusual to double major or create one's own course of study. Allegheny ensures that students develop wholeness across the divisions of knowledge (arts and humanities, social sciences, and natural sciences) as well as expertise in one or more fields. Each student must complete 131 semester credit hours; the major may require 32 to 48 semester credit hours, including a junior seminar and the distinctive Senior Comprehensive Project, while the remainder are electives and Liberal Studies Program courses. The innovative Liberal Studies Program includes two first-year seminars, with strong advising, writing, and speaking components; a sophomore writing and speaking course; and some in-depth study in a subject outside the division of the major. Writing proficiency is a central objective of the seminars. It is developed further in the sophomore writing course, after students have mastered some college-level material, and it must be demonstrated in all other courses. The Senior Comprehensive Project, a capstone of the Allegheny education, is not a mere report or semester paper but a significant piece of independent study, research, or creative work. An oral defense, required by most departments as the culminating point of the Senior Project, may involve a comprehensive examination of the student's departmental studies.

The College supplements the wide range of courses and programs offered locally with cooperative and special arrangements that increase the choices available to students. Faculty advisers working with their advisees usually find themselves consulting this section more often than any other part of the Catalogue.

Every first-year student is assigned both a student adviser and a faculty adviser (the latter teaches the first freshman seminar); students may choose a different adviser in later years. Entering students who have no commitment to a major field are encouraged to use the first two years to investigate the offerings of various departments. They also are offered special advising to help them identify a major by the start of the junior year.

Off-Campus Programs

Allegheny College recognizes the enormous value of off-campus study and offers a variety of programs and services to its students in order to facilitate participation in such opportunities. Allegheny's sponsored programs include direct enrollment programs at Lancaster University (England), James Cook University (Australia), University of Natal (South Africa), and Karls-Eberhard University of Tübingen (Germany); language and area studies programs in Seville (Spain), Angers (France), and Köln (Germany); an intensive language program in Queretaro (Mexico); and internship programs in London, Paris, and Washington, D.C. Programs geared to specific majors are also available, including programs in environmental studies at the Arava Institute for Environmental Studies (Israel) and the Center for Sustainable Development (Costa Rica), marine biology at the Duke University Marine Lab in North Carolina, and political science through the Washington Semester at American University. Allegheny faculty members have led domestic summer-study tours to locations that include New York, Yellowstone, Austria, Costa Rica, and South Africa. Individually arranged study abroad has taken students to Argentina, Canada (Nova Scotia), China, Cuba, Greece, Italy, Mexico, and Scotland.

An extensive array of undergraduate internships enable students to relate their academic preparation to associated career areas, often while earning college credit. The Allegheny College Center for Experiential Learning (ACCEL), established in 1998, uniquely coordinates student access to real-life opportunities, including internships, off-campus study, service-learning, and leadership development programs.

Academic Facilities

The library has a collection of 420,000 bound volumes, 227,000 titles on microform, 1,000 periodicals, and 261,000 U.S. government and Pennsylvania state documents. The library also houses noteworthy Americana and Ida Tarbell collections. A computer laboratory, an audiovisual center, and a music listening system are in the main library as well.

On campus, more than 200 PCs are networked and available 24 hours a day for students' use in all disciplines. All residence hall rooms provide direct high-speed access to the Internet and the campus network for students with their own computers. College facilities also include a 283-acre environmental research reserve, an observatory and planetarium, a state-of-the-art television studio, and the Bowman, Penelec & Megahan Art Galleries. Two science buildings serve as national models, and a $13-million sport and fitness center opened in 1997.

Costs

For 2003–04, tuition at Allegheny was $24,100, an inclusive fee that covered health service, activities and laboratory charges, and all extra charges except those for private instruction in music. The annual fee for room and board was $6180. Several payment plans are available.

Financial Aid

A large number of merit-based scholarships are awarded annually, making the College more affordable even to families who do not qualify for need-based financial aid. Trustee Scholarships, which award up to $60,000, are guaranteed for four years of study at Allegheny. Also, scholarships, grants, loans, and campus employment are awarded to students who need assistance to meet College expenses. The Free Application for Federal Student Aid (FAFSA), which establishes an applicant's eligibility for virtually all institutional, state, and federal assistance, must be submitted by February 15. Notices about the receipt of financial aid are sent to students shortly after their acceptance by the College.

Faculty

Allegheny's faculty is deeply committed to teaching, advising, and working closely with students. Ninety percent of the 134 full-time members hold terminal degrees in their respective fields, and there is a balance between highly experienced teachers and younger faculty members. All are active and highly regarded in their disciplines. The faculty includes authors of scholarly books (such as *Congressional Women* and *Comedy from Shakespeare to Sheridan*), research scientists, and performing artists.

Student Government

Through Allegheny Student Government (ASG), undergraduates assume an active role in formulating College policy, developing curricular changes and improvements, governing their personal conduct, organizing and promoting cultural programs, and implementing the social calendar. Through its administration of the student activity fee, ASG serves as coordinator of most campus activities. Nearly all committees of the faculty include students, so that the student point of view can be represented in the governance of the College.

Admission Requirements

The College actively seeks an academically able, geographically diverse, and ethnically varied student body with a broad distribution of special talents and individual experiences. This heterogeneous mix of first-year and transfer students enriches the learning process for all students, both in and out of the classroom setting.

In the selection process, all information available on each applicant is carefully considered. The College places more importance on performance in school than on standardized test scores or other criteria. Candidates for admission should follow a college-preparatory program in high school that includes four solid or major subjects, such as English, social studies, math, science, and foreign language, each year. Either the SAT I or ACT must be taken by January of the final year of high school.

Early decision, early admission, deferred entrance, and advanced standing programs are offered. Personal interviews are strongly encouraged. Transfer students are admitted both semesters.

Application and Information

The application for admission should be submitted by February 15 (January 15 for early decision), and the SAT I or ACT results should be forwarded to the College by each candidate. Applicants for early decision are notified on a rolling basis through January 31. Regular applicants are informed of the admission decision by April 1.

Office of Admissions
Allegheny College
Meadville, Pennsylvania 16335-3902
Telephone: 814-332-4351
800-521-5293 (toll-free)
E-mail: admissions@allegheny.edu
World Wide Web: http://www.allegheny.edu

Bentley Hall, completed in 1820 and still the main administration building.

ALLIANT INTERNATIONAL UNIVERSITY

SAN DIEGO, CALIFORNIA

The University

A multicultural, multinational focus is an integral part of all degree programs at Alliant International University (AIU). The University has a 60-acre campus in San Diego, campuses in Nairobi and Mexico City, and graduate programs in six California locations. Founded in 1952 as California Western University, the University became United States International University (USIU) and operated as such until 2001. In 2001, USIU combined forces with the California School of Professional Psychology (CSPP) to form Alliant International University. AIU offers students a chance to learn from a globally oriented faculty and to study with fellow students from nearly sixty countries. The University's mission is to educate citizens of the world, ensuring the acquisition of knowledge and competencies that are essential to live, lead, and solve problems in a global society.

AIU has an overall enrollment of approximately 6,000 students; undergraduates account for approximately 35 percent of the total student population on the San Diego campus. Classrooms at AIU are comfortable and are within a short walk of each other. Residence halls are designed as apartment complexes rather than as dormitories. Each complex has its own swimming pool and recreational area. Separate suites for men and women are set away from the classroom area. All suites are wired for online access. A variety of extracurricular programs are offered on the campus. The Office of Student Activities and the Office of Housing and Residence Life staff offer social functions, including karaoke parties, excursions, movies, and dances. On-campus recreational facilities include tennis courts, a soccer field, baseball and softball diamonds, an outdoor basketball court, sand volleyball courts, and a weight room. The SportCenter at AIU houses twelve indoor volleyball courts that are convertible to six basketball courts. AIU participates at the NAIA level of intercollegiate sports in men's and women's tennis, soccer, and cross-country and in women's volleyball; scholarships are available in these sports. A full range of intramural sports is offered for men and women. Placement, health, and counseling services are available on campus. Cars are permitted.

AIU offers graduate studies through its programs in business and management, education, organizational studies, social and policy studies, psychology, and international relations. Details about programs that lead to master's and/or doctoral degrees in various areas are available from the Office of Admissions.

Location

AIU's San Diego campus is set on rolling, wooded land within the northern boundary of San Diego. The city's central business district is a 20-minute drive away. San Diego offers many cultural and recreational attractions and activities: Sea World, the San Diego Zoo, sailing, boating, deep-sea fishing, and swimming are just a few. Concerts, dramatic productions, and museums are among the many cultural opportunities. Los Angeles is 2 hours to the north, Tijuana and Mexican beaches are an hour to the south, the beaches of southern California are 20 minutes to the west, and mountains and desert are to the east. The climate is excellent, with a mean temperature of 72 degrees Fahrenheit.

AIU's international campuses in Nairobi and Mexico City offer students the opportunity to easily transfer between campus locations for a semester or more while still continuing their chosen field of study. The Nairobi campus is located in the commercial and financial center of East Africa on a 20-acre campus. Students there enjoy modern classrooms, a computer center, a library, and on-campus residential housing. AIU–Mexico is located in the Reforma district, in the heart of Mexico City. While students have the opportunity to learn and study in the relative seclusion of the campus itself, the excitement, the cultural and social opportunities, and the chances to explore the city and surrounding attractions of Mexico City abound. A library and housing in the local community are also available.

Majors and Degrees

AIU students choose from a variety of disciplines in the University's bachelor's degree programs. Bachelor of Arts degrees are awarded in international studies and psychology. Bachelor of Science degree programs are offered in business administration, hotel and restaurant management, information systems and technology, international business administration, management, and tourism management. The University also has an extensive English as a second language program.

Academic Program

Bachelor's degree students are introduced to AIU beginning with the two-course First-Year Experience sequence, which provides the refinement of needed skills and the development of the intellectual framework needed for academic success. The general education program further introduces students to both the benefits and the demands of academic life. Finally, students are provided with a coherent, substantial, and challenging sequence of courses in the humanities, social sciences, and natural sciences that culminates with the three-course "capstone" sequence of the Senior Experience. Students' programs are planned in conjunction with academic advisers, using suggested lists of courses as guides. Diverse instructional methods include lectures, seminars, small-group discussions, case analyses, simulations, experiential situations, and internships. The opportunity to engage in closely supervised independent study is offered as a supplement to structured classes.

Academic Facilities

Academic facilities include the Walter Library, which has more than 160,000 books, 1,150 current print journal subscriptions, twelve electronic database subscriptions, approximately 995 psychological test titles, 1,700 audiotapes, and more than 1,200 videotapes available.

Costs

The cost for one academic year in 2002–03 at the University was $20,735 for undergraduates, which included tuition, room and board, and student fees but not books, travel, or personal expenses. Books cost about $810 per year.

Financial Aid

AIU offers financial assistance to eligible domestic and international students. Scholarships and grants are awarded to undergraduates based on their entering GPA. Assistance is provided by federal, state, and University funds and is offered in the form of scholarships, grants, part-time employment, and long-term loans. Applications submitted by March 2 receive priority consideration for funds; a student whose application is received later is awarded funds based on the availability of aid.

Faculty

Ninety-eight percent of AIU's faculty members have doctoral degrees, and many members are internationally known for their consulting work, publications, and professional stature. Faculty members teach both undergraduate and graduate courses, conduct independent study programs, and are available for academic counseling. Individual counseling by specially designated advisers and faculty members is a key feature of the University.

Student Government

The governing student body is an elected Student Body Government Association, with representatives from each of the University's academic departments. Through the council, students govern extracurricular activities and participate in other areas of student life.

Admission Requirements

The University seeks well-adjusted students with good academic backgrounds who show evidence of creativity and leadership potential. Students should also have a desire to participate in an academic community that emphasizes positive values and the sharing of experiences with people from other cultures of the world. The Admissions Committee selects students on the basis of their academic records and test scores. Requirements for American applicants include SAT I or ACT scores and transcripts. International applicants must submit school-leaving certificates and/or results from all schools previously attended and the Financial Guarantee Form, which is available from the AIU Office of Admissions. All transcripts must be in the original language and be accompanied by a certified English translation. Applicants are required to verify their English proficiency either through a TOEFL score or through participation in AIU's ESL program. Advanced standing and/or placement may be granted by the University to entering freshmen who submit AP, I.B., or CLEP test scores. This program enables students of high ability and motivation to accelerate their education. AIU also welcomes regularly admitted students who have not declared a major field of study and transfer applicants from accredited four-year colleges and universities and from community colleges. Campus visits are encouraged and may be arranged through the Office of Admissions.

Application and Information

First-year and transfer applicants may be admitted year-round. Applications and supportive data should be on file in the Office of Admissions at least thirty days prior to the term for which the applicant desires admission. Later applications are processed as quickly as possible on a space-available basis. The completed application form, a nonrefundable $40 application fee, and supporting documents should be sent to:

Office of Admissions
Alliant International University
10455 Pomerado Road
San Diego, California 92131
Telephone: 866-U-ALLIANT (toll-free)
Fax: 858-635-4739
E-mail: admissions3@alliant.edu
World Wide Web: http://www.alliant.edu

Graduates at AIU's commencement ceremony.

ALMA COLLEGE

ALMA, MICHIGAN

The College

Regarded as one of the nation's best liberal arts colleges, Alma College is in its third century of superior education and professional distinction. Founded by Presbyterians in 1886, Alma remains a private liberal arts institution committed to a values-oriented style of education. In a time when many professionals find that their technical training is already out of date, Alma's graduates are entering the job market with an education that will always serve them. Alma's academic philosophy, rooted in the liberal arts tradition and providing a broad educational base with flexible, innovative course work, has earned Alma a Phi Beta Kappa chapter. Classes are small—the average size is 20—enabling students to do more than just listen. Students enjoy the rigorous academic atmosphere; 88 percent of the faculty members hold the highest degree in their field.

In fall 2003, Alma College enrolled a total of 1,291 students (536 men and 755 women), of whom 1,249 were full-time. Alma's students are high achievers from the upper ranks of some of the best high schools in Michigan and its surrounding states. Current students come from twenty states and eleven countries. Entering freshmen have an average high school GPA of 3.43; their mean ACT composite score of 24.3 is approximately equivalent to a combined SAT I score of 1140. More than 70 percent of the freshmen enrolled in 2003 ranked in the top 25 percent of their high school class; 32 percent ranked in the top 10 percent. Nearly all of Alma's students live on campus. Housing units vary in size, accommodating from 10 to 200 students each. Single rooms, double-occupancy rooms, and 4-person suites are available. There are no all-freshman dormitories because the College believes that the interaction between freshmen and upperclass students is important. Each housing unit is supervised by a full-time director, who is assisted by student staff members.

The lifestyle that Alma students enjoy combines residential life with academic challenges. Flexible academic programs enable students to get involved in their favorite activities and to develop new interests. With more than 100 student organizations to choose from, students have the chance to put their talents to work. Organizations and activities include eighteen varsity athletic teams for men and women, the Student Congress, vocal and instrumental performing groups, symphony orchestra, national fraternities and sororities, theater and dance groups, intramural sports, the yearbook, the newspaper, and many more. Students enjoy Alma's Alan J. Stone Center for Recreation that features a climbing wall, fitness center, four courts, and a suspended three-lane track. The outdoor athletic complex features a multipurpose playing field of artificial turf, soccer and softball fields, tennis courts, an eight-lane track, and nearby Klenk Park for baseball. Even as students have fun, they develop valuable skills for their future. The Hamilton Dining Commons and downtown shops are a short walk from the main academic area on campus.

Location

Easily reached from Chicago, Detroit, Indianapolis, Milwaukee, Cleveland, and Cincinnati, Alma College is located in the heart of Michigan's lower peninsula. The city of Alma (population of about 10,000) is well-known as Scotland, USA, for its annual Highland Festival. Alma's relaxed, safe, small-town atmosphere enables students to concentrate on educational priorities, while both the metropolitan and recreational areas of Michigan are readily accessible. Tri Cities and Lansing airports are nearby.

Majors and Degrees

Alma offers four degrees: Bachelor of Arts, Bachelor of Fine Arts, Bachelor of Music, and Bachelor of Science. Departmental and interdepartmental majors are possible. Majors include art and design, biochemistry, biology, business administration, chemistry, communication, computer science, economics, English, exercise and health science, foreign service, French, German, history, international business, mathematical sciences, mathematics, music, philosophy, physics, political science, psychology, religious studies, sociology and anthropology, Spanish, teacher education, and theater and dance. Interdisciplinary majors may be designed in such fields as American studies, art history, cognitive science, electronics and computer engineering, environmental studies, gerontology, new media studies, public health, and women's studies. Preprofessional programs prepare students for further study and careers in dentistry, engineering, graphic design, law, medical illustration, medicine, the ministry, occupational therapy, and pre–physical therapy. Academic minors are available in American studies, art history, Christian education, cognitive science, environmental studies, gerontology, public health, women's studies, and many other fields.

Alma College offers cooperative 3-2 and 4-2 pre-engineering programs with the University of Michigan School of Engineering, Michigan Technological University, and Washington University in St. Louis. A 3-2 program in occupational therapy is offered in conjunction with Washington University in St. Louis.

Academic Program

The College operates on a 4-4-1 calendar—two 4-month terms in the fall and winter and one 1-month term in the spring. During the spring term, there are opportunities for international study as well as for on-campus instruction and research. In keeping with Alma's philosophy of educating the whole person, the College requires that all students complete liberal arts courses spanning the humanities, the natural sciences, and the social sciences. The B.A. and B.S. degree programs require the completion of 136 credits; the B.F.A. and B.M. degree programs, 148 credits.

Highly qualified students are challenged by Alma's honors program, featuring a specially designed freshman course that explores the methods of communication used in the liberal arts disciplines. The honors concept extends throughout the four years at Alma.

Alma accepts credits earned through the Advanced Placement (AP) Program and the International Baccalaureate Diploma (I.B.) program, and examinations designed by Alma's academic departments.

Off-Campus Programs

Numerous opportunities for international study are available through the College, including offerings in Australia, Austria, Bolivia, Ecuador, England, France, Germany, India, Italy, New Zealand, Peru, Scotland, South Korea, and Spain. A wide variety of options for housing, including placements in private homes, are featured. Alma's Program of Studies in France, a cooperative venture with the prestigious Alliance Française in Paris, can accommodate any student from beginner to advanced for periods of time from one month to one year. Students considering careers in international business may enroll in an international marketing or multinational business administration seminar held in Wollongong, Australia. Two spring term courses must be successfully completed, one of which must be a designated "S" course. These courses take advantage of the spring term format and cross-geographical, cultural, or disciplinary boundaries. Internships provide Alma students with experience related to their educational or career goals. On-the-job experience may be arranged in many fields through work in businesses, industries, and government and community agencies.

Academic Facilities

Twenty-five main buildings with up-to-date facilities and an outdoor sports complex are arranged around a scenic central mall on Alma's 125-acre campus. It is a short walk to the fully automated library, which houses more than 251,640 volumes. The Dow and Kapp Science Centers provide research and instructional facilities for biology, biochemistry, chemistry, and physics. Swanson Academic Center houses classrooms and faculty offices. The Eddy Music Building, Clack Art Center, and Oscar E. Remick Heritage Center for the Performing Arts offer rehearsal, exhibition, and performance space for art and design, music, theater, and dance. The Colina Library Wing houses stacks and additional study areas for students. The McIntyre Center for Exercise and Health Science has labs for cardiovascular physiology, human anatomy, and human performance testing. The Alan J. Stone Center for Recreation opened in the fall of 2001. The Center is a 53,000-square-foot, four-court facility with a suspended three-lane track and climbing wall.

Instruction at Alma is supported by computer technology. Students are encouraged to bring their own computers to the campus to best utilize available services. Access to the Internet, the campus network, the library, e-mail, and a variety of printers is available in all of Alma's eight residence halls. Student computer labs in academic departments throughout the campus provide access to Macintosh and IBM-compatible PC systems as well as Sun SPARCstations and Silicon Graphics UNIX systems. Computer classrooms in the library and Swanson Academic Center are staffed by student assistants.

Costs

Tuition for 2003–04 was $18,684. Room and board costs for the fall and winter terms totaled $6712. Students who attend during the spring term pay a $167 tuition charge and a $460 board charge but no room charge. A student activity fee of $170 is charged each year, and a charge of $258 for the Preterm is added to freshman-year costs. Books, supplies, and personal expenses (including travel, clothing, and entertainment) are estimated at $2100 per year.

Financial Aid

At Alma, students can achieve scholarship recognition regardless of need on the basis of outstanding scholastic achievement. Several academically competitive scholarship programs provide awards for eligible students, including a full tuition scholarship for National Merit Finalists. The College also offers performance scholarships in recognition of individual talent, as well as grants, loans, and deferred-payment plans. Up to 400 campus and community jobs are filled by Alma students yearly. To apply for aid, students are required only to file the Free Application for Federal Student Aid (FAFSA) in January of the year of prospective enrollment at Alma.

Faculty

A look at Alma's faculty shows a diversity of backgrounds; 88 percent of the 84 full-time faculty members hold the highest degree in their field. Superior undergraduate teaching is the first priority of Alma's faculty members; no graduate students teach classes, nor are there television lecture courses at Alma. Classes at Alma are small; the faculty-student ratio is 1:12.7. Faculty members are accessible and willing to assist students. They are also recognized as scholars in their fields; their research has been supported by such organizations as the Michigan Council for the Arts, the National Science Foundation, the Council for the International Exchange of Scholars (Fulbright scholarships), and the National Endowment for the Humanities.

Student Government

Alma encourages students to build leadership skills through involvement in student government and campus organizations. Members of the Alma College Student Congress represent all major student organizations as well as individual students. This group works as a liaison with the administration to implement or revise campus policies, develop a budget and coordinate the expenditure of student activity fees, manage the campus radio station and student publications, and resolve problems. Alma's Union Board, composed of students representing each residence hall, oversees most of the regular entertainment scheduled on campus. As a residential campus, Alma is governed by rules prohibiting academic dishonesty, gambling, cohabitation, infringements on others' rights, illegal use of alcoholic beverages and drugs, and damage to personal property.

Admission Requirements

To be considered for admission, applicants should have an average of B or higher in high school and a composite score of 22 or higher on the ACT or a combined score of 1030 or higher on the SAT I. All applicants are encouraged to schedule an admission interview on campus. Transfer students must have earned an average of C or higher at their previous institution. No more than 62 semester hours or 90 quarter hours of course work completed with a grade of C or better may be transferred to Alma. International students are asked to submit records of previous schooling and must show competence in English through the Test of English as a Foreign Language (TOEFL).

Application and Information

Students may apply at any time after completing their junior year of high school. Freshman applicants should send the completed application for admission along with a $25 nonrefundable application fee, high school transcripts, and ACT or SAT I scores. Students are required to submit a recommendation from their high school guidance counselor. Early action applications are due by November 1. Transfer students should submit transcripts from each institution attended, the completed application for admission, a $25 nonrefundable application fee, a financial aid transcript, and a Transfer Recommendation Form from the last institution attended. Applications are handled on a rolling basis; students should hear about admission decisions within three weeks after sending an application and records. Alma College's nondiscrimination policy includes age, color, creed, gender, national origin, physical ability, race, religion, and sexual orientation.

All records and forms should be mailed to:

Admissions Office
Alma College
614 West Superior Street
Alma, Michigan 48801-1599

Telephone: 800-321-ALMA (toll-free)
E-mail: admissions@alma.edu
World Wide Web: http://www.alma.edu
http://www.alma.edu/admissions/application.htm

ALVERNIA COLLEGE

READING, PENNSYLVANIA

The College

Alvernia College is a Catholic liberal arts college with a total enrollment of 2,311 men and women that stresses the development of the whole person—academically, emotionally, and spiritually. With a student-faculty ratio of 16:1, Alvernia offers a personalized environment where the faculty members know and care about each student. Located on a beautiful 80-acre campus on the outskirts of Reading, Alvernia offers a setting conducive to learning and is conveniently accessible. It is chartered by the commonwealth of Pennsylvania, fully accredited by the Middle States Association of Colleges and Schools, and sponsored by the Bernardine Franciscan Sisters.

Alvernia participates in a full range of intercollegiate sports, including baseball, basketball, cross-country, field hockey, golf, lacrosse, soccer, softball, tennis, and volleyball. The College is a member of the NCAA Division III, the ECAC, and the Pennsylvania Athletic Conference.

Student organizations include the American Chemistry Society, Athletic Association, Campus Ministry, Chorale, Foreign Language Club, Intercultural Club, Journalism Club, Math Club, Phi Beta Lambda, Science Club, Sigma Tau Delta, and Student Government Association. Formal and informal dances, formal and buffet dinners, informal club socials, picnics, parties, coffeehouses, and student entertainment all provide occasions for social development and friendly relationships. Resident students live in a coed dorm that has spacious rooms and several student lounges or in town houses for upperclassmen. A student center, used by both resident and commuting students, provides excellent study and recreational facilities. A campus center and a residence hall opened in fall 1999, and an additional residence hall opened in fall 2001.

Alvernia College's student body consists of people of all ages and walks of life. Alvernia offers both a traditional course schedule and a year-round continuing education program designed to give working adults the opportunity to earn a degree in fewer than four years. In addition, courses are offered on Saturday, in the summer, and in the evening under the traditional semester schedule. Alvernia College also offers five-year programs leading to the Master in Education, the Master in Business Administration, the Master of Arts in liberal studies, and the Master of Occupational Therapy. Alvernia offers a Master of Social Work through Marywood College.

Location

Alvernia College is located 3 miles from the center of the city of Reading, in the scenic Blue Mountain area of eastern Pennsylvania. Its campus overlooks Angelica Lake, noted for its rustic beauty. The College has easy access to the metropolitan areas of New York, Philadelphia, and Harrisburg, where students can take advantage of the cultural, historical, and educational attractions these cities have to offer.

Majors and Degrees

Alvernia College offers the Bachelor of Arts, Bachelor of Science, Bachelor of Science in Nursing, and Associate in Science degrees. Bachelor of Arts or Bachelor of Science candidates can major in the following baccalaureate degree areas: accounting, addiction studies, athletic training, biochemistry, biology, biology/medical technology, chemistry, chemistry/medical technology, communication, computer information systems, criminal justice administration, education (early childhood, elementary, special, and secondary, with major areas in biology, chemistry, English, general science, mathematics, and social studies), English, forensic science, general science, history, liberal studies, management, mathematics, nursing, occupational therapy, philosophy/theology, political science, psychology, social work, and sports management. Students can take double majors in areas that are closely related.

Academic Programs

The academic program is designed to help students to think logically and critically, to comprehend accurately, and to communicate effectively. The College concentrates on the personal development of its students by fostering academic integrity, social responsibility, and moral values. The educational program is based on a commitment to develop the whole person into a responsible individual. Therefore, students not only are required to demonstrate proficiency in those skills demanded by their chosen professional concentration but also are expected to take advantage of the opportunity to grow intellectually and spiritually and to be responsible to themselves and to society.

Alvernia offers an honors program designed to prepare students for graduate school. The course focuses on a current topic for study and discussion. During their junior year, students choose a topic for their thesis, which they present and defend.

To earn a bachelor's degree, students must complete a minimum of 124 credits, with 54 credits in the liberal arts, 40 in the major, and 30 in electives, although these requirements may vary according to the major program. Students must earn 68 credits in nursing to be awarded the Associate in Science degree.

Academic Facilities

Alvernia opened a library facility in 1991 that can hold more than 100,000 volumes, including reference works, books for general circulation, and bound periodicals. The library currently subscribes to 850 periodicals covering all areas of study taught at the College, and more than 1,440 volumes of back issues are in the microfilm collection. The library also houses the Audio-Visual Center, which has 23,000 pieces of audiovisual material, including more than 4,750 music records and scores. The science building houses several modern laboratories for science majors and research facilities for psychology majors. Alvernia also has an art studio.

Costs

For 2004–05, the basic tuition fee is $17,500; room and board are $6750.

Financial Aid

More than 85 percent of the students attending Alvernia receive some type of financial aid. The types of aid most commonly received are Pennsylvania Higher Education Assistance Agency grants for Pennsylvania residents, Federal Pell Grants, and numerous scholarships from private sources, as well as grants and scholarships from the College itself. This aid is awarded on the basis of academic performance and financial need. The deadline for application for Alvernia College aid is April 1. In addition, Alvernia participates in the federally funded Federal Work-Study Program. Student loans are also available.

Faculty

The faculty consists of 59 full-time and 125 part-time adjunct members, each dedicated to teaching and serving the needs of every student. The faculty is as diversified as the many fields of interest that its members represent. For example, the criminal justice administration program and the addiction studies program employ adjunct faculty members who possess expertise in their professional areas in addition to excellent educational credentials. The use of such faculty members is intended to enhance the theoretical portions of professional training with practical professional knowledge.

Student Government

The Student Government strives to promote responsible student action and to serve as a link between students, administration, and faculty. It is composed of a president, vice president, secretary, treasurer, and chief justice elected by the student body and is augmented by 2 representatives from each class.

Admission Requirements

Admission requirements normally include a high school diploma with 16 Carnegie units in the following subjects: English, 4 units; mathematics, 2 units; science, 2 units; social studies, 2 units; and modern languages, 2 units. The remaining units may be made up of academic electives. The College is willing to consider good students whose preparation does not include all of these subjects. Nursing students must fulfill the admission requirements established by the Pennsylvania State Board of Nurse Examiners. The State High School Equivalency Diploma is generally recognized as fulfilling the minimum entrance requirements. Applicants to the freshman class are required to take the SAT I; the ACT is also acceptable. Outstanding candidates are considered for entrance to Alvernia at the end of their junior year of high school on the basis of requests made by the candidate and the high school. With the approval of their school officials, students may also be admitted to certain courses during their senior year in high school, simultaneously earning credit toward the high school diploma and a college degree.

Application and Information

Applicants should submit an application for admission and enclose the nonrefundable $25 processing fee. The application form may be obtained from the Admissions Office or from the Web site listed below. Applicants should have an official copy of their high school record sent to the Admissions Office, along with the official results of the SAT I or ACT.

A personal interview, while not required, is often desirable for the prospective student. All interested students and their families are invited to visit the College for a tour of the campus and a personal interview with a member of the Admissions Office staff. It is advisable to make an appointment by mail or phone at least one week in advance. The College reserves the right to request an interview if certain aspects of an application need clarification.

Because the College has a rolling admission policy, an applicant is notified of acceptance by the director of admissions shortly after the necessary credentials are on file and have been reviewed, generally within one month of the time an application has been completed. To reserve a place in the freshman class, all students must make a $100 deposit by May 1. An additional $200 deposit is required of all resident students to reserve housing. These deposits are credited to the student's account for the first semester but are not refunded if the student fails to attend the College. All full-time students are required to return a medical history/health form to the health center. Residents need to submit this form before moving into the residence hall. Transfer students should have a grade point average of 2.0 or higher on a 4.0 scale and should be aware that only grades of C or better are eligible for credit transfer. Alvernia accepts a maximum of 75 transfer credits; at least 45 credits that are required for graduation must be earned at Alvernia and must satisfy all graduation requirements. A detailed analysis of credits to be transferred is done only after students have been accepted by the College. For more information or to schedule a visit, students should contact:

Director of Admissions
Alvernia College
Reading, Pennsylvania 19607
Telephone: 610-796-8220
888-ALVERNIA (toll-free)
Fax: 610-796-8336
E-mail: admissions@alvernia.edu
World Wide Web: http://www.alvernia.edu

Friends gather near the Student Center on the beautiful campus of Alvernia College.

ALVERNO COLLEGE

MILWAUKEE, WISCONSIN

The College

Alverno College is an internationally acclaimed, award-winning four-year liberal arts college for women known for an innovative, abilities-based, assessment-as-learning approach to education. Founded in 1887 by the School Sisters of St. Francis, Alverno College has one of the most diverse student bodies in the nation, both culturally and religiously. Currently, there are more than 2,100 students enrolled.

Alverno's mission is to promote the personal and professional development of women through four areas: creating a community of learning, creating a curriculum, creating ties to the community, and creating relationships with higher education. Alverno sets out to accomplish this by remaining focused on the student and higher education. The National Survey of Student Engagement (NSSE), an independent study that asks students to gauge the performance of their college or university and their own outcomes, placed Alverno in the 98th percentile overall nationally. This indicates that Alverno students are actually learning what they set out to learn at Alverno.

Alverno achieves a high level of success in its teaching through a comprehensive curriculum of abilities-based programs and an assessment process that provides each student with continuing evaluation of her performance, allowing her to make the adjustments necessary to succeed in her education. In every class, students learn by doing: they are participants and active learners. In addition, students are able to track their progress through Alverno's patented Diagnostic Digital Portfolio. This first-of-its-kind, Web-based system enables each Alverno student—anyplace, anytime—to follow her learning progress throughout her years of study. It helps the student process the feedback she receives from faculty members, external assessors, and peers. It also enables her to look for patterns in her academic work so she can take more control of her own development and become a more autonomous learner.

Faculty members have worked to create a more comprehensive approach to learning that places lessons into a framework that is relevant to today's changing world. The need to approach situations from a variety of perspectives, to weigh decisions, to engage in meaningful discussion, and to apply creative solutions in problem solving are all abilities women need for success.

Preparing students for real life, not just finals, is the hallmark of an Alverno education. *U.S. News & World Report* consistently ranks Alverno College as a top liberal arts college. At Alverno, each student is required to complete one off-campus professional internship. These internships are designed to complement the classroom experience, exposing each student to real-life work situations and providing insight into career options in each field of study. Alverno's Career Education Center is fully integrated into the learning process, providing students with numerous services, resources, training opportunities, and tools to assist them with their career planning. Within one year of graduation, 90 percent of Alverno College alumnae are working within their chosen field.

Students take advantage of a wide variety of social, athletic, cultural, and cocurricular academic activities on and off campus. Alverno Presents is one of the longest-running performing arts series in the Midwest, offering students the opportunity to see such top-notch performers as Wynton Marsalis, the Waifs, Kate and Anna McGarrigle, Baaba Maal, and many others.

The College's NCAA Division III athletics program provides students with five competitive sports, including basketball, cross-country, soccer, softball, and volleyball. Intramural sports are also available. The student center features the Mug Coffeehouse, run by students for students, as a place to relax and study with a latte or enjoy live music or lively discussions along with a variety of entertainment options, including large screen TVs and movie nights. There are more than thirty student organizations ranging from women's advocacy groups to professional business networking associations, including award-winning chapters of the Association of Women in Communications, Circle K, and Students in Free Enterprise.

Location

Alverno's 40-acre campus is nestled in the residential Jackson Park area of Milwaukee, just 10 minutes from downtown and beautiful Lake Michigan. Students are only minutes away from the world-famous Milwaukee Art Museum and the Calatrava addition as well as the Marcus Center for the Performing Arts and Summerfest grounds, the gallery and theater districts, and Miller Park, home of the Milwaukee Brewers. The city offers a mix of trendy nightspots and chic coffee bars and has a highly eclectic dining scene.

Internships and other cooperative programs with business, industry, and special-interest groups within the community give each student a variety of learning experiences off campus, enabling her to make a contribution through service projects in her areas of interest.

Majors and Degrees

Alverno College is a fully accredited four-year baccalaureate institution conferring Bachelor of Arts, Bachelor of Science, and Master of Education degrees. Alverno offers more than sixty majors and minors, including accounting, art, art therapy, behavioral science, biology, business, chemistry, professional communications, computer science, education, English, environmental studies, global studies, history, international business, Spanish, liberal studies, management, marketing, mathematics, music therapy, natural science, nursing, philosophy, political science, psychology, religious studies, secondary education, social science, and a host of preprofessional training programs. Alverno also offers educational licensure programs and a new licensure-to-master's degree program.

Alverno is also home to Wisconsin's original Weekend College program, one of the first in the nation. The program, which began in 1977, allows students to earn their degrees in professional communications, communication management and technology, community leadership and development, international business, management, management accounting, marketing management, and nursing (RN to B.S.N.) by attending class only twice per month.

Academic Programs

Alverno's learning process prepares students for success. The curriculum includes academic course work as well as external experiences such as internships and develops the student's abilities in eight specific core areas: communication, analysis, problem solving, value judgments, social interaction, decision making, developing a global perspective, and aesthetic engagement. Each student acquires the necessary knowledge to demonstrate learning in each of these areas, tying her studies into her personal and professional life.

Off-Campus Programs

The student's learning experience is enhanced by opportunities in the community and abroad through cutting-edge internship and international studies programs. Students are able to apply their knowledge to real-life situations in Alverno's internship program, working with mentors on job sites in business, industry, politics, nonprofits, and community organizations. Sites that regularly participate include Harley-Davidson, Miller Brewing, Milwaukee Art Museum, the mayor's office, and many others. Alverno's travel-abroad program provides students the opportunity to study for a semester or for a shorter term in such places as England, France, and Japan. In addition, travel courses, which culminate in a trip, are also available.

Academic Facilities

Alverno College remains one of the most technologically advanced campuses in the region, featuring SMART classrooms, a state-of-the-art Center for Instructional Communication, a video conferencing center that allows for long-distance learning, several computer labs, and many other multimedia capabilities. Even the residence hall features high-speed Internet access and cable television capability in each room. Alverno's library provides onsite and remote access to its print, audiovisual, and electronic holdings of more than 250,000 items as well as access to worldwide resources available through technology. The library's resources and services are further enhanced through a consortium of seven local college and university libraries.

The Teaching, Learning, and Technology Center is a 73,000-square-foot facility that features cutting-edge science labs, computer centers, and multimedia centers, including an on-campus digital production facility. The facility houses hundreds of networked, high-tech computers plus writing devices, the latest software, digital cameras, scanners, laptops, and more. The production facility houses nonlinear digital editing equipment, allowing students to produce and edit their own projects. All of these service areas are fully supported, so students have a resource on staff.

The Nursing Education Building provides resources dedicated to meet the needs of nursing students preparing for careers, including a library and a clinical nursing resource center. The center allows students to practice their nursing therapeutic skills and to participate in simulated clinical experiences. Computers are equipped with interactive nursing software. Registered nurses serve as mentors and assessors as they staff the resource center.

Alverno College also features several extra and cocurricular facilities on campus. Pitman Theatre is a beautiful art deco–style theater with seating for 930. The theater is the home of the Alverno Presents performing arts series and numerous concerts and functions each season. Wehr Hall, with seating for 375, is a state-of-the-art presentation hall designed for multimedia presentations as well as smaller performances. Alverno's Conference Center can accommodate seated dinners for up to 300 and is host to countless alumnae weddings and other celebrations each year.

Costs

For 2004–05, the tuition is $7080 per semester ($7452 for nursing), and room and board rates are $2700 per semester for first-year students. Books vary by course load but average $400 per semester for full-time students. Personal expenses vary greatly.

Financial Aid

Financial aid is readily available based on student need, academic performance, and other criteria. Aid can take the form of scholarships, grants, loans, and campus work-study programs. Approximately 85 percent of Alverno students receive some form of financial assistance, with an average award of $9494 per student per year.

Faculty

Alverno's coed faculty is made up of 104 full-time members, more than 90 percent of whom have earned the highest degree available in their fields. Faculty members also serve as academic advisers to students in their major areas of concentration. Class sizes are extremely small, averaging 20 per class.

Student Government

Students can join one of more than thirty student organizations and interest groups, including the Student Activities Planning Team. This gives students an active voice and leadership role in what happens on campus. Programming opportunities include events such as the Metropolitan Milwaukee Leadership Conference and the National Collegiate Alcohol Awareness Week. Some groups or activities, such as food and clothing drives, are also student initiated and supported by the professional staff.

Admission Requirements

Candidates applying for admission to Alverno College directly after high school must have completed at least 17 academic units. These units should include at least 4 units in English, with the rest distributed among foreign languages, history and the social sciences, mathematics, and natural sciences.

All students must complete an evaluation of their abilities through the Communication Placement Assessment before beginning classes.

Application and Information

Students who wish to apply for admission can apply online or they can write, call, or e-mail the Admission Office for the necessary forms. An application is considered complete on receipt of the application form, the application fee (waived if students apply online), a high school transcript, and ACT scores. Students may submit any additional evidence that they believe might help the College determine their capacity to benefit from an Alverno education.

Alverno's admission policy permits notification of acceptance within three weeks of receipt of all credentials. Acceptance is contingent upon satisfactory completion of the secondary school courses.

For more information about Alverno College, interested students should contact:

Admission Office
Alverno College
3400 South 43rd Street
P.O. Box 343922
Milwaukee, Wisconsin 53234-3922
Telephone: 414-382-6100
800-933-3401 (toll-free)
E-mail: admissions@alverno.edu
World Wide Web: http://www.alverno.edu

Studying on the campus of Alverno College.

AMERICAN ACADEMY OF ART

CHICAGO, ILLINOIS

The Academy

Founded in 1923, the American Academy of Art has been educating professional artists in the fine art and commercial art fields for eighty years. Beginning with a solid foundation of drawing and design, based on the classical academic tradition, the dedicated and distinguished faculty is committed to providing its students with artistic skills and knowledge of contemporary tools and techniques that enable them to build a successful career.

The American Academy of Art continues to build on its strong reputation of educating successful, professional artists. The Academy believes an artist must develop mastery of materials and understand how to depict the world in a realistic style. The American Academy of art prepares students to enter leading galleries, advertising agencies, and design and animation studios.

The Academy is granted authority by the Illinois Board of Higher Education to award the Bachelor of Fine Arts (B.F.A.) and Master of Fine Arts (M.F.A.) degrees. The Academy is an eligible institution under government-insured student loan and grant programs. It is authorized under federal law to enroll nonimmigrant alien students and is approved by the Veterans' Administration.

Location

The Academy is located at 332 South Michigan Avenue in the heart of Chicago's education and museum district. Four colleges and universities are within walking distance, as are the Harold Washington Library Center and the Chicago Cultural Center. Classes encourage outside research at nearby institutions such as the Field Museum, the Adler Planetarium, Shedd Aquarium, Terra Museum of American Art, and The Museum of Contemporary Art. Each summer the city is filled with festivals from the Taste of Chicago to Jazz, Blues, and Gospel Fests.

Majors and Degrees

The American Academy of Art offers the Bachelor of Fine Arts degree in several hands-on programs. Students can major in academic studies, design, foundations, illustration, life drawing, multimedia/Web design, painting, watercolor painting, and 3-D animation and modeling.

Academic Program

Unlike a traditional academically oriented college or university, the American Academy of Art focuses primarily on the fine arts, in particular, those in the visual artistic mediums as mentioned in the previous section. Students are required to complete 133 credit hours to obtain a Bachelor of Fine Arts degree in one of several different majors.

In academic studies, the student develops the necessary knowledge and skills to succeed in his or her chosen art career. Critical thinking, problem solving, and people skills are the cornerstones of the program. Students develop a historical perspective, learn professional standards and demonstrate interpersonal communication.

The design program focuses students on developing analytical skills and a critical eye for graphic design. Students work in teams to accomplish projects in print design, advertising design, and environmental graphics. Students produce professional-quality projects, including package design, posters, and logos.

In the foundations program, the fundamentals of art and life drawing courses give a thorough background in drawing the figure, composition, rendering, linear perspective, and color theory. Students are introduced to a variety of materials and techniques. Class projects include how to move from concept to sketch to thumbnail to finished work. The foundations year prepares students to think and work as artists and to continue into a chosen area of study.

The illustration program stresses mastery in all kinds of drawing techniques and media so that images convey emotions, tell a story, or market a product or idea. Students study various types of illustration, including editorial, advertising, and children's book illustration. Students develop an illustration style, a consistent body of work, and prepare a professional portfolio.

Professional artists are trained by drawing the human figure. The life drawing program emphasizes anatomical structure and its role in enhancing accuracy, rhythm, and meaning through projects involving the full figure, portraiture, and drapery studies. Attention is paid to the study of the styles and techniques of representational figurative work.

In multimedia/Web design, students learn the concepts, strategies, and techniques of working with digital media through the use and control of typography, images, animation, sound, and digital video. Students develop the conceptual framework to produce digital media along with the historical, legal, and social issues surrounding digital publishing.

The painting program emphasizes working with traditional oil painting techniques from life with special attention to painting the figure. Students learn composition, light and shadow, lines and edges, and depth of forms. The courses inspire the student to build an artistic style while building strong traditional skills.

Watercolor painting is tailored toward developing a high level of skill in this unique medium. Students develop mastery in drawing, composition, creativity, and technical refinement. Color, light, and translucency are some of the qualities explored as the student strives to attain a professional body of work.

Students in 3-D animation and modeling use software to create three-dimensional models and animations using lighting effects, camera angles, motion studies, digital video, and sound. The 3-D program trains students in both traditional skills, including sculpture and drawing, and 3-D digital skills.

Off-Campus Programs

The American Academy of Art offers a semester study-abroad program in Florence, Italy.

Academic Facilities

In addition to the studio areas provided by individual departments, the campus includes the Bill L. Parks Gallery, with revolving exhibitions, and the Irving Shapiro Library collection of specialized art resources. The Shapiro Library is filled with volumes supporting the curriculum, as well as computers with Internet and CD-ROM access. The Academy's archives contain more than seventy years of work by students, faculty members, and alumni. It contains, among others, works by Irving Shapiro, Thomas Blackshear, and Alex Ross.

Costs

Full-time tuition is $8890 per semester.

Financial Aid

It is the goal of the Academy to help every eligible student obtain financial assistance. The Academy participates in federal student financial programs. The level of financial assistance depends on demonstrated need as well as funds available, so it is wise to begin the process early. In fact, the Academy encourages the student to meet with the Financial Services staff even before enrollment is confirmed in order to assist the student in working out a plan to meet the cost of education.

Financial aid awards are based on a detailed analysis of need, taking into account many factors in addition to annual income. Also considered are total assets, debts, family size, marital status, additional family members in college, and recent changes in the family's financial status. In order to determine a student's eligibility, the student must complete the Free Application for Federal Student Aid (FAFSA) and the Academy's Application and Information Form and submit them to the Financial Services Office. Financial Services personnel are available to assist students and parents in the completion of the forms and to answer questions on the application process.

Faculty

The American Academy of Art is a professional community of artists, teachers, designers, support staff, administrators, and undergraduate and graduate students. The faculty brings professional work experience in art or a related field to their roles as mentors and educators; most are working professional artists. The majority of the 30 faculty members have master's degrees, and 90 percent of them work full time at the Academy. The student-faculty ratio is 15:1.

Admission Requirements

Applicants must be high school graduates. The Academy requires two rounds of interviews for all prospective applicants.

Application and Information

Prospective applicants must complete an application, which can be found on the Academy's Web site listed below, and submit the application along with a check or money order for $25. They must also demonstrate an advanced level of competence in studio arts through a portfolio review. The portfolio must demonstrate proficiency in the intended area of study. Two letters of recommendation are required. International students must demonstrate English proficiency by way of a minimum TOEFL score of 500 (paper-based test) or 173 (computer-based test).

For further information, please contact:

Stuart Rosenbloom
Admissions Office
The American Academy Of Art
332 South Michigan Avenue, Suite 300
Chicago, Illinois 60604-4302
Telephone: 312-461-0600
E-mail: stuartrnet@comcast.net
World Wide Web: http://www.aaart.edu

AMERICAN INTERCONTINENTAL UNIVERSITY

ATLANTA, GEORGIA; DUBAI, UNITED ARAB EMIRATES; FORT LAUDERDALE, FLORIDA; LONDON, ENGLAND; AND LOS ANGELES, CALIFORNIA

The University

American InterContinental University (AIU), part of the University Division of Career Education Corporation, is a coeducational, nondenominational institution with a reputation of academic excellence that offers global career-oriented education to a diverse student body. The University was established in 1970 and has since grown to an international network of six campuses. This international campus network gives students the opportunity to transfer between the campuses and provides them with the intercontinental experience that is important for their personal development and professional achievement.

American InterContinental University is accredited by the Commission on Colleges of the Southern Association of Colleges and Schools (SACS). The baccalaureate programs in interior design at the Atlanta and Los Angeles campuses are accredited by the Foundation for Interior Design Education Research (FIDER), and the advertising program at the Dubai campus is accredited by the International Advertising Association (IAA). AIU Online's degree-granting authority is authorized by the state of Georgia.

The University is recognized worldwide as a top educator in business administration (management and marketing), international business, fashion design and marketing, interior design, visual communication (graphic design, illustration, and photography), media production, and information technology. The student body is composed of students from all fifty states and more than 100 countries. Associate, bachelor's, and master's degrees are conferred by the University.

AIU offers comprehensive career counseling to students. The University has an active placement office that seeks to provide students with part-time employment opportunities during their studies at the University, as well as placement services to assist students who have graduated.

At the campuses in Atlanta (Buckhead), Los Angeles, London, and Dubai, students have the option of residing in modern, attractively furnished apartments with a variety of amenities, which may include swimming pools, tennis courts, and a clubhouse on-site. Living in college housing is encouraged, although not required, for nonresident students.

In addition to its undergraduate programs, AIU offers Master of Business Administration (M.B.A.) and Master of Information Technology (M.I.T.) degree programs.

Locations

AIU's six campuses are in some of the most dynamic cities in the world—Atlanta (Dunwoody and Buckhead), Dubai, Fort Lauderdale, London, and Los Angeles.

Atlanta is the home of many major corporations and is rapidly increasing its international profile as a result of the 1996 Summer Olympic Games and the success of its professional sporting teams. The Atlanta–Buckhead campus is located on Peachtree Road, only minutes from a number of the city's internationally recognized institutions. The Dunwoody campus is located in the growing business community just north of Atlanta.

The Los Angeles campus is located close to Marina del Rey. It is convenient to metropolitan Los Angelés attractions and destinations, including the city's downtown area and the beaches.

The metropolitan area of Miami-Fort Lauderdale has long been noted for its international flavor, global business activities, and tourism. The campus is located in the community of Plantation.

London is one of the world's most important capital cities. The attractive urban campus provides quick and easy access to places such as Buckingham Palace, Piccadilly Circus, and the West End, London's central theater district.

On the shores of the Arabian Gulf, Dubai is a leading center for business and tourism in the Middle East. Students experience a fascinating blend of modern amenities and colorful traditions. The campus is located in Jameira near beautiful beach and park facilities and is only a short drive from the city's thriving business center.

Majors and Degrees

AIU offers undergraduate associate and bachelor's degree programs in business administration (A.A. and B.B.A.) at all campuses. Associate and bachelor's degree programs in the fine arts (A.A. and B.F.A.) are offered in fashion design, fashion marketing, and interior design at the Atlanta-Buckhead, Los Angeles, London, and Dubai campuses; in media production at the Atlanta-Buckhead and London campuses; and in visual communication at all campuses. A bachelor's degree program in information technology (B.I.T.) is offered at the Atlanta-Dunwoody, Los Angeles, Ft. Lauderdale, and Dubai campuses. Atlanta-Buckhead also offers a bachelor's degree in criminal justice.

AIU's virtual campus, AIU Online, offers associate and bachelor's degrees in business, information technology, design, and education. AIU Online's interactive Web-based virtual campus and distance education services center located just outside Chicago offer students complete support throughout their degree program of study from admissions services, academic affairs, student affairs, financial services, career services, and technical support services. Online students can check the status of their account final grades, degree plan, and other information 24 hours a day through a secured Web site (http://www.aiuonline.edu).

Academic Programs

The academic year is divided into four to seven academic quarters of varying lengths. The University operates on a twelve-month scheduling plan, traditional quarters, and minisessions. Depending on the campus, two complete academic quarters are offered during the summer months (June 13 through September). Students can attend one or both summer quarters and earn full credit for an academic quarter in each summer session. In addition, the London campus offers two 4-week summer sessions during June and July that focus on European business, culture, and the arts as a part of the Study Abroad Program and regular academic schedule.

To qualify for the associate degree, a student must complete 100–130 credit hours with a cumulative grade point average of 2.0 or higher. To qualify for the bachelor's degree, a student must complete 190–200 credit hours with a cumulative grade point average of 2.0 or higher. For both degree programs, a minimum of the four final terms must be in residence at the University.

The normal academic load in the Undergraduate Program is 15 credit hours per quarter. Certain programs (B.I.T. and B.B.A. at the Atlanta–Dunwoody, Fort Lauderdale, and Los Angeles campuses) are accelerated, allowing qualified students to complete their degrees in less time than through traditional institutions.

Off-Campus Programs

AIU offers students the opportunity to participate in a number of University-sponsored internship programs. Eligible students who have completed 100 credit hours and have maintained a minimum overall GPA of 2.5 (3.0 for business majors) may, through practical experience, earn up to 20 credit hours toward their degree in an approved off-campus program. In the past, students have participated in internship programs at companies such as Brunschwig & Fils, Laura Ashley, Paramount Studios, and Merrill Lynch.

Students may also travel on University-sponsored study tours, earning up to 5 academic credit hours toward their degrees. They are required to complete sketchbooks, journals, and projects in order to receive credit. In the past, study tours have included Barcelona,

China, Florence, Hong Kong, Milan, New York, and Paris. The program is available through the Atlanta–Buckhead, Dubai, London, and Los Angeles campuses.

Academic Facilities

AIU's campuses in London, Atlanta–Buckhead, and Dubai maintain modern, well-planned, and well-equipped facilities. Each classroom provides a comfortable and aesthetically pleasing environment to facilitate students' educational growth. Fashion design and interior design studios contain sophisticated industry equipment. The visual communication facilities include Macintosh and PC labs and professionally equipped darkroom and photographic studios as well as classrooms with modern drafting tables and other studio supplies. Video production studios house state-of-the-art sound and video equipment. Collectively, the campus learning resource centers (libraries) include more than 80,000 volumes that support the major programs of study. Print and electronic subscriptions to international periodicals, and a varied collection of videotapes, DVDs, CDs, and slides are available. Students are provided electronic access to the card catalog, software applications, subject-specific databases, and the Internet. Special collections are maintained for the design academic programs including selections of carpet, wallpaper, fabric, paint and tile samples, and fashion forecasters.

The Atlanta–Dunwoody, Fort Lauderdale, and Los Angeles campuses feature more than 1,000 ports to deliver data, voice, and video throughout the building. Seats in classrooms and team rooms are wired, allowing students to connect their laptop computers to the Internet and AIU's network. Smaller team rooms provide space for collaborative learning, allowing students to work together to solve real business problems. Each campus houses a multimedia and learning resource center, including a library complete with the latest technology and media equipment.

The London campus is composed of eight buildings that house lecture rooms, Mac and PC computer labs, and art, design, photography, and video production studios. The Interior Design Resource Center contains a comprehensive collection of materials and catalogs of the interior design industry.

The new and expanded Dubai campus provides students with exceptional academic resources and state-of-the-art facilities, such as design labs, art studios, Mac and PC labs, a photographic studio and darkroom, an interior design resource room, a student union with food service, a campus bookstore, and the largest English library in the United Arab Emirates.

Costs

AIU's undergraduate tuition is priced between the tuition levels of nonprofit private universities and the comparatively lower tuition charged to resident students at public universities. The tuition is comparable to the tuition of public universities for nonresident and international students.

For traditional Associate of Arts and Bachelor of Fine Arts programs (interior design, fashion design, fashion marketing, media production, visual communication, business administration, and criminal justice) at the Atlanta-Buckhead, Los Angeles, and London campuses, the tuition ranges from $4935 to $5310 per full-time academic term (15 credits), or $14,805 to $15,930 for the full academic year, depending on campus location.

The total program cost at campuses offering accelerated programs (Atlanta-Dunwoody, Ft. Lauderdale, and Los Angeles) ranges from $39,630 to $65,950 for full-time enrollment.

Financial Aid

American InterContinental University offers a variety of scholarships, grants, loans, and part-time employment to help defray the cost of education. University-administered federal funding includes Federal Supplemental Educational Opportunity Grants and Federal Work-Study Program awards. Additional federal funding includes Federal Pell Grants, Federal Subsidized and Unsubsidized Stafford Student Loans, and Federal PLUS loans. University-administered state funding includes the HOPE scholarship (for Georgia residents only) and Cal Grants (for California residents only). The University also directly administers its own scholarship programs; for scholarship information, students should contact the individual campuses. The University also holds an annual high school/secondary school scholarship competition. Other sources of aid available to students may include vocational rehabilitation funds, Social Security and veterans' benefits, and private scholarships. For further information on financial aid, students should contact the Student Financial Aid Office on any campus.

Faculty

The faculty at the University includes qualified educators and distinguished leaders in their fields, such as award-winning interior and fashion designers, exhibiting artists and photographers, authors, illustrators, lawyers, accountants, business professionals, and information technology professionals.

Student Government

Students have a voice in the governance of the campuses through participation in the Student Government Association (SGA). SGA officers are elected by and represent the student body.

Admission Requirements

AIU welcomes candidates for admission who can profit from its programs and who present strong evidence of purpose and qualities of good character. The prospective student must have graduated from high school, must be pursuing high school graduation, or must have earned an equivalency diploma.

Application and Information

Candidates must complete and submit an application for admission, an official transcript of their high school record to date or proof of high school graduation, and two letters of recommendation supporting the applicant's suitability for attending the University. For additional information, students should contact:

Director of Admissions
American InterContinental University
6600 Peachtree-Dunwoody Road
500 Embassy Row
Atlanta, Georgia 30328
Telephone: 800-353-1740 (toll-free)
World Wide Web: http://www.aiudunwoody.com

American InterContinental University, Buckhead Campus
3330 Peachtree Road, NE
Atlanta, Georgia 30326-1016
Telephone: 888-999-4248 (toll-free)
Fax: 404-965-5701
World Wide Web: http://www.aiubuckhead.com

American InterContinental University
110 Marylebone High Street
London W1U 4RY
England
Telephone: 44-207-467-5600
Fax: 44-207-486-0642
World Wide Web: http://www.aiulondon.com

American InterContinental University
12655 West Jefferson Boulevard
Los Angeles, California 90066
Telephone: 310-302-2000
888-248-7390 (toll-free)
Fax: 310-302-2001
World Wide Web: http://www.aiula.com

American InterContinental University
Suite 1000
8151 West Peters Road
Plantation, Florida 33324
Telephone: 954-835-0939
888-248-3818 (toll-free)
Fax: 954-835-1020
World Wide Web: http://www.aiufl.edu

American University in Dubai
P.O. Box 28282
Dubai, United Arab Emirates
Telephone: 971-4-399-9000
Fax: 971-4-399-8899
World Wide Web: http://www.aud.edu
World Wide Web: http://www.aiuniv.edu (University-wide)

AMERICAN INTERNATIONAL COLLEGE

SPRINGFIELD, MASSACHUSETTS

The College

American International College opened in 1885. Today, the College has a wide geographic representation, and the 1,200 students come from twenty-eight states and forty-eight countries; the ratio of men to women is even. The majority are graduates of public high schools. About 48 percent are commuting students; all others live in the five residence halls. Students participate in a wide variety of activities that reflect their interests, ranging from volunteer work in the surrounding community to singing in the Chorale to sports. Varsity athletics include men's baseball, basketball, football, golf, hockey, lacrosse, soccer, tennis, and wrestling and women's basketball, field hockey, lacrosse, soccer, softball, tennis, and volleyball. There are forty separate student clubs and organizations.

Location

American International College is located in Springfield, Massachusetts, a city of 165,000 people, which is the seat of Hampden County and the metropolitan center for half a million people. Springfield is also the transportation center of western New England, easily reached by automobile on Interstate 91 and the Massachusetts Turnpike, by rail via major north-south and east-west lines, and by plane via Bradley International Airport. There are many cultural offerings in the area, including the Springfield Symphony, Civic Center, and City Stage Theatre Company.

Majors and Degrees

The Bachelor of Arts degree is offered in the School of Arts and Sciences. Students may select majors in the areas of biology, chemistry, communications, economics, English, history, interdepartmental science, liberal studies, mathematics, medical technology, philosophy, political science, public administration, sociology, and Spanish. Preprofessional programs in dentistry, law, medicine, optometry, physical therapy, podiatry, and veterinary science are also available. Minors are available in these disciplines as well as in the fields of journalism and athletic coaching.

The School of Business Administration awards the degree of Bachelor of Science in Business Administration. Majors include accounting, computer science, economics, entrepreneurship, finance, general business, hospitality management, human resource management, information systems, international business, management, marketing, marketing communications, and sports management.

The School of Psychology and Education offers the Bachelor of Arts degree with a major in psychology. The Bachelor of Science degree is offered in criminal justice, early childhood education, elementary education, human services, secondary education, and special education. Due to changing teacher certification requirements, students seeking certification must also complete the requirements of a second major from the School of Arts and Sciences.

The School of Health Sciences offers majors in nursing, occupational therapy, and physical therapy.

The nursing program awards a Bachelor of Science in Nursing degree through a four-year undergraduate program as well as through an upper-division program for registered nurses. The Division of Nursing is accredited by the National League for Nursing Accrediting Commission.

The occupational therapy program offers an accredited program leading to a combined Bachelor of Science in occupational science/Master of Science in Occupational Therapy (B.S./M.S.O.T.) degree.

The physical therapy program offers an accredited 5½-year program leading to a master's degree in physical therapy.

Academic Programs

General requirements are virtually the same for all majors. One year of Freshman Composition is required, as well as four semesters of physical education. Other general education requirements include 12 semester hours in the social sciences, 3 in literature, 6 in humanities, 8 in a laboratory science, 3 in a quantitative course, and one computer-oriented course. To graduate, students are required to complete a minimum total of 120 hours of academic credit with a C average or better.

A special four-year program, the Supportive Service Program, assists students with learning disabilities to function in a regular college curriculum.

Off-Campus Programs

Opportunities for international study are available. Individually designed courses of study can be arranged at international universities for a summer, a single semester, or a full year of residence. It is possible to transfer up to one full year of credit for such study.

Qualified students are allowed to participate in off-campus internships under the supervision and guidance of experienced personnel. The type of work and the amount of supervision a student receives are left to the discretion of the faculty member to whom the student is assigned. This program is designed to provide all students with an opportunity to gain practical experience in their field of study and is required of the students in the business disciplines and in communications, criminal justice, education, human services, nursing, and physical therapy.

Academic Facilities

James J. Shea Sr. Memorial Library (1980) houses 125,000 volumes, 519 current periodicals, 14,800 bound periodicals, 12,759 units of microfilm, and 3,423 sound recordings and tapes. An area for group study, a media center, and individual study carrels are provided for students.

Amaron Hall is the primary facility for liberal arts and business classrooms. It also houses a microcomputer laboratory and the computer center, which consists of a cluster of Digital VAXstations, Digital VT 320 terminals, and AT-class personal computers on an Ethernet network. Old Science and the newer Breck Hall of Science buildings provide up-to-date classrooms and laboratories for science, mathematics, preprofessional studies, and nursing. The Curtis Blake Child Development Center serves as a diagnostic center for children with learning difficulties and offers graduate-level courses in special education. The center also provides services for specially selected college-age students with learning disabilities.

Health Science Center is the academic center for the physical therapy, occupational therapy, and nursing programs. The 30,000-square-foot facility includes an amphitheater, several laboratories, classrooms, and faculty and administrative offices.

Costs

The comprehensive 2004–05 fee for tuition, room, board, and miscellaneous expenses is approximately $26,300. Books and supplies are approximately $500. Personal expenses average $1000 per year.

Financial Aid

American International College provides aid from institutional and external sources to assist 85 percent of the student body. The average financial aid package for the 2003–04 school year was $17,820. Scholarships and loans are available to those who demonstrate financial need and maintain an acceptable record of academic work and campus citizenship. Campus employment is available, and about 55 percent of the students earn a portion of their expenses. The College participates in the Federal Perkins Loan, Federal Supplemental Educational Opportunity Grant, Federal Pell Grant, and Federal Work-Study programs. Academic scholarships are available for eligible freshmen, and additional College grants are awarded on a need basis. Applications for scholarships and loans should be made to the Office of Financial Aid by April 15 for the following academic year, but they are accepted as long as funds are available. Applications for aid from early decision plan applicants must be received by October 15. Both the Free Application for Federal Student Aid (FAFSA) and the American International College financial aid form are required. Students should write to the Director of Financial Aid for additional information about financial aid or to the Admissions Office for information about academic scholarships.

Faculty

The emphasis of the faculty is on teaching. The full-time faculty members number 86, of whom 50 have doctorates. All teach freshman courses, and all faculty members, including department chairmen, serve as advisers to undergraduate students. The faculty-student ratio is 1:12.

Student Government

All students are members of the Student Government Association, and the elected officers play an important role in the administration of the College. Serious disciplinary problems are adjudicated by the various levels of the Student Judicial System, as well as by the Academic Dean and the Director of Student Affairs. In addition, students are largely responsible for social activities at the College.

Admission Requirements

Students applying for admission must be graduates of an approved secondary school and must have successfully completed 16 units of study or show evidence of equivalent education. Among subjects that should be a part of a student's secondary program are English (4 units) and a selection from mathematics, science, social studies, and foreign languages. Applicants should take the SAT I. The Committee on Admission also considers the applicant's class rank and a letter of recommendation in making its decision. Attention is given to the total course program and school attended by each applicant. American International College has no geographic or other quotas. Transfer applications are welcomed.

An interview at the College is recommended but not required of applicants to most of the programs; however, an on-campus interview is required of applicants to the Supportive Service Program. Guides offer campus tours to all guests; class attendance or an overnight stay may be arranged through the Admissions Office. Admission staff members also visit schools throughout the Northeast each year, and candidates who are unable to visit the campus are urged to meet with staff members or talk with alumni in their home area.

Application and Information

A completed application includes a transcript of the candidate's school work, scores on the SAT I, and a letter of recommendation. Everything should be sent to the address given below; a catalog or other information booklets may be requested from the same office. Decision letters are sent on a rolling basis.

The Dean of Admissions is glad to advise prospective students who wish to write or telephone for additional information.

Dean of Admissions
American International College
1000 State Street
Springfield, Massachusetts 01109
Telephone: 413-205-3201
800-242-3142 (toll-free)
E-mail: pmiller@acad.aic.edu
World Wide Web: http://www.aic.edu

Sokolowski Tower, a hub of student activity.

AMERICAN UNIVERSITY
WASHINGTON, D.C.

The University

American University (AU) is for academically distinctive and intensely engaged students who want to turn ideas into action and action into service. AU's rigorous curriculum enables students to combine serious theoretical study with meaningful real-world learning experiences.

American's unique core curriculum and Honors Program, its Washington, D.C., location, and its emphasis on the practical application of knowledge prepare students to be major contributors in their fields. Many AU students choose to study more than one field or design their own interdisciplinary major in order to prepare for their professional futures. For example, premed students can major in international studies in order to prepare for a career in international health. The University understands that tomorrow's careers require an understanding of a wide variety of fields, and it encourages students to transcend the traditional boundaries of academic disciplines.

AU's more than 5,000 undergraduates are a microcosm of the world's diversity. From across the United States and from more than 140 countries, they share a desire to shape tomorrow's world. AU actively promotes international understanding, and this is reflected in its curricula offerings, faculty research, and the regular presence of world leaders on campus.

The University's six smoke-free residence halls are modern and offer a choice of single-sex or coed floors and special interest options, such as the Honors Program floor. Sixty-five percent of the students live on campus. Dining options include a main campus dining facility as well as an on-campus Subway, McDonald's, Jamba Juice, Auntie Anne's Pretzels, and Chick-fil-A. Nonresidential fraternities and sororities, more than 140 students-run organizations, NCAA I athletics, and intramural and club sports offer students a range of choices.

Location

At the top of Embassy Row in northwest Washington, D.C., American University's traditional campus is an 84-acre home base. Students have easy access to the University shuttle, the subway, city buses, and taxis to all the incomparable resources of the nation's capital. AU is convenient to Ronald Reagan Washington National Airport, Dulles International Airport, and Baltimore Washington International Airport and to Union Station and interstate highways.

Majors and Degrees

The College of Arts and Sciences awards B.A., B.F.A., and B.S. degrees in the arts, education, humanities, sciences, and social sciences through its twenty academic units. Prelaw and premedical programs are also available.

The School of International Service offers the B.A. in international studies and in language and area studies.

The School of Public Affairs offers the B.A. degree in justice, law and society, and political science. The school also offers CLEG, a unique interdisciplinary program that combines courses in communication, law, economics, and government.

The School of Communication is a professional school that offers training in broadcast journalism, communication studies, foreign language and communication media, print journalism, public communication, and visual media.

The Kogod School of Business offers the the Bachelor of Science in Business Administration (B.S.B.A.) with specializations in accounting, economics, enterprise management, finance, human resource management, international business, international finance, international management, international marketing, management of information technology, marketing, and fields related to international service, including communications, development, economic policy, and regional area studies.

Academic Programs

In the General Education Program, AU's core curriculum, students choose ten classes from more than 150 specially designed courses. Two classes must be taken in each of the five following areas: social institutions and behavior, traditions that shape the Western world, global and multicultural perspectives, the creative arts, and the natural sciences. The first class in each area serves as the foundation course and must be followed by a second, more specialized course in an approved sequence.

These innovative courses are a vital part of students' intellectual and professional preparation: they improve writing and critical thinking skills; offer new and balanced scholarship on ethical principles, gender, race, class, and culture; and incorporate quantitative and computing skills as appropriate for that field. In addition, all students are required to complete two courses in English composition and one in college-level mathematics. Combined bachelor's/master's degree programs are available in most fields.

The educational goals of the College of Arts and Sciences include teaching students to examine Western and non-Western cultures, appreciate scientific inquiry, master written and oral expression, develop the ability to analyze and synthesize information, and build an understanding of the moral and ethical dimensions that underlie decision making. Working with faculty members and professional academic counselors, students select internships and develop courses of study in more than forty majors in the arts, education, humanities, mathematics, performing arts, sciences, and social sciences. The strong liberal arts curriculum of the college is enhanced by the educational, social, cultural, artistic, and scientific resources of Washington, D.C. The individual strengths of each department are heightened by students' ability to cross the lines between disciplines—expanding their educational horizons while acquiring the skills and knowledge required to be successful in graduate-level study or in their chosen careers.

American's School of International Service is the largest of its kind in the United States and is able to offer serious students a breadth of study in international relations. The international studies program begins with foundation courses and core field courses to provide students with the tools to explore specific areas of study in greater depth. Students select an area specialization from among Africa, the Americas, Asia, Europe, the Middle East, or Russia and Central Eurasia, and a functional field of concentration in business, comparative and international race relations, international politics, U.S. foreign policy, Islamic studies, global environmental politics, international communication, international development, international economic policy, or peace and conflict resolution. The language and area studies major provides a strong foundation in language and culture courses. Students choose one of four areas: French/West Europe, German/West Europe, Spanish/Latin America, or Russian Area Studies.

Students in the School of Public Affairs are engaged in learning about local, national, and international politics; public institutions; public policy; crime; justice; and law. These areas frame a comprehensive program that incorporates classroom learning, individualized research projects, relevant field studies, and professional training. Washington's facilities for scholarly research in public affairs and resources for work opportunities and personal enrichment are limitless. Students may participate in the school's leadership program, summer programs, and the Women and Politics, Public Affairs and Advocacy, or Campaign Management Institutes.

The goal of the School of Communication is to develop professionally trained communicators who are equipped intellectually and ethically to convey the issues of contemporary society. The curriculum benefits from the environment of Washington, D.C., one of the major communications centers of the world. The school emphasizes involving students with Washington's communicators and communication facilities. A strong liberal arts curriculum is required to ensure students' abilities to interpret the world around them.

The Kogod School of Business provides students with a solid foundation in business and preparation to be responsible citizens and assume leadership roles in a global business economy. Kogod is entrepreneurial, relevant to today's markets, and flexible in its strategies. The school offers a business curriculum derived from a multifunctional view of business that emphasizes critical skills and topics such as communication, e-commerce, teamwork, technology, ethics, and global business. Nearly every major U.S. corporation and many multinational firms have a presence in the Washington, D.C., area, providing Kogod students with limitless opportunities to enhance classroom learning through internship experiences.

Off-Campus Programs

The University's Career Center provides more than 500 students each year with internship experience in jobs related to their educational and career goals. Such professional training may be with arts organizations, museums, private business, industry, community and social service organizations, or local, state, or federal governments. Full-time faculty members from nearly all University departments serve as program coordinators.

American University administers its own exciting study-abroad program, called the AU Abroad Program. Students can study at more than thirty sites, including Andes to the Rainforests, Australia/New Zealand, Beijing, Berlin, Brussels, Buenos Aires, Copenhagen, Jerusalem, London, Italy (art), Madrid, Madrid and the Mediterranean, Moscow, Paris, Prague, Rome, Santiago, Southern Africa, and United Arab Emirates. Built into most of these study programs are opportunities to tour the country, meet and talk with national leaders and academicians, and participate in internships and homestays.

Academic Facilities

The University's facilities include a state-of-the-art language resource center, multimedia design and development labs, and science laboratories; well-equipped buildings for art, chemistry, and performing arts; and a sports center with indoor and outdoor tracks, soccer and intramural fields, an Olympic-size pool, and a state-of-the-art fitness center. There are fourteen classroom buildings, a 50,000-watt broadcast center, and an interdenominational religious center. The library is a member of the OCLC network, which gives students online access to 2,000 other member libraries. Each student receives an "EagleNet" user account, an "american.edu" e-mail address, and a personal Web page, if desired. Computing resources are delivered by a fiber-optic network with connections throughout campus, including all residence hall rooms, as well as through wireless access for laptops, PDAs, and phone/PDA hybrids.

Costs

Undergraduate tuition and fees for the 2004–05 academic year are $25,920. Room and board costs average $10,170 for the year. AU anticipates a 5 percent increase in tuition and fees for 2005–06. There are several installment payment plans.

Financial Aid

AU recognizes academic achievement and potential and offers merit scholarships to approximately 20 percent of each freshman class. These scholarships are not based upon financial need, and no separate application forms are required. The scholarships include awards of up to full tuition. Scholarships are also available for transfer students. The University also supports a multimillion-dollar financial assistance program. Families must apply by February 15 for priority consideration.

Faculty

The faculty represents a rich mix of academic and professional training. Its 487 full-time members are nationally and internationally recognized in their fields, and 96 percent have the highest degree in their field. An important part of American's academic program is the integration of practicing professionals into the faculty. The talent pool available in Washington, D.C., is enormous. Students have the opportunity to learn from professionals from such organizations as the World Bank, Discovery Communications, Associated Press, the National Endowment for the Arts, the John F. Kennedy Center for the Performing Arts, America Online, the National Aeronautics and Space Administration, and other private industries. These faculty members bring a real-world perspective to the classroom experience. The student-faculty ratio is 14:1.

Student Government

The Student Confederation is the representative student government for all full-time undergraduates. There are also school and college councils.

Admission Requirements

Admission to AU is selective and competitive. The University seeks accomplished, well-prepared students. Each freshman applicant is reviewed individually, with careful consideration given to the high school record, SAT I or ACT scores, the essay, extracurricular activities, and letters of recommendation. Special emphasis is given to leadership qualities, creative endeavors, volunteerism, and entrepreneurship. The middle 50 percent of admitted students have grade point averages between 3.1 and 3.7 (on a 4.0 scale) and combined SAT I scores between 1160 and 1320 or ACT scores between 25 and 29. Approximately 20 National Merit Finalists and Semifinalists enroll each year. Transfer applicants are welcome. A minimum GPA of 2.5 (on a 4.0 scale) on all university-level work completed is necessary to be considered competitive for admission. Transfer students should visit the University's Web site (http://aufax.american.edu/ST/registrar/articulations/) for more information.

Application and Information

The deadline for early decision freshmen is November 15, and notification is made by December 31. The regular decision deadline is January 15. While most freshmen are admitted for the fall semester, students may also apply for summer or spring semester entry. Transfer applicants apply for all three terms. Students should call or visit the Web site at the address listed below for application dates and requirements.

Undergraduate Admissions
American University
4400 Massachusetts Avenue, NW
Washington, D.C. 20016-8001
Telephone: 202-885-6000
Fax: 202-885-1025
E-mail: afa@american.edu
World Wide Web: http://admissions.american.edu

THE AMERICAN UNIVERSITY OF ROME

ROME, ITALY

The University

The American University of Rome is the oldest independent, four-year, degree-granting American university in Rome, Italy. The University fortifies students with knowledge and ideas through the liberal arts and professional disciplines in business administration, communication, international relations, and Italian studies. It offers cinema, opera courses, architecture, and archaeology. The American University of Rome prepares students for a global community by encouraging civil discussion and respectful dialogue in the classroom, public forums, and social activities. The University also enables students to participate in a semester or yearlong learning and living experience in Italy to enrich their knowledge and appreciation of ancient, past, and modern cultures.

Approximately half of the students are in the degree program and half are in the study-abroad program. The majority of the students are American. Approximately 10–15 percent are Italian and 20 percent are other nationalities. The typical student is between 18 and 23 years of age. The ratio of men to women is 35:65.

The University makes arrangements through designated local agents for students to rent apartments in the vicinity of the University. Apartments are quadruple or quintuple occupancy. The University also makes housing arrangements with a residence. Students may also make their own housing arrangements. Those who choose to work with University-designated agents receive the benefits of a housing agreement and are subject to regulations governing conduct in the apartments and are required to sign a pledge to this effect.

The American University of Rome is accredited by the Accrediting Council for Independent Colleges and Schools (ACICS) to award associate and bachelor's degrees. The ACICS is listed as a nationally recognized accrediting agency by the United States Department of Education.

Location

The University sits on the top of Rome's highest hill, the Janiculum, just a few minutes' walk from a wealth of educational and cultural resources in Rome's historic center. A lovely four-story villa contains offices, student lounges, classrooms, and studios for art, design, and architecture. Adjacent to the villa is a newly renovated building that houses the library, computer laboratories, faculty offices, and classrooms. With its own garden of historic Roman pines, the campus is located in proximity to the major parks of Villa Sciarra and Villa Pamphili and the renowned American Academy of Rome. The neighborhood offers a full range of amenities, including restaurants, shops, cafés, and an outdoor market. Located just off the ancient Via Aurelia, the University is easily reached by car and is connected to the center of Rome by several bus lines.

Majors and Degrees

The American University of Rome offers a strong undergraduate curriculum with an international perspective. The Associate of Arts degree is offered in business administration and liberal arts. The Bachelor of Arts degree is awarded in communications, Italian studies, international relations, and interdisciplinary studies. A Bachelor of Science degree is awarded in business administration.

Academic Program

All new and transfer students applying directly to the American University of Rome must take the City University of New York (CUNY) proficiency test in reading, writing, and mathematics, given at the beginning of each semester. These scores are used for English and mathematics placement.

All students are required to satisfy general education requirements by completing courses in three major academic areas: humanities, social sciences, and mathematics/natural sciences. Some degree programs also require students to complete general education electives outside their major area of study. All degree students must complete 1 year of English composition and conversation, although this requirement may be waived if a student has achieved a high score in Advanced Placement English. During the freshman year, students are expected to be enrolled in either developmental English or English composition and reading.

A student normally takes five courses (15 semester hours) each semester. A student is considered a sophomore after having completed 30 hours of credit, a junior once he or she has completed 60 hours of credit and officially declares a major field of study or enrolls in a degree program, and a senior after having completed 90 hours of course work.

One semester credit hour equals, at a minimum, 15 classroom contact hours of lectures, 30 hours of laboratory, and 45 hours of practicum. Internships also carry 3 semester credits and require 135 hours of work experience.

Off-Campus Programs

Freshman and sophomore students in Rome are enrolled for the first 60 credits in the American University of Rome–College of Staten Island articulation program so students in Italy may embark on a course of study that leads to a degree offered in the United States by one of the City University of New York's most innovative and technologically advanced campuses. The college offers more than sixty different degree programs, from accounting and computer science to economics and psychology and many more. Students in the program may complete general education requirements in Rome and then spend a period of residence at the College of Staten Island to complete their degree.

Academic Facilities

The American University of Rome possesses a specialized library of course-related books and periodicals. The American University of Rome also provides electronic library services to its students and faculty. These holdings are supplemented by a number of sizeable libraries in the city that are available to all students, including the Library of the British Council, the Library of the Church of Santa Susanna, and Centro Studi Americani. The University library can access a central catalog of the Italian National Library System and also participates in interlibrary loan programs.

There are two computer laboratories on campus available to students at scheduled times. All computers are IBM compatible and have access to e-mail, the Internet, and network printers. One laboratory is located in the library and is devoted principally to student research and term paper requirements. The other is open to student library research. A multimedia projector and laptop computer are available for classroom presentations using computer images and the Internet.

In addition to overhead and slide projectors, an extensive slide collection, and various stereo systems, the American University of Rome possesses tri-system videotape televisions for projecting films for cinema classes and other purposes. The videotape collection includes films that are essential to courses in Italian cinema and Italian opera as well as general cultural programs. Students also have access to a television linked to a satellite system.

Costs

The comprehensive tuition fee at the American University of Rome for the current academic year for full-time undergraduates is $10,910. A nonrefundable tuition deposit of $250 is required from all new students, payable by the deadline indicated on the acceptance letter. The tuition deposit is deducted from the final tuition payment, prior to the commencement of the semester. Some courses require travel or attendance at cultural events as required by the course instructor. The cost of these events and travel are not included in tuition and must be borne by the student.

Financial Aid

The American University of Rome is authorized by the United States Department of Education to participate in Title IV student financial assistance programs. Students who qualify may participate in the Federal Family Education Loan (FFEL) program. Financial aid available through FFEL includes subsidized and unsubsidized Federal Stafford Student Loans and the Federal PLUS Program. The school code is 031025.

Faculty

The American University of Rome has an international, culturally diverse faculty. Nearly 60 percent of the faculty members have received doctoral degrees and all professors either work professionally in their field or are active in scholarly research. The majority are bilingual and all faculty members act as teachers as well as advisers. The University also invites visiting professors from other universities for short-term residencies.

Student Government

Students are encouraged to take an active role in the student government as a way of contributing to the continued growth and development of the University. Elected officers of the student government meet regularly with the University administration to discuss matters of administrative and academic relevance. They also take responsibility for directing a variety of student social activities, athletic tournaments, club activities, and cultural events. The student government maintains funds for these activities, and the student officers enjoy a wide degree of autonomy in managing these financial resources.

Admission Requirements

The fundamental requirement for admission is a high school diploma or its equivalent. Students with a certain number of O levels may be admitted as well as students who have earned an Italian maturité, French baccalauréat, German abitur, or any other lyceum-equivalent diploma. Applicants for admission from high schools are required to submit an official transcript (including proof of high school completion); the application form, accompanied by a nonrefundable application fee; a personal recommendation from the principal, a guidance counselor, professor, or teacher; SAT scores; and a 200–500-word personal statement in which the candidate indicates how a study experience in Rome will help further his or her career and life aims.

Students who have completed their high school studies with the equivalent of a 2.0 grade point average on a 4-point scale are considered. However, students with a lower level of academic performance may also be accepted if letters of recommendation, personal interviews, and SAT or other standard test scores indicate that the student has the aptitude required to pursue studies at the University. The SAT requirement may be waived for non-U.S. nationals and for applicants who attend high schools outside the United States. If accepted, these candidates are generally admitted as probationary students. Transfer students with an equivalent of 60 semester credit hours of university study may seek a waiver for SAT and high school transcript requirements. The American University of Rome SAT institutional code is 0262.

Application and Information

Applicants are notified of the admission decision four to six weeks after the application, supporting credentials, recommendation, and $55 application fee are received.

Prospective students are encouraged to visit the campus. An application for admission and further information may be obtained by contacting the American University of Rome at either its U.S. address or its Rome address.

The American University of Rome
Via Pietro Roselli, 4
00153 Rome, Italy
Telephone: 39-0658330919 (direct dial from U.S.)
Fax: 39-0658330992 (direct fax from U.S.)
E-mail: aurinfo@aur.edu

The American University of Rome
1025 Connecticut Avenue, Northwest, Suite 601
Washington, D.C. 20036
Telephone: 888-791-8327 (toll-free)
Fax: 202-296-9577
E-mail: aur.homeoffice@dc.aur.edu
World Wide Web: http://www.aur.edu

ANDERSON COLLEGE

ANDERSON, SOUTH CAROLINA

The College

Anderson College, founded in 1911, is a private, coeducational, four-year liberal arts college sponsored by the South Carolina Baptist Convention. The College offers a clearly Christian educational program whereby students are provided opportunities to develop intellectually, physically, spiritually, socially, and morally.

Anderson College enrolls approximately 1,600 students, 80 percent of whom attend full-time. In addition, about one half of the student population lives in campus housing. In the typical academic year, the College enrolls students from more than twenty states and fifteen or more countries. The student body consists primarily of traditional-age students and of students from upstate South Carolina; however, many are nontraditional-age students and come from other geographic areas. Campus housing is available to international students.

A comprehensive program of student activities is provided, including varsity and intramural athletics, Christian ministry opportunities, theater, clubs and organizations, student government, and student-sponsored social activities. Intercollegiate sports programs for men include baseball, basketball, cross-country, golf, soccer, tennis, track, and wrestling. Intercollegiate sports programs for women include basketball, cross-country, golf, soccer, softball, tennis, track, and volleyball. The College also offers club sports in equestrian and cheerleader/dance, which comes under the umbrella of athletics. Anderson College is a member of NCAA Division II and of the CVAC (Carolinas-Virginia) conference.

The central campus of the College, which includes a small wooded park, athletic facilities, and student housing, occupies a 32-acre tract in an attractive, quiet neighborhood in the city of Anderson. In addition to the central campus, some buildings and parking areas are located on adjacent land.

Location

The city of Anderson is located in the northwestern section of South Carolina, halfway between Atlanta, Georgia, and Charlotte, North Carolina. The city serves as a shopping hub for a large area of northwestern South Carolina and northeastern Georgia. Anderson is served by Interstate 85 and the Greenville/Spartanburg Airport.

Majors and Degrees

Anderson College offers the Bachelor of Arts degree with majors in art (general studio, graphic design, interior design, painting/drawing), Christian ministry, church music, communications (journalism, speech/theater, writing), English, history, human services, music, psychology, religion, and Spanish. The Bachelor of Science degree is awarded in biology, business (accounting, computer information services, finance/economics, human resource management, and management), cytotechnology, education (early childhood, elementary, secondary), mathematics, and physical education (kinesiology). A Bachelor of Music Education is also offered. There are three degrees that may be obtained through the adult accelerated program: a Bachelor of Business Administration, a Bachelor of Business Administration with a concentration in computer information systems, and a Bachelor of Human Services and Resources. Teacher certification is offered in art education (K–12), elementary/early childhood education (K–8); music education (K–12); physical education (K–12); special education, and secondary education (7–12) in biology, English, mathematics, social studies, and Spanish.

Academic Program

The College follows the semester calendar and offers two summer sessions. A minimum of 128 credit hours is required for the bachelor's degree.

In order to graduate from any degree program of the College, a student must complete a general education component and a major studies component and must satisfy competence requirements in reading, writing, mathematics, and speaking. The ethical dimension of life is emphasized in all programs. Students have the opportunity to participate in internship experiences, study-travel, and overseas study.

Academic Facilities

Anderson College's Callie Stringer Rainey Fine Arts Center provides the finest facility in upstate South Carolina for art, theatrical, musical, and community functions and houses chapel services and other campus events. The Watkins Teaching Center contains most of the classrooms, a computer laboratory, conference rooms, and faculty offices. Other academic facilities on campus include the 60,000-volume Johnston Memorial Library, Merritt Administration Building, Merritt Auditorium, and Vandiver Hall.

Costs

Charges for 2003–04 were $9350 per semester, including tuition, fees, room, and board. For commuting students, the cost was $6600 per semester for tuition and fees. Books and supplies cost approximately $500 per semester. Charges for international students are the same as for regular boarding students. Personal expenses for transportation, recreation, and miscellaneous needs vary with the individual student. Students may keep cars on campus; there is a $30 fee for a parking permit.

Financial Aid

It is the intent of Anderson College to provide financial assistance to all accepted students who, without such aid, would be unable to attend. More than 95 percent of the College's students receive an average award of $5000 per year, and there are different sources of financial aid available to qualified students. It is best to complete and mail all required forms as soon as possible, since most aid is awarded on a first-come, first-served basis for qualified applicants. The first award deadline is March 15. The Financial Aid Office awards aid regardless of race, creed, place of national origin, or ethnic group.

Faculty

A faculty of 94 full-time and part-time professors brings the student-faculty ratio to 16:1, allowing for small classes and easy accessibility to professors and instructors. Sixty-three percent of the College's faculty members have a Ph.D. or other equivalent terminal degree.

Student Government

The entire student body is represented in the Student Government Association by 3 elected officers who form the executive branch of the association. Senators from each class are also elected and help plan student activities for social and educational enrichment.

Admission Requirements

Anderson College seeks to admit those who show promise of academic and social success at the College. Each applicant's record is examined for evidence reflecting potential for intellectual and social maturity, strength of character, and seriousness of purpose. The major factors considered in admission include graduation from high school, high school grades in college-preparatory courses, high school curriculum, and SAT I or ACT scores. In addition, the College may choose to examine further any applicant by use of personal interviews or tests administered by the College.

TOEFL scores are required of international applicants. A score of 550 is recommended. The SAT I is not required of nonnative English-speaking students. An I-20 (student visa) can normally be issued within two weeks of receipt of all required admission materials.

Anderson College admits students without regard to race, age, creed, color, gender, physical handicap, or national or ethnic origin.

Application and Information

Qualified students are encouraged to apply as early as possible during their final year of high school. The Admissions Office processes applications on a rolling basis, which enables the College to notify a candidate of the admission decision within two weeks after all credentials have been received. Interested students are encouraged to visit the campus.

For further information and application materials, students should contact:

Director of Admissions
Anderson College
316 Boulevard
Anderson, South Carolina 29621
Telephone: 864-231-2030
800-542-3594 (toll-free)
Fax: 864-231-2033
World Wide Web: http://www.AC.edu

The Merritt Administration Building, built in 1912, is the centerpiece of Anderson College's 32-acre campus.

ANGELO STATE UNIVERSITY

SAN ANGELO, TEXAS

The University

Founded in 1928, Angelo State University (ASU) is recognized as one of the United States' most outstanding regional public universities. A proud member of the Texas State University System, ASU subscribes to a proven traditional approach of undergraduate education while encouraging modern instructional techniques in intimate classroom settings. One of the University's major goals is to provide a stimulating educational climate that offers students maximum opportunities for academic achievement and personal growth. To achieve this goal, ASU maintains a distinguished student body and a superb faculty. Of the approximately 6,000 students enrolled, 5,600 are undergraduates. This diverse student population is drawn from throughout Texas, thirty-nine other states, and twenty-three countries.

Location

The 268-acre campus of Angelo State University is in San Angelo, an attractive and progressive city of 100,000 in the heart of Texas at the gateway to the scenic hill country. The attractively landscaped campus is located near the downtown business district in one of the city's finest residential areas. The cultural and entertainment offerings of the campus are complemented by those of the community, including a symphony orchestra, art museums, popular concerts, and a host of special events. Three recreational lakes and lakefront areas are available in and around San Angelo, providing a wide variety of facilities for picnicking, swimming, fishing, and many water sports.

Majors and Degrees

Angelo State University provides forty-six undergraduate programs in forty-five disciplines leading to eight baccalaureate degrees and one associate degree.

The Bachelor of Arts degree is offered in art, communication, drama, English, French, German, government, government with criminal justice option, history, journalism, mathematics, music, psychology, sociology, and Spanish. Programs for teacher certification at the elementary level are available as interdisciplinary programs in fine arts, language arts, and social studies.

The Bachelor of Business Administration degree may be earned in accounting, business, business with international option, computer science, finance, finance with a financial planning option, finance with a real estate option, management, and marketing. The University's undergraduate and graduate business programs are accredited by the Association of Collegiate Business Schools and Programs. A five-year integrated undergraduate/graduate program in accounting is designed to fulfill state requirements for eligibility for the Certified Public Accountancy (CPA) examination.

The Bachelor of Music degree and the Bachelor of Fine Arts degree are offered in music.

The Bachelor of Science degree is offered in animal science, applied physics, biology, chemistry, computer science, kinesiology, mathematics, medical technology, physics, and psychology. Programs for teacher certification at the elementary level are available as interdisciplinary programs in early childhood, math/science, and special learning and development.

The University also offers a Bachelor of General Studies degree, Bachelor of Science in Nursing degree, and an Associate in Applied Science in Nursing degree.

In addition, students may pursue courses and advising designed to help them meet entrance requirements to various professional schools, including dentistry, engineering, law, medicine, occupational therapy, pharmacy, physical therapy, and veterinary medicine.

Academic Program

The academic requirements at ASU are designed to give the student a broad background in the liberal arts and to enhance that foundation with discipline-specific courses. Curricula are continually evaluated to ensure the best and most current educational experience possible. Baccalaureate-seeking students must file a degree plan prior to the first semester of their junior year or the completion of 70 semester hours. Faculty advisers monitor students' progress from the beginning of the academic program until completion.

Two-year and four-year aerospace studies programs for men and women are also available. Completion of these programs leads to a commission in the U.S. Air Force. ASU has one of the most highly decorated detachments and can offer tremendous scholarships.

The college year consists of a long session and a summer session. The long session is divided into fall and spring semesters, each approximately 16 weeks long. The summer session is divided into two 6-week terms.

Off-Campus Programs

The International Studies Program provides academic study and travel opportunities in Mexico and in European and Central American countries. These arrangements carry college credit. Other off-campus programs include professional internships in education, government, journalism, and public administration and cooperative education programs in nursing and medical technology offered in conjunction with numerous local medical centers.

ASU operates a 4,643-acre multiple-purpose agricultural production and wildlife management area called the Management, Instruction, and Research (MIR) Center. Located near O. C. Fisher Lake and San Angelo, the MIR Center is one of the most complete domestic livestock and range and wildlife management facilities in the Southwest.

Academic Facilities

Attractive and well-maintained academic buildings enable ASU students to study in some of the most pleasant and modern facilities to be found. Classrooms range from the intimacy of seminar-oriented size to a small number of lecture halls. Specialized and general research laboratories serve many of the University's programs, including the applied sciences, nursing, communication, journalism, kinesiology, education, business, and computer science, among others. The Porter Henderson Library is the focal point of academic life at ASU. Containing more than 1 million holdings in bound volumes, government documents, and microforms accessible by an online cataloging system, the Henderson Library ranks among the finest libraries in Texas. The West Texas Collection of archival material admirably meets the genealogical and historical interests of students and faculty members desiring to learn more about the distinct West Texas heritage.

There are seven computer labs on campus that are available to students. One of these labs is open 24 hours a day during the week. The 20:1 student-to-computer ratio is extremely low. A radio/television studio, modular and proscenium theaters, a planetarium, musical rehearsal and recital halls, art studios, recreational facilities, and a Language Learning Center provide ASU students with exceptional opportunities for learning and fun outside the classroom. An extensive network of student-accessible microcomputer laboratories further complements the academic mission of the computer-intensive campus.

Costs

In 2003–04, state residents registered for a normal course load of 15 semester hours (full-time study) paid $1768 per semester for required tuition and fees. Room and board averaged $2445 per semester, depending upon the meal plans and residence hall selected. Tuition and required fees for out-of-state students were $5308 per semester. Books and supplies are estimated to cost from $300 to $400 per semester.

Financial Aid

To assist students toward meeting their financial responsibilities, the Office of Student Financial Aid administers a wide variety of programs from funds provided by the federal government and the state of Texas, including funds from the Federal Work-Study, Federal Pell Grant, Federal Supplemental Educational Opportunity Grant, Federal Perkins Loan, Federal Family Education Loan, Texas Public Educational Grant, and State Student Incentive Grant programs. In addition, numerous scholarships are awarded annually through the financial aid office in recognition of academic achievement, outstanding leadership, and exceptional promise or potential.

One of the most distinctive features of the University is the Robert G. Carr and Nona K. Carr Academic Scholarship Program. One of the largest privately endowed academic scholarship programs in the nation, this program provides scholarships ranging in value from $2000 to $6000 annually. Approximately 1,000 students enrolled at Angelo State University receive these awards. To compete favorably for one of these renewable scholarships, a student must normally rank in the top 15 percent of his or her class and present a composite score of 25 or higher on the ACT Assessment or a combined math and verbal score of 1140 or higher on the SAT I.

Students interested in the University's Air Force ROTC program may also apply for scholarships awarded through the Air Force ROTC detachment. These awards are funded by an endowment established by the late Mr. and Mrs. Robert G. Carr. This unique program provides scholarships ranging in value from $500 to $1500 annually to qualified cadets enrolled in the University's ROTC program.

Faculty

Angelo State University retains a distinguished faculty. In terms of academic preparation, the faculty ranks near the top of all colleges and universities in the South. Approximately 60 percent of the faculty hold earned doctorates in their teaching field. Faculty members are selected with great care; the University seeks to obtain the services of individuals who are prominent scholars and dedicated teachers who will merit the confidence of the students. Faculty members are associated with many of the nation's leading research universities, conduct special assignments in numerous countries, have acquired professional experience with some of the nation's leading business firms, conduct extensive applied and theoretical research, and travel internationally.

Student Government

The Student Senate is the official representative organization of the Angelo State University student body. As the primary forum for student opinion, the Student Senate provides a mutually beneficial communication link between the student body and administrative officials.

Admission Requirements

High school graduates are admitted to Angelo State University on a competitive basis. Applicants from accredited U.S. high schools must meet one of the following requirements: (1) they must satisfactorily complete the Texas Scholars Program or the Texas advanced high school program; (2) they must rank in the top half of their senior class at the time of application or graduate in the top half of their graduating class; (3) they must present a minimum composite score of 23 on the ACT Assessment or a minimum combined verbal and math score of 1030 on the SAT I if ranked in the third quarter or of 30 or 1270 if ranked in the fourth quarter; or (4) they must have a 50 percent or greater probability of earning an overall C average (2.0 GPA) during the freshman year at the University as computed from their high school grades and ACT or SAT I scores. Students who do not qualify for regular admission may qualify for provisional admission. Transfer students who have completed 18 or more hours of college-level work will be admitted providing they have maintained at least a 2.0 cumulative GPA. Students with less than 18 college-level hours must also meet the criteria established for high school students. The University welcomes applications from international students, who are considered on the basis of their secondary school record, their ACT or SAT I scores, and their Test of English as a Foreign Language (TOEFL) scores (550 minimum).

Application and Information

High school applicants are required to submit an application for admission, results of the ACT or SAT I, appropriate academic transcripts, and a $20 application fee. Requests for information and admission application forms should be made to:

Office of Admissions
Angelo State University
ASU Station #11014
San Angelo, Texas 76909-1014
Telephone: 325-942-2041
800-946-8627 (toll-free)
World Wide Web: http://www.angelo.edu

The Angelo State University Robert and Nona Carr Education–Fine Arts Building.

ANNA MARIA COLLEGE

PAXTON, MASSACHUSETTS

The College

Anna Maria College, a private, comprehensive, four-year, coeducational Catholic college, was founded in 1946 by the Sisters of Saint Anne in Marlboro, Massachusetts. In 1952, the College moved to its current 180-acre campus in Paxton, Massachusetts. Originally a women's college, the College has been coeducational since 1973. The 540 full-time undergraduate students come from thirteen states and 14 other countries.

The College is an unusually close-knit community. Small class sizes allow for mentor relationships to develop between faculty members and students. Freshman and sophomore classes generally have between 16 and 20 students; some upper-level classes have as few as 5 students. Faculty members teach and advise students based on their knowledge of each person as an individual, and classes are never taught by graduate assistants.

Criminal justice is the most popular program on campus, followed by education (early childhood, elementary, art, and music), business administration, social work, and psychology. A bachelor's degree in fire science is offered. The College also offers special majors such as music therapy and art therapy. Five-year programs are available in business administration (B.B.A./M.B.A.), psychology (B.A./M.A.), and criminal justice (B.S./M.A.).

The College is accredited by the New England Association of Schools and Colleges, the Council on Social Work Education, and the National Agency for Clinical Laboratory Sciences. The College is also approved by the American Bar Association, Massachusetts Department of Education, and the National Association for Music Therapy.

More than 70 percent of Anna Maria College's undergraduates reside on campus in the residence halls. Students enjoy a full social life both on campus and within the college-town atmosphere of nearby Worcester. A professional theater group, the New England Theatre Company, is in residence at the College. Annual events enjoyed by all students include the Variety Show, and Winterfest, Harvest, and Spring Weekends.

The College's NCAA Division III athletic program offers intercollegiate competition for men (baseball, basketball, cross-country, golf, and soccer) and women (basketball, cross-country, field hockey, soccer, softball, and volleyball). Intramural athletics and the coed club sport of cheerleading are also available to students who do not wish to participate on varsity teams.

The College is linked to the Internet. More than 500 computer hookups link classrooms, offices, the Academic Computing Center, computer labs, the library, and all residence hall rooms.

Location

Anna Maria College is located on a 180-acre wooded campus in Paxton, Massachusetts, 8 miles from downtown Worcester. The city offers numerous professional and cultural opportunities; Boston, Providence, and Hartford are only an hour away.

Local attractions include big-name entertainment and minor league hockey at the Worcester Centrum; art, history, and science museums; classical music performances at Mechanics Hall; the Worcester Common Fashion Outlets; theater; and day and night skiing at Wachusett Mountain.

Majors and Degrees

Anna Maria College offers a four-year curriculum of undergraduate instruction leading to the following degrees: Bachelor of Arts in art, art and business (interdisciplinary program), art therapy, teacher of visual art (N–8, 5–12), Catholic studies, English, English-language arts, fire science, graphic design, history, humanities (interdisciplinary program), legal studies/paralegal, modern languages, music, psychology, public policy, social work, social relations, and teacher preparation/licensure (available through the education program); Bachelor of Music in music education, music education and music therapy, music therapy, and performance (piano, voice); Bachelor of Science in business administration/management information systems, computer information science, criminal justice, environmental science, and fire science; and Associate in Arts in business administration.

Academic Program

When the Sisters of St. Anne founded Anna Maria College in 1946, their mission was to increase access to quality education, educational innovation, and respect for service to others through the development of the total human being. That mission has not changed in more than fifty years. As a Catholic college, the relationship between faith and reason is looked at closely. An Anna Maria College education is distinct because of its integration of rich tradition, diversity of knowledge, and the understanding of human history, institutions, and societies with Catholic teachings and traditions. The cornerstone of the Anna Maria College academic programs is the core curriculum, which integrates the Catholic character with a commitment to liberal arts education.

The academic programs are grouped into four divisions: Division I: Humanities, Arts, and International Studies; Division II: Business, Law, and Public Policy; Division III: Human Development and Human Services; and Division IV: Environmental, Natural, and Technological Sciences. Each division serves to illuminate and explore links between related areas of study so that the educational experience is broad-based and interdisciplinary. Students are encouraged to travel beyond their immediate interests to disciplines that may be connected by similar methods, history, theory, or application. The end result is a strong liberal arts foundation with a focused knowledge and professional preparation in a chosen area of concentration. Anna Maria College also encourages students to explore their own interest areas and design their own majors.

While at Anna Maria College, students can gain practical experience and explore career options through internship programs, fieldwork, and academic seminars and summer programs. They also learn through required practicums, part-time work, and community service.

Off-Campus Programs

Anna Maria College is a member of the Colleges of Worcester Consortium. Through this group of thirteen area colleges (Anna Maria College, Assumption College, Atlantic Union College, Becker College, Clark University, College of the Holy Cross, Massachusetts College of Pharmacy and Applied Health, Nichols College, Quinsigamond Community College, Tufts University School of Veterinary Medicine, University of Massachusetts Medical School, Worcester Polytechnic Institute, and Worcester State College), students may enroll in nonmajor courses at any of the member institutions and have credits transferred at no additional cost. The College offers several other off-campus opportunities for which academic credits are awarded. There is an exchange program with Holy Names College in California, where students may elect to study for one semester. The College participates, along with sixteen other New England colleges, in the New England–Quebec student exchange program. Through this program, students (especially those studying French language and literature) may choose to spend a year at one of a number of schools in Quebec. The College also provides opportunities for study abroad with additional programs in London, Seville, Rome, Latin America, and Nova Scotia. In addition, there is an Urban Seminar course with travel to Paris. Students are also eligible to apply for Army and Air Force ROTC programs, available through the Colleges of Worcester Consortium. A Washington, D.C., internship is offered for students in all majors, and a Disney internship is also available.

Academic Facilities

The Mondor-Eagan Library houses the College's volumes, stacks, periodicals, study rooms, computer center, resource centers, and language laboratory. The library also houses the main computer terminal, which links the combined material resources of central and western Massachusetts libraries, making more than 4 million books and periodicals accessible to students. Classrooms are located in Trinity Hall, Cardinal Cushing Hall, and Foundress Hall. Foundress Hall houses the Zecco Performing Arts Center. Trinity Hall also houses the learning center. Among the other buildings are St. Joseph's Hall for sciences and Miriam Hall for music, performance, and art.

Costs

Tuition for the 2003–04 academic year was $17,495. Room and board expenses were $6995. Tuition for music students was $19,995.

Financial Aid

More than 95 percent of the freshmen at the College receive financial aid in the form of scholarships, grants, loans, and work-study program awards. Some available sources of funds are the Federal Pell Grant, Federal Supplemental Educational Opportunity Grant, and Federal Perkins Loan programs. To apply for aid, students should submit the Free Application for Federal Student Aid (FAFSA) to federal student aid programs. Aid is awarded on the basis of need. Non-need-based scholarships are also available. For further information, students should call 508-849-3366.

Faculty

The College has 84 full- and part-time faculty members, 98 percent of whom are lay and 2 percent of whom are religious personnel. Faculty members have a deep respect for scholarship and research and are dedicated to teaching and to the success of the student. Graduate students do not teach classes at Anna Maria College.

Student Government

The Student Government Association (SGA) is the official representative of the student body, serving as the link between it and the administration. More than twenty clubs and organizations under the SGA offer many activities and opportunities to students, who are encouraged to participate in the government of student life at the College.

Admission Requirements

At Anna Maria College, every application is considered individually and weighed on its own merits. Emphasis is placed on the applicant's transcript, recommendations, and SAT I or ACT scores. Extracurricular activities and leadership positions are also important. Successful completion of a four-year college-preparatory program is required. Application for admission to the College is encouraged for all academically qualified candidates regardless of race, religion, age, gender, or creed.

Application and Information

To apply, students should submit a completed application form and an essay with the required $40 fee, request that an official high school transcript be sent to the Admission Office, forward the results of the SAT I or ACT, submit two letters of recommendation (one must be from a guidance counselor), and, if they wish, schedule a personal interview. The application priority deadline is March 1. To apply as a transfer student, the applicant must submit official transcripts of all postsecondary courses completed and a course-description catalog from each college or university attended in addition to following the steps given above.

Anna Maria College invites students to learn more about the College by visiting the campus. Students should call the Undergraduate Admission Office to schedule an appointment. For detailed information about the College's distinctive programs and campus community, prospective students should contact:

Wylie Culhane
Director of Admission
Anna Maria College
50 Sunset Lane
Paxton, Massachusetts 01612-1198
Telephone: 508-849-3360
800-344-4586 Ext. 360 (toll-free)
Fax: 508-849-3362
E-mail: admission@annamaria.edu
World Wide Web: http://www.annamaria.edu

Socquet House, built in 1750, is currently used as the residence for the Sisters of St. Anne.

AQUINAS COLLEGE

GRAND RAPIDS, MICHIGAN

The College

Located on the eastern edge of the city of Grand Rapids, Aquinas enjoys all of the advantages of Michigan's second-largest city and is just a 3-hour drive from Detroit or Chicago. The Aquinas College campus is an interesting blend of early-nineteenth-century architecture coupled with modern-day structures. The campus abounds with natural beauty; it has been called the most beautiful small campus in Michigan. Its ninety species of trees, winding woodland paths, and inviting creeks and ponds create a peaceful 107-acre environment that students of all ages find welcoming. Founded by the Dominican Sisters of Grand Rapids in 1886, Aquinas has a Catholic heritage and a Christian tradition. The Dominican tradition of working and serving remains alive at Aquinas. It is lived out by Aquinas students who volunteer their time and talents in the Grand Rapids community and by those who travel to places such as Oaxaca, Mexico; Appalachia, Kentucky; or any of a dozen other service learning project sites. An ability to see the world from different perspectives is the hallmark of an Aquinas-educated student. Aquinas, a coeducational liberal arts college, offers an approach to learning and living that teaches students unlimited ways of seeing the world. That is why every Aquinas student enrolls in the humanities program, a two-semester exploration of the best that has been thought, written, composed, and painted. And as students find their way in the world of thought, the core curriculum in natural science ensures that they discover the workings of the physical world as well. An Aquinas education makes graduates more employable. Each year, almost 200 Aquinas students find businesses, government agencies, and other organizations eager to offer field experience and internship opportunities. Students can write press releases, keep sports statistics, and travel around the country with such organizations as major league soccer; work on historic preservation projects with the Michigan Bureau of History in Lansing; or learn about politics from the inside as a congressional intern in Washington, D.C. Nine out of 10 applicants recommended by the Aquinas premedical advisory committee are admitted to medical school, and 19 of 20 are accepted into other graduate programs. In all, more than 90 percent of Aquinas seniors find jobs or enroll in graduate school soon after graduation. Aquinas sees a liberal arts education as career preparation. The Aquinas general education plan exposes students to the necessary skills that enable them to become critical thinkers, articulate speakers, strong writers, and effective problem solvers. Aquinas faculty members insist that students carry values as well as skills into the workplace. The College's curriculum, with its more than forty majors and cognates, is designed to provide students with both breadth and depth and to foster a thirst for knowledge and truth and a spirit of intellectual dialogue and inquiry. Coupled with nationally recognized co-op and internship programs, it prepares students to both live and work in the rapidly changing world of today and tomorrow.

Arriving from places as near as Grand Rapids, Chicago, and Detroit and as far as India and China, the 2,579 students include 1,412 full-time, 579 part-time, and 580 graduate students. The Insignis program at Aquinas encourages students of exceptional academic ability to participate in social and intellectual activities such as lectures and receptions for visiting scholars and trips to places of cultural interest. Aquinas offers more than forty student organizations, ranging from intramural teams and departmental clubs to a wide variety of musical groups, student publications, and service organizations.

In addition to its undergraduate degrees, Aquinas also offers Master in the Art of Teaching, Master in Education, Master in Science Education, and Master of Management (with concentrations in marketing, organizational development, health-care management, and international business) degrees.

Location

Aquinas' location in Grand Rapids allows students to reap the benefits of west Michigan's economic, educational, and cultural center. The city is one of the fastest-growing areas in the Great Lakes region. Grand Rapids combines big-city excitement and small-town charm. There are cosmopolitan amenities ranging from four-star hotels and restaurants to top-notch cultural facilities and entertainment venues. In addition to established attractions such as the Gerald R. Ford Presidential Museum, the Van Andel Public Museum, an expanded zoo, the 5,500-seat Fifth Third Park stadium for Whitecaps minor-league baseball, and the 70-acre Fredrik Meijer Gardens, recent attractions include the more than 12,000-seat Van Andel Arena, home to the Grand Rapids Griffins IHL hockey team and a venue for nationally known music concerts and performances. These major facilities add to the list of popular points of interest, festivals, and special events. With nearly half a million residents, there are abundant recreation, arts, and cultural opportunities available.

Majors and Degrees

Aquinas College offers the following undergraduate degree programs: Bachelor of Arts, Bachelor of Fine Arts, Bachelor of Arts in general education, Bachelor of Music Education, Bachelor of Science, Bachelor of Science in Business Administration, Bachelor of Science in environmental science, and Bachelor of Science in international business. A Bachelor of Science in Nursing degree program is offered in collaboration with the University of Detroit Mercy and St. Mary's Mercy Medical Center. Majors and programs of study are offered in accounting, accounting/business administration, art, art/business administration, art history, biology, business administration, business administration/communication arts, business administration/sports management, chemistry, communication arts, community leadership, computer information systems, conductive education, drawing, economics, education, English, environmental science, environmental studies, foreign language, French, geography, German, health, history, international studies, Japanese, journalism/publications, Latin, learning disabilities, mathematics, medical technology, music, not-for-profit management, organizational communication, painting, philosophy, photography, physical education and recreation, physics, political science, pre-engineering, printmaking, psychology, sculpture, social science, sociology, Spanish, studio art, sustainable business, theater, theology, urban studies, and women's studies. Preprofessional courses are available in dentistry, law, and medicine.

Associate degrees are also available, including the Associate of Arts and the Associate of Science.

Academic Program

In addition to their major and minor fields of study, students take an integrated skills course called Inquiry and Expression. This course spans the first semester freshman year and has an emphasis on writing integrated with reading critically, oral communication skills, critical thinking, library/electronic research methods, computer utilization, and basic quantitative reasoning. The thematic content is American Pluralism: The Individual in a Diverse America. Sophomores take a yearlong course in the humanities. As juniors they are required to take 3 hours in Religious Dimensions of Human Existence, with a choice among three categories: Scripture, Catholic/Christian

Thought, or Contemporary Religious Experience. Students are also required to be proficient in a second language through the 102 level. There also is a distribution plan in the general education plan covering social science; history/philosophy; natural world; artistic and creative studies; technology; and health, physical education, and recreation. A career/professional development component begins in summer orientation and is apportioned over four years; topics include assessment of students' strengths, skills, and interests; development of goals, a learning plan, and setting a direction; focus on the individual—wellness, personal finances, and leadership/team skills; awareness of careers, professions, and graduate study; information on making and maintaining a professional portfolio and resume; participating in a professional/career mentor program; career fairs and networking; and experiential learning (choices include co-op, internship, service learning, service trips, and study abroad). The College follows a two-semester calendar with a summer session. Aquinas also accepts credit through CLEP and Advanced Placement.

Off-Campus Programs

Students have the option of participating in the Dominican College Campus Interchange Program. Cooperating colleges are Barry University in Miami, Florida; Dominican College in San Rafael, California; and St. Thomas Aquinas College in Spark Hill, New York. Students can increase their foreign language skills through cultural-immersion programs in Costa Rica, France, Japan, Spain, or Germany. Two Aquinas faculty members accompany 25 students to Aquinas' study center in Tully Cross, Ireland. Students have the opportunity to earn a full semester of credit, travel abroad, and live in a rural Irish community. The curriculum is centered on several aspects of Irish studies.

Academic Facilities

The Woodhouse Library resources include a public access catalog, audiovisual materials, circulation and course reserve materials, reference services, and interlibrary loan services (free access to more than 27 million books and documents from libraries across the country). Students will find centrally located PC-based labs having more than 105 Pentium computers with additional PCs in such areas as residence halls and the Cook Carriage House. The lab technology works in a network environment to allow access to standard applications such as Windows 2000, Microsoft Office XP, and Web-based e-mail, as well as more than eighty-five discipline specific applications; printing to high quality laser printers; and access to multimedia technology. Labs are open seven days a week and are staffed by trained assistants. Albertus Magnus Hall of Science features the handicapped-accessible Baldwin Observatory and a greenhouse. Other facilities include the Cook Carriage House; a student center; and the modern Art and Music Center, featuring a dark room, a 200-seat recital hall, an art gallery, and a sculpture studio. The Jarecki Center for Advanced Learning offers network plug-ins every few feet and provides the latest in technology. Three new apartment buildings have opened, providing another housing option. The Aquinas Circle Theatre is a $7-million performance facility that opened summer 2003.

Costs

For 2003–04, tuition is $16,400, and room and board are $5494, for a total of $21,894. Other expenses, including books, travel, and personal supplies, average $2000.

Financial Aid

Aquinas College awards both merit-based financial assistance and traditional need-based assistance to qualified students. The Spectrum Scholarship Program was developed to recognize students' achievements in academics, leadership, and service. More than 90 percent of entering freshmen receive some form of financial assistance. The College administers the traditional grant and loan programs, including Federal Stafford Student Loans and Federal PLUS loans. Athletic grants are also available. The College participates in the Facts Tuition Management Plan. This plan assists students in paying costs over a period of time. To apply for financial assistance, students must complete the Free Application for Federal Student Aid (FAFSA).

Faculty

Aquinas faculty members are teachers first: while research plays an important part in the Aquinas faculty development, teaching remains the number one priority. In addition to teaching, faculty members serve as academic advisers, mentors, and advisers to various clubs and organizations on campus. With a student-professor ratio of 15:1, faculty members give individual attention and assistance to students. All classes and labs are taught by faculty members, not graduate assistants. Approximately 70 percent of Aquinas faculty members have doctoral or terminal degrees.

Student Government

The Student Senate is the governing body of Aquinas students. Senators are chosen by securing twenty-five signatures of students in support of their involvement. These students have both voice and vote on issues facing the College's Academic Assembly. The senate is responsible for many of the academic, social, recreational, and cultural activities brought to campus.

Admission Requirements

Freshman and transfer applications are received on a rolling basis. A candidate for admission to Aquinas is considered on the basis of academic preparation, scholarship, and character. Admission depends on a number of factors, including high school academic record and ACT or SAT I test scores. Transfer students must present a minimum 2.0 grade point average on a 4.0 scale. All applicants need to remit a $25 application fee. Online applications do not require an application fee. The admissions office reserves the right to review applications on a case-by-case basis. Curriculum, extracurricular activities, and any extenuating circumstances are considered in the decision. Letters of recommendation are encouraged but not required.

Application and Information

For further information, interested students should contact:

Paula Meehan
Dean of Admissions
Aquinas College
1607 Robinson Road, SE
Grand Rapids, Michigan 49506
Telephone: 616-732-4460
800-678-9593 (toll-free)
E-mail: admissions@aquinas.edu
World Wide Web: http://www.aquinas.edu

The Aquinas campus was once a private country estate.

ARCADIA UNIVERSITY

GLENSIDE, PENNSYLVANIA

The University

Founded in 1853, Arcadia University has the characteristics of a university yet retains a small-college atmosphere. Its diverse student population represents a cross section of cultural and socioeconomic backgrounds. Enrollment includes 1,570 full-time and 254 part-time undergraduates and 1,472 graduate students. At present, Arcadia students come from thirty-eight states and twenty other countries, and 70 percent of the full-time undergraduate population reside on campus. Adult students attend classes through Continuing Education, take noncredit courses through the Community Scholars Program, or pursue bachelor's degrees during the day or evening.

Campus life, including more than thirty clubs and organizations, athletics, and cultural and social events, is rich and varied. Community service is part of the Arcadia University experience. Students volunteer on neighborhood improvement projects, work at literacy or gerontology centers, and assist disadvantaged or disabled children. NCAA Division III intercollegiate competition is offered in field hockey, lacrosse, softball, and volleyball for women; in baseball for men; and in basketball, cross-country, golf, equestrian events, soccer, swimming, and tennis for both men and women. Intramural sports offer many other athletic opportunities.

Master's programs are offered in the fields of counseling, education, English, environmental education, forensic science, genetic counseling, health education, humanities, international peace and conflict resolution, physician assistant studies, and public health. A Doctorate in Physical Therapy (D.P.T.) and a doctorate in special education are also offered.

Location

Set on a beautiful former private estate in Glenside, a suburb of Philadelphia, Arcadia University offers urban resources in a countrylike setting. The focal point of the campus is the unique Grey Towers Castle, a National Historic Landmark. In 1995, the University completed a state-of-the-art Health Sciences Center. Knight Hall, a contemporary residence hall featuring suite-style accommodations, opened in 1997. The University completed expansion of the dining complex and student center and refurbished Murphy Hall, one of Arcadia's most historic buildings, at roughly the same time. Recent building projects include a new physician assistant and business facility and a multimillion dollar addition and renovation of the Landman Library, which doubled in size and now features a full range of information resources. Because the University is only 25 minutes from the center of Philadelphia, Arcadia students have ready access to the dozens of museums, galleries, performing arts centers, night spots, and historic, government, and commercial sites in this vital metropolitan area. New York City and Washington, D.C., are just a few hours away by car or train, as are recreation areas such as the New Jersey shore and the Pocono Mountains.

Majors and Degrees

The Bachelor of Arts is offered in art, art history, biology, business administration, chemistry, communications, computer science, computing technology, education (early childhood, elementary, and secondary), English, health administration, history, interdisciplinary science, international business and culture, mathematics, philosophy, political science, psychobiology, psychology, scientific illustration, sociology, Spanish, and theater arts and English. The Bachelor of Science is offered in accounting, business administration, chemistry, chemistry and business, computer science, finance, health administration, management, management information systems, marketing, mathematics, and personnel/human resources administration. The Bachelor of Fine Arts degree is awarded to students majoring in acting or studio arts with concentrations in ceramics, graphic design and illustration, interior design, metals and jewelry, painting, photography, and printmaking. Preparation for certification in art education is offered in conjunction with the B.F.A. program, as is preparation for graduate study in art therapy. A five-year program combines the Bachelor of Arts in education with a Master of Education in special education. Preparation for actuarial examinations comes through the Actuarial Science Program. The physician assistant 4+2 program provides a four-year undergraduate degree in a related field and is followed by two years of study in the Master of Medical Science, Physician Assistant program at Arcadia. Qualified candidates are assured admission to the program. The University offers a combined undergraduate and graduate (4+3) program leading to the Doctorate in Physical Therapy (D.P.T.). Arcadia University undergraduates who meet established criteria are assured admission to the graduate track. The International Peace and Conflict Resolution Program provides a four-year undergraduate degree followed by two years of study in the Master of Arts in international peace and conflict resolution. The forensic science program provides a four-year undergraduate program in a related field followed by two years in the Master of Science in forensic science program.

A dual-degree (3+2) program in engineering is offered in conjunction with Columbia University. An accelerated program with Pennsylvania College of Optometry leads to the Bachelor of Arts/Doctor of Optometry degrees. A 3+2 program in environmental science leads to a B.A. in psychology and Master of Arts in Education in environmental education. Preprofessional preparation is offered for dentistry, law, medicine, and optometry as well as in other areas.

The evening program offers part-time study leading to the Bachelor of Science in accounting, business administration, computer science, and management information systems as well as the Bachelor of Arts in corporate communications, English, health administration, and liberal studies. Postbaccalaureate certificates are also offered in business, computer science, communication, MIS, health administration, and health professions (sciences).

Academic Programs

The academic program provides students with a solid background of liberal arts and sciences integrated with courses in their chosen fields. Students explore a variety of interests and can engage in research, internships, or cooperative education placements. Such experiences enable students to gain relevant work experience while putting their academic training to use. The Cooperative Education Program, for instance, provides students with the opportunity to combine on-campus study with off-campus employment in a program that helps them earn both credit and income.

Highly qualified freshmen, sophomores, and juniors may enhance their education through the Honors Program, which includes special seminars, independent study, and cultural events.

Credit toward graduation is granted for scores of 3 or better on the Advanced Placement examinations of the College Board. Exemption from or credit for courses may also be earned through the College-Level Examination Program (CLEP) and locally administered examinations at the discretion of the department concerned.

The academic year is divided into two semesters. Summer sessions begin in May and continue through early August. Most students carry four academic courses in each regular semester; 128 semester hours are required for graduation.

Off-Campus Programs

Arcadia University operates one of the largest campus-based study-abroad programs in the country. Through this program, students may participate in any of more than 100 programs at locations in Australia, Equatorial Guinea, Great Britain (including the Universities of Aberdeen, Bristol, Edinburgh, London, and York), Greece, Ireland, Italy, Korea, Mexico, New Zealand, Northern Ireland, and Spain. London Preview is an opportunity available to freshmen in good standing to spend a week in London during spring break. The cost is $245 and includes round-trip airfare, housing, and programming. Off-campus study in the Philadelphia area includes internships and fieldwork in most majors. The University offers the Washington (D.C.) Semester at American University. Juniors and seniors may enroll for one advanced course each semester at the University of Pennsylvania.

Academic Facilities

Boyer Hall of Science houses the biology, chemistry and physics, genetic counseling, mathematics and computer science, psychology, and sociology departments. Individual laboratories are available for both faculty and student research.

The Health Sciences Center houses the Department of Physical Therapy. Taylor Hall is home to the education, English, history, philosophy and religion, and political science departments. Brubaker Hall houses the business department and the physician assistant studies program. Murphy Hall houses the fine arts, communications, music, and theater departments as well as video production and digital imaging studios. Students have easy access to campus computer facilities and to the Internet. Internet services include the World Wide Web, Telnet, ftp, and e-mail. Arcadia was recently awarded a special Tech Grant to implement Internet II broadband capability to foster interaction with classes abroad and make the whole campus wireless. The campus network extends to each room in the residence halls. Computer facilities include an Alpha mainframe with Ethernet connections to more than thirty on-site and dial-up workstations. There are also four computer labs and a Mac lab. The fine arts department offers a state-of-the-art computer graphics system to allow students to work with and master this technique of graphic design as well as desktop publishing and computer-aided design systems. A prime academic resource on campus is the Landman Library, which not only offers an extensive collection of books, journals, periodicals, microforms, and audio materials but also provides links to college and community library resources throughout the metropolitan area.

Costs

The charge for tuition in 2004–05 is $22,440. Student fees are $280 per year. Room and board charges are $8960 per year. Books and supplies are between $300 and $500 per semester.

Financial Aid

Every effort is made to see that students requiring financial assistance are able to attend Arcadia. Aid is awarded on the basis of need, as determined by the Free Application for Federal Student Aid (FAFSA) and the Arcadia University Financial Aid Application, and is available in the form of grants, loans, and part-time employment or some combination of the three. In 2003, 95 percent of the enrolled students received some form of financial aid, including need-based aid and merit awards. Scholarships are presented annually to students who have achieved academic distinction or have been recognized for outstanding extracurricular accomplishments. Distinguished Scholarships, ranging from $20,000 to $56,000 over four years, and the Arcadia University Achievement Awards, ranging from $4000 to $24,000 over four years, recognize academic excellence, leadership, and extracurricular accomplishments. A limited number of full tuition scholarships are available. Candidates have outstanding records of achievement, pursue competitive programs of study, and often excel in leadership, community service, and extracurricular activities. Transfer students are given special consideration. Financial Analysis Service Today (FAST) enables families to find out what the expected family contribution toward college costs and the estimated Arcadia University financial aid package will be. This service is available from September through January of the senior year of high school. To receive full consideration for financial aid, students should complete their applications and submit the FAFSA and the Arcadia University Financial Aid Application by March 1.

Faculty

Arcadia University has a faculty with a primary commitment to teaching. Most classes range in size from 15 to 20 people, and the ratio of students to faculty members is 12:1, so professors come to know and care about their students. This fosters an environment in which students and faculty collaborate on research and writing and engage in informal discussions, field trips, and other special activities outside the classroom. Eighty-five percent of the Arcadia faculty members hold doctorates or terminal degrees, and all courses are taught by faculty members.

Student Government

Student life is largely self-regulated by the Student Government Organization (SGO) through the Student Senate. Most students feel that the SGO has proved effective in working with the faculty and administration on matters of student concern, as well as in developing the social climate of the University. Students serve on most major faculty committees, and student leaders attend Board of Trustees meetings.

Admission Requirements

Students are carefully selected on the basis of educational preparation, intellectual promise, and potential. Each candidate's credentials are reviewed individually by members of the enrollment management staff. Particular emphasis is placed on the candidate's academic record, including the type of program followed and the grades and class rank earned. Standardized test scores, counselor and teacher recommendations, participation in school and community activities, and other supporting credentials are also considered.

Freshman applicants must submit an official high school transcript, standardized test scores (SAT I or ACT), and counselor and teacher recommendations. Applicants should pursue a college-preparatory program, usually consisting of 16 academic units. Early admission, early decision, deferred admission, and advanced placement are available. Students may be admitted through the Gateway To Success or Act 101 Program. Students are encouraged to visit the campus for a student-guided tour and an admission interview.

Transfer applicants may apply for the fall term or at midyear and must submit official college transcripts. In some cases, transfer applicants will be required to submit high school transcripts and SAT I or ACT scores.

Application and Information

Students are encouraged to submit their applications as early as possible in the senior year. Admission decisions are made on a rolling basis, and applicants are usually notified within a month of the date of completion of the application.

Requests for further information should be directed to:

Office of Enrollment Management
Arcadia University
450 South Easton Road
Glenside, Pennsylvania 19038-3295
Telephone: 215-572-2910
877-ARCADIA (877-272-2342, toll-free)
E-mail: admiss@arcadia.edu
World Wide Web: http://www.arcadia.edu/pet.asp

Grey Towers Castle, Arcadia University.

ART ACADEMY OF CINCINNATI

CINCINNATI, OHIO

The Academy

The Art Academy of Cincinnati is a small, independent college of art for students seeking a superior education in the creation and understanding of art. It is accredited by the National Association of Schools of Art and Design and the Commission on Institutions of Higher Education of the North Central Association of Colleges and Schools.

The Academy's origins reach back to the early nineteenth century, when individual artists offered classes in Cincinnati. In 1869 the school was established as the McMicken School of Art and Design. When the Cincinnati Museum Association was established in 1885, the school's founder suggested affiliating the art school with the museum. On November 26, 1887, the Art Academy was officially dedicated in its present location.

Students are attracted to the Academy for several reasons, particularly the closeness of the community of 225 full-time students. Faculty members are familiar with each individual's talents and needs, and there is a focus on the visual arts that only a professional art college can offer. Another outstanding advantage is the close relationship between the Academy and its neighbor, the Cincinnati Art Museum.

Location

The Art Academy of Cincinnati is located in Cincinnati, Ohio, a major metropolitan area. It is set in Eden Park, a 184-acre metropolitan park that also features an outdoor amphitheater, Mirror Lake, the Krohn Conservatory, the Playhouse in the Park theater, and the Cincinnati Art Museum. Like Rome, the city of Cincinnati is built on seven hills. As the Art Academy is located on one of the hills, it affords a spectacular view of the city, the Ohio River and its valley, and northern Kentucky. This scenery has inspired the images and styles of noted artists for the last century.

Greater Cincinnati is a center for social, cultural, and educational activities; there is something for everyone. The city is the home of the Reds (baseball), the Bengals (football), and the up-and-coming Cyclones (hockey). Kings Island, Coney Island, the Beach, Americana, and Surf Cincinnati are all amusement parks located near the city. The Academy itself is located minutes from downtown, where the nationally acclaimed Symphony Orchestra, Cincinnati Ballet Company, Cincinnati Opera, and May Festival Chorus perform. The Contemporary Arts Center, Taft Museum, Historical Society, Cincinnati Zoo, and Museum of Natural History are all a quick ride from the campus. Since the Academy is on the Metro bus line, students have easy access to Greater Cincinnati and northern Kentucky events.

Majors and Degrees

The Art Academy offers four-year programs leading to the Bachelor of Fine Arts degree in three areas: Fine Arts, with emphases in painting, printmaking, photography, drawing, and sculpture; Communication Arts, with digital multimedia, graphic design, photo design, and illustration; and Art History.

A five-semester Associate of Science degree in graphic design is available through an intensive, career-focused, accelerated program of study that enables students to enter the professional design market at an earlier date.

Academic Program

In completing the Bachelor of Fine Arts degree, a student is exposed to an integration of studio work, liberal studies, and art history, supporting the Academy's philosophy that the artist's strongest imagery and most effective visual statements come from a broad and rich mind.

Fine Arts students select a major area of emphasis and supplement their education with electives. The curriculum supports the understanding and benefits of the interrelationships of the various media, broadens students' visual concerns, and expands their self-expression. The Fine Arts Program is augmented by guest lecture series, seminars, workshops, visits to private collections, and field trips to museums and galleries in Cincinnati, as well as to institutions in Chicago, Cleveland, Columbus, Detroit, Indianapolis, New York, and Washington, D.C.

The Communication Arts Program offers professional career-oriented instruction in studio skills and seminars that integrate conceptual processes, media skills, technical methods, problem-solving theory, and social/historical references to applied design. The Academy is an educational leader in the integration of computer technology and the creative process of art and design. Students are introduced during their first year to the use of computers for solving problems and creating ideas. The Communication Arts Program gives students practical experience that will help them to move easily into business opportunities after graduation. Students in this program encounter the problems faced by the professional designer, illustrator, and photographer in today's business world.

Graduation requirements for the Bachelor of Fine Arts degree in Fine Arts and Communication Arts are 84 studio credit hours, 33 credits of liberal studies, and 15 art history credits, for a total of 132 credits. Graduation requirements for the Bachelor of Fine Arts in Art History are 66 studio credit hours, 33 hours of liberal studies, and 33 hours of art history for a total of 132 credit hours. Graduation requirements for the Associate of Science degree are 47 studio hours, 9 liberal studies hours, and 9 art history hours, for a total of 65 hours.

Academic Facilities

The Academy has three buildings. The first was designed specifically as an art school. The second is a school building that has been renovated to allow for the light and space needed for art classes. The Chidlaw Gallery is used for the professional display of students' works. In addition, there are exhibition areas in the lobbies of both Academy buildings, and students often show in other Cincinnati galleries and businesses. The third is a 6,000-square-foot sculpture facility with a hot glass shop.

Every student at the Academy is automatically a member of the Cincinnati Art Museum, which is one of the fifteen largest museums in the United States. As members, students are invited to exhibit openings, lectures, film series, special exhibits, and other museum-sponsored events. The resources of the museum's library are also available to students. The library has 66,400 volumes for circulation and reference, as well as an outstanding collection of clippings, monographs, and documents related to the visual arts.

Two computer labs are available to students. The computers have word processing, graphic design, and illustration capabilities.

Costs

Full-time instructional fees are $17,700 for 2004–05.

Financial Aid

Currently, 95 percent of Academy students receive financial aid. The Art Academy of Cincinnati participates in federal and state programs, including grants, loans, and scholarships. Institutional merit scholarships and institutional loans are also available.

Full-time freshmen or transfer students may apply for an Entrance Scholarship. The applicant's portfolio must be submitted by March 1 for judging. Those applying for financial aid through the federal government or the Art Academy must submit the Free Application for Federal Student Aid (FAFSA) by March 1 for priority consideration.

Faculty

There are 17 full-time faculty members; 16 have received a master's degree or its equivalent as their highest earned degree, and 1 has a doctorate. The Academy has 35 part-time faculty members. The student-faculty ratio is 12:1.

Student Government

Although the Art Academy of Cincinnati does not have a formal student government, its students have a strong voice in the arena of student issues and rights.

Admission Requirements

Applicants must have taken the SAT or ACT tests and should have a GPA of 2.0 or above. A portfolio review will be arranged unless the applicant lives more than 150 miles away (in which case slides may be sent).

The Art Academy seeks talented students dedicated to pursuing a degree in visual art. Applicants should demonstrate observational keenness, a strong sense of design, inventiveness, and technical ability. International and transfer students are welcome. The Office of Admissions accepts calls on specific questions regarding admission to the Academy. It is the policy of the Art Academy that no person shall be subject to discrimination as a student or employee because of race, color, sex, or national origin.

Application and Information

SAT I or ACT scores, transcripts from high school, and a $25 fee must be sent to the Office of Admissions by June 30 of the year prior to registration (March 1 for scholarship consideration).

For further information regarding admission, financial assistance, academic programs, and student/parent visits, students may contact:

Office of Admissions
Art Academy of Cincinnati
1125 St. Gregory Street
Cincinnati, Ohio 45202
Telephone: 513-721-5205
800-323-5692 (toll-free)

The Art Academy's Eden Park Building, which adjoins the Cincinnati Art Museum, dates back to 1887.

THE ART INSTITUTE OF BOSTON AT LESLEY UNIVERSITY
BOSTON, MASSACHUSETTS

The Institute

Founded in 1912, the Art Institute of Boston (AIB) is a professional college of visual arts that offers program and course work designed to prepare students to be professional illustrators, animators, graphic designers, Web designers, photographers, exhibiting fine artists, art teachers, and art therapists. AIB provides students with an intimate, challenging, and supportive environment that balances personal artistic expression with practical professional preparation.

AIB's 530 students come from thirty-five states and twenty-seven other countries, creating a global community of young artists with a stimulating variety of backgrounds and viewpoints. The nature of the college allows students to form close ties with other students and with faculty and staff members, most of whom are practicing professional artists. Studio classes are small and intimate—with an average of 14 students per instructor—which allows for personal attention and an emphasis on self-exploration and the development of an individual style. Students are prepared for professions in the arts by exposure to the most current trends and technology in their fields and internships and freelance opportunities that provide them with professional connections for career opportunities after graduation.

The University also offers activities such as major exhibitions, student exhibits, lectures, art auctions, special event–related parties, as well as a visiting artist program that brings prominent artists to the campus for lectures and workshops.

AIB's strengths as a professional college of the visual arts are combined with the resources of Lesley University, providing students with expanded educational opportunities that are not usually found at most independent colleges of art, yet preserving the character of a small, private art college.

The University provides a variety of dormitory housing options for students, including residences on the Cambridge campus of Lesley University, near Harvard Square (shuttle service provided).

The Career Resource Center at Lesley University provides career development and job search services to AIB degree candidates and alumni. Students are provided individual assistance and training in job search, career assessment, and decision-making skills that are used throughout a lifetime of employment. Workshops and special events are planned throughout the academic year on a variety of topics. The Artists Resource Center at AIB maintains current job listings and provides information on competitions, fellowships and grants, exhibition opportunities, and other resources for artists. Career counseling also takes place informally with faculty members and advisers within each department.

Master's programs in expressive therapies and art education are offered in conjunction with Lesley University.

Location

Boston is an extraordinary college town. Just under 225,000 students live and study here every year at seventy institutions of higher learning. The city offers all the human and institutional resources expected in a major cultural, educational, and commercial center. World-class art exhibitions, concerts, lectures, theater, sports, and popular entertainment are among its riches. The spirit is cosmopolitan, but the setting is distinctive of Boston, with its historic neighborhoods, parks, and nearby New England rural and coastal areas.

The Art Institute of Boston students use the city's extensive resources as a part of their learning environment in many ways—for artistic and academic research, for internships and job opportunities, and for personal recreation. Full-time students receive free admission to the Museum of Fine Arts, Boston.

Majors and Degree

The Art Institute of Boston awards the Bachelor of Fine Arts degree in design, fine arts, illustration/animation, and photography as well as combined degrees in fine arts/illustration and illustration/design. A three-year diploma program is available in each of the degree areas. A two-year professional certificate program is offered in illustration and design.

Candidates for the graphic design program can study advertising and corporate communications, package design, publishing and book design, and Web and multimedia design. The illustration program offers specializations in advertising, animation, book, and editorial. Fine arts students choose from drawing, painting, printmaking, and sculpture as concentrations, with courses available in ceramics, installation, and new media. Photography students specialize in either commercial, documentary, fine arts, or media. An intensive precollege program is available for high school students throughout the academic year and the summer.

Academic Programs

AIB's challenging curriculum is structured to provide students with an understanding of the process of visual communication and expression, along with the social, historical, and cultural influences that shape the world and inform their imaginations.

AIB's rigorous first-year foundation includes intensive study in drawing and visual perception. Photography students take a unique foundation, with a direct immersion in the conceptual, technical, and historic aspects of photography. The foundation supplies students with the skills, insights, and fluency of expression that are necessary to meet the challenges of further study in art.

After the foundation year, students choose a major that can include unique specializations, combined majors, and a wide variety of interdisciplinary courses and workshops. Students take core courses in their major and continue with more individualized instruction, working closely with the faculty of working professional artists, toward their personal and professional goals. Students prepare for careers in the visual arts with real world studio assignments and professional internships, giving them valuable firsthand experience in their intended fields.

As an integral part of their study, all degree and diploma students take a blend of required and elective liberal arts courses. These courses are designed to develop effective communication skills, give a firm academic grounding in the history of their major area of study, and allow students to pursue individual interests that stimulate their imaginations and interests.

AIB offers both day and evening degree credit courses during the fall, spring, and summer semesters. In addition, the continuing and professional education program offers evening and weekend courses, workshops, and intensive seminars in the areas of visual arts, liberal arts, and career development to be taken by artists, educators, and professionals.

Off-Campus Programs

The Art Institute of Boston at Lesley University offers a merit-based, semester-long illustration program in Rotterdam, Holland. Students also have the option to study visual arts and Italian language at The Art Institute of Florence or visual art at

Burren College of Art in Ireland; photography students can participate in an exchange program in Paris, France. Students may take an intensive yearlong course of study and studio work in New York City or spend their junior year at one of thirty schools in the Association of Independent Colleges of Art and Design (AICAD) located across the country. AIB also offers students the opportunity to take classes at the Boston Architectural Center and the Maine Photographic Workshop.

Academic Facilities

The Art Institute of Boston's facilities include three state-of-the-art Macintosh computer laboratories, an animation lab, a newly renovated photography lab with color and black-and-white printers, a printmaking lab with etching and lithography presses, a wood shop, a metals studio with welding facilities, and a clay lab with kilns. Senior fine arts students have their own individual studios in which to create.

The Art Institute of Boston was selected to join the New Media Centers Program, a consortium of higher education institutions and digital technology companies dedicated to advancing learning through new media. Plans for the AIB Center include expanded multimedia programs using state-of-the-art technology and equipment.

The AIB library collection is devoted principally to the visual arts and contains more than 9,000 books, seventy serial titles, 26,000 slides, a video viewing room, more than 250 art-related videos, and a picture reference file of 10,000 photographs and illustrations. The library has the National Gallery of Art's American Art Collection on videodisc, a visual reference of more than 26,000 images spanning three centuries.

In addition, the Eleanor De Wolfe Ludcke Library at Lesley provides a state-of-the-art multimedia resource center and a collection of 62,000 books, 700 current periodicals, 2,200 computer software and CD-ROM titles, 650 film and video titles, media material, and circulating media equipment. Students have borrowing privileges at six additional libraries through the Fenway Library Consortium.

The Art Institute of Boston sponsors a full program of exhibitions and lectures by visiting artists. The gallery presents major exhibitions of contemporary and historical work by established and emerging artists, including the alumni of the Art Institute of Boston. Students have the opportunity to assist in mounting exhibitions and to personally meet visiting artists. A student gallery and reserved areas show student work year-round. Gallery South exhibits the work of student photographers throughout the year, including group and senior exhibitions.

Costs

Tuition for the 2002–03 academic year was $16,210. Dormitory costs were approximately $9000 per year. Material and supply costs vary according to individual and departmental requirements. In general, foundation, fine arts, illustration, and design students spend approximately $1700 per year for supplies, while photography students can expect to spend about $2500 per year, with further expenses dependent upon the equipment chosen by the individual student.

Financial Aid

More than 60 percent of students receive aid each year through AIB's active financial aid program. Awards are made on the basis of need as determined by the United States Department of Education, which analyzes all the financial resources of the student. The Financial Aid Office's goal is to help students meet established needs through a combination of Federal Pell Grants, Federal Stafford Student Loans, Federal Work-Study Program awards, other federal grants, scholarships, and state programs.

Various merit-based and need-based scholarships are available. The Art Institute of Boston administers more than $4 million in scholarships, financial aid, and loans for students each year. The application deadline for scholarships is February 15; the deadline is March 15 for need-based awards.

Faculty

The Art Institute of Boston at Lesley University has 103 full- and part-time faculty members, 95 percent of whom have advanced degrees in their field; 90 percent are practicing artists, designers, illustrators, and photographers. The student-faculty ratio is 10:1.

Student Government

Each year, the student peer advisers and office staff are responsible for a full program of social events, lecture and film series, and out-of-town visits to important exhibitions. In addition, students can share their thoughts with the dean in monthly informal round table discussions.

Admission Requirements

In considering applications for admission, the Art Institute of Boston looks for artistic potential and personal commitment. A portfolio of original work is an important part of the application; academic grades, test scores, letters of recommendation, and extracurricular activities are also strongly considered. A school visit is encouraged, giving applicants the opportunity to present their portfolios, discuss their goals and interests with an admissions counselor, and determine how they may benefit from AIB's programs. SAT I or ACT scores are required of applicants who have graduated from high school since 1995.

Application and Information

To ensure a place in the desired program of study and in order to meet application deadlines for financial aid, students are encouraged to apply by the priority application deadlines of February 15 for fall and November 15 for spring admittance. After these deadlines, applications are accepted on a rolling basis as long as space allows. A complete application consists of an application form and fee, essay, resume of accomplishments and cocurricular activities, transcript(s) of all courses completed, SAT I or ACT test scores (B.F.A. candidates, U.S. only), an interview, and a portfolio. Transfer and international applications are accepted and encouraged.

For further information, students should visit the Web site listed below or contact an admissions representative at:

Office of Admissions
The Art Institute of Boston at Lesley University
700 Beacon Street
Boston, Massachusetts 02215
Telephone: 617-585-6700
800-773-0494 Ext. 6700 (toll-free, U.S. and Canada)
E-mail: admissions@aiboston.edu
World Wide Web: http://www.aiboston.edu

Studio classes are small and intimate, with an average of 14 students per instructor.

THE ART INSTITUTE OF PHOENIX

PHOENIX, ARIZONA

The Institute

The Art Institute of Phoenix was established in 1995 as a private postsecondary school and is accredited by the Accrediting Council for Independent Colleges and Schools (ACICS). The mission of the Art Institute of Phoenix is to accomplish its vision by providing employers with high-quality, skilled graduates prepared by an experienced faculty using market-driven curricula.

At the Art Institute of Phoenix, students learn how to use program-specific technology to bring their creative career goals to life. When they graduate, they have the specialized skills and competencies employers seek.

As of fall 2003, there were 1,216 students attending the school seeking Bachelor of Arts (B.A.) and Associate of Applied Science (A.A.S.) degrees or diplomas. There are 747 men and 469 women enrolled, of whom 1,045 are full-time and 171 are part-time students. The average class size is 20 students, and the faculty-student ratio is 1:20.

The Art Institute of Phoenix was recognized by the Arizona Private School Association as the "2001–2002 Outstanding School of the Year."

Location

The Art Institute of Phoenix is located in one of the fastest-growing metropolitan areas of the country. Located in the middle of the state of Arizona and in the heart of the beautiful Sonoran Desert, Phoenix is the gateway to cool pine forests, the red rock towers of Sedona, and nature's greatest wonder, the Grand Canyon. The nation's fifth-largest city, Phoenix offers sun-filled days and nightlife that ranges from top comedy and music clubs to such cultural icons as the Phoenix Art Museum and the Phoenix Symphony Orchestra. Professional sports teams include the Diamondbacks, Suns, Arizona Cardinals, and Coyotes.

Majors and Degrees

The Art Institute of Phoenix offers programs in four areas: animation, culinary arts, design, and media arts. The specific degree programs and specializations within those programs include an A.A.S. in culinary arts and a B.A. in advertising, digital media production, fashion marketing, game art and design, graphic design, interior design, media arts and animation, multimedia and Web design, and visual effects and motion graphics. Diplomas can be earned in baking and pastry and in the art of cooking. These programs are offered on a year-round basis, enabling students to work continually toward their degrees. The faculty members, many of whom are working professionals, strengthen students' skills and cultivate their talents through well-designed curricula.

Each program of study has its own technology needs. The media arts and animation program relies heavily on PC-platform computers and software used to produce 3-D animation, 2-D ink-and-paint, digital paint, and compositing effects. Game art and design students use much of the same equipment as the media arts and animation students, but with additional tools that allow game prototyping and simulations. Graphic design students have access to Macintosh and PC platforms to produce camera-ready and final copies of design projects. Interior design students work with PC-based computers and high-quality software to produce their design plans and renderings. Multimedia and Web design students concentrate on designing and producing interactive disks that may be educational, commercial, or entertaining in nature. Digital media production students use program-specific technologies to create, develop, and deliver content, combining traditional production techniques with digital tools as they prepare for a career where creativity and technology come face to face with the future.

The visual effects and motion graphics program offers students the opportunity to acquire skills in a specialization that focuses on communication arts for film, television, and the Web. By combining graphic design, filmmaking, animation, and sound, graduates of the program are qualified to create attention-grabbing visuals that inform and entertain.

Academic Programs

Programs range from 27 to 186 credit hours. Nine programs lead to the Bachelor of Arts degree. In the digital media production program, students learn to combine traditional production techniques with the latest digital tools to shoot, edit, refine sound, and develop special effects. In game art and design, the curriculum includes modeling (creating a character or object), scene and set design, motion capture, animation, texture mapping, and more; students become skilled in drawing, visualizing, and using color. In the graphic design program, students learn to package communication and commerce as art in order to enhance a company's image or to sell ideas, products, and services by coupling graphic design with advertising copy and concepts. Interior design students gain a strong foundation in the basics, including drawing, perspective, proportion, and color, and they use computer-aided drawing (CAD) to help plan residential and commercial spaces. As computer animators in the media arts and animation program, students work in 3-D to create characters with the subtleties and realistic motion of everyday life, learning to artfully blend creative vision with technology. Multimedia system and Web page design, video, animation, and scripting are just some of the key elements covered in the multimedia and Web design program's curriculum. Students in the visual effects and motion graphics program learn to deal with the interrelated fields of design, layering, and movement of digital elements and imagery to enhance or tell a visual story. Three culinary arts programs are offered. Both the art of cooking program and the baking and pastry program lead to a diploma; the culinary arts program culminates with an A.A.S. degree. The programs begin with the basics, from knife skills and kitchen procedures to nutrition, speed and timing, and presentation. Building on those basics, students progress to more advanced areas, such as baking and pastry, garde-manger (cold kitchen), international and American cuisine, à la carte, and dining room operations.

Academic Facilities

The Art Institute of Phoenix is located in a four-story building in the northwest corner of Phoenix, and the students can enjoy scenic mountain views from many of its large picture windows. With the sun streaming into the classrooms and computer laboratories, student creativity flows easily. Classroom and computer laboratory facilities are clean and well maintained, with a full-time technology manager located on-site. The culinary arts kitchens are spacious and filled with commercial equipment that students will work with in the real world. Digital media production students have a full television studio and control room at their command, along with editing suites to complete their work.

The Art Institute of Phoenix provides Internet access to its students throughout the school. Students can also avail themselves of multiple computer labs, a Learning Resource Center, student supply store, Career Services Center, and student lounge. Students can join student organizations and clubs and make friends with classmates who are also refining their creative talents.

Costs

Tuition is $340 per credit hour. School-sponsored housing costs are in addition to tuition. Through a special arrangement with select apartment complexes close to the school, the Art Institute of Phoenix can offer students the opportunity to live in furnished apartments with rent that includes the utilities. Students share these apartments with others studying at the Art Institute of Phoenix, and they are located just 1 mile from the school.

Financial Aid

Financial assistance is available for those who qualify. The Art Institute of Phoenix participates in federal, state, and other financial aid programs. Financial aid is divided into three general categories: gift aid, loans, and work-study. Gift aid includes grants, scholarships, and other benefits that do not have to be repaid. Loans need to be repaid, but repayment can usually be delayed until several months after the student leaves school. The Art Institute of Phoenix participates in the Federal Work-Study Program and also assists students in finding part-time jobs in the community.

Faculty

The Art Institute of Phoenix offers personal attention from knowledgeable, professional instructors. Many of the faculty members are working professionals who bring practical knowledge and real-world experience to the classroom. The Art Institute of Phoenix faculty members are available for student appointments and to discuss academic issues. They offer tutoring to those students in need of extra help.

Student Government

The President's Club is a school organization that promotes the philosophy of "students helping students." Those students selected assist new students with adjusting to life in Phoenix and at the Art Institute of Phoenix, as well as to school activities. Criteria for selection are a GPA of 3.0 or greater at the Art Institute of Phoenix, good attendance, completion of at least one full quarter, a desire to assist other students, responsible behavior, and being in good academic standing at the Art Institute of Phoenix.

Admission Requirements

An Assistant Director of Admissions is usually one of the first people prospective students speak with at the Art Institute of Phoenix. This person meets with students to talk about their future goals and assists them in navigating the admissions process. The Admissions Office sets up an appointment for a tour. For admission to the Art Institute of Phoenix, students are evaluated on the basis of previous education, background, and a demonstrated interest in one of the programs. Portfolios are encouraged but not required.

As part of the application process, applicants are required to independently conceive and write an essay of approximately 150 words stating how their education at the Art Institute of Phoenix will help them to attain their career goals. Successful admission into the Art Institute of Phoenix and a satisfactory program start is dependent on the level of accomplishment exhibited in the essay, all grade point averages as evidenced through transcript evaluation, an evaluation of GED scores, a review of the results of any nationally based exams (preferred but not required) such as the SAT I or ACT, and a personal interview with an Assistant Director of Admissions.

The Art Institute of Phoenix programs are technical in nature; therefore, international students are required to demonstrate proficiency in the English language and satisfy all admissions requirements and procedures. The English-language requirement is met when an applicant has submitted proof of a score of 480 or better on the TOEFL or has completed level 108 at an ESL Language Center or a recognized equivalent.

Application and Information

To arrange an interview or obtain more information, prospective students should contact:

The Art Institute of Phoenix
2233 West Dunlap Avenue
Phoenix, Arizona 85021
Telephone: 602-678-4300
800-474-2479 (toll-free)
World Wide Web: http://www.aipx.edu

The Art Institute of Phoenix.

ASBURY COLLEGE

WILMORE, KENTUCKY

The College

Founded in 1890, Asbury College is a Christian, multidenominational, coeducational institution founded in the Wesleyan-Holiness tradition. The College's mission is to provide a high-quality, Christ-centered, residential liberal arts education that equips men and women, through a commitment to academic excellence and spiritual vitality, for a lifetime of learning, leadership, and service to their professions, society, and family and the church.

A distinguishing mark of Asbury's Christian community is that the members are committed to a set of basic principles that are considered essential to maintain the spirit and health of the community. At Asbury College, the basic tenet of the community is found in Jesus's two great commandments in Matthew 22:37–40: "You shall love the Lord your God with all your heart, and with all your soul, and with all your mind . . . And . . . you shall love your neighbor as yourself." Thus, members of the Asbury community seek to love God and practice self-sacrificial love in relationship to others. Such disciplined community living is inherent preparation for servant-leaders who give their lives to fulfill a cause greater than themselves.

Citing the Christian and academic reputation of the College as their primary reason for selecting Asbury, 258 new freshman were enrolled in fall 2003. The current undergraduate enrollment is 1,191 students from forty states and ten countries. Kentucky, Ohio, Indiana, Pennsylvania, and Florida are the five states that are represented most. Asbury offers more than forty-five majors and programs of study within the liberal arts curriculum and confers the degrees of Bachelor of Arts and Bachelor of Science in education. The most popular majors are in the departments of communication arts, education, psychology, business and economics, and ministries and missions.

Organizations and clubs are an important part of student life at Asbury College. Positions on the *Collegian* (student newspaper) and the *Asburian* (yearbook) are open to all students. Students can become involved in the Ministerial Association, Christian Service Association, Fellowship of Christian Athletes, and Community Involvement, Art, Speech, English, Foreign Student, French, and Spanish Clubs. Students may also participate in the Women's Vocal Ensemble, Men's Glee Club, Jazz Ensemble, Concert Choir, and Concert Band. Student honor societies include Alpha Psi Omega (drama), Phi Alpha Theta (history), Phi Sigma Tau (philosophy), Sigma Zeta (science and mathematics), Sigma Tau Delta (English), and Sigma Delta Pi (Spanish). Among the professional organizations that students may join are the American Guild of Organists, the Music Educators National Conference, the Kentucky Intercollegiate Press Association, the Student National Education Association, and the Student Association for Health, Physical Education and Recreation.

Asbury recognizes the value of athletics and maintains a program of intramural and intercollegiate sports. Intercollegiate sports for men are basketball, cross-country, soccer, swimming, and tennis. For women, basketball, cross-country, soccer, swimming, tennis, and volleyball are offered. Intramural activities include basketball, flag football, golf, soccer, softball, tennis, volleyball, and walleyball. Asbury also sponsors a Christian witness gymnastics team that tours each spring semester.

Eighty-five percent of Asbury students reside in College residence halls. Duplexes for married students are available. Counseling and health services are available to all students. Asbury maintains a well-equipped clinic with a competent, experienced staff consisting of registered nurses and a physician.

In addition to the undergraduate degrees offered, Asbury College awards the Master of Arts in special education, instructional media, and English as a Second Language.

Location

Wilmore, a safe community of approximately 5,000, is located in the heart of the famous Bluegrass region, 15 miles southwest of Lexington, Kentucky, the second-largest city in the commonwealth. Surrounding Wilmore are reminders of the state's pioneer history, including Fort Harrod, Boonesborough, and Shakertown, a restored religious community dating from the 1800s. Near Lexington is the Kentucky Horse Park. Camping, rock-climbing, boating, and fishing are available at nearby Red River Gorge and Natural Bridge, and Mammoth Cave National Park is less than 2 hours from Wilmore.

Lexington has theaters, an opera house, a symphony orchestra, and Rupp Arena, where programs ranging from performances by well-known musicians to basketball games are presented.

Majors and Degrees

Asbury College confers the degrees of Bachelor of Arts and the Bachelor of Science in education. Undergraduate majors are available in accounting, applied communication, art, bible and theology, biblical languages, biochemistry, biology, business management, chemistry, Christian ministries, classical languages, computational science, elementary education, engineering (with the University of Kentucky), English, exercise science, French, Greek, health and physical education, health science, history, information technology, journalism, Latin, mathematics, media communication, middle school education, missions, music, philosophy, physical science, psychology, recreation, secondary education (art, biological science, English, French, health and physical education, Latin, mathematics, music, physical science, social studies, and Spanish), social work, sociology, Spanish, and sports management.

Academic Program

Asbury College operates on a sixteen-week semester system with two 4-week summer sessions. To qualify for graduation, students must complete a minimum of 124 semester hours with an overall grade point average of at least 2.0 and 2.5 in teacher education programs.

The liberal arts core requirements are as follows: Christian theology, 3 credits; communication, 3 credits; computer science/mathematics, 3 credits; English composition, 3 credits; English literature, 6 credits; foreign language, 12 credits; laboratory science, 6 credits; music and art appreciation, 3 credits; New Testament, 3 credits; Old Testament, 3 credits; philosophy, 3 credits; physical education, 3 credits; psychology/sociology/anthropology, 3 credits; and Western civilization, 6 credits.

Students may be granted college credit for satisfactory performance on AP tests in certain subjects. Advanced standing in foreign language is also available to qualifying students. Further detailed information is available from the College.

Off-Campus Programs

Qualified students may participate in the American Studies Program in Washington, D.C.; the Holy Land Studies Program in Israel; and the Wesleyan Urban Coalition Program in Chicago, as well as in the Latin American Studies Program.

Academic Facilities

College facilities that are available to students include a computer center and several well-equipped chemistry, biology, physics, computer, and language laboratories. The College also has a radio station and an outstanding TV studio with a 24-hour cable station. The Kinlaw Library, completed in 2001, is a 72,000-square-foot facility that houses the College's 168,000-volume collection, as well as the Kirkland Learning Resources Center. Computer, media, and curriculum labs are included in the building. More than 800 dataports are available throughout the facility.

Costs

For 2004–05, annual expenses are $17,660 for tuition, $148 for fees, and $4498 for room and board.

Financial Aid

More than 90 percent of the College's students receive some type of financial assistance. The various aid programs include academic scholarships, Federal Pell Grants, Federal Supplemental Educational Opportunity Grants, Kentucky Higher Education Assistance Authority Grants, Federal Perkins Loans, Federal Stafford Student Loans, state loans, United Methodist Student Loans, institutional grants and loans, institutional employment, and Federal Work-Study Program awards. Asbury offers honor scholarships, including a few full tuition grants. Merit Finalists receive 60 percent tuition scholarships.

To apply for aid, students should complete the Free Application for Federal Student Aid (FAFSA). Priority consideration is given to those who file before March 1. Financial need is defined as the difference between the amount a family can pay and the total expenses for the academic year. If there is a deficit, the student is considered to have financial need. The awards are made on the basis of financial need. Notification of awards begins early in April. For more information, students may contact the financial aid office at 859-858-3511 Ext. 2195 or 800-888-1818 Ext. 2195 (toll-free).

Faculty

Asbury has a full-time faculty of more than 90 members. The part-time faculty usually numbers 70 members. Each student has a faculty member as an adviser, who is personally interested in each student and is willing to assist advisees in any way possible. Many faculty members are hospitable and open their homes to students. Asbury's faculty-student ratio is 1:14. Approximately 77 percent of the full-time faculty members hold earned terminal degrees in their fields.

Student Government

The objectives of the student government organization are to act as a unifying force, bringing the institution as a whole into vital contact with current issues in college life; to help students find opportunities in college life in a mature Christian spirit, through recommendation and administration; and to promote an atmosphere for intellectual, spiritual, and cultural development. Regulations for student life are explained in the student handbook. The use of tobacco, alcoholic beverages, and illegal drugs is strictly prohibited.

Admission Requirements

The Asbury College faculty strongly recommends that applicants should have completed the following requirements in grades 9 through 12: 4 years of English, including 1 year of composition; 3 or 4 years of mathematics (algebra, geometry, advanced algebra, and other advanced math); 2 years of social studies, of which 1 year should be history; 2 or 3 years of laboratory science; and 2 years of the same foreign language. Applicants should have a grade point average of at least 2.5. Students should take the ACT examination or the SAT I and have a minimum ACT composite score of 22 or a combined SAT I score of 1030. Freshmen entering Asbury have had an average ACT composite score of 25, an SAT I combined score of 1165, and a high school grade point average of 3.56. Transfer students must have maintained an average of 2.5 or better at the college or university last attended.

Application and Information

Students may apply for freshman admission during the spring of their junior year or during their senior year in high school. Notification of admission decisions is given within 24 hours after the following have been received: the application and $30 application fee, transcripts, a pastor's recommendation, a high school counselor's recommendation (for high school students only), and a personal recommendation. Enrollment is cut off at resident capacity. Admission decisions are made and financial assistance is awarded by Asbury College without regard to race, color, sex, national origin, or handicap.

Further information may be obtained by contacting:

Stan F. Wiggam
Dean of Admissions
Asbury College
Wilmore, Kentucky 40390
Telephone: 859-858-3511 Ext. 2142
800-888-1818 Ext. 2142 (toll-free)
Fax: 859-858-3921
World Wide Web: http://www.asbury.edu

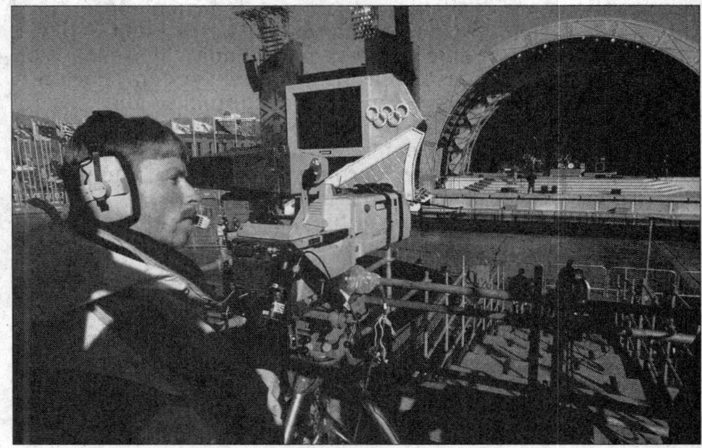

Media communications students participated in the 2002 Salt Lake City Winter Olympics and plan to operate cameras at the 2004 Summer Olympics in Greece.

ASHLAND UNIVERSITY

ASHLAND, OHIO

The University

Education at Ashland University (AU) goes beyond small classes, low student-faculty ratios, and personal attention. The campuswide philosophy of "Accent on the Individual" means that students are challenged to grow and change in a community of respect where they can discover their true potential.

Ashland University is a midsize regional teaching university, historically related to the Brethren Church. Its mission is to serve the educational needs of all students—undergraduate and graduate, traditional and nontraditional, full- and part-time—by providing educational programs of high quality in an environment that is both challenging and supportive.

The educational and social environment is built upon a long-standing commitment to Judeo-Christian values and a tradition that stresses the importance of each individual. In this environment, the members of the Ashland University community continually seek ways to challenge and support each other to develop intellectually, spiritually, socially, culturally, and physically.

Ashland University is home to 2,200 full-time undergraduate students, 85 percent of whom are from Ohio. Students also come from twenty-seven other states and twenty-three other countries. The University's total enrollment of 6,800 students includes students in graduate programs in business, education, and theology; a professional program in nursing; and thirteen off-campus degree-granting program centers throughout Ohio. Students of minority groups account for 6 percent of the student population. Twenty-five percent of the incoming class are transfer students.

Ashland is a residential campus, with men's and women's residence halls and options for coed divided housing, three-room suites, sorority suites, residential fraternity houses, and Scholar Floors. Fully furnished, 1,400-square-foot, two-bedroom apartments are available for seniors.

AU is a six-time recipient of an award for having the best student programming in the nation. More than 100 student organizations are available on campus. Ten men's teams and ten women's teams compete at the NCAA Division II level, several of which are in contention for national titles each year. The University's ever-increasing wireless system currently includes the student center, the quadrangle, and several residence halls, and laptop computers are available to students. Patterson Instructional Center features a large computer lab, teleconferencing, distance-learning classrooms, multimedia classrooms, and an instructional media center.

The campus features a beautiful 55,000-square-foot student center with several student lounges, a unique bookstore, a grill and snack bar, a game room, a health and aerobics center with locker rooms and showers, and many meeting rooms. This impressive building is now wireless and features laptop computers that can be used anywhere in the building. A 60,000-square-foot facility for the College of Business and Economics opened in spring 2004 and features an executive education center, two conference areas, a state-of-the-art trading room, three computer labs, a tiered lecture hall, a product development lab, a student lounge, a parent lounge, and M.B.A. and undergraduate staff offices.

Location

Ashland is an attractive community of 22,000, midway between Cleveland and Columbus. Recent FBI statistics show Ashland as having the lowest violent crime rate in the state for cities with populations between 10,000 and 24,999. *The Rating Guide to Life in America's Small Cities* lists the Ashland, Ohio, area as having the lowest crime rate of micropolitan areas in the U.S.

Majors and Degrees

Ashland University confers seven baccalaureate degrees: the Bachelor of Arts, Bachelor of Music, Bachelor of Science, and Bachelor of Science in Business Administration, Education, Nursing (completion degree for RNs), and Social Work. Undergraduate programs of study include accounting; American studies; art*; athletic training; biochemistry, biology*; business administration; business management; chemistry*; child and family studies; commercial art; computer art and graphics programming; computer science*; creative writing; criminal justice; economics; education: early childhood (preK–3), middle grades (4–9), grades 7–12, multi-age (preK–12), vocational, intervention specialist (special education), Christian education, and physical education; electronic media production: radio/audio production, television production and programming, and professional video production; English; environmental science; exercise science; fashion merchandising; finance; fine art; foods and nutrition; French*; geology; history; hotel/restaurant management; integrated language arts*; integrated mathematics*; integrated science*; integrated social studies*; international business; international studies; journalism*; management information systems; marketing; mathematics; music*; philosophy; physics; political science; predentistry; prelaw; pre–medical technology; premedicine; pre-optometry; prepharmacy; pre–physical therapy; preseminary; pre-veterinary medicine; psychology; recreation; religion; social studies*; social work; sociology; Spanish*; speech communication; sport management; sports communication; theater*; and toxicology. (Majors marked with * are education certification areas.) The University also awards the Associate in Arts degree in art, criminal justice, office administration, and radio-TV and in a two-year curriculum in general education.

Academic Programs

At Ashland, learning is about understanding new ideas, solving problems, and pushing limits. Through small classes, which allow individual instruction, field experiences in every academic area, academic support services, and an honors program for students with a minimum GPA of 3.5, AU's goal of helping students excel is achieved.

Institutional requirements are designed to allow for interdisciplinary opportunities in the students' programs. Basic degree requirements include English composition (6 hours), contemporary issues (4 hours), communications (3 hours), religion (3 hours), and physical education (2 hours). Distribution requirements in humanities (6 hours), social science (6 hours), science/mathematics (6 hours), fine/performing arts (6 hours), and business/economics (3 hours), or interdisciplinary seminars substituted for distribution requirements, complete the degree requirements.

There are two semesters in the University's academic year. Classification of students is based on progress toward meeting degree requirements in terms of semester hours earned, as follows: freshman, 1–29 semester hours; sophomore, 30–59; junior, 60–89; senior, 90 or more. A total of 128 semester hours of credit is needed for graduation.

Off-Campus Programs

Study semesters are available at both foreign and domestic universities. Commercial art and fashion merchandising students have the option of spending their junior year at one of the art institutes in Pittsburgh, Atlanta, Dallas, Fort Lauderdale, Houston, Philadelphia, Seattle, or Denver. Some art majors spend a semester in New York City through an affiliate program with Hunter College or Drew University. In cooperation with the Ohio Agricultural Research Center in Wooster, Ohio, selected science majors may spend one semester or more participating in the agriscience program. Ashland's classrooms extend around the world, with overseas student teaching opportunities, summer language classes, faculty-sponsored student tours, mission trips, and other special programs. Numerous study abroad opportunities are available.

Academic Facilities

Ashland's facilities include nine computer labs, modern science laboratories, fully equipped radio/TV studios, music studios and practice rooms, art studios and a gallery, a 750-seat theater, and a nursery and Montessori school. Physical education facilities include a natatorium, three basketball courts, a sauna, a training room, a fitness center, and a field house with an indoor banked track. The Ashbrook Center, a nationally known institute for the study of public affairs, publishes scholarly books, hosts academic forums, and sponsors lectures by famous political speakers. The new 60,000-square-foot Richard E. and Sandra J. Dauch College of Business and Economics building opened for spring semester 2004 and provides an innovative, world-class environment for business leaders of tomorrow. In addition, plans have been approved for the construction of an $18-million Sport Sciences/Recreation Center and an estimated $11-million renovation and addition to the Kettering Science Center. Both projects are to be completed by fall 2005. And by spring 2006, a new $10-million College of Education building is scheduled to be completed.

Costs

Tuition for the 2004–05 school year is $18,394, fees total $464, room is $3740, and board is $3224. The total cost of tuition, fees, room, and board is $25,822.

Financial Aid

Approximately 98 percent of Ashland University's students receive financial assistance, enabling them to receive the benefits of a private college education. Awards are based on outstanding scholarship, accomplishment, talent, and/or financial need.

To apply for financial assistance, students must file the Free Application for Federal Student Aid (FAFSA) with the federal government and submit the Ashland University Financial Aid Application to the AU Financial Aid Office.

Faculty

Ashland's teaching faculty includes 250 full-time members, 80 percent of whom hold doctorate degrees. The faculty's first priority is teaching, placing emphasis on individual instruction and helping students achieve. They listen, advise, coordinate internship and research opportunities, write letters of recommendation, and introduce professional perspectives into every class.

Student Government

Ashland University allows its students a role of major importance and responsibility in the conduct of all affairs relating to their lives as members of the University community. The Student Senate acts as the principal governing body and serves as a liaison between students and the faculty and administration. More than 100 other student organizations exist, ranging from Orientation Team to intramurals, from Campus Activities Board to community service. HOPE Christian Fellowship and the Fellowship of Christian Athletes are among the largest on campus. Thirty percent of AU students are involved in sororities and fraternities.

Admission Requirements

Ashland strongly recommends that applicants have 16 units of college-preparatory high school credit to ensure that they have sufficient background for college work. Freshman applicants must present an official transcript of courses and grades from secondary school and scores on either the SAT I or ACT examination. Each applicant is encouraged to visit the campus for an interview with an admission counselor. A visit provides the applicant with an opportunity to see the campus and ask questions of students and faculty members.

Transfer students from accredited institutions are considered for admission to Ashland provided that they are in good standing socially and academically (having at least a C average or a 2.0 GPA) at any institutions attended previously.

Applicants who complete their secondary education through an alternative program (e.g., home schooling) must present evidence that they have been adequately prepared for university work to be considered for admission to AU. Such evidence may include appropriate scores on ACT or SAT tests, a high school equivalency diploma (GED test), satisfactory achievement on state or nationally normed tests that evaluate achievement level in high school academic subjects, and adequate performance on AU placement tests.

Application and Information

Freshman applicants are encouraged to submit applications early in the senior year of high school. To be considered for admission, a student must submit a completed and signed application form; a secondary school transcript listing rank in class and all courses and grades, beginning with the ninth grade; scores on the SAT I or ACT; and a nonrefundable $25 application fee. Transfer students will be considered for admission after they have submitted the application form, an official college transcript from all colleges previously attended, and the nonrefundable $25 application fee. An enrollment deposit of $100 is requested thirty days after acceptance and is nonrefundable after May 1.

Additional information may be obtained by contacting:

Director of Admission
Ashland University
Ashland, Ohio 44805
Telephone: 419-289-5052
800-882-1548 (toll-free)
Fax: 419-289-5999
E-mail: enrollme@ashland.edu
World Wide Web: http://www.ashland.edu

The 55,000-square-foot Hawkins-Conard Student Center features several student lounges, a fitness center, a grill and a snack bar, an auditorium, and numerous meeting rooms.

ASSUMPTION COLLEGE

WORCESTER, MASSACHUSETTS

The College

Founded in 1904, Assumption College enters its second century championing the transformation of individuals and society through a liberal education that develops students as learned persons and responsible citizens. Catholic intellectual and moral traditions inform these transforming processes, with the College's Assumptionist heritage guiding its graduates toward lives of competent and compassionate service. The community at Assumption is held together by shared commitments to human dignity and difference, to social justice and global engagement, to the relationship of faith and knowledge, and to the transforming powers of a liberal education.

Location

Assumption College, located on a beautifully landscaped 175-acre campus in the residential Westwood Hills of Worcester, is just a short distance from downtown. Worcester, the third-largest city in New England, is a five-time recipient of the All-America City Award—the nation's oldest and most prestigious community recognition program. The city is a vibrant community, offering students opportunities for internships, service learning, and community service as well as for culture and recreation. Worcester boasts of its nationally acclaimed Worcester Centrum Centre, one of the country's busiest arenas for concerts, conferences, and shows. It is home to the renowned Worcester Art Museum and Higgins Armory Museum and unique Ecotarium. Nearby facilities for winter and summer sports include Wachusett Mountain and Lake Quinsigamond. Ethnic restaurants and shopping abound. Worcester is also centrally located, with Boston, Providence, Rhode Island, and Hartford, Connecticut, an hour's drive away.

Majors and Degrees

The College offers Bachelor of Arts degrees in accounting, biology, biology with concentration in biotechnology and molecular biology, chemistry, classics, computer science, economics, economics with business concentration, economics with international concentration, education (accompanying an appropriate major), English, English with concentration in writing and mass communications, environmental science, foreign languages, French, French with concentration in Francophone culture and civilization, global studies, global studies with business concentration, history, international business, Latin American studies, management, marketing, mathematics, organizational communication, philosophy, political science, psychology, social and rehabilitation services, sociology, sociology with concentration in criminology, Spanish, Spanish with concentration in Hispanic culture and civilization, theology, and visual arts

With the exception of environmental science and global studies, minors are available in the above list. In addition, minors are also available in anthropology, art history, community service learning, comparative literature, and English writing. Preprofessional preparation is available for dentistry, medicine and law. Joint seven-year programs are also available for those interested in podiatry and optometry. The College offers a first-year program, honors program, foundations of Western civilization program, study abroad, internships, cross-registration through the Colleges of Worcester Consortium, a 3-2 engineering program through Worcester Polytechnic Institute, and a new partnership with Columbia University at Biosphere II in Arizona. Air Force and Army ROTC programs are also available.

Academic Program

Father Emmanuel d'Alzon, founder of the Assumptionists, dedicated Assumption College to the "pursuit of truth, wherever it may be found." The College continues that pursuit of truth through the liberal education program. The students and faculty come together to contemplate the books, ideas, people, and events that have shaped civilization, so that the students might be better prepared to make their own contributions in the future.

Finding the truth about oneself and the nature of the surrounding world means learning not only how to ask questions but how to find the answers. That is why so many of the classes at Assumption are discussions, not lectures, and why the faculty assigns cooperative projects, frequent writing, and hands-on assignments designed to teach the student how to think, not memorize.

Assumption College follows a traditional two-semester calendar, running from late August to mid-May. The Continuing Education and Graduate School offers two summer sessions for its students.

Students must complete a core curriculum of two courses of English, one of which is composition; two courses of philosophy; two courses of theology; two of the following three courses: mathematics, a laboratory science, and a third year of a foreign language; and one each of literature, history, social science, and either art, music, or theater. A total of 120 semester credit hours must be completed, with 9 to 12 semester credit hours in the upper division of the major.

Off-Campus Programs

In 1967, Assumption College joined with the other institutions of higher learning in the Worcester area to organize the Colleges of Worcester Consortium. Through the cooperation of thirteen Worcester area colleges, Assumption students may cross-register for academic credit at any of the participating colleges and may enjoy cultural events through those colleges.

Assumption College encourages qualified students to spend a semester or year abroad as an integral part of their undergraduate education. In the past five years, Assumption College students have studied abroad in Australia, Austria, the Czech Republic, England, France, Germany, Greece, Ireland, Italy, the Netherlands, and Spain.

Students at Assumption practice classroom theories through internships designed to help them explore their professional choices and broaden their workplace skills. For example, local, national, and international sites where current Assumption students have recently completed internships include the Department of Commerce, Central America Bureau; the Department of State, NAFTA Agreement; Smith Barney; Fidelity; Dean Witter Reynolds; AT&T; and the Alliance Française in Paris.

Academic Facilities

Assumption College has recently completed a five-year, $50-million physical plant expansion program. The flagship of this building program is the new Science Center, which opened in

2003 and is home to the Department of Natural Sciences and includes biology, chemistry, environmental science, and physics. The facility features five multiuse classrooms (most of which have state-of-the-art technology), ten teaching laboratories, seven laboratories dedicated for faculty and student research, two conference rooms, a greenhouse, and inviting, open-air lounge areas. To ensure campuswide utilization, the south atrium has been outfitted with a sound system to be used for future lectures, receptions, and other special events.

The new Information Technology Center, which opened in 2002, houses public-access labs and technology-rich classrooms with more than 1,560 computers as well as help staff for the community. Equipment and software are available for standard applications and free laser printing as well as Web authoring, graphics and animation, digital video, and CD and DVD production. The College also has a new digital audio studio available for all students and faculty members. Resident students have unlimited Ethernet access to the Internet from their rooms. In 2003, Assumption College received a grant from the National Science Foundation for network infrastructure to connect to Internet2. The purpose is to develop and implement a high-performance network connection (Internet2) that is separate from the Internet and dedicated exclusively to research and education in all subject areas.

Costs

For 2003–04, tuition was $21,000 and room and board charges were $8210. The board plan is required for all freshmen and for all residents without cooking facilities. A student government fee costs $165. The total for tuition, room and board charges, and the fee was $29,605.

Financial Aid

Assumption College offers financial aid based on demonstrated need and scholastic promise. The College requires the Free Application for Federal Student Aid (FAFSA). This form should be filed by February 1 so that Assumption receives the processed application by the March 1 deadline.

The College offers merit awards to qualified students. Monies given through this program reflect the College's commitment to upholding a campus culture that champions academic excellence and student leadership. All applicants for admission are considered for these awards.

Faculty

Assumption College faculty members—92 percent of whom hold doctoral or terminal degrees in their field—represent diverse fields of specialization and a wide range of professional experience. They are distinguished by an unusually deep dedication to their students, putting in far more than the minimum requirement of 10 office hours a week.

Student Government

As a very active organization, the Student Government Association (S.G.A.) attempts to move closer to the fulfillment of the ideals of self-government. The elected representatives of the student body constitute the Student Senate of S.G.A. This group is responsible for the recognition and financing of student clubs and activities and for serving as the official means of communication and coordination with the Assumption College student community.

Admission Requirements

Admission to Assumption College is limited to men and women of character, intelligence, and motivation who are selected from applicants who have completed the prescribed secondary school requirements. Assumption College supports the efforts of secondary school officials and governing bodies to have their schools achieve regional accredited status to provide reliable assurance of quality of the education preparation of its applicants for admission.

Application and Information

Campus visits are strongly recommended. Appointments can be scheduled Monday through Friday. Group Information Sessions are held most Saturdays in the fall.

Applicants must submit a completed application, a $50 application fee, official transcripts, SAT I or ACT scores, a recommendation, and an essay. All applications for the freshman class, as well as all supporting credentials, must be filed in the Office of Admissions by March 1. Applications for early decision must be received by November 15. In addition to the Assumption Application, students may complete the Common Application and Supplement and may apply online at the Web site listed below or at http://www.commonapp.org.

For more information, students should contact:

Office of Admissions
Assumption College
500 Salisbury Street
P.O. Box 15005
Worcester, Massachusetts 01609-1296
Telephone: 508-767-7285
888-882-7786 (toll-free)
E-mail: admiss@assumption.edu
World Wide Web: http://www.assumption.edu

The flagship of Assumption's five-year, $50-million physical plant expansion program is the new Science Center, which was completed in September 2003.

ATLANTA COLLEGE OF ART

ATLANTA, GEORGIA

The College

Atlanta College of Art provides an educational environment for the career-minded student with a talent and passion for art or design. Founded in 1905, the College is an accredited institutional member of the National Association of Schools of Art and Design and the Commission on Colleges of the Southern Association of Colleges and Schools. Approximately 400 students from across the U.S. and from abroad compose a highly charged, creative community that nurtures the development of educated, effective, and successful professionals in the visual arts.

Atlanta College of Art is a founding member of the Woodruff Arts Center, the focus of the cultural life of the region. As the only art college in the United States that shares its campus with three other arts organizations—the High Museum of Art, the Alliance Theater, and the Atlanta Symphony Orchestra—the College is able to offer students access to a variety of art forms and resources on a working and thriving campus.

The Student Affairs Office provides career planning services and coordinates an internship program for students wishing to gain professional work experience to complement their academic and studio training. Recent internship sponsors have included American Museum of Papermaking, CNN Headline News, Coca-Cola, Georgia Pacific Corporation, IBM, Museum of Modern Art, Turner Publishing, and Zoo Atlanta.

Students are encouraged to become involved in the extracurricular life of the College. A variety of clubs and organizations are recognized and funded by the College to give students opportunities for enrichment beyond the classroom.

Location

Atlanta offers students the best of the Sun Belt: long, bright, crisp fall and spring seasons with short, mild winters in the largest cosmopolitan center in the Southeast. With one of the fastest-growing economies in the nation, Atlanta is a city bursting with newness and enormous energy while still retaining its traditions and flavor. The city has a flourishing grassroots art scene—an optimal environment for the emerging artist or designer. Atlanta has scores of galleries and alternative spaces that exhibit a broad variety of artwork; a ballet and opera; numerous movie houses showing new releases and foreign and classic films; a growing number of theater companies, large and small; many opportunities for rock, jazz, avant-garde music, and outdoor performances. In addition, Atlanta has a myriad of natural areas and parks, restaurants and coffee houses of every description, and four professional sports teams.

Atlanta College of Art is located in Midtown, the cultural heart of the city, a neighborhood where skyscrapers soar above tree-lined streets filled with restored older residences, some dating from the Victorian era. The Arts Center Station of MARTA, Atlanta's clean, safe, and efficient rapid transit system, is located just across the street from the College and offers easy access to many points of interest.

Majors and Degrees

Atlanta College of Art offers a four-year program leading to the Bachelor of Fine Arts degree in advertising, computer animation, drawing, digital art, digital multimedia, digital video, graphic design, illustration, painting, photography, printmaking, and sculpture.

Academic Programs

The College's first-year Foundation Program combines visual studies courses, which emphasize visual thinking and problem solving, with courses in drawing and liberal arts as well as work in a studio area of choice. In the sophomore year, students develop their own course of study with a faculty adviser, either electing an established major or designing their own individualized major program. During the course of study, studio work is combined with courses in art history and criticism, English, literature, philosophy, psychology, anthropology, sociology, science, and math in a ratio of 2:1. These liberal arts courses reflect the notion that the making of art and the making of the artist are imaginative and reflective tasks and not simply technical ones, and they embody the conviction that the best artists and designers are those who can appreciate how tradition influences their work and is affected by it.

Operating on a two-semester academic year with an optional concentrated summer session, the College requires that students complete 120 credit hours for the B.F.A. degree: 78 in studio (12 credits in visual studies, 12 credits in drawing, 30–36 credits in the major, and 18–24 credits in studio electives) and 42 in liberal arts (12 credits in art history, 18 credits in the humanities, 3 credits in natural science, 6 credits in social science, and 3 credits in math).

Off-Campus Programs

Atlanta College of Art is a member of the Association of Independent Colleges of Art and Design. The College's membership in this group allows students to study at other member schools for a semester or a year under a student mobility program. Because the College is also a member of the Atlanta Regional Consortium for Higher Education, students are able to take courses and attend lectures and events at other area colleges and universities, such as Emory University and Georgia Institute of Technology. Students may also study abroad in a variety of programs. Faculty members, the Student Affairs Office, and the Office of the Vice President of Academic Affairs assist in the choice of an appropriate program.

Academic Facilities

In spring 2003, the College opened a $14-million state-of-the-art residence hall and sculpture building. Designed by world-renowned Italian architect Renzo Piano, the project realizes the College's most ambitious dream—to create a true artists' community where students live and work, experiment and grow.

The residence hall is an urban-living arrangement including six floors of apartment-style suites for 150 residents. The suites address the basic needs of a community of artists with high ceilings and economy of space. Each furnished suite has two private bedrooms with a bed, sitting area, and a large desk providing ample space for working and producing art; a bathroom; a small kitchen; and dining area. The residence hall has a fitness center, game rooms, seminar spaces, television viewing rooms, and numerous residential social spaces.

The sculpture facility houses a woodshop, twenty-two individual student studios, a visual studies classroom, and an exterior covered courtyard for breakout working space. The building is flooded with natural light and provides a foundation from which all students can solve three-dimensional problems working in a variety of materials, including bronze, aluminum, wood, metal, clay, stone, resin, and fiberglass.

The residence hall and sculpture building are surrounded by a 10,200-square-foot campus courtyard where students gather, meet, interact, and collaborate.

Atlanta College of Art occupies space on all four floors of the Woodruff Arts Center. College facilities include visual studies studios; drawing studios; a photo shooting studio and darkrooms; silkscreen, lithography, and intaglio and relief printmaking studios; papermaking and bookbinding facilities; painting studios; design studios; video and computer studios; and academic classrooms. Advanced-level students in painting, design, and sculpture are allotted individual work spaces.

The two-story library, with its expanse of windows overlooking Peachtree Street, offers a view of Atlanta College of Art. The library has approximately 25,000 titles and 98,000 images and houses the Georgia Artists Registry, which has 550 files on Georgia artists. The library subscribes to more than 200 journals and houses a collection of 1500 nationally renowned artists' books, which is the largest collection in the Southeast.

The Rich Auditorium, which seats more than 400, is the scene of many events, including visiting artists' lectures, performances, film series, and other College gatherings.

The stunning Atlanta College of Art Gallery, a museum-quality space of 3,850 square feet, shows eight to ten exhibitions a year, including the annual faculty show, juried student and graduating senior shows, contemporary exhibitions organized by the gallery, and traveling exhibitions featuring works by internationally recognized artists such as Laylah Ali, Juan Perdiguero, John Bankston, and Shigeo Fukuda. Gallery 100 offers exhibits of student work that are changed weekly and is maintained by the students themselves. The High Museum of Art is an integral part of the College's academic life; faculty members often take classes to the museum, and visiting artists, critics, and curators give lectures and gallery talks there, often in conjunction with studio demonstrations, critiques of student work, and workshops at the College.

Costs

Tuition for the 2004–05 academic year is $16,900 for full-time students. The cost of a double-occupancy apartment in the residence hall is $5100. General fees total $384, and the housing activity fee is $50.

Financial Aid

Atlanta College of Art offers extensive financial assistance to students, combining institutional funds with funds from federal and state grant and loan programs. Each year, need-based grants, loans, and work-study jobs are awarded to students who apply for financial assistance using the Free Application of Federal Student Aid and the College's own financial aid form. While the priority deadline for applying for financial aid is March 15, awards are made on a first-come, first-served basis. The College also offers Merit Scholarships to both entering students and returning students. The Presidential Scholarship is awarded on the basis of the excellence of the portfolio and scholastic achievement. The School of Excellence award is given in recognition of the high quality of the student's high school or two-year college art program and the students' achievement in that program. The Portfolio Scholarship is awarded on the basis of the applicant's portfolio. Georgia residents are eligible for the Georgia Tuition Equalization Grant and the Hope Scholarship program.

Faculty

The 400 degree-seeking, full-time students at the College find that the 12:1 student-faculty ratio facilitates the personal attention and encouragement that are crucial to the development and nurturing of creative talent. The 24 full-time and 40 adjunct professors at the College are dedicated professionals who combine active careers as artists and designers with a primary commitment to teaching. Faculty influence is expanded by an extensive schedule of national and international visiting artists and designers, who lecture and critique student work.

Student Government

Representatives of the student body are organized in the Student Alliance for the purpose of governance. This group oversees the funding of other student organizations, acts as a liaison between students and the administration, and plans activities for the entire student body. The College is committed to student involvement throughout the campus.

Admission Requirements

Atlanta College of Art welcomes applications from high school graduates, recipients of high school equivalency certificates, and college transfer students. Applicants to the College must submit the following materials for evaluation: a completed application for admission, a $30 nonrefundable application fee, an essay, official transcripts from high school and all colleges attended, SAT I or ACT scores, two letters of recommendation, and a portfolio of twelve to fifteen pieces of work, including a minimum of five drawings from direct observation.

Application and Information

Students are admitted to the College on a rolling basis, and an admission decision is made as soon as the applicant file is complete. While there is no official deadline for submission of an application, students are encouraged to apply by March 1 for priority consideration for admission, financial aid, and scholarships.

For an application and more information, students should contact:

Vice President of Enrollment Management
Atlanta College of Art
Woodruff Arts Center
1280 Peachtree Street, NE
Atlanta, Georgia 30309
Telephone: 404-733-5100
800-832-2104 (toll-free)
E-mail: acainfo@woodruffcenter.org
World Wide Web: http://www.aca.edu

Students and faculty members at a gallery opening.

AUBURN UNIVERSITY

AUBURN, ALABAMA

The University

Auburn University was chartered in 1856 as East Alabama Male College. In 1872, the University was designated as a land-grant institution and has since evolved into a major comprehensive university, the largest in the state of Alabama. The campus consists of more than 1,800 beautiful acres, surrounded by farms and woodlands. The student body is composed of students from all fifty states, the District of Columbia, Puerto Rico, the Virgin Islands, and ninety countries. Auburn freshmen score well above the national averages; in 2001, Auburn averages were 23.5 on the ACT (composite score) and 1110 on the SAT I (combined score). About 16 percent of all undergraduates live on campus, and a wide variety of off-campus housing is available in the form of apartments, condominiums, and trailer parks. The campus offers numerous extracurricular activities, including nineteen sororities, twenty-eight fraternities, and more than 300 chartered and officially recognized organizations. Most are open to any interested student. Auburn offers an extremely active intramural sports and recreational services program in both team and individual activities. For students interested in musical organizations, Auburn offers a University Concert Choir, the University Singers, Gospel Choir, Men's Chorus, Women's Chorus, various ensembles, the University Orchestra, an Opera Workshop, and Marching and Concert bands. In addition, eight or nine theatrical productions are presented each year by the Auburn University Theatre. All students are welcome to audition for these productions, although casting priority is given to theater majors and minors. The Auburn Studio of the Alabama Public Television Network regularly produces programs for the Alabama Educational Television network, and a campus radio station, WEGL-FM, is operated by Auburn students.

Nationally recognized ROTC programs are available in three branches of service: Air Force, Army, and Navy/Marine Corps. Each of the three units is ranked among the top ten in the nation. Auburn is one of only seven schools in the Nuclear Enlisted Commissioning Program. It owns and operates the 334-acre Robert E. Pitts Auburn-Opelika Airport, providing flight education and fuel, maintenance, and airplane storage. The Auburn University Aviation Department is fully certified by the FAA as an Air Agency with examining authority for private, commercial, instrument, and multiengine courses.

Auburn University has been accredited by the Southern Association of Colleges and Schools since 1922, with specific programs accredited by the AACSB International–The Association to Advance Collegiate Schools of Business, the National Architectural Accrediting Board, the National Association of Schools of Art and Design, the National Association of Schools of Music, the Foundation for Interior Design Education Research, the American Council on Pharmaceutical Education, the Accreditation Board for Engineering and Technology, the Society of American Foresters, the National League for Nursing, the American Psychological Association, the National Council for Accreditation of Teacher Education, and many others. Auburn University offers, in addition to the undergraduate degree programs, more than 130 graduate-level programs. The Doctor of Pharmacy from the School of Pharmacy and the Doctor of Veterinary Medicine from the College of Veterinary Medicine are offered as first professional degrees.

Location

The city of Auburn (population about 35,000) is located in the east central part of Alabama, 60 miles northeast of Montgomery, 120 miles southeast of Birmingham, and 110 miles southwest of Atlanta, Georgia. Interstate 85 provides easy access to both Montgomery and Atlanta. Auburn is a small residential area and is often referred to as the "loveliest village of the plains." The University and the local community offer that rare blend of mutual support and cooperation evident only in a true university community.

Majors and Degrees

Auburn University offers 130 baccalaureate degree programs. The College of Agriculture confers the Bachelor of Science (B.S.) in agricultural business and economics, agricultural journalism, agricultural science, agronomy and soils, animal and dairy science, entomology, fisheries management, horticulture, poultry science, rural sociology, and several pre-veterinary medicine options. The College of Architecture, Design, and Construction offers Bachelor of Architecture (five-year) degrees in architecture and landscape architecture, the dual degree in architecture and interior design, the Bachelor of Science in environmental design, as well as a Bachelor of Industrial Design, Bachelor of Interior Design, and Bachelor of Science in Building Science. The College of Business and School of Accountancy grant a B.S. in business administration with professional option programs in accounting, aviation management, business economics, finance, human resources management, international business, management, management information systems, marketing, operations management, and transportation and physical distribution. The College of Education provides teacher preparation programs leading to a B.S. in early childhood education, elementary education, English/language arts, foreign language (French, German, and Spanish), health, mathematics, music, physical education, science (biology, chemistry, general science, and physics), social science (economics, general social science, geography, history, political science, psychology, and sociology), special education, and vocational education. In addition, Bachelor of Science programs that are not teacher preparatory are available in adult education, exercise science, health promotion, recreation and sports management, and rehabilitation services. The College of Engineering offers curricula leading to the degrees of Bachelor of Aerospace Engineering, Chemical Engineering, Civil Engineering, Computer Engineering, Computer Science, Electrical Engineering, Geological Engineering, Industrial and Systems Engineering, Textile Chemistry, Textile Engineering, Textile Management and Technology, and Wireless Engineering. In addition, the B.S. is offered in agricultural engineering, environmental science, and forest engineering. The School of Forestry grants the B.S. in forestry. The School of Human Sciences offers the B.S. in apparel merchandising, design and production, human development and family studies, hotel and restaurant management, interior design, and nutrition and food science. The College of Liberal Arts and School of Fine Arts award the Bachelor of Arts, Bachelor of Science, or Bachelor of Fine Arts in the following areas: anthropology, art, communication, communication disorders, corporate journalism, criminal justice/criminology, English, foreign languages–international trade, French, geography, German, health services administration, history, journalism, mass communication, philosophy, political science, psychology, public administration, public relations, social work, sociology, Spanish, theater, and visual arts. The School of Nursing provides study leading to the Bachelor of Science in Nursing. The College of Sciences and Mathematics offers the B.S. in applied discrete mathematics, applied mathematics, biochemistry, botany, chemistry, earth sciences, geology, laboratory technology, marine biology, mathematics, medical technology, microbiology, molecular biology, physics, wildlife science, and zoology. Preprofessional programs are offered in dentistry, medicine, occupational therapy, optometry, pharmacy, physical therapy, and veterinary medicine.

Academic Program

The academic year consists of two 15-week semesters (late August to mid-May). Additional summer semesters are in session from mid-May to late August. A common core curriculum is required. Undergraduate degree programs require at least 120 semester hours. Entering freshmen with extraordinarily high academic aptitude, an ACT composite score of at least 29 or an SAT I combined score of 1280 or more, and a minimum high school grade point average of 3.5 are eligible for consideration for admission into the honors program. The honors program provides individualized intellectual opportunities, smaller classes, and possible accelerated entry into graduate work. Advanced credit may be awarded on the basis of proficiency examinations, the Advanced Placement Program of the College Board, or the College-Level Examination Program (CLEP). A strong Co-op Education Program is available in agriculture, architecture, biological sciences, business, education, engineering, fine arts, forestry, human sciences, liberal arts, and science and mathematics in undergraduate as well as graduate programs.

Academic Facilities

The Ralph Brown Draughon Library is the main library on campus, with branch libraries located in the School of Architecture and the College of Veterinary Medicine. Computerized catalogs provide quick access to catalog records for most library items. Recently completed major projects include a $21-million expansion of the main library and the construction of a $10-million chemistry building, the $7.5-million Harbert Engineering Center for aerospace engineering, a $3.6-million biological research facility, a $15-million building for the College of Business, a 19,000-square-foot greenhouse complex costing $1.35 million, a 12,000-square-foot expansion of the Hoerlein Small Animal Clinic costing $1.5 million, an $875,000 veterinary research facility, a $20.8-million renovation of residence halls, the $10.5-million Martin Swim Center, an $8.9-million athletics center, a $1-million Satellite Uplink, a $550,000 educational television facility, the $1-million Ware Diagnostic Imaging Center in the Veterinary Medicine Complex, two residence halls costing $9.5 million, and the $12.5-million Rouse Life Sciences Building.

Costs

Undergraduate Alabama residents paid $11,399 for the 2002–03 academic year (two semesters). This figure included $3784 for tuition, $900 for books and supplies, $4500 for room and board, $729 for transportation, and $1486 for miscellaneous personal expenses. Out-of-state students paid an additional fee of $6520.

Financial Aid

Financial Aid: During 2001–02, more than 10,000 students received more than $65 million in student aid funds through the University and through Federal Stafford Student Loans from commercial lenders. Financial assistance includes University loans, scholarships, part-time employment, and federal programs, such as the Federal Pell Grant, Federal Supplemental Educational Opportunity Grant, Federal Work-Study, Federal Perkins Loan, Health Professions student loans, and Federal Student Loans.

Financial aid application packets are available in January for the following academic year from the Office of Student Financial Aid, 203 Martin Hall, Auburn University, Alabama 36849. Applications received by March 1 are given priority consideration.

Scholarships: Prospective freshmen with superior ACT or SAT I scores and a 3.0 high school GPA who are on file with the University's Office of Admissions by December 1 are given automatic consideration for academic scholarships. The University's most prestigious scholarships include the Vulcan Presidential Honors Scholarship ($4000 per year), the Blount Presidential Scholarship ($5000 per year), and the McWane Foundation Scholarship ($6000 per year). These scholarships are awarded in late January. The University also offers general and departmental scholarships ranging from partial to full tuition. These scholarships are open to all class levels and are typically awarded in February. For entering freshmen, these scholarships are awarded primarily based on test scores, high school GPA, and need (in some cases). Auburn University actively participates in the National Merit Scholarship Program and National Achievement Scholarship Program. In-state National Merit Semifinalists and National Merit Finalists who name Auburn as their first choice receive a four-year scholarship in the amount of in-state tuition. Excellent scholarship opportunities are also available in the Air Force, Army, and Naval/Marine ROTC programs.

Faculty

Approximately 93 percent of the 1,115 full-time faculty members hold terminal degrees in their field. The Auburn University faculty generates almost one fifth of the entire student credit hour production of the state of Alabama. Auburn's standing as a research university and the quality of its faculty are documented by the growth in research funds provided by contracts and grants—a 33 percent increase in the last five years. Auburn's Space Power Institute is the leading institute in a five-university consortium researching the large amounts of electrical power needed to operate space stations.

Student Government

The Student Government Association (SGA) is the controlling body of all student projects and organizations. All students become members of SGA after paying their tuition and fees. Active participation is encouraged, as all student activities are governed by the SGA. The SGA is the voice of the students, promoting cooperation and communication with the faculty, administration, the Auburn City Council, and the state legislature.

Admission Requirements

Freshman admission to Auburn University is based on either ACT or SAT I scores and high school academic grade point average. Transfer students with fewer than 48 quarter hours or 32 semester hours must also meet freshman requirements.

Application and Information

Applications are accepted with a nonrefundable $25 application fee ($50 international application fee). There is no provision for a fee waiver. The closing date is determined by the number of applicants accepted; admission is on a rolling basis. Students must be accepted before they can apply for their choice of campus housing.

For more information about Auburn University, interested students should contact:

Director of Admissions
202 Martin Hall
Auburn University
Auburn University, Alabama 36849-5145
Telephone: 334-844-4080
800-AUBURN9 (toll-free in Alabama)
E-mail: admissions@auburn.edu
World Wide Web: http://www.auburn.edu/admissions

AURORA UNIVERSITY

AURORA, ILLINOIS

The University

Aurora University was founded in 1893. The school has grown substantially over the years and has taken on many new challenges. In 1938, it was one of the first small colleges to achieve regional accreditation. In 1947, the college's evening program was instituted—one of the nation's first adult education programs at a liberal arts college. In 1985, Aurora College was reorganized as Aurora University, reflecting both the increased size of the institution and the needs associated with its many new programs. In addition to the College of Arts, Science, and Business, the University comprises the College of Education and George Williams College of Health and Human Services (social work, nursing, and human services). Today, the University enrolls 4,000 students in more than forty undergraduate programs and four graduate programs in business, recreation administration, social work, and education. An Ed.D. is offered in educational leadership. Courses are offered at other sites in Illinois, Iowa, and Wisconsin, in addition to the Aurora campus.

The University's student body includes 600 on-campus, traditional-age students; 1,000 undergraduate commuters; 1,800 graduate students; and more than 1,600 students at off-campus sites. The majority of Aurora's students come from the upper-Midwest region, but twenty states and five countries are also represented.

Social life is based on campus, and most activities are campuswide. Aurora has more than thirty musical, literary, religious, social, and service clubs and organizations. There are also three fraternities and sororities for students interested in Greek life. Aurora University has a long history of excellence in both intercollegiate and intramural athletics. A member of the NCAA Division III, Aurora fields intercollegiate teams in baseball, basketball, cross country, football, golf, soccer, softball, tennis, track, and volleyball, often with championship results.

Aurora University is accredited at the bachelor's, master's, and doctoral degree levels by the Commission on Institutions of Higher Education of the North Central Association of Colleges and Schools, and its programs are accredited by the Commission on Collegiate Nursing Education, National League for Nursing Accrediting Commission, Illinois Department of Professional Regulation, Council on Social Work Education, National Recreation and Park Association/American Association of Leisure and Recreation, and Association of Collegiate Business Schools and Programs.

Location

Aurora University is located in an attractive residential neighborhood on the southwest side of Aurora, Illinois, which has a population of more than 153,000 and is the state's second-largest city. The 27-acre main campus is located only minutes from the Illinois Research and Development Corridor, the site of dozens of nationally and internationally based businesses and industries. Located within an hour's drive or train ride is Chicago, one of the most vibrant cities in the world.

Majors and Degrees

The Bachelor of Arts degree is awarded in accounting, biology, business administration, communication (media studies and professional practice), computer science, computer science/business information systems, computer science/electronics, criminal justice, elementary education, English, history, management and innovation, marketing, physical education (K–12 teacher certification), political science, psychology, and sociology. The Bachelor of Science degree is awarded in accounting, biology, biology–environmental science, business administration, computer science, health science (predentistry, premedicine, pre–physical therapy, and pre–veterinary studies), management and innovation, marketing and mathematics, and physical education (athletic training and fitness and health promotion). The Bachelor of Science in human services is awarded in youth development, programming, and management. The Bachelor of Science in Nursing and the Bachelor of Science in Social Work are also offered. The University offers supplemental majors in prelaw and secondary education as well as the YMCA Senior Director Certificate Program.

Academic Programs

Aurora University offers academic programs combining a liberal arts foundation with majors emphasizing career preparation and selected concentrations. Graduates are educated to be purposeful, ethical, and proficient—equipped for worthwhile careers and productive lives and for venturing out into a changing world.

To earn a bachelor's degree, students are required to fulfill the general degree requirements of the University and the major requirements for an approved major; complete at least 120 semester hours with a GPA of at least 2.0 on a 4.0 scale, including at least 52 semester hours at a senior college; and complete at least 30 semester hours, including the last 24 for the degree and at least 18 semester hours in the major, at Aurora University.

Aurora University accepts credits earned through the CLEP, DANTES, ACT-PREP, and NLN Mobility testing programs. In addition, credit based on portfolio assessment is available to students who have significant prior learning from career experience or individual study.

The University observes a semester calendar (two sixteen-week semesters), with classes beginning in late August and concluding in early May.

Off-Campus Programs

Aurora University offers travel-study programs in Mexico and England. The University also has off-campus classes in various locations in Illinois and Wisconsin and several degree programs at the University's Lake Geneva campus in Williams Bay, Wisconsin.

Academic Facilities

The major buildings at Aurora are marked by the distinctive, red-tiled roofs specified by Charles Eckhart in his donation for the original campus. Dunham Hall houses state-of-the-art computer facilities as well as the Schingoethe Center for Native American Cultures. Other facilities include the fully equipped Perry Theatre, science labs, flora-fauna complex, and the College Commons. Music practice rooms, piano labs, and a spacious art studio are also available. Charles B. Phillips Library has more than 112,000 volumes, 190,000 microform units, and approximately 700 current periodical subscriptions. In addition, the library provides access to approximately 3,700 journals in electronic full text.

Costs

Tuition for the 2004–05 school year is $14,750 for full-time students (24 to 34 semester hours per year), while yearly room and board costs average $6100.

Financial Aid

Aurora University's financial aid program has been designed to make it possible for any academically qualified student to afford the benefits of a private education. The University works with students to determine the amount of their costs and to identify all available resources so that students can meet these expenses. Financial aid is awarded based on financial need as reported on the FAFSA. In addition to need-based financial aid, Aurora University offers academic scholarships, including the Board of Trustees Scholarship, Crimi Scholarship, Deans' Scholarship, Solon B. Cousins Scholarship, Aurora University Opportunity Grant, and transfer scholarships.

Faculty

The favorable student-faculty ratio of 15:1 ensures that students receive plenty of individual attention in class. Instructors also make time for students outside of class, acting as mentors, advisers, and friends who are eager to answer questions and to join students in sports and social activities.

Student Government

The student body is represented by the AUSA (Aurora University Student Association), which provides funding for various student groups on campus. Students are also active members of committees ranging from faculty searches to academic standards and are provided with certain voting privileges.

Admission Requirements

The Aurora University Committee on Admissions considers the complete record of a candidate for admission. The University seeks qualified students from varied geographical, cultural, economic, racial, and religious backgrounds. No single, inflexible set of admission standards is applied. Two general qualities are considered in each candidate: academic ability, enabling the student to benefit from a high-quality academic program, and a diversity of talents and interests that can contribute to making the campus community a better and more interesting place for learning. An application for admission to Aurora University is considered on the basis of the academic ability, achievements, activities, and motivation of the student. Transfer students with fewer than 30 semester hours of credit should apply in the same manner as freshman applicants. Transfer students with more than 15 semester hours may be admitted to Aurora University if they have a transferable overall GPA of 2.0 or higher. Aurora accepts a maximum of 90 semester hours of transfer credits from a combination of two- and four-year schools. A maximum of 68 semester hours may be transferred from two-year schools. For further information, students should contact a transfer counselor in the Office of Admission and Financial Aid.

Application and Information

To apply for admission to Aurora University, the following items should be sent to the Office of Admission and Financial Aid: a completed application form, an official transcript from the guidance counselor, and official ACT or SAT I scores. Transfer students should submit official transcripts from each college or university attended, along with the completed application.

For applications and further information, students may contact:

Office of Admission and Financial Aid
Aurora University
347 South Gladstone Avenue
Aurora, Illinois 60506
Telephone: 630-844-5533
800-742-5281 (toll-free)
E-mail: admission@aurora.edu
World Wide Web: http://www.aurora.edu

An aerial view of Aurora University in Aurora, Illinois.

AUSTIN COLLEGE

SHERMAN, TEXAS

The College

Austin College is considered one of the nation's finest four-year coeducational colleges of liberal arts and sciences. It is a thriving campus community and the majority of students live on campus, creating a dynamic living and learning environment. Founded in 1849, Austin College is affiliated through a covenant relationship with the Presbyterian Church (U.S.A.). The liberal arts and sciences foundation develops lifelong learning abilities, such as thinking critically, solving problems, and communicating with others. The College offers a comprehensive, values-centered education that develops the whole person through academic, co-curricular, and social involvement.

International education is a focus of the College, and more than 70 percent of Austin College graduates spend at least one month in international study during their college experience.

Austin College has an enrollment of approximately 1,300 students. The students are predominantly 18–21 years old, come from twenty-eight states and twenty-six countries, and represent a diversity of ethnicity, religion, and experience.

Opportunities for involvement include more than seventy student organizations, ranging from academic to special interest to local fraternities and sororities. Involvement in music, theater, and art programs is available to all students regardless of major. Intercollegiate athletics include six sports for men and five for women, and many students take part in intramural activities. The College maintains a 29-acre recreational area on Lake Texoma, about 20 minutes from the campus. All students are encouraged to participate in volunteer service and be involved in the community.

Austin College offers guidance to students through Career Services, the Academic Skills Center, and Health Services. The campus dining service offers many food options for students each day. The campus offers coed and single-sex residence halls, as well as apartments that are available to upperclass students. Students of German, French, Japanese, and Spanish may choose to live in the language residence, where the target languages are spoken in common areas.

Many students continue on to graduate and professional study and enjoy successful acceptance rates at these institutions. Austin College graduates can be found around the world in exciting and successful careers, and graduates regularly earn prestigious national honors.

Location

Austin College is located in Sherman, Texas, approximately 45 miles north of the greater Dallas metroplex. Sherman is a small city of approximately 35,000 that *Money* magazine includes among the top 15 percent of the 300 "most livable small cities" in the U.S. Sherman offers students plenty of cultural, religious, and social opportunities, and nearby Lake Texoma offers many additional recreational opportunities. For those seeking "big city" excitement, the Dallas–Fort Worth metroplex is an hour's drive south on U.S. Highway 75.

Majors and Degrees

The Bachelor of Arts degree is offered in American studies, art, biochemistry, biology, business administration, chemistry, classics, communication arts, computer science, economics, English, French, German, history, international economics and finance, international studies, Latin, Latin American studies, mathematics, music, philosophy, physics, political science, psychology, religion, sociology, and Spanish. In addition, the Special Degree Program allows students to design an individualized major.

Through the Austin Teacher Program, a special five-year teacher education program, a student earns both the Bachelor of Arts degree and the Master of Arts in Teaching degree.

Austin College also has excellent preprofessional programs in engineering, health sciences, law, and theology.

Academic Program

Courses in the humanities, natural sciences, and social sciences combine to provide students with breadth and depth in learning. Making connections across disciplines and discovering the "bigger picture" bring learning to life. All students, regardless of major, complete a number of courses that provide the foundation and exploration dimensions of the liberal arts experience at Austin College.

Austin College offers two programs that lead to the Bachelor of Arts degree: the Basic Program, which includes the foundation, exploration, and depth dimensions (plus electives) and the Special Program, which allows an individually designed nontraditional or interdisciplinary major.

Austin College has a 4-1-4 calendar year. Four courses are taken in the fall and spring terms, and one course is completed during the January term. Summer courses are also available. The January term offers an opportunity for in-depth study of one academic or special interest, travel courses, internships, and individualized study.

The College also offers the four-year Posey Leadership Institute, which combines course work, international study, volunteer service, an internship, involvement with a community mentor, and interaction with national and international leaders to develop awareness of leadership skills and styles. Membership in the Leadership Institute is competitive, limited in number, and includes a $10,000-per-year scholarship.

Off-Campus Programs

Students have opportunities for study in England, France, Germany, Spain, Japan, and other countries through the Institute of European and Asian Studies. They participate in the Washington Semester, Washington Summer Symposium, or the Austin College in Mexico programs as well. Students can also become involved in field study through the social sciences laboratory or individually arranged programs.

Academic Facilities

The College's excellent facilities include the Robert J. and Mary Wright Campus Center; well-equipped science classrooms and laboratories; a computer center; complete fine arts facilities, including two theaters; and the Robert T. Mason Athletic-Recreation Complex. A state-of-the-art library with more than 300,000 volumes and 900 periodicals maximizes research and learning opportunities. A campuswide fiber-optic computer network provides access to on-campus resources and the Internet. Three environmental research areas are all within a short drive of the campus.

Costs

The basic tuition charge for students entering in 2003–04 was $17,740; fees were $160, and room and board amounted to $6822, for a total of $24,722.

Financial Aid

Assistance is given in three forms: grants and/or scholarships, loans, and on-campus jobs. Students applying for need-based financial aid should request a financial aid application from Austin College and should also submit the Free Application for Federal Student Aid (FAFSA). Competitive awards, based on merit rather than on financial need, are also available. The application for admission serves as the application for most of these awards, which range in value from $2000 to $10,000. Separate applications are necessary for full-tuition Presidential Scholarships, Leadership Institute Scholarships, Hallam Citizen Scholarships, and Moseley Scholarships for Presbyterian Students. More than 90 percent of students receive some form of financial assistance.

Faculty

Of the full-time faculty members, 98 percent hold terminal degrees. Faculty members holding earned doctorates teach at all levels. In addition to carrying out their academic and professional responsibilities, faculty members participate in the governance of the College and serve as students' mentors. With a student-faculty ratio of 13:1 and an average class size of 23, the emphasis at Austin College is on classroom excellence.

Student Government

Under a community-government partnership plan, in which students and members of the faculty and administration are all participants, student involvement and leadership are important aspects of College governance. The College is committed to high principles in scholarship and general behavior.

Admission Requirements

Admission is competitive, with four times the number of applicants as places in the freshman class. Transfer students are subject to the same rigorous standards required of freshman applicants. Students who cannot fulfill these requirements are considered on an individual basis. Two admission deadlines have been established for freshman applicants for fall enrollment. December 1 is the Early Decision and Early Action I deadline and January 15 is the Early Action II deadline. Students are notified of an admission decision approximately four weeks after each deadline. After January 15, applications are considered on a rolling basis, with a March 1 recommended deadline, and are given consideration on a space-available basis. To reserve a place in the entering class, a $300 deposit is required by May 1. The College's early admission program allows qualified students to enroll after their junior year of high school. Admission to Austin College is on an equal basis, regardless of color, race, sex, religion, national origin, or handicap.

Application and Information

A completed application form, including a $35 nonrefundable application fee, SAT I or ACT scores, two letters of reference, and a transcript from each high school and college attended must be submitted to Austin College. Application forms for admission and financial aid should be requested from the Office of Admission or may be acessed via the College's Web site listed below. Students may request a complimentary loan copy of the *Austin College Video Visit* by calling Videc, Inc., at 800-255-0384 (toll-free).

For more information, students should contact:

Office of Admission
Austin College
900 North Grand Avenue, Suite 6N
Sherman, Texas 75090
Telephone: 903-813-3000
800-KANGAROO (526-4276) (toll-free)
Fax: 903-813-3198
E-mail: admission@austincollege.edu
World Wide Web: http://www.austincollege.edu

Austin College's tree-lined walkways and green expanses provide a backdrop for the mixture of historical and modern buildings on the campus of the more than 150-year-old college.

AZUSA PACIFIC UNIVERSITY

AZUSA, CALIFORNIA

The University

Celebrating more than 100 years of excellence in Christian higher education, Azusa Pacific University (APU) is a comprehensive university founded in 1899. Azusa Pacific earned university status in 1981. Committed to the goal of each student's personal, spiritual, and academic growth, APU provides extensive opportunities for student development with academic emphases in liberal arts and professional studies.

The University is divided into one college and five schools: the College of Liberal Arts and Sciences and the Schools of Music, Nursing, Education and Behavioral Studies, Business and Management, and Theology.

On-campus residential living is a distinctive feature of student life at APU, with several areas from which to choose. Each differs in size, location, structure, type, and activities. Each area sponsors individual and large-group events, academic and social activities, spiritual and cultural experiences, indoor and outdoor recreational opportunities, and both highly structured and spontaneous activities.

The University's 8,200 students (4,400 of whom are undergraduates) come from fifty states and seventy-two nations and represent forty-eight religious denominations. APU students are strong academically, entering with an average GPA of 3.6 and SAT score of 1102. They are often leaders in their high schools, churches, and communities. Azusa Pacific offers excellent leadership development programs that teach students how to be positive contributors to their communities, jobs, and society.

Twenty master's degree programs and four doctorates are offered in addition to the more than forty undergraduate programs listed below.

Location

Azusa Pacific University is located in the foothills of the San Gabriel Valley communities of Azusa and Glendora, 26 miles northeast of Los Angeles. APU is only an hour's drive from beaches, amusement parks, mountains, ski resorts, and cultural centers. The climate is moderate, mostly warm and dry throughout the school year.

Majors and Degrees

Azusa Pacific University grants the Bachelor of Arts degree in the fields of art, athletic training, biblical studies, biology, business administration, chemistry, Christian ministries, cinema and broadcast arts, communication studies, English, global studies, graphic design, history, liberal studies, mathematics, mathematics/physics, music, natural science, philosophy, physical education, political science, psychology, social science, social work, sociology, Spanish, theology, and youth ministries. The Bachelor of Science degree is awarded in the fields of accounting, applied health, biochemistry, biology, chemistry, computer information systems, computer science, finance, international business, marketing, mathematics, nursing, physics, and Web and information technology.

Preprofessional programs are available in allied health, dentistry, law, medicine, and veterinary medicine. Pre-engineering degree programs (3-2 and 2-2) are also offered.

The Department of Religion and Philosophy offers a ministry credential program that combines academic study with practicum and leads to the Bachelor of Arts degree.

Academic Programs

Azusa Pacific University's undergraduate program operates on the semester system and offers two summer sessions. Many graduate programs are on the quarter system.

The minimum number of credits required for a bachelor's degree is 126. About half of these units must be completed in general studies requirements, as follows: skills and University requirements, 43 units; aesthetics and the creative arts, 3 units; heritage and institutions, 6 units; identity and relationships, 3 units; language and literature, 3 units; nature, 4 units; God's Word and the Christian response, 18 units; and integrative electives, 6 units. Areas of concentration vary in their requirements, and many offer several emphases within the major.

The University grants credit for certain scores on Advanced Placement tests and College-Level Examination Program tests, college courses taken while in high school, and the International Baccalaureate.

Academic Facilities

Azusa Pacific's libraries include the William V. Marshburn Memorial Library, the Hugh and Hazel Darling Library, the James L. Stamps Theological Library, and six regional-center libraries. The libraries offer enhanced traditional services as well as state-of-the-art features that facilitate research. Apolis2, the libraries' automated catalog system, is searchable on the World Wide Web, providing increased ease and convenience to aid users in the search process. A unified catalog identifies more than 200,000 books, media, and 1,800 serial titles. More than 630,000 microforms include the Library of American Civilization, Library of American Literature, *New York Times*, and Educational Resources Information Center collections. The University provides access to more than 100 electronic databases, which include more than 12,000 full-text serial titles.

The holdings of the William V. Marshburn Memorial Library include collections supporting liberal arts and sciences, music, and business. Computer workstations and online services offer electronic access to materials from around the world. Special collections include many rare and valuable items. The Media Center has an extensive collection of scores, videocassettes, and compact discs as well as graphic art materials and equipment. Professional librarians are available for assistance.

The holdings of the Hugh and Hazel Darling Library include collections supporting computer science, education, nursing, and professional psychology and offer students a vast collection of printed books, reference materials, serials, and microfilm. Ninety-seven workstations offer access to more than 100 licensed databases and Web resources globally. There are also five classrooms equipped with video projectors, computers, and ISDN lines for distance learning; an auditorium with tiered seating; and a soundstage and TV control room. The design of the building is meant to meet the needs of the twenty-first-century learner.

The newest addition to the APU libraries is the James L. Stamps Theological Library, part of the $12.5-million Duke Academic Complex, which was completed in summer 2003. The library houses a three-story, 50,000-volume book stack dedicated to the APU theology collection; thirty-one workstations; and a number of periodicals. Denominational collections reflecting the rich traditions of the University's Christian heritage are available for research purposes. The rest of the 60,000-square-foot complex houses the eighteen technologically advanced classrooms, a lecture hall, forty faculty and staff offices, and two conference rooms. The School of Theology and Department of Art currently reside in the complex.

APU offers a number of technology options on campus, with computer labs in every library and dorm and in the student union. These labs offer PC and Macintosh computers and laser printers. All Access, the campuswide wireless network, provides

Internet access anywhere on campus to all students and faculty and staff members with laptops and wireless connectivity. A wide variety of software is available to fulfill students' needs.

Outstanding features of the Carl E. Wynn Science Center include an electron microscope facility with both scanning and transmission instrumentation for use in cellular and molecular biology, physiology, and ecology courses and practical facilities, such as a greenhouse and a cadaver lab. The Departments of Biology, Chemistry, Mathematics, and Physics offer vigorous programs with the support of the science center.

APU enjoys the state-of-the-art School of Music and chapel complexes. The two-story School of Music contains three large rehearsal rooms, a recording studio, twenty-two instrumental and voice practice rooms, classrooms, and faculty offices. The Munson Chapel seats 300 and is used for intimate group gatherings, choir and orchestra performances, and special chapel programs.

APU's attractive, landscaped, 103-acre campus houses many contemporary facilities, including Trinity Hall, a 350-bed, 103,000-square-foot residence hall that opened in fall 2003; the $5-million Wilden Hall of Business and Management; and a modern, lighted athletic complex. All facilities are barrier-free.

The 3,500-seat, $13.5-million Richard and Vivian Felix Event Center, designed to meet the University's and community's needs, opened in December 2000.

Costs

Expenses per year for 2003–04 were estimated as follows: tuition, $18,790; room, $3150 to $4280; board, $1970 (ten meals) to $2950 (twenty meals); and books and supplies, $1224.

Financial Aid

Azusa Pacific University offers financial aid in the form of employment, loans, grants, and scholarships. Approximately 90 percent of the student body receives some form of aid. Each year, approximately $8 million in institutional aid is awarded. Students must reapply for aid yearly. Financial aid for international students may be more limited due to government restrictions and differences in educational systems.

Faculty

The student-faculty ratio is 12:1. There are 329 full-time faculty members, 18 part-time faculty members, and 652 adjunct professors. Seventy percent of the faculty members possess terminal degrees. The faculty is primarily a teaching staff. No graduate students serve as undergraduate instructors. Faculty members are highly supportive of and involved in many student activities; they also provide academic advising.

Student Government

The Associated Student Body (ASB) is responsible for representing the students' needs and desires to the administration. Through an annual survey, the ASB can pinpoint major issues that need to be targeted on the APU campus. Elections are held annually in the spring. The student government is made up of a senate and an executive council. ASB also assists student groups requesting funds and participates in student activities on campus.

Students are asked to use personal discretion in activities that may be spiritually or morally destructive. In particular, students are expected to refrain from smoking, drinking, and using or possessing illegal drugs while in residence at the University.

Admission Requirements

Azusa Pacific seeks students who are committed to their own personal, intellectual, and spiritual growth. Consequently, these areas are considered in the admission evaluation. Applicants are required to have earned a minimum GPA of 2.8 in high school or a minimum GPA of 2.0 in previous college work. Minimum SAT I and ACT scores are 910 and 19, respectively. Both transfer students and international students who graduated from non-English-speaking schools also need a GPA of at least 2.8. Transfer, international, and older students are encouraged to apply.

Application and Information

Applicants must submit official transcripts of high school and/or previous college work, two references, a signed statement of agreement, and scores on either the ACT or SAT I. A nonrefundable $45 application fee must be submitted with the application. International students do not need ACT or SAT I scores, but a TOEFL score is required. A $65 application fee applies, and specific application deadlines are enforced. APU follows early action and rolling admission policies, depending on semester and class standing. Students should contact the Office of Undergraduate Admissions for enrollment application deadlines.

For further information, prospective students should contact:

Office of Undergraduate Admissions
Azusa Pacific University
901 East Alosta Avenue
P.O. Box 7000
Azusa, California 91702-7000
Telephone: 626-812-3016
800-TALK-APU (information requests, toll-free)
Fax: 626-812-3096
World Wide Web: http://www.apu.edu

For further information, international students should contact:

Mary Grams, Director
Office of International Student Services
Azusa Pacific University
901 East Alosta Avenue
P.O. Box 7000
Azusa, California 91702-7000
Telephone: 626-812-3055
Fax: 626-815-3801
World Wide Web: http://www.apu.edu/international

The $8-million Hugh and Hazel Darling Library and $12.5-million Duke Academic Complex offer a spectacular array of resources in an environment that is conducive to learning.

BABSON COLLEGE

WELLESLEY, MASSACHUSETTS

The College

Since its founding in 1919, Babson College has focused on educating business leaders capable of initiating and managing change, navigating ethical choices, and solving today's and tomorrow's problems. Students are immersed in an enriching environment that fosters leadership, teamwork, creativity, communication, and diversity. The 2003–04 undergraduate enrollment was 689 women and 1,028 men. An independent, coeducational institution, Babson is accredited by AACSB International–The Association to Advance Collegiate Schools of Business and by the New England Association of Schools and Colleges.

Babson is a residential college and is a 24-hours-a-day, seven days-a-week community alive with intellectual, cultural, athletic, and social activities. Approximately 85 percent of the undergraduate student body live on campus in twelve residence halls. Housing options include coed residence halls, fraternity and sorority housing, and substance-free, multicultural, entrepreneurial, and other-themed housing.

Babson College is an NCAA Division III school, and most of the College's intercollegiate teams compete in the New England Women's and Men's Athletic Conference (NEWMAC). There are twenty-two men and women's varsity sports teams, with additional club and intramural sports available to all students.

The Webster Center features an indoor, 220-meter, six-lane track; a field house; a gymnasium with three basketball courts; five squash and two racquetball courts; a 25-yard, six-lane pool with 1- and 3-meter diving boards; a fitness center; and a dance/aerobics studio. The Babson Skating Center features a 600-seat skating arena. Outdoor facilities include eight tennis courts, a new AstroTurf field, a game field, a renovated softball diamond, a baseball field, two sand-based varsity fields, and a club rugby field.

There were more than 800 extracurricular student activities and events on campus in the 2002–03 academic year.

Location

Babson's beautiful 370-acre campus is in Wellesley, Massachusetts, 14 miles west of Boston, a city renowned for its cultural and recreational opportunities. More than sixty colleges and universities bring more than 250,000 college students to the Boston area, making it one of the world's best college towns for cultural exchange and research.

Majors and Degrees

Babson offers a Bachelor of Science degree in business management, a Master of Business Administration degree, custom degree programs, and executive education programs for business professionals.

Academic Programs

The undergraduate curriculum integrates core competencies, key business disciplines, and the liberal arts into foundation, intermediate, and advanced programs. Babson's core competencies include rhetoric, numeracy and technology, ethics and social responsibility, international and multicultural perspectives, and leadership, teamwork, and creativity.

Foundation program courses include quantitative methods with calculus, probability and statistics, rhetoric, arts and humanities, history and society, business law, science, and the Foundation Management Experience (FME), a yearlong immersion into the world of start-ups, where student teams actually create their own businesses, receiving grants of up to $3000 to cover costs. Babson is the only U.S. school to teach the management core curriculum as an integrated three-semester course where all aspects of business are covered, including accounting, marketing, finance, management operations, strategy, organizational behavior, and economics.

In the Advanced Program, students are free to expand and fine-tune core competencies as they reflect on their own career and life goals. During this time, students take courses in advanced management and liberal arts electives. They also have the opportunity to participate in field-based experiences such as an internship or consulting experience. Special programs, such as the Honors Program, the Women's Leadership Program, the Management Consulting Field Experience, the Accelerated Curriculum for Entrepreneurship, and E-Portfolios allow students to take advantage of customized learning opportunities at Babson.

To earn the Bachelor of Science degree, students are required to complete a minimum of 128 semester hours with a C average or better, with a minimum of 64 credits in the liberal arts (including 20 credits in advanced liberal arts). Transfer students must complete a minimum of 64 semester hours at Babson. Once a student has earned 96 credits, all remaining credits must be earned at Babson, at a Babson-approved cross-registration program, or at a Babson-affiliated Study Abroad Program.

Entering students may be granted credit or advanced course placement for successful scores on either the College-Level Examination Program (CLEP) or Advanced Placement (AP) examinations administered by the College Board as well as some courses in the International Baccalaureate (IB) curriculum.

The College operates on a two-semester academic calendar; semesters run from September to December and from late January through May. An optional credit-bearing three-week winter session is offered in January, and a summer session is offered from late May to mid-July.

Off-Campus Programs

Babson students can also take a course each semester at one of the other area colleges, including Brandeis University and Wellesley College, for full academic credit. These off-campus programs offer greater access to liberal arts courses, including a wide range of foreign languages.

Located on a 70-acre site adjacent to Babson is the Franklin W. Olin College of Engineering, an independent institution that opened in 2001. Babson and Olin are collaborating academically in order to provide extraordinary opportunities in technology-based business, including joint academic and research programming, engineering, and entrepreneurial thinking.

Babson's vibrant study-abroad program enables students to spend either a summer or one or both semesters of their junior year overseas at a college or university. Currently, thirty-six programs are offered in twenty-one countries, and full academic credit is given for approved management and liberal arts courses.

Academic Facilities

Horn Library houses an extensive business collection of print, media, and computerized information resources. Students have campuswide access to newspapers, journals, investment analyst reports, corporate records, directories, and international information. They also benefit from numerous electronic research and news services that supplement a selection of the best business and liberal arts books, newspapers, journals, CD-ROMs, audiocassettes, videocassettes, and videodiscs.

Horn Computer Center is equipped with a lab that remains open 24 hours a day. All systems in Horn have active connections to the Babson network, and the entire campus has access to e-mail, the World Wide Web, and software. There are also more than 6,000 computer outlets on campus; all students have their own Web sites on the Babson intranet. Every incoming Babson undergraduate student receives a leased laptop computer as part of the College's technology initiative.

Other facilities are the Donald W. Reynolds Campus Center, the Richard W. Sorenson Family Visual Arts Center, the Richard W. Sorenson Center for the Arts, the Glavin Family Chapel, and the Arthur M. Blank Center for Entrepreneurship.

Costs

For 2003–04, tuition and fees were $27,248. The total estimated cost for a residential student was $37,226.

Financial Aid

Babson is committed to educating students from diverse backgrounds; applying for financial aid does not affect a student's chances of being admitted to Babson College. Financial assistance is awarded on the basis of merit and demonstrated financial need. Assistance for students begins with consideration for student loans and work-study. Those with need beyond the loan and work-study amounts are then considered for Babson grants.

In 2003–04, 42 percent of all first-year students received need-based Babson grants. Nearly half of Babson students receive some form of financial assistance. Students should note that need-based financial assistance is available to U.S. citizens and permanent residents of the United States. Babson's merit scholarships include Presidential Scholarships, the Women's Leadership Awards, and the Diversity Leadership Awards. Application for aid is made by submitting the Free Application for Federal Student Aid (FAFSA) and the Financial Aid PROFILE of the College Scholarship Service. The application deadline for first-year undergraduate students is February 15; for transfer students, April 15.

Faculty

Because of Babson's close-knit community, students are able to form close relationships with the faculty. Of the 247 faculty members, 164 are full-time, and 90 percent of the full-time faculty members hold a doctoral degree or its equivalent. Faculty members are accomplished entrepreneurs, executives, scholars, authors, researchers, poets, and artists, who bring an intellectual diversity that adds depth to Babson's educational programs and offers students a rich, challenging experience. Babson's student-faculty ratio is 13:1, with an average class size of 27. Most importantly, faculty members teach 100 percent of the courses.

Student Government

Students are encouraged to take an active role in campus activities and student government. The Student Government Association promotes students' interests; allocates funds to campus organizations for academic, social, and recreational activities; licenses student-run businesses; and helps formulate and maintain student regulations.

Admission Requirements

In selecting new students, the admissions office considers each candidate's biographical data, transcripts, test scores, personal statements, and references. Evaluation is based upon comparisons of the qualifications of those who apply. To a large extent, the degree of competition is set by the caliber of the applicants themselves. Consideration is given to the depth and rigor of each candidate's academic program, academic motivation and achievement, and progress from one year to the next. Prospective students are encouraged to have completed or be currently enrolled in a precalculus math class.

The Admission Committee carefully reviews courses taken, math aptitude, and standardized test scores. Reading and writing skills as well as verbal expression are measured using English grades, essays, and standardized test scores. Intangible personal qualities are also important—leadership, creativity, enthusiasm, and an overall good fit with Babson that includes a willingness to contribute to the community in meaningful and positive ways. There is no standard format for submitting this information, so Babson relies on letters of recommendation, references, and personal statements. In addition, the College evaluates extracurricular activities and work experience, seeking candidates who have exceptional leadership qualities and have participated in activities that have potential carryover to college. Efforts are made to enroll students with diverse backgrounds and experiences.

The College offers three application plans: regular decision, early decision, and early action. For more information about these plans and their deadlines, prospective students should visit the College's Web site at the address listed below. Campus visits and group information sessions with an admissions counselor are strongly recommended.

Application and Information

For further information or application forms, students should contact:

Lunder Undergraduate Admission Center
Mustard Hall
Babson College
Babson Park, Massachusetts 02457-0310
Telephone: 781-239-5522
800-488-3696 (toll-free)
Fax: 781-239-4006
E-mail: ugradadmission@babson.edu
World Wide Web: http://www.babson.edu/ugrad

BAKER UNIVERSITY

BALDWIN CITY, KANSAS

The University

Baker University was established in 1858 as the first four-year college in the state of Kansas. With 142 years of tradition, Baker embodies an unusual blend of innovation and tradition, quality, and community. Affiliated with the United Methodist Church, the University is dedicated to excellence in liberal and professional education, to the integration of learning with faith and values, and to the personal development of each community member.

Twenty-one buildings on a 26-acre tract make up the campus in Baldwin City. The buildings stand around the perimeter of the campus, leaving the interior for rolling lawns, winding walks, and traditional lamps under a canopy of towering trees. The beauty of the campus has been enhanced by the renovation of the campus's earliest buildings. The stained-glass windows and proud tower of Parmenter Hall, the stately neo-Gothic architecture of Mulvane Hall, and the early pioneer architecture of the Pulliam Center remind one of Baker's rich heritage. The George F. Collins Jr. Sports and Convention Center is an outstanding facility for student and community athletics.

There are 3,000 men and women enrolled in the University, with close to 1,000 undergraduates on the Baldwin campus in the College of Arts and Sciences. The University attracts the serious student who expects to encounter challenge in the classroom but also enjoys participating in the multitude of extracurricular activities—sports, debate, radio, the newspaper, theater, music, and departmental and special interest organizations. Five residence halls, including new student apartments, provide comfortable housing for all freshmen and upperclass students. After the freshman year residence hall experience, students may choose to live either in a residence hall or in one of Baker's eight fraternity and sorority houses.

Baker University is a pioneer in the development of accelerated degree programs tailored to meet the needs of the working adult. More than 1,800 men and women from the greater Kansas City area, Lawrence, and Topeka choose Baker's School of Professional and Graduate Studies for its blend of quality, efficiency, and convenience. Students have the opportunity to earn a Bachelor of Business Administration, a Bachelor of Science in Management, a Master of Science in Management, a Master of Business Administration, a Master of Liberal Arts, or a Master of Arts in Education degree. The Baker University School of Nursing offers the Bachelor of Science in Nursing.

Baker University is accredited at the bachelor's and master's degree levels by the North Central Association and is affiliated with the United Methodist Church. The B.S.N. program is accredited by the National League for Nursing Accrediting Commission; the Teacher Education Program by the Kansas State Board of Education; music programs by the National Association of Schools of Music; and business programs by the Association of Collegiate Business Schools and Programs.

Location

The main campus is in Baldwin City, a community of 3,000 people located 35 miles southwest of Kansas City. Baker students enjoy its college-town atmosphere but also take full advantage of nearby metropolitan areas. Kansas City offers many cultural and social attractions. Lawrence, Kansas, is only 15 minutes to the north, and Topeka, the state capital, is a 45-minute drive to the northwest. The School of Professional and Graduate Studies has its center in Overland Park, a suburb of Kansas City, and offers its programs in a number of locations. The School of Nursing is located at Stormont-Vail Regional Health Care in Topeka.

Majors and Degrees

Baker's College of Arts and Sciences confers the Bachelor of Arts, Bachelor of Science, Bachelor of Music, and Bachelor of Music Education degrees. Majors offered include accounting, art education, art history, biology, business, chemistry, computer information systems, computer science, economics, elementary education, engineering (in conjunction with Washington University and the University of Kansas), English, forestry (in conjunction with Duke University), French, German, history, international business, mass communication, mathematics, music, music education, nursing, philosophy, physical education, physics, political science, psychology, religion, sociology, Spanish, speech communication, studio art, theater, and wildlife biology.

Academic Program

The College of Arts and Sciences operates on a 4-1-4 academic calendar with two 5-week sessions of summer school. The month of January is set aside for Interterm, a period when students enroll in only one class. Interterm classes may be taken on campus or abroad, and internships are numerous. Baker emphasizes the liberal arts tradition through a general education program that develops fundamental intellectual skills and provides experiences and ideas that assist the student in making informed decisions as a member of society. Baker graduates include four Rhodes scholars (more than any private school in the state) and two recipients of the Pulitzer Prize in Journalism. Two recent graduates have been awarded the prestigious Goldwater Scholarship for their excellence in the area of science.

To complete a bachelor's degree at Baker, a student must successfully complete 132 semester hours with a Baker GPA of at least 2.0 (on a 4.0 scale).

The Baker honors program provides an opportunity for highly qualified students to complete advanced work in regular classes for honors credit and take special honors sections of courses. Honors participants are required to have a minimum 3.5 high school GPA and a minimum composite score of 27 on the ACT.

Off-Campus Programs

Students may study off campus during Interterm. Some study within the United States, while others participate in one of several Baker-sponsored Interterms abroad. The Harlaxton Semester program allows students to spend a semester studying in England, enjoying many travel and learning opportunities. The Department of Career Development assists students in exploring a variety of professional career options, either off campus for a semester or combined with regular course work, while academic credit is earned. The center also sponsors the Alumni Mentoring Program.

Academic Facilities

The College of Arts and Sciences in Baldwin City offers excellent academic facilities in a traditional campus setting. Three of its classroom buildings are on the National Historic Register. Parmenter Hall, built in 1865 and renovated in 1990, houses an art studio in the loft. Case Hall, built in 1904 and renovated in 1992, serves the humanities and social sciences. Pulliam Center for Journalism and Communications was constructed in 1868. Other classroom buildings include Mulvane Science Hall, Owens Musical Arts Building, Rice Auditorium, George F. Collins Jr. Sports and Convention Center, and Mabee Memorial Hall, which houses the Departments of Business and Economics, History, Physical Education and Recreation, Political Science, Psychology, and Sociology. Mabee Hall was completely renovated in 1995, adding considerable computer lab space and a state-of-the-art fitness center. Collins Library just underwent a $6.3-million redesign to make it one of the most state-of-the art facilities in the area. It has a computerized catalog with access beyond its own 65,000-volume collection to more than 2.5 million items in fourteen regional libraries. It provides more than 600 periodicals and makes more than 300 computerized databases available through membership in Dialog information retrieval service. The library houses several special collections, including the Quayle Rare Bible Collection and the Methodist Historical Library. On the lower level, the library houses Baker's continually growing computer laboratories and the Learning Resource Center. Computers in the library and in residence hall computer labs offer Internet and e-mail access.

Costs

Tuition for the 2003–04 academic year for undergraduates in the College of Arts and Sciences was $14,210. Double-occupancy room and board for the year were $5300, and the technological fees were $430. Full-time undergraduates should plan to spend up to $400 per semester for books and supplies.

Financial Aid

Ninety-five percent of the College's full-time students receive financial assistance. Special four-year academic scholarships, not based on need, are available for students with outstanding academic, leadership, and test records. These scholarships, up to $6000 in value, are renewable each year if the recipient performs in accordance with scholarship regulations. Baker leads the independent colleges in Kansas in the amount of Kansas State Scholar funds awarded to its students.

Financial assistance is available on both a need and no-need basis to full-time students in the University. Aid based on need is given to students who demonstrate genuine need, as determined by the Free Application for Federal Student Aid (FAFSA). Applications for financial aid should be submitted as early as possible, since aid is awarded on a rolling basis and may be exhausted by the summer months.

The University participates in all federally supported student aid programs, including the Federal Perkins Loan, Federal Pell Grant, Federal Supplemental Educational Opportunity Grant, and Federal Work-Study Programs. Approximately 42 percent of the students secure jobs through the campus-work program. Through the Kansas Comprehensive Grant Program and the Kansas State Scholar Program, special financial assistance is available for students who are residents of Kansas.

Faculty

The College's student-faculty ratio is 12:1. The average class size is about 20 students. Although Baker faculty members are primarily focused on teaching, most also conduct their courses in a way that integrates teaching research and services. This gives Baker students opportunities to participate in the research process and discover how their class content can be used to bring about positive change in their communities. More than two thirds of the faculty have terminal degrees in their fields, and all faculty members have advanced degrees. Professors are readily available outside of class for assisting students. As a residential community, faculty and student participation in extracurricular activities is extensive.

Student Government

The College's official student governing organization is the Student Senate. Members of the senate are elected from organizations on campus, and the president of the senate is invited to attend faculty meetings and general sessions of the Board of Trustees. The Student Senate allocates an ample student activity fund for campus events and student projects and plays a major role in ensuring that student opinion is heard within the University community. Faculty search committees also regularly involve students in the search for new faculty members.

Admission Requirements

Applications for admission are reviewed by an admission committee. In most cases, applicants with an ACT composite score of at least 21 (combined SAT I of at least 990) or a minimum 3.0 high school grade point average are admitted. Other applicants are evaluated on an individual basis. Transfers must have a minimum 2.3 transfer grade point average for admission. International students must also submit TOEFL scores (minimum score of 525 required) and a statement of financial support but are not required to submit ACT or SAT I scores.

Application and Information

Applications are considered in the order in which they are received, and an announcement of the admission decision is made immediately upon receipt of transcripts, ACT or SAT I results, and recommendations. When submitting the application for admission, the student must include a $20 fee or the application cannot be processed. After admission is granted, the student is asked to submit his or her residence hall contract and a $100 deposit. The deposit is nonrefundable after June 1.

Director of Admissions
P.O. Box 65
Baker University
Baldwin City, Kansas 66006
Telephone: 785-594-6451 Ext. 307
800-873-4282 (toll-free)
E-mail: admissions@bakeru.edu
World Wide Web: http://www.bakeru.edu

Baker's campus consists of twenty-one buildings on 26 acres.

BALL STATE UNIVERSITY

MUNCIE, INDIANA

The University

Ball State University was founded as a state institution in 1918, but its antecedents date from the late nineteenth century when the Ball family, prominent industrialists, purchased and donated to the state of Indiana the campus and buildings of the Muncie Normal Institute. In 1922 the Board of Trustees gave the school the name of Ball Teachers College, and in 1929 the school became Ball State Teachers College. In 1965 the Indiana General Assembly renamed the institution Ball State University in recognition of its phenomenal growth in enrollment, in physical facilities, and in the variety and quality of its educational programs and services. The buildings on the campus reflect the changing architectural styles of the twentieth century.

The total University enrollment stands at 18,059. In fall 2002, undergraduate enrollment was 47 percent men and 53 percent women. The majority of entering freshmen were 18 to 19 years old and single and from cities of moderate to large size; 7 percent belonged to a minority group. About 10 percent of Ball State freshmen came from outside the state of Indiana. There were 416 students from seventy-seven countries other than the United States.

There are more than 300 student organizations that provide extracurricular activities. These include leadership programs, departmental organizations, honorary societies, music groups, religious organizations, fraternities, sororities, governing groups, special-interest organizations, and service groups. The University Health Service staff members offer health education, provide care in cases of acute illness and injury while a student is in attendance, and serve as medical advisers for the University.

Location

The Ball State campus is in a pleasant, residential area of Muncie, an industrial city of 70,000 people in east-central Indiana, 56 miles northeast of Indianapolis. The city's cultural features include the Muncie Symphony Orchestra, the Civic Theater, and the Artists Series and Concert Series presented in the John R. Emens University–Community Auditorium located on the Ball State campus.

Majors and Degrees

Degrees are offered in the fields of administrative information technology (two-year), advertising, anthropology, architecture and planning (architecture, environmental design, landscape architecture, urban planning and development), art (ceramics, drawing, general, metals, painting, photography, printmaking, sculpture, visual arts education, visual communication (graphic design)), athletic training, biology (aquatic biology and fisheries, botany, cellular and molecular ecology, genetics, general, microbiology, wildlife, zoology), business (accounting, business administration, business information technology, business and marketing education, economics (business, liberal arts), finance (corporate finance management, financial institutions, financial planning), management (entrepreneurship and small business management, general management, human resource management, information systems, operations and manufacturing management), marketing, risk management and insurance), business administration (two-year), chemical technology (two-year), chemistry (biochemistry), classical culture, classical languages, communication studies, computer science (cooperative education, hardware systems, information systems), criminal justice and criminology, criminal justice and criminology (two-year), dance, dietetics, dietetic technology (two-year), early childhood education, earth science, earth/space science education, elementary education, English, English/language arts education, exercise science (aquatics, sport administration), family and consumer sciences (apparel design, family and child, family and consumer sciences education, general fashion merchandising, hospitality and food management, hospitality and food management (two-year), interior design, residential property management), French, French education, general studies, geography (comprehensive, geographic information processing and mapping, operational meteorology and climatology, travel and tourism), geology, German, German education, graphic arts management, health science, health education, history, industrial supervision (two-year), industrial technology (career and technical education, technology education), Japanese, Japanese education, journalism (graphics, journalism education, magazine, news-editorial, photojournalism), Latin American studies, Latin, Latin education, legal assistance (two-year), legal studies (business, public law), library media and computer education, life science education, manufacturing engineering technology, manufacturing technology (two-year), mathematical economics, mathematical sciences (actuarial science, applied mathematics, financial mathematics, mathematics, mathematics education, physics, statistics), mechanical engineering technology (two-year cooperative program with Purdue University), medical technology, military science (minor only), music (guitar, music composition, music education, instrumental and general music, music engineering technology, organ, piano, symphonic instruments, vocal and general music, voice), natural resources and environmental management (environmental communication/interpretation, environmental management, land management, natural resource studies, occupational/industrial hygiene, park and recreation management), nuclear medicine technology (two-year), nursing, philosophy, physical education, physical science education, physics, political science, printing technology (two-year), psychology, public relations, public service (two-year), radiation therapy (two-year), radiography (two-year), religious studies, social studies education, social work (B.S.W.), sociology, Spanish, Spanish education, special education (early childhood special education, exceptional needs, hearing impaired/deaf, mild interventions, severe interventions), speech-language pathology, telecommunications (media studies, news, production, sales and promotion), and theater (acting, design and technology, musical theater, theater education, theatrical studies).

Ball State also offers preprofessional programs in audiology, dental hygiene, dentistry, engineering (general, chemical, and metallurgical), law, medicine, optometry, pharmacy, physical therapy, physician's assistant, and veterinary medicine.

Academic Program

Undergraduate programs combine general studies with majors and minors. Most degrees require 126 semester hours, at least a 2.0 grade point average, and the last year in residence. The academic calendar consists of fall and spring semesters and two summer terms.

The Honors College, a four-year University-wide program

featuring special course offerings, colloquia, seminars, and independent study, is especially designed to challenge the talented student. University College is organized to provide support services to students undecided about their majors. The Learning Center provides free peer tutoring, small-group study sessions, and academic workshops to all Ball State students. Each year, more than 4,000 students, from freshmen through graduate students, use the Learning Centers service. Freshmen who attend tutoring or study groups earn higher grade point averages than those who do not.

The University, recognizing that there are other ways to obtain an education than through regular enrollment in a class, grants credit through any combination of credit for successful scores on Advanced Placement (AP) tests, IB and College-Level Examination Program tests, credit for military service, credit by departmental examination, and credit by departmental authorization.

Off-Campus Programs

Study-abroad programs are open to all Ball State students. It gives students the opportunity to explore intercultural issues outside the classroom. Programs vary in length, location, and cost, and credit is offered for most programs, so that students who participate are not required to delay graduation.

Summer programs are a popular option for students seeking short-term international experiences. The center works in coordination with the various colleges to develop discipline-specific field studies and special tours in all price ranges that appeal to students in all majors. Students receive course credit for most programs, and financial aid is applicable. Programs range in focus from ethnographic studies in British Columbia, student teaching in England, and business in Turkey or England, to architecture and urban planning in Germany and Italy.

Academic Facilities

Bracken library is one of the largest libraries in the state, with more than 1.5 million volumes. Professional collections are housed in the Architecture Library and the Science–Health Science Library. A K–12 school library is maintained at the Burris Laboratory School. Separate materials in the main library are the music collection, special collections, archives, government publications, maps, and educational resources.

Facilities on the campus also include an art museum, an observatory and planetarium, outdoor laboratories, a solar-energy research center, fully equipped science laboratories, a human-performance laboratory, state-of-the-art teaching classrooms, and music laboratories. University Computing Services provides a full range of computing and systems services for students, faculty members, and the administration.

Costs

Expenses for 2003–04 were $5532 for tuition for Indiana residents or $13,590 for tuition for nonresident (out-of-state) students, $5880 for room and board, and $800 (average) for books and supplies. Between $1800 and $2100 is considered reasonable for personal expenses and transportation.

Financial Aid

Through a program of scholarships, grants, loans, and employment, Ball State's Office of Scholarships and Financial Aid provides aid for deserving students. The Free Application for Federal Student Aid (FAFSA), obtainable from a high school guidance counselor, should be filed no later than March 10.

Faculty

Ball State's instructional programs are carried out by 868 full-time faculty members, 90 percent of whom hold earned doctoral degrees. Faculty members serve on the University Senate and on numerous senate and campus committees. Full-time academic advisers work with freshmen. Seven advising centers around campus work with departments and their faculty advisers.

Student Government

The all-campus student governing group is the Ball State University Student Association, composed of executive, legislative, and judicial branches. All students are encouraged to participate in such activities as proposing changes in University policy, working for expanded and improved educational programs at Ball State, and lobbying at the city and state levels. One student is appointed to serve on the University's Board of Trustees. In addition, representatives from the Student Association are appointed to serve on numerous boards, committees, and councils on campus, including the University Senate and its committees.

Admission Requirements

Undergraduate applicants are considered for admission to Ball State University after the Office of Admissions has received the application for admission, the $25 nonrefundable application fee, the secondary school record (official transcript) or GED high school equivalency scores and certificate, and scores on either the SAT I or ACT.

Transfer students must, in addition, submit an official transcript from each vocational or advanced educational institution attended beyond high school. The transcripts must be forwarded to Ball State directly from the institutions attended.

It is suggested that prospective applicants visit the campus and talk with a member of the admission staff.

Application and Information

High school students should complete an application in the fall of their senior year. Application materials must be submitted by March 1 for priority consideration for the autumn semester and by December 1 for the spring semester. Requests for appointments and information should be addressed to:

Dean of Admissions and Enrollment Services
Ball State University
Muncie, Indiana 47306
Telephone: 765-285-8300
800-482-4BSU (toll-free)
765-285-2205 (TDD users only)
E-mail: visitus@bsu.edu
World Wide Web: http://www.bsu.edu/admissions

BALTIMORE INTERNATIONAL COLLEGE

School of Culinary Arts
School of Business and Management

BALTIMORE, MARYLAND; VIRGINIA, COUNTY CAVAN, IRELAND

The College

The Baltimore International College, a regionally accredited independent college, was founded in 1972 to provide theoretical and technical skills education for individuals seeking careers as hospitality professionals. The College is committed to providing students with the knowledge and ability necessary for employment and success in the hospitality industry.

In 1985, the College was authorized by the state of Maryland to grant associate degrees. As part of the College's continued growth, restaurant and food service management and innkeeping management were added to its curriculum. In 1987, the Virginia Park Campus in Ireland was founded, enabling students to study under European chefs and hoteliers in a European environment. In 1996, the College was granted accreditation by the Commission on Institutions of Higher Education of the Middle States Association of Colleges and Schools. In 1998, the College was authorized by the state of Maryland to grant four-year baccalaureate degrees. In addition to classrooms, offices, and dorms, the College's campus in Baltimore includes a campus bookstore, a student union, a hotel, an inn, two restaurants, parking, student dining facilities, a Career Development Center, and a Learning Resources Center, which includes a library, two academic computer labs, and an art gallery.

Location

The College's main campus, located in downtown Baltimore, is just two blocks from the city's famous Inner Harbor, a location that puts the College in the midst of numerous hotels and restaurants. The city offers year-round cultural and entertainment opportunities, such as theater, opera, the Baltimore Symphony Orchestra, museums, sporting events, and festivals. Other attractions in Baltimore that are within walking distance of the College are the National Aquarium, Harborplace, Oriole Park at Camden Yards, Ravens Stadium, Maryland Science Center, and many historic sites, including Fort McHenry, the neighborhood of Mount Vernon, and the Walters Art Museum. Baltimore also has parks and miles of waterfront for those who enjoy outdoor recreation. Washington, D.C., the nation's capital, is just 30 miles from downtown Baltimore. The city of Baltimore is easily accessed by major highways and bus, rail, and air service. Baltimore/Washington International Airport is a short drive from the campus.

Majors and Degrees

Baltimore International College offers baccalaureate degrees in culinary management, hospitality management, and hospitality management with a concentration in professional marketing. The College also offers associate degrees in food and beverage management, hotel/motel/innkeeping management, professional baking and pastry, professional cooking, and professional cooking and baking. In addition, students can receive professional certificates in culinary arts, professional baking and pastry, professional cooking, professional cooking and baking, and professional marketing.

Academic Program

The College provides a comprehensive curriculum, which includes an honors study-abroad program at the Baltimore International College, Virginia Park Campus, near Dublin, Ireland.

The College's professional cooking program and the combined programs in professional cooking and baking and baking and pastry operate throughout the calendar year; new classes begin in the spring, summer, and fall. The College's business and management programs accept freshmen in the fall and spring semesters. The culinary arts certificate, which combines cooking and baking, is available through evening classes and begins in the fall and spring semesters.

To earn an associate degree in professional cooking, professional baking and pastry, or professional cooking and baking, the student must complete 62 to 64 credits. To earn an associate degree in food and beverage management or hotel/motel/innkeeping management, the student must complete 54 credits; this program is intended for students who already have a strong academic background. The associate degree program combines technical, hands-on courses with general education courses (such as nutrition, psychology, English, and mathematics) as well as an internship or externship.

The associate degree is offered separately and as part of the 2+2 program at Baltimore International College. In the 2+2 program, students receive their two-year degree and then continue to complete a four-year bachelor's degree in culinary management or hospitality management. Bachelor's degree programs require 125 to 133 credits.

Off-Campus Programs

The Honors Program has been developed for qualified culinary arts and business and management majors. The Honors Program is taught at the College's historic 100-acre Virginia Park Campus in County Cavan, Ireland. Culinary students who are selected for the Honors Program further enhance their skills in and knowledge of European cuisine, baking, pastry, and à la carte service. Business and management students selected for the Honors Program have the opportunity to learn the day-to-day operation of a hotel and restaurant, from reception to housekeeping and from restaurant management to accounting. Students fully enjoy the cross-cultural experience of living in an English-speaking foreign country.

Academic Facilities

The Baltimore campus includes kitchens, storerooms, cooking demonstration theaters, academic classrooms, multipurpose rooms, a library, two computer labs, a student union, and auxiliary services. Public operations that function as in-house training for students include the Mount Vernon Hotel and Bay Atlantic Seafood Restaurant, the Hopkins Inn, and the Bay Atlantic Club Restaurant.

The Virginia Park Campus is located on 100 acres, 50 miles from Dublin, and offers student housing, with laboratory kitchens and lecture facilities. The complex also includes the Park Hotel, with public operations that function as in-house training for students, including the Marquis Dining Room and the Marchioness Ballroom. The Park Hotel has thirty-six guest rooms. All students enjoy unlimited golf and fishing as well as hiking trails.

The College's Career Development Center offers students access to information about careers in food service and hospitality management. The College's Career Development Services are located in the Career Information Center, where coordinators organize on-campus recruiting and offer workshops and assistance in resume writing and interviewing skills.

The College's Learning Resource Center is a member of an interlibrary loan network that enables users to borrow from public, academic, and private libraries throughout Maryland. The library's current core collection has approximately 13,000 volumes, 200 periodicals, and almost 800 audiovisual selections. The library offers students access to the Internet, a worldwide network of electronic information. In-house services include two computer labs, electronic databases for research, and a photocopier.

The College's art gallery is part of the Learning Resource Center and features a permanent display of edible art. Student participation in all exhibits is encouraged. Culinary competitions are held in the gallery.

The College offers general academic counseling for all students, peer tutoring on request, and a variety of referrals for support services. In addition, Student Services provides many recreation and leisure activities, including the student union, a series of activities sponsored by the College, and information about cultural programs around the city. Student Services also provides ongoing support to the College's alumni through surveys, mailings about the College's growth, and involvement in College-sponsored events such as open houses, resume referrals, and career fairs.

Costs

Tuition for 2002–03 was $6371. Fees range from $150 to $2361, depending on a student's major. Student housing costs range from $2812 to $4713 per semester for dormitory-style housing, which includes a meal plan.

Financial Aid

Students receive financial aid from federal, state, institutional, and private sources and may be employed during their attendance as full-time students. The forms of financial aid available at the College through federal sources include the Federal Pell Grant, the Federal Supplemental Educational Opportunity Grant, the Federal Work-Study Program, the Federal Subsidized and Unsubsidized Stafford Student Loans, PLUS loans, and veterans' educational benefits. Students are encouraged to investigate the scholarship programs in their home state and apply for state scholarships if the grants can be used in Maryland. The College also offers its own series of scholarships and payment options. In 2002–03, College-funded scholarships averaged $2678 per academic year for in-state students and $4707 per academic year for out-of-state students. Students can request a financial aid application from the Student Financial Planning Office. The College employs the Federal Methodology of Need Analysis, approved by the U.S. Department of Education, as a fair and equitable means of determining the family's ability to contribute to the student's educational expenses, as well as eligibility for other financial programs.

Faculty

Baltimore International College faculty members include 29 chefs and academic instructors of high academic distinction. The student-faculty ratio averages 15:1 in culinary labs and 25:1 in academic classes. Each student is assigned to a faculty adviser who oversees the student's progress and answers questions about academic and career concerns. Students are encouraged to discuss program-related issues with the Director of Student Counseling.

Student Government

Many students become junior members of the Greater Baltimore Chapter of the American Culinary Federation. Membership is open to all students in good standing. Meetings, which are held monthly, are announced at the College.

Admission Requirements

Creativity and skill of students must be matched by dedication. The College seeks candidates who desire a professional career in the hospitality industry.

Individuals seeking admission to the College must have earned a high school diploma or have passed the GED. Applicants must either pass the College's Admissions Test, take developmental courses during their first semester, or have one of the following: a minimum SAT score of 430 verbal and 420 math, a minimum composite ACT score of 16, minimum CLEP scores in the 50th percentile in math and English composition with essay, a secondary degree, or 16 credit hours at the postsecondary level with a minimum average of C in math and English. Transfer students must submit an official college transcript as well as catalog course descriptions for credits they wish to transfer.

The College affords equally to all students the rights, privileges, programs, activities, scholarships and loan programs, and other programs administered by the College without regard to race, color, creed, sex, age, handicap, or national or ethnic origin.

Application and Information

Applicants are required to submit an application form along with a $35 nonrefundable fee. Requests by the College for additional information must be handled in a timely manner. An admission decision is made as soon as a file is complete. Upon acceptance, applicants are asked to submit a $100 tuition deposit.

For additional information, students should contact:

Office of Admissions
Commerce Exchange
Baltimore International College
17 Commerce Street
Baltimore, Maryland 21202-3230
Telephone: 410-752-4710 Ext. 120
800-624-9926 Ext. 120 (toll-free)
E-mail: admissions@bic.edu
World Wide Web: http://www.bic.edu

Small classes at Baltimore International College enable students to receive individual instruction that helps them perfect their skills.

BARNARD COLLEGE

NEW YORK, NEW YORK

The College

Barnard College was among the pioneers in the late nineteenth-century crusade to make higher education available to young women. Founded in 1889, it became affiliated with the Columbia University system in 1900 and today serves 2,300 students who come from nearly every state and more than thirty countries. It remains an independent affiliate of the university, and students at the two schools may cross-register for courses at either institution. Barnard students have access to Columbia University libraries and receive their degree from the University. Barnard College, however, has remained a small, independent liberal arts college, devoted solely to the undergraduate education of women. The College maintains its own Board of Trustees, faculty, and administrative staff; its own endowment, an independent admissions process, and sole ownership of its property and physical plant. It offers the intimacy of a small college with all the added advantages of access to a major university.

The self-contained Barnard campus occupies 4 acres of urban property along Broadway between 116th and 120th streets. Barnard Hall, with its newly renovated Ethel S. LeFrak '41 and Samuel J. LeFrak Gymnasium and Julius S. Held Lecture Hall, stands opposite the main gates of the College, while the south end of the campus contains the Brooks, Reid, Hewitt, and Sulzberger Hall residence hall complex. Additional housing is located nearby, and some options for coed housing are available; all students are guaranteed housing. Millicent McIntosh Center, the focus of student activities, has a cafeteria, lounges, and student leadership offices as well as other facilities.

Location

Barnard is located in New York City. In so cosmopolitan a setting, cultural, educational, and internship opportunities abound. New York is the College's laboratory and museum, its most constant and energizing resource.

Majors and Degrees

Students are recommended by the faculty members of Barnard College to the Trustees of Columbia University for the degree of Bachelor of Arts in the following subjects: American studies, ancient studies, anthropology, architecture, art history, Asian and Middle Eastern cultures, biochemistry, biological sciences, biopsychology, chemistry, classics (Greek and Latin), comparative literature, computer science, dance, economic history, economics, education, English, environmental science, foreign area studies, French, German, history, Italian, mathematics, medieval and Renaissance studies, music, Pan-African studies, philosophy, physics and astronomy, political science, psychology, religion, Slavic (Russian), sociology, Spanish, statistics, theater, urban affairs, and women's studies.

Barnard College also offers double- and joint-degree programs in cooperation with other schools within the Columbia University community. These include a five-year (3-2) program offered in conjunction with the School of International Affairs, in which a student earns both an A.B. degree and a Master in International Affairs (M.I.A.) degree, and a five-year (3-2) program combining undergraduate studies with the graduate public policy administration program in which a student earns both an A.B. degree and a Master of Public Administration (M.P.A.) degree. In cooperation with the School of Law, Barnard offers an accelerated program in interdisciplinary legal education; selected students can begin their legal studies after three years of undergraduate course work. The School of Engineering and Applied Science and Barnard College offer a five-year (3-2) program in all branches of engineering, including aerospace, civil, and electrical engineering, in which candidates receive both an A.B. and a B.S. degree. Outside the University, a student can earn both an A.B. degree and an M.M. degree in a five-year (3-2) program with the Juilliard School. In cooperation with the Jewish Theological Seminary, students can earn an A.B. degree from Barnard and another undergraduate degree from the seminary.

Academic Program

Two required courses, first-year seminar and first-year English, set the foundation for a Barnard education within small classes limited to 16 students. General education requirements are organized around the nine Ways of Knowing, which reflect the breadth and depth of a true liberal arts education while building the skills of analysis, independent thought, and self-expression. The nine Ways of Knowing offer a flexible structure and a wide array of courses under the following categories: reason and values, social analysis, cultures in comparison, language, laboratory science, quantitative and deductive reasoning, historical studies, literature, and visual and performing arts.

Advanced placement and I.B. credit are available, as are opportunities for independent or honors work. Barnard operates on a two-semester calendar, with classes beginning in early September. The fall semester ends in mid-December; classes resume for the spring semester in mid-January and end in mid-May.

Off-Campus Programs

Barnard College is an independent affiliate of Columbia University. As such, its students have open access to the courses, libraries, and other facilities of Columbia. With special permission, students may also register for classes in Columbia's graduate and professional schools. A program offered in cooperation with the Jewish Theological Seminary, located two blocks from Barnard, allows students to take courses for credit. In a similar exchange with both the Juilliard School and the nearby Manhattan School of Music, qualified Barnard students may take music lessons in a conservatory setting.

Under the auspices of Reid Hall in Paris, a Barnard-Columbia facility, several semester-long and full-year programs are offered. Students of classics are eligible to study at the Intercollegiate Center for Classical Studies in Rome. Qualified students may also study at Oxford (Somerville College), Cambridge (Newnham College), the University of London (University College, London School of Economics, King's College, or Queen Mary College), or the University of Warwick. Qualified students are also eligible to study in Germany, Italy, Japan, and numerous other programs in more than thirty-five countries. Students may also participate in exchange programs with Spelman College in Atlanta and Howard University in Washington, D.C.

Because of its location in New York City, Barnard offers its students a variety of work experiences through its extensive program of more than 2,500 internships. More than two thirds of Barnard students participate in internships throughout the academic year and summer; approximately one third of these internship opportunities receive stipends.

Academic Facilities

Milbank Hall, the oldest building on the campus, houses administrative and faculty offices, classrooms, the Arthur Ross Greenhouse, and the Minor Latham Playhouse. Millicent McIntosh Center includes music practice rooms, a student darkroom, and the Java City Café. Fourteen-story Altschul Hall, devoted mainly to the sciences, has classrooms, department offices, and the most modern laboratory equipment.

Wollman Library offers three floors of reading areas and more than 170,000 volumes in open stacks. Students also have access to the 8 million volumes of Columbia's Butler Library.

Costs

Tuition and fees for 2002–03 were $25,270. Housing costs were $10,140 for room and board.

Financial Aid

All financial aid supplied or administered by Barnard is awarded on the basis of demonstrated need, as determined by federal regulations and the College's Office of Financial Aid. Barnard gives no merit scholarships. College aid is supplementary to family resources. Once need has been established, it is Barnard's policy to cover 100 percent of that need for U.S. citizens and permanent residents through grants and self-help awards (work and/or loans). A student who is admitted to Barnard with a Barnard College Grant may expect grants in future years, provided she continues to meet economic and academic eligibility. Approximately 55 percent of the students at Barnard receive financial aid. A limited number of scholarships are available to international citizens.

Barnard College has a need-blind admission policy in which all applications are judged on merit without reference to the applicant's financial circumstances.

Faculty

Barnard College has 185 full-time teaching faculty members and 107 part-time members. The student-faculty ratio is 10:1. Although actively engaged in research and publication in their respective fields, Barnard faculty members regard teaching as their primary commitment. All students have faculty advisers who assist them in selecting courses and designing individual academic programs.

Student Government

Every Barnard student is a member of the Student Government Association, which sponsors numerous extracurricular activities. These include the College newspaper, the literary magazine, dramatic groups, political and religious organizations, and preprofessional and departmental clubs. Cooperation between Barnard and Columbia groups is common. Students, faculty members, and administrators serve on tripartite committees and share responsibility for policy recommendations on curriculum, housing, financial aid, orientation, and the library.

Admission Requirements

The Committee on Admissions selects young women of proven academic strength who exhibit the potential for further intellectual growth. Careful consideration is given to candidates' high school records, recommendations, writing skills, standardized test scores, and special abilities and interests. While admission is highly selective, no one criterion determines acceptance. Each applicant is considered in terms of her individual qualities of mind and spirit and her potential for successfully completing her program of study at Barnard.

Candidates for admission to the first-year class must have taken a college-preparatory program at an approved secondary school or have an equivalent level of education. A recommended program comprises 4 years of work in English, 3 or more years in mathematics, 3 or 4 years in a foreign language, 3 or more years in science (with laboratory), and 3 years in history. Barnard also requires candidates to submit scores on the SAT I and on three SAT II Subject Tests, including the SAT II: Writing Test or SAT II: Literature, or the ACT. An interview is optional.

Application and Information

Applicants for first-year admission should apply to Barnard in the fall of their senior year of high school. Applications must be received by January 1 and should be accompanied by a nonrefundable fee of $45. Students are notified of the admission decision in early April. Well-qualified high school seniors who have selected Barnard as their first-choice college may apply under the Early Decision Plan. Applications must be submitted by November 15. Barnard accepts transfer students to the sophomore and junior classes. Applications must be submitted by April 1 for admission in September and by November 1 for admission in January.

For more information about Barnard College, students should contact:

Dean of Admissions
Barnard College
Columbia University
3009 Broadway
New York, New York 10027
Telephone: 212-854-2014
Fax: 212-854-6220
E-mail: admissions@barnard.edu
World Wide Web: http://www.barnard.edu

A view of Milbank Hall from McIntosh Plaza at Barnard College.

BARRY UNIVERSITY

MIAMI SHORES, FLORIDA

The University

Graduates of Barry University say that the best part of their education was the unique sense of community in the Barry University family. Students at Barry receive personal attention from their professors, building one-on-one relationships that help prepare them to succeed. Many of the faculty members have extensive practical as well as academic experience, further enhancing students' education.

As a Catholic International University, Barry is widely known for recognizing the value of each person and for offering high-quality academics in an environment designed to promote growth. At Barry, students are encouraged to explore their individual interests and values and to develop the critical thinking skills needed to succeed in their careers.

Students also find South Florida's cultural diversity and the diversity of the Barry community a wonderful enhancement to their educational experience. *U.S. News & World Report* ranks Barry University number one for diversity among Southern Regional Colleges and Universities. Total enrollment is 9,042 (undergraduate, graduate, and adult and continuing education), which includes students from forty-nine states and sixty-seven countries. Just a few more than 3,000 full-time undergraduate students are enrolled at Barry.

More than sixty undergraduate programs, more than fifty graduate degrees, and several accelerated adult degree programs are offered through the Schools of Adult and Continuing Education, Arts and Sciences, Business, Education, Graduate Medical Sciences, Human Performance and Leisure Sciences, Law, Natural and Health Sciences, Nursing, and Social Work. There are seventeen honor societies, and a number of nationally recognized scholars present throughout the year. In many areas, students have the opportunity to work closely with faculty members on research projects.

Whatever a student's interest—biology, computer information sciences, e-commerce, exceptional student education, exercise science, information technology, nursing, or social work—their preparation includes high-quality academics, dynamic curricula, and close interaction with their professors and colleagues. Because of the University's ideal South Florida location, students have numerous opportunities for exciting internships and community service.

The University is accredited by the Southern Association of Colleges and Schools (1866 Southern Lane, Decatur, Georgia 30033-4097; telephone: 404-679-4501) to award bachelor's, master's, specialist, and doctoral degrees. Barry also holds a number of accreditations from professional organizations for specific programs.

Barry's beautifully landscaped campus and Spanish-style architecture offer the perfect environment for quiet reflection and study. Seven air-conditioned residence halls on campus and extended housing off campus accommodate residential undergraduate students. All students may keep cars on campus. Barry also has a Department of Commuter Affairs that serves as a resource center for commuters.

Student services available on campus include a Department of First-year Programs, an orientation team and peer assistants, counseling, career development and placement, campus ministry, and health services. The University has a snack bar, a cafeteria, a post office, a student center, a performing arts center, a television studio, a radio station, a game room, a health and sports center (complete with a strength and conditioning room), and an outdoor recreation center. There are more than ninety student organizations and a number of campuswide events.

The Barry Buccaneers field twelve athletic teams that participate in the NCAA Division II and in the Sunshine State Conference. Since 1984, the Buccaneers have participated in fifty-six national tournaments, twenty SSC championships, and five national championships. More than 50 percent of Barry's student-athletes achieve GPAs above 3.0. Intramural sports include basketball, flag football, 4-on-4 flag football, golf, sand volleyball, soccer, street hockey, tennis, 3-on-3 basketball, and volleyball.

Location

Miami Shores is located between the cities of Miami and Fort Lauderdale, giving students access to all the recreational facilities and cultural opportunities of South Florida. Golf, tennis, swimming, soccer, scuba and skin diving, waterskiing, and sailing are available all year long. Miami also offers football's Miami Dolphins; its NBA team, the Miami Heat; its National League baseball team, the Florida Marlins; its NHL team; and the Florida Panthers. The New World Symphony, the Opera Guild of Greater Miami, the Miami Film Festival, and the Miami City Ballet provide a full season of highly acclaimed performances, as do the Coconut Grove Playhouse and the Broward Center for the Performing Arts. Well-known personalities entertain regularly in the area. Also easily accessible are the Florida Keys, the Everglades, national parks, and marine and state parks.

Majors and Degrees

Barry University offers the Bachelor of Arts degree in advertising, art (ceramics, graphic design, and painting and drawing), broadcast communication, communication studies, English (literature and professional writing), environmental studies, French, general studies, history, international studies, philosophy, photography (biomedical/forensic, creative, digital imaging, and photo/communication), prelaw, public relations, Spanish, theater (acting, design/technical), and theology.

The Bachelor of Science degree is offered in accounting, athletic training (premedicine option and pre–physical therapy five-year seamless B.S. to M.S.), biology (biotechnology, ecological studies track, major for the medical laboratory technician, histotechnology track, marine biology track, predentistry, premedicine, preoptometry, prepharmacy, pre–physical therapy, pre–physician assistant studies, prepodiatry, pre–veterinary medicine, and three-year accelerated option), cardiovascular perfusion, chemistry (environmental track, predentistry, premedicine, and prepharmacy), computer information sciences, computer science, criminology, cytotechnology, diagnostic medical ultrasound technology, e-commerce, economics/finance, elementary education, pre-engineering, exceptional student education, exercise science (premedicine option, pre–physical therapy five-year seamless B.S. to M.S.), international business, management, management information systems, marketing, mathematical sciences (actuarial science, applied, and computational), medical technology, nuclear medicine technology, physical education (grades K–8 and 6–12), political science, pre–K through primary education, pre–K through primary education (Montessori), psychology, sociology, and sport management (diving industry and golf industry tracks).

The University also offers the Bachelor of Science in Nursing (accelerated option, accelerated B.S.N. to M.S.N. option, basic option, LPN to B.S.N. option, RN to B.S.N. option, RN/B.S. to M.S.N. option, seamless RN to M.S.N. option, three-year option, and two-year option).

The Bachelor of Fine Arts, the Bachelor of Music, and the Bachelor of Social Work are also offered.

Minor concentrations are available in specific subject areas as well as in the interdisciplinary areas of Africana studies, film studies, peace studies, and women's studies.

Teaching certification is available for pre-K through primary education, elementary education, exceptional student education, and physical education. A certificate program in the translation and interpretation of Spanish is offered.

Seven accelerated undergraduate degree programs are offered for working adults through the School of Adult and Continuing Education.

Academic Program

The University operates on a semester plan. The first semester extends from the end of August to mid-December, and the second semester extends from mid-January to early May. Two 6-week sessions are offered during the summer. Students must maintain a minimum cumulative grade point average of 2.0 (or C) and earn a minimum of 120 credits for a degree. Of these 120 credits, 9 must be in philosophy and theology, 9 in communication—oral and written, 9 in humanities and arts, 9 in physical or natural sciences and mathematics, and 9 in social and behavioral sciences. The traditional full-time academic load is 12 to 18 credits each semester and 6 credits each summer term. Candidates for degree programs may elect either a major area of specialization or a broad liberal arts program and must satisfy all requirements of the program that they choose to follow, including all professional preparation requirements. Exceptionally well-qualified seniors may earn up to 6 hours of graduate credit with the recommendation of the department chairperson and the dean. Internships are required for many majors.

An ELS Language Centers program is available to international students needing to increase language proficiency. The Clinical Center for Advanced Learning offers a program designed to assist students with learning disabilities who have the intellectual potential and motivation to complete a four-year degree.

The University also offers an active honors program designed to add breadth and depth to the educational experience. The approach is interdisciplinary.

Off-Campus Programs

Barry University offers summer programs in Europe. In addition, Barry is a member of the College Consortium for International Studies, enabling students to participate in programs in twenty-five countries offered by member colleges and universities. Barry University students may enroll in Air Force ROTC courses through cross-registration at a nearby university.

Academic Facilities

Students find the high-quality resources they need to support their education at Barry. Campus facilities include the Monsignor William Barry Library, an extensive library network, photography and digital imaging labs, a human performance lab, athletic training room, a biomechanics lab, a complete television production studio, academic computing center, multimedia business classrooms, art studios, a performing arts center, a nursing lab, the Classroom of Tomorrow, and a cell biology lab as well as several other well-equipped science labs.

Costs

For 2003–04, tuition for full-time undergraduate students for the academic year was $20,320. Student services fees are included in tuition. Room and board costs averaged $7000 (double room). Expenses such as books, supplies, laboratory or other special fees, and transportation are not included in these costs.

Financial Aid

Barry University offers an excellent scholarship and grant program, awarding scholarships each year to students who have demonstrated academic success and promise. These scholarships and grants may be renewed for up to four years as long as the students meet the renewal criteria. Barry need-based grants and athletic scholarships are also available.

The University also participates in the Federal Pell and Federal Supplemental Educational Opportunity Grant programs, the Federal Perkins Loan Program, the Federal Work-Study Program, the Florida Resident Access Grant Program, the Florida Student Assistance Grant, Florida Bright Futures Scholarships, and the Federal Family Educational Loan Program. Barry awards financial assistance on the basis of financial need and academic excellence. Applicants must submit the Free Application for Federal Student Aid (FAFSA) in order to be considered for aid. Ninety percent of undergraduate full-time students receive assistance from the University. Additional information may be obtained by calling the Office of Financial Aid at 305-899-3673 or 800-495-2279 (toll-free) or by e-mail at finaid@mail.barry.edu.

Faculty

Faculty members are easily accessible to students and are committed to providing individualized attention. The undergraduate faculty members of the Schools of Adult and Continuing Education, Arts and Sciences, Business, Education, Human Performance and Leisure Sciences, Natural and Health Sciences, Nursing, and Social Work participate in a dynamic academic advisement program. Doctorates are held by 81 percent of the faculty members, and the student-faculty ratio is 12:1.

Student Government

The Student Government Association serves as a liaison between the student body and the administration and faculty. All undergraduate students are members of the association, which is governed by an Executive Board that consists of 4 members and the Senate, which consists of 10 elected representatives. Six members are elected during the spring semester, and the remaining four places are filled early in the fall semester. Unless otherwise specified, meetings of the Senate are open, and students are invited and encouraged to attend the weekly sessions.

Admission Requirements

In reviewing the credentials of students seeking admission to Barry University, admissions considers an applicant's composite efforts. Candidates must present the following credentials: the completed application form, official high school or college transcripts, and the results of the SAT I or of the ACT.

Application and Information

The University reviews applications as they are completed. Students are advised of their acceptance once admissions has reviewed all required documents. Students may apply any time after completion of the junior year in high school. It is advisable to apply early. The student's completed application form and supporting credentials should be sent to the address below. Students may also apply online at http://www.barry.edu/ugapply.

Ms. Helen Corpuz
Acting Director of Admissions
Barry University
11300 Northeast Second Avenue
Miami Shores, Florida 33161-6695
Telephone: 305-899-3100
800-695-2279 (toll-free)
Fax: 305-899-2971
E-mail: admissions@mail.barry.edu
World Wide Web: http://www.barry.edu/success

Barry offers an outstanding environment for quiet reflection and study.

BARTON COLLEGE

WILSON, NORTH CAROLINA

The College

Founded in 1902 as the first degree-granting institution in eastern North Carolina, Barton College opened its doors to 107 students with one building on 5 acres of campus. Today, Barton welcomes approximately 1,300 students from thirty-one states and sixteen countries to a campus of twenty-five buildings on 65 acres.

The College offers several avenues of assistance for students, especially during the freshman year, including an innovative freshman advising program designed to assist students in making the transition from home and high school to college and residence hall life. All freshmen meet with their adviser three times a week in a classroom seminar setting. Outside the classroom experience, the First-Year Seminar program also offers exposure to a variety of cultural and social events, including concerts, lectures, art exhibits, drama productions, and sports events. Inside the classroom, Barton's student-centered core curriculum enhances academic success and provides students with an outstanding foundation from which the total liberal arts experience is achieved.

Barton's Student Development Program includes residence life programs, special activities, and counseling services that provide for the students' cultural, social, and emotional development. In addition, Barton has approximately thirty clubs and organizations in which students can be involved, including academic organizations, specialty clubs, fraternities, and sororities. Another vital component of student life is the Career Services Center. The center provides a vigorous on-campus recruiting program that brings approximately 100 recruiters to Barton's campus annually, representing corporations, government, and educational areas. In addition, several hundred other employers seek to hire Barton students each year. Barton's graduates rank exceptionally well in obtaining employment in their chosen field of study, and their salaries are competitive with those of students from other North Carolina colleges and universities.

On-campus housing is provided in four residence halls: Hilley, Hackney, Waters, and Wenger. All four facilities feature cable television and information technology access in each room.

Offering a strong, competitive sports program, Barton College's Bulldogs compete in the NCAA Division II and the Carolinas-Virginia Athletics Conference. The intercollegiate sports program includes women's basketball, cross-country, fast-pitch softball, soccer, tennis, and volleyball and men's baseball, basketball, cross-country, golf, soccer, and tennis. A wide variety of intramural sports are offered to the entire campus community. All students and especially those involved in Barton's intramural, physical education, and athletic programs benefit from the Kennedy Recreation and Intramural Center that features an indoor swimming pool, walking/jogging areas, an auxiliary gym, and a weight/fitness room. Barton also has a twelve-court tennis complex to add to its outstanding facilities package.

Location

Wilson is in the coastal plain region of eastern North Carolina. The city provides an excellent home for the College and is within easy driving distance of several metropolitan areas and scenic attractions. The state capital of Raleigh is a 45-minute drive to the west; to the north, Richmond is 2 hours away and Washington, D.C., is 4 hours away. The beautiful Atlantic coast of North Carolina is 100 miles from the campus, and the scenic Blue Ridge Mountains are easily accessible. Located on Interstate 95, Wilson is also accessible by U.S. Routes 264, 117, and 301 and North Carolina Routes 42 and 58. Wilson is 1 hour from Raleigh/Durham International Airport. Amtrak has daily service with one northbound and one southbound departure.

The College's historic neighborhood is just a few minutes from busy downtown Wilson. Banks, theaters, the shopping mall, and restaurants are close by. Many of Wilson's arts and cultural events take place on the College campus. The Wilson community (population 45,000) enjoys a mild climate that has an average annual temperature of 65 degrees.

Majors and Degrees

Barton College offers six baccalaureate degrees: Bachelor of Arts, Bachelor of Science, Bachelor of Fine Arts, Bachelor of Nursing, Bachelor of Social Work, and Bachelor of Liberal Studies. These degrees are administered by five schools. The School of Arts and Sciences offers programs in art education (K–12), art studio (with concentrations in ceramics, graphic design, painting, and photography), athletic training, biology (preprofessional programs in dentistry, medical technology, medicine, physical therapy, and veterinary medicine), chemistry (preprofessional program in pharmacy), English*, environmental science, fitness management, history, mass communications (concentrations include audio recording technology, broadcast/video production, print and electronic journalism), mathematics (preprofessional program in engineering), physical education (with teacher licensure), political science (concentrations include business and prelaw), religion and philosophy, social studies (with teacher licensure), Spanish*, sports management, and theater (concentrations include design, management, and performance). The School of Behavioral Sciences offers programs in criminal justice and criminology, gerontology, psychology, and social work. The School of Business offers programs in accounting, business administration, computer information systems, economics, and management of human resources. The School of Education offers programs in education of the deaf and hard of hearing (K–12), elementary education (K–6), middle school education (6–9), and special education–general curriculum. The School of Nursing offers a program in nursing. (Programs indicated with an asterisk (*) are available with or without a teacher licensure program.)

Minors can be earned in accounting, American studies, art (studio), biology, business administration, chemistry, communications, computer information systems, criminal justice and criminology, economics, English, geography, gerontology, history, physical education, political science, psychology, religion and philosophy, Spanish, strength and conditioning, theater, and writing.

Academic Programs

The major areas of study have a global focus, so students are assured of a high-quality academic program. Expanded travel opportunities and concentrated study are enhanced by Barton's 4-1-4 semester system featuring the January Term. Barton College offers a strong liberal arts tradition, and students follow a core curriculum during their freshman and sophomore years. In so doing, students are exposed to a variety of disciplines. Through a carefully guided advising program they declare a major area of study at the end of their freshman year or at the beginning of their sophomore year. At that point, they begin an intense and challenging program of study in their chosen field while completing general college requirements.

Barton College's nursing and education programs are ranked among the best in North Carolina. The School of Business majors (accounting, business administration, and management of human resources) continue to be popular areas of study. Barton is one of the few colleges on the East Coast to offer a program for the education of the deaf and the hard of hearing. Also unique is the recording technology program, which features a 32-track digital recording studio. The School of Behavioral Sciences offers a fully accredited social work degree program, gerontology and psychology majors, and a criminal justice and criminology major with law enforcement certification available to students choosing that track. Barton's athletic training education program has also received national accreditation.

Off-Campus Programs

Each year students participate in faculty-led trips to different areas of the world. Students recognize this travel as an excellent opportunity to enrich their college experience. Depending on the nature and destination of the travel, students may obtain college credit for their participation. Barton also has exchange agreements with colleges in Europe and Asia for extended overseas study offered in conjunction with the Global Focus international emphasis.

Academic Facilities

Barton College has a fiber-optic underground network that includes an infrastructure of data, voice and video wiring to selective classrooms, all faculty member offices, a majority of administrative offices, and two data connections in each residence hall room. The Willis N. Hackney Library is open 86.5 hours per week to serve the College community. BARTON LINC, the College's library information network center, offers a variety of services for users, including library information (hours, services, etc.), library online catalog, connection to other databases, connection to other libraries, and connection to subject-related Internet sites. The library's collection includes 190,540 total volumes, including more than 22,580 electronic books, and U.S. government documents, as well as a substantial collection of microfilm, maps, filmstrips, and pamphlets. It also subscribes to 434 periodicals and newspapers and 9,256 online journals. The Media Center, located on the basement level of Harper Hall, provides checkout service for audiovisual equipment. There are facilities for audiotape and videotape duplication as well as other production services.

Located on the first floor of J. W. Hines Hall are two computer labs for classes and individual student use. Computer labs are also available for student use in the Nursing Education Building, the Belk Education Building, and Moye Science Hall. The Nursing Education Building also has a multimedia center with a state-of-the-art projection system, installed for a broad range of lecture and teaching purposes, and the Belk Education Building houses the state-of-the-art Merck Science and Mathematics Instructional Lab. The Sam and Marjorie Ragan Writing Center supplements Barton's commitment to language and writing as vital components of the liberal arts curriculum. Students have access to more than 125 computer terminals on campus.

WEDT-TV, a local cable television station operated by Barton College and staffed by Barton students, is located in the Roma Hackney Music Building. The TV studio offers up-to-date equipment and facilities for study and use in television, videotape, and audiotape production. The Hackney Music Building also houses classrooms, the College's library for recordings and musical scores, and the Sarah Lynn Kennedy Recording Studio. Moye Science Hall provides classrooms, laboratories, a greenhouse, and research-related study areas for students. The Nursing Education Building houses classrooms and a laboratory for the nursing program. Case Art Building provides classrooms, private and class studios, and a museum with two art galleries for Barton's permanent art collection and for visiting exhibits. It also houses state-of-the-art computer graphics and darkroom labs.

Costs

Expenses for the 2004–05 year include tuition, $14,384; room, $2592; board plan, $2828; and combined fees, $979. These total $20,783 for the year. The estimated cost of books per semester is $600.

Financial Aid

The objective of the financial aid program at Barton College is to provide financial assistance to qualified students who would not otherwise be able to begin or continue their college education. Financial aid is awarded on the basis of need. (Financial need exists when the total cost of education exceeds the amount of money a student and family can reasonably make available from income and assets.) Barton College requires that all applicants for financial aid complete the Free Application for Federal Student Aid (FAFSA) as a means of determining financial need. Approximately 84 percent of Barton students receive financial aid. Aid comes from federal, state, and institutional resources and may be awarded as scholarships, grants, loans, or work-study. In addition, many students apply for part-time jobs on campus or in the community through the Career Services Center.

Students are encouraged to apply early for financial aid and should have their completed application in the Financial Aid Office by June 1 in order to ensure receipt of awards by the beginning of the fall semester. Every effort is made to process completed applications received after this date; however, earlier applications receive top priority in the awards process.

Faculty

Faculty members at Barton College recognize the importance of personalized attention for the students' learning experience. Because of the 12:1 student-faculty ratio, professors at Barton are able to teach small classes and have the opportunity to meet and to get to know their students as individuals. Faculty members make every effort to be accessible to students between classes and during regularly scheduled office hours. Professors at Barton are committed to the success of their students. Barton has 79 full-time faculty members. Approximately 55 percent of the full-time faculty members have obtained the highest degree available in their field.

Student Government

The Student Government Association (SGA) of Barton College provides students with opportunities to express themselves on issues of concern. Student government also provides a setting for studying the democratic process. The officers of the SGA are elected by the members of the student body, and the president of the SGA serves as an ex officio member of the College Board of Trustees.

Admission Requirements

To be considered for admission to Barton College, a student must have a high school diploma or its equivalent with a minimum total of 13 college-preparatory units. The following courses are recommended: English, 4 units; mathematics, 3 or more units (algebra I, geometry, and algebra II are required); natural sciences, 2 or more units (one lab science is required); social sciences, 2 or more units; and foreign language, 2 or more units (encouraged, but not required). A student applying for admission must also take the SAT I and achieve a score that, when considered along with the high school record, predicts probable success in college. ACT scores are also accepted.

Application and Information

To apply for admission to the College, a student must submit a completed application, a nonrefundable $25 application fee ($50 for international students), and an official transcript of high school credits. A copy of SAT I or ACT scores should be sent to the Office of Admissions by the testing agency. International applicants whose native language is not English must also submit the results of the Test of English as a Foreign Language (TOEFL). Students are encouraged to apply early and are usually notified of a decision within two weeks of the admission office's receipt of the completed application and information.

For further information, students may contact:

Office of Admissions
Barton College
Box 5000
Wilson, North Carolina 27893-7000
Telephone: 252-399-6317
800-345-4973 (toll-free)
Fax: 252-399-6572
E-mail: enroll@barton.edu
World Wide Web: http://www.barton.edu

BASTYR UNIVERSITY

SEATTLE, WASHINGTON

The University

Bastyr University offers two-year upper-division programs that lead to Bachelor of Science degrees. Undergraduates may choose degree programs in exercise science and wellness, health, herbal sciences, nutrition, psychology, or a combined B.S./M.S. program in acupuncture and Oriental medicine that is designed to meet the requirements for national licensure in acupuncture. In all degree programs there is a strong emphasis on broad education in the natural health sciences, preparing students to pursue graduate degrees in a variety of related areas. The University also offers graduate programs in nutrition and acupuncture, as well as doctoral programs in naturopathic medicine and in acupuncture and Oriental medicine. Undergraduates majoring in nutrition may complete the Didactic Program in Dietetics (DPD) designed to fulfill academic requirements for Registered Dietitian (RD) eligibility. Bastyr University is a small independent university with a strong sense of community that fosters both academic and personal support. Undergraduate students enjoy a collegial relationship with graduate and professional students, as well as with faculty and staff members.

Bastyr University was founded as a naturopathic medical college in 1978 to meet the growing need for scientifically trained naturopathic physicians, natural health–oriented care, and preventive medicine. Since 1984, as a part of its mission to provide comprehensive education in the natural health sciences, the University has added graduate and undergraduate programs. The Leadership Institute of Seattle (LIOS) became affiliated with Bastyr University in 1992. A Master of Arts in applied behavioral science is offered through this program.

Bastyr University is accredited by the Northwest Commission on Colleges and Universities. The Oriental medicine and acupuncture program is accredited by the ACAOM and meets the requirements of the national certification exam. Bastyr University's Didactic Program in Dietetics has been approved by the American Dietetic Association Council on Education.

The Natural Health Sciences campus total enrollment in 2003–04 was 1005; 22 percent were undergraduate students. Eighty percent were women. The undergraduate students' average age is 26. Twenty countries are represented, and 9 percent of the student body is international. The Bastyr University campus is situated on 50 acres of woods, fields, and trails on the northeast shore of Lake Washington, 30 minutes from downtown Seattle. The University also operates the Bastyr Center for Natural Health, an outpatient clinic where graduate students are involved in clinical training within their discipline.

Part of the University's mission is to pursue scientific research on the use of nutrition and natural medicine therapies to improve the management of health-care problems and to promote the prevention of chronic disease. Research at the University actively pursues research opportunities and publishes significant findings. Participation in research projects is available to a limited number of students.

Location

Seattle is one of the most attractive cities in the Pacific Northwest and has easy access to mountains, ocean beaches, lakes, and numerous national, state, and city parks. Several ski areas are within an hour's drive, and there are abundant opportunities for hiking, camping, and other outdoor recreation. The city offers a full range of museums, theaters, fine restaurants of many cuisines, a major opera company and a symphony orchestra, major-league sports, and outdoor activities. The Puget Sound area has a large number of academic institutions, including nine universities and many community colleges and professional schools.

Majors and Degrees

The degree programs provide the third and fourth years of an undergraduate program, offer a strong foundation in the natural health sciences, and provide an excellent preprofessional education for careers in nutrition, acupuncture, naturopathic medicine, health psychology, public health, and other health-care professions.

Academic Programs

The academic year is from September to June, with some summer classes available. The University is on the quarter system. There are vacations of three weeks after the fall term and two weeks after the winter term.

Students enter the program as juniors (having already completed a minimum of 90 quarter credits or 60 semester credits elsewhere) and should be prepared to declare their major upon entry to the University. Selected electives may be taken, with permission, from other programs in the University. This broadens students' exposure to the principles of preventive and holistic health care. At least one full year of credits must be completed at Bastyr University. At least 180 quarter credits are required to graduate.

The nutrition curriculum blends traditional nutrition education and a whole foods emphasis with the current advances in nutrition. This major emphasizes nutrient chemistry and metabolism, the personal and cultural aspects of food and their influence on nutritional status, dietary evaluation and modification, and the appraisal of current research. The exercise science and wellness major combines the nutritional science core with the basic sciences, exercise science, and additional courses in research methodology, activity classes, and a senior internship. Graduates in both majors are prepared for work with professional health-care providers as nutrition educators, for jobs with programs and businesses in the health and fitness industry, and for graduate work in related sciences. Graduates of the DPD program are eligible for an American Dietetics Association–approved dietetic internship or a preprofessional practice program that leads to the registered dietitian credential. Graduates in exercise science receive the educational foundation to achieve exercise certification from the American College of Sports Medicine and other professional exercise affiliates.

The health psychology curriculum explores the integration of mind, body, and spirit. The program is designed to enhance students' capabilities to blend the study of psychology with health, the healing arts, wellness, and fitness. This program also provides a solid undergraduate foundation for pursuing both professional studies and graduate degrees. Students may enroll in one of four tracks: health psychology, psychology and spirituality, psychology and human biology (psychology-premed), or psychology and human biology (psychology-premed), with an option for the summer massage intensive.

The herbal sciences degree program is designed to provide a thorough, scientifically rigorous, and inspiring exploration of herbalism and its applications. The curriculum does not include the diagnosis and treatment of disease but rather introduces the student to concepts of disease prevention and health maintenance using medicinal herbs. The curriculum addresses economic, historical, and sociopolitical perspectives regarding the herbal sciences. Additionally, issues related to herbal product manufacturing and quality assurance are introduced. Courses include basic sciences, herbal sciences, and exploration of research on medicinal herbs. Students complete an optional practicum in the herbal field. Graduates are uniquely qualified to enter the herbal industry or to pursue further education in a related field.

The combined B.S./M.S. option in acupuncture and Oriental medicine blends a basic science curriculum with the art of traditional Chinese medicine, modern approaches, and current research. Courses include fundamental principles of Oriental medicine, traditional Chinese medical diagnosis, medical pathology, meridians and points, acupuncture techniques, and clinical observation.

Academic Facilities

The University maintains a medical library with extensive resources for conventional and natural medicine. These include more than 250 journal subscriptions; special collections in the areas of nutrition, herbal sciences, psychology, and exercise science; and access to many health and natural medicine databases. Students at Bastyr University are also eligible to use the Health Sciences Library at the University of Washington.

Costs

Tuition for the 2003–04 academic year was $272 per credit (up to 15 credits); the cost for each additional credit was $200. The total cost of tuition and fees for a full-time student was between $12,000 and $16,700 for the academic year, depending on the number of credits needed to complete a program. Students spend approximately $900 per year on books and supplies.

The University has limited dormitory space. Many students live in shared housing facilities off campus; the average rent per person ranges from $400 to $800 per month. The Student Services Office maintains listings of available housing. The Washington Financial Aid Association estimates that living expenses, including transportation and personal expenses, average $1004 per month.

Financial Aid

Students are eligible to participate in state and federal financial aid programs, including the Washington State Need Grant, Washington State Education Opportunity Grant, Federal Pell Grant, Federal Supplemental Educational Opportunity Grant (FSEOG), Federal Stafford Student Loan, Federal Perkins Loan, and Federal Work-Study. Applicants seeking financial aid should complete the application process by May 15. Financial aid information is provided by the University on request.

Faculty

The Bastyr University student-faculty ratio is approximately 15:1. There are 19 full-time and 31 part-time faculty members, who also teach in the graduate programs. More than 70 percent hold doctoral degrees, and all faculty members are involved in teaching and are dedicated to providing students with a program of the highest quality.

Student Government

The Student Council makes decisions focusing on social activities as well as policies and budget items affecting students. Each class and program is represented. Students are represented on the University's Board of Trustees by an elected student, and 5 student representatives also serve on the University Council. Students also serve on the Curriculum Review, Library, and Resident Selection committees; the Appeals Board; and ad hoc committees.

The University relies upon this participation by students to create a more effective learning environment.

Admission Requirements

Admission is based on academic achievement, personal and social development, and demonstrated humanistic qualities. Credentials to be submitted include all official transcripts, a completed application form, and a $60 application fee. The minimum prerequisite for the bachelor's programs is two years of college-level general education (90 quarter or 60 semester credits), including those distribution and course requirements described below. Students must take the following distribution of general education courses, which are not counted toward any other requirements: arts and humanities, 15 quarter credits; social sciences, 15 quarter credits; and natural sciences and mathematics, 12 quarter credits. In addition, specific required courses include 9 credits of English composition and/or literature, 4 credits of college-level algebra, 4 credits of general biology, 3 credits of general psychology, and 3 credits of public speaking. A minimum 2.25 overall GPA and a C or better in all required courses are needed. Applications should be received by the University by March 15 for priority consideration for fall admission. Late applications are considered if space is available.

Application and Information

Prospective students are encouraged to visit the campus. Application may be made by submitting the Bastyr University undergraduate application with a $60 nonrefundable fee, and all official transcripts.

For further information, students should contact:

Admissions Office
Bastyr University
14500 Juanita Drive NE
Kenmore, Washington 98028–4966
Telephone: 425-602-3330
E-mail: admiss@bastyr.edu
World Wide Web: http://www.bastyr.edu

Students stroll through the inner courtyard on the Bastyr Kenmore campus.

BAYLOR UNIVERSITY

WACO, TEXAS

The University

Baylor University was chartered by the Republic of Texas in 1845 and is the state's oldest institution of higher education. The world's largest Baptist university, Baylor is affiliated with the Baptist General Convention of Texas. As one of the nation's major academic church-related universities providing liberal arts and professional education in a Christian environment, Baylor emphasizes high academic and personal standards. Excellence is a tradition, a practice, and a promise. Students come to Baylor from all fifty states and ninety other countries. Baylor has 11,712 undergraduates and a total of 13,937 men and women in attendance. More than 270 social, service, professional, religious, and honorary student organizations, including national fraternities and sororities, provide opportunities for recreation, the development of social skills, spiritual and intellectual stimulation, and pursuit of individual interests. Special University activities include numerous cultural events, including films, talks by prominent lecturers, and performances by musicians and entertainers. In addition to offering varsity sports as a member of NCAA Division I and of the Big 12 Athletic Conference, Baylor provides an extensive, balanced program of intramurals. A recreation center provides special facilities for boating, canoeing, sailing, swimming, and tennis. On-campus housing is provided in twelve residence halls. All freshmen are required to live on campus. Housing applications are not accepted prior to admission to the University. Priority for housing is based on the date the housing application is received in the Campus Living and Learning Office. For late applicants, priority is based on the date the housing deposit is received.

The Baylor School of Law offers the Juris Doctor degree. Graduate work is offered in the College of Arts and Sciences and the Schools of Business, Education, Engineering and Computer Science, and Music; in Institutes and Special Studies; in the School of Nursing at Dallas; and in the U.S. Army Academy of Health Sciences at San Antonio. The George W. Truett Seminary, in Waco, offers the Master of Divinity degree.

Location

Located on the banks of the Brazos River in central Texas, Waco has a metropolitan area population of 208,000 people. The city is very near the population and geographical core of the state; within 100 miles of Dallas, Fort Worth, and Austin; and within easy driving distance of Houston, San Antonio, and the Gulf Coast. Recreational and entertainment facilities, restaurants, and cultural activities of all kinds are numerous. Baylor University's 735-acre campus adjoins the historic Brazos River near downtown Waco.

Majors and Degrees

Baylor University's undergraduate programs are available in the College of Arts and Sciences; the Schools of Business, Education, Engineering and Computer Science, Music, and Nursing; and in the Honors College or Institutes and Special Studies. There are 163 baccalaureate degree programs and more than 100 major areas of study.

The College of Arts and Sciences, the Schools of Business and Education, and the Institutes and Special Studies offer departmental and intra-university programs leading to the Bachelor of Arts (B.A.), Bachelor of Science (B.S.), Bachelor of Science in Aviation Sciences (B.S.A.S.), Bachelor of Science in Education (B.S.Ed.), Bachelor of Science in Family and Consumer Sciences (B.S.F.C.S.), Bachelor of Fine Arts (B.F.A.), or Bachelor of Business Administration (B.B.A.) degrees. Undergraduate majors in these schools and colleges include accounting; administrative information systems; American studies; anthropology; applied mathematics; archaeology; architecture (with Washington University); art; art history; Asian studies; aviation sciences; basic business; biblical and related languages; biochemistry; biology; business administration; business–broadcasting; business–journalism; chemistry; child and family studies; classics; communication sciences and disorders; communication specialist studies; computer information systems; computer science; dentistry (combination program with an accredited dental school); design; earth sciences; economics; elementary education; English; entrepreneurship; environmental studies; fashion design; fashion merchandising; finance; financial services/planning; foreign service; forensic science; forestry (final year at Duke University); French; general family and consumer science; general studies in health, human performance, and recreation; geography; geology; geophysics; German; great texts; Greek; health; health/fitness studies; health science studies; history; human resources management; information systems; insurance; interdisciplinary studies; interior design; international business; international studies; journalism; Latin; Latin American studies; language and linguistics; law; life–earth science; management; marketing; mathematics; medical technology and biology; medicine (combination program with an accredited medical school); museum studies; music; neuroscience; nutrition sciences, operations management; optometry (combination program with an accredited optometry school); performance; philosophy; physical education; physical science; physics; political science; professional selling; professional writing; psychology; public administration; real estate; recreation; regional/urban studies; religion; risk management and insurance; Russian (9 hours required with another Russian program); science; secondary education; Slavic studies; social studies; social work; sociology; Spanish; special education; speech and language therapy; speech communication; studio art; telecommunication; theater arts; and university scholars. In addition, programs are available in predentistry, pre–dental hygiene, premedicine, pre–occupational therapy, pre-optometry, pre–physical therapy, prepharmacy, and pre–veterinary medicine.

The School of Engineering and Computer Science offers programs of study leading to the Bachelor of Science in Engineering (B.S.E.) degree with majors in electrical and computer engineering, engineering, and mechanical engineering. In addition, the school offers programs of study leading to the Bachelor of Science in Computer Science (B.S.C.S.) and the Bachelor of Science in Informatics (B.S.I.).

The School of Music offers programs of study leading to the Bachelor of Music (B.M.) degree in applied music, church music, composition, history and literature, pedagogy, and theory. The Bachelor of Music Education (B.M.E.) degree is designed for prospective teachers in public schools and offers concentrations in choral and instrumental instruction.

The School of Nursing combines a liberal arts curriculum and professional preparation in a four-year program leading to the Bachelor of Science in Nursing (B.S.N.) degree. Nursing majors complete their first two years on the Waco campus and then move to Dallas for two years in the professional component of the curriculum.

Academic Programs

Baylor, a Phi Beta Kappa university ranking in the top 1 percent in numbers of National Merit Scholars enrolled, operates on a two-semester academic year plus two 6-week summer sessions. In the first two years, students select courses that provide a broadly based liberal arts education. All students who are admitted to Baylor

University as freshmen enter either the College of Arts and Sciences, the School of Music, or a preprofessional program in the School of Business, the School of Education, School of Engineering and Computer Science, or the School of Nursing. Students pursuing degrees in one of the other professional schools may apply for admission to a specific degree program during the second year. Those students admitted to the University who intend to major in music should also qualify for admission to the School of Music at the time they enter the University in order to avoid undue delay in the completion of their degree program. Many of Baylor's students enter with credit hours earned through credit by examination. A number of these superior students elect to join the Honors College, which includes the Baylor Interdisciplinary Core (a set of comprehensive and cohesive interdisciplinary courses that are organized around world cultures, the natural world, and the social world), the Honors Program, University Scholars, and Great Texts.

Off-Campus Programs

Students may enroll in summer study-abroad programs in Cuba, Cyprus, Egypt, England, France, Germany, Greece, Israel, Italy, Scotland, Spain, Switzerland, Thailand, Turkey, and Wales. One-year exchange programs are available with universities in Argentina, Australia, Azerbaijan, Canada, China, England, Finland, France, Hong Kong, Indonesia, Japan, Korea, Mexico, the Netherlands, Slovakia, South Africa, Thailand, and Uzbekistan.

Academic Facilities

A brand new science building is opening in fall 2004, with 500,000 square feet of classroom, office, and lab space. The Mayborn Museum Complex, also scheduled to open in 2004, houses the Harry and Anna Jeanes Discovery Center, the Governor Bill and Vara Daniel Historic Village, and the Waco Mammoth Site as well as the Department of Museum Studies. Learning resource materials, housed in the six libraries on campus, total more than 1.5 million bound volumes. Modern scientific laboratories and equipment, computer science facilities, a speech and hearing clinic, the Castellaw Communications Center, and the Glasscock Energy Research Center offer students practical experience. The Hooper-Schaefer Fine Arts Center is available for work in the visual and performing arts.

Costs

The estimated direct total cost for 2003–04 was $26,336. Tuition was $17,900 (flat tuition rate for 12 hours or more), residence hall rooms are $3120, board (sixteen meals per week) was $3336, and required fees were $1980. The total figure does not include the cost of books, travel, or personal expenditures. Books and supplies are estimated at $1350 per year. Travel costs and personal expenditures vary with the individual. Costs are subject to change.

Financial Aid

Four basic forms of financial aid are available and are based on merit (as shown by achievement, National Merit status, and SAT I or ACT scores) and need (as determined by the FAFSA). These programs include scholarships, grants, loans, and on-campus jobs. About 75 percent of the students receive assistance. Students are considered for scholarships by virtue of the application for admission. Students may obtain a FAFSA from their high school counselor or local college or university.

Faculty

Baylor's faculty numbers 777, and 90 percent hold the highest degree offered in their fields. Ninety-two percent of all classes are taught by faculty members. Most faculty members are actively engaged in research, several hold special chairs in their respective fields, and all are dedicated to challenging and teaching students. All faculty members work with undergraduates and serve as academic advisers to the students. The student-faculty ratio is 16:1, and a typical class numbers 29 students.

Student Government

Baylor University Student Government, whose members are elected by popular vote, is a vital and influential force in campus activities. With more than 270 active student organizations, numerous traditional events, special involvement programs, entertainment programs, and leadership laboratories, there are plenty of opportunities for students to get involved in campus life.

Admission Requirements

Eligibility for consideration for admission to Baylor is established by competitive high school performance and by competitive scores on either the ACT or SAT. In connection with these admission criteria, Baylor students as a group demonstrate well above average academic achievement and potential. Other applicants who do not qualify for priority admission may be considered for admission at the discretion of the Admissions Committee. Such admission may require attendance in summer school and entrance with special requirements. Required high school units are English, 4; college-preparatory mathematics, 3; laboratory science, 2; foreign language, 2; and social science, 2 (1 in history). Prospective freshmen should take the SAT or ACT examination not later than the second semester of their junior year in high school and have the results sent to Baylor by the testing company. Freshman applications should be made at the end of the junior year or early in the senior year.

Students who wish to transfer to Baylor and who have completed at least 30 semester hours must present official transcripts from each college attended verifying a minimum overall grade point average of 2.5 (on a 4.0 scale) and must be eligible to return to the last school attended. Transfer students who seek admission with fewer than 30 semester hours must meet all the admission requirements for beginning freshmen. In addition, all transfer students must meet the same minimum course requirements for admission that are required for beginning freshmen. A student may present a high school transcript or a college transcript to verify that the course requirements have been fulfilled. Transfer students should plan to apply no later than the end of their sophomore year in order to meet the Baylor residence requirement of 60 semester hours.

Baylor offers admission to a limited number of superior high school students who have completed their junior year through an Advanced Studies/Early Admission Program. Applicants must rank in the top 10 percent of their class, score at least 1300 on the SAT or 30 on the ACT, and have recommendations from both the high school counselor and principal. Interviews and campus visits are recommended.

Application and Information

Notifications of acceptance are based on a review of an applicant's complete file and begin by mid-September on a rolling admission basis. The complete file includes a general application for admission with a $35 application fee, an official high school transcript giving the applicant's rank in class, and official scores on the SAT or ACT. To receive early consideration for admission, students are urged to apply in September, when the process begins. Requests for application forms and inquiries should be addressed to:

Office of Admission Services
Baylor University
One Bear Place
P.O. Box 97056
Waco, Texas 76798-7056
Telephone: 254-710-3435
800-BAYLOR-U (toll-free)
World Wide Web: http://www.baylor.edu

BAY PATH COLLEGE

LONGMEADOW, MASSACHUSETTS

The College

Founded in 1897, Bay Path College today offers baccalaureate and associate degrees for women. The College also offers a Master of Science degree in communications and information management as well as a Master of Science in advanced practice occupational therapy and a Master of Occupational Therapy for women and men. As a pioneer in innovative programs, the College educates students to become confident and resourceful contributors to an increasingly interdependent world through its focus on leadership, communication, and technology. Students are challenged to accept the responsibilities and to experience the rewards of leadership throughout their college careers. The College thoroughly integrates technological, analytical, and oral and written communication skills into the curriculum.

The core of the 44-acre campus is the site of the former Wallace estate, and the Georgian architecture of the buildings reflects that of the estate's mansion, Deepwood Hall, which is now the College's administration building. Attractive residence halls provide comfortable accommodations for students and are wired for voice mail, video, and data. The Blake Student Commons houses a spacious dining room, career development center, media theater, student lounges, game room, the College store, and a snack bar. The Fitness Center, fully equipped with exercise equipment and a dance and aerobics studio, provides both formal and informal fitness opportunities. Playing fields, a running track, and an athletic club house accommodate varsity sports.

Through the College's comprehensive extracurricular program, students have a choice of a wide variety of on-campus clubs, organizations, and athletic activities. Bay Path also sponsors an annual "Capitals of the World" trip; weekend or day trips to New York City, Boston, Montreal, and Cape Cod; and ski trips to nearby slopes and major New England resorts. Two full-scale musical productions are presented by students and professionals each year. The Bay Path Chorale, the Page Singers (a select singing group), and the Bay Path Dance Company appear both on campus and for clubs and other organizations throughout New England. Social events and other collaborative activities are scheduled with neighboring colleges. Although many of the 1,200 undergraduate women enrolled reside on campus, commuting students are fully involved in College life.

The College's Sullivan Career Development Center assists graduates who seek immediate employment; this service is available to them throughout their lives at no cost. In recent years, 90 to 95 percent of Bay Path's undergraduate students have obtained jobs in their fields upon graduation.

Bay Path is a member of the College Entrance Examination Board, the Association of Independent Colleges and Universities in Massachusetts, the College Board, the National Association of College Admission Counselors, the National Association of Independent Colleges and Universities, and the Women's College Coalition.

Location

Longmeadow, Massachusetts, is a residential town just south of Springfield, Massachusetts, and 20 miles north of Hartford, Connecticut. Located in the city of Springfield are shopping centers, restaurants and clubs, the Basketball Hall of Fame, a flourishing repertory theater, an excellent symphony orchestra, fine museums, and a civic center that is the site of numerous cultural and sporting events.

Transportation by air, bus, or rail is convenient. Bay Path is 20 minutes from Bradley International Airport in Windsor Locks, Connecticut; 1½ hours from Boston; and 2½ hours from New York City.

Majors and Degrees

Bay Path offers bachelor's degrees, associate degrees, and/or certificate programs for women in biology, biotechnology, business, child psychology, communications, computer information technology, criminal justice, early childhood education, elementary education, forensic psychology, forensic science, international studies, interior design, legal studies, liberal studies, management, marketing, occupational therapy, psychology, and therapeutic recreation.

The College is accredited by the New England Association of Schools and Colleges. The paralegal programs at associate, baccalaureate, and certificate levels are approved by the American Bar Association. The five-year occupational therapy program is accredited by the Accreditation Council for Occupational Therapy Education of AOTA.

Academic Program

Bay Path's undergraduate programs prepare women either for entry into careers or for continued studies. A minimum of 60 credits must be completed successfully to earn an associate degree, and a minimum of 120 credits are required for a bachelor's degree. The general education requirements are intended to provide students with a foundation for learning in the humanities and fine arts, mathematics, and the natural and social sciences, regardless of major. The innovative Communications and Information Technology Program provides all undergraduates with the opportunity to develop professional-level skills in reading and interpreting, writing, speaking, using technological support, managing information, and developing information literacy.

Internships are an integral part of all programs, and students are placed with professionals in local, regional, and national businesses, corporations, and organizations for on-the-job experience. Bay Path interns work in locations such as law firms, laboratories, decorating firms, insurance companies, social service agencies, correctional facilities, schools, and hospitals.

The Career Development Summit for seniors and the Senior-Year Experience, required of all majors, give students the opportunity to individually appraise their career potential and practice communication skills for their professional fields, through case studies, field projects, interactive workshops, networking opportunities, and addresses by leaders from the business community. Students who are undecided about a career path are advised throughout their years at Bay Path.

English as a second language is offered as a course and a program to help international students gain the necessary language skills to complete a degree program.

Off-Campus Programs

Through Bay Path's membership in the Cooperating Colleges of Greater Springfield, a consortium of eight colleges, interested Bay Path students may take courses at these neighboring colleges and can share networked library resources.

Academic Facilities

Carr Hall houses a fully equipped theater, presentation classrooms, computer labs, science laboratories, and faculty offices. D'Amour Hall features computer laboratories, a multimedia lab classroom, and technology-equipped presentation classrooms. A preschool on campus provides opportunities for laboratory training for education majors. The Catok Art Center is specifically designed for the study and practice of art and also serves as an art gallery, which contains only a portion of an extensive art collection on display throughout the campus. Hatch Library, an automated library system, has extensive book, periodical, tape, and record collections, as well as a "virtual library" with more than fifty full-text online resources available 24 hours a day from any computer with Internet access. Elliott House contains the occupational therapy laboratory and faculty offices.

Costs

Costs for 2003–04 were $16,890 for tuition and $8020 for room and board.

Financial Aid

Bay Path is keenly interested in admitting talented students who are serious about their education, and it encourages such students to apply regardless of their financial means. Scholarships, grants, loans, and employment opportunities are available. The Bay Path Scholar's Program for high-ability students provides scholarship assistance that is renewable for four years, based on meeting established criteria. Bay Path has a commitment to continue to aid qualified students who receive aid in their freshman year; every effort is made to maintain or increase the funding level to enable these students to graduate. Approximately 80 percent of current Bay Path students receive some form of financial aid. One hundred percent of those who apply for financial aid receive some form of assistance. Financial aid applicants are reviewed beginning on February 1.

Faculty

The small size of the student population encourages the development of close, professional interactions among students and Bay Path faculty. Faculty members, all experts in their fields, have teaching as their primary concern, but they devote many additional hours to participation with students in academic, social, and cultural activities. Sixty-five percent of the full-time faculty members have a doctoral degree or a terminal degree.

Student Government

The Student Government, composed of 4 officers and 40 student representatives, assists the administration in deciding a number of matters, leads the way in the observance of regulations, and helps to create a spirit of mutual understanding and cooperation between the student body and the College administration.

Admission Requirements

The satisfactory completion of a college-preparatory high school program or equivalent is required for admission. The Admissions Committee evaluates a student's academic record, class rank, recommendations, test scores, and essay. Official transcripts are required, and an interview is strongly encouraged. Transfer students are welcome and should submit transcripts of all previously attended colleges. Students are selected who are best qualified in ability, scholarship, leadership, and motivation to complete the College's program of study.

In accordance with state and federal laws, Bay Path College does not discriminate against any student who applies for admission or is enrolled at the College.

Application and Information

The College follows a rolling admissions policy and encourages students to apply early. Notification of decision is generally within two weeks of receiving the completed application and accompanying materials. The candidate reply is requested on or before May 1 for September enrollment. The College has an Early Action Program, wherein a student can apply after successful completion of her junior year, provided she has taken all necessary course work and tests. Decisions for Early Action are given within two weeks of receipt of all information. The Early Action Program is not binding; it simply allows a student to receive an early decision.

Students can apply online at the Web address listed below or mail in a copy of the completed application. The completed application should be sent to the Office of Admissions, together with a $25 nonrefundable application fee or fee-waiver request.

Director of Admissions
Bay Path College
588 Longmeadow Street
Longmeadow, Massachusetts 01106
Telephone: 413-565-1331
800-782-7284 (toll-free outside 413 area code)
Fax: 413-565-1105
E-mail: admiss@baypath.edu
World Wide Web: http://www.baypath.edu

Blake Student Commons.

BECKER COLLEGE

WORCESTER AND LEICESTER, MASSACHUSETTS

The College

Located in the heart of Massachusetts, Becker is a distinctive New England college. Becker College encompasses two individual campuses that are located 6 miles apart, each with its own residence halls, library, and academic facilities. The Worcester campus was founded in 1887 by E. C. A. Becker. The Leicester campus began as an academy in 1784 and is the nineteenth-oldest campus in the country. Both schools had sustained a long-standing tradition of high-quality education. In 1974, Becker and Leicester began working together to expand academic offerings and provide broader social and recreational opportunities for their students. As a result of their close cooperation, the two were formally consolidated in 1977 as the Worcester campus and Leicester campus of Becker College.

Today, with an enrollment of about 1,000 men and women from eighteen states and twelve countries, Becker College continues the tradition of excellence. The innovative programs at Becker College are a carefully crafted blend of professional and liberal arts courses that contribute to the development of competent professionals and informed citizens. The two beautiful campuses offer students a choice as to the living environment that best suits their personal tastes. On the Worcester campus, gracious older homes have been restored and serve as residence halls. In Leicester, students may choose to live in restored homes or contemporary residence halls. Whether they live on or off campus, students share in the strong sense of community spirit that prevails at Becker.

Extracurricular activities offered through student organizations and the campus activities office provide a rich and varied college experience. Becker strongly encourages student involvement and participation for enhanced learning, personal development, and enjoyment. Student clubs and organizations include the Black Student Union, Community Service Club, the *Becker Journal* student newspaper, Multicultural Club, and yearbook as well as a number of others. As a small college responsive to student needs, Becker makes every effort to support new clubs and student organizations. Since student interests vary from year to year, new ideas and suggestions are always welcome.

Athletics are an important part of extracurricular activities for Becker students. More than 50 percent participate in intramural or recreational sports. Becker College is a member of the NCAA Division III, ECAC. Varsity athletics for men include baseball, basketball, cross-country, soccer, and tennis. Women's varsity sports are basketball, cross-country, field hockey, soccer, softball, tennis, and volleyball. Equestrian riding is offered as a coed club.

Location

With campuses in Worcester and Leicester, Massachusetts, Becker College enjoys an ideal location and easy access. Becker's Worcester campus is situated in the Elm Park section of Worcester, a quiet area of tree-lined streets and lovely old homes that is a short walk from the downtown business district. With a population of 165,000, the city of Worcester is New England's second-largest urban center. The city is 1 hour from Boston, Massachusetts; Hartford, Connecticut; and Providence, Rhode Island and 3 hours from New York City. Air, rail, and bus transportation connect Worcester to all major points. The Worcester Regional Transit Authority provides regular bus service throughout the city.

Becker's Leicester campus surrounds the historic village green at the junction of Routes 9 and 56 in Leicester center. The town of Leicester is located 6 miles from the Worcester campus. Students on the Leicester campus have the opportunity to participate in the cultural, social, and recreational activities of the metropolitan area while living in a small New England town, rich in history that predates the American Revolution.

Becker's two campuses are linked via campus shuttle and Worcester Regional Transit Authority bus service.

Majors and Degrees

Becker College awards Bachelor of Science degrees in business administration, with concentrations in finance and accounting, hospitality and tourism management, human resources management, marketing, management, and sports management; criminal justice, with concentrations in criminal justice administration and policing; kinesiology, with concentrations in exercise science and health and fitness; legal studies; and veterinary science. Bachelor of Arts degrees are awarded in liberal arts, with a concentration in elementary education (grades 1–6) or a minor in English, management, or psychology; and in psychology, with a concentration in early childhood education (pre-K to grade 2). The Bachelor of Arts in design program offers concentrations in interior design, graphic design, and Internet communication. Associate in Science degrees are awarded in accounting, animal care, business administration, computer information systems, criminal justice administration, early childhood education, liberal arts, liberal studies, nursing (RN), paralegal studies, physical therapist assistant studies, and veterinary technology.

Academic Programs

To graduate with a Bachelor of Arts or Bachelor of Science degree, students must complete a minimum of 122 credits with a cumulative GPA of 2.0 or higher. For an Associate in Science degree, a minimum of 60 credits with a GPA of 2.0 or higher is required. Thirty percent of the total credits must be in the area of general studies. Many programs require clinical fieldwork or internships for graduation.

Becker College operates on a two-semester academic calendar. Classes begin in September and end in May.

Off-Campus Programs

Becker is a member of the Colleges of Worcester Consortium, an association of fourteen Worcester-area colleges and universities that sponsors interlibrary loan services, social events, and a course cross-registration system to broaden course offerings. Full-time students may take one course per semester free of charge at any other consortium institution with permission of their faculty advisers. Member institutions include Anna Maria College, Assumption College, Atlantic Union, Clark University, College of the Holy Cross, Fitchburg State, Massachusetts College of Pharmacy, Nichols College, Quinsigamond Community College, Tufts University School of Veterinary Medicine, the University of Massachusetts Medical School, Worcester Polytechnic Institute, and Worcester State College.

Academic Facilities

The Academic Center on the Worcester campus contains the Ruska Library, state-of-the-art computer labs, science labs, classrooms, conference facilities, and a lecture hall.

The Leicester campus academic center contains classrooms, a lecture hall, and science and computer labs. Other facilities include an animal health center, a preschool, and a video production center.

Academic Support Centers are located on both campuses. The centers are dedicated to helping Becker students achieve academic success. Services include one-on-one and group content tutoring, study skills instruction and workshops, and writing seminars. The purpose of the Academic Support Centers is to provide appropriate academic assistance to all students. Professional staff members, peer tutors, and faculty members work together to foster a supportive learning environment. The staff engages in a partnership with students to help them achieve their goals. Academic support is available to all students at no additional cost.

Costs

For current tuition and fees, students should visit the Admissions home page on the College Web site at http://www.beckercollege.edu.

Financial Aid

Financial aid is available for all eligible students through federal, state, and Becker College programs. Approximately 85 percent of all Becker students receive some form of financial assistance. Financial aid comes in the form of grants and scholarships, student loans, and work-study. Most types of financial assistance require that a student demonstrate financial need. All students who wish to apply for aid must complete the Free Application for Federal Student Aid (FAFSA). The application deadline is rolling; however, students are encouraged to apply as soon as possible after January 1. Incoming freshmen receive financial aid award announcements beginning in March.

Faculty

Becker College has a faculty of 126 members. Becker faculty members are committed to personalized teaching and are one of the College's greatest resources. The student-faculty ratio of 15:1 allows students to get the individual attention and recognition they deserve.

Student Government

The Student Government Association (SGA) is charged with overseeing all clubs and organizations and any activities funded by the student activity fee. SGA officers and members hold regular meetings to maintain and improve the quality of campus life, focusing on student needs and expectations. Membership may include elected representatives from each residence hall and the commuter population, as well as student leaders from many organizations.

Admission Requirements

To be considered for admission, students must submit a completed application, a $50 application fee, an official secondary school transcript, and SAT I or ACT scores. One letter of recommendation is required and an essay is recommended. Students applying to health science majors are required to demonstrate proficiency in math and science. Becker College recognizes that all students are individuals and considers each applicant's personal strengths and achievements.

Application and Information

Applications are accepted on a rolling basis and reviewed upon receipt of all required materials. Most applicants are notified of admission decisions within two to three weeks of completion of their application. For more information, prospective students should contact:

Office of Admissions
Becker College
61 Sever Street
Worcester, Massachusetts 01609
Telephone: 508-791-9241 Ext. 245
877-5BECKER (523-2537) (toll-free)
Fax: 508-890-1500
E-mail: admissions@beckercollege.edu
World Wide Web: http://www.beckercollege.edu

The Student Center.

BELLEVUE UNIVERSITY

BELLEVUE, NEBRASKA

The University

The community leaders who founded Bellevue College in 1966 had a vision that still resonates today: to provide high-quality, cost-effective business and liberal arts degree programs that meet the needs of busy working students, employers, and society.

From a small, one-building campus in the Omaha suburb of Bellevue, Nebraska, that original, down-to-earth vision has expanded worldwide. Today, Bellevue University (BU) attracts students from more than forty countries and has alumni spread around the globe. Bellevue University is recognized globally as an educational leader that values individual achievement, high productivity, and applied critical thinking in creating opportunities for undergraduate and graduate students. BU actively facilitates a network of strategic alliances and partnerships that build on its core strengths and enrich what it offers its students. Among educators and employers, the University has established itself as an important national force for high quality, growth, and innovation in classroom and online graduate degree programs.

The University is structured in four colleges, each targeting specific needs. The College of Arts and Sciences meets a need for high-quality, affordable degree programs in the arts, sciences, communication, and humanities. The Kirkpatrick Signature Series, General Education Core Curriculum, Master of Human Services, and Master of Communication Studies are offered by the College.

The College of Business provides undergraduate majors in accounting and business administration and offers a flexible M.B.A. degree with several concentration areas as well as a Master of Arts in management.

The College of Professional Studies provides accelerated undergraduate degree-completion programs for students with a two-year degree or equivalent earned college credit, and accelerated-format master's degree programs in leadership and health-care administration.

The College of Distributed Learning provides online degree programs and courses in a variety of disciplines incorporating the University's expertise in Cyber-Active® learning. Online instructional design, technical support, and faculty training are within the purview of the College.

The College for Information Technology, through the College of Business, actively engages learners to pursue a high-quality technical and business education and offers undergraduate degrees in computer information systems (CIS) as well as a graduate degree in CIS.

Location

The Bellevue University main campus, complete with ample parking, has some of the most modern facilities in the region. A historic river town nudging the banks of the Missouri River, Bellevue, Nebraska, is a small, safe, and friendly city, nestled amid a 1,300-acre forest.

Classes are offered at convenient times at the Bellevue University main campus in Bellevue; the Lozier Professional Center in West Omaha; a southwest Omaha location; Offutt Air Force Base; Central Community College in Grand Island; Western Iowa Tech Community College in Sioux City, Iowa; corporate locations; and a variety of satellite centers throughout Nebraska, western Iowa, and South Dakota.

Majors and Degrees

Bellevue University offers a variety of majors and degrees. In the College of Arts and Sciences, Bachelor of Arts degree candidates may choose from ten majors, including art, biology, and communication, and an accelerated 62-hour program in liberal arts and professional applications. Bachelor of Science degree candidates may select from seven majors, including psychology and sociology. Bachelor of Fine Arts degree candidates may select from ten areas of emphasis, including ceramics, computer graphic design, painting, photography, printmaking, and sculpture.

The College of Business offers a Bachelor of Arts degree and a Bachelor of Science degree in accounting and business administration. The Center for Information Technology in the College of Business offers Bachelor of Arts and Bachelor of Science degrees in computer information systems.

Academic Programs

Traditional programs are offered in a format following the conventional fall, winter, spring, and summer terms. The programs leading to a Bachelor of Arts are offered in the humanities and related disciplines. The Bachelor of Science degree programs place more emphasis on research and scientific method. Students are required to follow the General Education Core Curriculum for traditional programs, which furnishes background and foundation knowledge to build academic excellence and career flexibility. In addition to the General Education Core Curriculum, students complete a major in at least one academic area. Courses taken in a major area are accepted, where applicable, in meeting the requirements of the General Education Core Curriculum. A minimum of 127 hours is required for Bachelor of Arts and Bachelor of Science degrees.

Academic Facilities

The Bellevue University main campus features the University's Riley Technology Center, which houses the heart of the computer network where all campus data, communications, and Internet traffic come together. Classrooms in the Riley Technology Center house more than 172 computers that are connected by 9 miles of wire.

The Freeman/Lozier Library offers many services to its customers and is the primary center for support of academic research and information services. The collection includes more than 122,000 volumes in a variety of formats, including books, periodicals, microfilms, CD-ROMs, videotapes, and other media.

The library's collection is arranged according to the Library of Congress classification system and is shelved in open stacks to facilitate customer access to the collection. The library's collection is available through an online catalog, VTLS, which may be accessed through any of the workstations on the library's local area network.

The library is also an active participant in Online Computer Library Center (OCLC), an international computer network of library holdings. Customers can search a variety of databases on CD-ROM and through OCLC's First Search service. As an active participant in ICON, a consortium of health science libraries in Nebraska and Iowa, the library provides an electronic connection to databases housed at the University of Nebraska Medical Center.

Costs

For 2004–05, undergraduate tuition is $155 per credit hour. Application and general college fees total $95 (for non-international students). In addition, specialized instruction fees generally cover equipment, supplies, and access to all laboratories and are listed in the schedule of classes with the course listing. Some courses may require additional expenditures for materials.

Financial Aid

Financial aid is money available to assist students with the costs of attending college. This assistance comes from the federal and state government, the institution, and private sources. Financial aid includes grants, scholarships, work-study programs, and student loans. Grants and scholarships do not have to be repaid. Federal Work-Study allows a student to work and earn money. Student loans and loans to parents for the student must be repaid.

In general, all U.S. citizens and eligible noncitizens enrolled in an approved degree program may apply for financial aid. The student eligibility criteria is listed on the front of the Free Application for Federal Student Aid (FAFSA). Some scholarships are available to students who may not qualify for other forms of financial aid.

Faculty

The Bellevue University full-time and adjunct faculty consists of 132 men and 58 women teaching students from the freshman to the graduate level. The student-faculty ratio is 20:1.

Admission Requirements

Graduation from high school, preparatory school, or its equivalent is required, and submission of an official high school transcript, official GED transcript, or certification of home or high school completion is necessary. ACT or SAT I scores must also be submitted.

Students seeking admission more than two years after graduation from high school must submit an official high school transcript, official GED transcript, or certification of home or high school completion.

Students transferring from another institution of higher education must submit an official transcript from each learning institution previously attended and transfer in good standing from the last institution of higher education attended (associate and bachelor degrees, however, are transferred in full). To satisfy the minimum residency requirements for the degree, transfer students must complete a minimum of 30 hours at Bellevue University. Students dismissed from another institution during the past five years for academic or disciplinary reasons may be accepted for admission after one year has elapsed since dismissal from the other institution. In all cases of transfer, the credit evaluation is completed by the Registrar's Office under guidance of the Council for Higher Education Accreditation (CHEA).

Application and Information

The Bellevue University Admissions office is open from 8 a.m. to 5 p.m. weekdays. Prospective students may find additional information on the Internet at the site listed below, or by contacting:

Information Center
Bellevue University
1000 Galvin Road South
Bellevue, Nebraska 68005
Telephone: 402-293-2000
E-mail: info@bellevue.edu
World Wide Web: http://www.bellevue.edu

BELMONT ABBEY COLLEGE

BELMONT, NORTH CAROLINA

The College

The strong family nature of the community of Belmont Abbey College directly influences the campus and classroom atmosphere. Because the College is small, students know the faculty and administration, and the development of lifelong friendships is common.

Residence life gives the student opportunities to develop both social and academic ideals. The sense of community is featured in both the academic and social aspects of the College.

The student body of approximately 1,000 men and women represents thirty-five states and eighteen countries. This diversity adds a valuable dimension to the student's educational experience. The College is coeducational, and approximately 60 percent of the students live on campus. Cars are permitted.

There are many extracurricular activities for students. The College Union offers a full program of social events and entertainment, and the active intramural sports program involves more than 80 percent of the students. Intercollegiate sports for men include baseball, basketball, cross-country, golf, soccer, and tennis. Intercollegiate sports for women include basketball, cross-country, soccer, softball, tennis, and volleyball. Other campus activities include fraternities, sororities, the campus ministry, the student newspaper, the literary magazine, the Leadership Program, the Abbey Players theater group, student government, and more.

Location

The College is situated in rolling, wooded country on a 650-acre campus just on the fringe of Belmont, a small town of 6,000 people. Belmont is 10 miles west of Charlotte, a community of about 450,000 people, which offers many opportunities for entertainment and cultural and recreational activity. Ten miles west of Belmont is Gastonia, population 50,000. Lakes abound in the immediate area, and it is only a 2-hour drive to the mountains and winter sports areas. Charlotte International Airport is a 10-minute drive away, and I-85 is adjacent to the campus.

Majors and Degrees

The degrees of Bachelor of Arts and Bachelor of Science are offered with majors in the following areas: accounting, biology, business management, computer information systems, economics, elementary education, English, history, international business, philosophy, political science, psychology, sociology, sports management, and theology.

Preprofessional training in law, medicine, optometry, pharmacy, and veterinary medicine is available.

Degrees awarded through the Adult Degree Program (described in the Academic Programs section) are in accounting, business administration, computer information systems, economics, elementary education, and liberal studies.

Academic Programs

The academic program is built on a distinctive core curriculum that responds to the diverse nature and needs of the traditional-age student. The core reflects more than 100 years of commitment to liberal arts and Catholic and Benedictine values and emphasizes faith, truth, social justice, international studies, the use of primary sources in the pursuit of knowledge, and the place of the individual in community.

A cumulative average of at least C (2.0 on a 4.0 scale) is required for graduation.

The Adult Degree Program serves students who need to attend college in a program outside the traditional day school program. Students in the Adult Degree Program attend classes three nights a week and/or on the weekend. Students can earn up to 12 semester hours of credit (this is considered full-time), making them eligible to apply for federal, state, and institutional financial aid.

Off-Campus Programs

Through the Charlotte Area Educational Consortium, a cooperative group of twelve colleges and universities, students have free access to all course offerings not available on the home campus and to library holdings of all the colleges. Study abroad may be arranged on an individual basis with a departmental chairman and the academic dean. Internship programs with credit, especially in the social sciences and professional studies, are available.

Academic Facilities

The age of the College (founded in 1876) is reflected in some of its stately old buildings, all of which have been renovated. The library, science building, physical education center, and Student Commons Center are newer additions.

Costs

Tuition, room and board (nineteen meals per week), and required fees for 2004–05 are $23,325 per year. This cost is reduced by $1800 annually for North Carolina residents through the North Carolina Legislative Tuition Grant program. Books and supplies average $750 per semester.

Financial Aid

College-administered aid comes from the full range of federal programs—Federal Pell Grants and Federal Supplemental Educational Opportunity Grants, Federal Work-Study awards, Federal Perkins Loans, and Federal Stafford Student Loans. North Carolina students have access to state grant funds administered by the College. Scholarships based on academic promise are granted each year. About 90 percent of all students receive College aid in some form. All applicants for aid must file the Free Application for Federal Student Aid (FAFSA) with the Financial Aid Office at Belmont Abbey College by February 15. The two criteria for receiving aid are financial need and academic promise.

Numerous companies throughout the region have employees in Belmont Abbey College's Adult Degree Program. Many of these companies provide some form of tuition reimbursement. Belmont Abbey offers a tuition deferment program for students eligible for employer reimbursement.

Faculty

The faculty-student ratio is 1:17. All faculty members engage both formally and informally in student advising and counseling. A professional counselor is also available. Faculty members teach all class levels without regard to academic rank or length of service.

Student Government

There is a student government elected by the student body. This organization, set up with executive, legislative, and judicial branches, is very influential in campus affairs. In addition, students have voting positions on most standing committees of the College.

Admission Requirements

An applicant's high school preparation should include 4 units in English, 3 in mathematics, 2 in social sciences, 2 in science, and 2 in foreign language. For science and math majors, 4 units in mathematics, 1 in chemistry, and 1 in physics are also recommended. The College requires each applicant to submit a completed application, high school transcripts, and SAT I or ACT scores. For transfer students, a completed application and college transcripts are required. The combined SAT I scores of entering freshmen average 1012. Acceptance to Belmont Abbey is based on the high school record, grade point average, and SAT I or ACT scores. A written recommendation relating to academic abilities and participation in extracurricular activities is helpful but not required. Advanced placement and credit are granted on the basis of the CLEP and AP tests of the College Board. A physician's statement of good health is required as well as documentation of all immunizations. An interview is preferred but not mandatory.

Belmont Abbey College does not discriminate against persons on the basis of sex, age, race, color, mental or physical challenge, religion, national or ethnic origin, or status as a disabled or Vietnam Era veteran in the recruitment and admission of students, the recruitment and employment of staff and faculty members, or the administration of its educational programs and activities as defined by federal laws and regulations.

Application and Information

An application, together with a $25 nonrefundable application fee, may be submitted for either the fall or spring semester; the deadlines are August 15 and December 31, respectively, but early application is advised. Notification of acceptance is given December 1 and January 15, then on a rolling basis upon completion of application data. A $400 tuition and room-reservation deposit for boarding students or a $200 tuition deposit for commuting students is due thirty days after the notice of acceptance is received.

For further information, prospective students should contact:

Office of Admission
Belmont Abbey College
Belmont, North Carolina 28012
Telephone: 704-825-6665
888-BAC-0110 (toll-free)
Fax: 704-825-6220
E-mail: admissions@bac.edu
World Wide Web: http://www.belmontabbeycollege.edu

Classes at Belmont Abbey College average about 15 students, creating a setting where it is easy to jump into the dialogue, voice opinions, ask tough questions, and get direct answers.

BELMONT UNIVERSITY

NASHVILLE, TENNESSEE

The University

Nationally recognized programs thrive on the Belmont University campus, which is located in the heart of the state capital, known both as Music City, U.S.A., and the Athens of the South (for its many educational institutions). Nashville offers big-city advantages with small-town charm.

Belmont's vision is to be a premier teaching university, bringing together the best of liberal arts and professional education in a Christian community of learning and service. Central to the fulfillment of that vision are faculty members who have a passion for teaching and the belief that premier teaching is interactive, technology-supported, motivational, creative, and exciting.

With an enrollment of more than 3,600 students, Belmont is the third-largest of Tennessee's thirty-five colleges and universities. It is affiliated with the Tennessee Baptist Convention.

In addition to the twenty-nine international countries represented in the student body, Belmont University attracts students from every state in the United States. The culturally diverse institution is committed to listening and learning from everyone. Students of today are helping shape the way students of tomorrow will be educated.

Belmont's beautiful, antebellum campus reflects a long, rich history that dates back to the nineteenth century, when the grounds were Adelicia Acklen's Belle Monte estate. University buildings that were erected over the past 110 years flank the Italianate mansion, which is still used by the campus. On the way to classes that prepare them for the twenty-first century, students enjoy Victorian gardens, statuary, and gazebos that recall a treasured past.

Two prestigious women's schools preceded the comprehensive liberal arts institution: the original Belmont College (1890–1913) and Ward-Belmont (1913–1951). In 1951, the Tennessee Baptist Convention founded the second Belmont College (1951–1991), with an initial coeducational enrollment of 136 students. Soon after celebrating 100 years of education on the same campus, the institution became a university in 1991, culminating a decade of dramatic growth and progress.

In addition to seven baccalaureate degrees, Belmont University offers eleven graduate degrees: the Master of Accountancy, the Master of Arts in Teaching, the Master of Business Administration, the Master of Education in Sport Administration, the Master of English, the Master of Music, the Master of Music Education, the Master of Education, the Master of Science in Nursing, Doctorate in Occupational Therapy, and the Doctorate in Physical Therapy.

Location

Belmont University occupies a 62-acre campus in southeast Nashville. With more than 500,000 residents, Nashville is a cultural, educational, health-care, commercial, and financial center in the mid-South. Practical educational opportunities, offered through diverse curriculums, provide students with the hands-on experience they need in preparation for a meaningful career. The city's location halfway between the northern and southern boundaries of the United States, with three intersecting interstate highways and an international airport, makes it accessible to students from across the country.

Majors and Degrees

Belmont University is accredited by the Commission on Colleges of the Southern Association of Colleges and Schools to award baccalaureate, master's, and doctoral degrees. Belmont grants seven undergraduate degrees: the Bachelor of Arts, the Bachelor of Business Administration, the Bachelor of Fine Arts, the Bachelor of Music, the Bachelor of Science, the Bachelor of Science in Nursing, and the Bachelor of Social Work. Majors or concentrations are offered in accounting, art (art education, design communications, and studio art), audio and video production, biochemistry and molecular biology, biology, business administration, chemistry, classics, communication studies, computer science, early childhood education, economics, engineering physics, English, environmental studies, European studies, exercise science and health promotion, finance, French, German, health, health-care management, history, information systems management, international business entrepreneurship, journalism, management, marketing, mass communication, mathematics, medical imaging technology, medical technology, middle school education, music (church music, commercial music, composition, music education, music with an outside minor, musical theater, performance, piano pedagogy, theory), music business, nursing, philosophy, physical education, physics, political economy, political science, pre-professional programs, psychology, religion, science and engineering management, social work, sociology, Spanish, and theater and drama.

Academic Programs

Uniquely positioned to provide the best of liberal arts and professional education, Belmont University offers celebrated professional programs structured to provide an academically well-rounded education. Belmont University operates on a two-semester schedule with classes beginning in late August and ending in early May. Two summer sessions are also offered. The academic program is arranged by school: the College of Arts and Sciences, the College of Business Administration, the College of Health Sciences, the College of Visual and Performing Arts, the Mike Curb College of Entertainment and Music Business, and the School of Religion.

In addition to the degrees offered through the schools, Belmont University offers an honors program, which was created to provide an enrichment opportunity for students who have potential for superior academic performance and who seek added challenge and breadth to their studies. Students enrolled in the honors program are led in designing and working through a flexible, individual curriculum and interdisciplinary general education curriculum by a private tutor who is an honors faculty member.

The University's advancements in undergraduate research are credited to a faculty committed to helping students practice their disciplines. The annual Belmont Undergraduate Research Symposium puts Belmont at the forefront of this national movement by providing a public forum for in-depth research at the undergraduate level.

Off-Campus Programs

Belmont University has contracts for dual-degree programs with Auburn University and University of Tennessee, Knoxville. These programs require three years of study at Belmont University followed by approximately two years of study at one of the above institutions. The course of study at Belmont must be mathematics, physics, or chemistry. Following completion of the academic requirements at both institutions, a student is awarded a Bachelor of Science degree from Belmont University and the appropriate degree from the second institution.

Several programs at Belmont have agreements with area organizations to provide students practical training. Nursing students gain clinical experience at all fourteen local area hospitals and other clinical agencies. Education students gain classroom experience in Metro-Davidson County Schools. Music business students gain real-world experience through internships in the Nashville music industry and in the Los Angeles, California, area through the Belmont West program of study and internships.

Through a wide variety of international study programs, Belmont offers students the opportunity to broaden and deepen their education while earning credit hours toward their degrees. These programs, which range in duration from two weeks to a year, are available in Australia, the Bahamas, China, Costa Rica, England, France, Germany, Hong Kong, Ireland, Italy, Mexico, New Zealand, Russia, Scotland, South Africa, and Spain.

Academic Facilities

Belmont offers a quiet, secluded environment, and classes are held in nine buildings with the library and other facilities located in proximity to those classrooms.

The Lila D. Bunch Library includes a microcomputer center and has approximately 212,000 volumes. Adjacent to it is the 3,000-square-foot Leu Art Gallery. Located next to the library is the Leu Center for the Visual Arts, featuring state-of-the-art studios with natural lighting and spacious work areas.

The Sam A. Wilson School of Music Building houses classrooms, a resource room, seminar rooms, studio/offices, music practice rooms, a piano lab, and a music technology lab.

The Jack C. Massey Business Center, encompassing 115,000 square feet, provides classrooms, office space, study lounges, seminar and conference rooms, a copy center, a post office, and a convenience store. A state-of-the-art learning center includes five computer labs. In addition, Massey Business Center houses the 9,000-square-foot Center for Music Business, which provides classrooms, an academic resource center, two state-of-the-art recording studios and control rooms, four isolation booths, a MIDI pre-postproduction room, and an engineering repair shop.

Costs

Belmont's tuition and fees are $16,220 per academic year in 2004–05. Room and board in campus residence halls are $6080.

Financial Aid

The financial aid program at Belmont combines merit-based assistance with need-based assistance to make the University program affordable. Institutional merit awards range from full tuition Presidential Scholarships to performance scholarships. Also included are many levels of academic merit awards. Belmont University also administers traditional state and federal programs, including the Federal Pell Grant, Federal Stafford Student Loan, Federal Perkins Loan, Federal PLUS loan, and Tennessee Student Assistance Grants and Scholarships. Campus employment is available. Parents may arrange monthly tuition payments through an outside vendor. To apply for assistance, the student must complete the Free Application for Federal Student Aid (FAFSA).

Faculty

A highly competent faculty is the paramount attribute of a strong institution of higher education. Belmont University has faculty members who are dedicated to their profession and to the University. Of the more than 200 full-time faculty members, 65 percent hold terminal degrees. Another 30 percent of faculty members have completed formal studies beyond the master's degree.

The influence of the Belmont University faculty is felt beyond the campus. Faculty members are active in church, civic, professional, and academic associations; frequently speak to various groups; and often write for denominational and secular publications. Most faculty members have traveled extensively and many have experienced life in other regions of the United States and abroad.

Student Government

A liaison between the University and student body, the Student Government Association seeks to address educational, social, and spiritual needs of students. As a service organization for the student body, it offers opportunity for campus involvement, acts as the coordinating body for all student organizations, serves as a resource for the campus community, and represents student interests to the faculty and administration.

Admission Requirements

Applicants are considered based on the total picture a student's credentials present. High school students are considered competitive for admission if they present a rigorous course of college-preparatory academic studies. Students should have an above-average academic and cumulative grade point average and rank in the top half of their graduating class. Any college-level work is also expected to be at the above-average level. A strong correlation between high school grades and entrance examination scores is expected. The personal supplement information, a resume of activities, and recommendations are also strongly considered as positive indicators of success at Belmont. Additional requirements, such as portfolios or auditions, are considered in conjunction with the academic credentials for those programs that require them. Each application is considered on an individual basis. No two applicants present the same credentials or the same degree of "fit" with the University. The University desires to work with each student to determine the likelihood for that student to enroll, graduate, and benefit from the Belmont educational experience.

Application and Information

Further information and application materials may be obtained by contacting:

Office of Admissions
Belmont University
1900 Belmont Boulevard
Nashville, Tennessee 37212
Telephone: 615-460-6785
800-56ENROLL (toll-free)
Fax: 615-460-5434
E-mail: buadmission@mail.belmont.edu
World Wide Web: http://www.belmont.edu

Belmont University students enjoy a beautiful antebellum campus located in thriving metropolitan Nashville.

BELOIT COLLEGE

BELOIT, WISCONSIN

The College

Beloit College is an independent national college of liberal arts and sciences, whose foremost focus is on teaching. In small classroom settings, undergraduates work closely with faculty members in an academic community that values and emphasizes interdisciplinary thought, experiential learning, and global understanding. The College attracts students who are actively engaged in learning, who thrive in an atmosphere of discussion, and who are ready to make their mark.

Beloit is Wisconsin's first college, founded in 1846 to serve a frontier society. Today, a geographically diverse population of 1,235 students is drawn to Beloit's residential campus from forty-seven states and forty countries. Ten percent come from countries outside the United States, 1 in 5 students is non-Caucasian, and a variety of religious orientations and socioeconomic backgrounds are represented on campus. Beloit students are equally diverse in their academic choices. No more than 10 percent of the seniors are represented in any one of more than fifty majors available.

Beloit students are informed and experienced in political and social issues, and they place a premium on individual expression. The range of student extracurricular activities reflects a spectrum of their interests and involvement. Beloit students serve on the College governance committees, establish organizations, oversee the weekly Café Series, and host their own radio and cable TV shows. In a given week, students may have the choice of attending (or organizing) a lecture series, a movie. music performances, a poetry reading, or an environmental debate. Seventy percent of Beloit's students participate in club, intramural, or varsity athletics and use the College's $6-million athletic complex adjacent to the residential side of campus. Those who live on campus (93 percent) may choose to live in residence halls, on quiet floors or substance-free floors, or in one of the special interest houses, which include four foreign-language houses, the Alliance House, the Anthropology House, the Black Students United House, the Music House, the Interfaith House, the Outdoor Environmental Club, the Science Fiction and Fantasy House, Voces Latinas, and the Women's Center. A town-house complex, built in 2002, offers roomy, apartment-style living for upperclass students. Meals, served in two dining halls on campus, are offered on a twenty-meal weekly plan and include organic, vegetarian, and vegan meal options.

New students quickly become part of this active and diverse environment through First-Year Initiatives (FYI), an innovative program that places first-year students in interdisciplinary seminars taught by experienced professors and staff members. These seminars begin the first day new students arrive on campus and provide academic classes, a social base, and two-year faculty advisers to assist students in their adjustment to Beloit and to bolster campus involvement. FYI leads students into a curriculum that is open and collaborative.

Location

Beloit's 40-acre campus is located on the Wisconsin-Illinois state line 90 miles northwest of Chicago, 50 miles south of Madison, and 70 miles southwest of Milwaukee, in a small city that Margaret Mead once called "American society in a microcosm." Students may take advantage of the resources of the three major metropolitan areas, and Beloit's hospital, clinics, manufacturers, and various civic and service organizations provide numerous internship, job shadowing, enrichment, and community outreach opportunities as well. The academic buildings of Beloit College cluster around lawns dotted with North American Indian effigy mounds, while across campus, newly renovated residence halls encourage interaction among resident students. A 25-acre athletic field and Strong Memorial Stadium are located a few blocks east of the main campus.

Majors and Degrees

Beloit awards Bachelor of Arts and Bachelor of Science degrees in nineteen departments and more than fifty fields of study. In the natural sciences and mathematics division, students may choose majors from the departments of biology, biochemistry, chemistry, geology, mathematics and computer science, and physics and astronomy. In the social sciences division, students may choose majors from the departments of anthropology, economics and management, education, political science and international relations, psychology, and sociology. In the arts and humanities division, majors are offered in the departments of art and art history, classics, English, history, modern languages and literatures, music, philosophy and religious studies, theater arts, and women's and gender studies. Students are also able to create their own interdisciplinary major. The College offers departmental minors in biology and society, computer science, geology, integrative biology, international economics, management, mathematics, music, philosophy, physics, political economy, political science, and religion. Permanent interdisciplinary minors include American studies, ancient Mediterranean studies, Asian studies, environmental studies, European studies, health-care studies, journalism, Latin American studies, legal studies, linguistics, museum studies, performing arts, Russian studies, and women's and gender studies.

Beloit offers 3-2 cooperative programs for students interested in engineering and forestry and environmental management and 2-2 cooperative programs for students focused on medical technology and nursing. In addition, Beloit offers preprofessional programs in dentistry, law, and medicine. These programs, which have strong advisory and internship components, complement a major in an appropriate discipline. Beloit students may also earn teaching certification.

Academic Programs

Beloit's academic calendar consists of two 14-week semesters with one-week midterm breaks. Students are required to complete a major and may choose to add a second major, a minor, or teaching certification. In addition, Beloit's open curriculum requires two classes from each of the three academic divisions plus an interdisciplinary course, three writing-intensive courses, and significant contact with a culture not one's own. Thirty-one units are required for graduation, each unit representing the equivalent of a course of study involving 4 hours of class time a week per semester. Sophomore students work with faculty advisers to define academic and personal goals, including completion of graduation requirements and the declaration of majors, and develop a plan—which may include internships, independent research, or study abroad—for accomplishing them. A Comprehensive Academic Plan (CAP) allows students to shape their time at Beloit to ensure they will reach their goals.

Off-Campus Programs

Beloit has a century-old tradition of domestic and international study opportunities, and more than half of new Beloit graduates will have studied and/or conducted research in an off-campus program. Domestic programs include marine biological laboratory programs, the Oak Ridge National Laboratory, Chicago Semester in the Arts, the Urban Education and Urban Studies Programs, Northland College environmental and Native American studies programs, Newberry Library, and the Washington Semester. Internships, field terms, and summer employment opportunities are arranged through the office of Field and Career Services. Anthropology field training programs and geology field expeditions take students to domestic and international locations, and additional experiential opportunities exist through Beloit's membership in the Keck Consortium in Geology and the Pew Midstates Science and Mathematics Consortium.

At Beloit College, study abroad is more of an expectation than a luxury. Whether through Beloit's own extensive World Outlook Program or the Associated Colleges of the Midwest (ACM) and independent programs, Beloit students have studied in more than forty countries worldwide, including Australia, Brazil, Cameroon, China, Costa Rica, the Czech Republic, Denmark, Ecuador, England, Estonia, France, Germany, Greece, Hong Kong, Hungary, India, Indonesia, Ireland, Israel, Italy, Jamaica, Japan, Morocco, Nepal, the Netherlands, Norway, Poland, Russia, Scotland, Senegal, South Africa, Tahiti, Tanzania, Thailand, Turkey, and Zimbabwe.

Academic Facilities

Beloit's library collection is in excess of a quarter of a million holdings, which include books, periodicals, government documents, an international center, a science library, and other special collections. There are individual and group study areas, a computer lab, and an extensive listening and viewing area for use of audiovisual materials. The library is connected to a statewide interlibrary loan system, and Beloit students have access to the University of Wisconsin-Madison libraries. The Logan Museum of Anthropology and the Wright Museum of Art give students excellent resources for research and work experience. The 110,000-square-foot Science Center houses extensive laboratory facilities and equipment, student office space, and an observatory. Science students also perform research on the College's 25-acre woodland prairie. The Neese Performing Arts Theatre complex features a large thrust stage theater, a black box theater, a scenic design studio, a complete costume shop, and Beloit's cable access television studio. The World Affairs Center Language Lab includes eighteen student stations equipped with a multimedia PC and tape deck. An enclosed area is used for viewing international videotapes and TV programs and newscasts taken from the lab's satellite antenna. More than 900 student-accessible microcomputers and workstations are located throughout the campus, and every residence hall room, classroom, and office has access to the Internet through the campuswide fiber-optic network.

Costs

Tuition for the 2003–04 academic year was $24,166, fees were $220, a double room was $2672, and board (twenty-meal plan) was $2806, for a total comprehensive fee of $29,864. While the cost of books and incidental expenses varies, it is about $1300.

Financial Aid

Beloit College has a need-blind admissions policy and is committed to making the Beloit experience affordable to all qualified students. The financial aid program recognizes two criteria—scholastic ability and financial need—that may qualify students for awards. During the 2003–04 academic year, about 90 percent of Beloit College students received financial assistance through grants, loans, or work-study. The College also awards merit scholarships. The average need-based financial aid award for the members of the 2003 entering class was $18,635. Beloit's attention to providing students high value has won the College recognition. *U.S. News & World Report* and the *Fiske Guide to Colleges* have rated Beloit as among the nation's "best buys" in top colleges.

Faculty

The focus of Beloit's faculty is great teaching. Beloit professors are drawn to work in a setting that emphasizes discussion and collaborative learning in small classes. Of the 99 full-time faculty members, 95 percent hold the highest academic degree in their field. All classes are taught by professors. In classrooms, it is easy for students and faculty members to become immersed in their work, since the student-faculty ratio is 11:1 and the average class size is 15 students. All Beloit professors are also academic advisers involved in students' academic concerns as well as their adjustment to life at the College. Discussions begun in the classroom are often continued in an informal setting such as at a basketball game or over dinner at a professor's house.

Student Government

Students at Beloit are actively involved in the governance of the College. The Beloit Student Congress is the College's student government. Its committees (Governance Committee, Publicity Committee, Food Committee, Organization Task Force, and Programming Board) allow the Congress to focus on representing the student body and meeting its goals. In addition to this entirely student-run governing body, students are elected to the College's Academic Senate and serve as voting members of major College committees. Students also sit on all academic search committees.

Admission Requirements

Admission to Beloit is selective. Beloit seeks applicants with special qualities and talents, as well as those from diverse ethnic, geographic, and economic backgrounds. When reviewing applications, the transcript is the most important element. Beloit has no absolute secondary school requirements, but recommends a strong college-preparatory program. This includes 4 years of English, 4 years of college-preparatory mathematics, 4 years of laboratory science, 4 years of history or social science, and 4 years of a foreign language. Seventh-semester grades may be required. A counselor recommendation is a required part of the application. One teacher recommendation is also required. The essay component of Beloit's application is critical. There is no required topic, so students should write about a topic they believe will represent them well. Either SAT or ACT test scores are required, but they are the least important part of the application. Interviews are not required for admission but are encouraged. Off-campus alumni interviews can be arranged if a student would like to interview but cannot travel to campus. Transfer applications are considered for August or January entrance. Applicants must hold at least a B- average at an accredited college or university.

Application and Information

Beloit has modified rolling admissions, so students may apply at any time. For priority consideration, both in admissions and in financial aid, however, students should file their applications by January 15. Students who do apply by this date are mailed notification by early March. Early Action I applications are due November 15, with notification December 15; Early Action II applications are due December 15, with notification January 15. Transfer applications for the fall term are due by May 1, for the spring term by December 1. Notification for transfer applications is rolling. For more information, students should contact:

Admissions Office
Beloit College
700 College Street
Beloit, Wisconsin 53511
Telephone: 608-363-2500
800-356-0751 (toll-free)
Fax: 608-363-2075
E-mail: admiss@beloit.edu
World Wide Web: http://www.beloit.edu

Middle College, which houses the Admissions Office, is at the center of Beloit's New England–style campus.

BENEDICTINE COLLEGE

ATCHISON, KANSAS

The College

Benedictine College (BC) is a four-year, Catholic, Benedictine, residential, coeducational college that provides an outstanding liberal arts education for students of all backgrounds and faiths. Benedictine is distinguished by its unique Discovery College program that offers students exceptional opportunities for research and personal growth.

The College was established as the result of the 1971 merger of Mount St. Scholastica College (founded in 1924) and St. Benedict's College (founded in 1858). The sponsoring monastic communities of Mount St. Scholastica and St. Benedict's Abbey set the tone for the campus, where the dignity of all individuals is respected. Benedictine College fosters scholarship, independent research, and performance in its students and faculty members as a means of participating in and contributing to the broader world of learning.

Benedictine College, America's Discovery College, offers students—even freshmen and sophomores—the chance to collaborate with their professors on projects within the Discovery College program. On campus, discovery is a process; it's not a single idea, but a way of life. Students have the opportunity to discover important aspects of themselves and the world around them. This approach to education prepares students to be leaders in their careers and the community.

Every major offers unique, challenging opportunities to pursue outside of the classroom. Biology students may participate in Benedictine's nationally respected Wetlands and Wildlife Restoration Project, where they conduct field studies in a restoration area along the nearby Missouri River. History, business, chemistry, education, political science, and sociology faculty members, as well as others, have authored numerous books and articles, and many faculty members have received major grant funding for their research. The business administration program offers students a rare opportunity to learn to manage and take ownership of small businesses. These and other experiences lead students to become the next generation of managers, teachers, scientists, artists, and caregivers.

Benedictine College is fully accredited by the North Central Association of Colleges and Schools.

The College's ethnically diverse student population exceeds 1,300 students, including students from thirty-four states and fourteen other countries. Benedictine College does not discriminate on the basis of sex, race, color, religion, or national origin.

At Benedictine College, 3 out of 4 students live on campus. Students find the inviting, spacious residence halls offer convenient on-campus living with friendly, supportive staff members in a secure environment. Benedictine offers many different clubs and student organizations—more than thirty-five—to meet just about every interest, including student government, Students in Free Enterprise (SIFE), departmental clubs, Amnesty International, Hunger Coalition, Knights of Columbus, Chamber Singers, African-American Club, *Loomings* literary magazine, *The Raven* yearbook, and *The Circuit* student newspaper.

The Ravens compete in sixteen varsity intercollegiate sports (NAIA and Heart of America Athletic Conference), with men's teams in baseball, basketball, cross-country, football, golf, soccer, tennis, and track and women's teams in basketball, cross-country, golf, soccer, softball, tennis, track, and volleyball. Benedictine's cheerleading and spirit squads have been recognized nationally.

Both varsity and nonvarsity athletes can benefit by participating in fifteen intramural activities, including competition in men's and women's corecreational basketball, flag football, soccer, softball, and volleyball. All students are welcome to exercise their bodies and minds at the Student Union, with a gymnasium, athletic training rooms, and plenty of fitness-oriented equipment.

The Student Union features a comfortable 500-seat auditorium for concerts, plays, and lectures and also houses a gymnasium, coffee shop, snack and pizza bar, training and exercise rooms, TV room, student government and campus life offices, a Career Development Center, and plenty of space to relax and meet friends. Benedictine's Career Development Center offers students a variety of information and services to assist them in career preparation. Services include individual counseling, career testing, workshops, and seminars, as well as assistance with graduate and professional school applications, resume writing, interviewing skills, cover-letter writing, and job search strategies. In the natural sciences, 75 percent of graduates continue their education in graduate or professional schools, which is nearly double the national average for liberal arts college graduates. The College's record of acceptance into medical colleges is among the best in the Midwest. The Raven network of Benedictine alumni is a valuable resource for current BC students and new graduates. BC alumni can be found working in such prestigious places as the Federal Reserve Bank, Hallmark Cards, and the Mayo Clinic.

Location

Benedictine College is located on a peaceful, wooded campus in Atchison, Kansas, a picturesque town of 12,000 overlooking the Missouri River. The College is less than 1 hour's drive northwest of Kansas City and only 35 minutes from the Kansas City International Airport. Atchison offers shopping, beautiful parks, and a modern regional hospital across the street from the campus.

Majors and Degrees

Benedictine currently offers the following accredited degrees: Associate of Arts (business administration), Bachelor of Arts, Bachelor of Science, and Bachelor of Music Education. Every field of study at Benedictine College includes the opportunity for collaborative, hands-on training, a dynamic curriculum, internships, and a supportive faculty. The College offers four-year majors in accounting, astronomy, biochemistry, biology, business administration, chemistry, computer science, economics, education (certification, elementary, secondary, special education), English, French, history, mass communications, mathematics, music, music education, music marketing, natural science, philosophy, physical education, physics, political science, psychology, religious studies, sociology, social science, Spanish, theater arts, theater arts management, and youth ministry. In addition, the College offers preprofessional study programs in dentistry, 3-2 engineering, law, medical technology, medicine, nursing, occupational therapy, optometry, pharmacy, physical therapy, and veterinary studies. The College also offers certifications in athletic training and coaching. For those students who want or need the freedom to design a major to their unique interests, the College offers a liberal studies major.

Academic Programs

Benedictine College divides its academic year into two semesters and one summer session. The semesters are approximately sixteen weeks long. To earn a bachelor's degree from Benedictine College, a student is required to successfully complete 128 semester credit hours of courses numbered above 100. These courses must include courses specified by the student's major department, a total of 40 credit hours numbered 300 or above, and the general education requirements of the College.

Students must also achieve a minimum final grade point average of 2.0 in both the major and overall course work at Benedictine, successfully complete a comprehensive or standardized examination in his or her major at a level designated by the faculty, and finish the last two semesters of work in residence. The general education requirements for a bachelor's degree are divided into three categories: core requirements, disciplinary requirements, and proficiency requirements. Benedictine College offers opportunities for advanced placement, the College-Level Examination Program (CLEP), and credit for experiential learning to nontraditional students at least 23 years of age. The College also has a cross-enrollment agreement with Missouri Western State College and its Reserve Officers' Training Corps (ROTC).

Off-Campus Programs

Benedictine College sponsors a study-abroad program for students of Spanish in Cuernavaca, Mexico. For French students, the affiliation is with the Catholic University of the West at Angers, France. Benedictine students also can study at the Sorbonne in Paris and at the University of Granada in Spain. Students also may opt to study in China, England, Germany, Ireland, the Netherlands, and Wales.

Academic Facilities

The College enhances every student's educational experience with comprehensive facilities, including modern classrooms, nine science laboratories, and a modern computer network with Internet and e-mail access. The BC library is the designated federal depository for the area's congressional district and houses many rare books, including works on monastic history dating from the fifteenth century. The College also is a member of several library consortia, providing students with access to academic and public libraries locally and around the world. The College's Kansas area network (KANRAN) is one of the most sophisticated in America.

Costs

For 2004–05, tuition and fees are $14,576, room is $2650 and board is $3478. Other estimated expenses are books, $550; personal expenses, $1200; and travel, $800.

Financial Aid

More than 90 percent of Benedictine students receive some form of financial assistance. Benedictine College annually awards more than $5.3 million in institutional aid and offers a generous number of scholarships based on academic achievement, athletic ability, and other achievements and merits. The College participates in the federal grant, work-study, and loan programs, as well as ROTC and state of Kansas financial aid programs. Benedictine's priority deadline for financial aid consideration is March 1.

Faculty

More than 75 percent of Benedictine College faculty members hold terminal degrees, the highest degree in their fields. With a student-faculty ratio of 16:1, students have greater access to professors, who go out of their way to serve students on a personal level. Students are supported by instructors who are not only respected for their professional achievement but also for their commitment to student development. All Benedictine courses are taught by professors, not graduate or teaching assistants.

Student Government

The Student Government is designed to promote the general welfare of the student body in its academic, social, cultural, and religious needs. The executive officers of the student government and class officers are responsible for formulating and executing student government administrative policy.

Admission Requirements

Applicants must submit scores on the SAT I or ACT and all official high school and/or college transcripts. Sixteen units of college-preparatory work are recommended, including 4 units of English, 3 to 4 units of math, 2 to 4 units of foreign language, 2 to 4 units of natural science, 2 units of social science, and 1 unit of history.

Application and Information

The College employs a rolling admission policy. There is a $25 application fee. For further information or to request an application, students should contact:

Kelly J. Vowels
Dean of Enrollment Management
Benedictine College
1020 North Second Street
Atchison, Kansas 66002
Telephone: 913-367-5340
800-467-5340 (toll-free)
E-mail: bcadmiss@benedictine.edu
World Wide Web: http://www.benedictine.edu

Benedictine College faculty members understand the importance of a personalized education and are committed to lifelong learning. They prove their concern for students by relating to them on a personal level and collaborating with students in research and curriculum design.

BENEDICTINE UNIVERSITY

LISLE, ILLINOIS

The University

Benedictine University was founded in 1887 as St. Procopius College. One hundred sixteen years later, the University remains committed to providing a high-quality, Catholic, liberal education for men and women. The undergraduate enrollment is nearly 2,000 students. The student body comprises students of diverse ages, religions, races, and national origins. Twenty-eight percent of the full-time students reside on campus.

Benedictine University is situated on a rolling, tree-covered 108-acre campus of ten major buildings with air-conditioned classrooms and modern, well-equipped laboratories. A student athletic center features three full-size basketball courts, a competition-size swimming pool, three tennis courts, and training facilities. All of the residence halls are comfortable and spacious and have access to the Internet. On-campus apartments offer one-, two-, and four-bedroom residences. Other features include a scenic lake, spacious and well-kept athletic fields, and a student center with dining halls, lounges, a chapel, a bookstore, and meeting rooms.

At Benedictine University, the environment is strengthened by success, not size. Renowned faculty members know students by name and care as much about each student's progress as they do about their own research. Those personal relationships have produced superb results. Benedictine graduates are accepted into some of the most prestigious graduate programs in the country. Approximately two thirds of Benedictine graduates who apply to medical school are accepted, in addition to similar ratios for other health-related professional schools (optometry, pharmacy, physical therapy, and podiatry). The liberal arts curriculum has helped place the University among some of the finest small private schools in the nation.

U.S. News & World Report's 2004 rankings listed Benedictine University as one of the top schools in the Midwest. The magazine also ranked the school sixth in the region for campus diversity.

Benedictine University is highly competitive in varsity sports. Men's varsity sports are baseball, basketball, cross-country, football, golf, soccer, swimming, and track. Women's varsity sports are basketball, cross-country, golf, soccer, softball, swimming, tennis, track, and volleyball. Aside from varsity and intramural athletic programs, a variety of organizations exist, including student government, a student newspaper, an orchestra, a jazz group, an African-American Student Union, an Indian Student Union, the Coalition of Latin American Students, campus ministry, a drama club, and various other extracurricular and academic organizations.

The graduate division offers the following graduate degrees in the business, education, and health-care areas: the Doctor of Philosophy (Ph.D.) degree in organization development; the Master of Business Administration (M.B.A.); the Master of Arts in Education (M.A.Ed.); the Master of Education (M.Ed.); the Master of Science (M.S.) in clinical psychology, clinical exercise physiology, management and organizational behavior, and management information systems; and the Master of Public Health (M.P.H.).

Adult undergraduate accelerated programs, taught by distinguished faculty members, are available in the following areas: accounting (B.B.A.), business and economics (B.A.), computer information systems (B.S.), computer science (B.S.), health administration (B.B.A.), management and organizational behavior (B.B.A.), nursing and health (degree completion for B.S.N.), organizational leadership (B.A.), and psychology (B.A.). The University also offers an Associate of Arts degree in business administration in an accelerated format.

Location

Benedictine University is 25 miles west of Chicago, in suburban Lisle near Naperville, and is easily accessible from the city and suburbs via the interstate highway system. Metra trains stop in Lisle, and O'Hare International Airport is only a 30-minute drive away. In addition to the many social and cultural offerings of the Chicago metropolitan area, the University enjoys the proximity and use of Argonne National Laboratory, Fermi National Accelerator Laboratory, the Morton Arboretum, a ski hill, a riding stable, and several golf courses. The University's location in the high-tech East-West Tollway corridor gives students opportunities for internships and employment.

Majors and Degrees

Benedictine University offers programs leading to the Bachelor of Arts, Bachelor of Business Administration, and Bachelor of Science degrees. Programs are offered in accounting, arts administration, biochemistry, biology, business and economics, chemistry (concentrations in chemical business and marketing and forensic chemistry), clinical laboratory science, communication arts (concentrations in advertising and public relations, broadcasting and cable, journalism, and mass media), computer science, economics, elementary education, engineering science, English language and literature, environmental science, finance, health administration, health science, history, information systems, international business and economics, international studies, management and organizational behavior, marketing, mathematics (concentration in actuarial science), molecular biology, music (concentrations in instrumental and vocal), nuclear medicine technology, nursing (completion), nutrition (concentrations in dietetics and management), organizational leadership, philosophy, physics (concentrations in engineering physics and physics), political science (concentration in prelaw), prenursing, psychology (concentrations in pre–occupational therapy and pre–physical therapy), radiation therapy, social science, sociology (concentrations in criminal justice and social work), Spanish, special education (concentrations in learning disabilities and social-emotional disorders), studio art, world literature, and writing and publishing.

In education, the University partners with the Golden Apple Foundation. Students selected as a Golden Apple Scholar of Illinois have the opportunity to study elementary, secondary, or special education at Benedictine while receiving the $5000 scholarship through the foundation.

In many areas of study, students may opt for a double major. Preprofessional programs include chiropractic, dentistry, engineering, law, medicine, nursing, occupational therapy, optometry, pharmacy, physical therapy, podiatry, and veterinary medicine. Combined professional programs are available with cooperating institutions in clinical laboratory science, nuclear medicine technology, and engineering. A joint engineering program is offered with the Illinois Institute of Technology. A nursing program is offered in cooperation with Rush University in Chicago and the University of St. Francis; a registered nurse may earn a Bachelor of Science degree in nursing. Secondary education certification is available in the following majors: biology, business and economics, chemistry, English, mathematics, music education, physics, and social science.

Academic Program

For graduation, a student must earn at least 120 semester hours, 55 of which must be completed at a four-year regionally accredited college. At least the final 45 semester hours must be completed at Benedictine University. The University makes selective exceptions to the normal academic residency requirement of 45 semester hours for adults who are eligible for the

Degree Completion Program. Eligibility is limited to those who have nearly completed their undergraduate studies but who, for reasons of employment, career change, or family situation, found it necessary to interrupt their studies.

The Second Major Program is designed for people who already have a degree in one area and would like to gain expertise in another. This program allows the student to concentrate on courses that fulfill the requirements of a second major. The student receives a certificate upon completion.

Each year, a select number of talented and motivated prospective students are invited to participate in the Scholars Program. The program is designed to enhance the college experience by developing students' international awareness and strengthening their leadership ability.

Off-Campus Programs

Benedictine University is a member of a three-school consortium in the west suburban Chicago area through which students are able to take classes at the other member colleges. Study abroad and internships abroad are encouraged to complement a liberal education.

Academic Facilities

The Kindlon Hall of Learning and the Birck Hall of Science bring science and technology to new levels. The Birck Hall of Science houses state-of-the art computer labs, specialized science labs, a research center, and the Jurica Nature Museum.

The Kindlon Hall of Learning houses computer labs, classrooms, multimedia labs, offices, and student lounges. It is also home to the Benedictine Library, which houses more than 160,000 volumes and can be found in the building's impressive four-story tower. The library is also equipped with eleven group study rooms, a computer lab, and an instruction room.

Benedictine University has distance education classrooms that provide students with the capability to interact globally with other colleges and universities in a classroom setting. Scholl Hall was recently renovated and houses classrooms and faculty and administrative offices.

Costs

The cost of tuition for the 2003–04 academic year was $16,960. The average cost of room and board was $6145. Mandatory fees totaled $510 and included health, technology, and student activity fees.

Financial Aid

In 2002–03, Benedictine University freshmen received assistance totaling $3.88 million from sources that included loans, scholarships and grants, tuition remission, and employment opportunities. Ninety-eight percent of the freshman class received financial aid. The average package was $12,567. Benedictine University has dedicated more than $7 million of the annual budget to providing grants and scholarships to its students. Students who wish to apply for aid must complete the Free Application for Federal Student Aid (FAFSA), the Benedictine University application for financial aid, and the Benedictine University application for admission.

Faculty

The 13:1 student-faculty ratio allows for close interaction between students and faculty members. Of the 84 full-time faculty members, 86 percent hold a Ph.D. or the terminal professional degree in their respective fields. All students are assigned a faculty member as an adviser to help plan programs of study.

Student Government

All full-time enrolled students are automatically members of the student government. The Student Government Association (SGA) is a representative body elected annually by the students to represent their interests. The SGA is responsible for the annual allocation of the student activity fee.

Admission Requirements

The Benedictine University admission philosophy is to select students who are expected to perform successfully in the University's academic programs and become active members of the University community. Typically, Benedictine University's freshman students are in the top third of their high school graduating class, with about 50 percent in the top quarter, and report better-than-average ACT or SAT I scores. A minimum of 16 units in academic subjects is required, including 4 units of English, 1 unit of algebra, 1 unit of geometry, 1 unit of history, 1 unit of laboratory science, and 2 units of foreign language. Benedictine University does admit some students who fall below these standards. These applicants receive individual consideration by the Committee on Admission. When appropriate, the committee will place conditions and/or restrictions upon students to help them reach their academic potential.

Students interested in transferring to Benedictine University must have a minimum cumulative average of C (2.0 on a 4.0 scale) or better from all colleges previously attended. Official transcripts from high school and all colleges attended must be submitted directly to the Office of Admissions for evaluation. If fewer than 20 semester hours of transfer credit are submitted, an official high school transcript and SAT I or ACT scores are required, and the general admission high school curriculum requirements must also be satisfied. High school information is not required with A.A. or A.S. degrees. Credits transferred from other institutions are evaluated on the basis of their equivalent at Benedictine University. Grades of D are accepted as transfer credit but do not satisfy Benedictine University requirements, which demand a minimum grade of C.

Requests for admission are considered without regard to the applicant's race, religion, gender, age, or disability.

Application and Information

Applications are reviewed on a rolling basis. Students are encouraged to apply for admission at any time after completing their junior year of high school. Transfer students may apply for admission during their last semester or quarter before anticipated transfer to Benedictine University. Earlier applications are encouraged for scholarship and financial aid opportunities.

For further information, students should contact:

Enrollment Center
Benedictine University
5700 College Road
Lisle, Illinois 60532
Telephone: 630-829-6300
888-829-6363 (toll-free oustide Illinois)
Fax: 630-829-6301
E-mail: admissions@ben.edu
World Wide Web: http://www.ben.edu

The Kindlon Hall of Learning houses computer labs, classrooms, multimedia labs, offices, and student lounges.

BENNINGTON COLLEGE

BENNINGTON, VERMONT

BENNINGTON
COLLEGE

The College

Bennington College, a liberal arts college founded in 1932, began as and remains an invitation to learn. Bennington is committed to the belief that teachers should do what they teach and should bring their experience to the classroom. This same spirit continues to animate a faculty of working scientists, writers, scholars, and artists eager to teach, in the words of one, "what keeps them awake at night." Students study literature from published poets, design their own experiments alongside chemists engaged in research, study music with composers recording their own work, and explore international relations with a former diplomat. Faculty members teach both the disciplines they practice, such as science, dance, or architecture, and join together to create courses that study subjects from a combination of different disciplinary perspectives.

Because both students and teachers are actively engaged in the work at hand, the relationship between teacher and student is richly collaborative, more like coach to athlete, mentor to apprentice, and ultimately colleague to colleague than expert to nonexpert. Collaboration between faculty members and students works in both directions: faculty members participating in student work and vice versa.

Each academic year consists of three terms: two intensive fifteen-week on-campus terms during the fall and spring and an seven-week winter term of off-campus field work. During the winter term, students take their academic interests to the world beyond the College campus, where they pursue jobs and internships in fields that complement their studies, clarify their interests, and prepare them for their future. Students' written reflections on their work experience, as well as reports written by their employers, become part of their academic profile. The Field Work Term Office helps students find meaningful work experiences in areas ranging from publishing to politics and from arts administration to teaching. Students graduate from Bennington with a resume as well as a diploma.

There are 640 undergraduate and approximately 160 graduate students currently enrolled at Bennington. Virtually all undergraduates live in College housing.

On the graduate level, Bennington awards the Master of Arts in Teaching (M.A.T.), Master of Fine Arts (M.F.A.), and Master of Arts in Teaching a Second Language (M.A.T.S.L.) degrees. There is a one-year postbaccalaureate program in premedical and allied health sciences for students preparing to apply to medical or allied health sciences graduate schools. Students may enter the M.A.T. program in teaching as undergraduate, transfer, or graduate students.

Location

Bennington's 550-acre campus is nestled among the Green Mountains of southwestern Vermont, less than an hour from Albany and 3½ hours from both New York City and Boston. The central dining room looks out over the "end of the world," a wide commons stretching toward distant mountains, bordered by the whitewashed colonial houses that serve as dormitories. Wooded walking paths link the buildings on campus and lead to the campus fitness center, hiking trails, soccer fields, tennis courts, and a pond.

The region surrounding the College is renowned for its outdoor activities, including hiking, rock climbing, downhill and cross-country skiing, and canoeing.

Majors and Degrees

Students can pursue interests in all of the traditional academic disciplines within the liberal arts (e.g., history, literature, mathematics, philosophy, science, social science) and in the visual and performing arts (architecture, ceramics, dance, design, digital art, drama, music, painting, photography, sculpture, and video). In addition, Bennington offers a five-year bachelor's/master's degree in teaching. Graduates of this program are certified in early childhood, elementary, or secondary education and earn a license to teach in the state of Vermont. The degree is recognized in forty-four other states, including New York, California, and Massachusetts. Students may apply to this program after their freshman year.

Bennington's faculty members are more committed to providing students with resources for a life of independent thought and self-education than they are with designing majors. From their perspective, a genuine education is actively created rather than passively received. Throughout their education at Bennington, students are challenged to pursue questions and interests that matter to them and are taught the ability to pursue those questions wherever they may lead. It is not presumed that a student's progress need be the progressive elimination of all but one interest called the major; on the contrary, it is presumed that a student may well choose to explore a diverse range of disciplines in depth. Over the four-year period, students continually discuss with their faculty adviser and in writing what courses they intend to take and the reasons why. In these evolving statements of purpose, students design, chart, and argue their course of study. This individualized statement, called the "plan," replaces the traditional major. Student plans are presented at regular intervals to panels of faculty members for further discussion and review.

By taking an active role in crafting their own education, students learn what it takes to discover an intellectual identity and to pursue it. They learn to replace imposed discipline with self-discipline and to deal with a world where the requirements are imposed from within rather than from without. In the process of their education, every Bennington student must individually confront the question, "What is a real education?"

Academic Program

The programs of study that students design with their advisers are conceived more in the shape of an hourglass (starting broad, then focusing, then broadening again) than in the traditional pyramid structure with its progressive narrowing of focus. During their first year, students explore a wide range of possibilities, investigating the diverse forms of intellectual and imaginative life. In their second and third years, they increasingly immerse themselves in particular subjects, whether in the form of a craft, a discipline, or a question. In their final year, students look outward, extending and deepening the relevance of their own work through connecting it to the work of others and to the world at large. In this final year, students are also encouraged, once again, to explore new, emerging interests.

Faculty members regularly evaluate student performance through written reports that assess academic strengths and weakness, identify areas needing further work, and analyze overall progress.

Off-Campus Programs

The Field Work Term at Bennington requires students to spend seven weeks each year working off campus in jobs or internships relating to their academic and career interests. In addition, Bennington offers students a range of options for study abroad. These programs carry academic credit.

Bennington is a charter member of a consortium associated with the School for Field Studies (SFS). This program offers access to courses in field biology on five continents, providing hands-on education that addresses the world's most critical environmental issues. Bennington's affiliation gives students the opportunity to incorporate SFS courses into the fulfillment of degree requirements.

Academic Facilities

Most of the classrooms at Bennington are arranged for seminar-style discussions. In addition, classes are sometimes held in the campus café or in dormitory common rooms. Faculty members have offices throughout the campus where they meet regularly with students to discuss their work outside of class. The Dickinson Science Building includes fully equipped science labs, a computer center with audio/video digitizing and processing capabilities, and a language lab. The 120,000-square-foot Visual and Performing Arts Center (VAPA) contains three black box theaters with state-of-the-art technical support, the Usdan Art Gallery, and studios for music, dance, video, painting, architecture, ceramics, sculpture, printmaking, and photography. Bennington also houses one of the largest sprung wood floors in the world, especially designed for dance performance. Most facilities in VAPA are available for student use 24 hours a day.

New technologies play a central role in facilitating the dynamic relationships between diverse disciplines and between faculty members and student that define the College. Bennington's Center for Audio Technologies consolidates all campus music/audio technology; facilities include an electronic music studio, a computer instructional studio, a language laboratory that uses both existing technologies and creates new ones for the study of foreign language and culture, a digital audio studio, and a lab equipped for the production of graphics, computer art, and multimedia projects. Architecture and design programs are enhanced by computer-aided design (CAD). All dorm rooms are wired for Internet access. Notwithstanding the range of such resources, students and faculty members at Bennington are continually reminded that technologies, new and old, are designed to enhance the creative imagination, as opposed to replacing it.

Costs

For undergraduates in 2003–04, total charges were $35,910, including tuition, room, board, activities, and health services fees.

Financial Aid

Approximately 80 percent of Bennington students receive financial assistance in some form: need- and merit-based awards, College and federal grant funds, work-study programs, and student and parental loans.

Faculty

Because of its tradition of having a faculty of teacher-practitioners, Bennington faculty members are active artists, writers, and scholars. The average class size is twelve and the overall student-faculty ratio is 9:1. All faculty members teach first-year as well as advanced students.

Student Government

The responsibility students assume in planning a course of study extends to life outside the classroom. Bennington treats the idea and the ideals of self-governance very seriously. Students are expected to discover the balance between freedom and responsibility and to do so by meeting the challenges of self-governance in their academic and nonacademic lives.

Admission Requirements

Bennington looks for students who are alive to the possibilities of what a college education might be and whose passionate curiosity is matched by a capacity for self-discipline. While all parts of each student's application are considered with great care—essays, recommendations, transcripts, class rankings, test scores—the admissions interview is treated with particular seriousness. There are no formulas by which admissions decisions are calculated.

SAT I or ACT scores are required.

Students interested in early admission may apply for admission prior to the completion of high school. Transfer students are accepted for enrollment in the fall and spring terms.

Application and Information

The deadline for freshman applications is January 1; for transfer applications, the deadlines are January 1 (for the spring term) and June 1 (for the fall term). The early decision deadline is November 15, with notifications by December 1. Financial aid applicants should file appropriate financial statements as soon as possible and no later than March 1.

For more information about Bennington College, students should contact:

Office of Admissions and Financial Aid
Bennington College
One College Drive
Bennington, Vermont 05201
Telephone: 802-440-4312
800-833-6845 (toll free)
Fax: 802-440-4320
E-mail: admissions@bennington.edu
World Wide Web: http://www.bennington.edu

A student sits behind a state-of-the-art sound board in Jennings Hall, mixing down one of his latest compositions.

BENTLEY COLLEGE

WALTHAM, MASSACHUSETTS

The College

Bentley College is an outstanding business university, blending the breadth and technological strength of a university with the values and student orientation of a small college. It is to business education what technological universities such as Cal Tech and Worcester Polytech are to science and engineering education. Here, students gain knowledge and skills through an academic experience that combines a strong foundation in the liberal arts with the most advanced business education possible. Concepts and theories learned in the classroom come alive in several hands-on, high-tech learning laboratories—each among the first of its kind in higher education. Through course work, internships, jobs, campus activities, and study-abroad opportunities, students acquire the communication, teamwork, and leadership skills necessary for career success in today's global economy.

Bentley is the largest business school in New England, with an undergraduate population of approximately 4,250 students. Nearly half of the population comes from communities outside Massachusetts, with more than forty U.S. states and eighty countries represented. Approximately 7 percent are international students. Eighty percent of students live on campus and choose from fourteen residence halls and apartment-style buildings. Housing options include single-, double-, or triple-occupancy dorm rooms; apartments; or suites. In addition, a new hall opens in September 2004.

On-campus activities include a wide range of athletic events and music and theater programs and more than eighty clubs and student organizations. A state-of-the-art Student Center is the hub of campus activity. Students are welcomed into a large, inviting dining room where they enjoy an all-you-can-eat meal plan. The Student Center also has a games room, the 1917 Tavern, the campus radio station and newspaper, and office and meeting space for student organizations. Students take advantage of the Dana Athletic Center, which features an indoor track, volleyball and racquetball courts, a competition-size indoor pool and diving tank, a weight room, and other facilities. Situated next to the Athletic Center, student athletes compete on new baseball and soccer fields along with an outdoor track and six tennis courts.

An NCAA Division II institution, Bentley is a member of the Northeast-10 Conference and the Division I Atlantic Hockey League. The College fields twenty-three varsity teams for men and women, with teams and individual players routinely qualifying for postseason competition. Students may also take part in intramural sports such as floor hockey and flag football and in recreational activities that include dance and fitness training.

Location

With its beautiful landscaping and attractive buildings, the College represents the best of New England campuses and provides an inviting atmosphere for study and socializing. Bentley is located in Waltham, Massachusetts, just twenty minutes west of Boston, the country's premier college town. From theater to art exhibits, dance clubs to alternative rock concerts, championship sports to championship shopping, Boston has the proverbial "something for everyone." Students often use the Bentley shuttle, which facilitates access to Harvard Square and Boston.

Majors and Degrees

A strong curriculum focusing on business, technology, and the liberal arts provides students with many options for shaping an academic program that fits their skills, interests, and career goals. Bachelor of Science degree programs enable students to specialize in a specific business discipline: accountancy, accounting information systems, computer information systems, corporate finance and accounting, economics-finance, finance, information design and corporate communication, management, managerial economics, marketing, and mathematical sciences. Bentley also offers Bachelor of Arts (B.A.) degree programs, with majors in English, history, international studies, liberal arts, philosophy, and public policy and social change. Students may also receive a B.A. in mathematics or design their own arts and sciences concentration in areas such as behavioral sciences, communication, or environmental studies.

Minors and concentration programs give students the opportunity to develop expertise in an area outside their major. Bentley has a number of special programs, including those through which students can earn a bachelor's degree and a master's degree in five years.

Academic Program

With a focus on business, Bentley's resources are fully concentrated on providing the most advanced business education: more majors and minors, a focus on information technology, high tech learning facilities, business-related extracurricular activities, internships, and job opportunities. However, the Bentley education is broad in scope. A full 50 percent of required courses are in the liberal arts. Through a variety of these courses, students gain skills in critical thinking, decision making, and communication.

Known for distinctive programs at the intersection of business and technology, Bentley students learn to use information technology the way business does—as an important tool for planning, producing, marketing, and managing. Students gain a solid understanding of the latest technologies and develop the ability to analyze and manage information.

To strengthen its commitment to technology, Bentley was one of the first colleges in the U.S. to require students to have personal computers. Today, through the Mobile Computing Program, each freshman receives a laptop computer that is network-ready and fully loaded with software. Professors regularly require the laptops in class and most offer online access to syllabi, discussion groups, course assignments, and other materials. An advanced communication network allows students Internet access from just about anywhere on campus: dorm rooms, dining rooms, library, and classrooms. Students have immediate access to the library catalogue, centralized computing facilities, e-mail, and E-Campus, the internal computer network.

Bentley students gain hands-on experience through a variety of opportunities, such as internships, group consulting projects, or service-learning assignments.

Each year, through the Bentley Service-Learning Center, hundreds of students develop their business skills, while taking part in projects as diverse as offering tax assistance to area residents and helping immigrants apply for citizenship. The service-learning program has been recognized for leadership in the field of student character development in *The Templeton Guide*, which states, "Bentley's strong commitment to character development and the strength of its program make it a model for colleges and universities nationwide." In addition, the Service-Learning Center was recently ranked tenth nationwide by *U.S. News & World Report*.

Bentley offers an internship program through which students earn course credit toward their degree and gain valuable work experience in their field of study. There are many internship and career resources in Boston, which makes the city a valuable learning lab for Bentley students. Students have held internship positions in organizations such as IBM, Reebok International, Hewlett-Packard, and PricewaterhouseCoopers.

More than 90 percent of Bentley students find employment within six months of graduation. The Miller Center for Career Services offers comprehensive programs to help students explore careers, develop contacts, and find employment. Resources include an on-campus recruiting program involving some 250 national and international companies, an online job-listing service available to Bentley students and alumni, an online database of student and alumni resumes, career fairs, and workshops on topics such as effective resume writing, interviewing, and job search strategies.

Off-Campus Programs

Through the Joseph M. Cronin International Center, Bentley offers study-abroad programs in various countries, including Australia, Belgium, England, France, Italy, and Spain. Students may study abroad during the fall, spring, or summer term or for an entire year.

Academic Facilities

Bentley prepares students to meet the new demands of an information-rich, technology-driven workplace through a curriculum that integrates technology at every level. Supporting this curriculum is an array of academic resources, including classrooms equipped with multimedia computers and display technology, student computer laboratories with both IBM-compatible and Macintosh computers, and a virtual lab that offers online access to specialized software for courses.

Combining state-of-the-art technology and real-time data, the financial Trading Room offers firsthand exposure to financial concepts such as risk management and asset valuation. Students gain skills and expertise through Trading Room resources that include Reuters 2000 and 3000 products, Market Guide, Bridge, First Call, and Bloomberg.

The Center for Marketing Technology is a "best practices" center for studying the forces that drive buying and selling in an increasingly global, electronic economy. A range of high-end applications exposes students to the latest innovations in marketing. Equipped with powerful, networked desktop PCs and an array of specialized software, the showcase is an integral part of information-age marketing programs at Bentley.

The Accounting Center for Electronic Learning and Business Measurement introduces students to resources that foster the knowledge and skills needed for accounting tasks, such as developing a system and analyzing operational data for management decision making.

Information design programs at Bentley center on creating IT products and processes that users can intuitively understand and easily employ. The technological hub of these programs is the Design and Usability Testing Center, which offers unparalleled up-close exposure to the field and puts into students' hands the same applications employed by technical communicators, Web developers, user interface designers, and usability specialists.

The Center for Language and International Collaboration, a key resource for language students, international studies majors, and anyone with an interest in international issues, builds awareness of countries and cultures across the globe. Students and professors use the center's "global theater" to promote real-time collaboration with their counterparts overseas.

The Solomon R. Baker Library supports Bentley's curriculum with resources that include approximately 200,000 books and journals, 8,000 periodical subscriptions, an extensive collection of annual and 10K reports, and access to electronic databases such as LexisNexis, Westlaw, OCLC, Dialog, and Infotrac 2000.

Costs

Tuition for both resident and nonresident students for the 2003–04 academic year were $24,120. Room and board (double room with meal plan) costs were $9580. Additional costs include books, supplies, a laptop computer, and personal and travel expenses.

Financial Aid

More than $36 million in undergraduate financial assistance is administered every year. Bentley offers financial assistance in the form of scholarships, grants, loans, employment, and payment plans. Currently, 7 out of 10 Bentley undergraduates receive some form of financial assistance.

Faculty

Bentley's committed teacher-scholars combine the very best classroom skills with cutting-edge research acknowledged for its relevance and impact in the real world. By conducting research that relates to key concerns of business and society, faculty members are able to bring real-world problems into the classroom and develop an innovative curriculum that suits the needs of the modern age. A number of Bentley faculty members are consultants to leading local, national, and international corporations, ensuring students' perspectives on current practices and future directions in key business fields. Following the teacher-scholar model, classes are not taught by teaching assistants or graduate assistants. The average class size is 25 students and the student-faculty ratio is 13:1. Bentley has 422 full-time and part-time faculty members; 82 percent of full-time professors hold doctoral degrees.

Student Government

Bentley has a number of student governing organizations, including the Student Government Association, Senior Class Cabinet, Greek Council, Hall Council Advisory Board, Media Board, Panhellenic Council, and the Graduate Student Association.

Admission Requirements

Students applying for admission to the College are encouraged to complete a solid college-preparatory program. Bentley suggests that this program include 4 years of English, 4 years of mathematics (preferably algebra I and II, geometry, and a senior-year math course), and 3 to 4 years each of history, laboratory science, and foreign language.

Along with the application, students must submit a secondary school transcript, letters of recommendation from a teacher and a counselor, and official scores from either the SAT or ACT. All international students must file an international student application. Applicants who are nonnative speakers of English must also have official results of the Test of English as a Foreign Language (TOEFL) forwarded to the Office of Undergraduate Admission.

Application and Information

The application deadline for students planning to enter in September is February 1. For students planning to enter in January, the deadline is November 15. Candidates for the fall semester are notified by April 1; spring semester candidates are notified by December 5.

Students who have selected Bentley as their first choice may apply as candidates for early decision. The Early Decision Program is for freshmen who have shown excellent academic achievement and would like to find out early about admission and financial aid. Candidates participating in this program agree that if an offer of admission into Bentley is extended, they will withdraw any applications that have been made to other colleges. Students may also participate in the Early Action Program. This program is for students who would like an early answer about admission but would prefer to keep their options open. The application deadline for both programs is November 15. Bentley also accepts the Common Application.

For additional information, students should contact:

Office of Undergraduate Admission
Bentley College
175 Forest Street
Waltham, Massachusetts 02452-4705
Telephone: 781-891-2244
800-523-2354 (toll-free)
Fax: 781-891-3414
E-mail: ugadmission@bentley.edu
World Wide Web: http://www.bentley.edu

BEREA COLLEGE

BEREA, KENTUCKY

The College

Embracing a contemporary mission to educate service-oriented leaders for Appalachia and beyond, Berea College dates its founding to 1855 when a group of abolitionists established a racially integrated one-room school that was based on the biblical maxim "God has made of one blood all peoples of the earth." For the next fifty years, Berea was a monument to racial harmony and equality. Although Kentucky law prevented integration of the student body from 1904 to 1950, Berea College has a long and distinguished history of interracial education. Among the African-American students who attended Berea during its early days were Dr. Carter G. Woodson, founder of Black History Month, and Julia Britton Hooks, a musician who taught W. C. Handy and whose grandson, Dr. Benjamin Hooks, was the Executive Director of the NAACP for many years. Currently, 25 percent of Berea's 1,500 students are members of minority groups, and a large percentage of those students are African-American, international, and dual-nationality students.

Routinely at the top of its category in national rankings of colleges, Berea was ranked the number one comprehensive college–bachelor's in the South in 2003 by *U.S. News & World Report*. Among the special programs that contribute to the strength of Berea's academic program are extensive and well-funded undergraduate research opportunties; a universal technology access program that provides a laptop computer for every student; the Berea Term Abroad program that awards a scholarship worth one half of participation costs to all eligible students; the ceramics apprenticeship program; the January Short Term; the field-study opportunities available in all departments; and a quickly emerging program in sustainability and environmental studies. In recent years, Berea students have received national scholarship awards, including several Watson Scholarships, a Truman Scholarship, and a Fulbright Scholarship. One of the most unusual features of the College is a student work program, which requires all students to work on campus a minimum of 10 hours per week. The work program not only provides a way for students to earn part of their college expenses, but also provides excellent work-learning experiences and valuable on-the-job training.

Men and women participate in eight intercollegiate sports each: both participate in basketball, cross-country, soccer, swimming, tennis, and track; men in baseball and golf; and women in softball and volleyball. Berea had an Olympic bobsleigh competitor at the 2002 Salt Lake City Winter Games and has produced award-winning athletes on a regular basis, including All-Americans in basketball, cross-country, and track and field—most recently crowning a national champion in track. Berea has also visited the NAIA Division II men's national basketball tournament, placing in the "Final Four" in 1999. About 75 percent of the men and 50 percent of the women at Berea participate in one or more intramural sports. The Seabury Center, opened in 1995, is a physical education, athletic, recreation, and convocation facility housing two basketball courts, an indoor pool, racquetball courts, an indoor track, a weight room, a wellness center, and a multipurpose events forum.

The Berea College Concert Choir, the Black Music Ensemble, and the concert, stage, and brass bands provide many performance opportunities. The Berea College Country Dancers is a popular performance group that specializes in traditional Appalachian dance and folklore. The Theatre Laboratory presents three or four major productions each year and features a theater artist-in-residence for at least one term each year. The art department has excellent gallery space for the exhibition of work by students, faculty members, and guest artists. Worship opportunities and Christian outreach programs are coordinated by the Campus Christian Center, and Berea students take an active role in the congregations of many local churches. Service is an important dimension of the program at Berea, and many students participate in one or more of a variety of service organizations through Berea's Center for Excellence in Learning through Service (CELTS). In recent years, several Berea students have received national recognition for their work with Students for Appalachia (SFA), a group that provides a variety of services for surrounding communities, including tutoring and adult education.

Later-life achievers make up about 5 percent of Berea's student body. The majority of Berea's students live on campus in sixteen residence halls and a variety of theme houses. Berea also offers many family housing units, including several units that accommodate single parents and their children.

Location

Berea is a small city of approximately 10,000 located about 35 miles south of Lexington, Kentucky, the second-largest city in the commonwealth with a population of more than a quarter of a million. Recognized as Kentucky's folk arts and crafts capital, Berea is home to the new Kentucky Artisan's Center and is located on the edge of the Cumberland Mountains, a place described as "where the mountains meet the bluegrass."

Majors and Degrees

Berea College confers the degrees of Bachelor of Arts and Bachelor of Science. Majors are available in agriculture and natural resources, art, biology, business administration, chemistry, child and family studies, classical languages, economics, education studies, English, French, German, history, mathematics, music, nursing, philosophy, physical education, physics, political science, psychology, religion, sociology, Spanish, speech communication, technology and industrial arts, theater, and women's studies. Berea also provides preprofessional preparation for programs of dentistry, engineering, law, medicine, physical therapy, and veterinary medicine.

The College offers dual-degree programs in engineering with the University of Kentucky and Washington University in St. Louis, Missouri. This program of study leads to a Bachelor of Arts degree from Berea College and a Bachelor of Science degree in engineering from either the University of Kentucky or Washington University in St. Louis. A dual-degree program in computer science is also available through Washington University.

Academic Program

Berea operates on a 4-1-4 calendar. Students normally take four courses in the four-month fall term, one course in the January term, and four courses in the spring term. In all degree programs except nursing, a minimum of thirty-three courses is needed to graduate; nursing requires thirty-five courses. The courses taken must satisfy all general education, major, and major-related requirements.

Most courses in the General Education Program have a strong emphasis on cross-disciplinary learning. Some courses are arranged in sequences, with one course establishing a foundation for the next one. Such courses are taken in the prescribed order; others may be taken at a time of the student's choosing.

Courses in the General Education Program include Stories: Encountering Others through Literature; U.S. Traditions: Texts of Freedom and Justice; Introduction to Lifetime Wellness; Introduction to the Arts; Western Traditions I and II; Seminar in World Issues Since 1945; Seminar in Christianity and Contemporary Culture; an introductory course in the natural sciences; an introductory course in the social sciences; The Arts in Context; Natural Science; and the cultural area requirement. The cultural area requirement may be met by taking two courses in a foreign language or by taking two courses from Appalachian studies, Black studies, or world cultures.

Students may be granted college credit for achieving a score of 3, 4, or 5 on Advanced Placement (AP) tests. Advanced standing in foreign language is also available to qualifying students.

Off-Campus Programs

Berea encourages all students to take advantage of study-abroad opportunities by providing substantial financial aid to qualifying students. The Berea Term Abroad Program awards 50 percent of associated costs in outright scholarships for every participating student. Additional need-based aid is available to ensure that every Berea student has an opportunity to participate. Recently, students have traveled to Australia, Austria, Bolivia, the Czech Republic, Denmark, El Salvador, France, Germany, Greece, Guatemala, Iceland, India, Mexico, Nicaragua, Spain, the United Kingdom, and other interesting places.

Academic Facilities

The Hutchins Library houses both the library's collections and services as well as the Computer Center. The library has more than 350,000 volumes and subscribes to approximately 1,300 current periodicals. The Charles Martin Hall Science Building features up-to-date classrooms, state-of-the-art laboratory space, and a planetarium. The Jelkyl Drama Center offers excellent facilities for the active theater program. The Draper Building, built in 1938 and renovated in 2001, is the largest classroom facility on campus.

Costs

The College awards a full tuition scholarship, currently worth $19,900 per year, to every admitted student. Fees for 2002–03 were $350. Room and board cost $4500. Most students are eligible for additional financial aid, which brings the median first-year cost to about $1000. Many freshmen can pay all room and board costs through a combination of parental contributions and participation in the College's work program.

Financial Aid

All students accepted to Berea College are awarded financial aid based on need. The College assures that each student's need, as determined through a needs-analysis process, is met. This is accomplished through a combination of the student's and family's resources, the College's work program, public and private grants and scholarships, and a College grant or loan for any remaining need.

Faculty

Berea has 131 full-time faculty members—88 percent of whom hold doctorates or appropriate terminal degrees—and 19 part-time faculty members. The student-faculty ratio is 10:1. While professors consider teaching to be their first priority, they also find time to pursue their own scholarly work. Students are often involved in research. This sometimes leads to joint publications or presentations at professional meetings.

Student Government

The Student Government Association (SGA) oversees campus elections, provides student services, and maintains a loan fund and an accident fund. The SGA also works closely with clubs and organizations on campus and helps select representatives to serve on various committees, including College faculty committees, which help govern the student community.

Admission Requirements

Admission is limited to students whose families would have a difficult time financing a college education of Berea's caliber without significant assistance. Eligibility for admission from a need standpoint is determined by Berea's Family Resource Questionnaire or the expected parental contribution computed from the Free Application for Federal Student Aid. In recent years, most successful applicants to the College have ranked in the top 20 percent of their high school class and scored between 20 and 30 on the ACT and between 930 and 1350 on the SAT I tests. Preference in admission is given to students living in the Appalachian region of the United States, but 20 percent come from other parts of the United States and the rest of the world.

Application and Information

The College operates on a rolling admissions basis, and decisions are made as files become complete. Berea has a limited number of spaces for new students each year. Qualified early applicants for the fall term are more likely to gain admission if they complete the application process prior to November 30. The freshman and transfer classes are usually filled by May 1. Spaces are sometimes available for students who wish to enter in the spring term beginning in February. Applications for the spring term should be submitted by November 15. International students may apply for the fall semester only. International applications are due March 1.

The admissions office is open from 8 a.m. to 5 p.m. on weekdays and on Saturdays by appointment. For further information, a campus tour and interview, or an application form, prospective students should contact:

Office of Admissions
Berea College
CPO 2220
Berea, Kentucky 40404
Telephone: 859-985-3500
800-326-5948 (toll-free)
E-mail: admissions@berea.edu
World Wide Web: http://www.berea.edu

A laboratory class at the Hall Science Building.

BERKELEY COLLEGE

Berkeley College

WEST PATERSON, PARAMUS, AND WOODBRIDGE, NEW JERSEY

The College

Since its inception in 1931, Berkeley College has been committed to providing an exceptional undergraduate business education. Today, Berkeley College is recognized across the nation as a premier school, preparing students for successful careers in business in the twenty-first century. Berkeley College's strong academic program succeeds through a blend of traditional education, professional training, and real world experience.

At Berkeley, students benefit from small class sizes; personal, academic, and career counseling; and the chance to develop their analytical and creative skills. Berkeley believes that teaching should provide a practical perspective to traditional material, and Berkeley's distinguished faculty brings academic preparation and professional experience to the classroom. Teachers are chosen not just for their academic achievements, but for their applicable background in the business world as well.

All campuses are accredited by the Commission on Higher Education of the Middle States Association of Colleges and Schools. The New Jersey campuses are authorized by the New Jersey Commission on Higher Education to confer the degrees of Bachelor of Science, Associate in Applied Science, and Associate in Science. The American Bar Association (ABA) approves the paralegal studies program at all campuses. Bachelor of Science degrees are offered at all New Jersey campuses. Associate degrees are offered at all campuses except for the interior design program, which is offered only at the Paramus campus.

Berkeley's total enrollment of nearly 4,700 students at five campuses in New York and New Jersey, includes day and evening as well as full- and part-time students who represent seventy-six countries.

Berkeley offers a number of organizations, clubs, and activities designed to meet the educational, cultural, and social needs and interests of its students. Activities include, but are not limited to, picnics, intramural sports, ski weekends, theater events, and charity drives.

Berkeley's full-service Career Services Division has 20 placement advisers who specialize in each major field of study. Berkeley's Career Services' professionals work with students to identify career options, develop and refine resume and interviewing skills, secure internship positions, and schedule interviews in the areas surrounding the five New York/New Jersey locations. Lifetime career assistance is available to all Berkeley graduates. Last year, more than 96 percent of all graduates available for placement were employed in positions related to their studies at Berkeley College.

Berkeley programs provide the comprehensive foundation necessary to begin a successful business career or to advance in a current career. The Academic Resource Centers and Learning Labs provide students with a wide range of support services to help improve their study skills as well as their reading, writing, and mathematical abilities. Academic, career, and individual advisement and free tutorial services are also available. At Berkeley, the traditional undergraduate curriculum is enhanced with professional training and experience. Berkeley's internship requirement provides valuable work experience and often leads to a full-time position. Students work in their fields of study, earn academic credits toward their degree, establish a network of business connections for the future, and offset college costs.

Location

The West Paterson campus offers all the amenities of college life. Located on 25 acres of wooded countryside and situated atop Garret Mountain in the suburban West Paterson–Little Falls region, students enjoy the complete college experience with diverse student activities, residence halls, a student center, a full-service cafeteria, and the friendliness and warmth of the Berkeley community. The Woodbridge and Paramus campuses are ideal for students who prefer a smaller setting and the intimacy and extra-personalized attention that come with it. Berkeley's central New Jersey campus is located in downtown Woodbridge. It is within easy reach of Woodbridge Center, which is the focus for fashion, the arts, shopping, recreation, and government in the region. The Paramus campus is located in the heart of Bergen County's business district. The corporate atmosphere of the campus reflects the area. Internship and employment opportunities can be found nearby.

Majors and Degrees

Bachelor of Science degree programs are offered in accounting, business administration, fashion marketing and management, international business, management, and marketing.

Associate degree programs are offered in business administration, with specializations in accounting, information systems management, management, and marketing. Additional associate degree programs include fashion marketing and management, interior design, international business, network management, paralegal studies, and Web design. Prospective students should note that not all programs are offered at all campuses.

A highly student-supportive and flexible online program offering a bachelor's degree in business administration is also available for those whose busy lives and daily responsibilities do not allow them to attend classes on campus.

Academic Programs

Berkeley offers a wide range of career-focused bachelor's and associate degrees that prepare students for immediate marketability and professional growth. The academic curriculum combines leading-edge theory, real-world practicality, and extensive training in the latest computer technologies. Berkeley's commitment to excellence constitutes the primary objective of the College. Small classes, individualized advisement and counseling, and the development of the students' creative and analytical skills support this commitment.

Berkeley brings the classroom to students online with the same high standards of its on-site classes. With exceptional convenience and flexibility, the carefully developed program provides everything students need to pursue a wide range of bachelor's or associate degrees, backed by Berkeley's commitment to excellence in education and value. The Bachelor of Science degree in business administration is offered entirely online.

The College operates year-round on the quarter system, with quarters starting in September, January, April, and July. The flexible quarter system provides students enrolled in the day division the option of earning their bachelor's degree in as little as three years or in the traditional four years. An associate degree can be completed in only eighteen months. Evening/weekend students have the option of completing their bachelor's degree in less than four years or an associate degree in only two years.

Off-Campus Programs

Berkeley offers study-abroad programs in London and Paris.

Academic Facilities

Berkeley College maintains comprehensive libraries on each campus. Each library houses a collection of print and nonprint resources, periodicals, study areas, computers, and audiovisual equipment. The libraries provide a variety of services, including orientations, reference assistance, and course-related, course-integrated, and point-of-use instruction. A systemwide catalog encompassing the holdings of all Berkeley libraries consists of approximately 85,000 items. Library Web pages provide 24-hours-a-day, seven-days-a-week access to the online catalogs, electronic databases, reference tools, Internet search engines, library service and staff, and links to institution-wide portals. Throughout Berkeley's campuses are state-of-the-art computer labs with more than 700 classroom computer stations.

Costs

In 2004–05, full-time students pay $15,900 in tuition and fees for the academic year. Berkeley offers protection from any tuition increase to students who maintain continuous, full-time enrollment. A variety of housing options are available depending on the campus attended. Students who choose to live in residence housing pay an additional $5400–$7200 per academic year for a double- or single-room preference and an additional $3300 per academic year for fifteen meals weekly. Students are securely housed in Garret Hall and Knuppel Hall, which are three-story, brick, coed residence halls. Rooms are designed to house 1 or 2 students and are comfortably furnished. The buildings also include lounges, kitchens, and a laundry room as well as overnight security.

Financial Aid

Berkeley is committed to helping students find the financing options that make their education possible. Financial assistance programs are available from federal and state sources and through Berkeley in the forms of scholarships, grants, loans, and other awards. Berkeley College allocates approximately $12 million annually for student aid, based on need and/or merit. Financial advisers are available to meet one-on-one with students and their families to develop a plan that is best suited to individual goals and circumstances.

Faculty

Because Berkeley believes that teaching should encompass both a conceptual and practical perspective, faculty members are chosen for both their professional experience and their academic credentials. Their business experience brings an added intellectual reality to the classroom, resulting in a challenging and stimulating learning environment. Several of Berkeley's administrators are nationally recognized authors, lecturers, consultants, and leaders in business education.

Student Government

All students are members of the Student Government Association (SGA). Elected SGA officers meet regularly and act as liaisons between students and the administration concerning social and academic matters.

Admission Requirements

The basic requirements for admission to Berkeley College include graduation from an accredited high school or the equivalent and an entrance exam or SAT or ACT scores. A personal interview is strongly recommended. The following credentials must be submitted as part of the application process: a completed application form, a nonrefundable $40 application fee, and an unofficial transcript (for currently enrolled high school students) or a high school diploma or its equivalent (for high school graduates).

Students who graduated from an accredited high school or with the equivalent (GED) and then attended another college or university are considered transfer students. Transfer students must submit an application for admission and the nonrefundable $40 application fee, a final transcript from each college or university attended, and a final high school transcript or GED certificate.

Berkeley accepts transfer credits from regionally accredited postsecondary institutions for courses (minimum grade of C) that are applicable to a student's program at Berkeley. Academic advisers can also explore with transfer students the possibility of receiving credit for acceptable scores on national standardized exams and professional certification exams. Knowledge gained outside the classroom, through either work or life experience, can often translate into college credit at Berkeley. A prior-learning academic adviser counsels students, reviews the possibilities for credit recognition, and determines the best method for assessment.

Application and Information

Applications are accepted on an ongoing basis. All prospective students should contact the Director of Admissions at the campus that is most convenient to them or visit the College's Web site at the address below:

West Patterson Campus
Berkeley College
44 Rifle Camp Road
West Paterson, New Jersey 07424

Paramus Campus
Berkeley College
64 East Midland Avenue
Paramus, New Jersey 07652

Woodbridge Campus
Berkeley College
430 Rahway Avenue
Woodbridge, New Jersey 07095

To reach all campuses:
Telephone: 800-446-5400 Ext. G28 (toll-free)
E-mail: info@berkeleycollege.edu
World Wide Web: http://www.berkeleycollege.edu

Berkeley College's programs balance traditional academic preparation with professional training and hands-on experience.

BERKELEY COLLEGE

NEW YORK CITY AND WHITE PLAINS, NEW YORK

Berkeley College

The College

Since its inception in 1931, Berkeley College has been committed to providing an exceptional undergraduate business education. Today, Berkeley College is recognized across the nation as a premier school, preparing students for successful careers in business in the modern world. Berkeley College's strong academic program succeeds through a blend of traditional education, professional training, and real-world experience.

At Berkeley, students benefit from small class sizes, personal academic and career counseling, and the chance to develop their analytical and creative skills. Berkeley believes that teaching should provide a practical perspective to traditional material, and Berkeley's distinguished faculty members bring academic preparation and professional experience to the classroom. Teachers are chosen not just for their academic achievements, but also for their applicable backgrounds in the business world.

The Commission on Higher Education of the Middle States Association of Colleges and Schools accredits Berkeley College, and the New York State Board of Regents authorizes the New York City and Westchester campuses. Academic programs in New York and New Jersey are registered by the New York State Education Department and the New Jersey Commission on Higher Education, respectively. The paralegal studies program at all campuses is approved by the American Bar Association (ABA).

Berkeley's total enrollment of nearly 4,700 students at five campuses in New York and New Jersey includes day and evening and full- and part-time students who represent seventy-six countries.

Students are securely housed in Garret Hall and Knuppel Hall, which is a three-story, brick, coed residence hall. Rooms are designed to house 1 or 2 students and are comfortably furnished. The buildings also include lounges, kitchens, and a laundry room in addition to overnight security. Westchester students receive first priority for Cottage Place Apartments, a new six-story residence adjacent to the White Plains campus. Cottage Place comprises studio apartments with kitchenettes and two- and three-bedroom apartments with full kitchens and living rooms. All studios and bedrooms are designed for double occupancy, and the three-bedroom apartments have two bathrooms. Bright, cheerful, and attractively furnished, each apartment is air-conditioned and wired for voice, data, and cable TV. Amenities include overnight security, laundry facilities, and electronic key-card access. Cottage Place is within easy walking distance of commuter train and bus lines. Living expenses can vary considerably.

Berkeley offers a number of organizations, clubs, and activities designed to meet the educational, cultural, and social needs and interests of students. Activities include, but are not limited to, picnics, intramural sports, ski weekends, theater events, and charity drives.

Berkeley's full-service Career Services division has 20 placement advisers, who specialize in each major field of study. Berkeley's Career Services professionals work with students to identify career options, develop and refine resume and interviewing skills, set up and place students in internship positions, and schedule interviews in the areas surrounding the five New York/New Jersey locations. Lifetime career assistance is available to all Berkeley graduates. Last year, more than 96 percent of all graduates available for placement were employed in positions related to their studies at Berkeley College.

Berkeley programs provide the comprehensive foundation necessary to begin a successful business career or to advance in a current career. The Academic Resource Centers and Learning Labs provide students with a wide range of support services to help improve their study skills as well as their reading, writing, and mathematical abilities. Academic, career, individual advisement, and free tutorial services are also available. At Berkeley, the traditional undergraduate curriculum is enhanced with professional training and experience. Berkeley's internship requirement provides valuable work experience and often leads to a full-time position. Students work in their fields of study, earn academic credits toward their degree, establish a network of business connections for the future, and offset college costs.

Location

Berkeley College provides students with the choices and opportunities of both urban and suburban campuses. The New York City campus, found in the heart of Manhattan's east side next to Grand Central Station, is for students who want to take advantage of the total metropolitan experience. Berkeley's Westchester campus, which was recently relocated to the heart of the business district in downtown White Plains, is easily accessible and centrally located near commuter trains and bus lines.

Majors and Degrees

Bachelor of Business Administration degree programs are offered in accounting, e-business, general business, information systems management, international business, management, and marketing. Associate degree programs are offered in business administration, with specializations in accounting, information systems management, management, and marketing. Additional associate degree programs include e-business, fashion marketing and management, interior design, international business, network management, paralegal studies, and Web design. Not all programs are offered at all campuses.

Academic Programs

Berkeley offers a wide range of career-focused bachelor's and associate degrees that prepare students for immediate marketability and professional growth. The academic curriculum combines leading-edge theory, real-world practicality, and extensive training in the latest computer technologies. Berkeley's commitment to excellence constitutes the primary objective of the College. Small classes, individualized advisement and counseling, and the development of the students' creative and analytical skills support this commitment.

To add flexibility and convenience, Berkeley brings the classroom to students online with the same high standards of the on-site classes.

The College operates year-round on the quarter system, with quarters starting in September, January, April, and July. The flexible quarter system provides students enrolled in the day division the option of earning their bachelor's degree in as little as three years or in the traditional four years. An associate degree can be completed in only eighteen months. Evening/weekend students have the option of completing their bachelor's degree in less than four years or an associate degree in only two years.

Off-Campus Programs

Berkeley offers study-abroad programs in London and Paris.

Academic Facilities

Berkeley College maintains comprehensive libraries on each campus. Each library houses a collection of print and nonprint resources, periodicals, study areas, computers, and audiovisual equipment. The libraries provide a variety of services, including orientations, reference assistance, and course-related, course-integrated, and point-of-use instruction. A systemwide catalog encompassing the holdings of all Berkeley libraries consists of approximately 85,000 items. Each library has its own Web page, allowing the Berkeley community to access online catalogs, electronic databases, reference tools, and the Internet 24 hours a day, seven days a week. Throughout Berkeley's campuses are state-of-the-art computer labs with more than 700 classroom computer stations.

Costs

In 2003–04, full-time students paid $15,135 in tuition and fees for the academic year. Berkeley offers protection from any tuition increase to students who maintain continuous, full-time enrollment. A variety of housing options are available, depending on the campus attended. Students who choose to live in residence housing paid an additional $5100 to $6900 per academic year for a double- or single-room preference and an additional $3300 per academic year for fifteen meals weekly.

Financial Aid

Berkeley is committed to helping students find the financing options that make their education possible. Financial assistance programs are available from federal and state sources and through Berkeley in the forms of scholarships, grants, loans, and other awards. Berkeley College awards more than $9 million each year in scholarships and institutional aid based on academic achievement or financial need. Financial advisers are available to meet one-on-one with students and their families to develop a plan that is best suited to individual goals and circumstances.

Faculty

Because Berkeley believes that teaching should encompass both a conceptual and a practical perspective, faculty members are chosen for both their professional experience and their academic credentials. Their business experience brings an added intellectual reality to the classroom, resulting in a challenging and stimulating learning environment. Several of Berkeley's administrators are nationally recognized authors, lecturers, consultants, and leaders in business education.

Student Government

All students are members of the Student Government Association (SGA). Elected SGA officers meet regularly and act as liaisons between students and the administration concerning social and academic matters.

Admission Requirements

The basic requirements for admission to Berkeley College include graduation from an accredited high school or the equivalent and an entrance exam or SAT or ACT scores. A personal interview is strongly recommended. The following credentials must be submitted as part of the application process: a completed application form, a nonrefundable $40 application fee, and an unofficial transcript (for currently enrolled high school students) or a high school diploma or its equivalent (for high school graduates).

Students who graduated from an accredited high school or the equivalent (GED) and then attended another college or university are considered transfer students. Transfer students must submit an application for admission and the nonrefundable $40 application fee, a final transcript from each college or university attended, and a final high school transcript or GED certificate.

Berkeley accepts transfer credits from regionally accredited postsecondary institutions for courses in which the student earned a minimum grade of C that are applicable to the student's program at Berkeley. Academic advisers can also explore with transfer students the possibility of receiving credit for acceptable scores on national standardized exams and professional certification exams. Knowledge gained outside the classroom, through either work or life experience, can often translate into college credit at Berkeley. A prior-learning academic adviser counsels students, reviews the possibilities for credit recognition, and determines the best method for assessment.

Application and Information

Applications are accepted on an ongoing basis. All prospective students should contact the Director of Admissions at the Berkeley College campus that is most convenient to them.

New York City Campus
Berkeley College
3 East 43rd Street
New York, New York 10017
White Plains Campus
Berkeley College
99 Church Street
White Plains, New York 10601
Telephone: 800-446-5400 Ext. G28 (toll-free)
E-mail: info@berkeleycollege.edu
World Wide Web: http://www.berkeleycollege.edu

Berkeley College's programs balance traditional academic preparation with professional training and hands-on experience.

BERKLEE COLLEGE OF MUSIC

BOSTON, MASSACHUSETTS

The College

Founded in 1945, Berklee College of Music is the world's largest accredited music college and the premier institution for the study of contemporary music. The College's 3,800 students from seventy-eight countries and its more than 500 faculty members interact in an environment designed to provide the most complete learning experience possible, including all of the opportunities and challenges presented by a career in the contemporary music industry. Using Berklee's extensive facilities, students develop musical competencies in such areas as composition, performance, and recording/production and also learn to make the informed business decisions necessary for career success.

Berklee was founded on two revolutionary ideas: that musicianship could be taught through the music of the time and that students need practical, professional skills for successful, sustainable music careers. While the bedrock philosophy has not changed, the music has and requires that students evolve with it. For more than half a century, Berklee has demonstrated its commitment to this approach by wholeheartedly embracing change.

Berklee updates its curriculum and technology to make them more relevant and attract diverse students who reflect the multiplicity of influences in today's music. The College prepares its students for a lifetime of professional and personal growth through the study of the arts, sciences, and humanities and is developing new initiatives to reach and influence an ever-widening audience.

More than a college, Berklee has become one of the world's best learning labs for the music of today and tomorrow. It is a microcosm of the music world, reflecting the interplay between music and culture, and is an environment where aspiring music professionals learn how to integrate new ideas, adapt to changing musical genres, and showcase their distinctive skills in an evolving community. Berklee is at the center of a widening network of industry professionals who use their openness, virtuosity, and versatility to take music in surprising new directions. They focus on their musicianship, on the technologies that help shape this art form, on the intricacies and realities of the business and promotion of music, or on the leading thinking in music education and music therapy. Students start bands of their own, participate regularly in ensembles, go on tour, and take advantage of internships throughout the industry. They record student projects, score films, write, practice, and perform. What separates Berklee College of Music from other schools of music is the people—the faculty, the staff, the students, and the alumni who make up this extraordinary community.

Location

Berklee College of Music is located in Boston's Fenway Cultural District. An international hub of intellectual and creative exploration, the neighborhood includes treasure-filled museums and galleries and world-class performing arts centers such as Symphony Hall, the Wang Center, and the Berklee Performance Center. Boston is also home to many of the world's other great colleges and universities. In addition to the music made at Berklee, there is a lively club and concert scene in the area with coffee houses featuring folk and bluegrass music; neighborhood clubs offering jazz, reggae, and world music; and clubs specializing in rock, blues, dance, urban, and country-western music.

Berklee students participate in intramural sports and fitness programs at nearby institutions; watch Boston's professional sports teams play in the Fleet Center or at Fenway Park or other area sports venues; attend theater, club, and concert hall events year-round throughout the city; and walk, skate, or bike through the city's many scenic parks and public gardens. The College is located within walking distance of Boston's public transportation system, allowing students to take advantage of all that Boston has to offer.

Majors and Degrees

Berklee offers a Bachelor of Music (B.M.) degree program and a four-year program leading to the professional diploma. Students may choose to major in composition, contemporary writing and production, film scoring, jazz composition, music business/management, music education, music production and engineering, music synthesis, music therapy, performance, professional music, and songwriting. The College also offers a five-year, dual-major option in which students graduate with an even more marketable education that expands their career options in the music industry.

Academic Programs

The Bachelor of Music program offers a complete music curriculum combined with general education courses such as English, history, languages, mathematics, philosophy, and physical or social science. Intensive concentration in music subjects provides students with the necessary tools for developing their musical talents to the fullest and preparing for the multifaceted and ever-changing demands of today's professional music. The degree program is especially appropriate for students who wish to earn a formal degree, are interested in pursuing a career in music education, music therapy, or business/management or want to continue their studies at the graduate level.

The diploma is designed for students who want to focus exclusively on contemporary music studies and still get the benefits of a Berklee experience.

All students must complete the Core Music Curriculum, which consists of harmony, arranging, ear training, and introduction to music technology; instrumental studies; ensembles and instrumental labs; and the concentrate courses designated for each major. All degree candidates must complete the general education curriculum and traditional studies courses.

Off-Campus Programs

Through the Professional Arts Consortium (ProArts), an association of six area institutions of higher education dedicated to the performing and visual arts, Berklee students can take courses at leading Boston area arts institutions in such areas as communications, modern dance, visual arts, ballet, architectural and graphic design, theater arts, and liberal arts. The other members of the consortium are Boston Architectural Center, the Boston Conservatory, Emerson College, Massachusetts College of Art, and the School of the Museum of Fine Arts.

Students who major in music business/management may be eligible to receive credit for their Berklee course work toward an M.B.A. from Suffolk University.

The Berklee International Network is a shared endeavor designed to promote the effectiveness of contemporary music education among members and to advance the value of contemporary music education internationally. Berklee faculty and staff members visit network member schools annually to conduct workshops and clinics and to audition students for scholarships for full-time study at Berklee. There are currently twelve members of the network: Fundacio L'Aula de Musica Moderna i Jazz in Barcelona, Spain; Rimon School of Jazz and Contemporary Music in Ramat Hasharon (Tel Aviv), Israel; Phillipos Nakas Conservatory in Athens, Greece; American School of Modern Music in Paris, France; Pop and Jazz Conservatory in Helsinki, Finland; Koyo Conservatoire in Kobe, Japan; PAN School of Music in Tokyo, Japan; Jazz and Rock Schule in Freiburg, Germany; International College of Music in Kuala Lumpur, Malaysia; Academia de Musica Fermatta, Mexico City, Mexico; Conservatorio Souza Lima in Sao Paulo, Brazil; and Seoul Jazz Academy in Seoul, Korea.

Academic Facilities

Berklee students have the chance to work in the College's state-of-the-art music technology facilities, using some of the most sophisticated recording and synthesis equipment currently available, in addition to facilities specifically designed for the areas of composition, arranging, and film scoring. The facilities at Berklee are furnished with the instruments and equipment that are being used in the world beyond the classroom. Berklee's performance facilities include the Berklee Performance Center, a 1,200-seat concert hall hosting more than 300 student, faculty, and other concerts each year; four recital halls equipped with a variety of sound reinforcement systems; more than forty ensemble rooms; seventy-five private instruction studios; 300 private practice rooms; and an outdoor concert pavilion.

Technological facilities include the Recording Studio Complex, consisting of twelve studio facilities that include 8-, 16-, and 24-track digital and analog recording capability; synthesis labs, featuring more than 250 MIDI digitally equipped synthesizers, drum machines, sequencers, and computers, including hard-disk recording; Learning Center, equipped with forty computer-based MIDI workstations; Professional Writing Division MIDI Lab; and film scoring labs, providing professional training in the areas of film music composition, editing, sequencing, and computer applications.

Costs

Tuition and fees for the 2004–05 year are $23,532. Room and board fees are $10,900. While the cost of books tends to vary among students, it is estimated at about $500 per year.

Financial Aid

A very large percentage of the student body receives some form of financial aid, so no student should allow financial barriers to stop him or her from applying to the College. Funds are available from many different sources, including Berklee and federal and state programs. Students are eligible for merit-based scholarships and, in cases of demonstrated need, federal assistance is provided. Subsidized loans, a tuition-installment plan, and campus employment are also available. Financial aid counselors are available to students and their families to discuss the various options available to them. Students should be aware that there are specific deadlines for federal and state fund applications and for scholarships. Berklee awards $7 million in scholarships each year to students from all over the world who demonstrate the potential to succeed in today's music industry.

Berklee's Office of Scholarships and Student Employment provides extensive opportunities for both domestic and international students to apply for merit-based scholarships via in-person or recorded audition (entering students) or submission of an achievement portfolio (continuing and returning students who have successfully completed a minimum of two semesters).

Faculty

The personal attention students receive from teachers at Berklee guides them beyond the theoretical so that they can apply what they've learned in their next ensemble rehearsal, evening jam session, or gig. All instruction is administered by Berklee faculty members. Teachers are talented artists who demonstrate their commitment to music education in the classroom and beyond. Most faculty members also write and arrange music, perform in concert halls and clubs, make recordings, or perform on television and radio, and some do it all. All faculty members bring to the classroom a knowledge of music and the wisdom that comes from professional music experience.

Student Government

In recent years, student leaders have become more involved in the decision making of the College, and the Council of Students was created in response to the students' need for a student-run forum to discuss issues of importance to them as well as to prioritize their needs for presentation to faculty members and administration. The council provides adequate channels for expression of student viewpoints in areas of College life at Berklee and promotes the general welfare, interests, opinions, and activities of Berklee students.

Admission Requirements

To make sure that students are prepared for Berklee's exciting and challenging educational experience, all students must have a minimum of 2 years of formal music study on their principal instrument, covering standard methods and materials in preparation for college-level music study and/or significant practical experience in musical performance; knowledge of written music fundamentals (including rhythmic notation, melodic notation in treble and bass clefs, key signatures, major and minor scales, intervals, and construction of triads and seventh chords); a diploma from an accredited secondary school with satisfactory marks in college-preparatory courses; and, for degree candidates only, satisfactory scores on either the SAT I, ACT, or TOEFL (for international students).

Application and Information

Students intending to begin studies in September should submit their applications prior to February 1. This preferred filing date allows applicants to take full advantage of housing, financial aid, and scholarship opportunities at the College. Applications are permitted after March; however, the Office of Admissions (and other offices that serve students) can provide the best service to those who apply earliest. Applications are considered in the order in which they are completed.

Applicants considering the January or May semesters should apply at least three months in advance. International students should apply at least six months to one year in advance. All applicants are encouraged to visit the College and take part in a campus tour and information session; together, they provide an overview of the College and the admission process. Hours of operation are 9 to 5, Monday through Friday. Student-led tours take visitors through administrative buildings, the Berklee Performance Center, the Career Resource Center, and the Learning Center. Information sessions offer insight into Berklee's admission requirements and life at the College. The sessions are presented by admissions representatives. Open Houses are offered on selected Saturdays throughout the year. These include a campus tour, an information session, and special student ensemble performances.

For further information, students should contact:

Office of Admissions
Berklee College of Music
1140 Boylston Street
Boston, Massachusetts 02215
Telephone: 617-266-1400 Ext. 2222 (worldwide)
800-BERKLEE (toll-free in the United States and Canada)
Fax: 617-747-2047
E-mail: admissions@berklee.edu
World Wide Web: http://www.berklee.edu

Students performing at Berklee College of Music.

BERNARD M. BARUCH COLLEGE OF THE CITY UNIVERSITY OF NEW YORK

NEW YORK, NEW YORK

Baruch College
The City University of New York

The College

Baruch College, one of the best academic resources in the New York City area, has earned a reputation for excellence that extends to all parts of the world, attracting students from New York State, neighboring states, and abroad. A senior institution of the City University of New York (CUNY), Baruch offers students a broad array of majors through its three schools: the Zicklin School of Business, the Weissman School of Arts and Sciences, and the School of Public Affairs.

Baruch is accredited by the Middle States Association of Colleges and Schools. All baccalaureate and master's programs in business offered by the Zicklin School of Business are accredited by AACSB International–The Association to Advance Collegiate Schools of Business. In addition to the business accreditation, both the undergraduate and graduate accountancy curriculums have been awarded the accounting accreditation from the AACSB.

The student body is remarkably diverse, reflecting the extraordinary ethnic spectrum of the city. Baruch currently enrolls more than 15,000 students, of whom more than 13,000 attend the Zicklin School of Business. Eighty-three percent of those enrolled are undergraduates. There are more than 100 student clubs and organizations representing a wide range of interests: academic, artistic, cultural, ethnic, professional, and athletic. Intercollegiate sports include, among others, basketball, tennis, and volleyball. The Sidney Mishkin Gallery mounts notable exhibitions of photographs, drawings, prints, and paintings. Several music and theater groups are in residence at the College, including the Alexander String Quartet and the Orpheus Chamber Orchestra.

In addition to its extensive array of undergraduate majors, Baruch offers graduate programs leading to the M.B.A., M.P.A., M.S., M.S.Ed., M.S.I.L.R., and Ph.D. An M.B.A. in health care administration is offered jointly with the Mount Sinai School of Medicine; a J.D./M.B.A. is offered jointly with Brooklyn Law School.

The National Association of State Boards of Accountancy rated Baruch one of the top schools in the country for the number of candidates with advanced degrees who successfully take the CPA examination. Recent graduate business school surveys cited Baruch's M.B.A. program among the nation's top graduate programs in business for both quality and value.

Location

Baruch is located near the Flatiron section of Manhattan, which is easily accessible by public transportation from other boroughs, surrounding counties, and New Jersey and Connecticut. The College's central location in one of the most dynamic cultural and financial centers of the world gives students an unequaled learning environment and access to innumerable facilities.

Majors and Degrees

The Zicklin School of Business, the largest collegiate business school in the country, awards the Bachelor of Business Administration (B.B.A.) degree with majors in accountancy, computer information systems, economics, finance and investments, industrial/organizational psychology, management, marketing, operations research, and statistics. In addition, a five-year, combined bachelor's and master's program in accounting is offered.

The Weissman School of Arts and Sciences awards the Bachelor of Arts (B.A.) degree in thirteen major fields: actuarial science, business communication, economics, English, history, mathematics, music, philosophy, political science, psychology, sociology, Spanish, and statistics. It also offers interdisciplinary specializations in arts administration, business journalism, and management of musical enterprises. In addition, ad hoc majors allow students to design programs that combine two or more areas of interest.

The School of Public Affairs offers programs in both public affairs and real estate/metropolitan development, leading to a Bachelor of Science (B.S.) degree.

Academic Programs

Baruch College requires that all students take general liberal arts courses as the necessary preparation and framework within which specialized knowledge can be most effectively used.

Baruch's degree programs in business require 124 credits. Candidates for the B.B.A. are required to take at least half of their credits in the liberal arts and sciences. The business base is made up of 29 required credits, and students must take a minimum of 24 credits in the major field. The degree programs in the arts and sciences and public affairs require 120 credits. Candidates for the B.A. degree are expected to complete the base curriculum (at least 54 credits) in their freshman and sophomore years, select a major field of study by their junior year, and complete at least 90 credits in the arts and sciences. All students must maintain an overall C average or better and a C average or better in their major. Students can design a minor by using their free electives to take 12 credits in a specific discipline or 12 credits of intermediate and advanced courses outside their area of specialization. At least 60 percent of the credits in the major must be taken at Baruch.

College credits may be obtained through the University of the State of New York's Regents College Examinations and the College-Level Examination Program. Business students may obtain up to 6 credits for current business experience related to their major during their senior year.

Entering freshmen may receive a maximum of 16 credits for Advanced Placement (AP) examinations on which appropriate grades have been earned and for work completed in recognized prefreshman programs.

Baruch College participates in the Honors College–University Scholars Program. This is a select group of high-achieving students. These students have available to them the combined resources of the country's largest urban university and the world's most exciting city. Special funding provides a package that includes full-tuition coverage and stipends. A Cultural Passport provides entreé to the riches of the city, including concerts, theater, museums, and other cultural institutions. University Scholars participate in challenging honors programs through the Honors College Seminar, where they take part in a wide range of activities and common projects with honors college students from other CUNY campuses.

Off-Campus Programs

Students may study abroad for credit for a semester or a year through exchange programs with the University of Paris, Ecole Supérieure de Commerce of Rouen (France), Middlesex

University (England), Tel Aviv University (Israel), Mannheim University (Germany), and Universidad Iberoamericana (Mexico).

Academic Facilities

Baruch's Information and Technology Building houses the William and Anita Newman Library, one of the most technologically advanced facilities in New York. In addition to traditional holdings, the 1,450-seat library provides access to extensive print and electronic information resources, including several hundred online databases through the Dow Jones News/Retrieval, LexisNexis, and Dialog services, many of which are available to students via remote access from off-campus locations. Students and faculty members have access to the 4.5 million volumes in the CUNY library system. The Baruch Computing and Technology Center has 500 computer workstations with Web access and multimedia capability.

Baruch's award-winning Computer Center for Visually Impaired People provides access to specialized computer equipment and to data in such forms as Braille, large print, and synthetic speech. Staff members are available to translate class material to Braille. In addition, the center has a Kurzweil Reading Machine.

Baruch's College's new seventeen-floor, 800,000-square-foot vertical campus houses both the Weissman School of Arts and Sciences and the Zicklin School of Business as well as other programs and Student Life and Services. Classes are held in state-of-the-art classrooms, computer labs, and research facilities, and students enjoy a three-level sports and recreation center and a performing arts center.

Costs

For a New York State resident, the current undergraduate tuition for full-time attendance (a minimum of 12 credits or the equivalent) is $2000 per semester; for part-time study, tuition is $170 per credit. For nonresidents, tuition is $360 per credit. In addition, full-time day students pay a $75 activity fee; part-time day students pay a $37.50 activity fee. Tuition and fees are subject to change without notice.

Financial Aid

Financial aid is available for eligible students through various state and federal programs, which include the New York State Tuition Assistance Program (TAP), Federal Pell Grant, Federal Supplemental Educational Opportunity Grant (FSEOG), Federal Perkins Loan, and Federal Work-Study Program. To apply for aid, students must complete the Free Application for Federal Student Aid (FAFSA). Applications are processed as long as funds are available.

Baruch rewards academic excellence with generous scholarships to entering freshmen each year. The Presidential Scholarship, the Isabelle and William Brumman Scholarship, the Joseph Crown Scholarship, the Paul Odess Scholarship award, the Abraham Rosenberg Scholarship, and the Henry and Lucy Moses are the most selective and offer full tuition, fees, and most related expenses for four years. The Baruch Incentive Grant offers awards ranging from $500 to $1000 per year for four years.

Faculty

Baruch's faculty is recognized for leadership, academic honor, and distinction. Members include Yoshihiro Tsurumi, an expert on cultural and economic relations between the United States and Japan; Distinguished Professor David Reynolds, award-winning biographer of Walt Whitman; and E. S. Savas, an expert on privatization of public enterprises.

The faculty is made up of approximately 415 full-time and 350 part-time members. Eighty-seven percent hold doctorates. Full-time faculty members teach undergraduate introductory courses as well as advanced undergraduate and graduate courses. Faculty members also serve as advisers to student organizations and preprofessional programs. An ambitious faculty-hiring program is expected to bring more than 40 new highly credentialed professors to the Zicklin School of Business by 2004.

Student Government

The two student government organizations, which represent the undergraduate and graduate students, oversee the granting of club charters and the allocation of student activity fees and participate in campus educational and community affairs.

Admission Requirements

Freshman applicants are screened initially to select those with a minimum of 3 units of both high school English and math and a minimum of two lab sciences. Students who meet these criteria are admitted based on their overall high school performance and their performance on these index subjects. Alternately, the College admits students with a minimum combined SAT I score of 1150. Students with a GED score of at least 300 are considered, provided that they have satisfactorily completed the required high school units of English and math. Freshmen are required to submit SAT scores.

The best preparation for success at Baruch College is a full program of college-preparatory courses in high school completed with high grades. The College strongly recommends a minimum of 4 years of English, 4 years of social studies, 3 years of mathematics, 2 years of a foreign language, 2 years of lab sciences, and 1 year of performing or visual arts. Mathematics courses are especially important for Baruch's degree programs, and elementary algebra and geometry should be completed prior to enrollment. For students interested in majoring in business, mathematics, or science, 4 units of mathematics, including trigonometry and precalculus, are recommended.

Students who have attended a college or postsecondary institution must meet admission requirements based on the number of credits they have completed. Prospective transfer students must have a minimum GPA of 2.75 to be considered for admission to the Zicklin School of Business and a minimum of 2.5 for all other schools.

Application and Information

All freshman applications that are received complete with all official documentation and fees on or before October 15 for spring admission or December 15 for fall admission are processed first. Complete transfer applications received on or before October 15 for February admission or March 1 for September admission are processed first. Any freshman or transfer applications received after the dates indicated above are processed on a space-available basis.

Requests to schedule an appointment with an admissions counselor, to join a campus tour, or for application materials and additional information should be made to:

Office of Undergraduate Admissions
Baruch College of the City University of New York
One Bernard Baruch Way, Box H-0720
New York, New York 10010-5585
Telephone: 646-312-1400
Fax: 646-312-1363
E-mail: admissions@baruch.cuny.edu
World Wide Web: http://www.baruch.cuny.edu

BETHANY COLLEGE

LINDSBORG, KANSAS

The College

The mission of Bethany College is to nurture and challenge individuals in their search for truth and meaning as they lead lives of faith, learning, and service. Bethany, located on 62 landscaped acres, is a four-year, fully accredited liberal arts college affiliated with the Evangelical Lutheran Church in America. Graduates have excelled in graduate and professional schools and in diverse career fields such as the arts, education, engineering, economics/business, law, and medicine. Sixty-three percent of Bethany's 631 students are from Kansas. The College has students from nineteen other states and twelve countries.

Bethany enrolls a larger percentage of men than women students. Eighty-four percent of the students live on campus in five residence halls and five special interest houses. About 17 percent of the students belong to one of Bethany's three sororities or three fraternities. The average age is 19.

Students' involvement in their education is encouraged through extensive use of experience-based education such as internships. Small classes, personalized education, and caring faculty and staff members are Bethany College hallmarks.

Athletic facilities in the Stroble-Gibson Complex and Hahn Gymnasium include a sports medicine and training room, basketball and volleyball courts, the offices of the Athletic Director, classrooms and locker rooms, a weight room, a large multipurpose gymnasium, two handball/racquetball courts, offices for the Physical Education Department, and the Special Events Office. Anderson Field features an outstanding playing field, a press box, and composite-surfaced track and field facilities. Two softball fields, a baseball field, a soccer field, and the Anderson Tennis Courts round out the major athletic facilities.

The Pihlblad Student Union features a bookstore, a snack bar, a recreation room, meeting rooms, the main dining room, and the offices for the Dean for Student Life, the Residence Life Director, the Student Activities Director, and Director of Security. The Counseling, Career Services, and Health Offices are in Warner Hall.

Each resident student's room has telephone and cable television outlets. Students with computers capable of running Microsoft Windows may access the campus computer network from their rooms via modem. Each student has an individual, password-protected campus network and Internet account. All services are free and represent no additional charge to the room fee.

Location

Bethany is located in central Kansas in the Swedish-American town of Lindsborg, population 3,500, 3 miles west of Interstate 135. Lindsborg is 70 miles north of Wichita (the state's largest city, with a population of 350,000) and 20 miles south of Salina (population 45,000). The close college-community relationship provides a safe, friendly environment and easy access to both medium-size and large cities. Lindsborg has active art and music communities, numerous gift shops, art galleries, and several restaurants. Community ethnic and cultural events occur frequently.

The Bethany College Oratorio Society (composed of students and faculty and staff members as well as area residents) presents the annual Messiah Festival at Bethany College each Holy Week. The festival features Handel's *Messiah* on Palm and Easter Sundays and Bach's *St. Matthew Passion* on Good Friday. The Oratorio Society, a 275-voice choir and fifty-piece orchestra, has presented the *Messiah* annually since 1882. It is the longest-running annual presentation of the *Messiah* in the United States. The society performed the *Messiah* at New York City's Carnegie Hall in the spring of 1997.

The Midwest Art Exhibition, also a part of the festival, has been held annually since 1899 and is the oldest annual art exhibition in Kansas.

Majors and Degrees

The College grants Bachelor of Arts degrees in fifteen academic areas and twelve teaching areas. Majors include administration of justice, art, athletic training, biology, chemistry, Christian ministries, communication, contract, economics/business, education, English, history/political science, mathematics, music, psychology, and social work. Economics/business degree specializations are accounting, business/computer information systems, business management, economics, finance, and international management.

Bethany College offers an accelerated, three-year program in any of the economics/business specializations.

Education degree specializations include art (K–12), behavioral science (7–12), business (7–12), chemistry (7–12), elementary education (K–9), English (7–12), health and physical education (K–12 and 7–12), mathematics (7–12), social science (7–12), and special education (K–12).

Academic minors include administration of justice, church vocations, English, foreign language, information science, music, philosophy, religion, sacred music, and theater. The College has a 3+2 cooperative engineering program with Wichita State University (WSU) in Wichita, Kansas. Students can earn Bachelor of Arts and Master of Science degrees in engineering within five years by taking three years of coursework at Bethany followed by two full years of study at WSU. After the first year at WSU, the student receives a B.A. in mathematics from Bethany; after completion of the program at WSU, the student receives a Master of Science degree in aerospace, chemical, electrical, industrial, or mechanical engineering.

Academic Program

Bethany's course of study prepares men and women for life, with emphasis on the development of the student's social, intellectual, and spiritual potential. Bethany students gain knowledge and develop skills that enrich their minds and expand their vision while they develop a personal philosophy that recognizes the opportunities for self-fulfillment through service to God, society, and self. The College believes a liberally educated person is curious, sensitive to form, appreciative of beauty, imaginative, creative, and engages in rational inquiry. Liberally educated people work well alone or with others and can lead as well as follow. They take responsibility for their actions. A wide range of cocurricular and extracurricular activities augment classroom work and allow students to put what they learn in class into practice.

Students may be granted credit or advanced course placement for successful scores on either the College-Level Examination Program (CLEP) or the Advanced Placement examinations administered by the College Board. To earn the B.A. degree, students must complete between 38 and 54 hours of general education requirements as part of the minimum 128 required semester hours, with a grade of C or better. Transfer students must successfully complete a minimum of 64 semester hours at Bethany.

The College operates a 4–1–4 schedule, with a fall semester that runs from late August to December, a one-month Interterm in January, and a February-to-May spring semester.

Off-Campus Programs

Bethany shares a cooperative cross-registration program with the other five members of the Associated Colleges of Central Kansas. Foreign language courses, special education, and foreign study are popular cooperative program choices.

Academic Facilities

The Wallerstedt Learning Center contains 121,180 volumes and more than 350 titles on microfilm and is a member of the Kansas-wide interlibrary loan cooperative. A media center, a 24-hour study room, a study-skills resource center, and the College Archives are located in the center. The library has two of the College's four computer centers, with a Pentium (IBM)-equipped lab and a Macintosh lab with five machines. The Nelson Science Center computer laboratory has a twenty-four-computer, networked classroom used for instruction and individual study. The lab is connected to the LAN and the Internet from students' rooms if their computers have a modem and are capable of operating Microsoft Windows software.

The Nelson Science Center also houses the mathematics and science departments and has an auditorium, classrooms, laboratories, and a climate-controlled greenhouse. The music department has eight networked Macintosh computers optimized for musical composition. The Burnett Center for the Performing Arts and Religion includes a chapel and a 300-seat theater. The Mingenback Art Center features studios for ceramics, painting, sculpture, and photography as well as classrooms, faculty offices, and a gallery. Presser Hall, the main administrative building, houses the Offices of Admissions and Financial Aid, the Registrar, other administrative offices, and the music department. Presser Hall Auditorium seats 1,900 and features exceptional acoustics.

Costs

For 2004–05, tuition is $14,800, and room and board cost $5150. Books, supplies, and personal expenses are estimated at $2500. There are no other fees except for private music lessons and materials in some laboratory science and art classes.

Financial Aid

Consideration for financial aid is made outside of the admissions process and more than 95 percent of Bethany students receive some type of aid. Need-based aid is available to students who demonstrate financial need by submitting the Free Application for Federal Student Aid (FAFSA). The FAFSA application deadline is March 15 for Kansas residents and April 1 for all other students. Academic scholarships and performance awards are given to students meeting certain academic criteria. Both Federal Work-Study and Bethany work-study positions are available on campus, and part-time employment opportunities in the surrounding community are excellent. Bethany provides more than $3.3 million annually in scholarships, grants, and performance awards to eligible students.

Faculty

Twenty-five of Bethany's 41 full-time faculty members have doctoral degrees, the equivalent, or the highest degree offered in their specialty. Bethany faculty members challenge students to reach their potential, and faculty and staff members frequently mentor students. The strong relationships students form with faculty and staff members are fostered by small classes and personalized attention. The student-faculty ratio is 11:1 and most classes have fewer than 20 students.

Student Government

Elected representatives from the four classes, residential units, and special groups along with the student body officers constitute the Student Congress (StuCo), the governing body concerned with matters affecting student life and welfare. StuCo sponsors a wide variety of recreational and extracurricular activities throughout the year and funds more than thirty clubs and organizations. The College Board of Directors includes a StuCo representative as a voting member.

Admission Requirements

Admissions criteria include meeting two of the following three at the required level: grade point average, class rank, and standardized test scores on the ACT or SAT. Students denied admission can appeal before the Admissions Committee by submitting two letters of recommendation and an essay. Personal interviews can be required if the Admissions Committee deems them necessary. Each application receives individual attention and is considered on the basis of the student's probable success at Bethany. It is highly recommended that students have completed 4 years of English, 3 years of science (including 2 years of laboratory science), 3 years of mathematics and 3 years of social science in preparation for college. Bethany also evaluates extracurricular activities and work experience, seeking individuals who have demonstrated exceptional leadership qualities and have participated in activities that have carry-over potential for college success. Bethany admits students on the basis of individual merit without regard to sex, abilities, race, age, religion, veteran's status, or national or ethnic origin.

Application and Information

The deadline for application for new and transfer students for the fall semester is June 15; applicants are notified of a decision on a rolling basis. The deadline for application for admission to the spring semester is December 15. Campus visits and interviews with admissions staff members are highly recommended. For further information or application forms contact:

Office of Admissions
Bethany College
421 North First Street
Lindsborg, Kansas 67456
Telephone: 785-227-3311 or 3380 Ext. 8113
800-826-2281 (toll-free)
Fax: 785-227-2004
E-mail: admissions@bethanylb.edu
World Wide Web: http://www.bethanylb.edu

BETHANY COLLEGE

BETHANY, WEST VIRGINIA

The College

Bethany, a four-year private liberal arts college, is the oldest degree-granting institution of higher learning in West Virginia. The College was founded in 1840 by Alexander Campbell, educator, Christian reformer, celebrated debater, author, agriculturist, and businessman. Since its inception, Bethany has been affiliated with the Christian Church (Disciples of Christ). This religious body, of which Campbell was one of the principal founders, continues to support and encourage the College, although it exercises no sectarian control.

The student body represents a broad spectrum of economic, social, and religious backgrounds. Students from twenty-two states, the District of Columbia, and fourteen other countries live in the College's small chalet-style residences in the hills, overlooking the College and in larger dormitories in the heart of the campus. Campbell Village, Bethany's newest residential community, provides suite-style living. These residence halls also provide quarters for Bethany's five national fraternities and three national sororities.

Bethany's student union houses an activities area, a spacious lounge, an art gallery, and the College bookstore. Intercollegiate activities involve more than 44 percent of the men and women on campus. Approximately 40 percent of the students participate in intramural sports. There are forty clubs, organizations, and student groups. Student theater, choir, jazz, and wind ensembles offer numerous concerts and programs. The College brings an array of nationally known speakers and entertainers to the campus for in-depth conferences and seminars on current topics.

Townspeople, consisting mainly of faculty and staff families, are closely involved with the 900 Bethany students. Faculty-student interaction is natural in this environment and student-administration relations are friendly and informal. Student input is sought in both academic and extracurricular matters.

Location

The 1,600-acre campus is located in the Allegheny foothills in the northern panhandle of West Virginia, 2 miles from Pennsylvania and 5 miles from Ohio. The center of the Wheeling metropolitan area is 15 miles away, and Pittsburgh is 44 miles to the northeast. The Bethany community has a rich history, and the College has gained national recognition by having five sites placed on the National Register of Historic Places. Two sites are National Historic Landmarks. The cultural activities and attractions of Pittsburgh and Wheeling are readily available, as are professional sporting events. Parks and museums, as well as a zoo, are just a few miles away. Bethany's location combines the advantages of a rural campus with proximity to a metropolitan community.

Majors and Degrees

Bethany College confers Bachelor of Science and Bachelor of Arts degrees. Major work is offered in accounting, biochemistry, biology, chemistry, communication (with options for emphasis in advertising, electronic media, graphics, print media, and public relations), computer science, economics (with options for emphasis in financial economics, international economics, and managerial economics), education (elementary education, middle childhood education through individual department programs, and education in a nonschool setting), English, environmental science, environmental studies, fine arts, French, German, history, interdisciplinary studies, international relations, mathematics, music, philosophy, physical education and sports studies (with options for emphasis on sports communication, sports management, sports services and teaching physical education), physics, political communication, political science, psychology (with options for emphasis in scientific psychology, human services and pre–physical therapy), psychology and education, religious studies, social studies, social work, Spanish, theater arts (with options for emphasis in acting and technical theater), and visual art.

Students may include as part of their program of study one or more of the thirty-two optional minors offered.

Preprofessional study is available in engineering, the medical and health professions, law, ministry, and pre–physical therapy.

Academic Program

Bethany provides a four-year liberal arts education that combines freedom in designing individual programs with sufficient structure to ensure depth, breadth, and integration of knowledge. This plan includes a first-year seminar program, a writing requirement, a senior project, a senior comprehensive examination with oral and written parts, a seminar in biblical literature, a wellness course, a creative arts experience, and a foreign language requirement.

The academic calendar includes two 15-week semesters and a May term. The fall semester begins in late August and ends before Christmas; the spring semester is from mid-January to late April. Students may choose to use the May term for intensive study on campus or for working off campus. Some courses are offered for the full fifteen weeks, others for the first or second half of the semester. This division provides additional flexibility for students involved in off-campus study and internships. The College's Office of Career and Professional Development offers placement, interviewing, and counseling services.

Off-Campus Programs

Special arrangements with Case Western Reserve University, Columbia University, and Washington University in St. Louis provide opportunities for students interested in engineering. Students in history, political science, or economics can participate in a West Virginia legislative program and a semester in Washington, D.C.

Bethany's study-abroad programs are at the Padagogische Hochschule in Heidelberg, Germany; the Sorbonne program in Paris; the Seigakuin University program in Saitamaken, Japan; and the Spain program at the University of Navarra in Pamplona. Tuition and airfare allowance are included as part of the student's regular charges for most of these Bethany programs.

Exchange opportunities available through the consortium of East Central Colleges are those at the American College of Thessalonia, Greece; Beijing Institute of Petrochemical Technology in China; Blas Pascal University in Cordoba, Argentina; the Inter-American University in San German, Puerto Rico; Kansai Gadai University in Osaka, Japan; the University of Karlstad in Sweden; the University of Prince Edward Island in Charlottetown, Canada; the University of Quebec at any of its six campuses in Canada; and the University of Saskatchewan in Saskatoon, Canada.

Academic Facilities

The center for library services and resources is the T. W. Phillips Memorial Library, which also houses archives and special collections. The library assists in maintaining specialized library reading rooms for chemistry and law at other locations on campus. Other special facilities are a student-operated FM radio station and television station; student publication center; Kirkpatrick Hall, which has laboratories and classrooms for biology and psychology; Richardson Hall, which houses the computer center and facilities for chemistry, physics, and mathematics; and a modern recreation center. Steinman Fine Arts Center provides facilities for education, music, and theater and has a fully-equipped theater, teaching studios, studio-classrooms, a rehearsal room for choral and instrumental groups, and individual practice rooms. Mountainside Conference Center houses offices, seminar rooms, exhibition areas, and a circular conference room for education activities. The campus also maintains a high-speed fiber-optic network.

Costs

Tuition and fees for 2003–04 were $12,760; room ranged from $3200 to $4000, depending upon the particular housing arrangement; board was $3150. The Student Government Association fee was $375. The charge for tuition and fees includes tuition and activities and services such as athletics, health service, library, lectures, plays, concerts, publications, student union, student activities, and some laboratory services. It does not include the academic fees, course fees, music fees, and special fees.

Financial Aid

Bethany maintains an extensive scholarship and financial aid program. Approximately 90 percent of the College's students receive financial aid in the form of a package, which may include scholarships, grants, loans, and campus employment. Awards are made on the basis of need as determined by the Free Application for Federal Student Aid (FAFSA). The College attempts to provide adequate aid to enable all qualified students to attend Bethany.

Faculty

The College has a dedicated and talented faculty of 61 full-time members, who encourage free discussion and independent thought. Fifty-nine percent of the faculty members have terminal degrees, and many have published widely. The College's relationship with the town of Bethany allows an easy interaction between students and faculty members. Often what is started in the classroom is finished outside of that classroom and insight often comes in the informal, after-class meetings between professor and student that are an integral part of the Bethany education.

Student Government

The Student Government Association, with representatives from all residence groups, manages a substantial budget and appropriate funds for diverse student activities. Student representatives are appointed to many faculty committees, including those concerned with curricula, cultural programs, calendars, athletics, religious life, international education, student life, and the library.

Admission Requirements

Bethany accepts applications for admission from candidates who feel they would benefit from and contribute to a Bethany education. Admission is competitive and is based on a careful review of all credentials presented by the candidates.

The College seeks students who have prepared themselves for a liberal arts curriculum by taking at least 15 units of college-preparatory work. Students who have developed individual programs will be given special evaluation by the Committee on Admission. Prospective freshman students must take the SAT or the ACT examination.

Transfer and international students are welcome. Students who have received or will receive an Associate of Arts or Associate of Science degree are especially encouraged to apply.

An interview with an admission counselor is strongly recommended, but not required. Appointments for an on-campus interview, a tour of the College, and/or classroom visitations may be arranged through the Office of Admission. Students who are not able to visit the campus may be able to arrange for an interview with an admission counselor near their home.

Application and Information

Application for admission to the freshman class should be made during the final year of high school. Students are notified of their decisions by mail, beginning in October and continuing throughout the year as completed applications are received.

To be considered for admission, students must submit an application for admission, an application fee ($25), an official secondary school transcript, a personal profile, one recommendation, and SAT or ACT scores. Supporting documents that might be of help in the admission process (e.g., poetry, plays, music, artwork, photography, and journalistic writings) may also be submitted.

Requests for further information should be sent to:

Office of Admission
Bethany College
Bethany, West Virginia 26032-0417
Telephone: 304-829-7611
800-922-7611 (toll-free)
Fax: 304-829-7142
E-mail: admission@bethanywv.edu
World Wide Web: http://www.bethanywv.edu

Old Main, a symbol of Bethany College since 1858, is designated a National Historic Landmark.

BETHEL COLLEGE

NORTH NEWTON, KANSAS

The College

Founded in 1887, Bethel College is a liberal arts and sciences undergraduate college affiliated with the Mennonite Church USA. Students are encouraged to live and work together and become the kind of leaders who blend faith and learning. To these ends, Bethel maintains a residential environment designed to foster integrative learning experiences, including student organizations, campus worship services, public lectures, symposia, and cultural events. At Bethel, 85 percent of the freshmen and two thirds of the entire student body of more than 500 students live on campus. The sense of community afforded by the residential nature of the campus is invigorating.

Bethel's curriculum is founded on a general education program in the liberal arts and sciences and is geared toward students of moderate to high academic ability who want to be leaders. Distinctive elements include requirements in the study of religion and global issues. The College offers twenty-seven majors and ten specialized programs in traditional liberal arts and selected career areas. Bethel is a diverse community of learners, with students from twenty-three states, seventeen countries, and more than thirty religious denominations.

Bethel's programs are informed by four central values of the mission statement: discipleship, scholarship, service, and integrity. Bethel emphasizes faith, learning, and leadership.

The Bethel campus includes the historic Administration Building, two libraries, a performing arts center, a science center, a student center, two gymnasiums, a natural history museum, an art center, athletic fields, and three residence halls.

The Administration Building is the dominating landmark of the College. Home to the campus Chapel and its Dobson pipe organ, the Administration Building was built in 1888 and is listed in the National Register of Historic Places. Thresher Gymnasium (seating capacity of 2,000) is home to varsity women's volleyball and men's and women's basketball. The Schultz Student Center is a hub of student activity, with a cafeteria, snack bar, game room, bookstore, and meeting rooms. The campus facilities are clustered around an open, grassy area referred to as The Green. The Green, with its benches and fountain, is a gathering place for students.

More than two thirds of Bethel students live on campus in one of three residence halls: Voth Hall, Haury Hall, and Warkentin Court. Each residence hall is supervised by an on-site staff and offers recreational and lounge areas and laundry and vending facilities.

Location

The 90-acre, tree-lined Bethel College campus is in North Newton, which is adjacent to the city of Newton (population 20,000). Located in the rich agricultural and industrial region of south-central Kansas, Bethel borders Interstate 135 and Kansas Highway 15. Wichita, the largest city in Kansas, lies 30 minutes to the south, and Hutchinson is 30 minutes west of the campus. Between Newton, Wichita, and Hutchinson, a wide variety of services and attractions are available to students. These include the Kansas Cosmosphere and Space Center, a world-renowned space museum; several art museums; music theater; opera; symphonies; professional baseball, hockey, and soccer; an ice sports center; and multiple malls and shopping centers. Wichita is served by eleven major airlines, and Amtrak train service is available in Newton.

Majors and Degrees

Bethel College grants Bachelor of Arts and Bachelor of Science degrees. Majors include art, athletic training, Bible and religion, biology, business administration, chemistry, communication studies, computer science, computer system administration, elementary education, English, fine arts, German, global peace and justice, health management, history, history and social sciences, management information systems, mathematical sciences, music, natural science, nursing, physics, psychology, restorative community justice, social work, Spanish, and theater. Within these majors, students may concentrate in the following specialized areas: accounting, economics, environmental studies, finance, general management, marketing, mass media, software development, and speech. Preprofessional programs are offered in engineering, law, and medicine.

Academic Programs

Bethel operates on a 4-1-4 academic calendar. Four-month semesters in the spring and fall are supported by the one-month Interterm in January. Interterm allows for a time of focused study in one selected class, either on campus or through several off-campus options. Interterm study-travel options have included English literature in London, biology in the jungle of Belize, theater in New York, history in Russia, religion in Jerusalem, and art in a snowbound cabin in the Colorado Rockies. Through this multifaceted learning environment, Bethel is committed to the diverse educational goals of its students. Courses facilitate intellectual, cultural, and spiritual learning in the Bethel community. The general education requirement of 55 credit hours ensures development of academic skills and disciplines and of integrative learning. Graduation from Bethel requires at least 124 credit hours with a minimum grade point average of 2.0.

Off-Campus Programs

Bethel offers a wide variety of formal study-abroad programs. Students enrolled in these programs are considered to be enrolled as full-time Bethel students living off campus. Academic progress and financial aid are generally the same as for on-campus programs. Bethel students may participate in study-abroad programs at sixteen colleges and universities in thirteen countries.

Academic Facilities

The Mantz Library has a collection of 130,000 volumes and more than 500 periodical subscriptions. The library also houses the Career Development Office and the Center for Academic Development, which provides academic support in the form of tutoring and supplemental instruction. Additional support is available for postbaccalaureate placement exams, including the GRE, MCAT, and LSAT. Adjacent to the Mantz Library is the Mennonite Library and Archives, which houses more than 45,000 volumes of Mennonite historical and genealogical information.

The Fine Arts Center includes Krehbiel Auditorium, which is used for theater, concerts, and lectures. The Fine Arts Center also houses an art gallery; music rehearsal areas; a computerized music composition lab; studios of KBCU, the campus radio station; and offices of the *Collegian,* the student newspaper.

Krehbiel Science Center, opened in 2002, provides classrooms and laboratories for biology, chemistry, physics, and psychology. Two networked computer laboratories are available in the Academic Center.

Memorial Hall houses the nursing department (classrooms, labs, and research computers), the Wellness Center (exercise and weight rooms), the Academic Health Center (student clinic), Harms Sports Medicine Center (athletic training), and an auditorium and intramural gymnasium (seating capacity of 2,000).

The Franz Art Center has multiple art studios for painting, drawing, ceramics, and photography.

Costs

Tuition and fees for a full-time student for the 2003–04 academic year were $13,900; room and board costs totaled $5900. Interterm is included in these costs if a student is enrolled full-time for either the spring or fall term.

Financial Aid

Bethel College administers a broad spectrum of financial aid intended to make the educational experience affordable for qualified students. Through merit-based financial aid (academic and performance), students may receive assistance ranging from $2500 to $7400 per year. For qualified students, need-based aid is available in the form of Bethel, state, and federal grant and loan programs. More than 94 percent of Bethel students receive some form of financial assistance.

Faculty

Bethel has 44 full-time and 9 part-time faculty members. Of the full-time faculty members, 85 percent have terminal degrees. Faculty members of all ranks teach first-year students in addition to upperclassmen. Bethel faculty members are active in scholarly research and regularly enlist students as collaborators in their research. No classes at Bethel are taught by teaching assistants or graduate assistants. The student-faculty ratio is 11:1. As is consistent with the emphasis Bethel places on global awareness and service, more than half of Bethel faculty members have been engaged in overseas service and travel.

Student Government

Student government at Bethel is based on the federal model and consists of twenty-seven elected offices and several appointed positions. The executive branch comprises the Student Body President and Vice-President. The Senate has 5 senators from each class, 3 commuter senators, one senator from the International Club, and one from the multicultural organization. Bethel's active student government provides an opportunity for student advocacy and leadership development.

Admission Requirements

Bethel seeks to enroll a broad range of students with a demonstrated desire and ability to learn. Admission is competitive, and applicants must provide school transcripts and standardized test scores. Freshman applicants should present a minimum GPA of 2.5 and a minimum ACT score of 19 or SAT I score of 890. Transfer applicants should present a minimum college GPA of 2.0 on 24 hours or more of credit accepted in transfer. International applicants are required to present a minimum TOEFL score of 540 on the paper-based version or 207 on the computer-based version. All prospective students are encouraged to visit campus, either during a group-visit event or an individual campus visit. The College admits students without regard to race, color, sex, disability, or national or ethnic origin.

Application and Information

Interested students are invited to request an application for admission from the Admissions Office or to complete the application online at http://www.bethelks.edu/admissions/application.html. Although admission is granted on a rolling basis through the beginning of each semester, early application is encouraged for priority consideration for financial aid, class selection, and housing.

For more information, students should contact:

Office of Admissions
Bethel College
300 East 27th Street
North Newton, Kansas 67117
Telephone: 316-283-2500
800-522-1887 (toll-free)
Fax: 316-284-5870
E-mail: admissions@bethelks.edu
World Wide Web: http://www.bethelks.edu

Bethel College students in front of Memorial Hall.

BETHEL UNIVERSITY

ST. PAUL, MINNESOTA

The University

Bethel University began its Christian liberal arts program in 1945 but traces its roots to Bethel Seminary, founded in 1871. Bethel is a ministry of the churches of the Baptist General Conference. The University encourages growth and learning in a distinctly Christian environment, continually striving to help students discover and develop the skills God has given them. Campus lifestyle expectations have been designed to build unity within diversity. All Bethel students, faculty members, and staff members are expected to follow those expectations during their time as members of the Bethel community. Bethel's more than 3,000 students represent a range of national and international cultures. Most of Bethel's students are between 18 and 22 years of age, but older and younger students bring a welcome diversity to campus life. Bethel students are involved in a wealth of cocurricular activities, from music to ministry, Bible study to broadcasting, theater to tennis, and art to athletics. Bethel sports teams compete in NCAA Division III and the Minnesota Intercollegiate Athletic Conference. The Sports and Recreation Center is used almost continuously for intercollegiate and intramural sports events and personal recreation, and the Community Life Center provides a 1,700-seat performance hall and chapel.

The campus, built in the 1970s, is the newest among Minnesota colleges and universities. Versatile buildings are centers for the sciences, humanities, physical education, learning resources, and fine arts. A series of skyways and breezeways connect the facilities and make getting to and from class a pleasure—even in the heart of winter. Residence life at Bethel takes many forms. Traditional college dorm rooms, spacious suites, town houses—whatever their preference, Bethel students find a warm, family atmosphere in their living areas. All freshman and sophomore students, except those who are married or living with their parents while in attendance, are required to live in University housing.

In addition to the undergraduate degree programs described below, Bethel offers Master of Arts degrees in communication, counseling psychology, ethnomusicology, gerontology, nursing, organizational leadership, and teaching, and a Master of Education degree with programs in educational leadership and special education. Classes meet one evening a week for 4 hours, and course work is integrated with students' professional responsibilities.

Location

The Bethel campus borders Lake Valentine in Arden Hills and comprises 231 acres of beauty and tranquility, conducive to study and leisure. Just 15 minutes from downtown St. Paul or Minneapolis, Bethel enjoys the benefits of both cities, noted nationally for their high quality of life. The Twin Cities are home for the headquarters of most of Minnesota's large corporations as well as thirty-three major shopping centers and the world's largest shopping mall, the Mall of America. Culture thrives here with an international array of music, theater, and art. At the all-weather Metrodome, the Target Center, and the new Xcel Energy Center, sports fans cheer their favorite pro teams—the Minnesota Vikings, Twins, Timberwolves, and Wild. Abundant recreation exists year-round in this busy metropolis, which has more than 900 lakes and 500 parks.

Majors and Degrees

The Bachelor of Arts (B.A.) degree is offered with majors in art, athletic training, biblical and theological studies, biology, business, business and political science, business management, chemistry, communication, community health, computer science, economics, economics and finance, education, engineering science, English literature, English literature and writing, environmental studies, French, history, international relations, mathematics, media communication, music, music/sacred music, organizational leadership, philosophy, physical education, physics, political science, psychology, social work, sociocultural studies, Spanish, teaching English as a foreign language, teaching English as a second language, theater arts, Third World studies, writing, and youth ministry.

The Bachelor of Science (B.S.) degree is offered with majors in applied physics, biochemistry/molecular biology, biology, chemistry, computer science, nursing, and physics. The Bachelor of Music (B.Mus.) degree is offered in applied performance. The Bachelor of Music Education (B.Mus.Ed.) degree is offered with an emphasis in instrumental K–12 or vocal K–12.

Academic minors are available in most of the major disciplines listed above and in the following areas: art history, Asian studies, athletic coaching, biblical languages (Hebrew and Greek), cross-cultural missions, family studies, film studies, German, leadership studies, management information systems, modern world languages, religious studies, and social welfare studies.

The College of Adult and Professional Studies is a degree-completion program offering bachelor's degrees in business management, nursing, and organizational leadership and is designed for adults who have completed at least two years of undergraduate studies and seek to apply learning to professional interests. Students attend a 4-hour class one night a week and move through the program with the same group of 20 or fewer adults. The courses are taught by Bethel University faculty members.

Academic Program

Bethel was named among the top Midwestern universities by *U.S. News & World Report* in 2003. Bethel's general education curriculum has become a model for many other liberal arts institutions nationwide. Students are required to take classes that will give them a broad view of the world and their role as Christians. General education classes are grouped around the following themes: Bible and theology; Western culture; world citizenship; self-understanding; math, science, and technology; and health and wholeness. In addition, in order to graduate, all Bethel students must demonstrate competence in mathematics, writing, speaking, and computing.

Bethel University follows an early semester calendar consisting of two 15-week semesters and a three-week interim in January. A full-time academic load for each semester is 12 to 18 credits. To graduate, a student must complete a minimum of 122 credits with a cumulative grade point average of at least 2.0 and a minimum 2.25 grade point average in his or her major. Also required are 51 credits of general education. Bethel awards advanced placement credit in recognition of learning that has been achieved apart from a college or university classroom situation. A maximum of 30 advanced placement credits can be applied toward a degree program. Students may also individualize their academic program through directed studies with faculty members and through academic internships with off-campus institutions.

Off-Campus Programs

Bethel students may participate in a number of off-campus extension programs. The American Studies Program of the Council for Christian Colleges and Universities provides internship opportunities in Washington, D.C. The council also sponsors a Latin American Studies Program, which offers students an opportunity to study in Costa Rica. The Los Angeles Film Studies Center gives students of any major a semester of learning and working experience in Los Angeles, the world's film capital. The Christian College Consortium Visitor Program is designed to give students an opportunity to take advantage of course offerings and varied experiences on other Christian college campuses throughout the United States. The AuSable Institute in Michigan offers intensive courses in environmental studies. Through the Upper Midwest Association for Intercultural Education, Bethel students study abroad during the interim. In the spring semester of alternate years, Bethel students can study and travel in Great Britain under the direction of a faculty member from the Bethel University Department of English. Bethel is also associated with Jerusalem University College in Jerusalem, which offers undergraduate and graduate courses in archaeology, geography, history, languages, and literature.

Academic Facilities

Bethel's Community Life Center offers a beautiful auditorium with outstanding acoustical design that makes it one of the best performance halls in the upper Midwest. The Bethel University Library Web site serves as a portal to more than 170,000 volumes located in the library, including books, music CDs, and more than 7,000 videos/DVDs; interlibrary loan access to more than 2 million volumes within the consortium; more than 13,000 full-text periodicals online and 1,100 hard-copy journal titles; more than 65 online databases; a bibliographic manager; an e-mail reference service; a "Research Wizard"; and interactive tutorials. Services in the library include wireless access to the Internet, laptops for checkout, a full-service AV department, individual and small-group study areas, listening/viewing rooms, reference, and instruction. Bethel students are assigned computer accounts, allowing them access to a wealth of academic computing services, including word processors and Web browsing software. The Bethel science labs and music practice rooms are modern and well equipped. Approximately four plays are performed each year in the Bethel Theatre.

Costs

For 2003–04, tuition was $18,700, and room and board costs were $6380. Bethel University tuition costs are lower than average for Minnesota private colleges and universities. Bethel University housing costs are set each spring for incoming freshmen and transfer students. Freshmen living on campus must purchase the three-meal-per-day basic meal plan; upperclass students have a variety of meal plans from which to choose. The actual cost of attending Bethel depends on the amount of financial aid a student receives.

Financial Aid

Bethel University strives to make it financially possible for every qualified student to attend. Each year, more than 90 percent of the students receive some kind of financial aid, including scholarships, grants, loans, and assistance in the form of on-campus employment. Students who wish to be considered for financial aid must first be admitted to the University and then submit both the Free Application for Federal Student Aid (FAFSA) and a Bethel University Financial Aid Application. Bethel's priority deadline is April 15 of each year. Students who have completed and mailed all necessary forms by this date receive first consideration.

Faculty

Nothing determines the quality of a university more than the people who teach there. Bethel professors combine strong academic credentials with a commitment to Jesus Christ. Bethel faculty members are known for their warmth and caring. It's not hard to receive personal attention, since there are only 16 students to every faculty member. Professors are very accessible to students during regular office hours as well as at other times. Of Bethel's 165 full-time faculty members, the majority have earned doctorates. The Bethel faculty is complemented by 87 part-time instructors.

Student Government

As active and integral parts of the Bethel community, the Bethel Student Association functions in a variety of strategic campus areas. In addition to representing student needs to the administration, they oversee student publications and campus social activities and provide a forum for influential student-faculty committees. Guiding the affairs of the Bethel Student Association, the Executive Board is composed of the president, the vice president, and 6 executive directors.

Admission Requirements

Bethel University seeks students who desire an education based on strong academics in a Christian environment. To be considered for admission, the student must graduate from an accredited high school, rank in the top 50 percent of his or her high school class, and meet minimum test score requirements (92 on the PSAT, 920 on the SAT I, or 21 on the ACT). Transcripts, two references, and commitment to Bethel's covenant are also required. Bethel recommends that students take 4 years of English, 3 years of mathematics, 3 years of science, and 2 years of social studies while in high school. Transfer students are welcome. On-campus interviews are not required but are strongly recommended.

Application and Information

Students wishing to apply for admission to Bethel must send the following: a completed Bethel application form with a $25 nonrefundable application fee; test scores from the PSAT, SAT I, or ACT; transcripts of all course work completed at the high school and college levels; and references from a pastor and a school official. Students considering Bethel should apply in the fall of their senior year. The Office of Admissions reviews applications twice each year. Early action decisions are made for students who complete applications by December 1. Bethel's final application decision date is March 1. Applications received or completed after March 1 are considered on a space-available basis.

For further information about specific Bethel programs and campus visit opportunities, students should contact:

Office of Admissions
Bethel University
3900 Bethel Drive
St. Paul, Minnesota 55112
Telephone: 651-638-6242
800-255-8706 Ext. 6242 (toll-free)
Fax: 651-635-1490
E-mail: bcoll-admit@bethel.edu
World Wide Web: http://www.bethel.edu

Bethel's Community Life Center.

BETHUNE-COOKMAN COLLEGE

DAYTONA BEACH, FLORIDA

The College

Bethune-Cookman College is a private, liberal arts, career-oriented, coeducational, residential institution, which operates on a semester calendar and is affiliated with the United Methodist Church. The College is a result of a merger between the Daytona Educational and Industrial Training School for Negro Girls (founded by Mary McLeod Bethune in 1904) and the Darnell Cookman Institute for Men (founded in 1872). It is accredited by the Commission on Colleges of the Southern Association of Colleges and Schools to award the bachelor's degree, and by the Florida State Department of Education, the University Senate of the United Methodist Church, the AMA Committee on Allied Health Education and Accreditation, the National Council for Accreditation of Teacher Education, and the National League for Nursing Accrediting Commission. The College is approved by the Florida State Board of Nursing Licensure.

High academic standards, curriculum flexibility, concern for the individual student, and an emphasis on a broad Christian way of life are trademarks of the institution. The 2,800 students at Bethune-Cookman College come from forty-three states and thirty-five international countries. The campus cultural and social activities include choirs, band, drama, student publications, radio broadcasting, clubs, and Greek letter organizations, as well as intramural and NCAA Division I-A and I-AA intercollegiate athletics.

Location

Bethune-Cookman College is located in the Atlantic coast city of Daytona Beach, Florida, amid a metropolitan area that has a population of more than 160,000. Its location on Doctor Mary McLeod Bethune Boulevard provides easy access to local business centers, churches, theaters, museums, beaches, recreational facilities, and bus and air terminals. The College is within 100 miles of the Kennedy Space Center, Walt Disney World/EPCOT Center, Sea World, Universal Studios, Marineland, and other such attractions.

Majors and Degrees

The Bachelor of Science degree is awarded in accounting, biology, business administration, business education, chemistry, computer information systems, computer science, criminal justice, elementary education, gerontology, hospitality management, international business, mathematics, medical technology, nursing, physical education, physics, psychology, specific learning disabilities, and varying exceptionalities. The Bachelor of Arts degree is awarded in church music, English, history, international studies, liberal studies, mass communications, modern languages, music, political science, religion and philosophy, social science education, and sociology. The majors in biology, chemistry, English, mathematics, modern languages, music, and physics can carry teacher certification. A dual-degree program in engineering is offered in cooperation with University of Florida, University of Central Florida, Florida Atlantic University, Florida A & M University, and Tuskegee University. Army and Air Force ROTC programs are offered in cooperation with Embry Riddle Aeronautical University in Daytona Beach.

Academic Programs

The academic program follows an educational core-concept approach. Student progress is monitored by the Division of General Studies. Sequences are required in biology, English, general psychology, mathematics, modern languages, physical education, physical science, religion, and social science. A developmental program seeks to provide courses and growth experiences that develop student competence in communications and mathematics skills for those needing remedial assistance. Academic support and reinforcement activities include individual conferences, periodic academic evaluation, and access to five laboratories for tutoring in reading, writing, speech, mathematics, science, and study skills. The Bethune-Cookman College Honors Program is designed to broaden intellectual horizons and to integrate various areas of knowledge, individualized learning, and independent research. Student Support Service programs are designed to improve student retention as well as academic and personal development. These programs, designed to increase successful matriculation in major fields of study, enrich the curriculum by reinforcing academic skills and course content necessary for success. A cooperative education program and other career-related field experiences are major components in several fields of study.

To receive a degree from Bethune-Cookman College, a student must complete a major in an academic field of study with a minimum of 124 semester hours of work with a minimum cumulative grade point average of 2.0. Upon recommendation of the instructor, a student exhibiting outstanding competence in a given course may receive credit by examination in lieu of taking the course.

Off-Campus Programs

The College operates Continuing Education Program sites in Florida in Belle Glade, Bradenton, Fort Pierce, Gainesville, Lake Wales, Sanford, and West Palm Beach. A branch campus is located in Spuds, Florida.

Academic Facilities

Facilities on the 60-acre campus include twelve classroom buildings, a student union building, an infirmary, nine dormitories, a gymnasium, an athletic weightroom, a library resource center, five administrative buildings, and a new 2,500-seat performing arts center. The library resource center houses an open-stack collection of more than 156,861 volumes, 41,914 microforms, 5,355 films and slides, 1,792 audiocassettes and videocassettes, 800 journals and magazine subscriptions, and a special collection of African-American and Methodist historical materials. The campus Learning Resource Center includes a nonprint media center, a graphics studio, and an ITV studio. The College operates an academic computer center system, with outlets in all classroom buildings. There is also a telecommunications satellite network for mass communications majors. All residence hall rooms are wired for Internet access.

Costs

For the 2003–04 academic year, the basic cost for tuition and fees was $10,106, and room and board were $6252. The approximate cost of books and supplies is $600 per year. Other expenditures for travel, amusement, and incidentals vary according to individual needs.

Financial Aid

The financial aid program includes competitive academic, athletic, band, and choir scholarships; work study awards; and federal and state grants and loans. Applications should be filed by March 1. Notification of awards is generally made in the spring. Applicants for federal and state loans, a grant-in-aid, or a work-study award must file the Free Application for Federal Student Aid (FAFSA).

Faculty

There are 132 full-time teaching faculty members, 53 percent of whom hold the doctoral degree. The student-faculty ratio is 17:1. The faculty members participate actively in all phases of college life.

Student Government

The Student Government Association (SGA) is the representative body for students. The SGA president is the student representative on the College Board of Trustees. There are student representatives on virtually every college committee.

Admission Requirements

There is a ten-year restriction on accepting previously earned credits. Students accepted with an A.A. degree and passing scores on the College Level Academic Skills Test (CLAST) are admitted to the upper level, but they must have earned a C or higher in English, mathematics, reading, and speech. A.A. degree holders without a CLAST score must take the CLAST examination on the next available date. If the student takes the examination and does not pass one or more of the subtests, he or she must enroll in the course which corresponds with the failed subtest. Passing scores on the CLAST are a graduation requirement for all students

Application and Information

The college operates on a two-semester plan with an additional seven-week summer session. Qualified applicants may register at the beginning of any term.

The closing date for students applying for admission for the fall semester is July 30 and November 30 for the spring semester. For more information and application forms, students should contact:

Admissions Office
Bethune-Cookman College
640 Doctor Mary McLeod Bethune Boulevard
Daytona Beach, Florida 32114
Telephone: 386-481-2600
800-448-0228 (toll-free)
E-mail: admissions@cookman.edu
World Wide Web: http://www.bethune.cookman.edu

BIOLA UNIVERSITY

LA MIRADA, CALIFORNIA

The University

Biola is a private Christian university established in 1908 in Los Angeles with a mission of biblically centered education, scholarship, and service to equip men and women in mind and character to impact the world for the Lord Jesus Christ. More than 4,593 students, who are among the most ethnically diverse body of any Christian college in the U.S., are challenged yearly by faculty and staff members to integrate their faith and learning pursuant to their academic and vocational goals. Biola is a member of the Council for Christian Colleges and Universities (CCCU), an organization consisting of 100 Christian institutions across the U.S.

Location

Biola University's 95-acre campus is located in La Mirada, 22 miles southeast of Los Angeles on the border of Orange County. Centrally located in southern California, Biola is just a short drive to both the beaches and the mountains. Hollywood, the entertainment capital of the world, is just 30 minutes away, and unlimited cultural experiences are available in Orange County and Los Angeles. Los Angeles is the home of the Natural History Museum, Hollywood Bowl, Staples Center, the Great Western Forum, and Dodger Stadium. Disneyland, Anaheim Stadium, and the Arrowhead Pond are a short drive south of Biola. Five major airports, including LAX and John Wayne, are within an hour's drive of the campus. For internships and career opportunities, there are numerous choices.

Majors and Degrees

The Bachelor of Arts and Bachelor of Science degrees are offered with majors in anthropology, art, Bible, biochemistry, biological sciences, business administration, Christian education, communication studies, communication disorders, computer science, education/liberal studies, English, history, human biology, humanities, intercultural studies, journalism, mathematics, music, nursing, philosophy, physical education, physical science, prelaw, psychology, radio-television-film, social science, sociology, and Spanish. A 3-2 engineering program is offered cooperatively with the University of Southern California.

In all, Biola offers 145 programs ranging from the B.A. to the Ph.D. at six schools that include the School of Arts and Sciences, Talbot School of Theology, Rosemead School of Psychology, the School of Business, the School of Continuing Studies, and the School of Intercultural Studies. All are regionally and professionally accredited and based on evangelical Christianity.

Academic Program

The academic year consists of two 15-week semesters. There are also two summer sessions for three and five weeks each plus a three-week interterm each January. As a fully accredited national university, Biola University seeks to instruct Christian men and women in order to produce graduates who are competent in their field of study, knowledgeable in biblical studies, and equipped to serve the Christian community and society at large.

Religious and convocation requirements include 30 hours of biblical studies, attendance at chapel three times a week, and participation in student ministry.

Off-Campus Programs

Biola offers study-abroad programs in China; London, England; Israel; Japan; and Korea. The University also participates in the CCCU programs in Australia; Central America (Costa Rica, Honduras); Egypt; England; the Middle East; Russia; Washington, D.C.; the Au Sable Institute; the Contemporary Music Center at Martha's Vineyard; the Los Angeles Film Institute; and the Colorado Springs Focus on the Family Institute. Each program has unique requirements for admission.

Biola's Organizational Leadership Degree (BOLD) program, in which students who are 25 years or older can complete their college degree in eighteen months, has extension campuses in La Mirada, Aliso Viejo, Laguna Hills (Orange County), Vista (San Diego County), Palm Desert, Thousand Oaks, Inglewood, and Chino, California. Admission requirements are unique to the program and include completion of a minimum of 50 transferable semester units from an accredited college.

Biola offers courses to teachers in Hong Kong as part of the Biola-RICE (Research Institute for Christian Education) agreement.

Academic Facilities

Biola's Library Resource Center currently subscribes to more than 1,200 print periodical titles and has access to more than 12,000 titles online. The library provides access to its holdings on SCROLL, the online public access catalog and circulation system, and an increasing number of CD-ROM index databases available for patron searching. This 98,000-square-foot, state-of-the-art resource center features 950 study stations, twenty-three group study rooms, twenty multimedia stations, and forty-eight online reference stations.

Additional facilities include a media center, an on-campus radio station, a TV/film studio, an art studio, an art gallery, and an outdoor pool. Access to the Internet may be found by way of computers in the residence halls as well as throughout the campus. E-mail, Internet research, World Wide Web browsing, word processing, desktop publishing, multimedia presentation, graphic arts design, and application programming may all be accomplished at the computer center and in Biola's computerized classrooms and labs. Resources include two computerized classrooms equipped with Windows NT and Macintosh computers, plus a fully equipped computer lab with more than fifty computers (Mac and PC). Scanners and high-speed black-and-white and color laser printers are also available in the lab. Students can connect to the Internet via Ethernet or AppleTalk in all residence halls or by using the computer lab equipment. Connection to the Internet is via a high-speed T1 line.

Costs

Biola University holds the belief that every student, regardless of financial status, should have the opportunity to make an investment in his or her tomorrow. Therefore, the University strives to keep the cost of a Biola education within the financial reach of students and their families. For 2003–04, Biola tuition was $19,564, room averaged $3207, and board for a twenty-meal plan was $2760.

Financial Aid

Biola offers a generous financial aid program, with $12 million in institutional funds devoted to undergraduates alone. In addition, hundreds of University students receive state and federal grants and scholarships. Eighty-three percent of Biola students receive some level of financial aid, with the average award being $8200.

Institutional scholarships include the Academic Scholarship ($2000 to $7000), the Community Service Scholarships ($2700), and Scholarships for Underrepresented Students of Ethnicity (SURGE; $4000 to $6500), all of which are renewable. Other aid options include departmental scholarships (for athletics, music, and communications), international scholarships, dependent scholarships (for families where the primary income is in Christian ministry), and church-matching scholarships. Excellent loan programs and on-campus work opportunities round out the aid packages of most Biola students.

All students are urged to apply for financial aid by March 2, which coincides with the California aid deadline. Applicants should complete the Free Application for Federal Student Aid (FAFSA) and Biola's one-page form, the University Aid Application. In addition, California residents should complete the state GPA verification form.

Faculty

The University's faculty members are mentors and role models in addition to professors. Three fourths of all faculty members have earned doctorates. There are 177 full-time and 117 part-time faculty members. Some have won awards as Fulbright and National Endowment for the Humanities scholars. The student-faculty ratio is 17:1.

Faculty members remain on the cutting edge of their fields by continuing their education as they teach students. Research grants provide professors the time and resources not only to publish in their discipline but also to participate in seminars with topics such as Christianity and science and postmodernism. At these seminars, they consider how to integrate their faith within their fields and broaden their knowledge of other areas. This experience is brought back to their classrooms for their students' benefit.

Student Government

The mission of Biola University's Associated Student Government is to represent the student body on an administrative level, giving ear to the students' voices, providing services, and facilitating events necessary to foster a Christ-centered community.

There are two facets to the Associated Student Government. The Executive Council, comprised of 14 senators, represents residential students and commuters. The Services Council, comprised of nine service boards that provide various services and programming for students. These service boards include Chapel Board, clubs, multicultural relations, intramurals, social board, international student association, the *Chimes* (Biola's student newspaper), the *Biolan* (the yearbook), and marketing and public relations.

With a staff of approximately 50 students and a budget of more than $350,000 annually, the Associated Student Government not only provides high-quality programming but also a multitude of student leadership opportunities each year.

Admission Requirements

Biola seeks students who want to make a difference with their lives and impact the world for Jesus Christ. Candidate selection is based on SAT I or ACT scores, high school transcripts, and school recommendations. In addition, each applicant must be an evangelical believer in the Christian faith, must submit a reference letter from a pastor, and must go through an interview process. Freshmen who entered Biola in fall 2002 had an average combined SAT I score of 1127 and an average GPA of 3.55.

Application and Information

The Office of Admissions is open from 8 a.m. to 5 p.m. on weekdays. To visit the campus or to request information, students can call or write:

Office of Admissions
Biola University
13800 Biola Avenue
La Mirada, California 90639-0001
Telephone: 800-0K-BIOLA (toll-free)
E-mail: admissions@biola.edu
World Wide Web: http://www.biola.edu/undergrad

Students on the campus of Biola University.

BIRMINGHAM–SOUTHERN COLLEGE

BIRMINGHAM, ALABAMA

The College

Birmingham-Southern College (BSC) was created through a merger of Southern University (established in 1856) and Birmingham College (established in 1898). Since 1959, when *Harper's Magazine* called it "one of the leading small colleges in the South," Birmingham-Southern continues to be recognized as one of the nation's outstanding liberal arts institutions. Birmingham-Southern is ranked in the top tier of national liberal arts colleges in *U.S. News & World Report's America's Best Colleges 2004. U.S. News & World Report* also ranked Birmingham-Southern College as one of the best values in higher education and one of the most efficient schools; *Money* ranked Birmingham-Southern as one of the 100 best college buys. The College is also recognized by the John Templeton Foundation's Honor Roll as one of 100 schools nationwide that emphasize character building as an integral part of the college experience; as one of the 100 best values in private colleges by *Kiplinger's Personal Finance Magazine;* as being among the 100 colleges worth considering, as compiled by *Washington Post* staff writer Jay Mathews; as one of America's best Christian colleges by Institutional Research and Evaluation, Inc.; and as one of the nation's top thirty colleges by the *Washington Times.*

Birmingham-Southern is one of only six Baccalaureate Colleges–Liberal Arts, as classified by the Carnegie Foundation for the Advancement of Teaching, to hold both AACSB International–The Association to Advance Collegiate Schools of Business accreditation and the designation of Phi Beta Kappa.

Each year, Birmingham-Southern ranks number one in Alabama and among the nation's best in percentage of all graduates accepted to medical, dental, or health career programs; the College also ranks high nationally in graduates accepted to law school.

Birmingham-Southern competes in NCAA Division I athletics and supports fourteen different sports. The College has more than seventy clubs and organizations and intramural sports. Its enrollment averages 550 men and 750 women.

At the graduate level, Birmingham-Southern offers a Master of Arts program in public and private management and a Master of Music degree.

Location

Located in rolling country on a 197-acre campus in western Birmingham, the College is just 3 miles via I-59 from the downtown business district. Birmingham, Alabama's largest city, has been honored by the U.S. Conference of Mayors as the "Most Livable City in America," and offers fine restaurants, museums, city and state parks, and theater. Its offerings are supplemented by the activities of four other Birmingham colleges. Birmingham's 17,000-seat Civic Center Coliseum is the setting for many outstanding cultural and athletic events.

Majors and Degrees

Birmingham-Southern offers the undergraduate degrees of Bachelor of Arts, Bachelor of Science, Bachelor of Music, Bachelor of Music Education, and Bachelor of Fine Arts. Departmental majors include accounting, art, art education, biology, business administration, chemistry, computer science, dance, economics, education, English, French, German, history, international studies, mathematics, music, music education, philosophy, physics, political science, psychology, religion, sociology, Spanish, and theater arts. Individualized and interdisciplinary majors are also available.

Academic Programs

The College operates on a 4-1-4 calendar. Thirty-six units are required for the bachelor's degree; these comprise 32 regular term units and 4 Interim Term units. The minimum residence requirement is two years. In addition to its traditional liberal arts programs, Birmingham-Southern offers a number of individualized learning opportunities to meet students' special needs and career goals. These are the Honors Program, the Mentor Program, independent study, the student internship program, individualized majors, and the Interim Term. The College emphasizes international opportunities for students through course offerings, visitors to campus, and international travel/study programs. Through the Associated Colleges of the South, the College offers international programs in England, Brazil, and Central Europe.

Credit is available through CLEP and Advanced Placement tests. Credit may also be earned through a College-approved internship program.

Birmingham-Southern offers several special programs, including a six-week Summer Scholars Term for high school juniors, a one-week Student Leaders in Service program, and a dual-enrollment program that enables high school seniors to take college-credit courses.

Off-Campus Programs

The College sponsors an internship program through which students may earn credit for actual work experience. Depending on their major, students may be assigned positions in business, government, industry, human services, or other preprofessional areas of interest. Students may also take part in a cooperative exchange program that enables them to take courses at the University of Alabama at Birmingham, Miles College, or Samford University. They may also participate in Army ROTC at the University of Alabama at Birmingham or Air Force ROTC at Samford University.

Academic Facilities

Birmingham-Southern College features several new facilities including the Norton Campus Center, the Striplin Physical Activities Center, and the $25-million Stephens Science Center. BSC is home to the Meyer Planetarium, the first public planetarium in Alabama. The only split-lift revolving stage in the country is housed in the College Theatre. Academic year 2002–03 marked the opening of six new fraternity houses on fraternity row and a major renovation to Daniel Men's Residence Hall. The newly renovated Neal and Anne Berte Humanities Center was dedicated in September 2003.

Costs

For 2003–04, the total cost of attendance (tuition, room and board, books, personal expenses, and travel) was $29,830 and the total cost for commuting students was $23,930. These figures include fees for auto registration, student activity fee, computer usage fee, and an estimate for all other incidentals.

Financial Aid

Birmingham-Southern feels strongly that well-qualified students should have an opportunity for a college education regardless of economic circumstances. Approximately 90 percent of the College's students receive financial aid of some kind. Scholarships and grants range from $1000 to full tuition and may be renewed annually. Each student requesting financial assistance must submit the Free Application for Federal Student Aid (FAFSA). With the exception of the College's competitive scholarship programs and the Alabama Student Grant, all financial assistance awarded through the Office of Student Financial Aid is based on a demonstrated need determined from the required forms. Preference is given to those students who file by the March 1 priority deadline. The average award for those students who demonstrated need for the 2003–04 academic year was more than $14,000. In addition to the need-based programs, Birmingham-Southern awards more than $1.5 million in merit-based scholarships through a scholarship competition held in March.

Faculty

The faculty is composed of 96 full-time and 25 part-time teaching members; approximately 92 percent hold a Ph.D. degree or the terminal degree in their field. In addition to teaching, the faculty's major responsibility is advising students. Faculty members are actively involved in cocurricular activities planned primarily for students, and all are assigned a limited number of student advisees. They work closely with these students in planning and developing individual programs to fulfill the students' career interests. The student-faculty ratio is 12:1, and no freshman English class has more than 16 students.

Student Government

The Student Government Association of the College is chartered to operate under a constitution developed by the students, faculty, and administration. Through a large measure of self-government, this organization helps provide a well-balanced intellectual, educational, and social cocurricular program for all students. The Honor Code makes each student responsible for upholding the social and academic standards of the College. Students serve on numerous College committees, including recruitment, curriculum, fund-raising, and governance task forces.

Admission Requirements

Approximately 350 freshmen are selected for admission on the basis of high school record, ACT or SAT I scores, academic courses attempted, an admission essay, an interview, and recommendations of school officials. Applicants are expected to have completed at least 16 units of course work, 12 of which must be in academic subjects. Four units of English and at least two units each of mathematics, history, science, and social sciences are required, and two units of a foreign language are recommended. Students are encouraged to take more than the minimum units required in academic subjects.

Although an interview is not required except in the case of early admission, each applicant is encouraged to visit the campus and talk with an admission counselor or the vice president for admission services.

Transfer applicants must have at least a C average (2.0 on a 4.0 scale) on a full schedule of courses acceptable to Birmingham-Southern and a status of good standing with a clear academic and social record from the last college attended. If the applicant has attended more than one college, his or her overall average at these schools must meet the minimum academic-year grade point average required at Birmingham-Southern. Transfer students may enroll at the beginning of any term.

Application and Information

The College has an admission priority date of January 15. After January 15, the College continues to consider applications on a rolling admission basis.

Preview Days are held in October and November.

Inquiries concerning admission should be addressed to:

Sheri S. Salmon
Associate Vice President for Admission Services
Birmingham-Southern College
900 Arkadelphia Road
Birmingham, Alabama 35254
Telephone: 205-226-4696
800-523-5793 (toll-free)
E-mail: admission@bsc.edu
World Wide Web: http://www.bsc.edu

A view of the campus at Birmingham-Southern College.

BLOOMFIELD COLLEGE

BLOOMFIELD, NEW JERSEY

The College

Founded in 1868, Bloomfield College (BC) is an independent, four-year, coeducational college that offers programs in the liberal arts and sciences, creative arts and technology, and professional studies, which include accounting, business administration, computer information systems, criminal justice, education, Internet technology, materials management, nursing, prechiropractic, and the sciences. Bloomfield is accredited by the Middle States Association of Colleges and Schools, and the nursing program is accredited by the Commission on Collegiate Nursing Education and the New Jersey Board of Nursing. The College is chartered by the state of New Jersey, and its academic programs are approved by the New Jersey Commission on Higher Education. The accounting program is a Registered Accounting Curriculum for Public Accountancy in the state of New Jersey and meets the state's educational requirements for candidates applying to sit for the CPA examination. The College is affiliated with the Presbyterian Church (U.S.A.) through the Synod of the Northeast and is a member of the Association of Presbyterian Colleges and Universities.

With more than thirty-five organizations to choose from, students have many opportunities to engage in cocurricular programs that enrich their educational experience. In addition to student government, activities include the Nursing Student Association, the Association of Latin American Students, the International Student Association, and a variety of departmental clubs and social organizations. Campus publications include *In Print,* the College yearbook, and *Common Ground,* the honors literary magazine. The College Center is the social and recreational focus of the College community. Meeting rooms, a snack bar, lounges, a new Internet-based gaming center, and the Office of Co-Curricular Programs are all located there. Also located in the College Center, the bookstore is a convenient place to buy textbooks, school supplies, gifts, clothes, snacks, and personal items.

Bloomfield College has a full program of intercollegiate and intramural sports and recreational activities. Men's intercollegiate sports are baseball, basketball, cross-country, and soccer. Women's intercollegiate sports are basketball, soccer, softball, and volleyball. Bloomfield College is a member of NCAA Division II as part of the Central Atlantic Collegiate Conference (CACC).

In addition to general on-campus housing, the College provides special residence halls for first-year students. "Theme" houses are also available on campus. Housing priority is given to first-year students and students who live beyond a reasonable commuting distance. A complete residence-life program provides academic, social, and recreational programs for resident students. The Center for Academic Development offers individual tutoring and group workshops to all students. Academic advising is ongoing, and students meet with their adviser before registering each semester. Other support services include the First Year Experience, Educational Opportunity Fund Program, personal counseling, career counseling and placement, women's services, and the College Health Service. An extensive English for Academic Purposes program is also offered.

Location

Located in Bloomfield, New Jersey, a suburban, residential community just 15 miles from New York City, the College attracts resident students from many geographic areas as well as commuter students from the New Jersey/New York metropolitan area. Bloomfield is accessible by bus, train, or car from northern New Jersey and from the boroughs of Manhattan, the Bronx, Staten Island, and Brooklyn as well as Rockland and Westchester counties in New York.

Majors and Degrees

Bloomfield College offers the Bachelor of Arts and Bachelor of Science degrees. Majors and their concentrations include accounting (professional accounting and general accounting), allied health technology (diagnostic medical sonography, nuclear medicine technology, respiratory care specialization, and vascular technology), biology (environmental studies, general biology, prechiropractic studies, prepodiatric studies, and preprofessional studies), business administration (with specializations in computer information systems, economics, finance, human resource management, human resource training, management, marketing, and materials management), chemistry (biochemistry and general chemistry), clinical laboratory sciences (cytotechnology, medical technology, and toxicology), computer information systems, creative arts and technology (animation, digital video, graphics for print and digital media, interactive multimedia and the World Wide Web, music technology, and theater), education (elementary/early childhood and secondary), English (communications, literature, video/television production, and writing), history, Internet technology, mathematics (applied mathematics), nursing, philosophy, political science (general, public administration, and public policy), psychology, religion, and sociology (criminal justice and general sociology).

Bloomfield College maintains a joint Bachelor of Science/Doctor of Chiropractic degree program with twelve accredited chiropractic colleges. Three versions of the prechiropractic program are offered, each preparing students for admission to colleges offering the Doctor of Chiropractic (D.C.) degree. (See Academic Program section below.) Bloomfield offers certificate programs in digital video, diversity training, industrial/organizational psychology and materials management. The Advanced Technology Institute offers vendor-authorized certification training for Microsoft, Cisco, CompTIA, Sun, and Check Point. Web Master training is also available.

Academic Program

Degree candidacy requires the successful completion of at least 33 course units; a full course unit is equivalent to 4 semester hours. A minimum of 16 course units must be completed at an advanced level. Four categories of courses are offered at the College: general education courses, distribution courses, specific major and major required courses, and elective courses. Course requirements for the degree vary among majors. The prechiropractic program is a sequence of courses preparing the student for study for the Doctor of Chiropractic (D.C.) degree. The student may either complete graduation requirements for a bachelor's degree or transfer from Bloomfield College directly into a D.C. program after three years. Other special programs available at Bloomfield include an RN/B.S.N. transfer program for registered nurses who already have a two-year degree; the

Educational Opportunity Fund Program, a state-funded program of educational and special services for disadvantaged students; English as a second language; an honors program; a circus program, under the auspices of the division of creative arts and technology, in which students join a performing troupe; Weekend College, a complete degree program for adults that is offered on weekends; and various internship programs.

The Bloomfield College academic calendar consists of fifteen-week fall and spring semesters and an optional summer session consisting of a fourteen-week term or two 7-week terms.

Off-Campus Programs

Bloomfield College is a member of the College Consortium for International Studies (CCIS). Students have the choice of more than seventy-five study-abroad programs in thirty countries around the world, for a semester, a summer, or a full academic year.

Academic Facilities

The newly renovated Talbott Hall is the new technology hub and media center of the College. The lower level houses classrooms featuring laptop and desktop computers, conference rooms, a general computer lab, and a comfortable lounge area. A Web-based radio station, which is part of the College's communications program, occupies the lower mezzanine area level.

The Bloomfield College library opened in fall 2000 and houses a collection of more than 64,000 titles, including subscriptions to more than 400 periodicals and 1,000 electronic journals, an up-to-date reference collection, and thousands of reels of microfilm and microfiche, as well as musical recordings and scores, films, and videotapes. The library is particularly proud of its extensive audiovisual collection. The library has an online card catalog, offers access to 15 databases on the Internet, and holds a variety of CD-ROMs in the humanities, nursing, and social sciences. *Cybrary*, an online newsletter about library issues and events, is published monthly and is available to all users. Library instruction and research assistance make the library a complete learning center. The library is open Monday through Friday from 7:30 a.m. to 11 p.m., Saturday from 7:30 a.m. to 7 p.m., and Sunday from 4 p.m. to 11 p.m. The library also houses the Media Center, which consists of three electronic classrooms, a distance learning room, and a screening room.

Academic computing facilities consist of four laboratories in the Science Building, with more than seventy computers. The library houses six laboratories with more than 130 computers, including the Pollack Computer Center. All campus computers are networked, and all computers were updated in 2003. The College has a campuswide Microsoft licensing agreement as well as popular database and statistics packages and programming languages and packages used by specific disciplines such as biology, mathematics, and nursing. Graphics and desktop publishing packages are also available. Technical support is available, and laptops may be rented through the Media Center.

Costs

Tuition in 2003–04 for full-time students was $12,900 per year. Tuition for part-time students was $1300 per course. Room and board for resident students were $6150 per year. Fees total approximately $200.

Financial Aid

In 2002–03, Bloomfield College students received approximately $16 million in scholarships and financial aid, with more than 90 percent of the full-time day student population receiving some form of financial assistance. Academic scholarships are administered by the Office of Admission; athletic scholarships are administered by the athletics department. College, state, and federal programs, such as grants, loans, and work-study, are administered by the Financial Aid Office.

Faculty

A highly qualified and diverse faculty instructs more than 1,900 students of all ages in day, evening, and weekend sessions, with a student-faculty ratio of 14:1. Approximately 65 percent of the full-time faculty members have earned doctorates or terminal degrees.

Student Government

The Bloomfield College Day Student Government represents registered day students, all organized student groups and clubs, and the College's academic divisions. It also serves as a vehicle of communication for student concerns and interests. The Bloomfield College Evening/Weekend Student Government provides a means of communication among evening students, faculty members, and members of the administration and assists the College in meeting the educational needs of the evening student. The administrative staff and the College faculty serve as advisers to all student government activities and enterprises.

Admission Requirements

Bloomfield College admits qualified applicants who demonstrate motivation, desire, and the potential to benefit from and contribute to programs of study in the liberal arts and sciences, creative arts and technology, and professional studies. Applications are accepted throughout the year on a rolling basis, and applicants are notified within one week of the College's receipt of required materials. Once admitted, students are placed according to their academic preparation and achievement. The College's mission is to prepare students to attain academic, personal, and professional excellence in a multicultural and global society. Admission is open to all qualified students without regard to race, color, creed, religion, national or ethnic origin, sex, age, or physical disability. The College welcomes applications from high school seniors, transfer students, and adult students returning to school.

Application and Information

All applicants are encouraged to visit the College to discuss their academic and career plans with an admission counselor. Applicants may also spend a day on campus attending classes and talking with students, faculty members, and administrators about academic programs and student activities as well as the issues of admission and financial assistance. Recommended application deadlines are April 15 for the fall semester and December 15 for the spring semester. Applications received after these dates are considered on a space-available basis. Students may apply online at http://www.bloomfield.edu/admissions. For further information, students should contact:

Lourdes Mangual de Delgado
Vice President for Enrollment Management
and Dean of Admission
Bloomfield College
One Park Place
Bloomfield, New Jersey 07003
Telephone: 973-748-9000 Ext. 230
800-848-4555 (toll-free)
Fax: 973-748-0916
E-mail: admission@bloomfield.edu
World Wide Web: http://www.bloomfield.edu

BLUFFTON COLLEGE
BLUFFTON, OHIO

The College

Bluffton College is a fully accredited, four-year Christian liberal arts college in northwestern Ohio. Founded in 1899 by regional leaders of the General Conference Mennonite Church, it is today affiliated with the Mennonite Church USA. Shaped by the historic peace church tradition and coupled with its desire for excellence in all programs, Bluffton College seeks to prepare students of all backgrounds for life as well as vocation, for responsible citizenship, for service to all peoples, and ultimately for the purposes of God's universal kingdom.

More than 1,100 students from twenty states and eighteen countries study at Bluffton College, which is accredited by the North Central Association of Colleges and Schools (30 North LaSalle Street, Suite 2400, Chicago, Illinois 60602; 800-621-7440, toll-free). The College continues to receive national recognition in *Barron's Best Buys in College Education* for providing outstanding quality at a reasonable price. Bluffton is one of only a handful of Ohio colleges to be included in the prestigious *John Templeton Foundation Honor Roll of Character-Building Colleges.*

The student life program is rich with opportunities for personal and spiritual growth. Weekly chapel services and biweekly Sunday morning worship services provide a community context for joint worship. Examples of the many groups in which students participate include BASIC (Brothers And Sisters In Christ), Diakonia (Christian service/outreach groups), Habitat for Humanity, and PALS Drug Awareness programs. The Honor System, practiced in all classes and throughout campus life, promotes honest, open communication between all members of the campus community.

Students participate in many organizations and activities, including vocal and instrumental music, departmental and preprofessional clubs, student newspaper, student government, and many others. As a member of the NCAA Division III and the Heartland Collegiate Athletic Conference, Bluffton fields varsity athletic teams for both men and women. Men's sports include baseball, basketball, cross-country, football, golf, soccer, tennis, and track. Varsity teams for women include basketball, cross-country, golf, soccer, softball, tennis, track, and volleyball. Bluffton is the first NCAA Division III college in the nation to be selected for the NCAA Life Skills program, which helps prepare student athletes for life after college.

Residence life is integral to the campus community. All students are required to live in campus housing unless they are married or commuting from home. No self-selective fraternities or sororities are permitted, and students are expected to adhere to campus standards of conduct, which prohibit the use of tobacco, alcohol, and drugs. A satisfaction guarantee is offered to new residential students.

In addition to its undergraduate degrees, Bluffton offers a Master of Arts in Education and a Master of Organizational Management.

Location

Bluffton College is located just off Interstate 75, midway between Lima and Findlay, Ohio, in the Allen County village of Bluffton (population 3,900). Several restaurants and a movie theater are within walking distance of campus, and easy access to I-75 provides many additional opportunities in Findlay, Lima, Toledo, Dayton, and Columbus.

The campus is situated on 60 beautifully wooded acres and is adjacent to the 130-acre Bluffton College Nature Preserve.

Majors and Degrees

Bluffton College offers Bachelor of Arts degrees. Bachelor's degrees are available in accounting; adolescent/young adult, multiage, and vocational education; apparel/textiles merchandising and design; art; biology; business administration; chemistry; child development; communication; computer science; criminal justice; dietetics; early childhood education; economics; English; family and consumer sciences; food and nutrition–dietetics; food and nutrition–wellness, health, physical education, and recreation (HPER); history; information systems; information technology; intervention specialist studies (special education); mathematics; middle childhood education; music; music education; physics; premedicine; psychology; recreation management; religion; social studies; social work; sociology; Spanish; Spanish/economics; sport management; writing; and youth ministries and recreation. In addition, a number of minors, preprofessional programs, and special programs are available, including graphic design, prelaw, peace and conflict studies, TESOL studies, women's studies, and self-designed majors.

Academic Program

The Bluffton College curriculum is centered on a liberal arts and sciences general education program. The strength of this program lies in the many integrated courses in social science, humanities, fine arts, and natural sciences that build upon one another as students advance toward earning their degree. Courses in Bible and theology, an integrated cross-cultural course, and a capstone course titled Christian Values in a Global Community complete the general education program. Key components of the general education curriculum include the First Year Seminar for new students and the cross-cultural requirement. Students seeking a bachelor's degree must complete a minimum of 122 semester hours of academic work and maintain a minimum overall grade point average of 2.0.

Off-Campus Programs

Bluffton College offers several semester-long international and cross-cultural opportunities. Current programs include study in Central America, Mexico, Northern Ireland, and Vietnam. Bluffton is also a member of the Council for Christian Colleges and Universities, which offers study programs at various U.S. locations, including Washington, D.C., as well as international programs in the Middle East, Russia, and Central America. Many Bluffton students participate in short-term off-campus projects with organizations such as Habitat for Humanity, Witness for Peace, and the Urban Life Center in Chicago. In addition, Bluffton students may complete up to four supervised independent study courses, which may be used for off-campus study.

Academic Facilities

The Musselman Library, a 1930 building of Georgian colonial architecture, was the gift of Mr. and Mrs. C. H. Musselman. It holds approximately 150,000 volumes, 116,000 microfilm units, approximately 4,000 current periodicals, and more than 350 CD-ROMs. The library has about 4,500 maps and receives many important U.S. government publications as a selective depository library. The library is a member of both the OPAL (Ohio Private Academic Libraries) and the OhioLINK consortia. Through OhioLINK, Bluffton College students and faculty and staff members have access to more than 24 million library items held at more than seventy college and university libraries throughout the state, to more than 60 separate databases, and to hundreds of full-text periodicals.

One of the newest facilities on campus is the Centennial Hall academic center. The academic center is a multilevel building at the center of the campus and contains state-of-the-art computer facilities, a new media center, technology-enhanced classrooms, and faculty offices.

Completed in 1991, the Sauder Visual Arts Center contains an art gallery and classroom and offers studio facilities for printing, painting, drawing, sculpture, ceramics, woodworking, welding, and photography. Shoker Science Center is a unique underground science facility that houses integrated laboratories for all the sciences, a science library, and instructional computers. Historic College Hall serves as the main administrative building. Marbeck Center, with its new Bob's Place gathering area, is the student union.

Founders Hall is a complete physical education facility, containing a main gymnasium, a newly renovated auxiliary gymnasium, and a weight room. Other recent additions to campus include Salzman Stadium and Neufeld Hall, a suite-style residence hall for 109 students.

The Al and Marie Yoder Recital Hall provides a state-of-the-art performance facility for student recitals and guest artists. Weekly forums and chapel services are also held in Yoder Hall.

Primary student computer access is provided through the microcomputer center located in Centennial Hall. All students may have e-mail addresses, and Internet access is provided in the lab. In addition, computers are located in residence halls, academic departments, and other locations on campus. All residence halls are equipped for students who wish to bring their own computer.

Costs

Tuition for the 2003–04 school year (based on 24 to 34 semester hours per year) was $17,260. Board was $3272 and room was $2758, for a total of $23,290. There is also a $400 technology fee. Books and personal expenses are additional.

Financial Aid

Nearly 100 percent of Bluffton College students receive some form of financial aid. Some awards are based solely on financial need, such as the Bluffton College Grant, while others are tied to academic achievement or demonstrated leadership and service to others. Scholarships and grants unique to Bluffton include the Presidential Scholarship Competition; the Academic Honors Scholarship; the Academic Merit Scholarship; the Tuition Equalization Scholarship Program, for students scoring at least 23 on the ACT or 1050 on the SAT I and ranking in the top 25 percent of their class or achieving at least a 3.0 grade point average; the Bluffton College Incentive Scholarship, for students with at least a 2.8 grade point average and 21 on the ACT or 970 on the SAT I; Leadership/Service Grants, which are available to students who demonstrate significant contributions outside the classroom in school, church, and community activities; and Church Matching Scholarships to students whose church has awarded them a scholarship to attend Bluffton. Additional College awards include scholarships for music and art and need-based grants to dependents of ministers and those serving in foreign missions. The Learn and Earn program provides an opportunity for many students to work on campus to help with expenses and gain valuable work experience.

Faculty

A high-quality program depends on a superior faculty. Students at Bluffton are taught by 64 full-time faculty members and 37 part-time faculty members. More than 70 percent of the full-time faculty members have earned the doctorate or appropriate terminal degree, and all faculty members teach on a regular basis. Many faculty members continue to research and write yet remain committed to teaching. The faculty members are very approachable and work together with students to create a unique learning environment based on mutual trust and respect.

Student Government

A democratic atmosphere prevails in the Bluffton College campus community. The Student Senate is a very important part of the campus community and actively represents the interests of the student body to the administration. Composed of students elected from each of the four classes, the Senate has primary responsibility in the areas of cocurricular activities. Hall associations are organized for the purpose of self-government and social activities.

Admission Requirements

Requirements for admission to the first-year class include graduation from a secondary school or a GED certificate; satisfactory secondary school work, with preference given to students ranking in the top half of their class and who have taken the recommended secondary preparation of 4 units of English, 3 units of mathematics, and 3 units each of social sciences, science, and a foreign language; and satisfactory performance on either the ACT or SAT I. Also considered are participation in cocurricular activities, moral character, purpose for college study, and recommendations.

Application and Information

Application for admission should be made at the end of the junior year or early in the senior year of high school. The deadline for submitting the application for the fall term is May 31. For all other terms the deadline is fifteen days prior to the intended date of enrollment.

Applicants must complete and return the application with a $20 fee along with recommendations from the school guidance counselor and a teacher, a high school transcript, and scores from either the ACT or the SAT I. A personal campus visit and interview are strongly encouraged.

The Office of Admissions operates on a rolling basis and makes its decision and notifies the applicant soon after receiving the required items. Students wishing to receive additional information may contact:

Office of Admissions
Bluffton College
280 West College Avenue
Bluffton, Ohio 45817-1196
Telephone: 419-358-3257
800-488-3257 (toll-free)
Fax: 419-358-3081
E-mail: admissions@bluffton.edu
World Wide Web: http://www.bluffton.edu

Students enjoy Bluffton College's wooded campus.

THE BOSTON ARCHITECTURAL CENTER

College of Architecture
College of Interior Design
BOSTON, MASSACHUSETTS

The School

The Boston Architectural Center (BAC) has roots that can be traced to 1889, when the Boston Architectural Club established a formal school of architecture fashioned after the atelier teaching method. The atelier idea was practical: students would learn their profession by working for and being mentored by an architect. Today, the architecture and interior design programs at the BAC still offer this unique learning mode that integrates both academic study and professional experience. Most degree students work in the design profession during the day and attend classes at night, which allows students to gain professional training in their field while attending school. The BAC faculty consists of respected professionals from design firms in the Boston area, many of whom are at the college on a volunteer basis. This special relationship between the college and the profession allows the BAC to offer an exceptional education and maintain an affordable tuition. The fusion of education and practice provides BAC graduates with a solid preparation for a career in design, a professional network, and the most direct route to a professional license. Prior to graduation, architecture students can complete the intern requirements for NCARB (National Council of Architectural Registration Boards) licensing. Interior design students can fulfill some of the intern requirements for NCIDQ (National Council for Interior Design Qualification) certification.

The BAC is a private college that awards bachelor's and master's degrees in both architecture and interior design. The college is accredited by the New England Association of Schools and Colleges, and the architecture programs are accredited by the National Architectural Accreditation Board (NAAB). The interior design programs are accredited by the Foundation for Interior Design Education Research (FIDER) accreditation.

Location

Located in Boston's historic Back Bay, the BAC is close to many cultural and educational institutions and is easily accessible by public transportation. The college occupies three buildings on Newbury Street, known for its abundance of fine restaurants, shops, and art galleries. Within walking distance of the BAC are Symphony Hall, Fenway Park, The Museum of Fine Arts, the Isabella Stewart Gardner Museum, and Boston's Public Garden. Boston is a livable community that is rich in diversity and offers entertainment suitable to a variety of tastes.

Majors and Degrees

BAC awards bachelor's and master's degrees in architecture and interior design. In fall 2004, BAC will offer a Bachelor of Design Studies degree. Students wishing to complete professional studies at the master's level, but who come to the BAC without a prior bachelor's degree, may complete this new degree and then continue in BAC's Master of Architecture program. Concentrations will include architectural technology, design computing, and sustainable design. New programs in design studies and landscape architecture are scheduled to begin in 2004 and 2005, respectively.

Academic Programs

Like the careers of architecture and interior design, the BAC degree programs are demanding, rewarding, and multidisciplinary. Both programs combine classroom and professional learning to unite theory and practice. To graduate, a B.Arch. student must earn 124.5 academic credits and 54 practice credits; a student working toward a bachelor's in interior design must earn 118 academic credits and 40 practice credits. It is possible to complete the program in five years (interior design) or seven years (architecture). The BAC follows the traditional semester calendar, and a range of classes is offered in the eight-week summer session.

During the day, most students are employed in paid professional positions to fulfill the practice component of the degree requirement. BAC students enlist their supervisors as mentors, and together they endorse a statement of professional goals and objectives. Practice skill levels range from entry-level clerical support to design and project management. Practice credits, which are earned through contract learning as approved by the American Council on Education, may be completed in approximately two to three years of full-time work. After completion of the practice curriculum degree requirement, work credit may be applied to the NCARB intern requirement and the NCIDQ intern requirement. During the evening, most students participate in the academic portion of the curriculum, which consists of courses in history and theory, visual studies, technology and management, the arts and sciences, and design studios. At the heart of these studies is the design studio sequence. Instead of using terms such as freshman and sophomore, BAC student status is defined by the studio level.

Since fall 2002, the college has been offering new students with little, if any, academic and experiential background in design the opportunity to enroll in a primarily daytime, academic-only program for the first year. Students begin the concurrent curriculum, academic and practice, at the beginning of their second year at BAC. The Academic-Only First-Year Program includes course work in drawing, design, CAD, and other professional and liberal arts courses. Students benefit by shortening the length of their study by a semester, by gaining important skills and confidence in a concentrated period of time, and by entering practice at a more advanced level.

The academic portion of the curriculum is divided into three segments. In Segment I, or Foundation, architecture and interior design students participate in similar course work. Foundation studios focus on basic design principles and are supported by visual studies and CAD courses. Other Foundation classes focus on design history, construction technology, ethical issues in design practice, computer use, and structural systems. About half of the general education classes are completed in Segment I, including humanities, mathematics, physics, and writing. Rounding off the Foundation studies, students participate in a sketch problem, a 12-hour design charette. Segment I concludes with a portfolio review, which a student must pass before progressing to the next level of design studios. The two degree programs separate to focus on their respective disciplines via Segment II. Architecture design studios emphasize building design but also cover a wide range of topics, including urban design and the theoretical issues of form-making and design study. Interior design studios focus on the creation of meaningful interior space through layout and form, color, light, and finish and explore the challenges associated with institutional, commercial, retail, and residential environments. Segment II studios for both programs are complemented by advanced courses in technology and management, history and theory, arts and sciences, and visual studies. Segment II includes three sketch problems and concludes with a portfolio review.

Segment III begins with advanced design studios and professional electives related to the student's area of concentration. The final phase of Segment III is Thesis, a two-semester project conducted with the counsel of a thesis adviser and a panel of experts. Students conceptualize and frame their own Thesis design project, which not only highlights each student's personal design style but also unites the skills, education, and experience gained through both academic and practical learning. The final presentation of this rigorous exploration of design issues is an actual structure or interior. Progression through the BAC programs is measured by educational progress standards of the academic and practice curriculum, minimum credit requirements, and quantitative grade point average requirements. Students' work is qualitatively evaluated through a series of portfolio and progress reviews. Portfolios are evaluated on the basis of demonstrated growth and progress as well as the ability to synthesize learning from all educational settings and integrate that learning into design work.

Off-Campus Programs

Through the Pro-Arts Consortium, BAC students have the opportunity to register for one course per semester at one of the five nearby art and design schools, including Berklee School of Music, Boston Conservatory, Emerson College, Massachusetts College of Art, and the School of the Museum of Fine Arts. Students also have borrowing privileges at the libraries of all Pro-Arts institutions. The BAC and the Art Institute of Boston have a cross-registration agreement that includes a large selection of courses. The cost of both arrangements is covered by BAC tuition. BAC students may participate in a number of study trips offered periodically throughout the academic year. Recent destinations have included Havana, Cuba; Montreal, Canada; Paris, France; and Charleston, South Carolina.

Academic Facilities

The BAC Library houses an impressive collection of 25,000 books and 120 periodicals. Resources focus on architecture, interior design, urban planning, energy conservation, and architectural history. BAC also maintains a slide library, which contains approximately 40,000 architecture and interior design images that survey historical and contemporary designs. The Interior Design Materials Library houses a collection of reference materials that pertain to interior products and current samples of finishes, furniture, lighting equipment, and construction materials. Students make use of the Materials Library for research, specification, and actual samples.

Fully equipped computer facilities support an array of design-related applications. The facilities support several CAD applications, for both two-dimensional and three-dimensional work; modeling and rendering applications; desktop publishing; multimedia production; and Web development software. Word processing and spreadsheet software, as well as unrestricted high-speed Internet access, are also available. Additional equipment includes large-format plotters, scanners, color and black and white laser printers, and a laser cutter.

Media Services offers a wide range of audiovisual support. Equipment such as slide, overhead, and opaque projectors and videotape and DVD decks is available. Students also have access to a videotape library, photography studio, copy stand, and extensive digital photography capabilities. The BAC Woodshop contains hand and power tools, work benches, and a supply of wood stock suitable for small projects. Classes related to woodworking design are offered in this 700-square-foot facility.

Costs

For the 2004–05 academic year, BAC tuition is $4100 per semester for bachelor's students; tuition for undergraduate students participating in the Academic-Only First-Year Program is $5494 per semester. Additional administrative fees may apply. All students must pay a $10 student government fee. Massachusetts state law requires that all full-time students be covered by a qualifying health plan. In the case that a student does not already have coverage, a comprehensive health insurance package is available through the BAC at an additional cost.

Financial Aid

The BAC provides both institutional and federal or state-funded assistance to qualified students who demonstrate financial need. Sources of aid include federally funded subsidized loans and federal, state, and institutional grants and scholarships. Tuition, fees, food, housing, books, supplies, transportation, and personal costs are taken into account to determine need. Institutional aid is available to qualified students who have completed one semester. Numerous design scholarships and awards are also available.

Faculty

The academic faculty of the BAC consists of 275 dedicated practitioners of the design professions. Approximately 90 percent of the faculty members hold advanced or professional degrees. Students benefit from a tutorial relationship with instructors because of small class size. The overall student-faculty ratio is approximately 10:1 in lecture classes and 6:1 in design studios.

Also unique to the BAC is the Practice Curriculum Faculty, a group of dedicated architects and interior designers who counsel students on a one-to-one basis. Their function is to review students' progress through the practice component and assess their professional development. This personal advising nurtures the mentoring relationship that exists between BAC students and the profession.

Student Government

All full-time degree students are members of Atelier, the BAC student organization. Atelier's primary purposes are to expand students' educational opportunities through student-initiated activities, advocate concerns and interests of students to the administration of the school, and assist students in achieving their professional goals. Atelier holds the charter for the Boston region AIAS (American Institute of Architecture Students) and organizes social events and exhibits of art and student work. Officers of Atelier are voting members of the BAC Board of Directors and are represented on each of its committees.

All interior design students participate in the Interior Design Student Organization (IDSO). The IDSO develops and coordinates special events such as lectures and exhibits and focuses on issues that explore the students' interests in the design field.

Admission Requirements

The BAC remains dedicated to its founders' goal of allowing all who are interested to pursue a design education. Students may enter upon completion of high school or the equivalent. An official high school transcript or GED certificate, a complete application, and an application fee are the only admission requirements. Standardized test scores are not required. The BAC is restricted in its ability to admit international students and is only admitting international students at the master's level at this time.

Applicants interested in transferring academic credit from other institutions must submit official transcripts, copies of course descriptions, and a BAC Transfer of Academic Credit application. Although a portfolio is not required for admission, one that demonstrates fine arts and design ability can be submitted for possible advanced standing in the design studio sequence.

Application and Information

Applications are reviewed and letters of admission are issued on a rolling basis. Students are admitted to the entering class of their choice on a space availability basis. It is strongly suggested that students submit their applications to the BAC at least six months prior to the desired entering semester.

Admission Office
Boston Architectural Center
320 Newbury Street
Boston, Massachusetts 02115
Telephone: 617-585-0123
Fax: 617-585-0121
E-mail: admissions@the-bac.edu
World Wide Web: http://www.the-bac.edu

BOSTON COLLEGE

CHESTNUT HILL, MASSACHUSETTS

The University

Boston College (BC) was founded in 1863 by the Jesuits to serve the sons of Boston's Irish immigrants. Today a coeducational university on more than 200 acres in Chestnut Hill, BC may seem a world apart from the small school in the crowded heart of Boston that was its first home. Through more than fourteen decades of growth and change, however, BC has held fast to the Jesuit ideals that inspired its founders. A Jesuit education today, as a century ago, is grounded in the liberal arts and in a commitment to the service of others.

As the needs of its student body have grown, so have the university's offerings: twelve schools, colleges, and institutes now offer eleven degree programs and two certificate programs. Undergraduates may enroll in the College of Arts and Sciences, the Wallace E. Carroll School of Management, the Connell School of Nursing, or the Lynch School of Education.

BC's more than 8,900 undergraduates come from many backgrounds. The university draws from all fifty states and nearly 100 countries. Students' religious and cultural backgrounds are similarly diverse. Today, the university's AHANA (African-American, Hispanic, Asian, and Native American) and international students make up nearly 25 percent of the undergraduate student body.

In today's complex and increasingly diverse world, the university believes that the best education is one that broadens a student's capacity to reason, to think, and to make critical judgments in a wide range of areas. Thus, each BC student fulfills a core of liberal arts courses from which he or she can pursue degrees in more than fifty areas of study and choose from more than 1,400 class sections throughout the university.

According to several recent national publications, BC is in the top tier of the nation's colleges and universities. The foundation for that achievement is the university's scholars and researchers—645 full-time professionals who make up the faculty. The kinship between teachers and students is one of the hallmarks of a BC education; that relationship is nurtured by a student-teacher ratio of 14:1. The median class size at the university is 23 students.

At BC, learning continues beyond the classroom in more than 200 student-run organizations. These include student government, honor societies, language and cultural organizations, performance ensembles, political groups, preprofessional clubs, publications, and service organizations. BC also sponsors fourteen varsity teams for men and seventeen for women, all of which compete at the NCAA Division I level. The university also supports seventeen club and twenty intramural sports.

Location

Located in the Chestnut Hill section of Newton, BC sits on the doorstep of one of America's great cities, a center of culture and education for more than three centuries. It is an energetic, cosmopolitan city that draws life and enthusiasm from the more than 200,000 college students in residence during the academic year. Located just 6 miles from downtown Boston and with easy access to the city via the trolley system that stops at the foot of the campus, BC offers the best of both worlds: a scenic suburban setting neighboring an exciting metropolitan center.

Majors and Degrees

The College of Arts and Sciences (A&S) is the oldest and largest of the four undergraduate schools at BC. A&S students must complete thirty-eight 1-semester courses, thirty-two of which are in A&S departments. The normal course load is five courses per semester for the first three years and four courses per semester during the senior year. The undergraduate curriculum includes the university Core Curriculum and ten to twelve courses in the major field, with the remainder of courses chosen as electives. A&S offers degrees in the following areas: art history, biochemistry, biology, chemistry, classical studies, communication, computer science, economics, English, environmental geosciences, film studies, French, geology and geophysics, Germanic studies, Hispanic studies, history, international studies, Italian, linguistics, mathematics, music, philosophy, physics, political science, psychology, Russian, Slavic studies, sociology, studio art, theater, and theology. Preprofessional advisement is also available in medical, dental, veterinary, and legal programs. Students can also select from fifteen interdisciplinary programs.

The Carroll School of Management educates students to be leaders in business and industry and in public agencies, educational institutions, and service organizations. The Carroll School offers concentrations in accounting and information technology, computer science, economics, finance, general management, management information systems, marketing, operations and technology, and organization studies and human resource management, placing special emphasis on ethical management and international management.

The Lynch School of Education prepares students for education and human services professions. Programs provide a general education, professional preparation, and specialized education in the major field. Fieldwork in area schools is closely linked to course work in each specialization. The Lynch School awards degrees upon completion of thirty-eight courses, including the University Core, a major field of study in education, and a second major in a subject field or an interdisciplinary area in A&S that complements the student's program. Areas of specialization include early childhood education, elementary education, human development, secondary education, and a minor in special needs education.

The Connell School of Nursing offers a four-year program of study leading to a Bachelor of Science degree. The three major components to the curriculum are nursing major courses, electives, and the required University Core. In all courses, principles of wellness, illness, rehabilitation, and health maintenance serve as a theoretical basis in preparing students for professional nursing practice. Nursing courses include traditional classes, simulated and audiovisual laboratory activities on campus, and clinical learning activities in health-care settings.

Academic Programs

Every BC education is centered on a core curriculum—a set of required courses. BC offers a core curriculum because it believes in the unity of knowledge. While the core, which is continually reviewed by a committee of faculty members, varies somewhat by school, its common elements include literature, natural science, writing, philosophy, theology, social science, modern European history, mathematics, fine arts, and the study of a non-European culture.

There are a wide variety of extraordinary academic programs that BC students can participate in to enhance their educational experience. They include, among others, honors programs within each of the university's four undergraduate schools, Undergraduate Faculty Research Fellows, the Scholar of the College, PULSE, and Perspectives on Western Culture.

Off-Campus Programs

BC encourages all students to take part in internship programs. More than 70 percent of BC undergraduates participate in at least one internship during their college years. Internships can be paid or unpaid and may take place during the academic year or the summer; some carry academic credit.

BC students may take on the challenge of international study in one of 77 programs administered by BC at universities in more than thirty countries. BC students who study abroad typically do so in their junior year, but there is also a range of full-year and summer-abroad opportunities. The Office of International Programs helps students with program selection and applications and maintains a library of reference books and professional evaluations of international study programs.

Academic Facilities

BC's eight libraries contain 2.3 million printed volumes, more than 3.9 million items in microform, approximately 207,500 government documents, 6,735-linear feet of manuscripts, and a wide collection of films and archival items. The resources of the library system range from some of Europe's earliest printed books to hundreds of computerized databases. Students with personal computers have dorm-room access to these databases as well as to Quest and other library information sources through Agora, the campus information network.

Research laboratories in the state-of-the-art science facilities have been specially designed to accommodate the advanced instrumentation required for modern science and to provide flexibility for accommodating new equipment. The recent $85-million expansion to the Higgins Biology and Physics Center was carefully designed to place classrooms, laboratories, computer facilities, and office space in proximity and to facilitate interaction among faculty members, researchers, and students. In addition to the Center's seventeen new teaching laboratories, special working labs are designed and outfitted for research and teaching in the fields of biology and physics.

Costs

Tuition for the 2004–05 academic year is $28,940. The freshman room rate is $5970. The board plan, which is required for all resident freshmen, is $3650. Freshman mandatory fees, which include a charge for on-campus orientation, total $791.

Financial Aid

BC maintains a financial aid program to assist deserving and qualified students who might otherwise not be able to attend the university. Boston College is committed to providing funds to meet the full demonstrated need of every admitted student who applies for financial aid. Overall, 60 percent of students receive some form of financial aid. The average need-based award in 2003–04 was more than $20,000. Assistance for freshmen alone included more than $12.5 million in need-based grants. The university offers financial aid to students based on need as demonstrated by completion of the College Scholarship Service's Financial Aid PROFILE and the Free Application for Federal Student Aid (FAFSA). All requirements and deadlines and complete instructions are available in BC admission literature. An application for financial aid in no way affects a decision on admission.

Each year, BC chooses 15 incoming freshmen as Presidential Scholars to receive merit-based, full-tuition scholarships. Students are selected from all candidates who apply through the early action program.

Faculty

BC has 645 full-time faculty members. Of these faculty members, 97 percent hold doctoral degrees. The 110 Jesuits living on the BC campus make up one of the largest Apostolic Jesuit communities in the world. Nearly half of these members are active in the university's administration and teaching.

Student Government

The Undergraduate Government of Boston College (UGBC), formed in 1968, is led by the president and vice president, who are elected in the spring of each year by the entire student body. UGBC's goal is to serve the students by providing services and opportunities and by representing them in the best manner possible to the university community. To accomplish this goal, UGBC provides many educational, social, and cultural programs, such as concerts, lectures, roundtables, and other programs.

Admission Requirements

The undergraduate admission staff pays particular attention to students who have done well in a demanding college-preparatory curriculum, including Advanced Placement (AP) and honors courses when available. For the class of 2008, there were nearly 22,500 applications for 2,250 places. The majority of incoming freshmen ranked comfortably in the top 10 percent of their high school class. The SAT I scores of the middle half of admitted freshmen were 1260–1390. On the ACT, scores of the middle half were between 29 and 31.

Application and Information

Students applying to Boston College for a place in the freshman class must complete both the Common Application and the Boston College Supplemental Application. All applicants should submit the BC Supplemental Application as soon as they have decided to apply to Boston College. Students are encouraged to apply via BC's Web site at http://www.bc.edu/applications but may also apply at http://www.commonapp.org.

Students applying through the regular admission program must submit the Common Application and all other required forms, along with the $60 application fee, by January 2. Candidates are notified of action taken on their application between April 1 and April 15. Admitted students intending to matriculate are required to forward an acceptance fee to the Admission Office postmarked by May 1.

Students with superior academic credentials who view Boston College as a top choice may apply through the nonbinding and nonrestrictive early action program. These applicants must submit both application forms, along with the $60 application fee, by November 1. Candidates learn of their admission decision before December 25 but have the standard deadline (May 1) to reserve their places as freshmen.

BC accepts transfer applicants each semester. Transfer candidates should request applications for transfer admission from the Office of Undergraduate Admission or via the Web site at http://www.bc.edu/ugadmis. In addition to high school records and standardized test results, transfer applicants must furnish transcripts from all postsecondary institutions they have attended.

For more information, students should contact:

Office of Undergraduate Admission
Devlin Hall 208
Boston College
Chestnut Hill, Massachusetts 02467
Telephone: 617-552-3100
800-360-2522 (toll-free)
Fax: 617-552-0798
E-mail: ugadmis@bc.edu
World Wide Web: http://www.bc.edu

Located just 6 miles from downtown Boston, Boston College offers the best of both worlds: a scenic suburban setting neighboring an exciting metropolitan center.

BOSTON UNIVERSITY

BOSTON, MASSACHUSETTS

The University

A private, nonsectarian, coeducational university located on the banks of the Charles River, Boston University is an energizing community. As a major research institution, the University fosters creativity and innovation. As an undergraduate institution, its faculty comprises some of the world's foremost experts who are dedicated to the art of teaching. Of the classes held in the freshman and sophomore years, the vast majority contain fewer than 30 students. Together, the eleven undergraduate schools and colleges offer 250 major and minor areas of concentration. Students may choose from programs of study in areas as diverse as biochemistry, broadcast journalism, business, computer engineering, elementary education, international relations, physical therapy, and theater arts. With students from all fifty states and more than 100 countries, Boston University has one of the most culturally diverse student bodies in the United States. The campus community supports nearly 400 different student organizations, ranging from ice broomball teams to performing arts groups, community service activities to student government, and clubs with cultural and professional as well as academic affiliations.

Location

Boston is an international center of cultural and intellectual activity, with a concentration of facilities for higher education unrivaled throughout the world. Home to many fine museums, baseball's Fenway Park, an active theater district, and the Boston Symphony Orchestra, the city has a vibrant energy all its own. Because 1 in 5 residents is a college student, Boston is also the ultimate college town.

Majors and Degrees

Boston University grants the B.A., B.S., B.S.B.A., B.S.Ed., B.A.S., B.L.S., B.A.A., Mus.B., and B.F.A. undergraduate degrees. Of the University's fifteen schools and colleges, eleven offer opportunities for undergraduate study. The following information indicates the range of undergraduate programs available.

Students in the College of Arts and Sciences may concentrate in American studies, ancient Greek, ancient Greek and Latin, anthropology, archaeology, art history, astronomy, astronomy/physics, biochemistry, biochemistry/molecular biology, biology, biology with a specialization in ecology and conservation biology, biology with a specialization in marine science, biology with a specialization in neuroscience, chemistry, chemistry with a specialization in biochemistry, chemistry with a specialization in teaching, classical civilization, classics/philosophy, classics/religion, computer science, earth sciences, East Asian studies, economics, economics/mathematics, English, environmental analysis and policy, environmental earth science, environmental science, French/continental European literatures, French language and literature, geography, geology, German/continental European literatures, German language and literature, Hispanic/continental European literatures, Hispanic language and literatures, history, independent concentration, international relations, Italian/continental European literatures, Italian studies, Latin, Latin American studies, linguistics, mathematics, mathematics/computer science, mathematics/mathematics education, mathematics/philosophy, modern Greek studies, music (nonperformance), philosophy, philosophy/anthropology, philosophy/physics, philosophy/political science, philosophy/psychology, philosophy/religion, physics, planetary/space science, political science, psychology, religion, Russian/continental European literatures, Russian language and literatures, Russian/Eastern European studies, sociology, and urban studies/public policy. Special curricula include seven-year programs in liberal arts and dentistry and liberal arts and medicine; the Modular Medical Integrated Curriculum; a dual-degree program; and various combined B.A./M.A. degree programs.

The College of Communication offers major programs of undergraduate study in film and television, journalism (including broadcast journalism, magazine journalism, news-editorial print journalism, and photojournalism), and advertising, mass communications, and public relations.

Majors in the College of Engineering include aerospace, biomedical, computer systems, electrical, interdisciplinary, manufacturing, and mechanical engineering.

Areas of concentration in the School of Education include bilingual education, early childhood education, deaf studies, elementary education, English education, history and social science education, human movement (including physical education), mathematics education, modern foreign language education, science education, and special education.

The School of Hospitality Administration offers a rigorous program in the management of hotels, restaurants, food and beverage service, travel and tourism, and entertainment.

Concentrations in the School of Management include accounting, entrepreneurship, finance, general management, international management, management information systems, marketing, operations management, and organizational behavior.

The College of Fine Arts offers programs in the School of Music (history and literature of music, music education, performance, and theory and composition), the School of Theater Arts (acting; directing; scenic, costume, and lighting design; stage management; production; technical production; and theater studies), and the School of Visual Arts (art education, graphic design, painting, and sculpture).

Sargent College of Health and Rehabilitation Sciences offers programs in athletic training, communication disorders, exercise science, health science, human physiology, nutritional sciences, and rehabilitation and human services, as well as a five-year combined B.S./M.S. degree program in occupational therapy and a six-year B.S./D.P.T. program in physical therapy.

The College of General Studies offers a two-year liberal-arts-based program that features a core curriculum and intensive team teaching. It is designed so that students continue on at the junior level into select schools and colleges of the University.

The University Professors Program allows exceptionally able students to seek degrees in areas that combine, bridge, or fall between established University disciplines. Students follow a core curriculum for two years, then design their own course of study for the remaining two years.

The Metropolitan College Science and Engineering Program offers a five-semester program for those students who need additional preparation for studying the sciences or engineering.

Academic Program

A Boston University education combines the elements of a traditional liberal arts education with training for the professions. In addition, highly qualified freshmen and sophomores may be invited to participate in honors programs in the College of Arts and Sciences or the School of Management.

Boston University has twenty-nine programs that take students around the world. Internships, fieldwork, and study-abroad opportunities are offered on six continents in nineteen cities within sixteen countries. The University has a series of internships in Beijing, Dublin, London, Madrid, Moscow, Paris, and Sydney in art/architecture, business/economics, human health services, journalism/communications, and visual/performing arts. Fieldwork programs may be found in Belize and Ecuador, with study-abroad options in Dresden, Grenoble, Haifa, Madrid, Niamey, Oxford, Padova, and Venice. Summer study programs exist in Australia, China, England, France, Italy, and Spain.

Boston University operates on a calendar of two semesters and two summer terms. Students generally take four courses each semester; thirty-two courses are required for graduation. Most degree programs are built around a core of humanities and social and natural sciences. Concentrations require eight to thirteen courses. Electives generally total 30–40 percent of the courses taken, allowing for interdisciplinary study.

Academic Facilities

Two of the newest facilities on campus include the Photonics Center and the School of Management building. The Photonics Center features research labs designed to support industry partners who seek to develop new photonics-based products in addition to College of Engineering classroom and laboratory space. The School of Management building represents one of the most technologically advanced educational facilities in the country, with more than 4,000 data and communication ports as well as a dedicated career center and management library.

Boston University's newest building project, the John Hancock Student Village, is a multistage venture that is anticipated to include four high-rise dormitories and state-of-the-art fitness, athletic, and recreational facilities, including a 7,200-seat multipurpose arena. The arena and recreation center phase of the project, currently underway, is scheduled to be completed in the winter of 2005. Through the Office of Information Technology, students have access to public computing facilities equipped with workstations, terminals, and laser printers as well as a high-speed campus network interconnecting all computer resources and linking them to the Internet. An 850-seat proscenium theater, studio space for visual arts students, more than 100 practice rooms for music, and a 575-seat music performance center are indicative of Boston University's support for the arts. More than 2.2 million library volumes and 4 million microform units are contained in Mugar Memorial Library, where the Twentieth-Century Archives are held, including the papers of Martin Luther King Jr., Theodore Roosevelt, Robert Frost, and Bette Davis.

Costs

Tuition for 2003–04 was $28,512; estimated room and board costs were $9288. University and college fees were $394. These costs are exclusive of books, supplies, travel, and personal expenses.

Financial Aid

The Office of Financial Assistance offers both financial and advisory resources to students and their families who request help in meeting the expenses of attending Boston University. Information, counseling, and referrals are available to all families, regardless of income level or financial circumstances. In addition to providing both need-based and merit awards to many students, the office serves a much larger constituency of students and parents. Financial assistance officers review with students and their families the available means of financing an education, whether through the University or through external funding sources.

Financial aid can take several forms and may be awarded in a variety of combinations. Types of aid include scholarships and grants, state and federal grants and loans, and federal Work-Study and other part-time employment. When applying for financial aid, students should understand that University and federal student aid funds are limited. The University is unable to meet the full calculated need of every student offered admission. Those students with the strongest academic records are given priority for receiving available funds. In addition, as part of Boston University's commitment to excellence, the University recognizes academic achievement through a number of merit award programs.

Faculty

Students are taught by faculty members who distinguish themselves by their ability, experience, research, and publications. In addition to fulfilling their classroom responsibilities, faculty members are accessible as academic and career advisers who assist students in obtaining internships as well research opportunities.

Student Government

Each school and college has its own student government, which regulates student affairs within the school or college. The University-wide student governing body, the Student Union, has representation from all University schools and colleges. Each residence hall also has its own student government, composed of elected representatives from each floor.

Admission Requirements

The Board of Admissions considers each candidate individually. Primary emphasis is placed on the strength of the secondary school record, but required test scores (SAT I or ACT), character, breadth of interest, school recommendations, and other personal qualifications are also carefully evaluated. Secondary school graduation or an equivalency diploma is required of all candidates; for the College of Fine Arts, an audition or a portfolio is required. For certain programs, interviews and SAT II Subject Test scores are required. The *Undergraduate Bulletin* or the *Boston University Application for Admission* should be consulted for specific information.

Students with earned credit from other colleges may be admitted. Applicants are considered for September or January entrance. Transfer students are not eligible for admission to the Accelerated Liberal Arts Medical or Dental Programs, the College of General Studies, the Metropolitan College Science and Engineering Program, or Sargent College's physical therapy program. January admission to the College of Fine Arts (Schools of Theatre and Visual Arts) and Sargent College's occupational therapy and nutritional sciences programs are also not available to transfer students. Boston University does maintain programs of early decision (binding agreement), early admission, and deferred admission.

Boston University admits qualified students regardless of their race, color, national origin, religion, sex, age, or disability to all its programs and activities.

Application and Information

Application forms and information are available online or by writing to the Office of Admissions (addresses listed below). The deadline for applications is January 1, and early decision applicants must apply by November 1 (accelerated-program applicants and Trustee Scholarship nominees must file by December 1). Candidates for financial aid should complete the College Scholarship Service (CSS) Financial Aid PROFILE and the Free Application for Federal Student Aid (FAFSA) in time for the evaluation to reach the University by February 15. Transfer students applying for September admission should submit their applications, CSS/Financial Aid PROFILE forms, and Free Application for Federal Student Aid (FAFSA) forms by April 1 or by November 1 for January admission.

Office of Admissions
Boston University
121 Bay State Road
Boston, Massachusetts 02215
Telephone: 617-353-2300
E-mail: admissions@bu.edu
World Wide Web: http://www.bu.edu/admissions

BOWDOIN COLLEGE

BRUNSWICK, MAINE

The College

Students who come to Bowdoin will find a collaborative and meaningful college experience and the preparation they need for life and leadership in a changing world. In the process, they have a lot of fun. Founded in 1794, Bowdoin is one of the top liberal arts colleges in the country. It is a coeducational, private, nonsectarian, residential college with more than 1,600 students in residence each term from almost every state and from many countries around the world.

Academics at Bowdoin are rigorous, but the atmosphere is collegial, not cutthroat. Learning goes on not only in the classroom but also at club meetings and lectures and over dinner conversations with other students and faculty members. The flexibility of the curriculum allows students to take charge of their own educations, and they are constantly encouraged to explore something new and test their preconceived notions of what they want to study. For many, this kind of exploration begins with a first-year seminar. These classes introduce students to discussion-based college-level work and enable professors to examine a new area of study or look at a compelling contemporary issue. Limited to 16 students, first-year seminars guarantee some great discussions and the chance to get to know a professor right off the bat.

About 90 percent of students live on campus, and each is affiliated with a College House. The houses sponsor social activities, lectures, and other events. House activities depend entirely upon the interests of the students. Recently, a budding chef ran a restaurant in one of the houses, serving gourmet dinners to students and faculty and staff members every Tuesday. Good food is not limited to student cooks, however. Bowdoin has been nationally recognized for its delicious food, and there are always healthy food options, including vegetarian and vegan choices, as well as special class dinners, holiday celebrations, and theme nights.

Bowdoin's first president declared that the purpose of the College was to serve "the Common Good," an ideal that still influences the lives of students. Opportunities for community service are abundant, and about 70 percent of students are involved in such programs during their time at Bowdoin.

Opportunities to have fun outside of class are abundant. For most students, the difficulty is in deciding what to leave out rather than finding something to interest them. Among the more than 100 student organizations are the oldest continuously published college weekly in the U.S., a cable television station, the Bowdoin Outing Club (Bowdoin's largest club, it sponsors weekend trips for hiking, kayaking, skiing, and many other outdoor pursuits), a step team, music groups, and more. There are also organizations affiliated with religious beliefs, groups associated with ethnic and racial heritages, political clubs, and academic and athletic organizations—truly something for everyone.

Students do not have to wait for the weekend to find something to do; there is something going on nearly every night. Recent performers have included Mos Def, Rufus Wainwright, Jude, Dar Williams, Savion Glover, and Okay Go. Speakers have included Spike Lee, George Will, Doris Kerns Goodwin, Robert Reich, and other noted scholars.

Athletics are part of the Bowdoin experience for many students. Bowdoin fields twenty-nine varsity teams for men and women in eighteen sports and offers seven club sports and many intramural activities. The athletic and fitness facilities are open long hours for all students, and those not interested in organized sports have plenty of chances to work out or play games with friends.

Location

It would be hard to find a prettier backdrop for four years of study than midcoast Maine. Bowdoin's campus is one of the most beautiful in the country. Its buildings date from 1802 through 2003 and surround a central quad that is equipped with wireless technology, which allows students to sit outside and use their laptops under the trees. Brunswick is a coastal town that offers small-town charm with the amenities of a larger city. There are restaurants serving everything from Mexican to German to Indian cuisine, museums, shops, and movie theaters, and the town center is only a five-minute walk from the campus.

Freeport, 10 minutes away and known for its outlet stores and L.L. Bean (open 24-hours-a-day, 365-days-a-year), it is the destination for many late-night student excursions. Portland, Maine's cultural center and largest city, is just 30 minutes away. Portland is an ethnically and culturally diverse city with plenty to do. It is home to dozens of performing arts groups, professional sports teams, and a wide array of shops and restaurants.

Bowdoin is only a 2-hour drive from Boston, the business and cultural center of New England. Train service is available between Portland and Boston. Maine also provides a living laboratory for many of Bowdoin's courses; students in the sciences, economics, sociology, and other disciplines perform research in communities and locales around the state.

Majors and Degrees

Bowdoin offers the Bachelor of Arts degree in the following areas: anthropology, art history, biology, chemistry, classics, classics/archaeology, computer science, economics, English, French, geology, German, government, history, mathematics, music, philosophy, physics, psychology, religion, Romance languages, Russian, sociology, and visual arts. A coordinate major in environmental studies is also offered. The College offers interdisciplinary majors in Africana studies, art history and archaeology, art history and visual arts, Asian studies, biochemistry, chemical physics, computer science and mathematics, English and theater, Eurasian and East European studies, geology and chemistry, geology and physics, Latin American studies, mathematics and economics, neuroscience, and women's studies.

Bowdoin offers minors in dance, education, film studies, gay and lesbian studies, Greek, Latin, and theater. Students majoring in education may obtain teacher certification. A concentration is offered in Arctic studies, and courses are also offered in architecture. Bowdoin participates in joint liberal arts/engineering programs with California Institute of Technology and Columbia University and in a liberal arts/law program with Columbia University.

Students also have the option of designing their own major.

Academic Programs

Bowdoin gives students exposure to many disciplines and extensive knowledge in whatever major they choose. The curriculum is designed to allow students to test and expand their intellectual interests. Among the few requirements are at least two courses in each of the three divisions of the curriculum—natural sciences and mathematics, social and behavioral sciences, and humanities and fine arts—and two courses that focus on non-European cultures or societies.

Student-faculty interaction is at the center of intellectual life at Bowdoin. Students and faculty members often become friends and research associates, and it is not uncommon for students to publish papers with their professors. For many, this work is the most meaningful intellectual experience of their years at Bowdoin. As students increase their mastery of their chosen major, more than 60 percent of them participate in an independent study project.

Off-Campus Programs

More than 50 percent of Bowdoin students choose to study away from campus for a semester or a year in the U.S. or almost any other country in the world. Students also find opportunities for off-campus study through fieldwork in Arctic studies, biochemistry, biology, the classics, and other disciplines.

Academic Facilities

The intellectual heart of the campus is the Bowdoin College library, which contains more than 950,000 volumes, and in the science, art, and music libraries. The Bowdoin College Museum of Art, with more than 14,000 objects, holds one of the oldest and finest college collections in the country. The Peary-MacMillan Arctic Museum, named for two Bowdoin graduates, continues the College's historic link to Arctic exploration. Bowdoin boasts new and newly renovated theater and arts facilities, including a craft barn, a dance studio, and two state-of-the-art theaters. The science buildings have all been built or renovated within the past five years. The new outdoor leadership center is one of the finest in the country.

Bowdoin's off-campus research facilities include the Coastal Studies Center, with both marine and terrestrial labs and seminar and studio space, and marine and ornithological research stations near the campus and at Kent Island in the Bay of Fundy, Canada.

Costs

Tuition for 2003–04 was $29,470, fees were $650 (including the $310 student activities fee and the $340 health services fee), and room and board were $7670, for a total of $37,790. Books and supplies were estimated at $2010.

Financial Aid

Bowdoin does not want cost to be an obstacle to anyone who wants to attend the College. Financial aid at Bowdoin is need-based, and Bowdoin meets the full, demonstrated need of all admitted U.S. applicants for all four years. Aid may include grants, loans, and campus jobs. In 2003–04, more than 42 percent of Bowdoin students received about $16 million in need-based aid. Awards to entering students ranged from $500 to $36,800; the average award was $21,500.

Faculty

Bowdoin has a world-class faculty. Working with students is as important to Bowdoin's faculty members as their research. The student-faculty ratio is 10:1 and professors teach all courses. Professors routinely use knowledge from their research to keep students informed of the latest developments in their fields. Faculty members are also involved in the lives of students outside the classroom, serving as mentors to students and advisers to student organizations. They are willing to go the extra mile to help students thrive at Bowdoin.

Student Government

Bowdoin's student government is divided into two parts: the Student Assembly and the Executive Committee. The Assembly consists of class presidents, house officers, and open positions. The Executive Committee comprises 9 students elected at large. Students are also elected to serve as representatives to committees of the Board of Trustees and the faculty.

Admission Requirements

Academic accomplishments and talents are given the greatest weight in the admissions process. Extracurricular activities and written recommendations are also very important. Added consideration is given to demonstrated skills in leadership, communication, social service, the arts, and athletics. The College does not require SAT I, SAT II Subject Test, or ACT scores for admission, but scores are considered if submitted. About 20 percent of Bowdoin's accepted applicants each year have not submitted standardized test scores. In recent years, slightly less than 40 percent of the entering class is accepted under the College's early decision programs.

Application and Information

Application materials include the Common Application and Bowdoin Supplement. Both are included in the viewbook, available online, or are sent by the College's Admissions Office upon request. Also required are a school report, two teacher recommendations, a supplementary essay, a midyear school report, and a $60 application fee (or application fee waiver). An interview, either on campus or with an alumni interviewer living near the applicant, is strongly recommended but not required. Candidates should make appointments in advance.

Campus tours are available weekdays and most Saturdays throughout the year. Group information sessions are held several times a day throughout the spring, summer, and fall. There are two early decision options. Students who apply by November 15 under the early decision I option are notified in mid-December. Early decision II applications are due by January 1, and applicants are notified in mid-February. Regular applications are also due by January 1; candidates are notified by mid-April.

For more information, students should contact:

Admissions
Bowdoin College
5000 College Station
Brunswick, Maine 04011-8441
Telephone: 207-725-3100
Fax: 207-725-3101
E-mail: admissions@bowdoin.edu
World Wide Web: http://www.bowdoin.edu

BOWIE STATE UNIVERSITY

BOWIE, MARYLAND

The University

Bowie State University began as a normal school in the city of Baltimore in 1865, and it has evolved over the years into a four-year, coeducational, liberal arts institution. It is currently situated on a beautiful 312-acre campus in Prince Georges County, Maryland, and offers both graduate and undergraduate programs of study. Teacher education programs were established in 1925; in 1935, with state authorization, a four-year program for the training of elementary school teachers was begun and the school became the Maryland State Teachers College at Bowie. In 1951, with the approval of the State Board of Education, its governing body at the time, the college established a teacher-preparation curriculum for the training of teachers for the core program in the junior high schools. Ten years later, permission was granted to institute a teacher-training program for secondary education. A liberal arts program was established in 1963, and the institution's name was changed to Bowie State College. In 1988, Bowie State achieved university status and joined the University System of Maryland (USM).

Bowie State University received its first state funding of $5000 in 1908. Its physical plant is valued at more than $37 million, and its current enrollment is approximately 5,400 students, 1,450 of whom are in the Graduate School. The University has twenty-two buildings on campus with the addition of the new $21-million state-of-the-art Center for Learning and Technology that opened in fall 2000, and the new $11.8-million Computer Science Center that opened fall 2002. Two of the buildings, the Communication Arts Center and the physical education complex, were completed in 1973, and an administration building opened in 1977. Five residence halls, including Goodloe Hall, the honors students' residence, and Alex Haley Hall, a state-of-the-art residence hall, house approximately 800 students. In addition, a new 460-bed residence hall will be completed in fall 2004. The $2.6-million physical education complex houses a 3,000-seat basketball arena, an Olympic-size swimming pool with underwater viewing windows and facilities for 200 spectators, an apparatus gymnasium, a dance studio, a wrestling room, a weight-training room, eight handball/squash courts, a therapy room, and offices for instructors and coaches. The $5.5-million University Activities Center includes a cafeteria.

Bowie State University considers the student activities program a vital part of the total educational program. Students have access to more than forty different activities. These include student government, the student union, intercollegiate athletics, eight fraternities and sororities, numerous departmental clubs and preprofessional organizations, and music and drama organizations.

The Graduate School grants the Master of Education in elementary, secondary, and special education; guidance and counseling; reading education; and school administration and supervision; the Master of Arts in administrative management, counseling psychology, English, human resource development, organizational communications, and teaching; and the Master of Science in applied computational math, computer science, management information systems, and nursing. The Adler-Dreikurs Institute of Human Relations at Bowie State University is the first fully accredited master's-degree-granting Adlerian institute in the United States. A Doctorate of Education in education leadership began in spring 2000.

Bowie State University admits students without regard to sex, religion, or nationality, and the University does not discriminate on the basis of race, creed, color, national or ethnic origin, age, sex, or handicap. The University is accredited by the Middle States Association of Colleges and Schools and approved by the Maryland State Department of Education. Its programs in teacher education, social work education, nursing, business, and computer science are accredited by the National Council for Accreditation of Teacher Education, the National Council on Social Work Education, the National League for Nursing Accrediting Commission, the Maryland Board of Nursing, the Association of Collegiate Business Schools and Programs, and the Computer Science Accreditation Commission of the Computing Sciences Accreditation Board, respectively.

Location

Bowie, Maryland, is in a triangle formed by Annapolis (20 miles east), Baltimore (25 miles north), and Washington, D.C. (17 miles southwest). The suburban setting provides an ideal, safe environment for students and scholars, with access to all of the important cultural, governmental, and business activities in any of the three metropolitan areas.

Majors and Degrees

Bowie State University offers the Bachelor of Arts or Bachelor of Science degree with majors in biology, business administration, communications media, computer science, computer technology, early childhood education, elementary education, English, English education, fine art, government, history, mathematics, nursing, pedology, psychology, science education, social work, sociology/criminal justice, and technology. Dual-degree programs are offered in engineering and dentistry.

Academic Program

The University operates on a semester calendar. Academic offerings can be divided into four main areas: humanities, science and mathematics, social sciences, and education. To receive a bachelor's degree, a student must earn a minimum of 120 semester hours with a cumulative grade point average of 2.0 or better. Students are provided the opportunity to complete the General Education Program, acquire lifelong learning skills for a competitive world, and make a successful transition into their junior year. General studies requirements include communication skills, 9 hours; humanities, 9 hours; social sciences, 18 hours; science and mathematics, 9 hours; and physical education, 2 hours. The remaining credit hours can be electives or from major and minor areas of interest. Students must also pass the test of Proficiency in the English Language and must take the national standardized test in their major area.

The Honors Program is designed for students with outstanding academic records and potential and provides a special educational opportunity for young adults with exceptional talent. The program is comprehensive and multidisciplinary in structure and interdisciplinary in application. It has been designed to provide a creative approach to the teaching/learning process and to present activities that will encourage the shaping of students' own experiences.

The Special Services Project is a federally funded program designed to retain and graduate first-generation, low-income, and disabled students who have been admitted to Bowie State University. The purpose of the project is to help students overcome academic and nonacademic barriers to academic success, through participation in specially designed activities, including counseling, tutoring, and workshops on test taking and study skills.

Through the Cooperative Education Program, a student may choose either the alternate or parallel programs of study and work in business, industry, government, or a social-service agency. This program is open to Bowie State students who have completed at least one academic year with a minimum cumulative grade point average of 2.0.

The University participates in the College-Level Examination Program (CLEP), administered by the Educational Testing Service for the College Board, and in the Defense Activity for Non-Traditional Education Support (DANTES) program. The University also has a program for awarding students credit for learning acquired through life and work experience. Under this program, students document their backgrounds in a portfolio, which is reviewed by the faculty. Through all of these programs, qualified students may receive up to 30 credit hours toward their degree. In addition, the University offers an Army ROTC program. Two-year and three-year scholarships are available.

Academic Facilities

The Communication Arts Center, a $6.5-million building that houses the humanities division, contains classrooms, offices, conference rooms, and studio-laboratories and seats 450 patrons. The $8.8-million, 290,000-volume Thurgood Marshall Library is centrally located on campus and provides excellent equipment and reference departments for the student body. The microfilm file contains 500,000 items; periodicals number 1,400. Campus research facilities include science laboratories, television and radio studios, language laboratories, and the Adler-Dreikurs Institute. Access to the library collection is provided through Victor Web, the electronic catalog that also links users to millions of USM volumes. The new Center for Learning and Technology, the main classroom building, features fourteen electronic classrooms, two interactive lecture halls, three computer labs, one speech lab, and a 300-seat auditorium and conference center. In addition, the new Computer Science Center has five classrooms and thirteen labs.

Costs

In 2003–04, the annual cost of tuition, fees, board, and room for a freshman who is a Maryland resident averaged $11,000; for a non-Maryland resident, the cost averaged $17,000. The annual cost for a commuting student who is a Maryland resident was $4853; the cost for a commuting student who is not a Maryland resident was $12,464.

Financial Aid

Federal Pell Grants, Supplemental Grants, Work-Study, Perkins Loans, and Direct Loans are available. University scholarships, tuition waivers, and diversity grants are awarded. Most awards are based on need. Merit scholarships could be offered to students with cumulative grade point averages of at least 3.0 and minimum SAT I scores of 1100. More than 65 percent of all undergraduate students receive some form of financial aid. Scholarships and assistantships are offered through the Model Institutions for Excellence Program for Science, Engineering, and Mathematics. Deadlines are March 1 for the fall semester and November 15 for the spring semester.

Faculty

More than 75 percent of the 160 full-time faculty members have earned doctoral degrees. The faculty-student ratio is 1:18.

Student Government

All students are members of the Student Government Association, which, in cooperation with the administration, sets the standards for student life. Students are encouraged to assume leadership roles and to participate in the various programs and activities of the University. The Residence Hall Council provides opportunities for students to participate in the administration of residence life and in the cultural growth of the campus community.

Admission Requirements

Maryland residents applying for admission should have a minimum cumulative grade point average in their core high school courses of 2.0 (on a 4.0 scale) and a minimum SAT I score of 900 (or a minimum ACT score of 19). A sliding scale is used for students who have higher grade point averages or SAT I scores. Conditional admission may be offered to students with a minimum cumulative grade point average of 2.0 and minimum SAT I scores of 830 to 899 (or a minimum ACT score of 17). Applicants must have earned a high school diploma or a GED certificate. The following courses are required: English, 4 credits; social science/history, 3 credits; mathematics (algebra I, algebra II, and geometry), 3 credits; laboratory sciences, 2 credits; foreign language, 2 credits; and electives, 6 credits. A $40 application fee is charged, and a health certificate must be submitted before entering the University.

Transfer students must have a minimum 2.0 cumulative grade point average for a minimum of 24 transferable credits, or SAT I scores will be required. International students and mature adults are encouraged to apply.

Application and Information

The application deadline is April 1 for the fall semester and November 1 for spring. For an application form, students should contact:

Admissions Office
Bowie State University
Bowie, Maryland 20715-9465
Telephone: 301-860-3422 or 3423
410-880-4100 Ext. 3422 or 3423 (from the Baltimore-Columbia area)
877-77-BOWIE (toll-free)
Fax: 301-860-3518
E-mail: admissions@bowiestate.edu
World Wide Web: http://www.bowiestate.edu

Flags representing the international student population of Bowie State University frame the entrance to the 312-acre campus.

BOWLING GREEN STATE UNIVERSITY

BOWLING GREEN, OHIO

The University

Bowling Green State University (BGSU) offers an outstanding educational experience. At BGSU, academic learning is paired with a campuswide commitment to values exploration and prepares graduates to go out into the world as critical thinkers, skilled communicators, and ethical leaders in all areas of study. This vision uniquely distinguishes BGSU as a public university with a unified purpose.

BGSU combines the personal atmosphere of a small college with the opportunities of a major university. With more than 200 undergraduate majors and programs, BGSU's learning community provides high-quality faculty members who care about their students, an appreciation for diversity, and the latest in information technology. About 7,000 of BGSU's 20,400 students live on campus. BGSU attracts students who balance academic excellence with involvement in nearly 325 student organizations. Committed to ensuring that every student succeeds, Bowling Green challenges and supports students, both in and out of the classroom. Integral to campus life are the core values: respect for one another, cooperation, intellectual and spiritual growth, creative imaginings, and pride in a job well done.

BGSU's personal atmosphere is enhanced by its physically compact campus located within the Bowling Green community. Most restaurants and businesses are within walking or biking distance of residence halls. Bicycles are a popular means of transportation, but all students are permitted to have cars.

Of the 20,400 students enrolled at BGSU, 17,300 are undergraduate students, 10 percent come from outside the state of Ohio (including more than 550 from other countries), and more than 1,770 are African American, Native American, Hispanic, or Asian American. Students are actively involved outside of class, participating in student organizations and service learning opportunities and enjoying some of the more than 400 cultural and special events that are offered each month.

Residence halls reinforce the learning environment with a computer laboratory for each residence complex and one personal computer available for every 23 resident students. Every residence hall room has high-speed Ethernet connections to the University's computing backbone.

BGSU's Graduate College offers sixty-eight master's degrees, two specialist degree programs, and sixteen doctoral programs.

Location

The city of Bowling Green, Ohio, population 29,600 (including students), is located in northwest Ohio about 20 miles south of Toledo. It is within a comfortable driving distance of all major cities in Ohio and is within an easy commute from nearby towns.

Majors and Degrees

The University is fully accredited by the Higher Learning Commission and a member of the North Central Association of Schools and Colleges (30 LaSalle Street, Suite 2400, Chicago, Illinois 60602-2504; telephone: 800-621-7440, toll-free). BGSU offers more than 200 undergraduate majors and programs in seven undergraduate colleges: Arts and Sciences, Business Administration, Education and Human Development, Health and Human Services, Musical Arts, Technology, and the regional BGSU Firelands in Huron, Ohio. Numerous programs within these colleges are accredited by their respective national accrediting agencies.

Four-year undergraduate programs are available and lead to the following degrees: Bachelor of Applied Health Sciences, Bachelor of Arts, Bachelor of Arts in Communication, Bachelor of Fine Arts, Bachelor of Liberal Studies, Bachelor of Music, Bachelor of Science, Bachelor of Science in Business Administration, Bachelor of Science in apparel merchandising and product development, Bachelor of Science in child and family community services, Bachelor of Science in communication disorders, Bachelor of Science in criminal justice, Bachelor of Science in dietetics, Bachelor of Science in economics, Bachelor of Science in education, Bachelor of Science in environmental health, Bachelor of Science in nutrition sciences, Bachelor of Science in gerontology, Bachelor of Science in interior design, Bachelor of Science in journalism, Bachelor of Science in medical technology, Bachelor of Science in nursing, Bachelor of Science in social work, and Bachelor of Science in technology. BGSU Firelands offers fourteen programs that lead to associate degrees in applied business, applied sciences, nursing, science, and technical study, plus nine bachelor's degree programs.

Every entering student has the option of enrolling in an undergraduate college with a declared major or enrolling as an undecided student. Students who are undecided about a college begin their studies in premajor advising, where approximately 500 new students enroll each year.

Academic Program

The academic program at BGSU is designed to help all students achieve their full potential. All students, regardless of their major, take a core group of general education courses.

Classroom work is closely integrated with out-of-class experiences in the residence halls and off campus. Students can choose one of eleven smaller, special-interest housing and academic living-learning communities. In some communities, professors teach classes and have offices in the residence halls and extend experiential and service learning beyond the classroom. Community interests include the arts, music, health sciences, Hispanic and French language and culture, middle childhood and secondary education, international culture, and wellness. The Chapman Community and IMPACT (integrating moral principles and critical thinking) are open to all majors.

Bowling Green also offers a challenging honors program, honors housing, and the opportunity to complete a senior honors project for graduation with University or departmental honors. All students receive academic advising, and tutoring services are available. Bowling Green has Army and Air Force ROTC programs.

Off-Campus Programs

BGSU emphasizes education with a global perspective. About 275 BGSU students study abroad each year. Education-abroad programs range from a full academic year to a few weeks and are available at thirty sites in thirty countries.

BGSU participates in the National Student Exchange Program with 173 other colleges and universities in the U.S. The University is a leading partner in the Washington Center Internship program, which provides full-time internships and short-term academic seminars for college students in the nation's capital.

In all undergraduate colleges, BGSU students are given the opportunity for hands-on experiences that bring what they learn in the classroom to life. Every Bowling Green student can take advantage of at least one opportunity to gain practical experience related to his or her major.

Cooperative education, an "earn-while-you-learn" program, places students with more than 900 employers annually. Co-op participants earn an average of $11.03 per hour. The University's co-op program ranks in the top 10 percent in the country for number of placements and is open to all students regardless of their major.

Academic Facilities

Extensive state-of-the-art facilities support the work of faculty members and students at Bowling Green. BGSU's libraries provide a gateway to several million items on-site and online, including resources of the Music Library and Sound Recordings Archives, Popular Culture Library, Curriculum Resource Center, and Center for Archival Collections. The libraries are linked to the resources of all major colleges and universities in Ohio and can locate materials worldwide.

Recent completion of a $50-million infrastructure project brings far-reaching access to information and the latest technological learning and teaching resources to campus. Among the University's comprehensive computing resources are thirty instructional computing lab facilities located across campus. Several labs have highly specialized hardware and software for individual disciplines. Every residence complex has its own computer lab, and all residence hall rooms are wired for high-speed connection to the University's computing network, including e-mail, the Internet, and library resources.

Olscamp Hall, a classroom building with seating for 2,000, is equipped for teleteaching/distance learning, with capabilities for sending and receiving classroom activity to and from all parts of the world. BGSU also has a modern physical sciences laboratory building and planetarium, a recently renovated Fine Arts Center, and outstanding music facilities.

Costs

A full-time first-year student living on campus in standard housing and with the limited meal plan paid $13,300 in 2003–04. Out-of-state students paid a surcharge of $6960, for a total of $20,260. Students are encouraged to budget about $850 to $950 a year for books and supplies and an additional $2700 for other expenses, such as entertainment, clothing, transportation, and laundry.

Financial Aid

About 65 percent of BGSU students receive some kind of financial aid. In 2002–03, the University awarded academic scholarships that totaled $7.5 million. Bowling Green offers a renewable scholarship that is equivalent to 100 percent of the total cost of fees, room, and meals to National Merit Finalists, National Achievement Finalists, and National Hispanic Scholars with a minimum 3.3 grade point average. National Merit Semifinalists, National Achievement Semifinalists, and National Hispanic Honorable Mention Recipients with the minimum 3.3 GPA are offered renewable scholarships that cover fees only. Student employment, grants, and loans are other options that are available. BGSU employs about 4,500 students annually. Students apply for aid by completing the Free Application for Federal Student Aid (FAFSA). Students who are eligible for academic scholarships are automatically considered if their credentials are submitted to the Office of Admissions by January 15. Prospective students should contact the Office of Admissions for additional information.

Faculty

At the heart of Bowling Green State University are 839 full-time faculty members who devote their energies to teaching, research, and working closely with students. Many are national and international experts in their field, others are authors, and still others have won awards for both teaching and research. Their reputations as scholars, authors, and teachers complement the faculty's role as people who care about students and the future of the University. The personal attention students receive from the faculty and support staff contributes to the small-college atmosphere that is distinctive at BGSU.

Student Government

The Undergraduate Student Government (USG) is the representative body for Bowling Green's undergraduate students. Leaders and delegates are elected by the entire student body and carry the students' voice to both the University Board of Trustees and the Faculty Senate. Both an undergraduate and a graduate student are appointed each year by the governor to the University Board of Trustees.

Admission Requirements

High school seniors can apply to BGSU beginning August 1 before their senior year. Admission to the fall semester is competitive. Nonresidents of Ohio are considered for admission on the same basis as in-state students. To be admitted, a freshman applicant must be a graduate of a high school approved or accredited by the state or have earned a high school equivalency diploma. Results of either the ACT or SAT I are required (ACT preferred). An applicant is considered on the basis of high school course work, cumulative GPA, official ACT or SAT I results, and class rank. The University also considers the diversity of the student body and applicants' special abilities, talents, and achievements in making admission decisions.

Admission to the University for transfer students is determined by their college academic credentials. Several academic majors and programs have specific requirements for transfer students, but, in general, a minimum 2.0 GPA is required for students who have earned at least 60 semester (90 quarter) hours; a minimum 2.5 GPA is required for students who have earned fewer than 60 semester hours.

Application and Information

Prospective students are encouraged to apply to Bowling Green and have all admission credentials complete before February 1 of the year they intend to enroll. Notification of admission decisions begins on October 1 for those who have submitted all credentials, and continues on a rolling basis. Bowling Green does not discriminate in admission on the basis of race, sex, sexual orientation, color, national origin, religion, creed, age, marital status, mental or physical disability, or veteran status. Students may apply online at the Web site listed below or obtain an application for admission by contacting:

Office of Admissions
110 McFall Center
Bowling Green State University
Bowling Green, Ohio 43402
Telephone: 419-372-BGSU
866-CHOOSE-BGSU (toll-free)
Fax: 419-372-6955
E-mail: choosebgsu@bgnet.bgsu.edu
World Wide Web: http://www.bgsu.edu

BRADLEY UNIVERSITY

PEORIA, ILLINOIS

The University

Bradley University is a four-year, independent comprehensive university located on a tree-lined, 75-acre campus in Peoria, Illinois. Situated in the heart of Peoria's historic West Bluff neighborhood, Bradley offers a private residential environment in a medium-sized city.

Founded in 1897 by Lydia Moss Bradley, the University has a long and distinguished tradition of academic quality and dynamic campus life. For her part in establishing this reputation, and many other philanthropic and humanitarian achievements, Mrs. Bradley was recently inducted into the National Women's Hall of Fame. Her legacy lives on in today's highly-motivated and extremely active student body.

Bradley's five academic colleges and graduate school are fully accredited by the North Central Association of Colleges and Universities. Students may pursue more than 100 academic programs in the College of Education and Health Sciences, the College of Engineering and Technology, the Foster College of Business Administration, the College of Liberal Arts and Sciences, and the Slane College of Communication and Fine Arts. The Graduate School offers master's degrees in more than thirty areas of study. Bradley students are encouraged to take advantage of a wealth of internships, co-ops, practicums, and other "real-world" experiences offered by the University. Bradley's retention, graduation, and placement rates rival some of the most prestigious colleges and universities in the nation.

In addition to academic facilities—including the Cullom-Davis Library and newly renovated Olin Hall of Science—there are twelve residence halls, which house freshmen and upperclassmen; a student center that includes a food court, a cafeteria, and a movie theater; four student cafeterias; two performing arts facilities; a student recreation center with basketball courts, a fitness center, and a swimming pool; and the Robertson Memorial Fieldhouse, home to Bradley's NCAA Division I athletic programs.

Bradley's balanced, educational environment includes more than 220 student organizations, Greek life, a comprehensive student government system, and NCAA Division I athletic programs offering basketball, soccer, baseball, tennis, golf, and cross-country for men and basketball, volleyball, softball, tennis, golf, track and field, and cross-country for women.

Location

Bradley University is located in Peoria, Illinois, a diverse, metropolitan community of approximately 350,000 people located along the Illinois River. Peoria is home to several multinational corporations, businesses, and research centers and is the largest metropolitan area in downstate Illinois. In addition, Peoria offers an abundance of fine and performing arts, cultural attractions, shopping, entertainment, and professional sports teams. Both Chicago and St. Louis are less than 3 hours' drive.

Majors and Degrees

The College of Education and Health Sciences awards the Bachelor of Arts or Bachelor of Science degree in early childhood education, elementary education, family and consumer sciences education, foods nutrition and dietetics, general family and consumer sciences, health science (leads to Bradley's master's degree in physical therapy), nursing, retail merchandising, secondary education, and special education.

The College of Engineering and Technology awards the Bachelor of Science degree in civil engineering, civil engineering with environmental option, construction, electrical engineering, electrical engineering with computer option, engineering physics, industrial engineering, manufacturing engineering, manufacturing engineering technology (design and systems options available), and mechanical engineering.

The Foster College of Business Administration awards the Bachelor of Arts or Bachelor of Science degree in accounting (includes a 3/2 B.S./M.S. option), actuarial science–business, business computer systems, economics, entrepreneurship, finance, international business, management and administration (concentrations in human resource management and legal studies in business), marketing (concentrations in advertising, industrial marketing/sales management, marketing management, market research, and retailing), and risk management and insurance.

Bradley University's College of Liberal Arts and Sciences awards the Bachelor of Arts or Bachelor of Science degree in administration of criminal justice, actuarial science–mathematics, biochemistry, biology, cell and molecular biology, chemistry, computer information systems, computer science, economics, English, environmental science, French, geological science, German, history, international studies, mathematics, medical technology, philosophy, physics, political science, pre-law, pre-med, psychology, religious studies, social work, sociology, and Spanish.

The Slane College of Communications and Fine Arts awards the Bachelor of Arts, Bachelor of Fine Arts, Bachelor of Science, or Bachelor of Music degree in art (concentrations in ceramics, drawing, graphic design, painting, photography, printmaking, and sculpture), art education, art history, communication (concentrations in advertising, journalism, public relations, radio/television, and speech communication), multimedia, music, music business, music composition, music education, music performance, theater education, theater performance, and theater production.

Students may select minor areas of study from throughout the five colleges in African-American studies, applied ergonomics, art history, Asian studies, biology, business administration, business studies, chemistry, computer science and information systems, economics, English (literature, creative writing, and professional writing), decision analysis, family and consumer sciences, fine arts, French, geological sciences, German, health, history, journalism, Latin American studies, management, manufacturing, marketing, mathematics, multimedia, music, philosophy, physics, political science, psychology, quality engineering, Spanish, religious studies, Russian and East European studies, social informatics, sociology, speech, studio art, theater arts, Western European studies, and women's studies.

Academic Programs

Although Bradley is in session year-round, the official academic year consists of two traditional semesters. While the number of semester hours required for graduation varies with the program chosen, a minimum of 124 hours is required for a bachelor's degree. All students must fulfill the required semester hours in a major as well as complete the basic requirements of Bradley's general education curriculum. This curriculum blends course work from all major areas of study in order to provide each student with a well-rounded education. Students must complete a designated number of hours in composition, speech, mathematics, Western and non-Western civilization, literature, art, philosophy, the social sciences, and physical sciences. Considerable freedom is permitted in the selection of this course work.

Bradley also offers a dynamic honors program for qualified students and the Academic Exploration Program (AEP) for undecided students.

Off-Campus Programs

More than 30 percent of Bradley students take advantage of a study-abroad experience. Bradley has established formal relationships with universities around the world, and students may choose to study at these institutions for a few weeks, a semester, or a whole year. Most academic programs encourage international travel and assist students in scheduling foreign study.

Bradley students also enjoy collaborative learning opportunities in the city of Peoria, including laboratory research at Caterpillar, Inc.; the Downstate Medical Center of Illinois; and the USDA National Center for Agricultural Utilization Research. In addition, the Bradley men's basketball and baseball teams play in professional facilities located in downtown Peoria.

Academic Facilities

The Cullom-Davis Library supports all of the University's programs and offers extensive opportunities for print and computerized research, including online and wireless resources and a comprehensive Learning Assistance Center. The Michel Student Center hosts conferences, camps, and a variety of entertainers throughout the year. Inside the Caterpillar Global Communications Center, students have access to multimedia classrooms and labs, television and radio studios, video and audio editing suites, and a world-class telecommunication facility. Newly renovated Olin Hall of Science is home to some of the finest undergraduate laboratory facilities in the nation, while Jobst Hall includes robotic and automotive labs and a wind tunnel for engineering students. Several advanced labs throughout the campus provide access to Internet2. Bradley is one of only three, private, non-doctoral universities in the nation that is a member of the Internet2 research community. Historic facilities include Bradley Hall, Westlake Hall, Constance Hall, the Hartmann Center for the Performing Arts, and Dingeldine Recital Hall.

Costs

Tuition for the 2003–04 academic year totaled $16,800. Room and board for the year were approximately $5980. Students also paid a $130 health and activity fee. Books and supplies vary by major and year in school, but average approximately $750.

Financial Aid

The Office of Financial Assistance provides many resources to assist families in managing the cost of a Bradley education. Academic scholarships, which are competitive and renewable, are divided into four categories: the Presidential Scholarship, the Dean's Scholarship, the University Scholarship, and the Achievement Grant. Each of these awards is based on a comprehensive review of the student's high school academic record, standardized test scores, cocurricular involvement, letters of recommendation, and personal statement. Bradley also offers scholarships based on diversity, talent in the fine and performing arts, and athletic achievement. The University also participates in the following federally sponsored aid programs: the Federal Perkins Loan, Federal Pell Grant, Federal Supplemental Educational Opportunity Grant (FSEOG), Federal Work-Study, and Federal Stafford Student Loan programs. In order to be considered for these sources of financial assistance, students must submit the Free Application for Federal Student Aid (FAFSA).

Faculty

Bradley University is home to more than 375 teaching faculty members. More than 90 percent of Bradley's faculty members hold the highest degree in their field. The student-faculty ratio is 14:1, and the average class size is 23 students. Academic, vocational, and personal counseling is readily available to all students. Bradley University is nationally recognized for the excellence of its teaching faculty.

Student Government

Bradley's Student Senate is the principle body of student participation in University governance and is a visible contributor to the quality of student life on campus. Members of the senate are elected from the general student body and can serve as early as freshman year. The Student Senate is an active influence on University policy, and members of the Senate have frequent interaction with high-level University administrators and faculty members.

Admission Requirements

Bradley University is open to all qualified students regardless of ethnicity, religion, gender, national origin, age, or disability. Students who have demonstrated past academic achievement and who show promise and aptitude for successful performance at Bradley are encouraged to apply for admission. A student's potential for success in college is judged by the high school average, rank in class, standardized test scores (ACT or SAT), cocurricular involvement, letters of recommendation, and a personal statement or essay. Students who wish to be admitted to Bradley must have completed the college preparatory curriculum at an accredited high school or an equivalent program.

Transfer students in good academic standing are encouraged to apply for admission to Bradley. Transfer students must submit a completed application and official transcripts from all colleges or universities attended.

Bradley operates on a rolling admission basis, and students are typically informed of their admission status within four weeks of applying.

Application and Information

To be considered for admission, students must submit the Application for Undergraduate Admission with a $35 application fee, an official high school transcript, official standardized test scores (ACT or SAT), a personal statement or essay, and at least one letter of recommendation. Bradley strongly encourages students to apply as early as possible during the fall of their senior year. Applications received prior to January 1 are given priority consideration.

An application and additional information may be obtained online or by contacting:

Bradley University
Office of Admissions
1501 W. Bradley Avenue
Peoria, Illinois 61625
Telephone: 309-677-1000
800-447-6460 (toll-free)
World Wide Web: http://admissions.bradley.edu

BRANDEIS UNIVERSITY

WALTHAM, MASSACHUSETTS

The University

Brandeis combines two important traditions in higher education: the dedication to teaching that is characteristic of a small, selective college and the facilities and renowned faculty usually associated with a large research university.

Brandeis is a national and international, nonsectarian institution. From its founding in 1948 by members of the American Jewish community, the University has endorsed a religious pluralism that attracts bright and highly motivated students from culturally diverse backgrounds. The current student body consists of about 3,100 undergraduates, including men and women from nearly every state and fifty-four countries. Seventy-five percent of the students come from out of state. The Graduate School of Arts and Sciences offers programs in twenty-three fields and certificates in three postbaccalaureate programs and attracts an international group of graduate students. Brandeis's two graduate schools, the Heller Graduate School for Social Policy and Management and the International Business School, offer graduate degrees at the master's and doctoral levels.

Students participate in a wide range of activities, from sports to theater and government. The University's more than 215 clubs and organizations provide unlimited opportunities for a varied and extensive extracurricular life.

Brandeis competes at the NCAA Division III level and is one of eight top private universities that make up the University Athletic Association (UAA). Men compete in varsity baseball, basketball, cross-country, fencing, golf, indoor and outdoor track and field, soccer, swimming and diving, and tennis. Women compete in basketball, cross-country, fencing, indoor and outdoor track and field, soccer, softball, swimming and diving, tennis, and volleyball. There is a coed varsity sailing team. Club sports include bicycling, crew, field hockey, ice hockey, lacrosse, martial arts, rugby, skiing, softball, squash, tae kwon do, Ultimate Frisbee, volleyball, weight lifting, and wrestling. Students also play intramural sports and enjoy recreational activities that range from football to Frisbee. The Joseph S. and Clara Ford Athletic and Recreation Complex provides facilities for all of the above, including indoor and outdoor tracks and tennis courts, weight-training facilities, squash courts, a dance/aerobics room, and the largest field house on any New England campus.

More than 85 percent of the students live on campus. Freshmen and sophomores are guaranteed on-campus housing in eight of the nine residential quads. Every quad has a live-in professional staff person and upperclass peer advisers. Three dining halls serve the student body; these include a variety of alternate dining options, from kosher meals to deli-style, Mexican, and Middle Eastern fare.

Location

Brandeis is in Waltham, Massachusetts, a community of 58,000 just 9 miles west of Boston. The University's location combines the benefits of urban life with those of an active campus. The MBTA train line and campus shuttle give easy access to cultural, social, and athletic events in Cambridge and downtown Boston. The campus is also convenient to neighboring beach and mountain resorts. Perhaps the greatest advantage of the location is the social and intellectual interaction afforded by proximity to other Boston-area colleges and universities.

Majors and Degrees

Brandeis University offers forty-three different majors. The Bachelor of Arts (B.A.) degree is offered in African and Afro-American studies; American studies; anthropology; art history; biochemistry; biology; chemistry; classical archaeology and ancient history; classical studies; comparative literature; computer science; creative writing; economics; East Asian studies; English and American literature; European cultural studies; French, German, Greek language and literature; health: science, society, and policy; Hebrew language and literature; history; international and global studies; Islamic and Middle Eastern studies; Italian studies; Latin American studies; Latin language and literature; linguistics; mathematics; music; Near Eastern and Judaic studies; neuroscience; philosophy; physics; politics; psychology; Russian language and literature; sociology; Spanish; studio arts; theater arts; and women's studies.

The Bachelor of Science (B.S.) degree is offered in biochemistry; biology; biological physics; chemistry; computer science; health: science, society, and policy; neuroscience; and physics. Students may pursue double or independent majors.

In addition to choosing a major, undergraduates may follow minors or interdisciplinary programs in several fields: business; East Asian studies; education; environmental studies; film studies; health: science, society, and policy; history of ideas; international and global studies; Internet studies; Islamic and Middle Eastern studies; journalism; Latin American studies; legal studies; medieval and Renaissance studies; peace, conflict, and coexistence studies; religious studies; Russian and Eastern European studies; social justice and social policy; and women's studies. Students may also complete a minor in the following fields: African and Afro-American studies, anthropology, art history, chemistry, classical studies, computer science, creative writing, economics, English and American literature, French, German literature, Hebrew language and literature, linguistics, mathematics, Near Eastern and Judaic studies, neuroscience, philosophy (language, logic, and the philosophy of science; metaphysics and the philosophy of mind; philosophy; or value theory: ethics, politics, society, religion, and art), physics, Russian literature, Spanish, and theater arts. Creative writing is available as a major or minor in the English department.

A combined-degree program is offered with the Columbia University School of Engineering. Preprofessional advising in architecture, business and management, dentistry, law, and medicine prepares students for admission to professional schools after college.

Exceptional undergraduates may enroll in four-year combined B.A./M.A. programs in the departments of American history, anthropology, biochemistry, biology, chemistry, comparative history, mathematics, neuroscience, physics, and politics. Five-year combined B.A./M.A. programs are available in computer science, international economics and finance, and Near Eastern and Judaic studies.

Academic Programs

All first-year students take a seminar taught by Brandeis faculty members that allows them to discuss fundamental questions about human existence and meaning through the critical study of significant texts or artistic creations. A core curriculum is in place to maintain flexibility while ensuring exposure to course work in each of the four major schools: Creative Arts, Humanities, Sciences, and Social Sciences.

Students generally consult with a faculty adviser in the department of major interest to choose a major before the end of their sophomore year. To earn a bachelor's degree, undergraduates complete thirty-two semester courses, including the requirements of a major. Advanced Placement credit, credit for the International Baccalaureate and other international exams, and transfer credit are available upon approval of the registrar.

Brandeis offers numerous opportunities for independent research and fieldwork at the undergraduate level. Most departments offer honors and senior thesis programs, and students engaged in approved research work may apply for funding from the University. The Hiatt Career Center, a leader in the field of career placement, arranges internships in all areas of concentration.

Brandeis operates on a two-semester calendar. Classes for the fall term generally begin in early September, and examinations take place before the winter break. Classes for the spring term begin in late January and end in mid-May.

Off-Campus Programs

Opportunities exist for study abroad in more than fifty countries under the auspices of a variety of programs sponsored by international and American universities. Brandeis also has a special arrangement for a full-year study program at University College in London.

Through a cross-registration agreement, courses not offered at Brandeis may be taken at Tufts University, Boston University, Boston College, and Wellesley College. Students may also take business courses at Babson College and Bentley College.

Academic Facilities

The Goldfarb and Farber Libraries and the Gerstenzang Science Library together contain more than 1.1 million bound volumes, 893,000 microforms, 16,000 current serial subscriptions, and 500 electronic databases. Brandeis participates in the Boston Library Consortium, which allows undergraduates access to most major university libraries in the Boston area.

Forty-one academic facilities offer undergraduates substantial resources in the arts and sciences. The Berlin Premedical Center contains extensive laboratories devoted to preparing students for careers as physicians. The Volen National Center for Complex Systems hosts research in large, complex systems, with the brain and intelligence as the system of greatest interest. The University maintains twenty-seven technology-enhanced classrooms that are equipped with computers and AV equipment as well as seven public computer classrooms and clusters containing PC computers, public printing stations, and selected peripherals. The Instructional Technology Resource Center supports student course-related technology uses. Many laboratories and departments throughout the campus maintain specialized computing facilities and wireless technology. The Computer Science department has a network of Linux and Mac workstations.

The Spingold Theater Arts Center provides three theaters as well as dance and rehearsal rooms. Shapiro Campus Center, an undergraduate facility, provides opportunities for students to become involved in all aspects of theater production. The Slosberg Music Center hosts more than sixty performances by undergraduate musicians and visiting professionals each year. The permanent collection of American art of the post–World War II era at the Rose Art Museum is considered the finest at any university in the New England area.

Costs

Tuition costs, including fees, were $28,984 for the 2003–04 academic year, and the cost of room and board averaged $8320.

Financial Aid

Financial aid at Brandeis is based on need, as determined by information provided on the Free Application for Federal Student Aid (FAFSA) and the College Scholarship Service's Financial Aid PROFILE. However, a significant number of scholarships up to full tuition annually are available primarily on the basis of merit. Need-based aid packages generally include scholarship, loan, and work-study components. Last year, 70 percent of the student body received some form of aid. The University realizes that need is not necessarily determined strictly by income and designs each aid package individually.

Faculty

The faculty at Brandeis consists of men and women united by their commitment to undergraduate education. Ninety-eight percent of the 336 full-time and 82 part-time professors hold doctoral degrees or the highest degrees in their field. The student-faculty ratio of approximately 9:1 allows for a rigorous but personal academic environment. Graduate teaching assistants conduct a limited number of entry-level classes. The median class size is 16.

Student Government

The undergraduate student government, the Student Senate, consists of 8 elected class senators, 10 elected residential senators, and an executive board, who represent their constituents' interests to the University administration through the Dean of Student Affairs. The undergraduate student activity fee generates approximately $750,000 for distribution to more than 215 recognized organizations. Ninety undergraduates serve on thirty-four University committees. Two undergraduate students serve as student representatives to the Board of Trustees.

Admission Requirements

Brandeis places the most emphasis on the applicant's secondary school record. Teacher recommendations, the personal statement, and standardized test scores contribute to the evaluation as well. Prospective students should have followed a strong academic preparatory course while in high school, generally having completed four years of English; three years of a foreign language, including senior study when possible; at least three years of college-preparatory mathematics; and a minimum of one year each of history and laboratory science.

Brandeis expects its applicants to present scores on the College Board's SAT I and on three SAT II Subject Tests. The Writing Subject Test is required. Applicants may submit scores from the ACT in lieu of the SAT I and SAT II Subject Tests. The new SAT I, or the ACT with optional writing section, is going to be required of all students applying to Brandeis beginning with the fall 2006 semester. Students taking the SAT I will also need to take two SAT II tests from two different subject areas (for example, one math and one language). The ELPT exam is not an acceptable SAT II, so if English is not the native language of a student, the Test of English as a Foreign Language (TOEFL) should be taken.

Transfer students, while not required to submit Subject Test scores, are expected to send copies of their SAT I scores as well as transcripts of any credit-granting courses taken. High school transcripts are required.

All candidates for admission are reviewed individually. The Office of Admissions strongly encourages each applicant to arrange for an interview on campus or through an Alumni Admissions Council member in the student's home area.

Application and Information

Individuals interested in applying as early decision candidates should submit application materials before January 1. Regular applicants should submit part I of the application by January 1 and part II by January 15. Transfer students should submit their applications before April 1. The Office of Admissions notifies early decision candidates within four weeks after receiving completed applications. Regular admission candidates receive notification by April 1 and transfer candidates by June 10.

Requests for information and application materials may be directed to:

Office of Admissions
Brandeis University
Waltham, Massachusetts 02454-9110
Telephone: 781-736-3500
800-622-0622 (toll-free outside Massachusetts)
E-mail: sendinfo@brandeis.edu
World Wide Web: http://www.brandeis.edu

BRENAU UNIVERSITY
The Women's College of Brenau University

GAINESVILLE, GEORGIA

The University and The College

The Women's College of Brenau University is a four-year, private, nondenominational liberal arts college for women. The name *Brenau*, derived from German and Latin, means "refined gold." A constantly evolving educational program combines a broad base in the liberal arts with career-oriented majors for women of all ages. A student-teacher ratio of 13:1, a rich heritage of 125 years, and nationally recognized excellence attract more than 600 women from throughout the United States and abroad.

The University's Evening and Weekend College offers undergraduate and graduate instruction, both on and off campus. Approximately 1,500 students enroll in this program, which adds diversity in faculty expertise and library resources to the Women's College program. Qualified Women's College students may enroll in selected evening and weekend courses with the permission of the academic vice president.

The Women's College student is provided with opportunities to learn through participation. Many degree plans emphasize hands-on activities, laboratory experiences, and internships. Leadership experiences are plentiful in more than forty campus organizations, including seven national sororities (Alpha Chi Omega, Alpha Delta Pi, Alpha Gamma Delta, Delta Delta Delta, Delta Sigma Theta, Phi Mu, and Zeta Tau Alpha), special interest groups, and professional and honorary societies. Recreation activities abound in a geographic area rich in natural resources. There are intercollegiate competitions as well as plenty of outdoor activities nearby, such as hiking on the Appalachian Trail, camping, horseback riding, boating, swimming, waterskiing, snow skiing, golf, and tennis. Gainesville is a cultural and economic center of northeast Georgia, and Brenau is the center of much of this activity. A few examples of this are a version of "Meet the Press" called the Brenau News Forum, a weekly feature on the College's own WBCX-FM and area cable TV; nationally recognized artists and performers showcased in Pearce Auditorium (a lovely European-style opera theater) and the new John S. Burd Center for the Performing Arts; and a wide variety of events featuring award-winning students and faculty members. Special guests include current newsmakers, national leaders, writers, and scholars. These people bring a real-life perspective and in-depth knowledge to augment the academic preparation and extensive practical experience of the faculty.

Location

Brenau is located 50 miles northeast of Atlanta at the foothills of the Blue Ridge Mountains in Gainesville, Georgia. The metropolitan area, with a population of 100,000, has a wide variety of recreational opportunities. Gainesville is bordered by Lake Sidney Lanier, the largest freshwater lake in Georgia. Sky Valley, a modern snow-skiing resort, is only an hour's drive from the campus. There are six colleges and universities within an hour's drive.

Majors and Degrees

The School of Business and Mass Communication offers programs leading to the Bachelor of Business Administration degree with majors in accounting, management, and marketing. In addition, it offers the Bachelor of Arts and the Bachelor of Science in mass communications, with concentrations in broadcasting, corporate communications, journalism, and public relations.

The School of Education and Human Development offers programs leading to the Bachelor of Arts and Bachelor of Science degrees in early childhood education, middle grades education, and special education.

The School of Fine Arts and Humanities offers programs leading to the Bachelor of Arts degree in conflict resolution/legal studies and international studies. Programs are also offered leading to the Bachelor of Arts or Bachelor of Science degrees in English, fashion design/merchandising (a B.F.A. is also available), history/political science, and theater. The Bachelor of Arts and Bachelor of Fine Arts degrees in art and design (education, graphics, studio), arts management, dance (education, pedagogy, performance), interior design (B.F.A. only), musical theater, and theater are offered, as is the Bachelor of Music degree in music education, accompanying, and performance (piano or vocal).

The School of Health and Science offers programs that lead to the Bachelor of Arts or the Bachelor of Science degrees in biology, environmental science, and environmental studies. The Bachelor of Science in Nursing degree is offered by the Department of Nursing. The Department of Occupational Therapy offers a combination Bachelor of Science/Master of Science degree in occupational therapy. The Department of Psychology offers a B.A./B.S. degree in psychology.

Academic Program

To receive a degree, students must complete a minimum of 120 semester hours of college work, maintain an overall quality point average of at least 2.0 in all academic work not related to the area of concentration, maintain a minimum quality point average of 2.5 in all academic work related to the area of concentration, complete a minimum of 45 semester hours of academic work during that period, and complete the requirements in general education, the degree program and the upper-division concentration. Excellent laboratory experiences are offered in both lower- and upper-division courses, and internships are either offered or required in most academic areas.

Two summer sessions, special summer institutes, and continuing education programs provide additional opportunities for study.

Qualified entering freshmen may receive advanced placement and academic credit through the Advanced Placement Program, the College-Level Examination Program (CLEP), or an appropriate college achievement test.

Brenau's Learning Disability Program, designed for above-average students with a diagnosed learning disability, provides assistance and tutors where appropriate.

Brenau offers a Leadership Development Program, which provides students with essential leadership skills. Field projects, leadership retreats, internships, and courses in leadership are offered during the year.

Off-Campus Programs

The Women's College coordinates and sponsors various travel programs, which may be combined with a college credit program taken in the period preceding or following travel. Conducted during the regular academic year and during the summer, tours have included Mexico and the People's Republic of China, Africa and Europe, and places of interest within the United States. A junior-year-abroad program in Austria, England, France, the Netherlands, Spain, and the Yucatán peninsula is available.

Academic Facilities

Students have access to the Brenau Trustee Library, the Northeast Georgia Medical Center Library, libraries in the ARCHE system, science laboratories, five computer labs (including the Redwine Technology Center), a TV studio, and a radio station.

Costs

For 2004–05, the tuition for the Women's College is $14,610 and the room and board fee is $8060, for a total of $22,670. The charge per semester hour credit is $487. Students who are not yet 22 years of age or who are not residing with their parents locally are required to live in University housing.

Financial Aid

The University uses the Free Application for Federal Student Aid (FAFSA) to determine eligibility for all need-based financial assistance. Residents of Georgia enrolled as full-time undergraduate students are eligible to receive state tuition grants. Scholarship aid is offered for academic achievement and for special talent in such areas as art, athletics, communications, writing, dance, leadership, music, and theater. Other aid, provided on the basis of need, is available through the Federal Pell Grant, Federal Supplemental Educational Opportunity Grant, Federal Perkins Loan, Federal Work-Study, and Federal Stafford Loan programs as well as through institutional and private grant sources. Veterans' benefits are available also to those who qualify. Applications for institutional scholarships and grants should be submitted by May 1 for the following academic year. Applications for Federal Pell Grants and Federal Stafford Loans must be completed a minimum of six weeks before the student's beginning semester.

Faculty

All members of the faculty teach, and all counsel and advise students. Members of the faculty and professional staff hold degrees from major American and international universities; approximately 97 percent have doctoral or terminal degrees, and all hold membership in various professional organizations. No classes are taught by teaching assistants.

Student Government

An active student government association is responsible, in conjunction with the University administration, for making and maintaining social regulations concerning students. Brenau has an honor code administered by a student honor court, which is advised and reviewed by a faculty advisory committee. An executive council, composed of presidents of campus organizations, sororities, and dormitories, is responsible for coordinating activities and maintaining the University calendar, and it acts as a liaison among administration, faculty, and students. Student representatives sit on all major committees.

Admission Requirements

Students applying for admission to the Women's College should have completed a minimum of 16 units within a college-preparatory curriculum or the equivalent at an accredited secondary school. Applicants should submit a transcript of their high school work, an application for admission accompanied by a nonrefundable fee of $35, test results from the ACT or the College Board's SAT I. Admission decisions are made on a rolling basis.

Brenau welcomes applications from prospective transfer students and junior college graduates. In accord with recommendations from the American Council on Education and the American Association of Community and Junior Colleges, Brenau has adopted the following policy: all graduates of an accredited junior college with an A.A. or A.S. degree are admitted to upper-division status as juniors or seniors in the department of their selection, subject to the departmental and degree requirements; grades of C or better are assigned the same credit as those awarded by Brenau.

Application and Information

For additional information, students should contact:

The Women's College
Brenau University
One Centennial Circle
Gainesville, Georgia 30501
Telephone: 770-534-6100
800-252-5119 Ext. 6100 (toll-free)
E-mail: wcadmissions@lib.brenau.edu
World Wide Web: http://www.admissions.brenau.edu

Brenau University students.

BRESCIA UNIVERSITY

OWENSBORO, KENTUCKY

The University

Brescia University prepares its students for successful careers and for service to others. Brescia was founded by the Ursuline Sisters of Mount Saint Joseph in 1950 as a Catholic liberal arts college. It began as the Mount Saint Joseph College for Women at Maple Mount, Kentucky, in 1925. The school is committed to the concept of value-centered education with a strong emphasis on Christian values. The Southern Association of Colleges and Schools accredits Brescia to award associate and baccalaureate degrees, the Master of Science in Management degree, and the Master of Science degree in curriculum and instruction. The University of Louisville offers the Master of Science in Social Work on Brescia's campus. Students pursuing their master's in social work may also complete their field placement work locally where it is convenient for them. All of Brescia's teacher education programs are accredited by the Kentucky Department of Education.

Currently, 790 students are enrolled at the University. Thirty-eight percent are men; 62 percent are women. The average age of full-time students is 23. The cosmopolitan student body comes from as far away as Canada, Cyprus, Japan, Venezuela, and the West Indies, as well as states from Alaska to California. About 74 percent of the students live off campus. Students can choose from a variety of extracurricular activities, including the *Brescia Broadcast* (student newspaper), the Brescia Owensboro Student Catholic Organization, the Locke Society (students with interests in political science and history), the Alpha Chi National Honor Society, the Delta Epsilon Sigma National Catholic Honor Society, the Brescia Student National Education Association, the International Student Organization, and the Ichabod Society (students with interests in all forms of literature). Students may also participate in the Student Government Association, the Brescia Philosophical Society, the Brescia Science Association, the Brescia Writers Group, the Council for Exceptional Children, the Handbell Choir, the Psychology Club, the Spanish Club, the National Speech Language Hearing Association, the Social Work Club, the Math and Computer Club, and the choir. The Brescia Little Theater performs dramatic productions in an intimate setting. The Parents in Action club is open to any student who is currently a parent. Students and faculty members may enjoy lunchtime concerts featuring jazz, blues, and chamber music. Campus facilities include an indoor walking track, a racquetball court, fitness facilities, weight room, and an attractively furnished Study Pavilion.

Location

Brescia University's 9-acre campus is located near downtown Owensboro, Kentucky. The University is just 45 minutes from Evansville, Indiana; 2 hours southwest of Louisville, Kentucky (home of the Kentucky Derby); and 2 hours north of Nashville, Tennessee.

Owensboro is well known as the "Barbecue Capital of the World." Owensboro has a Barbecue Festival in May and a Summer Festival. The Riverpark Center in Owensboro offers a multitude of productions like *Grease, Chicago,* and *Cats.* The Executive Inn Rivermont features nationally known entertainers like Tanya Tucker, Loretta Lynn, and Toby Keith. These events are within walking distance of Brescia's campus.

Majors and Degrees

Brescia University offers an Associate of Arts degree in catechetical leadership ministry, human relations, liberal arts, and pastoral ministry. Brescia also offers the Associate of Science degree in business, engineering studies, and engineering technology. The Bachelor of Arts degree offers a variety of study areas, including art, art education, English, English: emphasis in professional writing, graphic design, history, integrated studies, pastoral ministry, pre–art therapy, psychology, religious studies, social studies, and Spanish. Minors for the Bachelor of Arts degree may be chosen from the following: English, history, pastoral ministry, political science, psychology, religious studies, Spanish, sociology, and women's studies. Majors for the Bachelor of Science degree are accounting, biology, business, business: economics and finance emphasis, business: human resource development or management emphasis, chemistry, communication sciences and disorders, computer and mathematical sciences, early elementary education, general studies, mathematics, medical technology, middle grades education, science with an area of concentration, and special education. Minors for the Bachelor of Science degree are accounting, biology, business, chemistry, computer studies, finance/economics, mathematics, and physics. Brescia also offers the Bachelor of Social Work degree and a dual-degree program in chemistry/chemical engineering through the University of Louisville.

Teacher certification/endorsement is offered in the following areas: art education; early elementary education; middle grades and secondary (8–12) education in English, mathematics, science, social studies, and Spanish; and special education in the areas of learning and behavior disorders and moderate and severe disabilities. Candidates graduate with a license to teach in Kentucky schools. The license is reciprocal in some other states.

Academic Programs

There are two semesters at Brescia—fall and spring. Intersession is offered in May. A summer session is offered in June and in July. In addition, Brescia has a Weekend College program that is divided into four modules. Candidates for the associate degree must earn a minimum of 63 credit hours, with a minimum of 27 hours of general education requirements. Bachelor's degree candidates must earn a minimum of 128 credit hours, of which at least 42 credit hours are in upper-division courses. They must also complete 57 credit hours of general education courses and complete a major program of study, with a 2.5 (C) grade point average or better in all upper-division courses in the major and minor. A cumulative grade point average of at least 2.0 on a 4.0 scale must be achieved. The Center for English as a Second Language (ESL) at Brescia University offers a variety of both full-time and part-time English language courses. The two levels (intermediate and advanced) in the Intensive Summer Session are content-oriented courses that focus on speaking/listening, reading, writing, and the study skills necessary for academic success. Brescia graduates should be committed to the following values: continued personal, intellectual, and spiritual growth; the welfare of others; respect for the physical environment; and respect for the appreciation of the diversity in cultures. Brescia's Ministry Formation Program is the only accredited undergraduate program of its kind in the nation.

Academic Facilities

The Brescia University campus consists of seventeen buildings within a two-block area near downtown Owensboro. Facilities include the library, science building, administration building, campus center, graduate center, and residence halls. The library, campus center, and classroom buildings are accessible to people with disabilities. The library has more than 180,000 volumes and is fully automated, with access to the Kentucky Library Network (300 libraries). Biology and medical technology students view the human body through computer simulations with the powerful ADAM, while mathematics students graph 3-D space curves and solve large systems of equations with Mathematica. Computer science and physics students learn from state-of-the-art IBM hardware and software packages, including the ability to analyze experiments by digital imaging. There are five computer labs available for students on campus. Every student may receive access to the Internet and e-mail. Students in Brescia's modern language classes and the English as a second language program have access to a state-of-the-art digital computer lab.

Costs

Full-time tuition at Brescia is currently $10,600, which is well below the national average. Room and board costs vary; the cost of a double room and a ten-meal plan is $4600. A technology fee of $60 per semester is assessed for each student, and the activity fee is $100 per year. Other fees vary according to the student's course work but are typically $50. New books are estimated to cost about $650. A $100 deposit is required for housing.

Financial Aid

More than 85 percent of Brescia students receive scholarships or financial aid. Students receive aid through the many federal and state programs in which the University participates and through the University's deferred payment plan. Brescia also awards scholarships annually to incoming students on the basis of academic excellence and leadership qualities. Students who wish to be considered for financial aid should complete the Free Application for Federal Student Aid (FAFSA). Preference is given to applications received by March 1. Students may obtain the FAFSA by contacting their high school counselor or the University's Web site listed below.

Faculty

Brescia's faculty consists of 72 full- and part-time members. There are almost equal numbers of men and women, and the faculty includes both lay and religious members. More than 70 percent of the full-time faculty members have earned terminal degrees. A 14:1 student-faculty ratio assures students of individualized attention.

Student Government

Brescia students participate in University governance through the Student Government Association. They are represented on the Board of Trustees committees as well as various other committees.

Admission Requirements

Applications to Brescia are reviewed on an individual basis. Grades and course work receive strong consideration. College-preparatory and liberal arts courses are recommended. Standardized test scores are taken into consideration. Students are asked to submit a high school transcript, showing proof of graduation date, or GED score report and an ACT or SAT score report. Transfer students must submit official transcripts from each college they attended. The Test of English as a Foreign Language (TOEFL) is required for nonnative English speakers.

Application and Information

Applications are considered as they are received. Applications and transcripts should be submitted with a $25 nonrefundable application fee. Admission is on a rolling basis. Applications must be received by March 15 for scholarship consideration. Students may e-mail the admissions staff, individual counselors, and financial aid staff members through Brescia's Web site at the address below.

For further information, students and parents should contact:

Admissions
Brescia University
717 Frederica Street
Owensboro, Kentucky 42301
Telephone: 877-273-7242 (toll-free)
E-mail: admissions@brescia.edu
World Wide Web: http://www.brescia.edu

Brescia Quad in the spring.

BREVARD COLLEGE

BREVARD, NORTH CAROLINA

The College

Brevard College offers a range of distinctive baccalaureate degree programs on a beautiful residential campus in Brevard, North Carolina. The curriculum combines small-classroom instruction with creative internships and immersion experiences. It also provides a strong core in the liberal arts and offers great strength in fine arts as well as in interdisciplinary programs that educate for leadership and service and draw on the natural resources of the College's mountain setting. Brevard has a diverse student population of 664 students, from thirty-seven states and twenty other countries.

Ranked among the top twenty-five Comprehensive Colleges in the South by *U.S. News & World Report,* Brevard offers close to forty majors and minors, including business and organizational leadership, religion studies, and wilderness leadership and experiential education. It also has one of the finest music and fine arts programs in the region.

Brevard offers an education that is supportive, flexible, and challenging. Every Brevard College student takes part in a one-semester course called the First-Year Forum (FYF). FYF allows students to learn about traditions, service opportunities, academic resources, and clubs and gives students a chance to meet weekly with a faculty mentor and other first-year students. Brevard's unique orientation program is ranked as one of the best freshman-year experience programs in the country by *U.S. News & World Report.*

The College's low 10:1 student-faculty ratio allows professors to design their classes based on student interest and to forge bonds with students that last the entire four years—if not a lifetime. Brevard also offers an honors program for students seeking greater challenges in the classroom as well as a Learning Enrichment Center that provides one-on-one academic support and weekly tutoring sessions.

Brevard has an active student government association and approximately twenty student-run clubs and organizations, including Omicron Delta Kappa, the national leadership honor society; Campus Crusade for Christ, a nondenominational fellowship group; and the Outing Club, which sponsors the Banff Mountain World Tour, an outdoor adventure film festival, each year. Service is a big part of the Brevard College experience, and almost every student club and organization is involved in volunteer work in the surrounding forests or at local schools, churches, and hospitals.

The residence halls are the center of student life at Brevard College. Most have all of the amenities of home: high-speed Internet access, free washers and dryers, and kitchens. All are located near the recently updated Myers Dining Hall and the new food court, which is housed within the student commons. The Annabel Jones women's residence hall recently completed a $1.9-million renovation. In addition to an updated heating and cooling system, residents enjoy new windows, carpets, and furniture as well as modern bathrooms, a fitness room and ballet practice room, and new student lounge and vending areas.

Recognized as a "Champion of Character Institution" by the National Association of Intercollegiate Athletics (NAIA), the Brevard Tornadoes are one of the best varsity sports teams in the region. More than half of the College's sixteen varsity teams have placed in the top twenty in the NAIA. The College boasts a new state-of-the-art tennis facility, which is one of the finest in the Southeast. Students also enjoy a variety of intramural sports, including an annual Frisbee Golf Tournament.

Location

Brevard College is located in Brevard, the county seat of western North Carolina's Transylvania County, renown as the "Land of Waterfalls." The College is less than 30 minutes from the Asheville airport (45 minutes from Asheville); 2 hours from Charlotte, North Carolina; and 3 hours from Atlanta, Georgia. Once students arrive on campus, they are surrounded by the forests and rivers of the Blue Ridge Mountains. Nearby Pisgah National Forest offers hiking and mountain-biking trails, white water, pristine trout waters, and some of the most challenging rock-climbing sites east of the Rockies.

Majors and Degrees

At Brevard, students can explore many fields of study, including majors in art (optional emphases in archaeology, art history, graphic design, painting, photography, and sculpture), business and organizational leadership (required emphasis in entrepreneurship and small-business leadership, information technology, management and organizational leadership, or sport and event management), ecology, English/interdisciplinary studies (required emphasis in art, communication/journalism, creative writing, environmental journalism, history, literary studies, music, natural sciences, prelaw, religion/philosophy, or theater arts), environmental studies (optional emphasis in archaeology), exercise science (required emphasis in allied medical fields, fitness leadership, or teaching/coaching), health science studies, history (optional emphases in art history and archaeology, environmental history, modern American history, and modern European history), integrated studies (emphases in prelaw, and pre–health professions), mathematics, music (optional emphases in composition, jazz studies, music teaching, music theory/history, and performance), psychology, religion studies (optional emphases in counseling and educational ministries, music ministries, outdoor ministries, philosophical studies, and youth ministries), theater studies, and wilderness leadership and experiential education. Minors are available in art, biology, chemistry, coaching, ecology, English, environmental art and design, environmental studies, fitness leadership, geology, history, information technology, management and organizational leadership, mathematics, music, natural history, personal fitness, prelaw, psychology, religion, sport and event management, theater, and wilderness leadership and experiential education.

Teacher licensure programs are available in English, math, science, and social studies at both the high school and middle school levels. K–12 teacher licensure programs are available in art, music, physical education, and theater. Brevard College is currently developing a licensure program at the elementary level.

Academic Programs

Brevard College uses a semester calendar and offers Bachelor of Arts degrees. The College's core curriculum provides a strong interdisciplinary base in literature and languages, religion, humanities, mathematics and analytical reasoning, history, natural and social sciences, fine arts, physical activity, and environmental studies. In addition to traditional disciplines, Brevard incorporates the surrounding natural resources into course work, taking students to study in the Pisgah National Forest, the Davidson and French Broad River ecosystems, the Great Smoky Mountain National Park, and the Cradle of Forestry in America. A special, selective academic program called "Voice of the Rivers" blends wilderness leadership skills with environmental studies. The College also offers strong programs in music and art, in which students benefit from performance and exhibition opportunities on and off campus in settings such as the Porter Center for Performing Arts at Brevard College, the Brevard Music Center, the Brevard Chamber Orchestra, and the Asheville Art Museum. Other opportunities for students include internships, study-abroad programs, and the honor societies Beta Beta Beta and Omicron Delta Kappa. Brevard College incorporates community service into the academic curriculum through a variety of service-oriented classes.

Academic Facilities

Brevard College's 120-acre campus within the city of Brevard reflects the beauty of its mountain setting, the balance of tradition, and the energy of change. Major buildings on campus include the McLarty-Goodson Building for the humanities and social sciences, the Bryan Moore Building for the natural sciences, the Porter Center for Performing Arts, the Dunham Music Building, the Sims Art Center, and the Beam Administration Building.

The College recently completed the first floor of its new Moore Science Building annex. The annex offers additional classroom spaces, including an ecology/environmental studies lab and a state-of-the-art chemistry/biochemistry laboratory. The expansion was necessitated by the growth of the College's programs in ecology, environmental studies, and the sciences. Plans are underway to add a second story to the annex to house additional classrooms.

Brevard recently dedicated the Lyday Natural Science Lab. Located on the banks of the French Broad River, the outdoor laboratory is designed to support eighteen of the College's field research courses as well as to provide boat access for College field trips.

The Porter Center, which houses a 700-seat auditorium, a magnificent 3,500-pipe organ, and an experimental black box theater, offers students their first chance to stage their own theater and music productions and to perform with nationally recognized artists. The Porter Center is a premiere site for performing artists of international acclaim, including Harry Belafonte, Peter Nero, the Beaux Arts Trio, Herbie Hancock, and the Stanislavsky Opera Company.

The Sims Art Building is the home of the College's Spiers Gallery, which hosts exhibitions by visiting artists, students, faculty members, and community artists throughout the year.

The James A. Jones Library provides access to diverse information resources, including more than 55,700 books, 300 periodicals, 3,000 microforms, and 3,800 audiovisual materials, such as compact discs and videos. Internet access is available to eighty databases containing indexes, abstracts, and thousands of full-text resources, including NC LIVE—a gateway to North Carolina's electronic information. The library also offers wireless Internet access to students.

In addition to its regular academic buildings and facilities, the College maintains several state-of-the-art computer labs on campus. The College also has several specialty labs, including a Macintosh-based lab for graphic design and a Macintosh-based music lab.

Costs

The College makes every effort to offer high-quality educational programs while keeping costs as reasonable as possible. At Brevard College, students are able to obtain an education for less than the actual cost of instruction and other student services. The difference, which averages about 35 percent of the total cost, is provided through the support of earnings on endowment investments and gifts from friends of the College.

For 2003–04, tuition, room, board, and fees cost less than $20,000 for students living on campus. Commuter students paid about $13,500. For North Carolina residents, total costs are reduced by the North Carolina Legislative Tuition Grant. For the 2003–04 academic year, the rate was $1800.

Financial Aid

The philosophy of the Financial Aid Office is to assist students in meeting their financial obligations to the College through need-based or merit-based grants, scholarships, loans, and work-study to the maximum extent possible, based on eligibility and available funds. Every student requiring financial assistance must file the Free Application for Federal Student Aid (FAFSA). Opportunities for student financial aid are available to every student who can show financial need, superior academic achievement, significant leadership and community service experience, or talent in athletics, art, drama, or music. Brevard College does not discriminate on the basis of sex, race, color, handicap, religion, or national or ethnic origin in the administration of its financial aid resources.

Faculty

Brevard College's faculty is an exceptional group of 61 full-time and 33 part-time instructors, characterized by their accomplishments and strong personal character. The faculty members are dedicated to undergraduate teaching and take pride in all aspects of their jobs, from instruction and lecturing to advising and mentoring. This dedication, along with the 10:1 student-faculty ratio, gives students an opportunity to form lasting and meaningful student-teacher relationships. The College's faculty members pride themselves on being as devoted to the teaching of freshmen and sophomores as to the mentoring of juniors and seniors.

Student Government

Brevard College makes a special commitment to experiential learning opportunities through the Student Government Association (SGA). SGA seeks broad representation from students so they can work together to make a difference in academic and campus life. This organization gives students invaluable experience in leadership and governance. SGA leaders meet regularly with the administration, faculty members, and trustees and are actively engaged in the shared governance of the institution.

Admission Requirements

Brevard College seeks to admit students who distinguish themselves by their talents, creativity, adventurous spirit, motivation, and concern for others. At Brevard, students have every opportunity to take advantage of educational programs, small classes, and caring faculty members in order to realize their potential as students and as leaders among their peers. The College is interested in enrolling students who give proof of academic curiosity, creativity, and community concern and actively seeks those who add diversity to the student body, welcoming students of any race, national origin, religious belief, gender, or physical ability. The College seeks students who display a willingness to exhibit personal initiative and leadership and are likely to contribute their energies to the campus community. An admissions staff of energetic and caring people invites all interested students to visit and learn about Brevard's special community. The application process is candidate-oriented; the admissions staff serves as the applicant's advocate.

When the applicant's file is complete, it is reviewed by an Admissions Counselor and/or Committee. The Admissions Counselor notifies the candidate of the decision. Decisions are made on a rolling basis, every week. A completed applicant file comprises a completed application; a nonrefundable $30 application fee; official transcript(s) showing all high school work, grades, and test scores; and official SAT I or ACT scores. Transfer applicants must also include transcripts of all college work attempted. International students for whom English is a second language must submit Test of English as a Foreign Language (TOEFL) scores as well.

For students wishing to be considered for degree programs in music or studio art, an audition with a Brevard College music faculty member or submission of a ten-slide portfolio of the student's artwork is required. For freshmen who have not successfully completed at least a semester of collegiate work, the high school transcript should show successful completion of college preparatory work, including 4 units of English, 3 units of mathematics, and courses in social studies, laboratory sciences, foreign language, and the arts. The program at Brevard College requires completion of core requirements that include studies in the above fields.

Specific guidelines for freshman, transfer, and international students can be found on the admissions Web site at http://www.brevard.edu/admissions.

Application and Information

For more information, students should contact:

Office of Admissions
Brevard College
400 North Broad Street
Brevard, North Carolina 28712
Telephone: 800-527-9090 (toll-free)
E-mail: admissions@brevard.edu
World Wide Web: http://www.brevard.edu

BRIARCLIFFE COLLEGE

BETHPAGE, NEW YORK

The College

Briarcliffe College was established in 1966 to serve the educational needs of Long Island residents. A suburb of New York City, Long Island experienced a rapid growth in population that resulted in a potential labor force that attracted many top corporations. The College has grown from an original enrollment of 18 women to the current coeducational enrollment of more than 3,100 students per year. Day, evening, weekend, and summer classes are offered.

A wide range of student activities is coordinated through the College's division of student affairs. Briarcliffe students have many opportunities to participate in college life through academic, social, service, and athletic programs. Typical events include theater trips, guest speakers, community service and charitable activities, concerts, and dances. Special interest clubs for law, broadcasting, computers, and other academic areas are active on campus. The athletic department sponsors intercollegiate and intramural sports. Scholarships are awarded for men's baseball and ice hockey, women's soccer and softball, and men's and women's basketball, bowling, cross-country, golf, and lacrosse.

A high-technology, small-business incubator is located on the main campus. The incubator provides up to twenty young companies with a supportive environment in which to grow. The companies are able to share resources, access the research and intellectual strengths of Briarcliffe College, and provide internship experiences for students.

Location

Briarcliffe College is located on Long Island, New York, with campuses located in Bethpage and Patchogue. Both campuses reflect the natural beauty of Long Island, including its world-renowned shoreline, yet are close enough to Manhattan to facilitate participation in the rich cultural experience that is New York City. Many students commute by car to Briarcliffe College. Housing is provided for out-of-state or international students. In addition, both the Bethpage and Patchogue campuses are only a short drive away from the major airports in the region. John F. Kennedy International, LaGuardia, and Long Island's Islip-MacArthur airport are all easily accessible from either campus.

Majors and Degrees

Briarcliffe College confers the Bachelor of Business Administration (B.B.A.), Bachelor of Fine Arts (B.F.A.) in graphic design, Associate in Applied Science (A.A.S.), and Associate in Occupational Studies (A.O.S.) degrees.

Program majors are offered in accounting, business administration, computer applications specialist studies, computer information systems, criminal justice, digital photography, graphic design, networking and computer technology, and office technologies.

The Bachelor of Business Administration degree offers concentrations in information technology, management, and marketing.

Academic Program

The multilevel structure of the academic program enables students to enroll immediately in four-year programs or to earn a credential by completing short-term diploma or associate degree programs. Briarcliffe College provides a rich, career-oriented curriculum that prepares students to initiate or advance in their careers.

A minimum of 120 credits is required to earn a bachelor's degree, and 60 credits are required for an associate degree. Diploma programs may be completed in two semesters of full-time study by successfully finishing prescribed course work.

In addition to courses directly related to the major field of study, there is a general education requirement for each degree program. A minimum of 42 general education credits is required for the B.B.A. degree, and a minimum of 21 credits in general education are required for the A.A.S. degree.

The College operates on a traditional two-semester calendar for day classes and an innovative evening schedule that enables students to begin classes at four points during the year to earn semester-hour credits.

Academic Facilities

The main campus building is a 240,000-square-foot facility that was purchased by the College in 1996. The size of the building makes it possible for Briarcliffe College to house lecture halls, computer labs, an electronics lab, conference rooms, faculty offices, counseling offices, and the College library all under one roof. The main campus is wired with fiber-optic cables and connected to the Internet through cable modems and T-1 lines. The branch campus is also served with a T-1 line that connects it to the main network. Computers throughout the College are connected using sophisticated network technology. Briarcliffe College has computer labs that operate on DOS/Windows, Macintosh, and UNIX platforms.

The Briarcliffe College Library supports the academic program with electronic and traditional bibliographic resources. The library is a member of the Long Island Library Resource Council and serves a New York State Electronic Gateway, enabling students and faculty members to access information and materials from libraries throughout the world. Software used throughout the curriculum is installed in computers available for student use in the library.

Specialized programs in networking technology and telecommunications are supported by an electronics laboratory. Student members of the Briarcliffe Amateur Radio Club (BARC) operate a short-wave radio station.

An art studio provides a setting for students to draw still-life and live models. Design software that students are likely to encounter when they enter the workforce is installed on Mac and PC platforms for use by graphic design and architectural design students.

Costs

The tuition for full-time students during the 2003–04 academic year was $5940 per semester. Full-time tuition charges apply to students enrolled in 12 to 18 credits. Tuition for part-time students is $530 per credit.

Financial Aid

Briarcliffe College offers a wide variety of financial aid programs, including scholarships, grants, loans, and work-study. Need-based and achievement-based awards are available. All applicants for financial aid are expected to complete the Briarcliffe College Financial Aid Application and the Free

Application for Federal Student Aid (FAFSA). New York State residents receive an Express Tuition Assistance Program Application (ETA), which must also be completed.

Briarcliffe College directly funds several scholarship programs. The Presidential Scholarship is awarded to first-time college students who have earned at least an 80 high school average and have cumulative math and verbal SAT I scores of at least 1075. Daniel Turan Memorial Scholarships are competitive awards for students who have completed a sequence of business courses in high school. An Alumni Scholarship exam is administered twice each year for high school seniors. Alumni Scholarships may award as much as $12,000 for a bachelor's degree program. Program-Specific Scholarships are competitive awards valued up to $6000 in each major program offered at Briarcliffe College. Athletic scholarships are awarded to outstanding athletes in baseball, bowling, golf, hockey, lacrosse, soccer, and softball.

Transfer Scholarships are available to students who have earned associate degrees at accredited community or junior colleges.

Faculty

The primary responsibility of all faculty members at Briarcliffe College is to provide effective learning experiences for their students. There are 49 full-time and 48 part-time faculty members. Faculty members set aside weekly office hours to meet with students and to provide academic advisement and program guidance.

Student Government

The Student Government Association (SGA), through its elected officers, is the official voice of the student body in campus governance. All matriculated students are voting members of the SGA. The SGA sponsors social, cultural, and athletic activities both on and off campus. The College views extracurricular activities as an important component of each student's education and relies heavily on the SGA to identify and support programs that inspire active participation by a broad cross-section of the College community.

Admission Requirements

Briarcliffe College has established admissions criteria that recognize the diversity of the college-going population. Regular admission as a matriculating student (one who is taking courses with the intention of earning a degree) requires a high school diploma or the equivalent.

Each applicant to the College is encouraged to meet with one of Briarcliffe's admissions counselors. Previous academic records, scores on standardized testing, and recommendations submitted by the applicant are all considered by the Admissions Office in making a determination of acceptance.

Transfer students are welcome at Briarcliffe College. Course work in which the student has earned at least a C grade at an accredited college is considered for transfer. International students should contact the Admissions Office or check the College Web site (listed below) for information on admission and obtaining an I-20A/B form.

Application and Information

Students who are applying for fall semester admission are encouraged to submit their applications before January 1. The College has a rolling admissions policy that permits admissions decisions to be made as applications and supporting documentation are reviewed, beginning in December. Applications for the spring and summer terms should be submitted at least sixty days before classes are scheduled to begin. Late applications are considered on a space-available basis.

Additional information and application materials are available by contacting Briarcliffe College at the following addresses:

Bethpage Campus:

Theresa Donohue, Vice President of Marketing and Admissions
Anna Lynskey, Director of Adult Admissions
Jeff Sacks, Director of National Admissions
Lancene Union, Director of High School Admissions
Briarcliffe College
1055 Stewart Avenue
Bethpage, New York 11714
Telephone: 888-333-1150 (toll-free)
Fax: 516-470-6020
E-mail: info@bcl.edu

Patchogue Campus:

Kathy McDermott, Director of Admissions
Maria Quigley, Director of High School Admissions
Briarcliffe College
10 Lake Street
Patchogue, New York 11772
Telephone: 866-235-5207 (toll-free)
Fax: 631-654-5082
E-mail: info@bcl.edu

World Wide Web: http://www.briarcliffe.edu

The picnic area near the main campus building is a popular spot to get together with friends.

BRIDGEWATER COLLEGE

BRIDGEWATER, VIRGINIA

The College

Bridgewater College was established in 1880 by Daniel C. Flory as a coeducational school affiliated with the Church of the Brethren. The founder's vision was "to aid young men and women to secure a good, practical education, and fit them for a higher sphere of usefulness in life (life after college)." Today, the College continues this tradition with its mission "to educate and develop the whole person," and an emphasis on providing a liberal arts education. Great importance is placed on maintaining academic rigor and quality. The College maintains a student-faculty ratio of 15:1 in order to facilitate effective interaction between faculty members and students, both in and out of the classroom.

Bridgewater has an enrollment of more than 1,400 students from a variety of backgrounds and religious affiliations. Students come mainly from Virginia and the mid-Atlantic states; twenty-one states and nine countries are represented. Members of minority groups comprise 13 percent of the student body. The majority of students are under age 25.

Seven residence halls, ten College-owned houses, and ten apartments are located on campus for resident students. A new 192-bed apartment complex opens on the campus in fall 2004. New students are assigned to a residence hall room with another new student of compatible interests through a nonautomated housing selection process. All residence facilities are wired to provide cable, telephone, and Internet access.

A large variety of clubs, societies, and organizations exist on campus to meet students' needs and interests. A complete schedule of intercollegiate sports for men and women is offered during each session, and an extensive intramural sports program promotes sportsmanship, leadership, physical health, and team play. The Funkhouser Center for Health and Wellness provides top-notch fitness facilities and offers a full range of programs that promote health and wellness.

The College is dedicated to meeting the needs of students. In addition to faculty and staff members, a writing center, career services, counseling services, and a chaplain are available to assist students with their academic, personal, and spiritual needs and to help with career planning. Reasonable and appropriate accommodations are provided to enrolled students with disabilities to ensure equal access to the academic program and College-administered activities.

Bridgewater College is accredited by the Commission on Colleges of the Southern Association of Colleges and Schools (1866 Southern Lane, Decatur, Georgia, 30033-4097; telephone: 404-679-4501) to award baccalaureate degrees.

Location

Bridgewater College is located in the town of Bridgewater in the scenic and historic Shenandoah Valley. The 190-acre campus has a complex of buildings with a modified Georgian architectural style. Facilities for boarding horses are adjacent to the campus. Bridgewater is located 7 miles south of the city of Harrisonburg and is convenient to the urban areas of Washington, D.C.; Richmond; and Roanoke. Air transportation is available at Shenandoah Valley Regional Airport, 13 miles from campus. The valley area is rich in the history of the early United States and the Civil War. Students can enjoy skiing, hiking, canoeing, bicycling, and other seasonal outdoor sports in the area.

Majors and Degrees

Bridgewater College awards the Bachelor of Arts degree in allied health science, art, applied physics, athletic training, biology, business administration, chemistry, communication studies, computer science, economics, English, environmental science, family and consumer sciences, French, health and exercise science, history, history and political science, information systems management, international studies, liberal studies (available only to students in the elementary and special education programs), mathematics, medical technology, music, nutrition and wellness, philosophy and religion, physics, physics and mathematics, political science, psychology, sociology, and Spanish. The College offers the Bachelor of Science degree in allied health science, applied physics, athletic training, biology, business administration, chemistry, communication studies, computer science, economics, environmental science, family and consumer sciences, health and exercise science, information systems management, liberal studies, mathematics, medical technology, nutrition and wellness, physics, physics and mathematics, political science, psychology, and sociology.

The College offers four-year curricula leading to the bachelor's degree and a state-approved program of teacher preparation at the PK–6 and 6–12 levels. Art education, teaching English as a second language (ESL), music education, foreign languages education, and physical education endorsement programs are offered for grades PK–12. A certification program (K–12) is offered in special education. Through reciprocity agreements, students complete Bridgewater's teacher education program may be certified to teach in many states.

Minors may be pursued in art, athletic coaching, biology, business administration, chemistry, communication studies, computer information systems, computer science, economics, English, equine studies, family and consumer sciences, French, German, history, mathematics, music, nutrition and wellness, peace studies, philosophy and religion, physics, political science, psychology, social work, sociology, Spanish, and theater.

Dual-degree programs are offered in engineering with George Washington University and Virginia Tech, forestry with Duke University, veterinary science with Virginia Tech, and physical therapy with Shenandoah University and George Washington University. Bridgewater is also associated with American University for internships/research programs in their Washington Semester and World Capitals program. Preprofessional programs are offered in dentistry, engineering, law, medicine, ministry, nursing, occupational therapy, pharmacy, physical therapy, and veterinary science.

Academic Programs

At Bridgewater, academic excellence is a commitment to provide an education that has breadth, depth, distinction, and discovery through a liberal arts foundation, the student's academic major, elective courses that are tailored to individual interests, and the Personal Development Portfolio (PDP) program. The general education curriculum focuses on developing the liberal arts: writing, speaking, reasoning, and thinking globally, analytically, and creatively. The PDP program is designed to enhance student development as whole persons in the four dimensions of personal development: citizenship and community responsibility, intellectual growth and discovery, emotional maturation and health, and ethical and spiritual growth. The centerpiece of the PDP program is the senior portfolio, which includes documentation of achievement in the four dimensions and participation in service learning, a resume meeting specific criteria, and evidence of career planning. The academic major courses add depth in one field to the breadth of knowledge that the student gains in the general education curriculum. The major enables a student to work effectively in a major field after graduation or prepares one for graduate or professional study. Elective options provide the student with the opportunity to take courses that increase skills and understanding in a field, address specific career interests, and meet professional or graduate school requirements. Students may also add to their curriculum by completing minor field requirements that are related to their major field of study.

A minimum of 123 credits must be earned to graduate; at least 48 credits must be chosen from courses at the junior and senior levels. A quality point average of at least 2.0 must be earned in all work attempted and in the major. Candidates for graduation must pass a written comprehensive examination in their major. Flexibility is added to the academic program through an internship program, honors projects, independent study, and an honors program. Bridgewater's academic calendar provides a January interterm experience. During the interterm, courses are offered giving the student the opportunity to travel in the United States and abroad.

Students may be exempted from certain requirements by demonstrating proficiency in written expression, quantitative reasoning, or foreign languages. Credit and advanced placement are awarded to students on the basis of scores on Advanced Placement tests of the College Board. In order to be considered for course credit and/or exemption from certain requirements, students must earn scores of 3 or higher on Advanced Placement tests.

Off-Campus Programs

The Brethren Colleges Abroad program gives students the opportunity to study in China, Ecuador, England, France, Germany, Greece, India, Japan, Mexico, or Spain. The program provides a firsthand knowledge of a foreign language and culture and an opportunity to become an active participant in the challenging task of creating a climate of mutual respect and understanding among the nations of the world. Brethren Colleges Abroad instituted a peace and justice program in fall 2003. Students have the opportunity to analyze some of the most fundamental issues confronting humanity through a series of programs in seven locations throughout Europe and another location in Cuba.

Academic Facilities

Bridgewater has outstanding classroom and scientific laboratory facilities. Each classroom building has computer laboratories with Internet and campus network access for student use. The Cole Hall auditorium seats approximately 650 people and is equipped with a modern stage, dressing rooms, a stage lighting system, motion picture and sound equipment, two artist grand pianos, and a fifty-one-rank Möller pipe organ. The Carter Center for Worship and Music includes a sanctuary, ten soundproof practice rooms, two Reuter pipe organs, and twenty-three pianos.

The Alexander Mack Memorial Library houses 181,197 volumes, 659 current subscriptions, and 412,460 microform units. Special collections include the Church of the Brethren Collection, Genealogy, and Virginiana. The Reuel B. Pritchett Museum contains more than 10,000 items of historical, cultural, and religious interest.

Health and physical education facilities include a large gymnasium, a 25-meter indoor pool, playing fields, and an all-weather track. The Funkhouser Center for Health and Wellness provides facilities for intramural and recreational activities, including basketball, volleyball, and racquetball courts; an indoor track; a cardiac and weight-training center; and a multipurpose room for aerobics, dance, and wrestling.

Costs

The basic cost for residential students for 2004–05 is $26,470. The estimated cost for books and supplies is $895. Estimated personal expenses are $990. Additional fees are charged for private instrumental or voice instruction. Accounts are payable by the semester or through a monthly payment plan arranged off campus.

Financial Aid

Scholarships, grants, loans, and on-campus jobs are available for qualified students through federal, state, institutional, and outside sources and are awarded in individualized financial aid packages. All applicants for any kind of financial aid must submit the Free Application for Federal Student Aid (FAFSA) by March 1. A work-study program provides jobs for qualified students. Early application is advised.

McKinney Achievement in a Community of Excellence (ACE) scholarships are awarded based on cumulative high school GPA and SAT scores. Applicants meeting all admissions requirements and having a cumulative high school GPA of 3.0 or better are eligible for ACE awards. Selected incoming freshmen who have a cumulative high school GPA of at least 3.8 and a combined SAT score of at least 1350 may receive a President's Merit ACE Plus Award for full tuition, based on academic achievement and standardized test scores.

Faculty

The faculty consists of 88 full-time members, 77 percent of whom hold a terminal degree. Several part-time faculty members bring unique skills to various departments. Faculty members also serve as faculty advisers, major professors, and sponsors of student organizations and activities.

Student Government

The Student Government acts as a representative of the student body by presenting student opinions and ideas to the faculty and administration and by interpreting the policies and standards of the College to the students. Through its own structure as well as the appointment of students to serve on College committees, the Student Government involves students in many aspects of the operation of the College. The student body president, vice president, and senators are elected by the students. The College Honor System is upheld by the Honor Council, a judicial body composed of 9 students appointed by the student body president and with a faculty member serving as an adviser.

Admission Requirements

Bridgewater College seeks students with above-average preparation who demonstrate a serious attitude toward studies. Although a majority of the students are from Virginia, College policy does not demand that Virginia applicants be accepted first. International students are welcomed at Bridgewater. The admissions policy for transfers is similar to the one for freshman applicants; a high school transcript is required, and students must have maintained a grade point average of 2.0 or better on previous college work. Decisions are made after a careful study of academic background (including rank in class, GPA, and course selection), SAT I scores, and letters of recommendation. An on-campus interview is strongly recommended. Rank in the upper half of the high school graduating class and strong SAT I scores are required. Scores on SAT II Subject Tests are not required but are strongly recommended. ACT scores are accepted in lieu of SAT I scores. The College seeks to enroll qualified students regardless of sex, race, color, creed, handicap, religion, or national or ethnic origin.

Application and Information

Information relating to Bridgewater College, including an electronic application, can be accessed through the College's Web site. Application may be made between completion of the junior year of high school and June 1 of the year of enrollment. Under the College's rolling admissions policy, students can expect notification of the admission decision within thirty days of the College's receipt of all records and credentials. Arrangements can be made for deferred entrance.

Linda F. Stout
Director of Enrollment Operations
Bridgewater College
402 East College Street
Bridgewater, Virginia 22812
Telephone: 540-828-5375
800-759-8328 (toll-free)
E-mail: admissions@bridgewater.edu
World Wide Web: http://www.bridgewater.edu

Students at Bridgewater College.

BRIDGEWATER STATE COLLEGE

BRIDGEWATER, MASSACHUSETTS

The College

Bridgewater State College was founded in 1840 and has grown from a teacher-preparation school of 28 students to a comprehensive liberal arts institution that enrolls more than 9,000 students each year (7,200 undergraduates) in day, evening, and summer programs.

The College offers students a lively cultural, social, and recreational life to enhance their learning experience. The new Adrian Tinsley Center, Rondileau Campus Center, and new East Campus Commons are the settings for many of the student-life activities. Cultural, educational, and entertainment programs, including lectures by guest speakers, concerts, exhibits, and movies, are regularly featured at the Campus Center, while a wide selection of fitness activities are available in the Tinsley Center. The College offers more than 100 student clubs and organizations in a variety of interest areas. Intercollegiate varsity athletic teams compete under NCAA Division III. Men's teams include baseball, basketball, cross-country, football, soccer, swimming, tennis, track and field, and wrestling. Teams for women include basketball, cross-country, field hockey, lacrosse, soccer, softball, swimming, tennis, track and field, and volleyball. A number of club sports are open to students, including men's lacrosse, Ultimate Frisbee, karate, cheerleading, men's ice hockey, and men's and women's rugby.

The Bridgewater State College campus has nine residence halls and thirty-four academic/administrative buildings spread over its 235 acre campus. The atmosphere at Bridgewater is friendly and informal, based on the concept that the College is a diverse community of people with shared interests and goals. A number of important student services (including career, academic, and personal counseling; disability and health services; and housing assistance) are available.

The College offers programs leading to master's degrees in fields such as management, criminal justice, public administration, computer science, psychology, and teacher education, which also offers certificates of advanced graduate study.

Location

Bridgewater State College is located in Bridgewater, Massachusetts, a community of more than 25,000 people approximately 30 miles south of Boston and 25 miles north of Cape Cod. The area is near many cultural, recreational, and historic sites. Commuter rail train service to and from Boston operates from early morning to late evening, seven days a week. The Bridgewater train station is located in the center of the College's campus.

Majors and Degrees

Bridgewater State College confers the Bachelor of Arts, Bachelor of Science, and Bachelor of Science in Education degrees.

Undergraduate majors are offered in accounting and finance, anthropology, art, aviation science (airport management, aviation management, and flight training), biology, business (see "management science"), chemistry, chemistry-geology, communication arts and sciences (communication studies, dance education, speech communication, theater arts, and theater education), computer science, criminal justice, early childhood education, earth sciences, economics, elementary education, English, geography, health education, history, management science (energy and environmental resources management, general management, global management, information systems management, marketing transportation), mathematics, music, philosophy, physical education, physics, political science, psychology, secondary education, social work, sociology, Spanish, and special education (including communication disorders).

Academic Programs

Bridgewater State College offers a full range of study in thirty degree areas. The goal of the academic program is to prepare broadly educated individuals in the liberal arts and the professions. The Academic Achievement Center provides academic counseling and assistance to all freshmen and transfer students. All students must complete the core program of general education courses to earn a bachelor's degree. Students must complete 120 semester hours of credit, of which at least 30–36 hours must be taken in a major field of study. Selected students may enroll in departmental or College-wide honors programs.

The College operates on a traditional two-semester calendar and offers two 5-week summer sessions and a number of intensive courses over the summer months.

Off-Campus Programs

Bridgewater State College participates in three programs that allow students to take courses for credit at other institutions of higher education. First, College Academic Program Sharing (CAPS) provides full-time students with the opportunity to take courses offered at any of the other state colleges in Massachusetts. The College is also a member of the Southeastern Association for Cooperation of Higher Education in Massachusetts (SACHEM), a consortium of public and private colleges that includes Bristol Community, Cape Cod Community, Dean, Massasoit Community, Stonehill, and Wheaton Colleges; Massachusetts Maritime Academy; and the University of Massachusetts Dartmouth. Finally, Bridgewater participates in the National Student Exchange Program, which allows students to spend a term at other public colleges and universities in the United States.

Students are encouraged to pursue internships within their major field that provide opportunities to earn college credit while gaining practical experience. Faculty advisers assist students in securing internships in which they work with professionals in business, industry, education, and government.

Academic Facilities

The John Joseph Moakley Center for Technological Applications, named in honor of the late congressman from Massachusetts, opened in 1995 and is the hub of the College's campuswide voice, data, and video network. Technological resources in the building include a series of technology-integrated classrooms, an open-access computer lab, a television studio and control room, a teleconference facility, and a large lecture hall with integrated, computer-based display technology.

The Clement C. Maxwell Library is a four-story facility that seats 2,500 and has more than 300,000 books, 1,102 periodicals, and 19,500 journals on its information network. Other major resources on campus include an astronomy observatory; radio and television production facilities; a Teacher Technology Center; and the new Tinsley Athletic Center, which houses classrooms, laboratories, a fitness center, an NCAA-regulation gymnasium and basketball court, and meeting areas.

Costs

For 2003–04, tuition for full-time study was $910 per year for Massachusetts residents and $7050 per year for out-of-state students. Fees averaged $3432 per year, books averaged $600, a room averaged $3334, and board averaged $2378. These costs are subject to change.

Financial Aid

Many sources of financial aid are available to Bridgewater students, including Federal Pell Grants, Federal Supplemental Educational Opportunity Grants, Federal Perkins Loans, Federal Stafford Student Loans, HELP loans, alumni scholarships, and Federal Work-Study awards. The Financial Aid Office has an informative brochure detailing methods of application and guidelines for qualification. For a copy, prospective applicants should write to the Financial Aid Office or telephone 508-531-1341. Students are required to submit the Free Application for Federal Student Aid (FAFSA). Applications for financial aid for the fall semester must be received by March 1.

Faculty

The College faculty has 263 full-time members and 212 part-time members; 91 percent of full-time faculty members hold terminal degrees in their area. Since the student-faculty ratio is 19:1 and the emphasis of the faculty is on classroom instruction, there are many opportunities for personal contact and interaction between faculty members and students at Bridgewater. Students discover that faculty members are interested in them as individuals and are eager to help them succeed. Graduate students do not teach any courses.

Student Government

Every Bridgewater student is automatically a member of the Student Government Association. Bridgewater's special philosophy of maintaining a College community means that all the people who are part of it—students, faculty, administrators, staff, and alumni—are partners in an educational program whose goal is academic excellence. The Student Government Association is the official representative of the students' point of view, and its officers, elected by the students themselves, organize activities and projects that benefit the student body and the College as a whole.

Admission Requirements

The basic aim of the admission requirements is to ensure the selection of students who have demonstrated intellectual capacity, motivation, and character and who have a record of scholastic achievement. Consideration is given to applicants regardless of their race, religion, national origin, sex, age, color, ethnic origin, or handicap. Three important factors are considered in the freshman admission process: secondary school preparation, College Board or ACT test scores, and personal qualifications. Prior to acceptance, secondary school students are required to pass 16 college-preparatory units: 4 years of English; 3 years of mathematics, including algebra I and II and geometry; 3 years of science, including 2 years of laboratory science; 2 years of history/social science, including 1 year of U.S. history; 2 years of the same foreign language; and two college-preparatory-level electives. High school students are encouraged to elect additional courses in music, art, and computer science. An essay/personal statement is required. Recommendations are not required but may be submitted with other application materials. Transfer students must submit an official transcript from each college previously attended.

The College also encourages qualified international students to apply for admission. A separate international-student application is required. The application procedures should be completed at least six months before the desired date of enrollment. Scores on the Test of English as a Foreign Language (TOEFL) are required from students whose first language is not English.

Application and Information

Applications for freshman admission should be filed with the $25 application fee on or before February 15 for priority consideration. Freshmen seeking on-campus housing should apply before February 15. Students who wish to transfer to Bridgewater from another college should apply by November 1 for January admission or by April 1 for September entrance.

Students choosing the early action option should submit an application and all supporting materials no later than November 15. Early action candidates are sent a decision letter by December 15.

Students are invited to attend on-campus Friday Admissions Information Sessions, which are followed by a student-led tour of the campus. Appointments can be scheduled by calling the Office of Admissions.

An application form and further information may be obtained by contacting:

Office of Admission
Bridgewater State College
Bridgewater, Massachusetts 02325
Telephone: 508-531-1237
Fax: 508-531-1746
E-mail: admission@bridgew.edu
World Wide Web: http://www.bridgew.edu

BROCK UNIVERSITY

ST. CATHARINES, ONTARIO, CANADA

The University

Brock University is celebrating its fortieth year of offering students a broad range of scholarly, innovative, and professional undergraduate and graduate programs. Recent years have constituted a period of unprecedented growth and transformation as Brock moves ahead to be a more broad-based, comprehensive institution. Brock's 47,000 graduates have applied their degrees to careers in Canada and around the world and enjoy the highest employment rate of all Ontario universities at 98.2 percent.

Currently the University has 15,527 undergraduate and graduate students representing all the provinces in Canada and more than eighty other countries around the world. In light of its unparalleled growth, Brock has invested more then $100 million to expand the campus, with the construction of academic buildings, students residences, and the Walker Complex, Niagara's largest recreational facility.

On-campus student residences are available for 2,400 students in traditional and town-house style housing. Residence is guaranteed to American students who are coming to Brock directly from high school. A wide variety of off-campus housing is also available in the surrounding community.

Students can participate in more than thirty clubs and organizations, relating to academic programs, faith, and student government. Athletics are also an important part of campus life. Students can choose to take part in intramural sports as well as varsity teams. Brock has one of the most successful athletic programs in Canada, capturing fifteen national and thirty provincial championships throughout its history.

Location

Located in the centre of Canada's beautiful Niagara peninsula in Ontario, 1 hour from Toronto, St. Catharines reflects the diversity of a rich rural and urban mix—combining the advantages of a prosperous urban area with the traditional touches and atmosphere of a small town. Known as the Garden City, St. Catharines prides itself on excellent community services, top-notch educational opportunities, and a strong health-care system. Families enjoy a high quality of life, a safe environment, and access to recreational and leisure activities for all ages. The Niagara region offers many attractions, such as Niagara Falls, twenty historical museums, and two reconstructed forts as well as more than forty golf courses, thirty private campgrounds, and fishing on Lakes Ontario and Erie.

Majors and Degrees

Students can pursue a variety of bachelor's degrees in the following faculties: Applied Health Sciences, with majors in child health, community health, health sciences, kinesiology, nursing, physical education, recreation and leisure studies, sport management, and tourism studies; Business, with concentrations in accounting and business administration (Co-op available for both); Education, with concurrent programs in child and youth studies (B.A./B.Ed., grades K–6), honours (B.A./B.Ed. or B.Sc./B.Ed., grades 7–12), integrated studies (B.A./B.Ed., B.Sc./B.Ed., grades 4–10), and physical education (B.Ph.Ed./B.Ed., grades K–6 and grades 7–12); Humanities, with majors in applied language studies, Canadian studies, classics, dramatic arts (Co-op available), English language and literature, French, German, great books/liberal studies, history, international studies (minor only), Italian, music, philosophy, Spanish, studies in arts and culture, and visual arts; Mathematics and Science, with majors in biochemistry (Co-op available), biological sciences, biomedical sciences, biotechnology (Co-op available), chemistry (Co-op available), computer science (Co-op available), computing and business (Co-op available), computing and mathematics (Co-op only), computing and solid-state device technology (Co-op available), earth sciences (Co-op available), environment (Co-op available), environmental geosciences (Co-op available), mathematics, neuroscience, oenology and viticulture (Co-op only), physical geography, and physics (Co-op available); and Social Sciences, with majors in business economics (Co-op available), child and youth studies, communication studies (Co-op available), economics (Co-op available), film studies (Co-op available), geography (Co-op available), international political economy, labour studies, policing and criminal justice, political science (Co-op available), popular culture (Co-op available), psychology (Co-op available), sociology, and women's studies.

Academic Programs

The University has a unique seminar system, in which almost every lecture has a weekly seminar or small group component. In these small groups, students explore the lecture material, develop teamwork and communication skills, and refine higher-order thinking skills.

Experiential learning is also an important element of a Brock degree. Many opportunities are available through the wide range of Co-op options; Brock has the second largest offering of Co-op programs in Ontario. Students gain a competitive edge in today's market by exploring career possibilities and developing key industry contacts.

Off-Campus Programs

Students have the opportunity to discover the world with Brock University by participating in Brock's many study-abroad programs. Each exchange program offers exciting educational and cultural experiences to enhance a student's degree. Students may travel to countries such as Argentina, Australia, China, England, Spain, France, Germany, Korea, and many more.

Other programs are designed to provide students with practical experiences and a means to highlight the skills they have developed during their time at the University. Med Plus is a noncredit, premedicine program that is unique in Canada. It provides students with a wide range of experiences, speakers, and skill-development workshops to enhance their chances of being accepted into their graduate program of choice. As a testament to the success of the program, the first class of Med Plus graduates all received offers to their graduate programs of choice, including medicine, dentistry, occupational therapy, and physiotherapy.

Experience Plus is a portfolio development program that allows students to highlight work- and volunteer-related skills and experiences on an official Brock transcript. This transcript clearly demonstrates to a potential employer the additional and highly valued skills a Brock University student has attained.

Academic Facilities

Brock's academic facilities include a range of state-of-the-art classrooms, computer labs, and resource centres. Classrooms feature rear-projection SMART boards and interactive white-boards, computer and Internet access, and multimedia stations. Brock's eight computer labs feature Pentium computers and laser printers, and select labs house scanners and CD burners.

The James A. Gibson library houses more than 1.5 million items, including books, government documents, special collections, sound and video collections, and more. A vast array of electronic databases and journals are also available to support the research and academic programs at the University.

Costs

For the 2004–05 academic year, tuition for American and international students is $2074.13 per full credit and $1037.06 per half-credit. All dollar figures are listed in Canadian currency.

On-campus residences range in cost from $3280 to $4540 per year, with an additional utilities fee of $270 to $385. Meal plans range from $2995 to $3790. Students living off-campus can expect to spend $350 to $450 per month for rent. Books and supplies cost $750 to $1000 per year for most programs. The cost of a bus pass, $126 dollars, is incorporated into student's tuition. On-campus parking is currently $20 to $60 per month.

Financial Aid

All students who apply directly from high school are eligible for a Brock Scholars Award. These awards range from $1550 to $10,000. Other donor scholarships are also available to incoming and returning students.

Faculty

The University has more than 490 faculty members, including 115 professors and 174 associate professors. The vast majority of Brock's faculty members hold a Ph.D., which reflects Brock's commitment to providing professors who are experts in their fields and who are actively involved in teaching and research.

Student Government

Representatives of the Brock University Students' Union stay in constant contact with students, the University administration, and the community to ensure that student issues are properly addressed.

Admission Requirements

American students are required to complete their high school education with high grades and a diploma. SAT scores are not required, but may be submitted to assist in the evaluation process. If English is not a student's first language, the student is required to submit proof of English proficiency.

Application and Information

Students may complete a Brock application form, which is available online at http://www.brocku.ca/registrar/forms/AppInter.pdf, or students may apply online through the Ontario Universities Application Centre at http://www.ouac.on.ca using the 105F application form. Students using the Brock application incur a Can$75 charge, while students applying through the OUAC are required to pay a fee of Can$85. Students who are applying to more than one Ontario university are encouraged to use the OUAC application process.

Students are strongly encouraged to visit the spectacular campus to see all that Brock has to offer. Tours are offered Monday through Friday, at 10 a.m. and 2 p.m. Limited Saturday tours are also available. Overnight accommodations are available on-campus from May through August.

Mailed applications may be sent to:

Office of Admissions
Brock University
500 Glenridge Ave.
St. Catharines, Ontario
Canada L2S 3A1

For further information, students should contact:

Recruitment and Liaison Services
Telephone: 905-688-5550 Ext. 4293
Fax: 905-988-5488
E-mail: liaison@brocku.ca
World Wide Web: http://www.brocku.ca

BROOKLYN COLLEGE OF THE CITY UNIVERSITY OF NEW YORK

BROOKLYN, NEW YORK

The College

Brooklyn College, since its founding in 1930, has fostered a tradition of academic excellence and achievement. Among its more than 120,000 graduates are many of the nation's outstanding men and women in the fields of education, the humanities, the performing arts, science and medicine, the social sciences, government and public service, law and justice, accounting, business and industry, athletics, and communications. Brooklyn College is the third-oldest senior college of the City University of New York (CUNY). It is housed in eleven main buildings on a 26-acre, tree-lined campus. The current undergraduate enrollment is about 15,000 men and women.

The Student Center is a focal point of social activity on campus. It contains lounges, conference and meeting rooms, a computer lab, game rooms, art displays, study rooms, music rooms, a television room, and a penthouse with a domed skylight. Brooklyn College's students participate in more than 140 chartered campus groups, including academic clubs, service and honor societies, athletics groups, special interest groups, and performing arts organizations. Special lectures, concerts, and events are scheduled throughout the year. On the campus quad and in the Student Center, fraternities and sororities provide social and community service activities. The Hillel Foundation, Intervarsity Christian Fellowship, and Newman Center are among the many special interest clubs on campus. Student publications include newspapers, magazines, and journals. Students also operate WBCR, the Brooklyn College radio station. Recreation and sports facilities consist of a swimming pool, seven outdoor tennis courts, an Astroturf-surfaced athletic field, six gymnasiums, an outdoor track, a fitness center, weight-lifting equipment, outdoor handball courts, and indoor racquetball and squash courts.

The Library Café is one of Brooklyn College's newest facilities for undergraduate students. It was funded by a $1.6-million grant from the City Council. The Library Café is available to assist students with their academic needs 24 hours a day. It is conveniently located on campus and provides a safe and friendly atmosphere. Equipped with state-of-the-art computers, laptops, Internet access, and data management programs, the Library Café provides a tranquil atmosphere in which students can enjoy a coffee break while attending to their studies.

The Office of Services for Students with Disabilities provides counseling and other assistance to students with disabilities to ensure that they have complete access to College programs and facilities. College and departmental counseling programs provide students with academic and personal counseling. Career, preprofessional, veterans', and psychological counseling services are also available. Other services include child care for students and a health clinic.

Location

Brooklyn College is located in the residential Midwood section of Brooklyn. The campus is near the Brooklyn Museum, the Brooklyn Botanic Garden, and Prospect Park. Within a short distance are all the cultural, recreational, and entertainment facilities of New York City. All major IND and IRT trains are easily accessible from the College.

Majors and Degrees

Brooklyn College awards the Bachelor of Arts (B.A.), Bachelor of Science (B.S.), Bachelor of Music (B.M.), and Bachelor of Fine Arts (B.F.A.) degrees. Majors are available in the following areas: accounting; Africana studies; American studies; anthropology; art; art history; biology; broadcast journalism; business, finance, and management; Caribbean studies; chemistry; classics; comparative literature; computer and information science; creative writing; economics; education (bilingual/bicultural education, childhood education, early childhood education, education of the speech and hearing handicapped, and secondary education with certification in fourteen subject areas); English; environmental studies; film; French; geology; health and nutrition sciences; history; Italian; journalism; Judaic studies; linguistics; mathematics; mathematics-computational; music; music composition; music performance; philosophy; physical education; physics; political science; psychology; Puerto Rican and Latino studies; religion studies; Russian; sociology; Spanish; speech (audiology, speech and hearing science, and speech-language pathology); studio art; television and radio; theater; and women's studies. Certificate programs are offered in accounting, computers and programming, and film production; credits earned in these programs are applicable toward a baccalaureate degree.

Students interested in economics and computer applications may apply to enter a 4½-year program that leads to both the Bachelor of Science and the Master of Professional Studies (M.P.S.) degrees.

Brooklyn College and the State University of New York Health Science Center at Brooklyn offer a coordinated eight-year honors program that leads to B.A. and M.D. degrees. The program is limited each year to 15 qualified students who are admitted only in the fall term following their graduation from high school.

Professional options include the opportunity for qualified students to earn a B.A. or B.S. degree from Brooklyn College by satisfactorily completing all requirements for graduation and by also satisfactorily completing at least one year's work in an accredited dental, engineering, law, medical, or veterinary school. Students interested in pursuing an engineering degree may participate in Brooklyn College's approved two-year coordinated engineering program. Students attend Brooklyn College for two years of pre-engineering studies and then transfer to Polytechnic University, City College, or the College of Staten Island for an additional two years of study to fulfill the Bachelor of Science degree requirements in a specific engineering field.

Academic Program

The liberal arts education at Brooklyn College consists of three kinds of study: the College-wide CORE curriculum, which provides a diverse educational experience in the liberal arts for all students; major studies, which comprise specialized, intensive study in one discipline; and elective courses, selected from more than seventy-five areas of study. The undergraduate curriculum aims to prepare students to make rational career and personal choices by developing their intellect in critical and independent thinking, their ability to acquire and organize large amounts of knowledge, and their ability to communicate in writing and speech with precision and force. Students pursuing a bachelor's degree must successfully complete a minimum of 120 credits.

The Scholars Program offers students who combine academic excellence with initiative and inquisitiveness the opportunity to take classes and special courses that are open only to members of the program.

The Honors Academy comprises eight units: the Scholars Program; the B.A./M.D. Program; the CUNY Honors College Program, which consists of a challenging honors curriculum and cultural experiences as well as a full-tuition scholarship, internship opportunities, and an academic expense account; the Mellon Minority Undergraduate Fellowship, a two-year program for members of minority groups who are considering scholarly study in the humanities; the Honors Academy

Research Colloquium; the Dean's List Honors Research Program; the Engineering Honors Program; and the Special Baccalaureate Degree Program. Applications for all eight programs may be obtained in the Office of Admissions.

Students who have completed college-level courses in high school may be considered for exemption, with or without credit, from equivalent college courses on the basis of Advanced Placement tests given by the College Board. Brooklyn College gives exemption examinations in subjects not offered by the College Board. Students completing 3 years of foreign language in high school are exempt from the College's language requirement.

TOCA (The On Course Advantage) offers eligible second-semester freshmen the opportunity to graduate in four years with priority registration and guaranteed availability of required courses.

The academic calendar consists of a fall and a spring semester. Two summer sessions are available. Classes are offered in day, evening, and weekend sessions.

Academic Facilities

The newly expanded and renovated Brooklyn College Library serves as the crossroads of the campus. Much more than a traditional academic library, it is a comprehensive and complex information center that includes substantial physical and digital collections, the College archives, a new media center, and both academic and administrative computing, all brought together in a single state-of-the-art building that doubles as the College's information hub. The library's physical collections total more than 1.3 million volumes, 4,200 journals, and around 25,000 audiovisual units (sound recordings, videotapes, and DVDs). The library's digital collections include 15,000 electronic subscriptions and works of reference, as well as several thousand electronic books. The new library comprises 277,650 square feet (6.5 acres), 2,317 student seats, 21.5 miles of shelving, twenty-two group-study rooms, five computer classrooms, and more than 500 computers for student and faculty access. Four of every ten seats include either a fixed computer or a net tap to which readers may attach their own laptops.

The Brooklyn Center for the Performing Arts at Brooklyn College, which presents music, dance, and theater productions, contains a 2,500-seat auditorium, a theater, a recital hall, and a workshop theater. The College Computer Center is a state-of-the-art facility that supports student course requirements as well as research. Other special facilities include microcomputer learning centers, a language laboratory, art studios, an advanced color-television studio, an early childhood education center, a speech and hearing center, psychology laboratories, laser laboratories, an astronomical observatory, an optical mineralogy laboratory, a greenhouse, an aquatic research center, and a nuclear physics laboratory.

Costs

In 2003–04, New York State residents paid tuition of $2000 per semester for full-time attendance (12 or more credits or the equivalent) or $170 per credit for part-time programs. Non–New York residents and international students paid tuition of $360 per credit without a limit. Tuition for the summer session was $170 per credit for New York State residents and $360 per credit for out-of-state and international students. The College is a commuter institution and does not have on-campus housing.

Financial Aid

Admission decisions and financial aid and scholarship decisions are made independently of each other, and an application for aid does not hinder a student's opportunity for admission. Financial assistance is available for eligible students through state and federal grant, loan, and work-study programs.

New students with strong SAT scores and strong high school or college academic records are encouraged to apply for annual scholarships. Continuing students may qualify for one of more than 400 scholarships, prizes, and awards that are given each year to Brooklyn College students. The requirements vary for each, but recipients are chosen based on academic performance, financial need, and other criteria stipulated by the donors. Scholarships range from $100 to $4000 per year. For more information, students should contact the Financial Aid Office (telephone: 718-951-5051) or the Office of Scholarships (telephone: 718-951-4796).

Faculty

The College has an outstanding faculty (476 full-time and 519 part-time) whose members have demonstrated excellence in teaching and scholarly research. More than 95 percent hold a doctoral degree or the equivalent in their field of study. Faculty members assist in the academic advisement of entering students and provide counseling to students majoring in their department. They also hold regular office hours and are generally available to support undergraduate as well as graduate student activities.

Student Government

Student governments are active in both the day, evening, and graduate divisions. Students are elected to positions on the Assembly/Council by the student body. Students also serve on the Policy Council, the major College-wide governing body.

Admission Requirements

High school students, students who want to transfer from other institutions, and adults returning to school are encouraged to apply. Freshman admission criteria involve a combination of a student's GPA, academic units, and SAT/ACT scores. Freshman applicants scoring 1100 or better on the SAT I are automatically admitted. Freshman students should demonstrate successful completion of at least 12 or more high school academic units (of which at least 5 units must include 2 or more years of English and 2 or more years of math). The recommended high school preparation for the College's curriculum is 4 years of English, 4 years of social studies, 3 years of mathematics, 3 years of science, and 3 years of a foreign language. Students seeking admission to the Scholars Program, CUNY Honors College Program, or the B.A./M.D. Program must present a high school average of 90 or better, exceptional SAT I or ACT scores, letters of recommendation, and an autobiographical essay and have a personal interview. Qualified high school juniors may apply for early admission. Students with special educational needs may qualify for admission into the Search for Education, Elevation, Knowledge (SEEK) program.

Application and Information

Application for admission to the undergraduate program for the fall or spring semester should be made on a standard CUNY application form, available from the Office of Admissions at any CUNY college. Application forms for the Honors Academy, including the Scholars, CUNY Honors College, B.A./M.D., and coordinated engineering programs; the Mellon Minority Undergraduate Fellowship; and the summer session are available only through Brooklyn College. Although applications for admission are processed by the City University on a rolling basis, applicants who apply before January 15 for fall admission and before October 15 for spring admission receive prompt notification of their admission status and have the best opportunity for comprehensive advisement and course registration. The CUNY Honors College Program applicants are required to apply by November 1 (early decision) and January 4 (regular decision) for fall admission.

For an application form, additional financial aid information, scholarship information, and brochures, students should contact:

Office of Admissions
1203 Plaza
Brooklyn College of the City University of New York
2900 Bedford Avenue
Brooklyn, New York 11210
Telephone: 718-951-5001
E-mail: adminqry@brooklyn.cuny.edu
World Wide Web: http://www.brooklyn.cuny.edu

BROWN UNIVERSITY

PROVIDENCE, RHODE ISLAND

The University

The history of Brown University reaches back over more than two centuries and tells of a university constantly undergoing change. Brown was established with a charter from the Colony's General Assembly in 1764, and the first men registered at the college in 1765. The first women were admitted in 1891, when the establishment of the Women's College in Brown University marked the beginning of eighty years of a coordinate structure for educating women within the University. Brown is now a coeducational institution, drawing men and women from all over the United States and many other countries to participate in the academic and extracurricular life of an Ivy League university. There are more than 7,000 students at Brown, of whom 5,600 are undergraduates.

A profile of the average Brown student is practically impossible to create. Here, the typical student is atypical and happy to be so. The diversity of Brown's student body is, in fact, one of the characteristics in which the University takes most pride. Given this diversity, however, there are still some generalizations that might apply to the Brown student body as a whole. One of them is that students have a deep concern for both the process and the quality of education. Another is the students' willingness, even eagerness, to become involved. Finally, it can be said that Brown students are highly motivated to seek advanced study after their undergraduate years.

Brown students feel a commitment to learn—and live—outside of the classroom. More than 200 clubs and activities thrive on the Brown campus. These range from athletic and recreational programs to community-service organizations and environmental-action groups; music, drama, and theater groups; literary publications; political organizations; clubs for vocational interests; and the nation's first college radio station. Specific activities vary from year to year according to student interest.

Brown's Graduate School and Medical School offer courses leading to the degrees of Master of Arts, Master of Science, Master of Arts in Teaching, Master of Medical Science, Master of Fine Arts, Master of Public Health, Doctor of Medicine, and Doctor of Philosophy.

Location

Providence, by virtue of its size, location, and diversity, offers many advantages to the college student. A city large enough to support a convention center and a large, active Civic Center that draws top entertainment and sports events, Providence is still small enough to offer involvement in local politics, community service, and cultural activities. Providence also offers an excellent repertory company and a major performing arts center as well as museums, concert halls, and a good commercial transportation system. It does not overwhelm the newcomer.

Majors and Degrees

Brown University offers the following degree programs for undergraduates: the Bachelor of Arts (A.B.), the Bachelor of Science (Sc.B.), a five-year program leading to the combined Bachelor of Science and Bachelor of Arts (Sc.B. and A.B.), and the Program in Liberal Medical Education, leading to a Bachelor of Arts or Bachelor of Science at the end of four years and an M.D. degree four years later (from the Brown Medical School).

Within a degree program, Brown students elect a concentration that is the focus of their undergraduate work. Standardized concentrations are available in the following areas: Africana studies, American civilization, ancient studies, anthropology, anthropology–linguistics, applied mathematics (applied mathematics–biology, applied mathematics–computer science, and applied mathematics–economics), architectural studies, art (applied art and art history), art–semiotics, biological and medical sciences (aquatic biology, biochemistry, biology, biomedical ethics, biophysics, human biology, molecular biology, and neuroscience), chemical physics, chemistry (biochemistry, geology–chemistry), classics (classics and Sanskrit, Greek, Greek and Latin, and Latin), cognitive neuroscience, cognitive science, community health, comparative literature, computational biology, computer science, computer science–economics, development studies, East Asian studies, economics (business economics, economics, economics–engineering, and mathematics), education studies, Egyptology, engineering (biomedical, chemical, civil, computer, electrical, materials, and mechanical engineering), engineering and economics, engineering and physics, English and American literature, environmental studies, ethnic studies, French studies, gender studies, geological sciences (geology–biology, geology–chemistry, and geology–physics/mathematics), German studies, Hispanic studies, history, history of art and architecture, international relations, Italian studies, Judaic studies, late antique cultures, Latin American studies, linguistics, literatures and cultures in English, mathematics (mathematical economics, mathematics–computer science, and mathematics–physics), media/culture (modern culture and media–German and modern culture and media–Italian), medieval cultures, Middle East studies, music, neuroscience, old-world art/archaeology, philosophy (ethics and political philosophy, logic and philosophy of science), physics, political science, Portuguese and Brazilian studies, psychology, public- and private-sector organizations, public policy/American institutions, religious studies, Renaissance and Early Modern studies, semiotics–French, sexuality and society, Slavic studies, sociology, South Asian studies, statistics, theater arts, urban studies, and visual art. In addition, each student at Brown may pursue study in any academic area through either independent study or an independent concentration program of the student's design.

Academic Programs

Brown's philosophy of education, promoted by students and endorsed by the faculty, can be simply stated: students will get more out of their education, and it will serve them better, if it is tailored to their individual needs and goals. Because Brown's curriculum has no distribution requirements, students have both the latitude and the responsibility to create an academic program that will reflect genuine and enduring personal accomplishment.

A student may register for and complete a maximum of forty semester courses; a minimum of thirty semester courses must be completed satisfactorily to earn a diploma. Course work can be evaluated by one of two grading systems at Brown: the ABC/No Credit option or the Satisfactory/No Credit option.

Work that is judged by the instructor to be unsatisfactory receives no credit, and the student's registration in the class never appears on a formal transcript. A written analysis of the student's work, in the form of a Course Performance Report, may be requested. The student must complete a concentration in order to graduate. This ensures an in-depth study that is centered on the unit provided by a discipline or disciplines, a problem, a theme, or a broad question.

Advanced Placement credit is available, as are opportunities for independent or honors work. Brown operates on a two-semester calendar. The first term begins in early September and continues through mid-December, while the second term runs from late January until mid-May.

Off-Campus Programs

Brown students can enroll in as many as four courses at the Rhode Island School of Design (Brown's neighbor on College Hill). Many students choose to study abroad for a semester or a year; Brown directly sponsors fifty-seven programs in eighteen countries.

Academic Facilities

The main campus of Brown University occupies an area of approximately 140 acres. More than fifty buildings are devoted to classroom, laboratory, research, library, office, and conference use by departments of instruction. The University Library, containing more than 5 million items, includes the John D. Rockefeller Jr. Library, the John Hay Library, the Sciences Library, the Orwig Music Library, the John Carter Brown Library, and the Ann Mary Brown Library. The University provides extensive modern laboratory and computer facilities designed for undergraduate and graduate instruction as well as research. The Performing Arts Complex, the Catherine Bryan Dill Center for the Performing Arts, includes the Leeds Theater, the Stuart Theater, and the Ashamu Dance Studio.

Costs

Tuition for the 2003–04 year was $29,200. The cost of room and board was $8096. Fees totaled $878. Books and personal expenses were estimated at $2306.

Financial Aid

Brown practices a need-blind admission policy. For applicants applying for financial assistance, the Financial Aid Office makes all awards on the basis of the candidate's need, as determined from the Financial Aid PROFILE analysis of the College Scholarship Service. A three-part package of aid is awarded, consisting of a scholarship, a loan, and a campus job (first-year students who are eligible for a University scholarship are not required to work). The University participates in the federally funded Federal Work-Study, Federal Supplemental Educational Opportunity Grant (FSEOG), and Federal Perkins Loan programs. Candidates should file the PROFILE application and the Free Application for Federal Student Aid (FAFSA) by February 1 and are notified of their award in April. Approximately 40 percent of students in each entering class receive University scholarship aid.

Faculty

Brown's faculty consists of 578 full-time and 198 visiting and adjunct teaching professors. Faculty members teach both graduate and undergraduate students, and each professor must teach an undergraduate class every year. The student-faculty ratio is 8:1, allowing for extensive counseling of students by the faculty. All professors have weekly office hours during which they are available to students. Faculty members and students serve jointly on approximately a dozen University committees concerning student affairs. While faculty members usually do not live in student dormitories, some members serve as dormitory liaisons, and the majority live close to the campus.

Student Government

The Brown Undergraduate Council of Students, a group of elected representatives, has primary responsibility for the disbursement of more than $500,000 in student monies. These funds are distributed among the more than 200 clubs, organizations, and activities that form the basis of extracurricular life at Brown. In addition, Brown undergraduates participate actively with faculty and administration on a host of campus committees concerned with University policies.

Admission Requirements

Individuals are considered for admission to Brown on the basis of academic and personal qualities. A strong scholastic background and the intellectual ability to meet the demands of a rigorous academic program are required. Secondary school records, teacher and counselor evaluations, and the results of standardized tests are all important factors in a decision. To obtain a diverse student body, Brown also reviews each candidate's credentials in light of the individual's strengths. Special interests, talents, and qualities are important; the Board of Admission is concerned with the extent to which each applicant might contribute in his or her own way to the total life of the University.

Application and Information

Students may apply to Brown by submitting an application for admission (Forms 1 and 1A) and the subsequent Forms 2 through 4, which include a personal statement, secondary school reports, and teacher references. The SAT I and three SAT II Subject Tests of the College Board or the ACT of the American College Testing Service must be taken. No interview is necessary. The application deadline for all forms is January 1. Notification is in early April. A fall notification plan, early decision, offers candidates the opportunity to apply in November (with a deadline of November 1 for all forms) and receive an admission notification in mid-December. Early decision is a binding early program for applicants who have selected Brown as their first-choice college and who will attend Brown if admitted as an early decision candidate.

Information and application materials may be obtained by contacting:

The College Admission Office
Brown University
Box 1876
Providence, Rhode Island 02912
Telephone: 401-863-2378
E-mail: admission_undergraduate@brown.edu
World Wide Web: http://www.brown.edu

BRYANT COLLEGE

SMITHFIELD, RHODE ISLAND

The College

Bryant College is a four-year, private New England college that focuses on helping students build the knowledge and develop the character needed to achieve success as they define it.

Founded in 1863, Bryant offers a student-centered learning environment, state-of-the-art facilities, and academic and cocurricular programming for diverse interests. Bryant has been educating business leaders for 140 years, and the College's rigorous academic standards have been recognized and accredited by AACSB International–The Association to Advance Collegiate Schools of Business.

Bryant is the college of choice for individuals seeking the best combination of a business and liberal arts education. Academic programs blend the practical with the theoretical—a combination essential to developing the character of success. Students learn in small classes with distinguished professors in superb facilities, obtaining an education of the highest academic quality.

Bryant's 2,700 full-time, undergraduate students come from thirty-one states and thirty-one countries. Bryant has all the advantages of a small community, with close relationships among students, faculty members, and college administrators. There are abundant opportunities for the exchange of ideas and dialogue between students and faculty members. Students learn how business decisions impact society and about the relationships between business functions and the larger spectrum of human need and well-being.

Students can find a balance to their academic and social pursuits at the Chace Athletic and Wellness Center. This state-of-the-art center boasts a 9,000-square-foot fitness center with the latest machines and free weights; a six-lane, 25-yard swimming pool; an exercise room for aerobics, karate, yoga, spinning, and other group exercise activities; and comfortable locker rooms that rival private fitness clubs. Over the past few years, the College has also updated its athletic fields, built a stadium, and added more parking.

Through the Graduate School, Bryant College offers a Master of Business Administration (M.B.A.) degree with concentrations in accounting, computer information systems, e-strategy, finance, general business, management, marketing, and operations management; a Master of Science in Information Systems (M.S.I.S.); a Master of Science in Taxation (M.S.T.); and a Certificate of Advanced Graduate Studies (C.A.G.S.).

Bryant's sixty student clubs and organizations benefit many social causes and provide recreational enjoyment and intellectual stimulation. From the Marketing Association to the Global Entrepreneurship Program to the Performing Arts Committee, Bryant provides activities for many areas of interest. The Student Programming Board organizes cultural and social programs for the Bryant community. The size of Bryant's campus allows easy access to all campus services, and there are many places for students to gather and enjoy bands, poetry, and comedians.

Location

The College is situated on 392 acres of beautiful New England countryside. Bryant is only 15 minutes from Providence, which offers access to a variety of restaurants, professional sports events, concerts, and a nationally acclaimed repertory theater. Rhode Island's geographic, historic, and cultural attractions include Newport's world-class sailing, jazz festivals, stunning mansions, and panoramic beaches. Bryant is only 1 hour from Boston and 3 hours from New York City and all the cultural and social amenities of these major metropolitan areas.

Majors and Degrees

Bryant College offers a Bachelor of Arts degree in applied psychology; a Bachelor of Science degree in international business; a Bachelor of Science in Business Administration degree, with concentrations in accounting, accounting information systems, applied actuarial mathematics, computer information systems, finance, financial services, management, and marketing; a Bachelor of Arts degree in communication; a Bachelor of Science degree in information technology; and a Bachelor of Arts in Liberal Studies degree, with concentrations in economics, English, history, and international studies. Students can pursue a minor in one of twenty business and/or liberal arts disciplines.

Academic Programs

Academic programs focus on the intellectual and professional development of each student, in preparation for leadership positions in a wide range of careers. Career exploration and planning begin as early as the freshman year.

Students pursuing a four-year baccalaureate degree must complete a core curriculum that includes business and liberal arts. Graduation requirements in the four-year programs include a minimum of 123 semester hours. Bryant College operates on a semester plan.

Entering students may receive credit through the Advanced Placement (AP) Program or the College-Level Examination Program (CLEP) administered by the College Board. Credit is also awarded for International Baccalaureate (IB) higher-level exams. The Honors Program is an excellent vehicle for highly motivated students to stretch their intellectual limits and experience exciting academic challenges.

Bryant participates in the Army ROTC Program.

Off-Campus Programs

Bryant College offers students many opportunities to expand their learning beyond the classroom. For internships or practicums, students can choose from more than 200 companies such as Walt Disney World; Fidelity Investments; PricewaterhouseCoopers; the New England Patriots; local NBC, CBS, and ABC television network affiliates; and a variety of nonprofit organizations.

The John H. Chafee Center for International Business links Bryant students directly to regional businesses that operate globally. Students can utilize the center's resources for research and reference and gain practical experiences through internships and assistantships.

By studying abroad for a semester, students learn about other countries, their cultures, and how they do business. Bryant students have studied in Eastern and Western Europe, Asia, Japan, Canada, Australia, and many other countries.

Academic Facilities

Bryant's modern campus is anchored by the Unistructure, which houses faculty and administrative offices, classrooms, Janikies Auditorium, and dining facilities. The Bryant Center houses the College bookstore, meeting places, a dining hall, a food court, and student services such as dry cleaning, copying, and a hair salon. The Koffler Technology Center offers 160 computer workstations, high-speed Internet connections, laser printers, and scanners.

The George E. Bello Center for Information and Technology is the hub of technological activity on campus, with thousands of wired and wireless data ports (1,536 wireless data ports) inside and outside of the building. A bank of high-speed computers provide access to numerous reference databases, including Bryant's own International Trade Data Network. The C. V. Starr Financial Markets Center receives real-time news, and information is transferred by feeds and interfaces through Reuters 3000, a system used by some of the largest financial organizations in the world. It also houses the Douglas and Judith Krupp Library, high-technology classrooms, the Grand Hall, team study rooms, and the Bulldog Bytes Café.

The Douglas and Judith Krupp Library contains more than 150,000 items in a variety of formats from publications to audiovisuals and subscriptions to more than 5,000 journals and newspapers in traditional hard copy or electronic format, making it one of the region's most comprehensive business library collections.

As part of their tuition, all freshmen receive new state-of-the-art IBM laptops that are network-ready and fully loaded with software. Prior to the beginning of junior year, this laptop is exchanged for a new model and can be purchased upon graduation. Every two years, instructional computers on campus are upgraded or replaced.

Costs

For 2004–05, the estimated tuition is $23,580, including personal use of an IBM laptop computer for entering freshmen. Estimated residence hall room and board fees are $9,630. Tuition and fees are subject to change. Housing at Bryant is guaranteed for four years; more than 80 percent of students live on campus. There is a variety of housing arrangements to choose from, including the First-Year Complex, suite-style residence halls, and the town-house villages for seniors. There are special fees for summer and winter sessions.

Financial Aid

Bryant has a comprehensive program of merit- and need-based financial aid. More than $44 million in financial aid is processed for Bryant students each year to cover educational expenses. The majority of freshmen receive financial aid through a combination of scholarships, loans, grants, and part-time jobs. Students interested in applying for financial assistance in the form of need-based grants, work-study, and education loans need only file a Free Application for Federal Student Aid (FAFSA). The FAFSA can be found online at http://www.fafsa.ed.gov. The paper version of the FAFSA is available in high school guidance offices or through the Bryant College Financial Aid Office. The FAFSA can be submitted as early as January 1; February 15 is the deadline. For more information, students should contact the Director of Financial Aid.

Faculty

Bryant professors are always adapting and optimizing their teaching methods in order to help students excel. With class sizes averaging about 28 students, there is a great deal of personal interaction between students and faculty members. Classrooms serve as forums for the presentation of theories and ideas and the enlightened exchange of opinions. Among the faculty members at Bryant are a practicing clinical psychologist, a nationally respected expert in advertising effectiveness and public policy, and the state poet laureate of Rhode Island. Bryant faculty members are also active in original research projects, publishing, consulting, and community service. Eighty-six percent of full-time tenured and tenure-track faculty members have the highest degree in their field.

Student Government

The Student Senate, the student governing body, serves as a channel of communication between students and faculty and administrators.

Admission Requirements

Bryant College seeks students who are motivated learners and have a history of academic achievement. Acceptances are based upon the quality of scholastic achievement shown by the individual applicant. Scores earned on the SAT I or on the ACT must be submitted. The Admission Committee considers recommendations from the secondary school guidance office and faculty members concerning character and personal qualifications not shown in the academic record. Interviews, though not required, may be scheduled in advance of a campus visit.

Application and Information

Applications must be submitted to the Office of Admission with a nonrefundable fee of $50. It is the responsibility of the applicant to request that the secondary school guidance office send a copy of the student's school record directly to Bryant and to have SAT I or ACT scores sent to the College. International applicants must also submit TOEFL scores and a completed Certification of Finances form. The early decision and early action deadline is November 15. The regular application deadline is February 15.

For admission information:
Director of Admission
Bryant College
1150 Douglas Pike
Smithfield, Rhode Island 02917-1285
Telephone: 401-232-6100
800-622-7001 (toll-free)
Fax: 401-232-6741
E-mail: admission@bryant.edu
World Wide Web: http://www.admission.bryant.edu

For financial aid information:
Director of Financial Aid
Telephone: 401-232-6020
800-248-4036 (toll-free)
Fax: 401-232-6319
E-mail: finaid@bryant.edu
World Wide Web: http://admission.bryant.edu

Bryant's scenic New England campus is located 15 minutes from Providence and 1 hour from Boston.

BRYN MAWR COLLEGE

BRYN MAWR, PENNSYLVANIA

The College

At Bryn Mawr, leadership doesn't mean simply being the president of this or the captain of that. Bryn Mawr women are leaders in the classroom, in the studio, in the laboratory, and on the field. They are women who share a profound intellectual commitment and a common desire to tackle complex concepts and bring about positive change in their lifetimes. They strive to develop clear and purposeful visions of themselves; they seize opportunities and accept eagerly the challenge and responsibility to contribute. Bryn Mawr women are leaders who expect to change the world.

Bryn Mawr women empower each other to make meaningful contributions far beyond campus, too, by testing the boundaries of knowledge in a number of ways. Through advanced research projects, summer internships, and collaborative research with faculty members, students are involved in Bryn Mawr's interdisciplinary Centers for 21st Century Inquiry. Praxis courses integrate fieldwork with theoretical study, and extensive opportunities for internships in Philadelphia allow students to apply knowledge far beyond the classroom. Many students pursue independent and interdepartmental majors with faculty permission. Joint academic programs also exist with Haverford, Swarthmore, and the University of Pennsylvania.

Bryn Mawr alumnae are physicians, economists, entrepreneurs, scholars, filmmakers, journalists, jurists, writers, and scientists whose achievements are marked by originality of thought and direction. Among Bryn Mawr's graduates are one of the first women to receive the Nobel Peace Prize, the first woman neurosurgeon, and the first and only woman to receive four Academy Awards. Bryn Mawr women have also been recipients of the MacArthur ("genius grant") Fellowships and Pulitzer Prizes and are continually awarded Fulbright and Watson Fellowships.

Bryn Mawr prides itself on diversity; students who are members of minority groups and international students make up more than a third of the undergraduate enrollment of more than 1,200 students. Bryn Mawr's student body is composed of women from forty-nine states and forty-one other countries. Above all else, Bryn Mawr women share a tremendous respect for individual differences, not merely a passive tolerance of other lifestyles and points of view. The result is a community that resounds with the energy, healthy friction, and range of perspective that can only come from true cultural and ideological diversity. These women share a commitment to a community that is based on inclusion and support and reinforced by Bryn Mawr's Honor Code, a set of principles stressing personal integrity and mutual respect. In the words of one graduating senior, "This is a place where being yourself makes you feel part of something larger than yourself. A strong sense of self is what we all have in common."

Bryn Mawr is home to varsity athletic teams in badminton, basketball, crew, cross-country, field hockey, lacrosse, soccer, swimming, tennis, track and field, and volleyball. Students participate in more than 100 active student organizations at Bryn Mawr. The tricollege community of Haverford, Swarthmore, and Bryn Mawr Colleges also sponsors many students groups and activities.

Location

Bryn Mawr College is located on a 135-acre suburban campus, 11 miles west of Philadelphia. Bryn Mawr's parklike campus is graceful and serene and has a deep engagement with the wider world. Bryn Mawr women enjoy a rich academic and social life on their own campus and at neighboring tricollege partners, Haverford and Swarthmore Colleges, and the University of Pennsylvania. This network allows Bryn Mawr students to experience the benefits of attending a small liberal arts college while also having access to nearly 5,000 courses. Bryn Mawr's relationship with Haverford College is particularly close. A 20-minute walk, or a 5-minute ride on the bicollege "Blue Bus," brings students from one campus to the other. There are nearly 3,000 course exchanges between the institutions each year, selected from a jointly published course list. Students may also choose to live on either campus and to participate in many bicollege extracurricular activities, including the orchestra, the chorus, the drama program, and one of the major newspapers.

Almost all students live on campus in one of fifteen main residence halls. These buildings, which include a multicultural residence for students interested in foreign languages and culture, range from university Gothic to postmodern in style. Two of the buildings are listed on the National Register of Historic Places, and one is also a National Historic Landmark.

Majors and Degrees

Bryn Mawr College grants the Bachelor of Arts (A.B.) degree with majors, minors, and concentrations in more than forty areas: Africana studies, anthropology, astronomy, biology, chemistry, classical and Near Eastern archaeology, classical languages, classical studies, comparative literature, computational methods, computer science, creative writing, dance, East Asian studies, economics, education, English, environmental studies, feminist and gender studies, film studies, fine arts, French and French studies, geology, German and German studies, Greek, growth and structure of cities, Hebrew and Judaic studies, Hispanic and Hispanic-American studies, history, history of art, Italian, Latin, mathematics, music, neural and behavioral sciences, peace and conflict studies, philosophy, physics, political science, psychology, religion, Romance languages, Russian, sociology, Spanish, and theater and theater studies.

Through an unusually broad cooperative arrangement with Haverford College, Bryn Mawr students may major in any of Haverford's coordinate departments or in astronomy, classics, music, or religion while earning a Bachelor of Arts degree from Bryn Mawr.

Academic Programs

Having the freedom to shape one's education is a central part of the Bryn Mawr experience—and excellent preparation for creating a purposeful life after graduation. The College's divisional requirements are designed to encourage students to explore extensively while allowing a good deal of flexibility in shaping their course work. A total of 32 units of work is required for graduation, including one course to meet the quantitative skills requirement, work to demonstrate proficiency in a foreign language, 3 units in the humanities and natural and physical sciences, 2 units in the social sciences, a major subject sequence, and elective units. Each student chooses and plans her major in consultation with her dean and faculty adviser. Some students take advantage of this freedom to design an independent major, while others fashion their own intellectual perspectives by enrolling in courses that span academic fields (such as The Growth and Structure of Cities) or assisting with a faculty member's research project.

Off-Campus Programs

Bryn Mawr is only 20 minutes by car or train from the vast cultural and professional resources of Philadelphia, the nation's fifth-largest city. Philadelphia is an incredible resource for Bryn Mawr—a truly accessible city rich with cultural and professional resources, including the Philadelphia Museum of Art, the Philadelphia Orchestra, the Pennsylvania Ballet, numerous theaters, professional and collegiate athletics, and some of the nation's most important historic sites, as well as internship opportunities in Center City law firms, art galleries, government agencies, hospitals, TV studios, banks, and schools. And when Philadelphia seems too small, 1 in 3 Bryn Mawr students participate in one of more than fifty study-abroad programs from Stockholm to South Africa.

Academic Facilities

Bryn Mawr students have unlimited access to libraries and laboratories equal to those of many graduate programs, allowing students to pursue independent research at a level unimaginable at most undergraduate institutions. These resources include more than 1 million volumes in a network of open-stack libraries at Bryn Mawr and an additional 400,000 volumes at Haverford available through cross-listed catalogs. Other resources include a language laboratory, computer facilities, and the Park Science Center, which has a recently renovated science library and chemistry wing. The Rhys Carpenter Library for Art, Archaeology, and Cities opened in 1997 and houses seminar rooms, research facilities, and a state-of-the-art Visual Resources Center. Special departmental research collections include American and European anthropological and archaeological artifacts; recordings of the music of native peoples from all parts of the world; an extensive and important geologic collection of minerals and maps; a study collection of Greek and Roman minor arts, especially vases and coins; Medieval manuscripts and late Medieval printed books (the third-largest collection of incunabula in the nation); and distinguished library holdings of American, Asian, and African books.

Costs

In 2003–04, Bryn Mawr tuition, room and board, and fees totaled $36,890.

Financial Aid

To apply for financial aid, students must submit the Free Application for Federal Student Aid (FAFSA) and the Financial Aid PROFILE from the College Scholarship Service, both available on Bryn Mawr's Web site. In addition, the College requires a copy of the family's most recent tax return and W-2 forms. Applicants who are not citizens of the U.S. must instead file the Foreign Student Financial Aid Application. Prospective freshmen are notified of the admission and financial aid decisions at the same time.

Faculty

The Bryn Mawr faculty has 146 full-time members, of whom 50 percent are women and 17 percent are members of minority groups. The College's student-faculty ratio is 8:1. Few colleges or universities can genuinely claim the intellectual curiosity, intensity, and passion found at Bryn Mawr. While many factors influence campus culture, to a large extent it exists because Bryn Mawr students and professors enjoy a special relationship. Classes are small (many have fewer than 15 students), and faculty members come to know their students as individuals. That means more than just being on a first-name basis. In fact, Bryn Mawr faculty members, world-renown leaders in their fields, regard their students as junior colleagues, fully capable of working at a high level, developing their own ideas, and making important contributions. It is in this way that, perhaps more than at any other school, Bryn Mawr feels like a graduate school on an undergraduate level.

Student Government

Bryn Mawr's culture of innovative leadership dates back to 1892. That year, the Self-Government Association, the oldest undergraduate governing body in the country, was founded, giving Bryn Mawr students the responsibility of running many campus organizations and activities and participating in discussion and resolution of important issues, such as curriculum and faculty appointments.

Admission Requirements

Bryn Mawr's freshman class of about 330 is selected from applicants from all parts of the United States and the world. The Admissions Committee, composed of admissions officers, professors, and current students, looks for an excellent school and test record and asks the applicant's counselor and teachers for an estimate of her character and readiness for college. Such qualities as integrity, vitality, a sense of humor, independence, and sensitivity to others are important, as are any special talents or interests. Early decision, early admission, deferred entrance, and advanced placement options are available to qualified students.

Basic high school academic requirements include 4 years of English, 3 years of mathematics, at least 1 year each of a laboratory science and history, and a solid foundation in at least one foreign language. However, most applicants are well prepared for the academic rigor of Bryn Mawr and have taken at least 3 lab science courses as well as mathematics courses that include trigonometry. The SAT I and SAT II Subject Tests in writing and two other areas must be taken by November of the senior year for early decision applicants and January for regular decision applicants. The ACT may be substituted. An interview, either at the College or with a local alumnae representative, is strongly recommended. Application forms should be submitted by November 15 for fall early decision applicants, by January 1 for winter early decision applicants, and by January 15 for regular decision applicants.

Transfer students must complete a minimum of two years' work at Bryn Mawr to qualify for the A.B. degree.

Application and Information

The Admissions Office is open from 9 a.m. to 5 p.m. on weekdays and, during the fall, from 9 a.m. to 1 p.m. on Saturdays. For further information, an application form, or the name of a local alumnae representative, prospective students should contact:

Jennifer J. Rickard
Dean of Admissions and Financial Aid
Bryn Mawr College
101 North Merion Avenue
Bryn Mawr, Pennsylvania 19010-2899
Telephone: 610-526-5152
Fax: 610-526-7471
E-mail: admissions@brynmawr.edu
World Wide Web: http://www.brynmawr.edu
http://www.applicationoptions.shtml
(to apply online)

BUCKNELL UNIVERSITY

LEWISBURG, PENNSYLVANIA

The University

As one of the top private liberal arts colleges in the nation, Bucknell University offers its students a solid foundation in the arts and sciences. Unlike many other liberal arts schools, however, Bucknell provides an unusual array of choices for its students. From traditional majors such as history, economics, and anthropology to programs in animal behavior, environmental studies, Japanese and East Asian studies, and international relations and from studies in the humanities, social sciences, and sciences to professionally oriented programs in engineering, education, business, and music, Bucknell students have many more options than are usually found in a school of 3,350 students. At the same time, Bucknell students enjoy the special attention usually associated with small, private colleges. Professors take time to know their students personally, both in and out of the classroom.

Bucknell attracts students from throughout the United States and abroad. Most live on campus in the residence halls and in special interest houses, such as the African-American Studies House. There are several recently completed residence halls on campus. Students spend time outside the classroom in a wide variety of activities, choosing from more than 120 clubs and organizations. A large number of students participate in intramural and intercollegiate (Division I) athletics; work on one of the several student newspapers or the radio station; are active in student government; help with community volunteer projects; perform with one of the music, drama, and dance groups; or join one of the twelve fraternities or seven sororities. Students also enjoy a new alcohol-free nightclub on campus.

Location

Students and faculty members study together in what has been described as one of the most beautiful campuses in the East. Located in central Pennsylvania in the scenic Susquehanna River valley, Bucknell is within 3 to 4 hours of most of the major Eastern cities, including New York City, Baltimore, Philadelphia, and Washington, D.C.

Majors and Degrees

Bucknell offers the Bachelor of Arts degree in animal behavior, anthropology, art, art history, biology, chemistry, classics (Greek and Latin), comparative humanities, computer science, East Asian studies (China or Japan), economics, education, English, environmental studies, French, geography, geology/environmental geology, German, history, international relations, Latin American studies, mathematics, music (music composition, music education, music history, and performance), philosophy, physics, political science, psychology, religion, Russian, sociology (general, human services, and legal studies), Spanish, theater, and women's and gender studies; the Bachelor of Music degree; the Bachelor of Science degree in animal behavior, biology, cell biology and biochemistry, chemistry, computer science, engineering (biomedical, chemical, civil and environmental, computer science, electrical, and mechanical), environmental geology, environmental studies, mathematics, and physics; the Bachelor of Science in Business Administration degree in accounting and management; and Bachelor of Science in Education degrees in early childhood development, elementary education, and secondary education. A five-year combined curriculum leads to the B.S. in an engineering field and a B.A. in another discipline.

Academic Program

Although requirements for each degree vary, all students are required to successfully complete three writing courses. Special programs are offered to encourage each student's personal and intellectual development. Examples are the first-year foundation seminars, an introductory engineering course open to students in the College of Arts and Sciences, an honors program, and the Residential Colleges. The Residential Colleges combine classroom and out-of-class activities, with each college centered on a theme, such as the arts, humanities, global affairs, environmental issues, social justice, or society and technology.

Bucknell prepares students for the challenges of the twenty-first century. Whether students plan to begin their careers immediately after graduating or go on to professional or graduate schools, professors strive to help them to use their skills and talents, to reason and comprehend, and to interact and communicate with global citizens in an increasingly complex society.

Off-Campus Programs

Nearly 40 percent of each graduating class has spent one or two semesters studying on approved programs in Europe, Asia, the Middle East, Africa, Australia, New Zealand, and Central or South America. Bucknell sponsors three of its own programs in England, France, and Barbados and is affiliated with programs worldwide. About 10 percent of those studying off campus attend internship programs in Philadelphia or Washington, D.C. All institutional financial aid is portable for off-campus study.

Academic Facilities

Bucknell provides unusually fine facilities to students, including a recently completed music building and psychology/geology center; a new athletics and recreation center that includes a new fitness center, pool, and 4,000-seat arena; an outstanding library; a performing arts center with a 1,200-seat concert hall; and computer labs throughout the campus. Extensive "electronic classrooms" (a computer for each student) are in use throughout the campus. The University is served by a dedicated, high-speed connection to the Internet. All student housing is connected to ResNet, the residence hall network.

Costs

The cost of tuition and fees for 2003–04 was $35,262, including $28,764 for tuition, $6302 for room and board, and $196 for student fees.

Financial Aid

More than $27.9 million in financial aid was awarded to freshman applicants in the fall of 2003, with an average award of $16,500. Financial aid applicants must file the Financial Aid PROFILE with the College Scholarship Service before January 1.

Faculty

Bucknell has 293 full-time and 24 part-time members on the teaching faculty; 95 percent hold doctorates or appropriate terminal degrees. The student-faculty ratio is 11.6:1. The most celebrated professors teach freshmen as well as advanced students; no classes are taught by graduate students.

Although professors consider teaching to be their first priority, they also find time to pursue their own scholarly work. Students are often involved in faculty members' research and special projects, which sometimes leads to joint publications or presentations at professional meetings.

Student Government

The Bucknell Student Government represents the student body, working with the faculty and administration to achieve student goals. It also dispenses funds for most student clubs and organizations. Its representatives serve on standing committees of the Board of Trustees and other University governance groups.

Admission Requirements

Admission decisions focus on the quality of preparation as demonstrated by achievement in rigorous high school courses, SAT I or ACT scores, talent and contribution to school or community, and evidence of strong character and integrity. The University actively seeks qualified students from throughout the United States and abroad.

Application and Information

Applications should be filed before January 1 of the senior year in high school for notification by March 25. SAT I or ACT results must be submitted before March 1. Early decision candidates may apply for Early Decision-Round One consideration by November 15 or Early Decision-Round Two consideration by January 1. Applications for transfer students should be submitted by April 1 for studies beginning in the following fall and by December 1 for the spring semester.

Mark Davies
Dean of Admissions
Bucknell University
Lewisburg, Pennsylvania 17837
Telephone: 570-577-1101
Fax: 570-577-3538
E-mail: admissions@bucknell.edu
World Wide Web: http://www.bucknell.edu

Bucknell students often say that they fell in love with the campus when they saw it for the first time. The Academic Quad, shown here, is one of their favorite spots on campus.

BUFFALO STATE COLLEGE, STATE UNIVERSITY OF NEW YORK

BuffaloState
State University of New York

BUFFALO, NEW YORK

The College

Buffalo State is the college of choice for students who want to develop close relationships with professors—a major contributor to college success. Most classes have fewer than 40 students; major courses average 12 to 16. And professors, not graduate students, teach even introductory courses. Buffalo State offers more than 120 programs for undergraduates, and a commitment to providing students with college degrees that put them on the road to success.

Buffalo State graduates are highly sought after by employers. Internships provide students with the real-world experience necessary for success in the marketplace. Buffalo State students gain experience in such places as museums, hospitals, political offices, schools, wildlife rehabilitation centers, police laboratories, banks and investment firms, advertising agencies, and engineering firms.

Of a total enrollment of about 12,000 students, approximately 9,600 are undergraduates. Most students come from New York state, but the College has a growing number of out-of-state and international students.

The College is known for its excellent teacher training programs. Until very recently, Buffalo State was the only SUNY college whose professional education programs were accredited by the National Council for Accreditation of Teacher Education (NCATE), a professional organization that evaluates teacher preparation programs to ensure that they meet rigid standards of excellence. Graduates from colleges with this accreditation are sought by school districts across the United States.

However, about two thirds of the College's undergraduate majors prepare students for careers other than teaching. Buffalo State students learn to become chemists, artists, or speech pathologists. They study urban and regional planning, psychology, television broadcasting, or business administration. They start careers immediately after graduation or go on to earn a master's degree or Ph.D.

The Sports Arena, housing Buffalo's only college ice hockey rink, is home to the NCAA Division III Bengals varsity teams, which include nineteen men's and women's teams. In addition, club and intramural teams involve students in friendly competition in various sports. A state-of-the-art student fitness center opened in fall 2002. The Sports Complex also includes outdoor fields, an indoor arena, a pool, dance studios, and weight rooms.

A variety of living and learning options are available on campus, including suite- and apartment-style housing and special floors for honors and international students. Attractive off-campus housing is readily available in surrounding residential neighborhoods.

More than 100 student organizations—from the radio station and volunteer groups to sororities and fraternities—allow students to meet new people, take breaks from classes, and develop leadership skills.

Location

Buffalo State is definitely not the place for students wishing to attend a school surrounded by cow pastures. Buffalo State is the only SUNY college located in a major city. The College is situated in the Elmwood Museum District adjacent to Delaware Park, the world-famous Albright-Knox Art Gallery, the Buffalo and Erie County Historical Society, Hoyt Lake, and the Buffalo Zoo. Students find trendy restaurants, shops, and cafés within walking distance of campus.

Buffalo is minutes from Niagara Falls, less than 2 hours from Toronto, and a day's drive—or an hour's flight—from New York City and Boston. The Buffalo Niagara International Airport is 15 minutes from campus, with daily service to major metropolitan areas.

Majors and Degrees

The Bachelor of Arts degree is available with majors in anthropology, art, art history, the arts, biology, broadcasting, chemistry, communication, economics, English, French language and literature, geography, geology, history, humanities, journalism, mathematics, music, philosophy, physics, political science, psychology, public communication, sociology, Spanish language and literature, and theater.

The Bachelor of Science degree is awarded in the following programs: art education, biology education, business administration, business and marketing education, career and technical education, chemistry education, childhood education, computer information systems, criminal justice, design, dietetics: coordinated, dietetics: didactic, early childhood education, earth sciences, earth science education, economics, English education, fashion and textile technology, forensic chemistry, French education, health and wellness, hospitality administration, individualized studies, industrial technology, interdisciplinary studies, mathematics, mathematics education, physics, physics education, physics-engineering (3-2 cooperative program), psychology, social studies education, social work, sociology, Spanish education, speech language pathology, technology education, and urban and regional analysis and planning.

The Bachelor of Fine Arts is awarded in design, painting, photography, printmaking, and sculpture.

The Bachelor of Music degree is offered in music education.

The Bachelor of Science in Education is awarded in exceptional education.

The Bachelor of Technology is awarded in electrical engineering technology (with concentrations in electronics and in power and machines) and in mechanical engineering technology.

Fifty-five departmental minors are available.

The College offers advisement programs for prelaw and prehealth students who are preparing for graduate study in dentistry, law, medicine, or veterinary science.

Academic Program

All Buffalo State undergraduate students must complete a minimum of 123 credit hours to qualify for a bachelor's degree. With general education courses and electives, the College provides a general framework for understanding the human experience and an intellectual context in which students evaluate personal and social values while building a foundation for a career.

Buffalo State offers an All-College Honors Program as well as honors sequences in eleven majors. Learning communities—open to all freshmen—involve small groups of students who take the same block of thematically related classes, taught by teams of faculty members. These students have access to special gathering places on campus, equipped with computers and kitchens, where they can meet and study with other students in the program and their professors.

The College operates on a semester basis, with a three-week intersemester term in January. A summer program of three 4-week sessions is also offered.

Off-Campus Programs

Several off-campus educational opportunities provide flexibility to broaden intellectual horizons and tailor learning to individual interests and career goals. These opportunities include internships, independent study projects, clinical practice, workshops, exchange opportunities at 177 other U.S. colleges and universities, study-abroad programs at more than 300 institutions around the world, credit for experiential learning, and the ability to cross-register or complete degrees at other schools through special arrangement. All options carry college credit.

Academic Facilities

The 120-acre campus is built for academic excellence, beginning with E. H. Butler Library. Its holdings include more than 525,000 volumes (including bound periodicals); 950,000 microforms; 20,000 audiovisual and nonbook items, including CD-ROMs and DVDs; and 7,500 periodical subscriptions, all easily accessed through the user-friendly online catalog.

Students have access to 875 computer workstations in sixty labs and classrooms throughout campus. Every student has a personal computer account with continuous e-mail and Internet access, as well as individual network accounts for file storage and Web pages. All residence halls are wired with high-speed Internet ports.

The Burchfield-Penney Art Center, accredited by the American Association of Museums, houses the world's largest collection of works by watercolorist Charles E. Burchfield. An 856-seat auditorium in stately Rockwell Hall houses the Performing Arts Center. Broadcast majors gain hands-on experience through the College's television studio and radio station (WBNY-FM 91.3). In summer 2003, the College dedicated the Warren Enters Theater, a $2.6-million state-of-the-art learning laboratory. The campus also offers several other "learning lab" opportunities for students: the Buckham Campus School (a K–8 Buffalo public school), Campus House (a private faculty-staff club operated by hospitality administration students), the Speech-Language-Hearing Clinic, and the Whitworth Ferguson Planetarium. Buffalo State's Great Lakes Center for Environmental Research and Education, located 1 mile from campus on Buffalo's waterfront, features a fleet of research vessels and an on-shore field station.

Costs

For academic year 2003–04, full-time tuition for in-state students was $4350; fees were $709. Out-of-state students paid $10,300 per year in tuition and $709 in fees. On-campus housing costs range from $1867 to $2626 per semester, and meal plans from $780 to $1170 per semester are offered. Books, supplies, and personal expenses, including transportation, were estimated at $2600 per year. Costs are subject to change.

Financial Aid

About 60 percent of Buffalo State undergraduates receive financial assistance through grants, scholarships, loans, and employment averaging $3037 per year. The Financial Aid Office helps students find ways to pay for their college education. The office oversees distribution of more than $32.5 million in federal and state grants, loans, and student employment annually. In addition, more than 125 scholarship funds are managed by the Scholarship Office.

For information on financial aid or scholarships, students may visit http://www.fafsa.ed.gov or the University's Web site, listed below. The recommended filing date for submission of aid applications for fall semester is March 15. Applications received after published deadlines are processed on a first-come, first-served basis, with awards subject to availability of funds.

Faculty

Buffalo State's faculty consists of 411 full-time and 305 part-time members. Eighty-two percent of the full-time faculty members have earned doctorates or terminal degrees in their fields. Faculty members are scholars, actively involved in research, publishing, and the arts. The College does not rely on teaching assistants or graduate students for classroom instruction. The College is especially proud of its 41 recipients of the SUNY Chancellor's Award and its distinguished professor, three distinguished service professors, and four distinguished teaching professors. Faculty members provide academic advisement for majors. Professional staff members provide academic advisement for undeclared students, tutoring, personal and career counseling, and health care.

Student Government

United Students Government (USG) represents the interests of all students and encourages their participation in educational, recreational, cultural, and social activities. USG offers a variety of services and programs, including concerts, a campus newspaper, the Whispering Pines college camp, and a dental clinic funded through the mandatory student activity fee.

Admission Requirements

Buffalo State accepts both proven and promising students who demonstrate the ability to complete college-level work. Admission counselors look for a broad, balanced high school education that includes study in English, foreign language(s), mathematics, science, and social studies.

Admission decisions are based on a variety of factors, including performance in rigorous college-preparatory course work, standardized test scores (SAT or ACT), rank in class, and recommendations from teachers and school counselors. Satisfactory results on the General Educational Development (GED) test are also acceptable. For transfer students, a minimum grade point average of 2.0 out of 4.0 is required for consideration, although some programs require a higher grade point average.

The College welcomes applications from international students (contact: International Student Affairs Office, telephone: 716-878-5331, http://www.buffalostate.edu/offices/isa).

Application and Information

Candidates must complete the State University of New York application, available from the Buffalo State Admissions Office, high school guidance offices, college transfer offices, or online at http://www.suny.edu/student. Decisions are made on a rolling basis beginning in mid-September for spring applicants, and in mid-December for fall applicants. Processing of applications continues until new-student enrollment goals have been met. On-campus interviews are encouraged.

Admissions Office
Moot Hall 110
Buffalo State College
1300 Elmwood Avenue
Buffalo, New York 14222-1095

Telephone: 716-878-4017
Fax: 716-878-6100
E-mail: admissions@buffalostate.edu
World Wide Web: http://www.buffalostate.edu

BUTLER UNIVERSITY

INDIANAPOLIS, INDIANA

The University

Celebrating its 150-year anniversary, Butler University has a proud tradition of excellence and innovation. Challenging and enabling students to meet their personal and professional goals has guided the University since 1855 and continues to do so as it embarks on the next century of its history. Today, Butler is an independent, coeducational, nonsectarian university with a total undergraduate enrollment of more than 3,800 students. Butler is accredited by the Higher Learning Commission of the North Central Association of Colleges and Schools.

Butler students represent almost every state in the nation and fifty-three countries, reflecting a diversity of cultures, interests, aspirations, personalities, and experiences. Students can choose from a number of housing options, including an apartment-style residence hall, a service-learning house, one all-women residence hall with an optional living-learning center, two coeducational residence halls with optional living-learning centers, fraternities, and sororities.

There are more than 100 student organizations, fifteen Greek organizations, and nineteen Division I varsity athletic teams. Students take advantage of Broadway shows at Butler's Clowes Memorial Hall, the city's premier performing arts center. Basketball fans cheer on the Bulldogs at the 11,000-seat historic Hinkle Fieldhouse, where the final game in the movie *Hoosiers* was filmed.

Located near the center of campus, Atherton Union serves as a natural gathering space for students. Atherton Union has numerous amenities including e-mail stations, wireless capabilities, a 24-hour computer lab, Starbucks coffee shop, fitness center, bookstore, food court, dining hall, and convenience store.

Location

Butler University is located on 290 acres of Indianapolis' historic Butler-Tarkington neighborhood, which is also home to Indiana's governor. The campus maintains its heritage with centuries-old trees; open, landscaped malls; curving sidewalks; and fountains. The majority of the University's full-time students call campus home and enjoy a nature preserve, prairie, historical canal, formal botanical garden, an observatory, and jogging paths.

Just 6 miles from downtown Indianapolis, Butler's urban location offers internship opportunities that provide excellent graduate school and career preparation. Indianapolis, Indiana's state capital and the twelfth-largest city in the nation, boasts a variety of cultural activities, including the Indianapolis Symphony Orchestra, the Indiana Repertory Theatre, the Indianapolis Museum of Art (just two blocks from campus), the Eiteljorg Museum, the Indiana State Museum, and the world's largest children's museum.

The Indianapolis Motor Speedway is the anchor of Indianapolis' professional sports, while basketball, football, hockey, and baseball have homes in three major sports arenas. Indianapolis is home to the NCAA headquarters and its Hall of Champions. Butler has been the proud cohost of the NCAA Final Four Championship in 1991, 1997, and 2000, and is scheduled to cohost again in 2006.

Majors and Degrees

As a comprehensive university with a strong liberal arts and sciences tradition, Butler is committed to graduating students who have a well-rounded yet focused education. A core curriculum affords students the opportunity to gain knowledge in the humanities, the arts, social sciences, natural sciences, and mathematics.

Baccalaureate degrees are offered through Butler's five colleges. Unique programs include the engineering dual-degree program, offered jointly by Butler University and the Purdue School of Engineering and Technology at Indianapolis. Students receive both a Butler Bachelor of Science degree in a selected liberal arts and sciences major (biology, chemistry, computer science, economics, mathematics, physics or science, and technology and society) and a Purdue Bachelor of Science degree in computer, electrical, or mechanical engineering.

For students who are undecided about their major field of study, there is an Exploratory Studies Program where students develop a personalized academic plan to help choose the major that best suits their interests and abilities. Butler also offers an individualized major that allows students to create their own major, such as women's studies.

The College of Education is dedicated to preparing outstanding teachers. The administration and the faculty and staff members of the College of Education are committed to providing the best possible learning experience for students. For the past seven years, the College has experienced a 100 percent placement rate for its students, an indicator that Butler students place first in education. Majors offered through the College are early and middle childhood (kindergarten to grade 6) and early adolescence (middle school)/adolescence young adult (high school).

The College of Liberal Arts and Sciences creates lifelong learners. The College affirms the central role of liberal arts education while offering opportunities for specialization. Majors include actuarial science, actuarial sciences/management (five-year B.S./M.B.A.), anthropology, biological sciences, chemistry, chemistry and pharmaceutical sciences, communications disorders, communication studies, computer science, economics, English, exploratory (humanities, natural sciences, social sciences), French, French and business studies, German, German and business studies, Greek, history, history and political science, international studies, journalism, Latin, mathematics, philosophy, philosophy and religion, physics, political science, psychology, public and corporate communications, religion, science technology and society, sociology, sociology and criminology, software engineering, Spanish, Spanish and business studies, and urban affairs.

The College of Business Administration prepares students to be tomorrow's business leaders through classroom work and two required semester-long cooperative education experiences. Majors include accounting, economics, exploratory (business), finance, international management, management information systems, and marketing.

The Jordan College of Fine Arts integrates intensive conservatory training with broad objectives and a strong academic curriculum. The College is well respected for its tradition of educating students as emerging professionals in the arts. Majors offered are arts administration, dance pedagogy, dance performance, exploratory (fine arts), music–Bachelor of Arts (applied, history and literature, and theory and composition), music–Bachelor of Music (music education, music performance, theory and composition, and piano pedagogy), telecommunication arts, and theater.

College of Pharmacy and Health Sciences graduates serve society as caring, ethical health professionals and community leaders. The College's professional programs combine intensive classroom education with clinical experiences in the professional phases of the degrees. Majors offered are exploratory (pharmacy and health sciences), pharmacy (Pharm.D.), and physician assistant (B.S.P.A.).

Butler offers preprofessional programs in dentistry, forestry, law, medicine, physical therapy, seminary, and veterinary medicine. Graduate programs include the M.B.A., the M.S. in school counseling, the M.S. in education administration, the M.S. in education, the M.A. in English, the M.A. in history, and the M.M. in composition, conducting, music education, music history, performance, and piano pedagogy and theory.

Academic Program

All candidates for the baccalaureate degree must complete the University core requirements and at least 45 semester hours of work. At least 30 of the 45 hours must be in the college granting the degree.

Eligible students may participate in the Honors Program. By the end of the sophomore year, honors course work is generally completed. Students then begin the next phase, an independent study to help them research, write, and eventually present their honors thesis. Butler is a sponsoring institution for the National Merit Scholarship Program. Butler also offers advanced placement with appropriate academic credit in most subjects covered by either the AP examinations or the CLEP tests. Students may choose to enroll in Air Force and Army ROTC programs.

Butler students have the chance to originate research projects and participate in them with faculty members and then develop these projects into professional presentations and publications. Hundreds of Butler students present their projects at the Undergraduate Research Conference, hosted by Butler every April. In addition, the Butler Summer Institute awards accepted students a $2000 grant plus housing while they work on summer research projects with faculty members.

Off-Campus Programs

One of the largest study-abroad programs in the United States is hosted by the Institute for Study Abroad–Butler University (IFSA), which sends students from American colleges and universities to Argentina, Australia, Chile, Costa Rica, England, Ireland, Mexico, New Zealand, Northern Ireland, and Scotland. In addition to the IFSA-Butler, students may also select their overseas opportunity from programs offered by fifteen other colleges, universities, and well-respected study-abroad organizations.

Academic Facilities

Butler has incorporated state-of-the-art technologies throughout its campus. These include Mac and PC computers, two Ethernet connections per residence hall room, seventeen networked computer labs, electronic and multimedia classrooms, Internet access and e-mail service, wireless capabilities, student home pages, language labs, international studies center, telephone systems with free voicemail, and 24-hour computer labs in Atherton Student Union and each residence hall.

Butler's public television station, WTBU, is housed in the Richard M. Fairbanks Center for Communication and Technology. Other facilities in the center include state-of-the-art classrooms, laboratories, conference rooms, television studios, graphics production and editing facilities, WRBU Internet radio station, recording studios, student newspaper offices, online magazine production space, and speaker labs.

Many student performances, including theater, dance, and music, can be seen in Butler's 2,200-seat Clowes Memorial Hall. The Holcomb Observatory and Planetarium houses the largest telescope in the state of Indiana, a 38-inch Cassegrain reflector. Butler's libraries house approximately 250,000 monograph volumes, 110,000 government documents, 1,500 current journal subscriptions, 14,000 audio-visual materials, and more than 17,000 musical scores. The library system also features a searchable computer database, rare books collection, archives, online catalog access, and research tools.

Costs

For the 2003–04 academic year, tuition was $20,990 for full-time undergraduate students. Average room and board were $7040 per year. Books are estimated at $300 per semester, and other fees are estimated at $250. Tuition for the professional pharmacy program was $22,430 and $24,910 for the sixth year. Tuition for the professional physician assistant program is $22,430 and $25,250 for the fourth year.

Financial Aid

Butler University offers a variety of financial assistance programs based on the demonstration of academic excellence, performance talent, or financial need. Butler awards merit-based academic scholarships to students who have displayed outstanding high school achievement and have excelled in leadership and community service. Performance awards are available in the areas of music, dance, theater, and athletics. Academic departments offer scholarships for students in selected majors. On-campus employment and work-study programs are also available. All students who seek need-based financial assistance are required to file the Free Application For Federal Student Aid (FAFSA) and the Butler University Application for Financial Assistance.

The University offers National Merit, National Achievement, and National Hispanic Scholarships. Semifinalists in these programs are guaranteed a minimum Freshman Academic Scholarship. However, based on academic screening, these students may qualify for a higher award. Finalists in these programs who designate Butler as their sponsor and file their FAFSA by March 1 are eligible for an additional award that ranges from $750 to $2000.

The University also offers Morton-Finney Leadership Awards and Latino Leadership Awards. African American students who exhibit leadership in their high schools and communities may be eligible. Awards are based on class rank, SAT/ACT scores, and leadership roles in school and the community. These awards include an expectation of continued campus and community leadership while at Butler.

Faculty

Teaching is the top priority for Butler's 269 full-time faculty members; 84 percent hold the highest (terminal) degree in their fields. Many are active in national research programs, write for publications, counsel in government and business, and participate in the arts. With a comfortable teaching load, Butler's faculty members have time to work with students individually. The student-faculty ratio is 14:1. All classes are taught by professors; there are no teaching assistants.

Student Government

As the official student governing body, Student Government Association (SGA) is the liaison between faculty and administration members. The organization is also responsible for budgeting funds from the student activity fee. These funds promote SGA's Program Board activities, including the film series, concerts, and all campus special events as well as the purchase of the Butler yearbook, *The Drift*.

Admission Requirements

Applicants are expected to complete a minimum of 17 academic units in high school, including four years of English, three years each of laboratory sciences and mathematics, two years each of history or social studies, and two years of foreign language. A candidate for admission typically ranks in the upper third of his or her high school class and should submit satisfactory results of the SAT I or the ACT. The Jordan College of Fine Arts requires an audition. In addition to these factors, the Admission Committee considers the applicant's leadership skills, motivation, and writing sample. Students who wish to transfer from another regionally accredited college or university are considered if they are in good standing and have a grade point average of 2.0 or better in their previous academic work. Transfer students must submit official transcripts of all college work.

Application and Information

Although regular admission is on a rolling basis, students may choose to apply for Early Admission. Butler offers two nonbinding Early Admission (not early decision) programs with specific benefits associated with each program. The application priority date for Early Admission I is December 1 of the senior year of high school and its benefits include early consideration for freshmen academic scholarships and departmental scholarships, early course registration, priority housing, and optional living-learning center participation. The application priority date for Early Admission II is February 1 and its benefits include early consideration for freshmen academic scholarships, early course registration, and priority housing. Scholarship notification is on a rolling basis and begins January 15. Campus visits and interviews are strongly recommended, though not required, and are arranged on a daily basis. Several open-house programs are also scheduled throughout the year. Interested students and their families are encouraged to call the Office of Admission to make arrangements for campus visits.

Office of Admission
Butler University
4600 Sunset Avenue
Indianapolis, Indiana 46208-3485
Telephone: 317-940-8100
888-940-8100 (toll-free)
Fax: 317-940-8150
E-mail: admission@butler.edu
World Wide Web: http://www.butler.edu/admissions/

CABRINI COLLEGE

RADNOR, PENNSYLVANIA

The College

Cabrini College, a Catholic institution for men and women, is concerned with the full intellectual, personal, and social development of each student. The College's programs are organized to help students welcome the changes in their lives with vigor, initiative, and confidence. While academic excellence is the priority at Cabrini, students are encouraged to participate in activities that will help them develop socially, culturally, and spiritually. Although founded as a private Catholic college, the institution is proud of its diverse student body and accepts students of all denominations. Cabrini enrolls approximately 2,100 men and women. The student community is a friendly one, characterized by close and long-standing ties to the faculty. Cabrini College is sponsored by the Missionary Sisters of the Sacred Heart of Jesus and is named for that institution's founder, St. Frances Xavier Cabrini, the first U.S. citizen to be canonized. Mother Cabrini's commitment to service to others and education of the heart are key parts of the College's programs.

More than 60 percent of Cabrini's full-time students live on campus in a variety of housing accommodations, including traditional residence halls for men and women, single-family homes, and a 120- bed, apartment-style complex. The College provides a full range of services to students, including placement, career, and personal counseling; a tutoring program; and health services. Students can participate in seventeen intercollegiate sports for men and women as well as an intramural sports program. Other popular extracurricular activities are the theater program, the College chorus, the ethnic student alliance, departmental clubs, and campus ministry. Students are encouraged to join the College's award-winning newspaper, the literary journal, and the yearbook. The campus radio station, WYBF-FM, and television studio are available to all students.

Cabrini also provides a Master of Education degree, a Master of Science degree in organization leadership, and a new Master of Science degree in instructional systems and technology.

Location

Cabrini offers students the best of both worlds—a wooded, spacious, 112-acre suburban campus near King of Prussia and a half hour away from Philadelphia. The College is close enough for students to take advantage of the many cultural, social, and educational opportunities of the city. Students may visit Philadelphia's art museums or historic sites or travel to the First Union Center to see national sporting events or performances by professional musicians. Cabrini also is close to many other Philadelphia-area colleges, which sponsor activities of interest to students.

Majors and Degrees

Cabrini offers the Bachelor of Arts degree with major programs in American studies, arts administration, communication, English, French, graphic design, history, liberal arts, organizational management (accelerated), philosophy, political science, professional communications (accelerated), psychology, religious studies, sociology, Spanish, and studio art. The Bachelor of Science degree is offered with major programs in accounting, biology/premedicine, biotechnology, business administration, chemistry, clinical laboratory sciences/medical technology, computer information science, finance, human resource management, Internet computing, management information systems, marketing, mathematics, and sports science. An individualized major, designed by the student using existing courses, can lead to a B.A. or B.S. degree. The Bachelor of Social Work degree, which is accredited by the Council on Social Work, is awarded to graduates completing the social work major. The Bachelor of Science in Education degree is available with majors in early childhood, elementary, and special education; these programs also lead to teacher certification in each of the three fields. Education majors are certified to teach in Pennsylvania and reciprocating states. Teacher certification for secondary education is offered in biology, chemistry, communications, English, mathematics, and social studies (concentration in history). Preprofessional programs in law, nursing, occupational therapy, pharmacy, and physical therapy are designed by faculty advisers to meet the needs of individual students. Academic concentrations include advertising, chemical technical management, computer-mediated communication, criminal justice, economics, human-computer interaction, international business, journalism and writing, management information systems, nonprofit management, professional communication, public administration, systems administration and management, systems training and technical support, theater, video/audio/recording arts/photography/new communication technology, and women's studies.

Academic Program

Cabrini College's academic program gives students a well-rounded educational experience—one that includes a strong liberal arts and science base as well as professional development in a specific career field. All students take core curriculum competency and distribution requirement courses to supplement the in-depth knowledge acquired within each major. The core distribution requirements include courses in the following areas: contemporary issues; cultural diversity; heritage; imagination, creativity, and aesthetic appreciation; natural science; the individual and society; religious studies; and values and commitments. In addition, students take two seminar classes, Self-Understanding and the Common Good, in their freshman and junior years, respectively. The Common Good seminar includes a service learning component. Cabrini's core curriculum has been developed by its faculty to help students understand themselves, their society, and the world around them. Within each major, Cabrini's curriculum is designed to help students develop professional skills in their chosen career field. Classroom instruction in all majors is supplemented by internships, through which juniors and seniors can earn credit and often a salary for working in a job related to their career interest. Cooperative Education at Cabrini College is an optional academic program in which students learn to apply theoretical principles in a professional environment while earning academic credit (based on the number of hours worked and the value of the work experience gained) and income.

All education majors participate in fieldwork beginning in the sophomore year. Social work majors spend 600 hours in direct practice before graduation. Cabrini students can choose a double major, and a free elective system encourages students to broaden their academic backgrounds.

Students may pursue their studies on a full-time or part-time basis during the school year. The College enables students to take courses in the evening, on Saturday, or during the summer and offers an accelerated degree program in organizational management.

Off-Campus Programs

Cabrini participates with area colleges in a number of cooperative programs that enrich educational opportunities. Through an exchange program with nearby Eastern College, Rosemont College, and Valley Forge College, full-time students may elect courses offered on the other campuses; no additional tuition fees are charged, and credit is automatically transferred. Cabrini also maintains affiliations with Thomas Jefferson University and Widener University for allied health programs, the Pennsylvania College of Podiatric Medicine for an accelerated medical program, and KAJEM Recording Arts Studio for communication. The clinical laboratory sciences/medical technology program is conducted in cooperation with major hospital schools of medical technology.

Academic Facilities

Cabrini's 200,000-volume library, which includes 8,132 microforms, serves as a comprehensive resource for students. The library has a complete microfilm collection and subscribes to 515 current periodicals. Cabrini is a member of the Tri-State College Library Cooperative and the Online Computer Library Center (OCLC), so additional resources at other libraries in the area are just a keystroke away. The College's computer laboratory, open to all students, and five state-of-the-art-computer classroom facilities are equipped with IBM or Macintosh computers. Research facilities include the biology, chemistry, and psychology laboratories. A modern, fully equipped communication center houses the College's television studio, FM radio station, newsroom (with facilities for desktop publishing), graphic design laboratory, and photography darkroom.

A great resource for education majors is The Children's School. Education majors have the opportunity to observe, do fieldwork, and student teach at the school. The College's educational resource center provides students with access to teaching materials, ranging from videos and transparencies to children's literature.

Costs

Tuition for full-time students in 2003–04 was $19,670; room and board were $8550 for the year. A general fee of $750 covers student registration, health services, activities, library use, testing, and publications. Textbooks and supplies are approximately $700 per year, and fees of $25 to $100 are charged for laboratory and other miscellaneous courses. Students with cars secure a $45 parking permit annually.

Financial Aid

Last year, 93 percent of Cabrini's undergraduates shared more than $11.3 million in financial aid in the form of scholarship, grant, loan, and work-study funds. The College's most prestigious academic scholarship is the Alumni Recognition scholarship, awarded annually to an outstanding student. A special application, due by December 31, is required. Achievement Scholarships are available to applicants with strong credentials. In addition to Cabrini College scholarships and grants, federal funds are available through Federal Pell Grants, Federal Supplemental Educational Opportunity Grants, Federal Work-Study Program awards, and Federal Perkins Loans. State grants are available through students' home states. Veterans are eligible for assistance under the G.I. bill. In addition, the College offers work-study and other employment opportunities through which a student may earn money to pay for college education expenses. Federal Stafford Student Loans are available through most local banks. Students may apply for such loans directly to the lending agency. All financial aid is offered for a one-year period but is renewable upon application as long as the student gives evidence of financial need. Applicants for financial aid must submit the Free Application for Federal Student Aid (FAFSA), ideally before February 15 in order to expedite processing of the request for financial aid and by April 1 at the latest.

Faculty

Cabrini's average class size is 18 students, and the College's faculty members are committed to developing and challenging the individual skills of each student. Faculty members are known for their dedication to teaching and getting to know their students personally. Each full-time student has a faculty adviser who assists in arranging a program designed to meet the student's objectives.

Student Government

The Student Government Association (SGA) of Cabrini College facilitates all communication pertaining to students within the College community. The association exists to make known the views of the student body and to look after its interests with respect to the faculty members, administration, and educational policies of the College.

Admission Requirements

The Admissions Committee considers applicants on the basis of their high school record, SAT I or ACT scores, class rank, and other indicators of potential to succeed in college-level studies, such as recommendations. Applications for admission are reviewed without regard to sex, race, creed, color, national origin, age, or handicap. Applicants should be graduates of an accredited high school (or present equivalent credentials) and have a minimum of 15 units of credit: 4 in English, 2 in a foreign language, 3 in college-preparatory mathematics, 3 in science, and 3 in social studies. Cabrini also conducts an early admission program through which students with superior ability and a sound academic background may begin college studies at the end of the junior year in high school. Applicants may apply for advanced standing at Cabrini through the Advanced Placement (AP) Program and the College-Level Examination Program (CLEP) of the College Board. The College's Graduate and Continuing Studies Office administers CLEP and DANTES tests.

Cabrini welcomes transfer students from other accredited institutions. Applicants should have a minimum GPA of 2.2 to be considered for transfer. Students transferring from Becker College, Bucks County Community College, Community College of Philadelphia, Manor College, Delaware County Community College, Montgomery County Community College, Harcum College, Harrisburg Area Community College, Peirce College, Reading Community College, or Valley Forge Military College with an A.A. or A.S. degree and a minimum 2.5 GPA receive credit for all previous course work. Two-year-college students are encouraged to follow a course of liberal and general studies during their first two years at another institution if they expect to continue their studies at a four-year college such as Cabrini.

A campus visit, while not required, is recommended for prospective students. The Admissions Office offers individual interviews and group information sessions on weekdays and select Saturdays. Students conduct campus tours, which may include class visits and informal meetings with faculty members and administrators. Those planning to visit the campus should contact a member of the Admissions Office staff for information. In addition, representatives of the College visit high schools in various cities.

Application and Information

Applicants for freshman admission are requested to have SAT I or ACT scores and official high school transcripts sent to the Admissions Office along with the application for admission. Transfer students must submit an application and high school and college transcripts. A nonrefundable application fee of $25 must accompany the application. The Admissions Committee maintains a rolling admission policy until the class is filled and takes action on an application when all the necessary credentials are on file. For more information, students may contact:

Gary E. Johnson, Dean for Enrollment Management
Cabrini College
610 King of Prussia Road
Radnor, Pennsylvania 19087-3698
Telephone: 610-902-8552
800-848-1003 (toll-free)
E-mail: admit@cabrini.edu
World Wide Web: http://www.cabrini.edu

CALDWELL COLLEGE

CALDWELL, NEW JERSEY

The College

Caldwell College is a Catholic, coeducational, four-year liberal arts institution rooted in a proud 800-year Dominican tradition of rigorous scholarship, committed teaching, and ethical values. Founded in 1939 by the Sisters of St. Dominic, Caldwell College's most popular offerings include undergraduate degrees in business, psychology, and education. The College offers an individualized major for students seeking a concentrated major to design their own course work with administrative approval. Caldwell College has twenty-eight undergraduate degrees, fifteen graduate programs, and a Caldwell Scholars Program. Also offered are an adult undergraduate program and a uniquely structured distance education program for adult learners. The College offers accelerated options that combine the curricular opportunities of the distance education program with traditional on-campus offerings. Master's degrees are offered in business administration, counseling psychology, curriculum and instruction, educational administration, and pastoral ministry. Specializations in art therapy and school counseling are open to students in the counseling psychology program. Specializations in special education, applied behavior analysis, and educational technology are open to students in the curriculum and instruction program. Educational administration is also offered in a fast-track Off-Campus Leadership Development version. Post-master's programs in art therapy, school counseling, professional licensing credits for counselors, and educational supervisor's certificate are also offered. Postbaccalaureate teacher certification, special education certification, and applied behavior analysis certification are also available.

The Office of Career Development provides ongoing career counseling, career education, interest testing, and graduate study information to assist students in clarifying personal goals and in exploring academic and career opportunities. A career library and a career-planning course offer additional resources.

Caldwell College sponsors work-based internship and cooperative education opportunities through the Office of Experiential Learning. These programs encourage students to integrate work experience with classroom learning. Approximately 40 percent of the students who participate in internship and cooperative education programs are offered full-time positions upon graduation. The office also assists students and alumni who are seeking full- and part-time employment. The College's Business Advisory Council, which includes about 40 members from major corporations throughout New Jersey, was formed in 1994 with the belief that business leaders and educators needed to share their resources so both students and the business community could prepare for the challenges of the global marketplace. Businesses benefit from the expertise of the College's business faculty members and through College-sponsored conferences related to current business trends.

Caldwell College enrolls 2,219 full-time, part-time, and graduate students each year. The College enrolled its largest full-time undergraduate population ever in 2003 and continues its tremendous growth while maintaining its liberal arts character. Fully qualified faculty members and a 13:1 student-faculty ratio provide students with close, personal attention. Approximately 94 percent of full-time students are from New Jersey. In addition, the College's rich cultural diversity attracts individuals from Northeastern and mid-Atlantic states and from more than twenty-six other countries. The cultural mix of students includes white, 66 percent; African American, 15 percent; Hispanic, 10 percent; Asian-American, 2 percent; international, 3 percent; and approximately 4 percent unknown.

About 35 percent of full-time students live on campus. Single, double, triple, and a few quad rooms are available. All students, including incoming freshmen, may have a car on campus. A rich program of student activities involves both residents and commuters in campus life. A variety of clubs and organizations, as well as publications, are available. Guest artists, musicians, authors, and speakers appear on campus regularly. Student social life features dances and other open activities. An on-campus fitness center provides students with health and exercise opportunities. The center is equipped with cardiovascular equipment, including treadmills, stationary bicycles, steppers, and combination weight machines. The College is a full member of the NCAA Division II. Caldwell fields intercollegiate teams in men's baseball, basketball, soccer, and tennis; women's basketball, cross-country, soccer, softball, and tennis; and coed golf. The College also sponsors a variety of intramural sports.

Location

Located on a beautiful, secure 70-acre campus 20 miles west of New York City, students participate in numerous educational, cultural, and social experiences while still enjoying the relaxed atmosphere of campus life. The center of Caldwell, with a variety of shops and restaurants, is within walking distance. Area attractions include theaters, museums, parks, ski resorts, malls, the Meadowlands Sports Complex, and the New Jersey shore. Many corporate headquarters are easily accessible and provide a variety of internship opportunities. The College is near major highways and can be reached by public transportation.

Majors and Degrees

Caldwell College offers twenty-eight undergraduate Bachelor of Arts (B.A.), Bachelor of Science (B.S.), and Bachelor of Fine Arts (B.F.A.) degrees. A multidisciplinary major is also offered. The B.A. is offered in art, biology, chemistry, communication arts, criminal justice, elementary education, English, French, history, an individualized major, mathematics, music, political science, psychology, religious studies, social studies, sociology, and Spanish. The B.S. is offered in accounting, business administration, computer information systems, computer science, international business, management, marketing, and medical technology. The B.F.A. is offered in art. The education department offers teacher certification programs in elementary education (nursery–grade 8) and for teaching grades K–12 in art, biology, English, French, mathematics, music, social studies, and Spanish as well as a P-3 certification. A certification program in school nursing and teacher of health is also available to registered nurses.

Academic Program

Eligibility for a degree requires completion of a minimum of 122 credits and a GPA of at least 2.0 (C). Students must also complete major courses with a minimum grade of C and satisfy all other departmental requirements. All programs require that students successfully pass a form of outcomes assessment in the senior year. To complete the liberal arts requirements, students must select courses from computer literacy, English, fine arts, foreign language, history, mathematics, natural sciences, philosophy, physical education, public speaking, religious studies, and social sciences. A Writing Across the Curriculum program systematically develops a student's ability to write well, regardless of his or her major. Opportunities for independent study, internships, co-ops, double majors, minors, and certificate programs are available. The Caldwell Scholars Program challenges exceptional students with both interdisciplinary studies and a directed honors project and is supplemented by guest lecturers.

Students must score a 3, 4, or 5 on the College Board's Advanced Placement test to receive advanced placement or credit for completed work. Students may receive credit for knowledge gained through independent study or experience through the College-Level Examination Program (CLEP). All students are encouraged to participate in internships. Proof of a TOEFL score of 550 (paper-based) or 213 (computer-based) is required with international student applications. Course selection is determined by placement test results, and international students may be required to enroll in credit-bearing, advanced-level English as a Second Language (ESL) courses.

Off-Campus Programs

In addition to a wide range of study-abroad opportunities, the College has a number of unique agreements with Korean institutions. The College signed its first exchange program agreement in 1995 with Duksung Women's University in Korea. Since then, 3 women have attended Duksung, and the College has hosted 6 women. In fall 1998, the College signed an exchange program agreement with the Catholic University of Korea, which provides men with broad international educational opportunities to better prepare themselves for the global marketplace. The latest articulation agreement enables both men and women to earn credits for business, education, music, science, and other courses while learning the Korean culture, economy, and language. In addition, the College has established both undergraduate and graduate affiliation programs for students in health-related majors to accelerate their career goals.

Academic Facilities

A recently completed comprehensive roadway project has enhanced campus parking, adding several hundred new parking spaces and an expanded dormitory parking area. An access roadway is planned to provide a main entrance to the campus from Bloomfield Avenue. In September 2002, the College opened the $8.2-million, 60,000-square-foot George R. Newman Student Activities and Recreation Center, which meets the needs of a growing student population.

Through an almost $2-million federal government grant to establish the Center for Excellence in Teaching on campus, Caldwell College recently renovated its biology, physics, and chemistry laboratories with a top priority of focusing on the need to excel in the teaching of math and science. The College plans to serve as a regional hub to implement innovative teacher preparation programs with an emphasis on the effective use of technology in classrooms, the refinement of math and science training, special education teacher training, and the development of programs for disadvantaged students.

Campus facilities also include a library, four classroom and administrative buildings, and a theater. An academic building, opened in 1997, is equipped with a 120-seat lecture hall, a spiral staircase, and faculty and administrative offices. A new psychology lab added to the building is equipped with computers and specialized state-of-the-art hardware and software for students to conduct psychological studies related to their class work and opportunities for independent student and faculty psychological research. The lab provides a camera and media equipment for the development of counseling skills, for student roleplaying, and for practice in the observation and data collection of behavior. Wide-screen video and computer graphic capability and satellite reception are available. Jennings Library contains 137,429 volumes and subscribes to more than 600 journals. Dial-up access is available from off-campus sites to both the online public access catalog and more than 25 online databases, including ERIC and the Wilson full-text indexes. Additional databases support other curricular areas, such as criminal justice, nursing, religion and theology, history, and literature. A curriculum laboratory has texts for grades K–12, visual aids, and other resources.

The art department contains a gallery studio featuring professional and student work. The Communication Arts Department provides a program of study that places special emphasis on broadcast journalism and on-air performance. The program also offers technical/production courses such as digital editing as well as film, communications theory, and public speaking courses. The facilities include a television studio, a digital editing suite, a public speaking lab, and a radio studio. Students may produce and perform TV and radio shows, which are broadcast to the entire campus community.

Computer labs, which include up-to-date personal computers installed with current software and multimedia equipment, offer free scanning and laser printing. Other computer labs dedicated to specific areas of study include the Art, Biology, Chemistry, Education, ESL, Foreign Language, Math, Music, Physics, Video Editing, and Writing Labs. There are two technology-rich classrooms, the Academic Computer Classroom and the Business Computer Classroom, and twelve technology-enhanced classrooms equipped with digital audio and video and computer equipment. All offices, classrooms, labs, and dorm rooms are connected to the campus network and the Internet.

Costs

For the 2004–05 academic year, full-time tuition and fees are $17,810, and campus room and board are $7350. Undergraduate tuition for part-time students is $428 per credit hour.

Financial Aid

Approximately 87 percent of current students receive financial aid. The federal financial aid program sources include the Federal Pell Grant, Federal Stafford Student Loan, Federal Work-Study Program, and Federal Supplemental Educational Opportunity Grant programs. Caldwell College offers scholarships for academic and athletic excellence. Special interest and privately sponsored scholarships, tuition grants, and campus employment are also available. New Jersey offers tuition aid grants for state residents. The New Jersey Educational Opportunity Fund (EOF) makes it possible for all students to pursue higher education, especially the educationally and economically disadvantaged, for whom college might otherwise be an unrealistic goal. All financial aid applicants must file the Free Application for Federal Student Aid (FAFSA). The priority filing deadline is April 15.

Faculty

There are 80 full-time faculty members, with 83 percent having earned their doctoral/terminal degree, and 14 part-time faculty members. There are 4 full-time ESL and Learning Center instructors and 91 adjunct faculty members.

Student Government

Caldwell College's students, through the Student Government Association and the Resident Council, shape many nonacademic policies and regulations. Students help determine total College policy through representation on several College standing committees.

Admission Requirements

The admission office reviews each applicant's high school record, including class rank, high school performance, and SAT I or ACT scores, to determine the student's ability to succeed at Caldwell College. A student must complete at least 16 high school academic units, including 4 years of English, 2 years of foreign language, 2 years of mathematics, 2 years of science, and 1 year of history. Caldwell College does not discriminate against applicants on the basis of race, color, creed, age, national or ethnic origin, or handicap.

Application and Information

Applicants are accepted throughout the school year through a rolling admissions policy; however, applicants are encouraged to apply early. A nonrefundable $40 fee must accompany each application. Applicants are notified of their admission eligibility after their credentials have been received and evaluated.

For further information, students should contact:

Director of Admissions
Caldwell College
9 Ryerson Avenue
Caldwell, New Jersey 07006-6195
Telephone: 973-618-3500
888-864-9516 (toll-free outside New Jersey)
Fax: 973-618-3600
E-mail: admissions@caldwell.edu
World Wide Web: http://www.caldwell.edu

Caldwell College's beautiful, secure 70-acre campus is 20 miles west of New York City.

CALIFORNIA COLLEGE OF THE ARTS

OAKLAND AND SAN FRANCISCO, CALIFORNIA

The College

Founded in 1907, California College of the Arts (CCA) offers a comprehensive approach to arts education, training students in a wide range of disciplines in fine arts, architecture, design, and writing. With an undergraduate population of about 1,500, CCA provides world-class resources and facilities in a small, private college environment. Students learn from a faculty of renowned practitioners in small classes (an average of 18 students per class). Faculty advisers, trained in assisting students in navigating their college experience, are part of a well-rounded first-year program.

CCA's two campuses, in San Francisco and Oakland, complement each other and create productive intersections among disciplines. CCA maintains close connections with the region's arts community. The CCA Wattis Institute for Contemporary Arts offers leading-edge programs, including exhibitions, lectures, artist residencies, performances, and symposia. The Center for Art and Public Life focuses on issues in community development, new models of practice in community-based art and design, and cultural diversity and youth development through the arts. The College offers continuing education courses for adults, middle school, and high school students.

CCA offers six graduate programs: the M.F.A. in design, the M.F.A. in writing, the M.A. in visual criticism, the M.A. in curatorial practice, the M.F.A. in fine arts, and the M.Arch. Concentrations in the fine arts program include ceramics, drawing/painting, film/video/performance, glass, jewelry/metal arts, photography, printmaking, sculpture, textiles, and wood/furniture. All inquiries and correspondence about the graduate program should be sent to the Assistant Director of Graduate Programs.

CCA is accredited by the Western Association of Schools and Colleges and the National Association of Schools of Art and Design. The interior design program is accredited by the Foundation for Interior Design Education Research, and the undergraduate architecture program is accredited by the National Architectural Accrediting Board.

Location

CCA is located in the San Francisco Bay Area—known for leading the way in technology development, ecological concerns, and creative innovation. The College comprises two campuses in San Francisco and Oakland. The San Francisco campus, set in the city's design district, houses programs in architecture, design, selected fine arts programs, and graduate programs. The Oakland campus, with the majority of the fine arts facilities, is set on 4 acres of landscaped grounds in a residential neighborhood 3 miles from the University of California at Berkeley. The San Francisco skyline and world-famous Golden Gate Bridge are visible from the Oakland campus.

First-year students may live in the new Oakland campus residence hall; CCA also offers apartments across from the Oakland campus. Transfer and continuing students may live in Webster Hall, 2 miles from campus in downtown Oakland. In the San Francisco Bay Area, CCA students enjoy endless educational, cultural, and recreational activities and events. Bus and Bay Area Rapid Transit (BART) are easily accessible. CCA operates a shuttle between the campuses and residence halls. Each campus offers a café open to the entire campus community.

Majors and Degrees

CCA offers four-year programs leading to the Bachelor of Fine Arts (B.F.A.) in ceramics, community arts, fashion design, film/video, glass, graphic design, illustration, industrial design, interior design, jewelry/metal arts, painting/drawing, photography, printmaking, sculpture, textiles, and wood/furniture.

CCA also offers four-year programs leading to the Bachelor of Arts (B.A.) in creative writing and visual studies. In addition, the College offers a five-year program leading to the Bachelor of Architecture (B.Arch.).

Academic Programs

The B.F.A. requires the completion of a minimum of 126 semester units, of which 75 must be in studio work and 51 must be in humanities and sciences. The B.A. requires the completion of 126 semester units, of which 51 must be in humanities and science, 36 in the chosen major, and 39 in studio work.

Undergraduates begin in a foundation—or core—program. Here, they begin mastering technical problem-solving and critical skills while being exposed to a variety of media, processes, principles, and imaginative strategies. Core courses are also offered in writing, literature, and art history. Students select a major after completing this program.

A diversified program of arts and humanities reflects CCA's philosophy that a professional art education occurs in the context of the education of the whole person. Students can explore a variety of media, change majors without changing schools, receive supplementary training in the arts, and develop programs related to individual interests, abilities, and long-range career goals. CCA also offers a new teaching concentration, open to students in all majors, which satisfies prerequisites for application to postgraduate art teacher credential programs.

The B.Arch., a five-year program, requires the completion of a minimum of 162 units, including the core program with an orientation to two-dimensional and three-dimensional media and a nine-semester major program.

CCA operates on the semester academic calendar, with the fall and spring terms constituting a full academic year. The summer term consists of a six-week session and a precollege program. Extended education programs are offered in fall, spring, and summer.

Off-Campus Programs

There are many supplementary educational opportunities for CCA students, including the ability to take courses at Mills College and Holy Names College in Oakland through cross-registration and to participate in the mobility program through the Association of Independent Colleges of Art and Design.

CCA is also supportive of students wishing to study abroad. Currently, the College has established study-abroad exchange programs with schools in Denmark, France, Germany, Italy, Japan, the Netherlands, and Sweden.

Academic Facilities

Most of CCA's instructional buildings house studio facilities. The Oakland campus features the Noni Eccles Treadwell Ceramic Arts Center and the Shaklee Building, which contains a foundry and sculpture, metal arts, jewelry, and glass studios. The Oakland campus also has an auditorium, a media center, and a silkscreen/papermaking facility. In San Francisco, the main campus building is a large, newly renovated, light-filled structure with classrooms, studios, a lecture hall, computer labs, model-making and wood/furniture studios, and fashion facilities. There is studio space for graduate students and undergraduate painters. Adjacent to the main building, a new graduate center houses studios, outdoor work space, and meeting/installation rooms. The CCA Wattis Institute is on the San Francisco campus; the Oakland campus is home to the Oliver Art Center.

In addition to informal exhibition spaces, CCA has galleries reserved for student work. The Oakland campus includes the Isabelle Percy West Gallery, Irwin Student Center Gallery, and North/South Galleries. On the San Francisco campus, the Long/Pollack Graduate Student Gallery and Tecoah and Thomas Bruce Galleries are dedicated to student exhibitions.

CCA has two libraries, Meyer Library in Oakland and Simpson Library in San Francisco. Together, the libraries house more than 60,000 cataloged items. Computer labs on both campuses offer the latest hardware and software for artists, architects, and designers. Students have access to scanning devices, video and audio sampling and editing capabilities, 3-D rendering and animation, digital cameras, graphic tablets, and CD recording. From the library's computers, students can search CCA's library catalog and library catalogs at other colleges and universities. The library computer labs have full Internet and e-mail capabilities. Students can also access the Internet, e-mail accounts, and campus software through CCA's wireless network.

The Oakland campus has three drawing studios, three painting studios, and a large print shop with litho presses, etching presses, Vandercook proofing presses, and a vertical graphic arts camera.

CCA has one of the most extensive glass facilities in the United States. It includes a 700-pound continuous-melt furnace, a pot furnace, slumping facilities, and a complete coldworking facility.

Sculpture facilities include a metal foundry and shop; studios for wax, plaster, and clay; a machine shop; welding facilities; woodworking equipment; and the Simpson Sculpture Studio, which supports the making of large-scale metal and glass sculpture.

The newly expanded photography facilities, available to students for more than 90 hours a week, include two large black-and-white and color darkrooms, twelve individual darkrooms for color printing, a mounting and finishing room, an artificial-lighting studio, a copy camera darkroom, printing and film-processing equipment, and large- and medium-format cameras.

CCA's film and video studios offer a wide range of equipment for digital video, Super-8, and 16-mm film production. The program has a digital emphasis; production tools include After Effects, Avid, Flash, Final Cut Pro, MAX/MSP, NATO.055, and Photoshop. The facility also features a sound booth, numerous digital video and sound editing stations, and a hybrid lab with the capacity for transforming physical phenomena via sensors into interactive media.

CCA's ceramics facility consists of 5,400 square feet of studio space, including two complete pot shops, fully stocked and equipped glaze rooms, sixteen large gas kilns, a car kiln, and electric kilns for outsized as well as regular firing.

Textile facilities include weaving studios, a variety of looms, a Macomber computerized loom, printing and silkscreening studios, dye rooms, and workrooms.

The jewelry/metal arts facilities include a metal foundry and equipment for metalsmithing, electroforming, photofabrication, and enameling.

Costs

Tuition and fees for the fall and spring terms in 2004–05 are $24,630 per year for full-time (12–18 units) undergraduate students. For part-time undergraduate students, tuition is $1015 per unit. California and out-of-state residents pay the same tuition. Residence hall fees (for room only) in 2004–05 range from $4620 to $5800 by contract for the fall through spring year. Estimated expenses for one academic year (two semesters) for a student living on campus are approximately $36,690. This covers tuition of $24,630, room and board of $8230, books and supplies of $1300, and miscellaneous expenses of $2530. The Enrollment Services Office maintains a local housing list to assist students in finding off-campus housing. Meals in the cafés are available on a cash basis.

Financial Aid

Scholarships, grants, loans, and work-study awards are available for students on the basis of merit and financial need. Students applying for aid should submit the Free Application for Federal Student Aid (FAFSA) to the Federal Student Aid Processing Agency by March 1 for priority consideration. CCA continues to fund students after the priority deadline as long as funds remain available. Applications for Federal Pell Grants and Federal Direct Student Loans may be submitted throughout the school year. CCA is approved for veterans attending under the Veterans Administration Educational Benefits Program. Approximately 77 percent of students attending CCA during 2003–04 received some type of financial aid. CCA offers an extended interest-free payment plan.

Faculty

The CCA faculty consists of 337 professional artists, designers, writers, and scholars (34 full-time and 303 part-time) who combine excellent teaching with active, visible work in their fields.

Student Government

CCA's Student Council organizes extracurricular activities and sponsor special events throughout the year. Student representatives serve on CCA's Board of Trustees.

Admission Requirements

All students admitted to the undergraduate programs leading to the B.F.A., B.A., and B.Arch. must have a high school diploma or its equivalent. The Admissions Committee considers the qualifications of each applicant on the basis of a balanced picture that includes an evaluation of academic achievement, the statement of purpose, and supporting documents such as test scores, letters of recommendation, and portfolios of applicant's art.

CCA admissions policy recognizes that not everyone has had equal access to art education before applying. Some applicants have limited art experience. In every case the total picture each applicant presents—including academic achievement, creative achievement, and personal goals—is taken into account.

Application and Information

Individuals interested in applying for CCA's merit scholarships should complete their applications by February 1. CCA's priority deadline for all fall semester applications is March 1. The priority deadline for spring applicants is October 1. Students meeting these deadlines are given priority consideration regarding admission, housing, and financial aid. CCA reviews undergraduate applications on a rolling admission basis; that is, applications are reviewed in the order in which they are received, and students are accepted and awarded financial aid after the priority dates. The application fee is $50. Persons who wish to take one or more individual courses may register as nondegree students on a space-available basis and receive College credit for courses completed. Students may apply online at the Web site listed below.

For undergraduate application forms, current College bulletins, or any additional information, students should contact:

Office of Enrollment Services
California College of the Arts
1111 Eighth Street
San Francisco, California 94107-2247
Telephone: 800-447-1ART (toll-free)
World Wide Web: http://www.cca.edu

CALIFORNIA INSTITUTE OF TECHNOLOGY

PASADENA, CALIFORNIA

The Institute

Caltech is a small, private research institution located in Pasadena, California. The Caltech community consists of 900 undergraduate and 1,100 graduate students, all sharing a passion for science, mathematics, and engineering. Caltech hosts 292 full-time tenure-track faculty members, which creates an extremely favorable student-faculty ratio across all undergraduate programs.

Housing is guaranteed for all Caltech students, and freshmen live on campus. Institute housing on and off campus is available all four years. Each undergraduate house on campus functions independently through a self-elected executive committee, which allows the house to establish its own rules as well as organize social and interhouse athletic events. All houses and students are represented equally within the student government organization, the Associated Students of the California Institute of Technology (ASCIT).

The Caltech Honor System is a code of behavior that applies to all aspects of campus life. It is an agreement that "no member of the Caltech Community shall take unfair advantage of any other member of the Caltech Community." It works because students believe in preserving the integrity of the scientific process, respecting their peers, and fostering a collaborative learning environment.

There are more than eighty-five extracurricular academic, cultural, musical, professional, religious, and social organizations in which to participate. The athletic program includes NCAA Division III, intramural, physical education, and ASCIT-sponsored athletic events. Last year, 80 percent of the undergraduates participated in at least one intramural sport, and a third played on at least one intercollegiate athletic team.

Location

Caltech is located in Pasadena, California, a city of approximately 135,000 inhabitants about 10 miles northeast of Los Angeles. The Institute is in the center of a residential district but within a few blocks of shopping facilities and "Old Town" Pasadena. Pasadena and Metropolitan Los Angeles provide abundant cultural and recreational opportunities.

Majors and Degrees

Caltech offers a four-year undergraduate program that leads to the Bachelor of Science degree with options in applied and computational mathematics, applied physics, astrophysics, biology, business economics and management, chemical engineering, chemistry, computer science, economics, electrical engineering, engineering and applied science, geobiology, geochemistry, geology, geophysics, history, history and philosophy of science, literature, mathematics, physics, planetary science, and social science. The program includes thorough instruction in the basic sciences of biology, chemistry, mathematics, and physics and requires a variety of courses in the humanities and social sciences. Near the end of the first year, students select an option; during the second year, they begin to specialize.

Academic Program

The first year of undergraduate study is essentially the same for all students at the Institute. Each student is assigned an individual faculty adviser for the freshman year. When a student selects an option (major), an option adviser is assigned. In conference with his or her adviser, the student then develops a program of study for the next three years. The program includes Institute-wide requirements in physics, mathematics, chemistry, biology, and humanities. Beyond these requirements, the student and adviser choose from a wide range of engineering and science electives to build a solid foundation for the student's prospective field of interest. A student may, with exceptional freedom, petition to change his or her major interest at any time. Many students decide to prepare for graduate study, while others choose to enter professional employment immediately after graduation.

Undergraduate students are encouraged to participate in research. Research activities are an important aspect of the faculty's work, and undergraduate students are given an opportunity to become involved in these activities.

In addition to research opportunities during the academic year, Caltech sponsors the Summer Undergraduate Research Fellowship (SURF) program. Each summer, approximately 400 undergraduate students conduct original research during a ten-week period. At the conclusion of the summer, students present the results of their work by submitting a paper and making an oral presentation. The fellowship carries a stipend.

Academic Facilities

All branches of science and engineering are served by the many superbly equipped laboratories on campus. Included among the many types of equipment available to undergraduate researchers are a high-current, high-stability particle accelerator; scanning electron microscopes; and a nuclear magnetic resonance spectrometer built around one of the world's most stable superconducting magnets that operates at one of the highest possible magnetic fields. Mead Laboratory, used for freshman chemistry, is the most sophisticated in the country. Off-campus installations are the Jet Propulsion Laboratory (JPL), which Caltech operates for NASA, and the Palomar Observatory, which houses the 200-inch Hale telescope. In cooperation with the University of California at Berkeley, Caltech operates the W. M. Keck Observatory in Mauna Kea, Hawaii. The 10-meter Keck Telescope is the world's largest. A modern computer network (Ethernet) has been installed on campus; it links the student houses, the computing center, and all the teaching and research facilities. Undergraduates use both the educational and research computers. The Caltech library system is a network of libraries with services that include electronic access to information sources, literature searching, document delivery, interlibrary loans, and an electronic catalog. The libraries collectively subscribe to more than 3,500 journals, contain more than 550,000 volumes, and have extensive collections of microfilm, government documents, archives, and maps.

Costs

Tuition, health plan coverage, and other student fees for the 2002–03 academic year were $21,903, books and supplies were $978, and personal expenses were $1797. Room and board in the student houses, including ten meals per week while the Institute is in session, cost approximately $6999. Meals not covered by board contract cost $1833. The total estimated cost was $33,510.

Financial Aid

Caltech admits students on the basis of academic and personal strengths without regard to their ability to meet the full cost of education. Caltech is strongly committed to meeting the demonstrated financial need of every admitted student. The calculated need, determined by an analysis of the appropriate federal and Caltech supplementary forms, may be met by a combination of grant, loan, and work. The Institute participates in the Cal Grant, the Federal Pell Grant, the Federal Supplemental Educational Opportunity Grant, the Federal Work-Study, the Federal Perkins Loan, and the Federal PLUS loan programs. In addition, the Institute offers several alternative financing options to assist families in paying for a Caltech education. All students who would be unable to attend Caltech without financial assistance are encouraged to apply for financial aid at the time they apply for admission.

Faculty

The faculty consists of 292 full-time and 32 part-time professors and approximately 810 members in the positions of emeritus, visiting professor, research associate, visiting associate, senior research fellow, instructor, lecturer, and research fellow. There is no distinction between the undergraduate and graduate faculty. Undergraduate students may enroll in graduate-level courses. Courses are taught by members of the full-time faculty. In some courses, graduate students provide some assistance in grading papers and in laboratory work.

Student Government

Undergraduate students are organized as the Associated Students of the California Institute of Technology, Inc. (ASCIT). This organization functions in relation to all student activities; it organizes social events and funds a variety of clubs and organizations. Its responsibilities include the honor system and board of control. ASCIT also sponsors a coffeehouse and weekly movies and publishes the *Research Opportunities Handbook for Undergraduates* as well as a weekly paper, *California Tech,* and an annual, *The Big T,* both of which are staffed entirely by students. Undergraduate students also sit with most of the faculty committees concerned with the governing of faculty matters.

Admission Requirements

Applicants should have four years of mathematics, three years of English, one year of physics, one year of chemistry, one year of U.S. history or government, and five years of other academic subjects. College Board tests required to be taken not later than the December series of the senior year of high school are the SAT I and the SAT II: Subject Tests in Mathematics (level IIC), Writing, and in Biology, Chemistry, or Physics. Caltech welcomes applications regardless of gender or ethnic or religious background.

California Institute of Technology complies with Title IX (Education Amendments of 1972), Title VII (Civil Rights Act of 1964), and Section 504 of the Rehabilitation Act of 1973 as amended, prohibiting discrimination on the basis of sex, race, creed, color, national origin, or handicaps in its educational programs and activities, including admission and employment.

Application and Information

An application for admission to the freshman class must be postmarked either before November 1 for early action or before January 1 for regular decision. Application forms for financial aid can be obtained from the Office of Financial Aid. Notification of the action of the Admissions Committee is sent by April 1. Students are admitted only once each year for fall matriculation. Requests for application material should be made to:

Office of Admissions
Mail Code 328-87
California Institute of Technology
Pasadena, California 91125
Telephone: 626-395-6341
800-568-8324 (toll-free)
E-mail: ugadmissions@caltech.edu
World Wide Web: http://www.admissions.caltech.edu

On the lawn in front of one of the seven undergraduate student houses.

CALIFORNIA INSTITUTE OF THE ARTS

VALENCIA, CALIFORNIA

The Institute

California Institute of the Arts (CalArts) is a single complex of six professional schools—Art, Critical Studies, Dance, Film/Video, Music, and Theater—conceived as a community of artists. The Institute is a training ground, an exhibition and performance center and a laboratory of the arts. It is one of the few degree-granting institutions wholly committed to contemporary and experimental directions in the arts.

Interaction among the arts is a fundamental premise of the Institute, and all six schools coexist within a 500,000-square-foot facility that was designed by architect Frank Gehry. This facility houses administrative offices, art galleries, cinemas, studio spaces, libraries, rehearsal facilities, classrooms, and theaters. The faculty members are all practicing artists and are renowned for their contributions to the contemporary arts. Students are accepted to the Institute as artists in their own right and come to develop their own artistic voices through intensive professional development and interaction with the members of the faculty.

CalArts was incorporated in 1961 as the first accredited institution of higher learning in the U.S. created specifically for students of both the visual and performing arts. The Institute was established by Walt and Roy Disney through the merger of two longstanding professional schools, the Chouinard Art Institute (founded in 1921) and the Los Angeles Conservatory of Music (founded in 1883). It moved to its present location in Valencia in 1971.

The total enrollment of the Institute is approximately 1,200 men and women, of whom 800 are undergraduates. The student body is geographically diverse, and students come from forty-eight states and forty different countries.

At the graduate level, the Institute grants the Master of Fine Arts degree in art, dance, film/video, music, theater, and writing.

Location

Thirty miles north of downtown Los Angeles, CalArts occupies 60 acres on hills overlooking the incorporated city of Santa Clarita, which encompasses the towns of Valencia, Newhall, Saugus, and Canyon Country. Rapid development in this suburban area has resulted in new residential communities and an ever-increasing population of more than 150,000.

Majors and Degrees

California Institute of the Arts grants the Bachelor of Fine Arts degree and certificates in art, dance, film/video, music, and theater. Certificates and advanced certificates are also offered.

Academic Program

Students must apply to and enroll in a specific program within a particular school. A modified grading system is in effect, and the curriculum of each school is determined by the special demands of its disciplines. Instruction proceeds according to the student's preparation and need, with the student receiving guidance from a faculty mentor. Continuation in programs depends on demonstrated ability.

Programs are designed to accommodate special projects, and each school organizes its own schedule to meet its particular needs. Undergraduate programs take four years or eight semesters and a minimum of 120 semester units to graduate.

All undergraduate students must fulfill the Critical Studies Requirements (40 percent of the total curriculum), which cover the humanities, social sciences, cultural studies, and natural sciences. These courses are intended to inform and influence each student's artistic practice. Graduate programs usually take two or three years to complete, depending on the individual program.

Academic Facilities

The Institute has extensive facilities for the visual and performing arts, which consist of studios, workshops, theaters, galleries, editing rooms, sound stages, electronic music and recording studios, computer art and animation labs, and performance spaces. Certain facilities, such as the Walt Disney Modular Theater, are among the most remarkable anywhere.

The library contains a collection designed especially for the visual and performing arts. In addition to holding more than 95,000 volumes, the library includes musical scores, sound recordings, films, videotapes, and slides that enable students to progress on their own in obtaining knowledge relevant to their specific studies.

Costs

Tuition for 2003–04 was $23,920 for the academic year. Room charges ranged from $2850 to $4300 per year, and board costs between $2600 and $3500. The cost of books and supplies varies according to major.

Financial Aid

CalArts offers the following financial aid programs: Institute scholarships and grants, Federal Pell Grants, Federal Supplemental Educational Opportunity Grants, Federal Work-Study Program awards, Federal Perkins Loans, and Cal Grants. The Institute is also eligible to certify Federal Stafford Student Loans from banks. Details of these financial aid programs are available from the Financial Aid Office upon request.

Faculty

The faculty numbers approximately 274, including both full- and part-time members. The student-faculty ratio is about 7:1. Faculty members maintain active careers in their respective disciplines and are sought out as unique artists who are pushing the boundaries of their art.

Student Government

Student government is conducted through the Student Council, whose members are elected by the student body. In addition, students are active participants in a variety of Institute-wide standing committees, the composition of which also includes a Board of Trustees, faculty members, and staff members.

Admission Requirements

Admission to the Institute is based primarily on an applicant's artistic talent and potential. This is demonstrated through an audition or submission of a portfolio. An artist statement, letters of recommendation and transcripts are also required. Admission to CalArts is based on qualifications and talent, without regard to the individual's race, color, creed, gender, sexual orientation, or age.

Application and Information

For application forms and additional information, prospective students should contact:

Office of Admissions
California Institute of the Arts
24700 McBean Parkway
Valencia, California 91355
Telephone: 661-255-1050
E-mail: admiss@calarts.edu
World Wide Web: http://www.calarts.edu

CalArts has extensive facilities for all the visual and performing arts.

CALIFORNIA LUTHERAN UNIVERSITY

THOUSAND OAKS, CALIFORNIA

The University

California Lutheran University (CLU) was founded in 1959, but its history goes back much farther than that. Cal Lutheran is part of a 500-year-old tradition of Lutheran higher education—a tradition begun on a university campus as a teaching and reforming movement, a tradition of thoughtful investigation and bold discovery. The Lutheran ideals were revolutionary 500 years ago, and they could not be more relevant today.

When Martin Luther posted his famous 95 Theses in 1517 as a theological challenge to the Roman Catholic Church, he created a new paradigm for intellectual and spiritual investigation. For the first time, an invitation had been issued for each person to study and ponder the Bible and pursue a personal exploration of what it means and to not simply accept the beliefs of those in authority. CLU considers this core value of diligent inquiry to be as relevant today as it was then, and it remains at the foundation of the educational experience the University offers.

CLU insists on wide-ranging, critical inquiry into matters of both faith and reason. Students are encouraged to investigate personal beliefs that impact their educational and career choices. Students are asked to reflect on how their intellectual and spiritual convictions come together to define them as a whole person. While fellow students and faculty members certainly bring the Christian perspectives to the table, personal convictions and commitments from all perspectives are respected and honored in discussions. Ultimately the goal of CLU is to educate capable leaders for a global society who are strong in character and judgment, confident in identity and vocation, and committed to service and justice. The individual exploration of truth is only a starting point for the whole educational experience by which students and professors work together to seek answers to the intellectual and professional questions that face world citizens.

CLU's 290-acre campus is home to 1,850 undergraduate students. The student body represents sixty-five countries and thirty-three states. CLU is large enough to provide access to a wide variety of organizations, sports (including new programs in swimming, diving, and water polo), and other activities, but small enough for students to have ample opportunities to develop their leadership skills. KCLU 88.3 FM, a National Public Radio affiliate based on the CLU campus, provides a valuable service to the community and a valuable resource and opportunity to students who are interested in communication arts and broadcasting.

More than 1,000 students are enrolled in CLU's graduate programs. Master's degrees are awarded in business administration, education, marriage and family counseling, psychology, and public administration. The School of Education offers an Ed.D. in educational leadership.

CLU is accredited by the Western Association of Schools and Colleges.

Location

Poised at the intersection of the Americas on the Pacific Rim, CLU's location helps prepare students for careers in a global society. Thousand Oaks, located in one of America's significant technology corridors known as the "101 Corridor," offers the conveniences of an urban area but is situated in an area of scenic natural beauty with open spaces and rolling hills. Because of its location midway between downtown Los Angeles and Santa Barbara and 15 miles inland from the Pacific Ocean, CLU offers students numerous recreational and cultural opportunities as well as internship and career opportunities in government, entertainment, and social services.

Majors and Degrees

CLU offers thirty-six majors within the College of Arts and Sciences, the School of Business, and the School of Education. In addition, undergraduate preprofessional preparation is available in dentistry, law, medicine, and optometry. Undergraduate degrees are offered in accounting, art, biochemistry and molecular biology, bioengineering, biology, business, chemistry, communication arts, computer information systems, computer science, criminal justice, drama, economics, English, environmental science, exercise science/sports medicine, geology, history, interdisciplinary studies, international studies, languages (French, German, and Spanish), liberal studies (education), marketing communication, mathematics, multimedia, music, philosophy, physics, political science, psychology, religion, social sciences, and sociology. Minors are offered in art, biology, business, chemistry, communication, computer science, drama, economics, English, environmental studies, French, geography, geology, German, Greek, Hebrew, history, international business, international studies, mathematics, music, philosophy, physics, political science, psychology, religion, sociology, Spanish, and women's studies.

Academic Program

CLU's integrated curriculum helps students comprehend issues from a variety of perspectives. Students learn to ask the right questions and to think critically in order to analyze, process, transform, and communicate information. With thirty-six majors and twenty-eight minors, students are encouraged to sample classes widely to build a broad base of knowledge. CLU feels that while planning for a career is important, the type of education that prepares students for a changing world is one of the greatest gifts a college education can provide.

At the heart of Cal Lutheran's academic program is a general education curriculum called Core 21. Students' view of the world expands as they learn how disciplines connect in this interdisciplinary approach. Core 21 extends through all four years, beginning with Freshman Seminar. CLU realizes that students' interests may not fit neatly into an academic box. Whether a student enters college with a definite major in mind or an awareness of the areas he/she wants to explore, CLU's curriculum offers distinctive ways to combine academic interests and goals with practical career preparation.

Students who wish to delve deeper into the life of the mind in smaller, seminar-style classes may also have access to the Honors Program. Honors courses bring students and faculty members together to contemplate issues of enduring human concern as well as contemporary problems facing society. Students who successfully complete the requisite honors courses over four years are awarded University Honors at graduation. A second honors program, Departmental Honors, is open to junior and senior students who wish to participate in prolonged, mentored scholarship with a faculty member in their chosen major field.

Off-Campus Programs

Students may take courses abroad while maintaining their student status at CLU by enrolling in one of the more than forty study-abroad programs offered. Among the countries in which students can study are Australia, Austria, Costa Rica, China, France, Japan, Mexico, the Netherlands, Spain, and the United

Kingdom. CLU also offers a Washington, D.C., semester for students in every field of study. This personalized program allows students to live, study, and complete internships in Washington, D.C., while earning a full semester of academic credit. Students take two academic courses while participating in an orientation to Washington, field trips, meetings with experts, seminars on current events, and a professional internship. Participating students live just across the Potomac River from Washington, D.C., in Arlington, Virginia, in condominiums furnished with appliances, furniture, kitchen accessories, and washer/dryer units.

Academic Facilities

The most recent additions to campus are the Spies-Bornemann Education Technology Center, home of CLU's School of Education and Communication Division, and the new Centrum café and coffee house. The campus is distinctive in its combination of mid-century modern and classic-contemporary architecture. The 600-seat Samuelson Chapel, with its towering wall of stained glass, mahogany carvings, and handcrafted Steiner-Reck organ, anchors the campus that also includes the state-of-the-art Ahmanson Science Center, Pearson Library, and Soiland Humanities Center. The Preus-Brandt Forum is a 250-seat lecture/performance center equipped with modern sound and lighting equipment. Construction was scheduled to begin in January 2004 on the first phase of the $80-million North Campus Athletic complex.

Costs

Tuition for the 2003–04 academic year was $20,200 (12–17 credits per semester). Room and board for the year totaled $7200. Student fees were $200 per year.

Financial Aid

Available assistance includes need-based and non-need-based University scholarships; low-interest, long-term loans from external sources; Federal Supplemental Educational Opportunity Grants; Federal Pell Grants; and Federal Work-Study. Part-time jobs are available both on and off campus. Applicants for aid should submit the Free Application for Federal Student Aid (FAFSA). The parents' and/or student's most recent IRS 1040 form must also be submitted. The priority application deadline is March 1. CLU scholarships are awarded based on the submission of a completed application. Presidential Scholarship semifinalists and finalists are chosen from those applications that are complete on or before January 13.

Faculty

At CLU, professors are free thinkers who care passionately about teaching and students. CLU's classes of 15 to 30 students enable faculty members to know their students and enable students to develop relationships with mentors. Students have lively, in-depth discussions with the highly trained faculty members who teach their classes. Ninety-four percent of CLU's faculty members have earned their doctorate or terminal degree. Many have taught at prestigious schools such as Harvard, Stanford, Yale, and Oxford. They bring a depth of intellectual expertise and academic curiosity to the classroom. Among the faculty members there are a former senior economist of the United Nations Development Programme as well as master scholars in everything from media law and Mexican narrative to artificial intelligence and classical and quantum chaos. The list of their areas of research and interests—the social psychology of moral development, molecular evolution, economic and business forecasting models, and politics in movies, to name a few—brings a broad and beneficial foundation to students' liberal arts experience.

Student Government

All undergraduate students carrying 9 or more units are automatically members of the Associated Students of California Lutheran University by virtue of their enrollment in the University. Student governance, including allocation of the student activity fee, is conducted by student body–elected officials.

Admission Requirements

Applicants for admission must complete the application form (the CLU application or the Common Application may be used) and submit a high school transcript, SAT I or ACT scores, one recommendation, an essay/personal statement, and a $45 nonrefundable application fee ($25 for online applications). An interview is not required but is strongly recommended. International students whose native language is not English must also submit TOEFL or IELTS scores. All students are expected to have followed the most competitive college-prep curriculum available to them at their high school. Transfer students must also send a transcript of all completed college work (if more than 28 semester units of college work have been completed, SAT I/ACT scores are not required).

Application and Information

Admission decisions for the fall begin December 1 and continue on a rolling admission basis. The priority application deadline is March 1. For additional information, interested students should contact:

Office of Admission
California Lutheran University
60 West Olsen Road #1350
Thousand Oaks, California 91360-2700
Telephone: 805-493-3135
877-CLU-FOR-U (toll-free)
Fax: 805-493-3114
E-mail: admissions@CalLutheran.edu
World Wide Web: http://www.CalLutheran.edu

Studying at CLU centers on critical inquiry and investigation.

CALIFORNIA MARITIME ACADEMY

VALLEJO, CALIFORNIA

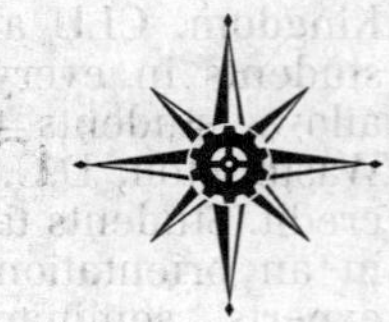

The Academy

Since its founding in 1929 as a college preparing students for work in the merchant shipping industry, the California Maritime Academy has grown to more than 650 students. Over time, the school began offering Bachelor of Science degrees, expanding its degree options. Today, it is the school of choice for students preparing for careers in shipping, logistics, international business, maritime policy, and engineering. It is the only school on the West Coast offering both the training and licensure required to work on U.S. merchant ships.

The Academy, California's best-kept secret in higher education, is the smallest campus in the California State University System. Cal Maritime is accredited by the Western Association of Schools and Colleges (WASC) and its mechanical engineering, marine technology, and facilities engineering technology degrees are accredited by the Accreditation Board for Engineering and Technology (ABET).

Located on the water's edge on Morrow Cove, the campus is beautiful, small, and community-like and includes just 650 students. Class sizes are small, with an average of 18 students per class. Students come from a variety of backgrounds, and most enroll directly from high school.

Although students come from varying backgrounds, they are attracted to Cal Maritime because of its solid academic programs, unmatched reputation with employers, stellar job placement rate, intimate campus atmosphere, hands-on training, and the opportunities that exist for adventure, excitement, and travel.

Students at Cal Maritime can have a rich and rewarding social life. The campus's small size makes for a tight-knit, family-like environment. Friendships flourish as students participate in a variety of campus activities, such as movie nights, comedy nights, a masquerade ball, formal dances, and trips to San Francisco to enjoy theatrical productions and museums. Cal Maritime has a robust outdoor activities program with students participating in outings such as skiing and snowboarding, whitewater rafting, camping, paintball, and spelunking.

The school competes in intercollegiate athletics through the NAIA (National Association of Intercollegiate Athletics). Team sports on campus include women's volleyball, basketball, crew, water polo, sailing, soccer, rugby and golf. Cal Maritime's crew team belongs to the Northern California Intercollegiate Association; the water polo team plays an independent schedule.

Location

Cal Maritime is located in Vallejo, California, a suburb of San Francisco. It has convenient access to the nearby international airports of San Francisco, Oakland, and Sacramento. Surrounding areas offer students a myriad of recreational opportunities, including shopping and sightseeing in San Francisco, skiing and snowboarding in the Sierra Nevada mountains, skateboarding at the skate park in Benicia, surfing in Santa Cruz and Half Moon Bay (Mavericks), and hiking or mountain biking on the Bay Area's many trails.

Majors and Degrees

Cal Maritime offers Bachelor of Science degrees in business administration, facilities engineering technology, marine engineering technology, marine transportation, and mechanical engineering, and a Bachelor of Arts degree in global studies and maritime affairs. In addition to their degrees, students also earn professional licensing in their particular field of study. Depending on their major, students earn their licenses in one or more of the following areas: Certified Plant Engineer-in-Training, Global Logistics Specialist, Management, Transportation Management, U.S. Coast Guard Qualified Member of the Engine Department, U.S. Coast Guard Third Assistant Engineer, or U.S. Coast Guard Third Mate.

Academic Programs

At Cal Maritime, an academic program combining intellectual learning, applied technology, and leadership development prepares students for success in their chosen fields. A solid foundation of academic theory provides the backbone for all programs—students learn the fundamentals of their subject area in classes taught by professors and experienced mariners. At Cal Maritime, there are no teaching assistants; the professors are the teachers.

Theories mastered in the classroom are applied during laboratory and simulator exercises, aboard the training ship *Golden Bear* (TSGB), and during internships with local, regional, national, and international companies. Every student at Cal Maritime sails on one or more training cruises aboard the *Golden Bear*, and all students participate in at least one internship during their tenure at the Academy.

The leadership development component of the program is implemented primarily through the Corps of Cadets. Every student at Cal Maritime is a member of the Corp. Part of the rich maritime heritage and tradition, the Corps instills the positive traits and skills of self-discipline, punctuality, responsibility, and initiative. The Corps is not for military training, but rather to develop it's members as leaders and decision-makers in their field. There is no military obligation upon graduation.

Academic Facilities

Cal Maritime's 67-acre waterfront campus, situated on the Carquinez Strait, includes a variety of facilities that assist students' academic and social development. Instructional and other facilities include a modern laboratory building, an engineering technology center, classrooms, state of the art simulators, library, residence halls, student center and Internet café, cafeteria, gymnasium, weight rooms, a boathouse, a beautifully refurbished indoor pool, the training ship *Golden Bear*, and other vessels.

Costs

Annual fees charged to all students attending Cal Maritime include the state university fee ($2046), health services ($500), housing and meals (double occupancy, $6750), associated student body ($210), instructionally related activity ($130), parking permit ($108), and campus ID ($10). There are one-time costs for orientation ($200), the initial issue of uniforms (approximately $1450), and the TSGB training cruise ($3000). Non-California residents are charged additional tuition up to $8460. All fees are subject to change. Total in-state costs are $14,296; total out-of-state costs are $22,756.

Financial Aid

Cal Maritime offers various federal, state, and private monies to students who qualify. Students can apply for federal aid beginning January 1 through the Free Application for Federal Student Aid (FAFSA), which is available online at www.csumentor.edu as well as at any high school or college, including Cal Maritime. California residents may apply for the Cal Grant using the GPA Verification form beginning January 1. Students who apply to Cal Maritime during its initial filing period (October 1 to November 30) are given priority for private scholarships.

Faculty

Students at Cal Maritime benefit from the instruction of highly educated faculty members as well as seasoned mariners with many years of industry experience. Sixty-five percent of the faculty are permanent, full-time members, and 65 percent have advanced degrees. Because Cal Maritime makes undergraduate education its focus, faculty members teach and instruct all classes; there are neither graduate students nor graduate or teaching assistants serving as instructors. The faculty members of Cal Maritime also serve as academic advisers to the students.

Class sizes are small, with an average of 18 students in lower-division courses. The faculty to student ratio is 1:15. Students receive one-on-one help from their professors in this supportive and close-knit environment.

Student Government

Students at Cal Maritime have many opportunities to assume leadership roles and participate in the governance of the Academy in response to both student-based issues as well as campuswide issues. Students are members on many important campus committees including the academic fee, dining, public safety, academic senate, accreditation review, and academic integrity committees.

The Associated Students of the California Maritime Academy (ASCMA) is the official voice of the students. It acts as an agent of change to represent the opinions and desires of the student body as a whole. The ASCMA offers students the opportunity to serve in elected offices as Executive President, Executive Vice President, Vice President of Finance, as well as President and Vice President of each class.

Finally, students can apply for appointment to positions in the Corps of Cadets. Corps officers assume significant responsibility both on campus and on the training ship *Golden Bear*. Their duties include teaching, instructing, and supervising other students, as well as developing, implementing, and evaluating the watch-standing program. Corps officers are selected based upon demonstrated academic and professional excellence and the ability to lead other student-cadets by example.

Admission Requirements

All applicants must submit scores on either the ACT or SAT I tests in order to enroll at Cal Maritime. In addition, prospective students must have successfully completed 4 years of English, 3 years of math (elementary algebra, geometry, and intermediate algebra), 2 year of a lab science (biology and chemistry, or physics), 1 year of an elective, 2 years of the same foreign language, 1 year of U.S. history, 1 year of a social science, and 1 year of visual or performing arts.

Mechanical engineering (ME) majors are required to take a fourth year of math. ME majors must also demonstrate readiness for calculus by scoring a 550 or above on the SAT I math section, 23 or above on the ACT math section, or pass a college-level algebra/trigonometry course at a community college or university with a C or better.

A fourth year of math is highly recommended, but not required, for engineering technology majors.

Application Information

Students may apply online at http://www.csumentor.edu beginning October 1 of the year before the fall in which they intend to enroll. November 30 is the deadline for Cal Maritime's initial filing period. Cal Maritime does not accept applications for spring or summer semesters.

Inquiries should be addressed to:

Cal Maritime Admission
200 Maritime Academy Drive
Vallejo, California 94590-8181
Telephone: 800-561-1945 (toll-free)
E-mail: admission@csum.edu
World Wide Web: http://www.csum.edu

The training ship, *Golden Bear,* moored at Cal Maritime.

CALIFORNIA STATE POLYTECHNIC UNIVERSITY, POMONA

POMONA, CALIFORNIA

The University

California State Polytechnic University, Pomona (Cal Poly Pomona) is located on the eastern edge of Southern California's San Gabriel Valley. Its 1,400-acre campus, featuring lush rolling hills, was once the winter ranch of cereal magnate W.K. Kellogg. While the land and its facilities were donated to the state in 1949, Kellogg's hilltop home and award-winning Arabian horses remain as lasting reminders of the University's heritage.

As one of a few polytechnic universities nationwide, Cal Poly Pomona integrates technology into a liberal arts education as well as into the applied sciences. This long-standing polytechnic approach is paired with a learn-by-doing philosophy that makes it unique among traditional universities and has earned Cal Poly Pomona the reputation of developing individuals who are among the most sought-after in today's marketplace.

A top western regional public university with a number of nationally ranked programs, Cal Poly Pomona is recognized for the high quality and wide range of its degree programs. The University offers more than sixty undergraduate majors in seven colleges and one professional school, including agriculture; business administration; education and integrative studies; engineering; environmental design; letters, arts, and social sciences; science; and the Collins School of Hospitality Management.

In addition, Cal Poly Pomona offers a Master of Architecture; Master of Arts in education, English, and history; Master of Business Administration; Master of Landscape Architecture; Master of Public Administration; Master of Science in agriculture, biological sciences, business administration, chemistry, computer science, economics, electrical engineering, engineering, engineering management, kinesiology, mathematics, mechanical engineering, psychology, regenerative studies, and structural engineering; a Master of Urban and Regional Planning; eleven teaching credentials/certificates; and a Doctor of Education (Ed.D.) in educational administration and leadership in partnership with the University of California, Irvine and three other California State University campuses.

Cal Poly Pomona is accredited by the Western Association of Schools and Colleges and is authorized by the California State Commission for Teacher Preparation and Licensing to recommend candidates for credentials in several areas. In addition, many of the degree programs are accredited by national organizations.

Students attending Cal Poly Pomona don't face overloaded classrooms or throngs of teaching assistants. In the belief that education should be a face-to-face interaction between real faculty members and students, the University strives to maintain a 20:1 student-teacher ratio, and most classrooms seat fewer than 50 students.

A wide variety of activities and opportunities abound on campus, with more than 200 organizations bringing students together based on academic and/or other common interests. Since 1949, student-constructed floats have appeared in the annual Pasadena Tournament of Roses Parade. About 800 students are involved in social Greek organizations, and the forty ethnically based organizations reflect the diverse student body. Students also enrich their educational experience through community service and volunteer opportunities. With twelve intercollegiate sports, Bronco men's and women's teams have won thirteen national championships and compete in the nation's premiere NCAA II conference, the California Collegiate Athletic Association. In addition, recreational sports involve nearly 2,000 students each year.

As part of the twenty-three-campus California State University system, Cal Poly Pomona's 2,670 faculty and staff members serve more than 19,800 students from forty-nine states and sixty-one countries worldwide. Nearly thirty percent of the students are Asian American, with 27.9 percent Hispanic, about 7.7 percent Filipino, 4 percent African American, and nearly .5 percent American Indian. The average undergraduate age is 22, with a student body that is 55 percent men and 45 percent women.

More than 13 percent of the student body lives on campus. Residence halls accommodate approximately 1,450 students, often in academic major, special interest, or lifestyle theme areas. The University Village, a residential complex adjacent to the campus, accommodates about 800 students. The new Residential Suites houses 400 students and offers suite-style accommodations as well as private balconies, an on-site café, and large study areas.

Location

Located just 35 miles east of downtown Los Angeles, Cal Poly Pomona offers the excitement of one of the world's most diverse metropolitan areas and Southern California's magnificent weather, while still retaining the serenity of a foothill community. The University's proximity to business and industry makes it ideal for internships and employment opportunities. And the campus is only a short drive from natural (beach, mountains, and desert), cultural (theaters, museums, and galleries), and recreational (Disneyland, Raging Waters, and L.A. County Fairgrounds) sites.

Majors and Degrees

Bachelor of Arts degrees include art; behavioral science; English; gender, ethnicity, and multicultural studies; history; liberal studies; music; philosophy; political science; psychology; sociology; Spanish; and theater. The Bachelor of Architecture is also offered.

Bachelor of Science degrees include aerospace engineering, agricultural biology, agricultural science, agronomy, animal health science, animal science, anthropology, apparel merchandising and management, biology, biotechnology, botany, business administration (majors include accounting; computer information systems; e-business; finance, real estate, and law; international business; management and human resources; marketing management; and technology and operations management), chemical engineering, chemistry, civil engineering, communication, computer engineering, computer science, construction engineering technology, economics, electrical engineering, electronics and computer engineering technology, engineering technology, environmental biology, food marketing and agribusiness management, foods and nutrition, food science and technology, geography, geology, graphic design, horticulture, hotel and restaurant management, industrial engineering, integrated earth science, kinesiology, landscape architecture, landscape irrigation science, manufacturing engineering, materials engineering, mathematics, mechanical engineering, microbiology, physics, social sciences, soil science, urban and regional planning, and zoology.

Academic Program

Classes are offered in four 11-week quarters. Candidates for Bachelor of Arts degrees must earn at least 186 quarter units. The Bachelor of Science degree requires at least 198 quarter units. A graduation writing requirement exists for all baccalaureate degrees.

Currently, architecture is an impacted program and is open only to California residents.

Cal Poly Pomona offers Air Force and Army Reserve Officers' Training Corps, a California Pre-Doctoral Program, an Educational Opportunity Program, an Honors Program, a Teacher Aide Path to Teaching, University Equity Programs, and other special programs.

The University features special centers and institutes, such as the innovative Lyle Center for Regenerative Studies, the Apparel Technology and Research Center, the Center for Turf, Irrigation and Landscape Technology, the Equine Research Center, the Ocean Studies Institute, and the Institute for Cellular and Molecular Biology, to name a few.

Off-Campus Programs

Affiliated with thirty-six recognized universities and institutions of higher education in sixteen countries, the International Center and Cal Poly Study Abroad Programs offer opportunities to earn credit while studying abroad. As active members in the National Student Exchange, students may complete courses at more than 100 participating institutions throughout the United States and its territories.

Academic Facilities

The library has more than 3.1 million resource materials as well as online databases and services.

There are dozens of computer labs, which are all staffed with trained personnel; some are open 24 hours per day.

Indicative of Cal Poly Pomona's hands-on learning are the Collins School for Hospitality Management and the University Farm. The Collins School houses a student-run restaurant, demonstration kitchens, and laboratories and features annual presentations by world-famous chefs. The University Farm has more than 700 acres devoted to pastures and livestock, crops, groves, and ornamental plantings.

A recent multimillion dollar building campaign to enhance campus resources resulted in the biotechnology building, the engineering lab, the Residential Suites, an expanded Bronco Student Center, and the AGRIscapes Research and Demonstration Center. Future projects include additional campus housing, an expanded University Library, and a new College of Business Administration.

Costs

In 2003–04, fees for full-time students (6.1 or more units) were $2046 for the year. Non-California residents paid an additional $188 per unit. Residence hall housing costs varied from $5801 to $6902 for the academic year, depending on choice of accommodations and meal plan.

Financial Aid

The University administers extensive financial aid programs, and more than 49 percent of Cal Poly Pomona students receive more than $53 million in financial aid each year.

Applications for academic and merit scholarships must be completed by January 30. Applications for financial aid should be completed as early as possible after January 1 and no later than March 2 for the following academic year. Applicants should contact the financial aid office for information and application materials or visit http://www.csupomona.edu/financial_aid.

Faculty

About three fourths of the faculty members have earned terminal degrees. Though research is actively conducted, the emphasis is on teaching students how to practically apply knowledge learned in the classroom. With a student-faculty ratio of 20:1, individual contact is common and encouraged. Faculty members serve as academic advisers for majors in their departments, and many advise cocurricular organizations.

Student Government

As a voice for student concerns in University governance, the Associated Students, Incorporated (ASI) provides leadership development opportunities through University-wide committee participation, campus event planning, student employment, and recreational sports leagues and tournaments. ASI also operates the Bronco Student Center and Children's Center, both of which are dedicated to enhancing the campus community.

Admission Requirements

Admission requirements and criteria are explained in detail in the CSU Application for Admission, the Cal Poly Pomona catalog, and online at http://www.csupomona.edu/admissions.

First-time freshmen must be high school graduates and must have completed the following college-preparatory courses with a C or better: 4 years of college-preparatory English; 3 years of mathematics; 2 years of social science (including 1 year of U.S. history or U.S. history and government); 2 years of laboratory science (1 biological and 1 physical); 2 years of a foreign language; 1 year of visual and performing arts; and 1 year of electives selected from the above areas. For first-time freshmen, qualification for admission is based on a combination of high school grades and scores on either the ACT or the SAT. Applicants must take the SAT I or ACT. Scores must be received by Cal Poly Pomona no later than January of the year for which the student is applying. For more information, students should go online to http://www.csupomona.edu/admissions/ftf_impaction.html and http://www.csupomona.edu/admissions/requirements/index.html.

Upper-division transfer students must have completed at least 60 transferable semester units (90 quarter units), have a grade point average of C or better in all transferable units attempted, must be in good standing at the last college or university attended, and must have completed at least 30 semester units (45 quarter units) of general education courses with a grade of C or better. The 30 semester units must include written communication, oral communication, critical thinking, and college-level mathematics. All 60 transferable semester college units must be completed by the end of the previous spring for the fall quarter, the end of the previous summer for the winter quarter, the end of the previous fall for the spring quarter, and the end of the previous fall for the summer quarter.

For international students, Cal Poly Pomona uses additional requirements to admit students who hold F-1 and J-1 student visas. Verification of English proficiency, financial resources, and academic performance are all important considerations.

All applicants, regardless of citizenship, whose preparatory education was principally in a language other than English must demonstrate competence in English. Undergraduate students who are required to take the TOEFL must score a minimum of 525 on the paper-based test or 195 on the computer-based test. Minimum scores for graduates vary by program.

Admission requirements may be subject to change, and students should consult the CSU application or access the Web site at http://www.csupomona.edu/admissions.

Application and Information

Applications are accepted for the following fall on October 1 of the preceding year and students are encouraged to apply during the priority application filing period. Applications may be requested from California high schools, community colleges, or CSU campuses; however, the University encourages students to apply online at http://www.csumentor.edu. Prospective students are also encouraged to fill out an online request card at https://vip.es.csupomona.edu. For further information, students should contact:

Office of Admissions & Outreach
Cal Poly Pomona
3801 West Temple Avenue
Pomona, California 91768
Telephone: 909-869-3210
World Wide Web: http://www.csupomona.edu

Cal Poly Pomona's lush, 1,400-acre campus provides students an ideal atmosphere for academic enrichment and social growth.

CALIFORNIA STATE UNIVERSITY, DOMINGUEZ HILLS
College of Health and Human Services

CARSON, CALIFORNIA

The University

Founded as South Bay State College in 1960, California State University, Dominguez Hills (CSUDH) is a multicultural, multi-ethnic, teaching and learning community dedicated to excellence. It is committed to educating a student population of unprecedented diversity for leadership roles in the global community of the twenty-first century. To further the goals of a democratic society through wide participation and civic responsibility in community, social, and economic affairs, the University maintains a commitment to quality and pluralism in higher education. It offers programs in a variety of modes, including online, that enable students to develop intellectually, personally, and professionally.

CSUDH, one of the twenty-two California State University campuses, offers an attractive, friendly, park-like atmosphere. The University is known for its generally small classes, which afford students the benefits of individualized attention from the faculty members. With its up-to-date facilities, excellent faculty and staff, accessible parking, and proximity to freeways and airports, Dominguez Hills has become an attractive alternative to other larger universities.

CSUDH is the most diverse campus in the West. The University's undergraduate enrollment of approximately 8,000 represents the wide diversity of the Southern California region. More than half of all undergraduate students are either African American or Hispanic. Approximately 60 percent of all students attend the University full-time. More than 62 percent of the students are women, and there is a strong attendance by older students. More than 55 percent of the students had high school GPAs of 3.0 or higher. Only 4 percent of the students are from out of state and more than 50 percent of the University's students are 25 years or older, with an average age of 26.

The University provides apartment-style housing for students who want to develop stronger relationships with their fellow classmates. In addition to fully furnished apartments with kitchens and baths, each residence hall has recreational facilities, a 24-hour staff, cable and Internet access, and other amenities. University Housing presents many programs and opportunities that bring students together in a relaxed, friendly setting. Those students who prefer to not prepare their own meals may take advantage of campus dining, including bistros, juice and coffee bars, and a food court that is open six days a week.

Students can participate in the more than sixty clubs and organizations that cover a wide array of interests, and they may join one of ten fraternities and sororities. In addition, the athletics department encourages participation in the campus' intercollegiate sports, whether as a player or as a supporter.

Through a commitment to the principles of economic, civic, and social responsibility, the University upholds its mission to become a viable part of its community by promoting partnerships that connect it to the community it serves. In particular, the University's efforts within the community focus on education, arts and culture, business, youth, health and wellness, and civic action.

In addition to its many bachelor's degree programs, CSUDH also offers undergraduate certificate programs, credential programs in numerous areas of education, graduate and postbaccalaureate certificate programs, and a wide variety of master's programs.

CSUDH is accredited by the Accrediting Commission for Senior Colleges and Universities of the Western Association of Schools and Colleges.

Location

The campus is located in Carson, California, just minutes away from downtown Los Angeles. Within 5 minutes of major freeways, CSUDH serves the South Bay area in Los Angeles and numerous other communities. Southern California's renowned warm temperatures and blue skies can be enjoyed right on the campus or at beaches along the Pacific Ocean, less than half an hour from campus. Entertainment options in the area include Universal Studios, Universal City Walk, Disneyland, Knott's Berry Farm, and a variety of professional sports venues, including the Home Depot Center.

Majors and Degrees

The College of Health and Human Services comprises the Division of Nursing, the Division of Health Sciences, and the Division of Human Services. The Bachelor of Arts is offered with majors in human services, physical education (options in athletic training certification, athletic training preprofessional, dance, fitness director, and teaching), and recreation and leisure studies (options in general recreation administration and in therapeutic recreation),

Bachelor of Science degrees are offered in clinical sciences (options in cytotechnology and medical technology), health science (options in community health, health-care management, orthotics and prosthetics, and radiologic technology), nursing, and occupational therapy.

Academic Programs

Students can earn a Bachelor of Arts or a Bachelor of Science degree in clinical sciences, health sciences, human services, kinesiology, nursing, and recreation studies. To earn a Bachelor of Arts degree, students must complete a minimum of 120 semester units of credit (132 for those earning a Bachelor of Science), including a minimum of 40 upper-division units and 54–60 units of general education. The remaining units are in elective courses.

Students must complete the requirements of at least one major but may also elect to complete a minor or a second major. This requirement can also be satisfied through the areas of concentration in interdisciplinary studies combined with a thematic project, a minor, or another major. In addition, students must demonstrate competency in writing skills by satisfying the Graduation Writing Assessment Requirement (GWAR).

The academic year is divided into spring and fall semesters, with summer classes also available.

Off-Campus Programs

Students have opportunities to study online (nursing courses) or off-site at approved clinical sites.

Academic Facilities

The James L. Welch Hall features five mediated-instruction classrooms, nine computer-based laboratories, two workstation rooms, and the 250-seat Claudia Hampton Lecture Hall.

The University Library is located in the Educational Resources Center (ERC) Building. Services and collections occupy the first four floors of the structure. The Library is also the site of the campus' first Internet café.

Other academic facilities include the University Theatre, Loker University Student Union, and the California Academy of Mathematics and Science (a comprehensive four-year high school).

Costs

Full-time tuition (7–21 credits) during the 2003–04 academic year was $1110 per semester for California residents; out-of-state students paid $1110 in tuition each semester, plus an additional $282 per credit. Room and board were $4032, and additional fees were approximately $100.

Financial Aid

Financial assistance is given to student in the forms of scholarships, grants, loans, and employment. Federal Pell Grants of $400 to $3750 per year are awarded to undergraduates who demonstrate financial need or are enrolled in a teaching-credential program. Cal Grants of up to $2000 are awarded to California residents, based on both GPA and financial need. Educational Opportunity Program grants are awarded to students who have been admitted through the Educational Opportunity Program; grants range from $400 to $800. Federal Supplemental Educational Opportunity Grants range from $200 to $750 per academic year. Federal Work-Study provides funds in exchange for up to 20 hours of campus employment per week. State University Grants are awarded to California residents who are in a regular degree program; the maximum award for full-time students is $1428.

Faculty

More than one third of the faculty members at the College of Health and Human Services at California State University, Dominguez Hills, are full-time professors. Approximately 400 faculty members hold a doctoral degree, and another 300 hold a master's. The student-faculty ratio is 21:1. The University system employs a policy of shared governance, with faculty members and administrators making joint decisions.

Student Government

The Division of Student Affairs provides services and programs in support of the educational development of students through a student-centered philosophy, student life activities, and an array of support and developmental services. Associated Students, Incorporated (ASI) is a nonprofit membership association and auxiliary organization of the University. Its mission is to improve the quality of campus life for students while enhancing their educational experience. ASI offers a number of campus programs and services for its members, including the Child Development Center, REC Sports, discounted movie tickets, scholarships, and more.

Admission Requirements

Admission to the University's programs requires a diploma from an accredited high school, a qualifiable eligibility index, and a C or better in each of the following high school courses: English (4 years), mathematics (3 years), U.S. history or government (1 year), laboratory science (1 year), foreign language (2 years), visual and performing arts (1 year), and electives (3 years). Interested students can find more detailed information at the University's Web site, listed below.

Students with a GPA of 3.0 or better (3.6 for out-of-state residents) are exempt from submitting test scores, though such score results are helpful for advising and placement purposes.

Application and Information

A completed application includes an Application for Admission; an official transcript of high school course work (and previous postsecondary course work, if applicable); official reports of SAT or ACT scores; and a nonrefundable application fee of $55. The deadline to apply for fall admission is June 1; the spring admission deadline is November 1. Late applications are charged an additional $15. Applications must be sent to the address listed below. Applications can also be submitted online.

For further information, students should contact:

College of Health and Human Services
Student Services Center
California State University, Dominguez Hills
1000 East Victoria Street
Carson, California 90747
Telephone: 800-344-5484 (toll-free)
Fax: 310-217-6800
World Wide Web: http://www.csudh.edu/soh

CALIFORNIA UNIVERSITY OF PENNSYLVANIA

CALIFORNIA, PENNSYLVANIA

The University

California University of Pennsylvania, a member of Pennsylvania's State System of Higher Education, recently celebrated its 150th anniversary. It traces its origin to the establishment of an academy in the town of California, Pennsylvania, in 1852. In the intervening years, the school progressed from a normal school to Southwestern State Normal College, to California State Teachers College, to California State College, and finally in 1983, to California University of Pennsylvania. California University began as a teacher-preparation school and has evolved into a multipurpose university that grants both undergraduate and graduate degrees.

The current enrollment is about 5,000 undergraduate and 950 graduate students. About 4,500 students commute, 700 live on campus in three recently completed residence halls, 750 live off campus in a new garden-style apartment complex affiliated with the University, and the rest live in off-campus fraternity or sorority houses, rental units, or private homes.

California University is included in the *Templeton Guide to Character Building Colleges* and the *Making a Difference College and Graduate Guide*, the distinctive guide for students who want to use their education to make a better world. The University adopted Integrity, Civility, and Responsibility as its core values in 1998 and encourages all members of the community to aspire to these high ideals in order to make the University community, and the world, a better place.

The campus, consisting of 90 acres with thirty-eight buildings, is nestled on a bend of the Monongahela River. The Natali Student Center, located in the center of campus, houses a student information center, dining facilities, a movie theater, a convenience store, a food court, a bookstore, an ATM machine, and a variety of student organizations, including the Commuter Center and the University radio (WVCS) and television (CUTV) stations.

A 98-acre recreational complex, Roadman Park, owned by the Student Association, Inc., is located just 2 miles from the campus. Tennis courts; running tracks; picnic areas; baseball, softball, and soccer fields; and the football stadium are located there. At the University, students have the opportunity to select the living arrangement that best fits their personal needs and preferences. On-campus residence halls provide the perfect environment for being in the center of all academic and recreational activities. On-campus living also provides an environment that offers structure, with tremendous convenience to classrooms, dining, Natali Student Center, and Manderino Library. A variety of room configurations allows students to choose from one, two, or three roommates or suitemates.

Great for more independent living, the apartments at Jefferson@California are located less than 1½ miles from campus, adjacent to Roadman Park. There are a variety of configurations, most of which have private baths. Jefferson also provides a clubhouse with a fully equipped fitness center, a recreation room with various games, a computer lab, and a media room. Other amenities include an outdoor swimming pool, sand volleyball, and basketball courts. A shuttle service connects Jefferson to the main campus.

The Health Center is open 24 hours a day, seven days a week, while the University is in session. A staff of full-time registered nurses is on duty at all times. A qualified physician is on duty Monday through Friday at specified hours.

The counseling center, also staffed by professionals, is available to all students and provides psychological services to students. The University also offers drug and alcohol education programs that include consultation, intervention, counseling, education, awareness programs, and substance-free activities.

Location

The campus is located in the borough of California, Pennsylvania, a community of 7,000 people. It is approximately 35 miles south of Pittsburgh in the foothills of the Allegheny Mountains, near Pennsylvania's Laurel Highlands recreational area. Professional baseball, football, and hockey, as well as a variety of cultural activities, are available in Pittsburgh. The area in which the University is located has a number of significant historical sites related to the pre–Revolutionary War era. The University also offers students the option of off-campus sites located in Canonsburg at the Southpointe Technology Park and at the Regional Enterprise Tower in Pittsburgh. Other outreach programs are being conducted in Somerset County.

Majors and Degrees

California University of Pennsylvania offers four baccalaureate degrees: the Bachelor of Arts, the Bachelor of Science, the Bachelor of Science in Education, and the Bachelor of Science in Nursing. Associate of Arts, Associate of Science, and Associate of Applied Science degrees are also offered.

The liberal arts majors include anthropology, art, communications studies (public relations, radio/television, and speech concentrations available), earth science (broadcast meteorology concentration available), economics, English (creative writing, journalism, and scientific and technical writing concentrations available), French, geography (geographic information systems and travel and tourism concentrations available), geology, history, international studies, parks and recreation management, philosophy, political science (prelaw concentration available), psychology (industrial-organizational psychology concentration available), sociology, Spanish, sport management, and theater.

The Bachelor of Science in Education includes majors in athletic training, communication disorders, early childhood education, elementary education, secondary education (biology, chemistry, communication, comprehensive social sciences, earth science, English, French, general science, mathematics, physics, and Spanish), special education, and technology education. Dual majors are available in many education programs. The College of Education and Human Services also offers bachelor's degrees in gerontology and social work and provides certification to teach art with one semester (15 credits) of work at Carlow College, Pittsburgh.

The Eberly College of Science and Technology offers majors in the areas of administration and management, applied computer science, business administration (accounting, business administration, business economics, computer-based systems management, finance, human resources management, management, and marketing), computer engineering technology, electrical engineering technology, environmental studies (environmental conservation, environmental pollution control, environmental resources, environmental science, and wildlife biology), graphic communication technology (electrographics, flexography, management, offset lithography, and screen printing), manufacturing technology (automation, computer numerical control, drafting and design, electronics, and industrial management), mathematics and computer science, medical technology, natural sciences (biology, chemistry, earth science, geology, mathematics, natural sciences interdisciplinary, and physics), and pre–health professions (pre-chiropractic medicine, predentistry, premedicine, pre–mortuary science, preoptometry, pre–osteopathic medicine, prepharmacy, pre–podiatric medicine, and pre–veterinary medicine). A cooperative nursing program is offered with the Community College of Allegheny County. The University offers an upper-division Bachelor of Science in

Nursing degree program for students who have completed an RN program. A cooperative pre-engineering program is offered with Penn State.

Academic Programs

Each bachelor's degree requires a minimum of 120 semester hours of credit. A general education requirement of 51 credits is distributed among the following areas: building a sense of community (1 credit), communication skills (9 credits), critical-thinking skills (3 credits), fine arts (3 credits), health and wellness (3 credits), humanities (3 credits), mathematics (3 credits), multicultural awareness (3 credits), natural sciences (8 credits), social sciences (6 credits), technological literacy (6 credits), and values (3 credits). An honors program provides an opportunity for an enhanced educational experience to students who meet the criteria. Honors students have the option of living in the new Honors Residence Hall, which offers numerous amenities, including a wireless Internet connection. Applications of all incoming first-year and transfer students are reviewed, and those with the highest indicators of past and future academic success are invited to participate in the honors program.

Academic Facilities

The University has traditional library holdings of more than 360,000 volumes, more than 1 million microform units, nearly 1,500 periodical titles, and U.S. government documents. It is a member of the Keystone Library Network, which provides access to library holdings, databases, and electronic resources among fourteen State System of Higher Education libraries. This virtual library electronically links users to a variety of information sources and delivers both text and multimedia sources immediately and seamlessly from any location. The 80,400-square-foot Eberly Science and Technology Center features state-of-the-art science and computer laboratories and is one of the premiere teaching facilities on campus. The Natali Student Center houses a movie theater complete with surround sound, a student-run radio station, and a cable television station, in addition to a food court and a bookstore. Every residence hall room is wired with fiber optics so that students can bring computers, plug them in, and have immediate access to the Internet and all of its resources. For students who do not have computers of their own, there is a computer lab on every floor of the residence halls. Numerous specialized computer facilities are available across the campus, including ones devoted to meteorology, math and computer science, word processing, accounting, CAD-CAM, robotics, teacher education, art, and chemistry.

Costs

The 2003–04 tuition for a resident of Pennsylvania attending full-time (12 to 18 credits) was $2299 per semester. For a full-time nonresident, tuition was $3449. Room costs for fall 2004 range from $2475 to $3070 per semester. In 2003–04, the nineteen-per-week meal plan was $1306. Fees for 2003–04 (based on a full-time schedule) included a $50 technology fee, an $85 service fee, a $175 Student Association fee, an $81 student union building fee, an $84 Student Center operations and maintenance fee, and a $229.90 academic support fee. The cost of books, materials, and supplies varies with each program but is estimated at $325 per semester.

Financial Aid

California University of Pennsylvania has available a number of types of financial aid, including student employment, grant and scholarship aid through the Pennsylvania Higher Education Assistance Agency, federal grants, and student loans. A number of non-need-based academic scholarships are available for talented students. All students must complete the Pennsylvania State Grant and federal financial aid application for need-based aid. The Director of Financial Aid at the University administers all student aid.

Faculty

Classes are taught by 268 full-time and 40 part-time faculty members; no classes are taught by graduate assistants. Doctorates are held by more than 65 percent of the full-time faculty members. Faculty advisers are assigned based on the student's major, department, or school.

Student Government

Student government at California University of Pennsylvania regulates cocurricular activities. It furthers the quality of student life by encouraging and funding diverse student activities, providing experiences in the principles and practices of democratic government, supplying a forum for general student interest, and improving and promoting the cultural standards of the University. Students sit on most important University committees and have a voice in most policy decisions.

Admission Requirements

California University of Pennsylvania welcomes applications from all qualified persons regardless of race, religion, or national origin. Admission standards have been established by California University of Pennsylvania for the purpose of ascertaining which prospective students are most likely to succeed at the University. An applicant for admission should have graduated from an accredited four-year high school or should possess an equivalency diploma issued by a state department of education. All applicants should submit to the University evidence of their ability to do college-level work, as indicated by such tests as the College Board's SAT I. All applicants are required to have a Social Security number.

Application and Information

Prospective students should obtain, complete, and return an application form, along with the Secondary School Record (which is completed by the high school guidance counselor). A nonrefundable application fee of $25 must accompany the application. Students can apply and pay online at the Web site listed below. A student who wants to transfer to California University of Pennsylvania should complete the application form (hard copy or online) and forward it to the Admissions Office with a nonrefundable check or money order for $25, or pay online. Official transcripts from all colleges and universities attended must be sent to the Admissions Office.

For additional information regarding admission, students should contact:

Director of Admissions
California University of Pennsylvania
250 University Avenue
California, Pennsylvania 15419
Telephone: 724-938-4404
E-mail: inquiry@cup.edu
World Wide Web: http://www.cup.edu

Students in the College of Science and Technology.

CALVIN COLLEGE

GRAND RAPIDS, MICHIGAN

The College

Calvin College is an institution that values both intellect and faith; this view affects every area of campus life from the content of each course to volunteer service and life in the residence halls. Calvin is one of the nation's largest and most respected evangelical Christian colleges. The 2003 fall enrollment was 4,332. Calvin maintains a strong affiliation with the Christian Reformed Church, and students from more than fifty other church denominations across North America and the world choose Calvin for its unique curriculum and faith-based mission.

Calvin is deeply committed to being a diverse community and is taking deliberate steps to increase opportunities for women, members of minority groups, and the disabled. Students are challenged not only to obtain a fine education and to prepare for a career but also to live lives of commitment and service.

Students come from nearly every state and forty-five countries. Most students are between 18 and 22 years old; however, those pursuing the Master of Education (M.Ed.) add to the age diversity on campus. The Broene Counseling Center offers career counseling and career resource services as well as personal counseling. Career Services assists students in finding internships and in searching for full-time employment upon graduation.

A wide variety of cocurricular opportunities are available, including music, theater, athletics, art, culture, service, and religious activities and events. Calvin's Service Learning Center provides opportunities for academically based service learning in addition to such programs as big brothers/big sisters, services for the elderly, and school tutoring. Calvin is an NCAA Division III school and participates in the Michigan Intercollegiate Athletic Association; Calvin's athletic teams regularly are ranked nationally in Division III. The men's basketball team won the national championship in 1992 and 2000; the women's cross-country team captured the national championship in 1998 and 1999. In 2000, the men's cross-country team won the national championship.

The 370-acre campus is a modern, well-planned community; its oldest academic building was erected in 1960. Fifteen residence halls, fifteen apartment buildings, and two spacious dining halls accommodate 2,600 resident students. The residence halls and campus apartments are all wired for high-speed computing. Knollcrest Fieldhouse seats 4,500 around its main court for sporting events or can be used as four separate gymnasiums for the school's many intramural events. It is often the site of conference and regional sports tournaments. The field house also includes a racquetball court; a strength and fitness facility; a six-lane, 25-yard swimming pool; and a diving pool with both one- and three-meter boards. Calvin's outdoor athletic sites include baseball and softball diamonds, a premier soccer field with seating for 1,500 and two practice fields, an eight-lane track, a six-court tennis facility, a paved jogging path, and two sand volleyball courts.

Location

Calvin's beautifully wooded campus, which includes an 85-acre ecosystem preserve, is located in the suburbs of Grand Rapids, a metropolitan area of more than 650,000 people. Hundreds of restaurants, dozens of theaters, seven shopping malls, and a fine selection of museums and parks are within a short drive. Lake Michigan beaches, ski areas, parks, and trails are within a 40-minute drive. Cultural and community activities take place weekly on the Calvin campus, on the campuses of six other local colleges, and at De Vos Hall and VanAndel Arena in downtown Grand Rapids. City buses regularly pass by the Calvin campus.

Majors and Degrees

The Bachelor of Arts or Bachelor of Science degree is offered with major concentrations in accounting, art, art history, biochemistry, biology, biotechnology, business, chemistry, classical civilization, classical languages, communication arts and sciences, computer science, Dutch, early childhood education, economics, education, engineering, English, environmental science, environmental studies, exercise science, film studies, French, geology, German, Greek, history, information systems, Latin, mathematics, music, nursing, philosophy, physical education, physics, political science, psychology, recreation, religion and theology, social work, sociology, Spanish, special education, telecommunications, and theater. The Bachelor of Fine Arts (B.F.A.) degree in art is offered in addition to the B.A. degree in art.

Professional programs include prearchitecture, engineering (chemical, civil, electrical/computer, mechanical), prelaw, premedicine/predentistry, natural resources, prepharmacy, pre-physical therapy, pre–seminary studies, social work, and elementary, secondary, and special education. Minor concentrations are available in archaeology, Asian studies, dance, English as a second language, environmental studies, gender studies, Japanese, journalism, medieval studies, missions, Third World development studies, and writing.

Academic Program

Calvin College maintains a strong commitment to a liberal arts curriculum as an integral avenue to help students understand God's world and their place in it. The College follows a 4-1-4 academic calendar, consisting of two 4-month semesters with a three-week Interim term during January. Typically, students take four courses each semester and one course during the Interim. Graduation requires the successful completion of 124 semester hours.

Calvin's core curriculum begins with a first-year gateway course, Developing a Christian Mind, and ends with a capstone course in the senior year. Core curriculum requirements include foreign language, history, literature and arts, mathematics, natural sciences, philosophy, physical education, religion, social sciences, and written and spoken rhetoric. Some requirements can be satisfied by advanced high school work in foreign language, literature, and natural sciences. Qualified students can earn course exemption and/or credit by completing college-level work in high school or by examination. Satisfactory scores on Advanced Placement (AP), International Baccalaureate (I.B.), and/or CLEP exams are also accepted.

Students with a cumulative grade point average of 3.3 or higher can apply to the Honors Program for advanced-level courses, interdisciplinary courses, and cocurricular opportunities. Students can also benefit from services offered by the Office of Student Academic Services, which provides academic counseling, tutoring, training in study skills, and review courses in key subjects.

Off-Campus Programs

Study-abroad programs for a semester or a year are offered in Austria, Belize, China, Costa Rica, France, Germany, Ghana, Great Britain, Honduras, Hungary, Japan, the Netherlands, and Spain. Students register for courses in various subjects, and the credits earned are applied toward graduation requirements. The Chicago Metropolitan Study Center, in cooperation with Calvin and other colleges, offers credit for internship experiences in Chicago. Students can also participate in the Oregon Extension Program of Houghton College and programs of the Council for Christian Colleges and Universities: the American Studies Program in Washington, D.C.; the Latin American Studies Program in Central America; a Film Studies Program in Hollywood; a Middle East Studies Program in Cairo, Egypt; and a Russian Studies Program in Moscow. Calvin's Study in Spain Program is one option students may choose to fulfill their foreign language requirement. Many courses offered during the Interim are also taught abroad. Along with several other liberal arts colleges, Calvin sponsors the Au Sable Institute of Environmental Studies, which offers creational stewardship experiences in a sylvan setting in the northern part of Michigan's lower peninsula.

Academic Facilities

The four-floor Science Complex features a center core of laboratories, an atom trapper, and an observatory. The Engineering Building provides space for engineering students and faculty members to do research and design work. The DeVries Hall of Science includes medical research laboratories and classrooms. The Spoelhof College Center houses administrative offices, a social research center, an art gallery, six art studios, and a 340-seat auditorium. In the Fine Arts Center, classrooms and offices surround a 1,000-seat auditorium.

The Hekman Library-Hiemenga Hall complex includes a five-level, computerized library containing more than 700,000 bound volumes, 2,750 periodicals, an extensive collection of microfiche, records and tapes, and government publications; more than 1,500 students can be comfortably seated at study carrels and tables. The complex also houses the Information Technology Center, the Calvin Center for Christian Scholarship, the Meeter Center for Calvinism Studies, a distance-learning classroom, a TV studio, a graphics production lab, and a curriculum center for teacher-education students. The 55,000-square-foot DeVos Communications Center is home to a 150-seat video theater, a television studio, an audio studio, digital audio and video editing labs, and a speech pathology and audiology clinic. The Prince Conference Center houses seminars, meetings, and retreats.

Costs

Tuition for 2003–04 was $16,775; tuition for the Interim was free for full-time students enrolled for at least one semester. Room and board charges were $5840 for resident students with a twenty-one-meal-per-week plan (ten- and fifteen-meal-per-week plans are also available). About $600 is needed for fees and textbooks.

Financial Aid

Sixty percent of Calvin students receive need-based financial aid; demonstrated need is the most important criterion in determining eligibility. Students wishing to be considered for financial aid must be admitted to the College and must submit the Free Application for Federal Student Aid (FAFSA) and Calvin's Supplemental Application for Financial Aid. February 15 is the filing deadline for maximum consideration. Financial awards to eligible applicants consist of state and federal grants, loans, Federal Work-Study funds, and institutional grants and scholarships. Part-time employment is available on campus, and placement preference is given to needy students. Calvin also helps students find off-campus employment and runs a job transportation service that drives them to and from their jobs for a fee.

Faculty

Calvin's outstanding faculty members have distinguished themselves through publication and research, yet each is available 10–15 hours per week outside of class for academic and personal counseling. More than 82 percent have earned the highest academic degree in their field. Each faculty member is a professing Christian, committed to the integration of his or her personal faith and discipline. There are 305 full-time and 77 part-time faculty members; the faculty-student ratio is 1:13.

Student Government

The 27-member Student Senate supervises most student activities and oversees the budgets for student publications, homecoming, the film arts, and the Service-Learning Center. Student members serve on most faculty committees governing the College. Each residence hall has its own governing council and judiciary committee. Campus rules are designed to build a Christian academic community. Calvin attempts to aid student development and responsible action by clearly expressing its expectations and de-emphasizing regulations.

Admission Requirements

Applicants should be graduates of an accredited high school program and should have completed satisfactorily at least 15 units of college-preparatory work, including 3 in English and 3 in algebra and geometry. Applicants with high school averages of C+ (2.5) or higher who score above 20 on the ACT composite or above 470 on both the math and verbal sections of the SAT I are normally given regular admission. Applicants with lower grades and scores, or those with deficiencies in their high school preparation, may be admitted under special conditions. International students for admission from other countries follow the customary entrance procedures. Students who come from a non-English-speaking culture must demonstrate proficiency in English by satisfactory performance on the Test of English as a Foreign Language (TOEFL).

Application and Information

Applicants must submit a completed application form, a high school or college transcript, results of either the ACT or SAT I, and an educational recommendation completed by a teacher or counselor. Admission decisions are made on a rolling basis beginning in mid-October. Applicants for fall admission are urged to complete their file before February 1, although there is no deadline as long as space remains in the entering class. Campus visits are strongly recommended. Students and parents are welcome to visit at any time that is convenient for them. The "Fridays at Calvin" program provides an excellent opportunity to experience life at Calvin first-hand. For more information about Calvin or about visiting the campus, students should contact:

Admissions Office
Calvin College
3201 Burton Street, SE
Grand Rapids, Michigan 49546
Telephone: 616-526-6106
616-526-8480 (TTY)
800-688-0122 (toll-free in North America)
Fax: 616-526-6777
E-mail: admissions@calvin.edu
World Wide Web: http://www.calvin.edu

Recognized as one of the finest research libraries in western Michigan, the Hekman Library is a hub of student and faculty activity on the Calvin College campus.

CAMBRIDGE COLLEGE

CAMBRIDGE, MASSACHUSETTS

The College

At Cambridge College, an innovative educational model combines peer teaching and learning with creative instruction. Its programs are known for offering academic substance and rigor in a highly supportive environment. The College has nearly 18,000 graduates in the Boston area, across the country, and around the world. Students choose Cambridge College for its distinctive focus on the needs of working adults and for the diverse community of lifelong learners it provides.

Founded in 1971, Cambridge College offers the degrees of Master of Education (in counseling psychology and in education), Master of Management, Bachelor of Arts (in multidisciplinary studies and in psychology), and Bachelor of Science (in human services and in management studies) to working adults. Sixty-five percent of the College's more than 5,100 students are women, and more than 40 percent are members of minority groups; the average age of Cambridge College undergraduate students is about 31. Classes take place in the evenings and on weekends and provide motivated adult students with an atmosphere of intellectual challenge, peer support, and respect for their professional and personal attainments.

Location

Cambridge College is located midway between Harvard and Central Squares in Cambridge, Massachusetts. This vital urban environment combines the diversity and richness of a major metropolitan area with the intellectual resources of a nationally known university community.

Majors and Degrees

Cambridge offers the Bachelor of Arts in multidisciplinary studies and in psychology as well as the Bachelor of Science in human services and in management studies.

Academic Programs

The bachelor's programs at Cambridge College support professional development in a wide variety of careers and graduate programs.

The Bachelor of Arts in psychology program is a liberal arts degree program that prepares people for careers in human services, management, administration, education, or community service; for professional advancement in their current work; or for graduate study.

The Bachelor of Science in human services highlights the dynamic interactions among individuals, families, and community institutions and develops expertise in working with them to make positive changes. Students develop knowledge and skills for a career, with concentration options in addiction studies, family studies, holistic studies, juvenile justice, community building, and medical interpreting. Many go on to graduate study in related fields.

The Bachelor of Arts in multidisciplinary studies provides a rich education in the arts and humanities, natural and physical sciences, mathematics, and social studies. This program provides the broad knowledge required of elementary teachers by the Massachusetts Department of Education. Students pursue educator licensure at the graduate level.

The Bachelor of Science in management studies equips adult students with broad-based marketable and transferable skills that focus on the management of people and systems. Students can become outstanding team members and managers of organizations. Graduates are ready to move into professional managerial and supervisory jobs.

Cambridge College also offers a Medical Interpreter Training Program that gives bilingual students the knowledge and skills necessary to provide effective interpretation in medical settings. Students learn how to bridge the perspectives and worldviews of both providers and clients by developing knowledge in both domains.

Cambridge College students join an active, diverse learning community of working adults in an environment of trust and shared vision. The bachelor's programs are shaped by an educational model in which advising, learning, teaching, and assessment work together as an integrated process.

Learners in this supportive community are empowered to synthesize academic and experiential learning with personal values and practical relevance. The Cambridge College learning experience transforms students' personal, professional, and social realities and enables them to participate more effectively in their communities.

Cambridge College provides an education for its students that, in addition to offering academic breadth and depth, goes beyond the traditional ways of organizing knowledge and traditional teaching methods that are often inadequate for adult learners in the contemporary world. Since its founding in 1971, Cambridge College has been offering distinctive programs designed especially for working adults. Its bachelor's programs are based on these years of experience about how they learn most effectively.

Cambridge College is committed to outcomes-based learning in all aspects of undergraduate study. Each program and each course have clearly defined, measurable skills and areas of knowledge to gain; understandings and perspectives to develop; processes to use; and projects to complete. Outcomes-based learning is centered on the learner. Clearly stated learning outcomes provide a baseline for learning and thus facilitate educational planning and enhance learners' abilities to achieve personal and career goals.

The College recognizes the importance and validity of prior learning for academic credit, program planning, shortening time spent in the program, and saving students money. Cambridge College assesses and awards appropriate credit to its students for courses completed at regionally accredited institutions, portfolios documenting prior or current learning, successful completion of nationally standardized subject-area and skills tests, and challenge examinations in writing and mathematics.

Academic Facilities

All Cambridge College students have the opportunity to use the Harvard Graduate School of Education's Monroe C. Gutman Library. Students who wish to borrow books may apply for a Special Borrower's Card. Students access Cambridge College's full-featured Online Library from their own computers. They get full-text scholarly articles and documents appropriate for research in education, counseling, psychology, management, health, and other academic areas. Students get online live reference librarian service, online tutorials, research guides, and instructional handouts. The College has computer labs for classroom instruction and student use of standard software and the Internet.

Staffed by members of the College's writing faculty, the Writing Center offers individual conferences to assist with writing projects in any course and support services in English as a Second Language. Students sign up at their own initiative or are recommended by faculty members. The Math Lab supports learners who need help with math problems, assignments, or exams.

Costs

Undergraduate course tuition was $300 per credit (2003–04). Students earning credit through portfolio assessment were charged a fee of $100 per credit hour attempted. Cambridge College also charges a nonrefundable application fee of $30 and a one-time degree processing fee of $110.

Financial Aid

Approximately 85 percent of undergraduate students receive some form of financial aid during the course of their work at Cambridge College. The College's Financial Aid Office offers a broad range of financial assistance, including low-interest loans, grants, scholarships, and work-study opportunities. Depending on their financial situation, income, and credit history, students may be eligible to receive federal assistance (including Federal Pell Grants, Federal Supplementary Educational Opportunity Grants, Federal Stafford Student Loans, and College work-study employment), Massachusetts state scholarships, and private scholarship funds.

Faculty

The student-faculty ratio of the Cambridge College bachelor's programs is 17:1. The College has a full-time core faculty of 30 members, with approximately 120 part-time senior and adjunct faculty members; 82 percent hold terminal degrees.

Student Government

Interested students have the opportunity to participate in a Student Advisory Board, which meets regularly to discuss issues of concern and to make recommendations to the College's faculty and administration.

Admission Requirements

Since its founding, Cambridge College has sought to provide academically excellent higher education to a diverse population of working adults. Students are admitted to the College on the basis of their understanding of their own educational and career goals, their commitment to a course of study, and the motivation demonstrated in their personal and professional lives. Three years of work experience beyond high school are recommended. Applicants to Cambridge College are not required to submit results from standardized tests; instead, prospective students are asked to demonstrate academic ability, commitment to succeeding scholastically and professionally, and capacity for clearly defining academic and career goals. Life and work experience are considered as an integral part of the admissions decision.

Application and Information

Students may enter Cambridge College in the fall, spring, or summer. For further information, students can contact undergraduate enrollment at:

Cambridge College–Cambridge (main campus)
1000 Massachusetts Avenue
Cambridge, Massachusetts 02138
Telephone: 800-877-4723 (toll-free)
E-mail: admit@cambridgecollege.edu (all locations)
World Wide Web: http://www.cambridgecollege.edu

Cambridge College–Lawrence
60 Island Street
Lawrence, Massachusetts 01830
Telephone: 978-738-0502

Cambridge College–Springfield
570 Cottage Street
Springfield, Massachusetts 01104
Telephone: 413-747-0204
800-829-4723 (toll-free)

CAMPBELL UNIVERSITY

BUIES CREEK, NORTH CAROLINA

The University

Founded in 1887, Campbell University has had the distinction of being North Carolina's second-largest private undergraduate institution. Graduate programs were established, and in 1979 the name of the institution was changed from Campbell College to Campbell University. Its current enrollment is about 9,700 students at all campuses. There are more than 3,950 students at the main campus in Buies Creek. In an average year, the student body comes from about ninety North Carolina counties, all fifty states, and fifty-six countries. Seventy-six percent of the students come from North Carolina. Members of minority groups make up 21 percent of the student body.

Campbell University has established a law school and schools of business, pharmacy, education, and divinity and now awards the J.D., Pharm.D., D. Min, M.Ed., M.A., M.B.A., M.S., and M.Div. degrees. Campbell now offers a Masters of Trust and Investment Management (M.T.I.M.) degree. These additions have increased interest in the general program of the undergraduate college. Completed projects include a $1.2-million classroom building, the Keith Hills housing development and golf course, an indoor swimming pool, a welcome center, and a $3.5-million fine arts complex. A $3.5-million addition to the Norman Adrian Wiggins School of Law, an addition to the Campbell University School of Pharmacy, and the 76,000-square-foot, $11-million Lundy Fetterman School of Business are the newest expansion projects that have been completed.

Campbell University is nonsectarian. Approximately 48 percent of its students are Baptist, but young people of twenty-two other faiths complete its student body. It is concerned with maintaining, for living and learning, an environment consistent with Christian ideals. Among the extracurricular activities available at Campbell are band, choir, and drama groups; religious, political, professional, social, and academic groups; and intercollegiate and intramural sports organizations.

In athletics, the University is a member of NCAA Division I (Sun Athletic Conference) for men and for women (with the exception of wrestling, which is in the Colonial Conference). Men's sports include baseball, basketball, cross-country, golf, soccer, tennis, track, and wrestling. Women's sports include basketball, cheerleading, cross-country, golf, soccer, softball, tennis, track, and volleyball. Women's swimming is scheduled to be offered starting in 2005, with limited scholarships.

A number of activities are available on campus during the summer for juniors and seniors in high school. Campbell University hosts an array of camps, such as band, basketball, golf, and volleyball, just to mention a few. During the ten-week period, Campbell accommodates more than 5,000 students.

The University also has campuses offering a variety of undergraduate and graduate courses at Fort Bragg, Raleigh/Morrisville, Rocky Mount, and Jacksonville, North Carolina, and in Kuala Lumpur, Malaysia.

Location

Buies Creek is a small, well-kept residential community surrounded by woods and farmland in Harnett County, where North Carolina's coastal plain and Piedmont meet just east of the center of the state. The region is one of the most progressive for education and research in the Southeast. Raleigh, the capital, and Fayetteville are 30 miles away from the campus; within about an hour's driving time are the Research Triangle Park and the city of Durham.

Majors and Degrees

Campbell University confers seven undergraduate degrees: Bachelor of Arts, Bachelor of Science, Bachelor of Applied Science, Bachelor of Business Administration, Bachelor of Health Science, and Bachelor of Social Work and an Associate in Arts degree. The major and/or the concentration may be in any one of the following fields: accounting, advertising, art, athletic training, biochemistry, biological sciences, business administration, chemistry, child development, church music, clinical research, composition of music, comprehensive music, computer information systems, computer science, criminal justice administration, drama and Christian ministries, economics, education, elementary education, English, exercise science, family/consumer science, family studies, fitness/wellness management, French, government, graphic design, history, international business, international studies, K–12 education, mass communication, mathematics, middle grades education, military science, music, music education, pharmaceutical sciences, physical education, piano pedagogy, predentistry, pre-engineering, prelaw, premedicine, prepharmacy, pre–physical therapy, pre–veterinary medicine, print media/journalism, professional golf management, psychology, public administration, public relations, radio/television broadcasting, religion, religion and Christian ministries, religion and philosophy, secondary education, social science, social work, Spanish, sports management, studio art, theater arts, trust management and financial planning, U.S. Army ROTC, and vocational education.

Academic Program

The curriculum of Campbell University is designed to meet individual needs and interests. During the first two years, students follow a general course of study, the General College Curriculum, to broaden their backgrounds in the basic fields of knowledge. By the end of the sophomore year, they should have selected a major subject for specialized study during the final two years. Basic curriculum requirements for the first two years in semester hours are math, 6; English, 12; social studies, 6; natural science, 8; religion, 6; music, art appreciation, or drama, 3; foreign language, up to 9, depending on high school credits and the program of study; and health and physical education, 3. Candidates for a bachelor's degree must earn a minimum of 128 credits, including the 3 in health and physical education, while maintaining at least a C average in academic course work; must complete a minimum of 32 semester hours in the departmental major at Campbell; and must average C or better in all courses required for the major. Candidates for the Associate in Arts degree must complete 64 semester hours of work and have at least a 2.0 GPA on all work required for graduation and at least a 2.0 GPA on 80 percent of all work attempted. The University calendar enables students to complete first-semester course work and examinations before Christmas vacation and end the spring session by the middle of May.

Campbell offers a complete curriculum of evening courses on its main campus and at its nearby Fort Bragg campus. The Fort Bragg campus is primarily a service for military personnel on active duty, but classes are open to civilian students.

Campbell offers the nation's first undergraduate program in trust management and since 1968 has been training prospective trust officers for the banks and trust companies of the region. Campbell also sponsors the Southeastern Trust School, a summer institute for trust officers.

Academic programs continue to expand at Campbell University. The charter class entered Campbell's School of Pharmacy in 1986. The school helps serve the health-care needs of North Carolina and beyond. Campbell's School of Education was formally established in 1985 in response to the need for fully qualified educators for the educational system of North Carolina and the country. The School of Education passage rate for the Praxis II exam in 2003 was 98 percent.

The Military Science Department offers Army Reserve Officer Training Corps (ROTC) classes leading to a commission as an officer in the Active, Reserve, or National Guard components of the United States Army. Campbell's ROTC program is one of the best in the nation, earning the MacArthur Award six times since 1989 as the premier leadership-training program in the nation. This annual award is given jointly by the MacArthur Foundation and the Commander, U.S. Army Cadet Command. The Campbell training program is one of the best preparation possible for the nation's future leaders.

Off-Campus Programs

Credit may be earned in off-campus settings through apprenticeships or internships in communications, government, public education, religious education, psychology, social work, and trust management. Campbell's philosophy on internships is departmental based. Departmental inquiries are welcomed. Other study-abroad opportunities allow students to study in Australia, China, Costa Rica, Egypt, England (Oxford), and Russia.

Academic Facilities

The Lundy Fetterman School of Business provides 76,000 square feet of state-of-the-art technology for educational enhancement. The Leslie H. Campbell Hall of Science provides the individual student with facilities for research projects, which the University encourages in four sciences. Campbell's own computer center (with an IBM System/4000 and IBM Personal Computers) is supplemented by more than twenty departmental computer labs. It is linked with the Triangle Universities Computation Center of the North Carolina Educational Computer Service. Campbell's Carrie Rich Library houses a collection of more than 208,000 volumes. The D. Rich Memorial Building, housing Turner Auditorium, and the four-story Fred L. Taylor Hall of Religion contain classrooms, laboratories, and faculty offices. The Taylor Bott Rogers Fine Arts Complex, containing 48,820 square feet of space, is well equipped for the wide range of events staged by active music, drama, and art groups. The closed-circuit television equipment of the school's audiovisual center enhances teacher training. The School of Pharmacy opened a 7,000-square-foot, $4-million research facility in March 2001. It supports both the Master of Science programs in Pharmaceutical Sciences and Clinical Research.

Costs

The estimated 2004–05 comprehensive fee for tuition and general fees is $13,900. On-campus students are provided with board and room at a minimum of $5000.

Financial Aid

Campbell University has private and institutional scholarships, federal grants, loans, and Federal Work-Study Program awards. Loans are available through the Federal Stafford Student Loan Program and the Federal Perkins Loan Program. Needs analysis forms (Free Application for Federal Student Aid) are available January 1 and are due in the Financial Aid Office by March 15 if the applicant wishes to be considered for a maximum award. Ninety-one percent of the student body received financial assistance in 2002–03. All assistance is offered without regard to race, creed, or national origin.

Faculty

The faculty consists of 302 teachers, of whom approximately 75 percent have earned the doctorate or have completed three years beyond the bachelor's degree. Ninety-seven percent of classes have less than 50 students.

Student Government

Through the Student Government Association (SGA), the student body has an opportunity for self-government and a means to channel ideas and wishes to the proper administrative personnel. The SGA is composed of executive, judicial, and legislative branches. The executive officers are the president, vice president, secretary, treasurer, advancement officer, parliamentarian, executive officer of the Disciplinary Committee, and the presidents of the women's campus, the men's campus, and the day students. The legislative branch includes the Student Congress, made up of representatives from each of the four classes elected by popular vote.

Admission Requirements

The minimum requirements for admission to Campbell include graduation from high school, or equivalent credentials, with at least 13 nonvocational units which must include 4 in English, 3 in college-preparatory mathematics (including 2 of algebra and 1 of geometry), 2 in foreign language, 2 in social sciences (1 must be in United States history), and 2 in natural sciences (1 must be a laboratory science). Two units of a foreign language are highly desirable. Acceptable scores must be earned on the SAT I or on the ACT.

Application and Information

An application for admission, accompanied by a $25 nonrefundable application fee, must be filed. Students may also apply on line at the e-mail address below. When all records are on file, the Admissions Committee notifies the student of its decision. Application forms and further information may be requested from:

Office of Admissions
Campbell University
P.O. Box 546
Buies Creek, North Carolina 27506
Telephone: 910-893-1320
910-893-1417 (international)
800-334-4111 (toll-free)
E-mail: adm@mailcenter.campbell.edu
World Wide Web: http://www.campbell.edu/

Students on the Mall in front of D. Rich Memorial Hall on the Academic Circle.

CANISIUS COLLEGE

BUFFALO, NEW YORK

The College

Canisius College is one of twenty-eight Jesuit colleges in the nation and is consistently ranked among the top regional colleges in the Northeast. Founded in 1870 by European Jesuits, Canisius is proud to share in the Jesuit heritage, which offers students a unique blend of academic, social, and spiritual growth opportunities to prepare them to be leaders in their professions, communities, and service to humanity.

Canisius offers more than seventy distinct academic programs through the Richard J. Wehle School of Business, the College of Arts and Sciences, and the School of Education and Human Services. Of the 5,095 students currently enrolled at Canisius, 3,535 are enrolled in the undergraduate program. The student body is divided almost equally between men and women.

Most students choose Canisius for its strong academic programs and reputation for personal attention. Canisius attracts students from thirty-two states, two territories, and fourteen countries. International students come from Europe, Asia, Africa, the Middle East, South America, and Australia. Canisius welcomes international students and appreciates the cultural diversity they bring to the campus. The director of international student programs is available to advise students and assist with their adjustment to Canisius and to American culture.

Students are encouraged to participate in the many academic, cultural, fraternal, social, and service-oriented organizations and activities of the College. Canisius is a member of the Metro Atlantic Athletic Conference and the National Collegiate Athletic Association. Intercollegiate sports offered are baseball, basketball, cross-country, golf, hockey, lacrosse, soccer, softball, swimming, synchronized swimming, and volleyball. Bowling, cheerleading, crew, fencing, field hockey, rifle, rugby, skiing, and men's volleyball are offered as club sports. Students and faculty and staff members may also participate in a variety of intramural activities that include basketball, flag football, floor hockey, indoor soccer, racquetball, softball, tennis, and volleyball (coed).

Comfort, state-of-the-art technology, and out-of-the-classroom learning experiences are all part of residence life at the College. Canisius housing is like a home away from home, not just a temporary living accommodation. The renovated Bosch and Frisch Residence Halls are the home to first-year students. A new residence hall that will be home to 270 students is scheduled to open in fall 2005. Apartment-style living is available to sophomores, juniors, and seniors in one of the newly built Delevan Townhouses or the College's other townhouse complexes and apartment buildings. Specialty housing is available for students enrolled in the All-College Honors Program. The Intercultural Living Center opened in fall 2003, housing nearly 50 students—both Americans and international students from more than ten countries. Nearly all of the resident accommodations at Canisius are fully wired; Internet service, cable television, and local telephone service with voice mail are part of the package.

Location

The Canisius campus consists of fifty-one buildings located on 36 acres in a residential neighborhood in north-central Buffalo. The Metro Rail rapid transit system connects the College with some of Buffalo's most exciting areas, including HSBC Arena, home of the National Hockey League's Buffalo Sabres, Buffalo Bandits lacrosse, and Buffalo Destroyers arena football. The arena also hosts college basketball with Canisius' Golden Griffins as well as major popular and rock music concerts. During the summer, students can catch Buffalo Bisons Triple-A baseball games at Dunn Tire Park, where postgame fireworks are part of the fun. At Ralph Wilson Stadium, in Orchard Park, the Buffalo Bills are a focal point throughout the football season.

Some of the finest skiing in the East can be found on the more than twenty slopes, which are a 45-minute drive from Canisius. The Buffalo Zoo and Delaware Park, a 350-acre park with a lake and a golf course, are located less than a mile from the campus.

The internationally known Albright-Knox Art Gallery holds one of the world's finest collections of nineteenth- and twentieth-century American and European works of art. Buffalo is also home to the Buffalo Philharmonic Orchestra and the Studio Arena Theatre, which provides a wide variety of theater experiences.

The central location of the College also provides many opportunities for students interested in community service, internships, and employment.

Majors and Degrees

The College of Arts and Sciences offers programs leading to the Bachelor of Arts (B.A.) degree in anthropology, art history, biochemistry, communication studies, computer science, criminal justice, digital media arts, economics, English, European studies, history, international relations, mathematics and statistics, modern languages (French, German, and Spanish), music, philosophy, political science, psychology, religious studies, sociology, and urban studies. The Bachelor of Science (B.S.) degree is awarded in biology, bioinformatics, chemistry, clinical laboratory science, computer science, environmental science, and physics.

The Richard J. Wehle School of Business offers programs leading to the B.S. degree in accounting, accounting information systems, economics, entrepreneurship, finance, information systems, international business, management, and marketing.

The School of Education and Human Services offers degrees in adolescence education, athletic training/sports medicine, childhood education, early childhood education, physical education, and special education.

Canisius also offers programs in fashion merchandising (in conjunction with the Fashion Institute of Technology), fine arts, and military science and certification programs in gerontology and women's studies. Preprofessional programs are available in dentistry, engineering, environmental science and forestry (in conjunction with the State University of New York (SUNY) College of Environmental Science and Forestry at Syracuse), law, medicine, pharmacy, and veterinary medicine. An early notification of acceptance agreement exists, for state (New York) residents only, between Canisius and the Schools of Medicine and Dental Medicine of SUNY at Buffalo and SUNY Medical School at Syracuse. Seven-year joint-degree programs exist between Canisius and the SUNY Buffalo School of Dental Medicine, the Ohio College of Podiatric Medicine, the New York College of Podiatric Medicine, and the SUNY College of Optometry. Joint-degree programs offered with Lake Erie College of Osteopathic Medicine include a seven-year program in osteopathic medicine and a five-year program in pharmacy. A five-year combined-degree program leads to the B.A. in a major in one of the liberal arts disciplines and a Master of Business Administration degree.

Academic Programs

To earn a bachelor's degree from Canisius College, students must complete forty courses and a minimum of 120 credit hours. Within each curriculum, the courses are distributed into three areas: the core curriculum, major field requirements, and free electives. The College requires that students complete a rounded program of humanistic studies embracing literature, the physical and social sciences, oral and written communication, philosophy, history, religious studies, and language.

An honors program is available for qualified students. The program includes rigorous exploration of the arts and sciences in an enriched curriculum with close faculty supervision and small classes. Students may also obtain college credit through the Advanced Placement Program of the College Board. Students with scores of 4 or better on Advanced Placement tests are considered for credit and advanced standing.

Off-Campus Programs

Canisius students have the opportunity to spend a semester or a year studying abroad, improving their fluency in another language and opening the doors to exciting opportunities, both personal and professional. Canisius administers semester-abroad programs in the cities of London, England; Oviedo, Spain; Lille, France; Dortmund, Germany; Morelia, Mexico; and Galway, Ireland. Canisius also works with other U.S. colleges and universities to make it possible for students to spend a semester or a year studying in Italy, Australia, Japan, Canada, and other countries. Some Canisius-sponsored programs also enable students to work as volunteers or interns in countries overseas. The Office of International Student Programs assists students in selecting a study-abroad program, organizes a predeparture orientation, and assists students upon their return to the United States.

Students majoring in international relations and political science may participate in programs in Washington, D.C., or Albany, New York, that have been designed to give students practical experience in their field.

Academic Facilities

Canisius has invested more than $90 million over the last ten years to create state-of-the-art technology classrooms, residence halls, and cultural and recreational spaces. The 96,000-square-foot Andrew L. Bouwhuis Library houses more than 800,000 books, periodicals, microforms, and other materials. The library also provides online database searching and has a number of computerized reference tools on CD-ROMs.

Instructional computing facilities include 276 Windows and Macintosh computers in general-purpose labs and teaching labs. Another thirty-two computers are located in residence hall computer labs, and thirty-four computers serve as e-mail and Internet stations at various convenient locations on campus. All College-provided computers have Internet access, and laser printers are available at all student-use computer labs.

Computer access and e-mail accounts are automatically created for all students upon registration. GriffMail, the College's Web-based interface, makes e-mail available to students on campus, at home, or when traveling to any place in the world that has Internet access. Students living in College dormitories can connect properly equipped personal computers to the campus Ethernet. Assistance in making such connections is provided by the Resident Computer Consultants. Dorm rooms are also equipped with cable TV service, including several Canisius-originated channels. Dormitory phone service includes voice mail and a variety of other services.

Costs

For the academic year 2003–04, tuition was $19,542, room and board were $7970, and fees were $651. Books and supplies were estimated to cost $500. An additional $1130 per year was recommended for travel and personal expenses.

Financial Aid

Of the class of 2006, 97 percent receive some form of financial aid, and the average award is $16,259. This aid includes Canisius College scholarships and grants, state grants, state and federal loans, federal grants, and Federal Work-Study Program awards. Application for financial aid should be completed by February 11. The Free Application for Federal Student Aid (FAFSA) and the TAP application (New York State residents only) must be filed before consideration can be given to applicants.

Faculty

The Canisius College faculty numbers 212 full-time teachers, including Jesuits and lay men and women; more than 97 percent hold doctorates or other terminal degrees. The primary emphasis of the faculty members is teaching, and many also serve as academic advisers. The student-faculty ratio is 14:1.

Student Government

The Undergraduate Student Association comprises the entire undergraduate student body and is represented by elected officers who serve on the Student Senate. The senate assists and supervises the student activities and represents the views of the student body to the College administration. In addition, students serve on many College committees.

Admission Requirements

Canisius College does not discriminate on the basis of age, race, religion or creed, color, sex, national or ethnic origin, sexual orientation, marital status, veteran's status, genetic predisposition or carrier status, or disability in administration of its educational policies, employment practices, admissions policies, scholarship and loan programs, and athletic and other school-administered programs. Their acceptability as students is judged by the Committee on Admissions and is based on a combination of factors, including a student's academic ability, strength of character, high school record, rank in class, an essay, aptitude tests (SAT I or ACT), extracurricular activities, and recommendations. An applicant to the College is encouraged to pursue a challenging college-preparatory program in high school. This program of studies should include 16 units of credit in the academic subjects of English, foreign language, mathematics, science, and social studies. Recommendations from teachers or guidance counselors are not required but are encouraged, and they are considered in reviewing applications for admission. Campus interviews are strongly recommended and in some cases may be required.

Transfer students are welcome and are admitted to Canisius in the fall and spring semesters. In addition to meeting the academic standards required of all entering students, transfer students are considered for admission if they have a minimum 2.0 cumulative quality point average when transferring from either a two-year or a four-year accredited institution.

Application and Information

Students are encouraged to submit their applications for admission in the fall of their senior year in high school. The completed application form should be presented to the high school guidance counselor, to be forwarded to the director of admissions with an official high school transcript, SAT I or ACT scores, and any letters of recommendation. Arrangements for interviews may be made by contacting the Office of Admissions at least one week in advance of the desired date for a visit.

Canisius considers applications under a rolling admission policy. Applicants are notified of the admission decision six to eight weeks after their application has been received.

For application forms and additional information, students should contact:

Admissions Office
Canisius College
2001 Main Street
Buffalo, New York 14208
Telephone: 716-888-2200
800-843-1517 (toll-free)
Fax: 716-888-3230
E-mail: admissions@canisius.edu
World Wide Web: http://www.canisius.edu

Canisius College is the ideal size for each individual to be an important part of campus life.

CAPITAL UNIVERSITY

COLUMBUS, OHIO

The University

Since its founding in 1850 by the Lutheran Church, Capital has earned a reputation for academic excellence and affordability, an accomplishment that earned Capital recognition as one of the top regional universities by *U.S. News & World Report.* The University's undergraduate and graduate programs prepare students for lifelong learning in the global environment of the twenty-first century. Students of all backgrounds and religions benefit from Capital's high-quality liberal arts education that is coupled with professional training. Students also benefit from the attention faculty and staff members pay to their moral, social, and ethical development. Students at Capital are part of the "CAP family," a family that cares about the total growth and well-being of each of its members.

Capital University is composed of four undergraduate colleges—the College of Arts and Sciences, School of Management, Conservatory of Music, and School of Nursing—and graduate programs offered through the Law School, School of Management, Conservatory of Music, and School of Nursing. The Centers for Lifelong Learning provide adults with alternative and effective learning experiences in Columbus, Cleveland, and Dayton. Capital offers six undergraduate degrees and eight graduate degrees, with more than eighty majors and forty minors. Of the approximately 3,900 students enrolled at Capital, more than 1,800 are traditional undergraduates. Approximately 65 percent of these students reside on campus in the University's four residence halls and apartment-style housing for upperclass students.

There are more than sixty student organizations, including a number of musical groups that are open to music and nonmusic majors alike. Other opportunities for involvement include student government, theater, the student newspaper and literary magazine, and the debate team. Numerous opportunities for volunteerism and service projects also exist. Approximately 20 percent of Capital's undergraduates are members of the nine social fraternities and sororities on campus.

Varsity and intramural athletics are offered for men and women. The eight varsity sports for men are baseball, basketball, cross-country, football, golf, soccer, tennis, and track. Women's varsity sports are basketball, cross-country, golf, soccer, softball, tennis, track, and volleyball. Capital's sports teams are sanctioned by the National Collegiate Athletic Association Division III, and the University is a member of the Ohio Athletic Conference. Intramural sports are also a big part of campus life. In addition, Capital's fitness rooms and activities such as aerobics provide options for students who want to develop their own individual fitness programs.

As a university affiliated with the Lutheran Church, Capital believes that the religious, social, racial, and ethnic diversity found on campus enhances each student's development. In this spirit, worship and study opportunities are offered in a cooperative, ecumenical way.

Location

Capital is located in the Columbus suburb of Bexley. Bexley is primarily a residential community with a number of small shops and restaurants. Downtown Columbus is just 4 miles from campus and easily reached by city buses. As part of a major metropolitan area, Columbus offers a wide variety of social and cultural opportunities. Students can enjoy performances by the Columbus Symphony Orchestra, BalletMet, Opera Columbus, or the Columbus Jazz Orchestra, or they may visit the more than fifty art galleries in the area. Students may follow professional sports by attending the games of the Columbus Crew (major-league soccer), the Columbus Blue Jackets (National Hockey League), or the Columbus Clippers (AAA franchise of the New York Yankees). There is also an expansive network of parks and recreation facilities, bike trails, and the Columbus Zoo. Many of the city's attractions are free or offer substantial student discounts. In addition, as Ohio's capital and largest city, Columbus is the home of many national and international corporations. These companies offer Capital students unlimited opportunities for internships and employment after graduation.

Majors and Degrees

Capital University offers the Bachelor of Arts degree in art, art therapy, athletic training, biochemistry, biology, business (accounting, economics, and management), chemistry (major approved by the American Chemical Society), communication, computer science, criminology, education, English (literature and professional writing), environmental science, exercise science, health and fitness management, health education, history, international studies, liberal and professional studies, mathematics, modern languages (French and Spanish), organizational communication, philosophy, political science, psychology, public relations, radio-television, religion, social work, and sociology.

Capital also offers the Bachelor of Fine Arts, Bachelor of Science in Nursing (approved by the National League for Nursing Accrediting Commission), and Bachelor of Social Work (approved by the Council on Social Work Education). For music students, Capital offers a Bachelor of Music in jazz studies, keyboard pedagogy (church music, organ, and piano), music education (vocal and instrumental), music industry, music media, music merchandising, music technology, music theater, performance (instrumental, organ, piano, and vocal) and composition. The Bachelor of Arts in music is also offered.

A program in engineering, which leads to dual degrees, is offered in cooperation with Washington University in St. Louis and Case Western Reserve University in Cleveland. A similar dual-degree program in pre–occupational therapy is also offered in conjunction with Washington University and the University of Indianapolis.

Academic Programs

The academic year consists of two semesters, the first of which begins in late August and ends in December. The second semester begins in early January and ends in early May. Summer classes are available.

For graduation, the College of Arts and Sciences requires the completion of a minimum of 124 semester hours; the School of Nursing requires the completion of 134 semester hours; and, depending on the major, the Conservatory of Music requires the completion of between 124 and 136 semester hours.

In addition to taking courses related to their field of study, all undergraduate students take courses that fulfill a set of general education goals and bring together the University's academic, scientific, religious, and artistic disciplines.

Learning is not confined to the classroom at Capital. All undergraduate students, regardless of their major, may participate in an internship that allows them to apply newly learned skills to on-the-job situations.

Faculty advisers help students select a major, choose appropriate classes, and suggest career options. In addition, staff members in Capital's Career Services Office help students plan careers, provide instruction in resume writing and interviewing, and share information about graduate schools. On-campus recruiting sessions and a job-referral service also enhance employment opportunities. In recent years, more than 96 percent of Capital's graduates who used the office's resources found employment or entered graduate school within six months of graduation.

Off-Campus Programs

At Capital, one way students learn more about other cultures and countries is through international study.

Capital is the only school in the country that offers a semester of undergraduate study at the Zoltán Kodály Pedagogical Institute of Music in Hungary for students in the Conservatory of Music.

In addition, Capital's Office of International Education offers overseas study opportunities in countries around the world, including France, Germany, Israel, Tanzania, Spain, Ecuador, China, and the Netherlands.

Closer to home, students may participate in a semester internship in one of nearly 500 agencies in the nation's capital through an arrangement with the Washington Center. In addition, cross-registration for enrolled students is available with Columbus College of Art and Design, Columbus State Community College, Ohio Dominican College, The Ohio State University, and Otterbein College.

Academic Facilities

Capital's campus consists of twenty-four buildings. Through CAPNet, Capital's campuswide voice, data, and video network, every residence hall room, classroom, and office is connected to the Internet and the World Wide Web. Through the library's connection to OhioLINK, students have access to more than 10 million items held by fifty libraries throughout the state. Information Technology provides a television studio and computer labs for student use. The Advanced Computational Science Laboratory includes an extensive array of computer hardware that allows students to access an extensive collection of scientific software and to simulate a parallel computing environment. A newly created state-of-the-art technology classroom enhances teaching and learning. Nursing students may also use the microcomputers and instructional software contained in the School of Nursing's Helene Fuld Health Trust Learning Resources Laboratory. For the art lover, Chagall, Picasso, and Warhol are as close as Capital's Blackmore Library, which houses the University's Schumacher Gallery and its 2,000-piece collection.

Costs

In 2003–04, tuition and fees were $20,500. Room and board fees were $6050.

Financial Aid

Approximately 95 percent of Capital's undergraduate students receive some form of financial assistance. To apply, a student must file the Free Application for Federal Student Aid (FAFSA).

University Scholarships of up to $10,000 and Challenge Grants of up to $6000 are awarded to incoming freshmen and transfer students on the basis of academic achievement (and standardized test scores for freshmen). Full-tuition scholarships (Collegiate Fellowships) are awarded to incoming freshmen based on academic achievement and an on-campus competition. Music scholarships and participation awards are granted based on music ability as demonstrated during an audition. Additional grants are available for leadership, students of color, and out-of-state residents.

Faculty

The University has 228 full- and part-time faculty members for its undergraduate programs. Student-faculty ratios are 16:1 in the College of Arts and Sciences, 4:1 in the Conservatory of Music, and 8:1 in the School of Nursing.

Student Government

There is an active and influential student government on the Capital campus. Students are elected in campuswide elections each spring. Through this organization, students have the opportunity to gain leadership experiences.

Admission Requirements

Capital University admits qualified students regardless of race, color, religion, gender, age, disability, or national or ethnic origin to all the rights, privileges, programs, and activities generally accorded or made available to the students at the University.

To be considered for admission to any of the undergraduate programs, students must submit copies of their high school transcript, ACT or SAT I scores, and a counselor recommendation. Applicants to the Conservatory of Music must also arrange for an audition, either in person or by videotape. Scores on Advanced Placement tests and College-Level Examination Program subject examinations are accepted as additional indicators of an applicant's ability, and course credit may be awarded for satisfactory scores on these examinations.

Campus visits are encouraged. Arrangements for a tour of the campus and an interview, class visits, and appointments with professors may be made through the Admission Office. When an admission representative visits high schools, interested students in the area are notified and encouraged to meet with the representative.

Transfer applicants must be in good social and academic standing and have a minimum grade point average of 2.25 at the institutions they attended previously. International applicants must submit official secondary school transcripts and photocopies of school leaving certificates, TOEFL scores, SAT I scores if available, and recommendation letters from a guidance counselor or headmaster and from a teacher.

Application and Information

Applications for admission may be submitted starting September 1 for the following year. Applicants are notified of their status as soon as their application is complete. The priority application deadline for the fall semester is April 15. Applications received after April 15 are reviewed on a space-available basis.

For additional information, the student should contact:

Director of Admission
Capital University
2199 East Main Street
Columbus, Ohio 43209-2394
Telephone: 614-236-6101
800-289-6289 (toll-free)
Fax: 614-236-6926
E-mail: admissions@capital.edu
World Wide Web: http://www.capital.edu

Capital's campus, located in a residential neighborhood, provides an excellent atmosphere for students.

CAPITOL COLLEGE

LAUREL, MARYLAND

The College

Capitol is a private coeducational college providing practical educational experiences that enable graduates to advance, manage, and communicate changes in the information age. Chartered in 1964, Capitol College offers degree programs in engineering, engineering technology, information technology, and management. The student body is composed of 483 men and 147 women who come from fifteen states and twenty-one countries. Capitol College is accredited by the Middle States Association of Colleges and Schools. The electrical engineering and all engineering technology programs are accredited by the Technology and Engineering Accreditation Commissions of the Accreditation Board for Engineering and Technology, Inc. (TAC/ABET, EAC/ABET).

Capitol sponsors a variety of extracurricular activities based on student participation and demand. Basketball, flag football, soccer, softball, and volleyball are offered on an intramural level. The Web Design Club and the student branch of the Institute of Electrical and Electronics Engineers (IEEE) provide professional and social development for their members. Student chapters of the Society of Women Engineers (SWE) and the National Society of Black Engineers (NSBE) promote educational and social growth through sponsored trips, guest speakers, and social activities. The Office of Student Development also plans trips and activities throughout the year. Scholarship and academic achievement are recognized through the Alpha Chi, Tau Alpha Pi, and Eta Kappa Nu national honor societies on campus.

Career development is an integral aspect of the College's mission, and graduates are in great demand by business and industry. Capitol is so certain of the quality of its programs and the market trend for high-technology employees that the College guarantees qualified B.S. degree candidates a job in their field at a nationally competitive salary within ninety days of commencement. For the past twenty-five years, 95 percent of Capitol College graduates have been offered full-time jobs in their fields of study or have chosen to continue on to graduate school within ninety days of graduation. The College's Cooperative Education Program arranges for paid work experience in jobs related to the student's major prior to graduation. Once hired, a student may work full- or part-time to supplement their academic program.

Capitol College's apartment-style residence facilities for men and women provide individual- and double-room accommodations. Students who live in the residence halls have access to complete kitchen facilities in each apartment plus Internet access via a T1 line and standard cable included in the room fee.

Location

Capitol College's 52-acre campus is located in Laurel, Maryland, halfway between Baltimore, Maryland, and Washington, D.C. The Baltimore/Washington metropolitan area is one of the fastest-growing technology markets in the United States. The campus is close to many high-technology corporations and a host of educational, cultural, and recreational attractions. The Smithsonian museums, the Library of Congress, the Kennedy Center for the Performing Arts, the MCI Center, FedEx Field, Baltimore's Inner Harbor, the Maryland Science Center, Oriole Park at Camden Yards, and PSINet Stadium are just a few of the sites that are a short drive or Metro ride away.

Majors and Degrees

Capitol College awards Bachelor of Science (B.S.) degrees in astronautical engineering, computer engineering, computer science, electrical engineering, management of information technology, network security, software and Internet applications, and software engineering. Capitol offers both the Associate of Applied Science (A.A.S.) degree and the B.S. degree in computer engineering technology, electronics engineering technology, management of telecommunications systems, and telecommunications engineering technology. Capitol also offers professional certifications in A+, Network+, I-Net+, MCSE, Cisco, and Check Point.

Academic Programs

Each department has its own sequence requirements for graduation. To earn a bachelor's degree, students must complete between 120 and 136 semester credit hours. To earn an associate degree, students must complete between 64 and 69 credits. Each degree program includes a core of courses in addition to classes within the major. The core curriculum consists of studies in humanities, mathematics, physical sciences, and social sciences. The average course load is 15 credits per semester.

Advanced standing can be earned through Advanced Placement (AP) and College-Level Examination Program (CLEP) tests. Credits can also be earned through institutional validation examinations.

At Capitol College, learning is centered both in and out of the classroom. Professors are available on a one-on-one basis, and tutors and lab aides are available for additional assistance. In the engineering and technology curricula, students reinforce their classroom lectures with assigned laboratory projects.

Academic Facilities

The campus is small in size but big in technological resources. Capitol College's Student Center, administrative offices, and classrooms are located in M/A-COM, MCI, and Telecommunications Halls. Also located in these buildings are Capitol's state-of-the-art laboratories. From electronics and computers to telecommunications and networking, Capitol stays abreast of the ever-changing trends in high technology.

Donated and wired by Bell Atlantic–Maryland, the Capitol Video Lab is a multimedia classroom equipped with eight televisions, three video cameras, a touch-screen control panel with a computer, twelve tables with microphones, a VCR, and a SoftBoard Digital blackboard. The Video Lab is currently used as an interactive classroom.

The John G. and Beverly A. Puente Library provides students with 100 monthly periodicals, nearly 10,000 volumes no more than 5 years old, more than twenty-five computer workstations, and a multimedia center with scanner and printer available for student use. The library is also home to the William G. McGowan Center for Innovative Teaching, a multimedia classroom with a network of fifteen interactive computer stations.

Alongside Telecommunications Hall is the Avrum Gudelsky Memorial Auditorium where Capitol hosts commencement and convocation. The auditorium is also used for special events such as educational seminars and student activities.

The McGowan Academic Center, a 40,000-square-foot building that is expected to be completed in 2004, is designed to combine high-speed multimedia and cutting-edge academic programs to provide an unparalleled learning center.

Costs

For the 2003–04 academic year, tuition for all degree programs was $16,850. Residential costs were $3850.

Financial Aid

Capitol College maintains an extensive program of financial aid to assist students in financing their education. Aid is available in the form of loans, grants, scholarships, and employment programs. Awards are based on financial need and/or academic ability. All students who wish to apply for aid must submit the Free Application for Federal Student Aid (FAFSA). Students are encouraged to contact the Director of Financial Aid at the College for assistance or for information about institutional scholarships.

Faculty

Teaching at Capitol College demands a focus on the student. The major concern is to challenge yet give students every opportunity to succeed in their programs. Capitol currently has 21 full-time and 63 part-time faculty members, who have amassed extensive teaching credentials and industry experience. Full-time faculty members not only teach, but also serve as academic advisers to assist students with planning their programs of study and achieving their academic goals.

Capitol College maintains a student-faculty ratio of 11:1. Individual attention and instruction are key elements of the academic program. Students are constantly encouraged to reach for their potential.

Student Government

Capitol Student Council plays an active role in both the academic and the social activities of the College. It is responsible for ensuring that an effective channel of communication remains open between students, the faculty, and the administration. Representatives of the student body are elected annually.

Admission Requirements

Admission to Capitol is based on educational preparation and the personal abilities necessary for academic success. Applicants must present evidence of having completed a high school course of study or its equivalent. Applicants to the technology programs must have 4 years of English, 3 years of mathematics (through at least algebra II), 2 years of a laboratory science, and 2 years of social sciences. Engineering majors must have a fourth year of math to prepare for college calculus and a third year of science. A foreign language is not a requirement for admission. Results of the SAT I or ACT are required of first-time freshmen. International applicants must submit scores on the Test of English as a Foreign Language (TOEFL). Transfer students must present transcripts of all postsecondary work.

Some applicants may be required to meet with the Admissions Committee. An admissions interview is strongly recommended for all applicants.

Application and Information

An application is considered when the student's file is complete, including a $25 application fee, the required test scores, and transcripts from each school attended. Application forms are available from the Office of Admissions or students may apply for free online. Capitol College maintains a rolling admission policy, and applicants are notified of the admission decision within one month of the completion of their file. To receive full consideration for financial aid and housing for the fall semester, students are encouraged to apply by March 1.

For more information, students should contact:

Office of Admissions
Capitol College
11301 Springfield Road
Laurel, Maryland 20708
Telephone: 301-953-3200 (from Washington, D.C.)
410-792-8800 (from Baltimore)
800-950-1992 (toll-free outside the Baltimore–Washington, D.C., area)
E-mail: admissions@capitol-college.edu
World Wide Web: http://www.capitol-college.edu

MCI and M/A-COM Halls.

CARDINAL STRITCH UNIVERSITY

MILWAUKEE, WISCONSIN

The University

Cardinal Stritch University is a comprehensive, coeducational institution rooted in the liberal arts and established in the Catholic tradition. Since its founding in 1937 by the Sisters of St. Francis of Assisi, Stritch has emerged as the largest Franciscan institution of higher education in North America and the second-largest private university in Wisconsin.

With a total population of more than 7,600 students on three campuses, Stritch's size can be deceiving. While the University provides all of the resources associated with large universities, it still offers the benefits of personal attention and one-on-one instruction associated with smaller institutions. The University keeps current with technological trends yet remains committed to maintaining the high-quality, value-centered education that has defined Stritch's history and continues to attract its diverse student body. At Stritch, a student-faculty ratio of 17:1 allows students easy access to faculty members who give students the personal attention needed to realize their full potential. A selection of more than forty undergraduate degrees means students can choose from a wide variety of majors to prepare themselves for future endeavors. For students who seek to continue their education after earning their undergraduate degree, the University offers nineteen master's degrees in a variety of specialty areas in business, education, nursing, psychology, and religious studies. Stritch was among the first institutions of higher learning in the state to offer both undergraduate and graduate degrees geared to meet the needs of working adults. These nontraditional programs meet once a week and are taught at an accelerated pace, with students taking one class at a time and progressing through their programs as a group. The University also offers a doctorate in leadership for the advancement of learning and service in an accelerated weekend/evening format.

With more than thirty student clubs and organizations and ten athletic teams, students discover social, cultural, and professional opportunities beyond the classroom. A member of NAIA Division II, Chicagoland Collegiate Athletic Conference, Cardinal Stritch University offers baseball, basketball, cross-country, soccer, and volleyball for men and basketball, cross-country, soccer, softball, and volleyball for women. Stritch athletes have a distinguished reputation for balancing their athletic and academic skills and have represented the University at the district, regional, and national levels. Service to the community and the world is an essential part of a Stritch education. Whether students are helping to build a house for Habitat for Humanity or leading health lessons in Tanzania, they are active in the social solutions that will ensure a better future.

A growing international student population and exchange programs with several universities abroad give students the opportunities to meet people from other cultures, develop a more global perspective of current events, and travel overseas to pursue studies.

The main campus, built in the early 1960s, houses a three-story residence hall, which is connected to several academic buildings and allows residents easy and climate-controlled access to many of the University's modern facilities. The student union, field house, bookstore, and auditorium are anchored by the Alfred S. Kliebhan Great Hall, where students study, visit with friends, or simply relax. Serra Dining Hall provides buffet-style meals with numerous menu selections. The chapel facilitates group worship at regular services and opportunities for personal reflection and individual prayer.

Location

Cardinal Stritch University's 40-acre, parklike main campus is situated in a quiet suburban neighborhood just north of Milwaukee. Downtown Milwaukee is a short, 15-minute drive from campus, while access to Lake Michigan is available within several blocks. The campus is conveniently accessible from Interstate 43, which offers a direct, easy route to Mitchell International Airport, the downtown Amtrak train station, and the Greyhound bus depot. The Milwaukee County Transit System provides students with a public transportation option when they are involved in off-campus pursuits. Interstate 43 also is a link to the excitement of downtown, which is home to numerous ethnic and American restaurants, specialty retailers, a downtown mall, the Milwaukee Art Museum, the Milwaukee Public Museum, several conference and performance centers, and cultural and sports entertainment.

Majors and Degrees

Cardinal Stritch University offers a wide variety of undergraduate degrees and encourages students to personalize their experience by creating a unique double major or minor to fit their specific career and educational goals. Personal advisers lead students through the process of choosing a major by answering questions and providing individual guidance. The College of Arts and Sciences offers Associate of Arts degrees in art, general studies, and women's studies and bachelor's degree programs in accounting, art, art education, biology, broadfield English/communication arts, business, chemistry, communication, computer studies, English, environmental chemistry, French, graphic design, history, integrated marketing communications, international business, jazz studies, management information systems/business, mathematics, music, music education, photography, political science, preprofessional programs, psychology, religious studies, social studies, sociology, Spanish, sports management, theater, and writing.

The College of Education offers bachelor's degrees in elementary and secondary education.

The College of Business and Management offers undergraduate degree programs exclusively designed to meet the special needs of working adults at on- and off-campus locations. Certificate programs and associate and bachelor's degrees are available.

The College of Nursing offers an associate degree in nursing for entry into nursing practice. Once completed, graduates of the program can take the exam to become a registered nurse and begin working in the field. The bachelor's degree in nursing is geared toward working nurses and is offered in a nontraditional format.

Academic Programs

The University strives to help students develop skills needed for a successful career as well as a personal code of ethics by which to live. Each degree program is based upon a foundation of liberal arts courses combined with a concentration in a major area of study. Courses in the general areas of communication, humanities, social and behavioral sciences, mathematics, and the natural sciences are common to all of the programs. The Associate of Arts degree is granted upon completion of 64 credits. The Associate of Science degree in nursing is granted upon completion of 70 credits, and the Associate of Science degree in business requires completion of 64 credits. The Bachelor of Arts degree and the Bachelor of Fine Arts degree require 128 credits, as do the Bachelor of Science degrees in business administration and management. The Bachelor of Science in Nursing degree requires 129 credits.

A dual-advising system for the undergraduate degree programs in the College of Arts and Sciences helps to ensure that students graduate in four years. Students work closely with a faculty adviser from the start of their Stritch education to determine required courses and electives. Advisers in the Academic Advising Center help students make their liberal arts core and elective course selections.

Off-Campus Programs

Opportunities to study abroad and participate in international service projects are available. Stritch students have studied in or traveled to such countries as England, India, Italy, Mexico, South Korea, and Spain as well as the continents of Africa and Australia.

Academic Facilities

An exceptional resource, the state-of-the-art library is easily accessible and contains a wealth of information necessary to complete in-depth research. The library is staffed by professional librarians; its holdings change daily and now include nearly 130,000 items in a variety of formats, as well as 630 current print periodical subscriptions and access to more than 3,000 periodicals in electronic format. The library offers the resources of eight college libraries through its collaborative Southeastern Wisconsin Information Technology Exchange (SWITCH) consortium and Topcat, a combined online public access catalog. The library offers an array of electronic databases, full-text and other resources, and interactive research services that are available to its community of learners, both on-site and from wherever learning takes place. The library's resources also include a number of laptop computers that are available for checkout for up to seven days at a time.

The Academic Computing Center gives students a competitive edge in today's computerized society. The three different computer labs house forty-five IBM and Macintosh personal computers. Laser printers and a document scanner are also available for student use.

The Career Services Center provides internship and job-search services to all Stritch students and alumni. Individual counseling and workshops offered throughout the year include career choices, job-search techniques, resume writing, interviewing, and choosing a major.

Other academic facilities include a 400-seat teaching theater, a spacious art gallery, photo labs, a dance studio, metal and woodworking shops, a graphic arts computer laboratory, and newly renovated biology and chemistry laboratories.

Costs

Full-time tuition for 2002–03 was $13,280; room and board were $4990. Part-time tuition was $415 per credit for all undergraduate programs except nursing, which was $470 per credit. Various meal plans are also available.

Financial Aid

A wide range of financial aid options is available at Cardinal Stritch University, including government-subsidized loan and grant programs as well as University scholarships, on-campus employment opportunities, and off-campus internships. About 80 percent of the full-time students receive financial aid, and the average financial aid package is approximately $9000. Eligibility for need-based grant and loan programs is determined after filing the Free Application for Federal Student Aid (FAFSA). Candidates for financial aid should complete and mail the FAFSA by March 1. The University also offers academic scholarships to those who qualify.

Faculty

Cardinal Stritch University faculty members play an active role in every student's life. Faculty members teach their own classes, so students can benefit directly from their knowledge, expertise, and open-door policy. As a result of the small class sizes, students grow from individual faculty member attention, gain opportunities to participate fully in class discussions, and are challenged to interact with and learn from their peers.

More than 60 percent of the faculty hold doctoral or other terminal degrees. Through their research, writing, and presentations, they keep abreast of the most current trends and continually update the subject matter and teaching techniques of the courses.

Student Government

All full-time undergraduate students are members of the Student Government Association (SGA) and are represented by a 30-member governing body. Student representatives, appointed by the SGA, sit on University academic committees and have a voice in issues related to educational policy and campus life.

Admission Requirements

The average student at Cardinal Stritch University graduated from high school with a B average, achieved a composite score of 23 on the ACT, and ranked in the top 40 percent of his or her high school class. The University considers for acceptance those students who achieve an ACT score of 20 or above or a combined SAT score of 930 or above; rank in the top 50 percent of their high school graduating class; graduate from high school with at least a 2.0 cumulative grade point average (on a 4.0 scale); and complete 16 high school academic units, broken down as follows: 4 years of English, 2 years of mathematics, 2 years of science, 2 years of social studies, and 6 units of academic electives. When applying for admission, students should send the completed application form, $25 application fee, high school transcripts, and ACT and/or SAT scores. On-campus interviews are not required but are recommended.

Transfer students who have fewer than 12 credits from another institution of higher education must submit their high school transcript and ACT or SAT scores. International students are welcome to apply. In addition to the application form and $75 fee, international students should also send a copy of their visa, certified copies of all high school and college transcripts, verification of a minimum score of 213 on the computer-based Test of English as a Foreign Language (TOEFL) or a minimum score of 550 on the paper-based TOEFL, the International Student Financial Aid Application, and verification of health insurance coverage.

Application and Information

The Admissions Office at Cardinal Stritch University accepts applications on a rolling admission basis. Applicants are notified of the decision two weeks after all records are complete.

Inquiries and application materials should be directed to:

David Wegener
Director of Admissions
Cardinal Stritch University
6801 North Yates Road
Milwaukee, Wisconsin 53217-3985
Telephone: 414-410-4040
800-347-8822 Ext. 4040 (toll-free)
E-mail: admityou@stritch.edu
World Wide Web: http://www.stritch.edu

Students on the campus of Cardinal Stritch University.

CARLETON COLLEGE

NORTHFIELD, MINNESOTA

The College

Since its inception in 1866, Carleton College has been a coeducational, residential, liberal arts college. Sponsored initially by the Congregationalists, Carleton opened its doors in September 1867 as Northfield College. Four years later, William Carleton of Charlestown, Massachusetts, donated $50,000 to the fledgling college, the result of which was the change of name from Northfield to Carleton. Binding church ties were dropped long ago, and the College continues to welcome students from a kaleidoscope of races, religions, and cultures.

Today, first-year classes number about 475 to 500, and the student body is approximately 50 percent men and 50 percent women. The on-campus enrollment of about 1,725 includes students from virtually every state and about twenty-five other countries. About a quarter are from Minnesota, and the next most represented states are Illinois, California, Wisconsin, New York, Massachusetts, Oregon, and Washington. About 18 percent are students of color, and 10 percent are the first generation of their families to attend college.

Most first-year students choose to take a first-year seminar, some of which deal with contemporary problems or concerns, others with more esoteric material. Many upperclass students do at least some independent study in their major, and a significant number of students take advantage of internship and work experience.

Though academic work takes top priority, Carleton students are actively involved in nearly 100 organizations, clubs, and other activities, ranging from the Carleton Singers (who performed at Carnegie Hall in February 1997) and the improvisational comedy troupe Cujokra to Ultimate Frisbee (Carleton's women's team won the national intercollegiate championship in 2000, and the men's team won in 2001) and one of the top Model United Nations teams in the country. Musicians can play in the orchestra or smaller ensembles or sing in the choir, the Carleton Singers, or the a cappella Knights or Knightengales. Athletes can participate in one of ten varsity sports for men or eleven for women, one of eighteen competitive club teams, or any of fifteen intramural sports.

Normally, 95 percent of Carleton first-year students return for their sophomore year. The most recent figures available show that 85 percent of first-year students graduated in four years or less, and 87 percent graduated within five years.

Location

Northfield is about 35 miles from the Minneapolis–St. Paul International Airport and 40 miles from the downtown Twin Cities. Once a traditional small agrarian community, Northfield is also the home of St. Olaf College and several multinational businesses, and a number of its residents now commute to the Twin Cities. Most of the buildings in downtown Northfield look much as they did at the turn of the century. A revitalized river bank and a core of downtown businesses and shops make for pleasant afternoon and evening strolls.

Majors and Degrees

Carleton grants only one undergraduate degree, the Bachelor of Arts. Majors offered are African/African-American studies, American studies, art history, biology, chemistry, classical languages, classical studies, computer science, economics, English, French, French and Francophone studies, geology, German, Greek, history, international relations, Latin, Latin American studies, mathematics, music, philosophy, physics, political science, psychology, religion, Romance languages, Russian, sociology and anthropology, Spanish, studio art, and women's studies. Students may also self-design their own majors.

In addition to a major, students may elect to study one of sixteen concentrations, integrated interdisciplinary programs that cut across traditional boundaries of academic disciplines and serve to both strengthen and complement the major: African/African-American studies, archaeology, biochemistry, cognitive studies, cross-cultural studies, East Asian studies, educational studies, environmental and technology studies, French and Francophone studies, Latin American studies, media studies, medieval and Renaissance studies, political economy, Russian studies, South Asian studies, and women's studies.

Special programs are available in biochemistry, educational studies, environmental and technology studies, Hebrew/Judaic studies, integrated general studies, linguistics, literary studies, media studies, studies in dance, and theater arts. Carleton offers a teacher education program leading to a secondary teaching license in art, English, French, German, mathematics, Russian, science, the social studies, or Spanish. Elementary licensure is available only in art. The joint liberal arts–engineering program, commonly known as the 3-2 program, is offered in conjunction with either Columbia University or Washington University (St. Louis).

Academic Programs

Carleton's avowed purpose is to provide a liberal arts education of the highest quality. The College teaches the basic skills upon which all higher achievements rest: to read perceptively, to write and speak clearly, and to think analytically. The Carleton education aims to nurture a sense of curiosity and intellectual adventure, an awareness of method and purpose in a variety of fields, and an affinity for quality and integrity wherever they may be found. These values prepare Carleton graduates to lead fully realized lives in a diverse and changing world.

To this end, the Carleton curriculum balances a traditional emphasis upon classic fields of study, or disciplines, with a complementary offering of distribution courses, electives, and interdisciplinary programs. To be awarded the Bachelor of Arts degree, a student must take at least thirty-five courses, two of which must come from arts and literature, two from the humanities, three from the social sciences, and three from mathematics and the natural sciences. In addition, everyone must take at least one course that is centrally concerned with a culture different from his or her own. All students must also satisfy two proficiency requirements: the writing of English and the learning of a second language.

Carleton students normally choose a major during the spring term of their sophomore year. In any given year, 12–15 students graduate with double majors, and about 15 graduate with special majors. All students must complete an integrative exercise, which could include a comprehensive examination, an extensive research project, a major paper, or a public lecture, in their major field, usually in the senior year. Carleton's academic year is composed of three 10-week-long terms: fall, winter, and spring.

Off-Campus Programs

Two thirds of Carleton students spend at least one term completing an off-campus program. During any one academic year, more than 350 students are involved in off-campus study in locations such as Australia, Japan, China, England, India, Mexico, Costa Rica, the Superior National Forest, and Washington, D.C. Each year the College sponsors as many as ten faculty-led off-campus seminars for Carleton students. Through membership in a number of consortia, Carleton students may participate in more than twenty additional international programs lasting from a semester to a full year. Students may also select from a list of programs sponsored by other institutions, consortia, and agencies that Carleton has evaluated and approved for academic credit, or they can request approval of a program that they and their academic advisers believe will further their educational goals.

Academic Facilities

The Carleton campus consists of more than 900 acres of land, about 450 of which are the Cowling Arboretum, a game and nature preserve used regularly as an outdoor laboratory for biology, chemistry, and geology as well as a recreational area. Twenty miles of running and skiing trails crisscross the "arb," which *Runner's World* has named the best place to run in the state of Minnesota.

Approximately forty buildings are found on the College's main campus of nearly 100 acres. Nine are student residence halls ranging in capacity from 110 to 205. A new $12-million, 80,000-square-foot field house/recreation center opened in April 2000. The Music and Drama Center offers a concert hall seating 500 and a theater seating 460, joined by a gallery, ensemble rooms, practice rooms, dressing rooms, and scenery and costume storage rooms. Recent construction has doubled the amount of art studio and gallery space and expanded the library to twice its original size and capacity. Three buildings are devoted to the sciences: Olin (physics and psychology), Mudd (chemistry and geology), and the newest, Hulings (biology), a $15-million, four-level building completed in 1995. Goodsell Observatory houses a 16-inch visual refractor telescope and an 8-inch photographic refractor telescope. The four-story Center for Mathematics and Computing (CMC) opened in 1993 and offers microcomputing labs open around the clock, with lab assistants available 16 hours a day. Along with six other labs distributed around campus, they provide easy access to a wide range of applications, free printing, and specialized multimedia equipment. The campus has more than 600 advanced workstations and personal computers, all of which are linked to the high-speed campus network. In the residence halls, every room provides Ethernet connections, allowing students to plug in their own computers for access to the campus network and a wide range of other information sources.

Costs

For 2003–04, tuition is $28,362; fees, $165; and room and board, $5868. Travel costs vary. Books, supplies, and personal expenses are estimated to be about $1200.

Financial Aid

Carleton meets the full demonstrated financial need of every student admitted to the College and continues meeting each student's need for four years or until graduation. An on-campus job of 8 to 10 hours per week and a loan opportunity are included in nearly every financial aid package. In 2003–04, about 80 percent of Carleton students received a total of more than $21 million in financial aid or scholarships from all sources. Fifty-eight percent received grant assistance; the average need-based grant was $16,997. The only non-need scholarships the College offers are sixty-five to seventy-five Carleton-sponsored National Merit, National Achievement, and National Hispanic Scholarships.

Faculty

All Carleton classes are taught by faculty members rather than graduate students or teaching assistants. Of the 207 faculty members, 184 are full-time, resulting in a student-faculty ratio of 9:1. Of those full-time faculty members, 95 percent hold the highest degree in their academic field. The average class size is about 18, and the average lab size is 15. Most faculty members also serve as academic advisers.

Student Government

Students are actively involved in the governance of the College. Directly below the Board of Trustees is the College Council, chaired by the President, which is composed of 5 faculty members, 5 students, 5 staff members, 1 trustee, and 1 alumnus. The three major policy committees, Education and Curriculum, Student Life, and the Budget Committee, are also made up of faculty members, students, and staff members. Every student is a member of the Carleton Student Association (CSA). Three officers and 16 senators are elected annually to serve as the CSA Senate, which, among other duties, manages the student activities budget.

Admission Requirements

Carleton normally receives about 4,700 applications for the approximately 500 places available in the first-year class. Admission is based on several considerations: superior academic achievement, personal qualities and interests, participation in extracurricular activities, and potential for development as a student and a graduate of the College. The Admissions Committee weighs all factors to ensure that those students offered admission are not only adequately prepared for the academic work but also will benefit from their total experience at Carleton and will add significantly to the College through their individual talents and personal qualities.

Application and Information

Students interested in applying for admission should contact the Office of Admissions to request an application. Interviews, with either a staff member or an alumni admissions representative, are recommended but not required. A visit to the campus is strongly encouraged. During the academic year, overnight stays, interviews, and class visits are usually available but must be scheduled in advance.

Students who decide that Carleton is their first-choice college are encouraged to apply for early decision by November 15, first round, or by January 15, second round. The application deadline for regular decision is January 15. Regular decision candidates are notified before April 15, and the candidate's reply date is May 1. For more information, prospective students should contact:

Office of Admissions
Carleton College
100 South College Street
Northfield, Minnesota 55057
Telephone: 507-646-4190
800-995-2275 (toll-free)
Fax: 507-646-4526
E-mail: admissions@acs.carleton.edu
World Wide Web: http://www.carleton.edu

An aerial view of the Carleton College campus.

CARLOW COLLEGE

PITTSBURGH, PENNSYLVANIA

The College

Carlow College was founded in 1929 in response to a local need for a Catholic women's college. The mission of the College is to involve people, primarily women, in a process of self-directed lifelong learning that frees them to think clearly and creatively, to discover and to challenge or affirm cultural and aesthetic values, to respond reverently to God and others, and to render competent and compassionate service in personal and professional life. While Carlow makes explicit its strong continuing commitment to the education of women, it welcomes men. The College's mission has been confirmed over the years by the growing number of students who come seeking a solid liberal arts education as well as strong career preparation. In addition to its undergraduate programs, the College offers graduate programs that lead to the Master of Education degree in art education, early childhood education, early childhood supervision, and educational leadership. A graduate program in professional leadership, management and technology, or professional counseling leads to a Master of Science degree. The Carlow Master of Science in Nursing program includes specializations in home health, gerontology, nursing case management, and nursing leadership and provides preparation for the nurse practitioner program.

Current enrollment exceeds 2,200 students. Carlow's students have various backgrounds and come mainly from the Middle Atlantic states; the majority are from western Pennsylvania. About 83 percent of current freshmen are graduates of public high schools, and approximately 65 percent of the freshmen live on campus in the College's modern dormitory. An active Resident Student Association strives to maintain a climate of responsibility and cooperation among the residents. The Commuter Student Association endeavors to serve the needs of commuting students.

Student support services are organized under a leadership model. Placement and career counseling, free professional and peer tutorial services, the Center for Academic Achievement, the Disabilities Service Office, student health, personal counseling programs, and campus ministry are support services available to students. The College has a large group of students involved in community service and volunteerism. Spring break service projects have taken students to Jamaica, the Virgin Islands, Arizona, Arkansas, Ireland, and many other locations. Cocurricular organizations include the Student Government Association, the Commuter Student Association, the *Critical Point* literary magazine, the International Student Association, the *Purple Menace* magazine, Rotoract, Yearbook, and United Black Students. Academically or career-oriented organizations include Alpha Phi Omega (national service/honor society), American Chemical Society, Beta Beta Beta (biology club), Business Leaders of Carlow, the Council for Exceptional Children, Kappa Delta Epsilon (for education majors), Social Work Organization, Student Nurses Association of Pennsylvania, Phi Chi Theta (business fraternity), and the Psychology Club. Special interest groups include the Pep Band, the Gospel choir Blessed, Student Athlete Association, the Theater Group, and Women in Communication (WIC). The College has a bookstore, dining facilities, gymnasium, swimming pool, and a wellness center. The athletic program includes intercollegiate basketball, soccer, softball, tennis, and volleyball as well as a selection of physical education courses, including aerobics, fitness and weight control, martial arts/self-defense, modern dance, water aerobics, weight training, and yoga. Wellness and fitness services include individual health assessment, fitness programming, and nutrition counseling.

Popular campus events include celebrity entertainment, film series, carnivals, Homecoming, Founder's Day, the Christmas concert, St. Patrick's Day celebration and parade, the International Festival, Black History Month events, Women's History Month events, Focus on Women lecture series, and drama productions.

The College's central location gives students opportunities for internships in various businesses and agencies. Students in health-related fields complete their clinical experiences in the many fine teaching hospitals, clinics, and private health-care facilities in the city of Pittsburgh. City buses stop in front of the campus, and campus parking is available for commuting students.

Location

Carlow College is located on a 14-acre campus in the heart of Oakland, one of the nation's biggest college towns and the educational, cultural, and medical center of Pittsburgh. Nine other colleges and universities at which students can cross-register at no additional tuition cost are within walking distance or just minutes away by bus. Schenley Park, Carnegie Institute and Museum, Phipps Conservatory, Carnegie Music and Lecture halls, the Scaife Galleries, and the Oakland shopping district are all a short walk from the campus. Downtown Pittsburgh—one of the nation's largest corporate-headquarters cities—is only a 10-minute bus ride away. Greater Pittsburgh International Airport is a 30-minute drive from Carlow, and exits from the interstates are about a quarter of a mile from the campus.

Majors and Degrees

Carlow College grants the undergraduate degrees of Bachelor of Arts, Bachelor of Science, Bachelor of Science in Nursing, and Bachelor of Social Work. Majors are accounting, art, art/art education, art/art history, art with a certificate in art therapy preparation, art/computer animation, art/graphic design, biology (with concentrations in forensic medical and legal investigations/autopsy specialization, human biology, molecular cell and biotechnology, and organismal/ecological), business management, business management/communication, chemistry, communication studies, computer science, creative writing, early childhood education, elementary education, English, health science (available to students who have previously earned an associate degree), history, human resource management and technology, information systems management, international business, liberal studies, mathematics, nursing, philosophy, professional writing, professional writing/business, psychology, scientific/medical marketing, social work, sociology, sociology–criminal justice, Spanish, special education, theology, and theology/psychology. An independent major, designed by the student, may also be arranged. Certification programs are offered in perfusion technology (biology majors only), school nursing, and secondary education (biology, chemistry, communication, English, general science, history, mathematics, and sociology). Preprofessional programs include dentistry, law, medicine, optometry, osteopathy, pharmacy, podiatry, and veterinary medicine. The College offers 3-2 programs in engineering in three areas: biology/environmental engineering, chemistry/chemical engineering, and mathematics/engineering. In addition, Carlow now offers a 2-2 program in athletic training, 2-3 programs in occupational therapy and physician assistant studies, a 3-2 program in environmental science, a 3-3 program in physical therapy, and a 3-3 B.A./J.D. law program.

Academic Programs

Carlow's primary concern is the development of the student as a lifelong learner. To this end, members of the Carlow community—students, faculty, and staff—try to help one another recognize the integrity and value of each person in the daily life and work of the College. The academic programs are broad and flexible, including opportunities for double majors, single majors with certification in education, minors, certificate programs, and changes of major. Transfer students are accepted into all programs. Persons already possessing a degree may be admitted to a second degree or certification program. The Carlow curriculum is based in the liberal arts, with significant emphasis on career preparation.

The College curriculum operates on the two-semester system, August to December and January to May. Summer sessions, a variable number of weeks in length, are offered every year. Most courses carry 3 credits (laboratory courses, among others, carry 4 credits). Students normally take five courses each semester. Each student must demonstrate basic competence in English composition, speech and interpersonal communication, reading comprehension, and mathematics. Required of all students is one course each in a lab science, history, literature, mathematics, social/behavioral science (such as psychology or sociology), theology, fine arts, philosophy, women's studies, and political science or economics, as well as one global perspective course. Students are also required to take an interdisciplinary course, which is selected from a variety of subject areas. Students in nursing, education, social work, psychology, management, and perfusion technology are required to do fieldwork as part of their program. Field placements and internships are guaranteed and encouraged in all areas of study. An honors program is open to eligible students. After the first semester of the freshman year, one course per semester (outside of the major) may be taken on a pass-fail basis. Some courses may be challenged, for credit or exemption, by passing an examination. CLEP general exam credits may be used for this purpose as well.

The College gives women and men the opportunity to return to the classroom at various stages of their lives. Adult learners may enroll in full-time and part-time degree programs, noncredit enrichment courses, seminars, and workshops. Scheduling options include day, evening, accelerated, weekend, and online courses.

Off-Campus Programs

After the first semester of the freshman year, full-time students may cross-register for one course per semester at any of the nine other area colleges and universities that are members of the Pittsburgh Council on Higher Education. There is no additional tuition cost for cross-registration.

Academic Facilities

Grace Library, a five-level multipurpose learning center in the heart of the campus, currently contains more than 100,000 books, subscribes to over 350 print journals, and offers access to more than 4,500 online journals. The library houses the offices of the President and Vice President for Academic Affairs. The Media Center, the Center for Academic Achievement, mail room, bookstore, Academic Affairs, Career Services, Copy Center, the International Poetry Forum, College Archives, and computer laboratories are also located here. Kresge Theatre, a 300-seat lecture/demonstration hall, and the Mellon Galleries—where students, faculty members, and local artists display their works—are located on the fifth level. Curran Hall is a facility for the nursing division and includes specially designed nursing skills labs and conference and seminar rooms. Frances Warde Hall houses the education division, art labs, student affairs offices, and the campus café. Antonian Hall houses the 1,000-seat Sister Rosemary Heyl Theatre, the social sciences and fine arts departments, and classrooms, as well as administrative offices for admissions, financial aid, advising, registrar, and student accounts. The cafeteria and the Carlow College Campus School (grades nursery through 8) are located in Tiernan Hall. St. Joseph Hall contains the gymnasium, fitness center, and swimming pool; and Aquinas Hall houses classrooms, the humanities department, the International Student Center, faculty and staff offices, and the Carlow Campus Montessori School. Carlow's A. J. Palumbo Hall for Science and Technology is home to the Dr. William A. Urrichio Division of Natural Sciences and Mathematics. This 95,000-square-foot complex contains state-of-the-art teaching/research laboratories in physics, organic and advanced chemistry, genetics, cell biology, and gross anatomy; an herbarium to store dry plant specimens; a greenhouse; an amphitheater for scientific presentations; and the Bayer Children's Science Learning Laboratory.

Carlow College's campus computer network features Internet accounts and e-mail addresses, network and Internet access from any location on campus, remote e-mail and Internet access for home users, and one network port per pillow in the residence hall. Carlow also offers a comprehensive e-portfolio to all undergraduate students to record their personal, academic, and professional development goals.

Costs

Tuition for 2003–04 was $14,776 for full-time students. Room and board charges for the year were $6110 for double occupancy. Fees totaled $488.

Financial Aid

Financial aid in the form of grants, scholarships, loans, and student employment is available to eligible applicants. More than 90 percent of all full-time students receive some type of financial assistance. Academic and/or leadership scholarships ranging from $1000 to full tuition are available for qualified students. The College expects that most aid recipients assume a portion of their expenses through loans and/or part-time employment. Job opportunities are available on campus in a wide variety of positions, and students are placed, whenever possible, in positions that coincide with their skills and interests. Basketball, soccer, softball, tennis, and volleyball scholarships are also available.

Faculty

The most valuable resource at the disposal of the Carlow student is a faculty whose primary commitment is to the education of undergraduates. The student-faculty ratio is 12:1, and faculty members are readily available to help plan individualized programs of study, to provide assistance relating to field placements and internships, and to assist in career preparation. The student's major adviser is normally a faculty member in the department. There are currently 229 faculty members, of whom 77 are full-time. A number of professional persons from the Pittsburgh area are among the part-time faculty members.

Student Government

All registered students are members of the Student Government Association (SGA). Through the SGA, students act as equal participants with the administration, faculty, and staff in general governance. The SGA promotes the general welfare of the students and is the advocate to ensure that the academic, social, and spiritual needs of students are met. SGA is empowered to charter all student organizations.

Admission Requirements

Generally, Carlow seeks applicants who rank in the upper 40 percent of their graduating class, who have attained at least a B average, and who have followed an academic or college-preparatory curriculum. Applicants are evaluated on the basis of their secondary school record, class rank, and scores on the SAT I or ACT. The Committee on Admissions recognizes that school curricula vary greatly and always gives careful consideration to the application of an able student whose course work or grading scale is more challenging or whose preparation differs from the traditional program. A personal interview is strongly recommended but not required. Overnight visits, a day of classes, campus tours, and meals, are available and are strongly encouraged. Throughout the year, the College sponsors programs that give candidates the opportunity to tour the campus and meet faculty and staff members and Carlow students.

Application and Information

Although Carlow subscribes to the rolling admission plan, high school students are encouraged to submit an application early in the first semester of the senior year. Students interested in early notification should apply by September 30. Notification of the admission decision for early notification candidates is made by October 30.

Students may apply online or request an application form by contacting:

Director of Admissions
Carlow College
3333 Fifth Avenue
Pittsburgh, Pennsylvania 15213
Telephone: 412-578-6059
800-333-CARLOW (toll-free)
E-mail: admissions@carlow.edu
World Wide Web: http://www.carlow.edu

CARNEGIE MELLON UNIVERSITY

Carnegie Mellon

PITTSBURGH, PENNSYLVANIA

The University

First envisioned in 1900 by steel magnate and philanthropist Andrew Carnegie, Carnegie Mellon University has steadily built upon its foundations of excellence and innovation to become one of America's leading universities. The University's unique approach to education—giving students the opportunity to become experts in their chosen field while studying a broad range of course work across disciplines—creates leaders and problem solvers for the changing marketplace of today and tomorrow.

Students in this private coeducational university come from all fifty states and more than 50 countries. Each year, Carnegie Mellon enrolls a diverse freshman class of approximately 1,350 students. The total undergraduate population is 5,347. Students come from a variety of different social and cultural backgrounds and also represent a wide range of academic and artistic interests. Approximately 10 percent of the student body identifies with an ethnic minority population such as African American, Hispanic/Latino American, or Native American.

Carnegie Mellon spans the best of both worlds. Its traditional 103-acre campus is located within the Pittsburgh city limits. Student activities include more than 130 clubs and organizations, varsity and intramural sports, fraternities and sororities, and student government. The University Center features state-of-the-art recreational and entertainment facilities. Off campus, students can take advantage of three culturally active neighborhoods within walking distance, the largest public park in Pittsburgh, urban and suburban shopping and sightseeing, professional sports, museums, art galleries, amusement parks, and more.

Approximately 75 percent of students live in the University's twelve traditional residence halls, fifteen houses, ten apartment buildings, thirteen fraternity houses, and five sorority houses. Freshmen are required to live on campus, and housing is guaranteed for four years, provided students remain in the University housing system.

Carnegie Mellon students come away from their undergraduate experience poised to be trendsetters, whether in the business world, the art community, or graduate school. Students not only gain the knowledge necessary to succeed professionally, but they also learn how to maximize their creativity, intellectual playfulness, and analytical skills in order to survive in an ever-changing global environment. The University strives to produce graduates who are adaptable, resourceful, and independent—graduates who communicate effectively, strive to be leaders, and understand their professional and social responsibilities.

In addition to bachelor's degrees, Carnegie Mellon offers master's and doctoral degrees.

Location

Carnegie Mellon is located in the Oakland neighborhood of Pittsburgh, 5 miles from the downtown area. As home to several of the city's colleges, universities, museums, and hospitals, Oakland offers many activities and resources to area students. While Carnegie Mellon has the collegiate feel of a suburban campus, the surrounding Pittsburgh community provides all of the cultural and social advantages of the big city. The University is 1½ hours from the mountains, which have some of the best skiing in the East, and a short plane ride away from many major metropolitan areas, including Boston, New York City, Chicago, Philadelphia, and Washington, D.C.

Majors and Degrees

Undergraduate majors at Carnegie Mellon include business administration, computer science, engineering (biomedical engineering, chemical engineering, civil and environmental engineering, electrical and computer engineering, engineering and public policy, materials science and engineering, and mechanical engineering), fine and performing arts (architecture, art, design, drama, and music), information systems, liberal arts and professional studies (economics, English, history, information systems, modern languages, philosophy, political science, psychology, social and decision sciences, and statistics), and the sciences (biological sciences, chemistry, mathematical sciences, and physics). The Bachelor of Humanities and Arts and Bachelor of Science and Arts degrees are available, as are many interdepartmental majors.

Academic Program

There is no core curriculum at Carnegie Mellon; the only required classes are Computer Skills Workshop and a first-year writing course. Each college has its own requirements for graduation.

Students at Carnegie Mellon have the freedom to design courses of study that cross over majors and disciplines. In fact, some students have double majors, minors, or concentrations in areas other than their principal major. It is not unusual to find an engineering student with a double major in music or an English major with a minor in business administration.

The Bachelor of Humanities and Arts and Bachelor of Science and Arts degree programs are unique nonperformance-based programs at Carnegie Mellon that allow students to pursue interdisciplinary programs in the fine arts and either the humanities and the social sciences or pure sciences. Other special programs include Army, Navy, and Air Force ROTC; a self-defined major and interdepartmental major options in the College of Humanities and Social Sciences; prelaw and premedicine advising programs; and five-year combined bachelor's/master's degree programs.

Carnegie Mellon also has nearly unlimited opportunities for students to participate in undergraduate research, sometimes as early as the second semester of the freshman year. Many departments offer research training courses and academic year and summer research programs. Students can work on research in groups, individually with a professor, or independently through Carnegie Mellon's Small Undergraduate Research Grant (SURG) program.

Off-Campus Programs

Carnegie Mellon students can take one course per semester at any of the following colleges and universities in Pittsburgh for full credit: the University of Pittsburgh, Carlow College, Chatham College, Duquesne University, La Roche College, Point Park College, Robert Morris University, Pittsburgh Theological Seminary, and the Community College of Allegheny County.

Carnegie Mellon has several study-abroad programs, including university exchange programs in Chile, Singapore, Mexico, Japan, and Switzerland. Students may also take advantage of study-abroad opportunities through their department or through another university.

Academic Facilities

Carnegie Mellon has a 103-acre main campus with a few outlying research buildings. The campus contains more than fifty academic and administrative buildings and three libraries. The Hunt, Engineering and Science, and Mellon Institute Libraries contain more than 906,000 volumes and 3,889 periodicals. An international online resource sharing system and reciprocal borrowing between Carnegie Mellon and other local universities provide students with almost unlimited library resources.

There are thousands of computers on campus, including Macintosh, IBM, and UNIX systems, which are housed in public clusters in almost every academic building and residence hall. In addition, most departments have their own computer clusters for students to use. For students with their own computers, all of the residence hall rooms are wired to the Andrew network, Carnegie Mellon's high-speed computer network linking the campus and providing access to the outside world. Carnegie Mellon was the first university campus to offer wireless networking in all administrative and academic buildings. Wireless Andrew, the largest installation of its type anywhere, connects thousands of students, faculty members, and staff members across campus.

In addition to academic facilities, Carnegie Mellon features the University Center with food court and recreational facilities, the historic Kresge Theater for Performing Arts, studio theaters and blackbox, art galleries, abundant studio and rehearsal space, a gymnasium, and numerous research laboratories. The Purnell Center for the Arts opened in fall 1999. The campus also borders the largest public park in Pittsburgh, Schenley Park.

Costs

Carnegie Mellon's costs for the 2003–04 academic year were tuition, $29,190, and room, board, and fees, $8560. The cost of books, supplies, and personal expenses was estimated at $2160. The total cost was $39,910. International students must also pay an additional $1980 for required health insurance.

Financial Aid

Carnegie Mellon is a need-blind institution; students' personal financial information is not considered in admission decisions. More than 60 percent of students receive some form of financial assistance.

Carnegie Mellon uses Federal Methodology to determine financial aid eligibility. The forms required to apply for financial assistance are the Free Application for Federal Student Aid (FAFSA), the Carnegie Mellon Form, parental W-2s, and both parental and student tax returns. Financial aid packages usually include a combination of loans, grants, and work-study allowances.

Four merit-based scholarships are offered, with awards ranging from $1000 to the cost of half tuition. Every student is eligible for merit-based scholarship consideration with no separate application process. Students are also encouraged to apply for outside scholarships as a source of aid.

Faculty

Carnegie Mellon has more than 1,200 teaching and research faculty members and a student-faculty ratio of 10:1. Faculty members are practicing professionals at the forefront of their respective fields. More often than not, faculty members teach both undergraduate and graduate courses. Carnegie Mellon's classes are taught by faculty members, not teaching assistants. Professors, instructors, and lecturers are in the classroom, lab, studio, or workplace creating new knowledge on a daily basis and passing that knowledge on to their students. Undergraduates have the opportunity to work on groundbreaking research projects with award-winning faculty members, many times one-on-one, through assistantships, internships, work-study positions, and extracurricular organizations.

Student Government

Carnegie Mellon's Student Senate is composed of representatives from each college at Carnegie Mellon and exists to promote the welfare of the campus community, distribute budget funds to student groups, provide a liaison between students and the administration, and inform the student body of proposals and changes.

Admission Requirements

Carnegie Mellon looks for strong students, both academically and socially, who have a wide range of interests and activities. There are no minimum grade requirements or standardized test scores, although most of Carnegie Mellon's students tend to have strong test scores and be at the top of their classes. The University uses standardized test scores, including the SAT I or ACT and SAT II Subject Tests, high school performance, evidence of leadership, honors and awards earned, and extracurricular activities to make admission decisions. Recommendations from a guidance counselor and a teacher are required along with a personal statement and essay.

Carnegie Mellon strives to build a class of students that is racially, socially, economically, and geographically diverse. Students come from all fifty states and more than fifty countries, and the University is committed to recruiting students from traditionally underrepresented backgrounds, including African Americans, Hispanic/Latino Americans, and Native Americans. Transfer students are also welcome.

Application and Information

Carnegie Mellon has three types of decision plans: early admission, early decision, and regular decision.

Early admission is for high school juniors who wish to skip their senior year to go directly to college. In addition to academic strength, early admission candidates must display maturity and have strong teacher and guidance counselor recommendations. The application deadline for early admission is January 1 (December 1 for fine arts), and candidates are notified of a decision between March 15 and April 15.

Early decision is for students who declare Carnegie Mellon as their first choice. The early decision plan is a binding agreement; if accepted, students are expected to enroll. The University offers two early decision plans. The deadline for Early Decision I is November 15 (November 1 for fine arts), and candidates are notified of a decision by December 15. The deadline for Early Decision II is November 15, and candidates are notified by January 15. There is no early decision for drama, and Early Decision II is not available for art, design, or music.

Regular decision is the most popular plan. Applications are due by January 1 (December 1 for fine arts), and notification occurs between March 15 and April 15.

Students interested in learning more about Carnegie Mellon can arrange to visit the campus. Throughout most of the year, the University offers group information sessions, campus tours, and personal interviews, which are recommended for admission. High school juniors can participate in Carnegie Mellon's six-week precollege programs.

Group information sessions and interviews are available for students who cannot come to Pittsburgh. University representatives travel across the United States during the fall of every year. The Office of Admission can provide more information on these options.

For more information about Carnegie Mellon, students should contact:

Carnegie Mellon Office of Admission
5000 Forbes Avenue
Pittsburgh, Pennsylvania 15213-3890
Telephone: 412-268-2082
Fax: 412-268-7838
E-mail: undergraduate-admissions@andrew.cmu.edu
WWW: http://www.cmu.edu/enrollment/admission/

Carnegie Mellon University, located in Pittsburgh, Pennsylvania, is one of America's leading universities.

CARROLL COLLEGE

WAUKESHA, WISCONSIN

The College

Carroll College was chartered by the territorial legislature of Wisconsin in 1846. Carroll College is affiliated with the Presbyterian Church (U.S.A.) but is nonsectarian and ecumenical.

The College realizes that personalized education is the special province of a small college and recognizes the variety of students' individual needs and preferences. Carroll's student body is diverse, with representation from thirty-two states and twenty-seven countries. The campus has more than 2,000 full-time men and women, as well as more than 700 part-time students. In addition, there are more than 250 graduate students on the Carroll campus.

Many opportunities exist for cocurricular involvement. Three fraternities and four sororities draw participation from about 13 percent of the students. A broad variety of special interest organizations provide a full program of campus activities in addition to the all-campus social, intellectual, and athletic events that are scheduled throughout the year. The College's facilities for recreation and athletics include the Van Male Fieldhouse, which has a basketball court; an indoor track; indoor facilities for badminton, tennis, and volleyball; and an Olympic-size pool. The adjacent Ganfield Gymnasium provides additional space for athletics and recreation. A football field, a soccer field, and a softball diamond are also available.

In addition to the bachelor's degrees Carroll offers, the College also grants the master's degree in education, software engineering, and physical therapy.

Location

The College is located in the city of Waukesha, a residential community of 64,000 people, which is 18 miles west of Milwaukee and 100 miles north of Chicago. The College's proximity to these two major urban centers and to the settings associated with Wisconsin's famous outdoor sports and leisure activities provides Carroll students with numerous opportunities for recreation, entertainment, and enrichment.

Majors and Degrees

Carroll College grants the B.A., B.S., and B.S.N. degrees. Areas of study include accounting; actuarial science; art; athletic training; biochemistry; biology; business administration (finance, human resources, management, management information systems, marketing, small business management); chemistry; coaching; communication; computer science (information systems, network applications, software engineering); criminal justice; education (early childhood, elementary, secondary, adaptive); English; environmental science; exercise science; forensic science; geography; graphic communication; history; human biology; international relations; journalism; marine biology; mathematics; music; nursing; organizational leadership; photography; physical education; physical therapy; politics; print management; psychology; public relations; religious studies; self-designed major; sociology; Spanish; and theater arts.

Academic Program

The College currently operates on a semester calendar. All students must complete 128 credits with a C average or better. A major, generally consisting of 40 credits, must be completed. General education requirements include the First Year Seminar, English, liberal studies distribution courses, and a capstone experience. B.A. students must take two years of a modern language or the equivalent. B.S. students must take mathematics and either a computer science or logic course. Students may also select a second major or they may select a minor, which generally requires 16 to 28 credits. The honors program offers intensive sections of courses in the arts and sciences for academically talented students.

Advanced placement or credit may be granted to students who have completed the appropriate College Board Advanced Placement examinations. Credit may be granted for a score at or above the 75th percentile on the humanities, natural science, or social science general examination of the College-Level Examination Program (CLEP). Scores on CLEP subject examinations may also qualify to be approved for credit. A total of not more than 48 credit hours may be awarded through CLEP general and subject examinations.

Off-Campus Programs

The New Cultural Experiences Program gives all Carroll students the opportunity to study in a different cultural setting. Students may plan an individual program or participate in a planned group experience involving other students and Carroll faculty members. Group experiences are offered in locations such as Australia, Belize, England, and Japan, and countries in Europe and Africa. Other off-campus programs include the Washington Semester, the United Nations Semester, and the Junior Year Abroad. In addition, career internships are provided in the Milwaukee-Waukesha area for students interested in gaining practical work experience in their proposed career field. All of these programs carry degree credit, the amount depends upon the nature and duration of the experience.

Academic Facilities

The College library houses more than 150,000 volumes, 18,000 microforms, and 400 periodicals. The Department of Education is in the Barstow Building with the Modern Language and Communication Departments. Rankin Hall houses the Departments of Biology, Psychology, and Religious Studies, as well as the psychology laboratories. Maxon Hall houses the Departments of Geography and Mathematics. It also contains the laboratories for advanced chemistry, the geography laboratory with independent-study booths and audiovisual instruments, a darkroom, a cartography laboratory, a map library, and a National Weather Service observation station. The chemistry and physics laboratories are in Lowry Hall. All science laboratories are provided with up-to-date equipment. The newly renovated Main Hall houses classrooms for all academic areas. MacAllister Hall is home to the Departments of English, History, Politics, and Philosophy and houses the Norman FitzGerald Civil War Collection.

The Shattuck Music Center houses a recital hall that seats 150, an auditorium that seats 1,350, and a Schantz seventy-two-stop pipe organ. The Department of Music has a large band-practice room, teaching studios, a multisensing room, a computerized music laboratory, and classrooms. The Humphrey Building houses the Art Department and Humphrey Memorial Chapel. The College's physical therapy program is located adjacent to the College's athletic complex. A new, state-of-the-art nursing lab is found in the lower level of the Theatre Arts Building.

Costs

For 2003–04, the tuition was approximately $17,020, and room and board were $5360.

Financial Aid

Approximately 98 percent of Carroll's students receive some form of financial aid. Aid is based on need, as determined by the U.S. Department of Education's Free Application for Federal Student Aid (FAFSA), as well as on scholastic ability and achievement. Generally, students receive a package consisting of a scholarship, a grant, a loan, and/or employment.

Various merit scholarships are available to students. Merit scholarships range from $20,000 to $30,000 over four years and are determined by a student's ACT or SAT I scores and class rank. Students who attend high schools that do not rank are not excluded from consideration for any academic scholarships. Additional scholarships are awarded to qualified students who are interested in music, journalism, nursing, theater, politics, business, physical therapy, computer science, international relations, history, art, math, or the sciences. Students should contact the Office of Admission for details.

Faculty

The student-faculty ratio at Carroll is approximately 16:1. More than 85 percent of faculty members hold a doctorate in their specialized area of study. There are more than 100 full-time faculty members at Carroll.

Student Government

Through election to the Student Senate and College Activities Board, students have responsibility for nonacademic matters affecting their lives at the College. In addition, there is voting student representation on all College committees, and there are student observers on the Board of Trustees.

Admission Requirements

Carroll's admission procedure is intended to ensure academic and personal success for accepted students. Each candidate is evaluated individually; evidence of the interest in and ability to do college-level work is important. The College exercises careful selection, but no candidate is disqualified because of race, color, religion, sex, national origin, age, disability, sexual orientation, or veteran status.

Application and Information

To be considered, each candidate for freshman admission must submit the following materials: a completed application for admission; a transcript from an accredited high school showing progress toward, or completion of, 15 units of work and graduation; a satisfactory personal evaluation from the high school; and scores on the SAT I or ACT. Transfer students must submit a transcript from every college attended previously and a statement of good standing. Admission decisions are made on a rolling basis until the class is filled. There are no deadlines, but early application is recommended.

Admission to the College may be granted following the completion of three years of high school work, provided that the high school indicates that this is in the applicant's best interest. The candidate may or may not have completed the course work required for high school graduation at the time of admission, but he or she must show unusual promise and achievement.

For more information about Carroll College, prospective students should contact:

Admission Office
Carroll College
100 North East Avenue
Waukesha, Wisconsin 53186
Telephone: 262-524-7220
800-CARROLL (toll-free)
E-mail: ccinfo@cc.edu
World Wide Web: http://www.cc.edu

CARROLL COLLEGE
HELENA, MONTANA

The College

Few colleges today are able to steer students toward their dreams as well as Carroll College can. With 1,450 students and an average class size of 20, Carroll's students receive rare personalized attention from professors who are always available to assist them with their academic and personal issues as well as their applications for jobs, research internships, and graduate schools. Carroll provides outstanding choices through its excellent academic offerings, specializing in not only a broad liberal arts education but also solid preprofessional programs and firm preparation for medical, law, and graduate school. For students seeking to get the most from their educational experience, Carroll's unique Honors Scholars Program fosters academic, social, and cultural excellence. Carroll students enjoy active and enriching social lives on campus as well.

In the science field, Carroll's professors opt for novel, student-led experiments into new areas that produce scientifically meaningful results. Students contribute to their field before even entering the job market. Biology and chemistry students performing original field work at Carroll have discovered new species, uncovered environmental contamination on public lands, and have been published in prestigious professional scientific journals. Biology and chemistry labs offer the most up-to-date equipment. While some schools reserve such resources for graduate students only, Carroll's undergrads use the most advanced facilities and tools of the trade everyday.

In fall 2003, *U.S. News and World Report* ranked Carroll as the fourth-best "Comprehensive Colleges–Bachelor's" in the West. This was Carroll's tenth year in the top ten for its category.

A member of NAIA Division I college athletics, the Carroll Fighting Saints teams are recognized as proven winners. In football, the Saints were crowned the 2002 NAIA national champions and won the 2000, 2001, and 2002 Frontier Conference championships. The men's basketball team ascended to the 2002 national playoffs and won the 2001–2002 Frontier Conference championship crown. In volleyball, the Saints were the 2002 Frontier Conference champions and 2001 Conference tournament victors. The women's basketball team had two players named as 2002 Daktronics–NAIA Division I Women's Basketball Scholar Athletes. The 2003 Women's Basketball Coaches Association ranked Carroll sixth out of the 275 NAIA institutions for combined overall grade point average of its team members.

Founded in 1909, Carroll College is a private, Catholic college, accredited by the Northwest Association of Schools and Colleges. The College is a member of the National Association of Independent Colleges and Universities, the American Council on Education, the Council of Independent Colleges, the Association of Catholic Colleges and Universities, and the Western Independent College Fund.

Location

Surrounded by epic views of unspoiled wilderness, Carroll students enjoy easy access to outdoor sports and a clean and healthy lifestyle year-round. Helena, the state capital, nestles in the heart of southwestern Montana's beautiful Rocky Mountains. Just a few miles from the Continental Divide and the headwaters of the Missouri River, Helena stands about halfway between Glacier and Yellowstone National Parks. Its location offers convenient and quick access to outdoor recreational opportunities, including downhill and cross-country skiing, hiking, mountain biking, world-class fishing, white-water rafting, canoeing, camping, and rock climbing.

The Great Divide Ski Area is about 45 minutes from the campus, and five other world-class ski resorts are within 2 hours of Helena. For those who love the water, Canyon Ferry, Holter, Hauser, and Park Lakes are short and scenic rides from the campus. Gates of the Mountains, a stop on the Lewis and Clark trail, offers boat tours throughout the summer. With Mount Helena City Park just 2 miles from the campus, students can enjoy study breaks on trails winding through wildflowers, evergreens, and the mountain's stony cliffs.

Majors and Degrees

Carroll College offers a four-year Bachelor of Arts degree program. Its majors and areas of concentration include: accounting; biology; biology for secondary education; business administration, with concentrations in economics, finance, and management; chemistry; chemistry for secondary education; civil engineering; communication studies; communication studies for secondary education; computer science; elementary education; engineering (see below); English; English for secondary education; English writing; environmental studies, with concentrations in science, community, and culture; ethics and value studies; French; health and physical education, with concentrations in community health and sports management; history; history for secondary education; international relations; mathematics for secondary education; mathematics, with a cognate concentration; nursing; performing arts/theater, with concentrations in acting/directing and performing arts technology; philosophy; political science; political science for secondary education; psychology; public administration; public relations, with concentrations in business and journalism; social science for secondary education; sociology; Spanish; Spanish education (K–12); teaching English to speakers of other languages (TESOL); TESOL (K–12); and theology, with concentrations in contextual and systematic.

Carroll offers a 3-2 program in engineering, with affiliations to Columbia, Gonzaga, Montana State, Montana Tech, and the Universities of Minnesota, Notre Dame, and Southern California. Under the 3-2 program, students attend Carroll for three years and then transfer to an affiliate school to complete specialized studies. Upon completion of the program, students receive two degrees—one from Carroll and one from the affiliate school.

Carroll offers preprofessional programs in dentistry, law, medicine, optometry, pharmacy, physical therapy, and veterinary medicine. Special programs and course offerings also include: anthropology; Carroll Intensive Language Institute (CILI); cooperative education and internships; the Honors Scholars Program; language, including French, German, Greek, Latin, linguistics, and Spanish; music; physics; military science (ROTC); and a study-abroad program.

Carroll also offers various two-year Associate of Arts degrees.

Academic Program

The academic year consists of fall and spring semesters and a limited summer term. Carroll's Bachelor of Arts degree program means all students study the arts, sciences, humanities, and social sciences for at least four of their eight semesters at Carroll.

Off-Campus Programs

Internships and hands-on experience form the cornerstones of the Carroll educational experience. These real-world experiences-for-credit help students choose their majors, focus on their future careers, discover what job paths to avoid, strengthen their resumes, and develop marketable skills. Carroll students pursue internships in federal, state, county, and city government; the legal system; local businesses; engineering firms; schools; and nonprofit agencies. Accounting students do not just crunch numbers in class; they also work in accounting firms to learn what the profession is all about. The editor and co-editor of the student newspaper, *Prospector*, create each issue from the ground up, from planning and assigning stories to editing, designing, and printing. Civil engineering students train on the same equipment used in the industry and work alongside engineers in private firms and in government.

Study-abroad opportunities round out Carroll's academic offerings. Since 1999, Carroll has provided students professor-led study-abroad opportunities to Belize, Chile, Ghana, Greece, Hong Kong, Ireland, Italy, Mexico, Swaziland, Thailand, Togo, and Vietnam. Students have also studied for full semesters in Australia, Canada, Chile, England, France, Germany, Ireland, Italy, Japan, Mexico, Scotland, Spain, Venezuela, and the Semester at Sea. Carroll also offers exchange programs with American State College, England; Cheju National University, Korea; Kumamoto-Gakuen University, Japan; National University of Ireland, Galway, Ireland; University of Aberdeen, Scotland; University of Caen, France; and University of East Anglia, England. Carroll's Study Abroad Office also arranges for students to perform independent study abroad at colleges and universities worldwide.

Academic Facilities

The Fortin Science Center provides classrooms and chemistry, organic biology, and engineering laboratories with the latest analytical tools, all specifically designed for hands-on student use. Completed in spring 2003, the College's new 4,290-square-foot Civil Engineering Laboratory houses a laboratory, a twenty-four-seat classroom, and extensive materials, hydraulics, machinery, and structures-testing capabilities. A network-affiliated television station is located on campus and includes a multimedia classroom. The College's spacious Arthur Vining Davis dance studio is equipped with a state-of-the-art spring floor for dancers' comfort, safety, and enhanced performance. Carroll's Corette Library houses an extensive collection of volumes, periodicals, and electronic research and referral systems. Nelson Stadium, built in 2001, is home to Carroll football and soccer and offers indoor seating and suites.

Of the College's four residence halls, the new South Hall, completed in fall 2003, offers juniors and seniors suite-style, apartment-type living with full kitchens and the most modern amenities. Also completed in fall 2003, the new, fully renovated Fitness Center in the Carroll Physical Education Center features the most up-to-date cardiovascular equipment, a comprehensive set of Hammer Strength equipment, group exercise bikes, and Broadcast Vision Fitness Cinema equipment for viewing television and listening to music with digital headphones.

Classrooms, laboratories, and residential halls are networked for access to the campus computer network, the Internet, and e-mail. Computer labs are located throughout the campus.

Costs

For the 2003–04 academic year, Carroll's tuition and fees totaled $14,466; room and board fees were $5810. Other general personal expenses include books, supplies, and transportation.

Financial Aid

In the 2003–04 academic year, Carroll awarded an average $11,000 financial aid package to 90 percent of its full-time, degree-seeking students in the form of College-sponsored scholarships, Federal Work-Study, and student loan programs, including Federal Pell Grants, Federal Perkins Loans, Federal Stafford Student Loans, Federal PLUS loans for parents, state grants, and Federal Supplemental Educational Opportunity Grants. Carroll's merit scholarships range from $2500 to $7500 annually.

More information on Carroll scholarships is available at the Web site address listed below. To receive priority consideration for scholarships, students must have a complete admission file by March 1. Carroll requires students interested in need-based financial assistance to submit the Free Application for Federal Student Aid (FAFSA), available from high school couselors or at http://www.fafsa.ed.gov, as early as possible after Jan. 1.

Faculty

At Carroll, 75 full-time and 50 adjunct faculty members help provide the resources, personal support, and academic challenge necessary to prepare students for academic and personal success. With an impressive 13:1 student-faculty ratio and modest class sizes (64 percent of classes have 20 or fewer students), Carroll offers students the opportunity to establish close relationships with their instructors and receive personalized attention from professors who maintain a sincere interest in their students' achievements.

Carroll's faculty is consistently recognized for its excellence. Ten professors currently on campus have earned Fulbright Scholarships. Professor and founder of Carroll's Environmental Studies Program, Dr. John Hart is a leader in the development and worldwide promotion of the United Nations' Earth Charter, an international document on environmental sustainability. Shirley Baker, Carroll's Director for International Programs, recently returned from ten months in Indonesia where she served as a Fulbright scholar and senior lecturer affiliated with the State University for Islamic Studies in Jakarta. History professor, Dr. Robert Swartout, has served as Montana's Honorary Consul for the Republic of Korea to the State of Montana since 1998. In June 2003, Dr. Swartout was reappointed to a second five-year term. Dr. Gerald Shields, Carroll's James J. Manion Endowed Chair of Biology, and Dr. John Addis, biology professor, recently discovered three new animal species. In 2001, psychology professor, Dr. Anne Perkins, was awarded a patent on her mathematical formula for assessing libido in all male mammals, including humans.

Student Government

The Associated Students of Carroll College helps students communicate with the administration and make important decisions about campus activities and student life. Each class (freshman, sophomore, junior, and senior) elects its own student officers, with each vice president serving as a student senator. Carroll's Student Senate consists of elected representatives from each floor of the residence halls, off-campus students, and nontraditional students. Students may also serve on a variety of committees.

Admission Requirements

Degree candidates are those who have applied through the Office of Admission for a course of study leading to the Bachelor of Arts degree. Degree candidates may be enrolled on a full-time or part-time basis. Admission decisions are based upon a student's performance during high school, verbal and quantitative skills, a secondary school report, letters of recommendation, demonstrated commitment to intellectual achievement, and performance on standardized college entrance examinations.

When applying for admission, candidates must submit the application form, official transcripts from the high school and all colleges previously attended, a secondary school report and/or a letter of recommendation, ACT or SAT I scores, and a $35 nonrefundable application fee, which is waived for applications submitted before December 31. Transfer students who have successfully completed more than 30 college semester credits with at least a C (2.5) grade average are not required to submit high school transcripts or ACT or SAT I scores.

Application and Information

Carroll College has a rolling admission policy with a priority admission deadline of March 1. Within three weeks of submission of all materials, the Office of Admission notifies candidates of acceptance, conditional acceptance, or denial. Students should note that late submission of material may jeopardize financial aid awards and course registration. Students can apply online at the address listed below.

For application forms or more information, students should contact:

Director of Admission
Carroll College
1601 North Benton Avenue
Helena, Montana 59625-0002
Telephone: 406-447-4384
800-992-3648 (toll-free)
E-mail:admissionstaff@carroll.edu
World Wide Web: http://www.carroll.edu

St. Charles Hall, the historic cornerstone of Carroll's campus, is known as "The Rock."

CARSON-NEWMAN COLLEGE

JEFFERSON CITY, TENNESSEE

The College

Founded in 1851 by Tennessee Baptists, Carson-Newman (C-N) is a private, coeducational, Christian liberal arts college. The College has an enrollment of 2,000 undergraduate and 200 graduate students. The average class size is 16 students, and the male-female ratio is 1:1. Each fall, Carson-Newman enrolls approximately 420 freshmen and 160 transfers. While Carson-Newman students come primarily from the Southeastern states, forty-four states are represented.

In addition to its outstanding academics, C-N also provides many opportunities for student involvement in various clubs and organizations, nationally recognized varsity athletics, intramural athletics, music and drama groups, an award-winning forensics team, and many other extracurricular activities. The majority of C-N students live on campus in one of the two men's and three women's residence halls.

Graduate programs in education are available leading to the Master of Arts in Teaching, the Master of Arts in Education, the Master of Education in school counseling, and the Master of Arts in Teaching English as a Second Language degrees. A Master of Science in Nursing program is also offered.

Location

C-N is conveniently located in eastern Tennessee, just 30 miles from Knoxville, which has a population of 450,000, and 45 miles from Gatlinburg, a gateway to the Great Smoky Mountains. Students appreciate the diverse opportunities available in the city and the outdoor areas. Shopping, dining, and entertainment opportunities are available near the College.

Majors and Degrees

The eight academic divisions of the College are Business, Education, Family and Consumer Sciences, Fine Arts, Humanities, Natural Sciences and Mathematics, Nursing, and Social Sciences. C-N awards the Bachelor of Arts, Bachelor of Music, Bachelor of Science, and Bachelor of Science in Nursing degrees. In addition, an Associate of Arts in Christian Ministries degree is also offered.

Majors are available in art (art and photography), athletic training, business (accounting, business administration, general business, international economics, long-term health-care management, and management), church recreation, communication arts and mass communication (advertising/public relations, drama, telecommunications, journalism, and speech), computer information systems (computer studies and data processing), computer science, education (athletic coaching, elementary education, leisure services, physical education/health, secondary certification, and special education), English (creative writing and film studies), family and consumer sciences (child and family studies, consumer services, foods and nutrition, interior design and retail, and vocational family and consumer sciences education), foreign language (French and Spanish), general studies, history (social studies), human services, individual directions, mathematics, military science/U.S. Army ROTC or U.S. Air Force ROTC, music (church music, music education, music theory, music with an outside field, piano and organ performance, and vocal performance), natural and physical science (biology and chemistry), nursing, philosophy (philosophy and philosophy/religion), political science, psychology, religion, and sociology.

The College offers extremely strong curricula in preprofessional programs and health professions. Preprofessional programs are offered in dentistry, engineering, health information management, law, medicine, occupational therapy, optometry, physical therapy, and veterinary medicine. In cooperation with several other institutions, C-N offers binary degrees (2-3 and 3-2 programs) in engineering, medical technology, pharmacy, and physical therapy.

Academic Program

The College operates on a traditional semester system. Mayterm is a three-week intensive period of study giving students the opportunity to earn 3 credit hours. Summer term is offered as a six-week program of study.

All baccalaureate degrees require completion of 128 semester hours. Students must complete 51 semester hours in general education requirements and a total of 36 semester hours at junior/senior level. Specific course requirements vary depending on major and degree program. Honors courses, independent study, and internships are available to students who qualify. Advanced credit is available for students who achieve required scores on AP exams, CLEP tests, and C-N departmental examinations.

New students are assigned a faculty adviser who assists with course selection and student concerns. Career planning services are also available. The College's exceptionally high placement rate in professional programs in medicine, law, business, and theological study is testimony to the excellence of its rigorous academic program.

Off-Campus Programs

Students have the opportunity to spend an entire semester abroad by participating in the London Semester and other study-abroad opportunities. C-N, along with International Enrichment, Inc., provides all academic and nonacademic support services.

The Washington Semester is available as an internship program primarily for political science and prelaw majors. Through the program, students earn credit for work in the nation's capital. Art and foreign language majors may earn credit while studying and traveling throughout Europe during the three-week Mayterm.

Academic Facilities

C-N offers the facilities and resources necessary for the enrichment of each student's education. Facilities include numerous computer labs; a campuswide computer network; a media service center; two theaters for drama production; Thomas Recital Hall, which is in one of the finest music facilities in the Southeast; two art galleries and twenty-three individual art studios; the Stephens Burnette Library, with more than 500,000 volumes; and an award-winning 96,000-square-foot Student Activities Center.

Costs

The annual cost at Carson-Newman, including room, board, and tuition, is well below the national average for four-year private colleges. Tuition in 2003–04 was $12,500, room was $2100, board was $3440, the student activity fee was $380, and the technology fee was $380. Total direct charges were $18,500. Students should allow approximately $800 for books per year.

Financial Aid

Carson-Newman allocates thousands of dollars each year to help supplement the resources of families. Financial aid awards are tailored to meet students' economic needs. Carson-Newman participates in all state and federal aid programs and awards aid based on demonstrated need as documented by a need analysis form, such as the Free Application for Federal Student Aid (FAFSA). Carson-Newman also awards academic scholarships based on achievement. Priority deadline for filing financial aid forms is March 1.

Faculty

Carson-Newman has 122 full-time and 65 part-time faculty members. Of these, 68 percent hold the Ph.D. The student-faculty ratio is 13:1. Faculty members are involved in scholarly pursuits such as authoring books, leading national scholastic organizations, and research, but their primary focus is teaching.

Student Government

The Student Government Association (SGA) represents the entire student body by voicing student concerns in campus affairs. The purpose of SGA is to promote the welfare of every student through justice, to protect individual rights and freedoms, to encourage high standards of conduct, and to train students in the general principles of self-government.

Admission Requirements

Carson-Newman College seeks applicants who demonstrate academic preparation and who possess an appreciation of and sensitivity to a Christian education and a liberal arts curriculum. Carson-Newman accepts applications for freshman and transfer admission for each term of enrollment (fall, spring, and summer). Freshman candidates must have a GPA of 2.25 or higher in the core curriculum and a minimum score of 920 on the SAT I or 19 on the ACT; they must also rank in the top half of their high school graduating class. Transfer applicants must have a minimum cumulative GPA of 2.0 in courses that transfer to Carson-Newman.

Application and Information

Applicants must submit an application for admission, official transcripts, and a nonrefundable $25 application fee. Admission decisions are made on a rolling basis, and students are notified within two weeks of receipt of all required documents. Application deadline is May 1 for fall semester, December 1 for spring semester. Applicants who wish to be considered for merit scholarships should apply by December 31.

For additional information, students should contact:

Office of Undergraduate Admissions
Carson-Newman College
Jefferson City, Tennessee 37760
Telephone: 865-471-3223
800-678-9061 (toll-free)
E-mail: sgray@cn.edu
World Wide Web: http://www.cn.edu

Students share unique learning relationships with faculty members at Carson-Newman.

CARTHAGE COLLEGE

KENOSHA, WISCONSIN

The College

Carthage is a four-year private college of the arts and sciences, committed to educating students in the liberal arts tradition. Founded in 1847, Carthage is affiliated with the Evangelical Lutheran Church in America. The College prepares its students for the challenges and complexities of life in the modern world.

Carthage's 1,956 full-time students come from all parts of the world, representing twenty-five states and fourteen other countries.

With an average class size of 19 students and a student-faculty ratio of 16:1, the College offers a nurturing, personal education in a way that most large universities cannot. Faculty members are hired from the top graduate schools in their fields, and they are valued for their commitment to teaching.

Carthage is primarily a residential campus, and life in the residence halls is an important component of the Carthage learning experience. All five residence halls have been recently renovated, and all rooms have free cable television and free T-1 Internet access in addition to outside phone lines.

Complementing the academic and residence-life programs are a wide range of extracurricular activities. There are more than eighty clubs and organizations, including social sororities and fraternities; fine arts performance groups; campus publications and media; social service organizations; student government; honorary, professional, and departmental organizations; religious life groups; and general interest organizations. In athletics, the College offers twenty intercollegiate teams that compete in the College Conference of Illinois and Wisconsisn (CCIW), one of the top NCAA Division III conferences in the U.S. Men's sports include baseball, basketball, cross-country, football, golf, soccer, swimming, tennis, and track and field. Women's sports include basketball, cross-country, golf, soccer, softball, swimming, tennis, track and field, and volleyball. Club sports are offered in women's bowling, co-ed ice hockey, men's volleyball, and women's bowling. Intramural and recreational activities are also available. The N. E. Tarble Athletic and Recreation Center opened in June 2001. This $23-million, 156,0000-square-foot facility features a 40-meter, sixteen-lane swimming pool; a six-lane, 200-meter indoor running track with multipurpose courts for basketball, volleyball, and tennis; a 5,000-square-foot fitness center; a climbing wall; an aerobics area; and racquetball courts.

Carthage is accredited by the North Central Association of Colleges and Schools and holds a variety of professional recognitions, including accreditation of its chemistry program by the American Chemical Society, its music program by the National Association of Schools of Music, its social work program by the Council on Social Work Education, and its business program by the International Assembly for Collegiate Business Education.

In addition to its undergraduate programs, the College offers a Master in Education degree with concentrations in classroom guidance and counseling, creative arts, language arts, natural science, reading, religion, and social science. In conjunction with Loyola University Chicago, Carthage also offers an executive M.B.A. program and a master's degree in social work.

Location

Carthage is located on the shore of Lake Michigan, 65 miles north of Chicago and 35 miles south of Milwaukee. The campus enjoys an idyllic setting on 84 parklike acres, including 2,850 feet of scenic shoreline. In addition to its beautiful natural setting, the College benefits from the cultural, educational, and internship opportunities offered by its two major metropolitan neighbors.

Majors and Degrees

Carthage awards the Bachelor of Arts degree. Areas of study include accounting; art; athletic training; biology; business administration; chemistry; classics; communications; computer science; criminal justice; economics; elementary/middle education (1–9); English; environmental science; French; geography; German; history; information systems; international political economy; marketing; mathematics; middle/secondary education (6–12); music; neuroscience; philosophy; physical education (K–12); physical education, sport, and fitness instruction; physics; political science; psychology; religion; secondary education; self-designed major; social science; social work; sociology; Spanish; special education; and theater and communication. Special programs are offered in Air Force ROTC; Army ROTC; art history; Chinese; coaching; creative writing; East Asian studies; engineering (3/2); health education; heritage studies; history of the arts; honors program; humanities semester abroad; Japanese; Mizuno Internship in Japan; music theater; occupational therapy (3/2); paleontology; piano pedagogy; predentistry; prelaw; premedicine; preministry; pre-optometry; prepharmacy; pre–physical therapy; preveterinary; ScienceWorks (entrepreneurial studies in the natural sciences); Smeds Executive Internship; Summer Undergraduate Research Experience; and women's/gender studies.

Academic Programs

Carthage is a liberal arts college that provides a strong foundation in liberal studies as well as career-oriented and preprofessional programs. Some of the course requirement areas are three freshman and sophomore heritage seminars, which emphasize critical thinking, reasoning, writing, speaking, and listening through cultural and international studies; one course each in social science, humanities, mathematics, and fine arts; two courses each in religion and foreign language; a Junior Symposium, which consists of three linked courses from multiple disciplines; and a senior thesis. A dynamic honors program gives outstanding students special opportunities for growth and learning throughout their four years at Carthage.

Carthage operates on a 4-1-4 academic calendar consisting of fall and spring terms separated by a January term. The monthlong January term provides opportunities for independent study, special course work, internships, travel for credit, and traditional courses. A summer pre-session and full summer term are also available but not required.

Off-Campus Programs

Carthage maintains several cooperative programs with other institutions, including a 3-2 program in occupational therapy with Washington University in St. Louis and 3-2 programs in engineering with the University of Wisconsin–Madison; University of Minnesota, Twin Cities; and Case Western Reserve University in Cleveland. Air Force ROTC and Army ROTC are offered in cooperation with Marquette University in Milwaukee.

Carthage students are able to secure internships with both large and small companies, government agencies, and nonprofit organizations. In addition, the College has an active study-abroad program that enables students to travel to various countries for month-, semester- or year-abroad studies.

Academic Facilities

Lentz Hall houses multimedia and traditional classrooms, the bookstore, and administrative and faculty offices. The recently renovated David A. Straz, Jr. Center for the Natural and Social Sciences includes the 400-seat Wartburg Auditorium, state-of-the-art undergraduate research laboratories, and multimedia and traditional classrooms, and it is home to the Clausen Center for World Business. The Johnson Art Center provides spacious art studios and individual and group music rehearsal studios. Above the Johnson Art Center is the 1,800-seat Siebert Chapel, the College's premier chamber music venue. The crown jewel of academic life on campus is Hedberg Library. Newly opened in January 2002, the $15-million, 65,000-square-foot library features electronic classrooms, videoconferencing capabilities, a media and technology AV production/presentation suite, off-campus access to reference databases, and an Einstein Bros./Freshens store located inside a 24-hour cyber-café. The library blends its 125,000-volume collection with extensive electronic resources including both wireless and wired computer access to the campus network and the Internet. Easily accessible to students, academic resources and support services designed to help every student reach his or her academic potential are strategically located in the residence halls. Comprehensive academic counseling services are also provided to all students by full-time professionals in the Advising Center and by faculty advisers. Each freshman is assigned to an adviser who is also available for counseling in all areas of college life.

Costs

For 2004–05, a comprehensive fee of $27,500 per year includes full-time tuition and fees ($21,250) and room and board ($6250). The cost of books is estimated at $350 per term.

Financial Aid

More than 90 percent of Carthage students receive some type of financial assistance. The College administers more than $20 million in financial aid each year. A wide range of aid is available, including both need-based and non-need-based scholarships and grants. Carthage participates in all federal and state student financial assistance programs and offers non-need-based student employment. In addition, Carthage awards more than twenty major scholarships per year through various scholarship competitions.

Faculty

More than 90 percent of the full-time faculty members hold a Ph.D. or other terminal degree. Their credentials include degrees from a broad range of highly respected graduate schools, and they are valued for their commitment to teaching. Many faculty members serve as academic advisers to upperclass students, enhancing the student-faculty interaction that is so valued at the College. Carthage students work closely with faculty members on independent research projects and present their research at local, regional, and national conferences.

Student Government

The Carthage Student Government, Residence Life Council, Hall Council, Interfraternity Council, Independent National Greek Council, and Panhellenic Council function as the voice of the students in issues pertinent to student life. Students may serve on a variety of standing committees that deal with specific areas of Carthage Student Government, such as Budget and Finance, Public Relations, Student Affairs, and Student Organizations.

Admission Requirements

Carthage selects its students on the basis of a variety of factors. Carthage strongly recommends that an applicant complete at least 16 academic units through four years of high school work in English, foreign languages, mathematics, science, and social studies. In addition, the College considers the student's grade point average and results of the ACT or SAT I. A personal statement, essays, and letters of recommendation are optional but are considered if submitted. A campus visit and on-campus interview are recommended. An interview is required in some cases.

Application and Information

To request an application and information, students should contact:

Office of Admissions
Carthage College
2001 Alford Park Drive
Kenosha, Wisconsin 53140
Telephone: 262-551-6000
800-351-4058 (toll-free)
E-mail: admissions@carthage.edu
World Wide Web: http://www.carthage.edu

Carthage is located on the shore of Lake Michigan in Kenosha, Wisconsin.

CASE WESTERN RESERVE UNIVERSITY

CLEVELAND, OHIO

The University

Formed in 1967 by the federation of Case Institute of Technology and Western Reserve University, Case Western Reserve University is today one of the nation's major independent universities. Currently, 3,587 undergraduates (2,172 men and 1,415 women) are enrolled in programs in engineering, science, management, nursing, the arts, humanities, and the social and behavioral sciences. Students have access to the facilities of a comprehensive university, including graduate and professional schools in applied social sciences, dental medicine, graduate studies (humanities, the social and natural sciences, and engineering), nursing, medicine, law, and management. Several undergraduate programs and majors combine the resources of the undergraduate colleges and the graduate and professional schools. Examples include biochemistry and biomedical engineering (Case School of Medicine) and accounting and management (Weatherhead School of Management). In addition, collaborative arrangements with neighboring cultural and health-care institutions enable the University to provide special opportunities in other fields. A six-year dental program leading to the D.M.D. degree is also available.

There are numerous college activities, including those of dozens of professional, religious, political, social, and academic organizations. Nearly every type of interest group, from political organizations to a film society, is represented on campus, and sports are offered at both the varsity and intramural levels. There are nineteen national fraternities and six sororities; approximately 30 percent of the students participate. Residence halls are coeducational, and 75 percent of the students reside on campus. Automobiles and motorcycles are permitted.

Students at Case Western Reserve enjoy an especially close interaction with the faculty.

Location

The University is located in University Circle, a cultural extension of the campus, which comprises 500 acres of parks, gardens, museums, schools, hospitals, churches, and human service institutions. The Cleveland Museum of Art, the Cleveland Museum of Natural History, and Severance Hall, home of the Cleveland Orchestra, are within walking distance; downtown Cleveland is 10 minutes away by RTA rapid transit. Partnerships in education and research among University Circle institutions enables students to make full use of resources beyond those of the University itself.

Majors and Degrees

Programs of study leading to the Bachelor of Arts degree comprise the following: American studies, anthropology, art history (joint program with the Cleveland Museum of Art), Asian studies, astronomy, biochemistry, biology, chemistry, classics (Greek and Latin), communication sciences (collaborative program with Cleveland Hearing and Speech Center), comparative literature, computer science, economics, English, environmental geology, environmental studies, evolutionary biology, French, French studies, geological sciences, German, German studies, gerontological studies, history, history and philosophy of science, international studies, Japanese studies, mathematics, music (joint program with the Cleveland Institute of Music), natural sciences, nutrition, nutritional biochemistry and metabolism, philosophy, physics, political science, prearchitecture, psychology, religion, sociology, Spanish, statistics, theater (dance and drama), and women's studies. Minor areas of concentration within the B.A. curriculum include artificial intelligence, art studio, childhood studies, Chinese, electronics, entrepreneurial studies, ethnic studies, history of science and technology, human development, Italian, Japanese, Judaic studies, management information and decision systems, public policy, Russian, and sports medicine.

Bachelor of Science degrees are offered in the following fields: accounting, aerospace engineering, applied mathematics, art education (joint program with the Cleveland Institute of Art), astronomy, biochemistry, biology, biomedical engineering, chemical engineering, chemistry, civil engineering, computer engineering, computer science, electrical engineering, engineering physics, fluid and thermal engineering sciences, geological sciences, management (business), materials science and engineering, mathematics, mathematics and physics (combined major), mechanical engineering, music education, nursing, nutrition, nutritional biochemistry and metabolism, physics, polymer science, statistics, systems and control engineering, and an undesignated engineering major. Course sequences emphasizing architecture, energy, environmental/water resources studies, and power are offered in conjunction with some engineering and science fields.

High school seniors who are exceptionally well qualified in some fields are eligible for the Pre-Professional Scholars Program offered in association with the Schools of Applied Social Sciences, Dental Medicine, Law, and Medicine. In addition to being admitted into the program, each student selected is also awarded conditional admission to the appropriate professional school upon completion of the entrance requirements set by each school.

Students may work toward a combined B.A./B.S. degree or integrate undergraduate and graduate studies to complete both the bachelor's and master's degrees in five years or less. Combined B.A./B.S. (3-2) programs in astronomy, biochemistry, and engineering are offered in conjunction with a number of four-year liberal arts colleges.

Academic Programs

Through a combination of core curricula, major requirements, and minors or approved course sequences, all undergraduates receive a broad educational base as well as specialized knowledge in their chosen fields.

The University offers students opportunities for independent research and internships or professional practicums in business, health-care, government, arts, or service fields. A five-year co-op option providing two 7-month work periods in industry or government is available for majors in engineering, science, management, accounting, and computer science.

The Undergraduate Scholars Program allows a small number of highly motivated and responsible students to pursue individually tailored baccalaureate programs without the normal credit-hour and course requirements. The program, administered by a faculty committee, must be one that cannot be accomplished within the regular curricula.

Candidates for the B.A. who have been accepted at a school of medicine or dentistry other than one of those at Case may exercise the Senior Year in Absentia Privilege, which permits them to substitute the first year of professional studies at an approved school for the final year at Case Western Reserve. The Senior Year in Professional Studies option allows B.A. candidates who are admitted during their junior year to Case's School of Applied Social Sciences, Dental Medicine, Management,

Medicine, or Nursing to substitute the first year of professional school for the final undergraduate year.

The Minority Engineers Industrial Opportunity Program offers a special orientation and support to minority students in secondary schools and academic and financial support to minority undergraduates in engineering.

The University has two 4-month semesters and one 8-week summer program.

Off-Campus Programs

Selected students may enroll as juniors and seniors in the Washington Semester, which is conducted each spring at the American University. Students with a B average or higher may participate in the Junior Year Abroad program. Up to 36 hours of credit may be granted for study at a foreign university. Students may also cross-register at other Cleveland-area colleges and universities for one course per semester.

Academic Facilities

The $30-million Kelvin Smith Library opened in 1997. Through reciprocal borrowing arrangements, Case students have access to the holdings of the Cleveland Public Library, as well as the libraries of five University Circle institutions; the members of OhioLINK, a network that includes state colleges and universities; the State Library of Ohio; and several private institutions. In addition to more traditional departmental research facilities, the University operates two astronomical observatories, a biological field station, and nearly 100 designated research centers and laboratories, many of them interdisciplinary. CWRUnet, the University's high-speed fiber-optic communications network with the switched gigabit to the desktop standard, links every residence hall room with computing centers, libraries, and databases on and off campus. Other computer facilities on campus offer various models of microcomputers and a wide variety of software programs.

Costs

For 2004–05, tuition and compulsory health and laboratory fees total $26,500. The student activity fee is $212. Room and board cost an average of $7800. Books and supplies come to about $1000, and incidental expenses are estimated at $1255. The approximate total cost for the year is $36,770.

Financial Aid

Financial aid consisting of grants, loans, and work assistance is awarded on the basis of a student's need. Last year, all students demonstrating need received financial aid. Applicants must file the Free Application for Federal Student Aid (FAFSA) and the Financial Aid PROFILE of the College Scholarship Service by February 1. A signed copy of the most recent federal tax return (Form 1040) is also required. The University also awards merit-based scholarships ranging from $500 to full tuition. These awards are based solely on the student's academic, creative, or leadership ability.

Faculty

The full-time instructional staff of 2,341, of whom 95 percent hold the Ph.D. or equivalent, is shared by all University students: graduate, undergraduate, and professional. The undergraduate student-faculty ratio is 8:1. Each college provides counselors who are always available for both academic and personal advice. Once a major has been chosen, a member of the department in which the student is majoring acts as his or her academic adviser.

Student Government

The Undergraduate Student Government of Case Western Reserve University represents all undergraduate students. The assembly acts as a liaison between undergraduate students and the faculty, administration, and other groups; grants recognition to undergraduate organizations; and has the responsibility and authority to allocate funds from student activity fees to student organizations.

Admission Requirements

The University requires at least 16 units of full-credit high school work in solid academic subjects, including 4 years of English or its equivalent. All applicants are expected to have completed 3 years of high school mathematics, and students interested in mathematics, science, or engineering majors should have 4. At least 2 years of laboratory science are required of all applicants, and prospective mathematics and science majors must present 3 years. For all engineering candidates, physics and chemistry are required. Two years of foreign language study are recommended for students considering majors in the humanities, arts, and social and behavioral sciences. An interview is not a required part of the admission process, but it is strongly recommended as the best way to learn about the University. Applicants should take the ACT or the SAT I not later than January of their senior year in secondary school. For candidates submitting the SAT I, three SAT II Subject Tests are strongly recommended, including the Writing Test for all students, the Level I or II mathematics test and physics or chemistry for engineering candidates, and two tests of their choice for others.

Application and Information

Freshmen matriculate in August. Students who wish to receive early notification of their admission status may apply for early action by November 15; they are notified by January 15. The final application deadline is January 15 for March notification. Application deadlines for transfer students are June 30 for fall admission and October 15 for spring admission. The application deadline for the Pre-Professional Scholars Program (medicine, dentistry, or law) is November 15. In addition to its own application form, Case Western Reserve University accepts the Common Application and offers online application options.

To obtain an application form and financial aid information, students should contact:

Office of Undergraduate Admission
Case Western Reserve University
10900 Euclid Avenue
Cleveland, Ohio 44106-7055
Telephone: 216-368-4450
E-mail: admission@case.edu
World Wide Web: http://admission.case.edu

Students at Case Western Reserve University in Cleveland, Ohio.

CASTLETON STATE COLLEGE

CASTLETON, VERMONT

The College

Castleton State College was founded in 1787 and was the first institution of higher learning in Vermont and the eighteenth in the United States. The 160-acre campus is located in Castleton, a historic Vermont village. Sixty-five percent of the 1,500 full-time undergraduate students at the College are Vermonters; the balance of the student population comes from the New England and Middle Atlantic states.

Castleton is committed to providing an undergraduate education in which the liberal arts and career preparation complement each other. Through an innovative program called Soundings, freshmen earn academic credit by attending a series of special events, which include theater, music, dance, film, debate, and opinion from influential people. New students also participate in the First-Year Seminar, giving them the opportunity to develop the skills of a successful college student. First-year students may apply for the College's Honors Program. Community service and internships play an important role in a Castleton education.

There are six major residence halls, with a seventh opening in fall 2004. Together, the residences accommodate nearly 900 students. Each residence hall room is equipped with at least two Internet hook-ups, which gives each student the opportunity to access the World Wide Web and e-mail using his or her own personal computer. There is no additional charge for this service. Each room is also equipped with cable TV connections and individual telephone lines. Off-campus housing is available in the Castleton, Fair Haven, and Rutland areas. Students who live on campus eat in Huden Dining Hall. All students are allowed to have automobiles on campus.

More than forty clubs and organizations provide a wide variety of student activities that include club sports, an FM radio station, the student newspaper, and an active outing club. Other clubs relate to college majors and future careers; still others serve the College or local community. Castleton is a member of the North Atlantic Conference of NCAA Division III. There are seventeen intercollegiate sports. Men compete in baseball, basketball, cross-country running, ice hockey, lacrosse, soccer, and tennis; women compete in basketball, cross-country running, field hockey, lacrosse, soccer, softball, and tennis. Varsity women's ice hockey begins in 2004–05. Intercollegiate competitive skiing and snowboarding for men and women are club teams organized by the athletic department. A majority of Castleton's students are involved in the intramural and recreational sports program.

Location

The campus is 12 miles west of Rutland, Vermont's second-largest city. Montreal, Boston, Hartford, Albany, and New York City are all within easy driving distance and are accessible by public transportation from Rutland. Killington and Pico ski areas, Lake Bomoseen, and the Green Mountains provide excellent recreational opportunities and an exceptional living and learning environment.

Majors and Degrees

Castleton State College offers B.A. or B.S. degrees in more than thirty areas of study: accounting, American literature, art, athletic training, biology, children's literature, computer information systems, communication, criminal justice, digital media, e-commerce, elementary education, environmental science, exercise science, forensic psychology, geology, health science, history, journalism, management, marketing, mass media, mathematics, music, natural science, physical education, psychology, public relations, secondary education, social work, sociology, Spanish, special education, sports medicine, theater arts, and world literature. Associate degrees can be earned in business, communication, computer programming, criminal justice, general studies, or nursing.

Academic Program

The Castleton curriculum is designed to provide the student with a strong liberal arts background plus the opportunity for career preparation in a specific area. All four-year students are required to complete a core of general education requirements during the four-year degree program. The first year of study can be used by the undecided student to explore various areas of interest. The student with a specific career interest may begin study in the major field as a freshman, although four-year students are not required to formally declare their major until the end of the sophomore year.

Castleton students typically enroll in five courses each semester. The academic calendar consists of two 15-week semesters and three 4-week summer sessions. Grading is traditional, and a pass/no pass option is available. Internships and field experiences complement many of the academic programs at Castleton and are required in the communication, criminal justice, social work, and education programs.

Students may transfer internally from two-year to four-year programs in business, communication, computer information systems, criminal justice, and general studies. Students who transfer to Castleton after graduating from an accredited two-year college are granted full transfer credit for all academic work up to 64 credits or the number required for the associate degree.

Freshman students achieving at least a 3.5 grade point average in their first year at Castleton are recognized by the Castleton Chapter of Phi Eta Sigma, a national honor society that recognizes freshman scholastic achievement in colleges throughout the country. Outstanding junior and senior scholars are recognized by the Castleton Chapter of Alpha Chi. Pinnacle, the honor society for nontraditional students, honors qualified candidates. There are honor societies in theater arts, education, psychology, and Spanish. Students who have achieved a 4.0 grade point average are named to the President's List of Outstanding Students, and those with a 3.5 grade point average or better to the Dean's List.

Academic Facilities

The Calvin Coolidge Library houses a collection of more than 500,000 books, periodicals, microforms, and nonprint media. Access to Castleton's library resources and outside scholarly sources is made possible through numerous online and CD databases; a sophisticated, networked electronic library system; the Internet; and strong consortial relationships within the state of Vermont. An audiovisual media facility provides a wide range of audiovisual equipment, including digital-video editing, digital cameras, and presentation equipment.

Castleton's Stafford Academic Center houses the Computing Center, a high-tech multimedia lecture hall, distance learning classrooms, and the Departments of Education, Mathematics, and Nursing.

Glenbrook Gymnasium houses the athletic training room, the Human Performance Center, the swimming pool, two racquetball courts, a fitness center, and a large indoor activity area.

The Fine Arts Center contains a 500-seat auditorium; facilities for art, drama, dance, and music; and television studios.

The Florence Black Science Center houses general classrooms and laboratories, a 200-seat auditorium, a precision-instrument room, an herbarium, a darkroom, a computing center, and an astronomical observatory.

There are more than 225 personal computers designated for student use located in labs across campus.

Costs

Costs for 2003–04 were as follows: tuition for Vermont residents, $5646; for nonresidents, $12,200. Room and board expenses totaled $6014. There was a student activity fee of $160. The orientation and registration for new students was also $160.

Financial Aid

Eighty percent of Castleton's full-time undergraduate students receive financial assistance from federal, state, College, or other sources. Grants, loans, and work-study jobs are available for qualified students. Applicants for financial aid should file the Free Application for Federal Student Aid (FAFSA) form by February 15 of the senior year in high school. All financial aid awards are based on need.

Most Castleton scholarships are awarded as part of the Castleton Fellows Program and are part of the College's Honors Program. Fellowships range from $1000 to $5000 per year. High school students who are in the top quarter of their class, have a combined SAT I score of at least 1100, or have a cumulative GPA of at least 3.25 on a 4.0 scale and transfer students with a 3.25 GPA are eligible to apply. There are also special scholarships for students wishing to study music or Spanish.

Faculty

The full-time faculty at Castleton consists of 86 men and women, 94 percent of whom hold terminal degrees in their field. Adjunct faculty members, many of them local businesspeople and members of the professions, complement the efforts of the full-time faculty. The student-faculty ratio is 13:1. Each student has a faculty member as an adviser.

Student Government

The Student Association is the chief vehicle of student government. All students registered for 8 or more credit hours are members. Elected representatives hold membership on most College committees, including the Curriculum and Cultural Affairs committees. Students are also able to develop leadership qualities by participating in the various clubs and other organizations on campus.

Admission Requirements

Applicants are evaluated on the basis of their secondary school records, standardized test scores, and recommendations. Admission is granted to those applicants who have demonstrated their ability and potential to meet the challenges of a postsecondary learning experience.

Application and Information

Students may apply for admission through the Castleton Web site below. Under Castleton's rolling admission policy, applications are processed throughout the year, and candidates are notified of the admission decision as soon as their folders are complete. Students are admitted in the fall and spring semesters.

For more information about Castleton State College or to arrange a campus visit, students should contact:

Director of Admissions
Castleton State College
Castleton, Vermont 05735
Telephone: 802-468-1213
800-639-8521 (toll-free)
Fax: 802-468-1476
E-mail: info@castleton.edu
World Wide Web: http://www.castleton.edu

Between classes, students gather on the patio near historic Woodruff Hall.

CATAWBA COLLEGE

SALISBURY, NORTH CAROLINA

The College

Catawba College is a senior coeducational liberal arts college that focuses on educating its students for productive careers and responsible citizenship. Founded in 1851 by German-American immigrants of the Reformed faith, Catawba provides an education that integrates the liberal arts and career preparation. This education is marked by academic challenges and a strong emphasis on enhancing leadership and character.

The College is situated on 276 wooded acres. The campus consists of thirty buildings and a 189-acre ecological preserve. The student body consists of 1,400 students from thirty-two states and twenty foreign countries. About 85 percent of Catawba's students are from the Eastern Seaboard. Seventy percent of the traditional-age students reside on the campus in one of nine residence halls.

Students can choose from a wide variety of campus activities, including theater productions, athletic events in seventeen intercollegiate sports, multiple choral and instrumental groups, academic clubs, community service organizations, the student government association, religious groups, and intramural activities. Excellent exercise facilities are available in the Lerner Wellness Center, and most campus organizations offer a variety of social activities both on campus and in the homes of faculty and staff members. Religious services organized by students and the campus minister are offered in the Omwake-Dearborn Chapel and are open to all faiths.

Location

Catawba is located in Salisbury, a historic Southern city of 35,000. The city is situated in the Piedmont section of North Carolina near Interstate 85. The Catawba campus is located on the western edge of Salisbury in a residential section within 5 minutes of downtown. The city has movie theaters, malls, restaurants, parks, and golf courses; other entertainment facilities are available in the immediate area.

Salisbury is located 30 minutes from the greater Charlotte area, one of the fastest-growing areas in the country, and approximately 45 minutes from the cities of Greensboro and Winston-Salem. These cities provide Catawba students with a wealth of cultural experiences and internship opportunities, plus opportunities to attend professional athletic events. Salisbury is a 4-hour drive from the Atlantic Ocean and about a 2-hour drive from the scenic Appalachian Mountains areas and ski resorts.

Majors and Degrees

Catawba College grants a Bachelor of Arts and/or a Bachelor of Science degree in the following majors: accounting, athletic training, biology, business administration, chemistry, chemistry education, communication arts, comprehensive science education, education (elementary (K–6), middle school (6–9), and secondary (9–12)), English (literature and writing), environmental science, environmental studies, French, history, information systems (accounting information systems and programming), marketing, mathematics, medical technology, music (music education, music management, music performance, and sacred music), physical education, political science (American politics, international relations, prelaw, and public administration), psychology, recreation, religion and philosophy (Christian education and outdoor ministries), sociology, Spanish, sports management, and theater arts administration.

The College grants the Bachelor of Fine Arts degree in the following majors: musical theater and theater arts.

Academic Programs

The College operates on the semester calendar and stresses rigorous academic courses, close contact between students and faculty members, and a supportive educational environment. The academic program allows the student opportunities to study in a wide range of fields while concentrating in one (the major). Catawba encourages students to actively pursue internship opportunities in their major.

Academic Facilities

Catawba College's Center for the Environment is a 20,000-square-foot classroom building that overlooks the College's 189-acre ecological preserve. This award-winning model of sustainable design opened in 2001 and is a teaching tool in itself. The College also owns a 300-acre wildlife refuge that is located 7 miles from the main campus. The building and these natural resources offer Catawba students endless opportunities for research and nature education. The Shuford Science Building offers state-of-the-art laboratories and classrooms for chemistry and biology students. Atop this building sits the Montgomery Observatory, which houses a 15-inch Fecker reflecting telescope.

Ketner Hall serves as a primary classroom area and houses the College's School of Business and the nationally accredited teacher education program. This facility is also equipped with computer laboratories that are available to students.

The Robertson College–Community Center includes the 1,500-seat Keppel Auditorium and the 250-seat Hedrick Theatre. The College's theater arts department uses both of these venues in staging its annual performances. In addition, the new Florence Busby Corriher Theatre, located adjacent to the community center, offers an intimate venue for student performances. The newly renovated Brodbeck Music Building offers individual practice rooms, recital halls, classrooms, and a music library.

The Corriher-Linn-Black Library resources include more than 300,000 volume equivalents. Library services include online database searching, individualized reference assistance, group library instruction, photocopying, and a document delivery system (including interlibrary loan service). The library is connected to the Internet and provides access to library and information sources around the world. The library also participates in the North Carolina Information Network (NCIN) for statewide library and information resources and the Online Computer Library Center (OCLC) via the Southeastern Library Network (SOLINET) for international online access to cataloging and reference services. All students have access to the Internet on the campus.

The Abernethy Physical Education Center houses three basketball courts, an indoor swimming pool, an athletic training room, racquetball courts, a weight room, and locker rooms for the indoor athletic programs. The College's new Hayes Athletic Field House is equipped with a weight room, an athletic training room, and locker rooms for the outdoor athletic programs. This facility is adjacent to the new Shuford Stadium (football stadium). A 20-acre athletic complex consists of two soccer fields, a hockey field, a softball field, a lacrosse field, and a football practice field. Six tennis courts, with lighting and spectator seating, are also available on the campus. These facilities and fields are available for extracurricular activities, as are training areas for the seventeen NCAA Division II varsity athletic teams (men's and women's).

Costs

For the 2004–05 academic year, tuition and fees are $17,600. Room and board costs $5900. The total fixed costs for attending the College as a commuting student are $17,600.

Financial Aid

Merit scholarships are available to students who have demonstrated high levels of academic achievement, leadership, and character. The College also provides departmental academic scholarships in the following majors: athletic training, biology, chemistry, environmental science, foreign languages, mathematics, psychology, and teacher education. Performance scholarships are offered in the fields of music and theater. Catawba also awards athletic scholarships to selected student-athletes in seventeen varsity sports.

Students applying for financial assistance must be accepted by the Admissions Office and must submit the Free Application for Federal Student Aid (FAFSA). Financial assistance includes federal and state grants, Federal Work-Study programs, campus employment, and a variety of student loans.

Faculty

The faculty members serve as advisers to students during registration periods and throughout a student's four years at Catawba. Faculty members are readily accessible to students and participate with them in activities on and off campus. More than 70 percent of the faculty members have doctorates.

Admission Requirements

Students seeking admission to Catawba must present evidence of outstanding educational achievement and be a graduate of an accredited public or private secondary school.

Members of the Catawba Admission Committee select from among the applicants those students whom they consider to be best qualified for success at Catawba. The factors they consider are grades for six or more semesters, course selection, standardized test results (including SAT I or ACT scores), an essay, and two letters of recommendations from school officials.

Transfer students are strongly urged to send their application and college transcript(s) along with their high school transcript two weeks prior to the term in which they plan to enroll. Official college transcripts must be mailed directly from the Office of the Registrar of all previously attended institutions. Grade point averages from prior institutions are used to determine admission to Catawba.

International students who are able to provide evidence of suitable academic preparation and adequate financial resources are encouraged to apply at least three months prior to the term in which they intend to begin their studies. Acceptable scores are a minimum of 525 for the TOEFL (computer equivalent of 197).

Application and Information

Application forms must be completed by the student and returned to the Admissions Office with a $25 processing fee ($50 for international students). The fee, which is nonrefundable, is not applied to any other college costs. An online application is available at the Web site listed below ($15 processing fee). The student's scholastic record forms should be prepared by the appropriate secondary school official and mailed directly to the Catawba Admissions Office. An applicant is also required to take the SAT I of the College Board or the ACT of American College Testing, Inc., as part of the Catawba admission procedure and to request that the test scores be sent to Catawba.

If applicants have successfully completed Advanced Placement (AP) courses in high school and received a score of 3, 4, or 5 on Advanced Placement tests administered by the College Board, they receive both credit and advanced placement at Catawba. The College recognizes International Baccalaureate–level work in the admission process and grants credit for examination scores of 4 or better on higher-level courses only. International Baccalaureate Certificate recipients receive one course credit (3 semester hours) for each higher-level score of 4 or better. Catawba also participates in the College-Level Examination Program (CLEP) and awards credit to students who receive a grade of C or better on the subject-matter examinations.

While Catawba does not have closing dates for the submission of applications, students are urged to apply during the fall of their senior year. The Admissions Office makes every effort to notify each applicant of the committee's decision within thirty days after the completed application has been received. After receiving notification of acceptance, the applicant should send a $400 enrollment deposit to the Admissions Office by May 1. The deposit is credited to the student's account and is deducted from the first payment of fees, which is made at the time of registration when the school term begins.

Chief Enrollment Officer
Catawba College
Salisbury, North Carolina 28144
Telephone: 704-637-4402
800-228-2922 (toll-free)
E-mail: admission@catawba.edu
World Wide Web: http://www.catawba.edu

Ralph W. Ketner Hall.

THE CATHOLIC UNIVERSITY OF AMERICA

WASHINGTON, D.C.

The University

The Catholic University of America (CUA) offers a strong liberal arts curriculum, small classes, and personal attention from faculty members in a values-based environment.

Founded in 1887 by the U.S. Catholic bishops, CUA is home to more than 2,700 undergraduate and 2,900 graduate students from all fifty states and ninety other countries. Students from all religious traditions are welcome.

While the University maintains a small-college atmosphere, with a student-faculty ratio of 12:1, it is a major research institution. Undergraduates learn from the same professors who conduct research and teach graduate students.

CUA maintains its green, tree-studded grounds through a commitment to ecologically sound practices and is noted for the beautiful architecture found on its 144-acre campus. The majority of undergraduates live on campus in seventeen residence halls, including an option of honors housing. Students are involved in more than 100 diverse student organizations in addition to extensive cocurricular, extracurricular, and social activities.

The University offers many venues for spiritual devotion and growth that enable students of all religious traditions to deepen their faith. Campus Ministry provides many opportunities for community service in the Washington, D.C. area; in other parts of the United States; and abroad.

A competitive NCAA Division III athletic program enables teams to compete with others who share similar standards of academic and athletic excellence. Intercollegiate teams for women are basketball, cross-country, field hockey, lacrosse, soccer, softball, swimming, tennis, track and field (indoor and outdoor), and volleyball. Men's sports are baseball, basketball, cross-country, football, lacrosse, soccer, swimming, tennis, and track and field (indoor and outdoor). Club sports are extensive, and they include crew, fencing, golf, ice hockey, rugby, and ultimate Frisbee. A wide range of intramural athletic programs is also offered.

The Raymond A. DuFour Center includes a main arena and stadium; swimming pool; handball, racquetball, and tennis courts; a dance and aerobics studio; a weight room; indoor and outdoor running tracks; and outdoor playing fields.

Services available to students include individual tutoring and general seminars on research techniques, writing, and study skills; career assessment and placement; disability support; and programs for minority and international students.

A state-of-the-art university center opened in 2003. A variety of food service choices and programs including concerts, seminars, and lectures are offered for the campus community.

Location

Located three miles north of the Capitol in residential Washington, D.C., CUA is in the same residential neighborhood as several other educational, medical, and research centers.

Majors and Degrees

Undergraduate degrees are offered in eighty-three major programs in six of CUA's ten schools: arts and sciences, engineering, architecture and planning, nursing, music, and philosophy.

The School of Arts and Sciences offers the Bachelor of Arts or Bachelor of Science degrees in the following areas: accounting, anthropology, art, biochemistry, biology, chemical physics, chemistry, classical civilization, classics, drama, economics, education (early childhood, elementary, and secondary), education studies (non-teaching), English language and literature, environmental science, finance, French, German, Greek and Latin, history, international business, international economics and finance, Latin and classical humanities, management, management information systems, marketing, mathematics, media studies, medical technology, medieval and Byzantine studies, music, philosophy, physics, politics, psychology, religion and religious education, social work, sociology, Spanish, and Spanish for international service. Predental, prelaw, premedical, and preveterinary programs are available. Students can also select double majors and minors. Accelerated degree programs are available to students who perform at exceptional levels. Possibilities include a three-year Bachelor of Arts program, a four-year bachelor's/master's joint-degree program, and a six-year joint Bachelor of Arts/Juris Doctor program with the Columbus School of Law.

The School of Engineering offers programs leading to the first professional degree in biomedical, civil, computer, construction, electrical, environmental, or mechanical engineering or in computer science. Students can also undertake a dual-degree program in civil engineering and architecture or in an interdisciplinary program such as computer science and engineering.

The School of Architecture and Planning offers the Bachelor of Science in Architecture—a four-year degree program—and the Master of Architecture—an additional 1½-year professional degree program. A dual-degree program is available in architecture and civil engineering.

The School of Nursing offers a four-year program leading to the Bachelor of Science in Nursing degree. Also offered is an accelerated B.S.N. program, a twenty-month sequence for students who have a bachelor's degree in another field.

The Benjamin T. Rome School of Music offers four-year programs leading to Bachelor of Music degrees in composition, music education, music history and literature, musical theater, and performance, including orchestral instruments, organ, piano, or voice.

The School of Philosophy offers two programs leading to the Bachelor of Arts degree, including the program of concentration and the prelaw concentration.

Academic Programs

Engineering, nursing, music, and architecture students follow study courses that provide professional training integrated with a broad range of academic disciplines. Students in the School of Arts and Sciences undertake a major course of study within a liberal arts curriculum that encompasses the humanities, languages and literature, philosophy, the social sciences, mathematics and natural sciences, and religion. Most majors require the satisfactory completion of forty courses that are 3 credits each for graduation. Certain majors under the Bachelor of Science degree may require additional credits. In addition to the major, students may complete a minor course sequence by utilizing the elective courses included in the undergraduate program.

CUA maintains small undergraduate classes, even for introductory courses. Faculty members who teach graduate students also teach undergraduates, enabling freshmen to engage in dialogues with teachers and scholars. CUA offers outstanding academic research and library facilities and exposure to graduate and professional-level programs.

Also provided is a University-wide honors program for outstanding undergraduates who seek intense intellectual challenges. The program draws from traditional liberal arts disciplines and professional curricula to offer comprehensive academic experiences.

Off-Campus Programs

CUA belongs to the Consortium of Universities of the Washington Metropolitan Area. Undergraduates, with the approval of their academic advisers, may undertake course work and research at member institutions. Earned credits are applied to the CUA baccalaureate degree.

Washington-area internships are available for students in almost every academic area. In addition to numerous internship and study opportunities in the Washington area, CUA students can take advantage of exciting study-abroad programs. These programs include British and Irish politics and society programs in London and Dublin, which include parliamentary internships. European studies are offered in Leuven, Belgium. Language and humanities programs are offered in Africa, China, France, Germany, Greece, Italy, Spain, and Venezuela. CUA also sponsors study-abroad programs in Hungary, Japan, and Poland.

Academic Facilities

More than 1.6 million volumes are available through the CUA library system. This collection is housed in the John K. Mullen of Denver Memorial Library and in six specialized libraries: chemistry; engineering, architecture, and mathematics; library and information science; music; nursing and biology; and physics. Students also have access to the libraries of the Washington Consortium and institutions such as the Library of Congress, the National Library of Medicine, the Folger Shakespeare Library, and the National Archives.

Catholic University's Center for Planning and Information Technology offers service and support for network, administrative, and academic computing. The center helps members of the University community use information technologies to deliver, access, process, communicate, and disseminate information.

In addition to a central computing cluster for faculty members and students, various labs, networked classrooms, and technology-equipped classrooms are located throughout the campus. VMS is the central operating system. A Compaq computer cluster is available for use by students and faculty and staff members. A high-speed fiber network links the entire campus to the Internet, including all academic buildings and all residence halls.

The Center for Planning and Information Technology issues a VMS and an NT account to all members of the University community. The VMS account can be used for e-mail and storage of files, and the NT account allows users to log on securely to any machine in an office or computer lab. A campus computing Information Center answers users' computing or information technology questions.

CUA is home to research facilities such as the Vitreous State Laboratory and the Centers of Excellence for Biomedical Engineering, Catholic Education, and other areas.

Costs

Tuition for the 2003–04 academic year was $22,200, except for the Schools of Engineering and Architecture and Planning, which cost $22,400. Room and board totaled approximately $8950.

Financial Aid

CUA administers two separate and distinct financial assistance programs: merit scholarships and need-based financial aid. A number of scholarships awarded on the basis of academic achievement are available. The University offers financial aid to students based on need as demonstrated by the Free Application for Federal Student Aid (FAFSA). Loans, work-study, and University grants are available. Candidates who complete the admission application process before February 1 of their senior year of secondary school are considered for academic scholarships and receive priority for financial aid.

Candidates apply for financial aid at the same time they apply for admission. CUA has a need-blind admissions policy and makes admission decisions without regard to financial aid status.

Faculty

CUA has 359 full-time and 311 part-time faculty members. More than 97 percent hold doctoral or appropriate professional degrees. Thirteen percent of full-time faculty members are in religious orders; 87 percent are laypersons.

Student Government

The Undergraduate Student Government (USG) is composed of the legislative, academic, and judicial branches and the treasury and program board. Through this organization, students serve on standing committees and send representatives to the University's Academic Senate and Board of Trustees. USG also governs and allocates student activities fees to student organizations, sponsors functions and social events, and protects students' rights.

Admission Requirements

CUA welcomes applications from men and women of character, intelligence, and motivation, regardless of race, creed, sex, ethnic background, or physical disability. CUA is most interested in students best qualified to profit from opportunities offered. For that reason, a selective admission policy is practiced. Successful candidates demonstrate achievement both in a challenging secondary school curriculum and on the standardized college entrance examinations.

Application and Information

Applicants for the Early Decision Program must apply by November 15 and are notified by mid-December. Regular decisions are made shortly after the February 1 deadline. Candidates for freshman admission must submit CUA's secondary school report, high school transcripts, letter of recommendation, scores on the SAT I or ACT, and a $55 application fee.

CUA accepts transfer applicants each semester. Transfer candidates should request applications for transfer admission from the Office of Admissions. In addition to the high school records and SAT I or ACT scores, transfer students must furnish a transcript from the school the student is attending (a minimum 2.8 GPA is recommended). Transfer applicants are notified of their status on a rolling basis. Financial aid is awarded on the same basis as for freshman students.

Office of Admissions
The Catholic University of America
Washington, D.C. 20064
Telephone: 202-319-5305
800-673-2772 (toll-free)
Fax: 202-319-6533
E-mail: cua-admissions@cua.edu
World Wide Web: http://www.cua.edu

The Catholic University of America's 144-acre residential campus provides an exceptional atmosphere for learning and living.

CAZENOVIA COLLEGE
CAZENOVIA, NEW YORK

The College

Cazenovia College, founded in 1824, is a small, private undergraduate college located in the lakeside community of Cazenovia, in central New York. The College was founded as a seminary. It later became a two-year women's college and finally became the four-year coeducational institution that it is today. One of the thirty oldest continuously operating independent colleges in the United States, the College offers innovative baccalaureate degree programs.

Cazenovia College is a residential institution drawing primarily traditional-age, full-time college students. The undergraduate student body is 70 percent women and 30 percent men. The majority of students live on campus. Freshmen are assigned housing based on an interest questionnaire; upperclass housing assignments are selected by lottery. Student dining facilities are open seven days a week, up to 12 hours a day, and continuously provide students with meals or snacks.

The main campus is located in the heart of the village of Cazenovia. All residence halls have been recently renovated and are fully wired for fiber-optic communications, including full Internet and e-mail capability. Nearby, the College's athletic complex, home to its NCAA Division III teams, features two gymnasiums, a swimming pool, outdoor playing fields, and tennis courts. Within walking distance, South Campus houses state-of-the-art computer facilities for interior design, commercial illustration, and advertising/graphic design classes. A short drive from the main campus, the 250-acre Equine Education Center is home to the College's nationally known equestrian program and champion riding teams. Cazenovia students enjoy the advantages of small-town life combined with nearby opportunities for urban cultural, athletic, and recreational activities. Social life focuses on activities sponsored by individual residence halls and campus clubs, as well as dances, professional and student performances, sports events, and intramurals. The College's health and counseling center offers a wide range of medical and counseling services.

Cazenovia College has always been committed to helping students prepare for real-life situations. Students combine career and liberal arts course work throughout their studies. Internships are a part of most academic programs. Students develop the skills and knowledge necessary to pursue a career or go on to further academic study. Cazenovia College is fully accredited by the Middle States Association of Colleges and Schools.

Location

Cazenovia College is situated in the picturesque lakeside village of Cazenovia, New York, a quiet village of 4,000 in central New York. Many structures in the village are listed on the National Register of Historic Places. The village retains much of its nineteenth-century charm with unique specialty shops, fine inns, and restaurants that cater to a variety of tastes. Cazenovia Lake is enjoyed for its beauty and for the opportunities it provides for summer and winter sports. Students have the opportunity to attend many cultural events on campus. In the city of Syracuse, a half-hour drive from Cazenovia, cultural attractions include a symphony orchestra, an opera company, several widely acclaimed regional theaters, museums, fine restaurants, and recreational events, among other social and cultural offerings. The Cazenovia area offers a wonderful living and learning environment.

Majors and Degrees

Cazenovia College offers the Bachelor of Arts degree in English, social science, and liberal studies, with specializations in theater arts, interdisciplinary social science, literature and culture, and communications.

The Bachelor of Fine Arts degree is offered in interior design; studio art, with specializations in studio art, photography, and fashion design; and visual communications, with courses in advertising design, graphic design, and Web design.

The Bachelor of Science degree is offered in business management; criminal justice; early childhood education and program administration; environmental studies; English; human services, with specializations in alcohol and substance abuse, counseling and mental health, criminal justice, social services for children and youth, and generalist studies; inclusive elementary education; psychology; social science (specialization in history and government); and liberal and professional studies, with specializations in theater arts, interdisciplinary social science, literature and culture, and communications.

The Bachelor of Professional Studies degree is offered in management, with specializations in accounting, business management, equine business management, fashion merchandising, and sport management.

Academic Programs

Part of what distinguishes Cazenovia College is the diversity and flexibility of its degree programs. Cazenovia offers a wide range of programs in art, business, early childhood education, equine studies, and human services, as well as in interdisciplinary liberal and professional studies. All students complete a common core grounded in liberal arts and sciences competencies. The general education core includes required course work in literacy and effective communication. Students select a major field of study and conclude their work by demonstrating the ability to integrate and apply their knowledge to a culminating senior capstone experience. All programs feature small classes and personal attention from faculty members. Interdisciplinary studies, the use of computer technology, and innovative instructional methods are hallmarks of College course work. Opportunities for internships and course work in Great Britain and Washington, D.C., are offered through the American Intercontinental University (London) and the Institute for Experiential Learning (Washington, D.C.). The College continues to develop additional opportunities for study abroad and internships across the United States. Students also have the opportunity to earn honors at graduation through the College honors program.

The Cazenovia College Center for Teaching and Learning staff provides workshops and individualized tutoring to help students improve their math, reading, writing, and study skills. The center's programs have been cited by the *National Directory of Exemplary Programs,* and it offers support services to all students. The center includes the Higher Education Opportunity Program, Collegiate Science and Technology Entry Program, Office of Special Services, and Title IV: Student Support Services. A strong job placement/transfer counseling program is also available on campus.

To earn a bachelor's degree, a student must complete 120 credits (except where otherwise specified) with a grade point average of at least 2.0 and must satisfy all additional program requirements. Sixty credits must be completed prior to the junior year. Arts and sciences credit requirements vary according to the degree sought. Advanced placement and credit by examination are offered to qualified students, and honors courses are available in selected areas. An independent study arrangement is possible for full-time students. The academic year is divided into two 14-week terms, January Intersession, and two 6-week summer semesters offering both academic course work and internships.

Off-Campus Programs

An increasing focus of the College is experiential education through internships offered in conjunction with classes and cocurricular service learning projects offered by the Office of Student Leadership. Students are able to integrate academic study and career development through these learning experiences. Each student learns the practical side of a career and develops the versatility to adapt to the competitive marketplace. Students gain valuable experience off campus in major corporations, banks, newspapers, hospitals, local businesses, government agencies, and radio and television.

Academic Facilities

The main campus consists of twenty-four buildings on 20 acres in the heart of the village. Classrooms, residence halls, and administrative buildings surround a centrally located quad that is a popular gathering place for students to study, relax, or join in a tag football game. A few short blocks away is South Campus, home of Cazenovia's art and design programs. A new art and design building featuring advanced computer technology is currently under development and opens in 2004.

The Witherill Library has holdings totaling more than 86,000 pieces, including bound volumes, extensive microfilm and video libraries, and subscriptions to hundreds of journals, newspapers, and index/abstract publications. Approximately 3,000 pieces are acquired annually. The library is a member of the national/international Online Computer Library Center (OCLC) Interlibrary Loan Network, which allows loans to and from libraries all over the United States and the world. In addition, the library's Web page includes subscriptions to eleven online databases, which include more than 2,600 full-text journals, indexes, and abstracts to be called up at a moment's notice. The library professional staff is available for assistance to groups or on an individual basis.

The College's computer resources rival the best-wired facilities in the nation. Two main campus computer classrooms and one open lab host seventy-six Pentium III–based Windows NT systems. Labs at South Campus dedicated to art and design host more than fifty G3 and G4 Macintosh workstations and an up-to-date AutoCAD/3-D Studio Viz Lab. All facilities support laser printers and scanners and (where appropriate) wide-bed printers and other specialized peripherals.

The College also has chemistry and biology laboratories and extensive art studios. The Gertrude T. Chapman Art Center Gallery exhibits the work of contemporary artists. The Howard and Bess Chapman Cultural Center houses changing exhibits of regional, historical, and general cultural interest, as well as art exhibits. The Cazenovia College Theatre is a resource for both the College and the community. Students produce plays and other entertainment, and the theater is also used for film showings and large-group lectures. Cazenovia College's nursery school, the Doug Flutie, Jr. Center for Early Childhood Education, attended by children from the village, enables students in the early childhood and inclusive elementary education programs to learn firsthand about the care and education of children. The College's 250-acre Equine Education Center, just a 5-minute drive from the campus, is one of the premier collegiate equestrian facilities in the nation.

Costs

For academic year 2003–04, tuition was $16,730 per year, room was $3740, and board was $3220. Books are about $800, and personal and travel expenses average $1300.

Financial Aid

Financial aid resources exist at Cazenovia College to bridge the gap between the amount the student's family can pay and the cost of attending the College. Ninety-one percent of students receive some form of financial assistance, either merit- or need-based. Need-based federal, state, and institutional sources include grants, loans, and on-campus work-study arrangements. About 50 percent of the students hold work-study jobs, and many are recipients of academic achievement scholarships designed to recognize and reward students for their scholastic achievements.

Faculty

Cazenovia has 48 full-time faculty positions. All full-time faculty members must possess a Ph.D. or other appropriate professional degree, and all faculty members must demonstrate proficiency in the discipline in which they teach. The faculty is more strongly committed to teaching than to research. In addition, many of the part-time faculty members pursue careers outside the College; their professional experiences enrich the College's programs. Faculty members also function as student advisers and academic counselors. The student-faculty ratio is 11:1.

Student Government

The Student Government Association (SGA) is elected and empowered to represent the student body in various aspects of their educational experience at the College. While all students are members of this association, voting membership consists of executive officers, class officers, representatives of the residential communities, commuter representatives, and the student chair of the Community Judicial Board. Responsibilities include allocation of funds to student clubs and organizations, representation of students in the campus governance structure, planning and sponsoring of campus events, and student contribution to the campus disciplinary process.

Admission Requirements

Cazenovia College seeks students whose high school and college records, standardized test scores, official recommendations, and qualities of mind and character promise success in college. Prospective students should send in a completed application, a transcript, test scores (where applicable), and a resume of extracurricular activities. A campus interview is strongly recommended. For freshman applicants, the SAT I or ACT is not required but is recommended. Freshman applicants should have completed a minimum of six semesters in a regular diploma program in an accredited secondary school. Students may be admitted for deferred entrance or to advanced standing. Transfer applicants must have a minimum overall GPA of 2.0.

Application and Information

The College has no application deadlines. Students are accepted on a rolling basis and are notified of a decision within thirty days of receipt of the application and all supporting documents. The College advises candidates to submit all materials before March 1 for admission in September. There is an application fee of $25.

Robert A. Croot
Dean for Enrollment Management
Cazenovia College
Cazenovia, New York 13035
Telephone: 315-655-7208
800-654-3210 (toll-free)
Fax: 315-655-4860
E-mail: admission@cazenovia.edu
World Wide Web: http://www.cazenovia.edu/

A lakeside study break.

CEDAR CREST COLLEGE

ALLENTOWN, PENNSYLVANIA

The College

Since its founding in 1867 as an independent liberal arts college for women, Cedar Crest has educated women for leadership in a changing world. Approximately 1,700 students come to the College annually from twenty-six states and twenty other countries. The 11:1 student-faculty ratio provides for small classes, individual advising, and independent work in an environment that emphasizes interdisciplinary, values-oriented education. The Honor Philosophy is the most compelling statement of each student's rights and responsibilities for her own academic and cocurricular performance.

Cedar Crest's science programs, including conservation biology, forensic science, genetic engineering, neuroscience, nuclear medicine, nursing, and nutrition, generate the largest student enrollment. Business, psychology, and education generate the next largest enrollments. The genetic engineering major was the first such program at a women's college and the second at an undergraduate institution.

Cedar Crest has a comprehensive wellness program for all students that includes a walkers/runners club, personalized sports training, and nutrition counseling through the College's Allen Center for Nutrition.

Student Affairs sponsors workshops and retreats on leadership and service throughout the year. More than fifty campus organizations offer opportunities in the performing arts, preprofessional areas, environmental awareness, cultural diversity, and much more. An active community service program is comprised of student and faculty volunteers with many groups from Habitat for Humanity to the Girls Club. Healthy lifestyle, community building, and innovative quality of life programs are held regularly in the four residence halls.

The Office of Career Planning offers placement opportunities, internships at nearly 350 companies worldwide, and four-year guidance in preparing for applying and interviewing for jobs and graduate schools.

The Cedar Crest Classics compete in eight NCAA Division III intercollegiate sports: basketball, cross-country, field hockey, lacrosse, soccer, softball, tennis, and volleyball. Intramural activities include badminton, basketball, soccer, softball, and tennis. The Equestrian Club competes in collegiate horse shows.

Cedar Crest's academic programs are fully accredited by the Middle States Association of Colleges and Schools, and, where appropriate, by the American Medical Association, American Dietetic Association, American Bar Association, National League for Nursing Accrediting Commission (B.S. only), and National Council on Social Work Education and by the Departments of Education of New York, New Jersey, and Pennsylvania.

Location

Cedar Crest's 84-acre campus, a nationally registered arboretum, is situated in a well-established residential section of Allentown, a mid-sized city (105,000) in the Lehigh Valley of eastern Pennsylvania. In Allentown, students enjoy the Allentown Art Museum, three professional orchestras, numerous community theater companies, and public parks with jogging paths, riding trails, picnic areas, and other recreational facilities. Sites for skiing, whitewater rafting, and hiking are nearby. By car or bus, Cedar Crest is less than 2 hours from New York City; 1 hour from Philadelphia; just under 3 hours from Washington, D.C.; and 2 hours from the Jersey Shore. The Pocono Mountains are less than an hour away. The Lehigh Valley International Airport, only 10 minutes away, is served by major airlines with connecting flights to most major cities in the United States.

Majors and Degrees

Cedar Crest offers B.A. and B.S. degrees in accounting, art, biochemistry, biology, business administration, chemistry, communications, computer information systems, conservation biology, dance, education (elementary and secondary), English, fine arts, forensic science, genetic engineering, history, international languages (Spanish), mathematics, music, neuroscience, nuclear medicine, nursing, nutrition, political science, psychology, social work, and theater. With committee approval, a student may pursue a self-designed major.

Preprofessional programs include dentistry, law, medicine, and veterinary medicine.

Certificate programs are offered in gerontology, human resource management, and nuclear medicine.

Certification programs include public school nurse studies (post-baccalaureate), elementary/secondary teacher studies, and social work.

A new five-year B.S./master's program in education began in spring 2003.

Academic Program

Self-designed majors, double majors, minors, independent study programs, and individual and group research projects support serious concentration at the undergraduate level. Working with her adviser, each student designs a program of study that meets the 120-credit College (nursing: 126 credits) and major requirements as well as her personal interests and professional goals. The College's curriculum is structured to provide course work in the areas that define a liberal arts education. Students can select or self design a theme to pursue their liberal arts course work. The Sophomore Ethical Life Course integrates applied ethics and service-learning opportunities. Science majors begin conducting advanced research at the freshman level, opening opportunities that often lead to internships at major research institutions.

Highly motivated students with records of academic excellence may participate in the four-year Honors Program. The program incorporates seminars not offered in the regular course schedule with off-campus activities and advanced creative and research projects.

Each major has a Capstone experience that reflects on previous learning and experience and explores issues emerging in the present and expected in the future. The academic program emphasizes independent and faculty-supported student research as a paradigm for dealing effectively with the information explosion.

Off-Campus Programs

Internship opportunities enable Cedar Crest students to explore career options and gain practical experience at major corporations, national nonprofit organizations, and health-care facilities. Students have completed internships as a CNN foreign correspondent with the United Nations, as an FBI honors intern working on a database for DNA fingerprinting, and as research assistants at Cold Spring Harbor Laboratory and other nationally recognized cancer research laboratories. Students may also participate in the Washington Semester at American University or study-abroad programs for a summer, semester, or an entire year or do fieldwork at nearby Hawk Mountain Wildlife Sanctuary.

At no added cost, Cedar Crest students may cross-register at Lehigh and DeSales Universities and Lafayette, Moravian, and Muhlenberg Colleges, all nearby schools.

Academic Facilities

Cressman Library collections include books, periodicals, and electronic and audiovisual resources. Access to the collections is through an online catalog that also provides access to the Library of Congress, OCLC, remote data and indexing sources, and 1.75 million volumes available with daily delivery through the local academic consortium. Campus-wide Internet/World Wide Web connections provide access to full-text reference tools and journals.

Other buildings on the campus house theaters, art galleries, sculpture gardens, student exhibit space, computer labs, multimedia classrooms, a multimedia development lab, music practice rooms, a video production studio, dance and art studios and workshops, a ceramics studio, a state-of-the art nutrition laboratory, spectrophotometry equipment, up-to-date genetic engineering laboratories, a greenhouse, dining services, a bookstore, a post office, a gymnasium, a fitness center, an aquatics center, and a new computational biology center. The campus also includes tennis courts and regulation fields for field hockey, lacrosse, soccer, and softball. In fall 2002, Cedar Crest opened the new Rodale Aquatic Center for Civic Health, which is a two-pool complex that houses health and fitness programming for the entire campus community.

Costs

For 2003–04, the comprehensive resident fee was $28,170, including $20,596 for tuition and $7274 for room and board.

Financial Aid

Cedar Crest offers a generous program of financial aid based on academic achievement and financial need, including scholarships, grants, loans, and employment. Federal funds available are Federal Pell Grants, Federal Supplemental Educational Opportunity Grants, Federal Perkins Loans, Federal Work-Study Program awards, and Nursing Student Loans. The size of an award varies with need. More than 80 percent of the students at Cedar Crest receive aid. Students applying for financial aid should file the Free Application for Federal Student Aid (FAFSA). Outstanding international students may also qualify for financial aid.

Applicants who rank in the top 20 percent of their class and score 1150 or higher on the SAT I (24 on the ACT) can qualify for a scholarship of up to one-half tuition per year. Sibling grants are awarded to students when 2 siblings are attending Cedar Crest full-time, concurrently.

Recipients of Girl Scout Gold awards, graduates of Governor's School of Excellence programs, and HOBY alumnae are also eligible for scholarship recognition.

Trustee Scholarships of full tuition for senior year are awarded to students with a Dean's List cumulative GPA of 3.75 at the end of their junior year at Cedar Crest. Students must be enrolled full time at Cedar Crest for three years prior to receiving this full tuition scholarship, net federal and state grants.

Students can receive an early estimate of aid eligibility by completing a Cedar Crest financial aid application/planner.

Faculty

Of the 67 full-time faculty members, 76 percent have doctorates or other terminal degrees in their field, and 55 percent are women. Excellence in teaching is the first priority of the Cedar Crest faculty. At Cedar Crest, research grows out of teaching and becomes part of the learning process. In the last six years, Cedar Crest faculty members have published books and many articles; won Fulbright fellowships, fellowships from the National Education Association and the National Endowment for the Arts, and grants from the National Science Foundation, Allen Foundation, Pennsylvania Department of Education, and the United Church of Christ; served as officers in national professional organizations; and presented research at conferences worldwide.

Student Government

Student Government is a strong and vigorous organization at Cedar Crest. Regular meetings are held to discuss policy, plan student activities, and initiate legislation. Students serve as voting members of College and faculty committees and on the Board of Trustees.

Admission Requirements

Cedar Crest seeks students who have shown academic achievement and promise and those with varied interests, talents, and backgrounds. An academic program providing a good foundation usually includes 4 years of English, 3 of mathematics, 3 of social science, 2 of a laboratory science, 2 of a foreign language, and 3 or 4 academic electives. The College considers good students whose preparation does not include all of these subjects. Through the Advanced Placement Program, qualified applicants may apply for advanced study credits at Cedar Crest.

Application and Information

Students need to submit the application form, an official transcript of the secondary school record, examination results from the SAT I or ACT, and a personal essay.

Cedar Crest has a rolling admission policy; applications are reviewed on a continuing basis. Students are encouraged to apply early in their senior year of high school. Admission is awarded for the fall or spring semester.

Transfer students applying to Cedar Crest must fulfill all of the requirements stated above. They must also submit official transcripts and a catalog from each college previously attended.

International students must complete the international student application form; students educated in non-English-speaking countries must also submit TOEFL examination scores.

An application form, the College catalog, financial aid forms, and additional information may be obtained by contacting:

Vice President for Enrollment
Cedar Crest College
100 College Drive
Allentown, Pennsylvania 18104-6196
Telephone: 800-360-1222 (toll-free)
Fax: 610-606-4647
E-mail: cccadmis@cedarcrest.edu
World Wide Web: http://www.cedarcrest.edu

CEDARVILLE UNIVERSITY

CEDARVILLE, OHIO

The University

Cedarville University is a four-year Baptist university whose mission is to "offer an education consistent with biblical truth." Because of its unusual ability to couple rigorous academic achievement with a conservative Christian world view, Cedarville consistently attracts sharp, Christian students.

More than 3,000 students from forty-eight states and eighteen other countries choose Cedarville. Two thirds of its students are from out of state. The typical Cedarville student is 18 to 22 years old, attends school full-time, lives on campus, and is at least 300 miles from home. As a result, student life is a high priority. The University sponsors more than sixty student clubs and organizations, forty intramural athletic programs, dozens of vocal and instrumental music performance groups, and three major drama productions per year. Cedarville also offers fourteen intercollegiate sports, including men's baseball, basketball, cross-country, golf, soccer, tennis, and track and field and women's basketball, cross-country, soccer, softball, tennis, track and field, and volleyball. These teams compete in the NAIA's American MidEast Conference.

All Cedarville students and faculty members testify to personal faith in Jesus Christ. The importance of spiritual development is evidenced through relevant daily chapel services, discipleship ministries, dorm prayer meetings, outreach ministries, and a required Bible minor. Students participate in more than 150 volunteer programs of community outreach and church ministry.

Cedarville University is accredited by the North Central Association of Colleges and Schools; the Commission on Collegiate Nursing Education; the Accreditation Board for Engineering and Technology, Inc.; and the Council of Social Work Education. In addition, the University is approved by the State Department of Education for the education and licensure of teachers.

The quality of Cedarville's graduates attracts more than 300 corporate employers each year. Graduates are also accepted to top graduate programs, law schools, and medical schools.

Because of its theological position and emphasis on spiritual growth, Cedarville is recommended by many evangelical groups, including the Southern Baptist Convention.

Location

The University's home is a beautiful 400-acre campus in Cedarville, Ohio, which is a small town that offers a safe learning environment. Students enjoy easy access to Dayton, Columbus, and Cincinnati.

Majors and Degrees

Cedarville University offers sixty-two majors. The Bachelor of Arts degree is available in accounting, American studies, applied psychology, athletic training, Bible, biology, biology education, chemistry, chemistry education, Christian education, communication arts, criminal justice, education (early childhood, middle childhood, secondary, and special education), electronic media, English, English education, exercise science, finance, graphic design, history, history education, history–political science, international studies, management, management information systems, marketing, mathematics, mathematics education, pastoral studies, philosophy, physical education, physical science education, physics, physics education, political science, prelaw, preseminary Bible, psychology, public administration, science education, social science, social studies education, sociology, Spanish, Spanish education, special education, sport management, technical and professional communication, theater, world missions, and youth ministries.

The Music Department offers a Bachelor of Music degree in church music ministry, keyboard pedagogy, music composition, and music performance. A Bachelor of Music Education degree is also available, with tracks in both choral and instrumental music.

Bachelor of Science degree programs include biology, chemistry, computer engineering (B.S.Cp.E.), computer science, electrical engineering (B.S.E.E.), mathematics, mechanical engineering (B.S.M.E.), nursing (B.S.N.), and social work.

Special programs include a computer/technology teaching endorsement, emergency medical technician training, environmental biology, honors, medical technology, one-year Bible certificate, TESOL teaching endorsement, and preprofessional programs in agriculture, medicine, pharmacy, and physical therapy. Army and Air Force ROTC programs are also available.

Academic Programs

The Cedarville University academic program is designed to meet the educational, moral, physical, social, and spiritual needs of students who desire to honor God with their lives. The program represents a blending of rigorous academic instruction, cocurricular activities, and spiritual development. In this setting, truth from Scripture is integrated with course content to provide effective learning and enduring life values. The knowledge and skills acquired at Cedarville provide students with professional competence in their chosen fields.

Although their work is still grounded in the traditions of a liberal arts education, two thirds of Cedarville's students are in professional programs such as business, education, science and mathematics, engineering, and nursing.

All degree programs require a minimum of 128 semester credits, consisting of major-specific courses plus general education requirements in Bible, communications, humanities, global awareness, physical education, science, mathematics, social sciences, and history. All students complete a Bible minor.

The University awards credit by testing through Advanced Placement, CLEP, and International Baccalaureate programs.

Off-Campus Programs

The University actively encourages students to enhance their classroom instruction with off-campus programs such as internships and study-abroad programs. Corporate and government internships are characteristic of programs such as Bible, business, communications, engineering, technical and professional communication, public administration, prelaw, and the social sciences.

Through its affiliation with the Council of Christian Colleges and Universities, Cedarville offers an American Studies Program, China Studies Program, Contemporary Music Program, Latin American Studies Program, Los Angeles Film Studies

Center, Middle East Studies Program, Oxford Honors Program, Oxford Summer Program, Russian Studies Program, and the Summer Institute of Journalism.

Additional off-campus programs include the Academic Residency and Research Internship for Baptists Abroad (ARRIBA), Au Sable Institute of Environmental Studies, and programs in Israel through cooperation with Jerusalem University College.

Academic Facilities

Cedarville has aggressively expanded its campus through both new construction and the modernization of existing buildings. The University has invested more than $100 million in academic facilities such as the Centennial Library, Technology Resource Center, Dixon Ministry Center, Stevens Student Center, Tyler Digital Communication Center, and Engineering, Nursing, and Science Center. These buildings are characterized by modern learning environments that exploit the pervasive computer technology on campus.

The University is recognized nationally as a leader in campus computer networking and instructional technology. The campus computer network, CedarNet, consists of more than 2,300 computers. In addition to computer labs, the library, and classrooms, networked computers are provided in every residence hall room. Each of these computers provides more than 150 software programs, online library resources, and e-mail and Internet access. Wireless network access is also available in all major academic centers and residence halls.

Cedarville offers extensive library resources through print and online collections. As a member of OhioLINK, Cedarville students can borrow from more than 9 million books and a collection of more than 20,000 electronic books and digital videos. In addition, the University library houses nearly 175,000 volumes, with access to 6,500 print and electronic full-text journals and approximately 128 online citation databases.

Costs

Tuition and fees for 2004–05 are approximately $16,032. Room and board are $5010 for the year. Books are estimated to cost $750 per year.

Financial Aid

Need-based scholarships, grants, and student loans are offered to students who demonstrate financial need using the Free Application for Federal Student Aid (FAFSA). No-need scholarships are available for achievement in academics, leadership, music, and athletics. Approximately 1,300 students are employed on campus annually.

Faculty

Cedarville faculty members are known for their academic achievement and devout Christian faith. They include 194 full-time and 50 part-time professors. Students enjoy personal attention from faculty members through academic advising and a 14:1 student-faculty ratio.

Student Government

The Student Government Association (SGA) is the representative assembly of the student body. It helps to provide a well-rounded program of extracurricular activities by supervising more than sixty student clubs and organizations. SGA also cosponsors the University's academic tutoring program.

Cedarville's faculty and staff members and students agree to live by a lifestyle statement, which is designed to honor Christ and demonstrate obedience to the Word of God. Accordingly, Cedarville students agree not to use alcoholic beverages, tobacco products, or non-medicinal drugs. In all things, they seek to serve Christ and avoid personal attitudes of dishonesty, selfishness, disrespect, racism, unethical conduct, and irreverence.

Admission Requirements

Cedarville University invites applications from high school and transfer students who are able to present strong academic records and a clear testimony of faith in Jesus Christ. Qualified applicants typically have 4 years of high school English, 3 to 4 years of college-preparatory math, 3 years of science, 3 years of history or social studies, and 2 to 3 years of foreign language. Applicants with the highest probability for admission have a GPA of 3.0 or better in college-preparatory courses and an ACT score of at least 22 or an SAT I score of at least 1050.

Applicants must submit autobiographical information, high school transcripts, ACT or SAT I scores, a guidance counselor's recommendation, the recommendation of a church leader, and a $30 application fee. Applicants must also provide transcripts of all college course work completed.

Cedarville does not discriminate on the basis of race, color, sex, or national origin.

Application and Information

Enrollment is limited, and qualified students are accepted on a rolling admissions basis. Therefore, freshman applicants are encouraged to apply between August and December of their senior year.

For more information, interested students should contact:

Director of Admissions
Cedarville University
251 North Main Street
Cedarville, Ohio 45314
Telephone: 800-CEDARVILLE (800-233-2784, toll-free)
E-mail: admissions@cedarville.edu
World Wide Web: http://www.cedarville.edu

The paths of many students cross at the Stevens Student Center.

CENTRAL CONNECTICUT STATE UNIVERSITY

NEW BRITAIN, CONNECTICUT

The University

Central Connecticut State University (CCSU) is a regional, comprehensive public university that is dedicated to learning in the liberal arts and sciences and to education for the professions. Founded in 1849, CCSU is Connecticut's oldest publicly supported institution of higher education. Comprising four schools—Arts and Sciences, Business, Education and Professional Studies, and Technology—CCSU offers undergraduate and graduate programs through the master's and sixth-year levels and a doctoral program (Ed.D.) in educational leadership. Committed to offering Connecticut citizens access to its distinctive academic programs of high quality, the University is also a responsive and creative intellectual resource for the people and institutions of the state. More than 85 percent of its graduates remain in Connecticut, contributing to the intellectual, cultural, and economic health of the state.

CCSU has earned designation as a statewide Center of Excellence in international education and in technology. Honoring the University's "visionary innovations in undergraduate education," the Association of American Colleges and Universities selected CCSU as one of only sixteen Leadership Institutions in the nation and the only one in Connecticut.

CCSU is the largest of four universities in the Connecticut State University system, enrolling 7,284 full-time and 4,807 part-time students. CCSU's student body represents the spectrum of ethnic and socioeconomic groups. Most students are Connecticut residents, with others coming from more than thirty states and forty other countries. Approximately 2,100 undergraduates live on campus in eight residence halls. Five meal plans are available and include options for different tastes and needs. Memorial Hall is the main dining hall.

The recently renovated Student Center houses the student newspaper, the radio station, dining areas, a game room, TV lounges, computer workstations, and other facilities. Students produce concerts, dances, film series, and other activities. The Student Government Association funds a yearbook, sports clubs, and cultural and special interest groups. More than 100 campus clubs and organizations are available, ranging from academic/career groups to religious, performing, and political clubs as well as fraternities, sororities, and honors and professional societies. Extracurricular activities include movies, intramural sports, lectures, musical and dramatic productions, and art exhibits. CCSU's eighteen NCAA Division I intercollegiate programs are a major source of excitement. Sports for men include baseball, basketball, cross-country, football, golf, indoor and outdoor track, and soccer. Women participate in basketball, cross-country, golf, indoor and outdoor track, lacrosse, soccer, softball, swimming and diving, and volleyball. Students interested in intramural sports enjoy basketball, flag football, floor hockey, softball, and volleyball. The modern Kaiser Hall Gymnasium offers an Olympic-size swimming pool, modern exercise equipment, a state-of-the-art fitness center, a weight-training room, and an athletic training center. The Kaiser Annex has a running track and tennis and basketball courts.

The Ruthe Boyea Women's Center is a multipurpose program and service center for women in the student body and on the staff and faculty. The University Police Department operates 24 hours per day, 365 days per year. Among the services they provide are day and night escort services, crime prevention and awareness programs, and an emergency phone system throughout campus. The CCSU Fire Marshal's office maintains computerized fire detection/alarm systems.

Location

CCSU is located in New Britain, home to a world-renowned art museum, a minor league baseball team, a 1,200-acre municipal park system, and a wide range of cultural activities. The University, located at the edge of the city, is in the heart of Connecticut, 15 minutes from the state capital of Hartford and its many restaurants, theaters, and sports and concert activities. One of the state's major shopping centers is West Farms Mall, 3 miles from campus. CCSU is 2 hours away from New York and Boston.

Majors and Degrees

CCSU offers the following degrees: Bachelor of Arts, Bachelor of Fine Arts, Bachelor of Science, Bachelor of Science in Engineering Technology, Bachelor of Science in Industrial Technology, and Bachelor of Science in Nursing.

The Bachelor of Arts is awarded in anthropology, art–ceramics, art–graphic design, art–illustration, art–painting, art–printmaking, art–sculpture, communication, criminology, economics, economics–operations research, English, French, geography, geography–planning, German, history, international studies (interdisciplinary), Italian, mathematics, mathematics–actuarial science, mathematics–operations research, mathematics–statistics, music, philosophy, philosophy–applied ethics, political science, political science–public administration, psychology, social work, sociology, Spanish, special studies (interdisciplinary), and theater (B.A./B.F.A.).

Bachelor of Science degree programs include accounting, athletic training, biology, biology–environmental science, chemistry, chemistry–biology, chemistry–business, chemistry–computer science, chemistry–environmental science, civil engineering technology, composites and polymer engineering technology, computer science, earth sciences, education (interdisciplinary), engineering (transfer program with University of Connecticut), entrepreneurship, exercise science and health promotion, finance, general science, graphic design (industrial technology), hospitality and tourism, industrial systems engineering technology, industrial technology, international business, international studies (interdisciplinary), management and organization, management information systems, manufacturing engineering technology, marketing, mechanical engineering technology, medical technology, nursing (B.S.N.), physics, science–environmental interpretation (interdisciplinary), science–physical sciences (interdisciplinary), social science, and special studies (interdisciplinary).

Certifiable programs in education for which a Bachelor of Science is awarded include early childhood education (preK–3), elementary education (1–6), secondary education (7–12), and special subject fields (nursery–12). Subject matter areas for early childhood education are English, general science, and mathematics. Single–subject matter majors for the elementary education program are English, geography, history, mathematics, science–biology, and science–earth sciences. Dual–subject matter programs include English/geography, history/linguistics, history/writing, mathematics/biology, and mathematics/earth sciences. Majors in secondary education include biology, chemistry, earth sciences, English, French, general science, German, history, Italian, mathematics, physics, social sciences, and Spanish. Special subject field majors are art education, music education, physical education, and technology education.

Preprofessional study is offered in prelaw and prehealth/premedical studies.

Academic Programs

The graduation requirements for a bachelor's degree are a minimum of 122 to 130 hours of credit. Majors consist of a minimum of 30 to 68 prescribed hours of credit in one specific, approved field. A total of 45 credit hours of general education studies must be completed and include writing, foreign language proficiency, and international requirements. Some of the professional B.S. degree programs enable students to develop a minor or a concentration in addition to the major.

Academically talented students can enroll in the Honors Program, in which interdisciplinary, team-taught courses focus on the themes of Western culture, science and society, and world cultures. Good academic standing and 30 earned academic credits at CCSU make a student eligible for the Cooperative Education Program. Students can earn between $8000 and $13,000 each work term by combining five months of on-campus study with six months of employment.

CCSU operates on a two-semester system. The fall semester usually starts the first week in September and ends in mid-December. The spring semester runs from the third week of January to mid-May. CCSU offers multiple summer sessions from June to August and two 3-week winter sessions in December and January.

The School of Technology's Pathway programs provide a seamless route between other institutions in the Connecticut State University System and Connecticut's community technical colleges without loss of credit or repeated courses.

Off-Campus Programs

Internships are available through government offices, newspapers, nonprofit agencies, and many businesses. In addition, off-campus internships are possible through study-abroad and consortium arrangements with the University of Connecticut and other institutions in the Connecticut State University System. The study-abroad program offers students a semester-long or yearlong exchange in which they enroll overseas and study via a cultural immersion program.

Academic Facilities

CCSU's forty buildings on a campus of 300 acres provide students with a full range of learning facilities. The Elihu Burritt Library contains nearly 700,000 volumes, more than 3,000 periodical titles, extensive research materials on microfiche and microfilm, and extensive online services and CD-ROM databases. CCSU's online public catalog provides access to the holdings of all four Connecticut State University libraries. The Marcus White Microcomputer Laboratory, a state-of-the-art facility, offers the latest PCs, Macintoshes, printers, scanners, and online capabilities. Other computer facilities are available in the residence halls. Some sixty-five smart classrooms and nine buildings offer multimedia technology that includes computers, DVD players, satellite teleconferencing capabilities, and other high-technology systems. The Samuel S. T. Chen Art Center's gallery area presents changing exhibits, lectures, and programs.

Costs

Annual tuition and fees for the 2003–04 academic year for Connecticut residents were $5384. Tuition and fees for out-of-state residents were $12,372. On-campus room (double occupancy) and board fees for the year were approximately $7000; costs vary slightly, depending on the meal plan selected and the particular residence hall. Annual costs for books, travel, and personal expenses vary but are estimated at approximately $2500. All costs are subject to change. Students may contact the Bursar's Office for the most current cost information.

Financial Aid

CCSU's Office of Financial Aid works with students and families to provide assistance to those who are unable to meet educational expenses entirely on their own. Financial aid is provided in three basic forms: grants, work-study employment, and educational loans, which must be repaid. The University offers Connecticut State University Grants, Connecticut Aid for Public Colleges Grants, Federal Pell Grants, Federal Supplemental Educational Opportunity Grants, Federal Direct Stafford Subsidized and Unsubsidized Loans, Federal Direct PLUS Loans (parent loans), and Federal Perkins Loans. Students may also visit Central's Financial Aid Home Page (http://www.ccsu.edu/finaid/) for additional information. Students are required to submit the FAFSA and other basic required documents by deadlines set by the school.

Faculty

Seventy percent of CCSU's faculty members hold doctoral degrees. Others have advanced degrees and are actively involved in research, publishing, and community service. CCSU's faculty members are dedicated to teaching; it is their prime concern and the basis of their students' successes. Due to CCSU's low 16:1 student-faculty ratio, students are better able to take advantage of their professors' expertise and to benefit from personal attention.

Student Government

All of CCSU's full-time undergraduate students are members of the Student Government Association (SGA). The SGA Senate is the representative body of the SGA, and the full-time undergraduates democratically elect its members, the Executive Officers and Senators of the SGA. It promotes student participation in various projects, committees, and organizations at the University and at state and national levels that help shape the University and education in Connecticut. The SGA Senate allocates the SGA portion of the student activity fee to promote and fund student clubs, activities, services, and issues that benefit students and their educational opportunities.

Admission Requirements

CCSU is selective in its admission policy, valuing excellence and achievement in academic scholarship, community and school involvement, and individual achievements. The University welcomes applications from students with a broad range of abilities, interests, and backgrounds and evaluates each student on the merits of his or her readiness to succeed, which is based on past demonstrations of academic and personal success. No applicant is denied admission because of race, color, religious belief, national origin, gender, sexual orientation, age, or disability. A candidate must be a graduate of an accredited high school or preparatory school or hold an equivalency diploma. First-year students' secondary school preparation should include at least 13 units of college-preparatory course work, including English (4 units), mathematics (3 units, including algebra I and II and geometry), science (2 units, including 1 unit of a lab science), social sciences (2 units, including U.S. history), and foreign language (3 units of the same language is recommended). Other factors include the student's academic performance in high school course work, competitive SAT I scores, and rank in class. A personal essay and letters of recommendation are required. Transferring students are encouraged to apply by contacting the Office of Recruitment and Admissions at the address below for details.

Application and Information

Fall semester candidates for admission should apply by May 1 and spring semester candidates by November 1. The Office of Recruitment and Admissions begins notifications by December 1 for fall semester candidates and continues notification on a rolling admission basis. Spring candidates are notified beginning in September. Early admission is recommended for those interested in housing and financial aid. An applicant should submit a completed application with a $50 application fee, an official high school transcript, SAT I scores, rank in class, recommendation letters, and other required documents by stated deadlines. Applications may be completed and submitted online at http://www.applyweb.com/apply/ccsu/menu.html.

To request an application, students should contact:

Myrna Garcia-Bowen, Director
Office of Recruitment and Admissions
Central Connecticut State University
1615 Stanley Street
New Britain, Connecticut 06050-4010
Telephone: 860-832-CCSU
888-733-2278 (toll-free in Connecticut)
860-832-2289 (tours)
E-mail: admissions@ccsu.edu
tour@ccsu.edu (tours)
World Wide Web: http://www.ccsu.edu

CENTRAL MICHIGAN UNIVERSITY

MOUNT PLEASANT, MICHIGAN

The University

Central Michigan University (CMU) is a vibrant community of scholars, students, and partners who are dedicated to achieving excellence in undergraduate and graduate learning and to addressing society's emerging needs in a wide range of academic areas, from health care to teacher education, business entrepreneurship, and nanotechnology research.

Founded in 1892 as a small college committed to training teachers and business professionals, CMU today is a doctoral research–intensive institution, offering more than 170 programs at all levels—bachelor's, master's, specialist, and doctoral.

A large, complex university with more than 28,000 students, CMU nonetheless maintains a friendly, small-college learning environment with distinguished professors who share a strong commitment to undergraduate teaching, research, and discovery. Its main campus is home to more than 19,000 students, including a freshmen class with a cumulative 3.36 grade point average.

CMU is a place where students experience learning through real-world problem solving and close interaction with their professors. Half of CMU students complete internships and cooperative work experiences, and many students are involved in research, leadership training, volunteer and community service, international study, and professional clubs and student organizations.

More than 5,900 students occupy CMU's twenty residence halls. Three new halls opening in 2003 provide additional first-class accommodations for the growing on-campus student population.

Location

Central Michigan's main campus is located in Mount Pleasant, a progressive city of about 25,000 residents in Michigan's scenic Lower Peninsula. To the north and west are the lakes, streams, ski resorts, beaches, and magnificent wilderness areas for which Michigan is famous. To the south and east lie rich farmland and larger metropolitan areas with numerous museums, theaters, art fairs, and shopping opportunities.

The city's quaint downtown district features specialty stores and boutiques of all types. These shops are within walking distance of campus. While this community is fond if its classic appeal, it also is proud of its many modern facilities. New governmental buildings, numerous churches, a modern hospital, a large community library, developed parks, and convenient shopping plazas blend comfortably with Mount Pleasant's heritage.

Majors and Degrees

Internationally and nationally recognized experts are found within the College of Science and Technology, the College of Communication and Fine Arts, the College of Humanities and Social and Behavioral Sciences, the College of Business Administration, the Herbert H. and Grace A. Dow College of Health Professions, the College of Education and Human Services, the College of Graduate Studies, and the College of Extended Learning.

Undergraduate degree programs include Bachelor of Arts, Bachelor of Applied Arts, Bachelor of Fine Arts, Bachelor of Individualized Studies, Bachelor of Music, Bachelor of Music Education, Bachelor of Science, Bachelor of Science in Business Administration, Bachelor of Science in Engineering Technology, Bachelor of Science in Education, and Bachelor of Social Work.

Business administration majors are offered in accounting, accounting information systems, advertising, business administration, economics, entrepreneurship, finance, global business, hospitality services administration, human resources management, international business, legal studies, logistics management, management, management information systems, marketing, operations management, personal financial planning, purchasing and supply management, retailing, and retail management.

Communications majors are offered in broadcast and cinematic arts, interpersonal and public communication, journalism, integrative public relations, and theater and interpretation.

Health-related program majors are offered in allied health, athletic training/sports medicine, communication disorders, dietetics, exercise science, health administration, health fitness in preventive and rehabilitative programs, industrial safety, medical technology and biology, nutrition, personal and community health, physical therapy/pre–physical therapy, psychology, public health education and health promotion, school health education, sport studies, substance abuse education, and therapeutic recreation/recreation.

Human services majors are offered in American Indian studies, apparel merchandising and design, child development, criminal justice/sociology, family life and human sexuality, family studies, food service administration, gerontology, human development, interior design, military science (Army ROTC), outdoor and environmental education, recreation, facility management, social work, sociology, women's studies, and youth studies.

Liberal and fine arts majors are offered in American ethnic studies; anthropology; art; art history; athletic coaching; dance; economics; English language and literature; European studies; foreign languages, literatures, and cultures; geography; history; humanities; international relations/comparative politics; Latin American studies; museum studies; music; music theater; philosophy; political science; public administration; public affairs; religion; social science; social studies; sociology; and theater and interpretation.

Preprofessional majors are offered in predentistry, pre-engineering, preforestry, prelaw, premedicine and preosteopathy, prenursing, pre–occupational therapy, preoptometry, prepharmacy, pre–physical therapy/physical therapy, and pre–veterinary medicine.

Science and technology majors are offered in actuarial science, astronomy, biology, chemistry, cognitive science, computer integrated manufacturing, computer science, computer science/mathematics, computer technology, earth science, engineering, engineering technology, environmental studies, geography, geology, hydrogeology/environmental geology, industrial safety, industrial technology management, information technology, mathematics, medical technology/biology, meteorology/earth science, natural resources, neuroscience, oceanography/earth science, physics, science, and statistics.

Elementary education majors are offered in art, bilingual/bicultural-Spanish/Ojibwe, biology, child development, classroom music, dance, earth science, English, English as a second language, family studies: life management education, French, geography, German, history, industrial education, language arts, mathematics, middle-level education, outdoor and environmental education, physical education, physical science, planned program, reading in the elementary grades, school health education, science, social studies, and Spanish.

Secondary education majors are offered in art, bilingual/bicultural-Spanish/Ojibwe, biology, business teacher education, chemistry, chemistry/physics, computer science, dance, earth science, English, English as a second language, family studies: life management education, French, general business, geography, German, history, industrial education, mathematics, outdoor and environmental education, physical education, physical science, physics, school health education, social studies, Spanish, and speech.

Special education majors are offered in teachers of students with emotional impairment and teachers of students with cognitive impairment.

Academic Program

CMU's academic year consists of two semesters, with two summer sessions available. The undergraduate program of study consists of at least 124 credit hours of academic work completed according to a planned program. The plan will largely be influenced by choice of major and the general education requirements. The student must complete a designated number of hours in the humanities, natural sciences, social sciences, and integrative and area studies. The student must also complete an English and a mathematics competency requirement.

The University Honors Program is available to all students of high ability. It provides a qualitatively unique learning experience through classroom and individualized study opportunities. Honors study is flexible and can fit into any degree, major, or minor.

Off-Campus Programs

CMU offers approximately 200 study-abroad programs in more than fifty countries. The programs are designed to provide interested students with the opportunity to live and study outside the United States for a summer, semester, academic year, or even a spring break. The Office of International Education assists students in choosing an appropriate study-abroad program and works to ensure that students receive academic credit for work completed outside the United States.

Academic Facilities

CMU's $50-million Health Professions Building, which will be ready for classes in spring 2004, will unite the University's highly acclaimed health professions programs in one technologically advanced environment that is conducive to learning, treatment, collaboration, and discovery. The facility features clinical, instructional, and research wings encircling a pair of aesthetically pleasing courtyards. Each wing houses state-of-the-art clinical facilities, laboratories, classrooms, and other resources to support CMU's growing health professions programs.

CMU's Student Activity Center was one of the first comprehensive recreation facilities in the nation and has received numerous program and facility awards from national organizations, including the National Intramural-Recreational Sports Association (NIRSA) and the Building and Design Construction Engineering Society.

CMU's newly remodeled and expanded $50-million Charles V. Park Library merges the traditional collections of a major academic library with advanced, computer-networked information resources and services. The new library features seating for 2,655 patrons, 33 miles of electronically assisted mobile shelving, more than 350 public computer workstations, and hundreds of open Web site connections. The library also houses Clarke Historical Library, which holds extensive genealogy, local, and Native American history collections.

Costs

Tuition and fees at Central Michigan University are $5218 annually for in-state students. Room and board costs average $5924 per year, depending on accommodations and food plans. Books and supplies cost an average of $750 per year. Costs are subject to change.

Financial Aid

College education is a major financial investment. Central Michigan University is one of the most affordable universities in the state of Michigan. It is CMU's goal to make it possible for students of all degrees of financial capacity to attend CMU by awarding financial assistance in recognition of achievement, as well as financial need, and by providing advice about other financing options.

Approximately 80 percent of CMU on-campus students receive some form of financial assistance from federal, state, University, and private agency sources. The Financial Aid Office has been designed to assist the student with the financial aid application process and to inform the student of the available sources of financial assistance.

Faculty

At the heart of CMU's success are outstanding faculty members who make teaching their top priority. Graduate students do not teach undergraduate classes. Faculty members bring an excitement to the classroom that often is complemented by substantial research and creative activities of national and international importance. There are 1,045 faculty members at CMU, of whom 69 percent are full-time. The student-faculty ratio is 22:1.

Student Government

The membership of the Student Government Association (SGA) represents the students of Central Michigan University by securing an active role within the University community through the creation and passage of legislation intended to support students' rights and interests. SGA creates and provides means for discussing issues relating to students and ensures that students' concerns are fairly and accurately represented. SGA promotes a spirit of unity among all students, the administration, faculty and staff members, and community and provides recommendations to CMU administrators for the enrichment of student life on campus.

In addition to student government, there are more than 200 different academic clubs, special interest groups, and Greek organizations to choose from.

Admission Requirements

Students who have graduated from a high school, academy, or the equivalent may be admitted, provided a prediction of success at CMU can be made from high school performance, ACT scores, and all other facts included in the application. Transfer students are considered for admission, provided academic records to date demonstrate the ability to successfully complete academic course work.

CMU strongly and actively strives to increase diversity and provide equal opportunity within its community. CMU does not discriminate against persons based on age, color, disability, gender, familial status, height, marital status, national origin, political persuasion, race, religion, sexual orientation, veteran status, or weight.

Application and Information

Interested students may obtain an application form from a high school counselor, the CMU Admissions Office, or online at http://www.cmich.edu/admit.html. An application is automatically sent to students who take the ACT, receive an adequate score, and indicate CMU as one of their top three choices.

Additional information may be obtained by contacting:

Admissions Office
Warriner Hall 102
Central Michigan University
Mount Pleasant, Michigan 48859
Telephone: 989-774-3076
888-292-5366 (toll-free)
E-mail: cmuadmit@cmich.edu
World Wide Web: http://www.cmich.edu

CMU students in the library.

CENTRAL PENNSYLVANIA COLLEGE

SUMMERDALE, PENNSYLVANIA

The College

Central Pennsylvania College's hallmark is high-quality career-oriented education, which is provided by a highly qualified and dedicated faculty and staff. The College's focus is on students and their educational development, thus enhancing their ability to think critically and succeed professionally. The College's educational goal is to provide its students with the knowledge, attitude, professional demeanor, and skills necessary to secure meaningful employment in their chosen career field.

Students prepare for professional success by demonstrating academic excellence in the classroom and through application of their newly learned skills in experiential educational activities. Central Penn students not only learn theory, they also learn by doing on the latest, state-of-the-art technology by participating in activities related to their major. Although the focus of education at Central Penn is on career preparation, all degree programs have general education requirements that help graduates develop traits that prepare them for the workforce.

The College seeks to create a stimulating learning environment in which students participate in their personal development through a variety of educational experiences. Central Pennsylvania College strives to instill in its students a lifelong desire to learn and to be a contributing member of society.

Approximately 700 students are currently enrolled at Central Pennsylvania College. Students from about thirty counties within Pennsylvania represent 97 percent of the student population. Out-of-state students, primarily from Maryland, New Jersey, and New York, represent 3 percent of the student body. The student ratio of women to men at Central Penn is 5:1. Students who are members of minority groups make up about 4 percent of the student body. Approximately 77 percent of students are traditional college age (ages 18 to 20), and 23 percent are nontraditional (age 21 or older) students.

A high-quality education includes more than just academics. Students are encouraged to become involved in campus life by participating in one or more of the many clubs, organizations, or athletic activities. Central Penn's small size makes it possible for everyone to participate in activities and assume leadership roles. Whether it's basketball, volleyball, golf, tennis, cross-country, or one of the many excellent clubs or professional organizations, the student affairs staff can assist in finding an activity that is right for each student. There are many special events throughout the year that give students opportunities to get involved and experience new and exciting things. Debit Debit Credit, Travel Club, and Marketing Club are some of the career-related clubs offered at Central Penn. In addition, throughout the year, students have many opportunities to experience new and exciting activities such as river tubing, Breakaway Weekend, golf outings, and trips to local attractions, including HersheyPark; Hershey stadium; Giant Center, a site of many sport events and concerts; soccer, volleyball, and minor-league baseball games on Harrisburg's City Island; trade shows and professional soccer at the state Farm Show Complex; plus concerts, museums, movie theaters, and malls all within a short distance of the campus.

In an effort to make Central Penn a positive living and learning environment, many facilities and services are available to students. On-campus town houses and apartments are available for resident students, and all campus housing has high-speed Internet access. The two-bedroom furnished apartments and the three-bedroom furnished town houses provide students with a complete kitchen and air conditioning and are wired for cable television service. The Scoozi Café is open for breakfast, lunch, and dinner, with a meal plan available for students. The student union, in the Advanced Technology Education Center, offers snack machines, a pool table, video games, and a place to study or just relax between classes. Coin-operated laundry facilities are available in key locations on campus. There are computer labs available for student use with extended weekend and late-night hours.

Location

Central Pennsylvania College's 35-acre campus is located in suburban Harrisburg just inside the Capital Beltway off I-81 at Exit 65. Harrisburg, the state capital, is just across the Susquehanna River from the campus, offering many social, cultural, and educational activities.

Majors and Degrees

Central Penn offers programs leading to the Bachelor of Science, Associate in Science, and Associate in Applied Science degrees. Students can complete a bachelor's degree in three years and an associate degree in eighteen months.

Bachelor of Science degree programs are offered in business administration (with concentrations in e-business, finance, health-care administration, management, and marketing), criminal justice administration (with concentrations in corporate security, financial crimes, governmental criminal justice, law enforcement, and legal studies), and information technology (with concentrations in application development, cyber security, database management, multimedia/Internet production, networking management, and office technology).

Associate in Science degree programs are offered in accounting, accounting information systems, child-care management, communications, computer information systems (with concentrations in application development, networking management, and database management), criminal justice, entrepreneurship and small business, finance, marketing, paralegal studies, and retail management.

Associate in Applied Science degree programs are offered in graphic design, hotel and restaurant management, medical assisting studies, medical secretarial studies, multimedia/Internet production, office administration (with a focus in legal studies), office technology, optometric technician studies, physical therapist assistant studies, and travel and tourism operations.

For a more detailed listing of all of Central Penn's academic programs, prospective students can visit the College's Web site listed below.

Academic Program

Students who enroll in a degree program at Central Penn can be assured that the course of study concentrates in the chosen field of study. The curriculum emphasizes hands-on learning, realistic experiences, and interaction with caring professionals who have worked in the field.

Every degree program at Central Penn stresses this learn-by-doing philosophy. The high-quality degrees focus on career preparation. Each program has its own advisory board of professionals who work in the field. These men and women review the program and provide recommendations that allow Central Penn to stay current with technology and other trends in the field. In addition, Central Penn's highly qualified faculty members ensure that their students receive a high-quality education.

Off-Campus Programs

All majors at Central Penn require students to complete an internship as part of the course objective. Internships provide real-life experience by allowing students to work directly with professionals in their field. This experience establishes invaluable business contacts and often results in full-time job offers. In the past, students have enjoyed internships at many sites, including Walt Disney World, the Pennsylvania state capital, travel agencies, and major Harrisburg-based accounting firms.

Academic Facilities

The Charles T. Jones Leadership Library provides a variety of educational resources to enhance the student's college experience. By using a Central Penn ID, students have access to electronic, book, and periodical resources as well as interlibrary loan agreements. The law library houses the legal reference collection to facilitate a legal learning environment.

Costs

For 2004–05, tuition (36 credits/12 credits each term) is $9900, housing is $4350 (for double-room occupancy), the meal plan (four meals per week) is $825, and the student fee is $540. For a complete listing of all costs for 2004–05, prospective students should visit the Web site at http://www.centralpenn.edu/admissions/financial_aid/.

Financial Aid

Central Pennsylvania College recognizes the need for financial aid to help students meet the cost of higher education. Therefore, the College provides grants, scholarships, loans, and work-study through federal, state, private, and institutional sources to help eligible students meet some of those costs.

The following programs are the major financial aid resources available to students: Federal Pell Grant, PHEAA State Grant, Federal Supplemental Educational Opportunity Grant (FSEOG), Federal Work-Study Program, Federal Stafford Student Loan (Subsidized and Unsubsidized), and Federal Parent Loan for Undergraduate Students (PLUS) programs. In addition, the College has agreements with several lending institutions to provide students and their parents with affordable alternative loans that can be used to supplement the student's financial aid award package. Students may receive assistance from any one of these or from a combination of all of these programs, in what is called a financial aid package. Eligibility for these programs is based on the student completing and submitting the forms described above. Awards are not automatically renewable. Students must reapply each year. For more information, students should call the Financial Aid Office at the telephone number listed below.

Many students choose to work part-time while going to college. The Career Services Director keeps a list of available part-time jobs and assists students in meeting their needs. On the average, students who do hold part-time positions work approximately 15 to 20 hours per week, so they are still able to devote adequate time to their studies.

Faculty

Attending classes at Central Pennsylvania College is a highly personalized experience. The class size averages 16 students to 1 faculty member. Students receive a high-quality education from a caring, talented, and dedicated faculty that takes pride in each student's educational accomplishments.

Central Penn believes in graduate success. In fact, 98 percent of Central Penn graduates find employment or continue their education within one year of graduating. The College makes every effort to help in the student's job search. The Career Services Director works with the student in the preparation of the resume and cover letter, assists with interviewing techniques, and points out career opportunities.

Student Government

At Central Penn, "student affairs" embodies all the educational and developmental aspects of a student's life that are not directly related to the classroom experience. Central Penn takes these responsibilities seriously, as it does its continued commitment to academic excellence and its long-standing success in preparing students for the workforce.

Students are expected to conduct themselves in an appropriate manner, which is defined in the Student Handbook and Residence Hall Lease Agreement. The students' living comfort, classroom atmosphere, and personal rights are considered important and should not be infringed upon; therefore, guidelines for conduct are seen as a benefit to the student. Central Penn follows a published judiciary process, which can result in appropriate disciplinary action. This process is published in the Student Handbook and can be discussed with the staff members in the Student Affairs Office.

Admission Requirements

To enroll in a degree program, an applicant must be a high school graduate or have earned a GED or Pennsylvania Home School Diploma. The College welcomes applications from traditional and continuing education students seeking to prepare for a career or a promotion. Prospective students should submit an application for admission and official copies of high school and/or college transcripts and attend a personal interview with the Admissions Office. Applicants should call the Admissions Office at the telephone number listed below to set up a campus visit for themselves and their families or friends.

Application and Information

Although the deadline for submitting an application for admission is ten working days prior to the first day of each term, Central Penn urges students to apply early, particularly if students wish to live on campus. For an application, applicants should call the Admissions Office at the telephone number listed below between 8 a.m. and 5 p.m., Monday through Friday. The application is also available online at the Web site listed below. There is no application fee for applying to Central Penn.

For further information, applicants should contact:

Central Pennsylvania College
Campus on College Hill and Valley Roads
Summerdale, Pennsylvania 17093
Telephone: 800-759-2727 (toll-free)
World Wide Web: http://www.centralpenn.edu

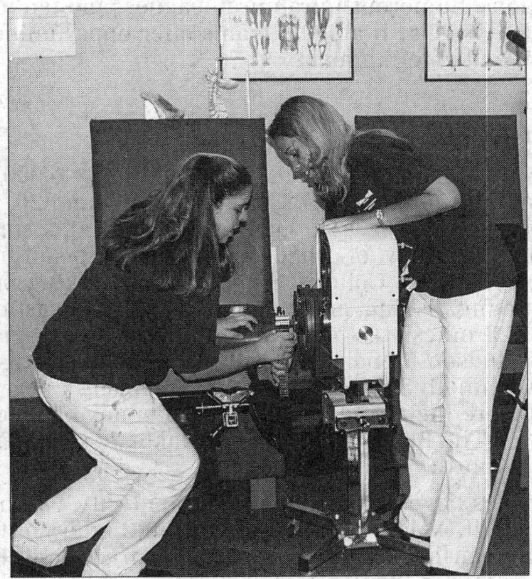

Students receive hands-on training at Central Penn.

CHADRON STATE COLLEGE

CHADRON, NEBRASKA

The College

Chadron State College (CSC) challenges and prepares students to realize academic, personal, and professional success. These successes are developed through experiences in activities on and off campus. Founded in 1911 as Nebraska State Normal School, Chadron State has a proven record of graduates who excel. The professors are approachable and work closely with the students. The total fall 2003 enrollment was 2,711 students. The student body is composed of students from various ethnic and racial backgrounds. The majority of the student population comes from Nebraska, Wyoming, South Dakota, and Colorado; twelve other countries are also represented on the campus. Forty-one percent of the undergraduate students are men.

A combination of academic offerings and faculty expertise enhances the rewards from students' efforts at Chadron State College. Chadron State offers Bachelor of Arts, Bachelor of Science, Bachelor of Applied Sciences, and Bachelor of Science in Education programs (four-year degrees) as well as the Master of Arts in Education, Master of Business Administration, Master of Science in Education, and Specialist in Education. The College is accredited by the Higher Learning Commission of the North Central Association of Colleges and Schools, the National Council for Accreditation of Teacher Education, the Council on Social Work Education, and the Nebraska State Department of Education.

A college campus environment in beautiful northwest Nebraska makes the location a great place to live and study. Tall, pine-clad buttes of a national forest extend across the south end of the campus. In addition, two state parks are within driving distance of the College. Chadron State College has six spacious residence halls, a physical activity center with an indoor track, three versatile basketball/tennis/volleyball courts, a weight-training room, five racquetball courts, and specialized classrooms for dance, cardiovascular exercise, and gymnastics. Chadron State also has a student center, a beautiful fine arts building with two theaters, an educational technology and distance learning center, a three-story library, and a media center. Sixty-nine campus clubs and organizations, numerous intramural leagues, and ten intercollegiate NCAA Division II athletic teams offer opportunities for involvement and entertainment.

Location

Chadron is a community of approximately 6,000 people. Located at the junction of U.S. Highways 385 and 20, Chadron has a low crime rate. The national forest and state parks surrounding the city of Chadron provide a beautiful recreational aspect to the College. Students enjoy hiking, mountain biking, hunting, fishing, and camping as favorite pastimes. Fort Robinson, 28 miles west, was once a colorful frontier military post. The Hudson-Meng Bison Kill Site, the Agate Fossil Beds, and the Mammoth Site are nearby. Neighboring Cherry County produces more high-grade beef cattle than any other county in this country. The Black Hills of South Dakota are only an hour's drive to the north.

Major airlines have connections into Rapid City, South Dakota, and Scottsbluff, Nebraska; both are within 2 hours of Chadron. A commuter airline connects Denver, Colorado, and Chadron. Bus service is also available in and out of Chadron. Six major fast food businesses and several fine dining restaurants provide numerous opportunities for eating out. Four theater screens provide movies each night of the week. Many other forms of entertainment can be found in Chadron, as the College brings entertainers and fine arts attractions to the city regularly.

Majors and Degrees

Bachelor of Arts degrees are awarded in applied history, art (with options in two-dimensional, three-dimensional, and graphic design), business administration (with options in accounting, agribusiness, economics, finance, management, management information systems, marketing, and office management), English, family and consumer sciences (with options in child development, design and merchandising, family and consumer studies, food management, and human services), history, industrial management (with options in agriculture, graphic arts, and manufacturing), journalism, justice studies (with options in criminal justice and legal studies), library media, music (with options in music performance and commercial music business), psychology (with options in general psychology and substance abuse), recreation (with options in fitness and exercise, leisure services, and sport leadership), social work, sociology, Spanish, speech communication, and theater.

Bachelor of Science degrees are awarded in biology (with options in environmental studies, general biology, and human biology), chemistry, clinical laboratory science (medical technology), health sciences, information science and technology, mathematics, physical science (with options in chemistry, geoscience, and physics), and range management (with options in rangeland business, rangeland livestock production, and range management).

A Bachelor of Applied Sciences (B.A.S.) degree is now available. This program is designed for individuals who have completed an Associate of Science or Associate of Applied Science degree from an accredited technical or community college. The B.A.S. degree is intended to enhance technical learning with general education courses and advanced technical support courses to meet individual career and education goals of the student. Options may be selected in agricultural operations, computers and electronics, health care, industrial trades, or management services.

The Bachelor of Science in Education is offered in art (K–12), basic business education, biology, chemistry, Earth science, economics, English, English (4–9), extended health education, family and consumer sciences (4–9 and 7–12), health and physical education (7–12), health education (7–12), history, industrial technology (7–12), language arts (7–12), mathematics (4–9 and 7–12), middle grades (4–9), music (K–12) and vocal music (K–8), natural science, physical education (K–8 and 7–12), physical science, physics, social science, Spanish, speech communication, speech communication and theater, theater, trade and industrial education (10–12), and vocational business education.

Chadron offers elementary education endorsements in early childhood education (Pre-K–3), elementary education (K–8), and mild/moderate disabilities (K–12 and 7–12). Supplemental endorsements are available in adapted physical education, coaching, computer science, driver education, and family and consumer sciences-related occupations (7–12). Endorsements to teach are offered in diversified occupations (7–12) and vocational special needs/school-to-work (7–12).

Academic Program

Chadron State College has an academic year divided into fall, spring, and summer semesters. Students seeking a baccalaureate degree from Chadron State College must complete the requirements for the program in addition to the general studies requirements. Bachelor of Arts and Bachelor of Science in education degrees are granted upon completion of a minimum total of 125 semester hours—45 of which must be at the 300 or 400 (junior or senior) level. A grade point average of 2.0 (on a 4.0 scale) must be maintained for the Bachelor of Arts programs, and a 2.5 GPA must be maintained for the Bachelor of Science in education programs. No more than 66 credit hours may be transferred or applied toward a baccalaureate degree from a two-year institution. Degree requirements for the B.A.S. degree include a minimum of 125 semester credit hours, 45 credit hours of upper-division course work (24 of the last 30 credit hours must be from CSC), 40 semester credit hours of CSC general studies, 36 semester credit hours of upper-division courses to support the student's chosen option, and at least a cumulative GPA of 2.0 (on a 4.0 scale).

Chadron State College offers alternative options for earning credit. Course work may be supplemented by internships and a cooperative learning program. Travel opportunities for credit during the school year and the summers are available. Independent studies and the College-Level Examination Program (CLEP) are available as well.

Off-Campus Programs

Several low-cost tours and field trips are arranged by the College, usually in the spring and summer months. Internships are encouraged for junior and senior students. Summer travel opportunities are developed for which students may receive credit. In the past, tours have gone to Europe, Japan, Canada, Nassau, and Mexico as well as various parts of the United States, including Alaska and Hawaii.

Academic Facilities

The Reta King Library currently contains 211,758 books, 361,172 microform titles, and 730 periodicals. The library provides a computer laboratory, duplicating machines, and microfilm/microfiche readers for student and faculty use. Students also have access to the card catalogs of the two other state colleges in Nebraska and an electronic database with access to 3,500 full-text and 6,000 indexed periodicals. The information highway of the Internet is readily accessible as well. The College has more than 175 terminals, including PCs and Macintosh computers for student use in the computer labs, classrooms, library, and residence halls.

Costs

For the 2003–04 academic year, the comprehensive cost of tuition, fees, room, and board for Nebraska residents was $6945. For nonresident students the cost was $9585. Other expenses such as books, travel, and supplies cost approximately $2475.

Financial Aid

Students seeking financial aid must complete the application for admission to Chadron State College and submit the $15 required application fee. Undergraduate students should file the Free Application for Federal Student Aid (FAFSA). After receiving the results from the processor, students should forward them to the College Director of Financial Aid. Undergraduate applications for financial assistance provide consideration for the Federal Pell Grant, Federal Work-Study, Federal Perkins Loan, Federal Supplemental Educational Opportunity Grant, Federal PLUS, and Federal Family Education Loan Programs as well as the State Scholarship Award Program and Student Assistance Program. A monthly payment plan is available through the Business Office. CSC provides electronic FAFSA processing.

Faculty

The College currently has a teaching faculty of 118 members (97 full-time, 70 percent of whom have terminal degrees). Ninety-nine percent of the faculty members advise undergraduate students. Each faculty member is involved in student activities. The vast majority of the undergraduate classes are taught by faculty members. The student–undergraduate faculty ratio of 19:1 allows close relationships between faculty members and students.

Student Government

A large number of students are actively involved in the student government. Numerous committees and organizations, including Student Senate, make an impact on the College. Students take part in decisions concerning scholastic, collegiate, intellectual, recreation, social, and cultural activities on and off campus.

Admission Requirements

Chadron State College welcomes inquiries regarding the College's programs and admission requirements. The College has an open admission policy for all students. To ensure a more successful college career, Chadron State recommends that a student pursue the following courses in high school: 4 units of English; 3 units of mathematics; 3 units of social studies, including 1 unit of American history and 1 unit of global studies; 2 units of laboratory science; and other academic courses selected from areas such as foreign language, visual or performing arts, and computer literacy. Applications for admission should be submitted by currently enrolled high school students between the beginning of their last year and one month prior to the beginning of the term for which they seek admission. Individuals who have completed high school should submit their application materials at least one month prior to the beginning of the term for which they wish to be admitted.

Application and Information

Freshman applicants should submit a completed application for admission; a $15 application fee; an official high school transcript reflecting a graduation date, class rank, and overall grade point average; and an official ACT or SAT I score report sent from the testing headquarters. Scores from the ACT/SAT I is not required for students who graduated from high school five or more years prior to enrollment at Chadron State. All students must show a physician-validated immunization record.

Transfer applicants should submit a completed application for admission, a $15 application fee, a physician-validated immunization record, and official transcripts from all colleges or universities previously attended. If the student has completed fewer than 12 semester hours of credit, he or she must also submit an official high school transcript and ACT or SAT I scores. Application forms, financial aid forms, and other information are mailed upon request. Campus visits are encouraged. For more information, students should contact:

Ms. Tena Cook Gould
Director of Admissions
Chadron State College
1000 Main Street
Chadron, Nebraska 69337-2690
Telephone: 308-432-6263
800-242-3766 (toll-free)
Fax: 308-432-6229
E-mail: inquire@csc.edu
World Wide Web: http://www.csc.edu

CHAMINADE UNIVERSITY OF HONOLULU

HONOLULU, HAWAII

The University

Chaminade University of Honolulu, a private, coeducational institution, was established in 1955 by the Society of Mary (Marianists). Named after Father William Joseph Chaminade, a French Catholic priest who ministered to his people during the late eighteenth and early nineteenth centuries and who founded the Society in 1817, the University today continues the Marianist mission of educating leaders through faith and reason. To achieve this mission, Chaminade forms a community encompassing people from diverse cultural origins, both traditional and nontraditional, who hold a variety of religious beliefs. The University encourages learning through cooperation, self-discipline, caring, and mutual respect while offering individualized attention that promotes personal and intellectual growth. A major goal of the University is to educate and train students for leadership both within Chaminade and in communities beyond the campus. The University advocates a personal concern for social justice, ethics, responsibility, and service to the community and exerts institutional leadership by promoting Chaminade's ideals outside the University community.

At any one time, 2,600 to 2,800 students are enrolled in a range of daytime and evening classes. Of this number, approximately 1,100 are full-time undergraduates, 1,200 are part-time undergraduates enrolled in the evening program, and 500 are graduate students. Nearly 60 percent of the full-time undergraduates are from Hawaii, 24 percent are from the mainland, 13 percent are from U.S. trust territories, and 3 percent are from other countries. Thirty-four states and thirty-one countries are represented in the student body.

Clubs and associations offer all Chaminade students a chance to pursue interests and extend their activities beyond the classroom. Student publications include the *Aulama,* a literary and art magazine; the *Silverword,* the monthly student newspaper; and *Ahinahina,* the Chaminade yearbook. Chaminade also sponsors chapters of Delta Epsilon Sigma, the national scholastic honor society for students at colleges and universities with a Catholic tradition; Phi Alpha Theta, the history national honor society; Delta Mu Delta, a national honor society in business administration; Sigma Tau Delta, the national English honor society; Pi Sigma Alpha, a national honor society in political science, and Alpha Phi Sigma, a national honor society for criminal justice.

Intercollegiate athletic teams are currently sponsored in men's basketball and water polo, women's softball and volleyball, and men's and women's cross-country and tennis. Intramural competitive and noncompetitive sports and recreation programs are open to all students, faculty and staff members, and alumni.

Chaminade University of Honolulu is accredited by the Accrediting Commission for Senior Colleges and Universities of the Western Association of Schools and Colleges. The University also has two sister universities on the mainland: the University of Dayton in Dayton, Ohio, and St. Mary's University in San Antonio, Texas.

Chaminade offers graduate degrees in business administration (M.B.A.), counseling psychology (M.S.C.P.), criminal justice administration (M.S.C.J.A.), education (M.Ed.), pastoral leadership (M.A.P.L.), and public administration (M.P.A.).

Location

Honolulu, a multicultural community, is enriched by a great diversity of ethnic activities and traditions. Chaminade is located on a hillside with a spectacular view sweeping across Waikiki to downtown Honolulu, from Diamond Head to the blue Pacific Ocean. This idyllic site is only minutes from the city, cultural activities, and the beach. The University also operates ten off-campus sites, primarily at military installations on the island of Oahu.

Majors and Degrees

The University offers twenty-one major programs of study at the undergraduate level as well as two associate degree programs. The Bachelor of Arts (B.A.) degree is offered in biology, chemistry, communication, English, historical and political studies, humanities, international studies, management, philosophy, psychology, religious studies, and social studies; the Bachelor of Fine Arts (B.F.A.) degree is offered in interior design; and the Bachelor of Science (B.S.) degree is offered in accounting, behavioral sciences, biology, computer information systems, criminal justice, early childhood education, elementary education, environmental studies, and forensic science. The Associate in Arts (A.A.) degree is offered in management; the Associate in Science (A.S.) degree is offered in computer science and criminal justice.

Preprofessional programs are offered in law, health sciences, nursing, and engineering.

Students may elect to pursue a minor program in most major programs as well as in anthropology, history, physics, political science, sociology, and studio art.

Academic Program

The core curriculum at Chaminade is in liberal arts. The University is committed to a broad liberal education for its students and believes that such an education provides a basis for long-term personal growth, a foundation for a career that may encounter job changes, and a background that allows students to rise to leadership positions in their chosen fields and communities. Through undergraduate programs based on the liberal arts tradition, Chaminade seeks to heighten cultural awareness. Coupled with understanding diverse methods of inquiry and participation in Chaminade's multicultural interdependent community, cultural awareness prepares all students for lifelong learning—about themselves, each other, and the world in which they live.

Undergraduate study is structured into four parts: practice in basic skills, liberal arts course work that provides a general education, intensive study in a chosen field of concentration (the major), and elective courses outside the major field to complement general and specialized knowledge. All baccalaureate degrees require a minimum of 124 credit hours of course work with a minimum of 45 hours in upper-division courses. Within these guidelines, the student selects a program of study appropriate to personal needs and interests. All appropriate courses at Chaminade require writing assignments from students. Upper-division courses in most fields train students to write in the style and format appropriate to the discipline.

In all fields of study at Chaminade, students are encouraged to apply their academic experience to on-the-job practice for academic credit. Faculty members may ask students to work with a specific organization, or students may develop internship possibilities on their own. Interns usually have at least junior-level standing, but in special cases sophomores are considered. Depending on the organization with which they work, students may or may not receive a salary for their internship experience.

The First Year Experience Seminar supports students in their transition from high school to college. The program provides an orientation to University functions and resources. This course also helps freshmen adjust to the University, gain a better understanding of the learning process and develop critical-thinking skills and provides a support group for students by examining problems that are common to the freshman experience.

Chaminade cooperates with two major programs that enable students to receive college credit prior to admission. These two programs, Advanced Placement and College-Level Examination Program, are sponsored by the College Board.

Off-Campus Programs

In 1990, Chaminade University and its sister universities signed an agreement through which any student at any of the three universities can enroll for their junior year at any of the other campuses. Full credit is given by Chaminade for approved courses taken at either university. Chaminade also encourages students to pursue part of their undergraduate education in another country.

Academic Facilities

Located in Henry Hall, Sullivan Library occupies three floors and houses a collection of approximately 74,000 volumes and 874 periodicals. Special collections include the Oceania Collection, the Catholic Authors Collection, the Julius J. Nodel Judaica Collection, and the David L. Carlson Japan Collection. Services offered include reference consultation, computerized information retrieval, and instruction in library use. Also in Henry Hall, the Computer Center provides students and faculty members with a variety of microcomputers, software programs, and reference materials for instruction, word processing, and programming. The multipurpose Audio Visual Media Resource Center provides instructional media technology support to all divisions of the University, student activities, special programs, and other events. The center is also a resource for films, slides, records, and videotapes.

Costs

Full-time undergraduate tuition for 2004–05 is $6925 per semester. Part-time undergraduate tuition is $462 per semester hour. Housing costs per semester range from $1468 to $2508, depending upon accommodations. Meal plans range from $1400 to $1960 per semester, depending upon the plan chosen. Various other fees for independent/individualized directed studies, parking, labs, and studios are also charged. The tuition charged by Chaminade University does not cover the total cost of instruction for each student. Gifts and grants are used to balance the difference. Tuition and fees must be paid at or prior to the time of registration.

Financial Aid

Those with a high school GPA between 3.5 and 4.0 are eligible for a $6000 yearly scholarship; between 3.0 and 3.49, a $5000 yearly scholarship; between 2.5 and 2.99, a $4500 yearly grant; and between 2.25 to 2.49, a $3000 yearly Father Chaminade Grant. The Hawaii Grant for new full-time day session students from Hawaii is $1500 per semester. Scholarships and grants, available to regular full-time undergraduate students, are renewable for four years and are awarded without regard to financial need. Students may obtain only one of the Chaminade scholarships or grants. When a first member of a family pays full-time day undergraduate tuition, additional members who are concurrently enrolled in the day undergraduate program may receive a tuition discount of 20 percent.

Faculty

The University is dedicated to teaching and to building the leadership skills of its students, and its major strengths lie in its relatively small size and its talented faculty. Classes are small, allowing faculty members to provide a significant amount of individual and small-group attention. Classes are taught by professors or professionals in their fields, not graduate students.

Student Government

The Chaminade University Student Association is the official representative of the student body. Each full-time student of Chaminade becomes a member upon payment of fees. Membership is open to all students at all instructional sites. The Senate, chaired by the student body president and composed of elected representatives, focuses on improving the quality of undergraduate student life and represents the needs, interests, and concerns of its constituents.

The Dean of Students, through the Assistant Dean of Students, initiates all disciplinary action. The committee is composed of administrators, faculty and staff members, and students. Chaminade does not condone activities on campus that violate state or federal regulations, including illegal possession of drugs or the illegal consumption of alcoholic beverages. Students found to be in violation of these regulations are subject to immediate disciplinary action.

Admission Requirements

Applications for admission are reviewed for specific majors or, when applicable, for "undecided" status. Chaminade considers several factors when assessing students' preparation for a selected area of study: grades throughout high school, selection of courses in preparation for college, scores from either the SAT I or ACT, and an essay that provides information about the applicant's character and record of leadership and service.

Application and Information

Chaminade University has a rolling admission process. As soon as all required information is received by the Admission Office, the application is reviewed by an application committee. Students are notified of the committee's decision usually within three to four weeks. Applications are accepted throughout the year. A $50 fee is payable upon application. Web site applications are also available for a $25 fee. All students desiring housing must file an application along with a $300 deposit applicable to the total cost per semester. Space and placement are not guaranteed without this deposit. A housing damage deposit of $100 is also required. Evidence of health insurance coverage from a U.S. insurer is required of all dormitory residents and international students.

To ensure full consideration for scholarships or grants, students are urged to complete the appropriate application by April 1. Award notices are mailed by April 30. For more information and application materials, students should contact:

Admission Office
Chaminade University
3140 Waialae Avenue
Honolulu, Hawaii 96816
Telephone: 808-735-4735
800-735-3733 (toll-free)
Fax: 808-739-4647
E-mail: admissions@chaminade.edu
World Wide Web: http://www.chaminade.edu

CHAMPLAIN COLLEGE

BURLINGTON, VERMONT

The College

Champlain College is a coeducational, private, nonprofit college founded in 1878. Its 21-acre campus, home to 1,668 full-time students, is nestled among the stately maple trees of Burlington's historic Hill Section, overlooking Lake Champlain and the Adirondack Mountains of New York to the west. Many of the College's buildings, including most of its dormitories, are restored Victorian-era private homes, which give students a unique atmosphere in which to learn and live. The newest dorm, 381 Main Street, offers suite-style housing and opened in 2003.

Champlain College is recognized as one of the leading career-focused colleges in New England, and has earned the respect of the business, technical, and human services professions for its outstanding education. For the past nine years, more than 97 percent of those graduates seeking employment found jobs within four months of graduation. Champlain's majors are designed to provide excellent preparation for employment in today's complex world as well as broadening and enriching experiences in the humanities.

Students are assigned three advisers: one each from the faculty, the Advising and Registration Center (Registrar's office), and the Career Planning Office. Confidential health and counseling services are provided on campus as well.

Champlain College is committed to involving its entire student body in extracurricular and cocurricular activities. The Champlain College Players and Champlain College Music Makers offer theatrical and musical opportunities. The student-run college newspaper, *ChamPlain Truth*, produces eight editions a year. Intramural programs are determined by student interest and currently include basketball, indoor soccer, ice hockey, golf, sailing, outing club, skiing/snowboarding, Ultimate Frisbee, and volleyball. Unique partnerships with nearby businesses offer indoor climbing, nautilus and free weight facilities, two swimming pools, indoor track, aerobics, and a gym. Organized weekend day trips take advantage of Vermont's four seasons and its numerous recreational and cultural opportunities.

Vermont is known as the ski capital of the East. The challenging slopes of Stowe, Bolton Valley, Mad River Glen, Smuggler's Notch, and Sugarbush are all within an hour's drive. The nearby mountains, lakes, and streams also provide seasonal opportunities for backpacking, hiking, fishing, camping, canoeing, sailing, mountain biking, and windsurfing. Great in-line skating, jogging, and bicycling are just 10 minutes from campus on the 7-mile-long recreation path that follows the spectacular shoreline of Lake Champlain.

Location

Burlington is a small city of 46,000 people and classic college town of nearly 15,000 students on the eastern shore of Lake Champlain. Covering 435 square miles, Lake Champlain is one of North America's largest lakes. The long ridgeline of the Green Mountains forms the eastern horizon and the Adirondack Mountains frame the western horizon. Montreal, Quebec is only a 1 ½ hour drive to the north. Burlington is one of the nation's most progressive cities, and it is the cultural center of Vermont. Five colleges are located in the area, along with one of the leading medical centers on the East Coast. There is an international airport; an Amtrak passenger train route with connections to Montreal, New York City, and Washington, D.C.; and a long-distance bus service, Vermont Transit Lines. The Church Street Marketplace, located just a few blocks from the campus, attracts both locals and tourists to its numerous shops, coffee bars, and restaurants. Three television stations, fifteen radio stations, and daily newspapers serve the area. The Arts and Entertainment Channel (A&E) has ranked Burlington as the nation's "Best Place to Live." Burlington also ranks as one of the best college towns in the country.

Majors and Degrees

Champlain College offers the Bachelor of Science degree with majors in accounting, advertising, applied psychology, broadcasting, business, computer information services, computer networking, criminal justice, digital forensics technology, electronic game and interactive development, elementary/early childhood education, e-business management, global networks and telecommunications, hotel-restaurant management, international business, management, marketing management, mass communication, middle school education, multimedia and graphic design, paralegal studies, professional writing, public relations and media communications, radiography, secondary school education, social work, software development, software engineering, travel and tourism management, and Web site development and management. Champlain also offers a Bachelor of Science degree in professional studies, with twelve different career concentrations that combine a practical liberal arts focus in communications, critical thinking, and ethics with career-centered marketable skills and prepare students for the competitive national and international job market. Students may pursue a course in prelaw.

Academic Programs

The "upside-down" curriculum format offers a four year bachelor's degree and allows students to concentrate on courses in their major in their first two years of college. Internships or on-the-job experiences are offered in 97 percent of the majors, many within the first two years of study, and a majority of students go directly into their chosen career field upon graduation. The mission of Champlain College is to provide motivated students with the opportunity, environment, and tools to achieve their goals for professional success and meaningful involvement in their community.

An Army ROTC program is provided in cooperation with the University of Vermont.

Off-Campus Programs

Ninety-seven percent of the College's majors require an internship experience, which may be done locally, nationally, or internationally. These interships give students practical job experience in a professional environment, often leading directly to permanent positions after graduation. The criminal justice major offers two options for the second semester of the fourth year. Students may apply to spend the term at the Vermont Police Academy or at the Federal Law Enforcement Training Center in Georgia. Hotel-restaurant management and travel and tourism management majors may do a fourth-year internship with Topnotch Resort and Spa in Stowe, Vermont, or the Wyndham Sugar Bay Resort in St. Thomas, U.S. Virgin Islands. Champlain students may also participate in the Walt Disney World College semester. Champlain has established international exchange programs with English-speaking universities in England, France, Sweden, and Switzerland. The College also offers a 4-plus-1 B.S./M.B.A. option with Clarkson and Southern New Hampshire Universities, allowing Champlain graduates to earn a Master in Business Administration degree after only one year of graduate study.

Academic Facilities

The Holly D. and Robert E. Miller Information Commons incorporates the features of a traditional library but showcases advanced technologies such as multimedia laboratories, integrated computer networks, specialized electronic classrooms, and online distance learning systems to enhance a student's ability to conduct research. The William R. Hauke Family Campus Center houses labs for the communications/public relations and hotel-restaurant management majors, accounting and math labs, multimedia labs, telecommunications facilities, the student life center, classrooms and faculty offices. Alumni Auditorium is attached to Hauke and houses audio-video labs and the stage. Freeman Hall includes science labs, a student teaching classroom for education majors, and faculty offices. Joyce Learning Center has the Statler Hotel-Restaurant/Travel and Tourism Teaching Lab online front desk simulator and classrooms. Cushing Hall houses the networking lab and classrooms for computer majors. Foster Hall includes the Mac lab for mulitmedia/graphic design majors and two other computer labs, plus the computer center and help desk. The radiography simulator is located in the Gallery.

Construction of the new Global Business and Technology Center is underway, with completion scheduled for fall 2004. Plans for the center include an international business resource room, market research rooms, video conferencing capabilities, an electronic lobby with global and financial news, and fully-wired, glass-walled classrooms. A new dining complex, fitness center, and student activities offices in the Student Life Center are scheduled to open in fall 2004. The gymnasium, locker rooms, and student lounges are scheduled to open in the fall of 2005.

The Office of Career Planning and Placement offers assistance to students before and after graduation.

Costs

Tuition for 2004–05 is $13,700; room is $5625, board is $3690, and activities fees are $150. Total tuition, fees, and room and board are $23,165.

Financial Aid

The financial aid program at Champlain College includes loans, grants, scholarships, and work-study awards. The College participates in the Federal Perkins Loan Program, Federal Work-Study, Federal Supplemental Educational Opportunity Grant Program, Federal Pell Grant Program, Federal Stafford Student Loan Program, Vermont Student Assistance Corporation, and state loan and grant programs. The College has budgeted more than $1 million of institutional money for financial aid.

Students interested in financial aid must complete the Free Application for Federal Student Aid (FAFSA) and the Champlain College Financial Aid application forms.

Faculty

Champlain's faculty members bring the requisite academic credentials to the classroom but also have built their careers in the workplace, bringing practical professional experience to provide what students need to know to in order to succeed professionally. In addition to the core of 74 full-time professors, the College seeks adjunct faculty who are actively employed in their profession and have an interest in teaching as well. Currently, there are 141 adjunct professors who bring their professional expertise and academic training to benefit Champlain's student body. The student/faculty ratio of 16:1. Champlain faculty members are noted for their accessibility and willingness to act as mentors for their students.

Admission Requirements

The College requires an official high school transcript, SAT I or ACT scores, and a completed application form in order to be considered for admission. Graduation from a recognized secondary school is required (or an equivalency certificate/GED), as a condition of acceptance. Letters of recommendation from the high school guidance counselor and current teachers are optional but strongly encouraged. A personal interview is highly recommended for all candidates, and may be required of applicants to certain majors. Students may earn advanced standing by submitting appropriate scores on AP, IB and CLEP exams. Champlain offers rolling admission, with no set application deadline. Students may apply for admission for the fall or the January term.

All completed applications for admission received before January 15 are reviewed by the Admissions Committee for consideration for Champlain College scholarships. No separate scholarship application is required. Scholarship recipients are notified in March.

All candidates for transfer admission are required to submit an official high school transcript with SAT or ACT scores, official college transcript(s), and a completed application form in order to be considered for admission with advanced standing. Transfer credit is given for academic courses from an accredited college completed with a grade of C or better.

Champlain College admits students without regard to race, creed, color, national and ethnic origin, religion, age, gender, sexual orientation, or qualified disability and does not discriminate in the administration of its educational and admission policies, scholarships and loan programs, or other College-administered programs. Champlain College makes reasonable accommodations to the disabilities of otherwise-qualified students, applicants, or employees. For additional information, interested parties should contact Dolly Shaw, Affirmative Action Officer.

Application and Information

Applicants should fill out the application form and forward it with the application fee of $40 to the Admission Office. Applications may be downloaded from the Web site listed below. Champlain College operates on a rolling admissions basis for its degree programs, processing applications as soon as they are received; notification of an admission decision is usually made within four weeks of receiving a complete application.

Mailing Address:

Director of Admissions
Champlain College
163 South Willard Street
P.O. Box 670
Burlington, Vermont 05402-0670
Telephone: 802-860-2727
800-570-5959 (toll-free)
Fax: 802-860-2767
E-mail: admission@champlain.edu
World Wide Web: http://www.champlain.edu

The Champlain College campus after a fresh snowfall.

CHAPMAN UNIVERSITY

ORANGE, CALIFORNIA

The University

During its 142-year history, Chapman has evolved from a small, traditional liberal arts college that was founded in 1861 by members of the First Christian Church (Disciples of Christ) into a midsize comprehensive liberal arts and sciences university that is distinguished for its nationally recognized programs in film and television production, business and economics, music, education, communication arts, and the natural and applied sciences. The mission of Chapman University is to provide personalized education of distinction that leads to inquiring, ethical, and productive lives as global citizens.

Chapman's parklike, ivy-covered, and tree-lined campus features a blending of fully refurbished historic structures with the newest in state-of-the-art Internet- and satellite-connected learning environments. Five residence halls and six on-campus apartment buildings are conveniently located on the edge of the campus. Also recently completed have been a five-story parking structure, the 100,000-square-foot School of Law facility, and Liberty Plaza, which features a large section of the Berlin Wall.

Chapman University's academic structure includes the Wilkinson College of Letters and Sciences, the Argyros School of Business and Economics, the School of Communication Arts, the School of Education, the School of Film and Television, the School of Music, and the School of Law. Programs of distinction include the A. Gary Anderson Center for Economic Research, which is internationally recognized for econometric forecasting; the nationally recognized School of Film and Television; and the ABA-accredited School of Law. Other nationally accredited programs include the School of Business and Economics, which is accredited by AACSB International–The Association to Advance Collegiate Schools of Business; the IFT-accredited program in food science and nutrition; the NASM-accredited School of Music; and the APTA-accredited graduate program in physical therapy. Chapman was also recently recognized by the Templeton Foundation as one of only 100 colleges nationally to be designated as a Templeton Foundation "Character-Building College."

In addition to approximately 4,800 undergraduate, graduate, and professional school students enrolled on the campus in Orange, Chapman also enrolls more than 5,000 undergraduate and graduate students annually through its Chapman University College and network of thirty University College centers that are located in California and Washington.

The University is electric, involving, and outdoor-oriented. In addition to taking advantage of the obvious benefits associated with the southern California climate, Chapman students enjoy a dynamic student activities program. Although predominantly from California, Chapman students come from forty different states; in addition, approximately 10 percent of its students come from thirty-four other countries. Over the past five years, Chapman students have been named Truman Scholars, Coro Fellows, *USA Today* All-USA College Academic Team members, NCAA All-Americans, and NCAA academic all-Americans. Chapman's long and distinguished heritage in intercollegiate sports includes five NCAA national championships in baseball, tennis, and softball. Chapman competes as an independent in the NCAA Division III level and fields teams in baseball, basketball (m/w), crew (m/w), cross-country (m/w), football, golf, lacrosse, soccer (m/w), softball, swimming (w), tennis (m/w), track and field (w), volleyball (w), and water polo (m/w). Approximately 20 percent of Chapman's student body participates in intercollegiate athletics, and last year, 4 student-athletes were honored as all-Americans and 14 as academic all-Americans.

More than seventy clubs and organizations are available, many with commitments to a wide range of community service efforts. Chapman's Greek system includes five nationally chartered fraternities and sororities. A comprehensive intramural sports program involves a myriad of sports activities for all campus community members throughout the school year. On-campus intercollegiate athletic events, music, art, and theater productions provide students with numerous ongoing extracurricular activity options. Chapman's proximity to area recreational and cultural opportunities allows Chapman students to enjoy the essence of what makes Orange County's south coast area an enviable environment in which to live and learn.

Prominent Chapman alumni include the Honorable Loretta Sanchez ('88), member of Congress; the Honorable David Bonior ('85), member of Congress and current House Minority Whip; television and film producer John Copeland ('73); UCLA head basketball coach Steve Lavin ('88); former San Diego Padre stars Tim Flannery ('80) and Randy Jones ('72); current U.S. ambassador to Spain/philanthropist George L. Argyros ('65), and star of Broadway's *Showboat*, Michael Bell ('68).

Location

Orange County, California, was recently rated by *Places Rated Almanac* as "the #1 place to live in North America," citing superior climate, cultural, recreational, educational, and career-entree opportunities. Los Angeles is 35 miles to the north, and San Diego is 80 miles to the south. Nearby entertainment venues include Disneyland, Knott's Berry Farm, the Orange County Performing Arts Center, major-league baseball, and hockey. Pristine West Coast beaches are less than 10 miles from the campus, and seasonal snow skiing is 90 minutes away. The average year-round temperature on campus is 71 degrees Fahrenheit, and the air is normally smog-free, due to a daily prevailing sea breeze from nearby southwest-facing beaches.

Majors and Degrees

Chapman awards the Bachelor of Arts degree in the fields of art, biology, chemistry, communications, dance, economics, English and comparative literature, film and television, French, health science, history, international studies, liberal studies (elementary education), movement and exercise science, music, peace studies, philosophy, political science, psychology, religion, social science, sociology, Spanish, and theater. The Bachelor of Fine Arts degree is conferred in art, dance, film and television, and theater. The Bachelor of Science degree is offered in accounting, applied mathematics, biology, business administration, chemistry, computer information systems, computer science, environmental science, food science and nutrition, health science, movement and exercise science, and natural science. The Bachelor of Music degree is granted in composition, conducting, music education (vocal and instrumental), music performance (vocal and instrumental), and music therapy.

Preprofessional or prevocational programs are offered in dentistry, law, medicine, physical therapy, social service, teaching, theology, and veterinary medicine.

Academic Program

The requirements for graduation are commensurate with the liberal arts philosophy of education maintained by Chapman. The program of studies is designed to ensure a breadth of subject matter selection in the liberal arts as well as depth of preparation in the student's major field. The minimum graduation requirements include successful completion (C average) of 124 semester credits, of which 36 must be earned in the upper division. Competence in reading, written communication, oral communication, computation, and library usage is required of all students. Chapman's general education sequence provides a broad introduction to the humanities, social sciences, and natural sciences. Students select general education classes with the guidance of their faculty adviser. A maximum of 32 credits may be gained through Advanced Placement (AP), College-Level Examination Program (CLEP), and departmental examinations.

Chapman's academic year operates on a 4-1-4 modified semester system. January is reserved for an optional Interterm, allowing a period for experimental, short-term course work or individual study.

Ample opportunities are available for alternative learning experiences. Internships and cooperative education programs are recommended. Students may also undertake in-depth individual study or research in their major field in conjunction with a faculty member.

Academic Facilities

The 90,000-square-foot Argyros Forum includes the primary campus dining area, conference and classroom facilities, and associated student offices. Bertea Hall is home to the School of Music. Memorial Auditorium seats 1,000 and is listed on the National Register of Historic Places. The Hutton Sports Center includes a 3,000-seat arena, a 5,000-seat outdoor stadium, four championship tennis courts, and training and fitness facilities for the campus and the surrounding community. Currently under construction, the Leatherby Libraries will feature five school-specific libraries in one five-story facility. Newly completed Beckman Hall for business and information technology houses the Argyros School of Business and Economics, including its endowed centers: the A. Gary Anderson Center for Economic Research, the Ralph W. Leatherby Center for Entrepreneurship and Business Ethics, and the Walter Schmid Center for International Business. The School of Communication Arts includes the Guggenheim Art Gallery and the 250-seat repertory-style Waltmar Theatre. The Hashinger Science Center features laboratories for nuclear science, radiation, crystallography, genetics, food science, and physical therapy.

Costs

For the 2003–04 academic year, full-time tuition and fees (including accident and sickness fee, health center fee, and associated student membership fee) were $24,590. Annual room and board averaged $8528. Books were estimated at $700 per year.

Financial Aid

More than 85 percent of Chapman students benefit from some form of financial aid or scholarship assistance. Need-based financial awards include a combination of grants, scholarships, loans, and work-study jobs. Awards are renewable, assuming that students complete the annual application process on time. The family contribution component of an award stays mostly the same annually if the family's financial circumstances remain the same. By using a combination of Chapman's internal resources and federal and state funding, an individual financial aid package can be tailored to meet the student's financial need. Merit and talent scholarship awards, regardless of financial need, round out the types of financial assistance that Chapman offers. Chapman offers an Early Aid Estimator service that gives students an up-front picture of what their prospective aid/scholarship eligibility is, rather than waiting for the postadmission, official aid-awarding period. Students asking for information about Chapman automatically receive the Early Estimator form, along with instructions for completion and submission.

Faculty

The University's faculty is composed of 222 full-time and 288 part-time members, more than 80 percent of whom hold doctoral or other terminal degrees. Their primary commitment is to undergraduate teaching, although most are also actively involved in scholarly research and publication. Many faculty members teach both undergraduate and graduate courses. Teaching assistants or graduate assistants are not used for the instruction of undergraduate classes. Chapman's favorable student-faculty ratio of 16:1 allows extensive interaction between the faculty members and students.

Student Government

Chapman has an associated student government that actively participates in the administration of the University.

Admission Requirements

Admission to Chapman is selective. In 2003, admission was offered to 60 percent of the applicant pool. The University is interested in admitting students whose prior records indicate that they will be successful in a competitive collegiate environment. Freshman applicants are considered for admission based primarily on the nature and sequence of their high school course work, the grade point average achieved, and their results on either the SAT I or ACT examination. Transfer candidates are considered for admission on the basis of their course work and cumulative grade point average earned at other regionally accredited post-secondary institutions.

Application and Information

When applying, candidates are strongly encouraged to visit the campus and meet with a member of the admission staff. Arrangements for an interview and a tour of the campus can be made through the Office of Admission at either of the phone numbers listed below. Freshman applicants can choose between a nonbinding November 30 early action application deadline or the January 31 regular application deadline. Transfer applicants must apply before the March 15 transfer deadline. Prospective freshmen who apply after the January 31 deadline are considered on a space-available basis.

For further information, students should contact:

Michael O. Drummy
Assistant Vice President and Chief Admission Officer
Chapman University
One University Drive
Orange, California 92866
Telephone: 714-997-6711
888-CUAPPLY (toll-free)
Fax: 714-997-6713
E-mail: admit@chapman.edu

CHARLESTON SOUTHERN UNIVERSITY

CHARLESTON, SOUTH CAROLINA

The University

Charleston Southern University is a fully accredited four-year liberal arts university. It's mission is to promote academic excellence in a Christian environment for students of all faiths. Charleston Southern is listed as one of *America's Best Christian Colleges*, identifying CSU as a school that provides students with the highest quality education in a Christian environment.

A coeducational university, Charleston Southern University's enrollment has grown from 500 students to nearly 3,000 students in its forty years and continues to change to meet the needs of a fast-paced society. CSU is affiliated with the South Carolina Baptist Convention.

Charleston Southern University seeks to develop the total person emotionally, intellectually, and spiritually. Programs are designed to prepare students for a successful and fulfilling life. Each major program is combined with a comprehensive liberal arts foundation. Courses in the humanities, the fine arts, natural science, and social science are included in this foundation. These subjects are designed to develop problem-solving skills and the ability to communicate effectively. A special career counseling center is designed to help students plan for the future.

Men's and women's athletic teams compete in the NCAA Division I Big South Conference. The University fields teams in baseball, basketball, cross-country, golf, soccer (women), softball, tennis, track and field, and volleyball as well as an NCAA Division I-AA football team. For outdoor recreation, there are NCAA-quality tennis courts, putting greens, and athletic fields; nature trails; and a lake for fishing.

Students are informed of campus activities through the University newspaper, *Buc in Print,* published by students under staff member supervision. In addition, the University yearbook, *Cutlass,* and the University literary magazine, *The Sefer,* are published by students under faculty and staff supervision.

Location

Situated on 300 acres, Charleston Southern University is strategically located near Charleston, South Carolina, in the center of the modern growth patterns of North Charleston. Students take advantage of the cultural, historical, and recreational opportunities the city offers. Nearby Interstate 26, with access to I-95, is conveniently located to the campus. Five airlines serve the Charleston area. Mild winters and long summers allow many opportunities for outdoor recreation. Charleston is a city famous for its well-preserved colonial houses, famous gardens and plantations, miles of wide sandy beaches, and major fine arts events, including the Spoleto Festival USA (a kaleidoscope of opera, dance, music, theater, and visual arts).

Majors and Degrees

Charleston Southern University awards the Bachelor of Arts degree with majors in business, communications and theater, English, English education, humanities and fine arts, music (with emphases in vocal performance and church music), music education (with emphases in choral and instrumental), music therapy, religion, Spanish, Spanish education, and youth ministry. The Bachelor of Science degree is offered with majors in applied math, athletic training, biochemistry, biology, business administration (with emphases in accounting, finance, information systems, management, and marketing), chemistry, computer science/mathematics, criminal justice, early childhood education, economics, elementary education, environmental management, history, mathematics education, mathematics, natural science, nursing, physical education, political science, psychology, science education, social science, social studies education, and sociology. Minors are offered in most of the above areas, and are also offered in aerospace studies (AFROTC), art, Christian leadership, and French. The School of Education offers a secondary education minor for several majors to meet teacher certification requirements. The Bachelor of Technology degree is offered to students who have completed an associate degree in a technical field prior to entry.

Preprofessional programs are offered in allied health science, dentistry, engineering, law, medicine, pharmacy, and seminary. Some of these programs require a four-year degree from CSU while others require two or three years of study at CSU before the student transfers to a professional school.

The Bachelor of Management Arts (B.M.A.) is a new program of study for adult learners in the Evening College. Students in this program can graduate in as little as twenty months after requirements are met.

The Graduate Studies Program offers Master of Education degrees in elementary education, secondary education, and school administration. In addition, there is a Master of Arts in teaching, a Master of Science in criminal justice, and a Master of Business Administration, with emphases in accounting, finance, information systems, health-care administration, and organizational development.

Academic Program

The purpose of Charleston Southern University is to help students to develop intellectually, socially, culturally, and spiritually. This is accomplished by ensuring that students receive a well-rounded education. The University requires all students to complete a core of liberal arts courses. The comprehensive course of study is subdivided into general education courses, including courses in English, the fine arts, history, mathematics, computer literacy, foreign language, natural science, religion and philosophy, and the social sciences. In addition, students are offered an opportunity to pursue a field of study in a major and minor area. Elective credits may also be taken to complete the minimum graduation requirements of at least 125 semester hours.

The academic-year calendar operates on a 4-4-1 system. The fall term begins in mid-August and ends in December, and the spring term begins in January and ends in early May. May is set aside as a one-month Maymester during which students may enroll in one course. Students also have the option of attending two 5-week summer sessions.

An award-winning Air Force ROTC program is available on campus.

Advanced placement credits are given for successful scores on approved tests of the Educational Testing Service. Credit may also be granted for successful scores on the College-Level Examination Program (CLEP) tests, the Defense Activity for Non-Traditional Education Support (DANTES), military experience, CSU challenge exams, A.P. credit, and I.B. credit.

Academic Facilities

The University has a modern library that contains more than 200,000 volumes, a modern chapel-auditorium with impressive fine arts facilities, and a multipurpose gymnasium. The Brewer Center, the wellness and activities building, houses state-of-the-art exercise equipment, a snack bar, social areas, an intramural gym, and meeting rooms for clubs and organizations. The music facility, Whittington Hall, includes a large music rehearsal hall, practice suites, a technology lab, and classrooms.

Costs

Tuition for the 2003–04 academic year was $14,426, and room and board were $5544 per year. Tuition and fees are subject to change.

Financial Aid

A comprehensive financial aid program, consisting of scholarships, grants, loans, and employment, has been established at Charleston Southern. Approximately 95 percent of the student body receives some type of financial assistance. The University participates in the Federal Pell Grant, Federal Supplemental Educational Opportunity Grant (FSEOG), and Federal Work-Study programs. Assistance is also available through Federal Perkins Loans and Federal Stafford Loans. Endowed or donated funds are available for many students; such awards are administered according to the provisions of the contributing agency or person. State tuition grants are available to eligible South Carolina residents.

Students may also be eligible to receive institutional scholarships and grants. Awards are not automatic and are subject to the availability of funds.

At Charleston Southern University, it is understood that financial concerns can often play a major role in the decision on which university to attend. The purpose of the financial aid program is to remove cost from the student's decision and allow the student to decide based on the academic and social environment offered at CSU.

Faculty

Charleston Southern University has a well-qualified and dedicated faculty. Faculty members combine teaching ability and scholarship with a concern for students. The majority hold doctoral degrees. Professors work directly with students in many phases of University life, including academic advising. Once the student selects a major course of study, he or she is assigned a faculty adviser in that major area. CSU offers small class sizes, which allow for individual attention and facilitates the pursuit of academic excellence.

The University encourages advanced study and research. Excellence in teaching is also recognized through an annual award.

Student Government

All full-time students become members of the Student Government Association upon enrollment. This organization enables students to develop leadership skills while achieving the goals the University has set for them.

Admission Requirements

The Enrollment Services staff works diligently to maintain a socially, economically, and culturally diverse student body. The University is a private, church-supported educational institution and is committed to a policy of nondiscrimination on the basis of race, sex, color, religion, national origin, or handicap.

Students may be admitted as first-time freshmen or as transfer students with acceptable credit. New freshmen must have official transcripts sent from their high schools and official SAT I and/or ACT scores sent from the appropriate testing service. Transfer students must have official transcripts sent from all colleges previously attended. Interviews are not required, but students are encouraged to visit the campus. Arrangements may be made by calling the Office of Enrollment Services.

Application and Information

Candidates for freshman admission are encouraged to submit applications in the fall of their senior year in secondary school. Transfer students are welcome to apply anytime during the academic year. A $30 nonrefundable application processing fee must be submitted with an application. An online application is also available at the Web site listed below. The University uses a rolling admission system, and students are notified of the admission decision as soon as all application materials have been received and evaluated.

Application forms and other information about Charleston Southern University may be obtained by contacting:

Office of Enrollment Services
Charleston Southern University
9200 University Boulevard
P.O. Box 118087
Charleston, South Carolina 29423-8087
Telephone: 843-863-7050
800-947-7474 (toll-free)
World Wide Web: http://www.charlestonsouthern.edu

CHATHAM COLLEGE

PITTSBURGH, PENNSYLVANIA

The College

Chatham College, founded in 1869, is one of the oldest women's colleges in the United States. Focused on preparing students for the future, a Chatham education emphasizes environmental awareness, global issues, and women's leadership. Chatham empowers women to assume their roles as leaders, World Ready Women®, as it has for more than 135 years.

Students' personal, professional, and leadership skills are developed to their fullest potential through Chatham's internship program, study abroad, service learning, leadership training opportunities, and personal development seminars. Chatham students may participate in up to six internships related to their major and career goals before they graduate. Recent examples include WorldBank, Pittsburgh Council of International Visitors, PPG Industries, H. J. Heinz History Center (affiliated with the Smithsonian Institution), Pittsburgh Children's Hospital, Carnegie Museum, the Pennsylvania Senate, the Washington Center Internship Program, Coro Center for Civic Leadership, WQED, Pittsburgh Zoo and Aquarium, YMCA Legal Resources for Women, Women's Law Project, UPMC Rehabilitation Hospital, UPMC Western Psychiatric Hospital, and numerous sites in Pittsburgh's corporate, nonprofit, government, health-care, and communications communities. Last year, 71 percent of Chatham seniors participated in service learning, more than twice the national average. Overall, the student body completed more than 46,000 hours.

The student body of approximately 1,250 represents twenty-five states and eighteen other countries. Members of minority groups represent 15 percent of the student body. Both resident and commuting students participate actively in the numerous professional, academic, social, and special-interest organizations at the College. Health services and personal and career counseling services are available on campus. The College offers NCAA Division III intercollegiate competition in basketball, ice hockey, soccer, softball, swimming, tennis, and volleyball and intramural and recreational competition in other sports. There are also several student publications, and the College sponsors frequent programs and speakers in the arts, environment, sciences, and public leadership.

Chatham offers coeducational graduate programs in biology, business administration, counseling psychology, landscape architecture, landscape studies, physical therapy, physician assistant studies, teaching, and writing.

Location

Chatham's 32-acre parklike, suburban campus is located in a beautiful, safe neighborhood minutes from downtown Pittsburgh. Steeped in history, the campus features towering trees, wandering paths, and period architecture, including century-old mansions, which serve as fully networked residence halls. Chatham also features a $10-million science complex and a new state-of-the-art $18-million athletic facility. The facility houses an eight-lane competition pool, a gym, squash courts, cardio rooms, a climbing wall, a running track, and exercise and dance studios.

Pittsburgh is one of the safest and most dynamic cities in the country. The city is headquarters to some of the country's major businesses and industries in finance, health care, and technology. Students enjoy eclectic city neighborhoods that reflect Pittsburgh's historic qualities yet appeal to a wide audience. Pittsburgh offers numerous arts and entertainment options, including the Pittsburgh Symphony; world-renowned opera, ballet, and theater companies; and two established lecture series, featuring some of the world's most prominent figures. Nearby parks and ski areas and the city's three rivers provide ample opportunities for hiking, biking, kayaking, skiing, white-water rafting, and numerous other recreational activities. Pittsburgh is also well known for its three professional sports teams: the NHL Penguins, MLB's National League Pirates, and the NFL's Steelers. Excellent bus, rail, and air connections are available to and from most major cities. (For more information, students should visit http://www.thecollegecity.com.)

Majors and Degrees

Chatham College offers the following departmental majors, leading to a Bachelor of Arts or Bachelor of Science degree: accounting, applied computer science, art (media arts, eco-art, photography, studio arts), arts management, biochemistry, biology, bioinformatics, chemistry, communication, cultural studies, economics, elementary education, English, environmental studies, exercise science, French, global policy studies, health care studies, history, history of art, international business, management, marketing, mathematics, multidisciplinary degree, music, physics, political science, psychology, public policy studies, social work, Spanish, theater, and women's studies. Students may choose a traditional departmental major, an interdepartmental major, a double major, or a self-defined major.

Preprofessional programs are offered in dentistry, education with teaching certification, law, medicine, physical therapy, and veterinary medicine. There is also a joint-degree engineering program with Carnegie Mellon University in Pittsburgh. Postbaccalaureate certificate programs are available in accounting, English as a second language, gerontology, landscape studies, and nonfiction writing.

Teacher certification is available through the education program in early childhood, elementary, environmental, foreign language, school counseling, special education, and secondary education. Well-qualified students can enroll in the College's dual-degrees program and earn both a bachelor's and master's degree in as few as five years in conjunction with nearly all of the College's graduate programs. They may also enroll in accelerated master's programs offered in conjunction with Carnegie Mellon University's H. John Heinz III School of Public Policy.

Academic Program

Chatham's general education curriculum includes seven required interdepartmental courses. Graduation requirements include the general education courses, a major, proficiency requirements, and the senior tutorial—an original research/capstone project. Students are mentored one-on-one by a faculty member throughout the tutorial process. The project provides an excellent bridge to graduate and professional schools and strong preparation for law and medical schools as well as science-based graduate programs.

The College's 4-1-4 academic calendar consists of fall and spring terms, plus a four-week Interim term in January. Interim programs include study abroad, concentrated study, experimental projects, travel and field experiences, internships, interdisciplinary study, and student exchanges with other colleges.

The First Year Student Sequence introduces students to the College community and its culture and provides opportunities to learn about the resources of the urban environment and study issues of concern to women. These courses provide students with the analytical and communication skills essential for successful college performance.

Chatham's Career Services coordinates student internships, placement, workshops, recruitment, and mentor programs as well as health and wellness issues and academic and personal counseling.

The Rachel Carson Institute honors Chatham's 1929 alumna and her commitment to the environment. The institute's focus is on global environmental issues, with a concentration on the impact of environmental degradation on women's health and societal roles and the promotion of women's leadership in the environmental movement.

The Pennsylvania Center for Women, Politics, and Public Policy introduces students to the world of politics, public policy, and civic engagement. It provides opportunities for one-on-one mentoring with local politicians, judges, state-level policy makers, and others. Students may also choose to participate in seminars and internships in Washington, D.C.

Off-Campus Programs

Chatham students may register for classes at any of Pittsburgh's eight other colleges and universities, including Carnegie Mellon University and the University of Pittsburgh, both of which are within walking distance of the campus. For journeys a bit farther from the campus, Chatham Abroad involves a three-week travel experience with faculty members during students' sophomore year and has taken students to Belize, the Galapagos Islands, Morocco, Egypt, Italy, Spain, France, Ireland, England, and Russia for an additional nominal fee. The Internship Program enables students to gain firsthand experience in field placements in a wide variety of agencies, businesses, and professional organizations.

Academic Facilities

All academic buildings have computer classrooms, labs, and smart classrooms connected to both the campus LAN and the Internet via fiber-optic connections. All residence halls have computer labs and high-speed network printers. Central computer equipment supports e-mail, computer-mediated courseware, personal Web pages, and file and print servers. Public computer labs in the residence halls and academic buildings supply high-end personal computer workstations, Macintosh G-4s, laser printers, scanners, and CD-ROM burners.

The modern Jennie King Mellon Library has 90,000 volumes and more than 600 current subscriptions, individual study areas, special seminar rooms, and a 285-seat theater. Chatham participates in campuswide software license agreements that permit students to install selected productivity software on their personal machines at no additional cost. Library facilities at neighboring colleges and universities are also available for Chatham students.

Buhl Hall houses state-of-the-art science laboratories and individual laboratory units. Psychology and language laboratories and audiovisual facilities are also available. The Media Center contains equipment used by students to gain experience with some of the sophisticated technology of audio, visual, and video presentations.

Costs

For 2004–05, full-time tuition is $21,780 per year, and room and board are approximately $7050. The student activity fee is $9 per credit. A one-time deposit of $100 for tuition and $100 for on-campus housing is paid by newly admitted students and is applied to first-semester charges. Regularly enrolled full-time students pay no additional costs for Interim courses, except for special supplies or travel. Additional fees are required for art supplies and music lessons. Students are required to have health and accident insurance.

Financial Aid

Financial aid is awarded on the basis of an individual's financial need, as determined through the Free Application for Federal Student Aid. The awards combine grants, loans, and employment. The priority financial aid deadline is May 1.

Sources of financial aid include Chatham grants and loans, state grants, Federal Pell Grants, Federal Supplemental Educational Opportunity Grants, federally funded student loans, and jobs provided under the Federal Work-Study Program. Chatham Merit scholarships for entering students are awarded on the basis of high academic achievement and an on-campus interview without regard to need. They range in value from $4000 to $10,000. Chatham also offers the World Ready Woman Leadership Award, ranging from $1000 to $4000, to students who demonstrate leadership potential, as evidenced in a required on-campus interview. Minna Kaufmann Ruud Scholarships are available for students with exceptional ability in vocal music, based on an on-campus audition. Approximately 90 percent of undergraduate students receive aid administered by the College.

Faculty

The Chatham environment features a student-teacher ratio of 12:1. Faculty members also advise students as they choose from more than thirty-five majors. The low student-teacher ratio ensures close student-faculty relationships and individual consideration of students by the faculty members. Each student is assigned a faculty member who serves as her adviser through the completion of her degree program. Ninety percent of all faculty members hold Ph.D.'s.

Student Government

The Chatham Student Government, of which every student is a member, coordinates student involvement in the affairs of the College, gives voice to student concerns, maintains student participation on College committees, and oversees various student boards and organizations. Chatham students serve as voting members on many of the College's planning and policy committees.

Admission Requirements

The prospective student must demonstrate academic strength, motivation, an enthusiasm for learning, and potential for growth. Evaluation of students is made on the basis of the student's academic record, recommendations, SAT I or ACT scores, involvement in activities, essay, and other submitted material. The College seeks to enroll students representing a variety of cultural, geographical, racial, religious, and socioeconomic backgrounds and with diverse talents in both academic and creative areas.

It is strongly recommended that candidates arrange to visit the College for a personal appointment, a tour of the campus with a student guide, observation of one or more classes, and conversations with faculty members, staff members, and students. Early entrance is available for well-qualified and mature students who wish to begin college at the close of their junior year in high school; early-entrance candidates are required to come to the College for interviews. The College also welcomes the opportunity to discuss future educational plans with transfer candidates, including junior college and community college graduates, in good academic standing. Chatham grants college course credit for grades of 4 or 5 on the Advanced Placement examinations of the College Board. Certain prerequisites in course offerings may be fulfilled by attaining scores of 3, 4, or 5.

Application and Information

Candidates for admission must file an application with the Admissions Office, together with a $35 nonrefundable processing fee. Students may also take advantage of the College's free online applications on the Web site (listed below). Applications are accepted on a rolling basis.

Vice President of Enrollment Management Services
Office of Admissions
Chatham College
Woodland Road
Pittsburgh, Pennsylvania 15232
Telephone: 412-365-1290
800-837-1290 (toll-free)
Fax: 412-365-1609
E-mail: admissions@chatham.edu
World Wide Web: http://www.chatham.edu

View of the Chatham College campus.

CHESTER COLLEGE OF NEW ENGLAND

CHESTER, NEW HAMPSHIRE

The College

Chester College of New England offers students a foundation in the liberal and fine arts and a thorough preparation for careers in the professional arts. The College offers majors in arts and humanities, creative and professional writing, graphic design and illustration, photography and media arts, and studio art. The College also offers minors in illustration and photojournalism and certification in art education. The programs are complementary. Students specialize in intersections among art, graphic design and illustration, photography, and the written word.

The low faculty-student ratio; artist/writer-in-residence programs; a robust program of guest lectures, exhibitions, art contests and shows, and internships; and relationships with professional associations complement and strengthen the College's offerings. The College's aim is to provide all students with the education, knowledge, skills, and experiences they need to become both thoughtful citizens and successful professionals.

Students at Chester College of New England find that the tranquil setting of the campus provides them with the kind of environment that is essential for creative inspiration, yet the College is close to Manchester and Portsmouth, New Hampshire, and Boston, Massachusetts—cities that are rich in history and culture. Students frequently travel to these cities to work at internship sites, visit galleries and museums, and attend an assortment of artistic performances.

Chester College of New England is a private, coeducational, nonsectarian institution. It is accredited to award the Bachelor of Arts degree and the Associate in Arts degree by the New Hampshire Postsecondary Education Commission and by the New England Association of Schools and Colleges.

The College has an enrollment of approximately 200 students. Although the ages of students range from 17 to 55, the average age of students is 19. Most of these students live on campus, but a number of students enroll as commuters. All resident students are full-time. Commuters may choose to enroll on a full-time or part-time basis. The classroom student-teacher ratio is very low, approximately 10:1, which allows for a great deal of personalized instruction. The College believes that this sort of interaction is critical, given its focus on the liberal and fine arts.

A new residence hall opened recently. This coeducational residence can house 102 students and has lounge areas, laundry facilities, and various recreational amenities. It is conveniently located near all academic and studio facilities.

The Dining Commons provides meals for students, faculty and staff members, and visitors. Breakfast, lunch, and dinner are served in this facility seven days a week during the academic year and for portions of the summer session as well.

Extracurricular programs are designed to enhance and enrich the learning experience, and students are expected to be active members of the campus community, both in and out of the classroom.

Location

Chester College of New England offers the aspiring artist a natural setting that nurtures both artistic and intellectual development. The campus is situated on 75 acres in the center of Chester, New Hampshire, a classic rural New England town near Manchester, New Hampshire, and just a short drive from the state's beaches and ski resorts. The campus buildings are a mixture of restored eighteenth-century houses and new buildings that preserve the feel of Colonial New England while providing modern conveniences and spaces appropriate for classroom learning and artistic creation. Many of the houses in the vicinity of the College are beautifully maintained antique homes from the Colonial, Federal, and Victorian periods. The town square, only a few hundred yards from the campus, includes a classic white Colonial church, the town hall, and a general store.

Majors and Degrees

The College offers a Bachelor of Arts degree with majors in arts and humanities, creative and professional writing, graphic design and illustration, photography and media arts, and studio art. Minors are offered in photojournalism and illustration. Those interested in art education can also complete an art education certification program.

Academic Programs

The arts foundation courses introduce students to the majors offered and provide the concepts, vocabularies, and insight that are essential preparation for further study. Foundation courses emphasize verbal, visual, technical, and written skills. The foundation curriculum is carefully sequenced to provide varied and complementary courses that interact with other foundation courses, as well as with the liberal arts component of the curriculum.

Close acquaintance with the liberal arts sharpens students' oral and written communication skills; provides them with opportunities to explore historical, social, and scientific contexts and concepts; and develops an appreciation of ideas and experiences that form the basis of all human endeavors. The liberal arts component of an education at Chester College of New England begins by establishing a foundation in English composition, art history, and the humanities. Students then move on to explore three traditional and challenging areas of study—the sciences, the social sciences, and history—and explore the liberal arts in greater depth by choosing from a variety of course offerings, some of them at the upper level.

The curriculum integrates courses in the liberal arts, fine arts, and professional arts throughout the undergraduate experience, along with opportunities to learn from and interact with a faculty of practicing professional artists, designers, photographers, and writers. The College's internship program and Student Success Center prepare students to enter their chosen professional fields with the appropriate knowledge, skills, experience, and preparation to succeed.

The programs leading to the Bachelor of Arts degree require a minimum of 120 credits; the Associate in Arts degree in liberal studies requires a minimum of 60 credits.

Chester College of New England follows a traditional academic calendar of two semesters. Summer-session courses are optional. Fall semester generally begins at the end of August; spring semester begins in early January.

Academic Facilities

Office, classroom, and living spaces on campus are relatively compact and create a comfortable environment for highly personalized interaction. The largest classroom holds no more than 40 people, and classes at the College rarely exceed 15 students.

The Photography Studio is located in the Photo Barn and includes a darkroom with multiple workstations for black-and-white and color printing. Separate studio areas are provided. In the exhibit areas, each student has the opportunity to have photography selected for display for the benefit and enjoyment of fellow students and the community.

Douglas Hall, a renovated governor's mansion, is the College's latest addition to its facilities. It currently houses art, drawing, graphic arts, and sculpture studios as well as three general-purpose classrooms and computer laboratories.

Wadleigh Library provides academic research support for the programs offered on campus. The library also provides individual study carrels, study space in the reference and other areas, meeting spaces for study groups, a computer design laboratory, and a small auditorium for lectures and presentations. The College's Student Success Center, also housed in the library, is intended to help students succeed not only academically, but also in their decisions about future career paths.

The graphic design computer classroom provides Macintosh computers for graphic design, digital imaging, and advertising classes, using state-of-the-art software. In addition, Wadleigh Library houses networked personal computers and printers specifically for student use. These machines are equipped with current releases of word processing software.

Each student is permitted to have one car on campus, and parking is provided for a $35 annual fee. The College provides occasional transportation to Manchester, Portsmouth, and Boston and to recreational sites.

Costs

In 2003–04, tuition for full-time students was $12,600. Room and board (double room) were $6900. Tuition per credit hour for full-time students, part-time students (8 to 11 credits per semester), and study-abroad students was $420. Photography majors should anticipate book and supply expenditures of $700 per semester ($400 per semester for other majors). Other charges included a semester service fee of $135, a technology fee of $130, a summer session fee of $250 per credit hour, a parking fee of $35, and a freshman-orientation fee of $90.

Financial Aid

Chester College of New England is dedicated to helping its students determine the best possible means for financing their educations and offers advice to students and their families regardless of income level. Through its programs of need- and merit-based financial assistance, the College makes every effort possible to assist students who wish to attend. These programs consist of loans, grants, work-study jobs, and scholarships. The College offers opportunities through federal financial aid programs (Federal Pell Grant, Federal Supplemental Educational Opportunity Grant (FSEOG), Federal Stafford Student Loan, Federal Work-Study Program, and PLUS loans). The College also offers merit scholarships to incoming students up to full tuition for up to four years of study. More than 85 percent of the students at Chester College receive some form of financial aid.

Faculty

The faculty is made up of both full- and part-time instructors who are master teachers and working artists and professionals. Faculty members participate in advising students in curriculum and career planning and act in supervisory capacities for internships.

Student Government

The Student Government members, in consultation with the Director of Student Services, plan and schedule activities and events for the academic year. The campus calendar offers numerous events, including dramatic performances, ski trips, art and photography exhibits, dances, musical performances, and lectures and discussion groups concerning important social and political issues.

Admission Requirements

Chester College of New England is a small college by design and enrolls limited-size classes of highly talented women and men in its Bachelor of Arts and Associate in Arts programs. The College admits freshmen and transfer students and seeks a diverse student body. Students may be admitted for the September and January semesters. Applicants for admission to either program are judged by many criteria, including academic performance, artistic achievements and potential, extracurricular accomplishments and activities, communication skills (both oral and written), standardized test scores (SAT I or ACT), energy and determination, and portfolio quality.

The College strongly encourages submission of SAT or ACT scores. Students who do not submit test scores are not penalized in the admission process. However, most Chester College of New England scholarships require the submission of test scores, so it is generally in the best interest of the student to provide official test results.

Admission requirements include submitting a completed application form (either paper or the online version, which is available at http://www.chestercollege.edu/apply), the $35 application fee, official copies of transcripts from all secondary schools and any colleges or universities attended, three letters of recommendation, and a written personal statement. A personal interview is required, either in person or via telephone.

Depending on the student's choice of major, artistic achievement may be a significant factor in the admission decision. Also, a number of scholarships are available that are based primarily on the student's artistic accomplishment. For these reasons, while the College does not require the submission of a portfolio, it is strongly recommended.

It is strongly recommended that the student arrange for a campus visit and tour, which provides an important opportunity to gain valuable firsthand knowledge of Chester College.

Application and Information

Chester College of New England operates on a rolling admissions basis. Students are notified of a decision within two weeks after they have completed the admission requirements. There is no application deadline; however, students are encouraged to submit applications no later than April 1 for fall admission and no later than December 1 for spring admission.

For more information, students should contact:

Director of Admissions
Chester College of New England
40 Chester Street
Chester, New Hampshire 03036
Telephone: 603-887-7400
800-974-6372 (toll-free)
E-mail: admissions@chestercollege.edu
World Wide Web: http://www.chestercollege.edu

CHESTNUT HILL COLLEGE

PHILADELPHIA, PENNSYLVANIA

The College

Chestnut Hill College (CHC) is a four-year, coeducational, Catholic liberal arts college. Founded in 1924 by the Sisters of St. Joseph, it is situated on a 45-acre campus overlooking Wissahickon Creek. Students come from fifteen states, thirteen countries, and many cultural heritages. In fall 2003, Chestnut Hill became fully coeducational with its first full-time admission of men to the College. Working adults are enrolled in the accelerated evening and weekend undergraduate program. In addition to its undergraduate degrees, Chestnut Hill awards the M.Ed., M.A., and M.S. in six fields, including administration of human services, applied technology, counseling psychology and human services, education, holistic spirituality, and holistic spirituality and health care. The College also awards a doctoral degree in clinical psychology (Psy.D.).

When it comes to student activities, students enthusiastically engage in the many clubs and organizations available and participate in everything from aerobics and horseback riding to golf and archery. The College is an NCAA Division III member and competes in basketball, lacrosse, soccer, softball, tennis, and volleyball. A swimming pool, a gymnasium, a fitness room, and tennis courts provide excellent athletic facilities for Chestnut Hill's students.

Location

Chestnut Hill College is situated in a beautiful historical area at the northwestern edge of Philadelphia. The College is bounded by the wooded hills of Fairmount Park, yet it is only a 30-minute ride by train or car to downtown Philadelphia where students can enjoy a wide variety of dining, cultural, and sporting events. Among the many attractions are the museums that grace Philadelphia, from its landmark Art Museum to the Rodin Museum, the Living History Museum, the Franklin Institute, and numerous others. The city's history is reflected throughout but is most prominent in the areas surrounding Independence Hall, Society Hill, and Penn's Landing. In addition, more than seventy colleges, universities, and medical schools in the area offer opportunities for socialization and an extensive range of activities.

One mile beyond CHC on Germantown Avenue is the well-known area of Philadelphia also called Chestnut Hill. Reminiscent of a Colonial village, this section of Philadelphia provides convenient opportunities for shopping, cultural experiences, and transportation to downtown Philadelphia. CHC is a school in a suburban setting with all the advantages of a cosmopolitan experience—located where the northwest corner of the city meets the suburbs.

Majors and Degrees

The Bachelor of Arts and Bachelor of Science degrees are offered with majors in accounting; biochemistry; biology; business administration; chemistry; communications and technology; computer and information science; computer and information technology; early childhood education (with an option of Montessori certification); early childhood and elementary education; elementary education; English; environmental science; French; history; international business, language, and culture; marketing; mathematics and computer science; molecular biology; political science; psychology; secondary education certification in various disciplines; sociology (with a professional option in criminal justice); and Spanish. Dual degrees (B.S./M.S.) are offered in education, psychology, and technology.

Chestnut Hill College also offers preprofessional programs in allied health fields, dentistry, law, medicine, and veterinary sciences. Cooperative studies are available with La Salle University.

Academic Program

The academic year consists of two 15-week semesters. There are also two 6-week summer sessions.

As a liberal arts college, CHC offers courses of study that provide the student with a broad background in the fine arts and humanities, a knowledge of science, and a keen awareness of the social problems of the day, as well as intensive, in-depth study in a major field.

CHC confers a B.S. or B.A. degree to students who earn 120 semester hours of credit and satisfy specific requirements set by the faculty. Distribution requirements are as follows: 11 semester hours in natural sciences (8 hours of which must be in a laboratory science), 9 semester hours in social sciences, and 21 semester hours in the humanities. In addition to these 41 hours of credit, every student must take 6 semester hours of religious studies, 6 hours beyond the elementary level in a classical or modern foreign language, and 3 hours in a writing course (unless exempted by the English department). As many as 45 of the 120 semester hours may be within the major area.

A student with the ability and proper motivation may be permitted to major in two departments. The student must consult with the chair of each department to determine the feasibility of the proposal and then submit it to the dean of the college for approval. It is understood that the student will satisfy the requirements of both departments.

Each year, selected first-year students and sophomores are invited into an interdepartmental honors program that challenges intellectual initiative and provides the opportunity for independent study and seminar discussion. The completion of the four honors courses and an honors paper satisfies all distributional requirements. Students may apply for admission at the beginning of their first year or sophomore year.

Sophomores of high scholastic standing are invited by their major departments to engage in a program of independent study during their junior and senior years. This opportunity for independent study and original research culminates in an honors thesis, which is a prerequisite for the conferring of honors at graduation.

The environmental studies, gerontology, international studies, and women in management certificate programs expose liberal arts students in any major to current principles and practices in business and management.

Off-Campus Programs

Students have the advantages of two campuses and two curricula through an agreement with La Salle University, which allows students from either school to register for courses at the other institution for full credit without paying extra tuition. Public transportation is available between the two schools.

At CHC, a student may take advantage of the monthlong interim between semesters by coordinating travel and study. Students, with the assistance of one or more of their professors, can use their imagination and interests to develop an off-campus program. Should the program be more lengthy than the interim allows, students may schedule their travel and study for the summer. Past intersession programs have included studies of French culture in Paris, women in English literature in London, and marine biology in Florida.

Chestnut Hill College participates in a consortium arrangement with ten colleges throughout the nation, founded by the Sisters of St. Joseph. As participants, students can study at any other member institution for a semester or a year, while maintaining status as full-time Chestnut Hill students.

An average of B or above and approval of the academic dean allow an upperclass student to pursue organized study in another country. The major department must approve the course of study. In recent years, Chestnut Hill College students have enrolled in institutions in London, Madrid, Rome, Salzburg, Vienna, and other European centers. Chestnut Hill College has an agreement with Regents College in London, England, for study abroad.

The growing interest of students in acquiring on-the-job experience while still in college has prompted the development of many departmental internship programs, which provide students with the opportunity to gain professional experience in their major while earning academic credit. Chestnut Hill has also established an office of experiential education, through which Chestnut Hill College students are assisted in finding jobs that correspond to their career interests and academic pursuits. Co-op students work and attend classes in alternate periods, earning academic credit for their practical experience.

Academic Facilities

CHC's Logue Library houses a collection of approximately 139,585 volumes and 544 current periodicals, a rare book room that contains first editions and special editions, the Gruber Theater, the fine Curriculum Library for elementary education, and an Irish literature collection. Well-equipped science laboratories, a math center, a multimedia technology center, a writing enrichment center, individual practice rooms for music students, a spacious art studio, a planetarium, and an observatory are among the many other outstanding facilities on campus. Martino Hall, which opened in 2000 and was designed to maintain the architectural history of the College, provides room for a performance center, gymnasium, or convocation center. The second and third floors house cutting-edge "smart" classrooms.

Costs

General expenses for 2003–04 were tuition and fees of $18,975 and room and board costs of between $7000 and $8000.

Financial Aid

Financial aid is available in the form of academic scholarships, guaranteed loans, work-study programs, federal grants, and Chestnut Hill College grants. Most of these are based on financial need and are awarded in financial aid packages that combine various forms of aid and are tailored to each student's need. More than 75 percent of CHC students receive financial aid to meet College costs. All applicants for aid should file a copy of the Free Application for Federal Student Aid (FAFSA). Merit-based scholarships and awards are granted for academic achievement.

Faculty

Evidence of Chestnut Hill's vitality can be seen in its faculty. While their primary interest is teaching, faculty members are also engaged in research, publication, travel, and other professional activities. Of the 109 members currently on the faculty, 57 are full-time, with more than 75 percent holding terminal degrees. The men and women who make up this group are deeply interested in both their subject and their students. Their qualifications include international degrees from Bangalore University (India), the University of London, and the University of Paris, and domestic degrees from Boston College, Bryn Mawr College, Catholic University of America, Columbia University, Creighton University, Duke University, Fordham University, Harvard University, Middlebury College, the New School for Social Research, New York University, Purdue University, Saint Louis University, Temple University, and the Universities of Arizona, Delaware, Massachusetts, Minnesota, Montana, New Mexico, North Carolina, Notre Dame, and Pennsylvania. CHC's faculty-student ratio is 1:12.

Student Government

A student at CHC has the opportunity to think independently and to approach decisions creatively. Judgments concerning all collegiate affairs are made by students in conjunction with the faculty and administration. Several organizations provide structure for the decision-making process. Students join members of the faculty and administration on the Curriculum Committee and the College Council. The Academic, Social-Cultural, and Student Affairs Committees of the Student Organization identify, represent, and meet campus needs.

Admission Requirements

CHC welcomes students whose aptitudes and academic records show a desire to accept a challenge. Applications are judged by the Admissions Committee on the basis of intellectual ability, academic achievement (class rank and performance in high school, including completion of 16 academic units), and SAT I or ACT results. CHC has early decision, early admission, and advanced placement programs.

Students should submit a completed application, application fee, SAT I or ACT scores, a high school transcript, an essay, and letters of recommendation. An interview is recommended and may be required. A student wishing to transfer to CHC is asked to submit a transcript from all colleges previously attended.

Application and Information

Applications are processed on a rolling admission system. To arrange an interview or to obtain more detailed information about the academic program, students should contact:

Director of Admissions
Chestnut Hill College
9601 Germantown Avenue
Philadelphia, Pennsylvania 19118
Telephone: 215-248-7001
800-248-0052 (toll-free)
E-mail: chcapply@chc.edu
World Wide Web: http://www.chc.edu

CHEYNEY UNIVERSITY OF PENNSYLVANIA

CHEYNEY, PENNSYLVANIA

The University

Cheyney University was founded in 1837 by Richard Humphreys, a Philadelphia Quaker. Since its inception, Cheyney University has continued to educate American and international students above and beyond the vision of Mr. Humphreys. His dream was a school of higher learning for African-American students "in order to prepare and fit and qualify them to act as teachers...." Cheyney University graduates still become teachers, but students also enter such fields as journalism, medicine, business, science, industrial arts, and communications. Today, Cheyney's students represent a variety of races, cultures, and nationalities. It is a coeducational university with an undergraduate enrollment of 1,535 students; 1,420 are full-time and 115 are part-time.

Students are Cheyney University's highest priority. Above all else, the faculty and staff are in the business of developing human potential and talent. Dedicated faculty members work closely with students and demand from them all that is necessary to prepare them for career success and responsible citizenship.

The 275-acre Cheyney campus is situated on rolling hillsides in southeastern Pennsylvania, an area that is changing from rural to suburban. The surroundings, small classes, and modern facilities provide an ideal atmosphere for learning.

Living on campus is desirable, particularly for first-year students. Off-campus housing is available in nearby communities. Resident students enjoy a rich cultural and social life as well as a sense of community. Facilities include five dormitories, a full-service dining hall, and a student/alumni center. Student interest groups include a drama club (the Cheyney Players), premedical and prelaw societies, the business club, the chess club, the choir, the band, cheerleading, Latino Students in Action, International Students Association, and about twenty other groups. Several honor societies and Greek-letter organizations are also active.

There are numerous opportunities for on-campus recreation. Cheyney has beautifully situated outdoor tennis, volleyball, basketball, and handball courts. The athletic building houses large and small gymnasiums and an Olympic-size swimming pool. The Cheyney Wolves have won national recognition in women's and men's basketball and in wrestling. Other sports include football, men's and women's tennis and track, and women's volleyball. Cheyney's open-tryout policy allows all interested students to try out for any team, provided that they maintain the grade point average required for participation. Students enjoy a full intramural program.

Cheyney is accredited by the Middle States Association of Colleges and Schools, and its programs in education are accredited by the Pennsylvania Department of Education. Graduate programs in education and teacher certification are offered at Cheyney's Urban Center in Center City Philadelphia.

Location

Cheyney is 25 miles west of Philadelphia. SEPTA bus service is available between the campus, Center City Philadelphia, Chester, and several sites in Delaware County. Lancaster is 1½ hours away, and Harrisburg is 2 hours from Cheyney. Wilmington, Delaware, is 15 miles south of Cheyney; New York City and Washington, D.C., are 2 hours away. The campus is easily accessible via the Pennsylvania Turnpike and Interstate 95.

Majors and Degrees

Cheyney grants the Bachelor of Arts degree in biology, chemistry, communication arts, computer and information sciences, economics, English, French, general science, geography, history, mathematics, political science, psychology, social relations (criminal justice and sociology), social science, Spanish, and theater arts. The Bachelor of Science degree is granted in business administration (accounting, management, marketing, office administration, small-business management, and tax accounting); clothing and textiles; hotel, restaurant, and institutional management; and recreation. The Bachelor of Science in Education may be earned in early childhood, elementary, and secondary education (majors in biology, business education, chemistry, English, French, general science, mathematics, social studies, and Spanish); home economics; and special education.

Academic Programs

The completion of 128 semester hours is required for a bachelor's degree. Of the 128 hours, 40 percent are in general education; the remainder are required in humanities, social sciences, natural sciences, mathematics, health and physical education, and electives. Army ROTC is available.

Qualified students may undertake independent study projects and internships. A cooperative education program enables students to work and study in alternate semesters. The Department of Sciences and Allied Health arranges summer research projects for science students at nearby medical colleges. The on-campus Head Start site and Academic Achievement Center offer opportunities for education majors to apply classroom concepts in real-life settings. A University internship program coordinator helps students secure internships and places students in accordance with their degree programs or personal interests.

The Academic Skills Center provides support services through tutors and counselors for students who seek academic support. The First-Year Studies Program ensures that each first-year student has the maximum potential to develop his or her academic skills through a series of placement tests in English, math, and reading.

Cheyney's Honors Program is open to all high school graduates, regardless of year of graduation. Students in the Honors Program are enrolled in several classes as a group and have their own special residence halls, complete with computer rooms and reading rooms. Honors students have opportunities to interact and be identified as a group while also participating in the activities of the overall student community.

Academic Facilities

The Leslie Pinckney Hill Library houses approximately 200,000 books plus a periodical collection of more than 23,000 bound volumes and 1,100 current subscriptions. Audiovisual media and CD-ROM full-text/images databases, Internet access, and World Wide Web access are available. The library also houses the famed Schomburg Collection of African-American history and culture on microfilm.

Cheyney's Telecommunications Center consists of a 240-seat auditorium with state-of-the-art satellite television capabilities, a cable television control facility, a television studio, and the

AT&T Distance Learning and Teleconferencing Center. AT&T has installed twenty fully loaded Pentium computers with network access in the Telecommunications Center. Used primarily for instruction of private and public school teachers in Pennsylvania districts in the use of the Internet, the facility is available for use by Cheyney students.

Cheyney has formed a partnership with Navigation Technologies, a company that designs databases for intelligent transportation, travel, and traffic markets. Students use highly sophisticated technology and programs that create economically efficient and environmentally sound transportation systems.

Students in the clothing and textile major have access to computer-aided design software for the creation of patterns for apparel, upholstery, and interior design, among others.

Costs

For the 2003–04 academic year, tuition for Pennsylvania residents was $5598 for full-time students and $192 per credit hour; for nonresidents it was $9196 for full-time students and $383 per credit hour. Required fees were $774 for full-time students. Room and board costs were $5382; room only was $2944. Room and board charges vary according to board plan. Deferred payment plans are available to those who qualify. Waiver plans are available for senior citizens, employees, and children of employees.

Financial Aid

The University makes every possible effort to enable interested and qualified students to take advantage of its educational opportunities. Financial assistance is available in the form of academic scholarships, grants, loans, and the Federal Work-Study Program. Financial aid packages are developed for qualified students based on individual student need. Students wishing to apply for financial aid must complete the Free Application for Federal Student Aid (FAFSA). Students should pay strict attention to all state and federal application deadlines.

Faculty

Cheyney's faculty members have earned degrees at such diverse institutions as Columbia; Fisk; Howard; Juilliard; Temple; Cheyney University of Pennsylvania; the Universities of California, Pennsylvania, and Wisconsin; Nagpur University; Punjabi University; the Universities of Madras and Kerala; and the Sorbonne.

Student Government

All students are members of the Student Government Cooperative Association (SGCA), which sponsors many cultural, educational, and social events and brings speakers and performers to the campus. SGCA and other student representatives sit on all University committees. A student representative is also selected to serve on the University's Council of Trustees.

Admission Requirements

Cheyney University seeks students who have not only academic ability but also talent and diversity. Students are encouraged to provide an overall view of themselves in their application, including extracurricular activities, interests, and academic goals. The Admissions Committee evaluates applicants on the basis of secondary school records, SAT I or ACT scores, and recommendations from teachers and counselors. As part of the State System of Higher Education, the University gives priority to residents of the Commonwealth of Pennsylvania. However, the University welcomes out-of-state and international applicants. The admissions office encourages visits to the campus and arranges tour and information sessions with members of the staff; students should call to make an appointment. Representatives from the admissions office visit many high schools during the year to increase contact with students.

Application and Information

In order to be considered for admission, students must submit a completed admission application, an official copy of the high school transcript, two letters of recommendation, SAT I or ACT scores, and a $20 nonrefundable application fee. Transfer students are required to submit official transcripts from all colleges or universities previously attended. A completed Dean's Recommendation Form is also required for transfer students. Prospective students may apply online or download an application form from the Web site listed below.

Cheyney encourages all prospective students and parents to visit the campus. For more information and to schedule an individual or group tour, students should contact:

Office of Admissions
Cheyney University of Pennsylvania
1837 University Circle
P.O. Box 200
Cheyney, Pennsylvania 19319-0200
Telephone: 610-399-2275
800-CHEYNEY (toll-free)
World Wide Web: http://www.cheyney.edu

Cheyney University does not discriminate on the basis of gender, race, religion, age, sexual orientation, or disability in educational programs, activities, employment, recruitment, or admission policies.

CHRISTOPHER NEWPORT UNIVERSITY

NEWPORT NEWS, VIRGINIA

The University

Christopher Newport University (CNU) was founded in 1960 and currently enrolls 4,800 students in more than seventy areas of study (including four master's degree programs). The University takes pride in its "student-first, teaching-first" community. Small classes taught by veteran faculty members, a beautiful and safe campus, and one of the nation's finest sports programs make CNU a distinctive choice among Virginia's public universities.

State-of-the-art residence halls and upperclass apartments accommodate 3,000 students on campus. CNU opened its $16-million Freeman Sports and Convocation Center in 2000, and completion of the $55-million Center for the Fine and Performing Arts, designed by I. M. Pei, is scheduled for 2005. A new $35-million Student Center is scheduled to be completed by 2006.

Location

CNU is located in suburban Newport News, adjacent to Mariner's Park, a pristine 600-acre nature preserve with miles of jogging trails around Lake Maury and along the James River. Newport News is the hub of high-tech industry in southeastern Virginia and home of the Jefferson Laboratory, the premier physics research facility in the world. CNU students have access to internships there and in many local firms and agencies in areas such as media, health care, education, and social services.

CNU ranks as one of the safest mid-size campuses in Virginia. Its picturesque 250-acre campus and superb residence facilities receive accolades from students and visitors alike. CNU is host to the annual Ella Fitzgerald Music Festival.

CNU is 35 miles from the pounding surf and rolling dunes of Virginia Beach, 25 miles from historic Williamsburg, 75 miles from Richmond, and 150 miles from Washington, D.C. Students enjoy the moderate climate year-round and appreciate the easy driving distance to the beach and the region's many recreational opportunities. The newest of these is the Virginia Beach Amphitheater, which attracts internationally known musical groups.

Majors and Degrees

The College of Liberal Arts and Sciences offers the Bachelor of Arts degree in communication studies; English (with concentrations in creative writing, journalism, language arts, literature, and technical writing); fine and performing arts (with concentrations in fine arts, music, music theater, and theater arts); foreign language (with concentrations in French, German, and Spanish); history (with an interdisciplinary prelaw program available); interdisciplinary studies; philosophy (with a concentration available in religious studies); political science (with a concentration available in international relations); psychology (with concentrations in early childhood psychology, general psychology, and industrial/organizational psychology); and sociology (with majors available in social work and sociology and a concentration available in culture, socialization, and society for sociology majors). Also offered is the Bachelor of Music degree (with concentrations in history/literature, performance, and theory/composition and emphases in instrumental music and choral music); the Bachelor of Science degree in interdisciplinary studies; and the Bachelor of Science in Governmental Administration degree (with concentrations in justice studies and public management). Minors are available in anthropology, art, childhood studies, English, film studies, French, geography, German, gerontology, government and public affairs, history, leadership studies, music, philosophy, professional writing, psychology, sociology, speech communication, Spanish, theater arts, and women's and gender studies. A certificate is offered in jazz studies.

Also offered in the sciences are the Bachelor of Arts degree in applied physics (with concentrations in technical writing and editing), biology, economics, interdisciplinary studies, and mathematics (with concentrations in computer science and physics) and the Bachelor of Science degree in applied physics (with concentrations in computation, instrumentation, and solid state/optics), biology (with preprofessional programs in dental, medical, and veterinary studies), computer engineering, computer science, environmental science, interdisciplinary studies, mathematics (with concentrations in computer science, mathematics education, and physics), and ornamental horticulture. Minors are available in applied physics, biology, business administration, chemistry, computer science, economics, finance, mathematics, and physics.

The School of Business offers the Bachelor of Science in Business Administration degree (with specializations in accounting, economics, finance, management, and marketing); and the Bachelor of Science in Information Science degree (with concentrations in management of information systems, networking and communications, and science of information systems).

A 3-2 cooperative program with the Duke University School of the Environment allows Christopher Newport University students to earn the Bachelor of Science degree from CNU and the Master of Forestry or Master of Environmental Management degree from Duke.

Academic Program

To be eligible for an undergraduate degree, students must successfully complete 120 academic semester hours. The last 45 semester hours of credit must be taken in residence.

The first two years of all students' academic programs require successful completion of general education requirements in such areas as English (writing), foreign language, history, humanities, laboratory science, mathematics, and social science. The last two years are devoted to the academic major and electives.

Off-Campus Programs

Christopher Newport University actively supports study abroad for all its students and sponsors a variety of international study programs each year. CNU students have recently participated with faculty members in study-abroad programs in Spain, England, France, and Guatemala. CNU offers up to a $1000 stipend for international study to students who participate in the President's Leadership Program. Students may also travel to Europe with the CNU Chamber Singers or worldwide with CNU's award-winning Model U.N. Club.

Academic Facilities

The Captain John Smith Library houses more than 600,000 books, micropieces, and bound periodicals and also offers students access to textual material, periodicals, and information recorded on film, microfilm, records, and tapes. Services include interlibrary loans and extensive computer-assisted bibliographical services. As part of the completion University's $300-million building campaign, it is planned that the library's size doubles by 2006.

Academic buildings contain a variety of small classrooms and auditoriums, computer laboratories, specialty laboratories, an art gallery, an instructional technology center, a theater, music recital halls and practice rooms, and a greenhouse/herbarium. CNU provides 1,200 computer workstations on campus as well as e-mail and Internet access in its residential facilities.

Costs

In-state tuition for full-time students for the 2003–04 academic year was $4600; nonresident tuition for full-time students was $12,300. Books and supplies average $600 per year. The room and board rate for the 2003–04 academic year was $6700.

Financial Aid

The University's financial aid programs serve about 50 percent of the student body. CNU offers every form of federally funded financial aid and a variety of renewable merit scholarships for freshmen, ranging from $1000 per year to full tuition.

Faculty

Eighty-five percent of CNU faculty members hold the highest degree in their professional field. In addition to providing high-quality classroom instruction, faculty members work with students to develop academic schedules, supervise independent programs, conduct a wide range of scholarly research, and provide a wealth of services to the community. CNU prides itself on the close, personal relationships between students and professors.

Student Government

The University encourages students to participate in the formulation of rules, regulations, and policies directly affecting student life. Students may get involved with the Student Government Association (SGA) and University committees and councils. SGA awards support monies to many of the eighty active campus clubs and organizations each year.

Admission Requirements

CNU welcomes applications from Virginia residents and out-of-state students whose education includes a strong college preparatory curriculum and a record of success. Of the students accepted into the freshman class, the midrange (middle 50 percent) SAT I score is 1080 to 1250 and the GPA range is 3.0 to 3.7. CNU admits less than half of its applicants.

Application and Information

Applications, a viewbook, and additional information may be obtained through the Internet at the address below or by contacting:

Admissions Office
Christopher Newport University
1 University Place
Newport News, Virginia 23606-2998
Telephone: 757-594-7015
757-594-7938 (TDD)
800-333-4CNU (toll-free)
E-mail: admit@cnu.edu
World Wide Web: http://www.cnu.edu

THE CITADEL

CHARLESTON, SOUTH CAROLINA

The College

The Citadel, founded in 1842, has a rich and storied history. Though it has been greatly expanded and modernized, it is basically the same distinctive institution it was when founded. The mission is to graduate leaders who excel in civilian professions and enterprises as well as serve their country in government and the military. The Citadel remains a stronghold of duty, self-discipline, and high ideals in a changing American society.

As a classic military college, The Citadel emphasizes the value of a strict indoctrination for first-year students, who are called knobs. The disciplined lifestyle that begins in the knob year binds cadets into a lifelong, close-knit camaraderie that is one of the strongest forces in their lives after graduation.

Citadel graduates have fought in every American conflict since the Mexican War. Cadets from The Citadel fired the first shots of the Civil War. The Citadel proudly displays on the Corps flag nine battle streamers earned in that war. Citadel graduates continue to serve their country with distinction in all branches of the armed services.

The Corps of Cadets numbers almost 2,000 and represents nearly every state in the union and many other countries. All cadets are required to reside in barracks. An ultramodern physical education center provides splendid facilities for physical education and individual and team sports unrelated to varsity events. An exceptional intramural program includes twenty-eight activities. The student activities building, named for General Mark W. Clark, the late president emeritus, houses the Honor Court room, reception lounge, Office of Cadet Activities, photograph darkroom, student publication offices, canteen, auditorium, billiard room, and post office. The beautiful Summerall Chapel, which is a shrine of religion, patriotism, and remembrance, is flexibly designed for use by major denominational groups.

The Citadel, a member of NCAA Division I (football division 1-AA) and the Southern Conference, fields fifteen men's and women's intercollegiate athletic teams. Club sports include bicycling, bowling, boxing, crew, fencing, gymnastics, judo, karate, lacrosse, pistol, rugby, sailing, scuba diving, skydiving, volleyball, and waterskiing. The Citadel has its own boating center and canoes, power boats, and sailboats.

Location

The Citadel is located in one of America's most historic cities, Charleston, South Carolina. The beautiful 100-acre campus is bordered by the Ashley River and historic Hampton Park. The climate is ideal, with an average temperature of 67 degrees. Many excellent ocean beaches are nearby. A Citadel beach club is located just a few minutes away on the lush Isle of Palms. Charleston is famous for its pre-Revolutionary houses and gardens, outstanding restaurants, golf courses, and cultural centers. Entertainment and nightlife abound.

Charleston is served by Amtrak, an international airport, two bus lines, seven taxi companies, a limousine service, and fifteen rental-car firms. The city's transit system stops at The Citadel's main entrance. The campus is readily accessible via Interstate 26 or U.S. Route 17.

Majors and Degrees

Organized into five schools, The Citadel offers twenty major and thirteen minor areas of academic concentration. This provides cadets with academic opportunities normally expected only at a university, combined with the personalized attention afforded only by a small college. Bachelor of Arts degrees are available in chemistry, criminal justice, English, history, mathematics, modern languages, political science, and psychology. Bachelor of Science degrees are offered in biology, business administration, chemistry, civil engineering, computer science, education, electrical engineering, environmental engineering, mathematics, physical education, and physics.

Academic Program

The Citadel provides a sound education reinforced by the best features of a disciplined environment.

All cadets participate in one of the Reserve Officers' Training Corps programs—Army, Air Force, or Naval/Marine Corps. These programs do not require students to accept a commission or be committed to active duty.

The educational requirements of all majors ensure that The Citadel graduate is conversant with literature, history, and the natural and social sciences. Students learn to evaluate and judge by confronting issues raised in challenging courses.

The Citadel Honors Program is a specially designed educational experience that meets the needs of students with an outstanding record of academic achievement and a sense of intellectual adventure. While pursuing any one of the twenty degree programs offered by The Citadel, Honors students take a series of general education Honors courses concentrated in their first two years and an Honors seminar in their third and fourth years.

The Citadel—a fully accredited, four-year, coeducational, comprehensive senior college—is a member of the Southern Association of Colleges and Schools, the American Council on Education, the American Association of Colleges for Teacher Education, and the Association of American Colleges. The business administration department is accredited by AACSB International—The Association to Advance Collegiate Schools of Business. The civil and environmental engineering and electrical and computer engineering departments are accredited by the Accreditation Board for Engineering and Technology. The chemistry department is accredited by the American Chemical Society. The education department is accredited by the National Council for Accreditation of Teacher Education and the National Association of State Directors of Teacher Education and Certification.

Academic Facilities

Twenty-four major buildings are efficiently grouped around a huge parade ground to provide maximum convenience for students. Among the College's academic facilities are the Daniel Library, two engineering buildings, and computer facilities located in all academic areas. The entire campus is linked to a fiber-optic network. Through a consortium arrangement, other local college libraries and facilities are available to cadets. Cadet barracks provide computer connections to the campus-wide network and the Internet in every room.

Costs

The Citadel's extremely competitive fee structure includes uniforms, room, board, books, dry cleaning, laundry, athletic events, student publications, infirmary care, and haircuts. The annual fees for 2003–04 by residence and by class were as follows: for residents of South Carolina, fees for first-year students were $15,655, and for sophomores, juniors, and seniors, $12,295. For out-of-state students, fees for first-year students were $24,066, and for sophomores, juniors, and seniors, $20,706.

Financial Aid

The Citadel offers two types of financial assistance: financial aid, which consists of loans and grants that are awarded on the basis of need, and scholarships, which are awarded on the basis of merit. In 2002–03, more than 76 percent of the Cadet Corps received financial aid and 49 percent received scholarships, ranging from several hundred dollars a year to a student's complete expenses for four years. To be considered for financial aid or scholarships, students must submit an application for enrollment. The deadline for applying for need-based financial aid is February 28 of the senior year in high school.

Faculty

All courses at The Citadel are taught by dedicated faculty members, more than 96 percent of whom hold doctoral degrees. The student-faculty ratio is 18:1. All faculty members are required to set aside time for counseling and assisting cadets with their studies.

Student Government

Cadets form a regiment, composed of a band and bagpipe unit, a ceremonial artillery unit, and four battalions of four companies each. Student authority is entrusted to the chain of command and the elected class officials.

A principal aspect of student government is the honor code. Under that code, a cadet does not lie, cheat, steal, or tolerate those who do. An Honor Committee elected by cadets administers the code.

Admission Requirements

Applicants must be unmarried, between 17 and 23 years of age, physically qualified for enrollment in ROTC, and graduates of an accredited secondary school or have satisfactorily completed the General Educational Development examination. The required high school subjects are 4 units of English; 3 units of mathematics (algebra I, algebra II, and geometry); 3 years of laboratory science; 2 years of the same foreign language; 2 units of social science; 4 units of electives; 1 unit of U.S. history; and 1 unit of physical education or ROTC. Other considerations include the applicant's rank in class, academic performance, and scores on either the SAT I or ACT. Extracurricular activities are viewed as indications of leadership and desirable character traits. All factors are weighed in the final determination of the applicant's qualifications. The Citadel actively seeks and encourages applications for admission without regard to gender, race, or ability to pay. Applicants are encouraged to apply upon completion of their junior year in high school.

Application and Information

Applications may be made at the end of the junior year in secondary school. Prospective cadets should arrange to have their SAT I or ACT scores forwarded to The Citadel. While applicants are welcome to visit the campus at any time, special programs are arranged on a designated schedule, during which the accepted applicants reside in barracks.

Inquiries should be addressed to:

Office of Admissions
The Citadel
171 Moultrie Street
Charleston, South Carolina 29409
Telephone: 800-868-1842 (toll-free)
E-mail: admissions@citadel.edu
World Wide Web: http://www.citadel.edu

Members of the Corps of Cadets stand in formation on the quadrangle within one of The Citadel's four battalions.

CITY COLLEGE OF THE CITY UNIVERSITY OF NEW YORK

NEW YORK, NEW YORK

The College

Since its founding in 1847, the City College of New York (CCNY) has stressed the dual goals of offering access to higher education combined with academic excellence. That policy has had remarkable results, making CCNY one of America's greatest educational success stories. For example, 8 Nobel Prize winners are City College graduates, placing CCNY's graduates among the nation's leaders. The College ranks ninth among public and private institutions in the number of graduates who have gone on to earn doctorates. It also ranks among the top dozen in the number of alumni who are members of the prestigious National Academy of Engineering and in producing graduates who have become America's leading business executives. Reflecting the College's commitment to equal educational opportunity, CCNY is also one of the nation's leaders in producing minority engineering graduates and in the number of black graduates who gain admission to medical school. Overall, CCNY graduates exceed the national average in obtaining admission to medical school. The College has more full-time doctoral students in campus-based programs than have all of the other City University of New York (CUNY) colleges combined. City College is internationally known for the research activities of its faculty, which were supported by grants totaling more than $50 million during 2002–03, the largest amount received by a unit of CUNY. The College houses several major centers and institutes, including the CUNY Institute for Transportation Systems, the Colin Powell Center for Policy Studies, and the New York State Structural Biology Center.

The College offers students a wide variety of social activities; more than ninety clubs are organized on campus. Students can also participate in numerous intercollegiate and intramural sports. There are sixteen varsity teams for men and women. The Herman Goldman Center for Sports and Recreation contains outstanding facilities for track and field, baseball, soccer, lacrosse, and softball.

Location

The City College campus occupies 35 acres in Manhattan along Convent Avenue from 131st to 141st Streets in the area known as St. Nicholas Heights. The surrounding neighborhoods are predominantly residential, although there are shopping areas west of the campus along Broadway and south toward 125th Street.

Majors and Degrees

The College of Liberal Arts and Science offers the Bachelor of Arts (B.A.), the Bachelor of Science (B.S.), and the Bachelor of Fine Arts (B.F.A.) degrees in the following majors: American studies; anthropology; art; art history; biochemistry; biology; chemistry; comparative literature; creative writing; earth systems sciences; economics; electronic art and graphic design; English; foreign languages and literature; history; international studies; Jewish studies; management and administration; mathematics; music (performance, sonic music arts, theory); philosophy; physics; political science; psychology; public policy and public affairs; sociology; theater; and women's studies. The School of Architecture, Urban Design, and Landscape Architecture offers a B.S. in architecture and landscape architecture, and a five-year program leading to the Bachelor of Architecture is available. The Sophie Davis School of Biomedical Education provides a seven-year B.S./M.D. curriculum for highly qualified high school graduates who reside in New York State. The Physician's Assistant Program, also part of the School of Biomedical Education, offers a B.S. degree and is a joint program between City College and Harlem Hospital. This is an upper-division (junior and senior years) program. The School of Education offers programs that lead to the Bachelor of Science in Education (B.S.Ed.) in the following majors: bilingual education, early childhood education, and elementary education. In addition, students are prepared to teach a wide variety of subjects in secondary schools. The School of Engineering offers the Bachelor of Engineering (B.E.) degree in the fields of biomedical, chemical, civil, computer, electrical, and mechanical engineering and the B.S. in computer science. The Center for Worker Education is an off-site program that helps adults return to college while continuing their full-time employment. Students can complete a bachelor's degree program in the evening.

Academic Programs

City College includes the College of Liberal Arts and Science and the largest complex of professional schools in the City University. These include Schools of Architecture, Education, and Engineering and the Sophie Davis School of Biomedical Education/CUNY Medical School. There are centers in performing arts and legal education, and special programs include four-year bachelor's/master's programs in economics, English, history, mathematics, mathematics education, and psychology. A Freshman Honors Program is available for qualified students who are interested in advanced research work and independent study. Cooperative education internships are also provided for interested applicants. Such programs as Minority Access to Research Careers (MARC), Minority Biomedical Research Support (MBRS), and City College Research Scholars (CRS) provide paid and volunteer opportunities to do research at various institutions.

City College has a core curriculum that is founded on a strong liberal arts base and is designed to ensure the continued quality and relevance of its academic programs. The core curriculum reflects a global vision of human achievement in an increasingly interdependent world and is designed to provide City College students with superior academic preparation while enhancing their capacity to think critically and creatively. The College has a long history of encouraging independent thought and initiative and continues to foster an educational atmosphere in which students can explore and develop their interests and talents.

For most bachelor's degree programs, the total number of credits necessary to earn a degree is 120; a bachelor's degree in engineering requires up to 136 credits. The College works on a semester calendar and offers three summer sessions—one 7½-week session and two 4-week sessions.

Off-Campus Programs

City College has exchange programs in Austria, China, England, Germany, and Morocco as well as a summer program in the Dominican Republic. Students are able to spend a semester, a full academic year, or a summer term at one of the cooperating schools. Through a cooperative arrangement, students are also able to take courses at the various branches of the City University System.

Academic Facilities

New facilities add a modern tone to the original neo-Gothic buildings, which have been designated state and national landmarks. In addition, a $200-million renovation of the neo-Gothic buildings is nearing completion. The thirteen-story Robert E. Marshak Science Building houses more than 200 teaching and research laboratories, a planetarium, a weather station, an electron microscope, laser research facilities, a science and engineering library, and a major physical education complex. The School of Engineering has more than forty research laboratories. Aaron Davis Hall contains a 750-seat proscenium theater, a 200-seat experimental theater, and a seventy-five-seat studio workshop for rehearsals. The North Academic Center occupies three full city blocks and has 2,000 classrooms, laboratories, lecture halls, offices, and dining and student activity areas. It includes the Morris Raphael Cohen Library, which houses more than 1.3 million volumes, the largest collection in the City University.

Computer facilities are extensive at City College. The Computation Center provides services to meet instructional, administrative, and research needs. Numerous computer labs are located throughout the College, utilizing microcomputers and minicomputers to provide research and academic services to students and faculty and staff members.

Costs

In 2003–04, for students who are residents of New York State, the tuition for full-time attendance (12 or more credits or the equivalent) was $2000 per semester, or $4000 per year. Part-time and summer-session students who were residents of New York State paid $170 per credit. Tuition for out-of-state and international students was $360 per credit. Tuition and fees are subject to change. Books, supplies, and commuting and personal expenses average $5685 a year for full-time students who live with their parents and $11,905 for students who live on their own, excluding tuition and moderate activity fees. All students commute to the College, since there are no dormitories.

Financial Aid

Financial assistance is available for eligible City College students through state and federal programs. Students who wish to apply for financial aid must file the Free Application for Federal Student Aid (FAFSA) and the TAP/APTS Application and CUNY Supplement. Among the forms of financial aid available are Federal Supplemental Educational Opportunity Grants, Federal Perkins Loans, and Federal Work-Study Program awards. A large percentage of City College students receive some type of aid. For information, students should contact the Financial Aid Office at City College (telephone: 212-650-5819). City College offers merit scholarships to students who have achieved superior performance in high school or college. The City College Scholars Award, worth $16,000 for four years, is available for qualified high school graduates of outstanding ability. Through the Division of the Humanities, the Isaacs Scholarship offers full tuition and expenses for students who plan to major in English. Finally, for students who wish to pursue a career in college teaching, the City College Fellowship, sponsored by the Ford Foundation, offers $2000 per year for undergraduate study, plus additional academic and financial support through graduate study. Although special aid programs have specified application deadlines, students who apply early for assistance have an advantage. For information about deadlines, eligibility, and credentials, students should contact the City College Office of Admissions.

Faculty

City College's outstanding faculty represents a broad range of disciplines, and many members have earned the nation's highest forms of recognition—Guggenheim and Fulbright awards as well as grants that amount to millions of dollars annually in support of their research and scholarship. Eighty-five percent of the faculty members hold Ph.D. degrees. The student-teacher ratio is 15:1.

Student Government

Students have traditionally played an active role in campus government. Each year, two different senates are elected at the undergraduate level: one each for the day and evening divisions. Student government funds pay for the activities of student organizations, which send representatives to a student-faculty administrative committee that advises the College president on matters of an extracurricular nature. Through their representatives, students are given a voice on departmental committees, and they vote on matters of educational policy, budget, and faculty appointments and reappointments.

Admission Requirements

In determining admission to City College, the following factors are considered: a student's overall high school academic average from 9th through 12th grade, the total number of academic units completed (New York State Regents courses), and the combined SAT I score obtained. These factors are weighted together to determine eligibility. The College recommends that students preparing to apply to programs at City College complete 4 years of English, 4 years of social studies, 3 years of sequential math (or its equivalent), 2 years of laboratory science, 2 years of a foreign language, and 1 year of performing or visual arts in high school as the academic preparation needed for success and admission to the College. Qualified high school juniors may apply for early admission. Students who take the General Educational Development test (GED) and receive a score of at least 3250 (325 old scoring) accepted to the City College. Students with special educational and financial needs may qualify for admission to the Search for Education, Elevation, and Knowledge (SEEK) Program. City College accepts students who wish to transfer from other postsecondary institutions. Requirements for admission vary according to the program and the number of credits completed. Applicants should contact the College for information about admission as a transfer student.

Application and Information

Applications to City College are processed through the City University of New York Processing Center. Although applications are processed on a rolling basis, students who wish a prompt response should adhere to the initial deadline dates of October 1 (spring admission) and March 15 (fall admission). Applications from qualified students that are received after these deadlines are processed on a space-available basis. Further information and application materials can be obtained from either:

Office of Admissions
The City College of the City University of New York
138th Street and Convent Avenue
New York, New York 10031
Telephone: 212-650-6977
E-mail: admissions@ccny.cuny.edu
World Wide Web: http://www.ccny.cuny.edu

Office of Admission Services (O.A.S.)
City University of New York
1114 Avenue of the Americas
New York, New York 10036
Telephone: 212-997-2869
World Wide Web: http://www.cuny.edu

CITY UNIVERSITY

BELLEVUE, WASHINGTON

The University

City University opened its doors in 1973 with one primary purpose: to provide educational opportunities for those segments of the population not being fully served through traditional means. City University believes that education is a lifelong process, and it is a pioneer in the concept of education unhindered by time, format, or location. City University is a private, not-for-profit institution of higher learning, open to anyone with the desire to achieve. Classes are offered in the day, evening, and on weekends in order to meet student needs without interrupting established lifestyles and associations.

City University's students are mainly working adults, drawn from all walks of life. In the 2002–03 school year, the University enrolled more than 4,300 undergraduate students. Of those, more than 50 percent were women and, for those reporting, 21 percent were members of minority groups. Although the majority of students attend classes near their homes in the Pacific Northwest, many live and study at locations around the globe. Often programs are available at the student's workplace through cooperative arrangements with progressive employers or professional associations.

City University is accredited by the Northwest Commission on Colleges and Universities. Graduate programs leading to the Master of Arts, the Master of Business Administration, the Master of Education, the Master of Public Administration, the Master of Science, and the Master in Teaching are offered.

Most City University students are already established in either a job or career and have chosen a path they are preparing to follow. As alumni, they are able to realize their career goals in business, in public administration, or in one of several professions.

Location

The University's mission statement specifies a commitment to education that is affordable, accessible, and practical as well as academically sound. Accordingly, the University owns or leases classroom space in metropolitan centers, smaller cities, military installations, or any other space that is convenient for students. Eight locations serve the Greater Seattle/Puget Sound area. Classes are also held in Bellevue, Renton, Everett, North Seattle, Tacoma, Yakima, Tri-Cities, and Vancouver in Washington; and Vancouver and Victoria, British Columbia and Calgary and Edmonton, Alberta in Canada. Classes are also offered around the globe through distance learning and from sites in Europe and Asia.

Majors and Degrees

City University offers a range of programs leading to Associate of Science, Bachelor of Science, and Bachelor of Arts degrees. Students are given a vast array of options and may choose the course of study best suited to their experience, prior learning, and the realization of their personal and professional goals.

The Associate of Science degree is offered in general studies.

City University offers the Bachelor of Science degree with a range of possible emphases. These include accounting, business administration, computer systems, general studies, and mass communication and journalism. The Bachelor of Arts degree in applied psychology or education is also offered.

Undergraduate certificate programs offer professional credentials for those whose immediate needs do not require the completion of a degree. Various preparation classes for industry certifications are available as part of the Bachelor of Science in database technology, e-commerce, information systems/technology, individualized study, and project management. Students can choose among classes geared toward accounting, Programming in C++, human resource management, marketing, networking/telecommunications, Web languages, and Web design. City University also offers Professional Human Resource/Senior Professional Human Resource Management (PHR/SPHR) certification.

Academic Programs

Students who live in other areas may complete a degree program through City University's online distance learning format, which serves students worldwide. Distance learning makes completing an education possible anywhere via the World Wide Web. These courses are on the traditional quarterly schedule.

Candidates for the bachelor's degree must complete 180 hours of credit by completing regular or distance learning classes or through recognized transfer credits or prior learning experience. Lower-division requirements total 90 credits, including a total of 55 general education credits in the broad areas of writing, mathematics, humanities, natural sciences/mathematics, and social sciences. For most bachelor's degree programs, upper-division course work consists of a series of common core courses that covers the areas of business, ethics, and critical thinking skills. Both B.S. and B.A. students then complete a series of competency courses respective to their degrees, followed by major required courses. Most undergraduate programs are designed to allow students to satisfy certain general education requirements through upper-division course work.

For the Associate of Science degree, students complete 90 credit hours, 35 of which are in general education. Each of these programs is wholly compatible with and transferable to baccalaureate degree study. Depending on the particular choice of program, students can complete an undergraduate certificate program with 24 to 45 credits.

The academic year is divided into four quarters. City University offers day, evening, weekend, and distance learning courses.

Academic Facilities

City University's library serves students throughout the Seattle area with a schedule of service that extends more than 68 hours per week. Extensive reference resources, indexes, journals, and online databases are made available by a professional staff at the main library in Bellevue. Reference and interlibrary loan services are offered to all students. For those residing outside the Seattle area, access is facilitated by the library's 800 telephone number and through e-mail. Most online databases are available 24 hours per day through the University's Web site. Student and faculty research is also supported by cooperative agreements with many libraries in the United States and Canada.

Costs

For 2003–04, tuition was $199 per undergraduate credit hour and $342 per graduate credit hour. Additional fees apply for certificate completion, graduation application, course registration and various tests or examinations that the student may request. Textbooks and other instructional materials are additional. All initial applicants to certificate or degree programs pay a nonrefundable application fee of $80. Tuition and fees are subject to annual review on July 1.

Financial Aid

To help qualified students achieve their educational and professional goals, City University participates in several financial aid programs. Federal Pell Grants, Federal Supplemental Educational Opportunity Grants, Federal Stafford Student Loans, Federal PLUS loans, and Federal Work-Study are available.

In addition, the University awards scholarships on the basis of financial need, demonstrated academic ability, and other criteria. Employer reimbursement programs and military tuition assistance programs are also available, and all programs are approved for veterans' education benefits.

Students interested in financial aid should contact City University's Financial Aid Office at the toll-free number listed below for more information.

Faculty

The University's senior administration and faculty have a University-wide role in quality assurance, academic policies and standards, curricular development, and instructional quality. City University's faculty is composed of distinguished practitioners in the fields of business, education, and government and in civic and research organizations and the legal community. They unite strong academic preparation with active professional careers in the fields in which they teach. Some of the University's approximately 50 full-time faculty members also serve as senior faculty members in charge of various academic disciplines. They oversee more than 800 adjunct faculty members instructing in both classroom theory and actual practice at more than a dozen locations around the world. The University draws on this faculty pool to achieve an average class size of 18 students.

Student Government

The philosophy and structure of City University do not lend themselves to the traditional student organization activities revolving around life on a fixed campus. The Student Code of Conduct creates an atmosphere conducive to an uninhibited, scholastically honest learning environment. City University encourages and responds to current and prospective students' comments in an effort to help maintain currency and relevance in its academic offerings.

Admission Requirements

Undergraduate degree programs are generally open to applicants over the age of 18 who hold a high school or GED diploma, who can benefit from postsecondary education. Students who began but did not complete academic careers at other postsecondary institutions are welcome to continue their education at City University. Course work completed at other recognized institutions is evaluated to determine its applicability to the selected degree and major objective.

To gain admission to the University, students must begin by contacting or meeting with an admissions adviser to select an educational objective and to complete initial enrollment. An application form must be filled out and an application fee submitted. Transcripts and other documentation may be required. International students and veterans find that additional requirements apply.

A rolling admissions policy governs most City University programs. That is, the University accepts applications and announce admissions decisions continuously throughout the year. Most degree programs may be commenced at the start of the fall, winter, spring, or summer quarters, or at the monthly start of distance learning courses.

Application and Information

Because of City University's rolling admissions policy, applications for admission may be submitted at any time. Response time is usually within two to four days of receipt of application or information requests.

For application forms or other information, prospective students may contact:

Office of Admissions and Student Services
City University
11900 NE First Street
Bellevue, Washington 98005
Telephone: 888-42-CITYU (24898) (toll-free)
425-450-4660 (TTY)
Fax: 425-709-7699
E-mail: info@cityu.edu
World Wide Web: http://www.cityu.edu

CLAREMONT McKENNA COLLEGE

CLAREMONT, CALIFORNIA

The College

Founded in 1946 as the third undergraduate college within the Claremont Consortium, Claremont McKenna College (CMC) occupies a unique place in American higher education. By infusing pragmatic sensibilities into an otherwise traditional liberal arts curriculum, CMC is committed to educating future leaders in business, the professions, and public affairs. Economics, government, and international relations are the most popular among twenty-three majors offered at CMC. The College is especially appropriate for students seeking to pursue careers in law, politics, government, international relations, business, management, and finance.

Claremont McKenna College is one of seven institutions—five undergraduate colleges and two graduate schools—that constitute the Claremont Colleges. The others are Harvey Mudd College, Pitzer College, Pomona College, Scripps College, the Claremont Graduate University, and the Keck Graduate Institute of Applied Life Sciences.

The current undergraduate enrollment at CMC is 1,050 (580 men and 470 women). Fifty-three percent of the student body are out-of-state residents and 5 percent are international. Forty-eight states and thirty countries are represented on campus. Thirty-one percent of the students at CMC are members of ethnic minority groups.

Because 96 percent of CMC students live on campus in coed residence halls and apartments, campus life is vibrant and active. Dorms provide the foundation for social life at CMC; the student-run government often plans field trips, movie nights, barbecues, dinners, and socials for each dorm or apartment group. Intramural athletic teams are typically formed by each residence hall.

One of the more distinctive features on campus is the Athenaeum, a facility that serves as a social, cultural, and academic center. Faculty members often arrange to meet their classes at the Athenaeum for lunch, dinner, and coffee hours. The Athenaeum program features guest speakers on a variety of topics four nights a week throughout the academic year. Other special resources at CMC include a center for religious activities, a bookstore that carries more than 40,000 titles, a professionally staffed counseling and medical center, the Office of Black Student Affairs, the Chicano/Latino Student Affairs Center, and an international center.

Claremont supports a wide variety of cultural events—concerts, plays, lectures, conferences, art exhibits, and films—and the Claremont Colleges cooperate to provide organized extracurricular activities. Although each campus is autonomous, many activities include students from several of the colleges. There are intercollegiate athletics programs, a four-college chorus, a five-college theater program, a five-college weekly newspaper, a five-college orchestra, and a five-college debate team. Five-college parties are also scheduled throughout the year.

Claremont McKenna College, Harvey Mudd College, and Scripps College are associated in a joint program of intercollegiate athletics, physical education, and recreation. Facilities include a football field, a track, a gymnasium (housing two gym floors, a squash court, a Nautilus and weight room, a fitness center, a boxing ring, offices, and locker rooms), a baseball field, a soccer field, a lacrosse field, three swimming pools, eight tennis courts, volleyball courts, intramural fields, and a climbing wall. The sports teams compete in the Southern California Intercollegiate Athletic Conference (SCIAC). The men's teams, known as the Stags, compete in baseball, basketball, cross-country, football, golf, soccer, swimming/diving, tennis, track, volleyball, and water polo. Women's teams, known as the Athenas, compete in basketball, cross-country, lacrosse, soccer, softball, swimming/diving, tennis, track, volleyball, and water polo. The Claremont-Mudd-Scripps intercollegiate athletics program is consistently at the top of the SCIAC All-Sports Championship race.

Location

Claremont McKenna College is in Claremont, California, a suburban community of 34,000 people about 35 miles east of downtown Los Angeles. It is a pleasant town with tree-lined streets and well-tended homes. Other educational resources in Claremont are the School of Theology, the Rancho Santa Ana Botanical Garden, the Blaisdell Institute for Advanced Study in World Cultures and Religions, and the Institute for Antiquity and Christianity.

"The Village," home to attractive restaurants, art galleries, and shops, is only a 10-minute walk from the College. All of the cultural, educational, social, and entertainment centers of greater Los Angeles are nearby, including major art museums, a ranking symphony orchestra, abundant theater productions, and a variety of professional sports teams. Mount Baldy is close by for skiing and hiking, and Pacific Ocean beaches and the Mojave Desert are each only an hour away. The weather throughout the academic year is usually warm, dry, and sunny.

Majors and Degrees

Claremont McKenna College grants the Bachelor of Arts degree in applied biology; biology; chemistry; economics; economics-accounting; the environment, economics, and politics; environmental science; French; German; government; history; international relations; Korean; literature; management-engineering; mathematics; neuroscience; philosophy; philosophy, politics, and economics; physics; psychology; religious studies; science and management; and Spanish.

In addition to these CMC-based majors, cooperative programs with the other Claremont Colleges allow students to major in American studies, art, Asian studies, black studies, Chicano studies, classics, film studies, music, and theater. Sequences, a series of courses related to a subject and selected from different disciplines, are offered in the areas of Asian-American studies, computer science, ethics, leadership, legal studies, and women's studies. Almost half of CMC students opt to pursue dual and double majors and/or to create individualized majors.

Academic Program

Students must satisfactorily complete thirty-two semester courses, including general education and major requirements, in order to graduate. General education requirements include one course in mathematics, one course in English composition and analysis, two courses in the natural sciences, two courses in the humanities, three courses in the social sciences, and a senior thesis. In addition, students must complete three semesters of a foreign language and a Questions of Civilization course.

Depending on the department, credit or advanced placement, or both, may be granted for college courses taken while in high school. Also, CMC may grant credit for scores of 4 or 5 on Advanced Placement (AP) examinations and for scores of 6 or 7 on higher level International Baccalaureate (I.B.) examinations.

CMC sponsors a joint science program with two other Claremont Colleges, Pitzer and Scripps. The Keck Science Center houses modern laboratories for teaching and research, and a large biological field station is located adjacent to the campus. Virtually all students in the joint science program do independent research, and reports on many student-faculty projects have been published in professional journals.

By intercollegiate agreement, CMC students may take courses not offered at Claremont McKenna at any of the Claremont Colleges. Up to one third of a student's courses may be taken at the other Claremont Colleges.

CMC operates on a semester calendar, beginning the first week in September and ending in mid-May.

Off-Campus Programs

Nearly 50 percent of CMC students elect to study off campus for a semester or a full year. Students may choose from almost 100 programs in thirty-eight countries; CMC's own Washington, D.C., Semester Program; college exchanges with Colby College, Haverford College, Instituto Tecnologico de Mexico, Morehouse College, McGill University (Canada), and Spelman College; and the Semester in Environmental Science at the Marine Biological Laboratory in Woods Hole, Massachusetts.

Academic Facilities

The Claremont Colleges pool their funds to support impressive central resources: libraries with more than 2 million volumes, a center for religious activities, medical and counseling centers, a 2,600-seat concert hall, a 700-seat theater, an Office of Black Student Affairs, and a Chicano/Latino Student Affairs Center.

Eleven research institutes within Claremont McKenna enrich the curriculum, attract distinguished scholars to the College, and give outstanding students research and internship experience and the opportunity to work closely with faculty scholars. The institutes are The Lowe Institute of Political Economy; The Reed Institute for Decision Science; The Keck Center for International and Strategic Studies; The Roberts Environmental Center; The Rose Institute of State and Local Government; The Salvatori Center for the Study of Individual Freedom in the Modern World; The Henry Kravis Leadership Institute; The Gould Center for Humanistic Studies; The Berger Institute on Work, Family, and Children; The Institute for Financial Economics; and The Center for the Study of the Holocaust, Genocide, and Human Rights.

Costs

Tuition for 2003–04 was $27,500. Room and board was $9180. Expenses for 2003–04, including tuition, fees, room and board, and personal expenses, totaled approximately $36,680. Travel expenses vary.

Financial Aid

Financial aid is awarded in the form of grants (nonrepayable gift aid), student loans, and part-time employment. Grants range from $1000 to $31,000 per year and average $25,780; loans for entering freshmen average $3000 per year. The total amount of aid a student is awarded is based on need.

The College offers approximately thirty McKenna Achievement Awards to members of each entering freshman class. These awards are valued at $5000 each and are renewable for each of the four years, provided the student earns at least a B average. To be considered for one of these awards, a student usually must rank among the top 5 percent in his or her high school class and earn a score of more than 690 on both the mathematical and verbal portions of the SAT I. Candidates must also have excellent school recommendations and strong extracurricular involvement, including leadership, and must have filed a completed application by December 20.

Faculty

CMC's faculty members are teacher-scholars who are dedicated to teaching undergraduates and to making contributions to their disciplines. Except in fields in which the doctorate is not the terminal degree, all tenured faculty members have doctorates. The student-faculty ratio is 8:1, and the average class size is 19.

Student Government

Officers of the Associated Students of Claremont McKenna College are elected each spring and serve a one-year term. Each residence hall is self-governing, and students sit on virtually all faculty, trustee, and staff committees. CMC has a history of active and responsible participation in student government.

Admission Requirements

College admission standards place CMC in the "highly selective" category. Eighty-three percent of the 2003 freshmen were in the top tenth of their high school graduating class; 94 percent were in the top fifth. The middle 50 percent of the class had SAT I math and verbal scores ranging from 660 to 740. CMC strives to enroll a class that is academically strong but also places a strong emphasis on extracurricular involvement, community participation, and leadership potential. Admission to CMC is need blind.

Early decision and deferred entrance are options. Students are strongly encouraged to visit the campus.

Applicants are expected to furnish transcripts of all academic work in high school and college; a recommendation from a guidance counselor, principal, or headmaster; recommendations from 2 academic course teachers; two essays; and scores on either the SAT I or ACT. Students whose first language is not English are strongly encouraged to take the Test of English as a Foreign Language (TOEFL).

Application and Information

Application materials must be received by November 15 or January 2 from applicants seeking early decision, November 15 for midyear entrance, and January 2 for those seeking entrance in the fall. CMC accepts only the Common Application and asks applicants to also complete a supplement to the Common Application.

Further information is available from:

Richard C. Vos, Vice President and
Dean of Admission and Financial Aid
Claremont McKenna College
890 Columbia Avenue
Claremont, California 91711-6425
Telephone: 909-621-8088
E-mail: admission@claremontmckenna.edu
World Wide Web: http://www.claremontmckenna.edu

View of the Claremont McKenna College campus, with the San Gabriel Mountain Range in the background.

CLARK ATLANTA UNIVERSITY

ATLANTA, GEORGIA

The University

Clark Atlanta University (CAU), incorporated in 1988, is a private, urban, coeducational, predominantly African-American institution of undergraduate, graduate, and professional education. Clark Atlanta University has inherited the historical missions and achievements of its parent institutions, Atlanta University, founded in 1865, and Clark College, founded in 1869.

As one of only two private, comprehensive, historically black universities in the nation that offer degrees from the bachelor's to the doctorate, CAU enrolls approximately 4,026 undergraduate and 1,178 full-time and part-time graduate students from forty states and fifty countries. The University is one of six institutions that make up the Atlanta University Center, the largest consortium of historically black educational institutions in the country.

Members of the faculty are known for their warm and dedicated spirit. They provide the quality of instruction necessary to ensure that their students become productive, creative, and socially responsible citizens. The family spirit at CAU is enhanced by the many traditions that are celebrated each year on campus, including the induction services for freshmen, the United Negro College Fund Drive, Homecoming, Consolidation Day, and the Spring Arts Festival. There are more than sixty chartered student organizations, special interest clubs, and academic honor societies on campus.

The athletic program at Clark Atlanta University receives the support of students, faculty, staff, and alumni. The University is an NCAA Division II school and is a charter member of the Southern Intercollegiate Athletic Conference (SIAC). Sports include baseball, basketball, football, golf, tennis, and track and field for men and basketball, tennis, track and field, and volleyball for women.

Location

One mile east of the campus lie the mirrored skyscrapers and modern expressways of Atlanta. The World Congress Center, the Civic Center, the Arts Alliance Center (home of the Atlanta Symphony Orchestra and the Atlanta Ballet Company), the Martin Luther King, Jr. Center for Nonviolent Social Change, the Atlanta Stadium (home of the Atlanta Braves baseball team), the Dome (home of the Atlanta Falcons football team), the Jimmy Carter Presidential Library, and outstanding entertainment features, such as Underground Atlanta, Stone Mountain Park, and Six Flags Over Georgia amusement park, mark Atlanta as the capital of the Sun Belt.

Majors and Degrees

Clark Atlanta University is made up of the School of Arts and Sciences and the professional Schools of Business Administration, Education, Library and Information Studies, and Social Work. The University offers undergraduate courses that lead to the Bachelor of Arts degree in twenty-seven majors, as follows: accounting, art, business administration, early childhood education, economics, elementary/middle grades education, engineering, English, fashion design and fashion merchandising, French, general science education, German, history, mass media arts, mathematics, music, music education, office administration, philosophy, physical education, political science, psychology, religion, sociology, Spanish, and speech communication and theater arts. The Bachelor of Science degree is offered with majors in biology, chemistry, community health education, computer science, health information management, mathematics, and physics. The Bachelor of Social Work degree and a dual-degree program in engineering are also offered.

Academic Program

Clark Atlanta University requires that each student becomes familiar with the technology of the future. Instructional programs in business administration make extensive use of computers, and business education programs are taught in labs equipped with the latest in office automation devices. A model quantitative skills lab has been established to expand the University's pace-setting instructional support system in mathematics, statistics, and computer science. The Mass Media Arts Department houses one of the most complete broadcast training and production facilities in higher education. Clark Atlanta University students are exposed to real-world experiences through internship and cooperative education assignments with some of the leading local and national corporations and agencies.

The minimum number of semester hours that are required for graduation is 122. The normal load for a full-time student is 15 to 18 credit hours. The minimum load that a student may take to be considered full-time is 12 credit hours. A student may take more than 18 hours only if he or she has a grade point average of 3.25 or above or if the department chairperson approves. Every student must take prescribed core courses in English, general mathematics, computer literacy, literature, and social science, as well as other courses that are included under the general education program.

Army, Naval, and Air Force ROTC programs are available.

Academic Facilities

CAU houses one of the most advanced microcomputer-equipped instructional centers of any university its size. This center is used heavily by students for review study in all of the general education courses at the University. The open-stack library that serves CAU is a cooperative venture of the Atlanta University Center; in addition to volumes, it houses audiovisual aids to study, periodicals, microfilm reader facilities, study carrels, and private study areas. Students in the natural sciences have access to modern laboratories operated by the Science Research Center, another facility operated jointly by the Atlanta University Center members.

Costs

For 2002–03, tuition was $12,312. Room costs ranged from $3710 to $4938 per year. Board for the year is $2280 for two meals per day and $2660 for three meals per day. The student center fee is $200 per year and the technology fee is an additional $200 per year.

Financial Aid

In order to be considered for financial aid, students must complete the Free Application for Federal Student Aid (FAFSA). This application determines eligibility for federal aid and institutional aid. Georgia residents should complete the Georgia Tuition Equalization Grant (GTEG) and Helping Outstanding Pupils Educationally (HOPE) applications. All out-of-state students should complete their state's application(s) for grants or scholarships available for students who will attend out-of-state postsecondary institutions. The FAFSA may be secured from high school guidance offices. All forms and current information about financial aid may be secured from the CAU financial office. The financial aid application deadline is April 1.

Faculty

The Clark Atlanta University faculty is characterized by its deep and abiding concern for students and their academic well-being. The faculty is composed of 361 full professors, associate and assistant professors, and instructors. The faculty-student ratio is 1:16, which allows for the maximum interaction between faculty members and students. Faculty members serve as advisers to all of the student-organized groups on campus and generally make themselves available for participation in activities beyond their teaching responsibilities.

Student Government

Elected representatives of the student body serve on the University Trustee Board to ensure that students' interests are voiced in the highest governing body of the University. Student government representatives are elected in the spring of each year by vote of the student body. The Student Government Association (SGA) traditionally assumes leadership in many matters that contribute to the overall effectiveness and quality of life in the University community. A partnership exists between the SGA and the University administration.

Admission Requirements

Admission is based solely on the qualifications of the applicant and is decided without regard to race, creed, or any other considerations irrelevant to scholastic aptitude, academic achievement, and desire to achieve in an academic community. The Admissions Committee considers, among other factors, the high school record, college entrance exam scores, letters of recommendation, and a one-page essay.

Application and Information

Clark Atlanta University admits students on a rolling admission basis. However, applications submitted by March 1 for the fall semester and by October 1 for the spring semester receive priority consideration. A processing fee of $35 must accompany the completed application to Clark Atlanta University. This fee is neither refundable nor transferable to another term regardless of the admission decision. It should be paid by cashier's check or money order made payable to Clark Atlanta University. Before action can be taken on an application, the applicant must submit an official copy of the high school transcript, SAT I or ACT scores, an essay, and two recommendations. Transfer applicants must submit official transcripts from all colleges previously attended and two letters of recommendation.

For more information and an application form, students should contact:

Office of Admissions
Clark Atlanta University
223 James P. Brawley Drive, SW
Atlanta, Georgia 30314-4385
Telephone: 404-880-6605
800-688-3228 (toll-free)
E-mail: admissions@panthernet.cau.edu
World Wide Web: http://www.cau.edu

Harkness Hall, CAU's main administration building.

CLARKSON UNIVERSITY

POTSDAM, NEW YORK

The University

Clarkson University, founded in 1896, is an independent technological university offering professional programs in business, engineering, liberal arts, and the sciences, including health sciences. Students benefit from a challenging, collaborative culture that develops the technical expertise, management skills, and versatility required in today's knowledge-based economy.

Clarkson has earned a reputation for developing innovative leaders in technology-based fields. It is also known for having a friendly campus where students enjoy personal attention. A rigorous curriculum emphasizes hands-on team projects and real-world, multidisciplinary challenges that develop skills in collaboration, communication, and creative problem solving. About 25 percent of the 2,725 undergraduates are women. Through a comprehensive Graduate School with 385 students, the University offers twenty-two master's degree and nine doctoral programs.

Many extracurricular activities are available to Clarkson students. Its more than 100 organizations include intercollegiate and intramural athletics, student publications (a newspaper and a yearbook), professional and honorary societies, outing club, pep band, jazz band, orchestra, religious clubs, chess club, amateur radio club, automotive association, and photo, drama, ski, cycle, bridge, rifle, international, outing, and table tennis clubs. The University's recreational facilities include a field house, with racquetball courts, a 3,000-square-foot fitness center, and a swimming pool, and a $13-million student center, including a 3,000-seat arena. An outdoor lodge was completed in 2000.

Location

Potsdam, New York (population 9,500), a college community, is located in the St. Lawrence River valley of northern New York. The community is the home of both Clarkson University and the State University of New York College at Potsdam. The village of Potsdam, with a combined student population approaching 7,000, is truly a college town. Students from both institutions attend events on either campus, and many combined social and cultural activities are scheduled during the year. Major international cities, such as Montreal, Quebec, and Ottawa, Ontario, are within a 2-hour drive.

Majors and Degrees

The Bachelor of Science degree is offered in aeronautical engineering, applied mathematics and statistics, biology, biomolecular science, business and technology management, chemical engineering, chemistry, civil engineering, computer engineering, computer science, e-business, electrical engineering, engineering and management, environmental science and policy, financial information and analysis, history, humanities, industrial hygiene–environmental toxicology (environmental and occupational health), information systems and business processes, liberal studies, mathematics, mechanical engineering, physical therapy (prephysical therapy leading to a master's degree), physics, political science, Project Aretè (liberal arts/business), psychology, social sciences, software engineering, and technical communications (telecommunications option). Choices that allow students to begin a general program and choose their major at a later date include business studies, engineering studies, science studies, and university studies. Clarkson offers both an honors program and an accelerated three-year bachelor's degree program. Special advising programs are offered in prelaw, premedicine, and pre–physical therapy, a program in which the University offers a master's degree. Preprofessional programs are available in dentistry, law, medicine, physical therapy, and veterinary sciences.

Academic Programs

Programs are flexible at Clarkson, enabling undergraduates to customize their studies according to individual interests and goals. Today, many of the most profound advances in knowledge and social progress are occurring at the intersections of previously distinct academic disciplines. Building on a tradition of collaboration, the University has developed an increasing number of interdisciplinary majors, while promoting opportunities for specialization and customization through double majors, minors, concentrations, and electives. Each student must achieve a cumulative GPA of at least 2.0 to qualify for graduation and must earn at least 120 credit hours.

The innovative interdisciplinary programs at Clarkson reflect not only the high quality of faculty members and resources, but also the flexibility and vitality of the highly collaborative academic environment. The curriculum in the interdisciplinary engineering and management program, established in 1954, was the first of its kind to be accredited at any college or university in the nation. Other interdisciplinary degree programs include biomolecular science, environmental science and policy, industrial hygiene–environmental toxicology (environmental and occupational health), Project Aretè (a double major program in business and liberal arts), and software engineering.

Undergraduates in all majors also have opportunities to join multidisciplinary academic teams that compete against intercollegiate peers as they tackle creative problem-solving challenges. Students can choose among fourteen different teams at Clarkson, organized through a program called Student Projects for Engineering Experience and Design (SPEED).

Recent recognition of quality at Clarkson includes the following: winner of the 2002 IBM Linux Scholar Challenge, a worldwide open programming project-based competition; winner of the 2001 Boeing Outstanding Educator Award for its SPEED program; top-twenty ranking in supply chain management in the 2003 and 2004 *U.S. News & World Report*'s "Best Business Programs"; and finalist for the 2002 and 2003 National Undergraduate Entrepreneurship Education Award from the U.S. Association for Small Business Entrepreneurship.

Off-Campus Programs

The Associated Colleges of the St. Lawrence Valley was chartered in 1970 to facilitate cooperative relationships among four distinct institutions: Clarkson University, St. Lawrence University, the State University of New York College at Potsdam, and the State University of New York College of Technology at Canton. Student-oriented objectives include improved coordination of cultural affairs, interlibrary exchange, and cross-registration that allows students to pursue two courses per year at other member colleges at no extra cost.

Academic Facilities

The University's 640-acre wooded campus is the site of forty-six buildings that comprise 1,224,000 square feet of assignable space. Eighty-five percent of these buildings have been built since 1970. Dedicated exclusively to instructional programs are

371,114 square feet, including 52,713 square feet of traditional classrooms and 166,334 square feet assigned as laboratory areas. In the Center for Advanced Materials Processing (a New York State Center for Advanced Technology), there are seventy state-of-the-art research labs. Other labs and research tools include the multidisciplinary engineering and project laboratory for team-based projects, such as the mini-Baja and Formulae SAE racers; a robotics laboratory; a high-voltage lab; electron microscopy; a Class 10 clean room; a polymer fabrication lab; crystal growth labs; and a structural testing lab. School of Arts and Sciences facilities include a virtual reality laboratory, a molecular design laboratory, a human brain electrophysiology laboratory, and other specialized facilities.

Bertrand H. Snell Hall, opened in 2000, houses the School of Business and School of Arts and Sciences administrative offices. Fully networked classrooms and study spaces, collaborative centers for team projects, and videoconferencing capabilities are among its state-of-the-art features. The facility includes three academic centers, available to all students: the Shipley Center for Leadership and Entrepreneurship, the Center for Global Competitiveness, and the Eastman Kodak Center for Excellence in Communication. The Center for Health Sciences at Clarkson is a regional center of excellence for education, treatment, and research in physical rehabilitation and other health sciences.

Costs

For 2004–05, tuition is $24,100; room (2 persons), $4728; and board (all options), $4340. Fees are $400, and books, supplies, travel, and personal expenses vary but may come to approximately $2000.

Financial Aid

More than 90 percent of the student body receive some form of financial aid. This aid includes Clarkson University scholarships; state scholarships and awards; state and federal student loans; industrial, endowed, organizational, and individual scholarships; federal grants; and Federal Work-Study awards. More than half of the freshmen receive renewable scholarships or grants directly from Clarkson.

Faculty

A full-time faculty of 175 serves both the undergraduate and graduate programs, thus enhancing the opportunities for interchange of knowledge among faculty members and students at all levels. The percentage of earned doctorates is high, and some departments are staffed completely by Ph.D.'s. Courses are taught by faculty members, while graduate students assist in laboratory and recitation situations. The faculty-student ratio is 1:16.

Student Government

The Student Senate and the Interfraternity Council combine to form the student government at Clarkson University. The former supervises all extracurricular activities (except athletics) and has responsibility for the allocation of student activity funds and for other appropriate business. The latter prescribes standards and rules for fraternities. Students are involved in the formation of University policies through membership, with faculty and staff representatives, on all important committees.

Admission Requirements

A thorough preparation in mathematics, science, and English is very important in the academic qualifications of a candidate for admission. Candidates for entrance to the Wallace H. Coulter School of Engineering or the School of Arts and Sciences should have successfully completed secondary school courses in physics and chemistry. All candidates for admission are required to take the SAT I or ACT. SAT II Subject Tests are recommended in Writing, Level I or Level II Mathematics, and either Physics or Chemistry (Physics is preferred). The high school record is the most important factor in an admission decision. International students for whom English is a second language must submit a minimum TOEFL score of 550 (paper-based) or 213 (computer-based).

Students achieving scores of 4 or better on the College Board's Advanced Placement examinations are considered for advanced placement and credit in virtually all academic areas. Advanced standing is most common in English, mathematics, and science.

An early decision plan is offered on a "first-choice" basis; this plan does not prohibit the student from making other applications, but it does commit the student to withdraw other applications if accepted at Clarkson. Early admission for students who have completed three years of secondary education is encouraged when the academic record, standardized test scores, and recommendations indicate the student has reached a sufficiently high intellectual and emotional level to perform successfully with other college students.

A personal interview is very helpful to the student in formulating his or her college plans. Interviews on campus should be arranged by letter or telephone at least one week prior to the intended visit. The interview is not required but is strongly recommended, especially for early decision candidates. The admission office is open Monday through Friday, from 9 a.m. to 4 p.m., and Saturday by appointment. The University welcomes visitors to the campus and makes arrangements, as requested, for families to tour and meet with academic and other departments on campus.

Application and Information

Office of Undergraduate Admission
Holcroft House
Clarkson University
P.O. Box 5605
Potsdam, New York 13699-5605
Telephone: 315-268-6479 or 6480
800-527-6577 (toll-free)
Fax: 315-268-7647
E-mail: admission@clarkson.edu
World Wide Web: http://www.clarkson.edu

Clarkson is a leader in project-based learning, providing students with strong communication skills, leadership ability, and technological skill in their fields.

CLEARWATER CHRISTIAN COLLEGE

CLEARWATER, FLORIDA

The College

Clearwater Christian College began in 1966 in response to a burden in the hearts of the founders concerning the trends in colleges away from standards of morality, historic biblical fundamentals, and casual attitude toward doctrine and discernment. From its inception, the need to inform others of the causes for the decline in doctrinal soundness, Christian responsibility in evangelism, gratitude and responsibility associated with the American heritage, and academic excellence and scholarship were distinctive emphases. Although nondenominational, the College stands without compromise for the fundamental teachings of the Word of God in a conservative theological environment. The College has enjoyed sixteen years of continued record enrollments while maintaining a small-college, big-family atmosphere.

In 1984, Clearwater Christian College received full accreditation from the Commission on Colleges (CC) of the Southern Association of Colleges and Schools (SACS). The College enjoys recognition and approval from the Florida Department of Education Teacher Education Continued Program Approval Review, Florida Office of Student Financial Aid, Immigration and Naturalization Service for international student admission, State Approving Agency for Veterans Benefits, State Board of Independent Colleges and Universities, and United States Department of Education for select financial aid programs.

Through association with NCAA Division II, Clearwater Christian College students compete in intercollegiate men's baseball, basketball, and soccer and women's basketball, soccer, and volleyball. Golf is also available as a coed sport. Previous teams have received recognition as regional champions. The Lady Cougar volleyball teams have been recognized four times in the last seven years as national champions.

Opportunities to develop leadership skills, to act on social and moral conscience, and to fellowship with students with like interests are available through the various clubs and organizations. At the hub of these organizations are thirteen organizations known collectively as the Greeks. These student-led groups are actively involved in providing social and service opportunities for the student body as well as organizing teams for the intramural sports programs. The Greeks include both men's and women's clubs and a coed group specifically for mature learners. Clubs focusing on specific academic or special interest concerns such as art, drama, history, music, politics, science, and foreign missionary service are also active on the campus.

Location

Clearwater Christian College is situated on Florida's central west coast in the tri-city metropolitan Tampa Bay area that includes Tampa, St. Petersburg, and Clearwater. From Tampa, access to the campus is over the Courtney Campbell Causeway, which spans Old Tampa Bay. Before students arrive on the Pinellas County peninsula, the outline of the campus facilities emerges on the horizon of the 130-acre campus, which is surrounded largely by the bay waters. Native plants and wildlife set off the Colonial-style buildings. The Clearwater Chamber of Commerce advertises an average year-round temperature of 72 degrees. The Tampa International and St. Petersburg/Clearwater Airports are within 10 minutes of the campus. The Tampa Bay area is home to professional sports teams such as the Buccaneers, Devil Rays, and Lightning and serves as the spring training center for fifteen major-league baseball teams. Local educational and cultural centers include the Ruth Eckerd Hall, Florida International Museum, St. Petersburg Holocaust Museum, and the Florida Aquarium. Clearwater Christian College is within easy driving distance of major central Florida attractions such as Disney World, Universal Studios, Sea World, and the Holy Land Experience.

Majors and Degrees

Clearwater Christian College offers thirty-one different associate and bachelor's degree programs through six academic divisions. Through the Division of Biblical Studies, the College offers degree programs in Bible, church ministries, and pastoral studies. Through the Division of Business Studies, majors include accounting, administrative office management, business administration, computer information systems, and secretarial science (A.S.). Students are able to train as teachers for both elementary and secondary education through the Division of Education. A degree program in special education–varying exceptionalities K–12 is also available. The Division of Fine Arts offers programs in church music, communication arts, and music. English, general studies (A.A./B.A.), history, humanities, interdisciplinary studies, and prelaw are programs offered through the Division of Humanities. Students interested in biology, mathematics, physical education with exercise science and sports management tracks, premed, and psychology can find satisfactory programs in the Division of Science.

Academic minors are available in most of the major disciplines listed above and in the following additional areas: biblical languages, coaching, computer information sciences, and missions. A one-year certificate in Bible is also available to students desiring concentrated instruction before going on to academic programs not available through the school.

Academic Programs

Clearwater Christian College has been recognized by *U.S. News & World Report* as one of the top liberal arts colleges in the South for the past six years. Formal instruction in Bible leading to an automatic minor allows graduates to leave with a basic understanding of overall content and the ability to apply biblical principles to daily living. Citizenship and patriotism are promoted through required instruction in the American constitution and in the lives of its early framers. Introductory and advanced computer course work ensures that graduates leave with basic computer literacy. Internships are available for some programs.

Clearwater Christian College follows a 4-1-4 academic calendar consisting of two fifteen-week semesters and a two-week interim in January. In addition, two three-week summer sessions immediately follow the spring semester. A full-time academic load for each semester is 12 to 18 credits. To graduate, a student must complete a minimum of 128 credits (depending on the program) with a minimum cumulative grade point average of at least 2.0 (premed and prelaw: 3.5, education majors: 2.5) and a minimum of 25 percent of their major course requirements completed through the College. A maximum of 24 credits can be applied toward a degree program from combined participation in the College-Level Examination Program (CLEP) and the Advanced Placement (AP) and International Baccalaureate (I.B.) programs.

Off-Campus Programs

Clearwater Christian College students may participate in Air Force, Army, Navy, Marine ROTC through detachments located on the nearby Tampa Campus of the University of South Florida. Both service branches offer two- and four-year programs that include minimal academic course work, leadership laboratory, and physical fitness training. Registration is handled through Clearwater Christian College, saving the student both valuable time and monies. Tuition scholarship programs are available on a two-, three-, and four-year basis, with possible matching room and board scholarships through Clearwater Christian College. Overseas mission trips are available each May through the Biblical Studies Division. Previous trips include visits to Antigua, China, Jamaica, Mexico, the Philippines, South Africa, Thailand, and the Alaskan wilderness. Trips sponsored through the Humanities Division to England, Ireland, Scotland, and Spain focus on major literary and historic sites as well as local culture.

Academic Facilities

Clearwater Christian College's buildings have all been erected since 1966. Cathcart Hall, the main reception area, houses the College's food service facility and administrative offices. Most classes are held in the educational areas of Dambach, Steele, and Rehearsal Halls. Dambach Hall also houses the Gospel Center Memorial Chapel, where fine arts performances are held. Easter Library contains more than 100,000 volumes. There are four residence hall facilities, including Emmons, Paden, Merritts, and Steele. The gymnasium serves the intercollegiate and intramural athletics programs and doubles as an auditorium for chapel and large campuswide events.

Costs

For 2003–04, tuition was $10,220, and room and board costs were $4820. Tuition remains the same for any enrollment between 12 and 16 credits. An additional per credit surcharge is added for enrollment exceeding 16 credits. Students can expect an average of $630 annually for required fees and $660 for textbooks. The board plan includes twenty meals per week. The actual cost of attending Clearwater Christian College depends on the amount of financial aid a student receives.

Financial Aid

A Clearwater Christian College education becomes more attractive in light of the financial aid offerings available to eligible students. Each year, an average of 85 percent of the student body receive some kind of financial aid, including scholarships, grants, loans, and assistance through the on-campus work program. The average financial aid packet is nearly $6000. Sample programs include federal and state need-based grants through the Federal Pell Grant, the Federal Supplemental Educational Opportunity Grant (FSEOG), and the Florida Student Assistance Grant (FSAG). Of premier benefit to Florida residents are the non-need-based grants and scholarships through the Florida Resident Access Grant (FRAG) and the Florida Bright Futures Scholarship Program. Eligible students can receive between $2600 and $5600 from these programs. Clearwater Christian College offers academic scholarships to first-time freshmen and transfer students through the Christian Leadership, General Academic, Presidents, and Transfer academic programs. Awards range between $1500 and $5000 annually, depending on the program. There are forty-three additional scholarship programs, including those designated for students pursuing specific academic programs such as business, education, ministry, and music. More than 37 percent of the student body participates in the campus work program. The Tampa Bay area provides excellent opportunity for off-campus employment because of the tourist and retirement nature of the community. Students wishing to receive financial assistance must complete the Free Application for Federal Student Aid (FAFSA) and the Application for College Funded Student Scholarships. Students who complete and submit all forms by the priority deadline of April 1 are given first consideration.

Faculty

Believing that the faculty has the greatest potential to change lives for the sake of Jesus Christ, Clearwater Christian College strives to secure the best academically and spiritually qualified professors for their classrooms. Personal attention is evidenced by the faculty-student ratio of 1:15. While providing the gift of service to the extended Clearwater Christian College community, the faculty members' main responsibility is to instruct their students. Accessibility is demonstrated by their regular office hours, fellowship during chapel and mealtimes, and sponsorship of student clubs and organizations. Of Clearwater Christian College's 36 full-time faculty members, almost half have earned doctorates. The Clearwater Christian College family is complemented by 17 part-time instructors who bring their unique experience and training to the classroom environment.

Student Government

Leadership from the thirteen Greek organizations comprises the Student Senate, whose responsibility is to oversee Greek activities and provide direction for community outreach and service projects.

Admission Requirements

Clearwater Christian College seeks students who desire a distinctive Christian education in the traditional liberal arts environment. The admissions process begins with the completion of the General Application for Admission. In addition, students are asked to provide a written essay regarding their personal faith and testimony. Current transcripts, ACT or SAT I scores, and two references are also required. Clearwater Christian College recommends that students take 4 years of English, 3 years of mathematics, 3 years of social science/humanities, and 2 years of a foreign language while in high school. To be considered for unconditional acceptance, the student must have a minimum high school grade point average of 2.0 on a 4.0 scale and meet minimum test score requirements of 18 on the ACT or a combined score of 870 on the SAT I. Interviews and campus visits are highly recommended but not required. Transfer students are welcome. Application packets may be obtained through the Admissions Office or downloaded from the College's Web site listed below. Interested individuals should carefully read the doctrinal statement, objectives, and distinctive emphases of the school as they consider applying. The College is committed to nondiscriminatory admission practices regardless of age, race, color, gender, or national or ethnic origin.

Application and Information

Students who wish to apply for admission to Clearwater Christian College must send in the following: a completed Clearwater Christian College General Application for Admission, along with a $35 nonrefundable application fee, the essay of personal faith, test scores from either the ACT or SAT I, transcripts of all course work completed at the high school and college levels, and references from a pastor and an academic counselor. Admissions decisions are made on a rolling basis. Priority consideration is given to individuals who apply and complete their files before May 1.

For further information about specific Clearwater Christian College programs and campus visit opportunities, students should contact:

Office of Enrollment Services
Clearwater Christian College
3400 Gulf-to-Bay Boulevard
Clearwater, Florida 33759
Telephone: 727-726-1153 Ext. 228
800-348-4463 (toll-free)
Fax: 727-726-8597
E-mail: admissions@clearwater.edu
World Wide Web: http://www.clearwater.edu

Clearwater Christian College.

CLEMSON UNIVERSITY

CLEMSON, SOUTH CAROLINA

The University

With a century of service to South Carolina, Clemson University has become one of the nation's leading land-grant institutions. The enrollment of the University has grown from 446 students when it was established in 1889 to more than 17,000 students in 2001–02. Approximately 67 percent of the students are residents of South Carolina; 33 percent come from all fifty states and ninety-seven countries. The University's diverse curriculum, combined with its 16:1 student-faculty ratio, means that students may enjoy the wide academic selection and special opportunities of a large institution without sacrificing the personal attention of a small one. The campus is conveniently designed for students to walk to and from their classes, and all campus residence halls and apartments are air conditioned.

In addition to seventy-two areas of graduate study, the University offers more than seventy fields of study in five undergraduate colleges: the colleges of agriculture, forestry, and life sciences; architecture, arts, and humanities; behavioral sciences; business and public affairs; engineering and science; and health, education, and human development. Students may participate in military training through Army and Air Force ROTC programs.

Clemson's academic programs are fully accredited by the Southern Association of Colleges and Schools as well as the Accreditation Board for Engineering and Technology, Inc.; AACSB–The International Association for Management Education; the Computing Sciences Accreditation Board; the National Architectural Accrediting Board; the National Council for Accreditation of Teacher Education; the National League for Nursing Accrediting Commission; and the Society of American Foresters.

Clemson's outstanding men's and women's athletic teams compete at the NCAA Division I level and are part of the Atlantic Coast Conference. The University fields teams in baseball, basketball, crew, cross-country, football, golf, indoor and outdoor track, soccer, swimming, tennis, and volleyball.

Location

The University is in Clemson, South Carolina (population 12,000), a friendly college town in the northwestern corner of the state. Clemson is less than an hour's drive from larger Anderson and Greenville in South Carolina and about 2½ hours from the major cities of Charlotte and Atlanta in neighboring states. The 1,400-acre campus is nestled in the foothills of the Blue Ridge Mountains and borders the shores of Lake Hartwell.

Majors and Degrees

The College of Agriculture, Forestry, and Life Sciences offers Bachelor of Science degree programs in agricultural and applied economics, with curricula in agricultural economics and community and rural development; agricultural education; agricultural engineering; agricultural mechanization and business; agronomy; animal industries, with curricula in animal, dairy, and veterinary sciences; aquaculture, fisheries, and wildlife biology; biochemistry; biological sciences; environment and natural resource management; food science; forest resource management; horticulture, with a curriculum in turfgrass; microbiology; and packaging science. The Bachelor of Arts degree is also offered in biological sciences. The college also offers prepharmacy, pre–rehabilitation science, and preprofessional studies.

Students in the College of Architecture, Arts, and Humanities may choose from bachelor's degrees in architecture, construction science and management, English, fine arts, history, landscape architecture, language and international trade, modern languages (French, German, and Spanish), performing arts, philosophy, and speech and communication studies.

The College of Business and Behavioral Science offers Bachelor of Arts degrees in economics, political science, psychology, and sociology. Bachelor of Science degrees are offered in accounting, economics, financial management, graphic communications, industrial management, management, marketing, psychology, and sociology.

The College of Engineering and Science offers the Bachelor of Science degree in agricultural engineering; ceramic engineering; chemical engineering; chemistry; civil engineering; computer engineering; computer information systems; computer science; electrical engineering; geology; industrial engineering; mathematical sciences; mechanical engineering; physics; polymer and textile chemistry; textiles, fiber, and polymer science; textile management; and textile science. Bachelor of Arts degrees are offered in chemistry, computer science, geology, mathematical sciences, and physics.

The College of Health, Education, and Human Development offers the Bachelor of Arts degree in early childhood education, elementary education, secondary education, and special education. The secondary education teaching areas are English, history and geography, mathematics, modern languages (French, German, and Spanish), political science and economics, and psychology and sociology. Bachelor of Science degrees are offered in health science; industrial education; mathematics teaching; nursing; parks, recreation, and tourism management; and science teaching. Teaching areas for industrial education are human resource development, industrial technology education, and vocational-technical education. The teaching areas for science are biological sciences, earth science, and physical sciences.

Clemson awards the Bachelor of Arts or Bachelor of Science degree in preprofessional studies to students who have satisfactorily completed three years of undergraduate work in an appropriate curriculum and the first year of an accredited medical, dental, veterinary, law, or other professional graduate program.

Academic Program

The academic year is divided into two semesters. The fall semester begins in mid-August, the spring semester in early January. Two summer sessions and one May-mester are also available. Students average 16 credit hours per semester. Clemson requires all students to complete 38 hours of general education classes specified by the University before graduation. The number of completed credit hours required for graduation ranges from 127 to 146, depending on the major. Army and Air Force ROTC provides 10 hours of military science or aerospace studies that can be counted toward the baccalaureate degree in any program.

Clemson awards credit by examination through the College Board's Advanced Placement (AP) Program. In 2001, 59 percent of the freshmen submitted AP scores, and more than half of them earned college credit. Credit is awarded for a score of 3, 4, or 5 on an AP examination. Placement and credit may also be earned by taking College Board Subject Tests or locally administered examinations.

Calhoun College, Clemson's honors program, is designed for bright students who thrive on achievement. Admission to Calhoun College for incoming freshmen is by invitation, based primarily on SAT I or ACT scores and the high school academic record.

Academic Facilities

Clemson University's modern laboratories and classrooms are well equipped for instruction, research, and lectures. The academic buildings, student housing, service facilities, and equipment are valued at $617 million. Beyond the main campus, stretching into Oconee, Pickens, and Anderson Counties are 24,000 acres of agricultural and forestry research lands that Clemson owns. Throughout the state, an additional 8,300 acres are devoted to its Agricultural Experiment Station research and 4-H Club activities.

A central feature of the campus is the Robert Muldrow Cooper Library with its large reflection pool. This beautiful structure houses more than 1.4 million volumes as well as 1.7 million equivalent pieces on microforms and other materials. Two college and four departmental libraries house additional books and periodicals in their disciplines, and Clemson students have access to even more information through a computer-based bibliographic network that links more than 11,000 libraries nationwide.

The Division of Computing and Information Technology (DCIT) supports the University's computing activities with an extensive network of computers. Facilities include several public-access labs that contain high-end PC, Macintosh, and printing equipment. All students are automatically assigned a computer ID to access a wide range of computing services, including electronic mail, word processing and spreadsheet software, the Internet and the World Wide Web, and student information services such as registration and financial aid. A wireless environment has been developed and laptop computers are required of students in two of the five colleges.

Costs

Tuition and fees for the 2002–03 academic year were $6034 for residents of South Carolina and $13,132 for out-of-state students. Charges for room and board were $4454 for both groups of students. These figures, which do not include the cost of books and miscellaneous additional expenses, are subject to change for 2003–04.

Financial Aid

The University annually awards approximately $75 million in financial aid to 11,900 students. Financial assistance includes more than 3,200 scholarships that range from $500 to full tuition and fees for scholastic ability and (in some cases) financial need, part-time employment on and off campus, and Federal Pell Grants, Federal Supplemental Educational Opportunity Grants, Federal Perkins Loans, Federal Work-Study, Federal Stafford Student Loans, and state programs. Applications for federal aid are accepted anytime, but those received by April 1 are given priority. All financial aid is awarded on an annual basis; a new application must be filed each year. Application forms for the upcoming academic year are available in January and may be obtained by writing to the Student Financial Aid Office, G01 Sikes Hall, Box 345123, Clemson University, or via electronic mail at finaid@clemson.edu. Clemson uses the Free Application for Federal Student Aid to determine eligibility for need-based scholarships and programs.

Faculty

Clemson's faculty, which is international in composition, has a reputation for excellence in teaching, research, and scholarship. Collectively, they have authored more than 21,000 articles and papers and 460 books. Of 1,248 faculty members, approximately 73 percent hold doctoral or highest terminal degrees. All students are assigned a faculty adviser in their curriculum to assist them with class scheduling and academic planning.

Among the activities of Clemson's professors outside the classroom are editing professional journals, chairing international conferences and symposia, sitting on boards of professional and curriculum registration, and serving actively in national learned societies. Many are licensed, practicing professionals with years of work experience in their fields, sometimes international in scope (some individuals have been advisers to the United Nations and foreign governments). At home, they are consultants to local, state, and national government agencies and to business, industry, and education.

Student Government

Student government provides services for the general benefit of students. It oversees homecoming activities, coordinates athletic spirit and charitable fund-raising drives, recognizes student organizations, allocates funds to organizations, hears cases involving the violation of regulations, reviews traffic violations, provides special minority representation, and periodically improves its constitution.

Student government also represents student opinion in the University committees on which student leaders sit. The power of student government in administrative affairs is primarily through its recommendations.

Admission Requirements

Admission to Clemson, moderately competitive, is based mainly on an applicant's high school record, class rank, and SAT I or ACT scores. The requirements in any given year are related to the number of applications received. There are no set cutoffs for grades, class standing, or SAT I or ACT scores. Clemson does not require an interview but auditions are required for those pursuing the performing arts. Transfer applicants must offer 30 semester (45 quarter) hours from an accredited institution, with a minimum grade point average of 2.5 on a 4.0 scale. International students must submit satisfactory high school credentials as well as TOEFL and SAT I scores.

Application and Information

General information and application forms are available online, or can be requested from the office of undergraduate admissions. For more information, students may call or write:

Undergraduate Admissions
105 Sikes Hall, Box 345124
Clemson University
Clemson, South Carolina 29634-5124
Telephone: 864-656-2287
Fax: 864-656-2464
E-mail: cuadmissions@clemson.edu
World Wide Web: http://www.clemson.edu/

THE CLEVELAND INSTITUTE OF ART

CLEVELAND, OHIO

The Institute

Established in 1882, the Cleveland Institute of Art (the Institute) has earned a reputation for being one of the finest fully accredited independent professional colleges of art and design in the country. Students seeking an intellectually stimulating and artistically challenging campus atmosphere are drawn to the Institute's location in the heart of University Circle, Cleveland's dynamic cultural and educational hub. The college's fundamental mission is to provide students pursuing professional careers in art and design with the most comprehensive visual arts education available. As an accredited founding member of the National Association of Schools of Art and Design (NASAD), the school's educational objectives include encouraging student artists to think originally and inventively within the creative possibilities of their chosen media, to achieve excellence in visual art techniques, and to experience increased powers of visual awareness and observation. The Institute also strives to provide a nurturing learning environment dedicated to the mission of the visual artist, mindful of the societal and cultural roles of the visual artist and the responsibility that lies therein, and to foster discernment in judgment and in values, both in art and life.

The Institute's consistent realization of these goals is the result of outstanding interaction among the students, faculty members, and administration. An undergraduate enrollment of about 550 students ensures intimate class sizes (students enjoy a 10:1 student-faculty ratio); a contemporary master-apprentice style of instruction ensures a higher level of collaboration between students and faculty members. The students at the Institute are guided on a daily basis by a faculty composed of some of the nation's most capable artists and craftsmen. In addition, the college's small population allows students to develop a productive and amicable rapport with administrators.

While sensitive to the student artist's need for individual experimentation, the Institute is built upon solid fundamentals. The Institute's two-year Foundation program develops skills in drawing, design, painting, and visual arts computer software while allowing student artists to explore any one of the college's sixteen majors through elective classes. The three years of major study that follow incorporate a professional practices curriculum during the fifth year that prepares the student artist for a smooth transition from college to a professional setting. The Institute also offers the studio courses necessary to earn a master's degree in art education from neighboring Case Western Reserve University (CWRU).

Location

The Institute's campus is nestled admist 488 acres of parks and buildings known as University Circle, an educational, civic, and cultural complex located 4 miles east of downtown Cleveland. The Cleveland Museum of Art is directly across the street from the Institute, Case Western Reserve University is next door, and the world-famous Cleveland Orchestra performs a block away in the internationally renowned Severance Hall. Within walking distance and offering a variety of cultural and social experiences are the Cleveland Museum of Natural History, Cleveland Botanical Garden, Western Reserve Historical Society, Cleveland Institute of Music, and twenty-two other institutions.

Majors and Degrees

The Cleveland Institute of Art offers a five-year program leading to a Bachelor of Fine Arts degree. A major may be chosen from one of sixteen studio areas: ceramics, drawing, enameling, fiber, glass, graphic design, illustration, industrial design, interior design, jewelry and metals, medical illustration, painting, photography, printmaking, sculpture, and the college's newest major, Technology and Integrated Media Environment (T.I.M.E.), which explores digital and time-based art. The Institute also participates in a four-year Bachelor of Science degree program in art education granted through Case Western Reserve University. The medical illustration program is offered in conjunction with CWRU's School of Medicine.

Academic Program

A comprehensive liberal arts program is an integral part of the academic curriculum at the Institute. The two-year Foundation program includes art history and world literature along with accompanying studio work in drawing, painting, design, and digital art and design. The remaining liberal arts requirements are distributed over the following three years, with study available in sociology, economics, philosophy, aesthetics, anthropology, music, psychology, and additional art history and literature courses. In the third year, with the beginning of study in a major art field, the student has increased opportunities to pursue personal artistic objectives. By the fifth year, studio work is essentially independent in nature, under the guidance of a faculty adviser.

Requirements for graduation are 150–153 credits: 102–105 studio and 48 liberal arts. Forty-two to 51 hours in a particular studio area constitute a major; optional minors are 9 hours.

Off-Campus Programs

As a member of the Association of Independent Colleges of Art and Design (AICAD), a consortium of the nation's principal private colleges of art and design, the Cleveland Institute of Art is able to provide a variety of unusual opportunities to students. One such opportunity, the Student Mobility Program, allows a student to spend up to two semesters at any of the other member schools. The foreign study program gives students the opportunity to study at a number of colleges, including Studio Art Centers International (SACI) in Florence, Italy; Edinburgh College of Art in Scotland; University of Newcastle, England; and Strate College in France.

Academic Facilities

The Institute has two main buildings, the George Gund Building and the Joseph McCullough Center for the Visual Arts. The McCullough Center formerly housed Ford Motor Company's Model T assembly line and is on Ohio's list of historical buildings. The facility has been renovated into studios and features large loft-like areas that provide excellent space and light. The campus offers approximately fifty studios, shops, and technical facilities supporting a full industrial-design studio, a sculpture foundry, ceramics and metalworking studios, fiber study in weaving and textiles, and graphic design facilities with state-of-the-art printing equipment as well as photography, printmaking, drawing, and painting studio areas. Spaces for glassblowing and papermaking are also available. The Institute makes every effort to ensure that its students have access to the latest technology used by professional artists and designers. To that end, the student-computer ratio is 3:1. Computer facilities include eight separate student labs supported by the following hardware: twenty-two Silicon Graphics Indigo2 and O2 workstations, sixty Macintosh G4 computers, thirty Macintosh G3 computers, thirteen Macintosh PowerPC 8500 computers, twelve Macintosh PowerPC 6500 computers, twenty-two PowerPC 7100 and 7200 computers, sixty-five NT and Windows 2000 workstations, flatbed and slide/film scanning stations in each lab, instructor projection capabilities for each lab, Tektronix Phaser 300i printers, LaserWriter and HP black and white laser printing in all labs, ten Epson Stylus Color 3000 printers, three HP color plotters, and three Axis milling machines. The software is continually upgraded to reflect professional standards. Currently, the college's computer labs have the following programs available: Alias/Wavefront Autostudio v8.5, Alias/Wavefront Studio Paint 3D v4.0, Adobe Photoshop 4.0 and 3.0 for both Mac and Silicon Graphics, Adobe Illustrator 7.0 and 5.5 for both Mac and Silicon Graphics, Adobe PageMaker 6.5, Adobe Premier, Rhino 3D, Studio Max, Macromedia Director, QuarkXpress, Microsoft Office 97 and Office 98, Macromedia Freehand, Macromedia Flash, Final Cut Pro and T1 Internet capabilities. Most of the Institute's majors take advantage of the technology available. For example, a computerized loom is used in the fiber major and a computerized lathe is used in metals.

The Jessica Gund Memorial Library, located in the Gund Building, houses 42,000 volumes, 260 periodical subscriptions, a visual reference catalog, an artists' book collection, 2,500 sound recordings, more than 300 video tapes, 85,000 slides, and other audiovisual equipment. Also in the Gund Building is the Reinberger Galleries, a very active public gallery that offers an extensive exhibition schedule each year.

Costs

Tuition and fees for academic year 2003–04 were $21,972 and $1490; room and board were $4600 and $2940, respectively. Other costs were estimated to be $2705. (These costs are subject to change.)

Financial Aid

The Institute participates in all of the federal assistance programs, including the Federal Pell Grant, Federal Work-Study, Federal Supplemental Educational Opportunity Grant, and Federal Perkins Loan programs. In addition, the Institute has its own grant program for new and returning students. The Institute makes every effort to offer financial assistance to students whenever possible. All aid is granted on the basis of financial need, as demonstrated through the Free Application for Federal Student Aid (FAFSA). A certified copy of the most recent federal tax return (Form 1040) and the Cleveland Institute of Art financial aid form are also required.

Merit scholarships, which currently range from $3000 to full tuition, are awarded in a scholarship competition for high school seniors based on outstanding portfolios and strong academic preparation.

Faculty

The Institute has 84 faculty members, of whom 16 teach in liberal arts and 68 in the studio areas. The latter are all practicing professionals in their respective fields who add the dimension of experience to the classroom.

Student Government

The Student Leadership Council is a volunteer organization designed to facilitate interaction and cooperation among the students, faculty members, and administration. It is made up of first- through fifth-year students and representatives from recognized student organizations. The council plans and coordinates student activities and officially represents the views of students to the faculty members and administration. One of its responsibilities is the sponsorship of the annual Student Independent Exhibition in the Reinberger Galleries. Other sponsored activities include managing display cases that exhibit student work, planning holiday parties and a spring picnic, and organizing intramural sports teams and out-of-town trips to museums and galleries. Recognized organizations include the Students Artists Association, United Nations Club, Nature and Hiking Club, Community Service Association, Gay and Lesbian Student Association, Student Activities Program Board, and the Student Independent Exhibition Committee.

Admission Requirements

At the Cleveland Institute of Art, admission officers counsel prospective students on an individual basis. If a student wants to attend, the Institute wishes to help; it also helps students find alternatives to this college. Any student who wants assistance is encouraged to contact the Office of Admissions.

Applicants must be high school graduates or must pass the high school equivalency examination. A high school transcript and transcripts of any subsequent college study must be filed in the Admissions Office. No credentials received for admission are released after the Institute receives them. A slide portfolio of at least twelve and no more than twenty of the applicant's most recent works must also be submitted for review. A personal interview is not a requirement, although it is recommended.

Application and Information

Applications for the fall term are accepted until July 1. The scholarship application deadline for the fall term is March 1.

Admissions Office
The Cleveland Institute of Art
11141 East Boulevard
Cleveland, Ohio 44106
Telephone: 216-421-7418
800-223-4700 (toll-free)
Fax: 216-754-3634
E-mail: admiss@gate.cia.edu
World Wide Web: http://www.cia.edu

Student studios in McCullough Center.

CLEVELAND INSTITUTE OF MUSIC

CLEVELAND, OHIO

The Institute

The mission of the Cleveland Institute of Music (CIM) is to provide exceptionally talented students from around the world an outstanding, thoroughly professional education in the art of music performance and related musical disciplines. The Institute embraces the legacy of the past and promotes the continuing evolution of music within a supportive and nurturing environment. The Institute also provides rigorous training in programs for gifted precollege musicians and serves as a resource for the community, with training for individuals of all ages and abilities.

A guiding principle at the Institute maintains that a liberal arts education contributes to a broad, humanistic perspective and is a vital component of the undergraduate curriculum. Equally important is the faculty's commitment to incorporating new technologies to complement and enhance the educational program.

The distinguished faculty of the Institute aims to develop the full artistic potential of all of its students. Through performance and teaching, the faculty and administration are dedicated to passing along their knowledge and love for this great art and to providing the bridge to an exciting and fulfilling career.

Founded in 1920, the Cleveland Institute of Music maintains its current size of approximately 360 undergraduate and graduate students and 90 full- and part-time faculty members by controlling the enrollment through carefully balanced admission policies, thus ensuring personal, individual attention for each student. In admitting the optimum number of students to each performance area rather than an unlimited number, CIM maximizes the performance experiences of its students so that they are well prepared to meet the challenges of professional life. The achievements of the Cleveland Institute of Music's alumni throughout the world are indicative of the Institute's commitment to high quality and professionalism. The distinguished-artist faculty includes the principals and other section players of the Cleveland Orchestra, a neighboring institution with which the Institute has a close relationship. Collegiate-level instruction is conducted by members of the CIM faculty and not by teaching assistants.

About 30 percent of CIM's students are in residence at Cutter House, the Institute's residence hall, which is adjacent to the school's main building. In addition to having the usual amenities, each room is connected to the extensive fiber-optic computer network operated by Case Western Reserve University (CWRU), whose campus borders that of CIM. Since all residents are CIM students, practice is permitted in the rooms of Cutter House. Residence hall accommodations are required for freshmen and sophomores.

In addition to the programs of study listed under the Majors and Degrees section, the Cleveland Institute of Music offers programs leading to the following graduate degrees and diplomas: Master of Music, Doctor of Musical Arts, Artist Diploma, and Professional Studies.

Location

CIM is located in University Circle, a cultural, educational, and scientific enclave situated approximately 3 miles east of downtown Cleveland. University Circle comprises more than thirty institutions that together constitute one of the largest diversified cultural complexes in the world. The complex includes museums, libraries, concert halls, colleges and universities, hospitals, gardens, churches, and temples. Occupying 500 acres in one of the most beautiful areas in the city, the facilities of University Circle offer extensive opportunities for serious study in many fields.

Located within easy walking distance of CIM are Case Western Reserve University, with which CIM cooperates in the Joint Music Program, and Severance Hall, home of the Cleveland Orchestra, whose rehearsals are open to CIM students by special arrangement. Students may also visit the Cleveland Museum of Art and enjoy its world-famous collections as well as its annual concert series, featuring world-renowned performers. Easily accessible to Institute students are numerous other University Circle institutions, such as the Cleveland Institute of Art, the Cleveland Playhouse, the Cleveland Museum of Natural History, the Western Reserve Historical Society, and the Cleveland Botanical Garden.

Majors and Degrees

Students may major in accompanying, audio recording, bassoon, bass trombone, cello, clarinet, composition, double bass, eurhythmics, flute, guitar, harp, harpsichord, horn, oboe, orchestral conducting, organ, piano, Suzuki violin pedagogy, theory, timpani and percussion, trombone, trumpet, tuba, viola, violin, and voice.

Through the Joint Music Program with Case Western Reserve University, five-year double-degree programs are available to CIM students. Of the two degrees earned by students in these programs, the Bachelor of Music is one component. Both B.M./B.A. and B.M./B.S. programs may be structured within music or with the CWRU component in a nonmusic field.

Academic Program

CIM programs offer intensive and comprehensive preparation for professional careers in music. All courses at the school revolve around a core of studies in theory, music history, and literature; the core is designed to provide a thorough musical education. At the undergraduate level, additional educational breadth is provided by required liberal arts courses.

An unusually intense performance environment involves students in a wide repertoire, including solo, chamber, orchestral, and operatic literature.

The development of the disciplines and skills required of a solo performer is an integral part of a student's training at CIM. This training, involving access to faculty members and visiting artists who are practicing professionals, is augmented by the many master classes, repertoire classes, and recitals offered annually. A concerto competition is held each semester, and approximately 6 to 8 students are selected for either public performances or readings with orchestra.

The orchestral training programs are designed to develop and maintain the disciplines and skills essential in making the smoothest possible transition from school to professional life. Sectional rehearsals and orchestral repertoire classes are conducted by principals of the Cleveland Orchestra. CIM's two symphony orchestras present approximately twenty concerts during the academic year, including multiple performances of two fully staged operas. The orchestras also provide a vehicle by which students in the Composition Department may hear and record readings of their works.

The sequence of opera courses is devoted to the principles of theory and practice of the various arts that combine to create an operatic performance. Emphasis is placed on vocal, musical, stylistic, linguistic, and dramatic techniques. Study stresses the application of these elements to role preparation for operas of different historical periods.

Started in 1969, the Joint Music Program between CWRU and CIM represents one of the strongest and most successful academic alliances in the U.S. It is a formal agreement for degree study at both the undergraduate and graduate levels. Each institution focuses on its strengths, which complement those of the partner institution. CIM concentrates on the education and training of professionals skilled in the art of performance, composition, and other related disciplines. CWRU concentrates on the fields of music history, musicology, music education, and early music performance.

Campuses for each institution are adjacent, allowing for easy access to classes and lessons and providing opportunities for regular exchanges of ideas of joint projects.

At its simplest level, the Joint Music Program provides CWRU music majors with instrumental, vocal, and composition lessons, as well as theory classes at CIM. It provides CIM students with music history and general education classes at CWRU. The program also provides a shared Audio Recording Degree Program; a partnership between CIM's library and CWRU's Kulas Music Library, with each collection complementing the other; academic advisement for D.M.A. candidates; and distance learning partnerships, with CIM adding an arts focus to CWRU's advanced Internet-2 network.

CIM operates on a two-semester calendar, with fall examinations preceding the Christmas holiday recess.

Academic Facilities

The CIM Library contains approximately 49,500 books and scores and 110 periodical subscriptions. The audiovisual facilities contain a sound-recording collection of 20,500 items, including CDs, DVDs, LPs, audiocassettes and videocassettes, reel-to-reel tapes, laser discs, and CD-ROMs. In addition, the library provides interlibrary loan service, enabling the faculty members and students to borrow materials from libraries nationwide.

Through the Joint Music Program with Case Western Reserve University, CIM students have access to the extensive resources of the CWRU libraries, especially those of the Kulas Music Library. The holdings of the CWRU libraries include 2,236,337 volumes, 2,475,337 microforms, and 17,506 current serial subscriptions. A shared online system with Case Western Reserve University permits the viewing of CWRU library holdings from online public catalogs in the CIM library. Through CIM's relationship with CWRU, there is access to OhioLink, a statewide information network.

The CIM main building, erected in 1961, includes classrooms, teaching studios, practice rooms, the CIM Library, an orchestra library, a specially designed eurhythmics studio, an opera workshop and studio, and a music store. Through connection of the entire CIM facility to Case Western Reserve University's fiberoptic computer network, CIM provides a Technology Learning Center that enables students to become aware of and accustomed to the ways in which music and technology go hand in hand. In addition, there are two concert and recital halls. Kulas Hall, the concert auditorium, houses three Steinway concert grand pianos and a Holtkamp three-manual tracker organ. Le Pavillon contains a recital hall with two Steinway grand pianos, additional classrooms, the electronic music studios, a meeting room, and a performers' lounge. All studios and practice rooms are equipped with Steinway grand pianos; there are two in every piano teaching studio. There are two Dowd French double harpsichords after Taskin, a Russell double-manual harpsichord after Blanchet, several concert harps, and comprehensive percussion equipment. Adjacent to CIM's main building is the Hazel Road Annex, an additional facility for chamber music, class recitals, individual practice, master classes, and rehearsal and coaching.

Costs

A comprehensive catalog, including information on costs as well as other areas of vital interest, is available upon request.

Financial Aid

The Cleveland Institute of Music offers outstanding professional training for talented musicians. While such training can be costly, CIM provides many forms of financial assistance, including scholarships, fellowships, work-study awards, and loans. Awards are available to full-time students and are based upon both musical capability and financial need. Entrance auditions as well as financial need serve as the basis for determining the eligibility of new students. More than 90 percent of CIM students receive some form of financial assistance. Further information is available by contacting the Institute's director of financial aid.

Faculty

The distinguished faculty of performers, composers, and teachers, headed by CIM President David Cerone, includes more than 30 members of the renowned Cleveland Orchestra and many other outstanding musicians. All liberal arts course offerings are taught by members of the faculty of Case Western Reserve University.

Student Government

The Student Government is the representative organization of the student body. Members are elected annually by the students. The organization carries on an active dialogue with the administration and addresses the daily and long-term needs of currently enrolled students.

Admission Requirements

Acceptance for study at the Cleveland Institute of Music is determined by musical talent and achievement and academic performance. The Institute expects applicants to have achieved a sufficient musical and academic background demonstrating their potential for successful completion of the intended course of study. Audition appointments are scheduled through the Admission Office upon receipt of the application. Candidates are required to submit two letters of recommendation from appropriate musically qualified individuals as well as all appropriate academic transcripts. Freshman applicants who are U.S. citizens or permanent residents must also submit scores on either the SAT I or American College Testing's ACT Assessment. International applicants for whom English is a second language must submit scores on the Test of English as a Foreign Language (TOEFL).

CIM does not discriminate on the basis of race, color, national or ethnic origin, citizenship, religion, age, sex, sexual orientation, or disability in its admission and scholarship policies, in the educational programs or activities it operates, or in employment.

Application and Information

The application deadline is December 1. An appointment for an entrance audition and the required admission examinations is scheduled by the Admission Office upon receipt of the application. The application process should be completed online at the Web address below. There is an application fee of $100.

Director of Admission
Cleveland Institute of Music
11021 East Boulevard
Cleveland, Ohio 44106-1705
Telephone: 216-795-3107
World Wide Web: http://www.cim.edu

CIM production of Mozart's *The Magic Flute*.

COE COLLEGE

CEDAR RAPIDS, IOWA

Coe College 1851

The College

Coe College is a private, coeducational, liberal arts college that specializes in turning good students into accomplished writers, scientists, musicians, ecologists, artists, bankers, and businesspeople. A unique sequence of activities, including a required term of practical experience, leads students step-by-step through their four-year program. Ninety-eight percent of Coe graduates are either working or in graduate school within six months of graduation.

The College's 1,200 students enter Coe with an average ACT score of 25 and an average GPA of 3.5; almost 50 percent graduate from Coe with two majors. Students represent thirty-four states and sixteen countries; 55 percent come from Iowa, 20 percent from other Midwestern states, 6 percent from abroad, and the remainder from across the U.S.

All students live on campus in one of five residence halls, which offer both single-sex and coed-by-floor options. The halls contain computer labs, vending machines, debit-card laundry facilities, kitchens, and television lounges. Roughly 35 percent of all students, including first-year students, bring cars to campus.

The list of active student clubs at any given time numbers sixty; interests range from literary to activist to social. Twenty-three percent of students belong to one of four national fraternities and three national sororities; nearly three quarters take part in intramural sports.

A member of the Iowa Conference, Coe competes at the NCAA Division III level in men's baseball, basketball, cross-country, diving, football, golf, soccer, swimming, tennis, track, and wrestling and in women's basketball, cross-country, diving, golf, soccer, softball, swimming, tennis, track, and volleyball. Intercollegiate and recreational athletes alike make year-round use of the K. Raymond Clark Racquet Center, which includes four racquetball courts, two squash courts, four indoor and six outdoor tennis courts, weight and exercise rooms, and a 200-meter indoor track. The softball field and football field (which is surrounded by an eight-lane all-weather track) can be found adjacent to the racquet center. In the well-equipped Eby Fieldhouse, the gymnasium, wrestling room, climbing wall, athletic training facilities, and eight-lane swimming pool and diving area can be found. Also housed in Eby is the recently renovated 8,000-square-foot fitness center. The weight-training area includes six supine benches, four squat racks, four Olympic platforms, five hammer strength machines, dumbbells, and twelve paramount station machines. Elliptical machines, stair steppers, stationary bikes, and treadmills are also available. Batting cages with natural pitching mounds for baseball and softball are located in lower Eby as well.

Location

Cedar Rapids, nestled in the rolling hills of eastern Iowa, is a safe and hospitable town of 175,000 people. A relaxed place to live in, the city is within a 5-hour drive of Chicago, Kansas City, Milwaukee, Minneapolis, Omaha, and St. Louis. The Eastern Iowa Airport, a regional airport served by five major airlines, is located in Cedar Rapids. The city offers a major museum of art, a nationally recognized symphony orchestra, and a strong community theater as well as malls, movie theaters, and dance clubs. Iowa City, just 25 minutes by car from campus, is a favorite destination for students in search of shopping, foreign films, and roving poets. Iowa has the highest literacy rate in the country and attracts more out-of-state college students than all but three other states.

Majors and Degrees

Coe awards the Bachelor of Arts, Bachelor of Science in Nursing, and Bachelor of Music degrees. Majors include accounting, African-American studies, American studies, art, Asian studies, athletic training, biochemistry, biology, business administration, chemistry, classical studies, computer science, economics, education, English, environmental science, French, French studies, gender studies, general science, German, German studies, history, literature, mathematics, molecular biology, music, nursing, philosophy, physical education, physics, political science, pre-architecture, predentistry, pre-engineering, prelaw, premedicine, psychology, public relations, religion, sociology, Spanish, Spanish studies, speech, theater arts, and writing. Students may combine courses from two or more academic areas to create an interdisciplinary concentration.

Student teachers may earn certification in art, elementary, music, physical, and secondary education.

Academic Programs

Coe's academic program couples the timelessness of the classics with the immediacy of hands-on learning. In addition to a major, students must complete the first-year seminar, two courses in the natural sciences, two in the social sciences, three courses in Western culture, and three in international culture. Students must also complete 5 hours of community service, attend issue dinners, and take part in career planning seminars. The sequence culminates with a practical experience requirement, which can be satisfied through an internship, research, practicum, or participation in one of Coe's many study-abroad options. An optional Leadership Program gives selected students advanced leadership training.

Coe follows a traditional two-semester calendar with an optional May term.

Off-Campus Programs

Coe's location in Cedar Rapids is a big benefit for students who opt to satisfy the practical experience requirement through an internship. Law firms, television stations, marketing agencies, art galleries, accounting firms, and major software and telecommunications companies are all just a few minutes from campus. St. Luke's Medical Laboratories is located across the street from campus. Students may also easily secure internships in Chicago, New York, Washington, D.C., or virtually any other major city in the country.

Those students who choose to study abroad have an equally wide selection. Coe students may earn credit for living and studying in Western and Eastern Europe, Asia, Africa, and Latin America.

Students of the natural and social sciences often satisfy Coe's practical experience requirement through research supervised by a Ph.D. faculty member. Recent topics have included the physical properties of glass compounds (physics), a comparative analysis of trees and grasses in decreasing the fertilizer runoff from farm fields (environmental science), and how EEG patterns differ between highly creative and normal people during problem solving (psychology).

Academic Facilities

Stewart Memorial Library gives students access to two commercial online services and dozens of microcomputers in addition to more than 216,000 books and bound journals and more than 15,000 periodicals, microfilm, and audiovisual materials. The library offers comfortable seating for more than 600, with well-lit group study tables, individual study desks, and conference rooms. The College's $4-million art collection, including works by Grant Wood and Marvin Cone, is displayed in the library galleries.

Coe's $3-million campuswide fiber-optic network connects students and professors with each other and the wider world via the Internet. Residence hall rooms are equipped with one network port for each student, giving students round-the-clock network access. In addition to the more than 260 computers available around campus for general use, Coe offers special computer labs for students of music, teacher education, art, theater, business, and life and physical sciences. Two general-use labs are open 24 hours a day.

Open 70 hours a week, the Coe Writing Center offers free coffee, computer disks, and advice on everything from grammar to writing style. It is staffed by student tutors who provide help on writing assignments that range from first-year English to senior honors papers.

Dows Fine Arts Center features a 300-seat theater with computerized light boards and a computer-aided design system; spacious fine arts studios for ceramics, painting, drawing, photography, printmaking, sculpture, fabric design, and graphic design; and a well-equipped computer graphics lab with animation capabilities.

In the Peterson Hall of Science, students have hands-on access to a laser with doubling and quadrupling crystals, liquid and gas chromatographs, a UV-visible spectrophotometer, a nuclear quadrupole resonance spectrometer, a Fourier transform infrared spectrometer, and global positioning system (GPS) equipment.

Costs

The costs for 2003–04 were $27,385, including $21,280 for tuition, $5780 for room and board, and $325 for activity fees. Annual miscellaneous costs—books, transportation, and personal expenses—typically range from $1000 to $1500.

Financial Aid

Coe awards renewable merit-based scholarships to students with strong records of accomplishment in academics, fine arts, foreign language, science, writing, and business/economics/accounting.

The average financial aid package offered to incoming students for fall 2003 totaled more than $20,000. To apply for aid, students must submit the Free Application for Federal Student Aid (FAFSA). Iowa residents should submit their forms before March 1 to qualify for the Iowa Tuition Grant. To request an early estimate form, interested students should call 319-399-8540.

Faculty

Coe's 74 full-time and 53 part-time faculty members teach classes with an average size of 16 students. Ninety-five percent hold the highest degree available in their field; all are committed to the students they teach. The student-faculty ratio is 12:1.

Student Government

The student body is governed by the Student Senate, whose members and officers are elected annually by students. In addition to planning campus activities and special events, the Student Senate appoints 2 students to serve as voting members of faculty committees. These committees deal with academic policies, admission and financial aid, athletics, public events, off-campus study, and the library.

Admission Requirements

Coe seeks dynamic students from across the country and around the world who can demonstrate strong academic achievement, intellectual curiosity, extracurricular participation, and community involvement. Coe requires a minimum 3.0 GPA (on a 4.0 scale), either an ACT score of 20 or a combined SAT score of 1000, and a ranking among the top 40 percent of the student's high school class for regular admission. While not required, an on-campus interview is strongly recommended.

Application and Information

In addition to a completed application, interested students should submit official SAT I or ACT results, an official high school transcript, a guidance counselor's recommendation, and a personal essay. For notification by January 15, students should submit all materials by December 1. For notification by March 15, the deadline is March 1. Coe requires a nonrefundable $200 deposit to secure a place in the entering class.

Interested students may attend one of Coe's high school visits, college days, and off-campus receptions or come for one of many visit programs and scholarship competitions. Both students and their parents are invited to contact:

Michael White
Vice President for Admission and Financial Aid
Office of Admission
Coe College
1220 First Avenue, NE
Cedar Rapids, Iowa 52402
Telephone: 319-399-8500
877-CALL-COE (toll-free)
Fax: 319-399-8816
E-mail: admission@coe.edu
World Wide Web: http://www.coe.edu

This senior art major satisfied Coe's practical experience requirement with three internships, all in New York City: one at the Leo Castelli Gallery, another with a printmaker, and the third at a senior center on the city's Upper West Side.

COGSWELL POLYTECHNICAL COLLEGE

SUNNYVALE, CALIFORNIA

The College

Cogswell Polytechnical College is dedicated to providing students with a superior education in engineering and the visual arts. Engineering theory combined with practical skills enables graduates to begin work immediately in their chosen areas of engineering and the visual arts.

Established in San Francisco in 1887 as a private, independent institution, Cogswell has developed new programs over the years to meet the emerging needs of technology industries. In 1985, the College moved from San Francisco to Cupertino. In 1994, the College moved to a permanent campus in Sunnyvale to be in proximity to the many technology companies located there. The College operates a day and evening class schedule, enabling students already working to complete their degree requirements. The student body of 400 brings together men and women of diverse ages, nationalities, and backgrounds who share a strong career orientation, a desire to make things function as designed, and a willingness to work together to achieve goals. Faculty members work closely with all students, enabling them to learn both the concepts and skills needed in technology. The independent study program for fire service professionals, Degree at a Distance Program, currently has 125 registered students.

Membership is available in clubs that are the student affiliates of the Institute of Electrical and Electronics Engineers (IEEE) and the Audio Engineering Society (AES).

Cogswell College is accredited by the Senior College Commission of the Western Association of Schools and Colleges.

Location

Sunnyvale, California, is in the Santa Clara Valley, at the south end of San Francisco Bay. Near the city of San Jose and 40 minutes south of San Francisco, the area offers students many cultural and recreational opportunities. Commonly referred to as Silicon Valley because of the high concentration of technology companies in the area, this location makes it easy for students to be a part of developments in engineering, technology, and digital art.

Majors and Degrees

Cogswell College offers seven degree programs, with each degree program containing specific concentrations. The Bachelor of Science degree in digital arts engineering has concentrations in animation, game, visual effects, and Web engineering. The Bachelor of Science degree in electrical engineering has concentrations in audio, computer, electrical, and software engineering. The Bachelor of Science degree in software engineering has concentrations in audio, computer, electrical, network, software, and Web engineering. The Bachelor of Arts degree in digital art and animation offers specializations in character animation, digital illustration, game design, modeling and animation, and technical director studies. The Bachelor of Arts degree in digital motion picture offers specializations in directing, technical design, and Web broadcasting. The Bachelor of Science degree in digital audio technology offers specializations in composing/arranging, Internet audio, synthesis and sound design, and studio recording.

Cogswell also offers the Degrees at a Distance program to students in California, Arizona, and Nevada. Through correspondence courses administered by the College, fire service personnel may earn a Bachelor of Science degree in fire science with concentrations in fire administration or in fire prevention/technology.

Academic Programs

Cogswell College has a trimester system, and the courses of study are carefully designed to provide a student with the theory and practical skills needed in technology industries. Students begin taking courses in their chosen area from the first trimester they enroll. General studies and communication courses round out each year and place technology in its human context.

In keeping with Cogswell's practical approach to education, a senior project is required. Students originate an idea and then design, build, and demonstrate it for faculty members and other students.

The Bachelor of Science in digital arts engineering and the Bachelor of Science in software engineering require 130 credits. The Bachelor of Science in electrical engineering requires 128 credits. The Bachelor of Arts in digital art and animation requires 127 credits. The Bachelor of Science in digital audio technology requires 128 credits. The Bachelor of Arts in digital motion picture requires 126 credits.

Off-Campus Programs

The College works with local industries to place students in employment positions appropriate to their major field of study. Many students graduate with actual working experience, and all Cogswell students graduate with the academic preparation necessary for immediate employment and advancement in their careers.

Academic Facilities

Cogswell has two high-powered PC 3-D modeling and animation labs, 2-D animation labs, 2-D design labs, and advanced computer programming labs. The College also has three Macintosh video editing labs, three audio recording studios, a sound design lab, and a MIDI lab. Students also benefit from the two traditional arts labs, the life drawing salon, and the clay modeling labs.

Cogswell's library of 12,000 volumes includes the most up-to-date publications in the engineering and imaging fields. The library also subscribes to more than 125 periodicals in the technological sciences as well as in general subject areas.

Costs

Full-time tuition for the 2003–04 academic year was $5640 per trimester for U.S. citizens, residents, and international students. Part-time students paid $470 per credit and may take up to 11 credits. The estimated cost of books and supplies is $1072 per year.

Cogswell is a nonresidential campus. Students have a range of housing options around Sunnyvale and in the Greater Bay Area. Cogswell offers student housing in commercial apartments under a corporate leasing plan. Students share a two-bedroom, two-bath apartment. Arrangements are made through the College Housing Officer. Costs average $800 per month, including basic furniture, utilities, and amenities.

Financial Aid

The Financial Aid Office enables students from diverse economic backgrounds to attend Cogswell, by putting together an aid package based on their need. In addition to federal and state loans and grants, qualified students may also receive aid from the Cogswell College Scholarship fund and many private scholarships unique to Cogswell. The College has jobs available on campus for work-study students. All programs are approved for veterans' training.

The state of California grants (Cal Grants) have an application deadline of March 2 for the following academic year. All other aid may be requested throughout the year.

For more information or to set up an appointment to discuss particular needs, students should contact the Financial Aid Office.

Faculty

The 16 full-time and 50 part-time faculty members are highly qualified in their fields and continue to be involved with business and industry. The student-faculty ratio of 12:1 fosters a personalized learning experience. Faculty members serve as student advisers and are eager to assist students in achieving their educational goals. The close working relationships among faculty, staff, and students encourage professional preparation in an environment of mutual respect.

Student Government

The Associated Student Body of Cogswell College is the general student membership organization. It gives students the opportunity to plan and direct their own programs, become involved with various aspects of College life, and influence decisions affecting the quality of education and student life at Cogswell.

Admission Requirements

Engineering students may apply for admission at any time during the year. High school students may apply after completion of their junior year. Students applying for the Bachelor of Arts in digital art and animation or digital motion picture or the Bachelor of Science in digital arts engineering or digital audio technology have these specific application deadlines: fall trimester, June 1; spring trimester, November 1; and summer trimester, March 1. Final acceptance is given when the official transcript confirms graduation and the completion of final semester grades.

Transfer students are asked to have official transcripts sent directly to the College. These are evaluated individually, on a course-by-course basis. Students from accredited two-year schools may transfer a maximum of 70 semester units; those from four-year schools may transfer a maximum of 94 semester units.

Digital art and animation, digitla audio technology, and digital motion picture students are required to submit a portfolio. Interested students should contact the College for portfolio submission guidelines.

Application and Information

For additional information and an application for admission, students should contact:

Admissions Office
Cogswell Polytechnical College
1175 Bordeaux Drive
Sunnyvale, California 94089-1299
Telephone: 408-541-0100
800-264-7955 (toll-free)
E-mail: info@cogswell.edu
World Wide Web: http://www.cogswell.edu

Cogswell College, located in Sunnyvale, California, emphasizes the fusion of art and engineering.

COLBY COLLEGE

WATERVILLE, MAINE

The College

Colby College, founded in 1813, enjoys a distinguished history as one of America's best private liberal arts colleges. The College offers outstanding value by combining a challenging academic program, an emphasis on undergraduate research, and a friendly and supportive atmosphere—all on one of the nation's most beautiful campuses. Colby's reach is global in its recruitment of a diverse student body and faculty, in the scope of its curriculum, and in the number of undergraduates who study abroad.

The College is guided by the belief that the best preparation for life, and for professions that require specialized study, is a broad acquaintance with human knowledge. Liberal arts students graduate with the competence and flexibility to thrive in an increasingly international and complex world. Colby has a superior record placing students who seek postgraduate study, and career opportunities for graduates are virtually unlimited.

Colby is a national leader at incorporating research into the curriculum in all disciplines. This approach to learning fosters strong critical-thinking skills, a lively imagination, and a capacity for independent work. It also contributes to faculty members' strong and supportive relationships with students. While many colleges lay claim to accessible faculty members, Colby ranks among the best in student-faculty interaction, both in and out of the classroom. Professors and students challenge assumptions and preconceptions together and consider the value and relevance of new information and ideas. Many academic programs incorporate fieldwork and independent learning, offer internships, sponsor service learning, and address global concerns. An extensive off-campus study program sees two thirds of Colby students studying abroad, among the highest rates in the nation. The 4-1-4 calendar includes a January term that offers exciting opportunities on and off campus to explore special areas of interest and expertise.

At Colby, 1,830 students from diverse backgrounds represent nearly every state and more than sixty countries. The student-faculty ratio is 11:1. There are more than 100 campus organizations, and each year students form new clubs. The most popular clubs include community service organizations, the Outing Club, choral and instrumental music groups, the International Club, and the FM radio station. Cultural opportunities abound, and most days see at least two or three events, including lectures, films, concerts, poetry readings, dance performances, exhibits, and plays.

Almost all students live on campus. A multiyear, $44-million project to add dorms and renovate all residence halls and dining facilities is almost complete. Notable facilities include the Pugh Center, designed as a hub of multicultural organizations; one of the nation's best college-based art museums; and the Alfond Athletic Center, one of the largest indoor athletic and fitness facilities in New England. The athletic center features an indoor track, swimming pool, ice arena, gymnasium, fitness center, aerobics studio, squash courts, tennis courts, and climbing wall. Outdoor facilities include 50 acres of playing fields, cross-country skiing and running trails, tennis courts, and an all-weather track. Colby fields sixteen varsity women's teams, fifteen men's teams, and one coed team. There are eleven club teams and many individual and intramural sports opportunities.

Location

Located in Waterville, Maine, an extended community of more than 40,000 people, Colby is just off Interstate 95, 20 minutes from the state capital and about an hour from Maine's two largest cities, Portland and Bangor. Maine's western mountains, including the Sugarloaf/USA ski area, are just over an hour to the north, and the Atlantic Coast is less than an hour to the east. Acadia National Park and Mt. Katahdin are both accessible as day trips. The 714-acre campus includes Johnson Pond and a 128-acre arboretum and bird sanctuary.

Majors and Degrees

Colby awards the Bachelor of Arts degree, with majors in African-American/American studies, American studies, anthropology, art, biology, chemistry, chemistry–ACS (accredited by the American Chemical Society), chemistry–biochemistry, classical civilization, classical civilization–anthropology, classical civilization–English, classics, classics–English, computer science, East Asian studies, economics, economics–mathematics, English, environmental studies–policy, environmental studies–science, French literature, French studies, geology, geology–biology, German language and literature, German studies, government, history, international studies, Latin American studies, mathematical sciences, mathematics, music, philosophy, physics, psychology, religious studies, Russian language and culture, sociology, Spanish, theater and dance, and women's, gender, and sexuality studies. Specific options within the above majors include art–art history, art–studio art, biology–cell and molecular biology/biochemistry, biology–environmental science, biology–neuroscience, chemistry–cell and molecular biology/biochemistry, chemistry–environmental science, economics–financial markets, geology–earth science, geology–environmental science, and psychology–neuroscience.

Minors are available in thirty-two fields of study, including administrative science, African studies, Chinese, creative writing, education, environmental studies, human development, indigenous peoples of the Americas, Japanese, Jewish studies, and women's, gender, and sexuality studies.

Academic Program

Colby's liberal arts program offers a broad educational foundation. In-depth study in a major provides a detailed understanding of at least one discipline's methods and perspectives. In addition to their major, students may complete a minor, a second major, a combined major, or an interdisciplinary major. A self-designed independent major or a senior scholars project of significant independent work may also be approved for qualified students. Secondary school teacher certification may be obtained, and a dual-degree engineering program is offered with Dartmouth College.

Area requirements include 4 credit hours of English composition, knowledge of one foreign language, 6 to 8 credit hours in the natural sciences, and 3 to 4 credit hours in each of the following areas: arts, historical studies, literature, quantitative reasoning, and the social sciences. Wellness and diversity requirements also must be filled. A minimum of 128 credit hours is required for graduation. Three January terms, including one during the first year, are also required.

Off-Campus Programs

More than two thirds of Colby students take advantage of international or off-campus domestic study opportunities. Many participate in Colby's own programs in Ireland, France, Spain, and Russia or in programs run cooperatively by Colby, Bates, and Bowdoin in London, South Africa, and Ecuador. Other students select approved non-Colby programs in countries throughout the world.

Domestic off-campus programs include the Washington Semester and exchange programs with Howard University in Washington, D.C., and Clark Atlanta University in Georgia. Colby's financial aid may be applied to any approved off-campus study.

Academic Facilities

Colby has three libraries on campus with access to almost 1 million books, microtexts, and other items, most of which are found in open stacks. In addition, Colby subscribes to more than 1,700 print periodicals and journals. An interlibrary loan program provides books and information from repositories across the nation. Miller Library, at the center of campus, has an audiovisual center, a 24-hour computer cluster, study space for more than half the student body, and an electronic-research classroom for teaching the use of electronic information resources. Special collections feature modern Irish literature, Edwin Arlington Robinson memorabilia, and an important collection of Thomas Hardy's works. The catalog is online, and many resources are available through the library's Web site.

In 2001, the Bixler Art and Music Center expanded with construction of the Crawford Art Studio wing. The center includes an art and music library, music practice rooms, and a 350-seat auditorium. The Colby College Museum of Art is one of the nation's finest college-based art museums.

The Runnals Building contains the 274-seat Strider Theater, a dance studio, and the Cellar Theater for improvisational workshops and small productions.

Four interconnected buildings contain science facilities, including teaching and research laboratories, environmentally controlled animal rooms, research greenhouses, exhibit space, and a 10,800-square-foot science library. A wide range of sophisticated science equipment is accessible to students beginning in their first year. The Collins Observatory features a 14-inch telescope equipped with a high-quality CCD camera and other research-grade equipment.

Computers are available for student use in clusters and teaching labs throughout the campus. Every classroom, dorm room, office, and laboratory is connected to the Colby network and the Internet through high-speed Ethernet connections. All classrooms are served by data-video projectors. An extensive software library is available to students. The Information Technology Services staff helps connect students' computers in the fall, runs a help desk for students, and assists with applications appropriate to each discipline. There are no fees for any of these services.

Costs

For the 2003–04 academic year, the comprehensive fee was $37,570. Personal expenses, books, and supplies average $1450 annually.

Financial Aid

Colby awards financial aid on the basis of need. About 70 percent of students receive some form of financial aid, and approximately 36 percent receive grant aid from the College's own funds. An average award includes a grant, a loan, and on-campus employment.

Faculty

Colby has 197 faculty members, 158 of them full-time. The student-faculty ratio is 11:1, and the median class size is 17. Ninety-five percent of faculty members hold doctorates or final degrees in their fields, and many have national or international reputations. A faculty-in-residence program provides housing for about a dozen faculty families in campus residence halls, and a faculty-associates program fosters further faculty involvement in campus life.

Student Government

Colby students have an unusual degree of autonomy through the Student Government Association (SGA) and the College's residential Commons system. Students also serve on most College boards and committees, including the Board of Trustees. The SGA deals with academic, cultural, and residential affairs and supports more than 100 clubs and organizations. It sponsors concerts, lectures, films, dances, and theater performances. The Student Judiciary Board has jurisdiction over most incidents that call for possible disciplinary action.

Admission Requirements

Colby seeks applicants from diverse geographical, racial, and economic backgrounds who have special qualities or talents to contribute to the College. Admission is highly selective. Evaluations are made on the basis of academic achievement and ability, interest and excitement in learning, character, and maturity. The quality of a candidate's preparation is judged by his or her academic record, references from school authorities, and College Board or ACT test scores. A minimum of 16 academic preparatory credits is recommended, including 4 years of English, at least 3 years of a foreign language, 3 years of college-preparatory mathematics, 2 years of a laboratory science, 2 years of history or social science, and 2 academic electives.

Colby offers early entrance and early decision options. Advanced standing may be established by examination, taken either through the department or through the Advanced Placement Program of the College Board, the International Baccalaureate, or other standard tests. Some transfer students are considered for admission each year.

Applicants are encouraged to visit the campus for interviews, tours, classes, meals, and, if possible, an overnight stay in the residence halls.

Application and Information

Applications for regular admission must be submitted by January 1. Those wishing to be considered for early decision may choose either the fall or winter option. Fall option applicants must complete the application process by November 15; winter option applicants, by January 1. For applications and admission forms, students should contact:

Admissions and Financial Aid Office
Lunder House
Colby College
4800 Mayflower Hill
Waterville, Maine 04901-8848
Telephone: 800-723-3032 (toll-free)
Fax: 207-872-3474
E-mail: admissions@colby.edu
World Wide Web: http://www.colby.edu/

Aerial view of the Colby College campus.

COLBY–SAWYER COLLEGE

NEW LONDON, NEW HAMPSHIRE

The College

Colby-Sawyer College, a coeducational, residential, undergraduate college founded in 1837, evolved from the New England academy tradition and has been engaged in higher education since 1928. The College provides programs of study that innovatively integrate the liberal arts and sciences with professional preparation. Through all of its programs, the College encourages students of varied backgrounds and abilities to realize their full intellectual and personal potential so they may gain understanding about themselves, others, and the major forces shaping our rapidly changing and pluralistic world. At present, students come from all over the United States and seven other countries, with 69 percent of the students coming from outside of New Hampshire. Within the last eight years, an apartment-style and two suite-style residence halls have been built to accommodate the College's steady growth in enrollment.

Student athletic involvement occurs at the varsity, club, intramural, and recreational levels. There are ten varsity sports for women (NCAA Division III basketball, diving, lacrosse, soccer, swimming, tennis, track and field, and volleyball; ECSC Alpine ski racing; and IHSA riding) and nine for men (NCAA Division III baseball, basketball, diving, soccer, swimming, tennis, and track and field; ECSC Alpine ski racing; and IHSA riding). Athletic successes include a nationally ranked men's basketball team that competed in the NCAA tournament in 2001, 2002, and 2003; a track and field team that sent individual qualifiers to the NCAA Championships in 2000, 2001, and 2002; and conference championships for men's baseball in 1998 and 1999; men's basketball in 2001, 2002, and 2003; women's volleyball in 1999; and women's basketball in 1997, 1998, and 1999. The women's basketball team also competed in the 2001, 2002, and 2003 ECAC tournament as well as the NCAA tournament in 1997, 1998, and 1999. The women's volleyball team also made appearances at the NCAA tournament in 1999 and 2003. Colby-Sawyer's equestrian team was the reserve national champion in 1998 and has sent riders to the IHSA national team every year since 1987. The Alpine ski racing team has competed in the USCSA National Championships for the past six seasons, sent one individual on to NCAA Division I Championships in 1998, and produced 13 All-Americans from 1999 to 2003. The Colby-Sawyer Chargers compete as a member of the Commonwealth Coast Conference.

The College is accredited by the New England Association of Schools and Colleges, and professional programs also carry the appropriate accreditations. Colby-Sawyer has consistently received recognition as one of the top colleges in its category.

Location

Colby-Sawyer's 200-acre campus is located on the crest of a hill in New London, New Hampshire. Its beautifully maintained grounds and stately Georgian architecture create a picturesque and safe environment that is conducive to learning. The College is located in the heart of the Dartmouth–Lake Sunapee region, a four-season recreational and cultural community known for the natural beauty of its lakes and mountains. Boston is only 1½ hours south and Montreal is 3½ hours north. Students have access to major cities by College van or public bus. The nearby seacoast at Portsmouth, and surrounding lakes, mountains, and state parks provide opportunities for biking, camping, canoeing, golf, hiking, ice skating, Nordic and Alpine skiing, swimming, and tennis. Arts and cultural opportunities can be found in New London as well as in nearby Concord, the state capital, and Hanover, the home of Dartmouth College.

Majors and Degrees

Colby-Sawyer offers bachelor's degrees in many fields. The Bachelor of Arts degree is awarded in studio art; biology; communication studies; English; history, society, and culture; and psychology. The Bachelor of Fine Arts degree is awarded in studio art and graphic design. The Bachelor of Science degree is awarded in business administration, child development, community and environmental studies, exercise and sport sciences (specializations offered in athletic training, exercise science, and sport management), and nursing. Teacher certification can be earned in art (K–12), early childhood (K–3), English language arts (5–12), or social studies (5–12) education. Highly motivated, academically strong students may receive approval to design their own interdisciplinary major program of study. An associate degree can be earned in the liberal arts and sciences. In addition, Colby-Sawyer offers sixteen academic minors.

Academic Programs

Colby-Sawyer College faculty and staff are excellent at working with students who are undecided on a major and they are highly qualified to help students explore their values, talents, and academic and career interests. At Colby-Sawyer College, it is believed that knowledge and experience nurture each other. Therefore, the combination of classroom learning and professional experience is an integral part of each student's education.

All students begin their liberal education at Colby-Sawyer by selecting a Pathway Seminar. Students choose a topic they are interested in learning more about, pose questions that are personally relevant, and search for answers through experiences in several liberal arts areas. They return to these themes in a seminar in their sophomore year, applying all they have learned to answer their own questions and share insights with classmates on such topics as "Money and the Meaning of Life."

Colby-Sawyer's Honors Program offers an environment conducive to intellectual exploration and creativity beyond that which is available in the general curriculum. This program is carefully designed to advance and polish critical skills of each participating student.

Through a carefully crafted program offered by the Harrington Center for Career Development, all students are encouraged throughout their four years of study to continue to clarify their interests and goals and to gain practical experiences through student employment, internships, and voluntary service to the community.

Internships are a key element in career development. Colby-Sawyer has an impressive roster of internship opportunities available, and through the internship experience, students often receive their first offer of a permanent position. During the internship, students have an opportunity to work directly with professionals in their field of study while developing valuable contacts who can serve as references and career mentors. Organizations that have recently accepted Colby-Sawyer interns include Merrill Lynch, Continental Cable, Beth Israel Hospital, Blue Cross/Blue Shield, Harvard University Athletic Department, the Buffalo Bisons, the New England Patriots, the Currier Gallery of Art, the Basketball Hall of Fame, the Olympic Regional Development Authority, Channel 7 (Boston), the Appalachian Mountain Club, and CNN.

Off-Campus Programs

Colby-Sawyer encourages students to study abroad for a semester or a year. The study-abroad adviser works closely with students to select an experience and a school best suited to their individual needs and interests. Students have studied in England, Australia, Spain, France, Italy, Ireland, Scotland, Switzerland, and many other countries.

Colby-Sawyer's membership in the fourteen-college New Hampshire College and University Council (NHCUC) allows students to enroll in other NHCUC institutions for a course or for an entire semester.

Academic Facilities

The Susan Colgate Cleveland Library/Learning Center contains 92,116 volumes, 4,148 periodicals, and 197,625 microforms. Access to these materials is provided by a Dynix automated catalog system and by 30 online and CD-ROM databases for periodical research. The library is housed in a unique five-level structure constructed from two pre–Civil War dairy barns masterfully transformed into a warm and inviting facility that has won regional and national architectural awards. The library/learning center also houses a curriculum lab, an audiovisual room, seventeen PC workstations for Internet and library database access, a computer lab with fourteen PCs, and a networked computer classroom with twenty-five PCs and interactive multimedia teaching equipment with CD-ROM capability. Interlibrary loan service provides access to an extensive array of library holdings throughout New England and the nation.

The magnificent 63,000-square-foot Dan and Kathleen Hogan Sports Center was designed to meet the athletic and recreational needs of Colby-Sawyer College students and members of the local community. This sports center contains a large field house with three multipurpose courts; a suspended walking/jogging track; a six-lane, competition-size swimming pool; and a fitness center furnished with equipment such as StairMasters, Body Master stations, treadmills, rowing ergometers, Nordic cross-country skiing tracks, a Universal gym, stationary bicycles, and a complete selection of free weights. The Hogan Center also houses the Sports Medicine Clinic, which is fully equipped with the latest technology to support the Exercise and Sport Sciences Program.

The Academic Development Center at James House provides academic support services for all students, including honors students. The staff consists of faculty members, learning specialists, and student academic counselors who work with students to strengthen their writing, math, and research skills, as well as their study skills, such as time management, note-taking, and exam preparation. Colby-Sawyer's English Language and American Culture Program provides support for international students and others whose first language is not English. Among the services available to students with diagnosed learning differences are classroom modifications, personal counseling, and professional as well as peer tutoring.

The nursing program features a Nursing and Health Laboratory containing resources that simulate clinical practice settings. Students also have access to a computer laboratory with software that helps to prepare them for clinical experiences. The nursing program is enriched by its relationship with Dartmouth Hitchcock Medical Center, one of the most well equipped and technologically advanced teaching hospitals in North America.

The Colby-Sawyer campus computing array includes a campus network with Internet access, five computer laboratory/classrooms, and six mobile multimedia teaching stations, which provide computer graphics, audio, and video capabilities employing the latest digital technology. Computing facilities are equipped with the latest Microsoft Windows applications and laser printers for student use. The College now has an 7.5:1 student-computer ratio.

The Frances Lockwood Bailey Graphic Design Studios are the center of the graphic design facilities. These studios are equipped with computers loaded with the latest versions of graphic design software programs and desktop publishing capability. Students create graphic images while working with digital scanning and optical character recognition, still video photography, and VCR, video camera, and other state-of-the-practice images. Advanced student projects are sent to professional imaging centers to create high-resolution hard copy.

Costs

Tuition, room, and board for 2004–05 are $32,260. Approximately $1500 should be allowed for books, supplies, personal expenses, and travel, depending on where students live.

Financial Aid

Through its Financial Aid Program, Colby-Sawyer encourages the attendance of students from a variety of ethnic and cultural backgrounds, economic levels, and geographic regions. Seventy-eight percent of the students currently receive some form of financial assistance, and Colby-Sawyer provides more than $7.4 million a year in grant assistance to its students. Both need-based and merit awards are available, including merit awards for outstanding academic achievement or student leadership. Merit awards are also available for students with special talents in art, the performing arts, or creative writing and for those students who have been significantly involved in community service. Applicants who wish to be considered for merit awards must be accepted for admission by February 1. Each applicant for need-based aid must submit the Free Application for Federal Student Aid (FAFSA) and the Colby-Sawyer Application for Financial Aid. Priority will be given to students whose completed forms are received before the March 1 deadline. A modest amount of financial assistance is available for international students.

Faculty

Colby-Sawyer has a distinguished faculty and staff dedicated to undergraduate teaching, and a personalized education is ensured by a 12:1 student-faculty ratio and average class size of 19. At Colby-Sawyer, senior faculty members teach first-year students as well as students in the upper classes.

Student Government

The Student Government Association (SGA) is structured to provide considerable interaction among students, faculty members, and staff, and the SGA allocates the resources that fund a multitude of involvement and leadership opportunities outside the classroom. Campus activities include the Campus Activities Board, Dance Club, Alpha Chi Honor Society, yearbook, radio station (WSCS 90.9 FM), Drama Club, Admissions Key Association, Art Students Society, Student Nurses Association, *The Courier* (student newspaper), community service, and numerous clubs and intramural teams.

Admission Requirements

The College requires prospective students to present at least 15 units of college-preparatory work. This would usually include 4 years of English, 3 years of mathematics, 3 or more years of social studies, 2 years of a foreign language, and 2 or more years of a laboratory science.

While an admissions interview is not required, every applicant is strongly encouraged to visit Colby-Sawyer for a tour and interview. Interviews often play an important part in the final admissions decision.

Application and Information

Colby-Sawyer receives and considers applications throughout the year. Beginning in December, applications are reviewed as soon as they become complete, and candidates are notified as soon as the admissions decision is finalized. A completed application includes a transcript of the candidate's high school work (including first-quarter grades for the senior year), SAT I or ACT scores, two letters of recommendation (one from a teacher and one from a guidance professional), a personal statement, and a $40 nonrefundable application fee. Application forms and additional information may be obtained by contacting:

Office of Admissions
Colby-Sawyer College
541 Main Street
New London, New Hampshire 03257
Telephone: 603-526-3700
800-272-1015 (toll-free)
Fax: 603-526-3452
E-mail: csadmiss@colby-sawyer.edu
World Wide Web: http://www.colby-sawyer.edu

COLGATE UNIVERSITY

HAMILTON, NEW YORK

The University

Founded in 1819, Colgate University is the sixty-sixth-oldest college in the United States. Originally a Baptist theological and literary seminary for men, and later an all-male university, Colgate today is a private, nonsectarian liberal arts college enrolling 2,750 men and women.

As a residential college in a small town, Colgate generates much of its own activity. Colgate students are doers, as a wide range of student-sponsored activities attests. The weekly student newspaper, campus radio and television stations, musical and drama groups, departmental clubs, religious and service organizations, and other special interest groups provide outlets for almost any student interest. Colgate is a regular lecture stop for nationally known speakers, and concerts and films are a regular feature of the weekly calendar.

Students at the University have traditionally placed a high value on athletic activity, and a high percentage participate in intercollegiate, intramural, and recreational athletics. Eleven men's and eleven women's teams are competitive in the Patriot League at the NCAA's highest level of play. Recreational facilities include cross-country trails, a boathouse on nearby Lake Moraine, an indoor skating rink, a complete gymnasium, a field house, a swimming pool, tennis courts, playing fields, a trap range, bowling lanes, a fitness center, and a golf course rated by *Golf Digest* as one of the five best on U.S. college campuses.

Residential education is an important part of a student's college experience, and Colgate offers a variety of programs and living accommodations through which students can learn the responsibilities implied in community membership. Traditional dormitories, campus apartments, special interest houses (such as Ralph Bunche House for Peace and World Order Studies, French House, and Ecology House), and fraternities and sororities are among the available living arrangements.

Colgate sponsors a complete range of student services, including career planning and counseling services, and there is a health center on campus.

Location

Colgate is situated on a 515-acre hillside campus in scenic central New York. Hamilton (population 2,500), which has old homes, tree-lined streets, a college inn, a coffeehouse, small shops, and municipal services, is reminiscent of a New England village. Its residents are active in Colgate activities, and there is an easy, friendly relationship between town and college. Rural areas surround Hamilton; Syracuse and Utica are within an hour's drive.

Majors and Degrees

Colgate offers the Bachelor of Arts degree with concentrations in Africana studies, art and art history, Asian studies, astrogeophysics, astronomy-physics, biochemistry, biology, chemistry, classical studies, computer science, computer science/mathematics, economics, educational studies, English, environmental biology, environmental economics, environmental geography, environmental geology, French, geography, geology, German, Greek, history, humanities, international relations, Latin, Latin American studies, mathematical economics, mathematics, molecular biology, music, Native American studies, natural science, neuroscience, peace studies, philosophy, philosophy and religion, physical science, physics, political science, psychology, religion, Russian studies, social sciences, sociology and anthropology, Spanish, theater, and women's studies. In consultation with faculty advisers, students may also develop their own concentrations, such as American studies and marine studies.

To combine education in the liberal arts with training in engineering, Colgate maintains cooperative agreements with Columbia University, Rensselaer Polytechnic Institute, and Washington University. A student typically studies for five years, two or three at Colgate and the remainder at the cooperating institution, to receive both the Bachelor of Science in engineering and the Bachelor of Arts degrees.

Academic Program

Colgate provides its students with a liberal education. In addition to course work in an academic concentration, the academic program for all undergraduates includes a liberal arts core curriculum, physical education, electives, and the requirement of two courses each in humanities, natural sciences, and social sciences. Before graduating, students are expected to demonstrate competence in a foreign language and in English composition. Some students elect to fulfill the requirements of two separate concentrations or of a concentration and a minor. The University requires the successful completion of thirty-two courses.

The liberal arts core curriculum comprises four courses that can be taken in any order. Two required courses examine continuity and change in the foundations of Western culture. Students choose a third selection from an array of courses dealing with historical, economic, and cultural aspects of non-Western societies. The final component of the liberal arts core includes one course in science perspectives that examines the historical and contemporary influences of science on the individual and society.

In addition to regularly scheduled courses, Colgate offers independent study through which undergraduates may study on their own for college credit with the approval and guidance of a faculty sponsor. About 300 students study independently each year.

Off-Campus Programs

Colgate offers twenty-four study groups at international and domestic sites away from campus. Each group is led by a member of the faculty and studies for one regular term. Nearly 60 percent of Colgate's students travel with at least one study group at some time during their undergraduate years. Recent groups have traveled to Australia, China, the Dominican Republic, England (three in London, one in Manchester), France, Germany, India, Italy, Japan, Russia, Spain, Switzerland, Wales, and the West Indies. The political science study group is centered in Washington, D.C., and a science study group works at the National Institutes of Health in Bethesda, Maryland. In addition to study groups, Colgate students may enroll in Sea Semester, a twelve-week program in which course time is divided between Woods Hole, Massachusetts, and the 250-ton staysail schooner *Westward*. Colgate also participates in the American Maritime Studies Program (in Mystic Seaport, Connecticut) and the Swedish Program.

Academic Facilities

Case Library and the Dana Addition contain more than 700,000 volumes and more than 1 million documents, journals, and other media and provide ample space for study and research. Cooley Science Library, which has a 70,000-volume capacity, provides additional space for reading and studying. Dana Arts Center is home for Colgate's art, music, and theater programs. In addition to classrooms and rehearsal and study areas, the center includes Brehmer Theater, Picker Art Gallery, and facilities for the study of electronic and non-Western music. Little Hall, the University's newest building, provides studio and exhibition space, faculty offices, and both digital and 35mm projection studios.

The computer center houses two Digital Equipment Corporation VAX 4000 computers that provide batch-processing and time-sharing capabilities on terminals throughout the campus. The computer science department has its own VAX-11/750 computer. Alumni Hall, home of the division of social sciences, has classroom and office space and a museum with an extensive collection of archaeological and ethnological materials relating primarily to the American Indian. Persson Hall (economics, geography, and political science) opened in 1994 and is equipped with electronic classrooms, a premier geography laboratory, and an auditorium.

The department of philosophy and religion maintains offices and classrooms in Hascall Hall, a renovated building listed on the National Register of Historic Places. Most offices and classrooms in the division of humanities are housed in Lawrence Hall, which has centers designed for the study of German, the classics, China, and Japan. The geology department and the department of physics and astronomy maintain offices, classrooms, and laboratories in Lathrop Hall. The geology department maintains collections of minerals and gems and Devonian fossils.

The department of computer science, the department of mathematics, the audiovisual center, and the Cooley Science Library are housed in McGregory Hall, along with several administrative offices. The Olin Life Science Building has classrooms, laboratories, and offices for biology and psychology. Facilities in Olin Hall include a greenhouse, animal cages, experimental rooms for psychology, two electron microscopes, the George R. Cooley Herbarium, and equipment and laboratories dedicated to the study of molecular biology and neuroscience. Wynn Hall houses facilities for chemical sciences. The Observatory, located on a hill above campus, has a Ferson 16-inch reflecting telescope with an electronic readout system.

Costs

Tuition for 2003–04 was $29,740, fees were $200, and room and board in college facilities were $3455 and $3700, respectively. Students should allow at least $1725 for books, supplies, normal travel, clothing, and incidentals.

Financial Aid

Colgate awards financial aid on the basis of need as determined by the Financial Aid PROFILE of the College Scholarship Service. While not all students who apply for aid receive assistance, the University is committed to helping as many students as funds will allow. Approximately 35 percent of Colgate students are aided with scholarship funds allocated from the University budget. More than 50 percent of all Colgate students receive some financial aid, which includes state or local scholarships, federal grants, work-study awards, student loans, or a combination from those resources. Award notifications are normally mailed with letters of acceptance from the admission office. The University also offers a variety of parent loan programs and payment options. Athletic scholarships are available in a limited number of sports teams.

Faculty

The 290 members of Colgate's faculty are distinguished teachers and scholars. While teaching is their primary responsibility, they are also active researchers, authors, artists, performers, and regular contributors in their academic disciplines. No graduate assistants teach at Colgate; from the first semester, students study with faculty members who may also be working on a new novel, researching the effects of acid rain, or investigating the role of women in history. Members of the faculty have attracted many significant grants, fellowships, and awards. The student-faculty ratio is 10:1. Faculty members hold regular office hours, serve as academic advisers to students, and are frequent participants in extracurricular activity on campus.

Student Government

The Student Association, comprising all students at the University, is governed by a senate of elected representatives. The Student Senate allocates funds in support of student activities and elects representatives to Colgate's campus governing boards and their committees.

Admission Requirements

Colgate seeks students who can be successful in a rigorous academic program and who demonstrate intellectual curiosity, academic talent, and the ability to contribute to the life of the college. The admission staff and the college are committed to attracting students who represent the widest possible diversity of economic, racial, social, and geographic backgrounds. While academic preparation is the single most important consideration in admission decisions, special interests, skills, and qualities of all kinds can be influential. Special promise in such areas as the arts, music, and athletics is recognized in addition to demonstrated academic achievement. Scores on the SAT I or ACT are required for admission. For students applying for entrance in fall 2005, SAT II exams will not be required but will be considered if submitted.

Although there is no prescribed distribution of high school courses, successful applicants typically show strong preparation in humanities (especially English and foreign languages), social sciences (particularly advanced history), mathematics, and physical and biological sciences. Honors work and advanced placement are opportunities for applicants to demonstrate intellectual maturity and curiosity, qualities highly favored in the admission process.

Application and Information

Colgate uses the Common Application form as its own. The closing date for regular applications is January 15, and notification is given by April 1. There is a $55 application fee, which can be waived if a student applies online. Candidates who decide on Colgate as a first choice may apply for early decision option I and complete an early decision agreement by November 15. Notification is mailed by December 15. Candidates who decide on Colgate as a first choice, apply by the January 15 deadline, and complete an early decision agreement will be considered on a rolling basis under option II. In addition, regular decision candidates may change their status to early decision by filing an early decision agreement prior to March 1. In both cases, notification is mailed within two to four weeks of receipt of the completed application. Accepted students are required to submit a $500 deposit by May 1 to ensure their place in the class.

Dean of Admission
Colgate University
Hamilton, New York 13346
Telephone: 315-228-7401
Fax: 315-228-7544
E-mail: admission@mail.colgate.edu
World Wide Web: http://www.colgate.edu

COLLEGE FOR CREATIVE STUDIES

DETROIT, MICHIGAN

The College

The College for Creative Studies (CCS) was established by the Detroit Society of Arts and Crafts. Founded in 1906, the society brought to Detroit exhibits by important artists from around the world. In 1916 it opened its first school, and in 1926 it was formally organized as the Art School of the Detroit Society of Arts and Crafts. The school began by offering course work in the fine arts; courses in crafts, advertising design, industrial design, and photography were added in the 1940s and 1950s. The general studies curriculum was introduced in 1961. The current enrollment is more than 1,200 men and women.

The school was granted membership in the National Association of Schools of Art and Design (NASAD) in 1972 and is accredited by the Higher Learning Commission of the North Central Association of Colleges and Schools. In 1975, the name of the school was changed to the Center for Creative Studies—College of Art and Design. The institution underwent another name change in 2001, becoming the College for Creative Studies. The new name better reflects the mission of the College: educating talented students to go out and shape the world.

The College is dedicated to providing an educational environment most conducive to the development of outstanding artists and designers. The teaching is directed not only toward developing technical excellence but also toward stimulating intellectual potential. Graduates are well prepared to join the professional world, have the overall ability to carry on their education as desired, are able to communicate effectively, and have a basic understanding of today's artistic, social, and intellectual world and its traditions.

Location

Situated within a 10½-acre complex of award-winning facilities, the College for Creative Studies is appropriately located in Detroit's Cultural Center. Twenty-eight major cultural and educational institutions are within easy walking distance. Students have full access to the Detroit Institute of Arts, one of the largest fine arts museums in the United States, and to the main branch of the Detroit Public Library, which possesses more than 2 million volumes. Other available facilities include the New Detroit Science Center, Detroit Children's Museum, Detroit Historical Museum, and the Charles H. Wright Museum of African American History.

Majors and Degrees

The College for Creative Studies offers a four-year program leading to the Bachelor of Fine Arts degree. Degrees can be earned in animation and digital media (concentrations: animation, character animation, digital cinema, and game), art education, communication design (concentrations: advertising design, graphic design, and interactive communication), crafts (concentrations: ceramics, fiber design, glass, and metalsmithing and jewelry design), fine arts (concentrations: painting, print media, and sculpture), illustration, industrial design (concentrations: furniture design, product design, and transportation design), interior design, and photography. Minors in art therapy and art history are also available. Interdisciplinary studies in crafts and fine arts are permitted upon departmental recommendation.

Academic Programs

The Bachelor of Fine Arts degree requires the completion of 126 credit hours: 84 in studio areas and 42 in general studies courses. All students are required to take core foundation course work in basic drawing, basic design, and figure drawing during their freshman year. They also begin work in their major department during the freshman year, or they may begin as an undeclared student. Typical weekly schedules for full-time students comprise 24 studio hours and 6 academic hours.

The Continuing Education Program permits individuals not pursuing a degree to enroll in daytime or evening classes in a broad array of high-quality programming in the visual arts. The Continuing Education Program also offers certificate programs designed for adults who are developing a new career, augmenting a current career, or seeking to expand their art or design skills. Once completed, these certificates acknowledge an individual's successful completion of a course of study.

Off-Campus Programs

Internships and independent study are available. Mobility programs, offered in cooperation with thirty-one other colleges in the Association of Independent Colleges of Art and Design (AICAD), allow students to take advantage of course offerings at other institutions while pursuing a degree at the College. In addition, seniors may study in a studio space in New York City to which CCS has access. Juniors and seniors also have the opportunity to spend a full year of study at an accredited institution abroad.

Academic Facilities

The College's instructional facilities total 597,039 square feet. The Kresge-Ford Building provides classrooms, studios, and workshops for painting, sculpture, printmaking, basic design, basic drawing and figure drawing, illustration, photography, and wood and metal working. The Yamasaki Building houses administrative offices and classrooms, studios, and workshops for ceramics, fabric design, glass, metals, and jewelry. The new 102,000-square-foot Walter B. Ford II Building houses the animation and digital media, communication design, industrial design, and interior design departments as well as computer labs and a 250-seat auditorium. Liberal arts courses are conducted in facilities located throughout the campus. The Academic Resource Center houses the library and Center Galleries, which encompasses the Main Gallery, the U245 Student Gallery, and the Alumni and Faculty Hall.

Costs

For 2004–05, tuition and fees are $21,376 for the academic year. Average charges for housing are $3500. The estimated cost of materials and supplies is $2000 in most fields of study.

Financial Aid

The College participates in the Federal Pell Grant, Federal Supplemental Educational Opportunity Grant, Federal Work-Study, Federal Stafford Student Loan, Michigan Tuition Grant, and Michigan Competitive Scholarship programs.

The College also awards scholarships, based on artistic ability and academic excellence, to currently enrolled and prospective students.

The College attempts to financially assist qualified students who apply, contingent upon the availability of funds.

Faculty

The College has 216 faculty members. All members of the studio art faculty are professionals in their individual fields who bring diverse backgrounds and experiences to the classroom.

Student Government

Students participate in the leadership of the school in several ways. The Student Coalition is composed of representatives from each department and takes an active role in areas affecting student life. The coalition works with the Student Programming Coordinator to organize dances and other events during the year. The coalition was active in the founding of U245, the student-run gallery, and continues to support its activities.

Admission Requirements

The Office of Admissions at the College for Creative Studies is dedicated to assisting students in evaluating educational alternatives and career possibilities in the visual arts. Applicants must have maintained a GPA of at least 2.5 in high school or successfully passed a high school equivalency examination and must submit SAT or ACT scores and a portfolio of representative work. Applicants who have had previous college experience are required to submit an official transcript from each institution attended. Personal interviews are available.

Application and Information

Applications for the fall term are accepted through August 1. Applications for the second semester should be submitted prior to December 1.

For application forms, catalogs, and additional information, students should contact:

Office of Admissions
College for Creative Studies
201 East Kirby
Detroit, Michigan 48202-4034
Telephone: 313-664-7425
800-952-ARTS (toll-free)
World Wide Web: http://www.ccscad.edu

The new Walter B. Ford II Building of the College for Creative Studies.

COLLEGE MISERICORDIA

DALLAS, PENNSYLVANIA

The College

College Misericordia is a high-quality liberal arts and professional studies institution. Founded by the Sisters of Mercy of Dallas, Misericordia offers undergraduate and graduate programs to resident and commuter students. Current enrollment is about 2,100 men and women; more than half the students range in age from 18 to 22 years old.

Misericordia provides an academic atmosphere designed to stimulate critical thinking, independent judgment, and creativity as well as encourage the development of curiosity, good study habits, and personal values. The College also cultivates a spirit of community service and a lifelong love of learning in its students through extracurricular activities and challenging academic programs. In the National Survey of Student Engagement and in surveys of freshmen by UCLA's Higher Education Research Institute, College Misericordia students have ranked the College in the top percentile in measures of student satisfaction.

The College is fully accredited by the Middle States Association of Colleges and Schools. Its programs in nursing, social work, radiography, occupational therapy, and physical therapy are accredited by the National League for Nursing Accrediting Commission, the Council on Social Work Education, the American Medical Association, the American Occupational Therapy Association, and the American Physical Therapy Association, respectively.

Misericordia operates three residential facilities and eighteen townhouse units with a total capacity for 700 students. Two special "theme" homes are reserved for students in leadership and service projects. Residents have a number of options, including single rooms and wellness housing, and students living in campus housing hold average GPAs of more than 3.2. Each residence hall offers study rooms, laundry facilities, and recreational lounges. The dining hall is located in the Banks Student Center, which also houses the Cougar's Den coffeehouse and snack bar.

There are numerous opportunities for students to become involved in campus activities. Besides Student Government, there are more than twenty-five chartered student clubs and organizations. Cultural events, Campus Ministry, intramural and intercollegiate athletic programs for men and women, performing arts shows, and many other social activities complement and reinforce the academic experience. In keeping with the College's tradition of mercy, justice, service, and hospitality, students also have opportunities to develop leadership potential through a variety of volunteer service projects that benefit the surrounding communities. The College's Service Leadership Center engages students in the development of lifelong civic responsibility through academic course work.

Campus Ministry provides opportunities to participate in campus and community programs. These programs are designed to promote social awareness in students. On spring break, students may elect to serve the poor in rural Appalachia or in the South Bronx. A six-week summer Cross-Cultural Ministry Experience in Guyana, South America, awaits selected participants.

Personalized attention is the key to the support available in the Learning Resource Center. A psychologist, counselors, therapists, and peer counselors form a dedicated team of professionals who conduct workshops for students each semester on a variety of topics, including test anxiety, stress management, time management, and goal setting. All services are free of charge to students, and contacts are strictly confidential.

First-year students may join the Guaranteed Placement Program through the Insalaco Center for Career Development. The program includes academic standards; cocurricular activities, such as leadership and service projects; internships; resume development; and interviewing skills. If a student fulfills the requirements of the program and is not employed in his or her field or enrolled in graduate or professional school within six months of graduation, a paid internship is assured. The center also co-presents the Choice Program, offering special guidance for students who have not chosen a major. Opportunities for career exploration, cooperative education, and internships are available for students to develop the knowledge and skills they need to enter the working world.

Student Health Services occupies a state-of-the-art facility. Healthcare staff members provide first aid, assessment and treatment of common illnesses, and referrals for more serious health conditions. Health center activities are directed by a registered nurse with a master's degree in nursing administration under the guidance of a physician. A nurse practitioner is also available. A self-care room offers reference materials and up-to-date information on personal health concerns. All services are confidential.

A rapidly evolving world and development of new technologies have increased the number of adults who seek higher education. Misericordia offers special undergraduate and graduate programs for adults, including the Expressway Program, an accelerated bachelor's degree program that is held at Luzerne County Community College; Women with Children, which provides housing and support services for single women with children; and evening and weekend formats for people with families and full-time jobs.

At College Misericordia, students can earn a master's degree by attending college classes in the evening and/or on weekends. The small-class format enhances critical thinking and decision-making skills and draws out a variety of viewpoints that help broaden the perspectives of the student. Master's degrees are available in education, nursing, occupational therapy, physical therapy, speech-language pathology, and organizational management.

Location

Located on a 120-acre campus in northeastern Pennsylvania, College Misericordia is the oldest institution of higher education in Luzerne County. Expansive lawns and thick stands of trees dominate the campus. It is 9 miles from the city of Wilkes-Barre. The area provides shopping centers, malls, cinemas, professional sporting events, and a variety of cultural activities. Pennsylvania's largest natural lake and two state parks are nearby, as are Pocono ski resorts. Metropolitan New York and Philadelphia are each within a 3-hour drive. Public and college-sponsored transportation is available to and from the campus.

Majors and Degrees

College Misericordia awards the Bachelor of Arts (B.A.) degree in English, history, and liberal studies. The Bachelor of Science (B.S.) degree is awarded in accounting, biochemistry, biology, business administration, chemistry, communications, computer science, elementary education, information technology, interdisciplinary studies, management, marketing, mathematics, math/computer science, medical imaging, medical technology, philosophy, professional studies, psychology, secondary education, special education, and sport management. A Bachelor of Science in Nursing (B.S.N.) is awarded to nursing majors, and a Bachelor of Science in Social Work (B.S.W.) is awarded to social work majors. Specializations in accounting, early childhood education, special education, pre-law, and preprofessional occupations are also available. Certification programs include addictions counseling, child welfare services, gerontology, new media, and secondary education and may be taken in support of several degrees offered by Misericordia or as stand-alone programs.

The College offers three 5-year majors in physical therapy, occupational therapy, and speech-language pathology. Students graduate with a master's degree in physical therapy, speech-language pathology, or occupational therapy and a bachelor's degree in health sciences.

Academic Program

Candidates for the B.A., B.S., B.S.N., or B.S.W. must fulfill a 48-credit liberal arts core curriculum in addition to the requirements of their chosen major to graduate. They must earn at least 36 credit hours in a chosen field. For regularly enrolled students, the average requirement for a baccalaureate degree is a total of 126 credits. Other options open to students include minors, specializations, certifications, and electives.

Courses are offered on a semester basis, beginning in August and January and ending in December and May. Summer, weekend, and accelerated courses are also available.

Academic Facilities

The chemistry, physics, and biology departments all have modern, fully equipped research laboratories available to students in these fields of concentration. State-of-the-art equipment includes high-performance liquid chromatography (HPLC), a rotary evaporator, an infrared spectrophotometer, and gas chromatography. The College also houses an energized radiation laboratory for the medical imaging program. The $5.5-million Anderson Sports and Health Center provides classrooms and laboratories for the occupational therapy, physical therapy, and nursing programs.

All residence halls are computer friendly and Internet ready. In addition, there are four main computer labs and a recently built "new media" lab for Web site development and multimedia. The Munson Center for Communications features the area's only all-digital television control room and editing bays, including the Avid nonlinear editing system. The Banks Student Center and Bevevino Library have more than 200 network access ports for Internet access. In 2003, the College introduced CM CENTRAL, a secure intranet portal where students can access e-mail, course schedules, group and chat functions, and student account and registration information from a single sign-on.

Mercy Hall, the College's original administrative building, underwent extensive renovations in 2002 with new multipurpose classrooms and facilities for the speech-language pathology program. In addition, many key student service departments, including the registrar, student accounts, and financial aid are now centralized in one area in Mercy Hall.

The three-story Bevevino Library covers 37,500 square feet and houses stacks for 90,000 volumes. Materials include state-of-the-art information and communication technology and a reference section that offers books, serials, and a variety of periodicals as well as reference search tools, CD-ROMs, and an electronic database and microfilm. The Bevevino Library is a member of the Northeastern Pennsylvania Library Network, which provides users access to the 1.5-million-volume collections of participating libraries via its new virtual online catalog.

Costs

Tuition for 2003–04 was $17,060 per year. The general fee was $830. The instructional technology fee (for full-time students) was $80. Housing options include traditional rooms, suites, town houses, and wellness housing. The average room cost was $4200. All resident students must participate in a meal plan. Residents may choose from a ten-, fourteen-, or nineteen-meal plan. In addition, townhouse residents are eligible to choose a five-meal plan. The average board cost was $3070.

Financial Aid

All students applying for financial aid must complete the Free Application for Federal Student Aid (FAFSA) by May 1. The application is used for Federal Pell Grants, Federal Supplemental Educational Opportunity Grants (FSEOG), Subsidized and Unsubsidized Stafford Loans, Perkins Loans, nursing loans, and Work-Study. This application is also the basis upon which state and institutional aid is awarded. The College also offers a no-interest monthly payment plan. In addition, many scholarships are available for qualified students, including $2.5 million in honors scholarships based on academic abilities and $4.2 million in McAuley Awards for students who have experience in leadership roles and volunteer service.

Faculty

There are approximately 184 teaching faculty members, 89 of whom are full-time. A student-faculty ratio of 14:1 results in students receiving a great deal of individual attention from a highly qualified faculty. Seventy-six percent of the faculty members hold doctorates. Besides student academic advising, the faculty members also serve as advisers to clubs.

Student Government

An active student government organization serves as a liaison between the students and the faculty and staff. The administration enables students to become involved by serving as student representatives on various college committees.

Admission Requirements

College Misericordia admits applicants based on their secondary school record, high school recommendation, extracurricular activities, and personal promise. The College requires SAT I or ACT scores. Although a personal interview is highly recommended, it is not necessary for all majors. Misericordia offers both early decision and early admissions programs.

Transfer students with a cumulative average of at least 2.0 (on a 4.0 scale) may be considered for admission and may receive advanced standing. Some majors require a 2.5 or higher cumulative average. Transfer students must submit official high school transcripts. A transcript of work completed at other colleges and universities and proof of honorable dismissal are also required.

Application and Information

Applicants must submit an official application form (available upon request), transcripts, and SAT I or ACT scores. Applicants may also apply for admission on line at the Web address listed below. There is a nonrefundable application fee of $25, which is waived for students who visit the campus.

The College considers applications on a rolling basis. Usually, candidates are notified of the admission decision within three weeks of receipt of all required materials.

Office of Admissions
College Misericordia
Dallas, Pennsylvania 18612-1090
Telephone: 570-675-4449
866-CM-AND-ME (866-262-6363, toll free)
Fax: 570-674-6232
E-mail: admiss@misericordia.edu
World Wide Web: http://www.misericordia.edu

Students at College Misericordia pursue their studies with an emphasis on academic excellence, service leadership, and professional preparation.

COLLEGE OF BIBLICAL STUDIES–HOUSTON

HOUSTON, TEXAS

The College

The College of Biblical Studies–Houston (CBS), formerly Houston Bible Institute, began as a burden in the heart of the late Rev. Ernest L. Mays, the founder of Houston Bible Institute. He sensed that large segments of the local Christian community were functioning without trained leaders. This was especially true within the inner-city minority groups. Out of this concern, Houston Bible and Vocational Institute was incorporated in 1976. A multiracial, interdenominational board of trustees was formed, and it began working to make the school a reality. Within a short time, a decision was made to focus on biblical and theological training because adequate resources for vocational training were already available in the area. In fall 1979, the first classes in Bible studies and theology were offered using the facilities of KHCB-FM, a Houston-based Christian radio network. Sixty-five students took courses that first semester.

The school has offered classes each semester since then and has grown to become the largest nationally accredited, multiethnic Bible college in the United States and Canada. Its mission is to provide college-level Bible education and biblically based general education for the body of Christ, with primary focus on African Americans and other ethnic minority groups, and to equip its students with a biblical worldview for ministry in and for the church and the world. CBS provides college-level training in Bible studies and theology for those individuals who have had little or no opportunity to receive such training by conventional means.

A commuter college, CBS is unique in several ways. First, instruction is provided six days a week, offering morning, afternoon, evening, and Saturday classes so that students can fit education into their life schedules without leaving their responsibilities in order to take classes, sharpen their ministerial skills, and pursue or finish a college degree. Second, tuition is kept low to broaden access to college education. Third, to enhance educational opportunities, instruction is offered utilizing both traditional and nontraditional methods. And, finally, all constituencies of the College consider its multiracial cultures and ethnicities an enriching and valuable strength in the educational process. The institutional philosophy is based on the biblical Scripture, 1 Timothy 1:5: the goal of the College's instruction is to love from a pure heart and a good conscience and a sincere faith. Its vision is to develop Christian leaders to serve a multiethnic community.

The College of Biblical Studies–Houston is denominationally unrelated and routinely has student representation from twenty-five to thirty-five different denominations. The College seeks to serve those individuals and churches of like biblical faith and welcomes to its student body qualified persons who are in general agreement with the school's doctrinal position. The College has historically held to a defined doctrinal statement and has a hermeneutical position defined as dispensational, premillennial, and pretribulational in form. The College of Biblical Studies–Houston (a private, not-for-profit, 501(c)3 corporation organized under the laws of Texas) is accredited by the Accrediting Association of Bible Colleges (AABC), a national accrediting body recognized by the Council for Higher Education Accreditation (CHEA), the U.S. Department of Education, and the Texas Higher Education Coordinating Board.

Thousands of students from the diverse Christian community, primarily adults attending classes part-time, commute weekly from all areas of the greater Houston metroplex. The school's trustees and faculty and staff members are multiethnic; the student body (51 percent women, 49 percent men) is composed of African-American, other black, Caucasian, Asian and more than twelve different Hispanic cultures. The school offers its educational programs through three 15-week terms: fall, spring, and summer. The majority of the student body is older than 35, married with a family, and working full-time. Ninety-five percent serve in Christian ministry. For some, CBS is their first college experience; many others have earned college credits at secular colleges and universities but have not had the opportunity to complete a college degree. Other students already have an earned vocational/professional undergraduate or graduate degree. No matter what their higher education background, all of the students come to make an in-depth, college-level, systematic study of the Scripture.

Location

CBS is located on approximately 10 acres in urban southwest Houston, two blocks off U.S. 59 at Hillcroft Street, in the Regency Square business complex. The Houston Metro bus system provides service to the area as well as close access to the Interstate 610 inner Loop and Beltway 8 outer Loop freeway systems surrounding the city.

Majors and Degrees

The College of Biblical Studies awards three Bachelor of Science degrees, all of them done in an accelerated degree completion program format: Bachelor of Science in leadership, Bachelor of Science in Christian ministry, and Bachelor of Science in biblical counseling. The first two baccalaureate programs require 120 credit hours composed of 36 hours of approved general education, 36 hours of approved general electives, and 48 hours of the CBS core curriculum. The Bachelor of Science in biblical counseling requires 123 credit hours. The College also awards the Associate of Biblical Studies degree and a Bible certificate in traditional program format (available in both an English- and a Spanish-language program).

Academic Program

The academic year consists of three full fifteen-week semesters during which 1-, 2-, and 3-credit-hour courses are offered (some flex-entry) for students in the 64-credit-hour associate degree and 32-credit-hour Bible certificate programs as well as non-degree-seeking students taking classes for personal enrichment. Typically, four new study groups in the 120-credit-hour accelerated bachelor's degree completion program begin two to three months apart each year, with the program continuing for a twenty- to twenty-two-month period.

Academic Facilities

The College library supports all of the College programs and offers opportunities for research, including online and CD-ROM resources.

Costs

Tuition is $85 per credit hour, with a $6-per-credit-hour library fee and a $20-per-term fee for lower-division courses in English. There is a flat rate of $50 per course for credit courses in Spanish. A full-time student in the English Bible certificate or Associate of Biblical Studies degree programs pays approximately $985 per term, including fees but excluding textbooks. A full-time student in the Spanish-speaking Bible certificate degree program pays $600 per term, not including textbooks. Tuition and program fees for the accelerated bachelor's degree completion program is $8000 ($8500 for the Bachelor of Science in biblical counseling option), with additional fees for installment or deferred-payment plans. The textbooks for this program average $1000 over the course of the twenty- to twenty-two-month period.

Financial Aid

The College has several scholarship offerings, including a new-student introductory scholarship for their first class, MS 401 Bible Study Methods. To qualify for any of the federal financial aid programs, the student must demonstrate financial need by submitting the Free Application for Federal Student Aid to the Financial Aid Office, and the student must be enrolled as a regular student in a baccalaureate program. The amount of aid disbursed from a federal program cannot exceed the cost of education. The educational programs have been approved by the Texas Workforce Commission, pursuant to 38 CFR 21.4253 for veteran education benefits.

Faculty

The instructional faculty for all divisions numbers 50 members, of whom 16 are full-time. Thirty-eight percent of the full-time faculty members hold doctoral degrees, and 30 percent of all faculty members have doctorates.

The student-faculty ratio is 22:1, and the average class size is 22 students.

Admission Requirements

CBS seeks to admit students who have a personal relationship with the Lord Jesus Christ.

Along with their application for admission, prospective students must submit a written testimony, telling when and how they became a Christian. The applicant must show evidence of being apprised of the doctrinal position of the College. A high school education or its equivalent is required. Demonstrated ability to benefit from college-level instruction is required of applicants seeking admission who are not high school graduates. General admission to CBS does not guarantee admission to all programs. Applicants must be able to fulfill the academic demands of college-level instruction as well as comply with individual program requirements.

The College of Biblical Studies considers itself a Christian ministry within Houston's multiethnic community. CBS does not discriminate against any qualified person on grounds of race, color, national or ethnic origin, age, sex, or because an otherwise qualified person is handicapped. This policy applies to all student admissions, academic policies, scholarships, and other school-administered programs, with noted exceptions.

Application and Information

To be considered for general admission, a student must first submit a completed application for admission and evidence of their highest educational achievement. An application and additional information may be obtained by contacting:

Office of Admissions
College of Biblical Studies–Houston
7000 Regency Square Boulevard, Suite 110
Houston, Texas 77036-3211

Telephone: 713-785-5995
Fax: 713-785-5998
E-mail: cbs@cbshouston.edu
World Wide Web: http://www.cbshouston.edu

THE COLLEGE OF MOUNT ST. JOSEPH

CINCINNATI, OHIO

The College

As a private liberal arts college founded in 1920, the College of Mount St. Joseph has a rich history of preparing students for the future. Today, the Mount is a coeducational college with more than 2,000 students, offering an outstanding liberal arts curriculum that emphasizes values, integrity, and social responsibility, as well as practical career preparation. Required courses in humanities, science, and the arts are complemented by opportunities for cooperative work experience, a universal computing requirement, specialized and professionally oriented courses, and extracurricular opportunities, which give students the broad-based background that is in high demand among employers.

Catholic in tradition, the Mount emphasizes a value-centered education and supports the personal growth of each student. A warm, close-knit campus community encourages students to exercise their talents to their fullest potential in academic, athletic, and leadership activities. Mount students come primarily from the Midwest, but many other regions of the United States and nearly fifteen countries are also represented. Spacious rooms are available in Seton Center Residence Hall. Resident students may keep cars on campus.

The College is accredited by the North Central Association of Colleges and Schools.

Campus organizations include the student government, student newspaper, academic honor societies, international club, departmental clubs, marching and concert band, chamber singers, and intramural athletics. The Mount offers a full intercollegiate athletics program in the NCAA Division III for men and women and is a member of the Heartland Collegiate Athletic Conference (HCAC). Women's programs include basketball, cross-country, golf, soccer, softball, tennis, track and field, and volleyball. For men, there are baseball, basketball, cross-country, football, golf, tennis, track and field, and wrestling.

Location

Located just 10 minutes from downtown Cincinnati, the College sits on a beautiful, 75-acre suburban campus overlooking the Ohio River. The campus is easily accessible from the airport, bus terminal, railway station, and interstate. Well known for its scenic and rolling hills, greater Cincinnati offers numerous parks, cultural and arts events, professional athletics, shopping areas, and a wide assortment of fine restaurants. In addition to their own on-campus activities, Mount students frequently participate in social and service activities with students from other area colleges.

Majors and Degrees

The College of Mount St. Joseph awards bachelor's degrees in the following areas: accounting, art, art education, athletic training, biological chemistry, biology, business administration, chemistry, chemistry/mathematics, communication studies, computer information systems, computer science with minor in math, education (early childhood, middle childhood, physical education, and special education), English, fine arts, gerontological studies, graphic design, history, interior design, liberal arts and sciences, mathematics, mathematics/chemistry, medical technology, music, natural history, natural science with biology or chemistry concentration, nursing, paralegal studies, paralegal studies for nurses, psychology, recreational therapy, rehabilitation science, religious education, religious pastoral ministry, religious studies, social work, and sociology.

Associate degrees are offered in accounting, art, business administration, communication arts, computer information systems, gerontological studies, graphic design, interior design, and paralegal studies.

Certificate programs are offered in gerontological studies, graphic design, interior design, paralegal studies, paralegal studies for nurses, and parish nurse/health ministries.

For state of Ohio licensure in education, the Mount offers programs in inclusive early childhood, middle childhood, adolescent and young adults, multiage, and intervention specialist/special education. Licensure programs in other states are also available.

Preprofessional programs are available in allied medical professions, law, and medicine.

Academic Programs

All majors are backed by a strong liberal arts curriculum that encourages students to develop skills in analytical thinking, problem solving, decision making, and communication. Students must earn 128 credit hours for a bachelor's degree, with 52 of those credits from the liberal arts and science core. For an associate degree, students must earn 64 credit hours, with 27–28 of those credits from the liberal arts and science core.

The academic year consists of fall and spring semesters and three summer terms, with classes offered in day, evening, or weekend time frames.

The Mount offers a highly respected Cooperative Education program, making available to students the benefits of hands-on work experience within their field of study as early as the second semester of their sophomore year. In addition to the financial advantage of being able to work through college, a student can also make the personal contacts that are so important in professional experiences. Students can also gain practical experience and career development before graduation through participation in programs such as the Kaleidoscope of Careers, Career Advising, e-recruiting, and on-campus recruiting.

Project EXCEL is a special program that offers tutorial services, audiotapes of textbooks, and self-instructional materials for students with learning disabilities. Students learn skills that facilitate success in the college environment. Project EXCEL carries an additional fee for testing and for services while in the program. Interested students must apply for admission through Project EXCEL.

The Mount's Academic Performance Center is a centralized system of support for the enhancement of students' academic skills. It encompasses a Math Center, Peer Tutoring Program, COMPASS testing, makeup testing, Skills and Reading Center, Listening Lab, instructional software, courses in basic academic skills, and academic support for students with disabilities.

Off-Campus Programs

Opportunities are available to study abroad in Heidelberg, Germany, through the Congress/Bundestag program; in London, England, at Thames Valley College and through the

Mount's affiliation with Huron University; and in Seville, Spain, through the Spanish American Institute.

Academic Facilities

The Mount's campus features modern buildings with state-of-the-art learning facilities. The Computer Learning Center offers all students access to IBM and Macintosh systems, supporting more than 500 different software packages. Students in the nursing department have access to on-campus laboratories and benefit from the department's relationship with nearby hospitals of outstanding quality and reputation.

The Harrington Center offers space for clubs and organizations and is home to the campus bookstore, food court, and entertainment center. Other recreation facilities include a running track, racquetball courts, a fitness center, a 2,000-seat gymnasium, and an athletic training center. A beautiful College theater seats more than 1,000 people.

Costs

For the 2003–04 academic year, tuition was $16,000 and room and board were $5990 (based on a semiprivate room and the fifteen-meals-per-week plan, with $150 flex dollars to use at the food court). The College offers private and semiprivate housing accommodations and a variety of meal plans. There are a $70 activities fee per semester and a technology fee of $450 per semester, which provides students with a wireless laptop/learning environment to use during their years at the Mount. The cost of books varies depending on course load and major.

Financial Aid

The College of Mount St. Joseph assists as many students as possible who require financial aid. About 94 percent of full-time undergraduate students receive some form of assistance, usually as federal, state, or College grants; work-study awards; and loans. In addition, part-time employment may be available in the metropolitan area for those students with transportation. The Mount offers academic scholarship programs in the areas of scholastic achievement and leadership based on merit or on a combination of merit and need.

Students who wish to apply for financial aid must complete, by April 15, the Free Application for Federal Student Aid (FAFSA). Most scholarships are awarded on a rolling basis. Interested students should inquire as early in their senior year as possible.

Faculty

Because the Mount is a small liberal arts college, the faculty's focus is on teaching. Many faculty members have been recognized regionally and nationally for their research and expertise outside the classroom as well as for their contributions as teachers, particularly in the fields of art, science, math, sociology, and education. The student-faculty ratio of 15:1 encourages personal interaction between students and professors.

Student Government

All matriculated students at the College of Mount St. Joseph are members of the Student Government Association (SGA). The SGA represents and serves as the voice of the entire student body. It strives to help students understand their rights, privileges, and responsibilities and to maintain effective communication among the students, faculty and staff members, and administration.

One of the functions of the SGA is that of appointing students to serve on various College committees to represent the common values of the Mount students and to participate in College government. The SGA works toward avoiding conflict by assisting with developing campus policies that directly affect student life.

The SGA supports and monitors all student club activities and functions through the Fiscal Committee. There are many opportunities for interested students to participate in SGA-sponsored programs and activities, including Campus Fair, movies, dances, fund-raising events, and community service activities.

A Student Affairs staff member serves as the adviser to the SGA.

Admission Requirements

Admission decisions are based on high school course selection, ACT or SAT scores, class rank, and grade point average. The College requires 4 units of English, 2 of math (algebra and geometry), 2 of social studies, 2 of science, 2 of foreign language, and 1 of fine arts. Two electives from the areas listed above may be substituted for foreign language. Students are encouraged to submit recommendation letters and personal essays.

Application and Information

Decisions on offers of admission are generally made within two weeks of the date the file is complete. The application fee is $25; the Project EXCEL fee is $60. Application fees are nonrefundable and do not apply toward tuition. Students who want to know more about the Mount may arrange a visit by contacting the Office of Admission. In addition to scheduling individual appointments, the College holds Get Acquainted Days throughout the year, giving students the opportunity to visit the campus, explore academic programs, and take a tour.

Office of Admission
College of Mount St. Joseph
5701 Delhi Road
Cincinnati, Ohio 45233-1672
Telephone: 513-244-4531
800-654-9314 (toll-free)
World Wide Web: http://www.msj.edu/admissions

The College of Mount St. Joseph provides a liberal arts and professional education that integrates life and learning while embracing excellence, respect, diversity, and service.

COLLEGE OF MOUNT SAINT VINCENT

RIVERDALE, NEW YORK

The College

The College of Mount Saint Vincent, a four-year, coeducational, liberal arts college, is a private, independent institution in a public trust. Founded as an academy by the Sisters of Charity of New York in 1847, it introduced postgraduate courses in the late 1800s and in 1910 expanded into a four-year college. It has been coeducational since 1974. The College currently enrolls students from sixteen states and twelve countries. About 50 percent of the students live on campus, although married students are required to live off campus. The current full-time undergraduate enrollment is more than 1,000 men and women.

Career counseling, personal counseling, and health services are available to all students. The Cahill Lounge features live entertainment and numerous student social events. Recognized campus organizations and Student Government committees sponsor a full calendar of events, including formal and informal dances and professional entertainment. Other groups include CAST (Culturally Aware Students of Today), CMSV Chorus, CMSV Players, Circle K, and the Student Nursing Association. Students can gain experience in broadcasting by participating in the work of the campus TV and radio stations, WMSV. Journalists are needed for College publications, such as the *MounTimes* (biweekly), *Fonthill Dial* (semiannual), and *Parapet* (annual). Fifteen academic honor societies have chapters on campus. Cyclists and joggers make good use of the picturesque campus. Facilities for athletics include a gymnasium, a state-of-the-art Fitness Center and Health Lounge, a 60-foot swimming pool, racquetball and tennis courts, a weight room, and a dance studio.

Varsity sports include women's and men's basketball, cross-country, lacrosse, soccer, tennis, and volleyball; men's baseball; and women's softball, swimming, and track. There is also an intramural sports program. The College is an active member of the National Collegiate Athletic Association (NCAA) and the Eastern College Athletic Conference (ECAC) on the Division III level.

Mount Saint Vincent students are involved in a wide variety of children's recreation programs and other voluntary community service projects, including tutoring, work in hospitals and senior citizens' homes, and participation in political campaigns. Many cultural programs sponsored by the College are extended to the surrounding community.

The College offers three graduate degree programs: the Master of Science degree in allied health studies, nursing, and teacher education.

The graduate allied health studies program offers six concentrations: addictions, child and family health, community health education, counseling, health-care management, and health-care systems and policy. This unique major is rooted in health psychology. It allows students with baccalaureates in diverse disciplines to pursue a career-oriented program that enables them to work in health-related settings, including positions in hospitals, clinics, private practices, health maintenance organizations, and pain clinics.

The graduate nursing program offers four programs of study: addictions nursing, nursing administration, adult nurse practitioner, and nursing of the adult and aged. These programs prepare nurses for the complex decision-making process necessary in today's health-care environment by incorporating three graduate business courses into their curriculum. A registered nurse license and baccalaureate degree in nursing are required for application.

The graduate program in teacher education is a Master of Science in urban/multicultural education. It is a values-centered program reflecting the belief that learning and culture are inseparable, as are relationships among learner, teacher, environment, and purpose for learning. A bachelor's degree and a provisional teaching certificate are required for application. Those who are in need of provisional certification can apply for the SPAN program and enter the master's program upon completion. In addition, a five-year combined bachelor's and master's program is available.

Location

The campus of Mount Saint Vincent encompasses 70 acres of beautiful rolling lawns, stone walls, wooded fields, and several buildings designated as landmarks of the city of New York. The campus is 11 miles from mid-Manhattan; this proximity offers unlimited cultural, social, and academic opportunities to students, all within a short bus or subway ride.

Majors and Degrees

The Bachelor of Arts is granted in biochemistry, biology, business, chemistry, communication, computer science, economics, English, French, health and human services, history, liberal arts, mathematics, modern foreign languages, psychology, sociology, and Spanish. The Bachelor of Science is conferred in biochemistry, biology, business, chemistry, computer science, health and human services, health education, mathematics, nursing and psychology. Students can pursue minors in creative writing, fine arts, and performance arts. Through a cooperative program with Manhattan College, CMSV students may also earn a B.A. in American studies, international studies, philosophy, physical education, political science, religious studies, or urban affairs or a B.S. in physics.

The Department of Teacher Education offers programs for prospective teachers of grades pre-K through 12. In addition to the B.A. and B.S. degrees, these programs lead to provisional New York State certification, which qualifies many out-of-state residents to apply for certification in their home states under the terms of the Interstate Agreement on Qualification of Educational Personnel. Concentrations in learning disabilities and the emotionally handicapped are also offered in addition to the majors in health and human services and physical education. Dual certification is available in special education and elementary education and in special education and secondary education. Certification is also available in biology, French, Spanish, English, mathematics, physics, chemistry, and social studies (grades 5–6 and 7–12) and in health education and special education (grades K–12).

Certificate programs are offered in addiction studies, adult nurse practitioner studies, nurse case management, and school nurse studies.

Academic Programs

The regular academic year is divided into two semesters, with intersessions in January and May. Three summer sessions are held during the months of May, June, and July. A core curriculum provides a foundation of knowledge for Mount Saint Vincent students, who also benefit from taking the core courses with fellow students all through their four years, regardless of individual majors. The core consists of foundation courses (generally in the freshman and sophomore years), area courses (by the junior year), and enrichment courses (in the junior and senior years).

Candidates for the B.A. must earn 120 credits, and candidates for the B.S. must earn 126 credits, distributed in accordance with the requirements of the curriculum pursued. Of the required credits, 54 are in the core curriculum, and at least 30 must be in the major field. The selection of courses for the remaining credits is planned, with guidance from the student's academic adviser, according to the student's aims and interests. Students who are preparing to teach after graduation follow a program outlined by the Department of Teacher Education.

Special curricular features include the January intersession; an interdisciplinary program in international business and economics; preprofessional programs in dentistry, law, medicine, occupational therapy, and physical therapy; the interdisciplinary liberal arts major, which allows students to tailor an individualized program combining two or three fields of study; and a College honors program as well as one in most academic areas. The College has an extensive internship program that enables students to combine course work with practical, job-related experience. There are more than 500 organizations currently participating in the College's internship program throughout the tristate area.

Off-Campus Programs

The College of Mount Saint Vincent has developed a cooperative agreement with nearby Manhattan College that allows both colleges to broaden their educational opportunities through the sharing of facilities, programs of study, and professional faculties. The College of Mount Saint Vincent also participates in the New York State Visiting Student Program and in international study programs in Austria, England, France, Germany, Italy, Spain, and Switzerland.

Academic Facilities

The library contains more than 170,000 volumes, 616 current periodical subscriptions, 9,850 microfilms, and 6,150 audiovisual units (recordings, films, and cassettes). Other facilities include the Audiovisual Center, the Special Collections room, a radio station, a video studio, a television studio, a small theater, a computer graphics center, and the Curriculum Center. The library has access via computer to bibliographic information in libraries across the country. The three-story Science Hall, which houses the joined biology department of Mount Saint Vincent and Manhattan College, contains well-equipped laboratories, a lecture hall, classrooms, darkrooms, and environmental research facilities. In the Administration Building are the Academic Resource Center and the Writing Center, open to all students needing academic assistance; a ceramics studio; photography studio; language lab; snack bar; bookstore; and a computer center, housing two classrooms equipped with full multimedia Pentium computers with access to the Internet and e-mail. These classrooms serve as open labs when classes are not in session. In addition to these computer facilities, there are also satellite computer labs with Internet and e-mail access in the biology, business, communication, nursing, and psychology departments that are available to all students on a limited basis.

Costs

Tuition for the 2002–03 year was $17,880; room and board were $7550. The motor vehicle registration fee ranges from $75 to $130 per year, depending on the parking lot the student selects. The cost of books, supplies, and personal items is approximately $1000.

Financial Aid

The College awards Academic Scholarships and federal, state, and institutional financial aid. Academic scholarships range from $6000 to $14,000. To apply for any scholarship or grant, students must have a completed application for admission on file with the Admissions Office by February 1 for freshman applicants. Freshman applicants should submit the Free Application for Federal Student Aid (FAFSA) by March 15; transfer applicants should submit the FAFSA by June 15. In addition to providing College scholarships, including the Corazón C. Aquino Scholarships, Mount Saint Vincent participates in all available federal and state programs of financial assistance, including Federal Pell Grants, Federal Supplemental Educational Opportunity Grants, Federal Work-Study awards, federal and New York State student loans, and New York State Tuition Assistance Program (TAP) awards. Eligibility for these programs is based on need. More than 90 percent of the students at Mount Saint Vincent receive aid from government or private agencies.

Faculty

The faculty is composed of 70 full-time and 89 part-time members who, in addition to their teaching responsibilities, act as academic advisers and moderate student activities. The student-faculty ratio is approximately 12:1. Of the full-time faculty members, 81 percent hold terminal degrees in their fields.

Student Government

Students participate in College governance through a strong Student Government with elected representatives on most major governing bodies of the College, including the College Senate, the Undergraduate and Graduate Committee, the Policies and Procedures Council, the Orientation Committee, and the Commencement Committee. Student Government leaders meet regularly with members of the Board of Trustees and make most decisions regarding the disbursement of student activities fees and budgeted funds for clubs and organizations. Students also play a central role in discipline through an elected Student Judicial Council. This constitutionally ensured involvement guarantees that students have direct access to information and multiple opportunities to present student views and articulate student needs to both faculty and administrators.

Admission Requirements

Applicants to the College of Mount Saint Vincent must have graduated from an accredited secondary school or possess a high school equivalency diploma, should rank in the upper half of their class, and must achieve satisfactory scores on the SAT I, ACT, or TOEFL. International students who qualify for admission are welcome. Students attending a community college or another four-year college may apply for admission with advanced standing. Qualified students may enter the College after three years of high school, either as accelerated candidates or as early admission freshmen. It is strongly recommended that prospective students telephone or write for an interview and tour. Students may apply online.

Application and Information

In order to be evaluated for admission, a candidate must present the following: a nonrefundable application fee of $35; a completed application; scores on the SAT I, ACT, or TOEFL; an essay; a letter of recommendation; and a high school transcript. Transfer applicants should submit all college transcripts. Students have the option of applying online at the Web address below.

The Admission Committee operates on a rolling admission basis. Decisions on regular admission are mailed shortly after December 15. Scholarship award letters are mailed within two weeks following decision letters. Students applying under the early action plan should do so before November 15. Recommended transfer application guidelines are June 1 for fall and December 1 for spring.

Information, brochures, and application forms for admission and financial aid may be obtained by contacting:

Timothy P. Nash
Dean of Admission and Financial Aid
College of Mount Saint Vincent
6301 Riverdale Avenue
Riverdale, New York 10471-1093

Telephone: 718-405-3267
800-665-CMSV (toll-free)
E-mail: admission.office@mountsaintvincent.edu
World Wide Web: http://www.mountsaintvincent.edu

THE COLLEGE OF NEW JERSEY

EWING TOWNSHIP, NEW JERSEY

The College

The College of New Jersey (TCNJ) welcomes students who have the talent and motivation to succeed in a rigorous academic environment. A public institution founded in 1855, the College enrolls about 5,700 full-time undergraduates, two thirds of whom reside on campus. Today it is one of the most competitive schools in the nation, public or private, and serves a diverse student body, preparing graduates to be leaders in their chosen fields.

Students report they find TCNJ large enough to provide a full range of academic and extracurricular choices, yet small enough to be a genuine residential community of friends and fellow learners. With professors easily available in and out of class and facilities of enviable quality, TCNJ today represents an exceptional value in higher education.

The College of New Jersey's academic approach combines those of both traditional liberal arts schools and professional schools. A liberal learning curriculum ensures that all students are grounded in the beliefs and values of a civic responsibility and intellectual and scholarly growth and that they receive a well-rounded education in the liberal arts. Interdisciplinary studies, internships, research, and faculty mentoring all are part of an educational approach designed to produce successful leaders. While a very high percentage of graduates find immediate employment related to their fields of study, more than 20 percent go directly into graduate schools across the country.

All first- and second-year students are guaranteed on-campus housing, and most juniors and seniors continue to live on campus. Rooming arrangements are quite flexible, from doubles in freshman residence halls to suites and single rooms in campus town houses or apartments for upperclass students. A nationally recognized residence life program and more than 150 student organizations offer numerous opportunities for friendship, personal growth, and leadership. An exceptional 96 percent of first-year students return for their sophomore year.

The arts flourish in two theaters, a recital hall, an art gallery, and numerous other campus venues. Student performances, professional groups on tour, and a large variety of films, lectures, local bands, and solo entertainers fill the academic year with cultural options—many of them free, the rest at low cost.

Student wellness has a high priority, with many facilities for recreation and physical conditioning. Most first-year students have a fitness room in their residence hall. In Packer Hall, the campus has access to a larger fitness center, a 25-meter swimming and diving pool, and a basketball court. The Student Recreation Center offers racquetball courts, four tennis courts that are convertible to basketball or volleyball use, a weight room, and an indoor track. Other facilities include a lighted Astroturf field, eight lighted outdoor tennis courts, an outdoor "beach" volleyball court, and numerous athletic fields.

As a Division III member of the National Collegiate Athletic Association, TCNJ offers twenty-one sports: eleven for men and ten for women. Since 1979, TCNJ student-athletes have amassed thirty-six national championships and twenty-nine runner-up awards, more than any other Division III institution in the country. In addition to its NCAA athletics, TCNJ offers a wide variety of recreation programs for intramural competition and self-governing sports clubs. More than 3,500 students play with these less demanding, but spirited and competitive teams, each year, some of which have intercollegiate schedules.

The College's undergraduate programs are accredited by the Middle States Association of Colleges and Schools and by professional associations in engineering, nursing, chemistry, music, education, education of the deaf, computer science, and business.

Location

The College of New Jersey is set on 289 acres in suburban Ewing Township, 5 miles from the state capital of Trenton. Woodlands and lakes surround the thirty-nine major academic and residential buildings. The campus is 30 miles from the theaters and museums of Philadelphia and 60 miles from those in New York City. Nearby Princeton and Bucks County, Pennsylvania, offer additional cultural activities.

Majors and Degrees

The College of New Jersey offers programs leading to the Bachelor of Arts, Bachelor of Fine Arts, Bachelor of Music, Bachelor of Science, and Bachelor of Science in Nursing degrees. The B.A. is awarded in art education; art history; communication studies; economics; English, including journalism and professional writing options; history; interactive multimedia; international studies; mathematics and statistics; philosophy; political science; psychology; sociology; Spanish; and women's and gender studies. The B.F.A. is awarded in digital arts, and fine art and graphic design. The B.M. is awarded in music (performance and education). The B.S. is granted in accountancy, biology, biomedical engineering, business administration (finance, general business, information systems management, international business, management, and marketing), chemistry, computer engineering, computer science, early childhood education, economics, education for the hearing-impaired, electrical engineering, elementary education, engineering science, health and physical education, law and justice, mechanical engineering, physics, special education, and technology education. Teacher preparation is available in many arts and science majors.

TCNJ offers a five-year combined Master of Arts in Teaching degree with dual certification in deaf and hard-of-hearing and elementary education. Students may also enroll in a seven-year B.S./M.D. degree program with UMDNJ—New Jersey Medical School (Newark) or a seven-year B.S./O.D. degree program with the State University of New York College of Optometry. Students may apply to TCNJ for a 4½-year combined B.S./M.A. program in law and justice with Rutgers, The State University of New Jersey (Newark). The College also offers a Medical Careers Advisory Committee for premed students and a Pre-Law Advisement Committee for students planning a career in law.

Academic Programs

In fall 2004, the College completed a transformation of its curriculum, requiring fewer, more in-depth courses. All courses contain a significant out-of-class requirement and provide for even more student-faculty interaction. All baccalaureate degrees require at least 32 courses including a core curriculum in the traditional arts and sciences.

The thirty-week year is divided into fall and spring semesters; the summer session offers courses in two 5-week sessions and one 6-week session. The average class size for freshman-level lectures is 24 students and for upper-division lectures, 22 students.

All first-year students participate in a program linking residential learning in small classes taught by full-time faculty members. Seminars, independent studies, and capstone courses give many students the opportunity for challenging advanced study in close collaboration with faculty members. TCNJ students publish the results of these endeavors or present them at national and regional conferences.

The honors program offers students the particularly challenging academic experiences that allow normal progress toward the degree. Whenever possible, honors courses have an interdisciplinary perspective and curriculum, concentrating on central themes within significant periods in the cultural development of civilization. Honors courses in the major consist of either specially designated sections or independent study. All honors classes are small, personal, and stimulating.

Off-Campus Programs

TCNJ offers students a variety of full-year and one-semester programs of study abroad as well as study at other state colleges and universities within the United States. Exchange programs are available in Australia, Austria, Canada, Denmark, France, Germany, Greece, Israel, Japan, Mexico, the United Kingdom, and twenty-three other countries. National exchanges are available at more than 130 participating institutions in the United States, the U.S. Virgin Islands, Puerto Rico, and Guam. The College of New Jersey hosts the New Jersey State Consortium for International Studies.

Academic Facilities

Supporting the efforts of students and faculty members are the Roscoe L. West Library, housing more than 500,000 volumes and receiving 1,563 periodical subscriptions; the media center; and a full range of laboratories to serve scientific, technological, and professional studies. Campuswide networking provides full Internet accessibility from all residence hall rooms and more than twenty student computing laboratories.

Costs

Costs are relatively low because of state funding. For 2003–04, full-time undergraduate tuition and fees were $8201 for New Jersey residents and $12,776 for out-of-state students. Room and board charges for the academic year, with a middle meal plan, averaged $7744.

Financial Aid

Approximately half of the full-time undergraduates receive some form of financial aid, such as federal, state, and institutional grants; merit scholarships; student employment; and loan assistance. The Free Application for Federal Student Aid (FAFSA) or Renewal FAFSA is used to apply for all types of aid.

Scholarships and grants include the College of New Jersey Merit Scholars Program, the New Jersey Outstanding Scholars Recruitment Program, the New Jersey Edward J. Bloustein Distinguished Scholars Program, the New Jersey Tuition Aid Grant, Federal Pell Grants, Federal Supplemental Educational Opportunity Grants (FSEOG), Educational Opportunity Fund (EOF), and Army and Air Force ROTC Scholarships, as well as other institutional scholarships. Loans include the Federal Subsidized and Unsubsidized Stafford Loans, the Federal Perkins Loan, the Federal Parent Loan for Undergraduate Students (PLUS), the New Jersey CLASS Loan, nursing loans, and short-term emergency loan funds. Student employment options include the need-based Federal–Work Study Program (on- and off-campus positions) as well as institutionally supported campus jobs.

Faculty

The approximately 335 full-time members of the College of New Jersey faculty are teachers and scholars. While teaching is their primary commitment, they are also active researchers, authors, artists, performers, and regular contributors in their academic disciplines. No classes are taught by graduate assistants. The student-faculty ratio is 12:1. From their first day, students study with faculty members who may be researching new ways to use solar energy; writing a new text, play, or novel; or investigating the life cycle of desert ferns. Members of the faculty have attracted many significant grants, fellowships, and awards, including the Bancroft Prize in history, Fulbright Scholarships, and grants from the National Science Foundation, the National Institute for Advanced Study, the Guggenheim Foundation, and the National Endowment for the Humanities. Faculty members mentor their students, preparing them for careers, graduate and professional schools, and prestigious fellowships such as the Fulbright, Truman, and Marshall Fellowships recently awarded to TCNJ students.

Student Government

The Student Government Association, comprising all undergraduate students at the College, is governed by elected representatives. The Residence Hall Association provides the mechanism for student input into campus housing policies, and members of the Student Finance Board oversee and administer approximately $500,000 in student funds. The College Union Board sponsors a wide range of special events, including visits by John Leguizamo, Cornel West, and George Carlin.

Admission Requirements

The College of New Jersey seeks students who can succeed in a highly selective academic program and who show intellectual curiosity, academic talent, and the potential to contribute to the life of the College. The College is committed to attracting students from diverse economic, racial, social, and geographic backgrounds. A high school record of at least 16 college-preparatory credits, high school class rank, and results of the SAT I are the most important considerations in admission decisions, but special interests, skills, and qualities of all kinds can be influential. Certain departments, such as art, music, and health and physical education, use additional criteria to evaluate candidates seeking admission into their programs. Students are required to take the SAT II: Writing Test for placement purposes only.

Application and Information

Application forms and a prospectus may be obtained by writing to the Office of Admission. The deadline for applications for January admission is November 15 and for September admission, February 15. There is a $50 application fee. Candidates who apply only to the College of New Jersey under the early decision plan may apply before November 15 and will be notified on or before December 15. For September admission, the College subscribes to the candidates' reply date of May 1 for payment of a $100 tuition deposit and a $100 room and board deposit.

For more information, students should contact:

Director of Admissions
The College of New Jersey
P.O. Box 7718
Ewing, New Jersey 08628-0718
Telephone: 609-771-2131
800-624-0967 (toll-free)
World Wide Web: http://www.tcnj.edu

Students take a break in front of Green Hall.

THE COLLEGE OF NEW ROCHELLE

NEW ROCHELLE, NEW YORK

The College

The College of New Rochelle (CNR), founded in 1904 by the Ursuline Order, is an independent college that is Catholic in origin and heritage. Its primary purpose is the intellectual development of students through the maintenance of high standards of academic excellence. The College is composed of four separate schools. The School of Arts and Sciences enrolls about 615 young women between the ages of 18 and 22 and offers baccalaureate degree programs in the liberal arts and sciences and a number of professionally oriented fields. The School of Nursing, founded in 1976 and accredited by the National League for Nursing Accrediting Commission, offers baccalaureate and graduate-level professional nursing programs that combine clinical experience with a liberal arts background. About 400 women and men are enrolled in the nursing programs. The School of New Resources, which maintains six branch campuses in New York City, offers a nontraditional baccalaureate program designed specifically for adults. The Graduate School offers professional degree programs in education, art, community/school psychology, gerontology, communication studies, career development, and guidance and counseling. The main campus includes four residence halls that provide guaranteed housing for all undergraduates. Other students live in Westchester County, and some commute from the Greater New York metropolitan area. Students come to CNR from twenty states and eight countries.

Location

The College of New Rochelle is located on a 20-acre historic campus in New Rochelle, New York, a suburban community in southern Westchester County, half an hour away from New York City and easily accessible by commuter trains. The area contains numerous parks and recreational areas, and the Long Island Sound, with its many beaches, is within walking distance of the campus. Four airports—Kennedy, LaGuardia, Newark, and Westchester—are all within an hour of the College, and Amtrak makes daily stops at New Rochelle. New York City provides countless opportunities, including shopping expeditions, museums, and Broadway plays. Manhattan and the four other boroughs of New York City also contribute immeasurably to the education of the College's students through various internship, honors, and cooperative education programs, which are conducted by CNR in New York City.

Majors and Degrees

The School of Arts and Sciences at The College of New Rochelle confers the Bachelor of Arts (B.A.) degree in art (studio), art history, biology, chemistry, classics, communication arts, economics, English, environmental studies, history, mathematics, modern and classical languages, philosophy, political science, psychology, religious studies, and sociology; the Bachelor of Science (B.S.) degree in art education, biology, business, chemistry, mathematics, and social work; the Bachelor of Fine Arts (B.F.A.) degree in art education, art therapy, and studio art; and a Bachelor of Arts in interdisciplinary studies, which offers the student the viewpoints of several disciplines, including American studies, comparative literature, general science, international studies, social studies, and women's studies. A series of field experiences and competency-based learning activities lead to certification in childhood education (grades 1–6) and adolescent education (grades 7–12). Childhood education allows for dual certification in early childhood (birth –grade 2), middle childhood (grades 5–9), and students with disabilities (grades 1–6). Adolescent education allows for dual certification in middle childhood and students with disabilities (grades 7–12). Certification is also available in art education (K–12). In addition, CNR offers a five-year sequence that leads to both the Bachelor of Arts and Master of Science degrees in community/school psychology or communication arts. The School of Nursing offers Bachelor of Science in Nursing (B.S.N.) and Master of Science (M.S.) degree programs. Preprofessional programs are available in art therapy, health professions, law, and medicine.

Academic Programs

The College emphasizes the importance of a liberal arts background. Each undergraduate in the Schools of Arts and Sciences and Nursing must complete a variety of courses focusing on philosophy and religious studies, social analysis, literature and the arts, foreign languages, and scientific inquiry. To earn a B.A., B.S., or B.F.A., students must complete 120 credits. Typically, a B.A. degree requires 90 credits in liberal arts and 30 credits in a major area; B.S. and B.F.A. degrees require 60 credits in liberal arts and 60 credits in major and elective courses. To earn a B.S.N. degree, students must complete 120 credits. It is possible to complete graduation requirements in three years. Students who earn successful scores on the College Board's Advanced Placement examinations may qualify for credit and course exemption.

Interdisciplinary studies and dual-degree programs can be designed. Independent study options and seminars play important roles in undergraduate programs as well. The Honors Program, which provides an alternative structure for the liberal arts curriculum, fosters the growth of intellectual independence and initiative, offers the opportunity for independent study and research, and encourages the pursuit of scholarly interests in a broad variety of disciplines. Participation in the Honors Program requires a minimum 3.3 cumulative index. The Learning Support Services staff offers tutoring programs, quiet study areas, professional tutors, and student-peer tutors to help students.

The academic calendar consists of two fifteen-week semesters; during each semester, students generally take five courses. The fall semester is in session from September through December; the spring semester runs from late January through May. Courses are offered during the January intersession but are not required. Two five-week summer sessions are also offered.

Off-Campus Programs

The College of New Rochelle offers an extensive internship program. Art students have opportunities to assist in the management of SoHo art galleries and the Metropolitan Museum of Art, while continuing to develop their artistic talents. Communication arts majors participate in internships at numerous radio stations, newspapers, film companies, advertising and public relations firms, and national and cable broadcasting networks. Social science majors are offered opportunities with government agencies in Washington, D.C.; Albany; New York City; and Westchester, New York. Social work majors complete their fieldwork at a variety of human services agencies, and education majors gain experience through fieldwork and student teaching in local school districts and institutions. Business majors put theory into practice at companies such as Merrill Lynch and IBM, as well as at the New York Stock Exchange.

Clinical experiences for School of Nursing students take place in some of the most modern and sophisticated health-care institutions in the world, including Memorial Sloan-Kettering Cancer Center, Columbia-Presbyterian Hospital, and the Albert Einstein College of Medicine.

Students of modern foreign languages are encouraged to study and travel abroad. The College is affiliated with the American Institute for Foreign Study and the Institute of European Studies.

Academic Facilities

The New Rochelle campus contains twenty buildings, including classroom and laboratory facilities, student residences, and centers for academic support services. The newly renovated Mother Irene Gill Memorial Library holds more than 200,000 volumes in open stacks. About 3,000 new volumes are purchased each year. Holdings in education, psychology, health sciences, gerontology, and art are extensive. Renovations to the library include the addition of approximately 200 data ports and forty computer stations offering a variety of computer capabilities, including Internet access. Gill Library is a member of an international network of libraries.

The Mooney Center provides technology and programs to assist students in the development of academic, professional, and personal lifetime goals. Facilities include state-of-the-art computer laboratories and classrooms, a computer graphics studio and desktop publishing facilities, photography laboratories, a television studio, the Romita Auditorium, art studios and gallery space, a model classroom for student teachers, and the H. W. Taylor Institute for Entrepreneurial Studies. More than a dozen laboratories are housed in Rogick Life Science Center and Science Hall. Facilities include a research microscope room, a radiation laboratory and counting room, a plant/animal tissue culture room, a computer room, a darkroom, a greenhouse, and laboratories set aside entirely for student research.

The Learning Center for Nursing is composed of a nursing laboratory, which simulates a hospital setting, and a multimedia laboratory equipped with four mobile television centers and a media library. The computer room in the nursing center contains computers and printers and COMMES, an artificial intelligence system that simulates a professional nursing consultant. The system supports clinical decision-making by students and professional nurses.

The Student Campus Center houses the food service operation, featuring a variety of hot and cold food choices and an attractive, comfortable seating area; a completely renovated bookstore; centralized mailboxes for all students on campus; student activity rooms; and meeting rooms and lounge areas designed to hold large groups of people for lectures and special events.

Costs

Tuition for the 2004–05 academic year is $19,100. Room and board costs are $7400. Total estimated annual costs, including travel, books, and personal expenses, are $27,450.

Financial Aid

Approximately 90 percent of all freshmen receive some kind of financial aid through Pell Grants, Supplemental Educational Opportunity Grants, Federal Work-Study Program awards, Institutional awards, and student loans. Financial aid awards are based on both need and superior academic performance. New York State residents are encouraged to apply for Tuition Assistance Program (TAP) awards. The College of New Rochelle also has numerous grants and scholarships available. The scholarships are all based on academic achievement, community service, and leadership qualities. Amounts vary from $1000 per year to full tuition. All students applying for financial aid are required to fill out a College of New Rochelle financial aid application and to complete the Free Application for Federal Student Aid (FAFSA).

Faculty

In no small measure, the College owes its growth and success to a highly committed faculty and administration. The faculty consists of dedicated scholars and teachers who have been recognized for excellence in teaching. Ninety percent of the faculty members hold doctoral degrees or the highest degree available in their field. No graduate students or teaching assistants teach undergraduates. Faculty advisers are available to students for consultation and guidance in academic and career planning. To supplement and complement its faculty, the College invites adjunct professors, artists, business executives, and social workers to teach courses in their areas of expertise. The student-faculty ratio is 10:1.

Student Government

The Office of Student Development and Programs oversees undergraduate extracurricular activities. The Student Government Association is comprised of elected officials and club and organization leaders.

Admission Requirements

The College is selective in its admission process and evaluates each candidate's secondary school record, class rank, grade point average, extracurricular activities, SAT I or ACT scores, and a counselor's recommendation. The secondary school curriculum should include 16 academic units in English, mathematics, foreign language, social science, and natural science. Applicants to the School of Nursing should complete biology and chemistry lab courses plus one other science course and three years of high school mathematics, including algebra I, algebra II, and geometry. Most applicants rank within the top half of their class and have maintained at least a B average. Students who will have completed 15 high school academic units within three years are invited to apply for early admission. While an admission interview is not required, it is recommended. First time and transfer students may apply for either the September or January term. The high school course of study is carefully considered, and the student must have maintained at least a 2.0 GPA at another institution. Students interested in the School of Nursing must have maintained at least a 2.5 GPA. Students interested in pursuing a major in social work or participating in the teacher certification program must maintain at least a 2.7 GPA. International students are welcome and must submit scores on the Test of English as a Foreign Language (TOEFL), when necessary. A minimum TOEFL score of 550 is required for admission.

Application and Information

Interested students should begin the admission process early in their senior year. The College accepts applications and renders decisions on a rolling basis. Students particularly interested in the College may apply for early decision; all credentials must arrive in the Office of Admission by November 1. Early decision candidates are notified by December 1. Applications for regular admission are accepted until all class spaces are filled. Housing is assigned according to the date of deposit. Enrollment deferrals are available.

For additional information about the School of Arts & Sciences and the School of Nursing, students should contact:

Stephanie Decker
Director of Admission
The College of New Rochelle
New Rochelle, New York 10805
Telephone: 800-933-5923 (toll-free)
E-mail: admission@cnr.edu
World Wide Web: http://www.cnr.edu

The College of New Rochelle students catch up on some studying while enjoying the beautiful weather and scenery.

COLLEGE OF NOTRE DAME OF MARYLAND

BALTIMORE, MARYLAND

The College

Founded in 1873, the College of Notre Dame of Maryland offers a four-year liberal arts undergraduate program for women. In 1895, it was established as the first Catholic college for women in the United States to award the baccalaureate degree.

Notre Dame was chartered by the state of Maryland and is accredited by the Middle States Association of Colleges and Schools and approved by the Maryland Department of Education. Overall enrollment at the College in fall 2003 totaled 3,021. There were 1,573 undergraduate students and 1,448 men and women in the graduate program, which offers the M.A. in contemporary communication, leadership in teaching, liberal arts, management, nonprofit management, studies in aging, teaching, and TESOL.

The 58-acre campus has nine major buildings. There are two residence halls: Doyle Hall for freshmen and sophomores and Mary Meletia Hall for juniors and seniors. Each hall has lounges and study areas, kitchen-dinette areas, laundry facilities, and televisions. First-year students are assigned roommates on the basis of their response to a questionnaire. Upperclass students choose their own roommates.

Other buildings on the campus house classrooms, labs, study and lounge areas, art and photography studios, music studios, a bookstore, a career planning center, auditoriums, a chapel, a planetarium, new TV and radio studios, a dance studio, a fitness center, a computer center, an international center, a state-of-the-art language lab, the Sports and Student Activities Complex, and a new addition to the science center. Campus sports facilities include a field hockey, lacrosse, and soccer playing field; four tennis courts; basketball, volleyball, and racquetball courts; and an indoor pool. Notre Dame competes in seven NCAA Division III sports.

Location

Baltimore, one of the largest cities on the East Coast, is in the national spotlight for its citywide renaissance, including the redeveloped Inner Harbor, which features the Harborplace shopping pavilions, the National Aquarium, the Science Center, and a busy schedule of concerts and ethnic festivals. The city's fine museums, theaters, and wealth of educational institutions, including the Johns Hopkins University, the Peabody Conservatory of Music, and Maryland Institute, College of Art, are just minutes from the campus. Washington, D.C., is accessible by train and is less than an hour's drive from the College. Historic Annapolis and the U.S. Naval Academy are only 45 minutes away, and Philadelphia and New York City can be easily reached by car, train, or plane.

Majors and Degrees

Notre Dame offers the Bachelor of Arts degree with concentrations in the following fields of study: art, biology, biology/psychology, business (emphases in accounting, computer information systems, finance, management, and marketing), chemistry, classical studies, communication arts, computer information systems, computer science, criminology and social deviance, economics, education, English, history, international studies, liberal arts, mathematics, modern foreign languages, philosophy, physics, political science, psychology, radiological sciences, and religious studies. A dual degree (B.A./B.S.) in nursing is granted in a cooperative program with the Johns Hopkins University. A dual degree (B.A./B.S.) in engineering is granted by Notre Dame in a cooperative program with the University of Maryland or the Johns Hopkins University. A B.A. degree in human services, an RN to B.S.N. program, a dual-degree program in radiological sciences, and a degree in nonprofit management are offered exclusively through the Weekend College.

Four-year preprofessional programs are offered in dentistry, law, medicine, and veterinary medicine, and two-year programs are offered in dental hygiene, medical technology, nursing, pharmacy, and physical therapy. The College also offers a five-year B.A./M.A. program in education and business.

Academic Programs

The curriculum is composed of three parts: general requirements, concentration requirements, and electives. Approximately one third of each student's program of study is made up of general education requirements—courses that Notre Dame considers essential in a liberal arts program. Students select a field of concentration on the basis of their interest and ability and choose one third of their courses in this specialized area. The remaining third of the curriculum enables students to broaden their intellectual and cultural backgrounds by choosing electives in fields of study outside their major. The Morrissy Honors Program challenges outstanding students.

Requirements for graduation include the successful completion of general education, concentration, and proficiency requirements and electives totaling 120 credits; a minimum cumulative grade average of C (2.0); and a minimum of two years, normally the last two, of course work at Notre Dame.

The Weekday College for Adult Women is open for full-time and part-time study.

The Accelerated College, Weekend College, and Center for Graduate Studies are primarily designed for part-time students and are open to women and men.

Notre Dame graduates have had a record of success in careers and in admission to graduate study at other institutions. The College's liberal arts program, which includes ample career preparation, works to strengthen that record. A comprehensive program, offered on an individual basis from the freshman year onward, helps students identify career goals and take practical steps toward achieving them. It is administered by professionals in the Career Center.

Off-Campus Programs

An internship program enables students to gain experience off campus—in major corporations, banks, newspaper offices, hospitals, local business offices, government agencies, and radio and TV stations, for example—and helps them integrate academic experience and career development. Internships are offered every term and are coordinated through the Career Center. More than 80 percent of the students participate in the highly regarded internship program.

Since 1963, Notre Dame has participated in an exchange program that enables students to take courses at any of the following colleges or universities, with permission of the dean: the Johns Hopkins University, Loyola College, Morgan State University, Towson University, Goucher College, Coppin State College, and Maryland Institute, College of Art. There is also an active social activities exchange program.

Academic Facilities

The award-winning Loyola–Notre Dame Library is the first library in the United States in which the entire collections of two undergraduate colleges have been combined for cooperative use. Constructed on land contiguous to the two colleges, the four-level structure houses more than 448,000 bound volumes and 1,700 periodicals. The library includes an audiovisual center containing 24,000 audiovisual materials and 348,000 microfilm and microfiche units; a reading deck overlooking a pond; study rooms, some of which have computers; and seminar rooms. The expanded Knott Science Center houses the biology, chemistry, physics, mathematics, photography, and psychology departments and contains fully equipped laboratories, lecture rooms, an auditorium, three darkrooms, and a planetarium. The Communication Arts Complex houses the communication arts department and contains a color television studio, a radio production studio, a soundproof control room, and filmmaking equipment. The College's Computer Center, open seven days a week, houses four classrooms and separate computer labs. The computer center features fifty Pentium PCs as a campus standard and twenty networked Power Macs. Students have access to the Internet and the electronic library system and may send e-mail around the world. The complex also includes a VAX cluster for administrative record keeping. The Sister Kathleen Feeley International Center houses the English Language Institute and the Office of International Programs.

Costs

The cost for the 2003–04 academic year at the College of Notre Dame was $26,675, exclusive of major travel expenses; tuition was $18,700 and room and board were $7600. Student fees were $375. Additional special academic and nonacademic fees, such as book fees and fees for instrumental lessons, are charged as they apply to a particular student. Fees are subject to change.

Financial Aid

Financial aid at Notre Dame is awarded to students who cannot provide the full cost of a Notre Dame education through their own and their families' reasonable efforts. Financial assistance consists of scholarships, grants, loans, and paid part-time employment. Awards are offered to students according to available funds and student eligibility. Eligibility is determined by documented financial need, as demonstrated by the Free Application for Federal Student Aid (FAFSA). Other qualifications considered include the applicant's high school record, scholastic aptitude and achievement as measured by the College Board tests, and special talents, contributions, and achievements. The application deadline for maximum consideration is February 15. For the 2004–05 academic year, tuition scholarships are available up to full tuition. A Notre Dame financial aid form and FAFSA must be submitted each year to reapply for aid.

Faculty

Notre Dame has 81 full-time and 5 half-time faculty members, all of whom hold as their highest degree a master's or doctoral degree. There are additional associate faculty members at the College. The undergraduate student–faculty ratio is 13:1.

Student Government

All full-time students are members of the Student Association at the College of Notre Dame and are encouraged to help determine College direction. The Student Senate officers and elected representatives from the Student Association have a strong voice in setting College policies. In cooperation with the administration and faculty, these students maintain and encourage those values that are considered important to the school as a whole. In addition, it is the policy of the administration that there always be a student representative at Board of Trustees meetings and on most College-wide standing committees.

Admission Requirements

The Admissions Committee selects students not only on the basis of academic records and test scores but also on the basis of personal character and accomplishments. The College of Notre Dame does not discriminate on the basis of race, color, religion, national or ethnic origin, or handicap in admission to, or treatment in, its educational programs and activities.

Because a strong academic program in high school is the best preparation for successful work at Notre Dame, the Admissions Committee places the greatest emphasis on the candidate's high school record. Applicants must graduate from an accredited high school and offer a minimum of 18 academic units distributed as follows: English, 4 units; foreign language, 3 units; college-preparatory mathematics, 3 units; history, 2 units; science, 2 units; and electives, 4 units. The committee recognizes variation in school curricula and reserves the right to admit students who lack one or more of the above requirements but give promise of doing acceptable college work.

The SAT I or ACT (SAT preferred) is required of all students. Application forms and information about the test are available from high school guidance counselors and from the College Entrance Examination Board, Box 592, Princeton, New Jersey 08541. International students may substitute the Test of English as a Foreign Language (TOEFL) for the SAT I. The TOEFL bulletin and registration form may be obtained by writing to TOEFL, Educational Testing Service, Princeton, New Jersey 08540. International students wishing to improve their English language skills may attend the College's English Language Institute.

Notre Dame admits with advanced standing those transfer applicants who have fulfilled the equivalent of freshman or sophomore class requirements in an accredited college. No credit is granted for a grade of D.

Personal interviews are recommended for admission, and all candidates who find it possible to visit the campus are encouraged to do so. The Office of Admissions is open for interviews, by appointment, from 8:30 a.m. to 4:30 p.m., Monday through Friday, throughout the year. Open house events are held for prospective students and their parents throughout the academic year. Interested students should check the College's Web site or phone for dates.

Application and Information

For maximum consideration, applications should be received by February 15 for fall semester admission and December 15 for spring semester admission. Applications completed after the deadline are considered on a space-available basis. Students who wish to enter the freshman class should submit the following credentials to the Director of Admissions: a completed application for admission, including an essay and a student resume, with a nonrefundable $25 application fee; an official transcript of the high school record; scores on the SAT I or ACT; a recommendation from the high school guidance director; and a letter of recommendation from an English teacher. International students should also submit TOEFL scores and a completed financial affidavit. Transfer students should submit high school and college transcripts along with a completed application, the $25 nonrefundable fee, and one letter of recommendation.

Additional information and application forms may be obtained from:

Director of Admissions
College of Notre Dame of Maryland
4701 North Charles Street
Baltimore, Maryland 21210
Telephone: 410-532-5330
800-435-0200 (toll-free)
E-mail: admiss@ndm.edu
World Wide Web: http://www.ndm.edu

COLLEGE OF SAINT ELIZABETH

MORRISTOWN, NEW JERSEY

The College

The College of Saint Elizabeth (CSE), which celebrated its centennial year in 1999–2000, is the oldest college for women in New Jersey. In addition, CSE is one of the first Catholic colleges in the U.S. to award degrees to women. A Catholic college in the liberal arts tradition, the College now includes a women's college, coeducational adult undergraduate degree programs, and coeducational graduate degree programs. An enrollment of nearly 1,800 students encourages considerable student-faculty interaction and fosters a spirit of campuswide friendliness and support. An emphasis is placed on opportunities for individual growth through academic, spiritual, cultural, leadership, and civic experiences.

Located on a 200-acre campus, CSE's buildings command a wide view of the surrounding hills. Sixty-four percent of the women's college students live on campus. The majority come from New Jersey, 4 percent from other northeastern states, 2 percent from other states, and 8 percent from other countries. Approximately 60 percent of those who begin as freshmen graduate, and about 47 percent go on to graduate study within five years of leaving college. Two attractive residence halls provide ample private and double rooms. Each residence hall has kitchenettes, laundry facilities, a mail room, lounges, and conference rooms. The student center contains a swimming pool, a gymnasium, a fitness center, a drama studio, an art studio, a dining room, and the College store.

Students may belong to extracurricular organizations associated with their academic interests, such as the cocurricular leadership program, the Elizabeth Singers, the International/Intercultural Club, the College Activities Board, Campus Ministry, the Students Take Action Committee, Volunteer Services, Student Government, and varsity athletics. NCAA Division III team sports include basketball, soccer, softball, swimming, tennis, and volleyball, plus an intercollegiate equestrian team. Other organizations include a number of Greek-letter honor and professional societies and student affiliates of the American Chemical Society. A rich calendar of social, cultural, and recreational events is available at the College of Saint Elizabeth. Students frequently socialize with their peers from Drew University and Fairleigh Dickinson University, College at Florham, two nearby coeducational institutions within walking distance of the campus. Career Services provides assistance with career preparation and graduate study. In addition to the majors and degrees listed below, the College offers the M.A. degree in education, educational leadership, counseling psychology, and theology and the M.S. degree in nutrition, management, and health care management.

Location

Morristown is located in the rapidly growing corporate center of Morris County. Neighboring towns and cities, only minutes from campus, offer facilities for shopping and recreation. The College is an hour from the cultural and social opportunities of New York City by car, train, or bus and is near the campuses of Fairleigh Dickinson, Seton Hall, Drew, and the County College of Morris. Newark Liberty International Airport is approximately 30 minutes and two New York airports are approximately 1 hour from the campus. Local bus routes are easily accessible, and New Jersey Transit, which has a stop at the campus gate, provides excellent rail commuter service from New York City, Hoboken, Newark, the Oranges, Short Hills, Maplewood, Millburn, Summit, Chatham, Madison, and Dover. Routes 287, 80, 280, 46, 78, 24, and 10 are located close by.

Majors and Degrees

The Bachelor of Arts is offered in American studies, applied science, art, biology, chemistry, communication, economics, education (early childhood and elementary education, secondary education, or special education), English, history, individualized major, international studies, justice studies (criminal justice, legal studies), mathematics, music, philosophy, psychology, sociology, Spanish, and theology. The Bachelor of Science is offered in biochemistry, biology (options for cytotechnology, medical technology, and toxicology), business administration (options for accounting, computer information systems, human resource management, management, and marketing), chemistry, computer science, and foods and nutrition. The Bachelor of Science in Nursing degree is offered as an upper-division nursing program.

Academic Programs

The requirements for a B.A., B.S., or B.S.N. degree are 128 semester hours of academic credit, competency in writing, First Year Seminar (not required of adult students), 2 credits in fitness/wellness, and successful completion of the comprehensive examination in the major subject. A minimum of 32 credits is required in the major, except for the major in elementary education, which requires 30 credits. The core curriculum requires that students take between 36 and 44 credits distributed among five cluster areas: Literature/Fine Arts/Language; Social and Behavioral Sciences; Natural and Physical Sciences and Mathematics and Computer Science; Philosophy, Theology, and History; and Perspectives on an Interdependent World. The remaining courses are free electives. With the exception of the sciences, mathematics, and nutrition, the major need not be declared until the end of the sophomore year.

Career preparation includes studies in accounting, business management, communication, computer information systems, computer science, criminal justice and legal studies, foods and nutrition, gerontology, human resource management, management, marketing, premedicine, pre–veterinary studies, secondary education, and social work. Education majors may obtain state certification and/or endorsement in early childhood or special education. The College has a highly successful leadership program.

Students interested in becoming registered dietitians may enroll in the dietetic internship program if they hold a baccalaureate degree and meet the current American Dietetic Association course work requirements.

Independent study, field experience, internships, study-abroad opportunities, honors, leadership, and accelerated programs, minors, and double majors are available for qualified students. Successful scores on Advanced Placement tests are honored for placement or credit. Credit is given for successful scores on CLEP subject examinations with essays, on the Thomas Edison College Examination Program (TECEP) examinations, on the Regents College Examination in nursing, DANTES, and ACE College Credit Recommendation, and on portfolio assessment of prior learning.

Courses are offered in the evenings and during the summer through the School of Graduate and Continuing Studies. Undergraduate degree programs are offered in business administration, communication, computer science, English, foods and nutrition, international studies, justice studies, nursing, psychology, and theology.

Off-Campus Programs

A cross-registration policy exists with nearby Fairleigh Dickinson and Drew universities. Qualified students may study abroad during the junior year or in the summer. A January Intersession Program and Summer Sessions provide opportunities for short-term courses and off-campus experiences. Students have opportunities in Morris County for volunteer service, field experience, and internships in local agencies, institutions, and the corporate headquarters of numerous multinational corporations.

Academic Facilities

Students majoring in biology and chemistry conduct independent research projects under the guidance of highly qualified professors and in conjunction with local research companies. The College has several well-equipped microcomputer laboratories and extensive software. Mahoney Library is a 300-seat, air-conditioned facility that provides group and individual study areas. The library's collection includes approximately 138,344 volumes, 1,642 audiovisual titles, 120,741 microforms, 718 periodical subscriptions, and a 4,750-volume curriculum collection for education students. The Phillips Library of Rare Books and Manuscripts houses a variety of special collections. The library is a selective depository for U.S. government documents. Seven Internet workstations provide access to the World Wide Web and to more than 90 online subscription databases, many of which include full text. A TV studio, an editing suite, an ITV classroom, and postproduction facilities are housed in the Media Services area.

Costs

Tuition in 2003–04 for incoming full-time freshmen was $16,450, and room and board were $8130. Academic fees are estimated at $890 annually, and other incidental expenses, such as travel, entertainment, clothes, books, and personal expenses, are estimated at about $3300. Part-time students pay $575 per credit.

Financial Aid

Approximately 95 percent of full-time undergraduate students at the College of Saint Elizabeth receive financial aid. Aid is available from the College itself in the form of scholarships, grants-in-aid, and campus employment and from the federal and state governments in the form of scholarships, grants, loans, and employment. Students who wish to be considered for grants, loans, and campus employment should apply to the College by March 1 for the fall semester and by November 1 for the spring semester. Campus employment is available in the residence halls, laboratories, the library, and College offices, and a limited number of work-study opportunities for qualified students are available both on and off campus. Transfer scholarships are also available.

Faculty

The faculty-student ratio is 1:10. Full-time instructional faculty members for 2003–04 included approximately 80 percent with doctorates and 20 percent with master's degrees. Several faculty members hold additional professional credentials. The goals of the faculty are to teach effectively, to be readily available to students, and to pursue research.

Student Government

Students participate in the governance of the College through the Student Organization. The Student Organization elects members to the student government, which serves as the student executive branch. Student views on residence life, day-student issues, student activities, and the operations of the student Rathskeller are expressed and acted on through a committee structure. The academic life, student life, and lectures and concerts committees of the College are composed of both faculty members and students and are engaged in determining methods of implementing institutional goals and increasing student satisfaction with campus life. Students are encouraged to participate fully in the academic community and to exercise considerable influence in social and extracurricular activities. There is an open atmosphere on campus, and students have access to the deans and the president.

Admission Requirements

The College looks for students whose aptitude and academic record demonstrate the ability to meet academic challenges. Normally, a student interested in admission to the College should complete 16 academic units by the end of her senior year, including 3 years of English; 3 years of college-preparatory mathematics, including algebra; 2 years of a foreign language; 1 year of U.S. history; 1 unit of laboratory science and 1 additional unit of science; and seven upper-level academic electives. Applicants must submit either SAT I or ACT scores. International students must send scores on the Test of English as a Foreign Language (TOEFL). Students applying to the College should submit a secondary school transcript, including courses currently in progress, plus two letters of recommendation from persons who can attest to their academic potential. Students are encouraged to have an on-campus interview and visit the campus. Open houses are held each spring and fall. Well-qualified students who are recommended by their high school principals may be accepted after three years of high school. Transfers from two- and four-year colleges are accepted for the fall and spring semesters. Through articulation agreements, an applicant who has earned an A.A. degree in a transfer program at an accredited two-year college is eligible for admission with junior-class standing. Adult students must admit secondary and previous college transcripts (if any) in addition to the application.

Application and Information

For further information, students may contact:

College of Saint Elizabeth
2 Convent Road
Morristown, New Jersey 07960-6989
Telephone: 973-290-4700 (Women's College)
800-210-7900 (Women's College, toll-free)
973-290-4600 (School of Graduate and Continuing Studies)
Fax: 973-290-4710 (Women's College)
973-290-4676 (School of Graduate and Continuing Studies)
E-mail: apply@cse.edu (Women's College)
theschool@cse.edu (School of Graduate and Continuing Studies)
World Wide Web: http://www.cse.edu

Students at the College of Saint Elizabeth.

The College of Saint Elizabeth has filed compliance with the Department of Education (formerly Department of Health, Education, and Welfare) under Title VI–Civil Rights Act of 1964, Title IX–Education Amendment of 1972, and the regulations issued by the then Department of Health, Education, and Welfare in implementation thereof, and Section 504 of the Rehabilitation Act of 1973, as amended.

THE COLLEGE OF SAINT ROSE

ALBANY, NEW YORK

The College

The College of Saint Rose is an independent, coeducational institution where academics and career preparation are top priorities. The College's progressive liberal education core prepares students to dive into one of the College's fifty-five undergraduate fields of study, most of which incorporate a field experience component. The College offers small class sizes, with a student-faculty ratio of 15:1 and an experienced, mentoring faculty. *Money* magazine and *U.S. News & World Report* have ranked Saint Rose as one of the top colleges in the Northeast and the nation, based on such factors as affordability and high academic quality. With the capital of New York as its convenient location and a distinctly friendly atmosphere on campus, The College of Saint Rose is a place where students realize that they have the ability to change the world.

Saint Rose was founded in 1920 by the Sisters of Saint Joseph of Carondelet and is located in a residential neighborhood. The College encompasses eighty buildings, including the new Thelma P. Lally School of Education, a state-of-the-art Science Center, a high-tech music studio, and the Hubbard Interfaith Sanctuary. The most recent transformation project at the College is the construction of a $7.5-million Events and Athletics Center. With the creation of this facility, the College of Saint Rose plans to provide an on-campus venue worthy of welcoming best-selling authors, Nobel Prize winners, and world-famous performers. This space is also designed to serve as a unique collegiate basketball venue in the Capital Region, large enough to accommodate the Golden Knights' loyal fan base.

Saint Rose students comprise a community of leaders. Most of the 2,898 undergraduates at Saint Rose come from New York State and New England, and there are international students who represent many countries. The College of Saint Rose actively seeks to enroll students of all backgrounds who can contribute to and benefit from the experience of shared learning and academic success.

Campus housing includes traditional- and suite-style residence halls as well as thirty historical homes. Each house has its own history, character, and uniqueness with wraparound porches and stained-glass windows.

Students participate in organized social activities as well as ten associations that are related to academic majors. The College of Saint Rose is a member of the National Collegiate Athletic Association (NCAA) Division II and the Northeast-10 Conference. Intercollegiate teams include men's baseball and golf; men's and women's basketball, cross-country, soccer, swimming, and tennis; and women's softball and volleyball.

While students ultimately attend Saint Rose to receive a superior education, they also participate in organized social activities that enhance the Saint Rose experience. Saint Rose students belong to thirty groups that include academic-related clubs as well as special interest clubs. They also play in ten to fifteen intramural programs and produce three publications—the *The Chronicle* weekly student newspaper, the *The Sphere* literary magazine, and *Reflections,* the College's yearbook.

Location

Saint Rose is located in the historic Pine Hills neighborhood of Albany. With more than 61,000 college students in the area, there are always things to do and people to meet. A wide variety of restaurants, shops, museums, and theaters are within walking distance or are easily accessible by buses that stop at Saint Rose.

Majors and Degrees

The College of Saint Rose offers programs of study in the fields of accounting, American studies, applied technology education, art education (K–12), biochemistry, biology, biology/cytotechnology, biology education (7–12), business administration, chemistry, chemistry education (7–12), childhood education, childhood education/special education, communication disorders, communications, computer information systems, computer science, criminal justice, early childhood education, early childhood/special education, earth science, English, English education (7–12), environmental affairs, exploratory, graphic design, history, history/political science, mathematics, mathematics education (7–12), medical technology, music education (K–12), music industry, prelaw, premedicine, preveterinary studies, psychology, religious studies, social studies education (7–12), social work, sociology, Spanish, Spanish education (7–12), studio art, and women's studies.

Academic Program

To earn a bachelor's degree, a student must complete a minimum of 122 credits, including, for most majors, the liberal education curriculum requirement of 42 credits, two courses in physical education, and the major requirements as specified. A minimum of 60 credits must be earned on the Saint Rose campus or at one of the colleges in the Hudson-Mohawk Association of Colleges and Universities through cross-registration. A cumulative index of 2.0 and an index of 2.0 in the major field are required for graduation in most majors.

Students are provided with assistance in planning their programs of study by faculty advisers in their major areas and by the Office of Academic Advisement. They may elect double majors or minors or may design their own programs within the guidelines set by the interdepartmental studies major.

The College of Saint Rose offers qualified students the opportunity to pursue an accelerated bachelor's/master's degree program, which can be completed in approximately five years of study. The College offers these option programs in accounting, business, English, and history. It also offers those who wish to enroll as early matriculation students the option to complete their senior year of high school and freshman year of college simultaneously.

The College's participation in the Hudson-Mohawk Association of Colleges and Universities provides an opportunity for students to enroll in classes at twenty participating colleges and universities in the Capital Region on a space-available basis.

Qualified students also may participate in special transfer programs: a 3+3 option with Albany Law School and a 3+2 engineering option with Union College, Clarkson University, Rensselaer Polytechnic Institute, or Alfred University. Students in these programs complete selected bachelor's degree programs at Saint Rose in three years and transfer to the cooperating institution to finish the professional program.

The College operates on a semester calendar with a fall term extending from August to December and a spring term from January to May. Two summer session programs offer undergraduate and graduate evening courses.

Off-Campus Programs

Saint Rose students can study in one of more than thirty countries, which is made possible by the school's affiliations with the College Consortium for International Studies, Regent's College in London, and the Center for Cross-Cultural Study. All study-abroad opportunities are offered for the same cost as Saint Rose tuition, including airfare, personal expenses, and Saint Rose financial aid packages. All credits count toward the student's degree.

Academic Facilities

A recent $3 million technology upgrade greatly enhanced the speed and performance of the College's network, providing the infrastructure for wireless networking, videoconferencing, streaming media, and Blackboard, the Web-based instruction tool. The campuswide network provides access to the College's Neil Hellman Library and all campus computer laboratories and residence hall rooms.

The Center for Art and Design, located about a mile from the main campus, houses the Saint Rose Art Gallery as well as extensive photography labs, graphic design computers, and one of the largest screen-printing facilities in the state of New York. The College's Music Center features the Saints and Sinners Sound Studio, a music library, a performance hall, and practice rooms. Science and mathematics majors have access to the latest equipment and research facilities in the College's 27,000-square-foot Science Center.

The newest facility at the College is the Thelma P. Lally School of Education. This new 56,000-square-foot building features a multimedia education forum, classrooms, computer labs, offices, an education and curriculum library, and a multidisciplinary services clinic. The School provides a learning and teaching environment in which technology plays a critical role and where teachers, parents, and students will exchange ideas on how to make the American education system second to none.

Costs

Tuition for 2004–05 is $16,230. Room and board costs range from $6562 to $7554 per year, depending on the meal plan chosen by the student. The estimated annual costs for books and personal expenses are $1000 and $1400, respectively.

Financial Aid

More than 90 percent of the students receive financial aid in the form of scholarships, grants, loans, and part-time employment. The College of Saint Rose participates in the Federal Pell Grant, FSEOG, TAP, and Federal Work-Study programs and in the Federal Perkins Loan and Federal Stafford Student Loan Programs. The College provides ample aid in the form of grants, service awards, and scholarships for need or academic achievement. Candidates for financial assistance must file the Free Application for Federal Student Aid. ISIR and SAR forms should be on file in the Financial Aid Office by March 1. Students interested in being considered for academic scholarships must apply to the College by February 1.

Faculty

Saint Rose has a full-time faculty of 174 members.

Student Government

The Student Association (SA) consists of elected students who want to make life at the College as enjoyable, interesting, and meaningful as possible. It budgets student funds, appoints representatives to College policymaking committees, and assists individual students and clubs in planning and carrying out projects. It also provides an organ of self-government, promotes an exchange of ideas within the College community, fosters opportunities beyond those offered in the formal curriculum, and advances the welfare of the entire College community. SA also oversees the College's thirty clubs and organizations.

Admission Requirements

The College wishes to admit students who show evidence of strong academic motivation and the ability to benefit from a challenging liberal and professional education. Admission decisions are made after careful study of all the data available for each candidate. Interviews are strongly recommended but not required. Freshman applicants should submit a high school transcript, a letter of recommendation from a teacher or guidance counselor, an essay, and scores on the SAT I or ACT.

Transfer applicants must submit high school and college transcripts, a letter of recommendation from a college instructor, and a written statement of the reasons for transfer.

Application and Information

Students are accepted for admission for the fall and spring semesters on a rolling admissions basis. Interested students must apply by February 1 to be considered for academic scholarships ranging from $1000 to full tuition for each undergraduate year. New students who are accepted for admission are asked to submit a tuition deposit of $150 and a residence deposit (where applicable) of $150. Information on all aspects of the campus and the academic programs can be obtained by contacting the Office of Admissions; this office also can arrange campus tours, classroom visits, and overnight accommodations.

Office of Undergraduate Admissions
The College of Saint Rose
432 Western Avenue
Albany, New York 12203
Telephone: 518-454-5150
800-637-8556 (toll-free)
Fax: 518-454-2013
E-mail: admit@strose.edu (admissions)
finaid@strose.edu (financial aid)
World Wide Web: http://www.strose.edu

Located in the historic Pine Hills neighborhood of Albany, New York, the Saint Rose campus features a mix of classic brick buildings and new stone and glass structures, with the Campus Green at its center. The border of the campus is outlined by more than thirty restored historic Victorian houses featuring wraparound porches and stained-glass windows.

THE COLLEGE OF ST. SCHOLASTICA

DULUTH, MINNESOTA

The College

The College of St. Scholastica provides intellectual and moral preparation for responsible living and meaningful work. An independent comprehensive college, it was founded in the Catholic intellectual tradition and is shaped by its Benedictine heritage. The College offers programs in the liberal arts and sciences and professional career fields. The entire St. Scholastica community is committed to an educational process that requires students to meet rigorous academic standards, to broaden the scope of their knowledge, and to be accountable to both self and society.

The College serves 2,850 students. The small, friendly community enables each student to participate in academics, extracurriculars, and recreational activities. A 13:1 student-teacher ratio makes it easy to seek individualized help and encouragement.

St. Scholastica graduates, well known for their academic and professional preparation, enjoy excellent placement opportunities. Last year, 99 percent of graduates either secured employment or enrolled in graduate school within six months of graduation. *U.S. News & World Report* magazine's 2004 "America's Best Colleges" rankings put St. Scholastica in the top tier of Midwestern colleges for academic excellence and affordability. The *Washington Post* calls the College a "hidden gem."

The College also offers innovative graduate programs, including the Master of Education, Master of Arts in management, Master of Arts in nursing, Master of Arts in occupational therapy, Master of Arts in physical therapy, Master of Arts in exercise physiology, and Master of Arts in health information management.

Today the campus includes the Mitchell Auditorium, an acoustically superb 500-seat music hall; the Science Center; Our Lady Queen of Peace Chapel; the Myles Reif Recreation Center; the College Library; the St. Scholastica Theatre; majestic Tower Hall; a state-of-the-art wellness center; Cedar Hall student apartment building; Somers Residence Hall (featuring a wing of suites); and three modular apartment complexes. Adjoining the campus are St. Scholastica Monastery, the home of the Benedictine Sisters; the Benedictine Health Center, which serves the needs of the Duluth area and provides many health science and behavioral arts and sciences students with opportunities to obtain practical experience; and Westwood, a continuous care facility for senior citizens.

Location

The 186-acre St. Scholastica campus is on a ridge overlooking Lake Superior in a residential area of Duluth, Minnesota. The location offers a safe and tranquil setting for scholarship amid exceptional natural beauty. The cultural and commercial offerings of Duluth, a regional center for shopping, the arts, and tourism, are only 10 minutes away. Duluth is in northeastern Minnesota, a 2-hour drive from Minneapolis–St. Paul. It is well served by Northwest Airlines as well as commercial bus lines. An intercity bus line provides efficient local transportation.

Duluth's low crime rate, economic stability, and natural beauty regularly earn it high rankings in national quality of life surveys. The city is an international seaport and a center of development for the health, education, and tourism industries. There are more than 15,000 college students in the Duluth-Superior metropolitan area.

The College's proximity to the Boundary Waters Canoe Area Wilderness, national parks, ski areas, lakes, and rivers allows students to enjoy the outdoors in a way few college students can. A student who values a highly cultured community where extracurricular activities abound will be happy at St. Scholastica. Music students take part in the Duluth-Superior Symphony Orchestra, and theater students feel at home at the Duluth Playhouse, one of the nation's oldest community theaters. Sports enthusiasts can play tennis, racquetball, and golf; use ice boats or snowmobiles; or ice-skate, ski, fish, hunt, and sail in St. Scholastica's backyard. Mont du Lac and Spirit Mountain ski areas are only 20 minutes from campus.

Majors and Degrees

The College of St. Scholastica offers a Bachelor of Arts degree in the following majors: accounting, applied economics, behavioral arts and sciences, biochemistry, biology, business communication, chemistry, communication, computer science/information systems, economics, education, educational media and technology, English, exercise physiology, health-care informatics and information management, health sciences, history, humanities, languages and international studies, management, marketing, mathematics, music, natural sciences, nursing, occupational therapy (entry master's program), Ojibwe language and culture education, open major/undeclared, organizational behavior, physical therapy (entry master's program), psychology, religious studies, self-designed major, social science/secondary education, and social work.

Minors are available in most of the major fields as well as in American Indian studies, art, French, German, gerontology, medieval and Renaissance studies, philosophy, Russian, self-designed minor, Spanish, theatre, and women's studies.

In addition, St. Scholastica offers preprofessional programs in dentistry, engineering, law, medicine, pharmacy, and veterinary medicine. St. Scholastica has a certificate program in gerontology, and the study of aging is a major initiative throughout the College. St. Scholastica offers a licensure program in teacher education.

Academic Programs

The curriculum prepares students for their responsibilities as working professionals, as citizens of a democracy, and as individuals who seek to live full lives. The program consists of three parts: general education requirements, a major, and open electives. The major prepares the student for graduate school or for a profession and is normally selected by the end of the sophomore year. Elective courses allow students to pursue particular interests. The general education component seeks to broaden the student's grasp of the accumulated wisdom of the past so that challenges of the present may be met with wisdom, faith, and imagination. At St. Scholastica, 128 semester credits are required for graduation, of which one third are general education credits. The general education program includes a system of area distribution requirements, a First-Year Program, and an upper-division writing course elective. The area distribution requirements cover cultural diversity, social sciences, world languages, literature, analytical reasoning, natural science, history, fine arts, philosophy, religious studies, and electives. The student's last 32 credits before graduation must be earned at St. Scholastica, and a minimum of 16 credits must be earned in a major field at St. Scholastica. The College offers an honors program for students to have enriched learning experiences and to provide a community of support for learners devoted to a vigorous life of the mind. Some majors require an internship that involves work, travel, or study related to a student's academic efforts.

Off-Campus Programs

The College offers its programs throughout the region. Accelerated degree evening programs for working adults are offered in Duluth, Brainerd, St. Cloud, and St. Paul. St. Scholastica also has consortium agreements through which students may enroll in courses at other colleges in the region. Clinical experience in the College's health sciences programs is offered at all health-care facilities in Duluth as well as in many other hospitals and health-care centers throughout the United States. The College also offers students the opportunity to study abroad at its study center in Louisburgh, Ireland; in a Russian language exchange program in Petrozavodsk, Karelia, Russia; and in exchange programs in Leipzig, Germany, and Lile, France. Service learning opportunities are available in many other countries.

Academic Facilities

St. Scholastica's three-story Romanesque library houses more than 120,000 volumes, with special strengths in the health sciences, nursing, Indian studies, and children's materials. Computer workstations link the library to other state and national libraries, the campus network, and the Internet. Library instruction is provided throughout the curriculum. The Science Center has interactive television classroom capabilities. College research facilities include general and physical chemistry laboratories, health sciences laboratories, anatomy laboratories, and two state-of-the-art 24-hour computer labs.

Costs

St. Scholastica's 2003–04 tuition was $19,192. Room and board were $5668.

Financial Aid

The College of St. Scholastica handles a wide variety of financial aid and attempts to meet the needs of any qualified student enrolled. More than 90 percent of full-time students receive some form of aid; the average award is more than $11,000. The College also offers academic scholarships (Benedictine Scholarships). These awards are made on the basis of academic and leadership excellence, not necessarily because of need.

Students desiring to apply for financial aid should file the Free Application for Federal Student Aid (FAFSA) and have the results sent to St. Scholastica. Applications are processed on a first-come, first-served basis only after a student has been accepted by the College.

Faculty

St. Scholastica faculty members are devoted to personalized instruction, and the 13:1 student-teacher ratio is important to them. Faculty members hold advanced degrees from colleges and universities around the world. Four faculty members have been recent Fulbright International Scholars.

Student Government

The College trains leaders by encouraging students to hold positions of responsibility. Students manage the Student Senate and are directly involved in policymaking within the College community. They establish policies for the student newspaper and serve on institutional standing committees.

Admission Requirements

The College of St. Scholastica seeks to identify and admit students who have a strong probability of success in a demanding curriculum and rigorous academic major. Historically, the student who successfully demonstrates academic aptitude in high school or in a home school curriculum, has above-average ACT and/or SAT scores, and ranks in the upper half of his or her senior class is admitted to the College. Transfer students must demonstrate similar success in the college-level environment, with a minimum cumulative GPA of 2.0 for admission consideration. The College is an equal opportunity educator and employer.

Application and Information

The College of St. Scholastica requires each applicant to submit an application and a $25 nonrefundable fee, test scores on the SAT or ACT (required prior to enrollment), and an official high school transcript or GED test score. The College admits students on a rolling basis and notifies the applicant of the admission decision as soon as his or her file is complete.

For application and financial aid forms, prospective students should contact:

Brian F. Dalton
Vice President for Enrollment Management
College of St. Scholastica
1200 Kenwood Avenue
Duluth, Minnesota 55811
Telephone: 800-249-6412 (toll-free)
TTY/TDD: 218-723-6790
Fax: 218-723-5991
E-mail: admissions@css.edu

Tower Hall is the center of the College of St. Scholastica campus, which is in one of the most beautiful areas of Minnesota. Nearby are the Boundary Waters Canoe Area Wilderness, national forests and parks, ski areas, and pristine lakes and rivers.

COLLEGE OF SANTA FE

SANTA FE, NEW MEXICO

The College

College of Santa Fe (CSF) is an independent, private liberal arts college with emphasis in the creative arts as well as social and conservation sciences. CSF was founded in Santa Fe, New Mexico, in 1874 by the Lasallian Brothers, a teaching order of the Catholic Church. The Lasallian tradition emphasizes close-knit learning communities, service to others, and personalized, diligent faculty advising. Classes are small—the average just 13 students—making active participation and student interaction a required component of instruction.

In fall 2002, CSF enrolled approximately 1,600 students at the Santa Fe and Albuquerque campuses. About 800 students are enrolled in the traditional, undergraduate program, 400 of whom live on campus. Freshmen and sophomores are required to live in campus residence halls, and upperclassmen can opt for the fully furnished campus apartments, each of which houses two students. The student body is diverse, hailing from forty-seven states and several other countries.

CSF has nationally recognized degree programs in theater, visual art, creative writing, and moving image arts (film studies). Programs in conservation science, documentary studies, education, political science, psychology, and business round out the liberal arts focus: no matter which major a student chooses, he or she learns across a broad range of subjects. Academic life enhances campus life—nightly readings, plays, gallery openings, concerts, and lectures are sponsored by academic departments as well as the Student Activities Office.

In addition to CSF's undergraduate programs, master's degree programs are available in business administration and education, with a focus on at-risk youth.

Location

CSF's 95-acre campus located in Santa Fe, the capital of New Mexico, is in the north-central section of the state. About 65 miles from Albuquerque—New Mexico's largest city—Santa Fe is a small town with an urban flair. With a population of 65,000 in town and 60,000 in the county, the numbers triple as tourists flock to the world-famous galleries, museums, wilderness areas, and the Santa Fe Ski Basin. The local population is made up of three main cultures—American Indian, Spanish, and Anglo.

Santa Fe is 7,000 feet above sea level, nestled in the foothills of the Sangre de Cristo Mountains. This region of colorful contrasts is the third-largest art market in the United States and has been called the most interesting 50 square miles in America. Hikers, historians, skiers, art lovers, fishermen, and opera buffs have equal opportunity for their interests. Santa Fe has about 300 days of sunshine per year—and it can snow as early as October and as late as May.

Majors and Degrees

College of Santa Fe offers Bachelor of Arts, Bachelor of Fine Arts, Bachelor of Business Administration, and Bachelor of Science degrees. Degrees are offered in more than forty subject areas and concentrations, including accounting, acting, art history, art therapy, arts administration, conservation science and studies, contemporary music, counseling psychology, creative writing, documentary studies, education, English, humanities, moving image arts, music theater, organizational psychology, political science, studio art (with concentrations in mixed media, painting, photography, printmaking, and sculpture), technical theater, and theater management. Students may also elect to design an individual program of study called a Self-Designed Major (SDM).

Academic Programs

All CSF students complete a liberal arts core curriculum regardless of major field of study. An interdisciplinary structure enables first-year students to combine multiple areas of study under cohesive themes. Interrelated courses called "maps" are designed by faculty members working together toward a common education goal, and all courses include a writing seminar component. The core paradigm encourages students to engage the world holistically; to be learners and thinkers in order to be effective creators; and address what it means to live in an information age, where critical and integrative thinking is key to discerning information's value, relevance, and application. Options may include "Origins: Literature and the Arts," which combines history, visual art, and writing to explore major figures in world literature, art, and antiquity; or "Media, Information and Freedom," which combines moving image arts, social science, and writing to study manifestos, artist statements, and sociological/political analysis of the media.

The College operates on a two-semester system and offers two 4-week summer school sessions. Internships and study-abroad options are available. CSF also participates in a study-abroad consortium, giving students a wide variety of international study opportunities. Documentary studies students spend a semester of their senior year in Brazil. CSF participates in the New York Arts Program, and art, music, film, theater, and creative writing students can spend a semester in New York interning with an artist or arts organization. Bachelor of Fine Arts majors in performing arts are eligible to apply to spend a semester studying theater in London.

CSF offers day, evening, and weekend classes; credit for life experience through the Prior Learning Portfolio; credit by examination through the College-Level Examination Program (CLEP); and Advanced Placement (AP) examinations. Course challenges and petitions are arranged individually with faculty members. In addition to the traditional program, classes are offered to working adults through the evening and weekend degree programs as well as at College of Santa Fe at Albuquerque.

Academic Facilities

CSF offers facilities for a wide range of cultural activities, study, worship, and recreation. The Visual Arts Center, designed by renowned Mexican architect Ricardo Legorreta, houses the Anne and John Marion Center for Photographic Arts, Tishman Hall (painting and studio fundamentals), the Thaw Art History Center, the Chase Art History Library, the Marion Center Library (containing the James Enyeart and Beaumont-Newhall collections), Tipton Hall (lecture center), and the Atrium Gallery. The Printmaking Center and sculpture area round out the Art Department facilities.

The Garson Communication Center (GCC) is the hub for moving image arts students. The GCC houses studios for student productions, an art-house cinematheque open to the campus and community, and a New Media Lab. Attached to the GCC are the Garson Studios, professional sound stages utilized by well-known filmmakers as well as smaller commercial productions. Films headquartered at College of Santa Fe include *All the Pretty Horses, The Missing,* and *The Hi-Lo Country,* as well as the cult science fiction television series *Earth 2.*

Performing arts students spend much of their time in the Greer Garson Theatre Center (GGTC), named after the Academy Award–winning actress and longtime friend of the College. The GGTC houses a 500-seat mainstage theater, a 90-seat black box studio theater, dressing rooms, scene shop, costume shop, dance studio, practice rooms, and classrooms. The theater lobby provides gallery space on two floors.

The Fogelson Library Center offers space for study, meetings, classes, and social events. The campus Digital Center is located on the top floor, and provides all the latest in software, from word processing and number crunching to digital editing and GIS remote sensing for geological mapping. The 53,000-square-foot library maintains more than 400 periodical subscriptions, 10,000 microfilms, and more than 150,000 volumes, including 8,000 in the College's outstanding Southwest Collection. Regarded locally as Santa Fe's finest library, the Fogelson participates in interlibrary loan and has several electronic research indexes and directories for student use.

The Driscoll Fitness Center (DFC) houses a gymnasium, a weight room, a multipurpose room containing aerobic and cardio machines, a motorized climbing wall, racquetball and squash courts, and locker rooms. The DFC offers a variety of for-credit and extracurricular classes, including yoga, tai chi, and belly dancing. The Outdoor Recreation Program, coordinated through the DFC, hosts day and weekend trips to regional sites, including Tent Rocks, Cochiti, Bandelier, and Canyonlands National Park in Utah, as well as skiing, hiking, and rafting excursions.

The new state-of-the-art Rosemarie Shellaberger Tennis Center features six indoor courts with a shadow-and-glare-free indirect lighting system, a clubhouse, a pro shop, an exercise room, and locker rooms, as well as an outdoor championship stadium.

Costs

Tuition for the 2003–04 academic year was $18,980. Room and board were about $6000, depending on the plan chosen. Students should expect to spend about $750 per year on books and supplies.

Financial Aid

CSF offers merit- and need-based financial aid, including the Presidential Scholarship and the Dean's Scholarship. Some academic departments offer talent scholarships to returning students. To apply for aid, students are required to fill out the Free Application for Financial Aid (FAFSA).

Faculty

CSF students learn from nationally and internationally recognized artists, writers, musicians, thinkers, and educators. CSF faculty members are practitioners in their fields rather than theorists, which makes class discussion relevant, immediate, and inspiring. Personalized education and faculty-student interaction are integral components of the CSF experience, rooted firmly in the Lasallian tradition of teaching excellence.

Student Government

All CSF students are encouraged to take an active role in the Associated Student Government (ASG). ASG oversees campus clubs and plans student events throughout the year.

Admission Requirements

Admission to CSF is based on a student's record of academic achievement and scholastic aptitude. All applicants must submit an official copy of their high school transcript or GED scores, copies of either SAT I or ACT scores (not applicable for students over 21), and official records of any college work previously attempted. All prospective students are encouraged to visit the campus.

Application and Information

CSF uses a rolling admissions system. Applicants must file an application for admission with a one-time nonrefundable fee of $35.

For more information about the College of Santa Fe, students should contact:

Admissions Office
College of Santa Fe
1600 St. Michael's Drive
Santa Fe, New Mexico 87505-5634
Telephone: 505-473-6133
800-456-2673 (toll-free)
Fax: 505-473-6127
World Wide Web: http://www.csf.edu

A view of the campus.

THE COLLEGE OF SOUTHEASTERN EUROPE, THE AMERICAN UNIVERSITY OF ATHENS

ATHENS, GREECE

The College

Founded in 1982, the College of Southeastern Europe (CSE) is a senior college accredited by the Accrediting Council for Independent Colleges and Schools to award bachelor's and master's degrees. It has an enrollment of approximately 1,000 students. Coeducational in all divisions, CSE has students from the U.S., Greece, and thirty-eight other countries. Students may choose from more than forty-five undergraduate majors in the three schools and later may pursue graduate degrees in eight specializations. The small-sized classes, the use of English in instruction, the highly qualified faculty members, the curricula, and the teaching methodologies reflect the educational philosophy and structure of an American university, thus making the College of Southeastern Europe a most competitive institution in Europe, especially in southeastern Europe. Major University divisions are the School of Business Administration, the School of Sciences and Engineering, and the School of Liberal Arts, as well as the Graduate School.

Location

The College of Southeastern Europe has three campuses located in the center of Athens, the ancient capital of Greece and home of the Olympic Games. It is a warm and exciting city belonging to that privileged class of historic cities of antiquity that offer students a fascinating selection of cultural events. Greece has the reputation of being one of the safest and most hospitable countries in Europe.

Majors and Degrees

The College of Southeastern Europe's undergraduate program in business administration is divided into three departments, all offering a bachelor's degree in business administration with various concentrations. In the Department of Accounting, Finance, and Economics, concentrations are available in accounting, economics, and finance. In the Department of Management, concentrations are available in hotel management, human resource management, management, management science and quantitative methods, shipping management, and travel and tourism management. In the Department of Marketing and General Business, concentrations are available in general business, international business, and marketing.

The School of Sciences and Engineering consists of two departments and awards Bachelor of Science degrees in various concentrations. In the Department of Computer Sciences and Engineering, concentrations are available in architectural engineering, civil engineering, computer hardware and digital electronics, computer information systems, computer science, electrical engineering, engineering science, manufacturing engineering, and mechanical engineering. In the Department of Natural Sciences and Mathematics, concentrations are available in biology, biochemistry, chemistry, mathematics, and physics. This department also offers a 2½-year program in premedical studies, preparing students for entrance into a school of medical or biomedical studies in the U.S.

The School of Liberal Arts has five departments, all leading to the Bachelor of Arts degree. The Department of Humanities has concentrations available in English literature and philosophy. The Department of Social Sciences has concentrations available in history, political science, psychology, and sociology. The Department of Communication has concentrations available in journalism and public relations. The Arts Department has concentrations available in art history and Byzantine studies. The Department of Applied Arts has concentrations available in fashion design and graphic design–3-D animation. The Department of Social Sciences also offers a four-year professional program in law studies in affiliation with the Institute of Legal Executives (ILEX) in the United Kingdom.

Students may select minor areas of study in art history, business, Byzantine studies, computer hardware and digital electronics, computer science, English literature, history, journalism, marketing for public relations students, philosophy, political science, psychology, public relations, and sociology.

Academic Programs

The academic year is made up of two semesters. A winter intersession and two summer intersessions are also available. A minimum of 129 semester hours of appropriate academic credit is required for a Bachelor of Science degree in all business concentrations. In order to graduate, a student must maintain a minimum 2.0 cumulative grade point average as well as a minimum 2.0 grade point average for each of the major courses.

While the number of semester credit hours required for graduation varies with each concentration in the School of Sciences and Engineering, a minimum of 131 hours are required for a degree. In order to graduate, a student must maintain a minimum 2.0 cumulative grade point average as well as a minimum 2.0 grade point average for each of the major courses.

A degree in the liberal arts concentrations requires a minimum of 126 semester credit hours. In order to graduate, a student must maintain a minimum 2.0 cumulative grade point average as well as a minimum 2.0 grade point average for each of the major courses.

CSE offers a special study-abroad program in Greek civilization. A particular feature of the program is that a number of courses include visits to historical and archaeological sites, museums, and theaters.

Academic Facilities

College of Southeastern Europe students have access to the CSE library, which contains a wide variety of reference books and slides. Electronic data retrieval is also available, allowing access to the main European or American libraries and data banks. The Computer Center provides computing resources to students and offers access to computers and software programs. There are also biology, chemistry, electronics, and physics laboratories with state-of-the-art equipment.

Costs

Tuition and fees for 2003–04 were €5636 per academic year. Housing costs in the residence centers averaged €2900 (double room) and €3300 (single room) per academic year. Books and supplies cost about €300 per semester. Food and miscellaneous personal expenses for twelve months were approximately €3000 for a student with a conservative lifestyle. There was also a €400 insurance charge.

Financial Aid

The College of Southeastern Europe offers an arrangement of financial assistance to full-time students through work-study programs. Successful candidates earn 40 percent of their semester tuition through completion of a 20-hour weekly work schedule during the fifteen-week semester.

Faculty

The faculty numbers 75 members, 85 percent of whom hold doctoral degrees. The student-faculty ratio is 6:1, and the average class size is 14 students. Academic, career, and personal counseling is available. CSE faculty members are creative, dedicated individuals who take the time to consider the welfare of their students.

Student Government

The Student Representative Council (SRC) is the governing body of the Student Association, which acts on behalf of the students, recommends changes, and refers problems to the appropriate heads. The council is made up of 8 elected members.

Admission Requirements

The College of Southeastern Europe seeks a student body that represents diverse backgrounds. A strong commitment to minority recruitment, equality of the sexes, and opportunities for the handicapped guarantee this diversity. CSE is proud of its history of providing opportunities for students from various educational and cultural backgrounds and from many geographic regions. International students are eligible to apply for admission if they have completed the equivalent of an American secondary school education (approximately twelve years of formal education starting at age 6) and have the appropriate diplomas or satisfactory results on exit examinations. It is strongly recommended, but not compulsory, that applicants submit a personal essay and two recommendation letters. Each candidate is required to have an interview. It is compulsory for freshmen who are not native speakers of English to take the CSE English Placement Test.

Transfer students in good academic standing are encouraged to apply to the College of Southeastern Europe. CSE grants transfer credits for courses to candidates with grades higher than C. Undergraduate transfer candidates are encouraged to file an application at least sixty days prior to the beginning of the semester of enrollment. Each applicant must arrange for official transcripts of all previous college records to be sent directly to CSE.

Application and Information

To be considered for admission, students are encouraged to file an application approximately sixty days prior to the beginning of the semester of enrollment. There is a €100 application fee. Subsequently, a copy of secondary school credentials must be filed with the Office of Admissions. The personal statement and recommendation letters are very important but not compulsory.

For application forms and additional information, students should contact:

Admissions Office
The College of Southeastern Europe,
the American University of Athens
17 Patriarchou Ieremiou Street
Athens 11475
Greece
Telephone: 30210-7259301-2
E-mail: information@southeastern.edu.gr
World Wide Web: http://www.southeastern.edu.gr

The College of Southeastern Europe, the American University of Athens.

COLLEGE OF STATEN ISLAND OF THE CITY UNIVERSITY OF NEW YORK

STATEN ISLAND, NEW YORK

The College and The University

The College of Staten Island (CSI) is part of the City University of New York, the largest urban university in the country. The College, like the University, is committed to both access and excellence. CSI's superb campus serves the pivotal endeavors of teaching and research that promote discovery and dissemination of knowledge while developing human minds and spirits. CSI was founded in 1976 by the union of two existing colleges within the City University: Staten Island Community College and Richmond College. Staten Island Community College, the first community college in the University system, opened in 1955. Richmond College, the University's first upper-division college, was founded in 1965. CSI's current undergraduate enrollment is slightly more than 11,000 men and women.

A general education is assured through requirements that allow students to explore a range of knowledge and acquire educational breadth in the arts and humanities, mathematics, science, and social sciences. Requirements for the associate degree provide a curriculum based on study in a specific area often directed toward a career. Requirements for the bachelor's degree provide a disciplined and cumulative program of study in a major field of inquiry.

CSI awards the Master of Arts degree in cinema studies, English, environmental science, history, and liberal studies; the Master of Science degree in adult health nursing, biology, and computer science; the Master of Science in Education degree in elementary education, secondary education, and special education; and a sixth-year professional certificate in education supervision and administration. The College offers a combined Bachelor of Science and Master of Science degree in physical therapy. CSI participates with the CUNY Graduate School and University Center and Brooklyn College in a doctoral program in polymer chemistry and with the Graduate School and University Center in doctoral programs in computer science and physics. With the Center for Developmental Neurosciences and Developmental Disabilities, the College participates in CUNY doctoral subprograms in neuroscience (biology) and learning processes (psychology).

Study-abroad opportunities are available through three Culture and Commerce programs emphasizing the study of Italian, French, or Spanish and through the Center for International Service.

The Campus Center incorporates facilities for a complete program of student activities. It contains the main dining facilities, the College health services, a bookstore, offices for student organizations, study lounges, a small performance/cafe space, game rooms, and the studios of WSIA, the student-operated FM radio station. The two-story rotunda space at the heart of the structure contains the dining areas and information services.

Location

The College occupies a 204-acre campus located near the center of Staten Island. The campus is the largest site for a college (public or private) within New York City. Set in a parklike landscape, the grounds and facilities create a rural oasis in an urban setting. In this attractive learning environment, classrooms and academic offices are located in ten buildings that form two quadrangles connected by the campus walk, which extends between the library building and the campus center. Five newly built and equipped buildings—the library building, the campus center, the biological sciences/chemical sciences building, the center for the arts, and the sports and recreation center—provide outstanding facilities for college and community activities.

The College's location offers students the best of two worlds. While Staten Island provides a suburban environment with some of the most interesting landscape in the metropolitan area, Manhattan, the center of cultural and social life of the city, is only 25 minutes from the island by ferry. The Verrazano-Narrows Bridge provides direct access to the island from Brooklyn.

Majors and Degrees

The Associate in Arts degree is offered in liberal arts and sciences. The Associate in Science degree is offered in engineering science, liberal arts and sciences, and liberal arts and sciences with a prearchitecture concentration. The Associate in Applied Science degree is offered in business, civil engineering technology, computer technology, electrical engineering technology, medical laboratory technology, and nursing.

The Bachelor of Arts degree is conferred in African-American studies; American studies; art; art with a photography concentration; cinema studies; economics; English; English with a dramatic literature concentration; history; international studies; music; philosophy; political science; psychology; science, letters, and society; sociology/anthropology; social work; Spanish; and women's studies. The Bachelor of Science degree is offered in accounting; art; art with a photography concentration; biochemistry; bioinformatics; biology; business; business with a finance concentration, an international business concentration, a management concentration, or a marketing concentration; chemistry; communications; computer science; computer science/mathematics; dramatic arts; economics; economics with a business specialization or a finance specialization; engineering science; information systems; international studies; mathematics; medical technology; music; music with an electronics concentration; nursing (upper-division program); physical therapy (combined B.S./M.S.); physician assistant studies; and physics.

The teacher education program prepares students for teaching at the early childhood, elementary, and secondary levels. The academic work and field experience meet the requirements for the certification and licensing examinations given by the state and city of New York.

Academic Program

A four-year senior college, CSI offers two-year programs in career areas and in liberal arts and sciences and four-year programs with majors in the traditional fields of study. General education requirements have been established for all degrees. The associate degree programs require 60–64 credits, depending on the field; the bachelor's degree programs require 120 credits, with a few exceptions. Credit may be awarded for experiential learning, internships, and independent study, and credit may be earned by examination. Minors may be taken in several fields, and double majors are permitted. Students may graduate with honors in their field of study in most bachelor's degree majors.

The College follows a semester calendar, with classes scheduled both day and evening; a summer session is also held. The

Weekend College, established to provide an opportunity for students with weekday commitments to pursue a college education, offers a variety of course combinations leading to associate and bachelor's degrees.

Off-Campus Programs

The College gives a number of courses for credit at off-campus locations throughout the city. These include employee-development programs for major corporations and other programs, supported by grants and by participating employers and unions that provide courses for city and state employees at agency or institutional locations.

Academic Facilities

The academic buildings are designed to house approximately 200 modern laboratories and classrooms. Each also houses a study lounge for students, department and program offices, and offices for faculty members. Academic and research programs are served by a computer network that allows students and faculty members full access to specialized software, the Internet, online library resources, and e-mail. All major computer languages and software packages are supported. The College houses an IBM 4381 computer, and students can access the University's IBM 3090/400 system.

The Center for the Arts complex provides facilities for teaching in the instructional wing and areas of public assembly in the public wing. The complex of public facilities includes a 900-seat auditorium, a 450-seat fully equipped theater, a recital hall, an experimental theater, an art gallery, and a conference center. Classrooms, lecture halls, studios, and offices for faculty members are located in the instructional wing fronting the campus walk.

The library is designed to house approximately 300,000 volumes, computer facilities for database searching, periodical subscriptions, and media services. Small study areas under skylights define a raised central area around a rotunda on the third floor, which provides space for readers within the expanse of the stacks. The collection also includes 1,700 current journal subscriptions, 600,000 titles in microform, and a wide range of audiovisual materials in various formats. The CSI Library is a member of the CUNY-wide integrated library system. Students and faculty members have free access to ERIC as well as various databases on CD-ROM or via the Internet.

The laboratory science building provides facilities for teaching and for two research centers: the Center for Environmental Science and the Center for Developmental Neuroscience and Developmental Disabilities. It consists of a research wing and an instructional wing. State-of-the-art laboratories serve students and faculty members in their teaching and research.

The 77,000-gross-square-foot Sports and Recreation Center is a multipurpose facility providing ball courts, locker rooms, instructional areas, an indoor 25-meter swimming pool, and offices for faculty. Recreational fields occupy the meadows in the northwest quadrant of the campus, providing a green and landscaped open area at the main approach to the campus.

Costs

For 2003–04, costs for first-time freshmen or non-CUNY transfer students enrolled after June 1, 1992, were $170 per credit (part-time matriculated) or $2000 per semester (full-time matriculated) for New York State residents and $360 per credit for out-of-state students.

Financial Aid

Financial aid is available through state and federal programs and includes the New York State Tuition Assistance Program (TAP) awards, Federal Pell Grants, Federal Supplemental Educational Opportunity Grants (FSEOG), Search for Elevation and Education through Knowledge (SEEK) awards, scholarships, Federal Work-Study Program awards, and student loan programs. Information about programs, application procedures, and deadlines is available from the Financial Aid Office.

CSI Presidential Scholarships are awarded annually to full-time students on the basis of academic proficiency and service. In addition, endowments have been established for scholarships in a number of fields. Further information about scholarships is available from the Office of Career Placement, Scholarships and Awards.

Faculty

The College has a full-time faculty of 300, of whom approximately 80 percent hold a doctoral degree or the equivalent. The faculty members have made significant contributions in many areas of scholarship, creativity, and public service. Numerous faculty members have received prestigious grants and awards, and 30 serve as members of the City University doctoral faculty.

Student Government

The Student Government is composed of 20 elected representatives, and it is through this structure that students are represented in the College's governance.

Admission Requirements

A freshman applicant for admission to a bachelor's degree program must pass the three CUNY Freshman Skills Assessment Tests unless he or she qualifies for exemption based on a satisfactory performance on the SAT I or ACT standardized tests or Regents Examinations. Admission to a bachelor's degree program is determined by an applicant's score on the College's admissions index. The index is based on the applicant's high school courses and academic average and the combined verbal and mathematics SAT I scores. An applicant whose score reaches or exceeds the College's minimum index number is admitted to a bachelor's degree program. A faculty admissions committee may consider the admission of applicants whose scores approach the College's minimum index number. Transfer students with fewer than 25 credits must have a GPA of at least 3.0; with 26 to 39 credits, a GPA of at least 2.5; and with 40 or more credits, a GPA of at least 2.0. Students must have passed the CUNY Freshman Skills Assessment Tests in mathematics, writing, and reading prior to enrolling in a bachelor's degree program or if they are transferring from another college in the City University.

Entering first-year students may be admitted to two-year programs if they have graduated from an accredited high school, have earned an equivalency diploma (GED) with a satisfactory score, or have completed at least six semesters of high school (eleventh grade) and are currently attending high school.

As a general rule, the College requires a grade point average equivalent to at least a C for transfer as a matriculated student into a two-year degree program.

Application and Information

Requests for further information and application materials should be directed to:

Office of Recruitment and Admissions
North Administration Building (2A-103)
College of Staten Island
City University of New York
2800 Victory Boulevard
Staten Island, New York 10314
Telephone: 718-982-2010
E-mail: admissionss@mail.csi.cuny.edu
World Wide Web: http://www.csi.cuny.edu

COLLEGE OF THE ATLANTIC

BAR HARBOR, MAINE

The College

College of the Atlantic (COA) was founded in 1969 to provide an ecological, problem-solving approach to education that combines academic rigor in the arts and sciences with practical application. The College's small size allows students to work closely with faculty members and to design an individualized program suited to their own particular interests. Enrollment during 2003–04 is 275: 170 women and 105 men. The oceanfront location of the campus allows students to take advantage of the abundant natural resources offered by the Atlantic Ocean and nearby Acadia National Park. The College also sponsors a regular film and speaker series, numerous concerts and dances, informal College parties, musical get-togethers, and recitals. Students, faculty members, and staff members form a close-knit College community.

In addition to its undergraduate degrees, the College also offers a Master of Philosophy (M.Phil.) in human ecology.

Location

The College is located in the town of Bar Harbor on Mount Desert Island, Maine, where Acadia National Park is also situated. Connected to the mainland by a causeway, the large, scenic island lies 300 miles north of Boston and 40 miles east of Bangor. In the summer, Bar Harbor teems with tourists. When students return in the fall, the traffic reverses direction and Bar Harbor becomes a quiet coastal Maine village. The Atlantic Ocean and Acadia National Park provide ample opportunities for such outdoor recreational activities as swimming, fishing, canoeing, kayaking, rock climbing, mountain hiking, cross-country skiing, and snowshoeing. Cooperative programs with the Jackson Laboratory, the Mount Desert Island Biological Laboratory, the national park, and the local public school system helps to broaden the scope of COA's educational activities. The College's two islands and 86-acre organic farm expand COA's resources.

Majors and Degrees

College of the Atlantic awards the Bachelor of Arts in Human Ecology. Human ecology emphasizes the understanding of interrelationships between humans and the social, technological, and natural environments. Within the degree focus, students may develop individualized programs in one or more of the following areas: environmental science, humanities, international and regional studies, landscape and building design, marine studies, natural-history-museum studies, public policy, sustainable agriculture and community development, teacher certification, and visual arts.

Academic Program

The academic program is designed to develop an ecological perspective through the understanding of social, biological, and technological interrelationships. With this perspective, students acquire the skills necessary to enter the fields of science, education, business, law, design, the arts, health, or journalism. Sixty percent of COA's alumni have pursued graduate or professional education at some of the country's leading institutions. Many different forms of study are available at COA, and small and informal classes are the foundation of the curriculum. Student-initiated workshops, independent studies, internships, and senior projects also provide important learning experiences. Applied learning is the norm, not the exception.

To qualify for graduation, students must complete required interdisciplinary course work, write an essay on human ecology, perform community service, and complete a one-term internship and a one-term senior project.

College of the Atlantic accepts up to two years of transfer credits from accredited colleges if the grades earned were C or better and were earned in courses of an academic nature.

Off-Campus Programs

The College's academic program is augmented by exchange agreements with the University of Maine at Orono; the Palacky University in Olomouc, Czech Republic; the Landing School of Boatbuilding in Kennebunk, Maine; and the Multiversidad Franciscana de Americana Latino in Uruguay. Students may also spend a term in COA's own study abroad program in the Yucatan Peninsula in Mexico.

Academic Facilities

Thorndike Library, with more than 35,000 volumes and 410 periodicals, also provides access to libraries throughout the United States, Great Britain, and Canada through OCLC interlibrary loans. COA has zoology, botany, and chemistry laboratories; a herbarium; greenhouses; design and ceramics studios; state-of-the-art computer facilities, including a Geographic Information Systems Lab and a design/graphics computer lab; research boats for marine research and to ferry students and faculty members to College-owned island research stations in the Gulf of Maine; and an 86-acre working organic farm.

Costs

The total cost for the 2003–04 academic year was estimated at $29,193. This included $22,266 for tuition, $3777 for room, $2310 for board, $480 for books and supplies, a $240 student activities fee, and $360 for personal expenses.

Financial Aid

More than two thirds of the College's students receive some form of financial aid. The Free Application for Federal Student Aid and the College's own form are required by the College to determine a student's eligibility for assistance. Aid is based on established need and academic merit. Financial aid packages generally consist of a combination of scholarships, work-study awards, and loans.

Faculty

With a faculty of 29 full-time and 13 part-time teachers, the student-faculty ratio is 10:1. Eighty-five percent of the full-time faculty members have Ph.D.'s or the equivalent. Courses offered by regular visiting faculty members supplement the curriculum. The primary commitment of the COA faculty is teaching and advising undergraduate students.

Student Government

The College governance system is a combination of pure and representative democracy. Students participate in all facets of decision making and serve on all standing committees. Major policy decisions are brought for review to the All-College Meeting, where members of the faculty, staff, and student body each have one vote.

Admission Requirements

The Admission Committee, composed of students, staff members, and faculty members, seeks students who have an enthusiastic and active approach to learning, a strong record of academic achievement, and accompanying intellectual strengths. These qualities should be supplemented with appropriate personal qualities enabling a student to learn in an environment requiring a high degree of self-motivation.

The COA application form contains a series of essay questions that require students to think carefully about College of the Atlantic's educational focus. The application is designed to encourage prospective students to reflect on and express personal reasons for choosing a small college with a focus on human ecology. The answers to these questions, teacher and counselor references, past academic records, and personal interviews are used by the Admission Committee in arriving at its decision. Standardized test scores are optional.

Admission procedures and standards are the same for transfer students as for freshman applicants. Special emphasis is placed on the transfer applicant's college transcript and recommendations. The transfer of credits is determined on an individual basis. All transferring students are required to complete a minimum of two years of study at COA. Applications are also accepted from students at other institutions who wish to spend time at the College as visiting students.

Application and Information

Prospective students are encouraged to visit the College in order to sit in on classes, talk with students and faculty members, and acquire an understanding of the College's individualized educational style. COA employs a deadline date of February 15 for fall admission for first-year students, but offers two early decision options with a December 1 deadline and a January 10 deadline. Transfer students must apply by April 1. Decisions for first-year students are mailed on or about April 1 and on or about April 25 for transfer students. Applicants for winter term should apply by November 15 and for spring term by February 15. Application materials may be obtained by writing to the College or by telephoning the Admission Office at the number below. The application fee is $45. COA endorses the policy set by the National Association of College Admission Counselors, whereby regular admission students have the right to defer accepting any offer of admission until May 1.

Director of Admission
College of the Atlantic
105 Eden Street
Bar Harbor, Maine 04609
Telephone: 207-288-5015
800-528-0025 (toll-free)
Fax: 207-288-4126
E-mail: inquiry@coa.edu
World Wide Web: http://www.coa.edu

Mount Desert Rock, 25 miles off Bar Harbor's coast, is owned by COA and serves as a research station for students.

THE COLLEGE OF WOOSTER

WOOSTER, OHIO

The College

One of the first coeducational colleges in the country, the College of Wooster was founded in 1866 by Presbyterians who wanted to do "their proper part in the great work of educating those who are to mold society and give shape to all its institutions." Today it is a fully independent, privately endowed liberal arts college with a rich tradition of academic excellence. That tradition defines student life at Wooster, beginning with the First-Year Seminar in Critical Inquiry and culminating in the Independent Study program.

The current enrollment is about 1,800 men and women. Almost all students live on campus, selecting from a variety of housing options. These include Babcock International House for students interested in international studies, Andrews Hall for students with an interest in the humanities and sciences, and Kenarden Lodge, a modern facility arranged in living suites. There are also thirty-three houses on the edge of campus, many of which serve as living-learning centers for those in community service and volunteer programs.

Wooster's 240-acre campus has forty major buildings. With its distinctive arch, Kauke Hall is instantly recognizable as an icon for Wooster. Kauke is home to many academic departments, classrooms, and faculty offices. Wooster has excellent facilities for physical education, including a fully equipped fitness center, a nine-hole golf course, an all-weather track, and eight hard-surfaced tennis courts. Wooster's newest structure, Bornhuetter Residence Hall, an $8.9-million structure, will house 185 students beginning in fall 2004. The 46,650-square-foot, four-story building is composed of two separate residential wings with double-loaded corridors scaled to house 21–31 students each. Student rooms are double occupancy with adjustable furniture, high-speed data lines for each occupant, and outlets for telephone and cable television. Three new buildings opened in 2002, beginning in March with the $2-million, 10,000-square-foot Longbrake Student Wellness Center. The Student Wellness Center is a state-of-the-art student facility that includes six treatment rooms, eight in-patient beds, and a pharmacy. The Gault Center for Admissions opened in June 2002, and the $8-million, 44,000-square-foot Burton D. Morgan Hall opened in fall 2002. Morgan Hall houses the Departments of Economics (including Business Economics), Psychology, and Education, and is the future home of the College's Information Technology Center. Other facilities include Severance Chemistry Building; Scheide Music Center; the Flo K. Gault Library for Independent Study, which adjoins the Andrews Library; the Ebert Art Center, which contains an art gallery and substantial facilities for studio art and art history; and the Timken Science Library.

Most of the social life at Wooster originates from Lowry Center, the student union. The Student Activities Board organizes dances, concerts, films, off-campus outings, and many other activities. The music and theater departments and local social clubs also contribute to the activities on campus. The student entertainment center (The Underground) hosts live bands, comedians, dance parties, and folksingers, and sometimes serves as a dinner theater.

Location

The College is located in Wooster, Ohio, a city of approximately 26,000. Wooster is 55 miles south of Cleveland and 30 miles west of Akron. An unusually close relationship exists between the College and the community. College-community activities include the Wooster Symphony, a college-community theatrical production, and a variety of volunteer and internship experiences.

Majors and Degrees

The College of Wooster offers the degrees of Bachelor of Arts, Bachelor of Music, and Bachelor of Music Education. A student may choose from thirty-seven possible majors, including seven interdepartmental majors: anthropology, archaeology, art history, art/studio, biochemistry and molecular biology, biology, black studies, business economics, chemical physics, chemistry, classical studies, communication sciences and disorders, communication studies, comparative literature, computer science, cultural area studies, economics, English, French, geology, German, history, international relations, mathematics, music, philosophy, physics, political science, psychology, religious studies, Russian studies, sociology, Spanish, theater, theater/dance, urban studies, and women's studies. In addition, minors are available in many of the areas above as well as physical education. Students also have the option of designing their own major, contingent upon the approval of the Upperclass Programs Committee. The Department of Education offers all courses necessary for either elementary or secondary teaching licensure.

Wooster offers combined-degree opportunities in cooperation with other institutions; such programs lead to either two bachelor's degrees (one from each institution) or a bachelor's from Wooster and a master's from the cooperating institution. Specific programs are in operation with Columbia University (law), Dartmouth College (business administration), the University of Michigan (economics, mathematics, and physics), Duke University (forestry and environmental management), Washington University (engineering), and Case Western Reserve University (dentistry, engineering, nursing, and social work).

Academic Programs

Wooster's academic program is designed to provide a liberal education that prepares undergraduates for a lifetime of inquiry, discovery, and responsible citizenship. In fall 2001, Wooster instituted a curriculum that focuses directly on these curricular goals. To be eligible for a Bachelor of Arts degree, a student must successfully complete thirty-two courses, including a First-Year Seminar in Critical Inquiry and three courses of Independent Study (IS). IS, as it is universally known on campus, gives each Wooster senior the opportunity to create an original research project, written scholarly work, exhibit of artwork or performance in a yearlong project, supported one-on-one by a faculty mentor. An overall grade point average of at least 2.0 (on a 4.0 scale) is required for graduation. Students may receive credit for work done at other colleges and for scores of 4 or better on the Advanced Placement tests offered by the College Board. Courses are graded A–D or No Credit unless the student exercises an option to take certain courses on a Satisfactory/No Credit basis.

Off-Campus Programs

Students who wish to enrich their undergraduate experience by overseas study may choose from a variety of fully accredited programs. Wooster sponsors a number of off-campus programs in the United States and abroad, and, as a member of the Great Lakes Colleges Association, offers off-campus study opportunities in thirteen countries on four continents. There are also programs available through the Institute of European Studies in seven university centers throughout Europe.

A variety of off-campus opportunities within the United States provide both academic and internship experiences. The Washington Semester and the Semester at the United Nations offer extensive possibilities in national and international government. Urban studies centers in Birmingham, Philadelphia, Portland, St. Louis, and San Diego provide many different experiential options. There is also a fine-arts semester in New York City. Other internship possibilities exist in business, the humanities, the natural sciences, and psychology.

Academic Facilities

The College libraries consist of the Andrews Library, the adjacent Flo K. Gault Library for Independent Study, and the nearby Timken Science Library in Frick Hall. Together, the libraries contain more than 1 million books, periodicals, microforms, electronic journals, videotapes, and audio recordings. As a member of CONSORT and OhioLINK, the libraries can provide almost any book from Ohio's academic libraries within two to three days. The libraries subscribe to a wide variety of electronic databases and to some 5,000 periodicals in electronic form, all available campuswide via the computing network. The libraries house more than 300 study carrels, each of which is equipped with electrical and data connections.

Computing is an important part of Wooster's academic environment. All academic buildings and every residence hall room are connected in an interactive computing network. The Taylor Hall computer center houses fifty-two terminals for student use while the Wired Scot, a cyber café that opened in fall 2003, features twenty-two PC workstations with Internet access, two large plasma-screen TVs, and wireless Internet access throughout the building to anyone with wireless capability.

The College's science facilities contain the most up-to-date laboratory equipment, libraries, computer terminals, and instrumentation, including ultraviolet, visible, fluorescence, and infrared spectrometers; a scanning electron microscope; an atomic force microscope; a nuclear magnetic resonance spectrometer; a mass spectrometer; an X-ray diffractometer; and various chromatographs.

Wooster's Learning Center provides academic support for students, and priority is given to students with identified learning disabilities. Adult tutors work with individual students on time management, organization skills, and effective study strategies. Wooster's Writing Center provides writing assistance through one-to-one tutorial sessions and group workshops covering all aspects of the writing process.

The Freedlander Theatre complex contains excellent technical equipment and a separate theater for students' experimental productions. The speech facility itself houses a radio station and a speech and hearing clinic that also serves the community.

The Scheide Music Center, a 35,000-square-foot complex, contains five classrooms, eleven teaching studios, twenty-three soundproof practice rooms, a music library, and a listening lab. The Timken Rehearsal Hall and the acoustically balanced Gault Recital Hall are "tunable" so that the halls can be rendered "live" to greater or lesser degrees.

The Ebert Art Center has expansive space for studio art and art history. The building includes classrooms, individual studios for senior studio art majors, and the Sussel Art Gallery.

Costs

The comprehensive fee (room, board, tuition, and fees) for 2004–05 is $33,200.

Financial Aid

Almost all financial assistance is awarded on the basis of need, as determined by the Free Application for Federal Student Aid (FAFSA). Aid is allocated when students are admitted to the College. Financial assistance information and forms should be requested at the time of application. Applications for aid should be submitted by February 15.

The College of Wooster believes in recognizing individual talent and hard work. Thus, Wooster offers merit-based scholarships that range from $2000 to $18,000 in a number of academic, leadership, and performance areas. All scholarship awards are applicable toward tuition only and are renewable for four years. Each year, the College awards about $16.5 million in competitive scholarship funds to the nations' top students. Students should call the Office of Admissions to request detailed information about scholarship opportunities.

Faculty

The faculty members and administration, 97 percent of whom (excluding those in performance areas) hold a doctoral degree or terminal degree in their field, are dedicated to meeting the educational needs of individual students; they strive to help them realize their inherent potential. The student-faculty ratio is 12:1.

Student Government

The Campus Council, which consists of representatives from the student body, faculty, and administration, is the main legislative body in the areas of student life and cocurricular affairs. The Student Government Association, the Black Students Association, and the International Student Association also contribute to policymaking at Wooster. Students may attend open meetings of the faculty and are represented on virtually all faculty committees; they may also send representatives to observe meetings of the Board of Trustees.

Admission Requirements

A candidate for admission to the College should have earned a minimum of 16 academic units in high school, with emphases in English, foreign language, mathematics, natural science, and social studies. The student must present satisfactory scores on either the SAT I or the ACT. No College Board Subject Test scores are required.

The deadline for regular admission is February 15. Students are notified of the decision by April 1 and must reply by May 1. Early Decision I applicants must apply by December 1 and are notified on December 15. Early Decision II candidates must apply by January 15 and are notified by February 1. Deferred admission is available, as is admission at the end of the junior year of high school. Students are encouraged to visit the campus and have a personal interview.

The College of Wooster does not discriminate on the basis of age, sex, race, creed, national origin, handicap, sexual orientation, or political affiliation in the admission of students or in their participation in College educational programs, activities, financial aid, or employment.

Application and Information

Dean of Admissions
The College of Wooster
Wooster, Ohio 44691
Telephone: 330-263-2000 Ext. 2270 or 2322
800-877-9905 (toll-free)
Fax: 330-263-2621
E-mail: admissions@wooster.edu
World Wide Web: http://www.wooster.edu

COLORADO CHRISTIAN UNIVERSITY

LAKEWOOD, COLORADO

The University

Located near the foothills of the Rocky Mountains, Colorado Christian University (CCU) is one of the members of the Council for Christian Colleges and Universities in the Rocky Mountain region. Founded in 1914, CCU is a private nondenominational institution committed to providing undergraduate and graduate students with a complete education that develops the whole person—academically, professionally, and spiritually. Through offering a variety of programs and activities, CCU challenges students to experience their faith in all aspects of life. As a result, CCU graduates are equipped to be effective leaders in their careers, communities, churches, and families and in the world.

CCU has high academic standards and works with students to help them achieve the highest success. Students are taught by mentors who are experienced practitioners and qualified educators committed to the Christian faith. All students are challenged to incorporate biblical concepts and integrity into the skills and knowledge they're gaining in the classroom, in every major. Through critical thinking and experiential learning opportunities in the classroom, CCU students are prepared to be successful in a wide range of careers.

Community service and personal development are integral parts of the educational program of the University. Through service to the community, students discover their gifts, develop skills, learn to lead and to work with others, and experience the joy and personal rewards of community involvement.

Campus housing provides apartment-style living for all students. Apartment units include kitchens, living rooms, basic furnishings, and balconies. In addition, the dining hall and food service plans are available to all resident students. Various meal plans are available to students to accommodate different schedules.

CCU competes in Division II of the NCAA and is part of the Rocky Mountain Athletic Conference. CCU offers men's and women's basketball, cross-country, soccer, and tennis; men's golf; and women's volleyball. For students who do not wish to participate in formal athletics, there are a variety of intramural sports and activities available. Academic and social clubs, discipleship groups, and University retreats provide informal opportunities for students and faculty members to spend time together in recreation, instruction, and fellowship. Both the band and the choir participate in annual tours in Colorado and the nation.

Colorado Christian University is accredited by the North Central Association of Colleges and Schools. The University is nondenominational and serves individuals and faculty members representing more than thirty Christian denominations. The University enrolls approximately 2,000 students from forty-eight states and sixteen different countries in its academic programs. The University offers graduate and adult degree-completion programs and has off-campus centers in Denver/Lakewood, Colorado Springs, Fort Collins, and Grand Junction.

Location

Located in the thriving Denver suburb of Lakewood, CCU is about 15 minutes from Denver's popular LoDo area, which is the home of coffee houses, international-style shopping, and major professional sports teams, including the NFL Denver Broncos, the NBA Denver Nuggets, MLB Colorado Rockies, and the NHL Colorado Avalanche.

Directly west of CCU and less than 2 hours away are many of the world's best skiing, snowboarding, bicycling, hiking, climbing, white-water rafting, and fly-fishing locations. Denver has more than 250 days of sunshine each year, moderate winters, and mild summer days with comfortably low humidity.

Majors and Degrees

Colorado Christian University offers bachelor's degrees in biblical studies, biology, business administration, computer information systems, elementary education, English, global studies, history, human communication, liberal arts, math (secondary education), music, music education, psychology, science (secondary education), secondary education, social science, theology, and youth ministries. Within these programs there are numerous emphases and concentrations. Students may also choose pre-law or premedicine courses of study. Academic minors include biology, business, English, history, human communication, leadership, music, outdoor leadership, psychology, Spanish, Young Life leadership, and youth ministries.

Academic Program

Colorado Christian University operates under a semester system offering fall, spring, and summer sessions. To qualify for graduation, students in all majors must complete the required minimum number of credits for their chosen major, including general education and elective courses. Colorado Christian University recognizes the importance of arts and sciences; therefore, the general education requirements include course work in behavioral and social sciences, communication, computers, humanities, mathematics, natural science, integrative studies, and biblical studies. The freshman year begins with an integration course providing information, activities, classes, and programs to help new students assimilate into University life. Except for students in teacher licensure and music programs, all students enrolled in Bachelor of Arts majors must complete a two-semester sequence in college-level foreign language courses or the equivalent.

Colorado Christian University may grant college credit for course work taken at another accredited college; through Advanced Placement, International Baccalaureate, College-Level Examination Program, DANTES, or Armed Forces Education; or by examination.

ROTC programs are available to students through cooperation with other colleges in the metropolitan Denver area. Specific ROTC information is available from the Office of Admission.

Off-Campus Programs

As a member of the Council for Christian Colleges and Universities, CCU offers students the opportunity to spend a semester abroad in programs designed to integrate Christian commitment in a world context. The American Studies Program places students in federal, public, and private agencies in Washington, D.C., where students can gain insights into government and public policy. Costa Rica is the setting for the Latin American Studies Program, where students can integrate their faith with knowledge and experience in a Third World country. Students involved in the China Studies Program have the opportunity to explore culture in Beijing, Xiian, and Shanghai and to learn about Chinese history, government, economics, and religion. The Middle East Studies Program in Cairo, Egypt, provides students with the opportunity to study cultures, religions, and conflicts within this diverse and strategic region. The Russian Studies Program affords students the opportunity to study Russian language, history, culture, and current events in the cities of Moscow, Nizhni Novgorod, and St. Petersburg. The L.A. Film Institute Program prepares students for the challenges and responsibilities of quality filmmaking, while the Focus on the Family Institute helps equip tomorrow's leaders for family, church, and society.

Other programs offer majors through cooperation with other state universities or institutes. Students complete general requirements at CCU and professional courses at cooperating institutions.

Academic Facilities

The CCU library includes a computer lab, a curriculum lab, and audiovisual equipment loan as well as book, video, and music collections. Students have access to 1,200 full-text journals via the Internet, which augment 400 print journals in the library. Religion, education, psychology, business, and periodical and newspaper indexes are offered through the CCU library with cooperative programs for borrowing materials from other libraries. Computer searching is performed for and by students to obtain the best resources for their assignments. The music facility has a separate music library and also provides multitimbral synthesizers, computer ear-training programs, Finale, Mosaic, Professional Performer, Tap Master rhythm laboratory, and facilities with grand pianos. Athletic facilities, a student center and bookstore, and other facilities all enrich academic life for CCU students.

Costs

The 2003–04 cost for tuition (12–16 credit hours) and fees was $7520 per semester for traditional undergraduate students. Room charges ranged from $1700 to $1850, and board charges ranged from $945 to $1295 per semester. All freshmen are required to live on campus and participate in a meal plan unless living at home in the Denver metro area with their parents or a legal guardian.

Financial Aid

Colorado Christian University provides a financial aid program to assist students who need additional resources to meet their educational costs. Students who qualify may be eligible for institutional scholarships and grants based on their talent in the areas of academics, music, or athletics or based on their financial need. Students may also qualify for assistance through federal grant, work, or loan programs. Students applying for financial aid must file the Free Application for Federal Student Aid (FAFSA).

Faculty

CCU faculty members teach primarily undergraduate courses. Small class sizes (most classes have fewer than 25 students), combined with a teaching rather than research faculty, assure students of personal, high-quality instruction. Faculty members teach all classes without the aid of undergraduate instructors. More than half of the full-time faculty members hold doctoral degrees. An advantage of CCU's faculty is that professors are practitioners in their field—they come with background and experience in the real world, not just from classroom textbooks. This element offers practical, relevant training for students. Faculty members also serve as advisers and mentors to students. They take a sincere and active role in the personal, academic, and spiritual lives of the students.

Student Government

The Associated Students of Colorado Christian University includes all registered students. Officers are chosen annually by election from within the student body and serve through the Student Government Association (SGA). Voicing the concerns and needs of the students to the University administration and providing opportunities for fun and fellowship are at the core of the SGA. SGA serves students through three distinct branches: the Executive Council, the Senate, and the Program and Activities Crew.

Admission Requirements

Applicants are evaluated on the basis of academic ability, personal and professional goals, character, and Christian commitment. For all programs, those applying are expected to have a high school diploma or the equivalent, with a satisfactory grade point average. Students applying as first-time freshmen or those with fewer than 30 transfer credits should submit the Application for Admission, a high school transcript, SAT I or ACT scores, and two character recommendations. Students applying for transfer admission should submit the Application for Admission, all college transcripts, and two character recommendations.

In order to provide a solid foundation for college-level work, it is recommended that the applicant present the equivalent of 16 academic units from an approved high school. Home school students are welcome to apply for admission by following the application procedures listed above. A GED diploma may be required of a home school student, at the discretion of the admission committee, if there is evidence of a discrepancy between the high school transcript and the standardized test scores.

Application and Information

For a viewbook and application, students should contact:

Office of Admission
Colorado Christian University
180 South Garrison Street
Lakewood, Colorado 80226
Telephone: 303-963-3200
800-44-FAITH (toll-free)
Fax: 303-963-3201
E-mail: admission@ccu.edu
World Wide Web: http://www.ccu.edu

THE COLORADO COLLEGE

COLORADO SPRINGS, COLORADO

The College

A private, four-year liberal arts and sciences college enrolling 1,900 students, the Colorado College (CC) is located on a 90-acre campus in downtown Colorado Springs near the base of the 14,110-foot Pikes Peak and about an hour from Denver. Consistently ranked in the top tier of national colleges and universities by *U.S. News & World Report*, CC is the only college of its kind in the Rocky Mountain region, the College is also one of only a handful of prestigious liberal arts and sciences colleges located in a metropolitan area.

The College's curriculum is as varied as its landscape. Best known for the innovative Block Plan, in which students take and professors teach only one course at a time, Colorado College offers first and foremost an excellent education in the liberal arts and sciences. The College encourages a spirit of intellectual exploration, critical thinking, hands-on learning, and personal responsibility within an environment of small learning communities where education and life intertwine.

Students come from every state in the nation and about twenty-five countries, and from many ethnic, religious, and socioeconomic backgrounds. The students are independent-minded adventurers who love a challenge. At Colorado College, they find the encouragement, opportunities, and inspiration they need to reach their greatest potential.

Students at Colorado College devote energy and effort not only to academics but also to interests outside the classroom. The small size of the campus community encourages and enables students to get involved. Most students participate in at least one extracurricular activity and many hold leadership positions, setting graduates up for success in their future careers. There are more than eighty clubs covering topics from athletics to the arts, media to debate, and community service to religious life. If students can't find a club that fits their interests, the Office of Student Life often has the resources and support they need to start their own.

CC feels that its community is integral to the learning process. This is why CC requires all students to live on campus for the first three years and guarantees housing for all four years. In the residential campus community, students form friendships and make connections that last a lifetime.

Location

A Colorado College education is made even more distinctive because of its location.

The College contributes actively to a city of about 500,000. Near the foot of Pikes Peak, the campus is located in a residential area near historic downtown Colorado Springs. Students enjoy being within walking distance of a variety of eclectic cafés, coffee shops, movie theaters, restaurants, clothing stores, and mountain outfitters. Colorado Springs is also the largest U.S. city within 20 miles of a national forest or wilderness area, so great outdoor adventures are close at hand.

Being in a metropolitan area allows students to take advantage of many amenities, such as sporting and cultural events. The World Arena is home to Colorado College Tiger hockey. Events ranging from the circus to rock concerts to a preseason Denver Nuggets basketball game are also held at the arena. The 2,000-seat Pikes Peak Center hosts more than 200 performances annually, including Broadway musicals, popular recording artists, and music and dance performances of all kinds. Collections of twentieth-century, Native American, and Hispanic art are on display at the Colorado Springs Fine Arts Center. The city also has a philharmonic orchestra, a 100-voice chorale, an annual opera festival, a dance theater that presents nationally and world-known ballet companies, art galleries, and several theater companies.

Denver (metropolitan population of 3.5 million), the state capital, is an hour's drive from campus. Students can also drive south about 5 hours to Santa Fe, one of the nation's great cultural centers.

Majors and Degrees

Students have more than thirty formal majors from which to choose, twelve of which are interdisciplinary. A student may also choose to double major, take a thematic minor, or even design an independent major. The College also offers a number of special programs for students to complement their liberal arts education. Preprofessional advising programs are available in law, business, medicine, and other health professions. Teacher certification is available through the Education Department, regardless of the student's major. The College also has 3-2 engineering programs with Washington University in St. Louis, the University of Southern California, Rensselaer Polytechnic Institute, and Columbia University.

Academic Program

The Block Plan, now in its thirty-third year, is one of the most innovative aspects of a Colorado College education. Unlike most small liberal arts colleges, Colorado College permits faculty members and students to pursue their interests at their own pace and in their own way. Students take eight courses between early September and mid-May (the same as at any semester-based institution), but take only one course at a time. Each course lasts for 3½ weeks and is called a block. While class schedules vary, many classes run from 9 a.m. until noon each day, with labs scheduled in the afternoons, but there's no bell to bring discussion to a sudden halt—and it often spills out of the classroom, across the quad, and into the dining halls and dorm rooms.

Off-Campus Programs

Students wishing to spend an extended period of time pursuing their quest for knowledge beyond the boundaries of the campus find that Colorado College offers many opportunities. The College encourages the study of cultures and peoples throughout the world, and the Block Plan provides numerous opportunities to study abroad. About 56 percent of graduating seniors have studied abroad, and many others have participated in off-campus study in the United States.

Understanding other cultures and traditions often necessitates the study of other languages, so language programs in China, France, Germany, Italy, Japan, Mexico, Russia, and other countries are central a CC liberal arts education. The study-abroad program also includes topical programs such as biology in Costa Rica. The College also cosponsors semester- or yearlong study-abroad programs with its sister schools in the Associated Colleges of the Midwest (ACM). If a program isn't offered in the student's country of interest, the international programs office can help find other options. In many of these programs, tuition is the same as studying on campus. Financial aid follows students participating in CC or ACM programs. Study-abroad program locations include Costa Rica, France, Germany, India, Japan, Mexico, Russia, Sweden, the Netherlands, Tanzania, and Wales.

Academic Facilities

Colorado College has some of the most modern equipment and technology available across every discipline. The natural sciences facilities have an electron microscope, a 16-inch reflecting telescope, a computerized microscopic interface, greenhouses with various climates, extensive lab space, and graphics workstations. Facilities for the humanities and social sciences include a language lab with video disk technology, several theaters, and extensive art studios and gallery space. More than 200 computers (PC and Mac) are available for student use. Three fourths of the students living in residence halls have high-speed network access in their rooms. The other fourth have modem access. Tutt Library has nearly 1,300 academic periodicals, more than a quarter of a million government documents, and numerous interlibrary loans. The College maintains two facilities for class retreats. The Gilmore-Stabler Cabin is situated in beautiful, rustic mountain surroundings, just 45 minutes from campus. The College also maintains the Baca Campus, which is located about 3 hours from campus near the base of the Sangre de Cristo mountains in the San Luis Valley.

Costs

Tuition, room, board, and fees totaled about $36,000 for the 2003–04 school year.

Financial Aid

Colorado College remains committed to the philosophy that cost should not deter a student from considering CC. The College administers a substantial financial aid program and uses financial need as the primary consideration in awarding aid. There is, however, a limited amount of financial aid available for non-U.S. citizens and transfer students. A financial aid award usually includes a combination of grants, federal loans (for U.S. citizens and permanent residents only), and possible work-study earnings. While the majority of college aid is need-based, some merit-based scholarships are offered as well. Students should contact the Financial Aid Office at 719-389-6651 for further details. In order to apply for aid, students must complete the both the Free Application for Federal Student Aid (FAFSA) and the CSS Profile form by February 15. (In order to do this, students need to register for the CSS Profile by January 15). Non-U.S. citizens applying for aid must fill out the International Student Financial Aid Application by January 15. For more information, students should visit the following Web sites: http://www.fafsa.ed.gov and http://www.collegeboard.com.

Faculty

The academic program at Colorado College is known for its extraordinary emphasis on teaching and learning. Outstanding faculty members, 97 percent of whom hold the highest degrees awarded in their fields, teach most classes, while others are taught by top-notch professionals as guest lecturers. There are no teaching assistants at Colorado College. With class sizes averaging 15 students, everyone has a chance to express opinions and be heard. The camaraderie that develops between students and professors often results in collaborative research projects and independent study projects.

Student Government

The Colorado College Campus Association (CCCA), the College's student government organization, probably has the highest profile among student clubs and organizations. The executive officers and the Student Senate fund student groups and events, discuss campus issues, and represent student opinion to the administration and community.

Admission Requirements

Every year, Colorado College enrolls an academically accomplished student body that encompasses a wide variety of interests, talents, and backgrounds. Its holistic evaluation process considers academic work, writing, letters of recommendation, test scores, extracurricular activities, and unique talents and personal qualities. Deadlines are November 1 for spring transfer postmark deadline; November 15, early action (non-binding) postmark deadline; January 15 for regular action postmark deadline; February 15 for priority deadline for financial aid paperwork; March 1 for fall transfer postmark deadline.

Application and Information

Regular action first-year applicants have a January 15 postmark deadline and receive a decision by early April. Early action first-year applicants have a November 15 postmark deadline and receive a decision by early January. First-year applicants may use the Common Application. Fall transfer applicants have a March 1 postmark deadline and receive a decision in mid-April. Spring transfer applicants have a November 1 postmark deadline and receive a decision by late December.

For more information, students should contact:

Admission Office
The Colorado College
14 East Cache La Poudre Street
Colorado Springs, Colorado 80903
Telephone: 719-389-6344
800-542-7214 (toll-free)
Fax: 719-389-6816
E-mail: admission@ColoradoCollege.edu
World Wide Web:
http://www.ColoradoCollege.edu/Admission

Students on the campus of Colorado College.

COLORADO STATE UNIVERSITY

FORT COLLINS, COLORADO

The University

In 1879, Colorado State University was designated Colorado's land-grant college. The land-grant concept of a balanced program of teaching, research, extension, and public service provides the foundation for the University's teaching and research programs. Today, Colorado State has a commitment to integrating first-rate academic programs with hands-on learning experiences inside and outside the classroom. Education at Colorado State encompasses the major areas of human knowledge—the sciences, the arts, the humanities, and the professions. The mission of the University is to graduate students who possess the knowledge and skills to compete in a global marketplace and to live full, rewarding lives. The University has historically had a reputation for excellence in its programs, from the baccalaureate to the postgraduate level, and has achieved a worldwide reputation in a number of important fields. Colorado State offers graduate degrees in all eight colleges.

The 25,000 students enrolled at Colorado State represent all fifty states and eighty countries. The variety of students broadens the educational experience for all and enables students to share their backgrounds and heritages and to learn about others in an atmosphere that encourages cultural exchange and an appreciation and respect for diversity. The University provides a wide range of programs to meet the social, recreational, and academic needs of its diverse student population. There are more than 300 clubs and organizations, including student government, honor societies, sororities and fraternities, athletic clubs, cultural and religious organizations, advocacy offices, and major-oriented or professionally oriented clubs. The Lory Student Center provides a focal point for student life on campus. Many students participate in intramural and club sports. For the more serious-minded athlete, Colorado State offers men's and women's athletics in the Mountain West Conference (MWC), Division IA of the National Collegiate Athletic Association (NCAA). All students have access to the sports facilities at the 100,000-square-foot Student Recreation Center, which is open daily for drop-in recreational use. This facility houses a gymnasium with multipurpose courts; an elevated running track; a 10-lane, 25-yard swimming pool and spa pool; and weight, fitness, aerobics, and locker rooms.

Colorado State has ten coed residence halls, each containing recreation and study areas, a laundry room, and vending machines. Residence Hall Dining Centers provide many dining choices for students. The halls provide a wide variety of activities, including educational programs, social gatherings, and recreational events. The University's residence hall system received top honors for outstanding programming, leadership development, and dedication shown toward students. Several floors within the residence halls are designated for either academic or leisure interests, providing the opportunity for students to live with others with similar interests. These community living options include honors, leadership, engineering, and pre–veterinary medicine. All residence halls are nonsmoking.

Location

Fort Collins, a city of more than 127,000, provides a unique blend of big-city amenities and small-town friendliness. It is scenically located at the western edge of the plains at the base of the Rocky Mountain foothills and conveniently located 65 miles north of Denver. The wide-open spaces and majestic Rockies make Fort Collins a very attractive place to live and learn. Areas for camping, hiking, skiing, swimming, boating, rafting, climbing, and fishing are within an easy driving distance of campus.

Majors and Degrees

Colorado State University offers bachelor's degrees through eight colleges. Bachelor of Science degrees are granted through the College of Agricultural Sciences in agricultural business, agricultural economics, agricultural education, animal science, equine science, horticulture, landscape architecture, landscape horticulture, and soil and crop sciences; through the College of Applied Human Sciences in apparel and merchandising, construction management, consumer and family studies, health and exercise science, human development and family studies, interior design, nutrition and food science, and restaurant and resort management; through the College of Business in business administration, with concentrations in accounting, finance–real estate, information systems, management, and marketing; through the College of Engineering in bioresource and agricultural, chemical, civil, computer, electrical, environmental, and mechanical engineering and in engineering science; through the College of Natural Resources in fishery biology, forestry, geology, natural resources management, natural resource recreation and tourism, rangeland ecology, watershed science, and wildlife biology; through the College of Natural Sciences in biochemistry, biological science, botany, chemistry, computer science, mathematics, natural sciences, physics, psychology, and zoology; and through the College of Veterinary Medicine and Biomedical Sciences in environmental health and in microbiology.

Bachelor of Arts degrees are offered through the College of Applied Human Sciences in social work and through the College of Liberal Arts in anthropology; art; economics; English; history; languages, literatures, and cultures; liberal arts; music; performing arts; philosophy; political science; sociology; speech communication; and technical journalism. The Bachelor of Fine Arts and Bachelor of Music degrees are offered through the College of Liberal Arts in art and in music.

Teacher licensure is available in early childhood education; at the secondary level in biology, biology/natural resources, chemistry, English, French, general science, geology, German, mathematics, physics, social studies, Spanish, and speech; and in grades K–12 in art and music. Vocational secondary education licensure is available in agricultural education, business education, consumer and family studies, marketing education, and trade and industrial education. Preprofessional programs are offered in dentistry, law, medicine (chiropractic, optometry, osteopathy, physical therapy, physician assistant studies, and podiatry), nursing, occupational therapy, pharmacy, and veterinary medicine.

Academic Programs

More than 150 undergraduate programs of study are offered within the eight colleges, allowing students to shape a course of study that best meets their personal and professional goals. Depending on their degree program, students are required to complete a minimum of 120 credit hours for graduation.

Colorado State provides students with a well-rounded education through the All-University Core Curriculum (AUCC), the centerpiece of Colorado State's integrated learning experience. All students are required to complete the AUCC. Students usually meet the AUCC requirements in their freshman and sophomore years and devote their junior and senior years to specialization in their major field. A concentration—a sequence of at least 12 semester credits of selected courses designed to accommodate the specific interests of a student—may be designated within some majors. Students may also choose to pursue a double major, a minor, or an interdisciplinary studies program.

The Colorado State Honors Program provides academically motivated undergraduates in all majors with intellectual stimulation commensurate with their abilities. It offers small classes and fosters a close intellectual association of students and faculty members.

Off-Campus Programs

The Office of International Programs provides information about and coordinates many study-abroad programs that allow students to study almost anywhere in the world. Study-abroad programs can range from two-week seminars to semester and yearlong periods of study in any major.

Academic Facilities

Colorado State comprises four campuses covering approximately 4,900 acres. The 579-acre main campus, with nearly 100 academic and administrative buildings, is virtually a city within itself. Classrooms and residence halls are in proximity. South of the main campus is the Veterinary Teaching Hospital (103 acres), one of the nation's top facilities for teaching and research in the clinical sciences. A 1,433-acre agricultural campus supports instruction and research in agronomy and animal science, including the Equine Teaching and Research Center. The Foothills Campus, a 1,715-acre facility located 2 miles west of the main campus, is home to many of the University's renowned research projects. A 1,177-acre mountain campus, Pingree Park, located 55 miles west of the main campus at an elevation of 9,000 feet and bordering Rocky Mountain National Park, is used primarily for summer educational and research programs in forestry and natural resources.

The William E. Morgan Library houses collections totaling more than 2 million items and provides reading areas for more than 1,500 people. The library collections include books, periodicals, newspapers, journals, manuscripts, microfilms, records, and other reference items. The collection is enriched by a wide selection of electronic resources. The library also offers more than 300 public computers that allow access to specialized indexes and Web-based sources.

Costs

All stated costs are per semester. For 2003–04, tuition and fees for full-time undergraduates were $1873 for Colorado residents and $7109 for nonresidents. The average cost of room and board in on-campus housing was $2828. Books and classroom expenses are estimated at $450. Freshman students, unless they are living at home, married, or over 21 years of age, are required to live on campus and are therefore guaranteed a space in the residence halls. Upperclass students may choose to live in the Colorado State residence halls (limited availability), in the on-campus apartment housing (for married students, single-parent students, single nontraditional-age students, or single graduate students), or in any of the numerous houses or apartments located nearby.

Financial Aid

Colorado State participates in and administers a wide variety of student financial aid programs, including loans, grants, scholarships, work-study, and student employment. Colorado State's Student Financial Services publishes the *Invest in Your Journey* brochure that describes in detail all scholarships and aid offered. Approximately 66 percent of the students at Colorado State received some type of financial assistance. Student Employment Services assists students with locating part-time positions both on and off campus.

Faculty

The Colorado State faculty teaches both graduate and undergraduate students. There are more than 1,500 faculty members; 89 percent of the regular faculty members hold advanced degrees. The student-faculty ratio is 17:1. Although faculty members are actively engaged in research, the majority of them teach undergraduate classes and serve as advisers.

Student Government

The Associated Students of Colorado State University (ASCSU) comprises all enrolled students. The ASCSU Senate acts as a liaison between the student body and the administration as well as the State Board of Agriculture, the governing body of Colorado State. The ASCSU also offers free legal, consumer, and other services to Colorado State students.

Admission Requirements

Colorado State University selects for admission students who demonstrate the greatest academic potential for successfully attaining a degree and who appear to be the best qualified to benefit from and contribute to the academic and cultural environment of the University. Applications are carefully and individually reviewed. Colorado State is a selective university. In fall 2003, the middle 50 percent of entering freshmen had a GPA range of 3.3 to 3.8, an ACT composite score of 22 to 26, and an SAT I combined score of 1020 to 1210.

Students applying as freshmen must submit a completed application form, a $50 application processing fee, official high school transcripts that include high school class rank, college transcripts for any college course work, and scores from either the ACT or SAT I. The personal essay and letters of recommendation from teachers, principals, or counselors are also encouraged. Several factors are considered, including the applicant's grades, class rank, number of completed academic units, scores on either the ACT or SAT I, rigor of high school curriculum, trend in quality of high school performances, leadership qualities, school or community service, and the ability to contribute to an appreciation of diversity on the campus. Minimum freshman admission prerequisites include the completion of 18 units, 15 of which are academic units. These 15 academic units must include 5 units of a social science/natural science combination, with a minimum of 2 units from each area; 4 units of English; 3 units of mathematics (algebra I, algebra II, and geometry).

Undergraduate students who wish to transfer to Colorado State must submit a completed application form, a $50 application processing fee, and official transcripts from all colleges and universities attended. The personal essay and letters of recommendation are also encouraged. To be a strong candidate for admission, transfer applicants should have college-level course work, e.g., college composition or mathematics, and at least a 2.5 cumulative GPA with a minimum of more than 12 semester credits after high school graduation. These credits must be earned from a college or university accredited by one of the six regional associations of schools and colleges.

Transfer applicants must also meet the admission requirement in mathematics. This requirement may be met by completing a transferable mathematics course, e.g., college algebra, with a grade of C or higher; completing intermediate algebra with a grade of B or higher; or completing algebra I, geometry, and algebra II with grades of C or higher while in high school (these students must also submit a high school transcript). Additional factors that are considered include academic rigor; trend in grades; involvement in campus, community, and/or family activities; and an ability to contribute to an appreciation of diversity on the campus.

Students may apply and pay the application processing fee via the World Wide Web at http://admissions.colostate.edu. Completed applications with all supporting documents must be received in the Office of Admissions by July 1 for the fall semester and December 1 for the spring semester.

Application and Information

The admissions office is open Monday through Friday, from 7:45 a.m. to 4:45 p.m. during the academic year and from 7:30 a.m. to 4:30 p.m. during the summer. Student-led campus tours and admissions/financial aid presentations are given every weekday. Students should visit the Office of Admissions Web site at http://admissions.colostate.edu for more information regarding on-campus visits. Additional information and application forms are available by contacting:

Office of Admissions
1020 Campus Delivery
Colorado State University
Fort Collins, Colorado 80523-1020
Telephone: 970-491-6909
World Wide Web: http://www.colostate.edu

COLUMBIA UNIVERSITY
Columbia College
NEW YORK, NEW YORK

The University

In 1754 King George II granted a charter to a group of New York citizens to found King's College, dedicated to instruction in "the Learned Languages and the Liberal Arts and Sciences." In its early days, King's College taught such students as Alexander Hamilton, John Jay, Robert Livingston, and Gouverneur Morris. After the Revolution, New York State issued the college a new charter with a more patriotic name—Columbia. In 1897 Columbia moved to a new site on Morningside Heights on the Upper West Side. The architectural firm of McKim, Mead and White, the preeminent architects of their day, designed an open central enclave six blocks long, with a majestic domed and colonnaded library at the center. It remains one of New York's most impressive settings.

Columbia College and the Fu Foundation School of Engineering and Applied Science (SEAS) today offer their students unique advantages; they are at the same time small selective colleges and integral components of a major research-oriented university.

The College enrolls approximately 4,000 students; the SEAS student body is about 1,250. Students come from all fifty states and several dozen countries. They represent a dazzling array of ethnic, social, economic, cultural, religious, and geographic backgrounds. The diversity of Columbia's student body reflects the diversity of New York City, the world's most international city.

Columbia guarantees four years of on-campus housing to all entering first-year students. More than 90 percent of the undergraduates remain for four years in the residence halls.

Columbia students take part in extracurricular groups of all kinds: artistic (e.g., many theater groups, musical groups, and dance groups), athletic (twenty-nine varsity sports and dozens of club and intramural sports), communications (the *Columbia Daily Spectator* and many other publications, the *Columbian* yearbook, WKCR-FM, a campus television station, and other groups), community service (e.g., Amnesty International, Big Brother/Big Sister programs, tutoring programs, a volunteer ambulance squad, service-to-the-elderly programs, and work in soup kitchens and homeless shelters), and preprofessional (e.g., the Charles Hamilton Houston Pre-Law Association and the National Society of Black Engineers). Other groups represent students' ethnic, religious, political, and sexual identities. There are twelve men's fraternities, five coed fraternities, and seven sororities. A new student center, Lerner Hall, opened in the fall of 1999.

Location

Columbia shares its Morningside Heights neighborhood with a number of other famous institutions: Barnard College, the Cathedral of St. John the Divine, Union Theological Seminary, Jewish Theological Seminary, and the Manhattan School of Music, to name only some of them. Most faculty members from Columbia and other schools make their homes in the neighborhood, and it is an area known for bookstores, wonderfully varied restaurants, and merchants that cater to student tastes, student budgets, and student hours.

Students are encouraged and assisted in making full use of New York's breathtaking variety of cultural, recreational, and professional resources. Columbia students can be found any day of the week exploring the Metropolitan Museum of Art, the Museum of Modern Art, the Guggenheim Museum, the Museum of African Art, the Museo del Barrio, the Asia Society, or another of the city's dozens of museums and galleries. Any evening, they might be discovering the theatrical offerings on, off, or "off-off" Broadway (or on campus); attending the opera, ballet, or symphony at Lincoln Center; taking in a movie on campus or in one of New York's 400-plus cinemas; enjoying jazz in Greenwich Village or blues at the Apollo; sampling *pai gwat* in Chinatown; or biking or boating in Central Park. Columbia's internship programs offer students opportunities to explore in depth a career possibility; nowhere else in the world does the concentration of industries allow such a range of possibilities. New York's public transportation system puts all of the city within easy reach of Columbia students; the campus is served by a subway line and five bus routes.

Majors and Degrees

Columbia College grants the B.A. degree in more than seventy-five majors in the humanities, social sciences, and pure sciences, including many interdisciplinary majors. SEAS grants the B.S. degree in about fifteen engineering fields. A five-year program that begins in either school allows students to receive both degrees.

Joint degree programs offer selected students the opportunity to combine their undergraduate work with study in Columbia University's schools of law and international affairs and with the Juilliard School.

Academic Program

Unlike many other colleges that are attempting to restore structure to their course offerings, Columbia has maintained a coherent and relevant curriculum since the time of the First World War, when it introduced the renowned Core Curriculum, a program of general education that has served as a model for hundreds of colleges around the country. One of the two oldest courses in the core is Contemporary Civilization, a year-long historical survey of western civilization's religious, political, and moral philosophies; the other is Literature Humanities, a year-long introduction to western culture's most seminal and meaningful literary works. A second year of humanities offers a semester each of music and art appreciation, encouraging students to experience the cultural treasures of New York City. The Major Cultures core courses enlarge the scope of inquiry beyond the Western focus in order to promote learning and thought about the variety of cultures and the diversity of traditions that interact in the United States and the world today. The Core Curriculum exposes Columbia's multicultural student body to a variety of disciplines, preparing them for the complex questions and issues of modern society.

One hallmark that distinguishes a SEAS education from that of other prestigious engineering schools is the number of nonengineering courses that every SEAS undergraduate takes; almost a quarter of a student's program is in the humanities and social sciences and includes components of the Core Curriculum. Alumni often cite this feature of their SEAS education as the most important reason for success in their careers.

Off-Campus Programs

Columbia maintains at Reid Hall, its Paris campus, several undergraduate programs. Courses at Reid Hall are quite varied, permitting students to work not only in the areas of French language, literature, and culture but also in several other fields throughout the range of the humanities and social sciences. There is additionally a year-long program that includes course work in the French university system.

Columbia was the first U.S. college to offer an integrated year-abroad program with the Universities of Oxford and Cambridge. Other programs allow students to work at the University of Kyoto in Japan or at the Free University of Berlin in Germany.

Columbia students may, with the help of a dean, choose from a variety of study-abroad programs around the world in addition to Columbia's own programs.

Academic Facilities

The Columbia University libraries constitute the nation's sixth-largest academic library system, with a collection of more than 6 million volumes and 4 million microunits. There are 26 million manuscript items in 2,500 separate collections. Twenty-six satellite libraries are within the campus. Five of Columbia's libraries are designated Distinctive Collections, so called because their holdings are of unusual depth and nationally significant excellence. All divisions are open to Columbia undergraduates. The Columbia Computer Center has five mainframe computers used for academic research and instruction as well as clusters of microcomputers, terminals, and printers; it has remote units and terminals all over campus, including in residence halls, to guarantee accessibility. The chemistry building, Havemeyer Hall, houses modern laboratory facilities for research and undergraduate instruction. Students may also make use of outstanding facilities throughout the University, including an electronic music lab, a cyclotron, an oral history collection, the facilities and programs of the Lamont-Doherty Earth Observatory, and oceanographic research ships.

Costs

Tuition for the 2003–04 academic year was $29,040. Room and board for all first-year students were $8750. With typical fees, books, and supplies, the total cost of a year at Columbia was approximately $39,990. This amount does not include travel to and from Columbia.

Financial Aid

All candidates who are U.S. or Canadian citizens or who have U.S. permanent resident status are considered for admission without regard to their financial need, and if admitted they receive financial aid packages to meet their full demonstrated and perceived need for the cost of a Columbia education. Financial aid documents must be filed by January 2 to ensure consideration for financial aid funds. All financial aid packages include a loan and a job (self-help); need not met by the self-help component will be met by grant. All financial aid at Columbia is based on need; no aid is given in the form of academic, athletic, artistic, or other merit awards. More than 50 percent of Columbia students are receiving some form of financial aid. The average financial aid package is more than $21,000. Students who are not U.S. or Canadian citizens and do not have U.S. permanent resident status should be aware that few such candidates may be admitted to Columbia with financial aid, for which the competition is intense.

Faculty

Given Columbia's enrollment, core curriculum classes are capped at 22 students and faculty members are not overwhelmed by the numbers of students they teach. The Columbia faculty is committed to both teaching and research, and students are taught by the most eminent professors as well as young assistant professors. All faculty members maintain office hours, and each student receives a faculty adviser from the department which he or she chooses as a major.

Student Government

Each undergraduate division has its own student council and elects representatives to the Columbia University Senate.

Admission Requirements

The Columbia first-year class of approximately 1,300 students is selected from a much larger pool of applicants by a painstaking process. Candidates for admission are expected to demonstrate the necessary ability and interest to do successful college work in a variety of disciplines as required for the Columbia degree. The following secondary school preparation is recommended: 4 years of English, including meaningful work in literature and writing; 3 (preferably 4) years of mathematics, including precalculus and calculus where offered; 3 (preferably 4) years of history and social studies; 3 or more years of the same foreign language; and 2 or more years of laboratory science (including chemistry and physics where available). The Admissions Committee recognizes that secondary schools vary in offerings and standards; consideration will be given to applicants whose preparations differ from the recommended course of study. Candidates for admission are required to submit test scores from either the SAT I or the ACT as well as from three SAT II Subject Tests, one of which must be Writing. For their other two, SEAS candidates must take any SAT II math test and either physics or chemistry; College candidates may take any two of their choice.

Transfer students may enter the College or SEAS in September only. The College also has a Visiting Students program, which allows students to attend for one or both semesters of their junior year.

Application and Information

The postmark deadline for applications is the first business day after January 1. Candidates are notified of the Admissions Committee's actions on or about April 1. Admitted candidates must respond to Columbia's offer of admission by May 1. Candidates for whom Columbia is their definite first choice may apply under the early decision plan; the deadline is November 1 for all application material, and a decision is rendered by December 15. Candidates admitted to Columbia under early decision are required to withdraw applications at any other colleges. The application fee is $65. The fee may be waived if a school official testifies that the fee would cause the candidate's family financial hardship. For further information or for applications, interested students should contact:

Office of Undergraduate Admissions
Columbia University
1130 Amsterdam Avenue MC2807
New York, New York 10027
Telephone: 212-854-2522
Fax: 212-854-1209
World Wide Web:
http://www.studentaffairs.columbia.edu/admissions

COLUMBIA COLLEGE

COLUMBIA, MISSOURI

The College

Columbia College is a four-year, private, coeducational college offering master's, bachelor's, and associate degrees. It was founded in 1851 as Christian College and is affiliated with the Disciples of Christ. The institution is accredited by the North Central Association of Colleges and Schools. Today, 920 students representing fifteen states and twenty-five other countries attend the College.

The College's 29-acre wireless campus, located four blocks from the downtown area of Columbia, Missouri, has twenty buildings, ranging from Williams Hall, constructed in 1851, through administration and classroom buildings erected in the early 1900s, to more modern residence halls and classroom facilities completed in the 1960s and 1970s. A gymnasium was erected in 1988, the Stafford Library was erected in 1989, and the Cultural Arts Center was remodeled in 1992. Brown Hall, the arts and humanities building, became operational in 1995. A new contemporary Student Commons is scheduled to open in August 2004.

Three spacious residence halls provide housing for students who live on campus. Miller Hall and Banks Hall offer coeducational housing. Banks Hall features a popular Wellness Floor. Every residence hall provides a computer lab, cooking and laundry facilities, individual phone lines, and cable TV and Internet access. Student academic programmers enhance the academic environment within the residence hall system through specialized programming, peer academic counseling, and research and referral information sharing. Every student is entitled to have an automobile, motorcycle, or bicycle on campus. Student service facilities include a Student Center, a central dining facility, a health center, a counseling center, and a career planning and placement center.

Recreational and athletic opportunities are furnished through the College's Southwell Complex, a remodeled fitness center, a gymnasium, a softball field, a soccer field, tennis courts, and also a large back-campus area for intramural sports programs, which are quite popular. The College is a member of the NAIA Division I and the American Midwest Conference, and its teams compete in men's basketball and soccer and women's basketball, softball, and volleyball.

Graduate degrees are available in business, criminal justice, and teaching.

Location

Columbia, Missouri (population 75,000 plus 25,000 college students), is situated halfway between St. Louis and Kansas City. Five hospitals, a major mental health center, social service agencies of all kinds, a large network of parks, and a well-educated populace accustomed to a rich cultural life make Columbia a pleasant place to live, work, and study. *Money* magazine has often ranked it as one of the top twenty cities in the nation.

Majors and Degrees

Columbia College awards the Bachelor of Arts and Bachelor of Science degrees with majors in accounting, art, biology, business administration, chemistry, computer information systems, computer science, criminal justice administration, English, financial services, forensic science, general studies, history, interdisciplinary studies, international business, management, marketing, mathematics, natural sciences, political science, psychology, social work, and sociology. Preprofessional programs in dentistry, law, medicine, and veterinary science are available. The BEACON and DAYSTAR are new, innovative programs in teacher education. The College also confers the Bachelor of Fine Arts and Bachelor of Social Work degrees. Students can choose minors in art history, ethics/philosophy/religion, music, geology, physics, Spanish, and studio art. Columbia College also awards the associate degree with majors in business administration, computer information systems, criminal justice administration, and fire service administration.

Academic Program

The academic curriculum supports the mission of the College to provide career degree programs based on a solid background in the liberal arts and sciences. Each of the degree programs can include an internship, enabling students to obtain practical experience in addition to the more theoretical classroom instruction.

The College follows a two-semester plan with an eight-week summer session. Each degree program sets its own sequence of requirements. To be eligible for graduation, students pursuing an associate degree must complete 60 semester hours with a cumulative grade point average of 2.0 (C) or better. Each associate degree program has a general education component. To receive a bachelor's degree, students must complete 120 semester hours of credit with a cumulative grade point average of 2.0 (C) or better. Students pursuing a baccalaureate degree must complete a series of general education courses, including 6 semester hours of English composition and an ethics course, and earn at least 39 semester hours of credit in junior- or senior-level courses.

Off-Campus Programs

Full-time Columbia College students may enroll, at no extra cost, in courses at two neighboring institutions through a cooperative arrangement. ROTC programs (all branches) are available through this arrangement as well. Study-abroad opportunities are also offered.

Academic Facilities

Stafford Library is fully automated and contains more than 70,000 volumes, 500 periodicals, 6,000 audiovisual materials, and innumerable electronic resources. Students also have access to materials through the College's interlibrary loan and exchange program with neighboring institutions and the statewide electronic MOBIUS system.

An art and humanities facility, completed in 1995, provides resources for the art degree programs and a public gallery for promoting cultural growth. The College has a large computer and Internet laboratory; science and psychology lab facilities; an educational curriculum/materials library; the Writing Center and Math Center, which have a variety of individual assistance and tutorial programs; and major classroom buildings for traditional instruction as well as numerous multimedia classrooms.

Costs

For 2003–04, student fees included $11,362 for tuition and $4777 for room and board. Students should plan to spend about $400 per semester for books, supplies, and incidentals. *The Student Guide to America's Best College Scholarships* has rated Columbia College as one of the top colleges with the lowest costs.

Financial Aid

Most Columbia College students receive some type of financial assistance. The College awards to students more than $4 million annually in federal, state, and institutional funds. Financial aid packages may include need-based and merit-based scholarships, grants, loans, and work-study opportunities in a variety of combinations. The most prestigious awards are the Columbia College Scholarship (full tuition, room, and board) and the Presidential Scholarship (full tuition). Five each are awarded annually. Many other competitive scholarships are available. Some awards and scholarships are automatic if certain criteria are met. Talent awards in athletics, art, and music are also available. Half-tuition scholarships are awarded automatically to upperclassmen who earn a 3.4 grade point average (GPA) with 30 hours earned annually. Renewal requires a 3.2 GPA with 24 Columbia College hours earned.

To be considered for financial assistance, students must complete the Free Application for Federal Student Aid (FAFSA) and submit the Columbia College financial assistance application.

Faculty

Excellence in teaching has been a common goal throughout the history of the College. Teaching is the faculty's primary responsibility. The faculty-student ratio of 1:14 fosters personal attention and animated discussion in the classroom. Faculty members also serve as advisers to students. The relatively small size of the student body promotes excellent communication and rapport among students and faculty members. Nearly 80 percent of the faculty members have terminal degrees.

Student Government

All students at Columbia College are members of the Student Government Association (SGA). The SGA Cabinet, elected from this body, serves as a formal liaison between students and the administration. One branch of SGA, the Student Activities Commission, plans and organizes social activities on campus, from programs of interest to specialized groups to campuswide recreational activities. Each residence hall has representation to SGA through its Hall Council, which is composed of elected students.

Admission Requirements

Columbia College evaluates each applicant individually on the basis of the total application, including academic records, ACT/SAT scores, activities, references, goals, and recommendations of high school counselors. A high school diploma or equivalent certification is required for admission. English and math tests are given on campus to appropriately place students. English and math ACT/SAT subscores are also used for placement. Admission requirements at Columbia College are moderately selective.

Transfer students must submit transcripts of all college work attempted and may need to submit high school academic transcripts. There are no restrictions on the number of transfer students accepted each semester.

Application and Information

Descriptive brochures and application forms are available from the Office of Admissions. A campus visit is highly recommended. The completed application should be returned along with a $25 nonrefundable application fee. There is no fee if the application is submitted before January 1 for the fall semester. Notification of the admission decision is made on a rolling basis following the fulfillment of all admission requirements.

For more information and application materials, students should contact:

Director of Admissions
Columbia College
1001 Rogers Street
Columbia, Missouri 65216
Telephone: 573-875-7352
800-231-2391 (toll-free in the U.S. and Canada)
E-mail: admissions@ccis.edu
World Wide Web: http://www.ccis.edu

Rogers Gates at the entrance of the historic Columbia College campus.

COLUMBIA COLLEGE CHICAGO

CHICAGO, ILLINOIS

The College

Columbia College was established during the World's Columbian Exposition of 1893. The College's original emphasis on communication arts has expanded to include media arts, applied and fine arts, theatrical and performing arts, and management and marketing arts. Today, Columbia College Chicago is the nation's premier visual, performing, and media arts college. The foundation of a Columbia education continues to include small class sizes that ensure close interaction with a faculty of working professionals, abundant internship opportunities with major employers in the Chicago marketplace, and outstanding professional facilities that foster learning by doing. All students are encouraged to begin course work in their chosen fields during their freshman year, allowing them four full years in which to master their craft and build professional portfolios, audition tapes, resumes, and clip books. The College provides a strong liberal arts background for the developing artist or communicator and supports student employment goals through a full range of career services.

Columbia's enrollment of more than 9,250 students is drawn from Chicago and its suburbs, the Midwest, across the United States, and more than forty-five other countries. The student body is almost equally divided between men and women. Creative students who enjoy a supportive but challenging environment thrive at Columbia.

Columbia College Chicago's residence halls extend the supportive philosophy of the College. There are a wide variety of available housing options, all with access to computer and study rooms, drawing and painting studio space, a fitness room, and a laundry room. Apartments, suites, and rooms are fully furnished. All facilities are conveniently located steps away from the main campus buildings and close to public transportation, all in the heart of downtown Chicago. Students have access to a wide range of services, including the student health center, counseling, and a variety of local and academic events. Columbia College students are immersed in a creative environment both in and out of the classroom.

Outside the classroom, students participate in activities that include the College's award-winning student newspaper, radio station, electronic newsletter, two student magazines, cable television soap opera, three theaters, dance center, photography and art museums, and film and video festival. Many of the fifty student clubs on campus are linked to an academic discipline and offer opportunities to expand social and professional networking experiences. The Hermann D. Conaway Multicultural Center and the Myron Hokin Center provide gallery/café environments in which students can relax or study between classes. These centers feature a variety of activities, including art exhibits, film screenings, lectures, and live performances of music, comedy, readings, or dance. The 11th Street and Glass Curtain Galleries and the Narrative Arts Center provide additional exhibition spaces for students, faculty members, and others.

At the graduate level, Columbia awards the Master of Arts (M.A.) in arts, entertainment, and media management; creative writing and writing instruction; dance/movement therapy; interdisciplinary arts; journalism; photography; photography–museum studies; and writing instruction. The College awards the Master of Fine Arts (M.F.A.) in architectural studies; creative writing; creative writing and writing instruction; film and video; interdisciplinary book and paper arts; interior architecture; and photography. The Master of Arts in Teaching (M.A.T.) is also offered in elementary education (K–9), interdisciplinary arts education (K–12), and urban teaching.

Location

Columbia's campus is set in Chicago's dynamic South Loop neighborhood, across from Grant Park and Lake Michigan. Close to the Art Institute, Navy Pier, the Adler Planetarium, the Field Museum, the Chicago Symphony, and several other colleges and universities, Columbia's faculty members and students utilize the city of Chicago as a social, educational, and professional resource. Convenient public transportation makes all cultural and educational opportunities easily accessible.

Majors and Degrees

Columbia College grants the Bachelor of Arts (B.A.) and the Bachelor of Fine Arts (B.F.A.) degrees and the Bachelor of Music (B.M.) degree in composition. The School of Fine and Performing Arts offers majors in art and design (advertising art direction, fashion design, fine arts, graphic design, illustration, interior architecture, and product design); arts, entertainment, and media management (arts entrepreneurship and small business, fashion/retail, media, music business, performing arts, and visual arts); dance (choreography, musical theater performance, and teaching); fiction writing; music (contemporary music, including composition, instrumental performance, and vocal performance, and jazz studies, including instrumental and vocal); photography; and theater (acting, directing, playwriting, technical theater, and theater design). The School of Media Arts offers majors in academic computing (digital media technology), audio arts and acoustics (recording, sound contracting, sound reinforcement, and sound technology), film and video (alternative forms, audio, cinematography, computer animation, critical studies, directing, documentary, editing, producing, screenwriting, and traditional animation), interactive multimedia (animation, graphic design, photography, programming, project management, sound design, video, and writing), interdisciplinary (self-designed major), journalism (broadcast, magazine program, news reporting and writing, radio broadcast, and reporting on health, science, and the environment), marketing communication (advertising, creative sports marketing, marketing, and public relations), radio (business and talent/production), and television (interactive, postproduction/effects, production/directing, and writing/producing). The School of Liberal Arts and Sciences offers majors in American Sign Language–English interpretation, early childhood education (center director, infant-toddler studies, language and culture, performing arts, and visual arts), English (poetry), and liberal education (cultural studies).

Academic Program

Columbia supports creative and integrated approaches to education and encourages interdisciplinary study. The B.A. degree is awarded to students who successfully complete 120 semester hours, and the B.F.A. degree is awarded to students who successfully complete 128 semester hours of study in designated programs. Of the required hours, 48 are distributed among courses in the humanities and literature, science and mathematics, English composition, oral communications, social sciences, and computer applications.

The College continues to expand its extensive internship program. Columbia's location allows students to intern with major employers in Chicago. Chicago provides professional settings, classrooms, and internship opportunities for Columbia students.

The Career Center for Arts and Media offers a full range of services designed to help students launch their careers. Services include career counseling; seminars on interviewing, resume writing, and job-search strategies; internships; placement assistance; job fairs; and alumni activities and assistance.

Off-Campus Programs

Columbia has an affiliation agreement with the American Institute for Foreign Study, which enables students to participate in study-abroad programs in numerous countries. Columbia also sponsors and participates in a variety of its own study-abroad programs.

These programs include trips to Moscow and Prague. Summer programs are also offered with Dartington College in Dartington, England; the Santa Reparata International School of Art in Florence, Italy; and the University of Guadalajara in Mexico. Open to all Columbia students, the Semester in Los Angeles program is a five-week immersion program in which the student maintains full-time status while gaining invaluable real-world experience. Located in Bungalow 25 on the CBS Studio Lot in Culver City, Columbia is the only institution of higher learning permanently located on a studio lot. Students are given Lot ID badges and enter the gates of the lot everyday just like working producers, directors, stars, and craft personnel.

Academic Facilities

Columbia College consists of thirteen campus buildings located primarily in the historic South Loop neighborhood of downtown Chicago. Advanced facilities for radio, television, art, computer graphics, photography, interactive multimedia, fashion design, and film are state-of-the-industry and include professionally equipped color and black-and-white darkrooms, digital imaging computer facilities, photography and film stages, film and video editing suites, and studios for painting, drawing, and 3-D design. The campus also includes the Museum of Contemporary Photography, one of only a few such facilities in the United States, and the Audio Technology Center, a recording production and research facility. In addition, Columbia has extensive computer facilities used by basic computer classes as well as dedicated computer facilities utilized by the departments. The centers for dance, music, and theater are separate but conveniently located and are designed for their specific performance needs, including individual and group rehearsal and specialized performance spaces.

The College's 200,000-volume library and instructional service center provides comprehensive information and study facilities. Reading/study rooms and special audiovisual equipment are available for use in individual projects and research. As a member of a statewide online computer catalog and resource-sharing network, Columbia's library provides students with access to the resources of forty-five academic institutions in Illinois, effectively creating an information base of several million volumes. The library also houses special collections, such as the George S. Lurie Memorial collection of books and resource materials on art, photography, and film; the Black Music Resource Center of books and sound recordings; the Screenwriters' Collection of film and television manuscripts; the History of Photography microfilm collection of books and periodicals; and a nonprint collection of 100,000 slides and more than 7,300 videotapes and films. The latest addition to the library is the Albert P. Weisman Center for the Study of Contemporary Issues in Chicago Journalism. The center includes a print and audiovisual collection and a learning center that explores the development of Chicago's political and social history.

Costs

For the 2003–04 academic year, full tuition (12 to 16 credit hours) averaged $7440 per each fifteen-week semester, or $14,880 per year. Part-time tuition (up to 11 credit hours) was $515 per credit hour. Summer school tuition was $400 per credit hour. Some courses require additional service or laboratory fees. Required nonrefundable fees charged each semester include the registration fee, $50; the student activity fee, $50 ($25 for part-time students); the U-Pass, $70 (for unlimited access to the public transportation system); and a health center fee, $25 ($15 for part-time students). There is also a one-time $30 library deposit that is refunded when the student leaves the College.

Financial Aid

Columbia College makes every effort to help students obtain financial assistance, including grants, on-campus work, and loans. The Office of Student Financial Services administers federal and state grant and loan programs. The College also provides information for students seeking part-time employment both on- and off-campus. On-campus jobs are available in technical, clerical, secretarial, and food service areas. Columbia offers institution-based scholarships, such as Presidential Scholarships for freshmen, scholarships for transfer students, academic excellence awards, leadership awards, and housing grants. The Fischetti Scholarships support the efforts of outstanding Columbia journalism students, and the Weisman Scholarships support special communication-related projects. Appropriate scholarship and applications forms for financial aid are available through the Office of Undergraduate Admissions.

Faculty

Many of Columbia's 1,267 full- and part-time faculty members are working professionals (artists, writers, filmmakers, dancers, etc.) with national reputations. The College is constantly seeking individuals who are both gifted teachers and talented professionals. Many faculty members work nearby in the disciplines in which they teach and share practical expertise with students in informal workshop settings and in the classroom. Interaction with faculty members who are practicing professionals provides students with invaluable access to the latest information in their fields. Students also begin developing their own professional network as faculty members share contacts and information on how to break into the market.

Student Government

Through the Student Government Association (SGA) and the Student Organization Council (SOC), students are able to address college-wide and departmental issues and sponsor services and activities. SGA and SOC work closely with the Office of Student Affairs and serve as liaisons to the administration and departments. The fifty campus clubs and organizations reflect the interests and the diversity of Columbia's student body. Film screenings, student-produced television shows, dance recitals, poetry readings, plays, campus radio, music concerts, and a national award-winning newspaper are just some of the campus events and activities available to students.

Admissions Requirements

Columbia College invites applications from all students with creative ability in or inclination to the arts, media, and communication disciplines in which the College specializes. To apply for admissions, students must submit high school transcripts, college transcripts (if applicable), a letter of recommendation, a personal essay, and a $25 application fee. ACT Assessment or SAT I scores are not required but are strongly encouraged. Graduation from high school or an earned GED is required prior to enrollment. Freshmen applicants whose application materials suggest they are likely to be underprepared to meet the College's standards are required to successfully complete the Bridge Program to be admitted to the College. Columbia has a liberal transfer policy.

Application and Information

Students are strongly advised to apply early. The priority date is July 1 for the fall semester, December 1 for the spring semester, and May 1 for the summer term. Applicants are notified within two to four weeks after the College receives all the required information and documents. Students who want to live in campus housing are strongly advised to apply early. Housing assignments are offered on a first-come, first-served basis until full occupancy is achieved.

All students are invited to tour the College and meet with an admissions counselor. To arrange for a tour and an appointment with an admissions counselor, students should call the telephone number below.

For more information, students should contact:

Office of Undergraduate Admissions
Columbia College Chicago
600 South Michigan Avenue
Chicago, Illinois 60605
Telephone: 312-344-7130
Fax: 312-344-8024
E-mail admissions@colum.edu
World Wide Web: http://www.colum.edu

COLUMBIA COLLEGE HOLLYWOOD

TARZANA, CALIFORNIA

The College

Columbia College Hollywood (CCH) is a leader in preparing students for careers in the film and television/video industries. Known as "the filmmaker's film school," CCH is where industry professionals nurture the talent of their future colleagues by emphasizing "hands-on" training. The technical and creative advances now being made in the motion picture and television industries make it imperative for aspiring film and video artists to receive cutting-edge training. Since its founding in 1952, CCH has offered that kind of training.

Columbia College Hollywood is a private, nonprofit institution accredited by the Accrediting Commission of Career Schools and Colleges of Technology (ACCSCT). CCH's goal is to turn out artists with technical proficiency and technicians who are also artists. The formula seems to be working: 2 CCH graduates recently produced Grand Prize winners at the Sundance Film Festival; others have won awards at the Hollywood and Palm Springs festivals. CCH is proud of the accomplishments of all its students.

Columbia College Hollywood's commitment to involving students in the professional film and television/video community is the reason why its campus is located right outside of Los Angeles, one of the world's centers for the motion picture and television industries. It has allowed the school to maintain close relationships with working industry professionals, studios, and production companies and encouraged them to become involved in the educational process at CCH. It also ensures access for CCH students to coveted internships and the networking opportunities that drive the entertainment business.

Location

Columbia College Hollywood makes the most of its location in Los Angeles's San Fernando Valley, the heart of the motion picture and television/video industry. CCH students are frequently invited to work on the many films that are produced daily in the L.A. area. The school's placement director arranges internships for students with production companies and studios, enabling them to gain invaluable experience and make all-important industry contacts. Apart from the excitement that comes from being at the visual media center of the world, there are the well-known physical attractions of Los Angeles itself: its temperate climate, beaches, mountains, and deserts. Los Angeles is a cultural center as well and is home to museums, galleries, concerts (both classical and popular), major-league sports teams, and live theater.

Majors and Degrees

Columbia College Hollywood offers the Bachelor of Arts (B.A.) degree in cinema, television/video production, and combined cinema/television. Students who wish may pursue an Associate in Arts (A.A.) degree in television/video production. The A.A. and B.A. degree programs can be attended on a part-time basis.

Academic Program

The Associate in Arts degree requires 96 units of study, of which 48 units are in general education and 48 units are in television production. The Bachelor of Arts degree requires 192 units of study, 48 of which are in general education and 144 of which are in the program major. In the B.A. programs, cinema and television/video students are enrolled in parallel courses of study for the first five quarters. These courses cover both film and video technology, which gives the student a solid foundation. This is beneficial because the two mediums are merging in the professional world. After the fifth quarter, students continue in their major area of study.

The program in television/video production is designed to provide students with knowledge and skills in the creative, technical, and operational aspects of the medium. The graduate from this course of study is well qualified for a variety of entry-level positions in a television broadcast facility, a nonbroadcast video production setting, or an allied industry. Examples of entry-level positions are production assistant, directorial assistant, camera operator, floor director, advertising and sales assistant, copywriter, assistant editor, tape operator, or video engineer.

Through the program in cinema, students learn about the technical and creative aspects of theatrical, documentary, and industrial film production. Graduates from this program are well qualified for entry-level positions such as camera assistant, lighting assistant, grip, dolly grip, budgeting and production assistant, sound recordist, assistant editor, postproduction sound mixer, and assistant director. In order to accommodate working students and the many instructors who hold entertainment industry positions, there are classes held at night and during the afternoon. Some weekend seminars are also offered.

Academic Facilities

Columbia College Hollywood has a nonresidential urban campus designed to cater to students' needs in their quest to become great filmmakers. Among its features is an equipment center that contains 16mm cameras, lenses, video cameras, lighting equipment, grip equipment, and sound equipment. Its television studio, currently being remodeled, is scheduled to open in fall 2004. CCH offers both Avid and Macintosh-based Final Cut Pro online-quality digital editing systems and a telecine machine that allows students to shoot in film and finish digitally. The campus also houses a student library of movie and television scripts, industry trade publications, DVD and VHS movies, and traditional literature and research material. There is a computer lab offering budget, planning, and scriptwriting software and an Internet lab for computers with Internet access. Additional features on campus include two projection theaters (twenty-four and seventy-three seats), study areas, a prop room, well-equipped classrooms, a "shooting gallery" workplace for student filming, and an ADR facility for postproduction sound editing.

Costs

For the 2004–05 academic year, tuition and fees for full-time attendance are approximately $13,000 per academic year. Laboratory fees vary from quarter to quarter. The estimated living costs for an independent student are approximately $8000 per academic year. Ample housing is available in the vicinity of the College.

Financial Aid

Columbia College Hollywood participates in the following federal and state financial aid programs: the Federal Pell Grant, Federal Supplemental Educational Opportunity Grant, Federal Work-Study, Federal Family Education Loan (which includes subsidized and unsubsidized Federal Stafford Student Loan), and Cal Grants A, B, and C. The school makes available scholarships for industry internships.

Faculty

The faculty consists of 35 members, the majority of whom hold positions in the television, motion picture, or educational fields during the daytime. The student-faculty ratio is 5:1.

Admission Requirements

Applicants for freshman-level classes must be high school graduates and at least 18 years of age at the time of enrollment. They must have earned a minimum cumulative grade point average of 2.0 or have maintained an overall letter grade of C or better during their high school studies. Transcripts must demonstrate high school graduation. Under special circumstances, a passing score on the General Educational Development (GED) test may be accepted by the College in lieu of high school graduation, provided that the applicant is at least 18 years of age. Applicants for admission to the College on any other level are required to furnish transcripts of previous course work to establish their academic standing. Applicants to the Upper Division programs are required to furnish transcripts verifying completion of an Associate in Arts degree or higher. All transcripts must be sent directly to Columbia College Hollywood by the educational institutions. Two letters of reference from people, other than relatives, who have been acquainted with the applicant for more than one year and are aware of the applicant's interest in the field of cinema, television, or communications media are required; these letters must be mailed directly to Columbia College Hollywood by the writers. A 250-word essay concerning why the applicant wishes to study either film or video and describing his or her career goals is required. SAT I scores may be submitted.

Students enrolling in Columbia College Hollywood for the first time are encouraged to attend an orientation session. Academic objectives and career goals are discussed, school programs and academic requirements are explained, and registration for classes takes place during the course of orientation. To guarantee enrollment, final registration should be completed at least one week prior to the beginning of the quarter.

Advanced standing may be granted to applicants for the programs in television/video production and cinema. Transcripts of the applicants' previous college-level study should be mailed directly to Columbia College by the institution previously attended for evaluation by Columbia College's Admissions Department.

Application and Information

Applications are accepted throughout the year, and applicants may apply to enroll in the fall, winter, spring, or summer quarters. Late registration can occur up to the close of the first week of the quarter; however, acceptance for enrollment in any particular quarter cannot be guaranteed unless the applicant has been fully matriculated at least one week prior to the beginning of that quarter.

A completed application for admission and an application fee of $50 should be mailed to the College or delivered in person by the applicant.

For more information, students should contact:

Admissions Office
Columbia College Hollywood
18618 Oxnard Street
Tarzana, California 91356
Telephone: 818-345-8414
800-785-0585 (toll-free)
Fax: 818-345-9053
E-mail: admissions@columbiacollege.edu
World Wide Web: http://www.columbiacollege.edu

At Columbia College Hollywood, students use professional equipment on location for a film production workshop class.

COLUMBIA UNION COLLEGE

TAKOMA PARK, MARYLAND

The College

Columbia Union College (CUC) was established in 1904 as the Washington Training Institute. In 1914, the College took the name Washington Missionary College, and in 1942, the College was given accreditation as a four-year, degree-granting institution by the Middle States Association of Colleges and Secondary Schools. In 1961, the College constituency voted to change the name of the school to Columbia Union College.

Columbia Union College is affiliated with the Seventh-day Adventist Church, and, as set forth in the College's Statement of Mission, aims to develop the talent of its students and to instill in them the value of service and the love of truth and learning. The College motto, "Gateway to Service," emphasizes CUC's intent to educate graduates who "bring competence and moral leadership to their communities."

Columbia Union College is a coeducational college that offers degree programs in liberal arts, sciences, and selected professional fields. The College is accredited for granting associate and baccalaureate degrees and has an M.B.A. program. CUC offers a combination of spiritual, cultural, academic, athletic, and employment opportunities. CUC is located just outside the nation's capital, which gives students an abundance of hands-on employment, educational, and entertainment opportunities.

Columbia Union College is committed to students. The faculty members of the College are qualified professionals with practical experience. Classes are small (13:1 ratio), and teachers have the time to give students individual attention and training for their futures. CUC takes pride in its graduates and those who instruct them and in its commitment to be more than an institution of higher education. It is a community of spiritual, cultural, athletic, and career opportunities under the spirit of Christianity.

Location

Columbia Union College is located in Takoma Park, Maryland. The College occupies 19 acres in this small community, just minutes from Washington, D.C. A RideOn bus stop is located on the campus, and a Metrorail station is just a mile down the road, allowing CUC students access to all parts of the nation's capital, Maryland, and Virginia. Shopping malls, restaurants, recreational resources, and entertainment abound around the campus of CUC. Students frequent the wide variety of interests in the local area and are also employed in prestigious internships and part-time positions in Washington, D.C. The list of employers of CUC students continues to grow and includes the Baltimore National Aquarium, the CIA, Children's Hospital, Seventh-day Adventist World Headquarters, IBM, NASA/Goddard Space Flight Center, National Institutes of Health, Smithsonian Institution, Walt Disney World, the White House, and WTTG–Fox Channel 5. Students and faculty members also take advantage of the educational resources that surround CUC. Visits to an exhibit at a Smithsonian museum or research conducted at the Library of Congress aid in classroom studies.

Majors and Degrees

Columbia Union College grants the Bachelor of Arts degree, with majors in biology, chemistry, education, English (emphasis in prelaw), English education, general studies, history (emphasis in prelaw), journalism (concentrations in broadcast, documentary production, and print; emphasis in media production), liberal studies, mathematics, mathematics education, music, philosophy and religion (emphasis in prelaw), political studies (emphasis in prelaw), psychology, public communication (concentrations in intercultural communication and public relations; emphasis in media studies), religion (concentrations in lay ministry, metropolitan ministry, and religious education; emphasis in prelaw), and theology (concentrations in metropolitan ministry and pastoral ministry; emphasis in prelaw). Bachelor of Science degrees are also offered, with majors in accounting, biochemistry, biology, business administration (emphases in entrepreneurship, finance, human resource management, international business, long-term health-care administration, marketing, and prelaw), chemistry, computer science, counseling psychology, general studies, health-care administration, information systems, mathematics, mathematics education, nursing, organizational management, physical education, physical education: teacher certification, and respiratory care. Bachelor of Music degrees are offered in music education and music performance. Associate of Applied Science degrees are offered in accounting, computer science, early childhood education, engineering, general studies, information systems, and respiratory care. An Associate of Science degree is offered in engineering. Columbia Union College also offers Associate of Arts degrees and a Bachelor of Science/Registered Nurse degree.

Students may select from several minor concentrations, including accounting, American religious history, behavioral science, biology, broadcast journalism, business administration, chemistry, computer science, computer business, English, French, forensic psychology, German, health-care administration, history, information systems, intercultural communication, intercultural studies, marketing, mathematics, media production, metropolitan ministry, music, organizational management, philosophy, physical education, physics, political studies, print journalism, psychology, public relations, religion, secondary education, Spanish, sports administration/coaching, and writing.

Academic Program

The academic year follows a semester schedule. To graduate, all students must take required core classes. Students must earn 120 to 128 credit hours, including 36 upper-division credit hours, with a minimum GPA of 2.0 and a GPA of 2.5 in the declared major. All traditional students must take general education classes that include 12 hours of religion; 9 of social sciences; 8 of physical sciences, natural sciences, and mathematics; 7 of humanities; 3 of physical education and health; and 6 of practical and applied arts. Courses in English, communication, and computer science are also required. A cooperative education program is required in the business, communication, computer science, English, mathematics, and nursing programs. The cooperative education program aids students in obtaining job placements and internships and also provides career counseling and courses in interviewing, resume writing, and job search strategies. Credit for life experience, nondegree study, and pass/fail options exist at the College. CUC also hosts an Adult Evening Program for degree completion as well as an external (correspondence) degree. Majors in business administration, health-care administration, information systems, and organizational management are available through the Adult Evening Program on CUC's main campus and at an off-site location in Gaithersburg, Maryland. Summer courses and special programs are available to give incoming first-year students preparation for college and to aid the progress of students who currently attend.

Off-Campus Programs

In conjunction with the University of Maryland, dual majors are available in engineering/chemistry and mathematics. Students may study abroad in Austria, France, and Spain through CUC and Adventist Colleges Abroad.

Academic Facilities

Advanced facilities for radio and television are available. Columbia Union College has its own television studio and audio and video postproduction suites. The communication department has several high-tech Electronic Field Production (EFP) cameras available for student use. WGTS-FM, a contemporary Christian radio station, is also located on the campus of CUC, and many students work there.

CUC has invested in extensive computer facilities that are used by all students. A large computer laboratory of PCs and Macs is available for student use, and there are many other computer areas on campus. Each dorm resident has Internet access from his or her room and a personal e-mail account.

Weis Library, on the campus of CUC, has a collection of nearly 130,000 volumes and subscribes to more than 400 periodicals. The library utilizes the services of the Online Computer Library Center (OCLC). OCLC's database contains approximately 38 million bibliographic records from library collections around the world. Interlibrary loan service is expedited through use of this online system. In addition, Weis Library provides Internet and CD-ROM access to many other electronic resources.

Costs

In 2003–04, full tuition (12 to 16 credit hours) averages $14,698 for the academic year, which consists of two semesters. Part-time tuition (up to 9 credit hours) is $612 per credit hour. The general fee is $375 per semester. Summer sessions vary in tuition prices. Some courses require additional service or laboratory fees. There is a nonrefundable application fee of $25.

Financial Aid

Columbia Union College makes every effort to help students seek out and obtain financial assistance, and it also provides information for students seeking part-time employment.

CUC offers institutional scholarships, such as those for musical and athletic groups on campus, as well as scholarships for proven academic excellence. Ninety-six percent of traditional students received some form of financial aid in 2002–03, and nearly $10.3 million in financial aid was awarded.

The Financial Aid Office of CUC administers federal and state grant and loan programs. Appropriate application forms for financial aid are provided by the financial aid office and are mailed to students who request them. Students who receive any form of aid, including scholarships, are required to fill out a Free Application for Federal Student Aid (FAFSA).

Faculty

There are 53 full-time and 3 part-time faculty members at Columbia Union College. More than 100 adjunct instructors are employed by CUC. The College prides itself on the integrity of its faculty members and the experience that they bring to the College. The ratio of full-time undergraduate students to full-time undergraduate faculty members is 13:1. Faculty members of CUC are the personal career advisers of students and guide students through their courses of study and preparation for the future. Faculty members share contacts from their professional fields to aid students in obtaining internships and career placement.

Student Government

The Student Association officers are elected yearly. This group leads special activities and plans feature events on and off campus. The Student Government takes interest in general assemblies on informational topics. The editor of the school newspaper, the *Columbia Journal*, and the editor of the College yearbook, *Golden Memories*, also function in the Student Government. Senate meetings are an activity of the Student Government. The Senate includes various representatives of the student body and discusses ideas and concerns of the College, which are then taken to the administration after debate. The vice president for student life and retention directs this special group of leaders as they represent Columbia Union College.

Admission Requirements

A minimum combined score of 900 on the SAT I (or at least 450 in each section) or a minimum composite score of 18 on the ACT is recommended. Applicants must be graduates of an accredited secondary school or have earned a GED certificate. Twenty-one Carnegie units are required, including 4 years of high school English and 2 years each of history, mathematics, and science. An essay is recommended, and an interview, as well as transcripts from previously attended colleges, is required.

Application and Information

Columbia Union College accepts applications on a continuous basis. Applicants must submit an application for admission, two recommendations, transcripts, and proof of high school graduation or successful completion of a GED certificate. Applicants are asked to submit a nonrefundable $25 fee at the time of application.

To receive an application booklet or for additional information, students should contact:

Enrollment Services
Columbia Union College
7600 Flower Avenue
Takoma Park, Maryland 20912
Telephone: 800-835-4212 (toll-free)
World Wide Web: http://www.cuc.edu/

Columbia Union College is located just minutes away from everything Washington, D.C., has to offer.

COLUMBIA UNIVERSITY, SCHOOL OF GENERAL STUDIES

NEW YORK, NEW YORK

The University and The School

One of the best kept secrets in American higher education, the School of General Studies of Columbia University is the nation's premier college for returning and nontraditional students. One of the four undergraduate colleges that grace Columbia, the School of General Studies is dedicated to those students who have interrupted or postponed their education for at least one academic year.

Unlike the division of the University dedicated to continuing education, the School of General Studies is a degree-granting liberal arts college. The School of General Studies is fully integrated into the Columbia undergraduate curriculum and provides an Ivy League education to the widest range of talented students with the demonstrated potential to succeed.

General Studies students come from all walks of life and from varied backgrounds, and for that reason may study full- or part-time. Many degree candidates hold jobs as well as study, and many have family responsibilities. Others attend full-time, experiencing Columbia's more traditional college life. The diversity in the student body makes attendance at Columbia highly attractive. The varied personal experience represented in each classroom allows for discussion and debate and, in turn, for the academic rigor and intellectual development that characterize a Columbia education. The School has more than 1,200 undergraduate degree candidates and about 300 postbaccalaureate premedical students. The average age of these students is 29. About half are full-time students. Between 80 percent and 85 percent of the School's students go on to graduate and professional schools after graduation. The acceptance rate for General Studies postbaccalaureate premedical students applying to U.S. medical schools is more than 85 percent.

In addition to its bachelor's degree program, the School of General Studies offers combined undergraduate/graduate degree programs with Columbia's Schools of Social Work, International and Public Affairs, Law, Business, and Dental and Oral Surgery, as well as with Teachers College, the College of Physicians and Surgeons, and the Juilliard School.

Location

Columbia University is located in Morningside Heights, on the Upper West Side of Manhattan. The University's neighbors include the Union Theological Seminary, the Jewish Theological Seminary, the Manhattan School of Music, St. Luke's Hospital, Women's Hospital, Riverside Church, and the Cathedral of St. John the Divine. The diversity of intellectual and social activities these institutions offer in the immediate vicinity is one of Columbia's great assets as a university; another is New York City itself, which offers students at Columbia an almost boundless and astonishingly rich variety of social, cultural, and recreational opportunities that are themselves an education.

Majors and Degrees

The School of General Studies grants the B.A. and B.S. degrees and offers the following majors: African studies; African-American studies; American studies; ancient studies; anthropology; applied mathematics; archaeology; architecture; art history; art history–visual arts; Asian-American studies; astronomy; biochemistry; biology; chemistry; classical studies; classics; comparative literature and society; computer science; dance; drama and theater arts; earth and environmental sciences; East Asian languages and cultures; ecology, evolution, and environmental biology; economics; economics–mathematics; economics–operations research; economics–philosophy; economics–political science; economics–statistics; English and comparative literature; environmental biology; film studies; French; French and Francophone studies; German literature and cultural history; Hispanic studies; history; human rights; Italian literature; Italian cultural studies; Latino studies; literature–writing; mathematics; mathematics–statistics; Middle East and Asian languages and cultures; music; neuroscience and behavior; philosophy; physics; political science; psychology; religion; Slavic languages; sociology; Spanish; Spanish and Portuguese; statistics; urban studies; visual arts; and women's and gender studies. Individually designed majors are also available. In addition, the School offers two undergraduate dual-degree programs: one in conjunction with Columbia's School of Engineering and Applied Science and the other in conjunction with the Jewish Theological Seminary of America.

Academic Program

The School of General Studies offers a traditional liberal arts education designed to provide students with the broad knowledge and intellectual skills that make possible continued education and growth in the years after college and that constitute the soundest possible foundation on which to build competence for positions of responsibility in the professional world. Requirements for the bachelor's degree comprise three elements: (1) core requirements, intended to develop in students the ability to write and communicate clearly; to understand the modes of thought that characterize the humanities, the social sciences, and the sciences; to gain some familiarity with central cultural ideas through literature, fine arts, and music; and to acquire a working proficiency in a foreign language; (2) major requirements, designed to give students sustained and coherent exposure to a particular discipline in an area of strong intellectual interest; and (3) elective courses, in which students pursue particular interests and skills for their own personal growth or for their relationship to future professional or personal objectives. Students are required to complete a minimum of 124 credits for the bachelor's degree; 60 of these may be in transfer credit, but at least 64 credits (including the last 30 credits) must be completed at Columbia. In addition to the usual graduation honors (cum laude, magna cum laude, and summa cum laude), honors programs for superior students are available in a majority of the University's departments.

Off-Campus Programs

Columbia students may enhance their academic experiences through various study-abroad programs around the world. General Studies students may spend a term at the Reid Hall Program in the Montparnasse district of Paris; the Free University of Berlin; the Kyoto Center in Japan; or in Beijing, China.

Academic Facilities

The Columbia University libraries constitute the nation's sixth-largest academic library system, with a collection of more than 6 million volumes, more than 4 million microform pieces, and 26 million manuscript items in 850 separate collections. There are twenty-two libraries in the system; five are designated Distinctive Collections because of their unusual depth and nationally recognized excellence. All library divisions are available to General Studies students. The University's Computer Center is one of the largest and most powerful university installations in the world and has remote units and terminals in several parts of the campus to enhance its accessibility. The Fairchild Life Science Building houses research facilities, laboratories, electron microscopes, and a vast amount of biochemical equipment used for teaching and research. The University's physics building has been the scene of many important developments in the recent history of physics, including the invention of the laser and the first demonstration in this country of nuclear fission.

Costs

For the 2003–04 academic year, tuition was $926 per credit, monthly living expenses were about $1200 for single students and about $1800 for married students, fees were approximately $1200, and books cost about $900 to $1200.

Financial Aid

The School of General Studies awards financial aid based upon need and academic ability. Approximately 70 percent of General Studies degree candidates receive some form of financial aid, including Federal Pell Grants, New York State TAP Grants, Federal Stafford and unsubsidized Stafford Loans, Federal Perkins Loans, General Studies Scholarships, and Federal Work-Study Program awards. Priority application deadlines for new students are June 1 for the fall 2004 semester and October 15 for the spring 2005 semester.

Faculty

The faculty of the School of General Studies, which is shared with Columbia College, the Graduate School of Arts and Sciences, and the School of International and Public Affairs, includes distinguished scholars in virtually every discipline. Of the School's more than 600 faculty members, more than 99 percent hold a Ph.D. degree. Students, whether full-time or part-time, have many opportunities to work closely with this faculty, both in small classes and in research projects. Faculty members also serve as advisers to students majoring in their area of study and maintain regular office hours to see students.

Student Government

One student of the School represents General Studies students in the University Senate, a decision-making body composed of students and faculty and administrative staff members from each division of the University. In addition, 2 General Studies students sit as voting members on the Committee on Instruction, which oversees the curriculum of the School. The General Studies Student Council elects officers each year and sponsors activities for students. *The Observer*, the School's student-run magazine, is published several times each year. The Postbaccalaureate Premedical Program Student Organization sponsors events related to the medical school admissions process.

Admission Requirements

The admission policy of the School is geared to the maturity and varied backgrounds of its students. Aptitude and motivation are considered along with past academic performance, standardized test scores, and employment history. The School's admission decisions are based on a careful review of each application and reflect the Admissions Committee's considered judgment of the applicant's maturity, academic potential, and present ability to undertake course work at Columbia.

Admission requirements include a completed application form; a 1,500- to 2,000-word autobiographical statement relating the applicant's past educational history and work experience, present situation, and future plans; two letters of recommendation from an academic or professional evaluator; an official high school transcript; official transcripts from all colleges and universities attended; official SAT I or ACT scores or scores on the General Studies Admissions Examination; and a nonrefundable application fee of $65.

Students from outside the United States may apply to the School of General Studies to start or complete a baccalaureate degree. In addition to the materials described above, international applicants must submit official TOEFL scores.

Application and Information

Application deadlines are March 1 for early action (nonbinding), June 1 for the fall semester, and November 1 for the spring semester. Applicants from countries outside the U.S. are urged to apply by August 15 for the spring semester and April 1 for the fall semester. Applications are reviewed as they are completed, and applicants are notified of decisions shortly thereafter.

For more information, students should contact:

Office of Admissions and Financial Aid
School of General Studies
408 Lewisohn Hall
2970 Broadway
Columbia University, Mail Code 4101
New York, New York 10027
Telephone: 212-854-2772
E-mail: gsdegree@columbia.edu
World Wide Web: http://www.gs.columbia.edu

The Low Memorial Library/Visitors Center.

COLUMBUS COLLEGE OF ART & DESIGN

COLUMBUS, OHIO

The College

Founded in 1879, the Columbus College of Art & Design (CCAD) is one of the oldest continuously operating art schools in the country. Located on a three-city-block tract of land adjacent to the Columbus Museum of Art in downtown Columbus, the College enrolls approximately 1,248 full-time students. The College is a member of the National Association of Schools of Art and Design.

The Canzani Center is the focal point of the seventeen-building campus. The structure houses a large exhibition area, a library and resource center, and an auditorium. A 250-student dorm located next to Kinney Hall houses all freshmen and first-year transfer students under 21 and offers full cafeteria service. This modern facility has suites that accommodate 4 students with adjoining kitchenettes and bathrooms.

In addition to the regular day-school program, the College conducts an evening program that is geared primarily to the adult learner, a Saturday program for children from 6 to 18 years of age, and summer school classes. The summer school courses are directed toward areas of major concentration. Students generally spend one summer acquiring knowledge in an area of particular interest. The College hosts exhibitions throughout the year, sponsors a visiting artist program, and conducts frequent workshops to ensure a rich and exciting environment for the growth of creativity.

Location

Columbus, the capital of Ohio, has a population of more than 1.3 million. Near the College are the Columbus Museum of Art; the Columbus Public Library, housing more than 500,000 volumes; Grant Hospital of Columbus; the Ohio Theatre, a center of cultural activity within the city that showcases the Columbus Symphony Orchestra and Ballet Metropolitan; and the downtown community, rich in social and cultural events.

Majors and Degrees

The Columbus College of Art & Design offers a four-year program leading to the Bachelor of Fine Arts degree. The curriculum features areas of major concentration either in commercial art through the Division of Fashion Design, the Division of Illustration, the Division of Industrial Design, the Division of Interior Design, the Division of Media Studies, and the Division of Visual Communication, or in the fine arts through the Division of Fine Arts, which offers work in ceramics, drawing, glassblowing, painting, printmaking, and sculpture. Integrated within the divisions are specializations in art therapy, computer graphics, fashion illustration, package design, photography, and product design.

Academic Program

The Bachelor of Fine Arts degree requires the completion of 129 semester credit hours (approximately 84 credit hours in art courses and 45 credit hours in general studies courses). During the first year of study, all students are required to take a sequence of core courses in anatomy, color concept, computer design, design, drawing, painting, and perspective. In the second year, students choose a major area of concentration and receive instruction in the fundamentals within a specific area. In the third and fourth years, students develop as professionals within their respective fields.

The educational goal of the Columbus College of Art & Design is professionalism. The curriculum is carefully structured so that courses taken at the same time complement each other and courses taken in sequence progress logically from the first year to graduation. Emphasis is placed on skill building, resourcefulness, versatility, and creativity to help students realize their full aesthetic potential. The College stresses the actual work methods used in today's professional art studio, agency, business, or industry, but the curriculum provides a thorough foundation in the methods and concepts of the finer realms of art expression. Students are encouraged to seek the ideal by experiencing the practical.

Qualified students may schedule work in dual divisions. The major divisions are integrated by having similar directions in creative design and related professional courses. The divisions are responsive to contemporary change and continually incorporate new areas of special interest into the curriculum.

Independent study is available in studio courses within the Division of Fine Arts. Specific areas include ceramics, drawing, glassblowing, painting, printmaking, and sculpture.

Academic Facilities

The facilities consist of seven large buildings for instruction and six buildings that house the administrative and faculty offices. Kinney Hall is the largest of the instructional buildings, consisting of space specifically designed for the education of the visual artist. Its features include classroom space; a supply store; glassblowing, ceramics, and printmaking studios; a print shop; a photography lab; exhibition space; and faculty and administrative offices. Battelle Hall, a large two-story building, houses a sculpture studio with an attached foundry and a welding facility on its first floor; on the second floor is a large open space for painting studios. Studio Hall contains two large classrooms for drawing, faculty offices, and the College's in-house print facilities. Beaton Hall is a distinctive building housing classroom space, exhibition areas, and some administrative offices. The Packard Library, located in the Canzani Center, has an open-shelf collection of books and bound periodicals on the arts and subjects offered at the College. The collection is supplemented by slides for classroom use and by circulating files of masterworks on print and picture clippings on all subjects. A copying machine, light tables, and a viewing room with audiovisual equipment are also available for use by students and faculty members.

Costs

The tuition for 2003–04 was approximately $17,880 for the academic year. Room and board for 2003–04 were $6300 for the academic year. Supplies and books are approximately $850 for the first year.

Financial Aid

The College participates in the Federal Perkins Loan Program, the Federal Work-Study Program, the Federal Pell Grant Program, the Federal Supplemental Educational Opportunity Grant Program, the Ohio Instructional Grant Program for Ohio residents, the Federal Stafford Student Loan Program, and the Federal PLUS Loan Program. For priority consideration, students should submit applications for these programs before April 3 for the following fall semester and before October 31 for the second semester.

The College also conducts a scholarship competition open to high school seniors entering the freshman class. Art submitted for this competition must be received between February 1 and March 1. Other scholarship programs include the Scholastic Art Awards, Battelle Scholars Program (for central Ohio students), Art Recognition Talent Search Scholarship, Ohio Governor's Show Scholarship, and industry and foundation scholarships. Applicants should contact the Admissions Office of the College for information about these programs.

Faculty

The College's faculty consists of 130 working professionals (67 full-time and 63 part-time members), which includes a large body of artist-designers who have had extensive professional experience and hold appropriate degrees in the divisions of art offered. Faculty members are professionally oriented, practicing artist-designers with broad teaching experience in diverse areas of the art world. In the Liberal Arts Department, experienced faculty members with graduate degrees teach a wide range of courses in the humanities and sciences. Faculty members take an active interest in the students and are involved in advising them on a one-to-one basis regarding both career decisions and curricular matters. The student-faculty ratio is 12:1.

Student Government

The Student Council is the officially recognized organization that represents the students at the College. Representatives are appointed by the council to sit on most major College committees to ensure that students have a say in the decision-making process. The council also plans social events and organizes art-related activities for the students. Meetings, held each week, are open to all students.

Admission Requirements

Applicants must be high school graduates with a minimum GPA of 2.0 or the equivalent certificate. An official high school transcript must be submitted before acceptance. The submission of ACT or SAT I scores is required. Transfer students must also request that an official transcript be sent from each college previously attended. In view of the school's professional goal, examples of artwork must be submitted to the Admissions Office for review. A personal interview is also recommended although not required. Application for admission may be made in advance for either the fall semester or the spring semester. Applications should be submitted well before the expected entrance date since the size of all classes is limited.

Application and Information

For information concerning the College and application to its programs, students should contact:

Admissions Office
Columbus College of Art & Design
107 North Ninth Street
Columbus, Ohio 43215
Telephone: 877-997-CCAD (toll-free)
World Wide Web: http://www.ccad.edu

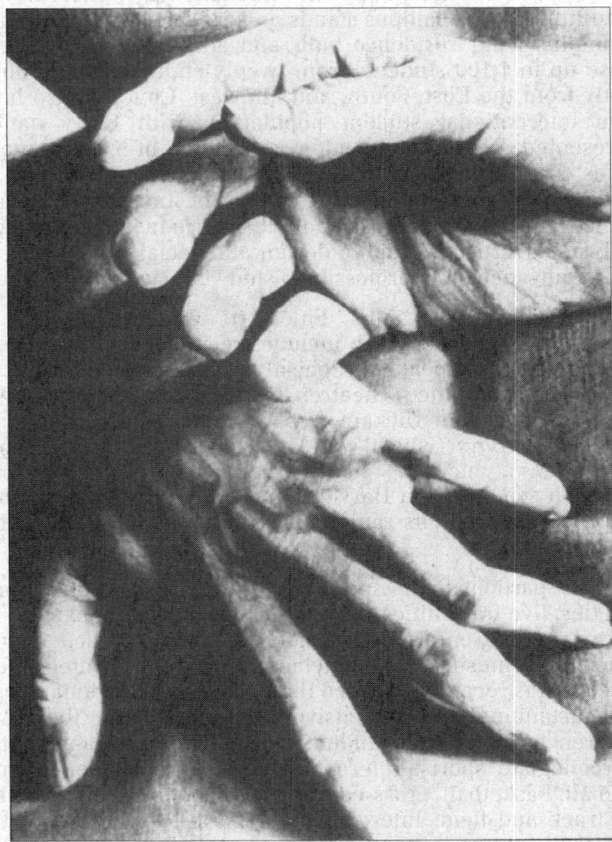

CCAD offers a distinctive education in the visual arts.

CONCORD COLLEGE

ATHENS, WEST VIRGINIA

The College

Concord College, a growing state-supported college committed exclusively to undergraduate instruction, was founded 129 years ago. Concord features accredited career-oriented education with a strong liberal arts base and focuses on the needs of the individual student as its fundamental concern. The beautiful 123-acre campus stands on a ridge of the Appalachian Mountains. Four residence halls and adult studio apartments house up to 1,100 students from twenty-eight states, predominantly from the East, South, and Midwest. Concord also has a large international student population, with thirty nations represented. With a total student population of 3,050, Concord serves the needs of active commuter students who join the residential students in following courses of study in the arts and sciences, business administration, teacher education, and such fields as advertising/graphic design and social work. Preparation for advanced and professional study is a Concord hallmark.

Each year, the Alexander Fine Arts Center presents the Artist-Lecture Series, which includes recitals, plays, art exhibitions, and guest speakers. Special events have included the North Carolina Dance Theatre; the West Virginia Symphony; lecturers Dr. Homer Hickam, NASA scientist and author of the book *Rocket Boys* (which was later made into the hit movie *October Sky*), and Dr. Cornel West, a preeminent African-American scholar from Harvard; and professional art exhibits. Theatrical productions range from Shakespeare and Chekhov to Woody Allen.

Students participate in special interest organizations, honor societies, five fraternities, four sororities, the yearbook, and the newspaper and enjoy many student activities, which include comedians, musicians, magicians, and other entertainers. Concord was recently awarded the Great Lakes Regional Award for Outstanding Comprehensive Programming at the NACA conference. In addition, students participate in intramural and intercollegiate sports. Intercollegiate sports for men include baseball, basketball, cross-country, football, golf, soccer, tennis, and track and field. Intercollegiate sports for women include basketball, soccer, softball, tennis, track and field, and volleyball.

Counseling and tutoring are strongly supported through Student Support Services; faculty-supervised developmental labs in English, reading, and mathematics; and twice-a-year individual counseling with faculty advisers. The Student Needs Assistance Program offers extensive academic support that ranges from time management to reducing stress anxiety to testing at the student's best level to perform.

Location

Athens is a small town in southern West Virginia near the Virginia border. Located near Princeton and Bluefield, West Virginia, Athens is 6 miles from I-77 and not far from I-64 and I-81. Athens has easy access to thriving population centers, such as Roanoke, Virginia; Charleston, West Virginia; and Charlotte, North Carolina. Shopping malls and entertainment are also available nearby, and Pipestem State Park Resort offers many recreational opportunities. WinterPlace ski resort is approximately 20 minutes north of the campus and white-water rafting is also nearby.

Majors and Degrees

Concord offers more than eighty-five majors, minors, and programs. The degrees offered at Concord are the Bachelor of Science in Computer Information Systems; the Bachelor of Arts in Communication Arts; the Bachelor of Arts/Bachelor of Science in Interdisciplinary Studies; the Bachelor of Social Work; the Bachelor of Science in Education (with a wide selection of teaching fields); the Bachelor of Science in Medical Technology; the Bachelor of Science in Business Administration; the Bachelor of Science, with majors in athletic training, biology, comprehensive chemistry, GIS and cartography, mathematics, mathematics comprehensive, mathematics/computer science, preprofessional biology, and preprofessional chemistry; and the Bachelor of Arts, with majors in advertising/graphic design, English (with emphases in journalism, literature, and writing), geography, history, history with a concentration in philosophy, political science, preprofessional mentoring programs for law and premed, psychology, sociology, and studio art. Concord offers the Regents Bachelor of Arts degree for adults who cannot interrupt their normal activities to attend college but have gained comparable knowledge outside the classroom. Concord also offers a two-year degree, the Associate of Arts in Office Supervision, and five structured interdisciplinary options, including environmental geosciences, health-care management, leadership and entrepreneurial studies, public administration, and sports management.

Academic Program

All students must complete a minimum of 128 semester hours with a grade point average of 2.0 (C) or better to receive a degree. A program of general studies, required of all students, includes courses in communication and literature, fine arts, social sciences, natural sciences, mathematics, foreign languages (optional in most majors), and physical education. Credit is awarded for satisfactory scores on the College-Level Examination Program (CLEP), Advanced Placement (AP), and International Baccalaureate tests. An outstanding honors program is also available to qualifying students. Honors courses and independent study projects are available in most departments. Semesters begin in late August and mid-January; there are summer terms as well.

Off-Campus Programs

The Concord College Beckley Center offers a wide range of academic opportunities, from freshman-level courses to the four-year degree in business administration, to students in Raleigh County, West Virginia. Summer internships, which provide valuable professional contacts and experience, are part of the program of study for students majoring in communication arts and advertising/graphic design. Medical technology students must complete a twelve-month internship at an approved hospital. An internship program is available for travel industry management students. Professional fieldwork placements form part of the social work program.

Academic Facilities

An open-stack library and a modern center for academic technologies facilitate research. Students have access to twenty-five computer labs, port-per-pillow fiber optics in the residence halls, the observatory, two spacious theaters, and physical education facilities, including gymnasiums, an indoor swimming pool, a dance studio, well-equipped weight rooms, and squash, handball, and racquetball courts. Laboratories are integral components of programs in the natural sciences, psychology, and geography. The Alexander Fine Arts Center houses facilities for art, music, communications, and dramatic arts studies.

Costs

For the 2003–04 academic year, the tuition and fees for West Virginia residents were $3198, room and board were $4938, books and supplies cost approximately $600, and personal expenses were nearly $1000. For nonresidents, tuition and fees are $7278 per academic year. All other costs were the same. These figures are subject to change.

Financial Aid

Concord College has the most generous scholarship program in the West Virginia State College System. Merit awards, athletic and talent scholarships, transfer scholarships, and scholarships for nontraditional students are readily available for qualifying students. Federal Pell Grants, Federal Supplemental Educational Opportunity Grants, Federal Perkins Loans, West Virginia Higher Education Grants, Federal PLUS loans, and Federal Stafford Student Loans are available through the College. The State Student Assistance Program and the Federal Work-Study Program offer opportunities for student employment. To receive priority, the Free Application for Federal Student Aid (FAFSA) must be on file by April 15.

Concord offers scholarships to international students. The average scholarship covers about 35 percent of the total institutional cost.

Incoming freshmen who are willing to perform community service may apply for the Bonner Scholars Program, which pays up to $3050 per year for four years as long as its criteria are met. Funded by the Corella and Bertram F. Bonner Foundation of Princeton, New Jersey, the award is primarily based on need and prior service.

Approximately 85 percent of freshman students receive scholarship, financial aid, or both. In addition, 65 percent of the entire student body receive some form of financial aid.

Faculty

All members of the faculty teach courses in the program of general studies, and all counsel and advise students. Terminal degrees are held by 61 of the 87 full-time faculty members. In addition, the College employs adjunct instructors who are experts in their fields. The average class size is 25 students.

Student Government

Concord's Student Government Association (SGA) budgets the student activity fee and plans entertainment. The SGA names students to voting membership on administrative councils and committees. Students also fund the SGA Memorial Scholarship. The College Center Board provides on-campus movies, dances, and special programs. The Concord Office of Student Residential Life offers numerous programs and activities in residence halls.

Admission Requirements

Applicants must have an overall grade point average of at least 2.0 (C) at an approved secondary school or a composite score of at least 17 on the ACT examination or 810 on the SAT I examinations, complete an application form, and send a high school transcript. Applicants may gain admission with advanced standing if they obtain qualifying scores on the College Board's AP tests, CLEP tests, or International Baccalaureate (IB) tests. GED test scores may be considered in lieu of the high school diploma.

Applicants must have completed the following secondary units: 4 in English, 3 in social studies (including U.S. history), 3 in mathematics (algebra I and higher), and 3 in laboratory sciences. Foreign language study is strongly recommended.

Transfer students are encouraged to apply for admission and may be eligible for scholarships. In addition, a limited number of talented high school students can be admitted to the summer school to earn college credit. Talented students who have completed the junior year of high school may be eligible for the College's early admission program.

Application and Information

Applications should be submitted by January 15 for early admission consideration and by August 1 for admission for the fall semester, which begins in late August and ends in December.

For further information, students may contact:

Michael Curry
Vice President for Admissions and Financial Aid
Concord College
P.O. Box 1000
Athens, West Virginia 24712
Telephone: 304-384-5248 or 5249
888-384-5249 (toll-free)
E-mail: admissions@concord.edu
World Wide Web: http://www.concord.edu
http://www.concord.edu/Pages/admissions/index.html (to apply online)

The Administration Building at Concord College.

CONCORDIA COLLEGE
BRONXVILLE, NEW YORK

The College

Founded in 1881, Concordia College is a four-year, coeducational liberal arts institution in suburban Westchester County, New York. The College is affiliated with the Lutheran Church and welcomes students of all faiths from twenty-four states and thirty-six countries. Concordia College is a Christian environment where students from many different cultures live, learn, and work together. As members of a close-knit community, Concordia students are mentored by a dedicated faculty and staff, most of whom live within a 10-minute walk of the campus. Students develop lifelong relationships as they prepare for fulfilling lives and careers. During their time at Concordia, students are encouraged to reach their full academic, spiritual, athletic, and artistic potential.

Concordia is intentionally small, with a population under 700, and its students are active and involved. The Student Government Association supports more than twenty clubs and organizations. Opportunities range from student publications to social-concern groups, Bible study to student government, and drama to intramurals. Concordia's talented choirs and ensembles perform on campus and throughout the United States and Europe. The College's ten varsity teams compete in the NCAA Division II. Teams repeatedly earn national ranking, and outstanding individuals are recruited in the professional drafts.

Concordia's beautiful campus is a pleasing mix of new and newly renovated buildings. A standout facility on campus is the Sommer Center for Worship and the Performing Arts, a 650-seat music center so acoustically well balanced that artists such as Itzhak Perlman, Yehudi Menuhin, and Harry Connick Jr. have recorded there. Other specialized facilities include the Schoenfeld Campus Center, Scheele Memorial Library, and Meyer Athletic Center, which includes a gymnasium, a weight room, a fitness center, two squash courts, three indoor tennis courts, and five outdoor tennis courts (three composite and two clay). Facilities include baseball, soccer, and softball fields.

Location

Concordia's 33-acre campus is set in the affluent and peaceful village of Bronxville. The village is home to 7,000 people, including UN diplomats, investment brokers, and a wide range of professionals. Entertainment, shopping, and employment opportunities are available within this safe and picturesque village. Students also benefit from of the limitless experiences offered in New York City, a 25-minute train ride from Bronxville.

Majors and Degrees

Concordia offers the Bachelor of Arts (B.A.), Bachelor of Science (B.S.), and Bachelor of Music (B.Mus.) degrees. The B.A. program includes majors in behavioral science, biology, education (New York State and Lutheran certification), English, history, international studies, mathematics, music (applied, church, and general), and religious studies.

B.S. degrees are offered in arts management, business administration, environmental science, music education, and social work.

The B.Mus. degree is offered in church music.

The College also offers special programs in prelaw, premedicine, and preseminary. Additional specializations include accounting, family life ministries, international management, and sports management.

Academic Programs

Concordia College provides students with an excellent education by building each degree program upon a foundation of basic skills, knowledge, and values. To graduate, students must complete the Concordia Distinctive (the College's popular core curriculum), a major, and general studies requirements. Multiple programs are integrated with field experience and internships in Westchester County and the New York area.

Concordia operates on a two-semester calendar. A minimum of 122 completed semester hours is required to earn a bachelor's degree.

Assistance is available via peer tutors. The staff of the Writing Center works with students at all levels and offers supplemental instruction to support Concordia's Writing Across the Curriculum Program. Concordia puts great emphasis on critical-thinking and communication skills.

The Career Development Center counsels students in career, vocational, and academic choices. The center coordinates resume and interview preparation, tutorial assistance, and postings for full-time and part-time jobs. Concordia alumni achieve significant roles in society: President of PaineWebber, Superintendent of Schools–San Francisco, star of the *Sopranos* cast, software engineers at PriceWaterhouse, social work manager, and publisher of *Business Week* magazine.

The Concordia Fellows Program (honors) is open via application to all students who demonstrate high academic achievement. Fellows are enriched through a variety of unique academic experiences, seminars, and travel.

The Concordia Connection Program is for students with diagnosed learning differences. Support services are provided to qualified students who meet regular admission requirements but need specific assistance in order to maximize their academic success.

Concordia offers an intensive English as a second language (ESL) program, serving students at a variety of proficiency levels. Concordia also offers an Accelerated Degree Program (ADP) for adult students over age 25 who have previously earned a minimum of 60 college credits. ADP students who meet the program requirements can earn their degree in one year of intensive study.

Concordia College is accredited by the Commission on Higher Education of the Middle States Association of Colleges and Schools and registered by the New York State Education Department.

Off-Campus Programs

Concordia is part of the national Concordia University System, which is made up of ten colleges and universities affiliated with the Lutheran Church–Missouri Synod. Students may enroll for up to one year at any of these sister institutions. Students may also study overseas at Oak Hill College in London and other international sites.

Academic Facilities

In addition to traditional holdings, the Scheele Memorial Library participates in a forty-library online system that gives students access to a multitude of academic resources. The library supports 467 active subscriptions and contains the Media Center, a distance learning classroom, a curriculum materials center, and the Concordia Gallery. New construction of a 19,000-square-foot facility, expected to begin in spring 2005, is planned to showcase sophisticated, computer-based, multimedia instructional space, an expanded art gallery, an auditorium-style classroom, a media-production center, and state-of-the-art computer and information technology installations. The new space is on the second floor of the library, which was designed in 1974 to accommodate a significant addition. The library is being renamed the Krenz Academic Center.

Brunn-Maier Science Hall houses science laboratories, the Writing Center, computer labs (PC and Mac), and the Halter Graphics Laboratory, which is equipped for graphics, desktop publishing, and music composition.

The Sommer Center for Worship and the Performing Arts includes a stunning recital/lecture hall, the College Chapel, and private rehearsal rooms for vocal, instrumental, and organ practice. Schoenfeld Campus Center, the hub of student life, provides a venue for student activities, intramurals, and dramatic performances. Historic Stein Hall houses the Concordia Conservatory, including individual and group studios and a keyboard lab.

Costs

Tuition and fees for the 2004–05 academic year are $18,700. Room and board charges are $7600. Costs are the same for in-state, out-of-state, and transfer students.

Financial Aid

Concordia strives to make a college education affordable to students from all backgrounds through an aggressive financial aid program. Need-based grants and merit-based and church vocation scholarships are available. Merit scholarships are awarded to students with academic, music, athletic, and leadership abilities. More than 90 percent of Concordia students receive financial aid.

A student's financial aid package may include a combination of grants, scholarships, employment, and student loans. To be considered, students must file the Free Application for Federal Student Aid (FAFSA). Concordia's FAFSA code is 002709.

Faculty

Concordia College's faculty members are committed to student success. The 14:1 student-faculty ratio enables students and faculty members to interact on a very personal level. The focus of Concordia faculty members is on teaching; teaching assistants are not utilized. Professors and students conduct research at all levels.

Student Government

All full-time students are members of the Student Government Association (SGA) and elect its representatives each spring. The SGA organizes and supports a host of campus events and provides a voice for all student concerns.

Admission Requirements

Concordia College admits students whose academic preparation, abilities, interests, and character show promise for success in college. Applicants are considered on the basis of academic record, class rank, test scores, and recommendations. Students may apply online. To apply, students should submit a completed application, an official high school transcript, SAT I or ACT scores, the School Report Form (part of the application form), letters of recommendation, and a $30 application fee. In addition, transfer students must submit official transcripts from all colleges and universities attended, plus SAT I or ACT scores (if they have earned fewer than 28 college credits). Concordia College is part of the Common Application Consortium of Colleges. Applications are available online at http://www.commonapp.org.

Prospective students are encouraged to visit the campus and meet with a faculty member in their area of interest. Open house events are regularly scheduled; Concordia is also happy to arrange individual visits, including overnight accommodations in residence halls.

Application and Information

Applications are accepted on a rolling basis. However, it is recommended that applications and supporting documents for first-year students be received by March 15 and for transfers by July 15. Applications may be accepted thereafter on a space-available basis.

Requests for information and applications should be addressed to:

Office of Admission
Concordia College–New York
171 White Plains Road
Bronxville, New York 10708
Telephone: 914-337-9300 Ext. 2155
800-YES-COLLEGE (937-2655, toll-free)
Fax: 914-395-4636
E-mail: admission@concordia-ny.edu
World Wide Web: http//www.concordia-ny.edu

At Concordia College, students from many different cultures live, learn, and work together.

CONCORDIA UNIVERSITY

PORTLAND, OREGON

The University

Concordia University (CU), Portland, is a private, four-year Lutheran university dedicated to the intellectual and professional development of the whole student. Founded in 1905 as an academy, Concordia grew from a junior college to a four-year college in the late 1970s, awarding its first bachelor's degrees in 1980 and graduate degrees in 1996. Concordia attained university status in 1995. The institution's mission statement is, "Concordia University is a Christian University preparing leaders for the transformation of society."

The University is composed of three academic colleges: the College of Education, the School of Management and the College of Theology, Arts, and Sciences. Programmatic development through the 1980s and 1990s increased the University's commitment to local and regional needs through several academic additions. These include a nationally recognized health-care administration program, a concentration in e-business within the bachelor's in business administration, and a progressive program emphasis in environmental management.

Concordia University further demonstrates its commitment to remain on the cutting edge of program development with its participation in the nationwide Concordia University System. An innovative intercampus partnership of the ten Concordia institutions of The Lutheran Church–Missouri Synod, the system has a combined enrollment of more than 15,000 students. Opportunities for enrollment in any one of the ten campuses and the benefits of high-tech distance learning and alternative timelines for degree completion are examples of the advantages of a small college within the framework of a nationwide educational system. Through the resource of compressed video, all system campuses are linked to provide academic offerings via a comprehensive telecommunications system. CU's electronic classroom increases educational accessibility and allows students to benefit from the academic expertise at other member institutions.

Concordia graduates meet the professional expectations of the academic, corporate, and church communities by presenting themselves in a focused, experienced, and ethical manner.

Academic focus is provided through the dedication of the University's faculty members, whose primary commitment is teaching and instruction. As educators, faculty members help students reach their full potential; as mentors, they make a conscious attempt to relate to each student's individual needs. Through interaction in and out of the classroom, students develop personal relationships with instructors who are well versed in their area of expertise.

Corporate internships lead directly to employment consideration and human services practicums that provide a supervised learning experience in a community agency, placing students directly in a career path.

Concordia's Lutheran heritage instills within all academic programs an intent to prepare professional leaders with personal attitudes of service and concern. Personal experiences, academic courses, and daily worship opportunities immerse students in a value-centered education grounded in Christian principles.

Concordia offers a full range of resources and activities that help to develop the whole student. Academic and professional needs are met through the Career Resource Center, which provides career advising and resume review services. The University's Writing Center assists students in many academic disciplines. Students who seek a residential experience at college can live in one of four residence halls, each providing a special living situation. Varsity student-athletes compete at the NAIA level in men's baseball, basketball, and soccer and in women's basketball, fast-pitch softball, soccer, and volleyball.

The College of Education offers a Master of Arts in Teaching, a Master of Education in curriculum and instruction, and a Master of Education in administration that is designed to meet the professional needs of certified teachers. In addition, the School of Management offers a case-based Master of Business Administration.

Location

Concordia University, Portland, is located in the Willamette Valley between the Cascade Mountains and the Coast Range. Situated in the heart of an established residential section of Portland that is minutes from downtown and Portland International Airport, Concordia utilizes the exciting resources of the city through internship opportunities, cultural events, and recreational activities. Outdoor recreation opportunities vary from windsurfing in the Columbia Gorge to year-round snow skiing on Mount Hood. The northeast Portland location is also minutes from the Rose Garden, home of the NBA Portland Trail Blazers and venue for major concerts and events. The campus is also well served by public transportation, which connects it to points of interest throughout the city.

Majors and Degrees

Concordia University awards the undergraduate degrees of Associate of Arts, Bachelor of Arts, and Bachelor of Science. The Bachelor of Arts degree is offered in arts and sciences, with emphases in biology, chemistry, English, history, humanities, interdisciplinary studies, psychology, social science, and theater; business administration, with emphases in accounting–CPA track, e-business, entrepreneurship, environmental management, finance, international business, marketing, and organizational management; education, with emphases in early childhood, elementary, middle school, and high school basic/basic advanced mathematics, basic marketing, biology, chemistry, general business, health, language arts, physical education, and social studies; health and social services, with concentrations in health and fitness management, health-care administration, nursing, and social work; and theological studies, with concentrations in the areas of church staff, Christian education, and pastoral studies. Concordia's professional church work programs provide opportunities for Lutheran elementary and secondary school teaching. A degree-completion program for the Bachelor of Science in management, communications, and leadership is available to returning adult students with previous work and college experience.

Academic Programs

Concordia operates on a semester calendar with two 15-week semesters. A summer session is offered in selected programs. Academic work is measured in semester hours, and courses are assigned from .5 to 5 semester hours each.

For a baccalaureate degree, 124 semester hours are required; for the associate degree, 63 hours are required. All degree-seeking students, regardless of their major, must complete the general education requirements, which include courses in communications, fine arts, humanities, physical education, religion, science, math, and social science.

In several academic areas, students may earn credit through successful completion of Advanced Placement and College-Level Examination Program (CLEP) tests.

Academic Facilities

Luther Hall contains state-of-the-art physical and life science laboratories, a science library, a greenhouse, an animal room, long-distance learning classrooms, and the University's administrative offices. The primary Luther Hall lecture hall seats 200 students and provides a reverse projection video system that enhances the quality of the learning process.

Hagen Campus Center houses the Sylwester Learning Resource Center, which includes the general library, Educational Media Services, and two student computer labs with Internet and e-mail access.

Costs

Within its commitment to providing a high-quality, affordable education, Concordia's tuition and fees for the 2003–04 academic year totaled $17,400; annual room and board charges were $5100. The total costs for a student living on campus vary, although average costs, including tuition and fees, room and board, supplies, and personal expenses, are approximately $23,300.

Financial Aid

The Free Application for Federal Student Aid (FAFSA) is used to determine a student's financial need for the awarding of scholarships, grants, work-study programs, and loans. Most awards are made in the spring for the following academic year. Approximately 95 percent of CU's first-year students receive some form of scholarships and grants. Merit-based scholarships are awarded based on academic history.

Faculty

Concordia's faculty members are dedicated scholars who are committed to the mission of the institution. Faculty members bring professional and personal experiences to the classroom, which takes learning beyond academic pursuits. Faculty members are also central to the academic advising and mentoring program.

Student Government

Students are elected to serve as hall presidents in the Resident Hall Association. Students also serve as leaders in the areas of intramurals, spiritual life, service and leadership, and student activities.

Admission Requirements

In keeping with its Christian commitment, Concordia University does not discriminate on the basis of sex, race, creed, color, national origin, age, or handicap. All high school graduates or transfer students who have fewer than 12 semester hours of college credit are eligible for admission if they have achieved a cumulative grade point average of at least 2.5 and earned a combined SAT verbal and math score of 930 or a minimum ACT composite score of 18. Transfer students with 12 or more semester hours of college credit should have a cumulative grade point average of at least 2.0. The selection criteria also include references submitted on behalf of a candidate.

Application and Information

Candidates for admission must complete a formal Concordia application for admission, submit test scores and/or high school/college transcripts, and furnish one reference. Applicants are encouraged to apply as early in the academic year as possible. Concordia follows a rolling admission procedure, and candidates are notified of a decision shortly after all the necessary credentials have been received. The application fee is waived for students who apply online.

For further information and application forms for admission and financial aid, prospective students should contact:

Office of Admissions
Concordia University
2811 Northeast Holman Street
Portland, Oregon 97211
Telephone: 503-280-8501
800-321-9371 (toll-free)
Fax: 503-280-8531
E-mail: admissions@cu-portland.edu
World Wide Web: http://www.cu-portland.edu

CONNECTICUT COLLEGE

NEW LONDON, CONNECTICUT

The College

Connecticut College, one of the nation's leading liberal arts colleges, is known for its innovative programs and tradition of academic excellence. Students and faculty members live and learn in a community committed to interdisciplinary collaboration, student-faculty research, international studies, and shared governance. Traditional courses are supplemented by opportunities for faculty members and students to travel together and conduct research in locations around the world. More than half of all students at the College study abroad at some point during their four years. In addition, well over 55 percent of students participate each year in summer research projects or funded internships, many of which are overseas. In addition to earning a degree in their major, students may also broaden their experience by earning certificates from one of four interdisciplinary centers: arts and technology, conservation biology and environmental science, community action and public policy, and international studies and the liberal arts. The College's Career Enhancing Life Skills Program and Web-based "e-portfolio" help students prepare for postgraduate life.

For the coeducational student body of 1,800, these learning experiences begin on a hilltop campus with panoramic views of the city of New London, the Thames River, and Long Island Sound. Founded in 1911, Connecticut College represents the best of a residential liberal arts education, with nearly all students living in twenty-one campus residences. Students and faculty members enjoy close interaction outside of the classroom setting. On a spacious central green that doubles as a playing field, the College community often gathers to cheer their nationally recognized athletic teams. Connecticut College competes in NCAA Division III and the New England Small College Athletic Conference (NESCAC).

The College has designated its entire 750-acre campus as an arboretum and manages its natural resources in an environmentally responsible manner. Students use this living laboratory, with its collection of plants from North America, Europe, and Asia, for research in the biological sciences and environmental studies.

Location

The College is located 2 miles from downtown New London, a city of 35,000 on the southeastern Connecticut seacoast. Frequently cited as one of the most beautiful college campuses in New England, it is 2 hours by train or car from the urban settings of New York City and Boston.

Majors and Degrees

Connecticut College awards the Bachelor of Arts degree in a wide range of majors and interdisciplinary programs, including Africana studies, American studies, anthropology, architectural studies, art, art history, astrophysics, behavioral neuroscience, biochemistry, biology, botany, cellular and molecular biology, chemistry, chemistry/biochemistry, Chinese language and literature, classics, comparative studies in culture, computer science, dance, East Asian studies, economics, English, environmental chemistry, environmental studies, film studies, French, gender and women's studies, German studies, government, Hispanic studies, Hispanic studies with teaching certification, history, human development, international relations, Italian, Italian studies, Japanese language and literature, Latin American studies, mathematics, medieval studies, music, music and technology, music with certification in music education, philosophy, physics, physics and engineering, physics for education, psychology, psychology-based human relations, religious studies, Slavic studies, sociology, sociology-based human relations, theater, urban studies, and zoology. Students may also minor in most of the above areas or the following additional areas: applied statistics, astronomy, cognitive science, geophysics, Greek, history of Christian thought, Judaism and culture, Latin, and linguistics.

Academic Programs

The College offers more than 1,000 courses in thirty-six academic departments and interdisciplinary programs and fifty-seven traditional majors plus opportunities for self-designed courses of study. Advanced courses such as the problems of environmental policy and law, the politics of refugees, bioethics, the Holocaust, and gender in architecture cross the traditional boundaries between academic fields.

Four interdisciplinary centers set Connecticut College apart: the Toor Cummings Center for International Studies and the Liberal Arts (CISLA), the Ammerman Center for Arts and Technology, the Goodwin-Niering Center for Conservation Biology and Environmental Studies, and the Holleran Center for Community Action and Public Policy. Each center pioneers new concepts in interdisciplinary learning and faculty-student collaborative research. Students participating in the centers complete a College-funded summer internship or research experience and a senior integrative project and receive a certificate upon graduation.

The College is a leader in creating opportunities for students in all disciplines to undertake original research. The Keck Undergraduate Science Program funds student research in the sciences and math, and the Connecticut College Social Science, Humanities and Arts Research Program (ConnSSHARP) funds undergraduate research in all other disciplines. Each year, scores of students and their faculty mentors copublish or present the results of their research at national conferences.

Connecticut College is also recognized for its scholarship in the arts. The theater department has a longtime partnership with the National Theater Institute of the Eugene O'Neill Theater Center, and its modern dance program builds on more than a half century of excellence dating to the era of Martha Graham. The Lyman Allyn Art Museum, located at the southern edge of the campus, offers hands-on instruction in museum studies.

Off-Campus Programs

Connecticut College has established relationships with institutions that offer programs of outstanding quality throughout the world. Students may choose from more than 100 institutions for study abroad and receive credit toward their degree. Over 50 percent of students study away from the College at some point in their four years.

In addition to traditional study-away options, Connecticut College offers an extraordinary range of innovative international experiences. Under the College's Travel Research and Immersion Program (TRIP), some courses include an expeditionary component.

Another option is the Study Away/Teach Away (SATA) program, in which small groups of students and professors spend an entire semester living and working together at an institution abroad. Recent SATA locations include Vietnam, Italy, the Czech Republic, India, Mexico, and South Africa.

Students have numerous opportunities for funded learning internships, either in the U.S. or overseas. These internships help students explore career paths, acquire research skills, interact with a wide range of mentors, and make connections between the classroom and the professional world.

Academic Facilities

The College library houses nearly 650,000 books, serial backfiles, electronic documents, and government titles that are accessible through the library's catalog. It is part of a three-college consortium that makes available more than 2 million titles.

Other facilities include a four-story arts center; two auditoriums, multiple performance venues, and four dance studios; a large athletic complex with a natatorium, a track, and cross-country trails; sailing and rowing facilities; computer laboratories; a student center; and a science triangle that includes buildings for the biological and physical sciences. One third of each class majors in science, and the F.W. Olin Science Center and observatory put freshmen in high-tech research labs and classrooms from the first day of school. The coastal location and Arboretum (which includes a salt marsh and an island) make marine biology and environmental science strong components of the curriculum. The College was one of the first in the nation to offer an environmental science major, and *Newsweek* has named it one of the best in the country.

Architectural styles range from the Gothic of the original granite dormitories to the latest face-lift for the residence halls of the Plex. A collection of contemporary sculpture also adds distinction to the spacious campus.

Costs

The comprehensive fee to attend Connecticut College for the 2003–04 academic year was $37,900. This figure includes tuition, room, and board.

Financial Aid

All financial aid is based on need, which is determined to be the difference between a family's ability to pay and the cost of education. Connecticut College requires that candidates file the Financial Aid/College Scholarship Service (CSS) PROFILE and the Free Application for Federal Student Aid (FAFSA). Copies of parents' and students' most recent income tax returns and W-2 forms should be sent directly to Connecticut College. Financial aid deadlines are November 15 for early decision 1 applicants and January 15 for early decision 2 and regular decision applicants. The College offers scholarships, grants, loans, and campus employment, with funds from endowment income, gifts, and budget allocations as well as state and federal programs. For the 2003–04 academic year, the average grant was $21,077 and the average award was $22,748. More than 46 percent of the College's undergraduates receive some form of financial aid.

Faculty

Connecticut College professors are superb teachers as well as renowned scholars and artists. A 10:1 student-faculty ratio facilitates the dynamics of learning both in and out of the classroom. Undergraduates routinely participate in collaborative research with faculty members, coauthor scholarly papers, and make presentations at academic conferences. The faculty is made up of 151 full-time and 67 part-time professors.

Student Government

Connecticut College's highly inclusive system of shared governance gives students a place on every administrative committee and a major role in decision making. A unique honor code, created in 1924, forms the foundation for all academic and social interactions and creates a palpable spirit of trust and cooperation between students and faculty members. Benefits of the code include the tradition of shared governance and self-scheduled, unproctored final exams.

Admission Requirements

Admission to Connecticut College is very competitive and selective. For the class of 2007, there were 4,396 applicants for a class of 510; 35 percent were offered admission. This low acceptance rate places the College among the twenty-five most selective national liberal arts colleges. Biographical information, extracurricular activities, the high school transcript, standardized test scores, an essay, recommendations, and an optional interview are all components that are taken into consideration when an application is reviewed for admission. The College requires either the ACT or any three SAT II Subject Tests. Submission of SAT I scores is optional. Of the admitted students who applied for the class of 2007, 77 percent ranked in the top 10 or 20 percent of their high school class. The median scores for the SAT I were 690 verbal and 670 math. The median score for the ACT was 28, and the median TOEFL scores were 634 (paper-based) and 267 (computer-based).

Application and Information

Applicants may choose to apply under one of the two early decision programs or as a regular decision applicant. Early decision is for students who have determined that Connecticut College is their first choice and who will commit to attending if admitted. Regular decision is a nonbinding process. Early decision I candidates must submit the Connecticut College Supplement and the Common Application by November 15. Early decision II and regular decision candidates must submit the Connecticut College Supplement by December 15 and the Common Application by January 1.

For information about obtaining application materials, students should contact:

Office of Admission
Connecticut College
270 Mohegan Avenue
New London, Connecticut 06320-4196
Telephone: 860-439-2200
Fax: 860-439-4301
E-mail: admission@conncoll.edu
World Wide Web: http://www.connecticutcollege.edu

Students at Connecticut College.

CONVERSE COLLEGE

SPARTANBURG, SOUTH CAROLINA

The College

Converse College is not for every woman. But for the student who is confident, adventurous, and talented—or who aspires to be—Converse is a place to grow and become.

Founded in 1889 as an independent, residential, liberal arts college for women in Spartanburg, South Carolina, Converse is consistently recognized by *U.S. News & World Report* as a top college and best value among colleges and universities in the South. Converse has also been named one of the *Best 201 Colleges for the Real World.* Throughout its history, Converse has produced strong leaders and thinkers who have used their Converse experience to expand women's roles in society and have significantly contributed to the advancement of the U.S.

Converse strengths range from the sciences, education, and interior design to music, politics, and theater. Nearly forty academic majors are offered in the College of Arts and Sciences and the Petrie School of Music—the nation's only comprehensive professional school of music within a liberal arts college for women.

In the coeducational graduate program, Converse offers master's degrees in education, the liberal arts areas, and music. Education specialist degrees are also available in marriage and family therapy, administration and supervision, and curriculum and instruction.

Small classes with individual attention are hallmarks of a Converse education, with the average undergraduate student-teacher ratio being an uncommon 9:1. The intimate classroom setting allows professors to challenge students through spirited and interactive discussions. Converse professors not only teach and advise, they know their students—as individuals.

Converse students use the world as their classroom, with opportunities to study on every inhabited continent of the world. The Nisbet Honors Program provides academically gifted students opportunities to conduct independent research with faculty mentors and gather socially to discuss intellectually challenging topics. An interdisciplinary program features seminars team-taught by faculty members from different fields who collaborate in the classroom throughout the course, enabling students to learn how different branches of learning approach collecting and interpreting evidence.

While academic quality receives top priority, Converse also places great emphasis on building community and involvement through campus and residential life programs. More than sixty student organizations at Converse make it easy to find things to do and meet other people. Spartanburg is home to six colleges who collaborate both academically and socially through the College Town Consortium, making interaction with students from other colleges abundant. The Converse Fine Arts Series features events on campus throughout the year; and the campus also actively supports the College's NCAA Division II athletics in basketball, cross-country, soccer, tennis, and volleyball.

Location

Located in the upstate region of South Carolina, Spartanburg is a city full of beautiful scenery, historically significant sites, and friendly people. Mixing Southern culture and hospitality with diverse traditions and cultures of other countries, Spartanburg is South Carolina's melting pot.

More than 100 international firms—including German automaker BMW—make Spartanburg an international and cultural center. The city offers a multitude of internship and job placement opportunities. In fact, many local and regional companies visit the campus each year to recruit Converse graduates.

Spartanburg's proximity to the North Carolina mountains, the South Carolina coast, and major cities such as Atlanta and Charlotte make it a very attractive place to live. Greenville-Spartanburg International Airport is served by six major airlines.

Majors and Degrees

Bachelor's degrees are in accounting; art (art education, art history, art therapy, and studio art); biochemistry; biology; business; business administration with concentrations in finance, international business, marketing, and organizational management; chemistry; computer science; economics; education (comprehensive special education, deaf and hard of hearing/interpreting, early childhood, educable mentally handicapped, elementary, emotionally handicapped, learning disabilities, and secondary); English; foreign language (French, German, and Spanish); history, interior design, mathematics; modern languages; music (composition, music business, music education, music history, performance, piano pedagogy, and theory); politics; psychology; religion; and theater.

Preprofessional programs include Army ROTC, arts management, predentistry, prelaw, premedicine, preministry, prenursing, prepharmacy, and publication and media.

Depending on the student's major and course of study, she can earn a Bachelor of Arts, a Bachelor of Science, a Bachelor of Fine Arts, or a Bachelor of Music degree.

The Individualized Major allows students to design an interdisciplinary degree program that links academic interests from at least three departments.

Academic Programs

A required core curriculum introduces Converse students to a variety of subjects, developing in them an appreciation of Western culture and the liberal arts. Students are then able to choose a major—or two—in which to specialize. The Converse College Institute for Leadership is an optional program that provides formalized leadership development, physical fitness, and service learning.

The academic calendar consists of two 14-week terms and a four-week January term. During January term, students can take classes on campus or take advantage of the many opportunities for off-campus study programs, including internships and study travel.

Off-Campus Programs

Converse offers full-year and semester-long study-abroad programs, through which students are able to study in Australia, England, France, Iceland, Spain, and many other countries. In addition, the Anne Morrison Chapman Study-Abroad Experience provides scholarships for students to participate in international study and travel programs led by Converse faculty members.

Academic Facilities

Converse's 86-acre campus includes seven residence halls, each with laundry facilities, study rooms, kitchens, and lounges with cable television. Each room has computer, cable TV, and telephone connections.

Phifer Science Hall is a new 26,000-square-foot facility designed for instruction in the natural sciences. Phifer contains cutting-edge laboratories, multimedia teaching technology, and computing equipment that allow faculty members to utilize new teaching methods and technology. Science majors are provided space for upper-level research.

The Sally Abney Rose Physical Activity Complex houses a soccer field, tennis courts, a multipurpose practice field, and the Weisiger Center—a 29,000-square-foot complex housing basketball and volleyball courts, fitness training rooms, locker rooms, coaches' offices, and physical education offices.

Blackman Hall houses the Petrie School of Music. It features more than thirty practice rooms—most with baby grand pianos—soundproof classrooms, faculty teaching studios, an electronic piano lab, and a music media lab with twenty-two iMacs and the latest in music software. Daniel Recital Hall is a 340-seat auditorium cited in *Chamber Music America* as an exemplary performance facility.

Milliken Fine Arts Building is home to the Department of Art and Design. Faculty studio lofts overlook classrooms, allowing students greater interaction with the work of faculty artists. The building houses a CAD and graphic design lab, darkrooms, ceramic kiln and sculpture yards, bronze casting, and a historic preservation studio. A permanent collection of fifty-two prints, includes works by Joan Miró, Salvador Dalí, Helmut Newton, and Andy Warhol. Milliken Art Gallery is filled with works by a wide variety of professional artists.

Wilson Hall houses the College's administrative offices, the Office of Admissions, Gee Dining Hall, Hazel B. Abbott Theatre, and the Laird Studio Theatre. The five towers on the front are named for the values held dear to Converse: friendship, loyalty, honor, service, and reverence. On display in the lobby of Wilson is the Converse Honor Pledge, signed by every new student.

Twichell Auditorium is home to Petrie School of Music performances and other campus events and also to community groups such as the Greater Spartanburg Philharmonic and Ballet Spartanburg. Built in 1899 and renovated in 1989, this 1,500-seat auditorium houses a fifty-seven-rank Casavant Freres organ with more than 2,600 pipes and is known for its outstanding acoustics. The auditorium has hosted such famed artists as Chet Atkins, George Burns, Duke Ellington, Burl Ives, Itzhak Perlman, and Yo-Yo Ma. It is named as a historic John Philip Sousa site.

The fully automated Mickel Library contains more than 180,000 books and subscriptions to more than 700 periodicals, the Gwathmey Music Library (one of the largest music libraries in the Southeast), and the Writing Center.

Two arts and sciences classroom buildings, Kuhn Hall and Carmichael Hall, complete the academic faculties on campus.

Costs

For 2003–04, tuition and fees were $18,915; room and board costs are $5795. Boarding students pay a comprehensive fee, which covers tuition and room and board. Therefore, students are not charged incidental fees throughout the year. The comprehensive fee includes free use of the laundry facilities located in each residence hall; student activities; unlimited Internet access through network connections in every residence hall room; e-mail; cable television hookup in each residence hall room; a microfridge provided in each residence hall room; local telephone service; a campus parking permit; health services, including counseling if needed; choice of meal plans; access to the fitness center and indoor swimming pool; 24-hour emergency assistance through Campus Safety; a Converse yearbook; and free admission to athletic, cultural, and other events offered on campus.

Financial Aid

Converse is dedicated to providing every capable student with the opportunity to experience a Converse College education. Approximately 95 percent of freshmen receive some form of financial assistance through scholarships, federal student assistance programs, loans, and work-study programs. Scholarships and grant awards range up to the full comprehensive fee. Residents of South Carolina may also qualify for South Carolina Tuition Grants, ranging up to $3360 for freshmen. The Free Application for Federal Student Aid (FAFSA) is required of all applicants for financial assistance.

Each year, Converse awards $5 million in scholarships in academics, athletics, leadership, music, theater, and visual arts. These awards are not based on financial need, so the FAFSA is not required. The awards are renewable for three additional years.

Faculty

Of the College's 76 faculty members, 85 percent hold the Ph.D. or other terminal degree, and full-time faculty members do all student advising. The student-faculty ratio in the undergraduate program is 9:1 overall and 7:1 in the Petrie School of Music. The College does not employ teaching assistants, and senior professors frequently teach freshman and sophomore classes. Faculty members are selected on the basis of teaching proficiency, scholarly competence, and ability to impart the excitement and value of learning.

Student Government

The Converse College Student Government Association (SGA) is the second oldest in the Southeast and has been active for more than ninety years. As an energetic student voice on campus, the SGA serves as an umbrella for sixty campus clubs and organizations. SGA also maintains important communication links between the College's administration and the students. The Converse Honor Tradition, which has been an integral part of student governance for more than eighty years, ensures that self-discipline, shared confidence, and community integrity are maintained on the campus.

Admission Requirements

Admission to Converse College is an individualized, informative, and interactive process. Students are encouraged to apply as early as possible in their senior year of high school. Early decision admission applications are due by November 15. Sixteen units of high school academic work are recommended. In addition to high school transcripts and SAT or ACT scores, personal interviews, previous extracurricular activities, demonstrated exceptional talent, and seriousness of purpose may be used as additional admissions criteria. Converse College participates in the Advanced Placement Program administered by the College Entrance Examination Board.

Transfer students are accepted each semester from accredited institutions. Limited scholarship programs are available to transfer students.

Application and Information

To begin the application process, students must send a completed application for admission, a $35 nonrefundable application fee, an official transcript of at least six semesters of secondary school, and official SAT I or ACT scores for freshmen, a teacher recommendation form, and a graded writing sample. Admissions information and online application are available from the Converse Web site, listed below.

All inquiries and requests for application forms should be addressed to:

Office of Admissions
Converse College
580 East Main Street
Spartanburg, South Carolina 29302
Telephone: 864-596-9040
800-766-1125 (toll-free)
E-mail: admissions@converse.edu
World Wide Web: http://www.converse.edu

Dr. Jeffrey Willis, Andrew Helmus Distinguished Professor of History, visits with Converse students outside of Carmichael Hall.

CORNELL COLLEGE

MOUNT VERNON, IOWA

The College

Cornell College is unique in U.S. higher education in that it offers the combination of liberal arts study within the One-Course-At-A-Time framework, an active residential community, an emphasis on service and leadership, and an ideal, wooded-hilltop setting that is one of only two campuses listed on the National Register of Historic Places.

Cornell College is a leader in educational innovation. A private, independent college founded in 1853, Cornell employs the One-Course-At-A-Time academic calendar; it is one of only four colleges in the United States to implement this advancement in postsecondary teaching and learning. Cornell is historically a place of "firsts": the first coeducational college west of the Mississippi, the first college in Iowa to grant a baccalaureate degree to a woman, the first college in the United States to confer upon a woman a full professorship with the same salary received by the male professors, and the first college in the nation to have its entire campus listed on the National Register of Historic Places. The College was among the first schools in the nation to offer its students a choice of degree programs, establish a teacher-education program, and introduce sociology into its curriculum. Cornell offers a strong leadership-training program and actively promotes community service opportunities. Nearly 70 percent of the student body take part in volunteer projects.

In 2003–04, 1,100 students from forty states and eleven other countries were enrolled at this residential college, which is situated atop a high hill overlooking the Cedar River valley. Centered on a pedestrian mall, the campus covers 129 acres and has more than forty buildings, including nine residence halls. A student center, the Commons, houses central dining rooms, a bookstore, meeting rooms, and recreation rooms. Cornell's sports and recreation center has facilities for wellness and fitness programs as well as year-round recreation and athletics space for practice and play. Cornell has 25 NCAA Postgraduate Scholars, ranking ninth in the nation among NCAA Division III schools. It competes in the Iowa Intercollegiate Athletic Conference in nineteen sports. Nearly 60 percent of students participate in sixty-six intramural sports. More than 100 clubs and organizations offer a wide range of activities, from participation in the KRNL-FM radio station to Habitat for Humanity to Greek social groups.

Location

Mount Vernon provides the best of both worlds—a classically beautiful campus in a small college town minutes from Cedar Rapids and Iowa City. These two metropolitan areas contain three additional colleges and universities and 350,000 people. Chicago, St. Louis, and Minneapolis can be reached in about 5 hours by automobile or in less than an hour by air from Cedar Rapids. Palisades–Kepler State Park, site of the annual Pal Day picnic, is 5 miles away. Cornell is 15 minutes from Cedar Rapids (airport, movies, malls) and 20 minutes from Iowa City and Hancher Auditorium, a regular concert and theater tour stop.

Majors and Degrees

Cornell College awards the Bachelor of Arts, Bachelor of Music, Bachelor of Philosophy, and Bachelor of Special Studies degrees. Majors are offered in art, biochemistry and molecular biology, biology, chemistry, classical studies, computer science, economics and business, elementary and secondary education, English, environmental studies, French, geology, German, history, international business, international relations, Latin American studies, mathematics, medieval and Renaissance studies, music education (general, instrumental, and vocal), music performance, philosophy, physical education, physics, politics, psychology, religion, Russian, Russian studies, sociology, sociology and anthropology, Spanish, theater, theater and speech, and women's studies. Prelaw and premedicine programs are available, as are programs to prepare for graduate study in social work/human services and theology. Students may design their own interdisciplinary majors.

Combined-degree programs include a 3-2 program in forestry and environmental management offered in cooperation with Duke University, 3-2 programs in engineering and occupational therapy, and a 3-4 program in architecture with Washington University in St. Louis.

The College also offers cooperative professional programs in nursing and allied health sciences with Rush University in Chicago and in medical technology with St. Luke's Hospital in Cedar Rapids. For students interested in dentistry, the University of Iowa College of Dentistry offers early acceptance into its program.

Academic Program

Cornell encourages the creative structuring of students' educational experiences by offering a choice of four degree programs within the framework of a liberal education. Programs range from a traditional curriculum, with course requirements designed to ensure both breadth and depth, to a nontraditional combination of courses, independent studies, and internships that meet specific goals. For the Bachelor of Arts, Bachelor of Music, and Bachelor of Philosophy degree programs, faculty members set the goals. The Bachelor of Special Studies degree program permits students to define their own educational objectives and design a curriculum to meet those objectives.

To increase the quality and intensity of a Cornell education, the College's academic calendar incorporates the One-Course-At-A-Time schedule. Cornell divides the traditional September–May academic year into nine 3½-week terms. During each term, students concentrate on one course chosen from the more than sixty offered and take one final examination. After a four-day break, the next term begins. Students take eight terms per year, which leaves a ninth term free for internships, off-campus programs, international study, travel, independent study, rest and relaxation, or another course.

The College's emphasis on One-Course-At-A-Time enhances the quality of liberal education offered by allowing students increased contact with faculty members, no interference from competing courses, and greater efficiency of study. It also provides rapid feedback to students about their progress. The work assigned on one day is discussed on the following day, when the material is fresh for both students and instructor. In addition, the pressure of having to prepare for several courses and examinations at the same time is eliminated.

Another liberalizing feature of One-Course-At-A-Time is the possibility of having classes meet for periods longer or shorter than the typical 50-minute period. Professors may opt to divide the day into a series of short meetings, with work assignments given and completed from one session to the next. Laboratories are not necessarily limited to one afternoon. Faculty members are also able to take students on daylong field trips or teach their courses off campus, either in the United States or abroad.

Recent Cornell College graduates are studying public health at Harvard, architecture at Washington University (St. Louis), medicine at Iowa, law at Loyola Chicago, and studio art at the Art Institute of Chicago, to name a few. Among the employers of recent graduates are the Peace Corps; Houston Grand Opera; Cheetah Outreach; Visa International; Wells Fargo; AT&T

Wireless; U.S. Agency for International Development; New York Life Insurance; RBC Dain Rauscher, Inc.; and the Red Cross.

Off-Campus Arrangements

Student internship experiences can be central to understanding the realities, demands, and rewards of the workplace. Internships arranged within Cornell's One-Course-At-A-Time academic calendar are distinctly different from those arranged within a semester system. Students are able to become immersed in the experience every day for an entire month without the distractions of other course demands. Employers/mentors can count on a full-time commitment. This availability earns the attention of many nearby Cedar Rapids businesses and corporations that have offered opportunities from engineering to telecommunications, health-related fields, and art history. More distant internships have also been completed. The intensive internship learning experience makes Cornell students very appealing to prospective employers.

Through Cornell courses abroad and College-affiliated off-campus programs, students may work and travel in other countries and become acquainted with other cultures. Recent classes have journeyed to Mexico to observe local potters, to Montreal to study French, to Mexico and Spain to study Hispanic and Spanish social development, to London for courses in English literature and drama, and to Brazil and Guatemala to experience firsthand the politics of revolutionary movements.

Cornell students have done tropical field research in Costa Rica, studied Chinese culture in Hong Kong, worked with Hispanic communities in urban Chicago, and visited Europe's great cultural centers through off-campus programs administered by the Associated Colleges of the Midwest, of which Cornell is a charter member, and the School for International Training.

Academic Facilities

Cornell's entire campus has been designated a National Historic District, and its carefully restored nineteenth-century academic architecture is combined with contemporary facilities on a fully wired campus, with Internet access in every residence hall room. King Chapel is the historic landmark of the campus and has a 130-foot clock tower. Armstrong Hall and McWethy Hall have recently been renovated and expanded for art, music, and theater. Law Hall Technology Center opened in 2000, and Cole Library was renovated recently.

Costs

The cost for 2003–04 was $27,825, including tuition, fees, and room and board. Students generally enroll for eight courses a year, but, at no extra cost, they may accelerate or broaden their studies by taking nine courses.

Financial Aid

Cornell is committed to making higher education available for all students. The majority of Cornell's students receive financial assistance, and the average aid package exceeds $18,000. A competitive scholarship program recognizes students with strong academic records or special talents. Federal aid programs include Federal Pell Grants, Federal Supplemental Educational Opportunity Grants (FSEOG), and student loans. Federal Work-Study Program awards can provide additional income through part-time, on-campus employment. Additional funds are available through the Iowa Tuition Grant Program and State of Iowa Scholarships. Need is determined by the Free Application for Federal Student Aid (FAFSA). An early financial aid evaluation is available from the College upon request. Students applying for Cornell-funded scholarships must complete their scholarship application by March 1.

Faculty

The members of the College's faculty are distinguished by their desire to teach undergraduates in a small, informal environment. Classes are capped at 25 students. Faculty members outside the department of physical education are required to have a Ph.D. or other terminal degree and are appointed, retained, and promoted based on their ability to teach. Many also distinguish themselves through scholarly and creative activities. The faculty-student ratio is 1:11, and only faculty members, not teaching assistants, teach classes.

Student Government

Student life at Cornell complements the academic program and provides a feeling of community at the College. Students participate actively in the governance of the College, serving on faculty-student committees, the Student Senate, the Residence Hall Council, and the Performing Arts and Activities Council.

Admission Requirements

The courses and degree programs offered at Cornell are intended for students who have been well prepared at the secondary school level, have obvious motivation and a desire to learn, and have the ability and potential to complete a carefully planned degree program and graduate from Cornell College. Admission to Cornell is selective. Applicants are judged on their high school records, test scores, interests, and achievements in such cocurricular activities as debate, student government, music, theater, athletics, and school publications as well as through personal recommendations and, in some cases, interviews. These are not exclusive criteria. Motivation, energy, and persistence are basic to Cornell. Students with the desire to succeed at Cornell and the motivation to benefit from a Cornell education may apply with confidence, knowing that these are important factors in the admission decision.

Application and Information

Cornell College follows a program of rolling admissions, and applicants are notified of admission decisions soon after their files are complete. Special consideration is given to students who apply by December 1. After March 1, applications are accepted on a space-available basis.

To apply for admission to Cornell, prospective students should obtain an application form online or from the Office of Admissions, complete and file the application with Cornell with a $25 application fee, have their high school forward an official transcript and a school recommendation, and have their ACT or SAT I scores sent to Cornell. Cornell welcomes transfer students from accredited two- and four-year institutions.

Additional information, catalogs, application forms, and financial aid forms are available from:

Office of Admissions
Cornell College
600 First Street West
Mount Vernon, Iowa 52314-1098
Telephone: 319-895-4477
800-747-1112 (toll-free)
E-mail: admissions@cornellcollege.edu
World Wide Web: http://www.cornellcollege.edu

Graduation time at Cornell College.

CORNELL UNIVERSITY
ITHACA, NEW YORK

The University

Cornell University is unique in American higher education. At once the largest, most comprehensive school in the Ivy League and the public land-grant university for New York State, Cornell is distinct in its combination of privately funded and state-assisted colleges. As a result, Cornell students benefit from outstanding educational programs and are nurtured by the prestigious intellectual tradition of the Ivy League. At the same time, they tap into the democratic spirit and sense of public service that energize the nation's great state universities.

Cornell's thirteen colleges and schools offer instruction in virtually every field, and the University's numerous interdisciplinary programs provide wide-ranging opportunities for study that cuts across traditional department boundaries. Students at Cornell arguably are exposed to the widest arrays of subjects and approaches to learning available anywhere. Moreover, they share the excitement of intellectual discovery with faculty members who are Nobel laureates, Pulitzer Prize winners, and researchers at the forefront of their fields—clear evidence of the University's commitment to undergraduate education. It is not uncommon to find prominent scholars teaching introductory classes and offering courses for general enrollment.

Cornell comprises people of all races, many nationalities, and every social and economic background, and the interplay of differences finds full expression throughout the University and in the surrounding Ithaca community. To put it simply, Cornell offers students the cultural diversity and intellectual vigor often associated with large metropolitan centers as well as the friendly atmosphere and livable pace of a smaller city environment.

Most faculty members live in or near Ithaca and take part in campus activities after classroom hours, and students and faculty members enjoy a sense of community not possible on urban campuses. More than 500 campus clubs and associations allow the development of leadership skills and provide opportunities for students who share interests, concerns, talents, or avocations to find each other.

Cornell's student body numbers more than 19,000 students, 13,800 of whom are undergraduates. About 51 percent are women and 49 percent are men. Nearly 34 percent of Cornell's undergraduate students are from New York State, 21 percent are from the Mid-Atlantic and New England states, 38 percent are from elsewhere in the United States, and 7 percent are from outside the country. Nearly one third of the students are members of a minority group, and the majority of students attended public high schools.

Students may live on or off campus. In addition to traditional residence halls, Cornell has more than 400 apartments for student families and a variety of small living units and residential program houses that provide an opportunity for cooperative living arrangements. The University has forty-three fraternities and sixteen sororities. About 46 percent of Cornell's students live in University residence halls or apartments, 14 percent live in fraternities or sororities, and 40 percent live off campus.

Cornell maintains one of the most extensive and diversified programs of physical education in the country. The teaching program, which each year offers more than fifty courses ranging from ballroom dancing to rock climbing, emphasizes recreational activities that students can continue to enjoy after they leave the University. The intramural athletics program—the largest in the Ivy League—provides opportunities for members of the University community to compete in more than thirty sports. Cornell also supports eighteen varsity sports for men and eighteen varsity sports for women.

Location

Cornell is on a hillside at the southern tip of Cayuga Lake, the longest of the Finger Lakes of central New York State. Within easy walking distance of the campus is the Cornell Plantations—a living laboratory of natural resources comprising 2,800 acres of woodlands, trails, streams, and gorges. Several ski areas, an extensive system of hiking trails, and three unusually scenic state parks with facilities for hiking, boating, swimming, and camping are a short drive away.

Majors and Degrees

Cornell University offers degrees at the baccalaureate level in seven undergraduate colleges (Agriculture and Life Sciences; Architecture, Art, and Planning; Arts and Sciences; Engineering; Hotel Administration; Human Ecology; and Industrial and Labor Relations). Undergraduates may choose from an impressive range of programs in fields such as agricultural sciences, animal science, architecture, art, behavioral sciences, biological sciences, business management, communications, design and environmental analysis, engineering, environmental studies, food science, government, history, hotel administration, human development, humanities, industrial and labor relations, languages and linguistics, mathematics and computer science, nutritional sciences, physical sciences, plant sciences, policy analysis and management, preprofessional studies, and social sciences.

Academic Program

Although degree requirements vary among the undergraduate units, students are encouraged to take courses in other divisions. This interdisciplinary approach is exemplified by Cornell's nationally recognized ethnic studies programs: Africana studies, Asian studies, Asian-American studies, Latino studies, Latin American studies, and Native American studies. In addition to offering courses, these programs promote multicultural understanding on campus by supporting lectures, conferences, seminars, exhibits, publications, and research projects. Honors programs, independent majors, double majors, and dual-degree programs are available in most areas of study. Entering freshmen may qualify for advanced placement or credit on the recommendation of the appropriate departments of instruction at Cornell.

The academic year is divided into two semesters, which run from late August to mid-December and from January to mid-May. There also are three consecutive summer sessions.

Off-Campus Programs

Students in many areas participate in fieldwork programs, internships, engineering cooperative programs, and research projects. They study in Albany; Washington, D.C.; New York City; and other places where they can best learn about the work of government, community organizations, businesses, and industry. Undergraduates participate in Cornell Abroad programs in many countries, including Australia, China, Denmark, Egypt, England, France, Germany, Greece, Indonesia, Israel, Italy, Japan, Kenya, Korea, Mexico, Nepal, Nigeria, Russia, Sweden, and Vietnam.

Academic Facilities

Cornell's library system is one of the ten largest academic research libraries in the United States. Two central libraries and an extensive system of thirteen libraries in the colleges contain more than 7.1 million volumes, subscribe to 65,000 periodicals, and add about 130,000 volumes to their collections each year.

The University's computer resources are important to students in almost every area of study. Cornell Information Technologies operates public terminals and microcomputers, produces documentation, and offers a variety of user education programs. In addition, all of Cornell's undergraduate residence hall rooms have direct Internet connections, enabling residents to log on around the clock.

Costs

Tuition and fees for the 2003–04 academic year for students enrolled in Cornell's state-assisted units (Agriculture and Life Sciences, Human Ecology, and Industrial and Labor Relations) were $14,634 for New York residents and $25,924 for nonresidents. Tuition and fees for those in the University's privately funded units (Architecture, Art, and Planning; Arts and Sciences; Engineering; and Hotel Administration) were $28,754. Typical room and board costs amount to $9580 per academic year, and personal expenses, including books, are about $1940.

Financial Aid

Admission decisions are not affected by a prospective student's need for financial assistance, and the University's comprehensive financial aid program offers a wide array of financial support options to students and their families. Sixty-four percent of all Cornell undergraduates receive some form of financial aid from University, state, federal, or other sources, and about 50 percent receive Cornell-allocated scholarships, jobs, and/or loans. All financial assistance is awarded on the basis of need, according to the standards of the College Scholarship Service.

Of particular importance to prospective students is Cornell's nationally recognized program of financial assistance known as the Cornell Commitment, which consists of three programs: the Cornell Tradition, which rewards students who demonstrate a commitment to working and funding a portion of their own education; the Meinig Family National Scholars, which rewards outstanding leaders in high school; and the Presidential Research Scholars, which recognizes students who have a strong interest in research.

Faculty

The more than 1,500 members of the Cornell faculty include many men and women who are recognized internationally as leaders in their fields. Among them are Nobel laureates, Pulitzer Prize winners, and scores of individuals who are members of the National Academy of Sciences, the National Academy of Engineering, or the National Academy of Education. Twenty-three members of the faculty have received Guggenheim Fellowships during the past five years, and 3 members of the faculty have received MacArthur Foundation "genius awards."

Nearly all teaching faculty members are involved in research, scholarship, or public service. Maintaining the quality of undergraduate programs is one of Cornell's highest priorities, and there is no distinction between the graduate and undergraduate faculty. Professors act as advisers and keep regular office hours to ensure their availability to students. The University community also enjoys a constant succession of visiting lecturers and professors from other institutions.

Student Government

Cornell students participate in governing the University through the Student Assembly (22 elected students), which has legislative authority over the policies of several campus life departments. Students may also be members of policymaking committees within each undergraduate college, and students sit as voting members on the University's Board of Trustees.

Admission Requirements

Cornell is among the most selective universities in the nation. There were more than 21,000 applications for the 2003–04 freshman class. Average combined SAT I scores of entering freshmen are about 350 points above the national average, and more than 80 percent of entering students are in the top 10 percent of their high school classes.

Each undergraduate unit has its own selection committee, and applicants compete only with other students seeking admission to the same division. Intellectual preparedness and evidence of the applicant's abilities in nonacademic areas are important considerations in admission decisions, as are work experience and other activities related to educational or professional objectives. The University seeks individuals with outstanding personal qualities, such as initiative and leadership. A few of Cornell's divisions also require or recommend interviews.

All seven undergraduate colleges offer an early decision plan to highly qualified high school seniors whose first preference is Cornell. A few students may be approved for early admission after only three years of secondary school.

Application and Information

Cornell has a two-part application. From freshman applicants, Part 1 is due well before January 1 and Part 2 on January 1. Applicants who wish to be considered under the early decision plan must file Part 1 well before November 1 and Part 2 by November 1; they are notified of decisions in mid-December. From fall transfer students, Part 1 is due well before March 15 and Part 2 on March 15. The spring transfer Part 1 application is due well before November 1 and Part 2 on November 1.

For additional information and application forms, students should contact:

Undergraduate Admissions Office
Cornell University
410 Thurston Avenue
Ithaca, New York 14850-2488
Telephone: 607-255-5241
World Wide Web: http://admissions.cornell.edu

A student studies in one of the libraries.

CREIGHTON UNIVERSITY

OMAHA, NEBRASKA

The University

Located in Omaha, Nebraska, Creighton University is a nationally recognized private, Jesuit, Catholic university. Multidimensional programs of study combine challenging academic courses with career development internships, service, and extracurricular opportunities. *U.S. News & World Report* recently ranked Creighton as the number one Midwest regional university.

The University has a total enrollment of 6,537 students, including 3,736 undergraduates and 2,801 graduate, law, medical, dental, pharmacy, and allied health profession students. Students come from nearly every state in the nation and from sixty other countries. Its size allows Creighton to offer ethnic and cultural diversity and a wide variety of course offerings and still provide individual attention with a student-faculty ratio of 14:1.

Creighton offers students many advantages and benefits. The University is grounded in 125 years of the Jesuit tradition of excellence in education and leadership and service to others. With an enrollment of 6,500 students, it is an ideal size, yet it offers fifty-one undergraduate majors, six professional and graduate programs, twenty-four master's programs, and three Ph.D. programs. Most universities with Creighton's quality of majors and professional schools are much larger, so at Creighton, students get the best of both worlds—a sophisticated curriculum, personal contact with faculty members, and a close-knit campus community in which students make friends for life. Students receive career and life planning preparation and counseling, and Creighton has one of the nation's highest placement rates of graduates into professional schools (medical, dental, law, pharmacy, physical therapy, occupational therapy, nursing, and business administration) and in graduate work in the sciences, education, or the arts.

Creighton University faculty members are internationally recognized for research in such diverse areas as cancer genetics, respiratory diseases, osteoporosis and hard tissue research, laser dentistry and implantology, health policy and ethics, photography, environmental science, international development, Biblical studies, economic forecasting, bankruptcy, and antidiscrimination laws. The University has privately endowed chairs in health sciences, Jewish civilization, communication, theology, accounting, managerial ethics, regional economics, information technology management, legal ethics, medicine, surgery, medical outcomes, humanities, and dentistry and the Clare Boothe Luce Faculty Chair for Women in Science.

The University is committed to and maintains facilities for a fourteen-sport Division I athletic program, including a nationally ranked men's soccer team. Each year, Creighton hosts the men's NCAA College World Series.

Creighton University is accredited by the North Central Association of Colleges and Schools. In addition, all undergraduate and professional programs are individually accredited by the appropriate national and state associations and boards.

Creighton offers doctoral programs in biomedical sciences and medical microbiology. Professional doctoral degrees are also offered in occupational therapy, pharmacology, and physical therapy.

Master of Arts degrees are offered in Christian spirituality, English, international relations, liberal studies, and theology. Master of Science degrees are offered in atmospheric sciences, biomedical sciences, counseling and education, mathematics, medical microbiology and immunology, nursing, pharmacology, and physics. Master's degrees are also offered in business administration, computer science, e-commerce, and information technology management.

Location

Creighton's 108-acre campus is intersected by a tree-lined brick mall. It is located within walking distance of downtown Omaha. Approximately 1,800 students live on campus.

Omaha is a great city with wonderful restaurants, high-quality shopping, world-class galleries and museums, large parks, an internationally known zoo, and competitive and entertaining sporting events. The city has invested more than a billion dollars into redeveloping the Missouri riverfront, including construction of a new Convention Center Arena and miles of new walking and biking paths and two new riverfront parks. These new venues offer exciting entertainment and recreational opportunities within walking distance to the campus.

With a metropolitan population of 767,000, Omaha's economy is thriving, offering numerous part-time jobs and internships throughout the city, including the businesses in the downtown area adjacent to Creighton's campus.

Majors and Degrees

The College of Arts and Sciences offers majors leading to the B.A., B.S., and B.F.A. degrees in American studies, applied computer science, art (history and studio), atmospheric sciences, biology, chemistry, classical civilization, computer science, economics, education, English (comparative literature, creative writing, and Irish literature), environmental sciences, exercise sciences, French, German, Greek, history, journalism (news, advertising and public relations, and design production), Latin, mathematics (applied and mathematics/computer science), music, organizational communication, philosophy, physics, political science (legal studies and public policy), psychology, social work, sociology, Spanish, speech communications, statistics, theater, and theology.

A bachelor's degree in emergency medical services is offered through the School of Pharmacy and Allied Health Professions.

Majors in the College of Business Administration lead to a B.S.B.A. degree in accounting, economics, entrepreneurship, finance, international business, management information systems, marketing, and prelaw business. Joint programs between the business college and the School of Law allow students to earn a B.S.B.A. degree and a J.D. in six years or a B.S.B.A., a J.D., and an M.B.A. in seven years. Undergraduate degrees in the College of Arts and Sciences and College of Business Administration are available to nontraditional students through Creighton's University College. Advanced technological training is taught in the Creighton Institute for Information Technology and Management.

A Bachelor of Science in Nursing (B.S.N.) is offered to undergraduates and RN students. The School of Nursing has an accelerated one-year program for students who hold nonnursing degrees and maintains a satellite campus in Hastings, Nebraska. It offers an RN-to-B.S.N. program and a nurse practitioner program.

Academic Programs

Undergraduate courses stress a well-rounded liberal arts education, with students fulfilling general education requirements in areas that include theology, ethics and philosophy, cultures and civilizations, natural science, and social and behavioral science and skills. A total of 128 semester hours is required for a bachelor's degree. The University offers unique community living and learning opportunities for upperclass students pursuing special research projects and accepts a select group of students in its honors program.

Academic Facilities

Creighton's campus is an exciting place to be these days. There are many changes taking place on the campus. A new state-of-the-art science complex houses multipurpose classrooms, lecture labs, high-tech teaching and research laboratories, offices, and student common spaces. A new stadium for the nationally ranked Bluejay soccer program, additional student housing, and landscaped green spaces have recently been completed.

Creighton offers students ample technological support. Campus housing allows for computer hookups as well as cable TV and satellite broadcast reception. Students have access to nearly thirty computer centers, with 24-hour online capability. There are desktop design and writing laboratories and broadcast facilities. The University's three libraries include the Reinert Alumni Memorial Library, the Health Sciences Library/Learning Resource Center, and the recently remodeled Klutznick Law Library. Together, they house 746,000 volumes, 7,131 different periodicals, and 1.4 million microforms, including U.S. government documents.

Creighton's health sciences schools are part of the Creighton Medical Center, which includes Saint Joseph Hospital and Creighton Medical Associates. The Ahmanson Law Center houses the School of Law, the local bar association, and the legal clinic.

Costs

Undergraduate tuition for the 2004–05 academic year are $20,354. The average room and board fees for the academic year cost $7020. There is also a University fee of $764.

Financial Aid

In an effort to keep high-quality Jesuit education affordable, Creighton consistently increases the total amount of scholarships and student aid. The student financial aid program totals more than $114 million, including all federal aid. About 85 percent of Creighton undergraduate students receive some type of financial aid.

Scholarships and grants are awarded on the basis of need, academic achievement, and leadership. The University participates in most federally supported financial aid programs. The Free Application for Federal Student Aid (FAFSA) or Renewal Application is to be filed by returning students by April 1 for the next academic year. Renewable, non-need-based scholarships are available to freshmen with outstanding academic and leadership records.

Faculty

Creighton has 722 full-time faculty members and several hundred others contribute service. The percentage of those having terminal degrees varies from 85 percent in the College of Arts and Sciences to 100 percent in the School of Law. Senior faculty members conduct most classroom instruction. Forty-three active Jesuit priests live and teach on the Creighton campus, providing spiritual direction as well as guidance in the classroom. Each student has a faculty adviser for individual academic counseling.

Student Government

The Student Board of Governors (SBG) is made up of 32 students elected from the undergraduate and professional schools. As the official student governing body, they serve on University committees, present entertainment events, and provide funding for college government and the more than 160 student clubs and organizations.

Admission Requirements

Creighton University invites men and women of all races, religious faiths, and nationalities to apply for admission. In fall 2003, the median ACT composite score for incoming freshmen was 26. Admission, however, is not based solely on scores but also on the student's personal qualities and leadership potential.

Requirements for freshman admission include high school graduation or equivalent credentials and an indication of college-level ability as reflected in high school grades, ACT or SAT I scores, and recommendations. Freshman applicants should present at least 16 units of high school credit, ideally in English, 4; foreign language, 2; American history, 1; American government, 1; mathematics, 3 (including 1 of algebra); science, 2; and electives, 3.

Students in good standing with a C+ (2.5) average or above at other accredited universities, colleges, or junior colleges may be accepted as transfer students. The College of Arts and Sciences and the College of Business Administration require a minimum of 48 hours to be completed at Creighton. Transfer students are eligible for financial aid.

Application and Information

Completed applications for admission should be submitted to the Director of Admissions. Applications may be submitted any time after completion of the junior year of high school. For priority scholarship consideration, students must apply before January 15. Applicants completing their files after that date are considered for merit scholarships based on availability of funds. The Committee on Applications usually notifies each applicant regarding the decision within three weeks after all credentials have been received by the admissions office.

Director of Admissions
Creighton University
2500 California Plaza
Omaha, Nebraska 68178-0055
Telephone: 402-280-2703
800-282-5835 (toll-free outside Omaha)
Fax: 402-280-2685
E-mail: admissions@creighton.edu
World Wide Web: http://www.creighton.edu

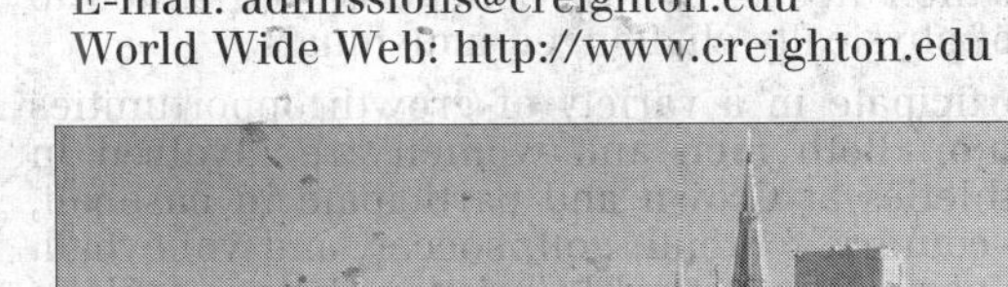

Creighton's tree-lined mall bisects a 108-acre campus that blends new and historic buildings.

CROWN COLLEGE

ST. BONIFACIUS, MINNESOTA

The College

Crown College is a Christian community of higher education dedicated to "Christ-centered" education and the development of servant leaders who will have an impact on their world in a positive and beneficial way. The institution was founded in 1916 in St. Paul, Minnesota, for the purpose of educating men and women for Christian ministry. The mission of Crown College today is to provide a biblically integrated education for Christian leadership in the Christian and Missionary Alliance, the church at large, and the world. It is the conviction of the College that the truth of God's Word is an essential ingredient in education. Students not only learn about life, they learn how to live. Crown College is a community of believers desiring to "grow in the grace and knowledge of our Lord and Savior Jesus Christ" (II Peter 3:18).

A recognized leader in biblical higher education, Crown College offers degrees at the associate, bachelor's, and master's levels, preparing students for professions in a variety of fields. A one-year Bible certificate and several teacher education licensures are also offered, the latter through extension courses. The College is accredited by the Higher Learning Commission and is a member of the North Central Association of Colleges and Schools and the Accrediting Association of Bible Colleges. Crown College continues to dedicate itself to the pursuit of educational excellence and to the perpetuation of spiritual fervency.

More than seventeen Christian denominations are represented in the diverse Crown student body that includes more than 1,000 students from approximately thirty states and several countries. Students and faculty and staff members are vitally involved in a mutual effort to build and maintain a community that reflects and magnifies Jesus Christ.

Most Crown resident students are between 18 and 23 years of age, and 39 percent live off campus (married or single living with family). Residence life at Crown College is intended to provide a meaningful experience in personal growth. By living with others in a residence hall, students can form new friendships, interact with people from different backgrounds, and learn more about themselves. Crown welcomes students with families and provides a fifty-four-unit on-campus housing complex to meet their needs. Crown College is well suited to serve the needs of physically challenged individuals.

Students may participate in a variety of growth opportunities regardless of major. Both men and women are involved in intercollegiate athletics at Crown and participate in baseball, basketball, cross-country, football, golf, soccer, and volleyball. Crown College is part of the National Christian College Athletic Association (NCCAA) and is a member of the National Association of Intercollegiate Athletics (NAIA) and the Upper Midwest Athletic Conference (UMAC). In addition to major music performance groups such as the choirs, Crown students may audition for several small ensembles that travel and perform throughout the year. Other leadership opportunities include student government, student publications, community service, and intercultural experiences.

Crown College offers two master's degrees—one in intercultural studies and the other in ministry leadership. Graduate courses are offered in modules that meet one evening each week for six to seven weeks or as course work available online. Additional information regarding the graduate program is available via e-mail (grad@crown.edu), telephone (952-446-4310 or 800-910-GRAD), and the World Wide Web at the site listed below.

Location

Situated on a beautiful 215-acre campus west of Minneapolis near the communities of Waconia and St. Bonifacius, Minnesota, Crown College is nestled among the rolling hills of the scenic lake-dotted region west of popular Lake Minnetonka. Just 20 minutes from the bustling Twin Cities of Minneapolis and St. Paul, Crown College offers a place of retreat for learning and growth.

Majors and Degrees

Students may select from more than twenty bachelor's degrees, six 2-year associate degrees, and several minors, certificates, and licensures. Majors include biblical and theological studies, biology, business administration, child and family ministries, communications, discipleship ministries, elementary education, English, English education, history, history education, intercultural studies, liberal arts, linguistics, management, music, music education, network administration, New Testament, pastoral leadership, physical education, prelaw, psychology, social studies education, sports management, youth ministry, and youth social ministry.

Since 1993, Crown College has offered adult degree completion programs for adults aged 25 and older. Six degree completion majors are available for the student who has completed approximately 60 semester credits of college. A major in Christian ministry is designed to equip students for leadership roles in the church and parachurch ministries. The early childhood major provides the course work leading to licensure for early childhood, which is designed to include birth through grade 3. The elementary education major is designed to provide course work leading to an elementary education licensure to serve children in grades K–6. The management and ethics major is designed to serve adults who are interested in the integration of faith and learning, equipping them for effective management and leadership roles in the marketplace or other contemporary leadership opportunities. The management and network administration major is designed to serve adults who desire leadership roles in information technology and certification as Microsoft systems engineers. The psychology/counseling major focuses on issues in development and diversity. The major is designed for students desiring entry-level positions or graduate-level work. Degree completion classes generally meet one evening a week or on weekends in a five-week modular format.

Associate degrees are available for adult students in six concentrations: business, Christian studies, early childhood, general studies, network administration, and psychology.

A certificate program is available to non-degree-seeking students in network administration, early childhood, and Bible. Crown College is an authorized IT Academy for Microsoft Corporation, and as such, it has designed various computer education programs to prepare the learner for Microsoft certification as a user specialist or systems administrator.

Crown College Online offers associate, bachelor's, and master's degrees in Christian ministry online. For more information or to apply online, students should visit http://www.crownonline.org or call 800-CROWN-OL (toll-free).

Academic Program

Crown College is uncompromising in its commitment to high-quality education with a solid base of studies in the humanities and sciences integrated with enthusiastic biblical studies. Every baccalaureate degree includes a general studies core curriculum and a Christian studies core curriculum in addition to the chosen major.

Practical hands-on experience is built into many of Crown's degrees. For example, the six-month cross-cultural internship for intercultural studies majors is unique at the undergraduate level. Pastoral, youth, and Christian education ministry majors also take a six-month internship during their junior year.

The academic calendar includes two 16-week semesters and two 4-week summer terms. Requirements for graduation are determined by respective departments of the College. The minimum hours required for a baccalaureate degree are 125 semester credits; an associate degree requires a minimum of 66 semester credits; and certificates require 32 semester credits. Students must attain a minimum cumulative grade point average of 2.0 (on a 4.0 scale) in work taken at Crown College.

Matriculated students at Crown College may earn up to 30 semester credits toward degree program requirements with satisfactory results in the following approved testing programs: Advanced Placement examinations of the College Entrance Examination Board (CEEB); College-Level Examination Program (CLEP); or the Crown College Proficiency Exams in math and computers.

Academically exceptional high school students in their junior or senior year may enroll in Crown courses to earn college credit while completing high school graduation requirements through the Post-Secondary Education Option (PSEO). The Learning Assistance Program helps students who need to improve their skills in reading, writing, and math through personal instruction and computer-based tutorials. Career services are available to all students and graduates for counseling concerning career preparation.

Academic Facilities

The Crown College Library provides access to approximately 220,000 volumes, including 70,000 books, 70,000 microcard books, and 80,000 e-books. The library contains a computer lab, providing access to millions of articles in more than 10,000 full-text electronic magazines and journals. More than 50 research databases are also available.

Costs

For the 2004–05 academic year, tuition is $14,354 based on 12–18 credits per semester, and room and board cost $6142. Students in the Crown Adult Programs (CAP) paid $289 per credit hour.

Financial Aid

About 90 percent of Crown students receive financial aid. The Financial Aid Office is committed to helping students obtain the maximum amount of financial aid available. The four main categories of aid are scholarships, grants, loans, and student employment. Students needing financial assistance must submit the Free Application for Federal Student Aid (FAFSA) and request that the information be sent to Crown College (school code 002383). The government uses the FAFSA to determine the amount the student and/or family is expected to contribute to that year's college costs. This amount is subtracted from a student's cost of attendance to determine the student's financial need. The Crown College Financial Aid Office uses this amount to put together a financial aid package for the student. A priority deadline for completion of financial aid applications is May 1. The FAFSA must be completed every year.

Faculty

Students find the men and women of Crown's faculty to be mentors, advisers, and friends. Their purpose is not merely to produce well-educated young professionals but to educate Christian leaders who make an impact for Jesus Christ in the world. Crown's faculty includes 69 full-time and part-time members; more than half have earned doctoral degrees and/or the appropriate terminal degrees in their field. The ratio of faculty members to students is 1:22.

Student Government

At Crown College, students have the opportunity to stretch their abilities as leaders by getting involved in any of the cocurricular activities on or off campus. Among the avenues for involvement are Student Services Board, Student Senate, residence hall councils, class offices, resident assistant positions, Global Impact Team, and various other organizations. Students also serve on various academic committees.

Faculty and staff members devote their energies to the formation of the next generation of leaders. Students meet voluntarily with faculty and staff members and upperclass students in mentoring relationships. The Leadership Center provides students, constituents, and the community with courses, seminars, and workshops that deal with such practical issues as fostering healthy team dynamics and resolving conflicts.

Admission Requirements

All applicants must have either graduated from high school or received a certificate of high school equivalency (GED) before registration day of the academic term for which application is made. In addition, all applicants must give satisfactory evidence of Christian conversion by both demonstrating quality Christian character in home and community and by making a positive contribution to the ministry of a local church. Applicants must submit the following: application for admission that includes a spiritual life essay, a Community Covenant response, and a $35 fee; two recommendations, one from a pastor and the other from either a teacher or employer; official transcripts from high school and all previous postsecondary institutions; ACT (preferred) or SAT college entrance exam scores. Standard acceptance requirements include a minimum 2.0 GPA, a rank in the top half of the graduating class, and an ACT composite score of 18. International students, other than Canadians, must also submit a TOEFL score.

Application and Information

Students may submit application for admission any time during the calendar year. Preference for class registration and room assignment is given to those who apply by May 1 for the fall semester. Admissions decisions are made on a rolling basis, and students are informed immediately. For further information on how to apply or to schedule a campus visit, students may contact:

Office of Admissions
Crown College
8700 College View Drive
St. Bonifacius, Minnesota 55375-9001
Telephone: 952-446-4142
800-68-CROWN (toll-free)
E-mail: info@crown.edu
World Wide Web: http://www.crown.edu

Crown College is situated on a beautiful 215-acre campus near Minneapolis, Minnesota.

THE CULINARY INSTITUTE OF AMERICA

HYDE PARK, NEW YORK

The Institute

The Culinary Institute of America (CIA) is a private, not-for-profit college dedicated to providing the world's best professional culinary education. The college provides students with the general knowledge and specific skills necessary to live successful lives and to grow into positions of influence and leadership in their chosen profession.

Originally called the New Haven Restaurant Institute, the college was founded in 1946 to give returning World War II veterans the opportunity to learn a new profession. Founders Frances Roth, an attorney chosen as the first director, and Katherine Angell, first chairman of the board, were instrumental in the college's early growth. A director, a chef, a baker, and a dietitian taught the first class of 50 students in the original sixteen-week program, and the college took off from there. In 1947, the school's name was changed to the Restaurant Institute of Connecticut, and in 1951, as students from all over the country were enrolled, it became The Culinary Institute of America.

In 1972, the college moved to its current home, St. Andrew-on-Hudson, a former Jesuit seminary in Hyde Park, New York. That same year, the Board of Regents of the State of New York granted the CIA the right to confer on graduates the Associate in Occupational Studies degree, and in 1993, the Bachelor of Professional Studies degree. The college currently enrolls more than 2,000 students from around the world.

The CIA offers numerous extracurricular activities, including those sponsored by a variety of student clubs. The college's Student Recreation Center includes a six-lane pool, a gymnasium, racquetball courts, an aerobics room, an indoor jogging track, a fitness center, a free-weight room, a game room, outdoor tennis courts, and a café. A number of fitness and intramural sports programs are offered year-round.

Special services include the Office of Career Services, the Craig Claiborne Bookstore, and the Learning Strategies Center. On-campus residence halls house approximately 1,325 students.

The CIA provides students with two meals per instructional day in specified kitchens and dining rooms, and there is an optional weekend meal plan available.

The Culinary Institute of America is accredited by the Commission on Higher Education of the Middle States Association of Colleges and Schools, 3624 Market Street, Philadelphia, Pennsylvania 19104 (telephone: 215-662-5606). The Commission on Higher Education is an institutional accrediting agency recognized by the U.S. Department of Education and the Council for Higher Education Accreditation (CHEA).

The CIA is also accredited by the Accrediting Commission of Career Schools and Colleges of Technology (ACCSCT). The certificate of accreditation is available for viewing on the wall of the President's Wing on the second floor of Roth Hall. Supporting documentation can be reviewed in the office of the Associate Vice President of Planning, Research, and Accreditation, located on the third floor of Roth Hall. Information related to tuition charges, fees, and length of comparable programs at other institutions may be obtained from the ACCSCT at 2101 Wilson Boulevard, Suite 302, Arlington, Virginia 22201 (telephone: 703-247-4212).

Location

The CIA's scenic 150-acre campus is nestled along the east bank of the Hudson River in Hyde Park, New York, conveniently located 1½–2 hours from New York City and Albany.

The Mid-Hudson region's numerous attractions and recreational opportunities offer something for everyone in both rural and urban settings. There are a number of state parks and historic sites throughout the area. Students can taste wines at local vineyards, visit farmer's markets, and pick apples at nearby orchards. Not far to the west lie the Catskill and Shawangunk Mountains, where opportunities for hiking, skiing, rock climbing, mountain biking, and sightseeing abound. Concerts, plays, films, and other cultural and special events are offered regularly at the many colleges, theaters, and community facilities throughout the Hudson Valley and Catskill regions. Students can take advantage of the campus's proximity to New York City and Albany to experience the culture, arts, and nightlife of those exciting cities.

Majors and Degrees

The Culinary Institute of America awards the degree of Bachelor of Professional Studies (B.P.S.) in baking and pastry arts management and in culinary arts management, as well as the degree of Associate in Occupational Studies (A.O.S.) in baking and pastry arts and in culinary arts.

Academic Programs

The core of the curriculum at The Culinary Institute of America is the hands-on teaching of cooking and baking as well as the managerial and creative elements that today's culinary professional requires. The unique Progressive Learning Year (PLY) system allows students to build essential culinary skills in a logical sequence during the first five semesters and enables a new class of 90 students to enroll every three weeks. In those five semesters, students take courses that include food safety, menu development, confectionery art, hearth breads and rolls, garde manger, and cuisines of Asia. They also gain invaluable experience in an eighteen-week externship by cooking and serving in the college's bakery café or in some of the four fine-dining public restaurants on campus. The junior and senior years build additional skills critical to career success through courses such as marketing, communications, foreign languages, computers in the food business, and management. Bachelor's-degree students also take a wine and food seminar in California.

Students must earn 132 total credits in culinary arts management or in baking and pastry arts management to graduate with a bachelor's degree. The A.O.S. programs comprise the first five semesters of the bachelor's degree curricula, including the externship. Students must earn 69 total credits in culinary arts or in baking and pastry arts to graduate with an associate degree.

Off-Campus Programs

All students work in externships for a minimum of eighteen weeks (600 hours). These externships provide students with valuable on-the-job experience at one of more than 1,600 top food service and hospitality properties—such as hotels, restaurants, and resorts—around the world. B.P.S. students also travel to California's Napa Valley for a four-week wine and food seminar, where they can learn from local purveyors and visit area wineries and vineyards.

Academic Facilities

The CIA campus features forty-one professionally equipped production kitchens and bakeshops and five student-staffed public restaurants. The Danny Kaye Theatre regularly hosts world-renowned chefs for lectures, cooking demonstrations, and discussions. Other valuable resources include the 69,000-volume Conrad N. Hilton Library, containing an outstanding collection of specialized culinary literature; the Learning Resources Center, which provides audiovisual programs to supplement course work; computer workstations; and a wireless network that allows students to access online resources from almost anywhere on campus.

Costs

For each semester in academic year 2004–05, tuition is $9310 for the A.O.S. programs and the first half of the B.P.S. programs and $6930 for the second half of the B.P.S. programs. Board is $1085, which includes two meals per instructional day. Housing costs range from $1695 to $2650 per semester, depending on the room to which the student is assigned.

Additional required fees for the first five semesters include a confirmation fee of $100, equipment fees of $850 for culinary supplies or $750 for baking and pastry supplies, a second-semester practical exam fee of $150, an externship fee of $360, a fifth-semester practical exam fee of $170, and an A.O.S. graduation fee of $250. B.P.S. graduates must also pay a $250 graduation fee. Student activity fees are $75 per semester in both degree programs. The CIA offers students a tuition installment plan. Details are available from the college's Bursar's Office.

Financial Aid

Approximately 85 percent of the CIA's students receive financial aid. Federal programs offered at the college include the Federal Pell Grant, Federal Supplemental Educational Opportunity Grant (FSEOG), Federal Stafford Loan, Unsubsidized Federal Stafford Loan, Federal Perkins Loan, Federal Work-Study Program (which provides a variety of on-campus and community service jobs to eligible students), Federal PLUS Program, and Veterans Administration benefits. Students should also investigate their own state's programs and apply if those grants or scholarships can be used in New York State.

Students who have applied for admission or who are currently enrolled at the CIA may apply for scholarships offered by various organizations in the food service industry. A list of these scholarships, which are administered by the college, is available from the Financial Aid Office.

Faculty

The college's faculty is composed of more than 130 chefs and instructors from fifteen countries whose credentials and industry experience are unmatched in culinary education. The faculty also includes the largest concentration of Certified Master Chefs anywhere. The 18:1 student-faculty ratio gives students the opportunity to work in an environment closely representative of the food service industry.

Student Government

All students in good standing are members of the Student Council. The council's Executive Board acts as a liaison between students and the administration. The Student Council helps support student activities and funds all student clubs and committees.

Admission Requirements

The Admissions Committee seeks candidates who have demonstrated a commitment to a culinary career and who have the personal initiative, confidence, and motivation to succeed. The basic requirements are successful completion of a secondary school education or its equivalent and some experience in the food service and hospitality industry. The applicant's educational record is evaluated on the basis of overall performance and the type of program taken. Academics and leadership ability are key requirements for the B.P.S. programs. Preference is given to candidates who have worked in food service, particularly in a kitchen that offers a varied menu. Before entering the program, students should have had about six months of hands-on food preparation in a non-fast-food environment.

Applicants must submit a formal application for admission, a nonrefundable $30 application fee, a secondary school report (high school students only), an official secondary school transcript (not a student copy), and an official college transcript, if applicable. The application requirements include an essay of at least 500 words for the B.P.S. or 150 words for the A.O.S. programs. In addition, A.O.S. candidates must provide one recommendation, which may be from an employer in the food service industry or a culinary educator, attesting to the applicant's interest in pursuing a culinary career. Two recommendations are required for B.P.S. applicants: one from a guidance counselor, professional character reference, or culinary educator describing their academic and leadership potential and the other from an employer describing their food service industry experience. Bachelor's degree candidates must also participate in an on-campus or telephone interview.

Application and Information

Students may apply for admission to the CIA year-round, as the college offers freshmen four enrollment seasons from which to choose—spring, summer/early fall, fall, and winter. Applicants should submit their materials according to the enrollment schedule (available at the Web site listed below) that corresponds to the season they are interested in beginning the degree program. Students are notified of an admission decision according to that schedule. For information or to schedule a tour, students should contact:

Admissions Office
The Culinary Institute of America
1946 Campus Drive
Hyde Park, New York 12538-1499
Telephone: 800-CULINARY (toll-free)
E-mail: admissions@culinary.edu
World Wide Web: http://www.ciachef.edu

Nestled along the banks of the Hudson River, the Culinary Institute of America's campus lies on 150 scenic acres in historic Hyde Park, New York.

CULVER–STOCKTON COLLEGE

CANTON, MISSOURI

The College

Culver-Stockton College (C-SC) was founded in 1853 as the first institution of higher learning west of the Mississippi River chartered expressly for coeducation. Affiliated with the Christian Church (Disciples of Christ), the College is personal (850 students) and provides a strong career-oriented education within a liberal arts setting. The College has one of the most attractive campuses in the Midwest and is home to one of the finest science center facilities in the region, which opened in fall 2002.

Principally residential in character, the College presents a full array of cocurricular activities, including course-related clubs and organizations, an active fraternity and sorority system, a fine intramural program, and a strong intercollegiate athletics program highlighted by baseball, basketball, football, golf, soccer, softball, and volleyball.

Culver-Stockton College has more than 9,000 living alumni, many of whom have achieved distinction in the arts, government, medicine, law, education, and other professional fields. With 150 years of history, Culver-Stockton College moves into the twenty-first century as one of the truly distinctive small liberal arts colleges of the Midwest.

Location

Canton, Missouri, a small Mississippi River town of 2,600, is surrounded by the rolling farmland of northeast Missouri. Culver-Stockton is statistically one of the safest college campuses in the United States. The College has close ties with Quincy, Illinois, a progressive, arts-oriented community of approximately 45,000, and is just north of historic Hannibal, the boyhood home of the famous American author Mark Twain. St. Louis is within a 2½-hour drive, and Chicago and Kansas City are close enough to be significant factors in the cultural life of the College. Culver-Stockton sits atop a hill from which three states can be seen and overlooks the city and the Mississippi River.

Majors and Degrees

Culver-Stockton offers Bachelor of Arts and Bachelor of Science degrees in twenty-four areas; the Bachelor of Fine Arts in art, arts management, and theater; the Bachelor of Music Education; and the Bachelor of Science in Nursing. Study areas include accounting, art, art education, arts management, athletic training, biology, business administration, chemistry, communication, criminal justice, early childhood development, elementary education, English, finance, history and political science, management, mathematics, medical technology, music, music education, nursing, physical education, psychology, recreation management, religion and philosophy, middle school education, secondary education, sociology, speech and theater education, and theater. Preprofessional programs are available in dentistry, engineering, law, medicine, ministry, optometry, pharmacy, physical therapy, and veterinary medicine. The College has cooperative arrangements with Washington University in occupational therapy. The College also has a pre-engineering program agreement with the University of Missouri–Rolla.

Academic Program

The Culver-Stockton emphasis on career preparation is enhanced by the liberal arts. The development of student skills in writing, speaking, critical thinking, and problem solving is a critical element in the liberal arts emphasis. In addition, core courses in composition, speech, and Christian heritage combine with student choices from among five distribution areas to ensure a wide breadth of study. Students must complete 124 credit hours for the bachelor's degree. Major programs require from 28 to 62 credits. Double majors and minors are encouraged, adding further diversity and breadth to graduates' qualifications as they approach the job market.

The College has committed itself to academic distinction. Students are challenged to achieve their maximum potential in learned skills, breadth and depth of knowledge, and understanding their own values. Students are assigned an academic adviser who is prepared to assist students in achieving their educational goals. An individualized plan is developed and then updated each semester until graduation.

For able and highly motivated students, including freshmen, the College Honors Program provides the opportunity to participate in certain specially designated courses and events, culminating in an opportunity for independent study or research in an area of the student's special interest. The program is especially helpful for students planning for graduate programs.

Exploratory and professional internships are available in all majors and are viewed as an important part of the career selection process. Combined with an active career counseling and placement service that includes computerized interest and preference testing, on- and off-campus internships are a key element in the Culver-Stockton approach to preparing students for employment after graduation.

Work completed at other colleges and universities is transferable toward Culver-Stockton graduation requirements, and various testing procedures (e.g., CLEP, AP, CPEP) allow credit for equivalent knowledge or experience. Individualized learning options are plentiful; they range from individually negotiated independent study to specially designed degree programs.

The College operates on a two-semester calendar, with the first semester concluding before Christmas and the spring semester ending in early to mid-May. Summer sessions of varying lengths are available to students who wish to overcome deficiencies or accelerate their programs. All programs and classes are characterized by individual attention to the needs and interests of the student.

Off-Campus Programs

Culver-Stockton students have continuing opportunities for international experience through an agreement with the Central College at Pella (Iowa) International Program. In addition, off-campus and international study experiences, as well as individually designed internship opportunities, are available. Groups of students have traveled with Culver-Stockton faculty members to Eastern Europe, Western Europe, Canada, the Dominican Republic, and Israel. The Concert Choir and the Wind Ensemble tour each year.

Academic Facilities

Culver-Stockton is one of only a handful of colleges its size to put computers at the fingertips of every student. Computer network outlets are available for each student in every residence hall room and provide connections for students' personal computers for continuous access to the Internet, the World Wide Web, e-mail, the College network, laser printers, and library holdings. Culver-Stockton offers Pentium computer clusters in every residence hall and maintains three computer labs with Pentium workstations, the Windows operating system, and Microsoft Office as well as four specialized labs. Faculty members have integrated computers into the classroom in almost every field, using dedicated computer labs equipped with major-specific software.

The computerized Johann Memorial Library has a collection of 151,979 volumes and also presents comprehensive collections of periodicals, journals, and other materials in both hard copy and microform. Extensive interlibrary loan and electronic bibliographical search capabilities are available to both students and the faculty. C-SC students have access to more than 6 million volumes through the College's link to a statewide library database.

The Robert W. Brown Performing Arts Center and Mabee Art Gallery house professional-quality art and performance studios, computer laboratories, and three performance stages where 200 to nearly 1,000 guests can attend theater and music performances.

The new $8-million Science Center is home to the departments of biology, chemistry, physics, mathematics, and computer information systems. Students can benefit from its state-of-the-art labs and technology, classrooms with full multimedia capabilities, and facilities designed specifically for student research.

Costs

The 2004–05 school year costs at Culver-Stockton College were $13,200 for tuition, $6775 for room and board, and approximately $600 for books and supplies. With the exception of students who are married or living with parents, all students receiving college financial aid are required to take room and board contracts. Variable board plans are available for the dining hall and "Cats Pause," the student restaurant.

Financial Aid

Culver-Stockton College has one of the best student financial planning programs available among colleges of comparable size and purpose. The College participates in all federal and state financial aid programs, presenting aid packages that are based on need and merit. The latter include performance—theater, music, art, leadership, and athletics—awards as well as those based on academic achievement. The College accepts the Free Application for Federal Student Aid (FAFSA). Several Pillars for Excellence full tuition scholarships are awarded on a competitive basis each year, and other academic scholarships are available to applicants who meet certain GPA and ACT criteria. Other awards are available for students in various other circumstances. All scholarships are renewable with minimum requirements. Application procedures are detailed in all admission materials and are subject to certain deadlines.

Faculty

Faculty members with diverse backgrounds, preparation, and interests provide instruction of high quality and individualized attention to students. Faculty members are active in scholarship, professional activity, and service and use College programs to maintain a keen interest and the highest competencies in their fields. Faculty members also take an active role in the advising and sponsorship of student organizations.

Student Government

An active Student Government Association regularly plans campuswide student events and, most importantly, deals with significant issues of student interest and communicates information about them to the faculty and administration. Students have voting representation on key faculty committees such as the Academic Council, the Student Services Council, the Academic and Cultural Events Committee, and others that have a direct impact upon the nature and quality of student life.

Admission Requirements

Prospective students are expected to have completed a college-preparatory course of study of 15 units at an accredited secondary school. A proper foundation to facilitate success in college studies includes 4 units of English, 3 units of history, at least 2 units of mathematics (algebra and geometry), and 2 to 4 units of science. Students who intend to major in the science disciplines may wish to select additional high school courses in science and mathematics, and those interested in the humanities and social studies areas typically present additional course work in literature, foreign language, and history. Applicants must submit ACT or SAT scores. Each applicant for admission is given personal attention and considered on the basis of academic performance, test scores, and personal attributes. An electronic application is available on the College's Web site at the address below.

Application and Information

Early application is recommended, as residence halls and classroom space may be limited. For further information, students should contact:

Enrollment Services
One College Hill
Culver-Stockton College
Canton, Missouri 63435
Telephone: 800-537-1883 (toll-free)
E-mail: enrollment@culver.edu
World Wide Web: http://www.culver.edu

Weldon Residence Hall, Culver-Stockton College.

CUMBERLAND COLLEGE

WILLIAMSBURG, KENTUCKY

The College

For more than 100 years, Cumberland College has been committed to providing a superior education in an exceptional Christian atmosphere at an affordable cost. Emphasis is placed on the growth of the individual student. The College strives to instill in students the desire to be agents of change in the world and to use knowledge for the benefit of others as well as themselves.

Cumberland is a four-year, coed liberal arts college offering a broad curriculum with more than forty programs of undergraduate study from which to choose. A graduate program leading to the Master of Arts in Education is also offered.

The student body consists of 1,700 students representing thirty-eight states and fourteen countries. Most students live on campus in the College's ten residence halls. Each hall is supervised by a director assisted by student staff members.

Extracurricular activities abound, including debate team, theater, musical performance groups, academic societies, Baptist Student Union, Appalachian Ministries, departmental clubs, and intramural sports. Cumberland participates in intercollegiate competition in women's basketball, cross-country, golf, judo, soccer, softball, swimming, tennis, track, volleyball, and wrestling; men's baseball, basketball, cross-country, football, golf, judo, soccer, swimming, tennis, track, and wrestling; and coed cheerleading. The O. Wayne Rollins Convocation/Physical Education Center houses a 2,700-seat athletic arena, a swimming pool, an indoor walking/jogging track, and classrooms. The James H. Taylor II Stadium complex includes a football field, an eight-lane all-weather track, and soccer fields.

Students benefit from such special services as the Career Services Center, Center for Leadership Studies, Student Health Center, Academic Resource Center, and free tutorial assistance.

Cumberland College is accredited by the Commission on Colleges of the Southern Association of Colleges and Schools (1866 Southern Lane, Decatur, Georgia 30033-4097; telephone: 404-679-4501) to award Bachelor of Arts, Bachelor of General Studies, Bachelor of Music, Bachelor of Science, and Master of Arts in Education degrees.

Location

Williamsburg is located in southern Kentucky, 185 miles south of Cincinnati, Ohio, and 70 miles north of Knoxville, Tennessee. The campus is easily accessible from Interstate 75, about 1 mile from Exit 11. Williamsburg is one of Kentucky's older towns and is known for its beautiful homes and the hospitality of its people. The College is situated on three hills above the town and has a panoramic view of the surrounding mountains and Cumberland River Valley, an area known throughout the country for its lovely waterfalls, forests, and lakes. Famed Cumberland Falls State Resort Park is just 20 minutes from campus.

Majors and Degrees

Cumberland College confers the degrees of Bachelor of Arts, Bachelor of Science, Bachelor of General Studies, and Bachelor of Music. Major fields of study are accounting, art, biology, business administration, chemistry, church music, communications and theater arts, computer information systems, education, English, health, history, mathematics, medical technology, movement and leisure studies, music, office administration, philosophy, political science, psychology, religion, social work, and special education.

Minor fields of study can be chosen from major fields or from biblical languages, French, philosophy, physics, and Spanish.

Preprofessional and special curricula are offered in medical technology, military science, predentistry, pre-engineering, prelaw, premedicine, prenursing, preoptometry, prepharmacy, pre–physical therapy, pre–veterinary medicine, and religious vocations.

Academic Program

Cumberland seeks to provide academic specialization within the broad framework of a liberal arts education. To supplement the in-depth knowledge acquired within each major, 47 semester hours of general studies from the areas of Christian faith and values, cultural and aesthetic values, the English language, humanities, leadership and community service, natural and mathematical sciences, physical education, and social sciences are required. Students must earn 128 semester hours to graduate with a bachelor's degree.

The academic year begins in late August, with the first semester ending in mid-December. The second semester runs from early January to early May. One 5-week undergraduate summer session and two 4-week graduate summer sessions are also offered. Orientation, preregistration, and academic advising by faculty members begin in the summer preceding entrance.

Students may receive credit for successful scores on the Advanced Placement examinations of the College Board, the College-Level Examination Program (CLEP), and special departmental tests. Through the honors program, highly qualified students have the opportunity to undertake advanced independent study.

Academic Facilities

Cumberland's campus contains thirty-two buildings, reflecting antebellum architectural style. The science building features well-equipped biology, chemistry, and physics labs providing graduate-level research opportunities.

The McGaw Music Building contains individual rehearsal and studio areas as well as a recital hall. The Norma Perkins Hagan Memorial Library houses more than 150,500 book titles, 1,630 periodical subscriptions, and 715,878 microform titles. Sophisticated computer equipment provides access to an additional 20 million or more items from many of the nation's outstanding libraries. The instructional media center includes a children's library, a computerized language lab, and a listening library.

Other special academic features include a computer center, an art gallery, a word processing center for English composition, a theater, the Career Services Center, a 600-seat chapel, two large lecture halls, and the Distance Learning Laboratory.

Costs

For 2003–04, the basic academic-year expenses were $11,458 for tuition and fees and $4926 for room and board, for a total of

$16,384. There are no additional fees for out-of-state students. The average cost for books and supplies is approximately $300 per semester.

Financial Aid

Cumberland sponsors a large financial aid program that coordinates money from federal, state, private, and College sources. Last year, 95 percent of Cumberland students shared more than $17 million in aid.

To apply for financial aid, it is necessary to complete the Free Application for Federal Student Aid (FAFSA). For further information about financial aid opportunities, students should contact the Director of Financial Aid at 800-532-0828 (toll-free). Applications made by March 15 are given priority for the fall semester.

Numerous scholarships and leadership grants are available.

Faculty

There are 95 full-time and 2 part-time faculty members who are respected scholars and whose primary responsibility is to teach. Courses are not taught by graduate assistants. The student-faculty ratio is 16:1, enabling students to receive ample attention and assistance from professors. Faculty members also serve as advisers to help students in planning their academic programs.

Student Government

The Student Government Association acts as a liaison between the students and the College administration. The organization also plans, implements, and governs various activities and special events each year to enhance the quality of campus social life. Members of the executive and legislative branches are elected by the student body.

Admission Requirements

In compliance with federal law, including provisions of Title IX of the Educational Amendments of 1972 and Section 504 of the Rehabilitation Act of 1973, Cumberland College does not illegally discriminate on the basis of race, sex, color, national or ethnic origin, age, disability, or military service in its administration of education policies, programs, or activities; admissions policies; or employment. Under federal law, the College may discriminate on the basis of religion in order to fulfill its purposes. The College reserves the right to discriminate on the basis of sex in its undergraduate admissions programs. Further, the College reserves the right to deny admission to any applicant whose academic preparation, character, or personal conduct is determined to be inconsistent with the purpose and objectives of the College. Where possible, the College will seek to reasonably accommodate a student's disability. However, the College's obligation to reasonably accommodate a student's disability ends where the accommodation would pose an undue hardship on the College or where the accommodation in question would fundamentally alter the academic program. Inquiries or complaints should be directed to the Vice President for Academic Affairs.

The purpose of the admission process is to identify applicants who are likely to succeed academically at Cumberland College and at the same time contribute positively to the campus community. The process considers such factors as high school records (including courses taken, grade trends, and rank in class), college records (if transferring from another institution), scores on the ACT or on the SAT I, application essay, letters of recommendation, extracurricular activities and honors, and personal contact.

Application and Information

Applicants for admission should contact the admissions office for an application form and return the completed form to the College, along with the appropriate application fee. Applicants should also have official transcripts of all high school and college work sent to the College, along with a copy of the ACT or SAT I scores. Each student is notified regarding official admission within ten working days after the application procedure has been completed.

Students accepted for admission must submit the required enrollment deposit.

Additional information may be obtained by contacting:

Office of Admissions
Cumberland College
Williamsburg, Kentucky 40769
Telephone: 606-539-4241
800-343-1609 (toll-free)
E-mail: admiss@cumberlandcollege.edu
World Wide Web: http://www.cumberlandcollege.edu

Students on the campus of Cumberland College.

CURRY COLLEGE

MILTON, MASSACHUSETTS

The College

The mission of Curry College, a private institution, is to develop liberally educated persons who are able to gain and to apply knowledge humanely, intelligently, and effectively in a complex, changing world. To achieve its mission, Curry College promotes individual intellectual and social growth by engaging its students in achieving these educational goals: thinking critically, communicating effectively, understanding context, appreciating aesthetic experience, defining a personal identity, examining value systems, and adapting and innovating. The College's curriculum and programs focus on the two hallmarks of the Curry education: a high respect for the individuality of every student and a developmental approach to learning that maximizes opportunities for achievement. One-on-one faculty-student relationships provide ample opportunities for personalized instruction and close interaction. Full student counseling and other support services are provided.

The current undergraduate enrollment is 1,600 men and women. Curry students have access to a wide range of cocurricular activities, including the Student Government Association, the student-run newspaper, the yearbook, the Curry *Arts Journal*, several organizations for the performing arts, and the award-winning, student-run radio station. The Office of Student Activities and the Student Program Board provide a variety of special events. A full schedule of men's and women's Division III and intramural sports is also provided. Varsity sports for men are baseball, basketball, football, ice hockey, lacrosse, soccer, and tennis; women's varsity sports are basketball, cross-country, lacrosse, soccer, softball, and tennis.

Now well into its second century of providing distinguished educational service, Curry College was founded in Boston in 1879. It was named in honor of its founders, Samuel Silas Curry and Anna Baright Curry. The College moved to its present site in Milton in 1952. In 1974, it absorbed the Perry Normal School, and, in 1977, it entered into a collaborative relationship with Children's Hospital Medical Center, which resulted in the establishment of Curry's Division of Nursing Studies. Curry College is accredited by the New England Association of Schools and Colleges; the nursing program is accredited by the National League for Nursing Accrediting Commission. Curry offers a Master of Education (M.Ed.) degree and a master's degree in criminal justice.

Location

Curry is ideally situated in Milton, Massachusetts, a largely residential suburb located near the exceptional resources of Boston. The Greater Boston area provides students with a diversity of cultural, educational, recreational, and sports activities. A wide variety of corporations, hospitals, agencies, broadcasting stations, and schools provide excellent opportunities for internships and jobs for Curry students. The College operates a shuttle bus to the MBTA trains, which provide easy access to Boston. Curry students have the benefit of a traditional, wooded New England campus and access to the excitement of a large city.

Majors and Degrees

Curry College awards the Bachelor of Arts (B.A.) and Bachelor of Science (B.S.) in nursing and health education degrees. Majors are biology, business management (with concentrations in accounting, entrepreneurship, finance, human resources, marketing, and sports management), communication (with concentrations in film studies, journalism, organizational communication, public communication, public relations, radio broadcasting, television, and theater), criminal justice, education (with concentrations in early childhood education, elementary education, special needs, and preschool education), English (with concentrations in English literature, American literature, creative writing, journalism, and professional writing), environmental science, health, information technology, nursing, philosophy, politics and history, psychology (with concentrations in counseling, developmental psychology, education, health, gerontology, and substance abuse counseling), sociology (with concentrations in ethnic and gender studies and service in the community), and visual arts (with concentrations in graphic design and studio arts). Special minors are available in applied computing, dance, music, religion, Spanish, Web development, women's studies, and writing. Provision is also made for students to design majors in areas in which they have a special interest.

Academic Program

A central liberal arts curriculum, required for all students, incorporates a variety of academic disciplines into every student's plan of study. Curry's programs also integrate theoretical classroom learning with a wide variety of field internships in the Greater Boston area.

Curry College operates on a two-semester calendar with a summer session. To graduate, students must complete at least 120 credit hours for a B.A. degree or 121 credit hours for the B.S. In both cases, a minimum 2.0 cumulative average must be achieved.

Curry allows students to gain advanced standing in a variety of ways: through successful scores on College-Level Examination Program (CLEP) tests, through credit earned at other accredited colleges and universities, and through end-of-course proficiency examinations. Credit may also be granted for educational experiences that have occurred outside the traditional academic environment.

Many academic programs enrich and facilitate the Curry education. The Freshmen Seminar, the Honors Program, the Women's Studies Program, the Essential Skills Center, and the Field Experience Program are representative of that focus on special interests and diverse learning needs.

The Program for Advancement of Learning (PAL) is a credited program designed to assist intelligent, motivated language-learning-disabled students to achieve at the college level. PAL provides individual or small-group instruction, textbooks on tape, and untimed examinations, as well as other services. Students may take advantage of PAL's services throughout their college careers.

Off-Campus Programs

Curry students may earn up to 30 credits for field internships with outside firms, agencies, radio stations, hospitals, schools, or similar organizations. In consultation with faculty members, students develop learning contracts that articulate their educational and personal goals and establish criteria for the evaluation of their field experience. Students may also arrange to study abroad or at another institution within the United States while enrolled at Curry.

Academic Facilities

The Levin Memorial Library houses more than 110,000 volumes, 650 periodicals, and 10,000 microforms. It is a designated depository for U.S. government documents. The library also houses the Essential Skills Center, where students may secure assistance in reading, writing, mathematics, and the development of study skills. Three computer laboratories contain more than 100 Macintosh and IBM computers, laser printers, color printers, and state-of-the-art optical scanning equipment. The entire campus is networked and linked to the Internet.

The Science Building includes five laboratories. The Kennedy Academic Center houses a simulated hospital room for use as a nursing laboratory, the Nursing Resource Center that is equipped with an interactive video lab, and a laboratory for experimental psychology equipped with biofeedback, computer control, and animal and human learning facilities. The Learning Center, with its own computer lab, maintains a complete tape library of all textbooks used at the College. The Hafer Academic Center houses the Experiential Education Office, the Career Planning and Placement Office, the Academic Advising Office, the Educational Technology Center, the Hirsh Communication Center, which features a state-of-the-art television studio, and the Parent's Lounge, which hosts student art exhibits. In addition, Curry students operate and maintain WMLN-FM, the College's 172-watt radio station.

Costs

Tuition for the 2003–04 academic year was $19,870. Room was $4400, and board was $3390 (fourteen-meal plan). The cost of the Program for Advancement of Learning was $4500. The cost of books, supplies, and personal expenses vary from $900 to $1200.

Financial Aid

Curry provides financial assistance for students who need funding in order to attend college. The financial aid program consists of federal, state, and Curry College scholarships, grants, work-study awards, student assistant jobs, and loans. Approximately 75 percent of the student body receive financial aid. All students applying for financial aid must submit the Free Application for Federal Student Aid (FAFSA) by March 1. Students applying for financial aid should contact the financial aid office.

Faculty

There are 91 full-time faculty members at Curry, many of whom hold earned doctorates. In addition, each year the College hires highly qualified part-time faculty members and visiting lecturers to augment its teaching staff. Although primarily a teaching faculty, many of Curry's faculty members are engaged in writing, research, and consulting.

Student Government

The general purpose of the Student Government Association (SGA) is the advancement of the College community and the promotion of the general welfare of the students. The SGA seeks to increase student involvement in the formulation of College policies, to communicate effectively with all constituencies of the College, and to promote student participation within the institution. Members of the SGA serve on the Joint Committee on Communication of the Board of Trustees.

Admission Requirements

Curry College accepts all students who have the necessary preparation and educational background to meet the requirements of the College, regardless of race, religion, national or ethnic origin, age, sex, sexual orientation, or physical handicap. Freshman students are selected on the basis of a combination of the following: secondary school record, scores on the SAT I or ACT, recommendation of the secondary school, and the candidate's readiness for college. To be considered for admission, students must generally present at least 16 units of high school work from an approved secondary school. A recommended program of studies includes 4 years of English, at least 3 years of mathematics, 2 years of a foreign language, 2 years of science (including at least 1 of a laboratory science), and 2 years of social studies. Applicants should contact the Admission Office to discuss any possible exceptions to these requirements. Nursing applicants are required to have taken high school biology and chemistry. A GED certificate is acceptable in lieu of a high school diploma. Curry College seeks well-rounded students who can contribute to the Curry community in athletic, artistic, and social endeavors as well as in the academic sphere.

Application and Information

Curry's recommended application deadline is April 1. Applicants to the learning disability program (PAL) must apply by March 1. Students are accepted on a rolling basis. Admission options, such as early decision, deferred entrance, and advanced placement, are also available. Students may apply for September or January entrance. Applicants must submit an application and fee, an official high school transcript, scores from the SAT I or ACT, and a counselor's recommendation. In addition, transfer students must submit official college transcripts, and international students must submit results of the Test of English as a Foreign Language (TOEFL). An interview is recommended. The Admission Committee evaluates each application as soon as all required credentials are received, beginning in January.

Applicants to the Program for Advancement of Learning must submit the application and fee, an official high school transcript, a counselor's recommendation, and the results of a recently administered Wechsler Adult Intelligence Scale (WAIS-R) test. Achievement testing in reading comprehension, written language, and math must also be submitted. Final decisions on admission to the program are made once all credentials are complete.

For more information about Curry College, students should contact:

Jane Patricia Fidler
Director of Admission
Curry College
Milton, Massachusetts 02186
Telephone: 617-333-2210
800-669-0686 (toll-free)
Fax: 617-333-2114
E-mail: curryadm@curry.edu
World Wide Web: http://www.curry.edu

The suburban campus of Curry College is only minutes from the city of Boston.

DAEMEN COLLEGE

AMHERST, NEW YORK

The College

At Daemen College, degree and student service programs are distinctly designed for the career-minded student. With a student body of 2,100, a low student-faculty ratio (15:1) is maintained in the belief that small classes encourage a better exchange of ideas and knowledge and promote the high-quality education for which the College is known. Providing more than forty career-oriented majors, this private, four-year, college provides career preparation with a liberal arts emphasis. Daemen is located on 39 acres in Amherst, New York, which is a suburb of Buffalo. The small, friendly campus offers a large selection of cultural, social, fraternal, athletic, and service groups to enrich the college experience, as well as the amenities of a big community nearby. Buffalo offers outstanding cultural and recreational resources plus exciting major-league sports.

On-campus housing is available to all students at any time. A complex of seven modern, two-story apartment-type buildings provides separate housing for men and women; there is also a five-story residence hall. The services of the Academic Computing and Resource Center and the Career Development, Health Services, Placement, and Cooperative Education Offices, as well as the Campus Ministry, are always available. Daemen has few architectural barriers; handicapped men and women using wheelchairs find it easy to move throughout the campus.

Along with its bachelor's degree programs, the College offers Master of Science degrees in adult nurse practitioner studies, palliative care, physician assistant studies, special education, elementary education, global business, and executive leadership and change. A Doctor of Physical Therapy degree is also available.

Location

Daemen is located on a 39-acre campus in Amherst, New York, a northern suburb of Buffalo. The campus is easily accessible by the major rail, plane, and motor routes that serve the city of Buffalo. The combination of a beautiful and safe campus and proximity to a bustling city is a definite asset. The area has a rich variety of participatory and spectator sports that range from skiing and swimming to major-league football. The wide range of cultural resources includes the Philharmonic Orchestra, the Albright-Knox Art Gallery, and the Studio Arena Theater. Buffalo, the second-largest city in New York State, is the focal point of the Niagara Frontier, an area that offers many historic and scenic points of interest. The metropolitan facilities offer opportunities in educational, cultural, business, and scientific areas. The many trees and wide open spaces on Daemen's suburban campus are a nice contrast to the nearby cities. Niagara Falls is a short 30-minute drive, and Toronto is only 2 hours away.

Majors and Degrees

Daemen College offers programs that lead to the Bachelor of Arts (B.A.), the Bachelor of Fine Arts (B.F.A.), and the Bachelor of Science (B.S.) degrees. Majors include accounting, adolescence education, art, art education, biochemistry, biology, business administration, business education, business weekend program, communications/public relations, drawing/illustration, early childhood, elementary education, English, environmental studies, French, global economics, graphic design, health-care studies, history and government, humanities, human resource management, human services, international business, marketing, mathematics, medical technology, natural sciences, nursing, operations management, painting/sculpture, physical therapy, physician assistant studies, predentistry, prelaw, premedicine, preveterinary, printmaking, psychology, religious studies, social work, Spanish, special education, and sport management.

Academic Program

The academic program followed by Daemen College was chosen to provide liberal breadth and great depth simultaneously. This plan is marked by four characteristics: (1) a generous number of courses in the major field; (2) the building of a sequential set of courses in this field so that knowledge is acquired according to a logical progression; (3) a reading list course in the junior year, in which the student reads widely in his or her particular field; and (4) a coordinating seminar in the senior year, which provides an interdisciplinary approach and relates the student's concentration to other components of the curriculum.

A minimum of 122 semester hours is required for a baccalaureate degree. One semester hour represents a lecture period of 50 minutes each week throughout a semester of fifteen weeks or a laboratory or studio period of 100 minutes each week throughout a semester of fifteen weeks.

Off-Campus Programs

Internships in various areas, including Washington, D.C., are available for students who major in history and government. Fieldwork at community social service agencies is an option for the psychology or social work major. Internships are available at area hospitals for outstanding applied science students. All students have the opportunity to study in Mexico and Montreal or spend an academic year abroad through the Junior Year Abroad Program. An international studies minor can be combined with most areas of study, and all students can take advantage of travel programs.

Cross-registration arrangements with other colleges and universities enable students to take courses for credit at twenty nearby colleges.

Job search workshops are offered to provide students with the opportunity to write professional resumes and cover letters and to practice effective interviewing and job search techniques.

Through Daemen's Cooperative Education Program, students gain hands-on experience in their chosen field while completing their degree. Academic credit is received for working, many times along with a salary. The program gives students the opportunity to relate classroom theory to actual work experience and, most importantly, enables them to acquire the workplace values that are basic for all career preparations.

Full- or part-time experiences are available in all areas of study, with placements available throughout New York and all over the United States. Co-op assignments include positions in business and industry, banks, hospitals, social service agencies, government agencies, schools and colleges, and cultural organizations. Field placements are incorporated into some of the College's degree programs, including the courses of study in medical technology, physical therapy, and social work.

Academic Facilities

The College's modern library has more than 139,000 volumes, more than 950 periodical subscriptions, a wide selection of musical scores and records, and a complete collection of American Enterprise Institute monographs. A learning resources center augments the library. Art department facilities include ten large studios and one of the largest bronze-casting foundries of any college in the country. Students of French and Spanish find a well-equipped language laboratory in the main classroom building. The beautiful and modern Business Building houses all of the business classrooms, including breakout rooms, which are used for smaller discussion groups. There is also a computer lab, which has fifty Pentium (IBM compatible) computers. All of the business faculty and staff offices are conveniently located on the second floor.

Costs

For 2002–03, tuition was $13,850, and room and board were $6400. The College fee is $420 per year. It is estimated that an additional $300 per semester for personal expenses enables students to enjoy a typical campus life.

Financial Aid

Daemen believes that students should be able to choose the college that offers the best range of educational opportunities. They should not have to select one simply because its tuition is lower than another. The College, therefore, makes a conscious effort to award financial assistance based upon academic achievement, academic achievement and financial need, and financial need. Ninety-two percent of all Daemen College students receive financial aid through the New York State Tuition Assistance Program, scholarships and grants, work-study awards, or loans, with the average award totaling about $9600. Daemen College participates in all federal and state financial aid programs and has private sources of scholarship monies to award to eligible students.

Faculty

Class size ranges from about 15 to 25 students, enabling faculty members to get to know the interests and goals of each student. There are 151 full- and part-time faculty members, 98 percent of whom hold terminal degrees.

Student Government

Through the elected Student Governing Board, students are responsible for all nonacademic matters that affect their life at the College. Students serve on advisory committees to the president, the academic dean, and others within the College community.

Admission Requirements

Students applying to Daemen College should have completed four years of college-preparatory studies in secondary school; however, Daemen considers applications from students who have completed only three years and have demonstrated academic strength and social and personal maturity.

Application and Information

For application forms, a catalog, or further information, students should contact:

Patricia Brown
Dean of Enrollment Management
Daemen College
4380 Main Street
Amherst, New York 14226
Telephone: 716-839-8225
800-462-7652 (toll-free)
E-mail: admissions@daemen.edu
World Wide Web: http://www.daemen.edu

While Daemen College is small enough so that all students receive individual attention, it still offers a broad range of programs and facilities.

No person shall, on the basis of sex, race, color, ethnic and national origin, handicap, religion, or age, be denied admission or be subjected to discrimination in admission to Daemen College.

DALLAS CHRISTIAN COLLEGE

DALLAS, TEXAS

The College

Located in the north Dallas suburb of Farmers Branch, Dallas Christian College (DCC) is one of the finest Christian colleges in the area. Graduates of the institution can be found in ministries all across the country and around the globe. Dallas Christian College educates students for Christian leadership in the church, community, and world.

As a Christian college, DCC understands the need for the integration of the Bible into every area of life. All of the courses are taught by professors who have clear biblical principles guiding them both in the classroom and in their personal lives. The College's ultimate goal is to develop Christian leadership in students.

Dallas Christian College is accredited by the Accrediting Association of Bible Colleges (AABC). While the College's primary support base is the Independent Christian Church, DCC is a nondenominational school, with more than a dozen denominations represented in the student body. Dallas Christian College is a small family in a big city. The enrollment is approximately 350 students.

There are a variety of social, athletic, and cultural opportunities available. In terms of intercollegiate sports, Dallas Christian College is a member of the NCCAA. The primary sports offerings are men's and women's basketball, men's soccer, and women's volleyball. There are a variety of intramural opportunities as well. The Student Government offers a number of service and social projects throughout the year.

Campus housing is provided in residence halls built in a suite format. In addition, there is a full-service cafeteria available to all residential and off-campus students.

Students may be involved in many ministry opportunities. Among them are some that are officially recognized by the College. Drama Team is a group of students who travel to church and youth functions with the expressed purpose of teaching the gospel of Jesus Christ through drama. Urban Team is a select group of students who go into the inner city of Dallas and strive for evangelistic excellence and racial harmony. This group of students was recognized by the North American Christian Convention's Urban Task Force as one of the most productive and evangelistic groups in the country. A music group, 4 The One, travels to church and youth functions in order to bring musical presentations.

Location

Farmers Branch, a quiet suburb of Dallas, is close to anything a student might wish to do in the Dallas–Fort Worth metroplex. The campus is just minutes from the downtown cultural district, which includes the Biblical Arts Center, the Meyerson Symphony Center, and the infamous Dallas Book Depository. There are many concerts at Reunion Arena, the Bronco Bowl, and the Dallas Zoo Amphitheater. Major professional sports teams are nearby, including the NFL Dallas Cowboys, the NHL Dallas Stars, the MLB Texas Rangers, the NBA Dallas Mavericks, the PISL Dallas Sidekicks, and the MLS Dallas Burn.

Majors and Degrees

Dallas Christian College's educational programs seek to produce graduates who take leadership in ministry, management, music, and classroom education.

To fulfill institutional goals, the College offers both Bachelor of Arts (B.A.) and Bachelor of Science (B.S.) degrees with double majors. Degrees are offered in Bible and preaching, business administration, Christian education, cross-cultural missions (foreign and urban), general studies, music, psychology, teacher education, worship and youth, and youth and family ministries. Degrees offered in the Adult Continuing Education Program (Quest) are education and ethics, management and ethics, and ministry and leadership. The degree in ministry and leadership is also available online. All degrees reflect the College's conviction that knowledge of Scripture is basic to education. DCC meets the AABC requirements of a balanced curriculum in Bible, general education, practical ministries, and specialized studies.

Academic Programs

Dallas Christian College's academic calendar is based on two semesters, each composed of sixteen weeks of classes, including one week of finals. Courses are offered on a credit-hour basis.

Eighteen credit hours are usually considered the maximum load. To complete a bachelor's degree (130 credit hours) in four years, the student should take 16 to 17 credit hours each semester. A class load of 12 credit hours or more constitutes a full-time load; fewer than 12 credit hours constitute a part-time load, with 7 to 11 credit hours considered a ¾-time load for financial aid purposes. Unless the student's program calls for more than 18 credit hours in a semester, special permission to enroll in additional courses beyond this maximum must be secured through the student's adviser and the Vice President for Academic Affairs. Certain courses in which outside assignments are minimal, such as choir and physical education, require additional class time, labs, or practice time for the credit hours awarded.

Those who must work to help meet college expenses should plan to reduce their credit-hour load. It is recommended that students who work more than 12 hours per week reduce their study load 1 credit hour for each 3 hours of self-support work.

Dallas Christian College welcomes a variety of students of all ages to the campus; many students bring a depth of knowledge to specific subjects. The College recognizes and honors such knowledge by accepting the following examinations through which a student may earn credit: the College-Level Examination Program (CLEP), the Defense Activity for Non-Traditional Education Support (DANTES), and the Advanced Placement (AP) examinations. Assuming that an acceptable grade is attained on an examination, the College grants full degree credit. CLEP, DANTES, and AP credits are accepted for transfer students as well.

Academic Facilities

The C. C. Crawford Memorial Library honors the memory of Dr. Cecil Clement Crawford, who, with Mrs. Helen Crawford, came to Dallas Christian College in August 1967. A popular professor during his years at DCC, Dr. Crawford was an honored scholar, educator, preacher, and writer. Before his death in 1976, Dr. Crawford donated his personal library to the College.

The Crawford Memorial Library contains a computer lab with Internet access and 60 online databases. There are approximately 36,000 volumes, 235 printed subscribed periodicals, 3000 electronic periodicals, and 2,000 audiotapes and videotapes on site. The library can be accessed at http://library.dallas.edu.

Costs

The 2004–05 cost for tuition is $210 per credit hour. Room and board charges are $2200 per semester. All freshmen are required to live on campus and participate in the meal plan unless they are living at home with parents or a legal guardian in the Dallas–Fort Worth metroplex.

Financial Aid

Dallas Christian College provides a financial aid program to assist students who need additional resources to meet their educational costs. Students who qualify may be eligible for institutional scholarships and grants based on their talent in the areas of academics and music or on their financial need. Students may also qualify for assistance through federal grant, work, or loan programs. Students applying for financial aid must file the Free Application for Federal Student Aid (FAFSA) and submit an institutional financial aid form to the Financial Aid Office.

Faculty

Small class sizes are combined with a teaching rather than research faculty to ensure students of personal, high-quality instruction. Most classes have less than 25 students. Sixty percent of full-time faculty members either hold or are completing their doctorates; the student-faculty ratio is 10:1. These elements combined translate into excellent teaching and personal attention. Another advantage of DCC's faculty is that professors are practitioners in their fields—they come with background and experience from the real world, not just from classroom textbooks. This element offers practical, relevant training for students. Faculty members also serve as advisers and mentors to students. They take a sincere and active role in the personal, academic, and spiritual lives of the students.

Student Government

The Student Government (StuGov) of Dallas Christian College represents all registered students. Officers are chosen annually from within the student body and serve through the Student Council. Voicing the concerns and needs of the students to the College administration and providing opportunities for fun and fellowship are at the core of StuGov.

Admission Requirements

Applicants are evaluated on the basis of academic ability, character, and Christian commitment. Those applying are expected to have a high school diploma or the equivalent with a satisfactory grade point average. Students applying as first-time freshmen or those with fewer than 12 transfer credits should submit the Application for Admission, a high school transcript, SAT I or ACT scores, and two letters of recommendation. Students applying for transfer admission should submit the Application for Admission, all college transcripts, and two letters of recommendation.

Home school students are welcome to apply for admission by following the application procedures listed above. A GED diploma may be required of a home school student at the discretion of the Admissions Committee if there is evidence of a discrepancy between the high school transcript and the standardized test scores.

Application and Information

For an application, catalog, or more information, students may contact:

Office of Admissions
Dallas Christian College
2700 Christian Parkway
Dallas, Texas 75234-7299
Telephone: 972-241-3371
800-688-1029 (toll-free)
Fax: 972-241-8021
E-mail: admissions@dallas.edu
World Wide Web: http://www.dallas.edu

DANIEL WEBSTER COLLEGE

NASHUA, NEW HAMPSHIRE

The College

Daniel Webster College (DWC) prepares its students for individual excellence through a commitment to individual attention. The College's innovative curriculums in aviation, business/management, computer science, information systems, social science, sport management, and engineering equip students with the knowledge and skills necessary to become tomorrow's industry leaders.

Daniel Webster College is accredited by the New England Association of Schools and Colleges and is a member of the New Hampshire College and University Council. The College holds Federal Aviation Administration Air Agency Certification PSE 15-21 as an approved pilot school. Courses are operated under Part 141 and Part 61 of the FAA regulations.

There is a diverse student population at Daniel Webster College, with twenty-five states and seventeen countries currently represented. A variety of living options promote comfort and enjoyment. Residential students are housed in five residence halls and in contemporary town house-style apartments on campus. The College Center houses the dining hall, the After Hours Café, the Center for Career Planning and Placement, and the Student Government and Student Life Offices. Movies, musicians, and other special events are held at The Common Thread, which contains a piano, pool tables, and houses a coffee bar. The Mario J. Vagge Gymnasium has facilities for volleyball and basketball, a weight room, and an aerobics facility. There are plenty of extracurricular activities, including the Student Activities Board, the student newspaper and yearbook, the Jazz Band, Theater Group, Film Society, the Professional Pilots Association, a variety of intramural athletics, and other exciting programs. The Leadership Initiative and Student Life Office annually bring nationally renowned speakers and visual performing artists to campus. A rigorous two- and four-year Air Force ROTC program is also available.

Home of the Eagles, Daniel Webster College's men's and women's sports teams compete in the Greater Northeast Athletic Conference at the NCAA Division III level. Men's sports include baseball, basketball, cross-country, lacrosse, and soccer. Women compete in basketball, cross-country, soccer, softball, and volleyball. Ice hockey and skiing are currently available as intercollegiate club sports.

Location

The College is conveniently located in southern New Hampshire in Nashua, the state's second-largest city and twice named "America's Best Place to Live." The city's municipal airport is adjacent to the campus. Nashua is home to a symphony orchestra, theater guild, arts center, and several fine restaurants, shopping areas, and craft centers. Several Fortune 500 companies are nearby, providing employment and internships.

Boston is just 36 miles to the south, and Manchester, New Hampshire, is 20 minutes to the north. Excellent skiing, snowboarding, hiking, and boating and the scenic New Hampshire seacoast are all within an hour's drive.

Majors and Degrees

Daniel Webster College awards Bachelor of Science degrees in aviation/air traffic management, aviation flight operations (professional pilot training), aviation management, business management, computer science, information systems, management and information technology, social science, and sport management.

Associate in Science degrees are awarded in aeronautical engineering, aviation operations, engineering science, general studies, and information systems.

Academic Program

The College operates on a semester system. Courses are designed to provide the highest quality educational opportunities. Independent study, a customized internship program, and advanced-placement programs are available to qualified students. The College is known for its commitment to individual attention.

The College's Aviation Division provides one of the country's most innovative and respected aviation programs and is one of only a few to introduce glider and aerobatic flight into its educational programs. Students can qualify for private single engine, private glider, instrument, commercial, multiengine, and instructor ratings. A student instructor internship is available to qualified juniors and seniors.

Academic Facilities

Daniel Webster Hall houses several classrooms, laboratories, the College Store, and administrative and faculty offices. The 25,000-square-foot Anne Bridge Baddour Library and Learning Center houses the College's extensive library, the Academic Support Center, and computer labs, including a CISCO networking lab. There are also conference and seminar rooms, audiovisual labs, classrooms, and staff offices. The computer facilities include Dual PIII 500 PCs and Rational Apex and Rose software as part of the College's effort and commitment to simulate the professional software engineering environment. The new Eaton-Richmond Center houses faculty offices, multimedia classrooms, and a 350-seat auditorium and features five new, state-of-the-art Windows XP computer labs. The computer facilities include Dual PIII 500 PCs and Rational Apex and Rose software as part of the College's effort and committment to simulate the professional software engineering environment.

The Tamposi Aviation Center is directly adjacent to Nashua Airport, with its 5,500-foot paved and lighted runway and operating control tower. The College's fleet of aircraft includes Cessna 172 Trainers, Grob G109B motorgliders, Mudry CAP-10 aerobatic trainers, Mooney 201 complex aircraft, Piper Arrows, Piper multiengine Seminoles, and Cessna 303 multiengine Crusaders. The Center is fully equipped with a flight dispatch area, classrooms, offices, and a lab with single- and twin-engine Aviation Simulation Technology flight simulators. It is one of the few aviation schools with its own Air Traffic Control simulators.

Costs

Tuition for 2003–04 was $19,600. Residence costs, including room and board, were $7890. Books, supplies, and miscellaneous personal expenses are estimated at $1650. There are some fees associated with flight activities. There are no laboratory fees.

Financial Aid

The College is committed to helping students it deems qualified to make a Daniel Webster College education a reality. It offers more than $3 million annually in institutional funds through a variety of financial assistance programs based on analysis of the Free Application for Federal Student Aid (FAFSA), which can be obtained through high school guidance offices. DWC also offers four-year renewable academic performance scholarships to students exhibiting high academic achievement through high school GPA and other test scores. These scholarships range from $500 to $7500. More than 90 percent of the students at Daniel Webster College receive some form of financial assistance.

In addition to providing aid through its own scholarship and work programs, the College administers both federal and local financial assistance programs. For more information, students should call or write the Director of Financial Assistance at the College.

Faculty

The student-faculty ratio at Daniel Webster College is 12:1. This provides the opportunity for individual attention and instruction, tutoring, and advising. While scholarship is encouraged and applauded, the prime focus of the faculty is quality teaching.

Student Government

The Student Activities Board and Office of Student Life coordinate a wide variety of student activities. Student Government represents students' views and facilitates meaningful dialog between the students and the College administration.

Admission Requirements

A student who has graduated from an accredited high school program will be considered for admission. The SAT I or ACT is required for all students interested in earning a Bachelor of Science degree. Consideration is based on high school performance and a letter of recommendation. Students may be admitted to the September and January semesters. Admission decisions are made without regard to race, color, creed, sex, physical handicap, or national origin.

Although not required for acceptance, a personal admission interview is strongly recommended. A campus visit, including an optional tour by air, provides an important opportunity to gain valuable firsthand knowledge of Daniel Webster College.

Application and Information

The application fee is $35. The College operates on a rolling admission basis, and students are notified of a decision within two weeks after their file is complete. Interested students are urged to arrange a campus visit while the College is in session.

For further information, please contact:

Office of Admissions
Daniel Webster College
20 University Drive
Nashua, New Hampshire 03063-1300
Telephone: 603-577-6600
800-325-6876 (toll-free)
Fax: 603-577-6001
E-mail: admissions@dwc.edu
World Wide Web: http://www.dwc.edu

Daniel Webster College is located in Nashua, New Hampshire—the only city in America twice rated "Number One Place to Live" by *Money* magazine.

DARTMOUTH COLLEGE

HANOVER, NEW HAMPSHIRE

The College

Dartmouth, America's ninth-oldest college, is rich in history and tradition. Founded in 1769 by the Reverend Eleazar Wheelock "for the education . . . of Youth of Indian Tribes, . . . English youth, and others," Dartmouth graduated its first class in 1771. The institution met its greatest challenge in 1819 when Daniel Webster, class of 1801, defended the College against government intervention. This famous dispute, which was finally resolved in the Supreme Court, came to be known as "The Dartmouth College Case." It was Webster's eloquent and convincing oratory that ensured Dartmouth's permanence as a private and independent institution of higher learning. Still appropriately called a college in view of its historic and continuing emphasis on undergraduate education, Dartmouth is actually a small university. Students aspiring to careers in medicine, business, or engineering may find special opportunities at Dartmouth's three professional schools: Dartmouth Medical School, the nation's fourth-oldest school of medicine; the Amos Tuck School of Business Administration, the nation's first graduate school of business administration; and the Thayer School of Engineering, founded more than a century ago.

Undergraduate education provided by an outstanding faculty dedicated to both teaching and research is at the heart of Dartmouth. The College seeks students of outstanding abilities who display curiosity and great intellectual potential and who bring to the community their particular talents and passions. Dartmouth strives for a heterogeneous student body representative of the world's diversity. The College's 4,300 undergraduates represent all fifty states and seventy-three other nations. All first-year students and a majority of upperclass students live in forty dormitories, all within easy walking distance of other College buildings and facilities. College housing is provided for all registered students, and dormitories contain a mixture of all four classes. All first-year students and many upperclass students maintain meal contracts through Dartmouth Dining Services.

Dartmouth offers many extracurricular activities, including more than 250 student organizations. Students participate in theater, music, dance, a daily newspaper, literary publications, student-run AM and FM radio stations, debate, foreign language clubs, service groups, fraternities and sororities, and ethnic, political, and religious organizations. Through the Dartmouth Outing Club, students enjoy bicycling, canoeing, hiking, kayaking, mountaineering, skiing, and other benefits of the North Country. Dartmouth's comprehensive athletics program includes thirty-four men's and women's varsity teams, extensive intramural offerings, and a physical education program.

Location

Set among the rolling hills of Hanover, New Hampshire, the College's beautiful 265-acre campus combines the educational opportunities of one of the nation's most prestigious institutions with an ideal New England setting. While the College itself provides many of the intellectual and cultural advantages usually found only in more urban areas, Dartmouth's proximity to the mountains and rivers of Vermont and New Hampshire allows for a range of outdoor activities. With its 10,000 residents, Hanover provides a comfortable small-town atmosphere for the College community, while the major metropolitan areas of Boston, New York, and Montreal are easily accessible by interstate highways and by regular bus, train, and air service.

Majors and Degrees

Dartmouth College awards a Bachelor of Arts (A.B.) degree in the following areas: African and African-American studies; ancient history; anthropology; art history; Asian and Middle Eastern languages and literatures; Asian studies; biochemistry and molecular biology; biology; biophysical chemistry; chemistry; classical archaeology; classical studies; classics; cognitive science; comparative literature; computer science; drama; earth sciences; economics; engineering physics; engineering sciences; English; English—literature and creative writing; environmental and evolutionary biology; environmental studies; film studies; French; genetics, cell, and developmental biology; geography; German; German studies; government; history; Iberian studies; Italian; Latin American and Caribbean Studies; Latino studies; linguistics; mathematics; mathematics and social sciences; music; Native American studies; philosophy; physics and astronomy; psychological and brain sciences; religion; Romance languages; Russian; Russian area studies; sociology; Spanish language, culture, and society; Spanish literatures; studio art; and women's studies. Interdisciplinary programs in education, Jewish studies, and neurosciences may be used to modify or expand on a departmental major.

Academic Program

All Dartmouth students study a broad spectrum of courses fundamental to higher learning and basic to a liberal arts education. Of the thirty-five courses needed for graduation, students must take ten courses distributed across eight intellectual fields: arts; social analysis; literature; quantitative or deductive science; philosophical, religious, or historical analysis; natural science; technology or applied science; and international or comparative study. In addition, students are required to take three courses in world culture, including the culture, ideas, or institutions of the United States, of Europe, and of at least one non-Western society; and a multidisciplinary or interdisciplinary course. All students must become proficient in at least one foreign language and must also complete a major. Majors typically comprise about one third of a student's total course count. Students of exceptional ability may undertake an honors program in the department of major study.

Dartmouth operates on an innovative year-round calendar, which provides unparalleled opportunities for each student to design a formal educational program closely suited to his or her personal goals. Under the Dartmouth Plan, students develop flexible enrollment patterns involving four 10-week terms in each academic year. Dartmouth students take three courses per term, which encourages more intensive study in each subject and allows enough academic variety for challenge and stimulation. Enrollment patterns may include off-campus study and vacation terms in addition to on-campus study.

Off-Campus Programs

Off-campus study is available in nineteen countries, and more than half of all Dartmouth students participate in at least one off-campus program. These programs are considered vital extensions of the regular Dartmouth curriculum, offering opportunities both to study other cultures and disciplines in depth and to gain new perspectives on American life. The programs are led by members of the Dartmouth faculty, and students earn full academic credit for their participation. Many of these programs also give students a chance to live with an international family. Foreign language programs are offered in Brazil, France, Germany, Greece, Italy, Japan, Mexico, Morocco, the People's Republic of China, Russia, and Spain. Other off-campus academic programs include the study of religion in Scotland; classics in Greece or Italy; geography in the Czech

Republic; government in England or Washington, D.C.; philosophy in Scotland; earth sciences in Mexico; biology in the Caribbean; art history in Florence, Italy; anthropology and linguistics in New Zealand; environmental studies in Zimbabwe; and drama, history, and music in England. Students can also participate in domestic exchanges at Stanford University, Tufts University, Morehouse College, Spelman College, Howard University, the University of California at San Diego, and through the twelve-college consortium.

Academic Facilities

Dartmouth's comprehensive library system includes more than 2.1 million volumes, 170,000 maps, and 2.4 million units of microtext. Collections are housed in Baker/Berry Library and in the eight branch libraries on campus. All libraries operate under a policy of open stacks, giving students direct access to their resources. The faculty members, students, and staff of Dartmouth have a long tradition—spanning nearly fifty years—of envisioning and embracing computing systems and information technologies. Dartmouth's far-reaching computing network touches nearly every activity on campus and allows for wide-ranging access to peers, colleagues, and research associates around the globe. Recently, Dartmouth was named "the most wired" campus in the nation by *Yahoo! Internet Life* magazine, in part because the campus is completely wireless. Personal computers, workstations, and central host systems are well integrated at Dartmouth through the computing network. More than 12,000 network ports provide service to more than 120 buildings on campus. All students are required to own personal computers, and Apple Macintosh computers (the recommended system at Dartmouth) number more than 10,000 at the College, professional schools, and the medical center.

Dartmouth's Hopkins Center for the Creative and Performing Arts offers every student participation in and exposure to a broad range of activities, including theater, dance, music, art, exhibits, films, and lectures. The 480-seat Moore Theater is complemented by the flexible, smaller Warner Bentley Theater. Facilities for curricular music and performing organizations include a 1,000-seat concert hall, four recital halls, twelve practice rooms, an extensive music library, and a multistation listening facility. The Student Workshops are fully equipped for woodworking, metalworking, jewelry making, and pottery. Three facilities have greatly enhanced the College's curricular offerings. Burke Laboratory, the $26-million chemistry facility, houses the most modern equipment and state-of-the-art research technology. The Rockefeller Center for the Social Sciences provides a forum for disciplines concerned with social and political issues. The Hood Museum of Art features additional gallery, classroom, and theater space. Recent construction on campus includes Moore Hall; among other offerings, the 100,000-square-foot facility includes "smart" classrooms and a research-dedicated MRI laboratory. Construction of the new $50-million Berry Library is now complete. This undertaking produced a companion facility to the existing Baker Library and created a new academic hall in the west wing of the Berry Library, which houses the History Department and several high-technology classrooms.

Costs

Expenses for the three-term first year in 2002–03 were as follows: tuition and fees, $27,600; room rent, $4932; board, $3395; and estimated books, fees, and personal expenses, $2267. Travel costs vary.

Financial Aid

Dartmouth is committed to providing students with the financial support necessary to enable their attendance. The College wishes to be accessible to the broadest range of students possible such that attendance is based upon an individual's talents and accomplishments, not the ability to pay. For many years, Dartmouth has operated with a need-blind admissions policy, which ensures that admissions decisions are made without regard to the financial circumstances of applicants. Furthermore, the College has guaranteed that 100 percent of an admitted student's demonstrated financial need is met for all four years of enrollment. Currently, 46 percent of the student body receives scholarship assistance, totaling more than $34 million, with an average financial aid package of approximately $22,800 per aid recipient.

Faculty

As an institution devoted to undergraduate education, Dartmouth prides itself on the fact that all senior faculty members teach introductory courses as well as more specialized offerings. For example, all entering first-year students participate in the First Year Seminar Program, which is designed to provide them with experience in independent research and small-group discussion, under the direction of an experienced faculty member.

Student Government

The Student Assembly, Dartmouth's student government, is broadly representative; its membership is drawn from all four classes. Students may also be elected to their respective Class Councils and are eligible for membership on several College-wide committees that have direct bearing upon student concerns, for example, the Trustee Committee on Student Affairs, the Committee on Standing, the Committee on the Freshman Year, and the Council on Budgets and Priorities.

Admission Requirements

Admission to Dartmouth is selective and highly competitive; approximately 12,000 candidates applied for 1,075 places in the entering class last year. Although there are no inflexible subject requirements for admission, candidates are urged to undertake the strongest program of preparation available at their secondary school. Evidence of intellectual capacity, motivation, personal integrity, and involvement in nonacademic areas are all of primary importance. Dartmouth requires all applicants, including all international citizens, to take three SAT II Subject Tests and either the SAT I or the ACT. All tests must be taken no later than January of the senior year in high school. An optional part of the admission process is the interview. All high school seniors are welcome to call the Admissions Office to arrange an on-campus interview during their visit to Dartmouth. In addition, most students will have the opportunity to interview with graduates of the College. Group Information Sessions, conducted by admission officers, are offered weekdays January through November on a walk-in basis. Student-guided campus tours are available Monday through Saturday throughout the year.

Application and Information

Under Dartmouth's application procedures, new students are enrolled only at the opening of college in September of each year. Applications may be filed up to January 1 of the calendar year in which the candidate expects to enter college. Admission decisions are announced in mid-April; candidates normally must respond to offers of admission by May 1. Candidates who definitely plan to attend Dartmouth if admitted may request an early decision on their applications, and such requests must be filed by November 1. By mid-December, early decision candidates are notified that they have been accepted, denied, or that a final decision has been deferred until mid-April. Requests for additional information and application forms should be addressed to:

Admissions Office
6016 McNutt Hall
Dartmouth College
Hanover, New Hampshire 03755

Telephone: 603-646-2875
E-mail: admissions.office@dartmouth.edu
World Wide Web: http://www.dartmouth.edu

DAVIDSON COLLEGE

DAVIDSON, NORTH CAROLINA

The College

Founded in 1837, Davidson College consistently ranks as one of the most competitive liberal arts and sciences colleges in the United States. Davidson's student body is made up of 1,600 students from forty-six states and twenty-eight other countries, chosen not only for their academic promise but also for their character and leadership.

The liberal arts curriculum at Davidson is designed to give students knowledge and skills that they can put to use throughout their lives. Davidson offers more than 850 courses in twenty major fields and in special interdisciplinary programs. Students benefit from the careful attention of 162 full-time faculty members who are dedicated to teaching and guiding undergraduates. Close relationships between faculty members and students are a hallmark of the Davidson experience.

The Honor System serves as a foundation for life at Davidson. The Honor Code represents a declaration by the entire College community—students, faculty and staff members, and alumni—that an honorable course is the most just and, therefore, the best.

Student life at Davidson is active and varied. Davidson students participate in a wide range of organizations of special interest and attend cultural and social events offered on campus. From student government to Amnesty International, from the United Community Action service organization to the Black Student Coalition, Davidson's more than fifty campus organizations provide students with opportunities to develop leadership skills, share their talents, and explore new interests. As one of the only colleges of its size in the nation competing in Division I of the NCAA, Davidson supports true scholar-athletes in twenty-one varsity sports. Approximately 25 percent of the student body play on varsity teams and 80 percent participate in intramural and club sports.

Opened in 2001, Davidson's Knobloch Campus Center houses, among other facilities, a fitness center, a 25-foot climbing wall, an amphitheater, a performance hall, a bookstore, a café, a post office, and offices for student organizations.

Location

Davidson's 450-acre campus is located in Davidson, North Carolina. Davidson students tutor children at the area elementary school, build houses for Davidson's chapter of Habitat for Humanity, bike and jog throughout the residential neighborhoods, or gather with friends at the local coffee house. Davidson owns 106 acres of waterfront property on Lake Norman, the largest lake in North Carolina, where students participate in a variety of water sports.

Charlotte, one of America's fastest-growing cities, the nation's second-largest banking center, and home to nearly 400 multinational corporations, is located 19 miles south of Davidson. From community service to internships, from cultural events to professional sports teams, Davidson students draw on Charlotte's advantages.

Majors and Degrees

Davidson grants the Bachelor of Arts and the Bachelor of Science degrees in twenty major fields: anthropology, art, biology, chemistry, classical studies, economics, English, French, German, history, mathematics, music, philosophy, physics, political science, psychology, religion, sociology, Spanish, and theater. Minors are available in anthropology, chemistry, economics, French, German, music, philosophy, Russian, Spanish, and theater. Students may double major or choose to complement their majors with an interdisciplinary concentration in applied mathematics, Asian studies, computer science, ethnic studies, gender studies, international studies, medical humanities, neuroscience, or Southern studies. Each year a number of students choose to design their own majors through Davidson's Center for Interdisciplinary Studies. Recent self-designed majors have included visual communications, bioethics, peace studies, and environmental economics.

Academic Program

The liberal arts curriculum at Davidson gives students a broad-based and rich education, exposing them to many different academic areas. Davidson requires a total of thirty-two courses to graduate. Through the required core curriculum, every Davidson student takes courses in six areas: the fine arts, natural sciences and mathematics, philosophy and religion, literature, history, and the social sciences. Additional courses are taken in composition, foreign language, cultural diversity, and physical education. In addition to the core curriculum, students choose a major by the end of their sophomore year. A major normally requires up to twelve courses, including at least five upper-level courses. The academic year at Davidson consists of two 15-week semesters. Notably, 90 percent of those who enroll at Davidson graduate within four academic years.

Off-Campus Programs

Davidson supports a vigorous program of international education and opportunity for all students. More than half of all Davidson students take part in off-campus study for a summer, a semester, or an academic year. Options include study abroad in England, France, Germany, Ghana, India, Italy, Mexico, Nepal, Spain, the former Soviet Union, and the Mediterranean region; internship programs in Washington, D.C., and Philadelphia; environmental research with the School for Field Studies in the Virgin Islands, Australia, or Kenya; Biosphere 2 Center in Phoenix, Arizona; marine biology off the coast of North Carolina; psychology study at Broughton Hospital in Morganton, North Carolina; exchange programs with Morehouse College and Howard University; and independently arranged programs elsewhere. Davidson's Dean Rusk International Studies Program provides grants each year to help encourage students to explore their international interests.

In addition to off-campus study programs, the Office of Career Planning and Placement helps students find internships in Charlotte and worldwide. Recent internship sites include the Carolinas Medical Center, the *Charlotte Observer*, Bank of America, the Philadelphia Museum of Art, and the Overseas Private Investment Corporation in Washington, D.C.

Academic Facilities

Davidson's campus features seventy-five academic and residential buildings. Chambers Building, the 1929 central academic building, is currently undergoing a complete renovation. The E. H. Little Library houses nearly 500,000 volumes, all listed in the online catalog, plus access to more than 5,000 journals and databases online. The new Baker-Watt Science Complex includes the 32,000-square-foot Watson Life Sciences building (with state-of-the-art biology and psychology laboratories) and the Dana Laboratories (housing physics and additional biology laboratories). A 7,000-volume chemistry library, laboratories, and classrooms may be found in the Martin Chemical Laboratories. The Belk Visual Arts Center contains two galleries, a computerized slide library, a lecture hall, and studios for sculpting, painting, and drawing. The Duke Family Performance Hall, completed in 2002, provides professional-caliber space for all performing arts. Sloan Music Building, renovated in 2002, provides performance, class, and rehearsal space as well as an extensive library and electronic studio. Cunningham Fine Arts Building houses performance and rehearsal space, a scene shop, and a script library. The campus computer network provides 100-megabit wired access from all campus locations and ample wireless hot zones on campus. All residence halls provide network and telephone ports for each student. More than 160 Windows and Macintosh computers are publicly available to students on the campus.

Costs

Required student charges (tuition, student activity fee, and laundry) for the 2003–04 academic year were $25,903. A room cost $3892, and full board cost $3479.

Financial Aid

Admission decisions are made without regard to a student's financial need. Through a combination of state, federal, and private sources, Davidson administers in excess of $20 million in student financial assistance. The instructions for applying for need-based aid are included with Davidson's application for admission. Students with financial need are assisted through a combination of Davidson scholarships, federal and state grants, loans, and work-study.

Davidson awards merit scholarships to approximately 15 percent of each entering first-year class. These awards recognize students' academic promise, special talents, and personal qualities. Recipients are selected based on the strength of their admission application. For some scholarships, selection may also be based on the outcome of an audition, interview, portfolio review, or writing sample. Merit scholarships range from $2500 to the comprehensive fee and include the following top awards: the Thomas S. and Sarah B. Baker Scholarship (four awarded, comprehensive fee), the John Montgomery Belk Scholarship (six to ten awarded to students from the southeastern U.S., comprehensive fee), the William Holt Terry Scholarship (two awarded to students with exceptional leadership qualities, full tuition), the Bryan Scholarship (two awarded to students who contribute in a superlative manner to their sport as well as to the academic and cocurricular life at Davidson), and the Missy and John Kuykendall Scholarship (three awarded to students who provide service leadership).

Faculty

Davidson's 162 full-time faculty members choose to teach at Davidson because they gain their greatest professional satisfaction from working with undergraduates. All classes are taught by full professors, and 100 percent of faculty members have a Ph.D. With a student-faculty ratio of 10:1, classes are small (the average class size is 13 students), and individual attention is the norm. Professors' ongoing involvement with students takes many forms: encouraging lively class discussion, including students in their research projects, inviting students to their homes for dinner, and participating in many facets of student life outside of the classroom. Each student is assigned a faculty adviser who provides guidance on academic choices throughout the student's four years.

Student Government

Davidson students have the opportunity to develop valuable interpersonal skills through leadership roles in the Student Government Association, the College Union, the Honor Council, United Community Action, and many special interest organizations. The Honor System governs Davidson's social and academic life, demanding the highest personal and community values and engendering an atmosphere of openness, mutual trust, and integrity among the entire Davidson community.

Admission Requirements

Davidson seeks students of outstanding academic ability and strong character who show promise of leadership. To be considered for admission, a student must have completed at least 16 high school academic units, including 4 units of English, 2 units of intermediate mathematics, 1 unit of plane geometry, 2 units of the same foreign language, and 1 unit of history. Electives should include 3 or 4 years of science and additional courses in mathematics, history, and the same foreign language. In addition to the SAT I or the ACT, the Davidson application requires three essay responses, an official transcript, and recommendations from two teachers, a peer, and a high school counselor. SAT II Subject Tests are recommended but not required. Davidson accepts the Common Application along with required supplemental information.

Admission to Davidson is highly selective. The selection process is composed of three major elements: the evaluation of academic performance and potential, the assessment of individual characteristics, and the recognition of outstanding interests, achievements, and activities. These three elements are used to gain an understanding of each student's academic and personal strengths and give an overall impression of the individual's eligibility for admission. As a college that welcomes students, faculty members, and staff members from a variety of nationalities, ethnic groups, and traditions, Davidson seeks students who are likely to bring diverse and unique talents and strengths to the College community.

Application and Information

Early decision—round one—has an application deadline of November 15 with notification by December 15. Early decision—round two—has an application deadline of January 2 with notification by February 1. Regular decision has an application deadline of January 2 with notification by April 1. Students are encouraged to visit Davidson for a campus tour and an information session with a member of the Admission Office staff. For additional information about Davidson, students should contact:

Nancy J. Cable, Ph.D.
Vice President and Dean of Admission and Financial Aid
Davidson College
Box 7156
Davidson, North Carolina 28035-7156
Telephone: 704-894-2230
800-768-0380 (toll-free)
E-mail: admission@davidson.edu
World Wide Web: http://www.davidson.edu

Members of the class of 2001 in front of Chambers, Davidson's signature academic building.

DAVIS & ELKINS COLLEGE

ELKINS, WEST VIRGINIA

The College

A comprehensive liberal arts and sciences education is the hallmark of Davis & Elkins College. Educational programs range from the highly professional, in nursing and teaching, to the innovative, in hospitality management and tourism management, to the traditional, in the liberal arts and sciences.

There are two fraternities and one sorority active on campus and a wide variety of extracurricular organizations, including the concert choir, jazz choir, radio station, theater, newspaper, and literary magazine.

An extensive schedule of intramural and club athletics is offered for men and women in addition to a sound program of varsity sports. Intercollegiate athletics for women include basketball, cross-country, soccer, softball, tennis, and volleyball. Teams for men include baseball, basketball, cross-country, golf, soccer, and tennis. The College holds membership in the NCAA Division II and WVIAC. A USCS coed ski team is also available.

Location

The College is located in Elkins, West Virginia, rated among the top thirty small towns in America. Elkins is situated at the entrance to the Monongahela National Forest in the center of one of the nation's most prosperous and fastest-growing outdoor recreation areas. Three nearby resorts provide a variety of recreational opportunities, including camping, golfing, hiking, fishing, tennis, and cross-country and downhill skiing.

Majors and Degrees

Davis & Elkins College offers programs of study leading to bachelor's degrees in accounting, art, art education, biology, chemistry, communication, computer science, elementary education, English, environmental science, exercise science, health education, history, hospitality and tourism management, management, management information systems, marketing, mathematics, music, nursing, physical education, political science, psychology and human services, recreation management and tourism, religion and philosophy, religious education, secondary education, sociology, Spanish, sports management, theater arts, and theater education.

Preprofessional programs prepare students for admission to schools of medicine, veterinary science, dentistry, forestry, church ministry, pharmacy, and law. An additional area of study is available in forestry (3-2 bachelor's-master's programs offered by special arrangement with the State University of New York College of Environmental Science and Forestry at Syracuse).

Associate degrees are available in accounting, computer business systems, marketing, and nursing.

Academic Program

Davis & Elkins College emphasizes a strong liberal arts and sciences foundation for all students. The Contract Degree Program provides opportunities to design individual programs of study under close faculty supervision. An honors program challenges the more advanced students. The William James Career, Academic and Personal Services (CAPS) Center provides academic, personal, and career support for all students. Included in the CAPS Center is the Supported Learning Program to support Davis & Elkins students with documented specific learning disabilities.

Off-Campus Programs

Off-campus and independent experiences include cultural studies of the Caribbean, England, Italy, Scotland, and Spain; marine biology courses in Florida; and internships and practicums at several sites throughout Maryland, New Jersey, New York, Pennsylvania, Virginia, West Virginia, and Washington, D.C.

Academic Facilities

An arts center/auditorium complex has a 1,300-seat auditorium for concerts, plays, and other cultural events. The complex also houses the music, art, and theater departments, a swimming pool, and the fitness center. A science center accommodates the business and natural science divisions. The center also contains a planetarium, rooftop greenhouse, computer center, and several microcomputer laboratories. The Booth Library opened in 1992 with a capacity of 300,000 volumes. The library includes a fully equipped media center with computer capabilities and an online computer catalog. One-day calls for materials can be made to three other Mountain State Association of Colleges libraries. Students may also use the resources of the West Virginia University library in Morgantown, West Virginia.

Costs

The comprehensive tuition and fees charge for 2003–04 is $14,668, and room and board costs are $5926. The tuition and fees cover the full cost of student publications, health service, laboratory classes, the Student Union, and athletic contests.

Financial Aid

Scholarships, grants, loans, and campus employment are offered to help students meet financial obligations; a student may be given one award or a combination of several awards. Most financial aid is based on need, but academic, honors, athletic, and performance scholarships are also available; 85 percent of the student body receives some form of financial assistance. Students applying for financial assistance should complete the Free Application for Federal Student Aid before March 1. Forms may be obtained from the Office of Financial Planning.

Faculty

The College has 45 full-time faculty members, of whom 77 percent hold terminal degrees. They include distinguished Fulbright scholars, authors, and lecturers. A student-faculty ratio of 12:1 provides students with ongoing opportunities to interact with instructors on a personal level.

Student Government

Davis & Elkins recognizes through its special governance system the value of student involvement in developing the academic and social policies of the College. Students work alongside members of the faculty and administration in planning and deciding policies in all basic areas of decision making (with the exception of finances) that affect students. Students participating in this process are elected to the Student Assembly by their classmates.

Admission Requirements

Davis & Elkins College seeks to enroll students with academic and personal qualities that indicate potential for intellectual, social, and spiritual growth. A basic premise of the admissions policy is that all applicants are reviewed individually to determine if they are capable of successfully meeting their responsibilities as a Davis & Elkins student and benefiting from the personalized educational experience the College provides. The Enrollment Management Committee establishes guidelines for admission that reflect the College's desire to identify academically capable students who demonstrate potential for further achievement; who are active at school and in the community, with a record of service; and who represent diverse cultures and backgrounds. Freshman applicants are required to submit scores from either the ACT or SAT I and an official high school transcript that demonstrates a solid preparation for college-level work. Transfer applicants are also required to submit official transcripts from all colleges and universities attended.

Davis & Elkins admits students regardless of race, color, sex, handicap, religious affiliation, or national or ethnic origin.

Application and Information

Along with the College application form, prospective students must submit a complete transcript of college-preparatory studies. SAT I or ACT scores are also required. In addition to regular freshman admission, early and deferred admission plans are available. Transfers may be admitted during both the August and January terms. They must have maintained a minimum overall average of C at all colleges attended and must submit satisfactory personal credentials.

Davis & Elkins follows a system of rolling admission (not applicable to international student applicants). Candidates whose files are completed during the early part of their senior year receive decisions first. Financial aid candidates are requested to complete the application process as early in the calendar year as possible. Admitted students have until May 1 or two weeks after admission (whichever is later) to present the required advance payment deposit that holds their place in the entering freshman class.

For further information, students should contact:

Office of Admissions
Davis & Elkins College
100 Campus Drive
Elkins, West Virginia 26241-3996
Telephone: 304-637-1230
800-624-3157 (toll-free)
E-mail: admiss@dne.edu
World Wide Web: http://www.davisandelkins.edu

Davis & Elkins College: giving you a competitive edge.

DEFIANCE COLLEGE

DEFIANCE, OHIO

The College

Defiance College (DC), founded in 1850, is a private liberal arts college related to the United Church of Christ, serving approximately 1,000 students. The College celebrated its sesquicentennial in 2000.

Defiance College is one of only 100 colleges and universities nationwide to be named to the Templeton Foundation's Honor Roll for Character-Building Colleges. DC was recently named as one of the top service learning colleges in the nation by the *U.S. News & World Report's America's Best Colleges*. Defiance is accredited by the North Central Association of Colleges and Schools and the Council on Social Work Education.

The College's beautiful campus is located on 150 acres in a residential area of Defiance, Ohio, a short walk from the center of the city. Many of the College's students are from Ohio, with the remaining students representing several states and countries. Fifty-three percent of the College's full-time students live on campus.

Student life is an important part of a Defiance College education. Activities include Greek social organizations; student government; musical and religious groups; theater; the student newspaper, yearbook, multicultural organizations, and service learning activities; honor societies; special interest groups; and intramural athletics. Defiance College is a member of the NCAA at the Division III level. A member of the Heartland Athletic Conference (HCAC), Defiance competes in men's and women's basketball, cross-country, golf, indoor and outdoor track and field, soccer, tennis, and volleyball as well as women's softball and men's baseball and football. The new Smart Fitness Center opened in February 2004.

In addition to bachelor's and associate degrees, Defiance College awards master's degrees in teacher education, business (organizational leadership), and criminal justice.

As a national leader in the field of service learning, DC strives to prepare its graduates not only for the world of work, but also to be active participants in their communities. Students are asked to commit to community service projects throughout the region; many of the students' experiences are tied directly to their major fields of study.

Location

Situated at the historic confluence of the Auglaize and Maumee Rivers, the city of Defiance has a population of about 18,000. Highly diversified industry and some of the richest farmland in the nation contribute to the area's prosperity. Defiance offers excellent shopping and a wholesome living environment. The city is served by daily bus transportation from the Greyhound Bus Lines (Detroit-Toledo-Fort Wayne-Indianapolis). Amtrak service is available into nearby Bryan, Ohio. The metropolitan centers of Toledo and Fort Wayne are approximately 55 miles away. Detroit, Michigan, is 2 hours away by car, and Chicago is a 4-hour drive from the campus. The College is located near the north city limits on Highway 66 just south of U.S. 24.

Majors and Degrees

Defiance College awards bachelor's degrees in forty majors and associate degrees in art, business administration, criminal justice, information technology, and religious education. Areas of study include accounting, art, arts and humanities, athletic training education, biology, business administration, chemistry, Christian education, communication arts, criminal justice, education, environmental science, finance, forensic science, graphic design, history, human resource management, information technology, management, marketing, mathematics, medical technology, multimedia communication, natural science, physical education, psychology, restoration ecology, religious studies and design for leadership, social work, sport management, and wellness/corporate fitness. A self-designed major is also an option. Also offered are preprofessional programs in dentistry, law, medicine, veterinary science, and seminary.

Special programs include Freshman Seminar, interdisciplinary studies, cooperative education, internships, field experience, and teaching certification. Recreation and economics are offered as minors only.

Academic Program

Defiance College operates on a semester calendar, consisting of two 16-week semesters. The fall semester runs from late August to mid-December; the spring semester runs from early January to early May. During the fall and spring semesters, students normally take four or five courses, totaling approximately 15 credits. Three 5-week summer sessions are offered. A minimum of 120 semester credits is required for a bachelor's degree; 60 semester credits are required for an associate degree.

Defiance College's academic experience includes studies in a major field as well as broad-based studies in the liberal arts. Studies in a major field allow an individual to achieve a level of competence in an area of interest, while studies in the liberal arts broaden the individual's understanding of the world. Core courses are required, and community service is incorporated into the curriculum for all students.

Academic Facilities

Completed in 1993, the College's state-of-the-art Pilgrim Library has shelving for 130,000 volumes and 550 current periodicals, as well as seating for 200 readers. The 30,000-square-foot facility also offers a public access computer lab and an advanced electronic library.

The Carma J. Rowe Science Hall, constructed in 1987, houses laboratories and classrooms. In February 1999, Rowe gained a new science and math computer laboratory. New computer labs have been constructed in Defiance Hall. The McMaster Center, completed in 1988, provides physical education and recreation facilities.

The Justin F. Coressel stadium, dedicated in 1994, features a 5,000-seat football stadium and an eight-lane all-weather track. Training facilities, meeting areas, and locker rooms are available on site.

The Hubbard Hall/McCann Student Activities Center opened in 1996. It features the campus bookstore, a fitness center, a dance room, a snack bar, offices, and meeting rooms.

The new student union, the Serrick Campus Center, was completed in spring 2000 and includes the campus dining complex, admissions and financial aid offices, the registration center, the student health center, and a distance learning classroom as well as banquet and conference spaces. A new coed apartment-style residence hall opened in fall 2001.

Costs

Tuition for the 2004–05 academic year is $17,780. Room and board have been set at $5590. There is an additional fee of $525 for the year to help cover student activity fees, technology fees, and a one-time residential fee. A student's personal expenses, including books and travel to and from the campus, average $1300 per year.

Financial Aid

Defiance College is committed to helping students invest in their future by providing scholarships, grants, loans, and work opportunities. Scholarship eligibility is based upon academic achievements in high school for freshmen and in college for transfer students. The Presidential Service Leadership Award recognizes students with a history of volunteer service. Some financial aid awards are made solely on the basis of merit (academic performance), some are awarded on the basis of financial need, and others are based on both merit and need. Approximately 80 percent of the College's students receive some form of financial assistance, which significantly reduces the cost of tuition and fees. The average financial aid package for an incoming full-time freshman is $17,460, including scholarships, grants, student loans, parent loans, and work eligibility.

Students requesting aid are required to submit the Free Application for Federal Student Aid (FAFSA). Although there is no application deadline, financial aid dollars are awarded on a first-come, first-served basis, so prospective students should file the aid applications as early as possible. DC's Title IV Federal School code is 003041.

Faculty

The 13:1 student-faculty ratio at Defiance College ensures close working relationships between students and faculty members. All of the students at Defiance, from freshmen through seniors, benefit from the faculty's expertise and experience. The College has 43 full-time and 44 part-time faculty members.

Student Government

Student government at Defiance College consists of the Student Senate and the Campus Activities Board. The Student Senate oversees the College's student organizations, while the Campus Activities Board plans and coordinates campuswide events.

Admission Requirements

Defiance College admits students without regard to sex, race, creed, age, national or ethnic origin, color, or disability. Applications are evaluated on an individual basis. Students must be high school graduates or hold an equivalency diploma. Preference will be given to students with a minimum 2.25 GPA and a score of 18 or higher on the ACT or 850 or higher on the SAT I. Other criteria considered are college-preparatory course work, extracurricular activities, the essay, letters of recommendation, and a personal interview. Transfer students will be considered according to their performance at the previous institution they attended. A combined GPA of 2.0 or higher is necessary to be admitted in good standing.

Application and Information

Applications are reviewed on a rolling basis; therefore, students will be notified of a decision approximately one week after all necessary material is received by the admissions office. Students may apply after completing six semesters of high school. A $25 nonrefundable application fee should accompany the application.

To obtain an application or to receive more information about Defiance College, students should contact:

Admissions Office
Defiance College
701 North Clinton Street
Defiance, Ohio 43512
Telephone: 419-783-2359
800-520-GODC(4632) (toll-free)
Fax: 419-783-2468
E-mail: admissions@defiance.edu
World Wide Web: http://www.defiance.edu

Students enjoy an afternoon with friends on the campus of Defiance College.

DELAWARE VALLEY COLLEGE

DOYLESTOWN, PENNSYLVANIA

The College

Founded in 1896, Delaware Valley College (DVC) is a private, coeducational four-year college enrolling approximately 1,350 full-time students. Over the years, the College has concentrated on producing graduates who can fill employers' needs. Today, DVC's curriculum has expanded to include a broad range of programs in agriculture, business, science, education, and liberal arts.

Students attend Delaware Valley College, first and foremost, to prepare themselves for a professional career. The placement record of Delaware Valley College graduates is outstanding, proving that the time-honored educational philosophy of "scholarship with applied experience" works. An extremely high proportion of graduates find employment in their major field of study or enter graduate school within six months of graduation.

In addition to its academic programs, the College offers a wide range of extracurricular activities and events. A total of thirty-three special interest organizations exist, many of which are linked with a specific major. Student publications include the weekly *RamPages* (newspaper), the *Cornucopia* (yearbook), and the *Gleaner* (literary magazine). The College band and chorale give students the chance to demonstrate their musical talents. There are active minority and international clubs on campus. The DVC Volunteer Corps lines up opportunities for student service to the community in a variety of settings relevant to the student's academic major. A-Day, the student-run campuswide fair, annually attracts 50,000 visitors who enjoy the festival, the entertainment, and the academically oriented projects. Such projects as livestock judging, plant sales, chemistry magic shows, computer-aided design demonstrations, a model rain forest habitat, and equestrian events all demonstrate the expertise of DVC students.

Seventy percent of students live on campus in twelve residence halls. A full range of intercollegiate and intramural athletics programs (NCAA Division III, ECAC, and MAC) for both women and men is offered. All elements of the College's educational and recreational programs are in place to develop students as open-minded professionals who are capable of expanding their horizons in a future of unlimited possibilities.

On the graduate level, Delaware Valley College offers a Master in Business Administration degree program jointly with La Salle University.

Location

The College is located in historic Bucks County, Pennsylvania, approximately 30 miles north of Philadelphia and 70 miles southwest of New York City. Bucks County is one of the fastest-growing areas in the United States, yet it maintains its rich historical and agricultural heritage. The central Bucks County area is also rich in libraries, institutions of higher education, museums, and additional cultural resources, further enhancing the educational opportunities of Delaware Valley College students. The Pennsylvania and New Jersey turnpikes provide quick access to the College. A commuter railway system links the College with Philadelphia, providing daily scheduled arrivals and departures. The College enjoys a mutually beneficial relationship with its surrounding community. Many students find convenient employment opportunities with local businesses, and the community benefits from the many events and activities that are held on campus.

Majors and Degrees

Delaware Valley College awards Bachelor of Science degrees in agribusiness, agronomy and environmental science, animal science, biochemistry, biology, chemistry, business administration, criminal justice, dairy science, environmental design, food science and management, horticulture, information technology and management, ornamental horticulture, and secondary education. A Bachelor of Arts degree is awarded in English. Within the degree programs, students are given the opportunity to focus their attention on a number of options, minors, and specializations, such as accounting, biotechnology, business management, computer information systems, ecological landscape design, ecology, equine science and management, equine studies, floriculture, food service systems management, food technology, landscape contracting and management, marketing, microbiology, plant biology, small animal science, sports management, and turfgrass management.

DVC also offers preprofessional preparation in dentistry, law, medicine, optometry, and veterinary medicine.

Academic Program

All courses are taught from a liberal arts perspective, which broadens the students' appreciation of their cultural heritage. The College is committed to producing graduates who are not only technically competent but also skilled in the use of language, mathematics, and computers. The entire academic program is designed to contribute to the total educational growth of the student and provides him or her with the opportunity to participate in special methods and techniques courses that coordinate theory with practice. The College stresses a practical, hands-on approach to learning. The curriculum includes a required 24-week Employment Program through which students gain practical work experience in their field while still in college. The Employment Program provides valuable entries on student resumes as it builds meaningful skills.

The academic calendar consists of two 15-week semesters, a January term, and two 6-week summer sessions.

Academic Facilities

Many of the courses taught at Delaware Valley College are laboratory or field oriented. Facilities include many lecture rooms, laboratories containing the most up-to-date equipment, and approximately 550 acres of cultivated and forested lands, which offer a variety of field laboratory situations. In addition, the recently acquired 174-acre Roth Farm is being developed and maintained with the help of students and various DVC departments as a "working history farm" to demonstrate agricultural and food production practices from the 1890–1910 era.

Delaware Valley College students benefit from the low student-laboratory ratio. This enables ready access to equipment, which is imperative to learning. Specifically, the College utilizes biology, chemistry, physics, plant science, and animal science laboratories. Facilities include a tissue culture laboratory, a food processing plant, a greenhouse-laboratory complex, a dairy, a small-animal science center, equine breeding barns, and an indoor equestrian center. The campus is itself a recognized arboretum managed by students and faculty members. These facilities are all supported by the Krauskopf Memorial Library, which houses some 80,000 publications.

Costs

For 2002–03, tuition and fees were $17,680, room was $3030, and board was $3550 for a twenty-one-meal plan.

Financial Aid

The College is committed to providing financial assistance so that every student is able to meet the costs of obtaining a college education. DVC offers to students of academic promise faculty scholarships and faculty grants. It participates with the federal government in the Federal Pell Grant Program, the Federal Supplemental Educational Opportunity Grant Program, the Federal Perkins Loan Program, and the Federal Work-Study Program. More than 90 percent of the College's total student body receives some type of financial aid; the average award package totaled $14,400 for 2002–03.

Faculty

All courses at Delaware Valley College are taught by faculty members who combine professional expertise with deep theoretical knowledge and are devoted to the teaching profession. Courses are never taught by graduate students. The faculty numbers approximately 80 instructors, who are friendly and accessible and always ready to help individual students make the most of the educational opportunities offered by the College. The teacher-student ratio is 1:16.

Student Government

Students are encouraged to make the most of extracurricular activities to ensure that their education includes as many different experiences as possible. The student government acts to coordinate the activities of all organizations on campus and sponsors a variety of mixers, movies, concerts, and speakers.

Admission Requirements

In reviewing applications for admission, the College takes into consideration the quality of a student's high school work, scores on the SAT I or ACT, class rank, the guidance counselor's recommendation, and the level of a student's motivation, as determined by extracurricular activities. A personal interview is recommended.

Application and Information

For more information about Delaware Valley College and its academic, athletic, and financial aid programs, the student should contact:

Office of Admissions
Delaware Valley College
700 East Butler Avenue
Doylestown, Pennsylvania 18901-2697
Telephone: 215-489-2311
800-2DELVAL (toll-free)
Fax: 215-230-2968
E-mail: admitme@devalcol.edu
World Wide Web: http://www.devalcol.edu

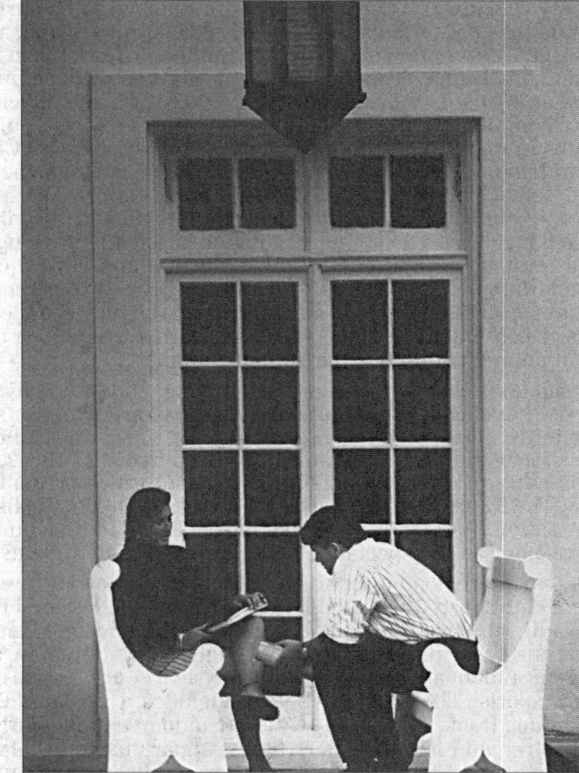

Students relaxing in front of Lasker Hall.

DENISON UNIVERSITY
GRANVILLE, OHIO

The University

Denison is a private, four-year, residential liberal arts university that provides a rigorous and challenging education while preparing students for lives of leadership and service. The University dates back to 1831, when the Ohio Baptist Education Society established the Granville Literary and Theological Institution. The University was given its present name and moved to its current location in the 1850s. Denison has nearly 26,000 alumni and, as of June 30, 2003, an endowment of $425 million. The Denison Annual Fund received a record $4 million through gifts from alumni, parents, and friends during fiscal year 2002–03. The University has just completed a $60-million construction project, its most ambitious in more than a quarter century. A 2-acre, grassy Campus Common is framed by two new buildings, the state-of-the-art Samson Talbot Hall of Biological Science and the Burton D. Morgan Center for student, faculty, and alumni-related activities. Denison has achieved a national reputation based upon its lengthy cultural heritage, the vitality of its intellectual and ethical concerns, and the performance of its graduates. Extensive personal, career and professional school counseling is available to students. Fifty-three percent of Denison's graduates earn a graduate or professional degree within ten years after graduation.

As a residential college, Denison requires its students to live in University housing all four years and offers a variety of housing options in its thirty-four halls. A full slate of social and cultural events is scheduled each semester. Forty percent of the 2,117 students join the different fraternities and sororities present on campus. The Denison International Student Association, the Black Student Union, the Asian American Association, and La Fuerza Latina respond to the special needs of multicultural students.

Twenty-two intercollegiate sports for men and women and a wide variety of club sports are available. The $7.2-million Mitchell Recreation and Athletics Center and the Physical Education Center serve as the focal point for intercollegiate sports for men and women, all student athletic recreation, physical education classes, and club sports. The Mitchell Center includes a six-lane, 200-meter indoor track, four state-of-the-art indoor tennis courts, a spacious strength room, a modern fitness apparatus room, a large multipurpose and aerobics room, and international squash courts. The Physical Education Center is home to the Alumni Memorial Field House with its recreational track and three hardwood basketball/volleyball courts; Livingston Gym, home of varsity basketball and volleyball with seating for 3,000; Gregory Pool, a six-lane, 25-yard competition and recreation facility; and five racquetball/handball courts. More than 75 percent of Denison students participate in athletics or recreational activities and DU's varsity teams have collected six consecutive North Coast Athletic Conference All-Sports titles since 1998.

Location

The 1,200-acre Denison campus is located on a ridge overlooking the village of Granville, in central Ohio. Founded in 1805 by settlers from Massachusetts, Granville bears a marked resemblance to a New England village. Columbus, the state capital, which has a population of 1.5 million and is 27 miles to the west, is the nearest large city and is served by numerous national airlines. Newark, 7 miles to the east, is an industrial city of 50,000 people. Granville has several fine restaurants and some shopping facilities, but those seeking the larger department stores go to nearby Easton Town Center or downtown Columbus. The University is a cultural and recreational center for the local community, and the Denison Community Association encourages student participation in community service activities, providing more than 13,500 hours of volunteer fieldwork each year. State parks, lakes, bike trails, and ski areas are nearby.

Majors and Degrees

Denison offers the degrees of Bachelor of Arts, Bachelor of Science, and Bachelor of Fine Arts. Departmental, interdepartmental, and individually designed majors, as well as concentrations within departments, are available within the degree programs. The B.A. can be earned through departmental programs in art (history or studio), biology, chemistry, cinema, communication, computer science, dance, economics, education (as a double major), English (literature or writing), environmental studies, geology, history, international studies (as a double major), mathematical sciences, modern languages (French, German, and Spanish), music, philosophy, physical education, physics, political science, psychology, religion, sociology/anthropology, and theater and through interdepartmental programs in black studies, classical studies, East Asian studies, educational studies, and women's studies. Interdisciplinary programs leading to a B.A. in philosophy, political science, and economics (PPE) and media, technology, and arts (MTA) have recently been added. The B.S. is offered in biochemistry, biology, chemistry, computer science, geology, mathematical sciences, physics, and psychology. The B.F.A. majors are art (studio) and theater. Concentrations can be arranged in astronomy, geophysics, Latin American and Caribbean studies, neuroscience, and queer studies. Certification is available in secondary education and organizational studies.

Preprofessional preparation is available in business, dentistry, engineering, environmental management, forestry, law, medicine, occupational therapy, and veterinary medicine. Denison offers 3-2 programs in engineering with Rensselaer Polytechnic Institute, Washington University, Case Western Reserve University, and Columbia University; in forestry and environmental studies with Duke University; in natural resources management with the University of Michigan; in medical technology with Rochester General Hospital; and a 3-4 program in dentistry with Case Western Reserve Dental School.

Academic Program

Denison expects its students to profit from exposure to a broad liberal arts education and to achieve proficiency in a major field. Its selective Honors Program has matriculated nearly 2,600 students in the last sixteen years. Degree requirements include successful completion of approximately thirty-five courses (127 semester hours) with a 2.0 or better average, both overall and in the major and minor fields; fulfillment of all general education requirements; passing comprehensive examinations if required in the major; and fulfillment of minimum residence requirements. About one third of a student's course work (thirteen courses) must be chosen from core course offerings in the humanities, sciences, social sciences, and fine arts. Another third is in the major field of study, and the remainder is in electives. There are opportunities for directed and independent study. Students may receive advanced placement or credit through College Board Advanced Placement (AP) tests or International Baccalaureate higher level examinations. Credit is automatically given for an AP score of 4 or 5. Denison's academic calendar consists of two semesters and an optional Internship Program, which includes internships and travel seminars. The academic year begins in late August and ends in early May.

Off-Campus Programs

Denison cooperates in off-campus study programs approved by recognized American colleges and universities and by the Great Lakes Colleges Association. Qualified students may participate for a semester or a year of international study in Europe, Latin America, Asia, Africa, Oceania, or the Middle East. Domestic programs, offered on a one- or two-semester basis, include the Washington Semester, the Philadelphia Semester, the New York Arts

Program, the Oak Ridge Science Semester, the Newberry Library Program in Chicago, the Border Studies Program, and linkages with historically black universities.

Academic Facilities

As a member of the Five Colleges of Ohio consortium, Denison offers access through a combined online catalog to a collection of more than 1.2 million volumes that can be accessed from computers anywhere on campus via the campus network. As a member of the OhioLINK statewide academic library consortium, library users also have ready access to more than 24 million titles from Ohio's library holdings. The William Howard Doane Library, one of eleven academic and administrative buildings on the academic quadrangle, has on-campus collections of more than 370,000 volumes, 340,000 government documents, 1,200 periodical subscriptions, 21,000 sound recordings, and 5,000 videocassettes. More than 200 microcomputers in eight student clusters, about 250 computers in departmental labs, and network outlets available to every student living in a residence hall provide access to computing resources and the campus network. Network services include central multiuser computers and servers, personal and departmental Web server space, free laser printing, hundreds of software packages, student and staff member Web portals, e-mail and access to the Internet and the World Wide Web. More than 80 percent of Denison's students own computers and connect to the campus network from residence hall rooms. For more information, students should refer to the library or computing links on the home page of the Denison Web site at the address listed below.

The Chemistry Center contains well-equipped laboratories and a 292-seat circular auditorium. Features of the seven-year-old $7.2-million F. W. Olin Science Hall include a 42-seat planetarium with a Zeiss Skymaster projector, a laser spectrometer, and computer-based learning centers for physics and astronomy, geology and geography, and mathematics and computer science. The Fine Arts Center is made up of six buildings containing classrooms and performance facilities for art, music, theater and cinema, and dance. Burke Hall contains a recital hall, the theater workshop, and an art gallery. Other buildings are the Theatre Arts Building; the Doane Dance Building; Burton Hall, that houses the Department of Music; Cleveland Hall, for studio art courses; the Art Annex; and the Cinema Annex, the center of Denison's nationally recognized cinematography program.

Costs

Annual charges for the 2004–05 academic year are as follows: tuition, $26,600; room and board, $7670; and student fees, $710. Personal expenses and books are estimated at $1800, bringing the total annual cost to $36,780.

Financial Aid

In 2002–03, Denison students received more than $33 million in financial assistance. Nearly $25 million was awarded from Denison funds. Financial aid packages based on need are composed of grants, loans, and employment on campus. Applicants for both federal and Denison grant aid must complete a Free Application for Federal Student Aid (FAFSA) as early as possible after January 1 and request that the information be sent to Denison. In addition to the institutional need-based grants, Denison offers more than 2,000 merit-based scholarships ranging from $6000 to full-tuition. Alumni and Dean's awards in the amounts of $6000 and $10,000, recognizing academic achievement, leadership, and talent, are also offered. The financial aid decision is entirely separate from the admission decision. For more information, students should write to Denison's Office of Financial Aid and ask for the financial aid brochure.

Faculty

Denison's 190 full-time faculty members are deeply committed to teaching and to students. Many have national reputations in their fields; each year faculty members win national awards for teaching excellence. Ninety-seven percent of faculty members have an earned doctorate or terminal degree in their field. The faculty-student ratio is 1:11. Small classes (average class size is 20) and unique opportunities for one-on-one research with a faculty member encourage active learning. All incoming first-year students are assigned a faculty adviser to assist with course selection and to ease the transition to college life.

Student Government

Through the Denison Campus Government Association, students budget and direct such campus organizations as the Student Senate, FM radio station, Denison Film Society, and campus newspaper. Students are strongly represented on the governance councils of the University.

Admission Requirements

Entering first-year students must have earned at least 16 academic credits in secondary school, including 4 years of college-preparatory English. Strongly recommended are 3 years each of mathematics, science, foreign language, and social studies. A candidate for admission must file a formal application and submit scores from either the SAT I or ACT. The Admissions Committee is particularly interested in the rigor of the academic program, the grade point average, and test results from the SAT I or ACT. Other selection criteria are written references from a college adviser and an academic teacher, extracurricular and personal accomplishments, and the student's essay on the application. An interview is strongly ecnouraged. It is Denison's goal to enroll academically talented students. Denison University admits students of any race, color, religion, age, personal handicap, sex, sexual orientation, veteran status, and national or ethnic origin.

Application and Information

First-Choice Early Decision candidates should apply by November 15, with a December 15 notification (Plan I), or by January 15, with a February 15 notification (Plan II). All admitted Early Decision candidates must send an enrollment deposit within two weeks of notification. Students interested in applying under regular status and for merit-based scholarship consideration are encouraged to apply by January 1. Candidates for regular admission should apply by February 1. Those deferred under Early Decision and all regular applicants are given a final decision by mid-March. Admitted candidates must respond to the admission offer by May 1.

Director of Admissions
Denison University
Box H
Granville, Ohio 43023
Telephone: 740-587-6276
800-336-4766 (toll-free)
E-mail: admissions@denison.edu
World Wide Web: http://www.denison.edu

Denison...preparing you for a lifetime of leadership and learning.

DEPAUL UNIVERSITY

CHICAGO, ILLINOIS

The University

Founded by the Vincentian Order in 1898, DePaul University is the largest Catholic university in the country and has a diverse student body enrolled on seven campuses. DePaul's location in Chicago—a world-class center for business, finance, government, law, and culture—as well as its partnership with the city provides students with exceptional career-related job experiences, internships, mentorships, services, and cultural opportunities.

The Loop campus, located in the heart of downtown Chicago, includes the DePaul Center, the Computer Science and Telecommunications Center, O'Malley Place, the Merle Reskin Theatre, and the Frank J. Lewis Center and is home to the Colleges of Law and Commerce, the School for New Learning, and the School of Computer Science, Telecommunications, and Information Systems. The College of Liberal Arts and Sciences, the School of Music, the School of Education, and the Theatre School are located on the 36-acre campus in Chicago's historic Lincoln Park neighborhood. Approximately 14,340 of DePaul's 23,227 students are undergraduates. Of the 2,261 freshman students in fall 2002, 32 percent were members of minority groups and 39 percent were first-generation college students. Though exhibiting a wide variety of backgrounds, DePaul students share a willingness to work hard in order to achieve their educational and career goals.

More than 130 student organizations provide opportunities for participation in personal, community, and University activities. Women's NCAA Division I sports include basketball, cross-country, soccer, softball, tennis, track, and volleyball. Men's NCAA Division I sports include basketball, cross-country, golf, soccer, tennis, and track. Intramural sports programs, as well as club athletics, are also available throughout the year. Facilities include two gymnasiums, a swimming pool, handball and tennis courts, basketball and volleyball courts, weight rooms, and a field for soccer and softball. The Ray Meyer Athletic and Recreation Center, a 120,000-square-foot facility, opened in fall 1999. In fall 2000, a state-of-the-art varsity athletic center opened. January 2002 marked the opening of a new student center designed to be the hub of student life on the Lincoln Park Campus. Fifteen residence halls and off-campus housing are available at Lincoln Park. Two semi-suite residence halls opened in fall 2000. Scheduled to open in fall 2004, the brand-new 18-story University Center of Chicago building offers a fitness center, cafeteria, and a landscaped terrace on the third floor as well as study and meeting rooms, laundry facilities, and more.

In addition to its baccalaureate programs, DePaul offers graduate degrees, including master's degrees in accountancy, business, computer science, education, liberal arts and sciences, and music; the Master of Fine Arts (M.F.A.) in theater; the Juris Doctor (J.D.); the Master of Law in taxation; and Ph.D.s in computer science, philosophy, and psychology.

Location

DePaul is located in a culturally and academically rich urban environment. The University has seven campuses: the Loop campus in downtown Chicago, the Lincoln Park campus, and five suburban campuses. The downtown campus is just blocks from the Art Institute, Orchestra Hall, Grant Park and Lake Michigan, and the LaSalle Street business district. Since 70 percent of DePaul's students work to help finance their education, they find that the downtown location provides many professional employment opportunities. At the Lincoln Park campus, the potpourri of stores, theaters, restaurants, and music clubs reflect the broad spectrum of interests of the people who live and work in the area. A short walk or ride on public transit enables students to browse through neighborhoods of unique shops and restored Victorian homes or to visit the area's conservatory, zoo, two museums, and professional sports arenas. DePaul's five suburban campuses (Naperville, Oak Forest, Rolling Meadows, Lake Forest, and Des Plaines) provide convenient locations for adult and graduate students to pursue degree programs. The University serves the needs of the Chicago community in many ways, such as providing the public with theater, music, and the resources of the Mental Health Center and its Learning Disabilities Center, the Legal Clinic, and the Monsignor John Egan Urban Center. There are also courses in several adult and graduate programs that are offered at all of the University's campuses.

Majors and Degrees

Bachelor of Arts and Bachelor of Science degrees are offered through seven undergraduate colleges. Double majors and minors may be taken in many areas of study.

The College of Liberal Arts and Sciences offers programs in American studies, anthropology, art and art history, biological sciences, Catholic studies, chemistry, clinical laboratory science, communication, comparative literature, economics, English, environmental science, environmental studies (urban studies), French, geography, German, history, honors, international studies, Italian, Japanese studies, Latin American studies, mathematical sciences, nursing (RN completion only), philosophy, physics, political science, preprofessional studies (dentistry, engineering, law, medicine, optometry, osteopathy, pharmacy, physical therapy, physician assistant studies, podiatry, and veterinary medicine), psychology, public policy, religious studies, sociology, Spanish, undecided major, and women's studies.

The School of Computer Science, Telecommunications, and Information Systems offers programs in computer graphics and animation, computer science (data analysis and database and telecommunications), computing (joint degree), e-commerce technology, human computer interaction, information systems, network technologies, and undecided major.

The School of Education offers programs in early childhood education, elementary education, physical education (fitness management and wellness), secondary education (art, biology, chemistry, computer science, English, French, geography, German, history, mathematics, physics, social science, and Spanish), and undecided major.

The College of Commerce offers programs in accountancy, business administration (prelaw), e-business, economics (business economics, environmental/resource economics, international trade, labor economics, prelaw, quantitative economics, urban economics), finance (banking and financial institutions, corporate financial management, investment management, and real estate management), entrepreneurship, human resource management, management information systems, marketing (advertising and promotion, international marketing, marketing management, marketing research, and sales and sales management), operations management, and undecided major.

The School of Music offers programs in applied music (performance), composition, jazz studies, music education, music/business, and sound recording technology.

The Theatre School offers programs in acting, costume design, costume technology, dramaturgy/criticism, general theater studies, lighting design, playwriting, production management, scene design, theater management, and theater technology.

The School for New Learning offers customized degree programs for adults.

Also available are a 3-2 option and a 2-3 option in pre-engineering, which result in a Bachelor of Engineering (B.E.) degree from the Illinois Institute of Technology, the University of Illinois at Urbana-Champaign and Chicago, the University of Detroit, USC, Northwestern, Iowa State, Ohio State, or the University of Notre Dame.

Academic Programs

To be eligible for a degree, a student must complete at least 192 quarter hours of college academic work with a grade point average of at least 2.0. Each college follows the common core liberal studies program consisting of courses taken in five divisions: English and history, philosophy-religion, fine arts and literature, behavioral–social sciences, and natural sciences–mathematics. Typically, thirteen courses are required for a major.

The academic year is composed of three quarters. Outstanding students may enter with credit earned through selected Advanced Placement (AP) tests. Up to 50 percent of the total credits necessary for graduation can be earned through CLEP, Advanced Placement, and University tests. In some cases, degree requirements can be completed in three years. Advanced undergraduates may take graduate courses. Honors programs are also offered in accountancy, computer science, finance, liberal arts, and marketing; an honors degree is awarded. The School for New Learning is DePaul's nontraditional college for adults 24 years of age or older. The School offers an individually customized undergraduate degree program. Students are responsible for designing their own programs and may receive credit for life experience.

Off-Campus Programs

The University has study-abroad programs that are available in Argentina, China, England, France, Germany, Greece, Hungary, Ireland, Israel, Italy, Japan, Malta, Mexico, Poland, Russia, South Africa, Spain, Thailand, Vietnam, and Zimbabwe.

Academic Facilities

The DePaul Center, a $70-million teaching, learning, research, and student services complex, is the cornerstone of the Loop campus. The DePaul Center Library at the Loop campus and the Lincoln Park Library contain 738,072 volumes, 15,890 periodical subscriptions, and extensive microcard and microfilm collections. The Law Library has 183,187 volumes and 10,356 periodical subscriptions. Among the outstanding holdings are the Dickens, Napoleonic, Horace, and Irish collections; the Farthing Collection of Illinois Sessions and Statutes; the antiquarian treasury of St. Thomas More's works; and the Verrona Williams Derr Collection of African American Studies. The libraries have reciprocal borrowing agreements with six other universities and are members of major cooperative lending groups.

DePaul offers students cutting-edge technology resources, including computer labs on every campus, with more than 800 computers for student use, free e-mail and Internet access, computers in most residence hall rooms, online registration and tuition payment services, and in-class technology resources designed to enrich course offerings. Among the other academic facilities are a 140-seat lecture/recital hall; the Concert Hall, with a seating capacity of 500; and the 1,400-seat Reskin Theatre for stage productions. In 1999, the McGowan Center for Biological and Environmental Sciences, a three-story state-of-the-art facility, was opened at the Lincoln Park campus.

Costs

For the 2003–04 academic year, tuition for the College of Liberal Arts and Sciences, the College of Commerce, the School of Education, the School for New Learning, and the School of Computer Science, Telecommunication, and Information Systems was $18,750. Tuition for the School of Music was $22,150, and it was $22,360 for the Theatre School. The tuition amounts for the Theatre School and the School of Music are guaranteed for four years. The registration fee (included in the tuition amount) was $30; books and supplies are estimated at $600. Average housing costs for 2002–03 were $6700 for room (double-occupancy) and $1700 for board. A required resident health-care fee is $126 per year; waiver of this cost is possible if the resident is covered by private insurance.

Financial Aid

DePaul has planned its financial aid program to assist as many students as possible. Scholarships, grants, loans, and work-study opportunities are awarded singly or, more commonly, are combined in a financial aid package to meet the demonstrated financial need of the student. About 68 percent of full-time DePaul students receive some form of financial aid; 75 percent of those recipients receive gift assistance. Merit scholarships for freshmen and transfer students, with values ranging from $3000 to full tuition for four years (approximately $56,000), are based on academic and extracurricular accomplishments. Institutional competitive scholarships are based on equal consideration of class rank, grade point average, and SAT I or ACT scores, without regard to need. Out-of-state and Illinois applicants are treated equally. All other financial aid programs, except athletic, music, and theater talent awards, are based primarily on need.

Students who wish to apply for aid must complete the Free Application for Federal Student Aid (FAFSA) and the DePaul application for admission. Applications and information can be obtained by contacting the Office of Student Aid. Application and notification of decisions are on a rolling basis. Financial aid programs are available to transfer students on the same basis as they are for regular upperclass students. Students are encouraged to apply before April 1 to receive maximum consideration.

Faculty

Approximately 88 percent of the full-time faculty members hold the Ph.D. or the terminal degree in their field. Faculty members are selected for their teaching ability and conduct all University classes. In addition to teaching, DePaul's faculty members are also engaged in research, publishing in their fields of expertise, and service. Graduate assistants do not teach classes at DePaul.

Student Government

The Student Government Association offers students the opportunity to become involved in representative government. The student-operated Activities Board also provides services and programs.

Admission Requirements

A candidate for freshman admission to DePaul should be a graduate of an approved secondary school and should have taken a minimum of 16 academic units. It is recommended that the academic work emphasize English, mathematics, laboratory science, social studies, and college-preparatory electives. Applicants should rank in the upper half of their class and present strong SAT I or ACT scores. Recommendations are required, and interviews are recommended. The School of Music and the Theatre School require auditions and interviews for admission. Early action, advanced placement, a cooperative high school–college program, and deferred entrance are available.

Transfer students are welcome. To be considered, transfers must be in good academic standing at the last college attended and must have earned a minimum cumulative GPA of 2.0 (C) in transferable courses at all colleges attended. College of Commerce applicants must have a cumulative GPA of 2.5 or better; School of Education applicants must have a cumulative GPA of 2.75 or better; registered nurses interested in the B.S.N. completion program must have at least a 2.5 cumulative GPA. At least 30 semester (44 quarter) hours of transferable credit must have been completed; those who have completed fewer than 30 semester hours must also meet the requirements of freshman applicants.

Rolling admission is on a space-available basis. The early action deadline is November 15. It is strongly recommended that freshman applicants apply by February 1.

Application and Information

Applicants are notified of the disposition of their applications soon after their application files are completed. Campus visits and overnight stays are regularly scheduled for prospective students. Interested students and their families are encouraged to call the admission office to arrange for an individual tour.

For further information, prospective students should contact:

Office of Admission
DePaul University
1 East Jackson Boulevard
Chicago, Illinois 60604-2287
Telephone: 312-362-8300
800-4DEPAUL (toll-free outside Illinois)
E-mail: admitdpu@depaul.edu
World Wide Web: http://www.depaul.edu/

DEPAUW UNIVERSITY

GREENCASTLE, INDIANA

The University

"DePauw is not a spectator sport" is the way one graduate described the DePauw experience. Indeed, DePauw students expect and seek a challenge. In small classes, students are challenged by professors who are leading scholars with a passion for teaching. There are countless opportunities to excel in more than forty programs of study, five honors programs, numerous leadership positions with student organizations and living units, athletic programs, and more. DePauw students have a tradition of volunteerism, as demonstrated by the fact that three fourths of the student body of 2,300 participate in community service each year. In the first annual *Guide to Campuses Where You Can Make a Difference*, DePauw ranked among the top fifteen colleges where students are truly making a difference in terms of service, both on campus and in the community. In brief, DePauw provides a broad, liberal arts education that is intended to serve as a foundation for the student's lifetime of learning and growth.

At DePauw, the traditional liberal arts curriculum is complemented by perhaps the largest per capita student internship program in the country. Eighty-five percent of DePauw students complete at least one internship during a semester, Winter Term, or summer, and many students complete at least two internships. As a result, DePauw offers a unique opportunity for students to explore various interests and career possibilities, which have a significant impact for students following graduation. More than 95 percent of DePauw graduates are employed or enrolled in graduate/professional school within nine months of graduation. The figure increases to more than 99 percent after one year. Of those students obtaining employment after graduation, approximately 1 out of 4 students accept jobs at companies and organizations where they served a student internship.

Much of DePauw's reputation for excellence can be attributed to the uncommon success of its alumni. DePauw ranked eleventh in the nation in terms of the likelihood that its graduates will become chief executive officers of major American companies, according to *Fortune* magazine in 1990. DePauw ranked eighth in the nation and first in the Midwest as the undergraduate origin of the nation's top executives, according to a 1994 study by Standard & Poor's Corp. DePauw also ranked sixteenth as a baccalaureate source for Ph.D. degree recipients in all fields, according to a 1998 survey by Franklin and Marshall College.

DePauw guarantees graduation in four years for students in forty standard programs, or the University waives tuition and fees for any subsequent course work necessary for graduation.

Location

DePauw is located in a town of 10,000 people set amid the gently rolling hills of west-central Indiana. The campus is exceptionally well maintained, blending new, state-of-the-art facilities with buildings, such as the historic East College, that exemplify the University's heritage. DePauw students are very active in the community, as indicated by the fact that about three fourths of the student body volunteers each year for public service in twenty-five community organizations. Greencastle is 45 miles west of Indianapolis and within a 3-hour drive of Chicago, St. Louis, Louisville, Cincinnati, and Columbus.

Majors and Degrees

DePauw offers the Bachelor of Arts (B.A.), Bachelor of Music (B.Mus.), Bachelor of Musical Arts (B.M.A.), and Bachelor of Music Education (B.M.E.).

DePauw offers majors in more than forty areas, including anthropology, art (history), art (studio), biochemistry, biology, black studies, chemistry, classical civilization, communication, computer science, conflict studies, earth science, East Asian studies, economics, elementary education, English (literature), English (writing), environmental geoscience, French, geography, geology, German, Greek, history, interdisciplinary, kinesiology (athletic training, sports medicine and exerise, and sports medicine), Latin, mathematics, music, music/business, music performance, music education, philosophy, physics, political science, psychology, religious studies, Romance languages, Russian studies, sociology, sociology and anthropology, Spanish, and women's studies. Preprofessional programs are available in dentistry, law, medicine, and secondary education. In addition, DePauw offers a 3-2 program in engineering.

Academic Program

DePauw is committed to providing its students with a traditional, liberal arts education complemented by internship opportunities, and degree requirements reflect this approach. The University follows a 4-1-4 calendar, with four-month fall and spring semesters and a January Winter Term. The normal course load in a semester is four courses, but course loads may vary from three to 4½ courses. During the January Winter Term, first-year students study on campus, and upperclass students participate in research, internships, and travel abroad. DePauw's distinctive honors programs include Honor Scholars, Information Technology Associates Program, Management Fellows, Media Fellows, and Science Research Fellows.

During the 1999–2000 academic year, DePauw began a new first-year experience program, called depauw.year1, that is designed to build a sense of community among first-year students. The program includes special seminars, speakers, programs, and other activities.

Thirty-one courses are required for students earning a Bachelor of Arts, Bachelor of Music, or Bachelor of Musical Arts degree. The Bachelor of Music Education degree requires thirty-two courses. Each student must complete a major, achieve at least a 2.0 GPA (on a 4.0 scale) in that major, and satisfy the senior major requirement. Students must attain a minimum cumulative GPA of 2.0, while students in the B.M.A. and B.M.E. programs need a minimum 2.5 GPA. Fifteen courses leading to a bachelor's degree, including six of the last eight courses, must be completed in residence at DePauw or in a University-approved program. Students in the College of Liberal Arts must achieve certification in writing (W), quantitative reasoning (Q), and oral communication skills (S). Students must complete three Winter Term projects with satisfactory grades, including an on-campus Winter Term for first-year students. A maximum of 3 internship course credits and five internship experiences (including Winter Terms) may be applied toward the bachelor's degree.

Off-Campus Programs

DePauw offers extensive off-campus study programs. Domestic programs include the Washington Semester, United Nations Semester, Sea Semester, New York Arts Program, Newberry Library Program, Oak Ridge Science Semester, and Philadelphia Urban Semester. Study abroad is available in Africa, Asia-Pacific, Australia, Austria, Belgium, Canada, the Caribbean, China, the Czech Republic, Denmark, England, France, Germany, Greece, Hungary, India, Indonesia, Ireland, Italy, Japan, Latin America, Mexico, the Middle East, the Netherlands, Poland, Russia, Scotland, Singapore, Spain, Switzerland, Vietnam, and Wales. Many students also participate in off-campus Winter Term projects. More than 40 percent of students study off-campus as part of their DePauw experience. In order to receive course credit, a student must have approval from the International Center; other restrictions may apply.

Academic Facilities

The new blends with the old on DePauw's 175-acre campus, which features thirty-nine major buildings and a nearby 40-acre nature preserve. DePauw's facilities provide an excellent environment for teaching and learning. The physical plant is equal to or superior to that of other liberal arts universities.

The centerpiece of the campus is historic East College, built in 1877 and listed on the Register of Historic Landmarks. New buildings on campus include the Indoor Tennis and Track Center, which opened in 2001 and was recognized by the United States Tennis Association as an outstanding public tennis facility for 2002. The Julian Science and Math Center is currently undergoing a $38 million expansion and renovation project, adding 110,000 square feet of new classroom and laboratory space, including the 361 degrees Technology Center. The new Peeler Art Center gives students a state-of-the-art space optimal to the teaching, creation, and presentation of art. The Pulliam Center for Contemporary Media has superb facilities and equipment for *The DePauw*, the oldest student newspaper in the state; student-operated WGRE-FM radio; and a television unit in which students produce programs for broadcast statewide and nationwide. The Performing Arts Center is home to the School of Music and features outstanding performance halls.

Costs

Expenses for the 2003–04 academic year included $24,000 for tuition, $7050 for room and board, and $530 in fees for health services and activities. Books and supplies are approximately $600 per year, and personal expenses are approximately $1000 per year.

Financial Aid

Admission to DePauw is need-blind. Ninety-five percent of all DePauw students receive scholarships, grants, loans, or work-study assistance. The average financial aid package covers slightly more than half of total costs. DePauw's financial aid program is designed to recognize achievement and potential and to assist students who otherwise would be unable to attend the University due to financial constraints. DePauw maintains its own scholarship, work, and loan programs and participates in all traditional forms of state and federal financial aid.

February 15 is the priority filing date for applications for fall financial aid. FAFSA and institutional financial aid applications are required. Scholarships/grants available include federal and state scholarships/grants, University scholarships/grants, private scholarships/grants, ROTC scholarships and academic merit scholarships. Approximately 40 percent of students work on campus during the academic year. DePauw participates in the Federal Work-Study Program, and 45 percent of students who receive financial aid participate in work-study.

Faculty

DePauw professors are devoted to teaching students. The University has 223 full-time faculty members, and 92 percent have the terminal degree in their field. The student-faculty ratio is 10:1. All classes at DePauw are taught by professors and not by graduate assistants. Ninety-seven percent of full-time faculty members serve as academic advisers to students.

Student Government

Leadership opportunities in a wide variety of organizations are an integral part of the DePauw experience. Students have numerous opportunities to be involved in student government as well as committees and councils representing student concerns. The president of the student body presides over the many committees of the Student Congress; each committee has several student representatives as members. Sororities, fraternities, and residence halls all have annual elections of officers and representatives to various campus organizations.

Admission Requirements

DePauw does not conduct admission by the numbers. Along with grades and SAT I or ACT scores, the University looks at the required student essays, record of other achievements, and examples of any special talent a student may have. Also considered are the quality of courses selected in the high school; the high school attended; the recommendations of high school counselors, teachers, coaches, and employers; and the personal interview. DePauw examines each individual's application carefully.

To be admitted to the first-year class at DePauw, students must have graduated from an accredited secondary school or offer evidence of equivalent education. Students should have completed the following work in a college-preparatory program: 4 units of English, 4 units of mathematics, 3-4 units of a foreign language, 3-4 units of social science, and 3-4 units of science (2 or more laboratory sciences). In addition, School of Music candidates must audition.

Application and Information

Prospective students can apply online or obtain an application for admission by calling or writing the Office of Admission. DePauw also is a member of the Common Application Group and gives the common application the same consideration as the University's application.

Students interested in early decision must submit applications by November 1, students interested in early notification must submit applications by December 1, and students interested in regular decision must submit applications by February 1. Admission decisions are mailed by mid-December for early decision applicants and by February 15 for early notification applicants. Regular decision applicants are notified by April 1. Early decision applicants who are admitted must respond by February 1; other admitted applicants who decide to enroll must submit an enrollment deposit by May 1. Students should contact:

Madeleine R. Eagon
Vice President for Admission and Financial Aid
DePauw University
P.O. Box 37
Greencastle, Indiana 46135-0037
Telephone: 765-658-4006
800-447-2495 (toll-free)
Fax: 765-658-4007
E-mail: admission@depauw.edu
World Wide Web: http://www.depauw.edu

Historic East College is the centerpiece of DePauw University's campus. The East College bell summons students to class and also signals victories in football.

DESIGN INSTITUTE OF SAN DIEGO

SAN DIEGO, CALIFORNIA

The Institute

Design Institute of San Diego is a private, independent college founded in 1977 and devoted exclusively to professional education in interior design. Enrollment is approximately 450 students.

The Bachelor of Fine Arts degree program at Design Institute is nationally accredited by the Foundation for Interior Design Education Research (FIDER). FIDER accreditation is important because it is recognized by the profession's principal design organizations, such as the American Society of Interior Designers (ASID), the International Interior Design Association (IIDA), the Interior Design Educators Council (IDEC), and the National Council of Interior Design Qualification (NCIDQ).

Design Institute is approved to operate under the Education Code of the State of California as a degree-granting educational institution. The Institute is accredited as a Senior College by the Accrediting Council for Independent Colleges and Schools.

Students are encouraged to join such organizations as ASID and participate as student chapter members. Student contact with working professional interior designers provides insight and understanding of professional standards and practices and serves as an important reinforcement of classroom learning.

Design Institute students have won numerous national and regional portfolio and design competitions, including the ASID Yale R. Burge portfolio competition, the ASID/Villeroy and Boch "Designing with Tile" competition, the Halo/Metalux Annual Lighting competition, the ASID Interior Design Excellence Award, and IIDA CALIBRE awards.

Location

Design Institute of San Diego is located within a few miles of the Pacific beaches of La Jolla. Southern California has always been a mecca for artists and designers who find the ocean, the desert, and the California sunlight conducive to the creative life.

San Diego has become one of America's largest cities, but it has retained the character of a small, seaside community. Its lifestyle is casual while offering a wealth of cultural and intellectual resources, including major museums, galleries, opera, dance, and theater.

Recreational opportunities abound. The city has long been the home and training ground for many of the world's finest athletes. Biking, surfing, jogging, boating, and hiking are a part of San Diego life.

The city is alive with visual interest, from its gracious old missions to the stark beauty of the Salk Institute designed by Louis Kahn. All of this, combined with an almost perfect climate, makes San Diego an ideal city in which to learn and work.

Major and Degree

Design Institute of San Diego offers a single program of study leading to a Bachelor of Fine Arts degree in interior design.

Academic Program

The Bachelor of Fine Arts degree program prepares students for careers in interior design. It balances the two most important aspects of the profession: interior design as creative and technical ability and interior design as professional business practice.

The creative aspects of interior design are part of an ongoing dialogue with culture. Through formal education, students gain insight into the historical development of furniture, decorative objects, and the interior architectural features of the built environment.

The social sciences have a profound influence on design. Design Institute students study the needs, values, behavior patterns, perceptions, and responses of people as the basis on which to create environments for living and working.

The design process requires more than aesthetic and social decisions. Specialized knowledge of structural principles, details and drawing, programming, building codes, energy conservation, safety regulations, lighting, and methods of construction are all part of the vocabulary of today's interior designer.

The curriculum at Design Institute is carefully organized to introduce these concepts in logical sequence, continually layering and overlapping basic design principles as their levels of complexity increase. This provides the student with a firm framework on which to build a professional practice.

Design Institute operates on a semester basis, fall and spring. The program is offered both day and evening.

Academic Facilities

Academic facilities are of a high-tech contemporary style and include spacious classrooms, drafting studios, exhibition space, a computer lab, a student lounge, and administrative offices. A library containing books, periodicals, samples, catalogs, and slides is available for student use. All facilities offer convenient parking.

Costs

Tuition for the 2004–05 academic year is $11,800. Books and supplies are estimated at $400 per semester. Beginning students should budget an additional $400 for the purchase of equipment.

Financial Aid

Approximately 50 percent of students attending Design Institute in 2003–04 received some type of financial assistance. Types of aid included Federal Pell Grants, Federal Supplemental Educational Opportunity Grants (FSEOG), Federal Stafford Student Loans, California Workstudy, and Cal Grants A and B. All awards are made on the basis of eligibility.

Faculty

The faculty at Design Institute includes 50 practicing interior designers, architects, artists, historians, environmental psychologists, lighting engineers, computer technologists, and business consultants—all working professionals who bring to the classroom practical instruction based on current professional knowledge.

Student Government

The college does not have a student government. All matters of interest to students are welcomed by the administration and faculty at any time.

Admission Requirements

All candidates for admission must possess a high school diploma or its equivalent. Previous training in art or design is not essential as this training is provided within the program. The school welcomes applications from those whose personal goals are consistent with the educational objectives of the school and whose previous background indicates a reasonable opportunity to benefit from the curriculum offered. A personal interview is advised but not required.

Transfer students may receive credit for courses, completed at an accredited institution, that are similar to courses at Design Institute. In some cases, the transferring student may need to submit actual work for evaluation. A grade of C is required to transfer credit, and official transcripts must be presented.

Design Institute welcomes applications from international students. Those from non-English-speaking countries must present evidence of English language proficiency at a level that allows them to proceed without difficulty. Certified translations of official transcripts are also required. A Certificate of Eligibility Form (I-20) is issued after the applicant has submitted all admissions material and has been accepted by the school.

Application and Information

Admission decisions are made on a rolling basis for both the fall and spring semesters. Applications are evaluated upon the receipt of the completed application for admission, the application fee of $25, and official transcripts. Applicants are notified of the school's decision in writing within thirty days of the completion of the admission procedures.

For a catalog and application, students should contact:

Paula Parrish
Director of Admissions
Design Institute of San Diego
8555 Commerce Avenue
San Diego, California 92121
Telephone: 858-566-1200
800-619-4337 (toll-free)
Fax: 858-566-2711
E-mail: admissions@disd.edu
World Wide Web: http://www.disd.edu

Design Institute's faculty of active professionals provides a wealth of exposure to diverse design philosophies and experiences.

DICKINSON STATE UNIVERSITY

DICKINSON, NORTH DAKOTA

The University

Student success, both inside and outside the classroom, has been the focus of Dickinson State University since 1918 when the University was established as Dickinson Normal School and Model High. The tradition continues today, allowing easy access and meaningful relationships with qualified professors, supportive and comfortable living arrangements on campus, and with student activities, providing something for everyone.

Dickinson State, with an enrollment of approximately 2,000 students, is the only comprehensive, four-year public university in West River North Dakota. The University is proud of its safe campus. Its location offers students a secure environment in which to pursue their educational and social interests.

The University's mission, as dictated by the North Dakota University System, is to provide high-quality, accessible programs; to promote excellence in teaching and learning; to support scholarly and creative activities; and to provide service relevant to the economy, health, and quality of life of the citizens of North Dakota. With a wide range of academic programs, Dickinson State University prepares students to live, learn, and lead in the twenty-first century.

Dickinson State University is accredited by the North Central Association of Colleges and Schools (NCA), the North Central Association for Teacher Education (NCATE), and the National League for Nursing Accrediting Commission (NLNAC).

At Dickinson State, there are approximately forty-five different organizations to help every student find a niche. Students choose from intramural sports, band, chorus, drama, art, forensics, student government, honorary societies, academic clubs, and cheerleading, to name just a few.

Living in a residence hall at Dickinson State offers many conveniences and countless opportunities to build friendships in an exciting environment close to classes and University activities. Meal plans are available on campus for five or seven days per week. For added ease, students can also opt to purchase meals at the snack bar. Rooms have free access to the campus computer network and cable television. Features in each hall include game room, exercise equipment, computer stations, laundry facilities, and kitchenette. Students can select to live in women's, men's, or coed halls, or student apartments. Family student housing complexes provide apartments at reasonable housing rates to nontraditional students.

Location

Dickinson State is located in Dickinson, North Dakota, near the rugged and beautiful Badlands. With a population of more than 17,000, Dickinson is the hub of West River North Dakota. The community lies only 30 miles from Theodore Roosevelt National Park, and it is just one hour's drive south of Lake Sakakawea. Dickinson is served by both commercial air and bus transportation.

Dickinson's location provides abundant opportunities for people to enjoy outdoor recreational activities year-round. The area's picturesque rivers, lakes, and Badlands are ideal for hiking, fishing, boating, hunting, cross-country skiing, and much more.

As the state's fifth-largest community, Dickinson offers a wide array of restaurants, shopping malls, specialty stores, historic landmarks, museums, movie theaters, and other entertainment outlets. The region offers abundant dinosaur fossils and geological phenomena for explorers of all ages. Many of these treasures are displayed in Dickinson's impressive Dakota Dinosaur Museum.

Health-care services are provided by a 109-bed acute-care hospital, two major clinics, and numerous specialty clinics. The University's Student Health Service provides prompt care on campus for routine health concerns.

Majors and Degrees

Programs offered at Dickinson State University include liberal arts along with specialized programs in education, business, health services, agriculture, and computer science. There are opportunities for preprofessional study and vocational training in selected areas as well.

Dickinson State offers Bachelor of Arts and Bachelor of Science degrees in ten departments, including majors and/or minors (indicated with a *) in accounting, agriculture (with options in natural resource management, integrated ranch management, and business/marketing), art, biology, business administration (with concentrations in accounting, agribusiness, banking and finance, business management, management information systems, manufacturing technology, marketing, office administration, and organizational psychology), business education, chemistry, coaching*, computer science, earth science*, elementary education, English, environmental health, geography*, graphic design*, history, journalism*, mathematics, music, music education, nursing, physical education, political science, psychology, science composite, secondary education, social science composite, social science (elementary education)*, sociology*, social work (linked with University of North Dakota), Spanish, theater and communication, university studies, and writing.

Associate degree and certificate programs include agriculture with specialty areas in agriculture sales and service (with options in agriculture business management and equine management) or farm and ranch management, nursing, office administration (with concentrations in accounting, agribusiness, computer science, legal, management, and medical studies), and university studies.

Preprofessional programs include athletic training, chiropractic, dentistry, dental hygiene, engineering, forestry, law, medicine, medical/lab technology, mortuary science, optometry, physics, seminary, social work, veterinary, and wildlife management.

Academic Program

While many of the majors that Dickinson State University offers have unique academic requirements, the basic baccalaureate degree academic curriculum consists of approximately 39 semester hours of general education courses from the areas of communications, scientific inquiry, expression of human civilization, understanding human civilization, multicultural studies, and physical education; a specific major core curriculum of 32 to 60 or more semester hours; approximately 24 semester hours of credit in a minor field of study (when a minor is required); and professional education course work for those students entering the teaching profession. Students seeking a Bachelor of Arts degree must also complete a minimum of 16 semester hours of a foreign language. A minimum of 128 semester hours is required for graduation in a baccalaureate degree program. Associate degree programs require 64 credit hours for graduation.

Academic Facilities

The commitment to technology at Dickinson State is evident in the number of cutting-edge computers provided for student use. There is an outstanding student-to-personal computer ratio, resulting in easy access to the type of technology students need to excel. Computer labs are located in academic areas, the library, and all residence halls. Students also have free access to e-mail and the Internet, including the World Wide Web.

Stoxen Library is proud of its highly sophisticated automated library. The On-line Dakota Information Network allows students to access resources from across the United States.

Costs

In 2003–04, tuition and fees were $1570 per semester for North Dakota residents; $1774 per semester for Minnesota residents; $1889 per semester for residents of Montana, South Dakota, Manitoba (Canada), and Saskatchewan (Canada); $2208 per semester for residents of Alaska, Arizona, California, Colorado, Hawaii, Idaho, Kansas, Michigan, Missouri, Nebraska, Nevada, New Mexico, Oregon, Utah, Washington, and Wyoming; and for residents of other states, tuition and fees were $3703 per semester. Room and board costs averaged $1675 per semester. Books were approximately $350 per semester. These figures reflect current costs, which are subject to change.

Financial Aid

College is a valuable investment in the future, and Dickinson State realizes financing it can be challenging. One of the best college buys in the region, Dickinson State's tuition and housing rates are among the lowest in the upper Midwest. In addition, attractive tuition rates are offered for students living in states and provinces bordering on North Dakota. Special rates also exist for students who live in those states participating in the Western Undergraduate Exchange (WUE) and the Midwest Student Exchange Program (MSEP). These include Alaska, Arizona, California, Colorado, Hawaii, Idaho, Kansas, Michigan, Missouri, Nebraska, Nevada, New Mexico, Oregon, Utah, Washington, and Wyoming.

The Office of Financial Aid is ready to help ease the cost of a college education through a number of financial aid programs, including scholarships, grants, loans, student employment opportunities, cultural diversity awards, and international awards. More than 85 percent of Dickinson State's students received financial assistance last year.

Faculty

Dickinson State University has 75 full-time and 70 part-time faculty members. Students develop close relationships with their teachers since three fourths of classes have fewer than 30 students.

Student Government

The Student Senate is the governing body and official voice of Dickinson State University students. The Senate is composed of a cross-section of students elected by the campus community. The Campus Activity Board (CAB) offers a broad range of social and recreational activities, including dances, films, comedians, and other special events. The Campus Programming Committee (CPC) provides a variety of educational, instructional, and cultural programs. Residence Hall Councils are made up of elected student residents and deal with matters relating to campus housing. The Student Policies Council is composed of students, faculty, and staff members. The Council recommends policies and programs related to student affairs.

Admission Requirements

Dickinson State's admission policy allows students to enroll if they are high school graduates or have successfully completed the GED examination along with completion of the ACT or SAT. The completion of a high school college-preparatory course core curriculum is also required for admission into a baccalaureate program.

The nursing program has special enrollment and admissions requirements. Students should apply early for this program.

All students under the age of 21 who have not completed 60 credit hours are required to live on campus. Exceptions to this policy include married students; students living locally with parents, grandparents, or a legal guardian; students who live with a brother or sister who is a head of a household; and single parents with one or more dependents.

Application and Information

The admissions staff is anxious to discuss the variety of programs the University has to offer and give a tour of the beautiful campus, its classrooms, facilities, and residence halls. When students are on campus, they should meet with the financial aid staff to discuss concerns about financing an education. Admissions representatives are available Monday through Friday, 8 a.m. to 4 p.m., Mountain Time. Students should contact:

Office of Student Recruitment
Dickinson State University
Dickinson, North Dakota 58601-4896
Telephone: 701-483-2175
800-279-HAWK Ext. 2175 (toll-free)
E-mail: dsu.hawks@dsu.nodak.edu
World Wide Web: http://www.dickinsonstate.com

Dickinson State University ensures student success with flexible schedules and by providing numerous group activities for students to live, learn, and lead as they grow together at Dickinson State University.

DOMINICAN COLLEGE

ORANGEBURG, NEW YORK

The College

Dominican College reflects the traditions of its founding Dominican order in its emphasis on a value-centered, liberal arts–based education. In 2002–03, Dominican College celebrated its fiftieth anniversary. The College offers undergraduate and graduate programs. Graduate degree programs include special education, occupational therapy, physical therapy, and nursing. Its 1,800 students represent a diverse ethnic population and include both campus residents and commuters.

Dominican's campus is growing. The Hennessy Student Center, completed in 1995, contains a 1,000-seat gymnasium, a physical fitness room, a suspended running track, athletic training facilities, athletic offices, and all-purpose meeting rooms. Hertel Hall, a residence center completed in 1996, contains social areas, computer-equipped study lounges, a kitchenette, student meeting rooms, and computer- and cable-equipped dorm rooms. The Granito Center, which was built in 1996, houses the cafeteria, health center, bookstore, and Global Communications Center. Seven other buildings make up the campus. Cooke Hall houses administration offices; the Admissions Office is in De Porres Hall. Doyle Hall is the teacher education facility, and the library is located in Pius X Hall. Casey, Rosary, and Forkel Halls contain classrooms. Casey Hall also houses the deans' offices and the offices of the arts and sciences, business administration, and allied health faculties. In addition, construction is underway for a new Center for Health and Science Education.

There are a number of social, athletic, and academic activities on campus through which students can satisfy personal interests. Student organizations include the yearbook, the College newspaper, the drama club, Alpha Chi honor society, the Council on Student Activities (COSA), and various academic clubs. To help students take advantage of the region, the College organizes outings, including ski trips to the Berkshires and theater evenings in Manhattan. Varsity sports include men's baseball, basketball, cross-country, golf, lacrosse, and soccer and women's basketball, cross-country, lacrosse, soccer, softball, and volleyball. Dominican College is a member of the National Collegiate Athletic Association (NCAA) Division II, and the Central Atlantic Collegiate Conference (CACC). In addition, many community service–oriented activities are available through academic departments of the College and through the campus ministry program.

In order to serve the adult and nontraditional student, the College offers an Accelerated Evening Program (eight-week terms), a Weekend College, and an Evening Program. Students enrolled in these programs may pursue full-time study while maintaining full-time employment. Academic support services, career counseling, internships, and placement opportunities are provided for all students.

In addition to its undergraduate degrees, Dominican offers a five-year Bachelor of Science/Master of Science degree in occupational therapy; a Family Nurse Practitioner Program leading to a Master of Science (M.S.) degree; a Master of Science in Education (M.S.Ed.) degree leading to certification as teachers of students with disabilities, including those with multiple and severe disabilities; a Master of Science in Education (M.S.Ed.) degree for teachers of the blind and visually impaired; and a Master of Science (M.S.) in physical therapy.

Location

Dominican College is located in Rockland County, New York, 17 miles north of New York City and approximately 3 miles north of Bergen County, New Jersey. This convenient, safe suburban location offers easy access to the outstanding cultural and educational resources of New York City.

Majors and Degrees

Dominican College awards B.A., B.S., B.S.Ed., B.S./M.S., and B.S.N., degrees. The areas of concentration in the liberal arts are American studies (with programs in education only), biology (which includes a premedicine track and pre–physical therapy studies), English, history, humanities, mathematics, natural sciences, psychology, and social sciences. In business administration, areas of concentration include accounting, computer information systems, economics, health service administration, and management, (including financial management, human resource management, information systems management, international management, and marketing management).

Other areas of concentration are childhood education, adolescence education, special education/childhood education, and special education/adolescence education.

Also offered are programs in athletic training and generic and upper-division nursing and an Accelerated Bachelor of Science in Nursing program (accredited by the National League for Nursing Accrediting Commission) as well as a B.S./M.S. program in occupational therapy (accredited by the Accreditation Council for Occupational Therapy Education) and a B.S. in social work (accredited by the Council on Social Work Education). A five-year integrated program in engineering offers a Bachelor of Arts degree in mathematics from Dominican and a Bachelor of Engineering degree from Manhattan College.

Academic Programs

The degree programs at Dominican College have been designed to give students the benefit of a study in the liberal arts disciplines and in professional preparation. The baccalaureate degree accommodates varied learning styles, previous academic backgrounds, divergent learning and career goals, and prior experience.

To receive a degree, students must complete a minimum of 120 semester hours, 30 of which must be earned at Dominican College. The College will grant up to 60 credits for achievement on proficiency examinations administered by American College Testing, Inc.; the New York State Regents' External Degree Program; and the College-Level Examination Program (CLEP). Learning acquired through experience may also be validated by the submission of a portfolio demonstrating that the student has acquired knowledge that corresponds to courses required at Dominican College.

Placement testing and a coordinated advisement process provide students with information and guidance for the effective use of the resources of the College. Support for the ongoing development of academic skills is provided through the Learning Resources and Writing Center, which offers tutoring in basic mathematics, writing, and other subjects. Opportunities for elective internships and independent study enable students to pursue a wide range of career and academic interests. An Honors Program provides innovative learning opportunities for students with superior academic preparation.

Academic Facilities

The College library, located in Pius X Hall, provides more than 103,000 volumes and approximately 640 periodical titles, with more than 14,300 volumes of additional back files on microfilm. The collection includes reference sources, basic indexes, and other bibliographic aids, including computerized search programs with remote access.

Forkel Hall contains science laboratories and a nursing practicum lab. Casey Hall houses the Learning Resources and Writing Center. Students may use computer labs in Casey and Rosary Halls; the residence center is also equipped with computers.

Costs

The tuition for 2004–05 is approximately $16,600 per academic year. Room and board costs are $8470 per academic year. For part-time and weekend students, the undergraduate tuition is $490 per semester hour.

Financial Aid

Dominican College administers four types of aid: scholarships, grants, loans, and work-study programs. Academic scholarships and grants are awarded on the basis of a student's academic record. Athletic scholarships and grants are awarded on the basis of athletic ability. Students applying for aid should file the Free Application for Federal Student Aid (FAFSA) by February 15. Transfer students are required to submit a transcript of all financial assistance received at institutions previously attended.

Supplementary aid opportunities are available through the New York State Tuition Assistance Program (TAP), the Federal Pell Grant Program, the Federal Family Education Loan Program, the Federal Supplemental Educational Opportunity Grant (FSEOG) Program, Nursing Student Loans, Nursing Scholarships, the Federal Perkins Loan Program, the Federal Work-Study Program, and veterans' benefits.

Faculty

The Dominican faculty has approximately 160 members, and the present student-faculty ratio is 13:1. Faculty members hold degrees from thirty different universities and colleges located in fourteen states and three other countries. Many have had varied experiences prior to teaching at the college level. Faculty members work with students as academic advisers and as advisers for nonacademic activities.

Student Government

The Dominican College Student Government Association is the official representative of the students. It approves charters for clubs and organizations, helps to plan the cultural and social calendar, aids in directing and coordinating social activities, and manages the student activity budget.

Admission Requirements

Entering freshmen are expected to have completed a secondary school program or its equivalent. The recommended preparation includes 16 academic units distributed among English, mathematics, natural sciences, social sciences, and foreign languages. All applicants for admission as freshmen should submit scores from the SAT I or the ACT. TOEFL scores are required for international applicants. Admission to the Honors Program is available to students who rank in the upper levels of their high school graduating class and who achieve acceptable scores on entrance examinations.

A minimum cumulative GPA of at least 2.0 is required for transfer students, with a maximum of 70 credits accepted from accredited two-year colleges and 90 credits from four-year colleges.

A personal interview is recommended in order to allow the applicant to become better acquainted with the College and to exchange information with a member of the admission staff. Dominican College does not discriminate on the basis of sex, race, color, age, national origin, religious affiliation, or physical limitation and is an Equal Opportunity/Affirmative Action employer.

Application and Information

Applicants should submit the completed Dominican College application form to the Office of Admissions.

For more information and application forms, students may contact:

Joyce Elbe
Director of Admissions
Dominican College
470 Western Highway
Orangeburg, New York 10962
Telephone: 866-4DC-INFO (toll-free)
E-mail: admissions@dc.edu
World Wide Web: http://www.dc.edu

Dominican College fosters relationships between students and faculty members through small, personal classes.

DOMINICAN UNIVERSITY

RIVER FOREST, ILLINOIS

The University

Dominican University is a distinctively relationship-centered educational community, rooted in the liberal arts and sciences and comprehensive in scope. The University is known for its rigorous and engaging academic programs, for the care and respect with which it mentors students, for its enduring committment to social justice, and for the enriching diversity of its students and faculty and staff members. Integral to Dominican's success and distinction is the ongoing exploration, clear expression, and shared experience of its Catholic Dominican identity.

The emphasis on a strong liberal arts curriculum began in Wisconsin in 1848 when Fr. Samuel Mazzuchelli, O.P., founded St. Clara Academy, a frontier school for young women. Father Mazzuchelli offered instruction in astronomy, logic, history, and natural philosophy—courses considered revolutionary for women at the time. Administered by the Dominican Sisters of Sinsinawa, St. Clara College was established in 1901. In 1918, on the invitation of Archbishop Mundelein of Chicago, the school was incorporated in River Forest as Rosary College. The institution has been coeducational since 1970. In 1996, the Board of Trustees formally approved changing the name of the institution to Dominican University.

The atmosphere on the 30-acre wooded campus is close-knit. The ivy-covered Gothic buildings are impressive, including a recently redesigned 287,000-volume library with cyber cafe, a Fine Arts Building with a recital hall and auditorium, two fully networked residence halls, and the Student Center, home to the men's and women's basketball and women's volleyball teams. Alive with activity, the center has an elevated running track, an indoor swimming pool, and a student grill that overlooks the glass-enclosed racquetball courts. Other varsity sports include men's baseball, cross-country, soccer, and tennis and women's cross-country, soccer, softball, and tennis. New intercollegiate and recreational soccer fields were recently constructed. A new residence hall was constructed in 2003.

Rosary College of Arts and Sciences offers more than fifty major fields of study. The University also has four graduate schools: Business, Education, Library and Information Science, and Social Work. Approximately 50 percent of the corporate librarians or information specialists in the Chicago area are graduates of Dominican University.

With Spring Fling, the Founder's Day Celebration, and the inspiring Candle and Rose ceremony, Dominican University's traditions make college life rewarding and memorable for students. A variety of clubs and honor societies also offer the opportunity for students to get involved. Students often travel off campus, perhaps to a Cubs baseball game at Wrigley Field or perhaps to a Chicago soup kitchen as a Campus Ministry volunteer. The University also sponsors a wide range of cultural programs on campus, ranging from lectures, plays, and concert performances by the Vienna Boys Choir and the Chicago Sinfonietta, the orchestra-in-residence, to an appearance by Ben Vereen. Recent theater productions include *Singin' in the Rain, The Sound of Music,* and *Much Ado About Nothing.*

At Dominican, opportunities to grow are limited only by a student's imagination.

Location

Dominican University is located in River Forest, a residential suburb just 10 miles west of Chicago's Loop. Students can take advantage of city offerings by using nearby public transportation, or they can enjoy the surrounding Oak Park–River Forest residential community, which, among other attractions, is home to the largest number of Frank Lloyd Wright houses in the country. These include Wright's first home and studio.

Majors and Degrees

Dominican University awards both the Bachelor of Arts and the Bachelor of Science degrees. Programs include accounting, addiction counseling, African/African-American studies, American studies, art, biology, biology-chemistry, business administration, business writing, chemistry, communication arts and sciences, computer graphics, computer information systems, computer science, corporate communication, criminology, economics, education (early childhood, elementary, and secondary), engineering, English, environmental science, environmental studies, fashion design, fashion merchandising, fine arts, food science and nutrition, food service management, French, gerontology, graphic design, history, international business, international relations and diplomacy, Italian, journalism, mathematics, mathematics and computer science, nutrition and dietetics, occupational therapy, pastoral ministry, pharmacy, philosophy, photography, political science, psychology, social science, sociology, Spanish, theater arts, and theology.

The Bachelor of Arts Honors Degree is awarded to students who complete the interdisciplinary Honors Program. Preprofessional programs are available in dentistry, law, library and information science, and medicine. In cooperation with Rush University, Dominican University offers an occupational therapy program. Engineering students complete a five-year degree program, earning a Bachelor of Arts degree from Dominican University and a Bachelor of Science degree from Illinois Institute of Technology.

Dominican University's Institute for Adult Learning (IAL) offers a unique, flexible means of degree completion for adult students who have been out of high school for at least seven years, have some college credit, and desire to complete their degree in an accelerated format. Designed for the fastest-growing segment in higher education today, the IAL offers programs compatible with adults' personal and professional needs, providing the services adult learners demand to achieve their specific goals. The IAL offers a Bachelor of Science in Organizational Leadership (B.S.O.L.), a Bachelor of Science in Computer Information Systems (B.S.C.I.S.) and a Master of Science in Organizational Leadership (M.S.O.L.).

Academic Programs

The curriculum of Rosary College of Arts and Sciences is built around a core of interdisciplinary seminars and liberal arts requirements. One interdisciplinary seminar is taken at each academic level. The liberal arts core requirements include history, philosophy, social sciences, natural sciences, literature and fine arts, and theology. In addition, students must demonstrate proficiency in writing, mathematics, computer applications, research, and a foreign language. The language requirement can be met in a variety of ways, including study abroad. Service learning and experiential learning opportunities are available to all students. Students must complete 124 credit hours to graduate.

The Honors Program is designed to adapt the strengths of a small institution to the special needs of superior students. In their senior year, honors students complete special projects in their major fields.

Off-Campus Programs

Students have a variety of opportunities to study off campus, ranging from the study-abroad programs described below to the

Washington Semester, a semester of study at the Washington (D.C.) Center for Learning Alternatives. Students in the sciences and mathematics have the opportunity to do research at Argonne National Laboratory, one of the outstanding research centers in the country. Juniors and seniors who have fulfilled any prerequisites set up by their major department may earn credit through internships. The internships provide on-the-job experience that gives students a realistic view of their field.

Students are encouraged to deepen their understanding of other peoples and cultures through study-abroad programs. The semester in London includes 6 to 8 semester hours of British life and culture and 6 to 8 semester hours of independent study. Other study-abroad programs are available in Florence, Milan, and Salamanca. In addition, Dominican University faculty members assist students who wish to study in other countries.

Academic Facilities

At the heart of academic life is the redesigned Rebecca Crown Library, with more than 287,000 volumes, 1,200 periodicals, and nearly 70,000 federal government documents. The library's membership in LCS (an online network of more than thirty academic libraries in Illinois) and ILLINET Online (a network of 600 public and academic libraries) provides access to more than 10 million volumes and nearly 10,000 current periodicals. A multimillion-dollar redesign of the library was completed in 2003. The University also provides computer laboratories and classrooms where students may do classwork or personal projects. In the Fine Arts Building, students attend lectures, plays, and musical performances in the auditorium and recital halls or view exhibitions in the art gallery. The Science Building is also home to the Junior Citizens' Child Development Center, a licensed day-care facility for children of students, community residents, and faculty and staff members.

Costs

Tuition for 2004–05 is $18,900 for full-time students. Room and board charges are approximately $5890, and costs vary depending on the type of room and meal plan selected. Part-time students are charged $630 per credit hour. The cost of books averages $800 per academic year.

Financial Aid

Dominican University supports both merit-based and need-based financial aid programs. Academic scholarships that range from $6000 to full tuition are offered to qualified full-time incoming freshmen based on class rank, grades, and ACT/SAT I scores. Full-time transfer students with a minimum cumulative GPA of 3.3 at previous institutions also qualify for scholarships. Parish Leadership Awards are available to full-time incoming students.

Need-based financial aid programs include grants, loans, and campus employment. Students may apply for financial aid by submitting the Free Application for Federal Student Aid (FAFSA). Aid awards are made on a rolling basis, but early application is encouraged.

Approximately 75 percent of undergraduate students receive some form of financial assistance.

Faculty

Excellent teachers ensure the excellence of education. At Dominican University, more than 85 percent of the faculty hold doctoral or terminal degrees. With a student-faculty ratio of 12:1, individualized attention is the norm.

All classes at Rosary College of Arts and Sciences are taught by faculty members of the University; there are no teaching assistants. The highest priority of the University is teaching. In addition, faculty members conduct research and publish works in their academic disciplines.

All advising is done by members of the faculty, who guide students in choosing their courses, selecting majors, and developing career interests. Close interaction between faculty members and students is the hallmark of the undergraduate program.

Student Govenment

Members of the Student Government Association (SGA) represent students on various official committees such as the board of trustees, educational policies committee, and judicial review board. In addition, SGA sponsors educational and social events for students and distributes student activities fees to the clubs and organizations.

Admission Requirements

Graduation from an accredited secondary school is required for admission. Most entering freshmen rank in the upper 25 percent of their graduating class and have an average GPA of 3.3 on a 4.0 scale. Transfer students with a GPA below 2.5 from a previous institution are required to present a high school transcript and come to the University for an interview before an admission decision is made. A transfer credit evaluation is made before a deposit is required.

Application and Information

Rosary College of Arts and Sciences operates on a rolling admissions program. However, early application is recommended to ensure that financial aid and housing are available. A $25 application fee is charged, and a $100 tuition deposit is required after acceptance. The IAL application fee is $45. A $100 housing deposit is required for students who plan to live on campus.

For more information, students may contact:

Office of Undergraduate Admissions
Dominican University
7900 West Division
River Forest, Illinois 60305
Telephone: 708-524-6800
800-828-8475 (toll-free)
Fax: 708-524-5990
E-mail: domadmis@dom.edu
World Wide Web: http://www.dom.edu

Dominican University's Lewis Hall.

DOMINICAN UNIVERSITY OF CALIFORNIA

SAN RAFAEL, CALIFORNIA

The University

Dominican University of California is an independent, learning-centered university of Catholic heritage. It offers a beautiful setting, a close-knit community of approximately 1,750 students, and an intimate social environment that is an important context for academic goals and personal development.

The Office of Student Development coordinates many services that support the University's educational programs. It provides tutoring, life-planning, career, and personal counseling without charge to Dominican students; offers housing, health, and job placement services; and helps students make the most of their college experience by its readiness to assist them in resolving problems.

The University and the Associated Students of Dominican University sponsor a number of campus activities each year for both resident and nonresident students. Dominican supports eleven intercollegiate teams that compete in the NAIA California Pacific Conference: men's lacrosse; men's and women's basketball, golf, soccer, and tennis; and women's softball and volleyball. Students can participate in the chorus, drama group, literary magazine, newspaper, campus ministry activities, special interest clubs, dances, and other social events.

Campus Ministry responds to the spiritual needs of Catholic and non-Catholic members of the University community. Catholic liturgies, ecumenical activities for students of all faiths, and community service projects are scheduled throughout the year.

Graduate degrees (M.A., M.S., and M.B.A.) and credentials are granted in counseling psychology, education, humanities, international business with a Pacific Basin focus, nursing, and strategic leadership.

Four residence halls of varied architecture accommodate more than 400 students; there is a dining hall for resident students and others who wish to purchase meals on campus. Forest Meadows, which comprises approximately 25 acres, is the site of the new Conlan Recreation Center, a soccer field, and an outdoor amphitheater where commencement exercises are held. The Recreation Center features regulation basketball and volleyball courts, two cross-courts for volleyball and basketball, and 1,285 spectator seats. It also features a weight-training and fitness room, a multipurpose room, lockers, athletic department offices, and conference rooms. Outside is a six-lane recreational swimming pool and grassy patio area.

Location

The University is located on 80 wooded acres in scenic Marin County, which is 11 miles north of San Francisco and within a half hour's drive of Pacific Ocean beaches.

Majors and Degrees

A broad range of degrees and certificate and credential programs are offered in letters, the arts and sciences, and professional and preprofessional disciplines.

Undergraduate degrees (B.A., B.S., B.S.N., and B.F.A.) are awarded in the academic areas of art, art history, biological sciences (with concentrations in premedical studies, neuroscience, and ecology), communications (with a concentration in journalism), digital art, e-business, English, English with a writing emphasis, environmental studies, history, humanities, interdisciplinary studies, international management, international studies, liberal studies, music, music with a performance concentration, nursing, occupational therapy, politics, psychology, and religion.

Minors are offered in chemistry, Latin American studies, philosophy, and prelaw.

Academic Programs

The General Education Program offers more than a brief exposure to the major areas of knowledge in the humanities, arts, and natural and social sciences. It is designed to provide a sequence of courses with a thematic focus that integrates the wisdom and perspectives of several disciplines. The focus assists students in discovering relationships between areas of knowledge, beliefs, cultures, and peoples that differ globally and historically, as well as in acquiring an awareness of tradition, a love of discovery, a respect for the diversity of the human condition, and a realization of human interdependence. Courses within the General Education Program also expose students to a variety of learning experiences that includes discussion, lectures, seminars, simulations, practicums, and quiet reflection.

A strong internship program offers students job experience in areas of their choice.

An evening degree-completion program (Pathways) for adult learners is also available.

The ELS Language Centers program provides intensive, high-quality English instruction to prepare international students to enter American colleges and universities. Completion of the ELS Language Centers program Level 112 satisfies Dominican's English requirement for admission.

Off-Campus Programs

Dominican offers exchange programs with Aquinas College, Grand Rapids, Michigan; Barry University, Miami, Florida; the College of New Rochelle, New Rochelle, New York; and St. Thomas Aquinas College, Sparkill, New York. These programs enable students matriculated at any one of the five colleges to spend a semester on a campus in a different part of the country, taking advantage of its location and programs. Students pay tuition on their home campus and room and board on the host campus. Further information about the program, recommended for students in the sophomore or junior year, is available in the campus Service Center.

Individualized programs for study in other countries may be planned in consultation with Dominican's Center for International Programs, the adviser, and the transcript evaluator. Dominican grants credit for international study only after a student who obtained prior approval of the program of study has returned to the campus and enrolled for the following year.

Arrangements are available whereby Dominican students can participate in Army ROTC at the University of San Francisco, Air Force ROTC at San Francisco State University, or Naval ROTC at the University of California at Berkeley. Students interested in the ROTC programs should request further information from the appropriate ROTC recruiting officer.

Academic Facilities

Archbishop Alemany Library houses more than 100,000 volumes in open stacks; 3,000 reels of microfilm; 500 videocassettes, audiocassettes, and compact discs; and subscriptions to

500 periodicals in print, in addition to another 1,200 in full-text online. The library also houses the Fletcher Jones Computer Laboratory, an art gallery, a listening room, and a fireplace corner.

Guzman Hall, Albertus Magnus Hall, Bertrand Hall, and the San Marco Art Gallery together house faculty offices, science laboratories, lecture halls, a computer center, art galleries and studios, and classrooms. Angelico Hall houses an 850-seat concert auditorium and theater, music studios and practice rooms, and faculty offices.

Costs

Undergraduate full-time tuition (12–17 units per semester) is $24,254 per year for 2004–05. Fees are $200; room and board (a nineteen-meal-per-week plan) are $9400 annually.

Financial Aid

Financial aid is awarded on the basis of need and merit. Dominican University participates in various federal and state need-based financial aid programs and also has its own financial aid funds, donated by generous alumni and friends, available to help meet University costs.

Need-based financial aid comes in the form of scholarships, grants, part-time employment, and loans. The federal and state financial aid programs are the Federal Supplemental Educational Opportunity Grant, Federal Pell Grant, Federal Work-Study Program, Federal Stafford Student Loan, CLAS/PLUS loan, and Cal Grants A and B. Eligibility for need-based aid is determined after the student, who must be a citizen or permanent resident of the United States, files the Free Application for Federal Student Aid (FAFSA). The need-based financial aid deadline for first priority consideration is February 1, although late applications are accepted. Student assistantship positions are also available for graduate students.

Faculty

Students find themselves intellectually challenged by the faculty members, who hold degrees from colleges and universities throughout the world and who are committed to individualized teaching and careful supervision of students' development. The majority of the faculty members hold Ph.D.'s. The student-faculty ratio is 10:1.

Student Government

The primary vehicle through which students plan and provide activities, distribute activity funds, and represent themselves to the University's administration and broader community is ASDU—the Associated Students of Dominican University. ASDU is the student association and the student government body. Through elected and appointed representatives to various Dominican committees and governing groups, students may voice their opinions on institutional matters.

Admission Requirements

Dominican University welcomes applications from prospective students of all ages, religions, races, and national origins. Although the University prefers that candidates have a grade point average of at least 2.7 (a minimum of 2.0 for non-nursing/occupational therapy transfer students), the University believes that academic potential is measured by more than grades alone. Each candidate for admission is given individual consideration and is evaluated by the Admissions Office on the basis of the student's past scholastic record, present motivation, and potential intellectual development as indicated by all of the admission materials submitted.

Recommended for undergraduate admission are graduation from an accredited high school with a total of at least 15 units in college-preparatory subjects, to include the following: 4 years of English, 2 years of the same foreign language, 2 years of college-preparatory mathematics (algebra, geometry, trigonometry), 1 year of laboratory sciences to be taken in grades 10–12, and 1 year of U.S. history (1 year of world history or Western civilization is an acceptable alternative for international students). The University encourages students to choose additional courses in at least two of the following areas: English, history, foreign language, social science, advanced mathematics, laboratory science, music, art, and computer science.

Dominican University admits highly qualified students after the completion of their junior year in high school if they have fulfilled all admission requirements for freshman standing or passed an equivalency exam and arranged a conference with a member of the admission staff prior to acceptance.

High school seniors wishing to take up to two Dominican University courses per semester to meet high school graduation requirements may do so with the written permission of their high school principal or counselor. Arrangements must be made through the Office of Admissions.

Application and Information

The Admissions Office makes its decision on each freshman candidate after receiving his or her completed application form with a $40 nonrefundable fee; an official high school transcript to date; one recommendation from a teacher, administrator, or counselor; scores from either the SAT I or the ACT; and a personal essay as described in the application. For information about the SAT I, students should write to Educational Testing Service, 1947 Center Street, Berkeley, California 94704 or P.O. Box 592, Princeton, New Jersey 08541. For information about the ACT, students should write to American College Testing Program, Operations Division, P.O. Box 168, Iowa City, Iowa 52243.

Transfer students must also submit the application form, a $40 fee, and their high school transcript if they have fewer than 24 transfer units. In addition, they must send official college transcripts to date, a personal essay as described in the application, and one academic letter of recommendation or one professional letter of reference.

International students should fulfill the admission requirements for native students; however, an SAT I or ACT score is not required. A score of at least 550 on the Test of English as a Foreign Language (TOEFL), administered by the Educational Testing Service, or official certification of achieving Level 112 in the ELS program may be submitted in lieu of SAT I or ACT scores.

An interview with a member of the admission staff is strongly recommended to enable the candidate and the University to become acquainted with one another.

Students may apply online at the Web site listed below, or they may obtain application forms and information by contacting:

Office of Admissions
Dominican University of California
50 Acacia Avenue
San Rafael, California 94901-2298

Telephone: 415-485-3204
888-323-6763 (toll-free)

Fax: 415-485-3214
E-mail: enroll@dominican.edu
World Wide Web: http://www.dominican.edu

DRAKE UNIVERSITY

DES MOINES, IOWA

The University

A Drake University education offers a unique mix of advantages for future success. More than seventy major programs of study—including top-notch professional and preprofessional programs and options for undecided students—create lively and diverse learning opportunities. Drake's outstanding faculty members are renowned scholars and experts whose top priority is teaching. The student-faculty ratio is 14:1, and no graduate assistants teach classes. Drake's 5,100 students, including 3,330 full-time undergraduates and 430 full-time graduate and law school students, represent forty-eight states and more than sixty countries. Approximately 1,700 students live on campus. Drake provides full high-speed connections to the University's telecommunications and fiber-optic systems, with an Ethernet port for every resident. Ninety-three percent of Drake graduates find career employment or enter graduate school within six months of earning their degrees.

In addition to its undergraduate degrees, Drake offers master's degrees in accounting, business administration, education, mass communication, and public administration, as well as the Doctor of Pharmacy, Doctor of Jurisprudence, and Doctor of Education degrees. The following joint degrees also are offered: M.B.A./J.D., M.B.A./Pharm.D., and M.P.A./J.D.

Location

Drake University's 150-acre campus is located in Des Moines, Iowa's capital and largest city. Des Moines offers numerous internship and employment opportunities in all fields, including government, banking, insurance, publishing, nonprofit organizations, and health care. More than 73 percent of Drake students graduate having had one or more internships. With a metropolitan population of approximately 450,000, Des Moines also offers diverse cultural and entertainment options, a convention center, a nationally known art center, a civic center, professional athletics, parks and bike trails, and a downtown skywalk system.

Majors and Degrees

The College of Arts and Sciences offers degree programs and liberal arts education experiences that equip students to apply knowledge and skills to the scientific, mathematical, literary, and artistic tasks that will confront them in all careers. The college awards Bachelor of Arts and Bachelor of Science degrees with majors in anthropology and sociology; astronomy; biochemistry, cell and molecular biology; biology; chemistry; computer science; English; environmental policy; environmental science; ethics; history; international relations; law, politics, and society; mathematics; mathematics education (secondary); neuroscience; philosophy; physics; politics; psychology; religion; rhetoric and communication studies; sociology; and writing. The college offers individualized majors and an open enrolled (undeclared) option. Preprofessional study and combined-degree programs are available in church vocations, dentistry, law, medicine and allied fields, and physics/engineering. Concentrations are available in aging studies, cultural studies, geography, Latin American studies, multicultural studies, and women's studies. Through the School of Fine Arts, the College of Arts and Sciences awards Bachelor of Arts, Bachelor of Fine Arts, Bachelor of Music, and Bachelor of Music Education degrees, offering programs in art, music, and theater arts with a dual focus on teaching excellence and artistic creativity. The Department of Art and Design, which is accredited by the National Association of Schools of Art and Design, provides degree programs in art history, graphic design, and studio art (drawing, painting, printmaking, and sculpture). The Department of Music provides degree programs in applied music (instrumental, piano, or vocal music performance), church music, music education, and piano pedagogy. Students may earn a Bachelor of Arts degree with a major in music, a Bachelor of Music degree with elective studies in business, and a music major with a jazz studies concentration. The Department of Theatre Arts offers majors in acting, directing, musical theater, theater, theater design, and theater education. The undeclared option is available in art, music, and theater arts.

Drake University's College of Business and Public Administration provides a four-year undergraduate program leading to the Bachelor of Science in Business Administration, with majors in accounting, accounting/other business major, actuarial science, actuarial science/finance, economics, finance, general business, human resource management concentration, information systems, information technology, insurance concentration, international business, management, and marketing. Interdisciplinary majors, combinations of majors, a concentration in insurance, and open business (undeclared) enrollment are also available. The college is accredited by the AACSB–The International Association to Advance Collegiate Schools of Business. Drake's College of Pharmacy and Health Sciences offers a six-year Pharm.D. degree program. First-year students are admitted directly into the college as prepharmacy majors. The college is accredited by the American Council on Pharmaceutical Education and is a member of the American Association of Colleges of Pharmacy. The School of Journalism and Mass Communication offers a Bachelor of Arts in Journalism and Mass Communication with majors in advertising (management and creative tracks), electronic media (broadcast news and radio/television), magazines, news/Internet, and public relations. An open enrolled (undeclared) option is also available. The school is accredited by the Accrediting Council on Education in Journalism and Mass Communication. In addition, the College of Arts and Sciences, the College of Business and Public Administration, and the School of Journalism offer combined 3+3 programs with Drake Law School. Students in this program can obtain their undergraduate degrees in three years in one of the aforementioned schools, then pursue a law degree for the next three years at the Law School. Drake's School of Education offers professional programs in elementary education, secondary education, and rehabilitation services. The University awards the Bachelor of Science in Education for teaching at the elementary level and the Bachelor of Arts or Bachelor of Science for teaching at the secondary level. Elementary and secondary education majors also may add middle school and coaching endorsements to their teaching credentials. Drake University has been a member of the American Association of Colleges for Teacher Education since the association's inception.

Academic Program

What makes the Drake experience so exceptional is the wide variety of accessible, hands-on learning opportunities students have both in class and out of class, beginning in their first year. Drake students conduct real research with top-notch faculty members, and many students present and publish their work. They student-teach in local schools; participate in and lead more than 160 campus organizations; perform in campus and community theater productions and music ensembles; and work on the campus newspaper, radio/TV station, and award-winning magazines. Students also gain invaluable experience in career-related internships in all fields, and they network with Drake's 45,000 alumni worldwide, many of whom are business and civic leaders in central Iowa and beyond.

A Drake education combines a foundation in the liberal arts and sciences with professional programs. The Drake curriculum offers extraordinary preparation for the varied challenges of career and life, with discussion-based first-year seminars, individualized plans for achieving educational goals, and a Senior Capstone—a research project, thesis, or other major work that demonstrates a student's ideas and abilities. Candidates for an undergraduate degree are required to successfully complete a minimum of 124 semester hours. Exceptional students may participate in Drake's Honors Program, a challenging interdisciplinary program of study. Students also have many opportunities for internships, undergraduate research, independent study, and combined bachelor's and master's degree programs.

Qualified Drake students may earn credit through the College Board's Advanced Placement Program, the International Baccalaureate, and the College-Level Examination Program.

The academic year is divided into two semesters; summer terms are also offered.

Off-Campus Programs

Through the Center for International Programs and Services, which maintains affiliations with several institutions and consortia, students can arrange to study overseas for a semester or a year. Programs are available in Argentina, Australia, Austria, Belgium, Belize, Bolivia, Botswana, Brazil, Cameroon, Canada, Central America, Chile, China, Costa Rica, Cuba, Czech Republic, Dominican Republic, Ecuador, England, France, Germany, Ghana, Greece, Guatemala, Hong Kong, Hungary, India, Indonesia, Ireland, Italy, Jamaica, Japan, Jordan, Kenya, Latin America, Madagascar, Mali, Malta, Mexico, Morocco, Namibia, Nepal, the Netherlands, New Zealand, Nicaragua, Northern Ireland, Poland, Russia, Samoa, Scotland, South Africa, Spain, Switzerland, Taiwan, Tanzania, Thailand, Tibet, Tunisia, Turkey, Uganda, Venezuela, Vietnam, Wales, and Zimbabwe and the Semester at Sea program is offered.

Academic Facilities

Cowles Library contains more than 400,000 books and has current subscriptions to more than 1,600 periodical titles. In addition, the library contains government publications and microforms and provides access to many electronic information resources. Specialized collections are also maintained by Drake's colleges and schools, including the Law School, the College of Pharmacy and Health Sciences, the Center for Teacher Education, and the School of Fine Arts. The Dwight D. Opperman Hall and Law Library contains a computer resource facility, study rooms, and more than 300,000 volumes. The multimillion-dollar Harmon Fine Arts Center includes the Studio Theatre, the Monroe Recital Hall, and the 600-seat Hall of the Performing Arts. The 775-seat Sheslow Auditorium in Old Main also provides a beautiful performance hall.

Costs

For the 2003–04 school year, tuition was $19,100, and room and board were $5700. Full-time students also pay an annual $220 technology fee and $100 student activities fee.

Financial Aid

Drake University's financial aid program is designed to offer, within the University's resources, all capable and deserving students the opportunity for higher education. The average financial aid package awarded to Drake students in 2002–03 was $16,400. Approximately 94 percent of full-time Drake students receive some form of financial aid; Drake provides more than 5,000 grants and scholarships on a merit and need basis and $50 million in financial assistance annually. Students interested in applying for financial aid should contact Drake's Office of Student Financial Planning and should file the Free Application for Federal Student Aid (FAFSA) by March 1. Students may apply for all federal, state, and institutional awards on this form.

Faculty

Drake's 244 full-time faculty members are accomplished in their fields and dedicated to their professions, yet they are primarily teachers. Full professors, including department chairs, regularly teach introductory-level courses. Each student works with a faculty adviser. The student-faculty ratio is 14:1.

Student Government

Drake offers students a wide variety of opportunities for campus involvement. Students play an active role in academic planning and campus governance through the Student Senate and its committees as well as through representation on some committees of the Faculty Senate. Students are elected to the senate by the student body. Students are also elected to the Student Activities Board, which plans cultural, social, educational, and special events. The Residence Hall Association is a network of student representatives who plan activities, address concerns, and provide information about residential life.

Admission Requirements

Admission to Drake University is selective. Because the University prefers students with varied talents and interests, there is no single, inflexible set of admission standards. The admission process involves a comprehensive review of a student's academic background (courses and grades), standardized test scores (ACT or SAT I), personal essay, recommendations, and activities in both high school and the community. Drake University admits students without regard to age, sex, sexual orientation, race, religion, color, national or ethnic origin, or disability.

To be considered for admission, first-year applicants must submit a completed application form, the $25 nonrefundable application fee (the fee is waived for those who apply online), the High School Report and Counselor Recommendation Form, an official high school transcript, ACT or SAT I scores, and a personal essay (not required but highly recommended). Transfer applicants are considered for admission on the basis of all college work attempted. Transfer students must provide official transcripts from all colleges and universities attended previously; high school transcripts may also be requested.

Application and Information

Application for admission to undergraduate degree programs, except the pharmacy program, may be made for any fall, spring, or summer term. Beginning October 1, students are notified of the admission decision within three weeks of the date that all materials are received. March 1 is the priority deadline for consideration for admission and merit- and need-based financial aid. Freshman applicants to the College of Pharmacy and Health Sciences must meet either the December 1 priority deadline or the February 1 final deadline. Transfer students are only admitted to the professional Pharm.D. program. Candidates should contact:

Tom Willoughby
Vice President for Admission and Financial Aid
Drake University
2507 University Avenue
Des Moines, Iowa 50311
Telephone: 515-271-3181
800-44-DRAKE Ext. 3181 (toll-free in U.S.)
Fax: 515-271-2831
World Wide Web: http://www.choose.drake.edu

DREW UNIVERSITY

MADISON, NEW JERSEY

The University

Drew prepares students for personal and professional growth in a rapidly changing world. It provides a rigorous liberal arts education characterized by inspiring teaching, close student-faculty relationships, the integration of modern technology into the study of the traditional arts and sciences, widespread opportunities for hands-on learning, and the cultivation of interdisciplinary and global perspectives. Students become fluent in the use of electronic information systems, explore the ideas and methodologies of diverse fields of study, sharpen the critical thinking and communications skills essential to success in all professions, and learn to place subjects of inquiry into larger intellectual and cultural contexts.

Ubiquitous computing, in which every student has a laptop computer and access to the campus network and the Internet, has been the foundation of the College's technology program for many years. Drew recently received a Pioneer Award from Educause for this program. The campus network includes ATTIC (Academic Technology Tools for Instructional Computing), an award-winning program that automatically provides shared network space as well as course management. Specialized facilities include thirteen mediated classrooms, a Multimedia Lab and a multimedia Language Resource Center, user labs and a computer classroom in the Academic Computer Center, a networked writing classroom, and many departmental facilities. Technology is used for teaching and learning throughout the curriculum, from music to statistics, and many faculty members participate in technology workshops and use a faculty lab to prepare digitized course materials. Students can also register and check their grades online. Residence halls offer students access to voice mail and cable TV.

Drew is committed to providing students with a global perspective through special off-campus programs, a variety of area studies programs, and curricular opportunities to investigate the history, economics, politics, literature, religions, and cultures of other nations and heritages. In addition, student-organized clubs and activities promote and celebrate the multicultural and international diversity of the campus community. Along with the faculty and staff members, Drew students (coming from thirty-nine states and ten countries) help create a stimulating and supportive campus community. Drew's enrollment totals more than 2,400 students, of whom more than 1,500 are undergraduates.

Ninety percent of Drew students live on campus in traditional residence halls or in special theme/language houses (ASIA Tree House, Umoja House, Environmental Concerns House, La Casa, Spirituality House, Islamic Culture House, and Womyn's Concerns House). Fourteen percent of Drew students are members of American ethnic minority groups. Drew students exert extraordinary influence on student affairs and provide leadership in more than eighty clubs and organizations, including an award-winning newspaper, a radio station, a television station, a literary magazine, a prelaw society and law journal, cultural clubs, a social committee, service organizations, an environmental action group, political clubs, fine and performing arts groups, and intramural sports programs. In addition, students may attend more than 300 free lectures, concerts, exhibits, conferences, films, dances, parties, and performances each year. Speakers appearing in Drew's Forum have included Presidents George Bush and Gerald Ford, Shimon Peres, Colin Powell, Leah Rabin, Mike Wallace, Henry Kissinger, Barbara Bush, Bill Moyers, Walter Cronkite, and Tim Russert. The University also sponsors varsity sports (NCAA Division III), which include men's and women's basketball, cross-country, lacrosse, soccer, swimming, and tennis; women's field hockey and softball; men's baseball; and coed equestrian riding (IHSA) and fencing.

Drew has maintained a historical affiliation with the United Methodist Church since the school's founding in 1867 and provides a chaplain who, along with Roman Catholic and Jewish clergy, conducts worship services and oversees various student religious groups, including Catholic Campus Ministry, Hillel, Hindu Gathering, Methodist Ministry, and others.

Drew also has a graduate school, which offers eleven master's and eight doctoral programs in the humanities, as well as a theological school, which offers five professional degrees.

Location

Drew's undergraduates enjoy a location that affords a wide variety of academic, cultural, and recreational opportunities. Just 30 miles west of New York City, the quaint, small town of Madison, New Jersey, provides a safe home to Drew's beautiful, heavily wooded, 186-acre campus. The immediate area has the highest concentration of headquarters for international corporations and research companies in the nation. Proximity to these resources, and to those provided by New York City, makes special semesters, academic internships, research assistantships, field trips, and guest speakers important parts of all department curricula. In addition, numerous parks and recreational areas, including the Jersey Shore, several ski resorts, Giants Stadium, and the Meadowlands, are all within a 1-hour ride by car, commuter train, or bus.

Majors and Degrees

The College of Liberal Arts awards the Bachelor of Arts degree in anthropology, art, behavioral science, biochemistry, biology, chemistry, classics, computer science, economics, English, French, German, history, mathematics, mathematics and computer science, music, neurosciences, philosophy, physics, political science, psychology, religious studies, Russian, sociology, Spanish, theater arts, and women's studies. Interdisciplinary and other special majors may be arranged. Minors are available in major subject areas (except behavioral science and neurosciences) as well as in African-American/African studies, American studies, archaeology, arts administration and museology, Asian studies, business management, Chinese comparative literature, environmental studies, European studies, Holocaust studies, humanities, Jewish studies, Latin American studies, linguistic studies, Middle East studies, Western heritage, and writing. Nonmajor offerings include international relations, marine biology, and foreign languages, including Arabic, Chinese, Greek, Hebrew, and Italian.

A seven-year, dual-degree program (including three years of study at Drew) leads to a B.A. from Drew and a medical degree (M.D.) from the University of Medicine and Dentistry of New Jersey–New Jersey Medical School (UMDNJ–NJMS) in Newark. An articulation agreement with the Graduate School of Management of Rutgers University offers qualified Drew graduates guaranteed admission to the M.B.A. program in professional accounting. Five-year cooperative programs lead to a B.A. from Drew and a master's degree in forestry or environmental management from Duke University, a B.S. in engineering from Washington University in St. Louis or Columbia University in New York, or a B.S. in chemical engineering from Stevens Institute of Technology. Through a cross-registration agreement with the College of St. Elizabeth, students may earn teacher certification in several areas.

Academic Program

Drew operates on a two-semester calendar. To graduate with the bachelor's degree, students must complete 128 credit hours, including a major, the First-Year Seminar, and, as part of the general education program, a minor. The major is chosen by the end of the sophomore year. Independent study, a regular offering in some departments, is an option in all departments. Up to 8 semester hours may be earned in off-campus internships for academic credit. General and specialized honors are awarded in the major field. Drew has one of New Jersey's three Phi Beta Kappa chapters as well as chapters of twelve other national honor societies: Alpha Kappa Delta (sociology), Beta Beta Beta (biology), Omicron Delta Epsilon (economics), Delta Phi Alpha (German), Phi Alpha Theta (history), Pi Delta Phi (French), Pi Mu Epsilon (mathematics), Pi Sigma Alpha (political science), Sigma Pi Sigma (physics), Psi Chi (psychology), Sigma Delta Pi (Spanish), and Dobro Slovo (Russian). There is also Epsilon Omega Psi, Drew's Educational Opportunity Scholars honors program, and Pinnacle, for nontraditional continuing education students.

Off-Campus Programs

The Drew International Seminars Program was established to allow as many students as possible to study, on location, a culture other than their own. In small groups, students and faculty members engage in course work on campus combined with three to four weeks of on-site, interdisciplinary study during January or May. Subjects and locations vary each year, depending on interest. In 2002–03, programs were held in Chile, Paris, Brazil, China and Southeast Asia, Eritrea, Iceland, and Italy. Students receive 8 credits for the entire program. The University subsidizes all travel, room, and board costs for the seminar; students are only charged tuition. Drew sponsors a summer program on the arts and culture of Western Africa and semester-long programs that offer on-site study of British politics, history, literature, and theater in London; American politics and public policy in Washington, D.C.; and theater, contemporary art, the United Nations, or Wall Street in New York City. Several of these programs include internship opportunities. Students may also participate in off-campus programs sponsored and supervised by other recognized American colleges and universities. University-approved marine biology programs are available at such institutions as the University of Miami, University of Hawaii, Duke University, and the Marine Biological Laboratory at Woods Hole. Closer to campus, credit-bearing internship opportunities in business, communication, industry, government, social service, and the arts and entertainment provide students with professional experiences to complement their studies.

Academic Facilities

The University library complex, which houses more than 480,000 volumes, 3,000 periodicals, and 363,077 microforms, is a federal, state, and United Nations depository. Drew's library is automated. Students and faculty have 24-hour direct access to the Drew library card catalog and selected journal indexes as well as to other bibliographic databases across the nation. In addition to the personal computer system given to each student, Drew maintains open computer labs for multimedia, foreign languages, computer graphics, and general use. The Hall of Sciences contains impressive research-grade equipment, including a scanning electron microscope; an observatory with solar radio and optical telescopes; a greenhouse; a laser holography laboratory; nuclear magnetic resonance, infrared, ultraviolet-visible, and mass spectrometers; and a chemistry and physics library. The William E. and Carol G. Simon Forum and Athletic Center is open to the entire University community. There is seating capacity for 4,000 people in its indoor forum, featuring a Cybex fitness room; an eight-lane, 25-yard pool; a six-lane, 200-meter indoor track; an indoor area with four multipurpose courts for basketball, tennis, or volleyball; and racquetball and squash courts. Other major facilities include the Lena C. Coburn Media Resource Center, the Elizabeth Korn Art Gallery, the Commons Theater, and the recently expanded and renovated Kirby Shakespeare Theatre.

The Dorothy Young Center for the Arts, newly opened in 2003, provides spacious state-of-the-art facilites that significantly expand the already strong offerings of the theater and art departments. A concert hall will be added by 2004.

Costs

Tuition for the 2003–04 academic year was $27,360, fees were $821, and room and board were $7644.

Financial Aid

Drew offers a comprehensive program of need-based and merit-based financial assistance. Last year, 95 percent of the first-year class received some form of assistance. Need-based aid is available in the form of University grants, campus employment, loans, or a combination of these. The Federal Pell Grant, Federal Supplemental Educational Opportunity Grant, Federal Work-Study, state grant, and federal and state loan programs are also sources of aid. A completed Free Application for Federal Student Aid (FAFSA) and a completed PROFILE form of the College Scholarship Service are required of all applicants for need-based aid. The on-time filing deadline is February 15; aid applicants are notified in early April. No special application is necessary for Drew's various academic merit awards, including academic scholarships of between $8000 and full tuition and Thomas H. Kean Minority Scholarships of between $1000 and $15,000. Students must submit a portfolio for the $10,000 awards for artistic talent.

Faculty

Of the University's 121 full-time faculty members, 95 percent hold the Ph.D. or highest degree in their fields. All college faculty members teach undergraduates, including the dean and the president, Thomas H. Kean, the former Governor of New Jersey, who teaches a course on state politics and government. In addition, the Charles A. Dana Research Institute for Scientists Emeriti (RISE) has brought 10 prominent scientists, recently retired from the area's corporate community, to campus to continue their work. With hundreds of patents and publications to their credit, RISE scientists serve as mentors and provide research assistantships for undergraduates.

Student Government

The student government is active in shaping institutional policy, academic and nonacademic. Students sit as voting members on the University Senate and on many college faculty committees, administer their own social program, manage the extracurricular budget, and participate in the judicial process.

Admission Requirements

Applicants for admission are strongly encouraged to complete a minimum of 16 academic units, including 4 in English, 3 in mathematics, 2 in foreign language, 2 in laboratory sciences, 2 in social studies, and 3 in other academic areas. SAT I or ACT scores are required. Admission is based principally on academic performance in high school. Nearly one quarter of Drew's first-year students graduated in the top 5 percent of their high school class; approximately 40 percent in the top tenth; and 75 percent graduated in the top 25 percent. Personal qualities and special talents are also considered. About 20 percent of each freshman class enter under Drew's Early Decision Plan, and early admission is also available. Applications from transfer and international students are encouraged. A campus interview is required for transfer students and is strongly recommended for first-year candidates. Interviews are offered between mid-April and January. Overnight accommodations are available on campus for visiting candidates. Tours are offered throughout the year.

Application and Information

The application deadline for first-year admission is February 15. Candidates are notified after mid-March. Accepted students are expected to respond to an offer of admission by May 1. The early decision application deadlines are December 1 and January 15. Transfer applications are reviewed on a rolling basis beginning April 1. The final deadline for transfer students for the fall semester is August 1.

Dean of College Admissions
Drew University
Madison, New Jersey 07940
Telephone: 973-408-DREW (3739)
Fax: 973-408-3068
E-mail: cadm@drew.edu
World Wide Web: http://www.drew.edu

DREXEL UNIVERSITY

PHILADELPHIA, PENNSYLVANIA

The University

Drexel, a private, nonsectarian coeducational university, has maintained a reputation for academic excellence since its founding in 1891. Its technologically focused academic programs prepare undergraduates for graduate school and a variety of careers. Full-time professional experience through Drexel's cooperative education program is a vital part of a Drexel education. Students gain professional experience in jobs related to their career interests by alternating classroom study with periods of professional experience. More than 1,500 employers from twenty-eight states and fourteen other countries participate in this program.

Drexel University grants bachelor's, master's, and doctoral degrees. The undergraduate enrollment is 11,000 full-time students, representing forty-four states and eighteen countries. Seven residential halls house more than 2,600 students on campus. Drexel offers its students social, cultural, athletic, and community service opportunities. In conjunction with Drexel's thirteen fraternities and six sororities, the Campus Activities Board sponsors events such as dances, lectures, excursions, and films. Students take part in a variety of extracurricular activities, including musical groups, a dance ensemble, theatrical productions, a student-run newspaper, a radio station, and a cable TV station. Drexel offers eighteen NCAA Division I varsity athletic programs, competing in the Colonial Athletic Association Conference, and produces some of the nation's top student athletes in both the academic and athletic arenas. The University sponsors intramural and club sports.

On July 1, 2002, Drexel's Board of Trustees voted unanimously to merge Drexel University and MCP Hahnemann University, one of the Philadelphia region's premier medical and health sciences schools. With the addition of the nation's largest private medical school, an outstanding college of nursing and health professions, and one of only two schools of public health in Pennsylvania, Drexel University now comprises eleven academic colleges and schools. The University offers 175 degree programs to some 11,500 undergraduates and 4,200 graduate students. Alumni number 90,000, and the size of Drexel's full-time faculty exceeds 1,000.

Location

Drexel is located in the University City area of Philadelphia, minutes from the heart of the city. The nation's fifth-largest metropolitan area, Philadelphia is home to world-class museums, theaters, restaurants, historic attractions, and recreational facilities, all easily reached from Drexel's campus. Year-round recreational opportunities can also be found in the Pocono Mountains and at the New Jersey shore, both within 2 hours of the campus. Drexel's main campus is located two blocks from Amtrak's 30th Street Station, providing easy access to New York; Boston; Washington, D.C.; and Baltimore, Maryland.

Majors and Degrees

The College of Arts and Sciences offers the bachelor's degree in anthropology, biological sciences, chemistry, communication, criminal justice, English, environmental science, general humanities and social sciences, history-politics, international area studies, mathematics, nutrition and food science, physics, preprofessional health, psychology, sociology, and unified science. The LeBow College of Business awards the B.S. in commerce and engineering, business administration, and economics. Commerce and engineering and business administration majors can pursue concentrations in accounting, economics, finance, general business, human resource management, international business, management information systems, marketing, and operations management. The College of Engineering awards the B.S. in appropriate technology, architectural engineering, chemical engineering, civil engineering, computer engineering, computer science, electrical engineering, environmental engineering, materials engineering, and mechanical and software engineering. The College of Engineering also offers a B.S./Ph.D. program. The College of Information Science and Technology awards a B.S. in Information Systems (B.S.I.S.) with concentrations available in areas such as analysis and design, distributed systems, information resource management, and knowledge-based systems. Qualified students can now pursue the accelerated degree option of B.S.I.S./M.S.I.S. The College of Media Arts and Design offers a Bachelor of Architecture program and B.S. degree programs in design and merchandising, digital media, dramatic writing, fashion design, film and video, graphic design, interior design, music industry, and photography. The College of Nursing and Health Professions offers undergraduate degree programs and certifications in addictions or behavioral counseling sciences, biomedical sciences, cardiovascular perfusion technology, emergency medical services, health sciences and general studies, health services administration, humanities and sciences, nursing (RN to B.S.N. degree completion), and radiologic technology. The Goodwin College of Professional Studies offers the B.S. in culinary arts, electrical engineering technology, hospitality management, manufacturing engineering technology, mechanical engineering technology, and sports management. The School of Biomedical Engineering, Science, and Health Systems offers a B.S. in biomedical engineering. The School of Education offers a B.S. in teacher education.

Academic Program

Drexel University is home to one of the nation's oldest and most established experiential education programs, Drexel Co-op: "The Ultimate Internship®". Combined with rigorous academic programs, this option provides students a way to bridge academic studies with the working world. Most academic degree programs are in either four- or five-year time frames, including up to eighteen months of co-op experience. Most of the media arts and design programs include six months of co-op. Business, humanities, and social science programs offer both four-year and five-year co-op/internship options.

Each college has its own sequence of graduation requirements, including a common core of subjects and the opportunity for specialization after the core is complete. All engineering and science students share a common program for the first year and part of the second. Specialization begins in the fourth term through elective course work, which also allows students to acquire background in related fields. In the LeBow College of Business, 40 percent of the graduation requirements are in business subjects and 40 percent are in liberal studies. The College of Media Arts and Design requires students to choose an area of professional specialization in the applied arts when applying for admission. The first year of study includes both foundation course work and an introduction to the professional discipline. The College of Arts and Sciences provides students with a broad and useful preparation for a variety of careers as well as preparation for graduate and professional schools. The College of Information Science and Technology provides a foundation program in the liberal arts, sciences, and computers. This foundation prepares students for a choice of specializations within the information systems major, which can lead to careers in such fields as computer education, database administration and design, and information management consulting in business and industry, health and medicine, government, libraries, or education.

Students who have demonstrated academic achievements can apply to the Pennoni Honors College, open to students in every major. Qualified students take part in special sections of general and required courses as well as in honors colloquia and seminars. These students take part in special living communities designed for the exceptional student. They are also encouraged to undertake ambitious independent projects under the supervision of a faculty adviser. Beginning in their third year, qualified students in most of Drexel's engineering and science specialties may take graduate courses along with their undergraduate curricula, graduating with an undergraduate and a graduate degree in an accelerated framework. Accelerated degree options include the B.S./M.S., B.S./M.B.A., B.S./Ph.D., B.S./M.D., B.S./D.P.T. (physical therapy), B.S./M.S.N. (nursing), B.S. (music industry)/M.B.A., B.S. (design and merchandising)/M.B.A., and the accelerated M.H.S. (physician assistant studies).

Academic Facilities

Drexel comprises three campuses: University City Main Campus, Hahnemann Center City Campus, and the Medical School Queen Lane Campus. Buildings contain dozens of state-of-the-art laboratories for classes and research. Drexel University's library system comprises a main library (W. W. Hagerty Library) on the University City Main Campus site as well as three health sciences libraries to serve the needs of students and faculty and staff members. The collections of each library emphasize subjects relevant to the spectrum of health science disciplines, with print resources distributed to meet the needs of the programs and departments at each location. The W. W. Hagerty Library, the University's central library, houses 400,000 volumes and maintains subscriptions to nearly 12,000 electronic journals. The library provides access via its Web site to these journals and 200 databases from library computers or remotely through the Internet. The library circulates laptops for use with its wireless network. Three libraries on the health sciences campuses provide additional study space, 75,000 books on a wide range of clinical and medical subjects, and network access to the same set of online journals and databases.

The LeBow Engineering Center forms a state-of-the-art engineering education complex with the Center for Automation Technology. The Design and Imaging Studio supports programs in the design arts. An electronic-music laboratory provides facilities for creating, modifying, and recording sound and music. In addition to clinical educational facilities, the College of Nursing and Health Professions has ready access to a network of hospitals in Philadelphia, including Hahnemann Hospital, less than a block from the Center City campus. The College of Medicine is home to state-of-the-art lecture halls and a multidisciplinary laboratory (including microscopes equipped with a networked video system) as well as a computer center and library.

As early as 1983, Drexel required incoming freshmen to have personal access to a microcomputer. By 2000, the University had created one of the nation's first fully wireless campuses, including all health sciences campuses. Since then the ubiquity of network access has changed the nature of the educational experience at Drexel. The University has most recently launched a new high-performance parallel computing facility available for faculty and student research. The parallel machine is an IBM RS/6000 S-80 Enterprise Server, which offers high-speed performance and scalability. This server provides a shared memory computing environment with low latency, high bandwidth communication between processors.

Costs

In 2003–04, tuition for full-time freshmen enrolled at Drexel ranged from $19,900 for a student in the five-year program to $24,800 for a student in the four-year program. Fees were approximately $1400 per year, depending on the degree program. The cost of on-campus housing ranged from $1900 to $2200. Board costs were $1300 per year. Books and supplies for 2002–03 were approximately $600 annually, and miscellaneous expenses were about $1800 for commuting students and $1300 for residential students.

Financial Aid

Approximately 87 percent of all freshmen receive financial aid. The aid package may contain academic, athletic, or performing arts scholarships; grants; loans; or part-time employment. Federal programs are also included. All students applying for aid must submit the Free Application for Federal Student Aid by May 1. Notification of incoming freshmen and transfer students begins about March 1. Drexel offers a unique achievement-based award, the A. J. Drexel Scholarship, to all qualified incoming freshmen and transfer students. With an annual award value of up to $19,000, the A. J. Drexel Scholarship is renewable on a yearly basis, provided the student maintains at least a 3.0 GPA and full-time status. Criteria include a strong academic record and involvement in extracurricular and community service activities.

Faculty

Approximately 94 percent of Drexel's full-time faculty members hold the Ph.D. or the highest degree in their field. Many of the engineering faculty members are registered professional engineers. As a matter of policy, faculty members engaged in research and graduate teaching are also required to teach at the undergraduate level. Thus, the undergraduate student benefits from the research activities of the faculty. Specially selected faculty members serve as advisers for freshmen.

Student Government

Drexel's student congress is composed of representatives from each of the colleges, student organizations, and special interest groups. The congress is structured so that all key administrators and deans in the University have student counterparts. Students take part in the governance and other decision-making processes of the University through joint committees and advisory boards.

Admission Requirements

All colleges within the University require completion of a college-preparatory program in high school that includes at least 3 years of mathematics and 1 year of laboratory science. Students applying to major in engineering, the sciences, and commerce and engineering are required to take 4 years of mathematics (through trigonometry) and 2 years of laboratory science; more advanced math, chemistry, and physics are strongly recommended. The quality of academic performance is more important than merely meeting minimum requirements. The strength of preparation is judged primarily by rank in class or relative grade point average, by the degree of improvement in the quality of the academic record, and by the comments and recommendations from principals, guidance counselors, or teachers. Freshman applicants are required to take the SAT I or the ACT. Transfer applicants must have a minimum 2.75 cumulative average for consideration and generally are expected to complete at least 24 credits at a four-year college or community or junior college in a program of study comparable to the one being sought at Drexel.

Application and Information

Applications to Drexel are available online (http://www.drexel.edu/apply) or from the address given below. Each application must be accompanied by a nonrefundable application fee of $50; however, the fee may be waived in cases of extreme hardship if requested by the secondary school or if the student visits the campus. Applications for regular full-time undergraduate status are accepted throughout the senior year. Drexel subscribes to the College Board's Candidates Reply Date of May 1. Transfer students should apply at least three months before the beginning of the term in which they wish to enroll.

Office of Undergraduate Admissions
Drexel University
3141 Chestnut Streets
Philadelphia, Pennsylvania 19104
Telephone: 800-2-DREXEL (toll-free)
World Wide Web: http://www.drexel.edu

DUKE UNIVERSITY

DURHAM, NORTH CAROLINA

The University

Duke University is an independent, comprehensive, coeducational research university that traces its roots to 1838, when it was established as Union Academy in Randolph County, North Carolina. Renamed Trinity College twenty-one years later, the school moved to Durham in 1892. In recognition of its primary benefactors, the Duke family, Trinity College became Duke University in 1924.

Duke offers a variety of outstanding undergraduate programs in two schools—Trinity College of Arts and Sciences and the Pratt School of Engineering. At the graduate level, the master's and doctoral programs in these schools (as well as the University's professional schools in business administration, divinity, the environment, law, medicine, and nursing) consistently rank at or near the top of their fields.

With a limited enrollment of 11,775 full-time students, Duke is among the smallest of the nation's major universities. Of these, 6,065 are undergraduates—5,099 in arts and sciences and 966 in engineering. Because of its size and the emphasis on meeting the needs of a diverse student body, the University maintains a commitment to individual education. At Duke, learning is a priority and teaching is personal. As a result, the student body, as a whole, reflects a quality of creativity and mental restlessness that goes far beyond excellent grades and testing. The University attracts students from all fifty states as well as eighty-five other countries, and about 85 percent of Duke's undergraduates come from states other than North and South Carolina.

Duke believes that to build a strong community students must live together. For this reason, all undergraduates are guaranteed housing as long as space remains available and are required to live on campus for their first three years. To accommodate students' widely varying interests, the residence halls provide diverse living styles, including single-sex or coed dorms, substance-free environments, and theme houses or other selective living groups. About 85 percent of undergraduates live on campus. All first-year students live on East Campus in a community designed to support the academic, residential, and recreational needs and interests of new students, and all sophomores live on West Campus. About 36 percent of undergraduates belong to fraternities or sororities. In addition to a rich campus living environment, students can enjoy a full calendar of activities through the University Union, the University-sponsored Artists Series, the Broadway at Duke Series, and 400 clubs and organizations focusing on everything from cultural and religious interests to intramural sports.

Location

Durham, located about 450 miles from Atlanta and 250 miles from Washington, D.C., is a city of about 223,000 with active research, medical, and arts communities. Together, Durham and nearby Raleigh and Chapel Hill, with a combined population of around 1 million, comprise the Research Triangle, one of the nation's foremost centers for research and high-tech industry. The Research Triangle has one of the highest concentrations of Ph.D.'s and M.D.'s in the world. Two interstates and the Raleigh-Durham International Airport, only 20 minutes from campus, make Durham easily accessible.

Majors and Degrees

Duke offers both a rigorous academic program and considerable flexibility in course selection and degree programs. Undergraduates can choose courses in nearly 100 different programs, including humanities, social sciences and natural sciences, mathematics, and engineering. Thirty-six majors are offered in Trinity College of Arts and Sciences, and students with interests that cannot be met within an established major are able to design their own curriculum with the help of a faculty adviser. In addition, students may pursue dual degrees, minors in most fields, and any of the University's sixteen certificate programs.

Trinity College of Arts and Sciences offers programs leading to the A.B. degree or the B.S. degree in African and African-American studies, art and art history, Asian and African languages and literature, biological anthropology and anatomy, biology, Canadian studies, chemistry, classical studies, comparative area studies, computer science, cultural anthropology, earth and ocean sciences, economics, English, environmental sciences, environmental sciences and policy, French studies, Germanic languages and literature, history, Italian and European studies, linguistics, literature, mathematics, medieval and Renaissance studies, music, philosophy, physics, political science, psychology, public policy studies, religion, Slavic languages and literatures, sociology, Spanish, theater studies, and women's studies.

Interdisciplinary nonmajor programs are available in applied science, architectural engineering, documentary studies, early childhood education studies, film/video/digital, health policy, human development, information sciences and information studies, Judaic studies, Latin American studies, markets and management studies, Marxism and society, neurosciences, policy journalism and media studies, primatology, and the study of sexualities.

The Pratt School of Engineering offers accredited four-year programs leading to the B.S.E. in biomedical engineering, civil and environmental engineering, electrical and computer engineering, and mechanical engineering and materials science.

Academic Program

The year is divided into two semesters with two optional summer terms; first-semester exams fall before the winter break. Students in the liberal arts plan their own courses of study, with the help of an adviser, according to guidelines rather than specific course requirements. Academic Writing, a one-semester class in expository writing, is the only course required of undergraduates. The Trinity College liberal arts curriculum of approximately 15 semester courses encompasses four areas of knowledge: arts and literatures, civilizations, social sciences, and natural sciences and mathematics. As students take courses in these areas, the curriculum provides significant exposure to cross-cultural studies, ethical inquiry, interpretive and aesthetic analysis, foreign language, and the relationships between science, technology, and society. Thirty-four courses are required for graduation.

First-year students are encouraged to participate in FOCUS, a group of programs of interrelated seminars spanning topics such as Biotechnology and Social Change, Changing Faces of Russia, Exploring the Mind, Forging Social Ideals, Modern America, and Visions of Freedom. FOCUS students in each program live together to expand the opportunities for discussion and learning. Also, in more than forty-five first-year seminars, offered in nearly every department, professors chosen for their outstanding undergraduate teaching lead classes of 15 or fewer students. In general, other than the occasional large lecture hall, classes at Duke contain between 16 and 35 students.

When students declare a major—no later than the end of the sophomore year in Trinity College and at the end of the first year in the Pratt School of Engineering—a faculty member from the major department becomes their adviser. Students who plan to continue their study in a professional school also work with career-specific advisers to plan a program of study that provides the appropriate foundation for advanced work and meets their unique interests.

Off-Campus Programs

Through internships and study-abroad programs, students are encouraged to take advantage of nearly 120 Duke-affiliated off-campus study opportunities. These range from oceanographic studies at the Duke Marine Laboratory in Beaufort, North Carolina; to arts programs in New York, Bombay, or Los Angeles; to a variety of overseas programs. Through the Office of Study Abroad, students can choose international programs from four weeks to a full year in length. In some cases, scholarship aid can be applied to study abroad. Approximately 40 percent of each graduating class studies away from campus on nearly every continent in the world.

Academic Facilities

With more than 4.8 million volumes, 16 million manuscripts, 1.4 million public documents, 3.9 million microforms, and tens of thousands of films, video recordings, and serials, Duke University's library holdings are among the most extensive in the nation. The University's most sophisticated research facilities, a phytotron, a hyperbaric unit, and a free-electron laser facility, while used primarily for graduate-level research, are available to undergraduates who have reached an advanced level of study. Duke students also may take advantage of additional nearby library and classroom facilities through reciprocal arrangements with the statewide University of North Carolina System.

All students have access to extensive computing facilities and services supported by the Office of Information Technology. Services include free accounts on Duke's main computer system, which provide access to high-speed Internet and e-mail and to eighteen campus-computer-clusters complete with computers, printers, and access to DukeNet, the campus-wide fiber-optic network. All undergraduate residence hall rooms are wired for DukeNet access.

Costs

For 2003–04, a year in Trinity College or the Pratt School of Engineering cost $40,030, with $29,295 allotted for tuition and fees and an average of $8205 for room and board (although costs varied with accommodations). The total yearly estimate included $2530 for books and miscellaneous expenses. All fees are subject to change, and up-to-date information is available through the Office of Undergraduate Financial Aid.

Financial Aid

Duke University believes that access to a high-quality private education should depend on a student's academic ability, not his or her family's financial strength. The University meets 100 percent of the demonstrated need for all admitted U.S. citizens and permanent residents, and applying for financial aid has no bearing on the admissions decision for these students. The University also makes need-based financial aid available for a limited number of international students who are not U.S. citizens or permanent residents. Duke meets the full demonstrated financial need for these students, as it does for admitted U.S. citizens and permanent residents, and financial aid is a factor in the admissions decision for these students. Foreign citizens applying for financial aid must apply under the regular decision plan.

The aid program includes honorary and need-based scholarships, grants, federal and institutional college work-study program awards, Federal Perkins Loans and Stafford Student Loans, and University-sponsored internships. Limited merit, ROTC, and athletic scholarships are available, and all admitted students are automatically considered for all appropriate scholarships.

U.S. citizens and permanent residents applying for financial aid should submit the PROFILE application provided by the College Scholarship Service and the Free Application for Federal Student Aid (FAFSA). Foreign citizens applying for financial aid should submit the College Scholarship Service's International Student Financial Aid Application along with a copy of their family's most recent national tax forms. Also, the parent(s)' employers must provide, in English, statements that outline annual income and benefits received in connection with their current employment. Further information is available through the Office of Undergraduate Financial Aid.

Faculty

Duke has a faculty of 2,491 full-time and part-time members in its undergraduate, graduate, and professional schools—958 of whom teach undergraduates, making the student-faculty ratio 11:1. More importantly, people of national or international prominence, members of major academic societies, state and national advisers, and faculty chairs honoring professors of extraordinary ability are found in every department or division. About 90 percent of tenured or tenure-track faculty members teach undergraduates, and many serve as first-year student and departmental advisers.

Student Government

Students at Duke are considered mature individuals capable of governing their own actions, while furthering the best interests of the broader University community. The Duke Student Government and various student-faculty-administration committees provide avenues for student interaction with professors and administrators. Undergraduates also serve as voting members of the University's Board of Trustees.

Admission Requirements

The Committee on Admissions selects students on the basis of their academic record and quality of their secondary school program, recommendations from teachers and counselors, extracurricular activities and accomplishments, the application essay, and standardized test scores. The University does not discriminate on the basis of race, color, national or ethnic origin, gender, handicap, or sexual orientation or preference in its admission policies. No geographic quotas are imposed. Applicants should have at least four years of English and at least three of mathematics, natural science, foreign language, and social studies. Most engineering applicants have four years of mathematics and four years of science, including physics and chemistry. Engineering applicants must have taken calculus before they enroll. Students are encouraged to enroll in advanced-level work as preparation for the Duke curriculum.

Students should submit either ACT scores or SAT I and SAT II scores in three areas, including writing. Engineering applicants who submit SAT scores must take the SAT II Subject Test in Mathematics. Personal interviews in the applicants' local areas by members of the Alumni Admissions Advisory Committee are recommended but not required. Limited on-campus interviews with student representatives are available from June 1 to November 30.

Application and Information

Application deadlines for first-year students are November 1 for early decision and January 2 for regular decision. Students who want to arrange an alumni interview should file Part I of their application by October 1 for early decision and by December 1 for regular decision. For transfer students, the application deadline for fall admission is March 15. Students must apply either to Trinity College of Arts and Sciences or the Pratt School of Engineering at the time of application. Required tests should be taken by January of the senior year; October for early decision applicants. Duke also gladly accepts the Common Application. For additional information, contact:

Office of Undergraduate Admissions
Duke University
2138 Campus Drive, Box 90586
Durham, North Carolina 27708-0586

Telephone: 919-684-3214
Fax: 919-681-8941
World Wide Web: http://www.admissions.duke.edu/

D'YOUVILLE COLLEGE

BUFFALO, NEW YORK

The College

D'Youville College is a private, coeducational, liberal arts and professional college that has offered students an education of high quality since 1908. The College was the first in western New York to offer baccalaureate degrees to women. Its current enrollment is 2,500 men and women. Students may choose from thirty undergraduate and graduate degree programs that are enhanced by a 14:1 student-faculty ratio. The College is committed to helping its students to grow not only in academics but in the social and personal areas of their college experience as well.

The multiple-option Nursing Degree Program is one of the largest four-year private-college nursing programs in the country. Available nursing programs include B.S.N., B.S.N./M.S. (five years), and RN to B.S.N. Ninety-two percent of D'Youville's 2002 graduates are employed in their field or are in graduate school.

Students residing in Marguerite Hall have a scenic view of the Niagara River and Lake Erie, which separate the U.S. and Canadian shorelines. The Koessler Administration Building contains the Offices of Admissions, Financial Aid, the President, Student Accounts, and the Registrar; the Learning Center; and the Kavinoky Theatre. The Student Center, the focal point of leisure and extracurricular activities, has a new gymnasium, a swimming pool, a weight-training room, a dance studio, a general recreation center, a pub, and dining facilities. Student organizations and regularly scheduled activities, including intramural sports, NCAA Division III intercollegiate sports (baseball, basketball, volleyball, golf, cross-country, soccer, and softball), a ski club, the College newspaper, the yearbook, and social organizations, as well as academic programs, all help to make up an active campus life.

Location

D'Youville is situated on Buffalo's residential west side. The College is within minutes of many local attractions, including the downtown shopping center, the Kleinhans Music Hall, the Albright-Knox Art Gallery, two museums, and several theaters that offer stage productions. Seasonal changes in the area offer a variety of recreational opportunities. Buffalo is only 90 miles from Toronto and 25 minutes from Niagara Falls, making it a gateway to recreation areas in western New York and Ontario. Holiday Valley, a skier's paradise, is an hour's drive away. The city is served by the New York State Thruway, Amtrak, Greyhound and Trailways bus lines, and most major airlines.

D'Youville enjoys a diversified interchange with the community due to its affiliations with schools, hospitals, and social agencies in the area. College students in the Buffalo area number more than 60,000.

Majors and Degrees

D'Youville offers the degrees of Bachelor of Arts (B.A.), Bachelor of Science (B.S.), and Bachelor of Science in Nursing (B.S.N.). Majors include accounting, biology, business management, chiropractic, dietetics, education (elementary, secondary, and special), English, exercise and sports studies, global studies, health services, history, information technology, international business, nursing, occupational therapy, philosophy, physical therapy, physician assistant studies, preprofessional studies (dental, law, medicine, and veterinary studies), psychology, and sociology. Five-year combined bachelor's/master's (B.S./M.S.) programs are offered in dietetics, education, information technology (B.S.)/international business (M.S.), international business, nursing, and occupational therapy. A six-year B.S./D.P.T. program is offered in physical therapy. A seven-year B.S./D.C. program is offered in chiropractic.

Academic Programs

The area of concentration recognizes individual differences and varying interests but still provides sufficient specialization in one discipline to form a foundation for graduate studies and professional careers. Students attending D'Youville are expected to complete the requirements of their chosen concentration while earning a minimum of 120 credit hours. Core requirements include humanities, 24 hours; social science, 12 hours; science, 7 hours; mathematics/computer science, 6 hours; and electives, 9 hours. A cumulative average of at least 2.0 must be maintained to meet graduation requirements. Sixteen credit hours, or five or six courses per semester, are considered a normal workload. Internships to meet specific career goals may be arranged in any major.

The College offers a Career Discovery Program that was purposely designed for the undecided student. This program, which can last for two years, offers credit courses and internships.

The academic year is composed of two semesters, each lasting approximately fifteen weeks. The first semester, including final examinations, ends before the Christmas holidays. During the eight-week summer sessions, programs of selected courses are given at all levels on a daily basis.

Off-Campus Programs

The baccalaureate program in nursing is affiliated with thirteen area hospitals and public health agencies. The education program is affiliated with local elementary, junior high, and secondary schools and with special education centers in the area for purposes of student teaching. The occupational therapy, physical therapy, and physician assistant programs are affiliated with appropriate clinical settings throughout the United States.

Academic Facilities

D'Youville's modern Library Resources Center, which was completed in fall 1999, contains 154,000 volumes, including microtext and software, and subscriptions to 870 periodicals and newspapers. The multimillion-dollar Health Science Building houses laboratories, including those for anatomy, organic chemistry, and gross anatomy; activity and daily living labs for the health professions; and additional laboratories for physics, chemistry, quantitative analysis, and computer science. It also houses classrooms, faculty member offices, and development centers, including one for career development. This is augmented by a new, modern academic center, which opened in fall 2001.

Costs

For 2003–04, tuition was $6960 per semester, and room and board cost $3480 per semester. A general College fee is required and is based on credit hours taken; a Student Association fee of

$40 per semester is applied toward concerts, yearbooks, activities, and guest lectures. A $100 deposit ($150 for dietetics, physician assistant studies, occupational therapy, and physical therapy programs), credited toward tuition, must be submitted by all candidates who accept an offer of admission.

Financial Aid

D'Youville attempts to provide financial aid for students who would not otherwise be able to attend. Determination of aid is based on the Free Application for Federal Student Aid. Aid is available in the form of grants, loans, and employment on campus. In addition, D'Youville offers scholarships for academic achievement to incoming students.

All students may qualify for D'Youville's new Instant Scholarship Program, which offers scholarships with total values up to $43,500. Students who apply, are accepted, and meet the criteria instantly qualify for one of these scholarships, all of which are renewable annually. These scholarships are not based on need. The three scholarship programs are the Honors Scholarship, the Academic Initiative Scholarship, and the Achievement Scholarship. The Honors Scholarship requires a minimum SAT I score of 1100 or an ACT score of at least 24 and awards 50 percent of tuition and 25 percent of room and board costs. The Academic Initiative Scholarship requires SAT I scores of at least 1000 or ACT scores of 21 to 23 and an academic average of at least 85. It awards 25 percent of tuition and 50 percent of room and board costs. The Achievement Scholarship criteria include SAT I scores of 900 to 1090 or ACT scores of 19 to 23 and an academic average of 80 to 84. This scholarship awards $1000–$4000.

Faculty

The ratio of faculty members to students is 1:14. All members of the full-time instructional staff hold a doctorate or another advanced degree. Faculty members act as advisers and are available for consultation with students.

Student Government

The Student Association (SA), a representative form of student self-government, seeks to inspire in its members dedication to the intellectual, social, and moral ideals of the College and works closely with the administration and faculty. All students of D'Youville are considered members of the SA and may be elected to the executive council and the student senate. There are seventeen academic and social clubs affiliated with the SA.

Admission Requirements

An applicant must be a high school graduate or have a high school equivalency diploma before matriculating. The applicant should have a college-preparatory background, including required English and history courses and a sequence in either mathematics or science. Scores on the SAT I or the ACT are also required for admission. High school advanced placement credit is acceptable and transferable. The admission decision is based on high school grade point average, rank in class, and scores on the SAT I or ACT. Students who have difficulty meeting normal admission standards may be admitted with a reduced academic load.

The College Learning Center offers academic assistance to students whose education has been interrupted or has not prepared them adequately for college courses. The Tutor Bank, a system of peer tutoring, offers the assistance of qualified students to those who need help in specific academic disciplines.

Application and Information

D'Youville admits students on a rolling admission basis; therefore, applications are reviewed as they are received by the admissions office. Transfer students who have a quality point average of at least 2.0 are encouraged to apply by December 1 for the spring semester and by July 1 for the fall semester. A brochure listing course offerings and giving details about costs and room and board is available upon request.

R. H. Dannecker
Director of Admissions
D'Youville College
One D'Youville Square
320 Porter Avenue
Buffalo, New York 14201-1084
Telephone: 716-881-7600
800-777-3921 (toll-free)
E-mail: admissions@dyc.edu
World Wide Web: http://www.dyc.edu

EARLHAM COLLEGE

RICHMOND, INDIANA

The College

Earlham College offers a challenging intellectual environment that attracts a diverse group of students with a variety of motivations—academic, political, social, athletic, ethical, and career-minded—who want to make an impact on the world. The College's 1,170 students—656 women and 514 men—represent forty-eight states and thirty countries. Students of many races, religious backgrounds, economic levels, and ethnic traditions join together on this Midwestern campus to create and experience the Earlham Effect.

They share an experience rooted in the Quaker values of tolerance, equality, justice, respect, and collaboration. They explore an unending desire to see the world differently and to bring about change when necessary. Earlham's commitment to engaging students in a changing world is at the heart of its own mission.

Students at Earlham get involved in a wide variety of associations and organizations, including numerous extracurricular programs in music, theater, dance, social and political action, ethnic and international awareness, and intramural and varsity athletics. Students manage an FM public radio station, a food co-op, an equestrian program, a newspaper, and a literary magazine. Activities are coordinated by the Student Activities Board, the Earlham Events Committee, and various special interest groups, such as the Black Leadership Action Coalition, Women's Program Committee, International Club, and Earlham Service Learning Center. Students are active in community service and donated more than 25,000 hours of time to the Richmond community each year.

Earlham, an NCAA Division III affiliate, is a member of the North Coast Athletic Conference. The College offers seven intercollegiate sports for men (baseball, basketball, cross-country, football, soccer, tennis, and track) and eight intercollegiate sports for women (basketball, cross-country, field hockey, lacrosse, soccer, tennis, track, and volleyball). Club sports include swimming, Ultimate Frisbee, lacrosse, and men's lacrosse and volleyball. Twenty-eight percent of the students participate in intercollegiate athletics, and many more participate in an extensive intramural program. Earlham athletic facilities include indoor and outdoor tennis courts; football, baseball, soccer, lacrosse, and hockey fields; an all-weather track; and a $13-million athletics and wellness center.

Earlham is a residential college. Students live in the seven residence halls and twenty-seven College-owned houses near the campus.

In 2002–03, Earlham initiated a Master of Arts in Teaching degree program. This eleven-month program for liberal arts and sciences graduates leads to certification in English/language arts, math, modern foreign languages, science, and social studies, all at the middle and high school level.

Location

Earlham's 800-acre tree-shaded campus lies in the southwestern edge of Richmond, Indiana, a city of 35,000. Richmond is 65 miles from Cincinnati, Ohio, and Indianapolis, Indiana, and 40 miles from Dayton, Ohio. Many students find opportunities to join in local activities. The city's arboretum and parks system, symphony orchestra, theater company, and art association all offer extra dimensions to student life.

Majors and Degrees

Earlham College awards the B.A. degree in more than thirty disciplinary and interdisciplinary programs. Academic majors include African and African-American studies, art, biochemistry, biology, business and nonprofit management, chemistry, comparative languages and linguistics, computer science, economics, education, English, French, geology, German, history, human development and social relations, international studies, Japanese studies, Latin American studies, mathematics, music, peace and global studies, philosophy, physics/astronomy, politics, psychobiology, psychology, religion, sociology/anthropology, Spanish, theater arts, and women's studies. Other special academic programs are offered in environmental science, Jewish studies, journalism, languages and literatures, legal studies, museum studies, outdoor education, Quaker studies, studio art, teaching English to speakers of other languages (TESOL), and wilderness. Excellent preprofessional programs are available in law, medicine, and the ministry.

Academic Programs

Earlham aims to educate for depth and breadth, believing that one's success in the twenty-first century depends heavily on an ability to understand and make well-educated connections across different intellectual and experiential boundaries. Earlham's General Education Program encourages students to develop competencies in the arts, quantitative reasoning, scientific inquiry, wellness, and perspectives in diversity (including domestic multiculturalism, interculturalism, or global historical awareness, and second language requirements). First- and second-year core courses (Earlham Seminars, Interpretive Practices courses, Comparative Practices courses, and Living and Learning in Community seminars) emphasize ways of knowing, critical reading and writing skills, and the first-year experience.

Students gain an in-depth understanding of one or more disciplines in their major area of academic concentration. An academic major usually consists of eight to ten courses in one department, a senior research project or seminar, and a departmental comprehensive examination. Earlham grants credit for Advanced Placement examinations and higher-level International Baccalaureate subjects. Students may also receive credit for independent studies and academic internships.

The academic year consists of two semesters plus an optional May Term. During the summer, the College sponsors a two-week academic experience for high school students called Explore-A-College.

Off-Campus Programs

Earlham believes that classroom learning must go hand-in-hand with experience in the richness of the wider world. More than 65 percent of Earlham students participate in at least one off-campus study program. Academic credit is earned and, except for transportation costs, no extra charge is incurred for off-campus study. Earlham students can study abroad in Austria, the Bahamas, China, England, France, Germany, Greece, India, Japan, Kenya, Martinique, Mexico, the Middle East, Northern Ireland, Russia, Scotland, Senegal, and Spain. Earlhamites also participate in American programs along the U.S.-Mexico border (Border Studies) in the southwestern United States; Philadelphia; New York; Chicago; Woods Hole,

Massachusetts; and Oak Ridge, Tennessee. The academic focus of these programs varies, and students in all majors are encouraged to participate in at least one off-campus program. Earlham offers a one-month wilderness experience backpacking in the Uinta Mountains of Utah or canoeing in the boundary waters of Canada.

Academic Facilities

The Earlham College library is composed of two internationally renowned teaching libraries—Lilly Library and Wildman Science Library. The combined collections contain more than 400,000 volumes and 9,150 current periodicals, as well as maps, music, and works of art. Special collections include the Herbert Hoover Peace Studies Collection, the Quaker Connection, and the Government Documents Collection.

The $15-million Landrum Bolling Center for Interdisciplinary Studies and Social Sciences opened in 2002, providing technologically equipped classrooms, offices, and common areas to enable pursuits in interdisciplinary programs, global outreach, experiential learning, collaborative projects, and networked information resources.

Modern, well-equipped science laboratories for biology, chemistry, geology, and physics are found in Stanley and Dennis Halls. Dennis Hall is also the location of the Joseph Moore Natural History Museum and the Ralph Teetor Planetarium. Earlham's observatory has a 14-inch Schmidt-Cassegrain telescope. Through updated computing and network resources, students have high-speed access to e-mail and the Internet. Seven microcomputer labs with 125 workstations (Macintosh-, Windows-, and UNIX-based) support word processing, programming, research, and Internet and e-mail access. One mixed-platform lab (Macs and Windows) is available to students and faculty and staff members 24 hours a day. All residence hall rooms are wired for Internet access, and wireless networking is available in all academic buildings and campus houses.

Music and art studios are found in the Runyan Student Center, which also houses a modern theater, the campus radio station, and the College bookstore. Other studios and Goddard Auditorium are located in Carpenter Hall.

Costs

Tuition, fees, and room and board charges for 2004–05 totaled $31,782. Students have free admission to the Earlham Artist Series, athletic events, speaker series, and numerous lectures, concerns, and dances.

Financial Aid

Most financial aid is awarded on the basis of demonstrated need; more than 75 percent of Earlham's first-year students receive financial assistance. Earlham usually meets the full need of all accepted students with a combination of Earlham Grants, endowed scholarships, loans, federal and state grants, and campus work. Students must file both the Free Application for Federal Student Aid (FAFSA) and a special Earlham form.

Scholarships are awarded without regard to financial need and recognize academic achievement. Earlham also offers scholarships through the National Merit Scholarship Corporation. Special scholarships are available to members of the Religious Society of Friends (Quakers) and to students who are likely to enhance the diversity of the student body. Scholarships and limited financial aid are available for international students.

Faculty

Earlham's faculty members are dedicated professionals whose first priority is teaching. Ninety-eight percent of the 92 teaching faculty members hold doctoral degrees or terminal degrees in their fields. In recent years their teaching, creative endeavors, and scholarly research have been recognized by numerous grants and fellowships from the Ford Foundation, Danforth Foundation, IBM, Woodrow Wilson Foundation, Fulbright-Hayes Program, Kellogg Foundation, Japan Foundation, Lilly Endowment Inc., National Endowment for the Humanities, National Science Foundation, and Carnegie-Mellon Foundation. The student-faculty ratio is 11:1.

Student Government

Earlham's distinctive approach to consensus governance recalls its Quaker roots. The philosophical system is summarized in a code of principles and practices based on the ideals of respect for both individuals and community, integrity, simplicity, peace and justice, and consensus governance. Campus organizations reach decisions by consensus rather than by parliamentary procedure or majority rule. The process emphasizes individual thought, group discussion, listening, and synthesizing.

Admission Requirements

Admission decisions are based on more than SAT I scores or high school grades, as important as these criteria are. Earlham pays close attention to the quality of the academic program, teacher and counselor recommendations, application essays, and personal interviews. Applicants should have had an academic or college-preparatory high school program. The SAT I is the preferred required test, although the ACT may be substituted. Interviews are strongly recommended, although not required.

Application and Information

Earlham offers several admission options. The early decision deadline is December 1 (notification on December 15); the early action deadline is January 1 (notification on February 1); the regular decision deadline is February 15 (notification on March 15); and the transfer deadline is April 1. International students (non-U.S. citizens) should apply by February 1. Applications are accepted after these deadlines as long as places remain in the entering class.

Students wishing additional information or materials on Earlham College should contact:

Office of Admissions
Earlham College
801 National Road West
Richmond, Indiana 47374-4095
Telephone: 765-983-1600
800-EARLHAM (toll-free)
Fax: 765-983-1560
E-mail: admission@earlham.edu
World Wide Web: http://www.earlham.edu

From Richmond, Indiana, Earlham College students engage a changing world and strive to make a difference.

EASTERN CONNECTICUT STATE UNIVERSITY

WILLIMANTIC, CONNECTICUT

The University

Eastern Connecticut State University, Connecticut's public liberal arts university, offers thirty undergraduate majors and graduate degrees in accounting, education, and organizational management. Eastern has all the advantages of a small school combined with "large-university resources." The University's concern for the individual student, along with its small classes, personalized counseling, and independent study opportunities, encourages intellectual and personal growth and development. The student body (3,631 full-time undergraduates) is heterogeneous, a mixture of various ethnic and socioeconomic groups. Students attending Eastern come from 164 Connecticut towns, twenty-three states, and thirty countries. There are six residence halls and three apartment complexes on campus. Housing is available to students who have been admitted to the University. Eighty-five percent of all freshmen and 54 percent of undergraduate students live in on-campus residence halls. The main cafeteria serves meals seven days per week. Cars are permitted for all students except for freshmen living on campus. There are more than forty special interest clubs and organizations on campus, as well as a student newspaper, a yearbook, and a literary and arts magazine. Extracurricular events include concerts, dances, films, intramural sports, lectures, musical and dramatic productions, and bus trips to Boston and New York City. Varsity sports for men include baseball, basketball, cross-country, lacrosse, soccer, and track. Women participate in intercollegiate basketball, cross-country, field hockey, lacrosse, soccer, softball, swimming, track, and volleyball. Sports facilities include an athletic center with a 2,800-seat gymnasium for badminton, basketball, tennis, and volleyball; a six-lane swimming pool; handball and squash courts; saunas; a fitness center and rooms for physical conditioning, modern dance, and gymnastics; and a new athletic complex that includes a state-of-the-art baseball field with a 1,500-seat grandstand as well as field hockey and multipurpose fields.

Location

Willimantic, Connecticut, a small city of diversified interests and many styles of living, has a population of 22,000. It has convenient shopping centers and a growing community of ambitious and ecology-minded individuals who are concerned with the city's future. The eastern Connecticut region is famous for its rolling hills, forests, state recreational areas, nature trails, clear lakes and streams, and beaches. Skiing areas are nearby. Hartford is 40 minutes away, and New York City and Boston are both less than two hours from Willimantic by car.

Majors and Degrees

Eastern offers four undergraduate degrees: the Bachelor of Arts, the Bachelor of General Studies, the Bachelor of Science, and the Associate in Science. The Bachelor of Arts degree is awarded with majors in computer science, economics, English, environmental earth science, fine arts (academic tracks in art history and criticism, dance, fine arts history, individualized major, interior design, music history and literature, music performance, music theory, theater, and theory and criticism), history, history and social sciences, mathematics, predentistry, prelaw, premedicine, psychology, public policy and government, social work, sociology and applied social relations, studio art, and Spanish. The Bachelor of Science degree programs include accounting, biochemistry, biology, business administration (concentrations in the areas of finance, management, and marketing), business information systems, communication, early childhood education, elementary education, physical education, secondary education, and sports and leisure management. Certification in secondary education is available in biology, English, environmental earth science, history, and mathematics. The associate degree program is available in the arts and sciences. The Bachelor of General Studies is a flexible degree program for adults who are 25 or older. Students may design a program integrating life experience into major or minor concentrations through a learning contract developed with their departmental adviser.

Academic Program

The basic graduation requirements for a bachelor's degree are a minimum of 120 hours of credit and completion of a major program (30–48 hours of credit in one specific field). In addition, all degree candidates must take a freshman English composition course and three physical education courses and fulfill specified credit hours in the humanities, natural sciences, social sciences, interdisciplinary courses, and computer competence (usually during the first two years). To earn an associate degree, students must complete 60 credit hours, which include credit hours in general education requirements, 15 credit hours in a concentration, and 5–9 credit hours in electives. The University operates on a two-semester system. The fall semester usually starts the first week in September and ends in mid-December; the spring semester, which includes a one-week vacation, runs from the third week of January to the middle of May. One 6-week and two 3-week sessions are offered during the summer. An Intersession program is offered in January of each year.

Eastern offers an Honors Program for academically talented students. This highly competitive program emphasizes independent study and special courses and offers tuition scholarships. The Contract Admissions Program (CAP) is an educational support service that offers counseling, tutoring, developmental courses, and financial assistance to highly motivated students who might otherwise have been denied admission on the basis of traditional criteria. Cooperative Education (Co-op) is an optional work-study program; students may choose to participate in the program for one or more periods.

The University grants credit for Advanced Placement Program examination in all the subject areas tested and accepts up to 60 credit hours earned through the College-Level Examination Program (CLEP). Persons with a minimum of five years of successful work experience in areas of specialization taught by the University may qualify for advanced placement through credit for life experience and learning.

U.S. Army and Air Force ROTC programs, offered by the University of Connecticut at Storrs, are available to qualified Eastern students.

Off-Campus Programs

Formal opportunities for off-campus study available through the University carry credit. These include off-campus internships, study abroad, and consortium arrangements with the University of Connecticut and other institutions in the Connecticut State University System. Internships are available in the academic areas of applied social relations, biology, business administration, communication, computer science, economics, education, environmental earth science, psychology, public policy and government, and Spanish. Biology majors may study in Belize or in Bermuda through the tropical biology program, which involves a ten-day trip. There are also opportunities to join international study groups for one semester, one academic year, or a summer session. Eastern also participates in the National Student Exchange program (NSE), which allows students to attend other public colleges and universities across the United States while still paying tuition and fees to Eastern.

Academic Facilities

The J. Eugene Smith Library contains more than 500,000 volumes and 127,000 square feet of educational learning space. The Media Building contains a color television studio, a recording studio, an FM radio station, an electronic auditorium, a computer center, darkrooms, and graphic arts areas and serves as the hub of the audiovisual distribution system. The planetarium contains two electron microscopes and a geology laboratory. The Science Building provides modern, well-equipped laboratories for biology, chemistry, and physics. There is a fully equipped early childhood center. A four-story, 72,000-square-foot classroom building and the library and clock tower serve as the main academic areas of the campus.

Costs

For 2003–04, tuition and fees for a Connecticut resident were $5045, and nonresident tuition and fees were $12,033 on an annual basis. The fees include a tuition deposit of $200, which is required to secure a place in the University, and a $250 housing deposit. Room is estimated at $3634 and board at $3118 for two semesters. Payments should be made as soon as possible after receipt of the bill for these charges. Books and supplies average $900 a year. The schedule of tuition and fees is subject to change as warranted.

Financial Aid

Financial aid includes grants and scholarships, low-interest loans, student employment opportunities, and special programs for veterans and their families. The University participates in the Federal Perkins Loan, Federal Pell Grant, Federal Supplemental Educational Opportunity Grant, and Federal Work-Study programs. In addition, it provides aid through alumni funds and other resources of its own. Approximately two thirds of all Eastern students receive financial aid. Awards are based primarily on demonstrated financial need. All students who wish to apply for financial assistance are required to complete the Free Application for Federal Student Aid (FAFSA) and send it to the processing agency by March 15 for the fall semester or by November 15 for the spring semester.

Faculty

The friendliness and approachability of the University's professors are usually noted by the students enrolled at Eastern. Faculty members are concerned primarily with teaching; many write and carry on significant research. Faculty members hold advanced degrees from leading American and foreign colleges and universities; 89 percent hold terminal degrees. All of them serve as academic counselors. Full-time advisers and counseling services are available to assist students in matters of personal and academic concern. The student-faculty ratio at Eastern is 16:1.

Student Government

An organized plan of student government and student representation on University committees permits students to be actively involved with important issues and develop basic policies for student life. The Student Senate is the governing body; it supervises and coordinates all student activities and serves as a liaison with the faculty, administration, and Board of Trustees.

Admission Requirements

Eastern maintains a selective admission policy, and applicants are considered on an individual basis. The criteria used are an applicant's the secondary school record, satisfactory SAT I or ACT scores, rank in in the upper half of the high school graduating class, personal accomplishments and motivation, and teachers' or guidance counselors' recommendations. Applicants must be secondary school graduates or have received a high school equivalency diploma. Their secondary school program should include 16 academic units of college-preparatory work, with the following divisions: English, 4 years; mathematics, 3 years; science, 2 years (including 1 year of laboratory science); social sciences, 2 years (including U.S. history); and foreign language, 2 years (3 years preferred). Students who are admitted without having fulfilled the language requirement must complete 1 year of a foreign language (6 credits) at Eastern. Deferred admission is also available. A campus visit is strongly suggested, although not required. A limited number of highly motivated students who do not qualify for admission if traditional criteria are used may be admitted in the summer Contract Admissions Program.

Application and Information

Applications can be made after the first quarter of the senior year of high school through May 1 for the fall semester. Applicants must submit an admission application, a $50 nonrefundable application fee, a complete transcript of high school grades and rank in class, two recommendations from guidance counselors or teachers, and an official copy of the SAT I or ACT score report. The University adheres to a rolling admission policy. Applicants are usually notified of the admission decision within one month after the application is complete. Application forms and information may be requested from:

Kimberly Crone
Director of Admissions and Enrollment Management
Eastern Connecticut State University
83 Windham Street
Willimantic, Connecticut 06226
Telephone: 860-465-5286
Fax: 860-465-5544
E-mail: admissions@Easternct.edu
World Wide Web: http://www.Easternct.edu

Eastern's J. Eugene Smith Library, with more than 500,000 volumes and 127,000 square feet of educational space, serves as the academic hub of the campus.

EASTERN MENNONITE UNIVERSITY

HARRISONBURG, VIRGINIA

The University

Eastern Mennonite University (EMU), a private Christian university founded in 1917, provides a high-quality liberal arts education that emphasizes spiritual growth and cross-cultural awareness. The nurturing environment of EMU's student-oriented campus not only prepares students for a wide variety of careers but also challenges students to experience Christ and follow His call to witness faithfully, serve compassionately, and walk boldly in the way of nonviolence and peace. The undergraduate experience is enriched by graduate programs in business administration, conflict transformation, counseling, and education. The University also has a seminary. EMU is accredited by the Southern Association of Colleges and Schools. In addition, the nursing, teacher education, and social work programs are accredited by their specialty organizations at the national level.

Undergraduate students make up about 900 of the 1,400 students. Of the undergraduates, 60 percent are women and 9 percent are American multiethnic students. Five percent come from international settings. Students represent thirty-five states and twenty-one other countries. Most students are traditional college age. Religious backgrounds vary widely, with 60 percent representing Mennonites.

EMU is a residential community in which students live on campus until age 21 (unless they are married or live at home). Housing options include traditional residence halls, coed buildings, suite arrangements, apartments for upperclass students, and group houses. An energetic residence staff provides a dynamic residential life program focused on education and support. After the freshman year, a housing lottery is used to determine certain housing options.

The cocurriculum at EMU affords numerous opportunities to develop skills, express creativity, or just have fun. Students are active in intramurals, music ensembles, theater, and the more than forty campus organizations that vary from Peace Fellowship to the Asian Dragon (martial arts) Club. Some students help operate the school radio station or edit the student newspaper or yearbook. Most students stay on campus on the weekend to enjoy movies, concerts, celebrative worship, and many other activities. Both men and women compete as members of the NCAA Division III and the Old Dominion Athletic Conference. EMU offers varsity teams for men and women in basketball, cross-country, soccer, tennis, track and field, and volleyball. Additional teams include baseball for men and field hockey and softball for women.

The dining hall offers many food choices and three meal plans. The snack shop, the Royals' Den, is the other eating facility on campus where students may use a Lion's Share account. Restaurants and a major grocery store chain are within walking distance of the campus. Other services provided by the University include career services, health and counseling services, an Academic Support Center, and multicultural and international student services. The Director of Career Services helps students to explore ways to use their education in the workplace.

Location

EMU's 92-acre campus on the edge of the growing city of Harrisonburg is located in the scenic Shenandoah Valley, with a spectacular view of the famous Blue Ridge Mountains. With only a 2-hour drive to the nation's capital or the state capital of Richmond, students have access to both urban and rural America. Skiing, hiking, the beach, and major cultural opportunities are all within easy reach. With its growing ethnic diversity, Harrisonburg's many restaurants provide a variety of cuisines. Local businesses and organizations are the sites for EMU student internships. Students also carry out numerous volunteer activities with local charities.

Majors and Degrees

The University offers Bachelor of Arts, Bachelor of Science, and associate degrees, as well as a one-year certificate. The Bachelor of Arts degree requires intermediate-level competency in a foreign language. Majors are offered in accounting; art; art education; biblical studies; biochemistry; biology; business administration; camping, recreation, and outdoor ministry; chemistry; clinical laboratory science; communication; computer information systems; computer science; congregational and youth ministries; culture, religion, and mission; economic development; economics; English; environmental science; French; German; health and physical education; history; history and social science; international agriculture; international business; justice, peace, and conflict studies; liberal arts; mathematics; music; nursing; philosophy and theology; psychology; recreation and sport leadership; social work; sociology; Spanish; and theater. Professional certification programs are available in early, elementary, secondary, and special education. Preprofessional programs are offered in engineering, law, and health sciences. A liberal arts major allows students to design their own programs. Minors include many of the above areas plus church music, coaching, exercise science, family studies, finance, journalism, marketing, missions, physics, political science, socioeconomic development, teaching English as a second language, and youth ministry. Associate in Arts degrees are offered in Biblical studies, general studies, and paraprofessional education. One-year certificates may be earned in Bible or general studies.

Academic Program

The academic calendar consists of two 15-week semesters from late August to late April. The baccalaureate degree requires 128 semester hours. All students complete a major, the Global Village general education curriculum, and electives. The Global Village general education curriculum features a number of team-taught, interdisciplinary courses, including a first-year seminar, colloquium courses focusing on various themes, a health/wellness course, and a senior seminar. Central to the curriculum are Bible/religion courses and a cross-cultural study experience (a variety of summer, semester, and year-long options are offered). Students meet requirements in writing, speech, and mathematics and take additional courses that refine writing skills and involve community learning. The curriculum allows flexibility for students to enroll in courses from a variety of disciplines to enhance their program of study.

Associate degrees require 64 semester hours of general education requirements, a concentration in a major, and electives. Thirty semester hours are needed to complete a certificate.

Cross-cultural studies take students to another culture for a semester or a three- to nine-week summer session. An honors program provides academic challenges and leadership opportunities for a select group of students through faculty mentoring, seminars, research opportunities, and special projects. Approximately 15 honors students are selected from each first-year class. Two of the students receive full tuition scholarships, and the remaining students are awarded half-tuition scholarships.

Other special academic opportunities include credit by examination and extension credit for special programs with outside organizations.

Off-Campus Programs

Eastern Mennonite is one of the few universities to include a cross-cultural study requirement of 9 semester hours as part of the general education curriculum. The program takes students and teaching faculty members to settings that include Latin America, the Middle East, Africa, Eastern and Western Europe, Asia, and Native American reservations. The program, which is community-based, usually includes living with local families. Students also study the historical, geographical, social, economic, religious, and artistic forces that shape the culture. Students may also elect to participate in the Washington Community Scholars' Center program in Washington, D.C. A dozen students live in a community and put knowledge into practice through internships, group living, and a student-centered seminar. Students also take courses at a local university. Other students spend a semester or year in the Brethren Colleges Abroad Program. Foreign language majors spend a full year in a country where the target language is spoken.

Academic Facilities

Academic facilities include the Suter Science Center, which is equipped with modern laboratories for study and research. The building also houses a planetarium and a museum with impressive collections of mounted animals and insects, minerals, fossils, and artifacts from distant locations. The library is fully automated with a state-of-the-art computer system. In addition to the usual resources, the library houses a large historical collection pertaining to Mennonite faith and life. Several campus buildings have laboratories equipped with computers for student use. Residence halls are connected to the campus network, providing students who own computers with access to the library and the Internet. The network accommodates both PCs and Macintosh computers. The University Commons houses student life services and athletic services, including an indoor track, a climbing wall, and a state-of-the-art fitness center.

Other special facilities and programs include a campus radio station, an arboretum, a music program for young children, a preschool for student practicums, an intensive English program, an adult degree-completion program, Summer Peacebuilding Institute, and the Shenandoah Valley Bach Festival.

Costs

Tuition and fees for 2003–04 were $17,530. Room and board are estimated at $5640. Additional expenses for books, transportation, and incidental costs are estimated at $1500. Special fees are charged for applied music instruction and certain physical education courses.

Financial Aid

More than 90 percent of EMU students receive financial aid. Scholarships include those given for academic achievement and an award of $1000 given to new first-year students who are children of alumni. EMU participates in the Federal Student Aid Programs, which include need-based grants, loans, and the work-study program. EMU also offers institutional need-based gift aid. Virginia residents receive the Virginia Tuition Assistance Grant, regardless of need, which amounts to $2000 annually. If students receive grants from their churches, EMU matches up to $1000 per year. No application is needed for academic scholarships except for honors awards. Students applying for need-based aid must complete the Free Application for Federal Student Aid (FAFSA). Applications should be completed by April 15.

Faculty

Faculty members at EMU are devoted first to teaching. More than 70 percent hold doctorates or terminal degrees in their fields. Most faculty members are full-time. A faculty-student ratio of 1:13 provides for small classes and out-of-class accessibility. All classes are taught by faculty members rather than graduate assistants, and 75 percent of classes have 25 or fewer students. In some disciplines, students participate in faculty research and publications. All faculty members serve as academic advisers to students.

Student Government

All students are members of the Student Government Association (SGA), which is led by the Senate and its Executive Committee. SGA coordinates student involvement in the campus community, communicates concerns to and from the administration, and aids in decision making. Students also hold representation on some faculty and administrative committees.

Admission Requirements

Admission to EMU is moderately competitive. Factors considered include high school or previous college GPA, SAT I or ACT scores, support from a reference, and commitment to uphold the lifestyle expectations of EMU. Applicants should rank in the upper half of their high school class. Some majors have specific GPA requirements to enter the upper-level courses. Recommended high school units include English (4), math (3), science (3), foreign language (2), social studies (3), and electives (6). Transfer students are welcome. The University seeks to be an inclusive community that welcomes students from diverse backgrounds and various religious and ethnic groups. Campus visits are encouraged. Students should apply by May 1.

Application and Information

The freshman application priority filing date is March 1. The final filing date is August 1. The application deadline for transfer applicants is thirty days prior to the start of the term for both fall and spring. Notification of admission is sent on a rolling basis. Inquiries and application materials should be sent to:

Lawrence W. Miller
Director of Admissions
Eastern Mennonite University
Harrisonburg, Virginia 22802
Telephone: 800-368-2665 (toll-free)
Fax: 540-432-4444
E-mail: admiss@emu.edu
World Wide Web: http://www.emu.edu

The campus of Eastern Mennonite University.

EASTERN MICHIGAN UNIVERSITY

YPSILANTI, MICHIGAN

The University

Founded in 1849 as a teacher's college, Eastern Michigan University (EMU) has not forgotten its roots, continuing to foster one of the nation's best teacher education programs. Today, Eastern Michigan University offers a wide variety of academic programs for its students through its five Colleges: the College of Arts and Sciences, the College of Business, the College of Education, the College of Health and Human Services, and the College of Technology. The University is fully accredited by many academic organizations, including the Higher Learning Commission of the North Central Association of Colleges and Schools, and in 2001 received an unqualified accreditation for ten years.

The campus now encompasses 457 acres, spreading across the south side of the Huron River west of the campus, where student residences, athletics facilities, and the Convocation Center are located.

In 2003–04, Eastern Michigan University had a total enrollment of 24,419 students: 19,668 undergraduate students and 4,751 graduate students. The students come from forty-two different states and 93 different countries; 61 percent are women. The average GPA for the 2003–04 freshman class was 3.2, the average ACT score was 21, and the average SAT score was 1006.

The Academic Advising Center, the Career Services Center, and the Holman Learning Center help students chart a course for success in their academic endeavors. Eastern Michigan University is dedicated to providing personalized instruction to its students through small class size, supplemental instruction, and individualized tutoring. The student-professor ratio is 20:1.

Eastern Michigan University offers its students an abundance of cultural, athletic, academic, service, and special interest organizations. The EMU Department of Recreation and Intramural Athletics hosts a number of athletic opportunities at the Olds-Robb Recreation Center and other venues on campus. Students have an opportunity to join a variety of clubs and organizations related to their academic field, including campus radio, theater, newspaper, and television.

Location

Established in 1823, the town of Ypsilanti, Michigan, is the second-oldest city in the state. It is a small town, just over 4 square miles in size, and is located in Washtenaw County. One of the physical features of Ypsilanti is the Huron River, which flows through the east side of town. Many of the homes were built in the 1800s. There is a depot town for shopping, seven parks totaling 85 acres, and many sports events. There are home tours during the Heritage Festival week, which is held during the third week in August. A variety of outdoor recreational activities are available in the area, including horseback riding, skiing, hiking, canoeing, and golf.

Majors and Degrees

Eastern Michigan University offers undergraduate degrees in the following programs: accounting; accounting information systems; actuarial science and economics; administrative management; advertising and sales promotion; African-American studies; anthropology; apparel, textiles, and merchandising; area studies; art; art education; art history; arts management; aviation flight technology; aviation management technology; bilingual-bicultural education; biochemistry; biochemistry–toxicology; biology; business; business services and technology; cartography and remote sensing; chemistry; children's literature and drama/theater for the young; classical studies; clinical laboratory services; coastal environment; communication; communication technology; computer information systems; computer science; computer-aided design; computer-aided manufacturing; conservation and resource use; construction management; criminology and criminal justice; cytogenics; dance; dietetics; early childhood education; earth science; economics; electrical engineering technology; elementary education; emotionally impaired; engineering physics; English as a second language; English language; facilities management; fashion merchandising; finance; foreign languages and bilingual studies; French; French for business; geography; geology; geophysics; German for business; German language and literature; gerontology; graphic design; health administration; health-care services; health, physical education, recreation, and dance; hearing impaired; historic preservation; history; hotel and restaurant management; human, environmental, and consumer resources; industrial distribution; industrial vocational education; interior design; international business programs; Japanese language culture; journalism; labor studies; language and international trade; language and world business; linguistics; literature; management; manufacturing; manufacturing technology; marketing; marketing education; mathematics; mathematics for elementary teaching; mathematics for secondary teaching; mathematics–statistics; mechanical engineering technology; mentally impaired; microbiology; military science/ROTC; music; music education–instrumental; music education–vocal; music performance; music therapy; nursing; occupational therapy; philosophy; physical education; physically and otherwise health impaired; physics; physics research; physiology; plastics; political science; polymers and coatings technology; prearchitecture; prechiropractic; predentistry; pre-engineering; preforestry; prelaw; premedicine; pre–mortuary science; prepharmacy; prepodiatry; preoptometry; preosteopathy; pre–religious careers; psychology; public administration; public law and government; public relations; public safety administration; recreation and park management; science; secondary education; social studies; social studies for secondary teaching; social work; sociology; Spanish; Spanish for business; special education; speech and language impaired; sports medicine–athletics training; sports medicine–exercise science; teaching English to speakers of other languages; technology education; technology management; telecommunications and film; theater arts; therapeutic recreation; travel and tourism; urban and regional planning; visually impaired; women's studies; and written communications.

Academic Programs

The academic philosophy of Eastern Michigan University ensures that students are offered a well-rounded education to prepare them for life's challenges and for functioning successfully in an increasingly global and dynamic society. Students take general education courses throughout their time at EMU to enhance the studies in their chosen field. The University offers classes during fall and spring semesters as well as accelerated winter, spring, and summer sessions. Students do not graduate if the GPA in their degree program falls below 2.0. Candidates for a bachelor's degree must earn a total of 124 credits. Students with credits from a junior or community college must earn a minimum of 60 hours from Eastern Michigan University. No more than 60 hours in any one academic department may be applied toward the minimum 124 credit hours needed to graduate. Students who have been in military service are granted credit in military science and leadership.

Off-Campus Programs

The Office of Academic Programs Abroad provides opportunities for students to enrich their education by studying abroad through the following programs: the Asian Cultural History Tour, the European Cultural History Tour, and the Japan Center for Michigan Universities. Students may also participate in exchange opportunities with schools in Australia, the Netherlands, and the United Kingdom. Business majors may participate in exchange programs at a college of business in Canada or Mexico.

Academic Facilities

Eastern Michigan's comprehensive facilities include fully equipped computer and science laboratories and classrooms. The EMU library offers a full range of information resources and instructional services for EMU students and faculty and staff members. It houses carefully selected materials, both print and electronic, to support student learning and research. The collection includes 700,000 print volumes; 4,400 journals; 140 online databases, many with full-text journal articles; 250,000 government documents; 52,000 maps; 965,000 microforms; and 7,000 videotapes and music CDs. Special collections include the Map Collection, the Government Documents Collection, the Children's Literature Collection, and the University Archives.

Costs

Costs for in-state residents in 2003–04 were tuition and fees, $4886; room and board, between $5850 and $7788, depending on residence hall and meal plan chosen; and books, supplies, transportation and other expenses, $2600 to $3600. Costs for out-of-state residents were tuition and fees, $13,524; room and board, $5850 to $7788, depending on residence hall and meal plan chosen; and books, supplies, transportation, and other expenses, $2600 to $3600.

Financial Aid

Financial assistance is given to qualified students in three different forms: scholarships, loans, or University work-study. The University offers several different scholarships to students who meet certain criteria. Applicants are evaluated for all the scholarship awards offered; recipients are awarded the scholarship that is most financially advantageous. Awards are dependent on the availability of funding and given in competitive rank order. They are offered by various departments as well as University-wide. Scholarships vary in amounts ranging up to $2600 per year. Seventy percent of students participate in on- or off-campus jobs. Eastern Michigan University also offers grants-in-aid to qualified athletes of selected sports programs. The University participates in all federal financial aid programs, including the Federal Stafford Student Loan and the Federal PLUS Loan.

Faculty

Eastern Michigan University has more than 1,200 faculty members, who come to the school with vast experience in their chosen field and the appropriate degrees, including doctorates, master's degrees, and certificates, where appropriate. Each faculty member strongly believes in the University's philosophy of keeping class sizes small, with a student-professor ratio of 20:1, and providing as much individual guidance as possible.

Student Government

The Student Government Organization at Eastern Michigan University is organized much like the federal government, with an executive office, a senate, a house of representatives, and a court system. The executive branch consists of the offices of the student body president and vice president and officers from other campus organizations. The senate passes resolutions and formulates bills that further causes of the student body. The house of representatives is a branch of student government focused on programming campus events. The court is responsible for making sure student government complies with any and all relevant statutes and the constitution.

Admission Requirements

Applicants who are not U.S. citizens or who have transferred from outside of the U.S. are subject to the deadlines for international students. International applicants who need an I-20 form should apply as early as possible. Applicants are strongly encouraged to apply early. Entering freshman and transfer students who are admitted to a first bachelor's degree program are automatically considered for a scholarship if they are admitted to the fall semester by the following dates: freshmen, February 15; transfers, May 15. The deadline for U.S. students for fall 2004 is August 2; for international students, the deadline is July 5. Admission to Eastern Michigan University is on an equal basis, regardless of color, race, sex, religion, national origin, or disability.

Application and Information

A completed application form, including a $30 nonrefundable application fee; transcripts from all high schools, colleges, or universities previously attended; and ACT or SAT scores must be submitted to the Admissions Office. All transcripts must be official transcripts sealed in an envelope from the institution. No ACT or SAT test scores are required for individuals over the age of 21. Individuals with 12 or more transferable credits apply as transfer students and usually do not need to send high school transcripts.

For more information, students should contact:

Admissions Office
401 Pierce Hall
Eastern Michigan University
Ypsilanti, Michigan 48197
Telephone: 734-487-3060
800-468-6368 (toll-free)
Fax: 734-487-6559
E-mail: admissions@emich.edu
World Wide Web: http://www.emich.edu

EASTERN NAZARENE COLLEGE

QUINCY, MASSACHUSETTS

The College

Eastern Nazarene College (ENC) is a coeducational liberal arts school, founded in 1900, that has been located in Quincy, Massachusetts, since 1919. It pursues a mission of educational excellence in an atmosphere of a Christian worldview and life view. It is one of nine liberal arts colleges supported by the International Church of the Nazarene in the United States and one of a network of institutions supported by the church around the world. The campus, three blocks from Quincy Bay, is located in a suburb of Boston, which is just a 10-minute walk from the Boston subway system and literally on the doorstep of the city.

Eastern Nazarene College offers resources and opportunities to students of all races, creeds, and colors. Approximately one half of ENC students come from Nazarene Church backgrounds; the remainder is comprised of students from more than twenty-eight denominations and some from other faiths. A school ENC's size, with a 15:1 student-faculty ratio, allows students to get to know their professors personally and fosters contact between student and teacher both academically and in matters of life and faith. An NCAA Division III athletic program and numerous other campus organizations, including service opportunities with ministry, are available to ENC students. The undergraduate student body of more than 1,200 is made up of an equal number of traditional students and nontraditional adult learners.

Location

Quincy, a city of more than 85,000, is a southern suburb of Boston within easy reach of the city by all modes of transportation, both public and private. As a result, many opportunities are available in this historic region, from cultural events and major-league sporting attractions to internships and joint ventures with major universities.

Majors and Degrees

The College offers Bachelor of Arts or Bachelor of Science degrees to students completing a prescribed four- to five-year course of study and Associate of Arts degree to those completing a two-year program. Major fields of concentration are accounting, advertising and public relations, biology, business administration, business management, chemistry, child and adolescent development, church music, clinical and research psychology, communication arts, computer engineering, computer science, early childhood education, electrical engineering, elementary education, engineering, English, environmental science, general science, general studies, health sciences, history, journalism, lay ministries, liberal arts, literature, marine biology, marketing, mathematics, middle-school education, movement arts, music, music education, music performance, pharmacy, physical education, physics, prelaw, premedical studies, premedical technology, psychology, radio and television broadcasting, recording arts, religion, secondary education, social relations, social work, sociology, special education, speech communication, theater arts, urban ministry, writing, youth and Christian education, and youth ministry.

The Division of Social Sciences offers the Bachelor of Arts with concentrations in accounting, business administration, child and adolescent development, clinical and research psychology, history, movement arts, prelaw, psychology, social relations, social work, sociology, and urban ministry in conjunction with the Division of Religion. The Associate of Arts is also available with a concentration in business administration.

The Division of Arts and Letters offers the Bachelor of Arts with concentrations in advertising and public relations, church music, communication arts, English, journalism, literature, music, music performance, radio and television broadcasting, recording arts, speech communication, theater arts, and writing. The Bachelor of Science with a concentration in church music is also available.

The Division of Natural Sciences offers the Bachelor of Science with concentrations in biology, chemistry, computer engineering, computer science, electrical engineering, engineering, engineering physics, environmental science, general science, marine biology, mathematics, physics, premedical studies, premedical technology, and psychology (in conjunction with Social Sciences). The Bachelor of Arts is also available, with concentrations in biology, chemistry, computer science, general science, marine biology, mathematics, physics, and psychology.

The Division of Religion and Philosophy offers the Bachelor of Arts with concentrations in religion and youth ministry and the Associate of Arts with concentrations in lay ministries and youth and Christian education.

The Division of Teacher Education offers teacher certification in conjunction with a liberal arts major in one of the following fields: elementary education, middle school education, music education, physical education, secondary education, and special education. An Associate of Arts is also offered in early childhood education.

Academic Programs

Each student seeking a bachelor's degree completes a general liberal arts core curriculum combining academics with a Christian education as part of a 128-semester-hour program. A grade of C or better must be obtained for all courses in the selected major. Electives completing the total number of semester hours needed must also be fulfilled. The senior year's work and that of the chief concentration of the major subject must be completed in residence at ENC. A comprehensive examination in the major field must be completed to the satisfaction of the major department, and a cumulative grade point average of 2.0 or better must be maintained. Dual-degree programs leading to both a B.A. and B.S. in a concentration require 153 semester hours. Most ENC students are able to complete bachelor's studies in four or five years.

The Associate of Arts requires the completion of a minimum of 62 total credits. A cumulative grade point average of 1.8 or better is required. Academic counseling is available through the Center for Academic Services to provide services to students who may need additional guidance to maintain satisfactory progress in their course work. Students who are interested in these services make an appointment with the director of academic services.

Off-Campus Programs

Through the Coalition for Christian Colleges and Universities, ENC is able to offer an American studies program in Washington, D.C.; a Latin American studies program in Costa Rica; a program at the Los Angeles Film Studies Center; an environmental studies program; and a summer semester at Great Britain's University of Oxford.

Academic Facilities

A center for on-campus study is the state-of-the-art Nease Library, which houses approximately 118,500 volumes, more than 500 periodicals, and 13,000 online periodicals. Reference service is available for all materials, and a full-service Resource Center, featuring Macintosh and PC computers, is available for student use.

Costs

Tuition for the 2003–04 academic year was approximately $16,052; room and board were $5638. Other student fees totaled $556. Various payment plans are offered. For information, students can contact the Office of Student Accounts at 800-510-3495 (toll-free).

Financial Aid

Eastern Nazarene College encourages any prospective student to consider its sources of aid. Both the Free Application for Federal Student Aid (FAFSA), which can be obtained from the ENC Financial Aid Office, and the ENC Application for Financial Aid must be submitted for priority consideration.

Nearly 400 institutional scholarships and grants dealing with academics, activities, and need are available, as are several open to members of the Nazarene Church. A family grant program also operates. These can be mixed with Federal Pell Grants, the FSEOG program, state grants, Federal Stafford Student Loans, Federal Perkins Loans, PLUS Loans, and work-study programs.

For further details, students can write to the Financial Aid Office, Eastern Nazarene College, 23 East Elm Avenue, Quincy, Massachusetts 02170 or telephone 800-88-ENC-88 (toll-free).

Faculty

At ENC, the faculty is committed to fostering excellence in students. The faculty members value their work with academics in a Christian environment. More than 60 percent hold terminal degrees in their field of concentration. Many faculty members have authored or contributed to numerous books and articles in addition to having presented at regional and national conferences.

Student Government

Student life and activities at ENC are entrusted to a large degree to the students themselves. The Executive Council of the student organization, a representative group of students and 1 faculty adviser, discusses campus problems and ideas suggested by the student body. The council works with the administration for the solutions to these problems and assists in coordinating and implementing the intramurals of the College.

Admission Requirements

All applicants are encouraged to have completed a high school curriculum that prepares students for college in English, history, foreign language, mathematics, social sciences, and sciences and must submit a high school transcript, SAT I or ACT scores, two letters of recommendation, and an essay or personal interview before an application for admission is reviewed by the admission committee. Admission is normally granted on a rolling basis to students who rank in the upper half of their high school class. Typically, students admitted to ENC have an average SAT score of 1060 or an average ACT score of 24. The Committee on Admissions, however, looks at the entire student profile, including class rank, high school GPA, SAT/ACT scores, TOEFL scores (where applicable), and recommendations in making the final decision.

Applicants who do not meet the above standards can be considered for admission through the College Achievement Program (CAP). The Committee on Admissions, before considering an application for the CAP, might require additional grade reports, placement testing, a campus visit, and an interview and references attesting that the student is ready for college. The number of applicants accepted through CAP is limited, and some may be denied admission or placed on wait-list status for the fall semester.

International applicants should consult the special admissions instructions for international students.

Application and Information

Applications are available online at the Web site listed below or from the Office of Admissions upon request. Applications mailed early in the senior year of high school help ensure priority consideration for fall registration, residence hall preference, and financial aid. An acceptance tuition deposit of $250 and a room deposit fee of $250 must be submitted by May 1 by all students accepted for, and planning to attend, the fall semester.

For additional information and application materials, students may contact:

Office of Admissions
Eastern Nazarene College
Quincy, Massachusetts 02170
Telephone: 617-745-3711
800-88-ENC-88 (toll-free)
E-mail: admissions@enc.edu
World Wide Web: http://www.enc.edu

On campus at Eastern Nazarene College.

EASTERN OREGON UNIVERSITY

LA GRANDE, OREGON

The University

Eastern Oregon University (EOU) is a public liberal arts and sciences university with an emphasis in undergraduate teaching and learning. Established in 1929 as a college to prepare teachers, EOU has evolved into a dynamic university offering twenty-seven undergraduate degree programs and one master's degree in education.

The University's 2,000 students come from thirty-five states and twenty-eight countries. With small, personalized classes taught only by faculty members, students have exceptional opportunities for interaction with both faculty members and peers. The faculty's dedication to student success is emphasized through hands-on research, advanced technology, and real-world practice through internships. Rigorous course work is the standard for EOU's baccalaureate and preprofessional programs and carries through to the University's innovative Honors Program. With personal attention and academic support, students at EOU have little trouble achieving the high expectations set by faculty members.

EOU requires that all first-year students live on campus. The residence halls become a community of peers, with students forming clubs and study groups and taking time out for day or weekend trips around the Northwest. Students who live on campus eat in Hoke Center, which provides an array of meal plans and options.

EOU has more than fifty different clubs and organizations, including a radio station, student government, theater, music, a newspaper, a literary magazine, and a science journal. Eastern Student Entertainment provides a variety of campus programs throughout the year.

EOU students compete in intercollegiate athletics at the NAIA Division II level in baseball, men's and women's basketball, men's and women's cross-country and track and field, football, softball, women's soccer, and women's volleyball. EOU Rodeo is affiliated with the National Association of Intercollegiate Rodeo. Club sports include downhill skiing, golf, polo, rugby, tennis, and men's volleyball. More than 50 percent of EOU students participate in intramural sports, including basketball, flag football, softball, and volleyball.

Location

Students at Eastern Oregon University live and learn on a campus of 142 acres surrounded by the Blue and Wallowa Mountains in the community of La Grande. With more than 12,000 residents, La Grande is a friendly, safe university community. The small-town atmosphere is the perfect setting for students to integrate into community life. The city has numerous lodging accommodations and a wide selection of restaurants for students and their visiting families.

Northeast Oregon is the perfect place for outdoor recreation. There are two ski areas, Anthony Lakes and Spout Springs, each within an hour of the campus. Both areas provide excellent downhill and cross-country skiing. Hiking, backpacking, kayaking, fishing, rock climbing, and biking are popular activities in the area. The Eagle Cap Wilderness, Hells Canyon National Recreation Area, and Wallowa Lake are all popular destinations for students searching for exceptional recreational opportunities.

Majors and Degrees

The University is organized into four schools: Arts and Sciences, Education and Business, Agriculture, and Nursing. Bachelor of Arts (B.A.) and Bachelor of Science (B.S.) degrees are available in the following areas: agriculture business management (with Oregon State University); anthropology/sociology; art; biochemistry; business administration (with concentrations in accounting; international business; leadership, organization, and management; and marketing); business/economics; chemistry; computer science/multimedia studies; crop and soil science (with Oregon State University); English/writing; environmental economics, policy, and management (with Oregon State University); fire service administration; history; liberal studies; mathematics; media arts; multidisciplinary studies (elementary education); music; nursing (with Oregon Health Science University); philosophy, politics, and economics; physical education and health; physics; psychology; rangeland resources (with Oregon State University); and theater arts.

Preprofessional programs include dental hygiene, dentistry, engineering, fisheries and wildlife, forestry, home economics, law, medical technology, medicine, nursing, optometry, pharmacy, physical therapy, and veterinary medicine.

Additional areas of concentration and minors include bilingual and Hispanic studies; economics; elementary and secondary education; engineering science; gender studies; geography; geology; German; interdisciplinary writing and rhetoric; international studies; military science; modern language; philosophy; political science; Spanish; and special education.

Academic Programs

All undergraduate students at Eastern Oregon University complete a general education program in addition to the course work for their major. General education helps develop skills and knowledge in communication and critical thinking, aesthetics and humanities, human behavior, the natural world, arts and the creative process, and logic, language, and culture. The general education program challenges students to become critical, creative thinkers and engaged, knowledgeable citizens, open to new ways of looking at the world.

The EOU Cornerstone Program offers a dramatically different way to learn. Cornerstone students complete substantial projects in four areas: international experiences, community service learning, internships, and research with faculty. EOU Cornerstone graduates are globally aware, committed to community, academically adept, and well prepared for the world.

Eastern Oregon University offers an Honors Baccalaureate degree for highly motivated students. The pursuit of an Honors Baccalaureate can enrich the educational opportunities available to EOU students and promote an environment for intellectual and personal achievement. EOU's Honors Program is designed to nurture talent by providing the opportunity to go further into an academic discipline, to broaden and deepen an education beyond the usual required work, and to cultivate and reward genuine intellectual curiosity. The Honors Baccalaureate requires the completion of six components in addition to the student's regular degree requirements: three academic projects, campus leadership, community service learning, and preprofessional conference participation/presentation.

The Learning Center provides academic support to all students in the form of peer tutors who are available to provide tutoring assistance for most first- and second-year courses. The math and writing labs are housed in the Learning Center, while the supplemental instruction and small-group study sessions take place across campus. The Learning Center also houses a small, networked computer lab for student use. Subject-specific programs are available for a variety of classes.

Off-Campus Programs

Eastern Oregon University offers a variety of study-abroad and overseas internship opportunities through participation in the Northwest Council on Study Abroad.

The University also participates in the National Student Exchange Program, allowing students to spend up to a year at one of more than 160 colleges and universities in the United States.

Academic Facilities

The EOU campus is a blend of traditional design with modern facilities. A state-of-the-art theater, music, and art facility allows students to hone their skills in a professional setting. The newest development on the campus is the Science Center. With completion scheduled for fall 2004, the Eastern Oregon University Science Center will house research and teaching laboratories, classrooms, faculty offices, and support areas in a unified facility, serving the University and regional education, health, science, and natural resource programs. In a unique research setting that places scientific agencies within the academic environment, students will receive a holistic yet practical approach to learning about and solving natural resource issues in the region.

EOU's Pierce Library is a common gathering place for students to study. The library houses approximately 250,000 volumes in the general collection. EOU is a member of Orbis, a unified library catalog made up of colleges and universities throughout the Pacific Northwest, providing students with access to 9 million books, sound recordings, films, videotapes, and more.

Students have access to several computer labs on the campus. The main computer labs are open more than 90 hours a week and have lab assistants to provide help and support to users. Other discipline-based and multimedia labs offer additional resources. Students living in the residence halls have access to T-1 lines in each dorm room. E-mail accounts and access to the Internet are free of charge.

Costs

Tuition and fees for the 2003–04 year were $4509 ($1503 per term). Eastern Oregon University does not charge out-of-state tuition; all undergraduate students, regardless of residence, pay one rate. The average cost for a residence hall double room and a meal plan was $5250.

Financial Aid

EOU offers a full range of scholarships, grants, work-study, and loans from federal, state, University, and foundation sources. To qualify for federal and state aid, students must apply for admission and must submit the Free Application for Federal Student Aid (FAFSA), listing EOU as one of their top six choices (Title IV code: 003193).

Through the EOU scholarship program, the University offers a variety of scholarships for new and returning students who have a strong record of academics, leadership, and motivation. Scholarships range from $500 to full tuition annually for up to four years.

Faculty

With a student-faculty ratio of 14:1, EOU students receive personal attention and outstanding one-on-one instruction from faculty members whose first priority is teaching. More than 90 percent of the more than 125 faculty members have Ph.D.'s or the highest degree in their field. It is common for faculty members to collaborate with students on research, academic papers, and presentations. Each student is assigned a faculty adviser to assist them in planning courses and mentoring them in their plans for graduate and professional school and careers.

Student Government

The Associated Students of Eastern Oregon University (ASEOU) is the officially recognized student government. ASEOU includes 6 executive officers and elected senators. The duties include representing the students in the University Assembly, working on current issues facing students at EOU, and working on state educational issues with the Oregon Student Association.

Admission Requirements

A minimum 3.0 high school GPA (on a 4.0 scale) in the fourteen core subject requirements (4 years of English, 3 of math, 3 of social science, 2 of natural sciences, and 2 of foreign language) guarantees admission to EOU. Applicants who do not meet the GPA or subject requirements may be considered for admission by submitting a portfolio. Students are considered on a case-by-case basis and may be required to make up specific deficiencies prior to fall admission.

Transfer admission requires successful completion of at least 30 transferable quarter credits with a minimum GPA of 2.25. Students must complete two courses in the humanities, natural sciences, or social sciences. Students with fewer than 30 transferable credits are considered for admission on the basis of their high school records in addition to their college credits.

Application and Information

Applicants must submit an application with a $50 nonrefundable application fee and official transcripts from each high school and/or college or university attended. Freshmen must submit official SAT I or ACT scores. Students may apply any time after the completion of their junior year for the following academic year. Admission is rolling, but the priority deadline for fall is June 1.

EOU encourages students to visit the campus. A visit, including a campus tour with a current student and an opportunity to talk with a faculty adviser and member of the coaching staff, can be scheduled by contacting the Office of Admissions/New Student Programs (listed below).

For an application or to request more information, students should contact:

Office of Admissions
Eastern Oregon University
One University Boulevard
La Grande, Oregon 97850
Telephone: 800-452-8639 (toll-free)
Fax: 541-962-3418
E-mail: admissions@eou.edu
World Wide Web: http://www.eou.edu

EASTERN UNIVERSITY

ST. DAVIDS, PENNSYLVANIA

The University

Eastern University is a Christian university committed to the integration of faith, reason, and justice in all of its undergraduate, graduate, professional, and international programs. The University's mission is to produce world Christians who are capable of confronting injustice and indifference with the character, competence, and commitment that Eastern has helped them develop. The power of the prophetic Word and the Lordship of Jesus Christ provide the context for Eastern's theological position. Sure of its Christian stand, the University encourages students to strengthen their faith by confronting serious contemporary issues. Eastern University values its affiliation with the American Baptist Churches USA and welcomes an interdenominational student body, faculty, and campus community. Eastern affirms and embraces Christians whose doctrinal positions may be broader or more restrictive. As a result, everyone at the University can actively pursue the full dynamic of abundant Christian life with freedom and confidence.

The academic curriculum emphasizes liberal arts and sciences foundational skills as well as the understanding and application of knowledge in an increasingly complex society. Classroom experience is intellectually rigorous. A creative core curriculum builds on basic truths and continually challenges the potential of an expanding mind. Practical experience is gained through a variety of internships and relationships with Eastern's Campolo School for Social Change in Philadelphia and the School for International Leadership and Development as well as ministries such as World Vision, Young Life, Youth for Christ, international missions, and Christian outreach programs.

More than 1,500 full-time undergraduates are enrolled at Eastern. The total enrollment, including adult and graduate programs, is approximately 3,000. Eastern offers graduate degrees in business, education, and counseling.

On-campus housing accommodates more than 1,000 students in seven residence halls (three were built within the last five years). Many air-conditioned suites and apartments are available, as are single rooms and the traditional double arrangement. For students who wish to connect a personal computer, each residence hall room is connected to the campus computer network. Intercollegiate teams for men are fielded in baseball, basketball, cross-country (club), golf, lacrosse (club), soccer, tennis, and volleyball (club). The intercollegiate program for women offers basketball, cross-country (club), field hockey, lacrosse, soccer, softball, tennis, and volleyball. An intramural program offers opportunities for participation in basketball, soccer, softball, touch football, and volleyball.

Eastern provides students with a well-developed Student Ministry Program that helps them develop their faith in Jesus Christ. Student ministries include weekly chapel, "Sunday Night Live" worship led by students, grow groups, and student chaplains. Among the outreach opportunities available are Evangelicals for Social Action, Fellowship of Christian Athletes, and Habitat for Humanity. Although it is an independent mission organization, the Evangelical Association for the Promotion of Education (EAPE) works closely with the Student Ministry Program and welcomes Eastern student volunteers to staff its programs in inner-city Philadelphia and Camden.

Location

Eastern University is located near Philadelphia, Pennsylvania, one of America's educational centers, and is within easy access of New York City; Washington, D.C.; and Baltimore, Maryland. Eastern's local community is on the Philadelphia Main Line, a residential area ½ mile north of Lancaster Pike (U.S. Route 30) in the town of Wayne. Eastern's convenient suburban setting provides easy access to Philadelphia via SEPTA trains that run every half hour from the St. Davids station to downtown Philadelphia. The traveling time is less than 30 minutes. Philadelphia offers a wealth of educational and cultural opportunities. Rare collections of historical and anthropological interest are displayed in the University of Pennsylvania Museum. The Franklin Institute and Fels Planetarium promote the physical sciences, while the Academy of Natural Sciences and Wistar Institute promote the biological sciences. The exhibits at the Museum of Art and the Pennsylvania Academy of Fine Arts are open to the public. Tickets to concerts by the world-renowned Philadelphia Orchestra are available to students at special rates.

Eastern has one of the most picturesque campuses in America, with its three lakes, wooded walking trails, and a historic, working waterwheel. Yet it is within minutes of a variety of intellectual and cultural resources, including Philadelphia, historic Valley Forge, and the Amish country of rural Pennsylvania. The seashore and the Pocono Mountains are an hour or two away.

Majors and Degrees

Undergraduate degrees include the Bachelor of Arts, Bachelor of Science, Bachelor of Science in Nursing, and Bachelor of Social Work degrees. Majors are offered in accounting, art history, astronomy, biblical studies (biblical languages/without biblical languages), biochemistry, biokinetics (exercise science, sports medicine, pre–occupational/pre–physical therapy), biological studies, biology, chemistry, communication arts (communication in society, dance, public relations/advertising, theater), dance, economics and finance, elementary education (early childhood, special education), English (literature, writing), environmental studies, French, history, information technology, management, marketing, mathematics, missions, music (church music, composition/electronic music, cross-cultural music, performance, teaching), political science, psychology, secondary education (five-year M.Ed. option), social work, sociology, Spanish, studio art, theological studies, urban economic development, urban studies, and youth ministry. Minors are offered in accounting, American history, anthropology, astronomy, biblical studies, biology, chemistry, communication arts, dance, economics, English literature, English writing, environmental studies, European history, finance, fine arts, French, French civilization, gender studies, Latin American studies, leadership, management, marketing, mathematics, missions, music, philosophy, political science, psychology, social welfare, sociology, Spanish, sports and coaching, teaching English as a second language, theological studies, and urban studies. Preprofessional programs are offered in dentistry, law, and medicine.

Academic Program

In the core curriculum, students take courses designed to fulfill the basic mission of Eastern: to provide a biblical foundation for all learning and action, to ensure the acquisition of basic skills, and to broaden the student's view of the world. The central themes of the Christian faith are integrated into the course content of the core curriculum, which includes courses such as Justice and Diversity in a Pluralistic Society and Science, Technology and Values.

The Templeton Honors College, "a college within the University," offers a rigorous, classically oriented curriculum designed to challenge the most academically gifted students and prepare them for leadership and service at the very top of culture and society and in the professions linked to their academic majors. The honors college includes a required study-abroad, study-away semester. Enrollment in the honors college is highly competitive and limited to 24 new students each academic year. Students qualify to apply to the Templeton Honors College by achieving a combined score of 1350 or higher on the SAT I or 30 or higher on the ACT or by ranking in the top 9 percent of their high school class.

Off-Campus Programs

Eastern students are encouraged to study abroad or participate in special programs recognized by the University. Academic study abroad is required of language majors, with study options in France, Spain, and Mexico. Nonlanguage majors may select from many options, including (but not limited to) Austria, Canada, England, Israel, Kenya, Peru, South Africa, and Uganda. At the AuSable Institute in Michigan, students may apply for certificate programs leading to the designation of naturalist, land resources analyst, water resources analyst, or environmental analyst.

The American Studies Program, sponsored by the Coalition of Christian Colleges and Universities, provides an opportunity for students to study or serve as interns in Washington, D.C., with the nation's leaders. In the Latin American Studies Program, students live with native families; study Spanish and the local culture, history, politics, economics, and religious life; participate in service projects; and travel in Central America. The coalition also operates a film-study center in California and offers Russian and Middle East studies programs.

The Oregon Extension offers a semester of community living and liberal arts studies in the Cascade Mountains of southern Oregon. The Honors Research Program at the Argonne National Laboratory in Chicago provides junior and senior biology, chemistry, and math majors an opportunity for advanced research at a nationally recognized laboratory. Through the Goshen Study Service Trimester, students and faculty members study the history and culture of Caribbean nations and engage in a service project. Exchange programs with selected American Baptist colleges allow upperclass students to spend a semester or a year at another college. May Term opportunities include special courses, semesters, and study tours. Eastern Baptist Theological Seminary offers students the chance to take selected course work.

Academic Facilities

Of Eastern's twenty-six buildings, the primary academic facility is the McInnis Learning Center. In addition to classrooms and offices for faculty members and administrators, the main floor includes a 300-seat auditorium and several music practice rooms. Other features are the biology center, a highly regarded curriculum laboratory for those preparing to be teachers, a technology classroom for distance learning, a planetarium, a media services center, a computer-assisted language laboratory, a fully equipped "smart" classroom, and two student computer centers. The state-of-the-art Bradstreet Observatory is located on the roof of the McInnis Learning Center. Heritage House offers an acoustically designed Great Room for music performances as well as "smart" classrooms with the latest computer technology. The Warner Library is a comfortable facility housing more than 155,000 volumes, 725 periodicals, and hundreds of microforms and audio recordings. In addition, Eastern students have direct access to libraries throughout the region and around the world via the computer and more than 50 electronic databases. Facilities for chemistry, physics, and computer science are located in Andrews Hall. In addition to offices and classroom space, Andrews houses six teaching laboratories, a computer center, and scientific equipment generally found only at larger colleges and universities.

Costs

For the academic year 2003–04, tuition was $16,780, and room and board were $7200. Total costs for the year were approximately $23,980.

Financial Aid

Eastern is committed to providing education to qualified students regardless of their means. The financial aid program offers scholarships, grants, loans, and employment. The University utilizes the Pennsylvania Higher Education Assistance Agency (PHEAA) for needs analysis forms processing. The student is required to complete the Free Application for Federal Student Aid (FAFSA) to determine financial aid eligibility. Overall, the University views financial assistance to students as a cooperative investment. If parents contribute to the maximum of their ability and the student contributes a fair share through earnings and personal savings, the University attempts to complete the partnership. Non-need academic scholarships ranging from $500 to full tuition are available. These scholarships are awarded on the basis of SAT I or ACT scores and high school class rank information. Music, leadership, honors college, and church matching grants are other University-based grant programs available.

Faculty

Eastern University employs more than 87 full- and part-time faculty members. More than 80 percent have earned doctorates. With an emphasis on teaching and a commitment to research, faculty members have authored more than 260 scholarly publications. Some faculty members teach both graduate and undergraduate courses, and almost all serve as academic advisers. Classes are kept small with a student-faculty ratio of 15:1.

Admission Requirements

The University seeks applicants who present acceptable academic records. Most applicants rank in the top half of their class and have combined SAT I scores of at least 1000 or comparable ACT scores. A campus visit and interview are recommended. Transfer applicants are welcome.

Application and Information

Applications are generally accepted until the beginning of each term. Admission decisions are made on a rolling basis. For more information, students should visit Eastern's Web site listed below. For further information, students may contact:

Dave Urban
Director of Undergraduate Admissions
Eastern University
1300 Eagle Road
St. Davids, Pennsylvania 19087-3696
Telephone: 800-452-0996 (toll-free)
E-mail: ugadm@eastern.edu
World Wide Web: http://www.eastern.edu

EASTERN WASHINGTON UNIVERSITY

CHENEY, WASHINGTON

The University

Established in 1882 as the Benjamin P. Cheney Academy, Eastern Washington University (EWU) has grown from a premier teachers' college into a comprehensive state university providing an excellent student-centered learning environment; professionally accomplished faculty members who are strongly committed to student learning; high-quality, integrated, interdependent academic programs; and exceptional student support services, resources, and facilities. The University retains the charm and personality of its founding on the parklike campus in Cheney. It also exhibits the distinctive marks of the modern comprehensive university in its newer facilities and the expansion of higher educational opportunities into downtown Spokane. Eastern is fully accredited by the Northwest Association of Schools and Colleges and by numerous professional accreditation agencies in specific disciplines. In addition to the undergraduate degrees that are listed, Eastern offers master's degrees in the arts and sciences, business administration, creative writing, education, nursing, public administration, social work, and urban and regional planning. Eastern also offers a doctorate in physical therapy.

Eastern's 9,500 students come from more than forty states and twenty-four countries. Nonwhite students make up 12 percent of the student body, and international students make up 2 percent. About 58 percent of Eastern's students are women. Educational and support services are available through the American Indian Studies, Chicano Education, and African American Education Programs; the English Language Institute; and the Academic Support Center. Seven residence halls can accommodate 2,086 students on campus. Additional housing is available for married students and students with children. Fraternity and sorority housing, as well as off-campus housing within walking distance in Cheney, affords a variety of housing options. All residence halls are smoke free. Students and the University community enjoy one of the Northwest's premier sports and recreation centers. The PHASE complex includes a 5,500-seat pavilion, an indoor aquatics center, a field house with indoor track and tennis, and the main PHASE building, which houses indoor courts for basketball, volleyball, and racquetball; dance studios; a fitness center; and a large, multisurfaced rock for climbing practice. These facilities, totaling 100,000 square feet, and Woodward Field are the venues for the NCAA Division I Eagles, who compete in the Big Sky Conference.

Location

The University's main campus is located in Cheney, a comfortable and compact city of 9,000, where students may find a variety of services, facilities, and shopping while enjoying the pleasant, secure feel of a small town. Spokane, one of the state's largest cities and a regional hub for manufacturing, business, transportation, and health services for more than 400,000 residents, is just 17 miles away and offers a full range of social, cultural, recreational, and consumer opportunities. The Inland Northwest region offers virtually unlimited scenic and recreational attractions in a four-season climate. More than seventy-five lakes lie within 50 miles of the campus, and the mountains and many rivers are easily accessible. Other outdoor activities include excellent skiing within a short drive in nearly every direction. The University sits amid fascinating geological and geographic diversity, with the arid high country to the west, the rich Palouse farming area to the south, and the fir-covered mountains climbing from Spokane into Idaho and Montana. The Spokane International Airport, rail and bus service, and interstate access serve the region.

Majors and Degrees

Electrical engineering is soon to become the newest degree program, pending final approval. EWU is responding to the needs of the state as defined by the Washington Council of the American Electronics Association. The following majors are available: anthropology; art; biology (including biochemistry/biotechnology, predental, premedicine, and preveterinarian); business administration (including accounting, economics, finance, general management, human resource management, international business, management information systems, marketing, operations management, and pre-M.B.A.); chemistry and biochemistry; communication disorders; communication studies (including interpersonal, organizational, public communication, and public relations); computer science (including computer information systems and multimedia programming and development); counseling, developmental, and educational psychology; criminal justice; dental hygiene; earth science; economics; education (including elementary and secondary options); electronic media, film, and theater; engineering technology and multimedia design (including computer engineering technology, construction design, electronics, graphic communications, manufacturing, and mechanical engineering technology); English (including creative writing, literary studies, and technical communication); environmental science; geography; geology (including environmental); government (including prelaw); health services administration; history; humanities; interdisciplinary studies; international affairs; journalism (including computer science, news editorial, public relations, and technology); mathematics (including computer science, economics, and statistics); military science; modern languages and literature (including French, German, and Spanish); music (including instrumental performance, liberal arts, music composition, piano performance, and vocal performance); natural science; nursing; occupational therapy; physical education, health, and recreation (including athletic training, coaching, community health education, exercise science, health, health and fitness/elementary or secondary education, health education, health promotion and wellness, outdoor recreation, recreation management, and therapeutic recreation); physics; psychology; social work; sociology; theater; and urban and regional planning.

Academic Programs

Eastern's mission is to prepare broadly educated, technologically proficient, and highly productive citizens to attain meaningful careers, to enjoy enriched lives, and to contribute to a culturally diverse society. Graduates must have well-developed skills in critical thinking and the ability to express themselves in oral, written, and quantitative forms of communication. The liberal arts core curriculum extends throughout the student's four-year program and includes both breadth and depth requirements as well as writing instruction and assessment in all areas of the curriculum. Small classes, a student-faculty ratio of 24:1, and facilities like the Writers' Center offer the student the resources to meet high expectations. Eastern's unique core curriculum and liberal arts goals were designed as a direct response to input from Eastern alumni, employers, and students. Minors are available in many areas of study, and teacher certification requirements and specific endorsements are available in conjunction with academic disciplines. The prestigious University Honors Program offers motivated students the opportunity to challenge their limits through special honors courses that are part of the core curriculum. University and departmental honor societies continue to provide these opportunities in the major fields. Career preparation is a focus during each student's entire program. Internships and career exploration opportunities for freshmen and sophomores assist in early career and major selection, enhanced employment skills, and locating professional internships as upper-division students.

Off-Campus Programs

Study-abroad opportunities are available for Eastern students as well as for students from other campuses. Programs are available in more than twenty-five countries. In addition, internships are available for students in the Inland Northwest, across the United States, and internationally. These programs provide countless training and research opportunities for graduate and undergraduate students.

Academic Facilities

Eastern's campus includes more than 300 acres in Cheney. The University also maintains classroom, office, and laboratory/clinic facilities in downtown Spokane and shares facilities at the Riverpoint Higher Education Center, also in downtown Spokane. The University libraries include the Kennedy Library on the Cheney campus, with more than 800,000 items, online catalogs, and computer search capabilities covering Eastern as well as other Washington State libraries. Eastern and Washington State University jointly support a downtown library facility. Student computer labs, including a multimedia lab, are located throughout campus. The Pence Union Building houses the main computer lab, with Macintosh and IBM-compatible systems, on-site assistance, DEC mainframe access with faculty sponsorship, and Internet access. The residence halls are wired for both voice and data communications. Additional facilities for learning and teaching include the planetarium, the Robert Reid Laboratory School (an elementary school directly on campus that includes observation facilities), a speech and hearing clinic, and the Turnbull Laboratory for Ecological Studies.

Costs

Annual undergraduate tuition and fees for 2003–04 were $3812 for Washington State residents and $12,668 for nonresidents. Students participating in the Western Undergraduate Exchange Program paid $5373 for tuition. Typical on-campus room and board cost about $5470.

Financial Aid

The Financial Aid and Scholarship Office assists students in identifying the most appropriate sources of funding for their college education. Students who are admitted to the University may apply for federal, state, and University funds by using the Free Application for Federal Student Aid and by applying before the priority deadline of February 15. Although most financial aid is based on need, a number of scholarships are available for students who meet competitive academic criteria. Academic scholarships also reward outstanding performance by continuing students at Eastern. A reduction of the nonresident tuition is available to qualified students from Idaho, Montana, Nevada, New Mexico, North Dakota, Oregon, South Dakota, Utah, and Wyoming through the Western Undergraduate Exchange Program. Applicants interested in need-based financial aid and academic scholarships should contact the Financial Aid and Scholarship Office, 102 Sutton Hall, Eastern Washington University, Cheney, Washington, 99004.

Faculty

More than 600 faculty members provide highly personalized instruction to undergraduates at Eastern. Faculty members are committed to keeping class sizes small and to helping students graduate in a timely manner. Eastern's faculty members are teachers and take pride in innovative curricula, in maintaining close relationships with the community and with professionals outside of the University for the benefit of their students, and in their research, which brings new information and methods into the classroom.

Student Government

All students are members of the Associated Students of Eastern Washington University. A president, executive officers, and a 12-member council are elected annually. The 12 council members represent the students' interest in every facet of student life at Eastern. The student government is responsible for budgeting and managing student fees collected from all students. These funds are used for the operation of the student union, the Pence Union Building, athletic and intramural programs, and the more than seventy-five clubs and organizations that provide opportunities for involvement of students both on campus and in the community.

Admission Requirements

Freshman applicants are admitted based on their high school GPA and test scores on the SAT I or ACT. Applicants also must meet the following core requirements in high school (having extra core classes is highly encouraged): English, 4; math, 3 (algebra I and II and geometry); social science, 3; science, 2 (including 1 lab science); foreign language, 2 (same language); and fine arts (or elective from above subject areas), 1. Transfer students with fewer than 40 transferable credits must meet the high school core and admissions index requirements and have a 2.0 cumulative GPA. Transfer students with more than 40 transferable credits must have a cumulative GPA of 2.0 and completed a minimum of precollege-level English and intermediate algebra with a 2.0 or better. Students who do not meet the academic criteria for admission may be considered on the basis of additional evidence of potential presented to the Office of Admissions. Many majors require considerably higher grade point averages for entry into the major field. Transfer students should consult the University catalog or contact the department for specific program requirements.

Application and Information

All freshman applicants should submit an application, complete high school (and any college) transcripts, and SAT I or ACT scores to the Office of Admissions. Decisions for fall freshmen are made on December 1 and on a rolling basis thereafter. Transfer students should submit an application, an official high school transcript, and official transcripts from all colleges and universities attended. A nonrefundable application fee of $35 is required of all applicants. A campus visit or participation in an overnight on-campus program is the best way to learn more about Eastern. Students should contact the Office of Admissions to find out more about these and other programs designed to provide an opportunity to explore Eastern Washington University. For additional information, students should contact:

Office of Admissions
101 Sutton Hall
Eastern Washington University
Cheney, Washington 99004
Telephone: 509-359-2397
Fax: 509-359-6692
E-mail: admissions@mail.ewu.edu
World Wide Web: http://www.ewu.edu

The state-of-the-art John F. Kennedy Library has fifty different databases available, 500 study carrels, wireless laptops that may be checked out, and more.

ECKERD COLLEGE

ST. PETERSBURG, FLORIDA

The College

Eckerd College, a liberal arts institution of distinctive quality, was founded in 1958 as Florida Presbyterian College. Its first freshman class entered in 1960. Eckerd College is related by covenant to the Presbyterian Church (U.S.A.), and it is governed by a self-perpetuating Board of Trustees. Dedicated to excellence, Eckerd College has established a national reputation as a leading innovative liberal arts college. Its student body, faculty members, and program attest to the high expectations of its founders and to a remarkable degree of fulfillment in the years that have followed. In addition, the College has been awarded a chapter of Phi Beta Kappa.

Eckerd College currently enrolls 1,606 students (730 men and 876 women) from forty-nine states and sixty-seven countries. Seventy percent of the student body comes from out of state. Campus life includes a multitude of activities that assist students with their intellectual, social, physical, and spiritual growth. Dormitory life is one hub of the College's social environment. More than 75 percent of students live in dorms and the majority live on campus all four years. The dorms are small and informal; friendships are easily developed in this setting. Upperclassmen may choose to live in the apartment-style town houses located right on campus. Through the Eckerd College student government, social and cultural programs are planned for the College community. Four buildings in the center of campus have been recently transformed into the Hough Campus Center, which includes a pub, snack bars, lounges, student offices and meeting rooms, and a fitness center. The Campus Center is designed to accommodate meaningful interactions between all members of the College community.

Many special interest clubs and a range of intramural sports programs are available. In addition, NCAA Division II intercollegiate athletics for men include baseball, basketball, golf, sailing, soccer, and tennis. For women, basketball, cross-country, sailing, soccer, softball, tennis, and volleyball are offered. Club volleyball is available for men, club golf is available for women, and club swimming and rugby are available for men and women. Students also have the opportunity to get involved with the campus television and radio stations, the yearbook, and the weekly newspaper.

Location

The 281-acre campus, bordered in part by a 1¼-mile waterfront, is located in a suburban setting on the southern tip of the peninsula that makes up Pinellas County. This peninsula is bounded on the west by the Gulf of Mexico and on the east by Tampa Bay. St. Petersburg is a city of approximately 425,000 people and is a major part of the rapidly growing Tampa Bay metropolitan area. The area has become the national and regional headquarters for many major corporations. Cultural and recreational opportunities are abundant, including art museums, symphony orchestras, professional theater and road-show engagements of Broadway plays, concerts, and year-round professional sports attractions.

Majors and Degrees

The Bachelor of Science is offered in biochemistry, biology, chemistry, computer science, environmental studies, marine sciences, mathematics, physics, and psychology. The Bachelor of Arts is offered in American studies, anthropology, biology, business administration, communication, comparative literature, creative writing, economics, French, German, history, human development, humanities, international business, international relations and global affairs, international studies, literature, management, modern languages, music, philosophy, political science, psychology, religious studies, sociology, Spanish, theater, visual arts, and women's and gender studies.

In addition to the list of approved majors given above, Eckerd offers flexible concentrations of study so that the student may design his or her own program, either in a traditional field or in an interdisciplinary field. Some typical concentrations include biological illustration, human services management, Latin American development studies, management information systems, organizational dynamics, and personnel and global human resources management. Preprofessional programs include dentistry, engineering and applied science (a 3-2 program), law, M.B.A. studies, medicine, theology, and veterinary medicine.

Academic Programs

The student pursues the study of a major field by joining a Collegium, a group of like-minded scholars who view their subjects, however diverse, in the same way. Each Collegium has its own decision-making group composed of professors and students. Eckerd operates on the 4-1-4 calendar system. Among the programs that illustrate the innovative nature of Eckerd are the mentorship program, a special training program for faculty members to enable them to help students in their academic progress, career planning, and personal growth; Autumn Term, a three-week orientation program for freshmen, which is designed to provide an intensive foretaste of college living and college academic work; Winter Term, a one-month midyear program especially adaptable to independent study and off-campus projects, first designed and implemented by Eckerd; a series of interdisciplinary seminars to explore issues related to aesthetics, cross-cultural interaction, environmental concerns, and social relations; and a senior capstone experience involving a choice of thesis, creative project, or comprehensive examination. Eckerd College has pioneered a residential Academy of Senior Professionals on campus, which prominent retired men and women from around the world are invited to join. These distinguished persons come from professions to which Eckerd students aspire and are available for lectures, advising, career counseling, and mentoring. The academy now comprises more than 350 distinguished professionals.

Off-Campus Programs

Various kinds of off-campus opportunities are available. Among the many options for international education are the Eckerd College Study Centre in London, yearlong exchange programs in Japan and Korea, and semester-long exchange programs on every continent through Eckerd's affiliation with the International Student Exchange Program. The Sea Semester Program is available for marine science students, and an exchange program with students on other campuses across the country can be arranged for January or for a semester. As part of Career Service and Applied Liberal Arts programs, many internship and field experience placements are available. These can be taken for credit upon satisfactory completion of an Independent-Study Contract.

Academic Facilities

The library at Eckerd has more than 140,000 volumes, 1,100 periodicals, and 13,000 items on microfilm. In addition, a new, state-of-the-art library opens in December 2004. Complete laboratory facilities are available for language, marine science, chemistry, physics, biology, and experimental psychology. Two state-of-the-art science buildings opened recently: a waterfront marine science laboratory and a marine mammal pathobiology laboratory. The 375-seat Bininger Theatre provides professional facilities for theatrical productions. The Roberts Music Center houses classrooms, practice studios, and acoustically insulated listening rooms. The Griffin Chapel has one of the finest Flentrop organs in the country, and a smaller Flentrop is located in the Music Building. Both instruments are used by students studying the organ. Facilities for physical education include a modern gymnasium and basketball court; a swimming pool; a renovated weight room; tennis and volleyball courts; a new complex for soccer, softball, and baseball fields; and a fleet of canoes, kayaks, sailboats, and waterskiing-equipped power vessels that are used in an extensive waterfront program. The waterfront program also includes the newly constructed Wallace Boat House and a fully equipped and nationally acclaimed Water Search and Rescue Team. The Ransom Center for Visual Arts provides studios for painting, sculpting, silkscreening, weaving, pottery, photography, video graphics, and other media. The Elliot Gallery is a part of the largest building in the art complex and features continuous showings of visiting exhibits as well as exhibits of work by students and faculty members. The Science Auditorium is equipped for films and demonstrations, and films are shown at Dendy McNair auditorium both for entertainment and for academic courses. The Information Technology Center houses more than twenty Sun Microsystem servers that are linked to more than 700 computers for Web site and data services. Students have access to more than 200 personal computers, both Macintosh and IBM-compatible, in several laboratories and in all the dormitory lounges throughout the campus. Each dormitory room is wired for access to the Internet and the campus intranet, which includes the library. A Writing Center featuring desktop publishing capabilities is also available to all students.

Costs

For 2003–04, tuition was approximately $22,538, and room and board totaled $5970. Books are nearly $900 per year. Student fees are $236.

Financial Aid

Thirty scholarships ranging from $11,250 to $22,500 per year are available to entering freshmen regardless of financial need. These Trustee, Presidential, and Dean's Scholarships are awarded to outstanding freshmen with strong scholastic records and leadership potential, as demonstrated in a special competition. Other scholarship programs for outstanding students include Church and Campus Scholarships for Presbyterian students recommended by their pastor, Byars Scholarships for Florida residents, and Honors and Special Talent Scholarships for outstanding applicants for admission. Additional details on these and other programs are available from the College's admissions office.

More than 88 percent of all students at Eckerd receive scholarships and/or financial aid. Academic performance, personal development, and potential contribution to the College community are important considerations. Financial need is determined by an evaluation of the Free Application for Federal Student Aid (FAFSA). A student's total financial aid package ordinarily consists of a scholarship or grant, work aid, and a loan. As a rule, the mix of grant and loan funding contains a more favorable grant component when the student's academic performance is strong.

Faculty

The faculty has 192 professors (147 full-time and 45 part-time). Ninety-five percent of faculty members have earned a Ph.D. or a terminal professional degree and average 48 years of age. The student-faculty ratio is 13:1. No graduate assistants teach courses.

Student Government

Student activities at Eckerd College are administered by the Eckerd College Organization of Students (ECOS). ECOS conducts campus social programs, including dances, concerts, and films; works to create special events and bring speakers to campus to address issues important to students; and represents student interests in academic policy decisions. Students have voting membership on all major faculty committees.

Admission Requirements

Scores on either the SAT I or ACT are required for admission. No specified high school subjects are required, but the following are recommended as minimal: 4 units in English, 3 in mathematics, 2 in a foreign language, 3 in science, and 3 in social studies. Although no minimum high school average or rank is required, students with less than a 2.5 average are seldom admitted. In last year's freshman class, more than 60 percent of the members ranked in the top quarter of their high school graduating class. An interview is recommended but not required. Geographical location and religious preference are not admission factors. Early admission is available to promising high school juniors. In addition, credit and advanced standing are offered through the Advanced Placement Program of the College Board or the International Baccalaureate Program.

Application and Information

Application may be made at any time and should include a $25 application fee. A rolling admission policy is practiced. For more complete information and to make arrangements to visit the campus, students should contact:

Director of Admissions
Eckerd College
4200 54th Avenue South
St. Petersburg, Florida 33711
Telephone: 727-864-8331
800-456-9009 (toll-free)
Fax: 727-866-2304
E-mail: admissions@eckerd.edu
World Wide Web: http://www.eckerd.edu

Eckerd's waterfront campus on Boca Ciega Bay.

EDGEWOOD COLLEGE

MADISON, WISCONSIN

The College

With a progressive and challenging curriculum, Edgewood offers the advantages of a small private college in a university-oriented city. The result is a stimulating learning environment rich in academic and recreational resources.

Edgewood's 55-acre wooded campus is situated on the shore of Lake Wingra in a residential neighborhood of Madison near parks and an arboretum. The College has three residence halls and one apartment building for students, a new student center/union, the state-of-the-art Sonderegger Science Center, a library, classrooms, athletic facilities, a chapel, and a theater. Campus organizations include the student newspaper, student government, professional groups, and a variety of clubs to meet personal interests. There are intramural athletics and intercollegiate teams in men's baseball, basketball, cross-country, golf, and soccer, and women's basketball, cross-country, golf, soccer, softball, tennis, and volleyball.

Edgewood has completed a major building program that has added several campus improvements, including the new Sonderegger Science Center and the Henry J. Predolin Humanities Center. The Sonderegger Science Center has been designed to be a national model for science education and collaboration. The Henry J. Predolin Humanities Center consists of state-of-the-art classrooms, offices, and, most importantly, a student center/union.

Edgewood collaborates with the University of Wisconsin–Madison, located only a few blocks away, in a program of shared resources that gives students opportunities that are not usually available at a college of Edgewood's size. Edgewood students may enroll in one university class per semester and have access to the university's library system and art museum. Guest lecturers, concerts, athletic events, and special programs are all readily available on a regular basis.

The current undergraduate population is approximately 1,800. The student body includes both residents and commuters. Although the majority of students come from the Midwest, about 15 percent are from states other than Wisconsin or from countries outside the United States.

The College is accredited by the North Central Association of Colleges and Schools, and its programs in education are accredited by the National Council for Accreditation of Teacher Education. The nursing program is approved by the Wisconsin State Board of Nursing and the American Association of Colleges of Nursing.

Location

Madison is a growing and exciting community, with a colorful assortment of art fairs, outdoor markets, festivals, sporting events, and concerts taking place throughout the year. As Wisconsin's state capital, Madison is home to a vigorous state legislature and a politically active community at all levels. The city has a stable economy driven by a broad base of educational, medical, and financial institutions as well as light industry. While Madison is renowned for its scenic beauty, it is also the gateway to hundreds of vacation, park, and lake areas in northern and central Wisconsin. Many students take advantage of the Madison community by gaining valuable work experience, participating in volunteer opportunities, and becoming involved in internships.

Majors and Degrees

Edgewood College offers baccalaureate degrees with majors in accounting, art, art therapy, biology, broad-field social studies (concentration in economics, history, political science, or sociology/anthropology), business (concentration in finance, management, or marketing), chemistry, child life, computer information systems, criminal justice, cytotechnology, early childhood–exceptional needs, economics, elementary education, English (writing or literature), French, graphic design, history, international relations, mathematics, medical technology, music, natural science and mathematics, nursing, performing arts, psychology, public policy and administration, religious studies, sociology, and Spanish. Preprofessional programs are available in dentistry, engineering, law, medicine, pharmacy, and social work. Individualized majors and minors may also be arranged. Minors include many traditional areas, plus computer science, environmental science, philosophy, secondary education, and women's studies.

Many people also attend classes for personal enrichment or professional development or participate in a separate continuing education program of noncredit short courses.

Academic Program

The goal of an Edgewood education is to develop intellect, spirit, imagination, and heart. The curriculum includes a foundation for all students in composition, logic, mathematics, speech, foreign language, arts, sciences, and perspectives, with an advanced sequence designed for honors students. Departmental course requirements for majors and minors are added to the above. The human issues project, a multidisciplinary study or activity, requires every student to apply knowledge and experience to the examination of a selected aspect of the human condition and the values involved.

Students are encouraged to participate in field experiences, internships, and independent studies, regardless of major. Education students begin classroom observation and practice as early as the freshman year. Nursing, medical technology, and cytotechnology students engage in clinicals in hospitals and laboratories as juniors and seniors.

The College is on a 4-1-4 calendar that consists of four months of classwork each semester and the Winterim, an optional educational and cultural program held each January between semesters, during which credit may be earned or independent pursuits followed. Two eight-week summer sessions are also available.

Edgewood offers alternative routes to credit for its degrees through the College-Level Examination Program (CLEP), the College Board's Advanced Placement (AP), the ACT Program's Proficiency Examination Program (PEP), locally administered programs of retroactive credit for foreign language proficiency, and credit for work experience that closely matches the content of a course.

Off-Campus Programs

Collaboration with the University of Wisconsin–Madison enables Edgewood students to take one course per semester at the university under Edgewood's tuition. This relationship greatly broadens the scope of courses, libraries, museums, and faculty members available to students of the College.

Edgewood encourages students to take advantage of community resources. Arrangements with a children's hospital, a local nursing home, a school for exceptional children, and a school for juvenile offenders provide education, psychology, and sociology majors with opportunities for off-campus experiences. Volunteerism at community meal programs, local prisons, shelters, centers for at-risk children, and public health agencies is also encouraged.

Qualified students may plan for special one- or two-week courses abroad or for a semester or year at an international institution of higher learning.

Academic Facilities

The College library is a comfortable facility with a reading atrium and group study rooms. Its collection includes books, periodicals, videotapes, audio recordings, and CD-ROM databases in several fields, including business. In addition, microcomputers, CD players, tape recorders, photocopiers, video equipment, and microform readers are available for student and faculty use. The library offers direct computerized access to the catalog of the University of Wisconsin libraries and to other library catalogs through the Internet. An interlibrary loan delivery service connects hundreds of libraries in the state. Computer labs on campus have both Apple and PC equipment that connects to a local access network. Student rooms in the residence halls are also joined to the network. The foreign language lab has audio and videotape equipment and receives international programs via satellite.

Costs

Edgewood's tuition and fees are $15,100 per year for 2003–04. The complete cost of room and board in a campus residence is approximately $5500 per year. Other expenses, including books, travel, and supplies, averaged $1500.

Financial Aid

Edgewood's financial aid program combines innovative merit-based assistance with traditional need-based assistance to make the Edgewood experience affordable. Institutional merit awards are available based on academic, leadership, science, and fine arts skills. More than 90 percent of freshman aid applicants receive some form of grant or scholarship. The College administers traditional federal and state programs, including the Federal Pell Grant and the Wisconsin Tuition Grant. Campus employment is available along with Federal Stafford Student Loans, Federal Perkins Loans, and supplemental loans. To apply for assistance, students must complete the Free Application for Federal Student Aid (FAFSA). Students may arrange with the College to pay tuition in monthly installments. Early aid eligibility estimates are available upon request.

Faculty

The College currently has a full-time teaching faculty of 81, of whom 79 percent have doctoral or terminal degrees in their fields. All classes and labs are taught by the primary professor and not by graduate students. The favorable student-faculty ratio allows good rapport between professors and students. Faculty members take a keen interest in their students, serving as academic advisers and becoming involved in student activities. The full-time faculty is supported by a cadre of part-time instructors who bring added expertise to the classroom.

Student Government

Through their participation in various committees and organizations and through the Student Government Association, students have the opportunity to take part in determining scholastic, intellectual, recreational, social, and cultural activities both on and off campus. Students have a voice and vote on the commencement, curriculum and education policy, library policies, student affairs, and teacher education programs.

Admission Requirements

Edgewood accepts applicants on the basis of the amount and kind of ability a student possesses, as reflected in scholastic standards that have been met, high school and community activities, and employment. Candidates for admission to Edgewood must submit 16 units of high school study, including 12 units in English, speech, mathematics, history, natural science, social science, and foreign language. High school grade point average, rank in class, ACT or SAT I scores, and recommendations are considered in determining the applicant's potential to do college work. Applicants from nontraditional high schools are welcome to apply.

Transfer students are evaluated on the college-level work they have done as well as on the standard criteria for admission. Each department determines transferability of credits, but a minimum of 32 hours must be completed in residence, including the major requirements.

Application and Information

Office of Admissions
Edgewood College
1000 Edgewood College Drive
Madison, Wisconsin 53713
Telephone: 608-663-4861
800-444-4861 (toll-free)
World Wide Web: http://www.edgewood.edu

Students in front of the Sonderegger Science Center, a state-of-the-art facility that has already become a national model for science and education collaboration.

EDINBORO UNIVERSITY OF PENNSYLVANIA

EDINBORO, PENNSYLVANIA

The University

Edinboro University, a part of the Pennsylvania State System of Higher Education, is located in the borough of Edinboro, Erie County, Pennsylvania. It is the oldest teacher-training institution in Pennsylvania west of the Allegheny Mountains and the second-oldest in the state. Edinboro Academy was chartered in 1856. After the passage of the State Normal Act in 1857, the school opened as Edinboro Normal School for the preparation of teachers. Under its original charter, the school was privately administered until 1861, when the commonwealth chartered it as a state normal school. The school was purchased by the commonwealth of Pennsylvania in 1914. The state recognized Edinboro State Teachers College as a four-year college in 1926 and granted it the right to offer a Bachelor of Science in Education degree in the areas of elementary, secondary, and art education. The name of the institution was changed to Edinboro State College in 1960. In 1983, university status was given to each of the state colleges, and a comprehensive commonwealth university system was established.

Edinboro's graduate school offers the Master of Arts, Master of Fine Arts, Master of Education, Master of Science, Master of Science in Nursing, Master of Social Work, and post-master's certifications.

The University is accredited by the Commission on Higher Education of the Middle States Association of Colleges and Schools (3624 Market Street, Philadelphia, Pennsylvania 19104; telephone: 215-662-5606). The commission is an institutional accrediting agency that is recognized by the U.S. Secretary of Education and the Commission on Recognition of Postsecondary Accreditation. Other University accreditations and program approvals include the National Council for Accreditation of Teacher Education, the Commission on Collegiate Nursing Education, the American Dietetic Association, the Association of Collegiate Business Schools and Programs, the Council on Rehabilitation Education, the Council for Accreditation of Counseling and Related Educational Programs, the American Speech-Language-Hearing Association, the Council on Social Work Education, the National Association of Schools of Music, the Pennsylvania State Board of Nursing, and the Pennsylvania Department of Education.

Of the 8,045 students at Edinboro, 7,029 are undergraduates. The University maintains six on-campus residence halls for approximately 2,500 students. Each residence hall is wired for digital satellite cable television services, two high-speed data connections, and a telephone connection. There are more than forty-three buildings situated on the spacious 585-acre campus, which includes open fields, a lake, and many acres of woods.

Edinboro University in Erie–The Porreco Center and Edinboro University in Meadville–The Meadville Access Center offers classes and University services at convenient off-campus locations.

Location

Located adjacent to the business district of Edinboro, Pennsylvania, the University is accessible by automobile from all sections of the state and is near the intersection of Interstates 90 and 79. Passenger service of all kinds operates on frequent schedules, connecting Edinboro with nearby cities and towns, including Erie, Pennsylvania's fourth-largest city. The Erie Airport is approximately 15 miles to the north. Within walking distance of the campus, the community of Edinboro has eight churches of various denominations.

Majors and Degrees

The University awards the Associate of Arts, Associate of Engineering Technology, Associate of Science, Bachelor of Arts, Bachelor of Fine Arts, Bachelor of Science, Bachelor of Science in Nursing, and Bachelor of Science in Education. These permit majoring in the following areas: anthropology, applied media arts (with concentrations in animation, cinema, graphic design, and photography), fine arts/crafts (with concentrations in ceramics, drawing, jewelry/metalry, painting, printmaking, sculpture, textile design, weaving/fibers, and wood/furniture design), art education, art history, biology, biology/premedical LECOM, biomedical equipment technology, broadcast journalism, business administration/accounting, business administration/administration, business administration/financial services, business administration/forensic accounting, business administration/marketing, chemistry, chemistry/forensic sciences, chemistry/industrial biochemistry, communication studies (with concentrations in broadcasting, organizational communication, and public relations/advertising), communication speech and hearing disorders, computer science, computer science/application, computer science/theoretical, criminal justice (A.A. and B.A.), drama, earth sciences, economics, elementary education, elementary/early childhood education, elementary/special education, English/literature, English/writing, environmental science/biology, environmental science/geology, environmental studies/geography, foreign language, general business administration, general studies, geography, geology, German, health and physical education (with concentrations in teacher education, health promotion, recreation administration, and sport administration), history, humanities, human services/social services, human services/developmental disabilities, industrial trades leadership, innovative nursing, Latin American studies, liberal studies, manufacturing engineering technology, mathematics, medical technology, music, music education, natural science and math, natural science and math/wildlife, nuclear medicine technology, nursing, nursing/RN, nutrition, philosophy, physics 3-2 engineering, physics/liberal arts, physics/theoretical, political science, preschool education, print journalism, psychology, secondary education (biology, chemistry, earth and space science, English, general science, German, mathematics, physics, social studies and Spanish), social science, social work, sociology, Spanish, special education, special education/elementary education, and specialized studies. Preprofessional programs are offered in dentistry, law, medicine, pharmacy, and veterinary science. Minors also exist in fifty-seven specializations.

Academic Program

Associate degrees require a minimum of 60 semester hours of credit, including a general education component.

Baccalaureate degrees require a minimum of 120 semester hours of credit. A general education requirement of 60 semester hours is distributed among the arts, humanities, and science and technology to ensure a basic liberal arts foundation. The remaining 60 semester hours are devoted to specialization and may include major and professional courses, a minor, and other concomitant courses.

Advanced Placement credit and honors courses are available.

The Office of Extended Learning offers a variety of workshops and special interest courses. The Office of Adult Student Information Services enables nontraditional students to enroll for academic programs at convenient times and locations on a full- or part-time basis.

An Army Reserve Officers' Training Corps (ROTC) program is available.

The Office for Students with Disabilities provides services essential for physically disabled, hearing-impaired, visually impaired, and learning-disabled individuals.

Academic Facilities

The seven-story Baron-Forness Library is the focal point of the University campus. The library houses more than 470,000 bound volumes and more than 1.3 million microform units. Technology and Communications supports and manages thirty-six computer labs.

Costs

For 2003–04, the tuition fee for a resident of Pennsylvania was $2299 per semester; for nonresident students, the cost per semester was $3449. For a semester, room rent was $1560, and meals were $983. Additional fees included a student activity fee of $119, a University Center fee of $125, a health fee of $60, an instructional service fee of $230, and an instructional technology fee of $50. The cost of books and supplies varies with the academic major. Costs are subject to change for 2004–05.

Financial Aid

The types of financial aid offered by Edinboro include student employment, loans, grants, and scholarships. In most cases, Pennsylvania State Grant and Free Application for Federal Student Aid forms are used to determine eligibility for these programs. Federal aid administered by the University is available for both the regular academic year and the summer sessions. The application deadline for upperclass students for these programs is normally May 1 for the following academic year. Freshmen may apply for aid upon acceptance by the University. Financial aid is also available through the University's ROTC program. For additional information, students should contact the Assistant Vice President for Student Financial Support and Services (888-611-2680, toll-free) or access the information online at http://piper.edinboro.edu/cwis/studaff/emr/finaid/.

Faculty

Edinboro's student-faculty ratio of 18:1 makes it possible to maintain close interaction between students and the highly qualified faculty members. A large percentage of the faculty have completed terminal degrees in their area of specialization.

Student Government

The Student Government Association is a vital and active organization on the campus and serves as the official student voice in all University matters. Student Government Association representatives serve on nearly all University committees and participate in the University governance system. This organization sponsors special events, activities, and student clubs to satisfy a variety of student interests. The Student Government Association participates in the annual budget recommendations regarding the budgeting of the student activity fund.

Admission Requirements

Edinboro University grants admission on the basis of general scholarship, character, interest, and motivation as they may be determined by graduation from an approved high school, home school or institution of equivalent grade or equivalent preparation as determined by the Credentials Division of the Department of Education; official scholastic records; aptitude tests; recommendations; and interviews. To fully prepare for a University program of study and increase the probability for academic success, students should pursue a college-preparatory curriculum at the secondary level and provide evidence of scholastic aptitude, as measured by scores on the SAT or ACT. Submission of aptitude scores can be waived for nontraditional, adult learners. An audition is required for all applicants to any music curriculum; music students are invited to participate in the audition some time after the application for admission is received by the Office of Undergraduate Admissions.

Application and Information

Students may make application for admission as early as July 1, after finishing the junior year of high school; the application for can be found online at http://iis1.edinboro.edu/pubrel/admissions/application.asp. Requests for application papers, viewbooks, financial aid forms, and further information should be addressed to:

Admissions Office
Biggers House
Edinboro University of Pennsylvania
Edinboro, Pennsylvania 16444
Telephone: 814-732-2761
888-8GO-BORO (toll-free)
Fax: 814-732-2420
World Wide Web: http://www.edinboro.edu

An aerial view of Edinboro University of Pennsylvania.

ELIZABETH CITY STATE UNIVERSITY

ELIZABETH CITY, NORTH CAROLINA

The University

Elizabeth City State University (ECSU) was founded on March 3, 1891, as a two-year normal school to train teachers of African-American heritage. In 1937, the institution became a four-year teacher's college and two years later was renamed Elizabeth City State Teacher's College. In 1969, the institution was dedicated as a regional university. In 1971, ECSU became a constituent institution of the sixteen-campus University of North Carolina system.

ECSU is a public university offering baccalaureate programs in the basic arts and sciences and in selected professional and preprofessional areas and the master's degree in elementary education.

Elizabeth City State University is accredited by the Commission on Colleges of the Southern Association of Colleges and Schools (1866 Southern Lane, Decatur, Georgia 30033-4097; telephone: 404-679-4501) to award the bachelor's degree. ECSU's Teacher Education Program is approved by the North Carolina State Board of Education and accredited by the National Council for the Accreditation of Teacher Education (NCATE). Its Industrial Technology Program is accredited by the National Association of Industrial Technology.

ECSU enrolls nearly 2,200 students: 76 percent of students are African American, 22 percent are Caucasian, and 2 percent are students from other cultural and ethnic backgrounds. Ninety percent of students are pursuing their education full-time. Students come from seventy-one of North Carolina's 100 counties, twenty-two states, the District of Columbia, and four other countries.

At ECSU, nearly half of the students choose to live on campus. These students live in a number of residence halls and one apartment complex. Each facility is staffed by administrators and student assistants who help provide and maintain a high-quality experience for students. Students who live on campus are automatically enrolled in a campus meal plan that provides all meals. The campus dining hall features an array of freshly prepared entrees, salads, sandwiches, and snack items. The Viking Den, a snack bar, is also located on campus. The Commuter Center gives students a place to relax or study between classes.

Participation in extracurricular activities enhances students' leadership skills. There are more than sixty officially recognized social, service, and interest-related organizations on campus. They range from professional and academic clubs to religious groups and service organizations, including fraternities and sororities. Activities like these bring students with similar interests together and add an extra measure of fun and camaraderie to the college years. Some of the organizations available include Greek fraternities and sororities, the Art Guild, Cheering Squad, Commuter Student Club, Criminal Justice Club, Dance Group, Residence Hall Council, Industrial Arts Club, NAACP, NABA, Panhellenic Council, Majorettes, University Band, University Choir, University Players, Gospel Choir, Viking Yearbook, Social Sciences Club, Spanish Club, Students in Free Enterprise, Student Government, and Usher's Guild.

ECSU is a Division II university and is affiliated with both the CIAA Conference and the NCAA. ECSU has one of the highest graduation rates of athletes attending NCAA Division II colleges. Men's varsity teams include baseball, basketball, cross-country, football, and tennis. Women's teams include basketball, cross-country, softball, and volleyball.

For students who want to play sports for fun, the campus offers numerous intramural sports and recreational and leisure activities. The campus also has an Olympic-size indoor swimming pool and a six-lane bowling alley.

Location

Elizabeth City State University is nestled in the historic Albemarle area near the mouth of the Pasquotank River in northeast North Carolina. This location is only minutes from Virginia Beach, Norfolk, and the Tidewater region. To the south lies the beautiful Outer Banks, a spot for vacationers from all over the country.

Majors and Degrees

The University currently offers thirty-five undergraduate academic majors. The School of Arts and Humanities offers the Bachelor of Science degree in criminal justice and music industry studies and the Bachelor of Arts degree in art, communication studies, English, history, music, political science, sociology, and sociology/social work. The School of Business and Economics offers the Bachelor of Science degree in accounting and business administration. The School of Education and Psychology offers the Bachelor of Science degree in elementary education (K–6), middle grades education (6–9), psychology, and special education (K–12); the Bachelor of Science degree with teacher licensure in biology, chemistry, health education, mathematics, and physical education; and the Bachelor of Arts degree with teacher licensure in art (minor in education, K–12), English, history, music (minor in education, K–12), political science, and sociology. The School of Mathematics, Science and Technology offers the Bachelor of Science degree in applied mathematics, aviation science, biology, chemistry, computer information sciences, geology, industrial technology, marine environmental science, mathematics, and physics.

The University offers an advanced master's degree in elementary education. ECSU also offers a host of concentration alternatives for students, designed to provide preparation for a specialty within the major discipline. Some examples include airway science, athletic coaching, black studies, environmental science, prelaw, and speech/drama.

Academic Programs

Elizabeth City State University awards thirty-four bachelor's degrees to students who have successfully completed all courses and other requirements prescribed by the major department and all of the general education courses prescribed by the University for all students. Credit hours required to earn an undergraduate degree vary from 124 to 130 semester hours. The University Honors Program is designed to challenge students with high academic potential at an accelerated rate and to provide them with exposure to a wide variety of in-depth academic experiences. The ROTC program is also available and is based on a four-year curriculum integrated with the normal baccalaureate degree program.

Academic Facilities

ECSU is an ever-growing campus, with more than fifty buildings spread over 114 acres in historic Elizabeth City, North Carolina. The beautiful and modern campus has many unique facilities, including the state-of-the-art G. R. Little Library, which utilizes a computerized catalog system and contains close to 1 million items, including books, microfilms, audiotapes, videotapes, films, and periodicals. Online services are also available to provide connection to the limitless resources of the Internet, scholarly research, and computer software. The Jimmy R. Jenkins Science Center houses the University's state-of-the-art planetarium, the first in the surrounding North Carolina area. Some of the building's most significant features include seminar and lecture rooms, instrumentation laboratories, an aquarium, and an appended greenhouse. For students in the music industry studies program, facilities include a comprehensive twenty-four-track recording studio. Capital improvements include the completion of the Fine Arts Complex in 1999, and the completion of the Information Technology Center and the Wellness Center in 2000.

Costs

Tuition and fees per semester in 2003–04 for North Carolina residents were $1431 for commuters and $3735 with room and board. Out-of-state tuition and fees per semester were $5563 for commuters and $7867 with room and board. Approximately $250 can be estimated per semester for books and other supplies.

Financial Aid

Of all ECSU students, 86 to 90 percent receive some form of financial aid. Assistance available to eligible students consists of grants, loans, scholarships, and part-time employment. Students applying for financial aid must complete the Free Application for Federal Student Aid (FAFSA). Deadline dates for priority consideration are March 1 (fall semester), November 1 (spring semester), and April 1 (summer semester).

Faculty

Elizabeth City State University employs 130 full-time faculty members; 68 percent hold doctoral degrees, while the remainder hold master's degrees. Many professors are nationally respected scholars who conduct in-depth research and have published numerous works. The faculty-student ratio is 1:15.

Student Government

The Student Government Association (SGA) of Elizabeth City State University is composed of students who are elected by the student body. The SGA's primary goal is to attend to the students' needs and development. It is the duty of the SGA to maintain a certain level of communication with students, faculty members, and the administration.

Admission Requirements

To be considered for admission to ECSU, applicants must have graduated from an approved or accredited high school and have achieved at least a 2.0 grade point average. Applicants should have a minimum SAT I score of 700 or minimum ACT score of 16 for in-state residents and a minimum SAT I score of 800 or minimum ACT score of 18 for out-of-state residents. Students who graduated from high school after June 1990 must meet the following requirements: 4 units of English, emphasizing literature, composition, and grammar; 3 units of mathematics (including algebra I and II and geometry); 3 units of science (including at least 1 unit of a life or biological science, at least 1 unit of a physical science, and at least one laboratory course); and 2 units of social studies, including U.S. history. Two units of the same foreign language are not required but are highly recommended.

Transfer students must satisfy all entrance requirements; their transcripts are evaluated in relation to the requirements of the specific program for which they are applying.

Application and Information

Elizabeth City State University is a constituent institution of the University of North Carolina and is committed to equality of educational opportunity. ECSU does not discriminate against applicants, students, or employees based on race, color, natural origin, religion, gender, age, or disability.

High school students should apply in the fall of their senior year. All students are encouraged to apply before May 1 for the fall semester and before December 1 for the spring semester. Summer session students may register up to the first day of classes.

Official notification of admission eligibility is sent to each applicant immediately after all credentials have been thoroughly evaluated.

The Office of Admissions is open Monday through Friday between 8 a.m. and 5 p.m. For further information about Elizabeth City State University, students should contact:

Office of Admissions
Elizabeth City State University
Campus Box 901
1704 Weeksville Road
Elizabeth City, North Carolina 27909
Telephone: 252-335-3305
800-347-3278 (toll-free)
E-mail: admissions@mail.ecsu.edu
World Wide Web: http://www.ecsu.edu

The Jimmy R. Jenkins Science Complex houses a state-of-the-art planetarium, the first of its kind in northeastern North Carolina.

ELIZABETHTOWN COLLEGE

ELIZABETHTOWN, PENNSYLVANIA

The College

Founded in 1899 to provide a high-quality higher education to men and women, Elizabethtown College maintains its commitment to an academic program that combines a traditionally strong liberal arts core curriculum with a career and professional orientation. The students at Elizabethtown come from thirty states and twenty-five countries, providing a diversity of backgrounds that enhances the College as a whole.

A residential college, 85 percent of E-town students live on the 185-acre campus in six dormitories and senior townhouses. Student-run residence hall councils plan programs and provide leadership opportunities. A wide variety of campus cultural events and other activities draw 80 percent student participation every weekend. The College maintains an active intramural sports program and fields ten NCAA Division III teams for men (baseball, basketball, cross-country, golf, lacrosse, soccer, swimming, tennis, track and field, and wrestling) and ten for women (basketball, cross-country, field hockey, lacrosse, soccer, softball, swimming, tennis, track and field, and volleyball), several of which contend for national titles each year.

The College offers an effective personal and career counseling service, which encourages students to make use of its office as early as their freshman year. The employment and graduate school placement rate for students within eight months after graduation has averaged 90 percent for the past several years.

Location

Elizabethtown is a community of 20,000 people, located in south-central Pennsylvania, within 20 minutes of Hershey, Lancaster, and Harrisburg, the state capital. Philadelphia and Baltimore are within 1 ½ hours of Elizabethtown; New York and Washington are within 4 hours. Elizabethtown is served by Amtrak train service from Philadelphia and Pittsburgh, and the Harrisburg International Airport is 15 minutes away.

Majors and Degrees

Bachelor of Arts degrees are awarded in art, communications, economics, English, history, modern languages, music, philosophy, political philosophy, political science, psychology, religious studies, social work, and sociology-anthropology. Bachelor of Science degrees are offered in accounting, biochemistry, biology, biotechnology, business administration, chemical physics, chemistry, chemistry management, computer engineering, computer science, criminal justice, early childhood education, elementary education, engineering physics, environmental science, industrial engineering, information systems, international business, mathematics, medical technology, music education, music therapy, occupational therapy, and physics. Fifty-two minors/concentrations as well as eight certification programs in secondary education are available.

The College offers joint institutional (3-2) programs with Duke University, leading to a master's degree in forestry or environmental management; 3-2 programs in engineering with Pennsylvania State University are offered, leading to a Bachelor of Arts in physics and a Bachelor of Science in engineering. Cooperative programs with Thomas Jefferson University in diagnostic imaging, laboratory sciences, and nursing lead to a Bachelor of Science, and programs in physical therapy lead to a doctorate. A joint program with Widener University also leads to a physical therapy degree.

Preprofessional majors are offered in dentistry, law, medicine and osteopathy, the ministry, and veterinary medicine.

The Pre-Medical Primary Care Program through the Pennsylvania State University College of Medicine at the Milton S. Hershey Medical Center provides options for Elizabethtown students pursuing careers in internal medicine, family practice, and pediatrics.

Academic Program

Elizabethtown's core program of traditional and innovative liberal arts areas complements both the intensive studies in the academic major/minor and the wide selection of elective courses. Students develop skills for critical analysis, effective communication, and habits of mind that ensure adaptability in the ever changing global job market.

Independent and directed studies and extensive internship and externship possibilities are available.

The College operates on a semester calendar. Freshmen arrive in the last week of August, and examinations are given prior to the winter break. The spring semester begins in the middle of January and runs through early May. Intensive summer-session courses are available for students who wish to accelerate their academic program. Students may earn credit toward graduation through Advanced Placement examinations, College-Level Examination Program tests, or tests administered by the individual departments.

Off-Campus Programs

Through the Brethren College Abroad (BCA) Program, students may spend all or part of a year studying in China, Ecuador, England, France, Germany, Greece, India, Japan, Mexico, or Spain. Study and internships in major U.S. cities and abroad are also available through cooperative programs with Boston, American, and Fordham Universities. Social work majors are required to complete 600 hours of field instruction in off-campus agency settings. Medical technology students spend their senior year studying at AMA-approved cooperative hospital programs. Both occupational therapy and music therapy students must complete six months of fieldwork in an approved health-care setting.

Academic Facilities

The nine academic buildings on campus include the Leffler Chapel/Performance Center, seating 900 for arts, religious, and cultural events; the High Library, with 161,989 bound volumes; two science halls, Esbenshade (biology, engineering, math, occupational therapy, and physics) and Musser (chemistry); a music building; and three other classroom buildings, one of which houses the College's VAX 3100 computer, which is connected to the $3.25-million campuswide network. Steinman Center houses the offices, classrooms, and facilities of the Department of Communications.

Costs

Tuition, room, board, and fees for 2003–04 were $28,800; $22,500 of this was tuition. Students should also plan on an additional cost of about $1500 for books, transportation, and personal expenses, for a total cost of about $29,500. Financial aid is based on this figure.

Financial Aid

Financial aid packages are typically a combination of scholarships, grants, loans, and student employment; 92 percent of the students receive some form of aid. To apply for financial aid, students must file the Free Application for Federal Student Aid (FAFSA) and the Elizabethtown College Verification Form. Estimated data should not be filed. Signed copies of the parent's (and student's, if applicable) most recent federal income tax form, including all schedules, must also be submitted to the financial aid office.

About 180 freshmen with the strongest academic credentials receive academic scholarships, awarded on a competitive basis and without regard to need. The deadline for all financial aid is April 1.

Faculty

Elizabethtown has a teaching faculty of 179 full- and part-time professors. The student-faculty ratio is 13:1. Ninety percent of the full-time faculty members hold a Ph.D. or the highest earned degree in their field. After the freshman year, students who have declared a major are assigned a faculty adviser within the department.

Student Government

Students play an active role in campus governance through the Student Senate, the Residence Hall Association, and other organizations. Members of the Student Senate are elected from each class to voice student concerns, coordinate special events, and allocate funds for student activities and more than sixty student-run clubs and organizations. The Activities Planning Board, also a student group, provides weekend programs, campus social activities, and entertainment for the College community.

Admission Requirements

Decisions about admission to Elizabethtown are made without regard to sex, race, religion, physical handicap, or place of residence. Fewer than 70 percent of all applicants are accepted. Students should have followed an academic curriculum, with the completion of at least 18 college-preparatory units recommended. Fifty-eight percent of the students admitted are in the top 20 percent of their high school class, and 37 percent are in the top tenth. Transfer students are encouraged to apply.

The College seeks diversity, and students who display leadership abilities or special talents are considered highly desirable. Campus interviews are recommended but not required for most students, although the College reserves the right to require interviews in special cases. Music students are required to have auditions, and occupational therapy students must have an interview at the invitation of the department.

Early acceptance is available for highly qualified high school juniors.

Application and Information

The College operates on a rolling admission basis and does not specify a deadline for application. Students can apply using the common application or on line at the Web site listed below. Applicants must submit a high school transcript, SAT I or ACT scores, two letters of recommendation, and a personal statement, essay, or graded paper. Early application is strongly recommended. Accepted students should notify the College of their decision to attend by May 1; matriculation after that date is on a space-available basis. Students interested in the Hershey Foods Honors Program must submit a completed application by January 15.

For more information, students should contact:

Office of Admissions
Elizabethtown College
One Alpha Drive
Elizabethtown, Pennsylvania 17022-2298
Telephone: 717-361-1400
Fax: 717-361-1365
E-mail: admissions@etown.edu
World Wide Web: http://www.etown.edu

The Elizabethtown men's soccer team, with forty-five winning seasons, won the NCAA Division III championship in 1989 and captured its record seventeenth Middle Atlantic Conference championship in 1996.

ELMHURST COLLEGE

ELMHURST, ILLINOIS

The College

Elmhurst College is a private, comprehensive liberal arts college located near the center of metropolitan Chicago. Founded in 1871, the College advances the practical and professional relevance of the liberal arts tradition. The academic programs are characterized by their connections with the professional world and their responsiveness to the intellectual needs of today's diverse student population. In forty-six undergraduate majors and seven graduate programs, Elmhurst students strengthen their skills of critical and creative inquiry and develop their capacity for lives of learning, service, and meaningful work.

The College enrolls more than 2,600 undergraduate and graduate students. Sixty-five percent are full-time undergraduates, 31 percent are over age 25, and 17 percent are minority students. Twenty-two states and seventeen countries are represented in the student body. More than one third of Elmhurst's full-time undergraduates live on campus in one of five residence halls.

The Center for Professional Excellence (CPE) is a distinctive component of an Elmhurst education. Established in 1997, the CPE offers internships, mentorships, international study programs, service-learning opportunities, guidance through career launches and transitions, and other student-centered programs. The goal of this innovative center is to enhance the traditional college experience with additional, purposeful challenges, both intellectual and professional, on campus and beyond.

While Elmhurst is small enough to offer students opportunities to make real contributions to campus life, it also is large enough to offer an extensive range of choices among cocurricular and extracurricular activities. Eighty-seven registered clubs, organizations, and athletic teams are active on campus. The jazz band, radio station, and student newspaper, *The Leader*, have a professional edge. The Mill Theatre presents dramas, musicals, and student-directed productions of original scripts. The Elmhurst College Jazz Festival is an annual, nationally recognized celebration of the supremely American artform. Eminent artists and business, political, and religious leaders regularly speak to campus audiences. Examples include Lech Walesa and Elie Wiesel, winners of the Nobel Prize for Peace; the acclaimed poets Maya Angelou and Gwendolyn Brooks; and the explorer Robert Ballard, who discovered the wreckage of the *R.M.S. Titanic*.

The College fields sixteen teams in NCAA Division III and is a charter member of the highly competitive College Conference of Illinois and Wisconsin (CCIW). During the 1990s, the Bluejays won CCIW championships in baseball, softball, and volleyball, and qualified for postseason play in men's basketball and women's volleyball.

Elmhurst is affiliated with the United Church of Christ. Like the church, the College is open, welcoming, and ecumenical. Nearly half of the students are Roman Catholic. Members of Jewish and Muslim religions, Orthodox beliefs, and many Protestant denominations are represented on the faculty and in the student body. In short, people of all creeds (and of none) come to the campus to learn and thrive.

Master's degrees are offered in seven disciplines: business administration, computer network systems, early childhood special education, English studies, industrial/organizational psychology, professional accountancy, and supply chain management.

Location

Elmhurst's lush suburban campus, located 16 miles west of Chicago's Loop, is a registered arboretum, with twenty-three red brick buildings and more than 600 varieties of trees and other plants. The students benefit enormously from the College's location near the heart of one of the world's most important and appealing urban regions. The Chicago area offers world-class opportunities for internships and other professional opportunities and for cultural, social, and sporting events. A commuter railroad stops two blocks from the campus, and city and suburban attractions are also accessible via several interstate highways. The city of Elmhurst, a charming suburb with more than 42,000 residents, is located on the eastern edge of DuPage County, which is 6 miles southwest of O'Hare International Airport.

Majors and Degrees

Undergraduates at Elmhurst can choose from among forty-six majors. Through the interdepartmental major, students can develop individualized programs of study with the guidance of a faculty adviser. The College awards the Bachelor of Arts, Bachelor of Liberal Studies, Bachelor of Music, and Bachelor of Science degrees.

Elmhurst offers undergraduate degree programs in accounting; American studies; art; biology; business administration; chemistry; communication studies; computer science; early childhood education; economics; elementary education; English; environmental management; exercise science; finance; French; geography and environmental planning; German; history; information systems; interdepartmental, interdisciplinary communication studies; international business; logistics and transportation management; management; marketing; mathematics; music; music business; music education; musical theater; nursing; philosophy; physical education; physics; political science; professional communication; psychology; secondary education; sociology; Spanish; special education; speech-language pathology; theater; theology; and urban studies.

The College offers preprofessional programs in actuarial science, allied health sciences, dentistry, engineering, law, library science, medicine, seminary, and veterinary medicine.

Academic Programs

About one third of Elmhurst students are transfers from other four-year institutions or community colleges. The Office of Admission addresses specific policies regarding transfer credit with students on an individual basis. Elmhurst provides alternatives by which students may obtain credit for areas of study in which they demonstrate prior competence. Such programs include Advanced Placement (AP), departmental examinations, the College-Level Examination Program (CLEP), credit for experiential learning, and credit for noncollegiate instruction.

Academic Facilities

The A. C. Buehler Library, the academic heart of the College, contains more than 225,000 books and subscribes to more than 1,000 periodicals. Through computer-supported consortia, students have access to nearly 20 million books and other resources. The campus has state-of-the-art academic technology. It includes PC and Macintosh laboratories; mainframe, graphics, robotics, and cartography laboratories; an instructional media center; a weather station; a 24-track digital music recording studio; and a 750,000-volt proton accelerator. All students have Internet access. The Deicke Center for Nursing Education occupies its own well-equipped building, Memorial Hall, and uses health-care facilities throughout metropolitan Chicago. One of the nine academic buildings, Old Main, is listed on the National Register of Historic Places.

Costs

Tuition and fees for full-time students totaled approximately $18,600 for 2003–04. Room and board were $6030; books and other expenses averaged nearly $1500. Part-time tuition was approximately $529 per semester hour. Graduate tuition was $590 per semester hour.

Financial Aid

In 2003, Elmhurst awarded approximately $15.6 million in grants and scholarships. Nearly 75 percent of full-time students received some type of aid. The typical package offered to eligible full-time students was $15,500. Approximately 65 percent of all aid is in the form of grants and scholarships. Nearly 45 percent of all freshmen were awarded scholarships based on prior academic accomplishments. All awards are renewable. To apply for financial aid, students should complete the Elmhurst Application for Financial Aid and the Free Application for Federal Student Aid (FAFSA). New students must be admitted before an aid offer is made.

Faculty

Elmhurst College has 113 full-time faculty members. More than 90 percent hold the highest academic degree in their fields. The College has 226 adjunct faculty members. The academic atmosphere attracts scholars who love to teach on a campus where they can work with students as individuals. The average class has 19 students; the largest class has about 35 students. The student-faculty ratio is 13:1. Faculty members and not teaching assistants teach every class.

Student Government

Elmhurst College believes in shared governance. Students are voting members of such important groups as the College Council. The Student Government Association (SGA) is the primary avenue through which students make recommendations to faculty members and administrators. The SGA consists of an elected student chairperson, 14 student members, 3 faculty members, 4 administrators, and the dean of student affairs.

Admission Requirements

Elmhurst seeks students whose academic profile provides a sound basis for success in the classroom and the larger College community. Typically, successful applicants for freshmen admission rank in the top half of their high school class; present a college-preparatory curriculum, including at least 3 units in English and 2 or more in laboratory science, in math, and in social studies (foreign language is recommended but not required); and score at or above the national average on the ACT or SAT I. The most important single element in admission review is the quality of a student's classroom performance. A faculty committee reviews applicants who fall short of the stated criteria. This committee may issue a positive decision with certain conditions, such as requiring the student to take a lighter full-time course load.

Transfer applicants should present an overall college grade point average of 2.4 or higher on a 4.0 scale and be in good standing at the college they most recently attended. High school records are required. As part of the admission process, the College provides an evaluation of previous credits in relation to both graduation requirements at Elmhurst and major department regulations. Thus, official transcripts from each college attended are required with the application.

Elmhurst College does not discriminate on the basis of race, color, creed, age, gender, disability, marital status, sexual orientation, national origin, or ethnic origin.

Application and Information

Elmhurst College admits freshman and transfer students to both the fall and spring terms. Most new students enroll in the fall. Admission decisions are made on a rolling basis. For fall term, the preferred application deadline is April 15 for freshman admission and July 1 for transfer admission. For the spring term, the preferred application deadline is January 15 for all applicants.

For additional information and admission materials, students are encouraged to contact:

Office of Admission
Elmhurst College
190 Prospect Avenue
Elmhurst, Illinois 60126-3296
Telephone: 630-617-3400
800-697-1871 (toll-free)
Fax: 630-617-5501
E-mail: admit@elmhurst.edu
World Wide Web: http://www.elmhurst.edu

The picturesque, traditional college setting at Elmhurst.

ELMIRA COLLEGE

ELMIRA, NEW YORK

The College

Elmira College is a small, independent college that is recognized for its emphasis on education of high quality in the liberal arts and preprofessional preparation. One of the oldest colleges in the United States, Elmira was founded in 1855. The College has always produced graduates interested in both community service and successful careers. Friendliness, personal attention, strong college spirit, and support for learning beyond the classroom help to make Elmira a special place. Elmira College is one of only 270 colleges in the nation to be granted a chapter of the prestigious Phi Beta Kappa honor society.

The full-time undergraduate enrollment is about 1,200 men and women. The students at Elmira represent more than thirty-five states, primarily those in the Northeast, with the highest representation coming from New York, New Jersey, Massachusetts, Connecticut, Maine, and Pennsylvania. International students from twenty-three countries were enrolled in September 2003. Ninety-five percent of the full-time undergraduates live in College residence halls.

The intercollegiate sports program includes men's and women's basketball, golf, ice hockey, lacrosse, soccer, and tennis and women's cheerleading, field hockey, softball, and volleyball. An intramural program is also available. Emerson Hall houses the student fitness center, a pool, and a gym capable of seating 1000, as well as the Gibson Theatre, which has a state-of-the-art sound and lighting system. Professional societies; clubs; music, dance, and drama groups; a student-operated FM radio station; and the student newspaper, yearbook, and literary magazine also provide numerous opportunities for extracurricular activity.

Location

Elmira College is located in the city of Elmira, which has a population of 35,000, in the Finger Lakes region of New York. The campus is a 10-minute walk from downtown Elmira. The relationship between the College and the local community is excellent, and numerous community activities and facilities are open to students, including the Elmira Symphony and Choral Society, the Elmira Little Theatre, clubs and civic groups, museums, movies, and a performing arts center. Excellent recreational areas are available in upstate New York and nearby Pennsylvania.

Majors and Degrees

Elmira College offers programs leading to the bachelor's degree in more than thirty-five majors, including accounting, American studies, art, art education, biochemistry, biology, business administration, chemistry, classical studies, criminal justice, economics, elementary education, English literature, environmental studies, fine arts, French, history, human services, individualized studies, international business, international studies, mathematics, medical technology, music, nursing, philosophy and religion, political science, psychology, public affairs, social studies, sociology and anthropology, Spanish, speech and hearing, and theater. Secondary teaching certification is offered in several areas. A 3-2 program in chemical engineering with Clarkson University is available, and 4+1 M.B.A. programs are available at Alfred University, Clarkson University, and Union College.

Preprofessional preparation is offered in education, medical technology, nursing, and speech pathology and audiology. Faculty advisers assist those who seek preparation for graduate study in dentistry, law, or medicine in choosing appropriate course work. More than 50 percent of Elmira graduates pursue graduate study.

Academic Programs

The College's calendar is composed of two 12-week terms followed by a six-week spring term. Students enroll for four subjects during the twelve-week terms, completing the first term by mid-December and the second during the first week of April. The 6-week term, from mid-April through May, may be devoted to a particular project involving travel, internship, research, or independent study. Students are required to participate in internships in order to gain practical and meaningful experience related to their program of study. Credit is awarded for these projects.

Special opportunities for outstanding students include participation in thirteen national honorary societies on campus and a chance to assist faculty members in teaching and research. The College also offers an accelerated three-year graduation option for outstanding students.

Army and Air Force ROTC are available.

Off-Campus Programs

Through the Junior Year Abroad programs, students may study in the United Kingdom, France, Spain, and Japan, as well as in other countries throughout Europe and Asia. Elmira students may study at the Washington Center for Learning Alternatives. Students from Elmira may spend the third term studying marine biology or doing sociological research on the island of San Salvador in the Bahamas. Education majors may work as student teachers in the Bahamas and in England.

Academic Facilities

The Elmira campus offers exceptional academic facilities in a beautiful setting. The modern Gannett-Tripp Library houses more than 389,000 volumes, receives 2,500 periodicals, and includes a special Mark Twain collection room and photography and audiovisual facilities.

The College Computer Center offers PC and Apple Macintosh microcomputers for student use. Dormitory rooms are equipped to provide direct access to the Internet.

A Center for Mark Twain Studies has been established at Quarry Farm, the author's summer home, which is located a few miles from campus. The College also operates a Speech and Hearing Clinic on campus, which serves the public and provides valuable internship experience for students. Excellent facilities for drama and music are available.

Costs

Tuition for 2004–05 is $26,130, room is $4950, board is $3380, and fees are $900.

Financial Aid

Financial aid is available for both freshmen and transfer students. Awards are based upon the Free Application for

Federal Student Aid (FAFSA) as well as the student's academic potential. Types of aid include grants, scholarships, federal loans, Elmira College loans, and work opportunities. In addition, superior students may qualify for non-need Elmira College Honors Scholarships, which are available to both freshmen and transfer students and range from $4000 to full tuition per year. For 2003–04, the average freshman aid package (including all types of aid) amounted to more than $20,000. About 80 percent of the full-time undergraduates receive financial aid.

Faculty

Members of the faculty are chosen for their ability in and dedication to teaching. All full-time faculty members serve as advisers, and the faculty approves all academic programs. Currently, the full-time faculty consists of 11 full professors, 25 associate professors, 32 assistant professors, and 10 instructors. Ninety-eight percent of the faculty hold the Ph.D. or highest degree necessary to teach in their field.

Student Government

Student government, an important part of the educational system at Elmira College, prepares students for active and responsible citizenship in society. Student government organizations include the Student Senate, the Judicial Board, and the Student Activities Board.

Admission Requirements

The Office of Admissions at Elmira College uses a rolling admission system. Each applicant is evaluated individually on the basis of his or her total application, including academic record, rank in class, SAT I or ACT scores, essay, activities, references, and goals. The College strongly advises a personal interview. The recommendations of teachers and guidance counselors are also important. Special consideration is given to applicants from distant states and other countries, applicants with special skills, and applicants who are prepared to become actively involved in designing their own programs.

Elmira has early decision, early admission, and advanced placement programs.

Application and Information

For further information, applicants should contact:

Dean of Admissions
Elmira College
Elmira, New York 14901
Telephone: 800-935-6472 (toll-free)
E-mail: admissions@elmira.edu
World Wide Web: http://www.elmira.edu

The Mark Twain Study is one of the most famous literary landmarks in America.

ELMS COLLEGE

CHICOPEE, MASSACHUSETTS

The College

Elms College is a dynamic, Catholic, coeducational liberal arts institution in Chicopee, Massachusetts, educating reflective, principled, and creative learners. Elms College has a 12:1 student-faculty ratio; small classes, all taught by faculty members; a challenging curriculum; successful and dynamic graduates; a thriving, inclusive athletic program; a safe campus; and faculty and staff members who are responsive to individual student's needs. Elms College educates learners for life through an integrated liberal arts curriculum that promotes critical thinking, effective communication, an appreciation of the arts and humanities, an ability to utilize technology for the advancement of knowledge, an understanding of faith, and a willingness to respond to global concerns of justice and peace.

Elms College offers Bachelor of Arts (B.A.) and Bachelor of Science (B.S.) degrees in twenty-eight disciplines as well as master's degrees in education (M.Ed.), liberal arts (M.A.L.A.), and applied theology (M.A.A.T.) and Certificates of Advanced Graduate Studies (C.A.G.S.) in education and communication sciences and disorders.

There are a total of 539 full-time students on a beautiful, suburban, 23-acre campus. The College's nine buildings are situated around a spacious quadrangle. Residential students live in two dorms on the campus, both completely wired for high-speed Internet access. One dorm, Rose William Hall, was completely renovated in 2002. Also facing the quad is the College Center, which houses the cafeteria, a bookstore, a theater and media studio, an art gallery, and an academic resource center. Elms' modern Maguire Center for Health, Fitness, and Athletics contains a gym with a suspended indoor running track, a 25-meter swimming pool, the Blake Aerobic Center, a weight-training area, and a full Health and Wellness Center.

An active student activities office plans cultural and social programs that provide entertainment, create multicultural and global awareness, and bring students together on campus. Elms College has a vibrant and expanding athletics program that gives students a safe environment in which to risk, compete, and be challenged. Elms belongs to the North Atlantic Conference in Division III and has varsity teams in women's basketball, cross-country, equestrian, field hockey, lacrosse, soccer, softball, swimming, and volleyball and men's baseball, basketball, cross-country, golf, soccer, swimming, and volleyball. In the past five years, Elms College has won a conference championship in softball, back-to-back conference championships in women's cross-country, women's basketball, and men's soccer. In addition, a popular intramural program and an extensive fitness center offer students who are not varsity athletes a chance to be part of the athletic program and work on their fitness goals.

Elms College is a member of the Cooperating Colleges of Greater Springfield (CCGS), a group of eight private and public colleges in the area that, through the sharing of programs, talents, and facilities, bring to Elms students the educational resources of a large university. CCGS offers students enriching educational experiences through shared library privileges, cultural events and social activities, jointly sponsored courses, and faculty member exchange. Most importantly, the cooperative endeavor provides direct academic exchange so that full-time Elms College students may enroll in undergraduate courses offered by the other seven member colleges.

Location

The Elms College campus is located just 2 miles north of the city of Springfield in the scenic and historic Pioneer Valley. The College's proximity to the city makes available a wide array of off-campus activities. The Springfield Civic Center is the site of many major concerts, sporting events, and other activities. Other nearby attractions include the Six Flags New England, the Quadrangle Museum area, the Basketball Hall of Fame, City Stage, and Symphony Hall. The College's proximity to the mountains of Vermont, New Hampshire, and the Berkshire Hills ensures easy access to great skiing, hiking, and other outdoor recreation. Nearby Northampton and Amherst, a 20-minute drive away, are home to a thriving arts community, numerous concert venues, theaters and restaurants, and the active Five College Consortium, which is made up of the University of Massachusetts and Amherst, Smith, Hampshire, and Mount Holyoke Colleges. The nearby junction of the Massachusetts Turnpike (Interstate 90) and Interstate 91 provides easy access from all directions. Boston is 1½ hours away; New York City, 3 hours. Springfield is accessible by Amtrak or by air into Bradley International Airport in Hartford, a ½-hour drive from the College.

Majors and Degrees

Elms College awards bachelor's degrees in accounting, biology, chemistry, communication sciences and disorders, computer information technology, education, English, fine art, health-care management, history, international studies and business, legal studies, liberal arts, management, marketing, mathematics, modern languages, natural sciences, nursing, paralegal studies, professional studies, psychology, religious studies, social services/paralegal studies, social work, sociology, Spanish, and speech language pathology assistant studies.

Minor concentrations are offered in most majors as well as in coaching, criminal justice (sociology or legal studies), legal nurse consulting, media management, philosophy, and sports management.

Academic Programs

Elms College offers a student-centered and value-oriented curriculum that teaches students to communicate effectively and think critically and creatively. It makes students aware of global issues and gives them an understanding of science, art, history, and themselves.

A minimum of 120 credits is required for graduation. These credits are distributed among core requirements, major requirements, and general electives that may be used for a minor. The College offers students the opportunity to qualify for credit and/or advanced placement through testing programs and a unique experiential learning program that awards credit for nonclassroom learning.

Transformational Leadership is an honors program that is designed to challenge students intellectually and through hands-on application of learning. The program involves rigorous honors-level courses and developmental service learning in the local community.

Elms College has special programs in academic assistance,

dance (with the New England Dance Conservatory), ROTC (Army and Air Force), Japanese and German language and culture courses, and an exchange program with Kochi Women's University in Japan. The campus is also home to an Irish Cultural Center and a Polish Center of Discovery and Learning.

Off-Campus Programs

Elms College recognizes that learning comes from outside as well as inside the classroom. The College has a strong internship program that offers students in all majors a valuable opportunity for field work and career exposure. Elms College has a partnership program with the American Institute for Foreign Study (AIFS), which provides overseas study and travel. Through this affiliation, Elms students can study in France, Ireland, or Spain for a semester, a year, or a summer.

Academic Facilities

Berchmans Hall, the main classroom and administration building, dominates the Elms College campus. Housed in this magnificent Gothic structure are a large auditorium, a gym, and state-of-the-art language, science, and computer laboratories. The Alumnae Library provides an ideal atmosphere for study and research. Its holdings include 109,000 volumes, 750 periodicals, and thousands of audiovisual items, CD-ROMs, and reels of microfilm. Provision is made for computer terminals and personal computers as well as areas for listening to, viewing, and recording various types of media. In addition, the library is one of four Federal Depository Libraries in the area and has a collection of 47,000 government documents. Remote access allows students to access the library's research databases from any computer.

Costs

For the 2003–04 academic year, tuition was $17,830, room and board costs were $7100, and fees were $720.

Financial Aid

Paying for a college education is a major investment, but Elms College strives to bridge the gap between the cost of attendance and family contribution by offering aid such as need-based and non-need-based scholarships; low-interest, long-term loans from external sources, the Federal Work-Study Program, and part-time jobs. The bottom line is that the cost of an Elms College education is usually not more than that of a public college or university once the generous financial aid is applied. More than 91 percent of the students receive some financial assistance. There are several non-need-based scholarships, including the Presidential Scholarship, for the strongest applicants with superior academic records ($6000 to $10,000 a year); the Elms Scholarship, for students with outstanding academic records ($1000 to $6000 per year); the Transfer Scholarship, offered to the strongest transfer candidates and based on GPA ($1000 to $8000 per year); and the Phi Theta Kappa Scholarship, offered to transfer candidates who are members of Phi Theta Kappa ($6000 to $10,000 per year).

Elms College also offers discounts of up to 50 percent of tuition to students admitted directly from high school in Chicopee (based on GPA), diocesan scholarship discounts of up to 50 percent of tuition for students from the area's Catholic high schools (based on GPA), Catholic school grants of $1000 per year for students from Catholic high schools outside the local diocese, Deanery Awards of 50 percent of tuition for 20 students in the Diocese of Springfield (based on involvement in the life of their parishes), and sibling discounts of 25 percent of tuition for families with more than 1 full-time undergraduate at the College in any given year.

Faculty

Elms College has 46 full-time faculty members, of whom 80 percent hold doctoral or terminal degrees, and 64 part-time faculty members, of whom 23 percent hold doctoral or terminal degrees. Faculty members, many of whom also serve as academic advisers, teach all of the classes. They take a personal interest in guiding each student toward his or her academic and career goals.

Student Government

Students are involved in campus governance through the Faculty-Student Senate (FSS) and the Student Government Association (SGA). Major policy decisions related to student life are made by the FSS, which is composed of 6 students and 6 faculty members, and the SGA, which is composed of an executive board, a student council, and a financial committee. These forms of governance allow for significant student involvement in all matters related to student life.

Admission Requirements

Elms College seeks women and men who have distinguished themselves inside and outside the classroom. In keeping with the College's commitment to a personalized education, the admissions committee carefully reviews the credentials of each applicant, considering the depth and variety of the academic program pursued, GPA, recommendations from teachers and/or guidance counselors, scores on the SAT or ACT, participation in student activities, and part-time employment.

Application and Information

Elms College requires a completed application, two letters of recommendation, high school transcript, SAT scores, TOEFL scores from international students, and an application fee of $30. A personal interview is not required but is strongly recommended. Interested students are encouraged to visit the campus and discuss their academic and career aspirations with an admission counselor. Several open houses and overnight programs are offered during the academic year, and tours and interviews are available year-round.

For further information and application materials, students should contact:

Joseph Wagner
Director of Admission
Elms College
291 Springfield Street
Chicopee, Massachusetts 01013-2839
Telephone: 413-592-3189
800-255-ELMS (3567) (toll-free)
Fax: 413-594-2781
E-mail: admissions@elms.edu
World Wide Web: http://www.elms.edu

Students at Elms College.

ELON UNIVERSITY

ELON, NORTH CAROLINA

The University

Elon was founded in 1889 by the United Church of Christ and remains a church-related rather than a church-controlled institution. The beautiful 575-acre campus is graced by ancient oak trees, well-kept lawns, brick sidewalks, a fountain, and two lakes. Visitors to Elon's campus often remark on the friendliness of the people and the strong sense of community. Elon is accredited by the Southern Association of Colleges and Schools. At the graduate level, it offers master's degrees in business administration and education, as well as a Doctor of Physical Therapy (D.P.T.) program.

With a student body of 4,400, Elon offers the varied opportunities of a university as well as small classes and individual attention. The members of the diverse student body come to Elon from forty-eight states and forty-one countries. Seventy percent of Elon's students come from out of state, primarily the Eastern Seaboard. Student satisfaction is consistently high: 84 percent of students eligible to return to Elon do so. Freshmen and sophomores are required to live on campus. Students are housed in one of the thirty residence halls on campus. In addition, there are thirteen fraternity and sorority houses. Students with at least junior standing may choose to live in nearby apartments. All students may have cars on campus.

In addition to a challenging academic curriculum, Elon encourages students to participate in five programs known as the Elon Experiences: student undergraduate research, study abroad, internships, service learning, and leadership. Elon is ranked number one nationally among comparable institutions for the percentage of students who participate in study-abroad programs. Seventy-eight percent of Elon graduates complete internships, compared to approximately 33 percent nationally, and approximately two thirds of Elon students volunteer in the community. Students can record their participation on an Elon Experiences transcript, which is issued as a companion to the traditional academic transcript.

Elon's exceptional sports facilities include two gymnasiums; a baseball park; a new, on-campus football stadium and field house; six athletic fields; and an Athletic Center. The Athletic Center features the 2,400-seat Alumni Gym, an aerobic fitness center with a weight room, racquetball courts, an indoor pool, and a dance studio. The Jimmy Powell Tennis Center is a twelve-court state-of-the-art complex. A member of the Southern Conference, Elon competes in NCAA Division I (I-AA in football). Before becoming a member of the NCAA, Elon won two NAIA national football titles as well as national championships in golf and tennis. When affiliated with NAIA, Elon teams won eight straight conference excellence awards, emblematic of the league's top athletic program. Intercollegiate sports are baseball, basketball, cross-country, football, golf, soccer, and tennis for men and basketball, cross-country, golf, indoor track, outdoor track, soccer, softball, tennis, and volleyball for women. Campus Recreation administers an extensive intramural program with seven multipurpose recreational fields. Other components include aquatics, fitness, open recreation, outdoor programs, special events, wellness, and competitive club sports such as field hockey, lacrosse, rugby, and swimming.

The University has more than 140 organizations, which include nine national fraternities, ten national sororities, the weekly student newspaper, the yearbook, an FM radio station, a student-run cable channel, a dance organization, the Black Cultural Society, the Student Union Board, Catholic Campus Ministry, Intervarsity Christian Fellowship, Elon Hillel, Model UN, Habitat for Humanity, and Elon Volunteers. Ninety-seven percent of seniors report having been involved in at least one organization, and 70 percent were involved in more than one.

Through the Elon Career Center, students can enroll in 1-credit-hour courses such as Choosing a Major and Securing a Job. The center also sponsors a Transition Tactics mentoring program, job fairs, and on-campus interviews with employers and helps students arrange internships and cooperative education experiences. More than 92 percent of the students who work with the Career Center have jobs within six to nine months of their graduation.

Location

The campus is located in the town of Elon, adjacent to Burlington, in the Piedmont region of North Carolina. The University is surrounded by a residential neighborhood yet is accessible to the major universities and private colleges of Greensboro, Durham, Chapel Hill, and Raleigh. Beaches and mountains are only 3½ hours away by car. Major bus, train, and airline transportation is nearby. Interstate 85/40 is within 2½ miles of the campus.

Majors and Degrees

Elon confers the Bachelor of Arts (B.A.) degree in art, biology, chemistry, communications (broadcast, corporate, and film), computer information systems, computer science, dance, economics, education (elementary, middle, secondary, and special education/learning disabled), English, French, history, human services, international studies, journalism, mathematics, music, music performance, philosophy, physics, political science, psychology, public administration, religious studies, science education, social sciences education, sociology, Spanish, and theater arts. An independent major is also available. A Bachelor of Fine Arts (B.F.A.) is offered in music theater and theater arts. The Bachelor of Science (B.S.) degree is offered in accounting, athletic training, biology, business administration (finance, information systems, international business, management, and marketing), chemistry, chemistry/engineering, computer science, computer science/engineering, engineering mathematics, engineering physics, environmental studies, environmental studies/engineering, exercise/sport science, health education, leisure/sport management, mathematics, medical technology, music education, physical education, and physics.

Elon offers preprofessional advising programs in dentistry, engineering, law, medicine, optometry, physical therapy, theology, and veterinary science.

Minor fields of concentration are offered in all major areas and also in African/African-American studies, anthropology, Asian/Pacific studies, cinema, classical studies, criminal justice, geographic information systems, geography, Latin American studies, multimedia authoring, nonviolence studies, professional writing studies, and women's/gender studies.

Academic Program

Elon's dynamic academic program is grounded in the traditional liberal arts and sciences and distinguished by a philosophy of learning that integrates academic and experiential activities. The curriculum features a general studies core in a 4-hour course design. Innovative teaching methods encourage independent thinking and active learning, especially through the Elon Experiences, a program that promotes the values of independent learning through research, intercultural understanding, work experience, volunteer service, and leadership. Students complete 132 hours of credit for the bachelor's degree.

Academic scholarship programs, known as the Elon Fellows programs, feature specialized courses, study/travel grants, mentor relationships, and some paid internships and research assistantships, as well as additional scholarships for selected participants. Programs include Elon College (the College of Arts and Sciences) Fellows, Honors Fellows, Journalism/Communications Fellows, North Carolina Teaching Fellows, Jefferson Pilot Business Fellows, and the Freshman Leadership Fellows.

Elon operates on a 4-1-4 academic calendar consisting of two 4-month semesters of classwork divided by a one-month winter term during January. The winter term allows students to gain added experience through additional course work, internships, study abroad, special research, or cooperative education programs in industry.

Off-Campus Programs

Elon offers numerous opportunities for international study/travel: a semester or year in places such as Argentina, Australia, Chile, Costa Rica, Denmark, Ecuador, England, France, Ghana, Japan, Scotland, Spain, or Sweden for the same tuition, room, and board cost as at Elon; winter term study/tours to Australia and Europe and countries such as Belize, Costa Rica, England, Ghana, Greece, Italy, Mexico, and New Zealand; summer programs in England, Greece, Hungary, and India; and exchange programs with universities in Japan and Sweden. In addition, the Office of International Programs assists students in joining study-abroad programs offered by other universities. Each year, more than 60 percent of the graduates have participated in a study-abroad experience, compared to 2 percent of college students nationwide.

Academic Facilities

Known for its beautiful campus, Elon has some of the finest academic facilities in the region. The most recent additions include the new Academic Village, with classrooms and housing for honors and international students; the 74,000-square-foot McMichael Science Building; the new 75,000-square-foot Belk Library; and more than 150,000 square feet of activity space in the Koury Athletics Center and Moseley Campus Center. A communications facility opened in 2000 and houses two television studios, nonlinear digital audio/video editing equipment, and cameras to support a student-run cable channel that features programs of news, music videos, sports broadcasting, and social issues. Classroom facilities offer interactive multimedia and teleconferencing capabilities with computer and satellite links, Internet access, laser disc technology, and cable television.

The Belk Library contains 214,727 volumes and 8,248 serial subscriptions and has an online catalog. It has 400 CD-ROM products and subscribes to twelve online commercial services. Facilities include spaces for private or group study, 150 PCs, exhibit areas, and microfilm and microfiche readers. The LaRose Resources Center in Belk Library provides free tutorial assistance in most academic areas, computer-assisted instruction, videotaping, satellite and cable television facilities, and an extensive variety of audiovisual equipment and materials. Computer resources on campus include IBM labs, Macintosh labs, and an Apple lab. There are more than 600 microcomputers linked to a Novell network and to a Hewlett-Packard (HP) system. All residence halls are wired to the campus and Internet networks. Many academic buildings have wireless technology.

The Center for the Arts features many outstanding theatrical and musical presentations. Classrooms for art, music, drama, and dance programs are located here, as well as a 600-seat theater, a 125-seat recital hall, and a black box theater.

The beautiful 75,000-square-foot Moseley Campus Center includes a concert/banquet hall, campus shop, food court, radio station, space for all campus organizations, post office, TV room, and lounge areas.

Costs

Elon is one of the most reasonably priced private universities in North Carolina. The 2004–05 tuition is $17,310, room is $2936, board is $3074, and fees are $245, for a total cost of $23,565, including the winter term. Additional estimated average costs for books, transportation, and personal expenses are $2748.

Financial Aid

Approximately 60 percent of Elon students receive some form of financial assistance. The CSS Financial Aid PROFILE is used to determine eligibility for institutional need-based aid. The Free Application for Federal Student Aid is used to determine eligibility for federal aid programs. Elon participates in all federal and state grant and loan programs, including the Federal Pell Grant, Federal Supplemental Educational Opportunity Grant, Federal Perkins Loan, Federal Stafford Student Loan, Federal Work-Study Program, North Carolina Legislative Tuition Grant, and several outside loan and payment programs. Scholarships are available for athletic and fine arts achievement and through Army and Air Force ROTC. Free room and board are provided for recipients of a four-year ROTC scholarship. Presidential Scholarships of $2000 to $3500 are awarded to approximately the top one quarter of each freshman class. Selected candidates are nominated by the Admissions Office. Such scholarships are renewable for up to four years. For further information regarding any aid programs, students should contact the Office of Financial Planning.

Faculty

Elon has 235 full-time and 69 part-time faculty members. Eighty-four percent have earned the highest degree in their field. The primary emphasis is on teaching, although faculty members also participate in research. Faculty members are known for their mentoring relationship with students. A 15:1 student-faculty ratio and an average class size of 22 students promote this high level of faculty participation in student learning.

Student Government

All Elon students are members of the Student Government Association (SGA) and have a vote through their elected executive officers, class officers, and student senate members. The SGA has the full support and cooperation of the faculty and administration. Students are encouraged to participate in the governance of the University and have an active role on all faculty administrative committees.

Admission Requirements

Every student who applies to Elon University is evaluated individually. Campus interviews are not required. Secondary school courses required for admission include 4 units of English, 2 or more units of one foreign language, 3 or more units of math (algebra I and II and geometry required), 2 or more units of science (including at least one laboratory science); 2 or more units of social studies, including U.S. history, are recommended.

Application and Information

An application should be accompanied by a nonrefundable $35 fee, SAT I or ACT scores, an official secondary school transcript, and a completed counselor evaluation form. Transfer students should, in addition, submit a transcript from every college previously attended and a dean's evaluation form. The minimum GPA for transfer students is 2.5. Elon University has a deadline admissions policy. Application deadlines for freshmen are November 1 for early decision (binding), November 10 for early action (nonbinding) and January 10 for regular decision. All deadlines are postmark dates. Notification dates are December 1 for early decision, December 20 for early action, and March 15 for regular decision. Elon applicants may apply by paper application, by using the University's online application, or by using the Common Application. Separate application must be made to the Fellows programs, with a deadline of January 10.

Susan C. Klopman
Dean of Admissions and Financial Planning
2700 Campus Box
Elon, North Carolina 27244
Telephone: 800-334-8448 (toll-free)
E-mail: admissions@elon.edu
World Wide Web: http://www.elon.edu

New facilities on the quad at Elon University.

EMBRY-RIDDLE AERONAUTICAL UNIVERSITY

PRESCOTT, ARIZONA

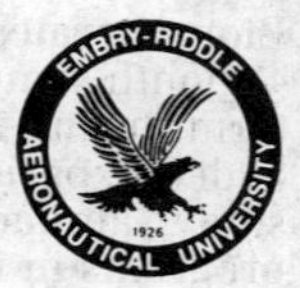

The University

Students at Embry-Riddle Aeronautical University–Arizona (Embry-Riddle/AZ) receive a comprehensive, technical, and applied education geared toward designing the next generation of aviation and aerospace vehicles and the systems that support them. Embry-Riddle's reputation is based upon its leadership role in aviation education as well as its commitment to a strong academic preparation and learning environment. Embry-Riddle is a private, independent four-year university and is accredited by the Commission on Colleges of the Southern Association of Colleges and Schools.

The campus team takes pride in providing Embry-Riddle/AZ students with a unique combination of features not readily found on other campuses. A sense of belonging exists, with the total focus on undergraduate education. Students share a love of aviation and a special motivation to succeed and become experts in their field. There is a close-knit residential atmosphere; nearly 850 students live in fourteen on-campus residence halls, which offer both suites and apartments. Housing priority is given to freshmen and sophomores. Most students take advantage of on-campus dining facilities and a variety of meal-plan options. The coed (17 percent female) student population of 1,700 undergraduates comes from fifty states and territories and thirty-two other countries. Seven percent of the students are international.

The students' pride in their campus experience is reflected in the enthusiasm and diversity of activities available. There are more than fifty student clubs and organizations, five professional associations, three fraternities and two sororities, three sports clubs, and thirty-five intramural sports. The NAIA men's soccer and wrestling teams, the NAIA women's soccer and volleyball teams, and the intercollegiate flight team compete with regional and national universities. The student precision flight team has consistently ranked among the top in the country in the SAFECON competitions, sponsored by the National Intercollegiate Flying Association (NIFA).

The extended Embry-Riddle family consists of more than 20,000 students and 38,000 alumni. The Embry-Riddle Daytona Beach, Florida, campus, with 4,500 undergraduate and 300 graduate students, offers additional resources. At Extended Campus Centers around the U.S. and the world, 9,000 undergraduate and 5,000 graduate students find Embry-Riddle's programs geared toward the needs of adult and part-time learners. Guided by its worldwide network of alumni, Embry-Riddle's reputation has grown steadily throughout the aviation, aerospace, and business communities. Embry-Riddle's placement rate for residential campus students one year after graduation is 91 percent. Since its inception in 1926, the flight-related school has added engineering and related majors, as well as six master's degree programs, to become the world-renowned university it is today.

Location

Just like its people, the University's location is warm and friendly. Prescott, a mile-high city on the Colorado Plateau, a beautiful geologic region, is home to the world's largest stand of ponderosa pine trees. The campus is about 100 miles northwest of Phoenix, 260 miles southeast of Las Vegas, and 375 miles east of Los Angeles. Prescott's climate reflects seasonable weather, with daytime averages of 80 degrees in the summer and 45 degrees in the winter. The local mountains exhibit the spirit of the rugged West, with students enjoying snow skiing, hiking, and tours of the Grand Canyon.

Known as a vacation getaway, Prescott offers shopping, entertainment, health, and recreational options and a friendly small-town atmosphere. For a flavor of city lights, Phoenix is a 2-hour drive away. The campus is situated on 557 acres, but campus life is centered within a 1-mile walking radius. Most of the eighty-four individual buildings are interconnected by walkways and indoor and outdoor lounging areas, making it easy to bump into friends and faculty members. The campus Flight Training Center is located nearby at the Prescott Municipal Airport.

Majors and Degrees

The B.S. in aeronautical science (professional pilot program) emphasizes multiengine training and prepares students for a career as an airline, military, or corporate pilot. The first two years include courses leading to FAA certification as an instrument-rated commercial pilot. The last two years stress professional-level courses in aircraft systems and flight methodology. Training in the late-model fleet is combined with the use of simulators, including two Level A Boeing 727 motion simulators. The program is accredited by the Council on Aviation Accreditation (CAA).

Aerospace engineering centers on the design of aircraft and spacecraft; electrical engineering focuses on circuits, communication and control systems, and electronic/avionics materials and devices. Embry-Riddle is consistently rated as one of the country's best engineering schools by *U.S. News & World Report*'s "America's Best Colleges." In the B.S. in computer science program, studies consist of graphics, simulation, computer architecture, database management, operating systems, software engineering, artificial intelligence, and applications to the aviation industry. The B.S. programs in aerospace engineering, electrical engineering, and computer engineering are approved by the Accreditation Board for Engineering and Technology (ABET).

The B.S. in science, technology, and globalization (STG) is an interdisciplinary program for the global work environment. The program is based primarily on humanities and social sciences in conjunction with the hard sciences and technology. STG students specialize in one of two significant areas for the aviation and aerospace industries: global aviation ecology and global management.

The B.S. in applied meteorology, new in 2004, provides a practical understanding of the physics and dynamics of the atmosphere and prepares the graduate for a range of meterologist positions in government or industry. Students use state-of-the-art Weather Center and computer-equipped classrooms to understand and forecast complex atmospheric phenomena ranging from severe thunderstorms and tornadoes, cyclones, fronts, and jet streams to the global climate and how it is changing.

The B.S. degree in aviation business administration prepares the student for managerial and business-related positions within the constantly evolving aviation and aerospace industries.

The B.S. in space physics, new to Embry-Riddle in 2003, consists of four areas of concentration: astrophysics, particle physics and cosmology, advanced propulsion systems, and remote sensing.

The B.S. in aerospace studies is an interdisciplinary program that draws upon a strong core of general education and advanced-level courses in a variety of areas to enhance communication, critical thinking, and technical skills; students also choose three minor areas of study.

Academic Program

The undergraduate academic preparation provides a strong foundation for all students, whether or not they choose a career in aviation. Each major is a combination of general education, specialized aviation focus, and applied technology. The general education component consists of courses in communication skills, social sciences/humanities, mathematics, computer science, and physical science.

Along with their major, students may opt to select a minor from the following fields: Asian studies, aviation safety, aviation weather, computer applications, computer science, environmental studies, humanities, mathematics, psychology, security studies, and technology, policy, and management. Army and Air Force Reserve Officer Training Corps (ROTC) courses are also available to all Embry-Riddle students and may lead to a position as a commissioned officer. Entering high school students with selected ROTC scholarships receive additional subsidies from Embry-Riddle.

Through participation in internships and cooperative education (co-op) arrangements, students in all fields of study gain valuable work experience with companies such as Continental Airlines, Delta Air Lines, Federal Aviation Administration (FAA), Honeywell, Gulfstream Aerospace Corporation, Lockheed Martin, NASA, Northwest Airlines, the Naval Air Systems Command, and Raytheon.

The academic year is divided into two semesters of fifteen weeks each. The average course load is 12–18 semester hours of credit. Two summer terms of approximately seven weeks each allow for additional enrollment. Many support programs exist to encourage students' development. The Student Success Center offers the college success course, orientation programs, academic advisement and counseling, and tutoring and supplemental instruction. In the Career Placement and Co-Op Services Office, students find assistance through job fairs, resume preparation and referral, the job bank and interviews, and the careers library.

Academic Facilities

Tucked into the rolling hillsides, the campus blends nature with the layout of the eighty-four buildings. Landmarks include the King Science and Technology Center; Davis Learning Center, with its auditorium and classrooms; the Bookstore; and the Visitor Center. Students and faculty members stroll down the many pathways and past outdoor lounging areas. The center of campus focuses on student life and services such as the library, cafeteria, the radio station and student government offices, student activities and financial aid offices, and the post office. The recreational and athletic facilities on campus include two gymnasiums, an athletic field, a weight room, an aerobic room, tennis courts, racquetball courts, a pool, sand volleyball courts, and several running trails.

Most of the classrooms, laboratories, and faculty offices are situated between the middle of campus and the hillside residence halls. These buildings house specialized labs, including the Airway Science Lab, Robertson Aviation Safety Center, Physics Lab, Engineering Graphics Lab, Aerospace Engineering Wind Tunnel, Aerospace Engineering Structures, and Aerospace Engineering Materials Lab.

Halfway up the sloping hillside stands the 22,000-square-foot King Engineering and Technology Center, which opened in 1995. The center's computer science classroom, the Computer-Aided Engineering Lab, and the UNIX Lab provide students with the latest in computer technologies. This center also houses the Linear Lab, Senior Design Lab, Electronics Power Lab, Honeywell Control and System Integration Lab, and Communications Lab. Here, too, the distance learning classroom connects Embry-Riddle/AZ students to faculty members and students at other Embry-Riddle sites as well as to worldwide teleconferencing facilities. The campus computer network links all student rooms, an e-mail system, library resources, engineering research labs, and distance learning facilities. The Embry-Riddle libraries are known for their outstanding aviation collections, which can be utilized by either visiting the facility or accessing the World Wide Web.

The University is currently building its new Academic Complex I, planned to house 46,000 square feet of classrooms, conference rooms, and offices.

Two miles from campus, the Embry-Riddle Flight Training Center occupies several buildings at the Prescott Municipal Airport. Embry-Riddle owns and maintains about fifty aircraft at Prescott. Currently, the Prescott fleet includes 2 Cessna 150s (flight team), 30 Cessna 172s, 4 Aerobatic Beechcraft Bonanza E33Cs, 2 Cessna 340s, and 8 Piper Seminole PA-44s. Cockpit procedural trainers include 3 PA-44 CPTs and 2 C-172 CPTs. Flight training devices include 1 Frasca PA-44 (FTD) with 220-degree visual, 2 Frasca C-172 FTD with 220-degree visual display, 3 Frasca 141 single-engine trainers, 1 Frasca 142 multi-engine trainer, 2 AST-300 multi-engine trainers, and 1 Boeing 727 full-motion simulator.

Costs

The 2003–04 academic year tuition for all programs is $10,350 per semester. Flight fees are charged in addition to tuition. On-campus housing accommodations range from $1570 to $1790 per semester, depending upon the accommodations; meal-plan options are an approximate $386 to $1284 per semester in addition to these charges. Students also need to include costs for books, transportation, and personal expenses. Since the tuition is similar for all students, in many instances these costs are lower than out-of-state tuition for state universities and are in the lower tier of costs for all national private universities.

Financial Aid

Students and their families find many sources of aid available to assist with paying the costs of a private university; more than 81 percent of students receive financial assistance. Embry-Riddle participates in all national and state assistance programs. The completion of the Department of Education's Free Application for Federal Student Aid (FAFSA) forms assures students consideration for these funds. In addition, Embry-Riddle/AZ provides assistance in the form of on-campus jobs, academic scholarships, veterans' educational benefits, and ROTC incentives.

Faculty

Easy access to faculty members is another strength of Embry-Riddle/AZ. Faculty members, not graduate students, teach classes. The average class size is 23, with an overall student-faculty ratio of 17:1. Faculty members keep regular office hours and consider it their most important role to enhance the individual learning of each student. As academic advisers, faculty members help in course selection and career guidance. Faculty members bring both teaching and industry backgrounds to the classroom; most have extensive practical experience in their field along with outstanding academic credentials. The faculty participates with members of Advisory Boards, consisting of experts from their field, to continually update the curriculum and technology.

Student Government

The Student Government Association (SGA) has an extremely important role. It provides many student activities, including service and community organizations, Activities Planning Board, *Horizons* newspaper, and representation and funding for clubs and committees. Also, the SGA is the key communication link to the University administration, and the council president serves as a member of the University Board of Trustees.

Admission Requirements

Each student receives individual consideration for admission based upon a variety of factors and circumstances. Completion of the Embry-Riddle/AZ Application for Admission begins this process; official transcripts and score reports for either the SAT I or ACT should also be submitted. Notification takes place throughout the year.

Application and Information

A virtual tour of Embry-Riddle/AZ is available on the World Wide Web (see address below). For additional information, including information on campus visits, and application forms, students may contact:

Embry-Riddle Admissions
3700 Willow Creek Road
Prescott, Arizona 86301
Telephone: 928-777-6600
800-888-ERAU (toll-free)
E-mail: dbadmit@erau.edu
World Wide Web: http://www.embryriddle.edu

EMBRY-RIDDLE AERONAUTICAL UNIVERSITY

DAYTONA BEACH, FLORIDA

EMBRY-RIDDLE AERONAUTICAL UNIVERSITY

The University

The purpose of Embry-Riddle Aeronautical University is to provide a comprehensive education of such excellence that graduates are responsible citizens and well prepared for productive careers in aviation and aerospace.

In addition to its traditional residential campuses in Daytona Beach, Florida, and Prescott, Arizona, Embry-Riddle serves the continuing education needs of the aviation industry through an extensive network of off-campus centers in the United States and Europe and through its division of continuing education's training seminars and management development programs. The total University enrollment (full-time and part-time) is more than 24,000. Approximately 4,500 undergraduate students are currently enrolled at the Daytona Beach residential campus, and more than 6,000 students are enrolled in graduate programs University-wide. Students come from all fifty states and more than 100 countries, which makes Embry-Riddle truly an international university.

Graduate programs leading to the degrees of Master of Science in Aerospace Engineering, Master of Business Administration in Aviation, Master of Aeronautical Science, Master of Aerospace Engineering, Master of Human Factors and Systems, Master of Software Engineering, and Master of Space Science are available at the Daytona Beach campus as well as at many college of continuing education locations.

Embry-Riddle provides cocurricular activities that appeal to almost every taste. Students take advantage of the many opportunities for personal growth and development through social and preprofessional fraternities and sororities and cultural and recreational activities. Embry-Riddle's award-winning Precision Flight Demonstration teams offer students the opportunity to compete nationally in air and ground events. Embry-Riddle also has the largest all-volunteer Air Force ROTC and Navy ROTC detachment in the country and one of the fastest-growing Army ROTC detachments. Embry-Riddle athletes participate in intercollegiate and intramural competitions in many sports, including baseball, basketball, crew, cross-country, golf, soccer, tennis, and volleyball.

Location

The year-round clear flying weather and the resort communities surrounding Embry-Riddle's residential campus in Daytona Beach, Florida, offer students an excellent environment in which to study, fly, and enjoy recreational activities. The campus, located adjacent to the Daytona Beach International Airport, contains more than twenty main buildings set on 211 acres and is only 3 miles from what is called the world's most famous beach. The high-technology industries located in Daytona Beach and in nearby Orlando provide the University with an outstanding support base. In addition, the Kennedy Space Center is less than a 2-hour drive away.

Majors and Degrees

The Daytona Beach campus of Embry-Riddle awards undergraduate degrees at the baccalaureate and master's levels. Bachelor of Science degrees are offered in variety of areas, each with a focus on the aviation and aerospace industries. In engineering, students can pursue a Bachelor of Science degree in aerospace engineering, civil engineering, and engineering physics. If business is the students' area of interest, they may elect aviation management, business administration, or management of technical operations. Degrees are offered in computer engineering and computer science. For those inclined toward technological pursuits, degrees are offered in aerospace electronics, aircraft engineering technology, aviation maintenance management, and avionics engineering technology. The College of Aviation awards degrees in aeronautical science (professional piloting), applied meteorology, safety science, and air traffic management. Other aerospace and aviation industry–related majors include aerospace studies, communications, and human factors psychology. Students entering Embry-Riddle with an undecided major have the opportunity to explore a variety of academic pursuits before making a commitment to a specific track.

The Extended Campus is specifically attuned to the educational needs and challenges of the adult, part-time student. Embry-Riddle's degree programs can be pursued at more than 120 locations throughout the United States and Europe. The department of independent studies offers Embry-Riddle undergraduate degree courses especially designed to serve the needs of the student who cannot attend regularly scheduled classes. These courses are used to fulfill the requirements of the A.S. and B.S. degrees in professional aeronautics and the Bachelor of Science in business administration. Embry-Riddle's center for professional programs offers a series of seminars, conferences, and hands-on training for the aviation professional.

Academic Program

Even a field as specialized as aviation requires a broad background. General education courses required of all students who are pursuing a baccalaureate program include communication skills, such as English composition, literature, and technical report writing; humanities; social sciences; mathematics; physical science; economics; and computer science. To ensure academic success, Embry-Riddle provides free tutorial services.

The calendar year is divided into two semesters of fifteen weeks each, with the summer session divided into two terms. The average course load for each fall or spring semester is 15 credit hours.

Academic Facilities

The College of Aviation building at the Daytona Beach campus provides an unsurpassed environment for aviation education and research. The multimillion-dollar simulation laboratories duplicate the components and functions within the national airspace system, including capabilities to replicate actual weather reporting, airports, airways, air traffic control, flow control, and pilot and aircraft performance as found in the national air transportation system. The simulator building, which is located in the greater College of Aviation complex, contains highly sophisticated aircraft simulators that provide realistic simulation training in aircraft used in flight training as well as the major airlines. Flight instruction is provided in the Embry-Riddle fleet of sixty-six aircraft and thirteen flight training devices.

The Jack R. Hunt Memorial Library is a 49,000-square-foot facility with a seating capacity of 800. The library houses more than 223,000 volumes and book titles and more than 311,000 items of microfiche, periodicals, documents, newspapers, and media programs. Among the library's resources is a historical aviation collection that includes materials dating from 1909 to the present. The library uses the Endeavor Integrated Library System and provides rapid interlibrary loan service and wireless access points as well as computer terminals for research.

The Advanced Flight Simulation Center gives Embry-Riddle students the opportunity to train in world-class simulators. The center, with more than 20,000 square feet of space and four high bays, currently houses an FAA Level "D" simulator of a Beech 1900D airliner. This simulator offers full-motion training and exactly duplicates the actual cockpit. It can duplicate adverse weather conditions, a full range of emergency situations, and virtually any flight pattern. In addition, several FRASCA 141 and 142 flight training devices (FTD) and a Canadair Regional Jet (CRJ) Level 6 FTD complement flight training done in actual aircraft. The center also offers briefing rooms, a conference room, classrooms, a self-learning laboratory, offices, an instructor bay, a reception area, a lounge, maintenance facilities, and space for computers and hydraulic systems for the simulators, of which all support flight training at the Sim Center.

The Samuel Goldman Aviation Maintenance Technology Center houses facilities to support instruction in maintenance and repair. Avionics maintains an FAA-certified repair station, which affords avionics students the opportunity to learn the theory and practice of the trouble analysis and repair of airworthy aircraft and equipment. The advanced reciprocating engine lab (FAA Certified Repair Station 708-55) overhauls engines for the Embry-Riddle fleet. Engine test cells allow students to check the effectiveness of their repairs.

The Lehman Engineering and Technology Center houses subsonic and supersonic wind tunnels and a smoke tunnel; structures, materials, and aircraft design and composite materials laboratories; and a computer-aided design/computer-aided manufacturing system. Embry-Riddle is also the country's first university to use its own rapid prototyping stereolithography for design instruction. Additional facilities to support instruction include the Lindbergh Center, which provides modern classroom facilities and chemistry and physics laboratories; the academic computing center, which provides hands-on experience with both mainframe and personal computers; and the Center for Aerospace Research, which supports both undergraduate and graduate research and other creative activities.

The 5,300-square-foot interfaith chapel accommodates the variety of faiths represented by the student body of Embry-Riddle. It consists of a 140-seat nondenominational worship area, four prayer rooms (Catholic, Jewish, Muslim, and Protestant), and administrative spaces for Campus Ministry's 2 chaplains and student assistants.

The 18,500-square-foot Capt. Willie E. Miller Instructional Center, a lecture auditorium and classroom complex, provides space for large audience events, including presentations by distinguished lecturers and speakers. A discussion/demonstration room is also equipped to facilitate distance teaching/learning and to enhance hands-on demonstrations.

The 66,000-square-foot ICI Center contains two full-size NCAA basketball courts, a fitness center, and a weight room. The ICI Center allows the University to consolidate its recreation/intramural activities and provide a place to host events and assemblies.

Costs

The 2003–04 tuition and fees are $10,645 per semester. Flight fees are charged in addition to tuition. On-campus room and board costs are approximately $3000 per semester. Personal expenses are in addition to the above. (Costs are subject to change.)

Financial Aid

Applicants for financial aid are required to complete the Department of Education's Free Application for Federal Student Aid (FAFSA) and any other documents requested by the University. Students are encouraged to apply early if they wish to be considered for all types of programs. Florida residents may also apply for several additional programs available through the state.

Faculty

The faculty members provide an excellent balance of professional experience and academic achievement. There is also a healthy balance between maturity and youth among the faculty. Faculty members who teach in the specialized and major programs have had professional experience in their areas of instruction. The student-faculty ratio is 18:1, and the primary concern of each faculty member is personalized teaching in classrooms and laboratories, on the flight line, and in student advising.

Student Government

The University places great emphasis upon student self-government. The Student Government Association has 2 voting members on the Board of Trustees and also supports publication of the weekly newspaper.

Admission Requirements

Admission is open to any qualified applicant, regardless of creed, sex, race, national origin, handicap, or geographical location. Admission decisions are based on high school work, college courses attempted, and SAT I or ACT scores. Embry-Riddle encourages every student to visit the campus and have a personal interview prior to making the decision to attend the University.

A student who is transferring from a community college or from a four-year institution and who has completed at least 12 semester hours immediately prior to applying at Embry-Riddle is considered a transfer applicant.

Application and Information

Embry-Riddle requires each applicant to submit an application form and fee, SAT I or ACT scores, and an official high school/college transcript. Flight students must provide an FAA Class I or Class II medical certificate. When a student is accepted for admission, tuition and housing deposits are required by May 1. For further information, interested students should contact:

Director of Admissions
Embry-Riddle Aeronautical University
P.O. Box 11767
Daytona Beach, Florida 32120-1767

Telephone: 386-226-6100
800-862-2416 (toll-free nationwide)
E-mail: dbadmit@erau.edu
World Wide Web: http://www.embryriddle.edu

Embry-Riddle Aeronautical University's Daytona Beach, Florida, campus.

EMERSON COLLEGE

BOSTON, MASSACHUSETTS

The College

Founded in 1880, Emerson is one of the premier colleges in the United States for the study of communication and the arts. Students may choose from more than twenty undergraduate majors and twelve graduate programs supported by state-of-the-art facilities and a nationally renowned faculty. The campus is home to WERS 88.9 FM, the oldest noncommercial radio station in New England; the 1,200-seat Cutler Majestic Theatre; and *Ploughshares,* the award-winning literary journal for new writing.

A pioneer in the fields of communication and performing arts, Emerson was one of the first colleges in the nation to establish a program in children's theater, which was founded in 1919. In addition, an undergraduate program in broadcasting was established as early as 1937. Professional-level training in speech pathology and audiology was inaugurated in 1935, educational FM radio in 1949, closed-circuit television in 1955, and a B.F.A. degree program in film originated as early as 1972. In 1980, the College created the country's first graduate program in professional writing and publishing.

Today, Emerson's 2,800 undergraduate and 900 graduate students come from more than sixty countries and forty-five states and territories. Approximately 1,200 students live on campus; some students live in special learning communities, such as the Writer's Block and Digital Culture Floor. The campus also has a 10,000-square-foot fitness center, the Health and Wellness Center, the Student Union, a 100-seat cabaret/multipurpose room, and Cultural Center. In addition, students are supported by several College offices, such as the Learning Assistance Center, the Office of AHANA Student Affairs, the Center for Spiritual Life, the Office of Off-Campus Services, the International Student Affairs Office, the Counseling Center, the Office of Residence Life, and the Career Services Office.

Emerson College is fully accredited by the New England Association of Schools and Colleges.

In addition to its undergraduate programs, Emerson College offers more than a dozen master's degree programs for its graduate students.

Location

Boston is arguably one of the country's best-known college towns, containing a wealth of diversions that range from scenic harbor cruises, Boston Pops concerts, and neighborhood festivals to baseball at Fenway Park and the legendary Boston Marathon. Emerson's campus is located on Boston Common in the heart of the city's theater district—within sight of the Massachusetts State House and walking distance from the historic Freedom Trail, Boston Public Garden, Chinatown, the financial district, and numerous restaurants and museums. Boston is also an international city with more than thirty foreign consulates, a busy international airport, and several multinational corporations.

Majors and Degrees

Emerson confers Bachelor of Arts, Bachelor of Fine Arts, and Bachelor of Science degrees. Students can major in acting, audio/radio, broadcast journalism, communication sciences and disorders, communication studies, film, marketing communication: advertising and public relations, media studies, musical theater, new media, political communication, print and multimedia journalism, production/stage management, television/video, theater design/technology, theater education, theater studies, and writing, literature and publishing. Interdisciplinary and self-designed majors, as well as an honors program, are available through the College's Institute for Liberal Arts and Interdisciplinary Studies.

Academic Programs

Emerson's academic calendar consists of two fifteen-week semesters, plus two six-week sessions during the summer months. The requirements for graduation combine general education and liberal arts courses with advanced, specialized classes that are specific to individual departments and majors. Internships for academic credit are available in almost every major and the Institute for Liberal Arts and Interdisciplinary Studies offers exciting first-year seminars, independent study options, and innovative courses that cut across academic disciplines.

Off-Campus Programs

Emerson College offers a unique study abroad program in Kasteel Well, the Netherlands. Housed in a brilliantly restored thirteenth-century castle, students have a convenient home base for excursions and study tours to the legendary centers of European culture and history, such as Paris, Amsterdam, London, and Florence.

The College also sponsors an exclusive study and internship program in Los Angeles and a summer film program in Prague. In addition, students can cross-register for courses at neighboring institutions through the Boston ProArts Consortium, whose members include the Berklee College of Music, the Boston Conservatory, the Boston Architectural Center, Emerson, the School of the Museum of Fine Arts, and Massachusetts College of Art.

Academic Facilities

Emerson possesses the highest quality visual and media arts equipment, including digital editing labs, Avid composers, publishing software, animation and optical printing, recording studios, a photography lab, and DVD-authoring suites. There are two radio stations, seven on-campus facilities and programs to observe speech and hearing therapy, and an integrated digital newsroom for aspiring journalists. Newest of all is the eleven-story Tufte Performance and Production Center, which houses expanded performance and rehearsal space, a theater design/technology center, makeup lab, and television studios with editing and control rooms.

The Emerson College Library houses more than 175,000 volumes, 13,000 serial subscriptions, 8,000 microforms, 9,000 audio/visual materials, and 7,000 e-books. An additional 2,400 films and videotapes are available in the College's Media Services Center. The library's Web pages are designed to serve as a gateway for research and can be accessed from the library's workstations, computers located throughout the campus, and dormitory rooms or off-campus apartments, using a student account. Emerson students can also access the resources of a dozen cooperating libraries through the College's membership in the Fenway Library Consortium.

Costs

The basic expenses related to attending Emerson College for the 2003–04 academic year were as follows: tuition, $22,144; room and board, $9828; fees, (including activity and orientation fees) $519; books and supplies, $680; and estimated transportation and personal expenses, $1500.

Financial Aid

Each year, more than 65 percent of Emerson students receives some form of financial assistanc, packaged in awards that typically combine grant and scholarship, loan, and college work-study. Academic scholarships ranging from $8000 to half-tuition are awarded on a limited basis to students who meet high academic standards. Special performance-based scholarships, averaging $4000, are available to exceptional students in the performing arts.

In order to apply for financial assistance, students must complete the FAFSA form, CSS PROFILE, and the Emerson College Application for Financial Assistance. Deadlines are March 1 for September admission or November 15 for January admission. More information about financial assistance at Emerson can be found online at http://www.emerson.edu/financial_services or by contacting the Office of Student Financial Services (telephone: 617-824-8655; e-mail: finaid@emerson.edu).

Faculty

With an average class size of 24, students at Emerson develop close relationships with a remarkably talented and active faculty. Faculty members are nationally recognized and award-winning authors, directors, producers, consultants, playwrights, and editors. The vast majority of the faculty members have earned doctorates or the highest degree obtainable in their field. The student-teacher ratio is 15:1.

Student Government

There are more than sixty student organizations and performance groups, thirteen NCAA intercollegiate teams, student publications, and honor societies at Emerson. The Student Government Association, in cooperation with the Office of Student Affairs staff, plans and executes student activities, allocates and supervises funding for clubs, and serves as a liaison between the student body and the College administration.

Admission Requirements

Emerson welcomes applications from students whose interests and abilities are congruent with a major in communication and the arts and who are well prepared to meet the challenges of a strong liberal arts curriculum. Admission is competitive. Each year, more than 4,000 applications are received for a class of 650. Selection is based upon academic promise as indicated by secondary school performance, academic recommendations, writing competency, and SAT I or ACT scores (or TOEFL if English is not the first language), as well as personal qualities as seen in extracurricular activities, community involvement, and demonstrated leadership.

The academic preparation for successful candidates should include four years of English and three years each of mathematics, science, social science, and a single foreign language. Candidates for programs offered by the Department of Performing Arts are required to submit a resume of theater-related activities and either audition or interview or submit a portfolio or essay. It is recommended that applicants for the film program submit a sample of creative work (a short video, script, or creative writing) and for the broadcast journalism, print and multimedia journalism, and writing, literature and publishing programs, a graded writing sample or SAT II Writing Test scores.

In addition to the application form and fee, students must submit an official secondary school transcript (or GED), official SAT I or ACT test results, application essay, and two letters of recommendation (one from a college adviser and one from a teacher of an academic subject, such as English, mathematics, social science, or science).

Application and Information

First-year candidates for early action admission should file their application by November 1, and notifications are mailed by December 15. The regular admission deadline for September admission is January 15, with notifications mailed by April 1, and November 1 for January admission, with notifications mailed by December 15.

Transfer students should submit their applications and supporting credentials by March 1 for September admission, or November 1 for January admission.

For further information, students may contact:

Office of Undergraduate Admission
Emerson College
120 Bolyston Street
Boston, Massachusetts 02116-4624
Telephone: 617-824-8600
Fax: 617-824-8906
E-mail: admission@emerson.edu
World Wide Web: http://www.emerson.edu

Emerson College: bringing innovation to communication and the arts.

EMMANUEL COLLEGE

BOSTON, MASSACHUSETTS

The College

Emmanuel College, founded in 1919 by the Sisters of Notre Dame de Namur, prepares men and women with the skills to succeed in tomorrow's world and the social conscience to make a difference in that world. An excellent liberal arts and sciences education, shaped by human values and a Catholic heritage, and a strong career development and internship program define the Emmanuel College experience.

At Emmanuel, students become engaged learners in small, interactive classes and develop leadership skills through participation in campus life. The city of Boston provides an extended classroom, opportunities for community service, and exciting internships with the city's most prestigious, leading-edge employers.

Enrollment in 2003–04 was more than 1,856 students, of whom 1,073 were undergraduates studying on the Boston campus. Emmanuel's diverse student population includes students from all over the United States and more than thirty-six other countries. Approximately 80 percent of the College's traditional undergraduate students reside in Emmanuel's residence halls on the campus, while the rest commute from the local area.

The Internship and Career Development Office offers a four-year career-development program for all Emmanuel students. Starting in their first year and continuing until graduation, students are exposed to career planning, assessment, and goal setting. Workshops on resume writing, job/internship search skills, the Internet job search, and interviewing skills are some of the services that are offered to students. The Internship and Career Development Office also maintains a Career Advisory Network of more than 300 committed alumni who are available to students for networking, career advice, and mentorship. Other services include job and internship postings, individual career counseling, and career planning programs and events.

Emmanuel College offers state-of-the-art computer classrooms and computer labs in a powerful campuswide communications network that provides students access to the Internet, voice mail, e-mail, and cable television. The classroom computers, both IBM and Macintosh, are used to teach basic computer skills as well as a wide variety of academic and industry software. Courses in calculus, communications, database design, digital imaging, graphic design, statistics, and Web design are taught in these classrooms. In the computer labs, students have access to powerful IBM and Macintosh computers and peripherals for their studies and outside interests. Other discipline-specific computer labs are equipped with appropriate hardware and software for students in the art, biology, chemistry, and education departments.

A wide variety of academic clubs, honor societies, media organizations, performance groups, leadership teams, and social and special interest organizations are available for student participation. Community service is a campus priority. Many students and staff members volunteer in neighborhood agencies and schools. Intercollegiate athletics include NCAA Division III sports for men and women. Women's athletics include basketball, cross-country, indoor track and field, outdoor track and field, soccer, softball, tennis, and volleyball. Men's athletics include basketball, cross-country, indoor track and field, outdoor track and field, soccer, and volleyball. In addition to athletics facilities supporting team sports, facilities for Emmanuel students include a fitness center, a dance studio, an aerobics room, and access to a swimming pool.

A leader in educating adults for nearly thirty years, Emmanuel College's Graduate and Professional Programs also offer accelerated courses leading to undergraduate and graduate degrees in education, human resources management, management, and nursing. These programs can be taken in flexible format at the Boston campus as well as satellite campuses throughout eastern Massachusetts.

Emmanuel College is fully accredited by the New England Association of Schools and Colleges.

Location

Emmanuel's 17-acre campus is located on the Fenway in the heart of Boston's cultural, medical, and educational communities. The College is within walking distance of the Museum of Fine Arts, the Gardner Museum, Fenway Park (home of the Boston Red Sox), Symphony Hall, and a variety of the world's most renowned medical institutions. Proximity to numerous colleges and universities as well as public transportation offers Emmanuel students additional academic, social, and cultural opportunities.

Majors and Degrees

Emmanuel College confers bachelor's degrees in American studies, art, biology, chemistry, educational studies, English, global studies, history, management, mathematics, political science, psychology, sociology, and Spanish. Students may also design individualized majors that reflect particular academic and career interests. The College confers a Bachelor of Fine Arts in graphic design and technology and painting/printmaking. Tracks within majors allow students with specialized interests to pursue concentrations in art therapy, biochemistry, communications, counseling and health psychology, developmental psychology, management–economics, management–global management, marketing–media and design, and medical technology. The education program provides provisional certification.

Academic Programs

The bachelor's degree requires completion of thirty-two courses, divided among general requirements, major requirements, and electives. Students may choose a minor within any department that offers a major and also in the following areas: information technology, music, philosophy, religious studies, speech, theater arts, and women's studies. Internships are an integral part of most majors and provide students with opportunities for career exploration and the acquisition of professional skills. The honors program provides highly qualified and motivated students with opportunities for additional intellectual exploration and challenge. Students with Advanced Placement scores of 3, 4, or 5 may receive credit and advanced placement.

Off-Campus Programs

Emmanuel College is a member of the Colleges of the Fenway collaboration, which allows Emmanuel students to take courses at five other institutions within close walking distance: Simmons College, Wheelock College, Massachusetts College of Pharmacy and Allied Health Sciences, Wentworth Institute of Technology, and Massachusetts College of Art. Students are encouraged to spend a semester or a year abroad in any approved program. In addition, the College participates in an exchange program with sister colleges in California and Japan and provides opportunities for internship and study semesters in Washington, D.C.

Academic Facilities

In addition to administrative and faculty offices, the administration building houses a chapel, an auditorium, a dance studio, lecture and conference rooms, a bookstore, art and music studios, computer classrooms (IBM and Macintosh platforms), and media classrooms.

The Cardinal Cushing Library, which holds 95,000 volumes, 400 journals, and 34 online databases to support student and faculty member research, also includes listening, viewing, and editing rooms; an art gallery; a language laboratory; and a state-of-the-art lecture hall, complete with satellite technology. The library participates with other local institutions in cooperative alliances to share resources and online catalogs and to exchange information. Library services include reference assistance, bibliographic instruction, interlibrary loan services, and electronic research.

The College's new state-of-the-art Student Center, which is scheduled to be completed in fall 2004, is designed to feature classrooms, laboratories, dining facilities, meeting and fitness spaces, and an NCAA-regulation gymnasium. Emmanuel is in the midst of developing joint academic programs in the sciences with Merck Research Laboratories, a division of Merck & Co. Merck is building its eleventh and largest research center on the Emmanuel campus. Upon completion in summer 2004, the facility should house more than 300 scientists and support staff.

Costs

Tuition for the 2004–05 academic year is $20,100. Room and board costs in the College residence halls are $9000 per year. There are additional fees of approximately $300 per year.

Financial Aid

Emmanuel College is committed to helping students pay for an Emmanuel College education by providing need-based grants, merit scholarships, low-interest student loans, and employment opportunities. Students' eligibility for need-based financial aid is determined through a careful analysis of information provided by students and their families regardless of race, color, religion, sex, age, national or ethnic origin, or the presence of any handicap. Entering students who seek financial assistance must complete the Free Application for Federal Student Aid (FAFSA) and the Emmanuel College Application for Financial Aid. The FAFSA may be obtained from a secondary school or the College or may be completed online at http://www.fafsa.ed.gov. The Emmanuel College Application for Financial Aid may be obtained from the College or can be printed from the College Web site listed below. The priority filing date for financial aid is April 1.

Students who complete the requirements for admission to Emmanuel College are considered for special scholarships that are awarded on the basis of academic achievement and specific eligibility requirements. These include the Presidential Scholarship (full tuition), the Dean's Scholarship (50 percent of tuition), the City of Boston Scholarship, and the Phi Theta Kappa Scholarship (for transfer students). Of special interest is the Sisters of Notre Dame Scholarship program, a $2500 scholarship awarded to students recommended, in writing, by a Sister of Notre Dame at the time of application. Also of special interest is the $2500 Friends of Emmanuel Scholarship, for which an alumnus or staff or faculty member from Emmanuel College recommends an incoming student. Students must submit the Friends of Emmanuel recommendation form with the written recommendation at the time of application.

Faculty

The College has 46 full-time faculty members, 85 percent of whom have a doctorate or other terminal degree. Faculty members hold degrees from prestigious national and international universities. The student-faculty ratio is 16:1. All classes are taught by faculty members, not teaching assistants.

Student Government

Emmanuel students have the opportunity to participate in decision-making processes that affect the College. The student governing body is the Student Government Association (SGA), which comprises student representatives from each class and an Executive Board. The SGA works closely with the College administration and presents the needs and opinions of the students to the College community.

Admission Requirements

An applicant's academic achievement, creativity, initiative, and involvement in the community are considered. No single standard measure for determining ability is used in accepting applicants to the College. The admissions committee reviews each applicant's high school curriculum and record, recommendations, and test results. It is recommended that applicants submit a strong academic program.

Candidates for admission as first-year students are required to take either the SAT I or ACT. A personal interview with a representative of the Admissions Office is suggested. Applicants are encouraged to visit the campus during their junior or senior year of high school so that they may visit classes and talk with students and faculty members.

Application and Information

To apply, a student must submit an application along with a $40 nonrefundable fee, an essay, SAT I or ACT scores, an official high school transcript, and two letters of recommendation. International students must submit the TOEFL score and Certification of Finances. The College operates on a rolling admissions policy; the applicant is notified of the admission decision as soon as the file is complete, after December 1. Emmanuel observes the College Board's Candidates Reply Date of May 1. The College also subscribes to the early decision plan. All admissions requirements should be completed before November 1 of the applicant's senior year to be considered for early decision.

Students who apply for transfer admissions must submit an application; an essay; a nonrefundable fee of $40; official secondary school and postsecondary school transcripts, including scores on the SAT I or ACT; and two letters of recommendation, at least one from a recent college professor. An interview with a transfer counselor is recommended.

For further information or an application, students should contact:

Sandra Robbins
Dean of Admissions
Emmanuel College
400 The Fenway
Boston, Massachusetts 02115
Telephone: 617-735-9715
Fax: 617-735-9801
E-mail: enroll@emmanuel.edu
World Wide Web: http://www.emmanuel.edu

Emmanuel students enjoy the campus setting of 17 secure acres in the heart of Boston's academic, medical, and cultural communities.

EMORY & HENRY COLLEGE

EMORY, VIRGINIA

E&H
FOUNDED 1836

The College

Founded in 1836, Emory & Henry College has enjoyed a solid reputation for inspiring students from all walks of life and guiding them toward personal success and lifelong achievement. Located on a pristine, historic campus in the highlands of Virginia, Emory & Henry enrolls approximately 1,000 students who represent a diverse group coming from rural areas, urban centers, more than twenty states, and many countries. The College provides a wide array of academic programs, including prelaw, premedicine, visual and performing arts, international studies, business, education, environmental studies, and public policy and community service, to name just a few. With a global perspective and an emphasis on service, excellence, and action, Emory & Henry encourages students to envision the world in which they would like to live and then challenges them to create it. The College is named for 2 men who symbolize this Emory & Henry dual emphasis on thought and action—Bishop John Emory, an eminent Methodist church leader at the time the College was founded, and Patrick Henry, a famous orator of the American revolution and Virginia's first governor. Emory & Henry graduates have found tremendous personal success, which they have used to improve the world around them. Through its comprehensive, four-year liberal arts education, Emory & Henry has produced leading scientific researchers, NASA engineers, well-known writers, and successful physicians, ministers, lawyers, educators and business people. Emory & Henry provides innovative programs in public policy and community service as well as international studies and environmental science.

Students have opportunities for involvement in a variety of campus activities: Christian fellowship, fraternities, sororities, sports clubs, honor groups, multicultural groups, and service clubs. Student staffs produce a yearbook, an online magazine, and a literary magazine; others operate an educational FM radio station. Musically talented students have opportunities to participate in a choral program and a pep band. The prestigious Concert Choir has toured throughout the United States and in parts of Europe. The Barter Theatre, a professional theater in nearby Abingdon, works with Emory & Henry College to provide a theater education program that integrates college-level drama study with the benefits of experience on a professional stage. The Appalachian Center for Community Service is available for students committed to community service. The King Health and Physical Education Center, which was recently expanded to include a new fitness center, enhances the College athletics program. Varsity sports for men are baseball, basketball, cross-country, football, golf, soccer, and tennis; women compete in basketball, cross-country, swimming, tennis, and volleyball. Several sports are played on a club basis.

Location

Emory & Henry is located in Emory, Virginia, which is approximately 25 miles north of Bristol, a city that offers large shopping areas, movies, and restaurants. The area surrounding Emory is known for its scenic beauty, recreational opportunities, and talented craftsmen. Within an hour's drive are slopes for snow skiing, lakes for waterskiing, the Appalachian Trail for hiking, and locations for horseback riding, canoeing, and many other sports. The historic town of Abingdon, Virginia, which lies just 7 miles south of Emory, is the home of the renowned Barter Theatre, the oldest professional theater in the United States. Abingdon's downtown district includes shopping areas, movie theaters, restaurants, and museums. The city also hosts the annual Virginia Highlands Festival, bringing together musicians, artists, and craftsmen for exhibitions and competition.

Majors and Degrees

Emory & Henry College offers programs of study in Appalachian studies, art, athletic training, biology, chemistry, computer science, economics and business, elementary and secondary education, English, environmental studies, French, geography, history, international studies, land-use analysis and planning, mass communications, mathematics, music, philosophy, physical education, physics, political science, psychology, public policy and community service, religion, sociology, Spanish, and theater. In addition, the College offers a cooperative program in engineering in conjunction with Tulane and North Carolina State. A cooperative program in forestry is available through an agreement with Duke University.

The Bachelor of Arts degree is awarded in all programs of study and the Bachelor of Science degree in selected areas. Individualized programs of study may be developed in consultation with a faculty adviser. Preprofessional preparation in dentistry, law, medicine, ministerial studies, pharmacy, and veterinary medicine may be completed within several of the programs.

Academic Program

Emory & Henry offers a liberal arts program with emphasis on writing, reasoning, value inquiry, and knowledge of global concerns, as well as a broad introduction to liberal arts subjects. All students complete a core curriculum, which includes a yearlong, interdisciplinary Western Tradition course and a writing course for all first-year students. Sophomores complete an ambitious Great Books program, and upperclass students take courses related to value inquiry and global studies. Along with the core curriculum, each student completes a major and a minor or a combined program referred to as an area of concentration. Students also have the opportunity to choose elective courses and to participate in international exchange programs.

Emory & Henry operates on a semester calendar from late August to mid-December and from mid-January to mid-May. A summer session runs from late May to early July. First-year students typically carry a four-course load of 13 to 14 credit hours per semester, including the yearlong course on Western tradition. Upperclass students carrying a full load complete five courses (15–17 credit hours) each semester. Thirty-eight courses are required for graduation. Classes meet on Monday-Wednesday-Friday or Tuesday-Thursday schedules.

One important feature of the Emory & Henry curriculum is its orientation toward helping students make a smooth transition from high school to college. A Center for Academic Support and Career Services aids students in developing strong study skills. The Writing Center helps students in every department to use writing for effective communication. Introductory courses in the modern foreign languages are taught by the Dartmouth Intensive Model, emphasizing concentrated study and drills that develop conversational skills in two semesters of work.

Off-Campus Programs

Many faculty members encourage students to get involved in community projects or research that benefit the region. Internship opportunities are available for students in most of the College's programs, providing academic credit for off-campus work in community agencies and businesses. Many students have completed internships in the surrounding communities, while others have opted for internships outside the region, including several in Washington, D.C., in positions related to congress or the federal government.

The College offers certain travel/study-abroad options regularly and can arrange other opportunities for interested students. Each year, a faculty member leads a monthlong study program in Rome, Italy, that provides 2 course credits in Roman art and archaeology. The College has exchange agreements with colleges and universities in Asia, Europe, and Central and South America. In addition, the Department of Modern Languages cooperates with the Vanderbilt-in-France program, which gives students the opportunity to live and study in France for varying periods of time. Students who desire other types of travel/study are assisted by faculty and staff members in locating suitable programs.

Academic Facilities

McGlothlin-Street Hall is a 70,000-square-foot academic center that houses the Departments of Biology, Business, Chemistry, Education, Environmental Studies, Geography, International Studies, and Psychology; a 104-seat auditorium; and a tiered sixty-seat auditorium. Classrooms and laboratories in McGlothlin-Street Hall are equipped with the most current technological equipment, including Internet access and interactive TV. Kelly Library currently holds more than 250,000 volumes and maintains subscriptions to 1,063 periodicals; the library features a computer center with PCs and terminals available for student use. Residence halls are wired for Internet access. Miller-Fulton Hall contains computerized classrooms used for instruction in such fields as accounting and computer science. Another computerized classroom in Byars Hall is used for instruction in writing, desktop publishing, and related fields. Science departments located in Miller-Fulton and McGlothlin-Street Halls feature a variety of equipment, such as a microcomputer-based laboratory for physics students, computerized chromatography for chemistry students, a DNA sequencer in the Biology Department, and biofeedback equipment. Art students have access to studios, an exhibition area, and printing equipment, and music students make use of practice rooms and a recital hall.

Costs

For 2003–04, the comprehensive fee for a resident student was $21,950 (includes tuition, room, and board). For a commuter student, the charge for tuition and fees was $15,800. There is a technology fee of $200 for resident students and $100 for commuter students.

Financial Aid

Forms of aid include need-based and non-need-based scholarships, loans, and part-time jobs. A Bonner Scholars program provides substantial scholarships for selected students who do volunteer work in the surrounding region. Virginia residents are eligible for a special grant based on residence. Merit scholarships are awarded based on academic performance, and many can be renewed based on continued academic success. Seventy-three percent of fall 2002 undergraduates received financial aid. The average aided first-year student received an aid package worth $13,114, meeting 83 percent of need. The priority application deadline for financial aid is April 1 and the deadline is August 1.

Faculty

Emory & Henry has 64 full-time faculty members, and the current faculty-student ratio is 1:14. Eighty-eight percent of the faculty members hold terminal degrees. Every student is provided with a faculty adviser who assists in the selection of courses. While the faculty members are encouraged to continue study and research, their primary function is teaching. Many professors live near the campus, and they make their homes open to students for special events, informal class meetings, or other activities.

Student Government

Students at Emory & Henry are encouraged to take part in campus decision making. They have voting representatives on nearly every faculty committee and on the Board of Trustees. The central body in campus government is the Student Senate, which brings together representatives of the student body, faculty, and administration.

Admission Requirements

Admission to Emory & Henry is determined on the basis of both academic achievement and personal qualifications. An applicant's secondary school preparation must include the following: 4 years of English, 3 years of mathematics (at least through algebra II), 2 years of laboratory sciences, 2 years of a single foreign language, and 2 years of history and social studies. It is strongly recommended that 1 year of study in the fine arts be included.

Application and Information

To apply for admission, students should submit the basic application form, an essay, a copy of the high school transcript, scores from either the SAT I or the ACT, and a nonrefundable $30 application fee. Transfer applicants must submit a transcript from any college previously attended. A rolling admission policy allows notification of the admission decision within two weeks after a file has been completed.

Students who have thoroughly researched their college options and have determined that Emory & Henry College is their first choice are encouraged to consider applying under the early decision plan. Although these students may file regular applications with other colleges, it is understood that they are applying for early decision only at Emory & Henry College and intend to enroll if admitted.

To be considered for early decision, a student should submit the completed Application for Admission, including the early decision agreement; the secondary school transcript; and a report of either SAT I or ACT test scores by December 1. The College agrees to notify candidates of their admission by December 20. The $200 enrollment deposit deadline for early decision is January 20. Under early decision, students are either admitted or deferred to regular admission.

Application forms and other information may be obtained by contacting:

Office of Admissions and Financial Aid
Emory & Henry College
P.O. Box 10
Emory, Virginia 24327-0947
Telephone: 276-944-6133
800-848-5493 (toll-free)
Fax: 276-944-6935
E-mail: ehadmiss@ehc.edu
World Wide Web: http://www.ehc.edu

Wiley Hall.

EMORY UNIVERSITY
Emory College
ATLANTA, GEORGIA

The University

Founded by the Methodist Church in 1836 as a college at Oxford, Georgia, Emory University received its university charter in 1915 and in the same year moved to the present campus in northeast Atlanta. The original campus is now Oxford College of Emory University, a two-year liberal arts division. The main campus occupies 631 acres. The original structures are of Italian Renaissance design and have red-tiled roofs and marble facades. In recent years, Emory has engaged in an extensive building and renovation campaign. The University is currently building nine new facilities ($250 million), including a performing arts center, physics facility, and residence hall complex.

Emory offers a stimulating intellectual environment in one of America's most exciting cities. The undergraduate college provides the advantages of a small college and the resources of a major university. Selective and innovative, with an emphasis on excellent teaching, Emory offers a rewarding environment for the student with serious intellectual and professional interests. Of the more than 11,000 men and women enrolled at Emory University, 5,500 are undergraduates. Geographic distribution of students is diverse; approximately 60 percent are residents of states outside the Southeast. Sixty-five percent of the students go on to graduate or professional school, and academic competition is keen. At the same time, the campus is a friendly one where students and faculty members may interact in a casual atmosphere. A majority of the students lives on campus in residence halls, fraternity houses, or sorority lodges. Extracurricular activities are plentiful and include lectures, concerts, movies, musical groups, theater, journalism, debate, volunteer groups, intramural sports, club sport teams, and intercollegiate athletics. There are more than 200 student organizations that encourage widespread involvement.

Emory athletes compete in ten varsity sports for men and women in the Division III University Athletic Association. Varsity sports include baseball (men's), basketball (men's and women's), cross-country (men's and women's), golf (men's), soccer (men's and women's), softball (women's), swimming and diving (men's and women's), tennis (men's and women's), track and field (men's and women's), and volleyball (women's). Seventy percent of the students participate in intramural, club, and recreational sports.

Emory ResNet provides Ethernet connections in each residence hall room, giving students access to the Internet via the campus computer network. Cable television is also available in each room. All first- and second-year students are required to live on campus. Housing is guaranteed for four years. Approximately 65 percent of undergraduates live on campus.

Other than Emory and Oxford colleges, major University divisions include the Graduate School of Arts and Sciences; the Schools of Business, Law, Medicine, Nursing, Public Health, and Theology; and the Division of Allied Health Professions.

Location

Emory University's wooded campus is in the rolling hills of Atlanta in an attractive residential section called Druid Hills. Adjacent to the campus is Emory Village, a small, neighborhood complex of shops and restaurants. Downtown Atlanta, easily accessible by rapid transit from Emory, provides an exciting, progressive atmosphere in which students can enjoy many recreational and cultural activities. In addition, Atlanta is just a few hours from the mountains of north Georgia and the Carolinas and from the beaches of Georgia and Florida.

Majors and Degrees

Emory College, the undergraduate arts and sciences school of Emory University, offers the B.A. degree in forty-four areas of study and the B.S. degree in nine areas. B.A. programs are offered in African-American studies, anthropology, art history, Asian and Asian-American studies, biology, chemistry, classical civilization, classical studies, classics, comparative literature, computer science, creative writing, dance and movement studies, economics, educational studies, English, environmental studies, film studies, French studies, German studies, Greek, history, interdisciplinary studies in culture and society, international studies, Italian studies, journalism, Judaic studies, Latin, Latin American and Caribbean studies, mathematics, medieval and Renaissance studies, Middle Eastern studies, music, philosophy, physics, political science, psychology, religion, Russian area studies, Russian language and culture, sociology, Spanish, theater studies, and women's studies. The B.S. degree is offered in anthropology and human biology, applied physics, biology, chemistry, computer science, environmental studies, mathematics, neuroscience and behavioral biology, nursing, and physics. Joint concentrations are available in anthropology and religion, art history and history, classical civilizations and religion, classics and English, classics and history, classics and philosophy, economics and history, economics and mathematics, English and history, history and religion, Judaic studies and religion, linguistics and Russian language, mathematics and computer science, philosophy and religion, and religion and sociology. Four-year combined bachelor's-master's degree programs are offered in chemistry, computer science, English, history, mathematics, mathematics/computer science, philosophy, political science, and sociology. Emory offers minors in African studies, applied mathematics, Arabic, Chinese studies, Hebrew, Japanese, Japanese studies, linguistics, Mediterranean archaeology, Persian, studio art, and violence studies. Emory offers undergraduate degrees in business and nursing through its Goizueta School of Business and Nell Hodgson Woodruff School of Nursing.

Combined degree programs in engineering are offered in cooperation with the Georgia Institute of Technology.

Academic Program

The Bachelor of Arts and Bachelor of Science degree programs combine general education in six broadly defined areas with advanced study in a subject of special interest to the individual student. The six areas of general education are (1) seminars and writing, including instruction in English composition and seminars representing a wide range of fields and topics designed to engage students in various aspects of inquiry and research; (2) natural and mathematical science (three courses); (3) social sciences (two courses); (4) humanities (two courses); (5) historical, cultural, and international perspectives, including courses covering Western and non-Western cultures, history, and a year of foreign language study; and (6) health and physical education (4 semester hours). To fulfill these area requirements, a student may choose from a wide variety of courses. In addition to the area requirements, a student must complete a concentration in at least one major field. To graduate, a student must complete satisfactorily a total of 132 semester hours.

The academic calendar is divided into two semesters from September to May, and there is a limited third semester during the summer. Several special programs are available, including honors programs, independent study, internships, combined-degree programs, and the opportunity to take courses in the graduate divisions of the University.

Off-Campus Programs

Emory participates in cross-registration with twenty colleges and universities in the Atlanta area. A semester in Washington, D.C., is available for economics and political science students. Internship programs are available for most majors. Study abroad is encouraged and can be taken in a wide variety of programs for a semester or a year.

Academic Facilities

Emory's five libraries hold 2.7 million volumes plus access to thousands of electronic information resources. Woodruff Library, the central library, which supports the social sciences and humanities, provides an integrated service environment, joining technology and media specialists with librarians. The facility includes an information commons, electronic classrooms, group-study rooms, and data-wired seating and is open 24 hours a day Sunday through Friday. Emory's $40-million Math and Science Center is the new home for the departments of physics, mathematics and computer science, and environmental studies. From the pristine physics laboraties in the basement to a rooftop environmental classroom and observatory, the building gives faculty members and students unprecedented opportunities for learning, teaching, and research. Among the Whitehead Biomedical Research Building's eight floors of office and state-of-the-art laboratory space are the departments of cell biology, human genetics, and physiology; two new entities, the Neurodegenerative Disease Center and the Center for Medical Genomics; and major research efforts in pulmonary and critical-care medicine, pathology and laboratory medicine, and digestive diseases. The 90,000-square-foot Donna and Marvin Schwartz Center for Performing Arts provides a central space for Emory's music, theater, and dance programs. The facility includes a world-class concert hall, a theater lab for the development of new works, and a dance studio. Equipped with an orchestra pit and choral balcony, the 825-seat Cherry Logan Emerson Concert Hall is the home stage for Emory ensembles, while the 135-seat theater lab is the home for the Emory Playwriting Center. The dance studio houses Emory's progressive and highly respected dance program.

Costs

For the 2003–04 academic year, tuition was about $27,600, and room and board were approximately $9620.

Financial Aid

Emory makes every effort to help students who need financial aid. Grants, loans, employment, and deferred payment plans are available. The amount of each grant is determined by financial need, and financial aid decisions are made independently of admission decisions. Merit scholarships (not based on need) are also available. In addition, Emory offers non-need institutional loans. The state of Georgia provides Tuition Equalization Grants to legal residents of Georgia who enroll at Emory; approximately 50 percent of the students in the College receive aid. More than 2,000 students have part-time employment at the University, including federally funded work-study. To be considered for financial aid, high school seniors should submit the CSS Profile and the Free Application for Federal Student Aid (FAFSA) by February 15.

Faculty

Emory College has more than 700 faculty members and a student-faculty ratio of 7:1. Senior faculty members teach courses at all levels, including first-year courses. Every student is assigned a faculty adviser for assistance in course selection and academic counseling. Faculty members are encouraged to work closely with students, as well as conduct research.

Student Government

Emory has always assumed that its students are responsible individuals. Students are involved at various levels of government in the University. Governing organizations with student representation include the Student Government Association (for the entire University), the College Council (primarily undergraduate), and the University Senate (predominantly faculty). Students also serve on all standing committees of the Emory College faculty. Students have a strong voice in residence life governments, social activities, and publications.

Admission Requirements

Admission to Emory is very selective. The Admission Committee evaluates applicants on the basis of secondary school records, SAT I or ACT scores, and recommendations from teachers and counselors. The College requires 4 years of high school English, 2 years of algebra and 1 of geometry, and at least 2 years of a foreign language. It strongly recommends that the remaining units include 2 or more years of history or social science, 3 years of laboratory science, and an additional year of mathematics. Students who wish to enter college before high school graduation are considered as early admission candidates. The middle 50 percent of freshmen entering in 2000 scored in the 640–720 range on the verbal portion of the SAT I and in the 660–740 range in the math section and completed high school programs with at least a B+ average. Average ACT scores ranged from 29 to 33. Emory seeks students who have not only academic ability but also talent and diversity. Students are encouraged to provide an overall view of themselves in their application, including extracurricular activities and interests and academic goals. The Admission Office encourages visits to the campus and arranges tours and focus sessions with staff members. Representatives from the Admission Office visit many high schools during the year to increase contact with students.

Application and Information

Applicants may apply as either early decision or regular decision candidates. Emory offers two rounds of early decision, both of which are binding. Early decision I postmarked deadline is November 1, and decisions are mailed by December 15. Early decision II postmarked deadline is January 1, and decisions are mailed by February 1. Regular decision applicants are encouraged to apply in the fall of the senior year of secondary school, but no later than the postmarked deadline of January 15. Applicants for regular decision are notified by April 1. Materials required for application include the completed application form, a $40 application fee, an official secondary school transcript, a letter of recommendation, and standardized test scores (SAT I or ACT). SAT II subject tests are recommended but not required. Test scores should be sent by the applicant's school or the testing center. Emory videos are available on a complimentary loan. Students may call 800-255-0384 (toll-free) or go to the Web site (http://www.videc.com) to order the video.

Daniel C. Walls
Dean of Admission
Boisfeuillet Jones Center
Emory University
Atlanta, Georgia 30322
Telephone: 404-727-6036
800-727-6036 (toll-free)
E-mail: admiss@learnlink.emory.edu
World Wide Web: http://www.emory.edu

Emory's Italian Renaissance campus is just 5 minutes north of downtown Atlanta.

EUGENE LANG COLLEGE, NEW SCHOOL UNIVERSITY

NEW YORK, NEW YORK

The College

Eugene Lang College is the distinctive liberal arts division of New School University, formerly known as the New School for Social Research. It is a major urban university with a tradition of innovative learning. The College offers all the benefits of a small and supportive college as well as the full range of opportunities found in a university setting.

Lang students are encouraged to participate in the creation and direction of their education. The desire to explore and the freedom to imagine shared by students and faculty members contribute to a distinctive academic community.

Eugene Lang College students currently come from forty-five states and thirteen countries. The ratio of men to women is approximately 2:3. About 45 percent of the College's 735 students come from outside the New York metropolitan area; 4 percent hold foreign citizenship and 23 percent are members of minority groups. The student body is composed of both residential and day students. The university operates residence halls within walking distance of classes; incoming freshmen and transfer students are given housing priority within these facilities, and housing is guaranteed for the first year for new students. Great diversity in interests and aspirations is found among the students. Through the Office of Student Services, students produce a student newspaper and an award-winning literary magazine. They organize and participate in dramatic, musical, and artistic events through the "Lang in the City Program," as well as numerous political, social, and cultural organizations at the university and throughout New York City.

The New School for Social Research was founded in 1919 by such notable scholars and intellectuals as John Dewey, Alvin Johnson, and Thorstein Veblen. It has long been a home for leading artists, educators, and public figures. For example, the university was the first institution of higher learning to offer college-level courses in such "new" fields as black culture and race, taught by W. E. B. DuBois, and psychoanalysis, taught by Freud's disciple Sandor Ferenczi. Among the world-famous artists and performers who have taught at the New School are Martha Graham, Aaron Copland, and Thomas Hart Benton. Today, such noted scholars as Robert Heilbroner, Eric Hobsbawm, Jerome Bruner, and Rayna Rapp are among the hundreds of university faculty members accessible to Lang College students.

The other divisions of the university include the Adult Division, which offers more than 2,000 credit and noncredit courses to students each semester; the Graduate Faculty of Political and Social Science (founded in 1933 as the University in Exile), which grants M.A. and Ph.D. degrees; the Robert J. Milano Graduate School of Management and Urban Policy, which awards the M.A. and M.S. degrees; Parsons School of Design, one of the oldest and most influential art schools in the country; and Mannes College of Music, a renowned classical conservatory. The total university enrollment in 2002–03 was approximately 7,500 degree-seeking students.

Location

The university is located in New York City's Greenwich Village, which historically has been a center for intellectual and artistic life. This slower-paced, more personal New York City neighborhood of town houses and tree-lined streets offers students a friendly and stimulating environment. Over and above the resources of Greenwich Village, New York City offers virtually unlimited cultural, artistic, recreational, and intellectual resources that make it one of the world's great cities.

Majors and Degrees

Eugene Lang College awards the Bachelor of Arts degree. Students are encouraged to design their own program of study, which includes an area of concentration, in consultation with their faculty adviser. Lang offers twelve areas of concentration: arts in context; cultural studies and media; dance; education studies; literature; philosophy; psychology; religious studies; science, technology, and society; social and historical inquiry; theater; urban studies; and writing. A student's concentration consists of eight to ten courses (32–40 credits) leading to relatively advanced and specialized knowledge of an area of study. In addition, students are encouraged to pursue an internship, where appropriate.

Students may also apply to a five-year B.A./B.F.A. program in conjunction with Parsons School of Design or in jazz studies at New School University, and advanced students may apply to the five-year B.A./M.A. programs offered in conjunction with the university's graduate divisions.

Academic Programs

When planning a program of study, Eugene Lang College students are encouraged to reflect on what their education means to them. Their program should parallel their own academic and personal development. By actively participating in the process of their education, students gain the knowledge to make informed choices about the direction of their studies with the help of their advisers and peers.

Small seminar classes serve as the focus of the academic program at the College. The maximum class size is 20 students. Classes are in-depth, interdisciplinary inquiries into topics or issues selected each semester by the College's outstanding faculty. Most importantly, the classes engage participants in the study of primary texts, rather than textbooks, and emphasize dialogue between teacher and student as a mode of learning. Here, not only is intellectual curiosity fostered by the small classes, but a genuine sense of community develops as well.

Although the College does not emphasize course requirements outside the area of concentration, freshmen are required to take one writing course and three other seminars of their choice in each of their first two semesters at the College. Upper-level students create their programs by selecting seminars from the College's curriculum, or they may combine offerings of the College with courses and workshops given by the New School's Adult Division, Graduate Faculty of Political and Social Science, Robert J. Milano Graduate School of Management and Urban Policy, and Parsons School of Design.

The College operates on a semester calendar; the first semester runs from September through mid-December and the second, from late January through mid-May. Students generally earn 16 credits per semester; a minimum of 120 credits is required for graduation.

Off-Campus Programs

Eugene Lang College recognizes the immense value of work undertaken beyond the classroom. The College arranges appropriate projects—internships with private and nonprofit organizations—which serve to strengthen the connection between theoretical work in the classroom and practical work on the job. Sophomores and juniors have the option of spending a year on a sponsored exchange with Sarah Lawrence College and the University of Amsterdam. Other exchanges, both American and abroad, are available.

Academic Facilities

Eugene Lang College is located on 11th Street between Fifth and Sixth Avenues in Greenwich Village. The university includes twelve academic buildings, including a student center, a Computer Instruction Center with more than seventy-five IBM personal computers and Macintosh systems, a 500-seat auditorium, art galleries, studios for the fine arts, classrooms, a writing center, and faculty offices. Lang College students have full and easy access to the Raymond Fogelman Library and the Adam and Sophie Gimbel Design Library. In addition, the university participates in the South Manhattan Library Consortium. Together, the libraries in the consortium house approximately 3 million volumes covering all the traditional liberal arts disciplines and the fine arts.

Costs

Tuition and fees for the 2003–04 academic year are $23,620. Room and board cost approximately $10,000, depending upon the specific meal plan and dormitory accommodations chosen. University fees are $100 per year.

Financial Aid

Students are encouraged to apply for aid by filing the Free Application for Federal Student Aid (FAFSA) and requesting that a copy of the need analysis report be sent to the New School (FAFSA code number 002780). Qualified College students are eligible for all federal and state financial aid programs in addition to university gift aid. University aid is awarded on the basis of need and merit and is part of a package consisting of both gift aid (grants and/or scholarships) and a self-help component (loans and Federal Work-Study awards). Aid is renewable each year as long as need continues and students maintain satisfactory academic standing at the College. Special attention is given to continuing students who have done exceptionally well.

Faculty

At Eugene Lang College, the faculty-student ratio is 1:10. Class size ranges from 10 to 20 students. Faculty members are graduates of outstanding colleges and universities and represent a wide variety of academic disciplines; 95 percent hold Ph.D.'s. College faculty members also serve as academic advisers, who are selected carefully in order to ensure the thoughtful supervision of students' programs and academic progress.

Well-known faculty members from other divisions of the university teach at the College on a regular basis. In addition, every semester, the College hosts distinguished scholars and writers as visiting faculty and guest lecturers who further enrich the academic program of the College and the university.

Student Government

There is a student union at the College, which is an organized vehicle for student expression and action as well as a means of funding student projects and events. Students are encouraged to express their views and concerns about academic policies and community life through regular student-faculty member meetings.

Admission Requirements

Eugene Lang College welcomes admission applications from students of diverse racial, ethnic, religious, and political backgrounds whose past performance and academic and personal promise make them likely to gain from and give much to the College community. The College seeks students who combine inquisitiveness and seriousness of purpose with the ability to engage in a distinctive, rigorous liberal arts program. Each applicant to the College is judged individually; the Admissions Committee, which renders all admission decisions, considers both academic qualifications and the personal, creative, and intellectual qualities of each applicant. A strong academic background, including a college-preparatory program, is recommended. An applicant's transcript; teacher and counselor recommendations; SAT I, ACT, or SAT II Subject Test scores; and personal essays are all taken into consideration. In addition, an interview, a tour of university facilities, and a visit to Lang College seminars are optional but highly recommended.

High school students for whom the College is their first choice are strongly encouraged to apply as early decision candidates and are notified early of an admission decision. Early entrance is an option for qualified high school juniors who wish to enter college prior to high school graduation. Candidates for early entrance must submit two teacher recommendations.

Students who have successfully completed one full year or more at another accredited institution may apply as transfer candidates. If accepted, transfer students may enter upper-level seminars and pursue advanced work. International students may apply for admission as freshmen or transfers by submitting a regular application to the College. If English is spoken as a second language, TOEFL scores are required. The New York Connection Program invites students from other colleges to Eugene Lang for a semester and incorporates an internship into their studies.

Students interested in applying for the combined B.A./B.F.A. degree program in fine arts or jazz studies are encouraged to apply for admission as freshmen to these special five-year programs. In addition to the admission requirements outlined above, a home exam and a portfolio are required for fine arts, and an audition is required for jazz studies.

Application and Information

Freshmen, transfers, and visiting students may apply for either the September (fall) or January (spring) semester. To apply for admission to the College, students must request an application packet and submit the required credentials and a $40 application fee by the appropriate deadline. (The application fee may be waived in accordance with the College Board's Fee Waiver Service.) For the semester beginning in January, the required credentials must be submitted by November 15, with notification by December 15. For the September semester, early decision candidates must submit the required credentials by November 15, with notification by December 15; for freshman candidates applying for general admission and freshmen early entrants, the deadline is February 1, with notification by April 1; for transfers and visiting students, the deadline is rolling to May 15, with notification rolling until July 1.

For further information, students should contact:

Terence Peavy
Director of Admissions
Eugene Lang College, New School University
65 West 11th Street, Third Floor
New York, New York 10011
Telephone: 212-229-5665
Fax: 212-229-5355
E-mail: lang@newschool.edu
World Wide Web: http://www.lang.edu

EUREKA COLLEGE

EUREKA, ILLINOIS

The College

Chartered in 1855, Eureka College was the first existing college in Illinois—and the third in the nation—to offer education on an equal basis to both men and women. In the years since its founding, Eureka has continued to be an innovative leader in coeducational liberal arts education. The College is fully accredited by the North Central Association of Schools and Colleges and is approved for teacher preparation by the Department of Public Faculty Instruction of the State of Illinois and the Illinois State Teacher Certification Board.

Eureka's campus is a wooded 112 acres at the southwest edge of Eureka, Illinois. In addition to the academic buildings, there are seven residence halls in which 91 percent of the students live; the Dickinson Commons food center; facilities for football, baseball, and tennis; the Cerf Center; and the Reagan Physical Education Center, which houses three basketball courts, a swimming pool, a weight room, and faculty offices. The College's stately Administration Building was built in 1858, and its Old Chapel was built in 1869. These two buildings are listed on the National Register of Historic Places.

Students come to the Eureka campus from a variety of areas: rural, urban, small town, and suburban. There is a rich mix of ethnic and racial backgrounds among the students, and a number of them come from other countries. A diverse student body on a small residential campus inevitably creates a community spirit that calls for cooperation, involvement, and interaction. This is a deliberate part of the Eureka program, providing opportunities for students to develop the potential for community leadership in their postcollege life.

Location

Eureka, in the heart of Illinois' fertile farmland, enjoys the best of two worlds. With tree-lined streets and a small population (4,500), the town is peaceful and secure. Yet, as a county seat with a large proportion of young residents, the town is every bit a part of the mainstream of American culture. The cities of Bloomington and Normal lie 20 minutes to the southeast, and the city of Peoria is 20 minutes to the west. Chicago is 140 miles to the northeast, and St. Louis, Missouri, is 190 miles to the southwest.

Majors and Degrees

Eureka College offers programs leading to the Bachelor of Arts and Bachelor of Science degrees. Major fields of study are accounting, art, arts and letters, biology, business administration, business information systems, chemistry, communication, computer science, elementary education, English, environmental sciences, history, mathematics, music, music education, philosophy and religion, physical education, physical science, political science and history, psychology, secondary education, social science, sociology, and theater arts and drama.

Academic Programs

The academic program at Eureka College seeks to maintain a balance between requirements that all students must meet and freedom for students to select those courses that best match and further their interests, skills, and life plan. The structure of the curriculum has been designed to reflect this balance.

The College believes that there are certain basic skills and a common core of knowledge that educated students must possess. Therefore, the College requires that each student acquire and display skills in composition, oral communication, and mathematics. The College also requires that each student devote a portion of time to the study of those disciplines in humanities, fine and performing arts, natural sciences, and social sciences. These distributional requirements insure that each student has the opportunity to explore the body of knowledge that is our common cultural heritage.

The College's academic program represents more than the accumulation of knowledge. Thus the College intends that students and faculty alike engage not only in the search for knowledge but also in the search for the higher goal of how to use that knowledge for the benefit of mankind.

The program at Eureka is rigorous both in its goals and in the efforts it demands, but the College believes that it is also exciting and satisfying.

Actual work experience—one of the most valuable educational tools of all—is normally available through internships and practicums in all fields. Independent study and pass/fail grading are available for qualified students in certain courses. The College also provides assistance to students, upon request, in determining vocational goals and finding employment after graduation.

Off-Campus Programs

A student may enroll for credit in travel-study projects sponsored by or acceptable to the College. Approval of registration for credit must be secured through the Dean of the College and the appropriate division chairman. Travel-study projects may be in this country or overseas, and must include readings, discussion, and a paper.

Academic Facilities

Most of the College's academic buildings are grouped together on the western half of the campus, including the Melick Library, completed in 1967; Vennum/Binkley Hall; Pritchard Performing Arts Center; and Burgess Hall, a classroom building that contains a newly developed "smart classroom." Located in the midst of the campus residence halls is a Learning Center available for students to receive assistance with class work or study skills or have a quiet place to study. Nestled in the wooded back-campus are the Rinker Amphitheater and the Lilac Arboretum.

Costs

The Eureka Idea has resulted in a 30 percent tuition reduction. For the 2003–04 academic year, tuition was $13,000, and room and board were $5880, for a total cost of $18,880 per year. *U.S. News and World Report* found Eureka College to be a best value among comprehensive colleges in the Midwest offering only bachelor's degrees.

Financial Aid

Eureka College administers an extensive financial aid program and encourages those who could not attend the College without financial assistance to apply for aid. Approximately 90 percent of Eureka's students receive some form of financial assistance, often as a package of scholarships, grants, awards, loans, and employment. Students can calculate their scholarship level by using Eureka's simple formula. If students wish to be considered for financial aid, they must submit the Free Application for Federal Student Aid (FAFSA) complete with the Eureka College school code of 001678. Federal and state aid make Eureka less expensive than the flagship state university.

Durward Sandifer Mentorships are available for entering freshman. If at the end of their sophomore year they have at least a 3.5 cumulative GPA and an established record of leadership and service at Eureka College, they will receive a mentorship anywhere in the world, paid for by the College.

Faculty

During the 2003–04 academic year, Eureka College's student-teacher ratio was 13:1. Sixty-three percent of the full-time faculty members of the College have a terminal degree in their field. The Eureka College faculty members are renowned for their excellence in teaching. However, they also recognize that the learning experience extends beyond the classroom. The faculty members play an active role in working toward the success of each student.

Student Government

Eureka College's Student Senate, which makes recommendations on administrative policy and oversees campus activities, comprises 8 senators-at-large and the presidents of the four classes. The senators elect the Chancellor from their own membership. Most campus events are directly sponsored by the Campus Activities Board, which is composed of students appointed by the senate. Student Residence Hall Councils, whose members are elected, control living regulations for individual dormitories.

Admission Requirements

Any person who feels that he or she has both the ability and desire to take advantage of Eureka College's small-campus, liberal arts education is encouraged to seek admission. Applications are welcome at any time after students have completed their junior year of high school. Admission is determined on the basis of prior performance in high school and on either the ACT or SAT I. Admission of applicants transferring from community colleges or other four-year colleges or universities is determined based on prior performance at the school from which they are transferring.

Application and Information

To obtain an application for admission, prospective students may visit the College Web site and either apply online or download the application. Students who wish to receive an application in the mail should write, call, or e-mail the address listed below.

The applicant must complete and return the application form and arrange for high school transcripts and ACT or SAT I scores to be forwarded directly to the College. Transfer students should have transcripts forwarded directly to the Admissions Office from each college or university attended. The applicant is notified of the decision as early as possible after all of the admission materials have been received. The application deadline for the fall is August 15.

Admissions Office
Eureka College
300 East College Avenue
Eureka, Illinois 61530
Telephone: 309-467-6530
888-4-EUREKA (toll-free)
E-mail: admissions@eureka.edu
World Wide Web: http://www.eureka.edu

THE EVERGREEN STATE COLLEGE

OLYMPIA, WASHINGTON

The College

"Unique," "innovative," and "challenging" are all words that have been used to describe the curriculum offered by the Evergreen State College, a public liberal arts and sciences college offering undergraduate and graduate studies. Established in 1971 to provide innovation in higher education, Evergreen is one of the smallest and newest four-year public institutions in the state of Washington. Since its beginning, Evergreen has designed and refined a format for higher education that has been recognized nationally and internationally as remarkable and exciting. Evergreen seeks qualified students who demonstrate a spirit of inquiry and a willingness to participate in their educational process within a collaborative framework. The College desires students who also express an interest in campus or community involvement, a respect and tolerance for individual differences, and a willingness to experiment with innovative modes of teaching and learning.

An education at Evergreen emphasizes interdisciplinary studies and collaborative learning. Instruction relies heavily on seminars—small discussion groups that involve students and faculty members in active participation. A state-supported college that offers the advantages of a small private liberal arts college, Evergreen is fully accredited by the Northwest Association of Schools and Colleges.

Graduate programs in public administration, environmental studies, and teaching are available.

Nearly 4,100 undergraduates from almost every state in the Union are enrolled at Evergreen; 43 percent are men, 57 percent are women, and 18 percent are members of minority groups. The average age of the student body is 25. About 1,000 students live on campus in apartment-style units. Accommodations include single and double studios as well as one- to six-bedroom apartments. Housing is within walking distance of classrooms and other campus facilities. Campus life is centered in academic programs, the residence halls, student clubs, and special-interest groups. On-campus activities include dances, plays, films, distinguished visiting speakers, concerts, and a variety of recreational activities. Notable among campus activities and services are those sponsored by the First Peoples Community, a network of minority student groups that offers peer support, guest speakers, and campus ethnic festivals.

Evergreen's women's and men's intercollegiate teams compete in the National Association of Intercollegiate Athletics (NAIA) in basketball, cross-country, and soccer. Intercollegiate volleyball is offered for women only. Numerous intramural sports are also available. The Campus Recreation Center is equipped with an eleven-lane swimming pool, a separate diving well, a sun deck, five racquetball/handball courts, a gymnasium, a wellness center, a challenge course, rock-climbing practice walls, two multipurpose rooms for dance and the martial arts, and exercise/weight-training rooms/classes with the latest in weight training equipment.

Location

The College is just outside Washington's capital city of Olympia in the midst of 1,000 acres of woods, with a 3,300-foot waterfront on Puget Sound. The campus is heavily forested with alder, maple, cedar, and Douglas firs and has trails for walking, jogging, and bicycling. The beachfront provides a delightful place for strolling, sunbathing, or marine research.

Olympia is a seaport community of about 81,760 located at the southernmost tip of Puget Sound. The Pacific Ocean is about an hour's drive to the west. The rain forests and mountains of the Olympic Peninsula lie to the north, and the Cascade mountain range is 2 hours east. Seattle, 60 miles north of the campus by freeway, offers all the cultural and recreational activities typically found in a large city, while Portland, Oregon, is a 2-hour drive south.

Majors and Degrees

Students are able to design undergraduate academic concentrations in anthropology, art, biology, chemistry, communications, community studies, computer science, creative writing, cultural studies, ecology, economics, energy studies, environmental studies, ethnic studies, film and video, history, humanities, journalism, languages (French, Japanese, Russian, Spanish), literature, management, marine studies, mathematics, Native American studies, performing arts, physics, prelaw, premedicine, psychology, public administration, social sciences, sociology, theater, and zoology.

Academic Program

Evergreen provides innovative academic programs that enable students to enroll each quarter in a single comprehensive program rather than in several separate courses. These coordinated programs bring a group of students and faculty members into extended contact, allowing them to work intensively in ways that encourage intellectual growth and friendship. The study of one topic at a time from a variety of perspectives provides students an excellent opportunity to combine the elements of an undergraduate education into a meaningful, cohesive whole.

The curriculum is founded on (1) collaborative, interdisciplinary teaching and learning; (2) small classes and close personal interaction of students and faculty members; (3) studies and group projects that encourage the understanding of theory as well as the development of practical applications; (4) narrative evaluations of the student's academic achievement; and (5) areas of concentration designed jointly by students and faculty members.

Studies at Evergreen are interdisciplinary. Students master one or more major fields of study by drawing knowledge from several different academic disciplines to develop an understanding of the relationships between the arts, the humanities, and the natural and social sciences. The academic program is based on the conviction that coordinated interdisciplinary study produces better conceptualizers, analysts, and problem-solvers and ultimately better citizens. A student's academic progress is assessed through narrative evaluations written by faculty members that describe in detail each student's academic activities, objectives, area of concentration, and degree of success in the attempted program. Narrative evaluations provide a comprehensive and insightful analysis of every student's work.

Each bachelor's degree requires the completion of 180 quarter credit hours. The academic calendar consists of three 10-week quarters and a summer session.

Off-Campus Programs

Evergreen offers an extensive internship program for advanced students. Placements are sponsored by faculty members and may be located anywhere in the world, although most are located in the Pacific Northwest. An international student exchange program exists with Miyazaki and Kobe Universities in Japan. Each year, Evergreen offers coordinated programs that enable students to spend a portion of the year overseas. Other study-abroad arrangements can also be made.

Academic Facilities

As one of the state's newest four-year colleges, Evergreen offers undergraduates some of the most modern academic facilities in the Pacific Northwest. The regional accreditation team that reviewed Evergreen described its scientific and artistic plant as "superior to that which can be found in any institution of which we have knowledge." Some of the resources available include a library containing 300,000 books, 15,000 reference volumes, 2,000 periodical subscriptions, and 4,000 items of media loan equipment. The science laboratory buildings house a lab supply store, a number of teaching and research laboratories, an advanced microscopy laboratory, and several instrument laboratories that feature spectrophotometers, chromatographs, ultracentrifuges, scintillation counters, and other equipment necessary for advanced work in the sciences. The computer applications lab is a facility designed to provide students in the laboratory science curriculum with language instruction, experiment and instrument interfacing, high-resolution color graphics, simulations, complex calculations, scientific software development, local networking, linear and digital electronics, and microprocessor applications.

The art facility includes ceramics, painting, and drawing studios; areas for weaving, batik, jewelry, drawing, and design; and a large high-ceilinged area for sculpture, casting, welding, glassblowing, lapidary work, spray painting, shop, and sheet-metal work. The communications laboratory building is a comprehensive instructional, performance, and production facility for audio and video communications, including dance, film, music, speech, theater, and two-dimensional design. This state-of-the-art facility also includes equipment for the performance of electronic music and for conventional filmmaking and previewing.

All Evergreen students have free access to computer facilities. The computer center's resources include microcomputer laboratories, clusters of microcomputers, 280 computer workstations, and minicomputers. Other on-campus computer facilities include NOVA minicomputers, micro-Plato workstations, plotters and graphic terminals, a hybrid analog/digital system, and additional scientific data acquisition devices. An extensive computer science teaching lab provides microcomputing resources and overhead display projection systems. The graphics imaging lab provides facilities for graphics and imaging projects.

Costs

Annual undergraduate tuition for the 2003–04 academic year was $3651 for Washington State residents and $13,329 for nonresidents. Evergreen is no longer a participant in the Western Undergraduate Exchange program. The estimated cost of books and supplies is $780. The cost of room and board is $5772, and personal living expenses are estimated at $2058.

Financial Aid

Evergreen's goal is to provide sufficient financial aid to make it possible for all qualified students to attend. Awards from Evergreen's aid programs, which are based on financial need, are designed to supplement the contribution of the student and his or her family. Once a student's level of financial need has been determined, his or her application is reviewed to evaluate eligibility for all programs. A financial aid package, which may combine a grant, scholarship, loan, and work opportunity, is then offered to meet the student's needs as closely as possible. Financial aid applications received by the processor by February 15 will have priority.

A variety of scholarships funded by the College's Foundation and private donors are available. Most of these scholarships are awarded on the basis of merit, high academic achievement, community service, and artistic or musical talent. For more information about these scholarships, students should write to the Office of the Associate Vice President of Enrollment Management or call 360-867-6310.

Faculty

Evergreen has a dedicated faculty committed to teaching. Seventy-three percent of faculty members hold the Ph.D. or other terminal degree; 49 percent are women, and 24 percent are members of minority groups. The favorable faculty-student ratio of 1:25 ensures close interaction between students and faculty members. Faculty members teach in one full-time program at a time, enabling them to have direct contact with a small group of students. Students work in small seminar groups from their freshman through their senior year and engage with academic content in unique ways. Faculty members strive to foster the environment of a learning community where common goals can include working across cultural and personal differences, engaging with difficult intellectual ideas through discussion, and making the abstract real and applicable to true-life situations. At Evergreen, students spend an average of 12–16 hours a week in the classroom, in direct contact with faculty members.

Student Government

Students at Evergreen have chosen to actively serve on a variety of campuswide committees and task forces rather than participate in a more traditional student government. With direct access to governance policies and resolutions, all Evergreen students are encouraged to become involved with campus issues. Students also directly administer the funds collected from the student services and activities fees, which are used to support a wide variety of student organizations.

Admission Requirements

First-year students are admitted on the basis of their high school GPA and test scores (SAT I or ACT). Essays and letters of recommendation are not required. First-year students are required to have completed the following college-preparatory program in high school: 4 years of English courses designed to develop college-level reading and writing proficiencies (composition, creative writing, and literature); 3 years of mathematics selected from algebra, geometry, trigonometry, advanced algebra, and higher-level courses; 3 years of social studies; 2 years of science, including 1 year of laboratory science (biology, chemistry, or physics); 2 years of the same foreign language; and 1 year in the visual/performing arts or in any of the aforementioned areas.

Students with at least 40 transferable credits are considered under transfer admission criteria. Transfer students are admitted on the basis of their cumulative college GPA, good standing at the last institution attended, and satisfactory completion of a variety of courses in the liberal arts and sciences.

Because Evergreen seeks to achieve a diverse student body, special consideration is given to applicants who are Vietnam-era veterans, adults 25 years of age and older, and students whose parents do not have a baccalaureate degree. In addition, special recognition is given to applicants who have 90 quarter credits of transferable work, an Associate in Arts degree from a Washington community college, or an Associate in Technical Arts degree from a Washington community college with which Evergreen has negotiated an "Upside Down" degree program.

Application and Information

Applications for fall entrance are accepted from September 1 to March 1; applicants are notified by April 1. Applications for winter entrance are accepted from April 1 to October 1; applicants are notified by November 1. Applications for spring entrance are accepted from June 1 to December 1; applicants are notified by January 1. Applications received after the deadline are considered on a space-available basis.

For more information about Evergreen, students should contact:

Office of Admissions
The Evergreen State College
Olympia, Washington 98505
Telephone: 360-867-6170
E-mail: admissions@evergreen.edu
World Wide Web: http://www.evergreen.edu

FAIRFIELD UNIVERSITY

FAIRFIELD, CONNECTICUT

The University

Founded in 1942, Fairfield University is a comprehensive Jesuit university. There are approximately 3,400 undergraduate full-time students attending Fairfield, with a total University enrollment of 5,200. The University has students from more than thirty-four states and thirty-seven countries. Students may choose from thirty-three undergraduate majors in four colleges and can later pursue graduate degrees in five schools. Fairfield is nationally recognized for providing a high-quality, personalized education rooted in the Catholic Jesuit tradition. Major academic divisions are the College of Arts and Sciences, the Charles F. Dolan School of Business, the School of Nursing, the School of Engineering, the Graduate School of Education and Allied Professions, and the School of Continuing Education.

Fairfield University also offers master's degree programs in American studies, business administration, finance, management of technology, mathematics, nursing, and software engineering.

Location

The University is located in Fairfield, Connecticut, a suburban community of 56,000, an hour from New York City and 5 minutes from Long Island Sound. The 200-acre campus, created from three private estates, retains a gracious, tranquil atmosphere with many wooded areas, lawns, gardens, pleasant walks, and broad views of Long Island Sound. Located in America's academic corridor, the short expanse from New York City to Boston that contains the world's largest concentration of colleges and universities, Fairfield provides access to hundreds of cultural, social, and intellectual programs on campus and at other institutions of higher learning.

Majors and Degrees

Fairfield's College of Arts and Sciences, the oldest and largest of Fairfield's six schools, offers the Bachelor of Arts degree with majors in American studies, communication, economics, English, history, international studies, modern languages and literatures (French, German, Spanish), philosophy, politics, psychology, religious studies, sociology/anthropology, and visual and performing arts (art history, music, studio art, theater). Students may also submit a curriculum proposal for a self-directed major allowing greater flexibility. The Bachelor of Science degree majors include biology, chemistry, computer science, economics, mathematics, physics, and psychology.

The Charles F. Dolan School of Business awards the Bachelor of Science degree in accounting, finance, information systems/operations management, international studies, management, and marketing. Internships are available to qualified students and are an integral part of the business program.

The School of Nursing is fully accredited by the National League for Nursing Accrediting Commission, the Connecticut State Board of Nurse Examiners, and the State of Connecticut Department of Higher Education. The four-year program leads to a Bachelor of Science degree with a major in nursing.

The School of Engineering offers undergraduate degrees in computer, electrical, mechanical, and software engineering. The undergraduate program can be completed in four years at Fairfield or in a 3-2 program where students complete three years at Fairfield University, followed by two years of engineering studies in one of Fairfield's partner institutions, Columbia University, Rensselaer Polytechnic Institute, the University of Connecticut, or the Stevens Institute of Technology.

Fairfield offers a preprofessional program in law. Students in the program are free to select any major of interest to them. The prelaw adviser assists students in course selection and preparation for law school.

The Health Professions Preparation Program (HP3) encompasses all Fairfield students, regardless of major, who are interested in a postgraduate health sciences profession requiring a graduate degree to practice. In addition to medicine, these include allied health fields, dentistry, health administration, optometry, osteopathy, podiatry, public health, and veterinary medicine.

Students may select interdisciplinary minor areas of study in applied ethics; Asian studies; biochemistry; black studies; business law, regulation, and ethics; classical studies; education with certification at the secondary level in English, history/social studies, mathematics, and modern or classical languages; environmental science; environmental studies; international studies; Irish studies; Italian studies; Judaic studies; Latin American and Caribbean studies; marine science; new media film, TV, and radio; peace and justice; Russian and East European studies; visual and performing arts; and women's studies.

Academic Program

The academic year consists of two semesters and a summer session. To graduate, students earn a minimum of 120 credits and complete at least forty 3- or 4-credit courses. The curriculum consists of courses that fall into the required categories of core curriculum, major, and electives, plus the optional categories of second major, minor, and concentration. With an emphasis on a liberal arts education, the curriculum has a primary objective: the development of the creative intellectual potential of its students within a religious context. The 60-credit core curriculum consists of a designated number of courses in foreign languages, the humanities, mathematics, philosophy, religious studies, sciences, and social sciences.

Faculty

The faculty consists of 207 full-time members. There are no teaching assistants or graduate students who do teaching. The faculty members hold degrees from more than seventy-five American and European colleges and universities, and 93 percent of them hold the highest degree in their discipline. Many have had practical experience in various careers and professions before becoming teachers. Fairfield University's faculty members are very student focused and enjoy the opportunity to mentor students regarding academic progress or personal opportunities. The student-faculty ratio is 13:1, and the average class size is 24 students. Academic, vocational, and personal counseling is readily available.

Off-Campus Programs

Students who wish to spend a year or semester abroad as part of their undergraduate education have a number of possibilities open to them. In addition to some ninety study-abroad program options, Fairfield has three direct overseas affiliates: Scuola

Lorenzo de'Medici (Florence, Italy), Harlaxton College (Grantham, England), and Herzen Institute (St. Petersburg, Russia).

Academic Facilities

The DiMenna-Nyselius Library is newly expanded and renovated. Students have open access to more than 300,000 volumes in addition to a reference department offering interlibrary loan, online and CD-ROM bibliographic search services, and access to the Internet. The library's media department contains DVDs, CDs, and video and audiocassettes. The Weil Café and 32-seat computer lab are accessible for 24-hour study. A major renovation to the Bannow Science Center was completed in spring 2002. The center now includes a 48,000-square-foot addition, new introductory labs, a computer-based academic resource center, and labs for faculty-student collaborative research.

Residential Facilities

At Fairfield, housing is guaranteed for all four years for incoming freshmen. Housing options expand each year, enabling students to select more independent living arrangements to accompany their personal and intellectual growth during their time on campus. First-year students typically live in one of eight residence halls, most in doubles, some in singles or triples. Sophomores may move to suite-style residence halls. Juniors may reside in town-house accommodations or the new apartment village. Seniors may elect any of the above options or choose to live off-campus. Town-house and apartment village residents do their own cooking and cleaning and pay their own electric and utility bills. All rooms have fiber-optic connection to e-mail, the library online catalog, electronic course bulletin boards, the Internet, the World Wide Web, and courseware on the central University computer. In addition, every room is wired for cable TV.

Costs

Tuition and fees at Fairfield for 2003–04 were $26,100; room and board were $8920 and fees were $485. Books and supplies cost approximately $500 per semester. Costs are subject to change.

Financial Aid

Fairfield University administers a comprehensive financial aid program offering assistance on the basis of need and merit, with funds derived from University, state and federal government, and private student-aid programs. Need-based funds are distributed based on a thorough analysis of a family's ability to pay for educational expenses. Merit-based awards are made to academically talented students as entering freshmen. About 70 percent of all freshmen receive some form of financial assistance. In order to apply for financial aid, students must complete the PROFILE and FAFSA forms.

Student Government

Fairfield University Student Association (FUSA) is the official undergraduate student government, and every student is a member. The student government is divided into four branches: executive, judicial, legislative, and programming. Each branch works individually and collectively to improve the quality of life for all students at the University. Students choose from more than ninety different clubs and activities. A 40,000-square-foot addition to the Barone Campus Center was completed in September 2001, allowing all student activities to be housed together in one location along with the bookstore, dining hall, mailroom, and late-night diner.

Admission Requirements

Fairfield is open to qualified men and women regardless of sex, race, color, marital status, sexual orientation, religion, national origin, or handicap. Admission to the University is highly selective and is based upon high school academic record, test scores (SAT I or ACT), recommendations, and accomplishments. The admission process, however, is not a simple review of test scores and grades, but a deliberate consideration of how a student's individual strengths, accomplishments, and character will enrich community life at Fairfield. An applicant must present 4 units of English, 2–4 units of a foreign language, 3–4 units of math, 3–4 units of laboratory science, and 3 units of history/social science.

Transfer applicants may apply for either the fall or spring term. To be considered, a student must be in good standing at their present college and have earned at least 15 credits with a minimum grade point average of 2.5 (2.8 for the Dolan School of Business).

Application and Information

Fairfield University uses the Common Application form as its own application. Students may also submit their applications online through the Fairfield University Web site. To be considered for admission, the University must receive the application, a $55 application fee, transcripts, and supporting documents. Admission deadlines are November 15 for early decision, December 1 for merit scholarship, and February 1 for regular decision. Deadlines for transfer students are November 15 for spring admission and June 1 for fall admission.

Additional information may be obtained by contacting:

Office of Admission
Fairfield University
1073 North Benson Road
Fairfield, Connecticut 06824-5195
Telephone: 203-254-4100
E-mail: admis@mail.fairfield.edu
World Wide Web: http://www.fairfield.edu

FAIRLEIGH DICKINSON UNIVERSITY

THE COLLEGE AT FLORHAM, MADISON, NEW JERSEY
METROPOLITAN CAMPUS, TEANECK, NEW JERSEY

The University

Founded in 1942, Fairleigh Dickinson University (FDU) is a center of academic excellence dedicated to the preparation of world citizens through global education. It comprises two strategically located and uniquely different campuses in northern New Jersey—the College at Florham in Madison and the Metropolitan Campus in Teaneck—offering both undergraduate and graduate programs. Building on its long history of international outreach and its proximity to New York City, the University strives to provide students with the multidisciplinary, intercultural, and ethical understandings necessary to participate, lead, and prosper in the global marketplace of ideas, commerce, and culture. Fairleigh Dickinson is the first university in the nation to require that all undergraduates complete as least one distance learning course a year as part of their educational requirements.

Location

Fairleigh Dickinson University's two campuses in northern New Jersey provide undergraduates with the choice of distinctively different living and learning environments.

The University's College at Florham, located on a former Vanderbilt-Twombly estate in suburban Madison (Morris County) about 45 minutes from New York City, offers undergraduates a classic experience for the contemporary world in a smaller college setting. Its focus is on providing outstanding on-campus and residential living opportunities, hands-on learning experiences, strong graduate and professional school preparation, and customized educational options—all framed by a global perspective.

The University's Metropolitan Campus for professional and international studies, located in the dynamic New York–New Jersey corridor less than 10 miles from New York City in Teaneck (Bergen County), features a university atmosphere with an international perspective, attracting students from the U.S. and around the world. Undergraduates have access to the resources of a major graduate center, and nearby New York City is an integral part of their learning experience. Accelerated bachelor's/master's options are among its many professional preparation programs.

Both campuses offer students a distinctive living and learning environment and a wide range of academic choices within an intimate university setting. Residence halls and off-campus housing are available on both campuses. There are nearly 100 active academic, social, political, and professional student organizations; sororities and fraternities; and sports at the varsity, intramural, club, and intercampus levels. Lectures, seminars, concerts, performances, and special events are also an intrinsic part of University life.

The University also owns and operates an overseas campus—Wroxton College—in Oxfordshire, England.

Majors and Degrees

Bachelor of Arts degrees are offered in art, communication, communication studies, creative writing, criminal justice, economics, electronic filmmaking and digital video design, English language and literature, fine arts, French language and literature, history, humanities, interdisciplinary studies, international studies, literature, mathematics, philosophy, political science, psychology, sociology, Spanish language and literature, and theater arts.

Bachelor of Science degrees are offered in accounting; allied health technologies; biochemistry; biology; business management; chemistry; civil engineering technology; clinical laboratory sciences; computer science; construction engineering technology; electrical engineering; electrical engineering technology; entrepreneurial studies; environmental science; finance; hotel, restaurant, and tourism management; information technology; marine biology; marketing; mathematics; mechanical engineering technology; medical technology; nursing (including a one-year accelerated program); radiologic technology; and science.

The QUEST five-year teacher certification program allows students to earn a bachelor's degree in a field of their choosing in the liberal arts or sciences as well as dual teacher certification in one or two high-demand specifications and a Master of Arts in Teaching (M.A.T.) degree. Preprofessional studies are offered in chiropractic, law, medicine, optometry, and veterinary medicine.

In addition, the University offers many other combined/accelerated degree programs, which enable students to earn both their undergraduate and graduate degrees in just five years in such fields as accounting, biology, business administration, civil engineering or construction technology/systems science, communication/corporate and organizational communication, computer science, computer science/computer engineering, criminal justice/public administration, electrical engineering, electrical engineering/computer engineering, environmental science/systems science, hotel and restaurant management/hospitality management, political science/psychology, psychology, and public administration.

An Associate in Arts degree in liberal arts is also offered.

Academic Programs

Candidates for the degree of Bachelor of Arts or Bachelor of Science must complete a minimum of 128 credit-hours of course work, maintain a minimum 2.0 CGPR (individual colleges have minimum CGPRs for course work within their majors), and complete the University Core Curriculum—a sequence of four courses designed to provide all FDU undergraduates with a solid foundation in the liberal arts, sciences, and humanities. The core provides students with a common base of knowledge; improves skills in communications and analysis; promotes understanding of individual, societal, and international perspectives; and inculcates an appreciation for the interrelationship among bodies of knowledge. Candidates for the B.A. must take 30 to 44 credits in the major, 40 to 63 credits in distribution requirements (19 to 23 credits in foundation courses, 15 to 30 credits in humanities and social and behavioral sciences, and 6 to 10 credits in laboratory science), and the University Core; the remainder of credits may be taken as free electives. Candidates for the B.S. degree must complete 54 to 60 credits in the major and the University Core; the remaining credits are taken in foundation and free elective courses. The undergraduate program includes all courses needed to meet graduate and professional school requirements.

The University offers an honors program and a cooperative education program, and many departments have internships and work-experience programs. More than forty undergraduate concentrations have been developed to enhance a student's major—including addictive behaviors, biochemistry, biological illustration, computer animation, international relations, journalism, and public relations. Mature adult students may participate in the SUCCESS program of personalized learning that leads to the B.A. in humanities.

Through the University's Regional Center for College Students with Learning Disabilities, students can receive academic support within the regular college curriculum (enrollment is selective and limited). The Freshmen Intensive Studies program is designed to assist a limited number of promising students who require focused support as they begin their college careers. The University also offers English Language Centers (a division of Berlitz, Inc.) on both campuses as a service to international students.

Off-Campus Programs

The University strongly encourages all students to incorporate an international learning experience into their education. For example, students can spend a semester or year at Wroxton College, the historic British campus located 70 miles from London that Fairleigh Dickinson has owned and operated since 1965. A variety of other international experiences are also available based on student interests and career goals. The University's requirements in distance learning further expand students' international learning experiences, enabling them to study with its "virtual faculty" of scholars and professionals around the world.

Domestic learning experiences available to students include the well-known Semester in Washington. In addition, the marine biology curriculum includes laboratory field experiences that are available at the University of Hawaii at Hilo, Shoals Laboratory of Cornell University, and Duke University's Marine Laboratory in Beaufront, North Carolina.

Academic Facilities

The University maintains comprehensive libraries on each campus as well as a business reference library on the Teaneck campus. The libraries have combined holdings of 470,000 volumes and subscriptions to 2,585 periodicals. Each library provides computer search services and access to subject CD-ROMs to augment in-house print resources. The University is a participating member of the Online Computer Library Center and maintains a University-wide online catalog to facilitate intracampus library loans. Each library has a number of distinguished special collections on subjects such as the Columbia film archives, the Kahn Memorial Collection on the History of Photography, and the Harry Chesler Collection of comic art, graphic satire, and illustration.

Students have access to nearly 2,000 minicomputers and microcomputers on campus as well as to programming languages and software. In addition, there are state-of-the-art computer graphics laboratories for the production of professional quality, computer-generated art. Computer, software, and Internet training is offered through the campus computer centers. Resident students with their own computers can link to the campus computer network from their rooms. Student e-mail and Internet access accounts are also offered to all students.

Costs

Educational costs (including the estimated cost of residence and meals) for 2004–05 for the College at Florham are $22,876 for tuition, $1145 for fees, $5098 for residence (based on standard double occupancy), and $3510 for meals (based on an eleven-meal plan plus a $300 flex plan). For the Metropolitan Campus, costs include $21,224 for tuition, $1145 for fees, $5546 for residence (based on standard double occupancy), and $3510 for meals (based on an eleven-meal plan plus a $300 flex plan).

Financial Aid

More than $23 million in financial aid is awarded annually, including a generous scholarship program for academically outstanding students. To be considered for financial aid, students should file the Free Application for Federal Student Aid (FAFSA) and Fairleigh Dickinson's University Financial Aid Application. Applications for aid should be filed by February 15 for priority consideration. Applications filed after this date are processed subject to availability of funds.

Faculty

There are 287 full-time and 657 part-time faculty members at Fairleigh Dickinson University. Of the full-time faculty members, nearly 80 percent hold a doctorate or the highest terminal degree in their field. The student-faculty ratio is approximately 18:1. All courses are taught by faculty members. Members of the faculty and administration participate in advising students as well as in planned activities that concern the student body as a whole. All first-year students are assigned faculty mentors to help develop class schedules and assess students' academic progress.

Student Government

Each campus has a student council that acts as the governing body to enforce student regulations and to plan social club activities. The student council serves as a liaison with the faculty and administration of both the campus and the University. It offers students' opinions as an aid in developing University curricular and extracurricular policies. The University Senate, which formulates University policies, includes voting representatives from the student body.

Admission Requirements

The University recommends at least 16 units of full-credit work from an accredited secondary school, including 4 years of English, 2 years of history, 1 year of a laboratory science, 2 years of college-preparatory mathematics, 5 to 7 elective units (4 should be academic), and 2 or 3 years of a foreign language. Additional science and mathematics units are required for some majors. The criteria that are used for University-wide admission are the high school record, SAT I or ACT scores, and counselor recommendations. SAT II Subject Test scores are used for placement only. Freshmen may submit scores on the SAT II: Writing Test. Foreign Language Subject Test scores may be submitted by those applicants who intend to continue study of the language they took in high school. The Mathematics Level I or II Subject Test may be taken by prospective chemistry, physics, mathematics, and engineering majors. The SAT I may be taken as early as July preceding the senior year and as late as March of the senior year, but the November or December test dates are preferred. Campus visits are strongly recommended. Interviews may be required in select cases.

Application and Information

Students must submit a completed and signed application form, a secondary school record form listing all courses and grades, SAT I or ACT scores, and a nonrefundable $40 application fee (which can be waived in cases of hardship). Freshmen and transfer students are admitted in September, January, and during summer sessions. Applicants for regular admission are reviewed on a rolling basis and are notified after receipt of all credentials. Information on filing an online application can be found by visiting the University's Web site (listed below).

For application forms, financial aid information, and other materials, students should contact:

Office of University Admissions
Fairleigh Dickinson University
1000 River Road, H-DH3-10
Teaneck, New Jersey 07666
Telephone: 800-FDU-8803 (toll-free)
E-mail: globaleducation@fdu.edu
World Wide Web: http://www.fdu.edu

FAIRMONT STATE COLLEGE

FAIRMONT, WEST VIRGINIA

The College

Fairmont State College has an enrollment of approximately 3,700 students. Founded in 1867, the College is located in the north-central portion of the state in the city of Fairmont, West Virginia. Fairmont State Community and Technical College has an enrollment of 3,128 students and was founded in 1974. In addition to the main campus, which includes thirteen major buildings, classes are also offered at the Robert C. Byrd National Aerospace Education Center in Bridgeport as well as at the Gaston Caperton Center, a 36,000-square-foot state-of-the-art facility in Clarksburg. The College also has satellite facilities reaching across the north-central region of West Virginia and at the Center for Workforce Education at the I-79 Technology Park.

Fairmont State College has a rich and proud athletic tradition. The College is a member of NCAA Division II and offers men's teams in baseball, basketball, cross-country, football, golf, tennis, and swimming. The College sponsors women's teams in basketball, cross-country, golf, softball, swimming, tennis, and volleyball. Fairmont State's cheerleaders are consistently among the top teams in the state and the nation. Fairmont State also has an extensive and well-organized intramural program and provides other recreational facilities across the campus.

Students who live on campus are housed in one of three residence halls and take their meals at a centrally located dining hall or at the food court in the student center. For those students who prefer to live off campus, private accommodations close to the College are available. Parents who are taking classes at the College may find it convenient to enroll their young children in the day-care center located on the main campus.

The Newman Center and the Wesley Foundation are available to minister to the spiritual needs of students; both organizations are adjacent to the Fairmont State campus. There are also various student organizations, honor societies, and social fraternities and sororities to enhance extracurricular life at the College.

Location

Fairmont is the county seat of Marion County and has a population of approximately 20,000. Located along Interstate 79 approximately 90 miles south of Pittsburgh, the city and College are easily accessible to all travelers.

Fairmont State and the city of Fairmont share a long history of mutual cooperation and respect. Shopping malls, restaurants, cultural entertainment, and nightlife are easily found throughout the city, while countless outdoor recreational pleasures are offered by such places as Pricketts Fort State Park, Valley Falls State Park, and a variety of city and county parks nearby.

Majors and Degrees

Fairmont State offers four-year baccalaureate degrees and several graduate programs. Fairmont State offers courses of study leading to baccalaureate degrees in the humanities, social and natural sciences, teacher education, business, industrial technology, and the fine arts.

Academic Program

Fairmont State College offers ninety bachelor's degree programs. These are offered in the areas of business, education, fine arts, health careers, language, mathematics, science, social science, and technology.

Special degrees such as the Regents Bachelor of Arts degree offer nontraditional approaches for individual career or personal requirements. Preprofessional studies are designed to prepare students for a wide variety of professional programs beyond a four-year degree.

Academic Facilities

The Ruth Ann Musick Library has a collection of more than 200,000 books and more than 15,000 bound periodicals, microfilms, and other materials, including a large collection of audiotapes and videotapes to supplement and enhance learning. The Computer Center allows students to use the latest in technology, including free access to the Internet. Music, theater, and other fine arts are showcased in Wallman Hall Theatre and the Gallery.

Costs

Fairmont State remains a very financially affordable institution. Tuition and fees for the 2003–04 academic year were $3130 for West Virginia residents and $7038 for out-of-state students. Average room and board costs were $4552 per year. Textbooks cost approximately $600 per year.

Financial Aid

Sixty-five percent of Fairmont State students receive some form of financial aid. Guidelines and forms for West Virginia and out-of-state residents are available from high school guidance counselors or Fairmont State's Financial Aid Office.

Faculty

Fairmont State employs more than 200 full-time faculty members, ensuring a student-teacher ratio of 17:1. Each student is assigned a faculty adviser who helps schedule courses, oversees classroom performance, and offers academic counseling.

Student Government

Student Government at Fairmont State actively seeks to supplement the academic atmosphere with intellectual, cultural, and social activities. Student Government members are involved in all aspects of life on campus and work cooperatively with the College administration.

Every segment of the student body is represented in the Government. Members are elected each spring by the student body and receive special training for these positions. Members include a president, vice president, secretary, treasurer, parliamentarian, and representatives of the four classes and other groups. An adviser is assigned by the Vice President for Student Affairs.

Admission Requirements

Students must indicate on the admission application their degree or program objective. Admission is granted to Fairmont

State College for baccalaureate degree programs and to the Fairmont State Community and Technical College component for associate degree and certificate programs.

Admission to Fairmont State does not guarantee admission to specific programs, which may be restricted based on qualifications and available space.

Application and Information

Campus tours are available Monday through Friday at 10 a.m. and 2 p.m. by appointment. Fairmont State also sponsors a Saturday Campus Visitation Day during the fall semester. For more information or to schedule a tour, students should contact:

Office of Admissions
Fairmont State College
1201 Locust Avenue
Fairmont, West Virginia 26554
Telephone: 304-367-4892
800-641-5678 (toll-free)
304-367-4213 (financial aid)
304-367-4216 (housing)
304-367-4000 (campus operator)
304-623-5721 (Caperton Center)
304-842-8300 (Aerospace Education Center)
E-mail: fscinfo@mail.fscwv.edu
World Wide Web: http://www.fscwv.edu

Fairmont State students have an opportunity to relax and socialize in the inviting plaza in front of the Education Building.

FARMINGDALE STATE UNIVERSITY OF NEW YORK

FARMINGDALE

STATE UNIVERSITY OF NEW YORK

FARMINGDALE, NEW YORK

The University

Farmingdale State University of New York is a coeducational, public college with nearly 6,000 undergraduate students. It is dedicated to educating students in the areas of business, applied arts and sciences, health sciences, and technology. A rich history of more than 77,000 graduates makes Farmingdale a college with a legacy of excellence. Farmingdale students enjoy small, personalized classes with dedicated faculty members who provide individual attention. Students are prepared for successful futures through real-life applications of knowledge, critical thinking, and a sound liberal arts education to help them pursue rewarding and successful careers.

Founded in 1912, Farmingdale State was Long Island's first public college. Farmingdale has a long and distinguished heritage of changing to meet the needs of the community it serves—Long Island and the greater metropolitan New York area. A four-year college with twenty-seven degrees, Farmingdale offers students the opportunity to study in small classes taught by distinguished professors. The relationship formed between student and professor ensures students of the individual attention necessary for a successful college experience.

While most of the students commute, they can also reside on campus in one of the four residence halls. Students can join one of the thirty student clubs, hang out in the Java City coffeehouse, work out in the fitness center, or find a peaceful place to study in the Greenley Library. Farmingdale's technology-enhanced classrooms provide unique learning experiences, while the athletics program offers a welcome distraction from the classroom. Making friends and building personal relationships are integral parts of life at Farmingdale.

Farmingdale offers unique courses of study that prepare students to assume responsible positions in a wide variety of careers. All programs operate within four schools: Health Sciences, Engineering Technologies, Business Administration, and Arts and Sciences. Because of its ideal location along the high-tech corridor on Long Island, many students combine their academic study with internships at local companies.

Farmingdale offers a comprehensive athletic program as an NCAA Division III school and as a member of the prestigious Skyline Athletic Conference. Athletic facilities include the 94,000-square-foot gymnasium, with a 4,000-seat athletic center, an indoor swimming pool, three regulation basketball courts, five volleyball courts, four tennis courts, and an indoor track. There are also four indoor racquetball courts, four indoor squash courts, and a weight-training complex. In addition, outdoors there are twelve all-weather tennis courts, a quarter-mile all-weather track, a twenty-station golf driving range, lacrosse/soccer fields, a softball field, and a baseball field.

The Farmingdale intercollegiate program is one of the finest in the country, with many teams receiving national and regional recognition. Teams include men's and women's basketball, cross-country, indoor track, outdoor track, and soccer; women's volleyball; and men's baseball, golf, lacrosse, and softball.

A new $2.5-million baseball stadium is scheduled to open in 2004. This 1,000-seat stadium, which features field turf, dugouts, lights, batting cages, two bullpen warmup areas, a press box, and a concession area, is Phase I of Farmingdale's master plan for the Department of Athletics. When completed, the Athletic Complex is anticipated to also include an oudoor 8-lane track encircling a new field for soccer and lacrosse. The softball field is scheduled to be expanded with new dugouts and bleachers. New tennis courts are scheduled to be built, and plans are underway for the renovation of the Nold Hall facility.

Location

At Farmingdale State, students can enjoy the benefits of a traditional 380-acre northeast campus that is rich in historical buildings. Its central location in the heart of Long Island allows limitless opportunities for recreational and cultural pursuits or internship opportunities with leading local companies. Unique to the campus are the ornamental horticulture teaching gardens, the Solar Energy Center, the Aviation Education Center at Republic Airport, the Institute for Research and Technology Transfer, and New Media Design, an in-house advertising agency. Farmingdale State is only 50 minutes from New York City, where students can revel in the unique cultural and social environment, and it is only 20 minutes from the beautiful ocean beaches for which Long Island is famous.

Majors and Degrees

There are currently eighteen bachelor's degree programs: aeronautical science–profesional pilot, applied mathematics, architectural technology, automative management technology, aviation administration, bioscience, computer engineering technology, computer programming and information systems, construction management technology, dental hygiene, electrical engineering technology, facility management technology, management technology (business administration), manufacturing engineering technology, mechanical technology, security systems, technical communication, and visual communications (graphic design). In addition, associate degree programs are offered in automotive engineering technology, business administration, computer science, criminal justice–law enforcement, dental hygiene, liberal arts and science, medical laboratory technology, nursing, and ornamental horticulture.

Academic Program

All programs operate within four schools: Health Sciences, Engineering Technologies, Business Administration, and Arts and Sciences. While graduation requirements vary by program, students must maintain a minimum GPA of 2.0. The University calendar consists of two semesters, a three-part summer session, and a winter intersession. Farmingdale State is fully accredited by the Middle States Association of Colleges and Schools, and all programs are approved by the New York State Department of Education.

Off-Campus Programs

Farmingdale teaches students success. Graduates are in high demand for their advanced technology skills, real-life experiences, and strong communications skills. Strategic partnerships with many Long Island companies result in active recruitment of students for internships and full-time careers. Farmingdale also focuses on applied research, such as solar energy, fuel cells, medical research, robotics, and manufacturing. Students may have an opportunity to be involved in cutting-edge research with faculty members and industry partners. With the new Broad Hollow Bioscience Park, students have an opportunity to interact with internationally acclaimed scientists.

In addition, there are several opportunities to study abroad and to participate in short-term international travel/study programs, such as art tours of Italy or horticulture programs in Costa Rica.

Academic Facilities

Within the campus, there are several buildings of particular note. Greenley Library houses an extensive collection of print and electronic resources. The Broad Hollow Bioscience Park provides internships for students interested in the dynamic biotechnology industry. The Institute for Research and Technology Transfer offers unique opportunities to complete research in fuel-cell development; for example, working with thermal spray and rapid prototyping technologies. The Center for Advanced Pavement Studies provides leading-edge technology transfer in transportation infrastructure. The Solar Energy Center provides training in residential photovoltaic systems and marketing alternative energy sources to the community. The L. I. Advanced Manufacturing and Applied Engineering Incubator provides students with real-world learning experiences with start-up companies. The 8-acre Ornamental Horticulture Teaching Gardens provide a living laboratory for students and faculty members and were recently highlighted in *House & Garden* magazine. The Security Systems Laboratories include four specialized teaching and research labs in access control, closed-circuit television, computer forensics, and intrusion detection. In addition, there are an on-campus child-care center, a cafeteria, a student union, a bookstore, a coffee bistro, and twenty-three other academic buildings.

Costs

A college education should be worth a fortune, not cost a fortune. Because Farmingdale is part of the State University of New York system, the University offers a high-quality college education at a very affordable cost. It also offers extensive financial aid for qualified students. For the 2004–05 academic year, annual costs for full-time attendance at Farmingdale are $4350 for tuition (plus nominal fees), $7680 for room and board, and about $600 for books and supplies. Tuition for out-of-state students is $10,300.

Financial Aid

Almost 55 percent of Farmingdale students receive some type of financial aid. Loans, grants, and scholarships are available through various federal, state, and private programs. To apply for financial aid, students must file the Free Application for Federal Student Aid (FAFSA) as early as possible, but no later than April 1.

Financial aid is based on a review of a student's financial circumstances. The FAFSA form should be completed soon after January 1. Farmingdale State is dedicated to providing high-quality, personal services to all applicants to assist them in funding their college education. An extensive network of services and resources is offered to help applicants with the financial aid process, and each student is assigned his or her own financial aid adviser. Financial aid advisers help students apply for financial aid and develop financial aid awards tailored to meet college expenses. Scholarships are available.

Faculty

Farmingdale offers small, personalized classes with dedicated faculty members. The relationships formed between students and professors ensure individual attention. The faculty is composed of more than 170 full-time and 120 adjunct faculty members ready to help students grow academically and personally. The faculty includes more than 70 Chancellor's Award winners, including 9 Distinguished Teaching/Service Professors. Farmingdale's faculty represents an outstanding group of individuals dedicated to teaching, research, and scholarship. Farmingdale State offers students a relatively small faculty-student ratio (1:18) in order to maximize the student's individual experience. All classes are taught by faculty members. There are no teaching assistants at Farmingdale State.

Student Government

The Farmingdale Student Government Association (FSG) has authority over all student organizational and elected officers. Sixteen senators and 7 executive board members compose the governing board, which acts in matters promoting the interests of the University and its students.

Admission Requirements

Farmingdale State seeks accomplished students with well-rounded backgrounds and competitive SAT scores. Applicants must have graduated from high school or hold a high school equivalency certificate. The SAT I or ACT is required. Decisions are based primarily on grades earned in academic courses. The review process takes into account the applicant's individual overall background, including available data such as test scores, rank in class, and teacher or counselor recommendations. A personal interview is not required. While the school offers rolling admissions, it is highly recommended that applications be submitted by December 1. With more than 7,000 applications a year, Farmingdale's admissions requirements are increasingly competitive.

Application and Information

Candidates must submit the State University of New York application form available online at the address below and in New York State high school guidance offices.

Requests for further information should be addressed to:

Admissions Office
Farmingdale State University of New York
Laffin Hall
2350 Broadhollow Road
Farmingdale, New York 11735-1021
Telephone: 631-420-2200
World Wide Web: http://www.farmingdale.edu

Students at Farmingdale State.

FASHION INSTITUTE OF TECHNOLOGY

NEW YORK, NEW YORK

The Institute

Today, to know the Fashion Institute of Technology (FIT) only by name is not to know it very well at all. The name reflects back sixty years to the college's origins, when it was devoted exclusively to educating students for careers in the apparel industry. But the name no longer tells the whole story.

A "fashion college" that offers programs in interior design, jewelry design, advertising and marketing communications, and even toy design; a community college that offers bachelor's and master's degree programs in addition to the traditional two-year associate degree, FIT is an educational institution like no other.

FIT is rooted in industry and the world of work. Industry visits by students and lectures by many different leaders in the field provide a cooperative and creative bridge between the classroom and the world of work. Although the college is now associated with many industries and professions, FIT's commitment to career education is still its hallmark and a source of pride to an institution whose industry connection is an integral part of its history. FIT counts among its alumni such luminaries as Calvin Klein and Michael Kors, as well as successful and talented professionals in advertising, packaging, television, the design fields, merchandising, manufacturing, public relations, retailing, and more.

Founded in 1944, FIT is a college of art and design, business, and technology of the State University of New York. More than fifteen majors offered through the School of Art and Design and ten through the School of Business and Technology lead to the A.A.S., B.F.A., or B.S. degrees. (The School of Graduate Studies offers programs leading to the Master of Arts or Master of Professional Studies degree.) FIT is an accredited institutional member of the Middle States Association of Colleges and Schools, the National Association of Schools of Art and Design, and the Foundation for Interior Design Education Research. The ten-building campus includes classrooms, studios, and labs that reflect the most advanced education and industrial practices. New as of fall 2004, the West Courtyard Food Pavilion includes a new dining facility and an expanded bookstore, and the East Courtyard Conference Center includes space for conferences, fashion shows, lectures, and other events. FIT serves more than 6,500 full-time and 4,000 part-time students, who come not only from within commuting distances, but also from all fifty states and seventy other countries. Three dormitories serve approximately 1,300 students and offer various accommodations. Student participation in campus life is encouraged through more than sixty campus clubs, organizations, and athletic teams.

With a consistent job placement rate of 92 percent, FIT graduates are well prepared to meet employers' needs. Working with both undergraduates and graduates, placement counselors develop job opportunities for full-time, part-time, freelance, and summer employment.

Location

The campus leaves behind the rolling green lawns of the more traditional college campus in favor of the culture and excitement of New York City. FIT's location in the heart of Manhattan on Seventh Avenue at 27th Street—where the worlds of fashion, art, design, communications, and marketing converge—permits an exceptional two-way flow between the college and the industries and professions it serves. Students are encouraged to participate in the cultural activities of New York, where opera, dance, theater, and the art world are readily accessible. Education, career direction, technical skills, and the liberal arts combine to take full advantage of New York's special offerings.

Majors and Degrees

The college offers both a two-year program leading to the Associate in Applied Science (A.A.S.) degree and an upper-division program leading to the Bachelor of Fine Arts (B.F.A.) or Bachelor of Science (B.S.) degree. Associate-level art and design majors are offered in accessories design, communication design, display and exhibit design, fashion design, fine arts (with a career-exploration component), illustration, interior design, jewelry design, menswear, photography, and textile/surface design. In the business area, majors are offered in advertising and marketing communications, fashion merchandising management, production management: fashion and related industries, patternmaking technology, and textile development and marketing. Bachelor of Fine Arts degrees are awarded in accessories design and fabrication, advertising design, computer animation and interactive media, fabric styling, fashion design, fine arts, graphic design, illustration, interior design, packaging design, restoration, textile/surface design, and toy design. (Transfer students wishing to enter B.F.A. programs may have to complete the one-year A.A.S. program described below prior to entry into the upper division.) The Bachelor of Science degree is offered in advertising and marketing communications; cosmetics and fragrance marketing; direct marketing; fashion merchandising management; home products development; international trade and marketing for the fashion industries; product management: textiles; production management: fashion and related industries; and textile development and marketing. The B.S. program is open to students who hold an associate degree from the college or an equivalent degree from another accredited institution. Graduates of other accredited institutions of higher learning or transfer students who have a minimum of 30 transferable credits and can satisfy the liberal arts requirements may enter one-year A.A.S. programs in accessories design, advertising and marketing communications, advertising design, fashion merchandising management, fashion design, jewelry design, textile development and marketing, and textile/surface design.

Academic Programs

Programs are designed to prepare students for creative and/or executive careers in the fashion and related professions and industries. To qualify for the A.A.S., a student must be in degree status, satisfactorily complete the credit hours prescribed for a given major with approximately one third of all required credits in the liberal arts, achieve a minimum GPA of 2.0, and receive the recommendation of the faculty. To qualify for the B.S. or B.F.A., a student must be in degree status, satisfactorily complete the credit and course requirements prescribed by the major, and receive the recommendation of the faculty. A minimum of 60 approved credits is required; at least half of the credits required in the major area must be earned in residence at the upper-division level. If the student has an appropriate Fashion Institute of Technology associate degree, a minimum of 30 approved credits must be earned in residence at the upper-division level. Most majors offer internship programs in their courses of study.

Precollege programs (Saturday/Sunday Live) are available during the fall, spring, and summer. More than forty-five programs offer high school students the chance to learn in a studio environment, to explore the business and technology sides of the fashion industry, and to discover natural talents and creative abilities. Classes are taught by a faculty of artists, designers, and other professionals. High school credit may be earned at the discretion of each student's high school.

Off-Campus Programs

FIT's International Programs in Fashion Design and Fashion Merchandising Management/Florence and New York provide international experience for students interested in careers in the global fashion industry. Offered to full-time, matriculated FIT students as two distinct programs leading to the A.A.S. and B.F.A. degrees, the curricula are taught in both New York City and Florence, Italy, with students completing a year of study in each city.

Textile/surface design majors may apply for a semester abroad at the Winchester School of Art or Chelsea College of Art and Design near London or at the Nova Scotia College of Art and Design in Halifax. Fashion merchandising management majors may apply for semester-abroad study in merchandising at RMIT in Australia, Manchester Metropolitan University in England, or Scuola Lorenzo de' Medici in Italy; seventh-semester advertising design students may study at the London College of Printing's School of Graphic Design or Nottingham Trent University in England; and seventh-semester students may study international marketing at the American University in Rome or business at Middlesex Polytechnic in London. A semester at the Institut Commercial de Nancy in Nancy, France, or at CELSA, Université de Paris IV, Sorbonne, is available for a limited number of advertising and marketing communications students with a working knowledge of French. Selected upper-division students majoring in fashion design may study for one semester at Nottingham Trent University, at Esmod, a college of fashion in Paris, or at the Polimoda in Florence, Italy. Brief off-campus courses are offered for credit during summer and Winterim semesters and include the fashion industry in Asia; French costumes and interiors in Paris; fashion and fabric in France and Italy; public relations in Britain; French in Paris; and art and design in Italy.

Academic Facilities

The campus, a modern plant with outstanding facilities for studying all aspects of a dynamic industry, covers almost two square blocks. The Fred P. Pomerantz Art and Design Center offers up-to-date facilities for design studies: photography studios with color and black-and-white darkrooms, painting rooms, a sculpture studio, a printmaking room, a graphics laboratory, display and exhibit design rooms, life-sketching rooms, and a model-making workshop. The Shirley Goodman Resource Center houses the Museum at FIT and the Library/Media Services, with references for history, sociology, technology, art, and literature; international journals and periodicals; sketchbooks and records donated by designers, manufacturers, and merchants; slides, tapes, and periodicals; and a voluminous clipping file. The Gladys Marcus Library houses more than 288,000 volumes, including books, periodicals, and nonprint materials. FIT also has many computer labs for student use. The Instructional Media Services Department provides audiovisual and TV support and a complete in-house TV studio. The Museum at FIT is the repository for the world's largest collection of fashion and textiles (with an emphasis on twentieth-century apparel), and is used by students, designers, and historians for research and inspiration. The museum's galleries provide a showcase for a wide spectrum of exhibitions relevant to fashion and its satellite industries. The annual student art and design exhibition is shown here, as are other student projects. Student work is also displayed throughout the campus. Fashion shows of menswear, womenswear, and accessories occur each academic year.

The Design/Research Lighting Laboratory, an educational and professional development facility for interior design and other academic disciplines, features more than 400 commercially available lighting fixtures controlled by a computer. The Peter G. Scotese Computer-Aided Design and Communications Facility provides art and design students with the opportunity to explore technology and its integration in the design of textiles, toys, interiors, fashion, and advertising as well as photography and computer graphics. Also located on the campus is the Annette Green/Fragrance Foundation Laboratory, an environment for the study of fragrance development.

Costs

An unusual program of sponsorship, shared by the city and State of New York, makes a comparatively low tuition rate possible. The 2003–04 tuition per semester for New York State residents was $1450 for associate-level programs and $2175 for baccalaureate programs; for out-of-state residents, it was $4075 for associate-level programs and $5150 for baccalaureate programs. Dormitory and meal plan fees were $3175 per semester. The Student Association fee was $105, books and supplies were $700, and personal expenses were about $500. Costs are subject to change.

Financial Aid

The Fashion Institute of Technology attempts to remove financial barriers to college entrance by providing scholarships, grants, loans, and work-study employment for students in financial need. Approximately 64 percent of the 6,400 full-time students receive some type of financial aid. The college directly administers its own institutional grants and scholarships, which are provided by the Educational Foundation for the Fashion Industries. College-administered federal funding includes Federal Pell Grants, Federal Supplemental Educational Opportunity Grants, Federal Perkins Loans, Federal Work-Study Program awards, and the Federal Family Educational Loan Program, which includes student and parent loans. New York State residents who meet state guidelines for eligibility may also receive TAP and/or Educational Opportunity Program grants. The college tries to meet students' needs by awarding a financial aid package from institutional scholarships and federal grants, loans, and Federal Work-Study Program awards. Financial aid applicants must file the Free Application for Federal Student Aid (FAFSA), on which they apply for the Federal Pell Grant, and should also apply to all available outside sources of aid. Other documentation must be requested from the Financial Aid Office. Applications for financial aid should be completed prior to February 15 for fall admission or prior to November 1 for spring admission.

Faculty

Those who do, teach at FIT. Members of the FIT community have considerable experience and are on the cutting edge of their various fields and industries.

Student Government

The Student Council, the governing body of the Student Association, gives all students the privileges and responsibilities of citizens in a self-governing college community. Many faculty committees include student representatives.

Admission Requirements

Applicants for admission must be candidates for or hold either a high school diploma or the General Educational Development certificate. Candidates are judged on class rank, grades in college-preparatory course work, and the student essay. Letters of recommendation from teachers and counselors are considered but not required. A portfolio evaluation is required for art and design majors only. Specific portfolio requirements are explained on FIT's Web site.

Transfer students from regionally accredited colleges must submit official transcripts for credit evaluation. Students can qualify for one-year A.A.S. programs if they hold a baccalaureate degree or if they have a minimum of 30 transferable credits from an accredited college, including a minimum of 24 credits that are equivalent to FIT's liberal arts requirements.

Students seeking admission to one of the upper-division majors leading to the Bachelor of Fine Arts or Bachelor of Science degree must hold an Associate in Applied Science degree from FIT or an equivalent degree from an accredited and approved college. They must also meet the appropriate prerequisites as required by the major and have completed FIT's liberal arts requirements. Further requirements may include an individual interview with a departmental committee, review of academic standing, and portfolio review for all applicants to B.F.A. programs. Any student who applies for transfer to FIT from a four-year program must have completed a minimum of 60 credits, including the requisite art or technical courses and the liberal arts requirements.

Application and Information

Candidates who have graduated from a New York State high school should obtain applications from the high school guidance office. Candidates from out-of-state high schools should obtain applications from FIT's Web site or by writing the Office of Admissions.

Office of Admissions
Fashion Institute of Technology
Seventh Avenue at 27th Street
New York, New York 10001-5992
Telephone: 212-217-7675
800-GO-TO-FIT (toll-free)
E-mail: fitinfo@fitnyc.edu
World Wide Web: http://www.fitnyc.edu

FELICIAN COLLEGE

LODI, NEW JERSEY

The College

Felician College is a Catholic/Franciscan college serving more than 1,700 men and women. Its mission is to provide a values-oriented education based in the liberal arts while it prepares students for meaningful lives and careers in contemporary society. To meet the needs of students and to provide personal enrichment courses to matriculated and nonmatriculated students, Felician College offers day, evening, and weekend programs. The College is accredited by the Middle States Association of Colleges and Schools, and carries program accreditation from the National League for Nursing Accrediting Commission and the National Accrediting Agency for Clinical Laboratory Sciences.

In addition to its undergraduate degree programs, Felician College offers the Master of Science in Nursing (M.S.N.) and the Master of Arts degree in religious studies and teacher education. A six-year doctoral program in physical therapy is also offered in conjunction with UMDNJ–SHRP.

Felician College competes in Division II of the National Collegiate Athletic Association (NCAA). The Felician teams, called the Golden Falcons, compete in men's baseball, men's and women's basketball, men's and women's soccer, men's and women's cross-country, and women's softball. The Athletic Department also sponsors numerous intramural sports activities, such as indoor soccer, faculty-student softball and volleyball games on the quad.

Students may elect to reside in one of the spacious suites in Elliott Hall or Milton Court Residence, both located on the new Rutherford Campus, a 10-minute shuttle bus ride from the main campus in Lodi. The campuses offer comfortable student lounge areas, student meeting rooms, dining halls, a gymnasium, a fitness center, and grassy areas for outdoor recreation.

Location

Felician College is located on two beautifully landscaped campuses in Lodi and Rutherford, in Bergen County, in northern New Jersey. Both campuses, nestled in suburban towns, are a 30-minute bus or train ride from New York City and a few miles from the New Jersey Meadowlands sports complex.

Majors and Degrees

Felician College offers programs of study in the arts and sciences, business and management sciences, health sciences, and teacher education.

A liberal arts program leading to the Bachelor of Arts, Bachelor of Science, Bachelor of Science in Nursing, or Associate in Arts degree is designed to provide students with a broad general education and concentrated preparation in a major area. For the B.A. degree, a student may choose a departmental major in art, biology, business administration, communications, computing science, English, history, management and marketing, mathematics, philosophy, psychology, or religious studies. A student may choose an interdisciplinary major in one of three liberal arts areas: humanities, natural sciences and mathematics, or social and behavioral sciences. Concentrations are available in accounting, communications, criminal justice, fine arts, general science, gerontology, graphic design, international education and foreign languages, mathematical sciences, political science, sociology, and teaching math P–12 certification. Bachelor of Arts degree programs in elementary education and special education enable students to seek New Jersey certification in elementary education (K–8) and teaching of the handicapped (K–12).

The Bachelor of Science degree is offered in nursing and in business administration. A program leading to the Bachelor of Science degree in clinical laboratory science and eligibility for national certification is offered in collaboration with the University of Medicine and Dentistry of New Jersey's School of Health-Related Professions (UMDNJ–SHRP). For this degree, a student may concentrate in cytotechnology, medical technology, or toxicology. Also offered in conjuction with UMDNJ–SHRP is a Bachelor of Science program in allied-health technology. Students may study medical sonography, nuclear medicine technology, respiratory care, or vascular technology.

Two-year programs are offered leading to the Associate in Arts degree in liberal arts and the Associate in Science degree in psychosocial rehabilitation.

Academic Programs

A candidate for the B.A. in liberal arts is required to complete an organized program of study comprising 120 semester hours distributed among prescribed and elective courses. Four interdisciplinary courses in the College's Core Curriculum are mandatory for all students. Each baccalaureate degree student in arts and sciences is required to prepare a written and oral senior research project. A minimum of 60 credit hours must be earned at the College. A student who pursues an A.A. degree is required to complete 64 to 66 credits in an approved program of study.

A candidate for the B.A. in elementary or special education is required to complete a program of 126 to 130 semester hours, including credits in general education, professional education, and a major in the arts and sciences. Field experience begins in the freshman year, students participate in a practicum in the junior year, and there is supervised teaching during the senior year in a public elementary school. The education programs are approved by the National Association of State Directors of Teacher Education and Certification (NASDTEC).

Evening and weekend classes provide adults with the opportunity to earn associate and baccalaureate degrees offered at Felician College. Students may take courses through the traditional semester format and through an accelerated trimester format. Distance learning courses are also offered.

The Honors Program for students with strong academic records provides an opportunity to conduct scholarly research and develop leadership skills through service learning. Upon successful completion of the program students graduate as Honors Scholars.

The Service Learning Program allows students to be of service to others while learning the value of citizenship and responsibility through action and reflection.

Academic Facilities

Seminar rooms, multimedia and learning resource centers, and laboratories in accounting, computers, psychology, science, and writing are updated annually the latest instructional technology. Through the Internet Laboratories, all students have access to e-mail and the World Wide Web. The College auditorium comfortably seats 1,500 people; its large stage with modern theatrical features hosts performing groups from all parts of the country. The College library has a selective collection of more than 110,000 volumes, as well as periodicals, cassettes, records, microfilms, and ultrafiche. A curriculum library serves as a resource center for the teacher education programs. The Child Care Center, the Felician School for Exceptional Children, the Lourdes Health Care Center, and the Nursing Skills Laboratory, all located on the Lodi campus, furnish convenient facilities for observation, application of learning, and field experiences.

Costs

Undergraduate tuition in 2004–05 is $15,900 per year for full-time students. The annual cost of room and board is $7500 (double occupancy).

Financial Aid

Felician College participates in federal, state, and institutional programs of financial assistance. To determine the amount and type of aid needed, applicants must file a Free Application for Federal Student Aid (FAFSA) with the Department of Education. The College participates in the Federal Work-Study, Federal Pell Grant, and Federal Supplemental Educational Opportunity Grant programs. Students who do not receive state scholarships may be considered for New Jersey tuition aid grants. Through a state-guaranteed loan program, students may also take out low-interest bank loans. A number of institutional scholarships are available for qualified students in need of financial assistance. The Office of Undergraduate Admission also awards merit-based scholarships to those who are eligible, regardless of need. Monies range from $3200 to full tuition based on GPA and SAT scores. To take advantage of federal financial aid programs exclusively for veterans, a certificate of eligibility should be submitted to the director of financial aid at Felician College. More than half of the students attending Felician receive financial aid.

Faculty

All courses are taught by fully qualified faculty members with advanced degrees, who are dedicated primarily to teaching, advising, and continued involvement in their disciplines. The student-faculty ratio of 15:1 facilitates a close working relationship, as well as individualized programs of instruction. The faculty is composed of lay and religious men and women.

Student Government

All students participate in the Student Government Organization (SGO). The governing body of the SGO, composed of elected representatives from various student groups, coordinates activities on and off campus, including community service, campus ministry, and social, cultural, civic, and athletic events. Student representatives also serve on College committees with faculty members and administrators.

Admission Requirements

Applicants must be graduates of an accredited high school and must present 16 academic units or the high school equivalency certificate, character references, satisfactory SAT I or ACT scores, and a physician's certificate of health. A personal interview is strongly recommended.

Students graduating with an associate degree from a recognized junior college are eligible for admission into the upper division of Felician College. Applications for transfer are considered for both fall and spring semesters. Admission requirements may be adjusted for adults on the basis of maturity and experience.

Felician College offers credit and advanced placement for acceptable scores on the College Board Advanced Placement tests and the College-Level Examination Program tests. Through Felician's Project Forward program, qualified students who have completed their junior year may take college-level courses upon recommendation by their high school principal and guidance counselor.

Application and Information

Applications, accompanied by a $30 fee, should be submitted during early fall of the senior year. The Office of Undergraduate Admission evaluates applicants' credentials on a rolling basis. However, applicants for the fall semester are strongly encouraged to apply as early as possible.

Office of Undergraduate Admission
Felician College
262 South Main Street
Lodi, New Jersey 07644
Telephone: 201-559-6131
Fax: 201-559-6138
World Wide Web: http://www.felician.edu

Felician College students on the lawn of the Rutherford campus's historic castle, which is targeted for renovation as a campus center to meet the needs of a student body that has more than doubled in the last decade.

FERRIS STATE UNIVERSITY

BIG RAPIDS, MICHIGAN

The University

At Ferris State University (FSU), students find small classes, leadership opportunities, and the personal attention they need to unleash their potential and achieve success. Ferris' small classes (80 percent have less than 25 students) are taught by professors, not graduate assistants.

Ferris has a well-deserved reputation for providing a top-quality education at competitive rates and lower fees than many other Michigan state colleges. Since 1884, the University has been recognized for its career-oriented majors that meet the technology and workforce demands of business, industry, health care, and education. The placement rate of Ferris graduates who are employed or continuing their education is 97 percent.

Some majors available to students at Ferris are not offered at any other university in Michigan or the United States. More than 170 undergraduate and graduate majors include two-year degrees that "ladder" into four-year programs; Bachelor of Science and Bachelor of Arts degrees; and seven master's degrees, including a Master of Education in curriculum and instruction, and a Master of Business Administration and Master of Science in information systems management, career and technical education, criminal justice administration, and nursing. A Master of Fine Arts is offered in drawing, painting, photography, printmaking, and dual concentration. Ferris also awards a Doctor of Optometry degree and a Doctor of Pharmacy degree.

International students from more than fifty countries and an 11 percent minority student population enrich the entire campus community of 11,800 students with a variety of perspectives and cultures. Students can join any of 210 student organizations; club, intramural, or varsity sports; or cheer on the Ferris Bulldogs who compete in Division I CCHA hockey and fourteen NCAA Division II sports.

Location

FSU's 880-acre campus is located in the mid-Michigan city of Big Rapids, just a few hours away from Chicago and Detroit, and about an hour from Lake Michigan beaches, downhill ski resorts, and the city-life attractions of Grand Rapids, Michigan's second largest city. Known as the "tubing capital of Michigan," the Big Rapids area provides a wide array of recreational activities and community celebrations.

Majors and Degrees

The College of Allied Health Sciences awards B.S. degrees in environmental health and safety management, health-care systems administration, medical record administration, medical technology, nuclear medicine technology, and professional nursing. Associate degrees are offered in dental hygiene, diagnostic medical sonography, environmental health and safety technology, medical laboratory technology, medical record technology, nuclear medicine technology, radiography (X-ray), respiratory care, and technical nursing.

The College of Arts and Sciences offers B.S. degrees in applied biology, applied mathematics, applied speech communication, biotechnology, public administration, social work, and technical and professional communication. The College offers B.A. degrees in biochemistry, biology, chemistry, communication, English, history, mathematics, psychology, and sociology and a Bachelor of Integrative Studies. Associate degrees are offered in applied speech communication, industrial chemistry technology, liberal arts, and ornamental horticulture technology. Preprofessional programs include engineering, law, mortuary science, optometry, pharmacy, and science.

The College of Business awards B.S. degrees in accountancy, advertising, business administration, business administration with legal studies, computer information systems (CIS), e-commerce marketing, finance, hotel management, human resource management, integrated resource management, international business, management, marketing, music industry management, professional golf management, professional tennis management, public relations, resort management, small business and entrepreneurship, and visual design and Web media. Associate degrees are offered in accounting, computer information systems, general business, legal studies, restaurant and food industry management, and visual design and Web media.

The College of Education and Human Services awards B.S. degrees in allied health education, biology education, business education, chemistry education, criminal justice, elementary education, English education, mathematics education, recreation leadership and management, social studies education, technical education, television and digital media production, training in business and industry, and wage-earning home economics education. Associate degrees are offered in early childhood education, pre–criminal justice, and preteaching in elementary and secondary education.

The College of Technology awards B.S. degrees in automotive engineering technology; automotive and heavy equipment management; computer networks and systems; construction management; electrical/electronics engineering technology; facilities management; heating, ventilation, air-conditioning, and refrigeration engineering technology; heavy equipment service engineering technology; manufacturing engineering technology; mechanical engineering technology; plastics engineering technology; printing management; printing and publishing, new media; product design engineering technology; quality engineering technology; rubber engineering technology; surveying engineering technology; and welding engineering technology. Associate degrees are awarded in architectural technology; automotive body; automotive service technology; building construction technology; CAD drafting and tool design technology; civil engineering technology; heating, ventilation, air-conditioning, and refrigeration technology; heavy equipment technology; industrial electronics; manufacturing tooling technology; mechanical engineering technology; plastics technology; printing and digital graphic imaging technology; rubber technology; surveying technology; and welding technology.

University College provides a variety of academic and career selection services and opportunities to students enrolled in the other seven colleges on the Big Rapids campus. Among those housed under the University College umbrella are the Honors Program, Career Exploration Program, University College Program, educational and career counseling, disabilities services, the Academic Support Center and Tutoring, the Structured Learning Assistance program, SCHOLAR program, and freshman seminars.

On the Ferris–Grand Rapids campus, Kendall College of Art and Design of Ferris State University awards Bachelor of Fine Arts (B.F.A.) degrees in art education, fine arts drawing, fine arts functional art, fine arts painting, fine arts photography, fine arts printmaking, fine arts sculpture, furniture design, illustration, industrial design, interior design, metals/jewelry design, visual communications–multimedia design, and visual communications–print media. A B.S. degree in art history is also offered.

Also on the Grand Rapids campus, the College of Professional and Technological Studies offers B.S. degrees in allied health education, business administration, computer information systems, construction management, criminal justice, digital animation and game design, elementary education, health-care systems administration, industrial technology and management, manufacturing engineering technology, medical records administration, nursing, product design engineering technology, quality engineering technology, and technical education. An associate degree is offered in medical records technology.

Academic Program

Ferris blends career-oriented professional training with a solid base of general education. The University is on the semester system, and the minimum requirement for a baccalaureate degree is 120 semester hours. The average major requires between 120 and 130 semester hours. The minimum number of hours required for an associate degree is 60. The University's academic year begins in August and ends in early May.

Off-Campus Programs

Off-campus sites include the Ferris–Grand Rapids location and the University Center for Extended Learning's (UCEL) network of centers and classrooms in Gaylord, Ludington, Petoskey, Traverse City, Clinton Township, Dearborn, Flint, Lansing, Midland, University Center, Dowagiac, Muskegon, Niles, Alma, and Big Rapids; at Red River College in Winnipeg, Manitoba, Canada; and also online. Through this network of sixteen locations, UCEL is able to provide an opportunity for approximately 900 working adult students to take classes in the evenings, on weekends, and online to obtain one of twenty-two degrees, four certificates, and three certifications available; many also take advantage of the professional development courses offered.

The University Center for Extended Learning offers Bachelor of Science degrees in accountancy; automotive and heavy equipment management; business administration, business administration: maritime; computer information systems; criminal justice; elementary education; environmental health and safety management; health-care systems administration; heating, ventilation, air conditioning, and refrigeration (HVACR) engineering technology; medical records administration; nursing (R.N. to B.S.N.); and secondary teacher education. Additional bachelor's degrees offered are the Bachelor of Applied Science in industrial technology and management and the Bachelor of Social Work. Associate degrees are offered in medical records technology and respiratory care, and certificates are available in human resource management, international business, medical coding/reimbursement, and nursing education.

Academic Facilities

FSU's strikingly attractive campus, with a spacious campus quad, beautiful landscaping, distinctive outdoor sculptures, carillon music, and 115 retro-style buildings, provides an atmosphere that inspires learning. The interior of new Granger Center, which houses the construction technology program and the heating, ventilation, air conditioning, and refrigeration program, is constructed of see-through material, allowing all to observe the color-coded inner workings and mechanics of the structure. The Ferris Library for Information, Technology, and Education (FLITE) provides state-of-the-art information technology, houses 300 computers, and has more than thirty individual and group study rooms. Collections include approximately 340,000 books and bound journals.

Costs

For 2003–04, tuition and refundable fees for undergraduate Michigan residents were $3093 per semester or $6186 per year and $12,230 per year for out-of-state residents. The 2003–04 yearly room and board rate for the nineteen-meal plan was $6326. Books and supplies were estimated at $1000 per year. Ferris State honors the Midwest Student Exchange Program (MSEP), which allows nonresident students from Illinois, Indiana, Iowa, Kansas, Minnesota, Missouri, Nebraska, North Dakota, Ohio, South Dakota, and Wisconsin to pay tuition in an amount equal to 150 percent of the resident tuition rate. Under the MSEP, nonresident students from participating states paid tuition and fees of $9066 per year and $6326 for yearly room and board.

Financial Aid

Approximately 82 percent of Ferris students receive some type of financial aid through federal, state, and University programs. In 2003–04, student financial aid included more than $71 million in scholarships, grants, loans, work-study, or a combination of these. The Free Application for Federal Student Aid (FAFSA) must be submitted by March 15 to receive priority consideration for need-based financial aid. The Woodbridge N. Ferris Scholarship Program offers competitive awards ranging from $2000 to $5500 per year to those who qualify. The Residential Life Scholarship offers $2000 per year for entering students who live in a residence hall on campus, have a 3.25 or better high school GPA, and have a minimum ACT score of 21 or SAT score of 980. Information and counseling are available from the Office of Scholarships and Financial Aid (telephone: 231-591-2110 or 800-940-4-AID, toll-free).

Faculty

There are 485 full-time and 166 part-time faculty members teaching at Ferris State University. Many have earned doctorates and have come to Ferris from positions with other colleges and universities, government, and business. Most of the faculty members in technical majors offer their students practical expertise derived from working in the fields they teach.

Student Government

The Associated Student Government is the elected student governing body that represents student concerns to the University administration and Board of Trustees and works toward improvement of student life.

Admission Requirements

The Office of Admissions and Records receives and reviews all applications and credentials for admission. Some programs are selective in nature and require the completion of specific courses and a minimum grade point average in high school or previous college work. High school applicants are encouraged to apply any time after the end of their junior year and are strongly advised to submit the application and all credentials during the first semester of their senior year. Applications should be completed carefully, with a $30 application fee (check or money order) attached, and returned to the high school guidance officer for processing. The high school completes the second page and attaches an official academic transcript before sending the application to Ferris. Freshmen are also required to submit their ACT test results (Ferris ACT code #1994) or SAT test results (Ferris SAT code #1222) to determine eligibility.

Transfer students should apply by the beginning of the last semester or quarter at their transferring institution. Completed applications for admission, the $30 application fee, and one official academic transcript from each college or postsecondary institution previously attended must be submitted. Transfer students are required to submit ACT or SAT test results for advising and course placement, except if the student (1) has had both a college English and algebra or higher math class, (2) has completed at least 60 semester hours or 90 quarter hours of college work, or (3) has an associate degree or higher from a regionally accredited college.

Application and Information

The application for admission, the $30 application fee, and academic credentials (high school and/or college transcript and official ACT or SAT scores) must be received no later than these deadline dates: December 1 for winter semester, April 19 for summer semester, and August 2 for fall semester. The University reserves the right to close admission earlier if warranted by enrollment limitations and the quantity and quality of applicants. Admission applications may be obtained from high school or college counselors, online at http://www.ferris.edu/admissions/application, or by contacting:

Office of Admissions and Records
Ferris State University
1201 South State Street, CSS-201
Big Rapids, Michigan 49307-2747
Telephone: 231-591-2100
800-4FERRIS (toll-free)
E-mail: admissions@ferris.edu
World Wide Web: http://www.ferris.edu

FERRUM COLLEGE

FERRUM, VIRGINIA

The College

Ferrum College is a four-year, independent, coeducational college situated on a 700-acre wooded campus in the heart of southwest Virginia's Blue Ridge Mountains. Ferrum is a self-contained community; 75 percent of the student body lives on campus, and many faculty members live on or near campus and are closely involved in campus life. Ferrum also provides in-room, fully networked Dell computers at no extra charge.

Founded in 1913 by the Methodist Church, Ferrum is a comprehensive liberal arts college accredited by the Southern Association of Colleges and Schools. Ferrum's student body of about 950 (59 percent men, 41 percent women) is a diverse group; while the largest contingent comes from Virginia, twenty-three other states and a number of other countries are also represented.

Ferrum's curriculum provides solid career preparation that includes rigorous academics, a strong experiential learning component, and a practical, broad-based, real-life emphasis. Ferrum students take what they learn in the classroom and apply it in the community through internships, volunteer opportunities, and fieldwork.

The result: a successful start to a meaningful career. Ferrum recently surveyed the graduating class of 2002 and nearly 100 percent of the respondents reported being either employed, attending graduate school, or both.

In addition to academic facilities—including Stanley Library and the Academic Resources Center, which offers tutoring services free of charge to all students—there are five residence halls that offer a number of housing options, including private rooms, an all-women's hall, and suite arrangements; a popular, busy student center and dining hall; a student fitness center with basketball and racquetball courts and a Nautilus weight and fitness room; several new athletic fields; a high and low ropes leadership training course; fine arts facilities; three student computer labs; and a comprehensive intercollegiate and intramural athletic complex.

Ferrum College students take advantage of a variety of extracurricular activities offered throughout the year. There are more than fifty student clubs and organizations, and many Ferrum students take part in the wide-ranging intramural sports program. Ferrum also has one of the region's top NCAA Division III athletic programs, offering baseball, basketball, cross-country, football, golf, soccer, and tennis for men; basketball, cross-country, lacrosse, soccer, softball, tennis, and volleyball for women; and coed cheerleading opportunities.

The Dell OptiPlex computers provided in each residence hall room feature an Intel Pentium 4 Processor and Windows 2000. Ferrum students now have free hardware and access to the best research libraries in the world, the most up-to-date databases, and computer word processing capabilities.

Location

Ferrum's residential campus, while just a 15-minute drive from the town of Rocky Mount and only 35 miles from the city of Roanoke, provides a measure of peace that is ideal for thoughtful study and quiet introspection. Opportunities for hiking, swimming, rock climbing, mountain biking, and camping are available minutes from campus; those seeking the amenities of urban life can find an array of shops, restaurants, and cultural offerings in Roanoke. Interstate 81 and the Roanoke Regional Airport are 45 minutes to the north, while Interstates 85 and 40 and the Piedmont Triad International Airport lie 90 minutes to the south.

Majors and Degrees

Ferrum College awards the Bachelor of Arts, Bachelor of Fine Arts, Bachelor of Science, and Bachelor of Social Work degrees. Students may choose from the following majors: accounting, agriculture, art, biology, business administration (concentration areas: decision support systems, financial management, management, or marketing), chemistry, computer science, criminal justice, dramatic and theater arts, English (concentration area: professional communication), environmental science, foreign languages (Russian and Spanish), history, horticulture, information systems, international studies, liberal arts (teacher education), liberal studies, mathematical science, medical technology, outdoor recreation, performing and visual arts, philosophy, physical education (concentration areas: exercise science, sports medicine, and teaching/coaching), political science, preprofessional science (concentration areas: predental, premedical, and pre–veterinary medicine), psychology, recreation and leisure, religion (concentration area: Christian ministry), social studies, social work, and sports management (concentration areas: sports information/journalism, sports marketing, and sports management).

Minors include accounting, agriculture, art, biology, business, chemistry, computer science, computer technology, criminal justice, drama, economics, educational theater, English, environmental science, foreign languages (Russian and Spanish), forensic science, history, international studies, journalism, mathematical science, music, outdoor recreation, performing and visual arts, philosophy, political science, psychology, recreation and leisure, religion, and sociology.

Students may also pursue certification in teacher education.

Academic Programs

Ferrum College's comprehensive approach to higher education provides the benefits of liberal arts education with solid, practical career preparation. To graduate, students must complete 127 semester hours of academic work, meet the appropriate distribution and major/minor requirements, and achieve a cumulative grade point average of at least 2.0.

Faculty members encourage students to take advantage of the wide variety of experiential learning opportunities available. Internships are required for programs such as agriculture, environmental science, outdoor recreation, teacher education, social work, recreation and leisure, sports management, and sports medicine and strongly recommended for all others, reflecting the College's belief in the value of hands-on learning. Ferrum students can also do volunteer work, join student government and/or the residence life staff, or work on campus in jobs ranging from student trainers to ropes course facilitators to public relations interns.

The College's innovative teacher education program is designed to encourage participants to develop a personal philosophy of education. In addition to rigorous course requirements, students receive a minimum of 300 hours in a public teacher education classroom and can become certified at the elementary, middle school, and/or secondary levels.

Ferrum operates on a two-semester academic calendar.

Off-Campus Programs

Through a number of cooperative programs, Ferrum students can study abroad in a range of countries, including England, France, Russia, and South Korea.

Academic Facilities

Ferrum's Stanley Library, which is currently being renovated and expanded, contains approximately 110,000 volumes and maintains subscriptions to 90 databases as well as more than 7,000 online journals. The library offers direct Internet access. Other campus facilities include Garber Hall, which has a science annex (housing a greenhouse, classroom, and laboratory space); a performing arts center; a chapel; and the Grousbeck Music Center. Direct access to the Internet and e-mail is available to all students, and a multiyear plan to network campus buildings and residence halls is complete.

Costs

The 2003–04 comprehensive annual fee for resident students was $21,240, which included tuition, room, and board. The comprehensive annual fee for commuting students was $15,640. There is no added cost to out-of-state students. Textbooks generally cost between $300 and $400 per semester.

Financial Aid

In 2003–04, 95 percent of Ferrum students were offered some form of financial assistance. Ferrum makes every effort to provide financial aid consistent with the ability of students and their families to meet college expenses. A comprehensive assistance program includes campus jobs, scholarships, grants, and loans. A typical package consists of 58 percent scholarships and grants, 34 percent low-interest loans, and 8 percent campus-based jobs.

Ferrum College is one of a small group of colleges nationwide that offers a unique financial aid opportunity known as the Bonner Scholars Program, which gives qualified students a chance to receive scholarship funds and to become involved in various service projects.

The Free Application for Federal Student Aid (FAFSA) and forms concerning grants and scholarships are sent to all applicants and should be completed and submitted no later than March 1 for priority consideration. Virginia residents are eligible for grants from the Tuition Assistance Grant (TAG) Program, and some out-of-state students receive a comparable award offered by the College.

Students that apply by January 1 receive priority consideration for grant aid and early estimates of packages.

Faculty

There are 68 full-time teaching faculty members, most of whom hold doctorates or terminal degrees in their fields. Faculty members are dedicated to providing students with in-depth, one-on-one assistance, and frequently involve students in their own research projects. Ferrum's "total community" concept makes close relationships between students and teachers possible. The student-faculty ratio is 12:1.

Student Government

The Student Government Association (SGA) enables students to assume a measure of responsibility in the organization of campus life. Through the SGA, students implement their own activity programs, enforce regulations governing student life, and assist in the development of College policy. Students are actively involved in the workings of the Honor Board, which deals with academic violations, and the Campus Judicial System, which has jurisdiction over nonacademic violations on campus.

Admission Requirements

Students who wish to apply for admission are encouraged to call, write, e-mail, or visit Ferrum College. The staff of the Admissions Office, which is open Monday through Friday, 8 a.m. to 5 p.m., and on Saturday from 9 a.m. to noon, welcomes the opportunity to talk and/or meet with applicants. Personal interviews are recommended and may be required for some students. Appointments for conferences and tours of the campus may be arranged by contacting the Admissions Office. The applicant's complete high school record is the most important factor considered by the Admissions Committee, and class rank, grades, courses completed, and test scores are evaluated. The College requires that each applicant for admission as a full-time student take either the SAT I or the ACT. The test should be taken either late in the junior year or early in the senior year, and the student should request that the results be sent to Ferrum College.

Application and Information

Applicants should submit a completed application (available on request from the Admissions Office or online at the Web address below), a high school transcript (and a college transcript, if applicable), and scores from the SAT I or ACT.

Further information may be obtained by contacting:

Director of Admissions
Spilman-Daniel House
Ferrum College
Ferrum, Virginia 24088-9000
Telephone: 540-365-4290
800-868-9797 (toll-free)
E-mail: admissions@ferrum.edu
World Wide Web: http://www.ferrum.edu/admissions

Schoolfield Hall, Ferrum College's performing arts center, is reflected in the water of Adams Lake in the center of Ferrum's campus.

FISHER COLLEGE

BOSTON, MASSACHUSETTS

The College

Fisher College, a private college for men and women, was founded in 1903 and has been a leader in preparing students for challenging careers. Currently, 550 students come from all parts of the United States and twelve different countries. The student body is composed of 200 men and 350 women. Five percent are part-time, 95 percent are full-time, 50 percent are state residents, and 60 percent live on campus. Ten percent of the students are international, 4 percent are 25 or older, 14 percent are Hispanic, 20 percent are African Americans, and 5 percent are Asian or Pacific Islander. Eighty percent of all students enter Fisher immediately after high school. Ninety-eight percent of all students find jobs upon graduation.

The Student Activities Office is the focal point of campus life and offers a full range of extracurricular activities, including the yearbook, the Volunteer Community Service Club, a fashion show, the Performing Arts Club, Phi Theta Kappa, the Women's Issue Support Group, the Multi Cultural Club, and the Honors Program.

Fisher College offers intercollegiate men and women's basketball. Men's baseball and women's softball are also available and compete as part of the NAIA Division II Sunrise Conference.

Fisher College is accredited by the New England Association of Schools and Colleges.

Location

Located in the Back Bay section of Boston, Fisher is a small college in a world-class city. Within a 6-mile radius of Boston, there are more than thirty-six schools and colleges that draw more than 250,000 students to the area each year. This creates an environment that is truly unique. Fisher provides the individual attention and structure that only a small college can offer, and the social, cultural, historical, and educational opportunities that make Boston famous.

The campus facilities, dormitories, and classrooms overlook either Beacon Street or the Charles River and the Esplanade. The Back Bay is one of the most exclusive and safe neighborhoods of Boston. The city itself becomes a part of the student's college experience. Many of the world-famous attractions are within walking distance of the campus, and there is nothing in Boston that is not accessible by the subway or bus.

Boston has an outstanding public transportation system; there is a subway stop within four blocks of the College. South Station and North Station offer bus and rail service for local and interstate travel, and both are only a few stops away on the subway. Logan International Airport is approximately 20 minutes away via taxi. Airport shuttle service is available.

Majors and Degrees

Fisher College awards a Bachelor of Science degree in management. Fisher also offers associate degree programs in administrative assistant studies, with a mass communication concentration; business administration, with an accounting concentration; computer applications for business; computer technology; early childhood education; e-commerce; fashion merchandising, with a fashion design concentration; legal studies; liberal arts, with humanities, social science with a justice studies option, and women's studies concentrations; psychology; and travel hospitality management. Certificate programs are also available.

Academic Programs

In 2003–04, 250 courses were offered. To earn a bachelor's degree, students must complete 121 credits. A faculty adviser is assigned to each student with the selection of courses.

Fisher College's location offers students a wide range of internship choices. Some internship locations include Walt Disney World, Boston Children's Hospital, the Park Plaza Hotel, and Saks Fifth Avenue.

Fisher College's Placement Office offers students a full range of professional services designed to help guide students along the path to a successful career. With a 98 percent effective placement rate and lifetime assistance, the Placement Office is an invaluable resource.

Academic Facilities

The Fisher College Library contains more than 35,000 volumes and 200 printed periodicals as well as a comprehensive supply of audiovisual materials. The library also provides students with Internet access. Students also use the Boston Public Library, located only a few blocks from the College.

Costs

In 2004–05, tuition for full-time students is $15,975. The annual room and board charge is $9975. There is a comprehensive fee of $1600. The total annual expense for resident students, including fees, is $27,550. The total annual expense for commuting students, including fees, is $17,575.

Financial Aid

A high percentage of students at Fisher receive some forms of financial aid. These include the Fisher Trustee Scholarship, merit-based scholarships, Federal Pell Grants, Federal Perkins Loans, Federal Stafford Student Loans, and the Federal Work-Study Program. All students who wish to apply for aid must submit the Free Application for Federal Student Aid (FAFSA).

Faculty

The faculty at Fisher is aware of and sensitive to students' needs and aspirations. Faculty members are chosen for their academic qualifications and experience. Students find that the faculty is involved in promoting the progress and success of each student. The student-faculty ratio is approximately 9:1, and faculty members and course advisers counsel students both during posted office hours and informally throughout the day. Of the 60 faculty members, 26 are full-time and 30 percent have terminal degrees.

Admission Requirements

The admissions process at Fisher may be best described as individualized. The College advocates an admission policy that accentuates positive attributes in a student's record. Applicants are evaluated objectively on the basis of their performance in their secondary school and their supporting credentials. They are evaluated subjectively on the basis of their character and motivation to attend college. Admission to the bachelor's degree program requires a minimum GPA of 2.5 in a college preparatory curriculum and a combined SAT score of at least 850. Admission to the associate degree program requires a minimum GPA of 2.0 in college preparatory classes. Applicants who have successfully completed the General Educational Development test (GED) are also considered for admission if they present evidence of the potential to perform successfully in college-level courses. Scores on the SAT I are not formally required. TOEFL scores are required for international students. An interview, SAT I or ACT scores, and placement exams are required for some applicants. Recommendations and interviews are strongly recommended.

Application and Information

Fisher College operates under a rolling admission program that enables the College to take action on an application as soon as a student's credentials have been received and reviewed. To obtain an admission application form and a College catalog, prospective students should contact:

Director of Admissions
Fisher College
118 Beacon Street
Boston, Massachusetts 02116
Telephone: 617-236-8818
Fax: 617-236-5473
E-mail: admissions@fisher.edu
World Wide Web: http://www.fisher.edu

FITCHBURG STATE COLLEGE
FITCHBURG, MASSACHUSETTS

The College

Fitchburg State College is a liberal arts institution where career-oriented and professional education programs thrive. The College guarantees that its graduates are qualified for jobs in their fields and continues to place more than 85 percent of its graduates in their chosen professions within six months of graduation.

Fitchburg State's excellent academic reputation and graduate placement can be attributed to a nationally recognized faculty and a strong commitment to teaching. The College enrolls approximately 3,500 undergraduate students in its day and evening divisions and another 1,500 students in its graduate programs. The average undergraduate class size is 25, and the overall student-teacher ratio remains low at 14:1. Each student is assigned to an academic adviser to assist with the planning of a program of study. In addition, each department has access to state-of-the-art equipment and an internship network that spreads throughout New England.

Student life at Fitchburg State is friendly and informal. There are numerous and varied opportunities for student leadership through the Student Government Association, the Athletic Council, the All-College Committee, the Campus Center Advisory Committee, the Residence Hall Councils, publications, and student-faculty-administration committees. More than sixty student-run clubs and organizations are open to all students, including the Dance Club, a student newspaper, the Falcon Players (theater), WXPL (student radio station), and the Black Student Union. Several sororities and fraternities contribute to the social and recreational life of the campus. Hundreds of popular and well-attended activities take place during the year, including films, lectures, concerts, seminars, coffeehouses, pub entertainment, recreational tournaments, a performing arts series, and visual arts exhibits.

In addition to the bachelor's degrees listed below, Fitchburg State confers the Master of Arts in Teaching (M.A.T.), the Master in Business Administration (M.B.A.), the Master of Education (M.Ed.) in several disciplines, and the Master of Science (M.S.) in communications media, computer science, counseling, and management. Several Certificate of Advanced Graduate Studies (C.A.G.S.) programs are available as well.

Location

The College is located in a residential area near the center of Fitchburg, a city with a population of 43,000, which serves as the hub of the commercial and industrial life of north-central Massachusetts. The Wallace Civic Center and Planetarium, located within walking distance of the College, provides a variety of activities, such as exhibits, fairs, performances, ice-skating, hockey, light shows, astronomy demonstrations, and lectures. Fitchburg offers many opportunities for study and practical experience in the areas of sociology, psychology, health, computer technology, business, industry, political organization, and community service. Outdoor activities, including skiing, camping, hiking, canoeing, and fishing, are just minutes from the campus.

The historic and literary centers of Lexington and Concord and the widely varied cultural advantages of Boston are approximately an hour's travel from the College. Worcester is a half hour to the south. Both train service and bus service are available.

Majors and Degrees

Fitchburg State College confers the Bachelor of Arts and the Bachelor of Science degrees in the following majors: accounting, architectural technology, biology, biotechnology, business administration, clinical exercise physiology, communications/media, computer information systems, computer science, construction technology, criminal justice, early childhood education, earth science, economics, electronics engineering, elementary education, energy engineering technology, English, environmental science, exercise and sport science, facilities management, film/video production, fitness management, geography, geo/physical sciences, graphic design, history, humanities, human services, industrial technology, interactive media, interdisciplinary studies, international business and economics, literature, management, manufacturing engineering, marketing, mathematics, middle school education, nursing, photography, political science, professional writing, psychology, secondary education, sociology, special education, technical communication, technical theater arts, technology education, and theater.

Academic Programs

The College's undergraduate programs operate on a two-semester calendar. The first semester begins in early September and ends in mid-December, and the second semester begins in mid-January and ends in mid-May.

The curriculum has a strong liberal arts and sciences requirement, providing a solid foundation for either further academic study or a career. Students may obtain practical experience through internships in social agencies, government offices, and businesses related to their interests. Some major programs require an extensive supervised practicum to complete degree requirements. For education and nursing majors, a broad spectrum of student-teaching and clinical experiences are incorporated in their respective programs of study. The four-year honors program, for students with excellent high school records, culminates in a senior thesis or project.

Off-Campus Programs

Fitchburg State is one of nine state colleges under the jurisdiction of the Massachusetts Board of Higher Education. Through this affiliation, students may participate in the College Academic Program Sharing program, which allows study for a semester or a year at another college. The Office of International Education at Fitchburg provides undergraduate students with the opportunity to study abroad at a variety of colleges and universities overseas. Programs may vary in length from as short as a few weeks to as long as a semester or a year. Over the past several years, Fitchburg State students have studied in England, Scotland, Italy, Spain, Australia, and Latin America.

Academic Facilities

The College has a number of special facilities. An unusually well-equipped Academic Success Center is part of the College library in the Hammond Building and includes offices for academic advising, career services, disability services, math and writing centers, and peer tutoring. The McKay Campus School Teacher Education Center is specifically designed for observing pupil development and instructional techniques. An Instructional Media Center is located in the Conlon Building. Modern, well-equipped shops support the industrial education and industrial technology programs. The nursing program utilizes an on-campus clinical lab that simulates a hospital setting with computerized training models. The communication media program owns a full range of late-model equipment, such as a full color dye-sublimation printer and CD recording and slide-scanning equipment, and supports multiple editing rooms, a production studio, darkrooms, and graphic design computer labs. Communications students at Fitchburg State have access to appropriate equipment and facilities as early as their freshman year.

Costs

Tuition for residents of Massachusetts was $970 per year in 2003–04; out-of state students paid $7050. Residence hall and meal plan costs were $5436. Required fees, including the student activity fee, Campus Center fee, and athletic fee, totaled $3216. Books and supplies were estimated at $750, depending on the student's major. Fees are subject to change.

The College also participates in a regional compact under the auspices of the New England Board of Higher Education, which provides New England residents with a tuition break when they study certain majors at public colleges and universities in other New England states (not available at public colleges in their home state). In 2003–04, out-of-state Fitchburg State students who met the criteria for this tuition assistance program paid tuition at a rate of 150 percent of the in-state tuition or approximately $1455.

Financial Aid

Many sources of financial aid are available to Fitchburg State students. The College participates in federal and state programs, including the Federal Direct Student Loan Program. Packages consisting of grants, loans, work-study awards, and scholarships are given to students demonstrating financial need. Financial aid applications for the fall semester must be completed by the preceding March 1 to be given priority consideration.

Faculty

More than 80 percent of Fitchburg State's 201 full-time faculty numbers hold earned doctoral or other terminal degrees. Full professors teach freshman sections as well as advanced courses and serve as academic advisers to students majoring in their respective programs.

Student Government

All full-time undergraduate students are members of the Student Government Association (SGA). The purposes of the SGA are to encourage responsibility and cooperation in democratic self-government; to form an official body for expressing the judgments of students and fostering activities and matters of general student interest; and to promote full understanding and cooperation among the students, the faculty members, and the administration in order to further the welfare of the College.

The governing body of the SGA consists of 6 SGA officers and a General Council, which includes these officers and 28 elected representatives of classes and residence halls, as well as the commuter student body. The SGA operates through a number of standing and ad hoc committees, membership on which is open to all students.

An 11-member All-College Committee, representing students, the faculty, and the administration, makes recommendations to the president of the College concerning matters of campuswide policy.

Admission Requirements

The College seeks to admit, without regard to race, religion, or ethnic background, students who are capable of success. To this end, significant attention is given to the student's high school record and SAT I or ACT scores. The record of achievement in high school is the single most important item in the applicant's academic credentials. Freshman applicants should have completed a college-preparatory program that includes at least 16 college-preparatory units, with 4 units in English, 2 units in a foreign language, 2 units in social studies, 3 units in mathematics, 3 units in the natural sciences, and two college preparatory electives.

An essay is required; however, interviews are not required. Applicants who have questions about the programs and procedures at the College or about matters of housing and financial aid are encouraged to request an interview through the Admissions Office.

Transfer students are welcome to apply to Fitchburg State. A transcript from each college previously attended must be submitted.

International students are encouraged to apply. Scores on the Test of English as a Foreign Language (TOEFL), evaluations of all foreign transcripts, and translations of foreign transcripts must be submitted. Additional information for international students is available at the Web site listed below.

Application and Information

Fitchburg State College reviews applications on a rolling basis, sending its first set of admission decisions for the fall semester by mid-December. On average, students receive an admission decision four to six weeks from the date their application file becomes complete. The priority deadline for applications is March 1. However, applicants to the Communications Media and Nursing programs are strongly encouraged to submit their applications by January 1. In addition, applicants who wish to be considered for merit scholarships must complete their admission and financial aid application process (i.e. submit all required materials) by February 1.

Transfer applicants for the fall are encouraged to apply by April 15 and by December 1 for the spring semester. International applicants for the fall semester must complete the application process by June 1 and by October 1 for the spring.

For further information, students should contact:

Office of Admissions
Fitchburg State College
160 Pearl Street
Fitchburg, Massachusetts 01420
Telephone: 978-665-3144
Fax: 978-665-4540
E-mail: admissions@fsc.edu
World Wide Web: http://www.fsc.edu

One of the hallmarks of education at Fitchburg State College is close student–faculty member interaction.

FIVE TOWNS COLLEGE

DIX HILLS, NEW YORK

The College

Located on Long Island's North Shore, Five Towns College offers students the opportunity to study in a suburban environment that is close to New York City. Founded in 1972, Five Towns College is an independent, nonsectarian, coeducational institution that places its emphasis on the student as an individual. Many students are drawn to the College because of its strong reputation in music, media, and the performing arts. The College offers associate, bachelor's, master's, and doctoral degrees. The College also offers programs leading to the Master of Music (M.M.) degree in jazz/commercial music and in music education as well as a master's in elementary education (M.S.Ed.) and a doctorate in musical arts (D.M.A.).

From as far away as England and Japan and from as close as Long Island and New York City, the 1,000 full-time students reflect a rich cultural diversity. The College's enrollment is 65 percent men and 35 percent women, with a minority population of approximately 34 percent. The College's music programs are contemporary in nature, although classical musicians are also part of this creative community. The most popular programs are audio recording technology, broadcasting, journalism, music performance, music business, music and elementary education, theater, and film/video production.

Coeducational living accommodations are available on campus. The Five Towns College Living/Learning Center is a brand-new complex containing modern dormitories. Each residence hall contains single- and double-occupancy rooms equipped with private bathrooms, broadband Internet access, cable television, and other amenities.

Location

The College's beautiful 40-acre campus, located in the wooded countryside of Dix Hills, New York, provides students with a parklike refuge where they can pursue their studies. Just off campus is Long Island's bustling Route 110 corridor, the home of numerous national and multinational corporations. New York City, with everything from Lincoln Center to Broadway, is just a train ride away and provides students with some of the best cultural advantages in the world.

Closer to campus, the many communities of Long Island abound with cultural and recreational opportunities. The College is located within the historic town of Huntington, which is home to the Cinema Arts Center, InterMedia Arts Center, Hecksher Museum, Vanderbilt Museum, numerous restaurants, coffeehouses, and quaint shops. The nearby shores of Jones Beach State Park and the Fire Island National Seashore are world renowned for their white, sandy beaches.

Majors and Degrees

The College offers the Associate in Arts (A.A.) degree in liberal arts, with concentrations in literature and theater arts; the Associate in Science (A.S.) degree in business administration; the Associate in Applied Science (A.A.S.) degree in business management and in jazz commercial music, with concentrations in audio recording technology, broadcasting, computer business applications, marketing/retailing, music business, and video arts; the Bachelor of Music (Mus.B.) degree in music education and in jazz/commercial music, with concentrations in audio recording technology, composition/songwriting, music business, musical theater, performance, and video music; the Bachelor of Fine Arts (B.F.A.) degree in theater, with concentrations in acting, film/video, and theater technology; the Bachelor of Professional Studies (B.P.S.) degree in business management, with concentrations in audio recording technology, music business, and video arts; and the Bachelor of Science (B.S.) in childhood education, with concentrations in an elective program, music, and theater. A Bachelor of Science (B.S.) in mass communication features broadcasting and journalism concentrations.

Academic Programs

The following describes some of the more popular programs at Five Towns College. For a complete description of the College's academic program, students should visit the Five Towns College Web site at the address listed below.

The music education program is designed for students interested in a career as a teacher of music in a public or private school. The undergraduate program leads to New York State provisional certification, while the graduate program leads to permanent certification. The course work provides professional training and includes a student-teaching experience. Music students are required to complete at least 40 credits, achieve a GPA of at least 3.0, and pass a piano qualifying examination before being admitted to this program. The audio recording technology concentration is designed to provide students with the tools needed to succeed as professional studio engineers and producers in the music industry. The music business concentration is designed for students interested in a career in entertainment-related business fields. The course work includes the technical, legal, production, management, and merchandising aspects of the music business. The composition/songwriting concentration provides intensive instruction in a core of technical studies in harmony, orchestration, counterpoint, MIDI, songwriting, form and analysis, arranging, and composition for those who intend to pursue careers as composers, arrangers, and songwriters. The performance concentration includes a common core of technical studies and a foundation of specialized courses, such as music history, harmony, counterpoint, improvisation, ensemble performance, and private instruction. The video music concentration includes professional training in music scoring and compositional techniques and in the artistic and technical skills required for the creation of synchronized music. The theater arts program is designed for students interested in careers as actors, entertainers, scenic designers, directors, stage managers, lighting or sound directors, filmmakers, and videographers. The film/video concentration includes extensive technical preparation in videography, filmmaking, linear and nonlinear editing, storyboarding, scriptwriting, producing, and directing. Elementary education students are prepared as teachers for grades 1–6, while those interested in journalism and broadcasting are prepared for careers in radio, television, and newspaper and editorial writing.

To earn a bachelor's degree, students must accumulate between 120 and 128 credits, depending upon the program of study, with a proper distribution of courses and a GPA of at least 2.0. To earn an associate degree, students must accumulate between 60 and 64 credits.

Off-Campus Programs

Off-campus internship opportunities are available to Five Towns College students who have fulfilled the necessary prerequisites, including a cumulative grade point average of at least 2.5., with a 3.0 in their major. In recent semesters, students have interned for major corporations such as MTV, Atlantic Records, Polygram Records, CBS, ABC, EMI Records, MCA Records, SONY Records, The Power Station, Pyramid Recording Studios, Channel 12 News, and many others.

Academic Facilities

Five Towns College occupies a multiwinged facility that comprises approximately 120,000 square feet and includes a 500-seat auditorium, production studios, athletic and dining facilities, classrooms, PC and Mac computer labs, and a student center. T-3 lines connect the College's completely fiber-optic computer network to the Internet. All students have access to this network and are provided with an e-mail account.

The Five Towns College Library has more than 35,000 print and nonprint materials. These include nearly 30,000 books and print items, 464 periodical subscriptions, and approximately 5,000 records, 2,500 videos and DVDs, and more than 2,000 CDs. Through its membership in the Long Island Library Resource Council (LILRC), students have access to other libraries around the country.

The Technical Wing at Five Towns College consists of eleven studio/control rooms. These facilities house the College's state-of-the-art 72-channel SL9000J audio board, 48-track SSL and 24-track digital recording studios and the Electronic Music-MIDI Studio. The Film/Video Studio utilizes Beta Sp, SVHS video formats, and the 16mm film format. Nonlinear edit suites utilize the Media 100 XS and XR operating systems on Macintosh G4 platforms. Students utilize these facilities to develop their skills while creating professional quality productions, both in the studio and on location, under the supervision of industry professionals. Student productions include CDs, music videos, documentaries, sitcoms, public service announcements, commercials, and talk shows, among many others.

The Dix Hills Center for Performing Arts at Five Towns College is an acoustically "perfect" venue, with digital lighting systems, digital sound reinforcement for concert production, and a Barco 6300 digital projection system for multimedia productions. The professional stage is 60 feet wide, with a proscenium opening of 16 feet and 32 feet of fly space. Students utilize this facility to produce live concerts, plays, musicals, and other performances and special presentations.

Costs

The tuition for 2004–05 is $13,200 per year. Miscellaneous fees are approximately $400, and books are about $700. Private instruction fees for performing music students are $675 per semester.

Financial Aid

The annual tuition at Five Towns College is among the lowest of all the private colleges in the region. Nevertheless, approximately 68 percent of all students receive some form of financial assistance. Need-based and/or merit-based grants, scholarships, loans, and work-study programs are available to qualified recipients, including transfer students. Prospective students are urged to contact the Financial Aid Office as early as possible.

Faculty

The College's growing faculty consists of 100 full- and part-time members. The student-faculty ratio is 13:1. While the faculty is more strongly committed to teaching than to research, many members continue to be active in their respective areas of expertise.

Student Government

The Student Council (SC) serves as the representative governance body for all students. The SC consists of an elected president and vice president and 9 elected at-large representatives who select from among themselves a secretary and a treasurer. The Student Council charters clubs and organizations, allocates student activity fees, and recommends policies that affect student life. There is also a Dormitory Council.

Admission Requirements

The College encourages applications from students who will engage themselves in its creative community and who will contribute to the academic debate with honor and integrity. Students seeking a seat in the entering class of students should have attained a minimum high school grade point average of 78 percent. The SAT I or ACT exam is required for all freshmen. Transfer students must also submit official transcripts of all college-level work attempted. International students from non-English-speaking countries must submit a TOEFL score of at least 500 or its equivalent. Students may be admitted for deferred entrance or with advanced standing. The College does not accept students on an early admissions basis, although early decision is available. Candidates for admission must submit a completed Application for Undergraduate Admission, official high school transcripts, at least two letters of recommendation, and a personal statement. International students must submit additional information and should contact the Foreign Student Advisor.

Application and Information

Admission into any music program is contingent upon passing an audition demonstrating skill in performance on a major instrument or vocally. Music students must also take written and aural examinations in harmony, sight singing, and ear training in order to demonstrate talent, well-developed musicianship, and artistic sensibilities. Admission into any theater program is also contingent upon passing an audition. In some cases, the Admissions Committee may request an on-campus interview with an applicant. Music, theater, video arts, and film/video students are encouraged to submit a portfolio tape or reel, if available.

Except for applicants applying on an early decision basis, new students are accepted on a rolling basis, with decisions for the fall and spring semesters mailed starting February 15 and October 15, respectively. There is an application fee of $25.

For further information, students should contact:

Director of Admissions
Five Towns College
305 North Service Road
Dix Hills, New York 11746-5871
Telephone: 631-424-7000 Ext. 2110
Fax: 631-656-2172
E-mail: admissions@ftc.edu
World Wide Web: http://www.ftc.edu

Five Towns College Studio A.

FLAGLER COLLEGE

ST. AUGUSTINE, FLORIDA

The College

Founded in 1968, Flagler College is an independent nonsectarian college that offers a four-year program leading to the baccalaureate degree in selected preprofessional and liberal studies. The College is coeducational, predominantly residential, and small by intent—enrollment is limited to 1,900 students. Flagler is governed by a Board of Trustees of 15 members and is accredited by the Commission on Colleges of the Southern Association of Colleges and Schools (1866 Southern Lane, Decatur, GA 30033-4097; telephone 404-679-4501), one of the six nationally recognized regional accrediting associations.

The campus is situated in the heart of historic St. Augustine, 4 miles from the Atlantic beaches. The focal point of the campus is Ponce de Leon Hall, formerly a famous resort hotel. Described as a masterpiece of American architecture, the Ponce de Leon is listed on the National Register of Historic Places. Ponce de Leon Hall contains a residence hall for 500 students, the dining hall, the student center, the infirmary, and some administrative offices. The 19-acre campus includes a men's residence hall, a technologically advanced library, and ten other buildings that are used for classrooms, faculty and administrative offices, and recreational and athletic facilities.

The College strives to develop the qualities that smallness fosters. These qualities include, but are not limited to, civility, integrity, loyalty, dependability, and affection. An atmosphere of friendliness and respect prevails throughout the College. Students come from forty-four states and twenty-three countries or territories; 67 percent of the students are from Florida. The student body is composed of traditional college-age students; most are between the ages of 18 and 22. Approximately 60 percent of the students live on campus. Students indicate that its size, location, cost, and programs of study are the major reasons for their choosing Flagler.

The College offers a wide range of extracurricular activities that are designed to enrich the student socially, culturally, and physically. There are twenty-one organizations and five honor societies for students to join. The clubs generally fall into the categories of community service, social interest, or those related to a student's major. In addition, some of the favorite pastimes of Flagler students are biking around town, walking through the restoration area, surfing at the beach, competing in a sports event or being a spectator, or just sunning by the pool. Students also make trips to the nearby cities of Jacksonville, Daytona, and Orlando. Athletics play an important role in campus life. Intercollegiate sports for men are baseball, basketball, cross-country, golf, soccer, and tennis. Intercollegiate sports for women are basketball, cross-country, golf, soccer, tennis, and volleyball. A lively intramural sports program is available for both men and women. Athletic and recreational facilities include a gymnasium, eight tennis courts, and a swimming pool. A 19-acre athletic field for baseball, soccer, softball, and intramurals is located 2 miles from the campus.

Location

St. Augustine is located on the northeast coast of Florida, about midway between Jacksonville and Daytona Beach. Famous as a tourist center, rich in history, and beautifully maintained in all its storied charm, St. Augustine provides an attractive environment for a liberal arts college. Community resources complement the programs offered by the College. Flagler is an important part of the St. Augustine community and seeks to use the educational, cultural, and recreational resources of the community to supplement and enhance the quality of life and the quality of education at the College.

Majors and Degrees

Flagler College awards the Bachelor of Arts degree in the following areas: accounting, art education, business administration, communication, deaf education, elementary education, English, exceptional child education, fine art, graphic design, history, Latin American studies–Spanish, philosophy-religion, political science, psychology, secondary education, sociology, Spanish, sport management, and theater arts. In addition, the College offers preprofessional programs in human services, law, and youth ministries.

Academic Program

The principal focus of the College's academic program is undergraduate education in selected liberal and preprofessional studies. The purposes of the academic program are to provide opportunities for general and specialized learning, to assist students in preparing for careers, and to aid qualified students in pursuing graduate and professional studies.

Flagler operates on a semester calendar with two 14-week semesters. The fall term is completed prior to Christmas, and the spring term ends in late April. All students must complete 33 semester hours in general education requirements, including 6 hours in English composition, 6 hours in mathematics, 3 hours in computer science, 3 hours in speech, and 15 hours in three broad areas: humanities, social sciences, and natural sciences/mathematics. The normal academic load is 15 semester hours, which generally represents five courses per term. The number of credits required for a major varies by department. Education majors are required to complete a highly prescribed course of study leading to certification in two or more areas (e.g., elementary education and specific learning disabilities). A student must complete a minimum of 120 semester hours to satisfy graduation requirements. Business administration and education are the two most popular majors at Flagler.

Advanced placement may be awarded to entering freshmen on the basis of scores earned on the tests of the College-Level Examination Program (CLEP) and/or the Advanced Placement Program (AP Program) of the College Board as well as the International Baccalaureate Higher Level exams.

Off-Campus Programs

Students majoring in deaf education have the benefit of working with faculty members and students at the Florida School for the Deaf and the Blind (FSDB), the largest school of its type in the nation. The FSDB is located in St. Augustine, approximately 2 miles from the College campus. Flagler is certified by the Council on the Education of the Deaf and holds membership in the Northeast Florida Consortium for the Hearing Impaired. In addition, Flagler serves as the Southeast Regional Extension Center for Gallaudet University.

Students may study abroad for a semester, a year, or a summer. The College offers organized trips each summer to Italy and England; however, students may choose their own program and many have traveled to a variety of other places, including Latin America, Spain, Mexico, France, and Australia.

Academic Facilities

The William L. Proctor Library building has three floors. The first two floors are devoted to the library with a capacity for 154,562 holdings. At present the library houses 82,692 volumes, 68,385 microform items, 3,003 audiovisual materials, and subscriptions to 476 periodicals. Interlibrary loan service is available for items that the library does not own. Also included on these two floors are study carrels, computer catalog stations, database stations, and an Internet lab. The third floor of building is devoted to computer laboratories for computer science and graphic arts courses.

There is also a computer lab for students' word processing needs. Overall, there are 200 computers available for student use. Students receive their own e-mail accounts through the College.

Costs

For 2003–04, costs were $7410 for tuition and fees and $4450 for room and board. While other costs vary according to the student's lifestyle, the estimate for books, supplies, and miscellaneous expenses is about $1500 per year.

Financial Aid

Financial aid is awarded primarily on the basis of proven need, as demonstrated by the information given by the applicant on the College application for financial aid and on the Free Application for Federal Student Aid (FAFSA). Awards may consist of grants, loans, campus employment, or some combination of the three. In addition to providing institutional grants, the College participates in all federal programs. Some aid may be awarded solely on the basis of academic achievement, talent, athletic ability, leadership, or character. Approximately 85 percent of the student body receives some form of aid from the College. Only those students who have applied for admission and have been accepted are considered for aid. It is recommended that all the necessary forms be submitted by March 15.

Students who have resided in Florida for at least one year are eligible to receive a tuition offset grant of approximately $2500 per year to attend a private college or university in Florida. Funds for the Florida Resident Access Grant are appropriated by the state legislature, and awards are not based on academic merit or financial need.

Faculty

Teaching is central to Flagler's mission. The College seeks to attract and retain a professionally competent faculty dedicated to the art of teaching and advising. Faculty members at Flagler are committed to high standards of performance and are concerned for the welfare of the College and its students. Faculty members are readily available and meet regularly with students outside the classroom. Many faculty members advise student clubs and organizations and take an active role in student life.

The teaching staff is composed of 60 full-time and 90 part-time faculty members. Half of the full-time faculty members hold earned doctorates. A favorable 20:1 student-faculty ratio ensures small classes, individual attention, and interaction between the faculty and students. The average class size is approximately 22 students; 93 percent of classes have 35 or fewer students.

Student Government

The Student Government Association (SGA) plays an important role in planning and implementing a varied program of campus activities at Flagler. Elected student representatives are responsible for voicing student ideas and opinions in matters of general student concern. The SGA also serves as the coordinating unit for many social, academic, and recreational activities. Members of the SGA serve on several committees of the College and participate in many community services and projects.

Admission Requirements

Flagler seeks students from diverse geographical backgrounds who can benefit from the educational experience offered by the College. Flagler welcomes applications from all qualified men and women without regard to age, sex, race, color, marital status, handicap, religion, or national or ethnic origin. Each applicant is evaluated individually, and admission is determined on the basis of the student's academic preparation, scholastic aptitude, and personal qualities. Other factors taken into consideration are the student's motivation, initiative, maturity, seriousness of purpose, and leadership potential. All admission decisions are made on a "need-blind" basis. The College offers an early decision plan.

For freshman applicants, the high school record remains the most important factor in determining admission to the College. The admission staff takes into consideration the quality of courses selected, grade point average, class rank, test scores, a recommendation from a secondary school counselor, a narrative, and participation in extracurricular activities. All freshman applicants are required to submit scores from either the SAT I or the ACT. A minimum of 16 high school units is required; at least 13 must be academic units. The College does not prescribe a particular course of study, but prospective applicants are advised to take 4 units of English, 4 units of social studies, 3 units of mathematics, 2 units of science, and 3 units of academic electives.

Transfer students who have completed at least 24 semester hours of transferable college credit are required to submit an official transcript from each institution attended. In addition, all transfer applicants are required to submit scores from either the SAT I or the ACT. Transfer students are expected to have a minimum 2.5 grade point average and may transfer up to 64 semester hours of credit from a community college. Those who have earned fewer than 24 semester hours of credit must satisfy requirements for freshman admission. In addition to fulfilling the above requirements, international students must submit scores from the TOEFL or demonstrate proficiency in the English language.

An interview is not required as part of the admission process, but many students regard on-campus interviews as valuable experiences because of the exchange of information. Arrangements for a campus visit should be made with the Admissions Office at least two weeks in advance.

Application and Information

Applications for admission should be submitted in the fall or the winter of the year prior to the desired term of enrollment. Applicants must arrange for transcripts and recommendations to be sent directly to the Admissions Office. The deadline for submitting an application is December 1 for early decision candidates and March 1 for all others.

Application forms and related materials should be sent to:

Director of Admissions
Flagler College
P.O. Box 1027
St. Augustine, Florida 32085
Telephone: 800-304-4208 Ext. 0 (toll-free)
E-mail: admiss@flagler.edu
World Wide Web: http://www.flagler.edu

Flagler students in front of Ponce de Leon Hall.

FLORIDA AGRICULTURAL AND MECHANICAL UNIVERSITY

TALLAHASSEE, FLORIDA

The University

For more than a century, the primary goals of the Florida Agricultural and Mechanical University (FAMU) have been to promote academic excellence and to improve the quality of life for those it serves. Founded in 1887 as the State Normal School for Colored Students, FAMU opened its doors with 2 instructors and 15 students. It was designated a land-grant institution in 1890 and became a university in 1953. It is a full and equal partner in the ten-member State University System. The FAMU campus, covered by lush shrubbery, flowering plants, and massive oaks, covers 419 acres. Valued at $119 million, the University campus has 111 buildings. Although historically black, the University seeks qualified students from all racial, ethnic, religious, and national backgrounds without regard to age, sex, or physical handicap. The current enrollment is 12,784 (84 percent black, 56 percent women). Graduate degrees in twenty disciplines are coordinated through the School of Graduate Studies, Research and Continuing Education. FAMU offers the law degree through its College of Law, located in Orlando, Florida.

The School of Journalism and Graphic Communication publishes a weekly student newspaper and operates an FM radio station. There are more than 100 student organizations on campus, including nationally affiliated fraternities and sororities, honor societies, religious groups, fashion/modeling clubs, the Literary Guild, Orchesis Contemporary Dance Theatre, the Playmakers Guild, and the FAMU Gospel Choir, which released its first album in 1985. The Marching 100, FAMU's 300-member marching band, has received national television and magazine coverage and, in 1985, became the first band outside the Big 10 Conference to earn the Sousa Foundation's prestigious Sudler Trophy. The University, a member of the Mid-Eastern Athletic Conference (MEAC), sponsors seventeen NCAA Division I teams for men and women and operates a I-AA football program within that division. Athletic facilities include Bragg Stadium (25,600), with a field house, locker rooms, weight room, and training facility; a track and field complex with an eight-lane, all-weather, 400-meter track; competition-grade tennis courts; two outdoor pools; baseball and softball fields; and a complex that serves as headquarters for the largest women's athletic program at any historically black institution in the country. The intramural sports program is divided into informal free play, competitive sports, and sports clubs.

Location

The University is located on the highest of seven hills in Tallahassee (population 200,000) among the heavily wooded, rolling hills of northwest Florida and only 22 miles from the Gulf of Mexico. There are more than 1,000 acres of public parks and land and numerous lakes nearby. Programs at FAMU, Florida State University, and Tallahassee Community College provide top-name entertainment, much of which is offered free, or at reduced prices, to students. Students in various disciplines intern or are employed in community businesses and agencies of all three levels of government. The University is located eight blocks from the Capitol Complex, and bus service is available from campus to shopping malls; state, county, and city offices; and recreational areas. An intercampus shuttle (between FAMU and FSU) and an on-campus shuttle run during class hours daily.

Majors and Degrees

The College of Arts and Sciences offers baccalaureate majors and degrees in Afro-American studies, chemistry, computer information systems, criminal justice, economics, English, fine arts, foreign languages, general biology, history, mathematics, music, philosophy and religion, political science and public management (prelaw and urban studies), physics, predentistry, premedicine, psychology, social work, sociology, and theater. The College of Education offers baccalaureate degrees in business teacher education; elementary education; health, physical education, and recreation; industrial arts education; office administration; secondary education; and vocational-industrial education. The FAMU/FSU College of Engineering offers baccalaureate degrees in chemical, civil, electrical, industrial, and mechanical engineering. The College of Engineering Sciences, Technology and Agriculture offers baccalaureate degrees in agribusiness, agricultural science, agricultural engineering, animal science (pre–veterinary medicine), architectural and construction technology, civil engineering technology, electronic engineering technology, entomology and structural pest control, landscape design, and ornamental horticulture. The College of Pharmacy and Pharmaceutical Sciences offers three professional degrees. The College of Law, located in Orlando, Florida, offers the Juris Doctor (J.D.) degree. The School of Allied Health Sciences offers baccalaureate degrees in health-care management, health information management, occupational therapy, physical therapy, and respiratory therapy and offers a master's degree in physical therapy. The School of Architecture offers a four-year, preprofessional baccalaureate degree in architectural studies and a five-year, professional baccalaureate degree in architecture. The School of Business and Industry offers baccalaureate and five-year M.B.A. degrees in accounting and business administration. The School of Journalism and Graphic Communication offers baccalaureate degrees in broadcast journalism, photography, graphic design, magazine journalism, newspaper journalism, printing management, printing production, and public relations. The School of Nursing offers a baccalaureate degree program in nursing.

Academic Program

The School of General Studies facilitates and monitors the general education of all matriculating undecided students. All students take core courses in English, mathematics, humanities, health, American history, natural sciences, and social and behavioral sciences. After completing these core requirements, students select an area of specialization in a major offered in one of the other colleges and schools. A minimum of 120 semester hours is required for the baccalaureate degree. Students who meet test and grade point average requirements and write an acceptable honors thesis are selected for the Honors Program, which enables them to accelerate completion of the basic requirements, enroll in classes of reduced size, develop leadership skills, have honor courses identified as such on their transcript, and be recognized at the annual All-University Convocation. FAMU offers Army, Naval, and Air Force ROTC.

Off-Campus Programs

The School of Architecture has a center in Washington, D.C., where students may study for one or two semesters. Architecture students have also worked on special projects in Florida and other parts of the continental United States. The College of Pharmacy and Pharmaceutical Sciences has a component in Miami, Florida, through which students receive clinical training in the hospitals of the Miami Medical Center. The College of Pharmacy also operates the Clinical Pharmacology Research Unit in Jackson Towers, Miami, Florida, for human drug studies and other research and research training. Through the University's Cooperative Education Program, students receive internships and other short-term work-study opportunities in business and industry, education, and government. The Cooperative Education Program has placed students in most of the fifty states. Individual schools and colleges provide undergraduate internships, usually for upper-division students. Students have interned in such places as London, England; San Juan, Puerto Rico; Sydney, Australia; and Geneva, Switzerland. FAMU has three cooperative programs with Florida State University, which is also located in Tallahassee. The general program enables students to take a limited academic load at the other institution. The Program in Medical Science (PIMS) provides a special route to medical school for students by allowing them to complete the first year of medical study in Tallahassee before transferring to a medical school. The School of Nursing offers the Ph.D. through the University of Florida in Gainesville, Florida. The joint FAMU/FSU College of Engineering program enables students to earn an engineering degree at FAMU while giving them access to course offerings at FSU.

Academic Facilities

The Coleman Memorial Library encompasses Library Service and Instructional Media Services. The library has 400,000 bound volumes, 3,640 periodicals, and 84,500 microfilms; a complete line of audiovisual equipment; a fully equipped television studio; and a photography laboratory. The Florida Black Archives, Research Center and Museum, located on campus, complements academic studies in history and has become a popular tourist attraction. Students have access to the R. A. Gray State Archives, the Leon County Public Library, the Robert Strozier Library at FSU, and the FSU Law Library.

Costs

In 2003–04, basic registration fees for Florida-resident undergraduates were approximately $90.09 per credit hour and for nonresidents, $435.26. The basic cost of University housing was approximately $1400 per semester. Other estimated expenses were board (Student Service Center), $980 per semester for nineteen meals; books, $250; orientation, $15; health fee, $59; and transportation fee, $45. For the most current information, students should contact the admission office.

Financial Aid

Financial aid is awarded according to each student's need in relation to college costs. Awards are available as need-based and non-need-based grants, loans, part-time employment (work-study), and scholarships. These awards may be offered singly or in various combinations. High-achieving high school and transfer students may be eligible for awards under special programs such as Presidential Scholars, Distinguished Scholars Award, and Life Gets Better scholarships. The priority deadline for financial aid application completion is March 1.

Faculty

Approximately 60 percent of the University's 463 faculty members hold doctoral degrees. Faculty members are expected to teach, conduct research, and provide public service. They are heavily involved with student affairs and serve as sponsors and advisers to clubs, student organizations, and professional societies. The overall student-faculty ratio is approximately 29:1; it varies by discipline and course level.

Student Government

Student Government Association officers are elected late in the spring semester and serve for the ensuing academic year. Representatives serve on University committees and advisory groups; each class has elected officers.

Admission Requirements

Florida A&M University encourages applications from qualified students of all national, racial, religious, and ethnic groups. Admission is selective; subject to limitations of curricula, space, and fiscal resources; and based on such factors as grades, test scores, educational objectives, pattern of courses completed, past conduct, recommendations, and personal records. Although requirements are subject to change without notice, current policy allows students to be considered for admission if they have graduated from an accredited high school or approved GED program and earned at least 19 units of academic credit, of which 4 must be in English (3 with substantial writing requirements), 3 in mathematics (algebra I and higher levels), 3 in natural sciences (2 with substantial lab requirements), 3 in social sciences, and 2 in foreign language. The remaining 4 elective units must come from these subject areas or other courses approved by the State Department of Education and the Florida Board of Regents. Students must submit ACT or SAT I scores. Applicants with at least a B average (3.0 on a 4.0 scale) in the required high school academic units who submit other evidence of successful academic progress are academically eligible for admission regardless of standardized test scores. Academic eligibility for students with less than a B average is determined on a sliding scale, published in the University catalog, that relates GPA to SAT I or ACT scores. Students who do not meet these requirements but who bring to the University other important attributes or special talents may be admitted by the University Admissions Committee. Outstanding students may submit an application for early admission during their junior year in high school (without having completed all credit requirements), along with a high school transcript (a B average or better), SAT I (at least 1010 combined) or ACT (at least 21 composite) scores, and a recommendation from the principal or designated representative.

Applicants who have attended any accredited institution of higher education and earned 12 or more semester hours are considered transfer students. Undergraduate transfers who enter FAMU with junior-class standing must have passed the College Level Academic Skills Test (CLAST) to be admitted to upper-level courses and degree programs. Transfer applicants with fewer than 60 semester hours of credit must meet first-time-in-college admission requirements. Undergraduate transfer applicants who have not earned the A.A. degree from a Florida community/junior college or from a state university must be in good standing and eligible to return to the last institution attended, must have earned a minimum of 60 semester hours and maintained at least a C (2.0) average, and must present passing scores on the Florida CLAST before admission to FAMU's upper division. Students who have earned an A.A. degree from an accredited state institution are automatically eligible for admission to nonlimited-access programs, under the Florida Community College–State University System Articulation Agreement. International transfer applicants who are not native English speakers must present a minimum score of 500 on the Test of English as a Foreign Language (TOEFL).

Admission to certain programs is highly selective. These limited-access programs tend to reach enrollment capacity before the cutoff dates for general admission, so interested students should apply early. Admission to the University does not ensure access to on-campus housing.

Application and Information

Office of Admissions
Florida Agricultural and Mechanical University
Tallahassee, Florida 32307

Telephone: 850-599-3796
866-642-1198 (toll-free)
E-mail: admissions@famu.edu
World Wide Web: http://www.famu.edu

FLORIDA ATLANTIC UNIVERSITY

BOCA RATON, FLORIDA

The University

Florida Atlantic University (FAU) is a midsize comprehensive university located on an 850-acre site near the Atlantic Ocean. It was established in 1961, making it the fifth-oldest university in the state system. As an upper-division and graduate state university, FAU admitted its first student in September 1964. In 1984 FAU admitted its first freshman class, instituting a comprehensive four-year undergraduate program. Enrollment has increased from 867 in the first year to 25,000 in 2003.

FAU is part of a rapidly expanding metropolitan area encompassing cities and towns from Fort Lauderdale to Port St. Lucie. Since the original Boca Raton campus was founded in 1964, the University has expanded to six other campuses in South Florida: Dania Beach (SeaTech), Davie, Ft. Lauderdale (two locations: Downtown Fort Lauderdale and Commercial Boulevard), Jupiter (John D. MacArthur Campus/Harriet L. Wilkes Honors College), and Port St. Lucie (Treasure Coast). The residential campus in Boca Raton accommodates 2,092 students in eight residence halls and a student apartment complex. The Student Services Building and two cafeterias are adjacent to the residence halls. On the west side of the campus is the Tom Oxley Athletic Center, with state-of-the-art training facilities. Nearby is a 5,000-seat gymnasium, field house, swimming and diving complex, and athletic fields and courts (baseball, soccer, softball, and tennis). The main academic areas of the campus are grouped around the centrally located library and learning resources buildings. A 24-hour study area is connected to the library. There are also computer labs, study lounges, a media center, and tutoring services to provide academic support for students. The Boca Raton Campus hosts art exhibits and theatrical productions in its two galleries and theaters. The University Center hosts student activities and meetings. In addition, its 2,400-seat auditorium enables students to enjoy performances ranging from rock groups to the Florida Philharmonic Orchestra. The south campus of Palm Beach Community College is also located on the University grounds.

FAU campuses can be found throughout the southeast Florida region. One of FAU's newest campuses is located in Dania Beach. Known as SeaTech, the campus is a marine and ocean engineering facility. There is a 110,000-square-foot classroom/office building in Davie, adjacent to the central campus of Broward Community College. In addition, an Education and Science building on the Davie campus is home to programs in education and science as well as state-of-the-art laboratories. The downtown Fort Lauderdale Campus primarily offers graduate programs in the busy city center. A third campus in Broward County is located on Commercial Boulevard. The Harriet L. Wilkes Honors College in Jupiter opened in fall 1999. It is the first public honors institution in the United States to be built from the ground up. To the north, the University provides classes and services at its Port St. Lucie campus and offers extension classes in Belle Glade and Okeechobee.

At the graduate level, FAU offers Master of Arts and Master of Science degrees in most academic areas. The Education Specialist degree is offered in curriculum instruction, educational leadership, and guidance and counseling. The Doctor of Education degree is awarded in administration and supervision, elementary education, and exceptional student education. The University also offers Ph.D.s in business administration; chemistry; comparative studies; complex systems and brain sciences; computer, electrical, mechanical, and ocean engineering; mathematical sciences; physics; psychology; and public administration.

Florida Atlantic University is accredited by the Commission on Colleges of the Southern Association of Colleges and Schools to award associate, bachelor's, master's, and doctoral degrees. In addition, it is accredited by fourteen professional agencies. FAU is also a member of the National Association of State Universities and Land-Grant Colleges and the Council of Graduate Schools in the United States. The University offers sixty-one bachelor's, fifty-four master's, three specialist, and eighteen doctoral degrees.

Location

The 850-acre Boca Raton Campus is located on a former U.S. Army airfield and is inhabited by a variety of wildlife, including burrowing owls. The University's NCAA Division I athletic teams have taken the feisty bird as their mascot. The campus was designated as a burrowing owl sanctuary by the Audubon Society in 1971. The FAU–Boca Raton campus is 3 miles west of the Atlantic Ocean and midway between Palm Beach and Ft. Lauderdale. The University is easily accessible from major highways. It is off I-95 on Glades Road, and the University is 25 miles from both the Palm Beach and Fort Lauderdale international airports.

South Florida's climate is subtropical, with an average year-round temperature of 75 degrees. FAU's campuses are within easy driving distance of some of the most beautiful beaches and recreational facilities to be found anywhere.

Majors and Degrees

Florida Atlantic University offers programs leading to the Bachelor of Arts and Bachelor of Science degrees as well as twelve specialized bachelor's degrees. A minimum of 120 credit hours is required for a bachelor's degree.

The College of Architecture, Urban and Public Affairs offers majors in architecture (upper division only), criminal justice, public management, social work, and urban and regional planning. The Dorothy F. Schmidt College of Arts and Letters offers a general college major and majors in anthropology, art, communication, English, history, languages and linguistics (French, German, Italian, Japanese, Spanish), music, philosophy, political science, social science, sociology, and theater. The College of Business offers majors in accounting, computer information systems, economics, finance, health administration, hospitality and tourism management, international business and trade, management, marketing, and real estate. The Harriet L. Wilkes Honors College in Jupiter offers a liberal arts education in a highly selective environment. The College of Education offers majors in elementary education, exceptional student education, the Genesis Teacher Education Project, and exercise science and wellness education. Secondary certification is also available. The College of Engineering offers majors in computer science and civil, computer, electrical, mechanical, and ocean engineering. The Davie Campus (upper division only) offers majors in biological sciences (biotechnology, ecology and organismic biology, marine biology, microbiology, and molecular biology), communication, English, geography, graphic design, history, interdisciplinary studies, music (chamber music/accompanying emphasis or piano performance emphasis), political science, psychobiology, psychology, social psychology, and sociology. The Christine E. Lynn College of Nursing offers the Bachelor of Science in Nursing degree. The Charles E. Schmidt College of Science has majors in biological science (biotechnology, ecology and organismic biology, marine biology, microbiology, and molecular biology), chemistry, geography, geology, mathematical sciences, physics, psychology, and social psychology. Preprofessional programs are available in dentistry, medicine, optometry, pharmacy, and veterinary medicine. Certificate programs are available in biotechnology, classical studies, community and economic development, environmental planning, environmental studies, ethnic studies, film, gerontology, Holocaust and Judaic studies, land development, Latin American studies, management, public administration, statistics, video, and women's studies.

Academic Programs

The University offers baccalaureate programs designed for highly motivated and well-qualified applicants. The rigorous core of courses prepares all students for the challenges of today's rapidly changing society.

Off-Campus Programs

Florida Atlantic University has established a work-study program between its colleges and cooperating businesses, industries, and government laboratories. This permits students to divide their programs into six-month periods of study at the University and on-the-job experience in the participating organizations for the duration of the course. Cooperative work-study classes normally start in the fall and spring semesters each academic year. FAU has exchange agreements with international schools in locations ranging from China to Germany. Students spend one or two semesters abroad, or they enroll in study tours or six-week summer programs. Arrangements must be made through the Office of International Programs.

Academic Facilities

The Boca Raton campus resources feature the five-story S. E. Wimberly Library with more than 1 million holdings. The Dorothy F. Schmidt College of Arts and Letters features a 75,000-square-foot three-building complex encompassing a performance arts center, art gallery, experimental theater, visual arts center, lecture halls, classrooms, and offices. The College of Business occupies a four-story classroom/office building. The College of Education's four-story, 90,000-square-foot facility houses its five academic departments and offers a teaching gymnasium, an early childhood center, and the A. D. Henderson University School, a public elementary school operated by the College of Education. There are six buildings devoted entirely to engineering and science disciplines. The Science and Engineering and Social Science buildings were recently joined by the Physical Science Building and the Charles E. Schmidt Biomedical Center. There is also a marine sciences center, Gumbo Limbo, located between the Intracoastal Waterway and the Atlantic Ocean; it provides teaching and research facilities.

Costs

For the 2003–04 academic year, in-state tuition was $98.09 per credit hour, and out-of-state tuition was $465.17 per credit hour. A full-time course load is 24 to 30 semester hours per academic year. Average room and board costs were $7528. Additional expenses are approximately $680 for books, $1352 for personal items, and $2200 for transportation for off-campus students. Fees are subject to change at any time by action of the Florida legislature. FAU offers one of the lowest tuition and expense costs available.

Financial Aid

Approximately $60 million in financial aid is awarded each year. A comprehensive program of student financial aid includes scholarships, grants, loans, and employment that may provide assistance from initial enrollment through graduate study. Assistance is tailored to fit each student's requirements and may vary during his or her enrollment. As a member of the College Scholarship Service of the College Board, the University is guided by the principles and policies of that organization. Students who are interested in applying for need-based aid must complete the Free Application for Federal Student Aid (FAFSA), which is available online at www.fau.edu/finaid/ and at all U.S. high schools, colleges, and universities. Students are strongly encouraged to complete the FAFSA in January for fall admission. The process of applying for aid normally takes six to eight weeks. The priority deadline is March 1. Students must be notified of their acceptance to the University before award allocations can be made.

FAU recognizes and rewards high achievement. There is a wide variety of scholarships available for academic, athletic, or artistic talent (detailed in the FAU catalog and on the Web site: http://www.fau.edu/finaid/).

Faculty

Recognizing that the excellence of its faculty is the true measure of the worth of a university, FAU has brought together a distinguished group of scholars who hold a balanced dedication to both teaching and research. Faculty members come from more than thirty states and several countries. The majority hold a doctorate or professional degree. They all represent a high level of professional experience and academic attainment and are committed to the development of a vigorous educational program of high caliber. The University community has benefited from the presence of 12 Eminent Scholars distributed over seven colleges. In addition, two Endowed Chairs have been fully funded and five others partially funded. The presence of these distinguished scholars and researchers has greatly enhanced the academic climate of the University and has provided focal points for the development of new programs, particularly at the graduate level.

Student Government

FAU gives students an active role on virtually all University and faculty committees, including the Curriculum Committee. They serve on the Board of Trustees and college advisory councils and operate the Student Government Association and Residence Hall Councils as well as the interclub, interfraternity, and Panhellenic groups. Students also serve on the University Senate along with members of the faculty and staff.

Admission Requirements

FAU welcomes applications from talented students. Applications are reviewed on a rolling basis. Preferred application filing dates are June 1 for the fall term, October 15 for the spring term, and March 1 for the summer sessions; international students must file by April 1 for the fall term and October 1 for the spring term. Freshman admission is competitive. Admission decisions are based primarily on a combination of the high school average and SAT I or ACT scores. Students must have completed a minimum of 18 academic units in high school to be eligible for consideration. These units should include English (4 units), math (3 units, algebra I and above), social science (3 units), science (3 units, 2 with a lab), foreign language (2 units, 1 language sequence), and academic electives (3 units). Electives are chosen from the above areas and from computer science, fine arts, and humanities. Students who have completed more demanding courses receive added consideration. Students may also be considered on the basis of outstanding abilities or extraordinary circumstances that indicate the potential to benefit from a competitive university curriculum and environment. The University is firmly committed to affirmative action policies and equal access.

Students who have completed fewer than 60 semester hours (fewer than 90 quarter hours) prior to entry into FAU must meet the freshman admission requirements and have maintained a minimum GPA of 2.0 (on a 4.0 scale) in the college or university previously attended. Students who have completed 60 or more semester hours (90 or more quarter hours) are eligible for admission as upper-division students (junior level or higher) if they have maintained a minimum GPA of 2.0 in their college-level work and are in good academic standing at each institution they have attended. Students with an A.A. degree from a Florida community college are guaranteed admission with upper-division status, with the exception of limited-access programs. Limited-access programs at FAU are the Honors College and nursing. These programs have a higher standard for admission.

Information sessions and tours of the Boca Raton Campus are offered weekdays at 10 a.m. and 2 p.m. and every Saturday at 10 a.m. Tours are not offered during University holidays. Students may access the University's calendar at http://www.fau.edu/registrar/acadcal.htm to determine the dates of University holidays.

Application and Information

Office of Admissions
Florida Atlantic University
777 Glades Road
P.O. Box 3091
Boca Raton, Florida 33431-0991
Telephone: 800-299-4FAU (toll-free)
World Wide Web: http://www.fau.edu

FLORIDA INSTITUTE OF TECHNOLOGY

MELBOURNE, FLORIDA

The Institute

Born in the age of space exploration and information technology, Florida Institute of Technology was founded in 1958 to offer continuing education to the scientists, engineers, and technicians working at what is now NASA's Kennedy Space Center. As the only independent technological university in the Southeastern United States, the university remains dedicated to providing a high-quality education that enhances knowledge through basic and applied research. In support of this mission, Florida Tech is committed to providing students with a world-class faculty; a hands-on, technology-focused curriculum; a high-quality, highly selective, and culturally diverse student body; and personal and career growth opportunities.

Florida Tech is a fully accredited, coeducational, independent, privately supported university that offers more than 145 degree programs in science and engineering, aviation, business, humanities, psychology, education, and communication. Doctoral degrees are offered in twenty disciplines, while master's degrees are offered in more than sixty-five areas of study.

Florida Tech has more than 2,300 undergraduate students and more than 2,300 graduate students from forty-nine states and eighty-eight countries. There are more than 100 student clubs and organizations and new ones are frequently added based on student interest.

Florida Tech competes in ten varsity sports and is a member of NCAA Division II and the Sunshine State Conference. More than twenty-five intramural sports are offered, and students can take advantage of the subtropical climate to participate in outdoor activities year-round.

Florida Tech is listed as a *Barron's Guide* "Best Buy" in college education. In addition, the university is named as one of the top fourteen technological institutions for engineering in the *Fiske Guide to Colleges 2002–2004*.

According to the last three surveys of Florida Tech graduates, 96 percent are working in their major or in graduate school within six months of graduation, and 53 percent of working grads have a starting salary of more than $40,000 per year.

Florida Tech was the recipient of a $64-million F. W. Olin Foundation grant, resulting in new facilities in engineering, life sciences, physical sciences, and sports and recreation.

Florida Tech's SAT scores are among the highest of any private university in Florida.

Location

Florida Tech is located along the Atlantic coastline of central Florida in Brevard County, better known as the "Space Coast." Situated within Florida's high-technology corridor, the area is home to more than 5,000 high-technology companies and the nation's fifth-largest high-technology workforce. It is home to NASA, Kennedy Space Center, United Space Alliance, and many other government agencies and technology companies.

The area's attractive business climate is matched only by its natural resources, many of them ideal for scientific study and research, including the estuarine habitats of the Indian River Lagoon; the Atlantic Ocean marine ecosystem; area beaches, marshes, and wetlands; thousands of acres of protected wildlife habitats; and a variety of tropical/subtropical Gulf Stream weather phenomena. Research and field projects spearheaded by Florida Tech professors often take students to exotic locations all over the world—from Peru to the Alaskan Arctic, Hungary to Australia.

Just beyond campus, students have plenty of opportunities to relax and unwind. Approximately 1 hour northeast of the campus is Orlando and 3 hours to the south is Miami. With the Indian River and Atlantic Ocean less than 5 miles from the campus, water sports such as swimming, sailing, surfing, diving, fishing, and boating are popular year-round activities. Central Florida attractions, such as Walt Disney World, Sea World, and Universal Studios are also nearby.

Majors and Degrees

Florida Tech offers bachelor's degrees in the following disciplines: accounting, aeronautical science (flight option available), aerospace engineering, applied mathematics, astronomy, astrophysics, aviation computer science, aviation management (flight option available), aviation meteorology (flight option available), aquaculture, biochemistry, biology, biology education, business administration, business and environmental studies, chemical engineering, chemical management, chemistry, chemistry education, civil engineering, communication, computer engineering, computer science, computer science education, earth/space science education, ecology, electrical engineering, environmental science, forensic psychology, general science education, humanities, information systems, information systems in business, interdisciplinary science, management information systems, marine biology, mathematics education, mechanical engineering, meteorology, military science, molecular biology, ocean engineering, oceanography, physics, physics education, premedical chemistry, preprofessional biology, preprofessional physics, psychology, research chemistry, software engineering, and the space sciences.

Academic Programs

The university operates on an academic year consisting of two semesters. Programs in the sciences prepare the student for graduate or professional work. Practical aspects of computer science and engineering may be combined with management science for the business minded, and a wide variety of programs are available for the environmentalist. Baccalaureate programs are completely outlined for each discipline. The opportunity for diversification is provided by the technical and humanities electives offered during the junior and senior years. All majors participate in hands-on educational activities such as research, cooperative education, internships, or interdisciplinary design projects.

In the School of Aeronautics, the bachelor's programs provide a strong business or science background in the first two years and concentrate on specialized knowledge in the aviation industry during the final two years. For students interested in flight options, training begins immediately within the first week of classes. Flight students earn their FAA commercial, instrument, and multiengine flight certificates and can earn their instructor, air taxi, and airline transport pilot ratings and flight dispatcher certificate.

Students at Florida Tech may qualify for advanced placement through English and mathematics examinations administered by the university. Advanced credit is awarded for Advanced Placement (AP) exams and higher-level International Baccalaureate subjects.

The university offers a four-year Army ROTC program and it rewards ROTC scholarship winners with a generous supplemental scholarship package. Prospective students should contact an ROTC representative at the university.

All students can participate in internships, cooperative education, research, or interdisciplinary design projects.

Academic Facilities

Florida Tech has more than 125 laboratories and state-of-the-art research facilities including Aquaculture Laboratory; Bioenergy and Technology Laboratory; Center for Airport Management and Development (CAMD); Center for Applied

Business Research; Center for Distance Learning; Center for EDA Software Engineering and Training (EDA-SET); Center for Environmental Education; Center for Remote Sensing; Center for Software Engineering; Claude Pepper Institute for Aging and Therapeutic Research; Dynamic Systems and Controls Laboratory; Geospace Physics Laboratory; Infectious Diseases Laboratory; Joint Center for Advanced Therapeutics and Research; Laser, Optics, and Instrumentation Laboratory; Microelectronics Laboratory; Research Center for Waste Utilization (RCWU); Research Vessel Delphinus; Robotics and Spatial Systems Laboratory; Southeastern Association for Research in Astronomy (SARA); Southeastern Center for Advanced Transportation Research (SCATR); Synoptic Meteorology Laboratory; Vero Beach Marine Laboratory (VBML); Wind and Hurricane Impacts Research Laboratory (WHIRL); Wind Tunnel Laboratory; and Wireless Center for Excellence (WiCE).

Computer facilities include Network Access, Harris Night Hawk (Ada environment under UNIX), Sun SPARC, and GS1 workstations. Programming languages include Ada, C, C++, COBAL, FORTRAN, Java, Lisp, ML, Pascal, Perl, Prolog, and Visual Basic. Available software includes matlab, MS Office, SPSS, and SIMSCRIPT. Databases include mySQL, Oracle, and SQL server. Graphics software includes Gimp, Java3D, OpenGL, Tcl/Tk, and X/Motif. Documentation systems include HTML, Office, Star Office, Tex, and Web systems. Additional teaching labs, virtual-reality labs, and online interactive classes with the latest multimedia and information technology are available in the F. W. Olin Building Complex.

Flight training is conducted at the Melbourne International Airport, 2 miles from campus, home to more than thirty modern aircraft and eight sophisticated simulators. The Florida Tech fleet includes Piper Cadets and Warriors, new Piper Arrows, twin-engine Piper Seminoles and a Piper Chieftan for multiengine training.

Costs

Tuition for the 2004–05 academic year is $23,730 for science and engineering majors and $22,260 for all other majors. Students pursuing aviation majors with flight training can expect an additional cost of $10,580 per year in flight fees. Room and board costs for the year are approximately $6,220.

Financial Aid

There are many different programs available to help cover the cost of higher education. Approximately 80 percent of Florida Tech students qualify for a combination of merit-based scholarships, need-based grants, educational loans, and school-year employment programs. Awards are based on academic promise, need, college costs, and the availability of funds. Monthly installment plans are available for tuition and other expenses. The priority deadline for financial aid is March 15. Students eligible for Veterans Administration benefits may contact the VA representative on the Melbourne campus.

Faculty

The student-faculty ratio is 12:1, and 93 percent of full-time faculty members have a Ph.D. or other terminal degree. The small average class size of 25 provides the opportunity to work one-on-one with some of the finest minds in education. In general, freshman- and sophomore-level instructors carry full-time teaching loads. They are closely involved with student life and serve as advisers and counselors. Upper-level and graduate instructors participate in teaching and research activities. Florida Tech's prime location amongst a vast array of high-tech corporations and scientific communities provides a wealth of adjunct faculty members, who bring skills and expertise from local business and industry.

Student Government

Student government at Florida Tech is the vital link between the administration and the student body and functions as the liaison between the university and the community as well as a catalyst for social change. The organization promotes new ideas and encourages students to participate at all levels of university involvement.

Admission Requirements

Applicants to Florida Tech must demonstrate the readiness to succeed in a challenging academic curriculum. The high school transcript is the most important element of the application. While no minimum grade point average, class rank, or standardized test score is specified, these measures must indicate a readiness for college studies in a chosen academic program.

An applicant who is a U.S. citizen must have earned a high school diploma or high school equivalency diploma by the date of first enrollment. Personal recommendations by counselors or faculty members are not required but are taken into consideration in certain circumstances. Transfer students are considered individually on the basis of transcripts and overall performance. Prospective applicants who do not meet the standardized admission requirements but are interested in attending Florida Tech are urged to arrange a personal interview with the admission counselor to receive individual attention.

Application and Information

Florida Tech encourages applicants from every social, ethnic, racial, and religious background. The university practices a rolling admission policy. Fees for applications are $50 when mailed or $40 when submitted online. Completed applications, high school and college transcripts, and standardized test results should be sent to the office below.

For further information, students may contact:

Office of Admission
Florida Institute of Technology
150 West University Boulevard
Melbourne, Florida 32901-6988
Telephone: 321-674-8030
800-888-4348 (toll-free)
E-mail: admissions@fit.edu
World Wide Web: http://www.fit.edu

Immersed in a thriving atmosphere of dedicated scientists, high-technology corporations, and natural habitats, Florida Tech responds to the educational and research challenges of the twenty-first century.

FLORIDA INTERNATIONAL UNIVERSITY

MIAMI, FLORIDA

The University

Florida International University (FIU) is Miami's public research university and one of America's most dynamic institutions of higher learning. The University offers more than 330 academic programs that lead to more than 190 bachelor's, master's, and doctoral degrees.

Major academic divisions are the Colleges of Arts and Sciences, Business Administration, Education, Engineering, and Health and Urban Affairs and The Honors College and the College of Law. In addition, there are the Schools of Accounting, Architecture, Computer Science, Hospitality Management, Journalism and Mass Communication, Music, Nursing, Policy and Management, and Social Work. The University is accredited by the Southern Association of Colleges and Schools. The professional programs of the respective colleges and schools are accredited or approved by the appropriate professional associations. The Carnegie Foundation classifies FIU as a Doctoral/Research University–Extensive. FIU is a member of Phi Beta Kappa, the country's oldest and most distinguished academic honor society. The University's priorities are to graduate a well-educated, technologically sophisticated, ethnically diverse student body whose members can think critically about a changing world to create greater understanding among the people of the Americas and the world.

FIU has two main sites: University Park campus in southwest Miami-Dade County, 10 miles west of downtown Miami, and Biscayne Bay campus located on Biscayne Bay in North Miami. In addition, the Pines Center offers services to students in adjacent Broward County. Both campuses and the center operate under a central administration.

The University has a diverse population of students. There are more than 33,000 men and women enrolled. Approximately 6 percent of the enrollment consists of international students who represent more than 125 countries. The University currently has more than 300 registered student organizations, which enrich campus life and contribute to the social, cultural, and academic growth of students. Nationally recognized lecturers appear regularly, and concerts and movies are offered, usually at no cost.

Athletic opportunities are numerous. Students can participate in intercollegiate, intramural, and recreational sports. Both campuses offer state-of-the-art recreational facilities. NCAA Division I intercollegiate athletics are available for men in baseball, basketball, cross-country, football, indoor and outdoor track and field, and soccer. Women can participate in NCAA Division I intercollegiate athletics in basketball, cross-country, golf, indoor and outdoor track and field, soccer, softball, swimming, tennis, and volleyball. Student Fitness Centers are available on both campuses.

The University offers apartment-style housing for students at both the University Park and Biscayne Bay campuses. The facilities provide students with the opportunity to live with others in a convenient and supportive residential setting. Most of the residence halls offer a full range of amenities for students, including cable TV, computer connectivity, study rooms, and computer labs as well as a swimming pool and various recreational areas. Recently completed structures include the President's house and Everglades Hall, one of three fraternity houses. Both campuses offer state-of-the art recreational facilities.

Location

Miami and FIU are comparable in their explosive growth, rich ethnic and cultural diversity, and quest for excellence. FIU is a leading institution in one of the most dynamic, artistically expressive, and cosmopolitan cities in the United States and is the gateway for Latin America and the Caribbean. The continued globalization of the world's economic, social, and political systems adds to the importance of FIU's mission and combines with its subtropical environment and strategic location to strengthen Southeast Florida's role as an information and transportation center.

Disney World, the Everglades, marine and state parks, Seaquarium, Metro Zoo, Fairchild Tropical Gardens, and the Parrot Jungle are popular student attractions. Other favorite year-round activities include swimming, waterskiing, scuba diving, sailing, tennis, golf, and horseback riding. Students can also head south for a weekend in the Florida Keys or the Bahamas.

Majors and Degrees

The School of Architecture offers a Bachelor of Science in architectural studies and a Bachelor of Science in interior design.

The College of Arts and Sciences offers programs of study that lead to the Bachelor of Arts in art history, Asian studies, chemistry, dance, economics, English, environmental studies, French, geography, geology, history, humanities, information technology, international relations, liberal studies, philosophy, physics, political science, Portuguese, psychology, religious studies, sociology/anthropology, Spanish, theater, and women's studies. The Bachelor of Science is offered in biology, chemistry, environmental studies, geology, marine biology, mathematical sciences, mathematics, physics, and statistics. A Bachelor of Fine Arts is offered in art, music, and theater. The School of Music offers the Bachelor of Music and a Bachelor of Science in music education. The School of Computer Science offers a Bachelor of Science in computer science.

The College of Business Administration offers a Bachelor of Business Administration, with majors in finance, human resource management, international business, logistics, management, management information systems, marketing, and real estate. The School of Accounting offers a Bachelor of Accounting. The School of Hospitality Management offers programs of study that lead to the Bachelor of Science in hospitality management and travel and tourism management. With the cooperation of industry executives, the school has an internship program that utilizes hotels, motels, restaurants, clubs, airlines, travel agencies, and cruise lines as practice labs for students.

The College of Education offers a Bachelor of Science in art education (1–12), biology education, chemistry education, elementary education, emotional disturbance education, English education, exercise and sports sciences, French education, health occupations education, home economics education, mathematics education, parks and recreation management, physical education (K–8 or 6–12), physics education, social studies education, Spanish education, special education, technology education, and vocational industrial education.

The College of Engineering offers programs of study that lead to the Bachelor of Science in biomedical engineering, chemical engineering, civil engineering, computer engineering, construction management, electrical engineering, environmental and urban systems, industrial and systems engineering, and mechanical engineering.

The College of Health and Urban Affairs serves as an umbrella for the School of Health, School of Nursing, School of Policy and Management, and the School of Social Work. Programs of study that lead to the Bachelor of Science are offered in criminal justice, dietetics and nutrition, health information management, health sciences, nursing, occupational therapy, and social work. The School of Policy and Management also offers a Bachelor of Health Services Administration and a Bachelor of Public Administration. The School of Nursing is accredited by the National League for Nursing Accrediting Commission and is open to generic and RN students.

The School of Journalism and Mass Communication offers a Bachelor of Science in communication.

Preprofessional programs are offered in dentistry, law, medicine, and veterinary medicine.

Academic Programs

At the undergraduate level, all students complete 36 semester hours of general education requirements before graduation. These consist of 6 semester hours each in the areas of humanities, mathematics, natural science, social science, and English composition and 6 semester hours in courses that require 6,000 words of writing. Students may tailor academic programs to fit their personal goals.

There are three terms in the academic calendar year: fall, spring, and summer. Two terms (or semesters) of full-time attendance constitute an academic year; a normal course load is defined as at least 12 semester hours per term. Mini-terms are also available within each semester.

Academic Facilities

At both the University Park and the Biscayne Bay campuses, buildings house high-tech media classrooms, lecture halls, computer facilities, and offices. University Park also has laboratories, auditoriums, music and art studios, an international conference theater, and an experimental theater. The state-of-the-art Kovens Conference Center and the Wolfe University Center, located at the Biscayne Bay campus, are multipurpose facilities with ballrooms, theaters, and seminar rooms. The University libraries contain more than 1.5 million bound volumes, over 3.2 million microforms, and periodical subscriptions in excess of 10,300. New buildings are in various stages of construction. Among them, a second Health Sciences building is nearing completion, and the new Frost Art museum recently broke ground at University Park.

Costs

Tuition for undergraduate courses during the 2003–04 academic year was $89 per credit hour for Florida residents and $457 for non–Florida residents. Additional fees assessed per-term include a $54 health fee, a $10 athletic fee, and a $51 parking fee. (These costs are subject to change.)

Financial Aid

The University adheres to the philosophy that a student is entitled to a university education regardless of his or her financial status. The financial aid program at the University includes scholarships, grants, loans, and employment. Awards are based on need, and individual attention is given to each applicant. To apply for aid, students should submit the Free Application for Federal Student Aid (FAFSA). Students are advised to apply before March 1.

Faculty

The University has more than 1,800 full-time and adjunct faculty members whose backgrounds reflect both quality and diversity. Nearly 90 percent hold terminal degrees in their fields. The faculty works across disciplinary boundaries in dealing with issues central to the environmental, urban, and international missions of the University. The University gives primary consideration to selecting faculty members who have a strong sense of commitment to teaching, research, and counseling students.

Student Government

FIU's Student Government Association (SGA) seeks to include all interested students on University-wide committees and task forces to ensure student representation. In developing the governing policies, the SGA strives to set up programs that entertain, educate, and challenge FIU's community.

Admission Requirements

The University has a rolling admissions policy. Fall applicants are, however, encouraged to apply and submit all required supporting documents by May 1, and all applicants, including those for the fall term, should submit their applications no later than two months prior to their intended term of enrollment. Due to the additional processing time required, international students should apply and submit the required supporting documents by the priority consideration date of April 1 for the fall semester, September 1 for the spring semester, and February 1 for the summer semester.

Applicants are notified of their admission status once a completed application, appropriate application fee, and all supporting documents have been received and the evaluation process is completed. It is the applicant's responsibility to request official transcripts and test scores, when applicable, from all previously attended institutions. All applicants are considered for admission without regard to race, creed, age, disability, gender, marital status, or national origin.

The University seeks highly motivated students with strong academic backgrounds and exceptional test scores. The quality and number of applicants create competition for a place in the freshman class. Freshman admission requires graduation from an accredited secondary school, 19 academic units in college-preparatory courses, and official SAT I or ACT scores. Decisions are based on the student's academic preparation.

Transfer applicants from accredited Florida public community colleges should have an Associate of Arts (A.A.) degree. Applicants who do not hold an A.A. degree must complete 60 semester hours of transferable credit, with a minimum grade point average of 2.0, based on a 4.0 scale. Applicants transferring from a Florida community college or university are required to take the College Level Academic Skills Test (CLAST) prior to admission. For students transferring from out-of-state or private colleges, the test can be taken during the first semester of enrollment. All applicants must meet the criteria published for limited-access programs and should consult the specific college and major for requirements.

International students must submit a Declaration of Finance that shows financial resources sufficient for attending the University and for all living expenses. Students from non-English-speaking countries must also submit a minimum TOEFL score of 500 on the paper-based test or 173 on the computer-based test.

Application and Information

Students are invited to visit the beautiful campus. Tours are available every day of the week and the first Saturday of the month, except on national holidays. For a complete schedule and to sign up for a tour, students should visit the Web site at http://www.fiu.edu/~admiss/visitus.

To apply online, students should go to http://www.fiu.edu/~admiss/apply. Additional information about the University may be found at the Web site listed below.

Office of Admissions
Florida International University
P.O. Box 659003
Miami, Florida 33265-9003
Telephone: 305-348-2363
Fax: 305-348-3648
World Wide Web: http://www.fiu.edu

FLORIDA SOUTHERN COLLEGE

LAKELAND, FLORIDA

The College

Florida Southern College was founded in 1885 by the Methodist Church and has remained an affiliate throughout its 119-year history. The original campus was in Leesburg, but the College moved to Palm Harbor in 1902 and finally settled in Lakeland in 1922. Florida Southern is an intentionally interactive, residential, coeducational college of liberal arts and sciences. Although 60 percent of the 1,800 students come from Florida, the remaining 40 percent represent forty-five states and forty-five other countries. All ages and economic strata are represented. Students come to Florida Southern because they want a liberal arts education and believe a smaller campus is the best place to find it. The atmosphere is relaxed and personal, fostering a very close-knit student body and faculty.

All members of the academic community take pride in the campus, a historic landmark and site of the largest collection of buildings designed by renowned architect Frank Lloyd Wright. Annie Pfeiffer Chapel, the first of the Wright buildings to be completed, hosts regular worship services where students of all denominations are welcome. Specific residence halls are reserved for freshmen. Upperclass students, whether members of fraternities and sororities or independent students, are housed in a variety of on-campus accommodations. Construction has been completed on the Miller Residence Hall, which includes seventy-six rooms. The George Jenkins Field House, which seats 3,000 people, includes a three-court gymnasium, a weight room, and a sports equipment room. Facilities for tennis, racquetball, dance, swimming, and waterskiing are also available. The Nina B. Hollis Wellness Center, which opened in 1997, features a fully equipped fitness center, an aerobics/dance studio, an intramural gymnasium, and a wide-screen TV/lounge area. There are branches of six national Greek fraternities and six national Greek sororities on campus. Each of these organizations defers rush to the second semester. Student activities include intercollegiate and intramural sports, drama and music groups, publications, and various clubs and organizations related to academic, political, religious, and social interests. In addition, many students are involved in volunteer programs and internships in the surrounding community.

Location

Florida Southern's campus consists of approximately 100 acres on the shore of Lake Hollingsworth in Lakeland, Florida, a pleasant community of about 90,000 residents in the heart of Florida's citrus belt. Lakeland is 45 minutes from Tampa and an hour from Orlando. Within an hour's drive of the state's major recreational attractions, including Disney World and major beaches, the College is ideally situated for internships and job opportunities with leading corporations that tap into one of the largest markets in the U.S. Members of the community come to the College campus to attend Fine Arts Series performances in music, the Child of the Sun Jazz Festival, dance, and drama; to hear distinguished speakers; and to participate in College and business symposiums. The Lakeland Center also offers many cultural and entertainment opportunities.

Majors and Degrees

Florida Southern College offers a Bachelor of Arts, Bachelor of Fine Arts, Bachelor of Music, Bachelor of Music Education, Bachelor of Sacred Music, or Bachelor of Science degree in the following majors: accounting, art (art education, art history, graphic design, and studio art), athletic training, biology, business administration (concentrations in computer information systems, finance, hotel/resort management, human resource management, international business, and marketing), chemistry, citrus and environmental horticulture, communication (advertising, news media, and public relations), computer science, criminology, economics, education (educational studies; elementary education, including specific learning disabilities; prekindergarten/primary/elementary education; and special education), English (dramatic arts, literature, and writing), history, mathematics, music (music composition, music education, performance, and sacred music), philosophy, physical education, political science, psychology, religion, secondary teacher certification (biology, English, mathematics, social science, and Spanish), sociology, Spanish, and theater arts (performance and technical). Divisional majors are available in humanities and social science.

Preprofessional programs are offered in dentistry, engineering, environmental studies, law, medicine, nursing, physical therapy, theology, and veterinary medicine. Interdisciplinary professional programs include music management, sports management, business-environmental horticulture, and marketing citrus. Programs in environmental horticulture include recreational turfgrass management as well as two tracks in production and landscape design. Students who wish to teach at the secondary level choose a major in a subject area and complete the requirements for certification by the state of Florida.

An honors program provides special opportunities for a select group of entering freshmen to explore topics of common interest in an integrated and interdisciplinary fashion. Selection to the honors program is highly competitive; the program is limited to approximately 10 percent of the entering class.

Academic Programs

All degree programs require the satisfactory completion of a minimum of 124 semester hours with a minimum grade point average of 2.0. Grading is traditional, with a pass/fail option available. The College operates on the semester system with two 15-week semesters, and three 4-week summer sessions. The average course load is 15 hours per semester. Students are required to complete a core curriculum of liberal arts and science courses in addition to their major course work. Credit by examination is awarded on the basis of successful scores on Advanced Placement tests, the International Baccalaureate (I.B.), and College-Level Examination Program (CLEP) tests.

Florida Southern has a Career Center that assists students in clarifying their career and life goals and that provides opportunities for them to explore these goals. Approximately 20 percent of Florida Southern graduates go immediately on to graduate work. Internship experiences help to place the vast majority of other graduates in field-related jobs within a few months of graduation.

Off-Campus Programs

The College sponsors a number of study-abroad opportunities, including May Option experiences Harlaxton Manor (England), Cuernavaca (Mexico), Salamanca and Alicante (Spain), and study-travel on an annually designated itinerary, such as Greece, Italy, and the Cities of Modernism in Europe. Other study-abroad options include Angers (France) and semester or yearlong programs in England, Northern Ireland, and Mexico or through one of the College's consortium programs.

Florida Southern participates in the Washington Semester of American University in Washington, D.C., through which selected students spend a semester in Washington studying government and international relations. Selected students may also spend one semester at Drew University in Madison, New Jersey, studying various aspects of the United Nations through Drew University's United Nations Semester.

Academic Facilities

Florida Southern's Roux Library houses a collection of 172,803 volumes; more than 650 periodical subscriptions; access to more than 2,000 full-text electronic periodicals and more than 10,000 electronic books; a 5,700-item media collection that includes videocassettes, CDs, DVDs, and CD-ROMs; a substantial microforms collection; and seating for more than 350 students. The Branscomb Memorial Auditorium seats 1,800 and is nationally known for its nearly perfect acoustical properties. The Ludd M. Spivey Humanities and Fine Arts Center includes the Marjorie M. McKinley Music Building, the Melvin Art Gallery, and the Loca Lee Buckner Theater. The theater seats 350 and is equipped with a hydraulic thrust stage, a computer-controlled lighting system, and laboratories for costume, makeup, and set design. The Polk Science Building houses the College's recently renovated, state-of-the-art science laboratories and one of the few planetariums in central Florida. The Pre-School Laboratory provides an opportunity for students majoring in prekindergarten/primary education to observe and teach preschoolers.

Costs

The comprehensive cost for 2004–05 is $24,650 ($18,240 for tuition and standard fees and $6410 for room and board). There are additional fees for individual music instruction and the use of practice rooms. Florida Southern estimates that another $500 is adequate for books and supplies, and $500 should cover personal expenses, exclusive of travel to and from home. Members of fraternities and sororities have additional expenses related to membership in these organizations.

Financial Aid

The Student Financial Aid Office offers students its counsel and assistance in meeting their educational expenses. Aid is awarded on the basis of an applicant's need, academic performance, and promise. Ninety-three percent of the students at Florida Southern receive financial assistance. To demonstrate need, an applicant is required to file the Free Application for Federal Student Aid (FAFSA). Various forms of aid, such as scholarships, grants, loans, and campus employment, are used to help meet students' needs. Merit scholarships are available, and awards are based on academic promise; performance ability in music, theater, or art; or athletic ability in baseball, basketball, cross-country, golf, soccer, softball, tennis, or volleyball. Applicants for aid must reapply each year. Florida Southern participates in the Federal Perkins Loan, Federal Supplemental Educational Opportunity Grant, and Federal Work-Study college-based programs. All applicants are expected to apply for any entitlement grant for which they are eligible, such as a Federal Pell Grant and, for Florida residents, a Florida Student Assistance Grant and the Florida Tuition Voucher. The Federal Stafford Loan Program is also available. There are extensive on-campus employment opportunities. The completed FAFSA and the College's financial aid application must be filed with the Student Financial Aid Office by April 1. Early application is encouraged for students seeking academic scholarships.

Faculty

Ninety percent of Florida Southern's faculty members have doctoral or other terminal degrees in their respective fields. The faculty is primarily a teaching faculty; all faculty members have posted office hours and are available for consultation and advising. Faculty members are selected not only for their teaching ability but also for their ability to relate to the needs and concerns of college students. The student-faculty ratio is 12:1.

Student Government

The Student Government Association represents the student body in matters involving the College administration, faculty, and student body and is responsible for coordinating student government. Each full-time student is a member of the association and has a vote in its affairs. The subsidiaries of the association are the Association of Campus Entertainment (ACE), the House of Representatives, the Student Senate, and the four classes: freshman, sophomore, junior, and senior.

Admission Requirements

Florida Southern looks for two things in applicants: performance and promise. The majority of applicants who have been admitted as freshmen have had a grade of B or better in college-preparatory courses (including four courses in English, three in mathematics, and the balance divided among science, foreign language, and social science), have ranked in the upper half of their graduating class, and have earned scores of at least 500 on each of the verbal and math portions of the SAT I or a composite score of at least 23 on the ACT. Nevertheless, the Admissions Office is committed to reviewing individual applicants on their own merits, based on the level of challenge attempted, patterns of grades over time, recommendations from appropriate references, and an applicant's own assessment of the learning environment ideally suited to his or her needs. Applicants must graduate from an accredited high school with a minimum of 19 credits, 16 of which must be academic. Qualified high school juniors may apply for early admission if they have the recommendation of their secondary school and have had a personal interview with the Director of Admissions. Applications from transfers are welcome, as are those from students resuming their education and from older students who have delayed their entrance into college. Transfer applicants should have a minimum 2.5 grade point average and be graduates of or eligible to return to their former institutions. Transfer students with fewer than 25 semester hours must submit high school transcripts and standardized test scores. Applicants who hold Associate of Arts degrees from regionally accredited two-year institutions are typically granted junior standing. Two references (1 academic and 1 personal) are required. All applicants are encouraged to interview; an interview may be required for some candidates.

Application and Information

An application is ready for consideration by the Admissions Committee when it has been received with the $30 application fee, required test scores and references, and transcripts from each school attended. Since all students are required to live on campus unless they are seniors, married, or living with their parents, early application is desirable to ensure that housing is available. The freshman application deadline is April 1. The deadline for applications for athletic training is February 1.

For more information about Florida Southern College, prospective students should contact:

Director of Admissions
Florida Southern College
111 Lake Hollingsworth Drive
Lakeland, Florida 33801-5698
Telephone: 800-274-4131 (toll-free)
E-mail: fscadm@flsouthern.edu
World Wide Web: http://www.flsouthern.edu

Joseph Reynolds residence hall.

FLORIDA STATE UNIVERSITY

TALLAHASSEE, FLORIDA

The University

Florida State University (FSU) is one of the nation's most popular universities, enrolling students from all fifty states and more than 100 countries. Its goals are to give students the best possible education while continuing a program of service to the people of Florida and to the nation. The University strives to maintain an intellectual climate of learning in which students develop respect for and become excited about discovery. Florida State's diverse student population participates in a Liberal Studies Program that has been nationally recognized for its effectiveness in fostering a spirit of free inquiry into human values and for developing strong written analytical skills. The University prides itself on achieving excellence in all pursuits. FSU is home of the National High Magnetic Field Laboratory, the Center for Materials Research and Technology (MARTECH), and other internationally acclaimed research centers. In addition, FSU has the country's newest College of Medicine and the fastest supercomputer in higher education. Florida State University's academic programs are fully accredited by the Southern Association of Colleges and Schools.

Florida State was originally established in 1851 as the Seminary West of the Suwannee. It was the Florida State College for Women from 1909 until 1947, when it became coeducational and was given its present name. Today, Florida State University is a nationally recognized comprehensive, public, coeducational research institution with a strong liberal arts base. Current enrollment is approximately 37,328, which includes 29,297 undergraduates. The average freshman is 18.6 years old; the average undergraduate is 21.2. Minority students make up 23.8 percent of the total undergraduate student population.

FSU's 463-acre main campus is well-designed and compact, making it convenient for students to get to and from classes. About 53 percent of the freshman class lives on campus in one of fourteen residence halls. On-campus housing is available for upperclass and transfer students as well. Students may also live in nearby fraternity and sorority houses or in one of the many scholarship houses surrounding the campus.

Florida State University offers a wide variety of extracurricular activities. Student clubs and organizations range from academic and professional to cultural and special interest, honorary and religious to recreational and athletic, political and theatrical to social and service. FSU has extensive facilities that support student activities and recreation, including a completely equipped University Union, a state-of-the-art Student Recreation Center, and the Seminole Reservation (a lakefront recreation area). Florida State's men's and women's athletic teams compete at the NCAA Division I level and are part of the Atlantic Coast Conference.

Location

Florida State University is nestled in the heart of historic Tallahassee, which is the capital of Florida and home to more than 250,000 residents. Tallahassee is a classic college town and is considered the "other" Florida because of its rolling hills, canopy roads, mild climate, and Southern hospitality.

Majors and Degrees

The College of Arts and Sciences offers baccalaureate programs with majors in actuarial science, American and Florida studies (American studies), anthropology, biochemistry, biological sciences (cell and molecular biology; ecology, evolution, and environmental science; marine biology; physiology and neuroscience; plant sciences; preprofessional health sciences; and zoology), chemical science, chemistry (chemistry and environmental chemistry), classics (classical archaeology, classical civilizations, classics, classics and religion, and Greek and Latin), computer and information science (computer science and software engineering), English (creative writing, English, English/business, linguistics, and literature), French (French, French/business, French and German, French and Italian, French and Russian, and French and Spanish), geology, German (German, German/business, German and Italian, German and Russian, and German and Spanish), Greek, history, humanities (humanities and women's studies), Italian (Italian, Italian/business, Italian and Russian, and Italian and Spanish), Latin, Latin American and Caribbean studies (Latin American and Caribbean studies and Latin American and Caribbean studies/business), mathematics (applied and computational mathematics, biomedical mathematics, and mathematics), meteorology, philosophy, physics, physics-interdisciplinary (physics/biology, physics/biology–premed, physics/biophysics, physics/computer science, physics/education, physics/environmental science, physics/geology, physics/government, physics/health physics, physics/management, physics/music technology, physics/oceanography, and physics/philosophy), psychology, religion (religion and religion and classics), Russian (Russian, Russian/business, and Russian and Spanish), secondary science and/or mathematics teaching, Spanish (Spanish and Spanish/business), and statistics.

The College of Business offers programs in accounting, business administration (business administration and entrepreneurship and small-business management), finance, hospitality administration, (hospitality administration and professional golf management), management (human resource management and management), management information systems, marketing, multinational business (multinational business operations), real estate, and risk management–insurance.

The College of Communication offers programs in communication (advertising, communication studies, general communication, mass media studies, media production, and public relations) and communication sciences and disorders.

The School of Criminology and Criminal Justice offers a program in criminology.

The College of Education offers programs in athletic training/sports medicine, early childhood education, elementary education, emotional disturbances/learning disabilities, English education, health education (community health education and health education), mathematics education (secondary mathematics education and middle grade mathematics education), mental disabilities, multilingual/multicultural education, physical education (physical education and sports management), professional golf management, recreation and leisure services administration, rehabilitation counseling (rehabilitation services), science education, social science education, and visual disabilities.

The College of Engineering offers programs in chemical engineering (bioengineering, biomedical engineering, chemical engineering, environmental engineering, and materials engineering), civil engineering (civil engineering, environmental engineering), computer engineering, electrical engineering, industrial engineering, and mechanical engineering.

The College of Human Sciences offers programs in clothing, textiles, and merchandising (apparel design and technology, clothing and textiles, merchandising, and textiles); family and consumer sciences education; family, child, and consumer sciences (child development; family, child, and consumer sciences; and housing); food and nutrition (dietetics, food and nutrition, and food and nutrition science); and human sciences (athletic training/sports medicine, exercise science, and human sciences).

The School of Information Studies offers a program in information studies.

The School of Motion Picture, Television, and Recording Arts offers a program in motion picture, television, and recording arts.

The School of Music offers programs in music composition, music education (choral music education, instrumental music education, and music education), music history and literature (music history), music–liberal arts (jazz and contemporary media and music–liberal arts), music performance (brass, guitar, harp, harpsichord, music performance, music theater–music, organ, percussion, piano, piano pedagogy, strings, voice, and woodwinds), music theory, and music therapy.

The School of Nursing offers a program in nursing.

The College of Social Sciences offers programs in Asian studies (Asian studies and Asian studies/business), economics (applied economics and economics), geography (environmental studies and geography), international affairs, political science, Russian and East European studies, social science, and sociology.

The School of Social Work offers a program in social work.

The School Theatre offers a program in theater (acting, design/technology, musical theater–theater, and theater).

The School of Visual Arts and Dance offers programs in art education, dance, graphic design, history and criticism of art (art history), interior design, and studio art.

Preprofessional programs are offered in dentistry, law, medicine, the ministry, optometry, pharmacy, physical therapy, and veterinary medicine.

Academic Program

The liberal studies program for undergraduates includes the study of the natural environment; the social sciences; the historical background of present-day civilization; and cultures, past and present, as expressed through language, literature, art, music, and philosophy. Undergraduate students may earn by examination a maximum of 60 of the minimum total 120 semester hours of credit required for graduation. Examinations may include departmental examinations administered by the academic departments in lieu of course work and examinations administered by national testing agencies. To encourage liberal education and to emphasize learning, the University permits limited enrollment in elective courses outside the major and minor fields on a satisfactory/unsatisfactory grading basis.

FSU recognizes scholastic excellence in a number of ways, including the announcement of deans' lists for undergraduates who achieve the required average for their school or college and honors programs for qualified upper-division students and qualified freshmen entering the Division of Undergraduate Studies.

The University seeks to facilitate the transfer of community college students at the upper-division level from public schools in Florida. Most students who earn an Associate in Arts degree from a Florida public institution in a university-parallel program, who have completed the foreign-language requirements, and who are applying for a nonlimited access program are eligible to be admitted to the upper division of Florida State University. In general, transfer credit is allowed for courses completed at all other regionally accredited institutions of higher learning.

Off-Campus Programs

The University maintains cooperative programs with Florida Agricultural and Mechanical University and Tallahassee Community College, both located in Tallahassee. These programs permit students to take courses that are not readily available at the home institution. Students may also study at FSU's international campuses in Italy, England, Spain, or Panama, or participate in summer programs in Costa Rica, Croatia, the Czech Republic, France, Germany, Ghana, Greece, Ireland, Russia, South Africa, South Korea, Switzerland, Trinidad and Tobago, or Vietnam. Participants can choose from a wide variety of liberal arts classes to satisfy graduation requirements while experiencing the rich cultures that these countries have to offer.

Academic Facilities

The Florida State University libraries are home to more than 2.6 million book titles, more than 9 million microforms, approximately 21,598 current serials, and 43,000 sound recordings. The Super FN accelerator plays an important role in the University's long-standing leadership in nuclear research. The Edward Ball Marine Laboratory on the Gulf Coast provides extensive facilities for teaching and research in the marine sciences. The FSU School of Computation Science and Information Technology serves research and training needs of the faculty and students in Florida and offers services to researchers throughout the country. In addition, the National High Magnetic Field Laboratory, which is the only national laboratory in Florida, plays a major role in the advancement of fields such as biology, medicine, physics, chemistry, engineering, superconductivity, and materials science.

Costs

Typically, the basic expenses for one semester in 2003–04 for an undergraduate student living in a University residence and participating in a campus food plan were as follows: a registration fee for Florida residents of $95.32 per credit hour ($462.92 per credit hour for non-Florida residents); books and supplies (estimated), $363; housing in residence halls, $1530–$2320; housing for married students, $320–$557 a month; and food (estimated), $1444–$1976.

Financial Aid

Florida State University believes that the primary purpose of financial assistance is to provide aid to students who, without assistance, would be unable to attend. Thus, financial aid is awarded based on an individual's need and the costs incident to attending the University. The Office of Financial Aid administers money from federal, state, and University sources in the form of loans, grants, scholarships, and part-time employment. Some merit scholarships are available for academically outstanding students.

Faculty

FSU employs 2,119 traditional faculty members, whose academic backgrounds reflect both diversity and quality. Approximately 92 percent of the teaching faculty members hold doctorates or other terminal degrees. Faculty members are expected to demonstrate an effective balance between classroom instruction and research.

Student Government

The student government plays an active and significant role in the development of policy. Elected and appointed officials are involved in all aspects of University life and have budget authority over activity and service fees, which total more than $6 million.

Admission Requirements

Most Florida residents accepted to the University have at least a B+ average in their academic subjects and a combined score of at least 1100 on the SAT I or a composite score of 25 on the ACT. Out-of-state students must meet higher standards. Freshmen must have earned at least 4 units of English, 3 units of mathematics (algebra I and above), 3 units of natural science (at least 2 units with laboratory), 3 units of social science, 2 units of the same foreign language, and 4 units of academic electives. Transfer applicants with fewer than 60 transferable semester hours must meet freshman admission criteria and have a cumulative college grade point average of at least 2.5 (on a 4.0 scale). Transfer applicants with 60 or more transferable semester hours must have a 2.5 minimum cumulative college grade point average unless they will receive an Associate in Arts degree from a Florida public institution immediately prior to transferring. All transfer applicants must have completed the foreign language requirement and submit official transcripts from each institution previously attended. Access to a number of degree programs is limited at the junior year to those students meeting additional criteria. They are programs in the College of Business; College of Communication; College of Education; School of Motion Picture, Television, and Recording Arts; and School of Nursing and the majors in computer science and psychology. Auditions are required for programs in dance, music, and B.F.A. theater.

Application and Information

Office of Admissions
Florida State University
Tallahassee, Florida 32306-2400
Telephone: 850-644-6200
Fax: 850-644-0197
E-mail: admissions@admin.fsu.edu
World Wide Web: http://admissions.fsu.edu

FORDHAM UNIVERSITY

NEW YORK, NEW YORK

The University

Fordham, New York City's Jesuit University, offers a distinctive educational experience that is rooted in the 450-year-old Jesuit tradition of intellectual rigor and personal respect for the individual. The University enrolls approximately 15,000 students, of whom 8,000 are undergraduates.

Fordham has five undergraduate colleges and six graduate schools. In addition to its full-time undergraduate programs, the University offers part-time undergraduate study at Fordham College of Liberal Studies and during two summer sessions.

Fordham College at Rose Hill and the College of Business Administration, located on the Rose Hill campus, are adjacent to the New York Botanical Garden and the Bronx Zoo. Rose Hill is a self-contained 85-acre campus with residential facilities for more than 3,000 students and ample parking for commuters. It is easily accessible by public and private transportation. Fordham also provides an intercampus van service to transport students to and from Manhattan. Fordham College at Lincoln Center is located in midtown Manhattan, overlooking the famous Lincoln Center for the Performing Arts complex. The Lincoln Center campus has a new 850-bed apartment-style residence called McMahon Hall, and is accessible via the West Side Highway and major subway lines.

In July 2002, Fordham added a third residential campus when Marymount College in Tarrytown, New York, consolidated with Fordham to form a new undergraduate college for women. Located in the historic village of Tarrytown and overlooking the Hudson River, the beautiful 25-acre Marymount campus of Fordham University is located just 25 miles north of New York City. Fordham and Marymount have enjoyed a relationship since 1975 when Marymount campus became home to Fordham's Graduate School of Education and Graduate School of Social Service.

The University has an extensive athletics program consisting of twenty-two varsity sports and numerous club and intramural sports. The newly renovated Murphy Field is the heart of intramural and recreational sports at Fordham, hosting softball, soccer, and flag football games. The Vincent T. Lombardi Memorial Center provides sports facilities to the campus for basketball, squash, swimming and diving, tennis, track, and water polo.

Location

As New York City's Jesuit University, Fordham can offer its students the unparalleled cultural, recreational, and academic advantages of one of the world's great cities. More than 2,600 corporations and organizations offer valuable work experience to Fordham interns. The University also provides unusual opportunities for participating in activities of direct service to the city, ranging from small-group community projects to large government-sponsored projects.

Majors and Degrees

Fordham University offers undergraduates more than sixty-five majors. Fordham College at Rose Hill offers programs of study leading to the B.A. or B.S. in African and African-American studies, anthropology, art history, biological sciences, chemistry, classical civilization, classical languages (Latin and Greek), communication and media studies, comparative literature, computer and information sciences, economics, English, fine arts, French language and literature, French studies, general science, German, German studies, history, information systems, international political economy, Italian, Italian studies, Latin American and Latino studies, mathematics, mathematics/economics, medieval studies, Middle East studies, music, philosophy, physics, political science, psychology, religious studies, Russian and East European studies, sociology, Spanish language and literature, Spanish studies, theology, urban studies, and women's studies.

Also at the Rose Hill campus, the College of Business Administration offers programs leading to the B.S. in accounting (public or management), business administration, and management of information and communication systems, with areas of concentration in business economics, finance, human resource management, information and communications systems, management systems, and marketing. The G.L.O.B.E. Program provides business students with an international study option that incorporates course offerings from both Fordham College at Rose Hill and the College of Business Administration.

Special programs at Rose Hill include a cooperative engineering program, double major or individualized majors, interdisciplinary studies, the B.S./M.B.A. program, and honors programs. Preprofessional programs are offered in architecture, dentistry, law, medicine, and veterinary medicine, and a program for teacher certification is offered in elementary and secondary education.

Fordham College at Lincoln Center offers the B.A. in African and African American studies, anthropology, art history, classical civilization, classical languages (Latin and Greek), communication and media studies, comparative literature, computer science, economics, English, French language and literature, French studies, history, information systems, international/intercultural studies, Italian, Italian studies, Latin American and Latino studies, mathematics, mathematics/economics, medieval studies, Middle East studies, natural science, philosophy, political science, psychology, religious studies, social science, social work, sociology, Spanish language and literature, Spanish studies, theater, theology, urban studies, visual arts, and women's studies. Special programs at Fordham College at Lincoln Center include extensive offerings in the performing arts (including a B.F.A. in dance with the Alvin Ailey Dance Company), a cooperative engineering program, creative writing, double major or individualized majors, independent study, and interdisciplinary studies. Preprofessional studies are offered in dentistry, health, and law. A teacher certification program is offered in elementary and secondary education.

Academic Program

Students in all the undergraduate colleges pursue a common core curriculum designed to provide them with the breadth of knowledge that marks the educated person. Drawn from nine disciplines, the core includes the study of philosophy, English composition and literature, history, theology, mathematical reasoning, natural science, social sciences, the fine arts, and foreign language. Business students benefit from the common core as well as from additional business core courses.

Off-Campus Programs

Fordham participates in an exchange program with other major U.S. universities and in special programs that provide opportunities to study abroad at universities in Australia, China, El Salvador, England, Ireland, Italy, Korea, Mexico, Spain, and many other countries. More than 250 Fordham students study abroad each year.

Academic Facilities

The outstanding libraries on the two campuses have combined holdings of more than 1.8 million volumes and 14,000 periodicals. On the Rose Hill campus, the William D. Walsh Family Library, which serves the entire Fordham community, has seating for more than 1,500 and a state-of-the-art Electronic Information Center, as well as media production laboratories, studios, and auditoriums. Students also have access to the vast library facilities of New York City, neighboring universities, and the various specialized collections maintained by numerous local museums and other institutions. Among laboratory facilities utilized by undergraduates are Mulcahy Hall (chemistry), Larkin Hall (biology), and Freeman Hall (physics and biology). The University has more than forty buildings that provide ample space for classrooms, science laboratories, theaters, and athletic facilities.

Costs

At the Rose Hill and Lincoln Center campuses, undergraduate costs for the 2003–04 academic year were $25,395 for tuition and fees and averaged $10,000 for room and board. Residence halls are available at each campus. Chemistry, physics, and biology fees were approximately $50 per laboratory course. Nominally priced meals are available in cafeterias on each campus. Such incidentals as transportation and laundry vary in cost. There is no difference in fees for out-of-state students.

Financial Aid

More than 75 percent of the entering students enroll with aid from Fordham as well as from outside sources. Among the major aid programs are the Federal Pell Grants, Federal Supplemental Educational Opportunity Grants, Federal Perkins Loans, work grants sponsored by both the government and the University, and University grants-in-aid. Outside sources of aid include state scholarships (more than 20,000 are awarded to students entering colleges in New York State each year), the New York State Tuition Assistance Program (TAP), privately sponsored scholarships, state government loan programs, and deferred-payment programs. The University also offers academic scholarships ranging from $7500 to the full cost of tuition and room.

Applicants for aid must submit the Free Application for Federal Student Aid (FAFSA) and the College Scholarship Service PROFILE. Inquiries should be directed to Fordham's Office of Undergraduate Admission or Office of Student Financial Services.

Faculty

The University has a full-time faculty of 601 and a student-faculty ratio of 11:1. Most members of the undergraduate faculty also teach at the graduate level, and 94 percent of the full-time faculty members hold doctoral or other terminal degrees.

Student Government

The traditional student governing body at Fordham has been the United Student Government, composed of undergraduates attending the University.

Admission Requirements

Admission is based on academic performance, class rank (if available), secondary school recommendation, and SAT I or ACT scores. Extracurricular activities and essays are also factors in the evaluation process. Religious preference, physical handicap, race, or ethnic origin are not considered. Out-of-state students are encouraged to apply. More than 57 percent of the students accepted for the freshman class ranked in the top fifth of their secondary school class. The average combined SAT I score for students entering in fall 2003 was approximately 1240. Recommended are 22 high school units, including 4 in English, 3 in mathematics, 3 in science, 2 in social studies, 2 in foreign language, 2 in history, and 6 electives. For regular admission, the SAT I or the ACT should be taken no later than the January preceding entrance. Candidates for early decision should complete the examinations by October of their senior year. The University participates in the College Board's Advanced Placement Program. Personal interviews are not required but may be arranged by contacting the Office of Undergraduate Admission.

Application and Information

Application may be made for either September or January enrollment. The application deadline is February 1 for fall admission. The completed application, the secondary school report, the results of the SAT I or ACT, all financial aid forms, and an application fee of $50 (check or money order made payable to Fordham University) should be submitted by this date. Students are notified beginning March 1. Candidates for early action should apply by November 1 and receive notification by December 25. Transfer students must apply by December 1 for spring admission or by July 1 for fall admission.

For additional details and application forms, students should contact:

Fordham University
Office of Undergraduate Admission
Thebaud Hall
441 East Fordham Road
New York, New York 10458-9993
Telephone: 800-FORDHAM (367-3426) (toll-free)
E-mail: enroll@fordham.edu
World Wide Web: http://www.fordham.edu

The William D. Walsh Family Library at Fordham University.

FORT VALLEY STATE UNIVERSITY

FORT VALLEY, GEORGIA

The University

Fort Valley State University, founded in 1895, is a unit of the University System of Georgia. Located in central Georgia, it is one of two land-grant universities in the state. Since its founding, the University has developed a comprehensive and stimulating curriculum that offers educational experiences in the liberal arts, education, and sciences as well as in selected vocational and technical fields. The student body (1,468 women and 1,069 men) represents more than fifteen states and five countries; the majority of the students come from Georgia. The University's physical facilities range from older buildings constructed by students in the early 1900s to the modern buildings constructed in the 1990s.

There are seventy-three approved organizations on campus through which students are able to make practical application of knowledge gained in the classroom or pursue a personal interest. Opportunities for travel, interaction with students from other colleges and universities, and participation in community affairs provide valuable experiences. Departmental organizations, service organizations, hometown organizations, scholastic honoraries, social fraternities and sororities, special interest organizations, religious organizations, and varsity athletics are among the areas of involvement provided for students.

Graduate degrees are conferred in counseling and guidance, early childhood education, environmental health, mental health counseling, middle grades education, and vocational rehabilitation. A collaborative Ed.D. program with the University of Georgia is also available.

Location

Fort Valley, Georgia, is located 12 miles west of I-75 between Macon and Perry. The area is known throughout the world for its camellias and peaches and pecan industry.

Majors and Degrees

Fort Valley State University awards the undergraduate degrees of Associate of Science, Bachelor of Arts, Bachelor of Science, Bachelor of Business Administration, and Bachelor of Social Work. Majors are offered in accounting, agricultural economics, agricultural education, agricultural engineering technology, animal science, biology, chemistry, commercial design, computer information systems, computer science, criminal justice, early childhood education, economics, electronic engineering technology, elementary education, English, family and consumer sciences/education, food and nutrition, French education, general business, health and physical education, history, infant and child development, management, marketing, mass communication, mathematics, mathematics education, middle grades education, music, music education, ornamental horticulture, physics, plant science, political science, psychology, social work, veterinary technology, and zoology.

Academic Programs

The academic year consists of two 16-week semesters. There are also three- and six-week summer sessions. A full academic load is 12–18 hours. Most courses are offered on a 2- or 3-semester-hour basis.

The foundation upon which all degree programs are built is the core curriculum of the University System of Georgia. Baccalaureate degree candidates must complete 60 hours in this general education program during the freshman and sophomore years in humanities, mathematics and sciences, social sciences, and other major-specific courses. The total number of hours required for graduation varies according to the program; however, most require 120 hours.

Credit may also be obtained through the College-Level Examination Program (CLEP) or through a proficiency examination administered by the department in charge of the discipline involved. A maximum of 30 semester hours of credit by examination may be applied toward graduation requirements.

Off-Campus Programs

Students at Fort Valley State may participate in cooperative training programs with local agencies and industries and receive up to 3 credit hours per semester for co-op experience or a maximum of 12 hours for the total program.

In addition, students may enroll in courses at Macon, Dublin, and Robins Residence Center, which operates as an educational consortium and offers courses to academically qualified military and civilian employees of Robins Air Force Base. As a part of this center, Fort Valley State University offers academic programs leading to the Associate of Science and Bachelor of Science degrees in electronic engineering technology and computer science.

Academic Facilities

The Henry Alexander Hunt Library/Learning Resources Center is the chief information/support services facility on campus. Located centrally to all dormitories and classrooms, it has a seating capacity of 625, open stacks, computers for word processing, and a 24-hour study room. The center, which includes the Curriculum Materials Center and Media Services, has approximately 190,062 volumes, 1,213 current periodical subscriptions, 50 newspaper subscriptions, CD-ROM computer workstations to access bibliographic information, a black heritage archival collection, and a growing video collection. The staff offers students point-of-use reference experiences, bibliographic instruction, and online capabilities for accessing databases for interlibrary loan.

Costs

In 2003–04, tuition was $2212 for state residents and $8848 for nonresidents.

Financial Aid

Almost 95 percent of all Fort Valley State University students receive financial aid through federal and state grants. Aid includes Federal Pell Grants, Hope Grants, Federal Supplemental Educational Opportunity Grants, Federal Perkins Loans, Federal Stafford Student Loans, Federal Work-Study awards, Georgia Incentive Grants, Georgia Higher Education Assistance Corporation awards, and work opportunities provided by the University. Presidential Scholarships are available to Georgia residents who demonstrate outstanding scholarship. CDEP scholarships are available to students in engineering, math, and geophysics. Students requesting financial aid are required to file the appropriate forms by April 15. Further information may be obtained from the Financial Aid Office.

Faculty

Fort Valley State University has a full-time faculty of 105 members and 9 part-time members, 70 percent of whom hold an earned doctorate.

Student Government

The Student Government Association (SGA) of Fort Valley State University is the official body through which students participate in the creation and administration of the policies and regulations by which they are governed. The SGA is the organization through which students make known their needs and wishes on all matters of concern to them. The SGA recommends students to serve on all student-faculty committees, the channels through which policy is formally initiated.

Admission Requirements

All applicants are required to present acceptable scores on the SAT I or ACT. A transcript of high school credits from an accredited secondary school or a high school equivalency certificate is required. In addition to meeting regular admission requirements, transfer students must submit transcripts of all college-level work.

Students may apply for temporary enrollment as transient students at Fort Valley State University. A statement of permission to enroll as a transient student must be obtained from the Registrar or dean of a student's home institution and submitted to the registrar at least ten work days prior to the beginning of the semester in which the student wishes to enroll.

Application and Information

All applications for admission should be received at least ten work days prior to the beginning of the semester in which the applicant wishes to enroll. A $20 application fee is required.

Office of Admissions and Enrollment Management
Fort Valley State University
Fort Valley, Georgia 31030
Telephone: 478-825-6307
877-462-3878 (toll-free in Georgia)
E-mail: admissap@mail.fvsu.edu
World Wide Web: http://www.fvsu.edu

The C. W. Pettigrew Farm and Community Life Center.

FRAMINGHAM STATE COLLEGE

FRAMINGHAM, MASSACHUSETTS

The College

Founded in 1839 as the first public college in the United States for the education of teachers, Framingham State College has a well-established tradition of academic excellence. Students discover a challenging curriculum firmly based in the liberal arts tradition, combined with many exceptional social and cocurricular activities designed to enhance their educational experience. Today, Framingham State College is known for its emphasis on undergraduate education and its commitment to "university learning in a college environment." It has become a comprehensive arts and science college with several career-related majors that serve an enrollment of more than 6,000 full- and part-time students. Forty percent of day-division students live on campus. Students of color represent 10 percent of the student body, while students over the age of 25 represent 17 percent of the undergraduates.

Framingham State College offers residential housing to 1,400 students in seven residence halls: five coed and two all-women. Resident students are required to purchase either a ten-, fourteen-, or nineteen-meal-per-week plan. Both the resident and commuter cafeterias are located in the D. Justin McCarthy College Center, the hub of all student activities. The College Center is the home for the campus art gallery, game room, meeting rooms, pub, radio station, college newspaper, club and organization offices, and offices for student services and student activities.

The Student Union Activities Board (SUAB) is one of the largest and most active clubs on campus. It plans the majority of campus events. There are several different committees, each with its own programming purpose, including concerts, films, special social programs, and travel and recreation. They have sponsored major concerts, dances, lectures, films, spring break events, cultural activities, and much more. SUAB also sponsors the Fall Street Fair and Spring Sandbox Weekend.

The College competes on the NCAA Division III level in a number of intercollegiate sports for men and women, including baseball, basketball, cross-country, field hockey, football, ice hockey, soccer, softball, and volleyball. A number of intramural sports are also offered. Several club sports are offered, including cheerleading, equestrian, and rugby. A state-of-the-art 65,000-square-foot athletic facility opened in 2001.

Location

Located in Framingham, the largest town in Massachusetts with a population of 68,000, Framingham State College is situated 20 miles west of Boston and is accessible from all major highways (Exit 12 on I-90, the Massachusetts Turnpike). Public transportation on both train and bus lines is readily available. The 73-acre campus is in a prime residential location, offering students a small to medium-sized suburban campus with access to the cultural, social, and educational opportunities of Boston and the New England region.

Majors and Degrees

Framingham State College confers the Bachelor of Arts and Bachelor of Science degrees. Undergraduate majors are offered in art history, biology, business administration, chemistry, communication arts, computer science, early childhood education, economics, elementary education, English, fashion design and retailing, food and nutrition, food science, French, geography, health and consumer sciences, history, mathematics, nursing (post-RN program), politics, pre-engineering, psychology, sociology, Spanish, and studio art. Within the twenty-five major programs are a variety of concentrations and minors. The following preprofessional programs are also offered: dental, law, medical, and veterinary.

Academic Programs

The mission of Framingham State College is to offer a dynamic and affordable program of educational excellence to its students. The College emphasizes a broadly based curriculum that blends the liberal arts and sciences with several professional fields.

Each student must satisfy a thirty-two-course requirement for completion of any degree program. Up to twenty courses form the basis of a student's major area of study. The other twelve courses are used to fulfill the general education requirement, which encompasses the humanities, social sciences, natural and physical sciences, mathematics, and computer science. The general education requirement ensures that students experience the benefits of a liberal arts education through familiarity with a variety of curricula. Each student is assigned a faculty member in his or her major as an academic adviser. Undeclared students are assigned advisers through the Center for Academic Support and Advising (CASA). Selected students may participate in departmental and College-wide honors programs.

The College operates on the traditional two-semester calendar, with two optional summer sessions as well as a winter intersession.

Off-Campus Programs

Framingham State College students may choose to participate in one or several College-affiliated programs, allowing them to take credit-bearing courses outside of the College. Among the most popular are internships, the CAPS (College Academic Program Sharing) program, the Massachusetts Bay Marine Studies Consortium, the Washington (D.C.) Internship, and study abroad.

Internships are available in most majors at the College. Annually, hundreds of FSC students serve as interns in the State House, town and city governments, museums, and a variety of businesses and high-technology firms in the greater Boston area. Internships allow students the opportunity to gain direct, practical experience while applying the knowledge and skills they have acquired in the classroom.

Through the CAPS program, Framingham State College students may take up to 30 semester hours of college credit at one of the other eight Massachusetts state colleges. Students who participate in the Massachusetts Bay Marine Studies Consortium may also attend a variety of credit-bearing classes and symposia at other schools.

For those students who seek an international dimension to enhance their undergraduate program, study abroad for a summer, semester, or academic year is an option. In the past, students have studied in Canada, England, France, Ireland, Italy, Mexico, New Zealand, and Spain.

Academic Facilities

The Henry Whittemore Library houses 200,000 bound volumes, 627,000 volume equivalents in microforms, and 409 current periodicals in subscriptions. Electronic databases supplement the library's in-house journal collection, and students have access to a variety of materials shared within the Minuteman Library Network. The College provides extensive computing capabilities for its students. The primary delivery vehicle is a LAN of nearly 100 486DX personal computers running under Novell NetWare version 3.12. The file server for the LAN is capable of storing 2 gigabytes of data. To ensure high availability, the server's disk drives are mirrored and the disk controllers duplexed. All workstations contain 8 megabytes of RAM and are Windows capable. Academic departments have computer systems and software available to their students.

A child-care center, planetarium, and greenhouse, housed in Hemenway Hall, provide students with the opportunity to gain practical experience in related studies. Likewise, the radio station and television studios serve as forums to apply textbook knowledge.

The Challenger Learning Center, established in memory of Christa Corrigan McAuliffe, the nation's first teacher astronaut and a 1970 graduate of the College, is located on campus. The Center provides a unique hands-on learning experience designed to foster interest in mathematics, science, and technology.

Costs

Tuition and fees for the 2002–03 academic year were $3420 for in-state students and $9500 for out-of-state students. Yearly residence hall charges were $2835, and the yearly meal plan was $1816. Students should anticipate additional expenses for books, supplies, transportation, and personal items. All costs are subject to change.

Financial Aid

Sources of financial aid available to Framingham State College students include federal, state, and institutional programs. Framingham State College students were the recipients of more than $10 million last year in loans, scholarships, grants, and work-study.

Federal programs include the Federal Work-Study Program, the Federal Pell Grant, Federal Supplemental Educational Opportunity Grant, the Federal Perkins Loan, and both subsidized and unsubsidized Federal Stafford Student Loans. State-funded aid includes state scholarship grants and a no-interest loan program. Institutional funds mainly provide scholarships.

All students applying for financial aid must file the Free Application for Federal Student Aid (FAFSA), designating Framingham State College as the recipient. Transfer students must submit financial aid transcripts documenting all previous aid received. The priority filing deadline for fall entrance is March 1.

Faculty

There are more than 165 full-time faculty members, all of whom are dedicated to upholding the undergraduate mission of the College. More than 70 percent of them hold the doctoral degree in their field. The active involvement of many professors in research and writing complements their primary commitment and dedication to teaching excellence at the undergraduate level. With an impressive student-faculty ratio of 15:1, Framingham is able to offer a variety of programs in a challenging academic atmosphere.

Student Government

The Student Government Association (SGA) is the center of all political and social activity of the students of Framingham State College. The primary duties of SGA are to provide funding for more than thirty organizations through the student activity fee, to ensure representation of the Framingham State College students in the state student organization, and to act on all other matters that concern the students of the College. SGA also plays a major role in the formulation of College policies, which are of mutual concern to the students, the faculty, and the administration, through the All College Governance system. All students who pay activity fees are eligible to seek one of the many positions within SGA and are encouraged to do so.

Admission Requirements

Framingham State College seeks to enroll students with a strong academic background who possess the necessary skills to succeed in college. Admission decisions are based primarily on the strength of the high school record and test scores. Secondary school students are required to pass 16 college-preparatory units: 4 years of English; 3 years of math, including algebra I and II and geometry; 3 years of science, including 2 years of laboratory science; 2 years of history/social science, including 1 year of U.S. history; 2 years of the same foreign language; and two college-preparatory-level electives. High school students are encouraged to elect additional courses in music, art, and computer science.

Students in the upper 50 percent of their class with a B average or higher are encouraged to apply. Recommendations, essays, and personal statements are not required but may be submitted as part of the applicant's materials. International and transfer students, as well as adults returning to college (ARC), are also encouraged to apply.

To be considered for admission to a degree program at the College, all applicants must submit a completed application along with the application fee, an official high school transcript, and official SAT I scores. Transfer students must submit official transcripts from all colleges previously attended.

Application and Information

It is recommended that students apply by the priority filing date of February 15 for fall admission and December 1 for spring admission. Interviews are not required, but students are encouraged to attend an admissions information session and tour. The information sessions are presented by a member of the admissions staff and are followed by a tour of the campus conducted by a student admissions representative. Students should call the Office of Admissions to arrange an appointment.

For further information and application materials or to schedule a campus visit, students should contact:

Office of Admissions
Framingham State College
100 State Street
P.O. Box 9101
Framingham, Massachusetts 01701-9101
Telephone: 508-626-4500
E-mail: admiss@frc.mass.edu
World Wide Web: http://www.framingham.edu

FRANCISCAN UNIVERSITY OF STEUBENVILLE

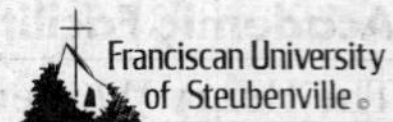

STEUBENVILLE, OHIO

The University

From unassuming beginnings as a college for World War II veterans, Franciscan University of Steubenville today is a prominent example of the renaissance underway in Catholic higher education. Operated by the Franciscan Friars of the Third Order Regular, the University attracts students from all fifty states and twenty-six countries. The University is listed in all six editions of Barron's *Best Buys in College Education* and ranked in the top tier in its division in the *2003 U.S. News & World Report's* list of America's Best Colleges. The school offers more than thirty undergraduate programs, including eight preprofessional programs, such as predentistry and premedicine, and seven graduate programs. Despite the recent enrollment growth to more than 2,200, the University maintains a low 14:1 student-faculty ratio, allowing for plenty of personal attention and direction.

The newest building on campus, Saints Cosmas and Damian Science Hall, has been a boon to science and math majors, while expanded facilities for the Nursing Program and a new legal studies major opens doors to careers in the medical and legal professions. And, as they have since 1991, students eagerly sign up to spend a semester abroad, studying and living in a renovated fourteenth-century monastery near the Austrian Alps.

The heart of the Franciscan University experience, however, is found in its mission to prepare the next generation of Catholic leaders—for business, society, home, and church life. Toward this goal, the University offers a wide range of programs within and outside the classroom.

Franciscan University sponsors the nation's only human life studies minor, which teaches students to think, speak, and act intelligently on human life issues. It also offers a unique humanities and Catholic culture major and a challenging Great Books Honors Program that introduces students to the most important writings of Western civilization. The combined religious education and theology programs are the largest in the country, allowing students to learn from professors whose writings and presentations on the Catholic faith are known worldwide.

Faith households, small groups of students whose members support, recreate, and pray with one another, break through the isolation that frequently permeates dorm life. Up to 600 students join households that foster Christian values and development of positive peer pressure. The campus is also known for its vibrant liturgies and strong turnout for retreats and spiritual talks. Hundreds make a weekly commitment to Eucharistic adoration, and most masses have standing room only, even on week days.

The popular Works of Mercy Program places students shoulder-to-shoulder with the poor and marginalized in inner city and rural communities. Many students join the pro-life group, Students for Life, while others sign up for evangelization and Christian outreach activities spearheaded by the Student Life Office, households, and other campus groups. A wide range of student-run academic clubs and a thriving athletic program that offers intramural sports, recreational sports, and outdoor adventures for every athletic ability round out a Franciscan education.

This combination of rigorous academics, Christ-centered social activities, and dynamic spirituality has earned Franciscan University high praise from church leaders and educators. The Templeton Foundation's Honor Roll for Character-Building Colleges describes Franciscan University as "a liberal arts school where faith and reason are allies, not enemies."

Location

Located on 123 acres of rolling hills overlooking the Ohio River, Franciscan University is an hour's drive west of Pittsburgh and 2½ hours south of Cleveland. Steubenville is a small urban community of 22,000. Because of the town's proximity to metropolitan areas, students have the advantages of a large city as well as the atmosphere of a small community.

Majors and Degrees

Franciscan University of Steubenville grants the Bachelor of Arts degree in biology, chemistry, classics, communication arts (journalism and TV/radio), economics, English (drama, British and American literature, Western and world literature, and writing), French, German, history, humanities and Catholic culture, legal studies, philosophy, political science, psychology, religious education, sociology, Spanish, and theology. The Bachelor of Science degree is granted in accounting, anthropology, biology, business administration (economics, finance, management, and marketing), computer information science, computer science, education (with twenty different licensure programs), engineering science, mathematical science, mental health and human services, nursing, and social work. Associate degrees are awarded in accounting, business administration, child development, general studies, and theology. Minors are offered in Franciscan studies, human life studies, and music. The special honors program in the Great Books of Western Civilization is offered to highly qualified candidates.

The University also offers a Master of Arts in Counseling, Master of Arts in Philosophy, Master of Arts in Theology and Christian Ministry, Master of Business Administration, Master of Science in Education, Master of Science in Educational Administration, and Master of Science in Nursing. The M.A. in Theology and Christian Ministry can be earned through the Distance Learning Program, with most courses available via audiotaped lectures. For undergraduate business majors, a 4+1 program allows for accelerated completion of an MBA.

The University offers the following preprofessional programs: dentistry, law, medicine, occupational therapy, optometry, pharmacy, physical therapy, and veterinary medicine. In addition, the University's Pre-Theologate Program is one of the few of its kind in the nation, offering a community of prayer, support, and study for men discerning the priesthood.

Academic Program

The academic curriculum is divided into three main categories: The Major Program, the student's area of specialization, consists of introductory courses and a minimum of 24 credit hours in upper-level courses. Grounded in the teachings of the Catholic Church and drawing upon important Franciscan themes and values, the Core Program exposes students to different points of view; challenges them to rethink their positions on questions of values, religion, society, nature, and self; and enables them to communicate their thoughts, beliefs, questions, and opinions effectively. Elective courses, the third main category, permit students to sample courses of their own interests that may complement their major or prepare them for alternative careers.

Students need a total of 124 credits for graduation. The number of electives varies with each major program. The University operates on the semester system. Three summer sessions also are available.

Many students select courses that fulfill requirements in a second field for a minor or double major. Internships in many majors provide hands-on field experience and give students a distinct advantage when seeking employment. Franciscan University of Steubenville participates in the Advanced Placement and College-Level Examination programs and gives credit by examination in a number of subjects.

Off-Campus Arrangements

A highlight of the Franciscan University experience for many is the "life-changing" semester spent at the University's program in Gaming, Austria. Located in a renovated fourteenth-century monastery in the foothills of the Austrian Alps, the Austrian Program features a four-day class schedule, so students may spend extended time visiting religious shrines and cultural and historical sites throughout Europe. The program also includes a pilgrimage to Rome and Assisi.

Academic Facilities

With its inviting design and spacious views, the John Paul II Library is the center of academic life on campus. The library's collection includes nearly 230,000 books, 30,000 bound periodicals, and more than 700 current periodicals. The OPAL Catalog and OhioLINK Network provide access to countless Web sites and databases and more than 7 million books and journals.

Egan Hall houses classrooms; a theater; television and radio studios; special laboratories for the education, computer science, and psychology departments; and computer workstations on each floor. In the newly remodeled nursing wing, a simulated clinic gives nursing students the opportunity to practice their skills.

Franciscan University opened Saints Cosmas and Damian Science Hall, an $11-million state-of-the-art science building, in fall 2000. This 43,000-square-foot, four-story campus addition contains extensive classroom and laboratory space for the departments of biology, chemistry, physics, and engineering science; and computer science and mathematical science. It has enormously enhanced the University's ability to give students the first-class education they need to thrive in the highly sophisticated and increasingly complex scientific fields.

Costs

For the 2003–04 academic year, tuition and fees for full-time students were $14,670. Room and board costs were $5250.

Financial Aid

Through a combination of grants, scholarships, loans, and student-worker opportunities, 85 percent of the students receive financial aid. Aid is offered to needy students as well as to students with high academic achievements. The goal is to provide maximum financial aid from federal, state, private, and institutional sources.

Faculty

There are full-time and part-time faculty members, both lay and religious, who make personal attention the rule rather than the exception. The student-faculty ratio is 14:1. Professors—not teaching assistants—teach at all class levels. Professors of all disciplines are committed to presenting Christian truths based on the teachings of the Roman Catholic Church and often present their material within a Catholic perspective.

Student Government

The heart of student participation in the decision-making process of the University is in the Franciscan University Student Association. The Student Activities Board, along with related groups, provides social and cultural activities. Chapel Ministry addresses pastoral concerns involved in meeting students' spiritual needs.

Admission Requirements

The University has a rolling admission policy. The application deadline for fall resident student enrollment is June 1. No single factor determines admission. The decision is based on a satisfactory high school record and recommendation and satisfactory entrance examination scores (SAT I or ACT), all in relation to the student's proposed major.

A student must present a minimum of 15 high school units, with at least 10 units in four of the following fields: English, foreign language, social science, mathematics, and natural sciences. The remaining 5 units may be in other subjects counted toward graduation. Students applying for admission with a major in chemistry, engineering science, or mathematical sciences should have 2 units in algebra and 2 units in geometry and trigonometry combined.

Transfer students must also submit a transcript from every college previously attended; once accepted, they may request preliminary evaluations of these transcripts. Full credit is given for courses transferred from an approved institution, provided the grade for each course is a C or better. No correspondence courses are accepted, but a maximum of 30 credits is allowed for extension work from an approved institution.

Application and Information

Prospective students are encouraged to apply as early as possible. Applicants must submit a completed application with the $20 application fee, official high school (and previous college) transcripts, and scores on the SAT I or ACT (which may be included on the high school transcript).

More information about Franciscan University of Steubenville is available by contacting:

Director of Admissions
Franciscan University of Steubenville
1235 University Boulevard
Steubenville, Ohio 43952
Telephone: 740-283-6226
800-783-6220 (toll-free)
E-mail: admissions@franciscan.edu
World Wide Web: http://www.franciscan/admissions.edu

Students at Franciscan University of Steubenville.

FRANCIS MARION UNIVERSITY

FLORENCE, SOUTH CAROLINA

The University

Francis Marion University (FMU), established by the South Carolina legislature in 1970, is a public four-year coeducational comprehensive institution with a growing number of graduate programs. Named for one of South Carolina's greatest heroes, General Francis Marion of Revolutionary War fame, the University has shown the same qualities of strength attributed to the patriot general.

The institution believes that all qualified South Carolina students and a number of out-of-state and international students should have the privilege of formal academic university training at Francis Marion University at a level consistent with their talents. This belief is the basis of the University's intention to attract students with a wide range of abilities and preparation and to provide them with academic experience that will permit them to contribute to the well-being of their community, state, and nation. To achieve these ends, Francis Marion offers numerous programs of study in the liberal arts and professional programs in education, business, the sciences, and technology. Although the teaching mission of Francis Marion University is paramount, research programs are also supported in order to sustain faculty vigor and to enhance the quality of teaching. Much of the University's research is related to faculty development.

Francis Marion is accredited by the Commission on Colleges of the Southern Association of Colleges and Schools (SACS) to award bachelor's and master's degrees. The business programs are accredited by AACSB International–The Association to Advance Collegiate Schools of Business. The teacher education programs of the University are accredited by the National Council for Accreditation of Teacher Education (NCATE) and approved by the South Carolina State Board of Education under standards developed by the National Association of State Directors of Teacher Education and Certification (NASDTEC). The chemistry program is approved by the Committee on Professional Training of the American Chemical Society. The graduate psychology program is accredited by the Masters in Psychology Accreditation Council (MPAC) and meets the standards of training approved by the Council of Applied Master's Programs in Psychology (CAMPP). The Master of Science in Applied Psychology Program is accredited by the Interorganizational Board for Accreditation of Master's in Psychology Programs (IBAMPP). The theater arts program is accredited by the National Association of Schools of Theatre (NAST), and the visual arts and art education programs are accredited by the National Association of Schools of Art and Design (NASAD). The University is approved by the South Carolina State Board of Education and is a member of the American Council on Education and the American Association of State Colleges and Universities.

The Francis Marion athletics program is a member of the NCAA Division II Peach Belt Conference, which consists of twelve member schools in Florida, Georgia, North Carolina, and South Carolina. The school sponsors seven intercollegiate men's sports (baseball, basketball, cross-country, golf, soccer, tennis, and track and field) and seven women's sports (basketball, cross-country, soccer, softball, tennis, track and field, and volleyball.) In addition to a 3,027-seat gymnasium, the Smith University Center houses an eight-lane pool, racquetball and handball courts, a fitness room, lockers and showers, a sauna, the University Center Cafe, a television lounge, and the Patriot Bookstore.

Students are informed through the campus newspaper, animated electronic signboards, a cable public-access channel, and a travelers' information radio station operated by the University. The institution also provides artistic, scientific, and literary programs for the public, both on campus and in the various communities the University serves.

Graduate degrees are offered in business administration, education, and applied psychology. The Medical School of South Carolina (MUSC) joins with the FMU School of Business to offer the Master of Business Administration degree with a concentration in health management.

Location

Located on a 300-acre tract of land originally included in a grant by the King of England and later made a cotton plantation, Francis Marion University is situated 7 miles east of Florence in the beautiful northeastern section of South Carolina. The University is located on U.S. Highways 76 and 301 and is just an hour's drive from Myrtle Beach and the Grand Strand and 4 hours from the Blue Ridge Mountains. With a metropolitan-area population of 125,000, the city of Florence is nestled alongside Interstate Highway 95, the main north-south corridor from the New England area to Miami, and at the eastern end of Interstate Highway 20. The city is served by Amtrak, bus service, and a regional airport.

Majors and Degrees

Francis Marion University offers four undergraduate degrees: Bachelor of Arts, Bachelor of Business Administration, Bachelor of General Studies, and Bachelor of Science.

More than thirty areas of study are available, including majors, cooperative programs with other institutions, and pre-professional programs. Students can choose to major in accounting, art education, biology, business economics, chemistry, computer science, criminal justice (concentration), early childhood education, economics, elementary education, English, finance, French, general business administration, German, history, international studies, management, management information systems, marketing, mass communication, mathematics, physics, political science, psychology, sociology, Spanish, theater arts, and visual arts. Students majoring in biology, chemistry, English, French, German, history, mathematics, political science, sociology, and Spanish may choose the teacher certification option in these areas. The MUSC satellite nursing program at FMU offers a bachelor's degree in nursing.

Academic Programs

The usual course load for Francis Marion University students is 15 to 17 hours per semester. The University offers four undergraduate degrees, each of which requires a minimum of 120 semester hours of approved credit. This includes those hours required for completion of the General Education Program and those required for majoring in a particular area or areas of concentration. To meet the special needs of students with superior academic ability, the University has an honors program, which is implemented through honors sections of regular courses; an interdisciplinary honors colloquium; and an honors independent study. Incoming freshmen are encouraged to take the Freshman Seminar course, an introduction to college life and the opportunities available at FMU.

The fall academic semester begins in late August and continues through early December. The spring semester begins in early January and runs through the end of April. A three-week late spring term is available for students to take one course. The University also offers two 5-week summer terms, one from early June through early July; the other from mid-July through mid-August.

The University gives credit for courses in which College Entrance Examination Board Advanced Placement Examinations have been given and in which appropriate levels of competence have been demonstrated. The score necessary for credit for a particular course is determined cooperatively by the Advanced Placement Committee of the University and the appropriate department or school.

Academic Facilities

The University's physical plant includes nine major buildings: J. Howard Stokes Administration Building, James A. Rogers Library, Robert E. McNair Science Building, Hugh K. Leatherman Sr. Science Facility, Walter Douglas Smith University Center, Founders Hall, John K. Cauthen Educational Media Center, Peter D. Hyman Fine Arts Center, and the Thomas C. Stanton Academic Computer Center. Francis Marion is also home to a two-story observatory, equipped with a 14-inch reflecting telescope, and a planetarium that offers public shows twice monthly.

Costs

In the 2004–05 academic year, tuition and other required fees for the regular academic year are $5082 for in-state undergraduate students and $10,029 for out-of-state undergraduate students. Housing fees per year are $2092 for a 4-person four-bedroom apartment, $2214 for a 2-person one-bedroom apartment, and $4282 for a 2-person dormitory room (including a meal plan). Private rooms are offered on a space-available basis at an additional cost. These figures do not include the cost of books and miscellaneous expenses and are subject to change.

Financial Aid

The University administers a variety of scholarship, grant, loan, and work programs. Presidential Scholarships, Francis Marion Scholarships, and Francis Marion Academic Excellence Scholarships in varying amounts are made possible by numerous organizations and individuals. Federal Pell Grants, Federal Supplemental Educational Opportunity Grants, Federal Perkins Loans, Federal Stafford Student Loans, Federal Work-Study Program, South Carolina Need-Based Grants, South Carolina Teacher Loans, and institutional work-study programs are also available.

Students must complete and file the Free Application for Federal Student Aid (FAFSA) as soon as possible after January 1 of the year in which they want to receive fall semester financial assistance. The FAFSA is required for most types of financial assistance and is available from high school counselors and the FMU Office of Financial Assistance after January 1. Priority processing is given to students who file prior to March 1. To be considered for an institutional scholarship, the FMU Application for Institutional Scholarship must be submitted to the Office of Financial Assistance by March 1, and students are encouraged to file a FAFSA.

Faculty

Francis Marion University employs 165 full-time faculty members, about 84 percent of whom hold doctoral degrees, and 42 part-time faculty members. The average class size is 20 students. All students are assigned a faculty adviser (in their curriculum) to assist them with class scheduling and academic planning.

Student Government

Upon enrollment, all full-time students automatically become members of the Student Government Association, the organization that represents all students in planning, organizing, and directing the student organizations and programs on campus. The Student Government Association consists of an executive council, a senate, and a judicial council and provides an early experience in self-government, which, in turn, serves as a useful background for later public service. The Student Government Association jointly participates with faculty members and the administration in certain designated areas of governance of the University.

Admission Requirements

Francis Marion University encourages all qualified students to apply. Equal educational opportunities are offered to students regardless of race, sex, religion, color, or national origin. Incoming freshmen are required to have a high school diploma or its equivalent and a satisfactory high school record, including completion of the following college preparatory courses: English (4 courses), mathematics (3), laboratory science (3), foreign language (2 of the same language), physical education or ROTC (1), social studies (3, including 1 unit of United States history), and academic electives (4). Applicants must also have satisfactory scores on the SAT I or the ACT, proper completion of all application material, and a recommendation from their high school. Transfer students must present proof of eligibility to return to the last school attended, satisfactory grades on all academic work attempted at previous institutions, and SAT I or ACT scores applicable to entering freshmen at the time of transfer. All international student applicants must meet regular admission requirements and must submit satisfactory scores on the TOEFL (Test of English as a Foreign Language) and verification that adequate financial resources are available for expenses while attending the institution. Francis Marion also offers admission for one or more courses to high school students of exceptional ability.

Although interviews are not required for admission, prospective students are encouraged to arrange a visit and tour of the campus by contacting the Office of Admissions. Tours are conducted Monday through Friday at 11:30 a.m. and 1:30 p.m. and at 10 a.m. on the second and fourth Saturdays of each month by appointment. The University holds open house programs for high school juniors and seniors in the fall and the spring. All new students are required to attend an orientation session prior to registering for classes.

Application and Information

Prospective students are required to take the SAT I or ACT (and request that the score be sent to Francis Marion University) and to complete and return to the Office of Admissions an application form with the $30 nonrefundable application fee. They should request that their high school principal or guidance counselor send a transcript of their high school record through their junior year, their class rank, courses enrolled in as a senior, and an evaluation and recommendation.

Application forms and other information about Francis Marion University may be obtained by contacting:

Office of Admissions
Francis Marion University
P.O. Box 100547
Florence, South Carolina 29501-0547

Telephone: 843-661-1231
800-368-7551 (toll-free)
Fax: 843-661-4635
E-mail: admissions@fmarion.edu
World Wide Web: http://www.admissions.fmarion.edu

FRANKLIN COLLEGE

FRANKLIN, INDIANA

The College

Founded in 1834 as one of Indiana's first and finest coeducational liberal arts institutions, Franklin College has a long tradition of excellence in education, leadership, and professional preparation. A Franklin education revolves around the broad goal of achieving wealth of mind, health of body, and strength of character while developing sensitivity to others through close personal relationships with classmates and faculty members. Franklin's commitment together with the faculty's support for this focus on leadership and professional development, curriculum, and internship programs support this goal. While the majority of more than 1,000 students come from Indiana, many other states and countries are represented. Seven residence halls provide a variety of living arrangements on the Franklin College campus.

The 105-acre campus currently includes seventeen buildings and the houses of four national fraternities. The Student Entertainment Board (SEB) is responsible for scheduling campuswide social events. The Eli Lilly Campus Center, with its student lounge, recreation room, snack shop, bookstore, and campus dining facility, serves as a center for numerous student activities. Franklin College sponsors more than seventy academic, social, and religious extracurricular groups. Additional campus involvement includes intercollegiate athletic competition at the NCAA Division III level for both men and women. Involvement in many activities enhances a student's personal growth and fulfills the "Franklin College Experience."

Location

An excellent relationship exists between the city of Franklin (population 15,000) and the College. The campus is a 20-minute drive south of downtown Indianapolis. The Indianapolis International Airport is a 25-minute drive from Franklin.

Majors and Degrees

Franklin College confers the Bachelor of Arts degree in the following areas: accounting, American studies, athletic training, biology, business (finance, general, international business, management/industrial relations, and marketing), Canadian studies, chemistry, computing/computer information systems, economics, education (elementary, middle school, and secondary), English, French, history, journalism (advertising/public relations, broadcasting, news-editorial, and visual communications), mathematics, philosophy, physical education, political science, psychology, religious studies, sociology (criminal justice and social work), Spanish, and theater. Minors are also offered in many of these areas and in fine arts and physics.

Students considering a career in dentistry, forestry, medical technology, medicine, nursing, optometry, or veterinary medicine arrange their program with the advice of the preprofessional advisor of the science division. Students seeking a career in law plan their program in consultation with pre-law advisors. Students planning a career in secondary education may elect an academic area of concentration that will satisfy the state requirements for a teaching major. The education department is endorsed and approved by the Indiana Professional Standards Board and the National Council for Accreditation of Teacher Education (NCATE).

Franklin College offers cooperative programming in various areas of study. A combined-degree program in medical technology is offered in cooperation with two nearby hospitals. A combined B.S. degree in nursing is available through a cooperative arrangement with Rush University, a combined B.S. and graduate degree program in public health is available through the University of South Florida, and a combined B.S. and graduate degree program in environmental studies and forestry is available through Duke University.

Academic Programs

The current academic program is the result of the faculty's plan to meet the express needs of students; the primary emphasis is on the unity of knowledge. Franklin believes in the importance of providing students with a liberal arts background while they develop talents for a particular professional career. Approximately one third of each student's total course work is composed of the prescribed and exploratory courses that make up the general education core curriculum.

All of Franklin's academic departments offer individualized study, allowing a student to pursue his or her field of interest in depth.

As part of the 4-1-4 calendar, students complete up to 8 hours of credit in a special four-week winter-term program in January. The winter term is designed to allow students to study in areas of particular interest to them, either within or outside their major field of study. A large number of internships are available during the winter term and the summer, offering practical experience under the supervision of a professional. The fall semester ends before Christmas; the spring semester begins in February and ends in May. An eight-week summer session beginning in mid-June allows students to take up to 9 additional credit hours.

Franklin gives credit in seventeen academic areas for successful scores on CLEP subject examinations; credit is also granted for successful scores on the Advanced Placement tests of the College Board. The Running Start Program enables talented high school students to get an early start on their college education.

Off-Campus Programs

Franklin College students participate in a variety of off-campus study experiences, including a year or a semester of study through Acadia University of Nova Scotia, Telemark University of Norway, and Hong Kong Baptist University. Other off-campus study programs include the American University Washington Semester; a junior year abroad; programs at Harlaxton College in England, Franklin College of Switzerland, and Brethren Colleges Abroad; and specific exchange programs in Japan and Taiwan.

Academic Facilities

Franklin College has two campus buildings listed on the National Historic Register. Old Main, the original home of the College, and Shirk Hall, home of the Pulliam School of Journalism, are footholds of the rich past and recent renovation of the Franklin College campus. Classrooms and administrative, business, and professorial offices, along with computer laboratories, occupy Old Main; Shirk Hall also houses classrooms and the radio and television stations.

A. A. Barnes Science Building houses all physics, biology, and chemistry department classrooms and laboratories. The Spurlock Center gymnasium and fitness center provides increased classroom and office space and weight room.

The Dietz Center for Professional Development is the home of the Professional Development Program. State-of-the-art conference rooms and computer facilities enhance Franklin's career programming commitment to its students.

The B. F. Hamilton Library, containing more than 117,000 volumes and collections of microfilm, slides, art reproductions, recordings, and periodicals, is a member of P.A.L.N.I. (Private Academic Library Network of Indiana). The Johnson Center for Fine Arts provides classrooms and practice and performance accommodations, and it houses the facilities and meeting rooms for the Leadership Program.

Costs

The direct cost of the 2003–04 academic year was $22,250. This amount was derived from tuition, which was $16,750; room and board, which was $5270; and the Winter Term fee, which totaled $230. In addition, the student activity fee is approximately $135 and entitles a student to admittance to all athletic contests and winter events.

Financial Aid

The Franklin College financial aid program assists students who might not otherwise be able to attend college and also rewards applicants for excellent academic achievement in high school. Awards are based on scholarship, curricular and extracurricular activities, and financial need. Aid involving financial need includes Franklin College grants, loans, and employment. Franklin participates in the Federal Stafford Student Loan, Federal Perkins Loan, and Federal Work-Study programs. Ben Franklin Distinguished Scholarships, President's Scholarships, Academic Excellence Scholarships, and Dean's Scholarships are awarded on the basis of academic performance, activities, and standardized test scores. The Ben Franklin Scholarship covers the full cost of tuition, room, and board; the President's Scholarship is a full-tuition award; and Academic Excellence and Dean's Scholarships are awarded on the basis of specified criteria. Scholarships are renewable for each of the recipient's four academic years at Franklin, provided students maintain a minimum GPA of 3.0 and advance in class status each year. The Free Application for Federal Student Aid (FAFSA) is required.

Faculty

The 13:1 student-faculty ratio allows Franklin faculty members to provide excellent instruction in small classes that promote participatory learning. Eighty percent of current faculty members have obtained the highest degree in their field. Faculty members serve as advisers and provide supplemental attention outside the classroom. While many faculty members carry on research and publish their work, their main emphasis is teaching. No classes are taught by graduate students or teaching assistants.

Student Government

The Student Congress is composed of representatives elected by the student body. The congress provides a forum for student concerns and is the most important governmental communication link among students, faculty, and administration. Student government also includes the Judicial Board and the Residence Hall Council. These groups have jurisdiction over certain questions concerning the social standards and regulations of the College.

Admission Requirements

Applications for admission to Franklin College are evaluated on an individual basis. A student's potential academic and personal contributions to the College, recommendations, school and community activities, academic record, and standardized test scores are taken into consideration by the Admissions Committee. A student should complete a strong college-preparatory program. Candidates for admission are urged to visit the campus in order to experience the College community.

Application and Information

To be considered for admission, an applicant must submit a completed application, a transcript of all secondary school and college work attempted, and either SAT I or ACT scores. A decision regarding acceptance is made after the College receives all necessary credentials. Notification is sent immediately after the Admissions Committee has acted.

For further information, students should contact:

Office of Admission
Franklin College
501 East Monroe Street
Franklin, Indiana 46131
Telephone: 317-738-8062
800-852-0232 (toll-free)
Fax: 317-738-8274
E-mail: admissions@franklincollege.edu
World Wide Web: http://www.franklincollege.edu

The bell tower on top of Old Main on the Franklin College campus.

FRANKLIN COLLEGE SWITZERLAND

LUGANO, SWITZERLAND

The College

Franklin College has a single specific mission: to provide students with an educational experience that is in every significant respect international. Students live in a vigorous Swiss city and mix freely with its population, as well as with their fellow students and faculty members who come from more than fifty different countries. Most of Franklin's courses are cross-cultural in content or perspective or both.

Named for the United States' first and most illustrious ambassador to Europe, Franklin College was founded in 1969 as a nonprofit and independent postsecondary institution that takes as its cornerstone Benjamin Franklin's vigorous support of intellectual interchange between nations. Franklin students want their college education to be international, partly because the need for people with an international competence is great. Many have a cross-cultural background from parents or relatives born or raised in another country; all share the desire to let their college studies take them beyond national boundaries. Franklin College is the "international alternative" in education.

Approximately 48 percent of the students come from the United States; 52 percent are from Europe, Asia, Africa, South America, and the Middle East. Bringing a variety of experiences and perspectives to college life, they live in College apartment residences on and near the campus. The apartments all have kitchens that are available, though the campus cafeteria also provides regular meal service. There is a residence supervisor for each of the eight buildings.

Campus activities are varied. The College Student Union promotes a student newspaper, a literary magazine, a theater group, language and sports clubs, and a variety of social events that take advantage of southern Switzerland's extensive recreational resources. For sports, the Dean of Students enrolls interested students in the considerable number of local Swiss clubs and teams that welcome newcomers—especially basketball, football, ice hockey, soccer, and volleyball teams, but also clubs for crew, fencing, flying, golf, hang gliding, ice-skating, judo, parachuting, riding, rock-climbing, sailing, swimming, tennis, track, and windsurfing. By joining the local groups, Franklin students become part of the region's life; they are themselves essential to the cross-cultural learning the College promotes.

Location

The Franklin College campus is in the Sorengo section of the city of Lugano, southern Switzerland's principal business, banking, medical, and cultural center. Accessible from campus either by public transportation or on foot, downtown Lugano and its surrounding lakeside villages are renowned for their scenic beauty and Mediterranean climate. Palm trees line lakefront piazzas, and an outdoor life-style is typical of Ticino, the Italian-speaking canton of Switzerland that best exemplifies Swiss versatility in all three of the national languages—Italian, German, and French.

Throughout the year, Lugano features outstanding cultural activities at the world-famous Thyssen art collection, the Swiss-Italian radio station with its own permanent symphony orchestra, and the International Convention Center, which attracts guest performers from around the world. Nine public museums, many art galleries, several movie houses, and a multitude of restaurants and discotheques make for a range of recreational choices normally found only in a large city. A covered ice rink, swimming pools, and a wide range of other sports facilities are maintained by local sports clubs; Lugano and the southern part of Switzerland offer access to an extraordinary variety of sports activities. In the spring and fall, Ticino's most popular recreation is hiking. In winter, skiing is available on Mount Tamaro, 20 minutes' drive from campus, or in the fabled St. Moritz, Davos, Klosters, and Zermatt.

Majors and Degrees

The Bachelor of Arts program offers majors in art history, European studies, history and literature, international banking and finance, international communications, international economics, international management, international relations, literature, modern languages, and visual and communication arts, with combined and double majors in two of nine subject areas. The Associate in Arts degree program provides a strong liberal arts foundation for students who usually continue their education in a baccalaureate degree program. The Institute for Modern European Studies, the Institute for International Management, and the Institute for Political Science and Economics offer specialized, one-year diploma programs for students coming to Franklin from colleges and universities in the United States.

Academic Program

Franklin's curricula promote international awareness and integrative thinking by being interdisciplinary in the highest tradition of liberal education. The courses of study explore the diverse disciplines that inform an educated human being. Students must complete at least 126 credit hours to be eligible for the B.A. degree (64 for the A.A. degree) and must maintain a minimum cumulative grade point average of 2.0 on a 4.0 scale.

As an integral credit-bearing part of the academic program, students participate twice a year (in mid-October and mid-March) in faculty-led academic travel-study programs to various destinations in Eastern and Western Europe, Africa, Asia, Latin America, and North America.

All degree candidates must demonstrate a foreign language proficiency equivalent to three years of university-level instruction in a language taught at Franklin. They meet this requirement, in a language other than their mother tongue, by successfully completing appropriate courses at Franklin or by passing an equivalency test administered by the language department.

In addition to their major field of study, students may add courses within another discipline to form a minor. The number of credit hours (12 to 15) and the program of courses are subject to departmental approval.

Students enrolled in one of the institutes must complete 30 semester hours in two consecutive semesters at the College with a minimum grade point average of 2.0. For students enrolling at Franklin for only one semester, completion of a specified distribution of courses with a grade point average of 2.0 or better leads to a Certificate of Studies.

The College operates on a two-semester calendar, with classes starting in late August and mid-January; two summer sessions are also available. A required orientation program for all new students is held in August and mid-January.

A cooperative agreement exists between Franklin College and the C. W. Post School of Business of Long Island University for a one-year (36-credit) graduate M.B.A. program. Students majoring in international management are treated on equal terms with C. W. Post students with regard to entry.

Off-Campus Programs

The Academic Travel Program is a fully integrated part of the regular curriculum. Each semester, students participate in two weeks of faculty-led academic travel. More than any other program of study, it gives students an opportunity to learn the "other way"—by experience. Travel destinations for 2003–04 included Rome and southern Italy, Sicily, England, Germany, Paris, Greece, Madrid, Prague, Budapest, southern France, Namibia, Cuba, Brazil, and China.

Internships are also available. Students with academic interest in any area may apply for an internship after two semesters of residence at Franklin, either by asking to be considered for one of the internships provided by the College or by arranging for an appointment themselves. The internship program is coordinated by a member of the Franklin faculty; a student may earn a maximum of 3 credit hours in an assignment.

Students in good standing who major in modern languages are eligible for study in a country where the target language is spoken; such study is limited to one semester at an approved institution.

Academic Facilities

The Franklin College Library contains 38,000 volumes and offers numerous English and foreign-language periodicals. The library also participates in the Swiss interlibrary loan system linking major Swiss university libraries. Two computer labs with Internet access are available for student use.

Costs

The comprehensive fee for the 2003–04 academic year was $33,900. This figure includes the cost of tuition, the room and board charge, academic travel, and student fees. The estimated cost of incidentals is $4000 per year. The estimated cost to fly round-trip from the United States ranges from $700 to $1100.

Financial Aid

Franklin College offers academic merit awards and need-based financial aid to qualified students. Applicants for financial aid must submit the FAFSA for evaluation. Veterans' and Social Security benefits are available to eligible students. Federal Stafford Student Loans and PLUS Loans may be obtained through local lenders. On-campus employment is available. Students interested in applying for on-campus employment should notify the campus Financial Aid Office at the beginning of each semester.

Faculty

The Franklin College faculty numbers 44 full-time and part-time teachers, approximately half of whom are American or British; the other half are of various European nationalities. The majority have advanced degrees from American universities, the others from English and Continental universities, and most have lived, studied, and taught in a variety of countries. The teaching staff represents the cross-cultural aims of the College. Faculty members are committed to the European arena of study, are familiar enough with particular countries to organize and lead academic travel, are competent in more than one language, and are dedicated to the personal, discursive style of teaching demanded by a small liberal arts college with small classes. These teachers also advise the various student activities, lead local excursions, and regularly contribute to the College's cocurricular program of lectures. In addition, each faculty member acts as academic counselor to a number of students. The faculty-conducted Academic Travel Program promotes the intellectual friendship between teacher and student essential to a liberal arts education. The student-faculty ratio is approximately 10:1.

Student Government

The student body elects the members of the Student Union. In addition to sponsoring interest groups and arranging social events, the Student Union appoints members to attend meetings of the College faculty and the Appeals Board.

Admission Requirements

Franklin College seeks students who are eager to meet the challenge of studying and living in Europe, serious about undertaking college-level learning, and prepared to contribute positively to the intellectual life of the College. To identify such students, and also to ensure a diverse student population, the College Admissions Committee considers both academic and personal facts, including the student's academic record, evaluations by teachers and counselors, test scores, extracurricular interests and talents, and academic distinctions. Admission to the College is limited and therefore competitive. To achieve the best match between the student and Franklin, a personal interview is strongly recommended; one can be arranged by contacting the Admission Office in Lugano or New York. Applicants to the freshman class must submit a completed application form and a nonrefundable fee of $50; an official transcript of their secondary school record; SAT I or ACT scores, either included on transcripts or forwarded by the testing service to Franklin College (code number 0922); and three letters of academic evaluation. Applicants are advised to take the College Board SAT II: Writing Test given in December. Applicants whose first language is not English must submit their score on the Test of English as a Foreign Language (TOEFL); a score of at least 217 (550) is required. Transfer applicants and institute applicants are required to submit a completed application and a nonrefundable application fee of $50, an official transcript of their college record, and one letter of academic recommendation.

Application and Information

The priority application deadline for fall entry is March 15 for applicants to the freshman class and June 15 for transfer and institute applicants. The application deadline for the spring semester is November 15. Admission decisions are made on a rolling basis. Applicants can usually expect a decision within three weeks from the time their application is completed. All inquiries and applications should be directed to the nearest Admission Office.

U.S. Admissions Office
Franklin College
91-31 Queens Boulevard, Suite 411
Elmhurst, New York 11373
Telephone: 718-335-6800
Fax: 718-335-6733
E-mail: info@fc.edu

Karen Ballard
Director of Admissions
Franklin College
via Ponte Tresa, 29
6924 Sorengo/Lugano
Switzerland
Telephone: 41-91-993-3906
Fax: 41-91-994-4117
E-mail: info@fc.edu
World Wide Web: http://www.fc.edu

FRANKLIN PIERCE COLLEGE

RINDGE, NEW HAMPSHIRE

The College

Franklin Pierce College (FPC) is a four-year, coeducational nonsectarian college located in the Monadnock region of New Hampshire. The College enrolls approximately 1,600 undergraduates on its main campus in Rindge and more than 2,500 adult learners at its six graduate and professional studies campuses across the state. The diverse student population represents thirty states and twenty-three countries. Franklin Pierce is accredited by the New England Association of Colleges and Schools, Inc. (NEASC).

Physical facilities of the main campus include modern classroom buildings (including a laboratory facility), the library, an academic services center, a campus center, residence halls and apartment houses, townhouse complexes, a field house, an air frame recreation complex, a fitness center, a health center, a boat house, and a theater. A wide range of services are offered to the students, including health-care services, counseling, and career planning and placement assistance.

Campus activities include a number of academic and special interest clubs, such as the Campus Activities Board, Law Club, Student Senate, *Pierce Arrow* (newspaper), *Raven* (yearbook), *Northern New England Review* (literary magazine), and the Crimson and Grey Cultural Committee. Bus trips to special events and malls are offered on weekends. The College's active adventure recreation and intramural programs offer a wide variety of activities on both the College's 1,200-acre campus and throughout the region's many natural recreational facilities. At the intercollegiate level, men compete in baseball, basketball, crew, cross-country, golf, ice hockey, lacrosse, soccer, and tennis. For women, basketball, cross-country, crew, golf, lacrosse, field hockey, soccer, softball, tennis, and volleyball are available.

Location

The main campus in Rindge, New Hampshire, is situated on 1,200 wooded acres on the shore of Pearly Pond near the base of Mount Monadnock. Rindge, which is in southwestern New Hampshire, is 65 miles from Boston, 112 miles from Hartford, and 236 miles from New York City. The area is an ideal setting for outdoor activities. There are many lakes and streams, including the Pearly Pond beach facility, which is ideal for fishing, swimming, and sailing, and there are also numerous trails for hiking, mountaineering, camping, and cross-country skiing.

Majors and Degrees

Franklin Pierce College offers Bachelor of Science and Bachelor of Arts degrees through five academic departments. The Department of Behavioral Sciences offers majors in anthropology/archaeology, art education, criminal justice, education (teacher conversion), elementary education, psychology, secondary education, and social work and counseling. In the Department of Business Administration, students can major in accounting-finance, arts management, management, marketing, and sports and recreation management. The Department of Natural Sciences offers majors in biology, computer science, environmental science, and information technology. In the Department of Visual and Performing Arts, students major in dance, drama, fine arts, graphic communications, mass communication (journalism, media production, media studies), music, and theater arts. Majors in the Department of Humanities are American studies, English, history, and political science. The College also offers preprofessional programs in dentistry, law, medicine, pre–physical therapy, and veterinary medicine. In addition to a major, students may also complete a minor area of study, and they also have the option of designing their own, interdisciplinary majors.

Academic Programs

Franklin Pierce College's curriculum is a blend of traditional liberal arts, preprofessional study, teacher preparation programs, and a nationally recognized core curriculum, The Individual and Community. In 1997, the College was the recipient of the Templeton Award for Character Building Colleges. Students receive much personal attention at Franklin Pierce College; the average class size is 19, and the student-faculty ratio is 15:1.

A total of 120 semester hours are required for graduation. These include the core, required courses; courses in the student's chosen major (generally 30 to 54 credits); and the required 42-credit Individual and Community Integrated Curriculum. The purpose of the Individual and Community program is to foster a common understanding of the questions and issues that lie at the heart of contemporary American life. The Integrated Curriculum begins with a one-semester, freshman seminar called The Individual and Community and continues with a sequence of courses culminating in the Senior Liberal Arts Seminar.

Franklin Pierce offers an Honors Program, which was established to help provide challenge and intellectual community to participants. The program offers honors sections of core courses, occasional honors electives, and honors options in major courses designed to appeal to the more academically committed student. Students are invited to participate in the freshman honors program based on their high school academic records.

Off-Campus Programs

Credit-bearing internships are available for qualified upperclassmen in several academic departments, and students may participate in the Washington Center for Internships and Academic Seminars, a comprehensive, credit-bearing learning experience in Washington, D.C.

FPC is one of twelve member colleges of the New Hampshire College and University Council (NHCUC). The NHCUC Student Exchange Agreement allows students to take courses at other NHCUC colleges at no extra tuition cost. Students may take courses at FPC and another NHCUC during the same semester, or they may spend up to two semesters in residence at a member school. Members of the NHCUC are Colby-Sawyer College, Daniel Webster College, Dartmouth College, Franklin Pierce College, Keene State College, New England College, Plymouth State College, Rivier College, St. Anselm College, the School for Lifelong Learning, Southern New Hampshire University, and the University of New Hampshire, Durham.

Franklin Pierce College holds affiliate status with Richmond College in London, England, which enables FPC students to take advantage of study in London for full credit toward their degrees. Another study-abroad opportunity is the Walk in Europe. This is a project that is unique to Franklin Pierce College and has been part of the curriculum since 1969. Approximately 25 students are chosen to participate in the semester-long project: a long-distance walk through several European countries. The sheer adventure and vitality of the project profoundly changes the participants' outlook on the world. The Walk is structured to facilitate engagement with Europeans and their cultures and with each member of the group. Students who have participated have described the Walk as the single most valuable learning experience of their years at Franklin Pierce.

Academic Facilities

The Franklin Pierce College Library provides a comfortable, open-stack environment for study and research. The 120,000-volume collection includes books, microforms, compact discs, DVDs, software, and audio and videocassettes as well as subscriptions to more than 13,000 electronic and print periodical titles. The Curriculum Library supports the education curriculum of the College and includes a wealth of resources related to K–12 teaching and learning and children's literature.

Costs

Basic charges for the 2003–04 academic year were $20,790 for tuition, $4000 for a double room, and $3330 for board. Other fees and deposits brought the total to $28,980 per year.

Financial Aid

Both need-based and merit-based financial aid is available in the forms of loans, grants, scholarships, and on-campus employment. Students should visit the College's Web site for details about the various aid programs.

Faculty

There are 72 full-time and 86 part-time professors at the undergraduate residential campus in Rindge, 79 percent of whom have terminal degrees in their field. All Franklin Pierce College students are taught by faculty members who are active professionally in organizations that span the academic disciplines. Over the years, their work has received the support of the Council for the International Exchange of Scholars (Fulbright Scholars), the Hewlett Foundation, the Whiting Foundation, the Lilly Endowment for the Arts, the National Endowment for the Humanities, the National Science Foundation, and the Kettering Foundation. Faculty members regularly contribute their work as researchers, writers, presenters, editors of professional journals, and performing artists.

Student Government

The Franklin Pierce College Student Government Association (SGA) is made up of dedicated student representatives working to make positive change for the student body. In addition to being an advocate for the student body, the SGA also funds the various clubs and organizations that enrich campus life and the Pierce experience.

Admission Requirements

Applicants are evaluated on an individual basis, with the student's potential and seriousness of purpose of primary concern. The trend toward improved grades, more difficult course work, and greater school involvement are weighed heavily in the student's behalf. Counselor support and supplementary recommendations are valued and are given special consideration. Class size and the campus environment are such that SAT results are generally a less valid predictor of success at FPC than ongoing classroom achievement.

Each entering student must submit evidence of adequate preparation for college. Sixteen credits of secondary school work are required of each candidate. The preferred distribution is English, 4 credits; mathematics, 3 credits; laboratory sciences, 2 credits; social sciences, 2 credits; and electives, 5 credits. Candidates deemed to have potential and motivation, yet not meeting all the admission requirements, may be accepted provisionally.

The application consists of the completed application form, official secondary school transcripts, official transcripts from each college attended, an official secondary school recommendation (guidance counselor, principal, or teacher), SAT or ACT scores, and a writing sample. An on-campus interview is recommended. Students whose native language is not English must also submit the Certification of Finances and an acceptable TOEFL score.

Application and Information

Students may apply to enter in the fall, spring, or summer sessions. Applications are processed on a rolling basis, but students are encouraged to apply and have their transcripts and recommendations sent early in their senior year.

Department of Admissions
Franklin Pierce College
20 College Road
Rindge, New Hampshire 03461-0060
Telephone: 603-899-4050
800-437-0048 (toll-free)
Fax: 603-899-4394
E-mail: admissions@fpc.edu
World Wide Web: http://www.fpc.edu

FRESNO PACIFIC UNIVERSITY

FRESNO, CALIFORNIA

The University

Fresno Pacific University, founded in 1944, is a Christian university of the arts and sciences professions. Fresno Pacific University (FPU) provides a complete education for students through excellence in Christian higher education. The academic program at FPU features a unique sequence of courses that challenge the student to develop academically, emotionally, and spiritually. Fresno Pacific University emphasizes faculty-student interaction, practical service, professional internships, and building a strong educational community in a Christian context.

Sponsored by the Mennonite Brethren Church, the University offers a distinctively Christ-centered vision of community and society. Through the pursuit of the knowledge of God and God's creation and using the tools of theology, science, and the arts, the University provides a stimulating center where students are challenged to shape their thought, character, and lifestyle in a way that prepares them for meaningful vocations and service in the world.

The 2,100 students at FPU (half undergraduates) form a rich community of different cultures, ethnicities, and religious denominations that bring the wider world to the student. Minority enrollment is 30 percent; international students make up 4 percent of the student body. On-campus living arrangements include apartments and residence halls as well as University-sponsored houses. Apartment living is available near the University. Host family arrangements can be made for international students. Students are involved in many clubs, organizations, and activities. Christian growth opportunities include various settings for worship, prayer, Bible study, and discipleship training. University Hour, a twice-a-week gathering of the campus community, offers students and faculty members a look at a variety of issues from a Christian perspective, as well as the sights and sounds of cultural and artistic presentations.

The Sunbird athletic teams of Fresno Pacific University are members of the National Association of Intercollegiate Athletics (NAIA) and compete at the intercollegiate level in men's basketball, cross-country, soccer, and track and women's basketball, cross-country, soccer, track, and volleyball. Intramural sports programs for both men and women are active throughout the school year. The theater department produces a variety of dramatic productions: full-length stage productions, readers theater, and one-act plays and hosts a traveling drama group. The music program offers a variety of musical opportunities: the Concert Choir, which takes a major tour each year, and many smaller vocal and instrumental ensembles.

The parklike 42-acre FPU campus has sixteen major buildings that include the Special Events Center/Gymnasium, a well-supplied bookshop, and a swimming pool. The campus provides convenient access for handicapped people.

The Student Life office provides personal, job, and career counseling and information on work and service opportunities as well as other support to students.

The graduate school offers five master's degrees, twelve credentials in education, and six graduate certificates.

Location

Fresno Pacific University is the only accredited, private, residential four-year Christian university of the liberal arts and sciences professions in central California. FPU is located in the heart of California, in the Great Central Valley. The Fresno metropolitan area has an ethnically and culturally diverse population of 500,000. Yosemite, Kings Canyon, and Sequoia National Parks; ski areas; beaches; and cultural and entertainment attractions of San Francisco and Los Angeles are all accessible from Fresno.

Majors and Degrees

Fresno Pacific University offers the Bachelor of Arts (B.A.) degree in applied mathematics, biblical and religious studies, biology, business accounting, business finance, business information systems, business marketing management, business nonprofit administration, chemistry, child development, church music, contemporary Christian ministries, English communication, English drama, English education, English literature, English writing, environmental science, environmental studies, history, intercultural studies, international business, mathematics education, music education, music performance/composition, philosophy, physical education exercise science, physical education health fitness, political science, psychology, social science education, social work, sociology, Spanish language and culture, and teaching/liberal studies. Preprofessional programs are available in law, medicine, and physical therapy.

Academic Programs

An FPU education begins with a broad foundation exposing the student to many areas of study. From this foundation, students learn the intellectual skills necessary to begin study in a major and a minor. Fresno Pacific University operates on a two-semester plus summer academic calendar. The academic year consists of an early fall semester, which ends before the Christmas holiday, and a spring semester, which concludes in May. The minimum number of units for a Bachelor of Arts degree is 124 units. The General Education Program includes four courses in biblical studies and religion. FPU grants credit for certain scores on Advanced Placement tests and College-Level Examination Program (CLEP) tests.

Off-Campus Programs

FPU offers special experiences in off-campus education. The University is part of several consortia that offer international and U.S. settings for education. Study-abroad programs are available in many countries of the world, including China, Ecuador, England, France, Germany, Greece, India, Japan, Mexico, Russia, and Spain, to name a few. An American studies program is available in Washington, D.C., as is a film study program in Los Angeles, California. Short-term study-abroad programs that are led by FPU faculty members are also available to various countries in May of each year.

Academic Facilities

Hiebert Library is owned and operated jointly with the Mennonite Brethren Biblical Seminary. There are currently 150,000 volumes, 2,200 journal subscriptions, 250,000 microforms, and an audiovisual collection of 10,000 items. Three computer laboratories are available to all students, where they can access word processing, e-mail, Internet, spreadsheet, database, and other software for their use in class work, research, and writing, using either MS-DOS or Macintosh equipment, including Power Macs.

Costs

The tuition for academic year 2004–05 is $18,500 and room and board are $5400. Other fees are additional.

Financial Aid

Fresno Pacific University offers a variety of federal, state, and private financial aid programs to assist students who would benefit from an education but need financial aid. Such students are encouraged to apply for assistance. More than 97 percent of FPU students receive financial assistance in the form of loans, grants, scholarships, and many on-campus employment opportunities. Merit scholarships are awarded to students based on academic achievement. Other scholarships include service/leadership, music, drama, and athletics awards. Students wishing to apply for financial aid must be accepted for admission and complete the Free Application for Federal Student Aid (FAFSA) and the FPU Financial Aid Application. California students should complete the FAFSA before the March 2 California Grant deadline and submit the Cal Grant GPA Verification Form in order to be considered for the Cal Grant program. Financial aid for international students is also available on a limited basis. International students should complete the FPU Financial Aid Application only.

Faculty

The FPU mentor-collegium program for incoming freshman students assigns a faculty mentor to each incoming student. This faculty member becomes an adviser/counselor, and the small group of students guided by the mentor forms a collegium. The collegium meets periodically for academic, social, and other activities. A special collegium—or core—course helps freshmen adjust to university life.

As a further expression of the conviction that interpersonal relationships are essential to the total educational process, the University encourages "Noon Hour Encounters," in which faculty members invite students to lunch for conversation in a local restaurant. Relationships that are developed in this informal setting are valuable to both faculty members and students.

More than 60 percent of the faculty members have earned doctorates. The student-faculty ratio is 16:1, with the average class size being 20 students. FPU's small class sizes promote discussion. Students know their professors up close and on a first-name basis.

Student Government

Fresno Pacific University is committed to helping students develop character and competence in order to become effective leaders who inspire, empower, and serve others. The Associated Students of Fresno Pacific University offers a variety of services, provides student representation to the University, and gives many opportunities for personal, social, spiritual, and political growth for students. Members of the Student Executive Council also serve as members of standing staff and faculty committees within the University governance structure. The Student Executive Council is composed of the following positions: president, vice president, business manager, student ministries, social affairs, commuter representative, secretary, and class senators. Appointment to these leadership roles is conducted through student body elections and personal interviews.

Admission Requirements

Fresno Pacific University welcomes students who qualify academically, who demonstrate the physical and emotional capacity for university work, who accept the purposes and standards of the University, and who would benefit from a Christian liberal arts education.

Acceptance for admission as a freshman student is based on an eligibility index score determined by a formula using the high school grade point average (excluding physical education, military science, and applied courses) and the total score from either the SAT I or the ACT. Applicants must also have a high school diploma or a GED.

Transfer students may bring in a maximum of 70 units of credit from an accredited postsecondary institution. To be granted admission solely on college-level academic work, a minimum of 24 transferable units must have been completed with at least a 2.4 academic GPA.

International students are valuable to the richness of the University's community. For those seeking improvement in their English language skills, the Intensive English Language Program (IELP) offers various levels of English language instruction. Students may receive university credits for language courses or may enroll in the Language and Culture Studies Program (LCS) to receive only a certificate. International students need good English skills in order to succeed in undergraduate studies. To study in regular undergraduate courses, students must reach a score of at least 500 (with 50 or higher on each section) on the TOEFL. SAT I or ACT scores are useful in considering students for scholarships. An application file can be complete without TOEFL and SAT I or ACT scores, although the University strongly recommends that they be submitted.

Application and Information

U.S. students entering directly from high school must submit an application for admission, a $40 nonrefundable application fee, official high school transcripts, SAT I or ACT scores, and at least one letter of recommendation.

U.S. transfer students need to submit an application for admission, a $40 nonrefundable application fee, official transcripts from high school verifying graduation, official transcripts from each college attended, and at least one letter of recommendation. Test scores are not required, but they are recommended.

Requirements for international students include the international application form, a $40 nonrefundable application fee, certified and translated transcripts from all secondary schools and postsecondary institutions certifying academically acceptable marks/grades, a completed financial certification form, two letters of recommendation, and a TOEFL score.

For more information, students should contact:

Dina Gonzalez-Piña, Director of College Admission
Fresno Pacific University
1717 South Chestnut Avenue
Fresno, California 93702
Telephone: 559-453-2039
800-660-6089 (toll-free)
E-mail: ugadmis@fresno.edu
World Wide Web: http://www.fresno.edu/

For international student information, students should contact:

International Programs and Service Office
Fresno Pacific University
1717 South Chestnut Avenue
Fresno, California 93702
Telephone: 559-453-2069
Fax: 559-453-5501
E-mail: ipso@fresno.edu
World Wide Web: http://www.fresno.edu/dept/ipso/

Fresno Pacific University provides a complete education for students through excellence in Christian higher education.

FROSTBURG STATE UNIVERSITY

FROSTBURG, MARYLAND

The University

A state-supported liberal arts institution, Frostburg State University has gone through a series of transitions since its founding in 1898. Established originally as a normal school, the University has expanded to a campus of more than 200 acres and a student body of more than 5,400. During the past decade, the most significant one in the University's history, the academic offerings have been expanded and enrollment has increased. Eleven residence halls provide sufficient on-campus housing to meet the needs of entering students.

The University offers extensive extracurricular activities. There are about 100 student organizations on campus, including sororities and fraternities, honor societies, professional organizations, communications and media-related groups, athletic clubs, Little Sister programs, and special-interest groups. The University offers twenty intramural sports. Intercollegiate sports for men are baseball, basketball, cross-country, football, soccer, swimming, tennis, and track and field; 10 percent of the men participate in these. Intercollegiate sports for women are basketball, cross-country, field hockey, lacrosse, soccer, softball, swimming, tennis, track and field, and volleyball; 5 percent of the women participate.

Location

Located in the mountains of western Maryland, the University campus is bordered on one side by the city of Frostburg (population 7,500), an attractive community that offers a range of activities, from dining at a gourmet restaurant to a community club social. Neighboring scenic and recreational areas are enjoyed throughout all four seasons of the year. Skiing is a popular winter activity, along with other traditional outdoor sports. The surrounding area has numerous historic sites, such as the C & O Canal and Fort Necessity. The history of the growth of Allegany County can be seen in the Allegany Museum, which is located in Cumberland, Maryland (population 25,000), just a short distance from the campus. Baltimore, Maryland, and Washington, D.C., are 150 miles east of the campus. Pittsburgh, Pennsylvania, is 100 miles to the northeast.

Majors and Degrees

Students completing an undergraduate program of study at the University may earn the Bachelor of Arts (B.A.), the Bachelor of Science (B.S.), or the Bachelor of Fine Arts (B.F.A.) degree. The diversity of the University's academic program is reflected in the majors that are available: accounting, actuarial science, art and design, athletic training, biology, business administration, business education, chemistry, communication studies, computer science, criminal justice, dance, early childhood/elementary education, earth science, economics, elementary education, English, environmental analysis and planning, exercise and sport science, foreign languages and literature, geography, health and physical education, health science administration, history, information technology management, international studies, interpretive biology and natural history, law and society, liberal studies, mass communication, mathematics, music, philosophy, physics, political science, psychology, recreation and parks management, social science, social work, sociology, theater, urban and regional planning, and wildlife and fisheries.

Frostburg offers preprofessional programs in dentistry, law, medicine, and diverse other areas. Frostburg also participates in cooperative preprofessional programs with the University of Maryland. These include several allied health programs (nursing, pharmacy, and physical therapy). These programs involve preprofessional study at Frostburg and professional training at the University of Maryland. Through a collaborative program with the University of Maryland, mechanical and electrical engineering majors are offered at Frostburg. This program offers the opportunity to attend a small university and receive a degree from the University of Maryland, College Park's established and nationally accredited engineering program.

Academic Programs

A student's program of study begins with the General Education Program (GEP), which is designed to provide the foundation for educational development. Through three components, a unified concept of general education is developed to meet the special needs of each student. The first of these components provides a common core of essential tools for further learning; primary among these tools are skills of verbal and symbolic communication. Another component of the GEP offers exposure to broad fields of knowledge through study of the humanities, social sciences, and natural sciences. The third component helps the student gain an understanding of the interrelationship of various disciplines. Each student selects specific courses and develops a common theme to aid in his or her understanding.

The significant distinction of the B.A. degree program is that it requires a student to become competent in a foreign language at the intermediate level. Students who are contemplating additional study beyond an undergraduate degree are strongly encouraged to obtain the B.A. degree, since it is of particular value in a graduate program. Many students are able to combine specific graduate school goals with their major by tailoring their program to meet specific needs. Serious students, with the assistance of their adviser, are able to arrange a program that will help them achieve a high degree of success in acceptance to a variety of professional and graduate schools.

The offerings of an honors program provide the challenge that will make the serious student aware of his or her potential as an individual. Superior performance in a secondary school program will encourage the student to participate in this demanding curriculum.

Off-Campus Programs

Frostburg State University offers students a variety of opportunities for off-campus learning. The largest of these is the internship program. Internships are a required part of several major programs (i.e., education, accounting, and political science) but are also available to students in most other majors. An internship allows students to gain practical experience and earn credit in their chosen field. Off-campus centers have been opened in Hagerstown and Frederick. For students who wish to study abroad, Frostburg participates in the International Student Exchange Program, which allows students to select the country in which they wish to study abroad and, if qualified, to be assigned to an institution in that country. Students majoring in education or physical education have the opportunity to study in England through special exchange programs in those majors.

Academic Facilities

As a residential campus, the University has grown physically in order to maintain pace with an expanding academic program. Academic facilities include eleven classroom buildings. The campus radio station, WFWM, was also renovated and electronically updated recently. An addition to the campus is the Nelson P. Guild Human Resources Center. This building houses the psychology, economics, political science, sociology, social work, and computer science departments. A beautiful performing arts building provides an exciting cultural center for the campus. The University was scheduled to open a modern science facility in fall 2003.

Costs

In 2003–04, the annual cost of tuition and fees was $4618 for Maryland residents and $10,424 for nonresidents. The cost of room and board was $5609 per year. Semester charges for room, board, tuition, and fees are payable at or prior to registration in the fall and in the spring.

Financial Aid

Financial aid available for eligible students includes need-based grants, merit-based academic scholarships, Federal Stafford Student Loans, and Federal Work-Study Program awards. Approximately 67 percent of the University's students receive financial aid.

Faculty

Frostburg's faculty consists of 233 full-time and 70 part-time members. Seventy percent of the faculty members hold a Ph.D. degree. The student-faculty ratio is 18:1. Eighty-six percent of classes have fewer than 30 students. All professors have weekly office hours during which they are available to students.

Student Government

A tripartite student government system allows students and members of the faculty and administration to become involved together in deciding the direction the University should take.

Admission Requirements

Applicants are considered for admission on the basis of their high school record and SAT I scores. A strong emphasis is placed on the high school transcript. High school equivalency certificates are accepted. An admission essay is required. An interview is not required, but the Admissions Office encourages students to visit the campus and talk with a member of the admission staff.

Application and Information

Students may apply to Frostburg State University by submitting an application along with official copies of their SAT I scores and high school transcript. Frostburg is on a rolling admissions program. The University must close admission when no further space is available. Students are strongly advised to make a college choice early in their high school career. Notification of admission decisions begins in mid-November for the fall semester.

For further information, prospective students should contact:

Admissions Office
Frostburg State University
101 Braddock Road
Frostburg, Maryland 21532
Telephone: 301-687-4201
Fax: 301-687-7074
E-mail: fsuadmissions@frostburg.edu
World Wide Web: http://www.frostburg.edu

A view of the campus.

GANNON UNIVERSITY

ERIE, PENNSYLVANIA

The University

Gannon University, consistently named one of America's Best Colleges by *U.S. News & World Report*, is dedicated to excellence in holistic education. The oldest part of the University is Villa Maria College, founded in 1925 by the Sisters of St. Joseph. In 1933, Archbishop John Mark Gannon established Cathedral College, a two-year institution, which by 1941 had evolved into a four-year college, the Gannon School of Arts and Sciences. The name Gannon College was adopted in 1944, and Gannon achieved university status in 1979. Villa Maria College subsequently merged with Gannon University in 1989.

Gannon's campus is located in the heart of downtown Erie, giving students the benefit of internships with businesses, law and law-enforcement agencies, health-care facilities, industries, and social service organizations. It is also within walking distance of stores, shops, restaurants, and theaters. The campus consists of thirty-four buildings located within six city blocks. Among these buildings is the Carneval Athletic Pavilion, which has a pool; three gyms; a running track; a weight room; courts for racquetball, handball, volleyball and basketball; and other facilities. Also on campus are an additional gymnasium, which is open to students during posted hours; two residence halls; eight apartment buildings; classroom and faculty office buildings; an administration building; and a multipurpose chapel building. The Waldron Campus Center is a focal point that gives students the opportunity to meet and socialize between classes with faculty members and other students. Each residence hall also has a game room and a laundry room.

Gannon offers students a broad intramural sports program that runs throughout the entire year. In Division II intercollegiate athletics, Gannon offers men's baseball, basketball, cross-country, football, golf, soccer, water polo, and wrestling and women's basketball, cross-country, golf, lacrosse, soccer, softball, volleyball, and water polo. There is also an intercollegiate coed swimming and diving team. Gannon's athletes utilize the newly constructed Gannon University Field, a multipurpose athletic facility that is conveniently located on campus.

There are approximately 3,400 students at Gannon, more than 2,600 of whom are undergraduates. The ratio of commuters to resident students is approximately 1:4. The University has a Career Development and Employment Services Office to aid students in locating internships and part-time work during school and full-time work after graduation.

Location

Erie is Pennsylvania's fourth-largest city and is located in the northwestern corner of the state on the shore of Lake Erie. Erie is approximately 120 miles north of Pittsburgh, Pennsylvania; 90 miles east of Cleveland, Ohio; and 90 miles southwest of Buffalo, New York. The campus is within 5 miles of Interstates 79 and 90 and 5 miles from Erie International Airport. Erie is also serviced by rail and bus transportation.

Majors and Degrees

The College of Humanities, Business and Education awards the Bachelor of Arts and Bachelor of Science degrees.

In the School of Humanities, the areas of study from which students may select a major are citizenship, communication arts, criminal justice, English (with concentrations in applied communications, literature, and writing), foreign language and business, foreign language and international studies, foreign language and literature, foreign language teaching, history, legal studies, liberal arts, mortuary science, philosophy, political science, prelaw, a 3-3 prelaw program that includes early admission to Duquesne University, psychology, social work, theater, theater and communication arts, and theology.

In the School of Business, students may choose to major in accounting, advertising communications, business administration, finance, international business, management, management information systems, marketing, and risk management.

In the School of Education, the areas of study from which students may select a major are early childhood education, elementary education, secondary education (in biology, chemistry, citizenship, communications, English, foreign language, mathematics, and science), and special education.

The College of Sciences, Engineering and Health Sciences awards the Bachelor of Science degree.

In the School of Sciences and Engineering, students may choose to major in biology, biotechnology, chemistry, chemical engineering, computer science, earth science, electrical engineering, electrical engineering (five-year co-op program), environmental science, mathematics, mechanical engineering, mechanical engineering (five-year co-op program), science, and software engineering. A minor is offered in environmental and occupational science and health. Preprofessional and accelerated programs of study are offered in chiropractic, dentistry, medicine, optometry, osteopathy, pharmacy, physical therapy, podiatry, and veterinary medicine; seven-year programs are offered in optometry and podiatry. A guaranteed medical school 4+4 program is available with the Lake Erie College of Osteopathic Medicine (LECOM).

In the School of Health Sciences and the Villa Maria School of Nursing, the areas of study from which students may select a major are dietetics, medical technology, nursing, occupational therapy, physician assistant, radiologic sciences, respiratory care, and sport and exercise science. A minor is also offered in athletic coaching.

The associate degree program offers Associate of Science and Associate of Arts degrees. Areas of study in which students may major are accounting, business administration, criminal justice, early childhood education, legal studies, radiologic sciences, and respiratory care.

Academic Program

Each undergraduate program has its own sequence of requirements. Students in all programs must complete credits in liberal studies. A faculty adviser is assigned to each student to assist with academic planning. A department chairperson and faculty adviser also assist each student in selecting courses that fulfill requirements and best meet the student's desired career objectives. The basic graduation requirements for bachelor's degree candidates are 128 credit hours, including completion of requirements for their major and the liberal studies program. Students must also have quality point averages of at least 2.0 in their senior year and 2.0 in their field of concentration. To earn an associate degree, students must usually complete 60 to 68 credit hours, depending on the program. Students may receive credit through the Advanced Placement Program.

Gannon offers a program for students with learning disabilities and an Army ROTC program that is open to interested students.

Gannon's academic calendar consists of two full semesters, running from August to December and from January to May. There are also optional summer classes.

Academic Facilities

The Nash Library currently has more than 250,000 bound volumes. The library subscribes to more than 1,000 periodicals and has book and periodical materials on various forms of microfilms and microcards. The newly wireless library contains a personal computer lab; a lecture room; a curriculum library; the Founder's Room for fine and rare books; the Cyber Café, containing personal computers, laptop ports, and cappuccino and juice machines; lounges; study rooms; typing rooms; an information-retrieval system; a TV studio; the latest audiovisual and tape equipment; and a multimedia studio classroom. In addition, students may use the facilities and resources of the Erie County Law Library and the Erie County Library. For specialized research projects, an efficient interlibrary loan service is available.

The A. J. Palumbo Academic Center houses the Schools of Health Sciences, Education, and Humanities and offers some of the finest laboratories, technology, and classrooms available today. From education to nursing and foreign language programs, the faculty members and facilities in Palumbo provide high-quality education. The University's Honors Program also has a home in the Palumbo Center. The Offices of Admissions and Financial Aid and the Career Development and Employment Services Center are also housed in this multilevel building.

The Zurn Science Center has laboratories for research in biology, anatomy, physics, chemistry, and engineering. The building also houses three computer laboratories, including the Computer Integrated Enterprise Center and an IBM PC lab. There are numerous classrooms and two auditoriums in the building. Among other University facilities are additional classroom buildings, a radio station, and a theater.

Costs

For 2003–04, full-time tuition was $8110 per semester ($8605 for engineering and health sciences), or $16,220 per academic year ($17,210 for engineering and health sciences). Tuition for part-time students was $370 to $410 per credit hour. Room and board were approximately $3255 per semester. The total cost for the academic year at Gannon, including books and supplies, was between $17,470 and $19,140 for commuting students and $23,980 and $25,650 for resident students, depending on the program of study.

Financial Aid

In order to bring a Gannon education to qualified students who could not otherwise afford it, the University offers an integrated financial aid program of scholarships, grants, loans, and employment. An application for financial aid must be filed with the admissions application. The filing has no effect on the decision of the Admissions Committee. Gannon's financial aid program is open to all full-time students attending classes during the period from August to May. All students seeking financial aid should file the admissions and financial aid applications no later than March 1.

Faculty

Gannon's faculty consists of 289 lay and religious men and women. Fifty-eight percent of the full-time faculty members have doctoral degrees. The student-faculty ratio is about 14:1, and there are approximately 25 students in each class. Most faculty members assist in the faculty adviser program, giving each student individual attention and counseling on academic and personal matters.

Student Government

The Student Government Association (SGA) is composed of students elected by members of their class. Through the SGA, students can play a responsible role in the planning and working of the University. SGA has voting representatives on all of the standing committees of the University. Members of the SGA not only research existing policies and problems, they also look for new ways to improve the academic life of students. The SGA also plans social events for the student body.

Admission Requirements

Gannon University actively recruits students of all races, creeds, and ages from all geographic regions. Transfer and international students are encouraged to seek admission. Applicants are required to submit scores (including senior-year scores) on either the SAT I or ACT; an up-to-date transcript of the high school record, showing rank in class (plus a college transcript for transfer applicants); a completed application form; and a nonrefundable $25 fee. Admission decisions are based upon numerous factors, central of which is the strength of the high school record, as demonstrated through grades and relative class standing. Less critical, although significant, are the SAT I or ACT scores and other test scores that may be available. Recommendations and personal statements also affect admission decisions. Transfer and international students should check with the admissions office for special application procedures.

Application and Information

Students applying for admission in the fall semester should start the application process at the beginning of their senior year in high school. Gannon operates on a rolling admissions basis, which means that there is no deadline for filing applications, with the exception of the physician assistant program and the LECOM 4+4 Medical Program, both of which have a deadline of January 15 for the fall semester. However, early applications are recommended, as are enrollment deposits.

For further information, students should contact:

Director of Admissions
Gannon University
109 University Square
Erie, Pennsylvania 16541
Telephone: 814-871-7240
800-GANNON-U (426-6668, toll-free)
Fax: 814-871-5803
E-mail: admissions@gannon.edu
World Wide Web: http://www.gannon.edu

Gannon University's faculty advisers are always available to help students chart their personal, educational, and professional accomplishments and potential.

GARDNER-WEBB UNIVERSITY

BOILING SPRINGS, NORTH CAROLINA

The University

Gardner-Webb University was founded in 1905 as a private high school by a group of Baptist associations. It became a junior college in 1928, was renamed Gardner-Webb College in 1942 in honor of former governor O. Max Gardner, and became a fully accredited senior college in 1971. Gardner-Webb moved to University status in 1993. Gardner-Webb's mission is to provide a high-quality liberal arts education in a Christian environment with the personal touch. The most outstanding characteristics of the University are its Christian environment, sense of community, and proven record of academic distinction. Its origins are obviously deep in Christian tradition, which is exemplified in the lives of staff and faculty members. Because the University is small, students can be well known by a large percentage of the faculty and administration. The cosmopolitan student body (more than 3,800 men and women, of whom nearly 2,700 are undergraduates) represents thirty states and thirty other countries and gives an added, valuable dimension to a student's educational experience. Cars are permitted for all.

The heritage of the University is reflected in its beautiful landscape and stately brick buildings. However, the University is constantly forging ahead with advanced technology and state-of-the-art facilities. There are several social and service clubs on campus, including the Drama Club, Fellowship of Christian Athletes (FCA), God and People (GAP), student government, and various University and student committees. There are many extracurricular activities for those who are interested. The Student Entertainment Association offers a full program of social events and entertainment. The Gardner-Webb Theatre offers a full season of plays. There are a student newspaper, a literary magazine, and a yearbook. Students may also participate in community projects or in various kinds of off-campus ministries, including those to the deaf and to prison inmates.

The Master of Arts degree is awarded in mental health counseling, school counseling, elementary education, middle school education, English education, English, school administration, and sport and science pedagogy. Gardner-Webb also offers the following degrees: a Master of Business Administration, Master of Accounting, Master of Science in Nursing, Master of Divinity, Doctor of Ministry, and Doctor of Education.

Intramural sports, in which all students are urged to participate, include basketball, racquetball, softball, tennis, touch football, and volleyball. Intercollegiate sports include baseball, basketball, cross-country running, football, golf, soccer, softball, swimming, tennis, track and field, volleyball, and wrestling. A modern physical education building, an indoor heated pool, and an athletic field amply accommodate these programs. A new wellness center and an Alpine Tower are available for student use.

The Program for the Blind at Gardner-Webb University has been developed to allow students with visual handicaps to receive a liberal arts education. Special support services and job opportunities are provided for every entering student who is visually impaired.

The Degree Program for the Deaf provides interpreters, note takers, and tutors skilled in sign language so that hearing-impaired students have full access to all University programs.

Location

The University is located at the foot of the beautiful Blue Ridge Mountains in Boiling Springs, North Carolina, a university town of about 3,000 people. The campus comprises 250 acres of land in an area of gently rolling, wooded hills. Nine miles away is Shelby, a town of about 30,000 people. There are a Greater Shelby Community Theatre and a Community Concert Series, and restaurants abound in the area. Charlotte, an area of about 400,000 people only 50 miles away, offers many other opportunities for cultural, social, and recreational activities. Several nearby lakes and Asheville and Beech Mountain, an hour and a half away in the heart of the mountains, provide facilities for summer and winter sports. Greenville, South Carolina, is 55 miles away and Spartanburg, 36 miles. Shelby is served by Greyhound-Trailways bus lines, and the Charlotte airport is served by major airlines. Interstate 85 is only 15 miles away, and Highway 74 runs through Shelby.

Majors and Degrees

The degrees of Bachelor of Arts, Bachelor of Science, and Associate in Arts are offered. Fields of concentration are available in the following subjects: accounting, American sign language, athletic training, biology, business administration, chemistry, communications, computer science, elementary education, English, finance, French, health/wellness, history, international business, interpreter training, management information systems, mathematics, medical technology, middle grades education, music, nursing, physical education, physician assistant studies, political science, psychology, public relations, religion, sacred music, social sciences, sociology, Spanish, sports management, and theater arts.

A dual-degree program is available in engineering with the University of North Carolina at Charlotte and Auburn University.

Preprofessional programs are available in dentistry, law, medicine, ministry, pharmacy, and veterinary medicine.

Academic Program

The total program is marked by flexibility for the student but encourages, through active faculty advisement, choosing a substantial course of study. Elements of the humanities, the social and physical sciences, and mathematics or related disciplines must be taken. A typical bachelor's degree program requires 128 semester hours for graduation: 59 to 63 in the core (humanities and social and physical sciences), 30 in the major, and 39 to 42 in supporting subjects and free electives. Requirements for science curricula vary somewhat. The associate degree requires the completion of 64 semester hours. A cumulative average of C (2.0 on a 4.0 scale) or better is required for graduation.

Gardner-Webb grants advanced placement and credit on the basis of the College-Level Examination Program (CLEP), the Advanced Placement (AP) tests of the College Board, and the International Baccalaureate Program.

Off-Campus Programs

Students in the Departments of Business, Fine Arts, Foreign Languages and Literature, and Religious Studies and Philosophy are given the opportunity to enrich their educational experiences through travel and study in Europe, Latin America, and the Holy Land.

Academic Facilities

The University's library currently holds 250,000 volumes. There are fully equipped biology, chemistry, and physics laboratories as well as computer and learning-assistance laboratories. A special-events/convocation center houses a theater and an athletics arena. The University also has a 50,000-watt FM stereo radio station.

Costs

Costs for the 2003–04 academic year were $14,160 for tuition and $5140 for room and board. Part-time tuition was $270 per semester hour for 1 to 9 hours. Books and supplies average $600.

Financial Aid

Gardner-Webb University makes available to its students a variety of scholarships, loans, grants-in-aid, and work-study awards. Prospective applicants with financial need should contact the financial aid director early in their senior year of high school for a financial need estimate. Applications received after April 1 can be considered only in terms of available funds. An applicant must be accepted for admission before being awarded aid. Students must file the Free Application for Federal Student Aid (FAFSA). Scholarships and other types of aid include academic awards, Christian service awards, endowed scholarships, and annual scholarships. There are several Gardner-Webb loan funds. The University also administers aid from the full range of federal programs: Federal Pell Grants, Federal Work-Study Program awards, Federal Perkins Loans, and federally guaranteed Federal Stafford Student and Federal PLUS loans. North Carolina students have access to state grant funds administered by the University. Scholarships based on academic promise are also granted each year. Of all students, 90 percent receive aid in some form. The two criteria for receiving financial aid are financial need and academic promise.

Faculty

The faculty-student ratio is 1:15. Faculty members engage both formally and informally in student advising and counseling. A staff of professional counselors is also available. Faculty members teach at all class levels without regard to academic rank or length of service. Graduate assistants are not used to teach classes.

Student Government

The University has a student government whose members are elected by the student body. This organization, set up with executive, legislative, and judicial branches, is very influential in campus affairs. In addition, students have voting positions on all standing committees of the University.

Admission Requirements

Although a fixed pattern of high school credits is not prescribed, the following minimum course distribution is recommended: 4 units in English, 2 in a foreign language, 2 in social science, 2 in algebra, 1 in geometry, and 2 in natural science, plus electives. The University requires each applicant to submit an application form, a high school transcript, and SAT I scores. ACT scores are also acceptable. Acceptance to Gardner-Webb is based on the applicant's high school record, rank in class, SAT I or ACT composite scores, and extracurricular activities. Transfer students' course credits are evaluated on courses as credit only, not on grade point average. An interview is recommended but not mandatory.

Gardner-Webb admits students of any race, color, and national or ethnic origin to all the rights, privileges, programs, and activities generally accorded or made available to students at the University.

Application and Information

Applications, together with a nonrefundable $25 application fee, may be submitted for either semester. Early application is advised. Notification of the admission decision is given on a rolling basis upon receipt of all application data. A $150 room deposit for boarding students is due thirty days after acceptance and is refundable until May 1. A $50 deposit is required of commuting students.

For further information, students should contact:

Director of Undergraduate Admissions
and Enrollment Management
Gardner-Webb University
Boiling Springs, North Carolina 28017
Telephone: 704-406-4GWU
800-253-6472 (toll-free)
World Wide Web: http://www.gardner-webb.edu

Gardner-Webb University students enjoy a safe, character-building Christian environment where people really care.

GEORGE FOX UNIVERSITY

NEWBERG, OREGON

The University

George Fox University was founded in 1891 by the Society of Friends (Quakers) with the purpose of providing students a challenging academic atmosphere within a community of Christian faith. Today, George Fox maintains the same mission and has grown to an enrollment of 2,700 students.

Students find George Fox to be a place where spiritual growth and intellectual challenge take place in a friendly, caring environment. This tradition of integration of faith and learning has been recognized by the Templeton Foundation, which named George Fox University to its honor roll of character-building colleges.

Seventy-five percent of George Fox students live in campus residence halls, suites, and apartments. Opportunities for extracurricular involvement are available in music, drama, journalism, student government, radio, clubs, and athletics. George Fox is a member of the NCAA Division III and competes in six men's sports (baseball, basketball, cross-country, soccer, tennis, and track) and seven women's sports (basketball, cross-country, soccer, softball, tennis, track, and volleyball). Intramural sports are also played.

Regular chapel services bring the campus community together in worship. Students have the opportunity to put their faith into action on volunteer mission trips and during community outreach activities.

In addition to its undergraduate degrees, George Fox confers the Master of Business Administration, Master of Education, Doctor of Education, Master of Arts in Teaching, and Doctor of Psychology degrees and eight graduate degrees through George Fox Evangelical Seminary.

Location

George Fox University is located in Newberg, a residential community of 18,000 people. The 75-acre tree-shaded campus is a 30-minute drive from the major metropolitan environment of Portland. The University is situated in the beautiful Pacific Northwest, with scenic Mt. Hood and the rugged Pacific coastline within short driving distances.

Tilikum Retreat Center, set on a 90-acre lake and just 10 minutes away, provides students a change of pace from the classroom. Students enjoy hiking, canoeing, and fishing at the camp. Tilikum has an extensive summer day camp program that employs many University students.

Majors and Degrees

George Fox confers the Bachelor of Arts and Bachelor of Science degrees. The following undergraduate majors are available: accounting, art, biblical studies, biology, business and economics, chemistry, Christian educational ministries, cognitive science, communication arts, communication/video production, computer and information science, electrical engineering, elementary education, family and consumer science, fashion merchandising, foods and nutrition in business, history, interdisciplinary studies, interior design, international studies, mathematics, mechanical engineering, music, philosophy, physical education, political science, religion, social work, sociology, and writing/literature.

Academic Program

The academic year at George Fox University is divided into two semesters of fifteen weeks. In addition to the two semesters, the University sponsors a three-week May Term. For graduation, students are required to earn 126 credit hours, including 54 general education and 42 upper-division credits.

Students may reduce the number of required courses and add flexibility to their undergraduate years with credit earned through Advanced Placement, International Baccalaureate (IB), the College-Level Examination Program, and credit by examination. All traditional undergraduates are given a personal computer to use and keep upon graduation.

George Fox demonstrates its commitment to freshmen by providing a Freshman Seminar Program to assist students as they integrate themselves into the academic and social life of the University community.

Off-Campus Programs

The importance of international study is shown through a variety of programs. Each year during May Term, George Fox sponsors a number of three-week study tours led by University faculty members. Transportation costs are subsidized by the University. These international learning experiences are designed for students completing their junior year. Through the Coalition for Christian Colleges and Universities, students are also given the opportunity to study for a semester in China, Costa Rica, England, Kenya, Russia, the Middle East, and Washington, D.C.

Membership in the Christian College Consortium enables George Fox University students to attend for a semester one of twelve colleges located throughout the United States.

Academic Facilities

The new Edward F. Stevens Center provides 40,000 square feet of office and classroom space. All student service-oriented offices are now housed under one roof that provides greater efficiency and access for students. The building has been selected as part of the "Ten Shades of Green" by Portland General Electric for its use of recycled materials and minimal environmental impact.

The three-story Murdock Learning Resource Center houses more than 175,000 books and periodicals. Its features include rare book collections, study carrels, computer and audiovisual laboratories, a recording studio, and a darkroom.

The Edwards/Holman Science Center is home to the University's science programs. The 36,000-square-foot building provides classrooms, offices, and laboratories for biology, chemistry, premedicine, mathematics, computer science, and engineering programs.

The William and Mary Bauman Auditorium seats 1,150 people in a facility that is among the finest in the Northwest. Rotating art exhibits appear in the adjoining Lindgren Art Gallery.

Costs

Tuition for the 2003–04 year was $19,500. Room and board were $6300. Fees cost $310. Books are estimated to cost $600 per year.

Financial Aid

George Fox maintains that every qualified student should be able to attend the university of his or her choice without letting limited finances stand in the way. To this end, federal, state, and institutional need-based funds are available, as are merit awards. About 87 percent of all students receive financial aid.

Faculty

The faculty at George Fox University fosters an atmosphere of discussion and independent thinking in the classroom. Faculty members have found a healthy balance between teaching and research by devoting a majority of their time to educating students. The University employs 120 full-time and 112 part-time faculty members. Seventy percent of the full-time faculty members hold earned doctoral degrees. Faculty members are personally committed Christians who are involved in the lives of their students. The student-faculty ratio is 15:1.

Student Government

The Associated Student Community of George Fox University serves as a unifying force and voice for the campus student community and plays a significant role in organizing cultural, social, and recreational activities.

Admission Requirements

Students admitted to George Fox University must show academic ability, high moral character, and social concern. These qualities are evaluated by consideration of each applicant's academic record, test scores, recommendations, interview reports, and participation in extracurricular activities. The priority application deadline is February 1. In order to provide a solid foundation for college-level work, it is recommended that the applicant present the equivalent of 16 academic units from an approved high school. The following units are suggested: English, 4; social studies, 2; science, 2; mathematics, 2; foreign language, 2; and health and physical education, 1.

Application and Information

For additional information, students should contact:

Office of Undergraduate Admission
George Fox University
Newberg, Oregon 97132-2697
Telephone: 800-765-4369 Ext. 2240 (toll-free)
E-mail: admissions@georgefox.edu
World Wide Web: http://www.georgefox.edu

GEORGETOWN COLLEGE

GEORGETOWN, KENTUCKY

The College

Chartered in 1829, but with origins dating to 1787, Georgetown College is one of the oldest Baptist-affiliated colleges in America. The coeducational undergraduate student body of about 1,350 comes primarily from Kentucky, Ohio, and Indiana, but twenty-seven other states and ten other countries are also represented. The standard of excellence maintained since the College began has helped to channel more than 10,000 alumni into medicine, law, diplomacy, teaching, business, the ministry, social work, and countless other occupations all over the world. In addition to its undergraduate programs, the College offers a graduate program leading to the Master of Arts in Education.

The academic reputation of the College is the primary reason given by freshmen for selecting Georgetown. The College's Christian commitment is another strong influence among a majority of students. By combining strong academics, a Christian emphasis, and a comprehensive extracurricular program that provides many opportunities for student involvement and leadership, Georgetown is able to offer a distinctive living and learning community. This program has brought Georgetown national recognition in publications such as *U.S. News & World Report,* Peterson's *Competitive Colleges, Barron's 300 Best Buys in College Education, The Student Guide to America's 100 Best College Buys,* and the Templeton Foundation's *Colleges That Encourage Character Development.* The Carnegie Foundation has also recognized Georgetown as a Baccalaureate I institution.

Membership in local chapters of national honoraries is available in most academic disciplines. Georgetown's chapter of Phi Beta Lambda (the honorary business fraternity) has achieved distinction on the state and national levels. The Association of Georgetown Students sponsors concerts, films, dances, and special events, and the Office of Campus Ministries organizes religious activities.

Kentucky's oldest drama group still resides on campus, along with a nationally recognized forensics team. One of Georgetown's choral groups performs on tour in Europe every third summer. Concert and pep bands, a weekly student newspaper, a yearbook, fraternities and sororities, and many other extracurricular activities provide opportunities for all students, regardless of major. The Academic Team has won the Kentucky state championship three out of the past five years.

More than 90 percent of Georgetown's students live on campus in the College's fourteen dormitories or four modern apartment-style townhouses. Most of these residence halls house fewer than 80 students each. This housing arrangement promotes a friendly, family atmosphere and demonstrates the College's personal approach to education.

The College fields athletic teams in eight NAIA intercollegiate sports for men (baseball, basketball, cross-country, football, golf, soccer, tennis, and track) and in eight NAIA sports for women (basketball, cross-country, golf, soccer, softball, tennis, track, and volleyball) and offers cheerleading and dance teams. Georgetown's teams regularly participate on the national tournament level, and in the 1990s, the Tigers captured two national championships. Team members regularly receive national recognition. The athletic facilities are among the best of comparable institutions. Rawlings Stadium and nearby apartments host the summer camp of the NFL's Cincinnati Bengals.

Location

Recognized as one of the safest cities in Kentucky, historic Georgetown is in the Lexington metropolitan area. Some of the world's most famous horse farms are very close to the campus, and the Kentucky State Horse Park (open the year round and offering 100 riding horses) is only 5 miles south of the College. Major industrial facilities are also located nearby. The Toyota Motor Manufacturing Company plant is 4 miles north of the campus, and LexMark's facility is about 11 miles to the south. The community is served by all major airlines at the Lexington Bluegrass and Greater Cincinnati airports and is readily accessible by the interstate highway system (I-75 and I-64).

Majors and Degrees

Georgetown College confers the degrees of Bachelor of Arts, Bachelor of Science, Bachelor of Music, and Bachelor of Music Education. Major programs are available in accounting; American studies; art; biological sciences; business administration and communication arts; business administration and ethics; chemistry; church music; communication arts; computer science; elementary education; English; environmental science; European studies; finance; French; German; history; international business management; kinesiology; management; management information systems; marketing; marketing/finance; mathematics; medical technology; music; music education; philosophy; physics; political science; psychology; religion; sociology; and Spanish. Preprofessional preparation is offered in dentistry, engineering, law, medicine, the ministry, nursing, pharmacy, physical therapy, and veterinary science.

Georgetown offers dual-degree programs in nursing (with the University of Kentucky), engineering arts (with Washington University and the University of Kentucky), and ministerial education (with Regent's Park College of Oxford University).

Academic Program

The College operates on a semester-hour system of two 15-week semesters, a summer session of two 5-week terms, and two miniterms. Students may study abroad in College-sponsored programs in England, France, Mexico, Chile, or Hong Kong. Arrangements through the Kentucky Institute for International Studies and the Consortium for Global Education provide additional study opportunities throughout Central and South America, Europe, Africa, and Asia.

To qualify for graduation, students must complete a minimum of 128 semester hours, including major and minor field requirements and up to 56 semester hours of general education. The general education requirements are distributed as follows: Christian faith and values, 6 hours; effective communication, 8 hours; natural sciences, 9 hours; social sciences, 6 hours in two fields; cultural and aesthetic values, 16 hours; foreign language and culture, 9 hours; and physical education, 2 hours. Any of these general education requirements may be satisfied by examination.

Students may be granted college credit for satisfactory performance on the Advanced Placement tests given by the College Board. They may also earn credit in twenty subjects and a waiver of certain requirements by taking the College-Level Examination Program (CLEP) subject examinations. The College also recognizes credit earned through the International Baccalaureate program.

Both Air Force and Army ROTC programs are available for Georgetown College students through an agreement with the University of Kentucky. Cadets are full-time students at Georgetown and take one course session weekly at UK. Applicants are considered on the basis of their ACT or SAT I scores, high school academic record, extracurricular and athletic activities, personal references, and a medical examination.

Academic Facilities

Georgetown's academic commons includes ten classroom buildings. From historic Pawling Hall, built in 1844 and completely renovated in 1991, to the modern Wilson Fine Arts Building, each facility has special features that enhance the learning process.

The George Matt Asher Science Center is the largest classroom building on campus. In addition to the eleven science laboratories located in the center, students also have access to a foreign language lab, a botanical greenhouse, a 24-foot-screen planetarium, and one of five computer science labs.

The Ensor Learning Resource Center (library), completed in 1998, encompasses more than 55,000 square feet, including space for 220,500 books and 1,050 periodicals, and features state-of-the-art electronic research technology. Other features include study tables with computer hookups and a replica of the Yale Law Library study room, complete with a 14-foot-high fireplace.

The Nunnelley Music Building, Wilson Fine Arts Building, and Wilson Theatre, all located on the campus's west side, provide a focal point for the arts. The Nunnelley Music Building's features include private-lesson studios, ensemble rehearsal rooms, and computer facilities for music students. The theater seats up to 150 and offers a fully equipped workshop for set construction. The Anne Wright Wilson Fine Arts Building, featuring lecture and gallery space, a sculpture yard, a modern computer graphics lab, and photography, printing, painting, and design labs, opened in 1996.

Costs

The 2004–05 academic-year expenses are $17,750 for tuition and $5450 for room and board for a total of $23,200.

Financial Aid

Approximately 94 percent of the College's students receive some form of financial assistance. Academic or need-based scholarships, departmental grants, Federal Perkins Loans, Federal Stafford Student Loans, Federal Pell Grants, Federal Work-Study Program awards, athletic scholarships, and Christian Service Grants are available. To be considered for assistance, students should file the Free Application for Federal Student Aid (FAFSA). Priority consideration is given to those who file before February 15. A number of awards, some paying up to the full cost of tuition, fees, and room and board, are made on the basis of academic ability alone; the application deadline for these is February 1.

Faculty

Georgetown has an outstanding faculty; 91 percent of its members hold the terminal degree in their area of expertise. The student-faculty ratio is 13:1, and the average class size is 18. No academic classes are taught by graduate students, and full professors teach freshman-level courses. Faculty members are readily accessible to any student both in and out of the classroom, and they interact freely with one another across disciplinary lines.

Student Government

The Association of Georgetown Students (AGS) actively represents the voice of the students in nearly all campus matters. It has a major responsibility in coordinating campus life and activities and regularly encourages interaction between students, faculty members, and the administration to enhance student development.

Admission Requirements

Applicants for admission to Georgetown are considered individually on the basis of a combination of academic records. All applicants must submit high school transcripts, official score reports of the ACT examination or the SAT I, and a brief written essay. International students must also present scores on the Test of English as a Foreign Language.

Other materials the student feels would be helpful in evaluating his or her potential for success, such as recommendations or tapes, are welcome. Evidence of creativity and leadership is also considered. Applicants should generally be in the upper half of their graduating class and have taken a strong college-preparatory program.

Admission and financial assistance are awarded by Georgetown College without regard to race, religion, sex, national origin, or handicap.

Application and Information

Application should be made in the senior year, and students are notified of the admissions decision on a rolling basis. Georgetown endorses the NACAC common Candidates Reply Date of May 1.

Further information may be obtained from:

Director of Admissions
Georgetown College
400 East College Street
Georgetown, Kentucky 40324-1696
Telephone: 502-863-8009
800-788-9985 (toll-free)
E-mail: admissions@georgetowncollege.edu
World Wide Web: http://www.georgetowncollege.edu

The Ensor Learning Resource Center contains more than 290,000 book volumes and microfilm and audiovisual titles as well as more than 170 computers and 185 data drops throughout the 55,000-square-foot building.

THE GEORGE WASHINGTON UNIVERSITY

WASHINGTON, D.C.

THE GEORGE WASHINGTON UNIVERSITY
WASHINGTON DC

The University

Located just four blocks from the White House, The George Washington University (GW) is the largest institution of higher education in the nation's capital. Founded in 1821 by an Act of Congress, GW is a private nonsectarian coeducational institution, accredited by the Middle States Association of Colleges and Universities. GW prides itself in being at the forefront of major research endeavors, while providing a stimulating intellectual environment for its diverse students and faculty.

The student population at GW consists of approximately 9,000 undergraduates and 10,000 graduates. Undergraduates hail from all fifty states, the District of Columbia, Puerto Rico, the Virgin Islands, and 139 countries. The undergraduate student body is 11 percent Asian American, 8 percent African American, 5 percent Hispanic American, and 8 percent international.

Both the Foggy Bottom and Mount Vernon campuses are located in historical and prestigious D.C. neighborhoods. The Foggy Bottom campus is situated in the heart of downtown D.C., neighbored by the Kennedy Center, the Watergate complex, the State Department, and the White House. The 26-acre Mount Vernon campus is home to athletic facilities and is surrounded by embassy and diplomatic residences. Both campus communities offer vibrant and distinctive residential options to freshmen and continuing students.

GW guarantees housing for entering freshmen and houses approximately 70 percent of undergraduates in thirty-one residence halls. GW offers a number of living arrangements, including apartment-style living for upperclassmen and residential town houses. GW's community living and learning philosophy guarantees that residence hall life is a valuable extension of the undergraduate experience. With nearly 97 percent of the entering class living in University housing, the atmosphere proves to be academically as well as socially stimulating.

GW hosts a strong intercollegiate varsity athletic program with twenty-two teams participating in the NCAA Division I and Atlantic 10 Conference. They include men's baseball, basketball, crew, cross-country, golf, soccer, swimming and diving, tennis, and water polo, and women's basketball, crew, cross-country, gymnastics, soccer, swimming and diving, tennis, volleyball, and water polo. Students interested in playing sports, but not quite up to the conference level may join a number of University-supported intramural sports.

There are more than 330 student-created and student-run organizations at GW. These organizations run the spectrum from academic to cultural, spiritual to recreational, and political to artistic. In addition to these special-interest organizations, GW is home to twenty-five national sororities and fraternities and nineteen honor societies, the Student Association (details in the Student Government section), the Program Board, the *Hatchet* (GW's independent newspaper), and WRGW (the campus radio station). The Student Activities Center plans large-scale events for students on campus, ranging from Welcome Week to Excellence in Student Life Awards to Fall Fest and Spring Fling.

Location

Many students at GW also choose to immerse themselves in the excitement of Washington, which has been called the most livable city on the East Coast. Washington, D.C., offers an infinite array of internships and cooperative education experiences, allowing GW students to explore their career aspirations outside of the four walls of the classroom. GW students have interned at the White House, the World Bank, AOL Time-Warner, the U.S. House of Representatives and Senate, NASA, the National Zoo, CNN, among many other world famous organizations.

The hordes of tourists that flock to Washington, D.C., every year experience the vibrant college town and young professional social scene in the nation's capital. There are more than 400,000 college students at forty-four colleges and universities concentrated in the metropolitan area.

Majors and Degrees

GW offers a wide range of undergraduate programs in six undergraduate schools: the Columbian College of Arts and Sciences, the Elliott School of International Affairs, the School of Business and Public Management, the School of Engineering and Applied Science, the School of Medicine and Health Sciences, and the School of Public Health and Health Services.

GW offers eighty-nine majors, more than 1,000 courses, and yet, the average class size is only 26. Students may earn an undergraduate degree in a single field of study, or they may choose to double major, major in one field and minor in another, participate in an interdisciplinary program, or create their own individualized field of study.

The University awards an array of bachelor's degrees, including Bachelor of Arts (B.A.), Bachelor of Science (B.S.), Bachelor of Fine Arts (B.F.A.), Bachelor of Accountancy (B.Accy.), and Bachelor of Business Administration (B.B.A.).

Several joint-degree programs are available to undergraduates. Five-year bachelor's/master's programs include the B.S./M.A. in economics, the B.S./M.S. in systems engineering/engineering management, the B.A./M.A. in art or psychology/art therapy, the B.S./M.S. in chemical toxicology (chemistry/forensic sciences), and the B.B.A./M.S.I.S.T., B.B.A./M.T.A., and B.B.A./M.P.A.

Academic Program

Most undergraduate students must complete 120 credit hours in order to be eligible for graduation, which means that the average student carries 15 credit hours (five courses) per semester. All freshmen at GW are required to take English composition. In addition, each school has general curriculum requirements, ranging from 17 to 45 credit hours.

GW is home to nineteen honor societies, including Phi Beta Kappa and Golden Key National Honor Society. GW offers a variety of specialized academic programs. The University Honors Program, which does not replace a regular program of study but rather enhances it with intellectually challenging analysis and discussion, consists of approximately 800 undergraduates. The University's Science Scholar Program in chemistry, physics, and mathematics combines nationally and internationally recognized faculty members, bright students, excellent on-campus facilities, and access to facilities in the Washington metropolitan area and beyond to give the future chemist, physicist, or mathematician the kind of head start that can make a difference in a scientific career. The seven-year Integrated B.A./M.D. Program is designed for students who wish to obtain a strong foundation in the liberal arts prior to becoming physicians, enabling them to accomplish that goal in a shorter amount of time than a traditional program of study. The Integrated Engineering and Medicine Program is an eight-year dual-degree program, combining four years of engineering, four years of medicine, a volunteer applied medical experience or an individual medical research project, and the opportunity to live on an exclusive floor of a GW residence hall. Similarly, the Integrated Engineering and Law Program offers highly qualified high school students the opportunity to earn a B.S. degree in engineering or computer science, and a J.D. degree in order to launch successful careers in such fields as patent law, intellectual property rights, and environmental law. The Presidential Arts Scholarship Program awards scholarships to, and encourages the work of, entering freshmen who have shown promise in the fine arts (ceramics, design, drawing, interior design, painting, printmaking, photography, sculpture, and visual communication), music, theater, technical theater, directing, dance, and choreography.

Off-Campus Programs

GW students are encouraged to study abroad in order to expand their world view and their educational opportunities. GW offers study abroad centers in Madrid, Paris, and Brasilia, as well as affiliated and exchange programs in more than fifty countries. During the 2002–03 academic year, 700 GW undergraduates were studying abroad.

Many GW students also take advantage of cooperative education (co-op), which provides students with an opportunity to gain valuable paid work experiences directly related to their major. The Career Center manages the program, in partnership with area employers, to ensure that co-op experiences are substantive and well-supervised. Similarly, many GW students engage in internships, which serve as a means for students to gain practical, professional experience and to augment their academic knowledge. Internships can be paid or unpaid, offered for academic credit, and can last for as long (or short) as the student and employer choose. The Career Center also acts as a clearinghouse for internship positions.

Academic Facilities

The Gelman Library owns more than 1.4 million volumes and 11,000 titles and, as a member of the Washington Research Library Consortium (WRLC), offers GW students access to more than 6 million volumes at eight area universities. Gelman Library is open 168 hours per week offering 24-hour study lounges, group discussion rooms, computer labs, walk-up reference consultation, and an interlibrary loan service. GW provides on-site and remote access to ALADIN, the shared online catalogue of WRLC libraries, plus databases indexing periodical articles and some full-text journals. GW is also home to the Eckles Library, the Jacob Burns Law Library, and the Himmelfarb Health Sciences Library.

Most academic buildings, libraries, residence halls, and the Marvin Center house computer labs, many of which are open 24 hours a day. In addition, most students who live on campus in residence halls have individual, high-speed Ethernet connectivity and Internet access.

Equipped with fiber-optic network, Internet access, and a state-of-the-art media center for print, broadcast, and online student media projects, the new Media and Public Affairs Building features a media auditorium that is home to CNN's *Crossfire,* a live hour-long news debate program that is aired five nights a week. The facility also features a press gallery, a newsmaker studio for faculty experts to hold media interviews, video archives, television and radio production facilities, and audiovisual laboratories.

Costs

Tuition for the 2003–04 academic year was $29,320. Room and board were approximately $10,070.

Financial Aid

The ability to finance a GW education is a priority, so the Office of Student Financial Assistance seeks to assist students and their families in meeting the costs to attend the University. The University budgets more than $85 million for undergraduate financial assistance, which includes scholarships and need-based assistance. In addition, GW offers families the opportunity to participate in a number of payment plans.

By applying for admission, students with outstanding academic credentials are automatically considered for Presidential Academic Scholarships ranging from $12,000 to $20,000 per year ($48,000 to $80,000 over four years). Approximately 23 percent of freshmen receive merit-based financial assistance. In addition, approximately 42 percent of GW's entering class receives need-based assistance totaling $10.2 million with an average package of $19,680 in 2003–04. More information about financial aid at GW can be obtained online at http://gwired.gwu.edu/finaid.

Faculty

There is 1 faculty member for every 12 students at GW. Of GW's 1,428 full-time faculty members, 92 percent hold a doctorate degree. Members of the part-time and adjunct faculty are often leaders in their field of expertise. GW professors are engaging, eminently qualified, and well connected, which allows for a robust intellectual community.

Student Government

The Student Association (SA) is an organization chartered by GW's Board of Trustees to represent students and their concerns. Any person registered for any academic credit at GW is a member of the SA. The SA undertakes initiatives related to academics, community service, neighborhood relations, and student activities.

Admissions Requirements

GW receives more than 18,000 applications for freshman admission and aims to recruit a class of 2,250. Admitted students have strong academic records and the demonstrated ability to achieve success in their college endeavors. To be considered for admission, applicants must submit the following credentials: application (part 1) and fee, application (part 2), high school transcripts, essay, letters of recommendation from a teacher and a guidance counselor, and either SAT I or ACT scores. Details can be obtained online at the Web site listed below. GW also accepts the common application, but requires a supplement to be included. On-campus interviews are not required, but may be helpful.

Application and Information

GW has a number of application options: regular decision, early decision I, and early decision II. Prospective students should consult the Web site listed below for the application and deadlines.

The George Washington University
Office of Admissions
2121 I Street, NW, Suite 201
Washington, D.C. 20052
Telephone: 202-994-6040
800-447-3765 (toll-free)
E-mail: gwadm@gwu.edu
World Wide Web: http://www.gwu.edu/~go2gw

Students on campus at The George Washington University.

GEORGIAN COURT UNIVERSITY

LAKEWOOD, NEW JERSEY

The University

Georgian Court University (GCU), founded in 1908 and sponsored by the Sisters of Mercy of New Jersey, is a Catholic comprehensive university with a strong liberal arts core and a special concern for women. The current undergraduate enrollment is 1,778. In 1976, the University expanded to include a Graduate School of Education. In 1979, the coeducational undergraduate Evening Division was established to provide both men and women the means to pursue a baccalaureate degree while being involved in full- or part-time employment; it now enrolls 489 students. The University's strong academic program aims not merely to educate competent professionals but, more importantly, to develop students' potential and to deepen their understanding of society and commitment to its future. Georgian Court students follow a curriculum broad enough to be truly liberal, yet specialized enough to provide preparation in depth for further study and future careers. The mission of Georgian Court is the education of creative and responsible leaders who have a firm sense of moral, spiritual, and intellectual values.

The University's beautifully landscaped 150-acre campus on the former George Gould estate provides an impressive setting for university life. The campus has seventeen buildings. The majority of the University's students come from New Jersey. A small percentage come from surrounding states and other countries. Twenty-one percent of the students enrolled in the women's university are resident students. The residence facilities, St. Joseph Hall and Maria Hall, provide private or semiprivate rooms situated around comfortable lounges. Kitchenettes are located on each floor.

Both resident and commuting students participate in a wide variety of activities, including numerous cultural and social functions. There are a number of University-sponsored trips to New York and Philadelphia to visit museums, attend the theater, and shop. In addition, social activities are planned on campus, with invitations extended to area colleges. The Patrick and Julia Gavan Student Lounge is the gathering place for all students. Seasonal parties, live entertainment, and special events make the student lounge a popular place to be. There are also thirty-five cultural, educational, honorary, and service-oriented clubs and organizations. Two student publications provide opportunities for students who enjoy photography or writing. For students who are musically inclined, the Court Singers, Court Notes, and the Georgian Court University concert and jazz bands and orchestra provide opportunities. Women's NCAA Division II intercollegiate competition is offered in basketball, cross-country, soccer, softball, tennis, and volleyball. The facilities at Georgian Court include a heated swimming pool, tennis courts, and landscaped acreage ideally suited for jogging and bicycling.

The Counseling Center staff assists students in adjusting to university life, helps them to budget their time, gives seminars on leadership and personal growth, and provides individual and group counseling and psychotherapy in addition to referral services. Career counseling and placement services are also offered to all students and alumni. Students needing extra assistance with course work may take advantage of the tutorial aides available through Student Support Services. The Health Center, staffed by registered nurses throughout the day and evening, provides general health care and arranges for medical treatment as needed. Campus ministers are available to provide spiritual counseling. The Eucharistic Liturgy is offered on campus. In addition, the Lakewood area has a wide variety of churches and synagogues to serve non-Catholic students. The Learning Center (TLC) is an assistance program designed to provide an environment for students with mild to moderate learning disabilities. Emphasis is placed on developing self-help strategies and study techniques. The newly established Academic Skills Development Center (ADC) provides free tutoring for any student on campus who needs assistance in a subject. Peer tutors, recommended by the faculty, aid students in a better understanding of the subjects they are studying.

Location

Bordering the north shore of Lake Carasaljo, the campus is situated in a quiet, residential neighborhood of Lakewood, New Jersey. Centrally located in the state, Georgian Court is convenient to the Route 9 corridor, the Garden State Parkway, and Interstate 195. New York City, Philadelphia, and Atlantic City are each less than 1½ hours by car from the campus. The distance to the seashore is approximately 10 miles.

Majors and Degrees

The Bachelor of Arts (B.A.) degree is awarded in art, art history, biology, chemistry, computer information systems, criminal justice, English, French, history, humanities, mathematics, music, physics, psychology, religious studies, sociology, Spanish, and special education. The Bachelor of Fine Arts (B.F.A.) is awarded in art with concentrations in general fine arts and graphic design/illustration. The Bachelor of Science (B.S.) degree is awarded in accounting, allied health technologies (a joint degree with the University of Medicine and Dentistry of New Jersey (UMDNJ)), biochemistry, biology, business administration, chemistry, clinical laboratory science, computer science, and physics. Students planning a career in social work can obtain the Bachelor of Social Work (B.S.W.) degree.

Teacher certification programs in elementary education, subject areas N–12 (secondary education), special education, and English as a second language are available at Georgian Court.

In the joint-degree program with UMDNJ, the allied health technologies student may choose to specialize in diagnostic medical sonography, vascular technology, respiratory care, or nuclear medicine technology. The student completes 93 credits at Georgian Court University and 41–50 credits at UMDNJ. The student earns a Bachelor of Science degree in allied health technologies with a minor in biology, jointly awarded by Georgian Court University and UMDNJ.

Academic Program

Successful completion of 132 credit hours is required for a B.A., B.F.A., B.S., or B.S.W. degree. With departmental approval, students may elect a second major. All students must complete general education requirements, which are designed to provide the breadth essential for complete development of the truly liberally educated person. These consist of nine approved semester courses in the humanities, five in the social sciences, and three in the natural sciences/mathematics.

Many departments offer minor field sequences, certification programs, or concentrations. These include anthropology, bilingual/bicultural studies, commercial art, communications, computer science, criminal justice, economics, English as a second language, gerontology, holistic health, marketing, medical technology, nuclear medicine technology, philosophy, and political science. Preprofessional programs include chiropractic, dentistry, law, medicine, and veterinary. In addition, interdisciplinary minors are available in American studies, international area studies, Latin American studies, and women's studies. Internships, externships, and practicums are offered in most majors, and independent studies are available.

Off-Campus Programs

Students are permitted to enroll in an accredited college or university offering a study-abroad program. Georgian Court University credits are offered for Autumn Semester in Quebec and study abroad in a Spanish-speaking country.

Academic Facilities

The Arts and Science Center contains classrooms, seminar rooms, offices, studios for the fine arts, the Little Theatre, a radioisotope laboratory, a computer laboratory, an anthropology laboratory, and modern laboratories and equipment for instruction and research in the biological, chemical, and physical sciences. The library houses a collection of more than 200,000 items in print and nonprint format, including more than 1,060 currently received periodical titles. An online library system and Internet capability provide students with access to a wide variety of information resources both local and worldwide. A multimedia classroom enhances instruction in the use of electronic resources, and a computer lab permits students to use these resources as well as e-mail, course-related software, and general software such as word processing and spreadsheets. The library catalog and many databases can be utilized from any networked computer on campus as well as off-campus users with a password to access library collections. The library is open 80 hours weekly, with reference assistance available at all times. Hamilton Hall houses the community education services in reading and diagnostics as well as some programs in special education. Residence halls are wired for room telephones, and data lines are connected by fiber-optic cable.

Costs

Tuition for the 2004–05 academic year for full-time students is $17,224. Residence and board are $7200 (seven-day meal plan) or $7050 (five-day meal plan). General fees are $700.

Financial Aid

Georgian Court University has endeavored to keep the cost of attending an independent university affordable. A large percentage of its students receive financial assistance. Financial aid consists of all scholarships, grants, loans, or campus jobs offered to the applicant to help meet education-related expenses. Eligible students may be aided through a combination of these items, called a financial aid package. Georgian Court offers both need-based and no-need financial aid. For example, some scholarships are granted on the basis of a superior academic record, SAT I or ACT scores, and financial need; other scholarships are based on academic excellence only. Athletic grants of variable amounts are available to students who qualify for admission and demonstrate the ability to participate in the sports program while advancing their college career. Georgian Court financial aid is available to U.S. citizens and eligible noncitizens. The University also participates in the New Jersey Educational Opportunity Fund program. In order to be considered for any financial aid, all students must submit a Georgian Court financial aid form to the Financial Aid Office. All applicants must also submit the Free Application for Federal Student Aid (FAFSA). This analysis indicates the student's degree of financial need. An award letter and acceptance statement are sent to students who qualify for aid, indicating the assistance provided to meet the student's financial need. Acceptance statements must be returned to the Financial Aid Office to finalize the awards. Financial aid information is included in the viewbook and on the GCU Web site (under Admissions).

Faculty

Seventy-four percent of the full-time teaching faculty members hold doctoral degrees. From the freshman year on, students have the opportunity to take courses with department chairpersons and other faculty members in the upper professional ranks. The student-faculty ratio is 14:1. The average class size is approximately 15. Individual counseling by the faculty adviser is an integral part of the educational process at Georgian Court.

Student Government

The Student Government Association, composed of elected students, organizes extracurricular activities for students. Through the student government structure, students take leadership roles in shaping student life and participate in all major University committees in conjunction with the faculty and administration.

Admission Requirements

Georgian Court University welcomes applications from students who desire a liberal arts education and have the necessary qualifications to benefit from the University's program. Entrance is based on individual merit. The high school record of achievement is of primary importance and must reflect solid performance in a college-preparatory program. Candidates for admission must have completed 16 academic (Carnegie) units. The majority of students attending Georgian Court ranked in the upper half of their senior class in high school. All candidates are required to take the SAT I or ACT, preferably by December of the senior year. Further consideration is given to the applicant's extracurricular activities and letters of recommendation submitted by teachers, counselors, employers, or similarly qualified people. A campus interview is highly recommended. The interview focuses primarily on a discussion of the student's experiences and interests and allows the interviewer to explain the University's current offerings. A guided tour of the campus is also offered.

Well-qualified applicants whose first choice is Georgian Court University and who apply no later than November 15 may be considered for early decision. A mature, well-qualified student who wishes to enter the University after three years of high school may apply for early entrance. Transfer students are accepted into the freshman, sophomore, and junior classes for the fall and spring semesters. All students must be in good standing at their former college. Applicants with fewer than 24 credits must fulfill all requirements for admission to the freshman class. International students in need of a student visa must present official documents at least six months prior to the semester's start and must have a minimum TOEFL score of 550. International students must complete a GCU financial support form and should be prepared to assume full financial responsibility for educational and personal expenses in the United States.

Application and Information

To apply for admission, regular freshman applicants should send an application, high school transcript, and nonrefundable $40 application fee. Transfer students should submit an application, the fee, and transcripts from high school and all colleges attended. Freshman applicants are urged to file an application as early as possible in their senior year of high school. Freshman and transfer applications must be received by August 1 for the fall semester and by January 1 for the spring semester. The University has a rolling admissions policy; however, transfer and freshman applications should be received by August 1 for the fall semester and December 15 for the spring semester for the best course selection. Printable and electronic applications are available on the Web site.

For further information, prospective students should contact:

Office of Admissions
Georgian Court University
900 Lakewood Avenue
Lakewood, New Jersey 08701
Telephone: 732-364-2200 Ext. 760
800-458-8422 Ext. 760 (toll-free)
Fax: 732-364-4442
E-mail: admissions@georgian.edu
World Wide Web: http://www.georgian.edu

GONZAGA UNIVERSITY

SPOKANE, WASHINGTON

The University

Gonzaga, founded in 1887, is an independent, comprehensive university with a distinguished background in the Catholic, Jesuit, and humanistic tradition. Gonzaga emphasizes the moral and ethical implications of learning, living, and working in today's global society. As a testament to this educational approach, Gonzaga's first-to-second-year retention rate tops 90 percent. Through the University Core Curriculum, each student develops a strong liberal arts foundation, which many alumni cite as a most valuable asset. In addition, students specialize in any of more than seventy-five academic areas of study.

Gonzaga's 110-acre campus is characterized by sprawling green lawns and majestic evergreen trees. Towering above the campus are the stately spires of St. Aloysius Church, the well-recognized landmark featured in the University logo.

Because personal growth is as important as intellectual development, Gonzaga places great emphasis on student life outside of class. Ranging in population size from 35 to 361 students and offering both coed and single-sex living, Gonzaga's sixteen residence halls and seven apartment complexes offer an intimate atmosphere and a lively campus experience. Each hall has one or more Residence Assistants and a chaplain or a resident Jesuit. Since freshmen and sophomores are required to live on campus and 40 percent of the total undergraduate student body also resides in Gonzaga's halls and apartments, campus-based activities ranging from residence hall government to current affairs symposiums to intramural sports keep students informed and entertained. Students in all academic majors integrate with the Spokane community through a variety of activities, such as volunteer opportunities and internships at numerous businesses and agencies. Gonzaga provides both career and counseling centers.

Gonzaga enrolls approximately 5,800 students, of whom about 3,990 are undergraduates. About 49 percent of the students come from Washington State, with forty-three other states and twenty-one other countries also represented. In addition to its undergraduate colleges and schools, Gonzaga University offers more than twenty master's programs, a doctoral program in leadership studies, and a School of Law.

Location

Located along the banks of the Spokane River in a quiet, turn-of-the-century neighborhood, Gonzaga University is just a 15-minute walk from downtown Spokane, a city with a metropolitan area population of 420,000. Spokane's beautiful 100-acre Riverfront Park, in the heart of downtown, is close to the Spokane Arena, Opera House, and Convention Center. Fine restaurants, a twenty-screen movie theater, and an assortment of shops and department stores, many of which can be reached through a convenient, weatherproof skywalk system, are also in the city's core. For mall shoppers, the Northtown Mall is a 10-minute drive from the campus.

Majors and Degrees

Gonzaga's undergraduate school awards the B.A., B.B.A., B.E., B.Ed., B.G.S., B.S., B.S.C.E., B.S.Cp.E., B.S.G.E., B.S.E.E., B.S.M.E., and B.S.N. degrees. Majors offered in the College of Arts and Sciences are applied communication studies, art, biochemistry, biology, broadcast and electronic media studies, chemistry, classical civilization, computer science, criminal justice, economics, English, French, history, integrated studies, international studies (including international relations and Asian, European, and Latin American studies), Italian studies, journalism, literary studies, mathematics, mathematics/computer science, music (including composition, literature, liturgical, performance, and education), philosophy, physics, political science, psychology, public relations, religious studies, sociology, Spanish, and theater arts. The School of Business Administration, accredited by AACSB International–The Association to Advance Collegiate Schools of Business, offers a Bachelor of Business Administration degree with a major in accounting or a major in business administration with concentrations in economics, entrepreneurship, finance, human resource management, individualized study, international business, law and public policy, management information systems, marketing, and operations and supply-chain management. As well as granting teacher certification on both the elementary and secondary levels, the School of Education offers degrees in physical education, special education, and sport management. The School of Engineering has degree programs in civil, computer, electrical, general, and mechanical engineering. The general engineering program includes numerous business courses and allows attainment of the M.B.A. in five years of study. The civil, computer, electrical, and mechanical programs are accredited by the Engineering Accreditation Commission of the Accreditation Board for Engineering and Technology, Inc. (EAC/ABET). The School of Professional Studies offers degrees in exercise science, general studies, and nursing.

Academic Program

Gonzaga University believes that it benefits all students, regardless of their chosen major or profession, to attain an education that goes beyond specialization. Therefore, all students attending Gonzaga receive a strong liberal arts background as well as depth in their major. The Core Curriculum is a very important component of the 128 semester units a student must earn for graduation.

The Honors Program challenges exceptional students with an integrated curriculum compatible with any major and most double majors. The program requires a separate application. The Hogan Entrepreneurial Leadership Program is for motivated and imaginative student leaders who are interested in creating new ventures and who want to make a difference in the world. A separate application is required. Gonzaga University Summer Term (GUST) offers motivated high school students intensive course work in a variety of academic disciplines. Academic and cocurricular activities are included in the six-week session. Credits earned through the Washington State Running Start Program or International Baccalaureate (I.B.) program are accepted on a class-by-class basis. College credit is given for certain test scores in most Advanced Placement (AP) subjects. The academic year follows a two-semester system, beginning in early September. Two summer sessions also are available.

Off-Campus Programs

Gonzaga University offers qualified students the opportunity to study abroad through programs in Australia, British West Indies, China, Costa Rica, England, France, Ireland, Italy, Japan, Kenya, Mexico, and Spain.

Academic Facilities

Gonzaga's "library of the future," the Ralph E. and Helen Higgins Foley Center, is a $20-million window to worldwide information resources. The library features more than 300 specialized databases, satellite capabilities, an advanced computer-controlled video editing system, a rare book room, computerized retrieval services, a wireless Internet connection, and beautiful views.

Foley Center holdings include 782,000 volumes and microform titles, with two special collections of materials especially rich in the areas of philosophy and classical civilization, as well as the nation's most extensive collection of works by the famous Jesuit poet Gerard Manley Hopkins. The School of Law maintains its own library of 130,000 volumes. The historic Administration Building houses the student-operated FM radio station, KAGU; a television broadcasting studio; the offices of the *Bulletin*, a weekly, student-published newspaper; the Russell Theatre; the Computer Center; a 24-hour computer lab; the University Chapel; and the main administrative offices and classrooms.

Campus computing services include more than 250 PC and Macintosh computers and Sun Workstations dispersed throughout a dozen computer labs across the campus. An HP9000/K100 minicomputer provides central academic services and student electronic mail. Students have sculpted T-3 cable access to the Internet, library, and central academic services from their dorm rooms and other University facilities. The Herak Center for Engineering houses a CAD/CAE center, general-purpose computer facilities, electronics and mechanical calibration rooms, and laboratories for physics, electronics, digital electronics/circuits, microprocessors, communications/controls, computer analysis, automation and embedded systems, power, mechanical design, mechanical engineering, materials testing, manufacturing engineering, rapid prototyping, water/wastewater, geotechnical engineering, and hydrology/hydraulics. The center also contains a large Fabrication Facility and extensive areas for the design and construction of student projects.

In 2003, the Hughes Hall Life Sciences Building added the newly created Inland Northwest Natural Resources Research Center. The Martin Athletic Center's 2003 facelift included a 13,000-square-foot fitness center, and 2004 marks the opening of the 6,000-seat basketball and concert arena. A 30,000-square-foot addition to the Jepson Center for Business Administration is anticipated to house classrooms, computer labs, the Ethics Institute, the Hogan Entrepreneurial Leadership Program, and a student lounge and café.

Costs

Tuition and fees for the 2003–04 academic year were $20,510. Room and board costs were $6380 for the year.

Financial Aid

Gonzaga University offers many different types of financial aid to qualified students, including scholarships, Federal Pell Grants, Federal Supplemental Educational Opportunity Grants, work-study jobs, Federal Perkins Loans, Federal Stafford Student Loans, and on- and off-campus employment. In order to apply for financial aid awards, a student must first be accepted by the University and must submit the Free Application for Federal Student Aid (FAFSA) by February 1. After this date, awards are made on a funds-available basis. Approximately 95 percent of the students at Gonzaga receive financial assistance.

Faculty

The student-faculty ratio is 13:1, and the average class size is 23, allowing close, mentoring relationships to develop. Only faculty members serve as academic advisers, and all classes at Gonzaga are taught by faculty members. Eight percent of the faculty members are Jesuits, and 83 percent of the 291 full-time faculty members hold the highest degree in their fields.

Student Government

The Gonzaga Student Body Association provides the means for students to participate in making decisions about student life at Gonzaga. The 5-member Executive Council, an elected board of students that administers and initiates programs, also serves as a liaison between the administration and the students. The Student Senate, a legislative body consisting of 24 senators, is responsible for sounding out the needs of the student body and directing this information to the Executive Council. Students also serve on the Board of Regents, search committees, budget committee, and many other University committees.

Admission Requirements

Gonzaga expects freshman applicants to have taken a challenging college-preparatory curriculum and to submit strong test scores on the ACT or SAT I. Transfer students who have earned 30 semester credits or 45 quarter credits do not need to submit a high school transcript or test scores. The admission process is selective, and applicants are considered through a pooling process. The Admissions Committee seeks motivated, well-rounded students and considers the rigor of academic study in high school, in addition to grades and test scores, as well as personal characteristics, awards and activities, and an essay.

Application and Information

Gonzaga University's nonbinding Early Action deadline for admission applications is November 15. Students who meet this deadline with a complete application are notified of an admission decision by January 15. The final deadline for freshmen to apply for admission under Regular Decision is February 1. Regular Decision applicants receive an admission decision by the middle of March. Transfer students are admitted on a rolling admission basis. Transfer students seeking financial aid are encouraged to apply for admission by March 1. Otherwise, to ensure a smooth transition to Gonzaga, transfer students should apply by July 1. After July 1, the University accepts transfer applicants only if space is available. Students may also apply by using the Common Application, APPLY!, CollegeLink, and the Catholic College Common Application. For priority financial aid, all students are encouraged to submit the FAFSA by February 1.

All requests for further information or materials should be addressed to:

Julie McCulloh
Dean of Admission
Gonzaga University
Spokane, Washington 99258-0102
Telephone: 800-322-2584 (toll-free)
E-mail: mcculloh@gu.gonzaga.edu
World Wide Web: http://www.gonzaga.edu

Gonzaga University: Education for the mind and spirit.

GORDON COLLEGE

WENHAM, MASSACHUSETTS

The College

Gordon College is a traditional New England liberal arts college where academic excellence and faith are considered complementary, not contradictory. Founded in Boston in 1889 as a missionary training institute, the College today offers the solid liberal arts foundation that distinguishes the best of New England's small colleges from others around the nation. Blending academic freedom with sincere, earnest faith, Gordon has developed a growing national reputation for graduating men and women known for intellectual maturity and Christian character. Students are well-grounded in what matters and become leaders in many occupations and organizations around the world. Gordon attempts to expand students' understanding of God and his purpose for their lives by encouraging them to ask the probing questions that lead to wisdom and understanding. One of the goals of the College is to be a place of personal integration where knowledge, faith, and character are a part of every class and the College community. Because of the close relationship between faith and learning, one national education observer says Gordon sees "...religious commitment as an enhancement rather than a threat to free and rigorous academic inquiry." In addition, the College has a commitment to a multicultural approach to learning that reflects the diversity of the world.

No less an authority than *U.S. News & World Report* ranks Gordon among the top liberal arts colleges in the nation. The John Templeton Foundation has selected Gordon as one of the 100 best colleges and universities in the country for character-building, and the well-respected *Edward Fiske Selective Guide to Colleges* has included Gordon for many years. The most recent edition of *Peterson's Top Colleges for Science* ranks Gordon as one of the 190 best schools in the country. Its premed students go on to some of the best medical schools in the United States. While academic reputation is important, residential life is also an important part of character formation and personal growth. Within its community there is incredible diversity: more than sixty denominations are represented, and the College draws students from forty-six states and twenty-five nations. Because of Gordon's emphasis on character and service, hundreds of Gordon students are involved in off-campus volunteer ministries such as hunger action, prison outreach, nursing home visitation, and working with the hearing impaired.

Gordon also offers a variety of recreational and social opportunities, including sixteen varsity sports in NCAA Division III, a strong intramural athletics program, active touring musical groups, a lively campus music scene, and four theater troupes (two of them professional). Concerts, movies, coffeehouses, and occasional day trips are scheduled on weekends.

In recent years, Gordon has built an athletics and recreation center, an arts and theater center, and a music building. Several buildings—including the student center—have been completely remodeled, and three new residence halls have been added. Gordon plans to add another residence hall and a new science center over the next few years.

Location

In 1955, Gordon moved to its current location—a beautiful 500-acre campus that has a lake for swimming and canoeing and miles of hiking, biking and cross-country ski trails. Less than 3 miles from the Atlantic Ocean, Gordon is situated in a suburban community near beautiful coastal towns such as the artist colony of Rockport and picturesque Manchester, a favorite location for Hollywood film crews. Boston, which is just 25 miles south and less than an hour away by train, offers numerous cultural and recreational opportunities as well as many historic attractions: the Boston Symphony, the Museum of Fine Arts, the Freedom Trail, the Isabella Stewart Gardner Museum, Copley Square, and colorful Faneuil Hall Market. Gordon's proximity to Boston and its high-technology metropolitan area provides many employment and internship possibilities.

Majors and Degrees

The Bachelor of Arts degree is awarded to students who graduate with the following majors: accounting, biblical and theological studies, business administration, communication arts, economics, English, foreign languages (combined), French, German, history, international affairs, international business, Jewish studies, leisure studies and recreation, music, philosophy, political studies, psychology, social work, sociology, Spanish, special education, theater, visual arts, and youth ministries. The Bachelor of Science degree is awarded to students who graduate with the following majors: biology, chemistry, computer science, early childhood education, elementary education, mathematics, middle school education, movement science, and physics. The Bachelor of Music degree is awarded to students who concentrate in music performance. In addition, the following programs are offered in conjunction with Thomas Jefferson University's College of Allied Health: cytotechnology, dental hygiene, medical technology, nursing, occupational therapy, physical therapy, and radiological technology. There is also a five-year program that allows students to earn a liberal arts degree at Gordon (A.B. or B.S.) and an engineering degree in selected fields from the University of Massachusetts at Lowell.

Academic Program

The four-year undergraduate degree program is divided into two 15-week semesters. Fifteen semester hours per term constitute a normal class load, and courses normally carry 3 semester hours of credit.

Graduation requirements include a minimum of 124 semester hours of credit, 32 of which must be taken at Gordon, the last 16 in residence; a grade point average of 2.0 or above; fulfillment of the liberal arts core curriculum; and fulfillment of the course requirements specified for the major, with no fewer than 18 semester hours in the major earned at Gordon.

For those with an eye toward graduate study, Gordon offers programs for teachers and music educators. The Master of Education program and the Master of Music Education give working educators and musicians the opportunity to receive an excellent education. The purpose of the academic programs is to bring faith and learning together, to be sure students are well-schooled in their area, and to prepare students for a wide variety of life's challenges.

Off-Campus Programs

One of Gordon's strengths is the number and quality of its off-campus programs, which include Latin American studies in Costa Rica and the International Seminar, a four-week summer course abroad. Students can also study in England, at Oxford University, through Gordon's program there. Several marine biology field courses are also offered for credit. Arts students can also take part in the special programs that are located in Orvieto, Italy. In addition, Gordon participates in the Christian College Consortium, the Council for Christian Colleges and Universities, and the Northeast Consortium of Colleges and Universities in Massachusetts. As a result, the following opportunities are available to students: American Studies Program, featuring political and governmental affairs internships in Washington, D.C.; study at Jerusalem University College in Israel; a Middle East Studies Program, based in Cairo; semesters at Daystar University College in Nairobi, Kenya;

Au Sable Trails Institute, a cooperative environmental studies program; and Urban Studies, a cooperative residential study program in San Francisco.

Academic Facilities

The Phillips Music Center is the newest academic building on campus. Opened in 2000, it contains an intimate recital hall, an instrument repair shop, electronic studios, and ample classroom, office, and practice space for the College's many music majors. In late 1999, Gordon opened the Barrington Center for the Arts. This building, home to the communications, theater, and visual arts departments, contains two art galleries, a studio theater, set construction space, a video screening room, and many other artistic touches that make this building one of the best of its kind north of Boston. The next new academic building will be a science center, tentatively planned for 2005. The campus is fully wired for individual student access to e-mail, the Internet, and the intranet.

Costs

The following rates are for the 2003–04 academic year, which is divided into two 15-week semesters. Annual tuition (12 to 18 hours per semester) is $19,334, board is $1898, room (double occupancy) is $3850, and the comprehensive fee is $900. The total for two semesters is $25,982.

Financial Aid

Students who demonstrate financial need normally receive a combination of grants, loans, and student employment opportunities. Nearly 70 percent of Gordon students receive financial aid, which includes federal, state, private, and institutional awards.

The A. J. Gordon Scholarship Program awards approximately twenty-five $12,000 scholarships per year to incoming freshmen who show promise of leadership and academic achievement. There is a separate application that requires a prearranged visit to campus on one of the special A. J. Gordon Scholarship days. Gordon has also begun a Choral Scholars Program, which provides a number of $6000 renewable scholarships to students who are focusing on choral studies and who have solid academic records. A competitive audition and an interview are required.

Faculty

Nearly 90 percent of the full-time faculty members have earned doctorates. Faculty members are professing Christians who seek to integrate their faith with their discipline. Although the first priority of the faculty members is teaching, many distinguish themselves in research and publications. A faculty-student ratio of 1:15 contributes to considerable interaction, both formal and informal, outside of class.

Student Government

The Student Government Association, whose primary officers receive stipends, plays a significant role in campus events, programs, and student publications. The student government president, a voting member of the Campus Advisory Council, represents student concerns directly to the president and administrative officers of the College.

As a Christian community, Gordon attempts to achieve a balance between individual freedom and the need for clear standards that are in harmony with the Christian character of the College. Practices clearly prohibited in Scripture are not condoned, and smoking and alcohol consumption are not permitted on campus.

Admission Requirements

A successful applicant must give evidence of both strong academic promise and a decision to follow Christ. Other factors that contribute to an applicant's chances of acceptance include musical, dramatic, or athletic experience; cross-cultural perspective; and proven leadership ability in service to church, community, or school. Applicants are expected to have successfully completed courses in the following areas at the college-preparatory level: English (4 years), mathematics (2 years), science (2 years, including at least 1 year of a laboratory science), social studies (2 years), and 5 units of acceptable electives. It is recommended that 2 or more years of foreign language be among these electives.

Credentials required for freshman applicants include an application, a $40 nonrefundable application fee, a transcript of grades, SAT I or ACT scores, a personal reference, and an admission interview. Applications from transfer and international students are welcome. Interviews are required of transfer applicants, who must also submit an application, a $40 nonrefundable application fee, a college transcript, a college catalog for transfer credit evaluation, SAT I or ACT scores, a personal reference, and a high school transcript if less than one collegiate academic year has been completed. International applicants must submit TOEFL or SAT I scores, the Foreign Students' Financial Aid Form of the College Scholarship Service, a second personal reference from a school official in lieu of an admission interview, and all other regular admission credentials. Canadian students may apply upon completion of grade 12 or 13. For music applicants, an audition is required in addition to the regular admission requirements. Visual arts applicants must submit a portfolio of their work.

Application and Information

Regular admission is on a rolling basis; the application deadline for early decision is December 1.

For further information, students may contact:

Nancy Mering
Director of Admissions
Gordon College
Wenham, Massachusetts 01984-9988
Telephone: 800-343-1379 (toll-free)
E-mail: admissions@hope.gordon.edu
World Wide Web: http://www.gordon.edu

Gordon's 500-acre campus provides scenic beauty, ponds, and hiking and biking trails in one of the most livable parts of the United States.

GOSHEN COLLEGE

GOSHEN, INDIANA

The College

Goshen College (GC) is a fully accredited national liberal arts college that is known for leadership in international education, service-learning, and peace and justice issues in the Anabaptist-Mennonite tradition. Founded in 1894 by the Mennonite Church, one of the historic peace churches, GC serves more than 1,000 students and encourages dialogue between students with different perspectives, backgrounds, and beliefs. While students from Mennonite backgrounds represent more than half of the student body, about sixteen denominations are represented. Students come from more than forty states, Canadian provinces, and more than thirty-five countries. Goshen College was recognized in *U.S. News & World Report*'s 2004 "America's Best Colleges" rankings as a "least debt college" for its graduates, for enrolling a high percentage of international students, and for adding to the sense of an international campus with its unique study/serve abroad program. Goshen's track record of sustained excellence has attracted national attention. Goshen is one of 300 schools included in *Barron's Best Buys in College Education* for offering a high-quality education at below-average prices. *Money* magazine listed GC fourteenth in the nation for educational value when financial aid is taken into account. For 2002, a study by *U.S. News & World Report* includes GC among the top 113 national liberal arts colleges. Ernest L. Boyer, in *Smart Parents' Guide to College,* praises GC's Study-Service Term (SST) program. GC ranks among the 100 Most Wired Colleges in *Yahoo! Internet Life* and was named one of *The 100 Best Colleges for African-American Students* in a book by Erlene B. Wilson. A study by Franklin and Marshall ranked GC in the top sixth of liberal arts colleges in the number of its graduates who go on to complete doctoral degrees. Among the top 100 schools in its category, GC has the lowest cost among national colleges in the Great Lakes region. Peterson's lists GC among its 190 *Top Colleges for Science.*

In a highly energetic, Christ-centered environment, students have plenty of opportunities to cultivate leadership skills and assume responsibility. Students edit a weekly newspaper and a yearbook, operate a radio station, produce a campus television program, serve on campus publishing editorial boards, and work and perform in theater and musical groups. Representatives of the student body are elected to serve on the Student Senate and Campus Activities Council. Campus groups also include the Student Women's Association, Black Student Union, Campus Ministries team, PAX, Latino Student Union, Nursing Students Association, Eco-PAX, Fellowship of Christian Athletes, Social Work Action Association, International Students Club, Business Club, and Pre-Med Club. GC belongs to the National Association of Intercollegiate Athletics and the Mid-Central College Conference and competes intercollegiately in men's and women's basketball, cross-country, soccer, tennis, and track and field; men's baseball and golf; and women's softball and volleyball. More than 60 percent of GC students participate in intramural athletics. All students have free access to the Roman Gingerich Recreation-Fitness Center.

Most Goshen students live in one of the College's five residence halls, which were made accessible, one port per pillow, to the campus computer network in 1997. Small-group housing is available to upper-level students. College-owned houses are available for married students and families.

With a long history of emphasis on experiential learning, Goshen College's programs encourage partnerships between the College and the community by placing students in practicum, internship, and service experiences. In addition, the College holds an annual Celebrate Service Day; classes are suspended so that students and faculty and staff members can participate in community service projects. Students also benefit from Multicultural Education Office programs that emphasize meaningful ways to address issues of diversity in order to prepare students for life in an increasingly interconnected, multicultural world.

Location

The campus is on the south side of Goshen, a city of 30,000 in north-central Indiana, 2 hours east of Chicago and 45 minutes east of South Bend. Known as the Maple City for its many maple trees, Goshen is part of Elkhart County, one of the fastest-growing counties in the nation during the 1980s and 1990s. The county enjoys its rich Mennonite and Amish heritage while serving as home to major corporations, with proximity to Chicago and Indianapolis.

Majors and Degrees

Goshen College offers seventy programs of study. The Bachelor of Arts is awarded in accounting; American sign language interpreting; art; Bible and religion; biology; business; business information systems; chemistry; communication; computer science; computer science and applied mathematics; early childhood education; economics; environmental studies; elementary education; English; environmental science; family life; French; German; Hispanic ministries; history; history and investigative skills; management information systems; mathematics; molecular biology; music; natural science; peace, justice, and conflict studies; physical education; physics; psychology; social work; sociology/anthropology; Spanish; special education; teaching English to speakers of other languages (TESOL); and theater. A Bachelor of Science in nursing or a Bachelor of Science in organizational management is also awarded. Interdisciplinary majors usually combine work in three different departments and allow students to tailor their studies to individual interests. Preprofessional programs in engineering, law, medicine, occupational therapy, physical therapy, seminary, and veterinary medicine are available as well. The College also offers minors in more than thirty areas.

Academic Program

The College calendar consists of two 15-week semesters and a 3½-week May term. A total of 120 semester hours (124 for nursing majors) is required for graduation. One third are usually in general studies courses, including art, Bible and religion, history, literature, philosophy, physical education, science, and social science; another third are courses in the student's major. Most majors require a practicum for graduation. All students must complete a course of international study. Most students choose to participate in the Study-Service Term (SST) program abroad, a thirteen-week term, including course work and field experience in a service assignment, in a significantly different country. Students also can fulfill the requirement by taking courses on campus or by participating in other study-abroad programs.

Off-Campus Programs

Goshen is one of the very few U.S. colleges that requires international education. Most students complete this requirement by going on SST, while others choose to take classes with an international emphasis on campus. GC's international education program ranks in the top sixteen both for quality and participation, according to *U.S. News & World Report.* Since the SST program began in 1968, more than 6,500 GC students have benefited from it tremendously, both academically and personally. The program has served as the model for international education programs across the country. In the SST program, students spend six weeks together focusing on the study of one country while immersed in its language and culture. The six-week SST field experience gives students a chance to develop interpersonal skills and to work alongside native residents in service to others. The field experience often relates to the students' major areas of study. During both parts of the program, students live with host families. Most SST units cost the same as a semester on campus. GC students earn 13–14 hours of credit for SST; however, the benefits continue for a lifetime. SST gives students a broader context for living their lives while helping them set an appropriate individual direction. The growing internationalization of U.S. business and culture amplifies SST's benefits; now, more than ever, foreign language skills and knowledge of other cultures are advantages in the job market.

Other off-campus programs include spring term courses in marine biology at the College's center in the Florida Keys and courses in Europe in theater history, art history, and literature.

Academic Facilities

On its 135-acre campus, Goshen College has eighteen major buildings and laboratories. The Roman Gingerich Recreation-Fitness Center features a swimming pool, running track, and gymnasium and houses the physical education department, student health center, and intramural and intercollegiate athletics. The 68,000-square-foot Music Center, which opened in 2002, features 1,000- and 300-seat performance halls, with some of the best acoustics in the nation. The building also holds a community music school, an art gallery and classrooms, and offices and practice rooms.

Another recent addition to the campus is an annex to the Science Building, which contains modern science classrooms, laboratories, and equipment. It also contains the Turner Precision X-Ray Measurements Laboratory and the Biological Research Laboratory. The Turner Laboratory gives physics majors a rare opportunity to assist in basic research on crystals. The Biological Research Laboratory, equipped with an electron microscope, Geiger system, climate chambers, incubators, and microtechnique systems, is also open to qualified students. The College regularly does research for larger universities and major industries.

The Harold and Wilma Good Library houses a collection of 120,000 volumes and 800 periodicals, the Mennonite Historical Library, and the Art Gallery.

At the GC Laboratory Kindergarten, psychology and education majors can observe and participate in activities. The Merry Lea Environmental Learning Center, an 1,150-acre nature preserve, offers internships in environmental and elementary education and is a key site for the College's environmental studies major and minor.

Goshen College has a progressive attitude concerning technology in an effort to encourage students to learn how to use technology intelligently and effectively. Computer facilities include three modern student labs, with one computer for every 7.6 students, as well as printers, scanners, digital cameras, wireless Internet access, and other equipment. Computers in student labs are upgraded annually. Multimedia classrooms feature integrated technology as well as media production facilities. All residence hall rooms are connected to the campus network and the Internet; account and course information is available on the College intranet.

The John S. Umble Center for the Performing Arts is recognized internationally for its exceptional theater acoustics. The Music Center, opened in 2002, has received awards for its design and acoustics in its 1,000 Sauder Performance Hall and 300-seat Rieth Recital Hall. The building also houses a Community School of the Arts.

Costs

Costs for 2003–04 included tuition, $16,320; room $3000; board, $2800; and tech fee, $330. The total for a residential student was $22,450. Costs included two 15-week semesters and one 3½-week May term.

Financial Aid

Ninety percent of the College's students receive some type of financial assistance through federal, state, and Goshen College programs. The average award exceeds $12,000. GC offers more than 130 different scholarships. College aid includes the President's Leadership Award, $10,000; Menno Simons Scholarship, up to $7000, Wens Honors Scholarship, up to $5500; Yoder Honors Scholarship, up to $4000, Grebel Honors Scholarship, up to $2500, and the Kratz Honors Scholarship, up to $1000. About 60 percent of incoming students receive renewable academic scholarships. Work-study jobs and other on-campus jobs are available.

Faculty

The faculty includes about 80 full-time and 30 part-time members. Most have lived or worked abroad. The student-faculty ratio is 13:1.

Student Government

The Student Senate acts as an advocate of student concerns and corresponding policy changes and works with the administration. The Campus Activity Council plans student activities. Most College committees include 1 or 2 voting student members.

Admission Requirements

Applicants should rank in the upper half of their high school graduating class and may apply for admission at any time after the junior year and up to one month before they wish to begin college. ACT or SAT I scores are required. Recommended high school work includes 4 years of English, 2 years of science, 2 years of social science, 2 years of mathematics, and 2 to 4 years of a foreign language. Prospective students are encouraged to visit the campus and meet with faculty members, students, and administrators. Special campus open houses scheduled throughout the year provide excellent opportunities for visits.

Application and Information

Students who would like more information may contact:

Office of Admission
Goshen College
1700 South Main Street
Goshen, Indiana 46526
Telephone: 574-535-7535
866-566-2637 (toll-free)
Fax: 574-535-7609
E-mail: admissions@goshen.edu
World Wide Web: http://www.goshen.edu

Research and hands-on learning serve students well, especially those who go on to graduate school.

GOUCHER COLLEGE

BALTIMORE, MARYLAND

The College

Goucher College is a small, private, coeducational liberal arts and sciences college with an international emphasis and an academic program that partners classroom learning with real, hands-on experience.

Since it was founded in 1885, Goucher has provided a truly global kind of education that puts learning in perspective against the events and developments of the entire world, encouraging students to test what they've learned against experience in service-learning, study-abroad, and internship programs around the nation and around the globe. It is a small college with a big view of the world—an educational community without boundaries.

Goucher's 1,270 undergraduates come from forty states and twenty other countries. They represent a tremendous variety of backgrounds, interests, and points of view. They live together in the center of the campus in five fieldstone residence halls with living spaces designed to blur the lines between the students' educational, cultural, and social lives. Each of the residence halls is divided into "houses" of 40 to 50 students, with each house setting its own rules and regulations based on how the students want to live together. Students can further tailor their residential experience by choosing to live in a special wellness-themed residence hall, on a special foreign-language floor, in a quiet area, in a nonsmoking area, or in a single-sex or coed house.

The residence hall buildings also house many of Goucher's academic and social resources, including the dining halls, the student union, a coffeehouse, health and counseling services, music practice rooms, and computer and language labs. Residence on campus is generally required of all students who do not live at home, and housing space is guaranteed for all four years.

The social center of campus is the Pearlstone Student Center (fully renovated in 1997), which houses a café, lounge, bookstore, post office, commuter study area, student activities office, game room, and the popular Gopher Hole, a coffeehouse offering space for casual conversations and featuring entertainment several nights a week. The campus' cultural center is the 1,000-seat Kraushaar Auditorium, where lectures and performances by leading actors, actresses, dancers, musicians, writers, and political and cultural figures attract audiences from the Baltimore–Washington area, around the nation, and around the world.

Athletic facilities include a 50,000-square-foot Sports and Recreation Center, the Welsh Gymnasium, and the von Borries swimming pool. The sports center features a field house, sauna, wellness laboratory, weight-training room, squash and racquetball courts, lockers, and offices. There are two dance studios, 4 miles of wooded riding and jogging trails, six tennis courts, riding rings, and stables. Goucher belongs to NCAA Division III. Varsity sports include basketball, cross-country, equestrian events, field hockey, lacrosse, soccer, swimming, tennis, track and field, and volleyball.

Location

Ideally located on 287 wooded acres just a few miles north of downtown Baltimore, Maryland, and an hour's drive from Washington, D.C., Goucher takes full advantage of its environs with a curriculum and programs that engage students directly in the lives of the communities that surround them—local, national, and international—and bring the best of those communities to the Goucher campus to enrich the cultural and intellectual life of the College.

Majors and Degrees

Goucher awards the Bachelor of Arts degree. Areas of study and concentration include American studies, anthropology, art, arts administration, biological sciences, chemistry, cognitive studies, communication, computer science, dance, economics, education, English, historic preservation, history, international and intercultural studies (British, European, Latin American, Russian), international relations, management, mathematics, modern languages (French, German, Russian, Spanish), music, peace studies, philosophy, physics, political science, prelaw studies, premedical studies, psychology, religion, sociology, special education, theater, and women's studies. Goucher students are encouraged to tailor their studies to their own goals and interests through traditional, double, or individualized majors or by taking a major and a minor. The College also offers a dual-degree program in science and engineering with Johns Hopkins University. Entrance to the Johns Hopkins Whiting School of Engineering is guaranteed for students with a minimum 3.2 GPA in Goucher science classes.

Academic Program

Goucher encourages students to plot their own course, offering degrees in twenty-nine different areas of study and enabling them to design their own majors. Thoroughly accomplished in all of the areas of study it has embraced, Goucher is particularly noted for its stellar programs in dance, the sciences, and creative writing. All education at Goucher takes an interdisciplinary perspective, encouraging students to assimilate the knowledge they gain throughout their academic careers into a cohesive whole.

Requirements for graduation include a demonstrated proficiency in a foreign language, English composition, and computer technology and successful completion of core courses in the arts, natural sciences, humanities, social sciences, and mathematics. All students complete a 3-credit off-campus experience, which may take the form of study abroad, an internship, or an independent project. The College offers an interdisciplinary honors program and honors courses in each department. Degree requirements include 120 semester hours of credit. A departmental major consists of at least 30 credits (about ten courses); a double major requires 60 credits. Goucher's calendar is based on the semester system.

Off-Campus Programs

Education at Goucher extends far beyond the classroom walls. Students test the lessons they learn in class against firsthand experience through internships, service-learning programs, and other off-campus opportunities tailored precisely to their course of study.

Goucher's 75-year-old internship program provides students with a view into potential careers, opportunities to apply classroom theory to working reality, and the chance to network with professionals in the field. Supported by advisers who work to ensure a close fit between internships and academic interests, Goucher students have worked with organizations ranging from the *Baltimore Sun* to the European Parliament.

Study-abroad options range from three-week intensive courses to semester-long and year-long programs. Many students build more than one complementary international experience into their course work. A full-time international-studies staff works with students to identify programs that neatly match their interests. Scholarship and other funds make study abroad possible even for students of limited financial means.

Through Goucher's student-founded Community Auxiliary for Service, students tutor at-risk students at area middle schools, serve meals at soup kitchens, and build houses with Habitat for Humanity, often for academic credit. The Hughes Field Politics Center offers high-quality internships in government, politics, and public service in Washington, D.C., and elsewhere, including recent placements with NATO in Brussels, the White House, CNN, and the Sierra Club.

For a number of years, Goucher College and Johns Hopkins University have had a reciprocal agreement by which qualified students at either institution may elect to take courses at no additional cost. The College has similar agreements with Loyola College; Maryland Institute College of Art; Towson University; Morgan State University; the College of Notre Dame of Maryland; Baltimore Hebrew College; and Essex Community College.

Academic Facilities

Goucher's campus is home to impressive facilities in technology, the sciences, and the arts, including a scientific visualization laboratory, a nuclear magnetic resonance spectrometer, and several computer, multimedia, and language labs. The campus is fully wired, featuring more than a dozen smart classrooms and providing widespread access to the Internet, cable television, and internal networks. Students have access to well-equipped laboratories and research facilities, superb performance and studio art spaces (including the Meyerhoff Arts Center and the Kraushaar Auditorium), and the Hughes Field Politics Center. The Julia Rogers Library includes a collection of more than 295,500 volumes, audiovisual materials, and 1,200 periodical subscriptions, along with several special collections and extensive access to Web-based resources.

Costs

Tuition for 2002–03 was $22,950 for two semesters. The cost per credit hour was $825. For two semesters, the cost for room was $5200, and the cost for board (240 meals-per-semester plan) was $3400. Students residing on campus also paid a health fee of $150 and a student activities fee of $150.

Financial Aid

Goucher's financial aid program is designed to put the College within reach of anyone who has the desire and ability to pursue an academic career there. Students and their families are expected to contribute to the financing of their education to the degree that they are able, but Goucher is committed to working with every qualified student to provide aid in covering the difference between the limits of their financial resources and the total cost of their education.

Goucher spent $13 million on financial aid in 2002–03. The College awards this aid in the form of packages based on each individual student's needs. Aid comes from a variety of resources that may include need-based grants, loans, merit-based scholarships, and work-study opportunities. Goucher makes a sincere effort every year to meet the need of every accepted student who meets the financial aid application deadlines.

Faculty

Goucher's faculty includes Danforth, Fulbright, Guggenheim, Newberry, and Woodrow Wilson fellows and a finalist for the National Book Award. All faculty members develop close, personal relationships with their students, often collaborating with them on nationally recognized, federally funded research projects of the kind most students at other colleges don't get to do until graduate school. With a student-faculty ratio of just 10:1 and 19 or fewer students in the vast majority (nearly 75 percent) of classes, nobody is ever just a face in the classroom at Goucher.

Student Government

The Student Government Association, to which all students belong, coordinates social activities, dispenses student activity funds, and formulates and enforces social regulations and the academic honor code. Students are represented on faculty and administrative committees. Students have founded a variety of departmental clubs in such fields as chemistry, computer science, French, history, math, political science, and Russian. Special interest groups include UMOJA–The African Alliance, Community Auxiliary for Service (CAUSE), International Students' Club, Environmental Concerns Organization (ECO), and Commuting Students' Organization. Student publications include a yearbook, literary magazine, and newspaper.

Admission Requirements

The Goucher Admissions Committee seeks to enroll students with strong academic ability who represent a variety of talents, ambitions, backgrounds, and experiences. Each candidate is considered individually. A complete application, ready for review, consists of the following: an application form (Goucher or Common Application); one essay; a nonrefundable $40 application fee (or fee waiver form); recommendations from 1 teacher who has taught the applicant in an academic subject and from a counselor or school principal; the official school transcript, including senior courses and first-term grades; and SAT I or ACT scores (TOEFL for international students), sent directly from the testing agency to Goucher. The SAT II: Writing Test is required for home-schooled students. Goucher accepts for admission to the freshman class a number of carefully selected students who have completed the eleventh grade and are ready to begin college a year early. Admission criteria are reviewed and weighed in the following order of importance: (1) the quality and level of secondary courses selected (a sound preparation includes at least 15 units of college-preparatory subjects, with AP or honors-level classes carrying more weight than regular classes); (2) grades received in grades 9–12; (3) the essay; (4) SAT I or ACT scores (the average score for entering freshmen is 607 verbal, 580 math); (5) letters of recommendation; and (6) activities, special interests, and awards. Applicants are encouraged to apply as early in the fall as possible. The application closing deadline is February 1. Applications are reviewed by the Admissions Committee, and the candidate is notified on or about April 1. The candidate reply date is May 1. Applications from transfer students filed by April 1 are given priority. Those filed after that date are considered on a rolling admissions basis.

Application and Information

Director of Admissions
Goucher College
1021 Dulaney Valley Road
Baltimore, Maryland 21204-2794
Telephone: 410-337-6100
800-GOUCHER (toll-free)
E-mail: admissions@goucher.edu
World Wide Web: http://www.goucher.edu

On the campus of Goucher College.

GRACE COLLEGE

WINONA LAKE, INDIANA

The College

Grace College is a Christian undergraduate college of arts and sciences founded in 1948 and affiliated with the Fellowship of Grace Brethren Churches, a conservative evangelical denomination. Grace College attracts students from a variety of conservative evangelical backgrounds and from around the United States and other countries. The College offers an environment and academic program that are conservative in theology and progressive in spirit and that emphasize three qualities for students as they reach adulthood—mature Christian character, academic and career competence, and a heart for service to mankind. Enrollment at Grace College is 1,189, providing an ideal atmosphere in which students can learn, grow, and develop lasting friendships.

Grace College has a campus of 165 acres. Approximately 69 percent of the College's students live on campus. The majority of students range in age from 18 to 23 years. More than 44 percent of the students come from Indiana; students also come from thirty-seven other states and seven countries. Approximately one third of the students are affiliated with the Fellowship of Grace Brethren Churches; the other two thirds are from other conservative Christian denominations, particularly Baptist and independent church backgrounds.

Grace College's intercollegiate sports are men's baseball, basketball, golf, soccer, and tennis and women's basketball, soccer, softball, tennis, and volleyball as well as cross-country and track and field for both men and women. The men's basketball team won the NAIA Division II national championship in 1992.

All major campus buildings at Grace College are centrally located, and most were constructed within the past thirty years. One exception is Westminster Hall, which was built in 1905 and is listed on the National Register of Historic Places and on the Indiana State Historical Register.

In addition to bachelor's and associate degrees, Grace College offers a Master of Arts degree in counseling.

Location

Grace College is located in the heart of historic Winona Lake. The town is in the midst of a major restoration that includes a boat-in restaurant, a hotel, and artisan shops as well as parks and museums. The lake itself offers a variety of activities, including waterskiing, swimming, and boating, and the region surrounding Winona Lake provides a number of recreational and cultural opportunities for students. The beaches of Lake Michigan and cities such as Chicago and Indianapolis are within 2 or 3 hours of the campus and make a great day trip.

The town of Winona Lake is approximately 40 miles west of Fort Wayne and 50 miles southeast of South Bend. Travel to the College is facilitated by the proximity of major highways and regional airports. The region has experienced unprecedented economic growth in recent years and offers a host of career opportunities, as well as excellent positions for part- and full-time student employment.

Majors and Degrees

Grace College offers the following majors leading to the Bachelor of Arts degree: biblical studies, Christian ministries, English, English education, French, French education, German, German education, international languages, music, Spanish, and Spanish education. In addition, all majors leading to the Bachelor of Science degree may also lead to the Bachelor of Arts degree, provided that the student fulfills the second-year proficiency in a foreign language requirement.

Grace College offers the following majors leading to the Bachelor of Science degree: accounting, art, art education, biology, business administration, business education, communications, counseling, criminal justice, general science, graphic design, international business, management information technology, mathematics, mathematics education, music education, music performance, physical education, psychology, science education, social work, sociology, and youth ministries.

Preparation for graduate study in professional programs is available in dentistry, medicine, pharmacy, and veterinary medicine through the Department of Biological Science. Preparation for law school is available through the Division of Social Sciences.

Grace College offers the Associate of Science degree in biblical studies and information processing.

Academic Program

The Christian liberal arts philosophy of Grace College pervades each program of study and reflects the College's recognition that a broad common core of course work is central to each student's education. When combined with detailed study in a major field, this core establishes the foundation for successful graduate study and for a career.

The requirements for the bachelor's degree include the successful completion of one major (36–56 semester hours) and one minor (20–28 semester hours) area of concentration in addition to the specified program of general education courses. Students are required to complete a total of 124 semester hours of course work.

Grace College operates on a two-semester calendar and offers a summer session. Advanced Placement (AP) and College-Level Examination Program (CLEP) test scores are considered for college credit and advanced placement.

One outstanding strength of Grace College is the Student Academic Counseling Center. The center offers academic advising and tutorial services.

Off-Campus Programs

Students majoring in a foreign language spend their junior year or its equivalent studying at a university located in a country where that language is spoken.

Academic Facilities

The Morgan Library contains classrooms, faculty offices, the Archives and Special Collections area, and the Computer Center, as well as the libraries of Grace College and Grace Theological Seminary. The combined collections total approximately 155,000 volumes. Students receive assistance through interlibrary lending and computer-based research services available in the library.

The Cooley Science Center serves the needs of the departments in the natural sciences, as well as those of the business and mathematics departments. The center houses faculty offices, classrooms, and laboratories.

The Education, Behavioral Science, and Art Departments are located in Mount Memorial Hall. The building also houses classrooms, offices, and a graphic design computer laboratory. The graphic design computer lab is among the most up-to-date computer graphics labs on any college or university campus in the United States and utilizes hardware and software based on the PowerMac computer system.

Rodeheaver Auditorium seats 1,400 and is used for special activities, including concerts, chapel services, and special conferences.

Costs

For full-time students, tuition for the 2003–04 academic year is $13,690. Room, board, and fees total $6135 for the two-semester academic year, which brings the total charges for tuition, room, and board to $19,825 for the academic year.

Financial Aid

The College offers extensive financial assistance to qualified students. Most students receive some sort of financial assistance—in the form of a scholarship, grant, loan, or campus employment—to help pay College costs. The average amount of financial aid awarded to a Grace College student totals $11,521 per year.

To be considered for financial assistance at Grace College, students must submit the Free Application for Federal Student Aid (FAFSA). Students may receive Federal Pell Grants, Federal Perkins Loans, Federal Stafford Student Loans, and Federal Supplemental Educational Opportunity Grants. In addition, students may be eligible for Federal Work-Study Program awards.

The FAFSA should be on file by March 1 for priority consideration. To renew financial aid, students must refile the FAFSA each year.

Faculty

Forty-two full-time and 42 part-time faculty members teach at Grace College; 29 full-time faculty members hold earned doctorates. Several Grace College faculty members are involved in various forms of research and writing, but their primary function is teaching. Every student has a faculty adviser in the academic major. Grace's student-faculty ratio is 19:1.

Student Government

Each of the four classes elects officers and plans activities. The College administration appoints one faculty adviser for each class and one for the student governing body. The Student Senate, consisting of student officers and representatives from each class, guides the student body by encouraging actions and activities beneficial to the College and students. Other student organizations are the Social Activities Board and Grace Ministries in Action, a group that coordinates student involvement in Christian service work.

Admission Requirements

Any individual who is in harmony with the evangelical Christian viewpoint of Grace College and possesses high academic and social standards is invited to apply. Graduation from an accredited high school or its equivalent is required. Each candidate completes an application that provides the Admissions Committee with pertinent information. The prospective student must secure recommendations from a guidance counselor and his or her pastor. All freshman applicants are required to submit scores from either the ACT or the SAT I. Students transferring from other colleges should request a transcript of their academic record from each college attended since high school.

Application and Information

Students may apply for admission to any semester. Applications are accepted on a rolling basis until December 15 for the spring term and August 15 for the fall term. There is a $20 nonrefundable application fee. Students may also apply on the Grace Web site at no cost.

Interested students and their parents are encouraged to visit the campus and to arrange for an interview at that time in order to get a clear picture of Grace College. Arrangements can be made for housing and meals for applicants by contacting the Grace College Visitor's Center.

Catalogs, application forms, and additional information may be obtained from the address below.

Grace College
200 Seminary Drive
Winona Lake, Indiana 46590
Telephone: 800-54-GRACE (toll-free)
World Wide Web: http://www.grace.edu

The Center for Intercultural Studies is a new facility that houses the Department of Foreign Languages and Cultures at Grace.

GRACELAND UNIVERSITY

LAMONI, IOWA

The University

Graceland University offers a strong academic program firmly rooted in the liberal arts tradition with an emphasis on career preparation. Since its founding in 1895 as a private, coeducational university, Graceland has maintained a tradition of academic excellence based on a commitment to the Christian view of the wholeness, worth, and dignity of every person. The University, sponsored by the Community of Christ, is nonsectarian and offers a varied religious life program for those who wish to participate. Thirty-one percent of Graceland students come from Iowa, and the remaining 69 percent represent forty-nine states and twenty-six nations.

Graceland believes that an important part of a student's learning experience is achieved through association with other students in residence hall living. This belief is supported by an on-campus housing system that provides students with the camaraderie of a fraternity or sorority without the competition. Within the residence halls, there are men's and women's houses. Members of each house elect a house council to plan social, intramural athletic, religious, and academic support activities. Residence halls are equipped with voice mail, e-mail, Internet connections, and cable TV.

The North Central Association of Colleges and Schools accredits Graceland as a bachelor's and master's degree–granting institution. Graceland's teacher-education program has been approved by the Iowa Department of Education and is accredited by the National Council for Accreditation of Teacher Education (NCATE). The nursing program is accredited by the National League for Nursing Accrediting Commission and is approved by the Missouri Board of Nursing and the Iowa Board of Nursing.

In addition to its undergraduate programs, Graceland offers a Master of Science in Nursing and an RN to M.S.N. course of study through the Outreach Program. The M.S.N. program has three tracks: family nurse practitioner studies, clinical nurse specialist studies, and health-care administration. Graceland also offers Master of Education, Master of Arts in religion, and Master of Arts in Christian ministries degree programs.

Location

Lamoni, in south-central Iowa, is on Interstate 35, 3 miles north of the Missouri border. It is 1 hour from Des Moines, 2 hours from Kansas City, and 3 hours from Omaha. Lamoni is the home of Liberty Hall Historic Center and antique shops. A county lake, Slip Bluff County Park, and Nine Eagles State Park are within 10 miles.

Majors and Degrees

Graceland awards the degrees of Bachelor of Arts, Bachelor of Science, and Bachelor of Science in Nursing. These degrees represent study in liberal arts with a concentration of courses in a major. The majors and concentrations offered in the Bachelor of Arts programs are accounting, art, athletic training, business administration, chemistry, cinema studies, communication, criminal justice, economics, elementary education, English literature, English writing, entrepreneurship and free enterprise, finance, German, health, history, human services, information technology, international business, international studies, management, management of information systems, marketing, mathematics, modern foreign language, music, music education, peace studies, philosophy and religion, physical education and health, political science, psychology, publications design, recreation, religion, secondary education, social science, sociology, Spanish, speech communication, theater, visual communications, and wellness program management. Bachelor of Science programs and majors are addiction studies, basic science, biology, chemistry, clinical laboratory science/medical technology, computer science, nursing, pre-engineering, premedicine/predentistry, and pre–veterinary medicine. In addition, a special liberal studies program is offered at Graceland allowing individualized program design by students. Nursing majors complete their last two years at the Graceland Independence Campus in Independence, Missouri.

Graceland offers four undergraduate Outreach Programs: a Bachelor of Science in addiction studies, a Bachelor of Arts in liberal studies (with emphases in health-care administration and health-care psychology), and an RN to B.S.N. program. (Applicants for the B.S.N. must be registered nurses.) These programs allow individuals to complete their degrees through a combination of directed independent study, preceptor-guided practicums, and short residences. For more information, students interested in the addiction studies major should call 800-585-6310 (toll-free); those interested in the nursing and health-care programs should call 877-471-1456 (toll-free).

Academic Programs

Graceland is committed to helping develop the lives of its students—intellectually, socially, physically, and ethically—through a curriculum that is strongly rooted in the liberal arts. General education requirements are based on ten core competencies and can be satisfied by course selections, internships, portfolios, proficiency exams, work experience, independent studies, and performance and achievement. Graceland offers majors that foster conceptual thinking, encourage team building, develop communication skills, and accommodate growth and enrichment.

Two programs at Graceland give attention to the special needs of students. The honors program is designed for highly motivated students who want to expand their learning beyond the regular academic curriculum. Honors students are required to develop and complete an honors thesis or project. Chance is a program for bright students who have the aptitude for university education but have experienced learning difficulties. The Lindamood and Bell clinical models are used for remediation in reading, spelling, and language comprehension.

The University operates on a 4-1-4 academic calendar. The regular semesters are separated by a one-month winter term in January. Full tuition for either the fall or the spring semester includes the winter term. This program is geared toward innovative and exceptional approaches and action-oriented learning experiences. On-campus programs vary from dance basics to science fiction to philosophy. Off-campus winter term experiences range from scuba diving in Grand Cayman to touring Italy. Winter term is also the ideal time to explore career interests through an internship.

Off-Campus Programs

Many students see the world during the winter term by visiting such places as Australia, China, England, France, Grand Cayman Island in the British West Indies, Hungary, Italy, India, Israel, Japan, and Mexico. Students who major in a foreign language may study abroad during their junior or senior year under the auspices of a recognized study program.

Academic Facilities

The Shaw Center for the Performing Arts includes an 800-seat auditorium, a 150-seat studio theater, a 40-foot proscenium stage with orchestra pit, a Casavant pipe organ, a full fly gallery, a spacious scene shop, an art gallery, classrooms, rehearsal rooms, and faculty offices. The Helene Center for the Visual Arts, which opened in January 2004, includes 29,000 square feet for classrooms, studios, and exhibits. The large north-facing windows, an important feature, provide optimum light for artists.

Computer facilities include three primary microcomputer laboratories with Macintosh and IBM-compatible computers. Students have access to equipment of commercial quality for desktop publishing and graphics design and to a music laboratory that provides computer-assisted tutoring, synthesis, and composition as well as professional-quality manuscript printing. The centerpiece of this laboratory is the Kurzweil synthesizer. Graceland's Enter.Net.C@fe provides 24-hour Internet access for student research and recreation.

The Frederick Madison Smith Library uses the latest technologies to provide the information services that students need. Ten fully networked computer workstations offer access to the Internet and many research databases, including 2 databases that provide full-text newspaper articles and periodicals for online reading. Access to LIBBIE, the computerized library catalog, is available from residence hall rooms. Articles and books may be ordered from a worldwide network of research libraries. Students log on to the library's home page to ask reference questions. Holdings include 119,615 books and bound journals, 3,383 audiovisual materials, 77,371 government documents, 569 magazine and newspaper subscriptions, and 5,322 items in the Teacher Curriculum Lab. Three microcomputer labs and the Iowa Communications Network (ICN) classroom are located in the library. Students across the state take classes from Graceland via the ICN.

Students have the opportunity to use the ABT 52 scanning electron microscope, nuclear magnetic resonance spectroscope, Fourier-transform infrared spectroscope, and a computer lab with PCs that provide access to a multiple-operating system environment.

The Eugene E. Closson Physical Education Center includes an indoor junior Olympic-size pool; an indoor track; a weight room; basketball, tennis, and volleyball courts; and a racquetball court. The Bruce Jenner Sports Complex contains the outdoor track, the football stadium, three soccer fields, five intramural fields, and eight tennis courts. The campus borders on a nine-hole golf course and two small ponds for fishing and canoeing.

Costs

Full-time tuition for 2004–05 is $15,000. All freshmen and sophomores are required to live on campus.

Financial Aid

Graceland's financial aid program is designed to assist qualified students attending the University. Ninety-three percent of Graceland's students receive financial aid such as academic scholarships, performance grants, work-study, federal and state grants, and government loans. Academic scholarships are based on the high school GPA and composite ACT or combined SAT I scores for entering freshmen and on cumulative GPA for transfer and continuing students. Grants are available for achievement in athletics and performing arts and for international students. The University matches a grant up to $1000 annually for a contribution made by a church and designated for a student attending Graceland.

Faculty

The majority of faculty members have earned a doctorate or the highest degree in their field. Faculty members are active in their professional fields, but consider teaching their primary responsibility. The student-faculty ratio is 14:1.

Student Government

Students are actively involved in the decision-making process of the University. Executive members of the Graceland Student Government attend faculty meetings and participate with voice and vote. Each academic department has student representatives who participate in business sessions and serve on faculty search committees. Students provide leadership for the housing system and for the campus social program. There are many avenues through which students can gain practical leadership experience.

Admission Requirements

Admission to Graceland is competitive. To be considered, high school graduates must qualify in two of the following three areas: (1) rank in the upper 50 percent of their class; (2) have a minimum 2.5 GPA, based on a 4.0 system; and (3) have either a minimum composite ACT Assessment score of 21 or a minimum combined SAT I score of 960. No one is denied admission to the University on the basis of race, color, religion, age, sex, national origin, disability, or sexual orientation. Prospective students and their families are encouraged to visit the campus.

Application and Information

Students are encouraged to apply as early as possible. For more information and application materials, students should contact:

Brian Shantz
Dean of Admissions
Graceland University
1 University Place
Lamoni, Iowa 50140
Telephone: 641-784-5196 (local)
866-GRACELAND (toll-free in the United States and Canada)
800-638-0053 (toll-free in Canada only)
Fax: 641-784-5480
E-mail: admissions@graceland.edu
World Wide Web: http://www.admissions.graceland.edu

From computer labs with Internet access to thousands of books, journals, and periodicals, the Frederick Madison Smith Library provides students with free access to a world of information.

GRAND CANYON UNIVERSITY

PHOENIX, ARIZONA

The University

Grand Canyon University is Arizona's only private, Christian, liberal arts university. The purposeful integration of faith and learning has made Grand Canyon the distinguished university it is today. Since the University's founding in 1949, professors at Grand Canyon have believed in a rare holistic approach to education wherein the mind, the body, and the spirit are seen as essential partners in the learning experience. With approximately 4,000 students, Grand Canyon University is committed to providing students with individual attention from faculty members and administrators. Grand Canyon offers more than sixty programs of study that all have their foundation in a core of liberal arts courses.

As a member of both the Council of Christian Colleges and Universities and the Council of Independent Colleges, Grand Canyon University belongs to an elite group. Less than 3 percent of all colleges and universities in the United States are Christ-centered, providing a value-added educational environment that synthesizes faith, learning, and life. At Grand Canyon, students seeking to learn and grow within a Christian value system find a sense of community, a demanding academic curriculum, and countless opportunities for community leadership and service both on and off campus. Grand Canyon University is open to students from all faith perspectives.

A degree from Grand Canyon University represents a well-rounded education. The Grand Canyon curriculum is challenging and radiates from a strong core of liberal arts and sciences. The University provides both traditional and innovative programs that enable students to think critically and creatively, solve problems through open-minded analysis, and communicate effectively. Academic habits acquired at Grand Canyon University stay with Grand Canyon graduates, enabling them to live flexible lives, to be open to new career opportunities, and to develop confidence in their ability to learn and adapt.

Grand Canyon University offers graduate degrees that include the Master of Arts in Education, Master of Arts in Teaching, Master of Education, Master of Science in executive fire service leadership, Master of Business Administration, Master of Science in leadership, and Master of Science in Nursing.

Location

Grand Canyon University is located just minutes from central Phoenix, Arizona's state capital and sixth-largest city in the United States. Phoenix is the nerve center of the Southwest, one of the fastest-growing regions in the nation. The greater Phoenix metropolitan area, known as the Valley of the Sun for its more than 300 days of sunshine each year, offers numerous educational, social, cultural, and recreational activities that enhance university life. Phoenix is a major-league city in many ways. The city is one of only eleven in the nation to be home to four major-league sports teams—the Phoenix Suns, Arizona Cardinals, Phoenix Coyotes, and Arizona Diamondbacks. The valley also provides opportunities for hiking, camping, cycling, golf, water sports, and virtually any other activity all year long. Also within a 2-hour drive of the Grand Canyon campus is some of the best snow skiing in the Western United States. Grand Canyon University students flourish in the school's southwestern environment. Surrounded by rugged mountains, lush valleys, and the arid beauty of the Sonoran Desert, Grand Canyon students feel a part of the larger human experience. Grand Canyon University and the Grand Canyon State are wonderful places in which to learn.

Majors and Degrees

Grand Canyon University awards bachelor's degrees in more than sixty areas of study. Specific degrees awarded are the Bachelor of Arts, Bachelor of Business Administration, Bachelor of Liberal Studies, Bachelor of Music, Bachelor of Science, and Bachelor of Science in Nursing.

Specific study areas include accounting, allied health, applied management, applied music, art education, athletic training, biochemistry, biology (environmental/general/human/secondary teaching), business administration, chemistry (general/secondary teaching), Christian leadership, Christian studies, communications (with emphasis in broadcasting/journalism/photojournalism/public relations), corporate fitness and wellness, elementary education, English literature, English teaching for secondary teachers, graphic design, history, international studies, justice studies, marketing, mathematics (engineering/general/secondary teaching), organizational sociology, piano performance, political science, predentistry, premedicine, pre–occupational therapy, pre-optometry, pre–osteopathic medicine, prepharmacy, pre–physical therapy, pre–physician assistant studies, prepodiatry, pre–sports health care, pre–veterinary medicine, psychology, public safety administration, recreation, science for elementary teachers, secondary education, sociology, special education (emotional handicaps and learning disabilities), speech teaching for secondary teachers, speech/theater, studio art, teaching English as a second language, theater/drama, and vocal performance.

Academic Programs

Grand Canyon University is accredited by the Higher Learning Commission of the North Central Association of Colleges and Schools (30 North LaSalle Street, Suite 2400, Chicago, Illinois 60602-2504; telephone: 800-621-7440, toll-free). Grand Canyon Bachelor of Business Administration and Master of Business Administration degree programs are additionally accredited by the Association of Collegiate Business Schools and Programs. The work of Grand Canyon students seeking certification as elementary, secondary, and special education teachers, or for the renewal of teaching certificates, is approved by the Arizona State Department of Education. Over the past ten years, 94 percent of Grand Canyon University College of Education graduates have been placed in teaching positions. Grand Canyon University Samaritan College of Nursing is accredited by both the National League for Nursing Accrediting Commission and the Arizona State Board of Nursing for the Bachelor of Science in Nursing degree. Over the past five years, 94 percent of nursing program graduates have passed the state board exams on their first attempt.

Graduates of Grand Canyon University's College of Science benefit from Grand Canyon's relationship with the Kirksville College of Osteopathic Medicine. Kirksville's southwest center, Arizona School of Health Sciences, reserves a large number of admission slots in each of its programs exclusively for qualified Grand Canyon students. These programs include physical therapy, occupational therapy, and physician assistant studies. Grand Canyon graduates are also in demand at a national level, with approximately 150 reserved admission slots in health-care programs across the country.

Off-campus internships are an important educational experience available to Grand Canyon students. Classroom sessions are more relevant when subject matter is seen in the light of the work environment. Students from all disciplines hone their skills through off-campus clinical and intern programs. Some internships result in permanent positions after graduation, an invaluable benefit.

While exploring a major field of study in depth at Grand Canyon, students are exposed to a wide range of experiences both on and off campus. This diversity is a key element of Grand Canyon's vision of educating students for successful careers and lives. Students benefit from Grand Canyon's blend of characteristics for a high-quality Christian education—small classes, accessible faculty members, a challenging curriculum, and hands-on learning experiences.

Academic Facilities

Grand Canyon University consists of thirty-six buildings on a 90-acre campus. The campus features the Fleming Library, which houses a collection of more than 166,000 volumes, 700 periodicals, newspapers, microfilm, and audiovisual materials. Fleming Library is a member of the CCLC network and as a designated depository receives a variety of government documents. Library holdings are expanded by CD-ROM databases, computerized database searches, and interlibrary loans. Computers housed in the library have Internet access to assist students.

The majority of classes are held in the Fleming Classroom Building, with additional classes held in the Weidenaar Classroom Building, Wallace Building, Williams Building, Tell Science Building, and Samaritan College of Nursing. Ethington Memorial Theatre sets the perfect stage for drama and other productions, with more than 300 seats. The C. J. and Thema Smith Arts Complex houses the A. P. Tell Gallery and other tailored creative spaces. The Tell Science Building and Samaritan College of Nursing are both equipped with state-of-the-art laboratory, computer, multimedia, and clinical learning spaces.

Grand Canyon University features two microcomputer laboratories utilizing IBM-compatible personal computers and a separate Macintosh computer laboratory.

Costs

In 2003–04, tuition and fees were $14,500 (24 to 36 hours), and room and board were $7130.

Financial Aid

Grand Canyon University has made a commitment to its students by keeping costs down year after year and focusing its dollars on what benefits students directly. The result of this effort yields an educational experience that offers high value and quality for the investment students make. The Office of Financial Aid and the Business Office at Grand Canyon University are committed to working with students and their families. They can help explain various options and ensure that every available resource is utilized to meet individual financial needs. More than 79 percent of Grand Canyon students receive some form of financial assistance to help meet the cost of their education. In addition to federal and state financial aid, Grand Canyon University has academic and other specific-criteria scholarships and aid available. Students wishing to apply for financial aid must be accepted for admission and complete the Free Application for Federal Student Aid (FAFSA) and have it on file in the Office of Financial Aid.

Faculty

Faculty members are drawn to Grand Canyon University due to a love of teaching. Rather than concentrating mainly on research and publication, Grand Canyon faculty members focus on assisting students to acquire knowledge and attain higher standards that help them reach their potential as people and as scholars. More than three quarters of Grand Canyon faculty members have earned doctoral or terminal degrees from some of the nation's most prestigious universities, and many are considered experts in their field. Beyond their academic qualifications, Grand Canyon faculty members are good friends. They help students become involved in the community and guide them through further explorations of their faith.

Student Government

Grand Canyon University understands that student involvement is essential in the university experience. Grand Canyon's Campus Leadership Council (CLC) is student-led and staff-supported. CLC is responsible for developing student leaders and programs that provide opportunities for contribution to the Grand Canyon campus and surrounding community. The election of Student Body President is held in the spring semester of each year. CLC positions for Chief of Staff, Director of Organizations, Director of Intramurals, Chief Financial Officer, Director of Marketing, and Director of Student Activities are determined through an application and interview process.

Admission Requirements

For admission to Grand Canyon University, students should submit an application for admission with a $50 nonrefundable application fee to the Grand Canyon University Office of Admission. Freshmen must submit their official high school transcript and/or GED scores plus have their ACT or SAT I scores submitted to Grand Canyon University. Transfer students must have their transcripts forwarded to Grand Canyon University. Both freshman and transfer students must bring a health history, with proof of immunization for mumps, measles, and rubella, to put on file.

Application and Information

Grand Canyon operates on a rolling admission system. Applicants generally receive an admission decision within ten days after all required documents are on file in the Office of Admission. It is to the student's advantage to apply as early as possible. Applications for financial aid and housing cannot be completely processed and transcripts are not evaluated until the admission application is complete.

For further information and application materials, students should contact:

Office of Admission
Grand Canyon University
3300 West Camelback Road
Phoenix, Arizona 85017
Telephone: 602-589-2855
800-800-9776 (toll-free)
E-mail: admissions@gcu.edu
World Wide Web: http://www.gcu.edu

Students in front of Fleming Library at Grand Canyon University in Phoenix, Arizona, experience the integration of faith in their learning process while surrounded by the beauty of the Southwest.

GRAND VALLEY STATE UNIVERSITY

ALLENDALE, MICHIGAN

The University

Founded in 1960, Grand Valley State University (GVSU) is a public institution dedicated to providing students with the highest-quality undergraduate and graduate education. Teaching in the liberal arts tradition, whether in general arts and sciences or the professional degree programs, has always been at the heart of Grand Valley's educational mission. Students at Grand Valley learn to think for themselves as they develop the skills of inquiry, reflection, critical analysis, dialogue, and expression. Grand Valley State University is characterized by and known for its superior student-centered teaching and learning. GVSU's 21,524 students, 17,885 of whom are undergraduates, experience rich learning environments, an average class size of 27, and classes taught by regular faculty members, not teaching assistants. Professors collaborate with students on advanced research projects, where they gain knowledge and skills more commonly associated with graduate-level study. As an investment, Grand Valley degrees are highly respected and valued by employers and graduate schools. GVSU has been recognized for eight consecutive years by Educational Research and Evaluation, Inc., as one of "America's 100 Best College Buys." Grand Valley's diverse environment promotes the development of intellect and creativity through teaching, scholarship, service, and a vibrant campus culture.

Grand Valley's residential living centers are the newest and most contemporary facilities in the state. More than 4,600 students live on campus, just steps away from classes, professors, campus dining, and extracurricular activities. Grand Valley competes in nineteen collegiate sports at the NCAA Division II level, and the football team won the 2002 and 2003 national championship titles. More than 160 clubs, societies, groups, and organizations make it simple to connect with other students who share common interests, academic goals, hobbies, ethnic backgrounds, and religious beliefs. Inspiring classroom and research facilities, modern living centers, wireless academic buildings, and convenient student services make Grand Valley a wonderful place to study, learn, and live.

Grand Valley State University has eight degree-granting colleges: the College of Community and Public Services, College of Education, College of Engineering and Computing, College of Health Professions, College of Liberal Arts and Sciences, College of University-wide Interdisciplinary Initiatives, Kirkhof College of Nursing, and Seidman College of Business.

Graduate degree programs are offered in accounting, biology, business general, communications, computer information systems, criminal justice, education general, engineering, English, health administration, health sciences, nursing, occupational therapy, physical therapy, physician assistant studies, public administration, reading/language arts, social work, special education, and taxation.

Location

Grand Valley State University's vibrant, residential main campus is located in Allendale, midway between downtown Grand Rapids (the second-largest city in the state of Michigan) and the lake shore. The dynamic, urban Pew campus, 12 miles to the east, is located in the heart of downtown Grand Rapids. Both campuses are safe and secure. The sandy beaches of Lake Michigan and the cultural opportunities of Grand Rapids are easily accessible from either campus.

Majors and Degrees

GVSU offers undergraduate degree programs in accounting, advertising and public relations, anthropology, art and design, athletic training, behavioral science, biology, biomedical sciences, biopsychology, broadcasting, business, cell and molecular biology, chemistry, city and regional planning, classics, communications, computer science, criminal justice, dance, earth science, East Asian studies, economics, education, engineering, English, film and video, finance, French, geochemistry, geography, geology, German, Greek, health communication, health sciences, history, hospitality and tourism management, information systems, international business, international relations, journalism, Latin, legal studies, liberal studies, management, marketing, mathematics, medical imaging, music, natural resources management, nursing, occupational safety and health, philosophy, photography, physics, political science, predental studies, premedical studies, preveterinarian studies, psychology, public administration, Russian studies, social work, sociology, Spanish, special education psychology, statistics, theater, therapeutic recreation, and writing.

Academic Programs

GVSU offers more than 200 areas of study in sixty-eight undergraduate degree programs. At Grand Valley, all students complete the University's general education curriculum, which enriches and complements the student's major and electives and is a significant part of the baccalaureate experience.

The Honors College, located on the Allendale campus, offers academically talented students an opportunity to participate in an exclusive community of scholars exemplifying intellectual achievement. Honors students develop high levels of proficiency in research, writing, and critical thinking, while taking their classes in the same building they call home, the Neimeyer Living Center.

Off-Campus Programs

The Office of Career Services has teamed up with hundreds of businesses and organizations to offer students internships in nearly every field. Each year, more than 2,000 students gain valuable work experience, often while laying the groundwork for employment after graduation.

Students in every major have opportunities to study in another country. The Padnos International Center sponsors summer, semester, and yearlong study-abroad programs through partnerships with universities in Europe, Asia, South America, and Australia.

Academic Facilities

On the 1,112-acre Allendale campus, the James H. Zumberge Library houses the more than 627,000 volumes and other materials necessary to effectively support instructional programs at Grand Valley. The Performing Arts Center houses faculty offices, classrooms, practice rooms, teaching studios for the performing arts, a music technology lab (using Macintosh computers), two new dance studios, the art gallery, and the 490-seat Louis Armstrong Theatre, for presentations of plays, operas, concerts, and other programs. The Calder Art Center contains two computer graphics labs and facilities for graphic design, painting, printmaking, art education, drawing, and ceramics.

Graduate degree programs and the upper-division courses for majors in business, criminal justice, education, engineering, public administration, and social work are located at the 29-acre Pew campus in downtown Grand Rapids. The 215,000-square-foot Cook-DeVos Center for Health Science, a $57.1-million state-of-the-art facility that opened in fall 2003, is the home of the Kirkhof College of Nursing, the College for Health Professions, and majors within the life sciences. It features cutting-edge training and laboratory facilities, project rooms to encourage group learning and interdisciplinary study, case-study classrooms, and faculty offices. The Richard M. DeVos Center, a 242,000-volume library, features a computer-operated robotic retrieval system and a New York–style reading room. The Eberhard Center has forty-three classrooms and labs, high-technology teleconference and conference facilities, and two interactive television rooms. The Keller Engineering Laboratories Building, located adjacent to the Eberhard Center, is a three-story, 27,000-square-foot facility built with its structural, mechanical, and electrical systems exposed to provide students with a living laboratory. The Meijer Public Broadcast Center houses Grand Valley's public television and radio stations.

Grand Valley's wide-area high-speed network provides a full complement of computer services and includes wireless locations throughout the campuses.

Costs

GVSU is one of the most affordable public universities in Michigan. During the 2003–04 academic year, freshman residents of Michigan carrying 12–16 credits paid $5353 for tuition; nonresidents paid $12,216. Students on full-service meal plans and living in University-owned on-campus housing paid about $5770 for room and board, depending on accommodations. Books and supplies were about $800 per year. On-campus parking and bus transportation between campuses are free. Approximately $1200 should be set aside for social activities and other personal needs. All costs are subject to change.

Financial Aid

Financial Aid at Grand Valley State University is awarded in the form of a package and generally consists of grants, scholarships, loans, and college work-study. Grand Valley participates in all applicable federal and state aid programs. During the 2002–03 academic year, Grand Valley students received more than $96 million in total assistance, with more than $28 million in scholarships, grants, and employment. Students should contact the Office of Financial Aid and Scholarships at the toll free number listed below for further information.

Faculty

Grand Valley prides itself on being a teaching institution dedicated to providing the highest possible level of quality instruction. The most crucial ingredient necessary for the achievement of this goal—the quality of the faculty—was judged "impressive" by the evaluation team of the North Central Association of Colleges and Schools' Higher Learning Commission. Doctoral degrees or other appropriate terminal degrees have been earned by 83 percent of the 902 regular faculty members.

The University promotes professional excellence in teaching and research. The Center for Research and Development focuses on the enhancement of faculty and student research and scholarship. Many faculty projects funded by this center actively engage students in research and creative processes to expand their learning experience. These projects include experimentation or observation in the laboratory, field, and library and initiatives in the creative and performing arts.

Student Government

The Student Senate is composed of 50 senators-at-large who represent the students of GVSU. The Resident Housing Association is a programming organization that sponsors campuswide programs for all Grand Valley students. In addition to programming, its members also serve as the governing body for all of the Community Councils on campus.

Admission Requirements

Admissions decisions are selective and are based on the secondary school record (grades earned and courses selected), the personal data submitted on the application, and SAT or ACT results.

A complete application for freshman admission includes a signed application, the nonrefundable $30 application fee, official high school transcript(s), and SAT or ACT test scores. Freshmen are normally expected to be graduates of accredited high schools or preparatory schools. The University recommends that high school students have taken college-prep courses that include 4 years of English (including composition), 3 years of science (including 2 years of laboratory science), 3 years of mathematics (including 2 years of algebra), 3 years of social sciences, and 2 years of a single foreign language. Elective courses in computer science and the fine arts are also recommended.

A complete application for transfer admission includes a signed application, the nonrefundable $30 application fee, and official transcript(s) for all previously attended colleges and/or universities. Transfer admissions are based upon the completion of at least 30 semester credit hours (45 quarter hours) and a cumulative grade point average of 2.0 or higher. If the student has less than 30 earned college credits, official high school transcript(s) and SAT or ACT scores are also required.

Application and Information

For an application or additional information, students should contact:

Admissions Office
Grand Valley State University
1 Campus Drive
Allendale, Michigan 49401-9403
Telephone: 616-331-2025
800-748-0246 (toll free)
World Wide Web: http://www.gvsu.edu

Opened in 2003, the Cook-DeVos Center for Health Sciences is located in downtown Grand Rapids, Michigan.

GRAND VIEW COLLEGE

DES MOINES, IOWA

The College

Grand View is a four-year liberal arts college affiliated with the Evangelical Lutheran Church in America. Founded more than 100 years ago, Grand View offered a high-quality education to all students who sought the opportunity. Today, Grand View continues the tradition, educating a diverse student body in a career-oriented, liberal arts–grounded curriculum at two campus locations in greater Des Moines. Grand View welcomes traditional students and adult learners representing a wide range of religious and cultural backgrounds.

At Grand View College, students find a winning combination of high-quality programs, experienced professors, and caring individuals. With 1,600 students and an average class size of 15, students get to know their professors and other students well. They learn independence and seek responsibility in Grand View's educational environment. Learning is an interactive process at Grand View—students engage in lively discussions, work on real-world projects, and participate in career-related work experiences.

Grand View College stands out from other colleges because of its partnerships with leading businesses and organizations in Des Moines, which has led to 100 percent of students finding jobs right after graduation or continuing their education for the past ten years. Grand View is known for its ability to connect students with exciting and challenging career opportunities.

Students are encouraged to develop leadership and team skills through involvement in campus organizations, which include intercollegiate and intramural athletics, speech and theater groups, major department clubs, student government, and the Grand View College Choir. Active honorary societies include Alpha Chi, Alpha Mu Gamma, Alpha Psi Omega, Alpha Sigma Lambda, Beta Beta Beta, Phi Eta Sigma, Sigma Theta Tau, and Theta Alpha Kappa. Grand View's student leadership program provides opportunities for students without leadership experience to seek and develop critical thinking, interpersonal, and networking skills.

Student athletes compete in men's baseball, basketball, cross-country, golf, and soccer and women's basketball, competitive dance, cross-country, golf, soccer, softball, and volleyball. Grand View participates in the Midwest Classic Conference of the National Association of Intercollegiate Athletics.

Two locations offer Grand View students convenient scheduling options for their program of study. Weekend and evening classes are offered at the main campus in Des Moines and also at Grand View's Camp Dodge Campus in Johnston, Iowa. For motivated students seeking to complete their degree quickly, an accelerated schedule leading to a business administration degree and an individualized degree in organizational and technical studies are offered at the Camp Dodge Campus in Johnston.

Location

Grand View is located in Des Moines, a metropolitan area of nearly 495,000 people in central Iowa. Des Moines is the state capital and serves as the communications hub for Iowa. Nationally recognized organizations that have their corporate offices in Des Moines include Pioneer Hi-Bred International, Inc.; the Principal Financial Group; Meredith Corporation; and the *Des Moines Register*.

Grand View College's campus is Des Moines—and as part of the Grand View community, students are not limited by the confines of a small college or small town. In a given day, students can catch an Iowa Cubs professional baseball doubleheader, head down to the Court Avenue district for great food and nightlife, or take in a concert at the Civic Center.

A thriving arts program in Des Moines features the Des Moines Metro Opera, Ballet Iowa, the Des Moines Symphony, the Des Moines Art Center, and the Des Moines Playhouse.

Des Moines features four distinct and beautiful seasons. Except for a month or so of bundle-up, see-your-breath weather, the climate is ideal for outdoor activities. Grand View students can take advantage of terrific recreational opportunities, including several golf courses, Saylorville Lake, and many city parks and state forests.

Easily accessible from Interstates 35 and 80, Grand View is 4 hours from Minneapolis, 6 hours from Chicago, and 4 hours from Kansas City.

Majors and Degrees

Grand View College grants the Bachelor of Arts degree and offers majors in accounting, applied math, biology, broadcast, business administration, computer science, criminal justice, elementary education, English, graphic design, graphic journalism, health promotion, human services, individualized major, journalism, liberal arts, management information systems, mass communication, organizational and technical studies, physical science, political studies, psychology, religion, secondary education, theater arts, and visual arts. Grand View also offers a Bachelor of Science degree in nursing. In addition, the College offers certificate programs in art therapy, in-house communication, Spanish essentials, and sport management and postbaccalaureate certificates in accounting and management in accounting.

Academic Program

Grand View operates on a 4-4-1 academic calendar. The first semester runs from September to December. The second semester begins in early January and ends in late April. Three 1-month summer sessions are offered in May, June, and July, as is a summer trimester evening program.

Grand View College has adopted a competency-based General Education Core. Requirements for the core are defined in student learning goals. Completion of the educational core enables students to achieve a measurable level of competency in key skill and knowledge areas, such as writing, critical analysis, oral communication, and computer proficiency.

The Logos Honors Program provides an alternative to the General Education Core. By invitation, freshman and sophomore students enrolled in this program complete a series of courses designed to challenge exceptional students.

The Grand View academic mission is to serve a diverse student body by providing a variety of learning environments and teaching techniques. In order to meet this commitment, Grand View provides academic support programs and services designed to enable students to master skills essential for success in college-level courses. Special programs and services include a mathematics lab for drop-in tutoring, a writing lab to assist students in honing their skills, reading and study skills assessment and planning, and individual tutorial programs.

Costs

For 2003–04, the comprehensive cost for freshmen on campus was $19,788, which included tuition, an activity fee, a technology fee, and room and board. Health services and Internet access were also included in the comprehensive fee.

Financial Aid

Last year, 99 percent of all full-time Grand View students received financial assistance. The average freshman full-time award package for 2002–03 was $17,730, with $9780 in grants and scholarships and the remainder in work-study and student loans. The amount of aid is determined through a combination of merit and analysis of need as determined through the Free Application for Federal Student Aid. The priority deadline for financial aid is March 1. Students receive notification of financial aid packages following acceptance of admission to the College and receipt of their financial aid analysis of need.

Faculty

There are 73 full-time faculty members and 62 part-time faculty members. Forty-four percent hold terminal degrees. All classes are taught by professors; no graduate or teaching assistants instruct Grand View classes.

Student Government

Students participate in College governance. The Student Activities Council and Viking Council plan student activities that promote educational, social, cultural, and recreational aspects of student life. Students serve as representatives on faculty and staff search committees, programming committees, and student life committees.

Admission Requirements

Applicants' files are reviewed to determine their preparedness for a Grand View education. Official high school transcripts and submission of ACT or SAT I scores are required for applicants with less than 24 semester hours of college credit. Applicants transferring from another college are required to submit official transcripts from all colleges previously attended.

Application and Information

For more information about Grand View, students should contact:

Admissions Office
Grand View College
1200 Grandview Avenue
Des Moines, Iowa 50316-1599
Telephone: 515-263-2810
800-444-6083, Ext. 2810 (toll-free)
Fax: 515-263-2974
E-mail: admiss@gvc.edu
World Wide Web: http://www.gvc.edu

Students on Grand View College's campus.

GREENSBORO COLLEGE

GREENSBORO, NORTH CAROLINA

The College

Established in 1838, Greensboro College is a four-year coeducational liberal arts college that is affiliated with the United Methodist Church. It is located in the College Hill Historic District of Greensboro, North Carolina. With an enrollment of approximately 1,250 men and women, the College stresses a small community atmosphere and maintains a student-faculty ratio of 14:1.

The College has completed an exciting $40-million building and renovation program that provides new classrooms and laboratories and transforms the gardens and grounds in a way that preserves and enhances the special character of the 60-acre campus. Its architecture is in the traditional Georgian style. The buildings include an indoor athletic center, four residential halls, classroom buildings, a chapel, a performing arts center, a library, and a main administrative building.

In the newly opened Royce Reynolds Family Student Life Center, students enjoy squash, racquetball, and basketball courts; a fitness facility; an indoor pool; an aerobics room; a Jacuzzi; a steam room; and a sauna. Intercollegiate sports include baseball, basketball, cross-country, football, golf, lacrosse, soccer, and tennis for men and basketball, cross-country, lacrosse, soccer, softball, swimming, tennis, and volleyball for women. Greensboro College is a member of the NCAA Division III and competes in the U.S.A. South Athletic Conference. An intramural program is also offered for students.

There is cultural, religious, and ethnic diversity at Greensboro College, where students come from more than thirty states and twenty-four nations. Many graduates have earned distinction in graduate and professional schools in all parts of the United States and abroad. Recent Greensboro College graduates have been accepted into the graduate schools of the College of William and Mary; Duke, Emory, Georgetown, Johns Hopkins, North Carolina State, Princeton, St. Andrews (Scotland), Temple, Vanderbilt, and Wake Forest Universities; and the Eastman School of Music. Most graduates pursue careers in business, education, health care, and the arts.

Extracurricular activities are designed to supplement and reinforce academic study at the College. More than 100 student leadership positions are available in more than fifty different student organizations, enabling most students to be as active in campus life as they wish.

Location

The city of Greensboro, located near the center of North Carolina, offers major industries, including insurance companies and textile manufacturers, and many cultural, social, and athletic opportunities. With a population of more than 1 million people in the Triad region, the city is a thriving business center that offers excellent internship opportunities. More than 24,000 college students study at the six colleges and universities within the city. Greensboro College is at the heart of this community.

Majors and Degrees

Greensboro College awards the Bachelor of Arts, Bachelor of Science, Bachelor of Business Administration, and Master of Education degrees. Students can major in the following areas: accounting, art, biology, birth-through-kindergarten teacher education, business administration and economics, chemistry, communications, education or special education, English, French, history, history and political science, mathematics, middle school education, music, physical education, political science, psychology, religion and philosophy, secondary education, sociology, Spanish, sports and exercise studies, and theater. Minors are available in child and family studies, computer science, dance, ethics, interdisciplinary studies, legal administration, women's studies, and other areas in which majors are offered. Combined-degree programs are offered in medical technology and radiological technology.

Academic Program

All students are required to take courses in the humanities, the natural sciences, the social sciences, and the arts. The general education requirements for both the B.A. and B.S. degrees total 52 semester hours. Graduation requires the completion of 124 semester hours.

Greensboro College offers an honors program for superior students who qualify on the basis of SAT I or ACT scores, high school grade point averages, or AP examination results. Students enrolled in the program must complete requirements in addition to those expected of students in the regular B.A. and B.S. degree programs.

Because Greensboro College recognizes that people must learn not only how to live but also how to make a living, the liberal arts curriculum and setting provide the context for a variety of professional programs, including accounting, business, and legal administration, as well as preprofessional programs in law, medicine, and theology. Besides providing career and academic counseling, the College seeks to ensure that its graduates acquire the basic intellectual and communications capabilities to cope with the changing demands of any career. An internship program during the junior and senior years places students in business and agency settings that are related to the major and to career aspirations. The College also seeks to develop in its graduates a philosophy of life and an appreciation of Judeo-Christian values that transcend particular vocational skills.

Off-Campus Programs

Greensboro College is a member of the Greater Greensboro Consortium and the Piedmont Independent Colleges Association, which provide for arrangements with Bennett College, Elon College, Guilford College, Guilford Technical Community College, High Point University, North Carolina Agricultural and Technical State University, Salem College, and the University of North Carolina at Greensboro. With permission from the academic dean, students at Greensboro College may take courses offered at any of the other campuses. Library resources are shared.

Academic Facilities

The James Addison Jones Library has approximately 103,000 volumes, periodicals, CD-ROMs, and microfilm reels. The computerized card catalog system allows students to access the holdings of other area colleges. Interlibrary loan among the colleges is permitted. There are reading rooms, periodical and browsing rooms, and a multipurpose meeting room.

One of the College's goals is to be sure that every student develops a broad range of technical skills in order to flourish in the twenty-first century. State-of-the-art computer labs are available for all students, and students can access the Internet and World Wide Web from most points on campus. All dorm rooms provide high-speed access to the Internet.

Other facilities include a computerized writing laboratory, natural science laboratories, the Annie Sellars Jordan Parlor Theater, and the Gail Brower Huggins Performance Center, one of the most elegant and state-of-the-art performance facilities in the area. Music facilities include a computerized music laboratory, practice rooms, two recital areas, thirty-nine pianos (including a 9-foot concert grand), and a concert stage. In addition, Greensboro College is one of only three colleges in the state to have a Fisk organ. There are two large art studios, one for the teaching of two-dimensional media and one for the teaching of three-dimensional media. Students in the education department are served by the Curriculum Materials Center, which contains audiovisual equipment, books, teaching kits, and a variety of other special supplies.

Costs

For 2003–04, the total cost of tuition, fees, room, and board was $21,750. A private room cost an additional $1500. Greensboro College estimates that an additional $800 to $1600 is adequate for books, clothing, entertainment, and other incidental expenses.

Financial Aid

Greensboro College participates in many federal programs of student aid, including the Federal Pell Grant, Federal Work-Study, Federal Perkins Loan, Federal Supplemental Educational Opportunity Grant, Federal Parent Loan for Undergraduate Students, and Federal Stafford Student Loan programs. Authorized state programs include North Carolina Legislative Tuition Grants, the State Contractual Scholarship Fund, North Carolina Prospective Teacher's Scholarships/Loans, and North Carolina Student Incentive Grants. Institutional programs funded by Greensboro College include the College work-study program, grants, scholarships, and loans. Full- and partial-tuition scholarships are awarded to students based on merit. United Methodist Church scholarships and grants, based on both financial need and merit, are available. Full merit-based Presidential Scholarships, valued at more than $87,000 each, are available. Approximately 90 percent of the students at Greensboro College receive some form of financial assistance. All students are encouraged to apply for financial aid, and the College accepts the Free Application for Federal Student Aid (FAFSA). Applications for United Methodist Church scholarships and grants are available from the financial planning office. A career development office on campus is available to aid all students seeking a part-time job, regardless of their financial need.

Faculty

Greensboro College has 105 full- and part-time faculty members. One-hundred percent of the full-time faculty members hold the highest degree in their areas of study. Although some faculty members have distinguished themselves by their research, scholarship, and creativity, all are deeply and primarily committed to undergraduate teaching and the personal welfare of the students. Every student has a faculty adviser; the average class size is 16, and there is a favorable student-faculty ratio of 14:1.

Student Government

The College's Student Government Association (SGA), acting within the policies and regulations of the College, is the main representative voice of the students. The SGA addresses various policy decisions that affect the students and acts as a sounding board for student opinions. The SGA is the communication link between student organizations, the student body, the administration, the staff, and the faculty. The Campus Activities Board plans and executes student events on campus.

Admission Requirements

Admission decisions are based on all available information. Although applicants are asked to submit scores from the SAT I and/or ACT, the high school record is actually the most important single factor. There is no exact formula that can be applied to all applications, but acceptable scores on the SAT I or ACT, rank in class, grade point average, and high school program form the basis for evaluation. Candidates for admission should demonstrate academic achievement in a select academic program in high school, although completion of a given program of study is not as important as evidence of intellectual curiosity and emotional and social maturity. A curriculum that provides good preparation for Greensboro College might include 4 units of English, 3 units of college-preparatory math (algebra I, II, and geometry), 2 units of science (including one laboratory science), 2 units of history, 2 units of the same foreign language, and electives chosen from art, music, physical education, and social science. An interview on campus is very helpful to the student and to the College. Arrangements may be made for the interview at the student's convenience.

Greensboro College accepts transfer credits on a case-by-case basis. Credit is given for courses successfully completed at accredited universities, senior colleges, junior colleges, community colleges, and technical colleges.

Application and Information

Students should submit an application for admission and immediately ask high schools and any colleges they have attended to forward official transcripts to Greensboro. SAT I or ACT scores should be forwarded to Greensboro College by the testing agency or the student's high school. Reference letters may be requested by the Admissions Committee, which reviews all applications on a rolling basis. As soon as a decision is reached, the student is notified. Greensboro College has no closing date for applications, but those received before March 31 are given priority.

Inquiries and application materials should be sent to:

Director of Admissions
Greensboro College
815 West Market Street
Greensboro, North Carolina 27401-1875
Telephone: 800-346-8226 (toll-free nationwide)
Fax: 336-378-0154
E-mail: admissions@gborocollege.edu
World Wide Web: http://gborocollege.edu

Greensboro College students frequently gather near the historic Main Building.

GRINNELL COLLEGE

GRINNELL, IOWA

The College

Grinnell College has been named one of the fifteen best liberal arts colleges in the country for the past fifteen years by *U.S. News & World Report.* The 130-acre campus is located in the heart of the Midwest, and its student body comes from fifty states and fifty-five countries. Founded in 1846—the first four-year liberal arts college west of the Mississippi to grant a B.A. degree—Grinnell is described today in the Yale publication, *The Insider's Guide to the Colleges,* as "one of the most enlightened, progressive colleges in the Midwest—or the entire country, for that matter." Innovative from the beginning, Grinnell was the first college to establish an undergraduate department of political science (in 1883), and the school's travel-service program preceded the establishment of the Peace Corps by many years. Examples of current innovations include first-year tutorials, cooperative preprofessional programs, and a comprehensive program in quantitative studies and the societal impacts of technology globally.

The College is a cultural and recreational resource for the local community as well as for its 1,450 students, the faculty, and the staff. More than 500 events during the academic year include plays, concerts, art exhibitions, dance recitals, lectures, discussions, and intramural and intercollegiate sports, all of which are free to the College community and general public. The Rosenfield Program in Public Affairs, International Relations, and Human Rights brings many outside lecturers to campus to enhance current-events programming. Facilities for sports and recreational activities are provided by the Physical Education Complex. The Bucksbaum Center for the Arts, which opened in 1999 with a $22-million addition, more than doubles existing arts space on campus, offering a new recital hall, art gallery, theater, scene shop, studio theater, and classroom and studio space.

Location

Named one of the twenty-five best small towns in America, Grinnell is located in central Iowa, 55 minutes east of downtown Des Moines, off Interstate 80, in a prosperous and picturesque agricultural area. Stores, personal and professional services, a modern hospital, churches, restaurants, and other community features are available in addition to opportunities for community involvement. A landscape of rolling hills is a ten-minute bike ride from campus, and nearby Rock Creek State Park offers hiking, swimming, and sailing.

Majors and Degrees

Grinnell offers a rigorous and highly interdisciplinary four-year undergraduate liberal arts program leading to the Bachelor of Arts degree. Majors available in the humanities are art, Chinese, classics (Greek and Latin), English, French, German, music, philosophy, religious studies, Russian, Spanish, and theater. In science, the majors are biological chemistry, biology, chemistry, computer science, general science, mathematics, physics, and psychology. Majors in social studies are anthropology, economics, history, political science, and sociology. Interdepartmental majors and independent majors may be arranged.

Nonmajor programs and concentrations are offered in alternative language studies, education (elementary and secondary certification), general literary studies, humanities/social studies, and physical education. Interdisciplinary concentrations include Africana studies, East Asian studies, environmental studies, gender and women's studies, global development studies, Latin American studies, linguistics, Russian and Eastern European studies, technology studies, and Western European studies.

In cooperation with other institutions, the College offers preprofessional programs in architecture, engineering, and law.

Academic Program

A Grinnell education is anchored in intense, active learning that occurs in one-on-one interactions between faculty members and students. The school is known for its rigorous academic and diverse extracurricular program. Its open curriculum enables students to learn initiative and leadership by assuming responsibility for their individual courses of study, which are developed under the guidance of a faculty adviser to reflect each student's goals for the future, including graduate school. This process challenges students to define and achieve their academic goals.

Outside of the First-Year Tutorial (a one-semester special topics seminar that stresses methods of inquiry, critical analysis, and writing skills), there are no core requirements. To graduate, students are expected to complete at least 32 credits in a major field and a total of 124 credits of academic work, with no more than 48 credits in one department and no more than 92 credits in one division. In the humanities, arts, and social and natural sciences at Grinnell, students have opportunities to conduct original research and undertake advanced study through independent and interdisciplinary projects that foster intellectual discovery. Course exemptions and advanced placement are also available. Students usually take 16 credits of course work during each of the two semesters in the academic year, which begins in late August and ends in mid-May.

Off-Campus Programs

Grinnell's commitment to the importance of off-campus study reflects the school's emphasis on social and political awareness and the international nature of its campus. Approximately 60 percent of all Grinnell students participate in more than seventy off-campus programs, including the Grinnell-in-London program and study tours of China, France, Greece, and Russia. These study programs in Europe (including Russia), Africa, the Near East, and Asia, as well as nine programs in Central and South America, provide the opportunity for research and enrichment in many disciplines, from archaeology to education. In addition to off-campus programs, Grinnell offers an extensive internship program in such areas as urban studies, art, and marine biology for students interested in field-based learning and experience in professional settings. Second- and third-year students may apply for summer internship grants and receive credit for the experience. Semester programs in the United States include those at the Oak Ridge National Laboratory, Newberry Library, National Theatre Institute, and Grinnell in Washington, D.C.

Academic Facilities

The eleven academic buildings on campus include the Grinnell College libraries—consisting of Burling Library, the Windsor Science Library, and the Music Library—which hold 455,000 volumes, 26,100 audio and video recordings, 16,100 microforms, 514,500 state and federal government documents, and subscriptions to 3,597 professional and academic journals, with an on-line catalog system and CD-ROM databases. In addition to the College archives and rare books collections, the library houses special collections in Africana Studies, East Asian Studies, and Latina/o Studies. A recent $15.3-million renovation and addition to the College's science facilities in the Noyce Science Center has equipped lab facilities and classrooms with research tools that encourage hands-on experience and collaborative work. These include sophisticated laboratories, aquaria, a herbarium, scanning and transmission electron microscope facilities, a nuclear magnetic resonance spectrometer, a physics historical museum, and other specialized resources. An observatory houses a computerized, research-quality, 24-inch reflecting telescope with sophisticated auxiliary devices and a lab, classroom, and darkroom. More than 1,000 PCs, Macintoshes, and workstations, linked to a variety of servers over a campus network, are used for teaching, research, and administrative computing. Near Grinnell, the biology department maintains the widely recognized 365-acre Conard Environmental Research Area, which has a fully equipped field-research laboratory for studies in ecology. Programs in art, music, and theater are housed in the new Bucksbaum Center for the Arts. The center includes the Roberts Theatre, the Flanagan Arena Theatre, the Scheaffer Gallery for art exhibitions, a studio for modern dance, music rooms, a scene shop, and art studios. The College Forum (student union) and the Harris Center, both centers for cultural activity and social and recreational events, serve all members of the College community.

Costs

The comprehensive fee of $31,060 for 2003–04 included $23,898 for tuition, $6570 for room and board, and $592 for activities, health, and other fees. Students should allow for the additional costs of books, supplies, travel, laundry, and personal expenses.

Financial Aid

Grinnell has a long-standing commitment to both a need-blind admission policy and to providing 100 percent of institutionally calculated need to each qualifying student. To that end, more than $15 million is budgeted annually for grants and scholarships. Grinnell also offers further assistance through campus employment opportunities, loans, and numerous payment options. Students wishing to be considered for financial aid should, along with their parents, file the Free Application for Federal Student Aid (FAFSA) and Grinnell's Application for Financial Aid and Scholarships by February 1.

Faculty

The Grinnell faculty consists of 141 men and women. Ninety-three percent hold Ph.D. degrees, and among the members are scholars, writers, and artists of established reputation who are active in producing original, significant scholarship. All classes are taught by professors, not teaching assistants, and the student-faculty ratio of 10:1 means that Grinnell students can work closely with their instructors, who view classroom teaching as their top priority.

Student Government

Self-governance is a guiding principle at Grinnell College. Students serve on departmental educational policy committees and the Faculty Curriculum Committee. Students regulate the residence halls in consultation with residence life coordinators and serve on committees that determine social policy and regulations. The organizational structure of the Student Government Association covers almost all aspects of student activity and campus life. There are no sororities or fraternities.

Admission Requirements

Academic promise and intellectual self-reliance are qualities sought in students applying to Grinnell. Requirements are a scholastic record and class standing that show ability to do college work; graduation from an accredited secondary school with 4 units of English, 4 units of mathematics, 3–4 units of laboratory science, 3–4 units of a foreign language, and 3–4 units of social studies; satisfactory results on the SAT I or the American College Testing (ACT) examination; recommendation of the secondary school counselor; and recommendations of 2 secondary school teachers. Interviews on campus or with alumni are strongly recommended.

Application and Information

Students may apply for early decision if Grinnell is their school of first choice. Students applying for early decision I should submit their applications by November 20; they will be notified by December 20 regarding both admission to the College and financial aid. For early decision II, applications must be submitted by January 1 with notification by February 1. Early decision is a commitment to enroll, and those accepted must withdraw all other applications.

Students may file applications for regular admission by January 20. Those filing by this date will be notified of the decision on admission and financial aid by April 1.

Grinnell College offers early admission to superior college-bound students who have completed the junior year of secondary school but who will neither complete their senior year nor receive a secondary school diploma.

For an application form and more information about Grinnell, students should contact:

Office of Admission
Grinnell College
Grinnell, Iowa 50112-1690
Telephone: 641-269-3600
800-247-0113 (toll-free)
E-mail: askgrin@grinnell.edu
World Wide Web: http://www.grinnell.edu

The Grinnell campus is considered to be one of the most attractive of American collegiate landscapes, as depicted in this photograph of North Campus near Gates-Rawson Tower.

GROVE CITY COLLEGE

GROVE CITY, PENNSYLVANIA

The College

The beautifully landscaped campus of Grove City College (GCC) stretches more than 150 acres and includes twenty-seven neo-Gothic buildings valued at more than $100 million. The campus is considered one of the loveliest in the nation. While the College has changed to meet the needs of the society it serves, its basic philosophy has remained unchanged since its founding in 1876. It is a Christian liberal arts and sciences institution of ideal size and dedicated to the principle of providing the highest-quality education at the lowest possible cost. Wishing to remain truly independent and to retain its distinctive qualities as a private school governed by private citizens (trustees), it is one of the very few colleges in the country that does not accept any state or federal monies. Affiliated with the Presbyterian Church (U.S.A.) but not narrowly denominational, the College believes that to be well educated a student should be exposed to the central ideas of the Judeo-Christian tradition. A 20-minute chapel program offered Tuesday and Thursday mornings, along with a Sunday evening worship service, challenge students in their faith. Sixteen chapel services per semester are required out of forty opportunities. Religious organizations and activities exist to provide fellowship and spiritual growth.

Ninety-one percent of the 2,300 students live in separate men's and women's residence halls. All others are regular commuters or married students. A full program of cultural, professional, athletic, and social activities is offered. An arena, Crawford Auditorium, and the J. Howard Pew Fine Arts Center are used for athletics, concerts, movies, plays, and lectures. The Physical Learning Center is one of the finest among the nation's small colleges. A student union, bowling alleys, handball/racquetball courts, playing surfaces, a bookstore, and Ketler Recreation Lounge are also available. There are more than 100 organizations and special interest groups, including local fraternities and sororities. No alcohol or drugs are permitted on campus. The athletics activities include an extensive intramural and recreational program and twenty intercollegiate varsity teams for men and women.

The College's well-established placement services are used constantly by students interested in business and industrial employment and by those seeking educational positions in the teaching field. A complete file of personal data, scholastic records, and recommendations is prepared for each registrant. These files are available to the scores of prospective employers who visit the campus annually to interview the graduating seniors. One of Grove City's strengths is placing students in business, industrial, and teaching positions, as well as in professional institutions such as medical schools.

Location

Grove City, a town of 8,000 people, is 60 miles north of Pittsburgh. Convenient to I-79 and I-80, Grove City is only a day's drive from Chicago, New York City, Toronto, and Washington, D.C. The municipal airport has a 3,500-foot runway, and there is bus service to Pittsburgh.

Majors and Degrees

Grove City College offers undergraduate degrees in liberal arts, sciences, engineering, and music. The Bachelor of Arts is offered with majors in Christian thought, communication, economics, English, English/communication, history, modern language (French, Spanish, and international business), philosophy, political science, psychology, secondary education, and sociology. Preprofessional students in Christian education, law, or theology usually earn the B.A. degree. Interdisciplinary major programs are also available for qualified students.

The Bachelor of Science is granted with majors in accounting, applied physics, applied physics/computer, biochemistry, biology, business, business management, chemistry, computer information systems, early childhood education, elementary education, entrepreneurship, financial management, industrial management, international business, marketing management, mathematics, mathematics/computer, and molecular biology. Preprofessional students often select one of these majors for dentistry, medicine, or other health fields.

The Bachelor of Science in Electrical and Computer Engineering degree is also offered. The Bachelor of Science in Mechanical Engineering major provides for mechanical systems design and/or thermal systems design. The electrical and computer and mechanical engineering programs are accredited by the Accreditation Board for Engineering and Technology, Inc. (ABET).

The Bachelor of Music degree is awarded to those who major in music. Programs may also include concentrations in business, education, performing arts, or religion.

Academic Program

Grove City College's goal is to assist young men and women in developing as complete individuals—academically, spiritually, and physically. The general education requirements provide all students with a high level of cultural literacy and communication skills. They include 38–50 semester hours of courses with emphases in the humanities, social sciences, and natural sciences and in quantitative and logical reasoning, as well as a language requirement for nonengineering and science majors. Degree candidates must also complete the requirements in their field of concentration, physical education, electives, and convocation. To graduate, a student must have completed 128 semester hours (136 in engineering) plus 4 convocation credits. About 78 percent of those entering as freshmen stay and receive a diploma in four years.

A distinctive liberal arts–engineering program includes engineering courses plus courses in the humanities to provide students with a well-grounded preparation for entering the engineering field, as well as the civic and cultural life of society. The economics program exposes students to all economic philosophies, yet strongly advocates economic freedoms and free markets.

Grove City follows the early semester calendar plan. Academic credit may be granted to incoming freshmen on the basis of scores on appropriate Advanced Placement tests, International Baccalaureate tests, or on the College-Level Examination Program tests. Honors courses, independent study, seminars, and the opportunity for juniors to study abroad for credit are also offered.

Academic Facilities

The Hall of Arts and Letters opened in January 2003. This state-of-the-art teaching facility features a 200-seat lecture hall; forty classrooms (including multimedia-equipped rooms and tiered "case study" rooms); eighty faculty offices; the Early Education Center; the Curriculum Library; and language, computer, and video production labs.

The College library houses 158,000 books and 270,000 microfilm/microfiche units. Modern, well-equipped laboratories for biology, chemistry, engineering, and physics are available, as are facilities for language and piano studies.

The Technological Learning Center, which consists of forty microcomputers and three big-screen projection systems, has received national recognition. All freshmen receive their own color notebook-sized computer.

The J. Howard Pew Fine Arts Center has art, photography, and music studios; a rehearsal hall; a little theater; a museum; an art gallery; music practice rooms; and an auditorium and stage large enough to accommodate the most elaborate drama productions and concerts. An addition completed in October 2002 contains additional classrooms, practice rooms, and a 188-seat recital hall.

Costs

As a relatively small, financially sound college, Grove City is able to charge an unusually low tuition in comparison to other independent institutions of similar quality. The 2004–05 annual tuition charge is $9952 for B.A. degree students, for B.S. and B.M. degree students, and for B.S.E.E. and B.S.M.E. degree students. The cost of a color notebook computer for all freshmen is included in the tuition fees. There is no comprehensive fee. Room and board are $5094. Expenses for books, laundry, transportation, and personal needs vary considerably with the lifestyle of the individual.

Financial Aid

Because the College's tuition charges are low, every student, in effect, receives significant financial assistance. Sixty-two percent of the freshmen receive additional aid from GCC. Students applying for financial assistance must complete Grove City College's financial aid form. Job opportunities are available both on and off campus.

Faculty

The focus of the Grove City faculty members is on teaching students, although many members are involved with research and writing. Seventy-seven percent of the faculty members hold doctorates. Most of the administrative staff also teach part-time in various departments. The student-faculty ratio is approximately 18:1. Faculty members emphasize teaching and attention to the students' individual needs; they also participate extensively in the College's extracurricular programs.

Student Government

The Student Government Association provides an opportunity for direct student interaction with the faculty members and administration in matters relating to campus activities. Students serve on regular College committees (library, publications, religious activities, and student activities) and also on the Men's and Women's Governing Board and the Discipline Committee.

Admission Requirements

An applicant for admission should be a high school graduate with the following recommended units: English, 4; foreign language, 3; mathematics, 3; history, 2; and science, 2. Engineering, science, and mathematics majors should have 4 units each in both mathematics and science. Auditions are required for music majors. An interview is highly recommended, especially for those who live within a day's drive.

The College seeks academically qualified students without regard to race, color, sex, religion, or national or ethnic origin. Grove City students generally come from middle-income families. The greatest number come from Pennsylvania, Ohio, New Jersey, and New York, although forty-six states and eleven countries were represented in 2003–04. Ninety percent of the women and 68 percent of the men in the most recent freshman class ranked in the top fifth of their high school class. Their average SAT I combined score was 1268; the average ACT composite score was 27.

Transfer students may receive advanced standing if they have been in good standing at their previous institutions and have maintained a minimum grade point average of 2.0 (on a 4.0 scale).

Application and Information

A regular admission applicant should take the SAT I or ACT by October or November of the senior year in high school. The application should include scores on the SAT I (preferred) or the ACT, a high school transcript, references, a recommendation from the student's principal or counselor, and a nonrefundable application fee of $50. An application may be submitted after the eleventh grade. An early decision applicant should take the entrance test in the eleventh grade, visit the College for an interview, and submit the application by November 15; notification of the admission decision is mailed on December 15. Approved early decision applicants must accept by January 15 and submit a nonrefundable deposit of $205.

Applicants seeking regular decision must submit the completed application and supporting documents by February 1 of their senior year. Notification of the admission decision is mailed on March 15. Students who are offered admission should reply as soon as possible, but no later than May 1, and include a nonrefundable deposit of $155. Applications received after February 1 will be considered as space permits. The College receives four applications for every freshman vacancy.

Additional information may be obtained from:

Jeffrey C. Mincey
Director of Admissions
Grove City College
100 Campus Drive
Grove City, Pennsylvania 16127-2104
Telephone: 724-458-2100
Fax: 724-458-3395
E-mail: admissions@gcc.edu
World Wide Web: http://www.gcc.edu

Crawford Hall.

GUILFORD COLLEGE

GREENSBORO, NORTH CAROLINA

The College

Founded in 1837 as the Quaker New Garden Boarding School, Guilford College, with its Georgian buildings set on 340 wooded acres on the western edge of Greensboro, North Carolina, retains a sense of tranquility and tradition. Guilford is the third-oldest coeducational college in the nation and has a long-standing history of commitment to the individual student and to Quaker values.

Guilford's 2,101 students come from more than forty states and thirty other countries. The College's size ensures the academic community's commitment to personalized education without giving up academic diversity. Students are encouraged to take an active part in extracurricular activities on campus, including seminars and lecture series, interest and service clubs, wide-ranging cultural opportunities as well as a program of intramural and intercollegiate athletics for both men and women. The Student Union, a student organization, sponsors many of the social, recreational, and cultural programs offered at the College. Many students participate in a variety of community service projects and volunteer programs.

There are frequent exhibitions featuring distinguished artists as well as College faculty members and students. Dramatic presentations range from *Romeo and Juliet* to *Waiting for Godot*. A touring choir and opportunities for individual lessons complement the music program. Each summer, Guilford is the home of the famous Eastern Music Festival. Orchestral, dramatic, operatic, and balletic opportunities are also available in the city of Greensboro.

Guilford's intercollegiate athletic teams compete at the NCAA Division III level and in the Old Dominion Athletic Conference (ODAC). The sports include women's basketball, cross-country, lacrosse, soccer, softball, swimming, tennis, and volleyball and men's baseball, basketball, cross-country, football, golf, lacrosse, soccer, and tennis. Sports programs are coupled with special academic opportunities in sports medicine, sport management, and physical education.

Guilford is primarily residential in nature.

Location

Greensboro, North Carolina, is a city of 234,000 people, located midway between Washington, D.C., and Atlanta, Georgia. The greater metropolitan area has a population of approximately 1.3 million. Greensboro is home to five colleges and universities, with a total student enrollment of approximately 27,000. The city is served by two interstate highways, and the Piedmont Triad International Airport is less than 5 miles from campus. Numerous historic sites as well as local, state, and national parks are within day-trip distance of the College. Greensboro's central location in the state allows easy access both to the coast and to several major ski areas in the mountains. The amenities of life in the Southeast—climate, pace, and friendliness—coupled with rich cultural opportunities and sound economic growth make the Sun Belt an attractive area in which to study and to live.

Majors and Degrees

Guilford College offers B.A. or B.S. degrees in accounting, African-American studies, art, athletic training, biology, business management, chemistry, community and justice studies, computer information systems, computing information technology, criminal justice, earth studies, economics, education studies, English, environmental studies, exercise and sports studies, forensic biology, French, geology and earth sciences, German, German studies, health science, history, integrative studies, international studies, life sciences, mathematics, music, peace and conflict studies, philosophy, physics, political science, psychology, religious studies, sociology/anthropology, Spanish, sport management, theater studies, and women's studies. The B.F.A. is offered in art.

Concentrations are available in accounting, African-American studies, African studies, anthropology, applied ethics, astronomy, business, business law, chemistry, communications, community studies, computing and information technology, criminal justice, dance, East Asian studies, economics, education studies, English, environmental studies, field biology, forensic science, French language and society, German language and society, history, human resource management, integrated science, international business management, international political economy, interpersonal communication, Japanese language and society, Latin American studies, mathematics for the sciences, medieval/early modern studies, money and finance, music, nonprofit management, organizational communication, peace and conflict studies, philosophy, philosophy of mathematics, physics, political science, psychology, Quaker studies, religious studies, sociology, Spanish language and society, sport administration, sport marketing, theater studies, visual arts, and women's studies.

A dual-degree program is available in forestry and/or environmental science with Duke University. Preprofessional programs are offered in dentistry, law, medicine, ministry, and veterinary science.

Academic Programs

Each student works closely with a faculty adviser to select courses that meet his or her individual educational and career goals. Thirty-two semester courses are required for graduation, eight of which are generally in the major field of study. Required courses are few but represent a distribution over the principal fields of the arts and sciences. Flexible requirements allow for interdisciplinary and double majors.

Incoming first-year students and transfer students have an opportunity to participate in Avanti, a summer preorientation program that includes computer training, learning skills, academic advising, self-awareness workshops, and outdoor experiences.

Independent study, off-campus internships, and off-campus seminars are open to all students. An expanded honors program includes a variety of honors courses for students with exceptional academic credentials and motivation. One pass/fail elective course may be taken each semester.

Entering students may waive courses through Advancestd Placement (AP) examinations in English, history, laboratory science, mathematics, and foreign languages. Advanced placement requires an AP score of 3 or better or a general CLEP score of 500 or better; credit requires an AP score of 4 or better or a general CLEP score of 550 or better. Subject CLEP scores must be at least 50 for advanced placement and at least 55 for credit.

Guilford College has a two-semester calendar. The first semester ends before winter break, and the second semester ends in early May.

Off-Campus Programs

Semester abroad programs enable students to study in Africa, China, England, France, Germany, Italy, Japan, and Mexico. Students may also participate in programs sponsored by other American colleges and universities. A full year of academic credit for study in Japan is available through a cooperative program with International Christian University in Tokyo.

Guilford participates in two consortia that allow open registration in seven area colleges and universities without additional fees. Other member schools are Bennett College, Elon University, Greensboro College, Guilford Technical Community College, High Point University, North Carolina A&T State University, and the University of North Carolina at Greensboro.

An on-campus programs director assists students who wish to study abroad. An internship director helps to place students who wish to study elsewhere in the United States. Course credit is given for all approved off-campus study. One-week off-campus seminars are sponsored by the College throughout the regular academic year in such locations as New York City, Washington, the Outer Banks, and Florida. These seminars focus on urban problems, education, government, the arts, religion, geology, ecology, and marine life. The Washington Semester in Washington, D.C., supplements the academic program and helps students develop professional skills and career potential through internships with the federal government, lobbying organizations, or public agencies.

Internships may be done in any discipline. Locally, students may pursue internships as part of their academic and career development in business, education, government, health services, law, medicine, scientific research, and social services. In addition, the Career and Community Learning Office sponsors a variety of community service activities, such as the Student Literacy Corps and Project Community.

Academic Facilities

Stately Georgian-style buildings in excellent condition house classrooms, a spacious auditorium, the library, a well-appointed student center, administrative offices, and residence halls. The 65,000-square-foot Frank Family Science Center opened in August 2000 and features fourteen laboratories (with twenty-four workstations each), 1,600 computer connections, a rooftop observatory with a computer-driven telescope, and a 150-seat multipurpose auditorium/planetarium. Multiple studio space is available to students in the fine arts. Guilford's Hege Library is one of the three largest private libraries in North Carolina. The library contains 250,000 volumes and includes an art gallery, a media center, and the only Friends Historical Collection in the Southeast. Hege Library is fully automated and is linked to buildings across the entire campus. Students also have library privileges at six colleges within 20 miles that have an additional 1.3 million volumes. Guilford is planning construction of a fitness and recreation facility that should complement the renovations made to the existing athletic facilities, which contain a swimming pool, racquetball courts, and additional multipurpose courts.

The state-of-the-art Bauman Telecommunications Center houses two computer-equipped classrooms, faculty offices, and three computer labs that contain ninety-one personal computers. In addition, there are 200 public terminals in the Center and other terminals in academic buildings around the campus. Fiber-optic hookups link Bauman Telecommunications Center to most academic buildings on campus, and all students living on campus can access the facility from their residence hall rooms. In addition, satellite connections make it possible to bring in foreign language programming from around the world. In 1995, Guilford acquired twenty state-of-the-art computers from AT&T to establish a multimedia learning center for cultures and languages. More than 500 students have PCs in their residence hall rooms, and the College has full Internet access. All students have e-mail accounts, and, through an interdisciplinary course, students play an active role in developing the College's Web site.

Costs

Basic expenses for the 2003–04 academic year were $19,100 for tuition, $5940 for room and board, and $345 for fees. Personal expenses, book costs, and transportation expenses vary according to individual need.

Financial Aid

Guilford College tries to meet the demonstrated financial need of all students, as determined by the Free Application for Federal Student Aid (FAFSA). More than $13 million in scholarships, loans, grants, and work-study opportunities was awarded to students last year. Academic scholarships are awarded on a competitive basis. Guilford offers six merit-based and special-interest scholarship programs. More than 90 percent of last year's student body received some form of merit-based or need-based assistance. The average need-based award was more than $14,000 a year per recipient.

Faculty

Guildord has 84 full-time faculty members, 90 percent of whom have terminal degrees. The College seeks faculty members who value the sense of community and concern for individuals that are part of Guilford's heritage. The student-faculty ratio is currently 15:1.

Student Government

Guilford entrusts its students with responsibility for governing their own actions and furthering the best interests of the entire College community. The student Community Senate is composed of representatives from residence halls and the day-student organization, a member of the administration, and 2 faculty members. Students serve on all faculty and administrative committees and on the College's Board of Trustees and Alumni Board. Since 1982, the student government has sponsored fund-raising activities to set up and maintain the first student-initiated loan fund in the country.

Admission Requirements

Each applicant is considered on an individual basis. The Admission Committee examines each applicant's academic potential as predicted by performance on the SAT I or ACT and by his or her high school record. The committee selects from among academically qualified students those whose particular backgrounds and talents might enrich the College's educational community. The committee looks for students whose energies and concerns promise constructive leadership and useful service in their own lives and in society. Interviews, although not required, are strongly recommended so that the applicant can become better acquainted with Guilford and so that the admission staff can better evaluate the candidate. Guilford is competitive with respect to admissions.

Application and Information

Admission plans include early action and regular decision. Early action and merit scholarship applicants must apply by January 15 and are notified by February 15. The regular decision priority deadline is February 15, and applicants are notified by April 1. After February 15, applications are considered on a space-available basis. Candidates admitted for regular decision must reply to their offers of admission by May 1.

Early entrance applicants are considered after their junior year of high school. They must have an outstanding academic record and must be sufficiently mature socially to adjust to college life.

Transfer candidates should apply for admission by December 1 for the spring semester and by April 1 for the fall semester.

The priority deadline for applying for financial aid is March 1.

For further information and application forms for admission and financial aid, students should contact:

Admission Office
Guilford College
5800 West Friendly Avenue
Greensboro, North Carolina 27410
Telephone: 336-316-2100
800-992-7759 (toll-free)
E-mail: admission@guilford.edu
World Wide Web: http://www.guilford.edu

GUSTAVUS ADOLPHUS COLLEGE

SAINT PETER, MINNESOTA

The College

Gustavus Adolphus College was founded in 1862 by Swedish Lutheran settlers for the education of teachers and pastors. Gustavus has since become a nationally ranked undergraduate college of the liberal arts and sciences. Affiliated with the Lutheran Church (ELCA), Gustavus is dedicated to helping students attain their full potential, developing in them a capacity and passion for lifelong learning and preparing them for fulfilling lives of leadership and service to society. Although the student body is primarily Midwestern, Gustavus draws its 2,509 students from forty-two states and seventeen other countries; 6 percent are persons of color. A Phi Beta Kappa institution, Gustavus typically sends 35 percent of each graduating class directly to graduate school. Gustavus students have won Fulbright, Goldwater, Marshall, Rhodes, Truman, Watson, and Younger Scholarships and National Science Foundation Predoctoral Fellowships. Students also benefit from the annual Nobel Conference on science and values, which brings world-renowned scholars to the campus for a two-day symposium. Nobel Conference XXXX, "The Science of Aging," will be held October 5–6, 2004.

Campus life is central to the Gustavus experience. More than 85 percent of the students live on campus in eleven residence halls and share their meals at the Market Place. "Gusties" are typically active in campus student groups, choosing from thirty music organizations (including concert bands, choirs, a symphony orchestra, and jazz bands); ten religious groups; local fraternities and sororities (20 percent of students are members); nine service organizations; student media, including a weekly newspaper, radio station, literary magazine, and yearbook; and more than sixty other special interest clubs. The student-run Campus Activities Board brings speakers, bands, and other entertainment to campus throughout the year. Gustavus competes at the NCAA Division III level and is a member of the Minnesota Intercollegiate Athletic Conference. Twenty-five varsity sports are offered for men and women, along with ten club sports and thirty-one intramural sports. All students may use the multimillion-dollar Lund Center, which contains an indoor track and forum, a 25-yard by 25-meter pool with ten lanes, a weight room, racquetball courts, gymnastics facilities, and an indoor ice rink. The nearby Swanson Tennis Center houses six indoor courts for year-round use. Additions to the 340-acre campus include an international education center and residence hall, a nine-lane outdoor track with access to an indoor track facility, an international soccer field, a forty-piece aerobic workout area, and new weight-lifting equipment. A new residence hall is scheduled to open in fall 2005.

Location

The 340-acre Gustavus campus overlooks the town of Saint Peter (population 9,000) and the scenic Minnesota River Valley, 65 miles southwest of the Twin Cities of Minneapolis and St. Paul. Saint Peter is a historic residential community set among river bluffs and rolling farmland, where the College serves as a cultural and recreational resource. Outdoor activities such as biking, running, hiking, skiing, camping, and canoeing are popular in the area. Ten miles south of Saint Peter lies Mankato (population 40,000), a regional business center providing nearby internship sites as well as a variety of shopping and dining choices. The campus "Gus Bus" offers transportation to the Twin Cities and Mankato on different weekends each month, although students may have cars on campus after their first year. Students arriving at the Minneapolis/St. Paul International Airport can reach Saint Peter by taking Land to Air bus transportation.

Majors and Degrees

Gustavus awards the Bachelor of Arts degree in accounting, art, art history, athletic training, biochemistry, biology, chemistry, classics, communication studies, computer science, criminal justice, dance, economics, education (elementary and secondary; coaching certification also offered), English, environmental studies, financial economics, French, general science, geography, geology, German, health fitness, history, international management, Japanese studies, Latin studies, management, mathematics, music, nursing, peace studies, philosophy, physical education and health, physical science, physics, political science, psychology, religion, Russian studies, Scandinavian studies, sociology/anthropology, Spanish, speech, theater, and women's studies.

Preprofessional programs are available in actuarial science, architecture, arts administration, church vocations, dentistry, engineering, law, medicine, ministry, occupational therapy, optometry, peace studies, pharmacy, physical therapy, veterinary medicine, and women's studies. Special degree opportunities include 3-2 engineering degree programs with the University of Minnesota and Minnesota State University, Mankato.

Academic Program

Gustavus operates on a 4-1-4 academic calendar. The first semester runs from September through December, followed by a monthlong January Term and a second semester extending from February through May. Students typically enroll in four courses each semester and one in January Term. To graduate, students must complete 35 credits (1 credit per full course) with a cumulative grade point average of at least 2.0, including three January Term courses, an approved major, and general education requirements. A major takes roughly one third of a student's courses, with another third required for distribution among the general education areas of the arts, religion, humanities, math and science, social science, foreign cultures, and personal fitness. Students may choose from two different tracks to fulfill general education course work. Curriculum I includes a First-Term Seminar and requires that students complete at least three writing-intensive courses; Curriculum II explores the interrelatedness of the disciplines and incorporates writing in every class. (Gustavus has gained national recognition for its Writing Across the Curriculum program.) Remaining classes are taken as electives. There are opportunities for independent study and individualized majors. Gustavus credit is granted to students who earn a 4 or 5 on the College Board Advanced Placement exams or to students scoring 4 or above on the International Baccalaureate higher-level exams. Gustavus offers Army ROTC through Minnesota State University, Mankato.

Off-Campus Programs

More than 50 percent of Gustavus students study abroad before graduating. Students may study abroad for credit for a full year, a semester, or a January Term. International study programs are offered in more than fifty different countries through Gustavus-sponsored programs, Gustavus exchange programs, and approved consortia programs.

Students may apply for a number of seminar/internship programs, including the American University Washington Semester Program; Metro-Urban Studies Term or City Arts Term in Minneapolis/St. Paul through the Higher Education Consortium on Urban Affairs; the Research Volunteer Program at the National Institutes of Health in Bethesda, Maryland; and European work experiences through Boston University International Programs. Internships may be conducted for credit during a semester, over the summer, or during January Term; they occur in the Twin Cities metropolitan area, the Saint Peter/Mankato area, and at other sites nationwide and worldwide. Gustavus has a comprehensive Career Center with three full-time professional staff members to assist students in securing internships and employment.

Academic Facilities

The Folke Bernadotte Memorial Library houses 260,758 volumes, 1,445 current periodical subscriptions, 31,381 microform items, 278,178 government documents, and 13,389 recordings and videotapes. Gustavus also subscribes to the PALS online catalog and LexisNexis, giving students access to additional millions of volumes and periodical holdings.

The Gustavus computing network is made up of 1,000 computers using TCP/IP protocols running over a fiber-optic backbone. Students have direct network access from any of 424 public access computers, the majority of them Macintoshes or IBM/PCs, but also including SGI, NeXT, and Linux machines. Computer labs or clusters are located in the library and in eight academic buildings (open 100 hours per week) and in all residence halls (open 24 hours a day); all residence halls are hardwired for direct network access from individual student rooms and provide full Ethernet connectivity from every student room on campus. The campus network gives students full access to library holdings, the Internet, and printing from laser printers in the computer labs.

Gustavus is recognized for having science facilities that are "the envy of other small schools in its class" *(National Review College Guide)*. Facilities include two electron microscopes, a 300-MHz NMR spectrometer, molecular biology and materials research laboratories, a five-section greenhouse, a herbarium, an automated DNA sequencer, and the 135-acre Linnaeus Arboretum. The 15,000-square-foot F. W. Olin Hall for Physics, Math, and Computer Science also provides student research offices, along with a 16-inch computer-guided Meade LX-200 telescope, an artificial intelligence laboratory, and laboratories in electronics and instrumentation, optics, solid state, and nuclear physics that have recently been enhanced by equipment grants.

Other facilities of note include the award-winning Christ Chapel, which seats 1,500 and is the site of voluntary daily chapel and the annual Christmas in Christ Chapel services, as well as concerts and lectures; the two-building Schaefer Fine Arts Complex, which features an art gallery, art and music studios, a MIDI computer lab, Björling Concert Hall, Anderson Theatre, Kresge Dance Studio, and an outdoor amphitheater; and the Culpepper Language Laboratory, which provides multimedia language study capability and SCOLA television programming in Confer Hall.

Costs

Tuition, room, and fees for 2004–05 are $28,850. This amount includes campus health service, technology, transcript, student government, and orientation costs. Private music lessons are $225 per semester; music majors receive instruction free of charge. Students should allow an estimated $1630 for expenses.

Financial Aid

More than 70 percent of Gustavus students receive financial assistance based on the College's analysis of the Free Application for Federal Student Aid (FAFSA) and Gustavus Supplement. Need-based packages in most cases contain a combination of federal (such as Pell) and/or state (for in-state residents) grants; scholarships and/or grants from Gustavus; subsidized federal loans; and student employment. The priority deadline for submission of the FAFSA is April 15.

Gustavus awards the following scholarships purely on the basis of merit, although they might be part of an overall need-based package: Partners in Scholarship Awards, which offer faculty mentorships for research and graduate school preparation ($9000 per year); Presidential Scholarships, awarded to students who, as National Merit Finalists, select Gustavus as their first-choice college ($15,000 to $16,000 per year); and Trustee Scholarships, which recognize academic achievement in high school ($1000 to $6500 per year). Other merit-based scholarships are given for music, service, and theater/dance.

Faculty

Gustavus has 170 full-time and 63 part-time faculty members; 88 percent have earned the Ph.D. or a terminal degree. Teaching is the first priority of the faculty. All classes are taught by professors, with a student-faculty ratio of 13:1 and an average class size of 17. Professors serve as academic advisers to first-year students as well as to majors.

Student Government

All Gustavus students are represented by the Student Senate, whose members are elected by class and by residence hall. The Senate serves as a student voice in campus policy by fielding student representatives for campus committees such as strategic planning, personnel, and academic policy. Members of the Senate also meet regularly with the Board of Trustees. The Senate annually administers a budget of more than $250,000, which is disbursed to petitioning student organizations.

Admission Requirements

Gustavus seeks academically well-prepared students from a broad range of backgrounds. Successful applicants should have completed a college-preparatory sequence of courses, including 4 years of English and social studies, 3 to 4 years of math and science, and preferably 2 or more years of a foreign language. While the difficulty of and achievement in high school classes are the most important considerations in admission, scores on either the ACT or SAT I, letters of recommendation, the essay, and out-of-class activities are also carefully considered.

Application and Information

Beginning November 15, applications are reviewed on a rolling competitive basis. Typically, more than 80 percent of all applications are received by January 31. Transfer and international students complete separate application forms and may enroll in either semester. Interviews on campus are recommended but not required. For more information about Gustavus, students should contact:

Mark H. Anderson
Dean of Admission
Gustavus Adolphus College
800 West College Avenue
Saint Peter, Minnesota 56082
Telephone: 507-933-7676
800-GUSTAVUS (toll-free)
Fax: 507-933-7474
E-mail: admission@gustavus.edu
World Wide Web: http://www.gustavus.edu

GWYNEDD-MERCY COLLEGE

GWYNEDD VALLEY, PENNSYLVANIA

The College

The dedication of the Sisters of Mercy to higher education led to the founding of Gwynedd-Mercy College in suburban Philadelphia in 1948. Gwynedd-Mercy is a four-year coeducational college with majors in both the liberal arts and professional fields of study.

Although it is intended that Gwynedd-Mercy remain a college of 2,400 students, its size does not inhibit its ability to innovate. Gwynedd-Mercy was the first Catholic college in the United States to establish a sequential associate degree to bachelor's degree program in nursing, and it has recently established the first such progressive program in health information technology.

Gwynedd-Mercy College is recognized in *U.S. News & World Report's Best Colleges* issue as having one of the highest graduation rates in the nation among institutions that have degrees up to and including the master's level. Students at Gwynedd-Mercy establish strong cooperative relationships, encouraging and tutoring one another at all levels. A high degree of interaction and cooperation is also evident between faculty members and students. This may help to explain the high retention rate.

Gwynedd-Mercy offers participation in eighteen NCAA Division III athletic teams—ten for women, eight for men. Two sports have conference Coaches of the Year. Men's basketball garnered its first-ever PAC Championship in 1999. Gwynedd-Mercy's recognized excellence in the health fields provides a basis for its commitment to physical as well as spiritual wellness.

A special effort is made to encourage the participation of all students in activities and student government. Opportunities are available through drama club, campus ministry, a nationally renowned choir, yearbook staff, and social committees. The first Catholic college chapter of Habitat for Humanity, endorsed by former President Jimmy Carter, gives students the chance to help in the actual construction of homes for the less fortunate. Students can write for the college newspaper, the *Gwynmercian,* which has received a first-place rating with special merit from the American Scholastic Press Association. Through the on-campus chapter of Mercy Corps, students can help the poor with fund-raising efforts and adopt-a-family programs at Thanksgiving and Christmas holidays. Some students decide to give a year of service after graduation to Mercy Corps' nationwide outreach program.

A student lounge dedicated as an International Center for Understanding and Culture (ICUC) was opened in 1986. It gives American students the opportunity to meet, socialize with, and get to know young people from other countries. This diversified international student group includes 63 international students representing thirty countries. The ICUC quickly became a popular campus meeting place for students to confide their hopes and dreams.

On the graduate level, Gwynedd-Mercy offers a master's degree program in education (educational administration, reading, school counseling, special education, and a Master Teacher program), nursing (geriatrics, oncology, and pediatrics), and an M.B.A. (in cooperation with LaSalle University).

Location

Gwynedd-Mercy's idyllic 160-acre campus is located in Gwynedd Valley, Pennsylvania, a suburb 20 miles from Center City Philadelphia. Old City, South Street, and sports arenas are a 25- to 30-minute car ride from the campus. The College is situated just minutes from several major highways, including the Pennsylvania Turnpike. The immediate area is rich in the history of Colonial America, and two of the oldest homes in Pennsylvania are located on the Gwynedd campus.

Majors and Degrees

Gwynedd-Mercy offers baccalaureate degrees in accounting, behavioral/social gerontology, biology, business administration, business education, computer information sciences, criminal justice, elementary education, English, history, mathematics, nursing, psychology, sociology, and special education. Seven certification options are available through the School of Education.

Associate in Science degrees are awarded in the allied health fields of cardiovascular technology, health information technology, and respiratory care. Associate degrees are also granted in accounting, business administration, computer programming, liberal studies, natural science, and nursing.

Academic Program

The school year is divided into two semesters, and most baccalaureate degree programs require the completion of a minimum of 125 credit hours. Gwynedd-Mercy maintains a strong liberal arts component in all its degree programs. Whether the student chooses to major in one of the liberal arts or to pursue a professionally oriented degree, courses are required in language, literature and the fine arts, humanities, and behavioral, social, and natural sciences.

Individualized internships and work-experience programs are available and recommended in all majors to give students first-hand experience in their chosen major. Nearby Fortune 500 companies offer a wide variety of experience to students in business and accounting. TAP, the Teacher Assistant Program, places every education major in the classroom one day a week beginning in the freshman year. All allied health and nursing programs require clinical experience. The 2+2 programs—those with an associate degree to bachelor's degree progression—offer allied health and nursing students the opportunity to gain employment in their field while continuing toward the baccalaureate degree. The School of Business and Computer and Information Sciences maintains a successful work-experience semester. Through this paid internship, students earn credit while gaining valuable experience in challenging positions.

The tutoring program begun for science and health majors has expanded so that free tutoring is now available in other academic areas for students who need it. This complements the close student-faculty relationship that is part of the Gwynedd-Mercy milieu.

Off-Campus Programs

The excellent on-campus laboratory facilities are extended by affiliations with more than 200 hospitals and health-care agencies in Pennsylvania, New Jersey, and Delaware, where students may complete their clinical experience. Merck provides a one-semester industrial laboratory experience for qualified biology majors. Gwynedd maintains a close relationship with nearby companies, such as Unisys, McNeil, and Sun Company, for work-experience programs.

Academic Facilities

Gwynedd-Mercy has expanded its physical facilities as its student enrollment has increased. The Sister Isabelle Keiss Center for Health and Science opened in fall 1999 and houses the Schools of Nursing and Allied Health Professions and the Division of Natural Sciences. The 50,000-square-foot state-of-the-art facility offers laboratories for areas such as nursing skills, respiratory care, cardiovascular technology, radiation therapy, health information technology, organic chemistry, and microbiology. The College's Griffin Complex houses the College's Student Union—equipped with a game room, a full gymnasium and track, racquetball court, and weight room. Two newly built residence halls have been added to the existing Loyola Hall. The College now offers three residence facilities that house 40 percent of the school population. The Lincoln Library, which is a large adjunct collection of books on Lincoln and the Civil War, is housed in Assumption Hall. Theaters include the Julia Ball Auditorium, a small in-the-round theater, and a TV production studio. One computer laboratory is reserved for computer majors. A separate facility is maintained for use by the general student body. Both are staffed and open at hours convenient to student use. Hobbit House, a private school for preschoolers, is situated on campus, where students in the School of Education are trained.

Costs

The 2003–04 academic-year tuition (two semesters) for full-time students (12 to 18 credits per semester) was $16,200. Allied health and nursing students paid $17,200. Room and board were, on average, $7500. Professional liability fees for students enrolled in clinical components and lab fees are extra. There is no parking or student activities fee.

Financial Aid

Gwynedd-Mercy's financial aid program is designed to provide financial assistance to academically qualified students whose resources are inadequate to meet the costs of attending the College. The student financial aid committee endeavors to assist as many students as possible, using Gwynedd-Mercy funds as well as federal, state, and other available funds. Aid is awarded on the basis of demonstrated financial need, academic proficiency, and responsible campus citizenship.

A financial aid packet is sent, with instructions, to those who request it on their application form. High school students should request the Free Application for Federal Student Aid (FAFSA) from their guidance office. In 2003–04, 91 percent of Gwynedd-Mercy full-time students received some form of financial aid. The average financial aid package for 2003–04 was more than $13,300. March 15 is the deadline for freshmen entering in the fall semester. The deadline for Academic Scholarships is February 15.

Faculty

The student-faculty ratio is 19:1, allowing for personal contact, advising, and after-class instruction. This is a widely acknowledged strength of the Gwynedd-Mercy experience. For nursing students in the clinical setting, there are never more than 8 students to 1 clinical adviser; in the allied health programs, there often is one-to-one instruction. The quality of teaching is enhanced by the diversified interests of the faculty. The 181 faculty members (90 part-time) teach both day and evening classes, allowing students the greatest flexibility in scheduling. Free tutoring is available in all disciplines.

Student Government

All students are encouraged to take part in the responsibilities of student government. This student participation and shared responsibility for the welfare of the College are promoted through a framework of committees. The student government president and 3 other students are members of the College Council, which is responsible for the continuing self-evaluation of the College and for policy formation. In addition, students share membership in the Educational Planning Committee, Faculty/Student Committee, Financial Aid Committee, and Library Committee.

Admission Requirements

Admission to Gwynedd-Mercy is based on a student's high school record, rank in class, SAT I or ACT scores, counselor's recommendation, and choice of major. Entrance requirements vary with the program. The rolling admission policy allows the student to be informed of the admission decision within two to three weeks after the file is complete.

Gwynedd-Mercy awards College credit for satisfactory completion of Advanced Placement courses. The exam score must be 3 or above.

A minimum 2.0 grade point average (on a 4.0 scale) is generally required to transfer from another college. Gwynedd-Mercy does, however, retain the right to require a higher GPA for admission to some programs.

Gwynedd-Mercy selects all students on the basis of academic achievement and does not discriminate on the basis of race, religion, gender, handicap, or sexual orientation.

Application and Information

All prospective applicants are urged to visit the campus to meet and talk with an admission counselor, a dean, or a program director. To apply for admission, applicants should complete the application form and submit it to the admissions office along with the required nonrefundable $25 application fee. First-time freshmen must also submit an official high school transcript or equivalency certificate; a written recommendation from a principal, teacher, guidance counselor, or employer; and results of the SAT I or ACT (for recent high school graduates). All applicants should verify that they meet the specific requirements and have the necessary high school prerequisites for admission.

Students wishing to transfer to Gwynedd should complete the application form and submit it to the admissions office along with the required nonrefundable $25 application fee, high school and college transcripts, and a letter of recommendation.

For additional information or to schedule campus tours and visits, students are encouraged to contact:

Office of Admissions
Gwynedd-Mercy College
1325 Sumneytown Pike
P.O. Box 901
Gwynedd Valley, Pennsylvania 19437-0901
Telephone: 800-DIAL-GMC (toll-free)
E-mail: admissions@gmc.edu
World Wide Web: http://www.gmc.edu

Students at Gwynedd-Mercy College.

HAMILTON COLLEGE

CLINTON, NEW YORK

The College

One of the oldest and most selective colleges in the country, Hamilton is capitalizing on its increasing popularity in recent years by investing more than $100 million in programs, personnel, and facilities for its 1,750 students.

The cornerstone of the College's investments in a new curriculum is the Hamilton Plan for Liberal Education, which provides highly motivated students with the freedom and responsibility to make educational choices. As one of the very few colleges that does not have distribution requirements, Hamilton has strengthened its advising system so that students work even more closely with their academic advisers to chart an individualized course of study that is tailored to each student's interests and learning styles.

At its core, a Hamilton education helps students learn to think critically and creatively; to write and speak clearly and cogently; to become conversant with a range of scientific, social, cultural, and artistic issues that make it possible for students to lead fuller and richer lives; and to contribute to society in meaningful ways. Hamilton believes that the capacities needed in the world its students are likely to encounter—a world in which there is a premium on solving problems and communicating one's ideas clearly; a world in which there is rapid cultural, technological, and political change; and a world in which they can expect to change careers several times—are best developed through a demanding liberal arts education.

Hamilton's residential environment is carefully designed to supplement the formal academic program. As such, more than 130 extracurricular and intercollegiate clubs and organizations abound. A weekly student newspaper, several literary and humor publications, a campus radio station, musical and drama groups, academic clubs, an active outdoor club, religious and volunteer service organizations, and other special interest groups provide opportunities for students to pursue personal interests and assume leadership positions. Lectures, films, and other cultural activities are an integral feature of the weekly calendar.

Many students at the College also participate in intercollegiate, intramural, and club sports. Fourteen men's and fourteen women's varsity teams compete in NCAA Division III competition, and the College is a charter member of the New England Small College Athletic Conference, a consortium of like-minded colleges that place academic excellence ahead of athletic performance.

Residential life at Hamilton provides opportunities for students to learn from classmates in a positive environment of community living conducive to academic achievement, personal growth, and a respect for the rights of all residents. The College provides some of the most diverse and attractive residential housing of any college its size. Traditional residence halls, suites, campus apartments, converted homes, substance-free housing, and quiet housing are among the many options. All housing is smoke-free.

Location

Hamilton is situated on a 1,250-acre hilltop campus overlooking the Mohawk and Oriskany Valleys of scenic central New York. Hamilton's two adjacent campuses, consisting of the original college campus and the former Kirkland College campus (which merged with Hamilton in 1978) reflect a blend of the traditional and the contemporary. The village of Clinton still retains much of the New England flavor brought to it by eighteenth-century settlers. While the city of Utica is within a 15-minute drive and Syracuse is situated less than an hour to the west, many rural areas also surround Hamilton's safe campus. The Adirondack Mountains, ideal for hiking and skiing, are within an hour's drive.

Majors and Degrees

Hamilton offers the Bachelor of Arts degree with concentrations in Africana studies, American studies, anthropology (archaeology or cultural anthropology), art, art history, Asian studies, biochemistry/molecular biology, biology, chemical physics, chemistry, Chinese, classical languages, classical studies, comparative literature, computer science, creative writing, dance, East Asian studies, economics, English, foreign languages, French, geoarchaeology, geology, German, government, history, mathematics, music, neuroscience, philosophy, physics, psychology, public policy, religious studies, Russian studies, sociology, Spanish, theater, women's studies, and world politics. In addition, Hamilton offers an increasing number of interdisciplinary concentrations, including American studies, East Asian studies, public policy, and women's studies, as well as minors in Africana studies, astronomy, environmental studies, Latin American studies, and medieval and Renaissance studies. In consultation with the faculty, students may design their own concentrations.

Academic Programs

The Hamilton Plan for Liberal Education emphasizes student freedom and responsibility by eliminating distribution requirements. In place of those requirements, Hamilton strengthened its advising system and created more opportunities for students to personalize their education. Unique to this plan are two distinct capstone requirements—one at the completion of the general education sequence (the Sophomore Program) and one at the conclusion of the concentration (the Senior Program)—that serve as integrating and culminating experiences for students at decisive points in their undergraduate careers. The College is well-known for its emphasis on writing and maintains a three-course, writing intensive course requirement. Faculty members of all disciplines require significant written work.

Off-Campus Programs

Each academic year, Hamilton offers many educational opportunities at international and domestic sites away from campus. The Junior Year in France, pioneered by Hamilton more than forty-five years ago, is today one of the most widely respected programs of its kind and enrolls students from many colleges. A parallel program allows students conversant in Spanish to spend a year or semester in Madrid, Spain. Hamilton's newest program, the Associated Colleges in China program (with Williams and Oberlin Colleges), offers intensive summer and/or semester-long study of Chinese in Beijing. Students also participate in programs sponsored by other colleges and universities, providing study-abroad opportunities in more than 100 countries.

Within the United States, the Term in Washington allows qualified students to spend a semester of their junior or senior year in the nation's capital, serving internships in the executive and legislative branches of the federal government. Hamilton's newest U.S. program is in New York City. The theme of the program is set each semester by the expertise of the professor in residence and includes course work, an independent research project, and an internship in a firm or organization. Approximately 40 percent of all Hamilton students study off campus at some point during their academic careers.

Academic Facilities

In summer 2004, Hamilton opened the first phase of a renovated and expanded science center that emphasizes student research and experimentation. Designed largely with the input of faculty members, the center should nearly double the amount of space for science instruction when the building is fully completed in the fall of 2005. Library facilities include the main Daniel Burke Library, the Dana Science Library, a music library, and the Audiovisual Services Division in the Christian A. Johnson Building. Circulation, reference, and interlibrary loan services are available to all in the community. Access to 577,000 volumes can be obtained through an online computer catalog. The Hans H. Schambach Center for the Performing Arts is home for much of the music program, containing ample classroom and rehearsal space, as well as the 700-seat Carol Woodhouse Wellin Hall. The adjacent List Studio provides rehearsal areas for dance and space for studio art. The campus computer network provides faculty and staff members and students with high-speed access to e-mail, College information, library databases, software, and information resources on the Internet. More than 950 institutionally owned computers and 1,200 student computers are connected to the network through 3,000 "information outlets" located in all College buildings, including one outlet per student in residence hall rooms. More than 475 computers are available to students in public and departmental computing facilities.

Costs

Tuition and fees for 2003–04 were $30,200; room and board in College facilities were $3800 and $3560, respectively.

Financial Aid

Hamilton awards financial assistance on the basis of need to more than half of its 1,750 students. In addition, eight to ten awards of half-tuition, offered as part of the Bristol Scholars Program—a $60,000 value over four years, are given to the most outstanding members of the first-year class. These awards are given without consideration of need. Through a comprehensive program of scholarships, loans, and jobs, Hamilton attempts to meet the full financial need of all admitted students. In addition to the PROFILE form of the College Scholarship Service, candidates for assistance must file the Free Application for Federal Student Aid (FAFSA) and a Hamilton financial aid form by February 1. Admission decisions are determined without reference to a student's financial need.

Faculty

The 193 instructional faculty members are committed to excellence in teaching, learning, and creativity. They are not only teachers and mentors, but are friends and academic colleagues who are admired and respected by their students. Often their scholarly achievements outside the classroom contribute to their disciplines. Professors frequently share research with students and encourage them to participate as well. For example, students have recently accompanied faculty members on scientific expeditions to the Antarctic and to present papers at professional meetings throughout the United States and abroad. Because the student-faculty ratio is 10:1 and because all courses are taught by faculty members, both students and professors do their best to meet each other's expectations. Faculty members are easily accessible to students needing help, for academic advising, or to those simply wishing to discuss their work or whatever else may be on their minds. Most students leave the campus having made at least one lasting friend among the faculty, and when compared to graduates of other colleges, more Hamilton alumni stay in contact with their faculty mentors ten years or more after leaving the campus.

Student Government

The Student Assembly, which administers a budget of nearly $500,000 for students programs, represents the functions of student government at Hamilton, and students often join with faculty members, administrators, and trustees on other College-wide committees to set policy.

Admission Requirements

Hamilton seeks to enroll intelligent, well-prepared, and strongly motivated students from as great a variety of backgrounds as possible. The admission staff and the College are dedicated to finding candidates who will contribute a wide diversity of talents, interests, and experiences to campus life. Applicants are expected to have taken advantage of the strongest academic curriculum available at their high schools. A strong record of personal accomplishment—taking into consideration the opportunities available—is also an important gauge of the candidate's ability to contribute to the life of Hamilton. Although a strong academic preparation is the most important consideration for admission, other special talents and interests may be considered. In 2001, Hamilton made the SAT I exam optional for admission. Students may now choose the stadardized testing option that presents their credentials most favorably. Candidates should keep in mind that while test scores are a part of Hamilton's evaluation, a student's overall academic record in high school is far more important.

Application and Information

Application materials may be requested directly from the College, or students may apply using the Common Application Form. The deadline for regular admission is January 1, and decisions are mailed by early April. There is a $50 application fee that is waived for students who apply online. Candidates who have chosen Hamilton as their first-choice college may apply for early decision by one of two possible deadlines, November 15 and January 10. Decisions are mailed by December 15 and February 15, respectively. Early decision acceptance is binding. A $400 deposit is required to ensure the accepted student's place in the class.

Dean of Admission
Hamilton College
198 College Hill Road
Clinton, New York 13323
Telephone: 315-859-4421
800-843-2655 (toll-free)
Fax: 315-859-4457
World Wide Web: http://www.hamilton.edu

The Bienecke Student Village provides a variety of opportunities for student interaction.

HAMPDEN-SYDNEY COLLEGE

HAMPDEN-SYDNEY, VIRGINIA

The College

Hampden-Sydney, a four-year liberal arts college for men, has been in continuous operation since November 1775, eight months before Jefferson wrote the Declaration of Independence. The tenth-oldest college in the country, Hampden-Sydney was formed with the guidance of such men as James Madison and Patrick Henry, who were members of the first Board of Trustees. The College was modeled after the Presbyterian College of New Jersey (now Princeton), and the same curriculum was chosen, except that at Hampden-Sydney there was to be a "greater emphasis upon the cultivation of the English language." Throughout its history, Hampden-Sydney College's mission has been "to form good men and good citizens."

Today, the College has a total enrollment of 1,000 students, representing forty-one states and several other countries. Students enjoy a complete and diverse campus life, with an active student government and honor court. Interest clubs, literary organizations, and performing societies, as well as intellectual and social gatherings, enhance the extracurricular offerings. Hampden-Sydney's Union Philanthropic Society is the oldest active debate club in the country. Approximately 30 percent of the students belong to the twelve social fraternities. Eight varsity teams enjoy spirited NCAA Division III competition as members of the Old Dominion Athletic Conference, while club and intramural teams draw strong participation.

As a wholly undergraduate institution, Hampden-Sydney is committed to the belief that liberal education provides the best foundation not only for a professional career but also for the challenges of life. Nearly half of the graduating seniors enter graduate or professional school within five years. Basic to the College's program and success are the faculty members, 76 percent of whom hold earned doctorates in their fields. The student-faculty ratio is 12:1, and the average class size is 15 to 20. It is in this setting that the true value of the Hampden-Sydney education shines through. Students work closely with professors, learning to think critically and analytically, to assimilate and interpret information, and to express themselves cogently and coherently. Beyond the classroom, faculty-student relationships flourish as well. Faculty members and students jointly contribute to the community in a wide variety of service activities and share social and enrichment opportunities.

Hampden-Sydney faculty members are nationally recognized as inspired teachers and productive scholars in such diverse fields as NASA-sponsored gamma ray research, environmental economics, and cetacean (whale and dolphin) evolution.

Hampden-Sydney is fully accredited by the Southern Association of Colleges and Schools and is a member of the Association of Virginia Colleges, the Association of American Colleges, the Southern University Conference, the College Entrance Examination Board, the American Chemical Society, and the College Scholarship Service.

Location

Hampden-Sydney is an hour from Richmond, Charlottesville, and Lynchburg. Its stately Federal-style buildings have earned designation as a National Historic Preservation Zone. Southern Virginia's rolling countryside and temperate climate are delightful year-round and especially in the spring and fall. The College's rural setting and tree-studded campus provide miles of jogging and bicycling trails and excellent fishing. Hampden-Sydney has a picture-perfect 660-acre campus, with a wonderful feel of community.

Majors and Degrees

Students may choose one of twenty-six established majors, plus custom programs, which lead to the degree of Bachelor of Arts or Bachelor of Science: applied mathematics, biology, chemistry, classical studies, economics, economics and mathematics, English, fine arts, French, German, Greek, Greek and Latin, history, humanities, interscience, Latin, management economics, mathematics, mathematics and computer science, philosophy, physics, political science, psychology, religion, religion and philosophy, and Spanish.

Academic Program

The curriculum is divided into three principal areas of study: humanities, social sciences, and natural sciences (including mathematics). The study of the humanities allows students to gain an understanding of the intellectual and literary influences that have shaped culture. Exposure to the humanities also increases students' appreciation of the importance of ideas and expands their ability to communicate. Studying the social sciences gives insight into human behavior and institutions and is central to the liberal arts education. The world's increasing reliance on scientific and technological advances—and the practical and ethical problems that accompany them—makes a general understanding of natural science indispensable.

To ensure that individual programs are broadly based, students are required to study in each division. Students take at least two semesters of English composition and rhetoric and study a foreign language through the second-year level. The College requires that students complete 120 semester hours for graduation.

In addition to the curriculum offerings, students may profit from one of Hampden-Sydney's special academic options, such as the Honors Program, study-abroad program, or business internship programs. Students may take courses at six other private colleges in Virginia, pursue a public service concentration, study foreign policy in Washington, or engage in international studies at Oxford University. Faculty advisers help develop programs suited to individual interests.

Academic Facilities

Hampden-Sydney is committed to providing state-of-the-art facilities. The J. B. Fuqua Computing Center contains a variety of computer systems for student use. Students can access the campus network and the Internet with their own computers from their dormitory rooms or by using one of the computing laboratories located in Bagby Hall, Eggleston Library, Gilmer Hall, Morton Hall, and the Computing Center.

Eggleston Library is one of the College's most valuable academic resources; its collection was specifically selected to support Hampden-Sydney's liberal arts curriculum. Eggleston Library contains 220,172 volumes, 58,000 periodical titles, microform, and government documents arranged in open stacks or computerized for ease of use. Also located in Eggleston, the Fuqua International Communications Center houses the newest electronic equipment to support learning. It maintains a collection of more than 10,640 videodiscs, videotapes, compact discs, sound recordings, and computer software programs. Study carrels and viewing-listening rooms hold a variety of hardware for individual and group use. Two antennae for reception of satellite television broadcasts from around the Western Hemisphere add an international dimension to the center.

Costs

Tuition for the 2003–04 academic year was $20,446. Other required College fees were a telecommunications fee of $496 and a student activities fee of $245. Room ($2968) and board ($4052) came to $7020. Books and miscellaneous expenses were estimated at $1600.

Financial Aid

Hampden-Sydney College offers financial aid to students who can make the most of the education that the College offers. Both academic achievement and promise, as well as financial need, are considered in the initial award of College funds. Similarly, financial aid for returning students is based upon both academic performance and demonstrated need. Approximately 88 percent of students receive financial aid based upon academic scholarship and need. The average need-based award of $15,872 consists of approximately 72 percent grant/scholarship funds. Financial aid in 2002–03 totaled nearly $14.9 million, including all federal aid awarded.

Entering students who wish to be considered for financial aid must complete two forms—the Free Application for Federal Student Aid (FAFSA), which determines eligibility for federal programs, and the CSS PROFILE, which is used for consideration for College funds. These forms may be obtained from high school guidance offices or Hampden-Sydney and must be submitted between November 1 (for early decision) and March 1 of the senior year.

Faculty

Hampden-Sydney has 113 faculty members (84 full-time and 29 part-time). While the College places primary emphasis on teaching skills, faculty research is encouraged as an aid to improving the quality of teaching. Seventy-six percent of faculty members have terminal degrees, and 90 percent are involved in academic advising. With more than 40 percent maintaining campus housing, faculty members are involved with students in a full range of academic, social, and recreational activities.

Student Government

Hampden-Sydney has a long tradition of student involvement in College affairs. Students serve as members of the faculty's Academic Affairs, Student Affairs, Lectures and Programs, and Athletic Committees. In addition, students are often named to various task forces, ad hoc committees, and search committees seeking key College officials. The Student Court, elected by classes, is the judicial arm of Student Government. The court tries cases arising from breaches of the Code of Student Conduct and Honor Code, assisted by a corps of student investigators and advisers. The College Activities Committee keeps an active calendar of events, planning dances, concerts, movies, and other activities for students.

Admission Requirements

Prospective students are expected to have mastered a solid, demanding college-preparatory program, including at least 4 units of English, 2 units of one foreign language, 3 units of mathematics, 2 units of natural science (one of which must be a laboratory course), and 1 unit of social science. In addition, a third unit of foreign language and a fourth unit of mathematics are recommended. Hampden-Sydney also considers SAT I or ACT scores and looks closely at recommendations from guidance counselors, teachers, and other people who know the applicant well. The records of successful applicants often include examples of impressive school and community extracurricular contributions in addition to their academic preparation.

There are three admission plans. If Hampden-Sydney is the student's first-choice college, he should apply under the early decision plan by November 15. The deadline for the early action plan is January 15. The deadline for the regular decision program is March 1. Application forms are available on request from the Admissions Office. Hampden-Sydney also accepts the Common Application in lieu of its own form and gives equal consideration to both.

Students may apply electronically at the Hampden-Sydney World Wide Web site or on the CollegeLink and Apply! computerized application forms. Though not a requirement, the College encourages campus visits as the one true way to witness the spirit and community of Hampden-Sydney.

The College also welcomes armed service veterans and students who wish to transfer from another college or university. Students must be in good standing, with a C average or above.

Hampden-Sydney College, while exempted from Subpart C of the Title IX regulation with respect to its admissions and recruitment activities, does not discriminate on the basis of race, color, sex, religion, age, national origin, handicap, or veteran status in its educational programs and with respect to employment.

Application and Information

Completed applications for admission should be submitted to the Dean of Admissions before the noted deadlines for each admission plan. Notification for early decision candidates is mailed on December 15. Notification for early action candidates is mailed on January 15. Regular decision notification begins on March 1 and continues through April 15. The candidate's reply date is May 1.

All requests for information or application forms are welcomed and should be addressed to:

Dean of Admissions
Hampden-Sydney College
Hampden-Sydney, Virginia 23943
Telephone: 800-755-0733 (toll-free)
Fax: 434-223-6346
World Wide Web: http://www.hsc.edu

Hampden-Sydney's campus has 660 wooded acres. Near several big cities, the campus is quiet, safe, and busy, with lots of room in which to work and play.

HAMPSHIRE COLLEGE

AMHERST, MASSACHUSETTS

The College

Hampshire College was founded in 1965 through the cooperative efforts of educators at Amherst, Mount Holyoke, and Smith colleges and the University of Massachusetts. These colleges comprise Five Colleges, Inc., one of the nation's oldest and most successful educational consortia. The mandate of Hampshire College was to provide a model of innovative liberal arts education. Individualized programs of study, close collaboration between faculty members and students, multidisciplinary learning, and an emphasis on independent research and creative work have been the foundation of Hampshire's program since its opening in 1970. Today, more than 9,500 Hampshire alumni provide convincing evidence of the soundness of the founders' vision. Nearly a fifth of Hampshire's graduates have started their own businesses, while others are pursuing successful careers in medicine, law, education, publishing, finance, public service, and the arts.

Hampshire's 1,200 men and women students come from across the United States and from Europe, Africa, Asia, and Latin America. Despite their varied backgrounds and career aspirations, they share a spirit of open-mindedness and intellectual curiosity and a strong desire to take part in Hampshire's distinctive approach to education.

Hampshire's campus consists of 800 acres of orchards, forest, and open land. Five residential areas provide both dormitory and apartment-style accommodations, most with single rooms. The Robert Crown Center, Hampshire's main athletic facility, houses a swimming pool, a playing floor, a bouldering cave, a rock-climbing wall, and weight-training equipment. The Multisports Center includes four indoor tennis courts, a jogging track, a weight-training room, and a playing area for soccer, volleyball, and aerobics classes. The Outdoors/Recreational Athletics Program offers courses in a variety of athletic activities, provides support to students who wish to play informal team sports such as soccer, basketball, and softball, and sponsors frequent backpacking, rock-climbing, bicycle, and canoe trips. Students also organize and participate in about eighty-five varied social and cultural organizations on campus.

Location

Hampshire College is located in the Pioneer Valley of western Massachusetts, an area known for its pastoral beauty and its extraordinary educational and cultural offerings. The nearby towns of Amherst and Northampton offer shops, restaurants, and entertainment, and the Five Colleges sponsor concerts, film series, lectures, theater and dance performances, and gallery exhibitions throughout the year. The surrounding New England countryside provides year-round opportunities for outdoor recreation. Hampshire is located 2 hours from Boston and 3 hours from New York City by car or public transportation.

Majors and Degrees

Hampshire College confers the Bachelor of Arts degree on students who successfully complete an individualized program of study that is designed and carried out in close collaboration with faculty members. Areas of study are organized within five multidisciplinary schools. The School of Cognitive Science includes aspects of biology (animal behavior and cognition, animal communication, evolution of behavior and cognition, and functional neuroscience and neural network theory); communications (sociology of information technology and new media study and practice); computer science; philosophy of mind, language, and science; linguistics; and several areas of psychology (cognitive psychology, cognitive development, cognitive neuroscience, experimental psychology, physiological psychology, and psychology of language). The School of Humanities, Arts, and Cultural Studies includes architecture and environmental design, art history, classics, comparative religion, critical theory, dance, digital imagery, film, history, journalism, literature, media and cultural studies, music, painting, philosophy, photography, and video. The Interdisciplinary Arts School encourages students and faculty members to work within and across the boundaries of such art forms as sculpture, painting, theater, and writing and to explore the relationship between artistic production and social action. The School of Natural Science offers study in agriculture, alternative technology, biomedical science, botany, chemistry, environmental science, geology, human and molecular biology, mathematics, physical anthropology, physics, physiology, science education, science and public policy, and women's health. The School of Social Science includes African-American studies, anthropology, Asian-American studies, economics, history, Latino studies, legal studies, political science, psychology, sociology, and urban geography.

Academic Program

Hampshire's distinctive academic structure offers every student the benefits of small classes, close contact with faculty members, individualized programs of study, and multidisciplinary learning. Students complete three divisions of study, rather than the traditional freshman–senior sequence. In Division I, Basic Studies, students explore their interests by taking courses and pursuing research or creative projects across Hampshire's schools. In Division II, the Concentration, they gain mastery of their chosen field through continued course work and independent study, internships, or study in other countries. Students are also expected to consider their Division II work from multiple cultural perspectives and to perform community service. In Division III, Advanced Studies, students complete a major academic or creative project—a written thesis, artistic exhibition or performance, or scientific experiment. Division III students are also required to participate in an interdisciplinary seminar with other advanced students or assist a faculty member in teaching a course.

Students at Hampshire receive extensive written evaluation of their work instead of traditional letter or number grades. Passage from one division to the next is marked by a final meeting in which a faculty committee reviews the student's activities and accomplishments. A transcript portfolio consisting of evaluations of course work and independent projects, as well as grades for Five College courses, provides a detailed record of the student's Hampshire education. The portfolio may also include letters of recommendation from faculty members and samples of the student's written work.

Off-Campus Programs

Hampshire students take courses and use the academic facilities at the other four schools of Five Colleges, Inc., at no extra cost; they regularly participate in theater and dance productions at the other colleges as well. A free bus system provides easy transportation among the five campuses.

The Five Colleges offer cooperative programs in African studies, astronomy, black studies, coastal and marine sciences, dance, East Asian languages, international relations, Latin American studies, Middle Eastern studies, Native American

Indian studies, peace and world security studies, and women's studies. Students have access to more than 8 million volumes in Five College libraries, and each year more than 5,000 courses are offered on the five campuses.

Academic Facilities

Hampshire's modern academic buildings provide superior facilities and equipment for a full range of intellectual and artistic activity. The Harold F. Johnson Library Center houses book and media collections, a computer laboratory, a fully equipped television production studio, and an art gallery. The Cole Science Center includes three floors of open laboratories with the most advanced chemistry instrumentation currently available in any undergraduate liberal arts college in the U.S. An attached 1,800-square-foot greenhouse supports research in aquaculture and energy use. The Longsworth Arts Village houses sophisticated film and photography facilities, art studios, and music and dance studios. In Emily Dickinson Hall, the Performing Arts Center includes two theaters. Franklin Patterson Hall contains classrooms, lecture halls, and faculty offices. Adele Simmons Hall houses a psychology research laboratory, a state-of-the-art video and film screening auditorium, computing facilities, and a digital design center. The Lemelson Fabrication Shop supports projects in innovation and applied problem solving. The Hampshire College Farm Center, a nationally recognized agricultural research and teaching facility, is located on 220 acres adjacent to the main campus.

Costs

In 2003–04, tuition was $28,832, room was $4904, board was $2785, and fees were $576.

Financial Aid

Hampshire has developed a generous financial aid program, which awards more than $10 million in grant aid annually. To be considered for an award, applicants must demonstrate financial need and submit all required materials by the stated deadline. Financial aid for international students is competitive, with maximum awards covering only up to tuition.

Approximately half of Hampshire's students receive financial aid with award packages that average about two thirds of Hampshire's total cost. Financial aid packages consist of income from on-campus employment (work-study), student loans, and grant assistance. In recent years, grant assistance has accounted for two thirds of the average aid package, and self-help funds (loans and employment) have made up the remaining third.

Hampshire also offers a merit scholarship program, consisting of several named scholarships designed to honor academic achievement, leadership, and a commitment to social concerns and the arts among students from all ethnic and socioeconomic backgrounds. Scholarships range from $1750 to $7500 per year over a one- to four-year period.

Hampshire was the first college in the country to offer matching grants to students who have earned National Service Education Awards. Hampshire matches National Service Awards, spread over a four-year period. Students can receive up to $4720 spread over a four-year period.

Students wishing to apply for financial aid at Hampshire College must do so at the same time they apply for admission. Any student applying for financial aid must complete the Hampshire financial aid application, a PROFILE application, a Noncustodial Parent Statement (if applicable), and the Free Application for Federal Student Aid (FAFSA). Applicants register to receive a customized PROFILE application from the College Scholarship Service (CSS) and return the completed PROFILE application to them. The FAFSA and PROFILE registration forms are available from high school guidance offices. All financial aid information is considered strictly confidential by the College.

Faculty

Hampshire's faculty has 103 full-time members, 86 percent of whom hold Ph.D. or other terminal degrees, and 8 part-time members. They are accomplished scholars and artists whose primary commitment is to teaching and academic advising. The student-faculty ratio at Hampshire is 12:1.

Student Government

Students at Hampshire serve with faculty, administrators, and staff on all of the College's governing bodies. Seven students serve on the College Senate, which approves the curriculum, academic calendar, degree requirements, and academic standards. Seventeen students are elected to Community Council, which oversees the quality of student life and manages a large student activities budget. The Judicial Council, which interprets the Hampshire Constitution and considers cases involving infractions of College regulations, includes 3 student members. Hampshire is one of the few colleges where students play a central role in the promotion and reappointment of faculty members. As members of Hampshire's schools, they also help determine curricular development and academic policy. One student is elected every two years to serve on the Board of Trustees, and students sit on seven committees of the board.

Admission Requirements

Hampshire College seeks students who are willing to assume substantial responsibility for shaping their own education. Applicants are asked to submit a personal statement, a critical essay or an academic paper, and a detailed description of their interests and activities, in addition to academic transcripts and recommendations. Transfer students must also provide a general outline of the program of study they intend to pursue at Hampshire. Interviews are strongly recommended; students who live far from Massachusetts may arrange an interview with a local Hampshire representative by calling the admissions office. Hampshire does not require SAT I or other standardized test scores for admission. Applicants are expected to demonstrate strong academic achievement and the potential to undertake Hampshire's individualized educational program.

Application and Information

Applications for September admission are due February 1 for first-year students and March 1 for transfer students. Notification is mailed on April 1; accepted students must respond to Hampshire's offer of admission by May 1. International students, whether first-year or transfer, must apply by January 15.

Hampshire offers Early Decision and Early Action plans for first-year students only. The Early Decision application deadline is November 15, with notification on December 15. Early Action applications are due by December 15, with notification after January 21. While Early Decision candidates promise to attend Hampshire if admitted, Early Action candidates have until May 1 to notify Hampshire of their intention to enroll.

Spring term admission is available to first-year and transfer students. Students should apply by November 15, with notification to follow on December 15.

Under its Early Entrance plan, Hampshire admits a limited number of high school juniors who show exceptional academic and personal maturity. An interview is required.

For complete information and application materials, students should contact:

Director of Admissions
Hampshire College
Amherst, Massachusetts 01002-5001
Telephone: 413-559-5471
E-mail: admissions@hampshire.edu
World Wide Web: http://www.hampshire.edu

HAMPTON UNIVERSITY

HAMPTON, VIRGINIA

The University

Hampton University is a privately endowed, nonsectarian, coeducational institution. Its almost 6,100 students come from nearly every state and thirty-five other territories and nations. The campus is one of the most picturesque in the South. Its 285 acres of waterfront property accommodate 120 buildings that include academic buildings, staff residences, historic landmarks, and state-of-the-art facilities. Founded in 1868, the University looks back on more than a century of outstanding contributions in higher education; it now has the buildings, the equipment, the faculty, and the administrative leadership to meet the challenges of its second century.

Challenge as a form of motivation is always present in a student's life at Hampton. Students' minds are stimulated and seasoned by contact with scholars, and learning to use the most modern tools available anywhere sharpens their skills.

The College of Continuing Education is a major academic unit of Hampton University. Its purpose is to provide instruction of high quality to the nontraditional student at the undergraduate and graduate levels, locally and at distant learning centers.

The programs of the Graduate College are designed to prepare students for professional competence in a specific field and for prospective graduate study. Graduate programs leading to the Master of Arts (M.A.) degree are offered in biology, communicative sciences and disorders, counseling, teaching, and special education. The Graduate College also offers the Master of Science (M.S.) degree in applied mathematics, biology, chemistry, computer science, nursing, and physics; the Master of Business Administration (five-year M.B.A. program) degree; the Ph.D. degree in physics and nursing; the Doctor of Physical Therapy (D.P.T.) degree; and the Doctor of Pharmacy degree (six-year Pharm.D. program).

Location

Hampton University is located in the Hampton Roads area of southern Virginia. The area's rich social heritage includes places and reminders of events that contributed to making our nation great. There are numerous opportunities for community involvement, and students are able to work on a voluntary or assigned credit basis on many of the problems in the surrounding community. Both faculty members and students participate in community planning and in ongoing community programs. The well-known annual Hampton Jazz Festival, which originated at and through the efforts of Hampton University, is now a community-wide event sponsored jointly by the city and the University. This marvelous musical experience, attended by thousands of patrons from around the world, annually revives and renews the best in the African-American cultural heritage.

Majors and Degrees

Bachelor of Arts (B.A.) and/or Bachelor of Science (B.S.) degrees are offered in the following majors: accounting, architecture, art, aviation (air traffic control, aviation computer science, electronic systems, flight education, and management), banking, biology, business management, chemistry, communicative sciences and disorders, computer science, electrical and chemical engineering, English, entrepreneurship, finance, history, marketing, marine and environmental science, mass media arts, mathematics, music, music engineering technology, nursing, physical education, physics, political science, psychology, recreation, sociology, sports management, and theater arts.

A Bachelor of Architecture degree is granted to those completing the five-year program in architecture.

The School of Pharmacy offers an innovative entry-level professional program leading to the Doctor of Pharmacy (Pharm.D.). The program requires six years for completion. The first two years consist of preprofessional pharmacy education, followed by four years of professional pharmacy education. For additional information, students should contact the School of Pharmacy (757-727-5071).

The School of Science offers an entry-level Doctorate of Physical Therapy (D.P.T.) program that may be completed in three years. The University has updated its plans for the D.P.T. program to meet the changes mandated by the American Physical Therapy Association requiring that the physical therapy degree be offered at the postbaccalaureate level by the year 2002. Therefore, all freshmen who are interested in pursuing a graduate degree in physical therapy must obtain a baccalaureate degree in another major while completing prerequisites for application to the doctorate program. Students who obtain undergraduate degrees at Hampton University are given preference for admission to the physical therapy program. For more detailed information on the D.P.T. program, students should call 757-727-5260.

Academic Programs

Requirements for receiving an undergraduate degree from Hampton University include completion of the following: a minimum of 120 semester hours with a cumulative grade point average of 2.0 or higher and a grade of no less than C in all courses in the major; courses in the general education sequence totaling 46–48 semester hours; and courses in the major field, related subjects, and free electives totaling at least 74 semester hours. The total number of semester hours required for the various majors differs from department to department. In each major program, students have a number of free electives. Students must be in residence the final 30 semester hours prior to the completion of degree requirements. English 101-102 and Speech 103 must be passed with a grade of at least C. Remedial or developmental work does not count toward graduation.

Students who plan to graduate with dual majors must satisfy all requirements in each major, including all related courses, with separate courses. The General Education sequence must be completed once. Entrance and graduation requirements for dual majors have been approved and are published in the University catalog.

Students who wish to declare a minor must complete one half of the credit hours for the major. Meeting the requirements for the minor should be independent of meeting the major requirements for graduation. Courses for the minor may not be taken on a pass/fail basis. The offering department determines the course requirements for the minor.

The University operates under a 4–4 academic calendar.

Off-Campus Programs

A cooperative work-study program is designed to tie together a student's education and his or her future employment.

Academic Facilities

Special research laboratories are available for faculty members and for advanced students in the natural sciences. The Peabody

Collection in the main library is one of America's outstanding sources of information on African-American culture and history. The Hampton University computer center is available for research purposes to faculty members and advanced students.

In projecting Hampton into the twenty-first century, the Academic Technology Mall (ATM) has been established. The ATM is located on the fifth floor of the Harvey Library, housing sixty-one computers for use by students, the public, faculty members, and staff members. Funded by a grant from the Kellogg Foundation, the ATM is designed to acquire and integrate a wide variety of technology resources. The five components of the ATM are the resource management system, telecommunications, multimedia productions lab, foreign language laboratory, and electronic classroom.

Costs

The annual costs in the 2002–03 academic year were $17,112 for on-campus students and $11,110 for off-campus students. Upon notification of acceptance, students must pay a $600 advance deposit fee.

Financial Aid

Students who are unable to meet the total cost of their college education may receive aid in the form of scholarships, grants-in-aid, loans, or part-time employment. Currently, 78 percent of the student body receives financial assistance (need- and non-need based). Of this number, approximately 13 percent have campus jobs. The most frequently awarded federal aid types include Federal Pell Grant, Federal Supplemental Educational Opportunity Grant (FSEOG) program, Federal Work-Study (FWS) program, Federal Perkins Loan program, and Direct/Stafford/PLUS program. Other types of aid include Virginia Tuition Assistance Grant (TAG) program and College Scholarship Assistance program (CSAP), both limited to residents of Virginia. The University participates in the Army and Navy/Marines ROTC scholarship programs and the Veterans educational benefits program. Scholarships awarded through the University include the Presidential Scholars and the Academic Achievers Scholarships, Leadership Institute Scholarships and other endowed scholarships, general undergraduate grants, the Native American scholarship program, athletic scholarships, and talent scholarships. All scholarships are awarded to students based on eligibility. The Financial Aid Office provides more information and details (800-624-3341).

Faculty

The members of the distinguished Hampton faculty come from the United States and from a number of countries around the world. The favorable faculty-student ratio permits a great deal of individualized instruction. The designers of Hampton's curriculums believe that living is learning and learning is living and that the learning process, as the Hampton faculty views it, must happen in the lives of the students.

Student Government

The Student Government, which is self-perpetuated by democratic student elections, is the recognized governing agency for the student body. The Student Government cooperates with the administration and faculty in the formulation of policies affecting the general welfare of the college, shares in the implementation of these policies, and works with all student organizations in stimulating student initiative and responsibility in campus affairs. Each year a student is democratically elected to serve as a representative to the Hampton University Board of Trustees.

Admission Requirements

A total of 17 Carnegie units of secondary school work are required for consideration as an applicant for admission (a unit represents a year's work in a subject-matter area). While the Committee on Admissions is more interested in the quality of the applicant's academic preparation and in his or her general promise as a college student than in the total number of such units offered, the core units must include 4 in English, 3 in mathematics (algebra 1, algebra 2, and geometry), 2 in science (biology and chemistry), 2 in social science, and 6 academic electives.

Hampton University requires that the student have a cumulative grade point average of at least 2.0 in the core requirements. A combined SAT I score of 920 is required. Those students taking the ACT must have minimum scores of 20 on the English section and 20 on the math.

Transfer applicants must submit official transcripts of all previous college work and their secondary school report along with SAT I or ACT scores. In addition, transfer students must have a minimum of 15 hours of college credit along with a 2.3 cumulative grade point average. All credits earned must satisfy Hampton University's entrance requirements and must be equivalent to the general average at the institutions previously attended.

Application and Information

Applications, furnished by the director of admissions upon request, should be filled in completely and returned with the required nonrefundable application fee of $25 (money order made payable to Hampton University).

Applications for the fall term must be submitted by March 15; notification of the admission decision is made on a rolling basis. Applications for admission to the second semester should be completed by December 1. The applicant is expected to reply within thirty-five days after receiving a statement of acceptance. Students who have satisfactorily completed courses at an accredited institution may be admitted with such advanced standing as their previous records warrant.

An application form, additional information, and literature may be obtained by contacting:

Ms. Angela Boyd
Director of Admissions
Hampton University
Hampton, Virginia 23668
Telephone: 757-727-5070
800-624-3328 (toll-free)
E-mail: admissions@hamptonu.edu
World Wide Web: http://www.hamptonu.edu

The University chapel.

HANOVER COLLEGE

HANOVER, INDIANA

The College

Hanover College is a private, independent, undergraduate liberal arts college related to the Presbyterian Church (U.S.A.). A Hanover education offers more than academic knowledge. It encourages students to explore ideas and make their own decisions. A Hanover education is preparation for the future. It stimulates the development of personal responsibility and sound judgment.

Hanover succeeds by emphasizing timeless standards: a strong, traditional liberal arts education; a rigorous curriculum within the academic community; and an open forum for spirited, independent discussion of ideas. For more than 175 years, Hanover College has remained an institution with a firm sense of its identity, its purpose, and its mission.

Those looking for a close, friendly relationship between faculty members and students will find just that at Hanover. The campus is truly an academic community, with 95 percent of the students and 50 percent of the faculty members and their families residing on the College grounds. In this setting of open dialogue and respect, students find many informal opportunities to discuss class work, career goals, and subjects of mutual interest. Interaction is not restricted to the hours spent in classes. The average size of classes is less than 16. Students find plenty of opportunities at Hanover for open group discussion and the informal sharing of ideas.

Hanover is committed to the liberal arts in the finest sense and for good reason. The College understands that there is more to higher education than facts, tests, and grades. Today's careers demand that students not only possess a broad range of human knowledge but that they also know how to apply that knowledge logically and independently.

Hanover provides an educational kaleidoscope for creating future opportunities. Students learn highly sought, adaptable skills required in the field of their choosing. A liberal arts education prepares them to think critically and communicate effectively.

Location

Hanover College is located on 650 acres overlooking the Ohio River. The campus consists of beautifully landscaped grounds, with thirty-eight major buildings designed in Georgian architecture. The town of Hanover is located in southeastern Indiana, a scenic area of natural beauty. Neighboring, historic Madison is minutes away; Louisville, 45 miles; Cincinnati, 70 miles; and Indianapolis, 95 miles from campus. Chicago, St. Louis, and Nashville are an easy day's drive from campus.

Majors and Degrees

The Bachelor of Arts degree is awarded in the following major fields of study: art, biology, business administration, chemistry, classical studies, communication, computer science, economics, education, English, French, geology, German, history, international studies, Latin American studies, mathematics, Medieval-Renaissance studies, music, philosophy, physical education, physics, political science, psychology, sociology-anthropology, Spanish, theater, and theological studies. Teacher certification is available in both elementary and secondary education.

Academic Program

Hanover's academic program includes a 4-4-1 yearly calendar of four courses during each of the fall and winter terms (fourteen weeks each). One course on or off campus during the spring term (four weeks) gives students the opportunity for intensive study of a subject.

Hanover students earn the Bachelor of Arts degree. The Hanover faculty placed the College in the forefront of national curricular reform by adopting a system of general degree requirements for students. The professors have ensured that the liberal arts core of an education at Hanover is both substantial and flexible, strong in fundamentals and full of opportunity for experimentation and innovation.

The faculty has also created a structure for multidisciplinary courses that allows students to complete two requirements with a single course. For example, a course in architecture jointly taught by an artist and a physicist might count toward the completion of the fine arts and natural science requirements. A course in Latin American social movements and literature jointly taught by faculty members in political science and Spanish might fulfill requirements both in literature and in cultures other than the West.

Major and minor programs provide students both breadth and depth of understanding within a given field. Majors culminate in either an internship, an independent study, or other form of directed or specialized study. All major programs prepare students for graduate studies. Preprofessional advising is available in dentistry, education, law, medicine, and other fields.

Off-Campus Programs

One aspect of Hanover's personal approach to education is the many specialized study opportunities that exist for students. Students are encouraged to apply to the College for funds granted from the Richter Trusts. These funds support study projects students have designed and planned. Projects are often undertaken during semester breaks or over the summer. These funds have allowed students to pursue specialized educational interests such as making stained-glass windows, building robots, studying koalas in Australia, and examining education in Soviet schools.

During the four-week spring term, many departments offer distinctive study programs. Students have studied Spanish in Spain and Latin America; Asian cultures in India and China; Dante in Florence, Italy; art, economics, and business in New York City; politics in Washington, D.C.; sociology at the East-West Center in Hawaii; theater in Canada and England; and international economics in Canada.

Exciting off-campus offerings include the junior-year-abroad program, the government-oriented Washington Semester Plan in cooperation with American University, and the Philadelphia Center Internship Program relating city and human interaction.

Hanover participates in a spring term consortium with seven other colleges and universities. Approved courses are taught on college campuses throughout the Midwest and East, as well as in Belgium, England, France, Italy, Greece, Germany, Spain, Mexico, and Canada.

Academic Facilities

The Haq Center, located in the heart of campus, serves the entire community as a support facility for students from other countries and for members of American minority groups. With its fully equipped kitchen, spacious lounge, and meeting and dining areas, the Center is ideal for dinners, lectures, studying, or getting together with friends. The student-operated center is open evenings and weekends.

The Writing Center and the mathematics centers offer students tutorial assistance in writing and mathematics at every stage of their undergraduate careers.

Hanover has three academic computing centers in addition to various departmental facilities. There are twenty-one pieces of equipment in each lab that are kept fully operational by the academic computing staff. Electronic mail accounts and "ports for every pillow" for on-campus housing provides access to the on-campus network and the Internet. Labs are open evenings and weekends and are staffed by student lab assistants. The Academic Computing Centers offer training and support services for both students and faculty members.

Costs

Hanover's costs reflect its commitment to providing a high-quality education at a reasonable cost. Direct student expenses for a year at Hanover, including tuition, general fees, room, and board, were $25,000 for 2003–04. The most current cost information is always available from the Office of Admission.

Financial Aid

More than 80 percent of Hanover students receive some form of direct financial assistance. College aid is available in the form of scholarships, grants, loans, and campus employment. Every effort is made to meet all demonstrated need of every student. The College offers three types of competitive scholarships based on merit, regardless of financial need. All Hanover scholarships are awarded on the basis of financial need and/or academic merit.

Faculty

Hanover professors are accessible, dedicated, and knowledgeable. Eighty percent hold a doctorate or other terminal degree. A third of the faculty members have been at the College for more than fourteen years.

The faculty members at Hanover want to teach. Though substantial scholars by any standards, they are not subjected to the "publish or perish" existence found on many campuses. To the contrary, Hanover's small-college experience offers one-on-one academic advising as an integral part of the student-faculty member relationship.

Student Government

Student Senate is the campuswide organization of student government. Through representative and advisory means, it provides input into the decision-making processes of the College. Student Senate promotes mutual cooperation among various campus constituencies in pursuit of its goals.

The Interfraternity Council and the Panhellenic Council are the governing bodies of the Greek social organizations at Hanover College. Composed of representatives of each fraternity and sorority, the councils promote a cooperative spirit and encourage mutual support among the organizations. They collectively serve the campus and wider community through activities and philanthropic projects.

Admission Requirements

To be considered for admission at Hanover, a prospective student must have the appropriate academic preparation and complete the required credentials by the dates listed below. The Admission Committee of Hanover College reserves the right to waive and/or alter requirements.

Students must graduate from an accredited secondary school and successfully complete a college-preparatory curriculum. The committee will consider applications from home-schooled students or others who have completed virtually all graduation requirements; an on-campus interview is always a requirement in such cases. The recommended curriculum for high school includes the following: English—4 units, with an emphasis on college-level writing; math—a minimum of algebra I and II and geometry (a fourth year of math is strongly recommended); science—2 units of laboratory science (a third unit is strongly recommended); foreign language—2 units of the same foreign language in consecutive years (a third unit is strongly recommended); social studies—2 units (3 units are recommended); and electives—a well-rounded selection, ideally including some units in the fine arts, religion, and philosophy.

Hanover accepts the SAT I or the ACT for admission purposes. Hanover will take the highest set of test scores; therefore, it may be advantageous to students to sit for these exams more than once. Standardized test scores are accepted directly from the test corporations or as a part of official transcripts mailed directly from the high school. SAT II: Subject Tests are not required but are considered if submitted.

Hanover offers two admission options, each with specific deadlines by which all required materials must be postmarked. Early Action (nonbinding) admission candidates who have submitted completed application materials postmarked by December 1 are notified of their admission status by December 20, although some candidates may be deferred for later consideration. The application for admission serves as the application for merit-based scholarships, including the prestigious Scholarships for Merit Competition. Those who qualify to apply for the merit competition must submit all admission materials postmarked by January 15.

Regular admission candidates who submit completed application materials after December 1 are notified of their admission status on a rolling basis, beginning February 1 until the freshman class is full. Applications received after the March 1 application deadline are considered on a space-available basis only.

Application and Information

For more information, students should contact:

Office of Admission
Hanover College
P.O. Box 108
Hanover, Indiana 47243-0108
Telephone: 800-213-2178 (toll-free)
812-866-7047 (TDD)
Fax: 812-866-2164
E-mail: admission@hanover.edu
World Wide Web: http://www.hanover.edu

Brown Memorial Chapel is a landmark on the Hanover campus and is one of thirty-five buildings designed in classic Georgian-style architecture that contribute to Hanover's reputation as one of the most beautiful campuses in the country.

HARDING UNIVERSITY

SEARCY, ARKANSAS

The University

Harding University is known for its outstanding liberal arts program and for its training of leaders. Students attend from every state in the Union and about forty countries. Affiliated with the Church of Christ, Harding is a selective-admission university with a total enrollment of 5,000.

Harding University was established as a senior college in 1924 when two junior colleges, Arkansas Christian College and Harper College, merged to form Harding College. Originally founded in Morrilton, Arkansas, the school moved to its present Searcy campus in 1934. Harding officially became Harding University in 1979 in order to better serve its constituency.

Harding has six divisions: the College of Arts and Humanities, the College of Bible and Religion, the College of Sciences, the College of Business, the College of Education, and the College of Nursing. Students can select from more than seventy undergraduate majors. The Master of Business Administration, Master of Education, Master of Science in Education, and Master of Science in Nursing are awarded. In addition, there are a number of graduate degree programs offered at Harding Graduate School of Religion located in Memphis, Tennessee. Many of the more than 30,000 alumni have pursued careers throughout the world.

Harding University is a member of the NCAA Division II. Men compete in baseball, basketball, cross-country, football, golf, soccer, tennis, and track. Women's teams compete in basketball, cross-country, soccer, track, and volleyball. The University also has an excellent intramural program that involves a large number of students.

Most students live in campus housing. The University has thirteen residence halls and several apartment complexes for student use. An application for housing should be filed when the student applies for admission.

Location

Harding is located in Searcy, Arkansas, a town of nearly 20,000. The small-town setting allows students to enjoy the beauty of the Ozark Mountains while being only 50 miles northeast of Metropolitan Little Rock, the state capital, and within 100 miles of Memphis. Camping, canoeing, backpacking, cycling, and a host of outdoor activities are available to Harding students. The Buffalo River, Greer's Ferry Lake, and Blanchard Springs Caverns are all located within a short driving distance of the campus. Proximity to Little Rock and Memphis allows students to enjoy the cultural and social activities associated with these cities.

Majors and Degrees

Harding University awards the Bachelor of Arts, Bachelor of Business Administration, Bachelor of Fine Arts, Bachelor of Music Education, Bachelor of Science, Bachelor of Science in Medical Technology, Bachelor of Science in Nursing, and Bachelor of Social Work. Majors are offered in the following fields: accounting, advertising, advertising art, American studies, art, art therapy, athletic training, Bible and religion, biblical languages, biochemistry, biology, business education, ceramics, chemistry, child development, communication, communication disorders, communications management, computer engineering, computer information systems, computer science, criminal justice, dietetics, economics, education (early childhood, middle level, secondary, and special), electronic media, English, exercise science, family and consumer science, fashion merchandising, food merchandising, French, general science, health-care management, history, human resources, information technology, interior design, international business, international studies, journalism, kinesiology, management, marketing, mass communication, mathematics, mathematics education, missions, music (voice and string instrument), music education (instrumental and voice/choral), nursing, oral communication, painting, physical education, physics, political science, professional sales, psychology, public administration, public relations, radio and television, religious education, social science, social work, Spanish, sports management, theater, theater management, and youth and family ministry.

Academic Program

Harding's academic year is composed of two semesters, an optional thirteen-day intersession following the spring semester, and two optional five-week summer sessions. The University grants college credit for Advanced Placement courses successfully completed with an examination score of 3 or higher. A maximum of 32 semester hours can be earned on the basis of the scores reported in the College-Level Examination Program. An honors program admits students by invitation. Harding has an Early Entrance Program for students who have not finished high school and who meet stated criteria.

Each student is assigned an academic adviser to help plan an individualized program of study. In order to graduate, 128 credit hours are required, including a core of general education courses.

Off-Campus Programs

Harding offers four outstanding study-abroad programs. Harding University–Florence gives students a chance to spend a semester in Europe. The University owns a sixteenth-century villa near Florence, Italy, that serves as the students' headquarters. Harding University–Greece is located in the seaside resort town of Glyfada just 45 minutes from Athens. This program focuses on the culture of Greece, Turkey, and Israel. Harding University–England is located in the Hyde Park area of London. Harding University–Australia is the most recent addition to the study-abroad program. It is located in Brisbane. All four programs set aside ample time for travel, which allows students the opportunity to acquire a world vision in the course of their academic studies.

Academic Facilities

Brackett Library is at the center of the academic training available to Harding students. With more than 500,000 volumes and 1,400 periodicals, the recently renovated library gives students immediate access to vast research sources. The campus has forty-seven buildings strategically placed on a beautiful 200-acre campus. These include the J. E. and L. E. Mabee Business Center, which houses the College of Business faculty and provides classrooms equipped with color video monitors; the John Mabee American Heritage Center, designed as a continuing education complex with an auditorium, a hotel that can accommodate 150 visitors, and facilities for seminars, workshops, and conventions; and the George S. Benson

Auditorium, which seats 3,539 and provides additional classroom space. There are three computer laboratories with extensive equipment available for student use.

Costs

Tuition and fees for the 2003–04 school year were $10,266 per year, based on a course load of 30 semester hours. Room and board cost $4770 per academic year. The total for the school year is $15,036.

Financial Aid

Approximately 80 percent of the students at Harding University receive some form of financial aid. Harding tries to meet all its students' demonstrated need. The College accepts the Free Application for Federal Student Aid (FAFSA).

Academic scholarships are given to students who show outstanding promise. Various departments award departmental scholarships to students who show a particular aptitude for a given subject.

Students may qualify for loans, grants, and work-study programs by submitting the FAFSA to the Harding University Financial Services Office. Upon filing this form, a student is considered for all the federal financial aid programs. It is recommended that a student apply for financial aid as soon as possible after January 1 and before May 1.

Faculty

The student-faculty ratio is 18:1. No graduate students teach any undergraduate courses. On staff there are more than 200 full-time faculty members, with approximately 75 percent holding earned doctorates or terminal degrees.

Student Government

The student government at Harding University is called the Student Association. Officers are elected each year to represent the student body. Class representatives are also selected to serve the interests of their respective classes. Various committees help to involve students in all aspects of student life and community service.

Admission Requirements

The Office of Admissions Services reviews several criteria in the selection of applicants. All students must submit the application with a fee of $25, a housing form with a housing confirmation fee of $125, official transcripts, official ACT or SAT I scores, and an educational reference and a character reference. All academic and personal qualifications are considered in granting admission.

Application and Information

Students should apply soon after the completion of the junior year of high school. Although the deadline for applications is May 1, all admission materials should be submitted early because of the limited number of places in the freshman class. To arrange a campus tour or to receive additional information, students should contact:

Office of Admissions Services
Harding University
Station A, Box 12255
Searcy, Arkansas 72149
Telephone: 501-279-4407
800-477-4407 (toll-free)
Fax: 501-279-4129
E-mail: admissions@harding.edu

The administration building on the campus of Harding University.

HARRINGTON COLLEGE OF DESIGN

CHICAGO, ILLINOIS

The College

Harrington College is dedicated exclusively to professional education in interior design and digital photography. It is a private, coeducational, urban college that enrolls more than 1,300 students. Since its founding in 1931, the College has consistently advanced its position to become internationally recognized for the quality of the education it offers and the success of its graduates.

The College is recognized by the Illinois Board of Higher Education as a private college authorized to award the Bachelor of Fine Arts degree in interior design and the Associate of Applied Science degree in interior design and in digital photography. The College is accredited by the National Association of Schools of Art and Design (NASAD). The bachelor's degree program is accredited by the Foundation for Interior Design Education Research (FIDER), the nationally recognized accrediting agency for interior design. The College is also authorized under federal law to enroll international (alien nonimmigrant) students.

The College attracts and maintains a diversified student body, which consists of high school graduates and transfer students who are preparing to begin a career, working adults who want to move ahead in the field or make a career change, and returning adults whose education was interrupted or postponed earlier in life. The student body reflects a rich variety of backgrounds and generates a spirit that is lively, collaborative, and informal. Although competition to excel is keen, individual talents, unique strengths, and creativity are respected. Opportunities for personal and professional growth, development, and advancement are plentiful. Students need bring only the initiative and determination to succeed.

The American Society of Interior Designers (ASID) sponsors a student chapter at the College, which offers students opportunities to meet practicing professionals and gain a firsthand understanding of professional standards and practices. Harrington College students are frequent award winners in national competitions sponsored by ASID, the Institute of Store Planners, and other professional organizations.

The College maintains a career development service that has an outstanding record in assisting graduating students and alumni to find rewarding positions in the profession.

Location

Harrington College's location in the heart of Chicago, a world center of design, is of inestimable value. Students have access to important designers' resources at the Chicago Merchandise Mart to supplement their studies. Its showroom galleries, exhibiting the best of contemporary furnishings, textiles, and accessories of every description, are a magnet for designers from around the world. Chicago, long known for its architecture, allows students to have daily contact with its finest examples, from landmark architecture to the most dynamic of twentieth-century design. The downtown Loop is a living museum of public art. Works of art by Picasso, Calder, Matisse, Bertioia, Chagall, and Miró further enrich the student's design experience. Libraries, galleries, museums, theaters, the Chicago Symphony Orchestra, and the Lyric Opera are within easy walking distance, and the proximity of the campus to Grant Park, Buckingham Fountain, and Lake Michigan enhances its atmosphere of beauty and tradition.

Majors and Degrees

Harrington College of Design offers full-time programs, with day, evening, and Saturday classes leading to either the Bachelor of Fine Arts in interior design or Associate of Applied Science in interior design or digital photography or a certificate in kitchen and bath design for advanced students.

Academic Programs

The exclusive mission of Harrington College is professional education in interior design and digital photography, serving students who seek career preparation. The goal of the College's curriculum is to produce practicing interior designers and commercial photographers who are proficient in their fields. Because successful practice is grounded in sound theory, instruction at Harrington College strives for balance between content and method, knowledge and skills, creativity and discipline, problem solving and decision making. Each course in the curriculum articulates with other courses in an intensive, structured, comprehensive, and integrated program of studies.

Classwork combines conventional methods of presentation, such as lecture, discussion, and audiovisuals, with studio courses in which an instructor guides students through a problem-solving process of experimentation and exploration of alternative solutions to a wide variety of design and photography-lighting problems. Field trips and guest lecturers augment classwork to take maximum advantage of Chicago's renowned architecture, commercial photography, and interior design resources. A variety of computer courses prepare students to generate graphic displays of design projects through hands-on computer training. Technology is an important part of the curriculum.

As the profession of interior design and commercial photography evolves, so does Harrington College's curriculum. It continues to undergo regular reevaluation to ensure the continuation of its reputation for high quality education.

The Bachelor of Fine Arts degree in interior design is awarded upon completion of 129.5 semester hours of credit, 36 of which are earned in liberal arts and general education courses. The Associate of Applied Science degree in interior design is awarded upon completion of 67.5 credit hours, including 21 in liberal arts and general education courses. The Associate of Applied Science degree in digital photography is awarded upon completion of 65 credit hours, including 21 in liberal arts and general sciences. Liberal arts and science courses are offered on campus to augment the interior design and photography curriculum.

Off-Campus Programs

Students are encouraged to participate in study-abroad programs in Paris and London and monthlong trips to Greece, Paris, and Italy.

Academic Facilities

In fall 2003, the College moved locations to 200 West Madison (Loop), tripling their space. Award-winning architects and designers from Torchia designed the new space as a working laboratory for teaching.

The Design Library's continually expanding collections consist of more than 22,000 volumes and 23,000 slides, which support every aspect of the curriculum. The library subscribes to ninety international and domestic professional journals, magazines, and indexes in interior design, architecture, photography, and art. Two full-time professional librarians and staff members serve students, faculty members, and alumni on an extended schedule. The library also houses the Products Library of current catalogs and product information. The new Design Atelier serves as a place for students to work and houses color and fabric samples, tile and laminate, and other interior samples from more than 3,000 manufacturers. Use of this collection of resources is integral to interior design studio course projects. The library holds memberships in ILLINET/ OCLC and the Chicago Library System, which enable staff to search and borrow nationwide, via computer, from the holdings of almost 5,000 libraries containing 14 million volumes.

Costs

Tuition for the 2004 academic year is $525 per semester credit hour, with additional fees. Students should budget an estimated $400 for textbooks and materials per academic year and an estimated $600 for the initial purchase of equipment and textbooks. A monthly tuition payment plan is available.

Financial Aid

In 2004, more than 75 percent of the student body received loans and/or grants to help them meet the costs of education. Harrington College administers these funds through the Federal Pell Grant, Federal Supplemental Educational Opportunity Grant, Federal Stafford Student Loan, and Federal PLUS loan programs as well as the privately funded Signature Student Loan program. International students are not eligible for federal financial aid or for part-time employment. Students should contact the Financial Aid Office for application materials.

Faculty

The Harrington College faculty is composed of more than 130 experienced educators, each of whom is also a professional interior designer, architect, artist, photographer, or computer technician. Because of the College's Chicago location, prominent practitioners who might otherwise be unavailable are able to serve on the faculty while continuing professional practice. The resulting mix of professional and academic involvement is one of Harrington's most valuable assets. Each faculty member is knowledgeable about his or her own specialization as well as its relationship to the total profession. Together, the faculty demonstrates an exceptional ability to motivate students to acquire and refine the knowledge and skills they will need to function as competent professionals.

Student Government

The Harrington College Student Council consists of elected representatives who serve to facilitate communication with the administration and to sponsor professional and social events.

Admission Requirements

The College maintains a selective admission policy and encourages students with creative aptitude to apply. No previous training in art, photography, or design is required because the program assumes progression from beginner to advanced and professional proficiency. A high school diploma or its equivalent is a prerequisite for admission. As part of the admission procedure, each applicant participates in a personal interview. Early application is advised.

Credits of transfer students are accepted as the courses apply to the Harrington College curricula. A grade of C or better from an accredited college is required for consideration as transfer credit.

International students are advised to complete admission procedures far enough in advance of the expected date of enrollment to fulfill all requirements. They must demonstrate proficiency in English by presenting an acceptable score on the Test of English as a Foreign Language (TOEFL). They must also provide certified English translations of official transcripts of credit.

Application and Information

To apply, each prospective student must submit a completed application for admission, attestation of high school graduation or equivalent, and a nonrefundable application fee. Students may apply online at the Web site listed below. To receive information and an application for admission, students should contact:

Director of Admissions
200 West Madison
Harrington College of Design
Chicago, Illinois 60606
Telephone: 877-939-4975 (toll-free)
Fax: 312-697-8005
E-mail: hiid@interiordesign.edu
World Wide Web: http://www.interiordesign.edu

Small classes provide students with individual faculty attention.

HARTWICK COLLEGE

ONEONTA, NEW YORK

The College

Hartwick College, a private college located in the northern foothills of the Catskill Mountain region of New York State, was founded in 1797 as the first Lutheran seminary in America. Hartwick became a four-year coeducational liberal arts and sciences college under its present charter in 1928. The current enrollment is 1,400 students (43 percent men and 57 percent women).

Approximately 64 percent of Hartwick's students come from New York State, and about 36 percent come from elsewhere in the Northeast or from outside the Northeast. The student body represents thirty-four states and thirty-seven countries. The majority of students live on campus and eat together in the College Commons. Residence halls are coeducational by floor or wing. Adjoining the campus are four special interest houses. As an alternative to downtown living, the College has twenty self-contained town-houses on campus that house 80 students. Each two-story unit has one double and two single bedrooms, two baths, a living room, a study area, and a kitchen. About 100 students live in the five fraternity and four sorority houses. Other off-campus housing includes facilities at the Pine Lake Environmental Campus.

There are approximately sixty student clubs and organizations on campus. A variety of social and cultural events, including special weekends, are offered throughout the academic year.

More than three quarters of the students participate in recreational, intramural, or intercollegiate sports. Hartwick is well known for its NCAA Division I men's soccer program, and its NCAA Division I women's water polo team is the premier team in the East in just its third year of competition. Women's track and field and field hockey and men's and women's basketball, lacrosse, and swimming are also successful programs among the College's twenty-four intercollegiate sports.

Career Services begins working with first-year students in developing career goals. One innovative program offered by the center is the Guaranteed Placement Program. If, after completing a checklist of activities and cocurricular experiences while maintaining a 3.0 grade point average, a student does not have a job within six months of graduation from Hartwick, the College's Board of Trustees guarantees the student a paid internship in his or her chosen field. The center also coordinates MetroLink, an award-winning program that connects students with Hartwick alumni and parents for shadow experiences and career networking. MetroLink is conducted in New York City, Boston, and Washington, D.C.

Hartwick continues to provide every student with a powerful notebook computer, printer, and software that is ready to link to Hartwick's award-winning campus network. Technology is integrated into the daily life of the College—in the classroom, library, and residence halls.

Location

The city of Oneonta, with a population of 14,000, is a college town. Hartwick College and the State University of New York College at Oneonta are located in the city. Students have access to the libraries on both campuses, and cross-registration for courses is also possible. Hartwick College is an integral part of the Oneonta community, and many area residents share in campus activities. Oneonta has a variety of shops, restaurants, and theaters. Many cultural and recreational resources exist in the city and throughout the area, including the Catskill Symphony Orchestra, the Catskill Choral Society, the Orpheus Theatre, several ski centers, city and state parks, golf courses, tennis courts, and lakes. Oneonta is also home to the National Soccer Hall of Fame and is near Cooperstown, the site of the National Baseball Hall of Fame.

Majors and Degrees

Hartwick students may select courses from thirty areas offered by nineteen departments. They may pursue independent study or create an individual student program, or they may take advantage of numerous special study options on and off campus available through Hartwick and cooperating educational institutions. Hartwick awards the B.S. degree in accounting, biochemistry, chemistry, computer science, information science, medical technology, music education, and nursing. It awards the B.A. degree in anthropology, art, art history, biology, chemistry, economics, English, French, geology, German, history, management, mathematics, music, philosophy, philosophy/religious studies, physics, political science, psychology, religious studies, sociology, Spanish, and theater arts. An accelerated B.A./B.S. option is available.

Twenty-two teacher certification programs are offered in adolescence, childhood, and middle childhood education in English languages, mathematics, science, social studies, and K–12 music. Preprofessional programs in engineering are offered in cooperation with Clarkson University and with Columbia University School of Engineering and Applied Science. Hartwick also participates in a cooperative 4+1 M.B.A./M.S. program with Clarkson University and a 3-3 cooperative law program with Albany Law School. Nursing students, upon graduation, are qualified to take the New York State Board Examination for licensure as registered professional nurses. Students graduating with a medical technology major are qualified to take the National Registry Examination for the professional certification MT (ASCP).

Academic Program

Hartwick's distinctive educational approach connects the best aspects of the liberal arts to experiential learning and individualized advising. Hartwick emphasizes the links between learning in the classroom and learning through real-world experiences. A Hartwick education is not about memorizing facts: it's about creating knowledge and developing skills. A Hartwick education happens in small classes taught by professors whose goal is to help students succeed both in the classroom and in course-related experiences outside the classroom. Hartwick's learning-by-doing approach has proven highly effective in producing engaged citizens and successful professionals who can apply their knowledge to practical problems. Independent study, directed study, internships, and off-campus programs are integral parts of the curriculum.

The College has a 4-1-4 calendar, consisting of two 15-week terms and one 4-week term in January. Hartwick's January Experiential Term allows students to participate in an internship, travel abroad, or take one intensive course during the month.

Hartwick offers both advanced placement and credit for scores of 3 or better on the Advanced Placement tests (4 or 5 in the departments of French and music). Advanced placement for credit is also offered through the College-Level Examination Program (CLEP) to students who have acquired mastery of a subject in ways other than the traditional classroom experience.

Off-Campus Programs

Hartwick is ranked fourth among liberal arts colleges in the nation for the percentage of students who engage in study-abroad programs. Hartwick offers numerous opportunities for off-campus study. Some of the program in which students participated in January 2004 included Golden Prague; Transcultural Nursing in Jamaica; Spain: A Cultural and Ethnic Mosaic; German Term in Vienna; Theatre in England; Irish Culture and Society; Anatomy of a Desert—Big Bend National Park, Texas; Madagascar: Culture, Conservation, and Natural History; Experience Writing in Australia; and Natural History of Costa Rica.

Academic Facilities

Hartwick's Science Center recently received a $12-million renovation and addition that provide shared spaces for cross-disciplinary teaching and student/faculty research. The facility includes new classrooms and laboratories, a tissue-culture lab, a greenhouse, an herbarium, cold room, biotechnology "clean lab," science communications center and graphics imaging lab, nursing lab and resource room, and a dark room. Clark Hall is home to English, the Writing Center, foreign languages, psychology, education, and the Technology Services Center. Yager Hall houses the College's 300,000-volume library; the Sondhi Limthongkul Center for Independence, which coordinates Hartwick's global programs; the Yager Museum; the College's archives; classrooms; a computing lab; and laboratory and office space. The Yager Collection contains more than 6,000 American Indian artifacts, covering a period of 10,000 years. It is one of the largest and most important collections of its kind in New York State. Arnold and Bresee Halls contain classrooms, faculty and administrative offices, and a black box theater. The Anderson Center for the Arts is a contemporary building that houses the fine and performing arts. The center includes studios and classrooms, soundproof practice rooms, a theater, and the Foreman Gallery. The Binder Physical Education Center provides facilities for recreation; physical education classes; intramural, club, and intercollegiate sports; a fitness center; a strength-training facility; and the Moyer Pool. The Pine Lake Environmental Campus, a 918-acre site 8 miles from the main campus, offers student housing and serves as an important resource for environmental study and recreation. The Ernest B. Wright 16-inch Telescope and Observatory is located at the top of Hartwick's multitiered campus.

Costs

Tuition and fees and for 2003–04 were $27,400, room was $3750, and board was $3500. The estimated cost of books, personal expenses, and transportation is $1200.

Financial Aid

Hartwick College grants financial aid on the basis of both academic merit and financial need. A large number of scholarships based on merit are awarded annually to prospective students, including transfers, and are based upon outstanding academic achievement and leadership in high school and/or college. The average amount of a financial aid award to first-year students is nearly $20,000. Approximately 78 percent of Hartwick students receive some form of aid.

Students requesting financial aid must file a Hartwick College financial aid application with the College, accompanied by a copy of their parents' federal income tax return and W-2 statement. They must also submit the Free Application for Federal Student Aid (FAFSA). The deadline is February 1. All forms should be mailed by early January. Some work opportunities are also available for students not receiving financial aid.

Faculty

Hartwick has 151 faculty members, of whom 104 are full-time. The Hartwick faculty is a teaching faculty, with principal responsibilities and commitments to students in the classroom. Faculty members serve as student advisers, share committee assignments with students and staff members, and act as advisers to student organizations. The student-faculty ratio is 11:1. Ninety percent of the faculty members hold the Ph.D. or other terminal degrees.

Student Government

The Student Senate serves as the central voice of the student body and carries out executive and legislative functions of the Hartwick College student government. Students share responsibilities with faculty, administrators, and trustees on a number of committees established by the faculty and Board of Trustees, as well as on the Judicial Board and the College Traffic Court.

Admission Requirements

Hartwick College seeks secondary school graduates who demonstrate academic competence and show evidence of being able to benefit from, and take full advantage of, the living and learning experience at Hartwick. Applicants are evaluated not only on class rank and test scores but also on personal qualities, activities, special talents, and recommendations. Applicants are required to submit a secondary school transcript, an essay, and two recommendations. Transfer students must submit official transcripts of work at other institutions, a secondary school transcript, and a letter of recommendation from an official of the college previously attended. On-campus interviews and scores on the SAT I or ACT are strongly recommended for all applicants but are not required.

Application and Information

Applications for regular admission must be filed by February 15 in the year of expected college entrance in the fall. Requests for an early decision may be made up to January 15 of the year of entrance (January 1 for early action candidates). Admission decisions for early decision are made within two weeks after the complete application is on file. Early action candidates are notified on or about January 25; regular decision candidates are notified on or about March 15. A nonrefundable fee of $35 must accompany the application. The College accepts the Common Application and online applications (on the College's Web site).

Prospective students may obtain application forms and additional information by contacting:

Office of Admissions
Hartwick College
Oneonta, New York 13820
Telephone: 607-431-4150
888-HARTWICK (toll-free)
E-mail: admissions@hartwick.edu
World Wide Web: http://www.hartwick.edu

HARVARD UNIVERSITY
Harvard College
CAMBRIDGE, MASSACHUSETTS

The University

Harvard University includes Harvard College and the following graduate and professional schools: the Graduate School of Arts and Sciences, the Business School, the Design School, the Divinity School, the School of Education, the John F. Kennedy School of Government, the Law School, and the Schools of Dental Medicine, Medicine, and Public Health.

The residential plan for undergraduate students is an essential part of the Harvard experience. Every student is assured a place in College housing for four years. Freshmen live in one of the several dormitories in Harvard Yard, the oldest and most central part of the campus. At the end of the freshman year, students move into residential Houses in which they will live for the remainder of their undergraduate careers. The House system provides a smaller community for students within the larger University environment. Each House has a resident senior faculty member who is called the master, a senior tutor or dean, a tutorial staff, a library, and dining facilities. All Houses are coeducational, and much of the social, athletic, extracurricular, and academic life centers on the House.

Harvard offers more than 300 student organizations. Some groups are long-established, such as the Hasty Pudding Club and Phillips Brooks House; others reflect the changing interests, attitudes, and politics of the times. Students find organized activities in dance, drama, government, journalism, music, religion, social service, visual arts, and a variety of other special interest areas.

The Department of Athletics offers forty-one intercollegiate sports programs for men and women—more than any other college in the country. In addition, there is a comprehensive system of intramural and recreational sports. The extensive athletic facilities include six basketball courts, forty squash courts, two swimming pools, and forty-eight tennis courts. Also available are facilities for aerobics, baseball, fencing, field hockey, football, hockey, lacrosse, martial arts, racquetball, rowing, soccer, track, water polo, weight lifting, and wrestling. Houses have their own intramural teams, and there are sports clubs run by students.

Location

Harvard College is located in Cambridge, Massachusetts, a city on the banks of the Charles River, across from Boston. Metropolitan Boston is a pleasant mixture of New England culture and urban vitality. Both Boston and Cambridge enjoy a history of tradition and innovation, as illustrated by their concert halls, libraries and bookstores, museums, theaters, coffeehouses, shops, and sports arenas. The cultural and recreational opportunities are countless and easily accessible. Beaches and mountains are both conveniently near.

Majors and Degrees

Harvard offers more than forty areas in which an undergraduate may specialize. Some of these fields of concentration are Afro-American studies, anthropology, applied mathematics, astronomy, biochemical sciences, biology, chemistry, classics, computer science, Earth and planetary sciences, East Asian studies, economics, engineering and applied sciences, English, environmental science and public policy, folklore and mythology, Germanic languages and literatures, government, history, history and literature, history and science, history of art and architecture, linguistics, literature, mathematics, music, Near Eastern languages and literatures, philosophy, physics, psychology, religion, Romance languages and literatures, Sanskrit and Indian studies, Slavic languages and literatures, social studies, sociology, statistics, visual and environmental studies, and women's studies. Within fields, there are various options for specialization, and it is possible to combine major fields or to devise special concentrations. Almost all undergraduates pursue an A.B. degree (only the engineering and applied sciences concentration offers an S.B. degree program).

Academic Program

Harvard's goal is to provide students with the freedom to design individual academic programs within the structure of a broadly based liberal arts curriculum. Students must complete at least thirty-two 1-semester courses during their four years, chosen from the more than 3,000 courses available in the humanities, social sciences, and natural sciences. A one-semester course in expository writing is required of all freshmen.

At the end of the freshman year, students choose a field of concentration. During the next three years, they take a minimum of twelve 1-semester courses chosen from that field and related fields. Except in a few fields, sophomores are assigned a tutor within their chosen field of concentration. The tutorial group meets weekly to investigate assigned topics or areas of special interest. Juniors and seniors may elect to pursue tutorials on an individual basis, thus enabling them to study an issue in depth. The culmination of the tutorial program is the senior thesis. Cross-registration in other faculties of Harvard University and with the Massachusetts Institute of Technology is also available.

The Core Curriculum courses are specially designed to fulfill students' requirements outside of their fields of concentration. Seven 1-semester courses are required, chosen from eleven areas of intellectual inquiry that include literature and arts, historical study, social analysis, moral reasoning, science, foreign cultures, and quantitative reasoning. This core program gives students an appreciation of disciplines other than their chosen concentration. Before graduation, students are also required to demonstrate proficiency in a foreign language and competence in certain areas of data analysis.

Harvard's Advanced Standing Program is designed for undergraduates who plan to graduate in three years or plan to complete the A.B./A.M. program in four years. This is a choice made at the end of two years of study at Harvard. To be eligible for this, students who have taken College Board Advanced Placement tests need a total of 4 full credits, earned by scoring a 5 on a minimum of four qualified AP exams.

Each year, about one third of the freshmen elect to participate in the Freshman Seminar Program. The seminar format is designed for those freshmen who are eager to work independently or within small groups on special topics, under the guidance of a professor well known in his or her field.

Off-Campus Programs

A large number of students receive credit each year for work done away from the Harvard campus under the auspices of a variety of programs that are sponsored by foreign and American universities. Undergraduates interested in study-abroad programs are counseled on an individual basis about program applications, academic credit, and financial assistance.

Courses (including ROTC programs) are also available through the Massachusetts Institute of Technology.

Academic Facilities

The University library system consists of the Harvard College Library and the libraries of the graduate and professional schools. Together these libraries house more than 15 million volumes, constituting the largest university library collection in the world.

The University Museum includes the Peabody Museum of Archaeology and Ethnology, the Botanical Museum, the Museum of Comparative Zoology, and the Mineralogical Museum. The Fogg and Sackler museums house a collection of paintings, drawings, and sculpture. Contemporary exhibits are featured regularly at the Carpenter Center for Visual Arts. The Loeb Drama Center seats 500 in the auditorium and houses a small experimental theater.

More than a dozen buildings are used exclusively for the classrooms, laboratories, and museums of the natural sciences. There are computers available for use in the science center and all residence halls. All student rooms have Internet network access.

Costs

Costs for 2003–04 tuition and fees were $29,060, and room and board were $8868. Estimated personal expenses, books, supplies, and similar costs were $2522; travel expenses vary.

Financial Aid

All admissions decisions at Harvard College are need blind, and all financial aid awards at Harvard College are based on need. Approximately two thirds of the undergraduates receive some form of financial assistance. Financial aid is provided in the form of scholarships, loans, and term-time employment. Family income and a number of other factors are considered in determining need. Any students who feel they may need financial assistance are encouraged to apply. Financial aid applicants who are U.S. citizens are required to submit the CSS Financial Aid PROFILE, the FAFSA, and copies of their family's tax returns by February 1. International students are required to file the Financial Statement for Students from Foreign Countries (FSSFC) by the same date. Applicants are usually notified of their aid awards at the same time they are notified of the admission decision.

Faculty

Harvard's faculty is an outstanding group of scholars, teachers, and researchers. The Faculty of Arts and Sciences consists of approximately 700 full-time members, all of whom hold the highest degree in their fields; they may be assisted by teaching fellows who are doctoral candidates. In a typical course, a faculty member teaches a group of nearly 25 students. Many of the courses with the largest enrollments are taught entirely in small sections of about 20. In contrast, the great majority of classes are taught with very small enrollments, and the tutorial system provides individual instruction. Because teaching and scholarship are both highly valued at Harvard, a freshman may well be taught by a Nobel Prize winner or a distinguished scholar.

Student Government

A freshman may participate in the Freshman Council. Representatives are elected from each dormitory in Harvard Yard. A freshman may also participate in the Undergraduate Council, the main student government organization. Upperclass men and women who reside in the Houses elect members for their respective House committees as well as for the Undergraduate Council, the Committee on Housing and Undergraduate Life, and the Committee on Undergraduate Education.

Admission Requirements

Undergraduates come from every state and nearly 100 countries. More than 20,000 applicants from both public and private schools compete for 1,650 places in the freshman class. The Admissions Committee seeks a diverse group of students who are intellectually capable, socially aware, and mature. The committee considers not only academic achievement but also students' extracurricular talents and potential for contributing to the Harvard community.

Applicants should present a high school transcript, two letters of recommendation from teachers, one letter of recommendation from a school counselor, and scores on the SAT I (or the ACT) and any three SAT II: Subject Tests. Students who are not native speakers of English should take the Writing (in English) test as one of their SAT II tests. Applicants must also submit a series of personal essays and, if at all possible, meet with an alumnus or alumna for an interview in their local area. The credentials of all applicants are considered in depth, and full attention is given to each candidate's particular strengths and abilities as well as personal qualities.

Application and Information

Students may apply to Harvard College under the early or regular action programs. Final application deadlines are November 1 and January 1, respectively. Early action decision letters are mailed in early December. Applicants who are deferred in the early action process are automatically considered in the regular action process. Regular action decision letters are mailed in early April. Students who apply to transfer into the sophomore or junior year should submit their applications by February 15. They may express a preference to enter in the fall or the spring. The College also accepts a few visiting students each fall and spring from well-qualified candidates who are currently matriculated at another college and wish to spend a term studying at Harvard. For application forms and additional information, students should contact:

Harvard College Office of Admissions
Byerly Hall
8 Garden Street
Cambridge, Massachusetts 02138
Telephone: 617-495-1551 (for freshman admissions)
617-495-9707 (for transfer and visiting student admissions)
617-495-1581 (for financial aid)
E-mail: college@fas.harvard.edu
WWW: http://www.college.harvard.edu/admissions

HARVEY MUDD COLLEGE

CLAREMONT, CALIFORNIA

The College

Harvey Mudd College was founded in 1955. Its mission is to educate undergraduate men and women in a rigorous academic environment, focusing on mathematics, science, and engineering, and also to provide a rich background in the humanities and social sciences. The faculty members are eminent, experienced professionals—humanists who are aware of technological needs and engineers and scientists who have an abiding faith in liberal learning. Small classes, the excellent faculty, and exceptional students create a setting that is conducive to both teaching and learning. An attitude of mutual trust prevails in all aspects of campus life and is amplified by a spirit of cooperation among students and faculty members and encouraged by the student-directed honor code. Harvey Mudd students deal daily with high standards, demanding course loads, and intense pressure, but in an atmosphere void of intimidation and unreasonable competition. The current undergraduate enrollment is 230 women and 465 men. In addition to the advantages that all small colleges share, Harvey Mudd has the advantage of being a part of the Claremont Colleges system, which has a total undergraduate enrollment of approximately 5,000. Students in the Claremont Colleges share many opportunities in course offerings, facilities, and extracurricular activities. The cluster of adjacent colleges also offers a well-integrated social life and a rich intellectual atmosphere, supported by lectures, concerts, dramatic productions, seminars, colloquia, and festivals. Harvey Mudd has a joint program of intercollegiate and intramural athletics, physical education, and recreation with Claremont McKenna and Scripps Colleges. The varsity athletic teams compete in the Southern California Intercollegiate Athletic Conference. Varsity teams compete in basketball, cross-country, soccer, swimming, tennis, track, and water polo, plus men's baseball, football, and golf and women's volleyball. Intramural teams are fielded in basketball, flag football, floor hockey, inner-tube water polo, paintball, soccer, softball, and volleyball. The culmination of the intramural season is a weekend playoff tournament, known as the Mudd Bowl. There are also club sports and recreational activities indigenous to the terrain and climate of the region. There is an active sailing club with a 30-foot racing sloop, located at Newport Harbor, and two other sailboats. Campus activities include the ballroom dance team; the ETC. Players, a dramatics group; the Forensic Society; the Symphony Orchestra; departmental organizations; religious activities; a stage band; a jazz band; a brass ensemble; the yearbook; two radio stations; and political clubs. The seven residence halls tend to be the center of social life on campus. All halls are coed and house students of all class levels. Freshmen are required to live on campus, and 97 percent of all students typically reside on campus.

Upon graduation, about 40 percent of Harvey Mudd's students enter graduate school at some of the nation's most prestigious universities. Virtually all of these students receive fellowships and assistantships. In a typical year, twice as many corporate recruiters visit the campus as there are seniors seeking employment, and it is not uncommon for seniors to have between ten and fifteen job interviews. More than 40 percent of Harvey Mudd alumni hold Ph.D.'s, the highest percentage in the country.

Location

The town of Claremont is located at the base of Mount Baldy. It takes 30 minutes to get to the ski slopes and 45 minutes to an hour to get to the Pacific Coast beaches, the desert, and the center of Los Angeles, where unlimited social, sports, and cultural activities are available. The town is served by the Ontario International Airport, a 15-minute drive away. With a population of 37,000, Claremont is known throughout southern California for its active support of educational and cultural programs. Adjacent to the Claremont Colleges is Claremont Village, a friendly community featuring sidewalk cafés, specialty shops, tree-lined streets, and Victorian homes. The weather in Claremont is warm and dry, with mild winters.

Majors and Degrees

The Bachelor of Science degree is awarded in biology, chemistry, computer science, engineering (nonspecialized), mathematics, physics, plus two joint majors (computer science/mathematics and mathematical biology). Also available are an off-campus major (at another one of the Claremont Colleges), and IPS (individual program of study). An IPS degree may be built around the College's programs and other interdisciplinary fields.

Academic Program

The College is an autonomous member of a much larger center of learning, the Claremont Colleges. Cross-registration at the other six Claremont Colleges (Claremont Graduate University, Claremont McKenna, Keck Graduate Institute, Pitzer, Pomona, and Scripps) is encouraged. Thus, students may experience the best that each Claremont College has to offer.

Harvey Mudd students devote one third of their study to a common technical core curriculum in mathematics, physics, chemistry, biology, computing, and engineering design. Approximately a third of the course work is devoted to the humanities and the social sciences, an emphasis that is unsurpassed by any accredited engineering college in the nation. The final third of the work is taken in the student's major, which is not declared until the middle of the sophomore year. The College uses a High Pass/Pass/No Credit grading system in the first semester of the freshman year.

Unique in higher education, Harvey Mudd's Clinic Programs expose advanced students to real, unsolved problems that require them to investigate alternatives, exercise judgment, and put into practice what they have learned. Clinic teams usually consist of 4 seniors and juniors. They work under the direction of a student leader, a faculty member, and a liaison from a sponsoring company and are responsible for conducting the work, monitoring the project's progress, managing a budget, and following it through to satisfactory completion. This hands-on experience has created numerous summer and full-time employment opportunities for students. More than thirty-five corporations participate in the Clinics annually.

A broad range of undergraduate research opportunities is available in theoretical and experimental sciences and mathematics, and all students must carry out research or clinic projects for at least one year. It is not uncommon for undergraduate students at Harvey Mudd to author or coauthor scientific papers that are published in national journals, and the majority of student researchers make presentations at academic conferences.

Academic Facilities

Classroom and laboratory facilities are modern and extensive and are available 24 hours a day. The academic buildings are within a 5-minute walk of all other facilities on campus. Central in both function and location is the Sprague Library, which houses more than 60,000 bound reference works and 6,800 periodicals in engineering, mathematics, and science. A computerized catalog system gives Harvey Mudd students immediate online access to all the holdings of both the Harvey Mudd library and the Seeley Mudd Science Library at Pomona

College. Altogether, Harvey Mudd students have open-stack access to more than 2 million volumes in the library system of the seven Claremont Colleges.

The College has a distributed model of computing, with some resources located centrally, but with specialized resources distributed to the various academic departments. The central facilities include Intel-based systems running Red Hat Linux, VAX and Alpha systems running Compaq's VMS, and Intel-based file servers running Novell NetWare and Microsoft Windows Server. Also available centrally are four public access laboratories housing more than seventy-five of the latest Apple Macintosh and Intel-based DELL personal computers. In addition, each of the academic departments has computing facilities, the three largest belonging to the computer science, engineering, and mathematics departments. Computer science's resources include a multiprocessor Sun SPARC 1000 and Sun UltraSPARC 3000 servers, two ATM switches, and clusters of SGI Indigo 2 and Sun SPARC workstations of various vintages. All are accessible from a local cluster of color X terminals as well as the campus network. The Engineering Computing Facility, which is part of the Engineering Design Center, includes two clusters of Intel-based systems running Microsoft Windows and supporting the latest engineering software. The mathematics department has a substantial high speed Linus computing cluster for use either in a classroom setting or by students individually. There are numerous other personal computers and workstations in the labs around the College. All resources are attached directly to the campus network. Although most of these resources are attached via fast Ethernet, some of the major resources have Gigabit Ethernet connections. Running through a fiber backbone, the network includes all the student residence and all academic and administrative buildings. It is also connected to the central library, the other Claremont campuses, the Internet, and Internet2. From their rooms, through a direct twisted-pair fast Ethernet connection, students can access any of these resources in addition to databases in the library, software on servers, compute cycles on supercomputers, and archives of public domain software, and they can send electronic mail and surf the Web. They can even create their own resources, such as a Web server, and attach it to the Net for others to access.

Physics laboratory facilities support student instruction and experimental research in astronomy, electronics, optics, condensed matter, low-temperature physics, atomic physics, nuclear physics, geophysics, and biophysics. Nearby Table Mountain Observatory is available for astronomy observation. Chemistry research in the areas of synthetic and physical chemistry, organic and inorganic chemistry, biochemistry, crystallography, and liquid crystals is supported by extensive research instrumentation. Biology facilities include apparatus for molecular biology, neurobiology, artificial intelligence, and robotics.

Costs

The total expenses for the 2003–04 academic year were tuition and fees, $28,660; room, $4790; and board, $4630 (sixteen-meal plan). The total cost was $39,780, including an estimated $1700 for personal expenses and books. Travel costs are additional.

Financial Aid

The College meets 100 percent of each student's demonstrated financial need. About 80 percent of the students at Harvey Mudd receive some type of financial aid. Scholarships and loans are awarded on the basis of financial need. All students are expected to contribute a portion of their summer earnings toward the cost of attending HMC. On-campus jobs are widely available. Harvey Mudd sponsors National Merit Scholarships, and one third of the current freshman class are Merit Scholars or participants in two other merit award programs. All aid applicants must file the Free Application for Federal Student Aid (FAFSA) and the College Scholarship Service (CSS) Financial Aid PROFILE. California residents applying for aid must also apply for the Cal Grant.

Faculty

Harvey Mudd's student-faculty ratio is 9:1. All courses, laboratories, and recitation sessions are taught by full-time faculty members with a Ph.D. Excellence in teaching is the primary criterion for the reappointment and promotion of faculty members, but most members are also actively involved with students in research. Professors are accessible, and close relationships are formed between students and faculty mentors.

Student Government

Elected officers participate in the Associated Students of Harvey Mudd College Council. The Student Affairs Committee coordinates most extracurricular and social activities in conjunction with the Dorm Affairs Committee. The student Judicial Board interprets the College's constitution and enforces the honor code. More than 10 percent of the student body is involved in some form of student government.

Admission Requirements

The most important aspects of a candidate's application are the courses that were taken and the grades that were earned in secondary school. To be competitive for admission, candidates must excel in a rigorous college-preparatory program, with a heavy emphasis on mathematics and science. Students interested in attending Harvey Mudd must take at least 1 year each of chemistry, physics, and calculus or a college equivalent course. Even though the major thrust of Harvey Mudd's program is in mathematics and science, particular attention is focused on a student's proven talents in English and communication skills. Typical candidates have taken several Advanced Placement (AP) or even college-level courses; however, candidates who have not had the opportunity to take honors, accelerated, or AP courses are given every consideration and should not hesitate to apply. Scores on the SAT I and three SAT II: Subject Tests are required for admission. Two of these SAT II tests must be Writing and Mathematics Level IIC. Because Harvey Mudd desires a multidimensional student body, serious consideration is given to an applicant's extracurricular and leadership activities. Interviews are not required, but a personal interview is strongly recommended and can influence a final decision. Teacher and counselor recommendations are essential to the admission decision.

Admission is highly competitive. For fall 2003, 1,773 applicants applied for admission to a freshman class limited to approximately 185 students. Of the entering freshmen in 2003–04, 47 percent were from California. Eighteen percent were National Merit Scholars and 27 percent ranked first in his or her high school class. Students who scored in the middle 50 percent (from the 25th percentile to the 75th percentile) on the SAT I achieved verbal scores from 650 to 750 and math scores from 720 to 790; Subject Test scores in the middle 50 percent ranged from 640 to 730 in Writing and from 730 to 800 in Mathematics Level IIC.

Application and Information

Early decision candidates must complete their application by November 15; notification is mailed by December 15. The postmark deadline for regular applications is January 15. Applicants for regular decision are notified April 1.

Deren Finks
Dean of Admission and Financial Aid
Harvey Mudd College
Claremont, California 91711
Telephone: 909-621-8011
Fax: 909-607-7046
E-mail: admission@hmc.edu

HAVERFORD COLLEGE

HAVERFORD, PENNSYLVANIA

The College

Haverford is the first college established by members of the Society of Friends (Quakers). Founded in 1833, Haverford has chosen to remain small, undergraduate, and residential to carry out its educational philosophy and to maintain a strong sense of community. An Honor Code is created and directed by students and is an important element of the Haverford community. The Honor Code allows students to directly confront academic and social issues in a spirit of cooperation and mutual respect.

Haverford's 1,100 students represent forty-five states, Puerto Rico, the District of Columbia, and twenty countries. Twenty-eight percent of the students are students of color, while an additional 6 percent are international students.

Haverford is a residential campus with 98 percent of the students and 70 percent of the faculty living on campus. Students may also choose to live at nearby Bryn Mawr College. Housing on Haverford's campus is single-sex or coed, and residence halls vary in accommodations from 4-person apartments to suites and singles. Other choices of residence facilities include the Ira De A. Reid House (Black Cultural Center), La Casa Hispanica, and an environmental house.

Haverford's athletic teams participate in Division III of the NCAA. Intercollegiate sports include baseball, basketball, cricket, cross-country, fencing, field hockey, lacrosse, soccer, softball, squash, tennis, track and field, and volleyball. Haverford also sponsors several junior varsity, club, and intramural sports teams. Athletic facilities include the Alumni Field House and Ryan Gymnasium.

Location

The College is located 10 miles (16 kilometers) west of Center City Philadelphia on a wooded campus of 204 acres. Haverford's proximity to the sixth-largest city in the United States allows its students to take advantage of the many social, cultural, and educational resources that this historic area offers. Extensive public transportation allows students easy access to the city and environs.

Majors and Degrees

Majors leading to a B.A. or B.S. degree are offered in twenty-nine departments: anthropology, archaeology, astronomy, biology, chemistry, classics, comparative literature, East Asian studies, economics, English, fine arts, French, geology, German, growth and structure of cities, history, history of art, Italian, mathematics, music, philosophy, physics, political science, psychology, religion, Romance languages, Russian, sociology, and Spanish. Students may minor, arrange an interdepartmental or double major, or design an individual major. Twenty-five to 30 percent of the students major in the sciences or mathematics, 30–35 percent in the social sciences, and 35–40 percent in the humanities. Approximately 15 percent have double, interdepartmental, or special majors. A 3-2 engineering program with Caltech is available to students who qualify.

Other programs in which students may incorporate into their curricula include Africana studies, biochemistry and biophysics, computer science, creative writing, dance, East Asian studies, education and education studies, environmental studies, feminist and gender studies, Hebrew and Judaic studies, international economic relations, Latin American and Iberian studies, linguistics, mathematical economics, neural and behavioral science, peace and conflict studies, prebusiness, prelaw, premedicine, and theater studies.

Academic Program

Students plan their programs using established guidelines and with the help of faculty advisers. They must have at least three courses in each of the divisions of the College: humanities, social science, and natural science. In addition, they must fulfill requirements in foreign language, social justice, writing, and quantitative course work. Flexibility in the curriculum allows opportunities for independent study, foreign study, and noncollegiate academic study. Haverford's curriculum has moved toward integrated learning and includes several centers where students and faculty members have opportunities to collaborate across disciplines and pursue innovative research. Centers include the Marion E. Koshland Integrated Natural Sciences Center, the John B. Hurford Humanities Center, and the Center for Peace and Global Citizenship.

Majors are selected at the end of the sophomore year. Normally, students take four courses per semester and thirty-two courses over four years. Scheduling is flexible, however, and students may arrange programs to meet individual needs, including six-semester, seven-semester, and five-year programs. Credit is given on the basis of Advanced Placement (AP) examinations, A-Level examinations, and International Baccalaureate Higher Level examinations.

One of Haverford's distinctive features is its extensive academic and social cooperation with Bryn Mawr College. Students may take courses or major at either school, live on either campus, and eat on either campus. There are more than 3,500 cross-registrations annually. Extracurricular activities, such as a weekly newspaper, a drama club, a radio station, an orchestra, social action groups, and intramural sports, operate jointly. A free bus service between the two campuses, which are a mile apart, facilitates cooperative arrangements. Haverford and Bryn Mawr also share library resources with nearby Swarthmore College. All three college libraries are linked electronically, and students have instant access to library resources through the campus computer network. Combined holdings are in excess of 1.5 million volumes.

Off-Campus Programs

Haverford students may take advantage of the course offerings at Swarthmore College and the University of Pennsylvania in addition to courses at Bryn Mawr. Students may also enhance their college experiences by arranging study abroad in forty-five programs overseas or study away at Claremont McKenna, Fisk, Spelman, or Pitzer colleges.

Academic Facilities

Major facilities include the James P. Magill Library (445,000 volumes); computer centers; the Koshland Integrated Natural Sciences Center for the physical sciences, biology, and psychology; the Strawbridge Observatory for astronomy; the Music Center; Gest Center for Cross-Cultural Study of Religion; the Fine Arts Center; Marshall Auditorium; and the Language Learning Center. Academic buildings and dormitories are linked by a campuswide computer network.

Costs

The total approximate costs for 2004–05 are $39,850 for new students and $39,690 for returning students. This consists of $29,990 for tuition, $9420 for room and board, and a student association fee of $280. New students have a one-time orientation fee of $160.

Financial Aid

The College has an extensive financial aid program. Approximately 40 percent of Haverford's students receive College grant aid. Candidates for Haverford College funded aid must file the Financial Aid PROFILE with the College Board, along with the FAFSA. Applicants may register for the PROFILE by completing a short form, available from their local high school guidance office, and sending it to the College Board or by calling the College Board at (800) 778-6888. Regular decision students should complete the PROFILE registration process by January 2, so the College Board can send the form and have students complete it by the January 31 deadline. The FAFSA is also available from high school guidance offices and must also be filed by January 31. Early decision candidates should complete the PROFILE registration process by October 15 and file the PROFILE form with the College Board by November 15.

Further details are given in the leaflet "Financial Aid at Haverford," which is included in the admission application booklet. Haverford's College Board PROFILE code number is 2289, and the FAFSA code number is 003274.

Faculty

The student-faculty ratio is 8:1. The faculty devotes its full teaching time to undergraduates. There are no graduate assistants. The regular faculty is supplemented by 90 to 100 scholars, artists, and public figures who visit the College annually under the auspices of seven specially endowed funds.

Student Government

The Students' Association has responsibility for nearly all aspects of student life. The Haverford Honor Code, established and administered by students, has been in existence since 1897. The Honor Code makes possible a climate of trust, concern, and respect, which produces a campus atmosphere conducive to learning and personal growth. The code provides for students' academic and social freedom within the confines of agreed-upon community standards. Exams are not proctored, and the students schedule their own final exams. The code is administered by an elected Honor Council of 16 students—4 from each class at the College. Each year, the students meet to discuss resolutions and changes in the Honor Code and to approve its adoption. The students also elect several members of the student body to serve on faculty committees and as nonvoting representatives to the Board of Managers (trustees).

Admission Requirements

Admission to Haverford is highly competitive. Admitted students have strong academic records and represent a diversity of backgrounds and interests. The primary criteria for admission are academic and personal qualities as shown by the school record, College Board test scores, extracurricular achievement, and personal recommendations. A combination of qualities that indicates academic and personal promise and potential for growth at Haverford is more significant than any single factor. Of the most recent first-year class, 98 percent rank in the top fifth of their high school class; their SAT I scores range from 400 to 800; the mean SAT I ranges are 640–730 (verbal) and 650–720 (math). All candidates are required to take the SAT I and three SAT II Subject Tests, including the Writing Test. The ACT may be substituted for the SAT I. A visit to campus to meet students, observe classes, and have an interview is strongly recommended, and students who live within 150 miles of the campus are required to arrange an on-campus interview. A first-choice early decision plan and a deferred matriculation plan are offered.

Admission of transfer students to Haverford is also highly competitive. A limited number of transfer students are accepted each year. Candidates must have completed one full year of college, with a minimum grade point average of 3.0 (B). Campus visits are strongly recommended for those wishing to transfer. A transfer student must spend a minimum of two years at Haverford in order to receive a degree.

Application and Information

The application deadlines for admission are November 15 for early decision candidates, January 15 for regular decision candidates, and March 31 for transfer candidates. Haverford also accepts the Common Application, which is available in school guidance offices. The admission office is open from 9 a.m. to 5 p.m. on weekdays (8:30 a.m. to 4:30 p.m. from June to August) and, during the fall, from 9 a.m. to noon on Saturday. For more information or to arrange an interview or tour appointment, students should contact:

Office of Admission
Haverford College
370 Lancaster Avenue
Haverford, Pennsylvania 19041-1392
Telephone: 610-896-1350
610-896-1436 (TTY/TDD)
Fax: 610-896-1338
E-mail: admission@haverford.edu
finaid@haverford.edu
World Wide Web: http://www.haverford.edu

HAWAI'I PACIFIC UNIVERSITY

HONOLULU, HAWAI'I

The University

Hawai'i Pacific University (HPU) is an independent, coeducational, career-oriented comprehensive university with a foundation in the liberal arts. Undergraduate and graduate degrees are offered in more than fifty areas. Hawai'i Pacific prides itself on maintaining strong academic programs, small class sizes, individual attention to students, an outstanding faculty, and a student population as diverse as the United Nations. HPU is accredited by the Western Association of Schools and Colleges and the National League for Nursing Accrediting Commission.

HPU is the largest private university in Hawai'i, with more than 8,000 students from every state in the union and more than 100 countries. The diversity of the student body stimulates learning about other cultures firsthand, both in and out of the classroom. There is no majority population at HPU. Students are encouraged to examine the values, customs, traditions, and principles of others to gain a clearer understanding of their own perspectives. HPU students develop friendships with students from throughout the United States and the world, important connections for success in the global economy of the twenty-first century.

In addition to the undergraduate programs, HPU offers several graduate programs: the M.B.A. (with ten concentrations), the Master of Science in Information Systems (M.S.I.S.), the Master of Science in Nursing (M.S.N.), and the Master of Arts (M.A.) in communications, diplomacy and military studies, global leadership, human resource management, organizational change, and teaching English as a second language.

HPU has NCAA Division II intercollegiate sports. Men's athletic programs include baseball, basketball, cheerleading, cross-country, and tennis. Women's athletics include cheerleading, cross-country, softball, tennis, and volleyball.

The housing office at HPU offers many services and options for students. Residence halls with cafeteria service are available on the windward Hawai'i Loa campus, while off-campus apartments are available in the Honolulu and Waikiki areas for those seeking more independent living arrangements.

Location

With two campuses linked by shuttle, Hawai'i Pacific combines the excitement of an urban, downtown campus with the serenity of the windward Hawai'i Loa residential campus, which is set in the lush foothills of the Ko'olau mountains. The main campus is located in downtown Honolulu, the business and financial center of the Pacific. Eight miles away, situated on 135 acres in Kaneohe, the windward Hawai'i Loa campus is the site of the School of Nursing, the marine science program, and a variety of other course offerings. Students may take classes on whichever campus is most convenient. The Hawai'i Loa campus is home to recreational facilities such as a soccer field, tennis courts, a softball field, a student center, and an exercise room. The beautiful weather, for which Hawai'i is famous, allows for unlimited recreation opportunities year-round. The emphasis on a career-related curriculum keeps students focused on their academic goals. The economy in Hawai'i makes cooperative education and internship opportunities hard to beat. Students desiring to expand their horizons in preparation for the changing global economy find Hawai'i an exciting learning laboratory where East meets West. The many opportunities available at HPU provide for a healthy combination of school, work, and fun.

Majors and Degrees

Hawai'i Pacific University offers programs that lead to the degrees of Bachelor of Arts (B.A.), Bachelor of Science in Business Administration (B.S.B.A.), Bachelor of Science in Computer Science (B.S.C.S.), Bachelor of Science in environmental science, Bachelor of Science in marine science, Bachelor of Science in Nursing (B.S.N.), Bachelor of Science in premedical studies, and Bachelor of Social Work (B.S.W.).

Undergraduate majors include the B.A. in advertising, anthropology, applied sociology, communication (concentrations in speech and visual communication), East-West classical studies, economics, engineering (a 3-2 program), English, environmental studies, history, human resource development, human services, international relations, international studies (concentrations in American, Asian, comparative, European, and Pacific studies), justice administration, political science, psychology, social sciences, and teaching English as a second language. The School of Business programs include the B.S. in accounting, advertising, business economics, computer information systems, corporate communication, entrepreneurial studies, finance, human resource management, international business, management, marketing, public administration, and travel industry management. The B.S. is also available in applied mathematics, biology, computer science, diplomacy and military studies, environmental science, marine biology, nursing, oceanography, and premedical studies. The Bachelor of Social Work is also available. Dual degrees, double majors, and minors are also offered.

Academic Program

The baccalaureate student must complete at least 124 semester hours of credit. Forty-five of these credits provide the student with a strong foundation in the liberal arts, with the remaining credits composed of appropriate upper-division classes in the student's major and related areas. The academic year operates on a modified 4-1-4 semester system, featuring a five-week winter intersession. The University also offers extensive summer sessions. A student can earn up to 15 semester hours of credit during the summer. By attending these supplemental sessions, a student may complete the baccalaureate degree program in three years. A five-year B.S.B.A./M.B.A. program is also available.

Off-Campus Programs

Hawai'i Pacific's academic and cocurricular programs are intertwined with the world of work. The University offers a comprehensive cooperative education/internship program through the Career Services Center, in which a student may enroll throughout his or her course of study. This program enables students to gain significant experience in a career-related position as well as earn academic credit and a salary. At the upper-division level, the position is generally an internship with a leading Honolulu firm. Recent internship employers have included Aloha Airlines; Bank of Hawai'i; the city and county of Honolulu; the state of Hawai'i; Hilton Hawaiian Village Hotel; IBM; KGMB-TV and Radio; Merrill Lynch; New York Life; Ogilvy & Mather; PricewaterhouseCoopers; Sears, Roebuck and Company; Sheraton; Starr Siegle Communications; and U.S. agencies and departments. The staff at the Career Services Center continues to work with students after graduation, from resume writing to job interview preparation.

Academic Facilities

The downtown campus comprises six buildings in the center of Honolulu's business district. HPU's newest facility is the Frear Center, which houses state-of-the-art classrooms, a communication lab, a robotics lab, and a graduate M.S.I.S. high-tech classroom. Hawai'i Pacific's Meader Library provides a large collection of circulating books, special reference resources, newspapers from around the world, and periodicals. A number of special collections are housed with extensive business collections and a separate career development section. Meader Library has a tutoring center that provides free tutoring in all core subjects, a graduate reading room, and ample study space. A computerized search system allows students access to information from libraries throughout the nation. The Learning Assistance Center is the home of language labs and an audiotape and audiovisual library as well as the multimedia lab with the latest in interactive computer and CD-ROM technology. The recently expanded computer lab has more than 420 IBM-compatible PCs.

On the suburban and residential windward Hawai'i Loa campus, academic life revolves around the Amos N. Starr and Juliette Montague Cooke Academic Center (AC). The AC houses faculty and staff member offices, classrooms, a theater, an art gallery, and the Atherton Learning Resources Center, which includes a library with extensive collections in the areas of Asian studies, marine science, and nursing. The Boyd MacNaughton Pacific Resource Room houses the Hawaiiana and Pacific special collections. The Academic Computer Center provides access to IBM computers.

Costs

For the 2003–04 academic year, tuition was $10,368 (for most majors), and books, supplies, and health insurance cost approximately $1865. For students who live in residence halls, room and board were $6610. Off-campus apartments, operated by Cadmus Properties Corporation, rented for between $2700 and $2900 per semester. There was an additional $500 refundable security deposit required for residence halls and off-campus apartments. Tuition for marine science majors was $12,320, and tuition for junior- or senior-year nursing majors was $14,840.

Financial Aid

The University provides financial aid for qualified students through institutional, state, and federal aid programs. Approximately 40 percent of the University's undergraduate students receive financial aid. Among the forms of aid available are Federal Perkins Loans, Federal Stafford Student Loans, Guaranteed Parental Loans, Federal Pell Grants, and Federal Supplemental Educational Opportunity Grants. To apply for aid, students must submit the Free Application for Federal Student Aid (FAFSA). The FAFSA may be submitted at any time, but the priority deadline is March 1.

Faculty

Hawai'i Pacific's dedicated professors put a priority on teaching. At HPU, teaching assistants are not found in the classroom, only qualified professors. Students receive the personal attention they need to excel. The student-faculty ratio is 18:1, and class size averages 25 students. Students get to know their professors as colleagues and mentors. HPU faculty members are actively involved in their academic fields and bring this experience to the classroom. Many of them are renowned leaders in their particular disciplines and come to HPU from leadership positions in business and industry. The University has 225 full-time and 220 part-time faculty members. Eighty percent have earned Ph.D.'s or terminal degrees in their fields. Hawai'i Pacific has a staff of professional academic advisers whose primary responsibility is to assist students with academic programs and help them choose the right courses in the right sequence to meet their individual goals. Students meet with an adviser prior to every semester's registration.

Student Government

All registered students are members of the Associated Students of Hawai'i Pacific University (ASHPU), which is headed by elected officers and class representatives. ASHPU supervises more than eighty clubs, organizations, and activities, including a literary magazine; a national award–winning student newspaper; a pep band; an international vocal ensemble; preprofessional, cultural, and social organizations; service societies; dances; luaus; and cheerleading.

Admission Requirements

Hawai'i Pacific seeks students who are motivated and show academic promise. The admissions office requires that applicants complete and forward the admission application and their high school transcripts. Transfer students should also submit college transcripts. SAT and/or ACT scores should be submitted if these scores are not posted in the transcripts. First-time freshmen are expected to have a minimum GPA of 2.5 (on a 4.0 scale) in college-preparatory courses. Students with less than a 2.5 may be considered for admission but should also submit three letters of recommendation and a short essay on educational and personal objectives. HPU recommends that students complete 4 years of English, 2 years of math and social studies, and at least 1 year of history and science. Transfer students with 24 or more postsecondary credits are required to have a GPA of 2.0 or above. For students with less than 24 credits, a combination of college and high school GPA is used.

The Marine Science and Environmental Science Programs require a high school GPA of 3.0 or above and 3 years of science, including biology, chemistry, and physics, as well as mathematics through precalculus (trigonometry). Transfer students must demonstrate ability in science and math at the college level. Students not meeting the above criteria are encouraged to enroll at HPU without declaring a major to demonstrate the ability to do college-level work in science and math.

Application and Information

Candidates are notified of admission decisions on a rolling basis, usually within two weeks of receipt of application materials. Early entrance and deferred entrance are available. For further information and for application materials, students should contact:

Office of Admissions
Hawai'i Pacific University
1164 Bishop Street, Suite 200
Honolulu, Hawai'i 96813
Telephone: 808-544-0238
866-CALL-HPU (toll-free in U.S. and Canada)
Fax: 808-544-1136
E-mail: admissions@hpu.edu
World Wide Web: http://www.hpu.edu/four

Students on the HPU downtown campus.

HEIDELBERG COLLEGE

TIFFIN, OHIO

The College

Heidelberg College, founded in 1850, is a selective, private coeducational liberal arts college that is affiliated with the United Church of Christ. Believing that a liberal education is the best career preparation a person can have to confront the challenges of the future creatively, Heidelberg College offers students a solid base on which to grow in their professional and personal lives. Heidelberg's dynamic community maintains a touch of its Old World heritage yet continually brings innovative ideas into the classroom.

The current undergraduate enrollment is about 1,200 men and women. Students come to Heidelberg from twenty-two states and nine other countries. This cross-cultural mix helps to keep the campus diverse and to broaden students' knowledge and understanding of ethnic and cultural differences.

Heidelberg has more than sixty campus organizations that offer opportunities for leadership, service, and fellowship. Included in these organizations are thirteen departmental clubs and fifteen departmental honorary societies that sponsor discussions, lectures, and field trips. Other cocurricular activities include a student-edited and student-managed newspaper, a television station that broadcasts daily news, forensic programs, choral and instrumental groups, and intramural sports. The Communication and Theatre Arts Department presents four or more dramatic productions each year.

A member of the Ohio Athletic Conference, NCAA Division III, Heidelberg offers nine varsity men's sports: baseball, basketball, cross-country, football, golf, soccer, tennis, track, and wrestling. The women's varsity sports program, among the first in Ohio to be affiliated with the NCAA Division III, fields eight intercollegiate teams: basketball, cross-country, golf, soccer, softball, tennis, track, and volleyball. Athletic facilities include a weight room, handball/racquetball courts, locker rooms, and an eight-lane, all-weather track, which is considered one of the finest in Ohio.

Heidelberg College also offers Master of Arts degree programs in counseling and education as well as a Master of Business Administration (M.B.A.) degree program.

Location

Heidelberg's 110-acre campus is located in Tiffin, Ohio, a town of 20,000. It is the center of a prosperous agricultural and business area. Downtown Tiffin, within half a mile of campus, is traditional in appearance; its charming brickwork stores and large lampposts trimmed in wrought iron resemble an old German town. Four metropolitan areas are within easy driving distance: Toledo, 50 miles; Columbus, 86 miles; Cleveland, 92 miles; and Detroit, 103 miles.

Majors and Degrees

Heidelberg offers a wide variety of undergraduate majors and several preprofessional programs within nineteen academic departments. It awards the Bachelor of Arts, Bachelor of Science, and Bachelor of Music degrees. Majors are available in accounting, anthropology, athletic training, biology, business administration, chemistry, communication and theater arts (communication/media, theater), computer information systems, computer science, economics, education (early childhood, middle childhood, adolescence to young adult, intervention specialist studies, multiage German, multiage Spanish, multiage health and physical education, multiage music education), English (literature, writing), environmental biology, German, health–physical education and recreation, history, international studies (international relations, cross-cultural studies), management science, mathematics, music, music education, music industry, music performance, music performance pedagogy, music theory/composition, philosophy, physics, political science, psychology (child and adolescent, mental health, biopsychology, general), public relations, religion, Spanish, sports management, and water resources (biology, chemistry, geology). Preprofessional and cooperative degree programs include dentistry, engineering, environmental management, law, medical technology, medicine, nursing, occupational therapy, optometry, osteopathy, physical therapy, physician assistant studies, podiatry, and veterinary science.

Academic Program

To graduate, a student must complete 120 academic semester hours, comprising 36–45 semester hours of general education, 40 semester hours in a selected major, and 35–44 hours of electives. Two credits in health and physical education and 1 credit for Total Student Development (TSD) are also required.

Off-Campus Programs

To supplement their course work, students may choose from a variety of off-campus study programs that provide practical, career-related experience. For example, students interested in studying habitats not found in northwestern Ohio may do on-site field research in Caribbean biogeography in Belize and on-site field research in the Appalachian mountains of West Virginia. Students may also participate in the excavation of an archaeological site.

Opportunities for practical experience in research are also available through Heidelberg's nationally recognized Water Quality Laboratory, which has ongoing research in water-quality studies involving both northern Ohio streams and Lake Erie. Heidelberg's internship program also enables students to participate in on-the-job internships in several area businesses and industries.

Students interested in studying in Washington, D.C., may take part in the Washington Semester at American University; those interested in studying abroad may participate in Heidelberg's own programs in Germany (at Heidelberg University) and Spain or may participate in programs arranged cooperatively with other colleges and universities in such locations as England, Latin America, Africa, and the Far East.

Heidelberg also has cooperative degree programs in engineering with Case Western Reserve University and in forestry with Duke University.

Academic Facilities

Beeghly Library, containing 154,000 volumes, is the intellectual heart of Heidelberg College. The three-story circular library holds a seventy-seat audiovisual room, a seminar and computer room, the Rickard-Mayer Rare Books Room, and the Besse Collection of Letters. Bareis Hall of Science has excellent laboratories and facilities where students may observe demonstrations and experiments. Also located in Bareis Hall are the computer center and the Heidelberg Water Quality Laboratory.

The computer center provides access to Macintosh and PC-compatible computers. All of these systems are connected to a campuswide network providing e-mail, file transfer, World Wide Web, and full access to the Internet. The high number of computers and terminals available for student use in addition to the convenience of the computer center hours are outstanding strengths of the College. Additional computer facilities are located in Brenneman Music Hall, the Pfleiderer Center for Religion and the Humanities, and the Aigler Alumni Building. Founders Hall houses a 250-seat performance theater and a rehearsal theater; an FM radio station, WHEI; television studio WHEI-TV; video taping rooms; costume rooms; a dance studio; and offices and classrooms for the Departments of Communication and Theatre Arts and the Languages.

Costs

For the academic year 2003–04, new student tuition and fees were $13,672; room and board were approximately $6275.

Financial Aid

More than 95 percent of the undergraduate student body at Heidelberg receive financial aid. College and government programs—including scholarships, grants, loans, and jobs—total about $14 million annually. Government assistance includes the Federal Pell Grant, direct loan programs, the Federal Supplemental Educational Opportunity Grant, and the Federal Work-Study Program. Heidelberg offers students who meet various academic requirements a number of grants and scholarships that are renewable if eligibility is maintained.

Faculty

Close personal interaction between students and professors is one of Heidelberg's primary strengths. Seventy-nine full-time professors serve the student body, and the student-faculty ratio is 13:1. More than 70 percent of the faculty members hold doctoral degrees in their disciplines. Heidelberg's faculty members are readily available to answer questions and meet with students outside of the classroom.

Student Government

Because students are voting members of 90 percent of the faculty committees, their concerns are heard and have an impact on academic standards, athletics, educational policies, and religious life. Heidelberg's Student Senate is made up of 25 students and a Student Affairs adviser.

Admission Requirements

Heidelberg's selective admission policy seeks to admit those students who will benefit from the educational offerings of the College and who will contribute to the shared life of the campus community. The Admission Committee considers each applicant individually to determine if the student will be able to successfully fulfill the academic responsibilities of a Heidelberg student. The applicant's high school achievement record is the single most important factor considered. Other factors considered are ACT or SAT I scores, cocurricular involvement, character, talent, and teacher recommendations.

Application and Information

Although Heidelberg follows a rolling admission policy, applicants are strongly encouraged to complete this process before January 1. Once all admission credentials are received, applicants are notified of the College's admission decision within two weeks.

For additional information, students should contact:

Office of Admission
Heidelberg College
310 East Market Street
Tiffin, Ohio 44883
Telephone: 419-448-2330
800-HEIDELBERG (toll-free)
Fax: 419-448-2334
E-mail: adminfo@heidelberg.edu
World Wide Web: http://www.heidelberg.edu

Founders Hall (1851), the oldest building on the Heidelberg campus, is one of ten listed on the National Register of Historic Places.

HESSER COLLEGE

MANCHESTER, NEW HAMPSHIRE

The College

The primary purpose of Hesser College is to provide a high-quality education that is personalized, cost-effective, and employment oriented. Hesser's innovative approach to higher education provides students with increased flexibility over traditional colleges. After two years of college, students earn an associate degree and are prepared to enter the workplace, or they can continue their studies in one of Hesser's bachelor's degree programs.

Hesser College was established in 1900 as Hesser Business College, a private, nonsectarian college. Over the years, Hesser has expanded and enriched its curriculum in keeping with its tradition of providing an affordable career education of high quality. The physical building encompasses more than fifteen different businesses, all of which create the Hesser Center of Commerce and Education. This is an unusual and beneficial partnership of business and education.

Nearly 85 percent of the students work in the afternoons, evenings, or weekends while attending Hesser College. The 890 men and women currently enrolled represent several states and more than fifteen countries. A large part of the student population are from the New England region.

Hesser offers intercollegiate sports in men's and women's basketball and volleyball, men's and women's soccer, men's baseball, and women's softball. The basketball and volleyball teams have consistently been a major power in the Northern New England Small College Conference. Students also participate in a number of intramural sports programs. Extracurricular activities are varied and include social activities, clubs, trips, and programs in the residence halls. A freshman orientation program is conducted each fall before classes begin.

The College has developed a number of learning assistance programs to help students succeed in their studies. Tutoring and special classes are provided by the faculty throughout each semester. In addition, several departments offer honors programs and special opportunities for independent study. The College also sponsors an active chapter of the national honor society, Phi Theta Kappa, which promotes scholarship and service to the College and the community.

Hesser College is fully accredited by the New England Association of Schools and Colleges. The association is the official accrediting agency for schools and colleges in the six New England states and is widely considered to hold the strictest academic standards. Students who choose Hesser are assured of a high-quality education.

Location

Hesser College is located in Manchester, New Hampshire. With a population of more than 100,000, Manchester is a medium-sized city that offers many cultural, historical, and social events. Hesser's central location provides easy access to entertainment, shopping, and a variety of part-time jobs and academic work experiences. Manchester is within 1 hour of Boston, and the mountains and major ski resorts are within 1 to 2 hours of Hesser's campus. Manchester has been called the "Gateway to Northern New England," and several major carriers serve the Manchester Airport.

Manchester was recently named by *Money* magazine as the number one small city in the Northeastern United States. In addition, Manchester was recently named one of the best cities in the United States for business. According to *U.S. News & World Report,* it is "at the hub of things" in the fast-growing high-technology and financial industries of southern New Hampshire.

Majors and Degrees

Hesser offers a wide range of associate degree programs that are intended to prepare students for high-demand careers. They include accounting; business administration; business computer applications; business science/individualized studies; communications and public relations; corrections, probation, and parole; early childhood education; graphic design; human services; interior design; law enforcement; liberal studies; marketing; medical assistant studies; medical office management; paralegal studies; physical therapist assistant studies; psychology; radio/video production and broadcasting; small-business management/entrepreneurship; and sport management.

In addition, Hesser College offers 2+2 Bachelor of Science degree programs in accounting, business administration, and criminal justice. Through this 2+2 academic model, Hesser's programs offer students great flexibility in their academic pursuits.

Academic Program

The primary goal of the curriculum is to prepare students for success in specific career areas. The general education requirements are designed to provide the skills necessary for career growth and lifelong learning. Internships, practicums, and opportunities for part-time work experience are available in all majors. An education from Hesser College provides a solid career foundation. The College's goal is quite simple: to prepare people for careers and career advancement.

Many of the Hesser College programs are for the career-minded student who wants to concentrate on the skills required to be successful in the workplace. Seventy-five percent of the courses that students take are directly related to their career choices.

Hesser College follows a traditional semester calendar.

Off-Campus Programs

The College offers opportunities for cooperative education and internships in most of its academic programs. The early childhood education program includes practicums and supervised fieldwork in the freshman and senior years, utilizing a variety of child-care facilities. In addition, the curricula of several programs incorporate short-term study tours: business program students study on a trip to Walt Disney World and criminal justice program students study on a trip to Washington, D.C. The physical therapist assistant studies program requires students to participate in at least 265 hours of clinical experience in a health-care setting under the direct supervision of a certified instructor or therapist.

Hesser College has relationships with many businesses, and internship sites have been located in the Hesser Center of Commerce and Education, in nearby downtown Manchester, and throughout the region.

Academic Facilities

The academic facilities located within the Hesser Commerce and Education Center include several networked computer labs, Mac-based graphic design labs, a medical assistant lab, a physical therapist assistant lab, and a radio/video production lab. The College library contains more than 40,000 titles. The Center for Teaching, Learning, and Assessment provides special tutoring and programs in study skills, reading, writing, math, and computer skills.

The College includes dormitories for approximately 70 percent of the 890 students. A wide range of resources are located on campus. Academic advising is coordinated through department chairpersons and the Center for Teaching, Learning and Assessment, and the size of the College allows for individual attention to the financial and career counseling needs of each student.

Costs

Part-time students are billed at the rate of $373 per credit (excluding information technology) for all majors. Full-time expenses per semester in 2002–03 were $5145 for tuition (12–16 credits) and $3400 for room and various optional meal plans.

Financial Aid

Hesser College offers financial assistance to students based on demonstrated financial need. Seventy percent of the students receive some form of aid. More than fifty scholarships are awarded each year to freshman and senior students. The College offers low-interest loans from both internal and external sources. Federal Supplemental Educational Opportunity Grants, Federal Work-Study, Federal Perkins Loans, Federal Direct Student Loans, and state scholarship programs are available to those who qualify. Awards are made on a rolling basis and are subject to availability. In order to apply for financial aid and scholarships at Hesser, students must complete the FAFSA form and a Hesser College Institutional Financial Aid Application.

Faculty

The faculty members of Hesser College consistently receive high student evaluations for their interests in each student's success and for the high quality of their teaching. The majority of the faculty members have completed programs of advanced study, and all have practical experience in business or other career fields. Faculty members participate in national and regional conferences and associations and are continually involved with program review and curriculum development. The student-faculty ratio is 18:1.

Admission Requirements

Admission to Hesser College is made by a committee of administrators and admission personnel. A high school transcript must be submitted, and international students must also submit TOEFL scores. SAT I scores are not required but may be considered in the admission decision if submitted. Transfer students are required to submit high school and college transcripts, with a minimum 2.0 grade point average for all previous college work.

It is required that applicants come to Hesser for an interview and that they submit at least one recommendation from counselors, teachers, or employers. The College operates on a rolling admissions basis, and notification is continuous.

Application and Information

Applicants must submit an application form with a $10 nonrefundable fee. Applications are reviewed on a first-come, first-served basis and normally take seven to fourteen days to be fully reviewed upon receipt of all required information.

Requests for additional information and application forms should be addressed to the following:

Director of Admissions
Hesser College
3 Sundial Avenue
Manchester, New Hampshire 03103
Telephone: 603-668-6660 Ext. 2110
800-526-9231 (toll-free)
Fax: 603-666-4722
E-mail: admissions@hesser.edu
World Wide Web: http://www.hesser.edu

Students at Hesser College.

HIGH POINT UNIVERSITY

HIGH POINT, NORTH CAROLINA

The University

High Point University is a private university related to the United Methodist Church. With more than 3,000 students, the University is large enough to guarantee high quality and diversity in programs and services, yet small enough to enable community among students, faculty members, and staff members. Approximately 2,500 students are enrolled at the High Point campus, and about 500 students are enrolled at the Madison Park campus in Winston-Salem, North Carolina. In a typical year, students come from forty-one states and thirty-four countries, making the campus a microcosm of the nation and the world, thereby creating an ideal learning environment.

The University fully recognizes its responsibility to provide the best liberal arts education possible, but faculty and staff members recognize that education, as often defined, is not sufficient. Therefore, the University intentionally seeks to develop character by encouraging personal responsibility and by inculcating values through curricular and cocurricular programs and services, including the University chapel, where services are offered each week. Attendance is voluntary.

In addition to the bachelor's degrees described below, the University offers four master's degrees: the Master of Business Administration (M.B.A.); the Master of Education (M.Ed.) in elementary education and educational leadership; the Master of Science (M.S.) in management, international management, and sports studies; and the Master of Public Administration (M.P.A.) in nonprofit organizations.

Location

Together, High Point, Greensboro, and Winston-Salem form the Golden Triad of North Carolina, a metropolitan area of approximately 1.4 million people, 85,000 of whom live within the city of High Point. Both Winston-Salem and Greensboro are 20 minutes from the campus, as is the Piedmont Triad (Greensboro-High Point) International Airport. Both Raleigh and Charlotte are 1½ hours away, the Appalachian Mountains are 2 hours away, and the Atlantic Ocean is 4 hours away.

The region is known nationally and internationally for the quality of its institutions of higher education. Within a 60-mile radius are Duke University, the University of North Carolina at Chapel Hill, and Wake Forest University, along with sixteen other colleges and universities. Obviously, such an area is replete with athletic, cultural, recreational, and social activities for young adults.

Majors and Degrees

High Point University awards the Bachelor of Arts degree in art, art education, criminal justice, elementary education, English: literature, English: media, English: writing, French, history, human relations, international studies, middle grades education, North American studies, philosophy, political science, religion, sociology: cultural studies, sociology: general studies, sociology: social work, Spanish, special education, and theater arts. The University awards the Bachelor of Science degree in accounting, athletic training, biology, business administration (accounting, economics, finance, information security and privacy, international management, management, and marketing), chemistry, chemistry: business, computer information systems, computer science, exercise science, forestry, home furnishings management, home furnishings marketing, interior design, international business, management information systems, mathematics, medical technology, physical education, psychology: general studies, psychology: industrial/organizational, psychology: mental health, recreation, and sport management. Within the liberal arts major, students can complete the requirements for admission to professional schools, including dentistry, law, medicine, pharmacy, theology, and veterinary medicine.

Academic Program

The academic program is administered through the College of Arts and Science, the School of Business, and the School of Education, which collectively offers fifty-one majors, primarily in the liberal arts. In addition, the University allows students with well-defined objectives that cannot be satisfied within the regular curriculum to design their own individualized majors. An honors program recognizes and encourages creativity and academic achievement.

The curriculum emphasizes the study of the liberal arts in the belief that there is no better way to encourage communication skills, critical thinking, and personal integrity and in the belief that in the process of acquiring these skills, students become self-learners who are equipped to succeed in life and work. Within the liberal arts framework, the University provides several professional programs, including athletic training, business administration, computer information systems, computer science, exercise science, home furnishings marketing and management, human relations (a program affiliated with American Humanics, Inc.), information security and privacy, international business, management information systems, and sport management. Cooperative baccalaureate programs are offered in environmental management, forestry, and medical technology.

The curriculum prepares students to pursue graduate programs consistent with the majors listed above and professional programs beyond the baccalaureate degree in areas that include, but are not limited to, dentistry, law, medicine, ministry, physical therapy, and sports medicine.

Through the Student Career Intern Program, juniors and seniors at High Point University are able to explore career opportunities outside the classroom. The program enables a student to assume the responsibilities of a regular employee in a local business or agency before graduating from High Point, thereby enabling the student to evaluate a career choice prior to graduation.

Students who have completed Advanced Placement courses in high school and who have achieved a score of 3, 4, or 5 on the Advanced Placement tests administered by the College Board may receive credit at High Point University. Applicants may also receive credit for university-parallel courses successfully completed prior to enrollment at High Point, including courses completed while in high school through dual enrollment or international baccalaureate programs.

Off-Campus Programs

Students may choose to study abroad for a year, a semester, or a summer through the High Point University in England program offered in cooperation with the University of Leeds or through the University's program at Oxford/Brookes. The University's affiliation with international-study programs administered by other institutions also makes it possible for students to study in Canada, France, Germany, Scotland, Spain, and Mexico. Subject to prior approval, transfer credit may be awarded for university-parallel work offered by institutions other than those with which the University has formal affiliation.

Students enrolled at High Point University may cross-register on the campus of any other member institution in the Greater Greensboro Consortium, including two state institutions and a women's college.

Academic Facilities

Smith Library, a fully electronically-integrated library system, supports fifty undergraduate majors and ten graduate programs. The Library contains over 290,000 print volumes, including more than 20,000 electronic books, and more than 20,000 electronic serials subscriptions. All electronic resources are accessible on line by students and other patrons, both on and off campus.

The Learning Assistance Center, located in the library, provides tutoring and other programs designed to facilitate learning. Although 76 percent of enrolled students own personal computers, more than 300 computers are available for student use in classrooms, laboratories, the library, the University Center, and other locations. A roaming profile enables students to save and access their personal documents from any campus PC, including their personal computers and those provided by the University. Computer laboratories in computer science and mathematics are equipped with Linux-based PCs connected to a Linux computing cluster.

The Horace S. Haworth Hall of Science provides science laboratories and modern equipment. The James H. and Jesse E. Millis Athletic and Convocation Center houses a state-of-the-art sports medicine center, along with facilities for physical education that include, but are not limited to, the Aerobic Center, an Olympic-size pool, racquetball courts, and tennis courts. The Charles E. and Pauline Lewis Hayworth Fine Arts Center includes a performance hall,the Sechrest Art Gallery, galleries for student exhibits, a laboratory for computer graphics, and studios for design, drawing, music, painting, photography, printmaking, and theater. Norton Hall, built on campus by the international furnishings industry, is a state-of-the-art facility which houses the Knabusch-Shoemaker International School of Furnishings and Design.

Costs

For 2004–05, tuition, room, board, and general fees for full-time boarding students amount to $22,480.

Financial Aid

Students who require financial assistance should complete the Free Application for Federal Student Aid (FAFSA). The FAFSA indicates how much the student and the parents/guardians of dependent students can contribute toward the cost of attending High Point University. The University subtracts that amount from the cost of attending and attempts to underwrite the difference through a financial aid package that consists of one or more of the following: scholarships, grants that do not have to be repaid, loans, and/or college work-study.

Presidential Fellowships, ranging from $6500 to full-tuition ($15,710), are awarded on a competitive basis to entering freshmen. The University awards up to fifty $4500 Presidential Scholarships to entering freshmen annually. Phi Theta Kappa Fellowships ($6500) are awarded automatically to members of Phi Theta Kappa who graduated from a two-year college with a cumulative GPA of 3.5 or higher. Students who qualify for the Phi Theta Kappa Fellowship are considered for one of two full-tuition Hallmark Fellowships ($15,710) offered annually.

Faculty

High Point University has a student-faculty ratio of 15:1 and an average class size of 22 students. More than 75 percent of faculty members have earned either the Ph.D. or another terminal degree. All members of the faculty teach classes and advise students, and faculty members routinely interact with students outside of class.

Student Government

High Point University intentionally seeks to involve students in campus life through Student Government, service on University-wide committees, and student activities, including sixteen NCAA Division I athletic teams, nine Greek organizations, and more than fifty other campus organizations. In addition, in a typical year, High Point University students provide more than 25,000 hours of voluntary service to the community of High Point.

Admission Requirements

Freshman applicants must be graduates of an accredited secondary school and must exhibit satisfactory performance in a college-preparatory curriculum of 16 units distributed as follows: English, 4; foreign language, 2; mathematics, 2; history, 1; laboratory science, 1; and electives, 6. Every freshman applicant must submit scores on the SAT I or the ACT. International applicants may submit TOEFL scores as an alternative to the SAT I or ACT; however, students who wish to play on an athletic team must take the SAT I. Campus visits and personal interviews are strongly recommended.

Application and Information

Application forms must be completed by the student and sent to the Office of Admissions, along with a nonrefundable $25 processing fee. Official transcripts (high school and college, where applicable) must be sent directly to the University by the appropriate school official. Students should request that a copy of their SAT I, ACT, or TOEFL scores be sent to the Office of Admissions at High Point University by the testing agency. High Point University operates under a rolling admission plan and accepts applications at any time. However, because enrollment is limited by available residential spaces, early application is encouraged. All requests for application materials and information should be directed to:

Office of Undergraduate Admissions
High Point University
University Station, Montlieu Avenue
High Point, North Carolina 27262-3598
Telephone: 336-841-9216
800-345-6993 (toll-free)
E-mail: admiss@highpoint.edu
World Wide Web: http://www.highpoint.edu

High Point University, located on a 77-acre campus, enrolls 3,000 students from forty-one states and thirty-four countries.

HILBERT COLLEGE

HAMBURG, NEW YORK

The College

Since its founding in 1957, Hilbert College has provided challenging academic programs and close personal attention to its students. The College is an independent, Catholic, four-year institution that grants degrees on both the baccalaureate and associate levels. There is a strong commitment to the philosophy of a liberal arts education being the cornerstone of any Hilbert graduate's success. In harmony with its Franciscan Spirit, the College provides individual counseling and support services for students whose diversified needs are best met in this small-college setting. Hilbert's campus consists of nine buildings: Bogel Hall, which is the academic building; the Francis J. and Marie McGrath Library; the Campus Center; three on-campus residence halls; one traditional-style and two apartment-style facilities; a grounds and maintenance building; the Hafner Recreation Center; and Franciscan Hall, which is the student services and administration building. Hilbert is also home to the Institute for Law and Justice, a local, regional, and national resource for law enforcement, crime prevention, and community well-being.

Hilbert College has a student body of approximately 1,050 students. There is an on-campus residential population of 135 students. All students are offered a myriad of social activities ranging from academic and student clubs to NCAA Division III athletics. Student government takes an active role in the planning and operation of most campus events. Hilbert also offers a select comprehensive Leadership Development Program as well as an Honors Program.

The College's Division III athletics program offers intercollegiate competition in men's baseball, basketball, cross-country, golf, soccer, and volleyball. Women's sports include basketball, cross-country, soccer, softball, and volleyball. Hilbert College competes as a member of the Allegheny Mountain Collegiate Conference.

Location

Hilbert College's nearly 50-acre campus is located in the town of Hamburg in western New York State on the shore of Lake Erie. The campus is approximately 15 miles south of Buffalo, a city of 350,000 people. Hilbert's proximity to Buffalo makes many cultural and recreational resources easily accessible to its students. Downtown attractions include Kleinhans Music Hall, Studio Arena Theatre, the Albright-Knox Art Gallery, the Museum of Science, and the Buffalo Zoo. The historic Shea's Theatre is also located downtown and is Buffalo's home to many concerts, operas, and Broadway shows. Niagara Falls, one of the nation's greatest natural attractions, is just a 35-minute drive from the campus. Buffalo also provides professional sports in football, hockey, lacrosse, and triple-A baseball. Hamburg also is located a short distance from several cross-country and downhill ski resorts.

Majors and Degrees

Hilbert College offers programs of study leading to a Bachelor of Arts (B.A.) degree in English, liberal studies (law and government), and psychology. The Bachelor of Science (B.S.) degree is offered in accounting, business administration, criminal justice, economic crime investigation, human services, and paralegal studies. The College also offers associate degree programs (A.A. and A.A.S.) in accounting, banking, business administration, criminal justice, human services, liberal arts, management information systems, and paralegal studies.

Academic Programs

The Bachelor of Arts and Bachelor of Science degrees are granted upon completion of 120 credit hours.

The Associate in Arts, the Associate in Applied Science, and the Associate in Science degrees are all granted upon successful completion of 60 credit hours.

Common to all programs is the completion of the Liberal Learning Core Curriculum. All students must fulfill the following graduation requirements: advanced communication skills, intercultural awareness, responsible local and global citizenship, an array of inquiry strategies, advanced research skills, the capacity for integrative learning, and a commitment to lifelong learning. The purpose of the Liberal Learning Core Curriculum is to provide students with a cumulative, holistic liberal arts education to complement and strengthen their professional training. The curriculum is designed to develop habits of critical examination, methods of critical investigation, and ethical perspectives that enable students to make sound judgments and increase their capacity for leading fuller lives. By studying the various liberal arts disciplines, students should achieve a greater awareness of their cultural and social identity while cultivating the intellectual skills and competence that allow them to perform successfully in their chosen careers.

Hilbert has developed a series of transfer articulation agreements with most two-year colleges in New York State. These agreements allow two-year college graduates to move directly into related four-year programs at Hilbert College as full juniors and with no course duplication. In addition, Hilbert is accredited by the Commission on Higher Education of the Middle States Association of Colleges and Schools. Therefore, its credits are readily transferable nationwide to other four-year colleges and universities.

Academic Facilities

Bogel Hall, the academic building, contains the Palisano Lecture Hall, faculty offices, two computer labs, a hands-on economic crime investigation computer lab, the Academic Services Center, the chapel, and most classroom space.

McGrath Library, an expansive building consisting of a two-level core housing the library collection, a seminar wing, and a conference wing, maintains a collection approaching 40,000 volumes, more than 340 periodicals, and a large selection of microforms and audio and video materials. The first floor houses the reference, index, and periodical collections. Computer workstations with the library catalog and numerous full-text databases, which enormously supplement the periodical collection, are also available on this floor. The circulating book collection begins on this level and continues in the stacks located on the second floor. The second level primarily houses the McGrath Library Law Collection in support of the paralegal studies and law and government programs on the campus. This collection ranks as one of the largest academic law collections open to the public in western New York State. The library's seminar wing has video-equipped classrooms and a legal research lab. Ample study space is available throughout the library with both private carrels and group-study tables available for student use.

Costs

For 2003–04, tuition and fees were $13,500, and room and board were $5355. The approximate cost for books and supplies is $700 and for travel and miscellaneous expenses, $1000.

Financial Aid

Ninety-two percent of the members of the current freshman class receive financial aid. Financial aid packages consist of loans, scholarships, grants, and jobs. Most awards are provided on the basis of need, as established by the Free Application for Federal Student Aid (FAFSA), and as funds are available. There are several merit-based scholarships for academic and leadership talents as well as transfer articulation and minority scholarships.

Faculty

Hilbert has a faculty of 87 men and women. Sixty-four percent of the faculty members hold doctoral or terminal degrees; 36 percent hold master's degrees. The student-faculty ratio is 14:1, with an average class size of 25.

Student Government

The largest student organization on campus is the Student Government Association (SGA). Headed by student-elected officers, this representative organization acts on the behalf of the entire student body. The SGA administers student funds to sponsor on-campus activities and events that range from intimate concerts to larger campuswide festivities. The SGA is composed of two bodies, the association and the student senate. The association comprises elected students who represent the needs of different classes, residents, and commuters. The student senate is a smaller group that consists of student government–elected officers and individual class representatives. The senate is responsible for the disbursement of funds to student-run clubs and organizations.

Admission Requirements

Hilbert College is open to men and women regardless of faith, race, age, physical handicap, or national origin. All students have an equal opportunity to pursue their educational goals through programs available at the College.

The College considers for admission to regular degree study those applicants who have been awarded a high school diploma or a New York State High School Equivalency Diploma.

Application and Information

The closing date for the receipt of applications is September 1. Admission decisions are made on a rolling basis.

For a catalog or an application, students should contact:

Office of Admissions
Hilbert College
5200 South Park Avenue
Hamburg, New York 14075
Telephone: 716-649-7900
800-649-8003 (toll-free)
E-mail: admissions@hilbert.edu
World Wide Web: http://www.hilbert.edu

Franciscan Hall, the Student Services Center.

HILLSDALE COLLEGE

HILLSDALE, MICHIGAN

The College

Hillsdale College is a private, independent, nonsectarian institution of higher learning founded in 1844 by men and women who described themselves as "grateful to God for the inestimable blessings" resulting from civil and religious liberty and as "believing that the diffusion of learning is essential to the perpetuity of those blessings." The College has maintained institutional independence since its founding by refusing to accept aid from or control by federal authorities. Far-reaching private support from a national constituency has enabled Hillsdale to continue its trusteeship of the intellectual and spiritual inheritance derived from the Judeo-Christian faith and Greco-Roman culture.

The current undergraduate enrollment is 565 men and 631 women. The College draws students from forty-eight states and thirteen countries. About forty percent come from Michigan. The entering freshman class in 2003 had an average high school grade point average of 3.63 and mean ACT and SAT I scores well above the national averages. Hillsdale students are housed in dormitories, fraternity and sorority houses, and various off-campus dwellings. Single and double rooms are available on campus; there are no coed dormitories. Each College-owned residence hall is supervised by a resident director and student staff members. All freshmen (except commuters) are required to live on campus; upperclass students seeking to live off campus must apply to the dean of men or dean of women for this privilege.

Hillsdale's athletes participate in fourteen intercollegiate varsity sports (the College belongs to the NCAA Division II and the Great Lakes Intercollegiate Athletic Conference), and a vigorous intramural program is also available. The College emphasizes the concept of the student-athlete and is proud of the national recognition won by a number of its athletes for academic achievements. Three national fraternities, three national sororities, and about forty other social, honorary, and service organizations provide Hillsdale students with an array of cocurricular opportunities. A resident drama troupe, a bagpipe and drum corps, a wind ensemble, a concert choir, a chorale, and a College-community orchestra constitute the College's performing arts organizations.

Special student services provided by the College include career planning and placement counseling, academic advising and tutoring, and a health service staffed by a physician and a resident nurse.

Location

Hillsdale College is located amidst the hills and lakes of south-central Michigan. The Indiana and Ohio turnpikes are each 30 minutes away, and the College is easily reached from such metropolitan areas as Detroit, Chicago, Cleveland, Toledo, and Indianapolis. The town of Hillsdale is a county seat with a population of 9,000. Stores, churches, restaurants, and a movie theater are all within walking distance of the campus.

Majors and Degrees

Hillsdale awards the Bachelor of Arts or Bachelor of Science degree in accounting, art, biology, chemistry, computational mathematics, economics, education, English, financial management, French, German, health and physical education, history, marketing management, mathematics, music, philosophy, physical education, physics, political science, psychology, religion, sociology, Spanish, speech, and theater. Interdisciplinary majors in American studies, Christian studies, classical studies, comparative literature, European studies, international studies in business and foreign language, and political economy are also available. Preprofessional programs are offered in dentistry, engineering, environmental sciences, forestry, journalism, law, medicine, optometry, osteopathy, pharmacy, theology, and veterinary medicine.

Hillsdale offers a 3-2 (B.A./B.S.) or 4-2 (B.A./M.S.) cooperative program in engineering science with Northwestern University and Tri-State University.

Academic Program

Hillsdale operates on a two-semester schedule, with the fall term beginning in late August and ending in mid-December and the spring term beginning in mid-January and ending in mid-May. Two 3-week summer sessions are also offered.

The College believes that a sound liberal arts education includes study in the humanities, natural sciences, and social sciences, and each student is required to complete core courses in these areas. Students are also required to declare a major by the end of their sophomore year. To graduate, they must complete at least 124 hours of course work and fulfill the requirements of at least one major field. It is not unusual for a student to complete two majors or a major and a minor. Each baccalaureate program is based on the completion of four years of study in the liberal arts. The B.A. program stresses language (and includes a foreign language requirement), literature, and the arts. The B.S. program stresses mathematics and the natural sciences. Both programs equally emphasize the social sciences.

The honors program enables exceptionally talented students to develop their intellectual potential through special honors classes, available all four years, and to participate in an honors program in the junior and senior years. Honors students are also required to write a thesis on a topic of their choosing.

The Center for Constructive Alternatives conducts four weeklong symposia during the academic year. These programs, dealing with themes that have contemporary significance and application, are of major importance in the intellectual life of the College. Each brings to the campus distinguished scholars and public figures chosen for their ability to contribute to the theme.

Off-Campus Programs

Two internship programs in Washington, D.C., place students at the ERI National Journalism Center or in congressional and government offices for a summer of work and study. Additional internships may be established in the fields of business and communication arts in consultation with the academic department concerned.

Hillsdale College is one of five American colleges affiliated with Keble College of Oxford University. This affiliation enables Hillsdale students to study abroad for a summer or a year at Oxford. Hillsdale offers a summer business program in cooperation with Regents College in London, England, and the opportunity to study subject areas ranging from ancient history to theoretical physics at the University of St. Andrews in St. Andrews, Scotland. The College also offers qualified students the opportunity to study in Seville, Spain, as well as France and Germany. Qualified individual students who wish to study in another country for a semester or a year are assisted by their faculty adviser and the registrar in planning a program that enables them to gain full credit as well as a rewarding experience. Students majoring in international studies are encouraged to participate in internships abroad.

Academic Facilities

Kresge Center for Traditional Studies contains classrooms, research facilities, language laboratories, faculty offices, and special laboratory facilities for experimental psychology. Mossey

Learning Resources Center, a library and learning center, houses more than 180,000 books and about 14,000 periodicals (both bound and microfilmed volumes), along with the Richardson Heritage Room, a special collections library for first editions. Hillsdale also participates in the general interlibrary loan program, which offers computerized access to 13 million bibliographical records (books, periodicals, and microfilm). Computer terminals for word processing and other functions, videocassette and videodisc players, record and tape players, and a large collection of recordings, audiotapes, and videotapes are available in the Mossey Center.

Strosacker Science Center has well-equipped facilities for biology, chemistry, mathematics, and physics. Special research areas and departmental libraries are also available. The recently completed, 32,000-square-foot Herbert Henry Dow Science Building provides additional classrooms, research laboratories, animal rooms, and a computer lab. Perhaps the most widely known of Hillsdale's academic facilities is the Mary Randall Preschool, a circular laboratory school in which nursery school children are taught by students specializing in early childhood education and psychology. Experts in the field have called this building "a model for the nation." The Hillsdale Academy, a K–12 private model school, provides additional opportunities for classroom observation. The indoor facilities of the Athletic Complex include a field house with a swimming pool, a six-lane indoor track, basketball courts, volleyball courts, tennis courts, and handball and racquetball courts. A prescription turf football field, ringed by an all-weather, Mondo surface, eight-lane running track, is in a lighted stadium that seats 7,000 people. Baseball and softball diamonds, one soccer field, and ten lighted tennis courts complete the outdoor facilities of the College's Athletic Complex.

The Sage Center for the Arts, which houses the departments of art, music, and theater, opened in 1992. The 47,000-square-foot facility features eight practice rooms, a 350-seat auditorium with a complete scene shop, makeup room, costume shop, and hydraulic orchestra pit that can be raised to provide additional seating for nonmusical events. The recently completed 29,000-square-foot Howard Music Building houses numerous practice rooms and studios, stately galleries, a large rehearsal hall, and a fine recital hall.

Costs

Tuition for 2003–04 was $15,750, room was $3040, board was $3260, and mandatory fees were $300. Books, supplies, and personal expenses (including travel, recreation, and clothing) are estimated at $1000 per year.

Financial Aid

Financial aid at Hillsdale is available in many forms. Academic scholarships are awarded on a competitive basis, regardless of financial need, to students who rank in the top 10 percent of their high school class and have standardized test scores in the top 10 percent according to national test norms. The priority deadline for academic scholarship consideration is January 2. Athletic scholarships are also available on a competitive basis in men's baseball, football, and golf; men's and women's basketball and track and cross-country; and women's swimming, tennis, and volleyball. To apply for aid on the basis of financial need, students are required to file Hillsdale's Confidential Family Financial Statement (CFFS) and (for Michigan residents) the Free Application for Federal Student Aid (FAFSA) in January or February of the year of prospective enrollment at Hillsdale. Grants and loans are available from the College and from state sources. Students may also earn up to $1000 per year in various campus jobs.

Faculty

The faculty consists of 90 full-time members (81 of whom have doctorates) and 40 part-time members. No classes are taught by graduate students. The size and closeness of the College community enable faculty members and students to get to know each other well in and out of the classroom. Each student has a faculty adviser who directs the program of study and provides academic and career counseling. Hillsdale's faculty is dedicated primarily to teaching and to students' personal development. Many faculty members also engage in research and scholarly writing, supported by summer and sabbatical leaves funded by the College.

Student Government

Hillsdale's student government and campus organizations offer students special opportunities to develop leadership skills that enrich their collegiate experience and their lives after graduation. The governing organization of the student body is the Student Federation, which is composed of 16 elected representatives. This group funds student organizations, sponsors all-College entertainment, and acts upon matters of concern to the student community. The Men's Council and Women's Council serve as legislative and judicial bodies within their respective domains in cooperation with members of the administration. The Leadership Workshop, which works closely with the administration, faculty, and community organizations, provides an additional forum for students to cultivate and perfect their leadership skills.

Admission Requirements

Admission is a privilege extended to students who are able to benefit by, and contribute to, the academic and social environment of the College. Important determinants for admission are intellectual curiosity, motivation, and social concern. Accordingly, grade average, test scores, class rank, strength of curriculum, extracurricular activities, interviews, self-evaluations, and recommendations from high school counselors or teachers are all reviewed carefully and are important in the evaluation process. Although some factors are necessarily more important than others, seldom is any single criterion, however important, decisive.

Transfer students must submit the standard application, including the high school record, SAT I or ACT scores, and transcripts from all colleges previously attended. Applications by transfers are evaluated similarly to nontransfers. A transfer form is also required from the dean of students of the most recent college attended.

Candidates for admission from other countries follow the customary entrance procedures. Students who come from a non-English-speaking culture must demonstrate proficiency in English by satisfactory performance on the Test of English as a Foreign Language (TOEFL) or the Michigan Test of English Proficiency or at an ESL Center.

Application and Information

Students may apply to Hillsdale College any time after the completion of the junior year of high school. A formal application includes a completed application form accompanied by a nonrefundable fee of $15 (free if submitted online) and all required credentials. Applications are accepted on a rolling basis, and applicants are usually notified of the decision of the Admissions Committee within six weeks after all necessary information has been received. Hillsdale College has been distinguished since its founding in 1844 by voluntarily adhering to a nondiscriminatory policy regarding race, religion, sex, or national or ethnic origin—long before government began regulating such matters.

All records and forms should be mailed to:

Admissions Office
Hillsdale College
Hillsdale, Michigan 49242-1298
Telephone: 517-607-2327
E-mail: admissions@hillsdale.edu
World Wide Web: http://www.hillsdale.edu

HIRAM COLLEGE

HIRAM, OHIO

The College

Founded in 1850, Hiram College cherishes its heritage as an institution of academic excellence and rare distinction. Hiram's 900 students come from twenty-six states and twenty-three countries and represent more than twenty-five different religions. SAT I and ACT scores of Hiram's entering freshmen exceed national norms: in 2003, SAT I medians were 570 (verbal) and 570 (math); the ACT composite median was 24. Between 50 and 60 percent of the College's graduates go on to graduate school or professional school within five years. The College was awarded a Phi Beta Kappa chapter in 1971.

Ninety-five percent of Hiram's students live in the eleven residence halls and eat their meals on campus. Newer College buildings are designed to complement Hiram's old, distinguished Western Reserve architecture. Student services include a health center, a fitness center, a sports medicine clinic, a career placement office, professional counseling on a wide range of personal and academic concerns, optional religious services and activities, and sports for everyone. There are honorary societies, social clubs, music and drama groups, student publications, religious groups, and student government and political and social-action groups. The campus radio station, TV station, and student publications are directed by the students themselves.

Location

Hiram's campus is in the scenic, rural Western Reserve area of northeastern Ohio. Located in Portage County, the campus is about 35 miles southeast of Cleveland. The area is served by excellent state and federal highway systems, which make the College easily accessible. Cleveland Hopkins Airport and the Canton Akron Airport are a 45-minute drive from Hiram. The campus is a day's drive or less from New England and northern East Coast cities, about a 6-hour drive from Baltimore, Chicago, and Washington, D.C., and less than 2 hours from Pittsburgh, Pennsylvania.

Majors and Degrees

Hiram College awards the Bachelor of Arts (B.A.). Areas of major concentration are: art, art history, biology, biochemistry, biomedical humanities, chemistry, classical studies, communication, computer science, economics, elementary and secondary education, English, English with a creative writing emphasis, environmental studies, French, history, integrated language arts, integrated social studies, management, mathematics, music, philosophy, physics, political science, psychobiology, psychology, religious studies, social science, sociology/anthropology, Spanish, and theater arts. Minors are available in most areas of study as well as in exercise and sport science, gender studies, Greek, international studies, Latin, and urban studies.

Preprofessional programs offer preparation for study in a wide variety of fields, including dentistry, engineering, law, medicine, physical therapy, and veterinary medicine.

Hiram also offers a cooperative, dual-degree program in engineering with Case Western Reserve University and Washington University, leading to a Bachelor of Arts degree from Hiram in a field of science or mathematics and a Bachelor of Science in engineering from the cooperating engineering school.

Academic Programs

Hiram's academic calendar, the Hiram Plan, is unique among colleges and universities. Each fifteen-week semester is divided into a twelve-week and a three-week session. During the three-week session, students take only one intensive course. The plan provides two formats for learning, which increases opportunity for small group study with faculty, study in special topics, hands-on learning through field trips and internships, and study abroad.

Hiram College's commitment to the liberal arts is manifested in a core curriculum required of all students. Required courses include the Freshman Colloquium, a small, seminar course on a special topic taught by a student's adviser; First Year Seminar, emphasizing critical thinking, effective writing, and speaking; and a sequence of interdisciplinary courses.

The course of study in most areas of major concentration is specified by the departments and divisions. Students generally take ten courses from within a department, as well as two or three courses from related or supporting departments. Alternatively, a student, with the assistance of the adviser, may develop an area of concentration that consists of related courses from different academic areas, crossing departmental lines to focus on particular needs or interests. A student may also submit a proposal for an individually designed program to the Area of Concentration Board.

Off-Campus Programs

A number of domestic and international off-campus programs and study opportunities are available. Programs in Australia, England, France, Germany, Italy, Japan, Mexico, Turkey, and other locations are conducted by the College's own teaching staff. Study-abroad programs are available to students regardless of their major discipline, and more than 40 percent of the College's graduates have participated. Hiram students may also spend a semester at the School of Social Sciences and Public Affairs of the American University in Washington, D.C. Another facet of Hiram's off-campus opportunities is study at John Cabot University, a Hiram affiliate, which is the major American university in Rome. Students may also take advantage of exchange programs with Mithibai College of the University of Bombay, India, and Kansai University of Foreign Studies in Osaka, Japan. Other opportunities are offered through the College's affiliation with the Institute for European Studies and the Institute for Asian Studies.

Internships with corporations and agencies are also available in all academic departments, and arrangements are made for students on an individual basis.

Other opportunities for off-campus study in marine science are described in the section below.

Academic Facilities

The Esther and Carl Gerstacker Science Hall opened in 2000. This state-of-the-art facility includes modern chemical laboratories specially designed for undergraduate instruction and research, plus a substantial amount of new chemical instrumentation. A $12-million addition to the Student Recreation Center is scheduled to open in August 2005. Plans for this addition include new classrooms, offices, and recreation areas. The five-level library contains nearly 180,000 volumes in open stacks and features a reference area that includes recent government documents (the library is one of only 1,400 federal depositories in the U.S.); a media center featuring a listening library, a videotape collection, and a video production room; a computer area equipped with CD-ROM and printers, with access to the Internet and other resources on the information superhighway; and an archival pavilion that houses a number of special collections relating to the history of the Western Reserve, including the papers of notable Hiram alumni James A. Garfield, twentieth president of the United States, and poet Vachel Lindsay.

Other resources include the Stephens Memorial Observatory; the Center for International Studies; the Center for Literature, Medicine, and the Health Care Professions; the Writing Center; InterVIEW™, a PC-based video conferencing and interview system; and SIGI Career Guidance System.

The computer facilities at Hiram include midrange Unix servers for administrative use as well as workstations and servers for academic use and general office work. Personal computers are available for student use in several computer labs located in the library, residence halls, and other locations throughout the campus. These computers are networked via fast Ethernet and wireless technologies to all campus buildings and offices, including the residence halls. Wireless laptop and PDA users are able to access the Internet from most campus locations. Hiram's connection to the Internet consists of a high-capacity, fractional DS3 line (12 megabits per second of bandwidth). The College is a member of the Internet2 initiative, which provides even greater network capacity among member academic institutions for applications such as real-time video conferencing.

Northwoods Field Station in upper Michigan, a day's drive from Hiram, offers an additional facility for field trips, summer course work, and research activities. Many independent and/or team research projects involving students and faculty members from a variety of disciplines take place at the Field Station and on campus.

Students interested in marine science have opportunities for advanced work at Shoals Marine Laboratory off the coast of New Hampshire and at the Gulf Coast Research Laboratory in Mississippi. The College's affiliations with these facilities provide students with field experience in Hiram courses and the opportunity to enroll in any of more than twenty specialized summer courses.

Costs

Hiram has instituted a new Tuition Guarantee program for incoming students beginning in fall 2004. Costs for 2004–05 are $21,970 for tuition and $7525 for room and board. There is also a general fee of $625.

Financial Aid

More than 80 percent of Hiram's students receive financial aid based on need. All financial aid awards are made on a one-year basis, and each year a new Free Application for Federal Student Aid (FAFSA) must be submitted to determine eligibility. Most financial aid at Hiram is a combination of grant-in-aid, scholarships, and work-study. Scholarships awarded on the basis of merit are also available and range from $3000 to full tuition per year. Aid includes Federal Pell Grants, Federal Supplemental Educational Opportunity Grants, Federal Perkins Loans, Federal Stafford Student Loans, state grants, Federal Work-Study awards, and veterans' benefits. Campus employment is available regardless of aid eligibility.

Faculty

Ninety-five percent of Hiram's faculty members hold earned doctorates or the appropriate terminal degree. The student-faculty ratio is 11:1. The ideal of a "community of scholars" thrives at Hiram, where students engage in research side by side with their professors, enjoy extracurricular activities with their teachers, and reach out with the faculty to serve the community. Faculty concern and guidance begin even before the formal opening of the academic year. One week prior to opening, faculty members work with their advisees, groups of about 15 freshmen, as part of the first-year orientation program. This one-week program, the New Student Institute, is followed by a semester-long seminar in which the freshmen continue to meet as a group. Seminar topics introduce students to scholarship in the liberal arts tradition. Approximately twenty seminars are offered each year.

Student Government

The student governing body, or Student Senate, composed in part of members elected from the academic departments and residence halls, is very active at Hiram. The Senate administers a $150,000 student activities budget and is involved in almost all aspects of college policymaking and governance. It holds seats with faculty, staff, and administrators on most College committees, the College Executive Committee, and the Student Life Subcommittee of Hiram's Board of Trustees. The Kennedy Center Programming Board, an arm of the student government, plans recreational and cultural activities for the campus community.

Admission Requirements

Admission to Hiram College is competitive. The admission process attempts to bring to Hiram students who have the ability and desire to benefit from the College's educational programs. Candidates should have pursued a strong secondary school program of college preparation in the humanities, sciences, and social sciences. All applicants are required to submit SAT I or ACT scores.

Application and Information

Application materials include the completed application form; a secondary school report, which must be completed and returned to Hiram directly by the high school guidance counselor; the results of the SAT I or ACT; and an essay. Teacher recommendations are also required. Hiram employs a rolling admission plan, but for maximum scholarship consideration, applications should be submitted by February 1. An early decision option is also available. Applicants are encouraged to visit the campus. The Office of Admission, located in Teachout-Price Hall, is open year-round for interviews from 9 a.m. to 4 p.m. on weekdays and from 9 a.m. to noon on most Saturdays.

Prospective students should address questions to:

Director of Admission
Hiram College
P.O. Box 96
Hiram, Ohio 44234
Telephone: 330-569-5169
800-362-5280 (toll-free)
E-mail: admission@hiram.edu
World Wide Web: http://www.hiram.edu

Esther and Carl Gerstacker Science Hall.

HOBART AND WILLIAM SMITH COLLEGES

GENEVA, NEW YORK

The Colleges

Hobart and William Smith are independent, coordinate liberal arts colleges in Geneva, New York. Hobart College for men was founded in 1822; William Smith College for women, in 1908. The two Colleges have the same faculty; men and women attend all classes together and share one campus. Each College, however, awards its own degrees, has its own dean's office, and maintains its own student government and athletic programs. More than forty residential options include both coeducational and single-sex housing, small houses, cooperatives, and theme houses.

Location

Geneva, New York, a city of 15,000 people, is located on the northern shore of Seneca Lake, the largest of the scenic Finger Lakes. Rochester, Syracuse, and Ithaca are all less than an hour's drive. Twenty-seven other colleges and universities are located in the Finger Lakes area.

Majors and Degrees

Hobart and William Smith Colleges offer Bachelor of Arts and Bachelor of Science degrees. Programs leading to provisional certification in elementary, secondary, and special education are offered. Departmental majors include anthropology, art (history and studio), biology, chemistry, classics, comparative literature, computer science, dance, economics, English, French, geoscience, history, international relations, mathematics, modern languages, music, philosophy, physics, political science, religious studies, sociology, and Spanish. Interdisciplinary and individualized majors have been developed in Africana studies; American studies; architectural studies; arts and education; Asian studies; critical social studies dialogues; environmental studies; European studies; Latin American studies; lesbian, gay, and bisexual studies; media and society; public policy studies; Russian area studies; urban studies; and women's studies.

The Colleges offer dual-degree programs in engineering in cooperation with Columbia University, Dartmouth College, Rensselaer Polytechnic Institute, and the University of Rochester. A 4-1 M.B.A. program is offered in conjunction with Clarkson University and the Rochester Institute of Technology. In addition, the Colleges offer a 3-4 degree in architecture with Washington University in Saint Louis and a five-year M.A.T. program is offered. The Blackwell Medical Scholars program, in cooperation with SUNY Upstate Medical University College of Medicine at Syracuse, offers students who meet the standards of the program a guaranteed seat in medical school.

Academic Program

At the heart of a Hobart and William Smith education is the requirement that each student complete a major and a minor or two majors, one of which must be disciplinary and the other interdisciplinary. The first option gives a student depth of knowledge; the latter gives breadth by reaching across traditional disciplines. Each student must also address the Colleges' educational goals and objectives, which represent an understanding of the skills, areas of knowledge, and qualities of mind and character that identify a liberally educated man or woman. Students must demonstrate the following abilities: critical reading and listening; effective speaking and writing; skills for critical thinking and argumentation; experience with scientific inquiry; quantitative reasoning; an appreciation of artistic expression based in experience; an intellectually grounded understanding of race, gender, and class; critical knowledge of the multiplicity of world cultures; and an intellectually grounded foundation for ethical judgment and action.

The academic year is divided into two 14-week semesters. Students normally take four courses each semester.

Off-Campus Programs

There are a number of opportunities for off-campus study. Hobart and William Smith offer terms abroad on six continents, with programs in Australia, Brazil, Central Europe, China, Denmark, the Dominican Republic, Ecuador, England, France, Germany, India, Ireland, Israel, Italy, Japan, Korea, New Zealand, Peru, Senegal, Spain, Switzerland, Taiwan, and Vietnam. Domestic programs are also offered in Boston, Los Angeles, New York, and Washington, D.C. Many off-campus programs include internships. Hobart and William Smith participate in cooperative programs in architecture and engineering and in a 4-1 M.B.A. program.

Academic Facilities

Among the major academic and administrative buildings on the campus is the Warren Hunting Smith Library. The library contains more than 370,770 volumes, 1,153 periodicals, and 77,258 microform titles as well as classrooms, study areas, and audiovisual facilities. As a member of the Rochester Regional Resources Library Council, the library provides students with access to holdings in excess of 5 million volumes in other library collections through the interlibrary loan system. Included among the Colleges' academic facilities are three of the newest buildings on campus: The Melly Academic Center, which greatly enhances the Colleges' ability to adapt and apply emerging technology; Rosenberg Hall, described as "one of the best-designed undergraduate science teaching/learning, research facilities"; and the Colleges' newest academic building, Stern Hall, housing the departments of economics, anthropology, sociology, political science, and Asian studies. The Colleges also own a 110-acre research preserve and maintain a 65-foot research vessel that is used for studies on Seneca Lake.

Costs

For 2003–04, tuition is $28,400, and room and board total $7588. Total costs of $36,536 include $548 in student fees.

Financial Aid

Nearly 70 percent of Hobart and William Smith students receive financial aid. Hobart and William Smith Colleges' Scholarships, Federal Pell Grants, Federal Supplemental Educational Opportunity Grants, Federal Perkins Loans, Federal Work-Study Program awards, loans through the Federal Family Education Loan programs, and part-time employment are the most frequent sources of financial aid. New York State residents may be eligible for the New York State Tuition Assistance Program.

To determine financial need, the Colleges rely on an evaluation of the Free Application for Federal Student Aid (FAFSA) and the College Scholarship Service's Financial Aid PROFILE. Both forms should be filed before February 15. Financial aid awards are adjusted annually to meet changing needs.

Faculty

The full-time teaching faculty numbers 169 members, of whom more than 95 percent hold Ph.D. degrees. The student-faculty ratio is 11:1.

Student Government

There are two student governments at Hobart and William Smith. All Hobart students are members of the Hobart Student Government. All William Smith students are members of the William Smith Congress. The students each maintain legislative, judicial, and committee functions that provide for student self-determination at the Colleges. The student governments are also responsible for appropriating student financial resources to support the numerous cultural and social activities on campus.

Admission Requirements

Admission to the Colleges is based on demonstrated potential to undertake college-level work and to contribute to life on campus. The Committee on Admission is most interested in students with comprehensive high school programs. Applicants are expected to have had a minimum of 4 years of English, 2 years of algebra, 1 year of plane geometry, 3 years of science (2 laboratory), and 3 years of a modern or classical language. Other units could come from social studies and from additional work in mathematics, science, literature, and languages. Two personal recommendations and scores on either the SAT I or the ACT examination are required. Candidates submitting scores on the SAT I are encouraged to submit the results of any SAT II Subject Tests. Campus tours and personal interviews are available throughout the year and may be arranged by contacting the appropriate admissions office.

Application and Information

Application should be made early in the senior year of high school and not later than February 1. A nonrefundable $45 fee must accompany each application. A campus visit, which may include an interview, is strongly recommended. First-year candidates are notified of their application results in late March and must respond by the Candidates Reply Date of May 1. Two early decision plans are offered to students who name Hobart or William Smith as their first-choice college. Under these plans, students must apply before November 15 of their senior year in high school and are notified of the admission decision by December 15; students applying before January 1 are notified by February 1. The Colleges also offer an early admission plan to selected high school juniors as well as a deferred entrance plan, under which students may delay the start of their college education for up to two years.

For more information, students should contact:

Mara O'Laughlin
Director of Admissions
Hobart and William Smith Colleges
629 South Main Street
Geneva, New York 14456
Telephone: 800-245-0100 (toll-free)
E-mail: admissions@hws.edu

Coxe Hall, on the campus of Hobart and William Smith Colleges.

HOFSTRA UNIVERSITY

HEMPSTEAD, NEW YORK

The University

Hofstra University is an independent, dynamic, private University offering more than 130 undergraduate and 140 graduate programs in liberal arts and sciences, business, communications, education and allied human services, law, and honors studies. With a student-faculty ratio of 14:1, professors teach small classes that emphasize interaction, critical thinking, and development of judgment. At Hofstra, students have the resources they need—high-speed, readily available access to the Internet, excellent library resources, and state-of-the-art classrooms and learning and laboratory facilities. With a diverse mix of students, Hofstra University's vibrant campus hosts a wide selection of cultural, social, and recreational activities, providing students with the full college experience.

Undergraduate students attending Hofstra come from forty-five states and sixty-one countries. The freshman class numbers almost 1,900. The total enrollment at Hofstra is approximately 13,400; there are almost 8,400 full-time undergraduates and 1,000 part-time undergraduates. Major University divisions are the Hofstra College of Liberal Arts and Sciences, the School of Communication, the Zarb School of Business, the School of Education and Allied Human Services, the Honors College, New College, the School of Law, the School for University Studies, the Saturday College, and the University College for Continuing Education. Residential facilities accommodate almost 4,200 students in modern on-campus residence halls. As a result of the Program for the Higher Education of the Disabled, Hofstra is 100 percent accessible to persons with disabilities. Necessary services are provided for wheelchair-bound and other disabled students who meet all academic requirements for admission.

With NCAA Division I athletic programs, Hofstra has a 15,000-seat stadium, a 5,000-seat arena, a 1,600-seat field turf soccer stadium, a physical fitness center, a swim center with an Olympic-size swimming pool and high-dive area, a softball stadium, a recreation center offering a multipurpose gymnasium, an indoor track, a fully equipped weight room, spacious locker rooms, a lounge area, cardio area, and mirrored aerobics/martial arts room. There are also extensive recreational and intramural sports available.

Location

A nationally accredited arboretum, Hofstra's campus covers 240 acres and is situated 25 miles east of New York City. The surrounding Long Island area offers recreation of all kinds and includes boating facilities, beaches, golf courses, and theaters. New York City is readily accessible by car or railroad.

Majors and Degrees

The Bachelor of Arts (B.A.) is awarded in adolescence education (dual enrollment required), Africana studies, American studies, anthropology, art education, art history, Asian studies, audio/radio, biology, broadcast journalism, chemistry, classics, comparative literature, computer science, computer science and mathematics, creative studies, dance, drama, early childhood education (dual enrollment required), economics, elementary bilingual education, elementary education (dual enrollment required), engineering science, English, film studies and production, fine arts, French, geography, geology, German, Hebrew, history, humanities, Ibero-American studies, interdisciplinary studies, Italian, Jewish studies, labor studies, Latin American and Caribbean studies, liberal arts, mass media studies, mathematics, music, music education, natural science, philosophy, physics, political science, psychology, public relations, Russian, social science, sociology, Spanish, speech communication and rhetorical studies, speech communication and education, speech-language hearing sciences, University Without Walls, and video/television. The Bachelor of Business Administration (B.B.A.) is awarded in accounting, business, business computer information systems, business education, entrepreneurship, finance, international business, legal studies in business, management, and marketing. The Bachelor of Science (B.S.) is offered in applied physics, athletic training, biochemistry, biology, chemistry, community health, computer engineering, computer science, computer science and mathematics, economics, electrical engineering, environmental resources, exercise specialist studies, fine arts, geology, health education, industrial engineering, mathematics, mechanical engineering, music, physician assistant studies, professional studies (Saturday College), school health education, University Without Walls, video/television, video/television and business, and video/television and film. The Bachelor of Science in Education (B.S.Ed.) is offered with specializations in fine arts, music, and physical education. The Bachelor of Engineering (B.E.) is offered in engineering science with specializations in biomedical engineering, civil engineering, and environmental engineering. The Bachelor of Fine Arts (B.F.A.) is awarded in theater arts.

Academic Programs

The requirement for the B.A. degree is 124 semester hours, of which 94 must be in liberal arts and 30 in free electives. Successful completion of at least 124 semester hours with a grade point average of 2.0 or better is required for graduation. For the major, each academic department defines the special pattern of required and suggested study that suits its discipline. Beyond this major requirement, seven general requirements in humanities, natural sciences and mathematics/computer science, social sciences, English, cross-cultural studies, interdisciplinary studies, and foreign languages must be fulfilled. A candidate for graduation with the degree of B.B.A. must successfully complete at least 128 semester hours with a grade point average of 2.0 or better, completing at least 58 hours in liberal arts subjects (humanities, mathematics, natural sciences, cross-cultural, interdisciplinary studies, English, and social sciences), 6 hours of general education, 40 hours in general business courses (accounting, BCIS, business law, finance, general business, international business, management, and marketing), and all major and additional requirements as listed under the department of specialization. Each of the scientific-technical programs leading to the B.S. degree requires 124 to 137 semester hours, of which approximately half must be in liberal arts courses exclusive of those offered by the academic department of major specialization.

The School of Education and Allied Human Services is a professional school to which undergraduate students are admitted only after they have established a broad liberal arts foundation. All undergraduate candidates for enrollment in the elementary education and adolescence education programs must have an overall grade point average of at least 2.75 at the time of enrollment in the School of Education and must complete a dual-major B.A. program with majors in elementary or adolescence education and a liberal arts area.

Founded in 1959, New College aims to provide multidisciplinary programs to fulfill the academic needs and interests of students within the traditions of the liberal arts. Emphasizing small, faculty-offered classes and independent study and off-campus education, New College has elective programs in the humanities, creative studies, social sciences, natural sciences, and interdisciplinary studies. Within this context of area studies, students may also participate in programs for preprofessional study and, through a coordination of resources from all area studies, programs emphasizing human services. To graduate from New College, a student must successfully complete 120 credits in a manner consistent with general graduation requirements and those contained within an area of study.

Hofstra University Honors College (HUHC) provides a rich academic and social experience for students who show both the potential and the desire to excel. HUHC takes full advantage of one of Hofstra University's most outstanding qualities—the wealth of opportunities associated with a small college in a large university. Honors students can elect to study in any of the University's more than 130 undergraduate programs; honors students are involved in all fields of advanced study, including pre–health professions, prelaw, engineering, business, communications and media arts, humanities, and social sciences.

College credit may be granted to qualified students passing such external examinations as the College Board Advanced Placement tests, the CLEP tests, and the New York State College Proficiency Examination. A maximum of 30 credits may be granted for external credit by examination.

A preprofessional adviser provides a direct link between students and medical, dental, and law schools.

Off-Campus Programs

Hofstra sponsors study-abroad programs during various sessions in such places as China, England, France, Germany, Italy, South Korea, the Netherlands, Spain, Jamaica, the West Indies, Singapore, Belgium, Australia, Austria, Ukraine, Russia, Taiwan, and Japan. Students wishing to pursue such study should consult the Study Abroad Office and may wish to also consult with the Advisement Office. Other overseas courses are organized by faculty members as part of credit-bearing courses. Recent courses have been held in Mexico and Egypt; similar courses are being planned for India and China.

Academic Facilities

Hofstra's fully computerized library has seating for almost 950 students and contains more than 1.6 million volumes and volume equivalents as well as 128 online databases providing access to 17,000 full-text journals. The library also has special units for periodicals, reserve books, documents, curriculum materials, special collections, and microfilm. Hofstra University's Student Computing Services provides students with a multitude of resources and learning opportunities. The Hofstra computer network provides individual accounts for all students for Internet, e-mail, and about 150 networked software programs. Almost 1,500 PC, Macintosh, and UNIX workstations are available to students in the various labs and classrooms on campus. The labs are staffed, and one computer lab is open 24 hours a day, seven days a week. All campus workstations have high-speed Internet access. All resident students are provided with Internet and e-mail access from their dorm rooms. The Language Laboratory has modern tape-recording and playback facilities for perfecting foreign language skills. Other facilities include an art gallery, museum, arboretum, bird sanctuary, writing center, career center, cultural center, language lab, technology lab, seven theaters, dance studios and performing arts classrooms, a rooftop observatory with powerful telescopes, and several computer labs for student use. The state-of-the-art facilities in Hofstra's School of Communication house a 24-hour student-operated radio station, one of the largest noncommercial broadcast facilities in the Northeast; audio production studios; a film/video screening room; and film editing rooms. The innovative new School of Education and Allied Health Services building is a completely wireless environment featuring assessment centers for child observation and mock counseling and a child-care institute.

Costs

Tuition per semester (12–17 credits) was $8705 for new students in 2003–04. A University fee of $392 per semester covered certain noninstructional University services. Tuition and fees totaled about $18,412 per college year; room and board averaged $8700. Off-campus housing is also available. New College tuition was $500 more per semester for 12 to 20 credits.

Financial Aid

Hofstra University awards both merit-based and need-based awards to incoming students. Seventy-six percent of full-time undergraduates receive aid. The average award for new freshmen is $10,980, and almost 1,000 freshmen receive merit-based scholarships from the University. A package of assistance may include grants, loans, or work-study programs. Hofstra encourages all students to apply for financial assistance using the FAFSA. Priority consideration for assistance is given to those students who file the FAFSA by February 15.

Faculty

Hofstra has 1,325 faculty members, including 524 full-time members; 90 percent of the full-time faculty members hold the highest degree in their field. The faculty consists of exceptionally talented men and women who are dedicated to excellence in teaching as well as scholarship and research. The faculty members, many of whom are nationally known in their disciplines, make it a point to be accessible to their students outside the classroom. The student-faculty ratio is 14:1. The average class size is 22. All classes are taught by faculty members; no courses are taught by graduate assistants.

Student Government

The chief instrument of government is the Student Government Association, which supervises and coordinates all student activities and serves as a liaison with the faculty and administration. The Student Government Association sends representatives to the committees of the University Senate. The Judiciary Board has responsibility for promoting justice in the conduct of student affairs.

Admission Requirements

Hofstra is a selective institution that seeks to enroll those students who demonstrate the academic ability, intellectual curiosity, and motivation to succeed and to contribute to the campus community. Typical applicants rank in the top third of their graduating class and present 16 academic units, including 4 of English, 3 of history and social studies, 2 of foreign language, 3 of mathematics, and 3 of science. Prospective engineering majors need at least 4 years of mathematics, 1 year of chemistry, and 1 year of physics. Campus visits are strongly recommended for applicants. Hofstra accepts applications from freshmen, transfers, and international students.

The University has an early action plan for students whose first choice is Hofstra. The completed application must be submitted by November 15. Early admission may be granted, on completion of three years of secondary school, to students with extraordinary maturity and promise. A personal interview is required for early admission. Transfer applicants are evaluated on an individualized basis, with admission decisions based on the quality of the student's academic record. Emphasis is placed on the most recent college course work completed. Transfer credit is granted for all appropriate courses completed with a grade of C– or better.

Freshman applicants must submit the application, a $40 application fee, their high school transcript, SAT or ACT scores, and a guidance counselor's recommendation. Transfer students must submit an application, the application fee, high school and college transcripts, and test scores (if fewer than 24 semester hours were attempted at the previous college). Hofstra accepts applications via mail or online and participates in the Common Application.

Application and Information

Peter Farrell, Dean of Admissions
Hofstra University
Hempstead, New York 11549
Telephone: 516-463-6700
800-HOFSTRA (toll-free)
Fax: 516-463-5100
World Wide Web: http://www.hofstra.edu

HOLLINS UNIVERSITY

ROANOKE, VIRGINIA

The University

Hollins University was founded in 1842 as Virginia's first chartered women's college. Today, Hollins is an independent arts and sciences university that enrolls approximately 1,100 students in its undergraduate programs for women and its coed graduate programs. Hollins is proud of its creative writing program, career internships, small class size, and study-abroad opportunities. Hollins prepares its students for career excellence in the social sciences, sciences, humanities, fine arts, and business. In addition to the Bachelor of Arts degree in twenty-nine major fields, Hollins awards a Master of Arts degree in children's literature, liberal studies, screenwriting and film studies, and teaching. In 2003–04, Hollins converted its one-year master's program in creative writing into a two-year Master of Fine Arts degree program. Its coeducational graduate creative writing program has long been acknowledged as one of the best of its size in the country. A 9:1 student-faculty ratio enables students to work closely with their professors both inside and outside the classroom.

Hollins structures the academic year to give students the month of January to focus on an internship, innovative course, senior thesis, independent study, or travel/study abroad.

Hollins' internship program gives students a head start on their careers while they earn academic credit. Eighty-two percent of Hollins students do at least one internship before graduation. Students have interned at the New York Stock Exchange; CNBC in London; Centers for Disease Control; ABC News; National Geographic Society; Time, Inc.; The *London Times*; National Zoological Park; the Metropolitan Museum of Art; and the Peace Corps, to name a few locations.

Situated on a 475-acre campus in the Shenandoah Valley of the Blue Ridge Mountains, Hollins is a quiet campus for the serious student looking to broaden her mind through a rigorous academic program. Students come to Hollins from forty-seven states and ten countries and bring with them cultural and ethnic diversity. Women returning to college can earn their bachelor's degrees in the Horizon Program.

Because approximately 89 percent of Hollins women live on campus in dormitories, language houses, or University apartments, a large family of friends develops in the first year and replaces the need for sororities. For those interested in group activities, there are more than thirty-five clubs and organizations, including a multicultural club, Black Student Alliance, a literary society, and political, environmental, women's, and volunteer organizations. Each year, many students volunteer in social service agencies locally and internationally, including a Hollins-directed Jamaica service project. The $14-million Wyndham Robertson Library features state-of-the-art technology and is a National Literary Landmark. The well-equipped athletic complex enables Hollins to compete and train its athletes effectively for NCAA Division III competition in basketball, cross country, field hockey, golf, lacrosse, riding, soccer, swimming, tennis, and volleyball. Hollins' strong riding program offers top facilities, including stables where collegiate riders may board their horses. The academic program is enriched by guest lectures, dance and theater productions, and the annual Literary Festival.

Location

Hollins is located on the outskirts of Roanoke, a cosmopolitan center with a population of approximately 225,000. Roanoke has its own opera, ballet, and orchestra. Mill Mountain Theatre, the Science Museum, and the Center in the Square cultural center provide entertainment for the area. The historic downtown market, with fresh flower and fruit stands and specialty shops, is a favorite spot on the weekends. Hollins is a 3½-hour drive from both Washington, D.C., and Richmond, 5 hours from Virginia Beach, and within easy driving distance of more than a dozen other colleges. The Roanoke Regional Airport is a 10-minute drive from campus. The campus has been described as "achingly picturesque." The Front Quadrangle is listed on the National Register of Historic Places. The Blue Ridge Mountains are minutes from campus and ideal for hiking the Appalachian Trail, camping, caving, and skiing.

Majors and Degrees

Hollins grants the Bachelor of Arts degree in art history, biology, business, chemistry, classical studies, communication studies, computational sciences, computer science, dance, economics, English, English and creative writing, film and photography, French, German, history, interdisciplinary studies, international studies, mathematics, music, philosophy, physics, political science, psychology, religious studies, sociology, Spanish, studio art, theater, and women's studies. Minors are offered in most major areas, and preprofessional programs are offered in education, law, medicine, and veterinary science. The Rubin Writing Semester offers women from other colleges and universities an opportunity to become visiting student writers.

Hollins has five- and six-year dual-degree programs in engineering with Washington University. Hollins also has an agreement with Monterey Institute of International Studies that streamlines entry in their M.B.A, M.P.A., translation and interpretation, and policy studies programs.

Academic Program

Candidates for the Bachelor of Arts degree normally follow a four-year program. They are required to complete 128 credits of academic work and 16 January Short Term credits. First-year students are required to take a seminar on campus during Short Term. Students may spend subsequent Short Terms pursuing career internships, independent study, abroad experiences, or service projects. Instead of a standard general education program, Hollins has ESP: Education through Skills and Perspectives. Students choose from a wide variety of classes that reinforce the basics of a liberal arts education. In addition, two regular terms of physical education or varsity sport participation are required. Students must choose a major by the end of their sophomore year and complete a minimum of 32 credits in the major field prior to graduation. Each first-year student must meet a writing requirement. Hollins grants 4 academic credits for Advanced Placement examination scores of 4 or 5 and in some cases for a score of 3. Hollins grants 8 academic credits for International Baccalaureate scores between 5 and 7 and up to 32 credits for an I.B. diploma with a score of 30 or higher.

Off-Campus Programs

In 1955, Hollins was one of the nation's first colleges to establish a program that enabled students to study overseas. For semester or full-year study, Hollins has its own programs in England and France and affiliated programs in Cuba, Ghana, Greece, Ireland, Italy, Japan, Mexico, and Spain as well as with the School for Field Studies. Fifty-six percent of Hollins students have an international learning experience before graduation. Domestic exchange programs are possible with members of the six-college exchange.

Academic Facilities

The Wyndham Robertson Library, which opened in 1999, has a collection of more than 250,000 titles. A fully equipped media center houses an extensive collection of recorded music and videotapes and provides a wide variety of recording and viewing equipment. The Robertson Library shares a Web-based library automation system with nearby Roanoke College. An active interlibrary loan/document delivery system ensures access to materials off site. Every seat in the library has its own network connection for easy access to the Internet. The library offers extensive media facilities, including a screening room, television studio and control room, composition and editing room with both digital and analog equipment, and viewing and listening booths.

More than 100 computers are available for student use, many 24 hours a day. The University's computer labs run Windows XP connecting to Windows 2003 servers and some Mac OSX servers. All student rooms and most classrooms have network (gig)/Internet (T3) access. Wireless connections are available in various areas on campus.

The Dana Science Building houses accessible labs and research facilities for computerized recording and analysis of physiological and behavioral data, plant and animal tissue culture, photomicroscopy and electron microscopy, biochemistry and molecular biology, chromatography, spectrophotometry, electrochemistry, gas kinetics, centrifugation, and EEG and biofeedback equipment.

The new Richard Wetherill Visual Arts Center, opening in fall 2004, will house the Eleanor D. Wilson Museum, which already has been named a Museum Partner by the Virginia Museum of Fine Arts (VMFA), a designation that helps bring world-class exhibitions and other arts programming to the campus.

Hollins also has a career development center, art gallery, writing center, theater, dance studio, and health and counseling center.

Costs

The 2004–05 costs are $21,200 for tuition and $7700 for room and board, which includes telephone, cable television, and computer network connections for each student's room. The Student Government Association fee is $275 and the student technology support fee is $200. The University estimates a budget of $600 for books and $850 for personal expenses, excluding travel costs.

Financial Aid

Financial aid is awarded on the basis of both academic merit and need. Sixty percent receive need-based aid in the form of grants, merit scholarships, low-interest loans, and campus jobs. The average award in 2003 was $17,513. The types of scholarships and grants available to undergraduates are Federal Pell Grants, Federal Supplemental Educational Opportunity Grants (FSEOG), state grants, University scholarships and grants, private scholarships and grants, academic merit scholarships, and aid for undergraduate students who are members of a minority group. Federal Perkins Loans, Federal PLUS, and Federal Stafford Student Loans are also available. Tuition Plan Inc., Knight Tuition Plans, and guaranteed tuition insurance ease tuition payments. A financial aid form should be filed with the financial aid office by February 15. Notification of awards is on a rolling basis.

Faculty

Faculty members are committed to teaching and are dedicated to their students. Although scholarly research and writing is emphasized, primary attention is placed on education. Currently, there are 74 full-time and 33 part-time faculty members, of whom 57 percent are women; 97 percent of the full-time faculty members hold the doctoral or corresponding terminal degree in their fields. With a student-faculty ratio of 9:1, students have considerable opportunity for personal attention. No courses are taught by graduate assistants.

Student Government

Each year, students sign the honor code, pledging not to lie, cheat, or steal. Hollins is thereby able to conduct daily operations with a great deal of trust. Final exams are freely scheduled and administered by students under the Independent Exam System. The campus judicial system is run by the students. Students who are elected to the Student Government Association have the authority to administer all student-related activities. Weekly Senate meetings are open to the entire campus. Students are represented on policymaking faculty committees and the Board of Trustees.

Admission Requirements

To be considered for admission, a student must have completed a minimum of 16 secondary school units in English, mathematics, science, social studies, and foreign language. All students must take the SAT I or the ACT. In addition to standardized test scores, the Admissions Committee takes into account an applicant's secondary school record, class rank, essay, recommendation, and personal interview. Transfer students are accepted in both semesters. International applicants can submit TOEFL scores in place of the SAT I or ACT.

At Hollins, the application process is very personal. The admissions officers go to great lengths to ensure that Hollins and the applicant are a good match.

Application and Information

Hollins has a formal early decision plan. The early decision application deadline is December 1; the deadline is February 15 for regular admission. Notification of admission is on a rolling basis beginning December 15 for early decision candidates and late January for regular admission candidates. The application fee is $35. A $400 tuition deposit must be made by May 1. For more information, students should contact:

Office of Admissions
Hollins University
P.O. Box 9707
Roanoke, Virginia 24020
Telephone: 540-362-6401
800-456-9595 (toll-free)
E-mail: huadm@hollins.edu
World Wide Web: http://www.hollins.edu

A view of part of Hollins' historic Front Quadrangle.

HOPE COLLEGE

HOLLAND, MICHIGAN

The College

Founded in 1862, Hope College has always promoted, in a liberal arts setting, the dual concept of preparation for life and vocation. The demanding academic program is supported by an accepting Christian campus community. Students from all walks of life are welcomed, respected, and given freedom to grow in this vibrant environment. Preparation for a career and for life in general involves both classroom and extracurricular activities. Hope sponsors seven local fraternities and six local sororities. Other activities include student publications, musical groups, and political organizations. Students manage an FM radio station, and their cable TV shows are broadcast weekly to the Holland community. There are four major theater productions each year as well as a film series, a Great Performance Series, and lectures by outstanding speakers. Many Christian activities broaden the range of student involvement, including Chaplain's Office Ministries, Fellowship of Christian Athletes, Intervarsity Christian Fellowship, and similar organizations. Voluntary chapel is offered three weekdays and Sunday, and is well attended. Intercollegiate sports include baseball, basketball, cross-country, football, golf, soccer, swimming, tennis, and track for men and basketball, cross-country, golf, soccer, softball, swimming, tennis, track, and volleyball for women. Club sports include lacrosse, ice hockey, sailing, men's volleyball, and Ultimate Frisbee. An extensive program of intramural sports is also maintained. An excellent health and recreation facility is available for student use. As Hope is a residential college, 75 percent of the students reside on campus. The College has eleven residence halls, with capacity ranging from 40 to 300 students. Styles include corridor, cluster suite, coed, and single-sex residence halls. In addition, upperclass students have the option of living in seven apartment buildings or fifty-five cottages, which are houses on or near campus that have been refurbished to accommodate students. The services of a well-developed Career Services Center are available to students and alumni for help with everything from assessing interests to arranging job interviews. The current enrollment is 3,035; 4 percent are part-time students. The student body represents thirty-six states and forty-two countries. Approximately 70 percent of the College's graduates become candidates for higher degrees within five years.

Location

Hope College's 45-acre wooded campus is in a residential area two blocks from the central business district of Holland, Michigan, a community that was founded by Dutch settlers and now has a population of 35,000 within city limits and a total area population of 100,000. The town is only a 30-minute drive from Grand Rapids and a 3-hour drive from Chicago and Detroit. An 85-acre biological field station is located on the shores of Lake Michigan, 5 miles from campus. Holland has long been known as a summer resort area, but it is also a fine spot for winter sports. Excellent relations exist between town and College. They have cooperated on the building of a municipal stadium for football and a Civic Center for Hope's intercollegiate basketball program.

Majors and Degrees

Hope College awards the Bachelor of Arts, Bachelor of Science, Bachelor of Music, Bachelor of Science in Engineering, and Bachelor of Science in Nursing degrees. Major programs include accounting, art, biology, business management, chemistry, classical languages, communication, computer science, economics, engineering, engineering physics, English, environmental studies, French, geochemistry, geology, geophysics, German, history, kinesiology (physical education, exercise science, and athletic training), Latin, mathematics, music (church music education, instrumental education, literature and history, performance, theory, and vocal education), nursing, philosophy, physics, political science, psychology, religion, social work, sociology, Spanish, special education, and theater. Hope is fully accredited for certification in elementary, secondary, and special (emotionally impaired and learning disabilities) education. Preprofessional programs are offered in dentistry, law, medical technology, medicine, the ministry, and physical therapy. Alternatives to departmental majors include the composite major and contract curriculum major. The composite major is concentrated study in any approved combination of majors related to a particular academic or vocational objective of the student that meets Hope's educational objectives. The contract curriculum major allows a student to develop his or her own plan of study within the educational objectives of the College.

Academic Program

To graduate, students must pass all College-required courses, earn at least 126 credit hours, and meet minimum GPA requirements. A Phi Beta Kappa institution, Hope is widely respected as a liberal arts college that balances academic excellence with a deep concern for the quality of life of its students and alumni. Hope's commitment to the Christian faith provides an incentive for academic excellence and rigorous inquiry and a perspective on the wholeness and value of life. A core curriculum brings teachers and students together for the purpose of facilitating student growth in seven areas: communication skills, social adaptation, an understanding of our heritage and society, a respect for science and discovery, an awareness of other cultures, an understanding and appreciation of the arts, and an understanding of religion and its impact on society. To accomplish this, students select course work in the following disciplines: English, fine arts, foreign language, kinesiology, mathematics, natural science, philosophy, religion, and social science.

Off-Campus Programs

Hope College participates in off-campus programs sponsored and supervised by the Associated Colleges of the Midwest (ACM), the Institute for Asian Studies (IAS), the Institute for European Studies (IES), and the Great Lakes Colleges Association (GLCA). Students may study for a semester or a year in fifty-two countries; some continents and countries included are Africa, Austria, China, France, Germany, Great Britain, India, Japan, Latin America, Russia, Spain, the Middle East, and the Netherlands. Hope also runs a summer school in Vienna, Austria. The College's director of international education assists students in arranging programs in other countries. Domestic programs of one or two semesters' duration include the Washington Semester, Urban Semester in Philadelphia, Semester at the Chicago Metropolitan Center, Arts Program in New York City, Oak Ridge Science Semester, and Newberry Library Program in the Humanities.

Academic Facilities

The campus library contains more than 320,000 volumes, 1,550 periodical subscriptions, approximately 290,000 microforms, 11,800 video and audio recordings, and a 19,000-volume set in ultrafiche from the Library of American Civilization. The Peale

Science Center, containing the most modern laboratory equipment available, facilitates close working relationships between faculty and students. The physics laboratories include a 2.7-MeV Van de Graaff accelerator. Students from many academic disciplines take advantage of state-of-the-art computer facilities. Access to computing facilities is excellent across the campus. Theater, music, dance, and art departments have excellent facilities. The DePree Art Center is a $1.3-million facility that contains a major art gallery, classrooms, and studios.

Costs

Annual charges for the 2003–04 academic year were tuition, $19,212; room, $2744; board, $3274; and activity fee, $110, for a total fixed cost of $25,340.

Financial Aid

Types of aid include academic scholarships, grants, loans, and campus employment. Approximately 60 percent of Hope's students receive need-based aid. All accepted students may be considered for federal and Hope-funded assistance. Michigan residents may apply for state-funded programs. Applicants for aid should be accepted for admission and should submit the Free Application for Federal Student Aid (FAFSA) and a Hope institutional form by February 15 to receive priority consideration for need-based aid. Hope sponsors National Merit Scholars with a $14,000-per-year tuition scholarship. Other academic awards range from $3000 to $14,000. Talent awards of $2500 are also available in the fine arts and creative writing. Thirty percent of 2003 freshmen received a merit award. Consideration for merit awards requires submission of all completed application for admission documents by February 15.

Faculty

Hope's 204 full-time faculty members hold degrees from more than 115 different universities; 84 percent hold a Ph.D. or terminal degree in their field. In addition, there are 84 part-time faculty members who teach in a broad range of disciplines, many of whom also teach, perform, and work outside the campus community. The student-faculty ratio is 13:1. Members of the faculty are dedicated to maintaining excellence in both teaching and scholarship and to taking a personal interest in students. Many conduct research programs in which students actively participate, sometimes as early as their freshman year. Faculty members also serve as academic advisers and frequently host student groups in their homes.

Student Government

Hope has an established community governance system. Decisions that concern the College community are made primarily by boards and committees composed of students, faculty, and administrators. The Academic Affairs, Administrative Affairs, and Campus Life boards bear the major responsibility for policy decisions, while subcommittees of each deal with more specific areas. Residence hall units elect representatives to Student Congress; these representatives are then appointed to the major boards. A Judicial Board of 7 students, 2 faculty members, and 1 staff person is charged with maintaining high standards of student life.

Admission Requirements

Hope is interested in students who seek the rigors of a proven, demanding academic program and feel comfortable in an open, supportive, Christian campus community. A complete admission file includes the completed application form, the application fee, high school/college transcripts, and either ACT or SAT I scores. Primary factors considered are the applicant's high school course selection, grades, rank, test scores, counselor's recommendation, essay, and involvement in extracurricular/leadership activities. The College prefers that its students enroll having completed at least four college-preparatory classes per semester in the ninth through twelfth grades, including a variety of subject areas. The minimum background includes 4 years of English, 2 years of mathematics, 2 years of foreign language, 2 years of history or social studies, and at least 1 year of laboratory science. For fall 2003, freshmen had a mean GPA of 3.72 (on a 4.0 scale), and their average rank was in the 79.5 percentile. Campus visits are not required but are strongly recommended for interested students and their parents.

Application and Information

Most students apply for the fall semester, but applications are accepted for the spring semester or other sessions. Admission decisions are made on a rolling basis as applicants' files become complete. Students must submit the application form, official high school transcript, results of the SAT I or ACT, and $35 application fee. Prospective freshmen are encouraged to submit applications during the first semester of their senior year in high school. Completed applications for admission must be on file by February 15 to ensure consideration for merit scholarships. A $300 deposit is requested by May 1. Prospective students may also apply online; application forms are available on the Web (http://applyweb.com/apply/hope/).

Hope College Admissions
69 East 10th Street
P.O. Box 9000
Holland, Michigan 49422-9000
Telephone: 616-395-7850
800-968-7850 (toll-free)
E-mail: admissions@hope.edu
World Wide Web: http://www.hope.edu

The Pull, an annual tug-of-war between freshmen and sophomores, has been called "the most unique sporting event in the nation" by *Sports Illustrated*.

HOUGHTON COLLEGE

HOUGHTON, NEW YORK

The College

Founded in 1883, Houghton College is one of America's most highly regarded Christian liberal arts colleges. Sponsored by The Wesleyan Church, Houghton attracts students from more than forty denominations. Houghton has an enrollment of 1,200 full-time undergraduate students who represent forty states and twenty-five countries. Most students live in College housing within the distinctly residential environment, while many faculty members live within walking distance of the campus. Houghton's 1,300 acres in the scenic Genesee Valley of western New York offer students various recreational opportunities. The College operates a 386-acre equestrian center and both downhill and cross-country ski facilities.

Accredited by the Middle States Association of Colleges and Schools and the National Association of Schools of Music, Houghton's selective admission ensures an academically able student body. Most students represent the top 20 percent of their high school's graduating class, possess SAT I or ACT scores commensurate with a competitive college, and are active in their churches and communities. Houghton offers more than forty majors and programs in an undergraduate-only atmosphere, a commitment that allows students to benefit from the instruction and guidance of experienced professors beginning with their first year of study.

Extensive cocurricular opportunities at Houghton include a competitive NAIA intercollegiate athletic program that fields ten teams for men and women, a wide array of intramural leagues, numerous Christian service organizations, student publications, music groups, and student government. Houghton's Artist Series brings well-known classical performers to campus several times a year. The student-guided Campus Activities Board sponsors regular Christian contemporary concerts and other student-oriented activities. Student chapel services meet three times per week. *The Star*, the College's weekly student newspaper, offers practical journalism experience.

The residential experience is at the heart of a Houghton education. First-year students and sophomores are required to live in a College residential hall. Juniors and seniors may also choose from several recently constructed town houses and approved community houses for off-campus living.

All resident students are required to participate in the College's board plan. Most students enjoy Houghton's twenty-one-meal-per-week plan, while those living in a town house may opt for a reduced plan.

Year after year, Houghton is commended by numerous national publications. For eleven consecutive years, *U.S. News & World Report* has cited Houghton as one of the nation's best liberal arts colleges. Among other publications that regularly recognize Houghton are *Barron's 300 Best College Buys* and *Fiske's Guide to Colleges,* which cite Houghton for solid academics, good social climate, and excellent quality of life.

Location

Houghton students benefit from the College's location in the rolling hills of western New York. The College's vast property—among the nation's leaders in campus acreage—offers numerous recreational opportunities, while nearby Letchworth State Park is one of the state's natural treasures. The metropolitan cities of Rochester and Buffalo, within an hour and a half drive of Houghton, offer cultural, entertainment, and shopping venues.

The West Seneca campus of Houghton College is located in a suburb of Buffalo, New York. This campus is used primarily as a residential and instructional location for academic internships and student teaching as well as for the College's adult degree completion program. The College's two campuses are connected via an interactive TV link.

Majors and Degrees

Houghton grants Bachelor of Arts, Bachelor of Science, and Bachelor of Music degrees. Majors and programs are available in accounting, adolescent education (grades 7–12), art, Bible, biology, business administration, chemistry, childhood education (grades 1–6), communication, computer science, educational ministries, English, environmental studies, French, general science, history, humanities, intercultural studies, international relations, mathematics, medical technology, ministerial studies, music composition, music education, music performance, philosophy, physical education, physics, political science, predentistry, pre–engineering, prelaw, premedicine, preoptometry, pre–physical therapy, preseminary, pre–veterinary science, psychology, recreation, religion, sociology, Spanish, and writing.

An adult degree completion program (B.S. in organizational management), designed for those with 62-plus credit hours and suitable work experience and who are at least 25 years old, is offered at the College's campus in West Seneca, New York, and at extension sites in Olean, Arcade, and Jamestown, New York.

A 3-2 engineering program is available through cooperation with Clarkson University in Potsdam, New York, and Washington University in St. Louis, Missouri.

Academic Program

Most bachelor's degrees at Houghton consist of 125 credit hours. As a traditional liberal arts institution, Houghton requires all students to complete an extensive integrative studies curriculum in addition to courses in their major and minor fields of study. Included in the 54-credit-hour integrative studies requirements are courses in composition, literature, communication, foreign language, social science, history, mathematics, natural science, Bible, religion/philosophy, and fine arts. Lecture and seminar courses with classes averaging 21 students create a positive learning environment and daily interaction between professors and students.

Houghton offers the First-Year Honors Program for approximately 25 students. Students spend the second semester of their first year studying in London, England, with Houghton faculty members. Independent study and honors projects are also available.

The College follows a 4-4-1 calendar. In addition to the fall and spring semesters, the College offers MayTerm, a two- to four-week term where students may enroll in one concentrated course. Both on- and off-campus courses are available during MayTerm.

Houghton accepts credit from the Advanced Placement Program of the College Board. Students must achieve a final exam score of 4 or higher to receive credit from Houghton. CLEP credit may also be accepted for subject exams only. Students wishing to challenge the College's foreign language requirement may take a College-administered placement test. A portion or all of the foreign language requirement may be waived, although no credit hours are granted.

Army ROTC is offered through cooperation with nearby St. Bonaventure University.

Off-Campus Programs

As a member of the Council for Christian Colleges and Universities, Houghton is able to offer many off-campus opportunities, including the American Studies Program in Washington, D.C.; the Latin American Studies Program in Costa Rica; the Film Institute in Los Angeles, California; the Russian Studies Program in Moscow; the Middle Eastern Studies Program in Cairo, Egypt; and the Oxford Summer School Program. Houghton also operates the Oregon Extension Program in Lincoln, Oregon, as well as programs in London, Tanzania, and Australia.

Academic Facilities

The Willard J. Houghton Library contains more than 225,000 volumes, 26,000 microfilm titles, and 3,036 periodical subscriptions. The College's online catalog, which uses the Virginia Tech Library Systems software, offers easy access to the College's holdings. Membership in a regional library consortium helps ensure optimum interlibrary loan service.

The Stephen Paine Science Building offers 65,000 square feet of animal, instructional, and research laboratories; a greenhouse; computer facilities; and lecture classrooms.

A comprehensive academic building offers 49,000 square feet of classrooms, learning resource facilities, laboratories, faculty offices, media services, and an interactive TV link with the College's West Seneca campus. Other major facilities include a modern, well-equipped athletic complex; four major residence halls and thirty town houses accommodating more than 900 students; the 1,300-seat Wesley Chapel; the Campus Center; the Stevens Arts Studios; a 386-acre equestrian center; and several outdoor athletic and recreational areas. Houghton's new Center for the Arts features an acoustically designed recital hall, a music library, numerous practice rooms, spacious teaching studios, an instrumental rehearsal hall, and a professional digital recording studio.

The Educational Technology Initiative is a campuswide commitment that provides Houghton students with their own laptop computer and printer and on-campus technical support. Students connect to the College network from their residence hall rooms and many other locations to communicate with professors and fellow students, obtain shared course work and information, and gain high-speed access to the Internet. Students benefit from one of the most accessible and easy-to-use technology programs on any campus.

Costs

Houghton's tuition and fees were $17,984 for the 2003–04 academic year, including a laptop computer and a printer. Room and board (twenty-one meals per week) totaled $6000. Other indirect expenses, including books, supplies, and travel, averaged $1500.

Financial Aid

Houghton administers more than $15 million in aid annually, benefiting nearly 90 percent of the student body. Traditional federal and New York State aid, including Federal Pell Grants, TAP, FSEOG, work-study, and Federal Perkins Loans, is available for students demonstrating need through the Free Application for Federal Student Aid (FAFSA) and the Houghton College Financial Aid Application. The priority application deadline for financial aid is March 1. Houghton also offers merit-based scholarships for excellence in academics, athletics, music, and art. Students should contact the Student Financial Services Office for specific information regarding merit-based scholarships.

Faculty

The College's faculty currently totals approximately 100 members, 80 of whom are full-time. More than 80 percent hold the terminal degree in their discipline. Since Houghton is an undergraduate institution, all courses are taught by qualified professors, not teaching assistants or graduate students. All full-time students work directly with a faculty adviser in their area of study. The College maintains a student-faculty ratio of 14:1, with classes averaging approximately 21 students.

Student Government

The Houghton Student Government Association (SGA) consists of elected student representatives. This College-sponsored organization allows students to have a direct impact on their college experience in areas ranging from academics to residence life to cocurricular activities. Most College committees include student representatives.

Admission Requirements

Houghton's competitive admission process seeks applicants who clearly possess the academic and spiritual qualities necessary for a successful experience at Houghton. Candidates for admission should submit a high school transcript indicating at least 16 units of college-preparatory course work. The academic evaluation of each applicant includes a review of the quality of the high school curriculum, grade point average, rank in class, and scores from the SAT I or ACT. Other important application materials include the applicant's pastor's recommendation and an essay regarding the student's desire to attend a Christian institution. Transfer students are evaluated on the basis of the above information in addition to the college-level course work completed to date.

The Admission Office responds to applications for admission on or about January 1 (for files completed by November 15) and on a rolling basis beginning February 1 for all other applications. The College subscribes to and supports the national Candidates Reply Date of May 1.

Application and Information

For application materials, students should contact:

Admission Office
Houghton College
1 Willard Avenue
Houghton, New York 14744
Telephone: 585-567-9353
800-777-2556 (toll-free)
E-mail: admission@houghton.edu
World Wide Web: http://www.houghton.edu

The quad at Houghton College.

HOUSTON BAPTIST UNIVERSITY

HOUSTON, TEXAS

The University

Houston Baptist University (HBU), an independent institution of higher learning related to the Baptist General Convention of Texas, is committed to fostering academic excellence in the context of Christian faith and teachings, promoting truth in learning, supporting personal and professional growth, and preparing undergraduate and graduate students for service and leadership in a diverse world. The University welcomes and extends its resources to those who strive for academic excellence. The faculty and staff members and administrators are committed to providing a responsive and intellectually stimulating environment that fosters spiritual maturity, strength of character, and moral virtue as the foundation for successful living; develops professional behaviors and personal characteristics for lifelong service to God and to the community; and meets the changing needs of the community and society. The University offers a broad range of programs and services committed to liberal arts education that are designed to promote the growth of the whole person. The integration of scholarship, service, and spirituality essential to liberal arts education is nurtured in an environment of open inquiry. Students are encouraged to think critically, to assess information from a Christian perspective, to arrive at informed and reasoned conclusions, and to become lifelong learners.

Founded in 1960, HBU is a comprehensive liberal arts university accredited by the Southern Association of Colleges and Schools. The University's academic programs are offered through five colleges: the College of Arts and Humanities, the College of Business and Economics, the College of Education and Behavioral Sciences, the College of Nursing, and the College of Science and Math. More than fifty majors and programs of study are available within the five colleges and the School of Music. The double-major program enables students to broaden and strengthen their academic and career preparation.

HBU students participate in numerous extracurricular activities throughout the year. There are more than forty-five student clubs and organizations, including five Greek fraternities and sororities and two award-winning student publications; a popular intramural sports program; and a distinctive Assisting Communities Through Students (ACTS) program, which encourages students to make a Christian response to human needs through service in nonprofit agencies and schools in greater Houston. HBU sponsors five varsity athletic teams and is a member of the National Association of Intercollegiate Athletics (NAIA) and the Red River Athletic Conference. The Huskies compete in basketball and baseball for men and volleyball, basketball, and softball for women. Each of the teams is perennially ranked in the NAIA top twenty-five. Admission to all Husky home athletic events is free to HBU students. In the last six years, more than 90 percent of student athletes have graduated.

Location

HBU is located in southwest Houston, Texas, the nation's fourth-largest city. Known as the Space City because of its connection to NASA's Johnson Space Center, Houston is also headquarters to almost two dozen of the largest corporations in the U.S. The Port of Houston is the nation's second largest, and half of the world's largest foreign companies have offices in Houston. The Texas Medical Center, the Museum District, professional athletics, and a strong heritage in the cultural arts make Houston a dynamic city in which to live, work, or study.

Majors and Degrees

HBU's College of Arts and Humanities awards the Bachelor of Arts or Bachelor of Science degree in art, biblical languages, bilingual education, Christianity, church music, communications, English, French, history, mass media, music (jazz studies), music (liberal arts), music performance, music theory and composition, Spanish, speech, and writing. Students may also pursue teacher certification in certain content areas within the college.

The College of Business and Economics awards the Bachelor of Business Administration to those students who choose both their majors within the college. It can be earned in accounting, computer information systems management, economics, entrepreneurship, finance, management, and marketing. The Bachelor of Arts or Bachelor of Science are awarded in accounting, business, computer information systems management, economics, entrepreneurship, finance, management, and marketing.

The College of Education and Behavioral Sciences awards the Bachelor of Arts or the Bachelor of Science in child development, interdisciplinary studies, kinesiology, multidisciplinary studies, pedagogy, psychology, and sociology. Certification or licensure programs are available in all-level (PK–12 in art, foreign language, music, or physical education), EC–4, generic special education, high school (8–12), middle grades (4–8), and secondary (6–12).

The College of Nursing awards the Associate Degree in Nursing and the Bachelor of Science in Nursing.

The College of Science and Math awards the Bachelor of Science in biochemistry–molecular biology, chemistry, engineering science, mathematics, and physics. Certification or licensure programs are available in high school (8–12) composite science, life science, mathematical studies, and physical science and in middle grades (4–8) composite science and mathematical studies.

Academic Programs

The academic year consists of three 11-week quarters and a summer session. Although operating on a quarter calendar, HBU grants semester hour credit. While the number of credit hours for graduation varies depending on the major, a minimum of 130 semester hours is required. The minimum undergraduate residence requirement is 32 semester hours, including at least 12 semester hours of upper-level courses in each major completed at HBU. No life experience, credit by correspondence or extension, or course received in transfer with a grade of D, F, or P is counted toward a degree.

The Departmental Honors Program provides highly qualified and motivated students with the opportunity to develop additional expertise in their chosen majors through independent investigation. HBU offers internship opportunities under the direction of the various academic colleges in awareness of the value of practical experience in the learning process. Various courses allow students the opportunity to travel both within the U.S. and internationally.

Students desiring to take course work at any other college must first secure prior approval from the University Registrar at HBU. Concurrent or transient enrollment may be permitted if the courses are taken at a regionally accredited institution. Only alphabetical grades of C or better are considered for transfer credit.

Academic Facilities

The Moody Library contains a collection of more than 296,000 bibliographic units, with 5,000 new titles added annually. The library subscribes to 2,000 journals. The catalog and circulation systems are fully automated. Computerized indexes and Internet access are available, as are several electronic databases. In addition to nearly 400 study spaces, the reference area, media area, offices, processing rooms, and open-stack collection area, the building houses the Bible in America Museum and the Museum of American Architecture and Decorative Arts.

Additional academic facilities include a television studio with full production capabilities; a state-of-the-art photography lab; a fully equipped newsroom with scanners, Adobe Illustrator, and Photo Shop; and a nursing skills lab, which provides the opportunity for students to practice their skills. Six labs house 142 computers, with an additional twenty-five computers located in the Moody Library and another 112 in classrooms.

Costs

Tuition at HBU for 2004–05 is $13,134 (33 credit hours at $398 per credit hour). Required fees are $1080 per year, and room and board costs start at $4845 per year. Books and supplies cost approximately $350 per quarter. Costs are subject to change.

Financial Aid

The question of cost is an important criterion for students and families in all income categories. HBU offers access to state and federal programs as well as institutional funds in the form of scholarships and grants. Academic scholarships, which are competitive and renewable, are divided into three levels: the Endowed Academic Scholarship, the Founder's Scholarship, and the Presidential Academic Scholarship. These scholarships are based on the student's academic qualifications. In addition, the Legacy Grant and talent-based grants in music, art, and athletics are available for students who can contribute specific talents to the University. Army and Navy ROTC scholarships are available through joint ventures with area colleges. In addition, HBU offers Ministerial Dependents Grants to dependent children of ordained or licensed Southern Baptist ministers and missionaries, while SERV Aid is awarded through the Center for Exploring Ministry Careers for students planning to enter a church-related profession. In order to be considered for need-based financial aid, students must complete the Free Application for Federal Student Aid (FAFSA). The HBU code on the FAFSA is 003576.

Faculty

There are 191 faculty members, 118 of whom are full-time. Of the full-time faculty members, 75 percent hold doctoral degrees. There are no teaching assistants, and graduate students do not teach. The student-faculty ratio is 16:1.

Student Government

The first student body wrote and adopted the "Constitution of the Student Association of Houston Baptist University." Student government at HBU is exercised through the Student Association. All full-time undergraduates (8 semester hours or more) become members of this association upon registering. Each spring, officers of the association are elected for the following year. The legislative body is the Student Senate, which is composed of representative students from all colleges of the University. Student officers serve as spokespeople for students and seek "to foster the recognition of privileges and responsibilities of the students of the college community."

Admission Requirements

The Office of Admissions accepts formal applications from all students for consideration of admission to HBU. Students who have demonstrated academic success and achievement are encouraged to apply for admission. High school curriculum, grade point average, rank in class, test scores (SAT I or ACT), personal essay, and recommendations are all considered when reviewing applications. Students with SAT scores of 1010 or above with a 480 on the verbal section or ACT composite scores of 20 or above with an English subscore of 20 or above are considered for regular admission. Students with scores below these levels are reviewed by the University Admissions Committee.

Transfer students who have completed 30 or more credit hours with a GPA of 2.0 or above at a regionally accredited college are considered for regular admission.

Admissions decisions at HBU are done on a rolling basis. Decisions are made upon the completion of the application file. There is a $25 application fee. The international application fee is $100. An online application is available on the Web site listed below.

Application and Information

To be considered for admission, a student must submit the application form and the $25 application fee; official transcripts and SAT I or ACT scores must be sent to the office from the school or testing agency. SAT I and ACT scores are considered official if they are on the high school record.

To request an application or additional information, students should contact:

Office of Admissions
Houston Baptist University
7502 Fondren Road
Houston, Texas 77074-3298
Telephone: 281-649-3211
800-969-3210 (toll-free)
E-mail: unadm@hbu.edu
World Wide Web: http://www.hbu.edu

An aerial view of the technologically advanced Hinton Center.

HOWARD UNIVERSITY

WASHINGTON, D.C.

The University

Howard University, founded in 1867, is a coeducational private institution of higher learning located in the northwestern section of Washington, D.C. Since its founding, Howard University has grown from a single-frame building to a campus of 241 acres with buildings and equipment valued at more than $820 million. The University has been expanded to include a 22-acre West Campus on which the School of Law is located, a 22-acre School of Divinity campus and support service facility in northeast Washington, and a 108-acre tract of land in Beltsville, Maryland. Howard University consists of twelve schools and colleges: the Graduate School; the Schools of Business, Communications, Divinity, Education, Law, and Social Work; and the Colleges of Arts and Sciences; Dentistry; Engineering, Architecture and Computer Sciences; Medicine; and Pharmacy, Nursing and Allied Health Sciences. The University offers baccalaureate, master's, Doctor of Dental Surgery, Doctor of Education, Doctor of Medicine, Doctor of Ministry, Doctor of Pharmacy, Doctor of Philosophy, Doctor of Social Work, and Juris Doctor degrees. Annual enrollment at Howard is approximately 10,700. Approximately 10 percent of the students are from Washington, D.C.; 73 percent are from other states; 12 percent are international students representing ninety-three countries and U.S. possessions; and 5 percent are international students who are permanent U.S. residents.

The University's physical plant consists of more than ninety buildings, including the Howard Plaza Towers and the Bethune Hall Annex, a theater, two dormitories for women, two dormitories for men, and five coed dormitories. Student organizations include religious groups, special interest clubs, honor societies, sororities, fraternities, bands, choruses, a string ensemble, student weekly publications, a debating group, and service clubs. Varsity athletics include men's baseball, basketball, cross-country, football, indoor and outdoor track, soccer, and wrestling; women's basketball, bowling, cross-country, indoor and outdoor track, and volleyball; and coed swimming and tennis. The intramural program includes all of these sports.

There are a variety of styles and locations of University housing, ranging from standard double rooms to shared apartments with full kitchens. Freshmen are encouraged to reside on campus. The residential life experience contributes to the educational and personal development of students. Students living in the local area and certain other categories of students may request an exception to the residential requirement. Certain residence halls (dormitories) are part of the combined room and board plan; residents of other halls may opt to purchase a meal plan. There are lively and diverse activities sponsored in the residence halls, and students in the residence halls are also encouraged to involve themselves in community service as part of their college experience. Each undergraduate residence hall has well-trained live-in staff members as well as front-desk monitors 24 hours a day. Residence counselors are aided by graduate assistants and resident assistants.

Location

The Howard University campus is situated on one of the highest elevations in the District of Columbia, overlooking downtown Washington. The White House, the Capitol, and all the cultural and historic institutions of the city are within minutes of the campus. Many of the University's academic programs are designed to make use of these institutions and to serve the needs of the immediate community as well as the entire Washington metropolitan area.

Majors and Degrees

The University offers the following undergraduate degrees: Bachelor of Architecture, Bachelor of Arts, Bachelor of Business Administration (nine options available), Bachelor of Fine Arts, Bachelor of Music, Bachelor of Music Education, Bachelor of Science, Bachelor of Science in Chemical Engineering, Bachelor of Science in Civil Engineering, Bachelor of Science in Clinical Laboratory Science, Bachelor of Science in Electrical and Computer Engineering, Bachelor of Science in Mechanical Engineering, Bachelor of Science in Nursing, Bachelor of Science in Nutritional Sciences, Bachelor of Science in Occupational Therapy, Bachelor of Science in Physician Assistant studies, Bachelor of Science in Radiation Therapy, and Bachelor of Science in Systems and Computer Sciences. The major areas of undergraduate study are accounting, administration of justice, African studies, Afro-American studies, anthropology, architecture, art, biology, chemical engineering, chemistry, civil engineering, clinical laboratory science, communication studies, computer-based information systems, dental hygiene, design, economics, education, electrical engineering, English, fashion merchandising, finance, fine arts, French, German, Greek, history, hospitality management, human development, insurance, interior design, international business, journalism, management, marketing, mathematics, mechanical engineering, music, nursing, nutritional science, occupational therapy, pharmacy, philosophy, physical education, physician assistant studies, physics, political science, psychology, radio/television/film, recreation, Russian, sociology, Spanish, systems and computer science, theater arts, and visual arts. The University offers degrees in more than ninety undergraduate areas and certificates in dental hygiene, health sciences, music therapy, and radiation therapy.

Academic Programs

The requirements for a bachelor's degree vary among the University's schools and colleges. A core of courses is required for each major.

The University awards credit for successful scores on Advanced Placement tests as well as credit for the International Baccalaureate program.

The University offers cooperative education programs in the College of Arts and Sciences; the College of Engineering, Architecture and Computer Sciences; the School of Business; and the School of Communications. Departmental honors programs are also offered for students with exceptional ability. Special support services are provided through the Center for Academic Reinforcement. Domestic and international exchange programs are also available for sophomores, juniors, and first-semester seniors.

Howard University is accredited by the Commission on Higher Education of the Middle States Association of Colleges and Schools, and its programs in specialized fields are accredited by numerous professional agencies.

Academic Facilities

There are separate classroom and laboratory facilities for each major discipline. The University library houses more than 2 million bound volumes, 26,000 current serial subscriptions, 3.5 million microforms, a media center, a microfilm preparation center, and the Moorland-Spingarn Research Center, which has the largest collection of black literature in the United States. The University also operates a radio station (WHUR-FM). The radio station and a TV station (WHUT-TV) serve as laboratories for the School of Communications.

Costs

Tuition was $10,840 and fees were $805 for the 2003–04 academic year. Room and board costs vary, depending upon the assigned accommodations and selected meal plan. The average annual cost of room and board is $5600. The approximate annual cost of books and supplies is $950.

Financial Aid

The University's financial aid program is designed to aid the maximum number of students. Every effort is made to assist students demonstrating merit and need through scholarships, loans, grants, and part-time employment. The amount of aid granted is determined by the availability of funds, the extent of the student's need, and his or her academic performance. Most financial aid awards are given for the academic year and are divided equally between the two semesters. Undergraduate students seeking financial aid must file the Free Application for Federal Student Aid (FAFSA), which can be obtained from the University's Office of Financial Aid and Student Employment. Applications must be filed by February 15.

Faculty

The University's faculty consists of 342 full professors, 376 associate professors, 299 assistant professors, 143 instructors, 180 lecturers, and 20 adjunct professors, making a total of 1,360. The normal teaching load is 12 credit hours, but faculty members also spend time advising, doing research and committee work, and undertaking administrative duties.

Student Government

Student government has many levels and branches and is concerned with all aspects of student life. Students hold voting memberships on the Howard University Board of Trustees.

Admission Requirements

All applicants must be graduates of accredited high schools and must present acceptable high school records, SAT I or ACT scores, and SAT II: Writing Test scores. Students who have studied a foreign language for 2 years and intend to continue study of that language should also take the SAT II Subject Test in that language. Applicants seeking admission to the Department of Music must audition in person or send a tape, those seeking admission to the Department of Art must submit a portfolio, and theater applicants must submit two letters of reference and a resume. Enrollment Management/Admission notifies applicants of any additional requirements upon receipt of an application.

Application and Information

Guided tours of the campus are conducted, by appointment, Monday through Friday, beginning at 10 a.m. The last tour begins at 3 p.m. Students who wish to schedule a tour should contact the Office of Admission at the number below. Students may apply for early action or traditional action. Early action applicants must submit an application for admission by November 1 and are notified of an admission decision by December 25. Traditional action students must submit a completed application by February 15 and are notified of an admission decision by April 15. Students seeking admission for the spring semester should apply by November 1. A nonrefundable application fee of $45 is required of all applicants. Howard University does not waive the application fee. Students interested in on-campus housing must submit the enrollment form, $300 enrollment fee, housing application, and $50 housing application fee by May 1.

For further information, students should contact:

Enrollment Management/Admission
Howard University
2400 Sixth Street, NW
Washington, D.C. 20059
Telephone: 202-806-2763
E-mail: admission@howard.edu
World Wide Web: http://www.howard.edu

HUNTER COLLEGE
OF THE CITY UNIVERSITY OF NEW YORK

NEW YORK, NEW YORK

The College

In 1870, Thomas Hunter founded Hunter College to train young women to become school teachers. Their contributions helped make New York City's schools among the most highly regarded public school systems in the world. Today, Hunter College is a coeducational liberal arts college serving 21,000 undergraduate and graduate students of all racial, ethnic, and cultural backgrounds. Wide offerings in the liberals arts and sciences and three professional schools—education, health sciences, and social work—meet the highest academic standards. A distinguished faculty encourages intellectual and personal growth in each student.

Location

Hunter students study in the heart of Manhattan. Many of the world's finest museums, libraries, concert halls, cultural centers, and theaters are just a quick walk away.

Majors and Degrees

Hunter College offers bachelor's and master's degrees in the arts and sciences, education, health professions, nursing, and social work, along with several combined (B.A./M.A. or B.A./M.S.) degrees. The following programs of study are available: accounting, Africana and Puerto Rican/Latino studies, anthropology, archaeology, art history, biological sciences, chemistry, Chinese language and literature, classical studies, community health education, comparative literature, computer science, dance, economics, elementary education, environmental studies, English, English language arts, film, French, geography, German, Greek, Hebrew, history, honors curriculum, Italian, Jewish social studies, Latin, Latin American and Caribbean Studies, Latin and Greek, mathematics, media studies, medical laboratory sciences, music, nursing, nutrition and food science, philosophy, physics, political science, psychology, religion, Romance languages, Russian, secondary education, sociology, Spanish, statistics, studio art, theater, urban studies, and women's studies. Secondary education programs are for grades 7–12 unless otherwise noted and include biology, chemistry, Chinese, dance (pre-K–12), English, French, German, Hebrew, Italian, mathematics, music (pre-K–12, accelerated B.A./M.A. program only), physics, Russian, social studies, and Spanish.

Special programs in anthropology, biological sciences/environmental and occupational health sciences, biopharmacology, biotechnology, economics, English, history, mathematics, music, physics, sociology/social research, and statistics and applied mathematics lead to the combined bachelor's/master's degree, enabling highly qualified students to earn both degrees more quickly.

Hunter College also provides preprofessional advisement and preparation for advanced study in chiropractic, dentistry, engineering, law, medicine, optometry, osteopathy, pharmacy, podiatry, and veterinary medicine.

Academic Programs

Hunter instills a rich and informed sense of the possibilities of humanity in its students and expects them to carry their liberal education forward in their careers, their public responsibilities, and their personal lives.

The College trains its students in the sciences, the humanities, and a number of professional fields. As they strive to achieve their career goals, students are expected to perceive their chosen fields of study as only a part of a wider realm of knowledge. Undergraduate programs of study at Hunter consist of five parts, totaling 120 credits: a general education requirement, a pluralism and diversity requirement, a concentration of in-depth study, elective courses, and a minor.

Undergraduate students at Hunter who exhibit intellectual curiosity and exceptional ability may apply to the Thomas Hunter Scholars Program, an interdisciplinary program that individualizes study according to needs and interests and grants a Bachelor of Arts degree.

Students may earn sophomore standing (up to 30 credits) if they score well on the College Level Examination Program (CLEP) subject tests, the Advanced Placement examinations of The College Board, and the Regents College Examination (RCE) Program of New York State.

Off-Campus Programs

Hunter College taps Manhattan to allow innumerable internships. Hosts have included Atlantic Records, CNN, The Council on Foreign Relations, DreamWorks SKG, Madison Square Garden, Metropolitan Museum of Art, New York City Council, Simon & Schuster, and many more. Interns perform curatorial and administrative work in museums, research and production work on TV news shows and newspapers, design work in commercial graphics, and booking, managing, and technical work in theaters.

Academic Facilities

The College comprises five sites in Manhattan. The largest, a modern complex of buildings connected by skywalks at 68th Street and Lexington Avenue, sits above a convenient subway stop. This campus offers programs in the arts and sciences and in teacher education.

Downtown, the Brookdale Campus on East 25th Street houses the Division of the Schools of the Health Professions, which includes the Hunter-Bellevue School of Nursing, one of the nation's largest nursing programs, and the School of Health Sciences.

Uptown on East 79th Street is the Hunter College School of Social Work, recently listed among the top ten schools of its kind in the nation by *U.S. News & World Report*.

On Manhattan's West Side, Hunter's Studio Art Building houses an 8,000-square-foot gallery and provides M.F.A. students with individual studios that are among the best in the city.

At East 94th Street, the Campus Schools house an elementary school and a high school for the intellectually gifted that are renowned, as is the College itself, for a long tradition of academic excellence.

All locations are minutes from Grand Central Terminal, Penn Station, and the New York/New Jersey Port Authority Bus Terminal, making Hunter easily accessible from Connecticut, Westchester, New Jersey, and Long Island.

The collections of the Hunter College libraries are housed in the Jacqueline Grennan Wexler Library and the Art Slide Library (located at the main campus), as well as at the branch libraries at the Brookdale Campus and the School of Social Work. The libraries hold 750,000 volumes, 2,300 periodicals, a nonprint collection of more than 1 million microforms, and 250,000 art slides in addition to records, tapes, scores, music CDs, and videos. Recently, Hunter installed new computer multimedia, and Internet labs and its first CD-ROM network. The CD-ROM network provides access to indexes, abstracts, and complete texts and multimedia resources, and Internet labs make the World Wide Web accessible.

Costs

Hunter College is affordable. In 2003–04, New York State residents enrolled as full-time, matriculated students paid $2000 per semester ($170 per credit part-time). Nonresidents enrolled as full-time, matriculated students paid $360 per credit. All students paid a Student Activity Fee ($159.50 per semester for full-time students and $91.95 per semester for part-time students) and a $5 per-semester Consolidated Fee.

Financial Aid

Hunter College participates in all state and federal financial aid programs. Financial aid is available to matriculated students in the form of grants, loans, and work-study. Grants provide funds that do not have to be repaid. Loans must be repaid in regular installments over a prescribed period of time. Work-study consists of part-time employment, either on campus or in an outside agency. More information is available from the Office of Financial Aid at 212-772-4820.

Entering freshmen whose high school records indicate a high level of academic achievement may apply to the CUNY Honors College at Hunter College. This prestigious program offers a generous financial aid package as well as extensive benefits, including a free room at the Hunter College Residence Hall. In addition, other scholarships are offered. More information on scholarships is available from the Director of Scholarships at 212-650-3550.

Faculty

Thanks to its location in the heart of New York City, Hunter College attracts a special kind of faculty member. Some are well-known scholars and researchers in their fields; for example, biologists involved in advanced research on genetic structure. Others are professionals with active careers in the city, including well-known painters, sculptors, architects, and urban design experts. Hunter's faculty also includes environmental health scientists who work on occupational health and safety issues, nursing administrators who work in the country's leading hospitals, and film directors, theater critics, and musicians who are engaged in New York City's cultural milieu. Many members of the faculty are nationally renowned; they maintain Hunter's reputation for academic excellence through outstanding teaching and cutting-edge publications and by securing millions of dollars in annual grants for research.

Student Government

Several governing assemblies involve students in Hunter's governance. The College Senate, the legislative body of the College, includes faculty members, students, and administrators. Two Student Governments (undergraduate and graduate) also play essential roles in the life of the College. Students with voting power sit on faculty and administrative committees.

Admission Requirements

Candidates for freshman admission are considered based on the overall strength of their academic preparation, grades in individual subjects, cumulative high school averages, and SAT or ACT scores. The College recommends 4 years of English, 4 years of social studies, 3 years of mathematics, 2 years of a foreign language, 2 years of laboratory sciences, and 1 year of performing or visual arts as the minimum academic preparation for success in college.

Transfer applicants with fewer than 24 credits must have a cumulative grade point average (GPA) of at least 2.3 and must meet the freshman criteria previously outlined. Those with 14–23.9 credits and a GPA of 2.5 as well as those with 24 or more credits and a GPA of 2.3 are eligible, regardless of high school average.

The School of Health Sciences and the School of Nursing offer several upper-division programs that have special admission criteria. For more information, applicants should contact the Office of Admissions.

Application and Information

Requests for further information and for application materials should be sent to:

Office of Admissions
Hunter College of the City University of New York
695 Park Avenue
New York, New York 10021-5085
Telephone: 212-772-4490
Fax: 212-650-3336
E-mail: admissions@hunter.cuny.edu
World Wide Web: http://www.hunter.cuny.edu

Students at Hunter College enjoy the convenience of skywalks, which connect all four buildings at the 68th Street campus. Hunter's Upper East Side location provides easy access to some of New York's finest offerings: Central Park and the Metropolitan Museum of Art are just blocks away.

HUNTINGDON COLLEGE

MONTGOMERY, ALABAMA

The College

To be successful in the twenty-first century, college graduates must be prepared to assume the role of world citizen, must be adept at using information and communication technology, and must have real-world experience in addition to a broad undergraduate education. Huntingdon College's outstanding liberal arts program provides travel/study, internships and hands-on learning opportunities, a computer for each entering freshman, and direct connections to the Internet and Campus Intranet in a port-per-pillow arrangement as part of its innovative Huntingdon Plan.

Founded in 1854, Huntingdon is a private liberal arts college related to the United Methodist Church. More than 700 students represent twenty-four states and twelve countries. Huntingdon has been recognized as a "Best Buy" by *Money* magazine, as an "up and coming" college by *U.S. News & World Report,* and as a "hidden gem" by Kaplan/*Newsweek* and has been included in *Templeton's Honor Roll of Character-Building Colleges.* In recent years, 96 percent of Huntingdon students applying to law school have been admitted and 88 percent of those applying to medical school have been admitted (the national averages are 56 percent and 41 percent, respectively). The mean grade point average for the 2002 freshman class was 3.28, the mean ACT score was 23, and the mean combined SAT I score was 1107; 75 percent of applicants were admitted.

Huntingdon provides a wide range of clubs, organizations, and activities, including national fraternities and sororities, special interest groups, performing groups, the Campus Ministry Association, service clubs, publications, and intramural sports. NCAA Division III intercollegiate athletics include men's varsity baseball, basketball, football, golf, and soccer and women's varsity basketball, soccer, softball, tennis, and volleyball. Huntingdon is a residential campus. About 70 percent of full-time students live in campus residence halls.

The College's Academic Services Center provides academic counseling, career planning, job placement, and internships. The center conducts workshops in personal growth and careers, maintains a library of graduate and professional school information, and offers computer-assisted career planning. Placement services range from summer jobs to permanent employment after graduation. Staff members provide resume assistance, career contacts, and background on employers. Representatives from government, business, and nonprofit organizations are invited to the campus to recruit. More than 90 percent of all Huntingdon graduates are either employed in their chosen fields or enrolled in graduate or professional schools within 6 months of graduation.

Location

Huntingdon's 71-acre campus is a naturally picturesque park. Centrally located in one of Montgomery's most beautiful neighborhoods, Old Cloverdale, campus buildings of primarily Gothic design extend along a semicircular ridge, overlooking a lush wooded area and natural amphitheater. Montgomery enjoys a pleasant climate with warm summers and mild winters and is not far from Gulf beaches, mountains, rivers, and parks.

A variety of cultural and educational activities take place in Alabama's capital city, just minutes from the campus, including the Alabama Shakespeare Festival, concerts, and performances of the civic ballet. State archives, state government offices and laboratories, the capitol building, the fine arts museum, and countless historic landmarks are also nearby. Montgomery is within easy driving distance of Birmingham (90 miles), Atlanta (170 miles), the Gulf of Mexico (160 miles), and New Orleans (300 miles).

Majors and Degrees

Huntingdon College offers the Bachelor of Arts degree with majors in American studies, art, art education, athletic training, biology, business administration, cell biology, chemistry, communication studies, computer science, creative writing, cultural and religious studies, digital art, drama, English, environmental chemistry, European studies, field biology, global leadership, history, human performance and kinesiology, international studies, mathematics, music, music education, musical theater, political science, psychology, public administration, public affairs, Spanish, and tri-subject. Huntingdon is the only college that offers tri-subject majors combining the study of political science with two of the following: economics, history, philosophy, psychology, and public communication.

Preprofessional programs in Christian education (youth and children's ministries), dentistry, law, medicine, optometry, pharmacy, physical therapy, theology, and veterinary medicine have excellent placement rates.

Secondary education programs are offered in chemistry, English language arts, history, and mathematics. Preschool through grade 12 programs in art, music, and physical education are also offered.

A dual-degree program in engineering is offered in cooperation with Auburn University.

Academic Program

Huntingdon's core curriculum includes unique interdisciplinary liberal arts courses, a senior capstone course, and freedom of choice in the selection of distribution courses within topic areas such as aesthetic expression, science and technology, and social and self-awareness. Credit is available for Advanced Placement and International Baccalaureate students.

Superb lecture and cultural programs bring current issues, topics of interest, and the arts to life for Huntingdon students. A long list of notable Huntingdon lecturers includes Elizabeth Dole, Janet Reno, Bob Hope, Beverly Sills, animal behaviorist Dr. Jane Goodall, Susan Rook, dinosaur expert Dr. Jack Horner, paleoanthropologist Dr. Donald Johanson, and Dr. Henry Kissinger. The College's Performing Arts Series offers dance, music, and theatrical performances throughout the year.

The College operates on a 4-1-4 system, with a two-week January Term and two 6-week summer sessions. Classes begin at the end of August. Freshman registration is held in August.

Off-Campus Programs

Huntingdon students may participate in the Marine Environmental Sciences Consortium on Dauphin Island in Alabama. Participation in Air Force ROTC at Alabama State University or in Army ROTC at Auburn University at Montgomery is also available to students enrolled at Huntingdon. Through a consortial agreement with local colleges, Huntingdon students may take courses at Auburn University at Montgomery and at Faulkner University.

The College offers a travel/study opportunity as part of the Huntingdon Plan. Students who enter as freshmen may choose from a menu of travel/study programs during the January term of the junior or senior year. Many opportunities are offered within regular tuition and fees, while others require marginal additional costs. Past study opportunities have included sites in the Caribbean; China; Australia; Mexico; New York; Washington, D.C.; the Bahamas; Los Angeles; England; Ireland; Italy; Spain; Belize; Peru; the Galapagos Islands; and the Holy Land. The College is also a member of the Center for Cooperative Study Abroad (CCSA), which offers study programs in English-speaking countries and a four-college archaeological consortium in Sepphorus. All study experiences sponsored through the Huntingdon Plan or through CCSA are faculty-directed and are offered for academic credit.

Academic Facilities

The Houghton Memorial Library holds nearly 150,000 volumes, periodicals, audiovisual materials, and microforms. The Wilson Center accommodates studies in business, mathematics, and computer science and houses state-of-the-art computing equipment, including a network of more than fifty PCs and Macintoshes available 24 hours a day. Since each student is also provided with a computer, the student-computer ratio is 1:more than 1. No extra charges are made for the use of these facilities. The Smith music building has a 120-seat recital hall, music studios, a library, rehearsal and practice rooms, four pipe organs, and twelve grand pianos.

Costs

Tuition for the 2002–03 school year (two semesters) was $14,560; room and board were approximately $5940. Books, supplies, and fees average about $700 per school year.

Financial Aid

At Huntingdon, financing an education is a cooperative effort. Through a variety of resources, Huntingdon College administers more than $6 million in aid to more than 90 percent of its students. These resources include institutional scholarships, gifts, and endowments as well as federal grants, loans, and work-study assignments. In addition, the school benefits from the Alabama Student Assistance and the Alabama Student Grant programs. To apply for financial aid, students must apply for admission, complete a Huntingdon College Financial Aid Application, and complete the Free Application for Federal Student Aid (FAFSA). Although the majority of financial aid is based upon demonstrated financial need, Huntingdon awards scholarships for academic merit, leadership, or performance skills in art, drama, and music. The priority deadline for the completion of the financial aid process is April 15. The scholarship application deadline is December 31.

Faculty

The faculty is composed of 49 full-time and 33 part-time teaching members; approximately 85 percent hold terminal degrees in their fields. In addition to teaching, the faculty's major responsibility is advising students. Faculty members work closely with students to plan and develop individual programs to fulfill the student's career interests. The student-faculty ratio is 10:1, and the average class size is 15 students.

Student Government

The Student Government Association, authorized by the College administration, embraces the entire student body. Based upon the honor system, it places responsibilities for the enforcement of regulations and the safeguarding of standards upon the individual. The association encourages student leadership and good citizenship through communication, cooperation, and endeavors among students, faculty members, administrators, and other officials. The legislative powers of the association are vested in the Senate, which is composed of representatives from other leading organizations on campus. The Executive Cabinet members are elected by the student body each spring. The Student Government Association and the College Programming Council, funded by the activity fee, present a variety of activities throughout the year. These include dances, festivals, parties, movies, special programs, and many other social events as well as such special events as the Presidential Banquet, Homecoming, pageants, and Parents Weekend.

Admission Requirements

Huntingdon College is an equal opportunity educational institution and, as such, does not discriminate in its admission policy on the basis of race, color, sex, age, creed, national origin, or handicap. Huntingdon places primary emphasis on the strength of the student's secondary school record. Required test scores (ACT or SAT), school recommendations, and other personal qualifications as demonstrated by extracurricular activities are also carefully evaluated by the Faculty Committee on Admissions. Secondary school graduation or an equivalency diploma is required.

Prospective students and their parents are encouraged to call the Admission Office to plan a visit to the campus, observe a class, and meet with an admission counselor.

Transfer applicants must meet freshman admission standards and have at least a C average (2.25 on a 4.0 scale) with a minimum of 15 hours of academic work. Applicants must be in good standing from the last college attended. If the applicant has attended more than one college, the overall grade point average obtained at these schools must meet the minimum academic average required at Huntingdon. Transfer students may enroll at the beginning of any semester.

Application and Information

Applications are processed and notification is given on a rolling basis. Early admission is available after the junior year of high school for students of exceptional ability. Materials to be sent include the completed Application for Admission, a $25 application fee, an official high school transcript, and scores on either the ACT or SAT I.

For more information, students should contact:

Office of Admission
Huntingdon College
1500 East Fairview Avenue
Montgomery, Alabama 36106-2148

Telephone: 334-833-4497
800-763-0313 (toll-free)
Fax: 334-833-4347
E-mail: admiss@huntingdon.edu
World Wide Web: http://www.huntingdon.edu

Social and academic activity flourish in the parklike setting affectionately known as "The Green."

HUSSON COLLEGE

BANGOR, MAINE

The College

Husson College was founded in 1898 as a commercial college committed to the development of business skills of a practical nature. The decades following the College's establishment were characterized by continuing growth and expansion. In 1968, the College moved to its present location, a beautiful 200-acre campus on the edge of the city of Bangor, approximately 1 mile from downtown. Modern residence halls provide comfortable living quarters for students. The total enrollment of 2,005 students includes 1,400 undergraduates.

Campus life accommodates a wide range of interests. Women's intercollegiate sports are basketball, cross-country, field hockey, soccer, softball, and volleyball. Men compete in baseball, basketball, cross-country, football, and soccer, and golf is a coed intercollegiate sport. The athletic teams have competed in national tournaments and have had an outstanding record of success over the years. There are honor societies, an a cappella choir, sororities, fraternities, professional business societies, a student government, a student newspaper and yearbook, two prayer groups, and WHSN, the campus radio station. Events at the College include concerts, movies, lectures, and similar activities. Residential life also plays an important role in the education of the students. On-campus housing is guaranteed for four years. Student residence halls are coeducational by floor, and there are no triples. Each residence hall room is equipped with a telephone jack, cable TV outlet, and two data ports. The College has a nearly barrier-free campus.

Husson is accredited by the New England Association of Schools and Colleges, the Commission on Collegiate Nursing Education, the Commission on Accreditation in Physical Therapy Education, and the Accreditation Council for Occupational Therapy Education.

The Husson College Dining Service, located in the Dickerman Dining Commons, has been recognized as one of the best in the business by the National Association of College and University Food Services for its efforts to meet the needs of a diverse student population.

Husson places a great deal of emphasis on equipping the student with marketable job skills. The professionally staffed Office of Career Counseling assists students in making career choices and in finding jobs. Husson College has an excellent placement record because employers appreciate the Husson educational program and the sound professional training of the College's graduates.

Master's degrees are offered in business (M.S.B.), nursing (M.S.N.), physical therapy (M.S.P.T.), and occupational therapy (M.S.O.T.). The M.S.B. program is designed for individuals in supervisory or administrative positions in business and education who have not had previous business or managerial training, as well as for business college graduates who desire more advanced education in their areas of expertise. The M.S.N. program (family and community nurse practitioner studies and advanced practice psychiatric nursing) reflects Husson's ongoing commitment to educate nurses for the challenges of the twenty-first century. Graduates are eligible to sit for the American Nurses Credentialing Center Family Nurse Practitioner certification exam. The M.S.P.T. and M.S.O.T. programs are five-year entry-level master's programs.

Post-master's certificates are offered for adult psychiatric mental health nurse practitioners, advanced practice psychiatric nursing, and family and community nurse practitioners.

Husson also offers a B.S./M.S.B. degree in accounting.

Location

Bangor is a city of 33,000 people on the Penobscot River, about 40 miles from the Atlantic Ocean and famed Bar Harbor and Acadia National Park to the south and equidistant from the Canadian border on the east and New Hampshire on the west. Mount Katahdin, Baxter State Park, Moosehead Lake, and several well-known ski areas are within a 1- to 3-hour drive of the campus. The region abounds in recreation opportunities.

Majors and Degrees

Husson College offers programs of study leading to the Bachelor of Science (B.S.) and Associate of Science (A.S.) degrees. B.S. degrees are offered in accounting, biology, biology teacher education, business administration (family business, finance, general, international, management, marketing, small business, sports management), business technology education, computer information systems, criminal justice, elementary education, hospitality management, nursing, occupational therapy, paralegal studies, physical education, psychology, and science and humanities.

In addition, Husson offers A.S. degree programs in accounting, business administration, computer information systems, criminal justice, and paralegal studies. A one-year undeclared major is offered.

Academic Program

A cooperative education option, allowing students to combine job experience with the opportunity to earn up to 12 academic credits, is available in most four-year programs.

Academic Facilities

Peabody Hall contains classrooms, computer labs, a library, administrative offices, a campus center, an art gallery, and a chapel. Bell Hall houses the Physical Therapy, Occupational Therapy, and Nurse Practitioner Labs. The Newman Athletic Center has a double gymnasium, an Olympic-size swimming pool, a new state-of-the-art fitness center, and tennis courts. The Communications Building houses the New England School of Communications.

The computer labs are open 24 hours a day and are equipped with Pentium computers; students work in a Windows NT environment. All students have e-mail addresses and access to the Internet. Computer kiosks are located in the administration building for easy access.

Costs

The basic academic-year expenses in 2004–05 are $10,800 for tuition, $5850 for room and seven-day board, and $250 for the comprehensive fee. Even though the cost of living in the area is somewhat lower than in other parts of the country, students should plan to have sufficient funds available for books and personal expenses.

Financial Aid

The majority of Husson students receive some form of financial aid. The dollar amount of financial aid to be offered to the student is determined by the Free Application for Federal Student Aid (FAFSA). On the basis of this review, financial aid is authorized in the form of Federal Pell Grants, Federal Supplemental Educational Opportunity Grants, Federal Perkins Loans, and Federal Work-Study awards. There are several academic scholarships awarded annually on a competitive basis. The College strives to help each student find whatever financial aid is available and appropriate to help reduce the cost of education. Part-time jobs off campus are also available.

Faculty

The Husson faculty is oriented toward teaching rather than research. There are 44 full-time and 27 part-time professors. The small size of classes enables students to develop academic relationships with their professors. Husson's small-college environment attracts and holds highly dedicated faculty members who share a commitment to the development of the whole student.

Student Government

There is an elected Student Senate, and students serve on many committees across the College. The President of the Student Senate is a voting member of the College Board of Trustees.

Admission Requirements

Husson College believes that all individuals who have the desire to further their education should have the opportunity to develop college-level competence. Admission is refused to applicants who do not demonstrate the potential to succeed in a college program. All applicants are considered on an individual basis.

Applicants to the freshman class are admitted on the strength of their secondary school curriculum, grade point average, class rank, counselor recommendations, and SAT I or ACT scores in relation to their intended major. Students whose high school transcripts show limited academic performance may be accepted on a conditional basis if they have a favorable recommendation from a high school guidance counselor or principal and show evidence of potential for success.

Transfer students are welcome and must present transcripts of their high school and college records. Transfer applicants should be in good academic standing and generally need a grade point average of at least 2.0 to be eligible for admission.

Application and Information

Husson College's rolling admission program allows applications to be reviewed as soon as they are complete. Application may be made for either the September or January term. There is a $25 application fee. All applicants should have copies of their transcripts sent to the Admissions Office as soon as possible after applying for admission.

Applicants are encouraged to get to know Husson College. Campus tours and open house programs, including the Fall Open House in November and the Spring Open House in March, provide candidates with an opportunity to visit the College and experience campus life. Prospective students may also visit at other times, and personal interviews are recommended.

Additional information and application materials are available by contacting:

Director of Admissions
Husson College
One College Circle
Bangor, Maine 04401
Telephone: 207-941-7100
800-448-7766 (toll-free)
Fax: 207-941-7935
E-mail: admit@husson.edu
World Wide Web: http://www.husson.edu

An aerial view of the Husson College campus.

THE ILLINOIS INSTITUTE OF ART–CHICAGO

CHICAGO, ILLINOIS

The Institute

The Illinois Institute of Art–Chicago is a leading institution for career preparation in the visual and practical arts, fashion, and culinary arts fields. It is a member of the Art Institutes, which also has several other locations throughout the United States. Founded in 1916 as the Commercial Art School, the Institute was one of the first applied art and design schools in the United States. The Institute became widely known in the 1930s as Ray Vogue School in recognition of its professional programs in fashion, art, and design. Renamed Ray College of Design in 1981 and joining the Art Institutes in 1995, the Institute offers the Bachelor of Fine Arts, Bachelor of Arts, and Associate of Applied Science degrees.

Students attend the Institute to prepare for and begin careers in creative industries. A strong faculty of working professionals strengthens students' skills and cultivates their talents through curricula that are reviewed often to meet the needs of a changing marketplace and qualify graduates for entry-level positions in their chosen fields. Programs are designed with the support and contributions of leading members of the professional community.

Chicago offers students an abundance of sporting, recreational, and cultural events that are world-class. When not in class, many Institute students participate in on-campus clubs such as the Student Animators Club, Fashion Focus, the American Institute of Graphic Artists, and the American Society of Interior Designers.

The Institute is dedicated to providing its students with safe, comfortable housing. Many students live in Pavillion Suites, school-sponsored apartments just a short train ride from the campus.

Location

Chicago, a world center of business, communication, and art, is located on the shores of Lake Michigan. The Institute is located downtown in the art and fashion center of River North in the heart of the city. City transportation is available nearby and also serves suburban locations, including Midway and O'Hare airports.

Majors and Degrees

The Illinois Institute of Art–Chicago offers eleven bachelor's degree programs in advertising, culinary management, digital media production, fashion design, fashion marketing and management, game art and design, interactive media design, interior design, media arts and animation, visual communications, amd visual effects and motion graphics. Associate of Applied Science degrees are offered in culinary arts, fashion merchandising, fashion production, graphic design, and multimedia production.

Academic Programs

The bachelor's degree programs require 180 quarter credit hours, which can be earned in three years of full-time study, while the associate degree programs require 96 quarter credit hours, which can be earned in eighteen months of full-time study. There are required core courses, depending on the program, which introduce students to the fundamentals and foundations of their chosen field, followed by hands-on projects providing real-world experience. The curricula offer a challenging blend of textbook study and actual on-the-scene training. All programs are offered on a year-round basis, allowing students to work toward their degrees in an uninterrupted fashion.

Academic Facilities

The Illinois Institute of Art–Chicago occupies approximately 70,000 square feet of space in the Apparel Center/Merchandise Mart complex in downtown Chicago. Classrooms, studios, computer labs with Internet access, administrative and student services offices, galleries, and the Resource Center are available for study and research. In addition, the fashion department contains a full complement of special equipment, such as power sewing machines and large cutting tables and steamers. Fashion merchandising classes utilize a walk-in window, props, mannequins, and other display materials. The Interior Design Resource Center has an extensive collection of fabric and wall- and floor-covering samples.

Located eight blocks from the Mart Center campus, the Loop campus includes the culinary facility occupying approximately 35,000 square feet. The facility contains kitchens, classrooms, and a full-service restaurant and dining lab, which serves lunch to the public. The Loop campus also has multiple computer labs and studios for recording, video shooting, and audio development.

Costs

Tuition is $351 per credit hour and $5616 per quarter for full-time study for all programs, not including a starting kit (with cost ranging from $185 to $660, depending on the program) and various monthly fees for books and supplies, which may range from $50 to $180 per month. Housing costs vary.

Financial Aid

The Illinois Institute of Art–Chicago offers several scholarship programs. Some are awarded by the Art Institutes to winners of various competitions. Six half-tuition scholarships are awarded to high school competition winners. Two scholarships are awarded to recipients of a Regional Portfolio Competition for high school seniors. The Institute also makes available a limited number of scholarships to international students and has a family assistance plan available when two or more family members are currently enrolled.

Various private and government loan programs and grant programs are also available. The Financial Services Department helps students and families develop individual financial plans to meet expenses, including tuition, fees, starting kit, and the cost of living.

Faculty

The Institute has 110 faculty members, the majority of whom hold a master's degree in their field. Many are professionals who have real-world experience in the subjects they are teaching.

Admission Requirements

A prospective student seeking admission to the Institute must be a high school graduate, hold a General Educational Development (GED) certificate, or have earned a bachelor's degree from an accredited college or university to be considered for admission. Each applicant is interviewed, either in person or by telephone. Exams such as the SAT and ACT are considered, but are not required. High school transcripts are required, and each applicant must write an essay (300 words if applying to a bachelor's program, 150 if applying to an associate program). A $50 application fee and a $100 registration fee are required. All applicants for whom English is not the native language must either score 480 or above on the TOEFL, successfully complete a Level 108 ELS course, or have graduated from a high school or university where the primary language of instruction is English.

Application and Information

For the 2004–05 academic year, start dates are July 12, 2004, October 4, 2004, January 10, 2005, and April 4, 2005. Applications should be made in advance of the quarter in which the student wishes to enroll. The Institute has an Early Acceptance program for high school seniors.

Students may request additional information from:

Janis K. Anton
Vice President/Director of Admissions
The Illinois Institute of Art–Chicago
350 North Orleans Street
Chicago, Illinois 60654-1510
Telephone: 312-280-3500
800-351-3450 (toll-free)
Fax: 312-280-8562
E-mail: janton@aii.edu
World Wide Web: http://www.ilic.artinstitutes.edu

ILLINOIS INSTITUTE OF TECHNOLOGY

CHICAGO, ILLINOIS

The Institute

Illinois Institute of Technology (IIT) is a private, Ph.D.-granting research university with undergraduate programs in architecture, engineering, humanities, psychology, and science. One of the seventeen institutions in the Association of Independent Technological Universities (AITU), IIT offers exceptional preparation for professions that require technological sophistication. Through a committed faculty and close personal attention, IIT provides a challenging academic program focused on the rigor of the real world. The internationally famous main campus is based on a master plan developed by the late Ludwig Mies van der Rohe, one of the most influential architects of the century, who served for twenty years as director of IIT's College of Architecture. An independent university, the Institute includes the College of Architecture, the Armour College of Engineering and Science, the Institute of Psychology, the Stuart School of Business, the Institute of Design, and the Chicago-Kent College of Law.

The more than 6,000 students at IIT (more than 1,500 of whom are undergraduates) are encouraged to participate in the many social, cultural, and athletic opportunities available. Student activities include the campus newspaper, the radio station, special interest clubs, theater and music groups, intramural and varsity athletics, fraternities and sororities, honor societies, professional societies, student government, residence hall organizations, and the student-run Union Board. Campus facilities include the new McCormick Tribune Campus Center, a convenience store and campus book store, a gymnasium, seven residence halls, six new residence halls, one resident sorority house, and seven resident fraternity houses. Counseling, job placement, and student health services are included in the various campus services.

Location

IIT stands in the midst of a developing urban area. It is 1 mile west of Lake Michigan and one block from the White Sox ballpark. The campus is located approximately 3 miles south of the Chicago Loop, offering students unlimited opportunities to enjoy art, music, drama, films, museums, and other entertainment. Also convenient to the campus are a number of recreational areas, including McCormick Place exhibition hall, Soldier Field, Grant Park, Lincoln Park Zoo, various bicycle paths, and lakefront beaches. IIT is easily accessible to the rest of Chicago via two major expressways. Bus and elevated train lines have stops on the campus, and the IIT shuttle bus provides free transportation between the campus and the university's Downtown Campus in Chicago's West Loop area.

Majors and Degrees

The Armour College of Engineering and Science offers the Bachelor of Science in Engineering with specializations in aerospace, architectural, biomedical, chemical, civil, computer, electrical, mechanical, and metallurgical and materials engineering as well as a Bachelor of Science degree in applied mathematics, biology, business administration, chemistry, computer information systems, computer science, humanities, Internet communication, molecular biochemistry and biophysics, physics, political science, professional and technical communication, and psychology.

The College of Architecture awards the Bachelor of Architecture degree through its five-year professional degree program.

There are various options and minors available within each curriculum, such as artificial intelligence, bioengineering, business, computer-aided drafting, law, management, manufacturing technology, military science, psychology, public administration, and technical communications. Other individualized specializations may be arranged with approval of the dean. Combined undergraduate/graduate degrees include those offered in conjunction with business administration (B.S./M.B.A.), law (B.S./J.D.), and public administration (B.S./M.P.A.).

Along with its traditional premed program, IIT has also established an honors combined program in engineering and medicine (B.S./M.D.) with the Finch University of Health Sciences/Chicago Medical School and Rush Medical College and an honors research program. IIT also offers an honors combined program in law (B.S./J.D.) with the Chicago-Kent College of Law and in pharmacy (B.S./Pharm.D.) with Midwestern University/Chicago College of Pharmacy. Students interested in an honors program must submit an undergraduate application and a supplemental application for the graduate portion of the program. All application materials are available online.

Academic Program

While requirements vary according to the major, all IIT students complete a general education core, which includes a minimum of 7 semester hours in mathematics and computer science, 11 semester hours in natural science or engineering, 12 semester hours in the humanities, and 12 semester hours in the social sciences. Students pursuing a Bachelor of Science in Engineering or in the physical sciences take, in addition, a program that includes further study in mathematics and computer science, chemistry, and physics.

IIT's mission is to educate students for complex professional roles in a changing world and to advance knowledge through research and scholarship. The Institute is committed to the educational ideal of small undergraduate classes and individual mentoring. IIT's unique Introduction to the Professions program brings students and senior faculty members together each week in small groups, where students interact with their advisers as both teachers and mentors. Throughout the curricula, the IIT interprofessional projects provide a learning environment in which interdisciplinary teams of students apply theoretical knowledge gained in the classroom and laboratory to real-world projects sponsored by industry and government. Many IIT students further enhance their education through a wide variety of research and entrepreneurial projects.

Cooperative education is encouraged. This career development program begins with a freshman year of full-time study and then alternates semesters of study and employment in industry for approximately four additional years. Placement services are provided by the university. Ninety-two percent of recent graduates were placed in jobs in the fields of their majors or went on to graduate or professional schools.

Study abroad is available in several academic disciplines.

Academic Facilities

As the central library, the Paul V. Galvin Library provides a broad range of services, including information on engineering, business, science, mathematics, the humanities, architecture, and design via the Internet; numerous electronic and paper-based databases; a document delivery service; interlibrary loan; and special collections. The main campus operates DEC minicomputers, a Silicon Graphics "Challenge" UNIX multiprocessor, and local UNIX servers. Terminals and microcomputers are located in most academic buildings across the campus, in residence halls, and in Galvin Library. Seminars, tutorials, and computer lab work are conducted in microcomputer classrooms. Among IIT's thirty-two research centers are the Center for Synchrotron Radiation Research, the Fluid Dynamics Research Center, and the Research Laboratory in Human Biomechanics. Most research centers offer undergraduates opportunities to participate on their projects.

Costs

Annual tuition for 2003–04 was $19,775. Other expenses are $6282 for room and board and approximately $1000 for books, $1200 for transportation costs, and $2100 for personal expenses. Additional fees are $100. The estimated annual total for freshmen is $29,482. Annual tuition covers the fall and spring semesters.

Financial Aid

Most full-time undergraduates at IIT receive financial aid from a variety of sources. IIT participates in the Federal Perkins Loan, Federal Work-Study, Federal Pell Grant, Federal Supplemental Educational Opportunity Grant, federally insured student loan, Illinois State Scholarship Commission Monetary Award, Illinois Guaranteed Loan, and Federal PLUS loan programs and similar programs. In addition, IIT provides generous merit-based and need-based scholarships and loans from its own funds and from those supported by a number of companies and other organizations. The Camras Scholarships range from $59,000 to $91,000 for the study of any major. A supplemental application is required for Camras Scholarships. All admitted students are automatically reviewed for tuition scholarships. More than 500 are awarded each year. Athletic scholarships are also available for qualified students. Two other programs may be utilized by students working to supplement their financial aid: on-campus employment and the cooperative education program. IIT requires the Free Application for Federal Student Aid (FAFSA). No additional applications or forms are required.

Army, Naval, and Air Force ROTC programs are offered. ROTC scholarship winners receive supplemental scholarships from IIT.

Faculty

There are 339 full-time faculty members and 196 industry professionals as part-time faculty members. The student-faculty ratio is approximately 12:1. All members of the senior teaching faculty instruct in both upper- and lower-division courses. Ninety-eight percent hold doctoral degrees or the highest professional degree in their area.

Student Government

The Student Government Association (SGA) is a vital force in the IIT community. It acts as the students' official voice in communications with faculty and administration, and it plans, develops, and supervises most of the activities pertaining to campus life. In addition to having its own standing committees, SGA is represented on seven of the ten institutional committees pertaining to undergraduates.

Admission Requirements

Admission evaluation is a thorough, personal process. Of paramount consideration is the student's academic performance in high school, specifically in areas that are vital to the student's major at IIT. Minimum high school preparation includes 16 units of credit, including at least 4 units in English, 4 units in mathematics through pre-calculus, and 3 units of science with 2 lab sciences. Calculus is encouraged but not required. Chemistry and physics are strongly recommended.

A completed application, recommendations, test scores—either SAT I or ACT—and an official high school transcript are required for admission. Interviews are not required. Supplemental applications and materials are required for the Honors Program in Engineering and Medicine, the Honors Law Program, the Honors Pharmacy Program, and for the Camras Scholarship Program. Special deadlines apply to these programs. All materials are available online.

Application and Information

Applications are reviewed on a rolling basis. Students are encouraged to apply as early as possible; an online application is available at http://www.iit.edu/~apply. In general, applicants can expect notification within two weeks after their completed applications are received.

For further information, students should contact:

Office of Admission
Illinois Institute of Technology
10 West 33rd Street
Chicago, Illinois 60616-3793
Telephone: 312-567-3025 (from Chicago)
800-448-2329 (toll-free outside Chicago)
Fax: 312-567-6939
E-mail: admission@iit.edu
World Wide Web: http://www.iit.edu

IMMACULATA UNIVERSITY
IMMACULATA, PENNSYLVANIA

The University

Immaculata, a comprehensive Catholic liberal arts university for students of all faiths, offers a high-quality education firmly grounded in values and tradition. Immaculata graduates are known for their skills and knowledge and also for their desire to serve. The University was founded in 1920 and has since grown to enroll 3,400 students in bachelor's, master's, and doctoral degree programs and accelerated degree completion programs.

Approximately 400 traditional-age students attend the College of Undergraduate Studies, with 85 percent of them living in campus housing. The College of Lifelong Learning includes undergraduate programs that are open to adult men and women, most of whom commute. Students represent eighteen states and fifteen countries, giving the campus both ethnic and geographic diversity. Eight percent of the students are members of minority groups. Resident students live in four dormitory buildings containing both double and single rooms. Both resident and nonresident students participate in more than thirty student clubs and organizations that represent interests in athletics, student government, academic disciplines, community action, music, dance, theater, and student publications.

Intercollegiate sports include women's basketball, cross-country, field hockey, lacrosse, soccer, softball, tennis, and volleyball. Men's sports for 2005 include basketball, soccer, and tennis; men's and women's golf (coed) is also planned. Athletic fields, gymnasiums, a weight room, and an Olympic-size swimming pool are available for student use and provide numerous opportunities for physical activities and wellness programs. The Student Association of Immaculata University provides the unity, enthusiasm, and leadership that are integral parts of the traditional undergraduate experience.

Immaculata University celebrates unique traditions as a part of the overall collegiate experience, such as Freshman Investiture, the academic capping of the newest members of the University community. Carol Night, one of Immaculata's best-loved traditions, involves students, faculty members, and alumni and families singing around the Christmas tree in the rotunda of Villa Maria Hall.

The main building, Villa Maria Hall, is of neo-Renaissance architecture in gray stone with a red tile roof. The other thirteen major campus buildings are also of gray stone with red tile roofs, unifying the aesthetic appearance of the campus. Renovations of the three main buildings, Villa Maria, Lourdes, and Nazareth halls were completed in December 2000.

Graduate degrees offered in the College of Graduate Studies include the Master of Arts in counseling psychology, cultural and linguistic diversity, educational leadership and administration, music therapy, nursing, nutrition education, and organization leadership. Doctoral degrees are offered in educational administration, clinical psychology, and school psychology. The ACCEL® degree completion program offers bachelor's degrees in financial management, human performance management, information technology in business, nursing, and organizational dynamics; this program also offers an Associate of Science degree in business administration.

Location

Immaculata's 400-acre campus is located in historic Chester County, 20 miles west of Philadelphia and 10 miles south of Valley Forge. The area is primarily suburban, with numerous colleges and universities offering a wide range of cultural and social activities. The many places of interest in Philadelphia and Lancaster are easily reached by car or train. Southern New Jersey shore resorts and New York City are within 2 hours by car, with Pocono Mountain ski resorts and Washington, D.C., only 2½ hours away by car or train. The University provides numerous opportunities for internships in the business, educational, and scientific communities throughout the area.

Majors and Degrees

The College of Undergraduate Studies at Immaculata offers the Bachelor of Arts, Bachelor of Music, Bachelor of Science, Associate of Arts, and Associate of Science degrees as well as certification in education for preschool through grade 12. Undergraduate major fields of study include accounting, biology, biology/chemistry, biology/psychology, business administration, criminology, dietetics, economics, education certification, English, exercise science, family and consumer sciences/home economics education, fashion marketing, finance, foods in business, French, general science, history, history–international studies, history–politics, information technology, international business/foreign language, international studies, mathematics, mathematics/computer science, music, music education, music therapy, nutrition/dietetics, prelaw, premedicine, psychology, public policy, sociology, sociology/social work, Spanish, Spanish/psychology, Spanish/social work, and theology. Most of the majors at Immaculata can be combined with certification in early childhood, elementary, secondary, or special education.

Academic Programs

Two factors are emphasized in the educational program at Immaculata: a comprehensive liberal arts background and a major field of concentration that prepares students to begin a career or to attend graduate school. Degrees in all majors require 126 credits. This number includes 54 credits in a liberal arts core, which is required of all students. The honors program, an option for gifted students, offers an array of courses designed to give those who participate a special involvement in the learning process.

The Mary Bruder Center houses the offices for personal, career, and graduate study counseling and for educational and career testing. Workshops and seminars in resume writing, interviewing, career options, internship opportunities, and graduate fellowships are offered at regular intervals.

The University operates on a four-day week class schedule, with Wednesday as an open day, allowing opportunities for educational observations and junior-senior internships. The academic schedule is traditional—spring and fall semesters with two summer sessions.

Off-Campus Programs

Both summer-abroad and junior-year-abroad programs combine travel with academic study to broaden the experience of students who seek these opportunities.

Every undergraduate major department offers internship opportunities for students in agencies, businesses, institutions, or corporations related to their study. Some majors—dietetics, nutrition, fashion marketing, and music therapy—require a multiweek internship for the degree.

Academic Facilities

The Gabriele Library, dedicated in 1993, houses 130,000 volumes and offers 714 periodical subscriptions and 3,609 units of microfiche. In addition to the computer center, students have access to networked computers in the library, an interactive language lab with a video screen, and a multifacet science lab with computer-simulated experiments; they also have Internet/Intranet access from their dorm rooms. Well-equipped laboratories, art studios, media centers, and a 1,150-seat theater give students more than adequate facilities in which to pursue their interests.

Eight state-of-the-art computer labs include the Campus Learning and Language Laboratory, the Sister Maria Socorro Studio Laboratory for Mathematics and Science, a new Biology Laboratory, and the Loyola Executive Technology Center. Classrooms and the library utilize wireless technology.

Costs

For 2004–05, tuition and fees are $18,000, and room and board are $8250. An additional $1000 is estimated to cover books and personal spending. A fixed tuition rate guarantees the same tuition cost for a maximum of four years for all full-time students that are entering the College of Undergraduate Studies.

Financial Aid

Financial aid is available in the form of scholarships, grants, loans, and part-time campus employment through the resources of Immaculata, federal and state governments, and private endowments. Scholarships are awarded for academic excellence. Approximately 90 percent of the students receive some form of aid, and all students who demonstrate need are offered financial aid packages. The University sends financial aid packages to accepted students as their files are completed after January 1. The Free Application for Federal Student Aid (FAFSA) reporting code is 003276.

Faculty

The faculty has 78 full-time and 199 part-time members, more than half of whom hold doctorates. All others have at least one master's degree. Although several members of the Immaculata faculty have conducted research and presented papers in various disciplines, both nationally and internationally, high-quality teaching is of the greatest importance to Immaculata's academic program. Full-time faculty members serve as academic counselors and activity moderators. The student-faculty ratio is 11:1.

Student Government

The Student Association of Immaculata University (SAIU) governs most aspects of student life for both resident and commuter students. The resident-assistant program moderates dorm life by holding open meetings to discuss safety issues and to set dorm regulations. Students serve on the various University policymaking committees and handle all student activity funds.

Admission Requirements

In order to be considered for admission to the College of Undergraduate Studies, students must submit an official secondary school transcript indicating course selection for the senior year and SAT I or ACT scores. The reporting code for the SAT I is 2320, and the reporting code for the ACT is 3596. Writing samples and an admission interview, while not required, can enhance a candidate's application. The Admission Committee requires a minimum secondary school GPA of 2.5 in 16 or more course units as follows: 4 units of English, 2 units of social science, 2 units of mathematics, 2 units of science (1 lab), and 2 consecutive years of the same foreign language. Most candidates exceed this curriculum.

All admission credentials should be sent to the address below. Students can apply online at the Web site listed below. The application fee can be waived for students with great financial need.

Application and Information

Applications are accepted from prospective freshman and transfer students on a rolling basis, and decisions are made three to four weeks after an applicant's file is complete.

For further information, students should contact:

The College of Undergraduate Studies
Immaculata University
P.O. Box 642
Immaculata, Pennsylvania 19345-0642
Telephone: 610-647-4400 Ext. 3015
877-428-6329 (toll-free)
Fax: 610-640-0836
E-mail: admis@immaculata.edu
World Wide Web: http://www.immaculata.edu

Students at Immaculata University.

INDIANA STATE UNIVERSITY

TERRE HAUTE, INDIANA

The University

Indiana State University (ISU) is a publicly assisted, comprehensive, residential institution offering instruction at the associate, bachelor's, master's, and doctoral levels. It was founded in 1865 as the Indiana State Normal School. Through the years, it evolved through successive stages as the Indiana State Teachers College and Indiana State College. It attained university status in 1965. University enrollment stands at 11,360. In fall 2003, undergraduate enrollment was 9,997 students. Graduate enrollment was 1,717. The Indiana State University educational experience is enriched by the presence of a diverse student body drawn from throughout Indiana and the rest of the country and more than sixty other countries.

Indiana State's identity and its vision for the future are based on a historic embrace of the values of opportunity and success for all of its students. In seeking to extend this vision into the twenty-first century, the University, through its Strategic Plan, is promoting excellence in areas such as technology; the student experience, particularly in the first year; teaching and learning; outreach; scholarships; and partnerships with educational institutions, government agencies, business and industry, service learning, and individuals.

ISU is committed to providing a high-quality educational experience in a student-centered learning environment. The student-faculty ratio is 19:1, and approximately 89 percent of classes at ISU have 39 or fewer students. Seventy-nine percent of classes are taught by full-time faculty members. Students can choose from more than 120 majors, ranging from criminology to packaging technology, athletic training to geography, teacher education to insurance and risk management, and safety management to nursing. The School of Graduate Studies offers master's and doctoral programs in a number of the areas listed in the Majors and Degrees section. Many of ISU's academic programs are nationally known, and some are the only ones of their kind in the state. The insurance and risk management program is listed as one of the top four programs in the nation by the *Journal of Risk and Insurance* in terms of the breadth of courses offered and as one of the top eight programs in the country by *Independent Agent* magazine. The campus's undergraduate and graduate programs in athletic training were the first in the nation to be accredited. ISU is also one of only a few institutions in the country that has accredited undergraduate and accredited master's programs in this field. The Doctor of Psychology in clinical psychology program is the only program of its kind in the state accredited by the American Psychological Association. The criminology program is one of the largest graduate programs in the state and houses one of only two criminalities laboratories in the state that foster education in basic, advanced, and forensic investigation techniques. The College of Education's Professional Development Schools Partnership received the 2002 Christa McAuliffe Award for Leadership and Innovative Teacher Education from the American Association of State Colleges and Universities. In the College of Technology, ISU's programs in industrial automotive technology and packaging technology are the only ones of their kind in the state.

The Hulman Memorial Student Union Board provides cultural, social, educational, and recreational programming for the Student Union and for the entire campus. As the primary all-campus programming board, the Union Board produces events that involve the whole student body, such as Homecoming and Tandemonia, a weeklong spring festival featuring a tandem bike race. Students at ISU can choose from among nearly 200 organizations and clubs. Students can compete in intramural sports. ISU's athletic teams compete in the NCAA Division I.

Location

Indiana State University's scenic campus is adjacent to the downtown area of Terre Haute, which comprises a metropolitan area of 100,000 people in west-central Indiana. The University's proximity to downtown Terre Haute helps to foster a number of partnerships between the campus and local businesses, government agencies, and civic organizations. Terre Haute serves as the fine arts, cultural, and athletic center of west-central Indiana and east-central Illinois. Terre Haute has the Sheldon Swope Art Museum, the Eugene V. Debs Museum, the Terre Haute Symphony Orchestra, Community Theatre, and the historic Indiana Theater. The city also has an extensive and excellent parks system. It is convenient to four major metropolitan areas: Indianapolis is within 75 miles, and St. Louis, Chicago, and Cincinnati are each only 180 miles away.

Majors and Degrees

Indiana State's undergraduate academic programs are offered through its College of Arts and Sciences and its professional Colleges of Education, Business, Nursing, Technology, and Health and Human Performance.

College of Arts and Sciences programs include African and African-American studies; anthropology; art; art history; chemistry; child development and family life; clinical laboratory science; communication studies; computer science; criminology (two- and four-year programs); dietetics; economics; English; English teaching; family and consumer science education; fine art; food and nutrition; food service management; foreign language concentration (international studies); French; French teaching; general family and consumer science; general studies (two-year program); geography; geology; German; German teaching; history; information technology; interdisciplinary studies; interior design; journalism; Latin; legal studies; liberal studies; life sciences; managerial communications; mathematics; mathematics education; music; music business administration; music composition; music education; music history and literature; music merchandising; music performance; music theory; philosophy; physics; political science; pre–dental hygiene; predentistry; pre-engineering; prelaw; premedicine; preoptometry; prepharmacy; pretheology; pre–veterinary medicine; psychology; public relations; radio/television/film; science education; social studies education; social work; sociology; Spanish; Spanish teaching; speech communication and theater teaching; study of religion; textiles, apparel, and merchandising; theater; visual arts education; and women's studies.

The College of Business offers programs in accounting, administrative office systems, business administration, business education, finance, insurance, management, management information systems, marketing, office support and technology (two-year program), and quality and decision systems.

The College of Education has programs in child development and early childhood education (two-year program); communication disorders; counseling; curriculum, instruction, and media technology; early childhood education; educational and school psychology; elementary education; kindergarten–primary education; school media services; special education; and speech-language pathology.

The College of Health and Human Performance has programs in athletic training, community health, environmental health, health-safety education, physical education, pre–occupational therapy, recreation and sport management, safety management, and sports studies–fitness and exercise science.

The College of Nursing has a four-year nursing program.

The College of Technology offers programs in aerospace administration, architectural technology (two-year program), biomedical electronics technology, computer hardware technology, computer-integrated manufacturing technology, construction technology, electronics and computer technology (two-year program), electronics technology, general aviation–flight (two-year program), general industrial technology, human resource development, industrial automotive technology, industrial supervision, industrial technology (two-year program), instrumentation and control technology, manufacturing technology, manufacturing supervision (two-year program), mechanical technology, packaging technology, printing management, professional aviation flight technology, technology education, trade and industrial education (two-year program), vocational trade-industrial teaching, and vocational trade-industrial-technical area.

Academic Programs

ISU's academic strength lies in its liberal arts and professional programs of study, its interdependent undergraduate and graduate programs, and its extensive student development programs. Undergraduate programs combine general education with majors and minors. All students working toward a bachelor's degree at Indiana State must take a minimum of 42 to 57 semester hours of general education course work, including 11 to 26 hours of basic studies and 31 hours of liberal studies. Most degree programs require 124 semester hours and a minimum 2.0 grade point average for graduation. Baccalaureate degree candidates must have earned at least 50 semester hours of residence credit at Indiana State. The academic calendar includes fall and spring semesters and summer sessions of varying lengths.

The University Honors Program, which offers special courses, colloquia, seminars, and independent study, is designed to challenge talented students and help them broaden and enhance their education. A variety of distance education programs are available. The transformation of student life through the development of learning communities is the result of the First-Year Experience Program, which was funded by a $2-million grant from the Lilly Endowment. The Student Academic Services Center offers a number of programs for students with special needs. Indiana State's Career Center helps students formulate career goals, gain career-related work experience while in school, and find employment. Air Force and Army ROTC programs are available.

Academic Facilities

Indiana State is committed to providing students with facilities that match the excellence of its academic programs. Over the past several years, the University, through its Campus Master Plan, has completed a number of building projects, including the Center for Fine and Performing Arts, which combines state-of-the-art performance facilities and an art gallery; the John T. Myers Technology Center, which features specially designed laboratories and classrooms in a high-technology setting; and Root Hall, a classroom building for the humanities. The Student Computing Complex offers students access to computers 24 hours a day. Computer clusters are also located in residence halls and other buildings throughout campus. All residence hall rooms are wired for Internet access.

With more than 1 million books and more than 5,000 subscriptions to periodicals and journals, the Cunningham Memorial Library ranks as one of the finest collegiate libraries in the Midwest. The library was one of the first in the state to computerize its card catalog and continues to be a leader in making information available in various electronic formats, including CD-ROM and the Internet.

The University also has laboratories and other learning resources such as computer-integrated manufacturing, a remote sensing and geographic information systems laboratory, the Writing Center, specially designed rehearsal rooms, fully equipped science laboratories, an observatory, and a human performance laboratory.

Costs

Fees for full-time undergraduate students are $10,844 per year for Indiana residents and $23,780 for nonresidents. On-campus housing costs and board are included in these figures.

Financial Aid

ISU awards financial aid to about 71 percent of its students. Indiana State University offers financial assistance to students in a number of forms, including loans, grants, scholarships, and work-study. Payment plans are also available. ISU awards more than $1 million in scholarships each year. Prestigious scholarship programs such as the President's Scholars and the Alumni Scholars are available to outstanding high school students. Those students who meet the minimum academic requirements for a scholarship are mailed a scholarship application after they have been admitted. Students also may be considered for financial assistance such as loans and grants after gaining admission to the University. Those who apply for assistance before March 1 are given priority. Students should file the Free Application for Federal Student Aid (FAFSA) and an Indiana State Financial Aid Application.

Faculty

Indiana State's instructional programs are carried out by its 458 faculty members. As a teaching university, ISU expects its faculty members to give highest priority to instruction and the intellectual and personal development of students. Faculty members, however, also are expected to be engaged in meaningful and productive scholarship and professional service and to integrate what is learned from these activities into their teaching. Faculty members also serve as student advisers and assist students in the planning of their academic programs.

Student Government

The Student Government Association (SGA), of which every student is a member, is the governing body for all ISU students. SGA operates under its own constitution and consists of three branches: legislative, executive, and judicial.

Admission Requirements

Admission applications are reviewed as they are received. Students are considered for admission after receipt of complete credentials—an application, a nonrefundable $25 processing fee, and official transcripts from all schools and colleges previously attended. Freshman and transfer students who have completed fewer than 24 transferable semester credit hours must submit scores from either the SAT I or ACT. In general, freshman applicants are expected to rank in the upper half of their high school graduating class, have completed Indiana Core 40, and have passed the ISTEP Graduation Qualifying Examination for Indiana residents for regular admission. Additional information is available from high school counselors or the ISU Office of Admissions. It is suggested that prospective students visit the campus and talk with a member of the admissions staff.

Application and Information

High school students should complete an application in the fall of their senior year. To ensure full consideration, applications and official transcripts must be received in the Office of Admissions by August 1 for the fall semester, December 1 for the spring semester, May 1 for the first summer session, and July 1 for the second summer session. Indiana State encourages all prospective students to visit the campus. Requests for appointments and information should be addressed to:

Director of Admissions
Tirey Hall
Indiana State University
Terre Haute, Indiana 47809
Telephone: 812-237-2121
800-742-0891 (toll-free)
E-mail: admisu@amber.indstate.edu
World Wide Web: http://www.indstate.edu

INDIANA UNIVERSITY OF PENNSYLVANIA

INDIANA, PENNSYLVANIA

The University

Founded in 1875, Indiana University of Pennsylvania (IUP) draws its enrollment of 13,868 from nearly every state and from scores of other countries. With three campuses located in the foothills of the Allegheny Mountains, IUP is the largest of the fourteen universities in the State System of Higher Education and the only one that grants doctoral degrees.

Recognized as a "public Ivy," the University sustains a tradition of high academic quality at an affordable cost. In forty-five academic departments located within six colleges and two schools, IUP offers more than 100 major fields of study. Graduate programs in many professional and applied areas are available, as are seven doctoral programs. IUP has one of the largest internship programs in Pennsylvania, providing students with professional experience to supplement their classroom learning.

The following publications have recognized IUP for its high academic standards and competitive costs: Arco's *Dollarwise Guide to American Colleges*; Barron's *300 Best Buys in College Education*; *The Best Buys in College Education* by Edward Fiske, education editor of the *New York Times*; *Changing Times* by Martin Nemko; *Kiplinger's Personal Finance* magazine's annual *100 Best Buys*; *Money* magazine's Money Guide; *Two Hundred Most Selective Colleges: The Definitive Guide to America's First-Choice Schools*; The Princeton Review's *The Best 331 Colleges*; and *U.S. News & World Report*.

Location

Located 50 miles northeast of Pittsburgh in the borough of Indiana, the seat of Indiana County, IUP is just three blocks from the town's business district. The University is easily accessible by automobile from all sections of the state. Passenger services of various kinds operate on frequent schedules, connecting Indiana with all nearby cities and towns, including Pittsburgh, Altoona, and Johnstown. Bus service connects Indiana with the main line of the Pennsylvania Railroad at Johnstown and Pittsburgh. The community of Indiana has more than thirty churches that represent all major faiths. All churches are within walking distance of the campus.

Majors and Degrees

IUP awards B.A., B.S., B.F.A., B.S.Ed., and B.S.N. degrees in approximately 100 majors in the areas of the arts and sciences, business, consumer services, elementary and secondary education, fine arts, food and nutrition, health and physical education, home economics, medical technology, nursing, respiratory therapy, and safety sciences. IUP also offers the Associate of Arts degree in business. Dual majors are available to students who wish to augment their academic background.

Academic Programs

IUP provides for the nourishment of the whole person through its Liberal Studies Program. In addition to fulfilling the 53-semester-hour Liberal Studies requirement, each student must complete the necessary major and minor requirements to reach the minimum total of 120 credits necessary for graduation.

Courses taken by students under the Advanced Placement Program of the College Board prior to admission may be recognized by the awarding of college credit or by the exemption of required subjects from the students' curriculum. For students who have acquired learning in nontraditional or other ways or who have advanced in a given field, an opportunity to gain exemption from a course is offered through examinations given at the discretion of each department.

The University offers an Army Reserve Officers' Training Corps (ROTC) program.

IUP operates on two 14-week semesters—September through December and January through May—plus two 5-week summer sessions.

Off-Campus Programs

The University participates in joint programs with other colleges and universities. Included in these cooperative programs are one in family medicine with Jefferson Medical College of Thomas Jefferson University, one in forestry with Duke University, two in engineering with Drexel University and the University of Pittsburgh, one in graphic arts with the Art Institute of Pittsburgh, one in jewelry with the Bowman Technical School, one in optometry with Pennsylvania College of Optometry, and one in podiatry with Philadelphia School of Podiatry.

The Office of International Affairs has arrangements for students to study in numerous countries. Each year, approximately 200 students study abroad. Other opportunities for off-campus study include the marine science consortium, the graphic arts exchange program, internships, and studies in the health services, which are offered through the University's affiliations with hospitals and other universities.

Academic Facilities

The Information Systems and Communications Center, established in 1963 on the ground floor of Stright Hall, provides computational support for undergraduate and graduate courses, faculty and student research, and the administrative requirements of the University. Terminals are located in the center and in various other locations on campus.

The University's campuswide cable system and fiberoptic backbone are fully connected to all academic buildings and each residence hall room, allowing immediate connection to the University's mainframe computer and access to the University's television station and educational programming.

The Stapleton-Stabley Library complex provides study space for about 1,200 students. The monograph holdings total more than 835,000 volumes. The general holdings are enhanced by the reference collection, which has more than 2,200 periodical subscriptions, 2.3 million items of microforms, and an extensive media collection. IUP is a designated select depository for federal and state publications and is currently housing more than 34,000 volumes of governmental publications. The Special Collections and Archives collections highlight the labor history and industrial heritage of western Pennsylvania. Media Resources provides children's and curricular material to support the teacher preparation programs. The Cogswell Music Library houses approximately 10,000 books, 15,000 scores, 10,000 recordings, and 2,000 CDs. There is a public computer lab in Stapleton. An increasing percentage of resources is available in full text electronically. The Industrial Design Center actively supports the growing distance education courses.

Costs

The basic costs that a student who is a resident of Pennsylvania could expect to incur per semester while enrolled at IUP in 2003–04 included $2893 for tuition and fees, $2351 for room and board, and approximately $500 for books and supplies. Additional costs include $500 to $1000 for personal expenses. Tuition for out-of-state students was $6367 per semester. All costs are subject to change.

Financial Aid

More than 80 percent of IUP students received some type of financial assistance during the 2002–03 academic year. The types of financial aid offered by IUP include student employment, loans, grants, and scholarships. In most cases, the Free Application for Federal Student Aid (FAFSA) serves as the application used to determine eligibility for these programs. Federal student assistance is available during the fall, spring, and summer terms. The application deadline for all students for the FAFSA is April 15, with award notifications to accepted freshmen beginning on March 15. Financial assistance is also available through IUP's Army ROTC program.

Faculty

There are 632 full-time and 62 part-time teaching faculty members. The student-faculty ratio is 19:1. While primarily serving as instructors, faculty members also aid students in course selections and career planning and advise student organizations and clubs.

Student Government

IUP students actively participate in the governance of the University through the Student Congress and through elected representatives to the University Senate.

Admission Requirements

Any graduate of an accredited four-year high school or holder of a high school equivalency diploma is qualified to apply for admission to IUP. Applicants are reviewed by the Admissions Committee on the basis of high school records, recommendations, and scores earned on the SAT I or the ACT. Applicants are expected to name their major field upon application, but a change in major can be made prior to or during the freshman year.

Application and Information

Applications are accepted for consideration for the fall and spring semesters after July 1 of the preceding year. Applications are reviewed on a rolling basis, beginning in September, until vacancies are filled.

To request an application or further information, students should contact:

Office of Admissions
117 Sutton Hall
1011 South Drive
Indiana University of Pennsylvania
Indiana, Pennsylvania 15705
Telephone: 724-357-2230
800-442-6830 (toll-free)
Fax: 724-357-6281
E-mail: admissions-inquiry@iup.edu
World Wide Web: http://www.iup.edu/admissions

INTERNATIONAL ACADEMY OF DESIGN & TECHNOLOGY

CHICAGO, ILLINOIS

The Academy

The International Academy of Design & Technology–Chicago is a postsecondary degree-granting institution with career-based curricula and professional staff members who contribute to students' development in their chosen fields. The Academy provides a high-quality education, prepares students for positions in fields related to their area of study, provides students with a professional environment that fosters cultural enrichment and personal development, maintains high-quality curricula that are sensitive to industry needs as defined by the Academy's advisory board, and offers career-planning services leading to employment opportunities for graduates to allow them to utilize their knowledge, skills, and talents.

The International Academy of Design & Technology was founded in 1977 by Clem Stein Jr. as a private coeducational institution. In 1983, the Academy opened a campus in Toronto, Canada. The Tampa, Florida, campus was opened in 1984, and in 1987, the fourth campus was opened in Montreal, Canada. In 1997, Career Education Corporation acquired the Academy. Career Education Corporation operates postsecondary institutions throughout the U.S. and abroad. In 2001, the Academy changed its name from the International Academy of Merchandising & Design to the International Academy of Design & Technology, which better reflects the infusion of technology into all of the program curricula.

The Academy sponsors a student chapter of the American Society of Interior Designers (ASID) and offers student memberships in the American Marketing Association (AMA) and the Fashion Group International Chicago, Inc. These student groups introduce students to the standards set by professional organizations and provide access to professional seminars and workshops. The Student Ambassador Program assists new students through their transition to the Academy and college life.

Other forms of student involvement include the Fashion Council, clubs organized by and for multimedia and information technology students, the International Students Organization, and the student-produced magazine *Mixed Media*.

The Academy is approved by the Illinois State Board of Education and authorized by the Illinois Board of Higher Education to grant the Bachelor of Arts degree in merchandising management; the Bachelor of Fine Arts degree in advertising and design, fashion design, interior design, and multimedia production and design; and the Associate of Applied Science degree in advertising and design, computer graphics, fashion design, interactive media, merchandising management, and PC/LAN.

The Academy is incorporated under the laws of the state of Illinois and accredited by the Accrediting Council for Independent Colleges and Schools (ACICS). The interior design program is accredited by the Foundation for Interior Design Education Research (FIDER).

Location

The Academy is located in Chicago's Loop at historic One North State Street. The campus is close to some of Chicago's famous and world-renowned landmarks. Within walking distance of the campus are the Merchandise Mart and Apparel Center complex in historic River North and the retail shops of North Michigan Avenue. Along the revitalized State Street are Marshall Field's, Carson Pirie Scott, and a multitude of nationally advertised retail outlets. More importantly, IADT Chicago is conveniently located in a region known for its internationally prominent advertising, graphic design, and interior design firms.

Nearby cultural and educational resources include the Art Institute of Chicago, the Harold Washington Library, the Chicago Cultural Center, the Athenaeum Museum of Architecture and Design, the Chicago Architecture Foundation, and the Goodman Theatre.

The natural beauty of Grant Park and the numerous public art works that are located throughout the Loop are the ideal complement to IADT Chicago's exciting urban location.

Majors and Degrees

All degree programs provide students with the opportunity for in-depth career preparation and a firm foundation in general education studies. In the bachelor's degree program, students benefit from advanced career courses and have the option of choosing elective courses to complete their general education requirements.

The International Academy of Design & Technology offers bachelor's degrees in advertising and design, fashion design, interior design, information technology, merchandising management, and multimedia production and design. Associate degrees are offered in advertising and design, computer graphics, fashion design, information technology, iteractive media, and mrchandising management.

Academic Programs

The programs of the Academy involve both classroom education and supervised activities off campus that are designed to prepare students for entry-level positions in their chosen field. Students must take a minimum of 180 quarter hours of study to earn the baccalaureate degree. Transfer credits are acceptable in all programs. Students must take a minimum of 90 quarter hours to earn the Associate of Applied Science degree and must complete all prescribed courses satisfactorily with a minimum grade point average of 2.0.

The curriculum for each program is reviewed periodically by the faculty members, program directors, and members of the faculty advisory council, who, along with the president and deans, constitute the Curriculum Advisory Committee. Members of the Faculty Advisory Council are experienced professionals in the fields of fashion, interior design, advertising, merchandising, multimedia production and design, computer graphics, interactive media, and information technology. The Faculty Advisory Council provides the Academy with counsel on a variety of subjects and also participates in seminars. These successful practitioners form an essential link between the academic world and the world that students enter upon graduation.

The Academy's programs are arranged into four quarters of eleven weeks each. A normal full-time load is 15 credit hours per quarter. As a result of the career-oriented emphasis of the Academy, course work is highly specialized and prepares students for entry into a career field. From the point at which they begin their studies at the Academy, and continuing through graduation, students are given personal one-on-one academic guidance. Students are regularly advised by the Academy's faculty members regarding their progress in classes.

Academic Facilities

Classrooms are designed to facilitate learning and consist of lecture rooms, drafting labs, design studios, and sewing and pattern-making rooms. Computer labs equipped with Macintosh and IBM-compatible personal computers are used for instruction and practice in computer-aided design (CAD), graphic design, word processing, database management, spreadsheet analysis, and computer-aided pattern drafting.

The library houses a growing collection of approximately 5,500 book volumes and 90 periodical subscriptions to support the major programs of study as well as general education courses. The library's multimedia resources consist of more than 500 videos, DVDs, and CDs with image and sound files. Other components of the collection are electronic resources with access to eBooks, full-text journals, magazines, and newspaper articles. A professional librarian manages the site and assists students in the use of the library's print collection and online databases. The librarian also facilitates student access to local libraries that participate in the INFOPASS program.

The bookstore sells books and supplies used in the courses taught at the Academy. The bookstore attempts to keep a balance of inventory between new and used books whenever possible. The bookstore also coordinates book buy-back periods at the end of each quarter.

Costs

Full-time tuition for the 2003–04 academic year was $13,800 for all programs. Books and supplies ranged from $300 to $2000.

Financial Aid

The Academy helps students find the financial resources they need to achieve their educational goals. The College participates in the Federal Pell Grant, Federal Supplemental Education Opportunity Grant (SEOG), Federal Stafford Student Loan, and the Federal PLUS loan program. In addition to state and federal aid, the Academy has its own scholarship programs.

Faculty

Faculty members of the Academy possess extensive academic and professional credentials. Their experience enables them to teach theoretical principles while emphasizing current practices in the field. Faculty members are sought and retained because they are committed to teaching at the undergraduate level. In and out of the classroom, the faculty is an integral part of the students' career preparation.

Student Government

The Student Council meets quarterly to discuss issues pertaining to student campus life at the college.

Admission Requirements

Pursuant to the mission of the institution, the Academy desires to admit students who possess appropriate credentials and have demonstrated the capacity or potential for successfully completing the educational programs offered by the institution. To that end, the institution evaluates all students and makes admission decisions on an individual basis. To assist the admissions personnel in making informed decisions, an admissions interview is required.

Transfer students meeting admission requirements are accepted. Students must have a transcript from the postsecondary institution previously attended forwarded to the Academy. Credit may be given for a course taken at the previous institution if it is comparable in scope and length to an International Academy course.

Application and Information

Prospective students should apply for admission as soon as possible in order to be officially accepted for a specific program and starting date. Prospective students must have an admissions interview and are given an opportunity to tour the Academy with their families to see its equipment and facilities, during which time, there is also an opportunity to ask questions relating to the Academy's curricula and a student's possible career goals.

At the time of application, the student must complete an enrollment agreement, pay a $50 application fee, complete an attestation of high school graduation or its equivalency or provide proof of high school graduation or its equivalency, and provide proof of immunization as required by Illinois law. Once an applicant has completed and submitted the enrollment agreement, the school reviews the information and informs the applicant of its decision.

For further information, students should contact:

Robyn Palmersheim, Vice President of Admissions
International Academy of Design & Technology
One North State Street, Suite 400
Chicago, Illinois 60602-3300
Telephone: 312-980-9200
877-222-3369 (toll-free)
Fax: 312-541-3929
E-mail: info@iadtchicago.com
World Wide Web: http://www.iadtchicago.com

INTERNATIONAL COLLEGE OF THE CAYMAN ISLANDS

NEWLANDS, GRAND CAYMAN, CAYMAN ISLANDS

The College

International College of the Cayman Islands (ICCI), situated in one of the world's premier banking and financial business centers, is ideally located to prepare students for careers in business. The College, founded in 1970, operates as a nonprofit, privately controlled, American-style senior college in Newlands, Grand Cayman.

The international student body is made up of about 200 men and women each quarter and usually includes representatives from other Caribbean islands as well as from countries around the world. The student body demonstrates intergenerational diversity, with students ranging in age from their late teens up to retired seniors. This diversity enhances class discussions and is an integral part of the educational goals of ICCI. ICCI offers the flexibility of allowing students to enroll for any one of the four quarters.

Caribbean flavor permeates the College campus, with its tropical bungalow–style buildings and colorful flowers and palm trees. The rich cultural heritage of the Cayman Islands, available to students through the National Museum, Heroes' Square, the Turtle Farm, Queen Elizabeth Botanic Park, the Blow Holes, the Wreck of the Ten Sails, environmental tours on land and sea, and local art and craft production of all kinds, enhances the educational experience at ICCI. No place is very far away from another on this 22-mile island. The sister islands, Cayman Brac and Little Cayman, are also popular tourist destinations. The bluff on Cayman Brac has a 150-foot-high limestone formation. Bloody Bay Wall, ranked by *Skin Diver* magazine in May 1999 as the world's premier dive site, is located in the waters off Little Cayman.

The island abounds in recreational activities such as running, swimming, SCUBA diving, golfing, volleyball, softball, netball, basketball, cricket, rugby, soccer, bicycle racing, and miniature golf. Soccer and cricket are two of the sports played professionally on the island. Three Caymanians have qualified to enter the 2004 Olympic Games in Athens, Greece. ICCI is less than 4 miles from Spotts Public Beach and 2½ miles from Pedro St. James Castle, the site of the "birthplace of democracy in the Cayman Islands." There are cultural events, such as plays, musicals, and concerts, at the Harquail Theatre as well as at the Prospect Playhouse. The National Gallery hosts local and international exhibits. The Student Activities Sub-Committee (SASC), as well as other student committees, plan boat cruises, beach picnics, banquets, and other activities for the enjoyment of students and faculty members. Annual festivities, such as the Agricultural Fair, the art show at the governor's mansion, Batabano Festival, and Pirates Week, are part of the island and campus life.

Students live off campus. Upon request, the College assists students in finding suitable accommodations.

The Accrediting Council for Independent Colleges and Schools (ACICS), Washington, D.C., accredits the College as a senior college to award associate, bachelor's, and master's degrees. In addition to its undergraduate programs, the College offers a Master of Business Administration degree program and a Master of Science degree program in management, with a human resources or education concentration.

Location

The Cayman Islands, located in the Caribbean Sea south of Cuba and west of Jamaica, are internationally famous for exceptional water sports. The clarity of the 80-plus-degree ocean waters makes underwater photography and fishing major attractions for the more than 1 million visitors to the Cayman Islands each year. The islands are an English-speaking British Overseas Territory, known for the friendliness of their approximately 40,000 citizens. The temperature averages 85 degrees year-round, with sunshine and gentle trade winds.

The College, located in the quiet, rural village of Newlands, is a 15-minute drive from the capital, George Town, and Grand Cayman's airport, Owen Roberts International.

Majors and Degrees

The Associate of Science degree is offered in business, with concentrations in accounting, banking, broadcasting, finance, hotel and tourism management, and information systems. General studies and office administration are also offered at the associate degree level.

The Bachelor of Science degree is offered with majors in business administration, community service, liberal studies, and office administration. Several concentrations are available within these major areas, including accounting, an interdisciplinary arts/science concentration for elementary school teachers, international finance, and Dean-approved liberal studies concentrations.

For those employed in the banking industry, the Bachelor of Science degree in business administration with a concentration in international finance meets the requirements for direct entry into the associateship program of the British Chartered Institute of Bankers (ACIB). The business administration program also has an accounting concentration.

Academic Programs

The academic year consists of four quarters—fall, winter, spring, and summer. A full academic load is 12–15 credits each quarter. A typical course is 5 credits.

A minimum of 180 credit hours is required for the Bachelor of Science degree, with no fewer than 60 credits earned in upper-division (300- and 400-level) courses and at least 55 credits in general education courses outside the major field. The specific requirements for each major vary. Credit by examination is available.

A minimum of 90 credit hours is required for the Associate of Science degree. No fewer than 25 credits must be earned in general education courses.

A cumulative grade point average of 2.0 or higher is required of all students in undergraduate programs at the College. To fulfill degree residence requirements, the equivalent of three quarters of full-time study must be taken at International College of the Cayman Islands.

The College also offers developmental courses in English, reading, math, and English as a second language.

Off-Campus Programs

Students who have earned at least 45 credits and meet additional criteria may participate, with approval, in internship programs with businesses and agencies and receive up to 5 credits for participation in the program. Each quarter, one or more seminars are offered over a long weekend in Miami. Two Miami seminars are required for graduation. Some of the many business and community service organizations that operate on the island are Rotary, Kiwanis, Lions Club, and Toastmasters.

Academic Facilities

A computer laboratory, equipped with Pentium 133 personal computers, is provided by the College. The library houses a constantly updated collection of books, 140 periodicals, CD-ROM subscriptions to ProQuest and SIRS, an Internet subscription to LIRN, and a multimedia center, which includes computers with CD-ROM and Internet access. The Cayman Islands' first radio station, ICCI-FM, 101.1 MHz, is owned and operated by the College and is staffed by students and community volunteers as a workshop for the school's Broadcasting Department. This department is one of the very few in the Caribbean that trains radio students for careers in this field and offers the Associate of Science degree in business with a concentration in broadcasting management.

Costs

In 2002–04, tuition per course for an associate or bachelor's degree was $468.75. A registration fee of $62.50 and other fees of about $20 were charged each quarter. Books cost approximately $1250 for the school year. (All costs are in U.S. dollars.)

Financial Aid

Four kinds of financial assistance are available for students who qualify when funding permits: scholarships, grants, grants-in-aid, and loans. (Grants-in-aid include campus work assignments.) Approximately 15 percent of the students at International College of the Cayman Islands receive financial assistance.

Faculty

International College of the Cayman Islands has a full-time and adjunct faculty of 40. Adjunct faculty members generally work full-time in the area in which they teach, giving students the benefit of current, hands-on business experience tested in the marketplace. About 65 percent of the full-time faculty members hold earned doctorates, and all full-time faculty members serve as academic advisers. Guest lecturers, drawn to the Cayman Islands from around the world, share their expertise with students. Most classes are small, enabling the instructors to know their students by name. The student-faculty ratio is 15:1.

Student Government

The Student Activities Sub-Committee (SASC) is a dedicated core group of students who also serve as a voice in student government. All students are invited to join this organization. In addition, the Academic Council includes student representation.

Admission Requirements

Admission to the College for undergraduate studies is determined on an individual basis. Generally, a student should be at least 17 years old.

Admission to an undergraduate degree program at ICCI requires submission of a completed, paid application form and graduation from high school or its equivalent. In addition, a student must meet one of the following criteria: have a minimum SAT I score of 1010 or an ACT cumulative score of at least 21; be a mature student (five or more years post–high school graduation with relevant work and/or business experience); have five General Certificate of Education (GCE), General Certificate of Secondary Education (GCSE), Caribbean Examinations Council (CXC), or other passes inclusive of English; or be a transfer student with credit(s) from an accredited, internationally recognized college or university. Transfer students must submit official transcripts. Applicants must also provide two letters of reference attesting intellectual and emotional readiness for college-level work. A satisfactory interview is required of local residents. In addition, a Test of English as a Foreign Language (TOEFL) score of at least 550 (paper-based) or its equivalent is required for international students whose native language is not English.

Each applicant is requested to visit the College and meet with one of the College admissions personnel or faculty members for a personal interview and to discuss plans and career goals.

Continuing education or transient students are required to provide a completed, paid application form. Overseas students should request a Student Visa Application Packet and return all completed application materials at least four months before the beginning of the quarter in which they wish to enroll. Cayman Islands immigration approval is a prerequisite for overseas students' enrollment. A one-year deposit is required.

Application and Information

Applications for any quarter are considered at any time up to the opening of the quarter; however, overseas students must submit an application at least four months before the quarter in which they wish to enroll. Overseas applications must be sent via international airmail and include a nonrefundable application fee of $37.50 (U.S. dollars).

For application forms and additional information, students should contact:

Director of Admissions
International College of the Cayman Islands
P.O. Box 136 SAV
Grand Cayman, Cayman Islands
Telephone: 345-947-1100
Fax: 345-947-1210

ICCI's Caribbean-style campus.

INTERNATIONAL UNIVERSITY IN GENEVA

GENEVA, SWITZERLAND

The University

The International University in Geneva is an American university in Europe that proposes undergraduate and graduate degrees in the areas of business administration and communication and media. The International University in Geneva emphasizes the importance of interpersonal skills, such as leadership, communication, and the ability to work in a multicultural team. These skills are encouraged through active participation and regular presentations in class.

The multicultural student body and faculty and the dynamic environment of the University contribute to the creation of a framework in which the students acquire global experience. The use of experiential learning methods such as case analysis and business simulations ensures the development of analytical skills, which are critical in today's competitive and rapidly changing world.

Students have access to several sport facilities, including basketball, volleyball, and tennis courts. Students have unlimited access to the Internet. The University provides personalized assistance for students looking for University housing or private apartments. An extensive range of student lodging is available in Geneva.

The University is accredited by the International Assembly for Collegiate Business Education (IACBE). The University is chartered by the Department of Education of the state of Delaware (U.S.A.) and is a Candidate for Accreditation with the Middle States Association of Colleges and Schools.

Location

The College of Business Administration and Media and Communication is located in a modern building in Geneva. Geneva belongs to a select group of truly "international" cities of the world, making it an ideal place to study international management. The city is host to the United Nations and specialized agencies such as the World Trade Organization and is often referred to as the capital of peace and diplomacy.

Many multinationals are located in the region due to the excellent logistical network and the central location of Geneva at the heart of Europe, only one hour by air from London, Paris, Brussels, and Milan. Geneva is well-known as one of the world's major international financial centers, especially for the management of private capital assets.

The quality and variety of Geneva's cultural life, with its numerous theatres, museums, and international conferences, makes it the right place to obtain a global education. The city is a showcase for the most celebrated names in fashion, jewellery, and watch-making and is home to Rolex and Patek Philippe, among others. Ideally situated on the shores of Lake Leman at the foot of the Alps, Geneva offers excellent outdoor sporting activities.

Majors and Degrees

The International University in Geneva awards the Bachelor of Business Administration degree and a Bachelor of Arts degree in media and communication. Two concentrations are offered: computer information systems and international relations.

Academic Program

The academic year consists of two semesters, and summer courses are available. Students in the undergraduate programs must achieve a minimum total of 128 credits. The minimum total can be reduced by transfer credits or waiver examinations. As part of the academic program at the undergraduate level, students are required to take a foreign language such as French, Spanish, or Italian. With an emphasis on management and media, the curriculum helps the student to prepare for a career in business and related areas.

Off-Campus Programs

International University in Geneva has developed educational affiliation agreements with DePaul University, Chicago; Fordham University, New York; Indiana University of Pennsylvania; Michigan State University (MSU); Monterey Institute of International Studies, California; and the University of Connecticut in the United States and with Anahuac University in Mexico City and the Universidad de San Ignacio de Loyola in Lima, Peru.

Academic Facilities

Most of the University's classrooms are equipped with state-of-the-art equipment including beamers, video equipment, and Internet access. All the computers have ADSL technology, allowing rapid Internet connections.

Costs

The 2003–04 tuition fees were 22,200 Swiss francs (or the equivalent in U.S. dollars) and include books. Access to the library and the computer center is free of charge. Room and board costs average 3,000 Swiss francs per semester.

Financial Aid

Each year, International University in Geneva sponsors several assistantships. The selection criteria for the assistantships include academic achievement and the financial need of the applicant. A student can apply for an assistantship by writing a letter, which should be included with the application form. Students receiving the assistantships are required to devote 15 hours per week to the University performing administrative duties.

Faculty

The faculty at International University in Geneva is multidisciplinary in professional training, international in experience, and practical in orientation, and its members are focused on their teaching. The full-time faculty is organised into unit coordinators, and the adjunct faculty is drawn from other educational institutions in the area and from the business community.

Student Government

The Student Council is the principal representation of student governance in the University. The Student Council is elected once a year and is organized into several subcommittees, including the Year Book Committee.

Admission Requirements

The International University in Geneva seeks a diverse student body and encourages applications from around the world. Admission to the University is competitive and emphasizes the applicant's previous academic performance and intellectual capacity. For the student's convenience, applications are considered on a rolling admission basis. The University has three starting dates throughout the academic year, in September, January, and May.

To enter the undergraduate program, the applicant must have successfully completed secondary education or high school with a minimum grade point average (GPA) of 2.3. In addition, the student is required to possess proficiency in English. The Test of English as a Foreign Language (TOEFL) is required of all applicants whose native language is not English. The minimum TOEFL score required is 213 (computer-based test).

Application and Information

To be considered for admission, a student must submit the application form with the application fee of 150 Swiss francs (or $100); an official high school transcript should be sent by the school. An application and additional information may be obtained by downloading an electronic application form from the University's Web site listed below or by contacting:

International University in Geneva
ICC, route de Pré-Bois 20
1215 Geneva 15
Switzerland
Telephone: (+41 +22) 710 71 10
Fax: (+41 +22) 710 71 11
E-mail: info@iun.ch
World Wide Web: http://www.iun.ch

IONA COLLEGE

NEW ROCHELLE, NEW YORK

The College

Iona College is a four-year, coed, comprehensive college in the suburbs of New York City. It is a medium-sized college with an average class size of 15 students. Iona offers more than forty majors. The most popular undergraduate majors are biology, business, computer science, education, and mass communication. Iona is also a Catholic college, founded by the Congregation of Christian Brothers, where ethical decisions and service to others are primary considerations.

Iona's overall enrollment is about 4,600, of whom 3,100 are traditional undergraduate students. The student body is talented and diverse, with students coming from thirty-five states and fifty-four countries. Thirty-three percent of the students are members of minority groups and contribute to a college environment that values different cultures.

Students are active and involved on campus. More than ninety clubs and activities are available for student participation, including student government, fourteen fraternities and sororities, intramural sports, community service organizations, an award-winning newspaper, radio and television stations, the yearbook, theater groups, a pipe band, ethnic-affinity groups, various honor societies, music groups, and many other possibilities.

Iona offers twenty-one NCAA Division I sports. Men's sports include baseball, basketball, crew, cross-country, football, soccer, swimming and diving, track (indoor and outdoor), and water polo. Women's sports include basketball, crew, cross-country, soccer, softball, swimming and diving, track (indoor and outdoor), and water polo.

The Office of Student Development operates two student clubs: the Gael Club, a nightclub; and The Isle at Iona, a coffeehouse. Student Development also organizes many activities for students to participate in each week. The activities include trips to New York City for theater, sports, and museums; movie nights; parties and dances; karaoke nights; wellness workshops; and other activities.

Iona offers five different residence halls, and 67 percent of freshmen live on campus. The College's board plan includes the normal campus dining hall, but also can be used at seven local eateries.

Location

Iona's campus is located in New Rochelle, New York, one of the oldest cities in the U.S. Founded in 1654, New Rochelle is a city of 70,000 on the shore of the Long Island Sound. It is a suburban community that borders New York City. Public transportation allows students to easily travel to Manhattan via commuter train in less than 30 minutes.

Majors and Degrees

Iona College offers the Bachelor of Arts, Bachelor of Science, and Bachelor of Business Administration degrees in majors including accounting, biochemistry, biology (general, preprofessional), business administration, chemistry, computer science, criminal justice, ecology, economics, education (early childhood, childhood, adolescence), English, finance, foreign languages (French, Italian, Spanish), history, information and decision technology management, interdisciplinary science, international business, international studies, management, marketing, mass communication (advertising, journalism, public relations, television and radio), mathematics, mathematics–applied, medical technology, philosophy, physics, political science, psychology, physical therapy (joint B.S./M.S. program with New York Medical College), religious studies, social work, sociology, speech communication studies (humanistic communication, theater and speech arts), and speech/language pathology and audiology. Five-year combined bachelor's and master's degree programs are offered in computer science, history, and psychology.

There are also minors available in accounting, biology, business, chemistry, classical humanities, computer science, criminal justice, economics, English, film studies, finance, fine arts, French, German, gerontology, history, information and decision technology management, international business, Italian, management, marketing, mass communication, mathematics, peace and justice studies, philosophy, physics, political science, psychology, religious studies, sociology, Spanish, speech communication, women's studies, and writing. A number of programs offer a business minor in combination with a major or concentration. For example, a student planning a career in theater management might major in theater arts and minor in business.

Academic Program

The College offers the B.A., B.S., and B.B.A. degrees to undergraduate students. The B.A. and B.S. degrees require a total of 120 credits for completion; for B.B.A. degrees, a total of 126 credits is required. As a general rule, the core curriculum fills one third of the student's credit total; a major fills the second third; and elective courses, a minor, or a second major fill the final third. During the fall and spring semesters, most students take five 3-credit courses. Classes are also offered during an intensive winter session and during two summer sessions.

An honors program is available for top students who want additional enhancement to their academic program. Special courses, seminars, mentoring, advising, and off-campus opportunities are part of the honors students' curriculum.

Off-Campus Programs

Iona College encourages students to broaden their educational experience through study and travel abroad. Iona sponsors summer, semester, and intersession programs in Australia, Belgium, France, Ireland, Italy, Mexico, Morocco, and Spain. The College also offers a wide range of internships in most majors. In recent years, students have held internships at some of the best-known corporate names in New York City and the surrounding area.

Academic Facilities

Outstanding physical facilities complement Iona College's beautiful 35-acre campus in Westchester County. Forty-seven buildings provide modern accommodations for student study. The campus features one of the first wireless computer networks in the U.S. and other significant technological advantages. The predominant style of architecture is red-brick Georgian. During the past few years, every major facility on campus has been renovated. The College has completed construction two new residence halls, and has broken ground on a new student union and a new fitness and health center.

Some of the major academic buildings, including John G. Hagan Hall, Myles B. Amend Hall, and Doorley Hall have been renovated recently to include seminar rooms and computer presentation facilities. Cornelia Hall, home of the Iona science programs, was completely renovated in 2000 and features state-of-the-art equipment for the study of biology and chemistry. The new Iona College Arts Center provides space for the study of art, dance, and music and includes the Brother Kenneth Chapman Gallery. The John A. Mulcahy Campus Events Center includes a multipurpose arena, an Olympic-size swimming pool, a Nautilus center, training facilities, and coaching offices. Mazzella Field is centrally located on Iona's campus and has an artificial turf surface for football, soccer, and other intercollegiate and intramural sports. The Murphy Science and Technology Center is a modern facility complete with communication and computer labs, classrooms, and a technological library. Overall, the College's computer labs have more than 800 computer stations available for student use.

The two campus libraries, Ryan Library and the Helen T. Arrigoni Library/Technology Center, house extensive collections and offer computer access to collections worldwide. The on-site collections, including more than 261,000 volumes, 687 periodical titles, audiovisual materials, and microforms, have been developed to support Iona's curriculum and special interests. They are readily available through the libraries' Web site, which offers subject databases with thousands of complete articles, electronic encyclopedias, and a link to the Internet. Students can access these resources from on and off campus, as well as from the libraries' eighty networked public computers and laptops.

The libraries can assist students with finding material in other libraries as well. With the libraries' Document Delivery Service, students can access and quickly retrieve materials from collections around the world.

Costs

For the 2003–04 academic year, tuition and fees were $18,520; room and board were $9698.

Financial Aid

Financial aid is critical to a student's decision to attend any college, and Iona College is no exception. Iona uses a system of academic scholarships in combination with need-based financial aid to help students enroll. For the 2002–03 academic year, 92 percent of Iona students received aid, with the average financial aid award near $14,000. To apply for financial aid, students should file the Free Application for Federal Student Aid (FAFSA) and the Iona College Financial Aid Application forms by April 15.

Faculty

Iona College has approximately 170 full-time and 80 part-time faculty members; 92 percent possess the terminal degree in their field. Faculty members conduct research and write books and articles, but their primary responsibility is teaching undergraduate students. All classes are taught by faculty members—there are no teaching assistants.

The student-faculty ratio is 16:1. Faculty members are readily available to meet for individual conferences. In addition, because of the College's proximity to New York City, many faculty members include regular trips to Manhattan as part of their classes and invite guest speakers to lecture about special topics.

Student Government

The Student Government Association (SGA) is a service organization that coordinates, supervises, and promotes student activities. The SGA also provides a necessary degree of leadership and coordination for the more than seventy student clubs and societies that are part of the student life at Iona College. Such student groups further the ideals and spirit of the College, attend to particular student interests, and present a definite opportunity for individual growth and development.

Admission Requirements

Admission decisions at Iona are based on a wide range of criteria. An applicant's previous academic record, including the curriculum taken, course level, and grades achieved, is most important. Also considered are SAT I or ACT scores, grade trends, a writing sample, extracurricular activities, work experience, and letters of recommendation.

Application and Information

In order to considered for admission, Iona requires students to submit an application (paper or electronic), a $40 application fee, an official transcript, SAT I or ACT scores, a counselor recommendation, and an essay. Transfer students must include official transcripts from all colleges and universities attended. Iona strongly believes that a rolling admissions policy best serves the needs of prospective students. Therefore, applications are accepted until March 15. Decisions are mailed out beginning January 15, usually within three weeks of the time that the application file is complete. When accepted, a student has until May 1 to tell Iona of his or her decision. If a student is highly interested in Iona, then it may be appropriate to apply under the Early Action Plan. Under early action, a student applies by December 1 and receives his or her decision by December 20. The student then has until May 1 to make a final decision.

Iona welcomes campus visits during any weekday that school is in session and on selected Saturdays. A visit can be scheduled by calling 914-633-2622.

For more information, students should contact:

Office of Admissions
Iona College
715 North Avenue
New Rochelle, New York 10801
Telephone: 914-633-2120
800-231-IONA (toll-free)
Fax: 914-637-2778
E-mail: admissions@iona.edu
World Wide Web: http://www.iona.edu/info

IOWA STATE UNIVERSITY OF SCIENCE AND TECHNOLOGY

AMES, IOWA

IOWA STATE UNIVERSITY

The University

Iowa State University of Science and Technology (Iowa State), a public, broad-based international university of 27,380 students, was established in 1858 as one of the first U.S. land-grant colleges. It is a member of the prestigious Association of American Universities and is accredited by the North Central Association of Colleges and Schools. All fifty states and 112 countries are represented in the student body, exposing students to ideas from other cultures both in and out of the classroom.

Iowa State has grown in size and reputation to become one of the nation's leading educational institutions and has made significant contributions to the development of the United States and the world. Revolutionary innovations include the world's first electronic digital computer, the digital encoding process that led to the development of facsimile machines, and LoSatSoy, a new cooking oil low in saturated fat. Iowa State's graduates include George Washington Carver, one of the nation's most distinguished educators and plant scientists; Carrie Chapman Catt, a leader in the women's suffrage movement; and John Vincent Atanasoff who, as a faculty member at Iowa State, invented the electronic digital computer.

Nearly 8,000 students live on campus in nineteen residence halls and twelve apartment-style buildings. Each of the nineteen residence halls is divided into houses, which are small-group living arrangements of about 60 residents. Wellness houses, learning communities, honors houses, and alcohol- and smoke-free houses are a few of the options available. The Department of Residence is in the midst of a $105-million renovation and improvement project. In addition, 3,000 undergraduates participate in Iowa State's national award-winning Greek system, which encompasses twenty-seven fraternities, thirteen sororities, and six National Pan-Hellenic chapters conveniently located near the campus.

More than 500 clubs and organizations provide unlimited leadership, social, and cultural opportunities. Annually, 3,000 teams participate in fifty intramural sports, 2,500 people participate in forty sports clubs, and 20,000 students, staff members, and faculty members participate in outdoor recreation activities. Facilities include the Lied Recreation/Athletic Center, which houses twenty courts for basketball and volleyball, a rock climbing wall, a 300-meter track, an artificial turf area, and a weightlifting and fitness center; Beyer Hall; the Physical Education Building; the State Gym; and many outdoor facilities. The Cyclones have eighteen Division I intercollegiate men's and women's sports and belong to the Big 12, one of the premier sports conferences in the country.

Outstanding facilities for the cultural and performing arts include the 2,700-seat Stephens Auditorium, the 452-seat Fisher Theater, and the 15,000-seat Hilton Coliseum. Iowa State attracts the top entertainment acts and world-renowned speakers. Recent performers include Shermie Alexie, Bill Cosby, the Dave Matthews Band, Simon Estes, Mae Jemmison, Jars of Clay, Prince, Wynton Marsalis, Nikki Giovanni, Michael W. Smith, Sarah McLachlan, Aerosmith, Dixie Chicks, Blue Man Group, Tool, Toby Keith, Cabaret, and John Mayer.

Personal support services, available to help students become their best, include the following: assertiveness training; career counseling; communication skills workshops; medical, physical, and learning disabled services; and stress management, study skills, and test-taking workshops.

Iowa State University offers 111 master's programs, eighty-two Ph.D. programs, and one professional degree program—the Doctor of Veterinary Medicine.

Location

Iowa State is located in Ames, just 30 minutes north of Iowa's capital, Des Moines. Minneapolis, Chicago, Kansas City, St. Louis, Omaha, and other metropolitan areas are a short drive from Ames or easily accessible by plane and train.

The campus environment rates high with students and faculty and staff members. The book *The Campus as a Work of Art* rated Iowa State among the twenty-five most beautiful campuses in the nation. The American Society of Landscape Architects recently chose Iowa State as a "medallion site," one of the three best central campuses in the nation. Iowa State students spend most of their time on the 24-acre central campus, part of the 1,984 acres.

Ames was ranked the second-best "micropolitan" area (population 50,000 or fewer) in the nation. Students take advantage of arts groups, recreational facilities, biking and hiking trails, more than eighty restaurants, a great downtown, many shopping areas, and a variety of movie theaters.

Majors and Degrees

Iowa State University offers 101 bachelor's degree programs. The College of Agriculture includes programs in agricultural biochemistry, agricultural business, agricultural education, agricultural extension education, agricultural studies, agricultural systems technology, agronomy, animal ecology, animal science, dairy science, dietetics, entomology, environmental science, food science, forestry, genetics, horticulture, international agriculture, microbiology, nutritional science, pest management, plant health and protection, public service and administration in agriculture, seed science, and zoology. The College of Business offers programs in accounting, finance, management, management information systems, marketing, and transportation and logistics. The College of Design offers programs in architecture, art and design, community and regional planning, graphic design, interior design, and landscape architecture. The College of Education offers programs in early childhood education, elementary education, environmental studies, exercise and sport science, industrial technology, and secondary education. The College of Engineering offers programs in aerospace engineering, agricultural engineering, ceramic engineering, chemical engineering, civil engineering, computer engineering, construction engineering, electrical engineering, engineering applications, engineering science, industrial engineering, mechanical engineering, and metallurgical engineering. The College of Family and Consumer Sciences offers programs in apparel merchandising, design, and production; child and family services; dietetics; early childhood education; family and consumer sciences education; family resource management and consumer sciences; food science; hotel, restaurant, and institution management; housing and the near environment; nutritional science; and studies in family and consumer sciences. The College of Liberal Arts and Sciences is the largest college and offers programs in advertising, African-American studies, American Indian studies, anthropology, astronomy, biochemistry, biology, biology/premedical illustration, biophysics, botany, chemistry, classical studies, computer science, earth science, economics, English, environmental science, environmental studies, French, genetics, geology, German, gerontology, history, interdisciplinary studies, international studies, journalism and mass communication, Latin, liberal studies, linguistics, mathematics, meteorology, music, naval science, performing arts, philosophy, physics, political science, Portuguese, psychology, religious studies, Russian, secondary education, sociology, Spanish, speech communication, statistics, technical communications, technology and social change, women's studies, and zoology.

Academic Program

Each college provides academic support through advising offices. Additional academic services include academic learning labs, learning communities, learning teams, peer education, supplemental instruction, and tutoring services. The University Honors Program provides academically talented students an opportunity to stretch their minds through individualized programs, special courses and seminars, unique off-campus opportunities, and 24-hour access to the Martin C. Jischke Honors Building, home of the Honors Program. The academic year is divided into two semesters of sixteen weeks each, beginning in late August and ending in early May. A program called Soar in Four guarantees graduation in four years in all majors except architecture and landscape architecture.

Off-Campus Programs

Students can take advantage of internships, cooperative education programs, and research programs, which provide the opportunity for professional work with national and international companies. International exchange programs are available at more than 100 colleges and universities in forty countries. The National Student Exchange program provides students an opportunity to study at one of 177 reciprocating universities around the country.

Academic Facilities

Iowa State's 173 campus buildings include several recent state-of-the-art additions. Among the newest are the Durham Center for Computation and Communication, the Molecular Biology Building, the Martin C. Jischke Honors Building, the Palmer Educational Building, and Howe Hall, the $61-million engineering facility that is the home of the Engineering Teaching and Research Center (ETRC). Construction is complete on Hoover Hall, a new engineering building, and the Gerdin Building, which houses the College of Business. Technology is utilized to provide students the resources to succeed in a competitive global market. Iowa State is home to C4 and C6, two of the world's most advanced virtual reality rooms. C6 is the only six-sided virtual reality environment in the United States and one of three worldwide. Students are provided free e-mail and Internet access and space to create their own Web pages. Students use AccessPlus via the Web for instant access to jobs, grades, schedules, and more. Computing resources include thousands of workstations, 24-hour availability, and mainframe/Internet access from residence hall rooms.

Costs

For the 2004–05 academic year, in-state tuition and fees are $5426 and out-of-state tuition and fees are $15,128 (based upon full-time undergraduate status for two semesters). Room and board are $6121 for two semesters. Books and supplies are estimated at $820 per year.

Financial Aid

Need- and merit-based financial assistance is available to qualified applicants. Approximately 66 percent of students receive some type of financial aid, such as grants, scholarships, loans, and jobs. Students should apply for admission early to receive maximum consideration for merit scholarships. All applicants are encouraged to file the FAFSA by March 1 (for fall semester enrollment). Links to scholarships and financial aid resources may be found at Iowa State's Web site at http://www.financialaid.iastate.edu.

Faculty

Iowa State has 1,751 faculty members, 77 percent of whom hold doctorates. The student-faculty ratio is 18:1.

Student Government

The Government of the Student Body (GSB) legislates and administers student policy and provides services to meet the needs of students. The functions of GSB are carried out by executives and senators elected by Iowa State students. GSB's primary function is the allocation of student activity fees, through which a number of diverse services and student organizations are funded.

Admission Requirements

Students seeking admission directly from high school must have a minimum of 4 years of English, 3 years of math (including 1 year each of algebra, geometry, and advanced algebra), 3 years of science (including 1 year each of courses from two of the following fields: biology, chemistry, and physics), and 2 years of social studies. In addition, students applying to the College of Liberal Arts and Sciences must have completed an additional year of social studies, for a total of 3 years, plus 2 years of a single foreign language. Grades, class rank, and quality of course work are the most important criteria in the admissions decision.

Transfer applicants are typically admitted if they have a minimum of 24 transferable credit hours and have earned at least a C (2.0) average in all college-level courses attempted. However, some programs may require a transfer grade point average higher than the 2.0 minimum. Higher academic standards may be required of students who are not residents of Iowa, including international students. Applicants who have not completed 24 transferable semester (or 36 quarter) hours prior to enrolling at Iowa State must submit a high school transcript and an ACT or SAT I score and meet all admission requirements for entering freshmen, as well as earn at least a 2.0 average in all college-level courses attempted.

Applicants must submit an application along with a $30 application fee ($50 for international students) and have their secondary school provide an official transcript of their academic record, including credits and grades, rank in class, and certification of graduation. Applicants must also arrange to have their ACT or SAT I scores reported to Iowa State directly from the testing agency. The Test of English as a Foreign Language (TOEFL) is required of international students whose first language is not English. Applicants may be required to submit additional information or data to support their applications.

Application and Information

Students interested in applying for the fall semester should apply during the preceding fall. Students should submit applications for the spring and summer terms six to nine months in advance. Interested students should contact the Office of Admissions at the toll-free number listed below or visit the Web site listed below for an application, a campus visit, financial aid, or other enrollment information.

Office of Admissions
Alumni Hall
Iowa State University of Science and Technology
Ames, Iowa 50011-2010
Telephone: 800-262-3810 (toll-free)
515-294-3094 (TTY/TDD)
Fax: 515-294-2592
E-mail: admissions@iastate.edu
World Wide Web: http://www.admissions.iastate.edu

ITHACA COLLEGE

ITHACA, NEW YORK

The College

Coeducational and nonsectarian since its founding in 1892, Ithaca College enrolls approximately 6,500 students. The College community is a diverse one; virtually every state is represented in the student population, as are seventy-five other countries. Students come to Ithaca College to get active, hands-on learning that brings together the best of liberal arts and professional studies. The program is offered in five schools—the School of Humanities and Sciences (2,500 students), School of Business (650 students), Roy H. Park School of Communications (1,300 students), School of Health Sciences and Human Performance (1,200 students), and School of Music (500 students)—and through interdisciplinary programs (100). There are approximately 250 graduate students.

Freshmen and most upperclass students (with some exceptions) are expected to live on campus. There are fifty-one residence halls, which range from garden apartments to fourteen-story towers. Extracurricular life abounds at Ithaca. There are approximately 130 student organizations, a strong Division III intercollegiate athletic program (twenty-five teams), extensive intramural and club sports programs, and dramatic and musical ensembles. A wide range of services are available, beginning with summer orientation for new students and including career planning and placement assistance, a counseling center, and a health center that is staffed by 4 physicians as well as numerous physician assistants and nurses.

According to College surveys completed in the past three years, 98 percent of first-year graduates are employed and/or are full-time graduate students.

Location

Ithaca College is in Ithaca, New York. Approximately 90,000 people live in the surrounding county, more than a quarter of whom are Ithaca College or Cornell University students. The city combines the cultural and commercial features of a diverse, multicultural, mostly youthful population with the spectacular scenery of central New York's Finger Lakes.

Majors and Degrees

Ithaca awards the Bachelor of Arts, Bachelor of Science, Bachelor of Fine Arts, Bachelor of Music, and the Master of Music, Master of Business Administration, and Master of Science degrees in the more than 100 degree programs offered through its five schools and its Division of Interdisciplinary and International Studies.

The School of Business offers a B.S. in business administration, with concentrations in accounting, finance, international business, management, and marketing as well as a B.S./M.B.A. degree in accounting for those pursuing CPA licensure. In addition, the School of Business also offers a one-year M.B.A. program.

The Roy H. Park School of Communications offers the B.A. in journalism. Also offered are the B.S. in cinema and photography; organizational communication, learning, and design; integrated marketing communications; and television-radio and the B.F.A. in film, photography, and visual arts.

Through the School of Health Sciences and Human Performance, students can earn the B.S. in athletic training/exercise science, clinical exercise science, community health education, exercise science, health education*, health and physical education*, health policy studies (B.A.), health sciences, leisure services, physical education*, speech-language pathology and audiology, sport management, sport studies, sports information and communication, teaching students with speech and language disabilities*, and therapeutic recreation, or they can enroll in the five-year B.S./M.S. clinical science/physical therapy or occupational science/occupational therapy programs.

The School of Humanities and Sciences offers the B.A. in anthropology, art, art education*, art history, biochemistry, biology*, chemistry*, computer science, drama, economics, English*, environmental studies, French*, German area studies*, history, mathematics*, mathematics–computer science*, mathematics-economics, mathematics-physics, philosophy, philosophy-religion, physics*, planned studies, politics, psychology, social studies*, sociology, Spanish*, speech communication, and writing; the B.S. is offered in applied economics, applied psychology, chemistry*, computer information systems, computer science, mathematics–computer science*, planned studies, speech communication, and theater arts management; the B.F.A. is offered in acting, art, musical theater, and theatrical production arts.

The * indicates areas that lead to teacher certification.

Students in the School of Music can earn the B.A. in music and the B.M. in composition, jazz studies, music education, music in combination with an outside field, performance, performance/music education, sound recording technology, and theory.

Special programs offered by Ithaca include the Exploratory Program for undecided majors; a B.S. and a B.A. in gerontology; accelerated programs with the Pennsylvania College of Optometry and the State University of New York College of Optometry; 3-2 programs in chemistry-engineering and in physics-engineering, offered in cooperation with Cornell University, Rensselaer Polytechnic Institute, and other schools; and M.B.A. 4+1 programs offered with Clarkson University, the Rochester Institute of Technology, and the American Graduate School of International Management (Thunderbird).

Academic Program

Undergraduate programs of study address two primary issues: the need for rigorous academic preparation in highly specialized professional fields and the need for students to prepare for the complex demands of society by acquiring an intellectual breadth that extends beyond their chosen profession. Each degree offered requires a minimum of 120 credit hours and a specified number of liberal arts credits. Minors, academic concentrations, and numerous teacher certification programs are available. Exceptionally qualified applicants to the School of Humanities and Sciences will be invited to apply to the honors program, an intensive four-year program of interdisciplinary seminars. The writing center offers assistance to students at any stage of the writing process, and Academic Computing and Client Services aids students in the use of personal and College computers. The Center for the Study of Culture, Race, and Ethnicity serves as a multidisciplinary clearinghouse for studying the experiences of groups that traditionally have been marginalized, underrepresented, or misrepresented in the United States as well as in college curricula. The Gerontology Institute provides opportunities for students to work with the elderly in a variety of community settings. The Center for Teacher Education serves to coordinate the courses of study leading to a teaching certificate.

The academic year comprises two 15-week semesters, from late August to mid-December and from mid-January to mid-May.

ROTC programs are offered in conjunction with Cornell University.

Off-Campus Programs

The College maintains a center in London, England, and offers courses in the liberal arts, business, communications, music, and theater arts. Study-abroad programs are also available in Australia, the Czech Republic, Ireland, Japan, Singapore, and Spain or in more than fifty countries through affiliate arrangements with the Center for Cross-Cultural Study, the Institute for the International Education of Students, the Institute for American Universities, and the School for International Training. Selected juniors and seniors in communications may study at the Ithaca College James B. Pendleton Center in Los Angeles, which offers outstanding internship opportunities. Students from all disciplines may participate in a new internship semester in Washington, D.C.

Academic Facilities

All academic facilities have been constructed since 1960, and three new major buildings have recently opened: a health sciences facility, a 69,000-square-foot addition to the music building, and a fitness center. The Roy H. Park School of Communications contains television and radio studios, a film and photography complex, and a variety of digital laboratories. The College's two science buildings house state-of-the-art physics, biology, chemistry, mathematics, computer, and psychology laboratories. Additional campus facilities include theaters, auditoriums, concert halls, an observatory, and research laboratories. Computing facilities include mainframes, several computer networks, and hundreds of computers in labs and classrooms across campus, allowing easy access to e-mail and the Internet. The library contains approximately 400,000 materials in various formats.

Costs

For 2003–04, tuition was $22,264, room was $4802, board was $4664, and the health and accident insurance fee was $340.

Financial Aid

Financial aid totaling more than $106 million from all sources is extended to approximately 80 percent of Ithaca students. To apply for financial aid, students should check the proper space on the College's admission application, and if seeking federal aid, submit the Free Application for Federal Student Aid (FAFSA) by February 1 with the U.S. Department of Education at the address indicated on the form. Early decision candidates should follow the time line outlined under the Application and Information section below. All accepted applicants are considered for merit aid in recognition of their academic and personal achievement. Programs providing grants and loans include the Federal Work-Study, Federal Pell Grant, Federal Perkins Loan, Federal Stafford Student Loan, and Federal Supplemental Educational Opportunity Grant.

Faculty

There are 453 full-time and 180 part-time faculty members; the overall student-faculty ratio is 12:1. Ninety percent of the full-time faculty members have a Ph.D. or a terminal degree in their field. While the faculty is principally devoted to teaching at all levels, there is also significant publishing and research in various disciplines. Faculty members serve as academic advisers to students and are active in the community.

Student Government

The student government is composed of the student congress, all-College committee representatives, executive officers and assistants, and the student government executive board. Students administer a budget of approximately $400,000. The student congress includes representatives from each residence hall and school as well as students who live off campus. There is a student member of the Ithaca College Board of Trustees, and the student government appoints representatives to several standing all-College committees, including the Academic Policies Committee. The College encourages and expects student participation in governance.

Admission Requirements

Admission is based on the high school record, personal recommendations, SAT I or ACT scores, and, for some programs, auditions or portfolios. Campus visits are recommended but not required. Admission is selective and competitive; individual talents and circumstances are always given serious consideration. Transfer students must also submit official transcripts from each college or university they have attended. Applicants whose native language is not English must take the Test of English as a Foreign Language. Typically, there are about 11,000 applicants for 1,550 places in the freshman class.

Application and Information

For freshman regular decision, prospective students should apply early in their senior year and no later than March 1; applicants are notified of a decision on a rolling basis no later than April 15 and must confirm their enrollment by May 1. Freshman applicants seeking institutional and federal aid should file the FAFSA by February 1 with the federal processor.

For freshman early decision, which is binding, students should apply by November 1; applicants are notified by December 15 and must confirm their enrollment by February 1. Early decision applicants seeking institutional and federal financial aid should submit the Financial Aid PROFILE, available from the College Scholarship Service, by November 1 and the FAFSA by February 1.

Students who want to transfer into Ithaca College should apply by March 1 for fall admission and by December 1 for spring admission. Applicants seeking institutional and federal financial aid should file the FAFSA by February 1.

All applicants must submit a $55 application fee. Ithaca's application for admission is available on the Web at http://www.ithaca.edu/admission.

For additional information and application forms, students should contact:

Paula J. Mitchell
Director of Admission
Office of Admission
Ithaca College
100 Job Hall
Ithaca, New York 14850-7020
Telephone: 800-429-4274 (toll-free)
607-274-3124
Fax: 607-274-1900
E-mail: admission@ithaca.edu
World Wide Web: http://www.ithaca.edu

The Ithaca College campus.

JACKSONVILLE UNIVERSITY

JACKSONVILLE, FLORIDA

The University

Jacksonville University (JU) is a private, independent, coeducational institution. Originally founded in 1934 as a junior college, the institution served local commuter students for the first twenty-eight years of its existence. In the 1950s, the institution moved to its current location and expanded its courses and degree offerings. With this change, the institution became Jacksonville University. The University's current enrollment is approximately 2,600 undergraduate and graduate students. Some 2,500 students who attend classes on campus come from forty-six states and more than sixty countries. JU accommodates more than 1,000 students in its residence facilities, which include apartments with kitchenettes, and guarantees housing for all four years. Fifty-one percent of the students are women. The average class size is 17 students, and most classes have less than 30 students.

Campus facilities include a gymnasium, tennis courts, a baseball stadium, intramural fields, a football/soccer/track complex, and handball/racquetball courts, all useable throughout most of the year. Ocean beaches are only minutes away by car. Students pursue their creative talents and special interests by participating in cocurricular activities, such as student publications, chorus, orchestra, band, dance, and theatrical productions. Four sororities and six fraternities, as well as numerous academic, service, and social organizations, are active on campus. NCAA Division I sports include men's baseball; women's crew, indoor and outdoor track and field, softball, and volleyball; and men's and women's basketball, cross-country, golf, soccer, and tennis. Intercollegiate athletics also include men's nonscholarship football, competing at the NCAA Division I-AA level. Active intramural sports competition is available to interested students.

Jacksonville University is accredited by the Commission on Colleges of the Southern Association of Colleges and Schools (1866 Southern Lane, Decatur, Georgia 30033-4097; telephone: 404-679-4501) to award bachelor's and master's degrees. Programs in music and dance are accredited by the National Association of Schools of Music and the National Association of Schools of Dance, respectively. The generic-track nursing program is accredited by the NLNAC and the Commission on Collegiate Nursing Education (CCNE). Teacher education programs are approved by the Florida Department of Education for the purposes of teacher certification.

Graduate programs are available leading to the Master of Science in Nursing with two options, the Master of Business Administration degree in five concentrations, and the Master of Arts in Teaching degree in eleven areas.

Location

The University occupies a 260-acre suburban riverfront campus across the St. Johns River from downtown Jacksonville and 12 miles from the Atlantic Ocean beaches. Jacksonville is the home of a professional symphony orchestra, a performing arts center, theaters, art museums and galleries, the NFL Jacksonville Jaguars, and minor-league baseball, soccer, and ice hockey teams. Major airlines serve the Jacksonville International Airport. The region's year-round climate is mild and pleasant, permitting outdoor activity throughout the year.

Majors and Degrees

Jacksonville University offers the following degrees through the Colleges of Arts and Sciences, Business, and Fine Arts: B.A., B.F.A., B.G.S., B.M., B.M.E., B.S., and B.S.N.

Undergraduate academic programs of study include accounting, art, art history, aviation management, aviation management and flight operations, biology, business administration, chemistry, communications, computer art and design, computing sciences, dance, economics, engineering (various disciplines through dual-degree programs), elementary education, English, environmental science, finance, French, geography, history, international business, management, marine science, marketing, mathematics, music, music education, music performance, nursing, philosophy, physical education, physics, political science, psychology, secondary education, sociology, Spanish, studio art, and theater arts. Students may also pursue preprofessional programs in dentistry, law, medicine, pharmacy, and veterinary medicine.

Academic Programs

Students enrolled in baccalaureate programs enjoy broad exposure to the liberal arts through a core curriculum. The core provides a foundation for study in the various major fields and is usually completed during the freshman and sophomore years. The core includes courses in English composition and literature, mathematics and computer science, the social sciences, the humanities, history, fine arts, philosophy or religion, the natural sciences, and foreign language. The core curriculum does vary based on the degree. The core also requires community service for graduation.

Baccalaureate majors require a minimum of 120 semester credits and varies based on the degree. Generally, students acquire these credits in four years, although year-round enrollment makes it possible to earn a bachelor's degree in three years. All programs require a minimum 2.0 (C) grade point average for graduation. A pass-fail option is also available. Undergraduate research, internships, study abroad, and an active honors program enhance the educational experience of JU students. Independent study programs enable promising students to pursue individual work in areas of special interest within and outside their major fields of study. In the departmental honors program, advanced study may be concentrated in the major.

JU also awards undergraduate credit through advanced placement and credit by examination. Such credit requires the achievement of satisfactory scores on the College Board's Advanced Placement tests or CLEP examinations.

Jacksonville University has a Naval ROTC unit. Successful completion of the program leads to an officer's commission in either the U.S. Naval Reserve or U.S. Marine Corps Reserve.

Off-Campus Programs

Approved study abroad may be integrated as a part of the baccalaureate program. The University coordinates study-abroad programs in countries such as Spain, France, Mexico, and Australia for students. Summer language programs are popular with many students. JU faculty members also lead travel-study courses to many countries and regions of the world. With the help of advisers, JU students may also plan individual programs of study abroad.

Academic Facilities

The Carl S. Swisher Library houses a collection numbering more than 700,000 holdings and a PC lab with more than forty computers. The Swisher/Merritt-Penticoff/Nelms science complex, along with the Millar Wilson Laboratory, Reid Medical Science Building, and Charter Marine Science Center, house modern laboratories and facilities for biological, chemical, and physics study and research. Marine science facilities include an operational wet lab. The Phillips Fine Arts Building houses the Alexander Brest Museum, two large rehearsal halls, music studios, and practice rooms. Terry Concert Hall is an acoustically balanced facility for orchestra, choral, and band concerts. Studios house painting, ceramics, glassblowing, photography, sculpture, and other art activities. The Alexander Brest Dance Pavilion includes two large dance studios, offices, and dressing rooms. The J. Arthur Howard Administration Building centrally locates most administration and student service offices. The J. Henry Gooding Social Science Building contains classrooms, offices, and the Urban Studies Center. Wilma's Little People's School, a child development facility, supports teacher education programs. The Davis Building houses the College of Business. The Lazarra Health Sciences Building houses the state-of-the-art School of Nursing and also the Dental School of Orthodontics.

Costs

For 2003–04, full-time (12–18 credit hours) tuition and fees per year were $17,700. For students taking more than 18 credit hours, there was an additional fee of $295 per credit hour. Residence hall room rental was $2800 per year, and a seven-day meal plan was available at $3300 per year.

Financial Aid

The University has a strong financial assistance program based upon both merit and need. Scholarships based on academic merit range in amounts from $500 to full tuition, room, and board. Fine arts scholarships are offered on a competitive basis to students excelling in art, theater, dance, and music. Athletic awards are offered based on talent and skill in NCAA Division I sports (except for men's football). JU also participates in a broad range of federal and state programs that include loans, grants, and work-study opportunities. The University requires financial aid applicants to complete the Free Application for Federal Student Aid (FAFSA). The deadline for submission of all forms to ensure the availability of aid for the fall term is March 15.

Faculty

Jacksonville University employs more than 129 full-time faculty members. Faculty members are readily accessible to students and take an active role in the lives of students as teachers, mentors, and friends.

Student Government

Student participation in University governance is a function of the Student Government Association (SGA), a constitutional legislative body composed of representatives elected at large by the student body. The SGA places student members on important University committees and boards. Dolphin Productions, operating under SGA auspices, schedules concerts, lectures, films, and other cultural and entertainment activities.

Admission Requirements

Jacksonville University seeks qualified students from diverse social, geographic, cultural, religious, and socioeconomic backgrounds. The Admissions Committee evaluates each applicant on an individual basis. Students applying as freshmen should have satisfactorily completed, or be in the process of completing, a standard college-preparatory curriculum. The University requires that applicants complete a minimum of 4 years of English, 3 years of mathematics, 3 years of science, and 3 years of social science. Freshman applicants also must submit scores from either the SAT I or ACT, the application form with essays, and at least one letter of recommendation. Admission interviews and campus visits are recommended but not required.

The University welcomes applications from transfer and international students; transfers comprise approximately one third of the entering class each year. To be considered for transfer admission, applicants must submit the application form with essays, one letter of recommendation, and official copies of transcripts from all colleges attended. Transfers must have a minimum 2.0 college GPA and be in good standing at their previous institution. International applicants should contact the Office of Admissions for further information.

Students interested in dance, music, or theater arts may be required to audition separately for admission to those programs. Students who plan to major in visual arts may be required to submit a portfolio of their work. Admission to nursing, teacher education, and fine arts programs occurs after the student is admitted to the University.

New students may enroll for the fall, spring, or summer terms. Students are notified of acceptance beginning on November 1 for the fall term, and on a rolling basis thereafter.

Individuals, families, and groups may visit the campus throughout the year, both during the week and on scheduled Saturdays. Campus visits include a meeting with an admissions counselor and a campus tour. Invitations to a series of open houses are extended to prospective students and parents. On-campus overnight visits are arranged for interested students. Students or parents should call the Office of Admissions to make visit arrangements.

Application and Information

Application for freshman admission should be filed as soon as possible after the completion of the junior year in high school. Forms are available from the JU Web site and the admissions office by calling or writing:

Office of Admissions
Jacksonville University
2800 University Boulevard North
Jacksonville, Florida 32211-3396
Telephone: 904-256-7000
800-225-2027 (toll-free)
E-mail: admissions@ju.edu
World Wide Web: http://www.ju.edu

JEWISH THEOLOGICAL SEMINARY OF AMERICA
Albert A. List College of Jewish Studies

List College
The Jewish Theological Seminary of America

NEW YORK, NEW YORK

The College

Founded in 1886, the Jewish Theological Seminary (JTS) includes five separate yet integrated schools: the Albert A. List College of Jewish Studies, the Davidson School of Education, the Graduate School, the H. L. Miller Cantorial School, and the Rabbinical School. The full range of programs available at JTS has established its reputation as a leading academic institution for Jewish studies on the undergraduate and graduate levels and as the academic and spiritual center of Conservative Judaism worldwide.

Albert A. List College of Jewish Studies, the undergraduate school of the Jewish Theological Seminary, is a four-year, private, coeducational college. It offers qualified men and women a full spectrum of courses in Jewish studies and grants the Bachelor of Arts degree. Students earn two undergraduate degrees: one in a field of Jewish studies from List College and one in the liberal arts major of their choice from either Columbia University's School of General Studies or Barnard College.

Students benefit from small classes and an intimate atmosphere that allow them the opportunity to interact with faculty members beyond the classroom. To complement the strong academic program, students participate in a wide array of extracurricular activities at List and Columbia. They are active in a cappella groups, student government, dance troupes, Greek life, campus radio and newspaper, theater, sports, and community service. In the residence halls, students have the opportunity to experience Shabbat and holiday celebrations.

More than 80 percent of List students graduate in four years. Having earned two undergraduate degrees, they continue their educations at some of the most competitive graduate and professional schools. Many have achieved prominence in the fields of business, law, medicine, education, the rabbinate, computer technology, and social work. List College alumni work throughout the world, from Israel to London and from Capitol Hill to San Francisco to Wall Street.

Location

List College is located on Manhattan's vibrant Upper West Side. Just blocks from Columbia University, Barnard College, Manhattan School of Music, Teachers College, and Union Theological Seminary, List is part of a dynamic community known as the academic acropolis. Students are encouraged to take advantage of New York's cultural offerings as well. They regularly explore the city, from the music and dance of Broadway to the museums of 5th Avenue and from the sports at Madison Square Garden to the clubs and galleries of SoHo and the Village.

Majors and Degrees

Students can major in a variety of Judaic subjects, including Bible, Jewish art and material culture, Jewish history, Jewish literature, Jewish music, Jewish philosophy, Jewish women's studies, Midrash, and Talmud and rabbinics. All majors at List consist of seven courses. Each department determines the specific distribution of courses required for the major. A Bachelor of Arts degree is granted for all of the majors listed above. As students progress through their requirements, it is not uncommon for them to discover new interests. Majors can be modified at any time prior to registration for the fall semester of the senior year.

List College offers unique dual-degree programs with Columbia University's School of General Studies and Barnard College. Through the Joint and Double Degree Programs, students pursue two major subjects that lead to two undergraduate degrees. Students earn a B.A. from List College and a second B.A. or B.S. from Columbia or Barnard. This exceptional opportunity allows students to pursue a Jewish studies passion without sacrificing their secular interests. Available majors at Columbia and Barnard range from architecture, chemistry, and dance to history, political science, and psychology. Astronomy, computer science, economics, physics, and urban studies are also among the dozens of majors offered. Two majors resulting in two degrees provide not only an enriched education but also a wider range of career opportunities.

Academic Programs

The course of study leading to a Bachelor of Arts degree is typically completed in four years. Students must take 96 credits in Jewish studies at List and a minimum of 60 credits in liberal arts at an accredited institution to qualify for the degree. Most courses are worth 3 credits.

Of the 96 List College credits, 51 are required of all students, 21 comprise the major, and 24 are taken as electives. The required credits come from six fields: Hebrew language, Bible, Talmud, Jewish literature, Jewish history, and Jewish philosophy.

Of the 60 required liberal arts credits, 6 each must be taken in the following areas: English, history, philosophy or social science, and math or lab science. The remaining 42 credits may be taken as electives.

Typically, students satisfy their liberal arts requirements through the Joint Program with Columbia or the Double Degree Program with Barnard. Students in either of those two programs may apply up to 18 credits, beyond the 60 required liberal arts credits, toward List College electives.

Students in the Joint and Double Degree Programs ultimately take about one third more courses/credits than they would in a standard university program. Many courses are double-counted; for example, Hebrew language taken at List satisfies the foreign language requirement at Columbia and Barnard.

Off-Campus Programs

Students may enhance their studies and enrich their educational experience by spending a semester or a year at a university overseas. Many students choose to study at Hebrew University in Jerusalem. Students have also studied in Australia, Brazil, Florence, London, and Paris. Faculty advisers work closely with students to ensure that they receive the maximum amount of credit for their semester abroad.

Academic Facilities

The library of the Jewish Theological Seminary houses the largest collection of Judaica in the Western Hemisphere. Equally impressive is Columbia University, home to the seventh-largest academic library system in the country. In addition to their extensive libraries, both campuses offer state-of-the-art computer facilities. Many students take advantage of the Columbia writing center and join various study groups. They also utilize the language lab and recording studio in the newly opened Kripke Tower on the JTS campus.

Costs

A student's budget typically includes tuition, fees, housing, meals, books, and personal expenses. These items are all factored into the total cost of education that is used to calculate financial aid. That figure is approximately $36,000. However, students never receive a bill for books, meals, or personal expenses. They are billed for tuition, fees, and housing. For 2003–04, List College tuition and fees were $11,200. Housing was $6700. In addition, students are charged for classes at Columbia or Barnard, which are billed per credit. Columbia/Barnard classes for the academic year 2003–04 were approximately $14,000.

Financial Aid

Helping students pay for college is a priority for the List College community and JTS is committed to meeting 100 percent of need for eligible students. In addition, every student who is admitted is automatically considered for a variety of merit awards. Financial aid awards are completely independent of admission decisions. Approximately two thirds of all List College students receive financial aid. To be considered for need-based financial aid, students must submit the JTS financial aid application and a copy of their own and their parents' income tax returns to the JTS financial aid office. They must also complete a Free Application for Federal Student Aid (FAFSA) and a PROFILE form from the College Scholarship Service. On both forms, they must designate JTS as a recipient. The school code for both forms is 2339. Women applying to the Double Degree Program with Barnard must also send both forms to Barnard. Their school code is 2038.

March 1 is the financial aid deadline for new students. Applicants should not wait for an admission decision to apply for financial aid.

Faculty

The dual-degree programs offer an excellent faculty and superb academic advising. JTS, with the largest faculty in North America devoted solely to Jewish studies, had such luminaries as Solomon Schechter and Abraham Joshua Heschel. This tradition of excellence continues today with noteworthy professors such as Neil Gilman and Burt Visotsky. Not only do 90 percent of the full-time faculty members have doctoral degrees from renowned universities, but many have written the major texts studied within their fields. The faculty members are accomplished scholars who are interested in the students' personal, religious, and intellectual growth. Students and faculty members may share a meal in the cafeteria or pray in the same synagogue. Columbia University is also home to some of the finest professors in the world, including several Nobel Prize winners and many bestselling authors. Small classes and dynamic discussions allow students to form lifelong relationships with their instructors.

Student Government

An active student government is responsible for coordinating social, cultural, educational, and community service programs. It also serves as a vehicle for List College students to express their ideas and concerns to the administration. Each class elects representatives to the Student Council and to the Student-Faculty Committee, which brings professors and students together to discuss matters of mutual concern. Many List College students also serve in student government at Columbia and Barnard.

Admission Requirements

High school graduates, regardless of race, color, religion, gender, or national origin, who have demonstrated academic promise, intellectual curiosity, and personal motivation are invited to submit an application to List College. Applicants should submit a completed application form, a $65 fee, and an essay directly to List College. An official transcript, SAT I and SAT II Writing Test or ACT scores, and two academic letters of recommendation should be provided by the appropriate sources. Applicants are strongly encouraged to arrange a personal interview with List College. Interviews should be arranged before March 1 of the year in which the student is applying. Interviews are followed by a tour of JTS, Columbia, Barnard, and the surrounding community.

For application to the Joint Program with Columbia University's School of General Studies, students must submit an application according to the instructions above. The final deadline for the Joint Program is February 15. Women interested in the Double Degree Program with Barnard must submit a List application as described above. In addition, they must submit a Barnard application to Barnard and arrange for an interview there. The final deadline for the Double Degree Program is January 1. Women are encouraged to apply for admission to both programs.

High school seniors who have selected List College as their first choice may apply under one of two early decision plans. Joint Program and Double Degree Program candidates may apply under the fall early decision plan. The deadline is November 15, and students are notified by December 15. Joint Program applicants may also apply under the winter early decision plan. The deadline is January 15, and decisions are mailed by February 15. Both early decision plans are for the fall term, and both are binding. Students may be admitted under early decision, denied admission, or deferred for later consideration.

Application and Information

Additional information and applications are available online at the Web site listed below. Students, parents, and counselors should also feel free to contact:

Director of Admissions
Albert A. List College of Jewish Studies
Jewish Theological Seminary of America
3080 Broadway
New York, New York 10027-4649
Telephone: 212-678-8832
Fax: 212-280-6022
E-mail: lcadmissions@jtsa.edu
World Wide Web: http://www.jtsa.edu

Students at the Albert A. List College of Jewish Studies.

JOHN CABOT UNIVERSITY

ROME, ITALY

The University

John Cabot University (JCU) was founded in 1972. The University concentrates on the liberal arts and social sciences, using the American system, with a distinctive European and international character. It is strategically located in one of the world centers of diplomacy and international organizations. That, coupled with its unique relationship with leading multinational corporations, embassies, media, and other organizations, gives degree-seeking students the opportunity to participate in exclusive internship programs and become first-run candidates for distinguished job openings around the world. The University has a truly international student body—about one fourth of the students are Italian, one half are American, and one fourth are from more than fifty other countries around the world. Classes are no larger than 30–35 students, and there are more than 50 full- and part-time faculty members holding advanced degrees from major universities in the U.S. and Europe. Working closely with professors and classmates in a small-class setting, students receive the individual attention needed to fully develop their talents and abilities. With a student-centered approach to both education and human relationships, the University offers an active learning environment while also teaching the ethical standards that are essential in dealing with social pressures and in deciding how best to fulfill one's own goals in life.

As a four-year American university in Italy, JCU offers a wide variety of study-abroad courses, taught in a truly international atmosphere. The Housing Office places students in off-campus apartments and in a residential hotel close to the University. Along with various campus activities, the Student Services and Activities Office organizes a wide variety of off-campus events, including educational travel throughout Italy.

The University is licensed by the Delaware Department of Education to award its degrees and is authorized by the Italian Ministry of Public Instruction to operate as an institution of American higher education in Rome. John Cabot University is accredited by the Commission on Higher Education of the Middle States Association of Colleges and Schools, 3624 Market Street, Philadelphia, Pennsylvania 19104; telephone 215-662-5606.

Location

Located in Rome, Italy, in the picturesque Trastevere quarter just down the river from St. Peter's Basilica and the Vatican, John Cabot University is housed in a former convent, which consists of a central main building of three floors and an adjacent wing connected by terraces and courtyards. The original separate chapel is now the student lounge. The property offers students a tranquil atmosphere in which to study and interact, while historic, bustling Rome is just a few steps away. Surrounded by the green gardens of the Accademia dei Lincei (Galileo was an early member) and next door to the Villa Farnesina of Raphael's famous frescoes, the University is buttressed by the Aurelian Wall of the Roman Empire. John Cabot is approached through the Porta Settimiana, which was built by Pope Alexander VI Borgia in 1498 and later restored by Pope Pius VI in 1798. But the walls of an old convent do not confine, nor completely define, the University. Across the Tiber, in the Centro Storico (Historic Center), John Cabot also has spacious classrooms in the Sacchetti Building, overlooking the river. JCU has use of the impressive library of the Centro Studi Americani (Center for American Studies) in the beautiful Renaissance palace Palazzo Mattei. Fine arts and art history classes often meet at famous monuments such as the Colosseum and the Forum, within easy reach of JCU. In effect, all of Rome is John Cabot University's campus.

Majors and Degrees

John Cabot University offers the Bachelor of Arts degree in art history, business administration, English literature, humanistic studies, international affairs, Italian studies, and political science. The University of Wales, in the United Kingdom, has validated JCU degrees in business administration, international affairs, and political science. As a result of this validation, students in these programs may work toward both an American degree from John Cabot University and a European degree (validated Honours) from the University of Wales. Students may select minors in art history, business administration, computer science, economics, English literature, history, international affairs, Italian studies, political science, and psychology.

John Cabot also offers the Associate of Arts degree in art history, business administration, computer science, economics, English literature, history, international affairs, and political science. Each of these programs is designed to develop the characteristics of the individual student by means of a unique learning and living experience in a setting rich in history, culture, and geopolitical interaction.

Academic Program

Unlike most European university systems, the American system of higher education encourages experimentation and breadth, particularly during the first two years of the university experience. The curricula of the University's programs are, therefore, divided into two basic categories: the general distribution requirements of the first two years of study, which give the student a broad exposure to the basic disciplines of the liberal arts educational experience, and the specified, additional requirements of each degree awarded by the University.

The general distribution and other introductory courses equip the student to select an area of specialization as a degree candidate in the junior and senior years. Within each degree program, there are specific requirements that must be met by the student who wishes to earn a degree at John Cabot. These requirements include ten to twelve core courses deemed by faculty members to be essential to the discipline of the degree and comparable to the requirements for the same degree at recognized and accredited colleges and universities in the American system of higher education. In addition to the core requirements, other requisites include elective courses that support the core program and offer opportunities to take courses in other discipline areas of particular interest or need.

The academic year is divided into two semesters of fifteen weeks each, beginning in September and January (students should see the academic calendar for more information). In one semester, a student normally enrolls in five courses, earning 15 credits in the semester and 30 credits in the year. A summer session of five weeks allows students to take one or two additional courses. To earn the Bachelor of Arts degree, a student must complete 120 credits (forty courses); to earn the Associate of Arts degree, a student must complete 60 credits (twenty courses).

Special programs include the Honors Program, internships, and the American Language Program (ALP).

Off-Campus Programs

Degree-seeking students also have the opportunity to study in the United States for credit for a semester or a year.

Academic Facilities

The Frohring Library, constructed in 1999, provides the latest in online access to academic journals and indexes and is the University center for research in support of the academic programs as well as a quiet place for study and pleasure reading. The new computer laboratories provide a central point for students to work on computer science projects, prepare business presentations, write compositions and papers, check and send e-mail, and surf the Web. The labs contain IBM and IBM-compatible personal computers equipped with the latest software as well as high-speed printers and a full-color scanner. The Aula Magna is the largest room in the University and serves as the theater for the drama club. The Aula Magna is also used for orientation, cultural and community events, concerts, and student activities. This great hall is named in memory of Regina Occhiena of Castel Nuovo Don Bosco, who was a great-niece of Saint John Bosco and a great-grandmother of Charles Norman Secchia.

Costs

Tuition is $6250 or €5850 per semester, and the student activity fee is $210 or €210. Housing is $2700 per semester. For study-abroad students there is a Visitors Inclusive Package for $10,375 or €9695 that includes tuition for up to 17 credits, housing, food coupons for some snacks and/or breakfasts, certain JCU-sponsored day and overnight trips, Italian emergency health insurance (for emergency care), airport transfer, and a cellular phone with initial limited credit for calls. The package does not include air or other travel costs to and from Rome, meals, books, personal expenses, or any travel except specifically included trips. Costs are subject to change.

Financial Aid

U.S. citizens attending a college or university outside the United States are eligible to apply for the Federal Family Education Loans (FFEL), including the Stafford Student Loan and PLUS loans. The Free Application for Federal Student Aid (FAFSA) form must be completed to apply for a Stafford Student Loan. Current U.S. government legislation prohibits U.S. citizens enrolled in colleges or universities outside the United States from receiving Federal Pell Grants, Federal Supplemental Educational Opportunity Grants (FSEOG), Federal Perkins Loans, and Federal Work-Study funds, even though they may be eligible for such assistance. The exception to this is a visiting student currently enrolled in a U.S. institution who will be returning to that institution after a semester or year abroad. Academic scholarships are awarded each year. Scholarships are awarded based on merit and need. John Cabot University is proud to participate in the Secchia Family Foundation's Secchia Scholars program, with the availability of up to $70,000 in tuition scholarships to be awarded each year for qualifying students. The four types of Secchia Scholarships are the Norman R. Peterson Scholarship, the Order Sons of Italy in America Scholarships, the Secchia–De Vos Merit Scholarships (up to nine awarded each year), the Economic Club of Grand Rapids–Secchia Scholarship. Other scholarships include the Presidential Scholarships, the Italian Merit Scholarships, the 100/100 Scholarships, the National Italian American Foundation (NIAF) Scholarship, the Balkans Presidential Scholarship, the Alitalia Scholarship, the Gallo Scholarship, and the Benjamin A. Gilman International Scholarship Program. A number of work-study assistantships are available for full-time, degree-seeking students who are interested in and capable of assisting the various administrative offices and academic departments of the University.

Faculty

The University has a distinguished faculty of more than 50 part- and full-time professors from around the world. The faculty members take part in academic advising, the careful planning and monitoring of a student's progress through the academic program, and other activities around the campus, such as academic field trips and support of the student government.

Student Government

Student government at John Cabot University contributes significantly to the quality of student life. A Student Senate is elected each spring to coordinate activities, and three Student Government committees—the Entertainment Committee, the Cultural Affairs Committee, and the Service Committee—are open to all students for participation. During the year, the Student Government sponsors a number of programs, such as Jazz Night, Opera Night, and JCU theater productions. The Student Government works closely with the faculty adviser, Gretchen Meyers, and the staff adviser, Anna Felberbaum, in planning social, cultural, intellectual, and sports activities to respond to students' interests and needs.

Admission Requirements

Admission to John Cabot University is selective. Successful applicants must have maintained a scholastic record demonstrating a serious commitment to their studies and the ability to succeed at college-level work.

Each applicant is considered as an individual, and no single factor can guarantee acceptance to the University. The previous school's documentation of the applicant's academic ability, motivation, character, and contribution to school life is very important. This information should be reflected in the student's academic record and letters of recommendation. The University does not prescribe a fixed secondary school course of study, but considers both the quality and breadth of the student's record. The University is open to all applicants without regard to race, national origin, religion, or gender. For applicants coming from the U.S. secondary school system, a standard college-preparatory program is expected. For applicants from other national systems, an essential requirement is successful completion of a secondary school program permitting university admission in the respective system. Students holding the Italian diploma di maturità, the International Baccalaureate, or other equivalent academic credentials may be granted advanced standing. Results of the SAT or the ACT are required for high school students graduating from an American secondary school. Applicants whose first language is not English or who did not attend a secondary school where classes were taught in English must demonstrate sufficient preparation in the English language. Standardized test scores, such as the Test of English as a Foreign Language (TOEFL) or the International English Language Testing System (IELTS), are useful in assessing a student's language capability. A minimum score of 550 on the TOEFL (213 on the computer-based exam), a minimum score of 6.5 on the IELTS, or an equivalent passing score on the John Cabot English Proficiency Test are accepted as evidence of sufficient preparation in the English language.

Application and Information

Admissions decisions are based on the review of official transcripts, results of standardized tests, the student's GPA, final examination results, a personal statement, and letters of recommendation from teachers or university professors. Students applying as transfer students from another university must be in good academic standing. An application form completed in its entirety must be accompanied by two recent passport-size photographs and a nonrefundable application fee of $50 or €50. Students may complete the application online or use the printable application. The University deadline is July 15 for fall admission and November 15 for the spring semester. Candidates are urged to submit their application and supporting documents as early as possible.

Students may apply online or obtain an application by contacting:

Admissions Office
John Cabot University
Via della Lungara, 233
00165 Rome
Italy
Telephone: 39-06-681-9121
Fax: 39-06-683-3738
E-mail: admissions@johncabot.edu
World Wide Web: http://www.johncabot.edu

International Education Division
105 Student Service Building
John Cabot University, U.S. Office
1 Campus Drive
Allendale, Michigan 49401
Telephone: 866-227-0112 (toll-free)
Fax: 616-331-3899
E-mail: usoffice@johncabot.edu
World Wide Web: http://www.johncabot.edu

JOHN CARROLL UNIVERSITY

UNIVERSITY HEIGHTS, OHIO

The University

In the Jesuit tradition of leadership, faith, and service, John Carroll University provides its students with a rigorous education, rooted in the liberal arts and focused on questions of moral and ethical value. The University wants its graduates to make a difference in their chosen careers and in bettering their communities. One of twenty-eight Jesuit colleges and universities in the United States, John Carroll offers degree programs at the undergraduate and graduate levels in fifty-four arts and sciences, business, and preprofessional fields.

John Carroll was founded in 1886 as St. Ignatius College. In 1923, its name was briefly changed to Cleveland College. Later it became John Carroll University, named after the first Catholic bishop of the United States. In 1934, the University moved from its original location on Cleveland's near west side to its current location in University Heights. Originally a men's college, the University and all its programs officially became coeducational in 1968.

In 2003–04, the enrollment was 4,242, with 3,279 students enrolled in full-time undergraduate programs and 793 in graduate programs. Students come from thirty-two states, the Virgin Islands, Puerto Rico, and seven other countries. The student body is 44 percent men, 56 percent women, and 9.4 percent minority group members. The University's eight residence halls house 1,925 students.

A well-rounded education includes learning and leadership activities outside the classroom. The University owns Thorn Acres, a 30-acre recreational facility used for fishing, canoeing, retreats, and student-group meetings. John Carroll offers more than eighty student organizations and clubs, as well as community volunteer-service opportunities, men's and women's varsity and intramural sports, and academic honor societies. A natatorium, racquetball and tennis courts, two gymnasiums, and weight-training and fitness facilities are located in the Student Center. Office space is set aside for a host of student activities, including the newspaper, radio station, yearbook, Student Union, fraternities and sororities, and various student organizations. University Counseling Services provides free personal and psychological counseling, therapy, in-depth analysis of academic and vocational concerns, and testing.

Students at John Carroll, in the Jesuit spirit of "making a difference," volunteer to help improve the local community. Each year, students paint the homes of the elderly or underprivileged, feed the homeless, and aid the dying. Student-organized Project Gold, a community service program, has supplemented University-run community service projects such as Christmas in April and Meals on Wheels.

The Graduate School at John Carroll offers Master of Science degree programs in biology, chemistry, mathematics, and physics; Master of Arts degree programs in communications management, counseling and human services, English, history, humanities, and religious studies; Master of Education; and Master of Business Administration degree programs. In addition, Economics America (the Cleveland Center for Economic Education), a nonprofit educational organization located on John Carroll's campus, provides advanced course work in economics for educators.

Location

Just 30 minutes from downtown Cleveland, John Carroll is located in the quiet, residential Heights neighborhood; it is surrounded by Shaker Heights, University Heights, and Cleveland Heights. The graceful walkways, rich landscape, and Gothic and contemporary architecture of the campus complement the surrounding community beautifully. The campus is easily accessible by bus, rapid transit, and car. Two shopping centers are within walking distance, so restaurants, theaters, banks, department stores, grocery stores, and specialty shops are all nearby. University Circle, 10 minutes from campus, is the home of the Cleveland Symphony Orchestra; Cleveland Museums of Art, Natural History, and Health Education; and Garden Center of Greater Cleveland. Downtown Cleveland offers comedy clubs; world-class shopping; theater at The Cleveland Play House; the Flats, an extensive entertainment district located on the Cuyahoga River; the Rock and Roll Hall of Fame; the Great Lakes Science Center; Jacobs Field, home to the Cleveland Indians; Gund Arena, home to the Cleveland Cavaliers; and the Cleveland Stadium, home to the Cleveland Browns.

Majors and Degrees

The Bachelor of Arts degree is awarded in art history, classical languages (Greek and Latin), communications, economics, education and allied studies (prekindergarten, elementary education, secondary education, and certain disabilities), English, French, German, Greek, history, humanities, mathematics teaching, modern languages (French, German, and Spanish), philosophy, physical education, political science (with an optional concentration in public administration and policy studies), religious studies (with an optional concentration in religious education), sociology, and world literature. The Bachelor of Science degree is awarded in biology, chemistry, computer science, engineering physics, mathematics, physics (with optional concentrations in computer engineering, electrical engineering, and engineering physics), and psychology. The Bachelor of Science in Business Administration degree is granted from John Carroll's Boler School of Business in accounting, business logistics, economics, finance, management, and marketing management information systems. Optional minors are offered in the American political system, art history, business, chemistry, communications, computer science, economics, engineering physics, English, foreign affairs, French, German, Greek, history, humanities, Latin, mathematics, philosophy, physical education, physics, probability and statistics, psychology, public administration and public policy, religious education, religious studies, sociology, and Spanish.

The University is well known for its preprofessional programs, including dentistry, engineering, law, and medicine. Interdisciplinary concentrations for students interested in exploring selected topics in several academic disciplines are available. These include East Asian studies, economics and mathematics, environmental studies, gerontology, humanities, international economics and modern language, international studies, neuroscience, perspectives on sex and gender, and public administration and policy studies.

Academic Program

In keeping with the Jesuit tradition of liberal arts education, every undergraduate takes a core curriculum that includes a single-theme first-year seminar course, four courses in humanities, four in science and mathematics, three in philosophy, three in social sciences, two in religious studies, one in English composition and rhetoric, and one in speech communication. Therefore all students enroll in the College of Arts and Sciences for their first two years. After the first two years, students select a major and are admitted to their respective degree programs.

To earn a degree, a student must complete a minimum of 128 credit hours with a grade point average of at least 2.0 (C) for all course work. The last 30 hours of instruction must be completed at John Carroll. Candidates for graduation must complete all the courses and proficiency requirements for the degree, and they must complete all the major requirements with an average of at least 2.0. All course work required for a declared minor or concentration must be completed with at least a 2.0.

A number of special programs are available, including ROTC and student exchange. The University operates on a semester calendar, with three 5-week summer sessions offered between academic years.

Off-Campus Programs

John Carroll offers many special educational opportunities. Exchange programs are available with two universities in Japan; The Center for Global Education works with students who hope to study abroad.

John Carroll University is a member of the Northeast Ohio Commission on Higher Education and offers students the opportunity to take one course per semester at one of the other sixteen area universities while enrolled full-time at John Carroll. There is no additional charge for tuition; the only stipulation is that the course may not be offered at the home institution. Students often take courses in the performance-based arts or in specific engineering fields through this cross-registration program.

Academic Facilities

The Dolan Center for Science and Technology, a $66.4-million, 265,000-square-foot building, opened with a grand celebration on September 6, 2003. This facility houses the biology, chemistry, psychology, physics, mathematics, and computer science departments, as well as laboratory and office space for business initiatives that will benefit the northeast Ohio community. With the Dolan Center, the University plans to advance its science and mathematics curriculum, upgrade instructional technology, and expand partnerships with area schools and employers.

A number of years ago, a $6.8-million expansion of the Grasselli Library doubled the capacity of the building and has enhanced accessibility of electronic databases.

The O'Malley Center for Communications and Language Arts features a television studio and an electronic newsroom, computer-assisted and audio language laboratories, and a center for writing instruction.

Costs

Tuition is $22,108 for the 2004–05 academic year. Room and board are $7236. The average cost for books and supplies is $800 per year.

Financial Aid

In 2003–04, 73 percent of the student body received some type of need-based financial assistance. Qualified students may be awarded scholarships, honor awards, grants, work-study employment, and loans or a combination of these to help offset the cost of their education. Merit-based scholarships, such as the President's Honor Award, National Merit Scholarship, and the Mastin Scholarship are given to a number of outstanding high school students based solely upon their academic achievement. Most students, however, apply for need-based aid by completing the Free Application for Federal Student Aid (FAFSA). The financial aid application deadline is March 1.

Faculty

The majority of John Carroll's 411 faculty members teach undergraduate classes, although some teach graduate programs as well. Of the full-time faculty, 94 percent hold doctorates or the appropriate terminal degree in their field, and 65 percent are tenured. The faculty's primary focus is teaching and scholarship. Counseling of students, research and publication, and community service are also important pursuits. John Carroll's faculty includes 8 resident Jesuit priests. The student-faculty ratio is 15:1.

Student Government

The John Carroll student body is self-governed, with the elected Student Union officers actively representing all students—undergraduate, graduate, full- and part-time, and day and evening—in all academic, social, religious, and disciplinary matters. Fifty-six men and women are elected to Student Union service for one-year terms.

Admission Requirements

Applications for admission from all serious candidates are welcome. John Carroll attracts students of diverse geographic, economic, racial, and religious backgrounds. Admission criteria in descending order of importance are the quality of the high school curriculum, grade point average, test scores on either the SAT I or ACT, extracurricular activities, and the recommendation of a high school counselor or teacher. Personal interviews are recommended, though optional, and are taken into consideration when admission decisions are made.

The deadline for applications to John Carroll is February 1. Candidates are informed of decisions on a rolling basis and should be notified within four weeks of applying.

Application and Information

John Carroll subscribes to the Candidates Reply Date of May 1. Accepted students who wish to reserve their place in the freshman class must submit their tuition deposit (and room deposit, if they wish to reserve on-campus housing) by May 1 to ensure their place in the class. All deposits are refundable by written request up to the May 1 deadline.

To request a viewbook and a current application, students are encouraged to contact:

Thomas P. Fanning
Director of Admission
John Carroll University
University Heights, Ohio 44118-4581
Telephone: 216-397-4294

Grasselli Tower stands behind the bust of Archbishop John Carroll, the University's namesake, along the main quadrangle.

JOHN JAY COLLEGE OF CRIMINAL JUSTICE OF THE CITY UNIVERSITY OF NEW YORK

NEW YORK, NEW YORK

The College

Founded in 1964, John Jay College of Criminal Justice is the unit of the City University of New York that emphasizes as its special mission criminal justice, fire science, and other related public service fields. The institution developed out of a recognition of the increasing complexity of law enforcement and the need for professionalization at all levels of the criminal justice system. Intended at its founding, as the College of Police Science, for members of the New York City Police Department, the College nevertheless has always welcomed civilian students with an interest in criminal justice. At present, approximately 20 percent of the College's 10,000 students are members of uniformed criminal justice and fire service agencies; the majority of the students are civilian preprofessionals, many of whom plan careers in these areas. John Jay College is accredited by the Middle States Association of Colleges and Schools.

Most of the College's students are residents of New York City and of surrounding communities in New York, New Jersey, and Connecticut. All students commute to the College directly from their homes or from their places of employment. To accommodate students, such as police officers, who work rotating tours of duty, both day and evening courses are offered. A student may attend a class in the daytime or, with the same professor covering the identical material, in the evening, depending on his or her work assignment. Weekend courses are also offered.

The College also offers master's degrees in criminal justice, forensic psychology, forensic science, protection management, and public administration. The Ph.D. in criminal justice is awarded through the Graduate School and University Center of the City University of New York and John Jay College of Criminal Justice.

Location

John Jay College occupies three buildings on the West Side of Manhattan at 59th Street and 10th Avenue—John Jay Square. One of the buildings was recently renovated and houses new classrooms, a theater, the world's largest criminal justice library, administrative offices, and an extensive athletic facility. Within a radius of a mile are Lincoln Center for the Performing Arts, the New York theater district, Carnegie Hall, and numerous other cultural facilities. The College's location not only makes access to major criminal justice agencies convenient but also offers all the aspects and resources of one of the most fascinating cities in the world as the background for its programs.

Majors and Degrees

The Bachelor of Arts degree is granted in criminal justice, criminology, deviant behavior and social control, fire service administration, forensic psychology, government, international criminal justice, judicial studies, justice studies, and public administration. The Bachelor of Science degree is offered in computer information systems, correctional studies, criminal justice, criminal justice administration and planning, fire science, forensic science, legal studies, police studies, and security management.

A B.A./M.A. program, which enables particularly well-qualified students to earn both degrees in a shorter time than would be required to earn them individually, is offered in criminal justice and forensic psychology. A similar B.A./M.P.A. program in public administration is available.

The A.S. degree is granted in correction administration, police science, security management, and criminal justice.

Academic Programs

As a specialized college, John Jay emphasizes the particular areas of its mission—all aspects of the broad fields of criminal justice and fire science—against a background of the liberal arts. Thus, the humanities, physical sciences, and social sciences contrast and integrate with the practical and theoretical components of the study of these public service fields. Since most students at John Jay College are planning to enter or already are employed in public service fields, the interdisciplinary approach to education that is the basis of the College's philosophy aims at a broadening and a further professionalization of their careers.

Candidates for the baccalaureate degree at John Jay College must fulfill certain broad educational requirements during the first half of their degree program (40–60 credits). In addition, all candidates must complete a major field of study of at least 36 credits. A minimum of 36 of the candidate's total credits and at least 50 percent of the selected major must be completed in residence. The associate degree at John Jay requires completion of basic distribution requirements and a specialization program (64–67 credits).

The Thematic Studies Program offers an alternative way of meeting basic course requirements and of completing the liberal arts portion of the baccalaureate and associate degree programs. Students who enroll in Thematic Studies take a package of classes related to a specific theme, combining literature, sociology, psychology, ethnic studies, history, writing, philosophy, government, and criminal justice. Each course centers on a broad topic or theme, to which all classwork and projects are related. These interdisciplinary courses are taught by teams of 6 to 8 professors. Students undertake individual or group projects, supplementary lectures, readings, discussions, and papers.

With departmental approval, students may be awarded credit for successful scores on the College-Level Examination Program (CLEP) subject tests, the Regents External Degree Examinations (REDE), and College Board Advanced Placement (AP) tests. Students may apply for and may be granted up to 30 credits for external and/or equivalent learning experiences.

The Certificate Program in Dispute Resolution is also available. This 30-credit, multidisciplinary program responds to the needs of personnel working in the criminal justice system as well as of those in other public and private sectors for training in the techniques of dispute resolution.

Programs are also offered in African-American studies and in Puerto Rican studies.

Off-Campus Programs

The College's location in midtown Manhattan and its special focus on criminal justice and related fields offer unparalleled opportunities for students to earn academic credits while gaining experience. Internship courses, which provide 3 credits each, combine classes and supervision with practical experience in criminal justice and government agencies, cultural organizations, private businesses, and health, research, and nonprofit institutions. Internships are available in such places as legislators' offices, hospitals, courts, New York City agencies, district attorneys' offices, juvenile-diversion programs, museums, legal societies, fire and police departments, social service agencies, and federal agencies.

The cooperative education program provides alternating periods of paid employment and college work. Juniors and seniors with satisfactory college records may enter into this program with such employers as IBM, the U.S. Customs Service, the U.S. Marshalls Service of the Department of Justice, and the Inspector General's Office of the Department of Health and Human Services. No college credit is offered for this off-campus employment.

Academic Facilities

The library collection consists of more than 250,000 books, periodicals, microforms, and cassette tapes and supports the full range of the College's curriculum and educational mission. The main strength of the collection is the holdings in the social sciences and criminal justice, public administration, and related fields and the growing bodies of material dealing with forensic science, fire science, and forensic psychology. Holdings in these areas are extensive and support the research needs of students and faculty members and of criminal justice agency personnel who are engaged in planning and development.

Five specially equipped laboratories are used to educate students in the professionally oriented forensic science program. In addition, research rooms are available for use by forensic science majors and faculty.

The Security Management Lab provides hands-on training in computer security and other modern security systems and techniques applicable in the field.

The Microcomputer Laboratory consists of four separate labs for classroom instruction and individual assignments. The labs are staffed with supervisors and consultants who assist students in their individual projects.

Costs

For New York State residents, tuition costs for 2003–04 were $170 per credit hour or a maximum of $2000 per term. Tuition costs for out-of-state residents were $285 per credit hour. Tuition may be increased at any time by action of the Board of Trustees.

Financial Aid

Financial aid programs are available to assist students who would not otherwise be able to obtain a college education. John Jay College makes every effort to help as many students as possible with a combination of financial aid awards, such as Federal Pell Grants, Federal Work-Study Program employment, Tuition Assistance Program (TAP) awards, Federal Stafford Student Loans, Federal Perkins Loans, Federal Supplemental Educational Opportunity Grants (FSEOG), and veterans' benefits. The College also awards scholarships in a variety of categories based on academic merit.

Faculty

The faculty consists of 285 full-time and 300 part-time members. All faculty members teach undergraduate courses, and teachers of graduate courses are drawn from the same group. Of the full-time faculty members, approximately 80 percent hold doctoral degrees.

While the John Jay College faculty has a representative background in the humanities, social sciences, and natural sciences, the special emphasis of the College has established as members of the faculty experienced practitioners in the fields of criminal justice and fire science, a large number of whom hold earned doctorates as well. Faculty members are encouraged to function as academic counselors to their students.

Student Government

The student government consists of an executive board of elected representatives from each class, including graduate students. Among the chief functions of the student government are the allocation of student fees, the chartering of campus clubs and monitoring of their activities and expenditures, and the selection of students to serve on College Council committees. Members also serve as student advocates before faculty and administrators.

The College Council is composed of faculty members, students, and administrators. Students are also voting members of College committees on personnel and budget, curriculum, retention, and other areas of College governance.

Admission Requirements

An applicant for freshman admission must present evidence of having received a high school diploma from an accredited high school or a New York State Equivalency Diploma or have passed a General Educational Development (GED) examination during or after June 1970. Students from non-English-speaking countries must submit TOEFL scores.

Effective as of September 2000, admission to the baccalaureate program for recent graduates of domestic high schools will be determined using an index that weights specific performance indicators. The indicators weighted include college admission average, number of academic courses completed in high school, and SAT I or ACT scores. SAT I or ACT scores are required for admission to the baccalaureate program.

Applicants to the baccalaureate program who are not recent graduates of domestic high schools must have a high school academic average of at least 80 and a minimum of 16 academic units with a combined total of 4 units of English and math, with at least 1 unit in each discipline, or an SAT I score of at least 1020.

Applicants who do not meet the baccalaureate criteria may be admitted to the associate degree program provided that they have an SAT I score of at least 900 or a minimum high school academic average of 72 or a GED score of at least 300. Associate degree applicants with lower academic averages may be considered provided that they have higher numbers of academic units, including English and math units. Course work in the associate degree program is applicable toward bachelor's degree requirements.

Students who have attended a college or postsecondary institution must have a minimum cumulative GPA of 2.0 based on the total number of credits attempted and completed. Prospective transfer students with fewer than 12 credits must have a minimum GPA of 2.0 and the prerequisite high school average and academic units for admission to the baccalaureate program.

Application and Information

Applicants who have attended college since graduation from high school may apply for admission with advanced standing.

For application materials and additional information, requests should be made to:

Office of Undergraduate Admissions
John Jay College of Criminal Justice
445 West 59th Street, Room 4205
New York, New York 10019
Telephone: 877-JOHNJAY (toll-free)
World Wide Web: http://www.jjay.cuny.edu

THE JOHNS HOPKINS UNIVERSITY
Krieger School of Arts and Sciences and Whiting School of Engineering

BALTIMORE, MARYLAND

The University

Privately endowed, The Johns Hopkins University was founded in 1876 as the first American university committed to the idea that knowledge should be discovered, rather than merely transmitted. Daniel Coit Gilman, the first president of Johns Hopkins, stated that the object of the University was "not so much to impart knowledge as to whet the appetite, exhibit methods, develop powers, strengthen judgment, and invigorate the intellectual and moral forces." Today, Johns Hopkins continues to stress creative scholarship by providing reseach-oriented education for undergraduates.

Johns Hopkins seeks diversity in its student body, which comes from all fifty states and from eighty-three other countries. Of the total undergraduate enrollment of approximately 4,000 students, about 43 percent are women and 57 percent are men. All out-of-town freshmen and sophomores must live in campus residence halls. In addition, University-owned housing, located directly across from the University on Charles Street, is available for juniors and seniors. Upperclassmen may also live in private housing or in Greek housing. Hopkins has eleven fraternities and seven sororities.

Films, concerts, seminars, and athletic events are regularly offered on campus. The Student Council runs a number of activities, including an annual Spring Fair featuring outdoor concerts, arts and crafts booths, food, carnival rides, and exhibits. Men's varsity teams compete in fourteen sports. In the fall, there are crew, cross-country, football, soccer, and water polo. In the winter, there are basketball, fencing, swimming, and wrestling. The big sports season at Hopkins is spring, with baseball, crew, indoor track, lacrosse, tennis, and outdoor track. The men's and women's lacrosse teams compete at the Division I level, and the men have won the NCAA lacrosse championships thirty-seven times. Women's varsity sports also include basketball, crew, cross-country, fencing, field hockey, indoor track, outdoor track, soccer, swimming, tennis, and volleyball. An extensive intramural program is also available. The recently completed O'Connor Recreation Center contains basketball and volleyball courts, a running track, racquetball courts, a rock-climbing wall, a weight room, and fitness and aerobic areas.

Location

Johns Hopkins University's Homewood campus is on 140 acres of lush greenery, bounded on all sides by residential areas. Hopkins offers the best of both worlds—the tranquil seclusion of the campus plus the adjacent urban environment. The Baltimore Museum of Art is on the southwest corner of the campus. The Walters Art Museum, a 10-minute drive away, has a collection that spans civilization from Egypt to the nineteenth century, and many smaller museums, galleries, and outdoor showings feature local artists. The University is located just 4 miles from the heart of downtown Baltimore; the theater, symphony, and opera are 10 minutes away, as are Oriole Park at Camden Yards and Ravens Stadium. Weekend activities include shopping at Harborplace, visiting the National Aquarium, enjoying an ethnic festival by the water, sailing on the Chesapeake Bay, and hiking around the Maryland countryside. Washington, D.C., is a 40-minute drive by car or a 50-minute train ride.

Majors and Degrees

Bachelor of Arts degrees are awarded in Africana studies, anthropology, behavioral biology, biology, biophysics, chemistry, classics, cognitive science, earth and planetary sciences, East Asian studies, economics, English, environmental earth sciences, film and media studies, French, German, history, history of art, history of science and technology, interdisciplinary studies, international studies, Italian, Latin American studies, mathematics, natural sciences, Near Eastern studies, neuroscience, philosophy, physics, political science, psychology, public health studies, Romance languages, sociology, Spanish, and The Writing Seminars. A Bachelor of Arts degree in engineering is available for students who seek preparation for professional careers (such as law or business) with a technological orientation. The B.A. in engineering is awarded in applied mathematics and statistics, biomedical engineering, computer science, electrical engineering, general engineering, and geography. Bachelor of Science degrees are awarded in applied mathematics and statistics, biomedical engineering, chemical engineering, civil engineering, computer engineering, computer science, electrical engineering, environmental engineering, materials science and engineering, mechanical engineering, molecular and cellular biology, and physics.

Accelerated bachelor's/master's degree programs are offered in biology, biophysics, German, history, international studies, mathematics, neuroscience, policy studies, psychology, public health studies, and Spanish. Accelerated B.S./M.S.E. programs are offered in most engineering departments. A dual-degree program leading to a Bachelor of Arts or Bachelor of Science degree and a Bachelor of Music degree is available in cooperation with the University's Peabody Institute and Conservatory of Music.

Academic Programs

The departments in the Krieger School of Arts and Sciences and the Whiting School of Engineering comprise four general areas for undergraduate programs: engineering, humanities, natural sciences, and social and behavioral sciences. If a student has special interests that fall outside the bounds of the departmental majors, an individual program can be devised, or a student may study independently with the guidance of a faculty member. Qualified students may complete their degree requirements in fewer than four years. In a number of departments, undergraduates of exceptional ability and motivation may in some cases engage in graduate work with the object of qualifying for the simultaneous award of the bachelor's and master's degrees at the end of four years.

Johns Hopkins has an extremely flexible program. There are no required freshman courses. All students must fulfill distribution requirements as well as the requirements for their major; the distribution requirements include a writing course. In most majors, 120 credits are required for graduation. Johns Hopkins has a 4-1-4 calendar.

The University offers the Army ROTC program on campus and the Air Force ROTC program in cooperation with the University of Maryland College Park.

Off-Campus Programs

If qualified, a student may undertake a program for study abroad, normally during the junior year. Programs are offered at Hopkins' international centers in Florence and Bologna, Italy, and Nanjing, China, as well as through the Berlin Consortium and through independent study-abroad programs with Johns Hopkins credit. The University participates in a cooperative program with the following colleges in the Baltimore area: Goucher College, Loyola College, Morgan State University, College of Notre Dame of Maryland, Towson State University, Baltimore Hebrew University, and Maryland Institute, College of Art. Undergraduates may also take courses at the other divisions of Johns Hopkins University, including the Peabody Conservatory, the School of Nursing, the Bloomberg School of Public Health, the Nitze School of Advanced International Studies, the School of Professional Studies in Business and Education, and the School of Medicine.

Academic Facilities

The Milton S. Eisenhower Library on the Homewood campus—housing more than 3.5 million volumes—is part of the University's Sheridan Libraries, which comprise the Milton S. Eisenhower Library, the John Work Garrett Library, the Albert D. Hutzler Undergraduate Reading Room, and the George Peabody Library. Together, these libraries provide one of the most comprehensive learning resources in the world, containing more than 3.5 million books, more than 30,000 periodicals, greater than 4 million microforms, more than 200,000 maps, and 3,000 electronic journals. The University's other libraries are the Welch Medical Library at the School of Medicine, the Lilienfeld Library at the School of Public Health, the Arthur Friedhem Library at the Peabody Institute, the Mason Library at the School of Advanced International Studies in Washington, D.C., the Bologna Center Library, the Hopkins-Nanjing Center for Chinese and American Studies Library in China, and the R. E. Gibson Library at the Applied Physics Laboratory.

Host systems, an academic computer lab, and user support are provided by Hopkins Information Technology Services. Students living in University dorms and apartments can connect directly to the Internet and the JHU network via a high-speed data jack. Wireless network coverage is also available throughout many areas of the campus with the use of a supported wireless LAN card. Those living off campus can remotely access University systems and library resources. The Homewood Academic Computing Lab is open 24 hours a day, has more than 115 computers, and provides student consultants who can assist with problems that arise. The Brown Foundation Digital Media Center offers an environment where students can bring artistic inspiration to life using digital tools. It features twelve high-end computers that enable digital and audio composition and editing, animation, virtual painting, and 3-D modeling. All campus buildings are networked with each other and the other Hopkins campuses.

The Bloomberg Center for Physics and Astronomy houses the Department of Physics and Astronomy, and it is also the site of the control center of the Far Ultraviolet Spectroscopic Explorer satellite, which was built at Hopkins in conjunction with NASA. The Mattin Student Arts Center contains a theater, practice rooms, film and digital labs, darkrooms, a café, art studios, and spaces for students to gather. The new Hodson Trust building includes classrooms, a meeting room for the Board of Trustees, the archives of the Hodson Trust, and a 500-seat auditorium, in which every seat is wired to the Internet. Clark Hall houses a state-of-the-art research and teaching facility for biomedical engineering. A new building for the chemistry department has recently been completed.

Costs

Costs for 2004–05 are $30,140 for tuition, $9576 for room and board, and $1650 for books and personal expenses. Travel expenses vary.

Financial Aid

Financial aid is based on demonstrated eligibility, as determined by the Free Application for Federal Student Aid (FAFSA) at the time of acceptance. Approximately 50 percent of students receive financial assistance. Students must reapply for financial aid each year with the FAFSA and the Johns Hopkins Application for Financial Aid. Johns Hopkins offers several merit-based scholarships, including the Hodson Trust Scholarship and the Charles R. Westgate Scholarship in Engineering. Hopkins also sponsors the National Merit and National Achievement Scholarships and offers Army ROTC scholarships worth up to full tuition.

Faculty

The University's intellectual reputation is based on the strength of its faculty, of whom 99 percent hold a doctorate. The student-faculty ratio is 9:1. The well-known professors at Johns Hopkins teach both undergraduate and graduate students, which means that students receive a great deal of personal attention both in and out of the classroom. Hopkins has a large number of notable professors, including Alice McDermott (professor of The Writing Seminars), winner of the 1998 National Book Award for Fiction; Saul Roseman (professor of biology), a molecular biologist who is a principal authority on the biochemistry of complex carbohydrates and on cell membrane functioning and serves as a consultant to the American Cancer Society and the National Academy of Science; and Charles O'Melia (professor of geography and environmental engineering), who specializes in aquatic chemistry, water and wastewater treatment, and modeling of natural surfaces and subsurface waters and is a member of the National Academy of Engineers. Faculty members are always accessible to advise and assist students and to work with them on independent research projects.

Student Government

Johns Hopkins students enjoy the benefits of a well organized and far-reaching student government, which is led by a powerful Student Council. The council is composed of elected class representatives and officers, but it relies on the active participation of many students in its numerous committees, boards, and commissions. Through the Student Activities Commission, the University encourages initiative and independence by giving students full responsibility and control of funds for various clubs and organizations.

Admission Requirements

In choosing from a large number of applicants, the University selects those men and women who will benefit from a Johns Hopkins education. A student's intellectual interests and accomplishments are of primary importance, and the Admissions Committee carefully examines each applicant's scholastic record, standardized test results, and recommendations from secondary school officials and other sources about the student's character, intellectual curiosity, seriousness of purpose, and range of extracurricular involvement. Scores on the SAT I and three SAT II: Subject Tests, one of which must be the Writing Test, are required; however, ACT scores are acceptable in lieu of these. The secondary school report and an essay must also be submitted. (One additional essay is required of applicants interested in engineering.) Every year, the University enrolls a first-year class of approximately 1,000 men and women from all parts of the U.S. and a number of other countries. In addition, transfer students from other colleges and universities are admitted to the sophomore and junior classes. Advanced-standing credit is granted from college-level work completed at an accredited college or through the Advanced Placement and International Baccalaureate programs.

Application and Information

Johns Hopkins uses its own application, but also accepts the Common Application with a Hopkins supplement. The application deadline is January 1. Notification is given by April 1. Students wishing to enroll in the biomedical engineering (BME) program must indicate BME as their first choice of major on their application. Freshmen who are BME majors are admitted specifically as such, although a limited number of transfer majors are accepted into the BME program, based on academic merit and space available, at the end of each academic year. If applicants consider Hopkins their first choice, they may apply under the Early Decision Plan. This requires that the application be filed by November 15. Students are notified of the decision of the Admissions Office by December 15. Accepted students who wish to postpone their college studies for one year after graduation from high school may do so provided that they notify the director of admissions and submit the nonrefundable $600 deposit by May 1.

Office of Undergraduate Admissions
The Johns Hopkins University
140 Garland Hall
3400 North Charles Street
Baltimore, Maryland 21218-2683
Telephone: 410-516-8171
Fax: 410-516-6025
E-mail: gotojhu@jhu.edu
World Wide Web: http://apply.jhu.edu

THE JOHNS HOPKINS UNIVERSITY
School of Nursing
BALTIMORE, MARYLAND

The University

Since its founding in 1876, The Johns Hopkins University has been in the forefront of higher education. Originally established as an institution oriented toward graduate study and research, it is often called America's first true university. Today, Johns Hopkins' commitment to academic excellence continues in its eight academic divisions: Nursing, Medicine, Public Health, Arts and Sciences, Engineering, Continuing Studies, Advanced International Studies, and the Peabody Conservatory of Music. With a full-time enrollment of approximately 6,570 students, it is the smallest of the top-ranked universities in the United States and, by its own choice, remains small. The School of Nursing attracts a national and international student body of approximately 575 students.

The School of Nursing was established in 1983 by Johns Hopkins University. By choosing to attend Johns Hopkins University School of Nursing, students will become leaders in the nursing profession. A Hopkins education will provide a solid foundation on which to base a lifelong career in the ever-growing field of nursing. Hopkins students enjoy the advantages of an education at an institution with a worldwide reputation and an outstanding network of alumni who are willing to serve as guides and mentors. Students at the School of Nursing are given the opportunity to participate in designing an educational program tailored to their individual needs. A rigorous academic curriculum, which includes a strong scientific orientation, gives students the background to understand the health-care decisions they will make as professionals. Students learn in an atmosphere where excellence is expected, valued, and reinforced.

The School of Nursing is one of only a few in the country that emphasizes undergraduate research. Its graduates are prepared for professional practice through an educational process that emphasizes clinical excellence, critical thinking, and intellectual curiosity. In addition to the undergraduate program, a graduate program is offered that offers a number of majors, including nurse practitioner studies.

Guest speaker programs, concerts, lacrosse, and other sports are just a few of the activities that enrich life at Hopkins. There are more than seventy student organizations on campus, including fraternities and sororities and social, religious, and cultural groups.

Location

The School of Nursing is located on the campus of Johns Hopkins Medical Institutions, including the School of Medicine, the Bloomberg School of Public Health, and Johns Hopkins Hospital. Located 10 minutes away is the Homewood Campus of Johns Hopkins University, which is accessible to students via a free shuttle service.

Often referred to as "the biggest small town in America," Baltimore has undergone one of the most successful transformations of any city in the nation. Baltimore's famous Inner Harbor and the National Aquarium are focal points of this revitalization. Washington, D.C., is less than an hour away by car or train.

Major and Degrees

The School of Nursing offers an NLNAC-accredited upper-division program that leads to a Bachelor of Science degree with a major in nursing. An accelerated program of study makes it possible for students who hold a bachelor's degree in another discipline to receive a nursing degree within thirteen months. Students who hold a bachelor's degree in another discipline are also eligible to apply to the Direct Entry Combined B.S./M.S.N. program.

Academic Program

Johns Hopkins University School of Nursing prepares students for professional nursing practice through an educational process that combines a strong academic curriculum with intensive clinical experience. The program is built on the University's commitment to research, teaching, patient service, and educational innovation and the consortium hospitals' commitment to excellence in clinical practice. The School's mission is to prepare its students academically and technologically for challenges of the future and to graduate professional nurses who can participate in all aspects of modern health care.

The upper-division courses in the baccalaureate nursing program are planned to meet the nursing needs of people in a complex and rapidly changing health-care system. The program is built on the liberal and general education prerequisites. The curriculum is planned to provide a balance among technologies, the theories of nursing, and the caring functions of the nurse. A high priority is placed on educating the nurse to practice in a variety of health-care settings as they exist today and in the future.

Johns Hopkins University School of Nursing has a collaborative program of study that integrates academic study at Johns Hopkins University and volunteer service in the Peace Corps. The Peace Corps Preparatory Program combines four semesters of academic course work followed by Peace Corps training and two years of volunteer service. Students who already possess a Bachelor of Science degree in a major other than nursing are eligible for the thirteen-month accelerated program at the School of Nursing prior to Peace Corps service. A Peace Corps Fellows Program is offered to returned Peace Corps volunteers.

The Army Reserve Officers' Training Corps (ROTC) is the principal source of commissioned officers for the Active Army, Army Reserve, and Army National Guard. All Army nurses are officers. Johns Hopkins University offers two- and three-year scholarships to students enrolled in Army ROTC, which is located on the Homewood Campus of Johns Hopkins University.

Academic Facilities

The William H. Welch Medical Library is the central resource library serving Johns Hopkins Medical Institutions. Students have free 24-hour-per-day access to the Welch Library Gateway, which leads users to local and remote bibliographic databases, full-text journals, and other resources available locally and on the Internet. The Nursing Information Resource Center (NIRC), located in the School of Nursing, is managed by the Welch Library. The NIRC maintains a core collection of books to support student course work, a reprint file of material used in the students' courses, a pamphlet file of material from the National League for Nursing, and clinical skills videocassettes. In addition, the facilities and 2 million volumes of the University's Milton S. Eisenhower Library, on the Homewood Campus, are available to School of Nursing students.

Three microcomputer, computer/interactive video laboratories are equipped with a computer network that contains seventy IBM-compatible microcomputers and laser printers. Several classrooms and the auditorium have PC hookup and distance learning capabilities. Additional computer resources are available throughout the campus.

Three nursing practice labs are available to provide the student with an opportunity to gain experience and confidence in performing a wide variety of nursing technologies. Students practice basic nursing technologies at numerous patient care stations designed to closely approximate hospital inpatient areas. Practice using actual medical equipment is an integral part of the laboratory experience, and patient simulators are provided to facilitate clinical skill mastery.

The clinical facilities of the three consortium hospitals, as well as a variety of other acute, long-term community and specialty health-care institutions, are available for student clinical education.

Costs

For the 2003–04 academic year, baccalaureate tuition was $20,776.

Financial Aid

Johns Hopkins University School of Nursing attempts to provide financial assistance to all eligible accepted students. The School of Nursing will assist those students who qualify for need-based aid. Such assistance is usually in the form of loans, grants, scholarships, and work-study programs. While most of the financial aid received by students is based on financial need, many students also benefit from awards based on academic merit and achievement.

Faculty

The faculty members view professional nursing as a unique health service offering effective, humane, and competent care to individuals, families, groups, and communities. Nurses function in independent, interdependent, and dependent roles to promote and improve delivery of health care. The faculty members view education as a process and as an enriching interaction in which both the teacher and learner must actively participate in an atmosphere of mutual trust. They believe that it is the responsibility of the teacher to guide the teaching-learning process and to develop the potential of each individual student to the highest level possible. The student-faculty ratio is 9:1.

Student Government

Each class within the School of Nursing has a government board and a president. There is also the Student Government Association (SGA), which includes all divisions of the entire University. Each class has 2 representatives to the SGA, and anyone may attend the meetings.

Admission Requirements

The School seeks individuals who will bring to the student body the qualities of scholarship, motivation, and commitment. The Committee on Admissions is interested in each applicant as an individual and will consider both academic potential and personal qualities. Therefore, school records, test scores, recommendations, a personal statement about goals and interests, and an interview are all important.

A complete application consists of an application form and nonrefundable $60 application fee; recommendations from 3 persons, 2 of whom must be instructors in current or recent courses; official college transcripts; an official high school transcript (unless the applicant has already completed a college degree); and SAT or ACT scores, if they are not more than five years old and the student does not already hold a bachelor's degree. A grade point average of at least 3.0 (on a 4.0 scale) is recommended.

Students are required to spend two years in a liberal arts setting either at Johns Hopkins University or another accredited university or college offering the prerequisite courses essential for entry into an upper-division nursing curriculum. This includes course work in anatomy and physiology, microbiology, the humanities, social sciences, chemistry, and nutrition. In addition, the School of Nursing has articulation agreements for direct transfer with the College of Notre Dame of Maryland; Gettysburg College, Pennsylvania; Juniata College, Pennsylvania; Mount Holyoke College, Massachusetts; Mount Saint Mary's College, Maryland; Randolph-Macon Woman's College, Virginia; State University of New York College at Oneonta; Virginia Polytechnic Institute and State University, Virginia; Washington College, Maryland; Wheaton College, Illinois; and Wittenberg University, Ohio.

International students must submit official test score reports of the Test of English as a Foreign Language (TOEFL). In order to be considered for admission, non–permanent residents must establish their ability to finance their education in the United States. International students must submit official records of all university-level course work. To be considered for transfer toward a degree, any courses listed on an international transcript must be submitted by the student to the World Evaluation Service (WES). International registered nurses may have their transcripts evaluated by the Commission on Graduates of Foreign Nursing Schools (CGFNS). WES and CGFNS must then send the official results to Johns Hopkins University School of Nursing.

Johns Hopkins University is an affirmative action/equal opportunity institution.

Application and Information

All inquiries concerning the School of Nursing should be directed to:

Office of Admissions and Student Services
The Johns Hopkins University
School of Nursing
Suite 113
525 North Wolfe Street
Baltimore, Maryland 21205-2110
E-mail: jhuson@son.jhmi.edu
World Wide Web: http://www.son.jhmi.edu

JOHNSON & WALES UNIVERSITY

PROVIDENCE, RHODE ISLAND

The University

Founded in Providence in 1914, Johnson & Wales University (J&W) is a private, career-oriented institution offering programs that are geared to the success of a range of students. The University's 15,886 students attend classes at campuses in Providence, Rhode Island; Charleston, South Carolina; Norfolk, Virginia; North Miami, Florida; and Denver, Colorado. The University expects to open a new campus in Charlotte, North Carolina, in fall 2004. Most students are recent graduates of high school business, college-preparatory, and vocational/technical programs and represent fifty states and ninety-six countries. The academic focus of the University is on two- and four-year degree programs in business, culinary arts, food service, hospitality, teacher education, and technology. M.B.A. programs include global business leadership (with a concentration in accounting, financial services management, international trade, organizational leadership, or marketing) and hospitality and tourism global business leadership (with concentrations in event leadership, finance, marketing, and tourism planning). M.A. programs in teaching (with or without certification) include business and food service. The University also offers a doctoral program in educational leadership.

Students are involved in a variety of extracurricular activities. The Student Activities Office and fraternities and sororities are among the many groups that schedule social functions throughout the academic year. Sports and fitness programs include aerobics, baseball, basketball, soccer, tennis, and volleyball.

The University maintains twenty-four residence halls throughout its five campuses. Student services include academic counseling and testing, a tutorial center, and health services. The University's Career Development Office provides extensive career planning and placement services. Within sixty days of graduation, 99 percent of J&W students have jobs in their chosen career field.

Johnson & Wales is accredited by the New England Association of Schools and Colleges. The hospitality programs in Providence are accredited by the Accreditation Commission for Programs in Hospitality Administration.

Location

The location of each of the University's campuses enables students to take advantage of internship and part-time work activities offered by many nearby businesses, community groups, and government agencies. All of J&W's city campuses retain a small-town feel and easy accessibility to students. The urban setting of the Providence, Rhode Island, campus provides students proximity to the city's many cultural and recreational facilities. The Charleston, South Carolina, campus is located in the Port City Center of that historic city, which is home to numerous special events each year. The Norfolk, Virginia, campus is in the heart of the Hampton Roads area. Norfolk is one of Virginia's most accessible cities, close to many annual regional festivals and activities. In North Miami, Florida, the J&W campus is a short trip from the sun and fun of Fort Lauderdale and the culture and diversity of Miami. Denver, Colorado, offers students great opportunities as the nation's sixth leading tourist destination and *Fortune* magazine's "second best city in America to work and live." The new Charlotte, North Carolina, campus is located in a vibrant urban setting that combines commercial and residential life. More than 300 Fortune 500 companies have offices in the Charlotte area, which is known as the second-largest financial center in the U.S.

Majors and Degrees

J&W's Providence campus offers Bachelor of Science degree programs in accounting, baking and pastry arts, computer graphics and new media, criminal justice, culinary arts, culinary nutrition, electronics engineering, engineering design and configuration management, entrepreneurship, equine business management, equine business management/riding, financial services management, food marketing, food service entrepreneurship, food service management, hospitality management, hotel management, information science, international business, international hotel and tourism management, management, marketing, marketing communications, network engineering, paralegal studies, retail marketing and management, sports/entertainment/event management, technology services management, travel-tourism management, and Web management and Internet commerce.

The Associate in Science degree is awarded in accounting, advertising communications, applied computer science, baking and pastry arts, business administration, computer/business applications, computerized drafting, computer graphics and new media, computing technology services, criminal justice, culinary arts, entrepreneurship, equine business management, equine studies (riding program), fashion merchandising, financial services management, food and beverage management, hotel management, management, marketing, paralegal studies, restaurant management, travel-tourism management, and Web site development.

In its Continuing Education division, J&W's Providence campus also offers diploma programs in baking and pastry arts and culinary arts; certificate programs are offered in computer-aided drafting, paralegal studies, and legal nurse studies (a bachelor's degree is required for acceptance into the paralegal studies certificate program, and a student must be a Registered Nurse or hold an associate degree for acceptance into the legal nurse certificate program).

The Charleston campus offers the Associate in Applied Science degree in baking and pastry arts, culinary arts, food and beverage management, hotel management, restaurant management, and travel-tourism management.

The Norfolk campus offers an Associate of Science degree in culinary arts and a one-year certificate program in culinary arts.

The North Miami campus offers Bachelor of Science degrees in accounting, criminal justice, culinary arts, food service management, hospitality management, hotel management, management, marketing, and sports/entertainment/event management. Associate of Science degrees are offered in accounting, baking and pastry arts, business administration, criminal justice, culinary arts, fashion merchandising, food and beverage management, hotel management, management, marketing, restaurant management, and travel-tourism management.

The Denver campus offers bachelor's degrees in accounting, financial services management, food service management, hotel management, international business, management, marketing, and sports/entertainment/event management. Associate of Science degrees are offered in accounting, advertising communications, baking and pastry arts, business administration, culinary arts, fashion merchandising, food and beverage management, hotel management, and marketing.

J&W's new Charlotte, North Carolina, campus is expected to open in fall 2004. Planned majors include Bachelor of Science degrees in accounting, food service management, hotel management, international hotel and tourism management, management, marketing, marketing communications, and sports/entertainment/event management. Associate of Science degrees include accounting, advertising communications, baking and pastry arts, business administration, culinary arts, fashion merchandising, food and beverage management, hotel management, management, marketing, and restaurant management.

Academic Program

Johnson & Wales offers programs in business, culinary arts, food service, hospitality, and technology within an academic structure of three 11-week terms. Classes generally meet four days a week,

Monday through Thursday. The "upside-down" curriculum of J&W provides immediate concentration in the student's chosen major. The associate degree is awarded after two years of successful study, at which time the student may continue studies toward the baccalaureate degree or seek immediate employment. Two degrees, the associate and the bachelor's, can result from a complete four-year course of study.

Learning by doing is an important part of career training at J&W, and many programs include laboratory studies as well as formal internship requirements. Special advanced-placement programs are featured for high school seniors with exceptional skills in culinary arts or baking and pastry arts. In addition, the University grants credit and/or a waiver of certain courses on the basis of CLEP and challenge examinations. All degree candidates must successfully complete the required number of courses and/or quarter credit hours, as prescribed in the various curricula, with a minimum average of 2.0.

Off-Campus Programs

Learning at J&W is not limited to the classroom. Many of the majors offer internships at University-owned facilities. The hotel-restaurant management program features an internship at the Johnson & Wales Inn, the Radisson Airport Hotel, or the Bay Harbor Inn and Suites; all are full-service hotel complexes owned and operated by the University (the Radisson is a corporate franchise). Fashion merchandising and retailing majors may spend their eleven-week internships at Gladding's, a women's specialty store also owned by the University. Students majoring in travel-tourism management may participate in an internship at American Express Travel Service, the University's travel agency. For all majors, optional selective career co-ops are available with cooperating businesses throughout the U.S. and worldwide, such as Marriott International, Hyatt Regency Hotels, Television Food Network, FleetBoston Financial, Foxwoods Resort and Casino, and Putnam Investments. Most internships and co-ops are one term in duration and carry 13.5 quarter hours of credit. Foreign exchange and term-abroad programs are also offered.

Academic Facilities

The facilities of the Providence campus are located throughout the intimate state of Rhode Island and in nearby Massachusetts. The downtown Providence campus is home to the University's College of Business, Hospitality College, and School of Technology. A number of academic and residential facilities are located at this campus as well as several training facilities. The Harborside campus, located a short distance away, houses the University's College of Culinary Arts. This campus has four student residence halls as well as specialized classrooms and laboratories, production kitchens, bakeshops, dining rooms, a storeroom, and meat-cutting facilities. This campus is also home to the Alan Shawn Feinstein Graduate School, the Center for Education, the University Recreation and Athletic Center, a student activities office, a bookstore, a gymnasium, a dining center, a snack bar, and an arcade.

The academic facilities of the Charleston campus are housed in a five-story brick building constructed in 1881 as part of the Reconstruction. Facilities include academic classrooms, demonstration/production kitchens, bakeshops, dining rooms, a storeroom, a mixology laboratory, a resource center, computer laboratories, and a public training food service facility. The University provides transportation between academic and residence facilities.

The Norfolk campus is located in the Westgate Center in the Norfolk Commerce Park and includes several classrooms, production/demonstration kitchens, a bakeshop, and a resource center. The University provides transportation between academic and residence facilities.

The North Miami campus' facilities include academic classrooms, production/demonstration kitchens, a bakeshop, residence halls and a specially designed conference center.

The Denver campus, located in the Park Hill neighborhood, combines old-world charm with the latest technological resources, including stately turn-of-the-century buildings and newer student centers in a quiet park setting. The traditional residential campus is fully wired with computers in every classroom and laboratory.

Costs

Tuition at all campuses for 2003-04 ranged from $15,222 to $18,444, depending on the program of study. The basic room and board plans ranged from $6777 to $8433. Each student was also charged a general fee of $750, and there was an orientation fee for new students. Books and supplies were estimated at $825, depending upon the program.

Tuition and room and board fees may vary at each campus. Students should consult the respective campus catalogs for further details.

Financial Aid

Johnson & Wales students are eligible to apply for a variety of financial aid programs, including the Federal Pell Grant, Federal Supplemental Educational Opportunity Grant, Federal Work-Study, and Federal Perkins Loan programs. They are also eligible for University-based student scholarship and loan programs and state-supported grants and scholarships. In the past, approximately 90 percent of J&W's entering students have received some sort of financial assistance. Students must submit the Free Application for Federal Student Aid (FAFSA) to the Federal Student Aid Processor to be considered for financial aid. Although there is no deadline, early application is strongly suggested for full consideration.

Faculty

The University's 429 full-time and 211 part-time undergraduate faculty members (all campuses) are oriented toward instruction rather than research. Many are chosen for their professional experience in business, culinary arts, hospitality services, and technology. The student-faculty ratio is 30:1.

Student Government

Student Government Association (SGA) representatives serve as the link among students, faculty, and the administration to bring students' concerns to the awareness of the University community.

Admission Requirements

J&W seeks students who are career-focused and have a true desire to succeed. Academic qualifications are important, but an applicant's motivation and interest in doing well are given special consideration. Graduation from high school or equivalent credentials are required for admission. It is recommended that students applying for admission into the culinary arts and baking and pastry arts programs have some prior education or experience in food service. Although no tests are required, all applicants are encouraged to submit scores from the SAT I or ACT. Students who wish to apply for the Honors Program must have either a score of 500 math and 500 verbal on the SAT or a score of 21 math and 21 verbal on the ACT. High school juniors may apply for early admission under the ACCESS Program. Transfer students are required to submit official high school and college transcripts and to have a minimum GPA of 2.0. Credits to be transferred from other institutions are evaluated on the basis of their equivalent at Johnson & Wales.

Application and Information

Johnson & Wales does not require an application fee. After submitting the application, the student is responsible for requesting that appropriate transcripts be forwarded to the Admissions Office of the University. While there is no deadline, students are advised to apply as early as possible before the intended date of enrollment to ensure full consideration of their application. Applications are accepted for terms beginning in September, December, and March and for the summer sessions.

Inquiries and applications should be addressed to:

Kenneth DiSaia
Vice President of Enrollment Management
Johnson & Wales University
8 Abbott Park Place
Providence, Rhode Island 02903
Telephone: 401-598-1000
800-DIAL-JWU (toll-free)
Fax: 401-598-4901
E-mail: petersons@jwu.edu
World Wide Web: http://www.jwu.edu

JOHNSON C. SMITH UNIVERSITY

CHARLOTTE, NORTH CAROLINA

The University

Founded in 1867 under the auspices of the Committee on Freedmen of the Presbyterian Church, U.S.A., Johnson C. Smith University (JCSU) is an independent, private, coeducational institution of higher learning. Located in the rapidly growing metropolis of Charlotte, North Carolina, "Queen City of the South," this historically African-American university has a residential campus with a familial atmosphere in which students are stimulated and nurtured by dedicated and caring faculty and staff members.

The present site contains 100 acres of land and more than 40 buildings. The University serves approximately 1,500 students and has more than 240 full-time faculty members, administrators, and staff members. As a liberal arts university, JCSU offers more than 30 fields of study.

JCSU's mission is to provide an outstanding education for a diverse group of talented and highly motivated students from various ethnic, socioeconomic, and geographical backgrounds. The University offers a liberal arts education in conjunction with concentrated study in specialized fields in preparation for specific careers and advanced study.

The University endeavors to produce graduates who are able to communicate effectively, think critically, learn independently as well as collaboratively, and demonstrate competence in their chosen fields. Further, it provides an environment in which students can fulfill their physical, social, cultural, spiritual, and other personal needs and develop a compelling sense of social and civic responsibility for leadership and service in a dynamic, multicultural society. Likewise, the University embraces its responsibility to provide leadership, service, and lifelong learning to the larger community.

Consistent with its Christian roots, the University recognizes the importance of moral and ethical values in undergirding intellectual development and all endeavors. JCSU believes in the unrelenting pursuit of knowledge and in the values of cultivating the life of the mind. The University assigns great significance to the development of self-confidence, to the understanding of ones' own heritage (as well as an awareness of the cultures of others), to the exploration of the myriad forces affecting people in today's complex technological age, and to formulating a sense of one's role in this schema.

From 2002 to 2004, JCSU has been consecutively ranked by *U.S. News & World Report* as one of the top-tier institutions in the southern region of the United States. With ThinkPad U. and other innovative programs, JCSU has begun to move into a new era of distinction.

The University is a fully accredited member of the Southern Association of Colleges and Schools (SACS). Its Department of Education is accredited by the National Council for Accreditation of Teacher Education (NCATE); the Department of Business Administration and Economics is accredited by the Association of Collegiate Business Schools and Programs (ACBSP); and the Department of Social Work is accredited by the Council on Social Work Education (CSWE).

Between the late 1990s and early 2000s, JCSU saw a burst of financial support from donors. In 1996, JCSU received a $1-million gift from Irwin Belk, a prominent Charlotte businessman, which was the largest gift from a living individual in the school's history. Between 1999 and 2002, JCSU received several million-dollar grants from funding agencies, including the Lilly Foundation, the Department of Interior, and The Duke Endowment, and a $2.57 million grant from the Kresge Foundation. In 2002, The Duke Endowment awarded JCSU $3.9 million, the largest grant in the school's history.

In fall 2000, JCSU launched the IBM Laptop Initiative, which made the University one of the few educational institutions in the country (and the first historically black college) to provide an IBM laptop computer to every student. The program, known as ThinkPad U., gives JCSU students and their computers complete access to the campuswide network and Internet services. The ratio of computers to students improved from 1:10 in 1994 to 1.2:1 in 2003. In addition, 3500 Ethernet ports have been installed campuswide; the ratio of connecting ports to students is 2.4:1. Since fall 2003, all JCSU students have wireless access on the campus. With this new initiative and the commitment to integrate technology throughout the curriculum, JCSU has gained national recognition.

Location

Charlotte, North Carolina, where JCSU is situated, is the largest city in the Carolinas. With a population of more than 500,000, Charlotte is a commercial, banking, and cultural center.

The city has an impressive skyline, a revitalized uptown, numerous industries and factories, and a diverse residential community. Rich in historic landmarks, Charlotte offers all the cultural and recreational facilities of any large city, including professional and other sports events; excellent shopping and dining facilities; rock, popular, jazz, and classical music concerts; theater; fine arts; and exceptional gardens. The area is served by an international airport, Amtrak railway, and Greyhound bus service. Major highways provide easy access to beach and mountain areas.

Majors and Degrees

JCSU offers the Bachelor of Arts, Bachelor of Science, and Bachelor of Social Work degrees. Majors are offered in applied mathematics, biology, business administration, chemistry, communication arts, computer science/information systems, criminal justice, economics, elementary education, English, English education, French, general science, health education, history, liberal arts, mathematics, mathematics education, physical education, political science, psychology, social science, social studies education, social work, sociology, and Spanish. Students may minor in most areas where majors are offered as well as in African-American and African studies.

Preprofessional programs are offered in dentistry, medicine, and law. Students may complete courses in military science as part of either the Army or Air Force ROTC programs.

Through collaboration with several other institutions, JCSU also offers programs leading to degrees in engineering, nursing, and pharmacy.

Academic Programs

To be eligible for a bachelor's degree, a student must complete a minimum of 122 hours, with a minimum overall grade point average of 2.0; earn a minimum grade of C in any course that counts toward the major; satisfy all requirements of the curricula in the Liberal Studies Program or the Honors College Program; complete all requirements for Community Service and the Senior Investigative Paper; and attend eight Lyceum events.

JCSU offers various special programs to assist students to both build upon their current understandings and expand into new areas of inquiry. Among them, the Freshman Through the Senior Year Experience (FSYE) program provides various support services to aid students with the academic demands of the college curriculum. The Honors College provides curricular and extracurricular experiences for students who are highly motivated, superbly prepared, and sufficiently dedicated to the highest level of academic achievement and scholarship. The Counseling and Testing Center offers 7/24 (seven days a week and 24 hours per day) services to the students. Student Support Services, a federally funded program, provides qualified students with peer and professional mentoring and tutoring.

Collectively, these programs create a dynamic learning community that promotes and enhances the student's ability to engage in interdisciplinary inquiry and build the intellectual foundation needed for a successful college experience. The programs eliminate technology barriers, foster inquiry and problems-based learning, and create mentors and apprenticeships.

Academic Facilities

The expansion of the physical plant, particularly the growth that occurred in the 1990s, reflects the growth of JCSU in the recent decade. Mainly, those improvements include the Robert L. Albright Honors College Center (1990), the Faculty Center (1991), the Edward E. Crutchfield Jr. Center for Integrated Studies (1993), new residence halls (1993), a Technology Center (1997), and the Irwin Belk Complex, a state-of-the-art academic and sports facility (2003).

In addition, a large scale of renovation enables JCSU to preserve some historical landmarks and improve the functionality of others. Among those efforts, the renovation of historic Biddle Memorial Hall was begun in 2001 after an aggressive campaign to raise more than $6.7 million. Upon its completion, this administrative building is planned to feature new computer systems, climate conditioning, modern lighting, and new electrical systems. The completion of the renovation of the James B. Duke Library in 1999 brought not only a new look but also new resources and technology to the facility. In fall 2003, the library's collection included 90,674 books, 164,553 microforms, 1,035 audiovisual materials, 292 serial subscriptions, and a large volume of online reference databases. Equipped with state-of-art technology, the library also has a great capacity to provide multimedia and other services to support instructional services and research activities.

Costs

To insure the integrity and stability of its status and the perpetuation of its rich legacy, JCSU has a firm resolve to maintain the fiscal and human resources requisite to be a truly distinctive institution—a hallmark of excellence in its students, faculty and staff members, administrators, academic and other programs, facilities, operations, and environment.

For school year 2003–04, the total cost of attending JCSU as a full-time student, including tuition, fees, room, and board, was $18,108.

Financial Aid

Loans, grants, and scholarships are available and are awarded on the basis of need or special achievement. In 2003, the average amount of aid awarded to qualified freshmen reached $5600 per student. Types of aid include Federal Pell Grants, Federal Supplemental Educational Opportunity Grants, Federal Perkins Loans, Federal Stafford Student Loans, Federal Work-Study awards, North Carolina state grants (for NC residents only), and institutional awards. There are also a variety of scholarships and other aid programs available. To be considered for financial aid, students must file the Free Application for Federal Student Aid (FAFSA). The form is available at high school guidance offices or through the JCSU Student Financial Aid Office.

All students are urged to file the FAFSA by May 1. JCSU's code (002936) should be used in the application.

Each year, a limited number of academic scholarships (Duke Scholars) are offered in the freshman year, primarily to participants in the Honor Program. Recipients of this scholarship are selected from high school seniors who earned high scores on the SAT I and who have a minimum GPA of 3.0.

In addition, for those students demonstrating outstanding academic achievement in the sciences, the Minority Biomedical Research Support Program and other programs provide a variety of opportunities, such as salaried positions during the academic year and summer, participation in research, and attendance at seminars and conferences of national scientific importance.

Faculty

Regarding teaching effectiveness as paramount in its educational enterprise, JCSU has a commitment to the recruitment and retention of an outstanding faculty. To this end, the University promotes faculty development, encourages faculty involvement in research and other creative activities, and endorses the principles of academic freedom.

During the school year 2003–04, JCSU employed about 90 full-time faculty members. Approximately 76 percent of them held doctorates or terminal degrees. The student-faculty ratio was 14.8:1.

To promote excellence in teaching and learning, JCSU has, since 1994, established joint research and student/faculty-exchange international relationships with Swinburne University of Technology in Australia, Al Akhawayn University in Morocco, and Moscow State Institute of Public Policy and Moscow State University in Russia. Such arrangements exist domestically with Providence College in Rhode Island.

Student Government

Opportunities for student participation in policymaking are provided through membership in the Student Government Association, the Student Christian Association, the Residence Halls Council, and the Pan Hellenic Council.

Admission Requirements

Candidates for admission should be graduates of accredited high schools; rank in the upper 50 percent of their high school classes; and have minimum averages of C. In addition, the candidates should have completed sixteen academic units consisting of 4 in English, 2 in mathematics, 2 in social science, 2 in science (at least 1 in a laboratory science), and 6 in electives. The recommendations and reputation of the applicant's high school, records in extracurricular activities and athletics, achievement in advanced placement or honors courses; evidence of leadership potential, and the impressions made during an optional interview are all factors that might affect the admission decision. Applicants must also have an official report of their SAT I or ACT scores forwarded directly to JCSU. The University's acceptance rate was 37 percent for the year 2003.

Application and Information

Application for admission should be submitted by June 15 for full consideration. Each student who is accepted must pay a $250 matriculation and room reservation fee.

Application and financial aid forms may be obtained by contacting:

Director of Admissions
Johnson C. Smith University
100 Beatties Ford Road
Charlotte, North Carolina 28216-5398

Telephone: 704-378-1010
1-800-782-7303 (toll-free)
E-mail: admissions@jcsu.edu
World Wide Web: http://www.jcsu.edu

JOHNSON STATE COLLEGE

JOHNSON, VERMONT

The College

Founded in 1828, Johnson State College served as a school for the training of teachers until the 1960s, when it expanded into the liberal arts and the sciences. The current enrollment is more than 1,750 men and women. Sixty percent of the College's students are Vermonters; 40 percent are out-of-state and come from more than from twenty-three states and ten other countries. The campus has modern facilities, including a state-of-the-art Library and Learning Center, Dewey Campus Center, the beautiful Dibden Center for the Fine and Performing Arts, a visual arts building, an excellent science facility, a health/athletics complex, an on-campus snowboard park, and newly renovated residence halls. The College is surrounded by 350 acres of meadowland and forest, and there are two ponds. Located on a hill overlooking the village of Johnson, the campus commands a breathtaking view of the Green Mountains. The College is accredited by the New England Association of Schools and Colleges and is approved by the Vermont State Board of Higher Education.

At the graduate level, the College offers the Master of Arts in Education degree with specializations in elementary licensure, gifted and talented, middle school licensure, secondary licensure, special education, and curriculum instruction. The curriculum instruction track allows students to choose from several strands: early childhood, literacy, and content specialist, as well as individually designed strands that can be negotiated by the student with a faculty adviser; the Master of Arts in counseling; and the Master of Fine arts in studio arts, in conjunction with the Vermont Studio Center.

More than thirty clubs and organizations provide a variety of student activities. These include *Basement Medicine* (the student newspaper), the *Gihon River Review* (the literary magazine), the Dance Ensemble, the Theater Club, the radio station (WJSC-FM), the College Concert Band, and the Outing, Earth Awareness, Snowboarding, and International Clubs. Varsity athletic competition is available for women in basketball, cross-country running, soccer, softball, and tennis and for men in basketball, cross-country running, lacrosse, soccer, and tennis. Many intramural and club sports, including indoor soccer, baseball, golf, hockey, lacrosse, rugby, swimming, and volleyball, are also available. Johnson State College's health education/sports complex includes two weight-lifting areas, a basketball court, a gymnasium, racquetball courts, a swimming pool, a training room, and a human performance lab. Also on campus are outdoor tennis courts, cross-country running and ski trails, a snowboard park, and large playing fields. The gymnasium and outdoor athletic facilities also provide recreational outlets for many individuals in the campus community. Stearns Hall houses a post office, the Summit Book Store, and a spacious dining room. The College has a Counseling and Health Center. The Dewey Campus Center houses the Dewey Commons Snackbar, the Advising Center, and a Career Resource Center.

Location

The College is just 20 minutes from Stowe, the ski capital of the East; 45 minutes from Burlington, Vermont's largest city; and 90 minutes from Montreal, Canada. Other attractions near the College are Smugglers' Notch ski area, Jay Peak ski area, Ben & Jerry's Ice Cream Factory, and Lake Champlain. The College can be reached by rail (Amtrak) or air (Burlington International Airport).

Majors and Degrees

Johnson State College offers major academic programs leading to the Bachelor of Arts or Bachelor of Science degree in anthropology/sociology, art, athletic training, biology, business management, drama and theater, English, environmental sciences, health sciences, history, hospitality and tourism management, integrated environmental science, journalism, liberal arts, mathematics, music, outdoor education, political science, psychology, and wellness and alternative medicine. The Bachelor of Fine Arts degree is offered in creative writing and studio arts.

The Bachelor of Arts or Bachelor of Science degree leading to state teacher certification is offered in art education (K–12), dance secondary education, elementary education, life sciences (biology) secondary education, mathematics secondary education, middle school education, music education (K–12), physical education (K–12), physical sciences (chemistry) secondary education, and social studies.

Associate of Arts or Associate of Science degrees are offered in general studies, management, and technical theater.

Certificate programs leading to business certification are offered in accounting, French for business majors, nonprofit management, and small-business management.

Minors are available in adventure education, anthropology/sociology, arts management, biology, business, chemistry, dance, drama, environmental education, French, gender studies, history, journalism, literature, mathematics, music, natural resources, political science, prelaw, psychology, Spanish, studio arts, and theater.

Academic Program

The Johnson State curriculum provides students with a general liberal arts background and the opportunity for career preparation in a specific area. All students in four-year programs are required to complete at least 120 credit hours in the selected program of study. Those studying for the associate degree must complete at least 60 semester hours of credit in the selected program of study. Students may transfer internally from two-year to four-year programs.

Transfer credit is awarded for college courses in which a grade of C– or above was earned. Accepted transfer students receive a credit evaluation.

The academic year consists of fall and spring semesters of fifteen weeks each and a six-week summer session. The College offers courses in the evening and on weekends through the External Degree Program.

Off-Campus Programs

Johnson State College provides internship opportunities in all degree programs, including student teaching for education majors.

The College offers study abroad opportunities through the National Student Exchange and the New England–Quebec Student Exchange. Other student-abroad opportunities are available.

Academic Facilities

The 350-acre, hilltop campus houses modern, well-equipped buildings. College facilities include an art gallery, art studios, dance studios, the Visual Arts Center, three computer centers, a library, a student center, the Child Development Center, and the Dibden Center for the Fine and Performing Arts, which contains a theater. The new Library and Learning Center contains more than 100,000 volumes, an audiovisual department, microfilm and microfiche units, government documents, periodicals, journals, records, the Vermont Room, the Art Room, the Ellsworth International Room, and the Children's Library. The Babcock Nature Preserve, a 1,000-acre tract of forests and ponds, serves as an outdoor laboratory for scientific and educational research.

Costs

Estimated tuition and fees for the academic year 2004–05 for Vermont residents are $5900 and for nonresidents, $12,876. Room and board expenses are $6282.

Financial Aid

Seventy-six percent of Johnson's students receive financial assistance from federal, state, College, or other sources. Grants, loans, and work-study jobs are available for qualified students. Applicants for financial aid should file the Free Application for Federal Student Aid (FAFSA) by March 1 of the year preceding anticipated enrollment. All financial aid awards are based on need. The College offers renewable academic scholarships for both freshmen and transfers. Special scholarships are also available.

Faculty

The full-time faculty at Johnson consists of 55 men and women, 91 percent of whom hold a Ph.D. or equivalent degree. Adjunct faculty members, many of whom are local professionals, complement the full-time faculty. The student-faculty ratio is 16:1. Each student has a faculty member serving as an academic adviser.

Student Government

The Johnson State College Student Association is a vital and active organization that has a strong voice in College affairs. Student representatives are elected to the Student Assembly, which helps plan curriculum and program developments. The association coordinates student social and cultural activities, including dances and numerous clubs.

Admission Requirements

Admission to Johnson State College is granted to applicants who have demonstrated the potential to succeed at the college level. They are evaluated on the basis of their high school transcripts, letters of recommendation, standardized test scores (SAT I or ACT), and class rank. The College emphasizes course selection, grades, and participation in extracurricular activities in reviewing applications.

All candidates should successfully complete a college-preparatory program that includes 4 years of high school English, 2 years of mathematics, 3 years of social science, and 2 years of science (one course with a laboratory). Applicants who do not qualify for regular admission may receive acceptance to the Transition Year Experience. A campus visit and an interview are strongly recommended.

Application and Information

The College has a rolling admission policy and processes applications throughout the year. However, high school students seeking fall enrollment are encouraged to apply early in their senior year. The College admits first-year and transfer students regardless of their state of residence. Notification dates are also rolling. Students may enter at the beginning of the fall or spring semester.

The student's application file is complete when the following items have been received: a completed application form, a $30 nonrefundable application fee, a transcript from the high school and any colleges previously attended, a writing sample, standardized test scores, and a reference from a teacher, a college adviser, or an employer. An enrollment deposit of $200 and a $100 housing deposit are required by May 1 or within two weeks of notification of acceptance if the applicant applies after May 1.

For application forms and further information, students should contact:

Penny P. Howrigan
Associate Dean of Enrollment Services
Johnson State College
337 College Hill
Johnson, Vermont 05656
Telephone: 802-635-1219
800-635-2356 (toll-free)
Fax: 802-635-1230
E-mail: jscadmissions@jsc.vsc.edu
World Wide Web: http://www.johnsonstatecollege.edu

A view from the campus overlooking the town of Johnson.

JONES INTERNATIONAL UNIVERSITY®

ENGLEWOOD, COLORADO

The University

Since 1993, Jones International University® (JIU™), the first fully online, accredited university, has been at the forefront of the online education revolution, creating relevant, content-rich graduate and undergraduate programs for motivated adult learners. In addition to its undergraduate programs, JIU offers twenty graduate programs and more than fifty certificate programs.

JIU courses are delivered via the Internet, letting students earn their degrees without putting the rest of their lives on hold; everything needed to complete a degree is online and easily accessible 24 hours a day, seven days a week. All that a student needs is a computer, access to the Internet, and any standard Web browser. In addition to convenience, JIU ensures quality, having received formal accreditation from the Higher Learning Commission of the North Central Association of Colleges and Schools, a U.S. regional accrediting agency, in March 1999. Regional accreditation is the highest level of accreditation a university can obtain and is recognized throughout the U.S. This accreditation ensures an outstanding and well-respected education from JIU.

In addition, JIU offers a global academic experience, employing a world-class faculty from leading U.S. and international universities. Content experts from such prestigious institutions as Cornell University, Purdue University, and the London School of Economics design all of the courses specifically for the Internet. At JIU, students expand their networks internationally and learn from a world of real-life experience. Residing in more than 100 countries, JIU students interact with a community of the world's leading business thinkers, peers, and executives.

Majors and Degrees

JIU awards a Bachelor of Business Administration degree with five specializations: corporate finance, information technology management, entrepreneurship, e-commerce, and generalist. The University also offers two degree-completion programs: the Bachelor of Science in Information Technology (B.S.I.T.) and the Bachelor of Arts in Business Communication (B.A.B.C.). Two degree specializations are available in the B.S.I.T. program, consisting of Enterprise Windows Systems Administration (e.g., Microsoft-Based Track) and Enterprise Unix Systems Administration (e.g., Solaris-Based Track). The three degree specializations available in the B.A.B.C. program comprise Applied Telecommunications, Communications Management, and International Marketing. Incoming degree-seeking B.S.I.T. or B.A.B.C. students must have a regionally or DETC-accredited associate degree or have completed 60 semester credit hours, including 39 credit hours of general education courses. JIU offers a selection of courses for those students who need to complete general education requirements.

Jones International University also offers a wide variety of certificate programs for individuals who want to gain professional and academic experience in specific areas. All courses within each certificate program are fully accredited and may be applied toward a degree at any time. Certificates in the Bachelor of Arts in Business Communication degree program are Using the Internet in Public Relations; Fundamentals of e-Marketing; Communication Skills for Managers; The Dynamics of Human Resource Management; Technology Tools for Managers; Managerial Communication; Communication and Motivation; Management Skills with a Human Directive; Fundamentals of Business Telecommunications; Applied Telecommunications Management; and Managing Global Communications. Certificates within the Bachelor of Science in Information Technology degree program are Strategic Network Planning, Quality Software Management, Enterprise Windows Systems Administration (e.g., Microsoft), and Enterprise Unix Systems Administration (e.g., Solaris). Certificates in the Bachelor of Business Administration degree program are Principles of Business Finance, Applied Information Technology, Entrepreneurship in a Global Context, and e-Commerce in the Global Market.

Academic Programs

JIU structures its degree programs to provide students with the skills and knowledge to innovate and implement rather than merely imitate and direct. For example, students in the Bachelor of Science in Information Technology degree program acquire the knowledge to design technical solutions to business problems, combined with the project management skills to interface with executives on their terms. The B.S.I.T. program consists of seven programming and development core courses, four systems architecture core courses, three business core courses, four technical degree specialization courses (one technical specialization area must be completed), one general education course, and one capstone experience (including portfolio). A total of 120 total credit hours are required for graduation.

The JIU Bachelor of Arts in Business Communication degree program is based on the widely accepted educational principle that adults learn best when they gain knowledge that is relevant and applicable to the demands of their lives. Through a unique combination of academic understanding and practical, applied strategies, JIU delivers the skills, knowledge, and confidence students need to succeed. The B.A.B.C. program consists of four interdisciplinary courses, twelve core curriculum courses, and four specialization courses. A total of 120 total credit hours are required for graduation.

The Bachelor of Business Administration program offers students the opportunity to complete their entire degree at JIU. To complete the program, students must take sixteen general education courses, ten business core courses, nine elective courses, four specialization courses, and complete a capstone course. A total of 120 credit hours are required for graduation.

JIU courses are offered in eight-week formats. New courses start every month. Applications for admission to the program are accepted on a continuous basis throughout the year.

Academic Facilities

While there may not be a physical campus for JIU, there is a strong sense of community among its students. In fact, JIU even holds online graduation ceremonies each May, where students walk down the virtual aisle and their degrees are conferred by JIU administration and prominent guest speakers. Graduation ceremonies include streaming audio and video in which students receive their commencement address and their degrees.

The JIU Library hosts a plethora of resources linking the virtual student to more than 100 research guides, 30 electronic databases, and nearly 7,000 content-rich Web sites that are selected, evaluated, and annotated by librarians with subject expertise. In addition, there is access to more than 325 federal government sites, categorized by subject, containing more than 150,000 documents and document delivery of up to five documents per course. This feature alone gives the online learner a convenient, competitive advantage. Jones International University students also receive reference assistance from librarians to help locate and research information. JIU also hosts a peer advisory program that establishes e-mail "buddies" to discuss the courses and requirements or provide study tips. There is also an online bookstore providing all necessary text materials for JIU courses and a variety of widely used forms.

This vast array of resources is available at all times, and JIU provides an online, user-friendly tutorial, Libraries 101. This tutorial guides students through different types of library resources, explains how they are organized, and demonstrates how to use them for research. JIU also offers Internet 101, an online guide that teaches students how to use the Internet effectively in their studies.

Costs

For the current tuition rates, prospective students should visit the JIU Web site listed below.

Financial Aid

JIU makes every effort to make education an achievable goal for its students. As a result, the University has aligned with organizations and agencies to make various financial aid options available.

JIU offers its students access to federal student aid. These loan and grant programs allow qualified students to take advantage of need- and non-need-based funds to help them finance their education. Other options for financing include SLM Financial loans and PLATO loans, which are available to U.S citizens and permanent residents who have demonstrated creditworthiness; corporate tuition assistance; VA benefits; JIU's special program for military personnel; and scholarships.

Faculty

As an institution designed to provide educational programs via the Internet, the JIU learning model represents a true best practice for online education. Committed to developing courses appropriate for the Internet rather than replicating traditional classroom lectures, JIU presents courses in exciting learning modules. They are rich in content and facilitate interaction between the participants and the instructors.

Faculty members are the cornerstone of an academic experience. That is why JIU works with some of the most highly respected experts in their fields. JIU's content-expert faculty members are professors at the world's most prestigious institutions. They are renowned for their knowledge in their fields and hold senior-level positions in some of the world's most cutting-edge universities, including prestigious institutions such as Stanford University, Columbia University, Michigan State University, and Rutgers University.

Admission Requirements

Students must complete an application for admission and submit a transcript from an accredited secondary school or a GED certificate, three letters of reference, a current resume, and an application essay.

Students order all textbooks and course materials from JIU Web page links. Upon registration, students are instructed on how to order course materials. The materials may include texts, articles, videotapes, and software. The course study guide is available for downloading from the course Web site and includes the course syllabus.

Hardware requirements include a 250-MHz processor (400-MHz recommended); 64 MB of RAM (128 MB recommended); a 15-inch VGA monitor (17-inch SVGA recommended); a 256-color monitor (65,000 color recommended), 800 X 600 resolution or better; a 56-K modem (faster speed is recommended); and a PostScript Emulation printer (PostScript recommended). The following additions are recommended for B.S.I.T. courses: 4 GB of free hard disk space, Metrowerks CodeWarrior, and Borland Jbuilder or Sun Java-2, Platform Standard Edition (J2SE).

Software recommendations include one of the following browser options: Internet Explorer 5.5 (Internet Explorer 5.5 Service Pack 2 recommended), Netscape Navigator 4.08, or Netscape Communicator 4.78 or 4.79; a word processing program (MS Word 97 or 2000 recommended); and an e-mail program (MS Outlook, MS Outlook Express, Eudora, or Eudora Pro recommended.) WinZip is also recommended, but not required. Recommended plug-ins are Adobe Acrobat Reader 4.0, Flash Player 6, and RealOne Player. No peripherals are required; however, speakers are recommended. Some courses require Flash 4.0 plug-in (free) and access to audio and visual equipment. Students enrolled in EDU 703 need PowerPoint software to complete their course project.

Application and Information

Admission applications are only required for degree-seeking students. A nonrefundable application fee is required. Admission applications are accepted on a continuous basis throughout the year.

Jones International University®
9697 East Mineral Avenue
Englewood, Colorado 80112
Telephone: 303-784-8247
800-811-5663 (toll-free in the U.S. only)
E-mail: info@jonesinternational.edu
World Wide Web: http://www.jonesinternational.edu

JUNIATA COLLEGE
HUNTINGDON, PENNSYLVANIA

The College

Juniata College is an independent, coeducational college of liberal arts and sciences, founded in 1876 by members of the Church of the Brethren to prepare individuals "for the useful occupations of life." Juniata College holds a place of national prominence in higher education. Recent studies rank the College highly in the percentage of graduates that eventually earn doctoral degrees; one, in fact, ranked Juniata in the top 10 percent in the nation among all four-year private undergraduate institutions. Juniata's national reputation is strongest in several fields, including biology, chemistry, environmental science and education, health sciences, peace and conflict studies, and prelaw. The College is known for the personal attention it gives students. Each student is assigned 2 faculty advisers, and the average student-faculty ratio is 14:1.

As a community that focuses on the whole person, Juniata recognizes the importance of both curricular and cocurricular aspects of student development. Juniata has bridged the traditional higher education dichotomy between academic affairs and student affairs by merging these two branches of the College, a structural move that integrates the student's total college experience.

Location

Juniata is located in Huntingdon, which lies in the scenic rolling hills of central Pennsylvania. The 110 acres on College Hill have allowed for careful expansion, and the forty campus buildings blend well with each other and the spaciousness of the campus. Juniata's campus also consists of a 365-acre field station and a 315-acre nature preserve. The surrounding area is suited for many outdoor activities, including swimming, boating, fishing, hunting, skiing, and hiking. Raystown Lake, the largest recreational lake wholly in Pennsylvania, is only 15 minutes from Juniata. Several major cities lie within a short drive of the campus—3 hours to Pittsburgh, Baltimore, and Washington, D.C.; 4 hours to Philadelphia; and 5 hours to New York City. The nearest commercial airport is in State College, the location of Penn State University. In addition, Huntingdon is on the main U.S. east-west railway line, with travel by train to East and West Coast cities available.

Majors and Degrees

Juniata awards B.A. and B.S. degrees in the arts, humanities, natural sciences, and social sciences. Rather than complete a traditional major, each Juniata student designs a Program of Emphasis (POE) that is tailored to the student's own goals and often crosses departmental lines. Working closely with 2 academic advisers, students select courses for either a designated or an individualized POE. Current areas of study include accounting, anthropology, art (art history; museum studies, with an art history focus; and studio fine arts), biological sciences (biochemistry, biology, botany, ecology, microbiology, molecular and cell physiology, and zoology), business management (international business, management, and marketing), chemistry, communication, computer science, criminal justice, early childhood education, early childhood and special education, economics, elementary education, elementary and special education, English, environmental science, environmental studies, exploratory studies, geology, health communication, history, interdisciplinary studies (humanities, liberal arts, natural sciences, and social sciences), information technology (business, computer science, and communication), international politics, international studies, languages (French, German, Russian, and Spanish), marine science, mathematics, peace and conflict studies, physics, politics, pre–health (biotechnology, cardiovascular technology, cytogenetics, diagnostic imaging/radiography, medical technology, nursing, occupational therapy, and physical therapy), pre–health professions (dentistry, medicine, optometry, pharmacy, podiatry, and veterinary science), prelaw, preministry, psychology, public administration, religion, secondary education (biology, chemistry, communication, earth and space science, English, French, general science, German, mathematics, physics, social studies, and Spanish), social work, and sociology.

Academic Program

Designed to foster individual responsibility, Juniata's flexible and academically rigorous program allows both acquisition of a broad range of knowledge and in-depth examination of a particular field. More than 50 percent of the students attending Juniata develop their own program through a flexible program of emphasis (POE).

Students must satisfactorily complete 120 semester credit hours. Writing, computer and bibliographic skills, and college transition issues are addressed in the freshman year. Graduation requirements also include a two-course cultural analysis sequence, advanced communication/writing skills, quantitative studies, social sciences, humanities, international, fine arts, and natural sciences and an optional service learning component. In addition, all students complete a 45–60 credit POE, and many choose to complete an integrative senior project to graduate with distinction.

Many students include independent study and independent research in their POEs. Participation in internships is also encouraged. The Juniata College Center for International Education provides excellent study-abroad opportunities that are taken advantage of by more than 28 percent of the junior class. Experiences include summer, semester, and year-long opportunities.

Academic Facilities

Juniata's academic programs are complemented by up-to-date technology, labs, and bibliographic resources. In addition to the College's academic computer center, the campus has high-tech classroom/laboratory and computer labs devoted specifically to business, education, psychology, and world languages. The College supports the Center for Entrepreneurial Leadership (JCEL), a unique opportunity for students of all academic areas to pursue developing their own business. JCEL provides students with hands-on experience in every aspect of entrepreneurial endeavors. A human interaction lab offers students the opportunity to study communication and group interaction. In addition, the College has a distance learning and teleconferencing facility, multimedia classrooms, and a teaching and learning technology center (TLT) for both student and faculty member use. The TLT center was designed to give faculty members and students the resources for utilizing advanced technology in their course work and presentations. The William J. von Liebig Center for Science is a new $20-million facility that provides state-of-the-art facilities for teaching and learning in chemistry and biology. The original Brumbaugh Science Center continues to house the computer science, environmental sciences, information technology, mathematics, and physical sciences departments.

For research projects, students in the natural sciences use laboratories equipped with sophisticated instrumentation typically reserved for graduate students. Juniata's Raystown Field Station serves as an ecology, zoology, and environmental science laboratory. The field station was awarded $4.5 million to expand facilities and allow students to live and learn at an on-site field laboratory. The first phase of new construction was completed in the spring of 2003. Juniata's Beeghly Library provides the College with an online public-access catalog that is accessible campuswide and an extensive CD-ROM network.

Costs

For 2003–04, the general fee was approximately $29,080, with tuition costs of $22,240, and room, board, and fee costs of $6840. Several special and occasional fees of $30–$100 for laboratory or studio use are also required.

Financial Aid

The Juniata College Office of Student Financial Planning is committed to building relationships with families striving to meet the long-term investment needs associated with quality education. Juniata succeeds by maximizing available assistance opportunities from Juniata programs as well as state and federal government programs in the form of grants, loans, and work-study initiatives. The College's commitment includes scholarship and loan programs. The Juniata College Plus Loan Program allows a family to borrow up to $20,000 over four years, interest free, while the student attends Juniata. Juniata's Academic Scholarship Program offers aggressive scholarship programs designed to recognize and reward academic achievement. Students who exhibit promise of future success may be eligible for academic awards ranging from $5000 to full tuition. Students who wish to be considered for Nomination Scholarships should have their admission applications postmarked no later than January 9 of their senior year.

Juniata representatives work with each family, matching their individual circumstances to all applicable aid programs. For need-based aid, individual plans are developed using the Free Application for Federal Student Aid (FAFSA) as the basis for determining need. The results of the FAFSA needs analysis should reach Juniata by March 1.

Juniata College offers all students who submit an application the opportunity to gain an early understanding of their eligibility for assistance through its Early Financial Aid Assessment (EFAA) Program. The EFAA is available in September; those submitting a completed form receive a response within two to three weeks. The financial assistance programs are designed to reassure students that a four-year commitment to Juniata College is reciprocated through the College's commitment to meeting the needs of its students.

Faculty

Juniata has 89 full-time and 31 part-time faculty members, of whom 94 percent hold a doctoral or terminal degree in their field. The student-faculty ratio is 14:1. Although faculty members engage in numerous scholarly pursuits and maintain professional ties to their academic fields, they consider teaching and advising their primary functions.

Student Government

Juniata seeks to provide an environment within which students can mature intellectually, socially, and personally in a manner consistent with academic programs. In campus life as well as in the classroom, many opportunities for growth and self-exploration exist. Students have a voice—and in most cases a vote—in all essential areas of campus governance.

Admission Requirements

Juniata seeks students who show strong academic promise, motivation, and maturity. The College seeks a wide geographic representation and a variety of cultural, social, and economic backgrounds. Selection is made without regard to race, sex, religion, creed, color, handicap, or the ability to afford a private college education. Careful consideration is given to the academic record, test results, and personal qualities of applicants. Applicants should have completed a minimum of sixteen college-preparatory courses in mathematics, social studies, world language, and laboratory science. SAT I or ACT scores are required. International student candidates may be required to submit TOEFL scores. Interviews and campus visits are strongly recommended.

Transfer students who have completed A.A. or A.S. requirements in an approved collegiate transfer program at an accredited community or junior college may enter Juniata with junior-class standing and receive transfer credit for two years of course work. Students who transfer without a degree receive credit on a course-by-course basis. Students whose college has a formal transfer agreement with Juniata College should consult with their transfer coordinator to review requirements for that agreement. It is strongly recommended that transfer students have an interview.

Application and Information

Students may apply to Juniata after completion of their junior year in secondary school. A nonrefundable $30 fee must accompany the application. A complete secondary school transcript that indicates courses and grades (with a list of senior courses, if required) must be sent from the applicant's guidance office along with SAT I or ACT scores, an essay, and a letter of recommendation. An on-campus interview is highly recommended but not required. Transfer students must complete the normal application requirements and submit an official transcript from each college previously attended.

Candidates for freshman admission can choose from two application deadlines. Early decision is designed for students who believe that Juniata College is their first choice. The early decision application deadline is November 15 of the student's senior year in secondary school, with notification no later than December 31. The student is asked to complete Juniata's institutional aid form in order to receive an early financial planning award. Students are required to submit a nonrefundable $200 matriculation deposit as soon as they have had the opportunity to inspect program and financial aid information. Students who wish to be considered for all merit awards offered by Juniata must have their application postmarked by January 9 of their senior year.

Juanita follows a modified rolling admission timeline. The application deadline is March 15 of the student's senior year. First decisions are released January 15. After January 15, students can expect an admission decision within three to four weeks of receipt of all necessary information. Financial award packages are determined after the FAFSA has been completed.

Juniata accepts applications for transfer admission for either the spring or fall semesters. The application due date for fall applicants is June 1; the due date for spring applicants is December 1. It is to the student's benefit to submit all application materials before the due date. Juniata's transfer admission policy is rolling. In most cases, transfer students receive an admission decision within one month of receipt of all credentials. Necessary credentials include an essay, a statement of interest, a secondary school transcript, SAT I or ACT scores, and college transcripts.

Application forms and additional information may be obtained from:

Enrollment Center
Juniata College
1700 Moore Street
Huntingdon, Pennsylvania 16652
Telephone: 814-641-3420
877-JUNIATA (877-586-4282, toll-free)
Fax: 814-641-3100
E-mail: admissions@juniata.edu
World Wide Web: http://www.juniata.edu/

On the campus of Juniata College.

KANSAS STATE UNIVERSITY

MANHATTAN, KANSAS

The University

Founded in 1863, Kansas State University (K-State) is a nationally recognized comprehensive university with more than 200 undergraduate programs and options, sixty-five master's degree programs, and forty-three doctoral programs.

K-State ranks first nationally among state universities in its total of Rhodes, Marshall, Truman, Goldwater, and Udall Scholars since 1986. K-State scholars have been awarded seven Rhodes, nine Marshall, nineteen Truman, twelve Udall, twenty-seven Fulbright, forty-eight Goldwater, and seventeen Phi Kappa Phi scholarships.

Approximately 3,600 students live in the nine residence halls, and more than 3,400 students are members of eleven national sororities and twenty-four national fraternities. Six national African-American and two Latino fraternities and sororities have K-State chapters. More than 375 student organizations are available, and 88 percent of K-State students participate in recreational activities. K-State is a member of the NCAA (Division I) and the Big Twelve Conference.

K-State's campus and students have ranked high in everything from best student government to best research project. Top rankings in 2002–03 included speech, number nine squad (American Forensics Association); yearbook, Gold Crown (Columbia Scholastic Press Association); Big 12 championships in football and volleyball; and crops judging team, national champion.

K-State is listed in the 2003 *Rugg's Recommendations on the Colleges* guide as a school where students can make the most of their education. K-State was listed in Kaplan's 2004 edition of *The Unofficial, Unbiased Guide to the 328 Most Interesting Colleges* and was ranked as one of the best public colleges in America, according to the sixth annual report by Institutional Research and Evaluation, Inc., an independent research and consulting organization. The University was ranked seventieth out of 351 top American colleges in Princeton Review's annual *Most Connected Campuses.*

The College of Arts and Sciences offers competitive programs in the natural sciences, communications, humanities, fine arts, social sciences, and the health professions. College of Engineering students have a high pass rate on the engineering licensing exam. The College of Business Administration is accredited by the AACSB International–The Association to Advance Collegiate Schools of Business, an honor shared by only 25 percent of the nation's business schools. The College of Agriculture offers the only programs worldwide in bakery, feed, and milling science and management, and the College of Education offers the most comprehensive teacher education program in the state. The College of Human Ecology is a founding member of the Human Sciences Undergraduate Research Community. The College of Veterinary Medicine is internationally recognized for the study of livestock diseases. The College of Technology and Aviation has the only FAA-approved bachelor's degree in aviation in the state and more than forty aircraft for training.

Location

The 668-acre campus is located in Manhattan, Kansas, a city with a population of approximately 45,000. A satellite campus, Kansas State University at Salina, is located 60 miles west in Salina and is the home of the College of Technology and Aviation. Nicknamed "The Little Apple," Manhattan is 125 miles from Kansas City. Local attractions include Aggieville, one of the oldest campus shopping areas in the nation.

Majors and Degrees

The College of Arts and Sciences offers majors in anthropology, art, biochemistry, biology, chemical science, chemistry, creative writing, criminology, dance, economics, English, fisheries and wildlife biology, geography, geology, history, kinesiology, mass communications, mathematics, microbiology, modern languages, music, music education, philosophy, physics, political science, psychology, social work, sociology, speech, statistics, theater, and women's studies. Interdisciplinary majors are humanities, life sciences, physical sciences, and social sciences. Secondary majors, which can be taken only in addition to a primary major, are American ethnic studies, industry and labor, international studies, Latin American studies, and natural resources and environmental sciences. Preprofessional programs are law and options in the health professions that include clinical laboratory science (medical technology), dentistry, health information management, medicine, nursing, occupational therapy, optometry, pharmacy, physical therapy, respiratory care, and veterinary medicine.

The College of Business Administration confers a B.S. with majors in accounting, finance, management, management information systems, and marketing. Management options available are general management, human resource management, and operations management. Marketing offers an agribusiness option. Finance options include financial services, financial management, and controllership. Also offered are a distance education major in general business and a certificate in international business.

The College of Engineering offers degree programs in architectural engineering, biological and agricultural engineering, chemical engineering, civil engineering, computer engineering, computer science, construction science and management, electrical engineering, industrial engineering, information systems, manufacturing systems engineering, mechanical engineering, and nuclear reactor technology. Options and concentrations are available in aerospace engineering, bioengineering, biomaterials processing, construction engineering, engineering materials, environmental engineering, nuclear engineering, and power systems.

The College of Agriculture offers degree programs in agribusiness, agricultural economics, agricultural education, agricultural communications and journalism, agricultural technology management, agronomy, animal sciences and industry, bakery science and management, feed science and management, food science and industry, horticultural therapy, horticulture, milling science and management, and park management and conservation. The College also has a preprofessional program in veterinary medicine, a specialization in golf course management, and a secondary major in natural resources and environmental sciences.

The College of Education administers programs in elementary, secondary, and special education. Secondary education programs are agriculture, art, biological sciences, business, chemistry, earth/space science, English, English/journalism, family and consumer sciences, journalism, mathematics, modern languages, music, physics, social studies, and speech. An additional endorsement in English as a second language is also available. Areas for K–12 licensure are art, foreign language (French, German, or Spanish), and music.

The College of Human Ecology offers majors in apparel marketing, apparel design and production, athletic training, communication sciences and disorders, a coordinated program and a didactic program in dietetics, early childhood education, family life and community services, general family studies and human services, general human ecology, hotel and restaurant management, human ecology and mass communications, interior design, life span human development, nutritional sciences (premedical), personal financial planning, and public health nutrition. Dual degrees are offered in family studies and human services and social work and in nutrition and exercise sciences. Family and consumer sciences education and early childhood education licensure programs and a secondary major in gerontology are offered.

The College of Architecture, Planning, and Design offers nationally accredited professional five-year degree programs in architecture, interior architecture and product design, and landscape architecture. Before entering one of the three professional programs, the student completes a one-year common environmental design studies program.

The College of Technology and Aviation offers the bachelor's degree in aeronautical technology, computer systems technology, electronic and computer engineering technology, mechanical engineering technology, and technology management and associate degrees in applied business, applied technology, aviation maintenance, civil and construction engineering technology, computer systems technology, electronic and computer engineering technology, mechanical engineering technology, professional pilot studies, and Web development technology. The College also offers a certificate in airframe and power plant.

Academic Programs

The common requirements for all curricula leading to an undergraduate degree are English composition and public speaking. To graduate, a student must complete a prescribed curriculum and 18 hours of approved general education courses. The total credit requirement for a bachelor's degree ranges from 120 to 167 hours, according to the curriculum taken.

Academic Facilities

The University's library system contains more than 3.4 million volumes, 11,187 journals and serials, more than 1.8 million government publications, and computerized information retrieval for all academic curricula. There are branch libraries for architecture and design, chemistry, math/physics, veterinary medicine, and technology (at Salina). Computing and Network Services provides four general computing labs that are open 24 hours a day, seven days a week. The residence halls offer twelve labs. The J. R. Macdonald Laboratory is one of the nation's leading laboratories in research in heavy-ion and atomic physics. Among K-State's research and laboratory facilities are the 8,616-acre Konza Prairie Biological Station, the Center for Basic Cancer Research, a NASA Center for Gravitational Studies in Cellular and Developmental Biology, the Center for Science Education, and an Environmental Protection Agency center for hazardous substance research.

Costs

Tuition for 2003–04 was approximately $3825 for Kansas residents and $11,190 for nonresidents. Books and supplies averaged $718, and room and board averaged $4800. All figures are subject to change.

Financial Aid

Approximately 70 percent of the University's students receive some form of financial assistance. During 2003–04, K-State students received more than $120 million through federal, state, and institutional student aid programs, including scholarships and veterans' benefits. About 80 percent of all scholarships are awarded on the basis of merit; in 2003–04, K-State awarded approximately $6.4 million in scholarships. K-State recognizes the importance of high-quality leadership by awarding a Leadership Scholarship for students with an ACT composite score of 26 or higher. National Merit Semifinalists and Finalists are considered for Presidential Scholarships, and other top scholars may receive the Putnam, Foundation, Honors, or Medallion scholarships. All federal need-based programs are available at K-State, and application for them should be made by filing the Free Application for Federal Student Aid prior to March 1 preceding fall enrollment. The freshman priority deadline for scholarship applications is November 1.

Faculty

K-State has 1,154 full-time instructional, research, and extension faculty members, of whom 85 percent have doctorates or comparable advanced degrees. A K-State professor was named the 1996 national Professor of the Year for research/doctoral universities by the Carnegie Foundation for the Advancement of Teaching.

Student Government

In 1994, 1996, and 1998, the National Association for Campus Activities honored K-State for having the nation's best large-school student government.

Admission Requirements

Students graduating from high school in 2001 or later are eligible for admission if they meet one of the following three academic criteria: an ACT composite score of 21 or higher or an SAT I score of 980 or higher, ranking in the upper third of the high school class, or a GPA of 2.0 or higher (Kansas residents) or 2.5 or higher (out-of-state students), on a 4.0 scale, in a set of prescribed core courses. All students are required to take either the ACT or SAT I regardless of the criteria used for admission, since the test results are also used for academic advising purposes. Up to 10 percent of the freshman class may be admitted based on academic criteria determined by the University.

Transfer students with 24 or more credit hours must have a 2.0 or higher GPA on their transfer work. Students with less than 24 credit hours are required to have a minimum GPA of 2.0 on their transfer work plus meet one of the three requirements for high school graduates.

International students must submit a $55 application fee and all required credentials before their academic records are reviewed. Students applying directly from their home country are encouraged to use the services of a reputable transcript evaluation service. Priority processing is provided to files with evaluated transcripts. International students applying after attending other U.S. institutions must demonstrate comparable academic potential.

Application and Information

Entering freshmen are encouraged to apply early in their senior year of high school. High school graduates must complete the application form and submit official ACT results. Transfer students should begin the application process at least one semester prior to their anticipated date of entry; they must submit a completed application form and official transcript from each institution previously attended. Only transcripts received directly from credit-granting institutions are considered official and acceptable for admission purposes. There is a $30 application fee for freshman and transfer students. All credentials are evaluated as they are received on a rolling basis. Students are notified in writing of their admission status generally within five working days of the receipt of all required documents.

For application forms and information, students should contact:

Office of Admissions
Kansas State University
119 Anderson Hall
Manhattan, Kansas 66506-0102
Telephone: 785-532-6250
800-432-8270 (toll-free in Kansas only)
E-mail: kstate@k-state.edu
World Wide Web: http://consider.k-state.edu

KEAN UNIVERSITY

UNION, NEW JERSEY

The University

Established in 1855, Kean University has undergone continuous growth. In 1958 it moved to its present campus, where modern facilities and spacious grounds help it to fulfill its many educational goals. A delightful contrast to the surrounding urban area, the campus consists of 120 acres of rolling lawns and wooded areas, bisected by a gracefully flowing stream. An additional 30 acres on the East Campus, located in Hillside, New Jersey, are used both for intercollegiate and intramural recreation and for other student activities.

The University's approximately 13,000 full- and part-time graduate and undergraduate students form a heterogeneous student body representing diverse cultural backgrounds. About 90 percent of the full-time undergraduates commute to school.

Kean University offers students a broad extracurricular program of cultural, social, and athletic activities. Among the offerings on last year's schedule were several guest-lecturer series; a program of classical and contemporary music, dance, and drama; jazz concerts with regional jazz artists; and monthly exhibitions in the Gallery. Varsity, intramural, and lifelong sports activities also enjoy wide popularity.

Location

Kean University is located in Union, New Jersey, which has been named an All-America City by the National Municipal League. New York City is approximately 10 miles away. All forms of surface and air transportation, including Newark International Airport, are within minutes of the campus.

Majors and Degrees

Kean University awards baccalaureate degrees in forty-six majors, with more than seventy options and collateral programs. In addition, the University offers twenty-seven graduate programs.

Bachelor of Arts degrees are offered in art history, bilingual education, biology, chemistry, communication, criminal justice, early childhood education, earth science, economics, education of the hearing impaired, elementary education, English, fine arts, foreign language (Spanish), graphic communications, history, industrial design, industrial education, interior design, mathematical sciences, music, music education, philosophy and religion, physical education, political science, psychology, public administration, recreation administration, sociology, special education, speech and hearing, speech and theater, studio art, teacher of the handicapped, and theater.

Bachelor of Science degrees are offered in accounting, biology, chemistry, computer science, finance, graphic communication, health information management, industrial technology, management science, marketing, medical technology, occupational therapy, psychology/psychiatric rehabilitation, and telecommunications/information technology. Bachelor of Fine Arts, Bachelor of Social Work, and Bachelor of Science in Nursing (for RNs only) degree programs are also offered.

Physical therapy is a joint B.A./Doctor of Physical Therapy (D.P.T.) program that is available to Kean University undergraduates; it is offered in cooperation with the University of Medicine and Dentistry of New Jersey (UMDNJ) in Newark, New Jersey.

Academic Programs

All degree programs include a 52-semester-hour general education requirement, including 18 credits in a humanities-based core curriculum and 34 credits distributed among courses that clearly meet the University's goals of a general education. These goals are designed to foster a broad liberal arts education as the foundation for specialized studies. Each degree program includes individual major requirements and free electives. A minimum of 30 semester hours is required for each major.

Internships are available to juniors and seniors in many degree programs.

The University calendar is based on a two-semester system with two summer sessions.

Off-Campus Programs

Kean University offers a variety of travel/study programs in which students may participate for a semester or for shorter periods of time. Programs include travel to all areas of the world and may be taken for credit or for personal enrichment. Selected courses are also offered in nontraditional formats, such as distance education and service learning.

Academic Facilities

The abundant resources of the Nancy Thompson Library are available to all Kean University students, in person or online. There are also more than thirty-five computer labs around campus, permitting students to submit papers to their professors by e-mail. In addition, smart classrooms give teachers and students access to the Internet; digital, audio, and visual resources; VHS media in the Instructional Resource Center; University libraries; modern office automation software; and specialized instructional software. Kean offers at least one modern workstation to every 3 students.

The Center for Instructional Resource and Technology (CIRT) provides a variety of nonprint materials, electronic and conventional audiovisual equipment, and comprehensive media services, all of which support the academic programs at the University.

Additional facilities include the Reading Institute, the Institute of Child Study, and the Clinic in Learning Disabilities. The University has an electron microscope and operates a meteorological station that includes the latest in global positioning system technology.

Costs

Undergraduate, full-time, matriculated, in-state students (12 to 19 credits) are charged a flat-rate tuition of $2224 per semester. Students taking more than 19 credits are charged an overload tuition rate of $148 per each additional credit.

Undergraduate, full-time, matriculated, out-of-state students (12 to 19 credits) are charged a flat-rate tuition of $3405 per semester. Students taking more than 19 credits are charged an overload tuition rate of $227 per each additional credit.

In addition to regular per credit fees, students taking off-campus courses are charges an off-campus fee of $20 per credit.

Housing costs are $2579 per semester for double occupancy and $2724 per semester for single occupancy. The meal plan is $1200 per semester.

Financial Aid

Approximately 60 percent of all full-time undergraduate students receive some form of financial aid. Federal aid is available in the form of Federal Perkins Loans, Federal Pell Grants, Federal Supplemental Educational Opportunity Grants, Federal Work-Study Program awards, and Federal Direct Loans. State aid includes Garden State Scholarships, Tuition Aid Grants, Educational Opportunity Fund awards, Edward J. Bloustein Distinguished Scholars awards, and Urban Distinguished Scholars awards. Students should complete and mail the Free Application for Federal Student Aid (FAFSA) to the processing center by March 15.

Faculty

Kean has 367 full-time faculty members, 8 part-time faculty members, and 625 adjunct faculty members. The faculty's regularly scheduled office hours and participation in virtually all areas of campus governance and operations ensure that they have continual interaction with students. Part-time and adjunct faculty members, including elected officials, business leaders, and industry representatives, provide valuable links with the community at large. Graduate assistants are not given primary instructional responsibility for any undergraduate course.

Student Government

The Student Organization of Kean University, Inc., a truly autonomous body, is incorporated and is composed entirely of students chosen through campuswide elections. Student officers administer an annual budget that is derived from student activity fees and receipts. The Student Organization supports the undergraduate student body with a wide array of service, culture and media programming, activities, and entertainment.

The University wholly supports the concept of students' rights of self-determination, and student participation in all areas of campus governance is traditional.

Admission Requirements

Admission to Kean University is based on a student's projected ability to complete a degree program, without regard to age, sex, race, color, creed, or national origin. Freshman applicants are expected to have a cumulative grade point average (GPA) of at least 2.8. SAT I scores are required; the suggested combined score is 1020. The student is also expected to have completed 16 high school units. Exceptions to standards may be made in some individual cases. Highly qualified high school juniors may apply for early admission if they have a recommendation from their high school guidance counselor; acceptance is contingent on final senior-year grades. Advanced standing based on CLEP scores and/or an evaluation of life experience may be available with approval from the director of admissions.

Transfer applicants are required to have a minimum GPA of 2.0, but some academic programs require a higher GPA; occupational therapy, for example, requires a GPA of at least 2.8.

Application and Information

The application deadline for freshman applicants is May 31 for fall admission and November 1 for admission in the spring. Students are accepted on a rolling basis. Application deadlines for all international (F-1 visa) students are March 1 for fall admission and November 1 for spring admission. The Kean University application, a $50 application fee, high school and college transcripts, and SAT I results (freshman candidates only) should be forwarded to the admission office. Campus visits are recommended. Tours are given on Friday at 9:30 a.m. from October to April and on Thursdays at 10 a.m. from May to August.

For additional information and application forms, students should contact:

Director of Admissions
Kean University
1000 Morris Avenue
Union, New Jersey 07083
Telephone: 908-737-7100
Fax: 908-737-7105
E-mail: admitme@kean.edu
World Wide Web: http://www.kean.edu

Kean students learn while benefiting from the University's vast commitment to technology.

KEENE STATE COLLEGE

KEENE, NEW HAMPSHIRE

The College

A public liberal arts college of New Hampshire, Keene State College (KSC) is a vibrant educational community that provides an extensive range of educational opportunities, awarding associate, bachelor's, and master's degrees. Students come to Keene State College for its small size and friendly atmosphere, the choice of thirty-five major programs, a location in the heart of New England, and a private feeling at a public price.

A member of the University System of New Hampshire, Keene State College is a coeducational residential college with an enrollment of approximately 4,000 full-time undergraduate students and 1,000 part-time and graduate students. Founded in 1909, the College enrolled 27 students its first year. From its original 20 acres, the campus has expanded to 160 acres and more than seventy-six buildings that feature an attractive blend of traditional and contemporary architecture.

The superb physical facilities on campus include living accommodations ranging from traditional older residence halls to apartments and suites. The College has three buildings registered as National Historic Landmarks and numerous recently completed facilities, including an expansive Recreation Center, the Pondside Apartments, the Rhodes Hall academic building, the Thorne-Sagendorph Art Gallery, and the Lloyd P. Young Student Center. KSC's most ambitious building project ever—a new Science Center—opens in 2004.

Keene State is affiliated with CoPLAC (the Council for Public Liberal Arts Colleges) and Campus Compact: The Project for Public and Community Service. Valuing service to the community, the College strives to prepare the next generation of leaders for the state, the region, and the nation.

Location

Keene, New Hampshire, at the geographic center of New England—only 84 miles from Boston and 200 miles from New York City—is a thriving, prosperous city of 22,000. The Keene State campus is bordered by Main Street on one side and the Ashuelot River on another. It is only four blocks from the historic downtown district, which offers a variety of shops, restaurants, and theaters. The surrounding New England landscape includes Mount Monadnock (the second-most-climbed mountain in the world), only 18 miles to the southeast of Keene. Opportunities for skiing, mountain climbing, camping, swimming, and hiking are all within a short drive of the campus.

Majors and Degrees

Bachelor of Arts, Fine Arts, Music, and Science degrees are granted in American studies; applied computer science; art; biology; chemistry; chemistry-physics; communication; computer mathematics; economics; education; English; environmental studies; French; general science; geography; geology; graphic design; health science; history; journalism; management; mathematics; mathematics-physics; music; physical education; psychology; safety studies; social science; sociology; Spanish; technology studies; theater, dance, and film; and vocational teacher education. An individualized B.A. or B.S. major is available for students who wish to design their own interdisciplinary program. Music education and music performance students are awarded the Bachelor of Music degree.

Minors in thirty-seven areas make it possible for students to supplement and strengthen their program. A strong cooperative education program provides work/credit opportunities in many majors.

Two-year degree programs offered are the Associate in Arts in general studies and Associate in Science in applied computer science, chemical dependency, general studies, and technology studies.

The College also offers a master's degree in education.

Academic Programs

Education in the liberal arts and sciences and in several professional fields is provided through associate and baccalaureate degree programs. These programs include three basic components: breadth and balance achieved through general education requirements, depth of scholarship developed through specialization in a major field, and an opportunity to elect a minor or courses in other areas of interest. The College's areas of emphasis include teacher education, science and technology, and the fine and performing arts.

All baccalaureate programs have general education requirements, which are intended to broaden, deepen, and integrate the student's understanding of the most significant aspects of humanity's heritage. These studies also enhance the capacity for aesthetic enjoyment, critical thinking, creativity, abstract and logical reasoning, and oral and written communication.

A total of at least 120 credit hours is required to graduate, including courses in English composition, arts and humanities, social sciences, and science/mathematics.

The academic year at Keene State consists of fall and spring semesters, plus two optional summer sessions.

Off-Campus Programs

Students are encouraged to study for a semester or a year in national and international exchange programs. The National Student Exchange is a domestic alternative to study abroad, with programs at 175 colleges and universities in the U.S., Guam, the Virgin Islands, and Puerto Rico. Keene State has eleven Direct Exchange Programs with institutions in Ecuador, England, France, Ireland, and Russia and more than sixty consortium programs in such popular destinations as China, Costa Rica, Greece, Italy, Scotland, and Spain.

Academic Facilities

The newly renovated Wallace E. Mason Library houses more than 300,000 paper volumes and has active subscriptions to nearly 1,200 periodicals, newspapers, and annual publications. The microform collection of more than 550,000 items includes the Library of American Civilization, the Library of English Literature, ERIC, Envirofiche, various newspapers, and a collection of college catalogs. Students also have access to the 100,000 volumes available at Keene Public Library. Mason Library has direct online access to thousands of libraries through OCLC, an international library network, and also subscribes to EPIC, which provides subject access to the OCLC database. The fully automated library supplies CD-ROM indexes and provides online access to more than 400 databases. Mason Library houses the Cohen Center for Holocaust Studies, with materials for those who wish to study, teach, or commemorate the Holocaust; it also houses the Curriculum Materials Library, which provides elementary and secondary education teaching materials for student teachers and classroom teachers across the state.

Other academic resources include the Arboretum, the BodyWorks Fitness Center, the Film Studies Center, the Language Learning Center, and the Writing and Math Centers.

The Redfern Arts Center on Brickyard Pond, which serves as a major regional performing arts center, houses classrooms and performance spaces for the art, music, and theater programs. The Thorne-Sagendorph Art Gallery hosts exhibits by KSC students and faculty members, as well as regional, national, and international artists.

Computer equipment is available in all academic areas. A network connects student rooms and the offices of full-time faculty members and administrative personnel to the online library catalog, e-mail, and the World Wide Web.

Costs

Tuition for the 2003–04 academic year was $4750 for New Hampshire residents and $10,800 for out-of-state students. Room and board cost $5682, and mandatory fees total $780. Books and supplies cost about $550 per year.

Financial Aid

Financial assistance is available in three basic forms: grants and scholarships, loans, and part-time employment. Grants and scholarships do not have to be repaid. Educational loans must be repaid, but such loans are made on a long-term, low-interest basis. Additional aid consists of part-time, on-campus employment. At Keene State, aid can be based on merit or need or a combination of both. Matriculated students are eligible to apply for assistance if they are enrolled for at least 6 credits per semester. Currently, approximately 70 percent of Keene State students receive some sort of financial aid. Interested students should write to Student Financial Services for more information.

Faculty

The resident faculty numbers more than 180 men and women who value personal attention to students and a commitment to academic advising. They are also active in their academic fields—writing books and articles, serving as consultants, presenting papers and seminars, participating in exhibits, and performing in concerts.

Student Government

The 27-member Student Assembly is the official student government organization of Keene State College. Its members are elected by the student body, with representatives for each academic class, off-campus students, and adult learners. A student body president and vice president are elected by the entire student body, while the chair of the Student Assembly, the secretary, and the treasurer are elected by Student Assembly members. Members of the Student Assembly serve on student committees and College Senate committees. The Student Assembly allocates student activity fee money and recognizes and sets policies for official student organizations.

Admission Requirements

The following requirements apply to all undergraduate programs except the Associate in Science in technology programs. Applicants should provide an application accompanied by the application fee; an official high school transcript and evidence of high school graduation or a satisfactory high school equivalency certificate; scores on the SAT I (applicants are responsible for making arrangements to take the test and for having the results forwarded to Keene State College); and a satisfactory evaluation from a high school guidance counselor, principal, or teacher. Applicants who have been out of high school for several years do not need to submit the evaluation, and questions regarding this requirement should be addressed to the Director of Admissions.

Applicants should have completed college-preparatory course work, ensuring competence in English grammar and composition, college-level reading speed and comprehension, and a distribution of courses in the humanities (English literature, a foreign language, history, and philosophy), the social sciences (political science, sociology, anthropology, psychology, economics, and geography), the sciences (3 years required, 2 of which must be a lab), and mathematics (algebra I, algebra II, and geometry).

A personal interview is not required, although all applicants are encouraged to visit the campus. Visits are arranged through the Admissions Office.

Application and Information

To receive an application form and additional information, students should contact:

Peggy Richmond
Director of Admissions
Elliot Hall
Keene State College
Keene, New Hampshire 03435-2604
Telephone: 603-358-2276
800-KSC-1909 (toll-free)
Fax: 603-358-2767
E-mail: admissions@keene.edu
World Wide Web: http://www.keene.edu

Appian Gateway serves as a gathering place for students and welcomes visitors to Keene State College's traditional New England campus.

KENDALL COLLEGE

EVANSTON, ILLINOIS

The College

Kendall College is a private, career-driven college located in the heart of Chicago that provides its students with a small, personal, and supportive academic environment. The school prepares its students for the "real world" with the skills and attitudes critical for success.

Internships are a key component of each degree program. As a result, Kendall students graduate with a solid liberal college education and hands-on experience in their chosen field. Each area of study is taught with the individual in mind and a low student-faculty ratio.

Outside of class, Kendall is also committed to providing an active social and cultural life for its students. The move to a new facility in Chicago, Illinois, offers students the rich resources of the city of Chicago. The new College residence is located at 320 North Michigan Avenue, just steps from world-class museums, shopping, and entertainment.

Kendall College is accredited by the Commission on Institutions of Higher Education of the North Central Association of Colleges and Schools (NCACS) and the University Senate of the United Methodist Church. The School of Culinary Arts is accredited by the American Culinary Federation (ACF) Accrediting Commission.

Location

Beginning fall 2004, Kendall College offers classes at its new Chicago campus. The 166,000-square-foot building has been redeveloped into a state-of-the-art academic facility. The eight-story tower is part of a 6-acre riverfront campus only minutes from some of the country's best restaurants, hotels, and companies, providing students prime access to internships and work experiences. The facility offers sweeping views of the Chicago skyline, access to newly developed areas on the Chicago River, and all the cultural and social benefits of the third-largest city in the United States.

Majors and Degrees

A Kendall education is designed to make students the most effective and well-rounded professional possible. Kendall College awards Bachelor of Arts (B.A.) degrees in business and technology, culinary arts, early childhood education, hospitality management, and human services. The College also awards the Associate of Applied Science (A.A.S.) degree in baking and pastry arts and culinary arts.

Kendall College offers six major degree programs from which students may choose an area of study: baking and pastry arts, business and technology, culinary arts, early childhood education, hospitality management, and human services.

Kendall also offers concentrations and certificates in each of its major programs. The business and technology program offers concentrations in business administration, marketing, and Web design, and certificates in entrepreneurship and e-marketing. The culinary arts program offers certificates in baking and pastry arts, professional catering, professional personal chef, and professional cookery. Early childhood education offers a concentration in special education approval. The hospitality management program offers one certificate in bed and breakfast operations and five concentrations: convention and meeting planning, culinary management, food and beverage operations, hotel management, and international hospitality management. Students may also pursue concentrations in human services in crime, justice and rehabilitation, gerontology, psychology, or substance abuse treatment studies.

Academic Programs

Kendall College operates on a quarter system. The first quarter term extends from September to early December, the second term extends from January to March, and the third term extends from April to June. Summer sessions are offered from July to September. Students must fulfill a minimum of 92 quarter hours for an associate degree and a minimum of 184 quarter hours for a bachelor degree, and maintain a 2.0 GPA.

Academic Facilities

The Chicago campus provides wireless Internet access, labs with the latest computer equipment, and two distance learning videoconference facilities. Classrooms and study environments are high-tech and flexible, designed to give students a first-class, state-of-the-art setting in which to learn. There are auditoriums and presentation spaces, student lounges, fifteen kitchens, 350 secure parking spaces, and a number of nearby health clubs. As Kendall College settles into the new campus, the College will operate several restaurants to augment the culinary and hospitality programs.

Costs

In 2004–05, full-time tuition and fees in the School of Arts and Sciences are $15,165 for three quarters (12–19 credit hours). Part-time tuition for the arts and sciences program is $460 per credit hour.

Full-time tuition and fees in the School of Culinary Arts are $24,480 for three quarters, including culinary facilities usage. Part-time culinary arts tuition is $475 per credit hour.

Housing is located at 320 North Michigan Avenue. Students may lease double- or triple-occupancy apartments for $9000 per eleven-month lease.

Financial Aid

The College works with each student and develops a needs analysis to determine student eligibility, which then culminates in a financial aid package. It is the goal of Kendall College to seek funding and to package aid to fully meet the needs of all applicants. The financial aid packaging process ensures effective use of available funds, providing fair and equitable treatment of all applicants. Priority is given to applicants who meet the April 1 preferential filing date.

The College administers aid for undergraduates, including need-based, merit-based, and curriculum-specific scholarships; state and federal awards; Federal Supplemental Educational Opportunity Grants (FSEOG); Federal Work-Study Program awards; and opportunities for campus employment.

Faculty

The academic faculty has 34 full-time and 45 part-time members. The student-faculty ratio is approximately 17:1. Faculty members at Kendall College believe students work best when they are actively involved in making choices about their own learning. As

Kendall students develop clear ideas of what they wish to study, they are provided with the opportunities to use tutorials to continue their education.

Student Government

Kendall College's Student Government Federation is designed to give students a leadership role and voice in building and improving their campus community. The Student Government Federation is elected annually in the fall term and is composed of a president, vice-president, and a group of senators. This group serves in an advisory capacity to the Board of Trustees, the Faculty Senate and various other faculty committees.

Admission Requirements

Kendall assesses its entrance difficulty level as moderate. Admission to Kendall College is open to men and women of all races and religious affiliations. Each applicant is considered on the basis of probable success at Kendall, as indicated primarily by high school grades, class rank, and ACT or SAT I test scores. A minimum GPA of at least 2.0 and an ACT score of 18 or an SAT I score of at least 850 are required for acceptance. If a student falls below either the minimum GPA or the standardized test requirements, the student must complete an entrance examination and submit two letters of recommendation. An essay accompanying the application is required. Qualities of character are also important at Kendall. Therefore, personal interviews and campus visits are encouraged, though not required, to help determine admission.

Application and Information

Prospective students may obtain applications from the Office of Admissions or via the College Web site listed below. Students may submit the admission application at any time. The Office of Admissions must be sent an official transcript. Some students may be admitted on probation after consulting with the Admissions Committee.

For further information, students should contact:

Office of Admissions
Kendall College
900 North Branch Street
Chicago, Illinois 60622
Telephone: 847-448-2304
877-588-8860 (toll-free)
Fax: 312-752-2248
E-mail: admissions@kendall.edu
World Wide Web: http://www.kendall.edu

A view of Kendall College's new Riverworks campus in Chicago.

KENT STATE UNIVERSITY

KENT, OHIO

The University

Kent State University has experienced tremendous growth since its founding in 1910. Today, Kent State is a multicampus network serving 35,433 students at eight locations throughout northeastern Ohio. The eight-campus network is anchored by a classic residential campus in Kent, Ohio. Throughout the network, students can pursue associate, bachelor's, master's, and doctoral degrees. The Kent Campus, serving 19,173 undergraduates and 5,069 graduates, offers 254 undergraduate study areas and numerous graduate degrees. Kent State's seven regional campuses are located in Ashtabula, Geauga, Stark, Trumbull, and Tuscarawas counties and the cities of Salem and East Liverpool.

As a residential campus, Kent State requires students to reside in one of thirty-one residence halls until junior academic standing is achieved. Exceptions include commuting and nontraditional students. Students can easily walk to any of the more than 100 academic, residential, administrative, and recreational buildings. The University has an eighteen-hole golf course, a 291-acre airport, a two-rink indoor ice arena, three on-campus theaters, and a new student recreation and wellness center. There are more than 200 student organizations, eighteen fraternities, nine sororities, and eighteen varsity sports. The Career Service Center provides career counseling and job placement assistance for students and alumni. In addtion to the undergraduate degrees listed below, Kent State offers a Master of Architecture degree.

Location

Kent, Ohio, a city with a population of 30,000, is within easy traveling distance of the major metropolitan areas of northeastern Ohio. Within a 20-mile radius are concerts, cultural events, numerous amusement parks, museums, nature preserves, recreational areas, and year-round sports.

Majors and Degrees

The College of Architecture and Environmental Design offers the Bachelor of Science degree. The School of Interior Design offers a Bachelor of Arts in interior design.

The College of Arts and Sciences awards Bachelor of Arts (B.A.), Bachelor of Science (B.S.), and Bachelor of General Studies degrees. Major fields of concentration are American Sign Language, American studies, anthropology, applied conflict management, applied mathematics, biological chemistry, biology, biotechnology, botany, chemistry, classics, computer science, conservation, (criminal) justice studies, earth science, economics, English, ethnic heritage studies, French, French translation, geography, geology, German, German translation, history, international relations, Latin, Latin American studies, management and industrial studies, mathematics, medical technology, Pan-African studies, paralegal studies, philosophy, physics, political science, psychology, Russian, Russian translation, sociology, Soviet and East European studies, Spanish, Spanish translation, and zoology. Numerous interdisciplinary and preprofessional programs are available, including general studies, integrated life sciences, predentistry, pre-engineering, prelaw, premedicine, preosteopathy, prepharmacy, and pre-veterinary medicine. Students may also design their own individualized major.

The College of Business Administration awards the Bachelor of Business Administration degree. Major fields of concentration are accounting, business management, computer information systems, economics, finance, marketing, and operations management.

The College of Communication and Information offers the B.A., Bachelor of Fine Arts (B.F.A.), and the B.S. degrees. Major fields of concentration are advertising, communication studies, news, photo illustration, public relations, radio-television, visual communication design, and visual journalism.

The College of Education offers the Bachelor of Science in Education and B.S. degrees, with licensure programs available in adolescence/young adult education, early childhood education, intervention specialist studies (majors include deaf education, educational interpreter studies, gifted education, mild/moderate educational needs, and moderate/intensive educational needs), middle childhood education, multi-age education, and vocational education.

The College of Fine and Professional Arts offers the degrees of B.A., B.F.A., Bachelor of Music, and B.S. The college also offers multiple-degree programs. The academic divisions are the Schools of Art; Exercise, Leisure, and Sport; Family and Consumer Studies; Fashion Design and Merchandising; Integrated Health Studies; Music; Speech Pathology and Audiology; and Theatre and Dance.

The College of Nursing awards the Bachelor of Science in Nursing degree. The four-year program includes clinical practicums in the Cleveland-Akron-Warren-Youngstown areas.

The School of Technology offers associate, bachelor's, and master's degree programs throughout Kent State's eight-campus system. Students can select from a number of specialized academic programs in aeronautics, industrial, electrical, manufacturing, or educational technologies.

Academic Programs

Kent State University's colleges and schools all maintain separate academic programs; completion of 36 credits of liberal education course work is a University requirement for all students. The number of credit hours required for graduation varies but is generally 121 semester hours. Credits can be transferred from previous college work satisfactorily completed or earned through courses taken at one of Kent State University's regional campuses. Credit by examination is available. Generally, to earn a degree, students must earn at least 30 semester hours in residence.

The Honors College provides opportunities for students and faculty members to develop and implement special learning experiences. It offers four-year programs of undergraduate study with concurrent enrollment in one of the University's degree-granting programs. In addition, the Honors College awards Advanced Placement credit, early admission to high school students, and specialized academic advising. Its Experimental and Integrative Studies Division offers nontraditional learning experiences for students and faculty members of the entire University community.

Support services are available for students needing assistance to ensure a successful college experience. The Academic Success Center Program offers tutoring, and Student Disability Services provides assistance to students with various physical disabilities and specific learning disabilities.

Army and Air Force ROTC programs are offered on campus.

Off-Campus Programs

Through the Center for International and Comparative Programs, Kent State University offers students a variety of overseas academic programs that provide a balance of academic, linguistic, and cross-cultural experiences and learning opportunities. Credit is granted toward degrees.

Academic Facilities

The collections of the University libraries total more than 2.6 million bound volumes, 12,420 periodicals, and 1.36 million microform pieces. Computer Services makes available an instructional laboratory that accepts FORTRAN, Pascal, BASIC, LISP, C, Ada, and assembly languages. An IBM 2003 mainframe computer is available for advanced work and research. The Department of Computer Science operates computer laboratories with Windows and UNIX workstations. These are connected to the campus network, which includes macrocomputer and microcomputer facilities. The Honors Center is a living-learning residential complex that houses undergraduate students as well as staff offices, a library-seminar room, a student computer facility, and an audiovisual center. The Center for Applied Conflict Management is an academic unit offering programs of study, research, and service activities that focus on the dynamics of change in human systems. The Instructional Television Service operates a closed-circuit, campuswide network and a production center for NETO, Inc., Channels 45 and 49, northeastern Ohio's public television stations. Audiovisual services support regularly scheduled classes with films and other educational materials. The Instructional Resources Center assists students in the production of educational media materials. The Language Laboratory provides tapes and other tools to assist students in foreign language studies. The Academic Testing Services Office offers test administration, test scoring, and research activities. The School of Fashion Design and Merchandising sponsors a working museum of fashion for students and the general public. This school houses classrooms, labs, a library, and a collection of costumes donated from the Silverman-Rogers estate for hands-on study.

As a recognized leader in liquid crystal technology, Kent State's Glenn H. Brown Liquid Crystal Institute is the nation's only center devoted solely to liquid crystal research. With a recent grant from the National Science Foundation, Kent State became the home of Ohio's first Science and Technology Research Center for the Study of Advanced Liquid Crystalline Optical Materials.

Costs

Instructional and other fees for Ohio residents for 2003–04 were $6882 per year. For students residing outside Ohio, instructional and other fees were $13,314 per year. Although room rates vary, costs for board and a double room averaged $6050 per year. The average student spends $990 per year for books and supplies and should budget extra money for personal needs and expenses. All fees and charges are subject to change.

Financial Aid

The University's financial aid program assists promising students who lack the funds necessary to finance a college education. This program, which serves nearly two thirds of Kent State's student body, consists of four basic sources of financial aid: scholarships, loans, grants-in-aid, and part-time employment. To be considered for financial aid awards, students must be admitted to the University and must submit the Free Application for Federal Student Aid (FAFSA). Ohio students should also check the Ohio Instructional Grant (OIG) box on the FAFSA if they are interested in being considered. Students planning to attend the fall semester as freshmen should apply for financial aid after January 1 and before March 1 of the same year. In order to meet the March 1 priority deadline, it is recommended that all financial aid forms be completed and mailed no later than February 1. Applications received after March 1 are considered, but sufficient funds to assist all late applicants may be lacking. Additional information and forms are available from the Office of Student Financial Aid, P.O. Box 5190.

Kent State University's Honors College awards merit scholarships to selected individuals who have the potential for superior scholarly and creative work at the University as determined by academic performance and creative artist competitions. For additional information, students should write to the Dean, Honors College, P.O. Box 5190. The Office of Student Financial Aid also administers numerous private scholarships, including the President's Scholarship for out-of-state students, the President's Grant for out-of-state students who are children of alumni, and various departmental scholarships. Kent State also administers the Oscar Ritchie Memorial Scholarship competition for qualified high school juniors who are members of underrepresented minority groups, including African Americans, Hispanics and Latinos, and Native Americans. Kent State offers the Founders Scholarship Program for academically talented freshmen entering the University in the fall. Qualified students are invited to campus to participate in an examination and meetings with faculty members. Scholarships range from full tuition, fees, room, and board to partial scholarships of varying amounts. Students should contact the Office of Admissions for a comprehensive scholarship application.

Faculty

The University's commitment to scholarship and teaching excellence is enhanced by a full-time faculty of approximately 1,100 members. Some of the faculty members are research oriented, and others publish widely.

Student Government

Students have leadership opportunities through residence hall and Greek organizations and the undergraduate Student Senate. The senate is responsible for allocating student activity fees to registered undergraduate organizations, appointing undergraduates to all University committees and to other positions, conducting elections, and polling student opinion. Two students serve on Kent State's Board of Trustees.

Admission Requirements

Kent State University's freshman admission policy differs for students with varying degrees of preparation for college studies. The students most likely to be admitted and to succeed at the Kent campus are those who have graduated with at least 16 units of the recommended college-preparatory curriculum in high school, achieved a high school grade point average of 2.5 or higher, and acquired an ACT score of 21 or better (or a combined SAT score of 980 or better).

Students who do not meet the above criteria but who have graduated with a cumulative grade point average of at least 2.2 (on a 4.0 scale) at a chartered or accredited high school or who have passed the GED may be admitted. High school course selection, class rank, recommendations, and ACT or SAT I scores are closely examined when making admission decisions for such students. Transfer students are required to have a cumulative 2.0 GPA for admission to the University.

Because special facilities and available faculties are limited, admission to certain academic programs requires special procedures and superior credentials. For freshmen, selective admission requirements apply to aeronautics flight technology, architecture, dance, education, fashion design and merchandising, interior design, journalism and mass communication, music, nursing, theater, and the six-year B.S./M.D. medical program with the Northeastern Ohio Universities College of Medicine. For transfer students, selective requirements apply to all of the preceding and to art and business. Students should contact the Office of Admissions for information.

Application and Information

Application forms are available from the Office of Admissions upon request. A $30 nonrefundable application fee is required. Application early in the senior year helps ensure priority consideration for fall registration, residence hall preference, and financial aid. Students may also access Kent State's online application at http://www.admissions.kent.edu. Applications are processed on a rolling basis.

Nancy J. DellaVecchia
Director, Admissions Office
Kent State University
P.O. Box 5190
Kent, Ohio 44242-0001

Telephone: 330-672-2444
800-988-KENT (toll-free)
E-mail: kentadm@kent.edu
World Wide Web: http://www.kent.edu
http://www.admissions.kent.edu

KENTUCKY STATE UNIVERSITY

FRANKFORT, KENTUCKY

The University

Kentucky State University (KSU) is a liberal studies public institution that offers a friendly, individualized education with excellence as its ultimate goal. Founded in 1886, the University is located in the historic capital city of Frankfort. While the University has changed to meet the needs of the society it serves, its basic goal has remained unchanged since its founding. It is a liberal studies institution of ideal size that is dedicated to the principle of providing the highest-quality education at the lowest possible cost.

Kentucky State University's enrollment for fall 2002 was 2,253 students. The primary source of students is the state of Kentucky, but more than thirty states and territories are represented on the campus; students also come from twenty-seven other countries and bring to the campus a regional, national, and global cultural and ethnic diversity. Nontraditional students may earn a degree at Kentucky State University through several programs.

The University believes that the on-campus residential experience is an essential part of student life. Freshman and sophomore students are required to live on campus. Residential living space is reserved for freshmen and other upperclass students who wish to live on campus.

KSU has about sixty student organizations—ranging from social fraternities and sororities to departmental clubs, literary groups, and political organizations. Students enjoy intramural sports as well as intercollegiate men's baseball, football, and golf; women's softball and volleyball; and men's and women's basketball, cross-country, tennis, and track. KSU offers convocations, special lectures, art exhibits, fine arts performances, and many other activities designed to complement classroom learning. It also offers personal and career counseling, helps students prepare resumes, arranges job interviews, and provides testing to help students assess their interests and abilities. Placement activities include an annual career fair. Health care is available on campus. KSU offers a Master of Public Administration degree program, and, through KSU's Interinstitutional Graduate Center, three other state institutions offer graduate classes and programs.

KSU offers a Master of Science in Agriculture.

Location

KSU is located at the western edge of the Bluegrass region in Kentucky's capital city (population 27,500). The Frankfort area offers historic, scenic, and recreational attractions. Activities in the area include boating, camping, fishing, golfing, horseback riding, and water and snow skiing. Frankfort is between Kentucky's two largest cities, 25 miles west of Lexington and 50 miles east of Louisville. It is on Interstate 64, less than an hour's drive from Interstates 71, 65, and 75, the Bluegrass Parkway, and the Mountain Parkway. Bluegrass Airport, near Lexington, is 20 miles from Frankfort; Standiford Field in Louisville is approximately 55 miles away. Bus transportation to and from both cities is available.

Majors and Degrees

Kentucky State University awards the degrees of Bachelor of Arts, Bachelor of Science, Bachelor of Music Education, and Bachelor of Music in Performance. Majors offered are applied mathematics (3-2 engineering); art (studio); art education; biology (options in general biology or health sciences); business administration (specialization in accounting, business administration, economics, management, or marketing); chemistry; child development and family relations; computer science; criminal justice; early elementary education (grades K–4); English; history; liberal studies (including a student-designed liberal studies major); mathematics; medical technology; microcomputers; music education; music performance (options in vocal or instrumental music); physical education (nonteaching or teaching); political science; psychology; public administration; social studies education; social work; sociology; and textiles, clothing, and merchandising (options in art or business). Secondary teacher certification is offered in biology, English, history, and mathematics. The Associate in Applied Science degree is offered in administrative support services, computer science, drafting and design technology, electronics technology, and nursing. An Associate of Arts degree is offered in liberal studies. In cooperation with various professional schools in Kentucky and other states, KSU offers preprofessional study in community health, cytotechnology, dentistry, engineering (3-2 program), law, medical technology, medicine, nuclear medicine technology, optometry, physical therapy, and veterinary medicine.

Academic Program

KSU provides a full liberal studies experience. Central to KSU's academic program are courses called the Liberal Studies Requirements. These 53 credit hours, required of all baccalaureate students, provide the broad, basic knowledge necessary in a rapidly changing world. The Liberal Studies Requirements include courses in English, speech, mathematics, and foreign language; in the behavioral, social, and natural sciences; and in health and safety education and physical activity. At least 128 hours are required for a bachelor's degree; at least 64 hours are required for an associate degree. KSU awards up to 64 credit hours based on examinations and certifications. The academic year is divided into two semesters—fall and spring—and a six-week summer session. KSU's Whitney M. Young, Jr., College of Leadership Studies is believed to be unique in U.S. public higher education. The college is a division in which students study the Great Books—enduring works of literature, including those on history, philosophy, mathematics, and sciences. Intensive work in writing is required. After two years, students may continue the study of the Great Books, which constitutes a liberal studies major, and minor in another area; they may major in an area in one of the University's other colleges and schools and minor in the Great Books study; or they may select both a major and minor in other areas after completing the equivalent of their Liberal Studies Requirements in Whitney Young College. Students may cross-enroll in Air Force ROTC classes at the University of Kentucky in nearby Lexington. Completion of the ROTC program leads to a commission as a second lieutenant in the appropriate branch of service.

Off-Campus Programs

Some students may qualify for internships in which they can test vocational preferences and develop job skills in work situations and may earn credit toward graduation. KSU also offers cooperative education opportunities that enable students to work off campus as a required part of an academic program. Students receive credit each semester for the paid work assignments. Through the Cooperative Center for Study in England, KSU students can study abroad between semesters, in the summer, or during their junior year.

Academic Facilities

The University has thirty-three buildings on its 485-acre campus. Blazer Library houses nearly 300,000 volumes and subscribes to hundreds of periodicals and journals. Students have access to the nearby Kentucky Historical Society Library, which has 50,000 volumes, and State Library of the Kentucky Department of Libraries and Archives, which has more than 125,000 volumes, 87,000 U.S. government documents, and hundreds of periodicals and journals. KSU also has four auditoriums, used for concerts, plays, lectures, films, and other cultural activities; biology, chemistry, physics, computer, music, and language laboratories; art studios; darkrooms; an art gallery; and a research farm and a fish hatchery.

Costs

In 2003–04, tuition, room (double occupancy), board, and fees totaled $9100 per year for full-time undergraduate residents of Kentucky. For full-time undergraduate out-of-state students, the total was $14,700 per year. Books, supplies, and personal expenses cost an estimated $700–$1000 per year. KSU offers one meal plan, required of students in residence halls. Certain laboratory courses require small additional fees.

Financial Aid

Eligibility for financial assistance is based on demonstrated financial need, scholastic ability, useful talent, training, and experience. Students can apply for State Student Incentive Grants, Federal Pell Grants, Federal Supplemental Educational Opportunity Grants, Federal Perkins Loans, Kentucky Stafford Student Loans, Federal PLUS loans, part-time employment awards, and Federal Work-Study Program awards. Approximately 90 percent of KSU's students receive some form of financial assistance. To be considered for need-based financial assistance, prospective students must submit a KSU financial aid application and a Free Application for Federal Student Aid (FAFSA) and signed copies of their and their parents' federal income tax return from the previous year. The FAFSA, which can be obtained from high school guidance counselors or the KSU Office of Admission, should be mailed directly to the College Scholarship Service in Cahokia, Illinois. Students who complete the application process by the priority date of February 15 receive consideration for both the fall and spring semesters. For students who do not qualify for need-based aid but who have demonstrated specific academic, artistic, musical, or athletic skills or talent, scholarships and grants-in-aid are available. Students may qualify for Full Presidential Scholarships (tuition, room, and board), Partial Presidential Scholarships (tuition, plus one half the cost of room and board), or Presidential Tuition Scholarships (tuition only). Residents of the Kentucky counties of Anderson, Franklin, Scott, Shelby, Owen, and Henry may qualify for Service Area Scholarships. Other scholarships are available as well. Prospective students must submit an Application for Scholarship and a FAFSA by March 15 of the year they plan to enter KSU. Application forms can be obtained from the Office of Admissions.

Faculty

KSU has 123 full-time and 7 part-time faculty members; 99 percent hold advanced degrees. Faculty members who teach graduate classes also teach undergraduate classes. Qualified professors, not graduate students, teach all classes. While faculty members represent a broad range at KSU, they share a commitment to close student-teacher relationships and to the value of a liberal education as preparation for graduate and professional school and career employment.

Student Government

The Student Government Association gives students a voice in campus affairs, plays a part in scheduling and sponsoring campus activities, and enacts legislation in matters of student concern, subject to ratification by the President's Cabinet and Board of Regents. SGA and the Cabinet have joint jurisdiction in regulating and promoting student activities and organizations. An SGA member serves as a voting member of the Board of Regents.

Admission Requirements

KSU seeks serious students who are committed to excelling in college studies. The University requires that all prospective students complete a precollege curriculum of 22 high school units, with at least 4 units in English; 3 in mathematics; 3 in sciences, including at least one laboratory course; 3 in social sciences; 2 in a foreign language; 1 in history and appreciation of visual or performing arts; ½ in health; ½ in physical education; and seven electives. Additional units in foreign languages, mathematics, sciences, arts, and computer literacy are highly desirable. New freshmen from Kentucky must have graduated from an accredited high school and taken the ACT. (Under recently enacted legislation, Kentucky State University may accept up to 10 percent of first-time freshmen, enrolled in baccalaureate programs, based on SAT I, rather than ACT, scores.) Any graduate of an accredited high school will be unconditionally admitted if they meet the precollege curriculum requirements established by the Kentucky Council on Higher Education and have an admission index of 430. The admission index is a numerical score determined by multiplying the cumulative grade point average (on a 4.0 scale) by 100 and the ACT Composite (or converted SAT I) by 10, and adding the two numbers. Nontraditional applicants (25 years of age or older) may substitute results of the Career Planning and Placement Test (CPP-II) for ACT or SAT I results if pursuing an associate degree. Students applying for admission to the Whitney M. Young, Jr., College of Leadership Studies should have taken sound academic courses in high school and have a strong interest in learning (transfer students will be considered, but they must start at the beginning of the Whitney Young program).

Application and Information

High school students should complete and submit an admission application early in their senior year. An official high school transcript and ACT or SAT I scores should be sent to KSU during the senior year. A final high school transcript, including class size and rank, grade point average, and date of graduation, should be sent to KSU after graduation and by July 1. Transfer students must submit official transcripts and statements of good standing from each college attended. Students dismissed less than honorably from other institutions may not enroll at KSU until they qualify for readmission to the college or university from which they were dismissed. Applicants are encouraged to visit the campus. Requests for a student prospectus, application forms, and further information should be directed to:

Office of Admission
Kentucky State University
400 East Main Street
Frankfort, Kentucky 40601-9957
Telephone: 502-597-6349 or Ext. 6813
800-633-9415 (toll-free in Kentucky)
800-325-1716 (toll-free outside Kentucky)
Fax: 502-597-5814
World Wide Web: http://www.kysu.edu

It is the policy of Kentucky State University not to discriminate against any individual in its educational programs, activities, or employment on the basis of race, color, national origin, sex, disability, veteran status, age, religion, or marital status. KSU is an Equal Educational and Employment Opportunity/Affirmative Action Institution.

KENTUCKY WESLEYAN COLLEGE

OWENSBORO, KENTUCKY

The College

Affiliated with the United Methodist Church, Kentucky Wesleyan College (KWC) stands among the foremost career-oriented liberal arts colleges in the Southeast. As a four-year residential college, Kentucky Wesleyan seeks students who show maturity, academic promise, and leadership potential. Students' learning is guided and their lives are shaped by faculty and staff members who are totally dedicated to undergraduate teaching and the success of each student. Learning takes place in an environment that affirms values of caring, integrity, honesty, respect, and hard work and encourages intellectual, physical, and spiritual development. The faculty and staff members proactively encourage learning outside the traditional classroom through leadership, travel, the arts, athletics, and community service.

Kentucky Wesleyan offers Leadership KWC, a nationally recognized program that utilizes liberal arts course work as its basis. Leadership KWC represents the College's belief that a solid liberal arts education provides the communication, problem-solving, and creative-thinking skills necessary for tomorrow's leaders. To specifically explore leadership, students may enroll in courses with special leadership emphasis, such as Profiles in Leadership, Women in Leadership, or the Psychology of Leadership. Students put leadership theory into practice through internships, community service, and workshops such as the College's sailing program. Students may choose to participate in Leadership XXI, a more extensive cocurricular leadership program that involves leadership courses, community service, leadership workshops, campus activity participation, and a senior thesis or project. Students who successfully complete Leadership XXI receive a leadership citation at graduation.

There are more than forty campus organizations, including two national sororities, three national fraternities, several campus ministries, the *Panogram* (newspaper), the *Porphyrian* (yearbook), a 5,000-watt student-programmed FM radio station (WKWC 90.3 FM), the Kentucky Wesleyan Singers, and the Wesleyan Players. The College also supports an intramural athletics program.

Kentucky Wesleyan participates in the NCAA's Division II and the Great Lakes Valley Conference, offering baseball, basketball, football, golf, and soccer for men and basketball, golf, soccer, softball, tennis, and volleyball for women. The men's basketball program is one of the top programs in the nation. With eight national championships, Kentucky Wesleyan is the only school in NCAA Division II history to win national championships in each of the past five decades. The College also leads the nation with ninety-one NCAA Division II tournament wins and twenty NCAA regional championships. In addition, KWC is the all-time leader in NCAA Division II wins, with 1,347 games won.

Kentucky Wesleyan is home to approximately 650 students from twenty-one states and several other countries. There are one women's, one men's, and two coed residence halls. Each residence hall room is air conditioned and has a cable television hookup and access to the campus computer network.

Location

Kentucky Wesleyan College is located on 70 beautiful acres in Owensboro, Kentucky's third-largest city. Owensboro is located on the southern bank of the Ohio River, and the College is in a safe, residential neighborhood. The College is 45 minutes east of Evansville, Indiana; 2 hours north of Nashville, Tennessee; 2 hours west of Louisville, Kentucky; 4 hours west of Cincinnati, Ohio; and 4 hours east of St. Louis, Missouri.

A growing community of nearly 60,000 people, Owensboro is the cultural and industrial center of western Kentucky. Owensboro provides students with many opportunities for part-time employment and internships as well as easy access to museums, parks, shopping facilities, theaters, and an excellent symphony orchestra. There are opportunities for outdoor activities such as fishing, hiking, cycling, and waterskiing.

Kentucky Wesleyan and the Owensboro community share a warm relationship. Many students are employed by local businesses, and some remain in Owensboro after graduation. In addition, many local businesses and shops offer discounts on goods and services to students.

Majors and Degrees

Kentucky Wesleyan College offers the Bachelor of Arts and Bachelor of Science degrees, with more than thirty majors, including accounting, art, art education, biology, business administration, chemistry, communication arts, computer information systems, criminal justice, education (elementary, middle grades, and secondary), English, fine arts (art, theater, and music), fitness and sports management, history, human services administration, journalism, mathematics, medical technology, physical science, psychology, religion and philosophy, sociology, and Spanish. Preprofessional programs are offered in Christian ministries, dentistry, engineering, environmental science, law, medicine, optometry, pharmacy, physical therapy, physician's assistant studies, and veterinary medicine.

Academic Programs

There are three academic divisions in the KWC curriculum: Natural Sciences, Humanities and Fine Arts, and Social Sciences. Requirements for the degrees of Bachelor of Science and Bachelor of Arts are based on the principle of a broad distribution of studies among the representative fields of human culture and a concentration of studies in a specific field. In most cases, 128 semester hours are required to obtain a bachelor's degree.

Students have the opportunity to develop and carry out individual programs of study related to their particular vocational or professional goals through the Interdisciplinary Studies (IDS) program. By combining courses from two or more departments, the IDS student works toward a specifically tailored area of concentration.

Kentucky Wesleyan operates on a semester calendar, with classes from late August to mid-December and from mid-January to early May. An interim May term (Maymester) is offered, as is a limited summer term from early June to early July. Credit and/or advanced placement is offered through CLEP, Advanced Placement courses, and the International Baccalaureate program.

Off-Campus Programs

Students have the opportunity to learn outside of the traditional classroom through a variety of off-campus study programs. Students may arrange to study overseas on an individual basis for a summer, a semester, or a year. During spring break, students may choose to study business institutions, take urban studies, or observe plays and playwrights in New York City for credit. An in-depth study of marine biology in Belize is also offered each year during spring break. Other coordinated trips have included travel to Estonia, Israel, London, Mexico, and France.

Academic Facilities

Academic facilities at Kentucky Wesleyan include the Library Learning Center, the new Center for Business Studies, the Ralph Center for Fine Arts, the PLUS Center, facilities for the FM radio station, the KWC Playhouse (theater), and extensive natural science laboratories.

The Library Learning Center houses more than 150,000 books, periodicals, government documents, and audiovisual materials. Online databases and other electronic resources are also available. The library houses two computer labs for student use. In addition, a campuswide computer network links all campus facilities. This Ethernet network supports Windows-based PCs and provides access to e-mail, the Internet, the campus intranet, and several popular office suite programs. Each residence hall room is equipped with two network connections.

The Center for Business Studies is equipped with new facilities and furnishings. The most up-to-date audiovisual equipment is readily available in each classroom, and computers in the center have Pentium 4 processors and individual student hard drives. There is a wireless thirty-laptop-unit cart system that is portable to any classroom, and videoconferencing is available for student and faculty member use.

The Ralph Center for Fine Arts centrally houses all facets of the arts on campus. The multipurpose facility houses the campus radio station, a small performance hall, classroom and office space, studio space for art students, and practice rooms for student use. There is also an art gallery for display of student artwork.

Natural science laboratory equipment includes a purge and trap gas chromatography system, a Fourier-transform infrared spectrometer, an atomic absorption spectrometer, a high-performance liquid chromatography system, and an ultraviolet/visible spectra photometer. Biology equipment includes an environmental chamber, a laminar-flow hood, a dual-viewing epifluorescence microscope, an inverted phase-contrast microscope, and an ultramicroscope and transmission electron microscope.

Costs

The total cost for attending Kentucky Wesleyan College is well below the national average for private colleges. Tuition for the 2004–05 academic year is $12,160. Annual room and board charges are $2500 and $2950, respectively. The student activity fee is $200 and the technology fee is $150. Students and parents should also consider expenses for books, transportation, and personal and miscellaneous items.

Financial Aid

Kentucky Wesleyan participates in all federal student aid programs and is committed to helping each student meet his or her demonstrated need. No student should hesitate to apply for admission due to financial reasons. Kentucky Wesleyan awards more than $6.2 million each year in financial aid to eligible students. Kentucky residents may also qualify for Kentucky Higher Education Assistance Authority Grants.

In addition to federal and state financial aid programs, KWC invests more than $2.7 million annually in scholarships and grants for its students. Academic scholarships range from $2000 to full tuition and are renewable annually. Students who demonstrate a strong record of leadership in their school, church, place of employment, or community may be eligible for Stanley Reed Leadership Awards, which are valued at $2000 per academic year.

For maximum financial aid consideration, students are required to submit the Free Application for Federal Student Aid (FAFSA) by March 15. Kentucky Wesleyan is need-blind in its admission process.

Faculty

Kentucky Wesleyan has 76 faculty members (39 full-time, 37 part-time). Eighty-nine percent of the faculty members have the doctorate or terminal degree in their fields. The faculty members at KWC combine scholarship and teaching ability with a genuine concern for students. Students' learning is guided and their lives are shaped by faculty members who are totally dedicated to undergraduate teaching and the success of each student. A student-faculty ratio of 13:1 and small class size (15–25 students) ensures that students and faculty members develop the rapport that is crucial to an effective learning environment. All faculty members teach and advise students; there are no graduate teaching assistants.

Student Government

Students elect at-large members and officers on an annual basis to represent the student body in all areas of College life. The president of the Student Government Association also serves as an ex-officio member of the College's board of trustees. All policy and disciplinary issues are reviewed by the Dean of Student Life and by elected members of the Student Judiciary Board. The student handbook contains established guidelines for student life on campus.

Admission Requirements

Each applicant is considered individually on the basis of his or her academic record, ACT or SAT I scores, extracurricular involvement, and recommendations. Freshman applicants should generally be in the top half of their graduating class and have taken a strong college-preparatory curriculum. A minimum ACT score of 19 or SAT I score of 890, along with a core GPA of at least 2.25, are required for general admission to the College. Applicants are considered for admission upon receipt of their completed application, a $20 application fee, an official high school transcript, and ACT or SAT I scores.

Kentucky Wesleyan also seeks to enroll transfer, international, and adult students who have demonstrated the ability to succeed in a competitive academic environment. Transfer applicants should submit a completed application, a $20 application fee, official high school transcripts, and official transcripts from all colleges attended. A GPA of at least 2.0 is required for general admission to the College as a transfer student. International applicants must submit a $50 application fee, TOEFL scores (500 or better required) and/or ACT or SAT I scores, and an English translation of their high school transcript.

Application and Information

The Office of Admission is open from 8 a.m. to 5 p.m., Monday through Friday, and by appointment on Saturday from 10 a.m. to 1 p.m. Interested students are encouraged to visit the campus during one of the College's weekend open houses in the fall and winter or by individual appointment during the week. Students who wish to stay on campus overnight are welcome to do so at no charge.

Students may apply for admission after completing their junior year of high school. Applications are evaluated on a rolling basis, and students can expect to be notified concerning admission to the College within two weeks of completing their application for admission.

To arrange a campus visit or request application materials, students should contact:

Office of Admission
Kentucky Wesleyan College
3000 Frederica Street
Owensboro, Kentucky 42302-1039
Telephone: 270-852-3120
800-999-0592 (toll-free)
E-mail: admitme@kwc.edu
World Wide Web: http://www.kwc.edu

KETTERING UNIVERSITY
FLINT, MICHIGAN

The University

Kettering University (formerly GMI Engineering & Management Institute) offers education for the real world. Nearly 100 percent of Kettering's students receive a job offer or are accepted by graduate schools before receiving their diplomas. Kettering University has a unique partnership that offers students, business, and industry an opportunity found at no other undergraduate college in America. Kettering, a professional cooperative engineering, management, science, and math university, is the only institution that assists incoming freshmen to be selected by companies for cooperative employment, a process initiated for all accepted students. Kettering University successfully integrates the practical aspects of the workplace into the world of higher education through its more than 700 corporate partners, corporations, and agencies located throughout the United States, Canada, and selected countries. Kettering's corporate partners represent most major industrial groups; many are recognized as worldwide leaders in business innovation and manufacturing technology. These corporations share a commitment to "grow their own" engineers and managers by employing exceptionally talented young men and women in one of the nine baccalaureate degree programs. Kettering's corporate partners invest in students' futures by providing a program of progressive work experience that exposes them to processes, products, corporate culture, and the technology necessary to compete in tomorrow's business environment.

Founded in 1919, Kettering University is private and enrolls more than 2,400 undergraduate students. The University is accredited by the North Central Association of Colleges and Schools. Its engineering curricula are accredited by the Accreditation Board for Engineering and Technology, Inc. (ABET). The management program is accredited by the Association of Collegiate Business Schools and Programs (ACBSP).

The combination of academics and professional, paid work experience offered through Kettering University is not only highly effective, it is without equal, even among other cooperative education programs. The advantages of a Kettering education have enabled thousands of graduates to rise to key executive leadership positions in the world's finest corporations.

A varied program of sports, fitness, and recreational activities is offered. A 445-student residence hall and a new apartment complex are located on campus. Recreation facilities include athletic fields, tennis courts, and a recreation center with an Olympic-size, six-lane swimming pool, aerobic fitness rooms, a full line of Nautilus equipment, and basketball, tennis, and racquetball courts. A public golf course is adjacent to the campus.

Professional counseling, support services, and health care are available.

Location

Located in east-central Michigan, 60 miles west of Lake Huron and Canada and 60 miles north of Detroit, Flint is a city of 135,000 residents with a metropolitan area population of 450,000. Flint is particularly proud of its distinctive College and Cultural Center Complex, which is about 1½ miles from campus. Built and endowed entirely by the gifts of private citizens, the center includes the Alfred P. Sloan Museum; the Whiting Auditorium, home of the Flint Symphony and host to leading stage shows and entertainers; the Robert T. Longway Planetarium, Michigan's largest and best-equipped sky show facility; the Flint Institute of Arts; the F. A. Bower Theatre; the Dort Institute of Music; the University of Michigan–Flint Campus; the C. S. Mott Community College; and the Flint Public Library.

Outdoor and indoor recreational opportunities are abundant. Within a few minutes' drive are downhill and cross-country skiing facilities, several fine lakes for the entire range of water sports, a wide selection of good golf courses open to the public, and excellent indoor and outdoor skating rinks.

Majors and Degrees

Kettering University offers a 4½-year, professional cooperative education program with curricula leading to designated Bachelor of Science degrees in Computer Engineering, Electrical Engineering, Industrial Engineering, and Mechanical Engineering degrees; a designated Bachelor of Science in Business Management degree with concentrations in accounting/finance, information systems, manufacturing management, marketing, and materials management; and designated Bachelor of Science degrees in applied mathematics, applied physics, computer science, and environmental chemistry. Minors are available in applied chemistry, applied mathematics, applied optics, computer science, liberal arts, and management.

Academic Program

Although each program at Kettering University has its own sequence requirements, 160 credit hours are generally required, including thesis credit hours. The program involves nine academic terms and nine co-op terms, two of which are focused on the capstone thesis project, which is done on behalf of the student's co-op employer. Students alternate between eleven-week periods of academic study on the campus in Flint and twelve-week periods of related work experience with their corporate employer. The academic year consists of two 3–month academic terms on campus and two 3–month terms of paid work experience. A typical Kettering University cooperative student may earn up to $65,000 in co-op wages through the complete program.

Academic Facilities

The C.S. Mott Engineering and Science Center—a $42 million facility—opened in summer 2003. This state-of-the-art facility houses a fuel cell lab, an emissions lab, and much more. Kettering University has the traditional laboratory facilities expected of any top engineering school, but also has labs to demonstrate and experiment with a wide range of technologies found in industry—from basic machining to emerging technologies. The instrumentation in some labs is generally found only in graduate school facilities at other colleges. There are manufacturing, laser, radioisotope, heat transfer, electricity and solid-state electronics, metallurgy, computer-aided design (CAD), computer-integrated manufacturing (CIM), acoustics, mechatronics, human factors, digital and analog computer, robotics, holography, and electron microscopy laboratories and the Polymer Optimization Center. The campus is fully networked and allows access to computer resources from dormitory rooms, dedicated labs, and other locations. Course materials are offered online through Blackboard. Each student has unlimited 24-hour access to computer resources and the World Wide Web. The library contains more than 94,000 cataloged volumes and currently subscribes to more than 540 periodicals and various online services. Special facilities include a microfilm area, database search services, record and tape listening and videocassette viewing facilities, and a special collection of SAE, SME, and ASME technical papers.

Costs

Tuition in 2003–04 was $21,184, and room and board were $4984 (nineteen meals per week).

Financial Aid

In addition to all traditional sources of aid, all Kettering students benefit from a special resource that is significant and not need based. One of the many advantages of attending Kettering University is the opportunity for students to earn a salary during their co-op work terms. Co-op income is substantial and can help cover part of the cost of a Kettering education by supplementing the family contribution and the standard forms of need-based and merit-based financial aid. Students who live at home during work experience periods are able to contribute a greater proportion of earnings directly to educational expenses. About 70 percent of students are able to live at home during work terms. The typical range of co-op earnings over the five-year program is $40,000 to $65,000.

Kettering University offers all the traditional forms of financial aid, both need- and merit-based. The new Kettering Merit Scholarship program rewards all qualified applicants. Because of their talents, many students win scholarships from agencies and organizations from their local communities. Michigan residents are often recipients of the Michigan Competitive Scholarship/Tuition Grant. Traditionally, more than 92 percent of the entering class receives some form of financial aid, making a private education at Kettering very affordable.

The primary purpose of financial aid at Kettering University is to supplement a student's unmet financial need after cooperative earnings and parents' contributions. Students who wish to apply for financial aid should complete the Free Application for Federal Student Aid (FAFSA) and request that a copy of the analysis be sent to Kettering University. Aid is given as grants, scholarships, loans, and work-study awards.

Faculty

Kettering University's full-time faculty of 144 members have teaching as their prime responsibility. Most professors in degree disciplines have industrial experience in addition to academic credentials and maintain contact with industry through consulting, sponsored research, and advising on student thesis projects. More than 80 percent of faculty members hold a doctorate. Because only half of the students are on campus at any one time, class sizes are small and opportunities for enrichment and extra help are readily available. Kettering faculty members find the challenge of teaching talented students who share their experiences from co-op especially refreshing and rewarding.

Student Government

Kettering University students enjoy an active college life with a wide range of clubs and organizations and an exciting intramural athletic program. Eleven professional societies are active on campus, and there are fourteen national fraternities and six sororities. More than half of all students are active in fraternities and sororities. Kettering students tend to enjoy competition, whether it be in service activities or on the athletic field. The student government represents the interests and needs of the students and contributes to their educational development in the areas of leadership skills, self-confidence, interpersonal relations, and organizational operations.

Admission Requirements

Admission to Kettering University is competitive and based on scholastic achievement and nonscholastic interests, activities, and achievements. Applicants are required to have earned the following credits (a credit represents two semesters or one year of study): algebra, 2 credits; geometry, 1 credit; trigonometry, ½ credit; laboratory science, 2 credits (physics and chemistry are strongly recommended for all students; at least 1 credit of chemistry or physics is required); and English, 3 credits. A minimum of 16 credits is required; however, the University encourages students to complete at least 20 credits. Applicants must submit results of the SAT I or ACT. (Kettering's ACT code number is 1998; the SAT I code number is 1246.) The staff of the Cooperative Education and Career Services Office initiates the process and assists all enrolled students with the process of securing cooperative employment. The process begins upon confirmation of enrollment and continues until each student is employed.

Most Kettering University students achieve at or near the top 10 percent of their graduating class on traditional criteria such as grades, rank, and test scores. Corporate employers are also very interested in activities, career goals, experiences, leadership, and other personal qualities. Kettering University also welcomes students wishing to transfer from other colleges and universities. The transfer alternative is an excellent way to gain admission for students who do not enroll as freshmen.

Application and Information

Prospective freshmen are encouraged to file their application early in their senior year. Admission decisions for transfer applicants are based on college record for those who have completed at least 30 credits. Applications are accepted all year long; however, early application greatly increases visibility for early employment possibilities in the co-op search process. The application fee is $35. Students can also apply online at the Web site listed below.

Admissions Office
Kettering University
1700 West Third Avenue
Flint, Michigan 48504-4898
Telephone: 810-762-7865
800-955-4464 (toll-free in the United States and Canada)
E-mail: admissions@kettering.edu
World Wide Web: http://www.admissions.kettering.edu

Kettering University graduates expect a good job or entrance into a top graduate school.

KEYSTONE COLLEGE

LA PLUME, PENNSYLVANIA

The College

Keystone College was founded in 1868 as Keystone Academy in Factoryville, Pennsylvania. Initially opened as the only high school between Binghamton, New York, and Scranton, Pennsylvania, Keystone flourished as a secondary school for more than sixty-five years. Rechartered as Scranton-Keystone Junior College in 1934 and then Keystone Junior College in 1944, the College served as one of the premier two-year institutions in the Northeast until 1995. In this year the school was again renamed, as Keystone College, and began its tenure as an "ideal" four-year degree-granting college. Keystone College has a current enrollment of 1,500, including students from fourteen states and seven countries. Students can choose from twelve different four-year majors and more than twenty-five different two-year degree and certificate programs.

Location

Located at the foot of the Endless Mountains in northeastern Pennsylvania, the 270-acre campus is both scenic and historic, with buildings dating back to 1870. Located 13 miles from Scranton, Pennsylvania, the campus offers easy access to major East Coast cities, including New York, Philadelphia, and Baltimore.

Majors and Degrees

The Bachelor of Arts degree is offered in humanities, professional studies–communication arts, and visual art. The Bachelor of Science degree is offered in accounting; business; business administration–human resource management; criminal justice administration; early childhood education; elementary education; professional studies–environmental resource management; professional studies–information technology; professional studies–natural sciences, with emphasis in forensic biology or general biology; professional studies–sport and recreation management; and teaching–art education (K–12).

The Associate of Applied Science is offered in accounting, culinary arts, hotel and restaurant management, and information technology. The Associate in Fine Arts is offered in art. The Associate in Arts is offered in allied health with emphasis in nursing, occupational therapy, physical therapy, and radiological technology/diagnostic imaging; biological science with emphasis in biology, biochemistry, premedicine, and prepharmacy studies; business administration; communications; computer information systems; criminal justice; environmental studies; forestry/resource management; human resource management; human services; landscape architecture; liberal studies; liberal studies–education emphasis; sport and recreation management; and wildlife biology. The Associate in Science is offered in early childhood education. In addition, there are one-year programs in computer information systems, forestry technology, information technology, Microsoft Certified Systems Engineer, Microsoft Certified Systems Administrator, and pre–major studies (undeclared major). Postbaccalaureate certification is available in elementary education, early childhood education, and teaching–art education (K–12).

Academic Program

The College runs on a two-semester schedule (fall and spring) and has night and weekend classes available. The number of credit hours required to earn a degree is dependent on the field of study chosen, and students must have attained a minimum cumulative GPA of 2.0. Every student must complete a set of general core curriculum requirements as well as the courses specific to his or her major course of study. All students are required to complete one internship or co-op before graduation, depending on the course of study.

Students have the opportunity to participate in both the Army and Navy ROTC programs in conjunction with other local participating institutions. There are opportunities for double majors as well as minors in various fields of study.

Academic Facilities

The Harry K. Miller Library is available on campus to all students. This facility offers standard print and online research opportunities. The Hibbard Campus Center is the setting for the student cafeteria, a full-service restaurant, The Chef's Table (a student-run restaurant), as well as a U.S. post office, a print shop, a student-run radio station, and reception halls. The campus also boasts an art gallery, a celestial observatory, and the Poinsard Greenhouse. Keystone College also serves as the home for the Urban Forestry Center, Willary Water Discovery Center, the Northeast Theatre (TNT), and the Countryside Conservancy.

There are more than 120 computers available on campus for general student use, and both the Internet and campus network can be accessed from all residence halls and most buildings on campus.

Costs

Tuition and fees for Keystone College for the 2003–04 year were $6925 per semester, while room and board costs averaged $3700 per semester. Books and general supplies averaged $500 per semester and vary according to major.

Financial Aid

The Financial Aid Office provides adequate funds and resources to meet the financial needs of students from all income categories. Scholarships are awarded based on merit, academic performance, and extracurricular involvement. Keystone College also participates in the following federally sponsored programs: Federal Perkins Loan, Federal Pell Grant, Federal Supplemental Educational Opportunity Grant (FSEOG), Federal PLUS Loan, and Federal Stafford Student Loan. The College also offers college employment programs to students and alternative loans as well as state grants and Keystone grants. In order to be considered for financial aid, students must complete the Free Application for Federal Student Aid (FAFSA).

Faculty

There are 59 full-time professors and 151 part-time adjunct faculty members. The student-faculty ratio is 10:1, and the average class size is 15 students. Counseling is available for academic, personal, and vocational issues. Keystone College is supported by strong interpersonal relationships among its students and faculty and staff members. All faculty members post regular office hours and are generally available outside of these hours.

Student Government

Student Senate is the central governing body of all student government organizations on the campus. It serves as the liaison between the student body and the College administration. Members of Student Senate are chosen by their peers and are responsible for improving and maintaining student life both on and off campus. Students may choose from more than twenty-five different clubs and organizations, including those with academic, service-oriented, and social interests.

Admission Requirements

Keystone accepts qualified students regardless of race, religion, handicap, or national origin, and admissions are on a rolling basis. Admission is based on prior academic performance and the ability of the applicant to profit from and contribute to the academic, interpersonal, and extracurricular life of the College. Keystone considers applicants who meet the following criteria: graduation from an approved secondary school or the equivalent (with official transcripts), satisfactory scores on the SAT or ACT (the SAT is preferred but is not required in all circumstances), one letter of recommendation, and evidence of potential for successful college achievement. All students are strongly encouraged to visit the campus for a personal interview with the admissions staff and a member of the faculty from the student's area of interest. Students applying to the art and teaching–art education programs are required to participate in a portfolio interview.

Transfer students in good academic and financial standing at their current institution are also encouraged to apply to Keystone. Transfer students should contact the Office of Admissions and may be required to submit either high school transcripts or transcripts from each college attended or both.

Admissions decisions are made within two weeks from the day all required materials are received in the Office of Admissions.

Application and Information

Students wishing to be considered for admission must submit an application and a $25 processing fee, along with official high school transcripts, college transcripts (if applicable), a letter of recommendation from someone other than a friend or relative, and scores from either the SAT or ACT (submitted directly to the Office of Admissions; Keystone's CEEB code numbers are 2351 for the SAT, 2602 for the ACT).

Applications and any additional information about Keystone College may be obtained by contacting:

Office of Admissions
Keystone College
One College Green
La Plume, Pennsylvania 18440
Telephone: 570-945-5141
800-824-2764 Option 1 (toll-free)
E-mail: admissions@keystone.edu
World Wide Web: http://www.keystone.edu

Students on the campus of Keystone College.

KING COLLEGE

BRISTOL, TENNESSEE

The College

King College is a four-year, Presbyterian-affiliated, coeducational college located in Bristol, Tennessee. King is a residential institution, with 46.3 percent of its students living in College housing. Many faculty and staff members live near the campus as well and are actively involved in campus life.

Founded in 1867, King College is a comprehensive Christian liberal arts college in the Presbyterian and Reformed traditions, with the core belief that because God is the Creator, Sustainer, and Redeemer of all life, knowledge of self, the world, and God are interrelated. The purpose of the vigorous and broad education at King College is to educate students so that they may live meaningful lives of achievement and cultural transformation in Christ. Transformation of culture in Christ requires the community of learners—students and faculty and staff members—to think critically about Western and non-Western cultures, to examine their own cultural captivities, to interact with diverse peoples, to be challenged by suffering and injustice, to understand belief systems that are hostile or indifferent to a Christian worldview, and to participate in civil society. King College seeks to foster a campus ethos that stresses the importance of exploration, personal initiative, character and integrity, collegiality, humane instincts, aesthetic sensitivities, and leadership. When students leave King they are intellectually proficient and disciplined, spiritually astute and mature, technologically competent and innovative, vocationally focused and adaptive, and socially confident and compassionate, and they possess a lifelong love of learning and service. Of recent graduates, 93 percent seeking employment are employed within six months of matriculation. Thirty percent of King College graduates attend a graduate or professional school upon graduation. Of those, more than 80 percent are accepted into their first choice of graduate schools. King College's School of Business and Economics offers a Master of Business Administration.

King has five residence halls, a newly constructed student center complex, a dining hall, a fine arts facility, three computer labs, and new athletic fields. A variety of extracurricular activities are available to King College students year-round. There are more then forty student clubs and organizations on campus. King also has active intercollegiate and intramural sports programs that utilize the gymnasium, the student center, six tennis courts, the soccer fields, the baseball diamond, and a nature trail. In addition, men's intercollegiate teams compete in baseball, basketball, golf, soccer, and tennis. Women's intercollegiate teams compete in basketball, soccer, tennis, and volleyball. Intramural programs include badminton, basketball, flag football, golf, soccer, softball, and volleyball.

Location

King College is located in Bristol, Tennessee. The 130-acre hilltop campus is 2 miles from the center of Bristol, a city of 43,300 residents. Bristol is actually two cities of almost equal size: Bristol, Tennessee, and Bristol, Virginia.

Bristol, recognized by the U. S. Congress as the "Birthplace of Country Music," is also noted for its historic sites, parks, natural beauty, the Paramount Center for the Arts, and the Bristol Motor Speedway. In 1999, Tri-Cities Tennessee/Virginia, made up of Johnson City, Tennessee; Kingsport, Tennessee; and Bristol, Tennessee/Virginia, was chosen by the National Civic League as a recipient of the All-America City Award.

Majors and Degrees

King College confers five undergraduate degrees: Bachelor of Arts, Bachelor of Business Administration, Bachelor of Science, Bachelor of Science in medical technology, and Bachelor of Science in Nursing. All majors in the Division of Natural Sciences and Mathematics receive Bachelor of Science degrees upon completion of graduation requirements. Students majoring in nursing receive the Bachelor of Science in Nursing (B.S.N.) degree.

Major subject areas in the School of Arts and Sciences include American studies (with concentrations in American art and culture and teachers of English language/American culture), applied science and math (engineering), behavioral science, Bible and religion, biochemistry, biology (with concentrations in cell and molecular biology, general biology, and a pharmacy 3+1 program), biology and business management, biophysics, chemistry, computer science, economics, education (elementary and secondary), English (with concentrations in communications, English/secondary education, literature, secondary education and theater, theater, and writing), French, health sciences chemistry, history, interdisciplinary studies, mathematics (with concentrations in mathematics and mathematics education), medical technology, modern languages, performing and visual arts (with concentrations in church music, music, and theater), physics, political science/history, psychology, and Spanish.

The School of Business and Economics offers majors in business administration and economics (with concentrations in accounting, accounting and finance, business administration, finance and economics, international business, management, marketing, and sport management) and online media and marketing. The Bachelor of Business Administration degree program is also available for working adults.

Major subject areas are also available in the Peeke School of Christian Mission, which offers degree programs in mission studies and youth ministry, and in the School of Nursing, which offers Bachelor of Science in Nursing and RN-to-B.S.N. programs.

Students may select minor areas of study in Bible and religion, biblical languages, biology, business administration and economics, chemistry, coaching, computer science, economics, elementary education, English, French, history, management and marketing, mathematics, mission studies, music, online media, philosophy, physics, political science, psychology, secondary education, and Spanish.

Academic Program

The academic year consists of two semesters, and summer courses are available. Requirements for individual programs are based upon the completion of general education requirements, the fulfillment of requirements in a major concentration (according to each academic department), and the completion of sufficient electives to make a total of 124 semester hours. The work must be completed with a minimum King College grade point average of 2.0. Nursing majors must complete a total of 125 or 126 semester hours of credit with a minimum grade point average of 2.5. Students majoring in behavioral science with teacher licensure must complete a total of 131 semester hours of credit with a minimum grade point average of 2.5.

Special programs include Honors in Independent Study, several international studies programs, summer research scholarships, an engineering dual-degree program in conjunction with

Vanderbilt University and the University of Tennessee, and the global health program offered through King's Peeke School of Christian Mission.

Off-Campus Programs

King College students wishing to take courses at other institutions for credit may do so with permission of the Dean of Faculty. King College accepts a maximum of 15 distance learning credit hours toward the degree. King College and Virginia Intermont College in Bristol, Tennessee, have approved a cooperative program whereby students enrolled at one institution may take certain courses at the other campus. King also has a cooperative agreement with Vanderbilt University and the University of Tennessee in its engineering dual-degree program.

Academic Facilities

The E. W. King Library serves the College through the acquisition and provision of access to numerous information resources to support the educational curriculum, research needs, and interests of students and faculty and staff members. The library contains more than 140,000 items, including book volumes, periodical subscriptions, bound periodical volumes, microforms, audio recordings, video recordings, government documents, and equipment. In addition, the library provides students and faculty members access to many electronic databases that provide full-text access to thousands of periodical titles that cover a wide variety of academic disciplines. The library's Web site serves as a Webliography and pathfinder for students to locate and use Internet resources.

Costs

Tuition and fees for 2004–05 are $22,500 for full-time resident students. Of that amount, room and board are $5460 and required fees are $1054. Books and supplies are an estimated $500 per year.

Financial Aid

Scholarships, grants, loans, a work program, and church matching grants are available for students needing assistance. The purpose of financial aid at King College is twofold: to provide financial assistance to students who, without such aid, would be unable to attend college, and to recognize and reward those students who have demonstrated superior achievement. More than $4 million in total financial assistance is made available each year to students. In addition to King College and private sources of assistance, the College also participates in the following federal and state programs of financial assistance: Federal Pell Grant, Federal Supplemental Educational Opportunity Grant (FSEOG), Federal Perkins Loan, Federal Stafford Student Loan, Federal Work-Study Program (FWS), Federal PLUS Loan for parents, and Tennessee State Grant.

Faculty

An 11:1 student-faculty ratio ensures that students receive personal attention in and out of the classroom and a vigorous and broad education. The 87 faculty members at King College are dedicated to transforming students so that upon graduation they possess a lifelong love of learning and service and are intellectually proficient and disciplined, spiritually astute and mature, and vocationally focused and adaptive.

Student Government

King College encourages student activity in government. The SGA offers opportunities to develop leadership qualities and learn the fundamentals of parliamentary procedure. The SGA Administrative Council is made up of 13 members who are dedicated to improving student life on campus. SGA representatives have the opportunity to sit on numerous King College committees.

Admission Requirements

King College welcomes students who desire an excellent education in a setting where Christian values are the foundation upon which a student's education is based. Admission is competitive and based on an overall evaluation of the ability to benefit from a King College education, rather than focusing on any single factor. Important criteria include demonstrated academic achievement, personal motivation, and the qualities of character and leadership ability. General requirements for admission include graduation from an accredited or recognized high school or secondary institution with a minimum of 16 academic units, distributed as follows: 4 units of English, 2 units of algebra (algebra I and II), 1 unit of geometry, 2 units of foreign language, 2 units of history or social science, 1 unit of natural science, and 4 units of academic electives. A student who does not present this pattern of preparation along with an academic grade point average of at least 2.4 (on a 4.0 scale) and a minimum ACT score of 20 or SAT I score of 1000 may be conditionally accepted with permission from the Admissions Committee of the Faculty.

Application and Information

To be considered for admission, a student must submit the application with the application fee, an official high school transcript sent from the school, and SAT or ACT scores.

An application and additional information may be obtained by contacting:

Office of Admissions
King College
1350 King College Road
Bristol, Tennessee 37620-2699
Telephone: 423-652-4861
800-362-0014 (toll-free)
E-mail: admissions@king.edu
World Wide Web: http://www.king.edu

KING'S COLLEGE

WILKES-BARRE, PENNSYLVANIA

The College

King's College is an independent four-year Catholic college with more than 2,200 men and women students. Founded by the Holy Cross Fathers and Brothers of the University of Notre Dame in 1946, King's prepares students for a purposeful life with an education that integrates the human values inherent in a broadly based liberal arts curriculum. The College encourages the religious, moral, personal, and social development of its students.

In addition to the undergraduate degrees, King's College offers graduate courses in health-care administration, a Master of Education (M.Ed.) degree (with a concentration in reading), and a five-year physician assistant studies program leading to a master's degree.

Academic advising begins before students enroll and continues with an innovative program of career development across the curriculum. King's Academic Skills Center includes a nationally certified tutoring program and a faculty-staffed writing center. More than 80 percent of King's first-year students return for their sophomore year, a percentage well above the national average. Sixty-one percent of King's students who enter as first-year students graduate within four years, and 99 percent are employed within six months of graduation.

Campus features include the Charles E. and Mary Parente Life Sciences Center, the Mulligan Physical Sciences Center, the William G. McGowan School of Business, and Robert L. Betzler Fields, a 33.5-acre athletic complex that includes a field house and fields for baseball, softball, men's and women's soccer, football, and field hockey. The 15-acre campus also includes the newly renovated Sheehy-Farmer Campus Center, which includes a gallery, an outdoor waterfall, student restaurants, and marketplace dining; the J. Carroll McCormick Campus Ministry Center; and the William S. Scandlon Physical Education Center, which includes a 3,200-seat basketball arena, wrestling facilities, racquetball and handball courts, an Olympic-size swimming pool, a rifle range, and a strength and fitness center as well as a state-of-the-art sports medicine facility. The College also has a 5,000-square-foot weight room with more than 13,000 pounds of free weights that is approved by the American Weightlifting Federation. The Student Health Center is located in Hafey-Marian Hall, a modern six-story building for classrooms and faculty offices, and a consulting physician is on call at all times. The six-story administration and science buildings form a unit that houses the College's theater, a cafeteria, administrative offices, science laboratories, and classrooms.

More than fifty student organizations provide King's students with the opportunity to explore interests outside the classroom. Student athletics include intercollegiate competition in men's baseball, basketball, football, golf, lacrosse, soccer, swimming, tennis, and wrestling; women's basketball, field hockey, lacrosse, soccer, softball, swimming, tennis, and volleyball; and coed cross-country, and cheerleading. Intramural and club sports include basketball, bowling, field hockey, flag football, racquetball, softball, street hockey, and volleyball. Other cocurricular activities include academic clubs in almost every department, the King's Players (theater), the nationally ranked debate team, Christian Voices, Cantores Christi Regis, Campus Ministry, the Experiencing the Arts Series, the *Crown* (student newspaper), the *Regis* (yearbook), and *SCOP* (literary magazine).

Location

The King's campus is located in a residential area near downtown Wilkes-Barre, a city of approximately 50,000 on the banks of the Susquehanna River in the Pocono Mountains. A growing city, Wilkes-Barre has developed both economically and culturally, yet it has avoided many typical urban problems. The crime rate in the city is one of the lowest in the nation. Local events include the Cherry Blossom Festival, a national ice carving competition, and the Fine Arts Fiesta. Shopping malls, multiplex theaters, parks, art galleries, and restaurants are nearby. Two blocks from King's is the F. M. Kirby Center, which has hosted national performances, music groups, traveling theatre, and more. National recording acts regularly perform in nearby venues.

King's is a short drive from several ski resorts, state parks, and major lakes, as well as the stadium of the Phillies' AAA baseball team, the Pocono International Raceway, and the Wachovia Arena, which is home to the Pittsburgh Penguins' minor-league ice hockey team and features regular concerts, is the site of the King's commencement. New York City and Philadelphia are within a 2½-hour drive; Harrisburg, Pennsylvania, and Morristown, New Jersey, are within 2 hours; and New England and Washington, D.C., are within 4 hours.

Majors and Degrees

King's awards Bachelor of Arts, Bachelor of Science, Associate in Arts, and Associate in Science degrees. The College's thirty-five major programs are offered in the arts and sciences and the William G. McGowan School of Business, which is a candidate for AACSB International–The Association to Advance Collegiate Schools of Business. Arts and sciences include the humanities and social sciences division (computers and information systems, criminal justice, English, French, gerontology, history, mass communication/media technologies, philosophy, political science, psychology, sociology, Spanish, theater, and theology); the education division (early childhood, elementary, secondary certification and special education), which is a candidate for NCATE accreditation; the science division (biology, chemistry, computer science, environmental science, environmental studies, general science, mathematics, and neuroscience); and the allied health division (clinical lab science, physician assistant studies, and athletics training education/sports medicine accredited by CAAHEP). Available majors in the William G. McGowan School of Business are accounting, business administration, economics, finance, human resources, international business, and marketing. King's offers preprofessional programs in dentistry, law, medicine, pharmacy, and veterinary science.

Academic Program

The general education program at King's is recognized nationwide by its peers. King's is included in *Barron's Best Buys in College Education* and eight consecutive issues of *U.S. News & World Report's Best Colleges Guide.* The College was also recognized by the John Templeton Foundation Honor Roll for Character-Building Colleges and is one of sixteen institutions nationwide named to the Greater Expectations initiative. The core curriculum is recognized as a model curriculum. It incorporates traditional and new concepts in liberal arts education, develops competence in such areas as communications and problem solving, and measures students' progress throughout the program.

The honors program offers highly motivated students the challenge of learning in discussion-centered courses that explore distinctive subject matter with exciting and innovative approaches. Sixteen honor societies encourage students to excel in their chosen fields and recognize students for their academic distinction; members are honored each year at the All-College Honors Convocation. Science students receive hands-on lab training much earlier than students at other institutions and work together with faculty members on real-world research projects.

Off-Campus Programs

Experiential learning (via internships) is available in conjunction with almost every major. Placement possibilities include CNN, Coopers & Lybrand, the New York Stock Exchange, the Pennsylvania Department of Education, the Pennsylvania State House of Representatives, the U.S. House of Representatives, U.S. Senators' offices, the U.S. Department of Energy, Walt Disney World, and Xerox Corporation. Every year students are placed with local, regional, and national companies around the globe.

The International Internship Program and Study-Abroad Program are also options for King's students who work in a variety of professions. An agreement with Webster University provides study opportunities on campuses throughout Europe and in Thailand.

Academic Facilities

King's facilities include the 51,000-square-foot, three-story D. Leonard Corgan Library, which contains several study rooms, a 100-seat auditorium, and a 160,000-volume collection accessed by a computerized catalog. The library uses its affiliation with the Online Computer Library Center to provide students and faculty members with access to college and research libraries throughout the United States. The library provides full-text databases from every computer on campus. Students and faculty members have direct access to more than 1 million volumes through the local library cooperative (NEPBC). Residence halls have cable television and individual phone service in rooms. King's features computer labs with more than 200 PCs; 24-hour labs in residence halls; e-mail accounts for all students; computerized library databases; multimedia classrooms with a variety of instructional aids; course discussions on electronic bulletin boards and chats via e-mail outside of the traditional classroom; a technology component of the core curriculum that requires all students to learn to access, process, and develop their own computer and information presentation skills; distance learning facilities for teleconferencing; satellite down-link capabilities in the 220-seat Burke Auditorium of the William G. McGowan School of Business; and cross-registration with area colleges that enables students to take courses complementary to their majors. The $6.4-million Charles E. and Mary Parente Life Sciences Center, which contains a molecular biology laboratory, includes computer facilities, instrumentation rooms, a rooftop greenhouse, and environmental chambers. The $6-million Mulligan Physical Sciences Center includes modern research laboratories, computer facilities, and state-of-the-art instrumentation used for molecular identification.

Costs

For the 2003–04 academic year, tuition for full-time students is $18,260. Room and board total $7930. There is a comprehensive College fee of $800.

Financial Aid

King's assists all qualified students through its financial aid programs. Currently, more than 85 percent of King's students currently receive financial aid in the form of scholarships, grants, work-study, or loans. Aid is awarded on the basis of demonstrated financial need, the difference between the total cost of education and the expected family contribution. Usually, a combination of financial aid sources and types are used in a student's financial aid package. Of all financial aid awarded to its students, grants and scholarships funded by King's comprise approximately 40 percent of the total aid awarded.

In addition to financial aid programs, installment payment plans are available, offering students and/or their families the ability to make monthly payments throughout the academic year. Students who wish to be considered for financial aid must fill out the Free Application for Federal Student Aid (FAFSA) and the King's College Financial Aid Application. The preferred filing deadline for new freshmen is February 15. Forms are mailed to students accepted for admission but can be completed prior to acceptance.

Faculty

King's College has 114 full-time and 69 part-time faculty members. Eighty-one percent of the full-time faculty have a Ph.D. or an equivalent terminal degree. Graduate assistants do not teach courses. The student-faculty ratio is 15:1.

Student Government

The student government coordinates and participates in numerous activities for both the student body and the surrounding community. It regularly holds open forums for students and senior administrators at the College, coordinates informal socials for the students with the College president, and makes presentations at each meeting of the Board of Directors. In addition, the student government sponsors events that foster awareness for social and justice issues and a celebration of cultural diversity. Community projects, a strong service component, include Cityserve, National Collegiate Alcohol Awareness Week, and fund-raisers for the United Way. The Association for Campus Events, a student-operated organization, also sponsors comedians, movies, and performers throughout the year.

Admission Requirements

King's encourages applications from qualified high school students and those who wish to transfer from another institution. To be considered for admission, students must be prepared to pursue successfully a program of study at the College, as evidenced by the quality of previous academic and extracurricular performance, the recommendation of school officials and character references, and the student's display of personal promise, maturity, and motivation. King's admits students of any race, sex, color, creed, or national or ethnic origin. Admission decisions are made for both high school students and transfer students with the understanding that all current courses and examinations will be completed satisfactorily. Candidates should complete four years of mathematics (through trigonometry or precalculus). One year of high school chemistry and physics is also strongly recommended. High school students must take either the SAT I or the ACT Assessment. Test scores are used primarily for advisement and placement.

Application and Information

Applicants should forward a completed application and the $30 fee to the Admissions Office or apply online at the address listed below. Secondary and postsecondary (if applicable) transcripts must be sent. High school students must also submit SAT I or ACT Assessment scores. Admission decisions are not made until these credentials are received. King's subscribes to a rolling admission policy. Decisions are announced within two weeks from the date of application. Upon notification of acceptance, a $200 nonrefundable deposit is requested to reserve a place in the class. The deposit deadline is May 1 but may be extended upon request. To schedule an interview, obtain an application form, or for more information, students should contact:

Admission Office
King's College
133 North River Street
Wilkes-Barre, Pennsylvania 18711
Telephone: 570-208-5858
800-955-5777 (toll-free)
888-KINGS-PA (toll-free)
E-mail: admissions@kings.edu
World Wide Web: http://www.kings.edu

KNOX COLLEGE

GALESBURG, ILLINOIS

The College

Knox College is a vital community of teachers and students that provides a challenging liberal arts curriculum, a faculty of national distinction, and a campus atmosphere noted for its informality. Knox invites students who seek a strong education and who relish the chance to explore their own ideas within a community of friends and mentors. Founded in 1837, Knox is one of the Midwest's great liberal arts colleges and among the nation's best. Site of the fifth Lincoln-Douglas debate, Knox has enrolled women and African-American students since the 1850s and international students since the 1860s. Knox has been known for its high academic quality since the nineteenth century and has many distinguished alumni in the professions—business, journalism, the natural sciences, and higher education.

Knox is an independent, coeducational four-year college. The student body of 1,120 comes from forty-five states and forty-two countries. Approximately 53 percent of students are women and 47 percent are men; 14 percent of students are students of color (5 percent African American, 5 percent Asian American, 3 percent Latino, and 1 percent Native American), and 8 percent are international students. Knox is very much a residential college, with more than 90 percent of students living on its spacious 82-acre campus. Most student residences are organized in 8- to 15-person suites with double and single rooms; options include coeducational residence halls, former private homes, and apartment-style units. Campus life is characterized by wide participation in more than 100 student organizations and extracurricular activities. The student-run Union Board provides a full entertainment calendar throughout the year. Musical groups run the gamut from rock, folk, and jazz combos to the Chamber Singers and the Knox-Galesburg Symphony. There are frequent theater productions and a modern dance ensemble. Knox has a 1,000-watt FM station, a biweekly student newspaper, and a student literary magazine twice named the nation's best. Student groups provide activities ranging from political activism to community service to religious meditation. There are five fraternities and two sororities. Knox competes at the NCAA Division III level in eleven men's and ten women's sports. Varsity sports are baseball, basketball, cross-country, football, golf, indoor and outdoor track, soccer, swimming, tennis, and wrestling for men and basketball, cross-country, golf, indoor and outdoor track, soccer, softball, swimming, tennis, and volleyball for women.

Location

Galesburg is an historic city of 33,500 located about 180 miles west of Chicago, 200 miles north of St. Louis, and about an hour away from the Mississippi River. It is accessible by transcontinental Amtrak trains, commercial airlines, bus lines, and interstate highways. Community service and internship and employment opportunities are available in local social service agencies, hospitals, financial institutions, and a variety of manufacturing firms. The campus is located three blocks from downtown shops, movie theaters, and restaurants. Notable features are the Orpheum Theater (a restored 1,000-seat concert hall), specialty shops on historic Seminary Street, and Lake Storey on the city's north side.

Majors and Degrees

Knox awards the Bachelor of Arts degree in the following major fields: American Studies, anthropology and sociology, art (history and studio), biochemistry, biology, black studies, chemistry, classics, computer science, economics, education (elementary, music, secondary, and social studies), English (creative writing and literature), environmental studies, French, gender and women's studies, German, history, integrated international studies, international relations, mathematics, mathematical finance, modern languages, modern languages and classics, music, philosophy, physics, political science, psychology, Russian, Russian area studies, Spanish, and theater. Students may also design their own interdisciplinary majors and minors. Minors are offered in American politics, anthropology and sociology, applied computer science, art history, behavioral neuroscience, biochemistry, biology, black studies, business, ceramics, comparative politics, computing systems, creative writing, dance, design and technology, directing, dramatic literature and history, English literature, environmental studies, French, gender and women's studies, German, history, international relations, jazz studies, journalism, Latin American studies, mathematics, mathematical finance, music history, music performance, music theory, painting, performance, philosophy, photography, physics, printmaking, psychology, religious studies, Russian, Russian area studies, sculpture, social services, Spanish, and theory of computing. Course work is also offered in Greek, Japanese, Latin, and sports studies. Preprofessional preparation is provided in architecture, engineering, law, and medicine. In addition, Knox offers teacher certification in elementary and secondary education.

Knox offers special programs in cooperation with several other institutions, including dual-degree programs in the following fields: architecture, engineering, environmental management, forestry, law, nursing/medical technology, and occupational therapy.

The Knox-Rush Early Identification Program identifies selected Knox first-year students for admission to Rush Medical College upon completion of their Knox degree.

Academic Program

The goal of Knox College is to provide students with a strong education in the liberal arts and to prepare them for rewarding professional and personal lives. The curriculum is designed to integrate the skills of critical inquiry and communication with study in breadth and depth. The required First-Year Preceptorial encourages students to engage the fundamental questions and concerns of a liberal education and fosters thoughtful debate, careful reasoning, and clear writing. Other requirements include enhancing specialized knowledge through a major, a second major or a minor, and the study of four broad areas of human inquiry—the arts, humanities, sciences, and social sciences. Students are also required to acquire competencies in writing, oral presentation, quantitative literacy, informed use of technology, foreign language, understanding diversity, and applying classroom learning through hands-on experiences such as internships, study abroad, community service, independent research, and teaching assistantships. The academic calendar is three 10-week terms, with a normal load of three 1-credit courses per term. Thirty-six credits are required for graduation.

The close relationship of faculty and students is key to Knox's program. Students work with faculty advisers to develop their programs of study; the ratio of first-year students to faculty advisers is held to no more than 8:1, while the overall student-faculty ratio is 12:1. Students with declared majors work with an adviser in their major field. Small classes (averaging 17 students) are the rule, and independent study is common in every department. Student research is a distinctive feature at Knox, which regularly sends one of the largest contingents to national conferences on undergraduate research. Promising students are encouraged to apply for one of the several available research opportunities, including the Ford Research Fellows, Richter Fellows, and ACM Minority/McNair Fellows Programs, to pursue an independent project under the supervision of a faculty mentor. Similarly, seniors are encouraged to pursue College Honors. Other special features worthy of note are the nationally recognized Writing Program, the theater department's Repertory Term, and the art department's Open Studio experience.

Off-Campus Programs

Knox maintains its own programs abroad in Buenos Aires, Argentina; Besançon, France; and Barcelona, Spain, in cooperation with the universities of those cities. In addition, Knox recognizes and gives credit for twenty-eight programs in nineteen countries as well as eight programs in the United States. Students normally participate in these programs during the junior year.

Academic Facilities

The Knox campus has forty-two academic and residential buildings. Old Main, built in 1857, is the sole intact site of the 1858 Lincoln-Douglas debates and is on the National Register of Historic Buildings. Library holdings include more than 291,000 volumes and 672 periodicals in addition to OCLC interlibrary loan, online databases, and an automated catalog accessible from remote workstations around campus. Seymour Library's Special Collections Center houses manuscripts and rare book collections of national importance, such as the Finley Collection on the Old Northwest and the Hughes Collection on Hemingway and the "Lost Generation." Umbeck Science-Mathematics Center contains spacious teaching and research labs, extensive research equipment including electron microscopes and NMR, and a science library. Computer technology features a campus-wide fiber-optic network, Internet access, five student computer labs (including 24-hour access), several specialized departmental labs, and more than 200 Windows and Macintosh workstations for student use. Davis Hall, housing the social sciences and modern languages, includes a data analysis microcomputer lab and a language center equipped with audio, video, and computer equipment. The Fine Arts Center contains two theaters, a recital hall, music rehearsal studios, and art studios for painting, drawing, sculpture, printmaking, and ceramics. In addition, there is a Student Union, an outstanding gymnasium, and a recreational field house.

Costs

The comprehensive fee for 2004–05 is $31,338. This includes $24,960 for tuition, $6102 for room and board, and a $276 student activities fee. Extra expenses for books, travel, supplies, laundry, and incidentals are estimated at $1200.

Financial Aid

Knox is committed to being accessible to all qualified students. Admission decisions are made without regard for ability to pay, and Knox awards need-based financial aid according to each student's eligibility. Financial aid awards may include federal and state grants, student loans, and campus employment. New students must file an official financial aid application by March 1 for priority consideration. Knox offers a number of supplemental loan options as well as a variety of payment plans.

Knox also awards merit-based scholarships not based on financial need to recognize outstanding academic achievement as well as special abilities in art, community service, dance, mathematics, music, theater, and writing.

Faculty

Knox has 94 full-time and 33 part-time faculty members, of whom 94 percent hold the Ph.D. or equivalent. Faculty members teach all courses. More than two thirds have published or presented scholarly or creative work in the past five years. National recognition includes major research awards from the National Science Foundation, the National Institutes of Health, and the National Endowment for the Humanities; an ASCAP Award–winning composer; and an NSF Shannon Award–winning geneticist.

Student Government

At Knox, students are treated as full members of the community. Students administer the campuswide honor and judicial systems, regulating academic and social behavior. They are appointed to all faculty committees (except two personnel committees), have formal observer status to the Board of Trustees, and are a majority of the members on the committee regulating student affairs. In addition, there is an elected Student Senate.

Admission Requirements

Applicants to Knox must demonstrate the ability to do successful college-level work and to make a positive contribution to the campus community. The fundamental requirement is successful completion of a challenging college-preparatory program. Of the first-year students in 2003, 29 percent were in the top tenth of their high school class and 67 percent were in the top quarter. The middle 50 percent of students scored between 540 and 660 on the mathematics portion of the SAT I and between 550 and 690 on the verbal; on the ACT composite, the mid-50 percent range was 24 to 30. Applicants must complete the application form, file a nonrefundable $35 fee, and provide Knox with their SAT I or ACT scores, their academic transcripts, and recommendations from a teacher and counselor. Interviews are strongly recommended. Applications from transfer and international students are strongly encouraged.

Application and Information

For more information, students should contact:

Paul Steenis
Director of Admission
Knox College
Galesburg, Illinois 61401
Telephone: 309-341-7100
800-678-KNOX (toll-free)
Fax: 309-341-7070
E-mail: admission@knox.edu
World Wide Web: http://www.knox.edu

Knox College's Old Main, the last remaining site of the Lincoln-Douglas debates of 1858.

KUTZTOWN UNIVERSITY OF PENNSYLVANIA

KUTZTOWN, PENNSYLVANIA

The University

In an independent survey, 93 percent of students and recent alumni rated their education at Kutztown University (KU) as excellent or good in regard to their overall college experience, the quality of instruction they received, and the quality of the faculty. KU offers excellent academic programs through its undergraduate Colleges of Liberal Arts and Sciences, Visual and Performing Arts, Business, and Education and through its graduate studies program. A wide range of student support services complements the high-quality classroom instruction.

Students have the advantage of a well-rounded program of athletic, cultural, and social events at KU. There are clubs, organizations, and activities to satisfy nearly every taste. Currently, more than 9,000 full- and part-time students are enrolled at the University. About half of the full-time undergraduates live in residence halls; the rest live at home in nearby communities.

Kutztown University's attractive 325-acre campus includes a mix of old and new buildings, including stately Old Main, the historic building known to generations of Kutztown's students; University Place, a modern residence hall in a courtyard setting; and the McFarland Student Union. A state-of-the-art science complex and a 500-bed apartment-style residence hall opened in fall 2003.

In addition to its Kutztown's undergraduate program, the University's graduate program awards master's degrees in a number of fields. The Master of Science is awarded in computer and information science and electronic media. The Master of Arts is awarded in counseling psychology and English. The Master of Education is awarded in art education, elementary education, elementary education (with extension of certification), elementary school counseling (certification and licensure), instructional technology, mathematics, reading, secondary education (with specializations), secondary school counseling (certification and licensure), and student affairs in higher education (administration and college counseling licensure). The Master of Library Science, Master of Business Administration, Master of Public Administration, and Master of Social Work are also awarded.

Location

The University is located in a beautiful rural Pennsylvania Dutch community midway between the cities of Allentown and Reading. Both cities are a short drive from campus and have major shopping and recreational facilities. Kutztown borough, an easy walk from the campus, has ample stores and shops to meet the needs of students. Philadelphia is about 1½ hours away, and New York City, about 2½ hours.

Majors and Degrees

Undergraduate degrees are offered in a wide variety of fields. The Bachelor of Arts is awarded in anthropology, English, French, geography, history, music, philosophy, political science, psychology, sociology, Spanish, speech communication, and theater. The Bachelor of Fine Arts is awarded in communication design, crafts, and studio art. The Bachelor of Science is awarded in art education, biology, chemistry, computer and information science, criminal justice, electronic media, environmental science, geology, marine science, mathematics, medical technology, nursing, physics, pre-engineering (with Penn State), psychology, and public administration. The Bachelor of Science in Business Administration is awarded in accounting, finance, general business, international business, management, and marketing. The Bachelor of Science in Education is awarded in elementary education with concentrations in early childhood development, English, French, instructional technology, mathematics, music, psychology, reading, Russian, science, social studies, Spanish, sports pedagogy, and urban education; in secondary education with specializations in biological science, chemistry, citizenship, communications, earth and space science, English, French, general science, German, mathematics, physics, physics and mathematics, Russian, social studies, and Spanish; in special education with concentrations in mentally/physically handicapped, speech-language pathology, and visually impaired; and in library science. The Bachelor of Social Work is also awarded.

The three most popular majors are business administration, elementary education, and psychology. The most popular minors are psychology and public relations.

Academic Programs

The University observes a two-semester calendar, and first-semester examinations are completed by late December. A minimum of 120 semester hours and a cumulative quality point average (QPA) of at least 2.0 are required for graduation. In the College of Liberal Arts and Sciences and College of Business, a quality point average of at least 2.0 in the major is also required.

Students seeking admission to teacher education must complete a three-stage process. (1) Applicants must have a projected grade point average (PGPA) of at least 2.0. Students with less than a 2.0 PGPA may be granted admission on a conditional basis and are required to schedule and pass appropriate developmental education courses. (2) During the fourth semester (or after completing 64 credits), applicants must present evidence of 30 hours of classroom observation, achieve at least a 3.0 overall average, pass a speech screening test, and complete basic speech, mathematics, English composition, EDU 100, student teaching, and professional education courses as determined by each major, with a minimum grade of C. (3) Prior to student teaching, applicants must complete a professional semester or early field experience, have achieved at least a 3.0 QPA as well as a 3.0 QPA in all courses in the major required for student teaching, and be recommended by the department screening committee. Students are required to pass the National Teachers Examination (three core batteries and a specialty area) at the end of their academic program before the Pennsylvania Department of Education will issue an Instructional I (Probationary) Certificate.

The distinctive University Honors Program is available to qualified students in all areas of study. Freshmen who have been identified as potential honors students based on their high school records and SAT scores, transfer students from other honors programs, and incumbent students who have at least a 3.25 GPA are invited to enroll in the program. The 21 credits in honors work, which include a senior thesis project, count toward the 120 credits required for graduation. Honors students select specially designed courses, independent study, and internships. The honors program awards several merit-based scholarships, and students who complete the program receive an honors diploma upon graduation.

Kutztown University and the Colleges of Engineering and Earth and Mineral Studies of Pennsylvania State University cooperate in a 3-2 program in liberal arts and engineering. Three years or the equivalent are spent at Kutztown University, where the student takes liberal arts courses along with pre-engineering courses. Upon satisfactory completion of this program and recommendation by the faculty, the student enters Pennsylvania State University and fulfills the specified course requirements. Successful completion of these programs leads to appropriate baccalaureate degrees from both institutions.

Kutztown University provides an opportunity for higher education for students who, because of economic need, cultural disadvantage, or inadequate preparation, have previously been unable to attend college. Students admitted to the University under the Developmental Summer Program attend a preparatory program designed to introduce them to university study and to provide supportive services in counseling and tutoring as well as special instruction in study skills, reading, and writing.

Off-Campus Programs

Students majoring in education spend one semester of their senior year student teaching in area schools under the guidance of an experienced teacher. Additional teaching field experiences are available in the junior year during the "professional semester." Internships in other programs provide students with one semester of practical experience in their specialty. For example, political science students may work in local, state, or federal government agencies; psychology students in area psychiatric hospitals, clinics, and rehabilitation centers; social welfare and criminal justice students in various social agencies; electronic media students in commercial or public broadcasting, cable television, and industrial, medical, or institutional television; and medical technology students in area hospitals.

The University has exchange and study-abroad programs with colleges and universities in fourteen countries. In addition, through the International Student Exchange Program, KU students may study for a year in any of sixty institutions in twenty-seven countries. Kutztown is now in its eighth year of a cooperative program with the Diplomatic Academy of the Russian Foreign Ministry, Moscow, in which prominent Russian scholars and foreign affairs experts visit KU to meet with classes and give public lectures. KU also has cooperative programs with institutions in England, Germany, the Netherlands, Hungary, Italy, Spain, and China.

Through consortium arrangements with colleges and universities in three states, Kutztown participates in the operation of a marine science research center at Wallops Island, Virginia, which has laboratories, research equipment, and coastal research ships. Through this facility, students in marine science classes are able to gain firsthand knowledge of the ocean environment. The University's participation in the Pennsylvania Consortium for International Education provides opportunities for study abroad during the summer.

Academic Facilities

The Rohrbach Library is a modern facility that provides many attractive and functional areas that greatly enhance the learning environment for all students. Its technologies are state-of-the-art, and it is the first completely wireless building on the campus. In addition to the 500 computer connection points installed when the building was expanded in 1998, students may bring their own laptops to access the Web or use one of the 100 available for circulation. The library has both Macintosh and PC public-access computers throughout the building. The library has more than 500,000 books and bound periodicals, subscriptions to 1,308 current periodicals and newspapers, access to 14,344 electronic full-text journals, and more than 1 million microform units. Electronic access to these library materials is provided through the online catalog, Quincy, and the library's Web page, which provides students with easy access to all its resources and links them to electronic resources available throughout the world. The map collection is one of the finest in Pennsylvania, with 40,379 sheets, and includes Braille maps, city plans, and geographic and raised-relief maps. The Audiovisual Center maintains a comprehensive collection of more than 15,000 items, including microcomputer software, films, filmstrips, videocassettes, records, audiocassettes, digital cameras, projectors, and laptops that circulate to students. The Curriculum Materials Center provides preservice and inservice teachers with current teaching and learning resources and includes one of the most coveted collections of children's literature in the country. Supplementing this collection is the Dornish Collection, which features first-edition signed books from top writers in the children's literature field. Kutztown's resources are supplemented by a traditional interlibrary loan service, a rapid document delivery service, and a direct borrowing system (PALCI) that links students with the collections of more than forty academic libraries in the state of Pennsylvania.

Other resources include a modern science complex, an astronomical observatory and planetarium, a seismic observatory, the Sharadin Art Gallery, a television studio, a modern language laboratory, and a speech clinic.

All residence hall rooms are wired for Internet usage, and multistation computer labs are available in buildings across the campus.

Costs

In 2003–04, tuition was $5860 for Pennsylvania residents and $12,808 for out-of-state residents. Room and board were $6820. Books and supplies averaged $1098. Clothes and travel expenses were additional.

Financial Aid

KU believes that no student who is eligible to enroll at the University should be denied the opportunity for an education solely because of lack of funds. Financial assistance is available through grants, private and institutional scholarships, military officer training programs, on-campus part-time employment, and loans. A booklet describing financial aid opportunities may be obtained by writing to the Director of Financial Aid. Any student wishing to investigate financial aid opportunities should do so when applying for admission, as most programs have application deadlines.

Faculty

Although many professors at KU are involved in important research and are leaders in their fields, their primary interest is in the classroom. The University has more than 320 full-time instructors and a favorable 18:1 student-faculty ratio. Upon enrollment in the University, each student is assigned a faculty adviser to help plan their academic career. Many faculty members are active in campus groups as members or advisers, creating a close and friendly working relationship with students.

Student Government

All students are members of the Student Government Association and elect representatives who form the Student Government Board (SGB). Students at Kutztown are regarded as mature individuals who can be, in great measure, responsible for the control of their own environment. For that reason, the SGB exercises considerable discretion in coordinating and funding student organizations. Most University committees, including the Council of Trustees, have student members with full voting rights.

Admission Requirements

The main criteria for admission are achievement as indicated on scholastic records, standardized and aptitude tests, and recommendations. Candidates must have graduated from an approved secondary school or demonstrate equivalent preparation. Scores on either the SAT or the ACT are required and are regarded as evidence of ability to do university-level work. It is the responsibility of the applicant to request that his or her scores be forwarded to the Admissions Office. Either test should be taken no later than the fall of the senior year; sitting for these exams during the junior year is encouraged. For admission to a special curriculum, the candidate may be required to take an appropriate aptitude test or to supply additional evidence of ability to succeed in the given field. Specific requirements and instructions are included in the admission application materials.

Application and Information

The completed application and all other required materials must be mailed to the Director of Admissions. No action will be taken by the Admission Committee until all necessary steps have been completed. For additional information and application forms, students should contact:

Dr. William Stahler
Director of Admissions
Kutztown University of Pennsylvania
Kutztown, Pennsylvania 19530
E-mail: admission@kutztown.edu
World Wide Web: http://www.kutztown.edu

LABORATORY INSTITUTE OF MERCHANDISING

NEW YORK, NEW YORK

The College

Situated in a lovely town house in the center of the fashion capital of the world, the Laboratory Institute of Merchandising (LIM) has been a major force in fashion and business education for more than six decades. Its graduates can be found throughout the reaches of the industry, and its high standards of education have earned LIM accreditation from the Middle States Association of Colleges and Schools.

LIM is a highly personal college where students learn about the business of fashion with an emphasis on academic and professional study. Lifelong friends are made at LIM as well as lifelong careers. While most students come to the college directly from high school or transfer from other colleges, there are also those of nontraditional college age who enter LIM. Students come to LIM from many parts of the country and the world. The current enrollment at LIM is 400.

LIM prides itself on its placement record. Prior to graduation, the Placement Office undertakes the important task of counseling each student with regard to her or his career. The Office has had outstanding success in helping both four-year and two-year graduates obtain positions relevant to their studies. More than 90 percent of the graduates available for placement have been placed in positions related to their studies within ninety days of graduation.

The unique nature of LIM's curriculum provides students with a foundation of core courses in liberal arts and business while offering diverse and intensive hands-on preparation in the fashion industry. This affords graduates the opportunity to accept executive training, merchandising, management, marketing, and communications positions in a wide variety of areas within the fashion and business worlds.

Support services are important at LIM. In addition to academic and career advising, personal counseling is provided through the Director of Student Services' office. Because of the college's small size and the close relationships between students and staff, any faculty member or administrator, including the president, is readily accessible to help and advise all students. LIM's advisory board members, all successful fashion industry executives, serve as mentors to junior and senior students, offering additional guidance and advice.

Aside from the Student Government and the Fashion Club, other clubs are formed in accordance with student interest. Students have responsibility for *LIMLIGHT,* the college yearbook, and for fashion shows and other social and cultural events.

While most students commute, many live in apartments and student residences near the campus. LIM recommends the de Hirsch Residence as well as several other private dormitory residences in New York City for off-campus housing. These facilities, which broaden the social experiences and friendships for LIM students, are safe, convenient, and located just minutes from the college.

LIM's unique open-house program, called Student-For-a-Day, offers students and their families the opportunity to tour the college and learn not only of LIM's unique academic programs, but also of the vast array of careers found in the fashion industry. The day also includes a special presentation on visual merchandising and financial aid information on a group or individual level. Current LIM students assist in hosting the event and are available to answer questions. Lunch is provided, and, immediately following, students are invited to stay for a personal interview, which is a requirement for admissions, and sit for the LIM Competitive Scholarship exam.

Location

LIM is fortunate to be able to call New York City its campus. A whole world of fashion is at the college's doorstep and includes such famous stores as Saks Fifth Avenue, Bloomingdale's, Henri Bendel, Armani, and Ralph Lauren. Some of the most exciting buildings in the world are within walking distance—Trump Tower, Rockefeller Center, St. Patrick's Cathedral, and the Metropolitan Museum of Art, with Broadway just a few blocks away. New York City is the headquarters for the garment, cosmetics, advertising, publishing, and textile industries, all of which are essential to the fashion industry and are visited regularly by LIM students. The college incorporates all of these resources into the curriculum. For example, the Fashion Magazines course includes trips to photography studios and modeling agencies, as well as tours of magazine and advertising firms. New York City offers LIM students an unparalleled learning experience.

Majors and Degrees

LIM offers four-year programs in fashion merchandising, marketing leading, and visual merchandising to a Bachelor of Business Administration (B.B.A.) or a Bachelor of Professional Studies (B.P.S.) degree and a two-year program leading to the Associate in Applied Sciences (A.A.S.) degree. Qualified transfer students may also apply to a one-year program (ACCESS) leading to the associate degree. Students also have the option to study visual merchandising as part of their curriculum.

Academic Program

LIM offers a combination of classroom education and supervised practical fieldwork that has been designed to prepare students for executive training programs and other entry-level executive positions in various areas of the fashion industry.

The curriculum has four divisions: fashion, visual, business, and arts and communications. Classroom study is supplemented by weekly field trips into the heart of the fashion industry and guest lectures by luminaries from the fashion world.

Work experience is an integral part of an LIM student's education. During the four-year bachelor's degree program, a student will enter the fashion industry three times. Each of the first two years of study contains a five-week, 3-credit work project. During Work Project I, freshmen are placed in paid, full-time selling positions in order to learn the basics of retailing. Work Project II, sophomore year, continues the retailing experience. Qualified sophomores may choose an internship in more glamorous areas such as cosmetics, magazines, designer showrooms, and fashion forecasting companies.

The third and most significant work experience is the Senior Co-op. Students spend one semester working full-time in the fashion industry in an area relevant to their career goals and ambitions. This program earns 13 credits and is required for graduation from the bachelor's degree program. The responsibility, challenge, and fun of this semester prepare students for their next step—the business world.

Students who are applying to the associate degree program follow the first two years of the bachelor's degree program, including the required Work Projects.

To graduate, students must complete 126 credits for the bachelor's degree or 64 credits for the associate degree (33 for one-year ACCESS students), achieve a grade point average of at least 2.0, and satisfactorily complete the cooperative work assignments.

LIM accepts qualified students as transfers throughout the four years. Those with an associate degree in fashion merchandising or related field or with 60 acceptable college credits from a regionally accredited college are usually eligible for junior-year status. Transfer students must complete a minimum of 33 semester hours in addition to the co-op semester at LIM.

LIM's calendar runs on a traditional semester format, offering both fall and spring start dates. Also offered is a summer program in July for both high school and college students. The specially selected courses, such as Display Workshop, Cosmetics Marketing, and Fashion Magazines, blend academics with hands-on experience. Three college credits can be earned for any of these courses.

Off-Campus Programs

Study-abroad options are available, including study in London, Paris, Milan, Barcelona, and China.

Academic Facilities

LIM's specialized resource center contains 11,000 volumes pertaining to the liberal arts, fashion merchandising, and related fields, as well as 110 professional and academic journals. The library connects to the Internet and accesses worldwide information sources. Videocassettes and other multimedia items useful for fashion-related studies are also at students' disposal. A distinctive feature of the video collection is a major group of tapes of the Institute's guest-lecture series, an important reference source for use by students and faculty alike. Personal computers are available for use in the library and classrooms. The student-to-computer ratio is 5:1. The Learning Center offers peer-tutoring and special computer programs to supplement and reinforce other learning.

Costs

In 2003–04, tuition is $14,900. Other expenses vary, depending on residence. Students who commute spend from $550 to $1500 for transportation. In 2002–03, off-campus room and board were about $10,000. Books, supplies, and fees were about $750. Personal expenditures are about $1000 a year.

Financial Aid

LIM believes that lack of funds should not keep students from attending college. Thus, admissions decisions and financial aid are totally separate, and a request for aid has no effect on admissions. About 79 percent of LIM's students receive some form of financial aid. Institutional scholarships, Federal Pell Grants, Federal Supplemental Educational Opportunity Grants, and New York State TAP grants are all available for eligible students. In addition, LIM is qualified to certify Federal Stafford Student Loans. The Free Application for Federal Student Aid (FAFSA) should be filed by all applicants by April 1. Aid is granted on the basis of need and scholarships on the basis of need and ability. Details of the financial aid program are available on request from the Financial Aid Office.

LIM features a Merit Scholarship Program for incoming freshmen and transfer students. These scholarship monies are awarded for academic achievement in high school or college. Students can remain eligible for their scholarship throughout their stay at LIM by maintaining a GPA of 3.2 or above. LIM's Fashion Education Foundation also administers a limited number of grants other than direct institutional awards.

Faculty

LIM prides itself on its faculty members. More than a third of the teaching staff, including all members of the liberal arts faculty, have advanced degrees; all professional subject faculty members have wide business and professional experience. Many, through their business contacts, bring guests to class to share in the lectures and discussions. The student-faculty ratio is 8:1.

Each student is assigned an adviser from the faculty or administrative staff. Work-study and career guidance is given to students by the Placement Office, with conferences held before, during, and after the cooperative work assignments and prior to permanent placement interviews. Students are always welcome to discuss career options at any other time as well.

Student Government

The Student Services Office is the center of all student activities at LIM. This facility supports student government and approves other student organizations and establishes their operating budgets.

Admission Requirements

Applicants must hold a high school or equivalency (GED) diploma and submit SAT I or ACT scores. International students must achieve a TOEFL score of at least 550. Great emphasis is placed on the required personal interview, which the college prefers to conduct on campus. Transfer students' records are evaluated individually with liberal interpretation placed on course equivalencies. Transfer students may enter LIM in either semester and with any amount of credits accumulated. Students applying for junior year status must hold either an associate degree or have at least 60 acceptable semester hours of credit. Transfer students with more than 30 acceptable semester hours of credit are eligible for the one-year ACCESS program. LIM's Admissions Committee recognizes that many intangibles go into the making of a successful fashion merchandising student, and it evaluates each application individually.

Application and Information

The application should be accompanied by the $40 fee, an official high school transcript, an official college transcript (if applicable), SAT I or ACT scores, and TOEFL scores (if applicable). Letters of recommendation are encouraged. Applicants must also make an appointment for a personal interview. The college uses a rolling admission policy. Applicants are informed of the admission decision within approximately two weeks after all admission requirements have been fulfilled. Application materials may be obtained from the address below:

Karen Hamill Iglio
Director of Admissions
Laboratory Institute of Merchandising
12 East 53rd Street
New York, New York 10022-5268
Telephone: 212-752-1530
800-677-1323 (toll-free outside New York City)
Fax: 212-421-4341
E-mail: admissions@limcollege.edu
World Wide Web: http://www.limcollege.edu

LAFAYETTE COLLEGE

EASTON, PENNSYLVANIA

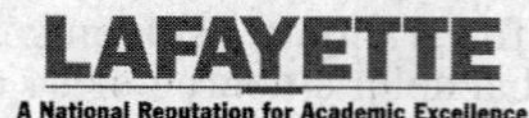

The College

Lafayette is classified as one of the nation's most academically competitive colleges and is committed to providing the best undergraduate education in the liberal arts, sciences, and engineering for men and women who can benefit most from the Lafayette experience. The current undergraduate enrollment is 2,300. Students from thirty-nine states and forty-one other countries currently attend Lafayette. They represent a wide range of interests, special talents, and aspirations. The College draws strength from the diversity of its students.

Primarily residential in nature, Lafayette guarantees on-campus housing to all students who choose to take advantage of the varied living options available to them. More than 96 percent of the students live on the 110-acre main campus in single-sex or coeducational residence halls, social residence halls, fraternities, or sororities, and another 2 percent live close to campus. An array of student organizations, cultural events, social opportunities, and varsity and intramural sports programs are available to all students.

Recent trends indicate that approximately two thirds of Lafayette graduates go on to obtain a graduate or professional degree. About 20 percent pursue full-time graduate or professional study immediately. A large and growing number obtain practical experience through employment and then undertake full-time study for an advanced degree, often with an employer's financial support. Others continue academic pursuits on a part-time basis.

Location

Lafayette is located in a picturesque setting atop a hill overlooking the Delaware and Lehigh Rivers and Easton, a progressive city of 30,000. Allentown and Bethlehem are located near Easton, and, together with the city and adjacent areas, they make up the Lehigh Valley, the third-largest metropolitan area in Pennsylvania. Various business establishments that serve the needs of students are available near the campus and in downtown Easton. Beyond Easton to the west and north are rolling farmland, beautiful countryside, and the Pocono Mountains. New York City is 70 miles east of the campus, and Philadelphia is 60 miles south.

Majors and Degrees

Lafayette awards the Bachelor of Science (B.S.) degree in the following fields: behavioral neuroscience, biochemistry, biology, chemical engineering, chemistry, civil engineering, computer science, electrical and computer engineering, geology, mathematics, mechanical engineering, physics, and psychology. The Bachelor of Arts (A.B.) degree is awarded in the following majors: American studies, anthropology and sociology, art, biochemistry, biology, chemistry, computer science, economics and business, engineering, English, French, geology, German, government and law, history, international affairs, mathematics, mathematics/economics, music, philosophy, physics, psychology, religion, Russian and East European studies, and Spanish.

In addition, Lafayette students may enroll in a five-year program leading to either a B.S. and an A.B. or two B.S. degrees.

Academic Program

Students work together one-on-one with faculty advisers to ensure the planning of a program that is both educationally sound and responsive to the student's individual interests and needs. Each academic department specifies core curriculum requirements for its majors. All A.B. candidates must satisfy a course-distribution requirement, which can be met through advanced placement, transfer credit, or a broad selection of college course work.

In combining arts, sciences, and engineering in one undergraduate institution and in having one faculty with a unified educational approach, Lafayette has a distinctive capability to exercise a broadening influence on all students. Approximately one half of Lafayette's students major in the humanities and social sciences, while the other half specialize in the natural sciences and engineering. Flexible curricular arrangements enable students to defer their final decision on a major until the end of the sophomore year.

In addition to the formal majors offered at the College, interdisciplinary minor programs are offered in ten areas: Black studies, classical civilization, East Asian studies, environmental science, ethical studies, health care and society, Jewish studies, Latin American and Caribbean studies, technology studies, and women's studies. A number of internships can also be arranged through the various academic departments.

Students planning to continue their study in a professional school are assisted by faculty preprofessional advisers in designing a program of study that provides an appropriate foundation for advanced work.

Army ROTC programs are offered for both men and women.

The College observes a two-semester academic calendar. An optional January interim session is offered. Classes are available on campus as well as off campus, including study overseas.

Off-Campus Programs

Students are encouraged to spend a semester or a year in a study-abroad program sponsored by the College or another institution. The College has recently established affiliations with four universities overseas. Groups of students led by Lafayette professors attend Vesalius College at the University of Brussels, l'Université de Bourgogne in Dijon, Middlesex University in London, the University College in London, and the Sweet Briar junior-year-abroad program in Paris.

Students also travel widely during the Lafayette interim session. Two faculty members have accompanied each group of students in their pursuit of knowledge in China, England, Germany, France, Israel, and Russia as well as in Eastern Europe and sub-Saharan Africa.

Lafayette is a member of the American Collegiate Consortium, an association of some sixty American colleges and universities that operates a prestigious study-abroad program at the Universities of Voronezh and Yaroslavl in Russia. Students may take a full semester of courses in the fields of their choice alongside Russian students.

Academic Facilities

Skillman Library, a building that has won awards for its architectural design and functional effectiveness, contains more than 525,000 hardbound volumes, as well as numerous pamphlets, periodicals, electronic databases, CD-ROMs, electronic journals, microfilms, audiovisual materials, and special collections. The library operates on an open-stack policy. Cooperative arrangements with other Lehigh Valley colleges make more than 1 million books available to Lafayette students.

Ten additional classroom, laboratory, and departmental buildings house specialized libraries, modern scientific and engineering equipment, studio rooms, galleries, classrooms, seminar rooms, and faculty offices.

The College's rapidly growing Academic Computing Services facilities include a campuswide network with connections in every residence hall, office, and classroom, and to more than 600 public microcomputers available for student use (many of them for 24 hours a day). At no charge, students can have access to electronic mail and the Internet and to general and course software from the computing sites or from their rooms.

Costs

The comprehensive fee for 2003–04 was $27,178. Additional costs included a room fee of $4740, a board fee of $3678, and an estimated $1625 for books, travel, and miscellaneous expenses.

Financial Aid

Substantial amounts of financial aid are available for students with demonstrated need. Approximately 60 percent of the student body receives financial aid: more than 40 percent of Lafayette's students receive financial aid directly from the College in the form of grants, loans, and work opportunities, and almost 20 percent are assisted by government grants or other awards not funded by the College. Detailed information regarding financial assistance is available from the Office of Student Financial Aid, Lafayette College, Easton, Pennsylvania 18042-1777 (telephone: 610-330-5055). Each year, through the Marquis Scholars Program, Lafayette offers merit scholarships to 60 entering first-year students who have demonstrated academic excellence. Each recipient is awarded a minimum of $12,500 each year with a scholarship to full need each year if need exceeds $12,500. In addition, 32 entering freshmen receive $7500 Trustee Scholarships.

Faculty

One hundred percent of the College's 186 faculty members hold the doctoral degree or the terminal degree in their fields. Many have earned wide recognition for their research and scholarship or have won awards for superior teaching. Some hold faculty chairs endowed to attract or retain professors of exceptional ability. Students benefit from a student-faculty ratio of about 11:1 and from the fact that all faculty members—full professors and heads of departments as well as junior faculty members—teach classes and advise students on an individual basis.

Student Government

Traditionally, students have contributed to major policy decisions at Lafayette. Student Government is responsible for formulating student activity policy, distributing funds to student organizations, and maintaining liaison with the Board of Trustees, the faculty, and the administration. Voting student members sit on four trustee committees and on almost all faculty committees, and student representatives participate in faculty meetings.

Admission Requirements

Lafayette admits students without regard to sex, race, religion, or physical handicap. All Lafayette students pursued a strong college-preparatory program of studies, and approximately one half graduated in the top tenth of their secondary school class. Many held leadership positions in school or community organizations or on sports teams. They are encouraged—and expected—to assume major responsibility for all aspects of their lives at the College and to continue to develop those attributes and talents on which their admission was based.

Lafayette requires submission of SAT I or ACT scores. Three SAT II Subject Tests, one of them Writing, are recommended. It is also recommended that B.S. degree candidates take Subject Tests in Mathematics and Physics or Chemistry in addition to the Writing Subject Test. Students are strongly encouraged to visit the Lafayette campus for an admission interview and a student-guided tour.

Application and Information

Applications for admission should be filed by January 1. Candidates are notified of the admission decision around April 1. If a student requests consideration of their application under the Early Decision Plan, a decision is normally made within thirty days of receipt of completed application forms. February 15 is the deadline to request early decision. Applicants accepted under early decision are obligated to enroll at Lafayette unless their financial needs are not met.

Office of Admissions
Lafayette College
Easton, Pennsylvania 18042-1770
Telephone: 610-330-5100
World Wide Web: http://www.lafayette.edu

A view of Lafayette College's campus.

LAGRANGE COLLEGE

LAGRANGE, GEORGIA

The College

Founded in 1831, LaGrange College is the oldest private college in Georgia. A four-year liberal arts and sciences institution affiliated with the United Methodist Church, LaGrange holds fast to its longstanding mission of challenging students' minds, inspiring their souls—and changing their lives. The College is ranked in the top tier and as one of ten "best values" among Southern Comprehensive schools by *U.S. News & World Report* and has an enrollment of more than 1,000 men and women. LaGrange College students come from thirteen states and thirteen countries, and they enjoy a student-faculty ratio of 11:1. Fully accredited, LaGrange provides a challenging and supportive academic environment. The Bachelor of Arts (B.A.), Bachelor Science (B.S.), Bachelor of Science in Nursing (B.S.N.), and Bachelor of Music (B.M.) degrees are offered in addition to the Master of Education (M.Ed.) degree and the Master of Arts in Teaching (M.A.T.) degree.

LaGrange College students can start their own special-interest group or join one of more than forty clubs and organizations, including student government, honor societies, service clubs, sororities and fraternities, performance groups, religious organizations, and student publications. Students also can get involved in service efforts, such as building homes through Habitat for Humanity, or traveling to Costa Rica or the Czech Republic on a mission trip. One of the more unique activities LaGrange students enjoy is "dive-in movies," in which popular films are beamed onto a 35-foot screen by the College's indoor pool, and students watch while drifting about in floats, inner tubes, and rafts. Other on-campus activities include intramural sports tournaments, theater performances, karaoke and open mike competitions, art exhibitions, "Vegas on the Hill," and Greek Week. Off-campus excursions are planned each semester, such as snow-skiing trips to North Carolina or visits to Atlanta Braves games.

LaGrange College's athletic facilities include an indoor competition swimming pool, an outdoor recreational swimming pool, a fully equipped fitness center, a recently completed $2-million baseball facility, two gymnasiums, two lighted softball fields, a lighted soccer field, and a training facility. Intercollegiate athletic teams for men include baseball, basketball, cross-country, golf, soccer, swimming, and tennis. Women's teams include basketball, cross-country, fast-pitch softball, soccer, swimming, tennis, and volleyball.

More than 60 percent of students live on campus in residence halls that include apartment-style facilities. Meal plan options are offered for the College's dining hall and student grill.

Location

The College is located in a residential section of LaGrange, Georgia, which has a population of 30,000 and was named Intelligent City of the Year by the World Teleport Association for its telecommunication infrastructure and Internet initiatives. LaGrange is home to Fortune 500 companies, unique shops and restaurants, and historic landmarks. Nearby are the world-famous Callaway Gardens, the Warm Springs Foundation, and Franklin D. Roosevelt's Little White House. The West Point Dam on the Chattahoochee River provides one of the largest lakes in the region; waterfronts and a marina are within the city limits of LaGrange. The city is located 65 miles southwest of Atlanta and 55 miles southwest of Hartsfield–Jackson Atlanta International Airport.

Majors and Degrees

LaGrange College offers the Bachelor of Arts (B.A.) degree in art and design, biochemistry, biology, business, chemistry, computer science, early childhood education, English, history, human development, human services, interdisciplinary studies, mathematics, middle grades education, music, political science, psychology, religion, Spanish, and theater arts, with concentrations available in church leadership, coaching, French, Latin American studies, philosophy, sociology, and women's studies. Students interested in secondary education careers first pursue a bachelor's degree in their preferred subject area (including art and music) and then enroll in the College's one-year Master of Arts in Teaching program. The Bachelor of Science (B.S.) degree is available in accountancy, business management, chemistry, computer science, and mathematics. The Bachelor of Music degree is available, with concentrations in creative music technologies, performance, and church music. The Bachelor of Science in Nursing (B.S.N.) degree also is offered. Preprofessional programs of study, as preparation for graduate and professional study, are available in dentistry, engineering, journalism, law, medicine and allied fields, optometry, pharmacy, physical therapy, theology/seminary, and veterinary medicine.

Academic Programs

Each program of study contains a substantial interdisciplinary core component. Providing a background in the natural and social sciences, arts, and humanities, the core helps students see how subjects interrelate, while developing the research and problem-solving skills employers and graduate schools seek most. A minimum of 108 semester hours is required to earn a bachelor's degree; 48 semester hours of liberal studies core courses are required for all bachelor's degrees. Most majors require an additional 36 to 56 semester hours of credit beyond the liberal studies curriculum. Students may be eligible for credit and/or exemption in certain areas through Advanced Placement (AP) tests or the College-Level Examination Program (CLEP).

The College operates on the 4-1-4 academic calendar, a schedule which allows for a one-month January interim term between fall and spring semesters. During January term, students focus on unique subject areas or participate in classes incorporating domestic and international travel.

Academic Facilities

The LaGrange College Library contains more than 135,000 volumes of books and other media. Print sources for 500 journal titles are provided through current subscriptions. GALILEO provides access to more than 75 databases, including several in full text (e.g., LexisNexis). JSTOR supplies access to more than 100 scholarly journals in electronic format. In addition, the library subscribes to subject-specific databases for education, religion, and music.

The campuswide fiber-optic network provides computer access in every dorm room, in all eleven computer labs on campus, and in designated classrooms where network connections are available by every seat. Students are able to access the College library's online catalog, the Internet and World Wide Web, e-mail, and other resources from any of these locations. Students majoring in biochemistry conduct research in the College's DNA fingerprinting lab, which was established with a National Science Foundation grant.

The Lamar Dodd Art Center is a premier facility for the study of art and design and includes a gallery for the College's permanent collection, which includes works by Picasso, Andy Warhol, Ansel Adams, and other famous artists. Price Theater provides a state-of-the-art proscenium theater with seating for 280, thirty-six fly lines, electronic sound and lighting systems, computer-design capabilities, a full costume and scenery shop, and an actors' lounge. The College's music facilities, which are home to the creative music technologies program, include a fully-equipped MIDI recording studio, MIDI workstations, isolation rooms, and an electroacoustic multimedia recital hall, while the entertainment/music library is home to many original Hollywood music scores.

A prime music performance space is now being completed through a multimillion-dollar renovation of the College's Callaway Auditorium.

Costs

Tuition and fees for 2003–04 were $14,482, and room and board were $6018 for the year, bringing the total cost to $20,500. Books and supplies averaged $1000 for the year.

Financial Aid

As a private college, LaGrange is committed to helping meet the difference between the funds any student has available and the cost of attending LaGrange College. More than 80 percent of LaGrange students receive some combination of financial awards, with more than $12 million awarded annually. These awards may include grants, loans, scholarships, and employment opportunities. Federal financial aid and institutional funds are available to all students who qualify. The state of Georgia provides additional funding for Georgia residents. All Georgia residents who enroll as full-time students receive the Georgia Tuition Equalization Grant in the amount of $909 per year. The HOPE Scholarship, which totals $3000 per year, is awarded to all Georgia residents who have graduated from high school with a B average and who enter as freshmen. Georgia residents who do not qualify for the HOPE Scholarship as freshmen may be able to obtain the HOPE Scholarship by earning a 3.0 cumulative grade point average. Academic scholarships that range from $1000 to full scholarships are also awarded. All accepted students are considered for scholarships; a separate application is not required. In 2003–04, all financial aid applicants were awarded financial aid.

Faculty

All courses at LaGrange College are taught by professors. Full-time faculty members number 66, 80 percent of whom hold the highest degrees in their fields; 26 are part-time. Faculty members are rewarded for teaching and are not required to conduct research, although many are involved in research efforts. All faculty members teach undergraduates and serve as academic advisers. The student-faculty ratio is 11:1.

Student Government

The LaGrange College Student Government Association (SGA) exists to serve as a medium for student expression, to coordinate campus activities, and to govern within the parameters granted by the president. Student publications are supported by the SGA, including the newspaper and literary magazine. The SGA oversees more than forty clubs and organizations in all, including three national fraternities and three national sororities, as well as service clubs, religious organizations, honorary organizations, and departmental/special-interest groups.

Admission Requirements

LaGrange College seeks to admit any qualified student who desires to study on the LaGrange campus. Preference is given to applicants who have had strong preparation in high school. A typical matriculant should have completed a minimum of 16 units of college-preparatory courses at an approved high school, including 4 units of English, 4 units of college-preparatory mathematics, 3 units of social science, 3 units of laboratory science, and 2 units of a foreign language.

Freshman applicants should submit a completed application for admission, a $20 nonrefundable application fee, official high school transcripts, and official SAT I or ACT scores. Transfer students should submit an application, the application fee, and official transcripts of all college work attempted. Transfer students who have earned fewer than 30 semester hours of credit must also submit official high school transcripts. International and transfer students are encouraged to apply.

Application and Information

Applications for admission are evaluated on a rolling basis and should be submitted at least one month prior to the beginning of the semester in which entrance is desired. Applicants can expect to receive notification within two to three weeks of the date that all documents are submitted. Weekday campus visits are encouraged, and appointments can be arranged by contacting the Admission Office. For additional information, students should contact:

Office of Admission
LaGrange College
601 Broad Street
LaGrange, Georgia 30240
Telephone: 706-880-8005
800-593-2885 (toll-free)
Fax: 706-880-8010
E-mail: admission@lagrange.edu
World Wide Web: http://www.lagrange.edu

The William and Evelyn Banks Library overlooks the College's main entrance.

LAGUNA COLLEGE OF ART & DESIGN

LAGUNA BEACH, CALIFORNIA

The College

The mission of Laguna College of Art & Design is to prepare women and men for careers as creative artists and designers in a culturally and ethnically diverse world through a curriculum that emphasizes the acquisition of skills based on observation, representation, and concept development. The College is committed to offering its curriculum through accredited degree programs that imaginatively combine studio work with academic studies and to sharing its resources with the broader community through continuing education and exhibition programs.

The spectacular seacoast of Laguna Beach has been a magnet for artists since the nineteenth century, and the city's famed beach, canyon, and luminous natural light still attract the attention of artists and visitors from all over the world, lending the area a truly cosmopolitan air.

Laguna College was founded as the Laguna Beach School of Art in 1961 under the auspices of the Laguna Beach Festival of Arts and the Laguna Beach Art Association (Laguna Art Museum) and was financed by a grant from the Festival of Arts and private contributions. The school opened on the festival's grounds in 1962 with the mission of providing the region with art education of the highest quality. In 1977, the school relocated to its present site in Laguna Canyon and was accredited by the National Association of Schools of Art and Design in 1981. In 1997, Laguna College was accredited by the Western Association of Schools and Colleges (WASC), bringing to it an even higher level of national recognition and respect. As of July 1, 2002, the College changed its name from The Art Institute of Southern California to Laguna College of Art & Design. It is the only four-year, fully accredited professional college of art and design in Orange County, and one of only four in southern California.

In fall 2004, Laguna College plans to introduce the Master of Fine Arts (M.F.A.) in drawing and painting.

Location

Laguna College of Art & Design occupies several acres in Laguna Canyon, approximately 1 mile from the Pacific Ocean. The contemporary wood architecture of the campus buildings blends with a mature grove of sycamore trees and the rugged hillsides. The temperate climate encourages swimming, surfing, and other year-round water activities, and there is a full range of outdoor recreation within an easy distance, including mountain skiing, desert and canyon hiking, biking, and more. Orange County, one of California's fastest-growing areas, offers a remarkable array of arts and entertainment activities.

The charming city of Laguna Beach itself is noted for its fine restaurants, its scores of artist's galleries and shops, the acclaimed Laguna Playhouse, and the Laguna Art Museum. Each summer, the famous Laguna Beach Festival of Arts and Pageant of the Masters draw people from across the nation and around the world, celebrating the unique artistic history of the city.

Within an easy drive are the Orange County Art Museum, the Bowers Museum of Cultural Art, and many other museums. The Orange County Performing Arts Center presents the world's finest ballet companies, touring Broadway shows, jazz, classical music, opera, and more, and South Coast Repertory presents award-winning plays. There are opportunities to attend numerous professional sports events in the area and many opportunities to participate in amateur sports. Libraries and bookstores abound in nearly every community, and Orange County has the largest population of home computer enthusiasts in the nation.

Within an hour's drive to the north is the excitement of Los Angeles, with the countless resources this cultural capital has to offer, such as the J. Paul Getty Center for the Arts, the Los Angeles County Museum, the Museum of Contemporary Art, the Norton Simon Museum, the Huntington Library and Gallery, the Los Angeles Music Center, and many more. Approximately an hour to the south is the beautiful city of San Diego, home of the San Diego Museum of Art, the La Jolla Museum of Contemporary Art, La Jolla Playhouse, and more. Just further south is Mexico, with its rich cultural and artistic tradition.

Majors and Degrees

Laguna College of Art & Design offers the Bachelor of Fine Arts (B.F.A.) degree in fine arts (drawing and painting) and in visual communication (feature animation, graphic design/multimedia, and illustration), with disciplines in printmaking and sculpture. Students can minor in any of the majors.

Academic Program

Laguna College gives the student the training and background necessary to develop the skills, knowledge, techniques, and critical thinking required of an artist or designer. Although studio work is the core of the curriculum, Laguna College believes that studies in the liberal arts are essential to the development of each artist and seeks to provide a program that offers new fields and challenges to the creative mind.

The College realizes that proper training and experience in art should include knowledge of contemporary theory, criticism, and the twentieth-century tradition. In order to further broaden students' knowledge, the College sponsors visits and lectures by artists, art historians, scholars, and art critics. These lectures and critiques are scheduled throughout the year and are also open to the public. A visiting artist residency program offers students an opportunity to work with an artist in a particular field, while the visiting art teacher lectures and exhibits his or her work in the galleries.

Academic Facilities

Laguna College's campus includes sixteen studios and an administration building. The studios are equipped for drawing, painting, illustration, graphic design, sculpture, computer art, and printmaking. The M. Paul Stiker Administration Building houses all staff offices, the Salyer Library, the Ettinger Gallery, and the Reynolds Gallery. Laguna College represents the work of accomplished artists and scholars in exhibitions in the Ettinger and Reynolds Galleries. Throughout the year, the College also sponsors public receptions and artist slide lectures to broaden knowledge of current developments in the arts. A full schedule of exhibitions is available at the Administration Building.

Costs

Laguna College is proud to offer the most affordable tuition of any of the four-year art and design schools in southern

California. Tuition for the academic year 2003–04 was $15,700. This included all texts and fees. Art supplies average $1800 annually. Room and board cost approximately $5800. The College does not offer dormitory facilities, but the Student Housing Coordinator assists students in locating housing. Students should allow $600 for transportation and $1400 for personal expenses.

Financial Aid

Laguna College offers a wide range of financial aid to its students. Federal aid to eligible students includes Federal Pell Grants, Federal Supplemental Educational Opportunity Grants, Federal Work-Study, Federal Stafford Loans (subsidized and unsubsidized), and Federal PLUS Loans. California state grants, which consist of Cal Grant A and Cal Grant B, have a deadline of March 2 each year for the following fall semester. Students must be residents of California to receive a Cal Grant. The College offers merit scholarships that are privately funded. For current information on financial aid, students should contact the Financial Aid Office at 949-376-6000 Ext. 223.

Faculty

The faculty is composed of professional artists and designers, art historians, scholars, and educators with distinguished professional and teaching experience. Classes are small, with an average student-faculty ratio of 10:1. These small classes enable students to receive personal attention from their instructors and to work actively with them. The majority of the members of the fine arts faculty have their own studios and exhibit their works regionally, nationally, and internationally. The feature animation, graphic design/multimedia, and illustration faculty is composed of professionals, each working in his or her area of expertise.

Student Government

Students have an informal organization for the purpose of promoting social activities, student exhibitions, and art sales. Students meet, as necessary, to plan events, coordinate field trips, and relay concerns to the faculty and staff. Students may request to speak at faculty meetings by submitting a written request to the Faculty Senate. One student is selected each year to serve as the student representative to the Board of Trustees.

Admission Requirements

Students who are interested in applying must complete and submit an application to the Office of Admissions, attaching a nonrefundable $45 application fee. Those seeking admission to the B.F.A. program must be high school graduates or the equivalent. Applicants must also present official sealed transcripts from their high school of graduation and colleges attended, plus one letter of recommendation and a two-page personal statement of intent (typed essay). Applicants are also required to submit a twelve-piece portfolio that must include a minimum of six observational drawings.

Transfer students who wish to apply credits to the B.F.A. program must request each institution formerly attended to forward an official transcript to the Office of Admissions. A transfer credit evaluation is carried out to determine which credits are accepted. Liberal arts course work completed with a grade of C or better may be accepted; a portfolio must be presented for transfer of studio credits.

The Admissions Committee reviews the qualifications of each student on the basis of a balanced picture that includes academic achievements, creative ability, and artistic and professional goals for the purpose of evaluating advising and placement. Based on the committee's decision, a written notification of acceptance or nonacceptance is mailed by the Vice President of Enrollment within three weeks of application. Students admitted to the program can expect to experience regular faculty review and evaluation of work completed in class as the measure of their progress.

Laguna College of Art & Design administers its programs without discrimination on the basis of race, creed, color, gender, national origin, or handicap.

Application and Information

A catalog introducing Laguna College and its programs is available upon request. For more information and an application form, students should contact:

Office of Admissions
Laguna College of Art & Design
2222 Laguna Canyon Road
Laguna Canyon, California 92651
Telephone: 949-376-6000
800-255-0762 (toll-free)
Fax: 949-376-6009
World Wide Web: http://www.lagunacollege.edu

Laguna College is located in the historic seashore artist colony of Laguna Beach.

LAKE ERIE COLLEGE

PAINESVILLE, OHIO

The College

Lake Erie College, founded in 1856, is an independent, coeducational institution located in the city of Painesville in northeastern Ohio. Instruction is provided at the baccalaureate and master's degree levels to academically qualified individuals. Programs of study, founded in the liberal arts, are offered in the arts and sciences, humanities, equestrian studies, teacher education, and business administration. Lake Erie College accommodates both residential and commuting students of various ages on a full-time and part-time basis. Local, national, and international students benefit from the College's traditional emphasis on intercultural programs.

Intercollegiate sports play an important role in student life. Lake Erie College athletics are exciting for competitors and spectators alike. The College is a member of the Allegheny Mountain Collegiate Conference and competes at the NCAA Division III level. Men compete in baseball, basketball, cross-country, golf, and soccer. Women compete in basketball, cross-country, soccer, softball, and volleyball. The College also sponsors an intercollegiate equestrian team.

Location

Lake Erie College is located on 48 acres of naturally wooded land in Painesville, Ohio. Painesville is an attractive community in northeast Ohio, which is 28 miles east of Cleveland and 3 miles south of Lake Erie. The Cleveland Museum of Art; Playhouse Square; Lake Metro Parks; Holden Arboretum; professional baseball, football, and basketball teams; theaters; comedy clubs; and other recreational attractions are located nearby. The area is served by two national highways: U.S. 90 and 20, and state routes 2 and 44.

Majors and Degrees

At the undergraduate level, Lake Erie College offers the Bachelor of Arts, Bachelor of Science, and Bachelor of Fine Arts degrees. Majors are available in accounting, arts management, biology (predentistry, premedicine, and pre–veterinary science), business administration, chemistry, communications, criminal justice, dance, early childhood education, middle childhood education, secondary education, English, environmental science, equestrian facilities management, equestrian teacher/trainer, fine arts (multidisciplinary), fine arts (with concentration), international business, legal studies, mathematics, modern foreign language, multinational studies, music, psychology, and social sciences (history, prelaw, sociology). Students may also pursue an individualized academic major.

Academic Programs

The philosophy of Lake Erie College is that the well-being and enrichment of society are dependent upon the abilities of individuals to think both creatively and critically, to make reasoned and informed decisions, and to assume responsibility for their personal actions and continuing education.

Education at Lake Erie College promotes the knowledge and understanding of various cultures and the growth of personal and social responsibilities associated with the acquisition of knowledge and the mastery of skills. The liberal arts and career-oriented disciplines the College offers are not mutually exclusive bodies of knowledge, and the best education is one that promotes the integration of both types of disciplines. The process of education is as vital as the subject matter communicated. It is through intercultural awareness, directed practice in discerning relationships among disciplines, and making informed judgments that a person becomes educated and acquires the flexibility necessary to meet the rapidly changing demands of the marketplace and the world.

One hundred twenty-eight semester hours are required to earn a bachelor's degree.

Off-Campus Programs

Through the College's Academic Program Abroad, students live and study with a native family in the Netherlands, France, England, Austria, Italy, or Spain while earning Lake Erie College credits. This affords students the opportunity to study within the special educational experience that is part of living in another country, speaking another language, and learning another culture. Academic experiences abroad range in duration from two weeks to an entire semester, depending upon individual schedules. Following the fourth semester of full-time study, students are offered a free study trip abroad.

Academic Facilities

The scenic and peaceful Lake Erie College campus provides the ideal setting to pursue an academic career; it reflects the College's commitment to provide a high-quality education in a personalized environment. The focus of the campus is College Hall, completed in 1859. College Hall is a center for classroom and office activities.

Lake Erie College features three newly renovated residence halls and one new residence hall that opened in November 2001. Every room is equipped with high-speed Internet access, individual phone lines, cable access, and furniture (desks, beds, and chairs). The College's residence halls have laundry facilities, computer labs, community lounges, and kitchens. Since many students bring their cars to campus, convenient parking is available near each residence hall.

The Arthur S. Holden Center houses a telecommunications center, a computer center, computerized classrooms, conference rooms, and faculty offices. In the Holden Center, students will also find the bookstore, Storm Café, a dining center, student life offices, student government offices, Lake Erie College security, and student mailboxes. Since its dedication in 1997, this facility has been Lake Erie College's premier student center.

The Fine Arts Building houses the 200-seat C. K. Rickel Theatre, the B. K. Smith Gallery, art studios, the dance studio, photography laboratories, faculty offices, and classrooms. The Austin Hall of Science includes laboratories, classrooms, and offices. The Jane White Lincoln Center for Physical Education and Recreation includes a gymnasium with pro-turf flooring, a conditioning center with a Universal weight room, a free weight room, first aid training rooms, classrooms, and offices. Adjacent to the center is Hitchcock Field, with a field for soccer and softball. Kilcawley Hall houses the President's Office and the Institutional Advancement offices.

The Lincoln Library/Learning Resource Center maintains a collection of more than 90,000 books and subscribes to more than 750 periodicals. Audiovisual services, educational media and media production centers, two computerized indexes, and three computer laboratories are also located in the library.

The 150-acre George M. Humphrey Equestrian Center is located just 5 miles from the campus. Served daily by the College van, the equestrian center includes an indoor arena of 100 feet by 225 feet, with seating for 1,000 spectators, and an indoor warm-up area of 75 feet by 130 feet. The Clarence T. Reinberger Equestrian Work Center has an additional indoor ring of 80 feet by 96 feet. Other facilities include the Equine Stud Farm Laboratory and breeding facilities as well as stabling for 100 horses. The equestrian center also features outdoor riding rings and a hunt field.

Costs

Tuition per semester for 2003–04 was $8440 for full-time students and $460 per credit hour for part-time students. The room charges per semester are $1560 for a double room and $2120 for a single occupancy. Semester costs for board are $1250 for ten meals per week, $1355 for fourteen meals per week, and $1460 for nineteen meals per week. Semester fees (student activity, library, and computer) are $420 for full-time students and $25 per credit hour for part-time students. At the established sites, the fees for the Academic Program Abroad are comparable to a semester's costs on the Lake Erie campus.

Financial Aid

Lake Erie College offers a number of competitive scholarship programs that are not based on need. Other forms of financial aid, all based on need, include scholarships, grants (federal, state, local, and College), loans (federal and state), and work-study programs; the application deadline for need-based aid is March 1. Approximately 85 percent of full-time students receive financial aid. Estimates of the expected family contribution are available from the Office of Financial Aid. To apply for aid, students must submit a Free Application for Federal Student Aid (FAFSA), Form 1040, and other documents required by Lake Erie. The deadline for priority consideration is March 1.

Faculty

The Lake Erie College faculty members are well qualified, capable, and eager to teach. Eighty-five percent of the faculty members hold doctoral or terminal degrees in their field. Many bring firsthand experiences in their disciplines to the classroom. They remain active in their respective academic disciplines and are able to provide students with information on current research, new trends, and career opportunities. Class size ranges from 4 to 30 students, and the student-faculty ratio is 15:1.

Student Government

Students at Lake Erie College play an important role in decision making in many aspects of campus life. Students retain membership on most faculty and administrative committees. The Student Government Association provides a means for students to govern their nonacademic lives and to maintain channels of communication with the faculty and administration.

Admission Requirements

A composite evaluation is made of each applicant, with special attention given to high school credentials. A college-preparatory background is necessary and should include 4 units of English, 3 units of mathematics, 3 units of science, 3 units of social studies, and 6 additional units from other academic areas; 2 units of foreign language are advised. Scores on the ACT or SAT I are required. Lake Erie College welcomes students of all races and backgrounds.

Application and Information

Lake Erie College operates with a rolling admission policy; however, application by March 1 is necessary for scholarship and/or financial aid candidates. Applicants are notified of the admission decision within two weeks of receipt of all materials.

For further information, students may contact:

Office of Admissions
Lake Erie College
391 West Washington Street
Painesville, Ohio 44077
Telephone: 440-375-7050
800-916-0904 (toll-free)
E-mail: lecadmit@lec.edu
World Wide Web: http://www.lec.edu

The Arthur S. Holden Center, dedicated in 1997, houses a telecommunications center, a computer center, computerized classrooms, conference rooms, faculty offices, student life offices, a dining center, student government offices, a bookstore, and study areas.

LAKE FOREST COLLEGE

LAKE FOREST, ILLINOIS

The College

Lake Forest College is a coeducational undergraduate community of 1,300 students that celebrates the personal growth accompanying the quest for excellence. Founded in 1857, Lake Forest provides a secure residential campus of great beauty and enriches its curriculum with the vibrant resources of Chicago.

A national liberal arts college, Lake Forest prides itself on diversity, with students representing forty-five states and forty-three other countries. International students and members of minority groups comprise more than 25 percent of the Lake Forest student body. With 86 percent of its students living in residence halls, Lake Forest fosters interaction and shared experiences among its diverse population. Lake Forest offers each student the opportunity to develop a variety of life skills.

More than seventy student organizations, groups, and clubs provide the campus with a wide range of extracurricular opportunities. These enriching experiences work in unison with Lake Forest's commitment to high standards of academic excellence and integrity. Ultimately, Lake Forest endeavors to help individuals develop lives of leadership, service, and personal fulfillment.

Location

Thirty miles north of Chicago on Lake Michigan's famed North Shore, Lake Forest College is situated on 107 scenic wooded acres in a residential community. The town of Lake Forest is 25 miles from O'Hare International Airport. Students are within an easy commute to Chicago, a world-class city of nearly 3 million people and a treasure of cultural locations. Chicago has become an extension of the campus. Internships, independent study, research projects, and field trips are readily available through Chicago's vast resources.

Majors and Degrees

Lake Forest College awards the Bachelor of Arts (B.A.) degree in nineteen departments and eight interdisciplinary majors spanning more than 500 courses. Departmental majors are art, biology, business, chemistry, communications, computer science, economics, education (in conjunction with another major), English, French, history, mathematics, music, philosophy, physics, politics, psychology, sociology and anthropology, and Spanish. The interdisciplinary majors are American studies, area studies, Asian studies (including beginning Chinese and Japanese languages), environmental studies, international relations, and Latin American studies. Course work is also available in religion and theater.

Students may create their own majors through the independent scholar program, which enables qualified and motivated students to design and pursue individual degree programs that focus on particular topics or themes rather than on single academic disciplines.

In addition, the College also offers minors. Students can declare a minor in those departmental and nondepartmental programs that have a major, as well as in religion, theater, African-American studies, French civilization, metropolitan studies, and women's gender studies. A minor requires at least four courses.

Lake Forest offers a cooperative degree (3-2) program with the Sever School of Engineering of Washington University (St. Louis). Students may receive a Bachelor of Arts degree from Lake Forest and a Bachelor of Science degree from Washington University.

Academic Program

Lake Forest College bases its academic calendar on two 15-week semesters, from late August through mid-December and from mid-January through early May. The curriculum establishes an integrated framework for the general education of undergraduate students across four years of study. The curriculum includes general education requirements, which ensure that students receive educational breadth as well as depth while allowing considerable latitude in designing individual programs of study. Also included are requirements for writing and cultural diversity. Students are expected to pass thirty-two courses, fulfill the general education requirements, and complete the requirements of a major.

Off-Campus Programs

In addition to the Internship Program, Lake Forest College provides students with a wide variety of opportunities for off-campus study, both domestic and international. Semester-long options in the United States include the Chicago Semester in the Arts, the Oak Ridge Science Semester, the Urban Studies Program, the Urban Education Program, the Newberry Library Program, and the Washington Semester Program at American University.

There are many options for international study, such as Lake Forest's own international internship programs in Paris and in Santiago (Chile), as well as the Ancient Mediterranean Civilizations Program in Greece and Turkey and the Marine Biology Program in the Bahamas. As a member of the Associated Colleges of the Midwest, Lake Forest also offers programs in such countries as Costa Rica, the Czech Republic, England, India, Italy, Japan, Russia, Tanzania, and Zimbabwe.

Academic Facilities

In fall 2004, Lake Forest College is scheduled to open the doors of a new, twenty-first century library and information technology center. An $18-million expansion and renovation project, the new facility will incorporate the latest concepts, ideas, and technological innovations pertaining to teaching and learning, while providing a comfortable environment for collaboration, including a 24-hour cyber café.

Currently, the Donnelley Library contains more than 300,000 books and government documents and 900 current periodical subscriptions. In addition, the library provides online access to articles from several thousand electronic periodical titles. The library features a strong literacy program where students can gain proficiency with a wide variety of information resources. Lake Forest students and faculty members have online access to the holdings of forty-five academic libraries statewide, and can borrow books online from any of those libraries. The library's Special Collections Unit includes the College Archives and houses rare books and manuscripts.

Information technology services works closely with library staff members to support the information and technology needs of the campus. There are more than 120 public-access computers available for student use in computing labs on campus. The Technology Resource Center, equipped with high-end computing hardware and software, is available for students and faculty members. All residence hall rooms, faculty offices, laboratories, and classrooms, are wired from connections to the College's fiber-optic network. From their residence hall rooms, students have full access to the Internet and all networked campus services. All students receive e-mail accounts and accounts on a College Web server.

Among the fifty-five buildings on campus is the Dixon Science Research Center, designed for student-faculty research. The modern three-story, 7,500-square-foot facility contains thirteen laboratories and two animal holding facilities. State-of-the-art equipment includes a nuclear magnetic resonance spectrometer with a 400-megahertz superconductivity magnet and an electron microscope.

Costs

Comprehensive fees for 2003–04 are $30,170: tuition and fees, $24,406, and room and board, $5764.

Financial Aid

Lake Forest College supports a comprehensive financial aid program. About 85 percent of the students receive need- and merit-based assistance. More than $14 million is awarded annually in Lake Forest College grant and scholarship assistance, with the average aid package totaling $20,650.

The College recognizes distinguished academic performance through the Trustee and Presidential Scholarship Competition. The Deerpath Scholarship Program honors achievement and talent in academics, art, foreign language, leadership, music, science, theater, and writing.

Faculty

At the core of the College stands its distinguished faculty of excellent teachers and accomplished scholars. The College seeks and retains faculty members principally because they enjoy and excel at teaching undergraduates. Faculty members, not graduate assistants, teach the College's courses and provide academic advising. A student-faculty ratio of 12:1 gives students easy access to their teachers, while providing opportunities for informed counsel about individual programs of study.

The faculty's tradition of teaching excellence is matched and supported by its achievement in scholarly research. More than 98 percent hold a Ph.D. or its equivalent. Faculty members have won national teaching awards and have spoken and consulted throughout the United States and abroad. More than 30 percent have published books in their disciplines. Lake Forest faculty members continually receive fellowships and grants from prestigious institutions and foundations in the U.S. and abroad.

Student Government

The first Lake Forest College student body self-governing organization was the Student Council, established in 1917. Today, Student Government is composed of the General Assembly and its subcommittees, the Executive Committee and the four Student Government officers: the president, vice-president, treasurer, and secretary. Student members of other College governing committees also play an active and important role in the Student Government.

Ultimate responsibility for guiding Lake Forest College rests with the Board of Trustees. The Student Government president and vice-president serve as voting members on the full board.

Students at Lake Forest College advise the administration through representation on a variety of committees that deal with the hiring of faculty members, allocation of the budget, department course offerings, and administering a judicial system while also taking a prominent role in enhancing the educational growth and social life of the campus community.

Admission Requirements

Admission to Lake Forest College is competitive and based on a record of achievement in academic studies and extracurricular activities. Selection includes assessment of a student's program of study, academic achievement, aptitude, intellectual curiosity, qualities of character and personality, and activities both within and outside the school setting. Lake Forest College unequivocally selects its students without regard to social background, religious affiliation, race, national origin, gender, handicap, or financial position. This admission policy is manifest in the diverse nature of the student community.

Students are urged to begin the application procedure early in their final year of secondary school. There is no formal closing deadline for receipt of the application. The early notification deadline is December 1. This option is nonbinding but allows the student to receive an admission decision as early as December 20. The early decision (binding) deadline is January 1. Admission decisions are announced no later than the third week of March for all freshman candidates whose applications are complete as of March 1.

Lake Forest recommends a precollege program that includes a minimum of 4 years of English; 3 or more years of mathematics, including trigonometry; in-depth study in one or more foreign languages; and 2 to 4 years of work in both the social and natural sciences. All candidates are required to present the results of either the SAT I or the ACT. The tests may be completed in the candidate's junior or senior year of secondary school. Although an interview is not required, the admission staff welcomes and encourages visits to the campus by prospective students and their families.

Candidates for undergraduate admission may obtain the required application forms by contacting the Admission Office. Lake Forest College also accepts the Common Application in lieu of its own form and gives equal consideration to both. Students may obtain copies of the Common Application from their high schools. Students who wish to defer enrollment should complete the application procedure during the final year of secondary school.

Transfer students are admitted at the beginning of each semester. Transfer applicants should have achieved an overall college average of at least a C or its equivalent and be eligible to return to their previous institutions. When a transfer student is admitted to the College, the maximum credit accepted in transfer is 60 semester hours. All transfer students are required to submit the following credentials: an application for admission, a secondary school transcript, transcripts of all college work completed through the most recent term, and a letter of recommendation from the academic dean or a professor at the current college.

Application and Information

The Admission Office is open from 8:30 a.m. to 5 p.m. on weekdays and 9 a.m. to 1 p.m. on Saturdays throughout the year. For further information, including a campus tour, interview, or an application form, prospective students should contact:

Admission Office
Lake Forest College
555 N. Sheridan Road
Lake Forest, Illinois 60045
Telephone: 847-735-5000
800-828-4751 (toll-free)
Fax: 847-735-6271
E-mail: admissions@lakeforest.edu
World Wide Web: http://www.lakeforest.edu

LAMBUTH UNIVERSITY

JACKSON, TENNESSEE

The University

Lambuth University is an independent, undergraduate, church-related liberal arts institution supported by the Memphis Annual Conference of the United Methodist Church. Lambuth has a limited enrollment with small classes and offers many activities on campus to augment academic and social life. One of the hallmarks of a Lambuth education is the way students are encouraged to think for themselves. Lambuth is committed to academic excellence, and the curriculum expands students' choices of careers. Liberal arts core courses enable students to become proficient in areas beyond their majors—from literature and writing to science and math, from religion and philosophy to economics and history. Through these core courses, students receive a well-balanced education that serves them throughout college and into the future. In providing an academic atmosphere for students, institutions must have a faculty that supports the purpose of the university and responds to students. Lambuth University knows that the student is the most important part of the University. Although faculty members participate in research and scholarship, their primary responsibilities are teaching and advising.

Lambuth's 900 students come from across the nation and the world, representing twenty-six states and twenty countries. Most students live on campus in modern, well-equipped residence halls, with a health center located on campus.

The Lambuth experience is not all study. The more than thirty clubs and organizations available on campus meet almost every interest. National fraternities and sororities, a wide variety of musical and theater activities, and special interest groups (including the Black Student Union) give students plenty of opportunities to participate, acquire leadership skills, and expand their horizons. Intercollegiate sports include basketball, cheerleading, cross-country, dance, golf, soccer, softball, swimming, tennis, and volleyball for women and baseball, basketball, cross-country, football, golf, soccer, swimming, and tennis for men.

On-campus facilities include an athletic center with an Olympic-size indoor swimming pool, two gymnasiums, a weight room, a handball/racquetball court, and outdoor lighted tennis courts. The Wilder Student Union houses a cafeteria, deli, bookstore, career center, and cardiovascular wellness center. The 50-acre campus provides a naturally beautiful setting, with broad expanses of green lawns shared by tall trees. The R. E. Womack Chapel sits in the heart of a parklike quadrangle that is bordered by buildings of Georgian Colonial design.

Location

Jackson, Tennessee, is a lively town of about 80,000 people, with five colleges and universities located in and around this growing community. Jackson's vitality can be seen in its symphony orchestra, bookstores, and civic center and coliseum. The West Tenn Diamond Jaxx, the AA minor-league baseball team for the Chicago Cubs, provides local sports entertainment. Jackson has been the home of such legendary figures as Davy Crockett, Casey Jones, Thomas Edison, and Carl Perkins. Nearby lakes, rivers, and state parks offer waterskiing, canoeing, hiking, and camping. Memphis and Nashville, both easily accessible by interstate highways, provide two different views of an exciting and revitalized mid-South.

Majors and Degrees

Lambuth University offers the degrees of Bachelor of Arts, Bachelor of Science, Bachelor of Business Administration, and Bachelor of Music. Majors and concentrations are available in accounting, art, biology, chemistry, church music, communication, computer information systems, criminal justice, economics, elementary education, English, environmental science, environmental studies, fashion merchandising, family and consumer science, foreign language, graphic arts, international business, health and human performance, history, interior design, international studies, management, marketing, mathematics, media studies, music (performance), music education, philosophy, piano pedagogy, political science, public relations, psychology, religion, sociology, special education, special major (self-designed), theater, and visual arts. Preprofessional programs are offered in dentistry, engineering, health information management, law, medical technology, medicine, ministry, nursing, optometry, pharmacy, physical therapy, and veterinary science.

Academic Program

To earn a bachelor's degree, students must complete core requirements in the liberal studies, consisting of three courses in English, one course in speech, two courses in religion, two courses in fitness/recreation, two courses in natural science, two writing courses, one math course, one course in computer science, and two interdisciplinary courses. A minor course of study is also required. Lambuth offers students with special career goals the opportunity to design their own interdisciplinary major by combining areas of specialization. Lambuth does accept credit through CLEP and Advanced Placement.

Honors study is available in most departments for students who have a cumulative GPA of 3.25 or higher at the end of the first semester of the junior year. The honors program consists of an 8-semester-hour sequence of research or the equivalent carried out over the last three semesters of study in a particular discipline.

Lambuth follows a 4-4-1 academic calendar, with a one-month optional May term. The University also offers two sessions of summer school.

Off-Campus Programs

Through a cross-enrollment arrangement that greatly expands course offerings, students may take courses at two other four-year colleges in the city of Jackson. Students majoring in interior design participate in the Interior Design Showhouse and also work for one semester as apprentices with professional interior designers. Under the Tennessee Legislative Intern Program, political science and prelaw students have the opportunity to work in the Tennessee legislature. Students in all disciplines are encouraged to engage in internships both in the Jackson area and further afield. Lambuth students also participate in study-abroad programs in various countries, including England and France.

Academic Facilities

The Luther L. Gobbel Library houses more than 237,000 items and is a depository for U.S. government documents. The M. D. Anderson Planetarium, adjacent to Hyde Science Hall, houses a Spitz Space System A3P projector, which can project more than

2,000 stars on a 10-meter dome. Other facilities and equipment in Hyde Science Hall include a gas chromatograph and ultraviolet and infrared spectrophotometers. The University offers multiple computer labs that contain various personal computers for student access. A fine arts wing, located in the chapel building, contains music studios, practice rooms, and rehearsal rooms. The Hamilton Center for the Performing Arts is home to musical and theatrical events throughout the year. Other campus facilities include the Learning Enrichment Center, Interior Design House, and Dunlap-Williams Log House Museum. The Oxley Biological Field Station, a facility located on Kentucky Lake and open year-round, is used by faculty members and students to study freshwater and terrestrial ecology in a natural habitat. Students also have access to the Gulf Coast Research Lab at Ocean Springs, Mississippi, which specializes in marine and estuarine biology.

Costs

For the 2004–05 academic year, tuition is estimated at $12,000 and room and board costs are estimated at $5200, for a total estimated cost of $17,200. Out-of-state students are not charged additional fees in any category.

Financial Aid

Lambuth University offers a comprehensive program of financial assistance to students who otherwise would be unable to continue their education beyond the secondary level. An essential part of the financial aid program at Lambuth is the individual attention given to students in their financial planning. Academic scholarships are awarded based upon ACT or SAT I scores and academic performance in high school. Performance awards in athletics, music, and drama are available on a limited basis. United Methodist scholarships are also available, as are preministerial grants. State and federal financial aid resources include Federal Supplemental Educational Opportunity Grants, Tennessee Student Assistance Awards, Federal Pell Grants, and loans (Federal Perkins, Federal Stafford Student, and Federal PLUS). The University also offers a variety of on-campus jobs. To enable the University to determine the level of need, financial aid applicants must submit the Free Application for Federal Student Aid (FAFSA) and request that a copy of the needs analysis report be sent to Lambuth. Financial need is not a factor in determining admission. The priority deadline for all types of aid is February 15.

Faculty

The student-faculty ratio is 14:1. No graduate teaching assistants conduct classes at Lambuth. The University has 70 full- and part-time faculty members, with the majority of the full-time faculty possessing terminal degrees. Faculty members have earned distinction by publishing, consulting, and lecturing on a national scale, yet they remain deeply committed to teaching. They have studied and earned degrees at more than eighty of the most prestigious institutions of higher learning. Many write textbooks and professional articles, and many share their time and knowledge by serving in professional and community organizations. Students have direct access to their instructors for advice and help in their studies.

Student Government

Lambuth has an active Student Government Association (SGA), which is divided into three branches: executive, legislative, and judicial. The SGA represents students on University committees and presents their interests and concerns to the Board of Trustees. The Student Activities Committee coordinates numerous activities of social and educational value each year.

Admission Requirements

In keeping with Lambuth's personalized approach to education, the University's Admissions Committee carefully evaluates each applicant's file for strengths, weaknesses, and exceptional circumstances. Items required for incoming freshmen include an application for admission, $25 application fee, an official high school transcript, ACT or SAT I scores, a personal essay, and at least one academic recommendation for admission (emphasis is placed on grades in college-preparatory courses). Transfer students must submit an application for admission, $25 application fee, an official college transcript from each college attended, a letter of good standing from the most recent college attended, and a personal essay. On-campus interviews are strongly recommended.

Application and Information

Lambuth has a rolling admission policy. Beginning October 1, students are notified of the admission decision as soon as all application materials have been received. Interviews and campus tours are available through the Office of Admissions.

For further information, students should contact:

Office of Admissions
Lambuth University
705 Lambuth Boulevard
Jackson, Tennessee 38301
Telephone: 731-425-3223
800-LAMBUTH (toll-free)
E-mail: admit@lambuth.edu
World Wide Web: http://www.lambuth.edu

Founded by the Methodist Church in 1843, Lambuth is one of the most time-honored universities in the South.

LANDER UNIVERSITY

GREENWOOD, SOUTH CAROLINA

The University

Lander University has been providing educational and cultural opportunities since its founding in 1872 as Williamston Female College. The college moved to Greenwood in 1904 and was renamed Lander in honor of its founder, Samuel Lander. Lander is now a four-year, coeducational, state-assisted university. When the college entered the state system in 1973, the Board of Trustees placed high priority on creating a master plan for campus development. In addition to six major buildings erected since 1973, campus improvements include extensive renovations to a number of older facilities and completely new housing complexes and athletic fields.

Full-time enrollment is approximately 2,400, and the student body represents twenty-five states and twenty-two other countries. The School of Business enrolls the largest number of majors, followed by the School of Education. Lander has an exceptionally strong science program, and more than 90 percent of students applying to medical school in recent years have been accepted. Students in Lander's engineering dual-degree program have a 100 percent acceptance rate at Clemson.

Lander's varsity athletic teams have reaped honors at both district and national levels, including nine national championships in men's tennis. A member of the NCAA Division II, Lander plays in the Peach Belt Athletic Conference and fields teams in men's and women's basketball and soccer, men's baseball and tennis, and women's cross-country, softball, and volleyball. The University's 130,000-square-foot John Drummond Complex offers basketball fans the opportunity to watch the Senators play in the new 2,500-seat Finis Horne Arena. In addition, the complex houses the Division of Physical Education and Exercise Studies and serves as headquarters for Lander's wellness program.

Lander University is accredited by the Commission on Colleges of the Southern Association of Colleges and Schools (1866 Southern Lane, Decatur, Georgia 30033-4097; Telephone: 404-679-4500) to award bachelor's and master's degrees. In addition, its baccalaureate program in nursing is approved by the State Board of Nursing for South Carolina and is accredited by the National League for Nursing Accrediting Commission (NLNAC). The School of Education is fully accredited by the NCATE. The music degree program is accredited by the National Association of Schools of Music (NASM). The visual arts degree program is accredited by the National Association of Art and Design (NASD). The mass communication and theater programs are accredited by the National Association of Schools of Theater (NAST).

Location

Lander University is situated on a wooded site of approximately 100 acres within the city limits of Greenwood, a town of about 25,000 in the Piedmont region of South Carolina. Lander serves as the cultural focal point of the area. In addition to housing Lander's fine arts programs, the University's Cultural Center is also the home of the Greenwood-Lander Performing Arts Series, which recently had its ninth consecutive sell-out season. Students enjoy easy access to local recreation facilities, including Lake Greenwood, shopping malls, and a variety of restaurants. The University is also within driving distance of Greenville and Columbia, South Carolina, and Augusta and Athens, Georgia.

Majors and Degrees

Lander offers more than sixty areas of undergraduate study. Major areas of study are art, art education (K–12), athletic training, biology, biology with an emphasis in genetics, biology with an emphasis in medical technology, business administration with a choice of four areas of emphasis (accounting, finance/economics, health-care management, or management/marketing), chemistry, chemistry/engineering dual-degree program with Clemson University, computer information systems with an emphasis in networking and telecommunications, computer science/engineering dual-degree program with Clemson University, early childhood education, early childhood education with an emphasis in Montessori, elementary education, English, English with an emphasis in applied English, English education (7–12), environmental science, exercise science, history, history with an emphasis in prelaw, history education (7–12), interdisciplinary studies, mass communication and theater, theater education (7–12), mathematics, mathematics education (7–12), mathematics/engineering dual-degree program with Clemson University, music, music education (K–12), nursing, RN–B.S.N. online completion for registered nurses, physical education (K–12), political science, political science with an emphasis in prelaw, political science with an emphasis in public administration, psychology, psychology with an emphasis in counseling, sociology, sociology with emphasis in criminal justice, Spanish, Spanish education (7–12), and special education.

Minors or certificates are available in African American studies, anthropology, art history, biology, business administration, chemistry, child and family studies, computer science, dance, electronic art, English, environmental science, French, gerontology, health-care management, international studies, Latin American studies, mass communication, mathematics, music, networking, political science, prelaw, public administration, psychology, sociology, Spanish, speech and theater, visual arts, and writing.

Nondegree programs in pre-medicine, pre-pharmacy, pre-dentistry, pre–occupational therapy, pre–physical therapy, pre-veterinary medicine, and pre-optometry are available for students interested in professional occupations. Through the University Center of Greenville, Lander offers bachelor's degree programs in political science with an emphasis in prelaw and public administration, psychology with an emphasis in counseling, sociology, and sociology with an emphasis in criminal justice. A Master of Business Administration (M.B.A.) degree is offered by Clemson University faculty on the Lander campus. A Master of Arts in Teaching (M.A.T.) degree is offered in secondary education with a concentration in art. A Master of Education (M.Ed.) degree is offered in elementary education.

Academic Program

The programs offered by the Division of Behavioral Sciences provide the tools for a scientific analysis of human behavior reinforced by an understanding of the origins and development of society and culture. An undergraduate degree in psychology prepares students for a number of opportunities, such as social work, counseling, mental health technician, and research technician. The program is also designed to help the highly successful student in the pursuit of graduate work, not only in psychology but also in other disciplines such as law, medicine, and social work. Students in the sociology program are provided with the tools for sociological analysis. An undergraduate sociology major prepares the student for a wide variety of occupational opportunities in such areas as social work, parole/probation, law enforcement, social survey, correction, vocational guidance, counseling, human relations agencies, and personnel management in industry and public health.

The faculty members of the Division of Biological and Physical Sciences have two primary missions. The first and most important is to provide excellent teaching through courses that are designed to support the various programs offered within the division. The second mission is to provide a variety of high-quality undergraduate research experiences that enhance the development of students as scientists and that prepare them for postgraduate careers. To support these missions, each faculty member is provided with a teaching laboratory and a research laboratory in a modern facility that is designed to support an array of technologies. Each classroom is equipped with multimedia capabilities and connections to the Internet.

The mission of the School of Business Administration is to provide high-quality undergraduate management education that prepares students for positions of leadership and responsibility in industry, government, and health care. The school offers an integrated curriculum that emphasizes discipline knowledge, communication skills, and technological skills; supports instructional innovations, professional development activities, and applied research by the faculty; and strengthens links with the community through service.

The conceptual model guiding the teacher education program at Lander University is that of the Professional Instructional Leader. The faculty of the School of Education, in conjunction with faculty associated with general education and content preparation of education students, developed this model to serve as a guide in planning, implementing, assessing, and improving the teacher education program. This is a comprehensive, innovative model. Its constructs and goals can be found on the University's Web site.

The Fine Arts Division offers visual arts, music, mass communication, and theatrical studies degree programs. Minors are offered in theater, media arts, music, visual art, dance, and a variety of other disciplines. Pop, rock, jazz, and classical styles are options in the music program. There are many opportunities in performance, including solo, ensemble, opera workshops, honors recitals, piano showcase, and music tours as well as in production work, designing, directing, scriptwriting, video, radio, and television production. Students also gain experience working in local community theaters, area radio stations, and touring productions.

In addition to preparation for professional careers in numerous fields, the History and Political Science Division provides undergraduate students an opportunity to explore the major political and governmental systems of the contemporary world and to examine the origins and development of civilizations and cultures.

The Division of Humanities is Lander's home for studies in American and English language and literature; foreign languages including French, German, and Spanish; and philosophy.

The Division of Mathematics and Computer Science offers students an opportunity to earn degrees in computer information systems and mathematics. In addition, a unique dual-degree program in mathematics and engineering is offered in conjunction with Clemson University.

The School of Nursing offers a baccalaureate nursing program that prepares students to provide high-quality, holistic nursing care in a variety of settings to diverse clients across the life span. The purpose of the School of Nursing is to prepare graduates for entry-level professional nursing positions and for graduate study. Students at Lander may complement their chosen degrees with one of twenty-nine minors offered by Lander University. Many nursing students minor in health-care agency management to strengthen their preparation for professional nursing with comprehensive knowledge of the health-care delivery system and fundamental skills in business administration. The curriculum is designed for completion in four academic years. However a three-year accelerated option that includes two summers is available.

The Joe V. Chandler Center, a $10-million facility that opened in 1993, serves as the hub for baccalaureate degree programs in physical education, exercise science, and athletic training. These programs prepare students for work in exercise-related fields such as physical education teaching and coaching, health fitness/wellness, cardiac rehabilitation, and sports medicine/athletic training.

The interdisciplinary studies program (IDS) is designed to accommodate students interested in fields that lie beyond the purview of traditional major programs. Students with an IDS major design their own programs of study in conjunction with faculty sponsors. Programs of study have included concentrations in scientific illustration, ministry, public administration, interior design, early child care, industrial technology supervision, and engineering technology supervision.

Many programs offer opportunities for internships.

Academic Facilities

A $13-million science/mathematics/computer science complex was completed in 1997 and houses the Division of Mathematics and Computer Science and the Division of Biological and Physical Sciences. In the Division of Biological and Physical Sciences, each faculty member is provided with a teaching laboratory and a research laboratory in a modern facility that is designed to support an array of technologies. Each classroom is equipped with multimedia capabilities and connections to the Internet. The University also has a state-of-the-art fine arts facility, media center, computer art lab, and distance learning classroom. There are up-to-date studios for design, drawing, sculpture, printmaking, photography, and ceramics, and there are individual painting studios for juniors and seniors. There is digital recording equipment for student recitals and ensemble concerts, a state-of-the-art fine arts facility, MIDI Clavinova lab, and a DAT recording facility. The Division of Mathematics and Computer Science recently moved into the newly renovated Laura Lander Hall. This building holds multimedia classrooms, normal classrooms, and an extensive computer laboratory.

Costs

In fall 2003, University fees were $2700 for residents and $5525 for nonresidents. Part-time tuition (fewer than 12 hours) was $225 per semester hour for residents and $462 per semester hour for nonresidents. Room and board ranged from $2399 to $2587 per semester. There is a $50 health-service fee.

Financial Aid

A variety of need-based and merit-based aid is available. Aid comes from federal, state, University, and private sources in the form of loans, scholarships, and grants.

Faculty

The undergraduate faculty has 114 full-time and 88 part-time members; 80 percent of full-time faculty members have doctoral/terminal/first professional degrees. The student-faculty ratio is 17:1. The library holds 156,550 books and 116,347 microform titles. Special programs include an honors program, cooperative education, and study abroad. The most popular majors are business administration/commerce/management, education, and behavioral science (sociology and psychology).

Admission Requirements

Applicants must submit the application (online application available), official SAT I or ACT Assessment scores, and high school transcripts. There is a $35 application fee.

High school course prerequisites can be found on the University's Web site. Students are encouraged to apply for admission on the Internet and may do so at the World Wide Web address given below.

Application and Information

The University operates on a rolling admission basis.

Office of Admissions
Lander University
Greenwood, South Carolina 29649
Telephone: 864-388-8307
888-4LANDER (toll-free)
Fax: 864-388-8125
E-mail: admissions@lander.edu
World Wide Web: http://www.lander.edu

LA ROCHE COLLEGE

PITTSBURGH, PENNSYLVANIA

The College

La Roche College invites students to experience learning that brings the world together. International in dimension, La Roche College is a growing global community of learners offering an education that enables students to reach their potential in an atmosphere of support and encouragement. Students at the College number nearly 2,000 and come from across the nation and around the globe.

Founded in 1965 by the Sisters of Divine Providence, La Roche is a Catholic, coeducational, international four-year institution and is fully accredited by the Middle States Association of Colleges and Schools. It is chartered by the Commonwealth of Pennsylvania, and its programs have been approved by the Pennsylvania Department of Education. The College holds memberships in the Council for Independent Colleges, the National Association for Independent Colleges and Universities, the American Council on Education, the Pittsburgh Council on Higher Education, and the National Collegiate Athletic Association (NCAA). La Roche's nursing program is accredited by the National League for Nursing Accrediting Commission (NLNAC). Its interior design and graphic design majors are accredited by the National Association of Schools of Art and Design (NASAD), and its interior design major is also accredited by the Foundation for Interior Design Education Research (FIDER). The Center for Teacher Education is fully accredited by the Pennsylvania Department of Education in early childhood education, elementary education, nursing education, secondary English, secondary mathematics, secondary science, Spanish (K–12), and special education.

Campus clubs and organizations give students an opportunity to participate in a variety of activities, including athletics, social clubs, academic societies, and student chapters of professional associations. In addition to intramural sports, La Roche participates in ten NCAA Division III intercollegiate sports, including men's varsity baseball and golf, women's softball and volleyball, and men's and women's basketball, cross-country, and soccer.

Students are encouraged to live on campus in one of four residence halls, where apartment-style suites promote group interaction and a sense of community. With the guidance of a residence life director, students plan a variety of programs, including guest speakers, recreational events, and social activities. All residence hall rooms are wired for the twenty-first century with Internet access. All residence halls provide students with microwave and refrigerator units and free laundry services.

Location

La Roche College's attractive 80-acre wooded campus is located in the North Hills of Pittsburgh, just 10 minutes from the center of the city. The College was recently named the thirteenth-safest college campus in the United States by the APBnews.com/GAP Index study. Pittsburgh is the second-largest city in Pennsylvania and the headquarters of several of the largest corporations in the United States, including USX and US Airways. A lively, dynamic city, Pittsburgh has outstanding facilities and attractions, including the Pittsburgh Symphony, the Civic Light Opera, Carnegie Music Hall and Museum, and Heinz Hall for the Performing Arts. Pittsburgh has a host of professional sports teams. The Pittsburgh Pirates make their home at PNC Park, and the Pittsburgh Steelers play in Heinz Field. Pittsburgh also has a professional hockey team, the Penguins. Proximity to a large metropolitan area offers students a number of internship and career opportunities.

Majors and Degrees

La Roche College awards the Bachelor of Arts, Bachelor of Science, and Bachelor of Science in Nursing degrees via two schools, with more tha fifty majors. In the School of Arts and Sciences, the following majors are offered: athletic training (2-2 program); biology (liberal arts); biology (sciences); biology education; chemistry; chemistry education; chemistry/chemical engineering (3-2 program); chemistry/materials science engineering (3-2 program); communication, media, and technology; comprehensive chemistry; computer science; computer science/industrial engineering (3-2 program); criminal justice; English education; English studies: language and literature; English studies: professional writing; environmental chemistry/environmental management (3-2 program); history; human services; international studies; liberal studies; mathematics (liberal arts); mathematics (sciences); mathematics education; mathematics/industrial engineering; occupational therapy (3-2 program); performing arts/dance; physical therapy (3-3 program); physician assistant studies (3-2 program); psychology; radiography (degree completion); radiologic technology; religious education/catechetics; religious studies; respiratory therapy (degree completion); sociology; speech and language pathology; and Spanish education (K–12).

In the School of the Professions, students can choose from these majors: accounting, computer information systems, early childhood education, elementary education, facility management, finance, graphic and communication design, information technology, interior design, international management, leadership and administrative development (degree completion), management, marketing, nursing–accelerated program (RN-B.S.N.), nursing–traditional program (RN-B.S.N.), professional studies (degree completion), and real estate.

Academic Program

La Roche College offers students a blend of liberal arts studies and professional preparation. This combination allows students to develop broad perspectives and understanding while acquiring professional skills. Students can gain practical field experience through an internship in one of Pittsburgh's many businesses or corporations. Study-abroad programs are also available.

In La Roche's highly individualized program, students work closely with faculty members who help identify and foster each student's talents and assist students in applying knowledge acquired at La Roche to the world of work. The student-faculty ratio at La Roche is 14:1. Students have faculty advisers who mentor and guide students during their time at the College.

Degree requirements in most majors include a minimum of 120 credits. Students must demonstrate competence in English, mathematics, and practical computer application and must complete a core curriculum.

Academic Facilities

The John J. Wright Library and Learning Center offers tutoring and academic support programs and a Writers' Center. The library is an official repository for government documents and participates in an interlibrary loan system that circulates materials through the ten higher education institutions in Pittsburgh.

La Roche College is positioned to prepare students for the information age and a twenty-first century global economy. The College employs "smart" classroom technology in many of its classrooms, which are wired for Internet access, telecommunications, data transmission, and cable TV. Students can bring their laptop computers to class and tap into the system. The "smart" classroom technology acts as a perfect complement to a dynamic and engaging faculty.

La Roche has three instructional computer labs and one general-purpose lab that each house IBM and IBM-compatible personal computers for student use. For graphic design students, two computer labs provide students access to Macintosh systems that use QuarkXpress, Illustrator and Photoshop, among others. Each student also has access to the Internet at any of La Roche's state-of-the-art computer labs and in their residence halls.

Costs

Full-time tuition for the 2004–05 academic year is estimated at $15,982. Room and board costs are approximately $6862. Updated figures can be obtained from La Roche's Web site, listed below.

Financial Aid

At La Roche, every student who qualifies and meets the appropriate deadlines is offered a financial aid package. The College strives to meet each student's demonstrated financial need. Ninety-four percent of La Roche's full-time students receive some form of financial assistance. Aid is available through various scholarships, grants, loans, work-study awards, and special benefits made available by the federal and state governments, La Roche College, and private organizations. In addition, the College awards full and partial tuition scholarships to students who qualify on the basis of academic achievements. Financial aid counselors are available to answer questions and assist students. La Roche also offers several payment plans. Information on these options can be obtained from the College's admissions office.

All students who intend to apply for financial aid must submit the Free Application for Federal Student Aid (FAFSA). Students who live outside of Pennsylvania should also submit their own state grant form, if applicable. All students are encouraged to submit the proper forms as soon after January 1 as possible so that they are processed prior to La Roche College's May 1 deadline.

Faculty

At La Roche, faculty members are an acclaimed group of scholars. They work closely with students, challenging them and encouraging them. In addition, they are experts in their fields. Many have earned distinguished honors, including a graphic design professor who was awarded a Fulbright Scholar Grant and a philosophy professor who was awarded a fellowship in Salzburg, Austria.

La Roche's faculty is engaged in research, but it is a teaching faculty. These highly trained and experienced people spend time in classrooms, labs and studios teaching students.

Student Government

The Student Government Association (SGA) is a central and vital organization at the College. It is a legislative body responsible for all areas of student life. All enrolled students are represented by the SGA, and all full-time students are eligible for election. Students are also represented on various administrative committees within the College, including the College Cabinet and the Academic Senate.

Admission Requirements

La Roche is selective in its admission process. The College seeks students who demonstrate a strong desire to fulfill their academic potential and have a clear commitment to personal growth and achievement. Because the College values a commitment to community and lifelong learning, the admission staff also considers a student's extracurricular and volunteer activities in such areas as school, church, and community.

The admission committee reviews each applicant individually, assessing personal and academic strengths in light of a student's background and opportunities. Committee members carefully examine high school records (course work, grade point average, and class rank), letters of recommendation, and SAT I or ACT scores. La Roche's code numbers are 2379 for the SAT I and 3607 for the ACT.

Application and Information

Candidates for admission should submit a completed application, a copy of their high school transcript, and a school report completed by a guidance counselor. There is also a $50 nonrefundable application fee. Applications can also be completed online. SAT I and ACT scores should be sent directly to the College. La Roche adheres to a rolling admission system by which students receive decisions once their application credentials are complete. To ensure appropriate financial aid and housing opportunities, students are encouraged to apply no later than March 31 for fall semester and December 31 for spring semester.

For additional information regarding La Roche admission, prospective students should contact:

Office of Admissions
La Roche College
9000 Babcock Boulevard
Pittsburgh, Pennsylvania 15237
Telephone: 412-536-1272
800-838-4LRC (toll-free)
Fax: 412-847-1820
E-mail: admissions@laroche.edu
World Wide Web: http://www.laroche.edu

Students on the campus of La Roche College.

LASELL COLLEGE

NEWTON, MASSACHUSETTS

The College

Founded in 1851, Lasell College is a coeducational, independent, nonsectarian institution of higher education and offers career-oriented bachelor's and master's degree programs. Predominantly a residential college, Lasell seeks to provide its students with the experience of living and learning in a community organized around a central educational purpose that Lasell calls "connected learning." Central to the Lasell plan of education is the belief that students acquire and retain knowledge most effectively when classroom theory is reinforced by regular application under direct faculty supervision. Students are supervised at any number of Lasell's on- and off-campus laboratories and internship and externship sites.

Lasell students are encouraged to participate in a wide variety of campus organizations and to take an active role in developing new interests. Among Lasell's organizations are the Business Club, chorus, the Drama Club, and the Center for Community Based Learning. All clubs organize and sponsor their own activities, including health fairs, fashion shows, trips, and various lectures and presentations. Lasell publications include the *1851* (the College's newspaper), yearbook, literary magazine, and fashion magazine. Each year the students and staff of the College plan a series of programs and events designed to inform and involve members of the Lasell community. These include lectures, Diversity Week, International Week, the Academic Colloquium, and highlighting the roles of men and women in society and the world at large. Other annual events include the Commencement Ball, the Torchlight Parade, and River Day. Athletic teams compete in a number of NCAA Division III varsity athletic programs, including men's basketball, cross-country, lacrosse, soccer, and volleyball and women's basketball, cross-country, field hockey, lacrosse, soccer, softball, and volleyball.

Resident students may choose to live in Victorian houses, modern residence halls, or suite-style residences. All rooms are cable- and Internet-ready. Each residence hall plans its own activities and participates in all College programs. Resident staff members are on hand to provide support when necessary. Special emphasis is placed on the advantages of the College as a close-knit community in proximity to Boston.

In addition to the undergraduate degree programs described below, Lasell offers a Master of Science in Management degree program with concentrations in marketing and elder care.

Location

Lasell's campus is 15 minutes from downtown Boston in the suburb of Newton, Massachusetts, just 8 miles from Boston. The "T," or Mass Transit, is conveniently located within walking distance of the campus. The College has 50 acres of land, with forty-seven residential and academic facilities. Students experience the advantages of a suburban setting with all of the social and cultural attractions offered in the city of Boston.

Majors and Degrees

Lasell offers Bachelor of Science and Bachelor of Arts degree programs in accounting, athletic training, business administration, communications, computer science, criminal justice, early childhood education, elementary education, English, exercise physiology, exercise science, fashion and retail merchandising, fashion design and production, finance, graphic design, health-care administration, history, hospitality management, humanities, human performance and physical education, human services, interdisciplinary studies, international business, legal studies, management, management information systems (MIS), marketing, psychology, secondary education, sociology, sport management, sport science, and undeclared major.

Academic Program

Candidates for a bachelor's degree complete between 123 and 128 semester hours of course work. Lasell College recognizes that students must be exposed to a wide breadth of liberal arts courses to have a well-rounded education and function in the twenty-first century. Lasell's core curriculum integrates writing across the curriculum, oral communication skills, critical and quantitative reasoning, computer literacy, and ethical development.

Academic Facilities

All of Lasell's academic and residential buildings are networked with fiber optic cable, providing high-speed access to the Internet and the College Intranet. Academic buildings include Wolfe Hall, the Wass Science Building, the Brennan Library, the Yamawaki Art and Cultural Center, and the Winslow Academic Center. These buildings house five state-of-the-art computer labs with a wide assortment of software, including graphics software, business applications, statistical packages, experimental programs, tutorials, and Microsoft Office.

Brennan Library houses a collection of more than 55,000 books, more than 70 electronic databases, and hundreds of periodicals. Lasell is a member of the Minuteman Library Network, which provides access to more than five million volumes from more than forty libraries. In addition, the Brennan Library is home to the Shoemaker Learning Center and Rosen Auditorium.

Wolfe Hall has a business computer lab, seminar room, board room, and spacious classrooms. Wass Hall accommodates laboratories for chemistry, anatomy and physiology, biology, physical sciences, exercise physiology, and athletic training.

The Yamawaki Art and Cultural Center, home of the Lasell Institute of Fashion Technology (LIFT), has undergone a multimillion dollar renovation but still retains its 1800s Victorian flair. The center has design labs with industry-standard pattern generation technology, lab space for ceramics and photography, and studios for painting classes. In addition, the center has a theater and an active gallery showcasing works from many media.

Two nationally accredited lab schools—the Holway Child Study Centers—are part of the College campus, and they provide valuable connected learning experiences for education majors.

The Athletic Center and recently completed athletic training labs provide not only a home for Lasell's NCAA Division III athletics, but serve as experiential learning sites for students majoring in athletic training and exercise physiology.

The Winslow Academic Center has seven classrooms with state-of-the-art audiovisual systems installed to maximize the effectiveness of faculty members and enhance the teaching and learning experience. Each classroom is equipped with an LCD projector, sound system, unified remote control system, and a SMART Board. The SMART Board can be used to project class notes and save them to the College Intranet, enabling students to focus on the lecture and discussion and download class notes later. The interactive technology assists in multiple teaching modalities, thereby enhancing student learning.

Costs

For the 2003–04 academic year, tuition for full-time students was $17,500. Room and board charges were $8500.

Financial Aid

More than 85 percent of the students at Lasell receive some form of financial assistance from the College. Programs include Lasell grants, Federal Pell Grants, Federal Supplemental Educational Opportunity Grants, Federal Perkins Loans, Federal Stafford Student Loans, Federal Work-Study, awards, state scholarships, and Lasell alumnae scholarships.

Lasell uses the Free Application for Federal Student Aid (FAFSA) and the Lasell Financial Aid Application to determine eligibility for programs. Applicants for aid who wish to enroll in September should mail the FAFSA to the appropriate processing centers as soon as possible after January 1. In 2002–03, the average financial aid package, including loans, grants, and work-study, totaled $15,000. Lasell guarantees all financial aid packages for four years if a family's financial situation and a student's academic record remain the same.

Faculty

Lasell has a total of 155 faculty members (48 full-time, 107 part-time), many of whom are practicing professionals in their respective fields and bring their experience to the classroom. The student-faculty ratio is 13:1. The student-faculty bond, strengthened by faculty members acting as academic advisers, is considered a vital element in the social, academic, and cultural growth and development of students. Faculty members serve as role models for success, and particular emphasis is placed on their availability for individual and group conferences.

Student Government

Students are elected in the fall and spring of each year to the association's Executive Council and Executive Board. The elected officials represent the student body and govern and coordinate College activities. All students are encouraged to participate in the association and to use it as an effective agency for communicating their concerns and interests.

Admission Requirements

Applicants are evaluated on the basis of their academic record, academic achievement, overall initiative, and SAT I or ACT scores. Prospective students are encouraged to visit the Lasell campus for a tour and interview. Appointments may be scheduled Monday through Saturday by calling the Office of Admissions.

Application and Information

Candidates for admission should submit an application and $40 application fee, a high school transcript, SAT I or ACT scores, and at least one letter of recommendation. Lasell offers rolling admission, and applicants receive decisions shortly after their applications have been completed. Transfer applicants must submit all college transcripts, their high school academic information, and at least one letter of recommendation.

For further information, students should contact:

Office of Admission
Lasell College
1844 Commonwealth Avenue
Newton, Massachusetts 02466
Telephone: 617-243-2225
888-LASELL4 (toll-free)
Fax: 617-243-2380
E-mail: info@lasell.edu
World Wide Web: http://www.lasell.edu

A view of Lasell College's campus.

LAWRENCE TECHNOLOGICAL UNIVERSITY

SOUTHFIELD, MICHIGAN

The University

Founded in 1932 as Lawrence Institute of Technology by brothers Russell and E. George Lawrence, Lawrence Technological University has more than 27,000 alumni worldwide. The curriculum at Lawrence Tech is diverse, but the University has traditionally given students a high-quality, affordable education with an emphasis on theory and practice. The University, including the graduate programs in business, architecture, and engineering, is accredited by the Higher Learning Commission and a member of the North Central Association. Appropriate national professional agencies provide additional accreditation to various degree programs in architecture, interior architecture/design, imaging, administration and management, chemistry, and engineering.

The University offers certificates and associate, bachelor's, master's, and doctoral degrees through colleges of Architecture, Arts and Sciences, Engineering, and Management. An independent university, Lawrence Tech offers a highly competitive tuition rate, modern facilities, and real-world application of textbook knowledge. The 120-acre campus is located at the hub of one of America's great technological and industrial centers and near sites of some of the world's most significant manufacturing and engineering accomplishments.

Around 5,000 students attend Lawrence Tech, of whom approximately 600 live in on-campus housing. Women make up 27 percent of the student body.

Numerous fraternities, sororities, and social and professional organizations sponsor a variety of activities during the year. Recreational facilities include the 38,000-square-foot Don Ridler Field House, which features a fitness track, a gymnasium, racquetball courts, a game room, saunas, and a weight and conditioning room. Intramural sports teams are active throughout the academic year. Lawrence Tech's campus includes nine major buildings, all built since 1955. The campus has more than doubled in size since 1981.

Location

Southfield is a suburb of more than 78,000 people, a center of corporate and industrial activity, and a city that provides a pleasant balance between big-city entertainment opportunities and a quiet residential atmosphere. Southfield's daytime population of commuting workers swells to 175,000. Oakland County has the fourth-highest per-capita income in the country. The Lawrence Tech campus is conveniently close to major freeways and about a 30-minute drive north of downtown Detroit. Southeastern Michigan offers a rich variety of recreational and cultural activities, with public transportation making most areas accessible to students. Within a few miles of the campus, students can find many restaurants, parks, shopping areas, and recreational facilities. Research, manufacturing, scientific, and business enterprises are also located nearby, aiding co-op students as well as those who work full- or part-time while attending classes. More than 200 Fortune 500 companies have headquarters or business operations in the metropolitan area.

Majors and Degrees

Lawrence Tech offers more than fifty majors or course concentrations. Most programs are available during the day and evening. Dual-degree programs combining either associate and bachelor's programs or bachelor's and master's programs are also available. Postgraduate preparation includes premedicine, predentistry, prelaw, and pre–biomedical engineering programs.

The College of Architecture and Design offers bachelor's degrees in architecture, facility management, and interior architecture and a Bachelor of Fine Arts degree in imaging, which includes digital arts and graphic design.

The College of Arts and Sciences awards bachelor's degrees in business management, chemistry, computer science, environmental chemistry, humanities, mathematics, mathematics and computer science, physics, psychology, and technical communication. Associate degrees are offered in chemical technology and university studies. Certificates can be earned in leadership and change management and technical communication.

The College of Engineering offers bachelor's degrees in civil engineering, computer engineering, construction management, electrical engineering, engineering technology, industrial management, mechanical engineering, and technology management. The college offers evening associate programs in construction engineering, electrical contracting, electrical engineering, manufacturing engineering, and mechanical engineering technology. Certificates are available in entrepreneurship and manufacturing systems.

The College of Management awards both a certificate and a Bachelor of Science degree in information technology.

Academic Programs

Graduation from Lawrence Technological University requires completion of a degree program, with an overall GPA of at least 2.0. Most disciplines combine a strong concentration in the major with basic science, humanities, and mathematics requirements. Engineering students share a core program the first two years, as do administration, industrial management, architecture, and interior architecture majors. The University operates on a semester calendar.

Off-Campus Programs

Lawrence Tech chemistry, computer science, engineering, and technology students may participate in a co-op program, alternating semesters of classes and work. Internships are also available.

Academic Facilities

Lawrence Tech is Michigan's first wireless laptop computer campus. All freshmen are provided custom-configured laptop computers. Other computers, workstations, and hundreds of terminals and microcomputers are located in various labs on the campus. Each student has his or her own account and is encouraged to make use of it. The library houses a broad selection of books, periodicals, electronic databases, and microforms and is part of a nationwide network of more than 6,000 libraries that share resources via computer. Lawrence Tech is also surrounded by numerous outstanding municipal and research libraries, many with reciprocal borrowing privileges. The campus houses many research labs. Lawrence Tech also owns a nearby Frank Lloyd Wright–designed home that is used as a study center. Plans for a new Student Services Center are underway.

Costs

The 2003–04 tuition for freshmen and sophomores majoring in arts and sciences and management was $503 per credit hour; for juniors and seniors, it was $525 per credit hour. In architecture, engineering, and engineering technology, tuition for freshmen and sophomores was $525 per credit hour; for juniors and seniors, it was $543 per credit hour. A normal course load was 12–17 credit hours per semester. The undergraduate registration fee was $100 each semester. International students on temporary visas must deposit the first semester's tuition and fees at the time of first registration. Additional fees for specific labs and studio courses vary.

Financial Aid

More than 70 percent of students receive some form of financial assistance, and the University awards nearly $22 million in scholarships, grants, loans, and work-study funds each academic year. Many privately funded scholarships are awarded to qualified students, based on need and/or scholastic performance. Part-time employment is available at the University on a first-come, first-served basis for full-time students. Student loans are also available from a variety of sources—state, federal, and private. Prospective students are urged to contact the Financial Aid Office for information on deadlines and requirements for eligibility (Web site: http://financialaid.ltu.edu).

Faculty

Approximately 420 full- and part-time faculty members teach at Lawrence Tech. Many part-time faculty members hold full-time jobs in industry and bring their real-world perspective to the classroom. More than 78 percent of the full-time faculty members hold a doctoral degree or the terminal degree in their field. Faculty involvement is extensive in student chapters of professional associations that meet on campus. Many faculty members are professional engineers or registered architects in Michigan and elsewhere. Reflecting the low student-faculty ratio of 12:1, approximately 70 percent of the undergraduate classes at Lawrence Tech have 19 or fewer students; less than 1 percent of the classes have more than 50.

Student Government

The Student Government sponsors and supports a variety of campus activities. It oversees expenditures, meets regularly to plan events, and is authorized to levy fines for minor, on-campus infractions. More than thirty-five student clubs and organizations, including fraternities, sororities, honor societies, and student chapters of professional groups, are active on campus.

Admission Requirements

A high school diploma or the equivalent is required of all students applying to baccalaureate or associate degree programs. Most baccalaureate applicants must have a minimum 2.5 overall GPA in academic subjects and a minimum 2.0 average in subject areas pertaining to the desired program of study. Applicants to associate degree programs are required to have a minimum 2.0 average in four academic areas (English, mathematics, social science, and natural science) combined. ACT or SAT results are required of all entering freshmen. Required high school courses vary with the curriculum, and Lawrence Tech offers a number of basic studies courses designed to augment incoming students' backgrounds if deficiencies exist.

Application and Information

Programs start in August and January. An optional summer semester begins in May or July. Entry in the fall semester is advised but not required. Students must submit transcripts from all schools attended, along with a nonrefundable $30 application fee. To obtain a University catalog and an application form, students should contact:

Admissions Office
Lawrence Technological University
21000 West Ten Mile Road
Southfield, Michigan 48075-1058
Telephone: 800-CALL-LTU Ext. 1 (toll-free)
248-204-4117 (TTY/TDD)
E-mail: admissions@ltu.edu
World Wide Web: http://www.ltu.edu

Lawrence Tech's University Technology and Learning Center offers state-of-the-art labs, studios, and high-technology learning facilities.

LAWRENCE UNIVERSITY

APPLETON, WISCONSIN

The University

Lawrence University offers a distinguished education in the liberal arts and sciences that blends study in the traditional disciplines with programs that address contemporary issues. Its 1,300 undergraduate men and women, from fifty states and forty countries, participate in a curriculum that not only promotes in-depth study within a single area but also invites exploration of the connections among different academic fields. Bright, motivated students are attracted to Lawrence by the exceptional level of student-faculty interaction both inside and outside the classroom.

Lawrence offers a number of meaningful differences that set it apart from other colleges. Among the most important are Freshman Studies, a two-term seminar-style course that, through major works of literature, art, and music, develops the ability to think critically, write cogently, and argue persuasively; Individualized Study, which encourages and requires intellectual maturity and self-direction and emphasizes the application of knowledge over the simple rote learning of facts; Bjorklunden, Lawrence's 425-acre estate on the shore of Lake Michigan, where students and faculty members gather every weekend of the academic year for relaxed yet focused discussions on issues and ideas covering a wide range of topics; the Conservatory of Music, which not only provides intensive training in performance, theory-composition, and music education, but also provides musical opportunities to all Lawrence students and supports performances of a quality and frequency not found in other colleges of similar size; and the Honor Code, which ensures academic integrity, promotes mutual trust and respect, and values cooperation and collaboration over competition in all aspects of campus life.

Lawrence offers an active social life and a full range of recreational and athletic opportunities. Seven residence halls on campus offer living arrangements from single and double rooms to 4-person suites. Formal group housing options provide alternate living arrangements for upperclass students. Twenty percent of Lawrence's students belong to five national fraternities and three national sororities. More than 80 student clubs and organizations provide a wide variety of activities ranging from performances by major music ensembles, an international film series, to the annual Trivia Weekend (the longest-running and most notorious trivia contest in the country), crew on the Fox River, and winter camping along Lake Michigan. The Buchanan Kiewit Recreation Center offers an indoor track; swimming pool; weight/exercise room; dance room; racquetball, handball, and walleyball courts; gymnasium; and saunas. Alexander Gymnasium, Whiting Field, and the Banta Bowl (a 5,300-seat football stadium) house twenty-three varsity and four club sports teams (NCAA Division III). The spirit of volunteerism flourishes at Lawrence, with more than ten campus organizations devoted to tutoring local school-age children, committing to Habitat for Humanity, serving as Big Brothers/ Sisters, and other volunteer activities. A staffed volunteer bureau assists students in finding volunteer opportunities.

Location

Lawrence is in Appleton, a city of 70,000 people, located on the banks of the historic Fox River in northeast Wisconsin. The Fox Cities area (population 250,000), of which Appleton is the center, has been considered one of the three best medium-sized metropolitan areas in the United States, based on "quality of life" indicators and has been cited as among the safest for cities its size. The 84-acre Lawrence campus overlooks the river and is situated adjacent to the city's downtown area. Appleton is accessible by car, bus, and plane and offers the commercial/ retail advantages of a larger urban area and the recreational opportunities and safety of a Midwestern town.

Majors and Degrees

Lawrence awards the Bachelor of Arts (B.A.), the Bachelor of Music (B.Mus.), and the five-year B.A./B.Mus. The more than thirty areas of study include anthropology, art history, biology, biomedical ethics, chemistry, Chinese, classics, cognitive science, computer science, East Asian languages and cultures, economics, English, environmental studies, ethnic studies, French, gender studies, geology, German, government, history, international studies, Japanese, linguistics, mathematics, mathematics-economics, music, music education, music performance, music theory-composition, natural sciences, neuroscience, philosophy, physics, psychology, religious studies, Russian, studio art, and theater arts. Preprofessional study is available in business, education, law, and medicine. Cooperative degree programs are available in engineering, environmental management, forestry, medical technology, nursing, and occupational therapy.

Academic Programs

The academic program not only emphasizes in-depth work within a single discipline but also encourages breadth by exposure to many fields of inquiry. Distribution requirements for both B.A. and B.Mus. candidates promote exposure to all areas of the arts and sciences. Working with their faculty advisers, students are encouraged to take initiative and responsibility for selecting a course of study best suited to them. More than 90 percent of Lawrence's students take advantage of tutorials and independent study, working one-on-one with faculty members. The Honors in Independent Study Program culminates in a written thesis or piece of work in the creative or performing arts and an oral examination.

Lawrence operates on a three-term calendar, with students taking three courses in each ten-week term. The academic year begins in late September and ends in mid-June.

Off-Campus Programs

More than half of all Lawrence students take advantage of a wide variety of both domestic and international off-campus study opportunities. The value of participating in off-campus opportunities is supported by the faculty through a resolution encouraging all students to do so. Many choose to attend Lawrence's program with its own campus in London, which operates all three terms of each academic year. Others choose from programs in cities such as Beijing, Florence, Melbourne, Rome, and Tokyo; countries such as the British West Indies, Costa Rica, the Czech Republic, France, India, Russia, Senegal, Spain, and Tanzania; and domestic programs in Chicago; Washington, D.C.; Woods Hole, Massachusetts; and Oak Ridge, Tennessee. Need-based financial aid is available to assist students with the additional costs of attending an off-campus program sponsored by or endorsed by Lawrence.

Academic Facilities

Seeley G. Mudd Library has 376,814 volumes, 300,000 government documents, 1,500 current periodical subscriptions, 21,000 recordings and videotapes, and more than 104,000 microform items. In addition to the online catalog, the library can access national computerized bibliographic databases. The library houses the Media Center, with its listening facilities, audiovisual equipment, and video studio, and the Career Center. There are more than 250 terminals and PC and Macintosh computers located across the campus, providing round-the-clock access to the campuswide computing system. Fiber-optic cabling interconnects all principal stations and residence halls by room and all halls have central computer lounges available around the clock. Science facilities include twenty-three general laboratories for student use; twenty-five special laboratories for research, including a laser physics lab; a graphics and computational physics lab; four environmentally controlled rooms; animal rooms for psychology and biology; a greenhouse; two electron microscopes; a nuclear magnetic resonator; and a variety of spectrometers. Briggs Hall, the new facility for the social sciences and math, opened in 1997. Science Hall opened in fall 2000. Main Hall houses humanities classrooms, seminar rooms, a computer text laboratory, a language acquisition center, and the Hiram A. Jones Latin Library. The Music-Drama Center and the Shattuck Hall of Music house private practice studios, classrooms, a recital hall, large and small ensemble rehearsal halls, a digital recording studio, performance facilities for the theater department, and WLFM, Lawrence's FM radio station affiliated with Wisconsin Public Radio. Lawrence has two theaters: the first, with a proscenium stage, seats 500 people; the second is an experimental theater, adaptable to arena- or thrust-stage productions. The Memorial Chapel seats 1,250 people and is the primary venue for convocations, performances by Lawrence's large ensembles, and other public events and concerts. The Wriston Art Center offers a first-rate facility for the studio art and art history programs. It includes an outdoor amphitheater, three galleries, and two- and three-dimensional art studios and houses the University's outstanding permanent collection.

Costs

For 2003–04, annual tuition was $24,900, room and board averaged $5652, and the activity fee was $189. Books, travel, and living expenses were estimated at $1800 per year.

Financial Aid

Lawrence adheres to a need-blind admission policy. For U.S. citizens and permanent residents, the Financial Aid Office makes awards on the basis of the candidate's need, as determined from the Free Application for Federal Student Aid (FAFSA) and the Lawrence University Application for Financial Aid. Lawrence is committed to meeting the full demonstrated financial need of every admitted student. Nearly two thirds of Lawrence's students receive grants, long-term loans, and work-study packages, totaling more than $12 million. In 2003, the average aid package exceeded $21,400. To apply for financial aid, students must submit the FAFSA and the Lawrence Application for Financial Aid. Non-need-based scholarships and conservatory performance awards ranging from $1000 to $10,000 per year are awarded primarily to strongly recommended applicants ranking in the top 5 percent of their class and to exceptional musicians by audition.

Faculty

Lawrence has 170 full-time faculty members; 93 percent hold a Ph.D. or the highest degree in their field; 30 percent are women. The student-faculty ratio is 11:1, and the median class size is 15. The faculty plays a central role in guiding students' experiences. Active scholars and artists, the faculty members encourage students to join with them in academic pursuits, many of which have led to collaborative faculty-student published works. Lawrence was recently ranked fifth nationally among 205 small, private undergraduate institutions in the total amount of awards received from the Research Corporation's Cottrell College Science Program for faculty and student participatory research. Members of the Lawrence faculty have received seven National Endowment for the Humanities fellowships in the last six years.

Student Government

The Lawrence University Community Council governs most nonacademic matters. It has a student president, vice president, and treasurer; 12 student representatives; and 4 faculty representatives.

Admission Requirements

The admission staff considers the strength of an applicant's course of study (16 units of English, math, history, social studies, physical sciences, and foreign languages are recommended), grades, standardized test scores (ACT or SAT I), recommendations, and extracurricular activities. Candidates for the B.Mus. degree are judged additionally on musicianship, performance potential, recommendations of teachers, and general academic ability. All music applicants must audition. More than half of Lawrence's students graduated in the top 10 percent of their high school class. A personal interview is not required, but a campus visit is strongly recommended and is required for merit award consideration.

Application and Information

One early decision plan (deadline November 15, notification December 1) as well as an early action application plan (deadline December 1, notification January 1) and a regular decision plan (deadline January 15, notification April 1) are available for high school seniors. International students should apply under the regular decision plan. A $200 nonrefundable enrollment deposit is due two weeks after notification of admission under the early decision option or on or before the Candidates Reply Date of May 1 under the early action or regular application procedures. A completed application consists of the personal application form with an essay, the secondary school report form and official transcript, the teacher's report form, official ACT or SAT I scores, and the application fee of $40. In addition, Conservatory of Music applicants must complete a supplementary music form, submit a music teacher's recommendation, and audition on campus or at a regional site. Transfer applicants are considered and notified on a rolling admission basis and should submit high school and college transcripts and ACT or SAT I scores. Lawrence accepts the Common Application form for high school seniors.

For more information, students should contact:

Office of Admissions
Lawrence University
P.O. Box 599
Appleton, Wisconsin 54912-0599
Telephone: 920-832-6500
800-227-0982 (toll-free)
E-mail: excel@lawrence.edu
World Wide Web: http://www.lawrence.edu

LEBANON VALLEY COLLEGE

ANNVILLE, PENNSYLVANIA

The College

With 137 years of tradition, an outstanding student body and faculty, and exceptional facilities make this private liberal arts college stand out among other schools. Founded in 1866, Lebanon Valley is steeped in a tradition of providing students with an educational foundation that transcends time and embraces new technology. The College has instilled in its graduates the desire and ability to think, ask questions, solve problems, and communicate effectively. These qualities, combined with a love for education and learning, prepare students to be competitive in a world that is constantly changing. A supportive community provides the final ingredient students need to achieve success in the job market and professional or graduate school.

The Lebanon Valley College family of 1,540 students is growing. The new freshmen and transfer students have become part of a student body that represents nineteen states and five countries. Technology wires them to the world and prepares them for the future. Beautiful spaces foster quiet reflection, where students work and play together, building friendships that last a lifetime.

Students' efforts and accomplishments are being recognized. Few other small colleges have received more Fulbright awards than Lebanon Valley College—thirteen awards in the past twenty years—with mathematics majors receiving five during that period. *U.S. News & World Report* ranks Lebanon Valley College as one of the top tier in "Northern Universities–Master's: Top Schools" and number thirteen in "Best Values: Northern Universities–Master's" in its America's Best Colleges rankings.

Lebanon Valley's tree-lined campus feels like a college of yesteryear—with twenty-first-century accoutrements. Students enjoy state-of-the-art facilities whether they are studying in the atrium of the Bishop Library or using a workstation in the molecular modeling lab. The College's forty buildings provide for every facet of college life with twenty-five residence halls, including four apartment-style halls; classroom buildings; two student centers; a recreational sports center; a new varsity gymnasium; a library; a music center; an art gallery and recital hall; an art studio; and a chapel. One of the keys to providing students with a rich, well-rounded experience is to offer a wealth of opportunities for learning and growth beyond the classroom. There are new athletic fields; gardens and plazas; soccer, baseball, field hockey, and softball parks; and a physical therapy facility. The baseball and soccer fields were each named National Collegiate Athletic Association (NCAA) field of the year in their respective categories, and the softball park is a two-time regional field of the year.

The staff of the Career Services Office helps students to research careers and establish contacts with potential employers. Seminars are offered on resume writing and interviewing skills. An alumni database provides students access to individuals who are working in their prospective field.

The College's mission is to continue to carry out the art of teaching and learning with the same dedication and love that has come to be identified with the educators of the Valley.

Graduate programs are offered in business administration, music education, physical therapy, and science education.

Location

Annville, founded in 1799, is a small town of approximately 5,000 people. Located in the heart of Pennsylvania Dutch country, the town is just 10 minutes east of Hershey and within a 2- to 3-hour drive of Philadelphia, Baltimore, New York, and Washington, D.C. Nestled in a valley, the College sits on 238 beautiful acres. A wide variety of cultural events and activities are offered on campus and within the community.

Majors and Degrees

The College confers five baccalaureate degrees. The Bachelor of Arts is available in the following major programs: American studies, art, art history, economics, English, French, German, historical communications, history, music, philosophy, political science, psychology, religion, sociology, Spanish, and certain individualized majors. The Bachelor of Science is available in the following major programs: accounting, actuarial science, biochemistry, biology, business administration, chemistry, computer science, cooperative engineering, cooperative forestry, digital communications, elementary education, health-care management, mathematics, music business, music education, physics, psychobiology, and certain individualized majors. The Bachelor of Science in chemistry, the Bachelor of Science in medical technology, and the Bachelor of Music (with an emphasis in music recording technology) are also available. In addition to its thirty-four majors, Lebanon Valley offers a doctoral program in physical therapy and preprofessional programs in dentistry, law, medicine, ministry, pharmacy, and veterinary medicine.

Academic Program

Lebanon Valley has long been known for the strength of its academic programs and the achievement of its faculty members and alumni. The science program is particularly strong, with exceptionally well-equipped laboratories. Peterson's identifies Lebanon Valley as one of 200 colleges and universities in America offering outstanding programs in the sciences and mathematics. Lebanon Valley's mission arises directly from its historical traditions and a relationship with the United Methodist Church. The College's aim is to enable its students to become people of broad vision capable of making informed decisions and prepared for a life of service to others. To that end, the College provides an education that helps students to acquire the knowledge, skills, attitudes, and values necessary to live and work in a changing, diverse, and fragile world. The general education core provides students with the breadth of knowledge and experience across the curriculum, in addition to their major course work. Each student's academic program is fully complemented by a wide range of extracurricular activities, including guest lectures; concerts; Division III athletics; trips to New York and Washington, D.C.; and a variety of cultural activities.

Off-Campus Programs

Domestic students are encouraged to take advantage of the numerous study-abroad opportunities in Australia, Costa Rica, England, France, Germany, Greece, Italy, the Netherlands, New Zealand, Spain, and Sweden. Scholarship money and financial aid can be transferred to the programs, making the cost of study abroad the same as the cost of attendance at Lebanon Valley. Students can focus on becoming fluent in a language or join their classmates and a faculty adviser in a classroom experience. Internships both abroad and in the U.S. are a very popular method for students to research possible professions, establish early contacts, and gain valuable experience within their professional field.

Academic Facilities

Lebanon Valley has beautiful facilities and provides a safe environment in which students can live and learn. The Bishop Library, built in 1995, houses more than 200,000 cataloged items, including books, journals, microfilm, and media collections. Most importantly, the library, residence halls, classrooms, and administrative offices are linked to the campus network, providing state-of-the-art technology and Internet access. A videoconferencing center not only brings guest lecturers "virtually" to campus but also allows students to interview with a company overseas or in another city. Well-equipped laboratories provide students with hands-on experience and numerous opportunities for research.

Costs

Annual tuition and fees for the 2003–04 school year were $22,510. Room and board charges were $6360.

Financial Aid

Lebanon Valley is committed to helping families finance a college education and has received national recognition for being one of the first colleges to offer merit-based scholarships. High school achievement is rewarded at Lebanon Valley. Students who graduate in the top 30 percent of their high school class automatically receive one of the College's academic scholarships for up to half of the cost of tuition. Additional need-based financial aid is available, and 98 percent of students receive some form of financial aid. The College has committed more than $13 million to institutional aid. The Free Application for Federal Student Aid (FAFSA) and the Undergraduate Financial Aid Application must be completed to determine eligibility. The priority deadline for filing for financial aid is March 1 of the senior year of high school.

Faculty

Lebanon Valley College's faculty members are dedicated to teaching. The close-knit community and an opportunity to be actively involved in the students' educational growth have drawn talented, multifaceted faculty members from all over the country. Many professors choose to live in the area and take an active role in supporting students' growth and development both in and out of the classroom. Faculty members are very involved in professional organizations and play an active role in helping students find internships and get started with research. Of the 100 professors at Lebanon Valley, 84 percent have earned a Ph.D. or equivalent terminal degree. The College is committed to maintaining a low student-teacher ratio of 14:1 (FTE). The average class size is 20.

Student Government

Lebanon Valley students participate in the College's governing system through the Student Government Association. This group includes 26 students who are elected from the student body each year for a one-year term beginning in September. Among the government's major responsibilities is fostering understanding, communication, and cooperation among the students, faculty members, and administration. It serves as the channel for all students' recommendations for establishing or changing policy and routes these recommendations to the appropriate administrative offices or faculty committees. The Student Government Association is a highly visible group on campus.

Admission Requirements

The admission process is selective, and the student's academic record is the most important factor. Lebanon Valley seeks students from diverse backgrounds and those who display leadership abilities, a commitment to community service, and special talents. All applicants should have completed 16 credit units and graduated from an accredited secondary school or present an equivalency certificate (GED). Of the 16 units, 4 should be in English, 2 in foreign language, 2 in mathematics, 1 in science, and 1 in social studies. Additional course work in math and science is strongly recommended. More than 75 percent of the freshman class rank in the top 30 percent of their high school class. Advanced standing is offered through CLEP and AP examinations.

Application and Information

To apply, students should submit a completed application, a $30 application fee, and official copies of their high school transcript and SAT I or ACT scores. Lebanon Valley has a rolling admission process. However, students are encouraged to apply during the fall of their senior year. The Admission Advisory Group gives careful consideration to scholastic credentials such as grades and test scores as well as to the nonacademic qualities of each applicant. Personal visits to the campus may also be arranged.

For more information, applicants should contact:

William J. Brown Jr.
Dean of Admission and Financial Aid
Lebanon Valley College
101 North College Avenue
Annville, Pennsylvania 17003-1400
Telephone: 866-LVC-4ADM (toll-free)
Fax: 717-867-6026
E-mail: admission@lvc.edu
World Wide Web: http://www.lvc.edu

"Hot Dog" Frank Aftosmes, who opened his hot dog shop a block from Lebanon Valley's campus in 1928, still keeps watch in the Peace Garden. Funded by hundreds of graduates, the life-size bronze statue recognizes his lifelong friendship with the Lebanon Valley community.

LEHIGH UNIVERSITY

BETHLEHEM, PENNSYLVANIA

The University

Lehigh University is among the nation's most selective, highly ranked private research universities, rich in tradition, with an inspiring history that spans more than 135 years. Lehigh offers a comprehensive education that integrates courses from four colleges and dozens of fields of study to create a dynamic learning environment. At Lehigh, students can choose from nationally recognized programs in the arts and sciences, humanities, business, engineering, and education. Students can customize their college experience to their personal interests by tailoring their majors and academic programs from more than 2,000 courses, with opportunities to take courses outside of their college or major field of study.

Lehigh is the right size—small enough to be personal, yet large enough to be powerful. The school combines learning opportunities found at larger research universities with the personal attention of a smaller, private college. Many students consider Lehigh as everything that college was meant to be. At Lehigh, students have easy access to world-class faculty members who are renowned in their fields but also offer their time and personal attention to help students learn and succeed. With a 9.9:1 student-faculty ratio, a college experience customized to the individual, close mentoring by faculty members, hands-on projects, extensive industry internships, and innovative study, Lehigh students emerge as leaders in careers and life.

The University's 4,685 undergraduate students come from nearly every state and more than sixty-five countries. Women comprise 40 percent of the student body, and minorities, 13 percent. More than half ranked in the top 10 percent of their high school class. Seventy percent live on campus in residence halls, in fraternity or sorority houses, in apartments, or in specialty housing.

At Lehigh, students gain hands-on, real-world experience and take part in a variety of activities, in and out of the classroom, that build confidence and help students develop as leaders. Lehigh prepares students to succeed in whatever careers they choose.

Twenty-five Division I varsity athletic teams compete primarily in the Patriot League. Lehigh is consistently among the leaders in NCAA graduation rates. Its athletics program was in the top twenty of *U.S. News & World Report's* "America's Best College Sports Programs." There are more than forty club and intramural sports, in which 80 percent of undergraduate students participate. Lehigh supports a vibrant campus life, offering many social and extracurricular activities outside the classroom, with more than 130 different clubs and social organizations to suit virtually any interest—from politics and student government to music, drama, journalism, and religion.

Location

Lehigh's metroburban location in Pennsylvania's Lehigh Valley, the state's third-largest market, provides the best of all worlds. It combines the comfortable, secure setting of a suburban town with convenient access to the excitement of major cultural centers, including Philadelphia (50 miles south) and New York City (75 miles northeast). Lehigh is situated in Bethlehem, Pennsylvania, an ethnically diverse community of 78,000 that offers a variety of cultural events, ethnic restaurants, and sources of entertainment to three quarters of a million people.

Lehigh offers a unique mixture of modern, state-of-the-art facilities and historic, ivy-covered stone buildings. Situated on the side and top of scenic South Mountain in the Saucon Valley, the University's three contiguous campuses, spread over 1,600 acres, rival the most beautiful parks. Amidst tall trees, wooded hills, and colorful landscaping, the Asa Packer Campus is home to more than 100 historic and contemporary structures. The Mountaintop Campus provides additional teaching and research space for the biosciences and the College of Education. The Murray H. Goodman Campus features the 16,000-seat Goodman Stadium for football; the 5,600-seat Stabler Arena for indoor athletics contests, concerts, and special events; Rauch Field House; Ulrich Sports Complex, with both natural grass and artificial turf fields; and extensive outdoor athletic fields for intercollegiate and intramural sports.

Majors and Degrees

The College of Arts and Sciences, the largest college with just under half of the University's faculty members and undergraduates, offers flexible curricula, personal attention to students, and a problem-solving culture. Students explore seventy-seven majors and minors in forty disciplines in eighteen departments spanning the arts, humanities, social sciences, and natural sciences. Departments team on joint ventures in the new Humanities Center, where courses, lectures, and informal gatherings embrace literature, languages, religion studies, philosophy, current events, the history of art, and architecture and music. Another example is the Lehigh Earth Observatory (LEO), in which teams of students work on real-world problems as they study environmental systems and their relationship with society. The modern Zoellner Arts Center is home to Lehigh's outstanding programs of music and theater. Cross-disciplinary programs like Africana studies, classical civilization, computer science and business, design arts, economics, women's studies, and science, technology, and society provide a well-rounded education and a rich variety of career opportunities. The college offers a four-year curriculum in arts and sciences, a five-year curriculum in arts-engineering, double-degree programs, and a combined bachelor's/master's degree program in education.

With its interdisciplinary approach to learning, the College of Business and Economics is powerfully positioned to develop leaders. It provides strong programs at both the graduate and undergraduate levels. Traditional undergraduate business majors, as well as a variety of niche-based, market-driven programs such as supply chain management, computer science and business, and integrated business and engineering, are offered. The Bachelor of Science degree is offered with majors in accounting, business economics, computer science and business, economics, finance, information systems, management, marketing, and supply chain management. The Bachelor of Science degree in business and engineering (BSBE) is offered to those completing the Integrated Business and Engineering (IBE) Honors Program. The business and accounting programs are accredited by AACSB International–The Association to Advance Collegiate Schools of Business.

In the College of Education, undergraduates discover new ways of learning with their world-renowned professors, fellow students, and the children and adults they serve. The College of Education has consistently climbed the ranks among U.S. graduate schools and offers some of the most competitive programs in the country. The college has a strong focus on the use of information technology in education, and faculty members are highly entrepreneurial in creating new learning experiences. The college offers a five-year combined-degree program leading to a B.S. or B.A. in a defined major and elementary or secondary education teaching certification.

The P.C. Rossin College of Engineering and Applied Science is internationally known for the quality of its professors and its research. Students receive a hands-on education and work on cutting-edge research projects with professors and with industry engineers. A co-op program allows students to work eight months for a company and graduate in four years. The college offers the B.S. degree in applied science, arts and engineering (five-year dual-degree program), bioengineering, chemical engineering, civil engineering, computer engineering, computer science, electrical engineering, engineering mechanics, engineering physics, environmental engineering, industrial engineering, information and systems engineering, materials science and engineering, and mechanical engineering. The College of Engineering, with the College of Business and Economics, offers the demanding and popular Integrated Business and Engineering Honors Program and a computer science and business degree. With the College of Arts and Sciences, the engineering college offers an arts/engineering dual degree and a B.S. in bioengineering. The three colleges also offer an award-winning one-year course in integrated product development (IPD), in which student teams make and market products for corporate sponsors.

Academic Program

Students are expected to maintain regular progress toward the baccalaureate degree by carrying the normal course load of 12 to 18 credit hours each semester. They may, however, accelerate the pace by using Advanced Placement credits, summer-session study, and course overloads, and by gaining credit for courses through examination. Students in good academic standing earn their degrees by meeting the requirements of their specific degree curriculum as well as general University requirements. Students should confer with their advisers on curricular matters.

Off-Campus Programs

Semester and yearlong study-abroad programs are available in Australia, Austria, Belgium, China, Costa Rica, Denmark, Egypt, England, France, Germany, Ghana, Greece, Hungary, Ireland, Israel, Italy, Japan, Kenya, Korea, Mexico, New Zealand, Russia, Scotland, Spain, Sweden, Taiwan, and Wales. Lehigh summer-study programs are available in London and Paris and at other locations in Europe and China. All programs are approved for credit. Internships in other countries are available. Credit for off-campus study may be earned through Urban Semesters in Philadelphia and Washington, D.C., and by cross-registration with a consortium of five other Lehigh Valley colleges.

Academic Facilities

From technology to the arts, Lehigh students learn in outstanding facilities as partners with professors in research and scholarship. The Zoellner Arts Center provides a laboratory for learning, performing, and visual arts for the University and the Lehigh Valley community. Lehigh was one of America's first "wired" campuses, with information network links in every residence, classroom, and office, and with large areas of wireless network access. Library and computing facilities provide access to more than 1.2 million print books and journals as well as a growing array of electronic databases and journals, computer software, and media collections.

Lehigh expects students to meet stringent academic demands, but the University provides support services to ensure each student ample opportunity to succeed. Lehigh's Dean of Students Office directs students toward help with academic or personal problems, legal issues, or general concerns. Lehigh offers a health center, fitness center, counseling service, drug and alcohol counseling service, testing service, and learning center. The University provides career planning and placement throughout students' undergraduate years and offers comprehensive support services for students who are members of minority groups.

Costs

Tuition in 2003–04 was $27,230; average room and board cost $7880.

Financial Aid

Lehigh offers merit scholarships each year based on academics, leadership, or talent in music or theater. Top Lehigh students who graduate and meet certain requirements can take a fifth year of courses, tuition-free, to earn a master's or second bachelor's degree through the President's Scholars program.

College selection should be based on educational growth opportunities, not on sticker price. Financial aid is designed to make college affordable for families unable to meet its costs. Lehigh is committed to providing need-based financial aid.

In 2002–03, Lehigh awarded more than $36 million in University grants and scholarships. Approximately 50 percent of freshmen receive financial aid awards. Financial aid packages are typically made up of a combination of scholarships/need-based grants, loans, and work-study. More than half of all incoming freshmen receive financial aid awards; the average freshman award for the 2002–03 school year was $19,156. Awards based on financial need ranged from $500 to $33,000.

In addition to providing students with extra cash to cover expenses, work-study jobs can also be a great opportunity to enhance a resume. At Lehigh, work-study positions can range from writing press releases in the Office of University Relations to working the front desk at the student health center.

Lehigh is a member of College Scholarship Service. To apply for need-based financial aid, the CSS/Profile and FAFSA are required. Financial aid application deadlines come early; the freshmen fall application deadline is January 1.

Faculty

Lehigh's 417 full-time faculty members and 572 total instructional faculty members, 99 percent of whom hold doctoral or other terminal degrees in their fields, are nationally and internationally known leaders in research and scholarship. They are committed first and foremost to undergraduate teaching and advising. It is common for a senior faculty member to teach a freshman course, and close student-faculty advising is the norm. Faculty members often meet with individual students and small groups outside of class, accompany students abroad, and participate in student governance and other activities.

Student Government

The Student Senate is an elected deliberative body that addresses student life and campus issues. Students are ensured access to the highest levels of decision making through two nonvoting representatives to the Board of Trustees.

Admission Requirements

Lehigh encourages men and women of all backgrounds to consider study at the University. All applicants should have completed 4 years of English, 3 or 4 years of mathematics, 2 to 4 years of history and social studies, 2 to 4 years of laboratory science, and 2 years of foreign language. An individual's potential cannot be fully reflected in the accumulation of units in a four-year college-preparatory program, so Lehigh considers a number of criteria in evaluating applicants, especially the strength of the high school record. The University requires either the SAT I or ACT, which must be taken by December of the senior year.

The middle 50 percent of students admitted to Lehigh score between 1210 and 1350 on the SAT I. However, the staff in Lehigh's admissions office works hard to move beyond the numbers and to look at a student's entire profile when making acceptance decisions. Admissions counselors review such factors as Advanced Placement or honors courses, evidence of special talent, and a student's leadership record. To provide prospective students with an opportunity to get to know the University and to determine if Lehigh is a good match, on-campus group or personal interviews are recommended.

Application and Information

Early Decision applications must be filed by November 15; regular applications must be submitted by January 1. For students who determine that Lehigh is their first choice later in the process, the University offers an Early Decision II option with an application deadline of January 1 and a declaration of intent to apply Early Decision II by February 1. Entrance exams should be taken by the January test date. Orientations for prospective students, consisting of general information sessions, campus tours, and personal interviews, are scheduled Monday through Friday. Interviews and tours are also available on some Saturdays. To schedule a visit, contact:

Bruce Gardiner
Interim Dean of Admissions and Financial Aid
Office of Admissions
Lehigh University
27 Memorial Drive West
Bethlehem, Pennsylvania 18015-3094
Telephone: 610-758-3100
Fax: 610-758-4361
E-mail: admissions@lehigh.edu
World Wide Web: http://www.lehigh.edu

LEHMAN COLLEGE OF THE CITY UNIVERSITY OF NEW YORK

BRONX, NEW YORK

The College

Established in 1968 as a senior college of the City University of New York (CUNY), Lehman offers nearly ninety undergraduate and graduate degree programs and specializations in business, business administration, computer graphics and imaging, liberal arts, natural and social sciences, education, nursing and health professions, and the fine and performing arts. Many programs provide training for particular careers and lead to professional degrees, preparing students for positions in private, nonprofit, and government organizations as well as for graduate study.

Lehman offers an active, diversified, and supportive campus life. Organized around various cultural, religious, political, academic, and personal interests, more than sixty clubs are housed in a Student Life Building that also features computer, conference, kitchen, and recreation areas. Many of these activities give students valuable experiences both for careers and for life. Through counseling and additional support services, students find the answers to academic and career questions, while a Child Care Center, Student Health Center, and Special Student Services help meet a variety of other needs.

Lehman serves as a regional center for the arts and recreation. The campus has a 2,300-seat Concert Hall, a 500-seat theater, a 150-seat recital hall, and an art gallery. In addition, the campus publishes several newspapers and hosts a radio station and a cable television station. The APEX, a sports and recreation facility, includes a fully equipped fitness center; a free-weight room; two full-size gymnasiums; four racquetball courts; a two-lane, 1⁄16-mile indoor track; an aerobics/dance studio; a ballet studio; an Olympic-size indoor swimming pool; and five outdoor tennis courts.

Location

Lehman College is located in a quiet residential neighborhood in the northwest Bronx. Convenient to major highways and multiple bus and subway lines, this location offers students easy access to the cultural, social, and academic resources of a city that is world renowned for its opportunities in almost every field of endeavor.

Majors and Degrees

Majors at Lehman College include accounting (specialties in industrial and government accounting and accounting and business practice); American studies; anthropology; anthropology (physical), biology, and chemistry; art (specialties in art history and studio art in ceramics, computer imaging, painting, photography, printmaking, and sculpture); biology; black studies; business administration; business education; chemistry (specialty in biochemistry); comparative literature; computer graphics and imaging; computer science; computing and management; dance; dance-theater; dietetics, foods, and nutrition; economics (specialty in business management); English (specialties in creative writing, literature, and professional writing); French; geography; geology; German; Greek; Greek and Latin (specialty in classical culture); health education and promotion (options in community health and community health and nutrition); health N–12 teacher studies; health services administration; Hebraic and Judaic studies (specialties in Hebraic and Judaic studies); Hebrew; history; Italian; Italian-American studies; Latin; Latin American and Caribbean studies; linguistics; mathematics; multilingual journalism; music; nursing; philosophy (specialties in ethics and public policy); physics; political science; psychology; Puerto Rican studies; recreation education; Russian; social work; sociology; Spanish; speech; speech and theater (specialties in communication arts—mass communications and public and group communications); speech pathology and audiology; and theater.

Academic Programs

Lehman College offers 120-credit Bachelor of Arts, Bachelor of Science, and Bachelor of Fine Arts degree programs in the liberal arts and sciences as well as a dual Bachelor of Arts/Master of Arts in mathematics. Many of these programs include course work and fieldwork that lead to professional certification. These programs include the B.S. in accounting–certified public accountant; dietetics, foods, and nutrition–dietitian; education (elementary)–elementary school teacher (N–6); education (secondary)–secondary school teacher in academic subjects; health education and promotion–health education specialist and health N–12 teacher; health services administration–nursing home administrator; professional nursing–registered nurse; recreation education–therapeutic recreation specialist and certified leisure professional; and speech education–teacher of the speech and hearing handicapped. Lehman also offers courses that lead to graduate programs for professional certification, including predentistry, prelaw, premedicine, prepharmacy, pre–veterinary science, and social work; these Lehman programs include a professional option that allows students to complete the undergraduate degree at an accredited professional school in their senior year. In addition, a pre-engineering transfer program is offered in cooperation with the School of Engineering at City College.

Lehman also offers an array of programs designed for specific needs and interests. These include the Freshman Year Initiative, which helps students make the transition from high school to college; the Individualized Baccalaureate Program for students who wish to design their own majors; the Lehman Scholars Program for honors students; the CUNY Honors College for exceptional students; the Adult Degree Program for returning students; ESL and Language Transition Programs; and study-abroad programs.

The 120-credit baccalaureate program includes core curriculum courses in the humanities, social sciences, the modern age, natural sciences, and problem solving through quantitative reasoning. Students must also complete distribution courses in seven major areas of study as well as courses in English composition, oral English, and foreign language. They also must fulfill major requirements, and minor fields of study are required of most students, although students in certain majors are exempt from the minor requirement. In addition, all students must be in compliance with CUNY testing requirements.

The academic calendar is divided into fall and spring semesters, with two summer sessions. Classes are offered days, nights, and weekends to accommodate students with work and family responsibilities.

Off-Campus Programs

Through a cooperative arrangement, students may take courses at other colleges within the City University of New York, one of the nation's most distinguished and extensive university systems. Off-campus internships are available through the academic departments and the Career Services Office. Opportunities for overseas study are available for an intersession, a semester, or an academic year through sponsored trips and the study-abroad and Paris/CUNY Exchange Programs.

Academic Facilities

Lehman's 37-acre campus is dominated by Gothic towers and tree-lined walks, where a blend of traditional and modern design helps reinforce the College's sense of community. This sense of community is further enhanced by the computers (including personal and multiuser systems) available for student use in the new Information Technology Center, the library, and departmental facilities. They provide access to general-purpose and specialized-application software, local and regional networks, and the Internet. Audio/video reception/distribution capability via satellite and other means is available in many classrooms, as are specialized facilities to support multimedia, distance learning, and high-end graphics capabilities. The library offers 546,000 books, 574,000 microforms, and 1,300 periodicals in open stacks and a fully automated CUNY-wide book catalog with a remote-access circulation system, periodical indexes, electronic full-text databases, a CD-ROM LAN, and large video and audio collections.

Costs

Eligible New York State residents who are matriculated students pay $2000 per semester for full-time study, which is at least 12 credits or credit equivalents, $170 per credit for matriculated part-time study, or $220 per credit for nonmatriculated study. Nonresidents and international students pay $360 per credit for full-time and part-time matriculated study, and $470 per credit for nonmatriculated study. Each semester, all students must pay a student activity fee. The fee is $55 for full-time students, $35 for part-time students for the fall and spring semesters, and $30 during the summer sessions with a $5 consolidated service fee. Also, each semester all students must pay a technology fee. The fee is $75 for full-time students and $37.50 for part-time students.

Financial Aid

Lehman College participates in federal and New York State financial aid programs. Students may request aid by filing a Free Application for Federal Student Aid (FAFSA), which may make them eligible for Federal Pell Grants, FSEOG, SEEK, the Federal Work-Study Program, and student loans. New York State residents may also file a Financial Aid Supplemental Information Request (FASIR), which may enable them to participate in New York State's Tuition Assistance Program (TAP). The College also offers various scholarships, including a renewable Academic Achievement Award Scholarship for entering students. Other scholarships and awards are tied to specific areas of study; students in eligible fields of study are given assistance in pursuing federal scholarship programs.

Faculty

The College has more than 300 full-time faculty members, of whom 85 percent hold doctoral degrees or their equivalent. Many have been recognized nationally and internationally for their scholarship and research through grants and awards; a significant number serve as faculty members at CUNY's graduate center. Most important, faculty members work closely with students outside the classroom in individual and group settings to support their academic, professional, and personal growth. The faculty-student ratio is 1:15.

Student Government

Lehman's student government is divided into the Campus Association for Student Activities (CASA), the programming arm of the student government, and the Student Conference, the legislative arm of the student government. CASA officers are responsible for the appropriation and management of student funds for clubs, cultural programs, entertainment, and other activities. The Student Conference makes up approximately one third of the Lehman College Senate, the decision-making body on matters of academic policy.

Admission Requirements

Students with combined SAT I scores of 1100 or better are admitted. Applicants with combined scores less than 1100 are determined eligible by SAT I scores and three other high school transcript components. The first of these three is the total number of College Preparatory Initiative (CPI) units. In evaluating high school transcripts, CUNY assigns CPI units to Regents-level courses indicated on the student's high school transcript. Second, CUNY evaluates the College Academic Average (the high school academic average earned only in CPI English, a foreign language, social studies, mathematics, science, and fine arts courses). Third, CUNY evaluates a student's earned average in English CPI courses. These four components are weighted to create an eligible admissions index.

Applicants who do not meet these freshman admission requirements but who satisfy particular academic and economic criteria may be eligible for admission through the SEEK program, the City University's opportunity program for senior colleges.

Transfer students who have earned at least 13 credits must have an overall cumulative index of at least 2.0 in all previous college work. Students transferring with fewer than 13 credits must have an overall cumulative index of at least 2.5 or meet the requirements for freshman admission. Students transferring from CUNY community or comprehensive colleges must also pass the Skills Assessment Tests prior to their admission to the College.

Applicants with student or other nonimmigrant visas who were not educated in an English system are required to score a minimum of 500 on the written TOEFL or 173 on the computerized TOEFL.

Application and Information

Applicants are encouraged to submit their completed applications with all official documentation and fees by March 15 for fall admission or by October 1 for spring admission.

The staff of the admissions office is available to answer questions and provide assistance with the admissions process. Students may request application materials, speak with an Admissions Counselor, or schedule a campus tour by contacting:

Office of Admissions
Shuster Hall, Room 161
Lehman College
250 Bedford Park Boulevard West
Bronx, New York 10468-1589
Telephone: 718-960-8713
877-LEHMAN-1 (toll-free)
E-mail: enroll@lehman.cuny.edu
World Wide Web: http://www.lehman.cuny.edu

LE MOYNE COLLEGE

SYRACUSE, NEW YORK

The College

Le Moyne College is a four-year, coeducational Jesuit college of approximately 2,500 undergraduate students that uniquely balances a comprehensive liberal arts education with preparation for specific career paths or graduate study. Founded by the Society of Jesus in 1946, Le Moyne is the second-youngest of the twenty-eight Jesuit colleges and universities in the United States. Its emphasis is on the education of the whole person and on the search for meaning and value as integral parts of an intellectual life. Le Moyne's personal approach to education is reflected in the quality of contact between students and faculty members. A wide range of student-directed activities, athletics, clubs, and service organizations complement the academic experience. Intramural sports are very popular with Le Moyne students, and nearly 50 percent of the students participate in athletics. Le Moyne also has sixteen NCAA intercollegiate teams (eight for men and eight for women). Athletic facilities include soccer/lacrosse, softball, and baseball fields; tennis, basketball, and racquetball courts; a weight-training and fitness center; practice fields; and two gymnasiums. A recreation center houses an Olympic-size indoor swimming pool, jogging track, indoor tennis and volleyball courts, and additional basketball, racquetball, and fitness areas. More than 75 percent of students live in residence halls, apartments, and town houses on campus. The Residence Hall Councils and the Le Moyne Student Programming Board organize a variety of campus activities, including concerts, dances, a weekly film series, student talent programs, and special lectures as well as off-campus trips and skiing excursions.

Location

Le Moyne's 150-acre, tree-lined campus is located in a residential setting 10 minutes from downtown Syracuse, the heart of New York State, whose metropolitan population is about 700,000. Syracuse is convenient to most major cities throughout the Northeast, New England, and Canada, and offers a wide array of shopping centers and restaurants, many near Le Moyne. Syracuse offers year-round entertainment in the form of rock concerts at the Carrier Dome and Landmark Theatre; professional baseball, hockey, and lacrosse; Bristol Omnitheatre; the Syracuse Symphony Orchestra; Syracuse Stage; Everson Museum of Art; and the Armory Square district downtown, offering one-of-a-kind eateries, pubs, and coffeehouses in addition to a wide variety of social and cultural events. All are easily accessible via the excellent public transportation service, which schedules regular stops on Le Moyne's campus. Just a few miles outside the city are the rolling hills, picturesque lakes, and miles of open country for which central New York is renowned. An extensive network of state and county parks, recreational areas, and other facilities offer an abundance of recreational opportunities, including swimming, boating, hiking, downhill and cross-country skiing, snowboarding, and golf.

Majors and Degrees

Le Moyne College awards the Bachelor of Arts degree in biology, communication, communication/advertising, communication/print journalism, communication/public relations, communication/television and radio, criminology and crime & justice studies, economics, English, English/creative writing, English/drama, English/literature, French, history, mathematics, mathematics/actuarial science, mathematics/operations research, mathematics/pure mathematics, mathematics/statistics, peace and global studies/general studies, peace and global studies/Latin American studies, philosophy, physics, political science, psychology, religious studies, sociology, sociology/anthropology, sociology/criminology and criminal justice, sociology/human services, sociology/research and theory, Spanish, and theater arts. The Bachelor of Science degree is awarded in accounting, biochemistry, biology, biology/physician assistant studies, business administration, business/applied management analysis, business/finance, business/information systems, business/leadership, business/marketing, chemistry, economics, industrial relations and human resource management, information systems, multiple science, physics, physics/pre-engineering, and psychology.

Students may minor in anthropology, Catholic studies, classic humanities, fine arts, Japanese, Latin, urban studies, or women's studies as well as in any of the major fields of study offered. Preprofessional programs are offered in dentistry, law, medicine, and optometry. Students may prepare for teaching careers through certification programs in adolescent education, dual adolescent/special education, dual childhood/special education, middle childhood specialist, and TESOL.

Formal accelerated 3-4 programs are offered in dentistry, optometry, and podiatry in cooperation with SUNY at Buffalo School of Dental Medicine, Pennsylvania College of Optometry, and the New York College of Podiatric Medicine. Predental students may also participate in an early assurance program with SUNY at Buffalo School of Dental Medicine. Cooperative 3-2 dual-degree programs in engineering are available with Clarkson University, Manhattan College, and University of Detroit Mercy. A 2-2 program in environmental science and forestry is available in cooperation with SUNY College of Environmental Science and Forestry in Syracuse.

SUNY Upstate Medical University in Syracuse offers students pursuing careers in the health-related professions a master's-level transfer program in physical therapy as well as two-year cooperative transfer programs in cytotechnology, medical technology, and respiratory care. Premedical students at Le Moyne are also offered the opportunity to participate in a medical school early assurance program. An early assurance program for premedical students is also available through SUNY at Buffalo School of Medicine.

Academic Programs

While each major department has its own sequence requirements for the minimum 120 credit hours needed for the Le Moyne degree, the College is convinced that there is a fundamental intellectual discipline that should characterize the graduate of a superior liberal arts college. Le Moyne's core curriculum provides this foundation by including studies of English language and literature, foreign language, philosophy, history, religious studies, natural sciences, mathematics, and social sciences.

For exceptional students, Le Moyne offers an integral honors program that includes an interdisciplinary humanities sequence as well as departmental honors courses. Le Moyne also offers a part-time course of study during evening hours through its Center for Continuous Education.

Le Moyne students may enroll in Army and Air Force ROTC programs at Syracuse University.

Off-Campus Programs

The study-abroad program allows students to spend semesters in Australia, China, Dominican Republic, Japan, and exciting European locations such as England, France, Ireland, Italy, Scotland, and Spain. Le Moyne is a participant in the sixty-member New York State Visiting Student Program. For career preparation, Le Moyne's strong emphasis on internships has been a continuing and expanding source of resume-building and real-world experiences for students from several different majors, all of whom have gained invaluable credentials to take to their first interviews. In addition, science interns have been given extraordinary access to research opportunities with some of the leading labs and companies. Externships allow students to observe alumni working in a particular area of interest. This program has taken students to places such as the White House and Capitol Building in Washington, D.C.; New York State's seat of government in Albany; and hospitals, Fortune 500 companies, and a wide array of small businesses. In addition, many student-teaching opportunities exist. In every education class, from freshman through senior years, students are required to spend time in a classroom.

Academic Facilities

Le Moyne students benefit from an ongoing commitment to technological excellence. The College's thirty-four buildings are equipped with accounting, biology, chemistry, computer science, physics, psychology, and statistics laboratories. The W. Carroll Coyne Center for the Performing Arts houses generous production, performance, and classroom space; the latest light and sound technology; scene and costume shops; an aerobics and dance studio; and rehearsal rooms for instrumental and choral music. Academic facilities also include an extensively renovated color television studio; a radio/recording studio; a receiver-antenna satellite dish; transmission and scanning electron microscopes; a nuclear magnetic resonance spectrometer; a gas chromatograph/mass spectrophotometer; a 240,000-volume, open-stack library; and extensive on-site computer facilities. A fiber-optic network enables students to access the library system, the campus network, and the Internet from several computer labs around campus or from their personal computers in their rooms. All classrooms have been converted to smart classrooms, with multimedia capabilities that expand and enrich the learning process. Le Moyne students have access to other libraries through the Central New York Library Resources Council, and the campus Academic Support Center is available to students for instructional support.

Costs

For 2003–04, Le Moyne's tuition was $18,440. Room and board charges were $7250. Additional fees amounted to approximately $500, and books and supplies cost approximately $550.

Financial Aid

Financial aid is offered to a large percentage of Le Moyne's students through scholarships, grants, loans, and work-study assignments. Le Moyne offers a generous program of merit-based academic and athletic scholarships as well as financial aid based on a student's need and academic promise. Federal funds are available through the Federal Pell Grant, Federal Work-Study, Federal Supplemental Educational Opportunity Grant, and Federal Perkins Loan programs. A student's eligibility for need-based financial aid is determined from both the Free Application for Federal Student Aid (FAFSA) and the Le Moyne Financial Aid Application Form. It is recommended that these forms be mailed by February 1.

Faculty

The Le Moyne full-time faculty numbers 149 men and women; 91 percent have earned the highest degree in their fields. With an average class size of 20 students, a student-faculty ratio of 13:1, and private offices for all full-time faculty members, the College promotes a personal as well as academic relationship between students and faculty. All classroom instruction is done by faculty members, and they are happy to assist and encourage students who wish to pursue undergraduate research through tutorials or senior research projects. These projects are carried out in an atmosphere free of competition from graduate students for books, laboratories, or professors' time. Le Moyne emphasizes advising and academic counseling for students throughout their four years.

Student Government

The College encourages student leadership in all activities. Positions of leadership are open to students in all class years. Students are represented by a Student Senate and have formal representation through the senate on most College-wide committees involved in decision making and policy formation.

Admission Requirements

Le Moyne seeks qualified students who are well prepared for serious academic study. Secondary school preparation must have included at least 17 college-preparatory high school units, 4 of which must be in English, 4 in social studies, 3–4 in mathematics, 3–4 in foreign language, and 3–4 in science. It is also recommended that prospective science and mathematics majors complete 4 units of mathematics and science. The SAT I or ACT is required and should be taken by December or January of the senior year in high school. Campus visits are strongly recommended, as the admission process is a personal one. As bases for selection, academic achievement and secondary school recommendations are of primary importance; SAT I or ACT scores are important as they relate to the record of achievement and to recommendations. Out-of-state students are encouraged to apply.

Application and Information

The Admission Committee reviews applications and mails decisions on a rolling admission cycle beginning January 1. The priority deadline for applications is February 1; all students who wish to be considered for academic merit scholarships should have a completed application on file in the Office of Admission before this date. Students who wish to be considered under the early decision program must have a completed application submitted by December 1. Early decision applicants are notified by December 15. Transfer students are encouraged to apply before June 1 for the fall semester and December 1 for the spring semester. A two-day orientation program takes place in midsummer.

Dennis J. Nicholson
Director of Admission
Le Moyne College
Syracuse, New York 13214-1399
Telephone: 315-445-4300
800-333-4733 (toll-free)
E-mail: admission@lemoyne.edu
World Wide Web: http://www.lemoyne.edu

Grewen Hall, the oldest building on campus, overlooks Le Moyne's beautiful 150-acre campus.

LESLEY COLLEGE

CAMBRIDGE, MASSACHUSETTS

The College

Lesley College, the undergraduate women's college of Lesley University, is a small, residential, four-year college where students enjoy the intellectual climate of a university community along with the small class sizes and engaged faculty they expect in a small college. The 550 full-time students live on a 5-acre campus, an urban academic village, just off Harvard Square in Cambridge and minutes from downtown Boston.

Lesley College students benefit tremendously from the resources and breadth of opportunities that come from being part of Lesley University, a comprehensive institution of more than 10,000 men and women. Students can cross-register for courses in the other schools at Lesley University, including the Art Institute of Boston, a coeducational college of art that merged with Lesley in 1998. Accelerated bachelor's/master's programs have been developed in conjunction with the School of Education and the Graduate School of Arts and Social Sciences. And the Lesley Dividend offers qualified Lesley College students a year of free graduate tuition when they continue with graduate study at the University.

At Lesley, the students share one thing in common: a passion for making a difference in the lives of others. Some may plan to have that impact through teaching, others through careers in human services or counseling, and others by working in not-for-profit organizations that serve the community. And it is through Lesley's unique integration of the liberal arts with professional course work and significant "hands on" internship experience that the students crystallize these goals.

The University is accredited by the New England Association of Schools and Colleges. The teacher certification programs have been approved by the National Association of State Directors of Teacher Education and Certification (NASDTEC), which offers a reciprocity agreement in which more than forty states and other organizations have established standards for granting certification.

Location

Lesley is located in a quiet residential area and is right around the corner from MIT and Harvard, a quick walk from Harvard Square and a short subway ride from Boston. Cambridge has everything: bookstores, cafes, theaters, concert halls, parks, festivals, restaurants, and students. In fact, nearly 250,000 students live in the Boston/Cambridge area. Metropolitan Boston is famous for its educational and business resources, and cultural life is rich and varied. More than 100 museums, dedicated to virtually every artistic, cultural, and scientific discipline, provide ample opportunities for student involvement on many levels. There are shops and restaurants of every ethnic variety, first-run films, theater, and famed professional sports teams. In addition, the Boston area has an efficient public transportation system for travel within the metropolitan area and easy, direct transportation to and from all regions of the United States.

Majors and Degrees

Lesley College offers Bachelor of Science degrees in the following professional areas: art therapy, child studies, communication technology, counseling, education, human services, and management. Although the majority of students do major in a professional area, there are also eight liberal arts majors that are designed to work especially well with the education programs. Liberal arts majors include American studies, the arts, English, environmental studies, global studies, history, human development and family studies, and natural science: mathematics and science.

Students interested in teaching concentrate in one of the following areas: early childhood education, elementary education, middle school education, secondary education, special education, or day-care leadership. Students majoring in one of these areas are also required to elect a double major in one of eight liberal arts areas. Completion of a major in education qualifies a student to be recommended for initial licensure in Massachusetts and the other states that are members of NASDTEC and have signed the Interstate Contract.

Students pursuing a major in other professional areas (art therapy, child studies, communication technology, counseling, human services, or management) combine a liberal arts minor with their professional studies.

Like all Lesley students, those who choose to major in one of the liberal arts areas integrate professional course work and internship experiences through an Individualized Professional Minor. This creates a liberal arts program that is designed for the real world—for real careers and real success.

In addition, the following accelerated bachelor's/master's degree programs are offered in conjunction with Lesley's graduate programs: a B.S./M.A. in counseling psychology or clinical mental health counseling; and a B.S./M.Ed. in early childhood education, elementary education, middle school education, or special education.

Academic Program

All of Lesley's academic programs are designed to integrate study in the liberal arts with professional course work and significant hands-on internship experience.

Internship experiences begin in the freshman year and are developmentally sequenced to complement classroom instruction throughout the undergraduate program. Internships are designed to show students what the workplace is like, challenge assumptions they may have about themselves and the world, and give the kind of experience that creates exceptional resumes. In fact, by the end of four years, Lesley students have spent from 400 to 650 hours out in the field. What's more, internships are integrated with seminar classes in which students discuss and evaluate their fieldwork, learning also from fellow students' experiences about workplace issues and emerging trends. It is this careful integration of theory and practice that Lesley believes really distinguishes its curriculum from those at other colleges.

Through a comprehensive general education program, all students also build a strong liberal arts foundation by taking courses in the arts, humanities, sciences, and social sciences. Through this liberal arts course work students develop their ability to think critically and strengthen writing skills, as well as ensure that they have a breadth of knowledge and skills that lead to success in graduate school and an interest in a life of learning.

Off-Campus Programs

Lesley College offers students the opportunity to participate in a number of Lesley-affiliated programs of off-campus study, in the U.S. and abroad, through which they may obtain Lesley College credit. In addition, each year a number of students choose to study abroad in non-Lesley programs, and a faculty adviser provides guidance regarding transfer of credit as well as advice about researching available programs.

Lesley-affiliated programs include the Orebro University Program in Sweden; the American University Washington and World Capitals Semester Program in Washington, D.C.; and several Lesley-sponsored study/travel opportunities. Current study/travel opportunities include the British Experience, Field Study in Europe: The Holocaust, Traditions and Cultures: Ireland, Traditions and Cultures of the Southwest: Santa Fe, and New England Field Studies: The Tall Ship *Ernestina*.

Academic Facilities

The Eleanor DeWolfe Ludcke Library is a state-of-the-art multimedia resource center supporting the academic programs of the university through a collection of books, journals, and multimedia and electronic resources. Located at the center of campus, the Ludcke Library also houses the Kresge Center for Teaching Resources as well as a computer lab and three computer classrooms.

The Kresge Center for Teaching Resources offers one of the finest collections of juvenile literature in the Northeast, as well as teaching aids; video, audio, and film collections; and media services. Students may produce teaching materials, using the center's equipment, and professional staff members offer support in children's literature, media materials, and production of teaching materials.

Ludcke Library offers a wide array of resources through the World Wide Web. On its home page, students may search the library catalog, identify and print journal articles and other documents, and search the Internet. A growing collection of full-text databases offers articles and documents in education, business, management, science, the humanities, and the social sciences. Students may access these resources both on- and off-campus via the Internet.

Ludcke Library is a member of the Fenway Library Consortium (FLC), a cooperative group of fifteen academic, special, and public libraries that offer reciprocal borrowing to the faculty and staff members and students of its member institutions.

The Instructional Computing Center consists of three classrooms and a lab area, with Macintosh and Windows-compatible computers, full Internet and e-mail access, scanners, laser printers, and other computer peripherals. Instructional Computing's educational software collection has more than 2,000 titles, ranging from pre-K through college level. In addition, the Mollye Lichter Block Computer Lab for word processing is open 24 hours a day.

Costs

Fees in 2003–04 for enrollment in Lesley College include tuition, $19,525; room and board, $8800; a health services fee, $1152; and a student activity fee, $175. Costs are subject to change without prior notice. (Students should call the university to confirm current expense figures.)

Financial Aid

No student should fail to consider Lesley because of financial considerations. More than 80 percent of Lesley College students receive financial aid from one or more sources. The average amount received by newly enrolled students is $16,000 in a combination of scholarships/grants, loans, and work-study jobs. The university participates in all federal aid programs, including the Federal Pell Grant, Federal Supplemental Educational Opportunity Grant, Federal Perkins Loan, and Federal Work-Study programs. Lesley also offers its own grants and need-based scholarships as well as an array of merit scholarships, ranging from $5000 to full tuition.

Students applying for financial aid must submit the Free Application for Federal Student Aid (FAFSA) and request that copies of the analyses be sent to Lesley University. In addition, students must complete the Lesley financial aid application, which is included in the application for admission. Students are advised to file all financial aid forms and documents as early as possible. The FAFSA should be filed by February 1 and the Lesley form by February 15.

Faculty

Lesley College faculty members hold teaching undergraduates as their highest priority. Even more important to a student's classroom experience, however, is the fact that many members of the faculty are trained practitioners, classroom educators, counselors, social workers, and business professionals. In fact, many continue to work in the field or as consultants and bring a wealth of real-world experience into their classroom teaching.

Of the 70 full- and part-time Lesley College faculty members, more than two thirds hold a doctorate or other terminal degree. Faculty members serve as academic advisers for students, and the student-faculty ratio of 16:1 allows for a close relationship to develop between students and their professors.

Student Government

The Student Senate is the representative governing body of the Lesley College student population. Through the sponsorship of the senate, numerous organizations, activities, seminars, and conferences are brought to the Lesley campus.

Admission Requirements

The College has designed the admission process to be reflective of the institution and its values. Lesley is an institution that values community and service to the community. Therefore, the College is interested in students who value making a difference in the lives of others and who have shown a commitment to community service. Lesley is also seeking students who, through a strong college preparatory curriculum, have gained the knowledge and skills that allow them to thrive and be successful in the academic programs. Graduates of accredited secondary schools with a total of 20 colleges-prep units of study are encouraged to apply for admission. Included in the 20 units are the following: English, 4 units; mathematics, at least 3 units; American history, 1 unit; and science, at least 3 units. Admitted freshmen typically have a 3.0 average or higher. All freshman applicants must submit SAT 1 or ACT scores. A personal interview is recommended.

Students who have been fully matriculated in a degree program at another college or university may apply for admission as transfers. The maximum number of hours that may be transferred is 65. Transfer applicants must present a minimum cumulative grade point average of 2.5. Advanced standing is determined by the nature and quality of the work offered for credit.

Application and Information

Applications are reviewed on a rolling basis beginning December 1, with a preferred freshman deadline of March 1 and a transfer application deadline of June 1 for the fall semester. All applications for the spring semester are due by December 15. A $35 application fee must accompany all freshman and transfer applications.

For further information about Lesley, students should contact:

Office of Admissions
Lesley College
29 Everett Street
Cambridge, Massachusetts 02138-2790
Telephone: 617-349-8800
800-999-1959 Ext. 8800 (toll-free)
E-mail: ugadm@mail.lesley.edu
World Wide Web: http://www.lesley.edu/lc

LEWIS & CLARK COLLEGE

PORTLAND, OREGON

The College

Founded in 1867 in a small town south of Portland, Lewis & Clark College moved to its present location in Portland's southwest hills in 1942. The 137-acre campus is situated in a wooded residential area 6 miles from the center of the city and overlooks the lush Willamette Valley and Mount Hood in the distance. The student body is known for its geographic diversity. In fall 2003, of the 1,792 undergraduates, 18 percent were from Oregon and 82 percent came from forty-nine other states and forty-six countries. Approximately 63 percent live in housing on campus, most of which is coed (91 percent). Residence halls allow for interaction among students, and the units are governed through student representation and hall councils. There are no fraternities or sororities. The College offers numerous cocurricular activities, including athletics and cultural events such as lectures, symposia, art exhibits, theater productions, concerts, recitals, and dance performances. Currently, there are eighteen NCAA Division III teams, eight club teams, and eight to ten intramural sports. Athletic facilities include three basketball courts, a competition-size swimming pool, a weight-training room, a stadium, a baseball/softball complex, and six tennis courts, three of which are covered by an airdome. The renowned College Outdoors Program offers backpacking, rafting, skiing, and sea kayaking in Oregon's nearby wilderness areas.

Location

Portland has long been known for its livability and its excellent transportation service. Public buses and a free College shuttle run from the Lewis & Clark campus to the center of Portland. The metropolitan area (population 1.8 million) is bisected by the Willamette River. Mount Hood, offering year-round skiing, is 50 miles away, and Oregon's rugged coastline lies 90 miles to the west. The city has 10,447 acres of parks, 33 music associations, 35 theater and dance companies, more than 90 galleries and museums, and more than 1,000 restaurants. Professional sports teams compete in baseball, hockey, indoor soccer, and NBA basketball.

Majors and Degrees

Lewis & Clark offers programs leading to the Bachelor of Arts degree. Academic majors include art, biochemistry, biology, chemistry, communications, computer science and mathematics, East Asian studies, economics, English, environmental studies, foreign languages, French, German, Hispanic studies, history, international affairs, mathematics, music, philosophy, physics, political science, psychology, religious studies, sociology/anthropology, and theater. Students may also design a major or pursue a double major and numerous minors. Preprofessional programs are available in dentistry, education, law, and medicine.

Dual-degree (3-2 and 4-2) programs in engineering are offered in cooperation with Columbia University, Washington University (St. Louis), the University of Southern California, and the Oregon Graduate Institute.

Academic Program

The liberal arts curriculum offers sufficient structure to ensure depth and breadth of study, but it also incorporates a high degree of freedom in order to promote creative and critical thinking. In the four-year plan of study, approximately one third of a student's time is devoted to general education, one third to a major program, and one third to elective courses. Students are also encouraged to participate in departmental honors programs, undergraduate research, independent study, and internships.

The academic calendar consists of two 15-week semesters. A normal load is four 4-semester-hour academic courses, plus one or more activity courses. By graduation a student is expected to have earned at least 128 semester hours—equivalent, roughly, to eight different classes a year. The fall semester begins early in September and ends before Christmas, and the spring semester begins in mid-January and ends in early May. There are also a limited number of courses offered during two summer sessions.

The community of scholars at Lewis & Clark College is dedicated to personal and academic excellence. Joining the Lewis & Clark community obligates each member to observe the principles of mutual respect, academic integrity, civil discourse, and responsible decision making.

Off-Campus Programs

Lewis & Clark offers nationally recognized international and off-campus study opportunities that have been in existence for more than forty years. Twenty-four to twenty-seven different overseas study programs and two domestic programs are available annually. Usually, 20 to 24 students, plus a faculty leader, participate in each program. More than 60 percent of the College's graduates have taken advantage of these outstanding programs, often satisfying General Education or major requirements at the same time.

Overseas study may have either a general-culture focus or a specialized academic focus. On general-culture programs, students become immersed in the everyday life of the host country by living with local families, traveling, studying in classes and seminars, and working on independent projects. Programs with a more specific academic focus may include studying German language and literature in Munich; perfecting language skills in France, Ecuador, Russia, Japan, or China; or studying literature in England. Sites for overseas study programs from 2004 through 2007 are Australia, Chile, China, Dominican Republic, Ecuador, England, France, Germany, India, Italy, Japan, Kenya/Tanzania, Micronesia, New Zealand, Russia, Scotland, and Senegal. Domestic programs are available in New York or Washington, D.C., for those interested in economics, political science, theater, or art. All programs, both overseas and domestic, are for credit and are similar in cost to full-time, on-campus study for the same period. Students with financial aid or scholarships can apply their assistance to the expenses of these programs.

Academic Facilities

The Aubrey R. Watzek Library (open 24 hours per day during the week when school is in session) houses approximately 280,000 volumes, 1,300 periodical subscriptions, 456,000 microforms, and 13,000 units of audiovisual materials. Its mission is to provide a solid core of materials designed to support the curriculum and the research needs of the Lewis & Clark community. The library offers individualized reference assistance in the use of both print and electronic resources. The library's Web site provides access to its catalog as well as to a full range of electronic databases and links to useful Internet resources. The library is a member of Summit, a consortium of twenty-six academic libraries that have a unified catalog that enables students to request and receive materials from member libraries within two days.

Music department facilities include Evans Auditorium, a 410-seat recital hall equipped with an orchestra pit and stage elevator; an extensive record, CD, and tape collection; twenty-two practice rooms; forty-three pianos, including several 6-foot and 7-foot concert grands and a 9-foot Steinway concert grand; two harpsichords; a Baroque organ; an electronic music studio with CD production capability; Zimbabwe marimbas; and an Indonesian gamelan orchestra. The 600-seat chapel houses an 85-rank Casavant organ. A $20-million construction project resulted in a new art building that is equipped with expanded studios for ceramics, sculpture, painting and drawing, calligraphy, design, and printmaking. The department also has a library of 50,000 art history slides. The arts center contains two gallery spaces as well. A three-story humanities center also opened its doors in 1996.

The natural sciences are housed in the Biology/Psychology, BoDine, and Olin Buildings, which are well equipped with modern instrumentation to support the College's emphasis on collaborative student-faculty research. These buildings contain numerous research laboratories and equipment, used by students in classes or research projects, in addition to teaching labs and classrooms. Among the notable facilities are a laboratory for the study of human-computer interactions, a scanning electron microscope, a modern greenhouse, an astronomical observatory with several telescopes, a molecular modeling laboratory equipped with high-speed computers, a laboratory for the study of parallel computing, a laboratory for studying the biomechanics of animal locomotion, and an astrophysics laboratory that is equipped to remotely operate and acquire data from a specialized telescope at Kitts Peak, Arizona. All labs are computerized for acquiring and analyzing data and are networked to allow sharing and acquisition of data remotely. Ecological investigations and studies of the environmental impacts of human activity can be conducted both on the College's heavily wooded campus and at the nearby Tryon Creek State Park.

Computer facilities include several computer laboratories in academic buildings that are for student use. More than 130 Macintosh, IBM, and compatible computers are available for student use, along with peripherals such as color scanners, color printers, digital cameras, and digital video editing. All residence halls have direct Internet access. Parts of the campus also have wireless network capability.

Costs

Tuition and fees for 2002–03 were $23,730. The room and board charge was $6630 for fourteen meals per week; other meal plans are also available. The estimate for books and personal expenses is $1800.

Financial Aid

In 2002–03, 70 percent of the College's students received some form of financial assistance. Institutional, state, and federal resources, including Federal Pell Grants, Federal Supplemental Educational Opportunity Grants, Federal Perkins Loans, and Federal Work-Study awards, may be part of an aid award. Other options include low-interest Federal Stafford Student Loans and opportunities to work on and off campus. To receive priority consideration for financial aid, students must meet appropriate deadlines for admission and should submit the Free Application for Federal Student Aid (FAFSA) by March 1. Merit-based awards are offered to exceptional students who are selected as Neely Scholars (up to ten full-tuition scholarships), Trustee Scholars (up to fifteen half-tuition scholarships per year), and more than a hundred Dean's Scholars ($4000–$8000 scholarships per year). In addition, nearly thirty $5000 Leadership and Service Awards are made annually. Students designated as National Merit Finalists with Lewis & Clark officially named as their first choice receive up to $2000.

Faculty

The 167-member faculty, which is committed to undergraduate teaching and advising, is also active in research, writing, and publishing. Involving students in the research process is of high priority. Ninety-eight percent of the full-time faculty members hold a Ph.D. or the highest advanced degree in their discipline. The student-faculty ratio is approximately 12:1. The average class size is 19, with an average size of 24 for first-year-level courses and 16 for upper-division courses.

Student Government

The Associated Students of Lewis & Clark (ASLC) has a decentralized structure that encourages cocurricular participation by students and places a high priority on participation with faculty and staff in the process of enriching the academic environment. ASLC consists of an Executive Council, governing boards, and appointed students who serve on faculty constitutional, standing, and special committees. The 24 members of the Student Academic Affairs Board (SAAB) are appointed on a departmental basis to solicit, evaluate, and support undergraduate and faculty research, instruction, curriculum, and program enhancement. One quarter of the total ASLC budget of more than $330,000 is used by SAAB in support of undergraduate research grants and speakers.

Admission Requirements

Lewis & Clark College seeks first-year and transfer applicants who are committed to academic excellence and personal growth. Admission is competitive. Applications are carefully reviewed and examined for degree of academic preparation, ability to express ideas in essay form, participation in activities, citizenship and community service, and support given by the school through recommendations. Interviews and campus visits are encouraged but are not required. Recommended high school preparation includes 4 years of English, 4 years of history or social science, 3 to 4 years of mathematics, 3 years of laboratory science, 2 to 3 years of foreign language, and 1 year of fine arts. The SAT I or ACT is required, unless the student is applying via the Portfolio Path.

Application and Information

First-year applicants should submit the Lewis & Clark or Common Application; a personal essay; an official academic transcript, including senior grades from the first marking period; one recommendation from a counselor; and at least one reference from an academic teacher. Lewis & Clark's application form can be found online at the College's Web site (address below). The application fee is waived if the applicant uses the College's online option or the online Common Application. Application deadlines are December 1 for early action (notification by January 15) and February 1 for regular admission (notification by April 1). The optional Portfolio Path Admissions Program provides an opportunity for applicants who have shown exceptional academic initiative to demonstrate the full extent of their pursuits by presenting a portfolio of their academic work. Under this plan, SAT I or ACT scores are optional. For more information about Lewis & Clark College or to arrange a visit, students should contact:

Office of Admissions
Lewis & Clark College
0615 Southwest Palatine Hill Road
Portland, Oregon 97219-7899

Telephone: 503-768-7040
800-444-4111 (toll-free)
Fax: 503-768-7055
E-mail: admissions@lclark.edu
World Wide Web: http://www.lclark.edu

LEWIS UNIVERSITY

ROMEOVILLE, ILLINOIS

The University

Lewis University is a coeducational, comprehensive, Catholic and Lasallian university located in the Midwest with an enrollment of approximately 4,400 students. Lewis continues to demonstrate its commitment to providing a high-quality, mission-based education while providing more than 85 percent of its new incoming students with some form of financial aid. The main campus is a picturesque 350-acre setting with eight residence halls that house nearly 1,000 students within easy walking distance of all campus buildings.

Lewis has been strengthened by the educational mission of the De La Salle Christian Brothers and their colleagues. Since they arrived on the campus in 1960, the Christian Brothers have been the providers of a quality education and personal attention based on the heritage of their founder, Saint John Baptist de La Salle. The student-faculty ratio of 15:1 assures that students experience some interaction with their instructors. Lewis is large enough to provide the resources of a university while maintaining personal contact with each student.

Part of the experience of a Lewis education includes small classes, service learning opportunities, a beautiful campus, free parking, a safe environment, an ideal location, and an active campus life. These elements combine to provide an educational experience that focuses on career preparation, academic choices, community service, and lifelong learning. Lewis has positioned itself as an academic leader and is quickly being recognized for its commitment to mission effectiveness.

The majority of Lewis students are Illinois residents, but the enrollment includes men and women from more than twenty-five states and thirty countries. Eight residence halls allow for various living styles, including apartment and suite arrangements. More than forty clubs and organizations offer students opportunities for a variety of social, athletic, academic, career, or hobby-related interests. Lewis residents report that the spirit of the campus community enhances the friendly and supportive environment.

Eighteen intercollegiate sports include men's and women's basketball, cross-country, golf, soccer, swimming, track, tennis, and volleyball, plus men's baseball and women's softball. All teams compete in NCAA Division II. In the past twenty-two years, Lewis teams have captured the Great Lakes Valley Conference All Sports Trophy twelve times. A high percentage of student athletes appear on the Deans' List and 95 percent of them earn a bachelor's degree.

On the graduate level, the University offers degree programs leading to the Master of Business Administration (M.B.A.); the Master of Arts (M.A.) in counseling psychology, education, organizational leadership, and school counseling and guidance; the Master of Science in Nursing (M.S.N.); the Master of Education; and the Master of Science (M.S.) in criminal/social justice and public safety administration. An M.S.N./M.B.A. option is also available.

Location

Located in Romeoville, Illinois, Lewis is only 30 minutes southwest of Chicago. This allows students to take advantage of the resources of one of the world's largest cities while enjoying the beautiful suburban campus. Shopping and recreational facilities are located nearby.

Majors and Degrees

Lewis University offers programs leading to the Bachelor of Arts (B.A.) degree in American studies, art studio, athletic training, biochemistry, biology, broadcast journalism, business studies, chemistry, communication technology, computer graphic design, computer science, contemporary global studies, criminal/social justice, drawing, education, English, environmental science, forensic criminal investigation, history, human communication, human resource management, illustration, liberal arts, mathematics, multimedia production, music, music merchandising, painting, philosophy, physics, print journalism, private security/loss prevention management, psychology, public relations, radio/television production, social work and human services, sociology, special education, speech education, sport management, theater, and theology.

Programs leading to a Bachelor of Science (B.S.) degree include accountancy, biochemistry, business administration, chemistry, computer science, economics, environmental science, finance, management information systems, marketing, mathematics, nuclear medicine technology, physics, political science, public administration, and radiation therapy. Preprofessional programs are offered in dentistry, engineering, law, medicine, meteorology, optometry, pharmacy, physical therapy, physician's assistant studies, and veterinary science. In addition to its more than sixty majors, Lewis offers interdisciplinary courses in women's studies and ethnic and cultural studies. Accelerated programs for working adults are available in business administration, health-care leadership, information technology management, management, social and community studies, and RN/B.S.N. completion. The Bachelor of Science in Nursing (B.S.N.) degree is offered in the College of Nursing and Health Professions.

The Scholars Academy allows eligible students in every major to enhance their educational opportunities through intensive projects arranged by contract with faculty members. To prepare students for careers in aviation, the University offers Bachelor of Science degree programs in aviation administration, aviation flight management, and aviation maintenance management as well as Associate of Science degree programs in aviation flight and aviation maintenance. Certificate programs are offered in aviation flight dispatch and aviation maintenance technology.

The Bachelor of Elected Studies (B.E.S.) degree and a liberal arts degree may be pursued by students whose educational and career goals lead them to combine course work from several areas. The B.E.S. degree allows students to develop their own major by choosing a concentration from any area of the University. The liberal arts degree permits them to combine two minors into a major.

Academic Program

The undergraduate curriculum has three parts: general education, major required courses, and elective courses. The general education requirements include specific courses in the humanities and the social or natural sciences designed to introduce the student to liberal culture. Requirements for the student's chosen major provide the opportunity for a greater depth of study in one academic field. Electives allow the student to select additional courses suited to his or her educational needs. The emphasis on humanities and communication arts in the undergraduate curriculum provides students with the knowledge of history and of the human experience necessary to develop an awareness of and responsiveness to contemporary social issues. Qualified students may receive academic credit through Advanced Placement, through CLEP testing, or for prior learning.

Students selecting majors in the College of Arts and Sciences discover that course work has been developed to foster critical thinking, open inquiry, precision in thought and expression, and familiarity with a broad range of knowledge. The College of Business seeks to educate individuals who are competent in the functional areas of business and who can recognize the responsibilities of business to the political, social, and economic segments of society. Many of the courses taken by business students are selected from the liberal arts area. Similarly, the College of Nursing and Health Professions and the newly established College of Education build on a foundation of liberal education. Nursing students take a concentration of natural and behavioral sciences, humanities, and electives during the first two years of the program. The nursing major course work is taken primarily at the upper-division level, with clinical experience acquired in hospitals and other health-care facilities. The nursing program prepares professional nursing practitioners who are competent to deliver health-care services in many situations.

The College of Education prepares future and current teachers and administrators to meet the diverse needs of all students. The College offers teacher education programs for certification in biology, chemistry, computer science, elementary education, English, history, mathematics, physics, psychology, special education, and speech education. Graduate programs include curriculum and instruction, elementary education, general administration, reading and literacy, secondary education, special education, and a Certificate of Advanced Study leading to a superintendent's endorsement.

The University operates on a semester system. The fall semester begins the Monday before Labor Day, and the spring semester starts in mid-January. Summer school sessions are six, eight, or ten weeks in length, depending on the program. Accelerated programs offer nine sessions per year in five-week and eight-week formats.

Academic Facilities

Lewis is committed to providing learners with access to modern educational technology. Technologies include computer labs, networks, Internet access, e-mail, classroom media, and distributed learning resources. Lewis University is connected to the Illinois Century Network (ICN), which provides reliable Internet access to schools and other educational entities throughout the state. The campus network includes a high-speed fiber-optic backbone to all buildings. Internet connectivity is provided in the dorms via an Ethernet connection at no additional charge to the residents.

All students are entitled to a campus e-mail address, which can be accessed through a Web-enabled interface. Staffed computer labs are available during generous hours in all major classroom buildings and provide access to a host of campus resources, including software applications, Web support for classes, library materials, and Internet searching. Lewis also provides specialized computer labs, which are supported for digital music, journalism, writing, graphic arts, nursing, aviation, computer science, and tutoring. Computer labs are also located at the extended campuses in Hickory Hills, Schaumburg, Oak Brook, and Tinley Park.

The University library houses nearly 150,000 volumes and an extensive microfiche and microfilm collection and is a depository for U.S. government documents. Besides housing a specialized music collection and an art-print collection, the library is home for the Archives of the Illinois and Michigan Canal Heritage Corridor. Online public-access terminals are available for use in the Lewis library. Patrons may access the University's card catalog as well as the holdings of more than forty other academic libraries in Illinois through this computerized system. More than 50 different periodical databases are also available through computer access; many of these full-text and more specialized databases are added each semester. More than 40 of these databases are available online.

The Aviation Department is housed in the $2.5-million Harold E. White Aviation Center next to the Lewis University Airport. The airport, which houses more than 300 aircraft, is the site of flight-training and management programs.

Costs

Tuition for 2003–04 for full-time students (24 to 36 credits) is $15,950, while yearly room and board costs average $7000, depending on room size and the meal plan chosen. General service fees and student activity fees are included in the tuition.

Financial Aid

Lewis University is committed to helping all students who need financial assistance. Besides assisting students in obtaining federal and state grants, Federal Work-Study jobs, or loans (repayable after graduation), the University offers academic and athletic scholarships as well as additional Lewis grants to students with demonstrated financial needs. To be considered for any aid, a student must apply for federal, state, and Lewis aid, using the appropriate forms. Additional information is available from the Office of Admission.

Faculty

The Lewis University faculty places a strong emphasis on scholarship and personal contact. The greater majority of the general faculty hold doctoral degrees, and 100 percent of the members of the aviation faculty hold FAA-approved licenses. In addition, because the student-faculty ratio is 15:1, classes tend to be close-knit, enhancing the opportunities for extensive interaction between faculty members and students, both in class and through office hours.

Student Government

The Student Governing Board (SGB) consists of presidents of each of ten councils: the Commuter, the Black Student Union, the Latin American Student Organization, Scholars, Interfratority, Interorganizational, National Pan Hellenic, International Student Association, the Student Athletic Advisory Board, and Residence Hall Councils. Four at-large members are appointed by the Office of Student Services. The SGB works to develop an effective activity program, reviews the quality of student life, oversees the effective functioning and financing of student organizations, represents student needs and concerns to the University's administration, and serves as the judicial body in overseeing organizational conduct.

Admission Requirements

Lewis University welcomes candidates for admission who present a strong record of academic success and/or high motivation. Freshman candidates are required to present ACT or SAT I results as well as a record of high school work. Students whose main language is not English must also present a score of at least 500 on the Test of English as a Foreign Language (TOEFL). Applicants for the nursing program must have also taken one year of chemistry, one year of biology, and at least one year of algebra.

Transfer students with fewer than 12 credits should apply in the same manner as freshman applicants. Transfer students who have completed 12 or more college credits may be admitted to the College of Arts and Sciences if they have maintained an overall GPA of 2.0 or higher. (The College of Nursing and Health Professions and the College of Business have additional transfer requirements. For more information, students should contact the transfer coordinator in the Office of Admission.) Most transfer students have all college credits accepted. However, for the Lewis degree, a maximum of 72 credit hours may be transferred from community colleges.

Application and Information

Application forms for admission and financial aid may be obtained from the Office of Admission. Freshman applicants should submit the application for admission, ACT or SAT I scores, and high school transcripts. Transfer applicants who have earned 12 or more credit hours should submit transcripts from each college or university attended and the completed admission application.

Director for Enrollment
Lewis University
One University Parkway
Romeoville, Illinois 60446-2200
Telephone: 800-897-9000 (toll-free)
E-mail: admissions@lewisu.edu
World Wide Web: http://www.lewisu.edu

The Learning Resource Center at Lewis University.

LIBERTY UNIVERSITY

LYNCHBURG, VIRGINIA

The University

Founded in 1971 by Dr. Jerry Falwell, Liberty University (LU) provides a Christian, comprehensive, coeducational environment committed to serious scholarship at the undergraduate and graduate levels. The University is situated on a 4,400-acre campus with complete classroom, dormitory, study, leisure, and recreational facilities. Liberty University is approved by the State Council of Higher Education for Virginia and is accredited by the Commission on Colleges of the Southern Association of Colleges and Schools to award associate, bachelor's, master's and doctoral degrees. There are more than 6,400 undergraduate and graduate students in the traditional resident program. The student body represents all fifty states and more than seventy-four countries, with 19 percent of the student population representing minorities and international students.

In addition to the 4,000-seat Earl H. Schilling Center, Liberty's facilities include the 12,000-seat football stadium and the 10,000-seat Vines Convocation Center. Also in use is Matthes-Hopkins Field, a superb outdoor track facility. Intercollegiate athletic competition is in NCAA Division I. Men compete in baseball, basketball, cross-country, football, golf, indoor track, soccer, tennis, and track and field. Women compete in basketball, cross-country, soccer, softball, tennis, track and field, and volleyball. Other sports programs at the club level include ice hockey, lacrosse, and volleyball for men; roller hockey and Ultimate Frisbee as coed sports; and ice hockey for women. Intramural competition is offered for both men and women in eight different sports.

New dorm rooms are currently under construction and offer apartment-style living within walking distance of the campus. Apartments include full furnishings, a kitchen, laundry facilities, gymnasiums, dining halls, fitness centers, and even a car wash.

Liberty offers several majors in a wide variety of degrees on the graduate level, in addition to its baccalaureate and associate degree programs. The Master of Arts degree is offered in counseling and religious studies. Students who are interested in education can pursue a Master of Education and a Doctor of Education through Liberty. The Teacher Licensure Option is available at the graduate level in early childhood (NK–3), elementary (K–6), and secondary (7–12) education; administration/supervision; gifted education; reading; school counseling; and special education. In addition, a Master of Nursing degree and a Ph.D. program in professional counseling and pastoral care are also offered.

Through the Liberty Baptist Theological Seminary, the University offers the following graduate degrees: Master of Arts in Religion, Master of Religious Education, Master of Divinity, Master of Theology, and Doctor of Ministry.

Liberty University's Law School is currently accepting application and expects to enroll its first class in fall 2004.

For international students, Liberty offers the English Language Institute. English grammar, comprehension, and reading are taught for those international students with little or no English skills. An English Language Institute certification is awarded, and students are invited to enroll as a student at Liberty University once completed or while enrolled in the institute. For more information, students should contact the University at the address listed below.

Location

The University is located in the heart of Virginia in Lynchburg (population 68,000), with the scenic Blue Ridge Mountains as a backdrop. The city is more than 200 years old and is noted for its culture, beauty, and educational advantages. Nearby are such sites as Appomattox Court House; Natural Bridge; Thomas Jefferson's Poplar Forest; historic Lexington; Washington, D.C.; and other places of interest.

The city of Lynchburg offers a wide variety of activities for recreation and entertainment. Excellent sports facilities and programs, cultural events at the Lynchburg Fine Arts Center, beautiful lakes and streams, and many other local attractions enhance the lives of Lynchburg residents. Lynchburg also has more than 2,000 hotel rooms, numerous outlets and malls, and a number of restaurants that serve a wide variety of cuisines. Lynchburg is accessible by air, train, and bus.

Majors and Degrees

The Bachelor of Science degree is offered in accounting, athletic training, biology, business (economics, finance, management, management information systems, and marketing), communication studies (advertising/public relations/media management, media graphic production, print and electronic journalism, and speech communication), computer science, English, exercise science and fitness programming, family and consumer sciences, general studies (elementary education and secondary education licensure), government (administration of justice, general, and prelaw), health promotion, history, interdisciplinary studies, mathematics, multidisciplinary studies, nursing, physical education, psychology (child/adolescent development, clinical/experimental, and human services/counseling), religion (biblical studies, missions, pastoral ministries, and youth ministries), social sciences, sport management, teaching English as a second/foreign language, and worship studies. Secondary teaching licensure is available in several degree programs.

The Bachelor of Arts degree is offered in English, general studies, history (international studies), interdisciplinary studies, philosophy, and religion (biblical studies).

The Bachelor of Music degree is offered in choral and instrumental music.

The Associate of Arts degree is available in general studies and religion.

Minors are available in accounting, athletic training, aviation, biblical Greek, biblical studies, biology, business, chemistry, coaching, communication studies (journalism and speech), English, exercise science, family and consumer sciences, French, government, health promotion, history, mathematics, missions, music, philosophy, physical education, psychology, Spanish, sport management, theater arts, theology, and youth ministries.

The Teacher Licensure Option is available at the elementary (K–6), middle school (6–8), and secondary levels (7–12) in biology, business, computer science, English, history/social sciences, mathematics, and work and family studies and at the comprehensive level (K–12) in teaching English as a second language, health/physical education, music (choral or instrumental), and special education.

Academic Programs

A minimum of 120 semester hours is required for the B.S., while a minimum of 123 semester hours is necessary for the B.A. In addition to the major, the student must complete general education courses in humanities, natural sciences and mathematics, social sciences, physical education, and religion. The A.A. requires a minimum of 64 semester hours.

Liberty is on the early semester calendar. During the summer, there are several one- and two-week modular classes offered. Winter modulars are also offered between semesters.

The University also offers higher education degrees for the adult learner through home study. Liberty's Distance Learning Program (DLP) is accredited by the Commission on Colleges of the Southern Association of Colleges and Schools to award associate, bachelor's, master's, and doctoral degrees. For more information on the Distance Learning Program, students should call 800-424-9595 (toll-free) or visit http://www.collegeyourway.net.

Academic Facilities

The Arthur S. DeMoss Learning Center, the academic hub of the campus, is a 500,000-square-foot Jeffersonian-style building that encompasses nearly all academic aspects of the University. All academic rooms are wired for the Internet, with large computer screens installed for interactive learning. This impressive facility is one of the largest academic buildings in central Virginia and houses the campus library, which currently contains 283,000 bound or microfilmed volumes. Students may find employment or volunteer their services in the University's 50,000-watt FM radio station or student-run radio and TV stations. The Fine Arts Hall houses the Lloyd Auditorium, which has a seating capacity of 315 as well as a recital hall and several practice rooms. The current student center, David's Place, provides a place for students to relax and offers such amenities as TV lounges; a game room; a multipurpose room for films, aerobics, and banquets; and a snack shop. A new $9-million student center is underway, including a movie theater, a drama stage, full indoor basketball courts, fitness centers, and a bowling alley.

In 2000, Liberty renovated the entire computer structure of the campus. The renovation included the installation of a computer network that allows each student to reach professors, various campus offices, and the Internet from individual dorm rooms.

Costs

Tuition for 2004–05 is $18,550 for 12 to 18 credit hours per semester, room and board (twenty-six meals per week), and telephone fee. A technology fee of $200 per semester provides each student with an e-mail address and high-speed Internet access in the dormitory. It also gives the student unlimited access to the many computer labs around the campus.

The estimated cost for books per semester is $350. Additional fees such as lab fees are required for specific classes and are listed in the class registration book. Automobiles are permitted if they are registered and a fee of $50 per semester has been paid.

Financial Aid

A variety of grants, scholarships, and on-campus jobs are available at Liberty. All federally funded student financial aid programs, except the Federal Perkins Loan Program, are available. Athletic, academic, merit, talent, Association of Christian Schools International (ACSI), National Merit, and other Liberty University assistance grants are also available for qualified candidates. Students are required to submit a Free Application for Federal Student Aid (FAFSA) to the U.S. Department of Education and include Liberty University's school code (010392) on that application. This is the student's application for all financial aid. Approximately 90 percent of the student body received some type of aid last year.

Liberty offers generous scholarships, grants, and other financial aid. Students should contact the University at the address below about financial aid opportunities. Liberty also partners with many Christian ministries around the world, offering scholarships to participating students.

Faculty

About 300 different colleges and universities worldwide are represented in the education of the Liberty faculty. The average Liberty faculty member has more than thirteen years of teaching experience. Courses are taught by faculty members, not graduate assistants. All members of the faculty serve as advisers to the students in their discipline, and many also serve as dorm parents.

Student Government

Students elect representatives to serve on the Student Senate. This group provides recommendations and suggestions to the student development staff. Student Senate members also organize and direct activities and civic programs.

Admission Requirements

All applicants should be familiar with Liberty's philosophy and expectations before applying. Applicants to the A.A., B.A., and B.S. programs must be high school graduates and must submit two official copies of the high school transcript, indicating graduation date (or GED test scores, if applicable). Applicants must also submit either ACT or SAT scores, which are used for academic counseling and placement. High school transcripts and SAT/ACT requirements are waived if the student transfers 60 hours or holds an associate degree. Test scores are waived if the applicant is 22 or older. The applicant must demonstrate the ability to do college work. Three personal references may be requested if needed. Although interviews are not required, prospective students are encouraged to visit the campus. Four "College For A Weekend" programs are available each year, giving prospective students an opportunity to participate in classes, attend social and athletic events, experience dorm life, and converse with students and faculty members.

Application and Information

Admissions decisions are made on a rolling basis, but June 30 is the preferred deadline for fall enrollment. However, applicants are encouraged to complete the application process by January 1 to be considered for maximum scholarship opportunities. Applicants for the spring term should complete the process by November 30, although early October is preferred.

To learn more about Liberty University, students should contact:

Office of Admissions
Liberty University
1971 University Boulevard
Lynchburg, Virginia 24502
Telephone: 800-543-5317 (toll-free)
Fax: 800-542-2311 (toll-free)
E-mail: admissions@liberty.edu
World Wide Web: http://www.liberty.edu/PS
(Advantage Code 00043)

An aerial view of Liberty University.

LIMESTONE COLLEGE

GAFFNEY, SOUTH CAROLINA

The College

Founded in 1845, Limestone is a fully accredited, private, coeducational liberal arts college. The College maintains a small student body and a well-qualified faculty in order to create an atmosphere in which each student develops intellectually, physically, and socially. The College endeavors to help students prepare for a satisfying, useful life through effective communication skills, responsible decision-making abilities, meaningful leisure-time activities, and lifelong aspirations. In addition to its programs on campus, Limestone offers several of its academic majors in an accelerated format called The Block Program at several locations throughout South Carolina. These programs are intended primarily for working adults. The College also has an impressive Virtual Campus Program on the Internet with many majors offered.

Extracurricular activities play a vital part in the development of all students at Limestone College. Among these activities are intercollegiate athletics in men's baseball, basketball, cross-country, golf, lacrosse, soccer, tennis, and wrestling and in women's basketball, cross-country, golf, lacrosse, soccer, softball, swimming, tennis, and volleyball. Students who are interested in music have the opportunity to participate in several instrumental and choral ensembles. A theater program is also available.

The 115-acre Limestone campus is well laid out for pleasant college living. The classrooms, library, laboratories, auditorium, bookstore, post office, and administrative offices are housed in buildings that border the central and circular drives, making each easily accessible to the others. The back campus has a plaza of four dormitories, and a dining hall is located nearby. The Timken LYFE Center is a physical education complex that houses the gymnasium, an AAU-size swimming pool, and athletic training facilities. The College also has eight lighted tennis courts, a baseball field, a softball field, a soccer/lacrosse field, and several practice fields.

Location

Gaffney, a small city with a population of 25,000, provides an ideal setting for a college campus. Whereas the distractions associated with a large city are absent from daily life, the cultural programs and services offered in Charlotte, North Carolina, and Spartanburg and Greenville, South Carolina, are all within a 50-mile radius of the campus. All are connected to Gaffney by Interstate 85.

The climate is free from extreme heat or cold. The well-known resort areas of the Blue Ridge Mountains, the Great Smoky Mountains, and the beaches of the Atlantic Coast are accessible for weekend visits. In the immediate area, facilities are available for all water sports, horseback riding, golf, tennis, and skiing.

Majors and Degrees

Limestone College offers the Bachelor of Arts, Bachelor of Science, Bachelor of Applied Science, and Bachelor of Social Work degrees with majors in athletic training, biology, business administration (concentrations in accounting, computer science, economics, general business, management, and marketing), chemistry, computer science (majors in Internet management, management information systems, and programming), counseling and human services, criminal justice, English, history, human resource development, liberal studies, mathematics, music, physical education (concentrations in athletic training and fitness/wellness), prelaw, psychology, secondary education, social work, sports management, studio art, and theater. Majors approved for South Carolina teacher certification are art education, biology education, elementary education, English education, mathematics education, music education, physical education, secondary education, and social studies education.

The Associate of Arts degree is offered with majors in business administration (concentrations in general business), computer science (majors in Internet management, management information systems, and programming), and liberal studies.

Academic Programs

The course of study leading to the B.A., B.A.S., B.S., B.S.W., or A.A. degree consists of four elements: requirements in communication and quantitative skills; a general liberal arts program, involving five different subject groups; courses in the major; and appropriate electives. The baccalaureate degree programs require the completion of a minimum of 120 semester hours.

Advanced placement and credit are given for scores of 3 or higher on the Advanced Placement examinations of the College Board.

An Honors Program involving special courses, seminars, and lectures is available for exceptional students. Admission to this program is contingent upon outstanding high school grades and scores on the SAT I of the College Board, the completion of a special application, and an interview. Almost 10 percent of all Limestone students are enrolled in this rigorous academic program.

A Program for Alternative Learning Styles (PALS) is available for qualified students with certified learning disabilities who might not otherwise succeed at the college level.

Academic Facilities

Limestone has outstanding computer facilities, including free e-mail accounts for all main campus students, residence hall high-speed Internet connections, and several well-equipped, state-of-the-art computer labs. There are also well-equipped science labs. The modern A. J. Eastwood Library houses approximately 90,000 volumes and is fully computerized, including student Internet access. Fullerton Auditorium, with a seating capacity of 975, serves for drama and musical productions and is one of the finest such facilities in the state of South Carolina.

Costs

The direct cost for a student at Limestone College for the 2004–05 school year is $18,600; the tuition is $13,200, and room and board costs are $5400. In addition, the cost of books, supplies, laundry, travel, and personal expenses is estimated at $4000 per year.

Financial Aid

Limestone College, one of the least costly private colleges in South Carolina, endeavors to meet the financial need of any qualified student through scholarships, grants, loans, work-study opportunities, or a combination of these. Limestone offers merit scholarships to students with outstanding academic, leadership, or athletic abilities as well as to those who have exceptional talents in such areas as art, music, and theater.

More than 90 percent of Limestone College day students receive some type of financial aid. Because institutional financial aid is limited, students are urged to submit their applications for admission and financial aid as early as possible.

Faculty

Personal attention to students and high-quality instruction characterize the faculty at Limestone College. Three-quarters of the faculty members hold Ph.D.'s or other terminal degrees in their fields. The student-faculty ratio is 12:1. Students and instructors work closely together in both learning and counseling situations. Each student has an assigned faculty adviser for assistance in course selection and for personal counseling.

Student Government

The Student Government Association exemplifies the College's democratic tradition and the principles of honor and individual responsibility. It is every student's privilege to participate in the government of the learning community of which he or she is a member. The more highly organized activities, including student organizations and social events, are coordinated through the Student Government Association. The College also has a literary magazine and a yearbook.

Admission Requirements

Limestone College does not discriminate on the basis of race, color, creed, national origin, financial need, or physical handicap. Each candidate for admission is evaluated as an individual. The College recommends that applicants have the following high school preparation: English, 4 units; social science, 3 units; mathematics, 3 units; and science, 2 units.

Applicants must submit an official transcript of the secondary school record, scores on the SAT I, and a nonrefundable $25 application fee. The application fee is waived if the student applies online at the College's Web site listed below. Transfer applications are encouraged.

Application and Information

Completed application forms for admission and for financial aid should be sent to the Director of Admissions at Limestone College. It is recommended that applications be submitted by May 1. Any admission applications received after that date are considered on a space-available basis. The College practices a rolling admissions policy. As soon as the application, high school transcript, and test scores have been received, the applicant is notified of his or her status. Upon acceptance, a student is required to submit a $100 tuition deposit.

Vice President of Enrollment Services
Limestone College
1115 College Drive
Gaffney, South Carolina 29340-3799
Telephone: 864-488-4554
Fax: 864-488-8206
E-mail: admiss@limestone.edu
World Wide Web: http://www.limestone.edu

The Winnie Davis Hall of History, named in honor of the daughter of Jefferson Davis, was completed about 1904 and is listed on the National Register of Historic Places.

LINCOLN MEMORIAL UNIVERSITY

HARROGATE, TENNESSEE

The University

Lincoln Memorial University (LMU) grew out of love and respect for Abraham Lincoln and his desire to provide the people of central Appalachia an opportunity to improve their lives through education. The University, a private, independent, liberal-arts school, today honors his name, values, and spirit. While the University has undergone rapid growth and change since its founding as a living memorial to Abraham Lincoln in 1897, it has retained its original mission of providing exceptional educational opportunities to deserving students not only from Appalachia, but to students from across the country and around the world.

Lincoln Memorial University is a values-based learning community dedicated to providing educational experiences in the liberal arts and professional studies. The University believes that one of the major cornerstones of meaningful existence is service to humanity. By making educational and research opportunities available to students where they live and through various recreational and cultural events open to the community, Lincoln Memorial University seeks to advance life in the Cumberland Gap area and throughout the region.

In addition to the undergraduate programs available, the LMU College of Graduate Studies offers masters degrees in Business Administration (M.B.A.) and Education (M.Ed.) and the Educational Specialist (Ed.S.) degree. These programs are specifically designed for working adults with classes offered in the evenings.

There are approximately 2,440 undergraduate and graduate students enrolled at LMU's Harrogate and extended-campus sites, representing twenty-two other countries and twenty-five states. The student body is slightly more than 70 percent women and slightly less than 30 percent men. LMU affords many opportunities for student involvement in campus life, including social fraternities and sororities, honorary societies, religious organizations, academic groups, and other clubs supported through the Student Organization Council.

Academic organizations include Alpha Chi (academic honor society for juniors and seniors), the Alpha Gamma Sigma Chapter of Sigma Tau Delta (English honor society), Phi Alpha Theta (history honor society), Phi Beta Lambda (business honor society), Psi Chi (national honor society in psychology), Psychology Club, Student Athletic Trainers Association, Student Nurses Association, Student Wildlife Society, and the Veterinary Technology Club.

Social organizations include Alpha Lambda Zeta fraternity, Delta Theta Sigma sorority, Gamma Lambda Sigma fraternity, Kappa Pi Omega sorority, Zeta Tau Kappa sorority, and Sigma Pi Beta fraternity.

Other organizations include Baptist Collegiate Ministries, Fellowship of Christian Athletes, First Priority, Inter-Greek Council, International Student Union, *Railsplitter* yearbook staff, Student Affairs Advisory Board, Student Alumni Association, Student Government Association, Student Organization Council, and the Wesley Foundation.

LMU is affiliated with the Gulf South Conference of NCAA Division II. Sports offered as part of the intercollegiate program include baseball, basketball, cross-country, golf, soccer, softball, tennis, and volleyball.

On-campus residency options are numerous and varied to meet the particular needs of single students and those with families. From individual rooms to shared rooms and small apartments, LMU's five residential facilities offer the resident student opportunities for learning-through-living on campus. The opportunity for meeting new people takes on a decidedly international flair by virtue of LMU's long-standing friendship with the Kanto School of Tokyo. Each fall and spring, a new group of Japanese students comes to the LMU campus to study English and other college skills and to share their remarkable culture. In addition to LMU's Japanese students, Lincoln Memorial University draws more than 50 other international students each year from many countries.

Location

Lincoln Memorial University's beautiful, historic, 1,000-acre wooded campus has thirty-two academic, administrative, and residential buildings on the grounds. It is located on U.S. Highway 25E in Harrogate, Tennessee, in the heart of Appalachia where Tennessee, Kentucky, and Virginia merge at the Cumberland Gap. It is adjacent to Cumberland Gap National Historical Park. The campus and the park create a natural recreational area for enjoying nature. Hiking, mountain climbing, and camping in the surrounding environs are activities available for all to enjoy.

Nearby Middlesboro, Kentucky, offers a shopping mall, movie theaters, restaurants, and other businesses and amenities. Harrogate offers several banks, restaurants, a variety and drug store, grocery stores, and physicians and dentists offices all within walking distance of the campus. For those desiring big-city entertainment, Knoxville, Tennessee, is approximately 55 miles south of the campus.

Majors and Degrees

LMU's Paul V. Hamilton School of Arts and Sciences awards the Bachelor of Arts or Bachelor of Science degree in American studies, art, biology, chemistry, communication arts, English, environmental science, history, humanities, interdisciplinary sciences, interdisciplinary social science, mathematics, and wildlife and fisheries management.

The Carter and Moyers School of Education awards the Bachelor of Science in Interdisciplinary Studies in human learning and development, psychology, and social work. Courses offered by the Department of Teacher Education lead to teacher licensure in Tennessee in elementary, secondary, and K–12 education. For licensure in secondary or K–12 education, students may select an accompanying major program.

The DeBusk School of Business awards the Bachelor of Business Administration (B.B.A.) with concentration areas in accounting, computer information systems, economics, financial economics, general business, management, or marketing. The Bachelor of Arts degree is also awarded in general business.

The Caylor School of Nursing and Allied Health awards the Bachelor of Science in athletic training, health, kinesiology, medical technology, nursing (B.S.N.), and veterinary science.

Associate degrees are awarded in applied science (veterinary technology), business administration (A.B.A.), and nursing (A.S.N.).

Academic Program

The academic year consists of two semesters. Summer courses are available. A minimum of 128 semester credit hours are required for the baccalaureate degree. A student must complete the required semester hours in a major as well as the general study requirements. The University's curriculum and commitment to high-quality instruction at every level are based on the beliefs that graduates must be able to communicate clearly and effectively in an era of rapidly and continuously expanding communication technology, have an appreciable depth of learning in a field of knowledge, appreciate and understand the various ways by which they come to know themselves and the world around them, and be able to exercise informed judgments.

Off-Campus Programs

LMU offers courses at extended-campus sites. The nursing program is offered in Knoxville, Tennessee, and Blount County, Tennessee; at Hiwassee College in Madisonville, Tennessee; and in Corbin, Kentucky. Business and education classes are offered in Knoxville and at Southeast Community College in Cumberland, Kentucky. Graduate studies are offered in Cleveland, Knoxville, Maryville, and Ducktown, Tennessee.

Academic Facilities

The 1,000-acre LMU campus—its grounds, buildings, equipment, and human resources—is one of the most strikingly beautiful and functional in the country.

The Harold M. Finley Learning Resources Center houses collections totaling more than 200,000 volumes. It also provides expanded library services through subscriptions to approximately 50 electronic databases and more than 19,000 electronic books. On-site technology facilities provide access for students to the Internet.

The Abraham Lincoln Library and Museum is home to a nationally recognized Lincoln and Civil War collection. This center for history, research, and public interest contains one of the nation's largest collections of Lincoln and Civil War artifacts. Scholars from every region of the globe have visited the library and museum to study the life and thoughts of the nation's sixteenth president.

The DeBusk School of Business houses the campus dining hall, snack bar ('Splitters' Lounge), and University Bookstore as well as the Business School's offices and classrooms. The Office of the President and the Office of Admissions are located inside the main entrance to the facility.

The Sigmon Communications Center is the home for radio stations WLMU-FM and WRWB-AM and television station, LMU-TV. The facility provides laboratory and classroom space to support the communication arts curriculum and production areas that allow student productions to be broadcast to the local community.

The 5,009-seat Tex Turner Arena is a state-of-the-art facility for intercollegiate basketball and for major concerts and special events. The multipurpose Mars Gymnasium provides classrooms, indoor swimming, and basketball courts. Outdoor athletic facilities include the Lamar Hennon Baseball Field, Gibbs Soccer Field, Neely Softball Field, Annan Tennis Courts, and walking trails.

Costs

The cost to attend LMU is substantially below the national average for private colleges and universities. Tuition and fees at LMU for 2003–04 were $5880 per semester. Room and board costs averaged $2190 per semester, depending on accommodations.

Financial Aid

Ninety-three percent of LMU students apply for and receive some type of financial assistance through a combination of scholarships and need-based financial aid. For many, the individual cost to attend Lincoln Memorial University is less than the cost associated with state supported institutions. The University participates in the following federally sponsored aid programs: the Federal Perkins Loan, Federal Pell Grant, Federal Supplemental Educational Opportunity Grant, Federal Work-Study, Federal Stafford Student Loans (subsidized and unsubsidized), and PLUS Loans programs. All financial aid applicants are required to submit the Free Application for Federal Student Aid (FAFSA). Academic scholarships are competitive and renewable. Students are strongly urged to apply for academic scholarships by the March 1 priority deadline.

Faculty

At Lincoln Memorial University, the faculty is dedicated to helping students succeed. Every effort is made to assist the individual student to accelerate a program of study or to master the developmental skills necessary for success. The student-faculty ratio at Lincoln Memorial University is 15:1. More than 70 percent of full-time faculty members teaching in bachelor's degree programs hold the doctorate or the highest degree available in the field.

Student Government

The Student Government Association (SGA) is the principle means for student participation in University governance and is dedicated to the well-being of the students. SGA is a student-based organization, composed of elected representatives from campus dormitories, social and academic organizations, and commuter students. LMU students serve on numerous University committees.

Admission Requirements

Application for general admission should be made as early as possible in the senior year of high school. Tentative acceptance is made during the senior year, but final acceptance is made only after receipt of the academic transcript confirming the high school diploma.

Transfer students in good academic standing are invited to apply to LMU. Transfer students must submit transcripts from their high school and each college attended.

Application and Information

All applicants must submit the following to the Office of Admissions: a completed application form with a nonrefundable $25 application fee; an official copy of the applicant's high school transcript or GED scores (upon graduation the student must forward a final transcript of his or her high school records); and a copy of the applicant's ACT scores (code 3982) or SAT scores (code 1408). Once these items are on file and reviewed, applicants receive prompt notification of the University's decision. Students are strongly encouraged to apply by the March 1 academic scholarship priority deadline.

An application and additional information may be obtained by contacting:

Office of Admissions
Lincoln Memorial University
6965 Cumberland Gap Parkway
Harrogate, Tennessee 37752
Telephone: 423-869-6280
800-325-0900 (toll-free)
E-mail: admissions@lmunet.edu
World Wide Web: http://www.lmunet.edu

LINDENWOOD UNIVERSITY

ST. CHARLES, MISSOURI

The University

An independent teaching university founded in 1827, Lindenwood is the oldest university west of the Missouri River. Lindenwood is a dynamic four-year liberal arts institution dedicated to excellence, delivering a quality education that leads to the development of the whole person and preparation for life and work after graduation, through eighty values-centered programs.

Lindenwood University (LU) is accredited by the Commission on Institutions of Higher Education of the North Central Association of Colleges and Schools and is a member of the Teacher Education Accreditation Council. The University has a historical relationship with the Presbyterian Church and is committed to the values inherent in the Judeo-Christian tradition. Lindenwood welcomes students from all religious denominations.

The University's athletic teams compete in the Heart of America Athletic Conference and the National Association of Intercollegiate Athletics (NAIA). Lindenwood's men and women athletes participate in baseball, basketball, bowling, cross-country, football, golf, ice hockey, lacrosse, soccer, softball, swimming and diving, tennis, indoor and outdoor track, volleyball, water polo, and wrestling. The men's wrestling team won the 2002 NAIA National Championship and finished as the national runner-up in the 2003 tournament. In addition, the University offers women's field hockey and men's roller hockey. The teams use the brand-new Robert F. Hyland Performance Arena, Harlen C. Hunter Stadium, baseball and softball fields, and a new eight-lane all-weather track. Students also participate in an assortment of intramural sports at the University's Fitness Center.

Student organizations and clubs provide avenues for extended personal growth, leadership, and community service. The University radio station, 35,000-watt KCLC-FM, is staffed by students.

Students wishing to live on campus may choose from residence halls, houses, and apartment-style living. Two new residence halls were opened to students in fall 2000. In addition, two new men's residence halls and two new women's residence halls are slated to open during the 2003–04 academic year. Sibley Hall, named in honor of founders Mary Easton and Major George C. Sibley, was built in 1856 to replace the original log cabin that served as the first University building. It is listed on the National Register of Historic Places and is now a women's residence hall. All residential buildings have easy access to University facilities.

Location

The 378-acre campus is located in St. Charles, Missouri, a city of about 55,000 people, situated 20 miles from downtown St. Louis. Resting on the banks of the Missouri River, just south of the Mississippi, St. Charles is the site of Missouri's first state capital. The area offers a wide range of opportunities for all types of interests and is particularly rich in state heritage and attractions associated with the history of America's westward expansion. Lindenwood's proximity to a major city allows students to enjoy theme parks, a world-class zoo, professional sporting events, Broadway plays and theater, performances of a world-renowned symphony orchestra, state parks, and lakes. St. Louis–Lambert International Airport is located just 5 miles from Lindenwood University on Interstate 70.

Majors and Degrees

With a foundation as solid as the campus' century-old linden trees, the academic programs of Lindenwood University have a tradition of excellence and innovation. Lindenwood awards Bachelor of Arts, Bachelor of Fine Arts, and Bachelor of Science degrees with majors in accounting, agribusiness, art history, art management, art (studio), athletic training, biology, business administration, chemistry, computer science, corporate communications, criminal justice, dance, early childhood education, elementary education, English, fashion design, fashion merchandising, finance, French, general studies, history, human resource management, human service agency management, information technology, international studies, management, management information systems, marketing, mass communication, mathematics, medical technology, music, performing arts, physical education, political science, psychology, public administration, religion, retail marketing, secondary education, social work, sociology, Spanish, special education, theater, theater management, and writing.

Preprofessional courses are offered in dentistry, engineering, law, medicine, and veterinary medicine. Also, programs in engineering are available in conjunction with Washington University in St. Louis and the University of Missouri–Columbia.

Academic Program

The emphasis at Lindenwood University is on an individualized liberal arts education with career-oriented preparation. Students fulfill general education requirements, participate in the University's Work and Learn Program when qualified, and acquire an in-depth knowledge of at least one area of study as a major. Lindenwood requires the completion of 128 credit hours to earn a bachelor's degree.

Academic Facilities

The Margaret Leggat Butler Library houses volumes, microfilm items, and a computer lab and subscribes to 450 periodicals. Roemer Hall serves as the main administration building and has classrooms and faculty offices on the upper floors. Roemer Hall is also home to the 450-seat Jelkyl Theatre. Young Science Hall houses an auditorium, laboratories, and classrooms for natural science, mathematics, and computer science, as well as a state-of-the-art television studio. Harmon Hall provides students with art, photography, dance, music, and performing arts studios; classrooms; practice rooms; a recital and lecture hall; the Harmon Theatre; and the Harry D. Hendren Gallery, which attracts local and national art exhibits. The Lindenwood University Cultural Center provides a 750-seat auditorium, classrooms, meeting rooms, and offices. It is home to the University's music department and is the site of theatrical productions, concerts, convocations, and lectures. In addition, the new Spellmann Campus Center opened in fall 2002. The facility was constructed in the same style as the two new men's and women's dormitories that opened in 2000 and the Performance Arena, which opened in 1997. The Campus Center serves as a student union and houses a state-of-the-art cafeteria, Macintosh and PC computer labs, conference rooms, networking and campus life offices, and career planning and placement services.

Costs

For the academic year 2003–04, tuition was $11,200. Students who chose to live on campus paid $5600 for room and board, plus $300 for communications service. There was a refundable $200 room deposit and a $150 activity fee. Books and other supplies were extra.

Financial Aid

Financial aid is available to all qualified students. A student must submit the Free Application for Federal Student Aid (FAFSA). To qualify for the full amount of financial aid, students must submit their federal financial aid forms before March 15. As determined by the evaluation, a student's financial need may be met with a combination of federal, state, and institutional sources of aid. In addition, institutional awards are available in the areas of academics, leadership, athletics, drama, yearbook/ newspaper, and music. Resident students may earn $1800 toward their expenses by working on campus.

Faculty

Lindenwood has 160 full-time faculty members, who serve as teachers, mentors, and advisers to their students. Faculty members advise students regarding majors and other matters to help them succeed academically.

Student Government

The Lindenwood Student Government Association (LSGA) is made up of representatives elected by the student body. LSGA has the responsibility of providing a balanced program of cultural, social, and recreational events and activities throughout the year.

Admission Requirements

To apply for admission, a student should submit a completed application form with a nonrefundable $25 application fee, a transcript of high school and/or college work, and ACT or SAT I scores.

Applicants are evaluated on an individual basis, and admission is based on an analysis of the student's grade point average, ACT or SAT I scores, extracurricular activities, recommendations, and personal qualifications. Students are admitted without regard to race, sex, or national origin.

Application and Information

Although admission to Lindenwood is on a rolling basis, students are encouraged to apply by April 15 for the fall semester and by December 1 for the spring semester. Notification of the admission decision is mailed soon after all required materials are received and evaluated by the Director of Undergraduate Admissions.

Applications for admission, financial aid, and scholarships and other information about Lindenwood University can be obtained by contacting:

Undergraduate Admissions
Lindenwood University
209 South Kingshighway
St. Charles, Missouri 63301-1695
Telephone: 636-949-4949
Fax: 636-949-4989
World Wide Web: http://www.lindenwood.edu

Students look over class notes in the shade of the linden trees at Lindenwood University.

LINFIELD COLLEGE

MCMINNVILLE, OREGON

The College

Linfield College (1858) is an independent, coeducational, residential, comprehensive liberal arts college dedicated to providing an educational environment conducive to learning and participation. There are 1,600 full-time students on the McMinnville campus. These students come primarily from the thirteen Western states (twenty-eight states overall) but also from twenty-four countries. Members of minority groups make up 11 percent of the student body, and 4 percent of students are international. Most students are between 18 and 22. Linfield is primarily residential, with one residence hall for men, three for women, and eleven that are coeducational, each accommodating between 10 and 100 residents. There are also four fraternity houses. Each hall establishes its own calendar of social, educational, and recreational events throughout the year. Students who reside on campus eat their meals in the College dining hall. Houses and apartments are available for upper-division students. Social clubs, professional organizations, sororities (one local: Sigma Kappa Phi, and three national: Alpha Phi, Phi Sigma Sigma, and Zeta Tau Alpha) and fraternities (one local: Delta Psi Delta, and three national: Kappa Sigma, Pi Kappa Alpha, and Theta Chi), service clubs, and almost forty other organizations play an important role in the daily life of a Linfield student. Linfield's winning athletics tradition fosters participation at all levels of competition. Women compete in intercollegiate basketball, cross-country, golf, lacrosse, soccer, softball, swimming, tennis, track and field, and volleyball. Men compete in intercollegiate baseball, basketball, cross-country, football, golf, soccer, swimming, tennis, and track and field. Water polo, Ultimate Frisbee, and men's lacrosse are club sports. Linfield also has an extensive and active year-round intramural program.

Linfield hosts the Oregon Nobel Laureate Symposium. (There are only five such symposiums worldwide.) At each symposium, several Nobel laureates come to share their backgrounds and expertise within the context of a basic theme.

The Linfield–Good Samaritan School of Nursing, an academic unit of the College at its Portland campus, prepares students for the B.S.N. or a degree in health science. This campus, at the Good Samaritan Hospital and Medical Center, has residence facilities, food service options, and a residence life program. The Portland campus median age is 24.

Location

Located in McMinnville, 36 miles southwest of Portland, Linfield College is a leader in the cultural, educational, and recreational events of the fast-growing community of 27,000. The seat of county government, McMinnville provides Linfield faculty and students with many opportunities to participate in community service activities. Cinemas, a community theater, bowling alleys, coffeehouses, and a wide variety of restaurants welcome Linfield students. Shopping is within walking distance. The central Oregon coast is an hour to the west, and the outdoor activity areas of the Oregon Cascade mountains, including year-round skiing at Mt. Hood, are 2 hours to the east. Salem, the state capital of Oregon, is 23 miles to the southeast, and Eugene is 80 miles south. Rainfall in western Oregon averages 42 inches annually, and the winter temperature averages 41°F.

Majors and Degrees

The Bachelor of Arts degree is awarded in art, communication, creative writing, English, French, German, history, music, philosophy, political science, religious studies, sociology, Spanish, and theater arts. The Bachelor of Arts or Bachelor of Science degree is offered in accounting, anthropology, applied physics, athletic training, biology, business, chemistry, computing science, economics, elementary education, environmental studies, exercise science, finance, general science, health education, international business, mathematics, medical technology, physical education, physics, and psychology. The College has programs to prepare students for advanced study in dentistry, law, and medicine. The education department offers a strong program of teacher certification at the secondary and elementary levels. A 3-2 engineering program is available with Oregon State University, Washington State University, and the University of Southern California.

Academic Program

The academic year is divided into two 15-week semesters (fall and spring) and an optional four-week winter term in January. (There is a $103 per-credit fee for January Term classes.) The January Term offers regular departmental courses and cultural-epochs study. Academic courses are assigned 1–5 semester credit hours each; 125 credits are required for a B.A. or a B.S. degree. Students divide their time equally among required general education courses, a major area of study, and elective subjects. The Linfield Curriculum courses, selected to provide a solid foundation in the liberal arts, require students to take 6 semester hours in at least two courses in each of the five areas of inquiry. These areas of inquiry are as follows: the Vital Past; Ultimate Questions; Individual, Systems, and Societies; the Natural World; and Images and Arts. In addition, students are required to take a writing-intensive course, a course addressing global diversity, and a course dealing with American pluralism. Major requirements differ from department to department. Individually designed majors are available with faculty approval. Students majoring in a foreign language spend an academic year in a country in which the language being studied is the native tongue. Language majors have recently studied in such cities as Avignon, Guadalajara, Nantes, Munich, Quebec, and Valencia. The Advanced Placement (AP) Program of the College Board is recognized, and up to 5 semester hours of credit are granted for a score of 4 or 5 on an AP test. AP examinations do not satisfy general education requirements. The College recognizes the International Baccalaureate (IB) Diploma and awards up to 30 semester hours of credit for higher-level courses on a course-by-course basis. Total credit awarded by AP or IB may not exceed 30 semester hours.

The College offers an intensive course in English as a second language. It is designed to help international students whose native language is other than English to achieve competence in academic and social English skills, so that they can work effectively in their undergraduate classes at Linfield.

Off-Campus Programs

Off-campus educational experiences include the Semester Abroad Program, involving four months of study in San José, Costa Rica; Paris, France; Vienna, Austria; Yokohama, Japan; Cuernavaca, Mexico; Oslo, Norway; Hong Kong, China; Seoul, South Korea; Galway, Ireland; or Nottingham, England. Sophomores, juniors, and seniors are encouraged to participate, and approximately 20 students are selected for each country each year. The program is designed to serve students who have successfully completed one year of study at Linfield in the appropriate language and who will return to the campus to share their international experiences with the College community. Transportation for the first round trip is included in the cost of tuition, and most of these study programs cost the same as a semester on campus. January Term study-abroad programs for four weeks are also offered. Recent offerings included the Emergence of Modern Ghana (West Africa); Mainland Southeast Asia History (Cambodia, Vietnam, and China); American Expatriate Writers in Europe: The Lost Generation Tour (nine European cities); and Australia: From Colony to Asian Power.

Academic Facilities

Murdock Hall houses the biology and chemistry departments and up-to-date laboratories and equipment. Laboratory and research space is provided for general and advanced chemistry and biology, organic chemistry, biochemistry, microbiology, bacteriology, immunology, ecology, botany, physiology, embryology, and gross and microscopic anatomy. Taylor Hall houses the economics department, a computer center, a resource library, a seminar room, and classrooms. The physics and mathematics departments are housed in Graf Hall. There are approximately 200 IBM and Macintosh computers on campus available for student use. Services on the network that students can use include the two UNIX hosts (available for programming, e-mail, and other communication services), a connection to the Internet, file servers, and both laser and dot-matrix printers. Linfield students benefit from a communications and technology network, including phone service, voice mail, e-mail, and Internet connections in each residence hall room.

The Health and Physical Education/Recreation Complex houses three gymnasiums; weight rooms; fitness laboratories with a hydrostatic weighing tank, a metabolic and pulmonary measuring system, and an electrocardiovascular exercise ECG system; an eight-lane, 25-yard-long indoor pool; handball and racquetball courts; classrooms; offices; and a 28,000-square-foot field house.

Since 2000, there have been many exciting changes at Linfield. The College has opened six new apartment buildings as well as the James F. Miller Fine Arts Complex. In July of 2003, Linfield opened its new library and theater and communication arts facility. The new library covers 56,000 square feet and combines traditional collections of books and journals with the new and changing digital and electronic technology to provide access to the Web and Web-based designs. There is seating for up to 500 students and 35 computer work stations as well as wireless access to the campus network, the Internet, and the World Wide Web for student who bring their own laptops or check out those available at the library. The new studio theater has an audience seating capacity of up to 140, more than double the former facility. It includes space for set construction and design as well as faculty offices. Other facilities include art galleries and studios, a 250-watt FM radio station, an experimental psychology laboratory, dance and music studios, a preschool, and a 425-seat auditorium that houses a three-manual, 48-rank Casavant pipe organ.

Costs

For 2003–04, tuition and fees were $20,770 per two-semester year. Board was $2920, and a double room was $3200.

Financial Aid

Eligibility for most of Linfield's assistance programs is based on need as determined by a federally approved needs analysis processor. The only form required for need-based programs is the Free Application for Federal Student Aid (FAFSA). Linfield participates in the Federal Perkins and Federal Stafford Student Loan programs, Federal Supplemental Educational Opportunity Grants, Federal Work-Study, and other forms of financial assistance on the basis of demonstrated need.

The College awards a number of scholarships to full-time students based on scholastic achievement, independent of financial need. These academic scholarships vary from 20 to 75 percent of tuition. To be considered, students must have a minimum GPA of 3.4. A number of other criteria are used when determining scholarships. Linfield sponsors special scholarships for National Merit finalists. The minimum award is 50 percent of tuition. Awards can range to full tuition, depending on financial need, provided the student has indicated that Linfield is his or her first-choice college. The College also sponsors the annual Academic Competitive Scholarship Program in early spring each year. Participation is limited to high school seniors who meet particular academic requirements. Each academic department offers prizes ranging from $10,000 to $16,000, divided over the student's four years at Linfield, provided the student maintains a grade point average of at least 3.0. Scholarships of varying amounts are awarded to entering students who are particularly talented in music performance. Amounts range from $1500 to $2500 annually. Interested students are required to audition either in person or by cassette tape by February 15. Financial assistance for non–U.S. citizens is limited to partial tuition scholarships and the opportunity to work part-time on campus. Other scholarships are available for students who demonstrate outstanding leadership and community service.

Faculty

There are 137 full-time faculty members, who are committed to undergraduate teaching and scholarship. Ninety-eight percent have doctoral or other terminal degrees within their field. The faculty-student ratio is 1:12. Faculty members serve as academic advisers. There are no teaching assistants.

Student Government

Students have a significant voice in establishing and changing College policies and regulations. The Student Senate, chosen through campus elections, is the focus of student opinion and debate. Students are represented on most College governing councils and committees, with faculty members and trustees, and are encouraged to express and implement their ideas on academic or extracurricular matters.

Admission Requirements

Admission to Linfield College is selective. Admission is granted to students who are likely to grow and succeed in a personal and challenging liberal arts environment. Each applicant is judged on individual merit. A faculty admission committee evaluates candidates in a number of areas that commonly indicate academic potential. These include high school performance, a writing sample, recommendations from teachers and counselors, and precollege standardized test results (ACT or SAT I). The committee also considers the depth and quality of an applicant's involvement in community and school activities. It reviews all applications as a group, selecting those students who show the greatest likelihood of benefitting from and contributing to the Linfield community. Linfield is a member of the Common Application Association.

International students whose education has been in a language other than English must submit certified English translations of their academic work. Proficiency in English is required, as demonstrated by an official TOEFL score report, including a Test of Written English (TWE) score. Admitted international students must show evidence of financial responsibility and submit a $2000 deposit.

Early action applicants must apply by November 15, and notification is made by January 15. The priority application deadline for regular admission is February 15, with notification made on or before April 1.

Application and Information

Interviews are not required, but students are encouraged to visit. Appointments should be made in advance. The Office of Admission is open Monday through Friday, 7:30 a.m. to 5:30 p.m. and on Saturdays during the school year from 9 a.m. to 2 p.m. The Linfield Web site provides students with information on student life, academic programs, and athletics. Students may also complete their application for admission online or ask for additional information. Interested students are encouraged to contact:

Director of Admission
Linfield College
McMinnville, Oregon 97128

Telephone: 503-883-2213
800-640-2287 (toll-free)
Fax: 503-883-2472
E-mail: admission@linfield.edu
World Wide Web: http://www.linfield.edu

LOCK HAVEN UNIVERSITY OF PENNSYLVANIA

LOCK HAVEN, PENNSYLVANIA

The University

Founded as the Central State Normal School in 1870, Lock Haven University (LHU) is part of Pennsylvania's state system of higher education. The enrollment is 4,500—an ideal size for a high-quality, personalized education. Students represent thirty-two states across the nation. The International Education program is one of the finest in the country, attracting students from thirty-nine countries. The University has seven residence halls, which house approximately 1,700 students. Six of the residence halls are coeducational and one is all women. All residence halls are equipped with kitchens, storage and vending areas, and both recreational and study lounges. Individual rooms receive basic telephone and cable TV service at no charge. In addition, Campus Village is reserved for upperclassmen. These on-campus apartments include 78 one-bedroom, double-occupancy apartments, two large triple-occupancy apartments, and twelve efficiency, single-occupancy apartments. There are also hundreds of apartments and houses for rent that are within easy walking distance of the campus. In addition to the full meal plan for resident students, the University dining hall offers flex accounts and several partial meal plans for off-campus and commuting students.

Social and extracurricular offerings at LHU are exhaustive and exciting. Lock Haven's nationally recognized athletic teams include NCAA Division I men's wrestling; Division II men's and women's basketball, track and field, and cross-country; men's soccer, football, and baseball; women's soccer, softball, lacrosse, volleyball, swimming, and field hockey. Other extracurricular offerings include an active student government and a residence hall council that both governs and promotes on-campus life, Greek life (six national fraternities, four national sororities, and a variety of honorary and professional Greek-letter societies), and more than eighty recognized clubs and organizations.

More than seventy-five academic programs are offered through the College of Arts and Sciences and the College of Education and Human Services. Widely respected programs in education, health sciences/athletic training, international studies, and recreation attract acclaim from across the state and the country. Master's programs are offered in education (curriculum and instruction), health science (physician assistant in rural primary care), and liberal arts. LHU is accredited by the Middle States Association of Colleges and Schools, the National Council for Accreditation of Teacher Education, the Commision on Accreditation of Allied Health Education Programs (CAAHEP), and the Council on Social Work Education.

LHU's branch campus in Clearfield, Pennsylvania, has grown steadily since opening in 1989. Currently, more than 445 students attend the Clearfield Campus. Several associate degree programs are also offered at this location.

Location

LHU is located on 165 acres in Lock Haven, Pennsylvania, a pleasant town of about 10,000 full-time residents. The town enjoys meticulously restored Victorian homes and turn-of-the-century architecture. Located on a hill overlooking the Susquehanna River, the campus is adjacent to all the outdoor wonders the area has to offer. During late spring and summer, the river is dotted with boats, rafts, and inner tubes. There are opportunities for swimming, fishing, hiking, hunting, skiing, camping, and hang gliding. The Millbrook Playhouse provides professional summer-stock theater, and the Ross Library is noted for its collection of artwork by John Sloan, a Lock Haven native for whom the University's fine arts and performing center is named. Lock Haven is within easy reach of Pittsburgh, Philadelphia, and New York City (about 3½ hours), and Washington, D.C. (about 4 hours). Lock Haven is accessible via Interstate Route 80 and U.S. Routes 15 and 220 and is served by the State College and Williamsport airports and by a Trailways bus station.

Majors and Degrees

The Bachelor of Arts degree is offered in art, communications studies, economics, engineering (a cooperative five-year dual-degree program with Pennsylvania State University), English, environmental geology, French, German, history, humanities (English, philosophy, and speech/theater), international studies, journalism/mass communication, Latin American studies, mathematics, natural sciences (biology, chemistry, and physics), philosophy, political science, psychology, social sciences (economics, history, political science, and sociology/anthropology), sociology, Spanish, and theater. The Bachelor of Fine Arts is offered in music and studio arts.

The Bachelor of Science degree is offered in accounting, applied geology, biology, biology/chemistry, biology/chemistry with a medical technology emphasis, chemistry, computer information science, computer science, criminal justice, DNA forensics, early childhood education, elementary education, geography, health and physical education (optional concentrations in aquatics, coaching, and sports and physical education in a correctional institution), health science (concentrations in community health, general (preprofessional), pre–physical therapy, pre–physician's assistant studies, and sports medicine/athletic training), paralegal studies, physics, preprofessional preparation (dentistry, medicine, pharmacy, and veterinary medicine), recreation (concentrations in fitness management, leisure and commercial management, outdoor management, and therapeutic recreation), secondary education (concentrations in biology, chemistry, citizenship studies, earth and space science, English, French, general science, German, mathematics, physics, and Spanish,) social work, and sports administration. The sports medicine/athletic training program at LHU is one of nearly ninety programs nationwide accredited by the CAAHEP.

Academic Programs

Candidates for graduation from LHU must have completed at least 120 credits, including a minimum of 52 credits of general education course work. The two-semester academic year is supplemented by optional summer sessions. Internships and independent study are frequently part of a well-balanced degree program. Credits from many regionally accredited institutions are accepted, contingent upon a minimum GPA of 2.0. Educational experiences gained while in the armed services are evaluated for credit. The University maintains a Veterans' Affairs Office to provide counseling and assistance in financial aid and other matters. The Army Reserve Officers' Training Corps offers a full program in military science to supplement the educational experience.

Off-Campus Programs

The Bachelor of Science in education degree program includes one semester of student teaching, which can be done in the Lock Haven area, elsewhere in Pennsylvania, or through the Office of International Education in Australia, Croatia, England, Scotland, or Spain. Students may study abroad for a semester or more and have those credits accepted toward graduation. Exchange programs exist with universities in Australia, Canada, China, Costa Rica, England, Finland, France, Germany, Italy, Japan, Mexico, Morocco, Poland, Russia, Scotland, Spain, Taiwan, Tunisia, and Ukraine. Students may apply for a semester overseas during any year at Lock Haven.

Academic Facilities

The Robinson Hall Learning Center is a multimillion-dollar research-learning facility that houses five academic departments as well as a full-production radio station, color-TV studio, the academic computing center, a multipurpose Model United Nations auditorium, and a psychological behavior laboratory outfitted for primate study. The Stevenson Library has more than 371,000 volumes and an extensive collection of periodicals, microfilm, and microfiche. LHU belongs to the state's interlibrary loan system, the Ohio College Library Center, and the Susquehanna Library Cooperative. Two large auditoriums are used for plays, concerts, and other performances. The John Sloan Fine Arts Center includes a theater, an art gallery, classrooms, art and pottery studios, and music practice rooms. Akeley Hall houses a complete student computing center. Sixty PCs attached to the University network are available for use by all students. Raub Hall and Robinson Hall each house an additional computer lab with thirty PCs for general student use. Each residence hall also houses computers. The Sieg Conference Center, several miles from the main campus, is used as a retreat by classes, clubs, and other campus organizations.

Costs

For the 2003–04 academic year, tuition was $4598 for in-state students and $9496 for out-of-state students. Room and board costs were $4936 for the year. In addition, students paid $1276 in fees ($1326 for out-of-state students), which included a student activity fee, the student center fee, and an educational services fee. Thus, in-state on-campus students paid a total of $10,810, and out-of-state on-campus students paid $15,758.

Financial Aid

Approximately 80 percent of students receive financial aid. Aid is divided into grants, loans, and work programs. Available grants include the Federal Pell Grant, a federally funded program that awards students from $400 to $3750 per academic year; the Pennsylvania Higher Education Assistance Agency (PHEAA) grant, through a state program that awards students (in-state only) up to $3200 per academic year; the University-administered Federal Supplemental Educational Opportunity Grant (FSEOG), which provides up to $600 per academic year in addition to other financial aid when a need still exists; and other state grant programs. Loans available through the Office of Financial Aid include Federal Perkins Loans, federally insured Federal Stafford Student Loans, and parents' loans, which vary according to the lending institution. Work programs are divided into the Federal Work-Study Program, which requires demonstration of financial need, and campus employment, which is open to most students to help with college expenses. Most aid may be applied for by filling out the Free Application for Federal Student Aid (FAFSA), found in most high school guidance offices. The deadline is March 15, but it is recommended that applications be filed sooner. A University financial aid form is sent to all newly admitted students and should also be filled out by March 15 for full consideration. Most award programs are operated on a first-come, first-served basis from a limited amount of available funds. Questions should be directed to Dr. William Irwin, Director of Financial Aid, at 877-405-3057 (toll-free).

The University Honors Program offers scholarships, including the Presidential Scholars Program for incoming freshmen who have exhibited exemplary academic and leadership performance in high school. Application forms for this scholarship program and information about other LHU Foundation scholarships, may be obtained by writing to the Honors Program, LHU, 401 North Fairview Street, Lock Haven, Pennsylvania 17745. Students may also e-mail the office at honors@lhup.edu or call 570-893-2053.

Faculty

The student-faculty ratio at Lock Haven University is 19:1. The faculty of 276 full- and part-time professors includes both career-long educators and professionals who bring experience to the classroom. Most faculty members have an advanced degree in their field and 60 percent of the faculty have earned a Ph.D.

Student Government

Upon payment of the activity fee, each student enrolled at LHU becomes a member of the Student Cooperative Council, Inc. (SCC), the governing student body. The SCC owns and manages the Parsons Union Building, the student bookstore, and the campus snack bar. The SCC also controls the budgeting of athletics and the on-campus clubs and organizations. Students are elected by popular vote to represent each of the residence halls and the commuting population. Many of the campus cultural and entertainment events, as well as campus improvements that affect the daily function of the University, are funded exclusively through the SCC.

Admission Requirements

Academic eligibility is based upon several variables. The most important factors are academic courses, class rank and grade point average, and standardized test scores (SAT or ACT).

For admission as a first-time freshman student, LHU requires a high school curriculum that includes preparatory courses in English, social studies, math, and science. Two years of a foreign language are preferred but are not mandatory. LHU does not consider technical, vocational, or applied courses as an acceptable college-preparatory curriculum. Although honors or Advanced Placement (AP) courses are not required for admission, they carry extra weight in the application review process. The Admissions Office looks closely at students' academic performance in the core subject areas throughout their high school career. A student's high school rank and GPA are highly considered in the application review process. It is not required that a student be involved in extracurricular activities, but the Admissions Office looks favorably upon students who have been active in high school clubs, organizations, and athletics.

Standardized test scores are evaluated after high school courses and grades have been reviewed. Students are encouraged to take the SAT or ACT at least twice, as LHU uses the highest verbal and math scores (SAT) or highest composite score (ACT). Students who graduated from high school three years prior to applying for admission to LHU are not required to submit SAT/ACT scores.

Transfer students with 24 or more transferable credits and a cumulative GPA of 2.0 or better may be considered for admission.

Application and Information

The Office of Admissions works on a rolling admissions basis. Students are encouraged to apply for admission in the fall of their senior year. Typically, students are notified of their admissions status within four to six weeks after their application and all required documents are received by the Admissions Office. During the busiest time of the year (November–January), the process may take six to eight weeks. To apply for admissions, students should submit the following documents: an application for admission, a $30 paper application fee (or a $25 online application fee), an official copy of their high school transcript (faxed copies are not official), and SAT/ACT scores (scores reported on high school transcripts or received directly from the College Board are considered to be official). Recommendations from teachers and/or guidance counselors are not required for the application process but are considered helpful for a more thorough evaluation of each applicant. In addition, the Office of Admissions often requests a student's senior grades before rendering a decision.

Transfer students must submit (in addition to the application form, high school transcript, and fee), transcripts from all colleges and universities attended. Students who have not been continuously enrolled in postsecondary education are required to submit a timeline/resume of their experiences since leaving high school. If fewer than 24 credits are being transferred, a copy of SAT or ACT results is requested.

International students must submit a TOEFL minimum score of 213. SAT scores may replace TOEFL scores for those students whose native language is English. International students must also submit an equivalent of a U.S. high school diploma, proof of financial support, a medical history report, a completed application, and $100 (U.S. dollars) for the application processing fee. International students wishing to have credits transferred from another college or university should also submit certified translations of their official postsecondary school transcripts. All transcripts are evaluated by an outside evaluation service.

For more information, students should contact:

Stephen Lee
Director of Admissions
Lock Haven University of Pennsylvania
Lock Haven, Pennsylvania 17745
Telephone: 570-893-2027
800-332-8900 (toll-free in Pennsylvania)
800-233-8978 (toll-free outside Pennsylvania)
E-mail: admissions@lhup.edu
World Wide Web: http://www.lhup.edu

LONG ISLAND UNIVERSITY, BROOKLYN CAMPUS

BROOKLYN, NEW YORK

The Campus

Students who wish to be in a metropolitan setting during their years of higher education make up the student body of Long Island University's Brooklyn Campus. The proximity of many cultural, commercial, educational, and governmental institutions is reflected in the University's curricula and activities. The more than 11,000 students represent every region of the United States and many other countries. Even though most students commute, many live and work on or near campus.

An integrative approach to undergraduate education known as The Long Island University Plan (LIU Plan) includes the Freshman Experience Program, comprehensive academic advisement, cooperative education and career development, and an innovative, integrative curriculum in the University Honors Program. Through workplace experiences, workshops, development of technological skills, consultation services, integrative seminars, and tools for self-assessment and exploration, the LIU Plan enables students to develop skills and talents that can lead to coherent, well-informed, and successful lives. Cornerstones of the LIU Plan are: (1) expanded academic and personal counseling from application to graduation; (2) enhanced academic and career opportunities—to give students decisive advantages in career fields of their choice by providing an option for well-paid, professional-level work or other types of special semesters that build professional connections, credentials, and experience; and (3) essential literacies—to hone students' analytic and writing skills and to familiarize them with the fundamental languages of culture and science. For further information about the LIU Plan, students should contact the Brooklyn Campus Office of Admissions at the number listed below.

In addition to its undergraduate degree programs, the Brooklyn Campus also offers eighty-six master's-level programs leading to the M.A., M.S., M.S.Ed., M.B.A., and M.P.A. degrees as well as doctoral programs in clinical psychology, pharmacy, pharmaceutics, and physical therapy.

Location

The 11-acre campus is located in downtown Brooklyn, 20 minutes from midtown Manhattan and convenient to public transportation that serves all parts of the metropolitan area. Within walking distance are excellent shopping areas, restaurants, and entertainment.

Majors and Degrees

The Bachelor of Arts degree is granted in the following areas: economics, English, English teacher studies (7–12), history, jazz studies, journalism, media arts, modern languages (French, Italian, Spanish), music (applied), music theory, philosophy, political science, psychology, social studies teacher studies (7–12), social work, sociology-anthropology, speech communications, and visual arts. The Bachelor of Science degree is granted in the following areas: accounting, adolescence urban education, bilingual teacher of special education studies, bilingual teacher of students with speech and language disabilities studies, biochemistry, biology, biology teacher studies (7–12), business finance, business management, chemistry, chemistry teacher studies (7–12), childhood urban education, computer science, cytotechnology, dance, dance education, health science, humanities, integrated information systems, marketing, mathematics, mathematics teacher studies (7–12), medical technology, molecular biology, nuclear medicine technology, nursing, physical education teacher studies (K–12), physician assistant studies, respiratory care, social science, sports science, and teacher of students with speech and language disabilities studies. The Bachelor of Fine Arts degree is granted in the following areas: art education, dance, music (jazz studies), and studio art. The Associate of Applied Science degree is offered in business administration; the Associate of Arts degree is offered in humanities, science, and social science. Five-year dual B.S./M.S. degree programs are offered in accounting, adult nurse practitioner studies, athletic training and sports sciences, nursing (executive program for nursing and health-care management), and occupational therapy. The Arnold & Marie Schwartz College of Pharmacy offers a six-year Pharm.D. program.

Academic Program

All undergraduate students are required to complete a core curriculum in the liberal arts and sciences in order to acquire the general background of ideas and knowledge that an educated person must have. The core curriculum consists of courses in the humanities, the natural sciences, mathematics, the social sciences, and now includes a 9-credit writing-intensive requirement (part of the core's new emphasis on writing across the curriculum). Specific requirements may vary depending on the major. Of the 128 credits required for graduation, a student must take 24 or more credits of advanced work in the major and have at least 48 credits in upper-division work. The minimum number of credits required in the liberal arts and sciences varies from 64 to 96, depending on the degree awarded. Qualified students in any major may arrange for independent studies and honors work.

The University Honors Program, open to all majors, offers academically qualified students core courses, designed for cross-disciplinary inquiry, and advanced seminars, which are theme oriented and field based. The program also allows for creative, as well as research, projects for independent study. Members of the program are eligible for Distinction in Honors when they write a thesis. All members may extend independent study beyond the stated limits through the Honors Program.

All students may enroll in the Cooperative Education Program, gaining valuable field experience and pay for employment related to their major field of study.

In the Arnold & Marie Schwartz College of Pharmacy and Health Sciences, degree requirements vary according to the individual program.

The commitment of the University to the support of each student's individual learning needs is reflected in the number of counseling and academic support services it offers. Instructional resources include the Academic Advisement Center, Achievement Studies, and Freshman Guidance, all of which are for students who require close program supervision and counseling, and the Academic Reinforcement Center, which provides free tutoring for nearly all undergraduate disciplines. Other academic support services include the Writing Center, the writing across the curriculum program, the Mathematics Center, the Academic Computing Center, and the Apple Macintosh Computer Skills Lab. Special programs include the Higher Education Opportunity Program (HEOP) and the Special Educational Services Program for Disabled and Academically High Risk Students. For specific academic majors, faculty advisers and/or professional academic counselors are provided. A 1-credit course, Freshman Orientation Seminar, familiarizes incoming students with the academic and cultural resources of the University and the community.

Academic Facilities

The Salena Library Learning Center combines the traditional materials of a library with modern educational technology. Database searching is available to students and faculty. Cooperative agreements make the resources of the Academic Libraries of Brooklyn (ALB) as well as the riches of libraries in New York City available to Long Island University students. The Brooklyn Campus of Long Island University is part of a University-wide electronically linked library/resource network of nearly 2.7 million volumes. Special library collections are in law, transportation, pharmacy, and the Weinberg Archives of Architecture and City Planning. The library includes a Media Center and a Library Cyber Lab.

The Department of Information Technology supports teaching, research, and student computer needs. Staff members are available to support the microcomputing environment and to help with connections to the wide-area network LIUNET, the CLSI library system, and Internet. On campus, there are thirty computer labs, including special labs for writing, science, and other disciplines, as well as general access labs utilizing the latest in Macintosh and IBM technology.

The state-of-the-art Health Sciences Center housing programs in pharmacy, physical therapy, respiratory care, and nursing was recently constructed on campus.

The newly built Pratt Building houses student services and the School of Education as well as the writing across the curriculum program and the Higher Education Opportunity Program.

Costs

Tuition for 2003–04 was $609 per credit hour plus University and Student Activity fees, which vary with the number of courses for which the student is enrolled each semester. The 2003–04 cost for a residence hall room ranged from $1545 to $3385 per semester, apartments ranged from $2870 to $3400 per semester, suites ranged from $2275 to $2520 per semester, and board costs ranged from $625 to $1350 per semester. Apartments, suites, and standard rooms are available on a first-come, first-served basis. The Residence Hall has a 24-hour study lounge, an IBM computer lab, and an on-site dining hall.

Financial Aid

Long Island University has a no-need-test scholarship program, which awards scholarships on the basis of academic qualifications or talent and skills. Financial aid is awarded on the basis of need and includes combinations of grants, loans, and work-study programs. Cooperative education placements are available to all students and serve as a valuable resource in meeting the cost of tuition. The entitlement programs of the Tuition Assistance Program (TAP) and Federal Pell Grant Program form the foundation of a student's financial aid package. Applicants must file a Free Application for Federal Student Aid (FAFSA), available on the Internet at http://www.fafsa.ed.gov. Students are assisted in securing part-time employment by the Office of Career Services.

Faculty

Most faculty members teach both graduate and undergraduate courses. Students have the opportunity to work with senior faculty members early in their college career. Although engaged in research projects of varying types, the faculty's primary focus is the students' academic development.

Student Government

The Student Government Association, the Campus's governing body of student life and its functions, consists of all registered students. The executive council includes president, vice president, treasurer, secretary, and 4 representatives from each academic class. Graduate, evening, and part-time students are represented on the council. The council's prime responsibility is to allocate funds to the various student organizations, thus assuring a full range of student activities.

Admission Requirements

It is recommended that incoming freshmen have a high school average of 80 or above and/or an SAT I combined score of at least 950. A limited number of students who present credentials below these minimums may be accepted in programs designed to assist them to reach their full potential. Students should present 16 units of high school work, including 4 years of English, 3 of social studies, and 2 of mathematics (including geometry). GED (high school equivalency) scores can be accepted in lieu of a high school diploma for older students or service veterans. Credit for life experience may be awarded to qualified applicants.

Long Island University does not discriminate on the basis of sex, handicap, race, national origin, religion, political belief, or sexual preference in any of its educational programs and activities, including employment practices and policies relating to recruitment and admission of students.

Application and Information

Admission applications should be completed by August 15. Late applications are considered.

Forms may be requested from:

Undergraduate Admissions Office
Long Island University, Brooklyn Campus
1 University Plaza
Brooklyn, New York 11201
Telephone: 718-488-1011
800-LIU-PLAN (toll-free)
Fax: 718-797-2399
E-mail: admissions@brooklyn.liu.edu
World Wide Web: http://www.liu.edu

An abandoned MTA substation gave way to a tower of education, Brooklyn's Pratt Center for Academic Studies.

LONG ISLAND UNIVERSITY, C.W. POST CAMPUS

BROOKVILLE, NEW YORK

The Campus

C.W. Post Campus is one of the six campuses of Long Island University (LIU), the seventh-largest private university in the U.S. Founded in 1954, the campus is situated on the North Shore of Long Island, approximately 25 miles from mid-Manhattan, on the former estate of cereal heiress Marjorie Merriweather Post. Ninety-one percent of the more than 4,700 undergraduates are from New York; the remainder come from all parts of the United States and forty-eight other countries. More than 1,600 students live in residence halls. On-campus organizations are numerous and include the traditional interest-oriented activities. Students also frequently take an active part in local or national public affairs. Two percent of the students join fraternities and sororities. Intercollegiate and intramural sports for men and women include basketball, football, horseback riding, and others. More than 1,000 cultural and entertainment activities are offered on campus throughout the year, and most are open to the general public. The Hillwood Commons campus center has an outstanding art museum and film theater. Musical and dramatic presentations are offered in the Little Theater, Great Hall, and Tilles Center for the Performing Arts. The campus features a state-of-the-art recreation center with an eight-lane swimming pool, indoor track, basketball and racquetball courts, and weight and fitness rooms.

Since 1959, Long Island University has also been offering undergraduate and graduate programs at its Brentwood Campus. Undergraduate programs at Brentwood combine courses in liberal arts and sciences with professional education in fields such as accountancy, business administration, and criminal justice. Master's degree programs include business administration (fast-track M.B.A.), criminal justice (fast-track M.S.), and education (M.S./M.S.Ed.) in the areas of school counseling, early childhood, childhood, childhood/special education, childhood/literacy, special education, literacy, and school district administrator. Graduate course are offered in conjunction with a number of different programs offered by the C.W. Post Campus, including library and information science, mental health counseling, school business administration, health-care administration, and public administration.

Location

C.W. Post's attractive 307.9-acre campus is nestled in the quiet, safe suburban community of Brookville. Bus transportation is available to the Long Island Rail Road's stations in Greenvale and Hicksville and to nearby communities. Two major shopping centers in the immediate area include good restaurants, movie theaters, and department stores. The cultural opportunities in New York City, only 40 minutes away, are also easily accessible to students.

Majors and Degrees

The major areas of study are accountancy, acting, anthropology, applied mathematics (with computer science), art, art education, art history and theory, arts management, art therapy, biology, biology education, biomedical technology, business administration, ceramics, chemistry, chemistry education, clinical laboratory sciences (medical biology), comparative languages, computer science, criminal justice, dance studies, digital art and design, earth science education, earth system science, economics, education, electronic media (broadcasting), English, English education, environmental science, film, finance, foreign languages, forensic science, French, French education, geography, geology, German, graphic design, health and physical education, health-care administration, health education, health information management, history, information management and technology, information systems, interdisciplinary studies, international business, international studies, Italian, Italian education, journalism (print and electronic), management, management information systems, marketing, mathematics, mathematics education, mathematics/physics, medical biology, molecular biology, music, music education, nursing (for RNs only), nutrition, painting, philosophy, photography, physical education, physics, political science, pre-engineering math, pre-engineering physics, prelaw, premedicine, prepharmacy, pre–respiratory therapy, psychology, public administration, public relations, radiologic technology, sculpture, social studies education, social work, sociology, Spanish, Spanish education, special education, speech-language pathology and audiology, and theater arts.

There are also accelerated five-year dual-degree programs: B.S./M.S. in accounting, B.S./M.S. in biology, B.A./M.S. in criminal justice, B.A./M.B.A. in international studies/business administration, B.S./M.S. in nutrition, B.A./M.A. in political science, B.S./M.P.A. in health-care administration, B.S./M.P.A. in public administration, B.A./M.P.A. in political science/public administration, B.S./M.S. in nursing/family nurse practitioner studies, and B.S./M.S. in nursing/advanced practice nursing. C.W. Post also offers thirty-six dual bachelor's/master's degree programs in education, which cover infancy, preschool, and elementary, middle, and high school.

Academic Programs

To be eligible for a bachelor's degree, a student must complete at least 129 credits, 44 of which must be taken in general core courses. The B.F.A. degree programs require between 134 and 136 credits. All students in good academic standing, including freshmen, may take two elective courses per academic year (including summer school sessions) on a pass/fail basis for regular credit. A total of 24 credits may be taken on this basis.

The Long Island University Plan (LIU Plan) offers students a complete counseling network that ties together all academic, career, and financial counseling for students, beginning before enrollment and extending throughout the undergraduate years. Freshmen meet with faculty mentors and peer counselors in a 1-credit freshman seminar, College 101. The plan also provides opportunities to earn income while gaining hands-on career experience. Through C.W. Post's award-winning, nationally recognized program in cooperative education, students build a resume, explore potential careers, establish contacts through networking, and earn money to defray the cost of a college education. C.W. Post places more than 250 students in paid cooperative education positions each year.

C.W. Post is liberal arts based, and all undergraduates, regardless of major, are exposed to different ways of thinking through courses in a broad range of subject areas, such as math, English, fine arts, history, and sociology. The campus's Writing-Across-the-Curriculum program offers courses in all majors to help students improve their writing skills.

An outstanding honors and merit scholarship program provides talented students with an academic environment designed to help them achieve their greatest potential. Approximately 9 percent of undergraduates who have demonstrated outstanding intellectual potential and academic achievement are selected to participate in this nationally respected program. Classes are usually limited to 20 students and run as discussion-style seminars in which the approach to the material is more sophisticated than in regular classes. Students also work independently with professors on tutorial and thesis projects and enhance their study with field trips to New York City, participation in national conferences, and lectures with noted guest speakers.

Off-Campus Programs

C.W. Post has affiliations with such institutions as Regents College in London and Franklin College in Switzerland. Post students can also participate in Long Island University's Friends World Program. This program operates throughout the world in places such as Costa Rica, India, Japan, and China and allows students to study in as many as four different countries throughout their college careers. For the 2004–05 academic year, Friends World is running a comparative Religion and Cultures program in Taiwan, India, Tunisia, Greece, and Italy. This respected program attracts individuals from every corner of the globe and brings them together for an academically and culturally rewarding experience.

Academic Facilities

The B. Davis Schwartz Memorial Library is one of the largest research libraries in New York and houses nearly 2.7 million volumes as part of the Long Island University System. The multilevel library is a digital powerhouse, with high-speed Web connections, online subscriptions, and more than 100 database services. The library features the nationally respected Center for Business and Information Research, Media Center, Rare Books Collection, and Government Information Department. All students have free e-mail and Internet access. More than 500 computers are available in several buildings and residence halls. Networked "smart classrooms" are located throughout the campus. Science, art, and education laboratories are fully equipped. Other facilities include an interfaith center, two modern student centers, and a world-famous concert hall that seats 2,200.

Costs

For 2003–04, tuition was $19,510, room and board averaged $3750 per semester, and student activity/University fees were $490 per semester.

Financial Aid

C.W. Post participates in all major federal and New York State financial aid programs. Aid includes Federal Pell Grants, Federal Supplemental Educational Opportunity Grants, Federal Perkins Loans, Federal Direct Loans, Federal Work-Study Program awards, and institutional grants and scholarships. C.W. Post awards $15 million in scholarships each year. Students should consult the admissions office for criteria and deadlines.

The LIU Plan combines scholarships and cooperative education to provide a high-quality education at an affordable cost. All C.W. Post students are strongly encouraged to participate in paid professional internships (also known as cooperative education). Students gain work experience related to their major, begin to build a resume, and help reduce their costs by supplementing financial aid with co-op earnings.

The C.W. Post Campus requires all applicants for financial aid to submit the Free Application for Federal Student Aid (FAFSA), College Scholarship Service PROFILE, and New York State TAP Application (New York State applicants only), in addition to the application for admission. All applicants seeking financial assistance are strongly urged to apply early in order to be assured of full exposure to the funding possibilities. The recommended submission date for application is March 15 in order to meet the University's deadline of May 15 each year. Financial aid is granted only after a student has been offered admission. All aid is granted for one year but is renewable, based on published criteria and federal and state eligibility guidelines.

Faculty

C.W. Post has more than 300 full-time faculty members. Approximately eighty-six percent of the full-time faculty members have the highest degree in their fields.

Student Government

The Student Government Association is the representative body of all students and is composed of three branches: the executive, the legislative, and the judicial. The Student Government Association works closely with the administration on many student-life issues such as recognition and funding of student clubs and organizations, special events, faculty evaluations, and campus issues that affect the academic life of the C.W. Post student.

Admission Requirements

Undergraduates apply from all parts of the United States and from more than forty-five other countries. Last year, 7,000 applicants from both public and private schools competed for 850 places in the freshman class and 700 in the transfer class. Each year, the Admissions Committee seeks a diverse group of students who are academically prepared for the college experience. The committee considers not only academic achievement but also a student's talent and potential to contribute to the C.W. Post community. Applicants should complete an admissions application and present a high school or previous college transcript, SAT or ACT scores, and a personal statement. The credentials of all applicants are considered carefully by the Admissions Committee, and attention is given to each candidate's individual strengths. On-campus interviews with admissions counselors are highly recommended.

Application and Information

Classes are offered year-round. Students may begin studies in the fall, winter, spring, or summer semesters. Campus tours are available Monday through Saturday and by appointment. Summer and holiday schedules vary. Admission decisions are made on a rolling basis, but those wishing to be considered for scholarships should consult with the admissions office for application deadlines. The Office of Admissions is open Monday through Thursday, 9 a.m. to 8 p.m.; Friday, 9 a.m. to 5 p.m.; and Saturday, 10 a.m. to 2 p.m. For additional information and to schedule interviews and campus visits, students are encouraged to contact:

Office of Admissions
Long Island University, C.W. Post Campus
720 Northern Boulevard
Brookville, New York 11548-1300
Telephone: 516-299-2900
800-LIU-PLAN (toll-free)
Fax: 516-299-2137
E-mail: enroll@cwpost.liu.edu
World Wide Web: http://www.liu.edu/

A view of the C.W. Post Campus.

LONG ISLAND UNIVERSITY, FRIENDS WORLD PROGRAM

SOUTHAMPTON, NEW YORK

The Program

With six program centers around the world and a student body and faculty drawn from more than twice that many countries, Friends World Program is uniquely international. Although actual enrollment varies from semester to semester due to visiting students, it hovers around 200. The Program is designed for students capable of assuming greater responsibility for their own lives and learning. The Program's worldwide facilities offer students the opportunity to live, study, and participate in three or more cultures while earning a B.A. degree; to design individual programs of study based on personal interests and goals; and to combine classroom study with field experience and internships. While acquiring a balanced liberal arts education, including the development of practical fluency in one or more foreign languages and an appreciation of the cultures of several world regions, students have the opportunity to carry out in-depth study and gain practical experience in their chosen field. In addition, they develop a deeper understanding of and a broader perspective on current world issues.

The Program began as Friends World College in 1965, under the sponsorship of the New York Yearly Meeting of Friends, and became part of Long Island University in 1991. While its beginnings were Quaker and North American, the Program is nonsectarian and its outlook decidedly global. The Program encourages students to consider the entire world their university, to take the most urgent human problems as one basis of their curriculum, to seek designs together for a more humane future, and to consider their responsibilities as citizens of the world.

Location

Since 1965, Friends World students have studied in more than seventy-five countries, making a reality of the phrase "The World is Your Campus." With its affiliation with Long Island University in 1991, the Program relocated its central offices to Southampton College in Southampton, Long Island, 90 miles east of New York City. The campus serves as the home of the Program's headquarters and the home base for students taking classes in the U.S. Graduating classes of 2006 and subsequent years will convene in Southampton for senior course work, including the all-important capstone experience. Southampton College occupies an old estate on the outskirts of Southampton Village, originally a colonial settlement. A full campus, Southampton College offers residence halls, sports facilities, a student center with evening and weekend programming, a library, and up-to-date computer labs. With New York City a day trip away, the campus provides an ideal balance between the distance needed to focus and reflect on one's learning and the accessibility to big-city resources. London, England, on the other hand, is the home base for the Program's first-year students. The European Center, as it is known, comprises a suite of offices and classrooms in a London neighborhood with easy access by "tube" (subway) to local sites. The European Center also supervises Friends World students on independent study projects throughout the British Isles and Europe. The Latin American Center is in Heredia, Costa Rica, just outside San José, that nation's capital. Down the street from a major national university, the neighborhood caters to students' needs. The ancient city of Kyoto, considered the "heart of Japan," is the location of the East Asian Center. Students enrolled in the South Asian Center are based in Bangalore, capital of the Indian state of Karnataka. The China Center is similarly located on a university campus, that of Zhejiang University in Hangzhou. Friends World's newest program, American Environmental Studies: Life in Balance, is based at the Southampton campus of Long Island University, which is nationally recognized for its strong environmental and marine science programs, for the first year. Students then move to the American Southwest, Costa Rica or India, and back to Southampton in years two, three, and four. Students have the opportunity to enroll for one or two semesters in any of the above centers. In addition, they may study in three distinct world regions in a single year by opting for the two-semester program in Comparative Religion and Culture. These students study values, beliefs, and religious practices and their effect on cultures of East, South, and West Asia. Countries typically visited include Taiwan, India, and Turkey. In addition, the Peace and Reconciliation program affords other students the opportunity to explore that theme in depth and within a global context. Thus, while students in Friends World Program are enrolled in an American university, they carry out their learning all over the world.

Majors and Degrees

Friends World graduates earn a Bachelor of Arts degree from Long Island University, accredited by the Commission on Higher Education of the Middle States Association of Colleges and Schools, 3624 Market Street, Philadelphia, Pennsylvania. All students matriculate as interdisciplinary studies majors and declare an area of concentration by their junior year. Areas of concentration have included such topics as activism and art, anthropology, business practices, communications (including journalism, photography, and video), community health, comparative health practices, comparative literature, criminal justice systems, cross-cultural studies, environmental studies, ethnomusicology, gay studies, human rights, indigenous peoples, international development, peace studies, schooling and socialization, sustainable development, and women's studies. Areas of concentration range from the traditional to the unique; courses of study are reviewed by faculty advisers to ensure students incorporate both interdisciplinary and international perspectives in their course work.

Academic Programs

The learning process is a carefully planned combination of classroom study, structured out-of-class experiences, and independent fieldwork in at least three regions of the world (including the student's own). Under the guidance of the faculty members, students develop skills and competence in their areas of concentration by combining reading and library research, direct experience, and analytical writing. For example, students have studied and compared Gandhian nonviolence in India and Buddhist responses to oppression among Tibetan refugees. Others have compared feminist movements in Africa, Europe, and the United States. Game parks and natural resource management in Africa and India have been studied from the perspectives of local residents, nongovernmental organizations, and national economic and political aims.

Freshmen spend the year in London engaged in a combination of required and elective courses designed to allow guided pursuit of individual interests while, at the same time, ensuring a high degree of intellectual rigor and providing a sound foundation for experiences to come. Throughout the year, freshmen work closely with a faculty adviser to define their educational interests and goals and to identify ways of extending and deepening their understanding of various issues. Cosmopolitan London offers exceptional resources to students as they begin planning their sophomore and junior years in their "world university." Seniors, as mentioned earlier, return to Long Island and reconnect with their freshman cohorts for guided reflection on their full experience as Friends World students and for the final preparation and presentation of senior projects. Drawing on their prior work and able to complement each other's experiences with their own, students graduate with the skills and knowledge to become truly effective global citizens.

As a record of their learning and growth, students maintain journals and submit assignments as required. In lieu of final exams, students prepare portfolios of their learning each semester. The portfolio contains the learning plan, thought pieces, and research papers; it serves as the basis for evaluation and the awarding of credits by the faculty adviser.

The B.A. degree is conferred upon successful completion of 120 credits appropriately distributed, the preparation of a senior project report or thesis, and an external evaluation by a specialist in the student's area of interest. Up to 60 semester credits may be accepted toward the degree from the following sources: transfer credits from other accredited institutions of higher education, College-Level Examination Program (CLEP) tests, military service, and College Board Advanced Placement examinations. Credit may also be awarded for learning acquired through life experience. Such learning must be documented and evaluated by the Friends World faculty.

Academic Facilities

Each regional center maintains a small library of books and materials relating to the regional culture, as well as a resource file of individual and institutional contacts and advisers that students use in developing and carrying out field studies. Centers also frequently make cooperative arrangements with local facilities in the region, such as libraries, language institutes, and specialized agencies and offices.

Costs

For 2003–04, tuition was $20,400 per year. Room and board costs vary from center to center. Program fees, which include the cost of special activities and excursions, also vary. Total costs, including the aforementioned as well as books, supplies, and personal expenses (but excluding international travel), averaged approximately $28,000 in 2003–04, with the multi-sited comparative religion program the most costly and the China Center the least.

Financial Aid

Aid is awarded on the basis of need, determined by the College Scholarship Service, using the Free Application for Federal Student Aid (FAFSA). Long Island University participates in most federal and New York State programs of aid for resident students, including the Federal Pell Grant, Direct Student Loan, and Perkins Loan programs. Students who are not permanent residents of the U.S. are ineligible for these aid programs. International students may be given partial tuition grants but need to provide the balance and all living and travel costs from their own resources.

Merit scholarships are awarded to students with exemplary academic credentials and a demonstrated commitment to community service and/or international and cross-cultural understanding.

Faculty

Friends World Program has a strong cadre of experienced faculty members at each of its centers around the world. The average student-faculty ratio is kept at 8:1, and depending on actual enrollment in any given semester, each center's academic director is able to call upon the services and expertise of experienced adjunct faculty advisers. In addition to permanent and adjunct faculty members (who frequently work with other institutions and professional groups in the region), dozens of field advisers provide supervision and support for individual students during field studies.

Student Government

Students and faculty members participate together in the governance of each regional learning community. The Program's biennial "World Conference" includes faculty and student representatives from each regional center. This weeklong gathering reviews operations and offers recommendations on educational and governance matters.

Admission Requirements

The Program seeks self-reliant, mature, intelligent, and world-minded men and women of all nationalities, races, and socioeconomic groups. Completion of a college-preparatory high school program is generally required, although applicants presenting a passing score on the GED test are also encouraged to apply. Transfer students, especially those at the sophomore level, are most welcome. Visiting students from other colleges who desire a semester or year of study abroad are invited to join Friends World students at regional centers and in the Comparative Religion and Culture program. Visiting students should work carefully with both the Program's admissions staff and their own advisers, however, to ensure a full, mutual understanding of the Program and any special requirements.

Application and Information

Friends World Program operates on a rolling admission basis with no application deadline. Further information can be obtained by contacting:

Admissions
Friends World Program
Long Island University–Southampton College
239 Montauk Highway
Southampton, New York 11968
Telephone: 631-287-8474
Fax: 631-287-8463
E-mail: fw@liu.edu
World Wide Web: http://www.liu.edu

Friends World Program offers students the opportunity to live, study, and participate in three or more cultures.

LONG ISLAND UNIVERSITY, SOUTHAMPTON COLLEGE

SOUTHAMPTON, NEW YORK

The College

Southampton College, with a current undergraduate enrollment of nearly 1,200, is one of three residential campuses of Long Island University, the seventh-largest independent university in the country. Its blend of strong academic programs, personal attention, and spectacular location has attracted students from the Northeast, across the United States, and around the globe. The campus is nestled in the Shinnecock Hills of beautiful eastern Long Island and is surrounded by pristine bays and the Atlantic Ocean. The campus's forty-three buildings house spacious classrooms, state-of-the-art laboratories, comfortable residence halls, and social and administrative facilities. Residence halls consist of suites with four (in most cases double) bedrooms, a living area, and a bath. Students have the option of choosing co-ed or single-sex dorms. Smoke-free and honors dorms are also available.

The College's gymnasium, with a capacity of 1,400, is the site of many concerts and athletic events.

A wide range of intercollegiate NCAA Division II sports are available, including basketball, lacrosse, soccer, tennis, and volleyball for men and basketball, cross-country, soccer, softball, tennis, and volleyball for women. Intramural and club sports are also available.

Students may have cars and motorcycles on campus. Student resident assistants are available at all times for assistance. Medical, counseling, and placement services are also available. In addition, Southampton's Student Activities Office provides students with the opportunity to organize on-campus events, ranging from informal poetry readings to large concerts.

A variety of noncredit continuing education courses and lectures are offered. At the graduate level, Southampton offers Master of Science degrees in accounting and in education (elementary, reading, and special education), a Master of Fine Arts in English and writing, and a five-year B.S./M.S. dual degree in accounting.

Location

Southampton's location offers the best of both worlds, the spectacular beaches, fine dining, and shopping of a world-renowned summer resort combined with the excitement, culture, and employment opportunities of New York City only 90 miles away (1¾ hours by car, 2 hours by Long Island Railroad). The surrounding Hamptons are a haven for famous artists and writers, many of whom teach at the College. During the fall, winter, and spring, Southampton's shops, restaurants, museums, and art galleries remain open, providing a sophisticated and stimulating yet peaceful environment for living and learning. As the oldest English settlement in New York State (1640), the town of Southampton also offers a rich historical setting to enjoy and explore.

Majors and Degrees

Southampton offers the Bachelor of Arts degree in fine arts, elementary education (N–6), English and writing, environmental studies, history/political science, liberal studies, psychology, secondary education (biology, 7–12; English, 7–12; social studies, 7–12), and sociology. The Bachelor of Science degree is offered in accounting, art education (K–12), environmental science and marine science (with concentrations in biology, marine vertebrate biology, and oceanography), and psychology/biology. Both the Bachelor of Arts and the Bachelor of Science degrees are offered in biology and business. The Bachelor of Fine Arts degree is offered in art and communication arts.

Students may minor in all major areas as well as in languages, music, and theater. Those who major or minor in secondary education are eligible to apply for certification from New York State upon graduation.

Academic Programs

Southampton's academic year is based on a two-term fall/spring calendar, with a winter intersession and two summer sessions offered from May through August.

The College's newly developed interdisciplinary core curriculum—the only one of its kind in the nation—emphasizes critical thinking, creativity, and global citizenship as the cornerstones of a well-rounded education. Requirements for graduation include 128 semester hour credits with a grade point average of at least 2.0 (on a 4.0 scale).

The Long Island University Plan (LIU Plan) offers Southampton students a program of classroom study combined with professional work experience to help them gain the hands-on experience that is so critical to prospective employers while defraying the cost of their college education. Academic, career, and personal counseling, as well as development of essential literacies in writing, technology, science, and culture, are also stressed. Cooperative education, a combination of classroom learning and major-related employment experience, is also available for all areas of study. Co-op students may choose from more than 3,000 paid professional positions.

Students who perform at a superior level are invited to be part of Southampton's Honors Program. The College's Freshman Program, designed to ease the transition from high school to the college environment and to enhance a student's opportunities for success, includes an extended 1-credit orientation course, intense advising, upperclass peer counseling, and freshman dormitory clusters.

Off-Campus Programs

Southampton offers a wide range of off-campus learning experiences, including the Friends World Program, which provides opportunities to study in China, Costa Rica, England, India, Israel, Japan, and across the United States; SEAmester, a nine-week sailing adventure aboard a schooner with ports of call from Maine to the Bahamas; Tropical Marine Biology, an exploration of Australia's Great Barrier Reef and other exotic South Sea environments through snorkeling, scuba diving, and lectures; Spring in Australia, the study of Australia's environment through field trips, site visits, research, and extended travel; Australearn, the study of the ecosystems of the tropical coastal regions of Australia; and exchange programs with Southampton University and Winchester College in England as well as Queensland University in Australia.

Internships that are specifically tailored for marine and environmental science students include work at Brookhaven National Laboratory, Skiowa Institute for Oceanography, Osborne Laboratories, National Oceanic and Atmospheric Administration, and Woods Hole Laboratories. Internships are also available for business, education, social science, English and writing, and science majors.

Academic Facilities

Southampton's library houses more than 145,000 volumes, 10,000 pamphlets, 168,000 microforms, and nearly 900 recordings and subscribes to 660 periodicals. Long Island University's nearly 2.7-million volume collection is also available to Southampton students through an automated information retrieval system.

The College offers state-of-the-art computer facilities, including the Academic Center Computer Lab, a twenty-five-station Pentium II lab; the Queen Anne Computer Center, with twenty-two Pentium PCs, four Macintosh Computers, and a Macintosh color scanner in addition to twenty Pentium 200MMX multimedia computers, a color flatbed scanner, and a PostScript Laser Jet printer; the Ada Lovelace Computer Off-center with a twenty-station Pentium, 200MMX multimedia classroom, LaserJet PostScript printer, a 37-inch-screen faculty presentation system, and a flatbed color scanner; the Business Center Computer Lab, which features ten Pentium multimedia computers; the Fine Arts Computer Lab, including fourteen Power Macintoshes, five Pentium PCs, a networked Epson Stylus Color 3000 printer, two flatbed scanners, and a slide scanner; the H.E.O.P. Computer Lab with eight Pentium PCs and a networked LaserJet printer; the Library Computer Lab, which contains four multimedia 586 class computers, four Pentium-class PCs, and a networked laser printer; and the Technology Center's Island Room, which has twenty Silicon Graphics workstations, a dedicated Silicon Graphics Origin200 server, and a large assortment of scanners, VCRs, and printers.

Southampton students can connect from their dorm rooms to the College's campuswide computer network, which offers Internet access at more than twenty times the speed of a modem connection. Students provide their own computers, and a one-time fee is charged for a network card and installation. No additional fees are charged for online time or usage.

Teaching facilities include Chancellors Hall, the academic center; an on-campus Marine Science Center; a fleet of twelve marine research vessels, including the 44-foot RV *Paumanouk*; psychology/biology laboratories; photography, sculpture, welding, painting, and ceramics studios; a metal-casting facility; music practice studios; computer laboratories; chemistry, biology, geology, and statistical laboratories; a learning laboratory; and WLIU, a 25,000-watt National Public Radio affiliate. The 440-seat Avram Theatre and the Avram Art Gallery are the sites of lectures, dramatic productions, concerts, and art exhibits.

Costs

The tuition for 2003–04 was $19,510. The standard room and board fee, based on a double-occupancy room and nineteen meals per week, was $8500 per year; other options are available. The cost of books is about $500 per year. Laboratory fees, travel expenses, and incidental costs vary.

Financial Aid

Scholarships based on academic merit range from $2500 to full tuition, renewable annually. Talent scholarships of $1000 to $6000 are offered in art and writing. Athletic scholarships are also available and are based on talent, determined by Southampton coaches. Community service–based awards are also available; awards range from $500 to $2000.

Other financial aid awards administered by the College are based on financial need and academic promise. These include special scholarships and state and federal assistance, including Federal Supplemental Educational Opportunity Grants, Federal Work-Study awards, and Federal Perkins Loans.

Candidates for admission requesting financial aid should submit their application, along with the College's aid form, well in advance of the March 1 deadline. All students applying for financial aid must also submit the Free Application for Federal Student Aid (FAFSA), which can be obtained from any high school guidance office or college financial aid office. Southampton's FAFSA code is 002755.

Faculty

Southampton has an accomplished teaching faculty with a strong sense of obligation to and interest in their students. Approximately ninety-six percent of the faculty members hold appropriate terminal degrees. Faculty members also serve as advisers to students. Most classes are small. Individualized attention from the faculty helps students realize their maximum academic potential. The undergraduate student–full-time faculty ratio of 18:1 allows for student-oriented courses and policies.

Student Government

Southampton has a representative student government that deals with all aspects of student life. Student committees meet with faculty committees to help formulate academic and fiscal policies. Students are also represented in a University-wide student government organization.

Admission Requirements

Admission to Southampton is based upon the College's evaluation of the applicant's potential for a successful experience. The Admissions Office feels it is essential not only that the applicant meet the College's standards but also that the College meet the applicant's expectations. Therefore, an interview is recommended. The applicant's performance in secondary school (and college, if applicable) and a counselor's remarks are perhaps the most important considerations for admission. SAT I or ACT scores are required for all students, and TOEFL scores are required for students whose native language is not English. In addition, an essay and letter of recommendation are required.

Southampton offers early admission to qualified high school juniors. Through prior arrangement with his or her high school, a student can receive a secondary school diploma upon completion of the freshman year of College.

New undergraduate applicants must have graduated from high school or have qualified for an equivalency diploma. Transfer students with an A.A. or A.A.S. degree receive credit for all courses (including grades of D) taken as part of the associate degree program. Transfer students without an associate degree receive transfer credit for all liberal arts courses completed with a grade of C (2.0) or higher. Up to 68 credit hours may be transferred from any accredited two-year institution. Up to 98 credit hours may be transferred from an accredited four-year institution. Transfer students must submit a transcript from every college attended as well as proof of high school graduation.

A total of 64 hours of credit by examination can be accepted under the following programs: CLEP (administered by the College Board) with a grade of C or above; CPEP (administered by the New York State Department of Education) with a grade of C or above; and the GED college-level examination (administered by DANTES, formerly the United States Armed Forces Institute) with a score in the 50th percentile or above. Credits earned by examination may lead to a waiver of course requirements or be accepted as elective credits. It is also possible to receive credit for life experience.

Application and Information

Applications for fall entry should be completed prior to August 15; for spring entry, by January 15. Completed applications for admission and financial aid, transcripts, SAT I or ACT scores, TOEFL scores for students whose native language is not English, school recommendations, and all inquiries should be sent to:

Admissions
Long Island University
Southampton College
239 Montauk Highway
Southampton, New York 11968
Telephone: 631-287-8010
800-LIU-PLAN (toll-free)
Fax: 631-287-8130
E-mail: admissions@southampton.liu.edu
World Wide Web: http://www.liu.edu

LORAS COLLEGE
DUBUQUE, IOWA

The College

Loras College, founded in 1839, is a four-year, coeducational, Catholic liberal arts college. Loras' liberal arts curriculum promotes learning of the broadest kind. The Catholic-Christian tradition of Loras nourishes heart and soul, while its small, comfortable size gives students room to discover themselves. The College's 1,764 students come from twenty-seven states and thirteen countries. All Loras students receive laptop computers for academic and personal use. Loras was named to *U.S. News & World Report's* top tier of Midwestern Comprehensive Colleges–Bachelor's. Of those students who received B.A. degrees from Loras over the last three years, 95 percent were either employed full-time or attending graduate school within one year of graduation.

In addition to its academic strength, Loras offers a variety of activities for students to engage in outside the classroom. More than fifty-five organizations encourage involvement and provide a sense of belonging for college students. Student services include the Intercultural Programs Office, the Wellness and Counseling Center, the Center for Experiential Learning (which includes study abroad and internship and career services), and campus ministry. The College Activities Board (CAB), a student-run organization, also plans weekly activities such as dances, contests, comedians, concerts, and guest speakers. Loras athletes compete in eleven men's and ten women's intercollegiate sports affiliated with the NCAA Division III. One of the nation's leading intramural sports programs is organized from the College's Graber Sports Center and offers more than ninety activities for students to participate in throughout the year.

Location

Loras College's 60-acre campus stands atop one of the Mississippi River's highest bluffs in historic Dubuque, Iowa, at the junction of Iowa, Illinois, and Wisconsin. The campus is situated in a residential area and is about a 3-hour drive from Chicago, Milwaukee, and Des Moines. The picturesque city of Dubuque (population 65,000), is a safe community in which to live. Home to a variety of restaurants, museums, theaters, antique and specialty shops, downhill skiing, parks, and trails, Dubuque offers natural beauty, historical significance, and year-round fun and excitement.

Majors and Degrees

Loras College offers four-year undergraduate programs based in a liberal arts tradition and leading to the Bachelor of Arts, Bachelor of Science, and Bachelor of Music degrees. Majors offered include accounting, athletic training, biochemistry, biological research, biology, business (finance, management, management information systems, and marketing), chemistry, communication arts (media studies and public relations), computer science, criminal justice, economics, education (early childhood, elementary, secondary, and special), electromechanical engineering, English (literature and writing), general science, history, integrated visual arts, international studies, liberal arts, mathematics, modern foreign languages (French and Spanish), music (applied and education), philosophy, physical education, physics–secondary teaching, political science, psychology, religious studies, social work, sociology, sports management, and sports science. In addition, individualized majors may be arranged.

Loras offers the following preprofessional programs: medical technology, nuclear medicine, chiropractic, dentistry, engineering, law, medicine, mortuary science, occupational therapy, optometry, pharmacy, physical therapy, physician's assistant studies, podiatry, and veterinary medicine.

Academic Programs

Requirements for the Bachelor of Arts and Bachelor of Science degrees include completion of core courses that demonstrate effective communication in critical thinking, oral expression, and written expression. Completing a minimum of 120 credit hours and maintaining a grade point average of at least 2.0 (C) are required for a bachelor's degree. Successful completion of a thesis and/or a comprehensive examination is required, according to the department or division in which a student takes an area of concentration.

Advanced standing, accelerated degree programs, honors programs, and graduate courses that are open to undergraduates for credit are all available. Most students take 15 credits of course work during each of the two semesters in the academic year, which usually begins in late August and ends in early May.

Off-Campus Programs

In addition to opportunities for internships in 80 percent of all academic majors, Loras provides a wide range of opportunities through its Center for Experiential Learning. The center sponsors programs for credit that combine classroom work, internships, and service learning nationally and internationally. Students may study abroad in Quetzaltenango, Guatemala; Dublin, Ireland; Amagasaki, Japan; Pretoria, South Africa; and Santiago de Compostela, Spain. Additional study-abroad programs are available through affiliate institutions.

Academic Facilities

The Academic Resource Center opened in fall 2002 and became the new home of the Loras College library. The library currently has one of the largest private collections in Iowa, with holdings of 431,903 items, subscriptions to 962 paper periodicals and 7,977 full-text electronic periodicals, a depository for state and federal documents, and a collection of maps numbering about 5,000. The library houses an outstanding rare-book collection that includes, among other items, a manuscript collection dating back to the twelfth century and sixty-one incunables printed through the year 1500, giving Loras College the largest such collection in the state.

In addition, the Academic Resource Center houses the Center for Dubuque History, the Loras College Barnes & Noble Bookstore, and several group-study areas and technology classrooms. The building is equipped for wireless network and Internet connectivity. Offering beautiful views of the city, this multimillion-dollar structure serves as the intellectual heart of the College.

Costs

Costs for 2003–04 were $17,370 for tuition and $5795 for room and board.

Financial Aid

Loras is committed to helping its students. Ninety-three percent of Loras students receive financial aid from a variety of sources, including scholarships, grants, loans, and employment. Both need-based and merit-based programs are available. Students seeking financial assistance should apply for assistance as soon after January 1 as possible and no later than April 15. Most types of financial assistance require completion of a need analysis form—the Free Application for Federal Student Aid (FAFSA). State of Iowa Scholarships, Federal Stafford Student Loans, Federal Perkins Loans, Iowa PLUS loans, Federal Pell Grants, Federal Supplemental Educational Opportunity Grants, Iowa Tuition Grants, and Iowa Supplemental Grants may also help make up a student's financial assistance package. Campus employment is available to those demonstrating financial need.

Faculty

The outstanding Loras teaching faculty of 122 full-time and 50 part-time members is primarily composed of laypeople. More than 70 percent of the full-time faculty members hold the highest degree in their field. The student-faculty ratio of 12:1 ensures students individual attention from instructors in an open, friendly, and responsive atmosphere.

Student Government

Students may serve on College-wide committees with faculty members and administrators. Leadership of the student body is vested in the Student Government and various class officers.

Admission Requirements

Each year, more than 1,300 applicants seek admission to Loras College. The first-year class has an average composite ACT score of 23. It is preferable that the high school program include 4 years of English, 3 three years in mathematics, and 2 two years each in natural science, social science, and additional academic courses.

Application and Information

Applications are processed on a rolling basis, and prospective students may apply to Loras anytime after their junior year of high school. Loras makes every effort to process applications within three weeks. Transfer students' credits are evaluated on an individual basis.

The College's innovative registration program allows first-year and transfer students to register on a one-to-one basis with their faculty adviser.

For more information about Loras College, students should contact:

Tim Hauber
Director of Admissions
Loras College
1450 Alta Vista
Dubuque, Iowa 52001
Telephone: 800-245-6727 (toll-free)
E-mail: admissions@loras.edu
World Wide Web: http://www.loras.edu

The benefits of being in a smaller college community include accessible classes, approachable professors, and the opportunity to make friends easily and get involved in a variety of activities.

LOUISIANA STATE UNIVERSITY AND AGRICULTURAL AND MECHANICAL COLLEGE

BATON ROUGE, LOUISIANA

The University

Louisiana State University (LSU), the state's oldest and largest institution of higher learning, was founded in 1860 and moved to Baton Rouge in 1869. The campus occupies 2,000 acres on the southern edge of the city, just east of the Mississippi River. More than 250 buildings make up the central part of the campus.

From its initial emphasis on agriculture and engineering, the University has evolved into a major research institution, the state's only Carnegie Research I University. LSU's Center for Advanced Microstructures and Devices, an Aquaculture Research Facility, a Students Recreational Sports Complex, the Life Science Building Annex, East Tiger Stadium Expansion, and a Computer Center are just a few examples of the rapid expansion the University is experiencing. LSU also holds the distinction of being one of a select number of universities in the country with both land-grant and sea-grant status.

The campus community offers a wide variety of social, cultural, and recreational opportunities and is enriched by the presence of a number of nationally recognized writers, musicians, and artists who serve on the humanities faculty. The University has a predominantly Louisianian student community, but many of LSU's more than 31,000 students come from all fifty states and 120 other countries. There are numerous extracurricular activities that range from billiards to sailing. LSU fields NCAA Division I men's and women's teams in basketball, golf, swimming, tennis, and track and field; women's teams in gymnastics, soccer, softball, and volleyball; and men's teams in baseball and football. Club sports include karate, rugby, soccer, tae kwon do, volleyball, and waterskiing. LSU supports one of the largest coeducational intramural sports programs in the country. The LSU Union's facilities provide areas for eating and studying, meeting rooms, two theaters, an art gallery, a bookstore, and a U.S. post office. More than 250 student organizations serve as focal points for specific interests and social activities. There are social fraternities and sororities on campus as well as churches, religious centers, and nondenominational units. LSU residence halls and apartments offer a variety of accommodations.

At the graduate level, LSU offers programs that lead to the degrees of Doctor of Musical Arts, Doctor of Philosophy, Master of Agriculture, Master of Applied Statistics, Master of Architecture, Master of Arts, Master of Arts in Liberal Arts, Master of Business Administration, Master of Education, Master of Fine Arts, Master of Landscape Architecture, Master of Library and Information Science, Master of Mass Communication, Master of Music, Master of Natural Sciences, Master of Public Administration, Master of Science, Master of Science in Biological and Agricultural Engineering, Master of Science in Chemical Engineering, Master of Science in Civil Engineering, Master of Science in Electrical Engineering, Master of Science in Engineering Science, Master of Science in Industrial Engineering, Master of Science in Mechanical Engineering, Master of Science in Petroleum Engineering, Master of Science in Systems Science, and Master of Social Work. In addition, the degrees of Juris Doctor, Master of Public Administration/Juris Doctor, Master of Laws, and Master of Civil Law are offered through the Paul M. Hebert Law Center, and the degree of Doctor of Veterinary Medicine is offered through the School of Veterinary Medicine; both schools are located on the campus. The University also awards the Certificate of Advanced Study in Library and Information Science and the Certificate of Education Specialist.

Location

LSU is located in Baton Rouge, Louisiana, the state's capital and second-largest city. Baton Rouge has a rapidly growing metropolitan area population of 500,000. The mild Baton Rouge climate makes it possible for students to enjoy outdoor sports and activities all year long. The city of New Orleans is within an hour's drive.

Majors and Degrees

Bachelor's degrees are awarded for the following general curricula (students should consult the LSU *General Catalog* for a complete list of curricula concentrations): accounting; agricultural business; animal, dairy, and poultry sciences; anthropology; architecture; biochemistry; biological engineering; biological sciences; chemical engineering; chemistry; civil engineering; communication disorders; communication studies; computer engineering; computer science; construction management; early childhood education: PK–3 teacher certificate; economics; electrical engineering; elementary grades education; English; environmental engineering; environmental management systems; family, child, and consumer sciences; finance; food science and technology; forestry (forest management); French; general business administration; general studies; geography; geology; German; history; industrial engineering; information systems and decision sciences; interior design; international studies; international trade and finance; kinesiology; landscape architecture; Latin; liberal arts; management; marketing; mass communication; mathematics; mechanical engineering; microbiology; music; music education; nutritional sciences; petroleum engineering; philosophy; physics; plant and soil systems; political science; psychology; Russian area studies; secondary education; sociology; Spanish; studio art; textiles, apparel, and merchandising; theater; vocational education; wildlife and fisheries; and women's and gender studies.

Preprofessional programs that do not culminate in a degree from LSU but that enable students to be placed in professional programs are dental hygiene, dental laboratory technology, medical technology, ophthalmic medical technology, physician's assistant studies, prenursing, rehabilitation counseling, and respiratory therapy.

Academic Program

LSU operates on a traditional two-semester plan with a multiple-session summer term. All students complete a 39-hour general education curriculum in English composition, analytical reasoning, arts, humanities, natural sciences, and social sciences. Freshmen are admitted to the University College Center for the Freshman Year, which is an academic division similar to a medium-sized college in a large university setting. The Center provides individual, academic, and career counseling as well as developmental education courses. Students remain in the Center until they have earned at least 24 semester hours of college-level credit and have met requirements for admission to a senior college. Credit-hour requirements for graduation vary between 119 and 160 semester hours, depending upon the curriculum chosen. Students with strong high school preparation can obtain University credit for Advanced Placement courses. An honors curriculum is available for superior students. A noncredit eight-week intensive English Language and Orientation Program that begins in January, March, June, August, and October is offered for international students.

Off-Campus Programs

LSU participates in a cross-registration program with Southern University in Baton Rouge and Baton Rouge Community College. Several cooperative programs either exist or are currently under development. The University also participates in the Academic Common Market, an interstate agreement among thirteen Southern states for sharing special programs. Up to one fourth of the number of hours required for the bachelor's degree may be taken through the Division of Continuing Education by correspondence study, extension courses, or both. The Evening school program provides educational opportunities for students not in residence, and the Office of Academic Programs Abroad administers a number of summer and exchange programs for undergraduate students in various fields and countries.

Academic Facilities

The University libraries offer students and faculty members strong academic support through collections that contain more than 3 million bound volumes, more than 5 million microform holdings, and a manuscript collection of more than 12 million items. The library catalog is computerized and accessible from terminals around campus. Supercomputer facilities are available on campus through the Technology Support Center (TSC), which provides computer resources for instruction, research, and administrative data processing. The staff conducts seminars, maintains a broad selection of software, consults with the center's clients, assists with and promotes the use of microcomputers and data communications, and manages distributed computer centers.

Computing supported by TSC includes microcomputers, superminicomputers, supercomputers, terminals, two major I/O rooms, and data communications. A VAX 8800 processor is available to support interactive graphics.

The LSU museum complex includes the LSU Museum of Art, the Museum of Geoscience, and the Museum of Natural Science. The University has extensive studios and practice rooms for the art and performance disciplines and two theaters for performances.

Costs

University fees for 2003–04 were $3910 for Louisiana residents and $9210 for out-of-state students. There are special fees for graduation, registration of motor vehicles, and advanced standing examinations. Louisiana resident expenses are estimated at $11,600 per academic year for fees, room and board, books, and personal expenses. Nonresident expenses are estimated at $16,900 per academic year.

Financial Aid

More than 75 percent of LSU's students receive financial assistance in the form of scholarships, federal and state grants, loans, and student employment. Students should submit the LSU Application for Admission and Scholarship as soon as possible after their junior year of high school. November 15 is the priority date for applying for scholarships. Those students who wish to apply for all of the federally funded financial aid programs (grants, loans, and Federal Work-Study) should complete the Free Application for Federal Student Aid (FAFSA) as soon as possible after January 1 of their senior year. Once enrolled, students are eligible to apply for a number of scholarships that are awarded by specific academic departments. Details are available from LSU's Office of Student Aid and Scholarships, which is located at 202 Himes Hall (telephone: 225-578-3103) or by using the University's Web site, listed at the end.

Faculty

LSU's faculty totals 1,344 members. The student-faculty ratio is 21:1. More than 80 percent of the full-time faculty members hold terminal degrees; many have earned national and international distinction. Members of the graduate faculty also teach undergraduate courses. Some undergraduate courses are taught by advanced graduate students who hold teaching assistantships.

Student Government

The Student Government Association is a policymaking body that is composed of students who represent most campus organizations and groups. The Board of Supervisors of the LSU System includes an elected student member. Students serve on a number of faculty senate committees.

Admission Requirements

Anyone who wishes to be considered for undergraduate admission to LSU should apply. Admission is granted to those students whose credentials indicate the greatest promise of academic success. Decisions are based on assessment of a combination of automatic criteria and a holistic review of the applicant's application package. Students are assured admission to LSU if they are eligible to enroll in university-level courses in mathematics (eligibility for college math is usually indicated by four years of college-preparatory mathematics courses or a minimum score of either 440 on the mathematics component of the SAT or 18 on the ACT) and meet the following requirements: 1) Students must have an academic GPA of at least 3.0 and 18 units and a minimum SAT score of 1030 or ACT score of 22 or rank in the top 15 percent of their high school graduating class; 2) Students must have 17 units and either a minimum SAT score of 1090 or ACT score of 24 and a minimum 3.0 GPA, or a minimum SAT score of 1060 or ACT score of 23 and a minimum 3.2 GPA, or an SAT score of at least 1030 or an ACT score of at least 22 and a 3.5 or greater GPA, or students must have a minimum 3.0 GPA and rank in the top 10 percent of their graduating class. Applicants who believe they do not meet the qualifications for assured admission should submit supporting documentation, such as recent grade reports and letters of recommendation as well as a letter outlining their qualifications for admissions with their initial application.

The Admissions Committee reviews an applicant's qualifications and application package to determine whether or not predictors of success exist as a basis for admission. LSU considers all components of an applicant's credentials. Factors such as rank in class, scores on required tests (SAT or ACT), credit in advanced placement and honors courses, pattern and quality of courses, grade trends, educational objectives, extracurricular activities, leadership abilities, and school recommendations are carefully evaluated in the admission process.

The specified high school units that are required for automatic admission to LSU are 4 years of English composition and literature, 3 years of college-preparatory mathematics (algebra I and II and geometry, trigonometry, calculus, or another advanced mathematics course—4 units of math are strongly recommended), 3 years of natural sciences (biology, chemistry, and physics), 3 years of social studies (1 unit in American history; 1 unit in world history, world geography, or history of western civilization; and 1 unit consisting of courses such as civics, free enterprise, economics, sociology, psychology and American government), 2 years of the same foreign language, 2½ years of approved academic electives and one semester of computer science or academic elective from those listed above. More detailed information is available upon request. LSU offers early and concurrent admission programs for exceptional students who choose to enroll on a full-time basis or who want to take University courses while in high school.

Students with previous college or university work from regionally accredited institutions are considered. Transfer students must have earned at least 30 semester hours of college-level credit (above remedial level), including a mathematics course and an English course (above remedial level), with a minimum 2.5 GPA from an accredited college or university. Students with less than 30 college-level semester hours need to meet the 2.5 transfer admission GPA requirement and the freshman admissions requirements to qualify for admission.

Application and Information

A nonrefundable application fee of $40 must accompany the application for admission. Application deadlines are April 15 for the fall semester and summer term and December 1 for the spring semester. The application deadline for international students is October 1 for the spring semester. Students are encouraged to apply well in advance of the deadlines. Prospective freshmen are advised to apply upon completion of their junior year in high school. Students may apply online at the Web site listed below.

For additional information, students should contact:

Office of Undergraduate Admissions
110 Thomas Boyd Hall
Louisiana State University
and Agricultural and Mechanical College
Baton Rouge, Louisiana 70803
Telephone: 225-578-1175
E-mail: admissions@lsu.edu
World Wide Web: http://www.lsu.edu

LOUISIANA TECH UNIVERSITY

RUSTON, LOUISIANA

The University

"At Tech you'll belong. Tech is family." That is how one graduate described the Louisiana Tech University experience. With its reputation for offering a private-college atmosphere at a public university price, Tech continues to rank as a "Best Value in the South" by *U.S. News & World Report*. Founded in 1894, this selective-admissions university is dedicated to challenging its students through the efforts of caring faculty members who are passionate about teaching, advising, and research. Tech offers more than eighty undergraduate majors and a wide variety of graduate degrees from within twenty-five master's and nine doctoral programs. Tech has the highest retention and graduation rate in the University of Louisiana system.

At this campus, 2,121 freshmen, of a total 11,975 students, thrive in a safe and supportive environment where collaborative research opportunities enhance learning alongside extracurricular and NCAA Division I athletic programs that enrich student life. Tech's campus brings together students from every state in the nation and from 57 different countries.

The pedestrian-friendly campus revolves around the oaks-shaded Quad and its gracious gardens, beckoning benches, and splashing Lady of the Mist fountain. Other campus highlights include a brick walkway that bears the names of all Tech grads, the 16-story Wyly Tower of Learning, the cutting-edge Institute for Micromanufacturing, and the imposing, round Thomas Assembly Center.

The 255-acre campus is also home to Tolliver Hall's state-of-the-art cyber café for students; an Olympic-size, T-shaped swimming pool; the Lambright Sports Center (housing basketball and racquetball courts, sauna facilities, weight rooms, and an indoor track; a nine-hole golf course); and soon, an on-campus, apartment-style community surrounded by shops and eateries and featuring a signature ballpark view.

With eleven residence halls, including one exclusively for honors students, campus life is fueled by excellent academic programs, 160 student organizations, and fourteen different varsity sports. (Students are admitted free of charge to all Tech sporting events.)

Tech is a state-supported university that is accredited by the Commission on Colleges of the Southern Association of Colleges and Schools.

Location

Louisiana Tech makes its home in the north-central Louisiana town of Ruston, which is at the intersection of Interstate 20 and U.S. Highway 167. Students can enjoy local eateries, stores, and activities, or they can take a drive (250 miles west to Dallas, Texas; 70 miles west to Shreveport; and 26 miles east to Monroe) for a wider range of dining, shopping, and entertainment experiences. Ruston, a friendly southern town of 23,000 and site of the annual Peach Festival, is close-knit, with its university neighbor sitting at the edge of the historical downtown. Tech students are active in cooperative projects with Ruston businesses and civic organizations.

Majors and Degrees

The College of Administration and Business awards the Bachelor of Science (B.S.) degree with majors in accounting, business administration, business economics, business management entrepreneurship, computer information systems, finance, human resources management, and marketing.

The College of Applied and Natural Sciences awards the B.S. and Bachelor of Science in Forestry (B.S.F.) degrees with majors in agribusiness, animal science, biology, environmental science, family and child studies, family and consumer sciences education, forestry, health information administration, medical technology, merchandising and consumer affairs, nutrition and dietetics, plant sciences, and wildlife conservation.

The College of Education awards the Bachelor of Arts (B.A.) and B.S. degrees with majors in art education, early/elementary education (preK–3), elementary education (1–6), health and physical education, middle school education-math (4–8), middle school education-science (4–8), music education, psychology, secondary education (agriculture, biology, business, chemistry, earth science, English, French, math, physics, social studies, speech), special education (elementary, early interventions, mild/moderate elementary, mild/moderate secondary, severe/profound), and speech, language, and hearing therapy.

The College of Engineering and Science awards the B.S. degree with majors in biomedical engineering, chemical engineering, chemistry, civil engineering, computer science, construction engineering technology, electrical engineering, electrical engineering technology, geology, industrial engineering, mathematics, mechanical engineering, and physics.

The College of Liberal Arts awards the Bachelor of Architecture (B.Arch.), B.A., Bachelor of Fine Arts (B.F.A.), Bachelor of General Studies (B.G.S.), and Bachelor of Interior Design (B.I.D.) degrees with majors in architecture, art-graphic design, art-photography, art-studio, aviation management, English, French, general studies, geography, history, interior design, journalism, music, political science, preprofessional speech-language pathology, professional aviation, sociology, Spanish, and speech.

Academic Program

All baccalaureate degree programs include a minimum of 120 semester hours. Minimum graduation requirements include a 2.0 GPA on all earned curricular course work. Additional GPA performance may be required in certain colleges. All curricula contain a general education core of 45 semester hours. Credit for selected courses may be earned through credit exams administered by the academic departments, through the Advanced Placement Program, and through the College-Level Examination Program (CLEP). Academically qualified students may seek admission to the Honors Program, which features smaller classes taught by prominent faculty members and enhanced with social and cultural programming. At the Career Center, students can schedule on-campus interviews with employers, get career and graduate school guidance, search job listings, attend resume and interview workshops, and meet company recruiters on Career Days. Tech awards semester hours on a quarter system. The fall, winter, and spring quarters equal two semesters.

Off-Campus Programs

Louisiana Tech offers an on-base degree program at Barksdale Air Force Base in Bossier City, Louisiana. Tech–Barksdale specializes in adult-oriented education for active-duty personnel and anyone seeking evening courses. The University also has a cross-registration program with Grambling State University and the University of Louisiana–Monroe.

Academic Facilities

The Prescott Memorial Library houses a media center, a computer lab with Internet access, classrooms with satellite teleconference downlink capabilities, an electronic reference center, and an electronic instruction classroom. The library collection numbers more than 3 million items. The Innovation Lab, featuring the most advanced information technology available, is a 24-hour-accessible space that encourages interdisciplinary innovation and entrepreneurship. The Honors

Program has a classroom equipped with a plasma board and technology table, which allows for a more interactive experience. All classrooms in the College of Administration and Business are equipped with LCD projectors, laptop stations, and full multimedia capabilities. Two presentation spaces are dedicated to the performing arts. The 40,000-square-foot School of Art has Macintosh labs that are the industry standard in graphic design and multimedia technology. The Center for Rehabilitation Science and Biomedical Engineering is recognized internationally for research ranging from the study of disabilities to the application of technology to assist disabled people.

Costs

Tuition and fees in 2004–05 are approximately $3500 for state residents and $7400 for out-of-state students. These figures are based on 8 semester hours, which is full-time status. The average residence hall costs $2025. The most frequently used meal plan costs $1650.

Financial Aid

Approximately 80 percent of Louisiana Tech students receive some form of financial assistance. Students may qualify for scholarship awards, need-based federal grants, or participation in federal loan programs. Students may also pursue regular or need-based campus job opportunities.

Four-year academic merit scholarships for talented entering freshmen range from $1000 to full tuition and additional incentives. The first step in being considered for financial aid is to complete the Free Application for Federal Student Aid (FAFSA) as early as possible. Tech's code number is 002008.

Faculty

Of nearly 400 faculty members, more than 80 percent hold the doctorate or equivalent degree. In addition to being excellent professors and researchers, the faculty members are known for their practical experience outside of academia. Software engineers, civil engineers, published authors, practicing architects, medical doctors, airplane pilots, and others bring hands-on expertise to the classroom to enhance learning. The student-faculty ratio is 22:1.

Student Government

Louisiana Tech's Student Government Association (SGA) serves as the official student voice to the administration, the Louisiana Board of Regents, University of Louisiana System Board of Supervisors, and the state legislature. Its mission is to continually represent the interests and opinions of students, increase student decision-making power, create and promote student leadership opportunities, improve campus life through the creation and continuation of effective student services, and support students in academic and community endeavors.

Admission Requirements

Freshmen applicants must graduate from an approved high school with a minimum 2.3 GPA (on a 4.0 scale) achieved in at least 17.5 units of prerequisite study, including 4 units of English; 3 units of mathematics (2 of algebra and 1 of geometry or a higher-level math for which algebra is a prerequisite); 3 units of science (biology, chemistry, and physics preferred); 3 units of social science (of which 1 unit must be U.S. history); 4.5 units of electives (foreign languages, social studies, science, mathematics, speech, advanced fine arts, and computer literacy recommended). No more than 3 elective units can be taken in vocational subjects. Otherwise, students must either rank in the upper 35 percent of their graduating class or have a minimum ACT composite score of 22 or combined SAT I score of 1020. No student with an ACT composite less than 15 will be admitted.

Homeschooled students must have a minimum ACT composite of 22 (SAT, 1020) and a high school transcript documenting completion of high school work.

International applicants must have a minimum 2.5 GPA on all course work and an official TOEFL score of 500 or greater on the paper-based test or a score of 173 or higher on the computerized test. Tech must receive the TOEFL score within two years of the test date. A waiver of the TOEFL may be possible if the international student has earned at least 24 hours from another approved U.S. university.

All students are encouraged to apply. The University may admit students not meeting all stated requirements. In such cases, the admission decision is affected by the student's potential for success and the need to enhance the University's population.

Transfer students with fewer than 24 semester hours of course work must meet the same requirements as entering freshmen and be eligible to reenter the institution from which they transferred. Students with 24 hours or more must have a minimum 2.0 GPA on all transfer work.

High school students may be considered for early admission if they have a 3.0 overall GPA on all course work pursued during three years of high school, a minimum ACT composite score of 25 or SAT I combined score of 1130 (to be submitted prior to June 1), and a recommendation letter from their high school principal. Upon completing a minimum of 24 semester hours at the University, the student will be issued a diploma by the high school last attended.

Tech's Summer Enrichment Program enables students to pursue college credit between their junior and senior high school years. The Summer Scholars Program for exceptional students awards scholarships to entering freshmen who want to get an early start by enrolling in the summer quarter.

Application and Information

The application and nonrefundable $20 application fee ($30 for an international student) should be submitted to the Office of Admissions. Priority will be given to those who apply by August 1 for admission to the fall quarter, Nov. 1 for the winter quarter, Feb. 1 for the spring quarter, and May 1 for summer quarter. Campus visits are encouraged. For materials and information, students should contact:

Office of Admissions
Louisiana Tech University
P.O. Box 3178
Ruston Louisiana 71272-0001
Telephone: 318-257-3036
1-800-LATECH-1 (toll-free)
E-mail: bulldog@latech.edu
World Wide Web: http://www.latech.edu

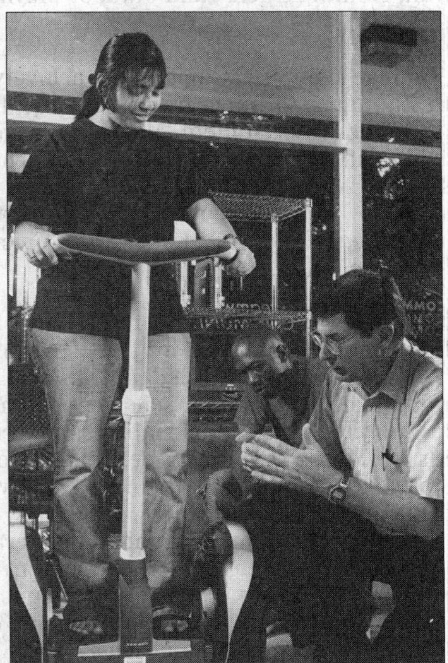

Students develop accessories for the Segway™ Human Transporter.

LOYOLA COLLEGE IN MARYLAND

BALTIMORE, MARYLAND

The College

Loyola College is a private, liberal arts college with the Catholic traditions of the Jesuits and the Sisters of Mercy. It is an educational community of students and faculty cooperating for the intellectual, spiritual, and professional enrichment of all its members and for the improvement of the local community and society in general. The intellectual enterprise is a joint creation of the faculty members and the students. Loyola's current full-time undergraduate enrollment is 3,400 men and women; more than 80 percent of the student body live on campus.

Loyola encourages cocurricular activities that contribute to the academic, social, and spiritual growth of the student. These include social and cultural organizations, Student Government activities, military science activities, national honor societies, and Division I athletic programs such as basketball, crew, cross-country, golf, lacrosse, soccer, swimming and diving, tennis, and volleyball. The majority of the student body participates in the wide variety of intramural sports offered.

In recent years, the College's campus has undergone significant expansion. Six apartment complexes and three freshman dormitories provide Loyola students with on-campus housing. Completed in fall 1999, the Andrew White Student Center provides more dining choices and expanded meeting and recreational space, making it a popular hub of the remodeled campus. The Student Center also provides facilities for athletics and the fine arts, including the McManus Theatre, the 4,000-seat Reitz Arena, and an Olympic-size pool. The center also has an art gallery, classrooms, and music, photography, and studio art labs. Adding to Loyola's sports facilities is the new Recreation and Sports Complex, completed in September 2000. This 110-square-foot athletic facility provides another Olympic-size pool, squash courts, a climbing wall, running tracks, and outdoor playing fields.

Location

The Loyola College campus is located in a lovely residential area of north Baltimore, 5 miles from the Inner Harbor area. This location offers the student the advantages of quiet residential living with the attractions of city life. The metropolitan area has a wide variety of theaters, museums, professional and intercollegiate sports events, and historical points of interest. Other colleges and universities in the vicinity help to expand the social calendar.

Majors and Degrees

Loyola College offers programs in thirty-two majors. The Bachelor of Arts degree is awarded in classical civilization, classics, communication, computer science, economics, education, English, fine arts, history, journalism, modern languages and literatures, philosophy, political science, psychology, sociology, speech pathology/audiology, theology, and writing. The Bachelor of Business Administration degree is awarded in accounting, business economics, finance, general business, international business, management, management information systems, and marketing. The Bachelor of Science degree is awarded in biology, chemistry, computer science, engineering science, mathematical science, and physics.

Academic Program

The curriculum at Loyola College is divided into three parts: the core, the major, and electives. The core contains those courses that Loyola College considers essential to the liberal arts curriculum. These courses, which are required of all students regardless of major, are completed during the four years. The core consists of a classical or modern language, English literature, writing, mathematics and natural science, social science, fine arts, history, philosophy, ethics, and theology. The major enables students to pursue in depth their specialized area of study. Electives give students the opportunity to broaden their intellectual and cultural background in areas of special interest. To prepare for graduate study, students may enroll in one of the four preprofessional programs: dental, law, medical, or veterinary.

An honors program and honors housing are available to outstanding students. The honors program stresses independent work by specially grouped students in many of the core courses. Honors housing provides an environment conducive to study and close social interaction.

Off-Campus Programs

Loyola College participates in a cooperative program with the College of Notre Dame of Maryland, Johns Hopkins University, Goucher College, Morgan State University, Towson University, the Peabody Conservatory of Music, and the Maryland College Institute of Art. Loyola students may cross-register at any of these area colleges and universities.

Students in good academic standing may pursue studies abroad through Loyola's programs in Leuven, Belgium; Bangkok, Thailand; Alcalá, Spain; Melbourne, Australia; Newcastle, England; Auckland, New Zealand; Beijing, China; Cork, Ireland; and Rome, Italy. Loyola has programs available in twenty-eight other countries in conjunction with other schools.

Academic Facilities

The Donnelly Science Center has recently been expanded, making it the largest academic building on the Evergreen campus. It features state-of-the-art laboratories for tomorrow's scientists and health-care professionals and new classrooms and offices that give faculty members even more space for instruction and research.

In the spring 2000 semester, Loyola welcomed the new Sellinger School of Business. For the first time since its formation in 1980, the School of Business and Management is headquartered in one central location on the Evergreen campus. Highlights of this newest academic addition include eleven classrooms, five seminar rooms, fifty-two faculty and departmental offices, and an information center. Also, 90 percent of Sellinger classes are taught in Internet-linked, multimedia classrooms.

A modern library shared by Loyola College and the College of Notre Dame of Maryland has a capacity of 349,000 volumes, making it one of the largest college libraries in the country.

Costs

For 2003–04, tuition for all undergraduate students is $26,010 per year. Room for freshmen is $5950; for upperclassmen, room costs range from $6290 to $7280. Optional board is estimated at $2400 and student fees are $570. The approximate cost of books and supplies is $400.

Financial Aid

It is the intent of Loyola College to assist qualified students who might not otherwise be able to provide for themselves an opportunity for higher education. Financial aid is awarded on the basis of academic ability and financial need. Two thirds of the student body receive financial assistance in the forms of Loyola College scholarships, state scholarships, Federal Pell Grants, Federal Supplemental Educational Opportunity Grants, Federal Perkins Loans, and Federal Work-Study Program opportunities. To apply for financial assistance, students must submit the Free Application for Federal Student Aid and the Financial Aid PROFILE through the College Scholarship Service in Princeton, New Jersey. The financial aid application deadline is February 1.

Faculty

Loyola College intends to remain a relatively small college and continue to have a faculty-student ratio similar to the current one of 1:12 in order to ensure interest in the individual student. The members of the administration and the full-time faculty of 272 hold degrees from seventy-three different colleges and universities. All of the full-time faculty members serve as student advisers. More than 90 percent of the course work in the Day Division of Loyola College is taught by full-time faculty members. No classes are taught by graduate students.

Student Government

The Student Government serves three chief functions, which make its existence not only valuable but necessary. These functions are to represent the student body outside the College, to provide leadership within the student body, and to perform services, both social and academic, for the students. Responsibility for budgeting activities also rests with the Student Government. The president of the Student Government is a member of the College Academic Council.

Admission Requirements

Applicants for admission to Loyola College are evaluated according to their academic qualifications. The most important academic criteria include the secondary school record, performance on the College Board's Scholastic Assessment Test (which is the College's required entrance examination), and the recommendations from an academic source. The College welcomes applications from men and women of character, intelligence, and motivation, without discrimination on the grounds of race or religious belief.

Application and Information

Interested students seeking to enroll at Loyola College may obtain the application form by writing to the address listed below. Each applicant must instruct the College Board to send his or her Scholastic Assessment Test scores to the Admissions Office. Applicants for all forms of financial aid must submit the Financial Aid PROFILE of the College Scholarship Service and the Free Application for Federal Student Aid. A $30 application fee must accompany the application for admission.

For additional information, students are encouraged to contact:

Undergraduate Admissions Office
Loyola College in Maryland
4501 North Charles Street
Baltimore, Maryland 21210-2699
Telephone: 410-617-2252
800-221-9107 (toll-free)
World Wide Web: http://www.Loyola.edu

Loyola's campus offers the freedom of a residential setting, yet it is only minutes away from the resources of a major metropolitan area.

LOYOLA MARYMOUNT UNIVERSITY

LOS ANGELES, CALIFORNIA

The University

Loyola Marymount University (LMU), situated on a picturesque campus, offers competitive students an education of high quality in a friendly and relaxed atmosphere. As successor of the oldest institution of learning in southern California, St. Vincent's College, the University is steeped in a tradition and history of dedication to academic excellence and the total development of its students. Although the emphasis is within the undergraduate school (full-time enrollment is approximately 5,001 and part-time enrollment is 357), 1,466 students attend the Graduate Division, primarily in the evening hours, working toward master's degrees in the fields of arts, arts in teaching, business administration, education, and science (including engineering). The School of Law, situated at a separate campus, has both day and evening divisions and offers the Juris Doctor degree. Law school enrollment is approximately 1,410.

Nearly 60 percent of the undergraduate students live on campus and are able to choose accommodations in one of ten residential halls or six apartment complexes. Students have access to a sports pavilion, two swimming pools, baseball and soccer fields, tennis and volleyball courts, and four indoor racquetball courts. A new recreation center includes three additional courts and a fitness center. LMU fields teams in eleven intercollegiate sports (baseball, basketball, crew, cross-country, golf, soccer, softball, swimming, tennis, volleyball, and water polo) and has club teams in lacrosse and rugby. More than 2,000 undergraduate students participate in the active intramural program, which includes coed sports. Student organizations include the AM/FM radio station (KXLU), Biology Society, Black Students Freedom Alliance, Chinese Club, MEChA, Pre-Legal Society, Student Activities Board, University choruses, fraternities and sororities, and various honor and service groups. The Debate Squad and LMU's Air Force ROTC detachment have received national recognition in their respective areas.

Location

LMU is ideally located on a 152-acre mesa that overlooks the southwest section of Los Angeles and the Pacific Ocean from Malibu to Santa Monica. The campus is close to the beach, and the University community enjoys a cool, clean, coastal climate. LMU is near the metropolitan complex, but it has the benefits of the slower pace of its residential community, Westchester. Los Angeles International Airport is 10 minutes away, and nearby freeways provide easy access to the city and its cultural and recreational activities.

Majors and Degrees

Loyola Marymount University offers the B.A. in the fields of Afro-American studies, animation studies, art history, Asian Pacific studies, biology, Chicano studies, classics, communication studies, dance, economics, English, European studies, film production, French, history, humanities, Latin, liberal studies, music, philosophy, political science, psychology, recording arts, screenwriting, sociology, Spanish, studio arts, television production, theater arts, theology, and urban studies. The College of Business Administration offers the Bachelor of Science degree in accounting and the Bachelor of Business Administration degree with emphases in business law, computer information systems and operations management, finance, international business, management, marketing, and tourism and travel. The College of Science and Engineering offers bachelor's degrees in biochemistry, biology, chemistry, computer science, engineering (civil, electrical, and mechanical), engineering physics, mathematics, natural science, and physics. Areas of emphasis can include such fields as computer engineering, environmental science, and marine biology.

Academic Programs

While premajor and major requirements differ with each area of study, a core curriculum is maintained as a degree requirement in the fields of American cultures, communication skills, fine arts, history, literature/psychology, mathematics/science, philosophy, social science, and theology, thus ensuring each student a balanced education. The maximum requirement in each of the core fields is 6 units of academic work. The interdepartmental honors program provides challenges for the exceptional student.

The academic calendar consists of two semesters and a six-week optional summer session. The fall semester begins in late August and ends before Christmas. The spring semester begins in mid-January and ends in mid-May. Students may earn credit through Advanced Placement (AP) examinations. In addition, it is possible for students to earn credit by examination for any course offered by LMU.

Off-Campus Programs

Students who are interested in studying abroad have a choice of several University-sponsored programs. LMU offers programs in Africa, China, England, France, Germany, Greece, Honduras, Ireland, Italy, Japan, Korea, Mexico, Spain, and the Phillipines. The University also has numerous affiliated programs, including the Rome Center of Loyola University of Chicago and the American Institute for Foreign Study. Choice of programs is made on the basis of the student's interest and ability or skill. Courses may be conducted in English, the language of the country in which the student elects to study, or both. In addition, LMU offers internship programs through which students can earn course credit for independent study that has been approved by the dean of the college in which the student is enrolled. The programs range from student involvement in political campaigns to the counseling of underrepresented youths to professional work at film/TV studios.

Academic Facilities

The completely automated Charles Von der Ahe Library contains the undergraduate library collections, which total approximately 375,000 books and bound periodicals, 140,000 microforms, 3,100 subscriptions, and nearly 17,000 recordings. Among the special collections are materials on St. Thomas More, Oliver Goldsmith, Spanish culture and civilization, and German and American philosophy. The library is also a federal depository for government documents. The undergraduate library includes a Learning Resource Center, a multimedia area for audiovisual materials and equipment. Study carrels are equipped for using a variety of formats, such as videocassettes, 8-mm and Super-8 film, audiotapes, turntables, filmstrips, and slides—both with and without cassettes. Instructional media related to classwork and individualized study are available. The

Law School Library, located within the School of Law in downtown Los Angeles, contains more than 540,000 volumes and microforms and is a depository for government documents of the state of California and the United States. It also has complete holdings of all publications relating to California law. All students have at their disposal an IBM 360/30 computer that is equipped to program five languages. The communication arts complex houses the Louis B. Mayer Motion Picture Theatre, a full-size color-television studio, a motion-picture soundstage, an HS-200 (instant-replay) machine, and other modern equipment. Strub Theatre offers excellent theatrical facilities for the performing arts of drama and dance.

Costs

Tuition for the 2004–05 academic year is $25,266. The cost of room and board varies with options that students select—for example, a full or partial meal plan, an apartment on campus, or a dormitory. However, the average yearly cost is approximately $8200. Students should expect to spend about $800 for books and supplies and $1850 for additional miscellaneous expenses.

Financial Aid

Approximately 78 percent of the University's undergraduate students receive some type of financial assistance. The total amount of financial aid awarded to students is approximately $84 million. Students applying for aid must file the Free Application for Student Aid (FAFSA) and the CSS PROFILE. All students are expected to apply for the Federal Pell Grant, and California residents must apply for the California grants. Most aid is awarded on the basis of need, but the University does offer merit scholarships (including full-tuition scholarships). The priority date for financial aid is February 15. Aid is awarded after that date on a funds-available basis.

Faculty

LMU's faculty is dedicated to undergraduate teaching and is easily accessible to students. Eighty-eight percent of the faculty members hold a Ph.D. in their area of instruction.

Student Government

The University believes that active student input is an essential part of the undergraduate years. Students sit on every University committee, including the Board of Trustees, with full voting rights. Students operate the campus recreation centers, manage the dormitories as resident advisers, operate a used-book store, and serve as advisers to their academic departments. Student actions have resulted in the development of such things as a campus recreation center, the water polo team, and the complete semester calendar.

Admission Requirements

Admission to LMU is selective, and a candidate is expected to present a better-than-average record in college-preparatory courses. Minimal achievement and limited preparation narrow the candidate's chances for acceptance into the University and into specific programs. In determining an applicant's eligibility, the University gives careful consideration to the student's academic preparation, national test scores, letters of recommendation, extracurricular activities, and family relationships to the University. A personal interview is not required but is recommended if it is convenient. Prospective candidates are always welcome to visit the campus, and personal tours or overnight stays can be arranged upon written request. Students who, for academic reasons, were not accepted for admission as freshmen may be admitted to advanced standing if they have completed at least the equivalent of 30 semester hours of transferable college work with at least a B average.

Application and Information

Applicants must submit official transcripts from the last high school attended and from each college attended, arrange for SAT I or ACT scores to be sent to the Office of Admissions, submit a recommendation form from an official of the last school attended, and file an application with the $50 nonrefundable fee. Applications are considered when all necessary documents have been received prior to the deadline of the semester for which application is made. The deadlines are February 1 for the fall semester and December 1 for the spring semester.

International students who are not legal residents of the United States must follow the same admission procedure but are required to submit all completed data before the following deadlines: fall semester, February 1; spring semester, December 1. International students must also submit scores on the Test of English as a Foreign Language (TOEFL), submit a statement of financial responsibility for all obligations covering the full period of time for which the student is making application, be certain all records of previous academic training are original or authentic copies with notarization, and have notarized English translations of all the required records.

For more information about Loyola Marymount University, prospective students should contact:

Matthew X. Fissinger
Director of Admissions
Loyola Marymount University
One LMU Drive
Los Angeles, California 90045
Telephone: 310-338-2750
800-LMU-INFO (toll-free)
Fax: 310-338-2797

Between classes at Loyola Marymount University.

LOYOLA UNIVERSITY CHICAGO

CHICAGO, ILLINOIS

The University

Loyola University Chicago is the most comprehensive Jesuit university in the United States. Founded in 1870 by priests of the Society of Jesus, Loyola continues the Jesuit commitment to education, which is well-grounded in the liberal arts and based on excellence in teaching and research.

Loyola attracts students from all fifty states and seventy-four countries to its nine schools and colleges: the Stritch School of Medicine, the School of Law, the College of Arts and Sciences, the School of Business Administration, the Niehoff School of Nursing, the School of Education, the School of Social Work, the Graduate School, and the School of Professional Studies (for adult and lifelong learning).

Each year, Loyola University Chicago enrolls more than 1,900 freshmen and more than 400 transfer students. These students choose Loyola because of its personal attention, its environment of academic excellence, and its reputation for career preparation. Loyola students take advantage of Chicago as an educational resource, often combining their studies with internships and part-time work experience.

The University seeks to provide an environment that will enhance the academic, social, and spiritual growth of students. More than 125 student organizations, including eleven fraternities and sororities, and extensive recreational sports programs and facilities are provided. NCAA Division I teams include basketball, cross-country, golf, soccer, track, and volleyball for men and basketball, cross-country, golf, soccer, softball, track, and volleyball for women.

Loyola provides thirteen undergraduate residence halls on the Lake Shore Campus. There are both coed and single-sex halls. Freshmen and sophomores are required to live on campus if they do not live at home. There is also convenient and affordable off-campus housing in the immediate vicinity of campus for upperclass students.

Location

The Lake Shore Campus is located 8 miles north of the city's center and sits on the shore of Lake Michigan in the Rogers Park/Edgewater area, a desirable residential neighborhood where many Loyola faculty and staff members reside. Students at the Lake Shore Campus also can take advantage of the city's vast business and cultural resources, with downtown Chicago being less than 20 minutes away via university-run shuttle bus or via convenient public transportation.

Loyola's Water Tower Campus is located on Chicago's "Magnificent Mile," a fashionable area on the near north side. Close to theaters, museums, major corporate and financial institutions, and some of Chicago's most elegant shops and boutiques, the Water Tower Campus is a vibrant educational center.

Majors and Degrees

Loyola's four undergraduate colleges offer the Bachelor of Arts (B.A.), Bachelor of Science (B.S.), Bachelor of Business Administration (B.B.A.), Bachelor of Science in Education (B.S.Ed.), and the Bachelor of Science in Nursing (B.S.N.) degrees. The College of Arts and Sciences offers majors in anthropology, biology, chemistry (biochemistry), classical civilization, communication (communication and social justice, journalism, and organizational communication/business), computer science, criminal justice, ecology, economics, English (creative writing), environmental studies, environmental sciences (chemistry), fine arts (art history, studio art, and visual communication), French, Greek (ancient), history, international studies, Italian, Latin, mathematics (operations research), mathematics and computer science, music, pharmacy, philosophy, physics, physics and engineering (theoretical physics and applied mathematics), political science, psychology (applied social psychology, human services, natural sciences, and social sciences), social work, sociology, Spanish, statistical science, theology, and women's studies. The School of Business Administration offers majors in accounting, economics, finance, human resource management, information systems management, international business (combined with a second major), marketing, and operations management. The School of Education offers a major in elementary education as well as secondary school certification in eleven majors. The Niehoff School of Nursing offers the Bachelor of Science in Nursing and a baccalaureate completion program for registered nurses, an accelerated B.S.N. program. Five-year dual-degree (bachelor's/master's) programs are available in applied social psychology, biology/M.B.A., business administration/accountancy, business administration/information systems management, computer science, criminal justice, environmental sciences/M.B.A., mathematics, political science, social work, and sociology.

Interdisciplinary studies include Asian studies, black world studies, Catholic studies, international studies, Latin American studies, medieval studies, neuroscience, peace studies, and psychology of crime and justice.

Preprofessional programs prepare students for future study in bioethics and health policy, cell biology, cell and molecular physiology, divinity, law, medicine, microbiology and immunology, molecular biology, molecular and cellular biochemistry, neurobiology and anatomy, pastoral studies, pharmacology and experimental therapeutics, religious education, and social work. A 3+3 Law Program, in conjunction with the Loyola University School of Law, allows talented undergraduates to enter law school at the conclusion of their junior year of college. An early assurance program to the Loyola Stritch School of Medicine provides students with an articulated admission to medical school.

Academic Program

Jesuit educators believe that a solid foundation in the liberal arts and sciences is essential for students entering all professions. Loyola's Core Curriculum is designed to give students this foundation. The core requirements vary by college but usually include courses in expressive arts, history, literature, mathematical and natural sciences, philosophy, social sciences, and theology. The core allows students who are undecided about their majors to explore all possibilities before deciding upon a field of study.

Most majors require 128 semester hours for graduation. Exceptionally well-qualified students may apply to the Honors Program. Students may receive credit through the Advanced Placement Program (AP Program) tests, the International Baccalaureate (I.B.), and certain College-Level Examination

Program (CLEP) tests are accepted. Loyola students may participate in the Army and Naval ROTC programs through neighboring universities.

Off-Campus Programs

Loyola offers more than thirty study-abroad programs in nineteen countries. Loyola's Rome Center in Rome, Italy, is the most popular student study-abroad destination. Students may also choose a reciprocal exchange program in Chile, China, England, France, Ireland, Japan, or Mexico, or they may participate in one of several other affiliate programs around the globe.

Academic Facilities

The University's library system, including the Cudahy Library at the Lake Shore Campus and the Lewis Library at the Water Tower Campus, contains more than 1.3 million books and 12,000 periodical subscriptions. Other academic facilities include extensive laboratories for the biology, chemistry, and physics departments; a nursing resource center; and computing facilities on all campuses. The School of Business is located in a $38-million building on the Water Tower Campus.

The Martin D'Arcy Gallery of Medieval and Renaissance Art is located on the Lake Shore Campus along with the Fine Art Department's gallery and studios. The theater department's facilities include the Mullady Theatre, where the most sophisticated computerized lighting system in Chicago was recently installed, and the Studio Theatre, an experimental black-box facility. Loyola's FM radio station provides communication majors with on-campus production experience.

The Medical Center Campus in Maywood, a suburb of Chicago, consists of the Foster G. McGaw Hospital and the Stritch School of Medicine as well as the Mulcahy Outpatient Center, the Russo Surgical Pavilion, and the Cardinal Bernardin Cancer Center.

Costs

For the 2003–04 academic year, tuition for full-time undergraduates was $20,544. Based on double occupancy, room and board costs average $7900. Books and fees total about $1715 per year.

Financial Aid

Loyola attempts to meet the financial need of as many students as possible. Ninety-four percent of Loyola freshman receive some form of aid, including University-funded scholarships and grants, federal and state grants, work-study, and loans. Students are encouraged to file the Free Application for Federal Student Aid (FAFSA) by mid-February in order to receive consideration for all types of aid.

Merit scholarships are awarded to entering freshmen who have outstanding academic records. Presidential, Damen, and Loyola Scholarships are awarded to students who rank at the top of their high school graduating class and score well on the ACT or SAT I. Scholarship amounts for these programs are $5000–$12,500 per year. These awards are renewable for up to three years.

Other scholarships available include competitive awards for students admitted to the Honors Program and students from Jesuit/BVM/Sisters of Christian Charity high schools, National Merit/National Achievement finalists, theater scholarships (awarded by audition), and debate, elementary education, leadership, and public accounting awards.

Transfer students who have completed 30 hours of college credit with an outstanding record of academic achievement may receive a Transfer Academic Scholarship. These awards are renewable for up to three years.

Faculty

More than 95 percent of the University's full-time faculty members hold the Ph.D. or the highest degree in their field. Faculty members generally teach both graduate and undergraduate students, and senior faculty members often teach Core Curriculum courses. At 13:1 the student-faculty ratio is far below the national average, giving undergraduates ready access to faculty members both as teachers and as advisers.

Student Government

Student government at Loyola provides a liaison between students and administration, emphasizes concerns for student rights, and provides a forum for debate, recommendation, and action on issues that pertain to students. Students also take an active role on University policy and advisory committees and as elected representatives in the residence halls.

Admission Requirements

Students seeking admission to Loyola University Chicago are evaluated on the basis of their overall academic record, including ACT or SAT scores. Most Loyola students rank in the upper quarter of their graduating class, but consideration is given to students in the upper half. Candidates should be graduating from an accredited secondary school with a minimum of 15 units, including courses in English, math, social studies, and science. Study of a foreign language is strongly recommended. Students must submit the application for admission along with high school transcripts, test scores, and a secondary school counselor recommendation. Admission counselors are available to meet and talk with students individually either before or after the application is submitted.

Transfer students with 20 semester hours or more of acceptable credit are evaluated on the basis of their college work only. Minimum acceptable grade point averages are 2.0 (C) for the College of Arts and Sciences; 2.0 (C) for the School of Education; and 2.5 (C+) for the Schools of Business Administration and Nursing. Candidates must also have been in good standing at the last college attended.

Application and Information

Applicants are notified of the admission decision three to four weeks after the application, supporting credentials, secondary school counselor recommendation, and $25 application fee are received. The application fee is waived for students who apply online.

Prospective students are encouraged to visit the campus. The Undergraduate Admission Office encourages students to schedule individual appointments and campus tours or to participate in one of the many campus programs offered throughout the year.

To obtain an application and further information and to arrange a visit, students should contact:

Undergraduate Admission Office
Loyola University Chicago
820 North Michigan Avenue
Chicago, Illinois 60611
Telephone: 312-915-6500
800-262-2373 (toll-free)
E-mail: admission@luc.edu
World Wide Web: http://www.luc.edu/undergrad

LOYOLA UNIVERSITY NEW ORLEANS

NEW ORLEANS, LOUISIANA

The University

Founded by the Jesuits in 1912, Loyola University's more than 35,000 graduates have excelled in innumerable professional fields for more than eighty years. Approximately 3,800 undergraduate students enjoy the individual attention of a caring faculty in a university dedicated to creating community and fostering individualism while educating the whole person, not only intellectually, but spiritually, socially, and athletically. Loyola students represent forty-nine states and forty-eight countries. This diversity is found in a setting where the average class size is 22 students. More than 49 percent of the students permanently reside outside Louisiana, and 30 percent belong to minority groups.

Loyola's 20-acre main campus and 4-acre Broadway campus are located in the historic uptown area of New Orleans and are hubs of student activity. The University's residence halls, equipped with computer labs, kitchen, laundry, and study facilities, are home to 34 percent of the undergraduate students. The Joseph A. Danna Center, the student center, houses five food venues, including the remodeled Orleans Room, Pizza Hut, N'Awlins Poboys, Smoothie King, and a gourmet coffee shop. Also found in the Danna Center are an art gallery, hair salon, concierge desk, and post office. Nationally affiliated fraternities and sororities are among Loyola's more than 120 student organizations. During the fall's Organizational Fair, students can join the award-winning newspaper, the Loyola University Community Action Program (a volunteer community service organization, the largest such club on campus), or one of the many special interest groups. Students can also take this opportunity to sign up for one of Loyola's club sports. Every year students participate in club cheerleading, crew, cycling, dance, and swimming, as well as men's lacrosse, rugby, and soccer. Loyola participates in the National Association of Intercollegiate Athletics (NAIA) men's baseball, basketball, and cross-country and women's basketball, cross-country, soccer, and volleyball. The Recreational Sports Complex offers six multipurpose courts, an elevated running track, an Olympic-size swimming pool, weight rooms, and aerobics and combat-sports facilities.

The career services offered by the Counseling and Career Services Center include career counseling and testing, assistance with choosing a course of study, recommendations about graduate and professional school, and assistance in securing internships and jobs. Career development services include individualized consultation and counseling, with personality and career-interest testing, a career exploration course, career-related speakers, and a career information library. Publications include information on a wide range of career choices, graduate school directories, scholarship and financial aid directories, and field-specific directories of employers.

The Joseph A. Butt, S.J., College of Business Administration is fully accredited at both the undergraduate and graduate levels by the AACSB International–The Association to Advance Collegiate Schools of Business and houses the Mildred Soule and Clarence A. Lengendre Chair in Business Ethics. The College of Music, founded in 1932, gives students the opportunity to combine liberal studies with professional music courses in the only college of music conducted by the Jesuit fathers in the United States.

Location

Loyola's main campus fronts oak-lined St. Charles Avenue in uptown New Orleans. Its red-brick, Tudor-Gothic buildings overlook Audubon Park, home of the famous Audubon Zoo. The downtown area is a 20-minute streetcar ride away, allowing students to take advantage of the city's broad cultural and artistic environment. Considering that New Orleans enjoys an average temperature of 70 degrees, students can enjoy year-round outdoor activities in a city famous for its food, music, and cultural festivals. Lake Pontchartrain is within the city limits and provides facilities for water sports.

Majors and Degrees

Loyola University grants degrees in four-year undergraduate programs. The College of Arts and Sciences grants the B.A. degree in classical studies, communications (advertising, broadcast journalism, broadcast production, communications studies, film studies, photojournalism, print journalism, and public relations), criminal justice, drama, drama communications, economics, English, English writing, French, German, graphic arts, history, philosophy, political science, psychology (also premedicine), religious studies, Russian, sociology, Spanish, theater arts, and visual arts and grants the B.S. in biology (predentistry, premedicine, and pre–veterinary studies), chemistry (premedicine), chemistry–forensic science, computer information systems, computer science, elementary education, mathematics, and physics. The College of Business Administration awards the B.B.A. degree in economics, finance, international business, management, and marketing, as well as the Bachelor of Accountancy. The College of Music grants the B.M. in jazz studies, music business, music education, music history, music therapy, piano pedagogy, theory and composition, and vocal and instrumental performance; the B.S. in music business; and the B.M.E. in instrumental and vocal performance. Minors are available in all disciplines offered as majors, except elementary education. American, African-American, Africana, environmental, women's, Latin American, medieval, and film studies and secondary education are offered as interdisciplinary minors addressing important areas of national and international concern.

Academic Program

Once enrolled at Loyola, students are introduced to the Common Curriculum, designed to give them a well-rounded preparation in their major field of concentration, as well as the ability to understand and reflect on disciplines allied to or outside their major. The curriculum is divided into four categories: major, minor, Common Curriculum, and elective courses. Students must meet the requirements of their degree program as specified by their particular college; the minimum four-year program requires 120 hours. Common Curriculum courses include seven introductory courses in English composition, math, science, philosophy, religion, literature, and history and nine upper-division courses in humanities, social science, and natural science. The College of Business Administration requires that all students with junior or senior standing complete an internship prior to graduation. Internships provide professional-level experience in area business firms and not-for-profit organizations, along with college credit for semester-long participation. The College of Arts and Sciences also requires a minimum of one year of study in a modern foreign language. The honors program and independent studies provide special opportunities for qualified students.

Off-Campus Programs

Through the international studies program, students may spend their junior year in Rome. Summer programs in Greece, Ireland, London, and Mexico are also available, as well as opportunities to study in Belgium, France, Japan, and Spain. Through consortium arrangements, students may cross-register for courses for credit at Xavier University, Tulane University, and Notre Dame Seminary and participate with these institutions in joint social-cultural events. In addition, the University offers a rigorous internship program in New Orleans at businesses, institutions, and schools to give students practical experience in their fields, including business administration, communications, education, modern foreign languages, music, and writing. Loyola offers a 3-3 program with the Loyola School of Law for students interested in pursuing a prelaw tract, as well as a 3-2 program in engineering with Tulane University and an early acceptance program with Tulane University Medical School.

Academic Facilities

A $13-million Communications/Music Complex includes classrooms, offices, specialized instructional facilities for the College of Music and the Department of Communications, and a 600-seat performing arts facility for the College of Music. It also houses fully equipped TV and radio studios. The communications department, which has one of the most comprehensive programs in broadcasting and print journalism in the United States, operates its own closed-circuit broadcasting studio in TV and radio and publishes its own newspaper.

Computing is an integral part of campus life at Loyola. The University provides more than 450 computers in seventeen computer labs throughout the campus. These labs consist of Windows- and Macintosh-based computers with a wide variety of application software and access to the Internet. Loyola's high-speed Ethernet network can also be accessed from locations such as residence halls, the library, and other public areas. A noteworthy characteristic of Loyola's computing resources is its student-centered emphasis. For example, specialized computer labs exist in the Writing Across the Curriculum Center, English and Math Basic Skills Labs, Poverty Law Clinic, and Business Solutions Center.

The Broadway campus, approximately two blocks down St. Charles Avenue, houses the Loyola School of Law, the visual arts department, the Twomey Center for Peace Through Justice, the Division of Institutional Advancement, and a residence hall.

Other facilities on campus include the J. Edgar and Louise S. Monroe Library, the region's most technologically advanced facility and the 2003 recipient of the Association of College and Research Libraries' Excellence in Academic Libraries Award, which contains more than 312,000 volumes and holds subscriptions to more than 2,000 periodicals and journals. The Monroe Library also offers more than 660,000 microform units and 2,500 media titles. There are also specialized libraries for music and law. The 150,000-square-foot Monroe Library contains 1,800 computer links, media/instructional technology services, a visual arts center, and the Lindy Boggs National Center for Community Literacy. The library also offers three 24-hour microcomputer labs, two multimedia classrooms, and sixteen group-study rooms.

Costs

For the full-time undergraduate student attending during 2003–04, tuition was $21,320 for the year, plus a $836 student activity fee. The cost of residence halls (double occupancy) and a complete meal plan was $7630 for the year.

Financial Aid

Loyola University's endowment provides money for financial aid in addition to that provided by federal funding. Assistance in the forms of merit- and talent-based scholarships, loans, work-study program awards, and grants is awarded on the basis of academic achievement and need. More than 450 scholarships are awarded annually to students with competitive grades and test scores. To apply for one of the scholarships, students must have a GPA of at least 3.2 and competitive standardized test scores. Offers of financial aid are not made until after admission. Notifications of awards are sent in early February. Awards of need-based financial aid packages are made on a first-come, first-served basis and are announced in mid-March.

Faculty

Behind every program at Loyola is a faculty of Jesuit and lay professors who are especially well qualified in their particular fields. The Jesuit Order, recognized throughout the world for its educational contributions over the centuries, administers the University's faculty of 277 full-time professors, of whom 91 percent hold the terminal degree in their field. Loyola also employs 160 part-time instructors. No graduate assistants teach classes. The student-faculty ratio of 13:1 emphasizes the University's special quality of personal involvement and concern for each student and his or her particular needs.

Student Government

Loyola's Student Government Association consists of representatives elected by the student body from each of the four colleges and the law school. The association conducts general meetings, elections, and student activities. Student representatives sit on nearly all University committees.

Admission Requirements

Prospective students must submit an application, resume, and essay; have a high school transcript or GED test results sent; submit ACT or SAT I scores; and have their counselor or teacher send a recommendation. Individual attention is given to each application form. Final selection is based on high school grades, test scores, and counselor or teacher recommendations. Significant community involvement and demonstrated leadership abilities are recommended. Auditions are required for final acceptance to the College of Music and the Department of Drama and Speech. Portfolios are required for final acceptance to the Department of Visual Arts.

December 1 is the priority deadline for freshman admission and scholarship consideration. January 15 is the regular deadline for freshman scholarship consideration. February 15 is the regular deadline for freshman admission consideration.

Transfer students are required to submit an official transcript for each institution previously attended along with their transfer application. Transfer scholarships are available only to students entering in the fall. Transfer students interested in competing for a scholarship should apply by March 1 if possible, and no later than April 15. For nonscholarship admission consideration, transfer students should apply no later than May 15 for the fall semester and no later than December 1 for the spring semester.

Application and Information

Interested students are encouraged to contact:

Office of Admissions
Loyola University
6363 St. Charles Avenue, Box 18
New Orleans, Louisiana 70118
Telephone: 504-865-3240
800-4-LOYOLA (toll-free)
Fax: 504-865-3383
E-mail: admit@loyno.edu
World Wide Web: http://www.loyno.edu

Loyola is located on beautiful, oak-lined St. Charles Avenue adjacent to Audubon Park.

LUTHER COLLEGE

DECORAH, IOWA

The College

Luther College, founded in 1861, is a four-year residential liberal arts college of the Evangelical Lutheran Church in America. The College, which was founded by Norwegian immigrants, is an academic community of faith and learning where students of promise from all beliefs and backgrounds have the freedom to learn, to express themselves, to perform, to compete, and to grow. The College, located in Decorah, Iowa, is home to 2,575 students from thirty-five states and thirty-seven countries. Thirty-six percent of the students are from Iowa; 86 percent come from the four-state area of Iowa, Minnesota, Wisconsin, and Illinois. Each year, approximately 130 international students choose to study at Luther.

In keeping with its liberal arts tradition, the College requires students to develop a depth of knowledge in their chosen major and a breadth of knowledge through exposure to a wide range of subjects and intellectual approaches (general requirements). Learning at Luther is about engagement: faculty members who are passionate in their teaching and scholarship, students who are active and involved, and a College community characterized by personal attention, hands-on experiences, academic challenge, and community support. At Luther, all students become immersed in the liberal arts through the College's common yearlong course for first-year students called Paideia. The course, which is uncommon in its approach, helps train students' minds and develop their research and writing skills as they explore human cultures and history. In addition, Luther offers a Phi Beta Kappa chapter and several departmental honor societies, evidence of the quality of teaching and learning on campus.

At Luther, students are encouraged to seek out connections between their lives in the classroom and their lives outside the classroom. The College provides a stimulating cultural and educational atmosphere by bringing distinguished public figures, theater groups, musicians, and educators to the campus. Cocurricular activities are an important part of College life. The College sponsors seven choirs, three orchestras, three bands, three jazz bands, and a full theater and dance program. Numerous student organizations and societies provide ample opportunities for student involvement in meaningful activities. As a community of faith, students can participate in daily chapel, weekly Sunday worship, outreach teams, and midweek Eucharist.

Nineteen intercollegiate sports are offered. Men may participate in ten sports: baseball, basketball, cross-country, football, golf, soccer, swimming, tennis, track and field, and wrestling. Women compete in nine intercollegiate sports: basketball, cross-country, golf, soccer, softball, swimming, tennis, track and field, and volleyball. Club sports include rugby and men's volleyball. Sixty-four percent of the student body is involved in an extensive intramural and recreational sports program. Available for recreational use and for the physical education program are nine outdoor tennis courts, an eight-lane polyurethane 400-meter track, numerous cross-country running and ski trails, and 15 acres of intramural fields. The well-equipped field house contains a 25-yard indoor pool, three racquetball courts, four hardwood basketball courts, a wrestling room, a dance studio, and a 3,000-seat gymnasium. A sports forum houses a six-lane, 200-meter indoor track; six indoor tennis courts; locker rooms; and athletic training facilities. The new Legends Fitness for Life Center provides the latest fitness equipment and a 30-foot-high rock climbing wall.

Location

The College is located in Decorah, a city of 8,500 people in the scenic bluff country of northeast Iowa. The Upper Iowa River, which runs through the campus, is designated as a National Scenic and Recreational River. Rich in Scandinavian heritage, Decorah is a popular recreation area, providing opportunities for canoeing, fishing, hunting, cross-country skiing, camping, hiking, cycling, and spelunking. Three airports are located within a 75-mile radius of Decorah: in Rochester, Minnesota; Waterloo, Iowa; and La Crosse, Wisconsin.

Majors and Degrees

Luther College grants the Bachelor of Arts (B.A.) degree and offers majors in accounting, Africana studies, anthropology, art, biblical languages, biology, business, chemistry, classical languages (Greek and Latin), classical studies, communication/linguistics, computer science, economics, elementary education, English, health, history, management, management information systems, mathematics, mathematics/statistics, modern languages (French, German, Norwegian, and Spanish), music, nursing, philosophy, physical education, physics, political science, psychobiology, psychology, religion, Scandinavian studies, social work, sociology, sociology/political science, speech and theater, and theater/dance. Interdisciplinary programs are available in arts management, international management, museum studies, Russian studies, Scandinavian studies, and sports management. Preprofessional preparation is offered in cytotechnology, dentistry, engineering, environmental management, forestry, law, medical technology, medicine, music therapy, optometry, physical therapy, theology, and veterinary medicine.

Academic Program

Luther operates on a 4-1-4 academic calendar. The first semester runs from September to December, followed by a three-week January Term and the second semester, which runs from February to May. Two four-week summer sessions are offered in June and July. Each candidate is required to complete a total of 128 semester hours of credit with a C average or better. At least 76 of the required 128 semester hours must be earned outside the major discipline. Each senior writes a research paper in his or her major. Students are required to complete the following number of semester hours of credit in designated areas: 12 of Paideia, an interdisciplinary course; 9–12 of religion/philosophy; 7–8 of natural science; 6–8 of social science; 3–9 of foreign language (proficiency based); 3–4 of fine arts; 3–4 of global studies; 3–4 of quantitative or symbolic reasoning; and 2 of physical education. Advanced placement and credit by examination are available. A qualified student may develop an interdisciplinary major with a faculty adviser.

Off-Campus Programs

Students may participate in off-campus programs during the fall and spring semesters, the January Term, and summer sessions. All of the programs carry academic credit. Luther participates in the Iowa General Assembly Legislative Intern Program during the spring semester of each year. Urban studies semesters may be arranged in conjunction with other colleges. The Washington Semester gives qualified juniors the opportunity to study at American University and work within one department of the federal government. Luther College also cosponsors a semester program in Washington, D.C., through the Lutheran College Washington Consortium. Students may elect to be exchange students at other colleges for one semester or a January Term.

Luther is an affiliate of the Institute of European Studies, which has centers in over twenty European and Asian countries; students studying at one of these centers receive credit in accordance with the provisions for transfer credit for study abroad under the Junior Year Abroad programs. A community studies program in Nottingham, England, is staffed by a Luther professor each year. In alternate years, a Luther professor directs on-site programs in Münster, Germany; Lillehammer, Norway; and in Sliema, Malta. In addition, opportunities for study are available in a variety of settings such as the Bahamas, China, Russia, Tanzania, and Norway.

Academic Facilities

The 800-acre campus includes the Preus Library, housing 350,000 volumes, 1,100 periodicals, and the College art collection. The library offers five online indexes and ten commercial online services and provides access to more than 480 other libraries. Modern, well-equipped laboratories in the Valders Hall of Science are supplemented by several other science-teaching facilities on campus: a planetarium, a greenhouse, an herbarium, a live-animal center, a human anatomy laboratory, a natural history museum, and a psychology sleep laboratory. The science facilities also include an extensive field study area and two electron microscopes. Within easy walking distance of the campus, the field study area offers an ideal setting for studies in aquatic biology, ecology, and field biology. Five ponds, two reestablished prairies, marshes, wooded areas, and agricultural lands are available for classwork and independent study. The College has a fiber-based campus network connecting a variety of PC and Macintosh computers (in several environments) to shared computing resources and to the Internet. More than 400 microcomputers and terminals are available for student use throughout the campus.

Luther College maintains radio station KWLC-AM, and the College's affiliate station, KLSE-FM, is part of the Minnesota Public Radio network. Luther also maintains the largest archaeological research center in Iowa. The Norwegian American Museum in Decorah, one of the finest ethnic museums in the country, provides an invaluable resource for museum and Scandinavian studies. The foreign language departments maintain a twenty-five-station electronic classroom, and the psychology department houses a twenty-station IBM interactive computer network.

The impressive F. W. Olin Building houses the economics and business, mathematics, and computer science departments. Among its technological wonders is the Luther Round Table Room, where students experience simultaneous decision making via a computer network.

The award-winning Jenson Hall of Music contains state-of-the-art computer facilities, a recording studio, and four pipe organs: 23-stop/34-rank and 42-stop/61-rank tracker organs for practice and performing and two Schlicker practice organs of 8 and 5 ranks, respectively. Jenson Hall of Music also contains 32,000 square feet of classrooms, studios, practice rooms, and rehearsal rooms for keyboard, vocal, and instrumental music. The Center for Faith and Life (CFL) houses a 42-stop/62-rank organ in the 1,600-seat auditorium for the performing arts. The CFL also houses the offices of the campus ministry, a 24-hour meditation chapel, a 200-seat recital hall, and one of four campus art galleries.

A new Center for the Arts, completed in 2002, serves as the home for theater, dance, and the arts.

Costs

For 2003–04, the comprehensive fee was $25,700, which includes tuition, general fees, facilities fees, room, board, subscription to student publications, and admission to College-supported concerts, lectures, and other events. A room telephone, cable TV, computer access from residence hall rooms, and a health-service program are also included. Private music lessons are $200 per semester. Luther estimates that an additional $2000 is adequate for books, clothing, entertainment, and other personal expenses.

Financial Aid

More than 97 percent of all Luther students receive financial aid in the form of grants, such as the Federal Pell Grant; scholarships from Luther and other sources; loans; and jobs on campus. Luther awards Regent and Presidential Scholarships to those demonstrating superior academic achievement. The amount of aid given is determined by the College's analysis of the Free Application for Federal Student Aid (FAFSA). The priority deadline for a financial aid application is March 1. Students receive notification of financial aid awards after their acceptance for admission.

Faculty

There are 191 full-time and 50 part-time faculty members; 74 percent hold a Ph.D., and an additional 8 percent hold other terminal degrees. The ratio of students to faculty is 13:1.

Student Government

Students share in the governance of the College and participate in social and cultural programming. They have full membership on most College committees, majority representation in the Community Assembly, and nonvoting representation on the Board of Regents.

Admission Requirements

Admission is selective. An applicant must be a graduate of an accredited high school and have completed at least 4 units of English, 3 units of mathematics, 3 units of social science, and 2 units of natural science. It is strongly recommended that the applicant have at least two years of a foreign language. Seventy percent of entering students rank in the top quarter of their high school class. Transfer students may enroll in either semester. Early admission and admission with honors are available. The priority deadline is March 1.

Application and Information

An application, SAT I or ACT scores, an educator's reference, a transcript of previous academic work, and a $25 application fee are required for admission. On-campus interviews are recommended but not required. For more information about Luther, students should contact:

Admissions Office
Luther College
Decorah, Iowa 52101-1042
Telephone: 563-387-1287
800-458-8437 (toll-free)
Fax: 563-387-2159
563-387-1062 (international)
E-mail: admissions@luther.edu (admissions)
lutherfa@luther.edu (financial planning)
intladmissions@luther.edu (international)
World Wide Web: http://www.luther.edu

Luther College's spacious 800-acre campus in the scenic bluff country of northeast Iowa.

LYNCHBURG COLLEGE

LYNCHBURG, VIRGINIA

The College

Lynchburg College is a fully accredited, coeducational, nonsectarian liberal arts college related to the Christian Church (Disciples of Christ). It offers undergraduate programs in the liberal arts, sciences, and professional disciplines (including business, communications, education, and nursing) and graduate programs in business and education. The College is committed to the principle that every individual is of infinite worth, and it endeavors to provide a program of liberal education consistent with the needs of contemporary society. It draws its undergraduate student body of 1,773 men and women from thirty-nine states and seventeen countries. The College community is largely residential, with approximately 67 percent of the full-time undergraduate student body living on campus. Approximately 45 percent of the undergraduates are from out of state.

The 214-acre campus has long been considered one of the most beautiful in the South. Thirty-two buildings of mostly Georgian Colonial design have the majestic Blue Ridge Mountains as a backdrop. The Claytor Nature Student Center, a 470-acre farm in nearby Bedford County, is utilized for environmental and educational purposes as a learning laboratory to promote the property as a model of environmental management in cooperation with various organizations locally and nationally.

A wide variety of activities are available in the Lynchburg College community: service and honor organizations, nearly seventy clubs, five fraternities, and five sororities as well as opportunities to participate in dramatic productions, student publications, religious activities, and musical performances. New Horizons provides adventure-based leadership and team-building opportunities for individuals and groups. Community service is a distinguishing feature of the Lynchburg College students, who annually contribute more than 20,000 volunteer hours to the community through such projects as Habitat for Humanity, Camp Jaycees, Special Olympics, and other programs.

The varsity athletics program is diverse and includes baseball, basketball, cross-country, equestrian sports, golf, indoor and outdoor track and field, lacrosse, soccer, and tennis for men and basketball, cross-country, equestrian sports, field hockey, lacrosse, soccer, softball, tennis, track, and volleyball for women. In addition, an intramural program exists for interested men and women. In 2001 and 2002, the College won the Commissioner's Cup for having the best athletic program in its conference. The Turner Athletic Facility has received a multimillion-dollar renovation that includes state-of-the-art exercise and fitness areas, a dance studio, and one of the top exercise physiology labs in Virginia. The gymnasium seats 1,500. The College participates in NCAA Division III and is a charter member of the Old Dominion Athletic Conference, which includes Bridgewater, Eastern Mennonite, Emory & Henry, Guilford, Hampden-Sydney, Hollins, Lynchburg, Randolph-Macon, Randolph-Macon Woman's, Roanoke, Sweet Briar, Virginia Wesleyan, and Washington and Lee.

Location

Lynchburg College is located in central Virginia, 100 miles from Richmond, 180 miles southwest of Washington, D.C., and 50 miles east of Roanoke. Greater Lynchburg is a growing business and industrial center with a population of more than 220,000. The city is noted for its climate, culture, and historic landmarks. It is within an easy drive of the Blue Ridge Mountains, where many popular lakes and resorts are located. Air, bus, and railroad transportation place Lynchburg within easy reach of any urban center.

Majors and Degrees

Lynchburg College offers the Bachelor of Arts in the following fields: accounting, art (graphic design or studio art), business administration, communication studies (journalism or speech communication), economics (financial or general), English (literature or writing), French, history, international relations, management, marketing, music, philosophy, political science, religious studies, sociology (criminology or general), Spanish, sports management, and theater. The degree of Bachelor of Science is offered in the following fields: applied physical science, athletic training, biology, biomedical science, chemistry (professional or technical), computer science, environmental science, exercise physiology, health and movement science, health promotion, human development and learning (elementary education or special education), mathematics, nursing, and psychology.

A candidate for a B.A. degree may elect to take a joint major in foreign language–business management, philosophy–political science, philosophy–religious studies, psychology–special education, religious studies–sociology, or religious studies and another major. Double majors and minors may also be taken in many areas of study. Advanced undergraduates may also take some graduate courses.

Preprofessional and professional courses are available for students who want preparation for careers in art therapy, dentistry, forestry and wildlife management, law, library science, medicine, the ministry and ministry-related occupations, occupational therapy, optometry, pharmacy, physical therapy, teaching, and veterinary medicine.

Academic Program

To be eligible for a degree, a student must complete at least 124 semester hours of college-level academic work. In addition, a degree candidate must have a grade point average of at least 2.0 on all work undertaken, plus an average of at least 2.0 on all work undertaken in the major field.

The curriculum at Lynchburg College is divided into two general areas; some additional hours are available for students to explore course work in free elective areas of their choice. The first of the two areas of study consists of General Education Requirements (GERs) selected from the broad disciplines of world literature, fine arts, philosophy, religious studies, mathematics, history, social science, laboratory science, foreign languages, and health and movement science. All students are exposed to each of these academic areas. The second of the two general areas is the major. The College offers thirty-eight majors, ranging from education and business to the sciences and the humanities, as well as thirteen preprofessional programs. This curriculum offers students breadth (GERs) as well as depth (the major). Students may devote their free elective hours to one of thirty-nine minor programs to further enhance their education.

Outstanding students may be selected to participate in the College's Westover Honors Program, the purpose of which is to attract, stimulate, challenge, and fulfill academically gifted students. The program offers a challenging curriculum that promotes intellectual curiosity and independent thinking and places strong emphasis on creative problem solving.

The College operates on an early semester calendar. The first semester begins in late August and ends before Christmas, and the second semester runs from mid-January to early May. An optional three-week winter term is also offered. An Advanced Placement Scholars Program permits some students to enter with advanced standing, credit, or both. Credit is also awarded on the basis of satisfactory scores on the CLEP subject exams. Early admission is available for the talented student. Eligible students who want to accelerate their program may meet degree requirements in three years.

Lynchburg offers entry-level computer courses to all students, and students are strongly encouraged to become computer literate. New students may bring a computer of their own or utilize one of the many available on campus. All students are assigned an e-mail account and have access to the Internet. In addition, all students are allowed to develop their own home pages on the World Wide Web, which they have access to through the computer resources provided by the College. All residence hall rooms are wired for network access and the Intranet, which serves the College community.

Off-Campus Programs

Various agency and intercollege exchange programs are available for interested students. Language students may engage in foreign-study programs and are encouraged to do so. In addition, any student who wishes to study abroad may do so as part of the College's study-abroad program.

Internships, organized through the Career Development Center, are available locally, nationally, and internationally. More than 800 internships are already established, and new sites are developed each year. Cooperative programs exist for some departments, such as political science, where full credit is granted for study at another institution. Specific guidelines for these programs are set forth by each department. In addition, Lynchburg College, Randolph-Macon Woman's College, and Sweet Briar College, as members of the Tri-College Consortium of Virginia, maintain cooperative relationships for the sharing of facilities and offerings. Students at each of the colleges have access to the libraries of the other two and may enroll in a course on either of the other campuses without payment of additional tuition.

Academic Facilities

As a result of a $6.1-million renovation and expansion, the Hobbs Science Center provides an outstanding learning environment for students pursuing studies in biology, chemistry, physics, biomedical sciences, environmental science, psychology, mathematics, and computer science. In addition to state-of-the-art research labs, including a cadaver lab, students studying environmental science can utilize the online weather station, GIS and remote sensing software, and digitizer. This modern facility is also used during the summer by the Virginia Governor's School for Math and Science to provide programming for selected high school students. Extending over 470 acres, the Claytor Nature Study Center is a hands-on learning environment with natural woodlands, grasslands, two lakes, wetlands, and a mile-long stretch of the Big Otter River, and an 8,000-square-foot education/research facility.

Scheduled to open in 2004, the $12-million Centennial Hall is designed to house the business and communication studies programs. This 67,000-square-foot facility includes a 250-seat auditorium and performance stage, technology-based classrooms, computer laboratories, and specialized teaching-learning settings, including a model stock exchange room, a digital darkroom, and a multimedia development center with television and recording studios.

The Daura Art Gallery is the major repository of more than 1,000 works of the Catalan-American artist, Pierre Daura. The expansion of this facility makes the Daura Gallery the largest visual art exhibit center in the city of Lynchburg. Each year, it is the site for the Senior Art Show in which chosen student works are exhibited.

Costs

For resident students who entered in the 2003–04 session, total charges were $26,195; this included $21,270 for tuition, $4800 for room and board, and $125 for a student activity fee.

Financial Aid

Lynchburg College administers a financial aid program of more than $20 million. These resources are awarded to students as a result of meritorious achievement and/or demonstrated need. Lynchburg College offers academic and achievement scholarships that range from $3000 to $12,000 and are based on performance and accomplishments at the high school or community college level. These awards are renewable each year until the student graduates, as long as the recipient maintains a qualifying minimum academic average each year. Students are identified to receive these scholarships through the admission application; no separate application is necessary. Free early aid estimates are available for students.

To determine eligibility for need-based financial aid, the student should complete the Free Application for Federal Student Aid (FAFSA), which may be obtained at most high schools and at Lynchburg College. The FAFSA results determine the student's eligibility for federally funded grants and loans and other support such as work-study opportunities. In addition, students from Virginia are eligible to apply for the Virginia Tuition Assistance grant.

Faculty

The Lynchburg College faculty has 124 full-time members, 81 percent of whom hold the doctorate or terminal degree in their field, and 46 part-time members. The student-faculty ratio is 13:1. While many faculty members are involved in research projects, it is a College policy that the faculty's top priorities must be in the classroom. Dr. Patty Hale, professor of nursing, is one of 4 national winners of the U.S. Professors of the Year Awards from the Council of Advancement and Support of Education (CASE) and the Carnegie Foundation for the Advancement of Teaching. The U.S. Professors of the Year Awards are the only national honors designed to recognize excellence in undergraduate teaching and mentoring.

Student Government

The student government of Lynchburg College is regulated by agreements determined by the students, faculty, and administration. It is felt that the College should not be run by the faculty alone, nor by students alone, but through the cooperative interest of all. Campus government is vested in the Student Government Association, the Judicial Boards, the Campus Life Policies Committee, and the Office of the Dean of Student Development. The Student Government Association is also responsible for the Academic Honor Code, a prominent part of campus life.

Admission Requirements

A candidate for admission to Lynchburg College should be a graduate of an approved secondary school with a minimum of 16 academic units or the equivalent, as shown by examination. It is strongly recommended that the academic work include major emphases in the areas of English, foreign language, social science, natural sciences, and mathematics. An applicant must demonstrate above-average academic ability in all areas of study, as admission is competitive. In support of the record, a student must present satisfactory scores on the SAT I or ACT. It is strongly recommended that all students have a personal interview and visit the campus before their first semester at Lynchburg College. Enrollment Office hours during the academic year are 9 a.m. to 5 p.m., Monday through Friday, and 9 a.m. to noon on Saturday.

Application and Information

Early decision admission applications must be received by November 15; notification of acceptance is made by December 15. All other applications are processed on a rolling admissions basis. Applicants are notified of the status of their application usually within two weeks of the date their application file is completed.

For information, students should contact:

Sharon Walters-Bower, Director of Admissions
Lynchburg College
1501 Lakeside Drive
Lynchburg, Virginia 24501
Telephone: 434-544-8300
800-426-8101 (toll-free)
Fax: 434-544-8653
E-mail: admissions@lynchburg.edu
World Wide Web: http://www.lynchburg.edu

LYNDON STATE COLLEGE

LYNDONVILLE, VERMONT

The College

Lyndon State College (LSC) was established in 1911 as a one-room teacher-training college. Lyndon has grown to a fully accredited, comprehensive four-year college, serving more than 1,400 students in liberal arts and preprofessional programs. Fifty-five percent of the 1,400 students at Lyndon are Vermonters; the remainder of the student population is from New England and states throughout the U.S. The 174-acre campus is located in Lyndonville, Vermont, the heart of the Northeast Kingdom; few campuses in the country can match the sheer beauty of Lyndon State's location.

Lyndon provides two- and four-year degree programs that prepare students for a wide variety of careers and graduate study. The hallmark of a Lyndon education is experience. Lyndon's dedicated faculty members have developed programs that offer a unique blend of experiential, hands-on learning with the traditionally structured lecture/discussion courses to give students optimum career preparation. New students participate in the First-Year Experience, a one- or two-day fieldtrip that serves as an introduction to their major. The students are accompanied by faculty members and upperclassmen from their major and visit sites related to their major. This trip is the students' first of many hands-on, real-life experiences. First-year students may also apply to the College's new Honors Program.

LSC is accredited by the New England Association of Schools and Colleges. Lyndon's three degree programs in recreation and ski resort management are accredited by the National Recreation and Park Association.

There are seven major residences halls, with an eighth opening in fall 2005. Together, the residence halls accommodate more than 550 students. Each residence hall room is equipped with Internet connections, giving each student access to the Web, e-mail, and the Vermont State College network through his or her own personal computer. Also, each room is equipped with cable TV connections and telephone lines. Students who live on campus eat at the Stevens Dining Hall and the Hornet's Nest Snack Bar. All students are allowed to have vehicles on campus.

The dedicated staff provides endless, high-quality support to students. Lyndon's Academic Support Center, Career Planning and Placement Office, Student Activities, and Health Services are a few of the key offices that serve the needs and promote the well-being of students.

More than twenty-five clubs and organizations provide a wide variety of student activities that include the campus radio station (91.5 FM The Impulse), the student newspaper (*The Critic*), sports clubs, and numerous social and academic clubs. Lyndon State is a member of the Sunrise Conference of NAIA Division II. There are ten intercollegiate sports. Men compete in baseball, basketball, cross-country, soccer, and tennis; women compete in basketball, cross-country, soccer, softball, and tennis. Intercollege competitive hockey and rugby for men and women are club teams. Lyndon's intramural program attracts the majority of the student body. Lyndon also has a new 6,700-square-foot fitness center, which is available to students and faculty and staff members.

Location

Lyndon State College is situated high on a hillside overlooking magnificent Burke Mountain and the picturesque Passumpsic Valley in the heart of Vermont's scenic Northeast Kingdom. It is located 1 mile west of Lyndonville and 9 miles north of St. Johnsbury and is easily accessible from all points by Interstate 91. The College is a 3-hour drive from Boston and Springfield, Massachusetts, and 2 hours from Montreal.

Facilities for such recreational sports as Alpine and cross-country skiing, hiking, fishing, and swimming are available within minutes of the College.

Majors and Degrees

Lyndon State College offers the Bachelor of Arts (B.A.) or Bachelor of Science (B.S.) degree in interdisciplinary studies (an individually designed program). The Bachelor of Arts degree is offered in digital media, English (literature and cultural studies, journalism and writing, and secondary education), graphic design, liberal studies, mathematics (applied mathematics, pure mathematics, secondary education 7–12), psychology, and social sciences (history, interdisciplinary, philosophy, political science, secondary education, and sociology). The Bachelor of Science degree is offered in allied health sciences (athletic training (4+2), health science, physical education, physical therapy (3+3), and sports management), business administration (accounting, business administration and information technology, and small business management and entrepreneurship), computer information systems (business and meteorology), education (early childhood education, elementary education, middle grades, reading teacher, secondary education, and special education), environmental science, human services, meteorology, natural science (natural science and secondary education 7–12), recreation resource and ski resort management (adventure-based program planning/outdoor education, natural resources/GIS mapping and planning, ski resort management), and television studies (broadcast news and broadcast design and production). The Associate of Science degree is offered in business administration, computer science, design and graphic communications, digital media, natural resource/GIS mapping and planning, nursing (offered jointly with Castleton State College to students employed in the state of Vermont), television production, and television studies. The Associate of Arts degree is available in general studies.

Academic Program

Lyndon operates on a two-semester calendar and a six-week summer-session schedule. To graduate with a bachelor's degree, a student must complete 122 semester hours of credit and meet College and program requirements. Sixty-two semester hours are required for an associate degree. Each student is tested for competence in writing and mathematics at entry to the College; any deficiencies noted must be made up in noncredit classes during the first two semesters. The College has a general education (distribution) requirement of 42 semester hours.

For two-year programs, students are accepted into a concentration upon admission; for four-year programs, in the fourth semester. Academic departments are responsible for advising and for planning the student's core courses within the concentration. In bachelor's degree programs, most concentrations require at least 42 credits of junior- and senior-level course work. The College requires that 30 of the last 39 hours toward any degree be spent in residence. Leaves of absence are granted to students in good academic standing.

Lyndon recognizes learning acquired from previous experience through an assessment course that documents nontraditional learning. The College offers fieldwork and practicums in most academic programs through the Cooperative Education Office.

Off-Campus Programs

A key component of a Lyndon State education is the variety of opportunities for off-campus study for credit, on either a full-time or part-time basis. Students can apply professional theories and principles through full-time cooperative education internships in behavioral sciences, business, design and graphic communications, education, environmental science, health sciences, interactive digital media, meteorology, nursing, physical education, psychology, recreation, social science, and television production or technical support programs. Students in elementary education participate in a sophomore-year exploratory field experience (a full semester of work blending on-campus study and off-campus experience), a junior-year field experience (two half-days a week), and a full semester of student teaching. Students majoring in psychology or human services complete required fieldwork related to their particular studies at least twice during their upperclass years.

Lyndon grants credit for study in other countries through an approved program such as the Experiment in International Living or the American Institute for Foreign Study.

Academic Facilities

Lyndon State College's exciting Academic Center—located atop the Samuel Read Hall Library—features state-of-the-art academic and computer classrooms and laboratories, including a fully equipped computer laboratory that is linked to the College's expanding computer information network.

The library maintains a collection of more than 100,000 circulating volumes as well as periodicals, audio and video materials, and microfiche collections. The library also participates in the Inter-Library Loan System, which allows students more extensive access to reference materials. The library's electronic catalog allows access to the collections of many other Vermont colleges, the Vermont Department of Libraries, and the University of Vermont. The language and science laboratories, the computer center and laboratories, and the music rooms are available to students for study, experimentation, and practice.

The state-of-the-art meteorology laboratory, staffed by a technician, prepares weather information and forecast information that is broadcast over Vermont radio and television stations. Meteorology students also operate a 24-hour weather-reporting telephone line.

Operated daily by students, LSCTV/News 7 is a noncommercial, public-service television facility that provides local news and educational, cultural, and public-service programs. Radio station WWLR-FM is staffed by student volunteers who provide local communities with programs of news, music, and interviews.

Costs

The 2003–04 tuition for Vermont residents was $5646 per year; for nonresidents, it was $12,200. Room and board (twenty-one-meal plan) for one academic year were $6014. Required College fees, including health and accident insurance, totaled $856. Total expenses for a Vermont resident living on campus were $12,646; for a nonresident, $19,200. Miscellaneous expenses were estimated at $1100. The estimate for these expenses is included in the financial aid budget.

Financial Aid

Financial aid is available in the form of loans, grants, and campus employment under the Federal Work-Study Program. Approximately 80 percent of the student population receives some type of financial aid from institutional and outside sources. Approximately 35 percent of the students are employed by either the Federal Work-Study Program or the College dining hall.

Applicants for aid are required to complete the Free Application for Federal Student Aid (FAFSA). In addition to filing the FAFSA, transfer students are required to have a financial aid transcript completed by the financial aid officer of each college they attended. For a student to be considered an on-time applicant, the FAFSA should be filed in early February in order to reach the College's Financial Aid Office by the March 15 deadline.

Faculty

Lyndon's excellent faculty consists of 57 full-time members and 76 part-time members. The student-faculty ratio is 17:1. The faculty is dedicated fully to undergraduate teaching. Full-time faculty members serve as academic advisers to students and as advisers to student organizations. Student evaluation of teaching is a formal process and is used in personnel decisions. Faculty members participate in dramatic, musical, and intramural athletic activities on campus and in many civic and community organizations.

Student Government

Students play an important role in Lyndon's internal organization. Students actively represent Lyndon on the Vermont State Colleges' Board of Trustees, in the Vermont State Colleges' Student Association, and on many campus committees.

The Student Senate heads the student organizations. It has jurisdiction over all student affairs and is responsible for addressing student issues and concerns, evaluating all campus clubs and organizations, and allocating Student Activities moneys.

Admission Requirements

Each application for admission is evaluated on its individual merits. Applicants for admission are expected to successfully complete a college-preparatory program and rank in at least the upper 50 percent of their graduating class. Recommended secondary school preparation includes 4 years of English and 2 to 3 years each of mathematics, science, and history. Admission decisions for first-year students are determined on the basis of the student's application, a copy of the secondary school transcript, the recommendation of the secondary school principal or guidance counselor, performance on the ACT or the SAT I, and, if possible, a personal interview. Although applicants' scores on the ACT or the SAT I are reviewed, more emphasis is placed on transcripts, class rank, and recommendations than on test scores.

Applicants who have completed examinations taken through the College Board's Advanced Placement Program with a grade of 3 or higher are granted both advanced placement and course credit after evaluation by the academic dean and appropriate department chairpersons. Advanced standing is awarded for successful performance on the tests of the College-Level Examination Program. Lyndon grants up to 60 college credits for scores above the 40th percentile on the five general examinations in English composition, humanities, mathematics, natural science, and social science/history and for scores at or above the minimum score established by the College Board for a wide variety of subject examinations.

Transfer students are encouraged to apply. A minimum 2.0 cumulative grade point average is recommended for consideration. Admission requirements for transfer students are the same as those for freshman applicants, but an official transcript must also be obtained from each college-level institution that the applicant has attended. Transcripts are required even if no credit is being transferred from a particular institution. Transfer credit may be given at Lyndon for courses completed with the equivalent of a grade of C or better at accredited or officially approved institutions.

The College may permit candidates to defer their enrollment for a period of two semesters.

Application and Information

A nonrefundable $32 fee must accompany each application. Lyndon uses a rolling admission system, and applicants may apply and be accepted throughout the year. All applications are given prompt attention, and applicants may expect a decision within two weeks of the date the application process has been completed.

For further information, students should contact:

Assistant Dean for Admissions
P.O. Box 919
Lyndon State College
Lyndonville, Vermont 05851
Telephone: 802-626-6413
800-225-1998 (toll-free in New England)
Fax: 802-626-6335
E-mail: admissions@lyndonstate.edu
World Wide Web: http://www.lyndonstate.edu

LYNN UNIVERSITY

BOCA RATON, FLORIDA

The University

Founded in 1962, Lynn University is a private, coeducational institution located in Boca Raton, Florida. The University, small by design, provides an environment within and outside the classroom in which a community of learners can pursue academic excellence. Faculty and staff members and students contribute to an atmosphere that nurtures creativity, fosters achievement, and values diversity.

Accredited in 1967 by the Southern Association of Colleges and Schools, Lynn University has steadily grown to become a comprehensive university offering undergraduate and graduate programs. The University's five colleges offer twenty-six majors. Lynn leads the country in offering majors in many of the world's fastest-growing professions, thus preparing its students to meet the career demands of the twenty-first century. The 2,100 students who are currently enrolled come from forty-six states and ninety-three nations.

Lynn is a residential institution with five air-conditioned residence halls that house 55 percent of the undergraduates. The residence halls include study lounges, computers, and recreation areas as well as health and fitness facilities that offer free weights, exercise machines, and cardiovascular equipment. The Lynn Student Center, the "living room" of the University, houses the dining room and the auditorium. Students study or relax outside on the patio or on comfortable sofas in the lounge. Also in the student center is the Knights' Court, a popular snacking spot for students and faculty and staff members. Laundry facilities, mailboxes, the University bookstore, and a variety of athletics facilities are all located on the campus.

University life is designed to provide a learning situation through which students are guided toward responsible decision-making and leadership. An extensive program of activities complements the academic program at Lynn, ensuring the development of the whole person. Students may choose from a variety of campus organizations and activities, including student government, the newspaper or yearbook, cocurricular clubs, leadership groups such as the Knights of the Roundtable, and fraternities or sororities. Lynn University holds membership in the National Collegiate Athletic Association (NCAA) Division II and the Sunshine State Conference. Lynn has won sixteen national championship titles in sixteen years in many sports. The intercollegiate athletic program includes men's and women's basketball, golf, rowing, soccer, and tennis; men's baseball; and women's softball and volleyball. An even wider range of athletic opportunities is available for students through the intramural athletic program.

Location

The University is located in Boca Raton, one of the most vibrant communities in the state of Florida. Its location provides a wide variety of cultural and recreational opportunities to students. Boca Raton is a progressive community with tremendous economic potential and is quickly becoming one of the nation's leading centers of commerce. Facilities of IBM, Siemens, Sony, Pratt and Whitney, Motorola, Sensormatic, and other companies are located just a few miles from the University, providing excellent opportunities for internships and for employment after graduation. The picturesque 123-acre campus is positioned 3 miles from the Atlantic Ocean and 2 miles from the heart of Boca Raton. The campus is set among freshwater lakes, palms, and lush tropical foliage, providing the peace and quiet needed to concentrate on academics. In addition, the cities of Fort Lauderdale, Palm Beach, and Miami are all less than a 50-minute drive away.

Majors and Degrees

The College of Arts and Sciences offers degrees in international relations with specializations in international business, international communications, and Asian, European, or Latin American affairs; in behavioral science; in criminal justice; and in English. It also offers a B.S.D. in graphic design, liberal arts, psychology, and visual design and a B.S. in biology. The College of Business and Management provides business administration degrees with specialization options in aviation management (flight and nonflight options), general management, fashion management, human resource management, international business, managerial electronic business, and marketing. The College of Hospitality Management offers programs in hospitality administration with specializations in hotel management; hotel, resort, and food service management; international golf management; international hotel and tourism management; and sports and recreation management. The College of International Communications offers B.S. degrees with specializations in broadcasting, film studies, international communications, and journalism. The college, established in 1996, has as its dean Mr. Irving R. Levine, the renowned NBC News Chief Economics Correspondent. Community service educational experiences, symposia, workshops, lectures by visiting scholars, and international internship opportunities are also offered within the degree. The Donald E. and Helen L. Ross College of Education and Human Services offers elementary and secondary education and human services. In addition, through the renowned Conservatory of Music, bachelor's degrees in music are available with specializations in bass, bassoon, cello, clarinet, double bass, flute, French horn, oboe, percussion, piano, trombone, trumpet, tuba, viola, and violin.

Academic Program

The University is committed to student-centered learning, where faculty and staff members provide personalized attention to students who have varying levels of academic proficiency and a motivation to excel. A full range of academic and support programs is coordinated to serve the increasingly diverse needs of all students. These are enhanced by the favorable 16:1 student-faculty ratio.

The First Year Experience is the cornerstone to freshman advising at Lynn and provides an introduction to college life for all first-year students. The course includes academic success strategies, time management, communication skills, study and test-taking techniques, academic advisement, and career development. The course is taught by select members of the faculty and staff, who serve as mentors to new students throughout their freshman year.

The Honors Program strives to create a dynamic academic environment that serves to heighten intellectual curiosity, promote free and active inquiry, and stimulate creative discovery among students with particularly strong academic promise. The innovative curriculum, team-taught by faculty members, encompasses the full breadth of the liberal arts and sciences while promoting both an in-depth exploration and a broad intellectual synthesis of the ideas and concepts that have shaped the dilemmas and choices of the past, present, and future.

The Probationary Support Program provides a smooth transition to college life for incoming students. Specialized assistance and support enable students to be successful in the first and most critical semester of their college careers. Students become involved in tutorials that provide the academic foundation of good study habits and meet weekly mentors who deal with any problems that arise. The Dean of Freshmen reviews the academic background and preparation of all incoming students in order to individualize learning by selecting a blend of university-level courses to address identified needs.

The Comprehensive Support Program is for students with specific learning differences who have the motivation and intellectual capacity for college-level work—students whose skill and performance levels indicate that without support their chances of success at the college level would be at risk. Various accommodations are available, including content area tutorials given in specific subjects by tutors with advanced degrees. Verbal examinations, tests that do not have a time limit, and lectures and textbooks on tape are also available. All students admitted to the Comprehensive Support Program are required to take a 3-credit course titled Language and Learning, and freshmen must participate in a minimum of two tutoring sessions per week.

Lynn University's approach to the development of academic programs has been one that focuses on the balance of a carefully selected core of liberal arts subjects within the framework of a curriculum that is career-oriented and provides both theoretical and practical preparation. Upon this solid liberal arts foundation, students build special competence in their chosen fields of concentration. The practical application of knowledge is a vital component of Lynn's academic program; therefore, residencies, student teaching, community service projects, and internships are required for many degrees.

The University follows a semester calendar and offers a summer session.

Off-Campus Programs

At Lynn University, great importance has been placed on bringing together students of various nationalities and cultures in an effort to foster greater understanding of diversity. Through a commitment to international education, students are empowered with the knowledge and understanding to effectively and peacefully deal with the challenges that face them in today's world. Enhancing each student's global awareness is an integral part of a Lynn University education.

The University instills a global perspective through a number of study-abroad programs and short-term, faculty-led study tours. Lynn University's sister school, American College Dublin, offers students the opportunity to study in Ireland for a summer, a semester, or even a year abroad. Both campuses provide high-quality international education to Lynn University students interested in expanding their horizons.

Lynn also offers what no other does—the Academic Adventure—an adventure at sea for all first-year students. Last year, students sailed to Central America and through the Caribbean to study different cultures and history and gain firsthand experience by actually seeing, touching, and experiencing the places and concepts studied in the classroom.

Academic Facilities

The Ritter Academic Center is home to the College of Business and Management and houses classrooms, computer labs, and faculty offices. The College of Professional Adult and Continuing Education can be found in the ASSAF academic center, where most of the classes for the College of Arts and Sciences are taught. The deHoernle International Center houses the College of Education, Health and Human Resources and contains classrooms, computer labs, the Center for International Programs and Service, and the Amarnick-Goldstein Concert Hall. The Academic Center for Achievement (ACA) is located in the Green Center building and the deHoernle International Center. The Eugene M. and Christine E. Lynn Library has its third floor dedicated to the College of International Communications, with classrooms, studios, computer labs, and faculty offices.

Costs

Tuition for the 2004–05 academic year is $23,100. Yearly room and board fees total $8400. The telecommunication and student services fee is $1000. Books are purchased separately.

Financial Aid

The University has a broad program of student financial aid, including scholarships, grants, work-study, and loans. Academic, athletic, and need-based scholarships are awarded. Inquiries may be made to the Office of Student Administrative Services.

Faculty

Faculty members are thoroughly committed to teaching and are readily accessible to students. The University has a very favorable student-faculty ratio of 16:1. Seventy percent of full-time faculty members hold doctoral degrees. Individualized attention is emphasized, and students are challenged as well as nurtured. A freshman mentoring program ensures a solid transition to University life.

Student Government

Officers of the student body, elected annually by the students, are involved in a wide variety of activities and interests.

Admission Requirements

All candidates for admission must be graduates of an accredited high school or must present formal evidence of having completed high school graduation requirements. Applicants are required to take the SAT I or ACT. Greater emphasis is placed on the recommendation of the applicant's guidance counselor than on standardized test scores. An early admission program is available for exceptionally strong students.

High school students who have taken an Advanced Placement test and scored 3 or higher may earn both credit and placement in a higher-level course. University credit may also be earned by taking the College-Level Examination Program (CLEP) tests. International Baccalaureate credit is also granted. All international applicants are expected to complete an undergraduate application for international admission. Applicants for whom English is not a first language must submit results from the TOEFL. All transcripts of previous academic work must be accompanied by certified English translations. Transfer students who have completed a minimum of 15 academic college credits are expected to submit an official transcript from each college attended, along with a recommendation from the Dean of Students at the institution most recently attended. Those who have accumulated fewer than 15 credits are asked to also submit high school transcripts. Every effort is made to facilitate the transfer of credit from other institutions, and a special transfer adviser is available to ensure proper placement.

Application and Information

There is no formal deadline for admission, and applicants are notified on a rolling basis upon receipt of all credentials. The application fee is $35. For additional information about admission, to obtain an application packet, or to arrange for an interview and tour of the campus, prospective students should contact:

Office of Admission
Lynn University
3601 North Military Trail
Boca Raton, Florida 33431-5598
Telephone: 561-237-7900
800-888-5966 (toll-free)
Fax: 561-237-7100
E-mail: admission@lynn.edu
World Wide Web: http://www.lynn.edu

A part of the campus of Lynn University.

Lynn University affirms the right of all individuals to equal treatment in education and employment, without regard to race, color, gender, religion, national and ethnic origin, disability or age.

MAINE COLLEGE OF ART

PORTLAND, MAINE

The College

Maine College of Art (MECA) is a dynamic college of art and design where nationally recognized faculty members, interdisciplinary programs, and expansive facilities create a visionary educational experience, building upon Maine's extraordinary legacy in the visual arts. Founded in 1882, MECA is a fully accredited, independent college with 450 students who come from across the United States as well as throughout the world. The College offers eleven studio majors (two new majors are scheduled to be added in fall 2004) and three minors.

Maine College of Art has state-of-the-art facilities with 24-hour access, small class sizes, and the kind of individual attention that students expect and enjoy. With a 9:1 student-faculty ratio and an average class size of 16 (the average major class size is 12), faculty support and close student-faculty relationships are the norm. MECA faculty members are accomplished in their fields and work closely with their students because they are uniquely dedicated to teaching. All students have 24-hours-a-day, 7-days-a-week access to professional-quality studio spaces. All juniors and seniors are guaranteed their own individual studio spaces. The College is located in the heart of Portland, on the southern coast of Maine. The primary studio building, the beautiful beaux arts Porteous Building, is a landmark in a hip city that is well known for its spectacular landscapes, numerous cultural advantages of an urban center, and a lively, contemporary art scene that embraces the work of new and emerging artists.

Student life is busy, and extracurricular activities include exhibition openings and visiting-artist workshops, a film series, music and cultural events, hiking outings to the ocean, day trips to Boston galleries, and parties and other celebrations. Students and staff members gather weekly for "Soup and Bread," a popular free lunch held Tuesdays in the College's student center. Student life at MECA begins with orientation, including a weekend at the renowned Haystack Mountain School of Crafts. Peer mentors provide a support system for new students at the College and advising is strong. Career services include both individual and small-group career counseling and workshops. The Learning Center provides academic assistance and support to all interested students.

Although undergraduates are the focus, MECA offers an innovative Master of Fine Arts degree in studio arts through a unique low-residency program.

Location

Portland is a city that revels in art and nurtures a diverse cultural community. One hour and 40 minutes from Boston, Portland has an urban sensibility and an energy that draws an eclectic population, from artists to entrepreneurs. A vibrant and diverse immigrant and refugee community makes up 10 percent of Portland's population. Downtown Portland, with its lively arts and Old Port districts, is home to numerous galleries, theaters, coffee houses, and performance venues. The Portland Museum of Art, housed in an award-winning building by I. M. Pei and Partners, features an extensive collection of fine and decorative arts and offers free admission to MECA students. Cosmopolitan and comfortable, Portland offers all the advantages of a small city, with easy access to beaches and the seacoast.

Majors and Degrees

Maine College of Art offers the Bachelor of Fine Arts degree in eleven majors: ceramics, graphic design, illustration (new), metalsmithing and jewelry, new media, painting, photography, printmaking, sculpture, self-designed, and woodworking and furniture design (new). Students may also minor in art history, drawing, and illustration. Art education is important to many MECA students, and a postbaccalaureate program in art education offers B.F.A. degree-holders a one-year course of study, in addition to hands-on experience in classrooms, museums, and community settings, that leads to certification as K–12 art educators.

Academic Programs

At MECA, students shape their own educational experiences, living and learning in a nurturing and diverse environment. The learning process is rigorous, challenging, personal, and creative. Students master the fundamentals of art, design, and critical thinking and apply them across multiple disciplines, traditional media, and emerging art forms.

MECA is noted for the strength of its Foundation Program in drawing and design, a program of studies that leads to individualized study in a chosen major. The Foundation Year, or first year, affords students comprehensive training for future creative work, and students acquire the language and skills vital to art making. In the second year, the Focus Year, students choose from a variety of electives to deepen fundamental skills within areas of particular interest. Students declare their major in the spring of their sophomore year and enter their major with the ability to choose the style, medium, and techniques that most effectively communicate and express their vision.

In addition to their studio courses, MECA students take a concurrent stream of liberal arts and art history courses throughout their four years, complementing their studio work and offering them a broader cultural context so critical to an artist's education. Reviews of studio work—completed and in progress—provide students the invaluable opportunity for more intensive feedback at the culmination of each semester, helping them to understand and evaluate their strengths and areas for growth.

MECA students are encouraged to explore the interdisplinary nature of contemporary art and to take courses in a wide variety of studio areas, both before and after declaring a major. Students can also design their own independent course of study. Students interested in an elementary or secondary teaching career can prepare for teacher certification. Internships are available in studio settings and in art administration offices as well as in social service and education-oriented organizations. The internships provide opportunities for students to explore first-hand the different venues in which their art knowledge and skills may be applied.

The academic year consists of two 15-week semesters. A comprehensive thesis exhibition of work accomplished in the student's major area is a highlight of commencement. MECA has a cross-registration program with Bowdoin College, 35 minutes from the campus, and also belongs to the Greater Portland Alliance of Colleges and Universities, an active consortium allowing cross-registration among five local colleges and universities.

MECA's summer Early College Program is an intensive visual arts program that provides high school students with in-depth studio foundation instruction, elective offerings, and the opportunity to strengthen their portfolios. College credit is available. Each year, MCA offers more than 150 continuing studies courses that, with special approval, may be applied toward B.F.A. degree requirements.

Off-Campus Programs

MECA students can study off campus through the Association of Independent Colleges of Art and Design (AICAD) Mobility Program, which provides students with the chance to study for a semester at thirty-five schools throughout the U.S. and Canada. Other study-abroad exchanges have recently included programs in England, Ireland, Italy, South Africa, and Vietnam. MECA students may also take summer courses at the Provincetown Fine Arts Work Center in Massachusetts.

Academic Facilities

Maine College of Art offers an ideal setting in which to explore the artistic process. Expansive facility spaces ignite and inspire creativity, and the technology that is necessary to turn visions into reality is at hand. Located within a four-square-block area in the heart of Portland, the campus consists of two studio and classroom buildings, three unique residence halls offering both dormitory and apartment-style housing options, and an administration building. All MECA students have 24-hours-a-day, 7-days-a-week access to the College's professional-quality studio space, and all juniors and seniors have their own individual studio spaces. The Porteous Building, the College's primary studio building, offers some of the finest facilities for art-making in the country. Its views of the Casco Bay islands to the south and the White Mountains to the north are breathtaking. Several excellent student-exhibition sites offer students the opportunity to exhibit their work in a variety of settings. The Baxter Building, which houses classrooms and studios, is the city's former public library and a unique example of Romanesque Revival architecture. The Clapp House is the original site of the Portland Society for Applied and Fine Arts (MECA's original name) and is listed on the National Register of Historic Places.

The Institute of Contemporary Art (ICA) at Maine College of Art is a nationally recognized gallery that features leading-edge exhibitions and public programs, showcasing new perspectives and fresh trends in contemporary art. A rich array of public programs enhances the exhibition schedule. Students and faculty members gather for provocative talks by leading artists and critics, timely forums on current issues in art and design, and interactive workshops.

MECA's Joanne Waxman Library offers a collection of 45,000 slides and maintains a specialized collection of nineteenth-century publications in the arts and a collection of artists' books. In addition, the library houses more than 18,900 volumes and 100 periodicals. The library's handsome quarters feature tin ceilings and large, Chicago-style windows that bathe its faculty-designed furniture in natural light.

Three computer labs offer more than fifty MacIntosh computers with complete Web, print, and design software; a selection of slide and flatbed scanners; and audio and video editing systems. Output capabilities include color laser and large-format drum printing.

Costs

The cost of tuition for 2003–04 was $20,623. The cost of books and arts supplies averaged about $1740 and room and board costs ranged from $5698 to $7856. Fees were $493. The total cost of attendance was estimated to range from $28,554 to $30,712.

Financial Aid

Maine College of Art is committed to doing all it can to make a unique and high-quality art education accessible to all qualified students. Actively participating in all federal and state financial aid programs, MECA offers both need-based and merit-based financial aid to assist students and their families. More than 85 percent of MECA students receive some form of financial assistance. Financial aid packages typically consist of a combination of grants, campus employment, and loans and are tailored to meet each student's needs. The Free Application for Federal Student Aid (FAFSA) is the only application required for both federal and institutional aid. The deadline for preferential consideration of financial aid requests is March 1.

Faculty

There are 50 full-time and 19 part-time faculty members teaching in the B.F.A. program. Faculty members are professional artists, designers, and scholars who are devoted to teaching and instruct at all levels of the curriculum. Faculty members also serve as academic advisers and build close relationships with students, actively assisting them in formulating and carrying out their career plans.

Student Government

The Student Representatives Association (SRA) is an active and lively group that serves as the official student voice and plays an important role at MECA. The SRA plans and carries out activities and events and works closely with College administrators on issues that arise throughout the year. SRA members include representatives from each of the majors as well as from both the first- and second-year classes.

Admission Requirements

A portfolio review is an integral part of the admissions evaluation process. Each applicant is required to submit a portfolio of his or her original art, and in-person reviews are a daily part of the campus visit opportunities. Students who are unable to visit MECA may have their portfolio reviewed at a National Portfolio Day, or may submit a slide portfolio. A personal statement, a high school transcript, two letters of recommendation (from an art teacher, a guidance counselor, an English teacher, or an employer), and SAT I or ACT scores are also required.

Applications are considered on a rolling basis for entry in both the fall and spring semesters. The priority application deadline for fall is March 1 and for spring it is November 15. Both full-time and part-time study are available. Academically advanced high school students who are completing their junior year may apply for early admission. Special student status is also available for qualified individuals who are not seeking a B.F.A. degree.

Application and Information

A complete packet of materials may be obtained by contacting:

Office of Admissions
Maine College of Art
97 Spring Street
Portland, Maine 04101
Telephone: 207-775-3052
800-639-4808 (toll-free)
E-mail: admissions@meca.edu
World Wide Web: http://www.meca.edu

All students have 24-hours-a-day, 7-days-a-week access to professional-quality studio space, and all majors have individual studio spaces.

MALONE COLLEGE

CANTON, OHIO

The College

Malone College is a Christian college committed to offering a high-quality education in a setting that encourages a solid devotion to God. The College was founded and established in 1892 by Walter and Emma Malone as the Cleveland Bible College. In 1957, the College moved to Canton, Ohio, and assumed the name Malone College. Today, Malone is one of four Christian colleges in Ohio that is a member of the Council for Christian Colleges and Universities (CCCU). Malone also belongs to the thirteen-member Christian College Consortium.

At Malone College, students are challenged to grow in three vital aspects of life. Spiritually, students are placed in an environment that lends itself to cultivating a deeper relationship with God. Academically, students encounter rigorous challenges offered by a strong faculty, of whom 63 percent hold doctoral, first professional, or terminal degrees. Socially, Malone offers students a chance to experience the real world through on-campus and off-campus activities in which they are exposed to almost every kind of social influence. This requires them to make vital personal decisions and to formulate their own ideas and moral values.

Malone's 2,210 students come from twenty-five states and twelve other countries. At Malone, the average undergraduate class size is 20 students. Of the total enrollment, more than 900 students live on campus in nine residence halls, the newest of which opened in fall 1999.

Students can participate in a variety of clubs and activities, including Christian organizations and fourteen intramural sports. Malone also offers strong varsity programs, including nine men's sports: baseball, basketball, cross-country, football, golf, indoor track, outdoor track, soccer, and tennis and nine women's sports: basketball, cross-country, golf, indoor track, outdoor track, soccer, softball, tennis, and volleyball. Students may also participate in the campus radio station, newspaper, yearbook, student government, marching band, symphonic band, chorale, and forensics and debate.

Malone offers the following graduate programs: Master of Arts (M.A.) in Christian ministries, M.A. in education (core areas in counselor education: community counseling and school counseling; core areas in graduate education: curriculum and instruction; curriculum, instruction, and professional development; instructional technology; intervention specialist; and reading), Master of Science in Nursing (tracks: family nurse practitioner and clinical nurse specialist), and Master of Business Administration.

Location

Malone College sits on a 78-acre campus in a quiet, residential area of Canton, Ohio. This setting lends itself to a variety of cultural experiences, including the Professional Football Hall of Fame; the ballet, symphony, and theater; museums; and professional sports teams. There is also easy interstate access to the metropolitan areas of Cleveland, Akron, and Youngstown.

Majors and Degrees

The Bachelor of Arts is offered in accounting, adult fitness, art, Bible/theology, biology, biology–clinical laboratory science, business administration, chemistry, church music, commercial music technology, communication arts, community health education, computer science, educational ministries, English, history, integrated language arts, integrated science, integrated social studies, liberal arts, life science/chemistry education, mathematics, music, outdoor leadership, philosophy, physical science, political science, psychology, social work, Spanish, sport management, sports ministry, sports science, and youth ministry. Combination majors in sports/educational ministries, youth/educational ministries, and youth/sports ministries are available. An individualized (student-designed) major is also an option.

Many of these majors and several other fields are available as secondary education fields.

The Bachelor of Science is offered in early childhood education, health education, intervention specialist education, middle childhood education, music education, nursing, physical education, Spanish education, and visual arts education.

Malone also offers adult degree-completion programs in nursing and management.

Academic Program

Since Malone is a college for the arts, sciences, and professions, there is a comprehensive general education requirement regardless of the chosen course of study. Students must meet requirements in each of Malone's academic areas, including communications, science, English, Bible/theology, and social science.

Malone students must meet a total of 60 semester credit hours in the aforementioned areas. A minimum of 124 credit hours is required to graduate. This is an accumulation of the major requirements, general education curriculum, and, in most cases, a series of electives. Malone offers forty-seven undergraduate degree opportunities, the most popular of which are education, nursing, and business administration.

Malone's academic calendar is based on two semesters, with a summer school that includes three sessions.

Off-Campus Programs

Malone students are given the opportunity to spend a semester on another Christian college campus through the Christian College Consortium Visitor Program. Other off-campus opportunities include the following programs sponsored by the CCCU: American Studies (Washington, D.C.), Australian Studies Centre (Sydney), China Studies (Shanghai), Latin American Studies (San Jose, Costa Rica), Middle East Studies (Cairo, Egypt), Russian Studies (Moscow, Nizhni Novgorod, and St. Petersburg), Los Angeles Film Studies (Los Angeles, California), Honour Programme at the Centre for Medieval and Renaissance Studies (Oxford, England), and studies at the Contemporary Music Center (Martha's Vineyard). In addition, numerous other programs are endorsed by or affiliated with the CCCU. Malone also provides international study opportunities in Costa Rica (for tropical ecology), Guatemala (for teacher education), and Kenya (at Daystar University).

Academic Facilities

The Cattell Library contains 161,899 books; 620,013 microfilm units; 1,193 periodicals; 330 CD-ROMs; and 10,943 audiovisual materials. Communication majors also have a television studio on campus. There are approximately 200 computers available for general student use in the library, residence halls, and the three computer labs.

Costs

The cost for the 2003–04 year at Malone was $20,995, which included $14,745 for tuition and $6240 in room, board, and fees.

Financial Aid

Affordability is one of the strengths of Malone College. The College holds the belief that a college education is a family investment that requires realistic support. More than 95 percent of traditional Malone students receive some form of financial assistance. This is offered through federal grants and loans, state grants, work opportunities both on and off campus, or Malone College scholarships. These scholarships are awarded on the basis of one or more of the following: need; academic, musical, or athletic talent; or Christian perspective and leadership ability. Malone requires the completion of the Free Application for Federal Student Aid (FAFSA). The average financial aid package amounts to approximately $11,350 per year.

Faculty

Sixty-three percent of Malone College faculty members hold doctoral, first professional, or terminal degrees. The undergraduate student-faculty ratio is 14:1. This allows students to learn and achieve in a comfortable setting and gives them easy access to assistance from professors.

Student Government

Malone's student organizations are directed by the Student Senate, which in turn is guided by a president and a vice president. The Senate is represented at nearly all of the institution's committee meetings, including the Board of Trustees' meetings. Working through committees, the Senate plays a significant role in shaping the total academic, spiritual, and social life of the Malone community. In addition, positions on the Senate are paid positions.

Admission Requirements

Malone welcomes applications for admission from bright, qualified high school graduates who want to attend college in an atmosphere of high academic standards and evangelical Christianity. Admission is based on objective evaluation of an applicant's motivation, maturity, and other personal qualifications and the applicant's academic credentials, with an emphasis on high school grade point average (2.5 or higher), ACT composite results equal to or above the national mean, class rank, standardized test scores, and depth of high school courses. Other applicants may be accepted by committee approval. A personal interview and campus visit are required in such instances. Malone admits students of any race, color, religion, sex, and national or ethnic origin who meet the academic requirements.

Application and Information

Applications for admission to Malone College are accepted until July 1, and there is a $20 fee required with the application. The Malone Admissions Center is open for campus visitation Monday through Friday from 8:30 a.m. to 5 p.m. The visitation includes a one-on-one interview with an admissions counselor and an individual tour of Malone's campus.

For more information about Malone College, students should contact:

John A. Chopka
Vice President for Enrollment Management
Admissions Center
Malone College
515 25th Street, NW
Canton, Ohio 44709
Telephone: 330-471-8145
800-521-1146 (toll-free)
E-mail: admissions@malone.edu
World Wide Web: http://www.malone.edu

The Brehme Centennial Center is home to Malone's cafeteria, bookstore, and instrumental music department.

MANCHESTER COLLEGE

NORTH MANCHESTER, INDIANA

The College

Manchester College, founded in 1889, is an independent, coeducational, liberal arts college of the Church of the Brethren. Throughout its history, the College has held that values are central in the study of all majors and that the liberal arts provide a foundation of critical skills and sound scholarship.

An emphasis on service produces exceptional graduates who possess both professional ability and personal convictions, prepared for responsible lives that make a difference in the world.

Located at the edge of North Manchester, Indiana, Manchester College is primarily a residential school; 75 percent of the students live on the beautiful 124-acre campus. The academic buildings are constructed around a tree-lined central mall, and manicured flower gardens dot the campus. In addition, the resource-rich 100-acre Koinonia Environmental Retreat Center is located 12 miles from the academic campus.

The undergraduate enrollment is 1,150. Most students are between the ages of 18 and 22. Approximately 85 percent of the full-time students are from Indiana. Students from twenty-three states and twenty-nine countries were also enrolled during 2002–03. Sixteen percent of the students are members of the Church of the Brethren, but many different religious backgrounds are represented, and all are welcomed.

At Manchester, students get to know the members of the College's well-trained, concerned faculty on both a personal and an academic level. Faculty members take the time to assist students in a caring way, both in the classroom and as advisers.

There are five residence halls on campus that provide a variety of living experiences for students to choose from.

Manchester is a member of the National Collegiate Athletic Association Division III and offers nine men's and eight women's sports. The Physical Education and Recreation Center houses physical education classes, a fitness center, intercollegiate and intramural sports, and recreational activities. The College has a very strong intramural program that involves about 80 percent of its students.

In addition to its undergraduate program, Manchester College offers the Master of Accountancy and Master of Arts in contemporary leadership degrees.

Location

Located in the heart of Indiana's beautiful lake country, North Manchester is a thriving community of 6,000 people. It is within a half hour's drive of the Fort Wayne metropolitan area and is only 3½ hours from Chicago. Wide streets with large shade trees, graceful homes, and a beautiful park combine to provide a setting for classic college living.

Majors and Degrees

Manchester College grants Bachelor of Arts and Bachelor of Science degrees. Areas of study include accounting, adapted physical education, art, athletic training, biology, business administration, chemistry, coaching, communication studies, computer science, corporate finance, criminal justice, early childhood education, economics, elementary education, engineering science, English, environmental studies, exercise science, French, gender studies, German, gerontology, health and fitness instruction, history, journalism, mathematics, media studies, medical technology, music, nonprofit management, peace studies, philosophy, physical education, physics, political science, prelaw, premedicine, prenursing, pre–occupational therapy, pre–physical therapy, psychology, religion, secondary education, small-business administration, social work, sociology, Spanish, and theater arts. Individualized interdisciplinary majors can also be arranged to meet a student's particular goals.

Academic Program

The curriculum reflects a commitment to sound training in a specific area of study, the major, and broad development of skills and understanding through the liberal arts. In addition, students may explore interests different from specific career or professional areas through elective courses. This combination prepares students for careers or graduate school immediately after graduation and equips them for the challenges and changes of the coming century.

Manchester College operates on a 4-1-4 calendar and offers three summer sessions. Qualifying scores on the Advanced Placement Program and College-Level Examination Program tests of the College Board are recognized for college credit or advanced placement.

Off-Campus Programs

Manchester College students may study abroad for a semester or year in thirteen countries: at Philipps-Universität Marburg in Marburg/Lahn (Germany), the Institut International d'Études Françaises of the University of Strasbourg (France), the University of Nancy (France), the University of Barcelona (Spain), St. Mary's College in Cheltenham (England), Hokkai Gakuen University in Sapporo (Japan), the Dalian Institute of Foreign Languages in Dalian (People's Republic of China), the University of La Verne Athens Center (Greece), the Catholic University of Ecuador, the Federal University of Ouro Preto (Brazil), Satya Wacana University (Indonesia), Marmara University (Turkey), Cochin (India), and Universidad Veracruzana (Mexico).

During January session, numerous classes are held off campus. In the past several years, professors have taken classes to India, Africa, England, Mexico, Russia, France, Ghana, Vietnam, Nicaragua, Haiti, Germany, Costa Rica, Cuba, and Hawaii as well as destinations in the continental United States.

Field experiences and internships are offered for credit in accounting, broadcasting, business, criminal justice, early childhood education, elementary education, forensic chemistry, gerontology, health sciences practicum, journalism, peace studies, physical education, political science, psychology, secondary education, and social work.

Academic Facilities

Manchester College has a local area network of 165 IBM-compatible workstations, one for every 6 students. In addition, the Clark Computer Center houses file servers, three computer labs, and an AS400 for student use. PC labs tied to the network are located in each residence hall and the library.

Cordier Auditorium, dedicated in 1978, seats 1,300 people and has modern facilities for staging, lighting, and sound.

The Holl-Kintner Hall of Science has extensive laboratory facilities for biology, botany, physics, and geology as well as four separate chemistry laboratories and a number of research laboratories. Students in astronomy use the 10-inch Newtonian reflector telescope in the Charles S. Morris Observatory.

The Funderburg Library is a newly renovated, three-story building that houses more than 170,000 books, 800 periodicals, and 4,500 audio recordings available for student use. Computer connections allow access to major libraries across the country.

Costs

Tuition for 2003–04 is $17,040 for full-time students. Room and board costs for the residence halls (double occupancy) are $6340. The total charges are $23,380 for the academic year.

Financial Aid

Manchester offers extensive scholarship and grant assistance through institutional resources. Academic awards include Honors, Trustee, Presidential, and Dean's Scholarships. Special scholarships based on academic merit and interest are awarded in art, broadcasting, journalism, music, theater, and the video arts. Service scholarships and modern language scholarships are also awarded. International students can receive scholarships based on academic accomplishments and financial need. Manchester awards significant need-based grants. More than $7 million in College funds were awarded in 2002–03.

Approximately 98 percent of Manchester's students have some type of financial assistance, whether it is a scholarship, a grant, a loan, or campus employment. Questions about financial aid should be referred to the Office of Admissions.

Faculty

Manchester's faculty consists of 72 full-time and 19 part-time members. Ninety-three percent of full-time faculty members hold the highest degrees in their fields, and 94 percent of all courses are taught by full-time faculty members. The primary emphasis of the faculty members is teaching, but many are actively engaged in research as well. Faculty members serve as academic advisers, with a specially trained group of faculty members acting as primary advisers for new students. There is a 14:1 student-faculty ratio.

Student Government

Students at Manchester assume responsibility for the governmental and judicial activities of the College. The Community Council provides a forum for discussion and investigation of community concerns and a channel for evaluating and solving community problems.

Each of the residence halls elects a governing body, which is responsible for providing leadership.

The judicial system of the College includes three courts: the Judicial Board, the Community Court, and an administrative hearing panel. The Student Budget Board is charged with responsibility for receiving requests for funds to support the activity program of the College and for making the necessary appropriations.

The Manchester Activities Council organizes programming of student events. Students are offered a wide variety of leadership and participation opportunities as part of the College's student development program.

Admission Requirements

Manchester College seeks to enroll students whose scholastic record, test scores, and personality give promise of success in college. Graduation from an accredited high school or its equivalent is required.

The College recommends that students take 4 years of English, 3 years of laboratory science, 3 years of mathematics, 2 years of foreign language, and 2 years of social studies in high school. Students may take either the ACT or the SAT I, and personal recommendations from a high school principal or guidance counselor are required.

For transfer students, transcripts of all previous college work are required.

Application and Information

Students may apply for admission prior to each term. Applications are accepted on a rolling basis. There is a nonrefundable $20 application fee.

Interested students and their parents are encouraged to visit Manchester College and meet faculty members, coaches, and current students; sit in on classes; and take a campus tour. Arrangements can be made by writing or calling the Office of Admissions.

For application forms and further information, students may contact:

Office of Admissions
Manchester College
North Manchester, Indiana 46962-0365
Telephone: 800-852-3648 (toll-free)
E-mail: admitinfo@manchester.edu
World Wide Web: http://www.manchester.edu

Students from the First Year Colloquium course Bodies in Motion lead residents of Peabody Retirement Community in Tai Chi.

MANHATTAN COLLEGE

RIVERDALE, NEW YORK

The College

Currently celebrating 150 years of excellence in Lasallian education, Manhattan College was founded by the Brothers of the Christian Schools in 1853 and chartered by the state of New York in 1863. The College has an enrollment of more than 3,200, of whom 2,500 are undergraduates. Approximately 72 percent of Manhattan's students come from New York State; 28 percent represent thirty-nine other states and the remainder represent fifty other countries. Approximately 1,500 housing units are available, consisting of on-campus residence halls and off-campus apartments. Seventy percent of the students reside on campus. Manhattan offers seventy extracurricular organizations and five student publications and fields twenty varsity and club sports teams. Of Manhattan's 40,000 living alumni, more than 18,000 work in the New York City area. Manhattan graduates are prominent leaders in business, government, education, the arts, the sciences, and engineering.

Location

The main campus of the College is located 10 miles north of midtown Manhattan in the suburban Riverdale section of the Bronx, about a mile from Westchester County. Riverdale is an upper-middle-class community, the home of many New York business, political, and education leaders. The area offers the calm and quiet of a residential, suburban setting as well as easy access to the many advantages of New York City. The College is easily accessible by subway, bus, or highway.

Majors and Degrees

The liberal arts curriculum of the School of Arts provides programs that lead to a Bachelor of Arts or Bachelor of Science with majors in the humanities and the social sciences, including communications, economics, English, fine arts, government, history, modern foreign languages, philosophy, psychology, religious studies, and sociology. Interdisciplinary majors include international studies, peace studies, and urban affairs. In the School of Science, programs lead to a Bachelor of Science or Bachelor of Arts with majors in biochemistry, biology, chemistry, computer science, mathematics, and physics.

The School of Engineering has a day session with programs leading to a Bachelor of Science in chemical, civil, computer, electrical, environmental, and mechanical engineering.

The School of Business has programs leading to a Bachelor of Science in Business Administration with majors in accounting, computer information systems, economics, finance, global business, managerial sciences, and marketing.

The School of Education offers a curriculum leading to a Bachelor of Arts for teachers of English, foreign languages, and social studies and to a Bachelor of Science for teachers of biology, chemistry, computer science, general science, mathematics, physics, and special education. The physical education curriculum leads to a Bachelor of Science in physical education in one of three concentrations: teaching, pre–physical therapy, or sports medicine. The health education curriculum leads to a Bachelor of Science in health education or community health. Curricula in radiological and health sciences lead to a Bachelor of Science in radiation therapy or nuclear medicine technology.

Academic Program

The core curriculum shared by the School of Arts and the School of Science studies some of the vital works of humankind, explores new ideas, examines the meaning of scientific experimentation, and encourages a student to develop his or her thinking and leadership abilities. The major programs offer advanced work in specific humanistic and scientific disciplines and opportunities to work on research projects in collaboration with faculty scholars.

In the School of Engineering, all engineering students follow a common core curriculum during the first two years and choose a major at the beginning of the junior year. Each curriculum includes a generous selection of courses in basic sciences, the engineering sciences, humanistic studies, and mathematics.

The School of Business prepares students for positions of executive responsibility in business, government, and nonprofit organizations. The business curriculum is based on a strong commitment to liberal education and is well balanced between professional business courses, humanities, sciences, and social sciences. This is a reflection of the School's belief that executives should be broadly educated and should involve themselves, as well as their organizations, in efforts to solve social problems.

The School of Education prepares students for teaching, counseling, and health professions. Students complete the College's core curriculum in liberal arts and sciences and then complete a major in various programs in the School's three departments: Education, Physical Education and Human Performance, and Radiological and Health Professions. All programs include internships/practicums in schools, hospitals, or other institutions. Graduates of the School's teacher-preparation programs receive New York State provisional teaching certification. The School also offers a five-year B.A./M.S. program in elementary or secondary education and special education.

Off-Campus Programs

Students in the liberal arts curricula who have demonstrated superior achievement in their first two years are encouraged to spend their junior year studying abroad. Manhattan College offers study-abroad programs; arrangements can be made to a country of choice. Students in the School of Business may participate in the International Field Studies Seminar. As participants in the seminar, students spend time in another country studying the effect of that environment on international firms. Career services and co-op education integrate classroom theory with the practical experience of a job in industry, business, the social services, the arts, or government. Portions of the education courses are conducted in New York City schools, in order that student teachers may gain experience in urban education at an early stage. Manhattan College and the neighboring College of Mount Saint Vincent collaborate in an exchange of students and facilities to provide more extensive opportunities for academic development.

Academic Facilities

There are more than forty scientific and engineering laboratories at Manhattan, including the Research and Learning Center, as well as a modern language laboratory and a computer information systems laboratory. Manhattan's new O'Malley Library is a state-of-the-art facility featuring modern accomodations for study and research. It is connected to the renovated and updated Cardinal Hayes Pavilion, formerly the Cardinal Hayes Library. The library combines Hayes' traditional neo-Georgian accents with strong contemporary lines. The five-story addition to the original building doubles the original square footage and connects the current library to the upper campus. Students and faculty members are able to enter directly from a brick walkway that starts at the Quadrangle.

Costs

For 2003–04, the tuition for all curricula is $17,800 per year. A fee that varies among programs is added. Room and board come to $8100 per year for the nineteen meals/week plan.

Financial Aid

Manhattan grants or administers financial assistance in the form of tuition awards to students on the basis of need and/or ability. Need is evaluated through the FAFSA. In addition to a general scholarship fund, Manhattan offers endowed scholarships, special-category scholarships and grants, student athletic grants, Federal Pell Grants, Federal Supplemental Educational Opportunity Grants, student loans, Federal Work-Study Program awards, and New York State financial assistance. A total of 1,650 students receive financial aid from Manhattan College, and approximately 87 percent receive financial aid from government or private agencies.

Faculty

Manhattan's faculty has 190 full-time and 82 part-time teachers. The faculty-student ratio is approximately 1:13. Nearly 95 percent of the faculty members hold doctorates. The maximum teaching load on the undergraduate level is 12 credit hours per semester. Faculty members serve on the College Senate, the Council for Faculty Affairs, and numerous faculty and campus committees. In addition, they are available to students for informal guidance and counseling and also serve as official moderators of many campus organizations.

Student Government

The Manhattan Student Government is composed of students elected annually by their peers to fill posts outlined in the Student Government Constitution. The Student Government allocates funds to all student organizations. Members of the Student Government are also full voting members of the College Senate.

Admission Requirements

Manhattan has a long-standing policy of nondiscrimination. No applicant is refused admission because of race, color, religion, age, national origin, sex, or handicap. All applicants must present an academic diploma from an accredited high school and must offer a minimum of 16 credits in academic subjects. Liberal arts candidates must be proficient in at least one foreign language. At the discretion of the Committee on Admissions, quantitative requirements may be modified for applicants with especially strong records who show promise of doing well in college. In the selection process, attention is given to scholastic ability as indicated by grades and rank in class, as well as to standardized test scores and recommendations from principals and counselors. All candidates must submit either SAT I or ACT results. An interview with a member of the admission staff is recommended. Applicants may submit scores on the General Educational Development test in lieu of a formal high school diploma. However, all such applicants must submit the results of the appropriate College Board tests. Manhattan College offers early acceptance for high school seniors, admission to advanced standing, advanced placement, and credit by examination. Junior college or other transfer students are welcome. There are also three special-status categories for students: nonmatriculated, nondegree, and noncredit. Manhattan College requires applicants whose native language is not English to take the Test of English as a Foreign Language (TOEFL) as well as the SAT I. The average SAT I scores of entering freshmen in 2002 were 566 in mathematics and 545 in the verbal portion.

Application and Information

Application forms are furnished by the Admission Office on request. The Common Application Form, which is available in many high school guidance offices, may also be used. After supplying the information required, students must send the application for admission to the Admission Office at Manhattan College. The high school report and the student evaluation and transcript must be submitted by the high school guidance counselor. This should be done after six terms of high school or right after the seventh term. There is a rolling admissions policy and a March 1 deadline for financial aid applications. A nonrefundable application fee of $40 is required.

William J. Bisset
Assistant Vice President for Enrollment Management
Manhattan College
Riverdale, New York 10471
Telephone: 718-862-7200
800-MC2-XCEL (toll-free)
E-mail: admit@manhattan.edu

Students entering the Quadrangle of the Manhattan College campus.

MANHATTAN SCHOOL OF MUSIC

NEW YORK, NEW YORK

The School

Since 1917, Manhattan School of Music has been preparing gifted young musicians to assume places on the great stages of the world. When they select Manhattan School of Music, students choose to work with faculty members who are themselves performers with international reputations. In addition, they choose to be with exceptional students from around the world who come together to create an environment remarkable not only for its intensity, but also for its genuine friendliness and sincere cooperation. When students choose Manhattan School of Music, they also choose New York itself, the very heart of music and art in America.

While all music conservatories of the first rank are acknowledged for their ability to develop talents and refine skills, Manhattan School of Music has a particular combination of strengths that makes it something more—an unrivaled place from which to launch a career.

Performance is the vital expression of a musician's life. At Manhattan School of Music, performance is not simply the goal for students, it is at the center of their lives. With extensive performance opportunities on campus and the chance to freelance and begin to develop a network of professional contacts, students undergo remarkable changes; they start to think and function as professional musicians while they are still in school. It is this powerful convergence of unmatched opportunity and rigorous training that gives these students the best chance to go as far as their talent, their intelligence, and their courage can take them.

Manhattan School of Music enrolls 852 students, approximately 45 percent of whom are undergraduates. They come from more than forty states and more than forty countries. Twenty percent of the students are people of color and 36 percent are international students.

Students must live in residence housing for the first and second years of their study and may apply to stay longer. The School opened a residence facility in 2001. The G. Chris and Sungeun Han-Andersen Residence Hall is a 380-bed facility that is attached to the main building. Double and single rooms are available, as well as approximately sixty practice rooms, an exercise room, a computer lounge, a multipurpose lounge, and a laundry facility for resident students.

Location

For musicians and other artists of great ability and ambition, New York is universally acknowledged as the best place to be. Around the corner and down every street there are opportunities to see and hear the best music in the world every night of the year. With Broadway and off-Broadway theaters, world-famous jazz clubs, and countless museums, New York remains what it has always been—the most extraordinary city on earth. The names of the legendary places and performers that make New York what it is are the very definition of excellence. Carnegie Hall, Lincoln Center, the Blue Note, the Metropolitan Opera, the New York Philharmonic, the American Ballet Theater, the New York City Ballet, the New York City Opera, the Alvin Ailey American Dance Theater, and the Metropolitan Museum of Art are all accessible from the campus.

As part of New York's "Academic Acropolis," Manhattan School of Music shares its student-oriented, Upper West Side location with Columbia University, Barnard College, Union Theological Seminary, Jewish Theological Seminary, Bank Street College, the Cathedral of St. John the Divine, and Riverside Church.

Majors and Degrees

Manhattan School of Music offers Bachelor of Music degrees in classical composition, classical performance (guitar, orchestral instruments, piano, and voice), jazz composition, and jazz performance.

Academic Programs

The degree requires completion of a four-year program of study, with a required humanities core sequence, a music history and music theory core sequence, required courses relevant to each instrument/major, and large and small performance ensembles. Faculty members provide weekly, private, one-on-one instruction in each major. The number of credits required to graduate depends on the instrument/major but is no fewer than 120.

Because the School is dedicated to training outstanding performing artists, performance is at the core of most courses. Appropriate assignments to symphony orchestras, opera studios and workshops, jazz ensembles, and chamber music ensembles evolve into more than 400 public performances per academic year by students. Performance opportunities include Symphony Orchestra, Philharmonia Orchestra, Chamber Sinfonia, Opera Theater, American Musical Theater Ensemble, Percussion Ensemble, Guitar Ensemble, Baroque Aria Ensemble, Jazz Orchestra, Concert Jazz Band, Afro-Cuban Ensemble, and more than seventy-five jazz combos and chamber music groups.

A cross-registration program between Manhattan School of Music and Barnard College of Columbia University enables qualified undergraduates to have access to a wide variety of academic courses. Musically qualified Barnard students may enroll in lessons with Manhattan School of Music faculty members.

Academic Facilities

Facilities at Manhattan School of Music include a 1,000-seat auditorium for symphony, opera, and jazz performances; a 250-seat recital hall; a 75-seat recital hall; a 35-seat recital hall/recording studio; three electronic music studios; and an 82,000-volume library, which includes more than 20,000 recordings.

Costs

Tuition for the 2004–05 academic year (12–18 credits per semester) is $24,500. Annual fees required of all students total $460 plus a health insurance fee. Housing costs are $7800 to $11,700 per year, and food costs are approximately $4200 per year.

Financial Aid

Manhattan School of Music offers federal and state financial assistance as well as its own institutional resources in the form of scholarships and grants. Federal and state aid is administered in accordance with federal and state laws and regulations. The majority of institutional scholarships are awarded on the basis of audition results, financial need, previous academic work, and the School's need for particular instruments/majors.

Each year the School also awards some of its resources on the basis of merit alone. Forty percent of the School's students receive scholarships. The financial aid deadline is March 15 for both government and institutional aid.

Faculty

The faculty forms the essential core of any school, but at a conservatory, faculty members take on an additional importance, for it is not simply what they know but what they do that helps to transform their students.

Manhattan School of Music's 250 faculty members are soloists and chamber and jazz artists as well as members of the New York Philharmonic, the Metropolitan Opera Company, the Chamber Music Society of Lincoln Center, New York City Opera, and the Orpheus Chamber Orchestra. Artists-in-residence include American String Quartet and Windscape.

Regular faculty members teach 98 percent of all courses and 100 percent of private lesson instruction.

Each year, Manhattan School of Music brings more than 50 internationally renowned conductors and performing artists to the School. Selected conductors during 2001–03 were Theo Alcantara, Pierre Boulez, Sergiu Comissiona, Graziella Contratto, JoAnn Falletta, David Gilbert, Miguel Harth-Bedoya, Manfred Huss, George Manahan, Kurt Masur, John Mauceri, Jorge Mester, Jean-Bernard Pommier, Julius Rudel, Gunther Schuller, Elizabeth Schulze, Gerard Schwarz, Jerzy Semkow, Claudio Vandelli, and David Zinman. Selected master classes during 2001–03 were conducted by Midori, violin; Charles Riecker, voice/auditioning; Martina Arroyo, voice; Yuri Bashmet, viola; Paul O'Dette, guitar; Shmuel Ashkenasi, violin; Martin Katz, voice/accompanying; Scott Tennant, guitar; Marna Street, viola; William Winstead, bassoon; Patti Monson, flute; Paul Galbraith, guitar; David Taylor, trombone; Rolando Morales, percussion; Wilfred Roberts, bassoon; Matthew Good, tuba; Darren McHenry, bass trombone; Douglas Howard, percussion; Nicholas Tsolainos, double bass; Steven Dibner, bassoon; Tim Day, flute; Mark Inouye, trumpet; Roberto Diaz, viola; Eugene Istomin, piano; Stephen Balderston, cello; Ronald Caravan, saxophone; Ubaldo Fabbri, voice; Gretchen Van Hoesen, harp; Jeffrey Turner, double bass; Shuku Iwasaki, accompanying; Glenn Dicterow, violin; Arnold Steinhardt, viola/violin/chamber music; David Kim, violin; Steven Schick, percussion; Wycliffe Gordon, jazz trombone; Sean Smith Quartet; Thomas Klaber, bass trombone; Max Dimoff, double bass; Duncan Patton, percussion; Tod Bowermaster, French horn; Frederic Macarez, percussion; Regine Crespin, voice; Pamela Frank, violin; Robert Vernon, viola; Anna Moffo, voice; David Leisner, guitar; Brian Zeger, voice; Yefim Bronfman, piano; Richard Albagli, percussion; Nancy Zeltsman, percussion; Fedora Barbieri, voice; and Lauren Flanigan, voice.

Student Government

The Manhattan School of Music Student Council serves as the voice of the student body. Made up of both undergraduate and graduate students, the council voluntarily serves a one-year, renewable term and serves as an advisory body to the administration. The council also sponsors various social activities at the School.

Admission Requirements

Manhattan School of Music requires an in-person audition in New York City during one of the two audition periods (March and May). Cellists, bassists, and tubists may submit a videotape in lieu of a live audition. A high school transcript or an official high school equivalency diploma is required of all applicants. Additional requirements can be found on the application.

Manhattan School of Music is a highly selective college and admitted only 36 percent of the freshman applicants for admission for the 2002–03 academic year. Manhattan School of Music seeks a geographically and ethnically diverse student body.

International applicants residing outside of North America may submit a videotape (U.S. format only) in lieu of a live audition. In addition, applicants whose first language is not English must take the TOEFL or the IELTS and submit their scores before consideration for admission.

Recognition of transfer credits from other institutions of higher education in theory, sight singing, dictation, keyboard harmony, required piano, and music history is determined by placement tests given during new student orientation before the first semester. Credit for other courses completed with a minimum grade of C or its equivalent depends upon the extent to which these subjects satisfy the curricular requirements of the School.

Application and Information

Applications for both freshmen and transfer students must be received by December 1 for the March audition period and by April 1 for the May audition period. Notification of admission status is sent by mail two to four weeks after each audition period.

For more information, students should contact:

Amy A. Anderson
Director of Admission and Financial Aid
Manhattan School of Music
120 Claremont Avenue
New York, New York 10027
Telephone: 212-749-2802 Ext. 2
Fax: 212-749-3025
E-mail: admission@msmnyc.edu
World Wide Web: http://www.msmnyc.edu

The Manhattan School of Music building and the Andersen Residence Hall as viewed from across Broadway.

MANHATTANVILLE COLLEGE

PURCHASE, NEW YORK

The College

Manhattanville, a coeducational, independent liberal arts college, attracts bright students who seek the challenge of a demanding curriculum at a small college that stresses individual attention and humanistic values. The College's mission is to educate ethically and socially responsible leaders for the global community, and faculty members and students find many ways to make that mission real, through academic course work, campus clubs, community service programs, and other ongoing activities. The College's population of 1,500 full-time undergraduates, who come to the college from across the United States and fifty-three countries, is extraordinarily diverse in terms of their interests, as well as their economic, ethnic, and geographic backgrounds.

Most students live on campus in one of four residence halls. More than fifty clubs and organizations center on particular interests and are open to all students. These groups include Amnesty International, Student Government, the Film Club, the Dance Ensemble, and Latin American Students Association. Students may also participate in fourteen NCAA Division III varsity athletic teams and intramural sports or may become involved in the newspaper, yearbook, literary magazine, or campus radio station. There are health services, 24-hour live food service (with free room service a few times per semester for each student), a fully equipped fitness center and pool, a campus café, and much more. The Career Services Office assists students with resumes and interviewing skills and in securing campus jobs, internships, and full-time positions at more than 350 area companies.

Location

Founded in New York City in 1841, the College moved to its present location in 1952, a beautiful 100-acre suburban campus in New York's Westchester County. The campus, in Purchase, New York, is just minutes from White Plains to the west and Greenwich, Connecticut, immediately to the east. It is 25 miles from the heart of Manhattan. Excellent shopping, dining, and entertainment facilities are minutes away, and many students find jobs and internships with companies whose corporate headquarters are nearby. The Valiant Express bus transports students to area shopping centers, directly to New York City on weekends, and to Manhattan-bound commuter trains on other days. Public transportation stops within the campus.

Majors and Degrees

Manhattanville College offers the full-time undergraduate degrees of Bachelor of Arts, Bachelor of Fine Arts, and Bachelor of Music. The College also offers part-time accelerated study culminating in Bachelor of Science degrees.

Students may choose from the following areas of study: African studies, American studies, art history, art (studio), Asian studies, biochemistry, biology, chemistry, classics, communications, computer science, creative writing, criminal justice, dance and theater, dance therapy, economics, education (including a 5-year B.A./M.A.T. program), English, environmental studies, film studies, finance, French, German, history, Holocaust studies, human resource management, international management, international studies, Irish studies, Italian, Latin American studies, legal studies, management, mathematics, music, music management, musical theater, neuroscience, philosophy, physics, political science, psychology, romance languages, social justice, self design, sociology, Spanish, women's studies, world literature, and world religions.

Students earning a Bachelor of Fine Arts may specialize in graphic design, painting, photography, printmaking, or sculpture. A professionally oriented Bachelor of Music is offered in music education. Other undergraduate programs include predental, pre–health sciences, prelaw, premedical, pre–physical therapy, and pre–speech-language pathology. To meet the growing demand from students interested in the liberal arts and the sciences, the College offers two 6-year programs with New York Medical College Graduate School of Health Sciences: a B.A./M.S. in speech-language pathology, and a B.A./M.S. in physical therapy. With Polytechnic University, the College offers two dual degrees in the computer science field: a B.A./M.S. in information technology, and a B.A./M.S. in computer science.

Academic Program

Manhattanville offers a traditional liberal arts program with the added benefits of very small classes and one-on-one teaching. More than 80 percent of classes have fewer than 20 students, and the student-teacher ratio is 10:1. At the core of Manhattanville's undergraduate curriculum is the portfolio. Working closely and meeting regularly with an adviser, the student discusses and plans his or her program to fulfill graduation requirements. Students establish a major and a minor from the different branches of the liberal arts, and they submit academic evidence of proficiency in written critical analysis and qualitative research. Study plans, annual evaluations, transcripts, and examples of the students' best work are part of the portfolio and are evaluated by a College-wide review board.

A special option open to B.A. candidates is the self-designed major. If students' interests direct them outside or beyond existing departmental majors, they may then propose a program of study to the Board of Academic Standards, delineating their goals and the means by which they will be achieved. A double major is also possible.

Off-Campus Programs

Manhattanville offers study abroad opportunities in hundreds of locations around the world, including Argentina, Belgium, England, Puerto Rico, Russia, and Zimbabwe. Students can choose from dozens of options through the College's own cooperative program, as well as countless others through its affiliation with American University's World Capitals Program.

Manhattanville conducts an exchange program with Sacred Heart University (Tokyo, Japan) and the Catholic University of Korea/Songsim (Seoul, South Korea). In addition, Manhattanville is affiliated with the New York State Visiting Students Program, through which students enrolled at a New York State college or university may spend a semester or a year at another participating institution. Manhattanville and the State University of New York College at Purchase also cooperate to enable students to enroll in courses on each other's campus that are not given at the home campus.

The College also offers a unique semester-long immersion in New York City, whereby a group of students live in the city and take courses taught by Manhattanville faculty members in subjects such as the sociology, history, architecture, and art of New York. Internships and service/leadership programs round out the popular program.

Academic Facilities

The Manhattanville Library is considered one of the foremost undergraduate teaching libraries in the country. In addition to a collection of more than 275,000 volumes and bound periodicals, the library offers access to hundreds of electronic journals, an impressive array of electronic and print reference materials, and a growing e-book collection. All resources are accessible to students anywhere, anytime, through remote data access. Its excellent reference facilities and extensive bibliographical holdings include the printed catalogs of such major libraries as the Bibliothèque Nationale, the British Museum, and the Library of Congress. The Menendez Language Laboratory includes tapes and record libraries that provide materials for class instruction and individual practice in French, Spanish, Russian, Italian, German, Chinese, Japanese, Hindi, Marathi, modern Hebrew, and English as a second language. The College provides a writing clinic, audiovisual facilities, a reading clinic, and a bibliographic instruction program.

The College has state-of-the-art computers, computer labs, and campus networking for student use and instruction. In addition, advanced music technology systems offer performing arts students limitless opportunities for creativity. Wireless access covering 75 percent of the campus is one of the reasons Manhattanville ranks as one of the top 100 wired campuses in the country.

Costs

For the 2003–04 academic year, tuition and fees were $21,430. Average room and board costs were $8730.

Financial Aid

Manhattanville offers both merit scholarships and need-based financial aid. More than 75 percent of Manhattanville students receive financial awards. The institutional form and the Free Application for Federal Student Aid (FAFSA) are required. The types of awards available are honors, merit, arts, and leadership scholarships; Manhattanville grants and scholarships; Federal Perkins Loans; Federal Stafford Student Loans; Federal Pell Grants; Federal Supplemental Educational Opportunity Grants; and Federal Work-Study Program awards as well as Tuition Assistance Program awards and Higher Education Opportunity Program awards for eligible New York State residents.

Faculty

At Manhattanville, student-faculty relationships are strong as a result of the advising system under which faculty members serve as advisers, guiding and counseling students throughout their undergraduate careers. Ninety-six percent of the faculty members hold a Ph.D. or terminal degree and a large majority serve full-time. Many faculty members live on campus in faculty housing.

Student Government

Students, in large measure, shape the quality of life on the Manhattanville campus. Elected representatives of the student body run the Student Government, which serves as a principal means of communication among the administration, faculty, and students. Its Board of Directors is responsible for formulating policy on student life and for implementing this policy through various committees. Student Government members also serve on the College's policymaking and ad hoc committees.

Admission Requirements

Manhattanville College admits men and women as candidates for undergraduate degrees if their academic records indicate the competence to engage in a challenging liberal arts curriculum. Admission to the College is selective, and the most important consideration is the student's secondary school performance. When weighing this aspect, the Admissions Committee evaluates the quality of the school, the strength of the student's program, and his or her success in those studies. Next, the committee considers the various recommendations that are submitted on behalf of the student along with scores on required standardized tests. The SAT I and/or the ACT are required. A campus interview is strongly recommended. Students who plan to specialize in music should come to Manhattanville for an audition or should secure permission to submit a tape. Students who plan to apply for the B.F.A. degree program should present portfolios to the art department for evaluation. The portfolios are not required for admission to the College.

Manhattanville offers both early decision admission and rolling admission. In both cases, advanced standing is given to accepted applicants who obtain scores of 4 or 5 on Advanced Placement examinations, have completed an International Baccalaureate program, or whose secondary school records warrant advancement.

Application and Information

The deadline for early decision applications is December 1, and the deadline for regular admission is March 1. The College subscribes to the Candidates Reply Date. Applications should be submitted as early in the senior year as possible. The application fee is $50. All application decisions are made without regard to race, religion, sex, national or ethnic origin, or handicap. Candidates may apply online at the Web site listed below.

For further information, students should contact:

Office of Undergraduate Admissions
Manhattanville College
2900 Purchase Street
Purchase, New York 10577
Telephone: 914-323-5464
800-32-VILLE (toll-free)
World Wide Web: http://www.manhattanville.edu

Reid Hall ("The Castle") at Manhattanville College.

MANNES COLLEGE OF MUSIC, NEW SCHOOL UNIVERSITY

NEW YORK, NEW YORK

The College

Training classical musicians is Mannes's main activity. The school's small size (fewer than 300 students) and small classes ensure personalized instruction and close interaction among students, faculty and staff members, and administrators. All students receive private lessons and participate in ensembles ranging in size from duos, trios, and quartets to full orchestra, chorus, scene productions, and fully staged operas.

Mannes offers its own undergraduate liberal arts curriculum focused on areas most pertinent to classical music. Students may choose to supplement this curriculum by taking courses at the other colleges of New School University. In addition, throughout their studies, students follow a program of instruction in the techniques of music. This program includes studies in ear training, sight singing, keyboard skills, theory, analysis, and dictation that is among the best in the world, all helping to train students to meet the unique challenges faced by musicians in the twenty-first century.

Graduate degrees offered include the Master of Music (M.M.), which is a two-year degree program offered in all orchestral instruments (violin, viola, cello, bass, flute, oboe, clarinet, bassoon, saxophone, horn, trumpet, trombone, tuba, harp, and percussion); piano, harpsichord, guitar, voice, composition, conducting, theory, and vocal accompanying. Students receive private lessons in their major field, performance classes (such as orchestra, opera, and chamber music), courses in the techniques of music, and chosen electives, which focus on specialized topics of the student's interest.

Mannes also offers the Professional Studies Diploma (PSD), which is an advanced course of study designed to enhance performance or compositional skills. The Professional Studies Diploma is generally pursued following an earned Master's degree or the equivalent. Individual programs are designed in coordination with the Associate/Assistant Dean. Orchestral instrument majors participate in orchestra during each semester of residency. Additionally, chamber music is a curricular component of some instrumental majors. All Mannes and some New School courses are available to qualified students; however, only graduate-level courses apply toward the Professional Studies diploma.

Total enrollment is 295, 52 percent of whom are international students. There are 156 faculty members, and the student-teacher ratio is 2:1. Average class size is 10 to 12 students.

Through New School University, Mannes is proud to offer housing facilities which include apartment-style dormitory suites equipped with full kitchens, full bathrooms, air conditioning, Internet service, and other amenities. Residences available to Mannes students are located in Greenwich Village, Union Square, and Lower Manhattan. All dormitories are equipped with a 24-hour doorman and resident advisers on every floor. All incoming freshman are offered on-campus housing, but it is not a requirement for admission. The housing office offers assistance with off-campus housing.

Location

Mannes is located in Manhattan's Upper West Side, one of the finest residential areas of New York City. It is within walking distance from the Museum of Natural History and Lincoln Center for the Performing Arts (home to the New York Philharmonic, the Metropolitan Opera, and other world renowned orchestras and ballet companies). Mannes students also benefit from and contribute to New York City's rich musical and cultural life.

Majors and Degrees

Undergraduate degrees offered include the Bachelor of Music (B.M.) in all orchestral instruments (violin, viola, cello, bass, flute, oboe, clarinet, bassoon, saxophone, horn, trumpet, trombone, tuba, harp, and percussion), piano, harpsichord, guitar, voice, composition, conducting, and theory. Students receive private lessons in their major field, performance classes (such as orchestra, opera, and chamber music,) course work in the techniques of music, and liberal arts courses and electives.

A Bachelor of Science (B.S.) is offered in all majors by completing the Bachelor of Music curriculum and taking or transferring from another institution an additional 30 academic credits.

The Undergraduate Diploma (UDPL) is offered in all majors and is equivalent to the Bachelor of Music degree, minus the liberal arts courses.

Academic Program

Some outstanding performance opportunities include the Mannes Orchestra, led by Samuel Wong and David Hayes; the Mannes Opera program, led by Joseph Colaneri; the Mannes Chorus; the Mannes Baroque Chamber Players; the Percussion Ensemble; NewMusicMannes; and numerous chamber music ensembles that perform year-round.

The Mannes Community Services Office employs students to perform in the widest range of New York settings such as official receptions, galas, and public and private settings, and are also encouraged to perform with many of New York's orchestras, choruses, and opera companies.

Mannes also offers concerto competitions for all performance majors, an audio recording facility, and career development advisement.

Academic Facilities

Degree candidates have access to the University's broad liberal arts curriculum, with offerings in the humanities, fine arts, and the social sciences. Mannes students share resources with New School University's other divisions, which include the New School, Eugene Lang College, Actors Studio Drama School, Parsons School of Design, Graduate Faculty of Political and Social Science, Robert J. Milano Graduate School of Management and Urban Policy, and the Jazz and Contemporary Music Program.

Mannes's home is a federal-style building on Manhattan's Upper West Side. The building houses classrooms, practice rooms, a state-of-the art computer lab, and the Harry Sherman Library, which offers access to more than 3 million books, 25,000 journals, a complete music and listening library, and study carrels. The New School University also offers the facilities of the Bobst Library at New York University through a consortium known as the Research Library Association of South Manhattan. The consortium's online catalog, Bobcat, is accessible over the Internet.

Mannes's two concert halls, seating 250 and 75 people, are the venues for hundreds of performances each year by students, faculty members, and artists-in-residence, as well as for Master Classes. The John Goldmark Practice Center, adjacent to Lincoln Center, provides additional practice rooms and an opera rehearsal room.

Costs

Tuition for the 2003–04 school year was as follows: for the B.M., B.S., M.M., and UDPL programs, $22,000; for the Professional Studies Diploma, $15,750; and for the ESL course work program, $3780. University fees were $1608. The average cost of one year of room and board was $12,960, and the average cost of books and supplies was $1950. A small percentage increase in costs is expected for the 2004–05 school year.

Financial Aid

Scholarships are available on the basis of merit and are determined at the time of the audition. Approximately 75 percent of Mannes students receive some form of scholarship. The average award ranges from 25 percent to 50 percent of tuition. In certain majors, opportunities exist for further assistance up to full tuition. Loans, grants, and work-study programs are available to students who fill out the Free Application for Federal Student Aid, the filing of which is required for U.S. citizens and permanent residents seeking financial aid of any type. A package of loans and information is sent along with the acceptance letter.

Faculty

Mannes is committed to providing broad and rigorous musical training in a friendly and supportive community that encourages artistic growth. The distinguished faculty includes some of New York City's most prominent musicians, as well as internationally known artists and ensembles. All students receive private lessons and participate in ensembles, and the 2:1 student-faculty ratio ensures personalized instruction and close interaction among, students, faculty and staff members, and administrators.

Admission Requirements

An application for admission to Mannes College of Music should consist of completed Unified Application for Conservatory Admission–Mannes Edition (available online at http://www.unifiedapps.org); a $100 nonrefundable application fee; official high school or college academic transcripts for all schools attended (graduate degree applicants need only send college transcripts); and one letter of recommendation from a recent music teacher or an evaluation from a professional musician. International students must submit a recent TOEFL score. Mannes's school code is 2398. A minimum computer-based TOEFL score of 213 and a successful English test taken at the audition is required. A minimum computer-based TOEFL score of 250 is required for all graduate theory, composition, and conducting majors.

Audition requirements vary by field of study and program sought, outlines of which can be found in the Mannes College catalog. During the audition period, musicianship skills are tested for all degree and UDPL applicants. These tests in dictation, ear training, piano, and theory are required in order to complete the application for entrance to the undergraduate and master's degree programs. English language testing is required of applicants for whom English is not their first language.

Application and Information

The application deadline for the main March entrance auditions is December 1. The application deadline for the late auditions in May is April 1.

For more information, students should contact:

Office of Admissions
Mannes College of Music
150 West 85th Street
New York, New York 10024
Telephone: 212-580-0210 Ext. 247
800-292-3040 (toll-free)
E-mail: mannesadmissions@newschool.edu
World Wide Web: http://www.mannes.edu

Mannes College of Music, New School University, located on Manhattan's Upper West Side.

MARIAN COLLEGE

INDIANAPOLIS, INDIANA

The College

Marian College, founded in 1851 by the Sisters of St. Francis, is a Catholic, ecumenical, coeducational, comprehensive liberal arts college. Located in the northwest suburbs of Indianapolis, the scenic 114-acre campus is composed of three turn-of-the-century estates, a lake, and a waterfall. Marian College provides an education that profoundly transforms lives and society. Faculty members are teachers who nurture students in an academic environment that is personalized for individual needs. As central Indiana's only Catholic college, Marian provides excellent teaching in the Franciscan and liberal arts traditions.

The close contact between students and faculty members at Marian College provides an exceptionally enriching experience for the approximately 1,500 students. Classes are small enough to permit seminars, group discussions, laboratories, and individual conferences. Marian's small population creates a friendly campus where students enjoy personal attention from faculty members. The student body is diverse, bringing with them the ideas and cultures of eighteen states and several other countries and representing many religious and ethnic traditions.

Extracurricular and social activities are an important part of life at Marian, giving students the opportunity to develop leadership abilities in a variety of ways. The theater club presents several productions annually. The madrigal singers, chorus, wind ensemble, and band may interest musically inclined students. Noteworthy films sponsored by student groups, as well as dances, mixers, field days, Homecoming, and sports, provide other social opportunities. Departmental clubs support classroom instruction. Student publications provide vital campus communication channels.

Marian College is a member of the National Association of Intercollegiate Athletics. The College provides opportunities for men to compete in intercollegiate baseball, basketball, cross-country, cycling, golf, soccer, tennis, and track. Women may compete in intercollegiate basketball, cheerleading, cross-country, softball, tennis, track, and volleyball. In addition to the intercollegiate sports program, the College provides numerous sports for both men and women through the intramural sports program. Nearly 90 percent of the students on campus participate in this College-organized program and have the use of all facilities. Located near the campus is the Major Taylor Velodrome, built for the 1982 Summer Sports Festival. Marian's team has won six national track championships and train at the Velodrome.

Location

Some of the necessities for a complete education can be found only in metropolitan areas. Despite its small-town atmosphere, the campus is a 10-minute drive from Indianapolis and such places as Clowes Hall, where Broadway plays and musicals, top entertainers, ballet, Shakespearean drama, and lecturers are scheduled regularly. Further exposure to the fine arts is provided by the Indianapolis Museum of Art, within view of the campus, and by the Indianapolis Symphony Orchestra, one of the best in the nation. Because Indianapolis is the state capital and also the largest city in the state, students interested in government and politics have superb opportunities to observe and participate. Professional basketball, baseball, football, and hockey are all 10 minutes away, and each May the city is the site of the Indianapolis 500. The NASCAR Brickyard 400 takes place at the Indianapolis Motor Speedway in August. Large shopping centers are also within minutes of the campus.

Majors and Degrees

The College offers programs leading to the Bachelor of Arts or the Bachelor of Science degree. Programs are offered in accounting, art, art history, biology, business administration, chemistry, communications, computer studies, economics, elementary education, English, finance, French, graphic design, history, international studies, management, management informations systems (MIS), marketing, mathematics, medical technology, music, nursing, pastoral leadership, philosophy, physical education, political science, psychology, religious education, secondary education, sociology, Spanish, sports management, and theology. Minors are available in most of these areas. Courses are also offered in humanities, journalism, and non-Western studies.

The Associate of Arts degree is offered in accounting, art, business administration, history, liberal arts, music, nursing, pastoral leadership, psychology, and religious studies.

Teacher education programs in elementary, secondary, and special education lead to certification. Combined programs in engineering are available with cooperating institutions. Preprofessional programs are available in dentistry, law, and medicine. Registered nurses (RNs) with one year of experience may earn a bachelor's degree in nursing.

Academic Program

Marian students build their major and minor areas of study on a foundation of courses in the humanities and the social and natural sciences. Students design their academic program with the help of their academic adviser. While general education requirements and those for major and minor fields of study are outlined by faculty members, students do arrange their schedules from a group of courses in fulfillment of the requirements. Because students enter college at differing levels of academic achievement, Advanced Placement or preparatory course work is available to freshmen and upperclass students. The Honors Program with its enriched curriculum also provides special opportunities for academically promising students.

Juniors and seniors may elect four courses (no more than two per semester) on a pass/fail basis. Seminars or comprehensives are required of seniors for academic assessment in their major field. Juniors and seniors may participate in a cooperative education program, which is designed to integrate classroom learning with practical work experience.

Freshmen who score well on the general examinations portion of the College-Level Examination Program (CLEP) test may receive up to 30 hours of credit toward their degree requirements. Other credit and Advanced Placement examinations are available.

Off-Campus Programs

Students interested in international study may spend a semester or two and/or a summer abroad. Marian College will assist these students in finding programs compatible with their degree requirements. Some courses not offered at Marian may be taken at any of the cooperating institutions in the Indianapolis area.

Academic Facilities

A 35-acre wetland ecological laboratory containing a small lake, a stream, a mature and second growth of hardwood forests, marshland, and a diverse assortment of wildlife is utilized by students. The area also serves as a resource for Marian's Environmental Studies Program. Laboratories in psychology, music, science, special education, and computer science are open to students for work in these fields. The library, containing more than 142,000 volumes and serving the Marian College community, could easily serve the needs of an institution many times the size of Marian. The Learning and Counseling Center offers such services as personal counseling, skill development, tutoring, and reentry support for nontraditional students.

Costs

For 2003–04, tuition was $16,800 per year, services and fees were $404, books and supplies were approximately $700, and room and board (twenty meals per week) were $5600 per year. A fifteen-meal-per-week plan is also available. Average personal expenses are $1260.

Financial Aid

The College awards yearly scholarships to outstanding students based on their academic records without regard to financial need. Athletic grants are awarded in all varsity sports for men and women. Indiana residents may qualify for state scholarships and grants. Marian College offers a full range of comprehensive academic scholarships. The College also participates in the Federal Pell Grant, Federal Perkins Loan, Federal Stafford Student Loan, Federal Work-Study, and Federal Supplemental Educational Opportunity Grant programs. Applicants for aid must file the Free Application for Federal Student Aid (FAFSA) to establish eligibility for these programs. The FAFSA may be obtained from a high school counselor or the Financial Aid Office of the College. The average 2003–04 financial aid package from all sources for enrolled freshmen was $17,000.

Faculty

Diversity in faculty members' educational and personal backgrounds contributes to the learning experience at Marian. Each faculty member, whether instructor or professor, teaches general education courses as well as specialized subjects; thus, that crucial initial contact of students and scholars begins in the freshman year. The faculty consists of 124 members, and the student-faculty ratio is 12:1. The close personal relationship among students, faculty members, and administrators is a particular strength of the education offered at Marian. The inclusion of part-time members—professional educators and businesspersons—in the faculty provides opportunities for students to become personally acquainted with leaders in the Indianapolis community.

Student Government

All students at Marian are members of the Student Association. The legislative arm of the association is the Executive Board, an elective body that chooses students to serve on various College committees, initiates activities of interest to students, and works for changes in College policies concerning students. The College believes that students should be involved in the affairs and decisions of the College community and encourages such involvement by inviting students to serve on its legislative body and on the majority of the College committees.

Admission Requirements

Marian College believes the goals and purposes of a liberal arts education are best attained within a diverse community and encourages applications from members of all cultural, racial, religious, and ethnic groups. Each year the Admissions Committee selects for admission men and women representing a wide variety of interests and backgrounds, from all parts of the United States and from several other countries.

Every applicant is expected to present 16 acceptable units of secondary school work, 4 of which should be in English, 3 or more in mathematics (algebra and geometry are recommended), 1 or more in a laboratory science, and 1 or more in social studies. Two years of a foreign language are strongly recommended. Important factors in considering the applicant for admission are the quality of academic achievement, including rank in the secondary school class; academic potential, as reflected by scores from the SAT I and/or the ACT; and evidence of leadership and service, as indicated by curricular and extracurricular contributions in the secondary school and community. Marian College also gives consideration to any student who has completed high school by passing the GED examination.

Transfer students are considered if they meet all the requirements stated above and are in good standing.

Application and Information

For admission applications and further information, students may contact:

Office of Admissions
Marian College
3200 Cold Spring Road
Indianapolis, Indiana 46222
Telephone: 317-955-6300
800-772-7264
E-mail: admissions@marian.edu
World Wide Web: http://www.marian.edu

Students enjoy Marian College's park-like campus.

MARIAN COLLEGE OF FOND DU LAC

FOND DU LAC, WISCONSIN

The College

Marian College is a community of students and faculty and staff members working together toward the pursuit of excellence in education. Founded in 1936 by the Congregation of Sisters of Saint Agnes as a private school for teacher education, Marian now offers more than forty majors and minors in professional and preprofessional programs. A strong liberal arts curriculum, combined with outstanding experiential education opportunities, gives students the reasoning, problem-solving, and communication skills essential for any career choice.

An active campus life provides many opportunities for the 1,203 traditional undergraduate students, 513 adult completion students, and 930 students pursuing master's degrees. The Marian community has many social organizations and clubs as well as twelve NCAA Division III athletic programs, including men's baseball, basketball, golf, ice hockey, soccer, and tennis and women's basketball, golf, soccer, tennis, and volleyball. Student life is further enhanced by a variety of programming that brings national entertainers to the Marian campus. Through its programming, Marian shows a continuous commitment to the service of diverse populations.

Students enjoy a variety of modern housing options while residing on campus. One traditional residence hall (completely renovated in 2000) and town house and courtyard complexes, with spacious living rooms, kitchens, bedrooms, and private bathrooms, are where Marian students make their home away from home. The Todd Wehr Alumni Center and coffee house and the atrium of the new Stayer Center for Technology and Executive Learning are two locations that not only enhance the beautiful 97-acre campus but also provide an atmosphere where students and faculty and staff members can relax and socialize.

In addition to the undergraduate degrees offered, Marian also provides executive education and degree completion programs for adults and master's degrees in education, nursing, and organizational leadership and quality.

Location

Situated in the heart of Fond du Lac (French for "bottom of the lake"), Marian College students have the privilege of living in a year-round recreational area where many people choose to vacation. Fond du Lac is a city of 40,000 that stretches from the southern end of Lake Winnebago, the largest lake in the state, to the rolling hills of southeastern Wisconsin. The College is located only 1 hour from both Milwaukee and Madison and 2½ hours from Chicago. Marian College has a long history of positive relations with the local community, which in turn takes great pride in the College and supports it greatly.

Majors and Degrees

Marian College of Fond du Lac awards bachelor's degrees with majors in accounting, administration of justice, applied information technology, art, art therapy, biology, broad field science, broad field social studies, chemistry, communication, cytotechnology, education (art, early childhood, elementary, music, and secondary), economics and finance, English, general business, graphic arts, history, interdisciplinary studies, management, marketing, mathematics, medical technology, modern languages, music, music industry, nursing, political science, psychology, radiologic technology, social work, sociology, Spanish, and sport and recreation management. Preprofessional programs are available in dentistry, medicine, pharmacy, and veterinary medicine along with a minor in law. Students may also design a major to fit their own needs and interests.

Academic Program

Six instructional divisions comprise Marian academic programming: the Division of Arts and Humanities, the Division of Business, the Division of Educational Studies, the Division of Mathematics and Natural Sciences, the Division of Nursing, and the Division of Social and Behavioral Science. In addition to classroom learning, more than 96 percent of Marian students receive hands-on work experience through internships, co-ops, and clinical programs prior to graduation. The classroom experience is further enhanced by the Marian Honors Program for exceptional students and the EXCEL Program for freshman students who need additional support for continued success in college.

All students, regardless of their specific degree program, must successfully complete 48 credits in the liberal arts general curriculum. Marian students must complete the requirements for at least one major and take at least 128 total hours of credit with a minimum average of 2 grade points for each credit hour. The senior year, or at least the last 32 credit hours, must be completed at Marian College. Credit is awarded for CLEP subject and general examinations according to current Marian criteria and policies. Details may be obtained from the Assistant Dean of Academic Affairs.

The College conducts traditional academic programs in two semesters, the first from late August to mid-December and the second from mid-January to mid-May. There is also a two-week Maymester in mid-May and a two-week Winterim in January. Students may also take advantage of extensive summer school sessions.

Off-Campus Programs

Marian offers a cooperative education program that allows students to integrate classroom theory with practical work experience. Students have extraordinary opportunities to test the appropriateness of their career choices to their interests, their abilities, and their temperaments while developing new knowledge, understanding, and skills. Cooperative education is open to all junior and senior students in good academic standing. Students must meet the specific requirements established by their major academic department. A student can earn a maximum of 12 credits for professional or paraprofessional work related to his or her academic and career interests. Students work under the close supervision of an employer, with coordination provided by a faculty member. In the professional programs of education, nursing, and social work, students complete extensive clinical experiences that prepare them to be skilled professionals upon graduation. There are also a number of immersion experiences available and a study-abroad program at Harlaxton College in England.

Academic Facilities

The Todd Wehr Alumni Center and coffee house, including the Marian College History Room, serves as the center for academic and social discourse on campus. Members of the Marian community enjoy the Common Grounds Coffeehouse for its rich beverages and entertainment offerings. In addition, 20 student baristas (servers) gain experience in this unique learning laboratory by serving in such internship roles as accounting manager, staff manager, and public relations and marketing specialist.

The Stayer Center for Technology and Executive Learning enhances the student academic experience. The first floor of the building houses computer labs and high-technology classrooms, as well as a 250-seat auditorium. Conference and executive training rooms are located on the second floor, and the third level provides additional visitor accommodations. In addition, a campuswide fiber-optic network keeps the College community connected by providing access to the Internet, e-mail, and a multitude of other information resources from every office, classroom, and residence hall room on the campus. Personal computers may be configured for direct access to the system, or students may utilize fully equipped computer labs around the campus.

The Cardinal Meyer Library is another intellectual center at Marian College. The library contains more than 91,000 volumes and microforms and subscribes to more than 750 periodicals, including electronic periodicals. The library subscribes to electronic databases of periodicals, including newspapers, and has a collection of more than 3,500 electronic scholarly and reference books. The library is fully automated, with CD-ROM and Internet access capabilities. Access to electronic library resources is available to members of the College community anywhere, anytime through the Internet.

Costs

Annual full-time undergraduate tuition for 2003–04 was $14,700. Housing costs ranged from $2600 to $3600, depending on the student's choice of accommodations. Students may select from a variety of meal plans, which in 2003–04 ranged from $2000 to $2400 per year. The cost of books is not included in the tuition figure.

Financial Aid

The Marian College Financial Aid Office coordinates an active program of financial assistance for students. More than 98 percent of students are recipients of aid, which is based on need and/or academic merit. The principal sources of aid include the Federal Pell Grant Programs, the Federal Work-Study Program, and Marian assistance. Academic scholarships, including the Academic Achievement Award ($7000), the Presidential Scholarship ($5000), the Trustee Scholarship ($4000), the Naber Leadership Award ($3000), the Sister Mary Shelia Burns Award, and numerous other renewable scholarships and awards are available to entering students.

Faculty

A hallmark of Marian College is its faculty's mission to teach. With a student-faculty ratio of 13:1, professors regard their students' success as a measure of their own and provide individualized attention to help students attain their academic, personal, and career goals. All classes are taught by faculty members with no use of graduate assistants.

Student Government

The Student Senate is the largest and most influential student organization on campus. It is the governing body of the students and their representative body in College governance. All registered students are members of the Student Senate. This body is responsible for initiating activities that are beneficial to the spiritual, intellectual, personal, and social development of every Marian student. Every registered student helps elect officers of the Student Senate to represent all other student groups, living units, clubs, and organizations. There are more than thirty student clubs and organizations represented in the Student Senate. A hallmark of the College is service to the community. Students are encouraged to participate and earn a service transcript indicating the hours provided.

Admission Requirements

Marian College encourages students who show evidence of academic motivation and ability to undertake baccalaureate-level studies to apply. In judging an applicant's eligibility, the College gives consideration to the entire secondary school record, ACT or SAT I test scores, and any academic credit earned after high school graduation. The ACT test is preferred. Admission decisions are made on a rolling basis, and, beginning October 2, applicants usually receive a response to their application within two weeks after all credentials have been received. When the application materials are reviewed by an admissions committee, the committee may direct the Admissions Office to accept the student, accept with provisions, or deny acceptance until evidence of academic potential is provided. Each applicant is considered on an individual basis, and an interview may be required.

Admission to freshman standing at Marian presupposes at least 16 units of high school credit, including at least 3 units of English, 2 of mathematics, 1 of laboratory science, and 1 of history. Biology and chemistry are prerequisites for the nursing program. Physics and a foreign language are recommended.

Students who have acquired academic credits at another accredited college may be admitted to Marian with advanced standing. Only college credits with a grade of C or better are accepted in transfer. The grade point average at Marian is based solely on courses taken at Marian College.

Marian College admits qualified students regardless of race, sex, creed, color, ethnic origin, or disability to all rights, privileges, and activities generally made available to students at the College.

Application and Information

For additional information regarding the application process or for other information, students may contact:

Stacey Akey
Assistant Vice President and Dean of Enrollment Management
Marian College
45 South National Avenue
Fond du Lac, Wisconsin 54935
Telephone: 920-923-7650
800-2-MARIAN Ext. 7650 (toll-free)
E-mail: admissions@mariancollege.edu
World Wide Web: http://www.mariancollege.edu

Marian College of Fond du Lac—a stimulating place to learn and grow.

MARIETTA COLLEGE
MARIETTA, OHIO

The College

Founded in 1835, Marietta College traces its roots to the Muskingum Academy, which was founded in 1797 as the first institution of higher learning in the Northwest Territory. Marietta's chapter of Phi Beta Kappa was the sixteenth in the nation, showing the College's early dedication to scholarship. Women were first admitted in 1897. About half of Marietta's 1,100 students come from a variety of states along the Eastern Seaboard, the South, and the Midwest; the rest come primarily from Ohio, the surrounding states, and nine other countries. More than forty states are represented in the Marietta student body. Situated on 120 acres within a block of downtown Marietta, the College has a number of academic and extracurricular facilities. Highlights of the campus include the McDonough Leadership Center, home to the most comprehensive program in leadership studies in the country; the McKinney Media Center, which houses two radio stations, a cable television station, and an award-winning student newspaper; and a pedestrian mall that enhances the central campus. A new recreation center features a 200-meter competition track, performance gymnasium, indoor rowing tanks, and more. The new Rickey Science Center opened in spring 2003, and it offers state-of-the-art science labs to house biology, chemistry, biochemistry, environmental science, math, computer science, and physics.

Marietta is one of the few colleges in Ohio with intercollegiate crew, a sport in which it has excelled. Marietta's premier men's baseball program has earned twenty-two conference championships, fifteen world series appearances, and three world series titles for NCAA Division III. Students become involved with the campus radio and television stations, the student newspaper, the literary magazine, the yearbook, drama productions, and musical groups, plus service and special interest clubs. National invitational art exhibits are sponsored annually by the College for the educational and cultural enrichment of students.

Location

Historic Marietta, Ohio, was the first permanent settlement in the Northwest Territory, settled by New Englanders in 1787. The city of 17,000 people retains a New England flavor with its wide, tree-lined brick streets, Colonial architecture, and large parks. Marietta is readily accessible by car via Interstate 77 (2 miles from campus) or by air from Wood County/Parkersburg Airport in West Virginia (6 miles from campus). The Ohio and Muskingum Rivers meet in Marietta, contributing to the economic, cultural, and recreational vitality of the area.

Majors and Degrees

Marietta offers all students foundation study in the liberal arts and sciences and the opportunity to gain concentrated study in either the traditional liberal arts disciplines or a number of preprofessional programs. Among the liberal arts are strong programs in biochemistry, biology, chemistry, English, physics, and psychology. Preprofessional programs include accounting, computer science, education, environmental science, graphic design, journalism, musical theater, petroleum engineering, radio/television studies, and a nationally renowned program in sports medicine.

Marietta College grants four baccalaureate degrees: the Bachelor of Arts, the Bachelor of Fine Arts, the Bachelor of Science, and the Bachelor of Science in Petroleum Engineering. Marietta is the only liberal arts college in the nation offering the petroleum engineering degree, which is accredited by the Accreditation Board for Engineering and Technology. Marietta also offers a major in sports medicine, the first such program at a small college to be accredited by the National Athletic Trainers Association. Students have the opportunity to be involved in the Bernard McDonough Leadership Program. The program, known as "the Marietta Model," allows students to study leadership through a multidisciplinary liberal arts perspective. Students involved in the McDonough Leadership Program have the option of completing a minor in leadership or receiving a certificate. Along with the core courses of problem solving, critical thinking, and leadership, the program also requires an internship and community service involvement at one of the many organizations in the Marietta area or throughout the world.

"Binary" programs—cooperative study programs with other institutions—enable qualified Marietta students to earn two degrees in such fields as engineering, forestry, natural resources, and nursing. Preprofessional programs are offered in dentistry, law, medicine, physical therapy, and veterinary medicine.

The College's Education Department is accredited by the State of Ohio Department of Education and offers programs leading to licensure in early childhood, middle childhood, and secondary school education. Ohio has reciprocity with many other states. In addition, the College's programs are accredited by the North Central Association of Colleges and Schools.

Academic Program

Marietta students are known for both their breadth and depth of study. Freshmen take a special first-year program that begins with the College Experience Seminar and includes courses in composition (English 101), oral presentation (Speech 101), and mathematics. Every student also completes a liberal arts core of sequence courses in the humanities, social sciences, science, and the fine arts. There is an honors program for students who are prepared for and desire an extra challenge and who wish to graduate with honors.

Off-Campus Programs

Students seeking international study experience may make use of Marietta's association with the Institute for the International Education of Students (IES), the international study program of Central College of Iowa, or the programs of the East Central College Exchange. The programs have centers in Austria, the British Isles, France, Germany, Mexico, and Spain and in Asia. Students may also choose other accredited international-study programs. Finally, the College has numerous exchange programs with the People's Republic of China and annually has both faculty members and students teaching and studying in China.

Students whose interests range from economics to government and politics may take advantage of programs offered through the College's affiliation with two institutions located in the nation's capital. Courses are offered through the Washington Semester program of American University, and internships are available through the Washington Center for Learning Alternatives.

Academic Facilities

Marietta's Dawes Memorial Library will undergo a $1-million renovation next year. The library houses 260,000 volumes, 1,500 periodicals, and an online card catalog. As a member of OhioLINK, the Library provides access to a substantial number of books, materials, and databases. Among the special collections are the Rodney M. Stimson Collection of Americana, a collection of rare fifteenth- through nineteenth-century books, and an extraordinary collection of historic documents pertaining to the Northwest Territory and early Ohio. The card catalog and database are computerized through OCLC (Online Computer Library Center). The Hermann Fine Arts Center includes a laboratory theater, providing study and performance facilities for the College's art, drama, and music departments. Modern computing facilities include 200 personal computers connected by campus network. The campuswide network provides e-mail, Internet, and World Wide Web access. Students can work in computer labs, the library, and the student center, as well as in five academic buildings. The College has well-equipped science labs and its own astronomical observatory and a state-of-the-art computer lab for graphic design students. For instructional and communications purposes, the College operates a media center with a 9,200-watt stereo FM station, a 10-watt FM station, and a television station that reaches more than 12,000 homes via a community cable system. All programs are run by students.

Costs

The total two-semester cost for 2003–04 for a student residing on campus was $26,836. This figure included $3176 for room, $2770 for board, and $536 for fees, but did not include the cost of books (approximately $500 per year) and personal expenses.

Financial Aid

About 85 percent of current Marietta students receive financial aid based on need. The average award for 2003–04 was $18,000. A number of merit-based scholarships are available in addition to funds allocated through College grants and federal and state sources. Members of the entering freshman class receive academic merit scholarships for three different levels of achievement. Students with a minimum GPA of 3.75, a minimum score of 30 on the ACT, or a minimum score of 1350 on the SAT I receive a Trustees scholarship ranging from $9000 to $13,000. Students with a GPA of 3.5, a score of 27 on the ACT, or a score of 1200 on the SAT I receive a President's scholarship ranging from $6000 to $9000. Finally, those students with a GPA of 3.25, a score of 25 on the ACT, or a score of 1150 on the SAT I receive a Dean's scholarship ranging from $4000 to $6000. Fine Arts Scholarships are awarded annually to winners of an art, music, and drama competition. Numerous work-study jobs are available to students in many campus departments. Grants are available for children and grandchildren of alumni.

Faculty

Close personal contact between students and professors is one of Marietta's primary features. All departmental faculty members, regardless of rank, teach courses. Full professors teach freshman courses. More than 80 percent of the College's full-time faculty members hold doctorates. Professors share their homes, outside interests, and hobbies with students. A 12:1 student-faculty ratio makes this possible.

Student Government

Through the Student Senate and its committee system, students have responsibility for the cocurricular aspects of College life. Students hold memberships on most faculty and trustee committees, as well as on various departmental committees. Housing boards in both men's and women's residence halls provide programming and dormitory governance. In addition, there are more than sixty-five active clubs and organizations on campus.

Admission Requirements

Admission decisions are based upon the high school record, scores on national exams (SAT or ACT), an essay, extracurricular involvement, and recommendations from guidance counselors or teachers. While admission is selective and competitive, individual consideration is given to each application. The admission committee seeks a cross section of students whose ability and past performance indicate that they can compete successfully. Credit is granted for Advanced Placement and International Baccalaureate higher-level 1B exams.

Application and Information

Students should apply early in their senior year of high school to guarantee a place in the fall. Marietta operates on a rolling admission plan, and students are notified of acceptance within one month after all application materials are complete. Students applying for financial aid should apply before March 1 of their senior year to be considered for merit scholarships.

To receive information about Marietta or to apply for admission, students should contact:

Office of Admission
Marietta College
Marietta, Ohio 45750-4005
Telephone: 800-331-7896 (toll-free)
E-mail: admit@marietta.edu
World Wide Web: http://www.marietta.edu

Erwin Hall (1850), the oldest building on the Marietta campus, is listed on the National Register of Historic Places.

MARIST COLLEGE

POUGHKEEPSIE, NEW YORK

The College

Marist College is located on the Hudson River, just north of the city of Poughkeepsie, midway between New York City and Albany. The 150-acre riverside campus comfortably accommodates 4,000 full-time undergraduates. The campus has twenty-eight buildings, including nine residence halls, three major classroom buildings, the James A. Cannavino Library, and a student center that includes a bookstore, music rooms, a theater, and a cafeteria. Town-house residences and garden apartments are also available for upperclass students. There are three major athletics fields and a boathouse and waterfront facilities for sailing and crew. The James J. McCann Recreation Center, one of the largest collegiate sports complexes in the Mid-Hudson Valley, houses a 4,000-seat field house and a natatorium with a diving well and spectator space for 700, as well as an indoor track, a crew tank, handball and racquetball courts, a weight room, a dance studio, and other facilities for recreation and competition.

Campus life accommodates a wide range of interests and talents. The student-administered Student Programming Council annually presents a full schedule of films, concerts, and social activities. More than seventy clubs and organizations are available in many areas, including theater, drama, music, debate, publications, and volunteer programs. Varsity sports for men are sponsored in baseball, basketball, crew, cross-country, diving, football, lacrosse, soccer, swimming, tennis, and track. Varsity sports for women are offered in basketball, crew, cross-country, diving, lacrosse, soccer, softball, swimming, tennis, track, and volleyball. Ice hockey, skiing, an equestrian team, rugby, and soccer are available as club sports. The Marist Red Foxes compete in NCAA Division I in the Metro-Atlantic Athletic Conference (MAAC). An extensive intramural program encourages all students to participate in athletic recreation, and more than 80 percent of Marist students take part in club or team activities.

Special student services are offered in the areas of academic advising, counseling, career development, campus ministry, veterans' affairs, financial aid, health, residence living, and support of disabled students.

Graduate degrees are available in business, computer science, counseling and community psychology, educational psychology, information systems, public administration, and school psychology.

Location

Marist's location in the historic and scenic Hudson River Valley provides access to many cultural and recreational opportunities. The Franklin D. Roosevelt Home and Presidential Library and the original plant of the IBM Corporation attest to the national and international significance of the region and its people and organizations. The river also serves as a focus for the College's Environmental Studies Program, while the nearby Catskill Mountains provide areas for such outdoor activities as hiking, skiing, and rock-climbing. A short distance from the campus, the city of Poughkeepsie offers a major civic center that consolidates many of the area's cultural programs and expands leisure-time choices. With Amtrak and Metro North railroad stations only minutes from campus, students also have convenient access to New York City, Albany, Boston, and other major metropolitan areas.

Majors and Degrees

The College is organized into the academic areas of the School of Computer Science and Math, the School of Social and Behavioral Sciences, the School of Communication and the Arts; and the School of Liberal Arts. The Bachelor of Arts is awarded in American studies, communication arts, computer mathematics, economics, English, fine arts, French, history, mathematics, philosophy, political science, psychology, psychology/special childhood education, and Spanish. The Bachelor of Science is offered in accounting, athletic training, biology, business administration, chemistry, computer science, criminal justice, digital media, environmental science, information systems, information technology, medical technology, and social work. The Bachelor of Professional Studies is offered in fashion design/fashion merchandising. Concentrations are offered in Jewish studies, Latin American studies, paralegal studies, and public administration, among others. In order to provide greater academic opportunities for students, the College offers two combined B.A./M.A. programs (one in psychology and one in teacher education) and two combined B.S./M.S. programs (one in information systems and one in computer science). These accelerated programs allow students to graduate with both degrees in five years.

Preprofessional programs in law, medicine, dentistry, and pre–veterinary medicine and other allied health professions are available. Marist's teacher education program qualifies students for secondary education teacher certification in biology, chemistry, English, French, history, mathematics, social studies, and Spanish and for teacher certification in special-childhood education.

Academic Programs

Central to academic planning at Marist is the core curriculum, a program that provides all students with a solid educational foundation in the liberal arts. Students can take advantage of the double-major option that allows equal study in two subject areas. They can also choose a major in one subject and a minor in another area of interest. The Emerging Leaders Program, the Dean's Circle, the Honors Program, the Marist Abroad Program, the Center for Estuarine Studies, and special academic advising are available for students wishing to enhance the academic experience. Faculty members help all students identify areas of academic interest and then continue to support students as that interest is developed and explored.

Off-Campus Programs

Through the international study options offered, students can spend their junior or senior year abroad. Marist students, representing a cross section of majors, have studied in many countries in Europe, as well as in Africa, Asia, Australia, and Latin America. Through the College's membership in the Associated Colleges of the Mid-Hudson Area, Marist students may cross-register at any one of four other institutions: Culinary Institute of America, Dutchess Community College, State University of New York College at New Paltz, and Ulster Community College.

A comprehensive program of off-campus internships is offered in all majors, and Marist has one of the largest communication arts internship programs in the Northeast. Cooperative education opportunities (paid work experiences) are currently available in a number of majors.

Academic Facilities

Marist College is consistently recognized for excellence in the use of digital technology in the classroom and was listed in *Yahoo! Internet Life's* "100 Most Wired Colleges." A partnership with IBM has provided the College with more than $30 million in computer technology, and the 4-year-old James A. Cannavino Library has been hailed by the *New York Times* as a model for digital libraries of the twenty-first century. This three-story landmark facility allows students and faculty members to access material stored on the College's powerful IBM S/390 mainframe as well as online sources of information from around the world. The $25-million library houses book stacks on its ground floor; research materials, periodicals, and an "e-scriptorium" on its main floor; and four state-of-the-art digital classrooms, a Center for Collaborative Learning, and the Weiss Language Center on its top floor. The Cannavino Library also offers more ports per student than any other college or university library in the United States; at any of the 860 seats—ranging from individual study carrels to soft-cushioned easy chairs overlooking the Hudson River—students and faculty members can plug in laptops and connect to sources of information from around the world. (In addition to the more than 200 desktop systems in place, IBM ThinkPad laptops are available for loan at the circulation desk.) Collaborative study rooms allow group discussions on projects, while quiet study areas with scenic vistas offer space from which to read and research. The Cannavino Library's two-story atrium entrance also features a coffee bar and is a popular gathering place for students, faculty members, and staff members.

The Lowell Thomas Communications Center links the study of communications with computer technology. It features two sets of television and radio broadcast studios, computer-equipped classrooms, and print journalism areas, as well as a public gallery displaying memorabilia of the late Lowell Thomas, the legendary broadcaster and explorer.

The Instructional Media Center's functions include consultation on media methods; production of films, slides, and videotapes; dispensing of audiovisual hardware; and distribution of video programming to classrooms. Group work and individual study in Arabic, Chinese, French, German, Italian, Japanese, and Spanish as well as in English for non-English-speaking students, are available.

The Margaret M. and Charles H. Dyson Center incorporates some of the most advanced technologies in education and houses the College's undergraduate and graduate programs in business, social and behavioral sciences, public administration, and public policy. The center is also used for innovative computer simulations and computer-assisted group learning and problem solving. In addition, it houses the School of Adult Education and the Office of Graduate Admissions.

Costs

Tuition and fees for 2003–04 were $19,354 for a full year. Room and board for a full year were $8950. The additional costs of transportation, clothes, and spending money usually amount to several hundred dollars. Students should plan on books and supplies costing an estimated $1200 per year.

Financial Aid

Approximately 70 percent of the College's full-time students receive aid from Marist and outside sources, including New York State Tuition Assistance Program (TAP) grants, Federal Pell Grants, Federal Supplemental Educational Opportunity Grants, Federal Perkins Loans, Federal Stafford Student Loans (Subsidized and Unsubsidized), and Federal Work-Study Program awards. Marist also has merit awards for outstanding students that are not based on financial need. Overall, Marist annually awards more than $10 million in grants and scholarships from its own funds. For a student to be considered for assistance, the Free Application for Federal Student Aid (FAFSA) should be filed as soon as possible after January 1. The financial aid staff is available to discuss financial aid possibilities with all prospective students.

Faculty

The College has 168 full-time faculty members, approximately 90 percent of whom either hold doctorates or are doctoral candidates. A strong working relationship between students and faculty members is an important aspect of the learning process at Marist. The student-faculty ratio is currently 16:1.

Student Government

Student representation in decisions affecting the College is a tradition at Marist. Through Student Government committees, the student body is given a role in both administrative and academic policymaking.

Admission Requirements

Applicants must have graduated from an accredited high school. Rigor of high school curriculum, grade point average, and rank in class are primary considerations; admission is based on a review of the high school transcript, scores on the SAT I or ACT, a personal essay, and the recommendation of the guidance counselor or college adviser.

Application and Information

Application may be made for either September or January enrollment, depending on the choice of the applicant. Students can apply on line through Marist's web pages at the address listed below. The College notifies regular candidates of the admission decision in mid-March. The completed application form, the secondary school transcript, results of the SAT I or ACT, the recommendation of the guidance counselor or college adviser, a teacher recommendation, and an application fee of $40 must be submitted before a decision on admission can be made. Candidates for early action should apply by December 1. Candidates for regular admission should apply by February 15.

Additional details and application forms are available by contacting:

Admissions Office
Marist College
3399 North Road
Poughkeepsie, New York 12601
Telephone: 845-575-3226
800-436-5483 (toll-free)
E-mail: admissions@marist.edu
World Wide Web: http://www.marist.edu

MARLBORO COLLEGE

MARLBORO, VERMONT

The College

Students come to Marlboro College with a passion for learning and a desire to create a course of study tailored to their own interests. Tucked away in the foothills of Vermont's Green Mountains, Marlboro offers a rigorous liberal arts curriculum that is taught in small classes and advanced one-on-one instruction, called tutorials. Marlboro's goal is to teach students to think clearly and learn independently, develop a command of concise and correct writing, and aspire to academic excellence, all while participating responsibly in a self-governing community. The College's 8:1 student-faculty ratio sparks dynamic exchanges between students and faculty members both in and out of the classroom and fosters a close-knit community in which asking the right questions is more important than knowing the right answers. Two thirds of all Marlboro students go on to graduate study.

Marlboro opened in fall 1947. The campus was originally a cluster of barns and other farm buildings that the first students converted into classrooms and dormitories. The fields and woodlands that make up its rural 350-acre campus are perfect for cross-country skiing and other outdoor activities. The College Outdoor Program offers instruction and equipment for canoeing, kayaking, rock climbing, backpacking, and other sports that bring students in touch with the surrounding environment. The soccer team competes with other colleges, and more impromptu volleyball, basketball, softball, and Ultimate Frisbee teams compete intramurally. In addition, Marlboro's broomball (a game akin to hockey) tournament takes place each winter, with prizes not only for the team that wins the most games but also for the team with the best costumes. Campus committees organize many events both on and off campus, including concerts, lectures, poetry and fiction readings, art shows, and trips to Boston, Montreal, and New York for museum visits, shopping, and baseball games. Other activities that enrich campus life include parties, dances, plays, and film screenings.

Marlboro is—and intends to remain—one of the nation's smallest liberal arts colleges, with some 330 students. Students come from nearly forty states and approximately six other countries. Transfer students—who make up one quarter of each incoming class—bring an important perspective to the campus community. More than 80 percent of all students live in campus housing, which consists of small dormitories (both single-sex and coed), several four-bedroom cottages, and a renovated country inn.

Location

The village of Marlboro, 2 miles from the College, consists of a post office, a town clerk's office, and an inn. About 1200 residents live within the 36-square-mile township. During the summer, the village swells to accommodate the famous Marlboro Music Festival. The town of Brattleboro, 12 miles away, is a lively cultural and commercial center located on the first Vermont exit off Interstate 91. The College is 2 hours by car from Boston and 4 hours from New York City and Montreal.

Majors and Degrees

Marlboro confers the Bachelor of Arts and Bachelor of Science degrees in thirty-three areas of study, which can be combined in an almost limitless number of ways. The College also offers Bachelor of Arts and Bachelor of Science degrees in international studies through its World Studies Program (WSP).

Majors offered at Marlboro include American studies, anthropology, art history, astronomy, biochemistry, biology, ceramics, chemistry, classics, computer science, cultural history, dance, development studies (in the WSP), economics, environmental studies, film/video studies, history, international studies, languages, literature, mathematics, music, painting, philosophy, photography, physics, political science, psychology, religion, sculpture, sociology, theater, visual arts, and writing.

Academic Programs

In the first two years, Marlboro students study broadly, discover new interests, and begin to see the connections that lead many to pursue interdisciplinary work later. Each new student is paired with a faculty adviser and joins an advising group of sophomores, juniors, and seniors as well as freshmen. Students learn from each other at Marlboro.

Marlboro believes that clear writing both reflects and engenders clear thinking. The College, therefore, requires each new student to pass a Clear Writing Requirement within three semesters of enrolling at the College. Designated writing courses, faculty advisers, and student writing tutors all help new students meet the requirement.

Marlboro's Plan of Concentration, more than any other academic component, sets the College apart from other undergraduate programs. Undertaken by all Marlboro students in their junior and senior years, the plan is the collection of related projects and papers that form the final product of the student's academic work at Marlboro. It is an individualized program of classes, research, experiences, one-on-one study, and original thought, driven by the student's interests and academic goals and designed in close collaboration with faculty sponsors. Final evaluation of the student's plan is conducted by his or her faculty advisers and an outside examiner who is a recognized expert in the student's field.

Off-Campus Programs

Students working on the Plan of Concentration often travel abroad or attend other institutions for a period of time to augment their academic work. Marlboro faculty members may help plan these pursuits and frequently aid students in securing internships in academic fields. The College sponsors several field trips each year, ranging from community service work in South Carolina and Costa Rica to interdisciplinary research in Cuba and Vietnam.

The World Studies Program is a four-year program leading to a Bachelor of Arts or Bachelor of Science degree in international studies. The program involves intensive study on campus, as well as a six- to eight-month internship abroad. In addition, WSP sponsors regular International Nights, which generally include a themed dinner, music from other countries, and lectures or films.

Academic Facilities

Marlboro's academic facilities offer small classrooms and oversized faculty offices for students to meet in small groups and individually with their professors. Facilities supporting student research and creative explorations include a new DNA lab, a state-of-the-art black and white/digital darkroom, a digital film editing studio, two pottery studios, and an astronomical observatory. Marlboro's ongoing campus renewal project has, to date, doubled the size of the library and added a suite-style dorm. Construction has begun on the Rudolf and Irene Serkin Performing Arts Center, which will offer dedicated spaces for rehearsing and performing music, dance, and drama.

Costs

Tuition and fees at Marlboro are $25,740 for the 2004–05 academic year. Room and board cost are $7800.

Financial Aid

No one should refrain from applying to Marlboro because of perceived inability to meet costs. More than 80 percent of all Marlboro students receive financial help. The College is committed to helping any student who qualifies for admission assemble the financial resources necessary to attend, and need is not a factor in the admission decision. Merit scholarships are also available.

Faculty

Marlboro's 40 full-time faculty members are committed first and foremost to teaching, rather than to publishing or research. The lively exchange of ideas between teachers and students is the cornerstone of the Marlboro curriculum.

Student Government

All students and faculty and staff members are equal members of the College Town Meeting. Since the opening of the College in 1947, the community has come together every few weeks to debate and decide budget initiatives, College policies, and other issues. A board of Selectpersons, elected by the College community, serve the College's interests and are responsible for drafting Town Meeting rules and regulations. Students serve with faculty and staff members on more than thirty College committees, including those that make admissions and faculty-hiring decisions. Other important committees include the social committee and the Community Court, which is responsible for enforcing campus regulations.

Admission Requirements

The admission committee seeks students with intellectual promise; a high degree of motivation, self-discipline, personal stability, and social concern; and the ability and desire to contribute to the College community. All applicants are considered without regard to race, creed, sex, sexual orientation, national or ethnic origin, age, or disability. Transfers and older or returning students are encouraged to apply.

Like most colleges, Marlboro requires students to submit a variety of documentation, from high school transcripts to teacher recommendations. Unlike most colleges, however, Marlboro's review process is conducted by an Admissions Committee composed of students and faculty and staff members. This committee evaluates each applicant as a unique individual who possesses qualities that are not necessarily quantifiable.

An interview is required of all applicants. When a visit to the campus is not possible, alternative arrangements can be made. Many campus interviews are conducted by faculty members in the applicant's area of interest. Marlboro does not use a formulaic approach in making admission decisions. Applicants are encouraged to demonstrate their particular strengths; the goal is a successful match between the student and the College.

Application and Information

New students and transfers are admitted for either the spring or fall semester. Applicants for the fall semester have a choice of three admission plans. Early decision is for those students who have thoroughly researched Marlboro and for whom Marlboro is the first choice. Applicants should be aware that early decision is binding. The deadline for submitting application materials is November 15, and applicants are notified by December 15. Early action, a nonbinding plan, has a deadline of January 15. These applicants are notified of a decision on February 1. The recommended regular admission deadline is February 15.

An application for admission must include a completed application form with a $50 fee, complete transcripts from all secondary schools and colleges, SAT I or ACT scores, an analytical writing sample, a personal statement, an interview, and two recommendations. Interviews and campus visits can be scheduled at any time during the application process. The Admissions Committee welcomes applications from home-schooled students. In lieu of a high school transcript, home-schooled students must submit a detailed description of their curriculum.

Office of Admissions
P.O. Box A, South Road
Marlboro College
Marlboro, Vermont 05344-0300
Telephone: 802-257-4333
800-343-0049 (toll-free)
Fax: 802-451-7555
E-mail: admissions@marlboro.edu
World Wide Web: http://www.marlboro.edu

On the campus of Marlboro College.

MARSHALL UNIVERSITY

HUNTINGTON, WEST VIRGINIA

The University

Marshall University is a public institution, established as Marshall Academy in 1837 and granted university status in 1961. Assigned a major role as an urban-oriented university by the West Virginia Higher Education Policy Commission, it is devoted to offering both undergraduate and graduate courses of study to accommodate both full-time students and employed persons who wish to pursue studies on a part-time basis. The Community and Technical College of the University provides two-year associate degree programs and prebaccalaureate courses. The health-care expertise of the medical staff and faculty has given rise to a concentration of undergraduate programs in allied health technologies and sciences. The school has been recognized as a "best value" based on academic quality and moderate cost.

The Graduate School offers various master's degree programs, a Ph.D. in biomedical sciences, and a Psy.D. in psychology; the M.D. is available at the Marshall University School of Medicine. Marshall offers a master's degree in adult and technical education; art; biological sciences; biomedical sciences; business administration; chemistry; communication disorders; communication studies; counseling; criminal justice; early childhood, elementary, or secondary education; educational specialist studies; engineering; English; environmental science; exercise science; family and consumer science; forensic science; geography; health and physical education; health-care administration; history; humanities; industrial and employee relations; information systems; journalism; leadership studies; mathematics; music; nursing; physical science; political science; psychology; reading education; safety; sociology; special education; teaching; and technology management.

Marshall now offers the Ed.D. degree in educational leadership. The Ed.D. degree in curriculum and instruction is offered in cooperation with West Virginia University. A master's degree in forestry and in environmental management is offered in cooperation with Duke University.

All of the University's academic programs are highly regarded by professional schools and educators and business, industry, and government. The University is fully accredited by the North Central Association of Colleges and Schools. AACSB International–The Association to Advance Collegiate Schools of Business accredits the Lewis College of Business.

Eighty percent of Marshall's students are residents of West Virginia. Approximately 2,200 live in campus housing. The informal and relaxed atmosphere of the six residence halls, single sex and coed, contributes an important focus to life at Marshall. The University offers more than 100 student organizations that provide excellent opportunities for extracurricular involvement. Twelve national fraternities and seven national sororities represent social organizations, with the majority having houses. Clubs, organizations, intramural athletics, theater, musical ensembles, student government, religious groups, and Black United Students provide many cultural and social activities. Marshall is a member of the NCAA-1A Mid-American Conference. Intercollegiate sports include men's baseball, basketball, cheerleading, cross-country, football, golf, soccer, and track and field and women's basketball, cheerleading, cross-country, golf, soccer, softball, swimming and diving, tennis, track and field, and volleyball.

Location

Huntington, with a population of 55,000, is the second-largest urban center in West Virginia. It is located on the banks of the Ohio River in the Tri-State region, bordering eastern Kentucky and southern Ohio. The area has many good shopping centers, theaters, parks, swimming pools, golf courses, churches, and art galleries. Huntington's Big Sandy Superstore Arena is host to some of the top names in entertainment. Many of these activities are within walking distance of the Marshall University campus. The city and the University work effectively together to provide the best educational and cultural opportunities possible. A regional airport, Amtrak, and Greyhound Bus Line provide transportation to and from the city.

Majors and Degrees

The Bachelor of Arts (B.A.) degree is offered in basic humanities, classical or modern languages (French, German, Latin, and Spanish), communication disorders, communication studies, counseling, criminal justice, economics, education (elementary and secondary), English, family and consumer science, geography, geology, history, international affairs, journalism and mass communications, multidisciplinary studies, physical education, political science, psychology, and sociology. The B.A. degree is also available through the Board of Regents External Degree Program. The Bachelor of Science (B.S.) degree is offered in biological science, botany, chemistry, computer science, cytotechnology, dietetics, environmental biology, geography, geology, integrated science and technology, mathematics, microbiology, park resources and leisure services, physics, physiology/molecular biology, safety technology, and zoology. The Bachelor of Business Administration (B.B.A.) degree is awarded in accounting, economics, finance, management, management information systems, and marketing. The Bachelor of Fine Arts (B.F.A.) is offered in music, theater, and visual arts. The Bachelor of Science in Medical Technology (B.S.M.T.), the Bachelor of Science in Nursing (B.S.N.), and the Bachelor of Social Work (B.S.W.) degrees are also offered.

The Associate of Applied Science (A.A.S.) degree is offered in banking and finance, electronics technology, health information technology, hospitality management, information technology, interior design, legal assistant studies, management technology, medical assistant studies, medical lab technology, physical therapist assistant studies, police science, radiologic technology, respiratory therapy assistant studies, and technical studies. The Associate of Science in Nursing (A.S.N.) degree is also offered.

Academic Program

Each undergraduate division specifies its own sequence requirements, but all baccalaureate degree students must complete a minimum of 128 credit hours with an overall GPA of at least 2.0. All students must complete general requirements in humanities, mathematics, science, and social sciences. To qualify as full-time, the undergraduate student must carry at least 12 credit hours per semester. Permission from the academic dean is required for students who wish to enroll for 19 hours or more in one semester.

Students may receive credit through Advanced Placement or College-Level Examination Program tests. Marshall University offers the following special programs: Public Service Internship, Honors Program, Semester Abroad Program, National Student Exchange, Academic Common Market, Cooperative Work-Study Program, U.S. Army Reserve Officers' Training Corps (ROTC), remediation services, academic assistance, counseling, and job placement.

The Marshall Plan for Quality Undergraduate Education went into effect in 1995. Designed to provide Marshall graduates with a competitive advantage, it includes science/computer literacy, global studies, intensified writing courses, and a capstone experience for all baccalaureate students entering at that time and later.

Academic Facilities

Facilities on the Marshall University campus include the Center for Academic Excellence; the Center for the Fine and Performing Arts; the Birke Art Gallery; the H.E.L.P. Center, for those with learning disabilities; the Center for International Programs; the Psychology

Clinic; the Fitness and Wellness Center; the Speech and Hearing Clinic; the Writing Center; the Learning Resource Center; language, mathematics, chemistry, and physics laboratories; WPBY-TV and WMUL-FM studios; and the Center for Academic Support. The John Deaver Drinko Library, an ultramodern library and information center that opened in 1998, provides 390 computer stations, group study rooms, a reading lab, a 24-hour computer lab, and a café among its many features.

Costs

Tuition and fees for the 2003–04 academic year were $3260 for West Virginia residents, $6004 for Metro students (residents of the counties adjacent to Huntington, West Virginia), and $8994 for out-of-state students. Room and board were $5856, and books averaged $800.

Financial Aid

Approximately 50 percent of the student body receives some type of financial assistance. Students who are admitted by February 1 and submit the application for financial aid by March 1 are considered for some type of financial aid. Marshall University participates in the following programs: Federal Pell Grant, Federal Supplemental Educational Opportunity Grant, West Virginia Higher Education Grant, Federal Work-Study, Federal Stafford Student Loans, Federal Perkins Loans, and Federal PLUS. Scholarships of $500 are guaranteed to students with a minimum ACT composite score of 20 (or an SAT I composite score of 930) and a 3.2 GPA. Scholarships of $750 are awarded to freshmen with either a 3.20–3.49 GPA and a minimum ACT composite score of 25 (or an SAT I composite score of 1130) or a 3.5 GPA with a minimum ACT composite score of 23 (or an SAT I composite score of 1050). Scholarships of $1250 are guaranteed to students with a minimum ACT composite score of 25 (or an SAT I composite score of 1140) and a 3.5 GPA; a tuition waiver and $1250 are guaranteed to students with a minimum ACT composite score of 30 (or an SAT I composite score of 1340) and a 3.5 GPA. There is no separate application for scholarships at the University; however, a student's application for admission must be received in the office of admission by January 31 to be eligible for an academic scholarship.

Faculty

Marshall University has 666 full-time faculty members. Seventy-nine percent hold a doctorate or terminal degree in their field. The student-faculty ratio is approximately 17:1.

Student Government

Marshall University sponsors the Student Government Association (SGA), a student-oriented organization that ensures practical and creative interaction among those students interested in administration and campus politics. The SGA consists of four executive members and representatives from all academic colleges. All officers and representatives serve from the spring of their election year until the following spring. The executive members receive a small monthly salary. Only full-time students with an overall GPA of 2.25 or higher are eligible for office. The goal of the SGA is to provide students with a number of important services, including off-campus housing assistance, a student consumer liaison, and various entertainment opportunities. The SGA appoints students in the University community to various planning and organizational positions and committees on campus. The SGA also accepts requests for special project funding from recognized groups or clubs throughout the year. The SGA is active and viable at Marshall University, helping students and the University to grow together.

Admission Requirements

The average ACT and SAT I scores of entering freshmen at Marshall University are 22.1 and 990, respectively, and the average cumulative high school GPA is 3.32. Students seeking a baccalaureate degree must have the following high school preparation: 4 units of English, 3 units of social studies, 3 units of science (2 units must be a laboratory science), and 3 units of mathematics (including algebra I and one unit higher). In addition, they must graduate from an approved high school with either a minimum GPA of 2.0 and a minimum composite score on the ACT of 19 (a minimum composite score of 910 on the SAT I). The Marshall University Community and Technical College has an open admissions policy for students desiring a two-year associate degree and/or career training. Applications from transfer students and nontraditional or returning students are welcome. Transfer applicants are required to have earned a cumulative GPA of at least 2.0 (C) on all previous college work. Academically superior high school juniors or seniors may be admitted to Marshall University on a part-time basis, provided they have a GPA of at least 3.0 (B) and the recommendation of a high school counselor or principal. Campus visits for prospective students are conducted through the Welcome Center by appointment, Monday through Friday, at 10 a.m. and 1 p.m. and on some Saturdays. Students may call the Welcome Center at 304-696-6833, or the toll-free number listed below, to make arrangements.

Admission to the University is not necessarily admission to a particular college or curriculum within the University. Applicants for the nursing program should apply a year in advance and show satisfactory scores on the ACT; an interview is required. Entry into the music program requires an audition.

Application and Information

Applicants to the freshman class should submit the Undergraduate Application for Admission and have their high school counselor or principal forward a transcript of grades to the Office of Admissions. Scores on the ACT should be forwarded to Marshall (code number 4526 on the ACT form). High school students who have not been admitted to Marshall and who have their ACT scores forwarded to the Office of Admissions are sent an application. The student should complete the application and take it to the high school counselor, who should then certify the student's GPA and return the form to Marshall. Transfer applicants should submit an application and request that official transcripts from each college previously attended be forwarded to the Office of Admissions. Prospective students are notified as soon as action is taken on their application. For more information, students should contact:

Director of Admissions
Marshall University
One John Marshall Drive
Huntington, West Virginia 25755-2026
Telephone: 304-696-3160
800-642-3499 (toll-free)
Fax: 304-696-3135
E-mail: admissions@marshall.edu
World Wide Web: http://www.marshall.edu

Drinko Library.

MARS HILL COLLEGE

MARS HILL, NORTH CAROLINA

The College

Mars Hill College (MHC), an academic community rooted in the Christian faith, challenges and equips students to pursue intellectual, spiritual, and personal growth. This growth is grounded in a rigorous study of the liberal arts, connected with the world of work, and committed to character development, service, and responsible citizenship in the community, the region, and the world. Mars Hill College is the oldest educational institution on its original site in western North Carolina. It was founded by a small group of pioneer citizens who were descendents of the original settlers of the area. The school opened in 1856 as the French Broad Baptist Academy. On February 16, 1859, the school was chartered by the North Carolina General Assembly as Mars Hill College, a name suggested from the verse in the Bible at Acts 17:22, "Then Paul stood in the midst of Mars Hill. . . ."

Students are at the center of the educational program at Mars Hill College. Mars Hill currently has approximately 1,351 students enrolled. As part of its strategic plan, the school plans to increase enrollment to 1,500 students by 2006. Committed to the academic, social, spiritual, and personal growth and development of students, Mars Hill College offers students a well-rounded education with programs that are tailored to meet the individual needs of each person. Through the general education program, students acquire the abilities and knowledge needed to be responsible and successful, providing a sound foundation for a major. Through a carefully chosen major, students gain the skills to be successful in a vocation or graduate study. Some students choose to major in more than one area or to minor or concentrate in additional areas in order to be more versatile.

Cocurricular activities support, and in some cases are responsible for, the goals of general and specialized education. Many such activities complement and enrich classroom studies. They also lead to individual growth and development in being responsible and accountable, setting priorities, developing leadership, and expressing creativity. The College's LifeWorks Learning Partnership involves students and faculty members in creating connections between faith and learning, between service and learning, and between learning in and out of the classroom. Through LifeWorks, students explore their roles in the community by tutoring and mentoring children, building a Habitat for Humanity house, participating in a community-based research project, doing an internship at one of more than seventy-five sites, or through many other opportunities. Making these connections helps students develop the knowledge, skills, and values that will enable them to make a life as well as to make a living.Athletics are a major aspect of campus life at Mars Hill College. Intercollegiate competition, including men's baseball, basketball, cross-country, football, golf, lacrosse, soccer, tennis, and track and field and women's basketball, cross-country, golf, soccer, softball, tennis, track and field, and volleyball, is offered through College teams that are affiliated with the NCAA Division II and the South Atlantic Conference. Hiking, snow skiing, white-water rafting, and golf are popular off-campus activities.

Social activities and entertainment are important to a student's life at Mars Hill College. There is a great diversity of student organizations at Mars Hill, through which a student can find personal, social, professional, and educational fulfillment. These include honor organizations such as Alpha Chi National Honor Scholarship Society, Beta Beta Beta, and the Business Honor Club. Professional organizations include Music Educators' National Conference, Music Teachers' National Association, American Guild of Organists, Alpha Psi Omega Theatre Fraternity, Delta Omicron Music Fraternity, and Phi Mu Alpha Sinfonia. Interest groups include Bailey Mountain Cloggers, Fellowship of Christian Athletes, Young Democrats, College Republicans, and Christian Student Movement. Greek organizations that are active in campus life include two national and four local fraternities and sororities.

Location

Mars Hill College is located in the mountains of western North Carolina, one of the most beautiful regions of the United States. The town of Mars Hill has a population of approximately 3,000. It is 18 miles north of Asheville via highway 19-23. The closest interstates are I-40, I-26, and I-240. Atlanta, Georgia, is 227 miles away; Roanoke, Virginia, is 264 miles away; and Charlotte, North Carolina, is 162 miles away. Asheville was recently named an All-American City and one of the top twenty-five cultural cities in America. Asheville has the sophisticated attractions of a major metropolis, including theater and a symphony, and is known for its high-quality arts, crafts, and musical offerings. Scenic attractions such as Mount Mitchell, Great Smoky Mountains National Park, Craggy Gardens, Linville Falls and Caverns, Biltmore House and Gardens, and the Blue Ridge Parkway are within easy driving distance.

Majors and Degrees

The College awards the Bachelor of Arts degree in art, education/elementary (K–6), education/middle grades (6–9), English, history, international studies, music, political science, psychology, religion and philosophy, sociology, Spanish, and theater arts; the Bachelor of Science in accounting, athletic training, biology, botany, business administration, chemistry, computer science, fashion and interior merchandising, mathematics, physical education/sports management, physical education/sports science, physical education/teacher education, recreation, and zoology; the Bachelor of Music in music education and performance; the Bachelor of Social Work; and the Bachelor of Fine Arts in musical theater. Preparatory programs for postgraduate study are available in dentistry, law, medicine, and veterinary medicine. Mars Hill also offers Bachelor of Arts degrees in English as a second language (ESL), secondary edication, and special education.

Academic Program

The academic program, which leads to a degree, is composed of four related parts: general education, community life, the major, and electives. Courses taken as electives may be in the student's major, in related disciplines, or in other areas of special interest. A maximum of 9 semester hours of credit for developmental courses may be applied toward graduation as electives. To receive a degree from Mars Hill College, a student must complete the general education and major requirements specified in the student's catalog of entry and earn a minimum of 128 semester hours of credit. Sixty semester hours, including 12 semester hours in the major, must be earned at a senior-level institution. The last 32 semester hours must be earned at Mars Hill. The student must earn a cumulative grade point average of 2.0 for all courses attempted at Mars Hill.

There are opportunities in most academic departments for students to engage in independent study, research, seminars, and directed readings. Such opportunities are open to all students in accordance with policies established by the Curriculum Committee. Independent study is defined as a program of study designed by a student and faculty member to achieve mutually agreed-upon objectives. Independent study and directed reading projects are designed to allow students to engage in research or study not available in regularly scheduled courses or to pursue in greater depth a subject or interest to which the student was introduced during a regular course.

Off-Campus Programs

The College recognizes the importance of global awareness and supports academic programs that emphasize international/intercultural education. Study-abroad opportunities are an essential feature of an international education, and students and faculty members are encouraged to participate in them. Students are eligible to study at more than 100 international universities through the International Student Exchange Program (ISEP). The College strongly encourages all foreign language majors to spend at least one semester of their training abroad.

Academic Facilities

Renfro Library supports the Mars Hill College curriculum by serving the research and information needs of the students, faculty members, and staff members of the College. The MHC computer network provides access to the Renfro Library catalog and direct access to encyclopedias, atlases, literary and biographical indexes, and other online information sources. The network is also used to search for indexes, abstracts, and full-text journals. The library contains more than 90,000 books and periodical volumes and provides in-house access to more than 700 journals. Interlibrary loan services are available through network agreements with regional and national consortia. The Harris Media Center is designed to serve the audiovisual needs of students and faculty members. The passive solar facility includes teaching darkrooms for photography classes and a projection room for viewing films, videotapes, multi-image programs, and computer presentations. Two viewing classrooms, an area for individual listening and viewing, a video studio with taping and editing facilities, and storage and maintenance facilities for audiovisual materials are also located in the Media Center. The College ranks high among North Carolina campuses with its computer-student ratio of 1:6. More than 180 computers are available for student use on the campus. Students with computers can access the network by modem from both on and off campus 24 hours a day.

Costs

For the 2003–04 academic year, tuition was $14,204 and room and board were $6760. Books were estimated at $600.

Financial Aid

Mars Hill College offers students a variety of grants, scholarships, loans, and employment opportunities to assist with the cost of college. Prospective students may contact the school beginning in the fall to inquire about the merit scholarship and award program. Students must file the Free Application for Federal Student Aid (FAFSA) in order to be considered for financial aid. The school code for Mars Hill College is 002944. Federal aid is administered through the following programs: Federal Pell Grants, Federal Supplemental Education Opportunity Grants (FSEOG), the Federal Work-Study Program, Federal Perkins Loans, Federal Stafford Student Loans, and Federal PLUS Loans. North Carolina residents qualify for the North Carolina Legislative Tuition Grant (NCLTG) and/or the need-based Contractual Grant (NCCG). Ninety-three percent of students receive some form of aid.

Faculty

The members of the faculty at Mars Hill College are very accomplished in their respective fields and skilled in the art of teaching. There are 81 full-time and 69 part-time faculty members. Of the full-time faculty members, 68 percent hold a doctorate or terminal degree in their discipline or specialty. The student-faculty ratio is 14:1.

Student Government

The students of Mars Hill College voted for a self-governing unit to be known as the Student Government Association (SGA). SGA is the students' voice to the faculty members, the administration, and those outside the academic community. The students are encouraged to support the organization and to communicate their needs to the elected leaders of the SGA. The Student Government Association is organized into three branches: the Executive, the Judicial, and the Legislative. The SGA constitution provides for 4 student body officers—president, vice president, secretary, and treasurer—and for other legislative, judicial, and programming units.

Admission Requirements

Candidates submit an application, a $25 application fee, an official high school transcript, and official SAT or ACT scores. A minimum of 18 units is required. These units should include 4 in English, 2 in history, 2 in natural science, and 3 in mathematics. It is recommended that the balance include 2 foreign language units and/or 1 computer science unit. Acceptance is based on the applicant's high school grade point average, rank in class, SAT or ACT scores, and extracurricular activities. Transfer candidates must submit an application, a $25 application fee, high school transcripts, and official college transcripts from all institutions previously attended. A General Educational Development (GED) certificate is accepted. All rights accorded to students are made without regard to race, color, national or ethnic origin, gender, or impairment of the student.

Application and Information

Applications may be submitted to Mars Hill College for either semester. Notification of the admission decision is given on a rolling basis upon receipt of all application data. A $250 deposit is required for boarding students, and a $150 deposit is required for commuting students. The deposit is due three weeks after acceptance and is fully refundable until May 1 for fall applicants and December 1 for spring applicants. For further information, students should contact:

Admissions Office
Mars Hill College
Mars Hill, North Carolina 28754
Telephone: 828-689-1201
866-MHC4YOU
Fax: 828-689-1473
E-mail: admissions@mhc.edu
World Wide Web: http://www.mhc.edu

On the campus of Mars Hill College.

MARYGROVE COLLEGE

DETROIT, MICHIGAN

The College

Marygrove College is a diverse Catholic, coeducational, liberal arts college located in historic northwest Detroit. The Sisters, Servants of the Immaculate Heart of Mary (IHM), founded Marygrove College in 1905 in Monroe, Michigan, as St. Mary College. When the College needed more room to grow, the new College opened in Detroit in September 1927 with 287 women students.

The Catholic intellectual tradition informs its general education curriculum and shapes the organizational culture of its community by educating the students toward the mission of the College. The College is proud, however, to practice its "catholicity" in the spirit of the Vatican Council II by welcoming and embracing persons from diverse ethnic and religious backgrounds, by supporting ecumenical and interfaith services and activities, and by striving to be as inclusive as possible in service to metropolitan Detroit. The fundamental purpose of Marygrove College is to educate each student toward intellectual and professional competence, toward career flexibility through grounding in the liberal arts, and toward active compassion and commitment.

Marygrove has approximately 450 full-time and 450 part-time undergraduate students. While many undergraduates arrive directly from high school and live on campus, many come with years of professional experience. Many students have jobs, families, and very full lives outside of class and enjoy the interaction with traditional-age students. Marygrove recruits purposeful, career-minded, highly motivated people who take their responsibilities and aspirations seriously.

Students have access to a coeducational residence facility, Florent Gillet Hall, which opened in 1958. The spacious suites are composed of two bedrooms, a bathroom, and a study area. Depending on availability of space, a student may arrange for private accommodations. Florent Gillet Hall also contains a large lounge area for student events.

The College offers a variety of academic and non-academic services, including career counseling and placement, an internship program, student support services, computer labs, a writing assistance lab, varsity basketball, intramural sports, study abroad, service learning, an honors program, and campus ministry.

Marygrove College is accredited by the Higher Learning Commission of the North Central Association of Colleges and Schools (NCA). The education unit at Marygrove College is accredited by the National Council for Accreditation of Teacher Education (NCATE).

Marygrove College offers the Master in the Art of Teaching (M.A.T.), Master of Arts (M.A.) degrees in human resource management and pastoral ministry, and Master of Education (M.E.) degrees in adult learning, educational leadership, reading, and teaching.

Location

The only small, private, liberal arts college in Detroit, Marygrove sits on 52 beautiful, wooded acres. Two classic Tudor Gothic buildings—the Liberal Arts Building and Madame Cadillac Hall—are set amid groves of towering trees and expansive lawns. This idyllic setting creates a perfect atmosphere for learning.

Located in the northwest corner of Detroit, Marygrove is within easy reach of cultural, entertainment, and sporting events. Students may visit the world-renowned Detroit Institute of Arts, famed Greenfield Village, or African American Museum or shop at local malls within easy access. They may also listen to cool jazz at one of the nearby jazz clubs or drive 10 minutes to the downtown area and observe a play at the State or Fox Theatre or watch the Tigers or Lions in their beautiful new stadiums. Students can even catch a Red Wings game.

Majors and Degrees

Marygrove College offers Bachelor of Arts (B.A.), Bachelor of Science (B.S.), Bachelor of Applied Science (B.A.S.), Bachelor of Business Administration (B.B.A.), Bachelor of Fine Arts (B.F.A.), Bachelor of Music (B.Mus.), and Bachelor of Social Work (B.S.W.) degrees.

The majors offered in the bachelor's degree program include accounting information systems; art; art therapy; biology; business; chemistry; child development; computer information systems; dance; early childhood education; English; environmental science; general science; history; international studies in language, business, and culture; language arts; mathematics; music; political science; psychology; religious studies; social science; social studies; social work; and special education. The education department certifies majors for elementary and secondary teacher education in more than sixteen major and minor areas of study. Preprofessional programs offered at Marygrove include law, medicine, and dentistry.

Marygrove offers Associate of Arts (A.A.) and Associate of Science (A.S.) degrees. Associate degree programs include accounting, business, child development, general science, and liberal studies.

Academic Programs

At Marygrove, the courses offered assist in the development of skills used in the personal and professional lives of students. They are designed to establish standards for the ethical decisions students will be called on to make, foster appreciation for the dignity of the individual, expand the essential skills needed for continued self-development and independent learning, and increase cognitive, communicative, judgmental, and interpersonal powers.

As part of the general education plan, the whole College curriculum includes the following emphases: writing, information literacy, oral/visual presentation, cultural diversity, critical thinking, social justice, and learning to learn.

Because Marygrove expects that each graduate should be able to effectively interpret and express ideas in writing, the College emphasizes writing across the curriculum.

Most majors require 128 semester hours for graduation. Exceptional students may qualify for the Honor's Program. Students may receive credit through the Advanced Placement (AP) Program, credit by examination and portfolio (CLEP), and the Proficiency Examination Program (PEP).

Off-Campus Programs

Study-abroad opportunities are offered each year. Numerous internships are available for students in selected programs. Students may also choose to attend classes through one of the College's satellite programs.

Academic Facilities

The Michigan Library Association honored the Marygrove Library program with two awards. In 1995, it received Outstanding Program Recognition for its excellent bibliographic instruction program, and in 1998, it was awarded the association's Information Literacy Award.

The library is a complete student resource center occupying a wing of the Liberal Arts Building. It is replete with a beautiful oak-paneled reading and group study room, a spacious reference/reading room, four floors of stacks, individual study carrels, a library instruction classroom, meeting rooms, and media facilities. Students have online access from the library or home to the library's catalog and electronic databases and its extensive print, electronic, microform, and audiovisual learning resources, which are carefully selected to support course-related endeavors.

Costs

For the 2004–05 academic year, tuition for full-time undergraduates is $12,190. Based on double occupancy, room and board costs average $6000. Books and fees total about $1500 per year.

Financial Aid

The Marygrove community believes that talent, not money, should open the doors of the College. By offering scholarships, work-study opportunities, grants, loans, and flexible payment plans, the College does all it can to make a Marygrove education financially available to all qualified students.

About 95 percent of Marygrove students (enrolled at least half-time) receive some form of financial assistance. Many students with limited personal resources receive enough financial help to cover their basic college costs, including tuition and fees.

Each fall semester, Marygrove awards scholarships to recent high school graduates and transfer students who demonstrate excellence in academics and the visual and performing arts. These awards range from $3000 to $12,190 and are renewable each year, provided the student maintains his or her grade point average.

Faculty

The undergraduate division has 67 full-time and 7 part-time faculty members. The student-teacher ratio is 14:1. The average class size is 12 students. Faculty members, not teaching assistants, teach all courses.

With about 900 undergraduates, Marygrove is an intimate learning environment—a place where every student counts. Faculty members and students often collaborate on college projects and committees. All students have faculty advisers to help them and challenge them to succeed. Faculty members are available to consult with students after class, during office hours, and by appointment.

Admission Requirements

Students seeking admission to Marygrove College are evaluated on their overall academic record, including ACT and SAT I scores. Applicants should submit a completed application and school transcripts. An interview is recommended.

Admissions counselors are available to meet students and give them tours of the campus on a walk-in basis or from scheduled appointments.

Transfer students with 24 semester hours or more of acceptable credits are evaluated based on their previous academic record. The minimum acceptable grade point average for admission to the College is 2.0 (C). However, students must adhere to each department's standards for specific majors. The Education and Social Work Departments accept a minimum grade point average of 2.7 and 2.5, respectively. GED candidates should have a score of 52 to be eligible for admission.

Application and Information

Applicants are notified of the admission decision one week following receipt of the completed application, supporting credentials, and payment of the $25 application fee.

The Office of Admissions encourages prospective students to visit the campus. Students may schedule individual appointments or tour the facilities during campus event programs scheduled throughout the year.

To obtain an application or arrange a campus visit, students should contact:

Office of Admissions
Marygrove College
8425 West McNichols Road
Detroit, Michigan 48221-2599
Telephone: 313-927-1240
866-313-1927 (toll-free)
Fax: 313-927-1399
E-mail: info@marygrove.edu
World Wide Web: http://www.marygrove.edu

MARYLAND INSTITUTE COLLEGE OF ART

BALTIMORE, MARYLAND

The College

Established in 1826, the Maryland Institute College of Art (MICA), is the oldest independent, fully accredited art college in the nation. Because of its belief in the vital role of art in society, the Institute is dedicated to the education of professional artists and to the development of an environment conducive to the creation of art. MICA has a well-equipped network of studio facilities, an exceptional faculty, extensive exhibition space, and an impressive art college library. A unique on-campus residential environment is provided, designed with the artist in mind. The College offers many options not fully available at a liberal arts college, including a visiting artists program that welcomes more than 100 artists a year to the campus; seven-days-a-week access to some of the most outstanding facilities and best equipped studios in the country; the opportunity to exhibit work in numerous galleries, starting in the freshman year; the opportunity to study, through College-sponsored programs, at art colleges throughout the United States and abroad; a challenging liberal arts program that is integrated into and expands upon the studio program; and the advantage of studying with other talented students in a rigorous program of art.

In addition to the undergraduate degrees described below, the Institute offers the Master of Fine Arts in painting, sculpture, photography, and graphic design; the Master of Arts in Teaching; the Master of Arts in Art Education; and the Master of Arts in Digital Arts.

The faculty comprises 210 professional artists, designers, art historians, writers, and scholars—an assemblage of dedicated, working professionals who share the insights and experiences they have gained as practicing artists and scholars.

The College's 1,500 students represent forty-five states and thirty other countries. They are marked by their intellectual curiosity, creativity, motivation, and self-discipline. Students develop a body of work that prepares them for a variety of career paths. The MICA experience, which includes internship programs and other reality-based opportunities, develops a firm base upon which students can launch and build their careers.

The Office of Multicultural Affairs coordinates programs, services, and activities for international students. The College provides specific services to international students such as orientation, immigration advisement, personal counseling, and host families.

MICA is a residential campus providing apartment-style housing that includes laundry and fitness facilities and is wired for high-speed Internet access. Additional benefits include many private rooms and studio space that are incorporated into the residences. MICA housing offers independence, privacy, and a lively sense of activity generated by a community focused on art. Student life is also focused at the Meyerhoff House, which houses the Center Café and meeting rooms for student organizations. The campus also includes a health center, and students have access to an athletic facility.

The College is accredited by the Middle States Association of Colleges and Schools and the National Association of Schools of Art and Design.

Location

MICA is an urban campus of twenty-five buildings that is located in a historic and beautiful neighborhood, surrounded by many cultural and educational institutions. These include the Meyerhoff Symphony Hall, the Lyric Opera House, and the Theatre Project. Baltimore has been cited as a city especially attractive to artists because of its vibrant and supportive atmosphere and its low cost of living. In addition to four world-class museums—the Contemporary Museum, the Walters Art Museum, the Baltimore Museum of Art, and the American Visionary Art Museum—Baltimore features a wide range of alternative art spaces and galleries that present classical and nontraditional works by acclaimed and emerging artists. It is also ideally situated for an artist because it is at the center of the Washington–New York art corridor. By train, Washington, D.C., is 40 minutes to the south; New York City, less than 3 hours to the north. The College offers inexpensive bus trips to New York studios, galleries, and museums every other week during the academic year.

Majors and Degrees

MICA offers the Bachelor of Fine Arts degree in the following studio majors: ceramics, drawing, environmental design, experimental animation, fibers, general fine arts, graphic design, illustration, interactive media, painting, photography, printmaking, sculpture, and video. Concentrations are offered in animation, book arts, environmental design, interactive media, and video. The College offers an art history minor, a language and literature minor, and a cross-disciplinary minor. Students may also pursue double majors. Five-year combined Bachelor of Fine Arts/Master of Arts degrees are offered in teaching and in digital arts.

Academic Program

To receive the Bachelor of Fine Arts degree, students must complete a minimum of 126 credits, including 42 liberal arts credits. Students participate in a foundation program during their freshman year and then select a studio major. During the first year, the curriculum is well structured to provide the conceptual and technical skills necessary for further specialized study. By the end of four years, students are expected to be able to work independently in their chosen medium. The program integrates writing and academic inquiry with studio practice. This combination reflects the need for artists to pursue intellectual concepts as well as aesthetic principles.

Off-Campus Programs

MICA participates in a cooperative exchange program with Goucher College, the Johns Hopkins University, Loyola College, the Peabody Conservatory of Music, and the University of Baltimore. This program makes it possible for full-time students at the College to enroll in one course per semester at one of the cooperating institutions without incurring an additional tuition charge. This option has proved to be exceptionally useful in offering studies not available at MICA, such as languages, the sciences, and business.

The Maryland Institute is a member of the Alliance of Independent Colleges of Art and Design (AICAD), which has cooperatively developed a program of study in New York City for eligible second-semester juniors and first-semester seniors.

The New York Studio Program's center, a loft facility in the Tribeca area of lower Manhattan, is home base for the semester-long program. Students may pursue either an independent study or, as apprenticeship students, they may work with a professional artist, museum, gallery, or an art-related business.

MICA encourages young artists to work and live in other cultural settings so that they will better understand the universality of the language of art. MICA offers a program for juniors in AIX-en-Provence as well as other junior-year-abroad opportunities in England, France, Ireland, Italy, Japan, Korea, the Netherlands, and Scotland allow third-year students to study for one semester at colleges and universities noted for their strength in the visual arts. Summer study abroad in specialized subjects has been designed to provide students an opportunity to work closely with senior faculty members in locations that offer diverse cultural, environmental, and philosophical experiences. Canada, France, Greece, Israel, Italy, Jamaica, Korea, and Mexico are the current sites for two- and four-week programs. Exchange programs in China and Germany are also options for students.

The director of career development arranges job internships for juniors and seniors. These internships provide educational experiences that bridge the worlds of academics and work. There are more than 1,000 local and national listings.

Academic Facilities

The campus includes twenty-five buildings with 385,000 square feet of studio and classroom space, creating a coherent and unified urban campus. The studios are fully furnished with state-of-the-art equipment for each area of concentration. The Decker Library includes more than 50,000 volumes, 300 current periodical subscriptions, and 250,000 slides of artwork. It is one of the largest art college libraries in the country.

MICA has taken a leadership role in integrating new technologies into its programs of study. Within a very short time, the oldest degree-granting college of art in the United States has developed its facilities to provide more than one computer and/or video workstation for approximately every 4 students. The College's faculty has introduced computer-based courses in all of the professional studio majors, and the computer is also an important resource in the liberal arts area, whether as a tool for word processing or as a research medium for accessing images and information in a variety of forms. In some departments, such as environmental design, graphic design, animation, interactive media, or photography, competency in the creative use of digital technologies is considered fundamental to the curriculum.

MICA has outstanding instructional facilities with specialized equipment for both traditional and new media. Independent and/or dedicated studio space is provided for seniors. Seven-days-a-week access is provided in all departments. Liberal Arts classrooms and lecture halls are intimately sized. A 550-seat auditorium provides programming for a full schedule of visiting artists and lecturers as well as for film, video, and performing arts.

The Meyerhoff Career Development Center houses a full staff of counselors providing services related to internships, job listings, alumni networking, corporate recruitment, and career development skills.

Exhibitions play a major role in the artistic and intellectual life at the Institute. Each year, more than ninety public exhibitions are featured in the Institute galleries, which are unrivaled by any art college. They bring the work of regional, national, and international artists, as well as faculty members and students, to the public year-round.

Costs

For the 2004–05 academic year, tuition is $24,474. Room is $5100 and board is $1980. There is an activities fee of $180, a health-center fee of $250, and a technology fee of $300.

Financial Aid

Each year approximately 65 percent of the full-time students receive $8 million in financial assistance. The College administers a variety of programs, including need-based grants and scholarships, government-related loans, and college work-study programs. The College also awards more than $300,000 through competitive, merit-based scholarship programs. Students who are not U.S. citizens or permanent residents are not eligible for financial aid.

Faculty

The faculty consists of 104 full-time and 106 part-time professional artists, designers, art historians, writers, and poets. Their work is represented in more than 250 public and private collections from the Museum of Modern Art to the Stedelijk Museum in Amsterdam and the Victoria and Albert Museum in London. They have won individual honors and awards from notable foundations, such as the National Endowment for the Arts and the Guggenheim Foundation. They are Fulbright Scholars and recipients of the Prix de Rome, the Louis Comfort Tiffany Award, and the MacArthur Fellowships. The faculty-student ratio is 1:10.

Student Government

The Student Voice Association represents the interests and viewpoints of students to the faculty, administration, and board of trustees.

Admission Requirements

Students applying to the Maryland Institute must have made a serious commitment to art; therefore, a portfolio of artwork that demonstrates talent, ability, and experience is required for admission to the College. The portfolio is very important; however, evidence of academic ability as determined by level of course work, grades, test scores, and class rank are also weighted heavily in the admission decision. Individual interests and accomplishments, revealed in the personal statement, letters of recommendation, and lists of extracurricular and volunteer activities beyond classroom instruction, strengthen the application. The required personal essay is seriously considered. A TOEFL score of 550 or above is required of students whose native language is not English.

Application and Information

Students interested in early decision must complete all requirements for admission by November 15. Freshmen applicants for the fall term should complete the application process by March 1 for priority admission and financial aid consideration. Those who wish to be considered for merit-based scholarships must complete the application procedures by February 15; transfer students have a March 15 deadline. Applicants for admission to the spring term are asked to complete the application process prior to December 1. For an application, catalog, and further information, students should contact:

Office of Undergraduate Admission
Maryland Institute College of Art
1300 Mount Royal Avenue
Baltimore, Maryland 21217

Telephone: 410-225-2222
Fax: 410-225-2337
E-mail: admissions@mica.edu
World Wide Web: http://www.mica.edu

MARYMOUNT COLLEGE OF FORDHAM UNIVERSITY

TARRYTOWN, NEW YORK

The College

Marymount College, founded in 1907, is an independent, four-year liberal arts college in the Catholic tradition that equips and empowers women to achieve their full potential, preparing them for leadership roles in a rapidly changing society.

Building upon a long relationship, Marymount College consolidated with Fordham University as of July 1, 2002, to create a new model of a Catholic women's college—one that enjoys the academic and administrative resources of a major university while retaining the character of a small liberal arts college. The new school—with a strengthened religious and intellectual focus—is now known as Marymount College of Fordham University.

Founded in 1841, Fordham is New York City's Jesuit University, enrolling approximately 14,000 students among its ten undergraduate, graduate, and professional schools. Fordham has residential campuses in the north Bronx and Manhattan, a graduate center in Tarrytown, and the Louis Calder Biological Field Station in Armonk, New York. Marymount College is the University's fifth undergraduate college.

Approximately 800 students are enrolled in Marymount College's undergraduate women's college. While both commuter and residential students attend the school, nearly 70 percent of Marymount College students live on campus in three residence halls.

Most students come to Marymount College of Fordham University from the New York metropolitan area as well as other areas of the United States. In fall 2002, students from thirty-one states came to Marymount College. Seven percent of Marymount students arrived from outside the United States, representing more than twenty countries, including Belgium, China, Ethiopia, Ghana, Japan, and Spain.

As members of the Fordham family, Marymount College students have access to clubs in such areas as academic, cultural, sociopolitical, social service, performing arts, and student government at all three campuses: Rose Hill, Lincoln Center, and Tarrytown. Specific clubs active on the Marymount campus in 2002 included Big Sister Little Sister, Black Student Union, Drama Club, Environmental Club, Irish Cultural Society, Italian American Club, Latinas Unidas, and Sisters of Universal Light.

Campus Ministry also coordinates a large roster of on- and off-campus volunteer programs that support the tradition of service embraced by Marymount College of Fordham University students. Programs include tutoring or teaching children; assisting the sick, aging, or disabled; and serving the poor and homeless.

Approximately 300 adult men and women attend classes in the evenings and on the weekends on the Marymount campus as part of Fordham College of Liberal Studies. The program was formerly known as Marymount Weekend College. In addition, Fordham's Graduate Schools of Business, Education, and Social Service also hold classes on the Marymount campus.

Location

From its scenic perch in the charming Westchester County village of Tarrytown, the Marymount College of Fordham University campus—one of the jewels of the Hudson River Valley—overlooks the Hudson River where it widens to form the Tappan Zee. Located 25 miles north of Manhattan, the school's proximity to the unmatched cultural and professional opportunities of New York City attracts many students.

Majors and Degrees

Students who attend Marymount College of Fordham University may earn either a Bachelor of Arts or Bachelor of Science degree. Majors (with concentration fields in parentheses) include American studies, art (studio, education, history) biology, business, chemistry, computer science, corporate training and development, education (elementary, inclusive teacher, secondary, special), English, family and consumer science education, fashion (design, merchandising), foods and nutrition, French, history, information systems, interior design, international business, international studies, legal and policy studies, mathematics, politics, psychology, social work, sociology, Spanish, and theater and media. Minors include acting and directing; anthropology; art history; arts management; biology; chemistry; cognitive neuroscience; communications; computer science; diversity and globalism; economics; English; ethics, religion, and spiritual values; French; home economics; information systems; international business; international studies; mathematics; music; natural science; philosophy; politics; psychology; race and ethnic studies; sociology; Spanish; studio art; and women's studies.

Academic Program

Supporting targeted work goals and rewarding intellectual curiosity require a carefully blended curriculum. The core curriculum—common to all majors at Marymount College of Fordham University—is crafted for this purpose, giving special emphasis to critical thinking, communication, and problem-solving skills.

The core curriculum is built upon a strong foundation of classic liberal arts courses. To meet the requirements, students complete courses in such areas as literature, philosophy, theology, history, foreign language, social science, natural science, fine arts, math, computer science, and American pluralism. In addition, students also participate in a first semester seminar, which offers students a choice of courses among a range of disciplines that apply feminist theory to discussions and analysis of common readings.

The goal of the core is to develop the habits of heart and mind that are the hallmarks of a liberal education. The core curriculum blends reverence for tradition with openness to new challenges and new ways of knowing and engaging the world. It is designed to nurture curiosity, inspire a love of learning, and provide students with the foundation they will need to engage in lifelong learning.

Candidates for either the Bachelor of Arts or Bachelor of Science degree must complete 120 semester credits, fulfill the requirements of the core, and complete the requirements of their major program.

Students are encouraged to participate in the internship program to earn college credit. Credit is awarded for successful scores on the College-Level Examination Program (CLEP) general and subject examinations. Students may also earn credit through Advanced Placement (AP) tests.

Off-Campus Programs

Marymount College of Fordham University offers study abroad opportunities in the United Kingdom and such countries as Austria, France, Italy, and Japan through affiliated programs.

Marymount maintains a London Centre, in which students can take courses taught by top British theatrical professionals.

The opportunity is also available to earn on-the-job experience and college credit through an extensive internship program, which places students both locally and internationally.

Academic Facilities

Students at Marymount College of Fordham University have access to the Fordham University Library collection, which houses more than 1.8 million volumes, 14,094 periodicals, 160 electronic databases, and 2.9 million microfilm units. On the Marymount campus, the holdings of the Gloria Gaines Memorial Library offer a collection of 117,100 volumes, 750 periodicals, and 7,529 microfilm units. A fully equipped multimedia interactive laboratory includes tapes and records for the study of French, Italian, Spanish, and English as a Second Language (ESL). The Marymount campus also houses a science building, a state-of-the-art CAD computer lab, audiovisual facilities, a writing center, mathematics laboratories, computer centers, a teacher education center, and art studios that include a darkroom for photography.

Costs

For the 2003–04 academic year, the total cost was $31,206. Tuition was $17,850, fees were $701, and room and board were $9260. The cost of books was estimated at $750. Personal expenses and travel costs were estimated to be $2645.

Financial Aid

In 2003–04, Marymount College students received approximately $8.9 million in student financial aid. Of this, $5 million came from federal programs, $982,000 came from state programs, and more than $3 million came from the College. Trustee grants and scholarships are also available. Financial aid applicants are required to file the FAFSA. It is recommended that the form be submitted by February 1. Early applicants can expect to receive their award notifications beginning April 15.

Faculty

The faculty includes 57 full-time members; 93 percent hold the terminal degree in their discipline. Faculty advisers support and guide students throughout their Marymount College experience. The student-faculty ratio is 12.5:1.

Student Government

Elected representatives from each of the four classes compose the Student Government Association (SGA). SGA members serve on policymaking committees with faculty members and administrators and represent the student body in planning aspects of student life at Marymount.

Admission Requirements

Candidates for admission must have a high school diploma and must submit a completed application for admission and generally have a B average or better. They also normally rank in the top two fifths of their graduating class and complete at least 16 academic high school units. For regular admission, the SAT I or ACT should be taken in the junior year of high school or in the fall semester of the senior year. Other factors important to admission officers are the reputation of the applicant's school, advanced placement or honors course work completed, and the student's involvement in school and community activities.

Application and Information

The application, a $30 fee, official high school records, and test scores should be submitted by April 15 for admission to the fall term or by December 1 for the spring term. Notification of the admission decision, given on a rolling basis, begins in late fall. Deferred admission and early admission are available.

For further information, prospective students should contact:

Office of Admission
Marymount College of Fordham University
100 Marymount Avenue
Tarrytown, New York 10591
Telephone: 914-332-8295
800-724-4312 (toll-free)
Fax: 914-332-7442
E-mail: admiss@mmc.marymt.edu
World Wide Web: http://www.marymt.edu

Butler Hall was named for the founder of the College, Mother Marie Joseph Butler, R.S.H.M.

MARYMOUNT MANHATTAN COLLEGE

NEW YORK, NEW YORK

The College

Marymount Manhattan College (MMC) is an urban, independent undergraduate liberal arts college. The mission of the College is to educate a socially and economically diverse population by fostering intellectual achievement and personal growth and by providing opportunities for career development. Inherent in this mission is the intent to develop an awareness of social, political, cultural, and ethical issues in the belief that this awareness will lead to concern for, participation in, and the improvement of society. To accomplish this mission, the College offers a strong program in the arts and sciences to students of all ages as well as substantial preprofessional preparation. Central to these efforts is the particular attention given to the individual student. Marymount Manhattan College also seeks to be a resource and learning center for the metropolitan community.

The social and extracurricular life of the student body of approximately 2,100 students centers on a number of clubs and organizations sponsored through the Student Affairs Office, including the International Students Club, Amnesty International, the French Club, softball and soccer clubs, the Nature/Science Club, the student newspaper and magazine, Student Government, the student volunteer organization, and the Student Development Committee. Students attend musical events, and MMC's own off-Broadway theater, the only one on the Upper East Side of Manhattan, offers students an opportunity to participate in student productions.

The Residence Life Office at Marymount Manhattan College is committed to providing residents with numerous opportunities and experiences that foster intellectual achievement and social and personal growth. Students are encouraged to become involved in the many activities that are sponsored by Residence Life and are assisted with assuming responsibility for their own lives and living environment. The College provides housing for approximately 650 students at three locations. The buildings offer suite-style, traditional dormitories, or apartment-style living, with classrooms, lounges, a laundry room, and rehearsal space. Additional off-campus facilities are obtained as needed.

The Office of Academic and Career Advisement serves the entire College community by providing an integrated program of academic and career counseling. The office helps students by offering internship opportunities and workshops in job placement, resume writing, and graduate school preparation. For the past five years, 90 percent of biology majors who apply are accepted to advanced professional schools, including Mt. Sinai School of Medicine and Cornell Medical College. Other College services include personal and financial aid counseling and campus ministry.

Location

Marymount Manhattan College is centrally located on Manhattan's Upper East Side at 221 East 71st Street between Second and Third avenues. Within walking distance of the campus are the Frick, Metropolitan, Whitney, and Guggenheim museums; the Asian Society, French Institute, and National Audubon Society; Central Park; New York Hospital and Sloan-Kettering Research Center; and public libraries. All forms of public transportation are easily accessible. Within minutes of the College are shops, restaurants, and movie theaters. This location gives students the opportunity to take advantage of New York City's rich culture and to explore a variety of neighborhoods.

Majors and Degrees

Marymount Manhattan College offers programs leading to the Bachelor of Arts, Bachelor of Science, and Bachelor of Fine Arts degrees. Majors are offered in accounting, acting, art, biology, business management, communication arts, dance (B.A. and B.F.A.), English, history, humanities, international studies, political science, psychology, sociology, speech-language pathology and audiology, and theater arts (B.A. and B.F.A.). Some of the minors offered are business, business communications, creative writing, education, French, media studies, religious studies, Spanish, and writing. Certificate programs are offered in substance abuse counseling, business management, computer information management, gerontology, industrial organizational psychology, and teacher certification.

Academic Programs

Marymount Manhattan College has designed its programs to enable students to meet the challenges of contemporary society. MMC is committed to the belief that a liberal arts education provides students with the ability and the flexibility to manage change and with broad understanding and the communication and problem-solving skills that are essential for success in any career and in life. To accomplish its goals, the College offers a liberal arts education, integrated with preprofessional training opportunities and individualized attention. The curricula are organized into five divisions: humanities, fine and performing arts, sciences, social sciences, and business management. Also offered are special-interest sequences that complement the student's major and minor with added concentration in such areas as prelaw, premedicine, social work, marketing, international business, finance and investments, and creative writing. The College's small size provides students with an individually planned academic career, reflects students' academic needs and interests, and supports their career goals.

Candidates for the Bachelor of Arts, Bachelor of Science, and Bachelor of Fine Arts degrees must complete 120 credits. To qualify for a degree, a student must maintain an overall scholastic average of at least 2.0. Requirements for certificate programs vary.

The College recognizes various types of nontraditional credit, including credit for acceptable scores on the Advanced Placement (AP), College-Level Examination Program (CLEP), and New York State College Proficiency Examination (CPE) tests and credit for life experience.

MMC encourages its students to participate in internship programs in New York City that range from work at hospitals, financial institutions, magazines, publishing houses, and off-Broadway theaters to HBO and CBS.

Off-Campus Programs

The College's Academic Year Abroad offers an opportunity for students to broaden their educational experience and to gain cultural perspectives through study at other colleges in the Americas and overseas. Students may spend one or both semesters of their junior year in this program. MMC summer sessions and January intersessions also offer students opportunities in travel/study-abroad courses in Egypt, France, Great Britain, Eastern Europe, Ireland, Russia, and Spain.

Academic Facilities

The Thomas J. Shanahan Library at MMC is a library/learning center. It contains more than 100,000 volumes in open stacks and maintains an extensive periodical collection. The media center, on the main library floor, houses nonprint materials, microfiche, microfilm, filmstrips, slides, tapes, videotapes, and records. Through the library's affiliation with the New York Metropolitan Reference and Research Library Agency, MMC faculty members and students have access to the materials of the member libraries. The library also participates in the Online Computer Library Center (OCLC), a computerized database of the holdings of some 4,000 libraries that is currently being used for cataloging and reference purposes.

The modern 250-seat Theresa Lang Theatre is equipped with an orchestra pit capable of accommodating 40 musicians. The theater has a special acoustical design, a sprung dance floor, a full technical balcony with equipment for lighting and sound, thirty-five counterweighted-line sets in the fly system, dressing rooms with showers, and a scene shop. Students benefit from exposure to the numerous professional dance, opera, and theatrical groups that perform at the College.

Recently, two completely remodeled laboratory facilities were opened to strengthen education in two areas in which MMC has always excelled—science and communication arts.

MMC's science facilities in biology, chemistry, and physics underwent a total reconstruction valued at close to $1 million, thanks to the generosity of the Samuel Freeman Charitable Trust and the Ira De Camp Foundation. The Samuel Freeman Science Center opens many new doors of opportunity to students who are biology/premedicine majors or who are interested in pursuing careers in other science or health-related fields.

The College's Theresa Lang Center for Producing features the latest in digital computer technology and is one of the most advanced facilities of its kind in New York City. With digital multimedia capability, a decor inspired by top television postproduction houses, and access to the public library's B. Altman Advanced Learning Superblock, the center further enhances students' skills in traditional video and television production and allows them to develop, design, and evaluate cutting-edge multimedia projects. In conjunction with the Communication Arts Department, the College offers students the Media Library, where many videos and screening computers are available to students.

The Writing Center at MMC provides a range of services and activities, including career-based courses, personal critiques and one-on-one assistance, lectures, workshops, and special events such as the Best-Selling Author Series and Annual Writers' Conference, as well as a minor in creative writing. This enables students to be a part of the highly respected New York City writing community.

Costs

For the 2003–04 academic year, full-time tuition was $15,592. The fee for a space in a residence provided by the College was approximately $9000 per year. For part-time students, tuition was $460 per credit. Additional fees are applicable for various laboratory and studio classes.

Financial Aid

The College administers a variety of financial aid programs, including scholarships sponsored by the College. Some of the awards are based on academic achievement; others are based on financial need. Students are also eligible for aid through a wide variety of state and federal programs. In addition, a number of jobs are available for students on campus, and the Offices of Financial Aid and Academic and Career Advisement can help students locate part-time off-campus jobs to help finance their education. More than 80 percent of MMC students receive some form of financial assistance. Therefore, limited finances alone need not prevent any student from attending the College. The suggested deadlines for applying for financial aid are February 15 for the fall semester and November 15 for the spring semester.

Faculty

Marymount Manhattan College's student-faculty ratio is 18:1. In addition to the staff of the advisement office, faculty members act as advisors to students. Full-time faculty members teach in all sessions and divisions (days, evenings, and weekends). Part-time instructors, who are drawn from the wealth of experienced teaching professionals in New York City, supplement the full-time faculty.

Student Government

The Student Government Association responds to three areas of concern at MMC. The association primarily serves the needs of its constituents by managing the student government budget, planning and publicizing events, and establishing organizations that reflect the interests of the students. In addition, the association assists faculty and administrative groups and committees in their policy and procedural tasks and communicates the results of committee work to the student body. Finally, the Student Government Association provides special representatives for students' rights and freedoms through established and clearly defined channels of authority.

Admission Requirements

Marymount Manhattan College seeks candidates with qualities that indicate potential for success in higher education and the ability to contribute to the College community. Admission is based on a combination of factors: the student's academic program, including scholastic average and rank in class; two recommendations from teachers, counselors, or employers; an essay; and activities. SAT I scores are required for general admission.

Each year the College enrolls an increasing number of transfer students. Transfer students may receive up to 90 credits for course work completed in an accredited postsecondary institution with a grade of C- or better. Transcripts are evaluated on a course-by-course basis.

Prior to registering, all new students are required to take placement examinations in the basic subject areas of English composition, reading, algebra, and mathematics.

Application and Information

The admissions application must be received by February 1 for MMC scholarship consideration. Students may apply online. For application forms and for more information about Marymount Manhattan College, students should contact:

Office of Admissions
Marymount Manhattan College
221 East 71st Street
New York, New York 10021
Telephone: 212-517-0430
800-MARYMOUNT (toll-free)
E-mail: admissions@mmm.edu
World Wide Web: http://www.mmm.edu

Marymount Manhattan College, in the heart of Manhattan.

MARYMOUNT UNIVERSITY
ARLINGTON, VIRGINIA

The University

Marymount University is a comprehensive, coeducational Catholic university. Located just 6 miles from the nation's capital, it serves a diverse student body of approximately 2,200 undergraduates and 1,600 graduate students, who represent more than forty states and seventy-five countries. The University offers a wide range of majors and graduate-degree programs through the Schools of Arts and Sciences, Business Administration, Education and Human Services, and Health Professions. Marymount is accredited by the Commission on Colleges of the Southern Association of Colleges and Schools.

The University takes full advantage of the resources in and around Washington, D.C. Government, business, and professional leaders are frequent visitors to the campus, enriching the learning experience. In addition, many students have internships with federal departments, international businesses, and technology companies. The State Department, Smithsonian museums, and Congressional offices are popular internship sites. The blending of academics with hands-on, practical experience serves as a cornerstone of a well-rounded Marymount education. The University emphasizes excellence in teaching, attention to the individual, and values and ethics across the curriculum.

Students enjoy NCAA Division III sports, a thriving student government, a strong campus ministry group, more than thirty clubs, and a wide range of service opportunities. The Activities Programming Board plans activities both on and off campus, including comedy nights, movies, and theater evenings in D.C. It also gets tickets to local sporting events and schedules outings to ski and beach destinations. The *Banner*, the student newspaper, keeps the campus informed and provides on-the-job learning for student participants.

The Lee Center serves as the hub of campus life. The Center has a 1,000-seat sports arena, café, bookstore, pool, recreational gym, fitness center, dance studio, meeting rooms, and lounges.

Living on campus is an important aspect of college life. Students who are under 21 and whose families do not live within commuting distance are required to live on campus for their first two years. Four residence halls house approximately 670 students. The rooms are wired with fiber-optic cable for Internet, phone, and cable-TV access. The campus also has wireless-access areas.

Location

With Marymount's proximity to the nation's capital, students enjoy the cultural and educational advantages of Washington, D.C. Museums, galleries, theaters, the Capitol, the Library of Congress, and the National Archives are all easily accessible. Marymount shuttle buses provide service to the Metro system. Union Station and Reagan National Airport are also within easy reach. The resources of Washington, whether for research, recreation, or internships, are right next door, while students enjoy the benefits of a peaceful, 21-acre campus.

Majors and Degrees

The University awards the undergraduate degrees of Bachelor of Arts (B.A.), Bachelor of Science (B.S.), Bachelor of Science in Nursing (B.S.N.), and Bachelor of Business Administration (B.B.A.). A Bachelor of Arts may be earned in art, biology, communications, criminal justice, economics and public policy, English, fashion design, fashion merchandising, financial economics, graphic design, history, interior design, liberal studies, paralegal studies, philosophy, politics, psychology (business, developmental, education, social, or human services), sociology, and theology and religious studies. An Associate of Arts degree is offered in liberal studies. A Bachelor of Science may be earned in biology (concentrations in ecology, human biology, and molecular and cellular biology), computer information systems, computer science, health sciences, mathematics, and psychology (health sciences). Bachelor of Business Administration specialties include accounting, business administration, business law, finance, international business, management, and marketing. Bachelor of Science and Associate of Applied Science programs are offered in nursing. Education licensure programs in the areas of early childhood education (pre-K–3), secondary education (7–12), and art education (K–12) are available to degree-seeking undergraduates who complete course work for education programs in addition to the courses required for the major discipline.

Marymount also offers preprofessional programs for law, medicine, and physical therapy.

Academic Programs

Marymount is dedicated to educating the whole person—to helping students develop every aspect of their potential. The college years are years of transformation. They are a time to explore interests and to grow in knowledge and understanding. Marymount is committed to preparing students intellectually and morally for the tasks ahead, enabling them to achieve success and make a positive impact on the world.

While students study a liberal arts core curriculum and the required elements of their chosen disciplines, they are able to work with their faculty advisers to tailor academic programs that fit their personal and career objectives. Requirements for earning a degree include a cumulative GPA of 2.0 or better and a minimum of 36 credits as a student at Marymount. The total number of credits required varies by program. Marymount operates on a semester system. Small classes and personal attention help ensure student success and a strong sense of community. An honor system guides academic and social conduct. The cultural and educational resources of the nation's capital add to the curriculum through off-campus activities.

Marymount's Honors Program is for students who are seeking significant challenges and rewards. New, current, and transfer students of all disciplines may apply. The Honors Program experience culminates in the completion and defense of an Honors Thesis. Admission is competitive and limited to 20 new students each year. Students in the Honors Program receive substantial scholarship support, priority registration, special courses and opportunities, one-on-one faculty mentoring, direct involvement with program governance, travel support for professional conferences, and recognition at graduation and on the diploma and transcripts.

Off-Campus Programs

Undergraduate degrees require completion of an internship in the chosen field, in addition to all necessary course work in the major and in liberal arts core courses. Marymount students intern regularly in Congressional offices, the State Department,

Smithsonian museums, technology and biotechnology companies, media organizations, and international businesses—just to name a few of the choices available. For many students, internships lead to full-time employment after graduation.

Through Marymount's Study-Abroad program, students have the option of studying and completing an internship in London. Overseas study opportunities include Rome and Florence in Italy; Limerick, Ireland; and many other exciting destinations.

Academic Facilities

The Main Campus has classrooms, computer labs and wireless-access areas, science labs, seminar rooms, language labs, nursing auto-tutorials, and studios for fine and graphic arts, fashion design, and interior design. The Emerson G. Reinsch Library is also located on the Main Campus. It houses more than 191,000 volumes and 1,100 journal titles, and thousands of searchable databases. Students have access to member libraries of the Washington Research Library Consortium and the Consortium for Continuing Higher Education in Northern Virginia. The Instructional Media Center (IMC) and the Learning Resource Center (LRC) are also in the Reinsch complex. The IMC provides audiovisual support for instruction, and the LRC offers group and individual tutorials and serves as a test center. The Reinsch Auditorium is used for a wide range of campus events, from a speaker series to theater productions. The Barry Art Gallery features a variety of juried exhibitions throughout the year.

The Ballston Campus, an eight-story building just minutes from the Main Campus by free shuttle bus, also houses classrooms, seminar rooms, and computer labs and wireless-access areas as well as physical therapy labs, the Truland Auditorium, and the Electronic Learning Center.

Costs

The undergraduate tuition for 2004–05 is $16,952 per academic year. Room and board for 2004–05 are $7520 per academic year for double occupancy; there is an additional fee of $707.50 per semester for single occupancy.

Financial Aid

Marymount has an extensive scholarship and grant program and participates in all federal and state aid programs. To be considered for aid, students must file the Free Application for Federal Student Aid (FAFSA) with the College Scholarship Service. In fall 2003, approximately 48 percent of full-time freshmen received need-based aid and 87 percent received some form of financial assistance. The financial aid includes scholarships, grants, loans, work-study awards, and on-campus employment. The average financial aid package for freshmen is $16,327.

Faculty

At Marymount, faculty members are committed to the success of each student. They make themselves readily available to discuss course work or career plans or to simply chat. The University has 128 full-time faculty members and a number of highly qualified adjunct faculty members. In addition, business and professional leaders often visit as lecturers. The undergraduate student-faculty ratio is 14:1. Marymount classes are small, so students and professors really get to know each other.

Student Government

The student government acts as the official liaison between students, faculty members, and the administration. It may make policy recommendations related to student issues. The Activities Programming Board plans and implements a variety of events, including comedy nights, movies, parties, dances, concerts, and trips.

Admission Requirements

The Admissions team reviews the strength of an applicant's academic record, national test scores, breadth of academic preparation, and letters of recommendation. Applicants to the freshman class are considered if a student's high school grade point average in academic courses is 2.5 or better on a 4.0 scale, the combined SAT score is within 100 points of the national average or better, and the student's academic preparation, recommendations, and character indicate that he or she is qualified to undertake Marymount programs. It is recommended that students have at least 4 years of English; 3 years of a foreign language, mathematics, and the social sciences; and 2 years of science.

A campus interview is not required but is strongly recommended. It gives students a chance to see if Marymount would be a good fit. The University holds Campus Visit Days in the fall and spring. Visitors are welcome at any time, and appointments with Admissions staff may be made in advance.

Application and Information

High school students seeking admission are advised to apply early during their senior year. They should submit an application (which can be completed online), a nonrefundable fee of $35, a high school transcript, SAT I or ACT scores, evidence of expected graduation from an accredited high school, and a recommendation from a high school counselor or an appropriate school official. Those who have attended another college or university must also submit transcripts of college-level study and a recommendation from the Dean of Students at the previous institution. The University has a rolling admission policy and notifies applicants soon after the application process is completed and a decision on admission has been made.

For more information, prospective students should contact:

Chris Domes, Vice President of Enrollment Management
Marymount University
2807 North Glebe Road
Arlington, Virginia 22207-4299
Telephone: 703-284-1500
800-548-7638 (toll-free)
E-mail: admissions@marymount.edu
World Wide Web: http://www.marymount.edu

Marymount University's historic 21-acre campus is only 10 minutes away from Washington, D.C.

MARYVILLE COLLEGE

MARYVILLE, TENNESSEE

The College

Founded in 1819, Maryville College is among the fifty oldest institutions of higher education in the United States and the twelfth-oldest in the South. Affiliated with the Presbyterian Church (USA), the College welcomes students of all faiths. Current enrollment is more than 1,050 men and women; students come from twenty-seven states; Washington, D.C.; and twenty-two countries. There is a strong community feeling on campus, and social activities include all students.

Facilities include twenty-five structures, of which ten are residence halls. Centrally located on the beautiful 320-acre campus is the Cooper Athletic Center, which contains three full-size gymnasiums, an indoor pool, racquetball courts, and a weight room. The College is a member of NCAA Division III. It fields men's varsity teams in baseball, basketball, cheerleading, cross-country, football, soccer, and tennis. Women's varsity sports are basketball, cheerleading, cross-country, soccer, softball, tennis, and volleyball. The College offers equestrian competition through its membership in the Intercollegiate Horse Show Association (IHSA). Dance team and wrestling are also available. A wide range of team and individual intramural sports are also offered. The College provides numerous social and special interest organizations.

Maryville College's Mountain Challenge Program is among the finest outdoor programs in the nation. On-campus facilities include a low-ropes course, an indoor climbing wall, and a climbing tower that is accessible to persons with disabilities. Equipment is available to students for rock climbing, hiking, camping, canoeing, biking, and white-water rafting in the nearby Great Smoky Mountains National Park.

Location

The city of Maryville is part of the metropolitan Knoxville area in eastern Tennessee. Maryville and Alcoa are side-by-side communities with a combined population of more than 30,000. The campus is 15 minutes south of Knoxville, a city of nearly 400,000 people and the home of the University of Tennessee. Fifteen minutes east of the campus are the Great Smoky Mountains, which provide ample opportunities for hiking, camping, snow skiing, and sightseeing. Maryville offers the best of both worlds—access to the city and to the mountains.

Majors and Degrees

Maryville College awards the Bachelor of Arts and Bachelor of Music degrees. Areas of study are American Sign Language and deaf studies, art, biochemistry, biology, business and organization management, chemical physics, chemistry, child development and learning, computer science/business, computer science/mathematics, economics, English, environmental studies, health care (nursing), history, international business, international studies, mathematics, music, outdoor recreation, physical education, physics–mathematics/teacher licensure, political science, psychology, religion, sign-language interpreting, sociology, Spanish, teaching English as a second language, theater studies, and writing/communication. Students may also design individualized programs that combine two or more disciplines. Certification is available in both elementary and secondary education.

Maryville College is one of very few colleges in the United States to offer four-year majors in American Sign Language and deaf studies and in sign-language interpreting.

Minors are offered in most major areas as well as areas in which majors are not available. They include accounting, American studies, Appalachian studies, French, German, medieval studies, philosophy, physics, and statistics.

Preprofessional study is offered in dentistry, law, medicine, ministry, pharmacy, physical therapy, and others. The College offers dual-degree programs in engineering in association with several regional universities. A dual-degree program is offered in nursing with Vanderbilt University (B.A. in health care and M.S. in nursing).

Academic Program

Course requirements for the baccalaureate degrees may usually be completed in four years. Maryville operates on a semester-hour system with a minimum of 128 hours required for graduation. Students must satisfy general education requirements, which account for about half the total number of courses. Each major has specific course requirements, which vary according to the program. Faculty academic advisers are assigned to all incoming students.

A senior thesis is required of every student. Internships and practicums are available in conjunction with all majors. All students must pass an English proficiency examination in their sophomore year and a comprehensive examination in their major in the senior year.

Credit by examination is available through CLEP tests, AP tests, I.B. courses, and institutional examinations.

The College calendar includes two traditional semesters with a three-week January term.

Off-Campus Programs

Affordable study abroad is available through sister school tuition arrangements in England, France, Japan, Korea, Mexico, Northern Ireland, Puerto Rico, South Africa, Venezuela, and Wales and through cooperative arrangements in Europe and Africa. The College is a member of the Oak Ridge Associated Universities, which affords multiple opportunities for research and study. Students participate in field study in biology and natural history in the Great Smoky Mountains and the lakes of east Tennessee. Internships and summer programs are available at such sites as the Woods Hole Oceanographic Institution in Massachusetts, the Savannah River Ecological Station in South Carolina, and several national laboratories, such as Argonne, Brookhaven, Lawrence Livermore, and Los Alamos, Pacific Northwest. Student interns also study in Washington, D.C., at the Washington Center for Learning Alternatives, in Nashville in the Tennessee State Legislative Intern Program, and with several international corporations in the United States and abroad. The International Programming Committee and the student's major department assist in arranging study abroad, internships, and other off-campus experiences.

Academic Facilities

The Sutton Science Center is a modern, well-designed, and well-equipped facility for the sciences, computer science, mathematics, and psychology. Private study carrels are available to many students in the sciences. The Fine Arts Center provides a 250-seat recital hall, an art gallery, classrooms, and private studios for both art and music students. Other classroom facilities are located in a mixture of older and newer buildings. The Lamar Memorial Library is fully automated with an online catalog and access to libraries throughout the world, as well as numerous electronic databases.

Costs

For 2003–04, tuition was $19,180; room and board costs were $3040 and $3140, respectively; and the student activity and technology fees totaled $600, for a total of $25,960. The College estimates a cost of $2000 annually for books, supplies, transportation, and personal expenses.

Financial Aid

More than 90 percent of Maryville's students receive financial assistance through scholarships, grants, loans, or employment. The Presidential Scholarships are the College's most prestigious merit awards; these renewable awards are full tuition scholarships. Merit scholarship awards ranging from $5000 to $12,000 are available to students with outstanding academic and personal achievement. Maryville participates in the Bonner Scholars program, which provides scholarship assistance in exchange for community service. Transfer students also have the opportunity to receive comparative scholarships, including the Phi Theta Kappa scholarship. The College also offers scholarships in art, music, and theater. Federal aid programs include the Federal Pell Grant, Federal Supplemental Educational Opportunity Grant, Federal Perkins Loan, and Federal Work-Study programs. Tennessee residents may qualify for the Tennessee State Grant. To apply for financial aid, students should complete the Free Application for Federal Student Aid (FAFSA) before February 1.

Faculty

The student-faculty ratio is 12:1; average class size is 20. Ninety-one percent of the 70 full-time faculty members hold doctoral or terminal degrees in their fields. Faculty members are committed to teaching in the undergraduate setting and are also involved in research and the publication of books and articles.

Student Government

The Student Government represents the entire student community and is involved in college-wide policy making, judicial issues, and student programming.

Admission Requirements

Admission to Maryville is selective. Students applying from high school are expected to have successfully completed a strong college-preparatory program. Factors evaluated in the admission decision include courses taken, grade point average, test scores (either SAT I or ACT), and teachers' recommendations. An admissions essay or a graded writing sample is also encouraged. The majority of entering students rank within the top 25 percent of their high school graduating class. An on-campus interview is strongly recommended but is not a requirement for admission.

Application and Information

To apply to Maryville College, a student should submit the application for admission, an official high school transcript, and scores on either the ACT or SAT I. The application fee is $25. Transfer students must submit a high school transcript plus official transcripts from each college previously attended. The application deadline for early action is September 15. The application deadline for early decision is November 15. The deadline for regular admission is March 1.

Maryville College does not discriminate on the basis of race, color, gender, ethnic or national origin, religion, sexual orientation, age, disability, or political beliefs in its admission procedures and educational programs.

For further information regarding admissions, financial assistance, academic programs, and campus visits, students should contact:

Office of Admissions
Maryville College
502 East Lamar Alexander Parkway
Maryville, Tennessee 37804
Telephone: 865-981-8092
800-597-2687 (toll-free)
Fax: 865-981-8005
E-mail: admissions@maryvillecollege.edu
World Wide Web: http://www.maryvillecollege.edu

Maryville students work together to reach the peak on the climbing tower.

MARYVILLE UNIVERSITY OF SAINT LOUIS

ST. LOUIS, MISSOURI

The University

Maryville University of Saint Louis is an independent, comprehensive, community-oriented institution founded in 1872 by the Religious of the Sacred Heart. The University, committed to the education of the whole person through programs designed to meet the needs of traditional and nontraditional students, offers programs in day, evening, and weekend formats. Primarily an undergraduate teaching university, Maryville also offers graduate programs in professional fields where there is evidence of need and corresponding institutional strength. The liberal arts and sciences are recognized as the foundation of all academic programs, including those leading to professional degrees. True to its heritage, Maryville ensures that excellence is preeminent in all endeavors. The Judeo-Christian tradition of the University is honored in symbol and in substance.

Maryville's integration of liberal learning and professional preparation results in an education valued for its high quality by employers throughout the St. Louis area and across the country. The University's liberal arts emphasis equips students with the ability to think analytically, solve problems creatively, and communicate clearly—skills needed throughout life.

The University is adjacent to Maryville Corporate Centre and St. Luke's Medical Center, providing convenient access to internships. Eight campus buildings have been constructed since 1997: the Anheuser-Busch Academic Center, the Art and Design Building, the University Auditorium, the University Center, and four student apartment buildings.

Maryville's education program is nationally recognized as one of the best in the country, with 100 percent of 2003 graduates employed as teachers. The actuarial science program is one of only thirty-five advanced undergraduate programs nationwide; 100 percent of graduates are employed. The University is an established leader in physical therapy, occupational therapy, and nursing education and offers one of only two music therapy programs in the state. The interior design program is one of only two in Missouri accredited by the Foundation for Interior Design Education Research (FIDER), with 100 percent of interior design graduates employed in their fields.

Maryville's enrollment of 3,200 students includes 1,550 undergraduates, 1,150 weekend college students, and 500 graduate students. Students who attend Maryville University are not required to live on the campus; an increasing number of students, however, choose not to commute. In fact, 25 percent of traditional students live on campus in one of two air-conditioned, coeducational residence halls or in one of four new student apartment buildings, which house 550 students. Both residential and commuter students are active in student government, intramurals and recreational sports, the NCAA Division III athletic program, more than forty other campus clubs and organizations, and enriching educational and cultural opportunities.

Location

Students appreciate the natural beauty and convenient West County location of Maryville's 130-acre campus. Its rolling hills, wooded areas, creeks, two lakes, and miles of walking trails are within 20 minutes of downtown St. Louis.

Majors and Degrees

Four schools compose the University: the John E. Simon School of Business, the School of Education, the School of Health Professions, and the School of Liberal Arts and Professional Programs. Through these schools, Maryville University offers the Bachelor of Arts; the Bachelor of Fine Arts; the Bachelor of Science in clinical laboratory science; the Bachelor of Science in music therapy, a 4½-year program that includes a six-month internship; a Bachelor of Science in Nursing; and certificates in American studies, health-care management, and gerontology. Majors include accountancy, accounting information systems, actuarial science, art and design, biology, business administration, chemistry, clinical laboratory science, communications, computer science, criminology, education, e-marketing, engineering, English, environmental science, environmental studies, graphic design, health-care management, health policy, history, information systems, interior design, liberal studies, management, marketing, mathematical modeling for business, mathematics, music, music therapy, nursing, organizational leadership, paralegal studies, physics, premedicine, psychology, psychology/sociology, science, and sociology.

Minors in international studies, women's studies, and writing are also available.

Academic Programs

All undergraduate programs at Maryville University ensure that graduates acquire the in-depth knowledge in a chosen major field of study and the skills and knowledge expected of a liberally educated person. The desirable characteristics of a Maryville graduate include communication, critical-thinking, technological, research, and data analysis skills; a multicultural awareness; a global perspective; a social awareness; and the qualities of a responsible citizen.

All bachelor's degrees require at least 128 credits, with full-time students taking 12–18 credits per semester. Other general requirements for a bachelor's degree include a 2.0 GPA (C average) or better, the completion of all general education and major requirements, and the satisfaction of minor requirements (if applicable). In addition, the last 30 hours of study must be completed at Maryville, and at least 60 of the 128 credits must be done at a four-year institution. Students should consult their adviser for specific program requirements.

Off-Campus Programs

Maryville University recognizes a special responsibility to prepare students to compete in an increasingly global economy and to promote mutual respect and understanding for cultural differences and divergent beliefs. Accordingly, Maryville faculty members encourage students to expand their horizons by studying abroad for a summer, a semester, or a year. Study abroad can help a student learn or improve in a foreign language, see other places, make new friends, and even progress toward graduation. In recent years, Maryville faculty members have arranged for students to take classes in countries from England and Austria to Japan and Australia. Financial aid is available for some study-abroad programs. Students interested in pursuing study-abroad opportunities should contact the Director of Multicultural Programs.

Academic Facilities

The Instructional Computing Department at Maryville University maintains sixteen computing lab facilities located at the main campus and two facilities located at the O'Fallon Campus and the Southwest Campus. The main computing facilities equip students to accomplish their academic work and further enhance their learning. In designing and delivering their courses, faculty members are supported by state-of-the-art tools in instructional computing and classroom technologies. Currently, a total of 250 microcomputers are available for use by students and faculty members campuswide.

The Maryville University Library, through a highly skilled and caring staff and a commitment to high-quality service and materials, strives to be a complete, responsive information resource gateway for the University community. The library supports research using traditional resources, emerging technologies, and resource-sharing opportunities; empowers students to become educated information users; and fosters a heightened community awareness of how the transition from information to knowledge enhances the quality of life, enriches values, and impacts rational decision making.

The Academic Success Center and the Advising Center offer individualized academic advising and career exploration if students are undecided about a major.

Costs

For the 2004–05 academic year, two semesters cost $23,400; $16,000 for full-time tuition, $400 for fees, and $7000 for room and board.

Financial Aid

Maryville's strong financial aid and merit scholarship programs make the overall cost comparable to that of a public institution. About 80 percent of Maryville's full-time students receive some form of financial aid. More than $17.5 million has been awarded, making Maryville University's high-quality education affordable. Many financial aid opportunities help offset the cost; both merit-based and need-based aid are available in the form of grants, loans, scholarships, and work-study programs. All full-time students are automatically considered for merit awards that range from $500 to $5000. There is also a competition for the University Scholars Program; awards range from the cost of tuition up to tuition, room, and board. Prospective art and design students can compete for scholarships ranging from $500 to $5000 a year.

Faculty

Maryville University prides itself on its accessible faculty members, 90 percent of whom have a Ph.D. or terminal degree. Professors are enthusiastic teachers with impressive academic credentials and professional experience in their fields as CPAs, artists, health-care professionals, and business leaders. Students benefit from their real-world perspective, the personal attention, and involvement in active learning. The student-faculty ratio is 13:1.

Student Government

Maryville Student Government (MSG) provides students with the opportunity to become involved in the Maryville community through a wide range of activities and responsibilities. MSG works with students and the administration in a continued effort to sustain and improve student life at Maryville. Membership in MSG is open to all Maryville students. Elections of officers and senators are held in the spring semester.

Admission Requirements

Freshman applicants must have minimum ACT or SAT scores of 20 and 950, respectively, and a high school cumulative GPA of at least 2.5 on a 4.0 scale. Students must submit the application for admission, a $25 application fee, high school transcripts, and either the ACT or SAT scores. Those who do not meet these requirements are encouraged to submit a letter of recommendation and a one-page personal statement. Additional documentation may be required, depending upon the major.

Transfer students must have a minimum GPA of a 2.0 on a 4.0 scale and must submit transcripts from all colleges or universities previously attended. In addition, applicants who have fewer than 30 transfer hours must submit an official high school transcript.

Application and Information

Most applications for admission to Maryville University of Saint Louis are reviewed on a rolling basis. The physical therapy program has a November 15 read date, after which files are reviewed until the program is filled. Applications should be submitted as soon as possible.

For more information, students should contact:

Office of Admissions
Maryville University of Saint Louis
13550 Conway Road
St. Louis, Missouri 63141-7299
Telephone: 314-529-9300
800-627-9855 (toll-free)
World Wide Web: http://www.maryville.edu

MARYWOOD UNIVERSITY

SCRANTON, PENNSYLVANIA

The University

Marywood University is coeducational, comprehensive, residential, and Catholic. Founded in 1915 by the Sisters, Servants of the Immaculate Heart of Mary, the University serves men and women from a variety of backgrounds and religions. The University enrolls more than 3,000 students in an array of undergraduate and graduate programs. Committed to enriching human lives through ethical and religious values and a tradition of service and motivated by a pioneering, progressive spirit, Marywood provides a framework for educational excellence that enables students to develop fully as persons and to master professional and leadership skills necessary for meeting human needs.

The central focus of the undergraduate curriculum is expressed in the phrase "living responsibly in an interdependent world." Students are encouraged to incorporate a concern for the responsible use of resources into their personal and professional lives. Marywood's historic concern for the enrichment of human life through honoring religious values and a tradition of service also extends to programs at the graduate level. Programs leading to master's and doctoral degrees are offered in the Graduate School of Arts and Sciences and the School of Social Work.

The athletic program for women and men at Marywood provides students with opportunities to play on competitive intercollegiate, club, and intramural teams. Students compete on an intercollegiate basis in baseball, basketball, cross-country, field hockey, soccer, softball, tennis, and volleyball. Marywood is a member of the NCAA Division III and the Pennsylvania Athletic Conference (PAC). Marywood's teams have been successful, winning titles in basketball, field hockey, softball, tennis, and volleyball. In addition, Marywood teams and individuals have participated in tournaments at the national level.

Marywood is fully accredited by the Commission on Higher Education of the Middle States Association of Colleges and Schools. Accreditations/approvals have been granted by Accreditation Review Commission on Education for the Physician Assistant, American Art Therapy Association, American Music Therapy Association, American Bar Association, American Dietetic Association, American Speech-Language-Hearing Association, Association of Collegiate Business Schools and Programs, Commission on Accreditation of Allied Health Education Programs (athletic trainer), Council for Accreditation of Counseling and Related Educational Programs, Council on Social Work Education, Middle States Commission on Higher Education, National Association of Schools of Art and Design, National Association of Schools of Music, National Council for Accreditation of Teacher Education, National League for Nursing Accrediting Commission (undergraduate only), and Pennsylvania Department of Education.

Location

Situated on a hilltop, Marywood's scenic 115-acre campus is part of an attractive residential area of the city of Scranton, in northeastern Pennsylvania. With a population of 78,000, Scranton is the fifth-largest city in Pennsylvania and is the county seat of Lackawanna County (the county population is approximately 213,000). Marywood is relatively close to many major cities of the Northeast; traveling by car, it is 1 hour to Binghamton, 2½ hours to New York and Philadelphia, 4 hours to Washington, D.C., and 5½ hours to Boston. Several airlines serve the Wilkes-Barre/Scranton International Airport, which is 20 minutes away from the campus. The Pocono Mountains, offering spectacular scenery and an abundance of outdoor recreational opportunities including downhill skiing, are only a few minutes away from campus.

Majors and Degrees

Marywood University offers a variety of majors and minors at the undergraduate level. Individually designed majors, developed with faculty guidance, and double and interdisciplinary majors are also available. Several five-year bachelor's/master's degree programs are offered.

At the undergraduate level, Marywood University awards the Bachelor of Arts (B.A.), Bachelor of Business Administration (B.B.A.), Bachelor of Fine Arts (B.F.A.), Bachelor of Music (B.M.), Bachelor of Science (B.S.), Bachelor of Science in Nursing (B.S.N.), Bachelor of Social Work (B.S.W.), and the Associate of Arts (A.A.).

Marywood offers majors and minors in the following areas of study: accounting, ad hoc (self-designed), advertising and public relations, art (studio: ceramics, painting, sculpture; design: graphic design, illustration, architecture/interior design, photography), art education, art therapy, arts administration (art, music, theater), aviation management, biology, biotechnology, church music, communication sciences and disorders (audiology, deaf studies, speech-language pathology), comprehensive social sciences (general, history, sociology), computer information and telecommunications systems, computer science (minor), criminal justice (2 years, 4 years), dance/movement (minor), digital media and broadcast production (broadcast, corporate), early childhood special education, education (elementary, secondary), English, environmental science, family and consumer sciences education, financial planning, French, general science education, health and physical education (athletic training, education, physical activity), health services administration, history/citizenship education, history/political science, hospitality management, industrial/organizational psychology, international business, journalism (minor), legal assistant (2 years, 4 years, postbaccalaureate degree program), management, marketing, mathematics, medical technology/clinical laboratory science, multimedia (minor), music, music education, music therapy, nursing (preservice, post-RN), nutrition and dietetics (coordinated program, didactic program), performance, performing arts, philosophy (minor), physician assistant studies, psychology, psychology/clinical practice, public administration, religious studies, retail business management, science, social work, Spanish, special education of the mentally/physically disabled, special education/elementary education (dual certification, theater, and women's studies (minor)).

Preprofessional programs are offered in chiropractic, communication sciences and disorders, dentistry, law, medicine, physician assistant studies, and veterinary medicine. A joint seven-year bachelor's/doctoral program in chiropractic involves three years of study on the Marywood campus and additional work at New York Chiropractic College, located in Seneca Falls, New York.

Academic Program

Marywood's programs are administered through four degree-granting schools. Undergraduate degrees are offered in more than sixty academic programs, including the arts, sciences, music, fine arts, social work, and nursing. All students are required to complete a core curriculum in the liberal arts in addition to the courses in their major. Opportunities for undergraduates abound through double majors, honors and independent study programs, practicums, internships, and study abroad. Army and Air Force ROTC programs are available.

Off-Campus Programs

Study-abroad opportunities are available in such countries as Australia, Canada, England, France, Mexico, and Spain. A visiting student program allows Marywood retail business management students to study at the Fashion Institute of Technology in New York City. Through Studio Art Centers International (SACI), art students may study in Florence, Italy. Students can also earn credits toward a degree through the distance learning program.

Academic Facilities

Marywood continues to expand its facilities with a new studio arts center and the Healthy Families Center. The McGowan Center for Graduate and Professional Studies includes three computer labs connected to the campus fiber-optic network. More than 360 microcomputers are found throughout the campus, giving students access to the library's online catalog, CD-ROM databases, software, and Internet resources.

Marywood's Learning Resources Center (LRC) houses library services, media services, and academic computing services. The library collection includes more than 216,000 volumes, nearly 1,000 current journal subscriptions, and more than 42,000 media items. The LRC provides the World Wide Web, CD-ROM, and full-text databases. It also participates in the interlibrary loan network with 8,650 libraries. The research collection includes many index and abstract services.

Costs

Tuition for full-time students (32 credit hours at $580 per credit hour) for the 2003–04 academic year was $18,560. There was also a general fee of $650 for full-time students. Costs for room and board for a full academic year were approximately $8134, depending on which meal plan is selected and the desired room occupancy. Costs of books and supplies were estimated at $700.

Financial Aid

Marywood offers a comprehensive program of financial aid to assist students in meeting educational costs. Eligibility for federal and state programs is based on demonstrated financial need, determined by a federal eligibility formula that analyzes family income and assets. In addition, nearly $11 million of institutional aid is awarded annually to Marywood students. Applicants to Marywood are considered for all financial assistance programs for which they qualify. Candidates are required to submit the Free Application for Federal Student Aid (FAFSA) and the Marywood application form, preferably by February 15.

Faculty

Of the 294 faculty members at Marywood, 130 are full-time, and 86 percent of these hold the Ph.D. or the highest degree in their field. The student-faculty ratio is 12:1. Faculty members are evaluated on their teaching and on their scholarly and artistic activities.

Student Government

All matriculated students in the undergraduate school are members of the Student Government Association (SGA). The SGA operates with a number of committees, including the Student Council, the Resident Committee, and the Commuter Committee. The association plays a key role in establishing a positive campus environment.

Admission Requirements

Candidates for admission should demonstrate reasonable progress toward graduation in an accredited secondary school, have graduated from a secondary school, or offer evidence of an equivalent secondary education. Each candidate should show satisfactory academic preparation in 16 units of subject matter, including 4 units of English, 3 units of social studies, 2 units of mathematics, 1 unit of science with laboratory, and 6 additional units. Either SAT I or ACT scores are required for those who wish to enter as freshmen.

In addition to fulfilling general admission requirements, candidates for admission to a degree program in art, education, music, nursing, and pre–physician assistant studies must meet special standards established by the department. Prior to enrollment, music, theater, and art candidates are required to audition or to present an art portfolio.

For certain programs, candidates without the recommended distribution of units may be eligible for admission if their course work as a whole and the results of their tests offer evidence of a strong foundation for college work. Candidates who are deficient in required course work may complete the appropriate work during the summer or the first year in college.

A student who demonstrates satisfactory academic performance at another college may apply for admission as a transfer student. Academic courses presented for transfer should be equivalents of courses required by the programs of study at Marywood. Students should have earned a grade of C or higher in their course work; C– will not transfer. A student should expect to earn a minimum of 60 credits at Marywood University; ordinarily at least one half of the credits required for a major must also be earned at Marywood.

International candidates are required to meet the academic standards for admission, demonstrate proficiency in the use of the English language, and submit documentation of having sufficient funds to cover educational and living expenses for the duration of study. To certify proficiency in the use of English, international applicants whose primary language is not English must submit scores from the Test of English as a Foreign Language (TOEFL).

Application and Information

Applications for admission are considered on a rolling basis; however, candidates are encouraged to submit applications by March 1. Applications received after March 1 are considered on the basis of available space in particular programs. To be considered for admission, applicants must submit to the Office of Admissions a completed application, a nonrefundable $30 application fee, an official high school transcript with an indication of class rank, an official report of scores from the SAT I or ACT, and at least one letter of recommendation. Students can also apply online at http://www.marywood.edu/apply.

Transfer students must submit a completed application, a nonrefundable $30 application fee, an official high school transcript, official academic transcript(s) reflecting all college course work for which the candidate has enrolled, and at least one letter of recommendation.

All submitted credentials become the property of Marywood and are not returnable to the applicant. Admission standards and policies are free of discrimination on grounds of race, color, national origin, sex, age, or disability.

For further information, interested students should contact:

Robert Reese, Director
Office of Undergraduate Admissions
Marywood University
2300 Adams Avenue
Scranton, Pennsylvania 18509
Telephone: 570-348-6234
800-346-5014 (toll-free)
Fax: 570-961-4763
E-mail: ugadm@marywood.edu
World Wide Web: http://www.marywood.edu

Students at Marywood enjoy a break between classes.

MASSACHUSETTS COLLEGE OF LIBERAL ARTS

NORTH ADAMS, MASSACHUSETTS

The College

Massachusetts College of Liberal Arts (formerly North Adams State College) was founded in 1894 as North Adams Normal School. There are approximately 1,500 undergraduate students enrolled and an additional 200 part-time students who are graduate students, evening students, and special program students.

Massachusetts College of Liberal Arts (MCLA), a four-year, residential, coeducational liberal arts college, offers numerous baccalaureate degrees and a Master of Education degree with concentrations in three areas.

The College is located on 80 acres and includes an athletic complex with softball, baseball, and soccer fields; tennis courts; and a cross-country course. There are three residence facilities that hold more than 1,000 students. Nine intercollegiate athletic programs including baseball (men), basketball (men/women), cross-country (men/women), hockey (men), soccer (men/women), softball (women), and tennis (women) are available. In addition, there are forty-five clubs, organizations, and intramural activities.

The Amsler Campus Center, a four-story complex, houses one of the three residence gymnasiums, a state-of-the-art fitness center, a swimming pool, a dance complex, racquetball and handball courts, two cafeterias, and a counseling center, as well as the bookstore and an athletic training center.

Additional services offered through the College include health services, academic support services, tutorial centers, and the First Year Seminar, an academic and social support service for incoming freshmen.

Location

MCLA is located in North Adams, Massachusetts, 1 mile from the downtown area of 15,000, in the northwestern corner of the state, bordering both Vermont and New York. Centered in the heart of the Berkshires, North Adams offers numerous cultural, historical, and recreational opportunities. Cultural attractions in the Berkshires include Tanglewood Theater, Jacob's Pillow, the Sterling and Francine Clark Art Institute, and the Williamstown Theater Festival. Approximate travel time from Boston is 2½ hours; from New York City, 3 hours; from Albany, New York, 1 hour; from Burlington, Vermont, 3 hours; and from Hartford, Connecticut, 2 hours.

Majors and Degrees

MCLA confers the Bachelor of Arts and Bachelor of Science degrees. Undergraduate programs are offered in biology, business administration, computer science, education, English/communications, environmental studies, fine and performing arts, history, interdisciplinary studies, mathematics, philosophy, physics, psychology, and sociology. Teacher certification is offered in the areas of early childhood education (grades N–3), elementary education (grades 1–6), middle school education (grades 5–9), and secondary education (grades 9–12).

Concentrations include accounting, anthropology, art, arts management, broadcast media, chemistry, computer science, corporate communications, criminal justice, finance/economics, journalism, literature, medical technology, music, political science, prelaw, premed, public relations, social work, sociology, sports medicine, theater studies, and writing. There are twenty-six minors offered through the College.

Academic Programs

MCLA operates on a two-semester basis with the first semester running September through December and the second running January through May. Classes are available to all students through both day and evening offerings.

A minimum of 120 semester hours of credit, including major requirements and achievement of a quality point average of at least 2.0, is necessary for completion of a bachelor's degree. At least 39 of the 120 credits must be in upper-division work. MCLA offers a course of study divided into three segments: a general education program, major and minor fields of study, and elective areas in which students have the opportunity to pursue additional academic interests. This program reflects the College's intention that its graduates acquire a sound general education foundation, master in considerable depth one or more integrated areas of human knowledge, and enjoy the freedom to explore fields of personal interest.

College credit is awarded to students with successful scores on the Advanced Placement examinations of the College Board and the College-Level Examination Program (CLEP) tests.

Off-Campus Programs

The College participates in the College Academic Program Sharing (CAPS), enabling a student to study at another state college and to earn up to 30 credits while maintaining degree status at MCLA. Students are also offered the opportunity to cross-enroll at Williams College and Berkshire Community College. Travel courses are offered during school breaks, and students are encouraged to explore other cultures while earning course credits. Internships are also offered to students in any major program, both on campus and off campus. Local businesses, such as General Electric, Community Development Corporation, Channel 7 in Boston (a CBS-affiliated station), the Museum of Contemporary Art, and the Berkshire Mall, routinely offer one-semester internships to qualified students.

As a member of the College Consortium for International Studies (CCIS), MCLA offers its students the opportunity to study abroad in sixteen countries throughout the world for a semester or for an entire year.

Academic Facilities

The holdings of the Eugene Lawrence Freel Library include 192,000 book volumes, 544 current journals and newspaper subscriptions, more than 300,000 microform units, and approximately 6,500 nonbook items. College facilities also include television and radio production facilities; biology, chemistry, and physics labs; three computer labs; two amphitheaters; a performance theater; the Career Services Center; and the Center for Academic Advancement.

Costs

In 2003–04, annual tuition and fees were for $5100 for in-state students, $5600 for residents of New York State and southern Vermont (based on specific criteria), and $14,200 for all other out-of-state students. Room and board per year were approximately $6500, fluctuating with the choice of housing and meal plans. Additional academic and miscellaneous expenses, including books and travel, average $2500 for the year.

Financial Aid

The Office of Financial Aid helps students remove financial obstacles that stand between them and their educational goals. The College's financial aid philosophy is that it should make every effort to enable attendance for students who have financial need remaining after their families have met as much of the cost as is reasonably possible. Need is calculated by subtracting the family's contribution from the total cost of attendance. Those students whose need is greatest may expect to receive priority in the awarding procedure if they meet published deadlines. Although the financial aid programs operate under specific federal and state constraints, every effort is made to consider each student's family financial situation individually. Typically, the student's financial aid award consists of a package composed of a combination of grant, loan, and part-time employment. The deadline for applying for financial aid is April 1 for priority review; however, applications will be accepted on a rolling basis until funds are exhausted.

Faculty

The College currently employs 77 full-time and 49 part-time faculty members; of these, 79 percent hold a doctoral degree. The student-faculty ratio is 13:1, and all classes are taught by faculty members. Working with a diverse student body, the faculty and staff aim to develop liberally educated individuals who have the knowledge, perspectives, critical thinking abilities, and ethical values necessary to become active citizens and leaders within their chosen field.

Student Government

The Student Government Association (SGA) has been in existence at MCLA since 1909. It was formed in order to coordinate and unify matters of student governance on campus, allowing students to have input in all College policies. The SGA administers the Student Activities Trust Fund to all recognized clubs and organizations and sponsors additional Massachusetts College events.

Admission Requirements

All freshman applicants must submit an official copy of their high school record, including at least the first-quarter senior grades. The primary emphasis in evaluating a candidate is on the total high school profile, consisting of overall grade point average, the applicant's curriculum, SAT I/ACT scores, and the level of competition in the individual high school. The unit requirements for freshman admission are English, 4; mathematics, 3; science, 3; history/social science, 2; foreign language, 2; and electives, 2.

Transfer students are strongly encouraged to apply for admission. To be eligible for admission, a student must have a cumulative grade point average of at least 2.0 on a 4.0 scale and submit an official transcript from each college attended. Transfer students are notified at the time of acceptance of the number of credits accepted and how they transfer into their program of study. MCLA has developed transfer articulation agreements with many community and junior colleges to ensure admission and maximum transferability of credit. MCLA offers joint admission to transfer students from Massachusetts community colleges.

International students must submit a record of secondary work, SAT I/ACT scores, and scores on the Test of English as a Foreign Language (TOEFL).

Consideration is given to applicants regardless of their race, religion, national origin, sex, age, color, ethnic origin, or handicap. Admission interviews are recommended for all applicants.

Application and Information

The application for admission to Massachusetts College of Liberal Arts requests information regarding a student's academic background, extracurricular activities, and personal data.

Applications are reviewed on a rolling admission schedule, and students are accepted by the College until all spaces are filled. Tours of the campus are provided daily and on specific weekends.

Application materials and additional information, including tour dates and times, may be obtained by contacting:

Office of Admission
Massachusetts College of Liberal Arts
375 Church Street
North Adams, Massachusetts 01247-4100
Telephone: 413-662-5410
800-292-6632 (toll-free)
Fax: 413-662-5179
E-mail: admissions@mcla.mass.edu
World Wide Web: http://www.mcla.edu

Historic Murdock Hall on the Massachusetts College of Liberal Arts campus.

MASSACHUSETTS COLLEGE OF PHARMACY AND HEALTH SCIENCES

BOSTON, MASSACHUSETTS

The College

Founded in 1823, the Massachusetts College of Pharmacy and Health Sciences (MCPHS) is well into its second century as one of the nation's oldest schools of pharmacy. One of only a few that remain private and independent, the College has the distinct advantage of quickly responding to change. That flexibility has allowed the College to expand its mission and programs over time to include a number of science and health-care programs.

With its distinguished history and an international reputation, the Massachusetts College of Pharmacy and Health Sciences is helping to redefine the roles of pharmacists, nurses, and health professionals in health-care delivery. The College's unique programs integrate theoretical and applied knowledge in the health professions with general education in the arts and sciences, so that graduates may become enlightened citizens as well as competent practitioners.

The curriculum at MCPHS is designed to develop active thinkers and learners who are prepared for fast-changing professions and a complex world. A core of liberal arts and sciences courses, or "science building blocks," are built into all bachelor's degree programs. Developed by scholars and working professionals, these courses are often custom-tailored to give students practical information and valuable insights into today's health-care concerns.

The Department of Sports, Recreation and Wellness offers opportunities for all students to participate in club sports, intramurals, wellness classes, and the Wellness Center. Baseball, basketball, cross-country, golf, soccer, softball, and volleyball operate as Student Government Association (SGA) clubs on campus and must comply with all SGA bylaws and regulations. The intramural program is open to all MCPHS students and faculty and staff members and is an ideal way for students to be involved with the College community. Other student activities include the Academy of Students of Pharmacy, the Black Student Union, the Indian Student Organization, the International Student Association, the Republic of China Student Association, the Vietnamese Student Association, the College yearbook, and the *Dispenser* (student newspaper). There are also five professional fraternities—two for men, two for women, and one coed.

At the Manchester, New Hampshire, campus MCPHS offers a two-year, six-trimester postbaccalaureate program that leads to a master's degree in physician assistant studies. It is a full-time day program that includes twelve months of didactic education and twelve months of clinical education.

Location

Dedicated solely to health education, the College is a highly respected institution in Boston's world-renowned Longwood Medical and Academic Area (LMA). Its location alone gives MCPHS students resources unmatched by any other program. The LMA is home to the nation's premier medical centers and educational and research institutions—a highly stimulating and inspiring environment in which to learn.

Boston is a college town in the best sense of the word—cultural, accessible, and pulsing with activity. Students can experience Boston's history along the Freedom Trail, enjoy its seafood on the waterfront, or explore its ethnic neighborhoods such as the Italian North End. Favorite spots include Faneuil Hall Marketplace; the Esplanade along the Charles River for outdoor concerts and movies, biking, jogging, and in-line skating; and the Public Gardens and Boston Common for walks, picnics, and just relaxing. The city's elaborate public transportation network (the "T") connects students to all these places and many more, such as Cambridge and Harvard Square, where students might browse in bookstores and enjoy a sidewalk performance; Newbury Street for shopping and distinctive galleries; the Fleet Center where the Celtics and Bruins play; Fenway Park, home of the Boston Red Sox; Symphony Hall, home of the Boston Pops; and the Boston Symphony Orchestra.

In September 2000, MCPHS opened a new school in Worcester, Massachusetts, the third-largest city in New England. Housed in a 60,000-square-foot, state-of-the-art facility, this school is located adjacent to the Worcester Medical Center and is close to the Fallon Clinic, St. Vincent's Hospital, and the medical school at the University of Massachusetts.

There is also a campus in Manchester, New Hampshire.

Majors and Degrees

MCPHS offers a six-year program leading to the Doctor of Pharmacy degree, along with the following undergraduate degrees and programs: Bachelor of Science degrees in chemistry, dental hygiene (Forsyth Program for Dental Hygienists), health psychology, pharmaceutical sciences, pharmaceutical marketing and management, pharmacy/chemistry (dual degree), physician assistant studies (six-year master's program), premedical and health studies, and radiologic sciences (accelerated three-year program in nuclear medicine, radiography, or radiation therapy).

MCPHS–Worcester and MCPHS–Manchester (beginning in September 2004) offer an innovative accelerated Pharm.D. program for students who have already completed two years of preprofessional requirements at MCPHS–Boston or at another undergraduate institution.

Academic Programs

Students in each of the undergraduate programs begin their studies in the basic sciences, humanities, and social sciences. First-year classes include two semesters of English, math, biology, and chemistry. After completing basic science courses, Bachelor of Science degree candidates progress to advanced courses in chemistry, psychology, pharmaceutics, and pharmacology. Students are also required to complete professional development courses such as interpersonal communications, ethics, and law courses. In addition, students must complete 12 semester hours of elective courses in the humanities, social sciences, and behavioral sciences, as well as 12 semester hours of general elective course work.

A significant aspect of every student's education at MCPHS is the application of theoretical knowledge in a clinical setting. For example, the sixth year of the Pharm.D. program is devoted to clinical clerkships consisting of required rotations in general medicine and ambulatory care and several elective rotations.

Off-Campus Programs

The externship/clinical experience is a very important part of an MCPHS education and is built into most programs. The programs place students in professional settings for firsthand learning and guidance as they work with a mentor from the sponsoring institution's staff. Students may choose from among more than fifty-five hospitals and 100 community practice sites in and around Boston. The College's affiliations with Boston's high-caliber medical centers, top teaching hospitals, and pharmacies ensure students the highest quality experience.

As part of its pharmacy curriculum, the College offers an optional radiopharmacy externship program in conjunction with the Massachusetts General Hospital. The program consists of an academic phase based at the College and an experiential component performed at the hospital.

In 1996, the College officially entered into a consortium called the Colleges of the Fenway. In addition to MCPHS, the Colleges of the Fenway include Emmanuel, Simmons, and Wheelock Colleges;

the Wentworth Institute of Technology; and Massachusetts College of Art. Students of each of the participating institutions may take courses at any of the others, as well as use the facilities of each. In effect, the collaboration has created a "mega-campus" for MCPHS students.

Academic Facilities

A new $30-million Academic Student Center is under construction and scheduled to open in August 2004. The first floor of the 93,000-square-foot building is planned to house a professional pharmacy practice lab and multipurpose chemistry lab. An expanded library and technology center is planned for the second floor, and the top four floors provide apartment-style residences for 230 students.

The present MCPHS Sheppard Library is a pharmaceutical and medical information center that maintains a working collection of more than 40,000 catalogued print and nonprint materials and an archives collection that documents the history of the College. The library receives approximately 700 serial subscriptions annually.

Costs

Tuition for the preprofessional curriculum is $18,800 per academic year. Tuition for the professional curriculum is $22,000. Room and board costs are $10,070. Additional fees and the cost of books are estimated at $1000.

Financial Aid

Financial aid is both merit- and need-based. A combination of various forms of aid is usually offered to meet the established needs of each qualified student. The College administers Federal Work-Study Program awards, Health Professions Student Loans, Federal Pell Grants, Federal Supplemental Educational Opportunity Grants, and Federal Perkins Loans as well as in-house scholarships. The priority deadline for application is March 1, and notification is made on a rolling basis. Approximately 90 percent of the students at the College receive financial aid.

Faculty

There are 130 full-time faculty members, with an additional 500 adjunct and clinical faculty members who support the programs. Ninety percent of the faculty hold the highest degree possible in their field. Classes are taught by regular and adjunct faculty members, not by team-teaching assistants.

Student Government

The Student Government Association is an elective body charged with appropriating funds for and monitoring student activities, overseeing class elections, and functioning as the voice of the students and their interests. Its membership includes the dean of students, 18 student representatives, and 2 faculty representatives.

Admission Requirements

No single standard is used in the admission decision-making process. All applicants are considered without regard to race, sex, color, or creed. Each applicant's high school record, curriculum, and class standing are evaluated along with official test scores. The required secondary school background is 4 years of English, 3 years of college-preparatory math, 2 years of a laboratory science (biology and chemistry), and 1 year of history. Applicants must also submit scores on the SAT I or the ACT. The TOEFL is required if English is not the applicant's first language. An interview is highly recommended.

Advanced standing of up to one year may be given on the basis of results on the College Board's Advanced Placement examinations. The College subscribes to the early decision plan.

Transfer students are accepted into all of the undergraduate majors, provided they have completed high school biology, chemistry, and algebra II (or its equivalent at the college level). Students must submit official transcripts from all colleges attended. Recommendations and personal statements are required. A student with less than 30 semester hours of college course work must submit a high school transcript. Application deadline is February 1 for freshmen and Worcester students. March 1 is the application deadline for Boston transfers.

Application and Information

For application forms or information, students should contact:

Office of Admission
Massachusetts College of Pharmacy
and Health Sciences
179 Longwood Avenue
Boston, Massachusetts 02115
Telephone: 617-732-2850
800-225-5506 (toll-free outside Massachusetts)
Fax: 617-732-2118
E-mail: admissions@mcp.edu
World Wide Web: http://www.mcp.edu

The George Robert White Building on the campus of the Massachusetts College of Pharmacy and Health Sciences.

MASSACHUSETTS INSTITUTE OF TECHNOLOGY

CAMBRIDGE, MASSACHUSETTS

The Institute

Massachusetts Institute of Technology (MIT) was chartered in 1861 to create a new kind of university with a mission to discover and apply knowledge for the benefit of society. Education and related research continue to be MIT's central purpose, with relevance to the practical world as a guiding principle. The campus is located on 153 acres in Cambridge, Massachusetts, bordering the Charles River for a mile and overlooking downtown Boston.

The total undergraduate enrollment at the Institute is 4,178 (1,727 women and 2,451 men). Ninety-eight percent of undergraduates live in a mixture of eleven residence halls and thirty-four independent and cooperative living groups. All students are guaranteed campus housing for four years.

Location

Located in Cambridge, directly across the Charles River from Boston, MIT is one of fifty colleges and universities within a 20-mile radius. As a result, in the area there is an extraordinary variety of young people from all over the world as well as an impressive range of facilities and activities available to all students. Within walking distance of the Institute are the Museum of Fine Arts, the Museum of Science, the New England Aquarium, Fenway Park, the Boston Common, Quincy Market, the Boston Symphony Orchestra, and the Boston Pops. All are easily accessible by greater Boston's safe, affordable, and wide-ranging public transportation. An hour or two from MIT by regional transit are the mountains of Vermont and New Hampshire, the ocean beaches of Cape Cod, and the lakes and rivers of Maine. The Boston area is where the American Revolution began, and historic sites are numerous.

Majors and Degrees

Some of the more common disciplines for which a B.S. is offered are aeronautics and astronautics; American studies; anthropology; archaeology and materials; architecture; art and design; biology; brain and cognitive sciences; chemical engineering; chemistry; civil engineering; computer science and engineering; earth, atmospheric, and planetary sciences; economics; electrical engineering and computer science; electrical science and engineering; environmental engineering science; foreign languages and literatures; history; humanities; Latin American studies; linguistics; literature; management; materials science and engineering; mathematics; mechanical engineering; music; nuclear engineering; ocean engineering; philosophy; physics; political science; psychology; Russian studies; theater; urban studies and planning; women's studies; and writing.

Many students earn a B.S. in either a preexisting interdisciplinary program or one of their own design; biomedical engineering is one of the most frequently chosen. Large numbers of MIT graduates go on to medical, law, and business schools.

Academic Programs

The undergraduate programs at MIT are designed to help students develop the understanding, maturity, and capabilities to meet the challenges of modern society. Students base their studies on a core of subjects in science, mathematics, and the humanities, usually begun the first year, and then slowly go on to concentrate in their departmental or interdepartmental programs. There is considerable time to take elective subjects each year. For most students, the program for the B.S. requires four years of full-time study. The first term at MIT is on a pass/no-record basis.

One of the most exciting features of undergraduate education is the opportunity for students to join with faculty members in ongoing research projects (Undergraduate Research Opportunities Program, or UROP). More than 80 percent of all undergraduates are involved in active research in the MIT tradition of learning by doing.

Advanced placement may be granted to entering freshmen through College Board Advanced Placement tests, International Baccalaureate exams, college transcripts, and advanced-standing examinations at MIT.

Air Force, Army, and Naval ROTC are all available at MIT.

There is a cross-registration program with Wellesley College, Harvard University, and the School of the Museum of Fine Arts.

Academic Facilities

At least sixty interdisciplinary and interdepartmental facilities provide opportunities for faculty members, students, and staff members to join together on projects that cross traditional disciplinary lines. Some of these are the Artificial Intelligence Laboratory, Bates Linear Accelerator, Center for Cancer Research, Center for International Studies, Center for Space Research, the Media Laboratory, and Whitehead Institute for Biomedical Research. The Institute has an extensive library system that includes 2.5 million volumes, more than 18,000 current journals and serials, and numerous back files. The Institute has well-equipped facilities to support all its programs.

Costs

The tuition for 2003–04 was $29,400. The standard cost for room and board was $8910, and $2720 can be estimated for books, materials, clothing, entertainment, and personal expenses. A range of options is available in housing and dining arrangements; the cost before financial aid for most students is about $41,030 per year, excluding travel expenses.

Financial Aid

Financial aid is awarded on the basis of need and is dependent on an objective analysis of family finances. Financial aid packages take into account the family contribution (including the parents' contribution, student's summer earnings, and student's assets), the student's self-help (loan and/or part-time job), and MIT grant money, if necessary, to meet the established costs. The CSS Financial Aid PROFILE and the Free Application for Federal Student Aid (FAFSA) are required to apply for financial aid. Approximately 75 percent of the undergraduates received financial aid last year.

Faculty

A single faculty of approximately 1,000 members teaches undergraduate and graduate students and engages in research. Ten members of the current faculty are Nobel laureates, and 15 are MacArthur Fellows. The Institute is characterized by one-on-one interaction between students and professors, and most of the faculty members participate in UROP. All students are assigned to faculty members who serve as their advisers throughout their undergraduate years.

Student Government

The Undergraduate Association is the major undergraduate governmental body. Its functions are divided among committees that allocate funds to student organizations, manage social and musical events, operate certain facilities on campus, improve classroom and living conditions in the dormitories, propose educational reforms, sponsor feedback programs, operate free computer services, and recommend student representatives for more than fifty faculty and administrative committees.

Admission Requirements

Ideal preparation for study at MIT includes English (4 years), history/social studies (2 or more years), mathematics through calculus (4 years), laboratory sciences (biology, chemistry, and physics), and a foreign language. Applicants are required to take the SAT I or the ACT, as well as three SAT II: Subject Tests—Writing or History, Science, and Mathematics Level IC or IIC. The December testing date is the last one for which SAT I, SAT II, and ACT scores are considered. Interviews are optional but highly recommended and are conducted in the applicant's home area by MIT alumni who belong to the Educational Council. All interviews must be completed between May 1 of the junior year and December 15 of the senior year in high school. The deadline for submission of regular admission applications is January 1.

Application and Information

Candidates who wish to apply for early action, which is nonbinding, must submit an application and all materials by November 1 and have tests completed on or by the November testing date. They can expect to hear from the admission committee by mid-December.

Freshmen are admitted for September only. Transfer students are accepted for September and February.

Requests for additional information and application forms should be addressed to:

Office of Admissions
Building 3-108
Massachusetts Institute of Technology
Cambridge, Massachusetts 02139-4307
Telephone: 617-253-4791
World Wide Web: http://web.mit.edu/admissions/www/

Spring in the Great Court, Massachusetts Institute of Technology.

MASSACHUSETTS MARITIME ACADEMY

CAPE COD, MASSACHUSETTS

The Academy

As the oldest continuously operating maritime academy in the United States, Massachusetts Maritime Academy is a coeducational state college with both maritime and nonmaritime curricula. Graduates of Massachusetts Maritime Academy have traditionally been recognized for their excellence. Naval admirals and government and business leaders are prominent among the Academy's alumni.

In addition to a Bachelor of Science degree and a professional license, students achieve a sense of self-confidence and competence—qualities important to success in any career.

A clear statement of approval regarding the Academy is made by employers within both maritime and shoreside industries. Nearly 100 percent of the senior class find high-paying employment within a few months of graduation.

The approximately 900 men and women have in common an interest in hands-on activities, an aptitude for mathematics and science, leadership potential, and an interest in, or experience on, the ocean. They recognize the value of a regimented campus life-style for developing decision-making skills, discipline, and the ability to assume responsibility. The Academy attracts most of its students from the Northeastern states, with Massachusetts residents making up two thirds of the total. However, students from across the nation as well as seven other countries are in attendance. The great majority of students live in traditional college dormitories as a part of the requirements to obtain a professional maritime license. Some students commute to the campus as participants in the Facilities and Environmental Engineering Program.

The Regiment of Cadets is divided into companies and is administered by student leaders as well as by full-time staff members. All students wear uniforms daily and participate in various activities, such as flag formation (morning colors) and inspection of quarters.

MMA has a fine athletics complex and a highly competitive athletics program; the Academy fields varsity teams in baseball, crew, cross-country, football, lacrosse, rifle marksmanship, sailing, soccer, softball, and volleyball. Academy teams have won All–New England titles in baseball and football. A vigorous intramural athletics program spans the academic year. The Academy also has active programs through the aviation, boxing, Catholic Newman, floor hockey, Knights of Columbus, minority awareness, photography, pistol and rifle, propeller, rugby, scuba, swimming, wrestling, and yachting clubs.

Massachusetts Maritime Academy is for the well-directed, environmentally conscientious, motivated young man or woman who loves the ocean and travel and who desires a thorough education to prepare for engineering, business, and maritime-related professions or for the armed forces. For students who are talented in mathematics and science, mature, and self-disciplined and who enjoy travel, the Academy can provide tradition, a fine education, and optimum hands-on training.

Location

The Academy is located on Taylor's Point, a peninsula at the western mouth of the scenic Cape Cod Canal where it joins Buttermilk Bay. Cape Cod is one of the most beautiful resort areas of the United States. Massachusetts Maritime Academy is located at the gateway to the cape, and it is less than an hour from the cities of Boston and Providence, Rhode Island, and from the Cape Cod National Seashore.

Majors and Degrees

Massachusetts Maritime Academy provides graduates with twofold credentials: a fully accredited Bachelor of Science degree and a professional license, which enables graduates to seek employment within the various maritime industries and within the stationary power plant industry. To achieve this end, students can major in facilities and environmental engineering, international maritime business, marine engineering, marine safety and environmental protection, or marine transportation. A five-year dual major program allows students to obtain both marine transportation and engineering licenses. The marine safety and environmental protection major, conducted with Woods Hole Oceanographic Institution, is designed to present the opportunity for preparation in the scientific, management, and legal foundations of environmental protection. A variety of minor concentrations in such areas as business management, commercial fisheries, mechanical engineering, and environmental/facilities engineering also broaden employment options for graduates.

Academic Program

Two academic terms on campus separated by a winter Sea Term make up the ten-month academic year. Approximately six months of sea time aboard the Academy's training ship are required. This time is divided into four cruises of approximately seven weeks each. Countries visited during Sea Term have included Barbados, Mexico, Portugal, England, Ireland, Italy, Germany, and Greece; cadets cruise to twelve to fifteen countries before graduating. During Sea Term, cadets apply classroom lessons to the operation of a large oceangoing vessel. The cadets have the opportunity to ship commercially with a variety of shipping companies or participate in paid co-op programs and internships throughout the world. Cadets have the summer off.

The academic program involves extensive study and emphasizes a blend of mathematics and sciences with technical and professional studies. Each career program provides a solid foundation in mathematics, physical science, humanities, and social studies in addition to a core of required professional subjects. Maritime majors are eligible to sit for U.S. Coast Guard license examinations as a Third Mate (Deck Officer) or Third Assistant Engineer of steam and motor vessels of unlimited tonnage. Facilities and environmental engineering majors are eligible for state licensure. Although there is no military obligation, some students select service in the U.S. Navy, U.S. Army, Coast Guard, or Marine Corps or in other military branches. Courses offered through the Department of Naval Science qualify cadets to apply for an officer's commission in the U.S. Naval or Coast Guard Reserve upon graduation. Graduates hold positions throughout the maritime industry as well as in government administration and land-based industries, and they have had great success in many fields unrelated to the maritime profession, such as power-plant operations and industrial and mechanical engineering.

Academic Facilities

Massachusetts Maritime Academy has facilities representing state-of-the-art technology in order to provide cadets with the finest training available. An All Weather Navigation and Radar Training Simulator coupled with a prototype of a "Schoolship"

Full-Function Video Shiphandling Simulator is the most modern instruction device for commercial marine navigation available in the world today. The system features not only video but also realistic radar, loran C, and depth-finding and radio-direction-finding capabilities. The Center for Marine Environmental Protection and Safety provides state-of-the-art oil spill response management and tanker liquid cargo simulators for student and industry training. The library computer lab makes personal-application equipment, along with modems, databases, and a wide variety of popular software applications, available to faculty, staff, and cadets.

Costs

For 2003–04, first-year tuition, fees, room, and board were $13,400 for residents of Massachusetts, Connecticut, Delaware, Florida, Maryland, New Jersey, Pennsylvania, Rhode Island, Virginia, and Washington, D.C.; $13,925 for certain New England residents; and $23,900 for out-of-region residents. These figures do not include uniforms, books, or incidental personal expenses.

Financial Aid

Massachusetts Maritime Academy offers its 900 students more than $350,000 per year in merit awards based on academic achievement, leadership, and community activities. Most of these awards are renewable for four years.

In addition, the Academy assists families with federal and state need-based programs, which include grants, scholarships, work opportunities, and student loan programs. Students apply for the need-based programs by completing the Free Application for Federal Student Aid (FAFSA). Prospective students should contact the Financial Aid office at 508-830-5087 with any questions concerning the financial aid process.

Faculty

The faculty is known for its high academic standards. Seventy-five percent of the academic faculty have doctoral degrees or top professional licenses. In the marine transportation department, there are 8 Ship Masters; in the marine engineering department, there are 8 Chief Engineers and 3 Ph.D.'s. These figures compare favorably with those at any similar academy in the country. The student-faculty ratio is a low 13:1 to ensure that all students receive personal attention commensurate with their academic and professional needs. The Academy also provides a strong support and tutorial program to ensure that every student may have an optimum opportunity for success.

Student Government

A student government is elected to help meet the extracurricular needs of the student body, and its members participate with faculty members and administrators on various all-Academy committees. Students are also represented on the Massachusetts Maritime Academy Board of Trustees.

Admission Requirements

Massachusetts Maritime Academy seeks applicants who have demonstrated an aptitude for mathematics and science. SAT or ACT scores are required of all applicants. In making admission decisions, the admission committee considers important criteria to be the applicant's class standing, SAT or ACT scores, and high school average, stressing college-preparatory mathematics and laboratory sciences (such as chemistry and physics). The rest of the evaluation considers the student's leadership potential, athletics or extracurricular participation, church and community involvement, employment, maritime experience, and letters of recommendation. At least two letters of recommendation are required. A personal interview is strongly recommended.

Application and Information

The application should be submitted as soon as possible but no later than June 1 for the class entering in September. Early decision deadline is November 1. Throughout the year, applicants and their families are invited to visit the Academy. Successful applicants receive a timely decision as well as follow-up communication throughout the year.

Application forms may be obtained by contacting:

Office of Admissions
Massachusetts Maritime Academy
101 Academy Drive
Buzzards Bay, Cape Cod, Massachusetts 02532
Telephone: 508-830-5000
800-544-3411 (toll-free)
Fax: 508-830-5077
E-mail: admissions@mma.mass.edu
World Wide Web: http://www.maritime.edu

Located at the gateway to Cape Cod, Massachusetts Maritime Academy is the oldest continuously operating maritime academy in the United States.

McDANIEL COLLEGE

WESTMINSTER, MARYLAND

The College

McDaniel College (MC) provides an ideal location for learning that brings together students from twenty-three states and nineteen countries. Its picturesque campus, including a nine-hole golf course, is situated on a hilltop in historic Westminster, just a short drive from two of the nation's major metropolitan centers, Baltimore and Washington, D.C. McDaniel was one of the first coeducational colleges in the nation and has been both innovative and independent since its founding in 1867.

Students are the focus of McDaniel's educational philosophy with its emphasis on teaching, strong tradition of studies in the liberal arts and sciences, and continuing revitalization of courses both at the undergraduate and graduate levels. Faculty members are engaged in research and professional writing; they are involved at the highest levels of their respective professions; they are sought after as consultants in many spheres, but their primary mission is teaching. McDaniel's close-knit community of about 1,600 undergraduates provides an environment in which every student receives personal attention. Small classes and more than 100 clubs, organizations, and athletic teams put leadership opportunities within every student's reach. Graduates leave McDaniel enriched by their classwork as well as by their meaningful interactions with one another.

A flexible curriculum in the liberal arts and sciences encourages critical and creative thinking, humane and responsible actions, and clear, thoughtful expression. McDaniel College is fully accredited by the Middle States Association of Colleges and Schools and is among the forty colleges in the nation highlighted in *Colleges That Change Lives* by Loren Pope. McDaniel is internationally recognized for its graduate program in training teachers for the deaf. Its chapter of Phi Beta Kappa is one of twenty honorary societies on campus.

Location

Sixty miles north of the nation's capital and 30 miles northwest of Baltimore's Inner Harbor, McDaniel College overlooks historic Westminster, Maryland, Carroll County's largest town and county seat. Within walking distance are gift boutiques, book and music stores, art galleries, and restaurants that line one of America's longest main streets. Both nearby metropolitan cities offer students opportunities for learning and leisure—art and history museums, internships on Capitol Hill, Baltimore Orioles and Ravens games, and bayside seafood and nightlife.

Majors and Degrees

The educational programs serve both students who enter with firm choices of majors or career ambitions as well as students who are undecided. All students take at least 30 percent of course work in the liberal arts and sciences: humanities, natural sciences and mathematics, and social sciences. The Bachelor of Arts degree is offered in twenty-four major areas of study: art, art history, biology, business administration, chemistry, communication, computer science, economics, English, exercise science and physical education, French, German, history, mathematics, music, philosophy, physics, political science/international studies, psychology, religious studies, social work, sociology, Spanish, and theater arts. Students may choose a dual major or design their own major if their academic interests and goals take them beyond an existing program. Recent student-designed majors include criminal psychology, medical and biological illustration, sports journalism, and women's studies. In addition, most departments offer minor programs (new are film and video studies, forensic science, jazz studies, and Latin) or particular courses to help students focus on or achieve specific goals.

The College also offers certification programs in social work and in elementary and secondary education (Maryland certification includes reciprocity with more than thirty-five other states), 3-2 programs in engineering with the University of Maryland or other engineering schools, and preprofessional programs in dentistry, law, medicine, the ministry, and museum studies. The College also offers an Army ROTC program.

Academic Programs

McDaniel's flexible curriculum encourages students to acquire a broad base of knowledge in the areas of humanities, natural sciences and mathematics, and social sciences and to pursue in-depth learning in one or more of the sixty fields of study. The program links wide-ranging educational experiences with strong career preparation through an extensive internship program. A total of 128 credit hours is required for graduation.

First-year seminars provide students with a unique opportunity to become better prepared for many facets of college life. Limited to 15 students, these courses on a variety of engaging topics emphasize important skills—writing, oral presentation, study skills, critical thinking, and time management.

Faculty advisers offer guidance across the curriculum and work closely with their advisees as they make decisions about course and major selections and planning strategies. Students may also request help from the Center for Career Services, which offers vocational testing, counseling, and guidance.

During the College's January Term, a three-week term between the fall and spring semesters, students and faculty members explore new areas and expand their intellectual horizons. Students choose from unconventional courses on campus and off. Students have studied art in Italy, architecture in Russia, marine organisms in the Bahamas, women in mystery novels in a McDaniel classroom, and, recently, log cabin construction starting from scratch in the woods near one student's home. Some students take advantage of January Term for independent off-campus study or join one of the popular international study tours.

Off-Campus Programs

Through its McDaniel–Budapest campus, the College offers a convenient option for students to study abroad. In tandem with American University, Drew University, and other colleges and universities, McDaniel offers opportunities for off-campus study in Washington, D.C.; at the United Nations in New York; and around the globe.

Academic Facilities

Among the forty buildings on the 160-acre campus are Eaton Hall, the $13-million state-of-the-art biology and chemistry lab building, which opened in fall 1999; the recently renovated Hoover Library, with access to materials from rare books to CD-ROMs and e-mail and Internet accounts to an audiovisual media and microcomputing center; Hill Hall, featuring the Writing Center and cutting-edge multimedia presentation classrooms; Peterson Hall, which offers a modern photography lab, a graphic arts computer classroom, and an art gallery for the College's permanent collection and visiting exhibitions; and Alumni Hall, home to the performing arts and summer repertory Theatre-on-the-Hill program.

Costs

McDaniel College offers an educational experience of outstanding value. Tuition charges include Student Health Service fees and Student Activities fees. A $150 technology fee is charged each semester. Tuition for 2004–05 is $24,500, room and board are $5600, and personal expenses (including books and transportation) are estimated at $800 per year.

Financial Aid

McDaniel College supports a program of financial aid to eligible students on the basis of both need and merit. The College awards more than $15 million each year in scholarships to academically talented students. Nearly 85 percent of McDaniel students receive financial assistance. Students who have been accepted by the College and can demonstrate financial need as required by the federal government may be eligible for assistance in the form of scholarships, grants, loans, and opportunities for student employment. Typically, an award is a package of these four resources, tailored to the student's needs.

Academic scholarships covering partial to full tuition are available for qualified students based on their academic record, SAT I or ACT scores, and extracurricular involvement. First-year students should apply by February 1; transfer scholarships are competitive, and preference is given to students who apply before March 15. The College also offers partial and full ROTC scholarships.

To apply, students should file the Free Application for Federal Student Aid (FAFSA) with the federal processor and apply for admission to McDaniel. Students also must submit a McDaniel financial aid application, which is available upon request.

Faculty

Faculty members—90 full-time professors, 95 percent of whom hold the most advanced degrees in their fields—devote themselves to classroom, lab, and studio teaching. Many conduct research; most involve students in their work. Professors teach a maximum of three courses each semester. This allows them ample time to spend with students outside of the classroom, helping them to plan academic programs, arrange internships, and prepare for careers; cheering along the sidelines of a football game; sharing a meal in the pub; or continuing a lively classroom discussion over pizza in town. An average class size of 17 students encourages discussion, and learning is collaborative rather than competitive. McDaniel's President, Provost, Dean of Students, and Financial Vice President may teach an undergraduate course. Faculty members also serve as advisers to many student organizations.

Student Government

All students are automatically members of the Student Government Assembly (SGA), which is the student body's central governing and coordinating organization. It consists of two main parts: the Executive Council, elected by the student body at large, and the Senate, composed of representatives from the classes. Students hold full voting membership on most policymaking College committees, serving with faculty members, administrative staff members, and trustees in dealing with issues such as the curriculum, academic policy, athletics, calendar, schedule, admissions, and financial aid.

Admission Requirements

McDaniel welcomes applications from men and women who desire the lifelong personal and professional benefits of a liberal arts education and who eagerly enter the partnerships necessary to achieve it. The College annually enrolls 400–500 first-year students, including international students and students beyond traditional college age. In addition, the College welcomes applications from students wishing to transfer from community colleges and other four-year colleges and universities.

Prospective applicants should have a broad secondary school program, including 4 years of English, 3 years of social studies, 3 years of a foreign language, 3 years of work in laboratory sciences (biology and chemistry), and 3 years of mathematics. In addition to the school record, McDaniel evaluates the potential academic success of each applicant by considering SAT I or ACT scores, class rank, application essay, recommendations, and participation in nonacademic activities. Each year, about 20 percent of new students transfer to McDaniel from two- and four-year colleges and universities. Transfer students must have a minimum GPA of 2.5 in college course work and submit an official transcript.

Personal interviews and campus tours are encouraged and are available Monday through Friday at 10:30 a.m. and 2 p.m. and on Saturdays by appointment. The College regularly holds open houses that include formal and informal presentations on academic programs, student life, financial assistance, and other topics.

McDaniel seeks diversity in its student population and does not discriminate in the recruitment, admission, and employment of students and faculty and staff members in the operation of any of its educational programs and activities as defined by law.

Application and Information

Deadlines for receiving completed applications are December 1 for early action and February 1 for regular admission and academic scholarship consideration. Applications from transfer students are accepted through the summer. Complete applications, along with a $40 nonrefundable application fee, should be sent to:

M. Martha O'Connell, Dean of Admissions
McDaniel College
2 College Hill
Westminster, Maryland 21157-4390
Telephone: 410-857-2230
800-638-5005 (voice/TDD; toll-free)
E-mail: admissions@mcdaniel.edu
World Wide Web: http://www.mcdaniel.edu

The brick pathways that front Hoover Library are a campus focal point.

McGILL UNIVERSITY

MONTRÉAL, QUÉBEC, CANADA

The University

Founded more than 175 years ago, McGill University is named for the Honourable James McGill, a Scottish fur trader who became a leading Montréal merchant and philanthropist. McGill College received its royal charter from George IV in 1821. Classes began in 1829 when the teaching wing of the Montréal General Hospital was incorporated into the College. The Faculty of Arts opened its doors in 1843. During the next ten years, the University added modern languages, commercial studies, and the sciences. In 1884, the first women were admitted, and classes for men and women gradually merged.

In 1906, Sir William Macdonald endowed a college at Ste. Anne de Bellevue, a village about 25 miles west of downtown Montréal. The Macdonald Campus buildings are now the site of the Faculty of Agricultural and Environmental Sciences, which includes the McGill School of Environment. The Macdonald Campus Farm, the Morgan Arboretum, the St. Lawrence Valley Ecomuseum, and the Avian Science and Conservation Centre provide the livestock and field facilities used in teaching and applied research and offer students the opportunity to gain hands-on knowledge in an agricultural milieu.

McGill is a comprehensive, publicly funded university with a diverse student population. The full-time undergraduate student body is 24,062 registrants: 57.5 percent from Québec, 30.1 percent from other provinces in Canada, and 12.4 percent from the United States and some 150 other countries. The language of instruction at McGill is English; however, as 1 in 5 students lists French as the mother tongue, students may write term papers and exams in French.

McGill is composed of eleven faculties, ten schools, and four institutes: the Faculties of Agricultural and Environmental Sciences, Arts, Dentistry, Education, Engineering, Law, Management, Medicine, Music, Religious Studies, and Science; the Schools of Architecture, Communication Sciences and Disorders (graduate programs only), Computer Science, Dietetics and Human Nutrition, Environment, Library and Information Studies (graduate program only), Nursing, Physical and Occupational Therapy, Social Work, and Urban Planning (graduate program only); and the Institutes of Air and Space Law, Comparative Law, Islamic Studies, and Parasitology. The University offers degrees at the bachelor's and master's levels and offers doctorates in all major areas. The professional degrees of Doctor of Dental Medicine and Doctor of Medicine/Master of Surgery are offered.

Residence accommodation is guaranteed for all first-year students. Downtown residences are available for 1,750 students in six buildings; all but one are coed. Accommodation is also provided in the buildings of the MORE network (McGill's Off-Campus Residence Experience), which occupies two apartment buildings and eleven smaller buildings. The Macdonald Campus has coed residence space for 340 students. Many students who live in residence for their first academic year move into apartments of their own for their following years of study.

Extracurricular activities are an important part of University life—they provide recreation and instruction, enhance a sense of independence, and offer experience in leadership. More than 170 student-run clubs support specialized interests, the largest being the McGill Outdoors Club, where members arrange skiing, canoeing, climbing, and hiking excursions. Indoor and outdoor men's and women's intercollegiate teams challenge the teams of other universities. Intramural athletics provide competition with fellow students, and instructional programs offer opportunities to improve standards and abilities in a wide choice of activities.

Location

Montréal is distinctly North American, yet it also has a very European atmosphere. The University gates open onto one of the main downtown avenues with restaurants and outdoor cafés, high-rise office buildings, boutiques, and underground shopping malls. On the north side, beyond the residences and sports facilities, a mountain park offers immediate access to the outdoors. Each of Montréal's four distinct seasons brings its own special pleasures of indoor and outdoor activities.

Majors and Degrees

The Bachelor of Arts degree is offered in African studies; anthropology; art history; Canadian studies; classics; computing (foundations of); East Asian studies; economics; English: cultural studies, drama and theatre, and literature; environment; French language and literature: linguistics, literature, and literature and translation; geography: geography and urban systems; German: contemporary studies, language and literature, literature and culture, and studies; Hispanic studies: literature and culture, languages, and studies; history; humanistic studies; industrial relations; international development studies; Italian: literature and studies; Jewish studies; Latin American and Caribbean studies: area and thematic; linguistics; mathematics; Middle East studies; music; North American studies; philosophy; political science; psychology; Québec studies; religious studies: Asian religions, scriptures and interpretations, Western religions, and world religions; Russian; sociology; and women's studies.

The Bachelor of Science degree is offered in anatomy and cell biology; atmospheric science; atmospheric science and physics; biochemistry; biology; biology and mathematics; chemistry: bio-organic, environmental, and materials; chemistry and biological sciences; chemistry and mathematics; computer science; earth and planetary sciences; earth sciences; environment; geography; immunology; mathematics; mathematics and computer science; mathematics, applied; mathematics, chemistry, and physics; mathematics, statistics, and computer science; microbiology and immunology; physics; physics and computer science; physics and geophysics; physiology; physiology and mathematics; physiology and physics; planetary sciences; probability and statistics; psychology; science for teachers; and software engineering. Also offered is a concurrent B.Sc./B.Ed. Internships are available. The Bachelor of Science (agriculture) degree is offered in agricultural economics: agribusiness, agricultural systems, and natural resource economics; agricultural science; animal biology; animal science; applied zoology; botanical sciences: ecology and molecular; environmental biology; microbiology; plant science; resource conservation; and wildlife biology. Bachelor of Science degrees are offered in agricultural engineering; architecture; food science; nursing; nutritional science: dietetics and nutrition; occupational therapy; and physical therapy.

The Bachelor of Commerce degree is offered in accounting; economics; economics and accounting; economics and finance; entrepreneurship; finance; information systems; international business; international management: faculty programs in East Asia, Latin America and the Caribbean, Western Europe (France, Germany, Italy, or Spain), Canada, and the United States; labor-management relations; management science; marketing; mathematics; operations management; organizational behavior and human resource management; psychology; and strategic management.

The Bachelor of Education degree is offered in kindergarten and elementary education (Jewish studies option), general secondary two-subject option; inclusive education; kinesiology; physical education; teaching of English as a second language (ESL) or French as a second language (FSL); and vocational secondary education (one subject). Concurrent B.Ed./B.Mus. and B.Ed./B.Sc. programs are also offered.

The Bachelor of Engineering is offered, with specializations in chemical engineering; civil engineering; computer engineering; electrical engineering; mechanical engineering; metals and materials engineering (co-op); and mining engineering (co-op). The Bachelor of Software Engineering is also offered. Internships are available.

A joint Bachelor of Laws/Bachelor of Civil Law degree program is offered in common and civil law. In addition, the Bachelor of Theology degree is offered in religious studies.

The Bachelor of Music is offered in composition; music education; music history; music technology; performance; performance: church music, early music, keyboard studies, or jazz; and theory. A concurrent B.Mus./B.Ed. is also offered.

The Bachelor of Social Work (B.S.W.) degree is offered. A special one-year B.S.W. degree program is offered for applicants who already hold a degree in another area (application deadline is December 1, entrance is in May).

The Centre for Continuing Education offers undergraduate and some graduate courses and/or diploma and certificate programs in career and management studies, education, general studies, information technology, and languages and translation.

Prospective students should consult the University's Web site for more detailed information about the programs listed above.

Academic Programs

The academic year has two regular semesters: fall term (September to December) and winter term (January to May). There are four months of summer sessions (May, June, July, and August). Applicants who have completed an appropriate level of education outside Québec may be considered for entrance to a University program that usually requires a minimum of eight semesters (four years), or 120 credits, of study. Some programs require longer periods of study. Applicants who have completed a Québec Diploma of Collegial Studies, Advanced Level Examinations, or the French or International Baccalaureate are typically eligible for admission to a three-year, 90-credit program.

Off-Campus Programs

McGill students may participate in a variety of official exchange programs with more than 500 universities worldwide or make independent arrangements to spend a year elsewhere.

Academic Facilities

With holdings of more than 6.1 million items, the McGill network of sixteen libraries is the largest in Montréal and the fourth largest in Canada. The six major areas encompass the humanities and social sciences, law, life sciences, medicine, music, and physical sciences and engineering. The network features easy physical access to all of the resources; automated computer entry into the catalogue from library, office, or home; quiet study areas; and workshops for new students. There are extensive computing facilities to meet undergraduate, graduate, faculty, and research needs. The campuswide mainframe service provides interactive and batch services and e-mail. A number of departments operate their own local systems to provide specialized services to their researchers, staff members, and students. Microcomputer laboratories and terminals connected to both the central mainframe and the departmental systems are located throughout the campus. The McGill high-speed fiber optics backbone network interconnects all these facilities and is available to all staff members and students. University archives, two major museums, and many unique and rare collections and exhibitions offer valuable resources for research. Most areas are open to the public.

Costs

For 2003–04, tuition fees for a normal full-time course load of 30 credits were Can$1668 for Québec residents, Can$4012 for non-Québec Canadians, and Can$9500 to Can$15,000, depending on the program, for visa students. There are other required University fees, such as student services, students' society, and course materials, and there is a compulsory health insurance for visa students. Residence costs for room and board ranged from Can$6686 to Can$9120 for 2003–04. Personal expenses, such as transportation, clothing, and amusements, are extra.

Financial Aid

Scholarship awards range in value from $2000 (renewable) to $15,000 (renewable) and are based on outstanding academic achievement or a combination of outstanding academic achievement and leadership qualities. Further information is available in the application for admission package or at the Web site.

Faculty

Research has always supported and enhanced teaching at McGill. Knowledge gained in the laboratory and in the library enlightens the practices of lectures and theoretical discussions. The great majority of McGill's full-time professors hold a Ph.D. degree, and almost all classes are taught by full-time, regular staff members.

Student Government

Students participate in the governance and administration of the University, with representation on both the Senate and the Board of Governors. The Undergraduate Students' Society manages its own building and all the various facilities it contains, including food services. Different academic areas also have their own undergraduate societies.

Admission Requirements

Admission is based on a review of the whole academic dossier, including academic performance over the past three years, strength of programs, rank in graduating class, and scores on standardized tests. Students are expected to have a minimum B+ average or the equivalent, depending on where they have completed their studies. Admission is competitive. Transfer applicants are evaluated on the basis of their university/college record and the criteria listed above.

Application and Information

Applications for admission in September should be completed and forwarded to McGill by January 15 for those studying outside Canada (except exchange students); by February 1 for those studying in Canadian high schools outside Québec; by March 1 for applicants from Québec CEGEPs; by May 1 for exchange students, transfer students from Canadian institutions, and non-Canadian special and visiting students; and by July 1 for Canadian special and visiting students. Some programs are available for January admission, primarily for Québec CEGEP students. For more information about January admission and the programs to which it applies, students should contact the Admissions, Recruitment and Registrar's Office.

McGill welcomes applications from all interested students regardless of race, religion, age, disability, nationality, or sex.

Admissions information and University calendars are available on the admissions Web site listed below. An online application can also be accessed, completed, and submitted at that site.

Prospective applicants are encouraged to visit the McGill campus. One-hour walking tours, which are conducted in the morning or afternoon, are led by McGill students. Applicants are also invited to attend selected classes in most faculties during the months of October, November, February, and March. For information about visits and tours, students should contact:

The Welcome Centre
Burnside Hall, Room 115
805 Sherbrooke Street, West
Montréal, Québec H3A 2K6
Canada
Telephone: 514-398-6555
Fax: 514-398-2072
E-mail: welcome@mcgill.ca
World Wide Web: http://www.mcgill.ca

To receive a regular application form or for additional information, students should contact:

Admissions, Recruitment and Registrar's Office
McGill University
845 Sherbrooke Street, West
Montréal, Québec H3A 2T5
Canada
Telephone: 514-398-3910
Fax: 514-398-4193
E-mail: admissions@mcgill.ca
World Wide Web: http://www.mcgill.ca/applying

McMURRY UNIVERSITY

ABILENE, TEXAS

The University

Founded in 1923 and affiliated with the United Methodist Church, McMurry University is a four-year, coeducational, liberal arts college that strives to maintain the highest academic standards possible while building its liberal and professional programs. Although most of the 1,400 students come from Texas and New Mexico, a total of twenty-three states and seven countries are represented in the student body. The students at McMurry also represent a wide range of religious affiliations: United Methodist, 30 percent; Baptist, 25 percent; Catholic, 12 percent; others and no preference, 33 percent.

Fifty-four percent of the full-time students live on campus in the residence halls. Approximately 39 percent of the eligible full-time students are members of local fraternities or sororities. All students are allowed to have cars.

McMurry University is active in the American Southwest Conference, a pioneering conference that has successfully implemented the student-athlete concept. The University is also a member of NCAA Division III. Baseball, basketball, cross-country, football, golf, soccer, swimming, tennis, and track are offered for men; basketball, cross-country, golf, soccer, swimming, tennis, track, and volleyball are offered for women. An active intramural sports program in both team and individual competition is available for students year-round.

All students are encouraged to try out for one of the choirs, the band, or theatrical productions. Each program offers a limited number of scholarships based on talent. Art exhibits of work by students and faculty members, as well as various invitational and traveling shows, are shown regularly in the art gallery of the Ryan Fine Arts Center and the Gypsy Ted Gallery.

Location

McMurry University is an important part of Abilene, Texas, a 114-year-old community of about 110,000 people. Abilene is centrally located in west-central Texas, 151 miles west of Fort Worth, 250 miles northwest of San Antonio, and 165 miles southeast of Lubbock.

Concerts; the Civic Ballet; the Philharmonic Orchestra; the Abilene Zoo; the Abilene Community Theatre; the Intercollegiate Orchestra and Opera; a children's, historical, and art museum; and the Abilene Repertory Theatre are some of the cultural and recreational resources to which McMurry students have access and in which many participate. Three local television stations and a morning newspaper provide excellent coverage of McMurry events. Abilene also has a shopping mall, movie theaters, and fine restaurants. Lakes in the area offer many opportunities for outdoor activities.

Majors and Degrees

Seven undergraduate baccalaureate degrees are offered: the Bachelor of Arts, Bachelor of Business Administration, Bachelor of Fine Arts, Bachelor of Music, Bachelor of Music Education, Bachelor of Science, and Bachelor of Science in Nursing.

The B.A. is offered in art, chemistry, communication, English, history, mathematics, music (church, instrumental, organ, piano, and vocal), philosophy, political science, psychology, religion, sociology, Spanish, and theater. The B.F.A. is offered in art education, ceramics, graphic design, painting, studio art, and theater. The B.S. is offered in biochemistry, biology, chemistry, computer science, education, environmental science, exercise and sports studies, mathematics, mathematics-computer science, natural science, and physics. The B.B.A. offers areas of concentration in accounting, computer information systems, economics, finance, general business, health-care administration, management, marketing, and multimedia applications. The B.Mu. is offered in music with an emphasis in church music. The B.M.Ed. is offered with concentrations in instrumental music (secondary level) and vocal music (all levels).

Preprofessional programs are offered in dentistry, engineering, law, medicine, occupational therapy, pharmacy, physical therapy, and veterinary medicine.

Academic Program

All degree programs at McMurry University are built upon a liberal arts core curriculum of three interdisciplinary courses as well as general education requirements in six areas: written and oral communication, health fitness, fine arts, humanities, science and mathematics, and social sciences.

Because the core curriculum was designed to expand students' choices in meeting basic degree requirements, students are strongly urged to consult with their faculty advisers regarding course selection. Core curriculum requirements in specific areas may be met by earning acceptable scores on the College Board's Advanced Placement (AP) examinations or College-Level Examination Program (CLEP) subject examinations.

Although requirements vary within departments, a candidate for the baccalaureate must complete satisfactorily a minimum of 126 semester hours of work, including the core curriculum requirements.

Opportunities for innovative and concentrated study are available to students in the May Term, a three-week miniterm following the spring semester. Courses are designed to explore, in experimental and innovative ways, academic areas not normally treated in the regular semesters. The May Term is followed by two 5-week summer terms.

The Servant Leadership Program promotes the idea that Servant Leaders will lead others by being servants first, seeking the best for those they lead. It is a unified curricular and cocurricular program, combining ethics, leadership, and service to the community.

Off-Campus Programs

Through a consortium agreement with Abilene Christian University and Hardin-Simmons University (both in Abilene), McMurry students may take course work for credit at any of the three institutions. In addition, library holdings at McMurry and the two other universities are available to students from any of the three institutions through a shared online computerized system.

Academic Facilities

The University provides excellent opportunities for academic growth, including a fully equipped Science Center that contains laboratory facilities for biology, chemistry, geology, and physics; fine arts facilities; two theaters, a recital hall, rehearsal rooms, and a band hall; and physical education facilities, including the physical education center, auxiliary gymnasium, football field, field house, track, tennis courts, a baseball field, an indoor swimming pool, and a new soccer field.

McMurry's Computer Center has a DEC computer system and microcomputer labs with Macintosh and PC-compatible microcomputers. There are student computer facilities in the Jay-Rollins Library; the Education Building; the Academic Enrichment Center; biology, chemistry, foreign languages, computer science, and psychology labs; and the writing and math classrooms. Numerous software packages are available for student use at these locations. The computer-to-student ratio on campus is 1:8. All students have access to the Internet through University labs and from their residence hall rooms.

The Jay-Rollins Library at McMurry University has more than 143,000 volumes and offers access to more than 900,000 additional volumes in Abilene through the Abilene Library Consortium. The library is also a member of the Online Computer Library Center and the AMIGOS Bibliographic Council. An interactive distance learning classroom, an observation classroom, and a faculty lab for interactive research were added in fall 1999.

The McMurry student affairs division provides most student services under the direction of the dean of student affairs. Among the offices and services provided are residential life, new student orientation, judicial affairs, the United Methodist Campus Center, the Office of Student Activities, campus recreation, career services, counseling, and handicapped student services. The health service, security office, international student affairs, and a Wellness Center also fall within student affairs. The University also provides an Academic Enrichment Center that provides both tutoring and access to state-of-the-art computing equipment.

Costs

The average yearly costs for a student in the 2003–04 academic year, including tuition, fees, books, supplies, and room and board are $18,646. Personal expenses and transportation costs obviously vary a great deal but are estimated at $2632 a year.

Financial Aid

Financial aid is awarded by the Office of Financial Aid and includes Federal Pell Grants, Federal Supplemental Educational Opportunity Grants (FSEOG), Texas Tuition Equalization Grants (TEG), TEXAS Grants, State Student Incentive Grants (SSIG), College Access Loans (CAL), academic scholarships, transfer scholarships, honors scholarships, ministerial scholarships, Federal Perkins Loans, Federal Work-Study awards, Texas Work-Study, Institutional Work Program, Federal Stafford Student Loans (subsidized and unsubsidized), PLUS Loans, and endowed scholarships. In addition, activity scholarships are available in art, music (instrumental and vocal), speech, and theater. An international scholarship is also awarded annually. Students applying for financial aid should submit the Free Application for Federal Student Aid (FAFSA), a McMurry Financial Aid Request Form, and be approved for admission.

Faculty

Classes and laboratories at McMurry University are taught by regular, top-notch faculty members, and those holding earned doctorates teach at all levels. Approximately 80 percent of the faculty has earned a doctorate or an equivalent terminal degree. The student-faculty ratio is 15:1. Each student is assigned a faculty member who serves as an academic adviser for individual counseling on degree planning, and members of the faculty are involved in many other phases of student life.

Student Government

The most inclusive of the McMurry University student organizations is the Student Association. Composed of all students at the University, this organization exists primarily to promote democratic expression and exercise of student opinion and to represent, serve, and assist students in matters relating to student social life, activities, and elections. The leadership of the Student Association is vested in the McMurry Student Government, which is divided into executive, judicial, and legislative branches. Student Government provides student representation on the University's Board of Trustees as well as on many faculty committees. All officers of the Student Association are elected by the student body or appointed by the Executive Council with Senate confirmation.

Admission Requirements

Candidates for admission should be graduates or prospective graduates of an accredited secondary school. Students are eligible to apply at any time after completion of the junior year in high school. A high school transcript and scores from the ACT Assessment or SAT I are required for consideration. High school grades and class rank, quality of the high school program, test scores, extracurricular activities, and leadership potential are all considered in the admission decision. Although not required, an on-campus interview is strongly recommended. Approximately 40 percent of the entering students graduated in the top quarter of their high school class. The College-Level Examination Program (CLEP) subject exams may be taken to earn course credit and advanced placement. McMurry University welcomes applications for admission from all qualified students regardless of sex, age, race, color, national origin, religion, or handicap.

Application and Information

A completed admission application form, a $20 nonrefundable application fee, scores on the ACT Assessment or SAT I, and a high school transcript or a transcript from each college attended must be submitted to McMurry University. Each application is considered as it is completed, and application deadlines are as follows: fall semester, March 15 (applications received after this date are reviewed on a space-available basis only); spring semester, January 5; and May and summer semesters, the first day of the intended semester. Housing and financial aid cannot be guaranteed until the student has been approved for admission.

Director of Admissions
Box 278
McMurry University
Abilene, Texas 79697
Telephone: 325-793-4700
800-460-2392 (toll-free)
Fax: 325-793-4718
World Wide Web: http://www.mcm.edu/admissions/admissions.htm

MCNEESE STATE UNIVERSITY

LAKE CHARLES, LOUISIANA

The University

Founded in 1939, McNeese State University is a comprehensive institution that awards undergraduate and graduate degrees. Named after the pioneer John McNeese, a southwest Louisiana educator, the University is committed to providing students with outstanding academic opportunities that prepare them to pursue their educational and career goals. McNeese State University is accredited by the Commission on Colleges of the Southern Association of Colleges and Schools and is a member of the University of Louisiana System, one of the largest public higher education systems in the United States. The system, which includes eight universities, serves more than 80,000 students and employs nearly 4,000 full-time faculty members. More than 8,000 students choose from more than eighty degree programs offered by the College of Business, Burton College of Education, College of Engineering and Technology, Dore School of Graduate Studies, College of Liberal Arts, College of Nursing, College of Science, and the Division of General and Basic Studies. Dedicated faculty members create an environment where students achieve their full potential, and McNeese has been rated as one of the top schools in the nation for the caring and friendly attitude of the faculty and staff members.

Students have access to state-of-the-art computer labs with convenient hours that are located throughout the campus. New residence halls provide comfortable and affordable housing for McNeese students and are available year-round. The new Recreational Sports Center offers and an Olympic-sized swimming pool, free weights, an indoor track, and state-of-the-art exercise equipment free to all students. Students may participate in a wide range of organizations, including student government, newspaper and yearbook staffs, social fraternities and sororities, religious organizations, and numerous honor societies. On-campus dining options range from homemade meals at Rowdy's cafeteria to international fare to fast food chains. The campus also features a convenience store, coffee shop, bookstore, post office, ATM machine, career services center, student health services and a counseling center. In addition to the main campus, today's physical plant includes the McNeese Farm, an athletics plant, student apartment complex, golf-driving range, and Burton Coliseum.

Location

Lake Charles and southwest Louisiana are historically and culturally rich. The year 2003 marked the bicentennial of the Louisiana Purchase, and Cajun culture is still very much alive in this region. The city of Lake Charles has a population of more than 75,000, and has important petrochemical, entertainment, and shipping industries. Contraband Days, the second largest festival in Louisiana, is held annually in May, and Mardi Gras is similarly festive in the spring. Perhaps the greatest local attraction is the Cajun food, which is the pride of southwest Louisiana. Lake Charles lies along the I-10 corridor with Houston, Texas, and Baton Rouge, Louisiana, just over 2 hours away and New Orleans nearly 4 hours away. This area offers a variety of outdoor activities, cultural events, and entertainment opportunities for students. The city is served by a regional airport with daily flights to Houston.

Majors and Degrees

McNeese State University offers students more than eighty degrees and majors. The degree programs are divided into six different colleges. The College of Business offers a Bachelor of Science degree in accounting, finance, finance with a concentration in economics, general business administration, management, management with a concentration in computer information technology, and marketing. The College of Business also offers a Master of Business Administration degree, and is nationally accredited by AACSB International–The Association to Advance Collegiate Schools of Business at both undergraduate and graduate levels.

The Burton College of Education offers many different degree programs, including administration and supervision, education technology, education (elementary, secondary, and special), health and human performance, and psychology. Each of these degree plans offer many different concentrations. Also offered are the Master of Education in school counseling and an Associate of Arts and Bachelor of Arts in early childhood education. All teacher education programs are accredited by the National Council for Accreditation of Teacher Education and approved by the Board of Elementary and Secondary Education, State of Louisiana.

Many different concentrations in engineering and engineering technology are available in McNeese's College of Engineering and Technology. The College is accredited by the Engineering Accreditation Commission of the Accreditation Board for Engineering and Technology.

The College of Liberal Arts awards a variety of degrees in history, languages, mass communication, music, social sciences, speech, theater arts, and visual arts. Each of these departments offers at least four different areas of concentration.

A Master of Science in Nursing degree is offered by the College of Nursing with the concentrations of clinical nurse specialist studies, nursing administration, nurse practitioner, and nurse education. An associate degree in nursing and a Bachelor of Science in Nursing are also offered. The College of Nursing is a member of the Intercollegiate Consortium for a Master of Science in Nursing, and is accredited by the National League for Nursing Accrediting Commission (NLNAC). In addition, the College is approved by the Louisiana State Board of Nursing.

Studies in environmental and chemical sciences, agricultural sciences, wildlife management, biological science, environmental science, medical technology, radiologic technology, chemistry, family and consumer science, mathematics, computer science and statistics, mathematical sciences, and physics are made available through the College of Science. Two-year programs in computer information technology, early childhood education, general studies, nursing, paralegal studies, and engineering technology are also available. Preprofessional training is also offered for chiropractic, dental hygiene, pharmacy, and physician assistant studies.

Academic Program

McNeese operates on a semester system (fall and spring) and summer classes are available. The number of semester hours needed for graduation varies according to degree program, with a minimum of 121 hours. General requirements emphasize the arts, humanities, social sciences, mathematics, and sciences, though students are given a wide variety of choices in selecting core courses. Special programs include the Honors College, which is designed for outstanding students with strong academic records who desire an alternative course of instruction. The program offers a substantial scholarship covering tuition, room and board, and a stipend for students who qualify as well as supplemented honors events, cultural opportunities, and social activities. The women's studies program provides special courses, a resource center, and an established lecture series.

Off-Campus Programs

There are a growing number of off-campus programs at McNeese. Programs are in Rome, Paris, and Greece and are organized directly through the University, allowing students to earn credits in areas such as art, literature, and classical studies. There is also a program in New York City through the Theater Department. Students may qualify for benefits through the CODOFIL program in Louisiana, which provides financial support for students who wish to study in a Francophone country. McNeese also has a Fulbright Advisery Committee dedicated to helping students secure grants to pursue study-abroad opportunities.

Academic Facilities

The Frazar Memorial Library holds over 400,000 volumes as well as room for study, library offices, and service areas. Several online systems are available through the library, as well as a computer room with Internet access for students, faculty members, and members of the community. Abercrombie Gallery hosts exhibits by students, faculty, and national and international artists. The Business Conference Center hosts seminars, workshops, and other University programs. Hardtner Hall is a $5-million state-of-the-art facility that houses the College of Nursing, a community clinic, and the Department of Mass Communication. There is a student health services center on campus, and all students who are enrolled in 7 or more semester hours are covered by the University's student accident and life insurance, which provides $10,000 of coverage.

Costs

Tuition and fees at McNeese are $1270 per semester for Louisiana residents and $4340 per semester for nonresidents. Books cost approximately $400 per semester. Costs are subject to change.

Financial Aid

More than $2.5 million in scholarships are awarded to McNeese students each year. Academic scholarships are awarded on a competitive basis to qualified full-time students who remain in good standing. Scholarships may be used to pay for University expenses and range from $100 to $2000 per semester. A limited number of scholarships are available to cover residence-hall room fees. The priority deadline for scholarship applications is December 1 for the upcoming academic year. The Office of Financial Aid also offers a variety of grants and loans to meet student needs, and the priority deadline is May 1. Programs such as the Federal Pell Grant and Federal Supplemental Educational Opportunity Grant offer federal money based on demonstrated need and does not have to be repaid. The Perkins Loan, the Parent Loan for Undergraduates, and the Federal Stafford Student Loan Program offer low-interest-rate loans for students who qualify. For students from the state of Louisiana, the State Student Incentive Grant and Tuition Opportunity Program for Students (TOPS) are available. McNeese also has a Work-on-Campus program that is open to all students regardless of income. However, funds are limited and upperclassmen receive first consideration, subject to deadline dates. Out-of-state students who meet specific criteria are eligible to receive a nonresident fee waiver. In order to be considered for financial aid, students must complete the Free Application for Federal Student Aid (FAFSA).

Faculty

McNeese has a faculty of 392 members, of whom 283 are full-time. Sixty-nine percent of full-time faculty members hold terminal degrees. Qualifying graduate students may serve as undergraduate instructors. The student-faculty ratio is 22:1. The average undergraduate class size is 25 students. McNeese is one of the top-ranked schools in the nation for individual attention to students. Faculty members serve as academic advisers in each degree program. Career and personal counseling and counseling for veterans and international students are also available. The University prides itself on its dedication to excellence with a personal touch.

Student Government

The Student Government Association (SGA) represents the student body to the faculty, administration, and the community. The SGA is staffed by students and aids the student body through several specific programs. The Student Union Board provides social, recreational, cultural, spiritual, and educational programs for students, faculty members, and alumni.

Admission Requirements

First-time freshmen students seeking admission to undergraduate programs at McNeese are required to submit an application for admission, $20 application fee, proof of immunization, official high school transcripts, official ACT or SAT scores, and proof of Selective Service Registration (males only, ages 18-25). Applicants must meet one of the following criteria: a minimum cumulative, unweighted high school GPA of 3.0 on a 4.0 scale; or a minimum ACT composite score of 20 (SAT) composite of 940); or a minimum of 39 on the admissions formula: high school GPA x 10 + composite ACT score. In addition to the regular admission criteria listed above, nonresident, first-time freshmen students must satisfy one of the following requirements: A minimum ACT composite score of 17 (SAT of 810); or a minimum ACT composite score of 16 (SAT of 760) and a minimum cumulative, unweighted high school GPA of 2.5 on a 4.0 scale and rank in the upper 50 percent of the high school graduating class; or a minimum ACT composite score of 15 (SAT of 710) and a minimum cumulative, unweighted high school GPA of 2.75 on a 4.0 scale and rank in the upper 40 percent of the high school graduating class.

Transfer students should be in good academic standing. Students who transfer to McNeese with less than 12 college-level hours must meet first-time freshmen admission criteria. Transfer students with more than 12 college-level hours must submit an application for admission, official college transcripts, proof of immunization, and proof of selective service registration (men only, ages 18-25).

Application and Information

To be considered for admission, students must submit a completed application for admission, nonrefundable $20 application fee, proof of immunization form, and submit official ACT and SAT scores and all transcripts of previous schooling, which must be sent directly to the Office of the Registrar by the institutions attended. For more information, students may contact:

Office of Enrollment Information
McNeese State University
P.O. Box 92895
Lake Charles, Louisiana 70609
Telephone: 337-475-5238
800-622-3352 (toll-free)
E-mail: info@mail.mcneese.edu
World Wide Web: http://www.mcnese.edu

MEMORIAL UNIVERSITY OF NEWFOUNDLAND

ST. JOHN'S AND CORNER BROOK, NEWFOUNDLAND, CANADA

The University

Memorial University is the only university in the Canadian province of Newfoundland and Labrador. Established as a college in 1925, the institution became a full-fledged university in 1949. Today Memorial is the largest Canadian center of research east of Montreal. Publicly funded, Memorial University recognizes in its mission statement a special obligation to educate the citizens of Newfoundland and Labrador. In meeting that obligation, Memorial has fostered groundbreaking research in areas ranging from marine biology to maritime history, folklore to aquaculture, and naval architecture to linguistics.

There are approximately 16,000 students at Memorial University. Nearly 90 percent come from Newfoundland and Labrador; the remaining 10 percent includes students from every province in Canada, the United States, and more than seventy other countries.

Most of the programs are based at the largest campus, in the center of St. John's, close to recreation, sports facilities, cultural outlets, and the city's historic downtown. Almost all the buildings are linked by a system of skywalks and underground tunnels, allowing resident students to wear shorts to class even in the middle of winter. Memorial's main campus also has a recreational complex of three facilities known collectively as The Works, the best university sports facility in eastern Canada.

Also located in St. John's is the Marine Institute, a center for training in ocean-related careers from navigation to aquaculture. Officially merged with Memorial University in 1992, the Marine Institute has won international acclaim for its innovation and research.

Sir Wilfred Grenfell College, in Corner Brook, is a small liberal arts college with about 1,200 students. Memorial's fine arts degree programs are offered here, as are interdisciplinary degrees in arts and sciences. The college is known for its intimate atmosphere and the personal attention and assistance given to each student.

Location

Newfoundland is Canada's easternmost province. Physically separated from the rest of the country, it has a distinct cultural identity. The music, art, and theater reflect a culture tied to the land and the ocean. St. John's, the capital at the extreme eastern edge of the country, has a population of about 175,000. Corner Brook, on the west coast of the island portion of the province, has about 25,000 people. The spectacular and unspoiled terrain draws tourists from all over the world for activities such as whale watching, hiking, skiing, canoeing, and photography. Newfoundlanders are famous for their friendliness, and the cultural and social opportunities are well known.

The province has a very low crime rate and numerous parks, and even from the densest urban centers, open country is never more than a few minutes' drive.

Majors and Degrees

The general Bachelor of Arts and the Bachelor of Arts (Honours) degrees at the St. John's campus are offered with majors in anthropology (archaeology/physical or social/cultural), Canadian studies (second major only), classics (classical studies, Greek, or Latin), computer science, economics, English language and literature (language and theater/drama specializations), folklore, French (language/literature option), geography, German, history, linguistics, medieval studies (general only), philosophy, political science, psychology, religious studies, Russian, sociology, sociology/anthropology, and Spanish. Degrees can be completed with joint majors or with a major and minor. Minors can be taken in most of the areas above as well as in aboriginal studies, Newfoundland studies, European studies (portion taught at the Harlow campus), women's studies, or any of Memorial's science departments.

The interdisciplinary Bachelor of Arts degree at Sir Wilfred Grenfell College is offered in English, environmental studies, historical studies, humanities, psychology, and social/cultural studies. The Bachelor of Fine Arts degree is offered in theater (acting or stagecraft/design) and visual arts. A Bachelor of Science degree in environmental science is also offered. The four-year Bachelor of Nursing Collaborative Program is available at the Western Regional School of Nursing in Corner Brook.

Memorial's Faculty of Business Administration offers the Bachelor of Business Administration as well as the Bachelor of Commerce, a cooperative option with concentrations available in accounting, finance, human resources and labor relations, information systems, management science, marketing, management science, and small business/entrepreneurship. In addition, a Bachelor of Arts/Bachelor of Commerce cooperative program and a Bachelor of Science (major in computer science)/Bachelor of Commerce cooperative program are now offered.

The Bachelor of Education is offered with degree options in primary/elementary education, intermediate/secondary education, music education, Native and northern education, postsecondary education, and special education.

The Bachelor of Engineering, a co-op degree, is offered in the disciplines of civil engineering, computer engineering, electrical engineering, mechanical engineering, and ocean and naval architectural engineering. All have an offshore oil and gas option.

The Bachelor of Music degree is offered with majors in music history and literature, performance, theory and composition, and general music studies. The conjoint B.Mus./B.Mus.Ed degree is available as a five-year program in cooperation with the Faculty of Education.

The Bachelor of Science and Bachelor of Science (Honours) degrees are offered in applied mathematics, behavioural neuroscience, biochemistry, biology, chemistry, computer science, computer science/statistics, earth sciences, environmental physics, geography, physics, psychology, psychology/biology, pure mathematics, and statistics. Bachelor of Science (Joint Honours) degrees are offered in applied mathematics/chemistry, applied mathematics/physics, biochemistry/behavioural neuroscience, biochemistry (nutrition)/behavioural neuroscience, biochemistry/psychology (behavioural neuroscience), biochemistry (nutrition)/psychology (behavioural neuroscience), biology/earth sciences, biology/psychology, chemistry/biochemistry, computer science/applied mathematics, computer science and geography, computer science and physics, earth sciences/chemistry, earth sciences/physics, geography/earth sciences, geophysics/physical oceanography, physics/biochemistry, physics/chemistry, pure mathematics/computer science, pure mathematics/statistics, statistics/biology, and statistics/computer science.

The University's School of Human Kinetics and Recreation offers the degrees of Bachelor of Kinesiology, Bachelor of Physical Education (general or teaching option), and Bachelor of Recreation (each with co-op components). The University also offers the degrees of Bachelor of Maritime Studies, Bachelor of Nursing, Bachelor of Science in Pharmacy, Bachelor of Social Work, and Bachelor of Technology.

Academic Program

The academic year has three semesters: fall (September to December); winter (January to April); and spring (May to August). Some programs admit students in September only, while others can be started in any semester. Two 6-week sessions in the spring semester offer concentrated study opportunities; however, course offerings in the spring semester are limited in number. Most programs take four years (eight semesters) to complete. Exceptions include the B.Eng., which takes six years, including six co-op work terms; the B.Comm., which takes five years, including three work terms; and the B.S.W., which takes a total of five years to complete.

Off-Campus Programs

In addition to its three campuses in Newfoundland, Memorial University has a campus in Harlow, England. The Harlow campus is used by various faculties to give students the opportunity of a semester's study abroad. Memorial also operates the Frecker Program on the French island of St-Pierre, just 14 miles off the coast of Newfoundland. The University is a member of CUSEC, an agreement under which students can spend a semester at another Canadian university. Memorial also has about a dozen formal exchange agreements with universities in other countries. Some programs, largely in arts and science, offer "field schools" for credit; students spend several weeks getting credit in other countries for program-related fieldwork. Past field schools have been held in Malta, Greece, Russia, Germany, and Barbados, among other areas.

Academic Facilities

The University has six libraries. The largest, on the St. John's campus, has 1.7 printed materials, 2.7 million micromaterials, and more than 120,000 nonprinted materials. Other Memorial libraries include those at Grenfell College and the Marine Institute, plus specialized libraries for education, medicine, and music. The University is home to several archives and collections. The on-campus computer network is among the most advanced of any educational institution in the world, with more than 100 courses that include some Internet component, and several offered entirely on line. Laboratory and research facilities include the Ocean Sciences Center, a wave tank, a marine simulator, and more. Theaters, used for student productions, are located in both Corner Brook and St. John's.

Costs

Tuition costs for Canadian students for the 2003–04 academic year were Can$1275 per semester for a normal five-course program; tuition for international students was Can$4000 per semester. Student organization fees, which include a health and dental plan, are Can$248 per semester for Canadian students; domestic students can opt out of plans if they have alternate health and dental coverage. International students must purchase health insurance, which costs approximately Can$496 per year. The cost of books and supplies varies by program. The cost of room and board in the St. John's campus residences is about Can$4186 (double room, fourteen meals per week) for two semesters for both Canadian and international students.

Financial Aid

Canadian students are eligible for government loans and grants. Memorial University offers scholarships in many areas; a complete listing is found in the University *Calendar*. Renewable scholarships valued up to Can$5000 per academic year are available and are generally awarded on the basis of academic merit. Memorial's award-winning on-campus work experience program provides students with jobs related to their areas of study. In extreme cases, emergency short-term loans are available through the Council of the Students' Union.

Faculty

Memorial University has 959 permanent and 752 contractual part-time faculty members, many of whom are world-renowned researchers; all teach at both the graduate and undergraduate levels. The faculty-undergraduate student ratio is about 1:15.

Student Government

There are several student unions at Memorial University. The largest is the Memorial University of Newfoundland Students Union (MUNSU) on the larger St. John's Campus. MUNSU has voting representation on the University's senate and board of regents. It also owns and operates a bar, games room, student-run newspaper, radio station, and child care center. The on-campus food court plays host to a wide variety of well-known restaurant names. MUNSU funds approximately seventy student organizations, with focuses from the academic to the political and including special interest groups such as student parents and international students.

Admission Requirements

A minimum 70 percent, computed from the grades received on selected final year high school courses (or their equivalents in other provinces and countries), is required for admission to the University. Complete information for specific provinces and countries is available in the University *Calendar* (available on the Web site). Applicants with a first language other than English must have a minimum TOEFL score of 550 (paper-based) or 213 (computer-based) or another recognized proof of fluency. Auditions, portfolios, or personal interviews are required for fine arts and music programs. Some programs require a separate application form in addition to the University General Application form. While most qualified applicants are accepted to the Faculties of Arts and Sciences, some departments may limit enrollment. Entry is competitive in other faculties and schools. In the Schools of Social Work, Nursing, Pharmacy, and Medicine, preference is given to applicants from within Newfoundland. Enrollment is also limited in the Faculties of Education and Engineering, so minimally qualified candidates are not always accepted.

Application and Information

The general deadline for application for September admission is March 1; applications received after this time are processed as time permits. Deadlines are earlier for some disciplines (e.g., medicine and social work) and later for others (e.g., B.Rec.). Students are advised to contact the University as early as possible to allow sufficient time for applications to be sent, completed, and evaluated and for supporting documentation, where necessary, to be gathered and evaluated.

To inquire or to request application materials, students should contact:

Office of Student Recruitment
Memorial University of Newfoundland
St. John's, Newfoundland A1C 5S7
Canada
Telephone: 709-737-8896
Fax: 709-737-8611
E-mail: new.students@mun.ca
World Wide Web: http://www.mun.ca

MENLO COLLEGE

ATHERTON, CALIFORNIA

The College

Menlo College, an independent, coeducational, nonsectarian institution, stands out among institutions of higher education in four exciting ways. First, rather than offer a traditional set of majors as many institutions do, Menlo concentrates on providing excellent programs in business management, liberal arts, and mass communications. Menlo's location in the heart of the Silicon Valley allows the College to train tomorrow's leaders in an intimate, student-centered, academically challenging environment. The College is small enough to be a real community but large enough to support a wide array of intercollegiate sports, student organizations, and internship opportunities, giving students the confidence and breadth of experience to flourish after graduation. The College's distinguished alumni provide a strong base of support for graduates, which helps students make the transition from college to career with great success.

A Menlo education is a process of training and cultivating leaders. This process begins with a broad-based liberal arts foundation in the humanities, mathematics, sciences, and social sciences. At the same time, students are challenged to enrich and develop their writing, critical-thinking, and decision-making skills. The result is rich programs staffed with seasoned practitioners who are experts in their respective fields. The advantage is a cutting-edge curriculum that equips students to succeed. Menlo's superior business program is renowned throughout the world. Other programs have been singled out by business executives, entrepreneurs, and industry leaders as illustrations of the type of preparation needed to succeed in the twenty-first century.

The learning process does not end in the classroom. Students are encouraged to participate in internships and study programs that bridge the gap between theory and practice. These opportunities range from Fortune 500 companies to innovative start-up enterprises, from San Francisco to South America, Asia, and Europe. Not only do participants gain hands-on experience, but they also grow personally as they encounter diverse peoples, cultures, and values, whether at home or 10,000 miles away.

As a whole, College-sponsored activities promote self-exploration and often lead to the discovery of hidden talents. Students can participate in a variety of clubs or organizations, ranging from the Alpha Chi National Honor Society and the Poetry, Art, and Music Society to the Menlo Oak Newspaper and the Outdoor Club. Leadership skills are cultivated through an activist student government and student life positions and special workshops that tackle pressing contemporary issues.

This commitment to personal and intellectual growth, coupled with Menlo's ideal location in a major metropolitan area, draws students from all across the United States and all around the world. The global village is a reality at Menlo, given the broad social, religious, cultural, and national makeup of the student body. The appreciation of different cultures that results becomes a tremendous advantages in the marketplace.

Menlo's warm, friendly atmosphere is enhanced by its residential status. Nearly two thirds of all students live in one of five residence halls. Off-campus apartments (for students who are older than 21 or married) are also an option.

For those who enjoy the exhilaration of intercollegiate competition, Menlo offers men's baseball, basketball, cross-country, football, golf, soccer, tennis, track and field, and wrestling, and women's sports include basketball, cross-country, softball, tennis, track and field, volleyball, and wrestling. The College competes in the NAIA Pacific Conference and the NCAA Division III. Intramural sports are also available. Almost 40 percent of all students participate in sports.

To meet students' health needs, the College provides care via the Menlo Medical Clinic. Counseling services are offered by faculty and resident life staff members and the Counseling Services Office.

Whether in the classroom, in the laboratory, or on the playing field, Menlo College nurtures students by creating programs, activities, and services that foster individual success.

Location

Menlo College is located on the San Francisco peninsula in the town of Atherton, a residential community near the cities of Menlo Park and Palo Alto. Major freeways do not pass near the campus, nor is heavy industry nearby. The area ranks among the most attractive and exciting in the world, with numerous cultural resources and a temperate climate. San Francisco lies 30 miles to the north. Many other important educational centers are within an hour's drive of Menlo, making the area an exciting place in which to study and live. To the south is Silicon Valley, where high-tech companies in the electronics, computer, aerospace, biotechnology, and pharmaceutical industries are literally transforming the world in which we live and work. Surrounding the San Francisco Bay Area is the great natural beauty of northern California, extending from the spectacular California coast to the majestic Sierra Nevada Mountains. Favorite spots such as Big Sur, Monterey Bay, Lake Tahoe, Napa Valley, and Yosemite National Park can be reached in a half day's drive from Menlo.

Majors and Degrees

Menlo College offers a Bachelor of Science in Business Management degree program with concentrations in general business management, international management, management information systems, and sports management. The Bachelor of Arts degree is offered in the fields of mass communications, with emphases in electronic communication arts and media studies, and in the field of liberal arts, with specializations in humanities and psychology.

Academic Program

Menlo College operates on a semester calendar. To earn a bachelor's degree, students must complete 124 units of credit and maintain good academic standing.

The Business Management Program provides a comprehensive management education based on a rigorous core modeled after the M.B.A. program.

The Mass Communications Program gives students a broad understanding of communication processes through a carefully selected core curriculum. Students are encouraged to pursue their studies with managerial and leadership goals in mind.

The Liberal Arts Program affords an interdisciplinary foundation and the intellectual essence of the management curriculum while integrating the humanities and social sciences.

The Academic Success Program and Learning Resource Center provide dynamic resources for increasing students' academic ability and morale. Included are innovative approaches to tutoring and developmental courses. The goal is to assist faculty members in meeting the needs of a varied student population using an assortment of individualized, small-group, and computer-based instruction. This method facilitates study and discussion of course material, tutoring, and test preparation.

Off-Campus Programs

The difference between obtaining an exciting professional position with opportunity for advancement and growth and settling for second best often comes down to experience. Internships enable students to apply theory to practice—to take classroom knowledge and test its relevancy. Through the Career Services Office and each academic department, qualified students are urged to participate in local, national, or international internships. Students spend one or more semesters working on or off campus in their fields of study obtaining academic credit and/or financial compensation and valuable insight. Menlo also has exchange agreements with Oxford University; Peking University, in Beijing, China; Anáhuac University, in Mexico City; and a program in Guangzhau, China.

Academic Facilities

Bowman Library maintains a superb collection of books and periodicals, supplemented by holdings in microform, computer software programs, and videocassettes. Networked CD-ROM workstations provide access to general and specialized periodicals and reference resources as well as the Internet and World Wide Web. Other workstations provide access to electronic databases offering abstracts and images of selected journal articles. Students can tap into the resources of academic, technical, and public libraries in the surrounding area and nationwide through Menlo's membership in a number of library cooperative networks. The library contains rooms for group study, viewing videocassettes and microforms, and photocopying.

Menlo College's four computer labs provide students with access to state-of-the-art PC and Macintosh hardware, software, and networking capabilities. All computer-lab equipment is connected to the campus network as well as the Internet and World Wide Web. Classroom labs include both individual workstations and presentation facilities. The Open Access lab is available more than 95 hours per week and is staffed by experienced monitors who are familiar with all lab equipment and applications and are able to provide students with the best possible technical and instructional services. With a 5:1 student-computer ratio, Menlo College offers students ample access to a wide range of computing resources for both classroom assignments and personal use.

Costs

Tuition for 2003–04 was $21,930. Residence costs, including room and board, were $9080.

Financial Aid

Menlo is noted for a strong program of merit and need-based aid. Approximately 70 percent of Menlo's students enroll with financial assistance, including Menlo scholarships, achievement awards, and on-campus employment as well as Federal Pell Grants, Federal Stafford Student Loans, State of California Grants, Federal PLUS loans, and others. Students transferring to Menlo are fully eligible to be considered for financial aid. Merit scholarships of up to $11,000 per year are available for both domestic and international students.

Faculty

Menlo's faculty members devote their full attention to teaching. The College faculty is composed of approximately 60 members, both full- and part-time. Guest lecturers from business, industry, and other professions add to the breadth of instruction. Faculty members are readily available to give students personal help and counseling. A student-teacher ratio of 10:1 allows for small classes and individual attention to students' progress.

Student Government

Students elect their own representatives to student government, which is responsible for legislative and executive decisions affecting student activities and the coordination of student affairs. At Menlo, students take the lead in shaping their education and the future of their College.

Admission Requirements

The Admission Committee considers each candidate individually, through the assessment of academic achievement and personal qualities, talents, and interests. There is an early decision plan for entering freshmen, and transfer students are welcome. Applicants are evaluated on the basis of their academic record (minimum 2.5 GPA), course of study, personal recommendations, school activities, essay, and scores on either the SAT I or ACT Assessment. A personal visit is strongly recommended but not required. The College looks for freshmen with both breadth and depth of academic background in college preparatory subjects. Transfer students are evaluated on the strength of their college programs. Applicants are considered without regard to age, race, color, creed, gender, sexual orientation, national origin, marital status, disability, or any other characteristic protected by law.

Application and Information

Students may enter Menlo College at the opening of the fall or spring semester. For further information concerning admission, students should contact:

Office of Admission
Menlo College
1000 El Camino Real
Atherton, California 94027-4301
Telephone: 650-543-3753
800-55-MENLO (toll-free)
Fax: 650-543-4496
E-mail: admissions@menlo.edu
World Wide Web: http://www.menlo.edu

MERCER UNIVERSITY

MACON, GEORGIA

The University

Founded in 1833, Mercer University is a private, coeducational institution of higher education with an enduring Baptist heritage. Offering more than twenty undergraduate, graduate, and professional degree programs in more than sixty major areas of study, the University is composed of ten colleges and schools: the College of Liberal Arts, the Eugene W. Stetson School of Business and Economics, the School of Engineering, the Tift College of Education, the Georgia Baptist College of Nursing, the School of Medicine, the Walter F. George School of Law, the Southern School of Pharmacy, the James and Carolyn McAfee School of Theology, and the College of Continuing and Professional Studies.

With its main undergraduate campus in Macon and its graduate and professional center in Atlanta, the University is accredited by the Commission on Colleges of the Southern Association of Colleges and Schools. Mercer has been recognized for thirteen consecutive years by *U.S. News & World Report* as one of the South's leading universities for quality and value.

Mercer's enviable reputation is built on its solid academic programs, outstanding faculty, and state-of-the-art facilities. Yet, tradition plays a key role in creating its unique identity as an institution committed to Judeo-Christian principles as well as the tenets of religious and intellectual freedom.

More than 7,300 students are enrolled in Mercer's nine schools, with 4,000 undergraduates attending classes on the historic main campus. The average class size at Mercer University is 25, with a student-faculty ratio of 15:1—unusually low for a major university. Although many students come from the southeast, thirty-eight states and thirty other countries are represented within the student body.

Students benefit from Mercer's welcoming atmosphere, small classes, and learning experiences guided by caring faculty members, not the teaching assistants found at many universities. The superb faculty, with credentials representing some of the world's greatest academic institutions, is distinguished for both teaching and research activities. More than 90 percent of faculty members hold doctorates or the highest attainable degree in their fields.

A variety of on-campus housing facilities, including residence halls, apartments, and Greek houses, are available to undergraduate students. The University's more than eighty on-campus organizations include a wide range of academic clubs and honor societies as well as performing arts and special-interest and religious groups. Seven sororities and ten fraternities create a vibrant social atmosphere and participate in numerous community service projects. Mercer also offers the U.S. Army ROTC program.

Mercer offers a full range of individual, intercollegiate, and intramural sports programs. The University is a member of the Division I NCAA Atlantic Sun Conference and competes in a complete schedule of men's baseball, basketball, cross-country, golf, riflery, soccer, and tennis and women's basketball, cross-country, golf, soccer, softball, tennis, and volleyball.

Location

Historic buildings and majestic magnolias provide the setting on Mercer's campus in Macon, Georgia—a welcoming community with small-town values and big-city amenities, just 1 hour from Atlanta. Mercer's convenient location in the center of the state also makes travel to Georgia's coast, Florida's beaches, and the Blue Ridge mountains an easy drive. Easily accessible from two interstate highways, I-75 and I-16, Macon is the fifth-largest city in Georgia and the educational, medical, cultural, and commercial hub of central Georgia.

Majors and Degrees

The College of Liberal Arts offers undergraduate programs of study leading to the Bachelor of Arts, Bachelor of Science, Bachelor of Music Education, Bachelor of Music in Performance, and Bachelor of Music in Sacred Music degrees. Majors and concentrations offered in the College of Liberal Arts include African-American studies, anthropology, art, biology, chemistry, Christianity, classical studies, communication and theater arts, computer science, criminal justice, drama and theater, economics, English, French, German, Greek, history, international affairs, journalism, Latin, leadership and community service, mathematics, media studies, music, music education, philosophy, photography, physics, political science, psychology, social science, sociology, Spanish, and women's and gender studies.

The Eugene W. Stetson School of Business and Economics offers undergraduate students a Bachelor of Business Administration degree through a self-designed program of business study called Managed Academic Path to Success (MAPS). Combining twelve core business courses with other academic areas, MAPS programs created have included music business, health-care management, advertising and marketing, accounting information systems, and political management.

The School of Engineering offers the Bachelor of Science in Engineering degree with specializations in biomedical, computer, electrical, industrial, mechanical, and environmental engineering and the Bachelor of Science degree with majors in industrial management and technical communication.

The Tift College of Education offers programs of study leading to the Bachelor of Science in Education degree in early childhood education (holistic child) and middle grades education. In conjunction with the College of Liberal Arts, the Tift College of Education offers secondary/grade certification programs in the following areas: art, English, foreign languages, history, mathematics, music, broad-field science, and broad-field social science.

Academic Program

The University's curriculum offers two academic tracks—the General Education Program and the Great Books Program. The General Education Program is broad in scope, requiring study in several areas. Students take courses that provide an introduction to some of the major areas of human knowledge and endeavor. Most of this work, which lays the foundation for continued study and for the student's own contribution to society, is completed during the freshman and sophomore years. During the junior and senior years, students take specialized courses in major fields in the upper-division curriculum.

The Great Books Program challenges students to examine the written works of the greatest minds of Western tradition—Plato, Socrates, Milton, and Freud. Students and faculty members engage these writings to learn more about themselves and their intellectual heritage. The sequence, consisting of eight 3-credit courses, begins the first semester of the freshman year and continues through the senior year.

Mercer University also offers an Honors Program for academically outstanding students to develop their talents and potential to the fullest, through intellectually enriched and stimulated learning experiences. In addition to the regular curriculum, qualified students in the undergraduate programs in the College of

Liberal Arts, School of Business and Economics, School of Engineering, and the Tift College of Education may be admitted to the Honors Program.

While students at Mercer University are required to complete a major, they are also encouraged to explore other fields of knowledge. Many departments offer courses in special topics, independent research, and independent reading. In addition, a student who has a special interest not filled by the traditional majors may apply for permission to complete an independent major, subject to approval of the dean of the college and a faculty committee.

The average course load is 15 semester hours (five courses) for students in the College of Liberal Arts, the Stetson School of Business and Economics, and the Tift College of Education, and 15 to 18 semester hours (five to six courses) for students in the School of Engineering. A student who maintains a B average may, with the adviser's permission, take an additional course. A student may receive up to 30 hours of credit through the College-Level Examination Program (CLEP) or International Baccalaureate (IB). Credit is usually awarded to those who score a 3, 4, or 5 on the Advanced Placement tests of the College Board.

Academic Facilities

The 130-acre Macon campus is a blend of tradition and innovation. Students walk among 100-year-old trees, yet state-of-the-art learning technology is at their fingertips. Opening in January of 2004 is the 230,000-square-foot University Center. From enjoying a lingering cup of mocha at the Coffee Shop to jogging laps around the indoor track to attending a concert or Division I basketball game in the arena, students will make memories in this facility that will enhance their college experience.

Costs

Costs for the 2003–04 academic year are $20,796 for tuition and fees and $6720 for room and board. The estimated cost for books and academic supplies is $600 a year.

Financial Aid

Mercer provides a wealth of financial assistance to every qualified student through scholarships, grants, loans, work-study opportunities, or a combination of these. Federal, state, and local funds are also awarded to students, helping make a Mercer education very affordable. In fact, more than 95 percent of Mercer students received some form of financial aid in the 2003–04 academic year. All applicants for financial aid are encouraged to submit the Free Application for Federal Student Aid (FAFSA) and the Mercer University financial assistance form. Georgia residents may be eligible for the Georgia Tuition Equalization Grant and the HOPE Scholarship, which are set by the state each year. Those students who are eligible for scholarships are notified by letter after acceptance to the University.

Faculty

With a student-faculty ratio of 15:1, Mercer professors know students not only by name, but also by professional ambitions and personal goals. The more than 500 full-time faculty members are among the nation's leading scholars, researchers, and practitioners in their respective fields of study. More than 90 percent have earned the Ph.D. degree or equivalent. Classes of all levels are taught by professors, not teaching assistants.

Student Government

Recognized student activities at Mercer are directed and sponsored by the Student Government Association. Elected representatives include the president, vice president, secretary-treasurer, and freshman adviser; representatives from each of the four classes and from the University at large; the editors of the student publications; and the Student Union Activities Board. All of these officers are chosen in a campus-wide election each spring. Liberal arts, business, engineering, and education students are equally represented on most major school committees.

Admission Requirements

Mercer admits students whose academic credentials and personal qualities are strong enough to give reasonable assurance of success in both the academic and social context of the campus. To be fully admitted into the University's traditional undergraduate program, first-year candidates should be in the process of completing or already have completed a college-preparatory course of study in an approved (by a state, regional, or official accrediting agency) secondary school program, with certain minimum academic units in the following courses: English (4), mathematics (4), laboratory science (3), social science (3), history (3), and foreign language (2). They should have achieved at least a 3.0 (B) academic grade point average, considering only grades in the following courses: English, mathematics, laboratory science, social science, and foreign language. They must have an SAT score of at least 1000 or a converted ACT composite score of at least 22. First-year applicants wishing to pursue studies in pre–health sciences (medicine, pharmacy, nursing, dentistry, etc.), mathematics, computer science, natural sciences, or engineering must have at least a 550 math score on the SAT or converted ACT. Finally, applicants must be in academic and disciplinary good standing at the current or last institution attended.

Application and Information

Candidates for first-year admission must submit an application for admission with a $50 nonrefundable application fee. Students may apply to Mercer through three application plans: Early Action, Early Decision, or Regular Decision. Many have advantages such as priority scholarship consideration, early admission notification, and advanced financial aid estimates. If a student applies through either of the early plans and is neither admitted nor denied, the application is moved to the Regular Decision plan. Applicants must submit an official high school transcript, with clear distinction of academic course subjects. All students intending to enroll must submit an official final high school transcript, indicating completion of senior courses and receipt of a high school diploma. Candidates must also include official score reports from the SAT I or the ACT. Scores on official high school transcripts are acceptable.

For more information, students should contact:

Allen London, Vice President of University Admissions
Mercer University
1400 Coleman Avenue
Macon, Georgia 31207
Telephone: 478-301-2650
800-840-8577 (toll-free)
E-mail: admissions@mercer.edu
World Wide Web: http://www.mercer.edu

The administration building at Mercer University is on the National Register of Historic Places.

MERCY COLLEGE

DOBBS FERRY, NEW YORK

The College

With six campuses throughout the greater New York metropolitan region and on the Internet, Mercy College offers more than ninety undergraduate and graduate degrees. The mission of the institution is to provide access to a high-quality education to students who possess the motivation and the abilities to succeed.

Availability of a quality education begins with financial assistance. In terms of affordability, Mercy's tuition is fourth in the state among all private colleges. Access is also measured by scheduling. Many of Mercy's 10,000 students work full-time and/or have family responsibilities. For this reason, convenient course scheduling is critical. The College offers its courses not only during the day but also in the evenings and on the weekends. In addition, entire degree programs can be taken online, enabling students to fit educational advancement into their hectic schedules. These courses are often more challenging, as the student-teacher ratio is kept at 17:1 and students are also graded on their participation.

Access also means locations that are close to where the students live and near public transportation. Mercy has campuses in Manhattan, the Bronx, White Plains, Dobbs Ferry, and Yorktown Heights. In addition, it has extension centers in Yonkers, Brooklyn, Queens, and Manhattan where students can pursue the first two years towards their degree.

Finally, access is characterized by not judging a student on his or her past academic history, but rather on present capabilities. For its undergraduate programs, Mercy College does not rely on high school class rankings or SAT scores. With an average age of 29 for its undergraduate students, these measurements often provide a distorted picture of a person's true capabilities. Instead, the school utilizes its own set of criteria and testing to determine if a student has what it takes to attain their dream of a college education.

Mercy's graduate programs, leading to a Master of Arts, are nationally renowned and allow students to attain the skills necessary to thrive in their current employment—or change careers entirely. The average age for the school's graduate program is 37.

Mercy is committed to providing every student with the supports that he or she may need to achieve success. This includes financial aid advisers, mentors, personal and career counselors, and computer support specialists.

Location

The campus in Dobbs Ferry is situated on 60 acres of beautifully landscaped grounds overlooking the Hudson River and is just a 40-minute train ride from Grand Central Station. A brand new campus, recently opened in midtown Manhattan directly across from Macy's, is conveniently accessible to public transportation. A major source of training teachers for the New York City school system, Mercy's Bronx Campus is home to more than 2,700 students. Plans are underway for moving to a newly renovated campus within the next year. The White Plains Campus features the newly renovated Center for Digital Arts, where students can study computer arts or music technology. The College's northern-most campus, located in Yorktown Heights, is easy to reach from Northern Westchester, Putnam, Rockland, Orange, Duchess, and Fairfield Counties. Mercy also has extension centers in Queens, Manhattan, Yonkers, and Brooklyn where courses are offered in the evenings and on the weekends.

Majors and Degrees

Mercy College offers programs leading to the Bachelor of Arts, Bachelor of Science, Associate in Arts, and Associate in Science degrees as well as certificate programs. The major degree-program offerings include accounting, behavioral science (specializations in community health, gerontology, and health services management), biology, business administration (specializations in banking, direct marketing, finance, general business administration, industrial and labor relations, international business, management, marketing, office information, and systems and technology), communication disorders, communications studies/television and media, computer arts and technology, computer information systems, computer science, criminal justice, English literature, film studies, history, interdisciplinary studies, journalism, mathematics (specializations in actuarial science, computer science, and operations research), medical technology, music, nursing (post-RN), occupational therapy, occupational therapy assistant, paralegal studies, physical therapy, physical therapy assistant, psychology (specialization in computer research applications), public accounting, public safety (specializations in occupational safety and health administration and in safety administration), social work, sociology (specialization in computer applications), therapeutic recreation, and veterinary technology. Interdisciplinary programs are available in American studies, business leadership, Third World studies, and women's studies. Preprofessional programs are offered in chiropractic, dentistry, law, medicine, optometry, osteopathy, and podiatry.

Teacher certification is offered in early secondary education, elementary education, secondary education, special education, teaching English as a second language, and teaching of speech and hearing to the handicapped. Tricertification is available in elementary education, bilingual education, and special education.

Career-oriented certificate programs include accounting, business management, child care, computer science, criminal justice, direct marketing, fire science, general business administration, gerontology, human behavior, journalism and media, liberal studies, management, marketing, occupational safety and health administration, personnel management, pet-assisted therapy facilitation, private security, public safety, Spanish language and culture, and substance abuse counseling. Mercy's innovative majors with unique scheduling also include five-year B.S./M.S. programs in acupuncture and oriental medicine, occupational therapy, and physical therapy.

Academic Program

Mercy College offers a full range of undergraduate programs. To be eligible for graduation with a bachelor's degree, a student must accumulate 120 academic credits and must fulfill one of the major curricular distributions. A dual major or a minor concentration is possible. To earn an associate degree, a student must complete 60 academic credits and must satisfy the appropriate curricular distribution.

The College offers a program for students with learning disabilities. A program in English as a second language offers instruction for those students whose native language is not English, and many courses are taught in Spanish and Korean through the Bilingual Education Program.

Students receiving satisfactory scores on College-Level Examination Program (CLEP) tests, the New York State Regents College Examinations, or College Board Advanced Placement (AP) examinations are eligible for advanced placement. Up to 30 credits for life achievement may also be awarded to qualified students. Entering students selected on the basis of past achievement and motivation may be invited to participate in the Mercy College honors program.

Off-Campus Programs

Through its membership in several interinstitutional cooperative programs, Mercy College is able to offer students a variety of off-campus learning opportunities. Arrangements with the Westchester Consortium of Colleges and the Westchester Conservatory of Music allow for the sharing of faculty members and resources in many programs. In addition, degree programs at Mercy College are enriched through joint ventures with private businesses, industries, and research facilities such as the New York Medical College Graduate School and the Karol Marcinkowski University of Medical Sciences in Poznan, Poland. Juniors and seniors are eligible to participate in the College's cooperative education program, through which they gain paid, professional work experience in conjunction with classroom work in their major fields of study.

Academic Facilities

Mercy's campuses feature science laboratories, psychology laboratories, audiological laboratories, a clinic for speech pathology, an acupuncture clinic, and a veterinary clinic. Mercy also features a T.V. studio, a radio station, a music recording studio, a center for the digital arts, and numerous computer and mentoring labs.

The library system houses more than 600,000 volumes. The system also includes extensive audiovisual materials, a federal depository for government publications, and interlibrary loan capabilities. Library materials are cataloged by means of a national, online computerized system (OCLC) using the modern COM (computer output microfilm) catalog.

Costs

Undergraduate tuition in 2003–04 for a full-time student was $10,700 per year (based on 12 to 18 credits per semester) or $450 per credit.

Financial Aid

Financial assistance is available in the form of scholarships, grants, loans, and employment for all eligible matriculated students. All students requesting financial assistance should file the Free Application for Federal Student Aid (FAFSA) by July 1 for the fall semester and by November 1 for the spring semester. Mercy College provides $2 million in scholarships and $4 million in grants to students per year.

Faculty

Of the 989 faculty members, 238 are full-time and 75 percent hold doctorates. Faculty members are actively involved in academic advisement and are dedicated to providing all students with teaching of the highest quality and preparing them for life. The student-teacher ratio of 17:1 ensures a personalized atmosphere and individualized attention.

Admission Requirements

To be considered for admission, freshman candidates must submit an application for admission, an application fee of $35, and an official high school transcript. Transfer students should submit their application, the $35 application fee, and an official transcript from each college or university previously attended. Transfer students who have completed fewer than 15 college credits must submit a copy of their high school record in addition to their college transcripts.

Qualified high school students may apply for early admission or advance study before completion of their high school education. Once admitted, an applicant's score on the College's placement examinations determine the level of English and math at which they begin.

Application and Information

All applicants are encouraged to visit the campus to discuss their college plans with an admission counselor or to have an interview by phone with an admission counselor.

An application form and additional information may be obtained by contacting:

Admissions Office
Mercy College
555 Broadway
Dobbs Ferry, New York 10522
Telephone: 914-674-7600
800-MERCY-NY (toll-free)
E-mail: admissions@mercy.edu
World Wide Web: http://www.mercy.edu

The College's main campus in Dobbs Ferry overlooks the Hudson River.

MERCYHURST COLLEGE
ERIE, PENNSYLVANIA

The College

Mercyhurst College is a fully accredited, four-year, Catholic liberal arts institution, offering a wide array of undergraduate and a limited number of graduate programs for men and women. Mercyhurst, founded in Erie, Pennsylvania, in 1926 by the Sisters of Mercy is now enrolling nearly 4,000 total students from more than forty states and nearly twenty countries. The College emphasizes the development of the whole person through a liberal arts education, focused programs in career preparation, and service-learning opportunities. At Mercyhurst, students gather the knowledge, insights, skills, and vision necessary to lead fulfilling and productive lives.

Students interested in Mercyhurst College should expect vibrant and challenging course work, as well as a unique collection of academic majors ranging from archaeology and forensic science to dance, and the Research Intelligence Analyst Program (RIAP), the original competitive intelligence program. Since its founding, Mercyhurst has also maintained a strong reputation of producing solid graduates in the fields of education and business, the College's two largest majors. Graduate programs leading to Master of Science degrees in the administration of justice, organizational leadership, and special education are currently ongoing, with additional graduate programs in forensic science, anthropology, and applied intelligence in the works for the 2004 or 2005 school year. In all, Mercyhurst offers 115 academic programs rooted in a liberal arts curriculum, and opportunities to actively participate in more than fifty clubs and organizations. Upon completion of their degrees, at least 95 percent of Mercyhurst graduates are employed or enrolled in graduate studies within six months of graduation.

Mercyhurst possesses a great sense of tradition and excellence, as reflected in its beautiful, Tudor-Gothic college setting. More than forty buildings surround stately Old Main, the College's epicenter since 1926. Facilities abound for academics, the arts, athletics, student services, student recreation, and student housing.

The College's athletic facilities include the Mercyhurst Athletic Center, the Student Recreation Center, the Mercyhurst Ice Center, Tullio Field, and several additional playing fields. The Athletic Center houses a gymnasium complex, rowing tanks, and a newly renovated and enlarged athletic training facility. The Ice Center includes a rink, four locker rooms, and seating for 1,500 people. The Recreation Center is home to most Mercyhurst intramural programs and contains a large physical fitness area, two all-purpose floors for basketball, volleyball, and other indoor uses. Mercyhurst fields twenty-five NCAA athletic teams, including its Division I men's and women's ice hockey teams. Division II sports include men's and women's basketball, cross-country, golf, lacrosse, rowing, soccer, tennis, volleyball, and water polo. Other Division II sports fielded are baseball, field hockey, football, softball, and wrestling.

Location

The College is comprised of more than 85 acres on a hill overlooking the city of Erie, Pennsylvania (population 250,000), and Lake Erie. The campus is within 3 miles of downtown and a bustling shopping and entertainment district. These areas are accessible to Mercyhurst students by using the Mercyhurst Shuttle Bus up to five days a week.

Majors and Degrees

Mercyhurst College awards the Bachelor of Arts degree (with concentrations in parentheses) in accounting; archaeology/anthropology; art (art education, graphic design, and studio); art therapy; biology (biology education, ecosystem conservation, predental, premedical, preosteopathy, prepharmacy, and preveterinary); business (advertising, business/chemistry, business computer and information technology, finance, management, marketing, and sport marketing); business/chemistry; chemistry (chemistry education and environmental science); communication (journalism, production, and public relations); computer systems (computer information systems, management information systems, and Web information systems); criminal justice (corrections, juvenile justice, and law enforcement); dance (performance and teaching/choreography); early childhood education; early childhood elementary education; early childhood special education; earth/space science education; elementary education; elementary education/special education; English (creative writing, secondary education, prelaw, and writing); general science education; geology (environmental geology/hydrogeology and geoarchaeology); history (citizenship education, public history, and research/intelligence analyst program); hotel, restaurant, and institutional management (facilities and property management, food and beverage management, hotel management, professional clubhouse and golf management, and professional convention management); mathematics (secondary education); music; philosophy; political science (environmental studies and politics and prelaw); premajor studies; psychology (neuroscience); religious education and lay ministry; religious studies; sociology; social work (criminology); special education; world languages and cultures; and world language education (French and Spanish).

The Bachelor of Science is conferred (with concentrations in parentheses) in applied forensic science (criminalistics, forensic anthropology, forensic chemistry and toxicology, and forensic wildlife investigation); archaeology/anthropology (archaeology and physical anthropology); biochemistry; biology (medical technology); chemistry; earth/space science education; family and consumer sciences (dietetics, family and consumer sciences education, fashion merchandising, interior design, and marriage and family studies); general science education; geology; and sports medicine (athletic training, health/fitness promotion, premedical, and pre–physical therapy).

The Bachelor of Music is awarded in applied music and music education.

Academic Program

Core requirements, which include a select, limited number of courses from the liberal arts disciplines, furnish students with a broad base of skills and knowledge. In addition to completing the core program, students must complete a major. Graduation requirements for the Bachelor of Arts, Bachelor of Science, and Bachelor of Music degrees range from 123 to 140 credits, depending upon the chosen major.

Mercyhurst College offers and honors program, cooperative education, contract majors, independent/tutorial study, and off-campus study. Students may earn credit or advanced placement through challenge examinations, life experience, Advance Placement tests (scores of 4 or 5 are accepted), and CLEP tests.

The College operates on a three-term calendar (fall, winter and spring), with an academic year that generally runs from the first week of September through the third week of May.

Off-Campus Programs

Mercyhurst College has an increasingly active study-abroad program that is open to all students, irrespective of the (academic) program. Up to half of a student's financial aid is available to transfer to the destination school. Mercyhurst students have studied all over the globe, including Australia, Europe, Central America, and Russia. Students may also choose to pursue internships abroad.

For further information, prospective students should contact Eric Evans, Director, International Admissions and Services, at the telephone numbers listed below, extension 2478, or by e-mail at eevans@mercyhurst.edu.

Academic Facilities

The spectacular new Mercyhurst College Bookstore opened in December 2003. One section of the new building is devoted to textbooks. A second section offers trade books and periodicals as well as a sizeable inventory of sundries, school needs, and clothing. A third area features a Starbucks coffee bar. Students enjoy the cybercafé aspect of the bookstore with its Internet connection capabilities.

The Audrey Hirt Academic Center, which opened in 2002, contains an atrium; technology-rich classroom and lecture halls; faculty offices; the Walker Recital Hall; special facilities for the graphic arts, communications, and the honors program; and studios and working areas for the College's newspaper, yearbook, and radio and television organizations.

Zurn Hall contains modern, well-equipped science laboratories and is home to the Mercyhurst Archaeological Institute (MAI). MAI is a teaching, research, and applied research entity composed of anthropology, archaeology, and geology departments. The MAI has two missions, which are to conduct the highest-quality research, while intensively training the next generation of anthropologists, archaeologists, and geoarcheologists. Also housed in Zurn are the College's forensic science and computational chemistry programs.

The Mary D'Angelo Performing Arts Center is a gorgeous facility built in 1996. The center seats 825 and has a performance stage of 3,400 square feet. As such, it is the only facility in the Erie-Cleveland-Pittsburgh-Buffalo area capable of handling the technical requirements of the most elaborate productions, including ballet and opera. Especially renowned for its acoustics, it was designed as a showcase for the performing arts. It is conducive not only to the cultural aspirations of the College and the Erie community, but also as a venue for students and faculty members to perform in a magnificent professional setting.

Costs

Tuition for 31 credits in the 2004–05 academic year total $17,298 ($558 per credit). In addition to tuition, various fees total between $1300 and $1500. Room and board total $6798. The total for room, board, tuition, and fees is roughly $25,500. Students should budget an additional $1500 for books, supplies and personal expenses.

Financial Aid

Mercyhurst is dedicated to assisting students with the cost of their education. Financial aid awards are both need- and merit-based. In addition to federal and state programs, Mercyhurst awards nearly $15 million in institutional scholarships, grants, and loans annually. More than 90 percent of Mercyhurst's students receive financial aid in the form of grants, scholarships, part-time on-campus employment, and/or long-term loans to be repaid after leaving the College. The typical student's financial aid award consists of aid from one or more of these sources.

Financing a college education is a challenging task and an important part of making a good enrollment decision. Mercyhurst's experienced admission and financial aid counselors look forward to assisting families in making Mercyhurst College affordable. Any questions that arise during the process should be directed to an admissions counselor at the telephone numbers listed below, extension 2202.

Faculty

There are 121 full-time and 75 part-time faculty members who staff undergraduate programs at Mercyhurst. More than 60 percent of the faculty members hold a Ph.D. or the terminal degree in their fields of study. The primary faculty function is teaching, but faculty members are also active in research, publishing, and service to their community. The faculty-student ratio is 1:17.

Student Government

A student government organization is designed to help meet the academic, cultural, and social needs of the student body and is financed by an activity fee. Student government comprises an Executive Committee, a Study Activities Committee, representatives from each major and club on campus, and 7 College senators.

Admission Requirements

In selecting a student for admission, Mercyhurst College looks for evidence of academic ability and readiness as demonstrated by high school course work, grades earned, performance on standardized tests, and personal characteristics that relate to a student's ability to succeed.

The College's entrance policy is free of discrimination on the grounds of race, creed, color, sex, or national origin. In fact, the student body reflects this diversity; students come from thirty-five states and five continents.

Application and Information

The College operates on a rolling admission cycle. Beginning in December, notification is given as soon as possible after all credentials reach the Admissions Office.

Students applying to Mercyhurst may apply on-line at the Web site listed below or complete the College's application and send it to the Admissions Office with the required application fee. Applicants must submit an official copy of all high school transcripts, official copies of SAT I and/or ACT scores, and two letters of recommendation. Applicants should also complete any required audition or portfolio review required by individual majors. If seeking consideration for an Egan Academic Scholarship, they should also submit the essay portion of the application.

While interviews are not required, students in their junior or senior year of high school are strongly encouraged to schedule a campus visit and an interview. Campus tours are available by appointment Monday through Friday at 9 a.m., 10 a.m., 11 a.m., 1 p.m., and 2 p.m. Saturday tours are scheduled at 9 a.m., 10 a.m., 11 a.m., and noon.

For additional information about Mercyhurst College, students should contact:

Mercyhurst College Admissions
501 East 38th Street
Erie, Pennsylvania 16546-0001
Telephone: 814-824-2202
800-825-1926 (toll-free)
E-mail: admissions@mercyhurst.edu
World Wide Web: http://www.mercyhurst.edu

MEREDITH COLLEGE

RALEIGH, NORTH CAROLINA

The College

Meredith College, chartered in 1891 by North Carolina Baptists to provide excellence in education for women, is today the largest private women's college in the Southeast. Even as the College has grown to 2,328 undergraduate degree candidates, the student-faculty ratio of 10:1 offers students individualized attention in all aspects of their experience at Meredith College. With a focus on the liberal arts, students are encouraged in all areas from career preparation to personal development. The College retains an appreciation of its Baptist heritage and is now independently governed. Degree candidates choose from nearly forty major fields, including preprofessional studies.

The faculty is dedicated to teaching and advising and to challenging the students to meet their academic and personal goals. Undergraduate students pursue programs leading to Bachelor of Arts, Science, Music, and Social Work degrees; the College also offers Master of Business Administration, Master of Education, Master of Music, and Master of Nutrition degrees. College programs are accredited by the Southern Association of Colleges and Schools, the National Council for the Accreditation of Teacher Education, the Council on Social Work Education, the Foundation for Interior Design Education and Research (FIDER), and the National Association of Schools of Music. The College has an approved American Dietetic Association Plan V Program. It is also the home of the Fletcher School of Performing Arts, which brings renowned performers and master classes to the campus.

The College focuses heavily on leadership development for women. Students are encouraged to participate in a wide variety of campus activities, including performing groups, sports, publications, academic and personal interest clubs, and student government. More than 500 leadership positions are available for women to fill. Rich with diversity with students from twenty-eight states and seventeen other countries, Meredith celebrates its student's uniqueness and potential to return to their communities as active participants in whatever capacity that they choose. A member of NCAA Division III, Meredith fields five intercollegiate sports teams in basketball, fast-pitch softball, soccer, tennis, and volleyball.

Location

Meredith's beautiful 225-acre campus is on the western edge of Raleigh, North Carolina's capital city, and is adjacent to the booming Research Triangle area of Raleigh, Durham, and Chapel Hill. A total of eleven colleges and universities that serve approximately 90,000 students can be found here. Raleigh, a city of 286,000 people, is centrally located between the North Carolina coast and the mountain ranges of the western part of the state. Two interstates and the Raleigh-Durham International Airport (15 minutes from the campus) make Raleigh easily accessible.

Majors and Degrees

Meredith confers four baccalaureate degrees. A candidate for the Bachelor of Arts degree can select her major from American civilization, art, biology, chemistry, communication, dance, economics, English, environmental studies, French, history, international studies, mathematics, music, musical theater, political studies, pre-art therapy, psychology, public history, religion, social work, sociology, Spanish, and theater. The Bachelor of Science degree is available in accounting, biology, business administration, chemistry, child development, clothing and fashion merchandising, computer information systems, computer science, exercise and sports science, family and consumer science, foods and nutrition, interior design, international business, and mathematics. The Bachelor of Music degree candidate can major in performance or music education. The Bachelor of Social Work degree is available in social work. In addition, a student may work with the faculty to create a self-designed major.

Licensure programs taken in addition to a major are offered in school social work and teacher education. Teacher education licensure is offered in birth to kindergarten (B–K), elementary (K–6), middle grades (6–9), secondary (9–12), art (K–12), business (9–12), dance (K–12), French/Spanish (K–12), home economics (7–12), music (K–12), and theater arts (K–12).

Preprofessional preparation is available in dentistry, law, medicine, pharmacy, physical therapy, physician assistant studies, and veterinary medicine. Minors are offered in most major fields and in some other areas such as professional communications, criminal justice, cross-cultural skills, physical education, philosophy, and women's studies. Concentrations are also available within most departments. A five-year Bachelor of Science and Master of Business Administration program is an option for outstanding accounting majors.

Academic Programs

Meredith's academic program blends a strong liberal arts foundation with opportunities for career and preprofessional preparation. To achieve breadth in her education, each student must fulfill general education requirements in humanities and arts, social and behavioral sciences, mathematics and natural sciences, and health and physical education. By the end of her sophomore year, she declares a major and begins to study her chosen field in depth. She may round out her program by completing options such as a second major, a minor or a concentration, a teacher education program, an experiential learning component (an internship, co-op, or field work), or a study-abroad program.

There are opportunities for advanced placement with credit for those who show by examination (AP, I.B., CLEP, and/or departmental examinations) that they have mastered the material for any college-level course. Each year approximately 25 entering students are invited to participate in the Honors Program. About 30 entering students participate in the Teaching Fellows Program, which provides special seminars, mentors, honors classes, and cultural opportunities for the winners of the prestigious North Carolina Teaching Fellows Scholarship/Loan.

Off-Campus Programs

Through the Cooperating Raleigh Colleges consortium, students may take courses with typically no extra cost at North Carolina State and Shaw Universities and at Peace and St. Augustine's Colleges.

Women who are interested in expanding their international horizons can participate in either summer or academic-year intercultural programs in almost any country. Every summer, students and faculty members travel to England, Italy, and Switzerland for five or ten weeks of study. It is possible to earn an entire semester of credit through this summer study at approximately the same price as a regular semester on campus in Raleigh. Art students above the freshman level may study in Florence, Italy. Students of French may study at the Université Catholique de l'Ouest in Angers, France, and students of Spanish may study at Universitas Nebrissensis in Madrid, Spain. Students of almost any major can study in the United Kingdom and Australia. Those seeking a less traditional venue can study at Meredith affiliates in the People's Republic of China or can work with the Office of Study Abroad to find a program appropriate to their academic or travel interests.

Students may take advantage of opportunities within the United States by completing a United Nations Semester at Drew University, a federal government semester through the Washington Semester program at American University, and a capital city semester in state government through Meredith's own program in Raleigh.

Academic Facilities

The Carlyle Campbell Library contains 140,634 volumes, 2,705 periodicals, 74,908 titles on microform, seventy-one electronic databases, and 12,232 records, tapes, CDs, and videos. As part of its academic department facilities, the campus also houses a music library, art galleries, a research greenhouse, music practice rooms, a state-of-the-art language lab, an autism lab, computer labs, a child-care lab, an indoor swimming pool, lighted outdoor tennis courts, a putting green, and a soccer field. The campus is also cabled to provide network and e-mail access in classrooms, computer labs, and residence halls as well as wireless Internet access throughout much of the campus.

Costs

For 2003–04, tuition and fees were $18,065; room and board were $5000.

Financial Aid

Meredith's financial aid program is designed to meet a high percentage of the analyzed need of the student. Approximately 50 percent of undergraduate students receive need-based assistance; when competitive scholarships and state entitlement grants are added, approximately 70 percent of Meredith students receive some form of financial assistance. The Free Application for Federal Student Aid (FAFSA) is used to determine eligibility for need-based federal, state, and institutional funds that include grants and scholarships, loans, and work-study. A freshman candidate may also file special application forms for the competitive scholarships that recognize students for superior academic ability and talent in art, music, or interior design. A North Carolina Teaching Fellow who is selected for Meredith's program may use her scholarship at the College and will have other gift assistance coordinated to match the stipend provided by the state.

Faculty

The College has 294 full-time and part-time faculty members. Eighty-three percent of the full-time faculty members have earned doctoral degrees. The student-faculty ratio is 10:1, and the average class size is 16. Sixty-seven percent of the full-time faculty members are women.

Student Government

Meredith has one of the oldest student government associations in the South and has an honor code that is a key ingredient of the Meredith community. All students assume primary responsibility for making and enforcing regulations; therefore, every student is a member of the Student Government Association (SGA). As members, students are encouraged to actively participate in branches of the SGA, such as the Association for Meredith Commuters, Elections Board, Honor Council, Residence Hall Board, Senate, Student Life, and Women in New Goal Settings.

Admission Requirements

Along with academic achievement, Meredith values individuality, integrity, and diversity. Each application is evaluated to determine how the student's academic preparation and ability match Meredith's requirements and challenges and to assess motivation, special talents, and commitment to learning. A freshman candidate is expected to have at least 16 units of credit earned in grades 9–12, with at least 15 in the academic subjects. Her program should include English (4 units), history/social studies (3 units), mathematics (3 units in algebra I, algebra II, and geometry or a higher level course), science (3 units), foreign language (2 units), and electives (1 unit from the academic subjects). Careful attention is given to an unweighted grade average on the academic subjects and to class rank; test scores (SAT I preferred, or ACT) are reviewed in relation to the high school record; recommendations from a school official and a teacher are also required. An interview may be requested in some instances, and students are encouraged to visit for an admissions conference and campus tour.

For transfer admission from an accredited college or university, the student needs at least an overall C average in transferable courses, must be eligible to return to the last institution regularly attended, and must be recommended by college officials. If the student has fewer than 30 semester hours of transferable work, she must also meet Meredith's freshman admission requirements. Nontraditional students and international students should contact the Office of Admissions.

Application and Information

An application for admission should be sent to the Office of Admissions along with a nonrefundable $35 processing fee (or acceptable fee-waiver request). Electronic filing is available. The student is responsible for requesting that her official high school transcript, SAT I or ACT scores, and recommendations be sent to the admissions office. A transfer student must file an official transcript from each postsecondary institution attended.

Meredith has two freshman admission plans: early decision and rolling admissions. An early decision candidate must apply by October 15; this "first choice" plan means that if accepted under early decision, the student fully expects to enroll and will withdraw any other pending applications. The student is notified by November 1. A candidate under the rolling plan is encouraged to file early in the senior year, with February 15 as the recommended deadline. Notifications under this plan begin in early November. The candidates' reply dates are December 1 for early decision and May 1 for rolling admission candidates.

Transfer applicants are encouraged to apply by February 15. Notifications begin in late January, and May 1 is the candidates' reply date. For admission to the spring semester, a freshman or transfer student should apply by December 1.

For additional information and for planning a campus visit, students should contact:

Office of Admissions
Meredith College
3800 Hillsborough Street
Raleigh, North Carolina 27607-5298
Telephone: 919-760-8581
800-MEREDITH (toll-free)
Fax: 919-760-2348
E-mail: admissions@meredith.edu
World Wide Web: http://www.meredith.edu

Meredith College's beautiful 225-acre campus is located on the edge of North Carolina's capital city near urban activity and eleven other colleges and universities.

MERRIMACK COLLEGE

NORTH ANDOVER, MASSACHUSETTS

The College

Founded by the Order of St. Augustine in 1947, Merrimack College is recognized as a superior Catholic coeducational institution of higher learning. The 2,100 undergraduates come from more than twenty-nine states and more than thirty-two countries. The College is located just north of Boston in the suburban towns of Andover and North Andover, Massachusetts. Merrimack is a small college of liberal arts and professions; however, it is its size, personalized academic and social environment, and campus location that attract many students. Eighty-five percent of the students reside on campus in the College's residence facilities, town houses, or apartment-style housing. The College strives to provide continued growth in its academic, professional, and support services. These services include Academic Support Services; the Faculty Advisement Program; a Career Services and Cooperative Education Office, which provides students with career development and job placement; the Counseling and Health Offices; the Campus Ministry Office, which is involved with social-action projects through its Merrimaction Corps; and the Student Activities Office. A writing center, a math resource center, and a science help center offer students additional assistance in academic areas.

The College offers a full calendar of academic, cultural, ecumenical, athletic, and social activities. The Student Government Association sponsors a film series and hosts leading musical artists and prominent lecturers on campus. Students also may participate in the On-Stagers, one of the College's more than fifty cocurricular activities; join a sorority or fraternity; or become involved in the many class-sponsored events. The College also has a student newspaper and a chorus. Athletic programs are offered at both the intercollegiate and intramural levels. As a member of the Hockey East Conference, NCAA, and Northeast Ten Conference, Merrimack has varsity teams in eight sports for men and eight sports for women. The S. Peter Volpe Physical Education Center has exercise rooms, squash and racquetball courts, a 3,600-seat hockey rink, and a 1,700-seat gymnasium for basketball. Outdoor facilities include athletic fields and eight tennis courts.

Location

Merrimack College is located in northeastern Massachusetts, 25 miles north of Boston. From campus, it's a 35-minute drive to the city of Boston, ocean beaches, or outlet shopping. Two hours north are the Lakes Region and White Mountains of New Hampshire. Cape Cod is two hours south. New York City is a four-hour drive. The area provides a wealth of interesting historical sites, cultural opportunities, and recreational pursuits.

The 220-acre campus offers a beautiful New England setting. The College has recently opened new residences. The Rogers Center for the Arts is a 600-seat, state-of-the-art auditorium and art gallery. Most recently, the Sakowich Campus Center opened with new dining areas, study lounges, and resident life and student activities offices. A multipurpose gymnasium, an indoor running track, and weight and aerobic rooms also enhance this center of student life.

Majors and Degrees

Merrimack College awards the B.A. and B.S. degrees through both day and evening programs, as well as the A.A. and A.S. degrees within the Division of Continuing Education. In addition, numerous certificate programs are offered through the Corporate Education Office. Bachelor of Arts degree programs in the liberal arts include communication, digital media art, economics, English, fine arts, French, history, philosophy, political science, psychology, religious studies, Romance languages, self-designed major, sociology, and Spanish. Teacher certification is available for elementary, middle, and secondary education.

Students in the sciences or engineering may attain the Bachelor of Arts degree in biology and mathematics and the Bachelor of Science degree in biochemistry, chemistry, civil engineering, computer science, electrical engineering, environmental science, health science, physics, and sports medicine.

Bachelor of Science degrees are offered in business administration with academic concentrations in accounting, finance, information technology, international business, management and organization studies, management operations, and marketing.

Merrimack College also awards a Master of Education (M.Ed.) in elementary education. The M.Ed. program offers both standard and advanced provisional certification for elementary teachers.

The Division of Continuing Education offers programs leading to either the associate or the bachelor's degree in accounting, computer and information sciences, human services administration, liberal arts, and management. The associate degree only may be earned in engineering science and the ministry. The bachelor's degree only may be earned in electrical engineering.

Academic Program

It is the mission of Merrimack College to provide students, in a Christian values-sensitive environment, the opportunity to develop a mature intellectual, cultural, social, emotional, and moral awareness. The College seeks to provide sound professional training with a commitment to an integrated liberal arts component in all courses of study.

The Merrimack College academic calendar consists of two 15-week semesters, beginning in early September and mid-January. Summer sessions are also available.

To receive a bachelor's degree, all students must complete forty semester courses with a final quality point average of 2.0 or better. Students usually take five academic courses each semester. All bachelor's degree programs revolve around a fifteen-course liberal arts core curriculum. The remaining semester courses in a student's program, following completion of core, major, and cognate requirements, are open electives. The liberal arts core curriculum consists of courses in religious studies and philosophy, humanities, the social sciences, and mathematics and science.

Merrimack College also offers interdisciplinary courses, study-abroad programs, and internships through the departments of English, history, management, political science, psychology, and sociology. Special academic programs include a double major in the Division of Arts and Sciences; a contract Bachelor of Arts or Bachelor of Science degree, consisting of a special interdepartmental program in two or more fields; and a double-degree program, usually involving five years, through which the student earns two bachelor's degrees (B.A. and B.S.).

Off-Campus Programs

Cooperative education (work-study) provides paid work experiences and may be elected by students majoring in biology, all business programs, chemistry, civil engineering, computer science, electrical and computer engineering, health sciences, math, physics, and select liberal arts. Internships are available and provide students with another avenue of hands-on experiential learning. The Stevens Learning Center provides students the opportunity to learn and develop through active participation in organized service at volunteer community sites while enrolled in traditional course work. While pursuing a full course load, students may immerse themselves in the history and culture of another country and study abroad for a year, semester, or summer. The classes taken abroad are approved for transfer credit and serve as part of the student's academic program.

Academic Facilities

The McQuade Library's book collection now stands at more than 130,000 volumes, and more than 900 journals are received, with access to the Noble Database, a source of more than seventy Boston libraries. The library offers a computerized catalog, circulation, and acquisition system. It provides 450 private study carrels, seminar rooms for small classes and group study, and a collection of tapes and records in audio rooms for either private or group listening. The library also houses Alumni Hall, a 200-seat auditorium that is used for film shows and lectures, and an art gallery, in which artwork by faculty members, students, and local artists is displayed. The Information Technology Center, which features a Digital Equipment Corporation VAXcluster, is located in McQuade Library. It accommodates multiple languages, including BASIC-Plus, FORTRAN, COBOL, APL, Pascal, C, Ada, MODULA-2, and LISP. The center is also equipped with microcomputers, Digital Equipment Corporation Gigi graphics terminals, and CRTs. The microcomputers can be used as stand-alone systems or as devices to access the VAX system. A group of twenty-five Macintosh personal computers are available to students for word processing. The Girard School of Business offers smart classrooms that are completely wired for Internet access; computer labs; and a technology auditorium with videoconferencing capabilities. The Gregor Johann Mendel, O.S.A., Center for Science, Engineering and Technology provides students with state-of-the-art laboratory equipment and facilities.

Costs

Tuition for the 2003–04 academic year was $20,625; room and board $8800. These costs were exclusive of books, supplies, travel, and personal expenses.

Financial Aid

Merrimack College sponsors financial aid through federally and state funded grants, loans, and work-study awards. Merrimack also provides scholarships and campus employment from College operating funds. To be eligible for any scholarship or financial aid program, an applicant must file the Free Application for Federal Student Aid (FAFSA) by February 15. Students who receive scholarships or other financial aid through Merrimack College are notified between March 15 and April 30. Currently, 75 percent of all Merrimack students receive scholarships and financial assistance through federal, state, and College funds.

Faculty

The Merrimack faculty is committed to the academic and personal growth of undergraduate students. There are 144 full-time faculty members, of whom more than 75 percent hold a Ph.D. degree. The faculty-student ratio is 1:14. Faculty interaction with students, through small classes and the availability of teachers, is a hallmark of the College. Faculty members also participate in a Student-Faculty Advisement Program to provide for students' individual academic guidance; they also serve on many College-wide academic and student affairs committees.

Student Government

The Student Government Association has a twofold purpose. This democratic body represents all students' rights by concerning itself with all policy matters that affect the student body and by serving as a primary liaison between students and the administration. The association also conducts and coordinates a varied program of social and cultural events for the College community.

Admission Requirements

Merrimack College seeks academically prepared students who are eager to improve themselves intellectually and socially within the College community. The Admission Committee considers each applicant on an individual basis and evaluates a candidate's strengths in light of personal accomplishments, motivation, and the academic major selected. The Admission Committee places primary emphasis on the secondary school record (courses selected and rank in class), SAT I or ACT scores, and teacher or guidance counselor recommendations. Applicants are encouraged, but not required, to visit the campus for an interview. The Admission Committee does not discriminate against applicants on the basis of race, sex, religion, or national origin; in fact, the College welcomes diversity among students. Applicants must have earned the following high school units: 4 years of college-preparatory English, 2 years of social studies, 3 years of mathematics (including algebra II), 2 years of science, and 5 electives. Applicants for the sciences or engineering programs, however, are expected to have at least 4 years of mathematics and 3 years of science (including physics for engineering) but need have only 3 electives.

Merrimack offers early action and deferred admission to properly qualified applicants. Merrimack also gives credit and advanced placement for scores of 3 or better on the Advanced Placement examinations sponsored by the College Board in certain academic areas.

Transfer applicants for the fall or spring semester should be in good academic standing at the institution last attended, not be on academic or disciplinary probation at that institution, and have a quality point average of at least 2.5 on the Merrimack College scale.

International applicants must also submit the results of the Test of English as a Foreign Language (TOEFL) or the English Language Proficiency Test (ELPT).

Application and Information

Early-action candidates applying for entrance for the fall term should apply by November 30. Regular-decision candidates should apply by February 15. All applications for the spring term should be made by December 1. Merrimack College adheres to the NACAC deposit deadline of May 1.

For more information, students should contact:

Office of Admission
Merrimack College
North Andover, Massachusetts 01845
Telephone: 978-837-5100
Fax: 978-837-5133
E-mail: admission@merrimack.edu
World Wide Web: http://www.merrimack.edu

MESSIAH COLLEGE

GRANTHAM, PENNSYLVANIA

The College

Messiah College is a place where students' minds are strengthened in unison with their character, where there is no separation between intellectual and spiritual life, and where students can make the connection between what they think and what they believe. At Messiah College, students are encouraged to engage both their heads and their hearts to pursue a higher education and discover a higher calling.

A coeducational Christian college of the liberal and applied arts and sciences, Messiah College takes its mission seriously: to educate men and women toward maturity of intellect, character, and Christian faith to prepare them for lives of service, leadership, and reconciliation in church and society. More than 2,900 students from thirty-eight states, thirty-four countries, and more than fifty denominations choose to take on the rigors of academic pursuit while strengthening their faith and putting it into action.

Alumni and faculty members include a Rhodes Scholar, a Marshall Scholar, and several Fulbright Fellowship and award recipients. In addition, Messiah has been listed for more than ten consecutive years on the Templeton Foundation's "Honor Roll of Character-Building Colleges."

At Messiah College, more than 90 percent of students live on campus, creating a vibrant community life and lasting friendships. More than sixty extracurricular activities, from national honor societies to special interest clubs to service and outreach teams, allow students the opportunity to enhance their classroom experiences and hone their leadership and team skills. In fact, in a recent year, students volunteered more than 88,000 hours in service and mission projects. Student government, the yearbook, the student-run weekly newspaper, the College radio station, theatrical productions, traveling musical groups, Habitat for Humanity, and residence hall activities are among the many opportunities offered by Messiah College for students to get involved.

Messiah encourages fitness for the body, mind, and spirit, offering active club and recreational sports programs as well as fielding twenty intercollegiate sports teams: ten for men and ten for women. Several of the NCAA Division III teams attain national rankings each year. In 2000 and 2002, the men's soccer team won the national championship. In 2002, the women's soccer and women's field hockey teams were national finalists. *USA Today* not only recognized the College for the success of its teams on the field, but also ranked Messiah fifth in the country for its high graduation rate of student athletes in Division III. Top-notch athletics facilities include a competition-size indoor pool, a diving pool, two gymnasiums, an artificial-turf field hockey field, a weight-training center, exercise machines, a human-performance laboratory, competition tennis courts, a demonstration tennis court, and an indoor track as well as an expansive soccer stadium, manicured baseball and softball diamonds, a high ropes course, a fitness trail, and an outdoor track and field stadium.

Location

Located just 12 miles southwest of the state capital, Harrisburg, Messiah College's beautiful, 400-acre campus provides an ideal setting for outdoor recreation with easy access to urban centers such as Baltimore, Philadelphia, and Washington, D.C. Students enjoy picnics and canoeing on the Yellow Breeches Creek that passes through campus. The thriving suburban environment of central Pennsylvania affords students the opportunity to participate in the cultural, internship, and service options provided by the state capital and other major East Coast urban hubs.

Majors and Degrees

Messiah College awards both Bachelor of Arts and Bachelor of Science degrees in more than fifty majors: accounting; art education; art history; athletic training; Bible; biochemistry; biology; broadcasting, telecommunications, and mass media; business administration; business information systems; chemistry; Christian ministries; communication; computer science; early childhood education (N–3); economics; elementary education (K–6); e-marketing; engineering; English; entrepreneurship; environmental science; family studies; French; German; health and physical education (K–12); history; humanities; human development and family science; human resource management; international business; journalism; marketing; mathematics; music; nursing; nutrition and dietetics; philosophy; politics; psychology; recreation; religion; social work; sociology; Spanish; Spanish business; sport and exercise science; studio art; theater; and therapeutic recreation. Individualized majors are also available.

Students may also pursue teaching certification in biology (7–12) and environmental education (K–12); chemistry, English, history, and mathematics (7–12); and French, German, and Spanish (K–12). Preprofessional programs of study include dentistry, law, medicine, physical therapy, and veterinary science.

In addition, students may choose from more than fifty different minors that include coaching, criminal justice, horticulture, peacemaking, and urban studies.

Academic Program

Messiah's unique approach to academics combines a solid liberal arts foundation with study in one or more academic major. In addition to courses required in their major, students complete required general courses in writing, the sciences, the arts, language and culture, Christian faith, and physical education as well as electives to broaden their understanding and skills; 126 credits are required to graduate.

The College's academic year consists of two semesters, fall and spring, with a monthlong January term offering concentrated study in a single course or numerous cross-cultural trips to expand horizons. The College Honors Program, independent study, service learning, and internships enrich students' academic studies.

U.S. News & World Report has repeatedly ranked Messiah College among the top ten best colleges in the Northern Comprehensive Colleges–Bachelor's category. But more importantly, Messiah's approach allows students to seek top-quality higher education to equip them for a higher calling. Ninety-nine percent of Messiah graduates are employed full-time, attending graduate school, or in voluntary service within six months of graduation.

Off-Campus Programs

Through the College's EpiCenter (experiential learning center), Messiah students have many opportunities for off-campus study. In fact, the *Open Doors Report* ranked Messiah sixth among the nation's undergraduate institutions in sending to students to study abroad.

In addition to a satellite campus in conjunction with Temple University in Philadelphia, students may also study in the following semester-long programs: American Studies Program (Washington, D.C.), AuSable Institute of Environmental Studies (Michigan), Central American Study and Service, China Studies Program, Global Stewardship Study Program, Jerusalem University College, Latin American Studies Program (Costa Rica), Los Angeles Film Studies Center, Oxford Semester (England), Russian Studies Program, Middle East Studies Program, Oregon Extension, and International Business Institute (Europe and Russia).

Messiah students may also participate in the Brethren Colleges Abroad program in locations such as China, Ecuador, England, France, Germany, Japan, and Spain. The College also participates in a student-faculty exchange with Daystar University College in Kenya. Annual cross-cultural study tours to locales including the

Bahamas, Greece, Guatemala, and Israel provide additional educational opportunities during January or summer terms.

Academic Facilities

Messiah College is committed to providing modern academic facilities with state-of-the-art technology and equipment for students in all fields of study. In addition to a 300,000-volume library with access to information, literature, and publications from around the globe, academic buildings include a new science center; a renovated and expanded nursing hall; a hall of engineering, mathematics, and business; a fine arts center; and a sports center, all constructed or renovated within the last twenty years. Two new facilities opened in the fall of 2003: a 95,000-square-foot academic building and a 35,000-square-foot student union. More than 500 computers in various academic and residence hall labs are connected to a campuswide network, along with fully wired residence hall rooms, enabling students to have access to research and important communication.

Costs

Tuition and fees for 2003-04 totaled $19,496 and room and board averaged $6340. Book costs are approximately $740, travel costs are approximately $580, and personal expenses cost roughly $1100.

Financial Aid

Keeping a Messiah education affordable for all students who desire it continues to be a high priority for the College. Tuition, room, and board costs remain competitive, ranking below about 75 percent of comparable four-year, private colleges in Pennsylvania. Financial aid counselors help students and families find available resources and create aid packages designed to meet needs. In addition to federal and state grants and loans and on-campus employment programs, Messiah students benefit from about $15 million in institutional merit scholarships and need-based aid. About 94 percent of Messiah students receive financial aid, with the average annual award per recipient (from all sources of aid) being nearly $14,000. Students should apply for institutional aid by the March 1 deadline for the following fall semester.

The College also offers both a semester and a monthly payment plan, allowing students and their families to choose the payment option most suitable to their needs.

Faculty

Professors, not teaching assistants, teach all classes at Messiah College. Representing nearly 150 graduate schools in five countries as well as a variety of denominational affiliations, more than 70 percent of the professors have earned the terminal degree in their field. While Messiah's faculty members are serious scholars who pursue original research, present findings, and publish widely, they are first and foremost committed to teaching. Chosen for their scholarship, Christian commitment, and teaching ability, Messiah's 158 full-time and more than 100 part-time faculty members lead by example, encouraging students to dig deeper, seek truth, pursue academic excellence, and grow in all areas of their lives. A low student-faculty ratio of 13:1 enables professors and students to forge close relationships while learning from each other.

Student Government

The self-governing Messiah College Student Government Association (SGA) is the vital force behind many campus activities. SGA also provides student services such as outreach opportunities, social events, and book sales. Encouraging trial by peers rather than the College administration, the student judicial council hears cases of rule violations on a regular basis. Messiah also values student input for critical College decisions, inviting student representatives to sit on almost every standing and ad hoc committee on the campus.

Admission Requirements

Messiah College seeks student applicants who are serious about their intellectual, spiritual, and personal development—those who strive to excel in many areas of their life and who will make a contribution to the campus community. Transfer, international, and ethnic minority students are welcome and encouraged to apply.

Selective in its admissions policy, the College examines academic achievement, extracurricular involvement, leadership skills, and Christian service. Thirty-five percent of last year's freshman class ranked in the top 10 percent of their high school class; 18 percent ranked in the top 5 percent. Sixty were valedictorians or salutatorians, 10 were National Merit Scholars, and 150 had SAT I scores of more than 1300 or ACT scores of more than 28.

Applicants should have taken at least 4 years of English, 3 years of mathematics, 2 years each of science and social studies, and 6 electives, preferably 2 in a foreign language. A large majority of students accepted at Messiah College exceed these minimum requirements. Students should take the SAT I or the ACT by January of their senior year in high school. Two recommendations are required. Students are invited to attend on-campus information sessions and tours.

Application and Information

Messiah College makes admissions decisions on the following dates: Early Decision, October 15; Early Action, November 15 and January 15; regular admission, February 15 and rolling thereafter. The Admissions Office is open from 8 to 5 on weekdays. For more information, to arrange a campus tour and an interview, or to request a catalog and application, students should contact:

Admissions Office
Messiah College
Box 3005
One College Avenue
Grantham, Pennsylvania 17027
Telephone: 717-691-6000
800-233-4220 (toll-free)
Fax: 717-796-5374
E-mail: admiss@messiah.edu
World Wide Web: http://www.messiah.edu

The spacious Murray Library provides a wide variety of learning resources in an architecturally striking atmosphere.

MICHIGAN TECHNOLOGICAL UNIVERSITY

MichiganTech

HOUGHTON, MICHIGAN

The University

Founded in 1885 as the Michigan Mining School, Michigan Technological University (MTU) has become famous for educational excellence in engineering, the sciences, forestry, computing, communication, and business. A total of 6,600 students from all fifty states and more than eighty nations enjoy beautiful Upper Michigan while pursuing associate's, bachelor's, master's, and Ph.D. degrees. Michigan Tech is rated among the nation's top 50 public national universities and top 100 doctoral universities in the 2004 *U.S. News and World Report's* "America's Best Colleges."

Current construction constantly improves the campus and includes a new computer science hall and library addition. Most importantly, Michigan Tech continues to expand its academic offerings. Recently, systems and network administration degrees were added, and students from many majors work together on real-world industry projects as part of the Enterprise program, from wireless to snowmobiles to alternative fuels.

More than 56 percent of students are enrolled in the College of Engineering, with the College of Sciences and Arts accounting for 20 percent; Graduate School, 12 percent; the School of Business and Economics, 6.7 percent; the School of Technology, 6 percent; the School of Forest Resources and Environmental Science, 3 percent; and distance education or other, 7 percent.

Michigan Tech has one of the nation's largest programs in technical communication and has top ten programs in enrollment in environmental, mechanical, and geological engineering.

Michigan Tech is accredited by the North Central Association of Colleges and Schools. Engineering programs are accredited by the Engineering Accreditation Commission of the Accreditation Board for Engineering and Technology (ABET), technology programs are accredited the Technology Accreditation Commission of ABET; and the surveying program is accredited by the Related Accreditation Commission of ABET. The forestry program is accredited by the Society of American Foresters, the chemistry program offers American Chemical Society–approved options, and the secondary teacher certification programs are approved by the Michigan Board of Education. The School of Business and Economics is accredited by AACSB International–The Association to Advance Collegiate Schools of Business, the premier business accrediting organization in the U.S. Only about 400 U.S. business programs (of 1,200 nationwide) have earned this distinction.

Michigan Tech's graduate programs continue to grow in stature. Enrollment is increasing while students gain access to the latest theories, equipment, and scholarship while working with faculty members who are acknowledged leaders in their fields.

Residence halls are close to classes and well connected. They feature T-1 Ethernet lines, and wireless zones abound. They also feature Finnish saunas (steam baths), their own cable TV system, lounges, and weightlifting and laundry facilities. First-year students must live in the residence halls, and they can from meal plans and numerous food options, choose the cafeterias in Wadsworth, McNair, or Douglass Houghton Halls. Some cafeterias are open later, especially during exams, and students can also eat, relax, and study at the Memorial Union, the center of campus life and home to many student organization offices. Guides to off-campus housing are also available.

In athletics, the hockey Huskies have been national champions three times and compete in the competitive NCAA Division I Western Collegiate Hockey Association. Football, men's and women's basketball, tennis, cross-country, track, and women's volleyball teams compete in the Division II Great Lakes Intercollegiate Athletic Conference against teams from Michigan, Wisconsin, Ohio, Pennsylvania, Indiana, and Illinois. The men's basketball team was rated the number one NCAA Division II team in the nation in during the 2002–03 season.

Most Michigan Tech students compete in intramural sports in everything from Ultimate Frisbee to wrestling to water polo. Club sports include lacrosse, women's hockey, and paintball.

Traditions include K-Day, which is an afternoon to enjoy McLain State Park on the shores of Lake Superior, the world's largest freshwater lake. The Parade of Nations is a celebration (including food) of all the nations of the world who have students and faculty and staff members at Michigan Tech. At Homecoming, students dress in their worst attire and parade through campus in autos that barely run. There's a football game, a Hobo Mixer, and various special events all weekend. At the Winter Carnival, massive snow statues emerge on campus and in the towns. Skits, queen competitions, first-class entertainment, and tourists everywhere make this a great event. Before hitting the books one more time for finals, students take a break on the campus mall for Spring Fling and celebrate with games, food booths, music, and more.

Location

Michigan Tech is situated on the Portage Waterway in the hills of Houghton in a safe, friendly environment, and the local area offers abundant opportunities for outdoor recreation, including the University's own ski hill; cross-country skiing, running, and biking trails; and a golf course. A waterfront jogging and biking trail cuts through campus.

Houghton is located about a 4-hours' drive time from Green Bay, 7 hours from Minneapolis, and 10 hours from Detroit. The Houghton County Memorial Airport (code CMX) has daily flights to Minneapolis that connect to other major cities and bus service to Houghton is also available.

Majors and Degrees

The School of Technology awards Associate in Applied Science degrees in civil engineering technology, electrical engineering technology, and electromechanical engineering technology. The College of Sciences and Arts awards a two-year associate degree in humanities.

The College of Engineering offers Bachelor of Science degrees in applied geophysics, biomedical engineering, chemical engineering, civil engineering, computer engineering, electrical engineering, engineering (mechanical design or manufacturing engineering), environmental engineering, geological engineering, geology, materials science and engineering, mechanical engineering, and software engineering.

The School of Business and Economics awards Bachelor of Science degrees in business administration with concentrations in accounting, finance, industrial marketing/management, and management information systems; and economics.

The School of Forest Resources and Environmental Science awards Bachelor of Science degrees in applied ecology and environmental sciences, and forestry. The School of Technology awards Bachelor of Science degrees in computer systems and network administration, engineering technology, and surveying.

The College of Sciences and Arts awards Bachelor of Science degrees in applied physics, bioinformatics, biological sciences, chemistry, clinical laboratory science, computer science, mathematics, physics, preprofessional programs (medicine, dentistry, pharmacy, and law), scientific and technical communication, and social sciences, and the Bachelor of Arts in scientific and technical communication and liberal arts.

Michigan Tech offers certificate programs in design engineering, industrial forestry, international business, media, mine environmental engineering, modern language and area study, an advanced certificate in modern language and area study, and writing.

Michigan Tech's minors are aerospace studies, American studies, art, astrophysics, biochemistry, biological sciences, chemistry, communication studies, computer science, earth sciences, ecology, economics, electronic materials, enterprise, environmental studies, ethics and philosophy, geological engineering, historical studies, international modern languages (French, German, or Spanish), international studies, journalism, mathematical sciences, microbiology, military arts and science, mining, modern languages (French, German, or Spanish), music, physics, plant biotechnology, plant sciences, psychology, remote sensing, state of Michigan secondary teacher certification, social and behavioral studies, speech presentation, structural materials, technical theater, theater arts, and engineered wood products.

Academic Program

Michigan Tech operates on a fall and spring semester system, and there are three options available for summer: two 5-week tracks and one 10-week track. Typically, it takes 128 credits to graduate, but the amount varies by department. Students must also complete the general education requirements, which seek to develop in each student fundamental scholastic habits of careful reading, communication, critical reasoning, balanced analysis and argument; the habit of applying multiple disciplinary perspectives in interpretation, analysis, and creative problem solving; respect for diversity and awareness of complex contexts of their study and their work; and knowledge of a broad range of topics and disciplines complementary to the major. Some graduate courses are open to undergraduates with faculty approval.

Off-Campus Programs

Distance education programs, focused on engineering, are offered through the Office of Extended University Programs. The Center for International Education helps international students adjust to life in Houghton and helps students study abroad in many different nations. The Career Center works with more than 200 industries, businesses, and organizations to help students find cooperative, internship, and summer employment opportunities. Co-op assignments earn academic credits; internships do not.

Academic Facilities

The J. R. Van Pelt Library contains more than 800,000 volumes and regularly receives approximately 10,000 serials and periodicals. The library is a designated depository for official international, U.S. government, and Michigan state documents, and for the U.S. Army Map Service. The archives maintain a collection of original materials concerning the history of the Keweenaw region, including the records of various copper mining companies. The Rozsa Center for the Performing Arts is within walking distance of all residence halls and features nationally renowned lecturers, musicians, comedians, and theatrical performers and Michigan Tech's own productions. The student-run newspaper, the *Lode*, has won national and state awards and the campus radio station, WMTU, allows students to be disc jockeys.

Costs

Tuition is $6810 for in-state and $17,700 for out-of-state students for an academic year; room and board are $5795. Required fees and computer fees total approximately $1000, and books and supplies total approximately $900.

Financial Aid

Currently, 84 percent of Michigan Tech's students receive financial aid. Four kinds of assistance are available to Michigan Tech students, including scholarships, which are awarded on the basis of student potential and, in some cases, financial need; grants, which are provided by the federal or state government or by MTU and do not need to be repaid; student loans, in which the interest charged is below regular interest rates and payment of the interest and principal on need-based loans does not begin until after students leave Michigan Tech; and part-time employment, which consists of on-campus student employment opportunities. The financial aid process begins with filing an application for admission. Students should apply for admission as soon as possible after September 1 preceding the academic year in which they plan to enroll.

Faculty

Most of the 424 undergraduate and graduate faculty members possess terminal degrees. Ninety-five percent of undergraduate classes are taught by faculty members, and the student-faculty ratio is 12:1. Faculty members balance teaching and research and have long been known for their student guidance.

Student Government

Undergraduate Student Government and the Graduate Student Council are the two agencies of student involvement in University governance. Fraternities and sororities maintain a large presence on campus, and there are more than 130 student organizations to choose from, including academic/professional, ethnic/cultural, service, religious, sporting, governmental, media, and honor societies. It is considered a great way for students to get involved and gain teamwork and leadership experience.

Admission Requirements

Michigan Tech has a selective admissions policy. The University admits only applicants who give definite evidence that they are qualified through education, academic fitness, aptitudes, interests, and character to complete the University's requirements. Once students are accepted for admission, every effort is made by the faculty and staff members to help students realize their potential.

Application and Information

To apply, students should complete the Michigan Tech application for admission any time after June 1 preceding the academic year for which they plan to enroll and include a $40 nonrefundable application fee (check or money order) made payable to Michigan Technological University. Freshmen should submit the application and fee to a high school counselor or principal. Transfer students should submit an application, official transcripts, and fee to the MTU Admissions Office. International students should contact the Center for International Education. Upon acceptance by MTU, students receive an acceptance packet containing, among other information, an acceptance letter, information regarding various University deadlines, and a request for the enrollment deposit of $100.

Admissions Office
Michigan Technological University
1400 Townsend Drive
Houghton, Michigan 49931-1295

Telephone: 888-MTU-1885 (toll-free)
E-mail mtu4u@mtu.edu
World Wide Web: http://www.mtu.edu/apply/

Overlooking the campus of Michigan Tech University.

MIDWAY COLLEGE

MIDWAY, KENTUCKY

The College

Midway College, Kentucky's only women's college, was established in 1847 as the Kentucky Female Orphan School to prepare financially disadvantaged women for teaching careers. Since 1988, Midway has served as an independent, residential four-year college that emphasizes career preparation based on a liberal arts background and is fully accredited by the Southern Association of Colleges and Schools.

An education at Midway is designed specifically to educate and empower women for achievement and leadership. The women's college offers twenty-eight baccalaureate degrees and four associate degree programs. Midway College is dedicated to providing a living and learning environment that enables students to assume roles of responsibility as contemporary women.

Learning at Midway is hands-on. Many of the College's programs require internships, which give students the opportunity to apply knowledge gained in the classroom in a professional setting. Experience gained at Midway is valuable when students begin their job searches after graduation.

Students continuously cite small, interactive classes and individualized faculty attention as their primary reasons for selecting Midway. Enrollment at Midway is approximately 800 traditional residential, commuter, and nontraditional students. Approximately twenty-five states and five other countries are represented in the College's student population.

Opportunity for involvement is one of the factors that makes an education at Midway such a rewarding experience. With various athletic teams, activities, clubs, and organizations at Midway, students have many opportunities to develop talents and leadership skills. The small-college atmosphere makes it easy for students to get involved in campus life or to assume leadership positions on campus.

Students can enjoy the competition and camaraderie that comes with participation in intercollegiate and intramural sports. A variety of athletic scholarships and grants are offered to talented young women in basketball, riding, soccer, softball, and tennis.

Location

Midway College is located in historic Midway (population 1,400) in the heart of scenic central Kentucky. Nestled among horse farms halfway between Lexington and Frankfort, the state capital, Midway is a picturesque, friendly community full of stately homes, restaurants, and antique and gift shops. Downtown Lexington is 15 minutes away and offers students many cultural and social opportunities, such as shopping, dining, movies, and theater. Louisville and Cincinnati are less than 80 miles away by interstate, and Lexington is served by major airlines through Bluegrass Field.

Majors and Degrees

Bachelor's degrees are available in biology, business administration, chemistry, English, environmental science, equine studies, liberal studies, mathematics, psychology, and teacher education. Areas of concentration include a liberal studies degree with concentrations in art studio, English, or music; an equine studies degree with concentrations in equine management, equitation instruction, or equine therapy; and a business administration degree with concentrations in accounting and equine business.

The College offers associate degrees in business administration, computer information systems, equine management, and nursing.

Academic Programs

The College calendar includes a fall and spring semester and a summer program. Midway College offers discussion and study groups, an Arts and Lecture Series, seminars, films, and chapel services to enrich the academic program of any student who wishes to participate. Students must complete requirements designed for a liberal knowledge of the major areas of learning in the humanities and arts, social and behavioral sciences, natural sciences, and mathematics. All incoming first-year students must enroll in a seminar entitled "College and Life Success Strategies for Women." Students may receive college credit or advanced course placement from the College-Level Examination Program (CLEP). Any student who wishes to receive credit from a CLEP or Advanced Placement (AP) examination should contact the Office of Student Development.

Off-Campus Programs

Qualified equine students at Midway may vary their studies and enrich their educational experience by studying abroad at prestigious Bishop Burton College or Hartpury College in England during their junior year. Bishop Burton specializes in show jumping, dressage, and combined training. Midway College is a member of the Kentucky Institute for International Studies, a consortium of colleges and universities that organizes and coordinates a group of summer and semester study-abroad programs for college students throughout the world.

Academic Facilities

Midway's 105-acre campus includes nine administrative, classroom, and residential buildings; an amphitheater; tennis courts; soccer and softball fields; and the Keeneland Equine Education Center, a 35,000-square-foot equine education complex with indoor and outdoor riding facilities and 50 acres for cross-country riding. Several of the College's Georgian-style buildings have been renovated in recent years.

The Little Memorial Library was completed in summer 1997. The state-of-the-art facility houses 72,000 volumes, 400 current periodicals, and 150 study stations and is home to the College computer center.

In October 2003, the $6-million Anne Hart Raymond Center for Mathematics, Science and Technology opened. The 44,420-square-foot structure contains eight laboratories, four classrooms, and five conference areas designed to stimulate teaching and learning. Large computer monitors, Internet access, and smart boards are just a few of the teaching aids featured in the new building.

Costs

Tuition for the 2004–05 academic year is $11,700. Room charges total $2800. Students have two board options; a nineteen-meal plan costs $2700, and a fifteen-meal plan costs $2600. Costs of books, travel, and personal expenses vary with each student.

Financial Aid

Families representing many income levels qualify for financial assistance at Midway. More than 90 percent of Midway students traditionally receive financial aid. In an effort to assist all families in budgeting their educational expenses, Midway offers a variety of payment plans, including a no-interest monthly payment plan.

Financial aid is available through scholarships, grants, loans, and campus work-study. Awards are based on scholarship potential, merit, and individual need. The size of each award may vary with need. Further information on special scholarships may be obtained from Midway's Office of Financial Aid.

Students seeking financial assistance at Midway College must complete the Free Application for Federal Student Aid (FAFSA). This form may be obtained from any high school guidance office or from the Office of Financial Aid at Midway College. The FAFSA should be filled out as soon as possible after filing taxes from the previous year. Forms completed by April 1 are given higher priority.

Faculty

Small classes guarantee personal attention from professors and create a comfortable environment for discussion and debate. Midway professors make every effort to help students succeed and graduate. Faculty members know their students well and work with them to ensure that their program of study meets their individual interests and career objectives.

Midway College faculty members come from a variety of graduate and professional schools, creating a well-rounded intellectual base for students. Approximately 70 percent of the baccalaureate and general education faculty members have a doctorate or terminal degree.

Student Government

Midway's Student Government Association (SGA) serves as an intermediary for the consideration of College issues that are of vital interest to students and faculty and staff members while developing principles of democratic self-government and encouraging and promoting cooperation between faculty, staff, administration, and students. All students enrolled at Midway College are members of the SGA. Elections are held throughout the year for representative positions. SGA meetings are held weekly, and student attendance is encouraged and welcomed.

Admission Requirements

Midway College considers the sum of a student's total experiences and achievements when considering admission. The College seeks students who have a strong academic background and varied talents, interests, and backgrounds. Every applicant is considered individually based on academic record, college entrance test scores, recommendations, interviews, and extracurricular background.

To apply, students should send a completed application, an official transcript and/or GED scores, and the results of her ACT or SAT I to the admissions office. Minimum admission requirements include graduation from an accredited high school with a minimum 2.2 grade point average (on a scale of 4.0) or satisfactory completion of the GED and an ACT composite score of 18 or its equivalent. Specific programs may have additional requirements. Applications are accepted on a rolling basis until the beginning of the fall and spring semesters.

Application and Information

Candidates for admission are encouraged to apply for admission at the end of their junior year or in the early part of their senior year. Students are encouraged to visit the College for a personal interview, a tour of the campus, and discussions with admissions staff members, faculty members, and students. The Office of Admissions is open Monday through Friday from 8 a.m. to 5 p.m. and by appointment on weekends and evenings. For more information or application materials or to arrange a campus visit, interested students should contact:

Director of Admissions
Midway College
512 East Stephens Street
Midway, Kentucky 40347-1120
Telephone: 800-755-0031 (toll-free)
Fax: 859-846-5787
E-mail: admissions@midway.edu
World Wide Web: http://www.midway.edu

Internationally known for equine studies, students at Midway College can concentrate on equine management, equitation instruction, equine therapy, or equine science (preveterinary).

MILLERSVILLE UNIVERSITY OF PENNSYLVANIA

MILLERSVILLE, PENNSYLVANIA

The University

Millersville University is a multifaceted public institution with a wide range of programs and a primary commitment to high-quality undergraduate instruction. Millersville's student body of approximately 7,600 is large enough for the University to offer a wide variety of programs. The University is small enough, however, to provide friendly service and individual attention. Students report that the relaxed, friendly campus atmosphere is one of the things they like best. The Millersville campus features a beautiful green and flowered landscape, a lake with two resident swans, and clean, well-maintained facilities.

Millersville University was established in 1855 as a normal school, the first one in Pennsylvania. It remained a teachers' college until 1962, when it was authorized to offer liberal arts degrees. It has been Millersville University of Pennsylvania since 1983.

The two reasons students most frequently cite for choosing Millersville are its excellent academic reputation and low tuition. The most popular majors are elementary education, business administration, biology, and psychology. Millersville's undergraduates are diverse; 1 in 8 students attends part-time, 1 in 10 is a member of a racial/ethnic minority, and 12 percent are more than 25 years old. Thirty-five percent of Millersville undergraduates are from Lancaster County, 60 percent from elsewhere in Pennsylvania, 4 percent from out of state, and 1 percent from other countries.

The University offers a wide range of intercollegiate varsity, intramural, and club sports; special interest clubs; and fraternities and sororities, to which 10 percent of undergraduates belong. A broad program of cultural events is offered, with alcohol-free nightclubs particularly popular.

Thirty-nine percent of undergraduates live in campus residence halls, with the rest commuting from home or living nearby. Women's and coed dormitories are provided. University-affiliated apartments are adjacent to campus. Noncommuting freshmen and sophomores are required to live on campus.

Special services provided for students include tutoring, academic advisement, career planning and placement, personal counseling, health services, wellness activities, child care, and special facilities for commuters.

Location

Millersville, in the heart of Pennsylvania Dutch country, is 3 miles from Lancaster, a growing metropolitan area. Lancaster County is an exceptionally friendly and beautiful area with a large number of stores, restaurants, theaters, parks, and tourist attractions. The campus is served by the area bus system, and Lancaster has train and air service.

Lancaster County is one of the fastest-growing counties in Pennsylvania and has one of the lowest unemployment rates in the state. The local economy is unusually sound and diverse. Sixty percent of Millersville graduates settle within the county.

Majors and Degrees

Millersville offers the Bachelor of Arts degree in anthropology, art, biology, chemistry, earth sciences, economics, English, French, geography, German, government and political affairs, history, international studies, mathematics, music, philosophy, physics, psychology, social work, sociology, and Spanish.

The Bachelor of Science degree is offered in biology, business administration, chemistry, communications and theater, computer science, earth sciences, geology, industrial technology, mathematics, meteorology, occupational safety and environmental health, oceanography, and physics.

The Bachelor of Science in Education degree with teaching certification is offered in art education, biology, chemistry, earth sciences, elementary education, English, French, German, mathematics, music education, physics, social studies, Spanish, special education, and technology education.

The University also offers the Bachelor of Fine Arts degree in art; the Bachelor of Science in Nursing degree; the Associate of Science degree in chemistry and in computer science; and the Associate of Technology degree in industrial technology.

Most majors offer several options that permit specialization. More than thirty minors are offered along with 3-2 engineering programs for chemistry and physics majors. Special advisement is available for students interested in premedicine and prelaw.

Academic Programs

Millersville University places a strong emphasis on the liberal arts. Half the courses required for all its undergraduate degrees, including those with technical or professional majors, are in the liberal arts. This prepares students for a lifetime of learning and gives them a background in writing, speaking, analysis, and critical thinking across a broad range of subjects.

Millersville's baccalaureate degree programs have four common curricular elements: proficiency requirements in English composition and speech; the general education program, which constitutes about half the curriculum; the major field of study; and elective courses if needed to meet the minimum of 120 credits required for graduation. Within this framework, students have many choices in developing programs of study.

The general education program has requirements in writing, speaking, humanities, natural sciences and mathematics, social sciences, and interdisciplinary and/or multicultural study. There is also a health and physical education requirement.

Millersville offers a University Honors College, departmental honors programs, independent study, a pass/fail option, remedial courses, and special advisement to students undecided about a major.

The University operates on a 4-1-4 academic calendar with summer sessions.

Off-Campus Programs

An exchange agreement with Franklin and Marshall College allows Millersville students to take Franklin and Marshall courses not offered at Millersville. Cooperative education internships are available to students in most majors, and some majors offer or require specialized internships. Millersville has study-abroad programs in Chile, England, Germany, Japan, Peru, Spain, and Scotland. Qualified students who wish to study abroad elsewhere may do so through cooperative arrangements with other colleges and universities.

Academic Facilities

Ganser Library houses more than 495,000 books and more than 558,000 other items and subscribes to more than 4,000 periodicals. Materials from other libraries are available through interlibrary loan. The library also houses computerized database-searching facilities, a curriculum center, a listening room, and archives.

Millersville's computing facilities include IBM and VAX mainframes and SUN Workstations. There are 450 terminals and microcomputers available, including IBM and Macintosh models. Users with their own microcomputers can access University mainframes through telephone lines. Access to the Internet is available for all faculty members and students.

Other University facilities include an extensive scientific instrumentation inventory, industry and technology laboratories, a variety of art studios, a large auditorium and a small theater, two gymnasiums and swimming pools, radio and television production facilities, and a language laboratory. The University's day-care center and prekindergarten provide field experiences in early childhood education.

Costs

Annual tuition and fees in 2003–04 were $5818 for Pennsylvania residents and $12,767 for out-of-state students. Annual room and board charges for 2003–04 were set at $5450. All students were expected to pay approximately $700 for books and incidentals.

Financial Aid

Approximately 67 percent of Millersville undergraduates receive financial aid through grants, scholarships, employment, and loans. Scholarships are available on the basis of academic performance. Federal Pell and Federal Supplemental Educational Opportunity grants and Pennsylvania Higher Education Assistance Agency (PHEAA) grants are awarded on the basis of need. Students may also qualify for Federal Perkins Loans and Federal Stafford Student Loans. On-campus and off-campus job opportunities are plentiful.

Students applying for a federal or state grant, Federal Work-Study, or a Federal Perkins Loan must complete the Free Application for Federal Student Aid, which is available from high school guidance offices or the Financial Aid Office. Deadlines are given in the forms' instructions.

Faculty

Millersville University faculty members are dedicated to teaching and to offering individual attention. They take a personal interest in their students' lives and careers and are solely responsible for providing academic advisement. The University keeps a relatively low student-faculty ratio of 18:1 and an average class size of 25. No classes are taught by graduate assistants. Ninety-two percent of the 325 full-time faculty members hold a doctorate or the terminal degree in their field.

Student Government

Millersville University students participate in University governance through the Student Senate, faculty-student committees, and representation on the Faculty Senate and the Council of Trustees. The Student Senate works with faculty members and the administration on major University policies.

The possession, use, or sale of alcoholic beverages and illegal drugs is prohibited on the University campus. Smoking is prohibited in all academic buildings on campus except for specifically designated areas. Freshmen and sophomores living on campus are not permitted to have motor vehicles.

Admission Requirements

Millersville University admits approximately half its applicants. More than 80 percent of its full-time freshmen rank in the top 40 percent of their high school class. Academic records are the most important factor in admission decisions. Applicants must have successfully completed at least 4 years of high school English, 3 years of social studies, 3 years of mathematics, 2 years of history, and 3 years of science (1 unit must be a lab). In addition, 2 years of foreign language and 1 additional year each of math and science are strongly recommended.

Because an important part of the college experience is meeting people with backgrounds and interests different from one's own, Millersville University is committed to recruiting a diversified student body. SAT I or ACT scores are required. Interviews, recommendations, and essays are not required. Out-of-state, international, and transfer applicants are welcome. Exceptional high school students may apply for early admission at the end of their junior year. Admitted applicants may defer their admission for one semester. Advanced standing is offered through CLEP and AP examinations.

Application and Information

To apply, students should submit a completed application form along with a $35 fee and official copies of the high school record and SAT I or ACT scores. The University has a rolling admission policy, and students are encouraged to apply early in their senior year for fall admission. Applicants are usually notified of a decision within a month after a completed application is received.

For application forms and additional information, students should contact:

Douglas Zander
Director of Admissions
Millersville University of Pennsylvania
P.O. Box 1002
Millersville, Pennsylvania 17551-0302
Telephone: 717-872-3371
800-MU-ADMIT (toll-free)
E-mail: admissions@millersville.edu
World Wide Web: http://www.millersville.edu

Millersville University's campus includes shaded lawns that invite students to study or relax with friends.

MILLIGAN COLLEGE

MILLIGAN COLLEGE, TENNESSEE

The College

Milligan College is a four-year private Christian liberal arts college in Northeast Tennessee. From its beginning in 1866, Milligan College integrates academic excellence with a Christian world view, and its mission is to educate men and women as Christian servant-leaders. A comprehensive humanities program and core curriculum is complemented by specialized training in more than twenty-five majors and several master's degrees. Christian perspectives are integrated throughout the curriculum and student life activities, as students are prepared intellectually and spiritually to change lives and shape culture.

Milligan's student body of 900 is from more than forty states and ten nations. Eighty percent of traditional students live on campus in one of six residence halls. More than twenty-five clubs and organizations provide opportunities to develop leadership skills. A wide variety of activities and campus events encourage social, cultural, and spiritual growth. Milligan College is affiliated with the Christian Churches/Churches of Christ, but the interdenominational student body is diverse.

Milligan is well recognized as an NAIA athletic powerhouse with a highly competitive athletic program in twelve varsity sports. Since 1995, Milligan has won more than sixteen conference titles and twelve national championship berths. Men's varsity teams include baseball, basketball, cross-country, golf, soccer, and tennis. Women's varsity teams include basketball, cross-country, soccer, softball, tennis, and volleyball.

Milligan is accredited by the Commission on Colleges of the Southern Association of Colleges and Schools (1866 Southern Lane, Decatur, Georgia 30033-4097; telephone: 404-679-4501) to award bachelor's and master's degrees. Milligan offers a Master of Education (M.Ed.) degree, a Master of Science in Occupational Therapy (M.S.O.T.) degree, and a Master of Business Administration (M.B.A.) degree. The M.Ed. and M.S.O.T. programs are nationally accredited by their professional organizations.

Milligan College is named among southern universities in *U.S. News & World Report*'s "America's Best Colleges" and is a member of the Council for Christian Colleges & Universities. More than 90 percent of its graduates are employed full-time, attending graduate school, or in voluntary service within six months after graduation, and more than 75 percent of premed students who take the MCAT are accepted to medical school.

Location

Milligan's 145-acre picturesque campus, which comprises more than twenty buildings of Georgian-Colonial architecture, is located in the beautiful mountains of northeastern Tennessee, just minutes from Johnson City and the dynamic Tri-Cities region. Students enjoy historical locations, theaters, parks, restaurants, and shops; explore the breathtaking Appalachian Mountains by hiking or camping in state parks near campus; visit local lakes and rivers for outdoor recreation; or ski the nearby North Carolina slopes. Because Milligan believes leadership is about service, students are encouraged to be active in the local community. Many are employed in internships or part-time work in area businesses.

Majors and Degrees

The Bachelor of Science, Bachelor of Arts, and Bachelor of Science in Nursing degrees are offered. Undergraduate majors include applied finance and accounting, Bible/ministry (children's ministry, missions, pastoral ministry, youth ministry), biology, business administration (accounting, economics, general, health-care administration, international business, legal studies, management, marketing), chemistry, communications (broadcasting, digital media studies, film studies, journalism, public relations/advertising), computer information systems, early childhood development, education (including professional teacher licensure areas, detailed below), English, fine arts (art, photography, theater), history, humanities, human performance and exercise science (exercise science, fitness and wellness, physical education), language arts, mathematics, music (applied study, fine arts, jazz studies), music education (vocal, instrumental), nursing, psychology, public leadership and service, and sociology. Professional teacher licensure areas include early childhood, K-12, middle grades, and secondary education. Preprofessional programs are available in dentistry, law, medicine, occupational therapy, optometry, pharmacy, and physical therapy. An adult degree completion program allows adults who have completed 60 or more semester hours of college credit to complete a business administration major in about eighteen months.

Academic Program

Milligan College offers students a liberal arts education taught from a perspective of God's activity with humanity. The College's strong core curriculum educates students toward the world in an open and constructive way. The candidate for the bachelor's degree must have completed a major and electives to total 128 semester hours of credit, with at least a 2.0 GPA. Core curriculum requirements include courses in humanities, the Bible, the social sciences, ethnic studies, laboratory science, speech communication, mathematics, and health/fitness.

Realizing that not all college-level learning occurs in a college classroom, Prior Learning Assessment programs provide a method by which other modes of learning can be evaluated for college credit. The Advanced Placement (AP) Program, the College-Level Examination Program (CLEP), and DANTES are available to all students interested in receiving college credit for studies or work experience already completed.

Milligan College operates on a semester system (August and January) with two 4-week summer sessions in June and July or one 8-week term. Also available are short-term classes during January term (one week before the onset of the spring semester) and May term (the weeks between the spring semester and the summer sessions).

Rising juniors are required to take a test covering general knowledge and graduating seniors are required to take a test to demonstrate knowledge in their major field of study.

Off-Campus Programs

Students can go beyond geographical and cultural boundaries and earn up to 16 hours of credit with Milligan's Study Abroad Program or with the many off-campus learning opportunities sponsored by the Council for Christian Colleges & Universities. These include an American Studies Program in Washington, D.C.; China Studies Program; Latin American Studies Program in Costa Rica; Contemporary Music Program near Martha's Vineyard; Los Angeles Film Studies Center; Honors Program and Summer Program in Oxford; Middle East Studies Program in Cairo; Russian Studies Program; and the Summer Institute of Journalism in Washington, D.C. Through an affiliation with the International Business Institute, business majors can earn college credit through an intensive ten-week summer program in Europe. Milligan also offers a four-week summer Humanities Tour in Europe, during which students explore the origins of Western civilization. In addition, internship opportunities offer students college credit and work experience in their field of interest.

Academic Facilities

A campuswide computer network system provides a high-speed data collection to the Internet in each residence hall room, office, and several computer labs. In addition to the more than 160,000 volumes in Milligan's library, students and faculty members have unlimited access to the holdings of four other local colleges through the Holston Associated Libraries (HAL), an interlibrary network on the Internet. Special collections within the library contain materials on the history of the College, the Restoration Movement, and the local area. The library also participates in resource-sharing agreements with Emmanuel School of Religion and East Tennessee State University. A Writing and Study Skills Center offers access to resources, instruction, and tutoring for academic success. Television and radio production studios and an FM radio station provide on-site training for communication students. A darkroom, a theater, and an art gallery feature works by fine arts students. Standardized laboratory facilities, including a gross anatomy lab, are available for general and advanced work in the sciences.

Recent on-campus projects include a $2.5-million renovation of the College's main classroom building and the addition of a new education center. As part of the College's Campaign for Christian Leadership, Milligan has also unveiled plans for a Campus Center, which should include a new theater, facilities for campus life, and a welcome center.

Costs

Tuition for 2003–04 was $14,750. Room and board were $4600. Additional fees were approximately $510. Typical annual miscellaneous costs (books, supplies, etc.) are approximately $1000 per year. As a private institution, Milligan supplements student fees with income from endowments and gifts from alumni, friends, and churches in order to keep tuition below the national average of similar four-year private institutions.

Financial Aid

Approximately 99 percent of all students at Milligan College receive federal, state, and/or institutional aid, including both academic scholarships and need-based grants. Each year, Milligan budgets more than $3.9 million in institutional scholarships, grants, and work-study programs. Financial assistance is allocated on the basis of need demonstrated by information supplied on the Free Application for Federal Student Aid (FAFSA), which should be completed by February 1 for priority consideration. Returning students must complete and submit a Milligan College Financial Aid Scholarship/Renewal Application. The Milligan College Office of Financial Aid begins mailing award letters between March 1 and March 15. The average aid package is approximately $13,100.

Faculty

More than 70 percent of Milligan's high-quality faculty members have earned the highest degree in their field from well-respected colleges and universities in the U.S. and abroad. Professors integrate Biblical truths into their classes and are active leaders both on and off campus. The low student-faculty ratio and small classes put the student at the center of attention and allow faculty members to cultivate special mentoring relationships with students. Professors serve as advisers to students from registration to graduation and are often instrumental in helping students find employment or gain admission to graduate school following graduation. Milligan's faculty members are mature and caring scholars who are committed to world-class scholarship, excellence in teaching, and their students.

Student Government

The Student Government Association (SGA) serves as the official representative voice of Milligan students and promotes academic, social, and spiritual activities for the campus community. SGA operates under a constitution approved and supported by the administration of the College, promotes well-ordered conduct among students, and enforces the regulations of the College. SGA leadership is provided by an executive council and representatives from throughout the campus. As a Christian college, Milligan adopts basic moral and social principles and expects students to serve Christ in an atmosphere of trust, encouragement, and respect for one another.

Admission Requirements

Character, ability, preparation, and seriousness of purpose are the qualities emphasized in considering applicants for acceptance to Milligan College. Overall excellence of performance in high school subjects as well as evidence of Christian commitment and academic potential provide the basis for admission to Milligan College. These qualities are evaluated by consideration of each applicant's academic record (based on transcripts), two personal references, ACT or SAT I scores, and participation in extracurricular activities. Some majors, such as music and theater, may require auditions and interviews. All applicants should have a high school diploma or equivalent and have completed a college-preparatory curriculum with course work in English, math, science, history and/or social sciences, foreign language, and some work in speech, music, or art in preparation for study in a liberal arts curriculum. Satisfactory scores on the ACT or SAT I are required of all applicants to the freshman class. The average ACT score for those enrolled is 23.8. Transfer students should have a grade point average of 2.5 or above and must follow the same application procedures as first-time students, with the addition of providing official transcripts of all previous college work. ACT or SAT I scores and high school transcripts are not required for transfer students with at least 24 earned semester hours.

Application and Information

Applications are processed on a rolling basis, and early application is encouraged. Notification is also given on a rolling basis. An application packet, complete with detailed instructions and requirements, can be obtained from the Admissions Office.

For further information, students should contact:

Admissions Office
Milligan College
P.O. Box 210
Milligan College, Tennessee 37682
Telephone: 423-461-8730
800-262-8337 (toll-free)
Fax: 423-461-8982
E-mail: admissions@milligan.edu (general)
visits@milligan.edu (for visits)
World Wide Web: http://www.milligan.edu

Milligan College is a Christian liberal arts college that unites humanities, sciences, and fine arts with a Christian worldview. It believes in encouraging the academic, spiritual, and personal growth of students so they can shape their futures successfully.

MILLS COLLEGE

OAKLAND, CALIFORNIA

The College

Mills is the only women's college among the many fine educational institutions in the San Francisco Bay Area. Founded in 1852 as the first women's college west of the Rockies, it is committed to remaining a women's college because it believes that such an environment offers women special advantages in preparing for new roles and responsibilities.

A small, liberal arts college, Mills enrolls more than 700 undergraduate women and 450 graduate women and men. The faculty is equally divided between women and men, and the ratio of students to faculty is approximately 10:1. The College has remained small because ideas and enthusiasm are more readily transmitted in a community of this size. Classes are normally small; 81 percent have 20 or fewer students. Faculty members observe each person's work closely, encouraging high performance and offering individual instruction when appropriate.

Although the College is a diverse community that serves many interests, it is built to a human scale. The 135-acre campus includes rolling meadows, peaceful woods, and a meandering creek. Mills is essentially a residential campus; 52 percent of its undergraduates live in four attractive residence halls, two small apartment buildings, and a co-op house. Undergraduate housing is guaranteed. Residence halls and classrooms are all within easy walking distance. The opportunities for discussion and discovery continue naturally outside the classroom: learning is at the center of everyday life. Conversations over dinner, in the residence halls, or during evening study in the library can sharpen and refine ideas that spring to life in a morning class. The Persis Coleman Organization and the Mary Atkins Organization provide a similar focus for commuting, older, and married students.

The student population offers many avenues for challenge and discovery. There is a variety of ethnic, national, economic, religious, and cultural backgrounds, which gives vitality and texture to campus life. Students come from forty states and twelve countries; 35 percent are women who are nonwhite, 3 percent are international students, and about 21 percent are women over 23 years old who are returning to college.

Academic, creative, and athletic abilities are cultivated and prized at Mills. Students participate in extensive intramural programs and six intercollegiate sports (crew, cross-country, soccer, swimming, tennis, and volleyball). Mills is a member of NCAA Division III. Athletic facilities include a well-equipped gymnasium, a sauna and weight room, outdoor tennis courts, a cross-country running trail, a soccer field, and the Trefethen Aquatic Center, which includes a state-of-the-art competition swimming pool. Other facilities include the Art Museum, a student center, restaurant, bookstore, and post office.

Location

The San Francisco Bay Area offers an exciting, cosmopolitan context for classroom work. Students may explore this larger "classroom" by taking internships with corporations and other organizations in San Francisco, Oakland, and elsewhere. They may also hike through the wild and beautiful East Bay parklands; enjoy symphonies, operas, theaters, and museums; or ski in the Sierras.

Majors and Degrees

The Mills curriculum includes more than thirty majors in the social sciences, English literature and creative writing, modern languages and cultures, the natural sciences, mathematics, and the fine arts. This breadth gives students chances to pursue interests outside their chosen academic fields as well as to test the waters of completely unfamiliar subjects.

Mills offers the Bachelor of Arts degree in American studies; anthropology and sociology; art (history and studio); biochemistry and molecular biology; biology; business economics; chemistry; child development (2); comparative literature; computer science; dance; economics; English (2); environmental science; environmental studies; ethnic studies; French studies; government; Hispanic studies; history; intermedia arts; international relations; liberal studies; mathematics; music; philosophy; political, legal, and economic analysis; psychology; public policy; sociology; and women's studies.

Students who choose to create their own major work with 2 faculty advisers to plan an individual program that draws courses from across the curriculum and knits them into a coherent whole.

Preparation for teaching and for California state teaching credentials is available at all levels, from nursery school to junior college. Special prelaw and premedicine advising is available.

Academic Programs

To earn a Mills B.A., students complete thirty-four semester courses (usually four courses each semester). Grading is traditional, and a pass-fail option is available outside the major.

The innovative general education program is guided by a set of learning outcomes, not a generic list of required courses. With the guidance of her faculty adviser, each student designs her own general education program, which ensures that her education is tailored to her specific needs and interests. The program places the work a student does in her major in a larger context, and ensures that she explores and appreciates realms of knowledge beyond her major. The general education requirements fall into three outcome categories: skills (written communication, quantitative and computational reasoning, and information literacy/information technology skills); perspectives (interdisciplinary, women and gender, and multicultural); and disciplines (creation and criticism in the arts, historical perspectives, natural sciences, and human institutions and behavior).

The Career Center offers a four-year counseling program to assist students in clarifying their career and life goals. Workshops, individual counseling sessions, an extensive internship program, a strong "old girl" alumnae network, and special opportunities to meet Bay Area business leaders and top professional women in every field all help students to focus their interests and plan career goals.

Off-Campus Programs

Mills has exchange or visiting programs with fifteen American colleges and universities: Agnes Scott, Barnard, Manhattanville, Mount Holyoke, Simmons, Spelman, Swarthmore, Wellesley, and Wheaton Colleges and Howard University. American University's Washington Semester program is available for qualified students.

Students with a spirit of adventure and a 3.0 GPA may participate in eleven study-abroad programs in Austria, England, France, Germany, Ireland, Israel, Italy, Japan, Scotland, Spain, and Wales.

Sophomores, juniors, and first-semester seniors may cross-register for one course per semester at the University of California at Berkeley, California College of the Arts, the

Graduate Theological Union, Holy Names College, and St. Mary's College of California, or they can pursue a subject as an independent study project under the supervision of a Mills professor who guides their work.

Academic Facilities

The beautiful, open-stack, computerized F. W. Olin Library attracts students to study as well as research among its 267,187 volumes and 22,000 rare books and manuscripts. A Web-based catalog and more than 80 databases, including Academic Search, LexisNexis, PsycInfo, and SocioFile are available 24 hours a day via the Library's Web site. The academic computer center (Mills was a women's college pioneer in computer study), electronic music studio, and excellent laboratory facilities in the physical and life sciences are widely used by students in all majors. The highly regarded Children's School provides a daily laboratory for students interested in early childhood education. Lisser Hall contains a flexible proscenium stage as well as a small experimental theater. The Art Museum is a wonderful resource with its collection of 6,000 works of art.

Costs

For 2003–04, tuition was $23,000, and room and board were $8930. Medical care, insurance, and Associated Student fees totaled $1441 for resident and commuting students. Students should calculate the costs of travel, books, and personal expenses on an individual basis.

Financial Aid

More than 80 percent of Mills students are awarded a financial aid package that includes a loan, campus work-study, and a scholarship grant from Mills, outside sources, or both. Awards are based on both need and academic merit. Scholarship grants range from $200 to full tuition per year. Mills makes a special effort to provide financial aid to members of minority groups who demonstrate need.

Almost 90 percent of Mills undergraduates who apply for financial aid are offered assistance. Financial aid applicants are expected to apply for assistance from appropriate outside sources, such as the National Merit Scholarship, Federal Pell Grant, and California State Grant programs. More than 40 percent of Mills students have some of their determined need offset by such outside awards. Loans may be obtained by most students, and 45 percent of undergraduates are offered campus work opportunities; some students take off-campus jobs.

All freshman and transfer candidates who are California residents must file the Free Application for Federal Student Aid (FAFSA) to be considered for all types of government aid and must also file the Cal Grant GPA Verification Form. Students who seek Mills scholarship funds must also file the Mills Financial Aid Form. Priority is given to applicants who meet the published deadlines.

Faculty

The Mills faculty is evenly divided between women and men and offers students the chance to work with professional women mentors in every academic area. Faculty members are selected for teaching ability and scholarly achievement; 95 percent of full-time faculty members hold the top degree in their fields.

Student Government

Student government plays a strong and active role in Mills life. Mills students establish the form of their own government and regulate all nonacademic aspects of their lives. The Honor System places the responsibility for upholding the social and academic standards of the College on the individual. Students serve as members of most faculty committees and also participate in curriculum planning.

Admission Requirements

Most freshmen admitted to Mills have a strong B average and have followed a full college-preparatory course in their secondary school, including English, 4 years; mathematics, 3 to 4 years; foreign languages, 2 to 4 years; social sciences, 2 to 4 years; and laboratory science, 2 to 4 years. Many have special talents or have taken course work in the fine arts. Mills is interested in individuals, not statistical averages, so each application is carefully reviewed. Credit for precollege courses is granted under certain conditions, and students are encouraged to take the College Board Advanced Placement tests. Applications from transfers are welcome, as are those from students resuming their education or older women who have delayed their entrance to college or who wish to continue work on the B.A. The SAT I requirement is waived if 24 or more transferable semester hours are presented. For international applications, both the SAT I and the TOEFL are required. Applications should be accompanied by transcripts, letters of recommendation, and SAT I/ACT test results. An interview, either on campus or with an alumna representative, is strongly recommended for all applicants.

Application and Information

The priority scholarship deadline for admission applications is February 1. All students are encouraged to meet this deadline; however, international students and merit scholarship applicants must apply by February 1. The regular decision deadline is March 1. Admission decisions are mailed approximately one month after the deadlines.

For admission to the spring term, the deadline is November 1.

For more information, students should contact:

Office of Admission
Mills College
5000 MacArthur Boulevard
Oakland, California 94613
Telephone: 510-430-2135
800-87-MILLS (toll-free)
Fax: 510-430-3314
E-mail: admission@mills.edu
World Wide Web: http://www.mills.edu

Mills students in front of Concert Hall.

MILWAUKEE SCHOOL OF ENGINEERING

MILWAUKEE, WISCONSIN

The School

Advancing beyond acquisition to the highly sophisticated application of knowledge has been the foundation of the Milwaukee School of Engineering's (MSOE) educational philosophy for more than 100 years. This approach, the university's educational niche, produces graduates who are fully prepared to begin their first jobs and pursue challenging careers. MSOE graduates start their careers as work-ready problem solvers and develop into leaders: creating new products, starting or heading companies, and working to better their communities. MSOE is governed by a Board of Regents of more than 50 members who are elected from leaders in business and industry nationwide who are members of the 200-member MSOE Corporation.

The student body of 2,600 men and women comes from throughout the United States and numerous countries. Since its founding, the university has encouraged the enrollment of students of any race, color, creed, or gender. Approximately half of the full-time students live in three high-rise residence halls.

Representatives from hundreds of firms from throughout the country, including representatives from Fortune 500 companies, visit MSOE during the academic year to interview graduating students for employment and to discuss career opportunities. The university had a 97 percent placement rate over the past five years.

MSOE's Counseling Services Office provides individual assistance for students with educational, personal, or vocational concerns. Free, on-campus tutoring is provided by the Learning Resource Center and Tau Omega Mu, an honorary fraternity founded in 1953 for the purpose of aiding students who need extra help with their studies.

The Student Life and Campus Center provides on-campus recreational activities. This facility houses student activity rooms, student organization offices, a TV viewing area, a marketplace eatery, and a game room. Additional recreation areas can be found in the residence halls and the MSOE Sports Center.

There are more than fifty professional societies, fraternities, and other special interest groups on campus. Many students participate in intramural sports programs. MSOE is a member of the National Collegiate Athletic Association (NCAA) Division III Lake Michigan Conference. The Athletic Department sponsors NCAA student teams in men's baseball, basketball, cross-country, golf, ice hockey, soccer, tennis, indoor and outdoor track and field, volleyball, and wrestling and women's basketball, cross-country, golf, soccer, softball, tennis, indoor and outdoor track and field, and volleyball that compete with teams from other private colleges and universities in the Midwest.

In addition to the undergraduate degree programs listed below, MSOE offers six Master of Science degree programs: engineering, engineering management (accelerated option available), environmental engineering, medical informatics (jointly offered with the Medical College of Wisconsin), perfusion, and structural engineering.

Milwaukee School of Engineering (MSOE) is a member of, and accredited by, the North Central Association of Colleges and Schools. Program-specific accrediting agencies are identified in the MSOE academic catalogs.

Location

The MSOE campus is located in the East Town section of downtown Milwaukee. Nearby are the Bradley Center, the Midwest Express Center, the Marcus Center for the Performing Arts, the theater district, churches of most denominations, major hotels and office buildings, restaurants, and department stores. Famous for its friendly atmosphere, Milwaukee offers students many opportunities for educational, cultural, and professional growth as well as ample employment opportunities. The metropolitan area has more than 15,000 acres of parks and river parkways and miles of bike trails. A few blocks east of the MSOE campus is Lake Michigan, a place of year-round natural beauty. MSOE also offers classes in several other locations in Wisconsin for students who wish to pursue select programs in the evening on a part-time basis.

Majors and Degrees

Four-year programs are offered that lead to Bachelor of Science degrees in business, construction management, engineering (architectural, biomedical, computer, electrical, industrial, mechanical, and software), engineering technology—transfer programs only (electrical and mechanical), international business, management, management information systems, and nursing. A Bachelor of Science or Bachelor of Arts degree is offered in technical communication. A five-year, double-major option is available in a combination of engineering, business, construction management, and technical communication programs. An engineering/environmental engineering dual degree (B.S./M.S. combination) is also available. An RN to B.S.N. program is available through the MSOE School of Nursing. International study opportunities also exist.

Academic Program

MSOE guarantees graduation in four years for full-time undergraduate students who start on track as freshmen, follow the prescribed curriculum, and meet graduation requirements.

The degree programs at MSOE combine study in degree specialty courses with basic study in sciences, communication, mathematics, and humanities in a high-technology, applications-oriented atmosphere. Students who are admitted with advanced credit to a program leading to a bachelor's degree must complete at least 50 percent of the curriculum in residence at MSOE. MSOE operates on a quarter system. Students average between 16 and 19 credits per quarter, which represent a combination of lecture and laboratory courses. Undergraduate students average 600 hours of laboratory experience.

MSOE offers students the opportunity to participate in the Air Force Reserve Officer Training Corps (AFROTC) program, the Army ROTC program, or the Navy ROTC program, which are offered in conjunction with Marquette University.

Academic Facilities

The Fred Loock Engineering Center adjoins the Allen-Bradley Hall of Science, forming a prime technical education and applied research complex. The Walter Schroeder Library houses more than 60,000 volumes, with collections that represent the specialized curricula of the university. Electronic technology enables the library to connect with libraries, government agencies, and other sources of information throughout the world. Full-time freshmen are required to participate in a Technology Package program that includes a notebook computer and affiliated services. A full range of software is available on these systems and via the local area network linked by a fiber-optic ring around the campus. State-of-the-art electrical, mechanical, industrial, and nursing laboratories complement the respective areas of study. The Rader School of Business has recently moved into a new facility, Rosenberg Hall, with computer technology integrated throughout. The Applied Technology Center™ (ATC) utilizes faculty and student expertise to solve technological problems confronting business and industry. The ATC is heavily involved in the transferring of new technologies into real business practice through the Rapid Prototyping Center (MSOE is the only university in the world to possess the five leading rapid prototyping technologies), Fluid Power Institute™, Photonics and Applied Optics Center, Construction Science and Engineering Center, and the Center for BioMolecular Modeling.

There are more laboratories than classrooms at MSOE, many with industrial sponsorship from such companies as Johnson Controls, Harley-Davidson, Rockwell Automation/Allen-Bradley, Master Lock, Snap-On, General Electric, and Outboard Marine Corporation. The key to the Rapid Prototyping Center's success is a high level of industrial parts design and fabrication activity using stereolithography, laminated-object manufacturing, and fused deposition modeling systems.

Costs

For 2004–05, tuition is $23,034 per year (same as 2003–04) plus $1140 for the Technology Package (notebook computer, software, insurance, maintenance, Internet access, and user services). The cost of room and board in the residence halls is approximately $5610 per year. Books and supplies average $400 per quarter but may be somewhat higher the first quarter.

Financial Aid

Qualified students are assisted by a comprehensive financial aid program, including MSOE and industry-supported scholarships, student loans, and part-time employment; Federal Perkins Loan, Federal Stafford Student Loan, Federal Work-Study, Federal Pell Grant, and Federal Supplemental Educational Opportunity Grant Programs; and state-supported grant programs. Students can also visit MSOE's Web site (listed at the end of this description) for a financial aid estimate.

Faculty

There are more than 200 men and women on the MSOE faculty (full-time and part-time). Many are registered professional engineers, architects, and nurses in Wisconsin and other states. They and their colleagues in nontechnical academic areas are active in related professional societies. The student-faculty ratio is 11:1. MSOE does not utilize teaching assistants.

Student Government

The MSOE Student Government Association (SGA) represents clubs and fraternities as well as residence halls and commuting students. SGA appoints representatives to the Campus Security and Disciplinary Hearing committees and the Alumni Association's Board of Directors.

Admission Requirements

Each applicant to MSOE is reviewed individually on the basis of his or her potential for success as determined by academic preparation. Admission may be gained by submitting an application for admission and the appropriate transcripts. High school students are encouraged to complete math through precalculus (including algebra and geometry), chemistry, biology (nursing), physics, and 4 years of English. All entering freshmen are also required to provide results from the ACT or the SAT.

Transfer opportunities exist into the junior year of the Bachelor of Science in electrical engineering technology, management, mechanical engineering technology, and technical communication programs with the appropriate associate degree or equivalent credits.

Application and Information

Classes start in September, November, March, and late May. Freshman and transfer students may enter at the beginning of any quarter; however, entry in the fall quarter is recommended. An application for admission may be obtained by contacting the address below or by visiting MSOE's Web site listed below. Applicants are encouraged to visit MSOE and have a preadmission counseling interview. Transfer students are required to submit transcripts from all prior institutions attended. An applicant's prior course work is reviewed to determine eligibility for admission. Required course work varies depending on the desired course of study.

Admission Office
Milwaukee School of Engineering
1025 North Broadway
Milwaukee, Wisconsin 53202-3109
Telephone: 414-277-6763
800-332-6763 (toll-free)
E-mail: explore@msoe.edu
World Wide Web: http://www.msoe.edu

MSOE's undergraduate students average 600 hours of laboratory experience—just one more advantage to an MSOE education.

MINNEAPOLIS COLLEGE OF ART AND DESIGN

MINNEAPOLIS, MINNESOTA

The College

The 117-year-old Minneapolis College of Art and Design (MCAD), along with The Minneapolis Institute of Arts and the Children's Theatre Company, occupies three square blocks in a residential neighborhood just south of the downtown district. The three institutions constitute one of the largest art centers in the nation.

There are currently 615 students enrolled in degree programs. The College maintains furnished apartments in modern residences on campus, which can accommodate approximately 265 students (35 percent of the entire student population).

In addition to its regular academic program, the College offers art-related films, lectures, and conferences through the Continuing Studies Office and community education courses online, in the evening, and on Saturdays.

The MCAD Gallery hosts national and regional exhibitions during the academic year, providing students and the general public with an excellent opportunity to view the work of important contemporary artists and designers. As part of a visiting artists program, nationally prominent artists, designers, and critics visit the campus for varying periods of time to teach, lecture, and work with students and faculty members.

Although there are a variety of campus social events each year, students who apply to the College should be aware that its standards of professionalism and performance demand a significant commitment.

In addition to its undergraduate programs, the Minneapolis College of Art and Design offers a Master of Fine Arts degree in visual studies and a postbaccalaureate program.

Location

Minneapolis and St. Paul have a combined population of more than 2 million. The Twin Cities are rich in arts cultural resources, which include the Guthrie Theatre, the Walker Art Center, the Minnesota Orchestra, the Hennepin Center for the Arts, and the University of Minnesota. The area has major-league sports teams in baseball, basketball, and football. There are beautiful city lakes, bike paths, ski slopes, and city and state parks.

Majors and Degrees

The Minneapolis College of Art and Design offers the Bachelor of Science degree in visualization and the Bachelor of Fine Arts degree with majors in advertising design, animation, comic art, drawing, filmmaking, fine arts studio, furniture design, graphic design, illustration, interactive media, painting, photography, printmaking, and sculpture.

Academic Programs

The B.F.A. program requires students to complete 120 semester credits. Eighteen of these are in the first-year Foundation Studies program, 39 are in the liberal arts department, and 63 are in the studio. To facilitate the growth of the perception and judgment necessary for meaningful creative endeavor, the College has developed a curriculum that stresses critical thinking, artistic inquiry, professional responsibility, and interdisciplinary dialogue. The goals of the first-year Foundation Studies program are to develop a student's ability to integrate verbal and visual communication skills and enhance personal expression while preparing for the major areas of study. Course work within the various majors provides students with a solid foundation in craftsmanship and offers both technical and conceptual information. All students are encouraged to expand their interests and technical abilities in other disciplines through elective courses. Complementing work in the studio courses, the liberal arts department offers study in history, criticism, literature, philosophy, religion, and the social and behavioral sciences.

In order to be awarded the B.S. degree, students are required to complete 120 semester credits, 36 of which concentrate in courses relating to visualization (e.g., communication theory and marketing: history, strategies, forms, and perceptions; media analysis; hypermedia) and 18 of which are taken within MCAD's studio offerings. Students are also required to participate in team-based projects, an externship or study-abroad program, and a senior project/exhibit. This degree program offers course work in visual persuasion and information techniques applicable to the fields of advertising/marketing, science/technology, entertainment, education, and corporate communications.

Off-Campus Programs

Professional internships, independent study, and externships are coordinated by MCAD Career Services. Mobility programs with other colleges in the Association of Independent Colleges of Art and Design, the four art colleges in Canada, Osaka University of Arts, and Macalester College allow students to take advantage of academic offerings at other institutions while pursuing a degree at the College. The College offers study-abroad opportunities in Denmark, England, France, Germany, Ireland, Italy, Japan, Mexico, and Scotland. MCAD also offers a New York studio semester program. In addition, a Student-at-Large Program permits students who are not pursuing a degree to enroll in day classes on a space-available basis.

Academic Facilities

The College's main building features a remarkable flexible architectural plan of more than 200,000 square feet that integrates studios, lecture-critique rooms, auditoriums, offices, a Media Center, and exhibition spaces. Personal, individual student workspaces are available to all students upon completing their foundation requirements. The College's nine computer labs, with more than 145 stations, offer a variety of software and hardware that support all academic areas with state-of-the-art equipment. Computers are connected to the Internet, which provides public information and e-mail access. The College library contains 50,000 volumes with emphasis on the visual arts; an extensive picture file; a collection of more than 130,000 slides; an audiocassette, videocassette, and CD-ROM collection; and periodical files. The Minneapolis Institute of Arts, a major American museum, and the Children's Theatre, an internationally acclaimed professional theater, are located adjacent to the College campus.

Costs

Tuition for full-time students in 2004–05 is $23,550 ($785 per credit). Art supplies and books average $1750, and housing is approximately $4090. Students should allow about $600 for personal expenses and about $300 for transportation locally.

Financial Aid

More than 87 percent of the College student body receive financial aid to meet education costs. Financial aid administered by the College comes from federal, state, and private sources and includes Federal Pell Grants, Federal Stafford Student Loans, Federal Supplemental Educational Opportunity Grants, Federal Perkins Loans, and Minnesota State Scholarships and Grants-in-Aid. College-controlled aid includes a variety of College grants, scholarships, and work-study contracts. Aid from private sources is also available. To qualify, applicants must submit the Free Application for Federal Student Aid (FAFSA).

Faculty

The College has a faculty of 108 working professional artists and designers (38 full-time, 70 part-time and/or adjunct). Seventy percent of full-time faculty members have earned terminal degrees. Members of the fine arts and media arts faculty generally have their own studios and exhibit works locally, nationally, and internationally. Members of the design faculty have professional responsibilities apart from their teaching, as many of them are employed by corporations, agencies, and design firms. The faculty-student ratio of 1:15 and the small size of the student body support excellent communication and rapport among students and faculty members.

Student Government

MCAD's student government includes a chairperson, a secretary, a treasurer, and the student representatives elected to the regular College standing committees. The government meets officially each week in open forum and sponsors a variety of activities and organizations, including membership passes to the Walker Art Center, film series, and social activities.

Admission Requirements

Admission to the College is based on a student's previous academic performance, creative abilities, and degree of personal motivation. All applicants for the B.F.A. and B.S. must have graduated from an accredited public or private secondary school or have received a certificate of equivalence. To apply for admission, every candidate must submit a completed application form, the application fee, and letters of recommendation. B.F.A. applicants are also required to submit a portfolio of creative work. SAT or ACT scores are also required. A B.F.A. applicant who has had art-related courses should submit one letter from an art instructor. An applicant who has had no art-related courses should submit a letter from an instructor in a different academic area or from a counselor. All freshman applicants who are applying for the first time must submit a high school transcript. Transfer applicants must submit high school and college transcripts. High school transcripts are not required for applicants who have received a four-year undergraduate degree. Portfolios are required of all B.F.A. transfer applicants desiring studio credit transferal.

Recognizing the value of a truly pluralistic academic community, the College strives to attract qualified men and women from all cultural, racial, religious, and economic backgrounds, from this country and abroad.

Application and Information

For a College catalog and an application form, students should write to the following address:

William Mullen, Director of Admissions
Admissions Office
Minneapolis College of Art and Design
2501 Stevens Avenue South
Minneapolis, Minnesota 55404
Telephone: 612-874-3760
800-874-6223 (toll-free)
Fax: 612-874-3701
E-mail: admissions@mcad.edu
World Wide Web: http://www.mcad.edu/

Facilities are among the best, featuring more than 200,000 square feet of classroom, studio, exhibition, 3-D, computing, auditorium, media arts lab, and academic support spaces.

MISSISSIPPI COLLEGE

CLINTON, MISSISSIPPI

The College

Founded in 1826, Mississippi College is a Christian college affiliated with the Mississippi Baptist Convention. The oldest college in the state, Mississippi College was the first private institution to grant a degree to a woman and the first to offer courses in chemistry. Mississippi College has been selected for six consecutive years by the Templeton Foundation as one of the country's top 100 character-building colleges. It is not the College's affiliation with a church that makes it a Christian institution; rather, it is the conviction of its administration, faculty, staff, and student body that they serve the greater society as part of the church's mission, including worship, evangelizing, ministry, missions, fellowship, and discipleship, that makes it a Christian center of higher education.

Mississippi College's academic programs are offered through six different academic schools: the School of Business; the School of Christian Studies, Communication, and Fine Arts; the School of Education; the School of Science and Mathematics; the School of Humanities and Social Sciences; and the School of Nursing. Each of the majors offered through these schools includes a balance of study in the humanities and sciences.

Location

Mississippi College is located in the town of Clinton, Mississippi, 20 miles from Jackson. A low cost of living, abundant housing opportunities on and off campus, and one of the nation's lowest crime rates make Clinton an ideal setting for students looking for a quieter college experience. Clinton has numerous parks and athletic fields for a variety of sports, a community recreation center, numerous houses of worship, and an outstanding educational system. Outdoor enthusiasts enjoy the miles of nature trails for hiking, while history buffs enjoy the historical landmarks that dot the town.

Majors and Degrees

The School of Business offers bachelor's degrees in accounting, business administration, business education, and marketing.

The School of Christian Studies, Communication, and Fine Arts offers bachelor's degrees in the following majors: art, Christian studies, church music, communication, education, general art, graphic design, interior design, music composition, music education, organ, piano, and voice.

The School of Education offers bachelor's degrees in elementary education, fitness management, physical education, psychology, secondary education, sports management, and sports medicine.

The School of Science and Mathematics offers bachelor's degrees in the following majors: biochemistry, biological sciences, biology education, chemical physics, chemistry, computer science, computing and information, computer science education, engineering, mathematics, mathematics education, and physics.

The School of Humanities and Social Sciences offers bachelor's degrees in American studies, criminal justice, English, foreign languages and international trade, French, French/Spanish education, history, modern languages, paralegal studies, political science, social science, social studies education, social work, sociology, and Spanish.

The School of Nursing offers a Bachelor of Science in Nursing (B.S.N.) degree.

Academic Programs

Mississippi College offers more than eighty undergraduate degrees and nearly twenty graduate degrees during its spring and fall semesters, along with optional summer sessions. Approximately 2,500 undergraduate and 1,000 graduate students attend Mississippi College, including the Graduate School and the School of Law, which are located in Jackson, Mississippi.

Off-Campus Programs

Mississippi College's study-abroad programs are designed to allow students to enhance their insights into the culture, history, economic systems, and politics of the host country; to engage in formal structured academic course work; to earn academic credit for that effort; and to develop their academic competence, maturity, self-confidence, and career qualifications to expand the horizon of cultural understanding and tolerance. The following study-abroad programs are available: British Summer Study Program, French Exchange Program, French Summer Program, Mainz Exchange Program, Holy Land Trip, Hong Kong Baptist University, London Semester Program, Nursing Mission Trip, Salzburg College, and University of Alicante, Spain.

Academic Facilities

In addition to the latest in software and hardware located in computer labs throughout the campus, Mississippi College has three libraries supporting its curriculum and degree programs: Leland Speed Library, Roger Hendrick Learning Resources Center, and the Law School Library. All faculty and staff members and currently enrolled students of Mississippi College have full borrowing privileges at each of these facilities.

Costs

Tuition and fees for the 2003–04 academic year were as follows: tuition, $10,880 (students taking more than 19 credits were charged $345 per credit); student publications and service fee, $168; fixed fee, $438; room, $2396 (the private room rate is two times the regular rate); new residence hall rate, $2830; and meals, $2566.

Financial Aid

More than 90 percent of students receive some form of financial aid. Work-study programs are available, allowing students to work up to 20 hours per week on campus. More than $22.5 million is awarded to students annually in institutional scholarships.

Faculty

Mississippi College employs 180 full-time faculty members plus highly qualified adjunct professors. A high percentage of the faculty members hold earned doctorates, and more than 50 percent of those who teach undergraduates also teach graduate courses. With a student-faculty ratio of 15:1, students and professors are able to cultivate relationships that extend outside the four walls of the classroom.

Student Government

Every undergraduate student has membership in and is represented by the Student Government Association (SGA). All students participate in the election of its officers each year. Composed of executive, legislative, and judicial branches, the SGA promotes student welfare, continues to foster College traditions and customs, and trains students in the principles of a democratic government. The SGA cooperates with the College's administration to enforce College regulations and appropriate conduct among its students.

Admission Requirements

Admission decisions are made by the Director of Admissions or the Dean of Enrollment Services. Admission is based on the high school or transferring university record, the essay, and ACT or SAT scores. Mississippi College selects students whose academic preparation and personal characteristics indicate they would contribute positively to the College environment and gain academically, socially, and spiritually from attending this institution.

Completed applications must be returned to the Office of Enrollment Services by August 15 for the fall semester and between September 15 and January 1 for the spring semester. Early application is encouraged because decisions regarding admission are made on a rolling basis as applications are received.

Applicants must have documented evidence of having had the MMR vaccine within the last ten years or evidence of having had two immunizations if they were born on or after January 1, 1957.

Application and Information

A nonrefundable $25 application fee, a completed application form, an essay, SAT or ACT scores, and a transcript from each high school or university attended must be submitted by the application deadline. For more information, students should contact:

Office of Enrollment Services
Mississippi College
Box 4026
Clinton, Mississippi 39058
Telephone: 601-925-3318
E-mail: admissions@mc.edu
World Wide Web: http://mc.edu

MISSOURI SOUTHERN STATE UNIVERSITY

JOPLIN, MISSOURI

The University

Missouri Southern State University is a four-year institution that features a liberal arts education with an international perspective. The University focuses on classroom teaching, resulting in a tradition of small classes and close, personal interaction between faculty members and approximately 5,600 students. This approach is maintained through an 18:1 student-teacher ratio. Southern's faculty members come from all over the world, with degrees from prestigious universities and professional experience in the disciplines they teach.

Southern stresses the development of independent learners and their ability to conceptualize, solve problems, manipulate thoughts and patterns, and work cooperatively. These elements, coupled with an international emphasis, enable Southern's graduates to compete successfully in the rapidly changing world. This international emphasis, a distinctive theme of the University's mission, is the focus of the Institute of International Studies, which coordinates all international programs and activities, including a pervasive global dimension in all curricula, study-abroad opportunities for faculty members and students, internships abroad for students, and expanded foreign language offerings.

A wide range of extracurricular activities, designed to support the academic experience and develop leadership abilities, is available for both resident and commuter students. More than 100 organizations, including departmental groups, Greek fraternities and sororities, religious and professional organizations, and honor societies, invite involvement and camaraderie. Also available are music and theater performance activities and many other opportunities. Varsity athletes in sixteen men's and women's sports compete in NCAA Division II. Athletic facilities include a multipurpose 80,000-square-foot athletic center with comfortable chair-back seating for approximately 3,500. The facility features a six-lane, 200-meter indoor track and is home to the Missouri Southern men's and women's basketball teams, who play on the arena's parquet floor. Other facilities include a new sprint turf stadium with an all-weather running track, a swimming pool, racquetball courts, and lighted tennis courts and softball and soccer fields.

The 600 students who live on campus enjoy air-conditioned residence halls. The Student Life Center offers a cafeteria, an aerobics room, a weight/exercise room, laundry facilities, a computer lab, a video game room, and a lounge with a big-screen television and surround sound.

Location

Missouri Southern's 341-acre campus is located in what has been known as the Crossroads of America. Two major cross-country highways intersect in Joplin—U.S. 71 north to south and I-44 east to west. This location allows easy access to major metropolitan cities around the Midwest. However, the University is also in ideal surroundings on the edge of the Ozarks, where recreational opportunities abound. The beautifully landscaped and extremely safe suburban campus rests on the edge of town within walking distance of the region's largest mall. Many movie theaters, restaurants, and athletic and cultural activities provide entertainment throughout the year. Students find employment in businesses throughout Joplin, which is Missouri's fourth-largest metropolitan region, and the surrounding communities. Area businesses also provide internships for students in a variety of disciplines and recruit graduates for permanent positions.

Majors and Degrees

Missouri Southern offers more than 100 degree options for the Bachelor of Science, Bachelor of Arts, Bachelor of Science in Business Administration, Bachelor of Science in Education, and Bachelor of General Studies. Also offered are a few Associate of Arts and Associate of Science degrees. Bachelor's degrees are awarded in accounting, art, athletic training, biology, chemistry, communications, computer-assisted manufacturing technology, computer information science, criminal justice administration, data processing, economics and finance, elementary education, English, environmental health technology, French, general business, German, health promotion and wellness, history, international business, international studies, management, management technology, marketing, mathematics, medical technology, music, nursing, paralegal studies, physical education, physics, political science, psychology, secondary education, social studies, sociology, Spanish, and theater. Associate degrees are awarded in accounting, computer-aided drafting and design, computer analysis, computer-assisted manufacturing technology, computer programming, dental hygiene, environmental health technology, law enforcement, pre-engineering studies, radiologic technology, and respiratory therapy. Certificate programs include basic police recruit studies, computer science and information systems, emergency medical technician studies, and EMT-paramedic studies. Preprofessional programs are offered in dentistry, engineering, law, medicine, optometry, pharmacy, and veterinary medicine.

Academic Program

Because graduates may change occupations and careers several times during their working lives, all students pursuing a degree complete the core curriculum, a series of courses carefully designed to instill certain lifelong thinking and learning skills. Core courses emphasize critical-thinking, problem-solving, and communications skills; a general understanding of scientific and artistic aspects of this culture; and the ability to function in a global society through knowledge and understanding of other cultures. In both the core and major studies, writing skills and computer literacy are developed, and an international perspective is stressed in every possible course. The baccalaureate degree requires 51 credit hours of the core and a total of 124 hours; the Associate of Arts degree requires 64 hours, with 42 hours from the core; and the Associate of Science degree requires 64 hours, with 26 hours from the core curriculum.

Many broad-based majors offer emphases that allow students a more specialized direction of study. A prestigious Honors Program provides special challenges and opportunities for qualified students who may receive full scholarships for their academic studies.

Off-Campus Programs

Study abroad is an integral part of the University's international approach to education. Three-week summer-study programs on various subjects are available at Oxford and Cambridge Universities in England to qualified students. Many other travel/study opportunities developed by departments last a week to a semester and include language studies, business practices, art, law enforcement, teacher education, and many other disciplines. A significant number of students receive financial assistance for these programs. In addition, students can pay Missouri Southern fees and study abroad for a semester or year at more than 100 colleges and universities throughout the world as part of the International Student Exchange Program (ISEP).

Academic Facilities

Students have access to the most modern facilities. More than $42 million in construction was completed in the last five years. New projects and facilities include a major expansion of the Spiva Library that doubled its size and wired it for the twenty-first century, an 80,000-square-foot athletic center, a new 250-seat black box theater, a major expansion of the Mills Anderson Justice Center, and an extensive refitting of the Ummel Technology Building.

Southern has a safe, modern, and beautifully landscaped campus. The George A. Spiva Library houses more than 238,000 books and 1,200 periodicals. A state and federal government documents collection, a law library, and a 584,000-item microform collection provide additional reference materials for student research. A world of materials and services are available through the library's link with a nationwide computer network of libraries. All functions of the library are automated, so students and professors can access library functions via modem. A vast array of resources is also available in CD-ROM format. State-of-the-art computer labs for student use are located in the library and throughout the campus.

Taylor Auditorium is a 2,000-seat facility equipped with state-of-the-art computerized sound and lighting systems. Theater students train and perform there, as do the University's music groups. Both Matthews Hall Auditorium and Mills Anderson Justice Center Auditorium have 300 seats and are equipped for multimedia presentations, films, and other events. Webster Hall Auditorium, which seats 400, provides performance space for small musical presentations, lectures, and satellite conferences. Webster Hall also has a variety of facilities that give students extraordinarily valuable experiences. Communications students have hands-on opportunities in the production studios of Missouri Southern Television, which broadcasts over the air and on cable. KXMS-FM broadcasts classical music to the region and around the world on the Internet, 24 hours a day.

Costs

Tuition for 2003–04 was $127 per credit hour for Missouri residents and $254 per credit hour for out-of-state students, the lowest in the state of Missouri. Residence halls cost $4000 per semester depending on the meal plan. An added cost-saving feature is the rental of textbooks for $6 per credit hour per semester.

Financial Aid

A wide variety of financial aid options assist students with college costs. More than $21 million is distributed each year to 80 percent of the students, with an average award of more than $3500. Federal programs include the Federal Pell Grant, Federal Supplemental Educational Opportunity Grant, Federal Work-Study Program, Federal Perkins Loan, and Federal Stafford Loan. Several state programs aid prospective teachers and students with high academic standing. In addition, the University provides a wide range of academic scholarships, performing awards, and student employment opportunities. Special scholarships are available for qualified junior college transfer students, and out-of-state tuition scholarships are offered to students in a designated surrounding area.

Faculty

The whole focus of Missouri Southern's faculty members is teaching and advising undergraduate students. With an 18:1 student-faculty ratio, close personal attention to the individual student's success is integral to the teaching process. Faculty members serve as personal advisers and mentors. Of the 197 full-time faculty members, 123 have doctoral or terminal degrees. Faculty members are actively involved in other campus activities as well as many community endeavors and encourage their students to participate in their communities.

Student Government

The Student Senate is the student governing body of the University. Senate members serve on various Faculty Senate committees as voting members, serve as liaisons with the University administration, and initiate new programs for the academic and cultural benefit of all students. The Campus Activities Board organizes social and cultural activities for the students.

Admission Requirements

Students are admitted to Missouri Southern if they are in the top 25 percent of their high school graduating class or have a minimum composite score of 21 on the ACT or a selection index score of 75. Students are strongly encouraged to complete a 16-unit high school core curriculum consisting of 4 units of English, 3 units each of math and social science, 2 units of science, 1 unit of visual/performing arts, and 3 units of additional core electives (2 years of foreign language is highly recommended). Students whose ACT scores and class rank are below those stated may request a review with the admission selection committee.

Application and Information

The University has a priority deadline of August 1. Students may apply any time during their senior year of high school. There is a $15 nonrefundable application fee. Information on specific academic areas and other University programs is readily available from the Admission Office and online.

Admission Office
Missouri Southern State University
3950 East Newman Road
Joplin, Missouri 64801-1595
Telephone: 417-782-6778
866-818-MSSU (6778) (toll-free)
Fax: 417-659-4429
E-mail: admissions@mssc.edu
World Wide Web: http://www.mssu.edu

MISSOURI TECH

SAINT LOUIS, MISSOURI

The College

Now primarily a college of computer technology, Missouri Tech has from its beginning specialized in educating students for technical professions. Determined to keep its offerings current, the faculty and staff have continually changed the college's programs to reflect technological developments. In 1932, Professor Charles J. Schwartz founded the college to teach what was then a new field of study—radio. During the 1940s television was added to the curriculum, and, during the 1980s, computer technology joined the subjects taught. Today Missouri Tech offers degree programs in information technology and networking, engineering management, and electronics, including instruction in programmable logical controllers. Students attend Missouri Tech because it provides hands-on training, offers tightly focused professional programs, hires highly qualified instructors with field experience, schedules small classes, and places graduates successfully in professional positions. Missouri Tech is a proprietary college with a student body of approximately 225, most of whom hail from Missouri, though some come from other states and countries. Enrollees include both traditional and nontraditional students. All live off campus, but the college sometimes arranges housing for students. Missouri Tech is accredited by the Accrediting Commission of Career Schools and Colleges of Technology.

Location

Missouri Tech is located in Creve Coeur, a suburb on the prosperous west side of Saint Louis. Situated less than 7 miles south of Lambert-Saint Louis International Airport, the college occupies a building in the Corporate Square Office Park, which is landscaped with lawns, trees, and a lake. The facilities include classrooms, a large computer lab, an activities room, a library, and administrative offices. Students can relax between classes on a deck overlooking the lake, where Canada geese often play.

The St. Louis metropolitan area offers many attractions. By the Mississippi River, the 630-feet-high Gateway Arch commemorates the city's historically significant role as the starting point for trips into the western frontier. The city still contains several historical neighborhoods and historical sites. Professional sports teams include the St. Louis Cardinals (baseball), Rams (football), and Blues (hockey). Among the area's cultural and entertainment organizations are the St. Louis Science Center, the Missouri Historical Society, the St. Louis Art Museum, the St. Louis Zoo, the St. Louis Symphony, the Missouri Botanical Garden, the Museum of Transportation, and the Six Flags amusement park. The city also offers an active night life and many excellent restaurants. The wooded and hilly countryside around the city contains several parks for outdoor recreation and appreciation of nature.

Majors and Degrees

Missouri Tech offers bachelor's degree programs in electronics engineering, engineering management, and software engineering; associate degree programs in electronics engineering, electronics engineering technology, information technology, network administration, and software engineering; and diploma programs in electronic service technician studies and network administration.

Academic Program

The college's programs are designed to prepare students for entry into technical professions, and they require few general education courses. Although each program has its own specific requirements, the shortest bachelor's program consists of 130 credit hours. Courses are taught in terms lasting eight weeks rather than the traditional fifteen or sixteen, providing an opportunity for students to begin an education every eight or nine weeks. Two terms constitute a semester, of which there are three per year.

In addition to providing students with knowledge, instructors try to develop students' problem-solving skills, recognizing that such skills are highly sought by employers. Instructors teach the basics of subjects and then assign hands-on projects that require students to find solutions. As they work on the projects, students develop the mental tools they need to solve a much broader array of technical problems. Missouri Tech instructors can present problems that are true to life, because they have tested their knowledge through first-hand experience. Instructors can also give plenty of personal attention, since the college has an exceptionally low overall student-teacher ratio of 12:1 and does not require instructors to publish.

The college's programs are built on the belief that students need confidence and motivation as well as a technical grounding in order to succeed professionally. Therefore, instructors encourage students to develop in the areas included in the five A's: Ambition, Attendance (responsibility), Academics, Attitude (engineering attitude), and Appearance (presence and confidence). The five A's converge to form the star that is Missouri Tech's logo.

Academic Facilities

Missouri Tech students find plenty of equipment for learning in the college's computer lab, which contains 100 workstations. Each workstation is connected as a client to the college's SQL server and operates under the Windows 2000 operating system. Visual Studio, which includes Visual C++ and Visual Basic; AutoCad; Visio; Publisher; FrontPage; Access; Excel; Word; and PowerPoint are installed on the lab computers. Electronics students may look forward to using circuit, hydraulics, programmable logic, and pneumatics trainers; logic analyzers; power meters; sweep generators; frequency counters; transistor checkers; curve tracers; L.C.R. bridges; signal generators; oscilloscopes; multimeters; component testers; logic probes; and simulators (depending on their course of study).

In the library, students can research technical and business topics or work on their homework. Students can also obtain books from other libraries with which Missouri Tech has made arrangements. In the computer lab, students can access the Internet to get information from sources all over the world. In addition, the Resource Library houses many computer programs, videotapes, and technical books that are available to students.

Costs

Tuition at Missouri Tech is $370 per credit hour, there is a lab/resource fee of $95 per term, and off-campus housing arranged through the college costs approximately $400 per month. The cost of books and supplies varies but averages approximately $200 per term for a student taking a full schedule of classes. Costs are subject to change.

Financial Aid

Financial assistance is available to students who are eligible. Missouri Tech participates in the Federal Pell Grant program, Federal Stafford Student Loan Program (subsidized and unsubsidized), and the Federal PLUS Program (loans to parents).

Believing that funding can be found for any person who sincerely wants an education, the Financial Assistance Department advises students about a variety of sources. Federal grants that do not require repayment are available to those who qualify. The U.S. Department of Education funds Pell Grants on the basis of financial need.

The college is approved by the Missouri Department of Veterans' Education, so United States citizens qualify for veterans' benefits, and Missouri residents qualify for state agency funds, such as Division of Vocational Rehabilitation and Job Training Partnership Act funds.

Missouri Tech can search nationally for other scholarships, as well, and advise students about corporate and institutional scholarships, company reimbursement, Non–Title IV Loans, College Aid Sources for Higher Education, and Veterans Administration, Division of Vocational Rehabilitation (DVR), and Job Training Partnership Act (JTPA) funds.

Faculty

At Missouri Tech, 85 percent of the classes are taught by full-time faculty members. The college employs 16 instructors, of whom 4 have earned Ph.D.'s and 4, master's degrees. The instructors' duties consist entirely of educating students, with the exception of 2 faculty members who have administrative responsibilities. All the instructors and the Director of Student Affairs are involved in advising students. The Dean of Education approves all student course schedules. The student-faculty student ratio is approximately 12:1.

Student Government

Students can voice their concerns collectively through their elected Student Council. Student Council members meet weekly with the administration to discuss problems and recommend solutions for the improvement of academic and student services. The college sponsors a chapter of the Instrumentation, Systems, and Automation Society (ISA) in which students are encouraged to participate.

Admission Requirements

Missouri Tech is open to qualified men and women regardless of religion, race, color, handicap, or national origin. The college encourages students who are interested in pursuing careers in computer technology, electronics, or engineering management to seek admission. Those who wish to apply should submit a completed application form, proof that they have graduated from high school or completed a GED, and the registration fee. Applicants must take and pass an entrance examination unless they have submitted an ACT score of 20 or better. In addition, applicants must complete an assessment instrument to determine their placement in courses. An on-campus admissions interview must be completed before the beginning of classes. Any applicant whose native language is not English must pass an English language proficiency test, such as the TOEFL, before enrolling.

Application and Information

Students can be enrolled as late as one week into each term, but prospective students ideally should apply at least one week before the beginning of classes. Students may apply online at the Web site listed below. Classes start every eight to nine weeks.

Application materials and further information can be obtained by contacting:

Bob Honaker
Missouri Tech
1167 Corporate Lake Drive
Saint Louis, Missouri 63132
Telephone: 314-569-3600
800-960-TECH (toll-free, Missouri only)
Fax: 314-569-1167
E-mail: b_honaker@motech.edu
World Wide Web: http://www.motech.edu

Missouri Tech.

MISSOURI VALLEY COLLEGE

MARSHALL, MISSOURI

The College

Missouri Valley College (MVC) is a private, coeducational, liberal arts college affiliated with the Presbyterian Church (U.S.A.). The College offers a rich tradition of personalized liberal arts education with a focus on career preparation. MVC is situated on 150 acres; its student body in 2004 is made up of 1,425 students from forty-three states and thirty countries. The College is committed to preparing young people to become active and contributing members of society.

Founded in 1889 by a group of Presbyterian and civic leaders in Marshall, Missouri, the College has been accredited by the North Central Association of Colleges and Schools since 1916. Missouri Valley College is approved by the Missouri State Department of Education and the Board of Christian Education of the Presbyterian Church (U.S.A.).

In addition to academic facilities, including the historic Baity Hall, the newly built Technology Center, Ferguson Center, and Collins Science Center, there are four men's dormitories, one women's dormitory, and numerous on-campus houses and apartments available for students. Built in 1991, the Burns Athletic Complex is recognized as one of the premier small-college facilities in the country. The building includes a full recreational area (basketball courts, indoor track, and other facilities) as well as classrooms, locker rooms, a concession area, the Missouri Valley College Athletic Hall of Fame trophy room, and seating to accommodate numerous events.

Missouri Valley College offers many opportunities to be involved on campus and within the community. The College is home to four nationally recognized fraternities and two nationally recognized sororities. The Greek system provides students with the opportunity to develop leadership skills, build career networks, and provide community service. Participants in Greek life also develop close bonds with fellow students through a variety of social activities.

Missouri Valley College competes in the NAIA as a member of the Heart of America Conference. Viking athletic programs include baseball (men), basketball (men and women), cheerleading (men and women), cross-country (men and women), football (men), golf (men and women), rodeo (men and women), soccer (men and women), softball (women), track (men and women), volleyball (men and women), and wrestling (men and women).

Location

Missouri Valley College is located in Marshall, Missouri, a town of about 13,000 residents. Marshall is 1 hour east of the Kansas City metropolitan area and 1 hour west of Columbia, Missouri.

Majors and Degrees

Missouri Valley College is divided into six academic divisions: Arts and Humanities, Business, Education, Human Services, Mathematics and Science, and Social Science.

The Arts and Humanities Division of Missouri Valley College offers Bachelor of Arts degrees in the areas of art, English, mass communication, philosophy and religion, speech communication, and theater. A Bachelor of Fine Arts degree in theater is also available. Courses in English as a second language, French, Latin, music, and Spanish are also offered, and dance, English, music, and theater minors are also available. The division collaborates with the Teacher Education Program to offer certification in English and speech/theater.

The College's Business Division offers Bachelor of Arts and Bachelor of Science degrees in accounting; business administration, with concentrations in agribusiness, finance, management, marketing, and small business development; and economics. The division also offers a two-year Associate of Arts degree in small business management. Students are encouraged to seek double majors within the division or in a complementary discipline, such as computer information systems. Minors are available in accounting, business administration, and economics.

Offered through the Division of Education and Physical Education, the Missouri Valley College Teacher Education Program is approved by the Missouri State Board of Education and accredited by the North Central Association of Colleges and Schools. MVC offers certification in the following areas: early childhood, elementary grades, middle school, secondary school, and special education cross-categorical. Missouri Valley Teacher Education Program graduates are well represented throughout the nation and have a 95 percent employment rate. MVC also has an athletic training major, and a physical education major is available with K–9, 9–12, and K–12 grade-level certifications.

The Human Services Division offers Bachelor of Arts degrees in human services/agency management and recreation administration. Students may apply for the specialized American Humanics Program, qualifying them to become certified American Humanics graduates. Academic courses stress the knowledge students need to become successful nonprofit youth agency administrators. American Humanics was founded at Missouri Valley College in 1948, and Missouri Valley College is the first institution to bring American Humanics into international light.

In the Mathematics and Science Division, Bachelor of Science degrees are obtainable in biology, computer information systems, and mathematics. MVC also offers a Bachelor of Arts degree in biology. Minors are available in biology, chemistry, and mathematics. The division collaborates with the Teacher Education Program to offer certification to teach science and mathematics.

The Social Science Division offers Bachelor of Arts and Bachelor of Science degrees in the following areas: alcohol and drug studies, criminal justice, history, political science/public administration, psychology, and sociology; a Bachelor of Science degree is offered in social studies education. A prelaw curriculum is an option for those interested in law school. Practicum and internship experiences are available, as are service learning and volunteer opportunities.

MVC also offers an Associate of Arts degree in liberal arts.

Academic Program

The academic program of Missouri Valley College has been formulated to promote the personal and professional development of every student. The program is intended to ensure the academic growth of the student within a framework of social, physical, and spiritual development.

The academic year consists of two semesters, with summer courses available. While the number of semester hours required for graduation varies with the program chosen, a minimum of 128 hours is required for a degree. A student must complete the required semester hours in a major as well as the basic requirements of the core curriculum. With an emphasis in liberal arts education, the core curriculum provides general education through approximately 40 hours of core classes.

Academic Facilities

The campus of Missouri Valley College has facilities that enhance the quality of the students' academic and social lives. The Technology Center provides students and instructors with classrooms, library space, and a computer lab equipped for the digital age. The new addition to the Technology Center hosts classrooms complete with wireless laptop computers, which have Internet access, and an instructor's station, where a professor can access everything from compact discs and DVDs to the Internet for sharing as part of a presentation. There is also a high-technology version of the old overhead projector that digitizes information and can even convert a three-dimensional object into a computer picture for sharing on the large screen at the front of the room.

Other major construction projects have included renovations of the old chapel on the upper floor of Baity Hall into the Learning Center, with computers and tutors available to students, and an extensive remodeling of Murrell Library.

The main library is located in the Murrell Memorial Library building, and the library annex is located in the Technology Center. This part of the library houses library collections that include art, business and economics, English, humanities, psychology, science and mathematics, and the social sciences. The Eckilson-Mabee Theatre also has been renovated into an extraordinary performance facility. The 274-seat theater is equipped with a Dolby 7.1 surround sound system, a high definition digital projection unit, and an ETC computerized lighting system.

Costs

Tuition and fees at Missouri Valley College for 2003–04 were $13,100 per year, and room and board averaged $5200. A nonrefundable deposit of $500 is required for resident students; a $250 deposit is required for commuter students.

Financial Aid

Financial need may be met through a combination of state, federal, and institutional aid, which is available to all qualified students. Institutional awards and grants are offered in many areas.

To be eligible for financial aid, a student must be admitted to the College. All students receiving federal or state-based program aid must file the Free Application for Federal Student Aid. New students need to file the financial aid application by the date of enrollment. International students are required to fill out a standard Affidavit of Support, in addition to their application for admission, to document their ability to pay their education expenses.

The College participates in the following federally sponsored aid programs: the Federal Pell Grant, Federal Supplemental Educational Opportunity Grant, Federal Work-Study Program, and subsidized and unsubsidized Federal Stafford Student Loan Programs. Missouri Student Grants are available to Missouri students carrying a minimum of 12 hours per semester who can prove financial need. Full-time resident students are able to defray a portion of their college costs by participating in the Missouri Valley College Work & Learn Program on campus. Generally, compensation for this work is credited toward the student's account.

A variety of scholarships are awarded to students who have excelled in fields of study, community activities, or athletic competition. Missouri Valley College's admissions counselors can advise prospective students of the full program of available scholarships.

Faculty

The total number of faculty members the College employs is 113, of whom 71 are full-time. The student-faculty ratio is 18:1, with more than 59 percent of the faculty members holding terminal degrees. The College prides itself on the good rapport and excellent personal relationships students and faculty members share.

Student Government

Students take an active leadership role in a wide variety of campus organizations and activities. Honorary, academic, athletic, and performance organizations and clubs, along with sororities and fraternities, contribute to the quality of student life at MVC. The Student Government Association (SGA), whose mission is to uphold and enhance all areas of student life on campus, also provides student leadership.

Admission Requirements

The College selects freshmen and transfer students who will benefit from the College's full-service program and who demonstrate the potential for academic success. Each application for admission is reviewed individually.

Students seeking admission to Missouri Valley College should earn at least a composite 18 on the ACT or a combined 860 on the SAT, be in the top half of their graduating class, and have at least a 2.0 GPA on a 4.0 scale. Students who do not meet these requirements are considered on a case-by-case basis.

Students should take the following steps to satisfy admission procedures: complete an application form and submit it in person or by mail to the Office of Admissions, along with a $10 nonrefundable application fee; provide the Office of Admissions an official high school transcript indicating graduation from high school (applicants may provide a copy of the General Educational Development (GED) certificate in lieu of transcripts); and provide a copy of the results of either the ACT or SAT. A student's high school counselor may assist in arranging for the test and obtaining the results. Students who have not taken the SAT or ACT by the time of their arrival on campus are contacted by the Office of Admissions and required to take the ACT during their first semester.

Students who wish to transfer from another institution, including those who have completed junior college work, should submit the following materials to ensure that their applications are processed promptly: the Missouri Valley College application for admission; a high school transcript or the recognized equivalent of a high school diploma; official transcripts of all previous collegiate work, including financial aid transcripts; and the ACT or SAT score (not necessary for students with more than 27 transfer hours). Students should provide a copy of the previous college's catalog to ensure proper credit transfer. If official transcripts are not received within a reasonable time, the student's academic and financial aid status may change.

Application and Information

An application and additional information can be obtained by contacting:

Office of Admissions
Missouri Valley College
500 East College Street
Marshall, Missouri 65340
Telephone: 660-831-4000 or 4114
E-mail: admissions@moval.edu
World Wide Web: http://www.moval.edu

Baity Hall, on the campus of Missouri Valley College.

MITCHELL COLLEGE

NEW LONDON, CONNECTICUT

The College

Mitchell is a private, coeducational four- and two-year residential college. With 800 full-time students and a 12:1 student-faculty ratio, the College provides a supportive student-centered learning environment that addresses the educational needs of all students, including those with learning disabilities. Mitchell is especially proud of its success in working with students who have yet to reach their full academic potential. To that end, the College maintains access for students with varied academic abilities who are highly motivated to succeed.

Mitchell's nationally recognized student support program, C.A.R.E.S. (Career Preparation, Academic Advisement, Retention, Education, and Support), includes extensive hands-on internship experiences; a First-Year Seminar helps students successfully make the transition to college; and career and transfer assistance helps students plan the next step in their learning adventure.

Nearly 90 percent of the full-time students live in three traditional residence halls, each housing 100 students. Each building has three floors with double rooms and common baths. The College also offers four historic Victorian and Colonial waterfront residence halls accommodating between 20 and 30 students each. Other facilities include a fully equipped gymnasium, a fitness center, athletic fields, a sailing dock, and indoor recreation areas.

Nearly all full-time students are of traditional college age, 18 to 22, and come from throughout the country and around the globe. Most students come from New England states, with about 60 percent from Connecticut, 30 percent from other New England states, and the remaining 10 percent from other states. International students and representatives of multicultural groups make up approximately 28 percent of the student population. About 150 part-time students, many of whom are adult commuters, enhance the classroom experience.

Clubs for students interested in biking, business, community service, choir, Hillel, music, the newspaper, the yearbook, skiing, multicultural affairs, psychology, and history bring together students with similar interests. Weekends are filled with guest comedians, bands, formal and casual dances, lectures, and organized trips to Boston and New York City.

Mitchell College is a member of the National Junior College Athletic Association and fields thirteen intercollegiate teams. Men play baseball, basketball, cross-country, lacrosse, and soccer; women play basketball, cross-country, soccer, softball, and volleyball; men and women compete together in cheerleading, golf, sailing, and tennis. The College has a history of athletic excellence, winning many national and New England championships. A full schedule of intramural sports is organized for students of all athletic experience and ability.

Location

New London, Connecticut, where Mitchell College makes its home, is a major center of activity in southeastern Connecticut, a region rich in historic significance. This small but sophisticated city, also home to Connecticut College and the U.S. Coast Guard Academy, is a maritime and resort center located midway between Boston and New York City on the main rail line.

The campus is situated in the city's most scenic residential section. Bordered by a long stretch of sandy beach, the campus consists of 65 acres of gently sloping hillside and forest. Places for shopping, banking, dining, and fun are within easy walking distance or can be accessed by buses that pass the College entrance. A major shopping mall, factory outlets, and fine and casual dining are minutes from the campus. The region is also home to major tourist attractions, such as the U.S.S. Nautilus and Submarine Museum, Mystic Marinelife Aquarium, Mystic Seaport, Olde Mystic Village, Ocean Beach Park, Stonington Vineyards, Foxwoods Resort and Casino, the Mohegan Sun Casino, and the Essex Steam Train.

Majors and Degrees

Baccalaureate degrees are offered in business administration, criminal justice, early childhood education, human development and family studies, liberal and professional studies, psychology, and sport management. Associate degrees are offered in athletic training, business administration–management, computer information systems, criminal justice, early childhood education, graphic design, human development, human services, liberal arts, marine science, physical education, and sport management.

Students undecided about their academic majors are enrolled in the Discovery Program, which is specially designed to provide special courses, additional advising, and services to explore their full potential and assistance in choosing a major.

Academic Program

The academic calendar consists of two full semesters that run from September to December and from January to May. A miniterm in January and five summer sessions are also offered.

All students must complete the core curriculum, which consists of expository writing, composition and literature, effective speaking, introduction to computer and information systems, an introductory psychology or sociology course, a mathematics course, a lab science, and either U.S. history I and II or Western civilization I and II.

If a student is having difficulty, it is recognized early. Mitchell grades at five-week intervals rather than just at midterms and finals. If a student is experiencing a problem, faculty members and the student's academic adviser work with the student to get back on course. Mitchell's Tutoring Center provides free, unlimited individualized tutoring by trained professionals (not peer tutors) in every academic discipline. It also offers assistance in improving writing, research, and computer skills as well as test and exam preparation and study skills development. Some of Mitchell's most successful students are regular users of the Tutoring Center, and they attribute much of their success to its programs.

Students with diagnosed learning disabilities may enroll in the College's nationally recognized Learning Resource Center, which provides instruction and support to complement a student's regular academic program. Each student is assigned two learning specialists to work one-on-one with the student and in small-group settings. The program is designed to teach the learning strategies a student needs to gain independence.

Following completion of their associate degree, 90 percent of the student body continue in one of Mitchell's baccalaureate programs or successfully transfer to the four-year college or university of their choice.

Off-Campus Programs

When not in class, Mitchell students gain the skills and experience they need to succeed in their careers and to make a difference in their communities. Nearly all academic programs require or encourage students to participate in volunteer opportunities, internships, or practical experiences as part of their curriculum.

Some of the opportunities include exploring the seacoast with a nationally recognized scientist, teaching at a local elementary school, partnering with a local police officer, helping to negotiate a bill through the state legislature, assisting with advertising campaigns, coaching developmentally challenged athletes and practicing the skills of injury prevention, and sparking the imagination of local school children through storytelling sessions.

Academic Facilities

Mitchell's unique 65-acre waterfront campus includes a 45,000-volume library and two primary classroom buildings. Students have full use of Mitchell's state-of-the-art computing facilities with high-speed, full T-1 Internet access. Open seven days a week and staffed with fully trained help-desk consultants, students may use the computer labs to e-mail, scan images, print documents, and complete academic assignments. This same high-speed network and Internet access is also available in each student's residence hall room. For those who do not own a computer, Mitchell offers a computer purchasing plan and service agreement.

Costs

Tuition, room and board, and fees for the 2003–04 year are $26,396. Additional annual miscellaneous expenses, including books, are estimated at $1500 per year. Students enrolled in the Learning Resource Center pay an additional $6000 per year.

Financial Aid

Mitchell annually awards more than $3 million in financial aid, both in need-based and merit-based scholarships and in grant programs designed to recognize academic, athletic, and leadership abilities. Accepted students may qualify for grants and scholarships that do not need to be repaid. They include the Connecticut Independent College Student Grant Program, Federal Pell Grants, Federal Supplemental Educational Opportunity Grants, and Mitchell Scholarships. Self-help aid in the form of loans is also available. They include Federal Stafford Student Loans (subsidized and unsubsidized), Federal PLUS Loans, and Federal Perkins Loan programs. On-campus job opportunities are plentiful for students regardless of their financial aid status.

Mitchell Valued Potential (MVP) scholarships are awarded based on an individual student's ability to contribute to the College. They may be given to students who demonstrate potential in leadership, volunteerism, and involvement in school activities. Athletic scholarships are available to students who participate in men's and women's baseball, basketball, soccer, and softball; women's volleyball; and men's lacrosse. Various payment plans are available.

Faculty

Twenty-six full-time and 30 part-time faculty members teach in Mitchell's classrooms. The student-faculty ratio is 12:1.

Student Government

The Student Government Association (SGA) is made up of officers and senators who represent the residents and commuters. It addresses issues with campus administration, organizes community projects, serves as the active voice for the student body, and sponsors at least one campuswide program each semester. The SGA also works in tandem with the Student Activities Office concerning club funding and overall programming.

Student involvement is not only encouraged but also expected of all Mitchell students. An active student leads to a well-rounded person. Students enhance their life with self-discipline skills, demonstrate selfless service, and become happier members of the College family through involvement in student activities, athletics, campus employment, and community service opportunities.

Admission Requirements

Each student is evaluated individually as soon as the completed application, along with the official transcript, is received. Admission is based on academic preparation, scholastic aptitude, personal character, and potential for academic success. Other important factors taken into consideration include the student's motivation, initiative, maturity, seriousness of purpose, and leadership potential. SAT I or ACT test scores are required. A campus visit and admissions interview are required. Open houses are held in October, January, and April.

Application and Information

Mitchell uses a rolling admission policy. Students can expect to be notified of decisions within weeks of the College's receipt of completed applications and official transcripts sent directly from the students' high schools.

For more information, students should contact:

Kevin Mayne
Vice President for Enrollment Management and Marketing
Mitchell College
437 Pequot Avenue
New London, Connecticut 06320-4498
Telephone: 800-443-2811 (toll-free)
Fax: 860-444-1209
E-mail: admissions@mitchell.edu
World Wide Web: http://www.mitchell.edu

Mitchell College's 65–acre campus is located in New London, Connecticut, where the Thames River meets the Long Island Sound.

MOLLOY COLLEGE

ROCKVILLE CENTRE, NEW YORK

The College

In 1955, 44 students became part of an exciting new tradition in higher education on Long Island. As the first freshman class of Molloy College, these young students made a commitment to academic excellence. So did the College, which had a distinguished faculty of 15 and a library containing 5,000 books.

Today, Molloy College has become one of the most respected four-year private coeducational institutions of higher learning in the area. It provides academic programs in both day and evening divisions. The Molloy population consists of recent high school graduates, transfer students, and graduate students whose average age is 24. Molloy College is accredited by the Board of Regents of the University of the State of New York and the Middle States Association of Colleges and Schools, and its programs in nursing and social work are accredited by the National League for Nursing Accrediting Commission and the Council on Social Work Education.

Despite its growth over the years, Molloy College retains an intimate and personal atmosphere. It encourages the 3,000 students to develop close working relationships with the faculty. The student body represents many ethnic and socioeconomic groups; to meet their varied needs, the College offers thirty-three undergraduate majors and programs.

The key word at the College is involvement. Student-run clubs and organizations offer a variety of planned activities. Student publications, which include the yearbook, a literary magazine, a newspaper, and a weekly newsletter, provide an outlet for students who want to share their literary and journalistic talents.

Molloy College offers opportunities for students to exercise their leadership abilities, contribute their special talents, utilize their initiative, and expand their social horizons through the variety of activities made conveniently available to them. Athletics, an integral part of student life, are represented at Molloy College on the varsity level by women's basketball, cross-country, soccer, softball, tennis, and volleyball. These teams compete in the NCAA, the ECAC, and the NYCAC. The equestrian team holds membership in the Intercollegiate Horse Show Association. Men's baseball, basketball, cross-country, lacrosse, and soccer are played at Division II level.

Student services include the Counseling and Career Services, the Campus Ministry, the Siena Women's Center, health services, and referrals for off-campus housing.

On the graduate level, Molloy College offers a Master of Science degree in nursing and education and post-master's certification in nursing. M.B.A. programs are available in both business and accounting.

Location

Located on a 30-acre campus in Rockville Centre, Long Island, Molloy College is close to metropolitan New York and all its diverse and rich resources. The College is easily accessible from all parts of Nassau, Suffolk, and Queens counties.

Majors and Degrees

Molloy College offers the A.A. degree in liberal arts; the A.A.S. degree in health information technology, nuclear medicine technology, and respiratory care; and B.A. or B.S. degrees in accounting, art, biology, business management, communications, computer information systems, computer science, criminal justice, English, environmental studies, French, history, interdisciplinary studies, international peace and justice studies, mathematics, music, music therapy, nursing, philosophy, political science, psychology, social work, sociology, Spanish, speech-language pathology and audiology, and theology. Teacher certification programs are available in childhood (1–6), adolescence (7–12), and special education.

Special advisement is offered for students interested in predental, prelaw, premedical, or preveterinary programs.

The internship program at the College offers students the opportunity for on-the-job experience along with the classroom exposure so essential to the completely educated person. Internships are available in accounting, art, business management, communications, computer science, criminal justice, English, history, IPJ studies, mathematics, music therapy, political science, psychology, social work, and sociology.

Academic Program

Molloy College, dedicated to the total development of the student, offers a strong liberal arts core curriculum as an integral part of all major fields of study. A minimum of 128 credits is required for a baccalaureate degree. Double majors can be chosen, and numerous minors are available.

Advanced placement credit is granted for a score of 3 or better on the AP exam. CLEP and CPE credit is also given. Qualified full-time students may participate in the Army ROTC program at Hofstra University or St. John's University on a cross-enrolled basis. Molloy students may also elect Air Force ROTC on a cross-enrolled basis with New York Institute of Technology.

Molloy has a 4-1-4 academic calendar.

Academic Facilities

Molloy's James Edward Tobin Library has 133,500 books, 700 periodical subscriptions, 13,500 bound periodicals, 2,950 microfilms, 1,200 microfiches, four OCLC computer terminals, and twelve microcomputers for student research. The Media Center houses 500 pieces of hardware, 9,700 pieces of software, and 2,700 videocassettes and DVDs.

The College computer labs house 260 microcomputers. In addition, many academic departments have their own computer labs. For example, the International Business Center has sixteen state-of-the-art microcomputers with Internet and e-mail accessibility, DVD drives, and zip drives for students to communicate internationally.

The Wilbur Arts Center features numerous art studios, music studios, a cable television studio, and the Lucille B. Hays Theatre.

Kellenberg Hall houses six science labs, a language lab, and the education resource center. Casey Hall houses two nursing labs and the behavioral sciences research facility.

Costs

For 2002–03, tuition and fees were $14,430. The cost per credit for part-time students was $480.

Financial Aid

More than 85 percent of the student body of Molloy College is awarded financial aid in the form of scholarships, grants, loans, and Federal Work-Study Program employment. Financial aid awards are based on academic achievement and financial need. Completion of the Molloy College Application for Financial Aid/Scholarship and the Free Application for Federal Student Aid (FAFSA) is required. No-need scholarships and grants are also available. Students who have attained a 95 percent or better high school average and a minimum combined score of 1250 on the SAT I are considered for the Molloy Scholars' Program, which awards full tuition scholarships. Partial scholarships are available under Dominican Scholarships, Encarnacion Amor Verde Scholarship, Girl Scout Gold Award, and the Fine and Performing Arts Scholarships. The Transfer Scholarship Program grants partial tuition scholarships to students transferring into Molloy College with at least a 3.0 cumulative average. Athletic grants (Division II only) are awarded to full-time students based on athletic ability in baseball, basketball, cross-country, equestrian, lacrosse, soccer, softball, tennis, and volleyball. The Community Service Award is awarded to full-time freshmen demonstrating a commitment to their community and their school.

Faculty

The 307 full-time and part-time faculty members at Molloy are dedicated as much to the students as to their respective fields. The 9:1 student-faculty ratio allows for small classes where students can receive the individual attention they deserve.

In addition to their teaching responsibilities, faculty members advise students in their fields to help them select courses that both satisfy major course requirements and lead to the attainment of career goals.

Student Government

Every member of the Molloy College student body belongs to the Molloy Student Association, whose elected leaders form the Molloy Student Government. This group of students provides the leadership necessary to keep extracurricular life at Molloy College alive, productive, and practical.

Admission Requirements

Recommended admission qualifications include graduation from a four-year public or private high school or equivalent (GED test) with a minimum of 18.5 units, including 4 in English, 4 in social studies, 3 in a foreign language, 3 in mathematics, and 3 in science. Nursing applicants must have taken courses in biology and chemistry. Mathematics applicants must have taken 4 units of math and 3 of science (including chemistry or physics). Biology applicants must have credits in biology, chemistry, and physics and 4 units of math. A portfolio is required of art applicants, and music students must audition. Social work applicants must file a special application with the director of the social work program.

The admissions committee bases its selection of candidates on the secondary school record, SAT I or ACT scores, class rank, and the school's recommendation. A particular talent or ability can be important. Character and personality, extracurricular participation, and alumni relationships are all considered. On-campus interviews are recommended but not required.

The St. Thomas Aquinas Program, which houses both HEOP and the Albertus Magnus Program, may be options for students not normally eligible for admission.

An early admission plan is available.

Application and Information

To apply to Molloy College, students should submit the following credentials to the Admissions Office: a completed application for admission, a nonrefundable $30 application fee, an official high school transcript or GED score report, official results of the SAT I or ACT, and official college transcripts (transfer students only).

The College uses a rolling admission system. Students are advised of an admission decision within a few weeks after the application filing process is complete.

For further information, prospective students should contact:

Director of Admissions
Molloy College
1000 Hempstead Avenue
Rockville Centre, New York 11570
Telephone: 888-4-MOLLOY (toll-free)
World Wide Web: http://www.molloy.edu

An aerial view of Molloy College.

MONMOUTH UNIVERSITY

WEST LONG BRANCH, NEW JERSEY

The University

Monmouth University is a private, moderate-sized coeducational institution committed to providing a learning environment that enables men and women to pursue their educational goals and realize their full potential for making significant contributions to their community and society. Small classes, which allow for individual attention and student-faculty dialogue, together with careful academic advising and career counseling, are hallmarks of a Monmouth education.

The student body is diverse, with a population of more than 4,400 undergraduates and 1,800 graduate students. Although most are from the Northeast, twenty-five states and forty nations are represented, and there is a rich ethnic mix. Of the nearly 3,900 full-time undergraduate students enrolled, approximately 1,600 live on campus in traditional residence halls and garden apartment complexes. Both resident and commuting students have a wide variety of extracurricular activities to choose from: an active Student Government Association; the campus newspaper and FM radio station; the yearbook and the literary magazine; the African-American Student Union; Hillel and Christian Ambassadors organizations; almost twenty-five special interest groups; theater; intramurals; and sororities and fraternities that engage in service work on behalf of the University and of the community. Many special events are planned each year, including art exhibits, concerts, lectures, sightseeing trips, and more.

The University's NCAA Division I intercollegiate athletics program includes nine men's teams—baseball, basketball, cross-country, football, golf, indoor track, outdoor track and field, soccer, and tennis—and ten women's teams—basketball, cross-country, field hockey, golf, indoor track, lacrosse, outdoor track and field, soccer, softball, and tennis. The gymnasium has an Olympic-size indoor pool, regulation-size basketball courts, and a training room and fitness center. Outdoor facilities include tennis and in-line skating courts, an all-weather track, and baseball, football, soccer, and softball fields.

Monmouth students are accorded many special services, including the full resources of the Life and Career Advising Center, which is staffed by academic and other professional personnel who offer academic advising in addition to individual personal and career counseling. Academic skills services, including the Math Center, the Reading Center, the Writing Center, and the Peer Tutoring Office, provide personalized academic assistance. There are offices to serve international students and students with disabilities. Employment counseling is available through the Placement Office. The Health Center makes available basic medical care.

In addition to its undergraduate degree programs, Monmouth offers numerous graduate degree programs in business administration, computer science, corporate and public communication, criminal justice, education, health-care management, history, liberal studies, nursing, psychological counseling, social work, and software engineering. There are also graduate certificate programs.

Location

The location of the University—in a residential area of an attractive community near the Atlantic Ocean, yet a little more than a one-hour drive from the metropolitan attractions of New York and Philadelphia—is an appealing feature. The University's safe and secure 153-acre campus, considered to be one of the most beautiful in New Jersey, includes among its fifty-four buildings a harmonious blending of traditional and contemporary architectural styles. The centerpiece building is Woodrow Wilson Hall, a National Historic Landmark that houses administrative offices and humanities classrooms. Monmouth's $6.5-million business administration building, Bey Hall; a $4-million renovation of the technology building, Howard Hall; and a $4.7 million renovation of the Edison Science Hall provide students with a first-class learning environment. The University recently completed the construction of the state-of-the-art Center for Communication and Instructional Technology and plans to begin construction of the Multipurpose Activity Center in the near future. Restaurants, shops, and theaters are within easy reach, and several large shopping malls and the PNC Bank Arts Center (an entertainment hub) are only a few miles away. Another advantage is proximity to many high-technology firms, financial institutions, and a thriving business-industrial sector. These provide not only employment possibilities for graduates but also the opportunity for undergraduates to gain practical experience through various internships and the cooperative education program conducted by the University.

Majors and Degrees

Monmouth University offers twenty-six baccalaureate degree programs within five schools. The School of Business Administration awards bachelor's degrees in business administration with concentrations in accounting, economics, finance, management, and marketing. The School of Education awards bachelor's degrees that allow students to earn certification as nursery and elementary teachers (N–8), as subject teachers (K–12), or as special education teachers. The School of Humanities and Social Sciences awards bachelor's degrees in the areas of anthropology, art, communication, criminal justice, English, foreign language, history, history–political science, music/theater arts, political science, psychology, and social work. The School of Humanities and Social Sciences includes the Department of Interdisciplinary Studies. The School of Science, Technology and Engineering awards bachelor's degrees in biology, chemistry, clinical lab sciences, computer science, mathematics, medical technology, and software engineering. The School of Nursing and Health Studies awards the Bachelor of Science in Nursing to upper-division transfer students. A preprofessional advising program is available for students who intend to pursue careers in medicine, dentistry, or other health-care fields. Monmouth also offers an accelerated degree program, the Graduate Scholars Program, to enable students to achieve both a bachelor's and master's degree in just five years.

Academic Programs

The curriculum is attuned throughout to today's globally oriented technological society while retaining a strong grounding in the liberal arts. Under the general education curriculum, students in all degree programs acquire a breadth of knowledge beyond their major fields of study, including an appreciation of world culture. Monmouth University also emphasizes writing, speaking, and other interpersonal skills that are critical to personal and professional success. Monmouth requires all students to fulfill computer literacy and experiential education requirements. Experiential education is a real-world experience related to the academic major.

Monmouth University believes that, while providing sound preparation for successful careers, a major goal of higher education is to help students develop important values. These include a keen sense of citizenship and social responsibility and the leadership qualities that will equip graduates to contribute actively to the democratic society in which they live. Academic programs at Monmouth prepare students for life in an increasingly complex, multicultural world. An honors program is available for all students who meet the academic requirements.

Genuine concern for the individual student characterizes the Monmouth University educational program. Professors—not teaching assistants—conduct all courses and supervise all laboratories. Students benefit from direct interaction with professors who are recognized for their scholarly expertise.

Cooperative education is available to students, enabling them to gain practical experience in jobs related to their majors while completing their studies. Internships are available in criminal justice, medical technology, and social work; special off-campus programs are offered for biology and political science majors; and all education majors are required to complete a semester of student teaching. All of these programs carry college credit. The University also participates in the Washington Center, which offers programs in which students may earn credit from their own institution for experiential learning gained through internships and symposia in the nation's capital.

Monmouth University offers a program for students who have not met regular admission requirements but who appear to have the potential for success in college. The Edward G. Schlaefer School is designed to give special attention to incoming students who need extra support and a more structured learning environment in the freshman year.

Academic Facilities

The Guggenheim Library holds approximately 253,000 volumes and nearly 12,000 print and electronic journal subscriptions. Academic programs are more than supported by state-of-the-art computer hardware and software and classroom/laboratory facilities. The major components supporting Monmouth's academic programs include UNIX, Windows NT, and Novell server systems connected by a sophisticated campus Ethernet network spanning twenty-three buildings and encompassing more than 1,000 workstations campuswide. Workstations that are specifically dedicated to student use are distributed among thirty instructional and open-use laboratories and include DEC-Alpha servers, Silicon Graphics servers and workstations, SUN servers and workstations, Pentium servers and workstations, and Macintosh workstations. Laptop plug-in ports are available in convenient locations across campus. A campus communications network (HawkNet) connects all Monmouth University computing resources to the Internet. All students receive a computer account that provides them with e-mail, World Wide Web browsing and authoring tools, and electronic access to the Guggenheim Library catalog. The Lauren K. Woods Theatre offers students an opportunity to experience all phases of the theater arts, from acting to lighting. All control of the various aspects of a theatrical performance is maintained by students. There are communications facilities for both radio and television, and the University supports a student-run FM radio station. There are also a student-run greenhouse and studios for art and music majors.

Costs

For 2004–05, tuition is approximately $19,108 per year. Room and board costs are $7804 per year, depending on the type of room and meal plan selected. Costs are subject to change for 2005–06.

Financial Aid

Monmouth University believes that qualified students should not be denied an educational opportunity due to lack of financial resources. The financial aid staff counsels students and their families and assists them in obtaining the maximum financial aid to which they are entitled. In a cooperative effort, the University utilizes institutional, federal, and state resources and expects a reasonable family contribution toward the student's cost of attendance. In developing each student's award package, all resources available are utilized to address individual circumstances and to provide equitable treatment for all applicants. A wide range of institutional scholarships and grants is offered to the incoming class each year. Award amounts vary according to the quality of the student's previous academic record and housing status. They range up to a maximum of $10,500. The scholarship and grant program is available to all prospective full-time freshman and transfer students. Award amounts are renewed at the same level each year for the student's four-year undergraduate career. Scholarship recipients are required to maintain a minimum 3.0 cumulative GPA; academic excellence grant recipients must maintain a minimum 2.5 cumulative GPA; incentive grant recipients must maintain a minimum 2.0 cumulative GPA. Grants and scholarships for this program are offered without regard to financial need. For some federal programs, resources are limited, and priority is given to students who are in full-time attendance and have filed in a timely fashion. All awards are subject to the availability of funds. Students and their families are strongly encouraged to call or visit the Office of Financial Aid for assistance.

Faculty

The University's professors are leaders in their fields and contribute through research, publishing, and consulting to their respective academic areas. There are 229 full-time and 264 part-time faculty members. Approximately 72 percent of the full-time instructional faculty members have doctorates. The average class size is 22, and the student-faculty ratio is 18.5:1. The largest class section at Monmouth is 41. Professors are able to know each student by name, and faculty members are available to students for office consultation and extra help.

Student Government

Monmouth's Student Government Association is an important and necessary voice in the University community. Seven senators from each class, along with certain elected officials, express clear and definite opinions and cast votes on University policy. Student representatives are present at all faculty meetings and other resolution-adopting events to present the opinions of the student body. All students are strongly encouraged to participate in these activities.

Admission Requirements

Many factors are considered when candidates are evaluated for admission. For freshman applicants, the committee evaluates grades and test scores. High school transcripts and SAT I or ACT scores must be sent with the application. Counselor recommendations and other information supporting the application are welcome. Admission interviews and campus tours are available. Transfer students must submit official transcripts from all colleges attended. If they have earned fewer than 24 transferable credits, they must fulfill freshman admission requirements as well.

Application and Information

The application deadline for early decision is December 1. The admission decision notification date is January 1. The early decision is for students who select Monmouth University as their first choice. Early decision is a binding commitment with Monmouth University. Housing and parking are guaranteed for students accepted for early decision only. The application deadline for early action is December 15. The admission decision notification date is January 15. Early action is for students with a strong desire to enroll at Monmouth. The application deadline for regular decision is March 1. The admission decision notification date is prior to April 1. Applications received after March 1 are considered on a space-available basis. Housing and parking are assigned on a first-come, first-served basis and are not guaranteed for early action and regular decision. Housing is prioritized by the date on which Monmouth University is in receipt of the student's enrollment deposit, housing contract, and housing deposit. Monmouth allocates housing spaces by class level. When all necessary materials have been submitted, a decision and notification are made as quickly as possible.

For further information, students should contact:

Office of Undergraduate Admission
Monmouth University
400 Cedar Avenue
West Long Branch, New Jersey 07764-1898
Telephone: 732-571-3456
800-543-9671 (toll-free)
Fax: 732-263-5166
E-mail: admission@monmouth.edu
World Wide Web: http://www.monmouth.edu

MONROE COLLEGE

BRONX, NEW YORK

The College

Founded in 1933, Monroe College is a private, coeducational, nonsectarian institution that offers bachelor's degrees, with the ability to earn associate degrees along the way in a unique 2+2 format. Both degrees are available in accounting, business administration, computer information systems, computerized office technologies, criminal justice, health office associate studies, and hospitality and tourism management. Monroe College is committed to providing a high-quality education, coupled with individualized attention and preparation for today's business world, to serious-minded students who understand the true value of such an education. The Monroe College student is given the opportunity to gain academic and professional competency through comprehensive curricula and is also offered a support system that provides those services essential for academic and professional success. Monroe College, which has campuses in both the Bronx and New Rochelle, is accredited by the Commission on Institutions of Higher Education of the Middle States Association of Colleges and Schools.

Monroe enrolls approximately 4,500 students on its two campuses and through distance learning. The diverse student population includes recent high school graduates as well as more mature students who are returning to the educational forum. International students, who have access to an International Students' Center and counselors at the New Rochelle campus, make up 5 percent of the total student body. Members of minority groups are well represented on both campuses, as well. The students are primarily commuters, but housing facilities are available at the New Rochelle campus.

Social activities are centered around the Student Activities Committee (SAC) and the athletic program. They seek to provide an opportunity for the future development of the whole student. The student-run newspaper and drama, cheerleading, and dance groups, as well as SAC, are open to all students. Monroe participates in intercollegiate basketball, soccer, and volleyball. Intramural sports include fencing, basketball, volleyball, track, and bowling. Cultural activities include Latino Month and Black History Month, among many others. Professional clubs are available for students in each major. The rich cultural treasures and tourist attractions found in New York City are easily accessible by public transportation.

Location

Monroe is part of the metropolis of New York City, with an urban campus in the Fordham district of the Bronx. The campus is easily accessible by car or public transportation. Its locale is near the Yankees, the Bronx Zoo, and the New York Botanical Gardens. A short train ride away is Manhattan, which is known for Central Park, Broadway, Wall Street and the Financial District, many museums, the Statue of Liberty, the Empire State Building, the Staten Island Ferry, and the South Street Seaport.

Monroe's suburban New Rochelle campus is located in the heart of the Sound Shore Corridor in bustling Westchester County. The campus offers convenient and spacious housing that is directly adjacent to the site of New Roc City, a multimillion-dollar development that includes recreational facilities, shops, and restaurants. Within a short distance is the Long Island Sound, with abundant opportunities for recreation and leisure-time activities. Students can make use of a multitude of cultural facilities in New Rochelle and the surrounding communities. Students can also easily travel into New York City by inexpensive public transportation.

Majors and Degrees

Monroe College confers the Bachelor of Business Administration (B.B.A.) degree in accounting, business management, computer information systems, and criminal justice and associate degrees in accounting, business administration, computer information systems, computerized office technologies, criminal justice, health office associate studies, and hospitality and tourism management.

Academic Programs

Monroe College's bachelor's and associate degree programs emphasize study in the liberal arts as well as in-depth immersion in each academic major. Applicants may be admitted to either the associate or bachelor's degree program upon acceptance. Upon the completion of 60 credits, all Monroe students receive an associate degree. Bachelor's programs, leading to the Bachelor of Business Administration, require completion of 60 credits beyond the associate degree. Those interested in continuing for a bachelor's degree must apply for admission to the upper division. Monroe operates on a three-semester calendar. The fifteen-week semesters begin in early September, early January, and late April.

In addition, there are distance learning opportunities through Internet courses.

Advanced placement is available for CLEP, transfer credit, prior learning experience (life experience evaluation), and proficiency examinations. Students can receive advanced-standing placement for up to 50 percent of the required credits for their chosen degree program.

Off-Campus Programs

Internship and co-op programs are conducted by the College in cooperation with businesses, industries, government agencies, and nonprofit organizations. They integrate on-campus study with off-campus work-study experience. The programs complement and reinforce the professional curriculum studied in the class, providing a broader comprehension of the context in which the student will be employed.

Academic Facilities

Both campuses have complete libraries with Online Computer Library Center (OCLC) access to other metropolitan New York and Westchester college libraries. The Learning Resource Centers, which are available to all students from early in the morning to late at night, are equipped with state-of-the-art computers and academic enrichment computer programs and videos. Staff tutors are available on a daily basis to reinforce classroom lectures in all subjects. In addition, Monroe has more computers per student than any other college of its size in the area. Student Services provides close educational advisement as well as health clinics and primary-level psychological counseling. Students are also urged to take advantage of the Lifetime Career Placement Service. This program evaluates the academic performance and personal attributes of the student in order to identify skills and career goals so they may obtain a position in their field of study upon graduation. Career services also assists students in obtaining part-time employment during their college careers. Workshops are provided on self-assessment, resume preparation, interview skills, and job search strategies. Currently, the College has a 95 percent placement rate.

Costs

Tuition for the 2003–04 academic year was $4200 per semester, and individual courses cost $1050, plus an administrative fee of $125 for up to 6 credits and $250 for more than 6 credits. Boarding students pay an additional residence fee of $2150 per semester (double room), with a nonrefundable $125 application fee. Books cost approximately $295 per semester.

Financial Aid

Financial assistance is determined by the need of the student along with the availability of funds from federal, state, and institutional sources. More than 90 percent of the students receive some type of financial aid. The College takes into account the objective facts and the financial circumstances of the student and family, recognizing the differences of each family situation. Available assistance includes Federal Pell Grants, Federal Supplemental Educational Opportunity Grants, Federal Stafford Student Loans (subsidized and unsubsidized), Federal PLUS loans, Federal Perkins Loans, and the Federal Work-Study Program. For those students who have been New York State residents for one year or more, TAP may also be available. In addition, the College offers institutional aid (grant-in-aid), scholarships, loans, and employment to students, as well as funding for the purchase of some special equipment and services for the disabled.

Faculty

Monroe has more than 250 full-time faculty members and adjunct faculty members who are experts in their fields, as well as an excellent tutorial staff. They work closely with their students, both inside and outside the classroom, to help them make the most of their talents, interests, and dreams. The student-faculty ratio is 15:1.

Admission Requirements

Monroe College seeks serious individuals who demonstrate that they have the interest, ability, and potential to successfully complete appropriate requirements for the course of study selected. Graduation from an accredited high school, two-year college, or the equivalent; a personal interview; and SAT I scores and/or an entrance exam are the basic requirements for admission to Monroe College.

Application and Information

Submission of the following credentials is required: a completed application, a transcript of all prior formal education, SAT I or ACT scores (optional, but should be submitted if available), two letters of recommendation, and an essay on a topic provided to all applicants. The College actively seeks applications from international students.

Applications are accepted on a rolling basis. Students are informed of the decision by the Admission Committee within two weeks of submission of all required documentation.

Students interested in applying to the Bronx campus should contact:

Luke Schultheis
Director of Admissions
Monroe College–Bronx Campus
2501 Jerome Avenue
Bronx, New York 10468
Telephone: 718-933-6700 Ext. 250
800-55-MONROE (toll-free)
E-mail: lschultheis@monroecollege.edu
World Wide Web: http://www.monroecollege.edu

Students interested in applying to the New Rochelle campus should contact:

Steve Schultheis
Director of Admissions
Monroe College–New Rochelle Campus
Milavec Hall
371 Main Street
New Rochelle, New York 10801
Telephone: 914-632-5462 Ext. 870
800-55-MONROE (toll-free)
E-mail: sschultheis@monroecollege.edu

International students should contact:

Gersom Lopez
Director of International Student Admissions
Monroe College–New Rochelle Campus
434 Main Street
New Rochelle, New York 10801
Telephone: 914-632-5462 Ext. 403
800-55-MONROE (toll-free)
E-mail: glopez@monroecollege.edu
World Wide Web: http://www.monroecollege.edu (select International Admissions)

Students interested in applying to the bachelor's degree programs should contact:

Alexis Safonoff
Assistant Director of Bachelor's Degree Admissions
Monroe College–Bronx Campus
2468 Jerome Avenue
Bronx, New York 10468
Telephone: 718-933-6700 Ext. 300
E-mail: asafonoff@monroecollege.edu

Emerson Phillips
Director of Bachelor's Degree Program
Monroe College–New Rochelle Campus
434 Main Street
New Rochelle, New York 10801
Telephone: 914-632-5462
E-mail: ephillips@monroecollege.edu

MONTANA STATE UNIVERSITY–BILLINGS

BILLINGS, MONTANA

The University

One-on-one relationships with faculty members, staff members, and classmates is what makes the difference for students at Montana State University–Billings (MSU–Billings). The academic experience is personalized, from the first campus visit to the last classroom discussion. In addition to receiving quality instruction, students participate in real-world experiences such as group projects, internships, and cooperative education programs to prepare them for their chosen career.

MSU–Billings continues to be a nationally recognized training ground for teachers and more recently has established its reputation for programs in business and allied health. Graduates from the College of Technology continue to be highly sought after by regional employers.

With an enrollment of 4,500 the University offers degrees in six colleges: Allied Health Professions, Arts and Sciences, Business, Education, Professional Studies and Lifelong Learning, and Technology.

The College of Arts and Sciences provides quality programs in the arts, humanities, and sciences that meet the needs of the state and region. This College also offers a rich menu of general education courses for the University's baccalaureate students.

As Billings has evolved into the major business center in the region, the business programs at Montana State University–Billings have grown and prospered. The College of Business has been accepted into AACSB International–The Association to Advance Collegiate Schools of Business candidacy. The College's graduates enjoy a high placement rate and outstanding success on the CPA exam.

The College of Education has earned a reputation as a regional leader. Faculty members and student teachers remain current in their fields through site work in area professional development schools that cover elementary, middle, and high school education. It has exclusive responsibility in the state of Montana for the undergraduate and graduate degree programs in special education and special education supervision. The College is accredited by the National Council for the Accreditation of Teacher Education and recently received national recognition with the Best Practice Award in Support of Teacher Education Accreditation by the American Association of Colleges for Teacher Education.

At the cutting edge of learning technologies, the College of Professional Studies and Lifelong Learning is home to MSUB Online University. Montana State University–Billings is the regional leader in providing online learning opportunities. The entire general education core is available online in addition to complete degree programs at both the undergraduate and graduate level. For more information, prospective students should visit the Web site at http://www.msubonline.org. In addition, the College offers continuing education, workforce training through the Yellowstone Development and Training Cooperative, and educational opportunities at the MSU–Billings Downtown campus.

The College of Allied Health Professions and its partnerships with health and human service organizations strive to enhance the quality of life of the regional citizenry by preparing students as health professionals. The College promotes excellence in teaching, research, and community service, and prepares students to assume professional responsibilities in health administration, health promotion, human performance, athletic training, rehabilitation and mental health counseling, health and physical education, and human services.

The College of Technology, located in west Billings, provides excellence in a wide range of associate and certificate programs. College of Technology graduates meet the employment market's demand within the state and region. In response to the community needs, the College of Technology is continuously updating and creating new degrees such as fire science, radiology, process plant technology, and Cisco certification.

The MSU–Billings Yellowjackets compete in NCAA II men's basketball, cheer team, cross-country, golf, soccer, and tennis, and women's basketball, cheer team, cross-country, golf, soccer, softball, tennis, and volleyball.

Location

Billings, the largest city in Montana, is the primary medical center for a multistate area and serves as a regional center for business, transportation, education, and agriculture. The Yellowstone Valley offers students educational, cultural, professional, and recreational opportunities that are as endless as the Big Sky. Hiking, biking, camping, canoeing, fishing, rock climbing, white-water rafting, skiing, snowmobiling, and many more activities are available to students. Within 45 minutes of the campus, the 12,000-foot Beartooth Mountains rise from the Yellowstone Valley and feature breathtaking views and incredible ski slopes.

Majors and Degrees

Bachelor's degrees are offered in accounting, applied science, art, art teaching (K–12), biology, biology teaching, chemistry, chemistry teaching, communication and theater, elementary education, English, English teaching, environmental studies, finance, general business administration, health administration, health and physical education (K–12), health promotion, history, history teaching, human services, information systems, liberal studies, management, marketing, mathematics, mathematics teaching, music, music performance, music teaching (K–12), psychology, public relations, rehabilitation and related services, social science teaching, sociology, Spanish, Spanish teaching (K–12), and special education (elementary and secondary).

Preprofessional programs are available in art therapy, engineering, law, medicine, nursing, pharmacy, and physical therapy.

Two-year associate degrees include accounting technology, administrative assistant studies, allied health, applied psychology, automotive collision repair and refinishing, automotive technology, computer desktop/network support, computer systems technology, data processing, diesel technology, drafting and design technology, education, environmental science, fire science, general studies, heating/ventilation/air-conditioning/refrigeration technology, human resources, medical administrative assistant studies, medical assistant studies, paramedic studies, practical nursing studies, process plant technology, rehabilitation and related services, radiologic technology, and word processing.

Certificates are available in accounting assistant studies, assistant drafter studies, automobile collision repair, automobile collision repair and refinishing, automobile collision refinishing, automotive technology, computer assistant studies, diesel technology, human resources, networking technology, office assistant studies, and welding/metal fabrication.

Academic Program

Access and excellence are fostered through quality instruction at Montana State University–Billings. Because the University is concerned that its graduates experience practical aspects of the subject matter in which they specialize, the University offers internships, research opportunities, teaching experiences, clinics, hands-on work assignments, and other practical activities. A Cooperative Education Program further increases students' opportunities to apply classroom learning to the demands of specific work assignments. The University is also strongly committed to providing developmental and other academic support programs necessary to assist promising students.

Academic Facilities

The senior campus, located under the Rimrocks on the northern edge of Billings, houses the Colleges of Allied Health, Arts and Sciences, Business, Education, and Professional Studies and Lifelong Learning. The MSU–Billings library features computerized library services as well as the Information Commons, an open lab where more than eighty computers can access the Internet. The offices of Career Services, Financial Aid, Admissions and Records, and the Advising Center are all conveniently located on the first floor of McMullen Hall. The Academic Support Center provides students with access to tutors and other educational tools. Cisel Recital Hall has soundproof practice rooms, an acoustic recital hall, and exceptional facilities for students. The physical education building houses Alterowitz Gymnasium, a new fitness center, a practice gym, a collegiate-size swimming pool, an enclosed running track, and racquetball courts. MSU–Billings students enjoy modern and spacious living quarters in Rimrock and Petro residence halls, which feature all the comforts of home, including Internet access, free cable television hookups, computer labs, kitchen facilities, comfortable lounges, and free access to laundry machines. The residence hall complex also includes The Rimrock Café, Stingers' Espresso Bar, the Student Union, Beezer's Book Store, and Petro Theatre. All twenty-two buildings are within a short walking distance across the senior campus.

The College of Technology is located on the west side of Billings, 7 miles from the senior campus. This 18-acre site contains a 100,000-square-foot-classroom, lab, and shop area.

Costs

The estimated 2003–04 annual tuition for Montana residents was $4180; for non-Montana residents, tuition was $11,540; for residents of states participating in the Western Undergraduate Exchange (WUE) program (Alaska, Arizona, Colorado, Hawaii, Idaho, Nevada, New Mexico, North Dakota, Oregon, South Dakota, Utah, Washington, and Wyoming) tuition was $5851. The WUE tuition rate is limited to a specific number of students. Other fees included an optional health insurance fee ($550), books and supplies ($800), room ($2510 for double occupancy), and meals ($1500).

Financial Aid

Approximately 85 percent of new Montana State University–Billings students receive some form of financial aid, including loans, grants, and work-study jobs. The scholarship deadline is March 1. Financial aid has a March 1 priority date for filing. Students applying for scholarships and financial aid need to complete the admissions process in advance of those dates. The University also has a job locator program to assist students in finding employment off campus.

Faculty

At Montana State University–Billings, students are taught and mentored by talented professors, not graduate assistants. The faculty members, 90 percent of whom have earned the highest degrees in their fields, are at the forefront of their academic disciplines. Each year, they receive Fulbright fellowships and other prestigious grants to further their professional development. They explore innovative teaching approaches and include students in their research, presentations, and published works.

Student Government

The Associate Students of Montana State University–Billings (ASMSU–Billings) represent student interests, needs, and welfare within the University system and provide for the expression of student opinion and interests to the community at large on issues affecting student life. ASMSU–Billings also serves to protect the privileges and rights of students.

Admission Requirements

For admission to the College of Allied Health Professions, the College of Arts and Sciences, the College of Business, the College of Education and Human Services, and the College of Professional Studies, applicants must submit an application for admission with a nonrefundable fee of $30.

Freshmen must submit their high school transcript (indicating class rank, graduation date, and cumulative grade point average) and scores from either the ACT or SAT I. A graduate of any accredited high school is eligible for admission provided he or she has obtained a minimum score of 22 on the ACT or 1030 on the SAT I, has at least a 2.5 grade point average, or ranks in the upper half of the graduating class and has completed the prescribed college-preparatory curriculum (4 years of English; 3 years of math, including algebra I, algebra II, and geometry; 3 years of social studies; 2 years of laboratory science; and 2 years of electives chosen from foreign languages, computer science, visual or performing arts, or vocational education). In addition, first-time students must earn a minimum ACT math score of 16 (SAT score of 390) or an AP Calculus AB or B score of 3 or higher.

Transfer students must submit their college transcript and have at least a 2.0 cumulative grade point average based on transferable credits from all colleges or universities previously attended.

For the College of Technology, applicants must submit an application for admission with a nonrefundable fee of $30. To be eligible for admission, applicants must have earned a high school diploma from an accredited institution or a GED certificate.

Application and Information

For further information and application materials, students should contact:

Office of Admissions and Records
Montana State University–Billings
1500 University Drive
Billings, Montana 59101-0298
Telephone: 406-657-2158
800-565-MSUB (toll-free)
Fax: 406-657-2302
E-mail: admissions@msubillings.edu
World Wide Web: http://www.msubillings.edu

Montana State University–Billings, "the University of the Yellowstone," provides students with serene surroundings and academic excellence.

MONTANA STATE UNIVERSITY–BOZEMAN

BOZEMAN, MONTANA

The University

Montana State University (MSU) in Bozeman is home to 12,135 students and offers a comprehensive array of programs and opportunities for students to study in one of America's most spectacular outdoor environments. Undergraduate and graduate programs are offered in the Colleges of Agriculture; Arts and Architecture; Business; Education, Health, and Human Development; Engineering; Letters and Science; and Nursing. Undecided students can explore all of their academic interests through the General Studies program prior to selecting a major.

"Mountains and minds" is a slogan especially appropriate to Montana State University. Nestled in the beautiful ranges and wilderness areas of the Rocky Mountains, the campus environment of clean air, uncrowded classes, and wide open spaces creates a collegiate atmosphere unrivaled in most of the United States.

MSU is unique in that it is not an overgrown and impersonal institution. The enrollment of 12,135 students (10,750 undergraduates) allows for much closer student-faculty interaction than is possible at many schools, ensuring each student the individual attention and academic counseling that are so important in achieving a meaningful college education. Its 1,170-acre campus and the surrounding area offer unlimited opportunities for combining academic and recreational experiences.

Location

Few geographical locations offer the broad range of recreational opportunities found in Bozeman. A community of about 63,000 people in a broad valley surrounded by the magnificence of the northern Rockies, Bozeman is a university town, the social and economic center for a large agricultural area, and a major tourist destination. Outstanding outdoor recreation is at the town's doorstep. Two challenging ski areas (Big Sky and Bridger Bowl), world-class fly-fishing streams, and a multitude of hunting, hiking, camping, mountain climbing, ice-skating, snowmobiling, boating, swimming, and waterskiing opportunities are within minutes of Bozeman. In addition, the gateway to the phenomenally breathtaking Yellowstone National Park is less than an hour away. The community, in cooperation with the University, offers a variety of cultural activities throughout the year, including opera, symphony, ballet, and various festivals. The Museum of the Rockies, which houses nationally known dinosaur exhibits, is also located on the campus.

Majors and Degrees

The College of Agriculture offers degrees in agricultural business, agricultural education (options in agricultural education broadfield teaching and extension), agricultural operations technology, animal science (options in livestock management, equine science, and industry and science), biotechnology (options in animal systems, plant systems, and microbial systems), environmental science (options in environmental biology and soil and water science), horticulture (options in horticulture and landscape design), land rehabilitation, land resource sciences (options in agroecology and land resources analysis and management), plant science (options in crop science and plant biology), and range science.

The College of Arts and Architecture offers degrees in architecture (five-year master's), arts (options in art education K–12 broadfield, liberal arts studio, and art history), environmental design, fine arts (options in graphic design and studio arts), media and theater arts (options in motion picture/video/theater and photography), music, and music education.

The College of Business offers degrees in business with options in accounting, finance, management, and marketing.

The College of Education, Health and Human Development offers degrees in elementary education (options in early childhood education, K–8 education, instructional media K–12, mathematics, reading K–12, science education, and special education), health and human development (options in community health, exercise science, family and consumer sciences, food and nutrition, health enhancement K–12, and pre–physical therapy studies), health promotion, secondary education (options in general science broadfield, social studies broadfield, and departmental teaching options), and technology education (options in industrial technology and technology education broadfield teaching).

The College of Engineering offers degrees in chemical engineering, civil engineering (options in bioresources and civil engineering), computer engineering, computer science, construction engineering technology, electrical engineering, industrial and management engineering, mechanical engineering, and mechanical engineering technology.

The College of Letters and Science offers degrees in anthropology, biological sciences (options in biology teaching, ecology and evolution, organismal biology, and fish and wildlife management), cell biology (options in biomedical science and cell biology and neuroscience), chemistry (options in biochemistry, chemistry professional, and chemistry teaching), earth sciences (options in geography, geohydrology, geology, paleontology, and snow science), economics, English (options in literature and English teaching), history (options in history and history teaching), mathematics (options in applied mathematics, mathematics, mathematics teaching, and statistics), microbiology (options in environmental health, medical laboratory science, and microbiology), modern languages and literatures (options in commerce, French, French teaching, German, German teaching, Spanish, and Spanish teaching), philosophy (options in philosophy and philosophy and religion), physics (options in interdisciplinary physics, physics teaching, and professional physics), political science, psychology (options in applied psychology and psychological science), and sociology (options in justice studies and sociology).

The College of Nursing offers degrees in nursing.

A new degree, the Bachelor of Liberal Studies degree, is avaiable beginning fall 2004. Bachelor of Arts and Bachelor of Science degrees are also offered in directed interdisciplinary studies. Nondegree programs are offered in military aerospace studies (Air Force), military science (Army), and general studies for students who are undecided about a major. In addition, minors are offered in Japan studies, Native American studies, and women's studies.

Montana State University offers direction in several preprofessional disciplines, including dentistry, medicine, optometry, physical therapy, and veterinary science.

An intensive English language program is also available to students.

The three smaller units of the Montana State University system: MSU–Billings, MSU–Northern, and the Great Falls College of Technology offer a wide variety of additional academic programs.

Academic Program

Core 2.0 is the new general education requirement at MSU, and its features include a freshman seminar, a diversity course, and an undergraduate research/creative experience for all students. Beyond the usual math and English requirements, students also choose a research or inquiry course in the fine arts, social sciences, natural sciences, and the humanities. The new core's mission is to enhance the students' use of multiple perspectives in making informed critical and ethical judgments in their personal, public, and professional lives through inquiry and research experiences.

An interdisciplinary University honors program is a significant addition to the curricular and community life of Montana State. Students from various academic fields take part in innovative seminars and research projects. Teaching is primarily Socratic in method.

MSU is ranked among the top in the nation for the number of Goldwater Fellowships in the sciences.

Included among the special programs at MSU are various internships and cooperative education opportunities.

The University operates on a semester system, and a summer session is available.

Off-Campus Programs

MSU offers opportunities for off-campus study, including the National Student Exchange Program, which allows students to attend one of more than 155 other colleges and universities for up to one year, and an international study program, which offers opportunities for study in 220 locations in fifty countries.

Academic Facilities

The University has many special facilities that are used for undergraduate education and research. The foremost of these is a 670,407-volume, recently renovated library that receives more than 6,600 periodicals on a regular basis and also serves as a depository for U.S. government documents. Montana State posted a record $82 million in research expenditures in 2003, putting MSU near the top 100 public universities based on its research volume. The University is home to numerous nationally and internationally acclaimed faculties, laboratories, institutes, and research centers, including the Center for Biofilm Engineering, the Center for Bio-Inspired Nanomaterials, the Center for Computational Biology, the Big Sky Institute, the Western Transportation Institute, the Geographic Information and Analysis Center, the Spectrum Lab, the Thermal Biology Institute, the Ag/BioScience Building (which houses one of the two largest biocontainment facilities in the nation), and the Molecular Bioscience Building. In addition, the area surrounding the University is utilized as a natural laboratory by students in many academic areas. Hundreds of students each year participate in cutting-edge research opportunities through the Undergraduate Scholarship Program. Projects range from developing experiments to be put on a satellite, to studying thermal features in Yellowstone Park, to original research on the history of Bozeman.

Costs

University tuition and fees for the 2003–04 academic year for out-of-state students were $12,707; board and a double room, $5370; and books and supplies, about $890. Personal expenses and transportation costs were estimated at $2420. The estimated total for an out-of-state student was $21,387 per year. Residents of Montana pay one third the cost in tuition and fees, with all other expenses remaining constant.

Financial Aid

Montana State University maintains a comprehensive program of financial assistance for both freshmen and upperclass students, including scholarships, loans, grants, and work-study opportunities. Such aid is intended to recognize and assist students who otherwise would not be able to begin or continue their education. Approximately 75 percent of the students attending Montana State University receive some form of financial aid. Approximately 25 percent earn part of their expenses through part-time employment.

Faculty

There are 825 resident faculty members at Montana State who are teachers and hold their scholarly relationship with their students as a priority above all else. For example, 5.1 percent of lectures/seminars are taught by graduate teaching assistants (GTAs) and 36.1 percent of labs are taught by GTAs. Members of the faculty serve as advisers to undergraduate and graduate students, and many also serve as faculty advisers for student clubs, organizations, and committees.

Student Government

Student government at MSU has a long history of responsible leadership and service to the campus. As a result, students actively participate in the administration of the University as well as of student organizations.

Admission Requirements

All applicants must file an application for admission with a nonrefundable $30 fee. Freshmen must submit their high school record (posting date of graduation and rank in class) and scores from either the SAT I or ACT. Transfer applicants must submit official transcripts from each college or university attended. Transfer applicants who have earned fewer than 12 postsecondary quarter or semester credits must also submit an official high school transcript and test scores.

A graduate of any high school that is accredited by the Board of Public Education is eligible for admission as a first-time full-time undergraduate student provided he or she has obtained a minimum score of 22 on the ACT or 1030 on the SAT I or at least a 2.5 high school grade point average or ranks in the upper half of the school's graduating class and has completed the prescribed college-preparatory curriculum. Entering students are required to have completed the following courses in high school in order to be eligible for admission: 4 years of English, 3 years of mathematics (algebra I and II and geometry), 3 years of social studies, 2 years of laboratory science, and 2 years of electives chosen from foreign languages, computer science, visual or performing arts, or vocational education.

Transfer students must present at least a 2.0 (C) cumulative GPA based on transferable credits from all colleges or universities previously attended.

Application and Information

Students should contact:

Office of Admissions and New Student Services
Montana State University
P.O. Box 172190
Bozeman, Montana 59717-2190
Telephone: 406-994-2452
888-MSU-CATS (toll-free)
E-mail: admissions@montana.edu
World Wide Web: http://www.montana.edu/wwwnss/

Montana State University in Bozeman.

MONTCLAIR STATE UNIVERSITY

UPPER MONTCLAIR, NEW JERSEY

The University

Founded in 1908 as a normal school for the education of future teachers, Montclair State University has evolved into a four-year comprehensive public university that offers a broad range of educational and cultural opportunities. Montclair State is composed of the School of Business, the School of the Arts, the College of Humanities and Social Sciences, the College of Science and Mathematics, the College of Education and Human Services, and the Graduate School and confers degrees in forty-seven undergraduate majors and thirty-six graduate majors. Through its diverse programs and services, Montclair State seeks to develop educated men and women who are inquiring, creative, and responsible contributors to society.

Montclair State has been designated a Center of Excellence in the fine and performing arts in New Jersey. It is accredited by the Middle States Association of Colleges and Schools, and its teacher education, administrative, and school service personnel programs are approved by the National Council for Accreditation of Teacher Education. The School of Business is also accredited by AACSB International–The Association to Advance Collegiate Schools of Business.

The total enrollment was 15,204 in fall 2003, 11,375 of whom were enrolled as undergraduates, 7,023 women and 4,352 men. The majority of students are from New Jersey, and approximately 65 percent commute. The remainder live in campus residence halls or apartments or in off-campus housing. Students participate in more than 120 campus organizations. Some of the organizations that are involved in student life are the College Life Union Board, which is responsible for coordinating all social, cultural, educational, and recreational student programs; the Intercollegiate Athletic Council, which provides men and women of all the schools with the opportunity to participate in many varsity sports; and the Department of Campus Recreation, which runs the student intramural programs.

Location

Montclair State has the advantage of being situated on a 275-acre suburban campus, only 14 miles west of New York City. This proximity to the city gives students the opportunity to take advantage of the unusually rich cultural, social, and educational environment of the metropolitan area, while Montclair's suburban setting offers a nice contrast to city life. Mountain resorts and ocean beaches are also nearby.

Majors and Degrees

Montclair State offers programs of study leading to the Bachelor of Arts degree in anthropology, broadcasting, classics, communication studies, economics, English, fine arts, French, general humanities, geography, history, human ecology, Italian, justice studies, Latin, linguistics, music, music therapy, philosophy, political science, psychology, religious studies, sociology, Spanish, theater studies, and women's studies. The Bachelor of Science degree is offered in allied health services, athletic training, biochemistry, biology, business administration, chemistry, computer science, geosciences, health education, hospitality management, human ecology, mathematics, molecular biology, physical education, physics, recreation professions, and science informatics. The Bachelor of Fine Arts degree is awarded in dance, fine arts, and theater. The Bachelor of Music is awarded in music, and there is a five-year combined B.Mus./B.A. program. There is a 4-year/5-year combined B.A./M.A. program in practical anthropology. Combined Bachelor of Science/Doctor of Dental Medicine and Bachelor of Science/Doctor of Medicine degrees are also offered with the University of Medicine and Dentistry of New Jersey–New Jersey Dental School and University of Medicine and Dentistry of New Jersey–New Jersey Medical School, respectively. Articulated programs in physical therapy and physician assistant studies with the University of Medicine and Dentistry of New Jersey are offered, as is an articulation leading to a Pharm.D. with Rutgers.

A teacher certification program is offered in many of the subject areas mentioned above, generally for grades K through 12. Nursery school and elementary certification (N–8) is also available through several majors.

Minors are available in many of the majors listed. There are also several interdisciplinary academic programs, such as African-American studies, archaeology, criminal justice, film, Hispanic community affairs, international studies, paralegal studies, prelaw studies, public administration, Russian, Russian area studies, and women's studies. Part-time bachelor's degree programs are available.

Academic Programs

Successful completion of a minimum of 120 semester hours is necessary for graduation. Course requirements include general education (34–58 semester hours), comprising communication, humanities and the arts, pure and applied sciences, social and behavioral sciences, a physical education requirement, and a multicultural awareness requirement; and courses in the major field of study (32–82 semester hours).

The academic calendar is organized into two semesters (fall and spring) and summer sessions.

Montclair State also offers undergraduate degrees through the Center for Adult Learning for students 25 years of age or older.

Off-Campus Programs

Through the Cooperative Education Program, a student may receive academic credit for a full-time job and earn a full-time salary. This program gives a student the opportunity to receive on-the-job training in his or her prospective career area. Internships—work for credit, not pay—are available through many major departments.

Through programs offered by the New Jersey State College Council for International Education, the International Student Exchange Program, and the College Consortium for International Studies, students have the opportunity to study abroad in the continent of Australia and such countries as Argentina, Austria, Belize, China, Colombia, Denmark, Ecuador, France, Germany, Great Britain, Greece, Hungary, Ireland, Israel, Italy, Jamaica, Korea, Mexico, the Netherlands, Portugal, Spain, and Uruguay. In addition, foreign language majors may spend a year, a semester, or a summer in French-, German-, Italian-, or Spanish-speaking countries.

The University is a charter member of the New Jersey Marine Sciences Consortium, through which students may take field-oriented courses in the marine sciences. The New Jersey School of Conservation, located in Stokes State Forest, is the largest university-operated environmental education center in the world. Through this facility, students may take courses relating to the environment in the humanities, social sciences, and natural and physical sciences and in outdoor pursuits.

Academic Facilities

The holdings of the Harry A. Sprague Library include 420,000 books, 3,400 periodical subscriptions, 24,359 government publications, and more than 1.3 million nonprint items. The nonprint department has equipment for viewing and listening to videocassettes, records, audiocassettes, compact discs, soundslide sets, and a variety of microforms. As a designated government publications depository, the library receives and makes available for use its collections of federal and New Jersey publications.

Sprague Library provides computerized access to its holdings, interlibrary services, and information retrieval. Online database searching and compact disc database searching are available for most subjects and disciplines.

Students are also encouraged to use the resources of the Technology Solutions Center, which provides audiovisual materials, equipment, and services. The center contains a film library, videotaping equipment, and a wide range of other audiovisual equipment and provides custom graphic and photographic services. The Information Technology Center offers computer services to students and incorporates the latest advances in technology in its facilities. Also included among the University's facilities are two modern theaters, a recital hall, a theater-arts workshop, and science, language, and computer laboratories.

Costs

In 2003–04, full-time tuition and fees were assessed at a flat yearly rate of $6410 for New Jersey residents and $9409 for out-of-state students. Part-time tuition and fees were $213 per credit for New Jersey residents and $313 per credit for out-of-state students. Approximate annual room and board for dormitory students were $7780 (costs are subject to change).

Financial Aid

Four major types of financial aid programs are available at Montclair State: loans, grants, scholarships, and employment. Within each of these categories, funding may be available through federal, state, and/or institutional sources. State aid programs include Tuition Aid Grants, Educational Opportunity Fund Grants, Bloustein Distinguished Scholars awards, Public Tuition Benefits awards, and N.J. CLASS loans. Federal sources of aid include Federal Pell Grants, Federal Supplemental Educational Opportunity Grants, Federal Perkins Loans, the Federal Work-Study Program, Federal Stafford Student Loans, Federal PLUS loans, and programs for veterans. Approximately 71 percent of undergraduates receive financial aid. Students should contact the Financial Aid Office regarding application materials and deadline dates.

Faculty

Faculty members teach both graduate and undergraduate courses, with few departments employing graduate assistants. Approximately 90 percent of the faculty members hold doctorates or the appropriate terminal degree in their disciplines. A faculty-student ratio of 1:18 permits considerable interaction between students and professors. All faculty members have posted office hours in order to provide students with assistance in course material and in planning a program of study. In addition, faculty members participate actively in student-oriented activities, serve as advisers to student clubs, and conduct extracurricular workshops and field trips.

Student Government

The Student Government Association (SGA), a parent corporation that includes within its structure various class organizations and services for the student body, is composed of all undergraduates. The substantial budget of the SGA allows for the development and financing of student activities and services, such as concerts, film series, intramural sports, a drop-in center, legal aid services, a student-run radio station, and a student newspaper. The Student Government Association Legislature acts as the final representative for the entire undergraduate student body and is composed of elected representatives from each class and major curriculum.

Admission Requirements

Montclair State is an Equal Opportunity/Affirmative Action institution and does not discriminate on the basis of sex, race, color, national origin, age, or physical handicap in providing access to its benefits and services, in compliance with relevant federal and state legislation.

Applicants must present a certificate of graduation from an approved secondary school (or a high school equivalency certificate), showing the following minimum college-preparatory units: English, 4; history, 2; mathematics, 3; laboratory science, 2; foreign language, 2; and electives in English, social studies, science, mathematics, or foreign languages, 3. Freshman applicants must take the SAT I or ACT; Subject Tests are not required. Admission to the programs in broadcasting, communication studies, dance, fine arts, music, and theater depends upon successful completion of departmental auditions, interviews, or portfolio reviews.

Application and Information

Applicants must submit a completed application form, a nonrefundable application fee of $55, a copy of their official high school transcript, and copies of their SAT I or ACT scores. Admission decisions are announced on a rolling basis until all spaces are filled.

For application forms and additional admission information, students should contact:

Office of Admissions
Montclair State University
Upper Montclair, New Jersey 07043-1624
Telephone: 800-331-9205 (toll-free)
World Wide Web: http://www.montclair.edu

MONTREAT COLLEGE

MONTREAT, NORTH CAROLINA

The College

Montreat College is a four-year Christian liberal arts college affiliated with the Presbyterian Church (USA). At Montreat, a student's experience is enhanced by an education of value, grounded in a strong liberal arts core, taught by an outstanding Christian faculty, and prized by today's employers and graduate schools. Students benefit from Montreat's small classes where their opinions matter, and they grow through one-on-one interaction with professors and classmates. Studies challenge them to integrate learning into their faith, while considering subjects in ways never thought possible. Hands-on experiences in the majors (internships, field studies, mission programs, community service, and independent research) enable students to gain practical career and life preparation.

Montreat College enrollment is rapidly growing. Enrollment is more than 1,000 in the traditional Montreat campus program and in the off-campus School of Professional and Adult Studies. The student body typically represents approximately thirty states and ten other countries.

The natural beauty of the Montreat campus both calms the spirit and awakens the senses. In a diverse and multicultural environment, students learn how to investigate the unfamiliar, think critically, and communicate and clarify their ideas. In the process, they develop the skills, personal values, and faith to take their places in the world with confidence.

Montreat College welcomes students of many denominations from diverse cultural backgrounds. In the residence hall or over dinner at a professor's house, students find themselves sharing perspectives and exchanging ideas. The distinct spirit of community goes beyond the faculty, staff, and students and extends to visitors to the Christian conference center, to residents of the neighboring towns of Montreat and Black Mountain, and to the "cottagers" who vacation in the area throughout the seasons.

Students enjoy living in the beautiful stone residence halls that provide views of the mountains surrounding the campus. The comfortable rooms are equipped with air-conditioning, cable TV, computer networking, and telephone installation, and residents have access to laundry facilities and kitchen areas.

Montreat College is also a place where students can set themselves apart through an extraordinary range of leadership opportunities. At Montreat College, a special emphasis is placed on the concept of servant leadership. Students participate in Servanthood and Leadership Training (SALT) Week each September. A nationally recognized Discovery/Wilderness Program takes advantage of the mountain location and offers a unique twenty-one day adventure for academic credit. Outdoor recreation opportunities ranging from hiking to white-water adventures to snow skiing are available to students. The students also choose from a variety of off-campus volunteer service opportunities such as area nursing homes, churches, children's homes, and shelters.

Montreat College is a member of the National Association of Intercollegiate Athletics (NAIA). Men compete in baseball, basketball, cross-country, golf, soccer, and tennis. Women compete in basketball, cross-country, soccer, softball, tennis, and volleyball. Students enjoy an active intramural program where exciting competition takes place throughout the year.

Location

Montreat College is located in the beautiful Blue Ridge Mountains of western North Carolina. The scenic main campus is nestled into sloping woods just 15 miles east of Asheville, North Carolina, and 2 miles from I-40. Students enjoy the proximity of Asheville, one of North Carolina's most architecturally and culturally diverse cities. Adjacent to Montreat is the historic town of Black Mountain, with picturesque avenues, stores, and restaurants.

Montreat College's off-campus School of Professional and Adult Studies has permanent campus facilities in Black Mountain and Charlotte and holds classes in a number of additional North Carolina locations, including Asheville.

Majors and Degrees

Montreat College is accredited by the Commission on Colleges of the Southern Association of Colleges and Schools to award degrees at the bachelor's, master's, and associate level. Traditional students can choose to pursue a Bachelor of Arts, Bachelor of Science, or Bachelor of Music degree with a wide variety of majors, minors, and concentrations. Teacher certification is available in elementary education.

Students pursuing a Bachelor of Arts degree may choose to major in American studies, Bible and religion, English, history, human services, and music business.

Majors available in the Bachelor of Science degree program are American studies, Bible and religion, biology, business administration, computer information systems, environmental studies, history, human services, and outdoor education.

A Bachelor of Music degree is offered with a major in music performance.

Montreat College's School of Professional and Adult Studies is designed specifically for the adult learner who has completed some college work and desires to finish a degree in an accelerated program. This off-campus program offers the Bachelor of Business Administration degree, the Master of Business Administration degree, the Associate of Science degree in business, and the Associate of Science degree in education.

Academic Programs

Upon enrollment, students are assigned a faculty adviser to assist them in clarifying their educational objectives and meeting the requirements for graduation. Students and faculty advisers work together in arranging a program of study leading to graduation. Graduation requirements are a minimum of 126 semester hours, cumulative quality point average of at least 2.0, completion of the general education core requirements, 33 semester hours in 300-level or above courses, completion of all requirements for a major, a grade of C or better in courses needed for the major or minor, and completion of the last 31 semester hours at Montreat College.

Students interested in careers in medicine, law, criminology, and other professional areas are reminded that the best preparation, according to graduate school advisers in these areas, is a solid liberal arts degree program such as that found at Montreat College.

Off-Campus Programs

Off-campus academic experiences are available to Montreat students through programs in Chicago, Illinois; Colorado Springs, Colorado; Washington, D.C.; Los Angeles, California; AuSable, Michigan; Oxford, England; Jerusalem, Israel; Cairo, Egypt; Moscow, Russia; Costa Rica; and China. Local and international service and internship opportunities are also available to students.

Academic Facilities

Classrooms are conveniently located close to residence halls. Morgan Hall provides modern classrooms and laboratory space for the environmental studies, science, and mathematics departments. The natural environment of Montreat, North Carolina, offers a broad, living laboratory close at hand for highly specialized majors in environmental studies and outdoor education. The library belongs to a coalition of college libraries, which greatly enhances study and research by making even more resources available from colleges throughout western North Carolina. The College has installed a campuswide fiber-optic computer network linking the campus and providing access to the Internet. The centrally located L. Nelson Bell Library houses one of the College's computer labs and the spacious Hamilton Gallery. The Belk Campus Center contains a computer lab, classrooms, campus store, lounges, and mailboxes. Gaither Hall houses the administration offices, the Chaplain's office, and state-of-the-art music laboratories and rehearsal rooms. The Christian Studies Center features the beautiful Chapel of the Prodigal, with an original fresco by internationally known artist Ben Long, and the McGowan Center for Christian Studies, which houses the Christian Ministries department. The Black Mountain Campus provides classrooms, laboratories, administrative and faculty offices, conference facilities, intercollegiate athletic facilities, a beautiful wooded preserve, and historical landmark buildings.

Costs

Tuition, room, and board for the 2004–05 school year are $19,970. This cost includes all standard fees. A few select courses require a separate registration fee. There is no out-of-state tuition fee. Basic fees for each semester are due at registration. Tuition payment plans are available through Academic Management Services (AMS).

Financial Aid

Through generous financial aid and scholarship packages, deserving students receive the quality academics of a private college at a modest cost. Each year, more than 95 percent of Montreat students receive some form of financial aid. Working individually with each student, the College awards financial aid packages that include scholarships, grants, loans, and work-study jobs. Scholarships are also made available to transfer students. All students must submit the Free Application for Federal Student Aid (FAFSA) and the Montreat College Application for Scholarship and Financial Assistance. To drastically reduce processing time, the FAFSA can be electronically submitted by the College to the federal government for students who have applied, been accepted, and submitted a $100 deposit. For more information, students should call the Financial Aid Office at 800-545-4656 (toll-free).

Faculty

Montreat College seeks to provide an education that is constantly informed by Christian insights. All faculty members are professing Christians committed to teaching, learning, and investing themselves in the lives and futures of their students. More than 70 percent of the full-time faculty members hold a doctorate or the highest degree in their field. Students benefit from small classes and the student-faculty ratio is typically 15:1.

Student Government

An active Student Government Association (SGA) is composed of all the full-time students at Montreat College. It carries out its responsibilities through its executive, legislative, and judicial branches, which operate at all levels of campus living. It plays a primary role in interpreting the needs of students and in determining the quality of student life. The SGA works closely with the Director of Student Services and holds the authority to implement and make effective its responsibility to the College community. Officers are elected by the students.

Admission Requirements

To be accepted, a student must have a minimum total score of 860 on the SAT I and a minimum cumulative 2.25 GPA (on a 4.0 scale). An ACT composite score of at least 18 is acceptable in lieu of SAT I scores. Montreat welcomes transfer students. Home-schooled students are also welcomed and encouraged to apply. International students from countries where English is not the primary language must score a minimum of 500 on the paper version of the Test of English as a Foreign Language (TOEFL).

Application and Information

Students are required to submit a formal application accompanied by a $15 application fee. The common application is accepted. An official transcript of high school credits must be submitted directly from the high school to the College Office of Admissions. SAT I/ACT verification is also required. Montreat College's school code is 005423.

For more information, students should write or call:

Office of Admissions
Montreat College
P.O. Box 1267
Montreat, North Carolina 28757-1267
Telephone: 828-669-8012 Ext. 3781
800-622-6968 (toll-free)
Fax: 828-669-0120
E-mail: admissions@montreat.edu
World Wide Web: http://www.montreat.edu

Students on the campus of Montreat College.

MONTSERRAT COLLEGE OF ART
BEVERLY, MASSACHUSETTS

The College

Students come to Montserrat College of Art for many reasons—to gain professional competence, to develop their own unique talents, and to engage in new areas of experience. Whatever the personal goal, students find an environment in which their visions, aspirations, and commitments are nurtured and refined.

Founded in 1970 by a group of artists questioning the status quo and seeking new solutions, Montserrat possesses a variety of advantages that distinguish it from the nation's other schools of art and design. With an enrollment of 390 students of diverse cultural and artistic backgrounds, the College is large enough to offer the wide array of courses and concentrations that make up a strong visual arts curriculum, yet small enough to provide the personal attention that is often difficult to find in larger educational environments. Montserrat is a residential college, which serves to enhance a student's sense of belonging to the college community and encourages a greater involvement in its cultural life. The College is accredited by the New England Association of Schools and Colleges (NEASC) and the National Association of Schools of Art and Design (NASAD).

Location

Many Montserrat students reside in apartments on campus in the historic city of Beverly, located 30 minutes north of Boston along the coast of the Atlantic Ocean. Beverly was founded in 1626 and was home to George Washington's naval base. Student housing is nestled among the homes of downtown Beverly and is within walking distance of all College facilities. The main academic building faces the newly landscaped public common and the Beverly Public Library. The Cabot Street Cinema screens popular, foreign, and art films and is the home of the Le Grand David Spectacular Magic Company. Shops, cafes, and restaurants line nearby Cabot Street where Montserrat's two other studio buildings are located. The public beach at Dane Street and tranquil Lynch Park, site of President Taft's summer White House, are just steps away. The renowned Peabody Essex Museum, the House of the Seven Gables, and other sites related to the infamous Witch Hysteria of 1692 are located in the neighboring city of Salem.

Boston and Cambridge are easily accessible by car or commuter train. More than 100 colleges and universities are located in the Boston metropolitan area. World-class museums, such as Boston's Museum of Fine Arts, galleries, libraries, shopping, sports, and a variety of entertainment options provide a stimulating intellectual, cultural, and social environment in which to live and learn.

Majors and Degrees

There are two 4-year options for study at Montserrat. Students may apply as a candidate for either the Bachelor of Fine Arts (B.F.A.) degree or the Diploma of the College. Both options offer the same challenging studio program but a different curriculum of liberal arts study.

Following the first year of art foundation studies, a student may choose to concentrate in fine arts, graphic design, illustration, new media, painting and drawing, photography, printmaking, or sculpture and can also prepare for a career in art education. To earn the B.F.A. degree, a student must earn 120 credits—78 credits of studio course work and 42 credits in liberal arts, including a minimum of 12 credits in art history and 6 credits in English. A student is awarded the Diploma of the College upon completion of 108 credits—a minimum of 78 credits of studio course work and a minimum of 6 credits in both art history and English. The balance of credits required for the Diploma of the College may be earned in either studio or liberal art courses. The art education program complements a studio concentration and prepares students to qualify for provisional certification with advanced standing in Massachusetts public schools and other states with reciprocity agreements.

Academic Program

Art is born of a rich variety of human experience and inquiry. Montserrat's unique curriculum engages both faculty and students in discovering new ways for the liberal and visual arts to work together to educate the total artist. During the first year of foundation studies, students are introduced to the various studio concentrations at Montserrat. The foundation curriculum is a carefully crafted sequence of varied but complementary courses that emphasize the visual, technical, written, and verbal skills essential to a successful art college experience.

Once a student has earned 90 credits, completed required course work, and demonstrated sufficient media skills in the chosen studio concentration, entry into the Senior Seminar is determined by a faculty panel. Students in Senior Seminar have the opportunity to delve independently into a significant, coherent body of work. Aided by a faculty mentor, students work intensely to articulate their unique voice and visual language. Seniors exhibit seminar work throughout the spring in the Montserrat Gallery at 301 Cabot Street. This revelatory experience helps students mature as artists and designers and, ultimately, make the transition into professional life.

Off-Campus Programs

Montserrat offers students a variety of opportunities to broaden their horizons and earn credits towards the B.F.A. degree or Diploma through, local, national, and international study.

The College is a member of the Northeast Consortium of Colleges and Universities in Massachusetts. Students may take classes and use the library facilities of member colleges.

Through Montserrat's affiliation with the Association of Independent Colleges of Art and Design (AICAD), students may spend a semester or a year in comparable studies at a member institution. Students remain registered at Montserrat, retaining residency and student aid eligibility. The AICAD New York Studio Program offers third-year students the opportunity to spend a summer in New York City either as a professional intern or attending weekly seminars while working independently in a semiprivate studio. Students may choose to spend a month in the walled, papal city of Viterbo in Italy while attending Montserrat's summer residential program. Intensive courses in painting, drawing, photography, art history, and writing are offered.

Academic Facilities

Montserrat's main building, the historic Hardie Building, houses four floors of newly renovated studios, classrooms, exhibition spaces, the Paul Scott Library, and offices. Specially equipped studios for printmaking, photography, painting, and illustration, as well as video and computer labs, are located here. Graphic design students work in an environment similar to a professional design studio, with computers, access to the Internet, and a meeting area. The Paul Scott Library contains a collection of more than 13,000 books, numerous art and related periodicals, videos, CD-ROMs, and other resources. The library also offers Internet access and houses a slide collection of more than 41,000 slide images. The library is a member of the North of Boston Library Exchange consortium of academic and public libraries, including the Beverly Public Library located across the street from Montserrat's Hardie Building.

The Montserrat campus offers four galleries that feature an exciting array of exhibitions by artists within the Montserrat community of students, alumni, and faculty and staff members and also professional artists of regional and national note.

Montserrat's Cabot Studio Building offers spacious facilities for sculpture students and semiprivate studios for seniors concentrating in painting, photography, printmaking, sculpture, and mixed media.

Across Cabot Street are the newly renovated studios for illustration students, including semiprivate studio spaces for seniors in the department. Adjacent to the studios are reproduction equipment and an extensive collection of research materials.

All students are entitled to free admission to the Boston Museum of Fine Arts, one of the finest collections of art in the world. The museum houses permanent exhibits of art and artifacts representing virtually all periods and civilizations, as well as changing exhibitions of art.

Costs

Tuition and general fees for the 2003–04 academic year were $17,850. Other annual direct costs of attendance, including supplies, health insurance, and on-campus housing in a shared room, were estimated at $6400. Indirect costs of attendance, such as food, transportation, and other personal expenses, were estimated at $5000.

Financial Aid

Nearly 80 percent of Montserrat students receive financial assistance (grants, loans, and employment). Sources include the federal government, state government, the College, and corporate and civic sponsors. Most financial aid is awarded on the basis of demonstrated need. To apply for financial aid, students must complete the Free Application for Federal Student Aid (FAFSA). Applications filed by March 1 receive priority consideration. Each year a select number of exceptional applicants for fall admission are selected for renewable talent scholarships. Candidates for scholarships must complete all requirements for admission and be accepted to the College by March 1.

Faculty

The faculty of Montserrat comprises professional artists and designers and accomplished scholars. There are 20 full-time faculty members and 47 part-time instructors. Fifty-nine percent of faculty members have earned a master's degree and 29 percent hold doctorates. The student-teacher ratio is 11:1.

Student Government

Students have a voice in College policies, events, and activities through the Student Council, which maintains close communication with College administrators and faculty members. Each year, a student elected by the Student Council serves as a representative at all faculty meetings. Student Council members are active in the programming and planning of social activities and College events designed to enhance student life.

Admission Requirements

The Admissions Committee is interested in the unique interests, experiences, and abilities of each applicant. The portfolio of artwork is the most significant part of a prospective student's application, and it is highly recommended that it be presented in person during an on-campus interview. Applicants who reside more than 150 miles from the campus may present the portfolio during an off-campus meeting or may mail the portfolio in slide form. Academic transcripts, standardized test scores, letters of recommendation, and an artist's statement help the Admissions Committee to assess an applicant's potential for success at the College.

Application and Information

Admissions decisions are made on a rolling basis, and applicants are notified of a decision within two to three weeks of completing all application requirements. For complete information on admission, financial aid, studio and academic programs, student and residential life, and campus visits, prospective students may contact:

Admissions Office
Montserrat College of Art
23 Essex Street
Beverly, Massachusetts 01915
Telephone: 978-921-4242 Ext. 1153
800-836-0487 (toll-free)
Fax: 978-921-4241
E-mail: admiss@montserrat.edu
World Wide Web: http://www.montserrat.edu

MOORE COLLEGE OF ART & DESIGN

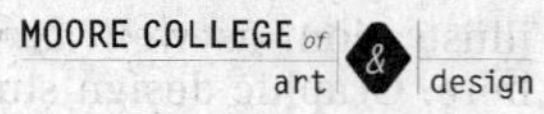

PHILADELPHIA, PENNSYLVANIA

The College

As the only women's college for the visual arts in the nation, Moore College of Art & Design sets the standard of excellence in educating women for careers in art and design. Moore students experience a singular educational expense within a small, supportive community and are taught by a dedicated faculty of exceptional artists, designers, and scholars.

Moore offers nine Bachelor of Fine Arts degree majors, emphasizing career and leadership skills throughout the academic and the cocurricular programs. Each major provides career preparation for the respective field and offers internships coordinated with the Locks Career Center for Women in the Arts. The Locks Center also provides extensive career resources for students and alumnae, such as one-on-one career counseling, mentoring, job bulletins, and workshops on topics ranging from networking to resume writing. On-campus leadership organizations provide the chance to learn about and utilize leadership skills and to develop self-confidence. Leadership fellowships provide financial support for students to work either with an individual leader in the arts community or within an innovative organization. Other experiences are available through community service or study abroad.

Approximately 70 percent of first-year students live in College housing, which includes Main Residence, Sartain Hall, townhouse apartments, and off-site College-contracted apartments. Some students choose to rent an apartment near the campus or in one of Philadelphia's other residential neighborhoods.

Moore alumnae are accomplished artists and designers who use their creativity, skills, and talent to excel in a wide variety of industries. Among Moore's notable graduates are fashion designer and business icon, Adrienne Vittadini; renowned twenty-first-century portraitist, Alice Neel; award-winning interior designer, Karon Daroff; and Pulitzer Prize-winning photojournalist, Sharon J. Wohlmuth.

Moore College of Art & Design is accredited by the Commission on Higher Education of the Middle States Association of Colleges and Schools (3624 Market Street, Philadelphia, Pennsylvania 19104-2680, telephone: 215-662-5606). The Commission on Higher Education is an institutional accrediting agency recognized by the U.S. Secretary of Education and the Commission on Recognition of Postsecondary Accreditation; by the National Association of Schools of Art and Design (11250 Roger Bacon Drive, Suite 21, Reston, Virginia 20190, telephone: 703-437-0700); by the Commonwealth of Pennsylvania, Department of Education (333 Market Street, Harrisburg, Pennsylvania 17126-0333, telephone: 717-787-5820); and by the Foundation for Interior Design Education Research (146 Monroe Center NW, #1318, Grand Rapids, Michigan 49503-2822, telephone: 616-458-0400).

Location

Moore is located in Center City, Philadelphia in the scenic Museum District. Neighbors on the Benjamin Franklin Parkway include the Philadelphia Art Museum, the Rodin Museum, the Academy of Natural Sciences, the Franklin Institute, and the Free Library of Philadelphia. The Parkway is also the future site of the new Calder and Barnes Museums. The city is home to famous historical sites, myriad art galleries, diverse neighborhoods, and shops and restaurants of every variety. This artistic and cultural vitality provides Moore students with a multitude of resources and recreation in a stimulating urban setting. Nearly eighty nearby colleges and universities form one of the largest higher-education communities in the nation, second only to New York City.

Philadelphia is 100 miles south of New York City and 133 miles north of Washington, D.C., a short journey practical by car or train. Faculty members regularly organize classroom trips to take advantage of these cities' additional galleries, museums, and designer showrooms.

Majors and Degrees

Moore College of Art & Design offers a four-year program leading to a Bachelor of Fine Arts, with concentrations in fashion design, fine arts (two- and three-dimensional), graphic design, illustration, interior design, general fine arts with art education certification, studio art with an art history emphasis, and textile design. Students can minor in any major offered as well as in photography. Students are required in most majors (and are encouraged in all) to participate in an internship to acquire practical experience in their chosen field. In addition to Bachelor of Fine Arts degree programs, Moore also offers postbaccalaureate certificates in art education as well as the other eight majors.

Academic Program

The College operates on a two-semester academic year. Of the total number of hours required for completion of the B.F.A. degree program, approximately two thirds are in a studio area and one third are in academic courses.

A student's first year includes a broadly based core of studies in art history, two- and three-dimensional basic design, color, drawing, computer applications, figure drawing, and the humanities. Introductory courses to the fine and design arts are also offered. Tutorial support is available for all students. At the end of the first year, the student chooses a design or fine arts concentration.

While instruction in the core studies is highly directive, advanced studio courses require more initiative and self-discipline, because the College provides each student with an increasingly personal program of study and assistance. Seniors in both the fine arts and design arts acquire practical experience in their fields through internships, apprenticeships, and the College's cooperative education program.

The College participates in the Association of Independent Colleges of Art and Design (AICAD) Student Mobility Exchange Program. A student who meets eligibility requirements may apply for one semester's study at an AICAD member school's program.

In addition to Bachelor of Fine Arts programs. Moore also offers leading programs for women and men through Continuing Education (CE), which is held mainly on evenings and weekends. The 81 year-old Young Artists Workshop (YAW) provides art education opportunities for girls and boys in grades 1–12. The Summer Fine Arts Institute is a four-week summer residency program for high school age women that earns 3 college credits. CE certificate programs include desktop publishing/computer graphics, Web design, and decorative arts for interiors. For CE information, students should call 215-965-4029 or contact CE via e-mail at ce@moore.edu.

Academic Facilities

A complex of interconnected buildings includes Wilson Hall, Sarah Peter Hall, and Main Residence. Sartain Residence Hall is located two blocks from the main campus. The main campus includes expansive studios and classrooms, technology centers, two auditoriums, Fox Commons, MAC and PC computer labs, a professional woodshop, ferrous and nonferrous metal workshops, ceramic studios with indoor and outdoor kilns, abundant student exhibition space, two contemporary art galleries, several outdoor courtyards, and the dining café. The Connolly Library's extensive holdings include 40,000 volumes reflecting subjects in the curriculum, artists' books, rare design folios, a slide collection of more than 125,000 images, reference materials, exhibition catalogs and annuals, and subscriptions to 185 local, national, and international periodicals.

The Galleries at Moore present a wide range of exhibitions and educational programs of both established and emerging artists. The Paley Gallery exhibits challenging and innovative work by national and international artists, while the Levy Gallery showcases artists from the Philadelphia area. The galleries also provide a professional exhibition space for shows by Moore students, faculty members, and alumnae. In addition, Moore has two galleries showing student, alumnae, and faculty members' work at Philadelphia's new landmark, the Kimmel Center for the Performing Arts.

Costs

Estimated tuition and fees for 2003–04 were $19,714; room and board fees for students living in College residence halls were approximately $7420. Books, supplies, and personal expenses (excluding transportation) are estimated to be between $2000 and $2200 per year for most students.

Financial Aid

The College offers financial aid based on financial need as established by information provided on the Free Application for Federal Student Aid (FAFSA).

The principal forms of financial aid are Federal Pell Grants, Federal Supplemental Educational Opportunity Grants, Federal Perkins Loans, and Moore College of Art & Design scholarships and grants. Assistance is also available through the Federal Work-Study program. For full consideration, students are encouraged to apply for financial aid by March 1.

Moore College annually grants $2 million in scholarship aid to incoming and continuing students who demonstrate excellence both academically and artistically. Awards are granted on the basis of the portfolio review and academic merit.

Faculty

Moore College of Art & Design has 111 faculty members, 25 in academic and 86 in studio areas. All studio classes are taught by practicing professionals. The student-faculty ratio is approximately 8:1.

Student Government

On-campus leadership organizations provide the chance to learn about and utilize leadership skills and to develop self-confidence participating in groups such as Student Government, Student Mentors, Residence Life Staff, and the Student Judiciary Committee. Students are trained in areas such as teambuilding, presentation skills, ethics, diversity, time management, and creating community on campus.

Admission Requirements

The admission decision is based on an evaluation of the following required materials: transcripts from high schools and any colleges attended, SAT I or ACT examination scores, and a portfolio of between twelve and twenty pieces of original artwork that must include six to eight drawings from direct observation. (International students should submit scores on the Test of English as a Foreign Language (TOEFL) instead of SAT I or ACT scores.) First-year students may enter in the fall and spring semesters.

Transfer students are encouraged to apply for advanced class standing at Moore. Class standing is determined on the basis of acceptable transfer credits and an evaluation of the applicant's portfolio. All transfers who are applying for advanced standing must submit their portfolio in slide form, accompanied by a detailed description letter. Upper-level transfer students may enter in the fall or spring semester.

Application and Information

Although Moore has no application deadline, students seeking admission in the fall semester are encouraged to submit applications to the Admissions Office by April 1.

For application forms, catalogs, and additional information, students should contact:

Director of Admissions
Moore College of Art & Design
20th and the Parkway
Philadelphia, Pennsylvania 19103-1179
Telephone: 215-965-4014
800-523-2025 (toll-free)
Fax: 215-568-3547
E-mail: admiss@moore.edu
World Wide Web: http://www.moore.edu

Moore College of Art & Design has the distinction of being the only art college for women in the United States.

MORAVIAN COLLEGE

BETHLEHEM, PENNSYLVANIA

The College

Moravian College is the nation's sixth-oldest college, tracing its origins to a women's program begun in 1742. Settlers from Eastern Europe, known as Moravians, founded both the College and the community of Bethlehem and brought to America a rich cultural heritage of architecture, music, scholarship, and craftsmanship. The strength of Moravian's music program and the community's famed Bach Choir are aspects of the continuing influence of this heritage. Moravian College is a selective, coeducational institution offering more than forty programs with foundations in the liberal arts and sciences. Among its strengths and distinctions are an outstanding faculty with a personal and professional commitment to teaching, a demanding academic program recognized for its excellence and high standards, and close working relationships among students, faculty members, and staff. Moravian has won national recognition for the depth and effectiveness of its career-counseling and placement programs. Opportunities for field studies and internships enhance career preparation in much the same way that independent study and honors programs enhance all aspects of the academic program.

The majority of the 1,490 students enrolled come from Pennsylvania and New Jersey, but approximately twenty-five states and twelve countries are represented in the student body. Moravian's students are involved in a wide range of activities and athletics. Men compete in intercollegiate baseball, basketball, cross-country, football, golf, lacrosse, soccer, tennis, and track and field; women compete in basketball, cross-country, field hockey, lacrosse, soccer, softball, tennis, track and field, and volleyball. Intramural sports include basketball, indoor soccer, softball, and touch football. Club sports include equitation, ice hockey, and skiing. Activities range from participation in an outing club to modern dancing. There are departmental clubs, honor societies, fraternities, sororities, and service organizations. Communications opportunities include a student newspaper, a yearbook, WRMC (radio station), a literary magazine, and work in the Media Center. Performance groups include the Moravian College Theatre Company, a wind ensemble, an orchestra, and the Moravian College Choir, which in recent years has toured Europe, including England, Germany, and Scandinavia; Israel; and the Caribbean and performed at the Kennedy Center in Washington, D.C. Nationally known lecturers, scholars, authors, and artists are brought to campus, and, through the College-Community Concert series, many major European and American touring orchestras have appeared on campus. Many students participate in volunteer activities related to political, social welfare, health, and teaching fields. Approximately 85 percent of Moravian's students reside on campus in housing that ranges from the traditional dormitory to apartment and town-house accommodations.

An M.B.A. degree is offered by the Department of Economics and Business through the Division of Continuing and Graduate Studies. As a corporate institution, Moravian College also includes a theological seminary, offering programs leading to the Master of Divinity (M.Div.) degree and Master of Arts (M.A.) degrees in theological studies and pastoral counseling; a cooperative program leading to the M.A. in Christian Education is also offered. While campus facilities are shared with the undergraduate program, the faculty, administration, and fee schedules are separate.

Location

Moravian College is located in Bethlehem, Pennsylvania, a city of 75,000 people. Bethlehem's location in the Lehigh Valley area (Allentown-Bethlehem-Easton) and its proximity to New York and Philadelphia allow it to combine the advantages of these cities with the accessibility and friendliness of a smaller community. Moravian shares its Lehigh Valley location with the world headquarters of Bethlehem Steel Corporation, Air Products, Mack Truck, Rodale Press, Agere Systems, and other businesses and industries as well as with five other private colleges: Lafayette, Muhlenberg, and Cedar Crest Colleges; and DeSales and Lehigh Universities. Bethlehem, with its distinctive history, is carefully preserving its past while engaging in twenty-first-century expansion.

Majors and Degrees

Moravian College offers the Bachelor of Arts, Bachelor of Science, and Bachelor of Music degrees with programs of study in forty areas. The following programs of study are offered: accounting, art, art education, art history and criticism, biochemistry, biology, chemistry, classics, clinical and counseling, computer science, criminal justice, drama and theater, economics, engineering, engineering (dual degree program), English, financial economics, French, geology, German, graphic and advertising design, history, information systems, international management, management, mathematics, medical technology, music, natural resource management, nursing, philosophy, physics, political science, psychology, religion, social science, sociology, Spanish, and writing. (Engineering, geology, medical technology, natural resource management, occupational therapy, and physical therapy are offered in cooperation with other institutions.) The College offers preprofessional programs in law, medicine, teacher education (elementary, secondary, and music), and theology. Students can also structure interdepartmental majors, individually designed majors, double majors, and minors in all areas.

Academic Program

The academic year consists of fall and spring terms of fifteen weeks each. The typical course load per term is 4 course units equivalent to 4 semester-credit hours per unit.

To earn a baccalaureate degree, students are required to complete 32 course units (128 semester-credit hours). By following Moravian's general education curriculum, Learning in Common, students are given a coherent introduction to the liberal arts and sciences. Special programs available include independent study, field study, study abroad and exchange programs, a special honors program in the senior year, and the Student Opportunities for Academic Research (SOAR) program.

The Learning in Common (LINC) curriculum includes a multidisciplinary approach designed to sharpen such critical skills as writing, computer competence, knowledge of economic and social systems, science experimentation, moral and ethical issues, international and historical perspectives, and quantitative reasoning.

Off-Campus Programs

Moravian students may participate in the Washington Semester, study at Oxford University, and experience a variety of other study-abroad opportunities for a summer, a term, or a full academic year. In addition, students may cross-register for courses offered by Lehigh and DeSales Universities and Lafayette, Muhlenberg, and Cedar Crest Colleges through the Lehigh Valley Association of Independent Colleges. Two- and four-year U.S. Army ROTC programs are available through cross-registration with Lehigh University. All programs carry academic credit. Students may also participate in courses and programs offered through the Lehigh Valley Center for Jewish Studies.

Academic Facilities

The Priscilla Payne Hurd Academic Complex, a $19-million technology-enhanced teaching facility, opened for the spring 2003 semester for the Departments of Education, Psychology, Sociology, Mathematics, and Computer Science. The facility is used for classroom teaching, conferences, laboratories, research, lectures, and special events.

Reeves Library houses 256,352 volumes and operates on an open-stack policy, with reading areas throughout the building. Cooperation with other Lehigh Valley colleges makes more than 2 million volumes readily accessible to Moravian College students. An automated online catalog with remote access is available, as are other online reference services. The library is open until midnight.

Collier Hall of Science, which has been recognized for its architectural design and function, provides lecture halls, teaching laboratories, specialized collections and reading rooms, a greenhouse, and individual research laboratories for faculty members and advanced students in physics, earth science, chemistry, biology, and computer science.

All members of the College community are provided a full range of computer network privileges, including e-mail, Internet access, and networked data storage. All residence hall rooms provide data network connections. Approximately 175 Windows, Macintosh, and Unix computers are available for student use in labs and classrooms. Standard office software, Web browsers, statistical packages, graphic design software, and miscellaneous courseware are available on these machines. Free laser printing is provided to all students as well. Seventeen of Moravian's classrooms have full multimedia capabilities. Course management software by Blackboard offers professors a full suite of teaching and communication tools for their classes.

The Center for Music and Art is located on the College's historic Priscilla Payne Hurd campus, in an area that reflects the grace of Colonial and Victorian architecture. The center has been extensively renovated for practice and performance needs and includes a changing-exhibition art gallery.

Costs

The cost of tuition and fees for 2003–04, including a student activity fee, was $22,028. Additional costs included a room fee of $3985 and a board fee of $3110. Books, travel, and miscellaneous expenses were estimated at $2370 for resident students, $4040 for students commuting from home, and $5270 for off-campus residents. International students' expenses are the same as those for resident students with additional expenses for airfare. A one-time freshman orientation fee of $30 is also charged.

Financial Aid

Moravian College, together with state and federal programs, offers financial aid to qualified students through scholarships, loans, grants, and employment. The purpose of these programs is to provide financial assistance to supplement that given by the student's family. Applications for financial aid, filed with the College and with state and federal agencies, allow students to be considered for each program for which they are eligible. All financial aid awards generally involve both grants and student self-help in the form of loans and student employment. Endowed scholarships are also available in several areas of study. Academic achievement, future promise, and leadership potential play a role in the type of award made. The College also offers limited funding to qualified international students each year.

The College awards approximately $20 million annually in financial aid (grants, campus jobs, and loans) to an average of 85 percent of the student body. Incoming freshmen and upperclassmen applying for need-based financial aid are required to file the College Scholarship Service Financial Aid PROFILE with signed copies of federal income taxes for both parents and student, and the Free Application for Federal Student Aid (FAFSA).

Moravian College offers merit scholarship programs, awarded to students without regard to financial need, based on superior academic performance. The scholarships range from $1000 to full tuition.

Faculty

More than 80 percent of Moravian's 114 full-time faculty members hold earned doctoral or other terminal degrees. The student-faculty ratio is 11:1. Many Moravian faculty members have distinguished themselves in research, publication, and public service, but the primary focus of their endeavors is on effective teaching and advising of students.

Student Government

The United Student Government represents students' interests, allocates activity funds to student organizations, and appoints students to student-faculty committees. Self-governance is developed through the appointment of an undergraduate resident staff and a student-dominated College Discipline Committee. Two students are elected annually as voting members of the Board of Trustees. The Haupert Union Program Board, composed entirely of students, provides a major part of the College's social program and, through its various committees, is a vehicle for the development of leadership.

Admission Requirements

Moravian welcomes students from diverse backgrounds and geographic locations. The Admissions Committee carefully evaluates the preparation and potential of each applicant, placing emphasis on academic achievement in secondary school. Other factors considered include a student's test scores, recommendations, extracurricular activities, major interests, and demonstrated interest in the College. Graduation from an accredited secondary school or a high school equivalency certificate is required. Eighty-one percent of the students entering Moravian in 2003 graduated in the top two fifths of their secondary school class, 52 percent in the top fifth. Of the 1,670 applicants, 1,143 were accepted. Of those that were accepted, 383 enrolled. Transfer and international students are welcome and are encouraged to apply. International applicants must demonstrate English proficiency and the ability to assume expenses and must provide transcripts (originals and certified translations) documenting secondary and postsecondary school study. Each transfer student's credentials are considered individually to determine the number of credits to be accepted. Transfer applicants must present a minimum 2.5 grade point average (4.0 scale). Students are strongly encouraged to visit the Moravian campus. Interviews, tours of the College, and visits with faculty members may be arranged by contacting the Admission Office prior to the visit.

Application and Information

Each prospective student should submit a completed application and a nonrefundable $40 application fee as early as possible in the senior year, preferably by January 1. The deadline is March 1. An official high school transcript, an essay, letters of recommendation, and reports from either the SAT I or ACT are required. The TOEFL is required of all applicants for whom English is not the native language. Applicants are notified of the Admissions Committee decision on March 15. Early decision applicants must apply by February 1. The committee notifies these applicants of its decision between December 15 and February 15.

For an application form or additional information, students should contact:

James P. Mackin
Director of Admission
Moravian College
Bethlehem, Pennsylvania 18018
Telephone: 610-861-1320
800-441-3191 (toll-free)
Fax: 610-625-7930
E-mail: admissions@moravian.edu
World Wide Web: http://www.moravian.edu

MORGAN STATE UNIVERSITY

BALTIMORE, MARYLAND

The University

Morgan State University, a coeducational institution, is located in a residential section of Baltimore, Maryland. The compact campus of forty-one academic buildings, service facilities, and residence halls covers an area of more than 157 acres. The University offers both graduate and undergraduate programs of study. Recently, emphasis has been placed on the urban orientation of the University. This emphasis has been incorporated in the graduate programs in particular. At the graduate level, the University offers the Master of Arts degree in African-American studies, economics, English, history, international studies, mathematics, music, sociology, and teaching. The Master of Business Administration is offered in accounting, finance, hospitality management, information systems, international business, management, and marketing and taxation. The Master of Science degree is offered in bioinformatics, educational administration and supervision, elementary and middle school education, science, sociology, telecommunications, and transportation. Professional master's degrees are offered in architecture, city and regional planning, engineering, landscape architecture, and public health. The Doctor of Education degree is offered in community college leadership, mathematics education, science education, and urban educational leadership. In addition, the Doctor of Philosophy degree is offered in bioenvironmental science, business administration, English, higher education, and history; the Doctor of Engineering degree is offered in civil, electrical, and industrial engineering; and the Doctor of Public Health degree is offered.

Morgan State University does not discriminate against applicants because of race, sex, religion, or nationality. The institution was chartered in 1867 and was built on its present site in 1890. From 1867 to 1890, it was known as the Centenary Biblical Institute; from 1890 to 1938 as Morgan College; and from 1938 to 1975 as Morgan State College. In 1975, the college became Morgan State University and was designated as the state's public urban university.

The McKeldin Center, often called the "living room of the campus," is the focal point of cultural and social activity for the University community. Its purpose is to provide all members of the University community with programs and facilities to satisfy a variety of out-of-classroom tastes and needs. The McKeldin Center is utilized according to individual interests for meetings, lectures, music, movies, reading, and other forms of indoor recreation, or simply for relaxing over a cup of coffee or casual conversation with friends.

The University is a member institution of several consortia, including the National Student Exchange, a consortium of twenty-two state colleges and universities across the country.

Location

The University has the advantages of both suburban life and proximity to an urban center. Built on two slopes, the campus is strategically located in the picturesque northeastern section of Baltimore, a city with a population of about 650,000, and is surrounded by rapidly growing residential communities. The center of the city is easily accessible from the University campus.

Majors and Degrees

The Bachelor of Arts degree is offered in economics, English, fine art, history, international studies, music, philosophy, political science, sociology, speech communication, telecommunications, and theater arts. The Bachelor of Science degree is offered in the fields of accounting, architecture and environmental design, biology, business administration, chemistry, computer science, economics, elementary education, engineering (civil, electrical, and industrial), engineering physics, family and consumer science, finance, food and nutrition, health education, hospitality management, information science and systems, management, marketing, mathematics, medical technology, physical education, physics, psychology, social work, and telecommunications.

Academic Programs

Students admitted to Morgan to study for a Bachelor of Arts or Bachelor of Science degree are generally expected to adhere to the accepted standards of higher education. Honors programs, independent study, and cooperative education programs are available in most areas. For those students who require special placement and/or special assistance, support services and programs are provided.

To earn a bachelor's degree, students must generally complete a minimum of 120 semester hours, depending on the program. Engineering students should expect to earn 135 semester hours to qualify for the degree.

Through the Continuing Studies Program, students can pursue an education outside traditional daytime classwork. Participants in the program include part-time students, as well as many full-time students who have been away from a formal educational experience for two or more years and want to pursue courses for personal fulfillment or career advancement. The Continuing Studies Program includes Summer School, Weekend University, Winter Session, noncredit courses, extension programs, conferences, and workshops.

Morgan State's Weekend University is designed for working adults and others who are unable to attend weekday classes. Classes are scheduled on Friday evenings and Saturdays, providing students the opportunity to earn a bachelor's degree in accounting, business administration, social work, or telecommunications in approximately five to six years.

Off-Campus Programs

The Cooperative Education Program is a special program that permits students to extend their chosen major program by working in business, industry, or government agencies, alternating a semester of study with a semester of work while studying for undergraduate and graduate degrees. This program enables students to gain experience in an area close to their chosen field and to understand the requirements of that chosen field. A cooperative work-study program allows students who qualify to gain financial support while learning.

Through cooperative education projects, students may participate in specific seminars cooperatively planned and implemented by the Maryland state colleges or may take courses on other state college campuses. In addition, a cooperative project with Goucher College, Towson State University, Loyola College, and Johns Hopkins University provides an opportunity for students to enroll in courses not offered on the home campus.

Academic Facilities

The Departments of Biology, Chemistry, Physics, and Mathematics and the School of Engineering have specialized research facilities. The Murphy Fine Arts Center and the renovated Hughes Stadium opened in fall 2001. The Richard N. Dixon Science Research Center is expected to open in fall 2003. The new communications building and the Library and Information Technology Center are scheduled to open in fall 2005.

Currently, Soper Library's holdings constitute more than 660,000 volumes, including works in special collections. One such collection includes books on Africa, with an emphasis on sub-Saharan Africa. The African-American collection is a body of historically significant and current books by and about African Americans and includes papers and memorabilia of such persons as the late Emmett P. Scott, secretary to Booker T. Washington, and Arthur J. Smith, who was associated with the Far East Consular Division of the State Department. The Forbush Collection, named for Dr. Bliss Forbush, is composed of materials associated with the Quakers and slavery. The Martin D. Jenkins Collection was acquired in 1980. Together, these collections provide both a contemporary and historical view of African Americans in education, military service, politics, and religion.

Costs

In 2002–03, tuition and fees were $4818 for residents of Maryland and $11,238 for nonresidents. Room and board with a nineteen-meal plan ranged from $6150 to $6360, depending upon the dormitory. Thus, tuition, fees, board, and room for a student who is a Maryland resident ranged from $10,968 to $11,178; for a nonresident student, they ranged from $17,388 to $17,598. Costs are subject to change without prior notice.

Financial Aid

Scholarships, loans, and campus employment are available, and awards are made on the basis of student merit and financial need. Information on these as well as on Federal Pell Grants, other federal grants, and Federal Work-Study awards may be obtained by writing to the Financial Aid Office.

Faculty

A majority of the University's 302 faculty members hold doctoral degrees. Many faculty members have attained national and international distinction for their research and creative work, and a number are officers of state, regional, national, and international professional organizations.

Student Government

Student government at Morgan State University is part of the student activities program, which is considered a vital element of the total educational program.

Admission Requirements

Applicants whose academic and personal qualifications show promise of success in college are considered on the basis of their high school grades, rank in class, personal recommendation, and scores on the SAT I or ACT.

Application and Information

Applications for August entrance should be submitted no later than April 15; those for January entrance should be submitted no later than December 1. Applications to Morgan State University are accepted as far as the facilities will permit. Transfer students must submit a transcript from every college previously attended. A limited number of out-of-state and international students may be accepted. All application forms must be accompanied by a $25 application fee and should be forwarded to:

The Office of Admissions
Morgan State University
Cold Spring Lane and Hillen Road
Baltimore, Maryland 21251
Telephone: 443-885-3000
World Wide Web: http://www.morgan.edu/

MORNINGSIDE COLLEGE

SIOUX CITY, IOWA

The College

The Morningside College experience cultivates a passion for lifelong learning and a dedication to ethical leadership and civic responsibility. For more than 100 years, the goal of Morningside College has been to provide students with an education of the highest quality. Morningside is rooted in a strong church-related, liberal arts tradition, and its challenge is to prepare students to be flexible in thought, open in attitude, and confident in themselves.

Founded in 1894, Morningside College is a private, four-year, coeducational, liberal arts institution affiliated with the United Methodist Church. The College seeks both students and faculty members representing diverse social, cultural, ethnic, racial, and national backgrounds.

At the graduate level, Morningside confers a Master of Arts in Teaching, with specialization in elementary education, special education, and technology-based learning.

Morningside College's approximately 1,000 students are encouraged to participate in a wide variety of activities, including departmental, professional, and religious organizations; honor societies; and sororities and fraternities. A newspaper, literary magazine, yearbook, and campus radio station are all under student direction. These activities provide students with many opportunities to develop leadership, interpersonal, and social skills. Since nearly all activities on campus are student initiated and student directed, ample opportunities for leadership development exist. Music recitals and concerts, theater productions, and an academic and cultural arts and lecture series are held each semester. Intercollegiate athletics are available for men in baseball, basketball, cross-country, football, golf, soccer, swimming, tennis, and track and field and for women in basketball, cross-country, golf, soccer, softball, swimming, tennis, track, and volleyball. A variety of intramural activities are available.

The Hindman-Hobbs Recreation Center includes a pool, saunas, racquetball courts, a weight room, three basketball courts, and a jogging track as well as classroom facilities and offices.

Location

Morningside College is located on a 41-acre campus in Sioux City, the fourth-largest city in Iowa. The campus is based in a residential section of the community, adjacent to a city park, swimming pool, and tennis courts and within 5 minutes of a major regional shopping mall. The Sioux City metropolitan area offers a blend of urban shopping, commerce, and recreation in a scenic, rural setting. Students find Morningside's Sioux City location to be advantageous in seeking internship opportunities and full- or part-time employment.

Majors and Degrees

The five undergraduate degrees conferred by Morningside College are the Bachelor of Arts, Bachelor of Science, Bachelor of Science in Nursing, Bachelor of Music, and Bachelor of Music Education. Career programs consist of accounting, art, biology, business administration, chemistry, computer science, corporate communications, elementary education, engineering physics, English, graphic arts, history, interdisciplinary studies, mass communications, mathematics, music, nursing, philosophy, photography, political science, psychology, religious studies, Spanish, special education, and theater. Students choosing to teach in secondary school may be certified in most academic majors.

In cooperation with other institutions, Morningside offers preprofessional programs in engineering, law, medical technology, medicine, the ministry, pharmacy, physical therapy, physician assistant studies, and veterinary medicine.

Academic Program

Morningside operates on a two-semester system; sessions are held from late August to December and from January to early May. Evening classes are offered each semester. A 3-week May interim and two 5-week summer sessions are also available.

Morningside College is committed to the liberal arts as a foundation for every field of concentration at the undergraduate level. Requirements in general education consist of a distribution of studies in the humanities, natural sciences, social sciences, and some interdisciplinary courses.

Special opportunities include a voluntary Honors Program, in which students meet weekly to discuss such focus topics as Ancient Rome and the Eighteenth Century. Friday is Writing Day is a weekly discussion format that allows students and faculty members to read aloud and react to one another's writing.

Every entering full-time student receives a laptop computer that is used in classroom work. Student technology services include high-speed Internet connection, ports in all residence halls and classrooms, Web-accessible personal e-mail accounts, a digital library accessible day and night, specialized computer labs to support academic programs, and wireless network access points in selected areas on campus.

Off-Campus Programs

Morningside students who qualify have the opportunity to take advantage of special programs for off-campus study. Programs are available for a semester or the entire school year. The College has agreements with schools in England, Japan, and Northern Ireland.

Students participate in exchange programs with Kansai Gadai University in Japan, Queen's University, the University of Ulster, and Belfast Institute for Further and Higher Education in Northern Ireland.

In addition, Morningside has opportunities for students to enroll for a semester at American University to study the U.S. government in action. Students may also be nominated for a semester at Drew University to study the United Nations. Students who participate in these programs maintain their enrollment at Morningside College.

Academic Facilities

The Hickman-Johnson-Furrow Library has more than 114,000 volumes, more than 5,000 audio recordings and video materials, and nearly 600 current print periodical subscriptions. Online accessibility includes student/faculty access to more than 10,000 full-text journals. The library's Web-based, integrated online system allows seamless access to numerous subscription databases as well as other online catalogs and Web sites. The library building also houses classrooms, the Mass Communication Department, a media center, and a computer lab.

The Eugene C. Eppley Fine Arts Building is one of the finest music and art facilities in the Midwest. The auditorium seats 1,500 people and is noted for its acoustical qualities and the majestic Sanford Memorial Organ. The MacCollin Classroom Building, adjoining the auditorium, houses offices, art studios, practice rooms, and classrooms for music and art students.

The Helen Levitt Art Gallery adjoins the Eppley Auditorium and is home to the Levitt art collection, which includes work by internationally famous artists.

The Robert M. Lincoln Center houses the College's division of business administration and economics and contains a library, auditorium, microcomputer lab, conference room, and several classrooms.

Costs

Tuition and fees for 2003–04 were $16,350, and room and board were $5260. These figures do not include books and personal expenses.

Financial Aid

In 2002–03, almost $14 million was awarded in financial aid to Morningside students, with an average financial aid package of $16,758. The financial aid resources of federal, state, and College programs are available to Morningside students through a combination of scholarships, grants, loans, and work-study employment. Morningside values students who achieve both in and out of the classroom—people who are thinkers and doers. Morningside Celebration of Excellence Scholarships recognize academic excellence and outstanding service, and awards of up to $10,000 per year are renewable for four years. Morningside also values its ties with alumni and the United Methodist Church, and those awards are also renewable for four years. Students are encouraged to submit the Free Application for Federal Student Aid (FAFSA) as early as possible. The College's code number is 001879. The annual priority deadline for need-based financial aid is March 1.

Faculty

Eighty-four percent of Morningside College's 63 full-time faculty members have earned the terminal degree in their chosen field. The College also employs 48 part-time instructors and has a 14:1 student-faculty ratio.

Student Government

Student government is directly responsible for regulation, supervision, and coordination of student campus activities. The president of the student body is a voting member of the Board of Directors, allowing for student input in decisions facing the Board.

Admission Requirements

Morningside College selects students for admission whose scholastic achievement and personal abilities provide a foundation for success at the college level. While the College seeks students who rank in the upper half of their graduating class, each application is considered on an individual basis. The student's academic record, class rank, and test scores are considered. Transfer students must have a minimum 2.0 GPA on previous college work to qualify for automatic admission. It is the policy and practice of Morningside College to not discriminate against persons on the basis of age, sex, religion, creed, race, color, national or ethnic origin, sexual orientation, or physical or mental disability.

Application and Information

Rolling admission allows for flexibility; however, prospective students are encouraged to apply as early as possible before the semester in which they wish to enroll. Transfer and international students are welcome. Catalogs, application forms, and financial aid forms are available from the Office of Admissions.

For further information, students should contact:

Office of Admissions
Morningside College
1501 Morningside Avenue
Sioux City, Iowa 51106
Telephone: 712-274-5111
800-831-0806 (toll-free)
E-mail: mscadm@morningside.edu
World Wide Web: http://www.morningside.edu

Morningside College provides a welcoming environment for art majors.

MOUNTAIN STATE UNIVERSITY

BECKLEY, WEST VIRGINIA

The College

Mountain State University (MSU) is a private not-for-profit university located in the scenic highlands of southern West Virginia. MSU is dedicated to providing students with an outstanding career-oriented education, firmly rooted in the liberal arts, in a relaxed environment that promotes academic excellence, self-esteem, personal growth, cultural enrichment, and aesthetic awareness. Mountain State University serves more than 5,000 students a year from across the United States and around the world, with degree programs offered at the associate, bachelor's, and master's levels. It is accredited by the Higher Learning Commission of the North Central Association of Colleges and Schools (telephone: 800-621-7440, toll-free; World Wide Web: http://www.ncahigherlearningcommission.org.

The School of Arts and Sciences offers degrees in a wide range of professional fields, including criminal justice, forensic investigation, and social work. It also offers degrees in general studies and an interdisciplinary studies program with concentrations in communication studies, ecology, prelaw studies, psychology, and a host of other subjects.

The School of Business and Technology prepares students for careers in traditional areas of business administration and accounting and in specialized fields, including aviation leadership and management, computer science and information technology, culinary arts, health-care administration, hospitality management, logistics and supply chain management, marketing, legal studies and business law, paralegal studies, travel, and sports and outdoor recreation management. These programs help students develop the managerial and technical skills they need to identify and respond to complex challenges in business.

The School of Health Sciences prepares students for a wide range of health-care professions, including nursing, occupational therapy assistant studies, physical therapist assistant studies, and health education and wellness. A prerequisite physician assistant studies curriculum prepares undergraduate students for the University's entry-level master's program. These health sciences programs prepare students to apply for certifications and licensures required for clinical practice and qualify them to pursue more advanced degrees in their specific field or a related discipline.

The School of Graduate Studies offers master's degree programs in criminal justice administration, health science, interdisciplinary studies, nursing, physician assistant studies, and strategic leadership. Some graduate programs provide for flexible study and distance learning with no residency requirement.

The School of Extended and Distance Education provides opportunities for undergraduate and graduate study through distance learning and other nontraditional options.

Student services include orientation, academic counseling, and a tutoring center. A variety of student organizations and activities are based on campus, and student life facilities include a student union and café.

All Mountain State University students receive a complimentary membership to the Beckley–Raleigh County YMCA, located within easy walking distance of the campus. A variety of individual and team sports are available to students through the YMCA and the University's intramural sports program. The University fields intercollegiate teams in NAIA Division I men's basketball and women's volleyball and softball.

Hogan Hall, a 192-bed residence hall, provides two-bedroom suites and apartment-style living in a central campus location. Renovated and refurnished in 2003, Hogan Hall's accommodations include lounges, study rooms, and laundry facilities. Three different meal plans are available for students to take advantage of campus dining facilities.

Location

Mountain State University is located in Beckley, West Virginia, a small metropolitan area of more than 50,000 people in the heart of the southern West Virginia highlands. The campus is within walking distance of downtown restaurants, retail stores, and services, with many additional options accessible by public transportation. Beckley is about an hour away by car from the state capital of Charleston; most major cities in the eastern United States are within a day's drive.

City, state, and national parks provide breathtaking panoramas as well as perfect settings for outdoor activities that range from mountain biking and rock climbing to hiking, picnicking, and swimming. In season, outdoor enthusiasts enjoy white-water rafting on the famed Gauley and New Rivers or hit the slopes of nearby ski areas. All are within a 20-minute drive of the campus.

Selected degree programs and courses are available through MSU's Eastern Panhandle Campus in Martinsburg, West Virginia.

Majors and Degrees

Bachelor's and associate degrees are offered in accounting; applied technology, aviation leadership and management; aviation technology; business administration (concentrations in accounting, business law, entrepreneurship, health-care management, international business, logistics and supply chain management, management, marketing, office administration, office management, public and nonprofit management); criminal justice; diagnostic medical sonography; elementary and secondary teacher preparation; emergency medical services; environmental studies; fire science; forensic investigation; general engineering; general studies; health education and wellness, hospitality (concentrations in commercial recreation management, culinary arts, hospitality management, therapeutic recreation management); information technology (concentrations in computer networking, computer science, information technology, Internet and e-commerce, Web site development); interdisciplinary studies (concentrations in biology, communication studies, ecology, English and literature, environmental studies, HAZMAT/occupational health and safety, health promotion, health sciences, health services management, humanities and fine arts, leisure studies, library science, media studies, natural sciences, prelaw studies, premedicine studies, psychology, rehabilitative psychology, social and behavioral sciences); legal studies; medical assisting; nursing; occupational therapy assistant studies; organizational leadership; paralegal studies; physical therapist assistant studies; public and nonprofit management; radiologic technology; respiratory care; social work; and surgical technology.

Academic Program

To earn a bachelor's degree, students must complete a minimum of 128 semester hours, including 36 hours of general studies and meet all program requirements. Most programs include an internship or practicum that provides hands-on experience and employment credentials.

Students in associate degree programs must complete a minimum of 64 hours, including 24 hours of general studies, and meet all program requirements. Some associate degrees fulfill the preprofessional studies requirement of the corresponding bachelor's program.

The School of Extended and Distance Education grants credit for nontraditional course work and demonstrated college-level learning. Students gain credit through transfer, Internet, and correspondence courses; proficiency examinations, including the College-Level Examination Program (CLEP) and Advanced Placement exams; demonstration of prior experiential learning; and independent study. A degree completion program allows adult students who have already earned at least 40 credit hours to earn a bachelor's degree in strategic leadership or criminal justice administration on a compressed schedule, and the Spectrum program of integrated general education helps students complete general education requirements conveniently.

Academic Facilities

Mountain State University's rapidly growing main campus currently encompasses nine main structures and four smaller buildings.

Academic facilities housed within the University's Robert C. Byrd Learning Resource Center, or LRC, include a library and media center. The library has holdings of more than 93,000 titles and networked access to more than one million titles. The core collection is supported by an online catalog and supplemented by electronic resources that include ProQuest, Cumulative Index to Nursing and Allied Health Literature (CINAHL), Social Issues Resources Index (SIRS), EBSCOhost, Westlaw, Wilson Web, NewsBank, and MEDLINE.

Computer stations include current software and broadband Internet access. Specialized learning resources include multimedia classrooms, a video lab, computer-assisted instruction, and science laboratories. The Technology Zone, a federally funded information technology initiative, provides a variety of technology resources campuswide, including a 3-D immersion classroom.

Costs

Mountain State University provides the educational advantages of a private institution at a financially accessible cost. Full-time tuition and fees for the 2003–04 academic year were $6300, or $210 for each credit hour. Tuition varies for some programs, and additional laboratory and clinical fees are sometimes required.

Financial Aid

Eligible students receive Federal Pell Grants, Federal Supplemental Educational Opportunity Grants, West Virginia Higher Education Grants, Federal Work-Study, and Federal Stafford Student Loans. Students must submit the Free Application for Federal Student Aid (FAFSA) for determination of eligibility. A number of scholarships based on academic merit and/or financial need are available to students.

Faculty

More than 200 full- and part-time faculty members provide students with personalized, high-quality instruction. Approximately one third of the University's full-time faculty members hold earned doctorates or other terminal degrees.

Student Government

The Student Government Association (SGA) links students with the University's administration and faculty. Governed by student-elected officers, the SGA works to improve the quality of student life, develops leadership skills in students, and provides representation of student views and opinions on University issues. A Residence Hall Association guides and develops aspects of campus residential life.

Admission Requirements

The University's overall admissions policy is open, although some programs have more competitive requirements. Prospective students who have graduated from an accredited high school or received a General Educational Development (GED) certificate are eligible to apply. Applications are welcome from all qualified students regardless of age, sex, religion, race, color, creed, national origin, or handicap.

Application and Information

Students apply for undergraduate admission by submitting an application, an official high school transcript or GED certificate, and a housing application or exemption form. Transfer applicants must also submit official transcripts for previous college-level course work. Applications are accepted on a rolling basis, and applicants are notified of their acceptance status as soon as the application process is completed. ACT or SAT scores are not required for University admission but are recommended for placement purposes. Competitive programs or courses may have minimum ACT or SAT scores, placement tests, or other requirements.

Mountain State University encourages prospective students and their families to arrange a campus visit. Campus tours and individual meetings are available.

For an application or more information, students should contact:

Mountain State University Information Center
Box 9003
Beckley, West Virginia 25802-9003
Telephone: 304-929-1433
866-FOR-MSU1 (866-766-6067) (toll-free)
World Wide Web: http://www.mountainstate.edu

MOUNT ALOYSIUS COLLEGE

CRESSON, PENNSYLVANIA

The College

Mount Aloysius College is a small, private, comprehensive, Catholic liberal arts college sponsored by the Religious Sisters of Mercy. Established in 1853, the College today specializes in both undergraduate and graduate education. Since the founding of the College, more than 10,000 students have become proud Mount Aloysius College graduates. The College is committed to small classroom size, providing a highly structured environment. Many Mount Aloysius College students are from the commonwealth of Pennsylvania, but other states represented on campus include Connecticut, Delaware, Maine, Maryland, New Jersey, New York, Vermont, Virginia, and West Virginia. Sixty-five percent of the College's students are women. There are approximately 1,100 full-time students and 500 students enrolled part-time.

Mount Aloysius College is one of eighteen Mercy Colleges nationwide. As part of the Mercy College curriculum, students are encouraged to evaluate ethical issues and form a sound character consistent with traditional, Judeo-Christian values. Social growth is seen as a vital element of a complete liberal arts education, encompassing the important ability to relate closely to people.

The College recognizes that student activities play a distinctive role in the total campus educational program. There are approximately eighty organized clubs, groups, honor societies, and intramural sports programs, including a newspaper, a yearbook, residence hall associations, student government, cheerleading, scholarship-funded theater and choir programs, and a student activities planning board. Student activities include many social events, intramural sports programs, NCAA Division III sporting events, comedians, cultural and educational events, campus forums, and lectures by guest speakers.

Beginning in fall 2004, Mount Aloysius College will compete as a provisional member of NCAA Division III. The following sports are available to both women and men: basketball, cross-country, golf, and soccer. Men's baseball and women's softball and volleyball are also offered. Both intercollegiate and intramural athletes benefit from the new Ray S. and Louise S. Walker Athletic Field Complex, which includes a softball field along with one of the finest soccer fields in the area. A baseball field and a multipurpose field are soon to be added.

Twelve buildings make up the 165-acre campus. The main building is a picturesque structure dating to 1897; it houses the admissions, financial aid, career services, security, health, and academic offices, along with the Office of the President, classrooms, telenursing research facilities, and the Wolf-Kuhn art gallery. Cosgrave Center is the main hub on campus, serving as the Student Union. The building contains the cafeteria, snack bar, bookstore, preschool (part of the elementary education/early childhood program at the College), lounges, recreational rooms, student affairs offices, and television lounge. The College's Health and Physical Fitness Center is adjacent to Cosgrave Center. Its main athletic arena has a seating capacity of approximately 2,000 and serves as the home to all Mounties fans. The facility provides space for three basketball courts, three volleyball courts, a tennis court, a weight and exercise room equipped with a sauna, two locker rooms, office areas, changing rooms for sports officials, public restrooms, a lobby, and a vestibule. Ihmsen Halls are key housing facilities for residential students. Alumni Hall is a historic, multipurpose room that is used for College drama, musicals, and many performing arts events. The College is in full operation twelve months per year and opens its facilities to the outside community as well.

Mount Aloysius is a comprehensive college that is fully accredited by the Middle States Association of Colleges and Schools and approved by the Pennsylvania Department of Education. All nursing programs and health studies programs are fully accredited by their professional accrediting bodies, including the National League for Nursing Accrediting Commission, the Commission on Accreditation in Physical Therapy Education, the American Association of Medical Assistants, and the Joint Commission on Accreditation for Programs of Surgical Technology.

In addition to its undergraduate programs, Mount Aloysius offers master's degrees in criminal justice management in correctional administration, health and human services administration, and psychology.

Location

Mount Aloysius College is located in the scenic southern Allegheny Mountains of west-central Pennsylvania. The College is located in the small town of Cresson, which is adjacent to U.S. Route 22. The College's setting is rural, with two middle-sized cities, Altoona and Johnstown, within a very short distance. The area has warm, beautiful summers; brisk, breathtaking autumns; invigorating, snowy winters; and cool, blooming springs. Facilities in the area are available for outdoor activities, including biking, golfing, swimming, horseback riding, waterskiing and water activities, hiking, spelunking, picnicking, and amusement and water parks.

Majors and Degrees

Mount Aloysius College awards bachelor's and associate degrees in the arts, sciences, and health-studies fields in both career-oriented and traditional liberal arts programs. Baccalaureate degrees are available in accounting, behavioral and social science, business administration, computer science, criminology, elementary/early childhood education, English, general science, history/political science, humanities, information technology, math/science, medical imaging, nursing (RN-B.S.N. program), nursing (2-2), occupational therapy (3-2), physical therapy (4-2), physician assistant studies (3-2), prelaw, psychology, sign language/interpreter education, and undecided/exploratory. Associate degrees are offered in applied technology, business administration, criminology, early childhood studies, general studies, legal studies, liberal arts, medical assistant studies, nursing, nursing (LPN to RN), occupational therapy assistant studies, physical therapist assistant studies, prenursing, radiography/medical imaging, and surgical technology. In addition, there is a unique three-year program in occupational therapy assistant studies and physical therapist assistant studies; in either major, students graduate with two associate degrees and two professional certificates. The College also has a one-year diploma program in surgical technology.

Academic Programs

Whether preparing students for careers upon graduation or for graduate school, Mount Aloysius recognizes the importance of a broad and liberal education. Thus, in addition to receiving solid preparation for a chosen career, every student at the College receives a foundation in the arts, sciences, and humanities through an outstanding core curriculum. Strong emphasis is placed on the specialized courses within each program of study, and many academic programs combine classroom experience with internships and related training at area clinical sites, agencies, and institutions. In addition to its regular academic programs, Mount Aloysius offers independent and directed study with a commitment to service, which is a key ingredient in a Mercy education. The College has an excellent honors program and Educational Enrichment Center. The academic calendar has two traditional semesters and two or three optional summer sessions.

Off-Campus Programs

An important feature of many academic programs is off-campus training. The majority of the College's programs of study require credit-yielding practicums, through which students work and receive training at local and regional hospitals, public and private schools, or health or human service agencies. Students in all health programs participate in required on-the-job training during their time at the College.

Academic Facilities

In 1995, Mount Aloysius College opened both a new library and a new era, signifying greater access to information for the College community. This state-of-the-art facility is the campus hub for technology and studying. With a Buhl Electronic Classroom and more than 70,000 print and nonprint titles, the library is an impressive, 31,000-square-foot facility with ample seating space, four group-study rooms, a reading lounge, a law library and classroom, and additional room for future expansion. This facility is also completely automated, with an online catalog and access to remote libraries and the World Wide Web at more than thirty public workstations. Also located in the library is the Information Technology Center, home to fifteen multimedia computer workstations and some of the latest offerings in educational software.

Pierce Hall serves as the science center on campus and is a state-of-the-art, 31,000-square-foot facility that was completed in 1997 and houses all science laboratories, health science centers, and offices of faculty members in the health studies programs. Academic Hall is an impressive facility that is home to the College Honors Program. It also has classrooms, labs, seminar rooms, faculty offices, and electronic rooms. The College is proud of its bridge to the past and its progress in providing twenty-first-century buildings.

Costs

Annual tuition and fees for the 2003–04 academic year for full-time students were $13,080, and room and board were $5700.

Financial Aid

Mount Aloysius recognizes the expense involved in acquiring a liberal arts education and encourages all students to apply for all available aid. Through the Office of Financial Aid, the College assists students in applying for state and federal grants, loans, work-study awards, and College merit scholarships and grants. The College awards academic monies based on GPA and SAT or ACT scores; these awards are renewable over a four-year period and range from $1000 to $8000 per year. Mount Aloysius College participates in all federal and state programs. In 2003, the College awarded more than $10 million in student financial aid. Ninety percent of the College's students receive some form of financial aid. *U.S. News & World Report* ranked Mount Aloysius College number one among private liberal arts colleges in the Northeast for the least amount of loan debt among students as they graduate.

Faculty

The Mount Aloysius faculty consists of approximately 60 full-time members, whose primary responsibility is teaching and advising students. Most full-time faculty members hold advanced or terminal degrees and are expected to maintain close instructional ties with students. Many professors hold national professional certificates in such disciplines as criminology, law, nursing, and occupational therapy. The Mount Aloysius student-faculty ratio of 14:1 allows close contact between students and faculty members, providing personal attention in a highly structured environment—a key ingredient in the College's academic philosophy.

Student Government

The Student Representative Government (SRG) represents students on all issues that concern the College. The SRG appoints student representatives to all student-oriented College committees. The College encourages active student participation in the general governance structure and in other matters concerning the development and implementation of policies on residential student life.

Admission Requirements

The College admits a freshman class of approximately 300 students, which amounts to a total class of 440 with transfer students. Admission is selective and is based on academic promise, as indicated by a student's secondary school performance and activities, standardized test scores, and special experience and talents. Applicants are required to have, or expect to earn, a diploma from an approved secondary school or a GED diploma. Submission of official transcripts and SAT or ACT scores is required. In addition to the general admission requirements, specific admission requirements exist for the health programs; students may visit the College's Web site, listed below, for further information. Prospective students are highly encouraged to visit the scenic 165-acre campus. The College is open Monday to Friday from 8:30 to 5 and on select Saturdays.

Application and Information

To apply for admission to Mount Aloysius College, candidates are encouraged to submit their application and $30 application fee to the Office of Undergraduate and Graduate Admissions. In addition, students may apply online.

For further information, students should contact:

Office of Undergraduate and Graduate Admissions
Mount Aloysius College
7373 Admiral Peary Highway
Cresson, Pennsylvania 16630
Telephone: 814-886-6383
888-823-2220 (toll-free)
Fax: 814-886-6441
E-mail: admissions@mtaloy.edu
World Wide Web: http://www.mtaloy.edu

The historic Main Building, located on the scenic campus of Mount Aloysius College.

MOUNT HOLYOKE COLLEGE

SOUTH HADLEY, MASSACHUSETTS

The College

Long distinguished for the quality of its curricular and cocurricular life as well as for the diversity of its student body and the success of its alumnae, Mount Holyoke is an independent college of liberal arts and sciences for women. The student body, numbering 2,100, represents fifty states and more than eighty countries. One out of every 3 students is an international student or an African American, Latina, Asian, or Native American. Ninety-three percent of all graduates are either employed or in graduate/professional school within six months of graduation. Of those who choose to pursue an advanced degree, 20 to 25 percent enroll within five years of graduation.

Mount Holyoke is committed to maintaining small classes and individualized academic advising. The College's student-faculty ratio is 10:1. More than half of Mount Holyoke's classes enroll fewer than 20 students, and one quarter enroll fewer than 10. All students are advised by faculty members. Non-Western cultures are a focus of the College's curricular life. Most students pursue interdisciplinary courses, some taught by teams of faculty members from different fields. Use of computers, proficiency in foreign languages, and development of speaking and writing skills are stressed throughout the curriculum. The College offers first-year students the opportunity to enroll in first-year seminars—small classes designed to introduce first-year students to Mount Holyoke's intellectual community and to help them develop essential skills in writing, speaking, and analytic and critical inquiry.

The College is distinguished in developing women leaders. The Weissman Center for Leadership and the Liberal Arts is devoted to increasing students' understanding of public policy issues and giving them the tools to create change. The work of the center focuses on enhancing students' ability to frame, articulate, and advocate positions constructively and effectively. A major component is the Speaking, Arguing, and Writing Program, which is a nationally recognized model among liberal arts colleges for training students to be powerful communicators. Other Weissman Center initiatives include community-based learning courses (combining course work with project-based field work in the community) and case method courses.

Mount Holyoke participates in the Five College Consortium, which also includes Amherst, Hampshire, and Smith Colleges and the University of Massachusetts Amherst. Students enrolled at any one of the Five Colleges can take the courses and participate in the cultural and social offerings of the other four. In addition, the five institutions' faculty and classes are coordinated in areas of common interest, such as African studies, Asian/Pacific/American studies, Latin American studies, Middle Eastern studies, and international relations. Dance and astronomy—the two Five College majors—both rank among the largest and most distinguished undergraduate programs nationally in their respective fields.

Forming a vital part of Mount Holyoke's offerings are diverse cocurricular opportunities—concerts, conferences, exhibitions, films, and social events. Noted actors, dancers, and musicians perform at Mount Holyoke and within the Five College area. In addition, there are performance opportunities through instrumental ensembles, dance groups, theater productions, and an active choral program. Groups such as the Five College Dance Department, the Five College Orchestra, and the New World Theatre supplement these opportunities. More than 100 clubs and organizations at Mount Holyoke provide creative outlets, leadership experiences, and service opportunities.

The residence halls complement the liberal arts experience, coordinating cultural and social events and providing a home away from home for all students. Almost all students live on campus in the residence halls, each of which accommodates between 65 and 130 students. All four classes are mixed in each hall, and housing is guaranteed for all four years. A variety of dining options are available across campus, including a full-service café and several coffee shops. A kosher/halal dining room serves the dietary needs of observant Jews and observant Muslims and is open to the entire campus community.

Other facilities include five cultural houses, a Japanese teahouse and meditation garden, a health clinic and counseling center, and a center for spiritual life and community service. Students of all religious traditions and spiritual paths are made welcome at Mount Holyoke. Four chaplains—Catholic, Jewish, Protestant, and Muslim—and a number of faculty advisers respond to the pastoral and liturgical needs of the College's diverse religious community.

The recent renovation of Blanchard Campus Center has transformed the building's interior into a center for dining, entertainment, and social activity. Highlights include a cyber café, coffee bar, art gallery, game room, performance space, and campus store. The radio station, student programs offices, and meeting rooms are also located here.

A comprehensive sports and dance complex has 130,000 square feet of facilities. The field house includes basketball, tennis, volleyball, squash, and racquetball courts; a 200-meter track; and an eight-lane swimming pool with a separate diving tank. The field house adjoins the gymnasium and dance studios. There are also twelve outdoor tennis courts, a 400-meter all-weather track, and six grass playing fields. An equestrian center provides a fifty-seven-stall barn and large indoor and outdoor riding arenas as well as three cross-country show courses. This center is widely considered one of nation's finest riding facilities. The College's eighteen-hole golf course, designed by Donald Ross, was the site of the 2004 USGA Women's Open. Mount Holyoke is an NCAA Division III school and offers fourteen intercollegiate teams as well as intramural and club sports.

Location

South Hadley, Massachusetts, is about 20 minutes from Springfield, 1½ hours from Boston, and 3 hours from New York City by car. Convenient bus, plane, and train service to the College is available. Bradley International Airport, 40 minutes away by car, serves Hartford and Springfield; Amtrak train stations are located in Amherst and Springfield. Bookstores, coffee shops, and restaurants are within walking distance of campus, and Northampton and Amherst are minutes away via the free Five College bus.

Majors and Degrees

Mount Holyoke offers the Bachelor of Arts degree. Majors include African and African American studies, American studies, ancient studies, anthropology, architectural studies, art (history and studio), Asian studies, astronomy, biochemistry, biological sciences, chemistry, classics, computer science, critical social thought, dance, economics, engineering, English, environmental studies, European studies, French, geography, geology, German studies, Greek, history, international relations, Italian, Latin, Latin American studies, mathematics, medieval studies, music, neuroscience and behavior, philosophy, physics, politics, psychology, psychology and educational studies, religion, Romance languages and literatures, Russian and Eurasian studies, self-designed studies, sociology, Spanish, statistics, theater arts, and women's studies. Students may also follow prelaw and premedical courses of study. In addition, students can earn both a B.A. from Mount Holyoke and a B.S. in engineering from Caltech, UMass' College of Engineering, or Dartmouth's Thayer School of Engineering in a five-year period.

Academic Programs

Within the framework of the liberal arts and sciences, Mount Holyoke offers students considerable freedom of choice in the academic program. The basic plan of study includes a distribution of courses among at least seven disciplines, courses in language, courses in a major and minor field, and at least one course dealing with an aspect of Africa, Asia, Latin America, the Middle East, or the nonwhite peoples of North America. A normal schedule is four 4-credit courses per semester, each meeting one to four times per week. By graduation, a student has completed 128 credits of academic work in courses that provide exposure to a variety of disciplines, as well as specialization in a major and a minor field. Independent study, honors work, and self-scheduled examinations are among the options available. The Frances Perkins Program is designed for women beyond the traditional undergraduate age who wish to initiate, continue, or enrich their undergraduate education.

The academic calendar consists of two semesters separated by an active January Term program. During January Term, students may take a single intensive course, pursue an independent project, or conduct a Career Exploration Project in a professional setting with alumnae or friends of the College.

Off-Campus Programs

The Mount Holyoke student lives and studies in an area where four independent colleges and a large university enroll a total of more than 30,000 students. Amherst, Hampshire, Mount Holyoke, and Smith Colleges and the University of Massachusetts Amherst participate in an extensive Five College cooperative exchange program. Free buses run among the institutions (all within a 12-mile radius) every 20 minutes from morning to late evening, seven days a week, during the school year.

Mount Holyoke is a member of the Twelve College Exchange, and students can spend a year or semester at any of the other participating institutions (Amherst, Bowdoin, Connecticut, Dartmouth, Smith, Trinity, Vassar, Wellesley, Wheaton, and Williams Colleges and Wesleyan University). The exchange also includes the Williams/Mystic Seaport Program in American Maritime Studies and the National Theatre Institute Program. Mount Holyoke also has its own exchange programs with Mills College in Oakland, California, and Spelman College in Atlanta, Georgia. Semester programs include the American University Washington Semester, Semester in Environmental Science at the Marine Biological Laboratory, Woods Hole, and Environmental Science and Policy Programs at Biosphere 2 Center. Each year, about one third of the junior class studies abroad for a semester or a year in such countries as Argentina, Australia, Chile, China, Denmark, France, Germany, Italy, Japan, Kenya, Korea, Republic of Georgia, Russia, Senegal, and the United Kingdom.

The College's Career Development Center assists students in developing both summer and January internships, which involve full-time work for six to twelve weeks over the summer or for three weeks during January Term. Internships have been undertaken in the fields of the arts, business and banking, communications, education, government, health, public policy, sciences, social services, and technology. Reflecting the College's internationalism and building on the College's extensive overseas ties, Mount Holyoke has a strong network of international internship opportunities around the world. Sponsoring organizations typically include the World Bank, UNESCO, and the United Nations.

Academic Facilities

In the past five years, the College has invested $75 million in the renovation and expansion of facilities and technology. The music and art buildings have been fully updated and expanded, including the Mount Holyoke College Art Museum, one of the nation's leading collegiate art museums with an active teaching collection. The new science center advances the College's international reputation as a leader in scientific education for women. A new, multistory, 40,000-square-foot environmentally sound building, connecting three science buildings, serves as the nexus for this academic center. The building features a four-story atrium that provides a gathering place for all members of the community. The science center houses classrooms, laboratories, and offices for eight departments—astronomy, biochemistry, biological sciences, chemistry, computer science, earth and environment, mathematics, and physics. It offers adjacent labs and offices, common spaces, and shared equipment for students and faculty members with overlapping research interest.

The 800-acre campus includes two lakes, wooded bridle trails, lawns, and forests. An undeveloped nature preserve covers 330 of these acres and serves as an environmental classroom for students and faculty members. Taking advantage of this "outdoor classroom," the Center for the Environment is a resource for students interested in using the campus and surrounding community to advance their studies of ecology and environmental studies.

The College's 700,000-volume library incorporates dedicated science and music libraries and computerized access to 6 million volumes through the Five College Consortium. Within the main library, the Information Commons has forty high-end computers and a help desk. The computer and language learning center uses state-of-the-art methods for teaching languages. Technology tools currently in use include wireless networking, video conferencing, and interactive, multimedia-based, curriculum-enhancing Web software. There are ongoing training opportunities for students to learn emerging technologies.

An extensive Career Development Center offers students assistance in clarifying their goals and in identifying internships, jobs, graduate schools, and fellowships.

Costs

For 2004–05, tuition is $30,770 and room and board are $9060, for a total of $39,830.

Financial Aid

Financial need should not discourage any student from applying to Mount Holyoke. Aid (grants, loans, and campus employment) is based on financial-aid eligibility as determined by the College. Mount Holyoke also offers a limited number of merit aid awards.

Faculty

Mount Holyoke's 200 faculty members are dedicated teachers as well as active scholars, research scientists, and creative artists. Half are women, and a fifth are persons of color. All courses are taught by faculty members; professors are also active in advising students about classes, cocurricular opportunities, and careers. Mount Holyoke professors have won numerous national and international awards, including National Science Foundation CAREER awards, MacArthur fellowships, Guggenheims, Fulbrights, the Pulitzer Prize, the Rome Prize, and the National Book Award.

Student Government

Mount Holyoke students, together with the faculty and administrators, have a strong hand in shaping campus life. Students sit on several committees, including the President's Commission on Diversity, the Academic Policy Committee, and the Board of Admissions. The Student Government Association allows students to govern their cocurricular lives and maintain communication with the faculty and administration. Students have an effective honor code of long standing.

Admission Requirements

Mount Holyoke seeks smart, ambitious students who value a liberal arts education and who are fired by a love of learning. Students who do well here tend to demonstrate a high level of maturity and independence. Mount Holyoke welcomes students of all economic, ethnic, geographic, religious, and social backgrounds. A high school program providing a good preparation for Mount Holyoke includes 4 years of English, either 4 years of one foreign language or a combination of 3 years of one language and 2 years of another, and 3 years each of mathematics, history, and laboratory sciences. SAT or ACT scores are optional. The Test of English as a Foreign Language (TOEFL) is recommended for students for whom English is not a primary language. Personal interviews are highly recommended for all candidates either on campus or with an alumna admissions representative.

Application and Information

Two rounds of early decision are available: the deadline for Round I is November 15, with notification by January 1; the deadline for Round II is January 1, with notification by February 1. The deadline for regular admission is January 15, with notification by April 1. Other admission options, such as early entrance, deferred entrance, and advanced standing, are available.

The admission office is open all year, Monday through Friday, from 9 a.m. to 5 p.m., and Saturday mornings from 9 a.m. to noon. Visitors may come to the admission office to take a campus tour, obtain admission materials, or meet with a staff member. For more information, students should contact:

Office of Admission
Mount Holyoke College
50 College Street
South Hadley, Massachusetts 01075-1488
Telephone: 413-538-2023
Fax: 413-538-2409
E-mail: admission@mtholyoke.edu
World Wide Web: http://www.mtholyoke.edu

MOUNT IDA COLLEGE

NEWTON CENTRE, MASSACHUSETTS

The College

Founded in 1899, Mount Ida College has been one of the Northeast's most innovative postsecondary institutions, evolving from a junior college to a four-year institution offering applied arts, sciences, and technology with a liberal arts core.

Approximately 1,300 students are enrolled at Mount Ida. About 75 percent of these students represent New England, New York, New Jersey, and Pennsylvania. International students represent approximately 11 percent of the full-time population. Approximately 750 men and women reside in five College residence halls, four of which are coed and one of which is all women.

Mount Ida's beautiful 72-acre campus was once an elegant country estate. Academic, administrative, and residential buildings are surrounded by playing fields, a pond, and wooded areas in a comfortable, self-contained environment. Over the last ten years, more than $16 million in new construction has been expended, providing residence halls, classrooms, and other buildings and an expansion of the Learning Resource Center. A new academic technology building and athletic center were completed in spring 1999.

At Mount Ida College, where each student is recognized as an individual, students find it easy to become involved. Students are encouraged to start new positive groups on campus that will enrich the College community. Campus organizations and clubs reflect the diversity of the student body and afford wonderful opportunities for creative expression and leadership development. Some of these are the Student Government, the Residence Hall Council, the Judicial Board, Phi Theta Kappa, Alpha Chi, and Phi Theta Delta Honor Societies, the International Student Club, the Drama Club, the student newspaper, the yearbook, the Veterinary Technology Club, A.S.I.D., the Fashion and Design Club, and the Communications Club. A variety of social, cultural, and recreational activities are also an important part of student life.

Various intercollegiate sports are offered during the school year, including basketball, football, lacrosse, soccer, and volleyball for men and basketball, cross-country, soccer, softball, and volleyball for women. There is also an equestrian team and club baseball for men. Mount Ida College is a member of the NCAA Division III. Many of Mount Ida's teams have enjoyed regional rank and tournament action.

Location

Newton, a city of 90,000, is located only 8 miles (13 kilometers) from the center of Boston. The College shuttle bus connects students with the Newton Centre business district, where there is MBTA subway service to Boston. The Boston metropolitan area is home to more than sixty other institutions of higher learning, numerous historic sites, a wide variety of shops, and diverse cultural and social opportunities. Local industrial parks, business districts, and shopping malls provide a wide variety of easily accessible employment opportunities.

Majors and Degrees

Mount Ida grants B.A., B.S., B.L.S., A.A., and A.S. degrees. Majors and areas of study include bereavement studies, business administration, child development, child study, communications, criminal justice, dental hygiene, equine management, fashion design, fashion merchandising, funeral service, graphic design, hotel/tourism management, human services, interior design, liberal arts, management, marketing, psychology, sports management, and veterinary technology. Mount Ida also offers a prelaw concentration and minors in child study, coaching, communications, criminalistics, criminal justice, forensic psychology, legal studies, and leadership studies.

Academic Programs

Mount Ida's academic and social support systems help students navigate the college world and maximize potential. Prime examples are the Learning Opportunities Program (professional and comprehensive support for learning disabled students) and the Academic Success Center (free tutoring and skills development). Each student has an academic adviser as well.

Off-Campus Programs

Most majors offered at Mount Ida include either a required or optional internship that provides the opportunity to gain valuable practical experience. For example, the Veterinary Technology Program includes several rotations at a variety of facilities, including the Tufts University School of Veterinary Medicine Teaching Hospital, Harvard Primate Center, New England Aquarium, and approximately seventy other sites.

Qualified students may also have the option of short-term, semester, and summer study abroad.

Academic Facilities

The Learning Resource Center and library houses more than 66,000 volumes, 560 periodicals, and a variety of media, including video disks and educational software programs. The Learning Resource Center is a member of the Minuteman Library Network, which also includes thirty-four public libraries, in a collaborative effort to provide excellence in information resources and services. Other on-campus facilities include a nursery school, a dental laboratory and clinic, computer laboratories, art studios, a communications laboratory, and facilities for veterinary technician studies and veterinary technology, including animal kennels, laboratories, and a surgical operating theater.

Costs

Tuition for the 2003–04 academic year was approximately $16,100. Room and board charges were $9000, and books and supplies ranged between $500 and $1000, depending on the program of study.

Financial Aid

Mount Ida supplements federal, state, and private funding with a substantial commitment of College funds. As a result, nearly 70 percent of Mount Ida's students received financial assistance during the academic year 2003–04. Grants, scholarships, campus employment, and loans are utilized to enable students to afford the College's opportunities. Mount Ida has a financial aid priority application deadline of May 1.

Faculty

Mount Ida's faculty consists of approximately 60 full-time members along with part-time and adjunct professionals. Each student is assigned a faculty adviser. There is a full-time career services counselor, a Health Center counseling staff, and a residence counseling staff. Most classes at Mount Ida have fewer than 25 students; such small classes are conducive to the individual attention to students for which Mount Ida is renowned. The student-faculty ratio is 9:1.

Student Government

Through the Student Government Association, the student body is able to share with the administration and faculty the establishing and administering of rules essential for successful group living. The system of student government is based on the assumption that each student will take responsibility for group behavior on the College campus and in the community. The College supports a Student Leadership Development Program, which includes both an academic and cocurricular component.

Admission Requirements

A composite evaluation is made of each applicant. Official high school and college transcripts (the latter where applicable) are required, as are recommendations and a personal statement. SAT I or ACT scores are required for bachelor degree candidates and preferred for associate degree candidates. Transfer students must submit official transcripts of all completed college course work. Transfer credit for fashion design, graphic design, and interior design studio courses may depend on a portfolio review.

Application and Information

Mount Ida has a rolling admissions policy. Although there is no deadline for the submission of applications, applicants are encouraged to apply as early as possible. Applications are considered as long as there is space in the desired program of study. Applicants are notified within three to four weeks after all credentials have been received.

For further information, students should contact:

Judith A. Kaufman, Dean of Admissions or
Nancy Lemelman, Director of Admissions
Mount Ida College
777 Dedham Street
Newton Centre, Massachusetts 02459
Telephone: 617-928-4553
Fax: 617-928-4507
E-mail: admissions@mountida.edu
World Wide Web: http://www.mountida.edu

Carlson Center at Mount Ida College.

MOUNT MARTY COLLEGE

YANKTON, WATERTOWN, AND SIOUX FALLS, SOUTH DAKOTA

The College

Mount Marty College (MMC), an academic community in the Catholic Benedictine liberal arts tradition, prepares students for a contemporary world of work, service to the human community, and personal growth. Founded in 1936 as a Benedictine, Catholic liberal arts college by the Sisters of Saint Benedict of Yankton, South Dakota, the College is named in memory of Catholic Bishop Martin Marty. The bishop came to Dakota Territory in 1876 as a Benedictine missionary to the Native Americans.

Mount Marty College, named one of the "Best Colleges for You" by *Time* and the *Princeton Review* in 2001, includes three campuses in Watertown, Sioux Falls, and Yankton, South Dakota. The Watertown campus offers a variety of degree programs that are in high demand in that area. The Sioux Falls campus is home to MMC's nurse anesthesia graduate program. The Yankton campus is the main residential campus. The total student population of the three campuses in fall 2003 was 1,185 students, with 600 at the Yankton campus.

The primary emphasis at Mount Marty College is the development of the total individual. That focus includes intellectual competence, professional and personal skills, and a composite of moral, spiritual, and social values. Service to humanity is a reflection of the strong Benedictine values of the College, which include a strong work ethic and personal development in each student. MMC has a well-known reputation for providing a value-centered education and high-quality preparation for professional careers.

Mount Marty is on the leading edge of instruction and learning, as defined by student achievement and the College's excellent graduate school and job placement rates. MMC's job placement rate is 94 percent.

Mount Marty students say that MMC is a place of opportunity—both in the classroom and in the real world. MMC provides the kind of environment that helps the student to excel, ensuring academic success, because the student is not lost in the crowd. Professors care about the student's success. Students know their professors and each other by name, allowing for the development of professional, academic, and personal support.

Students are attracted to Mount Marty College by its outstanding programs as well as its hospitable size. Regardless of their area of study, teaching faculty members (not graduate students) conduct classes. This allows students the luxury of learning from seasoned professionals while developing the social skills and professionalism required for their field. Students also benefit from the use of technology in the classroom. All full-time students receive a laptop to use while they are enrolled at Mount Marty.

Mount Marty has more than fifty student clubs and organizations, including varsity athletic teams, intramural events, performing and fine arts, trips, musical organizations, the student newspaper, and retreats.

The Yankton campus includes housing for students, dining facilities, a bookstore, and recreation facilities. Entertainment on campus may include theater events, guest speakers, art exhibits, and much more. Other services available at the College include free tutoring, professional career counseling, health services, 24-hour computer access, and religious services at Bishop Marty Chapel. As a member of NAIA and the Great Plains Athletic Conference, Mount Marty College is also host to intercollegiate athletics, including men's and women's basketball, cross-country, soccer, and track and field; women's softball and volleyball; and men's baseball.

Mount Marty College is accredited by the Commission on Institutions of Higher Education of the North Central Association of Colleges and Schools (30 North LaSalle Street, Suite 2400, Chicago, Illinois 60602-2504; telephone: 312-263-0456). Other accrediting groups have endorsed specific programs at the College.

Location

Mount Marty College is located on the bluffs of the Missouri River in Yankton, South Dakota (population 15,000). A thriving community, Yankton offers a variety of work and cultural activities and is home to one of the best-developed river recreation areas in South Dakota. Yankton is located within 1½ hours of Sioux Falls, South Dakota; within 3 hours of Omaha, Nebraska; and within 1 hour of Sioux City, Iowa. The main highways into Yankton include U.S. Highway 81 and South Dakota Highway 50 via Interstates 90 and 29.

Yankton is widely known for the popular recreational activities available at the Lewis & Clark Lake, which is within minutes of the Mount Marty campus. The available activities include swimming, boating, fishing, waterskiing, hiking, biking, dining, and much more. In this prosperous community, students find many recreation, shopping, dining, and cultural opportunities.

Majors and Degrees

Mount Marty College offers a Bachelor of Arts in accounting, applied technology management, behavioral science, biology, business administration, chemistry, computer science, criminal justice, elementary education, English, forensic science, graphic arts, history, information technology, math, music, nutrition and food science, psychology, recreation management, religious studies, secondary education, selected studies, and special education.

Bachelor of Science degrees are awarded in clinical laboratory science, nursing, radiologic technology, and selected studies.

Associate of Arts degrees are offered in accounting, business administration, criminal justice, religious studies, and selected studies.

Minors include accounting, art, biology, business administration, chemistry, computer science, criminal justice, English, environmental science, French, history, math, music, nutrition and food science, philosophy, physical education and recreation, political science, psychology, religious studies, sociology, Spanish, and speech and theater.

Preprofessional degrees are offered in a variety of disciplines, including chiropractic studies, dentistry, law, medicine, mortuary science, occupational therapy, optometry, pharmacy, physical therapy, and veterinary science.

Academic Programs

Mount Marty College operates throughout the calendar year with the usual nine-month academic year and summer sessions held May through August. The academic year includes a fall semester that commences in September and ends in December, a spring semester that commences in January and ends in May, and four summer sessions held in May, June, July, and August. The curriculum is scheduled in such a manner that a full-time student with an average workload may graduate with a bachelor's degree in four years.

Degree programs are enhanced with internships, extracurricular activities, outreach programs, clinical assignments, professional and industry visits, and firsthand experience.

Academic Facilities

All classes at Mount Marty make use of state-of-the-art technology systems that give students the opportunity to get the most out of their courses. Laptop computers are provided to each full-time student. Mount Marty's wireless campus provides easy access to computer applications, the Internet, and online assignments. The world is at the student's fingertips with MMC's wireless campus. Laptops, smart classrooms, and wireless connections across the campus are just some of the ways in which a student can take advantage of the latest technology.

Mount Marty's 24-hour computer access, convenient library hours, and study areas offer students ample opportunity to further their studies. A tutoring program provides assistance through peers and instructors to keep students on track in the classroom. Well-equipped laboratories with professional-level instruments also assist students in developing career skills in line with the industry.

The Scholastica Learning Center is new to Mount Marty College. This facility houses the library, academic achievement center, computer and distance learning center, Cyber Café, and the oratory.

Costs

The 2003–04 costs were $12,506 for tuition and $4670 for room and board, which included a meal plan, phone, cable, and Internet service. There were a program support fee of $20 per credit hour and a general fee of $1080, which included the use of a laptop, parking, student activities, a fitness center, a tutoring center, and counseling, placement, and health services. The approximate cost for books was $600 and for personal expenses was $800.

Financial Aid

Mount Marty College offers institutional and federal aid to 99 percent of its students. Mount Marty offers a vast array of scholarship and other aid opportunities to students. Awards ranging from several hundred dollars to full tuition are awarded as a result of interviews conducted during Scholarship Day. Other scholarships are awarded prior to and after Scholarship Day based on high academic achievement as well as athletic, musical, and theatrical talent.

MMC is dedicated to making high-quality education affordable. Mount Marty has several financial aid opportunities to acknowledge community service, outstanding academic achievement, leadership, and talent. Last year, the College gave more than $10.5 million in aid through scholarships, grants, loans, and employment. An average financial aid package for a freshman was more than $11,500. The priority deadline for financial aid is March 1. Mount Marty offers Presidential Scholarships, Trustee Scholarships, Deans Scholarships, Benedictine Scholarships, academic scholarships, Catholic Scholarships, MMC grants, athletic scholarships, talent scholarships, and several federal programs. The deadline for many academic scholarships is February 1.

Faculty

With campuses in Yankton, Watertown, and Sioux Falls, Mount Marty College employs 107 faculty members. Faculty members, not graduate students, teach all courses, so students learn from professional experts. The faculty-student ratio is 1:14, which enhances student interaction with faculty members.

Student Government

The Student Government Association at Mount Marty is composed of executive officers, student senate, and committees. The purpose of this association is to promote student activities and to advance the welfare of all students. Student government activities include Family Weekend, Homecoming, dances, live entertainment, and intramural activities.

Admission Requirements

Admission to Mount Marty College is open to students of all faiths, regardless of age, sex, race, national or ethnic origin, sexual orientation, veteran status, or physical ability. The admissions process is ongoing, and applicants are accepted based on academic record, experiences, and potential for growth. Applicants are eligible for admission if they have a cumulative high school grade point average of at least 2.0 and achieve a minimum ACT composite score of 18 or SAT score of 850. Applications for admission are available at the Mount Marty Web site listed below or by calling the Admissions Office. Students may visit the campus at any time by contacting the Admissions Office.

Application and Information

To be considered for enrollment, students must complete an application for admission and provide high school transcripts and official ACT or SAT I scores. A nonrefundable fee of $35 is required before students may register for classes. If students apply online, the application fee is deferred until registration. Transfer students should provide transcripts from their previous college as well as their high school.

For more information regarding admission, students should contact:

Director of Admissions
Admissions Office
Mount Marty College
1105 West 8th Street
Yankton, South Dakota 57078
Telephone: 605-668-1545
800-658-4552 (toll-free)
Fax: 605-668-1607
E-mail: mmcadmit@mtmc.edu
World Wide Web: http://www.mtmc.edu

Students enjoy visiting and studying with laptop computers in the new Cyber Café.

MOUNT MARY COLLEGE

MILWAUKEE, WISCONSIN

The College

Mount Mary College, Wisconsin's first Catholic college for women, was founded at Prairie du Chien on the Mississippi River in 1913 and moved to Milwaukee in 1929. Mount Mary is sponsored by the School Sisters of Notre Dame, traditionally recognized as excellent educators. A total of 1,500 undergraduate and graduate students from a variety of backgrounds attend Mount Mary. They represent more than a dozen states and many countries, although the majority of the students are from the Midwest. Students at Mount Mary are fully engaged in the classroom, learning not just the subject matter but also how to express opinions and develop leadership skills. Students are inspired, challenged, and motivated by excellent teaching. Dedication to excellence in teaching, seen as Mount Mary's finest tradition, always has remained the distinguishing feature of a Mount Mary education. Through exciting internships, club activities, community service, and campus ministry programs, students explore their interests and discover their skills. Special and professional interests are served by affiliates of national societies.

The College is situated on a beautiful 80-acre wooded campus with stately stone buildings. Caroline Hall, the student residence hall, provides accommodations for private occupancy and single and double suites. Every floor in Caroline Hall has a kitchen and a mini–computer lab with laser printers. Laundry and fitness facilities are located on the lower floor. All residence halls are wired for cable, telephone, and Internet connections.

Physical fitness and an interest in athletics are fostered through various activities, fitness programs, health and dance courses, and intramural and intercollegiate athletics. Mount Mary College is independent and affiliated with the NCAA Division III. The Blue Angels compete against NCAA and NAIA schools in soccer, softball, volleyball, basketball, and tennis. Facilities include a gymnasium, an indoor swimming pool, outdoor soccer fields, a fitness center, and sand volleyball courts. Bordering the campus is a large parkway for biking, jogging, cross-country skiing, and much more.

Of special note, Mount Mary has begun its first comprehensive capital campaign. With a goal of $19 million, funds raised go toward the development of two new buildings—the Science, Technology, and Campus Center and the Recreation Center—as well as toward scholarships, new and upgraded technology, women's leadership, and faculty development.

Mount Mary College sponsors many social activities, including performances by musicians and comedians, dances, and all-campus picnics. These events are sponsored by the Mount Mary Programming and Activities Council (MMPAC), Student Government, Hall Council, and other groups on campus. Other events include films, concerts, and lectures. Mount Mary students also attend social functions at area colleges and universities and invite students from those institutions to Mount Mary events.

Academic and professional student services are available to all Mount Mary students, including tutoring and assistance with tests through the Academic Resource Center; advising; resume writing; career planning through the Advising and Career Development Office; and personal counseling through the Counseling Center.

In addition to undergraduate programs, Mount Mary College offers five graduate programs: the Master of Arts in education and gerontology and the Master of Science in art therapy, dietetics, and occupational therapy.

Location

Mount Mary College is located in a residential area in northwestern Milwaukee, just 15 minutes from downtown and less than 5 minutes from a shopping mall. Students can access public transportation right in front of the campus. The city offers a major symphony, well-respected dance and theater companies, a beautiful lakefront, a newly expanded art museum, and a well-known zoo. Numerous professional and collegiate sports teams are based in Milwaukee.

Majors and Degrees

Mount Mary offers more than thirty undergraduate degree programs leading to bachelor's degrees in accounting, art, art therapy, behavioral science, biology, business administration, chemistry, communication, communication design, computer science, computer science management, computer science/professional communication, dietetics, English, English professional writing, fashion, French, graphic design, history, interior design, international studies, justice, liberal studies, marketing, mathematics, merchandise management, occupational therapy, philosophy, psychology/behavioral science, public relations, social work, Spanish, student designed, teacher education (early childhood/middle childhood, middle childhood/early adolescence, early adolescence/adolescence, early childhood/adolescence), and theology. The Columbia College of Nursing and Mount Mary College jointly offer a Bachelor of Science in Nursing (B.S.N.) degree. Special services for undeclared students help them find and focus on a major suited to their interests and talents. Preprofessional programs are also available in chiropractic medicine, dentistry, law, medicine, optometry, osteopathic medicine, pharmacy, and veterinary medicine. Mount Mary also provides a variety of minors to accompany any major.

Academic Program

Mount Mary's curriculum integrates leadership skills into each student's educational experience, developing leaders who take individual responsibility for social justice. The curriculum and cocurricular activities promote self-knowledge and competence, an entrepreneurial sense of vision, effective oral and written communication skills, and the ability to strengthen leadership in others. In their professions, churches, and communities, Mount Mary students model collaborative leadership, enabling them to work effectively both in leadership positions and as supportive team members. Mount Mary faculty members incorporate technology into the classroom through group projects and presentations. Students have access to the latest software and hardware in classrooms, labs, and residence halls and have Internet access throughout the campus.

The core curriculum consists of studies in five areas of the liberal arts: synoptics (12 credits in theology and philosophy), symbolics (8 credits in communication arts and mathematics), esthetics (12 credits in fine art), humanistics (12 credits in history and behavioral or social science), and empirics (4 credits of science). To qualify for graduation, baccalaureate degree students must complete a minimum of 128 credits that consist of 48 in core courses (a minimum of 24 in the major) and electives, with a minimum grade point average (GPA) of 2.0. Each academic department establishes its own requirements for the major and GPA needed for graduation. Students apply to a department at the end of their freshman year, with the exception of nursing students. Students pursuing a major in nursing, who meet the program requirements, are directly admitted to the program as freshmen. Transfer students at the sophomore level or above apply for admission to the College and the department of choice.

Two signature courses at Mount Mary College are Leadership Seminar and Search for Meaning. Leadership Seminar is a 3-credit course designed to introduce students to Mount Mary's mission and the College's leadership model. This interactive and reflective course focuses on leadership and issues of social justice and includes a justice-in-action component. The course emphasizes critical thinking, reading, writing, and speaking skills and provides both a context for subsequent courses and a foundation for search for meaning. Search for Meaning, a 4-credit course offering 2 credits in theology and 2 credits in philosophy, includes reading and discussion of classical and contemporary authors from philosophical and theological viewpoints and reflection on such elemental human concern as the possible sources of happiness, the role of conscience in personal integrity, the meaning of suffering and death, and the transcendent dimension of reality.

Many academic programs at Mount Mary College offer internships, which allow students to relate theory to practice and interact with professionals while learning life skills. The process encourages students to reflect on the skills and knowledge they hope to gain and allows them to tailor their practical experience to the career goals they have set for the future. Many of the programs incorporate a work experience into the curriculum. Work experience includes student teaching, clinicals, fieldwork, practicum, and internships.

Mount Mary College is committed to the academic success of each student. The Center for Educational and Professional Advancement strives to meet all adult students' needs, whether they are first-time college students or returning to complete or enhance a college degree, and provides assessment and placement testing, preliminary transcript evaluation, registration and orientation programs, as well as assistance with alternative means of earning credit (CLEP testing and credit for prior learning/portfolio). The Center has evening hours to assist the nontraditional student.

Off-Campus Programs

Mount Mary encourages its students to take advantage of a variety of study abroad opportunities. The College sponsors an annual summer study program in Rome. In 2001, the College signed an agreement with Catholic University–Santa Maria in Arequipa, Peru, in order to promote faculty and student exchanges between the colleges. While Spanish language study is a key component of the agreement, numerous options exist for students to combine language studies with service learning projects. In addition to these programs, the College also enjoys affiliate relationships with numerous international colleges and universities, including the American College, Dublin; the American Intercontinental University, London and Dubai; Nanzan College, Japan; and Notre Dame College, Kyoto, Japan. The Office of International Studies also aids students in finding an accredited program that meets their individual needs.

Academic Facilities

Located on 80 beautiful acres, Mount Mary offers students unlimited space to grow. Facilities include the Marian Art Gallery, the Walter and Olive Stiemke Memorial Hall and Conference Center, a Macintosh computer laboratory, two chapels, a fitness center, and an 800-seat theater. The Patrick and Beatrice Haggerty Library collection includes more than 110,000 volumes and 500 subscription periodical titles, along with a significant collection of audio-visual materials. As a member of the SWITCH library consortium, Haggerty Library is connected to six college and university libraries in the greater Milwaukee area. The consortium shares a common catalog, with complete exchange privileges for students and faculty members of member institutions; comprehensive subscription databases are available as well. The Web-based online catalog and an interactive library Web site provide services on and off campus.

Costs

For the 2003–04 academic year, tuition was $15,100 for full-time students and $440 per credit for part-time students. The undergraduate fee (including matriculation, student activities, library, computer lab, parking, and health services) for full-time students was $170 per year; part-time students paid $85 per year. Room and board costs averaged $5189 in 2003–04. Students should expect to spend $480 to $800 per year on textbooks and an estimated $1300 per year on personal expenses, not including travel costs. All costs are subject to change.

Financial Aid

The financial aid office at Mount Mary College develops a financial package on an individual basis for all qualified students. More than 90 percent of Mount Mary's full-time students receive some form of financial assistance. Students filing for financial aid should complete the Free Application for Federal Student Aid (FAFSA) and an early financial aid estimate, both available through the College financial aid office. Additional information on numerous merit-based scholarships, grants, and work-study opportunities are available for incoming freshmen as well as transfer students. Students should contact the Enrollment Office for more information.

Faculty

Faculty members holding advanced degrees do all the teaching; no classes are taught by teaching assistants. Faculty members are available to provide academic counseling. Mount Mary has 70 full-time and 90 part-time faculty members. With a total enrollment of 1,500, Mount Mary offers a low faculty-to-student ratio.

Student Government

Students are encouraged to participate in the governance of the College. Student government makes recommendations about College policies and other matters of importance to students and serves as a liaison to the Mount Mary administration, faculty, and staff.

Admission Requirements

Candidates for admission are considered on the basis of academic preparation, scholarship, and evidence of the ability to do college work and benefit from it. Sixteen secondary school units are required; of these, 11 must be academic (3 in English, 2 in college-preparatory mathematics, 2 in science, 4 in history, language, or social science) and 4 in electives. Students must have achieved a minimum composite score of 18 on the ACT (870 on the SAT I) and rank in the top 40 percent of their high school graduating class or have a minimum GPA of 2.5 (on a 4.0 scale). Students who do not meet the admission requirements are reviewed by an admission committee. International students must take the Test of English as a Foreign Language (TOEFL) and achieve a minimum score of 500. Mount Mary does not discriminate against any individual for reasons of race, color, religion, age, national or ethnic origin, or disability.

Application and Information

Mount Mary has a rolling admission policy. Early acceptance is available, and advanced placement is honored. An admission decision is sent as soon as all required materials, including a $25 application fee, have been received and reviewed by the Enrollment Office. After notification of acceptance, students wishing to enroll need to submit the $200 nonrefundable tuition deposit.

For further information, students should contact:

The Enrollment Office
Mount Mary College
2900 North Menomonee River Parkway
Milwaukee, Wisconsin 53222-4597
Telephone: 414-256-1219
800-321-6265 (toll-free)
Fax: 414-256-0180
E-mail: admiss@mtmary.edu
World Wide Web: http://www.mtmary.edu

Mount Mary College is located on 80 acres in a convenient Milwaukee neighborhood. Students have a safe, secure environment in which to live and learn.

MOUNT MERCY COLLEGE

CEDAR RAPIDS, IOWA

The College

Mount Mercy College is distinguished by a unique blend of career preparation and liberal arts, strengthened by a strong emphasis on leadership and service. A Catholic, coeducational four-year college, Mount Mercy is fully accredited by the North Central Association of Colleges and Schools.

Although the College offers a number of professional programs, its career preparation is not limited to those areas. Students majoring in English or history, for example, are just as likely to benefit from internships as students in business or social work. There is a focus on workplace skills such as group process and presentations—competencies that help graduates begin their careers. Mount Mercy believes strongly in a firm liberal arts foundation of analysis, critical thinking, and communication—skills that help graduates adapt to a changing world and find long-term career success.

Through its Emerging Leaders and Campus Ministry programs, the College supports the concept of servant leadership. This tradition of service is a legacy of the Sisters of Mercy, who founded the College in 1928. The College welcomes students of all faiths.

Mount Mercy's high academic quality and its relatively moderate cost make it one of the best values in Midwest higher education. The College offers thirty-five major fields of study, including several interdisciplinary majors. In the College's Partnership program, professors are paired with freshman students to support their transition to college and to enhance the intellectual growth needed to assure academic success.

Student activities include more than thirty clubs and organizations, a student newspaper, a choir, and a pom squad and cheerleaders, along with such annual events as Hillfest and Spring Fling. Each May, commencement exercises are followed by a celebration for graduates and their families on Mount Mercy's hilltop. During the school year, many student activities—including Club Friday, a Friday afternoon gathering of students, faculty members, and staff members—take place in the Lundy Commons, which houses a game room, fitness center, conference rooms, student organization offices, the *Mount Mercy Times* office, lounge areas, and a bookstore.

Mount Mercy College is a member of the National Association of Intercollegiate Athletics (NAIA) and the Midwest Classic Conference. The College offers intercollegiate competition in men's basketball, baseball, cross-country, golf, soccer, and track and field. In women's sports, the College offers basketball, cross-country, golf, soccer, softball, track and field, and volleyball. These programs have combined for more than twenty conference championship Mount Mercy teams and individuals that regularly qualify for regional and national championship events. In addition, Mount Mercy student-athletes are annually recognized as NAIA academic all-Americans. Intramural activities include basketball, cross-country, flag football, golf, softball, and volleyball.

About 400 of Mount Mercy's approximately 1,473 students live in campus housing. The College offers a variety of living arrangements. Mount Mercy's newest residence, which opened in fall 1999, houses 144 students in eight homelike, four-bedroom suites. A network of tunnels connects campus buildings; many students wear shorts all winter.

Location

Mount Mercy is just minutes from downtown Cedar Rapids' museums, malls, movie theaters, and restaurants. Local businesses offer numerous internships and employment opportunities. The 40-acre, tree-lined campus is tucked into a residential neighborhood of well-kept homes, neat lawns, and good neighbors. Mount Mercy's hilltop, with its sweeping view of the city skyline, is said to be the highest point in Linn County. The city bus stops at the College's "front door," providing convenient in-town transportation. Cedar Rapids is served by six major airlines and is just a 4- or 5-hour drive from Chicago, Minneapolis–St. Paul, Omaha, and St. Louis. Mount Mercy's location in a thriving Midwestern city helps students explore career possibilities and, when they graduate, find promising opportunities. Both economically and culturally, Cedar Rapids offers an outstanding quality of life.

Majors and Degrees

Mount Mercy awards the Bachelor of Arts, Bachelor of Science, Bachelor of Business Administration, Bachelor of Applied Science, Bachelor of Applied Arts, and Bachelor of Science in Nursing degrees.

The Bachelor of Arts degree is awarded to graduates who major in applied philosophy, art, biology, communication, criminal justice, criminal justice/business administration–interdisciplinary, English, English/business administration–interdisciplinary, history, international studies, mathematics, music, music/business administration–interdisciplinary, music education, political science, political science/business administration–interdisciplinary, psychology, psychology/business administration–interdisciplinary, religious studies, secondary education, social work, sociology, sociology/business administration–interdisciplinary, speech/drama, and visual arts/business administration–interdisciplinary.

The Bachelor of Science degree is awarded to graduates who major in biology, business, computer information systems, computer science, elementary education, health services administration, mathematics, medical technology, nursing, and secondary education.

Original endorsements, coupled with the secondary education major, may be completed in art, biology–education, business–marketing/management, English/language arts, history, mathematics–education, music–education, social science American government, social science American history, social science psychology, social science sociology, social science world history, and speech communication theater.

The Bachelor of Business Administration is awarded to graduates who major in accounting, administrative management, business–general (teacher education program), marketing, and secondary education. The Bachelor of Science in Nursing is awarded to graduates in nursing.

The Bachelor of Applied Science and Bachelor of Applied Arts degree programs are designed for students with technical training who wish to broaden their specialized background to include a liberal arts education. The Bachelor of Applied Science degree is awarded to graduates who major in accounting, administrative management, biology, business, computer information systems, computer science, health services administration, marketing, and mathematics. The Bachelor of Applied Arts degree is awarded to graduates who major in art, biology, criminal justice, history, mathematics, music, political science, psychology, religious studies, sociology, and speech drama.

Academic Program

Mount Mercy College requires 123 semester hours for graduation, with a cumulative grade point average of at least 2.0 (on a 4.0 scale). General education requirements include two courses in English, two in social sciences, and one each in fine arts, history, mathematics, multicultural studies, natural science, philosophy, religious studies, and speech. Students apply for admission to their major program in the spring of the sophomore year. The College gives credit for related experience based on portfolio presentations and for independent study arranged by the student and the instructor. Graduation requirements may vary according to the major field of study.

Special academic opportunities are offered to outstanding students through special honors sections of general education courses. Students graduating in the honors program receive special recognition at commencement.

Mount Mercy's academic year consists of fall and spring semesters, plus a winter term. This four-week term offers required courses as well as exploratory electives, allowing students to make more rapid progress toward their degrees. In addition, two five-week summer sessions are held.

Off-Campus Programs

Mount Mercy College has an exchange program with the University of Palacky in Olomouc, Czech Republic.

Academic Facilities

The Busse Library provides an inviting study and research environment. Internet access opens other major libraries to students as well. The library houses the computer center; a computer classroom used for instruction in writing, accounting, and computer skills; a media center; individual study carrels; group study rooms; and a variety of other comfortable study areas.

Basile Hall is a new business and biology building that opened in summer 2003, providing thirteen technology-ready classrooms and teaching labs, four seminar rooms, and a computer-teaching laboratory.

All on-campus student rooms and faculty/staff offices are connected to a campus network. The College also has an ICN (Iowa Communications Network) fiber-optics classroom, making it possible for students in more than one location to take the same course, interacting with other students and with the instructor.

Costs

Full-time tuition for the 2003–04 academic year was $16,070, about at the midpoint among Iowa private colleges. Major fees are included in this figure. Room costs were $2164 in residence halls and $2772 in apartments. Two meal plans are offered: the nineteen-meal-per-week plan, which cost $3166, and the fifteen-meal plan, $2944. Estimated annual costs for a resident student, including books, supplies, and personal expenses, were $25,894.

Financial Aid

Nearly all Mount Mercy's new, full-time freshmen receive some form of financial aid, including Mount Mercy scholarships or grants, federal or state grants, loans, on-campus employment, or a combination of these sources. The College awarded twenty-nine Presidential Scholarships of up to $6700 for the 2003–04 school year to high school seniors who had an ACT score of at least 26 and a high school grade point average of at least 3.5. Other awards also are made on the basis of ACT score and GPA. Each year, students who have been admitted to Mount Mercy and identified as Presidential Scholars are invited to campus to compete for the Holland Scholarship, a full-tuition award named for the first president of Mount Mercy. Three Holland Scholarships were awarded for the 2003–04 school year. Students may also apply for the Merit Award, given to entering freshmen and transfer students on the basis of their demonstrated leadership in school and community activities. In addition, scholarships are available to students with records of achievement in art, drama, and music and to those who are planning to major in social work. In 2003–04, the College awarded more than $5 million in institutional scholarships and grants to qualified students.

Students who show financial need may be eligible for the Federal Pell Grant, the Iowa Tuition Grant, Federal Stafford Student Loan, and on-campus employment. Students in work-study positions typically earn from $1000 to $1500 a year.

To apply for Mount Mercy scholarships and grants, students must first be admitted to the College. Early application is advised. The priority deadline for filing the FAFSA (Free Application for Federal Student Aid) is March 1. Students should check other deadlines with their high school counselors or call the Mount Mercy financial aid office.

Faculty

Most of Mount Mercy's 72 full-time and 45 part-time faculty members hold the terminal degree in their fields. Many have been recognized for their achievements: several have been Fulbright Fellows or have received grants from the National Endowment for the Humanities and the National Endowment for the Arts, and many others have been recognized by their professional organizations. With a faculty-student ratio of 14:1, Mount Mercy offers students the opportunity to know their teachers well and to learn from them in an informal, friendly, and supportive environment.

Student Government

The official voice of the student at Mount Mercy is the Student Government Association (SGA). Its officers serve on College committees, and SGA is represented at regular faculty meetings. An SGA petition to the faculty resulted in adding a fall break to the academic calendar. SGA is the body through which all other campus organizations are formed and funded.

Admission Requirements

Mount Mercy admits students whose academic preparation, abilities, interests, and personal qualities give promise of success in college. Applicants are considered on the basis of academic record, class rank, test scores, and recommendations. An Admission Committee reviews the applications of students with minimum qualifications. Students may apply online. To apply, students must submit an application for admission, a transcript of high school credits, scores from ACT or SAT examinations, and a $20 application fee. Transfer students must submit official transcripts from all colleges attended. Mount Mercy College has an agreement with several two-year colleges in Iowa through which degree graduates of these colleges may be admitted to Mount Mercy with junior standing.

Prospective students are encouraged to visit the campus and meet with a faculty member in their area of interest. Special campus visit days are scheduled each year, and individual appointments also may be made. Overnight accommodations in residence halls can be arranged.

Application and Information

Students who wish to be considered for Mount Mercy scholarships and grants should submit their applications for admission as early as possible after their junior year in high school. Admission decisions are made on a rolling basis, and the College notifies students of its decision within ten days of receiving the necessary forms.

Application forms and additional information may be obtained by contacting:

Office of Admission
Mount Mercy College
1330 Elmhurst Drive, NE
Cedar Rapids, Iowa 52402
Telephone: 319-368-6460
319-363-5270
800-248-4504 (toll-free)
E-mail: admission@mtmercy.edu
World Wide Web: http://www.mtmercy.edu

Students talk with a professor on the campus of Mount Mercy.

MOUNT SAINT MARY COLLEGE

NEWBURGH, NEW YORK

The College

Mount Saint Mary College is a private, four-year liberal arts college for men and women founded in 1960 by the Dominican Sisters of Newburgh.

The College has set the goal of preparing its students, within the environment of a small, independent, undergraduate college, to assume, by choice and preparation, their roles in an ever-changing cultural, intellectual, psychological, and social climate. According to the plan of its founders and the aims of the total college community, Mount Saint Mary College strives to produce alumni marked by intellectual acuity and professional competence who possess constructive attitudes toward the challenges of living in the world of their times. With its favorable student-faculty ratio of 16:1, the Mount provides an atmosphere that is warm and personal, and it also gives students an educational experience that will prove valuable throughout their lifetime. Mount Saint Mary College is a young, vibrant, growing school where group commitment is made to the individual student.

The current enrollment is more than 2,500 men and women. Students at Mount Saint Mary College come to the campus with various backgrounds and educational objectives. They are able to express individual desires and find an avenue for special talents not only in the academic environment but also through participation in extracurricular activities. A wide variety of choices make it possible for all students to find activities that fit their own interests. Intercollegiate athletics programs include baseball, basketball, soccer, softball, swimming, tennis, and volleyball. The 47,000-square-foot recreational facility features two NCAA basketball/volleyball courts, a cardiovascular fitness center, a weight room, an aerobics/dance studio, a swimming pool, a raised running track, training rooms, study lounges, a T.V. lounge, a snack bar, a game room, and four classrooms. Social programs, such as dances and other intercollegiate events, are held frequently in conjunction with neighboring colleges and the Military Academy at West Point. Students and their guests attend such social activities as Oktoberfest and Siblings' Weekend. Traditional College events include Parents' Weekend, Freshman Investiture, and One Hundredth Night.

The Mount provides twenty-eight garden apartment or townhouse-style residence halls, which include separate facilities for men and women as well as for freshmen and upperclass students. The halls are equipped with full kitchen facilities, lounges, and laundry facilities.

In addition to its undergraduate curricula, the Mount offers graduate programs leading to the Master of Science degree in elementary education, elementary/special education, secondary education, and special education; the Master of Business Administration; and the Master of Science in Nursing.

Location

Mount Saint Mary College is located in a residential section of Newburgh, New York, about 60 miles north of New York City and 15 minutes north of the United States Military Academy at West Point. The accessibility of New York City makes it possible for students to take advantage of a variety of cultural and social activities as well as the many attractions of the Mid-Hudson Valley. Recreational areas nearby provide facilities for skiing, boating, hiking, golfing, riding, and swimming. Shopping facilities are near the College. Many students are involved in some aspect of community service, often combining their academic interests with a community activity.

Majors and Degrees

Mount Saint Mary College awards Bachelor of Arts (B.A.) and Bachelor of Science (B.S.) degrees in such programs as accounting, biology, business management, chemistry, computer science, English, Hispanic studies, history, history/political science, human services, information technology, interdisciplinary studies, mathematics, media studies, medical technology, nursing, psychology, public relations, social science, sociology, and undeclared. Concentrations include counseling and client services, criminal justice, educational computing, finance, general concentration in human services, human resource management, international business, management information systems, marketing, networking, social and community services, and Web technologies. Certification programs are available in childhood education and childhood education and teaching students with disabilities (grades 1–6), childhood education with middle school extension and adolescence education with middle school extension (grades 5–6), adolescence education and adolescence education and teaching students with disabilities (grades 7–12). Preprofessional studies are available in dentistry, law, medicine, and veterinary medicine. Mount Saint Mary College offers a 4-3 physical therapy program and a 4-2 speech-language pathology program with New York Medical College. The Mount also offers a 3-2 mathematics-engineering program with Catholic University and a 3-2 social work degree program with Fordham University.

Academic Program

The Mount is dedicated to providing a diversity of programs to accommodate people with individual needs and specific objectives, while developing a total learning environment for all students. Each individualized program is geared to the complex and varied needs of each student seeking to become a whole person, ready for a rewarding career and ready to make full use of his or her leisure hours. A minimum of 120 credit hours is required for degrees granted by the Mount, including 90 credit hours in the liberal arts and sciences for the Bachelor of Arts degree and 60 credit hours in the liberal arts and sciences for the Bachelor of Science degree. A core curriculum of 39 credit hours is also required. Major requirements consist of 28 to 40 credit hours.

Advanced placement, credit for life experience, accelerated courses, and an honors program are available. Students are encouraged to take part in the Mount's study-abroad program. All students have the opportunity to gain practical experience within their major through cooperative education and internships.

Academic Facilities

Aquinas Hall, the main College building, has laptop-friendly smart classrooms with LCD projection and stereo sound systems; science, nursing, language, and state-of-the-art computer science laboratories; an art studio; administrative and faculty offices; the library; a theater; a multimedia digital production center; a video production studio; a photography lab; and the music department's facilities. The fully automated

Curtain Memorial Library, a trilevel wing at the southern end of Aquinas Hall, houses 120,000 volumes plus subscriptions to 1,129 current journals and periodicals. The Media Center contains recordings, cassettes, filmstrips, and tapes, along with individual listening areas and carrels to augment innovative courses and independent study. Internet access is available to all students in the Academic Computing Lab and throughout campus via the Wireless Academic Network. The Curriculum Library has been designed to meet the many needs of education students, and the Bishop Dunn Memorial School, an elementary and junior high school on campus, provides a place where education students can participate in observing and teaching. Individually guided instruction is conducted here, as well as a modified Montessori program and classes in special education. The on-campus Office of Academic Assessment and Developmental Instruction assists students in academic endeavors through tutorial services and skills development at no additional cost.

Costs

Tuition for the 2003–04 academic year was $13,830 for most full-time students. Room and board costs were $7080, including a room and a full weekly meal plan. Additional fees total approximately $420 annually.

Financial Aid

About 80 percent of the College's students receive financial aid from one or more sources. Scholarships, grants, loans, and work-study programs constitute most awards. The College provides aid from all federal aid programs, such as the Federal Pell Grant, Federal Supplemental Educational Opportunity Grant, Federal Perkins Loan, Nursing Scholarship and/or Loan, and Federal Work-Study programs. New York State residents may be eligible for Tuition Assistance Program (TAP) awards. The Mount also offers its own scholarship and grant programs. On-campus jobs are plentiful. All students are encouraged to apply for financial aid. Application may be made by filing the Free Application for Federal Student Aid (FAFSA) and the Mount Saint Mary College Supplemental Form (New York State residents should file the TAP Form) by March 15. For further information about financial aid, students should contact the director of financial aid. All students who apply for admission are eligible for consideration for half tuition Presidential Scholarships, Merit Grant Awards, and Mount Saint Mary College Scholarships.

Faculty

Mount Saint Mary College offers its students an environment that fosters close student-teacher interaction with the aid of a very committed faculty. The student-teacher ratio is 16:1, which allows for individualized advisement and instruction. The average class size is 25, and classes emphasize seminar and discussion-based learning.

Student Government

Students at Mount Saint Mary College participate in a very active system of student governance. Student representatives are members of every College committee. The Resident Living Council governs and represents the resident students of the College, while the Commuter Council focuses on the commuting population. Most student activities are generated by Student Government organizations, and the Student Government plays a leading role in the development of College policy; it is the main outlet for student participation in the College's decision-making process and in the planning of events. The Student Government manages its own student activities budget.

Admission Requirements

Mount Saint Mary College welcomes students whose potential for academic and social success is in keeping with the objectives of the College. Applicants are evaluated primarily on their past academic performance. SAT I scores and class rank are also considered. Transfer applicants should be in good academic standing at their previous college. Campus visits and interviews are strongly recommended. Early admission to the College is available.

Application and Information

Students who wish to apply to the Mount should submit a completed application and a $35 application fee to the Admissions Office. Students should also make arrangements for their high school transcript and SAT I scores to be forwarded to the same office. Letters of recommendation, while not required, are strongly advised. Mount Saint Mary College operates on a rolling admission policy. Once a student's file is complete, he or she is usually notified of the admission decision within two to four weeks.

For further information, students should contact:

Director of Admissions
Mount Saint Mary College
330 Powell Avenue
Newburgh, New York 12550
Telephone: 845-569-3248
888-YES-MSMC (toll-free)
E-mail: mtstmary@msmc.edu
World Wide Web: http://www.msmc.edu

Mount Saint Mary College, with the Hudson River in the background.

MOUNT ST. MARY'S COLLEGE AND SEMINARY

EMMITSBURG, MARYLAND

The College

As the nation's second-oldest Catholic college, Mount St. Mary's is blessed with a heritage that few can match. Founded in 1808, the Mount will celebrate its bicentennial in 2008, making it only the second Catholic college in the country to mark this distinction. Mount alumni include a Supreme Court Justice, a president of Mexico, and the founder of Boys' Town. Today, the Most Rev. Harry J. Flynn, Archbishop of St. Paul/Minneapolis; Susan O'Malley, President of the Washington Wizards NBA team; and Matt McHugh, who served nine terms in the U.S. House of Representatives, are counted among the Mount's 12,000 alumni. Most students come from Maryland and other mid-Atlantic states, but typically more than half of the U.S. states and nearly a dozen additional countries are represented by the 1,400 undergraduates.

Current Mount students are well prepared to join their predecessors in service to "the Church, the Republic, and the Professions." The Core Curriculum, which has received national recognition, provides a strong grounding in the liberal arts, developing reading, writing, and critical thinking skills—attributes needed for success in any career path. Academic majors and minors add specialized knowledge. Outside of the classroom the Mount offers even more: a full range of extracurricular and cocurricular activities and the opportunity to build people skills in a residential college environment. Among the more than seventy-five clubs and special interest groups are student media (radio, TV, newspaper, yearbook, and literary magazine), drama, campus ministry, and community service opportunities.

The Mount has one of the smallest enrollments of colleges competing at the NCAA Division I level, which gives students many opportunities for participation on the eighteen varsity sports teams. Club sports and intramurals are also available, as are indoor and outdoor recreation facilities. Of particular note is the 105,000-square-foot Knott Athletic Recreation Convocation Complex, with courts for tennis, volleyball, basketball, and handball/racquetball; a swimming pool; an indoor track; and aerobics and weight rooms (both recently outfitted with new weight-training equipment).

Student residences include traditional dormitories, suites, apartments, and special interest housing. Students are guaranteed housing for all four years. The recently renovated and expanded McGowan Student Center houses the dining hall, snack bar, and social gathering places, as well as the bookstore, mailroom, and offices for student organizations.

In addition to the undergraduate college, the Mount includes one of the country's largest and most successful Catholic seminaries, other graduate programs in business and education, and the National Shrine Grotto of Lourdes.

Location

The 1,400-acre campus is in north-central Maryland, 1 hour west of Baltimore and slightly farther northwest of Washington, D.C. Historic Gettysburg, Pennsylvania, is 12 miles north, and Frederick, Maryland's second-largest city and an attractive shopping and entertainment destination, is 20 miles south. Emmitsburg is a town of 1,500, with a variety of restaurants and shops. Elizabeth Ann "Mother" Seton, America's first native-born saint, began her religious order and the country's first parochial school here, and both survive to this day. Nearby attractions include Ski Liberty, national and state parks (including Catoctin Mountain National Park, home of the Camp David presidential retreat), and golf courses. Horseback riding is also available in the area.

Majors and Degrees

Majors leading to Bachelor of Arts or Bachelor of Science degrees are offered in accounting, art education, biochemistry, biology, business (concentrations in finance; international business, sports management, economics; management; and marketing), chemistry, computer science, economics, elementary education (including an option for dual certification in special education), English, fine arts (concentrations in art, music, and theater), French, German, history, information systems, international studies, Latin, mathematics, philosophy, political science, psychology, communications (concentrations in communications, creative writing, journalism, and professional and technical writing), secondary education (concentrations in English, mathematics, social studies, and other areas), sociology (concentration in criminal justice), Spanish, and theology. Students may also design their own majors. A 3-2 program in nursing with Johns Hopkins University, a 4-2 B.S./master's in occupational technology with Sacred Heart University, and a 3-3 B.S./master's in physical therapy with Sacred Heart University are also available. Minors are offered in all major areas and in African-American studies, gender studies, Latin American studies, legal studies, and non-Western studies. Predental, prelaw, and premedicine programs are offered.

Academic Programs

The academic majors offer strong preparation for a variety of careers, but Mount students take nearly half of the 120 credit hours required for graduation in the Core Curriculum, a carefully integrated four-year sequence of courses in Western civilization, American and non-Western culture, philosophy and theology, foreign languages, mathematics, and the social and natural sciences. This program helps students gain a broader perspective and a better understanding of themselves and the world around them and fosters the development and strengthening of a rational value system. After core and major requirements, students complete their course work with electives. The Mount accepts Advanced Placement and CLEP credits.

Mount St. Mary's yearlong Freshman Seminar is designed to build reading, writing, and critical thinking skills. Students are placed in seminar sections of about 18 students each, taught by their faculty advisers. Students with outstanding high school records are invited into the Freshman Honors Program; sophomores enter the College Honors Program. The latter includes an interdisciplinary honors seminar for juniors and a special senior project in a student's major.

The Mount sponsors its own international study programs in Costa Rica, England, France, Germany, Ireland, and Italy, and affiliated programs make it possible to study in other countries. At home, the Mount offers an aggressive internship program and a variety of career-preparation services.

Academic Facilities

Classes are held in two major academic buildings—the Knott Academic Center and the Coad Science Building—and in several other smaller or multiple-use buildings. Most classrooms are small because most classes are small. The science lab facilities are newly renovated, and continuous improvements are being made to computing facilities. PC and Macintosh labs are available, and online research resources are abundant through Phillips Library or any networked computer. Internet access is free. The library contains more than 200,000 books, including a reference collection of 3,000 volumes, CD-ROMs, and electronic databases. More than 2,000 periodicals are available in print, microfilm, or electronic form. Online access provides additional possibilities worldwide. Many special events are held in the 550-seat Marion Burk Knott Auditorium.

Costs

Tuition and fees total $21,430 for 2004–05; room and board are $7640. Books, supplies, laundry, transportation, and personal expenses average nearly $1600 per year.

Financial Aid

Mount St. Mary's offers financial assistance to qualified students in the form of scholarships, grants, loans, student employment, and special payment plans. Almost 90 percent of students attending the Mount receive some form of financial aid. Through its scholarship program and financial aid packages, the College attempts as much as possible to relieve the financial burden of attending college. The Mount participates in all major federal financial aid programs, including the Federal Pell Grant, Federal Perkins Loan, Federal Stafford Student Loan, and Federal Work-Study Programs. Federal PLUS loans may also be used.

The College awards a wide range of merit and merit-and-need scholarships. In 2003–04, about 325 were awarded to entering freshmen (400 total) at an average of more than $8000 per year. Three full-tuition Kuderer-Trustee Scholarships are awarded to qualified candidates on the basis of an essay exam competition. The full-tuition Marion Burk Knott Scholarships, usually one per year, is offered to qualified Catholic students residing in the Archdiocese of Baltimore. Mount Scholarships and Mount Merit Grants are offered to qualified students in amounts typically ranging from $5000 to $12,500 per year. Funston V. Collins and Bolivar–San Martin Scholarships and Grants-in-Aid are offered to qualified African-American and Hispanic-American students, respectively. All scholarships are renewable annually based on academic performance. In addition, as an NCAA Division I school, the Mount offers athletic scholarships to men and women in all intercollegiate sports.

The Free Application for Federal Student Aid (FAFSA) and the Mount St. Mary's College Financial Aid Application must be submitted by March 15 and should be filed as soon after January 1 as possible.

Faculty

More than 95 full-time faculty members—90 percent with Ph.D. or equivalent degrees—bring the Mount curriculum to life. All faculty members personalize the educational experience by working with and getting to know each student. The student-faculty ratio is 15:1, and the average class size is 21. Every professor serves as an academic adviser. No graduate assistants teach class. Faculty members are committed to teaching, but many are also active researchers, and opportunities exist for students to become involved in research projects.

Student Government

The Student Government Association (SGA) provides funding for other student organizations and is a conduit for student feedback to the Mount administration. The SGA President sits on the Mount Council, the College's governing body. The Campus Activities Board schedules dances, concerts, movies, bus trips, and other social events.

Admission Requirements

Candidates for admission to the College must be of good character and must show evidence that they have successfully completed a four-year college-preparatory program in high school. All students applying for admission should have a minimum of 16 academic units, including English, 4; social studies, 3; mathematics, 3; sciences, 3; and a foreign language, 2. Students must also present recommendations from a guidance counselor or a teacher in an academic course, as well as scores on the SAT I or ACT.

Application and Information

Students applying to the Mount should send test scores, high school transcripts, and recommendations to the Admissions Office along with a $35 application fee. Transfer students in good standing should forward both their college and high school transcripts. Information and forms are also available on the Mount's Web site listed below.

For further information, students may contact:

Director of Admissions
Mount St. Mary's College
Emmitsburg, Maryland 21727
Telephone: 301-447-5214
800-448-4347 (toll-free)
E-mail: admissions@msmary.edu
World Wide Web: http://www.msmary.edu

Students in front of the Coad Science Building on the campus of Mount St. Mary's College.

MOUNT UNION COLLEGE

ALLIANCE, OHIO

The College

Mount Union College was established in 1846 as a select school to meet the educational demands of a small community. Mount Union College offers a liberal arts education grounded in the Judeo-Christian tradition. The College affirms the importance of reason, open inquiry, living faith, and individual worth. Mount Union's mission is to prepare students for meaningful work, fulfilling lives, and responsible citizenship.

Mount Union is primarily a residential campus, and its residence halls mirror the variety of lifestyles and diversity of interests of the students. Students have the opportunity to select from large residence halls housing from 70 to 175, small houses, or fraternity houses. Upperclass students in good academic standing may be permitted to live off campus.

Student activities are an important complement to the academic program. From clubs allied with academic interests to those that are purely social, Mount Union has more than eighty student organizations in its cocurricular program, including chapters of four national sororities and four national fraternities. Nearly 85 percent of Mount Union students participate in the cocurricular program either on or off campus. There are facilities on campus for racquetball, volleyball, basketball, swimming, wrestling, tennis, track, and dance. The College also has a physical education complex, which includes the McPherson Wellness Center, the Peterson Field House, and the Timken Physical Education Building. Nearly 65 percent of Mount Union students participate in organized intramural or intercollegiate sports. Mount Union competes in twenty-one intercollegiate sports: baseball, basketball, cross-country, football, golf, indoor track, outdoor track, soccer, swimming, tennis, and wrestling for men and basketball, cross-country, golf, indoor track, outdoor track, soccer, softball, swimming, tennis, and volleyball for women.

Location

Mount Union College is located in Alliance, Ohio, a town of approximately 25,000 people. Alliance is situated 55 miles southeast of Cleveland, 75 miles northwest of Pittsburgh, 35 miles southeast of Akron, 40 miles west of Youngstown, and 15 miles northeast of Canton.

Majors and Degrees

The Bachelor of Arts is offered in accounting, American studies, art, business administration, communication studies, early childhood education, economics, English, French, German, history, international business and economics, international studies, Japanese, media computing, media studies, middle childhood education, music, non-Western studies, philosophy, physical education, political science, psychology, religious study, sociology, Spanish, sport management, theater, and writing.

The Bachelor of Science is offered in athletic training, biochemistry, biology, chemistry, computer science, environmental biology, exercise science, geology, information systems, mathematics, and physics-astronomy.

Mount Union offers three degrees in music: the Bachelor of Music in performance, which is a professional degree; the Bachelor of Music Education, which is a professional degree; and the Bachelor of Arts in music, which is a liberal arts degree.

Preprofessional programs are available in dentistry, engineering, law, medicine, and the ministry.

Academic Programs

The Mount Union education program is based on an academic year divided into two semesters of sixteen weeks each. The regular academic load is 12 to 18 semester hours per semester.

The Mount Union curriculum is designed with considerable flexibility to meet the needs of students who enter with widely varying educational backgrounds and objectives. The College has five basic educational plans: (1) a program geared toward specialization, with the student taking as many as sixteen courses in one department; (2) a program with a lesser degree of specialization, in which the student takes the minimum number of courses required for a major; (3) a program that permits concentration in interdepartmental areas, such as American studies, non-Western studies, or communications; (4) a preprofessional program that prepares students for entry into professional degree programs in dentistry, engineering, law, medicine, and the ministry; and (5) an interdisciplinary, individualized program, which students design in conjunction with a committee of faculty advisers to meet particular interests. While students have considerable latitude in determining their individual programs, the all-College comprehensive requirements ensure exposure to the fine arts, the humanities, the social sciences, the physical sciences, and mathematics. In addition, each student must complete a major requirement and a senior-year culminating experience.

Advanced placement, involving the awarding of credit or the waiving of certain prerequisites or requirements, is based on high school records, scores on College Board examinations or similar tests, scores and school reports on College Board Advanced Placement Program examinations, and tests devised and administered by departments within the College. Entering students are encouraged to take placement tests in applicable areas in order to begin course work at the proper level.

Academic Facilities

The library contains more than 230,000 volumes, receives more than 900 periodicals, and provides seating for 350 persons. The computer center, housed in the library, is equipped with the latest in computer and communications technology. The Kolenbrander-Harter Information Center houses two PC computer labs, a Macintosh computer lab, a language lab, several multimedia classrooms, and a 24-hour access to study space. There is also an eighteen-station PC lab in East Hall and a twenty-station PC lab in the Hoover-Price Campus Center. All residence halls are wired for computers and closed-circuit television. The Fine Arts Complex includes a 290-seat theater, an art gallery, a music library, an outdoor Greek theater, a large rehearsal hall, and a recital hall with a three-manual organ. The Eells Art Center contains classrooms, a printmaking area, a drawing and design studio, a kiln room, a sculpture and woodworking area, and a drama rehearsal hall.

Bracy Hall, a new natural sciences facility that opened in the fall of 2003, houses the departments of biology, chemistry, geology, and physics and astronomy. The 87,000-square-foot, $23-million structure has four floors and includes twenty-two laboratories of various types and sizes, three lecture halls, two classrooms, and twenty-one faculty offices.

The Clarke Astronomical Observatory is located on campus, and a nearby private observatory is also used by the College. Mount Union also has a 109-acre nature center, located 6 miles from the campus, for biology, chemistry, and ecology studies.

Costs

For 2004–05, the cost of a year at Mount Union College is $24,440, including $18,810 for tuition and fees and $5630 for room and board. This figure may vary slightly, depending upon the type of on-campus housing selected by the student. An additional $1000 should cover such expenses as books and transportation.

Financial Aid

Mount Union College believes that no student should fail to apply for admission to the College purely for financial reasons. Approximately 89 percent of students receive some financial assistance based on demonstrated need. The College also offers allocated institutional dollars to students as merit-based awards. In 2003–04, Mount Union students received financial aid in excess of $30 million. More than $15 million of that total was awarded in the form of institutional grants or scholarships. An additional $1.3 million was given in the form of various scholarships.

Faculty

Mount Union employs 128 full-time faculty members, 80 percent of whom hold a terminal degree. The student-faculty ratio is 14:1.

Student Government

Student government is a significant part of Mount Union's decision-making process. Students are represented on all major campus committees that discuss matters affecting student life, and they serve as representatives at meetings of the administration, faculty, and trustees.

Admission Requirements

Mount Union College does not discriminate on the basis of race, sex, religion, age, color, creed, national or ethnic origin, marital or parental status, or handicap in student admissions, financial aid, educational or athletic programs, or employment. Admission decisions are made with a view toward enrolling those students who are best qualified to participate intelligently and creatively in the total life of the academic community.

A $20 application fee is required. The admission packet contains instructions, an application form, a secondary school transcript form, and a reference request form. All candidates are required to submit either SAT I or ACT scores. Students can also apply on line via the College's Web site, listed below.

The qualifications of each candidate are evaluated on the basis of academic background, class rank, references, a required essay, recommendations, and entrance examinations. Candidates who find it possible to visit the campus are encouraged to schedule an interview, although this is not a requirement. Applicants should have pursued a strong college-preparatory course in high school.

The Office of Admissions is located in Beeghly Hall and is open throughout the year from 8 a.m. until 4:30 p.m. on weekdays and from 9 a.m. until noon on Saturdays throughout the academic year.

Mount Union welcomes applications from students wishing to transfer from other institutions.

Application and Information

Admission decisions are made on a rolling basis throughout the year. The first admission decisions are made in October. A $20 application fee is required. Students can also apply on line via the College's Web site, listed below.

Applicants may obtain further information by contacting:

Director of Admissions
Mount Union College
1972 Clark Avenue
Alliance, Ohio 44601
Telephone: 330-823-2590
800-334-6682 (toll-free)
E-mail: admissn@muc.edu
World Wide Web: http://www.muc.edu

Chapman Hall, built in 1864, serves as one of the main classroom buildings at Mount Union College.

MUHLENBERG COLLEGE

ALLENTOWN, PENNSYLVANIA

The College

Founded in 1848 and affiliated with the Lutheran Church, Muhlenberg College has the primary purpose of helping students develop those capacities of imaginative and critical thinking that make possible humane and responsible living within a free society. A secondary, but related, purpose is to provide students with excellent undergraduate preparation for socially useful and fulfilling occupations.

Muhlenberg students achieve the College's goals by assuming strong individual responsibility for intense involvement in vigorous academic work and for personal involvement within the College community. The more than 100 student organizations provide outlets for the diversified cultural, athletic, religious, social, leadership, and service interests of the students. The campus is primarily residential; more than 90 percent of the 2,100 students live on campus. A close sense of community develops naturally, one in which their diversified academic and personal interests enable students to contribute positively to the intellectual and personal growth of their peers.

Students are aided by an active Career Planning and Placement Service in relating academic and personal knowledge and skills to appropriate career goals and in obtaining positions upon graduation. About one third of a typical graduating class proceeds immediately to graduate or professional school.

Location

Muhlenberg College is located in suburban west Allentown, an area made up primarily of attractive family homes and parks. The central area of Allentown, a city of approximately 104,000 people, is a 10-minute ride from the campus. The College is located 90 miles west of New York City and 60 miles north of Philadelphia.

Majors and Degrees

Muhlenberg offers the Bachelor of Arts (A.B.) degree in the following fields: accounting, American studies, anthropology, art, business administration, communications, dance, drama, economics, English, French, German, history, history/government, international studies, music, philosophy, philosophy/political thought, political economy, political science, psychology, religion, Russian studies, social science, sociology, and Spanish. The Bachelor of Science (B.S.) degree is offered in the following fields: biochemistry, biology, chemistry, computer science, environmental science, mathematics, natural sciences, neuroscience, and physics. Students may also design their own major.

In addition, students may receive certification to teach at the elementary and secondary levels. Other opportunities include a 4-4 guaranteed-admission program with Drexel University College of Medicine; a 3-4 dental program with the University of Pennsylvania; a 3-2/4-2 combined program in engineering, offered in cooperation with Columbia University and Washington University; and a 3-2 combined program in forestry, offered in cooperation with Duke University.

Academic Programs

The A.B. and B.S. programs emphasize breadth of study in the liberal arts as well as in-depth study of a particular academic major. All students must fulfill requirements in foreign culture, the humanities, social sciences, and natural sciences. Strong achievement on Advanced Placement examinations may enable a student to receive advanced placement, possibly with credit. Scores of 4 or 5 earn automatic credit. Scores of 3 are evaluated by the appropriate department.

Students work closely with academic advisers to formulate programs well suited to their individual interests, abilities, needs, and goals. Generally, students are expected to declare their major at the end of the freshman year; however, many students later change their academic major with no difficulty. A double major is possible, and several fields are available as minor programs. These minor fields are accounting, anthropology, business administration, chemistry, computer science, economics, English, French, German, history, Jewish studies, mathematics, music, philosophy, physics, political science, religion, sociology, Spanish, and women's studies. In addition, independent study and research are available. The College also enriches the freshman-year experience through more than thirty special-focus Freshman Seminars.

Off-Campus Programs

Study abroad is available through Muhlenberg's Semester-in-London Program, Netherlands Semester, or more than thirty affiliate agreements with international universities all over the world. In addition, the Lehigh Valley Association of Independent Colleges sponsors summer study-abroad options in England, France, Germany, Israel, and Spain. Credit for study-abroad programs sponsored by other institutions or by private agencies may also be transferred to Muhlenberg by special arrangement.

Students may participate in a variety of internships in local businesses, health-care facilities, schools, public agencies, theaters, broadcasting stations, and magazines. Government internships in Harrisburg, Pennsylvania, and Washington, D.C., and an Ethics and Public Affairs semester in Washington, D.C., are also available.

Students may enroll in courses offered at any of the five other member institutions of the Lehigh Valley Association of Independent Colleges: Lafayette College, Lehigh University, Cedar Crest College, DeSales University, and Moravian College.

Academic Facilities

Muhlenberg's library collection contains more than 200,000 volumes as well as numerous government documents, periodicals, and microforms. The $12-million Harry C. Trexler Library, a state-of-the-art library facility, opened in 1988. Students may also use library materials owned by the other institutions participating in the Lehigh Valley Association of Independent Colleges.

The Baker Center for the Arts was designed for Muhlenberg by the well-known architect Philip Johnson. It houses a modern theater complex, a recital hall, classrooms, art studios, and a fine arts gallery. The Trexler Performing Arts Pavilion opened in 2000 and provides dance performance and studio space, a new theater, a Black Box, and additional arts spaces.

Life science facilities include numerous laboratories, classrooms, two electron microscopes, an isolation room used for growing and studying viruses, and a museum of natural history. Facilities supporting students in the physical sciences include equipment for optics, electronics, and atomic, nuclear, and solid-state physics. The College uses a UNIX/Windows computer system with Novell software.

Costs

The comprehensive tuition fee for 2003–04 was $24,945. The room and board fee was $6540. The total cost for a resident student was $31,485.

Financial Aid

Muhlenberg College endeavors to make its educational opportunities available to all qualified students regardless of their financial circumstances. While most financial aid at Muhlenberg is based on financial need as demonstrated by the College Scholarship Service Financial Aid PROFILE, there is also a limited amount of merit aid available. Typically, about 65 percent of Muhlenberg's students qualify for and receive financial aid.

Faculty

The Muhlenberg faculty consists of 154 full-time and 89 part-time members. Ninety percent of full-time faculty members hold doctoral or terminal degrees. While many faculty members are distinguished for their scholarly research, teaching is the main emphasis of their work. Professors at all levels work closely with students both inside and outside of the classroom. Most department heads teach introductory courses.

Student Government

Muhlenberg students are expected to demonstrate a high level of responsibility with regard to their own governance and to participate extensively in internal decision making and communication processes throughout the campus. These responsibilities are coordinated by the Student Council, which transacts all business pertaining to the student body. This organization is in charge of a $350,366 student activities budget. In addition, 2 students serve as representatives to the Board of Trustees, and students hold full voting privileges on many faculty committees.

Admission Requirements

The College selects students who give evidence of ability and scholastic achievement, seriousness of purpose, and the capacity to make constructive contributions to the College community. Approximately 65 percent of a typical freshman class ranked in the top fifth of their secondary school class. SAT I scores for entering freshmen average approximately 600 verbal and 610 math.

Submission of SAT I or ACT scores is optional. An on-campus interview is strongly recommended for all applicants and required for students who choose not to submit standardized test scores.

Application and Information

Students who wish to be considered for admission should submit a completed application form as early as possible during their senior year of secondary school and no later than February 15. Candidates receive notice of admission decisions in late March. Early decision and early admission plans and transfer admission are possible.

For further information, interested students should contact:

Christopher Hooker-Haring
Dean of Admission and Financial Aid
Muhlenberg College
Allentown, Pennsylvania 18104-5586
Telephone: 484-664-3200
E-mail: admissions@muhlenberg.edu
World Wide Web: http://www.muhlenberg.edu

The Bell Tower of the Haas College Center stands as the focal point of the Muhlenberg College campus.

NAROPA UNIVERSITY
Naropa College

BOULDER, COLORADO

The College

Naropa University is a private, nonsectarian, accredited liberal arts University providing a unique educational environment and a four-year undergraduate program in a wide range of majors. The undergraduate program at Naropa is referred to as Naropa College. The aim of education at Naropa College is to uncover wisdom, cultivate compassion, and develop the intellectual knowledge and skills necessary for effective action. Naropa's approach to learning is called "contemplative education," embodying the spirit of many contemplative traditions around the world and based in the practice of cultivating one's awareness of the present moment. Contemplative education teaches students to combine intellect with wisdom and encourages the desire to work for the benefit of others.

Naropa College grew out of an educational philosophy that dates back to Nalanda University, a major center of learning that was founded in India and that was presided over in the eleventh century by Naropa, a highly respected Buddhist scholar. Naropa College was originally founded in 1974 by the Tibetan meditation master and scholar Chögyam Trungpa. This Buddhist educational heritage has been the ongoing inspiration for the development of Naropa College.

Naropa's academic programs are rigorous. They are designed for students who are resourceful and willing to go beyond habitual patterns. The curriculum allows students to wholeheartedly train in a chosen field of study while engaged in a learning process that fosters precision, gentleness, spontaneity, and critical intellect.

Naropa College provides an atmosphere that is vital and dignified. The faculty members and student body at Naropa form a close-knit community, and this relationship between students and faculty members is a unique part of the educational experience. Drawn from more than forty-three states and nine countries, students at Naropa represent a wide range of life experiences, backgrounds, and ages. Of the 1,047 degree-seeking students at Naropa, 428 are undergraduate students enrolled in Naropa College.

Naropa provides limited student housing. The Office of Student Affairs also provides a variety of resources to assist students in finding the right living situation.

Accredited by the North Central Association of Colleges and Schools since 1986, Naropa offers a four-year undergraduate program through Naropa College, as well as M.A., M.Div., M.F.A., and M.L.A. degrees through Naropa University.

Location

Naropa College is located in Boulder, Colorado, a town nestled at the base of the majestic Rocky Mountain foothills. The city of Boulder, a town of 100,000, is located 25 miles northwest of Denver and was rated by *Outdoor Magazine* in 1997 as one of the top ten places to live for health and recreation. It is home to many theater, dance, and music companies, as well as to the University of Colorado. Boulder has bike paths all over town, and Boulder public transportation provides a frequent and comprehensive bus schedule throughout the day.

Naropa's main campus and surrounding grounds include a Performing Arts Center, a meditation hall, the Allen Ginsberg Library and Computer Center, Naropa Gallery, a student lounge, a bookstore, and Naropa Café.

Majors and Degrees

Naropa offers nine undergraduate programs leading to a Bachelor of Arts (B.A.) degree: contemplative psychology, early childhood education, environmental studies, interarts studies, interdisciplinary studies, religious studies, traditional Eastern arts, visual arts, and writing and literature.

Contemplative psychology has two main components: a contemplative core and areas of concentration, which include Buddhist and Western psychology, expressive arts and well-being, psychology of health and healing, somatic psychology, and transpersonal and humanistic psychology.

Early childhood education draws from the holistic and spiritual traditions of Montessori, Waldorf, and Shambhala. Graduates are preapproved by the state of Colorado for certification as preschool teachers, and private kindergarten teachers.

Environmental studies applies ecocentric, holistic, and systems science perspectives to ecological and cultural systems. Students may choose concentrations in anthropology, ecology, ecopsychology, horticulture, sustainable built environments, or American Indian studies.

Music provides an innovative environment in which students study composition, improvisation, and performance. Students are given the opportunity to study with leading innovators and artists, while concentrating in world music, jazz, music technology, theory, and ear training.

Interdisciplinary studies does not require a minor, allowing students to develop a varied curriculum from the College's majors for a personally directed educational experience.

Religious studies offers a nonsectarian, scholarly, and critical examination of the major religions of the world (Buddhism, Hinduism, Christianity, Judaism, Islam, Native American traditions, and the religions of East Asia) as living traditions.

Traditional Eastern arts is the only degree program of its kind, offering training and study in the traditional arts of Tai-chi Chuan, aikido, and Yoga, combined with sitting meditation.

Visual arts provides a hands-on studio approach. Students study traditional and contemporary artistic techniques from many world cultures, with an emphasis on meditative disciplines, art history, and portfolio/gallery presentations.

The writing and literature program fosters an environment of original writing combined with scholarship, contemplative study, and sharp-minded criticism. The curriculum includes writing workshops, literature courses, and training in oral presentations of creative work.

Beginning in the fall of 2003, Naropa College will also offer a conservatory-style ensemble training B.F.A. in performance. This degree, open for both first-year and transfer students, integrates contemplative practices, along with extensive community-based arts activism, multi-cultural/global perspectives, and teaching opportunities.

Academic Program

Undergraduate students in the B.A. program spend the first two years at Naropa College in the College Core Program, selecting courses from the following eight areas: contemplative practices, world wisdom traditions, cultural and historical studies, artistic processes, leadership and service, healing arts, communication arts, and complex systems. During this time, students receive support and advisement, while completing graduation requirements and exploring courses from all of Naropa's academic offerings. Upon completion of 45-60 credits, students declare a major.

Students must complete a total of 120 semester credits to earn an undergraduate degree.

Off-Campus Programs

Naropa College's study-abroad program provides a thorough introduction to the living traditions of Nepal, Bali, South India, and Prague. In addition to lectures, field trips, and classes, students experience these diverse cultures directly through community gatherings and cultural events. To apply, a minimum grade point average of 2.5 is required of degree-seeking students, and financial aid is available. Undergraduate and graduate students from other colleges are invited to apply and may inquire about financial aid through their home institutions. Study-abroad programs are also open to the public.

Naropa has also introduced a new distance education option for select students who prefer the flexibility of online classes. Naropa Online offers a sample of Naropa's courses via the World Wide Web, using the latest in Internet technology. Naropa Online offers ample opportunity for interaction with faculty members and fellow students through the use of threaded discussions, chat rooms, journals, e-mail, and collaborative workspaces.

Costs

Undergraduate tuition for the 2003–04 academic year was $543 per semester credit. In addition, there was a registration fee of $280 per semester.

Financial Aid

Naropa College makes every attempt to assist students who do not have the financial resources to accomplish their educational objectives. Naropa offers institutional grants and scholarships, as well as all types of federal student aid. Some financial aid for international students is also available. Approximately 70 percent of Naropa degree-seeking students receive financial assistance in the form of loans, student employment, scholarships, and grants.

Faculty

The Naropa College faculty is distinguished by a wealth of experience in the professional, artistic, and scholastic applications of their disciplines. They are committed to a heartfelt philosophy that brings out the individual insight and intelligence of each student. In addition to the outstanding core faculty, an international community of scholars and artists is consistently drawn to Naropa because of its strong vision and leadership in education. Classes range in size from 5 to 50 students, and Naropa's student-teacher ratio is 13:1.

Student Government

The Student Union of Naropa (SUN) was established in 1989. SUN allows students to participate effectively with faculty members and the administration to ensure that student concerns are addressed and to help shape school policy. Through the formation of student groups, SUN takes active steps to ensure an environment of dignity for all Naropa students.

Admission Requirements

Naropa College seeks students who have a strong appetite for learning and enjoy experiential education in an academic setting. The Admissions Committee considers inquisitiveness and engagement with the work, as well as previous academic achievement, when making admission decisions. A student's statement of interest, interview, and letters of recommendation play important roles in the admissions process. SAT I and ACT scores are not required but are highly recommended.

Application and Information

A completed application for admission into Naropa College includes the following: a completed application form, a $35 application fee (waived for international students), a two- to four-page statement of interest, two letters of recommendation, high school transcripts for all applicants with fewer than 30 semester college credits, and official transcripts from all previous college-level study. Many departments require supplemental application materials and may require a telephone or on-site interview.

Prospective students are strongly encouraged to visit the school. The Office of Admissions hosts a preview weekend each semester, and guided campus tours are offered throughout the year.

Naropa uses a suggested deadline as the initial deadline for receiving completed applications. Any application received after the suggested deadline will be reviewed on a space available basis. The suggested deadline for the fall semester is January 15, and the suggested deadline for the spring semester is October 15. For additional information, prospective students should contact:

Admissions Office
Naropa College
2130 Arapahoe Avenue
Boulder, Colorado 80302-6697
Telephone: 303-546-3572
800-772-6951 (toll-free)
Fax: 303-546-3583
E-mail: admissions@naropa.edu
World Wide Web: http://www.naropa.edu

A seminar group takes advantage of a fall day on the Naropa campus.

NATIONAL AMERICAN UNIVERSITY

RAPID CITY, SOUTH DAKOTA

The University

The mission of National American University (NAU) is to provide career education to students of diverse backgrounds, interests, and abilities. NAU is a private, multicampus institution of higher education committed to building a learning partnership with students by creating a challenging and effective educational environment. National American University offers educational programs that are responsive to the career interests and objectives of its students and to the needs of employers, government, and society.

The first campus of National American University (formerly called National College) was established in Rapid City, South Dakota, in 1941. The curriculum was focused on business administration. Since then, the curriculum has expanded to include a variety of high-demand career choices, such as athletic training, information technology, paralegal studies, and veterinary technology. The name change from National College to National American University was a natural evolution in the development and growth of the institution. National American University is accredited by the Higher Learning Commission of the North Central Association of Colleges and Schools.

Today, more than 400 students are enrolled at the Rapid City campus. The diverse student body consists of students from across the U.S. and around the world. National American University is about giving students the tools they need to pursue their dreams. Whether a student's career path leads to business administration or computer information systems, NAU prepares students to excel in today's competitive marketplace. Nearly every degree program requires an internship prior to graduation, and employment during college within a student's career choice is strongly encouraged and supported by faculty and staff members. Students also have the advantage of classes in their major during their freshman year.

In addition to its undergraduate offerings, NAU also offers a graduate degree in business administration.

Campus life revolves around student organizations, intramural sports, and varsity athletics. The National American University Mavericks are members of the National Association of Intercollegiate Athletics (NAIA) and the National Intercollegiate Rodeo Association (NIRA). Intercollegiate athletics include men's and women's rodeo and women's volleyball.

Location

National American University is located in a Midwestern community with a population of about 60,000 residents. Rapid City is a retail hub for several Midwestern states. Rapid City's shops, entertainment facilities, and wide array of dining establishments offer a big-city feel without the crime, pollution, and overcrowding. A strong Rapid City economy provides many part-time employment opportunities for college students.

Just 20 minutes away lies one of the most popular tourist areas in the world—Mount Rushmore. Nestled in the majestic Black Hills, Rapid City offers everything from Rushmore Mall and the Dahl Fine Arts Center to wilderness activities such as mountain biking and snow skiing. Rapid City offers the social and cultural diversity that students desire.

In addition to the main campus in Rapid City, NAU has other branch campuses in the following locations: Albuquerque and Rio Rancho, New Mexico; the Mall of America, Minnesota; Roseville, Minnesota; Brooklyn Center, Minnesota; Denver and Colorado Springs, Colorado; Sioux Falls, South Dakota; Kansas City, Missouri; Overland Park, Kansas; and the distance learning campus. An extension center is located at Ellsworth Air Force Base, South Dakota.

Majors and Degrees

At the Rapid City campus, bachelor's and associate degrees are offered in accounting, applied management, athletic training, business administration (with emphases in accounting, information technology, financial management, international business, marketing, prelaw, and management), equine management, health-care management, general education studies, management information systems, network management, Web developer/Webmaster (Microsoft certification), paralegal studies, programming, PC support specialist studies, and veterinary technology. NAU offers a veterinary assisting diploma, a Microsoft networking diploma, and a Webmaster professional diploma. Similar programs can be found at the branch locations.

Academic Program

In order to obtain a Bachelor of Science degree, students are required to complete all capstone courses with a minimum grade of C, finish with a minimum 2.0 grade point average overall in the major core, and complete 187 quarter hours of credit, with the final 48 coming in residence at NAU.

National American University accepts credits earned through the College-Level Examination Program (CLEP), the Defense Activity for Non-Traditional Education Support (DANTES), and ACT PEP. NAU also has its own credit-by-examination program.

National American University offers a strong English as a second language (ESL) program for international students.

Selected Internet courses are available to students, allowing them to take classes from around the globe on line.

Academic Facilities

National American University's on-campus library provides students with up-to-date business and paralegal resources. The computer laboratory gives students a state-of-the-art study aid with computerized library search capabilities and Internet access.

Costs

Tuition for the 2002–03 academic year was $9840 for full-time students (based on 16 credit hours per quarter). The residence hall charge was $1605, and board was $1920. All costs are per-year costs based upon three quarters.

Financial Aid

NAU understands that financing higher education is a concern, and the financial aid staff works with students on affordability options. The University provides assistance in the form of grants, scholarships, work-study, and low-interest loan programs through federal, state, and local sources. When students apply for federal student aid, the information reported is used in a formula established by the U.S. Congress that calculates Expected Family Contribution (EFC). This is an amount that students and their families are expected to contribute toward education. The EFC determines the student's eligibility for federal financial aid programs.

Merit-based academic and athletic scholarships are also available to qualified new and continuing students. In addition, many NAU students work part-time while attending the University.

Faculty

A 15:1 student-faculty ratio promotes individual attention in the classroom. Instructors are individuals with experience in their fields, providing real-world experience with textbook knowledge. Instructors also serve as academic advisers and student organization sponsors, providing invaluable interaction with students. Free tutoring is also available.

Student Government

The Student Senate provides funding for various campus student groups as well as school functions throughout the year.

Admission Requirements

It is recommended that applicants and their families visit National American University to become acquainted with the faculty, staff, and facilities of the University. A personal interview should be scheduled with a member of the admissions staff. The applicant is encouraged to contact the Director of Admissions in advance so that necessary arrangements can be made.

Graduation from high school is a requirement for regular admission to NAU for applicants who are seeking a diploma or degree. Those who have satisfied graduation requirements through the General Educational Development (GED) test are also eligible for regular admission.

If a student chooses not to attend full-time, a schedule may be arranged for one or more courses. Credits earned may be applied to degree or diploma programs.

A special student is one who is not enrolled in a diploma or degree program. Special students are not eligible for receipt of financial aid.

Students who have successfully completed course work at other accredited postsecondary institutions may apply for admission to NAU.

The international student admissions procedure requires that the student complete and submit an admission application along with a $45 application fee. International applicants must obtain official transcripts and diplomas, if earned, from all high schools and colleges attended (non-English documents must be accompanied by certified English translations). They must also present an official copy of one of the following: the Test of English as a Foreign Language (TOEFL) report with a minimum score of 500, an ESL Language Center score of 107 or above, or other comparable demonstration of English proficiency (students who have not yet taken the TOEFL or do not have an ESL proficiency are recommended to attend the ESL Center at the Rapid City campus or contact the respective branch campus for information on the ESL programs in their areas). International applicants must also provide a certified bank statement, an annual statement of earnings, and a letter of financial commitment that indicates the ability to meet financial obligations (students under contracted agreement or written verification of full sponsorship may be exempt from a portion of the above financial certification requirements). They must also provide proof of status with the Immigration and Naturalization Services if currently living in the United States.

National American University may be in contact with respective embassies in assisting students to maintain proper immigration status.

Application and Information

In order for students to apply for admission, an application for admission must be completed and mailed or personally delivered to the Director of Admissions. Application materials may be obtained and arrangements may be made for visiting the University through the Admissions Office. Students may also apply on line at the Web site listed below.

The application for admission must be submitted along with a $25 application fee. A letter of acceptance is mailed as soon as possible. If the applicant is not accepted, the application fee is refunded. Early application is encouraged, especially if campus housing (at the Rapid City location), financial aid, and/or part-time employment are desired.

For applications or more information, students should contact:

Director of Admissions
National American University
321 Kansas City Street
Rapid City, South Dakota 57701
Telephone: 605-394-4827
800-843-8892 (toll-free)
World Wide Web: http://www.national.edu

National American University students enjoy a break between classes outside the Thomas Jefferson Library.

NAZARETH COLLEGE OF ROCHESTER

ROCHESTER, NEW YORK

The College

Nazareth College is an independent, coeducational, comprehensive college that offers career programs solidly based in the liberal arts. Its suburban campus is located in Pittsford in western upstate New York, approximately 7 miles from the city of Rochester. Founded in 1924, the College has conferred more than 12,000 baccalaureate and master's degrees. Of the more than 3,200 men and women enrolled at Nazareth, more than 2,000 are undergraduates.

Twenty-two buildings of traditional and contemporary design are conveniently situated on the College's 150-acre parklike campus. The Otto A. Shults Community Center, housing a 20,000-square-foot gymnasium, the student union, a multifaith religious center, a 25-meter swimming pool, the newly expanded fitness center, and student personnel offices, is the hub of on-campus student life. The resident students, constituting two-thirds of the undergraduate population, are housed in eleven separate residence halls. As an alternative to traditional campus housing, foreign language majors may live in La Maison Française, which is maintained by the language department. The Casa Italiana, Casa Hispana, and German Cultural Center serve as facilities for social, cultural, and academic programs reflecting Italian, Spanish, and German heritages, respectively.

Intercollegiate and intramural athletics are fully represented in the areas of men's and women's basketball, equestrian, lacrosse, soccer, swimming and diving, tennis, and track and field and cross-country; women's field hockey and volleyball; and a variety of other NCAA-recognized sports programs.

Location

Rochester, a city of more than 300,000 people, is the third-largest city in New York State and the site of cultural, educational, and industrial centers. Located on the shore of Lake Ontario, the city is noted for the Eastman Theatre, the Strasenburg Planetarium, and the International Museum of Photography at the George Eastman House. Rochester is the world headquarters of Eastman Kodak and Bausch & Lomb and the site of a major Xerox facility. It is only 20 minutes from beautiful mountains, lakes, and recreational areas, where students can enjoy various outdoor activities, including skiing, hiking, water sports, and camping. The city supports professional sports teams in baseball, hockey, lacrosse, and soccer.

Majors and Degrees

Nazareth College awards the Bachelor of Music degree and Bachelor of Arts and Bachelor of Science degrees in accounting, American studies, applied music, art (studio), art education, art history, biochemistry, biology, business administration, business education, chemistry, economics, English, environmental science, fine arts, foreign languages (French, German, Italian, and Spanish), history, information technology, international studies, management science, mathematics, music, music education, music theory, music therapy, nursing, philosophy, physical therapy, political science, psychology, religious studies, social science, social work, sociology, speech pathology, and theater arts.

Preprofessional programs are available in dentistry, law, and medicine. Teacher certification (grades 1–9 and 7–12) is offered with many majors. Certification in learning disabilities is available through an undergraduate program in inclusive education. Certification for birth–12 is offered in art education, music education, and speech pathology (communication sciences and disorders).

Academic Program

To qualify for a degree, a candidate must fulfill the core curriculum requirements of the College as well as those of the major department or area of concentration. The candidate must also earn a minimum of 120 semester credits and satisfy a comprehensive test requirement in the major field during the senior year.

Off-Campus Programs

Nazareth College offers Junior Year Abroad programs in affiliation with the Université de Haute Bretagne in Rennes, France; the Institute of Spanish Students in Valencia, Spain; and the Universita degli G. D'Annunzio in Pescara, Italy. Students need not be language majors to take advantage of this exceptional program. Language students taking German or Japanese have the opportunity to study at the Studienforum in Berlin and Osaka University in Japan, respectively.

Nazareth College is a member of the Rochester Area Colleges, a consortium that includes Rochester Institute of Technology, the State University of New York College at Geneseo, and the University of Rochester, among others. Through this consortium, Nazareth College students can cross-register for credit in up to two courses per semester at any of the member institutions on a space-available basis.

Academic Facilities

Most of Nazareth's classrooms, laboratories, and studios are in Smyth Hall and the award-winning Arts Center, which houses art, music, and theater facilities as well as a 1,200-seat auditorium within its three wings. Recently expanded Carroll Hall houses speech pathology, physical therapy, counseling, and health services. Also recently expanded, Lorette Wilmot Library houses 233,736 volumes and has extensive resources in such areas as women's studies, education, minority issues, and religions in America. The library subscribes to approximately 7,000 periodicals and other serials. The building has seating for 450 students and includes a large number of individual carrels. The library also has a fine collection of lecture tapes and a growing collection of musical and spoken-word disks and tapes. The Rare Book Room is distinguished by special collections of works by Maurice Baring, Hilaire Belloc, Gilbert Keith Chesterton, and the Sitwells. The library is currently enlarging its resources and services in the nonprint media. In addition, the College's membership in the regional consortium and the Online Computer Library Center provides students with access to the resources of 1,300 other academic and research libraries.

Costs

Total costs for 2003–04 were $24,936. This included $17,020 for tuition, $7400 for room and board, and $516 for the required fees. The total does not include books, personal expenses, or transportation (if applicable). All fees are subject to change; up-to-date information can be obtained from the Admissions Office.

Financial Aid

Nazareth College endeavors to meet financial need as demonstrated on the Free Application for Federal Student Aid (FAFSA). The FAFSA should be submitted by February 15 of the year in which the student intends to enroll. The CSS PROFILE is required of early decision applicants only and should be submitted by November 15. Financial assistance is available through grants, loans, employment, and scholarships. Sources of aid include the Federal Pell Grant, New York Tuition Assistance, Federal Perkins Loan, and Federal Work-Study programs; the New York State Higher Education Services Corporation; and Nazareth College merit scholarships and grants.

Faculty

The full-time faculty members in the various academic departments hold advanced degrees from more than 100 institutions throughout the United States and abroad. Nintey-two percent of the faculty members hold the highest degree offered in their field of study. The student-faculty ratio of approximately 13:1 and an average class size of 25 ensure that students receive the individual attention that only a small college can offer.

Student Government

The Undergraduate Association of Nazareth College is the vehicle through which students can express the need for and initiate change within the College community. It is also responsible for the disbursement of funds, generated from the undergraduate activities fee, to various activities and social/cultural clubs.

Admission Requirements

Nazareth College welcomes applicants of all ages and educational backgrounds. Students of any race, color, sex, or national or ethnic origin are admitted to all of the rights, privileges, programs, and activities generally accorded or made available to students at the College. Nazareth College does not discriminate on the basis of race, color, sex, or national or ethnic origin in the administration of its educational policies, scholarship and loan programs, and sports and other school-administered programs.

Recommended academic preparation includes courses in English, college-preparatory mathematics, social studies, a foreign language, and science. Although the Admissions Committee gives primary consideration to academic achievement and potential for collegiate success, it also considers talent in art, drama, or music and involvement in cocurricular activities. A personal interview, although not required, is recommended, as it allows the applicant to view the campus and facilities, talk with students and faculty members, and meet with an admissions counselor.

Nazareth College is pleased to consider applications from students in good standing at accredited two- and four-year colleges and universities. A minimum GPA of 2.5 or better is expected. Transfer applicants who hold, or will hold prior to registration, the Associate in Arts (A.A.) or the Associate in Science (A.S.) degree from a fully accredited college may transfer a maximum of 60 semester hours of credit and enter with full junior status. Transfer applicants who hold, or will hold prior to registration, the Associate in Applied Science (A.A.S.) degree or the Associate of Occupational Studies (A.O.S.) degree from a fully accredited college or institute will have these credits evaluated on a course-by-course basis. Careful advisement on tailoring programs for holders of these degrees is offered by Nazareth College.

Application and Information

Regular decision applicants for the fall semester should submit the application form, transcripts, standardized test scores, an essay, recommendations, and a $40 application fee by February 15 (November 15 for early decision and December 15 for early action). Notification for regular decision begins February 15 (December 15 for early decision and January 15 for early action). For more information regarding the different application options, students should contact the Admissions Office.

For an application packet or information about a campus tour and interview, applicants should contact:

Vice President for Enrollment Management
Nazareth College
4245 East Avenue
Rochester, New York 14618-3790
Telephone: 585-389-2860
800-462-3944 (toll-free)

NEUMANN COLLEGE

ASTON, PENNSYLVANIA

The College

Neumann College, a Catholic coeducational institution in the Franciscan tradition, recognizes the value of developing intellectual excellence, professional competence, and strong community life. As a college that balances the liberal arts with the professions, Neumann was founded to meet and expand the educational and professional horizons of men and women through instruction that is based on values, ethical behavior, and service to others. With the addition of the Living and Learning Center, multimedia-capable residences, Neumann College serves a diverse geographic and demographic population.

Founded and sponsored by the Sisters of St. Francis of Philadelphia, the College is committed to a varied student body and welcomes students of all denominations. Current enrollment is 2,589.

The Life Center houses the Meagher Theatre, the Bruder Athletic Center, and the Crossroads Cafe dining facility. Intercollegiate sports include women's basketball, field hockey, ice hockey, lacrosse, soccer, softball, tennis, and volleyball and men's baseball, basketball, golf, ice hockey, lacrosse, soccer, and tennis. Neumann College competes as a member of the National Collegiate Athletic Association (NCAA) Division III, the Pennsylvania Athletic Conference (PAC), and the Eastern Collegiate Athletic Conference (ECAC). Intramural sports are available to all members of the campus community.

The Living and Learning Center is designed to provide a state-of-the-art residential experience, with a focus on education within a real-world living environment. Technologically smart, the center connects students to both faculty members and friends via the Internet, which is available in every suite and apartment. The system provides full access to campus resources and activities, as well as activities and resources worldwide. The center also houses a separate computer lab, a fitness center, a reflection room, various study rooms with warming kitchens for group study or meetings, and a laundry.

The College provides a full range of services to students, including career placement, which averages above 95 percent in the student's field of interest; career and personal counseling; a tutoring program; and health services.

Neumann students are involved in a wide variety of campus and community activities. Major and special interest clubs are available for student participation. Clubs bring together students who share common interests and help foster new friendships.

At Neumann, the spiritual dimension of one's life is recognized as integral to total human development. The Ministry Team provides a pastoral presence on campus and promotes a sense of community. The entire College community is invited to serve the needs of the poor and neglected in society through various outreach programs, with special attention to the need for peace and justice in the world today.

Neumann is well positioned to respond to the academic and extracurricular needs of students who are of traditional or nontraditional age, commuters or residents, and full-time or part-time.

In addition to undergraduate programs, Neumann confers master's degrees in education, nursing, pastoral counseling, physical therapy, sport management, and strategic leadership.

Location

Neumann, with a beautiful 50-acre suburban campus in Aston, Delaware County, Pennsylvania, is a short distance from Philadelphia; Wilmington, Delaware; southern New Jersey; and Maryland. It is easily accessible from major arteries such as I-95, Route 476, Route 1, and the Pennsylvania Turnpike.

Majors and Degrees

Neumann offers strong academic majors leading to a Bachelor of Arts degree or a Bachelor of Science degree in accounting, athletic training, biological science, business administration, communication arts, computer and information management, criminal justice, education, English, environmental science, environmental studies, international business, liberal arts, marketing, nursing, political science, psychology, and sport management. The education programs lead to teacher certification in Pennsylvania and reciprocating states, with secondary certification in biology/general science, English, or social studies. Preprofessional programs in law and medicine are also available. An accelerated evening program for adults using a 6-credit seminar format leads to an Associate of Arts, Bachelor of Arts, or Bachelor of Science degree in liberal studies.

Academic Programs

The academic program at Neumann College is composed of a core curriculum (required of all students), a major area of study (chosen by each student), and a wide range of elective offerings. Students may also choose a minor area of study. The College's broad base of liberal arts offerings prepares students for the intellectual and social challenges that they will face in the employment marketplace and throughout their lives. The core is intended to provide basic knowledge of the liberal arts and sciences; develop verbal, written, and symbolic communication skills; and stimulate interest in a broad range of topics for the purpose of enhancing the individual's contributions to society, thereby enabling the individual to realize full human potential.

Classroom instruction is supplemented by cooperative education through which juniors and seniors can earn credit for working in a job related to their career interest. Fieldwork and student teaching are required of all education majors. Clinical practice for the nursing major occurs in a variety of health-care facilities in the tristate area.

The honors program is an opportunity for academically talented students to explore imaginative and innovative perspectives on learning. It is also an opportunity to stimulate and motivate students to expand their knowledge and interest and to strive for greater excellence. Moreover, it is a reward for prior perseverance and dedication as well as an obligation to utilize skills and abilities in service to others. Admission to the honors program is by invitation.

Neumann College has transfer articulation agreements with numerous colleges throughout the area.

Academic Facilities

The Child Development Center is a state-of-the-art, octagonal-shaped building, specifically designed to house an educational program for preschoolers. As a state-licensed day-care facility, it enrolls children of Neumann students, the faculty, and the community. The Child Development Center is part of the Division of Education and Human Services. Students enrolled in education courses use the center for observation, practical experience, and student teaching.

The Academic Computer Center is located on the ground floor of the College. The computers are viewed as tools to support all fields of study and all students and faculty members. Neumann College has installed a wireless Local Area Network (LAN) that connects various computers and provides shared services such as printing, e-mail, and support for the instructional use of computers by providing for the sharing of files. Computers are available to all students. Both systems have CD-ROM drives. Software related to various academic disciplines are available. Access to the World Wide Web and the Internet is available.

The Academic Resource Center is a service that enables students to meet Neumann's academic standards and successfully attain their personal educational goals.

The College library contains a balanced collection of more than 70,000 volumes, 95,000 microfilm units, 1300 videos, and 700 periodical subscriptions. Private study rooms and conference rooms are available for both student and faculty use. In addition to traditional media services support, a full-color video studio and a graphics production area are available. Serving as a comprehensive resource for students, other holdings include Neumann's online catalog system, Francis, which is accessible via the World Wide Web; and a video, film, and sound recording collection of more than 52,000 items. The library is a member of the Tri-State College Library Cooperative, the Consortium for Health Information and Library Services, SEPCHE, and the Online College Library Computer, which provide additional convenient resources for students. The library subscribes to various online and CD-ROM computer research services.

Costs

Tuition for full-time students (12 to 18 credits per semester) in 2003–04 was $7910 per semester. There was a general fee of $250 per semester that covered library services, counseling and testing services, athletics, accident insurance, health services, special lectures, parking, the student government fee, and an I.D. card. Room and board were $3740 per semester.

Financial Aid

Typically, about 90 percent of Neumann students receive some form of financial aid (scholarships, grants, and student loans).

Neumann offers a variety of renewable scholarships each year to entering full-time freshmen. Interested applicants should contact the Office of Admissions and Financial Aid as soon as possible to determine eligibility.

In addition to Neumann scholarships, funds are available through the Federal Pell Grant, Federal Supplemental Educational Opportunity Grant, and Federal Work-Study Programs. Many states provide grant money to attend Neumann (non-Pennsylvania residents should check with their state's higher education agency for details). Veterans Administration benefits can be received by qualified veterans or their dependents. Federal Stafford Student Loans and Federal PLUS Program loans are available and can be applied for through Neumann's preferred lender or any participating bank. Neumann also offers institutional need-based grants. All students requesting financial aid must complete the Free Application for Federal Student Aid (FAFSA) each year to determine eligibility. In order to expedite processing, the FAFSA should be submitted by March 15 for the following school year. Financial aid funds are renewable annually based on need as determined by the FAFSA results.

Faculty

Neumann students describe faculty members as sincere, hard working, determined, and energetic. Faculty members view themselves, first and foremost, as teachers and are proud partners in their students' journeys toward self-discovery. Each student has a faculty adviser who assists in arranging a program designed to meet the student's educational goals; many faculty members serve as moderators of student clubs. The student-faculty ratio is 14:1.

Student Government

The Student Government Association (SGA) is the representative body for all students. Its function is to implement the aims and purposes of the College, foster cooperation in interstudent relationships, assist the College in being responsive to the needs of the student body, and encourage personal responsibility for an intelligent system of student self-government. Through the Student Activities Board, social functions are planned throughout the year. Students serve on various College committees, including Student Affairs Committee of the Board, Academic Advising Committee, Honors Program Committee, Registration/Orientation Task Force, and Student Judicial Board. For full-time students, a Student Government Association fee of $45 per semester is required.

Admission Requirements

Neumann has a rolling admission policy and accepts applications throughout the year. Applicants are considered on the basis of high school record, SAT or ACT scores, recommendations, class rank, and other indicators of potential to succeed in college-level studies. Applications for admission are reviewed without regard to sex, race, creed, color, national origin, age, sexual orientation, pregnancy, military status, religion, or disability. Applicants should be graduates of an accredited high school (or present equivalent credentials) and have a recommended curriculum of 16 units of high school course work distributed as follows: 4 in English, 2 to 3 in science, 2 in mathematics, 2 in social studies, 2 in foreign language, and 4 in electives. Students intending to pursue a major in biology or clinical laboratory science must have at least 1 year of high school biology and chemistry, and high school physics is also highly recommended.

Neumann participates in the Advanced Placement (AP) Program and the College-Level Examination Program (CLEP). Students with superior ability and a sound academic background may begin College studies at the end of the junior year in high school.

An interview and tour of the campus are highly recommended for all prospective students and parents. Visits can be arranged by contacting the Office of Admissions.

Application and Information

Applicants for freshman admission are requested to have SAT or ACT scores and high school transcripts sent to the Office of Admissions. A nonrefundable $35 application fee should accompany the completed application. A free application is available online at http://www.neumann.edu on the Web.

Neumann College welcomes applications from students who have attended or are currently attending either two-year or four-year regionally accredited institutions of higher learning.

For further information, students should contact:

Office of Admissions
Neumann College
One Neumann Drive
Aston, Pennsylvania 19014-1298
Telephone: 610-558-5616
800-9NEUMANN (toll-free)
E-mail: neumann@neumann.edu

NEWBERRY COLLEGE

NEWBERRY, SOUTH CAROLINA

The College

A private undergraduate liberal arts institution established in 1856, Newberry College is affiliated with the Evangelical Lutheran Church in America. With a mission focused on educating the whole person, Newberry epitomizes the small-college amenities of personal attention, easy rapport between students and faculty members, and a supportive environment for academic, personal, and social development.

Newberry College's student body is made up of about 750 men and women from twenty-four states and several countries. About 48 percent are women and 52 percent are men. Seventy percent of the students live in College residence halls; others live off campus or commute from home.

Students participate in a variety of College-sponsored activities, including five national fraternities and four national sororities; eight music-related organizations; three campus publications; musical theater and drama productions; intramural sports; ethnic, political, and religious organizations; honor, service, and leadership societies; the Newberry College Student Government Association (student government); the Newberry College Student Ambassadors; and special interest groups.

The Newberry College Indians maintain a full schedule of NCAA Division II intercollegiate athletic competition in men's baseball, basketball, cross-country, football, golf, soccer, and tennis and women's basketball, cross-country, golf, soccer, tennis, softball, and volleyball.

The College's buildings represent a pleasant combination of antebellum and contemporary architecture. Four buildings around the quadrangle make up the Newberry College Historic District and are listed on the National Register of Historic Places. Wiles Chapel, which contains the College Theatre, exemplifies modern Gothic architecture with some influence from the Prairie school. The physical education and athletic complex, including the 1,600-seat Eleazer Arena, was completed in 1982. The Casey Student Center, which adjoins the athletic complex on the northern edge of the campus, serves as the location for the Student Affairs Office, Career Services Center, College Bookstore, and Presidential Dining Room.

Location

Listed as one of the best 100 small towns in the United States in which to live and the safest city in South Carolina, Newberry is situated in the gently rolling hills of the South Carolina Piedmont, with average winter temperatures ranging from highs of 56 to 63 degrees. Newberry is home to approximately 10,000 permanent residents. The city was founded in 1794 and is replete with historically significant homes and buildings. It is easily accessible via three exits on Interstate 26 and lies at the juncture of U.S. 76 and South Carolina 34 and 121. Newberry's closest metropolitan neighbor is Columbia, the state capital and its largest city, which is approximately 40 miles southeast. The Greenville/Spartanburg metropolitan area is 1 hour northwest of Newberry. Other points of interest within easy driving distance are Myrtle Beach and the Grand Strand (3 hours); Charleston (2½ hours); Hilton Head (3½ hours); Charlotte, North Carolina (1½ hours); the Great Smoky Mountains (2 hours); and Atlanta, Georgia (3½ hours).

Majors and Degrees

The Bachelor of Science (B.S.) degree is awarded in arts management, biology, business administration, chemistry, early childhood education, elementary education, mathematics, mathematics/computer science, physical education (including leisure services, sports management, and teacher certification), and veterinary technology.

The Bachelor of Arts (B.A.) degree is awarded in art, communications, economics, English, foreign languages (French, German, and Spanish), history, international government and commerce, music (including applied music, music literature, and music theory), political science, psychology, religion and philosophy, sociology, and theater/speech communications.

The Bachelor of Music (B.M.) degree is awarded in music performance. The Bachelor of Music Education (B.M.E.) degree is awarded in choral music and instrumental music in teacher certification.

Preprofessional programs are offered in dentistry, environmental sciences, forestry, law, medicine, nursing, pharmacy, and theology. Nondegree programs of study are available in community service, military science, physics, and professional writing and editing.

Newberry offers 3-2 dual-degree programs in engineering with Clemson University and in forestry with Duke University. Special dual-degree programs in a number of health-related professions are available with the Medical University of South Carolina.

Academic Programs

A student must satisfactorily complete a minimum of 126 semester hours of course work with a minimum cumulative grade point average of 2.0 (on a 4.0 scale) to be eligible for a Newberry bachelor's degree. A core curriculum of 43 to 50 semester hours is required of all students regardless of their declared major(s) and includes course work in the following disciplines: history and social sciences, humanities, natural sciences, English, foreign language, mathematics, religion, speech, physical education, and College Life, a freshman experience course. In addition, students must also fulfill three fine arts and lecture requirements per semester. The Summerland Honors Community program, a four-year interdisciplinary core program, is offered to gifted students.

Students may receive Advanced Placement (AP) and college credit by participating in the Advanced Placement Program, the International Baccalaureate (I.B.) Program, or the College-Level Examination Program (CLEP). Students should consult the latest edition of the Newberry College catalog or contact the Office of Admissions for exact requirements.

The College operates on the two-semester calendar, consisting of a fall semester and a spring semester, each lasting sixteen weeks. The fall semester begins in late August and ends in mid-December; the spring semester begins in early January and ends in early May, with a one-week spring break in March. The College's summer session consists of two 5-week terms. During the fall and spring semesters, the normal class load ranges from 15 to 19 hours; for the summer session, two courses per term is normal.

Off-Campus Programs

Newberry's international studies program for sophomores and juniors gives qualified students the opportunity to study for a summer, a semester, or a full academic year in selected international colleges and universities as part of Newberry's regular academic program. Although this program is open to students in all majors, some proficiency in the language spoken in the host country is required.

Academic Facilities

Langford Communications Center contains state-of-the-art equipment and resources for the student of radio and television communications. As an Internet node with its own World Wide Web site, the College can extend free in-room Ethernet access for students using the Internet. Another modern building is dedicated to the study of music. Wessels Library contains nearly 100,000 books, sound and video recordings, CD-ROMs, and online electronic resources. Complete facilities for the use of audiovisual materials are provided. The library also subscribes to more than 450 magazines, newspapers, and scholarly journals. The College Archives are also displayed in the library. In addition to Wessels, students may use a smaller library that is housed in the Alumni Music Center's Music Department.

Costs

In 2003–04, tuition and fees were $17,251 and room and board were $5620. The total cost for a residential student was $22,871. The College estimated annual personal expenses (including books, supplies, automobile registration, and other costs) to be $2200. Once they are accepted for admission, students are requested to submit a $175 deposit, which is refundable through May 1 for fall semester admission and December 1 for spring semester admission.

Financial Aid

More than 90 percent of students at Newberry receive some form of financial assistance. Student aid counselors are available to work with students and families to design financial aid packages that make a Newberry education affordable. Assistance is available in the form of scholarships, loans, and campus employment based on need or merit. Newberry College awards more than 200 endowed scholarships, including the prestigious Trustee, Founders, and Presidential Scholarship awards. Music, theater, communications, and athletic scholarships are also available for men and women. Residents of South Carolina usually qualify for a South Carolina Tuition Grant. Communing members of a Lutheran church may receive a variety of tuition and scholarship grants from the Lutheran Scholarship Program. To apply for student aid, students should complete the Free Application for Federal Student Aid (FAFSA), which is available from high school counselors or from the Newberry Financial Aid Office.

Faculty

The student-faculty ratio is 12:1. Classes are small, and the easy interchange of ideas is a constant stimulus to both student and teacher. Seventy-four percent of the full-time faculty members have earned doctorates or terminal degrees. No classes are taught by graduate students.

Student Government

The Newberry College Student Government Association (NCSGA) is composed of students elected to the Newberry Student Senate. Through its committee assignments, it assists in the formulation and implementation of College policies. The NCSGA officers are selected through campuswide elections, and senators and other representatives are elected by the various campus constituencies.

Admission Requirements

In determining the admission status of all applicants to Newberry College, the following factors are taken into consideration: grade point average on academic courses, SAT I or ACT, high school rank, type of course work pursued, cocurricular activities, relationship(s) to Newberry College alumni, and other relevant factors such as part-time employment.

Students whose profiles fall below acceptable standards may be referred to the Admissions Committee. This committee, composed of members of the College faculty and administration, carefully deliberates before determining admission status.

Within two days following the admissions decision, the applicant is notified by mail. Acceptance of the applicant is always contingent upon successful completion of course work in progress. Following high school graduation, an additional official final transcript bearing the date of graduation is required.

Application and Information

The College operates on a rolling admission basis, notifying most applicants of their status within three weeks after the application is complete. The application for admission, along with a $30 nonrefundable fee, should be accompanied by official high school and/or college transcripts, SAT I and/or ACT scores, a secondary school report, letters of recommendation, and other supporting materials that may be required by the Director of Admissions. Students may also apply online for only $5.00.

Interviews can be scheduled through the Office of Admissions. Although walk-in visitors are welcome, a visitor's special needs and desires can best be met if he or she makes an appointment. Saturday morning visits are available by appointment only. In addition, the Office of Admissions hosts two open-house functions each year for the benefit of prospective students and parents.

Students are encouraged to apply for admission on the Internet and may do so at the World Wide Web address given below. The application fee is waived for students who apply through Newberry College's Web site.

For additional information, students should contact:

Office of Admissions
Newberry College
2100 College Street
Newberry, South Carolina 29108
Telephone: 803-321-5127
800-845-4955 (toll-free in the United States and Canada)
E-mail: admissions@newberry.edu
World Wide Web: http://www.newberry.edu

Newberry College's Holland Hall (Admissions Office).

NEWBURY COLLEGE

BROOKLINE, MASSACHUSETTS

The College

Newbury College is a private coeducational college that offers a four-year bachelor's degree program in selected areas as well as a host of two-year associate degree programs. Nearly 800 men and women are currently enrolled as full-time day students, and the total College enrollment is near 1,600. Approximately 20 percent of the College's day students come from states other than Massachusetts. The College provides housing for men and women on campus. Residence halls differ in age and design, providing a variety of styles. Approximately 37 percent of the day students live in the College's residence halls.

Founded in 1962, Newbury College has grown and changed dramatically in the past forty years. However, its educational philosophy remains the same: to prepare graduates to succeed in their chosen career. All of the College's accredited academic programs feature hands-on training to sharpen job skills. The College is accredited by the New England Association of Schools and Colleges. The interior design program is accredited by the Foundation for Interior Design and Education Research (FIDER).

Newbury College has an active student body and offers students a variety of cocurricular clubs and organizations to join. Newbury is a member of NCAA Division III and offers varsity sports in basketball, cross-country running, golf, soccer, softball, tennis, and volleyball.

Location

Situated only minutes from downtown Boston, Newbury College's Brookline campus encompasses 11 landscaped acres in a beautiful residential neighborhood with easy access to public transportation, first-run cinemas, and prestigious shopping centers.

Boston is the cultural, business, and education capital of New England. The city provides students with important educational resources and the opportunity to bring career goals into focus through internships and field trips. Just as important is that Boston is the home of the world's largest and most diverse population of college students.

Majors and Degrees

Degrees are offered within the School of Arts, Science, and Technology; the School of Business and Management; and the Roger A. Saunders School of Hotel and Restaurant Management. Bachelor of Science (B.S.) degrees within the School of Arts, Science, and Technology include a Bachelor of Science in legal studies, with concentrations in criminal justice, paralegal studies, and a 3+3 program in prelaw. Bachelor of Science degrees are also offered in computer science, communication, corporate communication, graphic design, interior design, and psychology. Bachelor's degrees within the School of Business and Management include concentrations in accounting, finance, general management, human resource management, international business management, marketing, retail management, and small business management. The Roger A. Saunders School of Hotel and Restaurant Management offers a bachelor's degree in hotel, restaurant, and service management, with concentrations in hotel administration and culinary management. Newbury College also offers a host of associate degrees.

Newbury's Continuing Education program offers both evening and weekend classes for adult learners at two conveniently located classroom centers.

Academic Program

Working with an adviser, students plan their course of study around a prescribed major core. Program requirements establish a framework that includes intensive study in the major area where hands-on training is stressed as well as course work in general education. By fulfilling the general education requirements and selecting courses outside the major, students receive a well-rounded education. At least 121 credit hours, usually five courses per semester, are required for graduation in most bachelor's degree programs. At least 60 credit hours are required for the associate degree.

Internships are an integral part of the academic programs and provide students with on-the-job experience in their chosen field.

The College observes a two-semester academic calendar, with first-semester examinations falling before the December holiday break. There are also two summer sessions.

Academic Facilities

The Newbury College Library, houses 31,825 volumes and subscribes to 127,000 periodicals. The College has also completed renovations to the dining hall, student lounge, and the bookstore, which is operated by Barnes & Noble bookstores. Special learning facilities include a staffed Center for Academic Services, a computer resource center, an in-house television and radio studio, a hospitality center equipped with state-of-the-art airline and hotel reservation systems, and seven fully equipped culinary arts kitchens.

Costs

For 2004–05, the total cost of a year in most programs at Newbury is as follows: tuition, $15,325; room and board, $7575. There is an annual $550 comprehensive fee. Part-time day students and Continuing Education students pay tuition on a per-credit-hour basis.

Financial Aid

It is the College's hope that all qualified and motivated students have the opportunity to pursue a college degree. To this end, Newbury endeavors to meet the financial needs of all students who qualify for financial aid. In order to apply for financial aid, applicants are required to complete the FAFSA. If eligible for federal financial aid, this could be in the form of grants, scholarships, loans, or a work-study program. The College also offers merit-based scholarships, which are determined by a Scholarship Committee. These scholarships are based on academic history, leadership potential, school or community involvement, and SAT scores. These include Presidential, Distinguished, and Newbury Scholarships.

Faculty

Newbury has a total faculty of more than 507 members, 54 of whom are full-time. A low student-faculty ratio of 15:1 encourages student and faculty interaction. Faculty members are skilled professionals with years of experience and expertise in their fields. They also serve as academic advisers, helping students explore career options outside of the classroom.

Student Government

The Student Government Association (SGA) at Newbury College has an elected president, vice president, treasurer, and secretary who represent the student body. Working with the administration and staff, representatives of the SGA help to plan activities and provide a means of communication within the College structure. The SGA has the responsibility of administering the calendar of school events, coordinating the expenditures of the activities budget, and planning the College activities program. All full-time students belong to the SGA.

Admission Requirements

The Admission Committee considers each applicant on an individual basis. Requirements include a $50 application fee, official transcripts from all previous secondary and applicable college study, an essay, and two letters of recommendation. SAT I scores are highly recommended. The TOEFL exam is required for all international applicants. Students must file the official Application for Admission, or they may apply online via the Web site listed below.

Application and Information

Application deadlines for freshmen applicants are as follows: early application deadline, December 1; regular decision and transfer applicants may apply on a rolling basis. A priority deadline of March 1 is set for those who wish to be considered for merit scholarships. In order to enroll in time for January admission, students must apply by November 1. If the application deadline has passed, students should contact the Office of Admission regarding space availability.

For more information, students should contact:

Office of Admission
Newbury College
129 Fisher Avenue
Brookline, Massachusetts 02445-5796
Telephone: 617-730-7007
800-NEWBURY (toll-free)
Fax: 617-731-9618
E-mail: info@newbury.edu
World Wide Web: http://www.newbury.edu

Newbury's low student-faculty ratio supports its philosophy of student-centered education.

NEW COLLEGE OF CALIFORNIA
School of Humanities

SAN FRANCISCO, CALIFORNIA

The College

Since its founding in 1971, New College of California has been a leader in alternative education, dedicating itself to integrating education with social change. New College fosters interdisciplinary learning and critical perspectives that place knowledge within social and historical contexts, encouraging a deeper understanding of humanity, social movements, and diversity. New College emphasizes community building and an activist orientation to empower students to work toward a just, sacred, and sustainable world. New College students are at the center of their learning process and are given significant opportunities to shape their education. New College's academic environment combines a pedagogy of critique, which emphasizes the development of a greater understanding of social problems and their historical origins, with a pedagogy of possibility, emphasizing ways to create a more just, sacred, and sustainable world.

Accredited by the Western Association of Schools and Colleges, New College of California offers a Weekday/Evening B.A. Program, a Weekend B.A. Completion Program, and graduate programs leading to M.A., M.F.A., and M.B.A. degrees.

The School of Humanities Weekday/Evening B.A. Program and Weekend B.A. Completion Program comprise an academic community of approximately 300 students. Through their mentoring/advising relationship with core faculty members, students are given guidance, understanding, and support for their academic work. Students' courses of study are tailored to their individual needs and/or interests. The Weekday/Evening B.A. Program offers an interdisciplinary curriculum with emphases such as activism and social change; arts and social change; interdisciplinary humanities; Irish studies; Latin American studies; psychology; writing, literature, and transformation; youth in society/education; or a self-designed emphasis area. The Weekend B.A. Completion Program is designed for people who want to complete their B.A. degree but have a less flexible schedule due to work and/or family. The Weekend B.A. Completion Program offers emphases in interdisciplinary humanities; activism and social change; and culture, ecology, and sustainable community.

The average age of students in the Weekday/Evening B.A. Program is 26. Students in the Weekend B.A. Completion Program tend to have a diverse age range from the late twenties to the late fifties. The majority of students at New College come from California and the Western states; however, a significant number come from the Eastern and Midwestern states as well as several European, Latin American, and Asian countries. Many New College students are committed to social change and hope to pursue public-interest careers upon graduation.

The New College of California School of Law, the oldest and most diverse public-interest law school in the country, is committed to teaching lawyers to be socially responsible as an integral part of political change.

The School of Graduate Psychology meets the requirements leading to Marriage Family Therapy (MFT) licensure and offers an M.A. in psychology with an emphasis in social-clinical or feminist-clinical psychology.

The Teacher Credential/M.A. in Teaching Program encourages understanding and examination of the political and social context of the institution of schooling.

The Science Institute, located at New College, offers prerequisite science classes for people interested in health-care professions.

The Experimental Performance Institute, located at New College, offers classes for students in the B.A. and graduate programs that support performing arts, particularly artistically potent and socially provocative interdisciplinary theater.

The Center for Education and Social Action (CESA), also located at New College, was created to promote ideas and action for social change. CESA links New College with community groups working for global justice, peace, and the environment.

Location

New College of California has three campuses: New College's oldest campus is located in the heart of the vibrant Mission District on Valencia Street in San Francisco. This urban campus offers the Weekday B.A. Program (with all emphases listed above), the Weekend B.A. Completion Program (with emphases in activism and social change or interdisciplinary humanities), the Teacher Credential/M.A. in Teaching Program, and graduate programs and is the home of the School of Graduate Psychology, the Experimental Performance Institute, and the Science Institute.

The New College School of Law is located in downtown San Francisco at the Fell Street campus, near the main branch of the public library.

The North Bay campus, located in Santa Rosa, California, focuses on environmental issues such as building sustainable and alternative ways of living. This campus offers the Weekend B.A. Completion Program, as well as graduate programs, in culture, ecology, and sustainable community.

Majors and Degrees

The Weekday/Evening B.A. Program offers a Bachelor of Arts in humanities with an emphasis in one of the following: arts and social change, interdisciplinary humanities, Irish studies, Latin American studies, psychology, writing and literature, youth in society/education, or a self-designed emphasis area.

The Weekend B.A. Completion Program offers a Bachelor of Arts in humanities with an emphasis in one of the following: activism and social change; culture, ecology, and sustainable community; or interdisciplinary studies. The student chooses his or her own concentration.

Academic Program

To graduate with a bachelor's degree, students must acquire a minimum of 120 semester hours. The Weekday/Evening B.A. Program and Weekend B.A. Completion Program emphasize a breadth of knowledge in the humanities as well as a refined level of skill and experience within a chosen emphasis area.

Some Weekday/Evening B.A. Program students enter with previous units from other colleges, but students can be admitted to this program with no prior units. To receive a bachelor's degree from New College in the Weekday B.A. Program, students are required to complete 3 units of the following: scientific reasoning, social science, literature, quantitative reasoning, hands-on art, expository writing, a second language, and a practicum. The practicum gives the student the opportunity to see the continuity between education and community work. Weekday/Evening B.A. Program students are required to complete 24 units in their emphasis area. Students can extend their studies through nontraditional forms of learning, including independent studies and tutorials. Students may earn additional units for life experience though the Prior Learning Program and/or by taking CLEP exams.

In the Weekend B.A. Completion Program, students complete their B.A. in one calendar year, which consists of three semesters. To enter the program, students must have at least 45 transferable units from an accredited college. Students may earn additional units for life experience through the Prior Learning Program and/or by taking CLEP exams. To receive a bachelor's degree from the program, students are required to complete 3 units of the following: scientific reasoning, social science, quantitative reasoning, hands-on art, and expository writing. The social science requirement is fulfilled by the humanities seminars that take place one weekend per month. Class topics vary each semester and may include literature, eco-psychology, gender studies, activism and social change, and queer studies. Weekend B.A. Completion Program students are required to complete 24 units in their emphasis area.

Off-Campus Programs

The Weekday/Evening B.A. Program requires students to complete a 3-unit practicum in a community organization. New College maintains a file of practicum placements, which include positions in health, Latino, environmental, peace, labor, and women's organizations, among others.

Academic Facilities

The Humanities Library, located at the Valencia Street campus in San Francisco, is small but specialized. It includes material of interest to New College students and faculty members, especially in the areas of literature, poetry, psychology, ethnic studies, and health studies. The library is also a member of the Online Computer Library Center (OCLC), an international library database with more than 20 million book titles, periodicals, and records that can be borrowed through interlibrary loan. The Holt Labor Library, located at the School of Law campus on Fell Street in San Francisco, has a rare collection of books and documents on labor history.

The computer lab, also located at the Valencia Street campus, has several computers and printers for student use.

New College's facilities also include a fine and graphic arts studio, a video editing room, a café, an information center, and two theaters.

Costs

For 2003–04, full-time tuition for the Weekday B.A. Program was \$5566 per semester, and yearly tuition was \$11,132. The Weekend B.A. Completion Program's tuition was \$5566 per semester or, with three semesters per year, \$16,698 for a year. Tuition is subject to change on a yearly basis.

Financial Aid

Financial Assistance is available to students who qualify. Nearly 75 percent of the students in New College's B.A. programs qualify to receive some form of federal, state, or local financial aid, including Federal Pell Grants, Federal Supplemental Education Opportunity Grants, Federal Perkins Loans, Federal Stafford Student Loans, Federal Work-Study Awards, Cal Grants, and Marin Educational Opportunity Loans. Students must submit the Free Application for Federal Student Aid (FAFSA) and a New College financial aid form. The priority deadline is March 1 for the following academic year. Forms are available from the Financial Aid Office by calling 415-437-3442 or by sending an e-mail to finaid@newcollege.edu.

Faculty

New College of California is dedicated to excellence in teaching. In New College's B.A. programs, the ratio of students to faculty members is 15:1, one of the best in the country. In addition to teaching, each core faculty member spends a significant amount of time advising students. New College faculty members have outstanding reputations in their field of expertise. Many have extensive ties to the community and experience in both practical and academic settings.

Admission Requirements

New College of California does not base its admissions policy on previous college or high school grades. Standardized test scores, such as ACT or SAT, are not required for admission. The B.A. programs require a high school diploma or a GED certificate.

New College recognizes that many excellent students do not always perform well in traditional academic environments. Instead, prospective students are evaluated on their enthusiasm for learning and their potential to achieve in an alternative, student-centered environment on the basis of their application, a five-page personal statement, and an interview.

Most Weekday B.A. Program students enter with previous units from other colleges, but students can be admitted to this program with no prior college units. The Weekend B.A. Completion Program requires at least 45 units from an accredited college.

The Weekday B.A. Program accepts new students for the fall and spring semesters. The Weekend B.A. Completion Program accepts new students for the fall, spring, and summer semesters.

Application and Information

Prospective students must submit a New College of California admissions application, official transcripts of all previous college work, an official high school transcript or GED certificate, a five-page personal statement (guidelines are on the application), and a \$50 application fee and participate in an interview with a faculty member or admissions counselor. Priority deadlines are one month before registration. The New College of California application can be downloaded at http://www.newcollege.edu/admissions/default.htm.

For further information, students should contact:

New College of California
Admissions Office
766 Valencia Street
San Francisco, California 94110
Telephone: 415-437-3460
888-437-3460 (toll-free)
Fax: 415-437-3470
E-mail: admissions@ncgate.newcollege.edu
World Wide Web: http://www.newcollege.edu

NEW COLLEGE OF FLORIDA

SARASOTA, FLORIDA

The College

New College of Florida offers serious students the opportunity to pursue rigorous academic study in an environment designed to promote depth in thinking, free exchange of ideas, and highly individualized interaction with faculty members. Throughout the history of New College, four principles have defined the College's educational philosophy: each student is ultimately responsible for his or her education; the best education demands a joint search for knowledge by exciting teachers and able-minded students; students' progress should be based on demonstrated competence and real mastery rather than on the accumulation of credits and grades; and students should have, from the outset, opportunities to explore, in depth, areas of interest to them.

Study is focused in the liberal arts and sciences and is highly accelerated and independent. More than 50 percent of the College's graduates pursue graduate or professional study, gaining admission to Harvard, Yale, MIT, Brown, Georgetown Law Center, Berkeley, and other major graduate centers. New College ranks among the top schools in the percentage of graduates earning the Ph.D.

New College was founded as a private institution in 1960 with a devotion to the values implicit in a liberal arts education and dedicated to creating an innovative academic community of talented scholars and outstanding faculty members. Affiliation with the state of Florida in 1975 served to strengthen and perpetuate the idealistic vision of the College's founders, which was furthered in 2001, when New College was officially designated the honors college of Florida's public university system. A public-private funding arrangement provides students with a private honors college experience at public cost.

The College's population is 671, 39 percent men and 61 percent women; approximately 25 percent are out-of-state or overseas residents. First-year and second-year students must live on campus, but many continuing students choose to live on campus as well. The Pei residence halls were designed by the eminent architect of the same name. The 131-room, three-court complex provides rooms with individual entrances, private baths, central air-conditioning, and various combinations of large picture windows, sliding glass doors, and/or balconies. The Dort and Goldstein dorms provide apartment-style housing with four single rooms, two bathrooms, and a common living room and kitchenette. A dining hall provides a full meal plan. The Counseling and Wellness Center offers basic health care and personal counseling as well as a variety of related services.

New College student life is informal. Activities are largely student initiated and include academic, artistic, religious, political, and recreational athletic pursuits. The College's 144-acre bayfront location on the Gulf of Mexico contains basketball, racquetball, and tennis courts; a multipurpose field; a running path; a volleyball pit; a 25-meter swimming pool; and a fitness center. Sailboats, sailboards, and canoes are available for use on Sarasota Bay.

Location

New College, situated on Sarasota Bay, serves as the northern gateway to Sarasota, a city of more than 50,000 located 50 miles south of Tampa on the west coast of Florida. Noted as a cultural and recreational center, Sarasota's beautiful public beaches and professional theater, art, and music, attract visitors and new residents from throughout the world. The climate is semitropical, consisting of long, warm autumns and springs and mild winters. Transportation from throughout the nation and within the city is readily accessible. Many major airlines serve Sarasota and within the city, buses link the campus to downtown, shopping malls, parks, and beaches. New College is in a residential neighborhood; mass transit is available, but the bicycle is a favored means of transportation among students.

Majors and Degrees

New College awards the Bachelor of Arts degree. Each area of concentration (major) at New College is an individualized program of study that a student designs in consultation with, and with the approval of, the faculty. Areas of concentration include anthropology, art history, biology, British and American literature, chemistry, classics, economics, environmental studies, foreign languages and literatures, French, German, history, humanities, international and area studies, literature, mathematics, medieval and Renaissance studies, music, natural sciences, philosophy, physics, political science, psychology, public policy, religion, Russian, social sciences, sociology, Spanish, urban studies, and visual arts. Partial areas of concentration may be pursued in gender studies and in theater. Students may also obtain permission from the faculty for self-designed concentrations. Premed, prelaw, and prebusiness advising and guidelines are provided by faculty and by Career Services.

Academic Program

The New College academic program aims to encourage academic excellence, creativity, and personal initiative and to provide essential tools for lifelong intellectual and personal growth. The College's distinctive curriculum enables students, in close consultation with faculty members, to develop programs of seminars, tutorials, independent research, and off-campus experiences that meet personal goals.

Students receive detailed narrative evaluations of their work as well as satisfactory/unsatisfactory assessments. In order to graduate, students must satisfactorily complete seven academic contracts (one per semester), three independent study projects, a senior thesis or project, and an oral baccalaureate examination. In addition to the requirements for the individual major, students must complete eight courses within the liberal arts curriculum with at least one course each in the humanities, social sciences, and natural sciences. All students must meet basic mathematics and computer literacy requirements, and pass or be exempted from Florida's College-Level Academic Skills Test. Finally, the New College faculty, in executive session at the last faculty meeting of the academic year, votes conferral of the Bachelor of Arts degree for each member of the graduating class.

The College operates on a 4-1-4 calendar, In January, students undertake independent study projects, which they design and complete under faculty sponsorship.

Off-Campus Programs

Internships, fieldwork, and independent research away from campus offer opportunities to gain new skills and test career interests. Exposure to other cultures provides new learning experiences and insights into one's own way of life. Because off-campus study can make a major contribution to an undergraduate education, the College facilitates such study through its flexible, individualized curriculum and special support services. New College is a member of the National Student Exchange, which provides access to more than 170 universities with programs in the U.S. and abroad (many with comparable tuition costs). Students may also participate in programs offered by independent providers, such as the School for International Training and AustraLearn as well as international programs available through the State University System of Florida and Center for Cross Cultural Studies. With faculty approval, students may pursue off-campus independent studies or participate in programs such as Living Routes, which offers non-traditional venues for study abroad.

Academic Facilities

The Jane Bancroft Cook Library, a $6-million facility, has an "open stack" arrangement that allows free access to most materials. Trustees, faculty members, students, and the New College Library Association have implemented an ambitious acquisition program to expand the current holdings of approximately 267,000 volumes. The library subscribes to more than 800 serial titles, including 700 magazines and journals and several state, national, and international newspapers. In addition, through computer networks and other cooperative programs, New College has access to hundreds of online databases and electronic journals and newspapers, as well as several online document delivery services. Through a comprehensive online interlibrary loan system, New College students have ready access to holdings throughout Florida;s public university libraries.

The Sudakoff Conference Center hosts visiting lecturers, meetings of campus and community organizations, and diverse special events. The Caples Fine Arts Complex includes the 264-seat Mildred Sainer Music & Arts Pavilion; the Lota Mundy Music Building, which houses eight practice rooms and the Benjamin and Barbara Slavin Electronic Music Studio; the Christianne Felsmann Fine Arts Building; the Betty Isermann Fine Arts Gallery and Studio; and the Sculpture Studio. Science facilities include the R.V. Heiser Natural Sciences Complex (laboratories, classrooms, offices, a computer lab, two electron microscopes, and an auditorium) and the $2.5-million Rhoda and Jack Pritzker Marine Biology Research Center, which has state-of-the-art culture rooms, laboratories, and aquaria with water drawn from Sarasota Bay. Saltwater effluent from the tanks is cleaned by means of a wetland constructed in 2001 as a senior thesis project.

Costs

For the 2003–04 academic year, in-state tuition and fees were $3240 and out-of-state tuition and fees were $16,473. Room and board costs were $5658. For the year, tuition, fees, room, and board for Florida residents totaled $8898. For out-of-state students, the total was $22,131.

Financial Aid

The actual cost of providing this highly individualized honors college experience is far greater than the state funding appropriated for support of the College. The New College Foundation secures independent funding designed to provide the difference. Part of the endowment produces income used for scholarships.

Approximately 87 percent of the College;s students receive some form of financial assistance, including scholarships from external programs and organizations. To apply for financial aid, students should file the Free Application for Federal Student Aid (FAFSA). March 1 is the priority date for need-based financial aid. For merit scholarship consideration, February 1 is the priority date to complete the application for admission. No additional application is necessary.

Faculty

One hundred percent of New College's faculty members hold the Ph.D. or terminal degree in their field. They have come to New College from the finest universities nationally and abroad, drawn by an environment that emphasizes excellence in teaching and fosters a close-knit community of scholars. Faculty members sponsor individual students in the formulation of their academic programs, gradually moving toward a form of mentorship through which joint research is sometimes pursued. An 11:1 student-faculty ratio is a key factor in the College's individualized approach to education.

Student Government

Student input is a decisive factor in campus governance. Student representatives, elected by their peers, serve on most major policymaking committees and are voting participants in divisional and campuswide faculty meetings. The New College Student Alliance has authority over funding for recreation, social events, and student organizations.

Admission Requirements

New College seeks highly capable students eager to take responsibility for their own education. The Admissions Committee reviews each candidate individually, assessing potential for success within, and contribution to, the College's special environment. Writing ability, academic record, and course selection are focal points of the committee;s review. The majority of freshmen entering in fall 2003 ranked in the top tenth of their high school class. The middle 50 percent of SAT I takers scored 1250–1390. The middle 50 percent of ACT takers scored 25–30.

All prospective students may apply for entrance to either the fall or the spring term. Candidates must submit a New College application and fee, official transcript(s), SAT I or ACT scores, a counselor recommendation, an academic teacher recommendation, and two essays. Applicants are encouraged to augment their applications with evidence of maturity, self-discipline, and motivation for rigorous in-depth study. Thorough research into the College is recommended for all those with serious interest in applying. Campus tours, interviews, and class visits are encouraged for all candidates.

Application and Information

Admission application materials and descriptive literature are available through the New College Office of Admissions. The College employs a rolling admission system. Candidates for the fall class are evaluated from September through May 1, or until enrollment goals are met. Notification of the admission decision occurs approximately two to three weeks after an application and all supporting credentials have been received.

Inquiries and application requests should be directed to:

Kathleen M. Killion
Interim Dean of Admissions and Financial Aid
New College of Florida
5700 North Tamiami Trail
Sarasota, Florida 34243
Telephone: 941-359-4269
Fax: 941-359-4435
E-mail: admissions@ncf.edu
World Wide Web: http://www.ncf.edu

College Hall, former home of circus magnate Charles Ringling, houses New College classrooms and faculty offices.

NEW ENGLAND COLLEGE

HENNIKER, NEW HAMPSHIRE

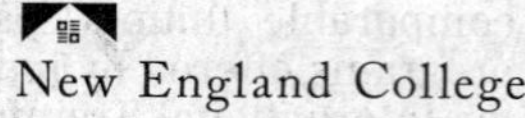

The College

New England College (NEC) is a place where students amaze themselves with what they learn and with what they can accomplish. A college that prepares students for the professional world, NEC also empowers its graduates with a broad knowledge base that results from a focus on the liberal arts. In addition, students develop strong analytical and communication skills that are vital to success in any career. The College's current enrollment stands at about 1,000 students (800 are undergraduates). The diverse student body, representing thirty-three states and twenty other countries, enriches the College curriculum's multicultural focus and global perspective. New England College prides itself on its commitment to each individual student and provides a strong support network to assist students with a variety of learning styles. The Pathways Center plays a key role in the academic and professional achievements of all students. It is an innovative combination of academic advising, study skills and support services, and career planning and placement. The Pathways Center is an integral part of academic life at NEC; students begin honing their academic and professional skills, planning for their future, and building their resumes from the moment they arrive on campus. Thus, NEC graduates are extremely successful in finding employment upon graduation. As an example, education majors have enjoyed 100 percent job placement over the last seven years.

The campus, which is nestled in the center of Henniker, a classic small New England town, consists of thirty-two buildings. Students take advantage of the many extracurricular activities available at NEC, ranging from outdoor recreation to theater productions and the student newspaper. There are thirteen Division III intercollegiate sports teams at NEC in addition to numerous club and recreational sports options. The campus offers 26 acres of playing fields, a new fitness center, a gymnasium, and a field house for student athletic activities. The Lee Clement Ice Arena, home of the NEC Pilgrims, provides some of the best hockey games in the region.

Location

New England College's location offers students the best of all worlds. Students have easy access to vibrant cities and the incomparable recreation and wilderness regions of New Hampshire. The College is located a short drive from the state capital, Concord, and about 45 minutes from the state's largest city, Manchester, and its airport. Portsmouth and Boston, as well as some of the best ocean beaches in New England, can be reached in less than 2 hours. Alpine and Nordic skiing opportunities abound. Pat's Peak, located only 3 miles from campus, provides free skiing to all NEC students. The College's 180-acre campus offers excellent trails for cross-country skiing and hiking. The Contoocook River flows through the center of campus, spanned by the College's historic covered bridge, a popular subject for photographers, especially during autumn. Almost all NEC students reside on campus in the six residence halls located adjacent to classroom buildings and the student center.

Majors and Degrees

The College offers thirty majors, a remarkable number for a small college. Such variety permits students to consider a number of options before selecting a major, which is encouraged. Graduates of the undergraduate program are awarded the Bachelor of Arts or the Bachelor of Science, depending upon their major. A number of concentrations are offered within the majors, further permitting students to develop expertise based upon their specific career goals. For instance, a student can major in art with a concentration in photography.

Majors available at NEC include art, art history, biological studies, biology, business administration, communication, comparative literature, creative writing, criminal justice, educational studies, elementary education, engineering (3+2 program with Clarkson University), English, environmental chemistry, environmental science, environmental studies, health and sport science, history, integrative health studies, kinesiology, mathematics, philosophy, physical education, political science, psychology, secondary education, sociology, special education, sport and recreation management, and theater. Students may elect an individually designed major, combining elements from several majors, subject to faculty approval. Many students pursue internship options in a wide range of disciplines, including business, fine and performing arts, government, health care and human services, law, media and communications, professional sports, and many others. Recent internship sites have included National Public Radio, Disney World, the Verizon Center, the Army Corps of Engineers, and the Manchester Monarchs. Education majors have many opportunities to interact with children and adolescents, from early on in their programs to their capstone student-teaching experience.

Academic Program

A comprehensive liberal arts college that also offers professional programs, NEC aims for its students to develop certain abilities: to think and communicate effectively, to understand the methods of the broad academic disciplines, to develop a strong sense of ethics, to respect other identities and cultures, and to develop a lifelong love of learning.

The First-Year Experience at NEC introduces students to college-level learning. It includes two writing courses, a computer technology course, seminars on human rights and cultural diversity, a course in science, and a course in basic mathematics. The New England College curriculum is rooted in the belief that students learn best when actively involved with their subject matter; thus, NEC courses focus on learning by doing. Students may also elect to participate in the honors program, where they work one-on-one with faculty members on research and student projects that earn extra credits. The academic year is divided into two main semesters, fall and spring. Additional sessions during January and the summer months offer students opportunities to take courses online or on campus. To graduate, students are required to complete a minimum of 120 credits as part of an approved program of study. CLEP and AP credits are accepted.

Off-Campus Programs

New England College encourages students to consider study-abroad options available to them via consortia agreements with a wide range of institutions located throughout the world. Students generally spend one semester when studying abroad, although some opt for a yearlong program. Participating institutions are located in Australia, Canada, England, France, Japan, and South Africa. Students may also choose to participate in travel courses, which are generally offered during the January term.

NEC's membership in the New Hampshire College and University Consortium (NHCUC) enables NEC students to take courses at any of the NHCUC member institutions and apply these credits to their degree program at the College.

Academic Facilities

The College's Center for Educational Innovation (CEI) was opened in 2001. A state-of-the art facility, the CEI provides networked data ports, Internet access, videoconferencing, and the full range of electronic and broadcast media access that enables professors to enhance their teaching by connecting to today's global network of information. The Simon Center, at the heart of the NEC campus, serves as the student center for the College. Both the Simon Center and the CEI have wireless networks, enabling students to access the College's network and the Internet from laptop computers at any location in those buildings. (The College also makes available fifty laptops for student use.) The H. Raymond Danforth Library provides a comprehensive research facility in addition to a comfortable reading and study space. The library holds more than 100,000 volumes, as well as a new thirty-three-station computer laboratory with Internet access. The science building serves as the home for the science departments, although classes for many other disciplines are scheduled in this large facility. Also located in the science building is the newly renovated Mainstage Theatre, where a number of plays are presented each year by NEC's outstanding Theatre Department.

Costs

For the 2003–04 year, tuition was $20,480. Room and board were $7740. Fees were $640.

Financial Aid

New England College offers a wide range of scholarships and grants for incoming students, ranging from $3000 to full tuition. The majority of these awards are merit-based, taking into account the student's academic achievement or other talents and accomplishments, such as participation in the arts, community service, and student government. Some need-based grants are available as well and are awarded to students based upon information provided on the Free Application for Federal Student Aid (FAFSA). All awards are renewable on an annual basis, depending upon the student's academic record and/or documented financial need.

Faculty

There are 53 full-time faculty members at New England College. More than 75 percent hold terminal degrees in their fields. The NEC faculty is highly accomplished and active professionally, publishing books and articles, participating in national conferences, conducting scientific research, and creating works of art. Yet the main focus of the NEC faculty members is teaching. They understand that students learn best by doing and so incorporate practical projects and activities into their course syllabi. The low student-teacher ratio (13:1) contributes to the friendly, highly personalized classroom experience. Students benefit from regular, personalized interaction with their professors, which helps them develop their knowledge and abilities beyond what they had ever thought possible.

Student Government

New England College's student government is actively involved in the academic, cultural, social, and organizational life of the institution. The Student Senate functions as a liaison between students and the NEC faculty, administration, alumni, and trustees. The Student Senate is responsible for its own budget, which funds numerous student-run clubs, organizations, social events, and recreational activities.

Admission Requirements

Freshman applicants must have received their high school diplomas (or equivalent) before attending New England College. A basic college-preparatory program is recommended, with course work in English, mathematics, science, social studies, and other academic electives. The Office of Admission takes into account the student's academic record, extracurricular activities and achievements, personal statement, and letters of recommendation, as well as the student's maturity and determination to succeed. Standardized tests (SAT or ACT) are not required, although most students submit scores. Students are encouraged to arrange an interview, conducted either in person or via telephone, with an admission counselor.

Application and Information

New England College has a rolling admission system; applications are reviewed as they become complete. All applicants must submit a completed application form, a $30 application fee, official high school transcripts, and letters of recommendation from high school teachers or guidance counselors. Most students receive decisions within two weeks of their file's completion. Students are encouraged to apply early, as scholarship decisions are made shortly after admission, and they are considered for the full range of scholarship opportunities at the early part of the application cycle. Students whose native language is not English must submit TOEFL scores. Those students who do not meet TOEFL score minimums may participate in the English as a second language (ESL) program at NEC. Transfer students must also provide official college transcripts and a supporting letter from their college's dean of students.

Application forms may be obtained from the Office of Admission or at the New England College Web site. Students may submit their applications online. For further information, interested students should contact:

Paul Miller
Director of Admission and Financial Aid
New England College
26 Bridge Street
Henniker, New Hampshire 03242-3297
Telephone: 800-521-7642 (toll-free)
Fax: 603-428-3155
E-mail: admission@nec.edu
World Wide Web: http://www.nec.edu/

Students relax in New England College's spectacular Simon Center.

THE NEW ENGLAND INSTITUTE OF ART

BROOKLINE, MASSACHUSETTS

The College

Founded as the Norm Prescott School of Broadcasting in 1952, the New England Institute of Art has been a member of both the academic and cultural community of Boston for more than fifty years, offering high-quality hands-on education to students in an urban environment.

The college has approximately 1,000 students and is authorized to award both Associate of Science and Bachelor of Science degrees by the Massachusetts Board of Higher Education and by the New England Association of Schools and Colleges.

The New England Institute of Art is student-centered, with an academic culture built on small classes and hands-on work in audio production, broadcasting (radio or television), graphic design, and multimedia and Web design. It is an intimate and challenging environment in which the student benefits from personalized attention from faculty members and close working relationships with fellow students. Student-centered also means that the student and his or her family work with experienced higher education professionals who provide supportive, user-friendly service at every step of the student's academic career, from the moment he or she first applies.

The New England Institute of Art's degree programs build academic strengths and technical and creative capacities on a foundation of general education courses that develop the student's ability to analyze and understand the factors that influence culture and technology.

A dedicated Career Services team assists students from entry through graduation in placement in internships and entry-level employment in their fields of study. Student counseling services are available, and approximately 200 students live in off-campus housing facilities. Students have the opportunity to apply their skills in cocurricular activities, including an in-house record label, literary magazine, video club, and Internet radio station. An on-site, *Boston Globe*–recognized art gallery allows for the display of student work.

Location

The New England Institute of Art is located on the border of Brookline and Boston, Massachusetts, and is easily accessible by car and public transportation. Proximity to Boston allows for a rich cultural experience, including world-class museums, music performances, sporting events, and a thriving artistic and media community. The Boston area is also home to more than eighty institutions of higher learning, offering free lectures, gallery exhibits, and activities to enrich the college experience.

Majors and Degrees

The New England Institute of Art offers Bachelor of Science degrees in audio and media technology, graphic design, and multimedia and Web design. The college also offers Associate of Science degrees in audio production and in broadcasting, with a concentration in either radio or television.

The Bachelor of Science degree in audio and media technology is for students who are serious about the audio industry and their future. Students get a solid grounding in critical listening, computer music, and the physics of sound, plus exposure to the actual situations that they run into in their professional career. Students are able to submit some of their projects to the college's student-run record/CD label, Naked Ear Records.

The Bachelor of Science degree program in graphic design is the first step toward a career in commercial design. Initially, students develop an understanding of color and composition, design and typography, and drawing skills. As they progress through the program, students are trained in creative problem solving and learn to offer solutions that are effective in the business of graphic design.

The Bachelor of Science degree program in multimedia and Web design offers hands-on experiences in everything from designing streaming media to managing Web site growth and exploring new dimensions with electronic shopping and interactivity. Students can study a wide range of areas, from designing virtual worlds to marketing on the Internet. Students learn to develop and manage Web activities and create e-commerce applications. Students work in the college's Internet labs, where they learn about Web site development and management, marketing and e-commerce, measuring the success of online activities, and protecting secure access. Students graduate with skills in building and maintaining Web sites and developing Internet-based strategies to help organizations integrate the Web into their operations.

The Associate of Science degree program in audio production allows students to learn a basic skills set covering the fundamentals of various audio applications. Included are courses that require the student to produce projects that demonstrate their creative and technical abilities.

In the Associate of Science degree program in broadcasting, students can concentrate in either radio or television. Students acquire essential skills of radio or TV broadcasting, from announcing and videography to editing and producing. Students also learn to produce a high-quality product and bring it to market, with assignments built around real-world broadcast situations such as shooting, writing, and editing a TV news story or producing a music video under deadline. Students can get involved in an Internet radio station and a video club.

Academic Programs

Bachelor of Science degree candidates must complete 121 credit hours, including 40 in general education. Students must take 57 credits in core courses and 18 credit hours within their concentration and may use 6 credit hours toward electives.

Associate of Science degree candidates must complete a minimum of 61 credit hours, with 21 credit hours in general education courses, with a cumulative GPA of 2.0 or higher.

Students must also receive a passing grade or credit for all required course work, meet portfolio or other requirements, and complete a 120-hour internship or capstone project.

Academic Facilities

The campus includes a variety of student and faculty accommodations, administrative offices, a student lounge, and a performance space and growing library equipped with Internet access. Academic facilities at the college include four recording studios, two television studios, editing suites, radio production studios, MIDI facilities, multimedia and computer laboratories, and an Internet radio station as well as a record label company. Audio studios B and C share a 570-square-foot performance space. The college also takes advantage of learning spaces and classrooms in neighboring organizations to complement student learning and experience.

Costs

Yearly tuition and fees at the New England Institute of Art for 2003–04 were $16,140. Technology fees, books, and supplies are additional and vary according to program. Housing costs are approximately $9000 per year.

Financial Aid

Many students receive some form of financial aid to assist them in financing their education. Programs include loans, grants, and work-study assistance and are based, in part, on eligibility. The New England Institute of Art provides financial planning for its students, providing payment plans to allow budgeting for the entire program.

The goal in Student Financial Services is to make monthly payments as affordable as possible. After a student completes the application forms, a Financial Aid Officer (FAO) reviews them using a federally required calculation to determine eligibility for financial aid. The FAO then works with the student and families to devise a student financial plan, based on financial aid eligibility and family circumstances, to help him or her cover educational expenses.

Faculty

The faculty members at the New England Institute of Art bring years of teaching and professional experience to the classroom. There are 30 full-time faculty members and 65 adjunct faculty members, with 45 percent holding advanced degrees. The student-faculty ratio is 17.5:1.

Admission Requirements

The New England Institute of Art is dedicated to admitting men and women of any age, creed, ancestry, race, color, religion, national origin, sex, sexual orientation, or disability.

Applicants are reviewed on the basis of individual interests as well as academic and professional promise. Additional qualities such as seriousness, purpose, leadership, and an understanding of and commitment to the mission and educational objectives of the college are also considered in the admissions review process.

Application and Information

The New England Institute of Art's admissions policy allows applicants to apply for admission at any time to attend semesters beginning in September, January, and May. Scholarships, financial assistance, and payment programs are available to qualified students for each of these semesters. The New England Institute of Art notifies applicants of a decision on the application soon after they complete the admissions procedures. Applications are accepted at any time by mail or online. To apply or request more information online, prospective students should visit the Web site listed below.

For general information, application forms, and catalogs, students should contact:

Admissions
The New England Institute of Art
10 Brookline Place, West
Brookline, Massachusetts 02445
Telephone: 800-903-4425 (toll-free)
Fax: 617-582-4500
E-mail: neia_admissions@aii.edu
World Wide Web: http://www.neia.aii.edu

NEW HAMPSHIRE INSTITUTE OF ART

MANCHESTER, NEW HAMPSHIRE

The Institute

The New Hampshire Institute of Art has been devoted to the education of artists for more than 100 years. Founded in 1898 as the Manchester Institute of Arts and Sciences, the Institute provides educational opportunities for a broad regional audience to learn about and experience the arts. In 1996, the Institute's Board of Trustees voted to rename the organization the New Hampshire Institute of Art. In that same year, the Institute was authorized by the state of New Hampshire to grant the Bachelor of Fine Arts degree. The Institute received national accreditation through the National Association of Schools of Art and Design in November 2001.

The Institute functions as an important cultural resource for the state of New Hampshire. Several fully accessible gallery spaces support a free and widely varied exhibition schedule throughout each year, featuring student, faculty member, special artist, and community exhibits. The Institute's French Auditorium offers significant opportunities for visiting artist presentations and political and critical forums of regional and national importance. In recent years, speakers have included Bob Smith, Dan Quayle, Pat Buchanan, John Sununu, Al Gore, Bill Clinton, and Richard Gephardt.

Location

The Institute is located in Manchester, New Hampshire, a medium-sized, cosmopolitan city of 100,000 people, with a lively downtown. Manchester, recently named the number one city in America by *Money Magazine*, is a northern New England cultural center, featuring the Currier Gallery of Art, the Manchester Historic Association and Millyard Museum, and the SEE Science Center. In addition, Manchester offers the Palace Theatre, the Verizon Wireless Arena, the New Hampshire Symphony Orchestra, the Granite State Opera, the New Hampshire Philharmonic Orchestra, and the Opera League of New Hampshire. There are six other colleges in the greater Manchester area. Students can hike, fish, golf, and ski without leaving the city. Manchester is centrally located, allowing easy access to Boston, Portland, and the seacoast areas.

Majors and Degrees

The Institute offers a four-year Bachelor of Fine Arts degree in ceramics, general studio, painting, photography, and illustration. Certificate programs and lifelong learning classes are also available.

Academic Program

The mission of the New Hampshire Institute of Art's Bachelor of Fine Arts degree program is to provide a traditional program of study in the fine arts, emphasizing the importance of integrating creative, aesthetic, technical, and critical skills in artistic expression. The creation and study of art is central to the mission and to the student's educational experience at the Institute.

The B.F.A. degree allocates 75 percent to course work in studio and art history courses and 25 percent to liberal arts courses. All of the Institute's resources, programs, faculty members, facilities, and student services focus on the needs of the developing artist. Liberal arts courses support the studio programs and develop an understanding of creative expression. For example, a science course may focus on color in light and pigment, or a philosophy course may explore the thought and inner reflection of the creative process.

During a student's first year in the B.F.A. program, required courses focus on drawing two- and three-dimensional design, color theory, art history, and writing courses. Specific introductory studio, art history, and liberal arts courses are required in the sophomore year to prepare students for the intermediate- and advanced-level courses to follow.

The student's final year at the Institute focuses on the student's ability to create a culminating body of work and a senior paper addressing the issues posed in the student's original entrance essay. This serves as the capstone to the student's experience in the B.F.A. program.

Academic Facilities

The Main Building is home to the drawing and painting program, the ceramics and sculpture program, and a metalsmithing studio in addition to two exhibition galleries and the main administration offices. In Gallery 7, a student exhibition gallery offers students the opportunity to exhibit their works during the academic year. Shows are organized, curated, and installed by a student committee. The historic French Auditorium is located on the upper level of the Main Building.

Fuller Hall houses an up-to-date photography facility; studios for foundations, painting, and printmaking; liberal arts classrooms; the Institute's library; and gallery space. The student lounge, store, and student service offices are on the main floor.

Costs

For the 2003–04 academic year, tuition for full-time B.F.A. students was $4950 per semester. A full-time course load was 12 to 18 credits per semester. Estimated fees for full-time students were $400 per semester. Costs are subject to change.

Financial Aid

The Institute was recently approved to offer federal financial aid programs to its B.F.A. students beginning in fall 2002. In addition, the Institute offers several merit- and need-based scholarship opportunities to help students and their families defray the cost of education. All B.F.A. students seeking financial aid at the Institute must complete the Free Application for Federal Student Aid (FAFSA). The Institute's priority deadline is May 1. Students are encouraged to submit their FAFSA online at http://www.fafsa.ed.gov.

Faculty

Most faculty members have terminal degrees and have achieved significant recognition in their fields. Their extensive studio experience and strong educational backgrounds enable them to assist students in the development of artistic skills and the professional skills required to be a practicing artist. Institute faculty members serve both as mentors and as academic advisers to students.

The faculty members of the New Hampshire Institute of Art are a diverse group of practicing artists who are highly experienced in their fields and dedicated to the educational experience. Works by Institute faculty members are exhibited in major museum collections, including the Art Institute of Chicago; the Museum of Fine Arts, Boston; the Museum of Quebec; the

Currier Gallery of Art; and the De Cordova Museum and Sculpture Garden. Museum and gallery exhibitions include Dartmouth College's Hood Museum; the Renwick Gallery in Washington, D.C.; New York City's American Craft Museum; the Whistler House Museum; the Fitchburg Art Museum; McGowan Fine Art; and numerous Boston, New York, and San Francisco galleries. Faculty members' works also appear in many private and corporate collections all over the world.

Student Government

Through the Student Activities Council (SAC), students participate in a wide variety of college and community activities. SAC officers are elected and serve as exhibition coordinators for the student-run Gallery 7. They plan social activities, identify student initiatives, and improve the quality of the student experience at the Institute.

Admission Requirements

The New Hampshire Institute of Art is a private, not-for-profit educational institution that maintains a policy of equal opportunity for all. The Institute does not discriminate on the basis of race, color, religion, national origin, sex, sexual orientation, age, veteran status, or disability in admissions, access to, or employment in its educational programs. Students who demonstrate artistic promise, potential, and aptitude for successful artistic endeavor are encouraged to apply for admission. A student's potential for success at the Institute is judged by the submission of a complete application and portfolio.

A complete application contains two letters of recommendation from a present or former teacher and/or guidance counselor or person who is familiar with the student on a professional basis; a 500-word essay on an artist, an artistic work, a movement, or an issue that has significance to the student as a developing artist and the reason for the significance; official transcripts from every high school or college attended; and a nonrefundable $25 application fee. Transcripts must be requested from each institution and sent directly to the Institute. Applicants currently in high school must submit either SAT or ACT scores. Applicants who have not graduated from high school must submit GED forms.

Portfolios usually contain between ten and twenty examples of the student's work and observe the following guidelines: drawings made from direct observation (not copied from photographs of published artwork); two or more self-portrait drawings ranging from representational to conceptual or expressive renderings; still-life drawings in any medium; interior studies, architectural renderings, or any other drawings that demonstrate the use of perspective; works that demonstrate the use of color; landscape, cityscape, portrait, or still-life paintings; and works that refer to the student's personal interests and strengths, including works in photography, printmaking, ceramics, sculpture, metalsmithing, or other mediums.

A slide portfolio can be submitted and should observe the following guidelines: 2" x 2", 35mm slides (standard mount) in a clear plastic slide page; the student's name, address, and phone number and an identification number and a notation indicating the top of the slide in permanent marker on each slide; and a slide identification sheet listing the size, the medium, and the year each work was created (titles and a brief description of each piece are optional). Two different views should be submitted of three-dimensional work (these two slides equal the representation of one work.) Students should prepare their slide portfolios carefully and include postage if they want them to be returned.

Transfer students in good academic standing are invited to apply to the New Hampshire Institute of Art.

Application and Information

The Institute has a rolling admissions policy; however it is recommended that applications be completed by April 1 to be considered for merit-based and need-based financial aid.

To be considered for admission, students must submit the completed application and the required nonrefundable $25 application fee to:

Admissions Department
New Hampshire Institute of Art
148 Concord Street
Manchester, New Hampshire 03104-4858
Telephone: 603-624-2456
866-241-4918 (toll-free)
E-mail: lsullivan@nhia.edu
jlanglois@nhia.edu
jgirvin@nhia.edu
World Wide Web: http://www.nhia.edu

The campus of the New Hampshire Institute of Art.

NEW JERSEY CITY UNIVERSITY

JERSEY CITY, NEW JERSEY

The University

There is much to discover at New Jersey City University (NJCU). This vital, 75-year-old liberal arts institution (formerly Jersey City State College) offers an incomparable educational experience at an affordable price.

At the heart of the University is a strong academic program that is recognized by a host of accrediting institutions. NJCU has an esteemed and caring faculty and extensive student support services. Twenty-five undergraduate degree programs are offered, as are graduate studies and teacher certification programs. NJCU provides unparalleled opportunity for academic and personal growth through such study options as its nationally recognized Cooperative Education Program, which enables undergraduates in all majors to earn income and academic credit while experiencing field study at one of hundreds of participating corporations, agencies, and organizations.

There is a sense of excitement on the 47-acre, tree-lined campus, which is located in the midst of one of the world's largest metropolitan areas. The University community is rich in diversity; people from many cultures come together and learn from each other. The student population includes high school graduates pursuing the four-year degree sequence, part-time and weekend students, nontraditional older students, and students seeking job retraining—all of whom are able to take advantage of the University's flexible class scheduling. While drawn primarily from northern New Jersey and the New York metropolitan area, students from fifteen other states, some as distant as California and Florida, and the Virgin Islands are enrolled. International students, who come to the University from more than fifty-one countries around the globe, enrich the multicultural nature of the campus.

The total undergraduate and graduate enrollment for full- and part-time students at the University is 10,000. An average class size of 20, smaller than that of most universities, enables students to work closely and directly with faculty members and classmates, encouraging intellectual exchange and fostering successful mentoring relationships.

The richness of university life at NJCU is seen in the extracurricular activities, services, and facilities that are available. Most student activities take place in the spacious, modern Michael B. Gilligan Student Union. Special features of the facility include quiet study lounges, a game room, a TV lounge, the University bookstore, a cafeteria, indoor parking, small and large meeting rooms, a private dining room, and a multipurpose room, which can accommodate banquets, special events, lectures, festivals, and fairs. The Gilligan Student Union is also home to the Student Government Organization, the student newspaper and radio station, and many clubs, organizations, fraternities, and sororities.

All students can participate in sports through the University's extensive varsity, intramural, and recreational athletic programs, which include baseball, basketball, cross-country, flag football, racquetball, soccer, softball, tennis, and volleyball. The University's Athletic and Fitness Center is a 72,000-square-foot state-of-the-art facility that houses a 25-yard, six-lane swimming pool; saunas; a 2,000-seat basketball/volleyball arena; an elevated jogging track; a fitness center and training facility; and three racquetball courts.

The Thomas M. Gerrity Athletic Complex, home to NJCU's outdoor sports and located a mile southwest of the main campus, is a 14-acre facility that features a 3,000-seat stadium, an enclosed press box, and a natural grass surface. The University campus also houses six composition-surface outdoor tennis courts, which are available to the NJCU community.

Location

New Jersey City University is located in Jersey City, New Jersey, within minutes of New York City. While the University's location in the urban center of the Northeast affords students all the cultural and intellectual stimulation of the metropolitan area, the campus has retained a quiet atmosphere for study. The University's urban setting also makes travel to and from campus convenient, providing easy access by car, train, and bus. An international airport is located minutes away.

Majors and Degrees

Undergraduate programs at New Jersey City University lead to the Bachelor of Arts (B.A.), Bachelor of Music (B.M.), Bachelor of Science (B.S.), Bachelor of Fine Arts (B.F.A.), or Bachelor of Science in Nursing (B.S.N.) degrees.

NJCU's College of Arts and Sciences offers major programs leading to a bachelor's degree in art (B.A. or B.F.A.); biology (B.A. or B.S.), geoscience/geography (B.A. or B.S.), and physics (B.A. or B.S.); chemistry and computer science (B.S.); and economics, English, history, mathematics, media arts, music, philosophy, political science, psychology, sociology, and Spanish (B.A.). A B.S. in clinical laboratory sciences is offered jointly with the University of Medicine and Dentistry of New Jersey (UMDNJ).

The College of Education offers major programs leading to a Bachelor of Arts degree in early childhood education, elementary education, and special education. Also offered are undergraduate programs that lead to certification, such as New Jersey Department of Education certification in secondary education. The College of Professional Studies offers major programs leading to a Bachelor of Science degree in business administration, criminal justice/fire safety/security administration, and health sciences and a Bachelor of Science in Nursing (B.S.N.).

Academic Program

An institution committed to the liberal arts, New Jersey City University requires 12 credits of core courses that prepare students for the required 42 credits of general studies for all degree programs. Students select courses from each of six clusters: natural sciences, social sciences, fine and performing arts, humanities, communications, and the contemporary world. Students must also fulfill an all-University requirement of 12 credits in communications, mathematics, and computers. There are specific major requirements as well as electives in each degree program. In addition, students may use general electives to complete a minor or a second major, strengthen a major, or pursue areas of personal interest. In their junior and senior years of study, students have ample opportunity to engage in fieldwork in their major. The University calendar is based on a two-semester system with two summer sessions.

Off-Campus Programs

NJCU, the premier cooperative education university in New Jersey, offers sophomores, juniors, and seniors in all academic areas the opportunity to study for a degree while working in salaried positions in related fields. NJCU's Cooperative Education Program works with more than 550 local and international employers.

Academic Facilities

The Congressman Frank J. Guarini Library houses 250,000 books and monographs, subscribes to 1,579 periodicals and journals, receives approximately 5,000 selected U.S. government publications per year, and maintains a collection of official state of New Jersey publications. The library has a complete file of microfiche issued by the Educational Research Information Center, a clearinghouse for research in all areas of education, and more than 500,000 fully indexed publications on microfilm. The library also maintains an online system catalog for academic reference. Upon reopening in September 1999 after undergoing a complete renovation, the library is now a state-of-the-art research facility, fully wired for Internet access. NJCU's Electronic Learning Laboratory provides computer laboratory support services to students.

NJCU's Media Arts Center is a 16,000-square-foot facility that houses two full-color broadcast-quality television studios, a radio and audio production studio, a complete 16-mm production studio and processing laboratory, two large projection/seminar rooms, an animation laboratory, a graphic production studio, individual student editing space, and work rooms. The Media Arts Center is the home of the Black Maria Film Festival, a 19-year-old international showcase for alternative film and video.

The University's A. Harry Moore Center for Special Education is comprised of the A. Harry Moore Laboratory School, the A. Harry Moore Special Education Camp at Stokes State Park, and the University's Department of Special Education.

NJCU's Center for Public Policy and Urban Research designs conducts basic and applied research on issues related to urban education, urban development, and public policy.

The University has established the Center for HIV Educational Studies and Training through funding from The Centers for Disease Control and Prevention (CDC). Under the aegis of the CDC, the University is participating in a two-year cooperative agreement, gathering formative research data and developing a pilot behavioral intervention plan.

NJCU's Asian Institute addresses economic, political, and cultural issues through conferences that bring together prominent scholars and business and civic leaders. The institute also sponsors exchange programs and funds special projects.

The Peter W. Rodino Institute of Criminal Justice at NJCU serves as a major avenue for the exchange of ideas between the community, criminal justice professionals, and the University. The institute sponsors conferences and seminars; provides technical assistance to local police, court, correctional, probation, parole, and juvenile justice agencies; conducts innovative research and demonstration projects; and assists in the development of student internships at criminal justice agencies.

The NJCU Women's Center offers a range of services to women, and presents programs on women's issues for NJCU and the community. The center provides a supportive atmosphere, informal counseling and referrals, and various education services.

NJCU's Medical, Counseling and Psychological Services Center provides medical care, counseling, and psychotherapy services.

The Career Development Center provides career counseling services and placement assistance to recent graduates.

NJCU's Early Childhood Learning Center provides educationally focused child care to foster the development of the children of students.

Costs

Undergraduate tuition and fees for the 2002–03 academic year were $5556 for New Jersey residents and $9508.50 for nonresidents. Room and board in NJCU's Vodra Hall Dormitory, Cooperative Education Dormitory, or apartment complex were $6198.

Financial Aid

NJCU strives to offer students maximum opportunities for financial aid. Financial aid available for eligible students includes needs-based grants, merit-based Corporate Scholarships, Federal Perkins Loans, Federal Stafford Student Loans, and jobs provided under the Federal Work-Study Program. Applicants for aid must submit the Free Application for Federal Student Aid (FAFSA). Approximately 75 percent of NJCU full-time undergraduates receive financial aid.

Faculty

Seventy-one percent of NJCU's faculty members hold the highest degrees attainable in their fields. A student-faculty ratio of 19:1 supports the development of close mentoring relationships and fosters the academic, social, and cultural growth of undergraduates. This student-faculty ratio also enables NJCU professors to be very accessible to their students.

Student Government

NJCU's Student Government Organization (SGO) charters and regulates all student clubs and organizations funded by student activity fees, providing a necessary degree of leadership and coordination. The SGO is administered by the Student Council, which is composed of the Student Executive Committee and class representatives. Members of the SGO serve in the University Senate to represent the interests and concerns of students.

Admission Requirements

Admission to New Jersey City University is based on a student's projected ability to complete a degree program. All admission decisions are made without regard to race, religion, sex, age, handicap, or national origin. It is desirable that freshman applicants rank in the top half of their high school class and complete a college-preparatory program that includes 4 units of English, 3 units of mathematics, 2 units of social science, and 2 units of laboratory science. A student's combined SAT I score or ACT score is taken into account in determining acceptance in individual cases. In addition, New Jersey residents who demonstrate financial need and do not meet traditional admissions requirements but have the academic potential and motivation to succeed in college may apply for admission through NJCU's Opportunity Scholarship Program (OSP). The University also accepts students who have been identified as learning disabled through its Project Mentor Program. Transfer applicants are required to have a minimum grade point average of 2.0. Students are accepted for transfer primarily into the sophomore and junior classes; a limited number are accepted with senior class standing.

Application and Information

Application for admission may be made by submitting a completed application, a $35 application fee, an official high school transcript, and SAT I or ACT scores. Transfer students must submit all college transcripts. Applications for the fall semester should be received by April 1; applications for the spring semester should be received by November 1. These dates are subject to change. Admission decisions are made on a rolling basis.

For additional information and application forms, students should contact:

Director of Admissions
New Jersey City University
2039 Kennedy Boulevard
Jersey City, New Jersey 07305
Telephone: 888-441-NJCU (toll-free)
World Wide Web: http://www.njcu.edu

The Hepburn Building's Gothic tower at New Jersey City University.

NEW MEXICO INSTITUTE OF MINING AND TECHNOLOGY

SOCORRO, NEW MEXICO

The Institute

New Mexico Institute of Mining and Technology was founded in 1889 as the New Mexico School of Mines. The school's name was changed in 1951 to reflect a broadened curriculum that included the sciences and more fields of engineering. Referred to as New Mexico Tech by its students and faculty members, the university still celebrates its mining heritage with the annual 49ers Celebration.

New Mexico Tech is a research-oriented public university specializing in science and engineering. Students who choose Tech are serious, career-oriented students who go on to become successful engineers, scientists, computer systems analysts, business managers, researchers, college professors, doctors, and other medical and professional personnel. Tech expects its students to work hard and take their education seriously. About 80 percent of Tech students graduate with work experience in a research environment.

Tech students benefit from the low tuition of a public university and the same personal attention of an expensive private college. A verdant, tree-filled campus with Southwestern-style architecture; a small-town setting; sunny weather; and easy access to the spectacular outdoors of New Mexico add to Tech's allure.

New Mexico Tech has an enrollment of about 1,800 students, approximately 60 percent of whom are full-time undergraduates. Eight percent of all undergraduates are transfer students. Hispanics are the largest minority group on campus, comprising 20 percent of undergraduates. Eight percent of undergraduates belong to other minorities, including African-Americans, Asian-Americans, and Native Americans. Nearly 3 percent of undergraduates are from other countries. The gender breakdown for undergraduates is 70 percent men, 30 percent women. The average age of full-time undergraduate students is 21.4 years, and 11 percent of undergraduates are age 25 or older.

New Mexico Tech is accredited by the North Central Association of Colleges and Schools. All engineering programs, except the newly established civil engineering program, are accredited by the Accreditation Board for Engineering and Technology, Inc.

Socorro and its environs appeal to mountain bikers, runners, astronomers, geologists, hikers, campers, rock climbers, birders, rock hounds, nature photographers, and people who like the slower pace of small-town life. Tech's Performing Arts Series brings a variety of entertainment to the campus each semester. Students can participate in the Music Program's vocal or instrumental performing groups and the Theater Program's productions. (Music and theater, however, are not offered as majors.) Tech students enjoy an active intramural sports program, a year-round swimming pool, and a championship 18-hole golf course, with golf lessons available.

Tech students participate in numerous clubs, from major-related ones (such as the Astronomy Club and the Institute of Electronic and Electrical Engineers student chapter), to clubs for specific groups (such as the Society of Women Engineers, Society of Hispanic Professional Engineers, the American Indian Science and Engineering Society), to interest-related groups (such as the Ski Club, Scuba Club, and the Juggling Club).

Tech has a student apartment building, residence halls, and student family housing units located on campus. Nearly half of all undergraduate students live on campus, although this is not required. Apartments, rental houses, and mobile homes are available in town for students who desire to live off campus. Rent and other costs of living are typically lower in Socorro than in most college towns.

The campus dining room and canteen snack bar, both located on campus, provide a variety of convenient and nutritious meals, all prepared fresh daily. The dining room features many theme dinners and special events throughout the year, including special meals for Halloween, Chinese New Year, and Mardi Gras. Students living in residence halls without kitchens are required to purchase a meal plan of at least 175 meals per semester. The meals may be eaten at any time, but may not be carried over to the next semester. Plans with more meals are also available. Students who require special dietary plans because of health or religious reasons are accommodated through a special menu developed with the student's and food service provider's input.

Student services provided by Tech include an on-campus health center, academic advising and tutoring, a first-year program to help students adjust to college, career placement services, short-term personal counseling, and programs for international students and students who are members of minority groups. Special services for disabled students are available through the Counseling Office.

Location

Tech students enjoy small-town life with access to the big city. Socorro has a population of 9,000 and its prime industries are education and research. It is located on I-25, 76 miles south of Albuquerque and 194 miles north of El Paso. Air travelers can fly into Albuquerque's International Sunport and take a shuttle to Socorro. Commercial bus service is available from both Albuquerque and El Paso.

Students can easily get around Socorro by bicycle. A car is not necessary, but it can be handy for trips to Albuquerque or exploring New Mexico. Socorro has no public transportation.

Majors and Degrees

New Mexico Tech offers Bachelor of Science degrees in biology, chemistry, computer science, environmental science, geology, geophysics, information technology, management, management of technology, mathematics, physics, psychology, and technical communication and also in several fields of engineering: chemical, civil, electrical, environmental, materials, mechanical, mineral, and petroleum.

Academic Program

Tech has a two-semester academic calendar, with an eight-week summer session. All departments offer senior-level independent study courses. Engineering departments require yearlong senior design courses in which students work in teams.

Depending on the major, students earn 130 to 139 hours of credit to graduate. All students must satisfy general degree requirements, which include English, technical writing, humanities, social sciences, physics, chemistry, and mathematics. Engineering students must also satisfy a depth requirement in the humanities and social sciences. Most majors do not require a foreign language.

Students may receive credit for course work by passing a challenge exam. Undergraduates with appropriate prerequisites may take graduate courses.

Academic Facilities

The library's collection of more than 600,000 books, periodicals, government documents, microforms, maps, videos, audiocassettes, and computer files reflects the specialized research interests of the Tech community. The library offers access to more than 65 five databases and specialized indexes on CD-ROM. As a selective depository of U.S. government documents, the library receives more than 34,000 federal documents each year. It also contains a collection of state and international documents concentrating on geology and mining.

The Tech Computer Center (TCC) offers computer access to students, faculty members, and staff. Most departments have computer systems for their own use. The campus network is connected to the nationwide National Science Foundation computer network, giving Tech access to thousands of other sites worldwide. All residence hall rooms are hardwired for Ethernet access.

Costs

For 2003–04, tuition and fees were $3073 for New Mexico residents and $9510 for nonresidents. Room and board in a traditional residence hall were $4600, and books and supplies were approximately $800. Student apartments, which are available only to upperclassmen, were $3350 per semester for a 4-bedroom and $3600 for a 2-bedroom. Miscellaneous and personal expenses were estimated at $2120 for residents, not counting travel for nonresidents. Total expenses were $10,593 for residents and $17,030 for nonresidents.

Financial Aid

New Mexico Tech offers many merit scholarships based on an applicants' high school GPA and scores on either the SAT or the ACT. Merit scholarships are also available for transfer students, based on their college GPAs. All students who apply for admission are automatically considered for merit scholarships; there is no separate application.

Deadline for the two highest-valued scholarships is February 1 of the year before the student plans to enter. Other scholarships have a deadline of March 1. For in-state students, New Mexico Tech is the only state university that stacks a merit scholarship on top of the Lottery Success Scholarship.

Financial aid available includes Federal Pell Grants, Federal Supplemental Educational Opportunity Grants, New Mexico Student Incentive Grants (for in-state students), and Federal Student Perkins, PLUS, and Stafford Student Loans.

Many Tech students are able to obtain on-campus jobs in research areas, providing them with valuable experience as well as income.

Faculty

Nearly all (99 percent) of Tech's faculty members have a Ph.D. and conduct research. Most classes are taught by full-time faculty members rather than graduate students. A 12:1 student-faculty ratio allows extensive interaction with professors in the classroom and laboratory. Most professors live in Socorro and participate in Tech's social life along with their students. This extraordinary level of contact between faculty members and students promotes mentoring, which Tech alumni say is a key factor in their subsequent career successes.

Student Government

All full-time undergraduates are members of the Student Association. Any student may run for a seat on the Student Senate, the representative body that regulates student activities and organizations and provides funding for campus clubs and special events. Elections are held twice a year for one-year terms, with half the Senate elected each time.

Admission Requirements

First-time students must complete Tech's Application for Undergraduate Admission and Scholarship. They must provide an official high school transcript and an official ACT Student Profile Report or an SAT College Report and pay a $15 application fee.

Transfer applicants must fulfill the requirements listed for first-time students and provide official transcripts from all colleges attended.

Application deadlines are August 1 for the fall semester, December 15 for the spring semester, and June 1 for the summer session.

Application and Information

For more information, students should contact:

Mike Kloeppel
Director of Admission
New Mexico Tech
801 Leroy Place
Socorro, New Mexico 87801
Telephone: (505) 835-5424
(800) 428-TECH (8324) (toll-free)
Fax: (505) 835-5989
E-mail: admission@admin.nmt.edu
World Wide Web: http://www.nmt.edu

NEW MEXICO STATE UNIVERSITY

LAS CRUCES, NEW MEXICO

The University

Founded in 1888 as Las Cruces College, New Mexico State University (NMSU) was designated the state's land-grant institution in 1889 and was renamed New Mexico College of Agriculture and Mechanic Arts. In 1960, the present name was adopted. NMSU has been accredited since 1926 by the North Central Association of Colleges and Schools as a degree-granting institution and now has 16,174 students from all fifty states and seventy-one countries. In addition to its six undergraduate colleges, the University has a graduate college that offers fifty master's, three educational specialists, and twenty-four doctoral major areas. NMSU is ranked as one of 151 top research universities in the nation by the Carnegie Foundation for the Advancement of Teaching.

University housing is available on campus in residence halls for men and women, family housing, and fraternity and sorority houses. The residence halls have space available for 2,500 single students, and housing assignments are made on a date-priority basis; more than half of the rooms are reserved for incoming freshmen. Students are encouraged to apply early for housing.

There are approximately 200 professional, social, academic, religious, and service groups on campus as well as an eighteen-hole golf course, lighted tennis courts, indoor and outdoor swimming pools, playing fields, and a track surfaced with rubberized asphalt. The activity center has dance rooms, a climbing wall, weight-training equipment, an indoor track, and basketball, volleyball, and racquetball courts. NMSU has one of the best intramural programs in the country, offering more than fifty events. New Mexico State is a member of the NCAA Sun Belt Conference. Men's teams compete in baseball, basketball, cross-country, football, golf, and tennis. Women's teams compete in basketball, cross-country, golf, softball, swimming, tennis, track, and volleyball.

Location

Las Cruces, the second-largest city in New Mexico, is a pleasant blend of its tricultural (Indian, Spanish, and Anglo) past and modern technology. The space shuttle *Columbia* landed at nearby White Sands Missile Range, just 45 miles from Old Mesilla, the stately Spanish plaza where the Gadsden Purchase was signed in 1853. The Organ Mountains are to the east, and the Rio Grande is to the west. Bordering the city are fertile farmlands. Only an hour and a half away are the ski resorts of Cloudcroft and Ruidoso, and Albuquerque is just a 3-hour drive. The largest cities on the border—El Paso, Texas, and Juárez, Mexico—are 40 minutes away. With an average of 350 days of sunshine a year, residents enjoy year-round biking, hiking, swimming, golfing, rock climbing, camping, and sunset strolls.

Majors and Degrees

New Mexico State University's main campus offers undergraduate degrees through the Colleges of Agriculture and Home Economics, Arts and Sciences, Business Administration and Economics, Education, Engineering, and Health and Social Services. The following majors are offered, leading to the bachelor's degree: accounting; agricultural and extension education; agricultural biology; agricultural economics and agricultural business; agronomy; animal science; anthropology; art; athletic training education; biochemistry; biology; business computer systems; chemical engineering; chemistry; city and regional planning; civil engineering; clothing, textiles, and fashion merchandising; communication studies; communication disorders; community health; computer science; criminal justice; dance; early childhood education; economics; electrical/computer engineering; elementary education; engineering physics; engineering technology; English; environmental and occupational health; environmental science; family and child science; family and consumer sciences education; finance; foreign languages; general agriculture; general business; geography; geology; government; history; horticulture; hotel, restaurant, and tourism management; human nutrition and food science; individualized studies; industrial engineering; international business; journalism and mass communication; kinesiology; management; marketing; mathematics; mechanical engineering; microbiology; music; music education; nursing; philosophy; physics; psychology; rangeland resources; recreational areas management; secondary education (with endorsements in bilingual education, business education, foreign languages, general science, language arts, mathematics, physical education, and social studies; social work; sociology; soil science; special education; studio art; surveying; theater arts; and wildlife science. Preprofessional programs are offered in chiropractic, dentistry, forestry, law, medicine, pharmacy, physical therapy, and veterinary medicine. Two-year associate degree programs are offered in arts, criminal justice, and prebusiness.

Academic Programs

New Mexico State offers courses during two semesters and two 6-week summer sessions. NMSU awards both a designated and an undesignated associate degree following completion of 66 semester credits. The last 15–30 credits, depending on the requirements of the college in which the degree is pursued, must be completed at NMSU or one of its branches. To earn the bachelor's degree, students must meet the University's basic skill requirements in English and mathematics, successfully complete general education or constant courses as required in their particular college, complete a minimum of 128 credits (including at least 55 in upper-division courses), and have a cumulative grade point average of 2.0 or higher. Students may receive credit for scores of 3, 4, or 5 on the Advanced Placement examinations of the College Board. A total of 30 credits may be obtained through the College-Level Examination Program general or subject examinations.

An honors program is available to entering freshmen with a minimum ACT composite score of 26. Students must maintain a minimum GPA of 3.3 in the freshman year and 3.5 in the sophomore, junior, and senior years. Students who attain higher overall GPAs and complete 18 credits of honors work are eligible to graduate with University Honors or with Distinction in University Honors.

Through the Distance Education program, students can opt to take some courses and degrees online.

Off-Campus Programs

NMSU enjoys a national reputation for its Cooperative Education Program. Elements of the program include voluntary participation, three types of work-study schedules, and possible academic credit. Through the National Student Exchange, students who qualify may study at any of 150 colleges and universities across the nation for credit while paying NMSU tuition. Students can explore a world beyond New Mexico and the United States by choosing to study abroad for a year, a semester, or even just a month.

Academic Facilities

Although New Mexico State's campus is one of the largest in the world (5,800 acres), the academic, administrative, and residence buildings are conveniently located close together. Each undergraduate college has a research division, and there are various specialized research institutes on campus, including the Southwest Technology Development Institute and the Water Resources Institute. More than 1.6 million volumes and almost 6,000 current periodicals are available in the two libraries, along with hundreds of thousands of government documents, maps, and archival materials. The library is open approximately 95 hours a week and provides a number of special services, including computerized literature searching and interlibrary loans.

Costs

Expenses for the 2003–04 academic year (two semesters) were as follows: tuition and fees, $3372 for New Mexico residents and $11,550 for out-of-state residents; room and board, $4632, depending on the housing and meal plan selected; and books and supplies, $380. Travel and personal expenses are additional. (All charges are subject to change.)

Financial Aid

The University has a broad financial aid program for students, including scholarships (academic need and non-need, activity, and athletic). Tuition scholarships are awarded on the basis of ACT scores and GPA; in-state recipients may be granted a full waiver of tuition and fees, while out-of-state recipients may be eligible to pay in-state tuition. Students wishing to apply for scholarships should complete the NMSU scholarship application, available from the Financial Aid Office. All scholarship applicants must be admitted to the University by March 1 to be given consideration. NMSU participates in all federal programs, including the Federal Work-Study, Federal Perkins Loan, Federal Stafford Student Loan, Federal Pell Grant, and Federal Supplemental Educational Opportunity Grant programs, and in New Mexico state financial aid programs. Students may apply for these by completing the Free Application for Federal Student Aid (FAFSA) and must meet the March 1 deadline to be eligible. In the 2002–03 academic year, 80 percent of the enrolled undergraduate students received aid. A wide variety of part-time jobs for students are available on campus; students should contact the Placement Office for further information.

Faculty

New Mexico State employs 665 full-time faculty members, 84 percent of whom hold doctoral degrees. The student-faculty ratio is 19:1. There is generally no distinction between the graduate and undergraduate faculty members, many of whom are engaged in research projects. They consistently receive teaching and research awards, and many are nationally and internationally renowned. A faculty member from the department in which a student is majoring serves as the student's academic adviser. No major classes are taught by graduate students.

Student Government

There are six college councils that work closely with the dean of each college. The Associated Students of New Mexico State University is the student governing body and has an annual budget of approximately $700,000 (of which about $100,000 is for campus entertainment). The *Student Handbook* describes students' rights and responsibilities.

Admission Requirements

Prospective freshmen should apply during their senior year. Course work in high school must include 4 units in English, 2 of which must be in composition (1 of these must be at the junior/senior level); 3 units of mathematics, from algebra I, algebra II, geometry, trigonometry, or advanced math; 2 units of science beyond general science; and 1 unit of a foreign language or the fine arts. Students are eligible for regular admission if they graduate from a regionally accredited high school with the previously listed courses, have submitted an ACT or an SAT score, and meet one of the following conditions: (1) have a cumulative high school GPA of 2.5 (on a 4.0 scale) or higher, or (2) an ACT composite score of 21 or higher, or (3) a cumulative high school GPA of at least 2.0 and an ACT composite score of at least 20. If a student has met all but one of the high school course requirements previously listed and has a minimum GPA of 2.25 and an ACT score of 20 or higher, he or she is also eligible for regular admission. Once admitted, students receive an invitation to one of the summer orientation/registration programs.

Transfer students must have a cumulative transfer grade point average of 2.0 (on a 4.0 scale) or higher. Transfer students who have not completed 30 credits must meet the freshman requirements. Official transcripts must be sent from each college or university attended. Transfer students who were suspended from the institution previously attended are not considered for admission until the terms of the suspension have been met.

Application and Information

The application and all required materials must be received by the Office of Admissions prior to registering for course work. New Mexico State has a rolling admission policy.

Inquiries should be addressed to:

Angela Mora-Riley
Director of Admissions, MSC 3A
Box 30001
New Mexico State University
Las Cruces, New Mexico 88003-8001
Telephone: 505-646-3121
800-662-6678 (toll-free; for admissions only)
E-mail: admissions@nmsu.edu
World Wide Web: http://www.nmsu.edu

NEW SCHOOL BACHELOR OF ARTS
NEW SCHOOL UNIVERSITY

NEW YORK, NEW YORK

The University

New School University, formerly the New School for Social Research, was founded in 1919 by a small group of renowned American scholars and intellectuals, including John Dewey, Alvin Johnson, and Thorstein Veblen. They sought to develop a new kind of academic institution—a school of advanced adult education that would be free to address the real problems facing society in the twentieth century. Since 1944, the New School has offered adult students the opportunity to pursue course work in the liberal arts leading to the Bachelor of Arts degree. Established to meet the needs of students returning to college after World War II, the New School Bachelor of Arts Program allowed working adults to complete an undergraduate degree part-time or full-time during either the day or the evening. The approach was new, but very much in keeping with the commitment of the New School to adult education and to the idea of learning as a lifelong endeavor.

The student body, numbering approximately 628, represents a particularly diverse group of individuals. While a significant number of students attend full-time, an even larger group attends on a part-time basis. The New York metropolitan area accounts for three quarters of the student body; international students and students from other states make up the remainder. Although the majority are in their twenties and thirties, students of all ages are present. Most students hold jobs while attending school and many have family responsibilities.

The New School has long been a home for leading artists, educators, and public figures. The New School was the first institution of higher learning to offer college-level courses in such "new" fields as psychoanalysis, taught by Freud's disciple, Sandor Ferenczi in 1926; African-American culture and history, taught by W. E. B. DuBois in 1948; and women's studies, offered by Gerda Lerner in 1962. It also was one of the first colleges or universities to offer instruction in art forms that flourished during the twentieth century, such as photography, film, jazz, and modern dance. Among the world-famous artists and performers who have taught at the New School are Martha Graham, Berenice Abbott, Aaron Copland, Frank Lloyd Wright, and Thomas Hart Benton. Today, many noted scholars and creative artists are among the hundreds of instructors who teach at the New School.

The New School, the founding division of New School University, offers graduate programs in media studies, international affairs, and creative writing in addition to the Bachelor of Arts Program.

The other academic divisions of New School University are the Graduate Faculty of Political and Social Science (founded in 1933 as the University in Exile), which grants M.A. and Ph.D. degrees; the Milano Graduate School of Management and Urban Policy, which awards the M.S. and Ph.D. degrees; Parsons School of Design, with programs in the fine arts and design on the undergraduate and graduate levels; Eugene Lang College, an undergraduate degree program for traditional-age students; the Mannes School of Music, with undergraduate and graduate programs in performance and theory (including both classical and jazz); and the Actors Studio School of Dramatic Arts, which offers an MFA in acting, directing, and playwriting. In 2003–04, the University served approximately 20,000 students (part-time and full-time) annually.

Location

The New School is located in New York City's Greenwich Village, which historically has been a center for intellectual and artistic life. Over and above the resources of Greenwich Village, New York City offers virtually unlimited cultural, artistic, recreational, and intellectual resources.

Majors and Degrees

The New School offers the Bachelor of Arts degree in liberal arts. There are no majors, but formal concentrations are available in democracy and cultural pluralism, the city, film, literature, media studies, psychology, and writing. Most students develop individualized concentrations in a wide variety of academic fields as well as in interdisciplinary areas. In addition, professional certificates are offered in the following fields: creative arts therapies, English language teaching, and film production.

Academic Program

Fully integrated with the curriculum of the New School, the Bachelor of Arts serves a broad range of adult students who are committed to learning in an environment that is flexible and intellectually challenging. While three quarters of the 120 credits applied toward the degree must be in liberal arts, students are encouraged to develop a program appropriate to their own needs. Choices are made from more than 1,000 courses offered each semester in the humanities, social and natural sciences, fine arts, performing arts, foreign languages, writing, communication, and business. In consultation with a faculty adviser, students plan a program of study that enables them to explore their intellectual and career objectives. The primary organizing principle is determined by the individual interests, talents, and goals of each student. Within this context, students may elect structured concentrations of course work in a particular field or may design their own course of study.

Credit may be awarded for prior learning based on a portfolio assessment process.

Most classes are small, with 15 to 25 students, and are conducted through a combination of lecture and discussion. Classes are scheduled during a variety of times, allowing adults with work and family responsibilities to choose class times that are convenient for them. Classes are offered every weekday, beginning at 9 a.m. and continuing until 9:30 p.m., with the majority scheduled in the late afternoon and early evening. Online courses are also available. The New School operates on a semester system, with fifteen-week terms during the fall and spring and an intensive summer session that begins in early June and ends in July.

For students planning to go on to a graduate program at the university, the New School offers an accelerated bachelor's/master's option. Students may apply for bachelor's/master's status upon completion of 60 college credits and at least one semester of satisfactory work in the Bachelor of Arts Program. Students admitted to an accelerated degree program may apply up to 12 graduate credits toward the 120 undergraduate credits required to earn the B.A. degree. These same graduate credits apply toward completion of the graduate degree when the student matriculates in the designated master's program.

Accelerated B.A./M.A. options are available in anthropology, economics, historical studies, international affairs, liberal studies, media studies, philosophy, political science, psychology, and sociology.

Accelerated B.A./M.S. options are available in health services management, human resources management, nonprofit management, and urban policy analysis.

Off-Campus Programs

In addition to traditional classes, the New School offers an alternative approach to adult education through New School Online University (NSOU). Using asynchronous computer conferencing, students can participate in their classes any time and any place they have access to the Internet. All students matriculating in the Bachelor of Arts Program can include NSOU courses in their programs. Students living outside the New York area who meet special admissions requirements can take all of their courses through NSOU.

Qualified students are also able to participate in independent study, internships, and study-abroad programs.

Academic Facilities

The Bachelor of Arts Program is situated in the main academic center at 66 West 12th Street.

New School Bachelor of Arts students have full access to the Raymond Fogelman Library (New School/Graduate Faculty), the Adam and Sophie Gimble Design Library (New School/Parsons), the Cooper Union for the Advancement of Science and Art Library (Cooper Union), and the Elmer Bobst Library (New York University). Together, these libraries house approximately 3 million volumes that cover all the traditional liberal arts disciplines and the fine arts.

New School Bachelor of Arts students also have access to additional university facilities that include a University Computing Center with both Macintosh and IBM-compatible computers, laser printers, and software; a 500-seat auditorium; various galleries; darkroom and filmmaking facilities; and studios for the fine arts as well as classrooms and faculty offices.

Costs

Tuition for the 2004–05 academic year is $696 per credit. Students pay a $100 registration fee each semester, and there is a student services fee of $15.

Financial Aid

B.A. degree candidates enrolled for 6 or more credits are eligible to apply for federal, state, and institutional aid. All applicants must file the Free Application for Federal Student Aid (FAFSA). The Title IV code for the New School is 002780. Students may begin the process of applying for financial aid prior to admission. Financial aid awards are made on a rolling basis after the applicant has been accepted into the program. Institutional aid is awarded on the basis of both need and merit. Financial aid is renewable each year as long as need continues and students maintain satisfactory academic standing.

Faculty

Instructors at the New School come from diverse fields within and outside the field of education. They all share one common motivation: teaching what they are most interested in and what they consider most valuable to know. In addition to academic scholars, many are working professionals who bring to the classroom the benefit of their experience. Writing workshops are taught by published authors, film production workshops by filmmakers, theater arts courses by actors and directors, and business courses by professionals with substantial business and corporate experience. The combination of interest and professional competence makes for a rich classroom experience.

Student advising is an essential feature of the Bachelor of Arts Program. A small number of instructors in the humanities and social sciences hold special appointments as core faculty members. These faculty members work closely with students in planning the students' academic programs and are available throughout the year for educational advising.

Student Government

Students are encouraged to participate in the governance of the program and the School in a number of ways. Student advisory committees serve at the university level. Students are invited to serve on many university committees, such as diversity, food services, library, and student life.

Admission Requirements

The New School welcomes applications from individuals who have the maturity necessary to be responsible for their own learning process and who can demonstrate their ability to work successfully in an intellectually rigorous and challenging environment. Most applicants have completed at least one year of liberal arts study (30 credits) at an accredited college or university. Applicants who are 24 years old or older and have fewer than 30 transfer credits may apply for special admission. Applicants who live at a distance from the New School and plan to complete their course work through NSOU must have completed at least 60 credits at an accredited college or university prior to admission. All applicants must submit transcripts from each college previously attended; an application form, including essays and a statement of purpose; and a nonrefundable $40 application fee. An interview, either in person or by telephone if the applicant lives at a distance, is required of all applicants.

Application and Information

Application deadlines are August 1 for the fall semester and December 1 for the spring semester. Admissions decisions are made as applications become complete. It is the responsibility of the applicant to ensure receipt of all materials by the stated deadline. A Bachelor of Arts Program brochure and the *New School Bulletin* will be sent upon request. Information sessions are held approximately once a month.

For further information, students may contact:

Office of Admissions
New School Bachelor of Arts Program
New School University
66 West 12th Street, Room 401
New York, New York 10011
Telephone: 212-229-5630
800-862-5039 (toll-free)
E-mail: nsadmissions@newschool.edu
World Wide Web: http://www.nsu.newschool.edu/ba/

NEW YORK SCHOOL OF INTERIOR DESIGN

NEW YORK, NEW YORK

The School

The New York School of Interior Design (NYSID) is an independent, coeducational, nonprofit college accredited by NASAD. It was established in 1916 by architect Sherrill Whiton and chartered by the Board of Regents of the University of the State of New York in 1924. Throughout its history, the School has devoted all of its resources to a single field of study—interior design—and has played a significant role in the development of the interior design profession. Enrollment is approximately 700.

NYSID continually updates its curriculum to reflect the many changes taking place in interior design. Today's students learn not only the colors and materials appropriate to period residential interiors, but also how to design hospitals and restaurants and offices with barrier-free access. Whether learning the importance of historic preservation or the latest programs in computer-aided design, NYSID students learn a wide range of skills and techniques taught by faculty members who work in the field. The area's professional design studios, art and antique shops, showrooms, and museums are all an exciting part of the college's "campus."

The atmosphere of the college is cosmopolitan, not only because of its excellent location but also because it attracts students from all areas of the United States and abroad. International students make up approximately 10 percent of the student population. Students also transfer from other colleges in order to obtain a more professional, career-directed education.

Because of its select faculty and established reputation, the School continues to maintain a close relationship with the interior design industry. This provides an excellent means for students to develop associations that offer opportunities to move into the profession after completing their degree program at NYSID.

In addition to the three programs in interior design listed below, NYSID also offers a postprofessional Master of Fine Arts (M.F.A.) degree in interior design.

Location

The New York School of Interior Design is located on Manhattan's upper East Side, where many of the major interior design studios are located. Many of the world's most important museums, galleries, and showrooms are close by, most within walking distance. The city is world-renowned for its cultural activities, architecture, historic districts, and cosmopolitan urban experience. The college can be reached easily by bus, subway, train, and car.

Majors and Degrees

The New York School of Interior Design offers three programs in interior design: a four-year Bachelor of Fine Arts (B.F.A.) degree accredited by FIDER, a two-year Associate in Applied Science (A.A.S.) degree, and a 24-credit nondegree Basic Interior Design Program.

Academic Program

The New York School of Interior Design is a single-major college. It devotes all of its resources to providing a comprehensive education in interior design, and the carefully organized curriculum is constantly evaluated by professionals in the field.

The various academic programs compose an integrated curriculum covering interior design concepts; history of art, architecture, interiors, and furniture; technical and communication skills, materials and methods, philosophy and theory; and professional design procedures and design problem solving.

The Basic Interior Design Program consists of a 24-credit required sequence of foundation courses in which all students enroll. These courses provide a general, cultural, and professional introduction to the field of interior design. Although completion of the Basic Interior Design Program may be the major goal for some, for most students it serves as the foundation for matriculation into the degree programs.

The A.A.S. degree program provides the minimum educational requirement to become a certified interior designer in New York State. The 66-credit program includes professional, design, and liberal arts courses.

The 132-credit Bachelor of Fine Arts degree program provides the education that, with practical experience, enables the graduate to take qualifying exams for interior design certification in many states and to join national and local professional associations. Studies focus on the development of a broad array of technical skills, conceptual analysis, creative problem solving, and relevant cultural developments. Students are required to take 32 credits of liberal arts courses in addition to 100 credits of professional design-related courses.

The program planning is flexible and permits students to take courses on a full-time or part-time basis during the day, evening, and on Saturday. The School maintains an active job placement service. Students may be placed in a wide variety of positions that reflect the full spectrum of job opportunities in the interior design profession.

Academic Facilities

The NYSID campus occupies two buildings on Manhattan's Upper East Side. The college has a first-rate physical plant with light-filled studios; a unique lighting laboratory; a centralized computer facility for computer-aided design (CAD); a large atelier for independent work furnished with drafting tables, computers, and a materials collection for use in projects; a lecture hall and seminar rooms; a well-stocked bookstore; and a handsome auditorium. The library contains more than 12,000 volumes devoted to design, 100 periodical subscriptions, a product literature collection, and a select collection of 35 mm slides illustrating the history of interior design and decorative arts.

Costs

Tuition for 2004–05 is $580 per credit, plus a $100 registration/technology fee each semester. There are additional costs for supplies and textbooks, depending on the courses for which a student registers. Typical full-time expenses for the first year (exclusive of room and board, which the college does not provide, and personal expenses) are as follows: tuition, $18,560 (16 credits per semester); registration fees, $200; and supplies and textbooks, $1000.

Financial Aid

The New York School of Interior Design makes every effort to provide assistance to students with financial need. Several institutional scholarships are available for students who meet the criteria. Students are encouraged to apply for the New York State Tuition Assistance Program (TAP—for New York State residents only), the Federal Pell Grant, and Federal Education Loans. The college also participates in the Federal College Work-Study Program, which offers opportunities for on-campus employment.

Faculty

The college's programs are supported by an excellent and dedicated faculty of 85. In addition to teaching, faculty members have active professional careers in interior design, architecture, lighting design, fine arts, furniture and fabric design, history, psychology, decorative arts, law, and appraising.

Student Government

The college has an active student chapter of the American Society of Interior Designers (ASID). ASID organizes lectures, tours, workshops, and other events throughout the school year, providing an inside view of the interior design industry.

Admission Requirements

All applicants must submit an application, an official secondary school transcript, SAT I or ACT scores, and two letters of recommendation. Applicants to degree programs must meet the visual requirements by providing a portfolio or sketchbook described in the catalog; transfer students must also submit college transcripts.

Interviews are recommended for all applicants.

International applicants should contact the college's International Student Adviser for assistance in applying.

Application and Information

Admission decisions are made on a rolling basis. However, for processing purposes, it is recommended that the Admissions Office receive an application for fall admission by March 1. An application for spring admission should be received by November 1. Applicants are notified of the Admission Committee's decision by mail shortly after all required documents have been received and visual requirements fulfilled.

Inquiries and applications should be directed to:

Director of Admissions
New York School of Interior Design
170 East 70th Street
New York, New York 10021-5110
Telephone: 212-472-1500 Ext. 204
800-33NYSID (toll-free)
Fax: 212-472-1867
E-mail: admissions@nysid.edu
World Wide Web: http://www.nysid.edu

The campus of the New York School of Interior Design is centered on its building at 170 East 70th Street in the Upper East Side Historic District.

NEW YORK UNIVERSITY

NEW YORK, NEW YORK

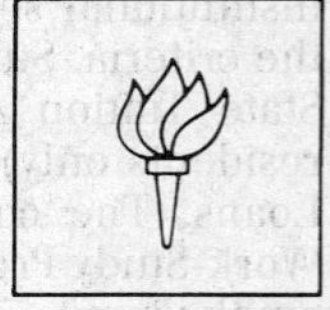

The University

New York University (NYU) was founded in 1831 by Albert Gallatin, Secretary of the Treasury under Thomas Jefferson; he believed that the place for a university was not in "the seclusion of cloistered halls but in the throbbing heart of a great city." NYU draws top students from every state and more than 140 countries. The distinguished academic atmosphere attracts the teachers, and the teachers and the atmosphere together attract the students who are capable of benefiting from both. Within three years of graduation, 80 percent of NYU's students go on to postbaccalaureate work. Of those who apply for admission to medical school, 85 percent are accepted, placing NYU well above the national average. The faculty includes world-famous scholars, researchers, and artists, among them Nobel laureates, winners of the Pulitzer Prize, and members of the National Science Foundation. NYU is a member of the prestigious Association of American Universities. A study sponsored by the National Science Foundation placed NYU among the top four universities in the country in the number of "leading intellectuals" on the faculty. Full professors teach on both the graduate and undergraduate levels. Seven undergraduate divisions provide extensive offerings in a wide range of subjects: more than 2,500 courses in 160 major fields are available to NYU's full-time undergraduates. The average class size is under 30, and the faculty-student ratio is 1:12—benefits generally associated with a much smaller institution.

NYU's residence hall program is an important aspect of the total educational experience. Approximately 11,000 undergraduate students live in twenty-one University residence halls. All freshmen who request housing on their admission application and meet all deadlines are guaranteed housing accommodations during all their years of undergraduate study. Freshmen are not required to live on campus, and many students live in private apartments off campus.

The traditions of campus life—more than 250 clubs, eleven fraternities and eleven sororities, and athletics and other activities—are very much a part of the University. Students have the opportunity to write for the campus newspaper and to work with the University's radio station, WNYU-FM. The Jerome S. Coles Sports and Recreation Center and the Palladium Athletic Facility serve the recreational needs of all students. Coles provides the setting for a full intramural sports program, and is home to NYU's twenty intercollegiate teams. NYU and eight other private, urban research universities have formed a varsity league, the University Athletic Association. The athletic program includes men's basketball, fencing, golf, soccer, swimming and diving, tennis, track and cross-country, volleyball, and wrestling and women's basketball, cross-country, fencing, soccer, swimming and diving, tennis, track, and volleyball.

Location

NYU's undergraduate center is located in historic Greenwich Village, which is virtually an extension of the University. Greenwich Village, traditionally a community of artists and intellectuals, is famous for its contributions to the fine arts, literature, and drama and for its small-scale, European style of living. NYU's campus is within minutes of off-Broadway drama and dance, boutiques, art galleries, coffeehouses, restaurants, clubs, bookstores, record stores, Little Italy, Chinatown, and world-renowned museums and libraries. Intellectual stimulation abounds. Through course work and through outside activities, students can enjoy all of the advantages of New York City. As an international center of finance, culture, and communications, New York City offers unmatched educational, internship, and social opportunities. NYU's campus is perhaps one campus in America that could not be mistaken for any other.

Majors and Degrees

The College of Arts and Science awards B.A. and B.S. degrees in Africana studies; ancient studies; anthropology; anthropology-linguistics; Arabic; art history; Asian/Pacific/American studies; astronomy; biochemistry; biology; chemistry; Chinese; cinema studies; classical civilization and Hellenic studies; classics; classical civilizations-anthropology; classics (fine arts); comparative literature; computer science; creative writing; dramatic literature, theater history, and the cinema; earth and environmental science; East Asian languages; East Asian studies; economics; economics and computer science; economics and mathematics; education; engineering (chemical, civil, computer, electrical, environmental, and mechanical); English; English and American literature; European studies; fine arts; French; French and linguistics; gender and sexuality studies; German; German and linguistics; Greek; Hebrew language and literature; Hellenic studies; history; Irish studies; international studies; Italian; Italian and linguistics; Japanese; Jewish history and civilization; journalism and mass communication; Korean; language and mind; Latin; Latin American studies; Latin and Greek; law and society; linguistics; literature in translation; Luso-Brazilian language and literature; mathematics; mathematics and computer science; medieval and Renaissance studies; metropolitan studies; Middle Eastern languages; Middle Eastern studies; music; neural science; Persian; philosophy; physics; politics; psychology; public policy; religious studies; Romance languages; Russian; social work; sociology; Spanish; Spanish and linguistics; Turkish; urban design and architecture studies; West European studies; and women's studies. Preprofessional programs are available in dentistry, law, medicine, optometry, and podiatry. A B.S./B.E. program in engineering, a seven-year B.A./D.D.S. program, and an eight-year B.A./M.D. program are available.

Stern School of Business awards the B.S. degree in accounting, actuarial science, economics, finance, information systems, international business, management and organizational behavior, marketing, and statistics and operations research. An accelerated B.S./M.P.A. program and a five-year B.S./M.S. program in statistics and operations research are available.

The School of Education awards the B.S. degree in arts professions (with majors in studio art and educational theater), communications studies, education (with majors in early childhood and childhood/special education and secondary education with a teaching specialization in English, foreign language, mathematics, science, or social studies), health and nursing (with majors in nursing; nutrition and food studies; speech-language pathology and audiology for teachers of speech and language disorders; and applied psychological studies, for juniors and transfer students only), and music (with majors in classical and jazz instrumental, music business, music technology, music education, music theory and composition, piano, and voice).

Tisch School of the Arts awards the B.F.A. degree in cinema studies (film history, theory, and criticism), dance, theater (acting, musical theater, directing, and technical management), dramatic writing, film and television (film, television, radio, and animation), photography and imaging, and recorded music. The School of Social Work awards the B.S. degree in social work. The Gallatin School of Individualized Study awards the B.A. degree. The School of Continuing and Professional Studies offers a two-year liberal arts (general studies) program leading to the Associate in Arts degree, the B.S. degree in sports management and leisure studies, the B.S. degree in hotel and tourism management, and the B.A. degree for adults.

Academic Program

Requirements for graduation vary among departments and schools. A liberal arts core curriculum is an integral part of all areas of concentration. The baccalaureate degree requires completion of at least 128 credits. The University calendar is organized on the traditional semester system, including two 6-week summer sessions. Some divisions offer part-time programs during the day and evening and on weekends.

Off-Campus Programs

Through its seven undergraduate colleges, the University administers a number of programs abroad, including those at NYU sites in Paris, Madrid, Florence, London, Prague, and Ghana. Exchange programs with several historically black colleges in the U.S. and eighteen exchange programs with urban universities around the world are also offered.

Academic Facilities

NYU's Bobst Library, one of the largest open-stack research libraries in the world, has more than 40 miles of open stacks housing some 3 million volumes. Among the collections in Bobst are the Avery R. Fisher Center for Music and Media, the Microfilm Center, and the largest official depository of United Nations records and publications outside of the UN itself. Bobst is one of eight NYU libraries that together hold more than 4.5 million volumes. La Maison Française, the Deutsches Haus, the Lewis L. and Loretta Brennen Glucksman Ireland House, the Hagop Kervorkian Center for Near Eastern Studies, the Casa Italiana, the King Juan Carlos I of Spain Center, and the Lillian Vernon Center for International Affairs broaden the range of international programs on campus. The Grey Art Gallery and Study Center, the University's fine arts museum, presents six or seven innovative exhibitions each year that encompass all aspects of the visual arts.

Costs

For 2003–04, tuition and fees cost $28,496, and average room and board costs were $10,910. Books and supplies cost about $450, and personal expenses total between $500 and $1000.

Financial Aid

Financial aid at NYU comes from many sources. All students are encouraged to apply for financial assistance or one of NYU's innovative financing plans. Seventy-five percent of NYU's full-time undergraduates receive financial assistance. Each year more than 2,700 entering freshmen are awarded scholarships based on academic promise and/or financial need. The University may offer a package of aid that includes scholarships or grants, loans, or work-study programs. NYU requires the submission of the Free Application for Federal Student Aid (FAFSA). The deadline for filing this financial aid form is February 15 for the fall semester and November 1 for the spring semester. An estimated financial aid is available to early decision admitted students. The financial aid application is included in the admissions packet or online at http://www.nyu.edu/financial.aid.

Faculty

NYU employs 3,891 faculty members (1,815 full-time and 2,076 part-time). Ninety-nine percent have the doctoral degree. The faculty-student ratio is 1:12. The faculty devotes equal time to teaching and research. All faculty members keep office hours, and each student meets regularly with a faculty adviser. Seventy percent of the faculty reside on campus. Faculty honors include 137 Guggenheim Fellowships, 3 Nobel and Crafoord prizes, 12 MacArthur Foundation Awards, 3 Pulitzer Prizes, 7 Lasker Awards, 22 elected to the National Academy of Sciences, 19 elected to the American Academy of Arts and Sciences, and numerous Tony, Obie, and Academy awards.

Student Government

Each of NYU's schools and colleges has a student council, organized by its respective students, that represents those students. The University Senate, the major policymaking body for all matters relating to academic concerns not delegated to the separate schools and colleges, has 20 student members.

Admission Requirements

Admission is highly selective. The Committee on Admissions carefully considers each student's high school record, recommendations from guidance counselors and teachers, and scores on standardized tests (the SAT I or ACT). NYU actively seeks students who have a variety of interests, talents, and goals and looks for a diversity of social and economic backgrounds. Consideration is also given to participation in meaningful school, community, and work activities. Portfolios, creative materials, or auditions are required for some majors. Applicants to the premedical, predental, and pre-engineering programs typically have 1 unit each from at least two of the major sciences—physics, chemistry, and biology. It is recommended that applicants submit three SAT II Subject Test scores: English writing and two other examinations. Applicants to the B.A./M.D. program must submit scores from the SAT II Subject Tests.

Application and Information

For entrance in the fall term, the application for admission—including all supporting credentials—must be received by November 1 (early decision freshman candidates), January 15 (freshmen), or April 1 (transfer students). For entrance in the spring term (transfer students only), the application materials must be received by November 1. For entrance in the summer (transfer students only), the application materials should be received by April 1. Applications for admission received after these dates are considered only if space remains. Official notification of fall admission is made on April 1 and on a rolling basis thereafter. A campus tour or an appointment for an information session can be arranged by calling 212-998-4524 or on the Web site (listed below).

Office of Undergraduate Admissions
New York University
22 Washington Square North
New York, New York 10011
Telephone: 212-998-4500
World Wide Web: http://admissions.nyu.edu

NIAGARA UNIVERSITY

NIAGARA UNIVERSITY, NEW YORK

The University

Niagara University (NU), founded in 1856, is a private, independent university rooted in a Catholic and Vincentian tradition. The suburban 160-acre campus combines the old and new; both ivy-covered buildings and modern architectural structures are among its thirty-three buildings. The University is easily accessible from every major city in the eastern and midwestern United States via the New York State Thruway, Buffalo International Airport, and rail and bus service.

There are 2,600 undergraduate and 800 graduate students enrolled at Niagara. A large percentage of these students take advantage of the more than seventy extracurricular and cocurricular activities offered. Volunteer work in the community is popular among the students and enhances community relations. Students work with numerous organizations including: Habitat for Humanity, Big Brothers/Big Sisters, Maranatha (a shelter for homeless men), and the Skating Association for the Blind and Handicapped. University teams compete on the Division I level and are members of the NCAA, the Eastern College Athletic Conference, and the Metro Atlantic Athletic Conference. Intercollegiate sports include baseball, basketball, cross-country, golf, ice hockey, lacrosse, soccer, softball, swimming and diving, tennis, and volleyball. Club sports include hockey, lacrosse, martial arts, and rugby. The Kiernan Center offers a variety of sports and recreational facilities, including a multipurpose gymnasium, a swimming and diving pool, an indoor track, racquetball courts, free-weight and Nautilus rooms, and aerobics rooms. There are several outdoor athletic fields and basketball and tennis courts.

Special student services include the Health Center, which provides inpatient and outpatient care during the day; the Learning Center, which provides free tutoring services; and the Career Development Office, which offers professional and career counseling. Other services include counseling, orientation, academic planning, career planning, and job placement.

Niagara University's housing accommodations include five residence halls, a grouping of four small cottages, and a student apartment complex. Both coed and single-gender accommodations are available.

The University offers graduate studies in business, counseling, criminal justice, and education.

Location

Niagara University is situated on Monteagle Ridge overlooking the gorge of the Niagara River, which connects the two Great Lakes of Erie and Ontario. Niagara's suburban campus setting is just a few miles from the world-famous Niagara Falls. Millions of visitors view the scenic majesty of the Falls every year. NU is located 20 minutes from Buffalo, which offers a variety of cultural events, sports, and entertainment opportunities. Toronto, Canada's largest metropolitan area, is just 90 minutes north of Niagara's campus and offers an even wider variety of experiences for NU students. In addition, the University is minutes away from the quaint village of Lewiston, New York, and the city of Niagara Falls, New York.

Majors and Degrees

The College of Arts and Sciences offers the Bachelor of Arts degree in chemistry, communication studies, English, French, history, international studies, liberal arts, life sciences, mathematics, philosophy, political science, psychology, religious studies, social sciences, sociology, and Spanish. The Bachelor of Science degree is awarded in biochemistry, biology (concentration in biotechnology), chemistry, computer and information sciences, criminal justice and criminology, mathematics, and social work. This division also offers the Bachelor of Fine Arts degree in theater studies. Preprofessional programs are offered in dentistry, law, medicine, pharmacology, pharmacy studies, veterinary medicine, and Army-ROTC. Pre-engineering is offered as a two-year A.S. degree transfer program. An Associate of Arts degree is available in liberal arts. In addition, Niagara offers an environmental studies concentration to supplement a degree in biology, chemistry, or political science. Enrichment courses in fine arts and languages are also available.

The College of Business Administration grants a B.B.A. and a combination B.B.A./M.B.A. degree in accounting. This division offers a B.S. degree in commerce with concentrations in economics and finance, general business, human resources, international business, management, marketing, and transportation and logistics. In addition, an A.A.S. degree can be earned in business. Through various innovative programs and courses, such as the cooperative education programs and the small-business institute, students have the opportunity to gain valuable work-related experience.

The College of Education offers bachelor's degree programs leading to New York State initial certification in early childhood (birth–grade 6), childhood (grades 1–6), childhood and middle childhood (grades 1–9), middle childhood and adolescence (grades 5–12), adolescence (grades 7–12), and certification for teaching students with disabilities (grades 1–6 childhood and grades 7–12 adolescence). All education majors pursue an academic concentration to establish expertise in one of the following subject areas: biology, business, chemistry, English, French, mathematics, social studies, and Spanish. Business education is offered only at grades 5–12. Most other states, and Puerto Rico, have reciprocity agreements with New York, meaning that an NU education would qualify education majors to teach in those states as well. In addition, the Canadian province of Ontario recognizes Niagara graduates as qualified for the Letter of Eligibility to teach in that province.

The College of Hospitality and Tourism Management provides a career-oriented curriculum leading to a B.S. degree in two specific areas: hotel and restaurant management (concentrations in hotel and restaurant planning and control, foodservice management, and hotel entrepreneurship) and tourism and recreation management (concentrations in tourism marketing and sports and recreation management). NU offered the world's first bachelor's degree in tourism when it was founded in 1968. NU's hotel and restaurant program, the second oldest in New York State, has the distinction of being the seventh program nationally to be accredited by the Accreditation Commission for Programs in Hospitality Administration by the Council of Hotel, Restaurant, and Institutional Education. The College introduces students to a comprehensive body of knowledge about the hotel, restaurant, tourism, and recreational areas and applies this knowledge to current industry challenges. The College requires that its students accumulate 800 hours of industry-related experience. These and other practical experiences offer NU students the knowledge necessary to advance in the field. Students work with industry leaders in classroom projects, join academic clubs and professional organizations, and participate in special field trips to trade shows and conventions and specially designed study-abroad experiences, making NU a national leader in the area.

For students who are undecided about which major to choose, Niagara University offers an Academic Exploration Program (AEP). AEP provides a structured opportunity for students to participate in a thorough, organized process of selecting a major that meets their academic talents and career goals.

Academic Program

Niagara University's curricula enable students to pursue their academic preferences and to complete courses that lead to proficiency in other academic areas. Courses that have been considered upper-division courses are available to all students. This provides students with the opportunity to avoid introductory and survey courses and permits motivated students to take advantage of more challenging courses early in their collegiate career. The honors program provides special academic opportunities that stimulate, encourage, and challenge participants. In addition, an accelerated three-year degree program is offered to qualified students.

Students pursuing a bachelor's degree must complete a total of 40 or 42 course units (120 or 126 hours) to meet graduation requirements. Niagara grants credit for successful scores on the Advanced Placement and College-Level Examination Program tests.

Internships, research, independent study, and cooperative education are available in many academic programs. An Army ROTC program is also offered.

The University operates on a two-semester plan (fall and spring). A comprehensive summer session offers a diversity of courses.

NU is fully accredited by the Middle States Association of Colleges and Schools. Its programs in the respective areas are accredited by the National Council for Accreditation of Teacher Education, AACSB International–The Association to Advance Collegiate Schools of Business, the Council on Social Work Education, and the chemistry department has the approval of the American Chemical Society. The travel, hotel, and restaurant administration program is accredited by the Commission for Programs in Hospitality Administration.

Off-Campus Programs

For those students who wish to study abroad, the University offers semester and summer programs in Chile, England, France, Ireland, Mexico, Spain, and Switzerland. Upon request, programs may be offered in other countries. NU is also affiliated with Western New York Consortium. Through this program, students may take courses at other colleges and universities and apply the credits to Niagra's graduation requirements.

Academic Facilities

The University's open-stack library includes 200,000 books and more than 7,500 periodicals in paper and electronic format. In addition, the library holds 78,833 units of microfilm. The library is housed in a modern facility that includes seating for 500 people, including individual study carrels. The library is affiliated with the Online Computer Library Center (OCLC) network.

The prize-winning Dunleavy Hall, outstanding both educationally and architecturally, includes a behavioral science laboratory, a computerized lecture hall, and TV production rooms. The University's facilities also include the Computer Center; DePaul Hall of Science; St. Vincent's Hall; the Kiernan Center, NU's athletic and recreation center; the Leary Theatre; the Castellani Art Museum; Bailo Hall, which houses the Office of Admissions; and the Dwyer Arena, a dual-rink ice hockey complex.

Costs

Tuition for 2003–04 was $16,700. Room and board (with a choice of meal plans) cost an additional $7670 per year. Fees were estimated at $680 per year. Niagara estimates that an additional $1500 per year is adequate for books, laundry, and other essentials, exclusive of travel to and from home.

Financial Aid

Ninety-eight percent of the incoming students who enrolled at NU received a financial aid package. They receive assistance in the form of merit scholarships, loans, grants, or campus employment. Students seeking financial aid should file the Free Application for Federal Student Aid (FAFSA). New York State residents should also file a Tuition Assistance Program (TAP) application.

Faculty

Niagara University has a dedicated, accessible faculty who genuinely cares about the academic and personal growth of their students. Their commitment to teaching is their primary concern. A student-faculty ratio of 16:1 and an average class size of 25 allow personal attention and classroom interaction.

Student Government

The Student Government represents all parts of the student body equally. It coordinates and legislates all student activities, serving as both liaison to and a participating member of the University as a whole. In addition, students serve on all major departmental committees and on the University Senate, which is the major advisory committee to the president and Board of Trustees.

Admission Requirements

The University welcomes men and women who have demonstrated aptitude and academic achievement at the high school level. Either SAT I or ACT test scores are required. International students are required to submit the results of their TOEFL examination. Interviews are recommended. Transfer students are accepted in any semester. (Transfer credit is evaluated individually by the dean of each division.) Students who complete high school in less than four years are eligible for early admission. Students may also apply under an early action program. Economically and educationally disadvantaged students from New York State are eligible to apply for admission through the Higher Educational Opportunity Program (HEOP).

Application and Information

Niagara operates on a rolling admission basis and adheres to the College Board Candidates Reply Date. A visit to the campus is encouraged, and overnight accommodations in a residence hall are available.

Information on all aspects of the University can be obtained by contacting the Office of Admissions.

Mike Konopski
Director of Admissions
639 Bailo Hall
Niagara University, New York 14109-2011
Telephone: 716-286-8700
800-462-2111 (toll-free)
Fax: 716-286-8710
E-mail: admissions@niagara.edu
World Wide Web: http://www.niagara.edu

The main campus of Niagara University.

NORTH CAROLINA AGRICULTURAL AND TECHNICAL STATE UNIVERSITY

GREENSBORO, NORTH CAROLINA

The University

North Carolina Agricultural and Technical State University was founded in 1891 as one of two land-grant institutions in the state. Originally, it was established to provide postsecondary education and training for black students. Today, the University is a comprehensive institution of higher education with an integrated faculty and student body, and it has been designated a constituent institution of the University of North Carolina, offering degrees at the baccalaureate, master's, and doctoral degree levels. Located on a 191-acre campus, the University has 110 buildings, including single-sex and coeducational residence halls. Of a total undergraduate population of 8,715, 4,165 students are men and 4,550 are women. The total population is approximately 10,030.

North Carolina Agricultural and Technical State University (A&T) provides outstanding academic programs through five undergraduate schools, two colleges, and a graduate school.

The mission of the University is to provide an intellectual setting in which students may find a sense of belonging, responsibility, and achievement that prepares them for roles of leadership and service in the communities where they will live and work. In this sense, the University serves as a laboratory for the development of excellence in teaching, research, and public service. As a result, A&T today stands as an example of well-directed higher education for all students.

Student life at the University is active and purposeful. The broad objective of the program provided by Student Development Services is to aid students in attaining the attitudes, understandings, insights, and skills that enable them to be socially competent. The program places special emphasis on campus relationships and experiences that complement formal instruction. Some of the services available are counseling, housing, health, and placement services. There is a University Student Union, and there are special services for international and minority students, veterans, and handicapped students. The University also provides a well-balanced program of activities to foster the moral, spiritual, cultural, and physical development of its students.

Location

Greensboro, North Carolina, is 300 miles south of Washington, D.C., and 349 miles north of Atlanta. It is readily accessible by air, bus, and automobile. The city offers a variety of cultural and recreational activities and facilities. These include sports events, concerts, bowling, boating, fishing, tennis, golf, and other popular forms of recreation. There are major shopping centers, churches, theaters, and medical facilities near the University. The heavy concentration of factories, service industries, government agencies, and shopping centers provides many job opportunities for students who desire part-time employment.

Majors and Degrees

North Carolina Agricultural and Technical State University grants the following degrees: Bachelor of Arts, Bachelor of Science, Bachelor of Fine Arts, Bachelor of Science in Nursing, and Bachelor of Social Work.

The School of Agriculture and Environmental Sciences offers programs in agricultural and biosystems engineering, agricultural economics, agricultural economics (agricultural business), agricultural education, agricultural education (agricultural extension), agricultural science–earth and environmental science (earth and environmental science, landscape horticulture design, plant science, soil science), agricultural science–natural resources (plant science), animal science, animal science (animal industry), child development, child development–early education and family studies B–K (teaching), family and consumer science (fashion merchandising and design), family and consumer science education, food and nutritional sciences, laboratory animal science, and landscape architecture.

In the College of Arts and Sciences, programs are available in applied mathematics, biology, biology–secondary education, broadcast production, chemistry, chemistry–secondary education, criminal justice, electronic/media journalism, English, English–secondary education, French, French–Romance languages and literatures, French–secondary education, history, history–secondary education, journalism and mass communications, liberal studies, mathematics, mathematics–secondary education, media management, music education, music–general, music–performance, physics, physics–secondary education, political science, print journalism, professional theater, psychology, public relations, sociology, social work, Spanish–Romance languages and literatures, Spanish–secondary education, speech, speech (speech pathology/audiology), visual arts–art education, and visual arts–design.

The School of Business and Economics offers programs in accounting, business education, business education (administrative systems, vocational business education, vocational business education–data processing), economics, finance, management, management (management information systems), marketing, and transportation.

In the School of Education, programs are available in elementary education, health and physical education (fitness/wellness management), health and physical education (teaching), recreation administration, and special education.

In the College of Engineering, programs are offered in architectural engineering, chemical engineering, civil engineering, computer science, electrical engineering, industrial engineering, and mechanical engineering.

The School of Nursing grants the Bachelor of Science in Nursing (B.S.N.) degree.

The School of Technology has programs in construction management, electronics technology, graphic communication systems, manufacturing systems, occupational safety and health, technology education, and vocational industrial education.

Academic Program

Students must complete a minimum of 124 semester hours to earn a bachelor's degree; the exact number varies with the program. Students are also required to demonstrate competence in English and mathematics.

As complements to the academic programs, the University's Army and Air Force ROTC programs and cooperative education program provide excellent opportunities for students to enrich their educational experiences. The ROTC programs are designed to prepare college graduates for military service careers. The cooperative education program provides an opportunity for qualified students to alternate periods of study on campus and meaningful employment off campus in private industrial or business firms or government agencies.

Academic Facilities

The University library has current holdings that include 507,036 book volumes and bound periodicals, as well as 5,446 current serials. As a select depository in North Carolina for U.S. government documents, the library contains a collection of more than 250,000 official publications. Among the library's other holdings are a collection of audiovisuals and 1,038,474 microforms, archives, and special collections in black studies and teacher-education materials. Special services are provided through formal and informal library instruction, interlibrary loans, and photocopying facilities.

The University's educational support centers are the Learning Assistance Center, the Audiovisual Center, the Closed Circuit Television Facility, a 1,000-watt student-operated educational radio station, the Computer Center, the Reading Center, the Language Laboratory, and the Center for Manpower Research and Training. The H. Clinton Taylor Art Gallery and the African Heritage Center are two exceptional art museums on campus. Throughout the year, these museums have on display a number of special exhibits of sculpture, paintings, graphics, and other media.

Costs

In 2003–04, tuition and fees for North Carolina residents were $2714 per year; for nonresidents of the state, they were $11,635. Board and lodging for the academic year were $4845.

Financial Aid

Through the student financial aid program, the University makes every effort to ensure that no qualified student is denied the opportunity to attend because of a lack of funds. Students who demonstrate financial need and have the potential to achieve academic success at the University may obtain assistance to meet their expenses in accordance with the funds available. Financial aid is awarded without regard to race, religion, color, national origin, or sex. The University provides financial aid for students from four basic sources: grants, scholarships, loans, and employment. To apply for aid, students must submit the Free Application for Federal Student Aid (FAFSA). The priority filing deadline is March 15 for fall semester. North Carolina residents may call 800-443-0835 (toll-free).

Faculty

The University's teaching faculty consists of 600 highly qualified members, of approximately 90 percent hold the doctoral degree or the first professional degree in their discipline. Faculty members are recruited from many areas and backgrounds, thereby bringing together a diverse cadre of academic professionals from many nations.

Student Government

The Student Government Association (SGA), composed of senators elected from the student body, is primarily a policy-recommending group and represents the views and concerns of the students. The president of SGA reports directly to the vice-chancellor for student affairs. In addition, each student organization is represented by a senator, and these senators sit on the Faculty Senate.

Admission Requirements

Applicants for undergraduate admission are considered individually and in accordance with criteria applied flexibly to ensure that applicants with unusual qualifications are not denied admission. However, admission for out-of-state freshman students is competitive due to an 18 percent out-of-state enrollment cap. Students who are applying for admission as freshmen are expected to have completed a college-preparatory program in high school and taken the SAT I or the ACT. General requirements include graduation from an accredited high school with 16 units of credit, with no more than 4 units in vocational subjects and with at least 2 units in physical education; a satisfactory score on the SAT I or ACT; and a respectable GPA and/or class rank. The General Educational Development (GED) test score results or a high school equivalency certificate from the state department of education may be submitted in lieu of the high school transcript for applicants receiving equivalency before January 1988.

North Carolina A&T State University welcomes applications from graduates of accredited community, technical, and junior colleges and from students who wish to transfer from other senior colleges.

Application and Information

The suggested application deadline for students who expect to live on campus is February 1; for commuting students, it is June 1. Applications are processed upon the receipt of the completed application form with the application fee of $35, official transcripts, and SAT I or ACT scores. Out-of-state admission is limited; therefore, applications for admission should be filed by February 1.

To arrange an interview or a visit to the campus, students should contact:

Office of Admissions
B. C. Webb Hall
North Carolina Agricultural and Technical State University
Greensboro, North Carolina 27411
Telephone: 336-334-7946 or 7947
800-443-8964 (toll-free in North Carolina)
World Wide Web: http://www.ncat.edu

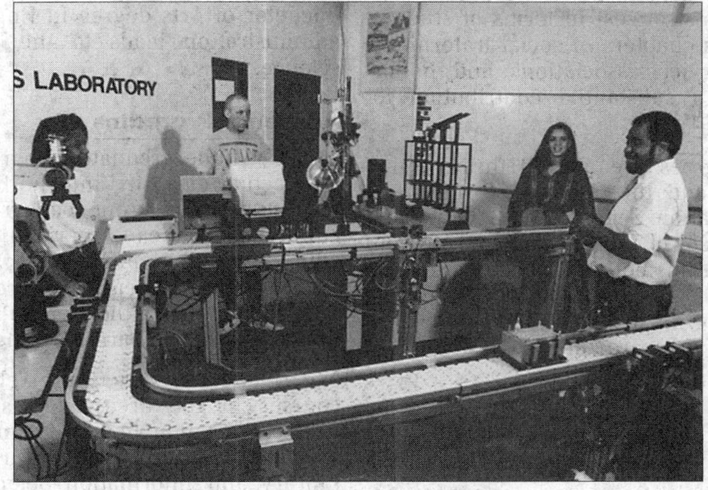

A professor and students in the chemical engineering lab.

NORTH CAROLINA CENTRAL UNIVERSITY

DURHAM, NORTH CAROLINA

The University

North Carolina Central University (NCCU) is a comprehensive public university, a constituent institution of the sixteen-campus University of North Carolina System. NCCU was founded in 1910 by Dr. James Edward Shepard, a pharmacist and political leader. In 1925, the institution became America's first state-supported liberal arts college for African Americans. Today, NCCU enrolls 7,291 students in undergraduate, graduate, and professional programs. Predominantly black (13 percent of the students are Caucasian), NCCU enrolls slightly more than 2 women to every 1 man. The average age of full-time undergraduate students is 23 years. Only 17 percent of freshmen are from outside the state of North Carolina, the percentage that prevails at almost every one of the sixteen state institutions. Approximately 50 of these students are from outside the United States. About 41 percent of the students are from Durham, Wake, and Mecklenburg Counties, and most of these are commuting students. On-campus housing is available for approximately 2,000 students.

NCCU's motto is "Truth and service," and over the years, the University's alumni have taken leadership roles in political life and the law. The governor holds a degree from NCCU, as does the former chair of the Board of Governors for the University of North Carolina and the U.S. Ambassador to the Central African Republic. NCCU graduates have served as district attorneys in the federal and state courts and as judges of state appellate courts, including a state supreme court. Other NCCU graduates are outstanding teachers at all levels of academic life, lawyers of national reputation, corporate vice presidents and executives, and school and university administrators.

NCCU is a member of the Central Intercollegiate Athletic Association and fields teams in football; men's and women's basketball, cross-country, tennis, and track; and women's softball and volleyball. NCCU has strong student ensembles in choral music, band music, and jazz, and NCCU's dramatic arts department is among America's strongest in terms of student productions. The University has chapters of social fraternities and sororities, as well as service associations and honor societies, all of which make a substantial contribution to campus life.

Graduate and professional degrees are offered through the College of Arts and Sciences and the Schools of Business, Education, Library and Information Sciences, and Law. The School of Business and the School of Library and Information Sciences offer joint degree programs both with each other and with the School of Law (Juris Doctor/Master of Business Administration and Juris Doctor/Master of Library Science). Several teacher licensure programs are offered through the School of Education.

Location

Durham is at the center of North Carolina's Research Triangle, which incorporates three major research universities in addition to NCCU, as well as three senior liberal arts colleges, two private junior colleges, and two state-funded technical community colleges. Several major corporations, particularly electronics and pharmaceutical operations, have large facilities in the Research Triangle area, whose total population is approximately 500,000. Durham itself is called the City of Medicine, with a quarter of the population employed in the field of health care.

Majors and Degrees

NCCU offers the following degrees and their respective majors: the Bachelor of Arts in art (general), art education, dramatic arts, dramatic arts (secondary education), early childhood education, economics, elementary education, English, English (concentrations in media journalism and secondary education), fine arts, French, French (secondary education), history, history (secondary education), middle grades education, music, music education, political science, political science (concentrations in criminal justice and public administration), psychology, social sciences, sociology, Spanish, Spanish (secondary education), theater arts, theater arts education (K–12), and visual communications; the Bachelor of Business Administration in accounting, business administration, computer information systems, finance, management, and marketing; the Bachelor of Music in jazz; the Bachelor of Science in biology, biology (secondary education), chemistry, chemistry (secondary education), community health education, computer science, family and consumer sciences, family and consumer science education (birth through kindergarten), geography, health education, mathematics, mathematics (secondary education), physical education, physics, physics (secondary education), and recreation administration; and the Bachelor of Science in Nursing.

NCCU has a cooperative arrangement with Georgia Institute of Technology and Duke University that enables a student, over a period of approximately five years, to earn a bachelor's degree in physics from NCCU and a bachelor's degree in engineering from Georgia Tech or Duke University.

There are organized preprofessional programs in dentistry, law, and medicine. The English department offers a substantial curriculum in media journalism as an alternative route to the Bachelor of Arts degree in English. A concentration in public administration leads to the bachelor's degree in political science.

Academic Programs

NCCU's undergraduate program is designed to stimulate intellectual curiosity and the habit of disciplined learning, to give students a strong background in both general Western culture and African-American culture, and to equip students with marketable intellectual and professional skills. Credit hours required to earn a degree may range between 124 and 128, depending on the student's choice of major or concentration and desire to earn teaching certification.

NCCU offers a variety of Web-enhanced distance education courses in the areas of business administration, criminal justice, education, hospitality and tourism, human sciences, and social work. Internet courses are offered through the Schools of Library and Information Sciences, Nursing, and Recreation. Several new Internet courses and programs are being developed to meet student demand.

Special honors seminars are open to qualified freshmen and sophomores. ROTC is available by cooperative arrangement with neighboring institutions.

Academic Facilities

NCCU's James E. Shepard Memorial Library has a collection of some 6 million volumes, not including serials; microforms; manuscripts; or graphics, audio, film, or video materials. A Learning Resources Center provides technical assistance and support for academic programs, including the production of audiovisual materials. The University's academic facilities include a variety of laboratories and 147 classrooms.

Costs

In 2004–05, the cost per semester, including tuition, for in-state students residing in a residence hall is $3766; out-of-state students residing in a residence hall pay $8450. In-state students not residing in a residence hall pay $1609; out-of-state students not residing in a residence hall pay $6293. There is a residence hall security deposit of $100. Costs are subject to change by the state legislature.

Financial Aid

NCCU's financial aid program has the primary purpose of helping families find resources to cover the cost of tuition, fees, housing, meals, and books. The burden of financing a college education has been eased due to the availability of grants, scholarships, work assistance, and loans. While most families initially seek funds that are free, such as grants and scholarships, low-interest student and parent loans are also available to help cover the cost of education. Some students are also afforded the opportunity to work and earn funds for personal expenses. Regardless of income, there are funds available at NCCU to assist students with college expenses. The most widely distributed federal and state grants and loans are Pell, SEOG, NCCU, Eagle, Federal Work-Study, Perkins, Direct Stafford, and Federal PLUS. Generally, the financial aid process begins when the Free Application for Federal Student Aid (FAFSA) is filed. Students should file the FAFSA as early as possible after January 1. Awards to new students are typically made after April 1 for the ensuing fall semester.

Faculty

NCCU's teaching faculty members number approximately 414, of whom about 289 are full-time teachers. (Specific numbers vary from semester to semester.) Of the full-time faculty members, 65 percent hold a doctorate. An additional 6 percent hold degrees considered to be the terminal degree in their discipline or specialty. Departments and schools offering undergraduate programs assign all of their faculty members to teach undergraduate courses.

Student Government

Undergraduate students elect class representatives to the Student Congress and the president and vice president of the Student Government Association. Also elected by student vote are Miss NCCU and officers of the four undergraduate classes. The Student Government Association recommends policies and regulations governing student life to the vice chancellor for student affairs. From the vice chancellor the recommendations go to the chancellor and the institutional Board of Trustees, to which the general authority to set regulations and policies affecting student life and discipline has been delegated by the Board of Governors of the University of North Carolina System. The president of the Student Government Association is a voting member of the Board of Trustees. The Student Government Association has substantial authority in managing the expenditure of student activity fees collected from undergraduates.

Admission Requirements

North Carolina Central University practices rolling admissions. Applications are accepted up to twelve months before the beginning of the semester in which a prospective student wishes to enroll. Applicants for entry as freshmen must provide evidence (a complete transcript) of graduation from an approved or accredited high school and a satisfactory score on the SAT I or ACT. Students who graduated from high school after spring 1990 must present in their high school transcripts 4 course units in English, emphasizing grammar, composition, and literature; 3 course units in mathematics, including algebra I, algebra II, and geometry or a higher-level mathematics course for which algebra II is a prerequisite; 3 course units in science, including at least 1 unit in a life science, at least 1 unit in a physical science, and at least one laboratory course in science; and 2 course units in social studies, including 1 unit in U.S. history. Two units of the same foreign language are required, and students are encouraged to take a math class and a foreign language class during the senior year. NCCU and other North Carolina state universities are required to limit out-of-state freshman enrollment. In practice, out-of-state students admitted have higher SAT I scores and higher class standing.

For a transfer student at the undergraduate level seeking admission to the University, several standards are considered. The transfer applicant must not presently be on probation at the last or current school of attendance and must submit the required confidential statement form. The transfer applicant must not have been suspended or dropped from the last or current institution attended. The transfer applicant must have a cumulative average of at least a C at the institution from which they are transferring. Evidence of the applicant's participation in scholastic, community, and civic organizations, including leadership participation, is also considered. Transfer students who have attended another college or university but have earned fewer than 24 semester hours of specific acceptable credit must meet all freshmen requirements.

Application and Information

Students should submit applications for the fall semester by July 1 (March 1 for out-of-state students and for students seeking on-campus housing or financial aid) and for the semester beginning in January by November 1. Early application with partial transcripts is encouraged, but final admission is deferred until all required documents are received and reviewed. International applicants must submit applications and other required materials at least ninety days before registration for each semester. Application forms and additional information are available from:

Director of Undergraduate Admissions
North Carolina Central University
P.O. Box 19717
Durham, North Carolina 27707
Telephone: 919-530-6298
877-667-7533 (toll-free)
Fax: 919-530-7625
E-mail: admissions@nccu.edu
World Wide Web: http://www.nccu.edu

NORTH CENTRAL COLLEGE

NAPERVILLE, ILLINOIS

The College

Founded in 1861, North Central College has a distinctive heritage as a comprehensive college that educates students in both the liberal arts and sciences and in preprofessional fields.

A private, United Methodist–affiliated institution, the College has long been recognized for academic excellence, with its educational philosophy of incorporating leadership, ethics, and values into academic and cocurricular activities. North Central's 2,500 students include traditional-age undergraduate, part-time, and graduate students. Master's degree programs are offered in business administration, computer science, education, information systems, leadership studies, and liberal studies. New graduate certificates are now available in business foundations, change management, dispute resolution, finance, gender studies, history and nature of science, human resource management, investments and financial planning, leadership studies, management, marketing, multicultural studies, and organizational ethics.

North Central's 56-acre campus has more than twenty major buildings. Facilities include the historic Old Main, built in 1870 and renovated in 1998; the state-of-the-art Cardinal Stadium, which seats 5,500 and is the home to football, soccer and track; and Pfeiffer Hall, a 1,050-seat auditorium. Kaufman Dining Hall serves the entire campus.

Twenty-five states and twenty-five other countries are represented (86 percent of the students are Illinois residents). Twelve percent of the members of the 2003 freshman class were members of minority groups, and 82 percent of freshmen live in one of nine residence halls.

Cocurricular programs parallel many academic majors and include the nationally acclaimed Students in Free Enterprise, Cardinals in Action (a community service organization), campus radio station WONC, Mock Trial, Model United Nations, and forensics. North Central student athletes compete in nineteen NCAA Division III intercollegiate varsity sports within the College Conference of Illinois and Wisconsin. The varsity sports include baseball, basketball, cross-country, football, golf, soccer, swimming, tennis, track and field, and wrestling for men. Women participate in basketball, cross-country, golf, soccer, softball, swimming, tennis, track and field, and volleyball. Students have many options for social activities: programmed events through the College Union Activities Board, residence life activities, an active intramural program, and travel to both downtown Naperville and Chicago. Student services include centers for academic advising, counseling, writing, foreign language, and career development.

Location

North Central is located in a charming historic district in the heart of Naperville, Illinois, a fast growing community of 140,000 residents in the west-suburban area of metropolitan Chicago. The city is a residential community with excellent community services and has become the Midwest center of scientific research and development. It is in the "Silicon Prairie" center of the high-technology Illinois Research and Development Corridor, where some of the nation's largest companies (e.g., BP Amoco, Metropolitan Life, and Ondeo-Nalco Chemical Company) are located. Nearby are Argonne National Laboratory, Fermi National Accelerator Laboratory, and Morton Arboretum. All of these facilities and industries represent unique resources for North Central students—for internships, jobs, and joint research opportunities.

Chicago is just 29 miles away, and the cultural, artistic, and entertainment venues in this great city make it a rich resource for a North Central education. Students can catch the Burlington Northern Railroad just two blocks from campus for an easy commute.

Majors and Degrees

North Central College awards the Bachelor of Arts (B.A.) degree in accounting, art, art education, arts and letters, athletic training, biochemistry, biology, broadcast communication, chemistry, classical civilization, computer science, East Asian studies, economics, education (elementary and secondary), English, entrepreneurship and small business management, exercise science, finance, French, German, history, human resource management, humanities, international business, international studies, Japanese, management, management information systems, marketing, mathematics, music, musical theater, music education, organizational communication, philosophy, physical education, physics, political science, print journalism, psychology, religious studies, science, social studies, sociology, sociology and anthropology, Spanish, speech communication, sports management, theater, and urban and suburban studies. The Bachelor of Science (B.S.) degree is awarded in actuarial science, applied mathematics, biochemistry, biology, chemistry, computer science, mathematics, and psychology and in all economics and business areas.

Preprofessional-professional programs are offered in engineering, health sciences, medical physics, medical technology, nursing, and law. A 3-2 engineering program is offered in cooperation with the University of Illinois at Urbana-Champaign, Washington University in St. Louis, Missouri, Iowa State University and the University of Minnesota. Both 2-2 and 3-2 programs in nursing are available in cooperation with Rush University in Chicago. Students may also design other majors that bridge two or more areas of study.

Academic Program

North Central provides a comprehensive education with the goal of preparing students to live free, ethically responsible, and intellectually rewarding lives. Each student must complete a minimum of 120 credit hours, including all general education requirements and an approved major. CLEP, AP, and IB exams are considered for college credit and/or advanced course placement.

The academic year comprises three 10½-week terms and a monthlong Interim Term between Thanksgiving and the beginning of the new calendar year. Students usually take three courses during each term, while the Interim Term is used for independent study, taking courses, travel, research, work, or simply relaxation. The College actively supports internships as part of career preparation, and the College Scholars Honors Program is open to select students.

Off-Campus Programs

North Central College provides many opportunities for students to study abroad. Students interested in engaging in intensive Spanish study may travel to Costa Rica each fall term for 13 weeks. The 13-week London term allows students to explore European history and understand the changing contemporary English and continental cultures. Other study-abroad possibilities include exchange programs to Japan, China, Korea, Taiwan, Northern Ireland, and France.

North Central is also one of only twelve colleges and universities in the nation to offer the distinctive Richter Independent Study Fellowship Program, which provides funds of up to $5000 for a single specialized project. Richter Independent Study projects have included travel and research on every continent.

Academic Facilities

WONC (89.1 FM), the College's 1,500-watt radio station, is one of the most powerful student-staffed stations in the Midwest. The station, with three state-of-the-art studios for on-air and audio production work, has won 20 Marconi Awards—more than any other college radio station in the country.

All students and faculty and staff members have access to a voice, video, and data network, including full Internet access from their residence halls, classrooms, computer laboratories, and offices. Ten MB of Web space has been made available to every enrolled student for personal pages, and 55 MB of hard drive space for file storage.

Science equipment available for student research projects includes a fourteen-CPU LINUX parallel processor, computer networking and multimedia labs, a 300 MHz magnetic resonance spectrometer, a gas chromatograph/mass spectrometer, a liquid chromatograph, a pulsed nitrogen laser, a phase-contract video microscope, PCR thermal cyclers, and environmental chambers. North Central also has state-of-the-art language and market research laboratories.

Costs

For 2004–05, tuition at North Central College is $20,160. Room and board are $6747. Resident students pay a $225 technology fee. The student activity fee is $180, and estimated additional expenses are $425 for books and supplies. Students should also budget personal expenses and transportation costs.

Financial Aid

The Offices of Administration and Financial Aid are committed to assisting students throughout the process of applying for financial aid. Scholarships, loans, grants, and work-study assistance are awarded on the basis of demonstrated financial need and the academic record. Students are required to submit the Free Application for Federal Student Aid (FAFSA). Funds are also available through the Illinois State Monetary Award Program (for Illinois residents only), the Federal Pell Grant Program, Federal Supplemental Educational Opportunity Grant, and the Federal Stafford Student Loan Program. The College awarded more than $12 million from institutional sources for 2003–04. A large portion of those funds was allocated through the academic-based Presidential Scholarship Program. Awards range from $5000 to full tuition, renewable annually. Students may also interview and/or audition for scholarships in science, theatre, forensics, vocal and instrumental music, as well as submit art portfolios.

Faculty

Members of the North Central faculty, 89 percent of whom hold the Ph.D. or another terminal degree, are first—and foremost—teachers. A student-faculty ratio of 14:1 and an average class size of 19 students ensure opportunities for a stimulating exchange of ideas. All faculty members also serve as academic advisers to provide guidance and counseling for students. Students get to know their professors on a personal basis, and the list of independent study projects is extensive. Faculty members teach both undergraduate and graduate courses.

Student Government

All undergraduates are members of the Student Association, which is governed by its elected officers. The Student Association is a vital and influential force in campus activities, and it takes an active role in the development and implementation of policies concerning student life on campus. Representatives of the student body have a voice on faculty, trustee, and administrative committees, while the College Union Activities Board plans social and service events.

Admission Requirements

New students are accepted individually on the basis of their overall academic preparation, character, and potential for success at North Central College. Graduation from an accredited secondary school is a basic requirement for admission. Other criteria used in the selection of prospective students are the high school academic record, personal recommendations of high school counselors, ACT or SAT I scores, and involvement in extracurricular activities. Members of the North Central freshman class of 2003–04 scored an average of 24 on the ACT and ranked in the 75th percentile of their high school graduating class. North Central does not discriminate on the basis of sex, race, ethnic background, age, or physical handicap.

Application and Information

North Central College operates on a rolling admission basis, which allows students to apply at any time during or after their senior year in high school. Students can complete and submit an application for admission on the College's Web site. Applicants receive notification within three weeks after the College receives all documentation. Early application is recommended to ensure availability of campus housing. The application must be accompanied by a $25 fee, an official high school transcript, and official reports of ACT or SAT I scores from the testing agency. For additional information or application forms, students should contact:

Office of Admission
North Central College
30 North Brainard Street
Naperville, Illinois 60540
Telephone: 630-637-5800
800-411-1861 (toll-free)
Fax: 630-637-5819
E-mail: ncadm@noctrl.edu
World Wide Web: http://www.northcentralcollege.edu

Historic Old Main, built in 1870 and renovated in 1998, houses the Offices of Admission, Financial Aid, and the Registrar.

NORTHEASTERN UNIVERSITY

BOSTON, MASSACHUSETTS

The University

There is a certain energy about Northeastern. It comes from bright, ambitious students with a sense of purpose. In the classroom, in the workplace, in campus activities, and in the city of Boston—the ultimate college town—Northeastern students stimulate their minds, investigate career options, participate in community affairs, and graduate personally and professionally prepared for their future careers or for graduate school.

Northeastern students not only acquire knowledge, they learn how to apply it. Through Northeastern's innovative cooperative education program—cited for excellence for the past two years by *U.S. News & World Report*'s annual guide "American Best Colleges" for programs that require students to combine classroom learning with real-world experience—students alternate classroom learning with periods of full-time, usually paid work or other types of practical learning related to their major or interests. Graduates accumulate as many as two years of professional experience, professional contacts, and the social confidence that gives them a significant edge in the job market over new graduates without experience. Each year, students graduate from Northeastern with a solid sense of themselves and their relationship to the community and with a valuable head start on their careers or graduate school.

By working in varied jobs and settings, students learn what they like—and don't like—before committing to a permanent position. Many Northeastern students even go to work for a co-op employer after graduation. Northeastern students graduate knowing what they could have learned only on the job: how to conduct themselves, what to wear, how to interpret a company's culture, how to get things done, and how to write a resume and interview successfully. Co-op is an education in itself.

The current undergraduate enrollment of 14,492 is made up of students of all backgrounds, interests, and tastes, giving Northeastern its distinctive, urban style. This diversity shows in the range of available activities. Students can join a cultural club, write for the *Northeastern News*, perform with the Silver Masque, go on a ski trip, play basketball, tutor local children, learn to ballroom dance, and much more. Students have many opportunities to make friends, try something new, become a leader, or simply have fun. Students can also find quiet corners of the campus that feel far from city streets where they can read or just relax, sprawled on a wooden bench under a shade tree; sip gourmet coffee from a nearby campus café; or listen to a midday jazz performance behind the Curry Student Center amid the art of Northeastern's sculpture park. The 67-acre campus is dynamic and welcoming, a beautiful stretch of leafy green in the heart of Boston. Its compact size lets students get to class on time or rush back for a forgotten book. Yet it contains many needed services, from a hair salon to a travel agency.

Location

Though in the midst of the hustle and bustle where Boston's Back Bay meets the Fenway, Northeastern is an increasingly residential campus and has built, in the past five years alone, a host of new on-campus residence halls, more than doubling the amount of housing available to undergraduates. The newest residence halls offer apartment-style living with modern kitchens complete with dishwashers, disposals, and full-sized appliances; cable hookups; and data jacks. Many have amazing views of the Boston skyline.

The Back Bay area, known for its many cultural and educational institutions, is steps from Symphony Hall, the New England Conservatory of Music, the Museum of Fine Arts, and the Isabella Stewart Gardner Museum. The Fenway area, with its beautiful rose garden, bicycle and jogging paths, and Fenway Park (home of the Boston Red Sox), is just a few blocks away. The campus comprises sixty-eight buildings in an area of 67 acres.

Majors and Degrees

Northeastern's academic programs are divided among six colleges: the College of Arts and Sciences, the Bouvé College of Health Sciences, the College of Business Administration, the College of Computer and Information Science, the College of Criminal Justice, and the College of Engineering. Top-notch faculty members with a variety of research interests personally guide students through their studies.

The College of Arts and Sciences awards undergraduate degrees in African-American studies, American Sign Language and English interpreting, anthropology, applied physics, architecture, art (including concentrations in animation and photography), behavioral neuroscience, biochemistry, biology (including a concentration in marine biology), biomedical physics, chemistry, communication studies (including concentrations in media studies, organizational communication, and public communication), economics, English, environmental geology, environmental studies, geology, graphic design, history, human services, international affairs, journalism, linguistics, mathematics, modern languages, multimedia studies, music (concentrations in music industry, music literature, music literature and performance, and music technology), philosophy, physics, political science (including concentrations in international relations and comparative politics, law and legal issues, and public administration), psychology, sociology, and theater. In addition, preparation programs in elementary education and early childhood education (both including a specialization in special education) and a minor in secondary education are available.

The Bouvé College of Health Sciences awards degrees in athletic training, cardiopulmonary and exercise sciences (with concentrations in clinical exercise physiology, exercise physiology, and respiratory therapy), medical laboratory sciences, nursing, pathways (open option, available to freshmen interested in the health professions who have not yet decided on a specific major), and speech-language pathology and audiology. The College also offers a six-year Doctor of Pharmacy degree and a six-year program leading to a Master of Science in physical therapy.

The College of Business Administration offers two tracks: the Bachelor of Science in Business Administration (B.S.B.A.) or the Bachelor of Science in International Business (B.S.I.B.). The B.S.I.B. programs includes language instruction and international study and work. The College offers concentrations in accounting, entrepreneurship and small business management, finance and insurance, human resources management, management, management information systems, marketing, and supply-chain management.

The College of Computer and Information Science awards degrees in computer science and information science and also offers dual-major degrees combining computer science with cognitive psychology, mathematics, or physics.

The College of Criminal Justice awards an undergraduate degree in criminal justice, with concentrations in criminology and corrections, legal studies, and policing and security.

The College of Engineering offers degrees in chemical, civil and environmental, computer, electrical, industrial, and mechanical engineering. In addition, the School of Engineering Technology offers degrees in computer, electrical, and mechanical engineering technology.

Academic Programs

Northeastern's internationally known cooperative education program enables students to gain practical and lively workplace or other experience integrated with their academic studies. Students alternate semesters of work and study (after completing their freshman year) and can earn their bachelor's degree in either four or five years. Co-op employers include some of the country's largest and most reputable companies, such as Pfizer, John Hancock, Fidelity Investments, General Electric, Massachusetts General Hospital, and *The Boston Globe*. Students also enjoy international placements for a semester or a year abroad; co-op employers recruit from Australia, Scotland, Italy, and Spain, among many other countries.

A University-wide honors program gives students opportunities to participate in enriched educational experiences and offers opportunities that include honors sections of required academic courses, honors seminars, independent research, and study abroad. The Ujima Scholars Program is a freshman-year access program that recruits students who are members of minority groups who have demonstrated ability to succeed in University studies but need additional academic support, particularly during their first year. NUPRIME is a program committed to helping historically underrepresented students fulfill their potential—academically and professionally. The University also offers Army, Naval Nursing, and Air Force ROTC. The Disability Resource Center provides many support services that enable students with disabilities to participate fully in the life of the University community.

Academic Facilities

Northeastern is home to a variety of research centers, including the Center for Labor Market Studies, the Institute of Molecular Biotechnology, the Nano Manufacturing Research Institute, the Race and Justice Research Institute, and many others. Students have ample opportunities to work alongside their professors to aid and conduct research on a variety of topics.

University libraries contain 984,443 volumes, 2,260,556 microforms, 160,834 government documents, 7,654 serial subscriptions, and 22,205 audio, video, and software titles. The libraries have licensed access to more than 12,954 electronic information sources. A central and branch library contain technologically sophisticated services, including Web-based catalog and circulation systems and a Web portal to licensed electronic resources. The University is a member of the Boston Library Consortium and the Boston Regional Library System, giving students and faculty members access to the region's collections and information resources.

Northeastern University provides a broad range of academic and administrative computer resources available to students and faculty and staff members. Many computing resources are available, including Internet connections for all offices and University-owned residence halls, technology-assisted classrooms, computer labs, and the myNEU portal, which allows student to access many administrative and academic functions online.

Costs

For 2003–04, freshman tuition was $25,600, room and board were $9810, and other mandatory student fees were $296.

Financial Aid

The University operates a substantial aid program designed to make attendance at Northeastern feasible for all qualified students. By coordinating the resources of the University and various public and private scholarship programs, the Office of Student Financial Services was able to provide more than $100 million to more than 10,000 students last year. About 81 percent of the freshman class received some form of financial aid. Financial aid is based on need and academic merit and may consist of grants, loans, work-study employment, or any combination of the three. To apply, students must file a Free Application for Federal Student Aid (FAFSA) and a CSS PROFILE form with the College Scholarship Service by the priority filing date of February 15.

Faculty

The University has 830 full-time faculty members with a wide variety of research and teaching interests and specialties and a staff of academic counselors in each college who work closely with students to assist them in developing programs suited to their interests and abilities. Each student is assigned both an academic and a a co-op adviser. The co-op adviser aids in resume building, interview skills and tactics, and contacts with business and co-op employers as well as networking and eventual job searches.

Student Government

The Student Government Association, a group of students from the various colleges, is the official liaison between undergraduate students and the administration. Providing advice and opinions on a wide variety of issues, the association strives to improve the quality of life at Northeastern.

Admission Requirements

Great emphasis is placed on secondary school achievement. In addition to the application for admission, prospective freshmen must submit official high school transcript(s) (or official GED score reports), including their first-quarter, senior-year grades; official transcripts for any college-level course work taken while a secondary school student; written recommendations from their secondary school guidance counselor and a teacher; and scores on the SAT I (Northeastern's College Board code is 3667) or ACT. Students may enter the University with advanced credit on the basis of test scores on Advanced Placement (AP) examinations, the College-Level Examination Program (CLEP), or the International Baccalaureate (I.B.) or on successful completion of accredited college-level courses before enrollment at Northeastern.

Application and Information

Admission to Northeastern is selective and competitive. For the 2003–04 academic year, the University received 21,500 applications for 2,800 places in the freshman class. In building a diverse and talented class, Northeastern seeks to enroll students who have been successful academically and who have shown a strong commitment to school and community through extracurricular activities. Students who have earned strong grades in a rigorous college preparatory program, are innovative and creative, and who possess leadership abilities are most successful in the admission process.

January 1 is the deadline for priority consideration for freshmen for September admission, merit scholarships, and admission to the Honors Program. February 15 is the general deadline for September admission. Freshmen who apply for the fall entrance date by February 15 are mailed a decision between March 1 and April 1. If accepted for fall admission, freshmen are required to send a tuition deposit by May 1 to secure a place in the class. For transfer students, the priority deadline for the fall is May 1. March 1 is the deadline for transfer Pharmacy applicants for the fall. Admission decisions for transfer applicants are made on a space-available, rolling basis. October 1 is the deadline for international applicants for January admission. October 15 is the deadline for international transfer applicants for January admission. November 1 is the deadline for January transfer admission for both freshman and transfer applicants. Admission decisions for spring applicants are made on a space-available, rolling basis. Campus tours and group information sessions are held daily and are available without an appointment.

For more information, students should contact:

Office of Undergraduate Admissions
Northeastern University
150 Richards Hall
360 Huntington Avenue
Boston, Massachusetts 02115
Telephone: 617-373-2200 (voice)
617-373-3100 (TTY)
E-mail: admissions@neu.edu
World Wide Web: http://www.neu.edu

Northeastern University students in a West Village residence hall enjoy spectacular Boston vistas.

NORTHERN ARIZONA UNIVERSITY

FLAGSTAFF, ARIZONA

The University

Northern Arizona University (NAU) is a fully accredited, state-supported, four-year institution with approximately 13,390 full-time students on its main campus. Since 1899, the University has made a major commitment to undergraduate education, and its goal has been to preserve a friendly campus atmosphere and close student-faculty relationships through classroom teaching of the highest quality and faculty guidance for each student.

The University is composed of the Colleges of Arts and Science, Business Administration, Education, Engineering and Technology, Fine and Performing Arts, Health Professions, and Social and Behavioral Sciences and the Schools of Communication, Forestry, and Hotel and Restaurant Management. Undergraduate, master's, and doctoral degrees are offered in more than 150 major areas and in a number of interdisciplinary and preprofessional curricula. A graduate degree is available in physical therapy.

Ten advisement centers assist the University in realizing its strong commitment to one-on-one advising, and regular office hours are maintained by faculty members. The new Gateway Student Success Center offers academic advising services and career exploration assistance for all students who are undecided in terms of a degree program. An average class size of 29 is another example of the institution's attention to high-quality education.

Nonacademic facilities include seven buildings listed on the National Register of Historic Places. In addition, there are three student unions, a student health center, an Olympic-size swimming and diving complex, a 16,230-seat multiuse wooden dome, and a multipurpose recreational facility.

As a residential campus, NAU provides an atmosphere of friendship and community. Fifty percent of the undergraduate students live in the sixteen residence halls and 346 family housing apartments located on the campus. Of the 11,487 full-time undergraduates enrolled in the 2003 fall semester, 4,432 were men and 6,648 were women.

Northern Arizona University is an Equal Opportunity/ Affirmative Action institution.

Location

Northern Arizona University's 730-acre mountain campus is located in Flagstaff, which is a community with 58,000 residents. Flagstaff is located at an elevation of 7,000 feet, just south of the 12,600-foot-high San Francisco Peaks, a major winter-sports center. The University is at the junction of Interstate Highways 40 (U.S. 66) and 17, less than a 3-hour drive from Phoenix and about a 5-hour drive from Tucson, Arizona; Albuquerque, New Mexico; and Las Vegas, Nevada. The city is served by Amtrak, Greyhound buses, and a commercial airline. The campus is surrounded by scenic beauty and natural wonders, such as the Grand Canyon and a student favorite, Oak Creek Canyon. The varied northern land of mountains, gorges, forests, and lakes provides the University with natural classrooms and laboratories for research as well as recreation.

Majors and Degrees

Northern Arizona University offers baccalaureate degrees in approximately ninety major areas, embracing most of the recognized fields in the arts and sciences and a number of interdisciplinary majors. NAU also offers a number of special programs, including arts management, criminal justice, dental hygiene, forestry, hotel and restaurant management, and parks and recreation management.

Academic Program

A four-year baccalaureate degree program at Northern Arizona University requires the successful completion of 120 semester hours of course work, including 35 hours of liberal studies courses. The liberal studies program consists of foundation studies and studies in various disciplines designed to assist students in cultivating their abilities to recognize significant problems and to define, analyze, and defend solutions in a variety of contexts. Major-field requirements vary from 35 to 73 semester hours. Students may combine a major field with one or more 18-hour minors, take two majors or an extended major of 63 to 65 hours in a field of their interest, or select the merged major programs.

NAU has a long-established honors program designed to challenge the talented student. This leads to graduation with honors, and honor students may elect to take the special degree of Bachelor of Arts: Honors. The program provides special courses and seminars and offers superior students opportunities for independent study and research.

A three-year bachelor's degree program is available in forty-six majors. The program offers intellectual and academic challenges for well-prepared and motivated students, allowing them to take the fast track to graduation and graduate programs.

Off-Campus Programs

NAU actively cooperates in the work and research programs of several major scientific institutions that are located close to its campus. These include the Lowell Observatory; the U.S. Naval Observatory's Flagstaff station; various facilities of the U.S. Geological Survey, including its space-oriented Astrogeology Center; the U.S. Forest Service Rocky Mountain and Range Experiment station; and the Museum of Northern Arizona and its multidisciplinary Colton Research Center. The specialized libraries, laboratories, and other facilities of these institutions are available to qualified students at the University. NAU sponsors a marine biology camp in Mexico on the Gulf of California, as well as scientific field trips to many of the distinctive natural areas of northern Arizona, including an annual geological study tour through the nearby Grand Canyon.

The Northern Arizona University Centers in London, England; Tübingen, Germany; Granada, Spain; Montpellier, France; and Shanghai and Beijing, China, offer students an opportunity for exciting enrichment programs for one or two semesters in Europe or Asia. Students may also study for one semester in Cuernavaca, Mexico. Through field trips, students explore the history, literature, and culture of these regions. All students except freshmen may enroll.

Through the National Student Exchange program, NAU students have an opportunity to broaden their educational horizons by attending a college or university in another state for one semester or one year while paying tuition and fees at NAU. There are more than 150 participating institutions nationwide from which students may choose.

Academic Facilities

NAU's facilities for education and research are extensive. The University library contains more than 1.6 million volumes, approximately 6,253 current periodical titles, a media center, and a number of special research collections of original documents relating to the history, economy, and culture of Arizona and the Southwest. The facility now has an online public access catalog and a book capacity of 2 million volumes.

Well-equipped general and specialized laboratories serve students in the basic sciences and health professions. Specially designed studios, workrooms, theaters, auditoriums, and an art gallery are available to students in the creative arts. Closed-circuit television hookups, student-paced audiovisual systems, language laboratories, an observatory, and a major computer center are used regularly by students for both learning and research. The Bilby Research Center augments NAU's research facilities.

NAU makes extensive use of the spectacular Colorado Plateau country surrounding its campus as a natural laboratory for anthropology, biology, ecology, geology, geophysics, paleontology, and other sciences. Prehistoric Indian ruins and the living cultures of the Navajo, Hopi, and many other Indian peoples of the Southwest provide rich resources for students of archaeology, ethnology, and linguistics. The University also maintains a 4,000-acre research forest for forestry students. The area's 7,000-foot elevation and unusually clear, dry air have made it a major center for astronomy and the atmospheric sciences.

Costs

For 2003–04, the charges for an academic year of two semesters for an in-state student were tuition and fees, $3594, and average board and room, $5374. Books and supplies averaged $750. The total cost for Arizona residents was $9718 per academic year. The out-of-state tuition and fees were $12,114, for an academic-year cost of $18,238. This does not include travel or personal expenses, which vary for each student. All costs are subject to change by the Arizona Board of Regents.

Financial Aid

Northern Arizona University maintains an extensive program of financial assistance to aid students in pursuing their educational goals. The amount of financial aid awarded to a student is based upon the student's need level, as computed from the Free Application for Federal Student Aid (FAFSA). However, some scholarships are awarded on the basis of a student's demonstration of academic excellence and/or participation in various University activities.

In the 2003–04 academic year, more than $120 million was available for loans, scholarships, grants, veterans' benefits, and work-study programs. About 60 percent of the students at NAU received some form of financial aid.

Along with grants, loans, and scholarships, on- and off-campus employment is available to help students meet financial obligations. More than 4,500 NAU students are currently employed in a wide variety of jobs on the campus.

Faculty

NAU's faculty is made up of outstanding and dedicated professionals. More than 85 percent of the 698 full-time and 630 part-time faculty members hold doctoral degrees. Many are nationally distinguished scientists and scholars. The student-faculty ratio is 17:1, with more than 80 percent of the classes taught by faculty members rather than graduate assistants.

Student Government

Each student who enters NAU is a member of the Associated Students of Northern Arizona University (ASNAU), which represents the students' interests in all matters that affect them.

Besides ASNAU, other student governing groups are the Associated Women Students, Association of University Residence Halls, Panhellenic Council, and Inter-Fraternity Council. About 50 percent of the students belong to one or more of the 192 student groups and organizations.

Admission Requirements

Applicants for admission must complete both general aptitude and basic competence requirements. Conditional admission for non-Arizona residents is granted on a space-available basis. Participation in some form of assistance program may be required for those admitted conditionally.

For unconditional admission, the general aptitude requirements for new freshmen are any one of the following: a cumulative GPA of 3.0 or better (on a 4.0 scale), a class rank in the upper quarter, a minimum ACT composite score of 22 (24 for non-Arizona residents), or a minimum combined SAT I score of 1040 (1100 for nonresidents). For conditional admission, the requirements are a cumulative GPA between 2.5 and 2.99 or a class rank at least in the upper half with test scores below the previously stated minimums. The GPA to meet the general aptitude requirement for admission is calculated using only the sixteen required core courses. Transfer students with fewer than 12 transferable academic semester credits must meet the same standards as new freshmen. If 12 or more semester credits have been earned, then the cumulative GPA must be at least 2.0 for unconditional or conditional admission for Arizona residents. Non-Arizona residents must have a cumulative GPA of at least 2.5 for unconditional admission or between 2.0 and 2.49 for conditional admission.

Basic competency requirements must be met by all freshmen and transfer students, either through high school course work and/or transferable higher education courses. Generally, one 3-hour college course equals one year of high school study. Core course requirements include 4 years of English, 4 years of mathematics, 3 years of laboratory science, 2 years of social science, 2 years of foreign language, and 1 year of fine art. There are specific course requirements within these areas, and some requirements may be met by achieving minimum scores on standardized tests. Students should contact the Admissions Office for more information.

March 1 is the priority deadline for the summer and fall semesters; December 1 is for the spring semester. Applications and supporting documents received after these dates are processed on a space-available basis.

Application and Information

The NAU information booklet, which includes an application for admission and information about financial aid, housing, and academic programs, may be obtained by contacting:

Admissions Office
Box 4084
Northern Arizona University
Flagstaff, Arizona 86011-4084
Telephone: 888-667-3628 (toll-free)
E-mail: undergraduate.admissions@nau.edu

A friendly residential campus and the four-season climate of Flagstaff, Arizona, attract about 12,000 undergraduate students each year to Northern Arizona University.

NORTHERN KENTUCKY UNIVERSITY

HIGHLAND HEIGHTS, KENTUCKY

The University

Northern Kentucky University (NKU) was founded in 1968 and is the newest of Kentucky's eight state universities. The atmosphere of the campus is futuristic, emphasizing a high-quality education by supporting the liberal arts. Thirteen major buildings are of modern, contemporary architectural design and are set on 300 acres of rolling countryside. NKU has an enrollment of approximately 14,000 students from forty-three states and seventy-two countries and is accredited by the Southern Association of Colleges and Schools. The Salmon P. Chase College of Law is accredited by both the American Bar Association and the Association of American Law Schools.

There are more than 100 student organizations. NKU competes in the NCAA Division II Great Lakes Valley Conference. Intercollegiate sports are offered for men and women in basketball, cross-country, golf, soccer, and tennis; for men in baseball; and for women in fast-pitch softball and volleyball. Intramural activities are archery, badminton, basketball, canoeing, flag football, inner tube water polo, racquetball, soccer, softball, track and field, volleyball, water basketball, and water volleyball.

Location

NKU is located in the largest metropolitan area of any state university in Kentucky. It is located at the junction of U.S. Highway 27 and Interstates 275 and 471 in Highland Heights, Kentucky, 8 miles southeast of Cincinnati, Ohio. NKU is only 60 miles from Dayton, 79 miles from Lexington, 93 miles from Louisville, and 114 miles from Indianapolis. While the immediate surroundings are suburban, NKU is part of the metropolitan area of greater Cincinnati.

Majors and Degrees

Northern Kentucky University awards the Bachelor of Arts, Bachelor of Fine Arts, Bachelor of Music, Bachelor of Science, Bachelor of Science in Nursing, and Bachelor of Social Work degrees. NKU also offers preprofessional programs, secondary education teacher certification, and the Associate of Applied Science degree.

The B.A. and B.S. degrees are offered in accounting, anthropology, applied sociology–anthropology, biological sciences, business education, chemistry, computer science, criminal justice, economics, electronics engineering technology, elementary education, English, environmental science, finance, French, geography, geology, graphic design, history, industrial and labor relations, industrial education, industrial technology construction, industrial technology manufacturing, information systems, international studies, journalism, management, manufacturing engineering technology, marketing, mathematics, mental health–human services, middle grades education, organizational studies, philosophy, physical education, physics, political science, psychology, public administration, public relations, radio-TV, recreation-fitness, sociology, Spanish, special education, speech, sports marketing, studio arts, and theater.

The B.F.A. degree is granted in art and in theater arts. The B.Mus. degree is offered in music. The B.S.N. degree is offered in the nursing major and the B.S.W. degree in the social work major.

Preprofessional programs are available in dentistry, engineering, forestry, law, medicine, optometry, pharmacy, physical therapy, veterinary medicine, and wildlife management. In addition, the University offers majors, minors, and areas of discipline for secondary education teacher certification.

The University also awards the A.A.S. degree in aviation administration, construction technology, criminal justice, human services, liberal studies, prebusiness studies, radiologic technology, and respiratory care.

Academic Programs

NKU operates on a semester calendar. To receive a bachelor's degree, students must complete a minimum of 128 credit hours. At least 64 credit hours are required for the associate degree.

The University offers a variety of career planning and placement, internship, independent study, work-study, and cooperative education programs. There is also an Advising, Counseling, and Testing Center available. Other programs include an honors program, a program that allows for the dual enrollment of high school students, a program where students can combine their career interests in the liberal arts and engineering fields, and University 101, an orientation program for freshmen.

NKU recognizes credit earned through the Advanced Placement (AP) Program and the general, subject, and institutional tests of the College-Level Examination Program (CLEP). A maximum of 45 credit hours may be applied toward the bachelor's degree from the AP and CLEP examinations. The International Baccalaureate Program allows students to earn credit in science, mathematics, psychology, and languages.

Off-Campus Programs

A variety of study-abroad opportunities are available to NKU students through membership in several consortia and through NKU exchange agreements with international universities.

Study in Australia, Canada, England, Ireland, New Zealand, Scotland, and South Africa is possible in a wide range of courses and programs available through NKU's membership in the Cooperative Center for Study Abroad (CCSA), which is headquartered at NKU.

The Kentucky Institute for International Studies (KIIS) offers students academic language programs in Austria, China, Ecuador, France, Germany, Greece, Italy, Mexico, and Spain. The NKU International Programs office has expanded its own international offerings to include student and faculty exchanges in Aarhus, Denmark; Gifu, Japan; Glasgow, Scotland; Munich, Germany; and Leon, Spain.

Academic Facilities

Among the academic facilities at NKU are an anthropology museum, a biology museum, and a geology exhibit at Landrum Hall. The University also has nursing, respiratory care, and radiologic technology laboratories and an art gallery with rotating exhibits. The W. Frank Steely Library at NKU contains 218,734 book titles and maintains 1,526 periodical subscriptions. Computer laboratories offer students opportunities to learn a variety of software programs.

Costs

Tuition and fees for 2003–04 were $3744 for Kentucky residents and $7992 for out-of-state students. Room and board costs were

$4776 a year. The cost of books and supplies amounted to about $650. Transportation costs were $700, and miscellaneous expenses were $800.

Financial Aid

Last year, 51 percent of undergraduates received some form of financial assistance. To receive financial aid, applicants must complete the Free Application for Federal Student Aid (FAFSA). Academic, athletic, music-drama, and art scholarships and scholarships for members of minority groups are available at Northern Kentucky University.

The application deadline for all academic scholarships is February 1. There is no deadline for the University's financial aid application; however, students who wish to receive institutional aid must apply by March 1 for priority consideration. Applicants are notified of acceptance on a rolling basis.

Faculty

More than 82 percent of the faculty members at NKU hold a doctoral degree or the terminal degree in their field. Classes are small, with a student-faculty ratio of 17:1. All classes are taught by faculty members; no classes are taught by graduate assistants.

Student Government

Student Government (SG) is the elected student assembly at Northern Kentucky University. It is the official student voice on campus and represents the student viewpoint on University committees. All SG meetings are open, and students are encouraged to attend.

Admission Requirements

Incoming freshmen must submit an application for admission; arrange for the official ACT, SAT, or COMPASS score report to be sent; and request that the high school send an official transcript. Students must meet precollege curriculum requirements for Kentucky. Out-of-state applicants must also meet the Kentucky precollege curriculum requirements, with the exception of the world civilization requirement.

Application and Information

There is a $25 fee that may be waived for applicants with demonstrated need. The fall semester early action and scholarship deadline is February 1; the priority application deadline is May 1. The priority application deadline for the nursing program is January 31. The deadline for the radiologic technology program is February 15. The priority application deadline for the respiratory care program is April 15.

For more information, students should contact:

Office of Admissions
Northern Kentucky University
Highland Heights, Kentucky 41099
Telephone: 859-572-5220
800-637-9948 (toll-free)
E-mail: admitnku@nku.edu
World Wide Web: http://www.nku.edu

Northern Kentucky University's modern campus is set in Highland Heights, just minutes from downtown Cincinnati.

NORTH PARK UNIVERSITY

CHICAGO, ILLINOIS

The University

North Park University began its tradition of academic excellence in 1891 and traces its roots to first-generation Swedish Americans. Formerly North Park College, the institution changed its name to North Park University in 1997 to more accurately and inclusively describe academic programs, especially to graduate and international students. North Park University was from the beginning, and continues to be, affiliated with and generously supported by the Evangelical Covenant Church. North Park believes that a liberal arts education should prepare students for a rich, morally responsible life and equip them with the intellectual and social skills necessary to succeed in any vocation or pursuit.

To serve this end, North Park has created a comprehensive education experience entitled the North Park Dialogue. This program provides many opportunities throughout the academic and cocurricular experience to explore questions of broad human significance from a wide range of perspectives. The North Park Dialogue occurs within the University's distinctively international/multicultural, urban, and dialogical Christian environment. Thus, the Dialogue and the three distinctive characteristics provide the framework within which all students are prepared for lives of significance and service. North Park University is committed to ensuring that all of its graduates have experience with international issues in the global culture and economy; understand urban challenges in a society where cities are the center of culture and multiculturalism; interact comfortably with people from a wide variety of Christian traditions, other religions and philosophies, and the broader culture while being confident of their own faith; and have explored the deep questions of life that affect everyone, despite age or background.

North Park students are involved in and committed to a wealth of cocurricular activities that develop them personally, morally, and socially. North Park's Outreach Ministries program attracts students from around the country; hundreds of North Park students volunteer in one of twenty programs on a weekly basis. Music, theater, and student government as well as athletics and religious involvement play an important role in the daily lives of the students, who are challenged to examine their values, define their potential, and maximize their personal growth. North Park University is a member of the NCAA Division III and the College Conference of Illinois and Wisconsin (CCIW); men and women participate in national and regional competition in Division III. Competition in intramural sports is open to the entire campus community.

At the graduate level, the University offers a Master of Arts in Community Development (M.A.C.D.), a Master of Arts in Education (M.A.Ed.), a Master of Business Administration (M.B.A.), a Master of Management (M.M.), a Master of Management (M.M.) in nonprofit administration, a Master of Music in vocal performance, and a Master of Science (M.S.) with a major in nursing with various concentrations; joint graduate degree programs between the seminary, business, and nursing departments; and seminary degrees, including Christian education, Christian ministry, divinity, and theological studies.

Location

Located in a pleasant residential neighborhood on the northwest side of Chicago, North Park's beautifully landscaped, 30-acre campus has small-town flavor and warmth, yet its intimate environment is within one of the largest and most exciting metropolitan areas of the world. Chicago offers a multitude of cultural, recreational, and service opportunities—everything from the Art Institute of Chicago and the Chicago Symphony Orchestra to the Chicago Cubs and Bulls to homeless shelters. The North Park campus hosts regular appearances by professional musicians and guest speakers. The impact of the city on the University's education program is significant. Several hundred student internship sites have been identified in the city. Easily accessed by public transportation, city life is available on demand.

Majors and Degrees

North Park University offers the Bachelor of Arts with major concentrations in advertising, anthropology, art, biblical and theological studies, biology, business administration, chemistry, communication arts, constructed majors, economics, education (early childhood, elementary, secondary (certification only)), English, exercise science, French, general science (secondary education only), history, human development, management of information technology, mathematics, music, organizational management, philosophy, physical education, physics, politics and government, psychology, Scandinavian studies, social studies (secondary education only), sociology, Spanish, Swedish, and youth ministry.

The Bachelor of Science is offered with major concentrations in accounting, athletic training, biology, business administration, chemistry, clinical laboratory science, constructed majors, exercise science, finance, international business, marketing, mathematics, nursing, physical education, and physics.

A student may earn the Bachelor of Music or the Bachelor of Music Education by choosing a major in music performance.

GOAL, a degree completion program for adults, offers accelerated B.A. degrees in human development, management of information technology, and organizational management. Classes meet in the evenings and on weekends.

Preprofessional programs are offered in dentistry, law, medicine, ministry, occupational therapy, pharmaceutical science, physical therapy, and veterinary medicine. North Park participates in a 3-2 engineering program whereby a student receives a baccalaureate degree from North Park and an engineering degree from one of four participating universities.

Academic Programs

The North Park Dialogue is integrated into all curricula, thus providing a consistent link among general education, major programs, and elective courses. Through general education, students learn how to reason, examine values, and communicate, which are skills as important as the knowledge gained in the courses. The general education curriculum is made up of interdisciplinary courses during the first two years, as well as courses in biblical and theological studies, fine arts, languages, mathematics, and science.

North Park operates on a calendar year consisting of two

16-week semesters and a ten-day interim between the winter and spring terms. Students are considered full-time if they are enrolled in a minimum of 12 semester hours. To graduate, a student must complete 120 semester hours with an overall grade point average of 2.0 or better. There are also requirements for the major and minor.

North Park recognizes high school graduates who have completed college-level courses in high school and have taken the Advanced Placement tests of the College Board. Students who have completed their junior year in high school, rank in the upper fourth of their class, have been enrolled in a college-preparatory curriculum, and show an aptitude test score that ranks at or above the mean score at the University may apply for early admission. Homeschooled students are also encouraged to apply.

North Park seeks and attracts students of superior high school backgrounds and academic aptitude. A scholars program is offered to qualified first-year students and continues throughout their academic career. The North Park Honors Scholars Program provides such students with enriching curricular and cocurricular supplements to their undergraduate experiences.

Off-Campus Programs

North Park students may participate in a number of off-campus programs. The American Studies Program of the Council for Christian Colleges and Universities provides work-study opportunities in Washington, D.C. Other coalition programs are available in Los Angeles (for film studies), Costa Rica (for Latin American studies), Egypt, and Russia. North Park also provides study-abroad programs in Ghana, Israel, Korea, Mexico, and Scandinavia.

Academic Facilities

Library services at North Park support and extend the academic instruction of the University. Students have immediate access to more than 215,000 bound volumes, 1,500 titles on microform, 1,000 periodical subscriptions, and 5,000 records and tapes. In addition, North Park students have access to the resources of Northeastern Illinois University and all sixteen of the LIBRAS Colleges in the Chicago area. In addition to computer classrooms, North Park offers a full computer center and two student labs with nearly sixty Apple Macintosh and IBM-compatible microcomputers available. The Center for Africana Studies, Center for Korean Studies, Center for Latino Studies, Center for Middle Eastern Studies, Center for Scandinavian Studies, and Archives for the Swedish American Historical Society are research centers located on the campus that can be used by students.

Costs

Tuition and fees for the 2004–05 academic year are $20,350. Room and board are $6510 for full-time students. Books and supplies are estimated at $900 but vary according to each student.

Financial Aid

At North Park, it is desired that no qualified student be prevented from obtaining a college education because of financial inability. In the 2003–04 academic year, 90 percent of North Park students received some form of financial assistance. The University offers comprehensive academic merit scholarships for those students who demonstrate high academic performance.

Upon submission of the Free Application for Federal Student Aid (FAFSA), North Park awards financial assistance to eligible applicants through a combination of scholarships, grants, loans, and work-study. A student must be admitted to the University before financial aid is awarded.

Faculty

One of the most vital characteristics determining the quality of an institution is its faculty members. The North Park faculty members are committed to relating the values and understandings of Christian faith to the academic fields it represents. Eighty-five percent of North Park's 100 full-time faculty members have earned doctorates or terminal degrees for their profession in the arts, sciences, and professional disciplines. Coming from a variety of denominational and educational backgrounds, faculty members share a commitment to North Park's goals as a Christian liberal arts university and are highly regarded in their scholarly fields.

Student Government

The North Park University Student Association represents the undergraduate student body in all areas of University life. Its elected and appointed members work in cooperation with the administration and the faculty in shaping both academic and other areas of student life.

The association operates through three main branches: the Student Senate, a legislative body of elected representatives; the Executive, whose function is to recommend and execute policy as well as to coordinate the activities of the association; and the Judiciary, which renders interpretations of the Student Association constitution. The association encourages campus dialogue via four student publications and sponsors cultural and social events via the Student Senate, a late-night café, various departments (including Academic Affairs, Social Awareness, and Social Events), and eight special interest student organizations (including associations for African-American, Asian, Catholic, Latin American, Middle Eastern, and Scandinavian students).

Admission Requirements

North Park gives consideration to students who have demonstrated their readiness for college by presenting superior or above-average high school records and satisfactory SAT I or ACT scores. The University also considers evidence of serious purpose, the character of the applicant, and participation in extracurricular activities as demonstrated through the application, essay, and personal reference. An interview is recommended but not required. North Park University admits students regardless of race, creed, sex, national or ethnic origin, or disability.

North Park welcomes applications from transfer students. The student seeking transfer admission must have a cumulative grade point average of at least 2.0 from an accredited institution.

Application and Information

Admission decisions are made on a rolling basis, with a first priority deadline of January 15 and a second priority deadline of March 15.

To be considered for admission, students need to submit the following: a North Park University application, high school or college transcripts, ACT or SAT I test scores, a personal essay, and two personal references.

Students are strongly encouraged to visit the campus. Those interested in more detailed information are invited to contact:

Mark Olson, Dean of Enrollment
North Park University
3225 West Foster Avenue
Chicago, Illinois 60625-4895

Telephone: 773-244-5500
800-888-6728 (toll-free)
World Wide Web: http://www.northpark.edu

NORTHWOOD UNIVERSITY

WEST PALM BEACH, FLORIDA

The University

Northwood University was founded in 1959 by Dr. Arthur E. Turner and Dr. R. Gary Stauffer in order to teach business and management infused with practical experience, based upon the concepts of freedom and free enterprise. Since the early days, the University has grown systemwide to include campuses in Michigan, Texas, and Florida as well as thirty-seven satellite centers throughout the United States, with a system enrollment of more than 7,000 students. Northwood is a private, independent, coeducational institution and is accredited by the North Central Association of Schools and Colleges.

The Florida campus, which opened in the mid-1980s, has grown to its current enrollment of more than 1,000 students. Attracting students from all over the globe, the campus is host to students who come to Northwood from twenty-nine different states and thirty-two different countries. Approximately 300 of the students reside on campus in attractive apartment-style residence halls.

The campus architecture is quite unique. The buildings are directly influenced by the work of noted architect Alden B. Dow (a student of Frank Lloyd Wright). The low and rounded modern buildings create the feel of a corporate campus surrounded by lakes and dotted with palm trees. It has been described as a corporate campus in paradise.

Outside of the classroom, Northwood offers its students a broad spectrum of activities and clubs in which to participate. Clubs include Delta Epsilon Chi (DECA), Student Government, Fellowship of Christian Athletes (FCA), the Investment Club, the drama club, the dance club, the cycling club, and organizations linked to major fields of study. Activities include cultural awareness programs, concerts, Big Brothers/Big Sisters, Northwood's Outstanding Business Leader Forum, intramural sports, and many others.

Athletics play an important role in student life. Northwood's Florida campus competes in the National Association of Intercollegiate Athletics (NAIA). Men's intercollegiate sports include baseball, golf, soccer, and tennis. Women's sports include golf, soccer, softball, tennis, and volleyball. Several of the teams have been nationally ranked and are most competitive within the Florida Sun Conference.

Facilities for tennis, racquetball, swimming, basketball, and fitness are in proximity to the student residence halls.

Location

The beautiful 90-acre campus is located in West Palm Beach, Florida. West Palm Beach is a 1-hour drive from Ft. Lauderdale, 30 minutes from Boca Raton, and within a 2½-hour drive from Orlando. The Palm Beach International Airport, 10 minutes from the campus, provides easy access to students and visitors.

West Palm Beach offers students a vast array of opportunities for both work and play. Great weather year-round and easy access to outdoor activities ranging from scuba and snorkeling to spring training major-league baseball and concerts at south Florida's premier outdoor concert venue supplement a very active on-campus activity program.

Majors and Degrees

The Florida campus of Northwood offers the Associate of Arts (A.A.) degree and the Bachelor of Business Administration (B.B.A.) degree. Degree programs are offered in accounting; advertising/management; automotive aftermarket management; automotive marketing/management; banking and finance/management; computer-management information systems; entertainment, sport, and promotion management; hotel, restaurant, and resort management; international business/management; management; and management/marketing management.

Off-Campus Programs

Recognizing that the business world is truly global, the University offers several exciting study-abroad programs for its students. The Term in Europe is a ten-week, traveling study-abroad program that explores the likes of France, Germany, Greece, Hungary, and Italy. The Term in Asia program is a residential study-abroad program in partnership with universities in Southeast Asia.

Northwood University's Margaret Chase Smith Library in Skowhegan, Maine, also offers a unique learning experience. The private library is open to serious students who are interested in the compatible, constructive coexistence of government and the private sector. The library, in addition to its invaluable collection of twentieth-century American politics and government, serves as an arena for free discussion of the economic ideas and ideals upon which the nation was founded.

Academic Facilities

At the heart of Northwood's academic facilities is the DeVos-Cook Academic Center. One of the newest buildings, this facility contains 23,000 square feet of space and houses state-of-the-art classrooms, faculty offices, and computer labs for both instructional and general student use.

Supplementing the DeVos-Cook Center is the Johann M. and Arthur E. Turner Education Center. This modern 38,000-square-foot facility houses the library, an art gallery, administrative offices, conference rooms, classrooms, and an auditorium.

Costs

The annual fee structure for the 2004–05 academic year is $13,989 for tuition, $540 for fees, and $7261 for room and board. Northwood estimates that annual books and supplies cost $1211. As Northwood is a private university, the tuition and fee charge is the same for both in-state and out-of-state students.

Financial Aid

Approximately 70 percent of students at Northwood's Florida campus receive some form of financial assistance. The University makes available academic merit scholarships, athletic scholarships, and general need-based aid.

Merit scholarships are based upon academic performance and standardized test results (ACT or SAT). The Freedom Award is $5000 per year for new students who present a grade point average of 3.0 or higher and test scores greater than 1150 on the SAT or 25 on the ACT. The Free Enterprise award is $4000 per year for new students who present a grade point average of 2.7 or higher with test scores greater than 950 on the SAT or 20 on the ACT. Several other merit-based scholarships are available to those who qualify and are not need-based. Examples include grants for students who have participated in organizations such as DECA, FBLA, BPA, and Junior Achievement.

In order to be considered for all need-based aid programs, students must file the Free Application for Federal Student Aid (FAFSA). Need-based aid is available to those who qualify in the form of federal, state, and Northwood grants, loans, and work-study programs.

Faculty

The student-faculty ratio at Northwood is currently 20:1. This affords the student not only small classes but also the opportunity to work closely with faculty members. The faculty is dedicated to bringing current business practices into the classroom. In addition to the fact that the vast majority of the faculty members hold advanced degrees, more than 90 percent have had prior experience in the business or management world. It is their practical experience in the real world, coupled with small classes, which creates a learning experience that combines both theory and practical skills.

Student Government

The Student Government Association (SGA) assists in the personal, social, and political development of Northwood students, both individually and collectively. The organization consists of 5 major officers, class presidents, and several subcommittees and/or appointed positions. SGA has representatives to confer with Student Services and campus administrative leaders throughout the academic year.

Subcommittees include the Diversity and Cultural Committee, the Peer Education Network, BACCHUS–Alcohol and Drug Education and Awareness, the Food Service Committee, and the Commuter Advisory Board.

Admission Requirements

Northwood University seeks to enroll students who have an interest in pursuing business, management, or entrepreneurship and who have demonstrated that desire through performance in the classroom. When reviewing a candidate for admission, the University takes into consideration the applicant's high school record, the results of the SAT or ACT, and a host of other factors, including extracurricular activity, recommendations, and involvement in business-related activities or clubs.

Northwood strongly encourages students who have followed an approved course of study at another college or university to apply for admission. The University's transfer program is designed to allow each student to transfer the maximum number of credit hours into their program of study. Transfer students with fewer than 40 hours must submit high school transcripts and standardized test scores. All students who apply should be in good academic and social standing at the college from which they are transferring.

All international students are required to take the TOEFL examination, unless they have taken the SAT or ACT. A minimum score of 500 (173 electronic) on the TOEFL exam is required for regular admission. Official transcripts of all secondary (high school) and college work must be provided with the application.

Application and Information

An application is ready for consideration by the Admissions Committee when it has been received with the $25 application fee, required test scores, and transcripts from each school attended. Northwood encourages students to apply via the Web site. For online applications, the application fee is waived.

For more information about Northwood University, prospective students should contact:

Office of Admissions
Northwood University
2600 North Military Trail
West Palm Beach, Florida 33409
Telephone: 561-478-5500
800-458-8325 (toll-free)
E-mail: fladmit@northwood.edu
World Wide Web: http://www.northwood.edu

The Northwood University campus has been described as a corporate campus in paradise.

NORTHWOOD UNIVERSITY

MIDLAND, MICHIGAN; CEDAR HILL, TEXAS; AND WEST PALM BEACH, FLORIDA

The University

Northwood University was founded in 1959 by Dr. Arthur E. Turner and Dr. R. Gary Stauffer, who had decided that the liberal arts approach to business did not really expose students to the wealth of opportunities the world of work had to offer. Established originally in Alma, Michigan, the school moved to Midland in 1961. The Texas campus was opened in 1966. Other expansions include the Florida campus in West Palm Beach and the Northwood University Margaret Chase Smith Library Center in Skowhegan, Maine.

Northwood University also coordinates a nontraditional program, University College, headquartered at the Midland, Michigan, campus; extension centers are located on all three campuses and in Carlsbad, New Mexico; Chicago, Illinois; Fort Worth, Texas; Detroit, Flint, and Lansing, Michigan; Tampa, Florida; Indianapolis, Indiana; Louisville, Kentucky; New Orleans, Louisiana; and Selfridge ANG Base, Michigan. University College is dedicated to providing nontraditional options for earning management degrees for students who are balancing work schedules, family responsibilities, community involvement, and educational goals.

Executive, managerial, and full-time M.B.A. programs are offered at the University through the Richard DeVos Graduate School of Management, which adds to a series of bachelor and associate degree programs that offer an exceptionally wide array of free-market-based degrees in management and entrepreneurship.

In terms of facilities, the Michigan campus is the most fully developed. The 268-acre campus is heavily wooded, and all of the buildings were designed by Alden B. Dow. About 60 percent of the students live on campus. Important activities on campus include the student government, advertising club, ski club, Free Enterprise Group, radio station, fraternities, sororities, service clubs, intramural sports, and the drama club.

The Michigan campus has a well-developed athletic program, headquartered in the Bennett Sports Center. Outstanding teams are fielded every year in men's varsity baseball, basketball, football, golf, soccer, tennis, and track and field. Women's varsity teams include basketball, soccer, softball, tennis, track and field, and volleyball. The Sports Center has a six-lane pool; facilities for basketball, dance, and indoor tennis; and a state-of-the-art fitness center that features Nautilus weight machines. Northwood's Michigan campus is a member of the National Collegiate Athletic Association (NCAA, Division II), and the Florida and Texas campuses are members of the National Association of Intercollegiate Athletics (NAIA).

The Texas campus is located near the Dallas–Fort Worth metroplex. Students participate in intercollegiate baseball, cross-country, the Student Senate, newspaper and yearbook, Auto Club, DECA, field trips, and the annual ribfest and chili cook-off.

Current facilities on the Florida campus comprise more than 26,000 square feet of classroom, office, and library space and include a 38,000-square-foot multipurpose building. On-campus housing for students is also available.

Even though Northwood's campuses are in different locations, with students coming from more than forty states and many countries, all have one goal in common: the preservation and promotion of the American free enterprise work ethic. Students come to Northwood to develop entry-level skills for management positions in business and industry.

Location

Midland, a professional town, is the site of the world headquarters of Dow Chemical U.S.A. It has 2,600 acres of parks and forests, the impressive Center for the Arts, the Chippewa Nature Center, and the Dow Gardens. The famous Michigan North Country begins in Midland County, and students have easy access to skiing, camping, hiking, fishing, and hunting. A large number of students work in the surrounding area.

The campus in Cedar Hill is located in the cedar-covered hills and valleys south of Dallas. Students work and have access to activities and facilities in Dallas and Fort Worth, including football games, shopping, and symphony concerts.

The Florida campus is located in the rapidly developing area of West Palm Beach. Numerous cultural and recreational facilities are available.

Majors and Degrees

Northwood University offers programs leading to the Associate of Arts degree in accounting; advertising; automotive aftermarket management; automotive marketing; banking and finance; business management; computer science/management; entrepreneurship; entertainment, sports, and promotions management; fashion marketing and merchandising; hotel, restaurant, and resort management; international business; and rapid text entry. Not all degree programs are offered at all campuses and extension centers.

Qualified graduates of an associate degree program may enter directly into the Bachelor of Business Administration program, which is available at all campuses and at the extension centers. This degree program offers majors in accounting; automotive aftermarket management; banking and finance/management; computer information management; entertainment, sports, and promotions management; hotel, restaurant, and resort management; international business; management; management/automotive marketing; management/computer science; management/economics; management information systems; management/marketing; and verbatim systems.

Academic Program

Northwood University's programs have been designed to prepare men and women for specific career goals. The courses for the major (approximately 30 percent of the total requirements) are reinforced by classes in general business (30 percent) and the humanities (40 percent). Associate degree candidates are required to complete 90 term hours with a minimum GPA of 2.0. Bachelor's degree candidates must complete 180 term hours with a minimum GPA of 2.0.

Northwood's terms last ten weeks. The fall term runs from September through November, the winter term from December through February, and the spring term from March through May. In addition, the college offers three 3-week summer sessions.

Northwood believes strongly in the free enterprise system and, accordingly, has designed its curriculum to reflect this belief. All students must satisfactorily complete core courses in accounting, business law, economics, management, and marketing. No matter what the ultimate career goal of a student may be, he or she will have acquired a set of basic skills as preparation for the productive world of work. This academic program, however, does not prohibit students from appreciating the arts. Northwood strongly promotes the interrelationship between the business and art worlds by providing on- and off-campus voluntary programs.

Employers of Northwood University graduates constantly stress their need to have employee candidates who demonstrate experiences, attitudes, and leadership abilities beyond those provided in the classroom and those reflected on the academic transcript. The EXCEL program goes beyond the curriculum to enhance the employability of Northwood University graduates and provide valuable experiences and dimensions beyond the classroom. Through EXCEL, students participate in valuable, documentable activities, resulting in a Student Development Transcript that is issued along with the academic transcript. Students document a minimum of five extracurricular activities per year; honors and awards are reflected on this transcript as well. The Student Development Transcript has no bearing on meeting degree requirements reflected through the academic transcript, but the EXCEL program provides opportunities to expand and document students' Northwood University education well beyond the classroom requirements and to enrich students' lives and prospects for employment.

Off-Campus Programs

In keeping with its interest in the world marketplace, Northwood University offers its students an optional opportunity each fall to participate in the Term-in-Europe program. Formal classes are supplemented by student tours, industry and cultural visits, and opportunities to meet with students and industry leaders from host countries such as the Czech Republic, France, Germany, Greece, Italy, and the Netherlands.

Academic Facilities

The Strosacker Library contains 47,000 volumes, receives 410 periodicals, and has an especially strong reference division on business management. The Griswold Communications Center has full-color videotape capability and a closed-circuit television-monitor system. The National Auto Dealers Association Center is equipped with a twenty-five-room hotel, classrooms, and a conference center. All students receive training in business computer application and IBM PC–compatible computers. Additional facilities are available on the Texas and Florida campuses.

Costs

The 2002–03 costs for the Michigan campus for both in-state and out-of-state students attending full-time were $13,461 for tuition and fees, $2976 for a room, and $3030 for meals. Students spend about $825 per year for books. Costs vary slightly on each campus.

Financial Aid

Students should file the Free Application for Federal Student Aid (FAFSA). Available aid includes Federal Pell Grants, Federal Supplemental Educational Opportunity Grants, state and institutional grants and scholarships, Federal Stafford Student Loans, loans for parents, and Federal Work-Study awards. Approximately 70 percent of students receive some type of financial aid.

Faculty

The faculty members at Northwood not only have academic credentials (90 percent have earned an advanced degree) but also bring to the classroom a wealth of business experience. These professionals are hired from business and industry to impart not only the theoretical concepts but also the practical, real-world aspects of a discipline. Faculty members are not engaged in research; their primary duty is in the classroom. In addition, each member is involved in at least one extracurricular activity with students. The student-faculty ratio is approximately 26:1.

Student Government

In keeping with Northwood University's philosophy of training future management leaders, the student government has these responsibilities: to provide for the formulation and expression of student attitudes and opinions, to represent the student body in discussions with the faculty members and administration, to provide student activities, to appropriate and disburse funds, and to investigate and resolve complaints from faculty members, students, and the administration.

Admission Requirements

Northwood is fully committed to maintaining diversity among its student population. Young adults from a variety of social, geographic, and economic backgrounds have begun their careers at Northwood. Interested students should design their high school program to include 4 years of English, 3 years of mathematics, accounting, and typing. Candidates must submit a complete high school transcript, and ACT or SAT I scores are required. Personal interviews are recommended.

Application and Information

There is no deadline for submitting applications for freshman-year admission. Transfer students are admitted year-round.

For more information, students should contact the appropriate location:

Director of Admissions
Northwood University
4000 Whiting Drive
Midland, Michigan 48640
Telephone: 989-837-4273
800-457-7878 (toll-free)
World Wide Web: http://www.northwood.edu

Director of Admissions
Northwood University, Florida Campus
2600 North Military Trail
West Palm Beach, Florida 33409
Telephone: 561-478-5500
800-458-8325 (toll-free)

Director of Admissions
Northwood University, Texas Campus
1114 West FM 1382
P.O. Box 58
Cedar Hill, Texas 75104
Telephone: 972-293-5400
800-927-9663 (toll-free)

Director of Admissions
University College
4000 Whiting Drive
Midland, Michigan 48640
Telephone: 989-837-4411
800-445-5873 (toll-free)

Students in Northwood's interactive classrooms in Florida and Michigan listen to author Clive Chajet talk about his book *Image by Design*.

NORWICH UNIVERSITY

NORTHFIELD, VERMONT

The University

Norwich University was established in 1819 as the first private military college in America. It was at Norwich that the idea of the citizen-soldier developed and eventually evolved into the Reserve Officer Training Corps (ROTC). Norwich was the first private college to offer civil engineering, and many University alumni were involved in the construction of the nation's continental railway system. In 1974, Norwich became one of the first military colleges to admit women into its Corps of Cadets, preceding the Federal Academies.

Norwich University offers a diverse blend of disciplines, teaching styles, and viewpoints. Students enrolled in the Corps of Cadets have a more disciplined, challenging, and structured path through college, while their civilian student classmates lead a more traditional collegiate lifestyle. However, both groups are coeducational and attend classes and participate in sports and other activities together.

In keeping with its mission, Norwich provides opportunities for all its students to develop leadership skills with a strong commitment to community service. Both groups gain skills such as leadership, honor, and integrity, which are required to be successful in today's job market. These two diverse groups of students are very different and yet have much in common—they are Norwich.

Norwich University has an enrollment of 1,800 students from more than forty states and twenty countries. The University's minority enrollment is consistently higher (by percentage) than that of any other Vermont university or college.

Location

Norwich University is located in the heart of the Green Mountains of Vermont right in the middle of ski country. Some of the nation's most popular resorts, such as Stowe, Sugarbush, and Killington, are located within an hour's drive. Vermont is world-renowned as one of America's most beautiful states. Nature's playground is just outside the dorm room—skiing, snowboarding, telemark skiing, cross-country skiing, snowshoeing, rock climbing, hiking, mountain biking, canoeing, kayaking, and more are available.

The University campus is located in the small town of Northfield, Vermont. Northfield is 10 miles south of the state capital of Montpelier and is 50 miles from Burlington, the largest city in Vermont. Both Montpelier and Burlington are cultural centers for the arts. Burlington International Airport is within an hour's drive. In addition, the cities of Boston and Montreal are only a 3-hour drive from the campus.

Majors and Degrees

Norwich offers students twenty-nine academic majors from which to choose. The Bachelor of Arts degree is awarded in communications; criminal justice; English; history; international studies; peace, war, and diplomacy studies; political science; and psychology. The Bachelor of Science degree is awarded in accounting, architecture, biochemistry, biology, biomedical technology, chemistry, civil/environmental engineering, communications, computer engineering, computer information systems, computer science, economics, electrical engineering, environmental science, geology, management, mathematics, mechanical engineering, physical education, physics, and sports medicine. Teacher licensure, prelaw, premedical, and dental programs are also available.

Norwich has the only professional five-year Master of Architecture program in northern New England. The University also offers online graduate degrees in business administration, diplomacy, information security assurance, and justice administration.

Academic Programs

Norwich University is dedicated to the discovery, preservation, and dissemination of knowledge and the search for truth. Norwich is distinctive in that it maintains a strong emphasis on the development of leadership in both military and civilian pursuits and in providing for the educational needs of students. The University's mission is to foster in each student the growth of self-discipline, personal integrity, social responsibility, physical fitness, respect for law, and intellectual ability essential for full and effective participation in a free society.

For students enrolling in the Corps of Cadets, six semesters of Reserve Officer Training Corps (ROTC) are required. Norwich is considered the birthplace of ROTC and therefore all four service branches can be found on campus. Prior to their junior year, cadets may elect to contract with their ROTC program and be considered upon graduation for a commission as officers in the Army, Navy, Air Force, or Marine Corps. Cadets not on an ROTC Scholarship are not required to join the military.

Students typically take an average of five classes per semester. Each semester is sixteen weeks long, with holiday breaks at Thanksgiving, Christmas, New Year's, and in March during spring break. The academic year normally begins the last week in August and ends after the first week in May.

Academic Facilities

Opened in 1993, the Kreitzberg Library is an attractive, 58,000-square-foot, multistoried facility that offers plenty of work space and study areas for students to work individually or in groups. The library houses a collection of 280,000 volumes, more than 900 periodical subscriptions, and electronic resources, which provide sources of information necessary to complete assignments and research papers. Internet connections and interlibrary loan service provide access to many more resources from around the world. The state-of-the-art, Web-based Voyager online library catalog and an increasing number of databases are networked and accessible from computers in the library and from sites both on and off campus. Recreational books, videocassettes, and audiocassettes are available for circulation. Informed and approachable library staff members are always present to assist with reference needs and library instruction.

Students may research the Norwich facilities on the University's Web site and may view individual buildings at http://www.norwich.edu/maps/northfield.html.

Costs

For 2003–04, tuition and fees were $17,629. The cost of room and board was $6722. Books and personal expenses averaged $700 per semester. Cadets paid a one-time uniform fee of $1120.

Financial Aid

Most families assume they cannot afford a private college education and fall victim to "sticker shock," but a Norwich education is often as affordable as a local state college. Last year 92 percent of Norwich students, with an average family income of $42,000, shared in more than $23 million of financial aid from all sources. This included an aggressive need-based financial aid program that enabled deserving students to secure a private education at Norwich.

Norwich awards academic scholarships on a competitive basis to students who are placed in the top 10 or 20 percent of their high school class. These scholarships pay from 33 to 50 percent of the student's tuition for four years. Students are required to maintain a specified GPA in order to renew the scholarship each year. Students whose high schools do not rank should contact the University admissions office and ask to speak with a counselor.

Norwich also offers a vast array of leadership and merit scholarships based on a student's record of demonstrated leadership as well as their participation in sports, community and school organizations, employment, volunteer work, and other extracurricular activities. Students who bring a three- or four-year ROTC scholarship to Norwich are eligible for the General I. D. White Scholarship, which covers the cost of room and board. Students interested in applying for an ROTC scholarship should visit the individual ROTC detachment's Web page on the Norwich University Web site.

Faculty

The student-faculty ratio is 14:1. Faculty members are full-time instructors with advanced degrees; 80 percent hold a doctorate. Small classes help promote a close relationship between faculty members and students. Students are assigned faculty advisers within each academic division.

Student Government

The Norwich University Corps of Cadets is a military organization made up of and led by cadets under the supervision of the Commandant of Cadets. Members of the corps and student body preside over the University Honor Council. The University's honor code binds all Norwich students. Members of the corps and student body also participate on the Student Affairs Committee, whose members include the Dean of Students, members of the faculty, and the Senior Vice President and Commandant of Cadets. This committee serves as the voice of the Norwich community and provides a channel of communication for change.

Admission Requirements

Admission to Norwich is based on a review of the applicant's academic record, personal essay, letters of recommendation, and extracurricular activities. Students at Norwich are heavily involved in community service and leadership development activities. Applicants should be able to demonstrate participation in activities both inside and outside of their high school.

Norwich is looking for students who want to become leaders, serve others, and give back to their communities. While the admissions office uses a rolling admissions system (meaning applications may be submitted at any time), there is a priority deadline of March 1. Students applying for admission or financial aid after March 1 are admitted on a space-available basis.

Application and Information

Students can visit the University's Web site or contact the University at the address, phone number, e-mail address, or fax number listed below.

Dean of Enrollment Management
Norwich University
27 I. D. White Avenue
Northfield, Vermont 05663
Telephone: 800-468-6679 (toll-free)
Fax: 802-485-2032
E-mail: nuadm@norwich.edu
World Wide Web: http://www.norwich.edu

Norwich University's Kreitzberg Library is the pride of the Northfield campus.

NOTRE DAME COLLEGE

SOUTH EUCLID, OHIO

The College

Notre Dame College was established in 1922 by the Sisters of Notre Dame of Cleveland. The College exists today largely because of the spirit of the foundress of the Notre Dame order, St. Julie Billiart, an eighteenth-century pioneer in education. The College believes that truly progressive education selectively blends traditional values with new ideas that represent real growth. Within the scope of a career-oriented liberal arts education, students can grow to meet the challenges of the present and the future. The College is accredited by the North Central Association of Colleges and Schools. It is registered for the awarding of State Teachers' Licenses by the State of Ohio Department of Education.

A variety of clubs and activities enrich the educational experiences of the College's 1,200 students. Student clubs include chapters of the American Chemical Society and the American Institute of Biological Sciences. The Masquers promotes talent in the performing arts and provides entertainment for the College community and general public. Campus publications include the *Notre Dame News* and *PIVOT*, the literary magazine. Faculty members and students schedule and coordinate lectures, plays, performances, and concerts. Most on-campus events are free, and students may purchase tickets at reduced rates for off-campus programs such as performances of the world-famous Cleveland Orchestra, the Cleveland Opera, and road shows of Broadway productions at the Palace Theatre, State Theatre, and Ohio Theatre at Playhouse Square. Performances at the Cleveland Play House are also available.

Men's and women's intercollegiate basketball, soccer, track, and cross-country, are offered along with men's tennis and women's softball and volleyball. New sports introduced in 2004 include men's and women's golf, women's lacrosse, and men's baseball. Notre Dame College is a member of the National Association of Intercollegiate Athletics and competes in the American Mideast Conference.

The beautiful 53-acre wooded campus provides the perfect setting for the Clara Fritzsche Library; the Administration Building, housing all of the classrooms and offices; Connelly Center, the cafeteria and student center; the Keller Center, the recreational and fitness facility; and three residence halls.

A Master of Education degree, designed for classroom teachers, is offered with concentrations available in special education, reading, and critical and creative thinking.

Location

The College is located in South Euclid, 25 minutes from downtown Cleveland and only 5 minutes from Legacy Village, Cleveland's new lifestyle retail center. The area combines the excitement and cultural wealth of a major urban and educational center with the relaxed atmosphere of a suburban setting. University Circle in Cleveland, a 500-acre complex containing an unusual blend of cultural, educational, medical, religious, and social service institutions, is easily accessible from the College.

Situated on the shores of Lake Erie, Cleveland is the home of the Rock-and-Roll Hall of Fame, professional sports, and the Flats entertainment district. The Cleveland Metroparks offer a variety of activities and recreational opportunities. Snowy winters provide abundant opportunities for skiing and tobogganing, and popular ski areas are located a short distance from the city.

Majors and Degrees

The College awards the Bachelor of Arts degree in accounting; communication; education, including early childhood (PK–3), middle childhood (4–9), and secondary education; English; graphic communications; history/political science; human resource development; information systems; management; marketing; prelaw; psychology; public administration; sports/recreation manangement; studio art; and theology. The Bachelor of Science is awarded in biology, chemistry, and mathematics. A student can also design his or her own major that leads to a Bachelor of Arts or Bachelor of Science degree by combining two or three academic areas, such as graphic design, human resource management, and public relations.

Certification programs are offered in business and environmental technology. Teacher licensure is available in elementary school education, kindergarten, prekindergarten, and secondary education (grades 7–12). A multiage license is also available.

The Associate in Arts degree is awarded at the completion of two-year programs in business management and pastoral ministry.

The Center for Pastoral Theology and Ministry grants a two-year catechetical diploma and the Bachelor of Arts degree.

Academic Program

All students pursue a career-oriented liberal arts education. For the bachelor's degree, students must earn 128 semester hours of credit, with a minimum cumulative grade point average of 2.0. From 36 to 68 semester hours of credit are required in the major field of study.

Through a cooperative education program, students may receive up to 6 semester hours of credit for paid or volunteer work experience related to their academic field of study.

Advanced Placement credit is awarded to students who have demonstrated the ability to pursue course work beyond the level of entering freshmen, as indicated by their scores on the Advanced Placement (AP) or College-Level Examination Program (CLEP) tests of the College Board. College credit is given on the basis of a decision made jointly by the academic dean and the department involved.

Academic Facilities

The Clara Fritzsche Library, housing the modern Media Center, has a capacity for 100,000 volumes. As a member of Ohiolink, the College also has online access to members throughout the state, with access to more than 31 million library items and more than 90 research databases. The newly renovated science wing includes new state-of-the-art biology and chemistry labs. The Science Research Center houses $1 million in sophisticated instrumentation and computers that allow students to work side-by-side with faculty members on research projects. Undergraduates learn to operate such equipment as a Fourier-transform infrared spectrometer, Fourier-transform nuclear magnetic resonance spectrometer, and gas chromatograph/mass spectrometer, allowing science majors to develop independence and confidence in laboratory practices.

The $1-million Dwyer Learning Center is the computer hub of campus, with forty-eight computer stations for student use. The center includes an electronic classroom, areas for peer tutoring, a writing lab, and curriculum-specific software in science, math, history, and foreign languages.

The new Multi-Media Lab for graphic design majors offers PC and Mac technology for advanced multimedia production capabilities.

The Center for Professional Development offers course work for educators on a variety of topics. The center offers seminars and short, flexibly scheduled courses for teachers and social workers throughout the year as well as new certificate programs in business leadership and athletic coaching.

Costs

For the 2003–04 academic year, tuition charges were $16,990. Room and board costs were $6200 for double occupancy. Part-time tuition was $405 per hour. Student fees were $500.

Financial Aid

A comprehensive financial assistance program of approximately $2.2 million assists nearly 90 percent of all full-time students.

Students applying for aid must submit the Free Application for Federal Student Aid (FAFSA). Forms are available from the College's Office of Student Financial Assistance.

Faculty

The faculty has 24 full-time and 40 part-time members; 70 percent of full-time faculty members have doctoral/terminal/first-professional degrees. The faculty is augmented by highly qualified instructors in special areas. Faculty members hold advanced degrees from more than thirty universities in the United States, Canada, and Europe.

Student Government

The Undergraduate Student Senate and the Resident Association Board are the active student governing bodies. In addition, students have representation on various College committees.

Admission Requirements

In fulfilling its mission, Notre Dame College seeks to attract students of diverse religious, racial, and economic backgrounds. Candidates for admission as first-time, full-time freshmen are reviewed on an individual basis, and decisions are based on a broad range of criteria. The most important consideration is the candidate's high school performance, as demonstrated by her/his overall grade average, class rank, grade trends, and level of courses completed. Aptitude for verbal and mathematical reasoning, as measured by performance on standardized tests, is also considered. In addition, counselor and teacher recommendations are reviewed.

Notre Dame College requires at least 16 units of high school credit in academic subjects as a prerequisite for matriculation in the College. The distribution of these subject areas and the units are as follows: English, 4; mathematics, 3 (to include algebra I, geometry, and algebra II); science, 3 (with laboratory experience); social studies, 3; foreign language, 2 (from the same language); and fine arts, 1. Applicants should generally rank in the upper half of their high school graduating class and have a minimum average of C+. Either ACT or SAT I scores are accepted.

Students wishing to transfer from other regionally accredited colleges and universities are admitted to advanced standing upon presentation of satisfactory evidence of scholarship and character.

Special consideration may be granted to an applicant whose academic preparation is not consistent with the requirements stated above.

Notre Dame College strongly recommends that prospective students schedule an appointment to visit the campus and talk with an admissions counselor. Open houses throughout the year also give prospective students the chance to visit the campus.

Application and Information

The College maintains a rolling admission policy. To apply, students should submit the completed application for undergraduate admission, an official transcript of their high school record that includes class rank, results of the ACT or SAT I, a letter of recommendation, and a nonrefundable $30 application fee to:

Office of Admissions
Notre Dame College
4545 College Road
South Euclid, Ohio 44121
Telephone: 216-373-5355
800-NDC-1680 Ext. 5355 (toll-free)
Fax: 216-373-5278
E-mail: admissions@ndc.edu
World Wide Web: http://www.notredamecollege.edu

The Science Research Center allows undergraduate students to conduct research with faculty members.

NOTRE DAME DE NAMUR UNIVERSITY

BELMONT, CALIFORNIA

The University

At Notre Dame de Namur University (NDNU), formerly College of Notre Dame, students gain the knowledge, expertise, and values that develop them and prepare them to excel professionally. In addition, students practice their talents through undergraduate research and internships as well as in roles of campus leadership and service.

Notre Dame de Namur University has been providing students of all backgrounds and beliefs with an individualized liberal arts education for 153 years. Founded by the Sisters of Notre Dame de Namur in 1851, NDNU was one of the first four colleges in California chartered to grant the bachelor's degree. It is the mission of the University to help students develop both a broader understanding of the world and the tools required to flourish personally and professionally.

NDNU's total enrollment is approximately 1,800, allowing for closeness among students, faculty members, and staff members. Classes are kept small; many have only 10 to 15 students, while the largest classes have 25 to 40 students.

The University's population is composed of people from diverse ethnic and religious backgrounds. Students come from throughout the U.S. and more than forty countries. NDNU's size enables the University to guarantee housing for all new students in either residence halls or apartment complexes. There is a residency requirement for freshmen and sophomores. NDNU is composed of buildings reflecting a variety of architectural styles interspersed with green lawns and trees.

There are many extracurricular opportunities available at NDNU. Students take part in a wide variety of campus organizations, including Alianza Latina, the *Argonaut* (student newspaper), the Biz-Com Club, the Black Student Union, the *Bohemian* (literary magazine), the Computer Science Club, the Hawaiian Club, the International Club, the Science and Medical Careers Club, and Sanlahi (Filipino Club).

There are five main stage theater productions each year for students interested in drama, and musicians perform with an orchestra, a choir, and smaller ensembles. NDNU competes in the National Association of Intercollegiate Athletics (NAIA) and is a full member of the California Pacific Conference, with six men's and six women's teams.

In addition to the undergraduate degrees shown below, the University offers master's degrees in art therapy, business administration, computer science, counseling psychology, education, English, music, public administration, systems management, and eBusiness management, and credentials in education.

Location

Notre Dame de Namur University's campus covers 50 acres of forested hillside in the safe and peaceful community of Belmont, California—only 25 miles south of San Francisco at the northern edge of Silicon Valley. The San Francisco Bay Area is home to one of the world's most dynamic cities and the technological heart of the nation as well as some of the premier centers of cultural, recreational, and athletic attractions in the country. Students often plan short trips to the beach in Santa Cruz, to the Napa Valley wine country, and to the Sierra Nevada mountains for skiing.

Majors and Degrees

Notre Dame de Namur University offers the Bachelor of Arts degree in art, art/graphic design, biology, communication, English, history, humanities, liberal studies, marketing-communication, music, musical theater, philosophy, political science, psychology, religious studies, social science, sociology (including concentrations in behavioral science and social action), and theater arts.

The Bachelor of Science degree is awarded in biochemistry, biology, business administration (including concentrations in accounting, economics and finance, international management, marketing, sports and leisure management, and technology management), computer science, human services, and software engineering and management. The Bachelor of Fine Arts is offered in studio art; the Bachelor of Music is offered in music performance.

Students interested in dentistry, law, medicine, teaching (elementary and secondary), pharmacy, physical therapy, and veterinary medicine may enroll in preprofessional programs. Double majors are quite common, and individually designed interdisciplinary majors are encouraged. Minors are offered in environmental studies, film studies, French, Latin American studies, mathematics, Spanish, technical communication, Web design, and women's studies, as well as in the major fields. Students may enter Notre Dame de Namur University undeclared and are guided by a faculty adviser in selecting a major.

In addition to the undergraduate and master's degrees, the University offers elementary and secondary school teaching credentials.

Academic Programs

As a comprehensive college with a liberal arts history, the University requires that students complete a core of general education courses designed to strengthen analytical abilities and develop skills in critical thinking and effective communication. General education courses range from the arts to English composition to intercultural studies to natural science.

The University encourages students to conduct mentored research and offers distinctive opportunities for interdisciplinary course work, experiential and service learning, integration of project-based and cocurricular activities, Web-based learning, career and service internships, and professional portfolio development to enhance career advancement and job placement.

Notre Dame de Namur University operates on a traditional semester system, with two semesters of fifteen weeks each, plus an optional summer session. The graduate and evening degree completion programs operate on a trimester system. Students pursuing an undergraduate degree must complete a minimum of 124 semester units. Entering freshmen are granted credit for each Advanced Placement exam passed with a score of 3 or higher.

Off-Campus Programs

NDNU's Study Abroad Program places interested students (preferably as juniors) in colleges and universities in many countries around the world, including Ecuador, England, France, Japan, Mexico, and Russia. Students may also take advantage of exchange programs with the University's sister schools: Emmanuel College in Boston and Trinity College in Washington, D.C.

Academic Facilities

NDNU's beautiful campus in the wooded hills of Northern California provides an ideal setting in which to study and learn.

The University offers modern science laboratories, computer centers, and a fully equipped 600-seat theater. The spacious library holds a collection of more than 100,000 volumes, 722 periodical subscriptions, and 9,500 audio recordings. Special features include the multimedia computer lab and the music technology lab. The Madison Art Center (located in a historic mid-1800s carriage house) is home to modern art studios, a viewing theater, and the Wiegand Art Gallery, which hosts exhibits by students and nationally known professional artists.

Costs

Tuition costs for 2004–05 are $21,350. The cost of room and board for the academic year is estimated at $8800, depending on the meal plan chosen by the student, and includes all utilities except for telephone. The total cost of one year (including books and other expenses) is estimated at $34,000.

Financial Aid

Notre Dame de Namur University is committed to making high-quality education affordable for every accepted student. Some form of financial assistance is given to approximately 80 percent of the University's full-time students. Need-based grants, loans, and work-study programs are available through the federal and state governments and the University itself. Merit-based scholarships are offered for students with demonstrated high academic achievement, community service, and leadership experience. Scholarship information is included on the NDNU admission application.

All students are encouraged to apply for need-based financial assistance. Each applicant for financial aid must submit the Free Application for Federal Student Aid (FAFSA) and California residents must submit the Cal Grant GPA verification form by March 2. Students should contact the college counselor at their school or the NDNU admission office for these forms.

Faculty

Notre Dame de Namur University's distinguished faculty is committed to helping each student reach his or her highest potential. All students are assigned a faculty adviser with whom they meet one-on-one each semester. Advisers and instructors also hold weekly open-office hours. The student-faculty ratio is 12:1, and the average class size is 15. More than 90 percent of the full-time faculty members hold doctoral or other terminal degrees.

Student Government

The Associated Students of Notre Dame de Namur University (ASNDNU) provides many opportunities for participation in student government and the planning of campus activities. Each student is eligible to take part in ASNDNU as a student representative, and each of the University's governing committees has a student member, thereby ensuring student involvement in the making of administrative decisions.

Admission Requirements

Notre Dame de Namur University welcomes applications from interested students without regard to religious preference, financial need, or ethnic background. The completion of a college-preparatory course pattern, including courses in English, mathematics, natural science, social science, foreign language, and the arts is required for freshman applicants, along with the submission of SAT I or ACT scores. Students whose first language is not English must submit TOEFL scores in lieu of ACT or SAT I scores. Each applicant is considered individually, taking into account the application essay, a letter of recommendation, and service and extracurricular achievements in addition to the academic record. Approximately 79 percent of each year's applicants are offered admission.

Transfer students are accepted at all class levels in both fall and spring semesters. Students who have completed more than 30 transferable units are not required to submit high school transcripts or SAT I or ACT scores. Transfer students considering Notre Dame de Namur University may request a preapplication transfer credit evaluation to determine what course work is needed to complete a bachelor's degree. Concurrent enrollment agreements are in place with nearby community colleges.

Application and Information

Notre Dame de Namur University operates on a rolling admission basis. For fall freshman applicants, the early action deadline is December 1 and the priority deadline is February 1. Transfer students should apply by July 1 for the fall semester and December 1 for the spring semester.

All interested students are encouraged to visit the University for a campus tour and admission counseling.

For an application packet, to arrange a visit, or for more information, students should contact:

Office of Admission
Notre Dame de Namur University
1500 Ralston Avenue
Belmont, California 94002
Telephone: 650-508-3600
800-263-0545 (toll-free)
E-mail: admiss@ndnu.edu
World Wide Web: http://www.ndnu.edu

Students on the campus of Notre Dame de Namur University.

NOVA SOUTHEASTERN UNIVERSITY

FORT LAUDERDALE, FLORIDA

The University

Nova Southeastern University (NSU) is the largest independent or non-tax-supported university in the Southeast. Based upon fall enrollment, it is the tenth-largest independent university in the United States. Nova Southeastern University is a nonsectarian, nonprofit, and nondiscriminatory university, and it accredited by the Southern Association of Colleges and Schools.

Unusual among institutions of higher education, NSU is a university for all ages: the University School for children, numerous undergraduate and graduate degree programs in a variety of fields, and nondegree continuing education programs are all available at NSU. The traditional population in the undergraduate program is approximately 1,200 students. With students from all fifty states and thirty-three other countries, NSU is a university of national and international scope.

Student activities include more than twenty-five faculty-sponsored clubs; events sponsored by the student government; NCAA Division II sports such as baseball, basketball, cross-country, golf, soccer, softball, and volleyball; a newspaper; a radio station; intramurals; five national fraternities and seven national sororities; and a variety of sport clubs.

Location

The main campus of Nova Southeastern University is located on a 300-acre site in Fort Lauderdale, Broward County, Florida. Broward County is a principal coastal area in south Florida and a rapidly growing community for business, industrial, electronics, and computer opportunities. The climate is subtropical and has an average year-round temperature of 75 degrees. Natural areas for outdoor activities such as sailing, fishing, golf, tennis, and swimming are easily and quickly accessible from the University. With tourism as a major industry, Fort Lauderdale provides the best in shopping, dining, and cultural offerings, which include concerts, opera, ballet, museums, theater, and professional sporting events.

Majors and Degrees

Nova Southeastern University offers B.S. degrees in accounting; applied professional studies; athletic training; biology (premedical); business administration; computer information systems; computer science; education (prekindergarten/primary education, elementary, and exceptional); environmental science/studies; finance; legal studies (prelaw); marine biology; paralegal studies; psychology; and sport and wellness studies. The B.A. degree is offered in English, history, and humanities. Also offered are a number of certificate programs as well as a variety of credit and noncredit courses, workshops, and institutes.

NSU offers a dual-admission program for a select number of highly motivated, qualified students interested in pursuing both undergraduate and graduate studies in business, computer sciences, conflict analysis and resolution, dental medicine, education, family therapy, law, marine biology, mental health counseling, occupational therapy, optometry, osteopathic medicine, pharmacy, physical therapy, psychology, or speech-language pathology. Students who successfully meet all program requirements have a seat reserved for them in one of the specified NSU graduate or professional schools.

Academic Program

The undergraduate program for NSU's daytime population combines a general education curriculum with a set of majors designed to prepare students for work in graduate school or a professional career. Through a small, intimate classroom setting, NSU's program provides a cooperative form of learning in which students are encouraged to help each other achieve competence while they receive close personal attention and support from individual instructors.

The academic year is divided into six terms of eight weeks each, permitting students to enroll for up to 9 credits of time-intensive course work per term. Each course of study leads to the Bachelor of Science or Bachelor of Arts degree.

Other Nova Southeastern University programs are organized for the adult working population. Courses are offered in the evenings and on weekends at the main campus, as well as at off-campus locations convenient to students and online. Although course content is designed to satisfy traditional educational requirements, courses are scheduled to meet the needs of employed students and are taught by utilizing a blend of University professors and knowledgeable practicing professionals. Most students are employed and have passed the traditional age of undergraduates; many have families. Credits may be awarded for prior learning experiences after a faculty committee has approved a student's application for such credit. Additional credit may be earned through PEP and CLEP general and subject examinations. Credit toward a degree may also be transferred from regionally accredited institutions.

Academic Facilities

Students enrolled in academic programs at Nova Southeastern University have numerous academic facilities available to them. Computer labs provide courses and programs in applied microcomputer technology. The University Computing Center provides data processing facilities and services to meet the instructional, research, and administrative needs of the University and is available to qualified students for computer-oriented course work. Other facilities within the University include the University School (prekindergarten through grade 12), the Family Center, the Shepard Broad Law School, the Oceanography Center, the Health Professions Division, and the Center for Psychological Studies. The NSU Alvin Sherman Library, Research, Information, and Technology Center offers twenty electronic classrooms, 700 workstations, 1,000 user seats equipped with Internet access, and the 500-seat Rose and Alfred Miniaci Performing Arts Center. The library has the capacity to house 1.4 million volumes of reference materials, making it the largest in Florida.

Costs

Tuition for undergraduate students at Nova Southeastern University varies according to the academic program. For the 2003–04 academic year, tuition for the full-time day program was $15,000. Textbooks cost approximately $600 per year, and on-campus housing was approximately $3800 for the year. Meal plan costs were approximately $2400 per academic year.

Financial Aid

Nova Southeastern University offers a comprehensive program of financial aid to assist students in meeting their educational expenses. Financial aid is available to help cover direct educational costs such as tuition, fees, books, and supplies as well as indirect costs such as food, clothing, and transportation. The following forms of financial aid are available to qualified undergraduate students: Federal Pell Grants, Federal Supplemental Educational Opportunity Grants, Florida Student Assistance Grants, Florida Academic Scholars Fund awards, Florida Tuition Vouchers, Federal Stafford Student Loans, Federal Perkins Loans, Federal PLUS loans, Federal Work-Study awards, and Florida College Career Work Experience Program awards. In addition, many academic scholarships are available. Deferred-payment plans and veterans' benefits are also offered.

Applicants for financial aid are required to submit the Free Application for Federal Student Aid (FAFSA) to be considered for all campus-based aid programs. Students who apply before April 1 are given priority consideration for funds; however, applications are accepted all year.

Faculty

The undergraduate faculty at Nova Southeastern University is full-time and resident. In addition, faculty members are drawn from qualified professionals in the community, as well as from other centers and programs within the University. Most of the faculty members have backgrounds in professional, industrial, managerial, civic, educational, or other private and public sectors of the community. For example, lawyers and judges teach criminal justice courses; accountants, personnel managers, and others teach in their respective fields; and principals and teacher curriculum specialists teach education courses. All faculty members are dedicated to the philosophy that contemporary higher education combines theory and practice and that the education of working professionals and adult students requires the active participation of both the student and the instructor.

Student Government

All Nova Southeastern University students benefit from the services of the Student Government Association (SGA). The SGA has proved to be an influential organization in campus affairs; it instills a sense of community in the student body. Students in the undergraduate programs enjoy the same rights and services as all other Nova Southeastern University students, including use of University study and recreational facilities, access to all support services, and participation in student affairs.

Admission Requirements

Admission requirements vary according to the program. A counseling session is recommended. Freshman applicants must submit official high school transcripts and SAT I or ACT scores.

Transfer applicants must submit official college transcripts. Each student's record is evaluated individually to determine the number of transferable credits. There is a maximum of 90 transferable credits, and students must complete 30 semester hours at Nova Southeastern University.

Application and Information

The application should be submitted with a nonrefundable $50 application fee. There is no closing date for applications for the fall term. Applicants are notified of the admission decision on a rolling basis.

For further information, prospective applicants are invited to contact:

Farquhar College of Arts and Sciences
Office of Undergraduate Admissions
Nova Southeastern University
3301 College Avenue
Fort Lauderdale, Florida 33314
Telephone: 954-262-8000 (local tri-county)
800-338-4723 Ext. 8000 (toll-free)
E-mail: ncsinfo@nova.edu
World Wide Web: http://www.undergrad.nova.edu

Nova Southeastern University's Library, Research and Information Technology Center is Florida's largest library.

OAKLAND UNIVERSITY

ROCHESTER, MICHIGAN

The University

Pioneering the Future is the best way to describe the excitement building at Oakland University (OU) today. The comprehensive campus is in its forty-fifth year and continues to increase its programs, facilities, resources, and enrollment. Oakland University was created in 1957 when the late Alfred G. and Matilda R. Wilson donated their 1,500-acre estate and $2 million to Michigan State University to begin a new college in Oakland County. Named Michigan State University–Oakland, the new campus enrolled its first students in 1959. In 1963, its name was changed to Oakland University, and in 1970 the Michigan legislature recognized the maturity and state of the University by granting it autonomy. From its beginning, the University has flourished, emphasizing academic quality and concentrating on providing its students with a broad liberal arts education by a nationally recognized faculty.

Dedicated to preparing learners for the twenty-first-century workplace and society, the university today is organized into the College of Arts and Sciences and the Schools of Business Administration, Education and Human Services, Engineering and Computer Science, Health Sciences, and Nursing. Oakland offers undergraduate programs in more than 100 areas, with master's and doctoral programs in sixty-three areas. OU also features an active Honors College for students looking for a more challenging academic experience. Oakland was rated twenty-fourth in academic reputation among the 123 top Midwestern regional colleges and universities for 1998 by *U.S. News & World Report*.

Enrollment at Oakland University continues to set new records, reaching 16,059 students in 2002–03. Oakland retains the best features of a small-campus setting even as the University grows and changes to meet enrollment demands.

Oakland is committed to preparing students for a rapidly changing work environment. The University has major institutes and centers in eye research, wellness, biochemistry technology, and international studies. Students use multimedia applications and interactive learning to reach their potential. Through innovative, technology-enriched delivery of educational services, Oakland University is preparing a community of learners for the opportunities of today and tomorrow.

OU is home to approximately 1,200 students who live on campus in six residence halls and a 48-unit apartment complex. All rooms are equipped with phones with voice mail and cable TV. Cars are allowed for all class levels.

Oakland University has ninety-five recognized student organizations, including thirty-six academically oriented organizations and fifteen Greek letter organizations.

In 1999, OU's athletic programs moved from Division II to Division I competition. OU joined the Mid-Continent Conference and competes in six men's sports and eight women's sports.

Oakland's cultural enterprises attract more than 500,000 visitors to the campus each year. Students can enjoy events offered through OU's Meadow Brook Theatre, Meadow Brook Art Gallery, and Meadow Brook Hall. Meadow Brook Music Festival stages a variety of summer concerts.

Location

Oakland University's 1,441-acre campus is conveniently located in suburban Rochester, Michigan. The University's location in Oakland County offers many cultural and recreational opportunities, such as the Palace of Auburn Hills and the Pontiac Silverdome. Oakland County, the fastest-growing county in the state, plans to add about 40,000 new jobs within the next two years, which will mean more opportunities for Oakland's students and graduates.

Majors and Degrees

The College of Arts and Sciences offers bachelor's degrees in anthropology, applied statistics, art history, biochemistry, biology, chemistry, communication arts, East Asian studies/China, East Asian studies/Japan, economics, English, environmental health, French, general studies, German/German studies, history, international studies, journalism, Latin American languages/civilization, Latin American studies, linguistics, mathematics, medical physics, modern languages, music, music education, performing arts (music, theater, and dance), philosophy, physics, political science, predentistry, prelaw, premedicine, preoptometry, psychology, public administration and public policy, Russian language/civilization, Slavic studies, sociology, South Asian studies/India, and Spanish. The School of Business Administration offers bachelor's degrees in accounting, economics, finance, general management, human resource management, management information systems, and marketing. The School of Engineering and Computer Science offers bachelor's degrees in computer engineering, computer science, electrical engineering, engineering chemistry, engineering physics, mechanical engineering, and systems engineering. The School of Health Sciences offers bachelor's degrees in industrial health and safety, medical laboratory sciences, medical physics, physical therapy, and radiation therapy. The School of Education and Human Services offers bachelor's degrees in elementary education, human resource development, and secondary education with certification in biology, chemistry, English, French, German, history, mathematics, music, physics, and Spanish. The School of Nursing offers a bachelor's degree in nursing.

Academic Programs

While each school has its own sequence requirements, all students must satisfy the following requirements: 32 credits in general education, writing proficiency, and one course in ethnic diversity. Students must also have a cumulative grade point average of at least 2.0 in courses taken at Oakland University. In certain programs, additional GPA requirements must be met. Finally, students must successfully complete 32 credits in courses at the 300-level or above. Students at Oakland have the unique opportunity to conduct research at the undergraduate level.

Off-Campus Programs

Oakland prepares students for the twenty-first-century workplace by offering meaningful challenges and experiences. Oakland is one of four Michigan colleges participating in the federally funded Americorps program, patterned after the Peace Corps.

At Oakland, students have opportunities to gain paid work experience. Many students work in internships and cooperative job placements in government, business, and industry throughout southeastern Michigan.

Oakland also offers study-abroad opportunities in England, France, Italy, Japan, and Vienna.

Academic Facilities

To accommodate ongoing growth, several capital improvements are underway at Oakland. A new science and engineering complex, an Honors College, a new business administration building, a new education building, and a $31-million recreation and athletic center have opened recently.

Oakland University's Kresge Library includes a 1.7-million-piece collection of books, microforms, and periodicals. The library also houses private study rooms, a major computer lab, and an interlibrary database so students can access materials at other libraries.

Computer labs are located in various campus buildings, offering current software and applications, high-quality printers, and advanced computer graphics.

Costs

Tuition for the 2002–03 academic year was $144.25 per credit hour for freshmen and sophomores, $158.75 per credit hour for juniors and seniors, and $364 per credit hour for out-of-state students. A typical full-time semester schedule consists of 12 to 16 credit hours. The 2002–03 room and board cost was $5252. Books and supplies averaged $475.

Financial Aid

Oakland offers two programs of assistance to students: scholarships based on academic achievement and financial aid based on need. Students must submit the Supplemental Application for Scholarships and Financial Aid for consideration.

Faculty

Oakland's faculty members encourage curiosity, foster critical thinking, and help students develop skills that allow them to analyze an increasingly complex world. Of the University's 371 faculty members, 90 percent hold a doctoral degree in a specialized field of study from many of the nation's finest research institutions. Virtually all courses (99 percent) are taught by faculty members. The student-faculty ratio is 19:1. Small classes contribute to Oakland's student-focused learning environment.

Student Government

Oakland's student government, University Student Congress, is an elected, campuswide governmental body that serves students' needs. In addition to its administrative duties, University Student Congress provides funding for the Student Activities Funding Board, which allocates money to recognized student organizations, and for the Student Program Board, a student committee responsible for programming films, lectures, concerts, and other recreational activities. The elected student leaders also lobby on behalf of students at the state and national level.

Admission Requirements

Freshman applicants should have completed a high school college-preparatory program and have a B average or better. The ACT is required. Transfer students must be in good academic standing at the time of transfer and have at least a 2.5 GPA. For both freshman and transfer applicants, required grade point averages vary for certain programs.

Application and Information

For more information, students should contact:

Office of Admissions
101 North Foundation Hall
Oakland University
Rochester, Michigan 48309-4475
Telephone: 248-370-3360
800-OAK-UNIV (toll-free)
E-mail: ouinfo@oakland.edu
World Wide Web: http://www.oakland.edu

Students enjoy a break between classes at the newly renovated food court at the Oakland Center.

OBERLIN COLLEGE

OBERLIN, OHIO

The College

Oberlin College, founded in 1833, is an independent, coeducational, liberal arts college dedicated to recruiting students from diverse backgrounds. Oberlin comprises two divisions: the College of Arts and Sciences, with roughly 2,350 students, and the Conservatory of Music, with about 550 students. Students in both divisions share one campus; they also share residence and dining halls as part of one academic community. Many students take courses in both divisions. Oberlin awards the Bachelor of Arts and the Bachelor of Music degrees. In Oberlin's unique double-degree program, students pursue the B.A. and the B.Mus. degrees in a unified, five-year program. Selected master's degrees are offered in the Conservatory.

Oberlin was the first college in the country to admit women, and one of the first to admit African Americans. By 1900 nearly half of all the black college graduates in the country—128 to be exact—had graduated from Oberlin. This core of Oberlin-educated men and women formed the first black professional class in the country.

Today, Oberlin's progressive history lives on in the idealism and conviction of its students. Students are united by a commitment to social justice and a willingness to confront social issues that many would prefer to ignore. As the *New York Times* noted in an article marking Oberlin's 150th anniversary, "In its century and a half, while Harvard worried about the classics and Yale about God, Oberlin worried about the state of America and the world beyond."

Oberlin seeks a diverse and promising student body. Recognizing that diversity broadens perspectives, Oberlin is dedicated to recruiting a culturally, economically, geographically, and racially diverse group of students. Interaction with others of widely different backgrounds and experiences fosters the effective and concerned participation in the larger society so characteristic of Oberlin graduates. Among primarily undergraduate institutions, Oberlin ranks first for the number of graduates who go on to earn Ph.D. degrees. Its alumni, who include three Nobel laureates, are leaders in law, scientific and scholarly research, medicine, the arts, theology, communications, business, and government.

Oberlin has several distinctive academic programs. During the four-week Winter Term, students create independent projects (group or individual) that can be pursued on- or off-campus. These projects may have an academic or career focus and need not be connected to a student's major. Oberlin's Experimental College, a student-run program, offers courses for limited academic credit taught by Oberlin students, townspeople, administrators, and faculty members.

Oberlin offers a small-town atmosphere, and is located not far from Cleveland. There is never a lack of something to do. More than 400 concerts and recitals take place on campus annually, from ticketed events like the Cleveland Orchestra to free student and faculty recitals. Each year the Conservatory stages two operas, and the theater and dance program presents several productions. Numerous lectures and readings feature guests prominent in a variety of disciplines.

Location

Oberlin College is an integral part of the city of Oberlin, a town of about 8,000 residents located 35 miles southwest of Cleveland. The town is primarily residential, with tree-lined streets and fine old clapboard houses. The College is located in the center of town, close to the business district, and virtually everything a student needs is within walking or biking distance.

Majors and Degrees

Oberlin offers the Bachelor of Arts degree (awarded by the College of Arts and Sciences), and the Bachelor of Music degree (awarded by the Conservatory of Music). Oberlin also offers a unique "double-degree" program, a five-year course of study leading to the B.A. and B.Mus. degrees. Students wishing to enter the double-degree program must be accepted by both the College of Arts and Sciences and the Conservatory of Music.

The B.A. is awarded in African-American studies, anthropology, archaeological studies, art (history and studio), biology, biopsychology, chemistry, cinema studies, classics (Greek, Latin, and classical civilization), comparative literature, computer science, creative writing, dance, East Asian studies, economics, English, environmental studies, French, geology, German, Hispanic studies, history, Jewish studies, Latin American studies, law and society, mathematics, music, neuroscience, philosophy, physics, politics, psychology, religion, Russian, Russian and East European studies, sociology, theater, Third World studies, 3/2 engineering, and women's studies. In addition, many students pursue interdisciplinary individual majors.

The B.Mus. is awarded in composition, electronic and computer music, historical performance, jazz studies (performance or composition), music education, music history, and performance (baroque cello/viola da gamba, baroque flute, baroque oboe, baroque violin, bassoon, clarinet, classical guitar, double bass, flute, harp, harpsichord, horn, lute, oboe, organ, percussion, piano, recorder, saxophone, trombone, trumpet, tuba, viola, violin, violoncello, and voice). A major in music theory is only offered as part of a double major.

The Conservatory of Music also offers combined 5-year B.Mus. and M.Mus. degrees in opera theater, conducting, and music education and teaching as well as an M.Mus. in historical performance and a four-semester Artist Diploma.

Academic Program

To receive the B.A. or the B.Mus. degree, students must complete a major; nine credit hours in each of Oberlin's three divisions: humanities, natural sciences, and social sciences; and three Winter Term projects. Students must also demonstrate quantitative proficiency and writing proficiency. For the B.A., 112 credit hours are required for graduation; for the B.Mus., 124 hours are required. The recommended semester course load is 14 credit hours for students in the College of Arts and Sciences and 15 or 16 credit hours for students in the Conservatory of Music.

Academic Facilities

Oberlin's four libraries contain more than 1.75 million items, including 1.1 million catalogued volumes— an unusually large collection for a college of Oberlin's size. Other features include an online catalog, connections to several networks, and access to numerous online and CD-ROM databases. The College's Allen Memorial Art Museum is considered one of the top college or university art museums in the nation. Seventeenth-century Dutch and Flemish painting, European art of the late nineteenth and twentieth centuries, and contemporary art are especially well-represented among the more than 14,000 objects spanning the range of art history in the museum.

The Conservatory of Music contains 153 practice rooms—all with windows—and houses 168 Steinway grand pianos and 18 uprights. The Conservatory also has two concert halls, numerous instrument collections, state-of-the-art electronic music studios, and recording facilities.

Oberlin's Irvin E. Houck Computing Center provides more than 250 Macintosh and Dell computers for student use in several locations on campus. In all of the residence hall rooms, students have direct access to the Internet and the campus network from their personal computers. Computer accounts are automatically given to all students at no charge. Although it is becoming more wireless, Oberlin is considered to be one of the most wired colleges in the country.

Oberlin's new Science Center was designed to accommodate contemporary methods in science education. Everything is interconnected, promoting communication across disciplines and collaborative research relationships for which Oberlin is so well known. The new Science Center complex is a testament to Oberlin's long-held belief that the best liberal arts education has a strong science component and that the best science education occurs in a liberal arts environment.

The Adam Joseph Lewis Center for Environmental Studies is an integrated building-landscape system that incorporates several ecological technologies, including solar cells on the roof that produce a portion of the building's electricity needs, an engineered wetland that treats and recycles wastewater, a restored native wetland, and orchards and vegetable gardens that demonstrate urban-scale organic agriculture.

Costs

Tuition for the 2002–03 academic year was $27,880. Double-room and board fees were an additional $6830. The student activity fee was $170.

Financial Aid

In an average year, Oberlin commits more than $30 million, more than one-fifth of the College budget, to financial aid. The Office of Financial Aid works to develop financial aid packages that meet the demonstrated financial need of all regularly admitted students who comply with the filing deadlines. Canadian citizens are treated as U.S. citizens for financial aid purposes. Limited financial aid is also available for other international students.

To apply for assistance, students must submit the Financial Aid PROFILE of the College Scholarship Service and the Free Application for Federal Student Aid (FAFSA).

Faculty

Of Oberlin's 339 faculty members, 253 teach in the College of Arts and Sciences and 86 teach in the Conservatory of Music. They are eminently qualified for their positions with more than 95 percent having earned doctoral or terminal degrees in their field, many from the world's finest graduate institutions. The faculty-student ratio is 12:1 in the College and 8:1 in the Conservatory.

Student Government

By serving on Oberlin's Student Senate and in other ways, Oberlin College students have the opportunity to influence College policy on academic and student-life issues. Student representatives sit on nearly every faculty committee, and allocation of the student activity fee is determined by a committee composed solely of students.

Admission Requirements

Admission to both the College of Arts and Sciences and the Conservatory of Music is highly selective. Candidates for admission must submit the results of the SAT I or ACT. The College also recommends that three SAT II Subject Tests be taken. For the class of 2005, the median SAT I scores were 684 verbal and 652 math. The median ACT score was 29. Of those students who attend high schools that rank their students, 61 percent were in the top tenth of their high school class and 79 percent were in the top fifth. For admission to the Conservatory of Music, the most important factor is the performance audition, or in the case of composition and electronic and computer music applicants, the compositions, tapes, and supporting materials submitted.

Application and Information

For more information or to request an application, students should write to:

Office of Admissions, College of Arts and Sciences
Oberlin College
Oberlin, Ohio 44074
Telephone: 440-775-8411
800-622-OBIE (toll-free)
E-mail: college.admissions@oberlin.edu

Office of Admissions, Conservatory of Music
Oberlin College
Oberlin, Ohio 44074
Telephone: 440-775-8413
E-mail: conservatory.admissions@oberlin.edu
World Wide Web: http://www.oberlin.edu

Office of Financial Aid
Carnegie Building
Oberlin College
52 West Lorain Street
Oberlin, Ohio 44074
Telephone: 440-775-8142
800-693-3173 (toll-free)
E-mail: financial.aid@oberlin.edu

OGLETHORPE UNIVERSITY

ATLANTA, GEORGIA

The University

Standing as a landmark in north Atlanta since the beginning of this century, Oglethorpe University is located on 126 acres of unquestionable beauty. Only 10 miles from the heart of downtown Atlanta, the campus, with its classic neo-Gothic architecture, maintains an Old World charm. The current undergraduate enrollment is approximately 1,120, with nearly 60 percent women and 40 percent men. Approximately half of the full-time students live on campus in the seven residence halls. The ethnic and religious backgrounds of the student body are diverse; students come to Oglethorpe from forty states and approximately twenty-two countries. Oglethorpe students learn to make a life, make a living, and make a difference. Its graduates become community leaders who are distinctive in their ability to think, communicate, and contribute.

Numerous activities are offered on campus, such as concerts, exhibits, and social affairs. The University has a student center, six tennis courts, a Reslite track, a swimming pool, an intramural field, a recreational sports facility and a basketball arena with seating for 2,000. There is an extensive intramural program. Intercollegiate sports are offered for men in baseball, basketball, cross-country, golf, soccer, tennis, and track and field and for women in basketball, cross-country, golf, soccer, tennis, track and field, and volleyball.

There are many avenues for development of leadership potential, including the Rich Foundation Urban Leadership Certificate Program. Omicron Delta Kappa, a national leadership organization, recognizes outstanding leadership on campus. Alpha Phi Omega, a national service fraternity that is open to both men and women, is one of Oglethorpe's largest organizations; its purpose is to serve the school, the community, and the nation. Alpha Phi Omega emphasizes service, friendship, and leadership as qualifications for membership. Students also have excellent opportunities to develop their extracurricular interests. More than sixty clubs and organizations are open to students, including fraternities and sororities, honor societies, academic societies, and special interest groups. One of the distinctive features of Oglethorpe is the interest and support the University gives to such activities. This is in keeping with the goals of the institution, which are to build a community of leaders and to stimulate personal and intellectual growth and development.

In addition to its undergraduate programs, Oglethorpe also offers a Master of Arts in Teaching degree and a Master's of Business Administration degree.

Location

Students enjoy the many benefits of being on a small suburban campus near a large metropolitan cultural center. Metropolitan Atlanta's population is more than 4 million, and the community offers all the entertainment advantages of a large city, including professional athletics, world-renowned museums, concerts by well-known artists, theaters, and restaurants. Cultural centers and recreational facilities are easily accessible, and good transportation is available. Home to one of the busiest airports in the world, Hartsfield Atlanta International Airport, the city is a major international transportation hub. Transportation within the city is connected by four major interstates and the Metropolitan Atlanta Rapid Transit Authority (MARTA), which provides bus and rapid rail service to and from Oglethorpe.

Majors and Degrees

Oglethorpe University confers the Bachelor of Arts (B.A.) and Bachelor of Science (B.S.) degrees. Majors leading to the B.A. are offered in American studies, art, business administration and behavioral science, communications, economics, English, French, history, individually planned major, international studies, philosophy, political studies, psychology, sociology, sociology–social work, and Spanish. Majors leading to the B.S. are accounting, biology, business administration, business administration and computer science, chemistry, economics, mathematics, mathematics/computer science, and physics. Preprofessional programs are offered in dentistry, law, medicine, optometry, and pharmacy. Dual-degree programs are offered in art in conjunction with Atlanta College of Art and in engineering in cooperation with Georgia Institute of Technology, Auburn University, the University of Southern California, and the University of Florida.

Academic Programs

Each new student is assigned a faculty adviser, who is responsible for assisting the student with academic and other matters. Close relationships between students and teachers are the heart of Oglethorpe's educational approach. Fresh Focus, a seminar for freshmen, provides a way for new students to get to know each other and to explore academic programs, career interests, and academic resources.

The program for undergraduates is viewed as a process of personal and intellectual development. The liberal arts and sciences provide the forum for increasing competence in reading, writing, speaking, reasoning, and the fundamental fields of knowledge, the arts and sciences. A core curriculum constitutes about 25 percent of each student's requirements. The core encourages students to reflect upon and discuss matters fundamental to understanding who they are and what they ought to be, forging a community of learners. This includes how they understand themselves as individuals and as members of society, how the study of the past informs a sense of who they are as human beings, and the ways in which the practice of science informs them on the physical and biological processes influencing human nature. The product of the core is a well-rounded student who is able to make a life, make a living, and make a difference. Readings are based on primary sources rather than textbooks.

Off-Campus Programs

Study-abroad programs in Europe, Moscow, South America, Mexico, and Asia award academic credit. The University also offers excellent internship programs with various scientific, government, and business organizations; sites include CNN, the Centers for Disease Control and Prevention, major accounting firms and corporations, and state government. Students may earn a maximum of 15 semester hours of credit through these programs.

Academic Facilities

The Philip Weltner Library was dedicated in 1992. The 56,000-square-foot facility houses an art museum, a 24-hour study area, and a viewing room with state-of-the-art equipment. Current library holdings include more than 150,000 books, an extensive collection of movies on videodisc, the *New York Times* on microfilm, and more than 800 periodicals. Oglethorpe participates in a library sharing program with several other colleges and universities in the Atlanta area. Several computer laboratories are available for student use. Through GALILEO, students have online access to any college library in Georgia.

Costs

The comprehensive fee for 2004–05 is $28,000. This fee includes $20,700 for tuition, $7100 for room and board, and a student activity fee of $450. An additional $1800 should be sufficient for books, supplies, and personal expenses.

Financial Aid

The University offers aid from various federal programs, including the Federal Perkins Loan, Federal PLUS loan, Federal Pell Grant, Federal Supplemental Educational Opportunity Grant, and Federal Work-Study programs. Applications for these funds should be received by March 1. The James Edward Oglethorpe Scholarship Competition for freshmen awards the winners full tuition, room, and board. The University also offers the Oglethorpe Scholar Awards for outstanding students. These scholarships are based on scholastic performance, participation in activities, qualities of leadership and citizenship, and potential for success. Institutional need-based awards and campus employment are other possibilities. Approximately 95 percent of the University's students receive some type of assistance.

Faculty

Oglethorpe has an outstanding faculty; 96 percent of the members hold doctoral or other terminal degrees, many from the finest graduate schools in the country. The student-faculty ratio is 13:1, and no graduate assistants serve as undergraduate instructors. Although Oglethorpe is primarily a teaching institution, faculty members are engaged in various research projects and scholarly pursuits. Professors are available for student counseling and generally take an active role in campus activities.

Student Government

Undergraduate life at Oglethorpe University is, in a large sense, that of a democratic community; student government is mainly self-government. The Oglethorpe Student Association is the organization that guides and governs student life. The Executive Council is made up of a president, a vice president, a secretary, a treasurer, a parliamentarian, and the presidents of the four classes. They work in conjunction with a student senate. The Oglethorpe Honor Code contains the responsibilities that students and faculty members accept by becoming members of the community that is committed to high standards of academic honesty.

Admission Requirements

Throughout its history, Oglethorpe has welcomed students from all sections of the country as well as from abroad. Admission to the University is selective. It is the policy of the Admission Committee to accept those students who present the strongest evidence of purpose, maturity, scholastic ability, and potential for success. In making these judgments, the committee considers the applicant's high school program and grades, high school rank if available, SAT I or ACT scores, a personal essay, and the recommendations of counselors and teachers. Students entering Oglethorpe should have completed 4 units of English, 4 of mathematics, 3 of science, and 3 of social studies; 2 units of language are recommended.

The SAT I score range of the middle 50 percent of accepted applicants in 2000 was 1110 to 1300. The median ACT composite score was 27. Candidates for regular decision admission may apply at any time. Applications are reviewed on a rolling basis, beginning immediately after early action reviews (late December) and continuing as long as space in class is available. Early action applicants must apply by December 5. Notification letters are mailed no later than December 20. Transfer applicants and students applying for joint enrollment are welcome.

Application and Information

For additional information, students may contact:

Office of Admission
Oglethorpe University
4484 Peachtree Road, NE
Atlanta, Georgia 30319
Telephone: 404-364-8307
404-261-1441 Ext. 8307
E-mail: admission@oglethorpe.edu
World Wide Web: http://www.oglethorpe.edu

Oglethorpe's history, dating back to 1835, is reflected in its architecture.

OHIO DOMINICAN UNIVERSITY

COLUMBUS, OHIO

The University

Ohio Dominican University is a private, Catholic liberal arts university guided in its educational mission by the Dominican motto, "To contemplate truth and to share with others the fruits of this contemplation." Founded in 1911 as the College of Saint Mary of the Springs, its name was changed to Ohio Dominican College in 1968 when it became a coeducational campus. The college changed to university status in July 2002 as part of a commitment to increase enrollment, offer graduate studies, and be one of the preeminent Catholic universities in the country.

Ohio Dominican's campus spans 62 beautifully wooded acres, mixing the charm of older buildings featuring federalist architecture with contemporary buildings. The University has launched the first phase of a master plan that includes a new campus center, study center, expanded recreational facilities, and additional residential facilities to support the University's continued growth.

More than 2,500 students currently are enrolled in Ohio Dominican's day, evening, and weekend programs. Students come from across the nation and more than twenty countries, creating an enriching cultural experience on campus. Ohio Dominican offers students a high-quality, career-oriented liberal arts education in a setting that is conducive to intellectual exchange, personal growth, and the development of enduring values. It is a place where diversity is embraced and individualism is celebrated.

State-of-the-art technology in a student-centered environment opens the door to learning collaboration among students and instructors. In Ohio Dominican's intimate atmosphere, faculty members know their students by name, and every student realizes that he or she is a top priority. At the core of the University are the Dominican principles of caring, learning, and truth. Students are in an environment where they can benefit from moral guidance, spirituality, and contemporary thinking.

A full calendar of academic, cultural, and social events is provided for student enjoyment. A student newspaper, student government, academic clubs, cultural events, and religious organizations are just a few of the many activities offered on campus. The University offers a wide range of sports opportunities as a member of the American Mideast Conference (AMC) of the National Association of Intercollegiate Athletics (NAIA). Intercollegiate sports offerings include men's and women's basketball, golf, soccer, and tennis; women's softball and volleyball; and men's baseball and football. Students also have a variety of intramural activities from which to choose, including flag football, sand volleyball, basketball, tennis, and softball.

Ohio Dominican's Career Services Office is a valuable resource for students, alumni, and employers. The office maintains contacts with a large number of companies seeking to hire Ohio Dominican graduates. In addition to these services, Career Services houses a Career Resource Center and assists students with internships, resume writing, interviewing skills, and career counseling. Ohio Dominican is a sponsor of the Collegiate Job Fair of Greater Columbus, held at the University. More than seventy-five employers from around Ohio attend the job fair, providing students with a great opportunity to network and search for a job right on their own campus.

Graduate degree programs include Master of Arts in Theology, Master of Business Administration, Master of Arts in Liberal Studies, and Master of Education.

Location

Ohio Dominican is located just minutes from downtown Columbus. A 5-minute drive from campus is Easton Town Center—a shopping, restaurant, and entertainment center with a thirty-screen movie theater and more than 150 stores and entertainment establishments. As Ohio's state capital, Columbus is one of the fastest-growing cities in the nation (nationally ranked fifteenth largest) and offers a wide range of cultural opportunities, such as Broadway theater, Opera Columbus, Ballet Met, the Columbus Museum of Art, and the Columbus Symphony Orchestra. Located less than 5 minutes from Port Columbus Airport, Ohio Dominican is also easily accessible from Columbus's major highways.

Majors and Degrees

Ohio Dominican confers master's, bachelor's, and associate degrees, as well as certificates, in a variety of disciplines.

Major programs of study offered within the Bachelor of Arts degree are art, business administration, communication studies, criminal justice, cross-disciplinary studies, economics, education (integrated language arts, integrated social studies, and visual arts), English, graphic design, history, international business, liberal studies, philosophy, political science, political science with environmental issues concentration, psychology, public relations, social justice, social work, sociology, sports management, and theology.

Major programs of study offered within the Bachelor of Science degree are accounting information systems, biology, biology–pre-allied health track, business, chemistry, computer information management, computer science, computer systems development, cross-disciplinary studies, education (chemistry, earth science/chemistry, integrated mathematics, integrated science, life science, life science/chemistry, life science/earth science, life science/physics, and physical science), finance, management, and mathematics.

Within the Bachelor of Science in Education degree, major programs of study offered are early childhood, intervention specialist (mild/moderate educational needs, K–12), and middle childhood.

The University offers major programs of study within the Associate of Arts degree in cross-disciplinary studies, gerontology, legal studies, library services, and theology. Major programs of study within the Associate of Science degree are business and chemistry.

Special program tracks include pre-engineering, prelaw, and reading endorsement for teachers. Certificates are offered in administrative management, coaching, communication studies, criminal justice, gerontology, and teaching English to speakers of other languages (TESOL).

Academic Programs

The Ohio Dominican University liberal arts curriculum teaches skills and competencies valuable in every career and life—the ability to think critically, write proficiently, and communicate clearly. The University's nationally acclaimed humanities program is at the core of every student's academic study at Ohio Dominican.

Ohio Dominican has invested heavily in technology. The University's goal is to integrate technology into the learning process, making students' education the priority while helping them become more comfortable with technology, which is crucial in today's competitive job market.

Students are encouraged to take advantage of study-abroad and internship programs to enrich their University and educational experiences at Ohio Dominican. These programs can be very beneficial to future career plans. The honors program also provides students with the opportunity to graduate with distinction through a combination of seminars, honors-designated course work, and senior research and thesis projects.

The Ohio Dominican University academic calendar is based on the semester. The academic calendar consists of two 16-week semesters beginning in late August and running through mid-May. Summer courses are also offered.

Students come from all over the world to Ohio Dominican for its academic programs. The English as a second language (ESL) program has been an integral part of the campus community for more than twenty-five years.

Academic Facilities

Academic excellence is the result of an outstanding faculty working with students in state-of-the-art facilities. Ohio Dominican's Spangler Learning Center houses a library, Multimedia Center, Academic Center, and Information Services Department and computer classrooms. Spangler Library houses more than 150,000 volumes, as well as CD-ROMs and several online databases, such as OhioLink, Business and Company Resource Center, GroveArt, Hoover's Online, Mental Measurements Yearbook, NewsBank, Proquest Religion, Standard & Poor's Net Advantage, Social Work Abstracts, and Philosopher's Index. The Multimedia Center is equipped with scanners, CD burners, laminators, lettermakers, and many more technologies for students to use. The Academic Center offers students a wide range of academic assistance, such as tutoring, workshops, and graduate school test-preparation materials. Information Services supports the campus computer network, including the Microsoft Office suite, full Internet access, e-mail, and other software packages.

Ohio Dominican is networked for computer access throughout the campus. In addition to computers available in labs, computers are conveniently located in the student lounge and residence halls.

Costs

Tuition at Ohio Dominican is modest in comparison with other private universities. Tuition and fees for the 2004–05 academic year are $18,000. Room and board are approximately $6000 per year. Personal expenses and transportation costs vary depending on individual lifestyle and location of residence.

Financial Aid

Education is an investment. While Ohio Dominican's tuition is modest in comparison to most private universities, many families from a wide range of incomes benefit from the University's financial assistance programs. Nearly 90 percent of Ohio Dominican students received some form of financial assistance in 2002–03. More than $17.6 million was awarded to Ohio Dominican students from University, federal, state, and private resources in that year alone. The average aid offer, including scholarships, grants, loans, and employment, was $12,467. Aid offers ranged from $1038 to $23,980. Ohio Dominican's merit-based scholarship programs are particularly helpful to students who may not qualify for need-based aid programs. To be considered for need-based aid, students must complete the Free Application for Federal Student Aid (FAFSA), found on the Internet at http://www.fafsa.ed.gov.

Faculty

More than 60 full-time and 100 part-time professors make up Ohio Dominican's faculty. The student-faculty ratio is 17:1. Approximately 99 percent of the full-time faculty members hold a master's or doctoral degree, and no courses are taught by teaching assistants. Sabbaticals ensure that teaching faculty members remain experts in their academic field. The faculty members believe that the personal attention they give their students is a significant benefit of study at Ohio Dominican.

Student Government

Student leadership and involvement at Ohio Dominican are fostered through the College Council. College Council consists of students, faculty members, and administrators who join together to discuss and make decisions that have an impact on student life at the University. Each spring, campuswide elections are held for class officers and representatives, club and student organization officers, and student representatives on standing University committees.

Admission Requirements

To be considered for admission to Ohio Dominican University, students must complete an application for admission. There is no charge for completing an application online, but there is a $25 fee for paper applications. Official transcripts, ACT or SAT scores, and an interview are required. A campus visit is an important part of the application process. Students are encouraged to visit the campus, talk with faculty members, visit with coaches, and attend a class in addition to meeting with an admission counselor.

A significant number of students transfer to Ohio Dominican each year. Along with official transcripts from all colleges previously attended, transfer students must submit a high school transcript if they have completed fewer than 30 semester credits of college work.

Students may be considered for admission following the completion of their junior year of high school.

International applicants must submit the International Student Application Form, the Declaration and Certification of Finances form with supporting documentation, transcripts or certified true copies of original transcripts for all academic preparation beyond age 15, and a $25 application fee. A minimum 550 TOEFL score is required for admission into the regular curriculum, and a minimum 500 TOEFL score is required for admission to the ESL-based curriculum.

Application and Information

Ohio Dominican University uses a rolling admission process whereby students are notified of the admission decision as soon as their application is complete.

For additional information, students should contact:

Director
Office of Admission
Ohio Dominican University
1216 Sunbury Road
Columbus, Ohio 43219-2099
Telephone: 614-251-4500
800-955-OHIO (toll-free)
E-mail: admissions@ohiodominican.edu
World Wide Web: http://www.ohiodominican.edu

Erskine Hall at Ohio Dominican University.

OHIO NORTHERN UNIVERSITY

ADA, OHIO

The University

Founded in 1871, Ohio Northern University offers a dynamic learning environment, with its four undergraduate colleges, the College of Law, and a combination of professional and liberal arts programs. The University is related to the United Methodist Church and is committed to promoting spiritual as well as intellectual values. With a student population of more than 3,350, ONU is small enough to provide a personalized atmosphere but large enough to attract students with many different educational goals. Students attending Ohio Northern are presented with many opportunities to explore a wide range of activities—academic, social, spiritual, and physical.

Residence hall living is considered to be an integral part of the educational program, and the residence halls' professional staff, facilities, and programs contribute to students' personal development. The residence halls serve as key places for study sessions and student activities. There are ten residence halls on campus as well as the new campus village apartments, which house mainly juniors and seniors. The dining hall is located in the student union. There are also eight national fraternities and four national sororities, as well as thirty-eight honorary societies that recognize scholastic achievement or service.

The University is a member of the Ohio Athletic Conference and fields intercollegiate teams in men's baseball, basketball, cross-country, football, golf, indoor and outdoor track, soccer, swimming and diving, tennis, and wrestling and in women's basketball, cross-country, fast-pitch softball, golf, indoor and outdoor track, soccer, swimming and diving, tennis, and volleyball.

In addition to the undergraduate programs, the University offers a Juris Doctor, Doctor of Pharmacy (Pharm.D.), and Master of Education in Teaching.

Location

Surrounding the campus is the town of Ada, a small, quiet, friendly community of 5,000 residents. Located in northwestern Ohio, Ohio Northern and Ada are easily accessible by major highways. Students have convenient access to Columbus, Dayton, and Toledo while enjoying the hospitality and comfort of Ada's hometown atmosphere.

Majors and Degrees

Ohio Northern University offers the undergraduate degrees of Bachelor of Arts, Bachelor of Fine Arts, Bachelor of Music, and Bachelor of Science. Majors are offered in accounting, art (graphic design and studio arts), athletic training, biochemistry, biology, chemistry, civil engineering, clinical laboratory science (formerly medical technology), communication arts (broadcasting and electronic media, musical theater, professional and organizational communication, public relations, and theater), computer engineering, computer science, creative writing, criminal justice, early childhood education, electrical engineering, environmental studies, exercise physiology, French, German, health education, history, international business and economics, international studies, journalism, language arts education, literature, management, mathematics, mathematics/statistics, mechanical engineering, medicinal chemistry, middle childhood education, molecular biology, music, music composition, music education, music performance, music with elective studies in business, pharmacy, philosophy, philosophy/religion, physical education, physics, political science, professional writing, psychology, religion, social studies, sociology, Spanish, sport management, technology, technology education, and youth ministry.

Special programs are available in predentistry, prelaw, premedicine, pre–occupational therapy, pre–physical therapy, pre–physician assistant studies, preseminary, and pre–veterinary medicine. Interdisciplinary degree programs are available in arts/engineering and arts–business/pharmacy. Additional programs are offered in athletic coaching and reading validation. Teacher licensure programs are offered at the adolescent, early childhood, and middle childhood levels and in thirty-two program areas.

Academic Program

In the College of Arts and Sciences, the first two years of study are usually devoted to a program of general education. Work in a major is usually taken at the advanced level during the junior and senior years. To graduate with a Bachelor of Arts, Bachelor of Fine Arts, or Bachelor of Science degree, students are required to complete a minimum of 182 quarter hours, which includes appropriate general education courses, completion of an approved major, and a cumulative grade point average of at least 2.0. To graduate with a Bachelor of Music degree, students are required to complete a minimum of 182 quarter hours in music education, performance, composition, or music with elective studies in business. To fulfill the minimum residence requirements, all students must spend the last three quarters of their program in residence and complete 45 quarter hours with at least 90 quality points in courses elected mainly from junior- and senior-level courses. The Bachelor of Science in clinical laboratory science has different requirements.

In the College of Business Administration, the first two years of study are devoted to general education courses plus introductory courses in several of the business disciplines. To graduate, a student must satisfactorily complete a minimum of 182 quarter hours of appropriate course work for the specific major(s) and maintain at least a 2.0 grade point average. Students in all three majors are encouraged to participate in an internship program in either the junior or senior year.

The College of Engineering offers degrees in civil engineering, computer engineering, computer science, electrical engineering, and mechanical engineering. The courses for the first academic year are essentially the same for each degree program, offering students an easy track to move from one program to another if they are initially uncertain which disciplines they prefer to study. Students are required to maintain a minimum cumulative grade point average of 2.0 as well as a minimum GPA of 2.0 computed for all engineering, math, and science courses. An optional five-year co-op program is available for students in each engineering program provided they maintain a minimum 2.5 GPA. A minor in computer science and options in environmental studies and business administration are available to engineering students provided they maintain at least a 2.5 GPA.

The College of Pharmacy offers the six-year Doctor of Pharmacy program, and admission may be granted to students directly out of their high school programs. After three years of course work in the physical sciences, social sciences, humanities, and professional areas, students spend two years studying the practice of pharmacy through a patient-care-oriented curriculum that utilizes body system and disease-based modules as well as modules with an administrative and practice-based focus. The last year is experiential and takes place in a variety of clinical settings throughout the country. The College also offers a nontraditional Doctor of Pharmacy program for pharmacists holding the B.S. degree. The didactic portion of this curriculum is Internet based. Resident students have available a strong undergraduate research program and may pursue minors or dual majors in biochemistry and medicinal chemistry.

The University offers a special prelaw program, which guarantees Ohio Northern graduates admission to the Pettit College of

Law if they complete the specially designed program with a grade point average of at least 3.4 in any of ONU's undergraduate colleges.

Off-Campus Programs

Many majors may take part in study-abroad programs developed in consultation with faculty members. Field experiences and internships are available in most majors. Externships are required of all pharmacy majors and place students in retail and clinical experiences. Teacher licensure requires one quarter of primary or secondary classroom teaching experience under the supervision of practicing teachers. Additional opportunities include computer science and mathematics co-op programs (professional practice), engineering co-op programs (professional practice, domestic and international), an honors program, and a nontraditional pharmacy doctorate program. All of these off-campus learning experiences carry credit.

Academic Facilities

ONU's Heterick Memorial Library and the Taggart Law Library provide information resources and services to support course offerings and foster independent study. In addition to books and periodicals, the library houses microforms, CD-ROM services, state and federal documents, records, audiotapes, videocassette tapes, films, filmstrips, and slides. Facilities include individual study carrels, study rooms, microform reading and printing equipment, copy services, audiovisual equipment, personal computers, and access to the University's computer network. An online catalog system, compact disc indexing, and abstract services are readily available in the library and through the campus computer network.

The Freed Center for the Performing Arts features a 550-seat theater/concert hall, a 120-seat studio theater, and television and radio production facilities. WONB-FM is the commercial-free 3,000-watt voice of ONU. The facility accommodates the entire Communication Arts Department in state-of-the-art style.

The University is among the leaders in offering the creative and efficient application of information technology in support of teaching, learning, administrative, and student services. Information technologies are integrated into all aspects of University life, enhancing classroom, laboratory, research, and living experiences as well as recreation and communications.

The University provides a heterogeneous environment of computer equipment integrated by local area networks. The campus network is attached to the Internet and Internet2 through high-speed fiber-optic connection. The campus network is available in every academic building and residence hall room. In addition, wireless networking is available in most academic and administrative buildings. More than 580 computers are available to students in academic areas.

Costs

Charges for the 2003–04 year were $30,465 for tuition, room, and board for the Colleges of Arts and Sciences and Business Administration, $33,510 for the College of Pharmacy, and $32,130 for the College of Engineering. The cost of books and supplies is approximately $900 per year.

Financial Aid

Ohio Northern University makes every effort to ensure that no qualified applicant is denied admission because of inability to pay the total cost. More than 90 percent of the student body receive some type of financial assistance. To be considered for financial assistance, the student should submit the FAFSA and the ONU financial aid application to the University along with the admission application. Both merit and need-based aid are available to students.

Faculty

Students are served by 207 full-time and 68 part-time faculty members whose full responsibilities are to the undergraduate students. The primary interest of the faculty is teaching, although research as an adjunct to good teaching is pursued by many faculty members in order to maintain current professional awareness. Most of the faculty members live near the campus and participate in some area of cocurricular student activities. Emphasis is placed on careful advising of students in academic and personal matters. The student-faculty ratio is 13:1.

Student Government

The Student Senate provides self-government in many areas of student life and seeks to further ideals of character and service to the University. Officers of the Student Senate are elected by the students, and the group meets on a weekly basis. The Student Senate serves as the official representative group of the student body to the University administration and agencies in matters pertaining to the student body.

Admission Requirements

High school students applying for admission to the University should present an official transcript indicating at least 16 total units, including work in the academic areas indicated by each college, as follows: College of Arts and Sciences, 12 units—4 in English, 2 in mathematics (algebra and geometry), and 6 in history, social studies, language, or natural science or any combination thereof; College of Business Administration, 13 units—4 in English, 3 in mathematics (including algebra and geometry), and 6 in history, social studies, language, or natural sciences; College of Engineering, 10 units—4 in English, 4 in mathematics (algebra I and II, geometry, and at least ½ unit in trigonometry or its equivalent), and 2 in science (1 in physics and preferably 1 in chemistry); and College of Pharmacy, 18 units—4 in English, 4 in mathematics (algebra I and II, geometry, and trigonometry, precalculus, or calculus), 4 in science (including biology, chemistry, and physics), and 6 units of history, social studies, languages, or any combination thereof. Applicants are also required to submit scores on the ACT of American College Testing. (Scores on the SAT I of the College Board may be substituted for the ACT.) An interview on campus is recommended.

Application and Information

Completed applications should be sent along with a $30 nonrefundable application fee. It is recommended that students apply for admission at the end of their junior year in high school or early in the senior year. The University operates on the rolling admission plan, and applications are processed immediately upon receipt of all necessary information. Requests for catalogs, application forms, or additional information should be directed to:

Office of Admissions
Ohio Northern University
Ada, Ohio 45810
Telephone: 888-408-4668
Fax: 419-772-2313
E-mail: admissions-ug@onu.edu
World Wide Web: http://www.onu.edu

Students outside the Dukes Memorial building.

OHIO WESLEYAN UNIVERSITY

DELAWARE, OHIO

The University

An unusual synthesis of liberal arts learning and preprofessional preparation has set Ohio Wesleyan University (OWU) apart. It is one of the country's five independent four-year colleges to rank among the top twenty in both the number of graduates earning Ph.D.'s and the number who are U.S. business leaders. Founded by the United Methodist Church in 1842, the University is strongly committed to developing the service ethic in students, to fusing theory with its practical applications, and to confronting specific issues of long-range public importance.

Undergraduate enrollment is about 1,850 men and women. Students come to Ohio Wesleyan from forty-four states and forty-five countries, and most reside on the attractive 200-acre campus. OWU ranks fourth in the nation (among schools in its class) in the proportion of students with international origins. Housing options include six large residence halls with special-interest corridors; a number of smaller special-interest units, such as the Tree House and the Peace and Justice House; and eleven fraternity houses. The five sorority houses are nonresidential.

There is a wide range of cocurricular activities. Students initiate discussion groups, service projects, and intramural athletics. Other activities include a fully independent student newspaper, cultural- and ethnic-interest groups such as the Student Union on Black Awareness and the Christian Fellowship, crisis intervention work, the College Republicans and Young Democrats, and prelaw and premed clubs. In the course of a year, students may enjoy more than 100 concerts, plays, dance programs, films, exhibits, and timely speakers. The Theatre and Dance Department stages four major productions and much additional studio work each year, while the Music Department sponsors four large groups and other small ensembles. An impressive campus center is the hub of cocurricular life on campus.

There are twenty-three varsity athletic teams—eleven for men, eleven for women, and a coed sailing team. Many teams often earn NCAA Division III national ranking; recent rankings have included the men's teams in baseball, golf, lacrosse, soccer, and tennis, and the women's cross-country, field hockey, soccer, swimming, and track teams. In 2001 and 2002, the OWU women's soccer team was the NCAA Division III national champion. In recent years, individual All-Americans have been named in these sports and in football, men's cross-country, and men's track. Intramural programs are extensive, and all students have access to racquet sports, swimming, and weight-lifting facilities in the Branch Rickey Physical Education Center. Fitness equipment and health services are housed in the Health and Wellness Center, conveniently located near the residence halls. Off-campus opportunities for backpacking, boating, camping, golf, skiing, and swimming are abundant.

Location

Delaware combines the small-town pace and maple-lined streets of the county seat (population 25,000) with easy access to the state capital, Columbus, the fifteenth-largest city in America. Thirty minutes south of the campus, Columbus provides rich internship opportunities, international research centers, fine dining and shopping, and cultural events that complement campus life. Delaware, founded in 1808, retains a stately, post-Colonial charm in many of its sections. Because the campus is in the town, students find a degree of solitude but not a sense of isolation. About half of the faculty members live a short walk from campus.

Majors and Degrees

Ohio Wesleyan offers the Bachelor of Arts degree in accounting, astronomy, biological sciences (botany, genetics, microbiology, and zoology), chemistry, computer science, economics (including accounting, international business, and management), education (elementary and secondary licensing in seventeen areas), English literature and writing, environmental science, fine arts, French, geography, geology, German, history, humanities-classics, journalism, mathematics, music (applied or history/literature), neuroscience, philosophy, physical education, physics, politics and government, psychology, religion, sociology/anthropology, Spanish, and theater and dance. Fifteen interdisciplinary majors include black studies, East Asian studies, environmental studies, international studies, urban studies, and gender studies, as well as prelaw and premedicine. Students may also design majors in topical, period, or regional studies.

Two professional degrees are awarded: the Bachelor of Fine Arts in art history, arts education, and studio art, and the Bachelor of Music in music education and performance. Combined-degree (generally 3-2) programs are offered in engineering, medical technology, optometry, and physical therapy.

Academic Program

Ohio Wesleyan provides opportunities for students to acquire not only depth in a major area but also knowledge about their cultural past through the insight provided by a broad curriculum. At Ohio Wesleyan, education is placed in a context of values, and students are encouraged to develop the intellectual skills of effective communication, independent and logical thought, and creative problem solving. To these ends, students are required to demonstrate competence in English composition and a foreign language (often through placement testing) and to complete distributional study in the natural and social sciences, the humanities, and the arts. With few exceptions, the major requires the completion of eight to fifteen courses; double majors and minors are encouraged. Completion of thirty-four courses is required for graduation.

Advanced placement is available with or without credit. Under the four-year honors program, freshmen may be named Merit Scholars and work individually with faculty mentors on research, directed readings, or original creative work. Upperclass students are also encouraged to participate in independent study. Phi Beta Kappa is one of more than twenty scholastic honorary societies with chapters on campus.

The objectives of an Ohio Wesleyan education are crystallized in the distinctive Sagan National Colloquium, a program focused annually on one issue of compelling public importance, such as "Food: A Harvest of History, Culture, Politics, and Science." Through weekly speakers and semester-long seminars, the colloquium stimulates campuswide dialogue and encourages students to integrate knowledge from many different disciplines and apply what is studied to life. Participants should discover not only what they think about the issue but also why they think as they do and how to make important decisions based on their beliefs.

Off-Campus Programs

Full-semester internships and apprenticeships, as well as programs of advanced research, are actively developed through most departments. Many are approved by the Great Lakes Colleges Association, Inc. (GLCA), a highly regarded academic consortium of twelve independent institutions. Programs include the Philadelphia Center, the GLCA Arts Program in New York, and the Oak Ridge National Laboratory Science Semester. Other cooperative arrangements include the Newberry Library Program, Wesleyan in Washington, and the Drew University United Nations Semester. Research is done locally at the U.S. Department of Agriculture (USDA) Laboratories in Delaware, the nearby Columbus Zoo, and several other sites.

Ohio Wesleyan has been long committed to education for a global society. Consequently, the curriculum has an international perspective, a significant portion of the student body is drawn from other countries, and a wide variety of opportunities are offered overseas.

Individual work may be arranged elsewhere, but formal programs are offered in more than twenty countries. These include Ohio Wesleyan's affiliation with the University of Salamanca in Salamanca, Spain, and its program in Strasbourg, France, as well as programs in Africa, China, Colombia, England, India/Nepal, Japan, Russia, and Scotland.

Academic Facilities

The University has recently completed, and exceeded the goal of, a $100-million campaign. This campaign, which has substantially enhanced the endowment, has also provided funding for extensive building renovations, athletic facility enhancements, and technology improvements. The Beeghly Library houses 517,646 volumes, one of the largest collections in the country for a private university of Ohio Wesleyan's size. The library's federal documents depository is among the nation's oldest and largest, providing an additional 200,000 reference publications. Beeghly also offers the Online Computer Library Center's most advanced cataloging system. The collection is enhanced by OhioLINK and CONSORT membership.

The comprehensive academic computing system is accessible to students 24 hours per day, and all residence hall rooms are wired for network and Internet access. University-wide computing systems at Ohio Wesleyan include Linux-based IBM xSeries and RS/6000 servers for e-mail, administrative data processing, Web hosting, and timesharing as well as a Compaq ProLiant server running Windows 2000. Approximately 300 Windows-based microcomputers in more than a dozen public computer laboratories are accessible to the campus community. In the summer of 2003, a new, massively scalable fiber-optic Internet connection (owned by OWU) was installed for the campus.

The first phase of the $34-million new Science Center opened in January 2003. Now completed, it includes a 145,000-square-foot three-level building that houses a wide variety of state-of-the-art instrumentation, including a scanning electron microscope and scanning and transmission electron microscopes, which are co-owned by the USDA Labs. The Woltemade Center for Economics, Business, and Entrepreneurship; the Department of Economics; the Learning Resource Center; and Information Systems are located in the R. W. Corns Building. The University has a state-of-the-art Geographic Information Systems Computer Laboratory. Perkins Observatory houses a 32-inch reflector telescope and two smaller instruments. Two University wilderness preserves cover a total of 100 acres. Other special facilities are the multistage Chappelear Drama Center; Sanborn Hall, home to the Music Department; and Gray Chapel, which houses a Klais concert organ.

Costs

The general fee for 2003–04 was $32,550. This amount covered tuition ($25,080), room ($3530), board ($3580), and fees ($360). Books and personal expenses averaged $1100. Nominal fees are charged for some studio art courses, off-campus study, private music lessons for students who are not majoring in music, and student teaching.

Financial Aid

Nearly all freshmen who demonstrate need have been awarded an aid package. Packages include grant, loan, and employment assistance from Ohio Wesleyan and the standard federal and state programs (such as Federal Pell Grant, Federal Stafford Student Loan, Federal Perkins Loan, and Federal Work-Study). More than two thirds of the student body receive some form of need-based aid, and another quarter receive merit- or non-need-based aid. More than 75 percent of all aid is provided by grants and scholarships. On the average, students on financial aid at Ohio Wesleyan receive more scholarship and grant assistance and rely less on loan support than do students at most other institutions.

Several merit scholarship programs worth as much as $25,080 per year, private loan programs, and flexible payment plans are available without regard to financial need. This year, more than 140 enrolling freshmen received merit awards.

Faculty

The full-time faculty numbers 135, providing a student-faculty ratio of approximately 13:1. All of the full-time faculty members hold the highest degree in their fields. Although committed first to teaching and advising, most faculty members maintain active research programs and publish important articles and books. Some members of the faculty are practicing artists whose contributions include the creation and exhibition of original works of art and theater.

Student Government

Students have a significant voice in the government of campus life. The Wesleyan Council on Student Affairs, more than two thirds of whose members are students, formulates basic policy. Students also sit on judicial boards and nine faculty committees and are represented at all meetings of the Board of Trustees.

Admission Requirements

The admission process is competitive. Each application is carefully studied on an individual basis. Although the applicant's academic record is most important, followed closely by teacher and counselor evaluations and SAT I or ACT scores, many other factors are considered, such as evidence of creativity, community service, and leadership. A sixteen-course preparatory program is required. Four units of English and 3 each of mathematics, social studies, science, and foreign language are recommended, but variations of this program are considered. SAT II Subject Tests are not required but may qualify students for advanced placement. Candidates for the B.Mus. degree must audition (tapes are accepted). Early action, early decision, and transfer admission are offered. Campus interviews are strongly recommended but not required. In 2003, approximately 2,600 applications were received; about 1,900 of the applicants gained admission.

Application and Information

Students are urged to complete the application process as early as possible in the senior year of secondary school, especially if they are applying for financial aid. Once complete credentials (application, transcript, recommendations, and SAT I or ACT scores) are received, decisions are made on a rolling basis after January 1. The student's response is required by May 1. The deadline for early decision application is December 1; the deadline for early action application is December 15. Notification is given within four weeks. After April 1, students are admitted on a space-available, rolling admission basis.

For further information, students should contact:

Office of Admission
Ohio Wesleyan University
Delaware, Ohio 43015
Telephone: 800-922-8953 (toll-free)
Fax: 740-368-3314
E-mail: owuadmit@owu.edu
World Wide Web: http://www.owu.edu

The Hamilton-Williams Campus Center is a magnificent meeting place for the campus community.

OKLAHOMA CITY UNIVERSITY

OKLAHOMA CITY, OKLAHOMA

The University

Oklahoma City University (OCU) takes pride in its dual role as the city's university and as the university for the United Methodist Church in Oklahoma. Located in the geographic center of Oklahoma's capital city, OCU provides a wide variety of educational, social, and cultural opportunities for the campus community. OCU has more than 3,800 full- and part-time students who represent forty-eight states and sixty other countries. With a 100-year tradition of church-related service and academic excellence, OCU continues to be a vital and growing institution.

Oklahoma City University is accredited by the North Central Association of Colleges and Secondary Schools and approved by the University Senate of the United Methodist Church, the National Association of Schools of Music, the American Bar Association, the Association of Collegiate Business Schools and Programs, the Supreme Court of the State of Oklahoma, and the Oklahoma State Board of Education. The Kramer School of Nursing is approved by the Oklahoma Board of Nursing and is accredited by the National League for Nursing Accrediting Commission.

Oklahoma City University is ranked in the company of elite colleges and universities across the nation. *U.S. News & World Report*'s "America's Best Colleges" directory places OCU in the top tier of universities in the West. *Money* magazine named OCU one of the 100 best college buys in the United States. The University is also included in *Student Guide to America's 100 Best College Buys* and is rated as one of the top fifty-eight liberal arts colleges in America in *The National Review College Guide*. Most recently OCU was recognized as one of the eighty-seven colleges and universities included in *America's Best Christian Colleges*.

The Prior Learning and University Studies (PLUS) program is an alternate undergraduate program for adult learners in which credit is accepted for life experience. In addition to its undergraduate programs, OCU offers the M.A. degree in religion; the M.S. in accounting and computer science; the Master of Business Administration, Criminal Justice Administration, Education, Liberal Arts, Music, Performing Arts, and Religious Education; and the J.D. degree.

All single full-time students under the age of 21 must live on campus unless they are living with their parents or legal guardian. There are five residence halls on campus. The Cokesbury Court apartment complex includes options of one-, two,- and four-bedroom apartments, with a swimming pool and Jacuzzi, as well as parking and laundry facilities. Both environments are excellent for living and learning. Students living in residence halls are required to participate in one of the University board plans. Students are encouraged to participate in activities both on and off campus. There are more than thirty-five social and academic organizations, intramural sports, dramatics, student publications, music ensembles, dance companies, and a wide range of cultural enrichment events available to all OCU students. The University is a member of the National Association of Intercollegiate Athletics (NAIA) and sponsors ten competitive sports programs. The tradition of OCU's sports programs is known nationwide.

Location

Oklahoma City offers a wide variety of cultural, civic, religious, entertainment, and sports events in a unique setting of modern facilities and Southwestern hospitality. With more than 1 million people in the metropolitan area, the city is a dynamic location offering a wide range of opportunities. From the State Capitol and the center of Oklahoma's political and governmental activity to the cultural offerings of the Oklahoma City Philharmonic, Lyric Theatre, and Ballet Oklahoma to the attractions of the Oklahoma City National Memorial, National Cowboy Hall of Fame, the Firefighters' Museum, the Oklahoma City Zoo and Omniplex, and professional baseball and hockey, Oklahoma City stands as a vibrant metropolitan center of the Southwest. OCU students are involved in city life through internships in governmental and social agencies and extracurricular activities that involve the city's many resources and facilities. The many opportunities and activities available in this growing metropolitan area add another dimension to the high quality of education available at Oklahoma City University.

Oklahoma City is linked by interstate highways to other major cities in the region, and the city's Will Rogers International Airport, one of the busiest in the region, provides coast-to-coast jet service and international flights to Europe, Asia, and South America. The campus is located near the center of Oklahoma City. While close to the business community, the State Capitol, and all the conveniences of a major city, the OCU campus environment is quiet, sheltered, and natural.

Majors and Degrees

The Bachelor of Arts degree is offered in the following subject areas: biology, business, chemistry, criminal justice, education, English, French, German, history, history/political science, humanities, mass communications, math, music, philosophy, philosophy/religion, political science, sociology, psychology, religion, religion/philosophy, Spanish, speech, studio art, and theater. The Bachelor of Science degree is offered in the following subject areas: biochemistry, biology, biophysics, business, chemistry, computer science, criminal justice, dance management, education, entertainment business, history, history/American studies, kinesiology and exercise studies, math, nursing, physics, political science, sociology, psychology, science, and technical theater. The Bachelor of Fine Arts degree includes programs in graphic design, photography, and studio art. The Bachelor of Science in Business is offered in the following subjects: accounting, business administration, economics, finance, management, and marketing. The Bachelor of Music is available in applied piano pedagogy and composition, with elective studies in business administration, guitar, musical theater, orchestral instrument, organ, piano, and voice. Other degrees include the Bachelor of Music Education, instrumental and vocal; the Bachelor of Performing Arts in dance; and the Bachelor of Nursing.

Academic Programs

All undergraduate degree programs require a minimum of 124 semester hours, including the general education curriculum, which represents requirements that must be fulfilled by all undergraduate students. OCU believes that the experience of value-conscious education makes a difference. The curriculum has been specially designed to place a premium on teaching students how to learn rather than merely what to learn. As an integral part of the general education curriculum, the University has established an Honors Program designed to meet the special interests and needs of intellectually gifted students. Honors sections of general education curriculum courses feature limited enrollment with greater emphasis placed on the seminar format and interdisciplinary design. All honors classes are weighted an additional .25 grade point higher than regular classes. Upon completion of 25 hours of honors courses with a 3.5 cumulative University GPA, an honors student receives special recognition at graduation and a special designation on his or her diploma.

OCU operates on a two-semester calendar.

Off-Campus Programs

Departments offering international study include German, biology, and sociology and the Meinders School of Business. The Washington Semester Program, at American University, provides students with the opportunity to conduct an intensive inquiry into the institutions and policymaking processes of their chosen fields. OCU also sponsors overseas trips for performing arts majors.

OCU offers programs that identify and match students to study-abroad/internship opportunities in England, Germany, and Argentina. Relationships exist with the University of Göttingen, Germany; Edge Hill College, England; Ulyanovsk State University, Russia; and Tianjin University of Finance and Economics, People's Republic of China. In the past, OCU students have studied in England, Mexico, France, Republic of China, Japan, Germany, Russia, Ecuador, Chile, and Italy. OCU is a member of the Council on International Education.

Academic Facilities

The University continues to improve facilities and services to accommodate its students. In summer 2002, ground was broken on three campus improvements designed to enhance the student experience: a $1.2-million expansion to the Norick Art Center, a new $18-million building for the Meinders School of Business, and the $30-million Wanda L. Bass Music Center. In November of 2003, the $1.3-million admissions and visitors center was completed. A task force is looking at ways to make the C. Q. Smith Student Faculty Center (SFC) the hub of campus life.

During the past eighteen years, seven academic classroom facilities have been constructed. The Loeffler Math and Science Building, Jones Administration Building, Gold Star Building, and the Margaret E. Petree School of Music and Performing Arts have all had major renovations in the last seven years. The research center for the campus, the Dulaney-Browne Library, has more than 306,844 items, including books, videos, cassettes, bound periodicals, microfiche and microfilm periodicals, periodical CD-ROMs, government documents, and more than 900 current periodical subscriptions. The C. Q. Smith Student Faculty Center houses the snack bar and Marriot Food service. Also in the SFC are the University Book Store and Placement Office. Campus religious life functions around the Bishop Angie Smith Chapel, an award-winning architectural structure.

Costs

The typical expenses for one term include tuition, which is $6670 for undergraduates taking 12 to 16 hours; room and board, which is $2785 for a double room and eighteen meals per week; $345 in fees; and an estimated cost of $500 for books.

Financial Aid

The University is committed to making the utmost effort to assist students who are seeking an education at OCU. The Financial Aid Office assists any admissible student in working out a financial aid package to help meet basic education expenses. In granting aid, the student's demonstrated financial need is considered, together with academic potential and personal qualities. Academic ability and other talents may be recognized through non-need-based scholarships.

To be considered for any kind of financial assistance, a student must first complete the application procedure for admission to the University. The student should then file the FAFSA and designate Oklahoma City University to receive a copy. The FAFSA may be obtained from high school guidance offices, the Financial Aid Office, or the Undergraduate Admissions Office. The suggested priority deadline for scholarships and financial aid is March 1.

Faculty

OCU has 168 full-time and 184 part-time faculty members. Of the full-time faculty members, 71 percent hold doctorates or terminal degrees in their fields. The student-faculty ratio at OCU is 14:1. No classes are taught by graduate assistants or teacher assistants.

Student Government

Each student at Oklahoma City University is a member of the OCU Student Association. The Student Senate is composed of 20 students who are elected by their peers. Each class is represented in the Senate, and at-large seats are held by graduate and law students. The Student Senate is funded through fees assessed to each student and sponsors social, cultural, and recreational events both on and off campus. Senate members meet regularly with the University administration to ensure that communication lines remain open. They also serve as voting members of many university committees. OCU is recognized as an institution that provides many outstanding leadership opportunities.

Admission Requirements

All incoming freshmen must take either the ACT or the SAT I; the results are used in admission determination, student evaluations, and awarding scholarships. OCU's SAT code number is 6543; the ACT code number is 3416. Students must meet two of the following three criteria to be considered admittable: a minimum score of 22 on the ACT or 1030 on the SAT I, a minimum cumulative GPA of 3.0, and a class rank in the upper half.

Transfer students must have a minimum GPA of 2.0 from an accredited college or university to be considered for admission to the University. Transfer students who have earned fewer than 29 college hours are required to provide the Admissions Office with their high school transcripts and test scores.

Application and Information

Entering freshmen must submit an application for admission, accompanied by a $30 nonrefundable fee, to the Undergraduate Admissions Office. An official high school transcript or GED certificate should also be submitted; the student's high school counselor or principal must send an official copy of the transcript. An official final high school transcript with graduation date posted must be received prior to the start of classes.

Transfer applicants must submit an application for admission, along with a $30 nonrefundable fee, to the Undergraduate Admissions Office; an official transcript from each institution attended is also required. Students should request that the proper official send an official transcript directly to the Undergraduate Admissions Office. A high school transcript is required for transfer students who have earned fewer than 29 hours of college credit.

For answers to questions or for an application, students should write or call:

Undergraduate Admissions Office
Oklahoma City University
2501 North Blackwelder
Oklahoma City, Oklahoma 73106
Telephone: 405-521-5050
800-633-7242 (toll-free)
E-mail: uadmissions@okcu.edu
World Wide Web: http://www.youatocu.com

The Gold Star Building on the campus of Oklahoma City University.

OLD DOMINION UNIVERSITY

NORFOLK, VIRGINIA

The University

Old Dominion University (ODU) was founded in 1930 as the Norfolk Division of the College of William and Mary. It became an independent public institution in 1962. Old Dominion University is a state-assisted doctoral research–extensive institution that embraces diversity and has a global perspective on higher education. Old Dominion enrolls about 21,000 students (13,900 of whom are undergraduates), who hail from all fifty states and U.S. territories as well as 108 countries. Old Dominion offers sixty-six bachelor's degree programs, sixty-seven master's degree programs, and twenty-three doctoral degree programs and is accredited by the Commission on Colleges of the Southern Association of Colleges and Schools. Each degree program is housed within one of the University's six colleges: Education, Engineering and Technology, Arts and Letters, Business and Public Administration, Health Sciences, and Sciences. Through the Career Advantage Program, ODU is the only doctoral-degree-granting university in the United States to guarantee each of its students an internship in their field of study. Old Dominion offers a wide variety of activities, creating an energetic campus environment. The 1,400 international students and the 193 student organizations reflect the diversity that exists. As a member of the Colonial Athletic Association, ODU has sixteen intercollegiate Division I athletic teams and has won twenty-nine national titles.

Location

Old Dominion University is located on 188 acres in a residential section of Norfolk, one of the five cities that comprise what is known as Hampton Roads, Virginia's most populated region, at approximately 1.5 million. Norfolk is well known as a major cultural center for its abundance of museums, historic sites, sporting venues, festivals, concerts, shops, and restaurants. Norfolk is ideally situated, as the Virginia Beach oceanfront is within a 20-minute drive and historic Williamsburg is within a 40-minute drive.

Majors and Degrees

The College of Arts and Letters confers B.A. and B.S. degrees for students in the following majors: acting; art education; art history; art studio; communication; criminal justice; English (creative writing, journalism, linguistics, professional writing, teacher preparation); fine arts (drawing and design, fibers, graphic design, metalsmithing and sculpture, painting, print and photo media, teacher preparation); foreign languages (French, German, Spanish, teacher preparation); geography; geography, teacher preparation; history; history, teacher preparation; interdisciplinary studies (early childhood (pre-K–3) and special elementary education (pre-K–6), individualized studies, professional writing, work and professional studies, zoological parks management); international studies; music composition; music education; music history; music performance; philosophy (government education, political/legal studies, religious studies); political science; sociology (anthropology, social welfare); theater and dance (dance education, theater education); and women's studies.

The College of Business and Public Administration confers B.A. and B.S. degrees for students in the following majors: accounting, decision sciences (accounting, economics, finance, insurance, management, marketing, operations management, real estate), e-commerce, economics, finance (insurance, real estate), information technology, international business (East Asia, Europe, Latin America), management, and marketing.

The Darden College of Education confers B.A. and B.S. degrees to students in the following majors: human services counseling, occupational and technical studies (fashion, industrial technology, marketing education, technology education, training specialist), physical education (exercise science, sport management, teacher preparation), recreation and tourism studies (recreation and tourism management, therapeutic recreation), and speech-language pathology and audiology.

The College of Engineering and Technology confers B.A. and B.S. degrees to students in the following majors: civil engineering, civil engineering technology (construction management, structural design, surveying/site development), computer engineering, electrical engineering, electrical engineering technology (computer engineering technology, electrical systems technology), environmental engineering, mechanical engineering, and mechanical engineering technology (manufacturing systems, mechanical system design, nuclear engineering technology).

The College of Health Sciences confers B.A. and B.S. degrees to students in the following majors: dental hygiene; environmental health; health sciences (requires licensure or associate degree): cytotechnology ophthalmic technology; medical technology; nuclear medicine technology; and nursing (postlicensure, prelicensure).

The College of Sciences confers B.A. and B.S. degrees to students in the following majors: biochemistry; biology (marine biology, teacher preparation); chemistry (teacher preparation, prepharmacy track); computer science; mathematics (applied mathematics, statistics/biostatistics, teacher preparation); ocean and earth sciences: earth science education; physics; physics, teacher preparation; and psychology.

Academic Program

Old Dominion provides each student with a broad, liberal arts core curriculum that ensures the students have a well-rounded foundation before they move into their upper-level classes within their chosen majors. Old Dominion runs on a traditional semester calendar, with numerous summer sessions. The Honors College is open to exceptional students from all majors, and accepted students must maintain a minimum 3.0 GPA in their course work. With some of the largest military installations in the United States located in the region, Old Dominion is a prime choice for students interested in an Army or Navy ROTC program.

ODU also offers various accelerated programs in which students can attain both a bachelor's and master's degree in a condensed period of time. Students may choose from the following programs: B.A./M.A. applied linguistics; B.A./M.A. English; B.A./M.A. history; B.A./M.A. international studies; B.A. or B.S. communication/M.A. humanities; B.A. or B.S. individualized interdisciplinary studies/M.A. humanities; B.A. or B.S. women's studies/M.A. humanities; B.S./M.S. engineering; B.A. or B.S./M.B.A. (business administration); B.S. dental hygiene/M.S. dental hygiene; B.S.N. postlicensure/M.S.N. (nursing); B.S. health sciences/M.S. community health; bachelor's/M.S. programs in biology, chemistry, geology, and oceanography; and a bachelor's/Ph.D. program in engineering.

Old Dominion University offers regular degree programs at numerous locations away from its Norfolk campus. In Virginia, students may attend classes at the Peninsula Higher Education Center in Hampton, the Virginia Beach Higher Education Center, the Northern Virginia Center in Sterling, and the

Tri-Cities Center in Portsmouth. Old Dominion offers regular degree programs to students in every region of the commonwealth and to students in various states across the U.S. via TELETECHNET distance learning. Students may take classes that are broadcast from the ODU Norfolk campus to locations in their respective communities (often a local community college). Currently, Old Dominion broadcasts to distance learning sites at all community colleges in Virginia and to sites in Arizona, North Carolina, Georgia, Washington State, and Indiana. In addition, Old Dominion offers classes streamed in real time, over the Internet, so students can take classes from their home computers.

Off-Campus Programs

The Old Dominion Study Abroad Program allows students to spend a semester of study at one of numerous overseas locations.

Academic Facilities

The Patricia W. and J. Douglas Perry Library at Old Dominion is a state-of-the-art facility that houses more than 2 million volumes and is fully automated. There are eight computer labs on campus that are free and accessible to all students. The following resources are available for individuals with particular needs: Disability Services, Writing Center, Testing Center, Advising Services, Center for Professional Training and Development, Dragas International Center, and the Career Management Center. University support facilities provide hands-on experience that complements the education received inside the classroom. For instance, special education, early childhood education, or speech pathology and audiology majors may utilize the Child Study Center. Other academic facilities are the University Theater, Experimental Theater, Diehn Fine Arts Center, Nuclear and Particle Physics Facility, Benthic Ecology Lab, Engineering Learning Center, Applied Research Center, Center for Advanced Engineering Environments, Langley Full-Scale Wind Tunnel, Technology Applications Center, Virginia Modeling Analysis and Simulation Center, and the Virginia Space Flight Center at Wallops Island.

Costs

Tuition and fees for average full-time undergraduates in 2001–02 were $4110 for in-state students and $13,140 for out-of-state students (based on 30 credit hours per year). Room and board were $5498.

Financial Aid

Nearly 55 percent of Old Dominion students receive financial aid in the form of grants, loans, work-study, and academic merit–based scholarships. Often students find it easy to attain part-time employment on campus or in the local area. Old Dominion offers more than 350 merit-based scholarships each year, amounting to nearly $3 million in academic support. All incoming freshmen who submit their applications and credentials by the December 15 early action deadline and transfer students who submit their applications and credentials by March 15 are automatically considered for merit-based scholarships. To be considered for endowed scholarships, the Free Application for Federal Student Aid (FAFSA) must be submitted to the Department of Education by February 15.

Faculty

The number of faculty members at Old Dominion totals 931, of whom 603 are full-time. The student-faculty ratio is 16:1, and 85 percent of the faculty members have attained the terminal degree in their field. The average class size is 25. Old Dominion faculty members are largely responsible for the $50 million in research grants that the University receives each year. All faculty members are required to keep office hours, which makes professors readily available to meet out-of-class student needs. Faculty members also serve as academic advisers and as supervisors of independent study programs, and they often counsel students in their educational and professional endeavors.

Student Government

The Student Senate is the primary body of student governance at Old Dominion. The Student Senate consists of 24 senators chosen by the student body as representatives. Student senators are assigned to committees and must attend meetings. The student body elects 3 senators as Executive Officers, including the Student Body President. The Senate was designed to assist the University in its effort to increase the quality of student life at Old Dominion.

Admission Requirements

Old Dominion University is a selective university that reviews applications on an individual basis. Each application is read and reviewed by the admissions staff. While academic performance is a vital factor in the decision-making process, Old Dominion also takes into account any athletic, student organization, or community service involvement. Admitted students are those who have a zest for higher education and career development. The average freshman admitted to Old Dominion ranks in the top third of his or her graduating class; earned a minimum of 16 high school academic units in English, math, science, foreign language, and social studies; and is actively involved in school and/or community-based clubs, organizations, and athletics. Approximately 50 percent of the transfer students have earned an associate degree or have completed 60 semester hours at another institution prior to enrolling at Old Dominion.

Application and Information

For students who wish to apply for the fall semester, the deadline for application is March 15. A completed application includes a completed official application, a $40 nonrefundable application fee, official high school transcripts, SAT I or ACT scores, a student activity resume, an essay, and a letter of recommendation. The deadline for transfer applications is May 1.

Applications and additional materials should be sent to:

Office of Admissions
Old Dominion University
108 Rollins Hall
Norfolk, Virginia 23529-0050
Telephone: 757-683-3685
E-mail: admit@odu.edu
World Wide Web: http://www.odu.edu

A view of the campus at Old Dominion University.

OLIVET NAZARENE UNIVERSITY

BOURBONNAIS, ILLINOIS

The University

Olivet Nazarene University (ONU) is a Christian, private, liberal arts university with a strong emphasis on both academic excellence and Christ-centered living. ONU offers one of the finest liberal arts educations in the Midwest, world-class facilities for learning and entertainment, and an atmosphere that promotes fun, relationship building, and spiritual growth.

Olivet's high retention, graduation, and employment/placement rates demonstrate the University's commitment to students' success. The faculty, staff, and administration are dedicated to teaching, encouraging, and mentoring each student as a whole person—academically, socially, and spiritually.

With 4,300 total students (2,200 undergraduates), Olivet offers an ideal student population for a private institution, maintaining diversity without sacrificing personalized attention. Half of the student body comes from the Nazarene denomination, while the remainder come from some thirty other denominations. Most U.S. states are represented, as are twenty-one countries.

The campus offers a championship-caliber athletics department (eighteen intercollegiate men's and women's sports in all) and a large intramural sports program. Music and drama groups involve hundreds of students, and many clubs are organized for a wide variety of interests. Olivet students are also heavily involved in dozens of ministry groups and volunteer efforts, small-group Bible studies, and weekly student-led services.

The University recently completed a number of campus renovations, including construction of the 56,700-square-foot Weber Center, home to the University's Divisions of Education and Social Sciences; a new entrance to the football field; and outdoor athletic facilities. Larsen Fine Arts Center, housing Kresge Auditorium and the Brandenberg Gallery for showcasing students' and outside artists' work, received a complete renovation in 2002. Future plans call for a new chapel and performing arts center.

The University is home to the Chicago Bears' summer training camp and Shine.fm, a 35,000-watt station ranked among the top stations in the nation and staffed by Olivet's broadcasting students.

Location

The University is located just 50 minutes south of Chicago's Loop in the historic village of Bourbonnais. The area includes mall shopping, restaurants, entertainment, and natural recreation centered on the Kankakee River State Park system. Olivet students enjoy many activities nearby and often make the quick trip north to sample the limitless offerings of Chicago and its surroundings.

In addition to recreation, students find numerous opportunities for employment and internships in the area, which is ranked as one of the top locations in the nation for small businesses, and the vast professional resources of Chicago. Students, faculty members, and staff members also find themselves working side by side in local and regional ministry projects. Olivet students are recognized professionally and ministerially as a valuable commodity by area businesses, churches, and parachurch organizations.

Majors and Degrees

Olivet confers Bachelor of Arts (B.A.) and/or Bachelor of Science (B.S.) degrees in the following fields of study (includes all majors, minors, and concentrations): accounting, art, art (education), athletic coaching, athletic training, biblical languages, biblical studies, biochemistry, biology, business administration, chemistry, child development, children's ministry, Christian education, church music, clinical laboratory science, communication studies, computer science, corporate communication, counseling, criminal justice, cross-cultural ministries, dietetics, digital media: graphics, digital media: photography, digital production, drawing/illustration, early childhood education, earth and space science, economics and finance, electrical engineering, elementary education, engineering, English, English (education), environmental science, family and consumer sciences, family and consumer sciences (education), film studies, finance, French, general science, general studies, geobiology, geochemistry, geoengineering, geology, geomathematics, Greek, health education, history, hospitality, housing and environmental design, information systems, international business, journalism, literature, management, marketing, mass communication, mathematics, mathematics (education), mechanical engineering, music, music education, music performance, nursing, painting, personnel psychology, philosophy, physical education/health, physical science, physics, political science, practical ministries, predentistry, prelaw, premedicine, preoptometry, prepharmacy, pre–physical therapy, pre–physician's assistant studies, pre–veterinary medicine, psychology, public policy, radio, religion, religion and philosophy, science (education), secondary education, social science, social science (education), social work, sociology, Spanish, Spanish (education), sports management, systems programming, television/video production, theater, youth ministry, and zoology.

Academic Programs

Olivet seeks to offer an "Education with a Christian Purpose." The University believes this commitment to Christ mandates nothing less than the highest-quality academic programs. Olivet's liberal arts curriculum requires that students complete 53 to 61 hours of general education courses. With the addition of major and minor programs of study, students must complete a minimum of 128 credit hours to obtain a bachelor's degree. Credit may be earned through AP and CLEP tests. Students may also participate in ROTC.

Olivet operates on a two-semester schedule, from August to May. Two summer sessions are also available.

Off-Campus Programs

Olivet students are encouraged to participate in the various off-campus study programs offered each semester. International locations include Beijing, China; San José, Costa Rica; Cairo, Egypt; Oxford, England; western Europe; Irian Jaya, Indonesia; Tokyo, Japan; Moscow, Nizhni Novgorod, and St. Petersburg, Russia; and Sighisoara, Transylvania (Romania). Domestic opportunities include the American Studies Program in Washington, D.C.; the Los Angeles Film Studies Program in Burbank, California; Focus on the Family Institute in Colorado Springs, Colorado; and the AuSable Institute (environmental science) in northern Michigan. Costs are usually comparable to a semester at Olivet, and credit is given for these programs. In addition, financial aid is applicable.

In addition, many Olivet students participate in numerous educational and missions-oriented short-term trips, which are available during the Christmas, spring, and summer breaks.

Academic Facilities

Olivet's 200-acre, $150-million campus offers leading-edge academic facilities. These include high-quality performance halls and athletic arenas; excellent natural science, engineering, and nursing laboratories; "smart" classrooms in most departments; and an observatory. It is one of only a handful of small college campuses in the nation to have a planetarium. Each department uses the top software in its field. More than a dozen campus computer labs are available for student use, and two network ports in each dorm room give students access to e-mail, the Internet, and classroom applications 24 hours a day.

Benner Library and Resource Center provides unlimited access to any material a student needs, either on-site from its more than 225,000 volumes, 1,000 periodicals, more than 250,000 government documents and CD-ROMs, or through the interlibrary loan system.

Costs

Tuition, based on 12 to 18 credit hours, was $14,160 in 2003–04. Room and board, based on double occupancy and the twenty-one-meals-per-week plan, were $5655.

Financial Aid

More than 95 percent of Olivet students receive some form of financial aid each year. Merit- and need-based scholarships range from $500 to full tuition. The Olivet Nazarene University Leadership Scholarship for Freshmen provides a significant award for those students who qualify through an application and essay process.

Olivet's cost is below average for private colleges nationwide, and more than 95 percent of ONU students receive financial aid. The University also participates in all federal and state financial aid programs. The priority deadline for filing the Free Application for Federal Student Aid (FAFSA) is March 1. To apply for aid, students must fill out the FAFSA as well as Olivet's application for financial aid. The student must be an accepted applicant before a financial aid package can be created. Olivet offers a monthly installment plan in addition to the traditional three-payment plan. Olivet believes funding a student's education is a partnership between each family, Olivet, and the state and federal governments. The friendly staff is committed to making an Olivet education affordable to every young person.

Faculty

Olivet's more than 100 full-time faculty members are the key to excellence in and out of the classroom. Teaching is a ministry for these dedicated Christian individuals, and Olivet's student-faculty ratio gives them an opportunity to teach, mentor, and encourage students on a personal level. To that end, the faculty is heavily involved in campus life, whether sponsoring social organizations or participating in talent shows.

Within the traditional liberal arts curriculum, more than 75 percent of Olivet's faculty members have terminal degrees.

Student Government

The Associated Student Council is the student government organization on campus. Its Executive Council consists of a president, vice president of finance, vice president of spiritual life, vice president of social affairs, vice president of women's residential life, vice president of men's residential life, vice president of office management, the *GlimmerGlass* (student newspaper) editor, and the *Aurora* (yearbook) editor. They work alongside the University's administrative team to ensure the health and promotion of campus activities and organizations.

Admission Requirements

Admission to the University is moderately difficult. Students are considered for admission on the basis of their high school GPA, ACT or SAT I scores, and personal recommendations. An ACT score is required for placement in courses. For international students, TOEFL results are an additional factor in the admission decision. Students with low test scores and GPAs may be admitted on a provisional basis. A campus visit and interview are strongly recommended for all prospective students.

Application and Information

Admission is on a rolling basis, although an early decision is required for some scholarships. Students may apply at Olivet's home page on the World Wide Web or in print. The application process includes the written (or electronic) application, high school transcripts, two letters of recommendation, ACT or SAT I scores, and a health form. There is no application fee, but a $30 room deposit places the student on the list for housing.

For more information or to arrange a campus visit, students should contact:

Office of Admissions
Olivet Nazarene University
One University Avenue
Bourbonnais, Illinois 60914
Telephone: 800-648-1463 (toll-free)
E-mail: admissions@olivet.edu
World Wide Web: http://www.olivet.edu

A view of the campus at Olivet Nazarene University.

OREGON STATE UNIVERSITY

CORVALLIS, OREGON

The University

Exceptional students, an outstanding faculty, and a challenging curriculum combine to make Oregon State University (OSU) a nationally and internationally recognized comprehensive university.

OSU has earned the Carnegie Research Doctoral designation for commitment to education and research. Widely recognized research programs add to the quality of teaching by bringing new knowledge into the classroom and by encouraging undergraduate students to work with faculty members on research projects in many fields.

The University's 19,000 students come from all fifty states and more than eighty-eight countries around the world to pursue a wide choice of undergraduate programs that prepare them for careers and leadership positions in science, engineering and computer-related fields, natural resources, government, teaching and social service, pharmacy, and other professions. One hundred seventy-six valedictorians joined the 2003 freshman class. Employers from across the nation recognize the value of an OSU degree, and more of them recruit at Oregon State University each year than at any other university in the state. Oregon State also ranks twenty-fifth nationally in Peace Corps volunteers.

OSU is committed to offering students the resources they need to be successful in their education. In 1997, Oregon State was named the leading institution in the U.S. and Canada for electronic services to students. In presenting the award, the American Productivity and Quality Center recognized OSU for innovative programs, including bringing Internet access to every residence hall room on campus. OSU has earned the distinction of being named one of "America's 100 Most Wired Colleges" by *Yahoo! Internet Life* (May 2000).

Students also benefit from more than 300 cocurricular activities on campus. These include student government, student media, theater and music, intramural and club sports, and numerous social, academic, cultural, and professional clubs and organizations. In addition, Dixon Recreation Center offers opportunities for swimming and diving, weight training, aerobic exercise, and recreational sports on campus. A campus child-care facility offers educationally oriented day-care programs for children of students and faculty and staff members.

OSU offers a wide range of housing and dining options, including special program residence halls, cooperative houses, student family housing, and fraternity and sorority housing. Many apartments and houses are available within biking or walking distance of OSU for students who choose to live off campus. There are more than fifteen restaurants on campus.

In fall 2001, OSU opened the door to a new campus located in Bend, Oregon. The OSU Cascades Campus represents a unique educational partnership involving eight distinguished institutions, creating an innovative and collaborative university to serve the needs of central Oregon.

Graduate degrees are offered through the Colleges of Agricultural Sciences, Business, Engineering, Forestry, Health and Human Sciences, Liberal Arts, and Science. Graduate and professional degrees are also offered through the Colleges of Oceanic and Atmospheric Sciences, Pharmacy, and Veterinary Medicine, and through the School of Education.

Location

The OSU main campus is in Corvallis, which is consistently ranked as one of the safest university communities on the West Coast. With about 52,000 residents, Corvallis offers a friendly, university-oriented atmosphere. Miles of bike lanes and free city bus service make it easy for students to get around town. Within a couple hours of Corvallis are the Oregon Coast; the Cascade Mountains, with skiing, hiking, camping, and snowboarding; and Portland, Oregon's largest city.

Majors and Degrees

Oregon State is a comprehensive university, with more than 200 academic programs. Undergraduate degrees are offered through the Colleges of Agricultural Sciences, Business, Engineering, Forestry, Health and Human Sciences, Liberal Arts, and Science.

Students in any undergraduate major can strengthen their transcripts by earning an Honors Degree or an International Degree. Almost 600 top students are enrolled in the University Honors College, which offers a small-college atmosphere within the larger University. The University also offers twenty-eight preprofessional programs that prepare students for graduate programs and careers in fields such as health sciences, law, and education.

The OSU Cascades Campus offers a variety of undergraduate and graduate degree opportunities. Geology, wildlife biology, botany, business, nursing, education, computer science, engineering, museum studies, outdoor recreation leadership, and tourism are among the many programs available.

Academic Program

All undergraduate students at Oregon State complete the Baccalaureate Core, which helps develop skills and knowledge in writing, critical thinking, cultural diversity, the arts, science, literature, lifelong fitness, and global awareness, ensuring that as graduates they will be well prepared for life as well as a career.

Many students take advantage of OSU's first-year experience program, called Odyssey, which offers opportunities for new students to interact with faculty members and other students throughout the year, thus easing the transition to college life. The year begins with a five-day "connect" orientation that features small group meetings between faculty members and students, a barbecue, outdoor movies, open houses, and more.

Undergraduate research is an important component of many academic programs, and more than 2,000 OSU undergraduates participate with faculty members and graduate students on research projects each year.

OSU has more majors, minors, and special programs than any other college in Oregon and offers a University Exploratory Studies Program for students who want to try various options before choosing a major field. Oregon State uses the quarter system for its academic year. Most majors require between 180 and 192 credit hours for a bachelor's degree.

Learning and resource centers around campus help OSU students deal with problems and develop the skills they need in college and beyond. The Center for Writing and Learning, the Mathematics Learning Center, and departmental resource centers assist students in preparing for assignments in specific areas, while the African-American, Hispanic-American, Asian-American, and Native-American education offices, along with the Educational Opportunities Program, help ensure that specific groups of students have successful college careers. University Counseling and Psychological Services offers learning resource materials and professional assistance to help students deal with problems, both in and out of the classroom. Career Services assists students in locating internships and in finding jobs when they graduate.

Off-Campus Programs

Through the International Degree, study-abroad, and international internship programs, OSU students can study, work, or conduct research almost anywhere in the world. Programs, which range from a term to a full year, are offered in Australia, Canada, China, Denmark, Ecuador, England, France, Germany, Hungary, Italy, Japan, Korea, Mexico, New Zealand, Norway, Russia, Spain, Thailand, Tunisia, and Vietnam.

OSU also participates in the National Student Exchange Program, allowing students to spend up to a year at one of more than 160 colleges and universities in the U.S. and its possessions while paying in-state tuition and fees.

Academic Facilities

OSU's Valley Library is a state-of-the-art facility that offers modern electronic services, including a wireless computer network, and unique special collections as well as traditional library services to students and the community. The OSU library is the first academic library to be named "Library of the Year" by *Library Journal* (1999). Library holdings include more than 2.5 million books, periodicals, and government documents on paper or microform. A reciprocal agreement makes more than 5 million additional volumes in the Oregon University System available to OSU students and faculty members. OSU's special collections include the papers and memorabilia of Linus Pauling, the only winner of two unshared Nobel prizes, and the Atomic Energy Collection. The Valley Library is an official depository for U.S. government and state of Oregon publications.

Students at OSU have access to more than 2,200 computers at labs around campus, including some that are available 24 hours per day. In addition, all rooms in campus residence facilities are wired for high-speed access to the Internet. All students have Internet and e-mail accounts. Facilities also include the Northwest's only stereographic classroom, which shows scientific principles in 3-D format; a fully equipped multimedia classroom; and modern laboratories, including an undergraduate biology lab that allows students to explore a wide range of studies, from analysis of DNA molecules to the nature of cancer cells. Special research facilities include OSU's Mark O. Hatfield Marine Science Center, the Forest Research Laboratory, the Radiation Center, and the Hinsdale Wave Research Lab.

Costs

In-state undergraduate tuition and fees were $4620 for the 2003–04 academic year, while nonresident charges were $17,376. The average cost for a residence hall double room and meal plan was approximately $6000, while the room and board cost in University-owned cooperatives averaged $3600. Students who live in a fraternity or sorority house pay about the same for housing and meals as those students who live in residence halls.

Financial Aid

OSU offers the full range of scholarships, grants, work-study, and loans from federal, state, and University sources. Every effort is made to offer students the best package possible. To qualify, students must have applied for admission and must submit the Free Application for Federal Student Aid (FAFSA), listing OSU as one of their top six choices (Title IV code: 003210). Some students help meet educational expenses with one of the many part-time jobs available on or near campus. For financial aid information, interested students should contact the Office of Financial Aid and Scholarships, 218 Kerr Administration Building, Corvallis, Oregon 97331 (telephone: 541-737-2241, World Wide Web: http://oregonstate.edu/admin/finaid/).

Through the OSU Scholars Program, the University offers a variety of scholarships for new students who have strong academic records. Scholarships range from $500 to $6000 annually for up to four years. In addition, most OSU colleges offer scholarships to new students, and the financial aid office has a number of University-wide scholarships.

Faculty

Undergraduate education is a priority at OSU, and nationally prominent scholars and scientists regularly teach undergraduate courses at all levels. Students receive individual attention and the chance to know their professors both in and out of the classroom. Faculty members consistently receive awards for teaching and research, and many of them are nationally and internationally renowned. The more than $100 million in external research funds received annually by OSU faculty members exceeds that of all other Oregon public universities combined. With more than 1,300 teaching faculty members, OSU has a student-faculty ratio of 16:1.

Student Government

The Associated Students of Oregon State University (ASOSU) plays a major role in making policy and regulating activities for students and in governing the University through student participation on more than fifty University-wide committees. In recent years, ASOSU has become more involved with local, state, and national issues that affect the welfare of students.

Admission Requirements

A minimum 3.0 high school GPA (on a 4.0 scale) guarantees freshman admission to OSU when all subject requirements are met. Applicants for first-year undergraduate admission for fall 2004 are required to complete an "Insight Resume", a written assessment designed to evaluate students' non-cognitive attributes. These attributes include self-concept, realistic self-appraisal, handling the system, ability to set long-range goals, leadership, connections with a strong support person, community engagement, and nontraditional learning. High school subject requirements are 4 years of English, 3 years each of mathematics and social studies, and 2 years each of science and of the same foreign language. Students who do not meet the subject requirements may be considered for admission by earning a 1410 total score on three SAT II Subject Tests or by successfully completing course work to make up specific deficiencies. The alternatives must by completed by the time of high school graduation.

Transfer admission requires successful completion of at least 36 graded, transferable credits (24 semester credits) from accredited U.S. institutions, with a minimum GPA of 2.25. Grades of C- or better are required in college-level writing and mathematics. Students with less than 36 transferable credits are considered for admission on the basis of their high school records.

Application and Information

An *OSU Viewbook*, with an application form and information on specific academic programs, housing, financial aid, scholarships, and activities are sent to students upon request. Additional information and an online application are on the OSU World Wide Web site (listed below).

Prospective students are encouraged to visit OSU to determine for themselves whether the University meets their needs. A visit, including a campus tour and an opportunity to talk to faculty members in the student's area of interest, can be arranged by calling the Office of Admissions (listed below).

For an application or to request more information, students should write or call:

Office of Admissions
104 Kerr Administration Building
Oregon State University
Corvallis, Oregon 97331-2106
Telephone: 800-291-4192 (toll-free)
Fax: 541-737-2482
E-mail: osuadmit@orst.edu
World Wide Web: http://www.oregonstate.edu

OTIS COLLEGE OF ART AND DESIGN

LOS ANGELES, CALIFORNIA

The College

Founded in 1918, Otis College of Art and Design offers an interdisciplinary education for artists and designers who shape the future. Its programs embrace new technologies and emerging disciplines, uniting these practices with established strengths in fine arts, design, and fashion. Otis' reputation attracts students from thirty-nine states and twenty-six countries, making it the most diverse private art college in the U.S. The College's diversity is its strength; it prepares students to imagine what lies ahead and benefits employers who know the value of creativity. Otis graduates shape the visual world, from museum and exhibition design to the Hollywood screen, from the clothes people wear to the toys children play with. Otis alumni are cultural and economic leaders, working in high-level positions in companies such as Disney, Mattel, Paramount Pictures, Nike, Guess?, DKNY, Sony Pictures, the Los Angeles County Museum of Art, Industrial Light and Magic, and Warner Bros.

Otis began when *Los Angeles Times* founder and editor Harrison Gray Otis bequeathed his property in MacArthur Park to create an art institute. Today, Otis has three campuses and state-of-the-art facilities for its programs in communication arts, digital media, environmental design, fashion design, fine arts, toy design, and interactive product design. On the graduate level, Otis offers programs in fine arts and writing. Otis' newest building, the Galef Center for Fine Arts, is an "art factory" in which students research painting, sculpture, photography, and new genres in light-filled loft spaces. The building also houses two large museum-quality art galleries.

Otis' approximately 1,000 students earn degrees accredited by both the Western Association of Schools and Colleges and the National Association of Schools of Art and Design. The College also enrolls approximately 1,000 weekend and evening students through its continuing education programs. Among Otis' alumni are artists John Baldessari, Philip Guston, Robert Irwin, Billy Al Bengston, and Alison Saar; costume designer Edith Head; and Jim Rygiel, visual effects supervisor for *The Lord of the Rings: The Return of the King*.

Location

Otis' main 5-acre campus is on Los Angeles' west side in the midst of Southern California's dynamic film, digital imagery, and toy design industries. The proximity of art museums, studios, and galleries allows students to experience some of the most significant fine art in the country. The School of Fashion Design is in the heart of downtown L.A.'s garment district. The third campus, in the beach community of El Segundo, houses individual studios for graduate fine arts majors.

Majors and Degrees

In the School of Design, students choose from five majors. Communication arts (advertising, graphic design, and illustration) focuses on the connections between applied art and design concepts and current and emerging technologies. Students gain an essential understanding of drawing, painting, typography, narrative sequence, storytelling, visual literacy, and history.

The digital media major includes five components: two-dimensional (image creation and manipulation, text as image, and typography), three-dimensional (character design and animation, props, vehicles, and virtual sets), motion graphics, interactive design, and Web design.

The environmental design program is concerned with the space that people inhabit, both external and internal, through the exploration of architecture, landscape, interiors, and environmental graphics.

The toy design major combines product design, marketing, and engineering. Each year of the program focuses on a specific category such as plush, action figures, preschool, vehicles, dolls, or games.

Interactive product design, the newest major at Otis, encourages students to integrate their artmaking and creative thinking skills with engineering and cutting-edge technology to create products with sports, fashion, medical, and lifestyle applications.

In the School of Fashion Design, the year follows the same calendar as the professional seasons, allowing students to work on three collections annually. In the final two years of the program, students interact with professional designers through the Mentor Program.

The School of Fine Arts offers three areas of concentration (painting, photography, and sculpture/new genres) that encourage students to discover their own artistic vision. Faculty members and visiting artists work with students in a cross-disciplinary approach (e.g., painters work with photographers, and video artists interact with sculptors).

The two-year M.F.A. programs in creative writing and fine arts allow advanced independent work. Fine arts students focus on methodology and artmaking skills through critiques with their peers and resident and guest faculty members. Writing students participate in critical practice seminars. These students concentrate on either poetry or fiction. In both graduate programs the emphasis is on an interdisciplinary approach to developing artistic vision.

Academic Programs

The Foundation Year helps new students master a vast array of studio skills, including life drawing, form and space, color and design, and drawing and composition. Liberal studies and art history courses are carefully designed to complement the studio curriculum. At the end of the year, having developed both a creative vocabulary and a grounding in liberal arts, students select a major.

Within each major, the curriculum reinforces creativity through integrated learning. Students take advantage of a coordinated set of offerings and disciplines to gain deep training in each discipline. They graduate with cross-boundary thinking and the ability to formulate transdisciplinary solutions to problems that may not even exist at the time of their matriculation.

Off-Campus Programs

Otis participates in a mobility program with the Association of Independent Colleges of Art and Design (AICAD). Participating colleges include premier AICAD art colleges in the United States as well as selected colleges in Europe (such as London, Paris, and Stockholm) and Canada. The Mobility Program at Otis College of Art and Design allows students to study for one semester at another art college during their junior year. Application procedures and deadlines are available through the Registration Office.

Academic Facilities

Each of the campuses features state-of-the-art tools and equipment. Facilities range from well-equipped wood, plastic, and metal shops and metal foundry; a CNC milling machine; a complete letterpress lab; color and black-and-white photo labs with mural capability; a printmaking studio; and both analog and digital video editing. Students have access to cutting-edge software across several platforms in more than 300 computers, scanners, and output devices, including a 3-D printer and large-scale output. The library holds an excellent collection of books on the arts, subscribes to more than 150 periodicals, and offers a wide range of electronic resources, such as full-text databases and e-books. The 40,000-square-foot Galef Center for Fine Arts, known as the "art factory," is a light-filled facility that houses painting, sculpture, and photo/video lighting studios as well as dedicated senior studios, work space, classrooms, and galleries for student exhibitions. The museum-quality Ben Maltz Gallery, which presents group and 1-person exhibitions by local, regional, and international artists, is also located there. The Fashion Campus occupies 18,000 square feet of prime space at downtown's California Mart, the headquarters for the West Coast's fashion design industry. Students design with the latest equipment, study in a dedicated library, and use current computer technology—all in proximity to the professional design studios of Los Angeles' fashion district.

Costs

Tuition and fees for the academic year 2003–04 were $23,420. Housing and cost of living and other incidental personal expenses vary depending upon individual circumstances. These costs are estimated to run from $2400 to $7000 per year.

Financial Aid

Otis is proud to award more than $4 million in scholarships to its students. In addition, aid from other sources, such as the state and federal governments, provides aid monies to more than 75 percent of the student body.

Students must complete the Free Application for Federal Student Aid (FAFSA). Applicants for fall admission are encouraged to file on or before the February 15 priority date; applicants for January admission should submit all forms before December 1. California residents should file the Cal Grant GPA Verification Form and FAFSA before February 15. Financial aid is awarded on a first-come, first-served basis according to availability. All aid is based on artistic and academic merit and a student's financial eligibility as determined by the United States Department of Education.

Faculty

The Otis faculty comprises practicing artists and designers who have chosen to enrich their professional experience by sharing their expertise with new generations of artists and designers. There are currently 32 full-time and more than 150 part-time faculty members.

Student Government

In the Student Government Association, students from every department of study play an active role in student life and produce a wide variety of student-oriented lectures and events.

Admission Requirements

Admission to Otis is based on artistic and academic preparation. Applicants should have solid academic credentials and basic artistic skills. Required materials for students applying directly from high school (no college experience) are the application and fee, high school transcript, standardized test score (SAT or ACT), essay, and portfolio of original work. Required materials for students applying who have prior college experience are the application and fee, transcripts from all colleges attended, an essay, and a portfolio of original work. (In some cases, high school transcripts and/or test scores may also be required for students who have some college work.) Additional requirements for students who are citizens of countries other than the United States (for both the B.F.A. and the M.F.A.) are the TOEFL score (or appropriate equivalent), certified and translated copies of transcripts from all work completed outside the U.S., and verification of sufficient funds to pay for tuition and fees and all related expenses.

Application and Information

Students can apply for the B.F.A. program for the fall or spring semester. The priority deadline for the fall semester is the preceding February 15. For the spring semester, it is the preceding December 1. To apply online, students should visit the College's Web site listed below. For a viewbook, prospective students should call the toll-free number listed below. For information and requirements on applying to the M.F.A. programs in fine arts and writing, students should contact the College directly.

Students are encouraged to visit Otis. Tours of the campus, appointments with admission staff members, and opportunities to talk with current students and faculty members are available Monday through Friday throughout the year and on some Saturdays between January and May (holiday weekends are excluded). Saturday appointments should be scheduled at least one month in advance. For more information about Otis or to schedule an appointment, students should contact:

The Office of Admissions
Otis College of Art and Design
9045 Lincoln Boulevard
Los Angeles, California 90045-9785
Telephone: 310-665-6800
800-527-OTIS (6847; toll-free)
Fax: 310-665-6821
E-mail: admissions@otis.edu
World Wide Web: http://www.otis.edu

Otis College of Art and Design is located on the west side of Los Angeles on a 5-acre campus.

OTTERBEIN COLLEGE

WESTERVILLE, OHIO

The College

Otterbein College, a private, coeducational institution affiliated with the United Methodist Church, blends the traditional and contemporary and continues to pride itself on offering a broad-based liberal arts education. Its 1,969 full-time and 1,095 part-time students come from all over the United States and several countries, but the majority, including 440 graduate students, are from Ohio. Founded in 1847 with only two buildings on 8 acres of land, Otterbein has since grown to twenty-seven buildings on 140 acres in the heart of historic Westerville, Ohio, a suburb of Columbus.

The College offers a wide range of extracurricular activities. They include theater productions, vocal and instrumental ensembles, religious programming activities, the ca weekly student newspaper, the campus radio station (WOBN), the Otterbein-Westerville television station (WOCC), and intramural and intercollegiate athletics. Otterbein men and women compete in the Ohio Athletic Conference, NCAA Division III. There are eight varsity sports for men and eight for women. The Rike Physical Education–Recreation Center is the home for men's and women's athletics and physical education facilities and includes racquetball and tennis courts, an indoor track, a weight room, and seating for 3,000. The $9.5-million Clements Recreation Center opened in fall 2002. Five local fraternities and six local sororities attract approximately 27 percent of Otterbein's students. Roush Hall, a multipurpose, handicapped-accessible building, houses academic departments, multimedia classrooms, contemporary conference rooms, a gallery, and a computer center.

A Master of Science in Nursing program is offered for students who have completed a four-year baccalaureate program.

A Master of Arts in Teaching (M.A.T.) degree program is available to qualified liberal arts graduates to prepare for teacher certification in elementary education or secondary education—biology (life science), computer science, English, and mathematics. A Master of Arts in Education (M.A.E.) degree program is available to certified teachers. Majors are offered in curriculum and instruction, reading, and teacher leadership and supervision.

Otterbein also offers an M.B.A. program.

Location

Otterbein is located in Westerville, Ohio, 20 minutes from downtown Columbus, one of the fastest-growing cities in the Midwest and Northeast. The College's proximity to Columbus means more than access to entertainment and recreation; as a thriving business center, the city provides many internship opportunities for students that often lead to full-time employment after graduation. The College is easily accessible from Interstates 71 and 270 and is close to the Port Columbus International Airport.

Majors and Degrees

The Bachelor of Arts degree is offered in accounting, broadcasting, business administration, chemistry, computer science, economics, English, equine science, French, health education, history, international studies, journalism, life science, mathematics, music, organizational communication, philosophy, physical education, physics, political science, psychology, public relations, religion, secondary education, sociology, Spanish, speech communication, sports medicine, sports wellness and management, theater, and visual arts. The Bachelor of Science degree is offered in accounting, business administration, chemistry, computer science, equine science, life science, mathematics, physics, psychology, and sports medicine. The Bachelor of Fine Arts is offered in theater with concentrations in acting-directing, design-technical, and musical theater programs. The Bachelor of Music Education prepares students for teaching careers in music. The Bachelor of Science in Education is awarded in early childhood education and middle childhood education. The Bachelor of Science in Nursing degree is also offered. The Bachelor of Music is offered for students interested in performance careers.

Preprofessional programs are offered in dentistry, law, medicine, optometry, and veterinary medicine.

A dual degree in engineering is offered in conjunction with Washington University in St. Louis and Case Western Reserve University in Cleveland.

Minors are offered in accounting, athletic training, black studies, broadcasting, business, chemistry, coaching, computer science, dance, economics, English, French, geology, health sciences, history, mathematics, music, philosophy, physical education, physics, political science, psychology, public relations, religion, sign language, sociology, Spanish, speech communication, visual art, and women's studies. In fall 2002, minors were added in sound production and arts administration.

Academic Program

Otterbein College offers a program of liberal arts education in the Christian tradition. The College encourages serious dialogue so that students will develop to serve within the community. The fulfillment of this purpose requires students to read well, write well, think clearly, and identify ideas; know how to discuss, listen, and seek data; and have the abilities of synthesis and creativity.

Graduation with a bachelor's degree from the College requires successful completion of 180 quarter hours, of which 50 quarter hours are in core requirements offered under the title of Integrative Studies in Human Nature. The College's quarter calendar lends itself to the wide variety of internships and other off-campus educational opportunities offered by the College. The academic year begins in mid-September and ends in early June.

Through other academic opportunities, students may design an individualized major as well as receive advanced placement by examination and credit through CLEP examinations in some academic areas.

Off-Campus Programs

A variety of off-campus programs are available, including foreign language study in Dijon, France. Semester at Sea, a shipboard-campus program offered in cooperation with the University of Pittsburgh, enables students to take a variety of liberal arts courses while cruising. Study opportunities also exist with the Washington Semester Plan, operated through the American University in Washington, D.C., and with the Philadelphia Center. The Roehampton Exchange, located in the Wimbledon area of London, England, consists of a federation of four institutions, providing the student with many cultural opportunities.

Academic Facilities

Roush Hall houses state-of-the-art computer labs, classrooms, a multimedia room, a two-story art gallery, and faculty and administrative offices. The Courtright Memorial Library houses 300,000 volumes and 1,015 periodical subscriptions and has an outstanding learning-resource center that includes the studios of the Otterbein-Westerville television station, WOCC. The McFadden-Schear Science Hall has modern laboratories and classrooms and a renovated planetarium and observatory. Cowan Hall houses modern facilities for speech and theater, including WOBN-FM, the campus radio station. The Battelle Fine Arts Center is the home for programs in music, art, and dance and also houses an electronic music laboratory. Historic Towers Hall, a campus landmark since 1870, had an $8.5-million renovation in 1999–2000 and houses classrooms, faculty offices, and updated math and computer science labs.

Costs

For 2003–04, Otterbein's tuition and fees were $20,133. Room and board cost $5952 per year. Books and supplies amount to approximately $600–$700 per year.

Financial Aid

Otterbein offers a wide variety of scholarships and grants, including Presidential Scholar Awards, Otterbein Scholar Awards, Endowed Scholarships, Dean's Scholarships, community service awards, talent awards, Federal Pell Grants, Ohio Instructional Grants, and Ammons-Thomas minority scholarships. In addition, Federal Perkins Loans, Federal Stafford Student Loans, and United Methodist Student Loans are available. To be considered for need-based College financial aid, students must file the Free Application for Federal Student Aid (FAFSA). Otterbein's financial aid policy is to attempt to meet the financial need of each full-time dependent and independent student offered admission who files financial aid forms by April 1.

Approximately 95 percent of Otterbein's students receive some form of financial aid. In addition to its need-based awards, the College offers scholarships to students on the basis of academic ability and proven talent.

Faculty

Otterbein has a faculty of 144 full-time and 105 part-time members (giving a student-faculty ratio of 13:1). Ninety-two percent of the full-time faculty members hold a doctorate or appropriate terminal degree. Faculty members are actively involved in campus governance, committees, and activities. The extensive sabbatical plan at Otterbein helps ensure that the faculty members constantly update and improve their classroom teaching.

Student Government

Otterbein's governance program gives students a voting voice along with faculty and administrators on all campus policymaking and decision-making bodies. Students are elected to the College Senate, to all governance committees, and to the College's Board of Trustees.

Admission Requirements

To be considered for admission to Otterbein College, students must complete and sign an admission application, submit an official copy of their high school transcript, and provide the College with their scores on either the ACT or SAT I. Applicants should have a solid high school academic record with at least 16 college-preparatory units. Otterbein does not discriminate on the basis of sex, race, gender, sexual orientation, age, political affiliation, national origin, or disabling condition in the admission of students, educational policies, financial aid and scholarships, housing, athletics, employment, and other activities. Inquiries regarding compliance with federal nondiscrimination regulations may be directed to the chairperson of the Affirmative Action Committee, the vice president for academic affairs, or the vice president for business affairs.

Students can gain a fuller understanding of student life at Otterbein by spending a day on campus. Prospective students are welcome to visit classes, eat in the Campus Center, and talk informally with Otterbein students and should simply notify the Office of Admission in advance so arrangements can be made.

Application and Information

Students are urged to begin the application process early in their senior year of high school. Applicants are notified of their admission status as soon as their application file is completed. Otterbein College's application is available on the Web at http://www.otterbein.edu.

For further information, students should contact:

Office of Admission
Otterbein College
Westerville, Ohio 43081
Telephone: 614-823-1500
800-488-8144 or 877-OTTERBEIN (toll-free)
E-mail: uotterb@otterbein.edu

Students on the campus of Otterbein College.

OUR LADY OF THE LAKE UNIVERSITY OF SAN ANTONIO

OurLady of the Lake University

SAN ANTONIO, TEXAS

The University

Our Lady of the Lake University (OLLU), founded in 1895 by the Congregation of Divine Providence, is a coeducational liberal arts institution. There are more than 3,300 students enrolled in fifty-eight undergraduate, forty-eight graduate, and two doctoral programs in the College of Arts and Sciences, the School of Business, the School of Education and Clinical Studies, and the Worden School of Social Service. The University's combination of historic Gothic buildings and modern facilities is the setting for innovative academic programs. OLLU is proud of its emphasis on service to others, its tradition of academic excellence, and its personal, student-centered atmosphere.

The University's student body ranges from recent high school graduates to working adults who are returning to college. The University offers Weekend Degree programs in San Antonio, Dallas, and Houston. A majority of the students are from Texas, but sixteen states and eight other countries are represented on campus. The average age of new freshmen is 18. More than 63 percent of the University's students are Hispanic, 9 percent are African American, and 1 percent are international. Seven residence halls are available, with space for more than 600 students.

The Campus Activities Office sponsors events throughout the year. Students are encouraged to join campus organizations to foster a well-rounded education by developing leadership skills through out-of-the-classroom involvement. Our Lady of the Lake University has four types of organizations to meet the needs of students: special interest groups, academic organizations, honor societies, and chartered organizations.

Campus Ministry serves the entire University and offers prayer services on campus as well as off-campus retreats, providing students a forum for spirituality and bonding. During the fall and spring semesters University liturgies are celebrated on weekdays and Sundays. Special liturgies are celebrated in the Sacred Heart Chapel throughout the year, and weekday liturgies are celebrated in Constantineau Chapel. Other opportunities for spiritual growth are offered through Bible study and special rosaries. A new OLLU program, La Llamada, also offers students the opportunity to integrate their faith into educational and career choices.

Intramural sports include basketball, football, racquetball, soccer, softball, tennis, and volleyball. Campus athletic facilities include playing fields, tennis courts, sand volleyball courts, an outdoor track with fitness-trail equipment, indoor and outdoor swimming pools and basketball courts, and the University Wellness and Activities Center, which houses a gymnasium, aerobics room, weight room, racquetball courts, lounge/study areas, and other facilities.

Location

The University's 72-acre campus is located in a residential area 3 miles west of downtown San Antonio, the nation's ninth-largest city. City bus routes link the campus to downtown. With a mix of Mexican, Spanish, German, and other heritages, San Antonio is known for Fiesta, the rodeo, Spanish missions (including the Alamo), the beautiful RiverWalk, a Mexican market, world-class museums, the 2003 NBA World Champion San Antonio Spurs basketball team, the San Antonio Rampage hockey team, an annual arts festival, the third-largest zoo in the United States, a symphony orchestra, and a sunny climate. San Antonio is less than 3 hours by car from the Gulf Coast and Mexico and a short drive to the state capital.

Majors and Degrees

Undergraduate degrees are offered in accounting, art, biology, business, chemistry, communication and learning disorders (speech pathology), communication arts, drama, early elementary (concentrations in generic special education and in bilingual education), electronic business and entrepreneurship, electronic commerce/information systems, English, finance, fine arts, generic special education, history, human resources management, human sciences, liberal studies (including an engineering dual degree with Washington University), management, marketing, mathematics, Mexican-American studies, music, natural sciences (including a core in environmental science), organizational leadership, philosophy, political science, professional accounting, psychology, religious studies, social studies, social work, sociology, and Spanish.

The applied studies degree is available for students who have 18–30 hours of transfer credit, life or work experience, or credit-by-examination in a technological specialization. Secondary Texas teacher certification is available in art, biology, chemistry, drama, electronic commerce/information systems, English, history, mathematics, political science, social studies, and Spanish. Preprofessional programs include dental, law, medical, nursing, occupational therapy, optometry, pharmacy, physical therapy, physician's assistant studies, and veterinary medicine. Interdisciplinary majors are available in six fields. Bilingual students who speak in English and Spanish may also choose to study in a biliterate-track degree program in business, broadcasting, communication and learning disorders, psychology, or social work. The degree program prepares undergraduate students to provide professional services to English and Spanish-speaking populations.

Academic Program

The requirements for a bachelor's degree at OLLU include a minimum of 128 semester hours (36 of which must be on the advanced level), a cumulative grade point average of at least 2.0, an average of at least 2.0 on all work taken at the University, a minimum of 32 semester hours in residence, and computer literacy requirements as specified by the student's major or area of concentration. General education requirements are listed in the University's Undergraduate Bulletin. Applicants may have their prior learning experiences evaluated for credit according to the methods approved by the University and the Council for the Assessment of Experiential Learning. The University offers computer-assisted learning, internships, practice in professional fields, and independent study. Army and Air Force ROTC courses are available.

Academic Facilities

The Electronic Commerce Lab and Technical Center, the Grossman Computer Instructional Laboratory, the Sueltenfuss Science/Math Computer Laboratory, and the English Computer Laboratory are equipped with computers and printers. All residence halls have network connections, and all students have access to the Internet and e-mail. The new $10-million 49,000-square-foot Sister Elizabeth Ann Sueltenfuss Library houses most of the University Library system's holdings, including ERIC microfiche, a Texana collection, and several rare book collections. It also contains state-of-the-art technology classrooms, conference rooms, study areas, group study areas, and a 24-hour computer and study laboratory. Other libraries include the Media Services Center, the Worden School of Social Service Library, and the Old Spanish Missions Historical Research Library.

Modern laboratory facilities are available in general chemistry, general biology, bacteriology, physiology, organic chemistry, analytical chemistry, and physics. The Science Research Laboratory is designed to enable undergraduate science majors to perform research projects under the supervision of two new research faculty members. The lab contains a wide variety of new instruments and, as the lab is not used for teaching classes, students are allowed to leave projects set up. Communication arts students have access to a fully equipped small-format video studio. The Decision Theater, a simulated boardroom arena with one-way observation galleries, is used to teach decision making and problem solving courses for business students.

As part of its research and student practicum facilities, the University maintains the Harry Jersig Center for communication and learning disorders; the Community Counseling Service for marriage, family, and individual counseling; the St. Martin Hall Elementary School; the Child Development Center for training and studying developmental learning; the Kliesen International and Cultural Center; the Center for Women in Church and Society; and the Center for Sociological Practice.

Costs

Full-time (12–19 semester credit hours) undergraduate tuition for 2003–04 was $7325 per semester plus fees. Part-time undergraduate tuition was $475 per credit hour, plus fees. The tuition rate applies to both in-state and out-of-state students. University housing costs vary, but averaged $2982 for the academic year 2003–04. All students who reside in University housing must participate in one of four meal plans ($650, $850, $950, or $1050 per semester).

Financial Aid

Most of OLLU's dependent undergraduate students receive some form of financial assistance. The University awards scholarships and academic grants on the basis of the student's composite score on the ACT or combined score on the SAT I and their high school or college grade point averages. Freshmen and transfer students accepted for admission are automatically considered for awards.

Students can apply for additional financial assistance. Federal and state grant and loan programs are available. Work awards are available through the federally funded Federal Work-Study Program and the University's Campus Employment Program. To be considered for financial aid, students must complete the Free Application for Federal Student Aid (FAFSA). On the FAFSA, students should list Our Lady of the Lake University, code number 003598. OLLU receives the FAFSA data electronically and then calculates a financial aid award. Financial aid applicants must be accepted for admission to the University before the award can be made. More documentation may be needed for government programs. All financial aid is awarded on a first-come, first-served basis.

Faculty

OLLU has 186 full-time and 124 part-time faculty members. Seventy percent of the full-time faculty members hold a doctoral or other terminal degree. The student-faculty ratio is 10:1. Freshmen are advised by the Advising Center staff. Faculty members advise sophomores, juniors, and seniors; serve as sponsors of student clubs and organizations; and are available to students in person and via e-mail.

Student Government

The Student Government Association (SGA) provides a forum for students to examine issues affecting the welfare of students and to propose solutions for positive change. It provides students an opportunity to stay involved in campus issues and activities and to build leadership skills. SGA consists of a 7-member executive board, which oversees two legislative branches: the Senate, with elected student representatives from each academic class, and the House of Representatives, with representatives of each recognized student organization. The president of the SGA is the student representative to the University's Board of Trustees. Students and faculty members share faculty-student policymaking and advisory committees. Students are represented on University planning councils and search committees for administrative positions.

Admission Requirements

OLLU seeks a diverse student body and offers equal educational opportunity to all students regardless of race, color, creed, sex, age, national or ethnic origin, or disability.

Prospective students should send a completed application form, a nonrefundable $25 application fee, and SAT I or ACT scores to the Admissions Center. OLLU's ACT code number is 4140; the SAT code is 6550.

Entering freshmen must also give evidence of their academic preparation and aptitude: either a transcript indicating graduation from an accredited high school with 16 units of credit (including 4 in English, 3 in social science, 2 in mathematics, 2 in a laboratory science, and 2 in a foreign language—or 2 additional units in English, math, social science, or natural science) or evidence of successful completion of the GED test. Also required are either a satisfactory combination of SAT I or ACT scores and high school grade point average or the successful completion of college-level work at another accredited postsecondary institution.

Transfer students must send a completed application form, a nonrefundable $25 application fee, and an official transcript from each institution attended. Transfer students with fewer than 30 transferable college credit hours must also submit SAT I or ACT scores and an official high school transcript if the college/university transcript does not indicate high school credits.

Application and Information

Entering freshmen must submit a transcript of high school credits (this may be done as early as the completion of the junior year). Students should submit their credentials prior to May 1 for the fall and summer semesters and December 1 for the spring semester. Admission decisions are made within two weeks of receiving completed application forms and all required documents. Students planning to live on campus must complete and return the housing application and the $100 housing deposit to the Residence Life Office by June 1.

To arrange a campus visit and tour, students should contact the Admissions Center.

Inquiries and application materials should be directed to:

Admissions Center
Our Lady of the Lake University
411 S.W. 24th Street
San Antonio, Texas 78207-4689
Telephone: 210-431-3961
800-436-OLLU (800-436-6558) (toll-free)
E-mail: admission@lake.ollusa.edu
World Wide Web: http://www.ollusa.edu

Our Lady of the Lake University is located in beautiful San Antonio, the nation's ninth-largest city with a small-town atmosphere.

PACE UNIVERSITY

NEW YORK CITY AND PLEASANTVILLE, NEW YORK

The University

Pace University was founded by two brothers, Homer and Charles Pace, in 1906. Their vision is reflected in Pace's motto "Opportunitas." A comprehensive, diversified, coeducational institution, Pace provides an array of opportunities for learning, living, and working at two distinct campus locations: metropolitan New York City and suburban Pleasantville, New York. More than eighty majors and 3,000 courses of study are offered through five undergraduate schools and colleges: the Lubin School of Business, the Dyson College of Arts and Sciences, the School of Computer Science and Information Systems, the School of Education, and the Lienhard School of Nursing. Pace University is chartered by the New York State Board of Regents and is accredited by the Middle States Association of Colleges and Schools.

Many student-led clubs and organizations are active on campus, including Model United Nations, Black Students Organization, the Chinese Club, the Caribbean Students Association, and the Collegiate Italian American Organization. Pace also offers many campus activities, including student government associations, fraternities and sororities, two campus newspapers, two literary magazines, two yearbooks, and two campus broadcasting systems. Athletic facilities are available for students, and intercollegiate sports include baseball, basketball, cross-country running, equestrian sports, football, golf, lacrosse, women's soccer, softball, tennis, track and field, and volleyball.

In 2003–04, approximately 9,000 undergraduate students enrolled at Pace University. The student body is diverse, representing forty-eight states, five U.S. territories, and more than seventy countries.

Location

Pace University is a multicampus institution with campuses in both New York City and Pleasantville, New York. Both locations are within reach of cultural, business, and social resources and opportunities. The New York City campus is located in the heart of downtown Manhattan, adjacent to the financial district and City Hall and within short walking distance of Wall Street and the South Street Seaport. Lincoln Center, Broadway theaters, museums, and many world-famous attractions are minutes away by public transportation. Located 35 miles north of New York City, the Pleasantville campus is located in suburban New York and includes an environmental center, riding stables, and a new athletic center. The town of Pleasantville houses gifted resident artisans and local musical and theater groups, and museums surround the campus. The campus is within easy reach of the resort and ski areas of the Catskills, Berkshires, and Poconos, as well as all that New York City has to offer. Both campuses are accessible by car and public transportation.

Students can take courses at either campus, and housing is available in both New York City and Pleasantville. Pace provides intercampus bus transportation to students free of charge. Resident facilities feature Internet connectivity, voicemail, and cable TV access.

Majors and Degrees

The following programs are offered at both the New York City and Pleasantville campuses.

The Bachelor of Business Administration (B.B.A.) is offered with majors in finance, general accounting, information systems, international management, management (with concentrations in business, entrepreneurship, hotel management, human resources, and operations management), marketing (with concentrations in advertising and promotion, database marketing, e-business and interactive media, management, and international marketing), and public accounting (CPA preparation). In addition, five-year combined B.B.A./M.B.A and B.B.A./M.S. programs in public accounting are available for qualified students. The Bachelor of Arts (B.A.) degree is granted in applied psychology and human relations, childhood education, computer science, economics, English and communications, French, history, language culture and world trade, liberal studies, mathematics, modern languages and cultures, political science, psychology, social science, sociology/anthropology, Spanish, teaching adolescents (with concentrations in English, French, social studies, and Spanish), technology systems, and theater arts; the Bachelor of Science (B.S.) degree in biology, chemistry, computer science, criminal justice, earth science, information systems, mathematics, medical technology, nursing, teaching adolescents (with concentrations in biology, chemistry, and earth science). Programs leading to combined B.A./M.B.A. or B.S./M.B.A. are available. The Associate of Science (A.S.) is available in applied information technology. The Associate of Applied Science (A.A.S.) is available in general business.

The following programs are available at the New York City campus only: the B.B.A. in general business, management with a concentration in operations management, and management science; the B.A. in art history, communication sciences and disorders, speech communication, teaching adolescents with concentrations in math and speech/language disabilities, and theater arts; the B.S. in business education, early childhood development, office information systems, and allied health; the A.S. in general science; the A.A.S. in banking; and the Bachelor of Fine Arts (B.F.A.) in theater. The Physician Assistant Program is offered at the New York City campus in cooperation with Lenox Hill Hospital.

The following programs are available at the Pleasantville campus only: the B.A. in biological sciences, communications, environmental studies, human services, Italian, philosophy and religious studies, teaching adolescents Italian, art, biochemistry, physics, and teaching adolescents physics and the A.A. in design, fine arts, and general arts and sciences.

Pace University offers two 5-year engineering programs in cooperation with Manhattan College and Rensselaer Polytechnic Institute. In the first program, electrical engineering, students attend Pace for three years and Manhattan College for two years, leading to a B.S. degree in science with a concentration in physics from Pace and a B.S. degree in electrical engineering from Manhattan. In the second program, chemical engineering, students attend Pace for three years and either Manhattan College or Rensselaer for two years. Upon successful completion, students receive a B.S. degree in chemistry from Pace and a Bachelor of Chemical Engineering (B.C.E.) in chemical engineering from Manhattan or a B.S. degree in engineering from Rensselaer.

Academic Program

At Pace University, the core curriculum emphasizes educational breadth. Students enroll in prerequisite courses in the first two years and major courses and electives in the junior and senior years. Selective academic programs in the University are preparatory for professional training in dentistry, law, medicine, and veterinary science.

The University Honors Program is designed to foster the intellectual life of outstanding students by enabling them to take greater responsibility and initiative in their academic work. The Open Curriculum privilege permits Honors Program members to choose courses in arts and sciences with a greater degree of freedom. The Independent Study Program encourages qualified students to undertake research and study to a depth beyond the normal course requirements.

The Cooperative Education Program is nationally recognized and offers qualified students the opportunity to gain experience in their field of study while earning a four-year degree. Students can choose full-time, part-time, or summer positions working in an area directly related to their major course of study. Students are recommended to enroll in the program during their first year at the University.

Academic Facilities

The Pace University Library is a comprehensive teaching library and student learning center, a virtual library that combines strong core collections with ubiquitous access to global Internet resources to support broad and diversified curricula. Reciprocal borrowing and access accords, traditional interlibrary loan services, and commercial document delivery options supplement the aggregate library. Pace offers Instructional Services librarians, a state-of-the-art electronic classroom, digital reference services, and multimedia applications. Pace's computer resource centers are linked to high-speed data networks and feature sophisticated hardware and software to facilitate active learning. Recognized as one of America's most wired universities, Pace supports high-speed Internet and Internet2 access on every campus; resident facilities are "wired," and most public areas are enabled for wireless connectivity. Full motion videoconference facilities enable remote delivery of instruction between campus sites for synchronous learning applications. Many courses are Web-assisted with state-of-the-art software, and some courses and programs are completely Web-based.

Costs

For the 2003–04 academic year, undergraduate tuition was $20,540 per year for full-time study. Tuition for part-time study was $590 per credit. Tuition is increased each year for incoming freshman students; however, students are guaranteed no tuition increases for up to five years if they remained enrolled as matriculated full-time students. The cost for an on-campus double-occupancy room was $5600. However, there are several housing options available. The cost of the meal plan was $2320. Additional fees cost approximately $500, and books and supplies average $720 per year.

Financial Aid

Pace University strives to provide opportunities to students of diverse backgrounds and varied circumstances and is committed to offering financial aid to students to the fullest extent of its resources. Scholarships are awarded to students in recognition of superior academic achievement and are available for full-time and part-time study. Pace's comprehensive student financial aid assistance program includes scholarship, graduate assistantships, student loans (federal and alternative plans), and tuition payment plans. Pace participates in all federal financial aid programs and the New York State Tuition Assistance Program (TAP) and honors awards from other states' incentive grant programs.

Students should submit the Free Application for Federal Student Aid (FAFSA) by February 15 for priority consideration for the fall semester. Further information about any financial aid programs can be obtained by contacting the Office of Financial Aid at any campus location.

Faculty

The undergraduate faculty at Pace is outstanding. Senior staff members, including department heads, teach freshman- and sophomore-level courses as well as upper-division classes. Approximately 90 percent of full-time faculty members hold a doctoral degree; many act as professional consultants to other educational institutions, businesses, and government. Adjunct faculty members pursue professional careers while teaching their specialty part-time.

Student Government

The Day Student Government Association is a major instrument for self-government on all campuses. On the New York City campus there is also an Evening Student Council. The University Senate, which operates on behalf of the entire institution, is composed of representatives from the student body, the faculty, alumni, and the administration representing all campus locations. The Senate plays an active role in the formulation of University policy.

Admission Requirements

A minimum of 16 units from an accredited secondary school, or equivalent, are required. Academic subjects in high school should be distributed as follows: 4 units of English, 3–4 units of college-preparatory mathematics, 2 units of foreign language, 4 units of history/social science, 2 units of laboratory science, and 4–5 units of academic electives. It is recommended that students applying to the Lubin School of Business complete 4 units of preparatory mathematics. Applicants to the Lienhard School of Nursing should complete 3–4 units of science (2 of which should be laboratory science) and 3–4 units of college-preparatory mathematics. All applicants are required to take either the SAT I or ACT examination and have results forwarded to the University.

Application and Information

The freshman application deadline is March 1. Transfer applications are reviewed on a rolling basis. Requests for application forms and information for both the New York City and Pleasantville campuses should be addressed to the Enrollment Information Center at the address below.

Enrollment Information Center
Pace University
1 Pace Plaza
New York, New York 10038
Telephone: 800-874-7223 Ext. UPG1(toll-free)
Fax: 212-346-1821
E-mail: infoctr@pace.edu
World Wide Web: http://www.pace.edu

PACIFIC UNIVERSITY

FOREST GROVE, OREGON

The University

Pacific University is a private, fully accredited four-year liberal arts university that encompasses an undergraduate College of Arts and Sciences and six graduate programs: five in the health professions and one in teacher education. Founded in 1849 by Congregational pioneers, Pacific is still a frontier institution, proud of its tradition in liberal arts and sciences and innovative in its programs for the rapidly changing health-care professions.

Pacific's 2,200 students come from all over the United States and twenty-eight countries, creating a diverse and dynamic student body. Students are taught by the University's 147 full-time faculty members, each of whom is chosen for his or her distinctive devotion to teaching and an emphasis on individual mentoring.

The College of Arts and Sciences is noted for its exceptionally personalized approach to education that is grounded in a philosophy of service. It is recognized for outstanding programs in the natural sciences, education, business, psychology, world languages, and the humanities.

Pacific's select group of graduate health profession programs includes the Pacific Northwest's only college of optometry as well as schools of physical therapy, occupational therapy, clinical and counseling psychology, and physician's assistant studies. In addition, a school of education offers undergraduate and master's-level programs leading to teacher licensure.

The lively and vigorous campus springs from the college's residential nature. Freshmen and sophomores under 21 are required to live in one of the University's coed residence facilities. Students who choose to live off-campus may live in the University-owned housing units or other nearby apartment complexes. On campus, the University Center is a hub of activity that houses the campus bookstore, the dining commons, a new lounge, student government offices, Macintosh and IBM lab facilities, the campus radio station, and the newspaper office. The Associated Students of Pacific University (ASPU) provides funding to twenty-seven student interest groups ranging from the Outback program to the Hawaiian Club to the Politics and Law Forum. The Pacific Outback program provides a multitude of outdoor activities for interested students, such as kayaking, hiking, cross-country and downhill skiing trips, camping, and outings to Portland-area events.

In athletics, Pacific is a member of the Northwest Conference of Independent Colleges and the NCAA Division III. Men's intercollegiate sports are baseball, basketball, cross-country, golf, soccer, tennis, track, and wrestling. Women compete in basketball, cross-country, golf, soccer, softball, swimming, tennis, track, and volleyball. Pacific athletes train and compete in the Pacific Athletic Center, which includes a gymnasium; a multipurpose field house; racquetball, handball, and squash courts; saunas; a dance studio; a weight room; and a complete sports medicine training facility.

Location

Situated in the northwest corner of Oregon between metropolitan Portland and the Pacific Ocean, the University is located in Forest Grove (population 17,000). The 60-acre, oak-covered campus is surrounded by green countryside and the foothills of the Coast Range Mountains, beyond which is the 300-mile stretch of Oregon coast. Opportunities abound in Oregon for hiking, skiing, camping, fishing, beach combing, and bicycling. The climate is temperate throughout the year with winter rainfall tapering off to a pleasant spring and sunny summer.

Majors and Degrees

Major programs leading to the B.A. or B.S. degree are offered through the College of Arts and Sciences in anthropology/ sociology, applied science, art, bioinformatics, biology, business administration (with an emphasis in accounting, finance, management, or marketing), chemistry (with an emphasis in biological chemistry, chemical physics, or environmental chemistry), Chinese studies, computer science, coordinated studies in humanities, creative writing, economics, education and learning, environmental biology, exercise science (with an emphasis in sports medicine or human performance), French studies, German studies, history, international studies, Japanese studies, literature, mathematics, media arts (with an emphasis in film production, film studies, integrated media, journalism, or video production), modern languages (with an emphasis in Chinese, French, German, Japanese, or Spanish), music (with an emphasis in education or performance), philosophy (with a bioethics emphasis), physics, political science, psychology, social work, sociology, Spanish, and theater. The B.M. degree is offered in music. Secondary education certification is available in art, biology, English, French, German, health education (combined endorsement only), integrated science, Japanese, mathematics, music, reading (combined endorsement only), social studies (secondary education students only), and Spanish.

Pacific offers five programs in the health professions that require undergraduate study. These include optometry (O.D.), professional psychology (M.A., M.S., and Psy.D.), physical therapy (M.S. and D.P.T.), occupational therapy (M.O.T.), and a physician's assistant studies program (M.S.). Programs in teacher education include the fifth-year M.A.T., M.A.T. Flex, M.Ed., and the M.Ed. in Visual Function and Learning (in conjunction with the optometry program). Physical therapy students must complete three years of undergraduate prerequisite work before being admitted into the program. Optometry students spend three years in undergraduate prerequisite work before being admitted into the four-year doctoral graduate program. Occupational therapy students spend three years in undergraduate prerequisite work and 2 ½ years in the master's program. The physician's assistant studies master's program is a twenty-seven-month consecutive program.

Pacific offers 3-2 programs in computer science, electrical engineering, and environmental science through a cooperative program with the nearby Oregon Graduate Institute. At the completion of the program, the student receives both a bachelor's degree from Pacific and a master's degree in their specialty from Oregon Graduate Institute.

Academic Program

Pacific provides an excellent education in the liberal arts and sciences. The undergraduate core curriculum emphasizes writing, reasoning, and communication skills with attention given to cross-cultural education and work in the natural sciences and the fine arts. All freshmen participate in a semester-long first-year seminar program designed to introduce students to college-level writing and research expectations. Pacific has a long tradition of ethical concern that is reflected in its undergraduate courses and its many opportunities for service both on-campus and within the broader community. As a small college, Pacific maintains small classes that ensure close contact among students and faculty members.

Special programs in the College of Arts and Sciences include the Senior Capstone thesis research project, the Peace and Conflict Studies Program, and a minor in feminist studies.

Basic requirements for the B.A. or B.S. degree are 124 semester hours of credit, completion of a major, and completion of the core requirements in the College of Arts and Sciences. The year is divided into two semesters with a three-week winter term between the two semesters. Students typically take 15 credit hours during each semester and three credit hours during the winter term.

Pacific grants credit for both subject and general CLEP examinations. Each department or school at Pacific University determines whether or not a specific examination may substitute for a specific course. Students who score 4 or better on the Advanced Placement examinations of the College Board are given advanced placement and credit toward graduation. Pacific recognizes the International Baccalaureate program as providing college-level work. Six semester credits are awarded for each higher examination passed at a score of 5 or higher.

Off-Campus Programs

Pacific offers study-abroad programs with thirty-three schools in fifteen countries, including Austria, China, Denmark, Ecuador, France, Germany, Hungary, Italy, Japan, Korea, Mexico, Netherlands, Spain, Thailand, and Wales. Foreign language and international studies majors are required to spend at least one semester studying abroad and may use financial aid toward their foreign study. Pacific also emphasizes internships, which are regularly arranged for students in business, communications, political science, psychology, sociology, and other fields. The internships, which may be arranged for periods lasting from fourteen weeks to an entire academic year, offer the opportunity to become thoroughly acquainted with professional work and often lead to employment upon graduation.

Academic Facilities

The 60-acre campus, a picturesque setting with green lawns and tall shade trees, has eighteen major buildings. Historic Marsh Hall, which was originally constructed in 1893 and completely refurbished in 1977, holds classrooms, offices of faculty members, and administration facilities. Old College Hall, built in 1850, was the first permanent structure of Pacific University. This building contains museum galleries, historic exhibits, and the campus chapel. The Douglas C. Strain Science Center and the Taylor-Meade Performing Arts Center were additions to campus in 1993. Students live in one of three residence halls or in the Vandervelden apartments. All on-campus rooms are connected to the campus computer network linked to the Internet. The Harvey W. Scott Library has 133,329 bound volumes, documents, periodicals, microfilm, microfiche, and musical recordings and scores. Pacific is part of OCLC (Online Computer Library Center), which allows students access to libraries all over the nation. Also available are a foreign language laboratory, a study-skills center, a rare books room, and various audiovisual services.

Costs

Tuition and fees for the 2003–04 school year were $19,330. Room and board were approximately $5540 for a double room and a nineteen-meal-per-week plan. Books and supplies are estimated at approximately $700.

Financial Aid

Financial assistance at Pacific is awarded on the basis of demonstrated need, academic merit, and talent. The Free Application for Federal Student Aid (FAFSA) is used in evaluating need. Prospective students are encouraged to apply for financial assistance by submitting the FAFSA to the federal processor as soon after January 1 as possible. Pacific provides financial assistance through grants, scholarships, loans, and part-time employment. Further information is available via e-mail at financialaid@pacificu.edu.

Faculty

Pacific's outstanding faculty members provide the foundation for the University's academic program. A student-faculty ratio of 13:1 allows for personal attention by the professors. Pacific's faculty is made up of 147 dedicated educators, of whom 96 percent hold terminal degrees in their field. As professionals, they uphold the University's standard of academic excellence. Pacific does not use graduate or teaching assistants in any course.

Student Government

Participatory government at Pacific enables students to help shape the campus community in which they live and work. Students are encouraged to voice their opinions and to pursue new ideas that not only further personal growth but also the overall growth and development of the University. The official student government body manages activity funds, reviews and supports student issues, and coordinates student participation within the system.

Admission Requirements

Pacific University is selective in considering new students. Primary consideration is given to a candidate's academic preparation and potential for successful study at the college level, as assessed by evaluating the student's transcripts of college-preparatory work, counselor and teacher recommendations, personal essay, SAT I or ACT scores, and other student-submitted information, such as teacher recommendations. Transfer students must submit high school records and test scores if they have completed less than 30 semester hours, plus official transcripts from any institution previously attended.

Application and Information

Students may apply early and may be notified early through the modified rolling admissions plan. The regular priority deadline for admission is February 15.

For additional information, interested students should contact:

Office of Admissions
Pacific University
2043 College Way
Forest Grove, Oregon 97116
Telephone: 503-352-2218
800-677-6712 (toll-free)
E-mail: admissions@pacificu.edu
World Wide Web: http://www.pacificu.edu

PAIER COLLEGE OF ART, INC.
HAMDEN, CONNECTICUT

The College

Paier College of Art, Inc., founded in 1946 as Paier School of Applied Arts, has educated artists in advertising, illustration, design, interior design, photography, and graphics, as well as in other applied art fields. Upon receiving a charter in 1982, the College expanded its commitment to provide as wide a range of art education as possible while maintaining its focus on preparing its students for professional careers in the arts. At Paier a professional art education occurs in the context of the education of the individual as a whole. The College maintains close relations with the professional art community as well as with the community at large. Instructors and full-time faculty members are all active professionals in their fields and provide an invaluable resource in terms of professional experience and expertise. The curriculum combines career skills with a background in the liberal arts. This approach to instruction—with its expectations of study in the fine arts through drawing, painting, composition, and computer skills, and in the mastery of procedures of the specialized field and development of portfolios geared to the workplace—has attracted students seeking rigorous preparation and has resulted in graduates of Paier College of Art finding rewarding careers in the professional world.

Students participate in semiannual shows and sales sponsored by the Student Association. These shows provide the student with exposure and reviews from the community at large, peers, and professionals in the field. Paier College of Art is approved by the Connecticut Board of Governors for Higher Education and accredited by the Accrediting Commission for Career Schools and Colleges of Technology and is a member of the International Council of Design Schools.

The current undergraduate enrollment is 292 men and women. The College provides no on-campus living arrangements. Private houses and apartments near the campus offer accommodations for both men and women. A list of rooms may be obtained from the admission office.

Location

Paier College of Art is located on the edge of New Haven. Public transportation provides students with easy access to other area colleges and universities. New Haven and the surrounding communities contain many centers of art display and activity. The Yale Gallery, the Peabody Museum, and the Mellon Center for British Art are examples of the art collections available locally. The Greater New Haven area supports many galleries, theaters, and dance and musical organizations. New Haven also supports a variety of shopping facilities, hotels, and restaurants. The rolling, picturesque Connecticut countryside is only a short distance away and is complemented by the fine beaches that dot the length of New England's coastline. All of New England, rich in the tradition of early America and alive with the creative energy of a well-educated population, surrounds the Paier student with countless opportunities for cultural experiences. Students are also within easy reach of New York, Hartford, and Boston.

Majors and Degrees

Paier College of Art offers programs of study leading to the Bachelor of Fine Arts (B.F.A.) degree in the following studio majors: fine arts, graphic design, illustration, interior design, and photography. An Associate of Fine Arts (A.F.A.) degree is available in photography. Paier College also offers programs of study leading to a diploma in fine arts, graphic design, illustration, interior design, and photography. Certificate programs are offered in graphic production, interior design, portrait and figure painting, and sharp focus/trompe l'oeil painting. Students completing certificate programs may apply the credits earned toward a Bachelor of Fine Arts degree or diploma in their field.

Academic Programs

Degree and diploma candidates begin with a foundation year of required study. A progressive, contemporary philosophy is shared with a respect for classical tradition and structured discipline. The foundation year of study reflects this philosophy and is and has been directed and staffed by outstanding practitioners since the school's inception a half century ago. Classes are mixed, with candidates for degree, diploma, and certificate programs working together. The same degree of professionalism is demanded of and shown to all students regardless of their program of study. The B.F.A. requires 130 semester hours of study, of which 88 must be in studio work and 42 must be in the humanities and sciences. The diploma requires 104 semester hours, of which 92 must be in studio work and 12 must be in the humanities and sciences. The A.F.A. in photography requires 43 semester hours of studio work and 21 semester hours in the humanities and sciences. The diploma in photography requires 43 semester hours of studio work and 9 semester hours in the humanities and sciences. Certificate programs require from 28 to 34 semester hours of study, consisting almost entirely of studio work.

Paier College of Art operates on the semester academic calendar. Spring and fall semesters are also supplemented by a summer session.

Academic Facilities

The campus is situated at the corner of Circular and Gorham Avenues. Administration activities, including admissions, personnel matters, consideration and disbursement of financial aid, maintenance of student records, and general administration, are conducted at 20 Gorham Avenue. Instructional activities in classrooms, studios, and laboratories designed for the College's purposes are conducted in four buildings that include the library, the auditorium, the computer lab, and exhibition spaces. The library contains 13,000 volumes, subscribes to 70 periodicals, houses a picture reference file of more than 30,000 images, and has a slide library containing more than 24,000 slides. In addition to extensive holdings in the field of the arts, the library contains a well-balanced collection of volumes in the humanities, social sciences, and physical sciences.

Costs

Tuition for 2004–05 is $11,200 per year for full-time degree students and $9400 per year for full-time diploma students. Part-time tuition is $360 per semester hour. Fees and supplies vary by program of study.

Financial Aid

Paier College of Art has a program of financial aid for those who are eligible that includes the Federal Pell Grant, Federal

Supplemental Educational Opportunity Grant, and Connecticut Independent College Student Grant. Loans may be obtained through the following programs: Federal Perkins Loan, Federal Stafford Student Loans, Universal Education Loans, and Federal PLUS. Further information may be obtained from the Office of Financial Aid at Paier College of Art.

Faculty

Faculty members at Paier College of Art are all professionals in their fields. As such, their level of expertise in preparing students to enter their chosen profession is invaluable. There are 40 faculty members, including both full-time and part-time practicing professionals. The student-faculty ratio is 6:1.

Student Government

Every member of the College student body is encouraged to participate in the Student Association, which is a vital and influential force in campus activities. The officers of the Student Association act as a liaison between the students and the College administration. Activities include socials, exhibitions of student and faculty work, field trips to major exhibits in Boston and New York, and cultural presentations.

Admission Requirements

Paier College of Art maintains a rolling admission system in which decisions are made throughout the year. Students may apply for full-time or part-time program status or for full-time or part-time nonmatriculated status. All high school and college transcripts, scores on either the SAT I or the ACT (for BFA students only), and two letters of recommendation are required. A nonrefundable application fee of $25 must accompany the completed application materials. An interview is required and is a vital part of the application process. A portfolio of recent artwork should be presented at the interview. Students with earned credit from other colleges may be admitted with advanced standing.

Application and Information

Application forms and additional information are available by contacting:

Office of Admissions
Paier College of Art, Inc.
20 Gorham Avenue
Hamden, Connecticut 06514
Telephone: 203-287-3031
Fax: 203-287-3021
E-mail: paier.admin@snet.net
World Wide Web: http://www.paiercollegeofart.edu

Students interact with 3-D sculptures.

PAINE COLLEGE

AUGUSTA, GEORGIA

The College

Paine College is private, four-year, coeducational, and residential college. Established in 1882 by the United Methodist Church and the Christian Methodist Episcopal (C.M.E.) Church, Paine offers a broad-based educational program in the liberal arts. Historically black in enrollment, Paine is one of the forty-one colleges and universities associated with the United Negro College Fund.

The mission of Paine College is to provide a high-quality liberal arts education that emphasizes ethical and spiritual values, social responsibility, and personal development. Paine is committed to timeless standards of instructional quality within a curriculum that responds to the needs of its students. Paine's excellent academic environment, small size, and competent, caring faculty members form the matrix of an extraordinarily nurturing experience.

Paine's attractive 57-acre campus provides a thriving yet relaxed social center for college life. Central to the campus setting is a beautiful tree-lined quadrangle, with Haygood-Holsey Hall, the administration building, and the Gilbert-Lambuth Memorial Chapel as its anchors. There are approximately 900 students enrolled at Paine. Sixty percent of the students live on campus in seven residence halls. Represented among the more than forty clubs and organizations are eight fraternities and sororities. Planned recreational activities are usually held at the Peters Campus Center or the Randall A. Carter Gymnasium. The chapel is the setting for assemblies, formal convocations, religious services, and commencement exercises. The newly renovated Candler Memorial Library includes a conference center for meetings, receptions, and other special events.

Paine competes in the Southern Intercollegiate Athletic Conference (SIAC), which is affiliated with the National Collegiate Athletic Association (NCAA) Division II. Athletic programs include men's and women's basketball, cross-country, and track; women's softball and volleyball; and men's baseball.

Location

Located in Augusta, Georgia, Paine is situated in the heart of the state's second-largest metropolitan area. Augusta is located 150 miles east of Atlanta on the west bank of the Savannah River. The riverbank is a hub of activity, including the $4-million Riverwalk—a complex of shops, restaurants, and entertainment spots. Augusta is known internationally as the host city for the Masters Golf Tournament, which draws spectators from around the world. The city has numerous shopping centers and a major mall. The Augusta–Richmond County Civic Center and the Bell Auditorium offer a variety of entertainment, including national performers and cultural events. Public transportation is available to all parts of the city. Augusta is easily accessible by car or air.

Majors and Degrees

Paine College offers thirteen majors leading to the Bachelor of Science or Bachelor of Arts degree. The College's major areas of study are biology, business administration, chemistry, early childhood education, English, history, mass communications, mathematics, middle grades education, music education, psychology, religion and philosophy, and sociology. Concentrations or emphases include computer science, criminology, information systems, and secondary education. Many majors may be selected as minors, or students may choose from several areas designated as minors only, including art, economics, French, music, physical education, physics, and political science.

Academic Programs

A challenging academic program offers numerous opportunities for development and preparation for a diverse and flexible future. Paine's comprehensive curriculum is continually enhanced to challenge and stretch the mind of every student. While the curriculum is grounded in the liberal arts, the College recognizes the changing career patterns its graduates face in the twenty-first century and offers expanded opportunities in new technologies. The curriculum is designed to provide opportunities for sound physical, intellectual, moral, social, and spiritual growth under Christian influences.

The academic year is divided into fall and spring semesters. There is also a summer session. Credit for courses is recorded in semester hours, with a minimum of 124 hours required for graduation. The 61-hour general education requirement includes courses in English, fine arts, physical education, mathematics, natural sciences, social sciences, philosophy, religion, and a foreign language. A core of at least 34 hours is required for each major.

Special programs include ROTC, an honors program, cooperative education, and a preprofessional sciences program that prepares students for graduate and professional study in medicine, dentistry, pharmacy, and veterinary medicine. The preprofessional sciences program also offers students early acceptance to the Medical College of Georgia in nursing and eleven allied health fields. In addition to the health sciences programs, Paine offers a strong program in teacher education, which has been cited by the state of Georgia as a model. Teacher education has a 100 percent placement record, and the demand for graduates has surpassed the number of students in the program. The College has received several grants to support the growth of the teacher-education program.

Enhancement courses and the Tutorial and Enrichment Center supplement the academic program. The College is accredited by the Southern Association of Colleges and Schools.

Academic Facilities

Paine College's academic buildings include Haygood-Holsey Hall, Mary Helm Hall, Warren A. Candler Building, Walker Science Building, and the Gilbert-Lambuth Annex. The Collins-Callaway Library is a state-of-the-art library and learning resources center. The two-story, 30,000-square-foot facility is equipped to house more than 123,000 volumes. In the learning resources center, students have access to more than 150 microcomputers and more than 500 computer programs.

Costs

Tuition for the 2003–04 academic year totaled $8448. Room and board charges were $3940. Fees were $634. An optional meal plan is available for commuter students. Tuition fees, room, and board are subject to change annually.

Financial Aid

It is Paine College policy to provide every eligible student with the maximum amount of financial aid available. In fact, 90 percent of Paine College students receive some form of financial assistance. Paine College offers scholarships, grants, loans, and part-time employment, from various funding sources, to assist eligible students in meeting their educational expenses. The largest amount of support comes from the federal government through Federal Pell Grant, Federal Perkins Loan, Federal Supplemental Educational Opportunity Grant, Federal Work-Study, Federal Stafford Student Loan, and Federal PLUS Programs.

A student's eligibility for federal financial aid is determined by the information the applicant and his or her family provide on the Free Application for Federal and Student Aid (FAFSA). Paine College recommends that every student complete and submit the necessary financial aid forms as soon as possible. The priority deadline for applications is April 15.

Faculty

Paine College has 65 full-time and 11 part-time faculty members. A student-teacher ratio of 12:1 enables Paine's talented and energetic faculty members to provide the kind of individualized attention for which the College is known. Approximately 50 percent of Paine's faculty members have earned doctorates; all have advanced degrees.

Student Government

Once enrolled, students automatically become members of the Student Government Association (SGA). The SGA is the chief agent between the students and the faculty. Paine College believes that student input is important. The president of the SGA is a member of the College's Board of Trustees, and a student government representative serves on the Committee on Strategic Planning.

Admission Requirements

Students are admitted on the basis of scholastic achievement, academic potential, seriousness of educational purpose, and leadership. To that end, Paine is committed to giving all who qualify an opportunity to learn and grow. New freshmen are expected to have at least a 2.0 average on a 4.0 scale in 16 units of college-preparatory courses from a school accredited by a state or regional accrediting agency. The courses must include English (4 units), mathematics (2 units), social sciences (2 units, including 1 in history), natural science (2 units), and electives (6 units). An early admission program is available to students of superior ability and maturity who have completed the eleventh grade.

Application and Information

Candidates for admission must submit a Paine College Application for Admission, the $20 application fee, Graduation High School Test scores (if applicable), SAT I or ACT scores, an autobiographical essay, three letters of recommendation, and a high school transcript or passing scores on the GED test. Application deadlines are August 1 for the fall semester, December 1 for the spring semester, and June 1 for the summer session.

For an admission and financial aid packet, students should contact:

Office of Admissions and Financial Aid
Paine College
1235 Fifteenth Street
Augusta, Georgia 30901-3182
Telephone: 706-821-8320
800-476-7703 (toll-free)
World Wide Web: http://www.paine.edu

Paine College's small setting and strong academic program promote an atmosphere for intellectual growth and discovery.

PALM BEACH ATLANTIC UNIVERSITY

WEST PALM BEACH, FLORIDA

The University

Palm Beach Atlantic University (PBA) was founded in 1968 by concerned Palm Beach County residents who felt the need for a distinctive institution of higher learning that would stress not only academic quality but also character development and spiritual maturity. Chartered as a Christian liberal arts college, Palm Beach Atlantic offers a high-quality education for students of all faiths. In 1972, the University was accredited by the Southern Association of Colleges and Schools to award bachelor's degrees.

By 2003, PBA had grown to serve nearly 3,000 students in a variety of traditional and nontraditional programs. Four master's degree programs also are offered: Master of Business Administration, Master of Science in Organizational Leadership, Master of Education in Elementary Education, and Master of Science in Counseling Psychology. In 2001, PBA enrolled its first class of pharmacy students in its Pharm.D. program.

For both undergraduate and graduate students, Palm Beach Atlantic seeks to promote intellectual, moral, and spiritual growth. The undergraduate may opt for a variety of ways to get involved in college life, including service and leadership organizations, intercollegiate and intramural sports, fine arts, religious groups, and professionally oriented organizations such as Kappa Delta Epsilon and Phi Beta Lambda. In 2002, the University dedicated an additional 250,000 square feet of campus facilities as part of its comprehensive campus growth plan. The DeSantis Family Chapel provides exciting opportunities for multiple weekly chapels on the PBA campus. Oceanview Residence Hall and Dixie Garage add additional freshman housing and offer convenient access to the University's educational and cultural programs. Vera Lea Rinker Hall houses PBA's School of Music, accredited by the National Association of Schools of Music (NASM).

Location

Palm Beach Atlantic University occupies nearly 25 acres in the heart of West Palm Beach on the Intracoastal Waterway across from Palm Beach, approximately 1 mile from the Atlantic Ocean. Palm Beach County provides a broad spectrum of cultural activities in music, theater, fine arts, and sports. The cosmopolitan area of the Palm Beaches, with its shopping, recreation, and service opportunities, is at the University's doorstep.

Majors and Degrees

The Bachelor of Arts is offered in art; art education (K–12); biblical studies; Christian leadership; Christian social ministry; communication; dance; elementary education, with specializations in middle grades English and middle grades social sciences; English; history; ministry; music; musical theater; philosophy and religion; political science; religious studies; secondary education, with specializations in drama (6–12), English (6–12), social science/history (6–12), and social science/political science (6–12); and theater arts (dance). A Bachelor of General Studies is also available.

The Bachelor of Music degree is offered in church music, instrument performance, keyboard performance, music composition, music education, and voice performance.

The Bachelor of Science is offered in applied finance and accounting; athletic training; biology (with concentrations in biotechnology, botany, environmental science, field biology, marine biology, molecular biology, pre–health professional preparation, and zoology); computer information systems; elementary education, with specializations in pre-K primary, middle grades general sciences, middle grades mathematics, specific learning disabilities (K–12), and varying exceptionalities certification; international business; management; marine biology; marketing; mathematics; nursing; organizational management; psychology; secondary education, with specializations in biology (6–12), mathematics (6–12), and physical education (6–12); and sports management.

Minors are offered in accounting, art, athletic training, biblical studies, biology, business administration, chemistry, Christian leadership, Christian social ministry, communication, communication/performance studies, computer information systems, computer science, dance, English, history, marketing, mathematics, ministry to the child, missions, music, musical theater, oceanography, philosophy, physical education, political science, psychology, public relations, religion, sociology, Spanish, theater arts, and youth ministry.

Preprofessional programs are offered in engineering (a 2-2 program with the University of Florida), health, and legal studies.

Academic Programs

A minimum of 120 semester hours of academic work with a minimum overall grade point average of 2.0 is required for graduation. The student must complete a major of 30 or more semester hours and a minor of 15 or more hours. Double majors are possible. The major and minor are usually declared by the midpoint of the sophomore year, although changes after this time may be allowed.

Culture is the unifying force in the general education program that is required of all degree programs. The Unified Studies program is designed to give students a "wide-angle lens" on the world with an interdisciplinary focus on four areas: Faith and Culture, Communication and Culture, History and Culture, and Science and Culture. The program is a collaborative effort among faculty members, not only from within the department of instruction but also from related areas. Guest lectures and team-teaching are integral components, and students shape their own experiences by becoming participating, active learners.

College-Level Examination Program (CLEP), International Baccalaureate (I.B.), and Advanced Placement (AP) test credits are accepted, and advanced standing is granted to qualified students. Opportunities are available for independent and directed study.

The academic year is divided into two semesters, one running from September through December, the second from January through April. A six-week summer term is offered as well.

Off-Campus Programs

Several courses during the May and summer terms include opportunities for study abroad that carry academic credit. Semester-abroad programs are also available.

Academic Facilities

PBA is committed to state-of-the-art academic facilities. Every classroom is designated a smart classroom with wireless network access and a projection screen, and every residence hall room has a high-speed Internet connection via PalmNET, the campuswide fiber-optic network.

The Blomeyer Library contains more than 130,000 volumes, over 2,000 active subscriptions, and access to over 2 million volumes in the South Florida Library Information Network (SEFLIN).

In 2002, the University completed construction on 250,000 square feet of new facilities. A 40,000-square-foot building to house the Gregory School of Pharmacy is scheduled to be dedicated in July 2004.

Costs

The tuition, room, and board costs make PBA an affordable institution in comparison with other colleges across the country. The cost for a full-time student attending Palm Beach Atlantic University during the 2003–04 school year was $14,690 per year (12–18 hours). Room and board costs were approximately $5600 per year. Expenses for books, personal items, and travel should be considered when estimating the total cost of attending the University.

Financial Aid

More than 90 percent of the undergraduate students at PBA receive some type of financial aid. Each student should submit the Free Application for Federal Student Aid (FAFSA). Students may be eligible for federal and state grants, federal loans, and work-study programs as well as institutional grants and scholarships.

Faculty

The University has an outstanding faculty of 192 full- and part-time members who are dedicated to Christian education. Approximately 70 percent hold earned doctorates, and individualized attention results from the favorable student-faculty ratio of 16:1. The University's family atmosphere allows for a great deal of student-faculty interaction in and out of the classroom. No graduate assistants teach at PBA.

Student Government

An active Student Government Association represents student opinion and plans student activities at the University. Students are represented on most faculty and board committees and are active in setting the direction of the University.

Admission Requirements

High school graduates are required to submit an application with a personal essay, one academic and one character recommendation, official transcripts indicating at least a 3.0 grade point average in college-preparatory studies, and a minimum score of 960 on the SAT I (combined) or 20 on the ACT (composite). An interview with an admission counselor is required. International students must also demonstrate English proficiency on the Test of English as a Foreign Language (TOEFL).

Transfer students must be eligible to return to their previous college or must have been out of school for at least one semester. One academic and one character recommendation are required in addition to official transcripts indicating a grade point average of 2.5 or better in previous college work.

Application and Information

Both freshmen and transfer students are admitted in either semester. December 1 is the Early Action deadline. February 1 is the deadline for priority decision.

Applications are accepted throughout the year, but students who wish to live in residence halls on campus are encouraged to apply early because of housing capacity limitations. Candidates must submit an official University application to the Admissions Office along with a $25 nonrefundable application fee and the required materials (transcript, test scores, and recommendations).

For materials and additional information, students should contact:

Admissions Office
Palm Beach Atlantic University
P.O. Box 24708
West Palm Beach, Florida 33416-4708
Telephone: 561-803-2100
888-GO-TO-PBA (toll-free)
E-mail: admit@pba.edu
World Wide Web: http://www.pba.edu

Palm Beach Atlantic University offers the best of both worlds: the diversity of an urban setting coupled with the recreational activities and stunning vistas of Florida's waterways.

PAUL SMITH'S COLLEGE

PAUL SMITHS, NEW YORK

The College

Paul Smith's College was named for an entrepreneur whose famous resort on Lower St. Regis Lake was synonymous with Adirondack hospitality. Many of the rich and famous of the late nineteenth and early twentieth centuries gathered at the resort to enjoy the mountain wilderness and the comfortable accommodations provided by Paul Smith and his wife, Lydia. Vast land holdings, acquired over the years, were passed on to Smith's son Phelps, who, upon his death in 1937, bequeathed the bulk of the estate to the establishment of a college in his father's name. Paul Smith's College was chartered as a college of the arts and sciences; however, in the tradition of Paul Smith, who believed in "learning by doing," the school provides students with the opportunity to gain practical experience in a chosen field, while obtaining the academic background necessary for a well-rounded education. Today, the College-owned Hotel Saranac, in nearby Saranac Lake, provides students of hotel and restaurant management, culinary arts, and travel and tourism with experience in many aspects of the hospitality industry. Furthermore, the immense expanse of woodlands, lakes, and streams surrounding the campus offers students of forestry, ecology and environmental technology, and environmental studies a large-scale laboratory in which to practice. The combination of "hands-on" and classroom learning that Paul Smith's prescribes has attracted students from across the country and throughout the world to the campus.

Student activities are an important part of life at Paul Smith's. Popular organizations include the Forestry Club, Adirondack Experience Club, Travel Club, American Junior Culinary Federation, yearbook, campus radio station, and Emergency Wilderness Response Team.

For those interested in athletics, Paul Smith's has a swimming pool, basketball courts, a fitness center with Universal and free weights, an archery and rifle range, a padded aerobics room, a rock-climbing wall, and a multiple-use court for badminton, volleyball, and other indoor sports. Outside, the College has tennis courts, sand volleyball courts, and miles of wooded trails for the cross-country runner or mountain biking enthusiast. Paul Smith's participates at the intercollegiate level in men's and women's basketball, cross-country, soccer, and woodsmen's competitions and men's ice hockey.

Paul Smith's College of Arts and Sciences is approved and chartered by the Regents of the University of the State of New York and the Commissioner of Education of New York State. The College is accredited by the Commission on Higher Education of the Middle States Association of Colleges and Schools. Paul Smith's is accredited additionally by the Society of American Foresters (forest recreation and forest technician); the Technology Accreditation Commission of the Accreditation Board for Engineering and Technology (surveying technology); and the American Culinary Federation Educational Institute Accrediting Commission (culinary arts).

Location

The College is located in the midst of approximately 14,200 acres of College-owned forests and lakes on the shore of Lower St. Regis Lake in the Adirondack Mountains of northern New York State. Students have access to 23 miles of navigable water for boating and fishing, while nearby forests and mountains provide sites for hiking, climbing, and more. The campus is located 22 miles from Lake Placid, site of the 1932 and 1980 Winter Olympics. Students go there to shop or to watch athletes train in luge, bobsled, ski jumping, and other winter sports. Whiteface Mountain, Big Tupper Ski Area, and Titus Mountain provide skiing venues for the beginner as well as the expert.

Majors and Degrees

Paul Smith's College awards Bachelor of Science (B.S.), Bachelor of Professional Studies (B.P.S.), Associate in Science (A.S.), Associate in Arts (A.A.), and Associate in Applied Science (A.A.S.) degrees. Bachelor's degree programs of study include biology (concentrations in conservation science, ecology and field biology, and general biology) (B.S.); culinary arts and service management (B.P.S.); forestry (concentrations in ecological forest management, forest biology, industrial forestry operations, recreation resource management, and vegetation management) (B.S.); hotel, resort, and tourism management (B.S.); natural resources (with a concentration in either environmental science or management and policy) (B.S.); business management and entrepreneurial studies (B.S.); and recreation, adventure travel, and ecotourism (B.S.).

Associate degree programs of study include business administration, culinary arts, culinary arts baking track, environmental studies, fish and wildlife technology, forest recreation, forest technician studies, hotel and restaurant management, hotel and restaurant management (travel), liberal arts, outdoor recreation, preprofessional forestry, surveying technology, and urban tree management. Paul Smith's also offers a one-year certificate program in baking.

Academic Programs

Students in the baccalaureate program in natural resources have the option of pursuing either an environmental science or a management and policy concentration. In the environmental science concentration, students use scientific exploration to better understand human impact on the environment and provide the scientific base for rational decision making. In the management and policy concentration, students gain an understanding of the policy implications of protected areas of management and models of land-use management.

Biology majors who are interested in postgraduate studies in the health sciences can choose general biology as their concentration. Those interested in conservation or in field studies can choose either ecology and field biology or conservation science for a concentration.

The Bachelor of Science degree in hotel, resort, and tourism management prepares students for professional positions in the hospitality and tourism industries. At the same time, the program makes them aware of the economic and environmental implications of a burgeoning travel and resort industry and the growing interest in the "greening of the industry."

The Bachelor of Professional Studies program in culinary arts and service management develops a student's ability to research, understand, analyze, and manage contemporary restaurant and food service operations. The hospitality industry continues to evolve as the need increases for managers of facilities, who can produce high-quality food, embrace and effectively use computer technology, and employ personnel management strategies consistent with the twenty-first century.

Students in the business management and entrepreneurial studies program are well-suited for a wide range of career possibilities, from opening their own small business to being an executive with a multinational corporation. The combination of a strong traditional business curriculum and the entrepreneurial focus of other required courses prepares students to enter the job market or pursue an M.B.A. degree with confidence upon graduation.

The recreation, adventure travel, and ecotourism program prepares students for professional positions in the field of participatory, nature-based tourism through courses such as Adventure Skills Development, Expedition Planning, and Interpreting the Environment. Tropical destinations such as Costa Rica are the setting for an ecoadventure practicum, and students complete an externship at a site that relates most closely to their ultimate career goals.

Information on the associate degree programs can be found in *Peterson's Guide to Two-Year Colleges.*

Off-Campus Programs

Cooperative work experiences for credit are required in the following programs: baking, culinary arts, hotel and restaurant management, surveying technology, tourism and travel, and urban tree management. Students in these programs have the opportunity to practice what they have learned at locations throughout the country.

Academic Facilities

Thousands of acres of College-owned lands and waterways in the Adirondack Mountains provide the natural laboratories for students in the forestry and environmental programs. The ninety-two-room Hotel Saranac, with its restaurants, banquet and catering facilities, lounge, and gift shop, offers occupational experience for hotel and restaurant management, culinary arts, and tourism and travel students. Located in the College's more traditional classroom buildings are state-of-the-art laboratories for chemistry, biology, physics, computers, graphic arts, photography, mechanical drawing, and culinary arts. The Forestry Division's resources are augmented by a permanent Lane sawmill complex, a mechanical skidder, recreational campsites, and a sugar bush. Paul Smith's library houses 56,000 volumes, 430 periodicals, a computer lab, audiovisual equipment, and four study rooms. Paul Smith's also provides for its students a Student Health Center, 24-hour campus security, a job placement and college transfer office, personal counseling, and campus ministry.

Costs

In 2004–05, yearly tuition is $15,330, board is $3360, and housing is $3360. Summer sessions are required for some programs, and the costs vary by program. Additional fees to cover lab charges, student activities, and other costs vary from $510 to $1620 per year, depending on the program. The cost of books and supplies is estimated at $750 to $1450 per year.

Financial Aid

Federal programs available at the College include the Federal Pell Grant, Federal Supplemental Educational Opportunity Grant (FSEOG), Federal Stafford Student Loan, Federal Perkins Loan, and Federal Work-Study programs. The Federal Work-Study awards provide work for more than 70 percent of the student body, and more than 98 percent of the students receive some form of financial aid. The Financial Aid Office encourages students to apply for aid with the Free Application for Federal Student Aid (FAFSA) by the end of January to be processed by March 15. A financial aid brochure is available. State programs processed through the College include New York State Tuition Assistance Program (TAP), Vermont State Assistance Program, and Rhode Island Educational Assistance Program.

Faculty

Paul Smith's College faculty is composed of 85 full-time and 10 part-time members. Most faculty members live on or near the campus and participate in all phases of academic life. The student-faculty ratio is approximately 14:1.

Student Government

The Student Government is primarily responsible for the sponsorship and funding of a variety of campuswide activities, such as freshman orientation, concerts, dances, talent nights, and weekly movies.

Admission Requirements

Admission requirements vary by program. Each candidate is evaluated individually based on the requirements of the program applied for. Assuming all course prerequisites have been fulfilled, admissions decisions are based on academic performance, extracurricular activities, and a personal interview, if possible.

Application and Information

Applicants for either the associate or bachelor's degree programs must submit a formal application for admission, a $30 application fee, SAT I and/or ACT scores (unless applying for the associate degree program in culinary arts), and an official high school transcript. Recommendations, a personal interview, and an essay are strongly recommended. Transfer students must submit an official copy of their college transcript from any college attended; letters of recommendation and an essay are recommended. Non-native English-speaking international students are required to submit scores from the TOEFL examination. Because the College operates on a continuing admissions system, applicants are urged to apply as early as possible. Prospective students normally receive a decision within three to five weeks of receipt of all application materials.

For more information, students should contact:

Admissions Office
Paul Smith's College
Paul Smiths, New York 12970
Telephone: 518-327-6227
800-421-2605 (toll-free)
(Monday through Friday, 8 a.m. to 5 p.m.)
Fax: 518-327-6016
E-mail: admiss@paulsmiths.edu
World Wide Web: http://www.paulsmiths.edu

Students learning in Paul Smith's outdoor classroom.

PEACE COLLEGE
RALEIGH, NORTH CAROLINA

The College

Peace College is a baccalaureate college of arts and sciences that challenges women to an adventure of intellectual and personal discovery, preparing women for graduate and lifelong learning, for meaningful careers, and for ethical lives of purpose, leadership, and service. The institution was founded in 1857 and named for founding benefactor William Peace, an elder of the First Presbyterian Church of Raleigh.

The main campus setting is in a 19-acre grove of native oaks. Attractive brick and wrought-iron fencing extends around the campus. Facilities include five air-conditioned residence halls, an athletic field, six all-weather tennis courts, and an indoor swimming pool.

Location

Peace College is located at 15 East Peace Street in historic downtown Raleigh, North Carolina. The State Capitol, Legislative Building, State Library, North Carolina Symphony, Exploris (a global learning center), and several museums (art, history, and natural sciences) lie within a few blocks of the campus. Also, Raleigh is one of the cities that comprise North Carolina's Research Triangle Park. Duke University, North Carolina State, and the University of North Carolina at Chapel Hill are all located within the Triangle. Such a location provides many opportunities for personal enrichment and professional development.

Majors and Degrees

Bachelor of Arts degrees are offered in biology, business administration, child development, communication, English, human resources, leadership studies, liberal studies, music performance, politics and public affairs, psychology, Spanish, and visual communication. The teaching licensure option is available through a partnership with the local consortium, Cooperating Raleigh Colleges (CRC).

Academic Programs

The B.A. degree requires a minimum of 125 semester hours for graduation. All degree programs require a strong general education component. Requirements include 19 hours of "Essential Skills" (developing written, oral, computing, mathematical, and analytical competencies) and 25 hours of "Essential Knowledge" courses (liberal arts and sciences). In addition to the hours required for each major, all B.A. programs have a third category of "Advanced Skills and Knowledge," including a required internship related to the major; a senior seminar course, "Ethics in the Modern World;" and 9 hours of additional general education courses chosen to complement the declared major. A liberal number of electives and Peace College's participation in a consortium of local colleges and universities provide students with an opportunity to build desired credentials by taking double majors, concentrations, and minors. Honors, independent study, research, and special topics courses are available, as are career exploration internships for lower-division students. There are no off-campus credit programs except international programs. Peace College supports a variety of international programs through its Ragland endowment. An ROTC program is available through CRC.

Academic Facilities

The Lucy Cooper Finch Library contains a total of 51,788 titles, including 8,366 volumes of 390 periodicals and 950 recordings, videotapes, and computer disks. The library provides electronic and interlibrary loan access to collections of other colleges and research universities in Raleigh, the Research Triangle, and the state. The library also subscribes to online database resources to meet the information needs of students and faculty members.

All academic facilities are networked and provided with Internet service. Computer laboratories, the library, and the student publications area are equipped with Pentium-based platforms. Macintosh laboratories are also available in the biology, music, and visual communication departments. Student laboratories in the chemistry, general biology, and molecular and cellular biology departments are available. A recital hall in the music building, the Leggett Theater, and a dance studio are available for students in the fine arts department. In fall 2000, a classroom and faculty office building opened, making $500,000 of instructional technology available to students and faculty members. This academic building features an 84-seat amphitheater/lecture hall for campus and public events, a communication media laboratory, a psychology/anthropology laboratory, a psychology observation room, a business/human resources laboratory, and additional computer laboratories for student use.

Costs

For 2003–04, tuition and fees for full-time study totaled $7963 per semester. The charge for part-time study was $400 per credit hour. Room and board were $2967 per semester.

Financial Aid

Students and/or their families are expected to pay for educational expenses, to the extent that it is possible. However, it is the goal of Peace College that no student is denied the opportunity to attend because of financial need. Accordingly, the College administers a generous program of financial aid, including Federal Work-Study opportunities, Federal Pell Grants, Federal Supplemental Educational Opportunity Grants, and North Carolina State Contractual Scholarship Grants. The College administers loans under the Federal Family Education Loan Program. The College offers both scholarships and grants to all eligible first-year and transfer students.

To apply for financial aid, students must submit a completed FAFSA, either to the processor or to the College, for electronic processing. Applicants must demonstrate financial need and show evidence of academic promise or academic achievement to receive assistance from federally funded programs. Students may also apply for Peace College scholarships by completing an application form that is available from the Financial Aid Office. North Carolina residents are eligible for the North Carolina Legislative Tuition Grant (NCLTG), which is currently valued at $900 per semester. The NCLTG is awarded to students who have resided in North Carolina for a minimum of twelve months prior to enrolling, who meet state residency requirements, and who complete and submit to the Financial Aid Office an application for the grant. Out-of-state students receive a tuition offset grant that is funded through the College.

Faculty

There are 41 full-time faculty members who teach 75 percent of all courses. Approximately 30 part-time faculty members teach courses for curricular enrichment and when a full load for a new full-time member does not exist. Because Peace is an undergraduate institution that focuses on excellent teaching, all classes, including laboratories, are taught by its regular faculty. Although faculty members are expected to sustain a scholarly interest, the most important factor in all evaluations for promotion, tenure, and merit pay is the quality of teaching. The role of faculty members is to teach, supervise student research and internships, and advise students. Faculty members are also expected to show support for the extracurricular activities of their students. Some faculty members have some release time when serving as division chairs or program coordinators, but the substantial majority of their workload is instruction-related, not administrative. All Peace faculty members have advanced degrees (except those who teach an occasional physical education activity class, such as skiing or scuba diving). Seventy-four percent of the full-time faculty members hold terminal degrees in their disciplines. It is the policy of Peace College to maintain a student-faculty ratio of less than 14:1.

Student Government

The Student Government Association (PSGA) at Peace College is an organization of student leaders, both elected and appointed, who focus on the individual and collective needs of the student body. PSGA works cooperatively with the faculty and administration of the College to create positive avenues of change and growth. PSGA promotes responsibility for upholding the highest standards of College life through honor and integrity. In addition to being the voice of the student body, PSGA is actively engaged in sponsoring and encouraging participation in a number of traditions and student activities throughout the year. These include Stunt Night, Honor Week, Fall Fest, and Spring Fling.

As the governing body for Peace students, PSGA has approximately 35 voting members representing various campus constituencies. Every student is a member of PSGA. Meetings are open to students, and the association meets every week. The main branches of PSGA include the Christian Association (PSCA), the Recreation Association (PSRA), and the Judiciary Board. All students are responsible for their self-governance at Peace under the Honor System.

Admission Requirements

Peace College recruits and admits women who are likely to benefit from the College's various academic programs and who are also likely to contribute to the life of the Peace College community. The College encourages women with varied talents and interests representative of all social, economic, ethnic, and racial backgrounds to apply.

Applications are reviewed individually. Decisions are based on the following credentials: course selection, grade point average in academic courses (see minimum required courses, below), SAT I or ACT scores, and class rank.

Further consideration is given to an applicant's personal qualifications, potential for success, and ability to add to the social, cultural, and spiritual environment for which Peace College is known. The major criteria for admission are the strength of the high school courses taken, the grades in the academic courses, and scores on the standardized tests.

To meet the minimum academic requirements, applicants must complete 4 units of English; 3 units of mathematics (algebra I, algebra II, and geometry); 2 to 3 units of science; 2 units of social science, and 2 units of the same foreign language. Students are encouraged to take additional courses in math and science when possible.

Application and Information

Admissions decisions are made on a rolling basis. The Admissions Committee begins reviewing applications in September for the following fall. Applications received after April 1 for the fall semester and after November 1 for the spring semester are reviewed on a space-available basis.

The College requires each freshman applicant to submit an application, a nonrefundable $25 fee, SAT I or ACT scores (senior year scores are preferred), and an official high school transcript of all courses taken in high school. Transfer applicants must also submit official transcripts from all colleges attended.

Inquiry cards and application forms may be completed at the Web site, listed below. Application forms and additional information may be obtained by contacting:

Admissions Office
Peace College
15 East Peace Street
Raleigh, North Carolina 27604
Telephone: 919-508-2000
800-PEACE-47 (toll-free)
Fax: 919-508-2306
World Wide Web: http://www.peace.edu

Peace College's Main Building is the centerpiece of a picturesque 16-acre campus in the heart of downtown Raleigh, North Carolina.

PENNSYLVANIA COLLEGE OF TECHNOLOGY
An Affiliate of The Pennsylvania State University
WILLIAMSPORT, PENNSYLVANIA

Pennsylvania College of Technology
PENNSTATE

The College

Pennsylvania College of Technology (Penn College) is a special-mission affiliate of the Pennsylvania State University (Penn State). As Pennsylvania's premier technical college, Penn College is committed to applied technology education. The school has a national reputation for the high quality and diversity of its traditional and advanced technology majors. Partnerships with industry leaders provide students unique opportunities to build relationships with future employers who can advance their careers.

Graduate surveys indicate a placement-success rate that exceeds 90 percent annually (100 percent in some majors). Among the keys to graduate success are Penn College's emphasis on small classes (18 students is the average size of freshman classes), personal attention, and hands-on experience using the latest technology. State-of-the-art classrooms and laboratories reflect the expectations of the twenty-first-century workforce. A number of campus buildings, including a conference center, a Victorian guest house, an athletics field house, and a rustic retreat used for professional gatherings have been designed, constructed, and maintained by students.

In fall 2003, 6,255 students attended Penn College. Another 4,659 students took part in the extensive noncredit and continuing education program, which includes customized business and industry courses offered through the Technology Transfer Center.

Location

Penn College is located in beautiful north central Pennsylvania. The main campus is in Williamsport, a city known around the world as the home of the Little League Baseball World Series. Penn College offers credit classes at three other locations: the Advanced Automotive Technology Center in the Wahoo Drive Industrial Park in Williamsport, the Aviation Center at the Williamsport Regional Airport in Montoursville, and the Earth Science Center, 10 miles south of Williamsport near Allenwood. Noncredit classes are offered from locations in Williamsport and Wellsboro.

Majors and Degrees

Bachelor of Science (B.S.) degrees focus on applied technology in traditional and emerging career fields. Majors include accounting; applied health studies; applied human services; automotive technology management; aviation maintenance technology; building automation technology; business administration (concentrations in banking and finance, management, human resource management, management information systems, marketing, and small business and entrepreneurship); civil engineering technology; computer-aided product design; computer information technology (concentrations in IT security specialist, network specialist, technical support specialist, and Web and applications development); construction management; culinary arts technology; dental hygiene (concentrations in health policy and administration and special population care); electronics engineering technology; environmental technology management; graphic communications management; graphic design; heating, ventilation, and air conditioning (HVAC) technology; legal assistant/paralegal studies; manufacturing engineering technology; nursing; physician assistant studies; plastics and polymer engineering technology; residential construction technology and management; technology management; and welding and fabrication engineering technology.

Associate degrees (A.A.S., A.A.A., A.A., or A.S.) are offered in accounting; advertising art; architectural technology; automated manufacturing technology; automotive service sales and marketing; automotive technology (including Ford and Toyota industry-sponsored majors); aviation technology; baking and pastry arts; building construction technology; building construction technology (masonry emphasis); business management; civil engineering technology; collision repair technology; computer-aided drafting; computer information systems (emphases in Cisco technology, information technology technician, network technology, technical support technology, and Web and applications technology); culinary arts technology; dental hygiene; diesel technology (including a Mack Trucks industry-sponsored major); early childhood education; electric power generation technology; electrical technology; electromechanical maintenance technology; electronics technology (emphases in Cisco systems, communications/fiber optics, computer-automation maintenance, electronics engineering technology, industrial process control, and semiconductor processing technology); environmental technology; floral design/interior plantscape; forest technology; general studies; graphic communications technology; health arts; health information technology; heating, ventilation, and air conditioning (HVAC) technology; heavy construction equipment technology (emphases in Caterpillar industry-sponsored, operator, or technician); hospitality management; human services; individual studies; landscape/nursery technology; landscape/nursery technology (turfgrass management emphasis); legal assistant (paralegal) studies; mass media communication; nursing; occupational therapy assistant; office information technology (emphases in medical office information, specialized office information, or Web design); paramedic technology; physical fitness specialist; plastics and polymer technology; radiography; surgical technology; surveying technology; toolmaking technology; and welding technology.

Certificate majors are offered in automotive service technician, aviation maintenance technician, cabinetmaking and millwork, collision repair technician, computer applications technology, construction carpentry, diesel technician, electrical occupations, machinist general, plumbing, practical nursing, and welding.

Academic Programs

Penn College offers unique bachelor's degrees that are designed to prepare students for employment or serve as the basis for additional educational opportunities. The bachelor's degree offerings either parallel or build upon two-year majors or stand as their own unique majors. Five B.S. degrees are offered via distance learning: applied health studies, automotive technology management, dental hygiene, residential construction technology and management, and technology management.

While associate degrees primarily emphasize practical applications, the bachelor's degree curricula complete a larger educational base by adding advanced practical applications, broader liberal arts study, systematic problem solving, writing-enriched courses, cultural diversity, senior-year capstone projects, and interdisciplinary courses that develop appreciation for the relationships between science, technology, and society. In addition to regular B.S. degree offerings, evening/weekend courses allow students to complete selected bachelor's degree majors on a part- or full-time basis.

Off-Campus Programs

Penn College students earn academic credit for real work experience if they choose to participate in cooperative education (co-op) and internship experiences. Many majors require internships. Penn College co-op students have worked throughout Pennsylvania as well as in eighteen other states, the District of Columbia, Canada, and Puerto Rico.

Academic Facilities

The hands-on experience offered at Penn College creates a need for a variety of special academic facilities. Students enjoy access to an advanced computer network through both on-campus and dial-in services. On-campus computer labs offer an average of one computer for every 5 students. Besides extensive, accessible computer labs, the main campus has an automated manufacturing center, a plastics manufacturing center, a printing and publishing facility, a dental hygiene clinic, an automotive repair center, a machine shop, a welding shop, a building trades center, an architectural studio, computer-aided drafting labs, a broadcast studio, modern science laboratories, a fine-dining restaurant and campus guest house, an aviation and avionics instructional facility located at the regional airport, greenhouses, a working sawmill, a diesel center, and a heavy-equipment training site.

Off-campus sites include the Aviation Center, one of the nation's finest aviation and avionics instructional facilities, located at the regional airport; the Earth Science Center, located on 180 acres of wooded land and featuring greenhouses, a working sawmill, a diesel center, and a heavy-equipment training site; and an Advanced Automotive Technology Center, with motorsports and other advanced laboratories.

The library on the main campus is open every day during the academic semesters and offers an impressive selection of print and electronic resources. Services available include a professional reference staff, a well-developed instructional program, reciprocal borrowing at twenty-two regional libraries, interlibrary loans, and paper and electronic reserves.

Costs

Tuition and related fees are based on a per-credit-hour charge. Yearly tuition and fees, based upon 15 credits per semester for 2003–04 (not including housing, food, and living expenses, lab fees, books, tools, uniforms, supplies, and major personal expenses), were $8940 for in-state students and $11,250 for out-of-state students. In 2003–04, costs ranged from $1843 to $2500 per semester for on-campus housing. All on-campus housing is apartment-style (kitchen, living room, bedrooms, and bathroom). On-campus housing is alcohol free, drug free, noise controlled, and secure. The Residence Hall Association is a student-run organization in which all on-campus students are considered to be members. Resident and nonresident students may purchase meal plans, which are accepted in the College's dining facilities, including the main dining hall, a bistro-style restaurant, a gourmet restaurant, two convenience stores, a coffeehouse, and on-campus pizza delivery.

Financial Aid

Approximately 4 out of 5 Penn College students receive financial assistance. Types of aid available include Federal Pell Grants, Pennsylvania Higher Education Assistance Agency grants, Federal Supplemental Educational Opportunity Grants, Federal Work-Study awards, Federal Stafford Student Loans, Federal PLUS loans, veterans' benefits, and Bureau of Vocational Rehabilitation benefits. A deferred-payment plan allows students to spread their tuition over two payments each semester. Penn College offers a variety of academic, need-based, and technical scholarships to qualified students. Detailed information on scholarships can be obtained from the Financial Aid Office or on the Web at http://www.pct.edu/scholarships.

Faculty

Penn College's 455 faculty members (269 full-time and 186 part-time) provide the kind of individual attention students need to be successful in the classroom and in the workplace. Faculty members are both educated and experienced in their field. Penn College recognizes excellence among the faculty members through distinguished faculty award programs. Small class sizes (student-faculty ratio of 18:1) provide individual attention and promote student success. In addition, advisory committees of business and industry leaders and faculty and staff members work together to ensure that programs of study meet current workplace needs.

Student Government

Student Government Association (SGA) and Wildcat Events Board (WEB) represent the student body in matters related to College policy and social activities. All enrolled students are members of SGA and WEB. Active participation offers the opportunity to develop leadership skills while contributing to the well-being of the College and the student body. In addition, more than forty student organizations offer opportunities for organized campus activity.

Admission Requirements

Penn College offers educational opportunities to anyone who has the interest, desire, and ability to pursue advanced study. Due to the wide variety of majors, admission criteria vary according to the major. At a minimum, applicants must have a high school diploma or its equivalent. Some majors are restricted to people who meet certain academic skills and prerequisites, who have attained high levels of academic achievement, and who have achieved acceptable scores on the SAT I or ACT. Questions regarding the admission standards for specific majors should be directed to the Office of Admissions, listed below.

To ensure that applicants have the entry-level skills needed for success in Penn College majors, all students are required to take placement examinations, which are used to assess skills in math, English, and reading. The College provides opportunities for students to develop the basic skills necessary for enrollment in associate degree and certificate programs when the placement tests indicate that such help is needed. International students whose native language is not English are required to take the TOEFL, submit an affidavit of support, and comply with test regulations of the Immigration and Naturalization Service, along with meeting all other admission requirements.

Penn College offers opportunities for students to transfer course credit earned at other institutions, college credit earned before high school graduation, service credit, DANTES credit, and credit earned through the College-Level Examination Program (CLEP). The College offers equal opportunity for admission without regard to age, race, color, creed, sex, national origin, handicap, veteran status, or political affiliation.

Application and Information

College catalogs, viewbooks, financial aid information, and other informative brochures as well as applications for admission are available from the Office of Admissions. The College invites prospective students and their families to contact the Office of Admissions to arrange a personal interview or campus tour. Fall and spring visitation events are held annually.

All inquiries should be addressed to:

Office of Admissions
Pennsylvania College of Technology
One College Avenue
Williamsport, Pennsylvania 17701-5799
Telephone: 570-327-4761
800-367-9222 (toll-free)
E-mail: admissions@pct.edu
World Wide Web: http://www.pct.edu

Banners representing each of the eight academic schools at Penn College adorn lampposts on the road leading from the new main entrance to the heart of the campus.

THE PENNSYLVANIA STATE UNIVERSITY ABINGTON COLLEGE

ABINGTON, PENNSYLVANIA

The College

Penn State Abington offers the resources of one of the nation's premier teaching and research universities combined with a small-college atmosphere in a suburban setting. The mission of Penn State Abington is to provide high-quality teaching in a wide array of programs in the arts, humanities, and sciences. Eleven 4-year baccalaureate degree programs and two 2-year associate degree programs are offered, as are the first two years of most baccalaureate degrees that can be completed at other Penn State locations.

Penn State Abington was established in 1950 when Abby A. Sutherland, principal and owner of the elite Ogontz School for Girls, gave the campus and facilities to the Pennsylvania State University. The campus is located on a picturesque 45 acres in a northern suburb of Philadelphia.

The campus currently has 3,220 undergraduate students attending classes in its modern academic buildings and labs. There are no housing facilities at Penn State Abington; however, the Office of Student Life provides an online housing directory of rooms for rent and apartment complexes in the surrounding community.

Penn State Abington participates in a variety of varsity sports and is a member of several local athletic conferences, including the Commonwealth Campus Athletic Conference, the Eastern Pennsylvania Collegiate Conference, and the Pennsylvania Collegiate Athletic Association. Varsity sports include softball and volleyball for women; baseball, soccer, and golf for men; and basketball and tennis for both men and women. The intramural athletic program includes badminton, basketball, flag football, softball, street hockey, tennis, volleyball, and weight lifting. Opportunities also exist to participate in noncompetitive programs, such as aerobics, dance, and fitness.

Location

At Penn State Abington, students benefit from a convenient location less than a half mile from Route 611. The community of Abington is about 15 miles north of Center City Philadelphia and 4 miles south of the Willow Grove exit of the Pennsylvania Turnpike. The campus is easily accessible by car, public transportation, and the free Penn State Abington shuttle.

Majors and Degrees

Penn State Abington offers the Bachelor of Arts degree in administration of justice; American studies; corporate communication; English; history; integrative arts; letters, arts, and sciences; and psychological and social sciences. The Bachelor of Science degree is offered in administration of justice, business, information sciences and technology, psychological and social sciences, and science. The Associate in Arts is awarded in one major: letters, arts, and sciences. The Associate in Science is offered in business administration.

Penn State Abington also gives students the opportunity to complete the first two years of most of the more than 160 University degrees before changing location to the University Park Campus; Penn State Erie, the Behrend College; Penn State Harrisburg, the Capitol College; or any other Penn State location where students can complete their degrees.

Academic Programs

Each baccalaureate program has two components: at least 46 credits in general education and at least 78 credits in specific requirements for the major. Students must complete a minimum of 124 credits to earn a bachelor's degree; the exact number depends on the program. Associate degrees require a minimum of 60 credits. All baccalaureate degrees offered at Penn State Abington require an overall grade point average of at least 2.0 and a grade of C or better in upper-level courses in the major. An honors program and the Schreyer Honors College program are available to students who demonstrate exceptional promise.

Several majors serve as excellent preparation for law or medical school. Special prelaw and premed advisers assist students in planning their programs. The Division of Undergraduate Studies enables those who have not yet decided on an academic major to explore several areas of study before selecting a specific program.

The fall and spring semesters are each fifteen weeks in length. Registration and advising take place before the first week of classes, and the final examinations are given after the last week. There are also two summer sessions of six weeks each. The campus provides a comprehensive orientation program, which includes individual academic and career advising and is popular with students and their parents.

Penn State Abington wants students to succeed, not only in getting a degree but also in having a rich, fulfilling future. The campus provides many avenues to help students achieve their goals, including honors studies through the Schreyer Honors College program or the Penn State Abington Honors program; research projects (ACURA) with faculty members at the forefront of their fields; independent study; internships through the Career Development Center; cooperative (co-op) education through the College of Engineering; the Educational Opportunity Program, which offers a strong program of academic support and personal counseling; and Army ROTC.

When students enroll at Penn State Abington, they are assigned an academic adviser who assists them with scheduling, interpreting degree requirements, and matching their interests and abilities to their career goals. In addition, professional advisers are available in the Division of Undergraduate Studies. The Career Development Center staff is committed to helping students in all stages of their career planning—from choosing a major to gaining an internship to interviewing for jobs.

Academic Facilities

The Penn State Abington Computer Center houses both IBM and Macintosh computers, which can access the IBM mainframe system at the University Park Campus, the Library Information Access System (LIAS), and the Internet. AutoCAD workstations for graphic design are also available. The computer center has evening and weekend hours to accommodate student schedules. Additional Macintosh computers are accessible in the Computer-Assisted Learning Center, where students can familiarize themselves with computer applications in an informal environment. The Penn State Abington Learning Center offers free professional and peer tutoring to all students who want to improve their skills in math, sciences, English composition, and many other subject areas. At Penn State

Abington, students have access to an extensive library system. The Penn State University Libraries comprise a vast collection of more than 3.5 million books, periodicals, and other documents available either on site or through interlibrary loan. The College is linked electronically to every library in the University Libraries system through the computerized LIAS.

Costs

For the 2003–04 academic year, tuition for an in-state student for one year was $8620 full-time or $348 per credit part-time. An out-of-state student's tuition for one year was $13,250 full-time or $552 per credit part-time. Mandatory computer fees and student activity fees ranged from $65 to $194 per semester, depending on the number of credits scheduled. Other costs were a nonrefundable $50 application fee, a nonrefundable $100 enrollment fee, and a $100 general deposit.

Financial Aid

Student financial aid awards are based on an analysis of the student's financial need. Students should file the Free Application for Federal Student Aid (FAFSA) by February 15 of their senior year of high school. Students are encouraged to seek grant assistance from their home state. Financial aid applications are available from high school counselors and financial aid offices at colleges and other institutions. Students are strongly encouraged to complete the form online at http://www.fafsa.ed.gov. These forms and the application for admission are the only forms that incoming freshmen need to complete to be considered for federal, state, and University aid. Aid includes Federal Pell Grants, Federal Work-Study Program awards, Federal Perkins Loans, Federal Supplemental Educational Opportunity Grants, Federal Stafford Student Loans, and Penn State awards and scholarships. Students at Penn State Abington receive nearly $3.2 million in scholarships and grants each year. Many of the campus-based scholarships have been created through the generosity of alumni, corporations, faculty members, staff members, and friends who try to help students who demonstrate academic merit or financial need.

Faculty

The faculty members at Penn State Abington are well known in their fields of research. They take great pride in the honors they have received for their teaching excellence, and they pass their knowledge and enthusiasm on to their students in the classroom. Because Penn State Abington is a small, close-knit campus, students have the advantage of a one-on-one relationship with their professors on both a teaching and an advising level. Penn State Abington has 107 full-time faculty members, of whom 82 percent have terminal degrees. The College has no teaching assistants.

Student Government

Penn State Abington offers a wide variety of student organizations that involve leadership, community service, ethnicity, and social events. The Student Government Association is the official representative of the student body. In addition to representing students to the administration and faculty, the Student Government Association charters all student organizations and allocates funds to support and promote student activities. The association also appoints student representatives to serve on all key administrative and faculty committees and the appropriate adjudicatory boards.

Admission Requirements

As part of the Pennsylvania State University, in compliance with federal and state laws, Penn State Abington is committed to the policy that all persons shall have equal access to admission without regard to race, religion, sex, national origin, ancestry, color, sexual orientation, handicap, age, or status as a disabled or Vietnam veteran. Each applicant is evaluated on the basis of his or her high school record and the results of the electronic SAT I. The high school grade point average, when combined with the SAT I score, produces an evaluation index, and students are admitted on the basis of this index.

Application and Information

Students interested in freshman admission to Penn State Abington may obtain an admission application form from any Penn State campus or by writing to Penn State Abington. Application forms are available in late summer. The recommended date for submitting an application is November 30. Students are strongly encouraged to use the Web application at http://www.psu.edu/dept/admissions/apply. Applicants admitted to Penn State Abington are notified approximately four to six weeks after the application and credentials are received. The student must make certain that the Educational Testing Service forwards the SAT I scores to the Undergraduate Admissions Office, Pennsylvania State University, University Park, Pennsylvania 16802. Scores must be submitted electronically. This description is available in alternative media upon request.

Students interested in scheduling a campus tour of Penn State Abington should call 215-881-7351. For an application form or additional information, interested students should contact:

Admissions Office
The Pennsylvania State University Abington College
1600 Woodland Road
Abington, Pennsylvania 19001-3990
Telephone: 215-881-7600
Fax: 215-881-7655
World Wide Web: http://www.abington.psu.edu/

Penn State's mascot is the Nittany Lion.

THE PENNSYLVANIA STATE UNIVERSITY AT ERIE, THE BEHREND COLLEGE

ERIE, PENNSYLVANIA

The College

Penn State Erie, The Behrend College, is committed to providing the best possible education in the disciplines of business, engineering, engineering technology, the humanities, science, and the social sciences. Students benefit from the resources and opportunities provided by a major research institution while they enjoy the advantages of lecturing in a small university setting. The College offers thirty 4-year baccalaureate degree programs, five 2-year associate degree programs, and three graduate degree programs.

Among all public colleges and universities in Pennsylvania, Penn State Behrend ranks in the top three in the student-to-faculty ratio, freshman retention rate, and SAT scores.

More than $100 million in new facilities are transforming the Penn State Behrend experience, including three new residence halls, an athletics center, a chapel, an observatory, a child-care center, a baseball and softball complex, intramural fields, a research center, and a high-technology park.

The College was established in 1948 when Mary Behrend donated her Glenhill Farm estate in memory of her husband, Ernst, the founder of Hammermill Paper Company. The campus is magnificent with 725 acres overlooking Lake Erie and Presque Isle State Park. The park has miles of sandy beaches and some of the most beautiful sunsets in the world. Penn State Behrend's campus has extensive woodlands, deep gorges, and beautiful streams, and it features cross-country ski trails and fitness trails.

More than 3,600 students attend classes in modern academic buildings and labs. The College provides on-campus housing for 1,650 students. Two residence halls, Ohio and Almy Halls, have opened in recent years, and a third new facility, Senat Hall, is scheduled to welcome students in fall 2004. Undergraduates also live in traditional student housing, four-bedroom suites, and two-bedroom apartments. On-campus housing is not guaranteed, but assistance is offered in securing accommodations off campus.

A multifaith chapel and carillon is designed to inspire quiet reflection and offer enrichment opportunities provided by campus ministries.

Penn State Behrend participates in twenty-one varsity sports and is an NCAA Division III member. Varsity sports include ten teams for men (baseball, basketball, cross-country, golf, indoor track, soccer, swimming, tennis, track and field, and water polo) and eleven for women: (basketball, cross-country, golf, indoor track, soccer, softball, swimming, tennis, track and field, volleyball, and water polo). More than 65 percent of students participate in a comprehensive intramural program. A new Athletics and Recreation Center, featuring a swimming pool, gymnasium, and exercise equipment is available.

Knowledge Park at Penn State Erie is a 200-acre research and development park housing knowledge-based companies that benefit from the site's technological infrastructure and the University's strengths in applied research and technology transfer. A number of students work as interns for companies in the park.

Location

Penn State Behrend students benefit from the college's convenient location near I-90 (and close to I-79 and I-86) in a suburb of Erie, Pennsylvania. The population of the area is more than 280,000.

Public transportation departs from campus every half hour to other points throughout the Erie area, including dozens of movie theaters, ethnic restaurants, a philharmonic orchestra, museums, theaters, and a zoo. A convention center in downtown Erie features Broadway plays and top-name performers in rock, classical, and country music. Erie is located within 2 hours of Buffalo, Cleveland, and Pittsburgh and is a comfortable 4-hour drive from Toronto.

Majors and Degrees

Penn State Behrend confers the Bachelor of Arts degree in communication, economics, English, general arts and sciences, history, political science, psychology, and science.

The Bachelor of Science degree is offered in accounting; biology; business economics; business, liberal arts and science; chemistry; computer engineering; computer science; electrical engineering; electrical engineering technology; finance; international business; management; management information systems; marketing; mathematics; mechanical engineering; mechanical engineering technology; physics; plastics engineering technology; psychology; science; and software engineering.

The Associate in Arts degree is awarded in one major—letters, arts, and sciences. The Associate in Science degree is offered in business, and the Associate in Engineering degree is offered in electrical engineering technology, manufacturing technology, mechanical engineering technology, and plastics engineering technology.

The College's graduate degree program offers a Master of Business Administration (M.B.A.), a Master of Project Management (M.P.M.), and a Master of Manufacturing Systems Engineering (M.Eng.).

Academic Programs

Each baccalaureate program has two components: at least 46 credits in general education and at least 78 credits in specific requirements for the major. Students must complete a minimum of 124 semester hours to earn a bachelor's degree; the exact number depends on the program. Associate degrees require a minimum of 60 semester hours. All Penn State Behrend majors require an overall grade point average of at least 2.0 and a grade of C or better in all upper-level courses in the major. An honors program and the Schreyer Scholars Program are available to students who show exceptional promise. Several majors serve as excellent preparation for law or medical school. Special prelaw and premed advisers assist students in planning their programs. The Division of Undergraduate Studies enables those who have not yet decided on an academic major to explore several areas of study before selecting a specific program.

For two of the last three years, Penn State Behrend faculty members received the University-wide Teaching Fellow Award, selected from among 4,000 Penn State colleagues.

The Plastics Engineering Technology program and its facilities are among the nation's best. The program is one of only four in the country to earn accreditation. The School of Engineering and Engineering Technology also has nationally accredited programs in electrical engineering technology, mechanical engineering technology, and electrical, mechanical, and computer engineering.

The College's chemistry program has earned approval from the American Chemical Society, making Penn State Behrend one of only 619 colleges and universities in the United States to achieve such approval.

The Sam and Irene Black School of Business is the first and only school of business in the Erie region to receive accreditation from AACSB International, the premier accrediting agency for programs in management and accounting. The school was named for Sam and Irene Black in 2003 following a $20 million endowment bequest.

The fall and spring semesters are each fifteen weeks in length. Registration and advising take place before the first week of classes, and the final examinations are given after the last week. There are also three summer sessions. The Division of Undergraduate Studies provides a summer preregistration and counseling service for all entering freshmen and their parents.

Many students present their undergraduate research at regional and national conferences, and others publish in refereed journals. This provides Penn State Behrend students with an advantage when looking for a job or applying to professional or graduate school. The Career Development Center works closely with employers, and each fall it hosts recruiters on campus at its successful engineering and business career fairs.

Academic Facilities

Penn State Behrend features a mix of contemporary and traditional buildings in a parklike setting. Facilities include an engineering complex, library, academic building, observatory, and science labs. A Research and Economic Development Center is being designed and will house the School of Business and the School of Engineering and Engineering Technology.

In addition to Penn State Behrend's library collection, students can use the resources of the entire Penn State University Libraries collection through the computerized Library Information Access System. The collection comprises 4.3 million cataloged items, 38,500 serial titles, and 2.5 million government documents. Materials are available by mail from other Penn State locations and the Big Ten libraries. Computers connect students to major databases throughout the world.

The General Electric Foundation Computer Center provides a sophisticated, high-speed electronic link from Penn State's mainframe computer, one of the most up-to-date in the country, to supercomputing. Students benefit from T-3 Internet access, new technology classrooms, and e-Lion, the University's online student advising system. In addition, the College has ten microcomputer labs with IBM and IBM-compatible personal computers, Silicon Graphics workstations, and computer-aided design systems.

Costs

Educational costs at Penn State Behrend vary depending on whether the student is a resident of Pennsylvania, whether enrollment is in the upper or lower division, and whether he or she lives off campus or in a residence hall. The 2003–04 tuition and fees at Penn State Behrend for Pennsylvania residents (lower division) were $9034 for the academic year. For out-of-state students, the tuition and fees were $16,652 for the academic year. On-campus rooms are a fixed cost, but board and all other costs are variable and fluctuate according to each student's spending habits. These variable costs are approximately $6000 for room and board, $800 for books and supplies, and $1200 to $2400 for personal expenses, including clothing, laundry, travel, and miscellaneous items. Other costs are a nonrefundable $50 application fee, a nonrefundable $100 enrollment fee, a $100 general deposit, and a $100 housing deposit for students living in on-campus residences.

Financial Aid

Students benefit from more than $500,000 in annual Penn State Behrend scholarships, and more than 75 percent of students receive some form of financial aid. Awards are based on an analysis of the student's financial need. Students should file the Free Application for Federal Student Aid (FAFSA) by February 15 of their senior year of high school. Penn State's school code is 003329. Students are encouraged to seek grant assistance from their home state. Financial aid applications are available from high school counselors and financial aid offices at colleges and other institutions. These forms and the application for admission are the only forms that incoming freshmen need to complete to be considered for federal, state, and University aid. Aid includes Federal Pell Grants, Pennsylvania Higher Education Assistance Agency Grants, Federal Work-Study Program awards, Federal Perkins Loans, Federal Supplemental Educational Opportunity Grants, Federal Stafford Student Loans, and Penn State awards and scholarships.

Faculty

A first-rate faculty is at the heart of the Penn State Behrend experience. Of the 266 faculty members who teach both graduate and undergraduate students, almost all have earned the terminal degree in their major field. There are no graduate teaching assistants, and part-time professors are very limited. The faculty members are distinguished scholars and superb teachers. They are extensively involved in research and publishing, and they are caring people with a record of excellence in advising students. Professors and students know each other. Such close relationships have many educational and career advantages.

Student Government

The Student Government Association is the official representative of the student body at the Penn State Behrend. In addition to representing students to the administration and faculty, the Student Government Association charters all student organizations and allocates funds to support and promote student activities. The association also appoints student representatives to serve on key administrative and faculty committees and the appropriate adjudicatory boards.

Admission Requirements

As part of the Pennsylvania State University, and in compliance with federal and state laws, Penn State Behrend is committed to the policy that all persons shall have equal access to admission without regard to race, religion, sex, national origin, ancestry, color, sexual orientation, handicap, age, or status as a disabled or Vietnam veteran. Each applicant is evaluated on the basis of his or her high school record, the results of the SAT I, or scores from the ACT. The high school grade point average, when combined with the SAT I score, produces an evaluation index, and students are admitted on the basis of that index.

Application and Information

Students interested in freshman admission to Penn State Behrend may obtain a Web application at the site listed below. Students who are unable to obtain a Web application can obtain an admission application form from any Penn State campus or by writing to Penn State Behrend. Application forms are available in late summer. The recommended deadline for submitting an application is November 30. Applicants admitted to Penn State Behrend are notified approximately four to six weeks after the application and credentials are received. The student must make certain that the Educational Testing Service forwards the SAT I scores to the Undergraduate Admissions Office, Pennsylvania State University, University Park, Pennsylvania 16802.

This description is available in alternative media upon request. For application forms, more information, or a campus visit, interested students should contact:

Office of Admissions
Penn State Erie, The Behrend College
5091 Station Road
Erie, Pennsylvania 16563-0105
Telephone: 814-898-6100
866-374-3378 (toll-free)
E-mail: behrend.admissions@psu.edu
World Wide Web: www.pserie.psu.edu

The library at Penn State Behrend features access to all of the holdings in the Penn State system.

THE PENNSYLVANIA STATE UNIVERSITY WORTHINGTON SCRANTON CAMPUS OF THE COMMONWEALTH COLLEGE

DUNMORE, PENNSYLVANIA

The University

Penn State Worthington Scranton (PSWS), a regional campus of Penn State University, combines the vast resources of this premier teaching and research university with the personal attention and close faculty association of its small college learning environment of 1,650 students. Students at Penn State Worthington Scranton often collaborate with faculty members in research and publish and present their findings at conferences while they are students.

Innovative classes allow students to work in teams, using state-of-the-art computer and telecommunication technologies. Since internships are an integral part of the curriculum in most majors, students gain important experience integrating theory and practice in their academic studies. Students gain practical experience and earn academic credit simultaneously. Optional internships may be taken for elective credit to supplement a major discipline and are arranged on an individual basis. Required internships fulfill a major discipline requirement.

PSWS's Career Services Center offers an array of services to help students gain cocurricular experience outside the classroom, determine and clarify their career goals, and prepare them for careers. Counselors work with students in individual and group sessions in career information research, goal setting, career-related experience, resume and cover letter preparation, networking, and interviewing techniques. The center posts employment, internship, volunteer, and educational opportunities; sponsors career-related activities, workshops, educational programs, and on-campus employment recruiting; and participates in local and regional job fairs that help students to secure competitive employment opportunities and to promote valuable networking experiences.

Penn State University is accredited by the Middle States Association of Colleges and Schools, and its numerous academic programs are accredited by the accreditation commissions for their fields.

Penn State Worthington Scranton's goals are to achieve excellence in scholarship, education, and university life; to fulfill with distinction the commitment to the people of the commonwealth; and to foster a caring university community that provides leadership for constructive participation in a diverse, multicultural world.

With an average class size of 20 and a student-faculty ratio of 10:1, PSWS students have close interaction with faculty members. Many students are involved in valuable research projects. Outside the classroom, Penn State Worthington Scranton offers many cultural events and entertainment and social activities. Students may join more than fifteen active student clubs, organizations, and professional organizations for specific careers. Varsity sports include men's and women's basketball and cross-country; men's baseball and soccer; and women's softball and volleyball, with men's basketball and women's volleyball as the new four-year eligibility programs. Several club and intramural sports are also offered.

The Educational Opportunity Program (EOP), which offers a strong program of academic support and personal counseling, is available to PSWS students who are first-generation college students who meet the federal income and eligibility criteria. Penn State Worthington Scranton is a great value for high-quality education at an efficient price.

Location

Conveniently located just 2 hours from New York City, Philadelphia, Albany, Syracuse, and Danbury, the campus is nestled on 45 acres on a picturesque hilltop outside Scranton, a city of 81,000 in the larger metro area of 750,000. PSWS sits at the crossroads of Interstates 81, 84, and 380 and is easily accessible by highway, Scranton International Airport, and extensive local and national bus lines that service Scranton. The campus is located in the Pocono Mountains in a major ski resort area with extensive cultural attractions, shopping, and entertainment.

Majors and Degrees

PSWS offers bachelor's degree programs in business, human development and family studies, information sciences and technology, and nursing and, projected for fall 2004, American studies; letters, arts, and sciences; and communication arts and sciences. Associate degrees are offered in architectural engineering technologies; business administration; human development and family studies; information sciences and technology; letters, arts, and sciences; and nursing. PSWS also offers the first two years of course work for the University's more than 160 bachelor's degrees, which students can complete at University Park or other PSU locations.

Academic Programs

PSWS combines the intimacy of a small college with the vast resources of the Penn State community. Innovative classes allow students to utilize state-of-the-art computer and telecommunications technologies, with access to one of the largest academic libraries in the United States and an award-winning faculty.

Outstanding students may be invited to participate in the University-wide Schreyer Honors College. Qualifying students may take part in the PSWS Honors Program. In these programs, high-achieving students can enrich their general education by taking special courses and participating in research and extracurricular events that add depth to the college experience.

The Division of Undergraduate Studies advises students who have not yet decided on an academic major, encourages them to explore several areas of study before selecting a major, and assists students with academic concerns and educational plans, including the First-Year Testing, Counseling and Advising Program (FTCAP). The Learning Center provides peer tutoring, study skills workshops, and test accommodations.

Penn State Worthington Scranton offers students the ROTC program through a cooperative agreement with local universities.

Bachelor's degrees are awarded after a student has completed 120 credits of course work in a designated field of study, which includes courses in the field of study as well as general education requirements. Students who are enrolled in a minor program must complete at least 18 credits in a single area or from several discipline areas. A specialization within a major should involve at least one third of the course work credits required for the major, but need not be more than 18 credits. All options within a major must have in common at least one fourth of the required course work credits in the major. A student can only be enrolled in an option within his/her own major.

PSWS students can enroll in Penn State World Campus courses, developed and taught by the Penn State faculty members and offered online. World Campus electronic courses appear on Penn State academic transcripts together with all credit courses. Penn State Worthington Scranton offers a variety of courses delivered online each semester to students with an active access account.

In addition to spring and fall semesters, PSWS offers three summer sessions and accelerated eight-week terms of evening courses throughout the year. New students are assigned to an academic adviser, who provides counseling about their academic progress. Students are encouraged to meet with advisers twice each semester.

Off-Campus Programs

PSWS students who wish to enrich their academic experience by studying abroad join the Penn State University Study Abroad program.

Academic Facilities

Penn State Worthington Scranton's facilities include state-of-the-art labs and classrooms, AutoCAD workstations, cutting-edge computer and telecommunications technology, and a renowned library. PSWS students access the Penn State Library, ranked thirteenth in holdings of all university research libraries in the U.S. and Canada with nearly 4.7 million volumes, plus the campus collection of more than 70,000. Through the University library's portal, students have direct access to all library resources, electronic indexes, periodicals, and reference tools and services.

Worthington Scranton students have many choices for accessing the Penn State network on campus or from home. On campus, students can use any of the computer labs or bring in their own laptop for use on campus. Student computer labs are open evenings and weekends. Wired and wireless access to the Penn State network is available for student-owned equipment at different locations throughout the campus. Penn State students can register for courses online, check their academic records, and perform most services directly through ELion. The Penn State Worthington Scranton's Study Learning Center includes classrooms and the Learning Assistance Center, which offers free professional and peer tutoring to all students who want to improve their skills in math, sciences, English composition, and other subjects.

Costs

Tuition per credit for 2003–04 at PSWS for Pennsylvania residents was $348 for lower-division students and $368 for upper-division programs excluding business, science, engineering, and information technology, which were $394 per credit. Although PSWS has no on-campus housing facility, affordable housing near the campus is available. The Office of Student Affairs provides off-campus housing information. Local bus service provides easy access to the campus.

Financial Aid

Approximately 70 percent of PSWS students receive financial aid in the form of loans, grants, work-study, and scholarships. More than 170 scholarships are available. Students are encouraged to seek grant assistance from their home state. All Penn State students must complete the Free Application for Federal Student Aid (FAFSA) as the first step in applying for student aid each year. Some scholarships are based on academic success and financial need, while others are awarded to students enrolled in a specific major. New students should apply by February 15 for maximum student aid consideration (forms are available after January 1). Returning students should apply by April 1. Students must fill out the FAFSA to be considered for maximum aid and scholarship opportunities, including federal aid. Students are strongly encouraged to complete the form online at http://www.fafsa.ed.gov. These forms and the application for admission are the only forms that incoming students need to complete to be considered for federal, state, and University aid. Aid includes Federal Pell Grants, Federal Work-Study Program awards, Federal Perkins Loans, Federal Supplemental Educational Opportunity Grants, Federal Stafford Student Loans, and Penn State awards and scholarships. Students who are eligible to receive Veterans Educational Benefits should contact the Financial Aid Coordinator (Veterans Coordinator).

Faculty

The 62 full-time and 46 part-time faculty members at Penn State Worthington Scranton are involved in research, the community, and supporting and teaching students. Faculty members at the campus have impressive academic credentials, with the vast majority holding doctorates and professional certification. They share this expertise and enthusiasm in and out of the classroom and are dedicated to teaching in interactive small classes. The average class size is 23 students, so faculty members can offer individualized attention to each student.

Student Government

PSWS offers a variety of student organizations that involve leadership, community service, academic and social interest areas, and social events. The Student Government Association (SGA), the official representative of the student body, promotes student welfare. Students are invited to attend SGA meetings and make comments or suggestions. In addition to representing students to the administration and faculty, the Student Government Association charters all student organizations and allocates funds to support and promote student activities. The association also appoints student representatives to serve on all key administrative and faculty committees and the appropriate adjudicatory boards.

Admission Requirements

Admissions decisions for first-year students are made on the basis of final grades reflected in their high school records and the results of the electronic SAT I. The high school grade point average, when combined with the SAT I score, produces an evaluation index; students are admitted on the basis of this index. The index includes weighted average/class rank for students who have taken AP/honors courses, and required Carnegie (H.S.) units standardized test scores (SAT I or ACT). Approximately two thirds of Penn State's evaluation is based on a student's high school GPA. Transfer admissions decisions are based on a student's cumulative collegiate GPA and completion of appropriate prerequisite courses.

Students are considered equally, regardless of residence; no preference is given to Pennsylvania residents. On average, students have a GPA of 2.8 to 3.3 and SAT I scores of 950 to 1140 or ACT scores of 20 to 25. Prospective students are encouraged to visit the campus, but interviews are not required. The application can be completed and submitted online or downloaded from the PSWS Web site.

Application and Information

The best way to learn more about Penn State Worthington Scranton's programs and campus life is to visit the campus, talk with an admissions counselor, meet students, and attend classes. Students should contact the PSWS Admissions Office to schedule a campus visit and tour, which are offered daily all year. Applications for admission to PSWS are considered on a rolling admissions basis; however, students are encouraged to apply by March 1, especially when they are applying for campus scholarships. Once they have applied for admission, applicants can track their application status directly online. Penn State University encourages all students to apply online (http://www.psu.edu/dept/admissions/apply). Applicants are notified of their admission decision approximately four to six weeks after their application and credentials are received. Students must ensure that their SAT I or ACT scores are electronically sent directly by the appropriate agency to the Undergraduate Admissions Office, Pennsylvania State University, University Park, Pennsylvania 16802. Scores must be submitted electronically.

Office of Admissions
Penn State Worthington Scranton
120 Ridge View Drive
Dunmore, Pennsylvania 18512
Telephone: 570-963-2500
E-mail: wsadmissions@psu.edu
World Wide Web: http://www.sn.psu.edu

PEPPERDINE UNIVERSITY
Seaver College
MALIBU, CALIFORNIA

The University and The College

Pepperdine University is committed to providing education of high academic quality with particular attention to Christian values.

Seaver College is the liberal arts college of the University. Fifty percent of Seaver's 2,900 students come from California, 42 percent from the other forty-nine states, and 8 percent from other countries. The 2003–04 freshman class had a median high school GPA of 3.6. Housing is guaranteed for the first two years. Students who live on campus may live in the twenty-two residence houses, in Towers Hall, or in University apartments.

A wide range of student organizations and activities are available, including social, honor, service, spiritual, professional, divisional, and special interest clubs; a campus radio station; a weekly student newspaper; and a television studio. Pepperdine participates in intercollegiate sports, including baseball, basketball, cross-country, golf, tennis, volleyball, and water polo for men and basketball, cross-country, golf, soccer, swimming, tennis, and volleyball for women. The University is a member of the West Coast Conference, the NCAA, and the Southern California Women's Intercollegiate Athletic Conference. Both men's and women's teams compete in Division I and have been very successful in regional and national competitions. Sports facilities include a 3,500-seat gymnasium, an Olympic-size swimming pool, a tennis pavilion and sixteen additional tennis courts, an intramural field, a baseball diamond, and a 2,000-seat baseball stadium.

The Master of Arts degree is offered at Seaver College in American studies, communication, history, and religion; the Master of Science degree is offered in ministry. The School of Law awards the J.D. degree, and the School of Public Policy offers the master's degree; both schools are located on the Malibu campus. The Graduate School of Education and Psychology and the George L. Graziadio School of Business and Management offer graduate degrees at five locations in the Los Angeles area.

Location

Nestled in the Santa Monica Mountains and overlooking the Pacific Ocean, yet less than an hour from Los Angeles, Seaver's campus offers both the serenity of a tranquil setting and the advantages of proximity to a major metropolitan area. Malibu has a movie theater, excellent restaurants, and two small shopping centers complete with banking facilities and a variety of shops and services. The winding seashore, the rugged beauty of Malibu Canyon, and the clean air provide an environment conducive to study, while the moderate climate permits year-round outdoor recreation. In addition to making use of the physical education facilities on campus, students can enjoy swimming, surfing, horseback riding, fishing, boating, and other activities in the vicinity. As an international center for trade, recreation, culture, industry, and education, Los Angeles provides students with a wide range of opportunities.

Majors and Degrees

Seaver College awards the Bachelor of Arts in advertising, art, biology, chemistry, communication, economics, English, French, German, history, humanities, international studies, journalism, liberal arts, music, philosophy, political science, psychology, public relations, religion, sociology, Spanish, speech communication, telecommunications, and theater. The Bachelor of Science is awarded in accounting, biology, business administration, chemistry, computer science/mathematics, international business, mathematics, natural science (engineering 3-2), nutritional science, physical education, and sports medicine. A teacher education program offers credentials in single or multiple subjects.

Academic Programs

The academic programs at Seaver College provide students with a liberal arts education in a Christian atmosphere and relate it to the dynamic qualities of life in the twenty-first century. Students must complete 128 units for the B.A. or B.S. degree, including 64 units in general education requirements and 40 or more in upper-division studies. Major requirements may be fulfilled through three basic arrangements. Students who specialize in a discipline must complete at least 24 units of upper-division work in one discipline. Students may choose an interdisciplinary major, entailing at least 40 units of upper-division work, with courses ranging broadly across disciplinary lines within a division and on occasion crossing divisional lines, in one of the following fields of study: communication, English, humanities, international studies, liberal arts, or religion. Alternatively, students may initiate a contract major by presenting an application for specific upper-division courses to the Dean of Seaver College.

The College functions on a semester plan, and the regular academic year consists of two semesters, from late August to April. In addition to the regular academic year, summer sessions run from late April to early August.

At Seaver, instruction and study are adapted both to students' abilities and to the nature of the course content, instead of utilizing only the traditional lecture method. Programs involve several types of learning experiences: seminars, integrated lectures, individual study, fieldwork, and laboratories. The Dean's List of undergraduate students in the top 10 percent of the class with a grade point index not lower than 3.5 is published each semester. Other honors include cum laude for students graduating with a scholastic level of at least 3.5, magna cum laude for 3.7, and summa cum laude for 3.9.

Off-Campus Programs

Seaver offers students the opportunity to study abroad in Buenos Aires, Argentina; Florence, Italy; Heidelberg, Germany; Hong Kong, China; London, England; and Lyon, France. The academic program emphasizes European or Latin American history and culture. Serious study and the daily experiences of living in another country give students a special depth of understanding of other people and their cultures. Classes are taught in English by Seaver faculty members. A four-day class schedule permits extensive weekend travel throughout Europe and Latin America. Seaver also offers summer language programs in Spain and France, an archaeological dig in Israel, and study tours in the Far East, Asia, and Russia. Sports medicine majors have the opportunity to pursue studies in Canberra, Australia, and a Mediterranean Biblical Studies Tour allows students to visit significant biblical sites.

The Heidelberg program has space for approximately 50 students at Moore Haus, located near the city's famous castle. Classes are held in modern facilities in downtown Heidelberg, and students have full access to a 20,000-volume library of books in English at the nearby Amerika Haus. The London program has space for approximately 40 students at 56 Prince's Gate in the Knightsbridge area. In addition to living quarters, the facility includes classrooms, a library, a computer room, offices, and a student center. The Florence program accommodates approximately 55 students. Students reside in a University-owned Florentine Villa and residential complex with classrooms, a library, a microcomputer facility, and recreational facilities. The Latin American program houses approximately 40 students who live in the homes of carefully chosen host families.

Academic Facilities

The Payson Library houses a collection of approximately 475,000 volumes. Students have access to an additional 227,000 volumes at the law school. Reading rooms and periodical and stack space facilitate use of library materials. The 300-seat George Elkins Auditorium is used for public presentations and lectures. Six academic complexes contain seminar and lecture rooms, art studios, a museum, communication facilities, workshops, science and computer laboratories, minitheaters, a recital hall, and administrative offices. There is also a theater arts and music complex.

Costs

Charges for the 2003–04 academic year were $27,430 for tuition, $8730 for room and board, and $90 for the student government fee.

Financial Aid

Approximately 77 percent of Seaver's students receive some form of financial assistance through scholarships, loans, grants, work-study programs, or jobs within the University or community. To be eligible for financial assistance from institutional resources, an undergraduate student must be enrolled in at least 12 units. An applicant must be admitted to the University before being awarded assistance, but the financial assistance application may be submitted with an admission application. To ensure full consideration, the Pepperdine financial assistance application should be submitted by February 15 for the fall semester and October 15 for the winter semester. Students are also responsible for applying for the California State Scholarship (California residents only) and Federal Pell Grant by submitting the Free Application for Federal Student Aid (FAFSA) in addition to Pepperdine's one-page financial assistance form.

Faculty

Seaver College's faculty includes 312 men and women of high academic distinction, 100 percent of whom hold an earned doctorate or the terminal degree in their field. The teaching faculty of Seaver College is committed primarily to the instruction of undergraduate students. The student-faculty ratio of 12:1 allows ample individual assistance through classroom instruction and counseling. Upon enrollment, each student is assigned an academic adviser from among the faculty members. A qualified counseling staff is also available to serve personal and professional academic needs.

Student Government

The Student Government Association (SGA) is composed of student leaders and works in coordination with the Campus Life Office in establishing activities and maintaining school policies. SGA coordinates on-campus movies, sightseeing trips, guest performances, dances, and speakers and serves as the voice of the students to the Seaver administration.

Admission Requirements

Applicants are admitted on the basis of their academic record, SAT I or ACT scores, and personal information and references. Admission decisions are made without regard to race, religion, sex, or national background. Students who have completed at least 30 transferable semester units with a minimum grade point average of 3.0 are considered for admission as transfer students. Students who apply with fewer than 30 units are classified as freshmen with transfer units. To ensure full consideration, students should apply by January 15 for the fall semester and October 15 for the winter semester. Decision letter dates are announced in the current application form.

Application and Information

For the bulletin or application forms, students should contact:

Paul A. Long
Dean of Admission and Enrollment Management
Seaver College
Pepperdine University
Malibu, California 90263-4392
Telephone: 310-506-4392
Fax: 310-506-4861
World Wide Web: http://www.pepperdine.edu

The 830-acre Malibu campus of Pepperdine University, Seaver College, overlooks the Pacific Ocean, 35 miles west of Los Angeles, California.

PERU STATE COLLEGE

PERU, NEBRASKA

The College

Peru State College offers a high-quality education at a minimum personal cost to the student. Students receive substantial personal attention with a 16:1 student-teacher ratio and thrive in a supportive learning environment designed for students with diverse abilities.

Peru State College was founded in 1867 as Nebraska's first college. It operates as a public state-assisted institution that offers Bachelor of Arts, Bachelor of Science, and Bachelor of Technology degrees in the principal areas of teacher education, business, humanities, and science and technology as well as numerous preprofessional programs and a Master of Science in Education. The College is accredited by the North Central Association of Colleges and Schools and the National Council for Accreditation of Teacher Education.

Nearly 600 of Peru State's full-time students live in the eight residence halls on campus. Residence life options include single-sex halls as well as coed buildings and married student housing.

Students enjoy high-quality campus facilities, and an active social life is available on campus. The College offers more than thirty social and academic clubs, a fine arts theater, Benford Recital Hall, a coffeehouse, the Student Center, and an activities center/natatorium. Many students participate in the fifteen intramural sports offered. The Peru State Bobcats field NAIA Division II teams in women's basketball, cross-country, golf, softball, and volleyball and in men's baseball, basketball, football, and volleyball. The football program competes in the Central States Football League. All other sports teams are members of the Midlands Collegiate Athletic Conference.

Location

Peru State College, a prominent feature of the historic town of Peru, Nebraska, overlooks the Missouri River Valley. "The Campus of a Thousand Oaks" offers students the rural beauty of southeastern Nebraska only 65 miles from the state's two largest cities, Omaha and Lincoln. International airlines, passenger trains, bus service, and major highways provide convenient transportation for travelers to the area.

Peru State students enjoy four distinct seasons, from the red-gold blaze of autumn to lush green fields in spring. Many students enjoy hiking, mountain biking, camping, hunting, and fishing at nearby Indian Cave State Park.

Movie theaters and a variety of fast-food restaurants in nearby Auburn and Nebraska City provide students with additional entertainment opportunities.

Majors and Degrees

Peru State College awards the Bachelor of Arts and/or Bachelor of Science degrees in art; business, with options in accounting, computer information systems, management, and marketing; education, with endorsements in art, biology, business, chemistry, English, graphic design, history, language arts, liberal arts, mathematics, physical science, psychology, and special education; elementary education, with endorsements in early childhood education, middle school education, preschool handicapped, and special education; physical education, with an option in sports management and teaching endorsements in athletic coaching, physical education (K–6), and physical education (7–12); English; mathematics; music, with options in music performance and music marketing and teaching endorsements in elementary vocal music education (K–6) and vocal/instrumental music education (7–12); natural science, with options in biological science, natural science, nuclear technology, physical science, and wildlife ecology; psychology/criminal justice; and social science, with an option in history. The College also offers Bachelor of Technology degree in management.

Minors are available in biology, chemistry, mathematics, and music.

Academic Program

Peru State College provides a strong liberal arts education designed to produce graduates who are literate critical thinkers with the social and technological skills needed to apply their knowledge effectively as they pursue their social and civic roles in a complex and changing world.

The academic year at Peru State College is divided into two 15-week semesters (fall and spring) with two optional 5-week summer sessions. Students who are seeking a Bachelor of Arts or Bachelor of Science degree must earn a minimum of 125 semester credit hours, at least 40 of which are upper-division 300- and 400-level courses. All bachelor's degree candidates must complete the general studies program, which is designed to provide students with a solid foundation in the liberal arts; a major (or for teacher education candidates, one field endorsement or two subject endorsements); and elective courses that support their educational objectives.

A minimum cumulative grade point average (GPA) of 2.5 is required for all teacher education degrees. A minimum cumulative GPA of 2.0 is required for all other degrees and for all courses used to fulfill requirements in an academic major. In addition, no grade lower than a D+ (or C for transfer credits) may be used to fulfill requirements in an academic major. A maximum of 66 semester credit hours may be transferred from a two-year institution toward requirements for a bachelor's degree program. A minimum of 30 semester credit hours must be earned from Peru State College; 24 of the last 30 semester credit hours must be earned in residence unless earned from another Nebraska state college or from a college with an official cooperative agreement with Peru State College.

An Honors program is offered to challenge academically gifted students. Honors courses are designed to stimulate critical thinking through an interactive seminar structure.

Students who are seeking a Bachelor of Technology degree from Peru State College must first complete a technical associate degree or its equivalent from a regionally accredited institution. The Bachelor of Technology program requires a minimum of 125 semester credit hours, at least 20 of which are at the 300 level or higher. A minimum of 59 semester credit hours must be earned at an accredited institution of higher education, and 30 semester credit hours must be earned through Peru State College. A maximum of 66 semester credit hours may be transferred into the program from the technical associate degree program. A minimum cumulative GPA of 2.0 is required for all courses earned at Peru State College.

Students may earn credit toward degree programs through several standardized examination programs, including the College-Level Examination Program (CLEP), the Proficiency Examination Program (PEP), and Defense Activity for Non-Traditional Education Support (DANTES). Credits earned through examination are considered transfer credits.

Off-Campus Programs

Career Services offers students individualized career planning assistance. A resource library, Cooperative Education Internship information, computer technology and equipment, employment directories and search magazines, and major newspapers are available to students. Open and closed credential files are maintained for students and alumni. Individual assistance is provided in such areas as career counseling, designing an internship experience, job-search correspondence, interviewing, and negotiating job offers. The staff assists students in developing resumes, cover letters, and job search skills, and provides help in using electronic job search information.

Cooperative Education Internships are encouraged for students in every academic area. Students earn credit hours and gain applied work experience through field internships with outside organizations. The Cooperative Education Internship Program provides students with the opportunity to explore their chosen field of work and to gain valuable work experience while earning academic credit in their major or area of career interest. The maximum number of hours allowed for graduation is 12.

Academic Facilities

The Peru State College Library offers students access to several online databases and research utilities in addition to 105,615 bound volumes, 46,554 titles on microfilm, 7,070 audiovisual materials, and more than 1,500 print and full-text, online periodical subscriptions. Students have free access to the Internet from computer labs throughout the campus, including labs in each residence hall.

The Benford Recital Hall and the Art Gallery provide outlets for vocal, instrumental, and fine art presentations. Wheeler Activity Center houses an indoor running track as well as tennis, basketball, and volleyball courts; a weight room; and an Olympic-size swimming pool.

Costs

Tuition, fees, room, and board for a Nebraska resident for the 2003–04 school year totaled approximately $8800 (based on 30 semester credit hours, a semiprivate room, and a fifteen-meal plan). Additional expenses for books, supplies, and travel were estimated at $1100. Residents from adjacent states may benefit from reduced tuition if they qualify for the Student Opportunity Scholarship Program or the Midwest Student Exchange Program. Nonresident annual costs are $11,400.

Financial Aid

Currently, more than 85 percent of Peru State's full-time students are receiving financial aid. The College tries to meet the financial needs of all qualified students through a combination of federal, state, and institutional funds. In addition, merit-based scholarships are awarded for academic achievement, leadership, and demonstrated ability in the areas of art, drama, instrumental music, vocal music, and athletics. Nonresident scholarships are also available to qualified candidates.

All students should file the Free Application for Federal Student Aid (FAFSA) to be considered for the Federal Pell Grant, Federal Work-Study, Federal Supplemental Educational Opportunity Grant, Federal Perkins Loan, and Federal Family Education Loan programs.

Faculty

Peru State's student-faculty ratio of 16:1 ensures students personal interaction and an individualized education from 50 full-time and 50 part-time faculty members who are committed to undergraduate teaching and academic advising. Approximately 50 percent of full-time faculty members hold the highest degree in their field.

Student Government

The 23-member Student Senate, which consists of delegates elected from each class, is actively involved in decisions regarding the College's academic calendar, programs, and civic and cultural activities. The Campus Activities Board organizes hundreds of social, cultural, and recreational activities on campus each year.

Admission Requirements

Peru State College offers open admission to the state's residents who hold a Nebraska high school diploma or GED and who have not previously attended college. Admission is also granted to qualified transfer students, non-Nebraska residents, international students, and personal enrichment students. High school students may apply for admission as early as the first semester of their senior year, and all applicants should submit materials at least one month prior to the beginning of the semester they wish to be admitted.

Articulation agreements with twelve community colleges and technical schools provide efficient transfer of credits for students who wish to apply their Associate of Art, Associate of Science, or Associate of Applied Science degrees toward a bachelor's degree program at Peru State. Transfer students may apply for admission during their last year of attendance at another college or university.

Application and Information

Freshman applicants should submit a completed application for admission; an official high school transcript that lists cumulative grade point average, class rank, and graduation date; official ACT or SAT I score reports sent from the testing organization; and a Peru State College Medical/Immunization Form.

Transfer applicants should submit a completed application for admission, official transcripts from every postsecondary institution attended or enrolled in, official high school transcript (if applicant has completed fewer than 30 transferable semester credits), and a Peru State College Medical/Immunization Form. Online applications are available on the World Wide Web at the Internet address http://www.peru.edu/admissions/application.html.

To receive application forms, a College catalog, or additional information, students should contact:

Office of Admissions
Peru State College
P.O. Box 10
Peru, Nebraska 68421
Telephone: 402-872-2221
800-742-4412 (toll-free)
E-mail: admissions@oakmail.peru.edu
World Wide Web: http://www.peru.edu

PHILADELPHIA BIBLICAL UNIVERSITY

LANGHORNE, PENNSYLVANIA

The University

Philadelphia Biblical University (PBU) is the result of the merger of two Bible schools: the Bible Institute of Pennsylvania and Philadelphia School of the Bible. In 1951, the schools became the Philadelphia Bible Institute, which offered a three-year Bible diploma. In 1958, Pennsylvania granted the institute approval to offer the Bachelor of Science in Bible degree. The institute then changed its name to Philadelphia College of Bible. In 2000, Pennsylvania granted the college approval to become a university, and the college became Philadelphia Biblical University.

PBU is regionally accredited by the Middle States Association of Colleges and Schools and is professionally accredited by the Accrediting Association of Bible Colleges. PBU is an institutional member of the National Association of Schools of Music. The Bachelor of Social Work program is accredited by the Council on Social Work Education, the teacher education programs are accredited by the Association of Christian Schools International, and the business program is accredited by the International Assembly for Collegiate Business Education. PBU was approved in 1958 by the State Council on Education, commonwealth of Pennsylvania, to confer Bachelor of Science and Master of Science in Bible degrees, and by the Department of Education to confer the remaining bachelor's degrees listed below and to offer both public and private school teacher certification. The University is listed in publications of the United States Office of Education, the Office of Chief of Chaplains, and the Justice Department and is approved for veterans' education. PBU maintains appropriate relationships with the Pennsylvania Association of Colleges and Universities, Council for the Advancement and Support of Education, National Association of Independent Colleges and Universities, Commission for Independent Colleges and Universities, and the Council for Christian Colleges and Universities.

In addition to the undergraduate degrees described below, PBU offers the following graduate degrees: Master of Divinity; Master of Science in Bible, Christian counseling, educational leadership and administration, organizational leadership, and teacher education; and the Doctor of Ministry (Dallas Theological Seminary extension program).

PBU has an intercollegiate athletic program for both men and women. PBU participates in the National Collegiate Athletic Association Division III, the National Christian University Athletic Association, and the North Atlantic Christian Conference. Sports include men's baseball, basketball, cross-country, soccer, tennis, and volleyball and women's basketball, cross-country, field hockey, soccer, softball, tennis, and volleyball. Intramural sports include a variety of individual and team sports for both men and women. Recreational facilities include a fitness center and four tennis courts.

The dormitories at PBU are at two locations: the main campus and neighboring Penndel Borough. There are five main campus residence halls and sixty-six Penndel apartment units. The Dining Commons seats more than 500 people and provides a comfortable, casual atmosphere in which to enjoy a wide selection of food.

Location

PBU's main campus is a 112-acre facility located in Bucks County. It is 30 minutes from Center City Philadelphia; 15 minutes from Trenton, New Jersey; and 2 hours from New York City. The Langhorne train station is within walking distance, and Philadelphia International Airport is a 45-minute drive.

Majors and Degrees

The School of Biblical Studies offers biblical studies and Bible ministries programs leading to a Bachelor of Science in Bible degree.

The School of Church and Community Ministries offers a Bachelor of Social Work* degree program and Bachelor of Science in Bible degree, with programs in camping ministries, children's ministries, church ministries (interdisciplinary), counseling, Jewish missions, missions ministry, pastoral ministries, pre-seminary, social service (interdisciplinary), and youth ministries.

The School of Music and Performing Arts offers Bachelor of Science in Bible degree with a church music minor as well as a Bachelor of Music degree, with programs in church music,* composition,* music education,* and performance.*

The School of Education has programs leading to a Bachelor of Science in Bible degree in Bible education, early childhood education–preschool/kindergarten, and secondary education–Bible and history. An additional degree, the Bachelor of Science in education, can be earned in elementary education,* elementary education–early childhood,* health and physical education,* music education,* secondary education–English,* secondary education–math,* secondary education–social science,* and secondary education–citizenship.*

The School of Business and Leadership offers a Bachelor of Science in business administration* degree program.

An * designates double bachelor's degree programs.

Bachelor of Science in Bible degree programs in accounting, computer application development, networking technology, office administration and technology, and PC and end-user support are offered in cooperation with Bucks County Community College (BCCC).

Academic Programs

Students choose PBU for its emphasis on biblical and practical education. Each student receives a core curriculum of Bible classes in addition to those in their areas of professional study. PBU students are expected to apply the knowledge gained in the classroom to their spiritual lives and to practice godly character. The undergraduate degree programs are structured to provide every student with a thorough grounding in Bible, doctrine, and church history. Up to 6 additional elective credits may be stipulated for graduation. The curriculum also provides the student with a foundation in general education through a knowledge of the history, language, behavior, expression, and thought of both past and present cultures. Students take a cross section of general education subjects, totaling 48 credits. To complete the undergraduate curriculum, the student specializes in an elected professional area. These professional programs are designed to equip the student with a foundational knowledge of the history, philosophy, content, literature, and skills in each respective field.

The Honors Program seeks to develop Christian scholars who integrate their biblical studies with their general and professional education. Students must take the four designated Honors courses (Philosophy, History of Christianity, Politics and Society, and Literary Classics), participate in the Honors Colloquia and special activities every semester in the program, and submit a thesis or special project at the end of their senior year. Honors students must maintain a minimum cumulative GPA of 3.5 to continue in and graduate from the program.

At the Institute of Jewish Studies (IJS), students study the Scriptures from a Jewish perspective and take courses in Jewish history, culture, and the geography of the land of Israel, both ancient and modern. Students engage in practical outreach courses taught by experienced Friends of Israel staff members and have opportunities to be involved in ministries to Jewish people.

PBU students are eligible to participate in the Air Force Reserve Officer Training Corps (AFROTC) through a collaborative agreement with Saint Joseph's University. The AFROTC program enables a college student to earn a commission as an Air Force officer while concurrently satisfying requirements for the baccalaureate degree.

Off-Campus Programs

The Wisconsin Wilderness Campus (WWC) of PBU offers an accredited alternative to a traditional college year. The curriculum is primarily biblical with some general and professional studies. The enrollment is limited in order to provide increased opportunities for personal guidance and discipleship, formal and informal interaction with professors, the development of interpersonal skills, and involvement in outdoor recreational/educational experiences.

Since 1993, the University has offered a program of Biblical education at its New Jersey Campus (NJC) in Liberty Corner, New Jersey. The Bible Certificate Program continues this commitment to residents of Central New Jersey and the Greater New York area.

Academic Facilities

The Masland Learning Resource Center offers approximately 100,000 volumes in the main collection, along with reference works, periodicals, sound recordings, microforms, and other media. Two computer labs are available for use by students and staff members. A teacher education curriculum lab is available for study and instruction, and two conference rooms are available for group study.

Costs

In 2004–05, tuition is $6595 per semester for full-time students (12–18 credits). Part-time students pay $397 per credit (1–7 credits) or $550 per credit (8–11 credits). Room and board costs (21 meal plan) are $2927.50. Other fees vary by program.

Financial Aid

Admitted students who complete the FAFSA are considered for PBU Grants. These grants are awarded in various amounts (up to 50 percent of tuition) based on demonstrated need after considering all other sources of aid available. PBU Grants are renewable each year for full-time students whose annual FAFSA results document continuing financial need.

Students with outstanding academic records and SAT I or ACT scores who are accepted for admission by December 20 are invited to compete for the PBU Honors Scholarship ($8000 for 2004–05). Students should contact the University Admissions Office for competition details and dates. Other PBU academic scholarships include the President's Scholarship and the Dean's Scholarship, with awards ranging from $1000 to $4000 per year. The Scholarship Committee considers admitted students and notifies them on a rolling basis throughout the year. Students with a high school GPA of 3.2 or above and an SAT I score of 1100 or above (ACT 24 or above) are considered. Transfer students are also considered for these scholarships. Students awarded scholarships for 2004–05 must enroll full-time for the fall 2004 semester. Students who are dependents of a full-time Christian worker (pastor or church staff, missionary, Christian school, or para–church organization employee) may also qualify for the PBU Christian Worker Scholarship. This scholarship is a supplement to other types of aid, with awards ranging up to $3,000 or 50 percent of unmet need after all other aid is considered. Admitted students are eligible to be considered if the parent in the full-time Christian vocation is the primary wage earner of the family.

On-campus employment is available in many areas, including maintenance, security, food service, housekeeping, and clerical services.

Faculty

Of the 153 faculty members, most are engaged in full-time teaching and service to the student body. The majority possess doctoral degrees. The faculty-student ratio is 1:8.

Student Government

Students at PBU have an opportunity to influence the decisions that are made on campus and provide leadership for their fellow classmates through involvement in student government. The umbrella for government leadership is the Student Senate Cabinet. This group exists to present student concerns to the administration and to improve the University as a whole. The cabinet promotes school functions, helps to acclimate new students, and plans student gatherings. Involvement in student government can also be accessed through serving one's class. Each class has a cabinet that works to improve the students' experience and serves as a mediator between the Student Senate and the class. One role of the class leadership team is to organize activities, plan class chapels, and voice the concerns of those with whom they come in contact.

Admission Requirements

Three factors are considered in relation to the applicant's high school grades: overall grade point average, class rank and school size, and grade pattern from freshman to senior year. It is normally expected that the applicant should rank in the upper half of the high school class and have at least a 2.0 grade point average. To determine whether the applicant can benefit from the programs and environment of the University, three areas are reviewed: conversion, lifestyle, and beliefs. It is expected that students at the University have confessed faith in Jesus Christ as personal Savior. It is also expected that the applicant understands the theological perspective of the University, and the applicant's lifestyle should reflect Christian principles. A personal interview with an admissions counselor is recommended if an applicant is visiting the campus. On occasion, an interview is required in order to clarify personal or academic issues pertaining to the application.

Applicants must submit an application form with an autobiography and a $25 application fee, along with official high school transcripts, official SAT I or ACT scores, and a pastor's reference. Transfer students should enclose official transcripts for work completed at other colleges. International students should also submit TOEFL scores, an International Financial Aid Form, and proof of financial support.

Application and Information

For more information, prospective students should contact:

Academic Communications Office
Philadelphia Biblical University
200 Manor Avenue
Langhorne, Pennsylvania 19047
Telephone: 800-366-0049 (toll-free)
Fax: 215-702-4248
E-mail: inquiries@pbu.edu
World Wide Web: http://www.pbu.edu

PHILADELPHIA UNIVERSITY

PHILADELPHIA, PENNSYLVANIA

The University

Founded in 1884, Philadelphia University (formerly Philadelphia College of Textiles and Science) is a private institution of higher learning for students with high motivation and academic ability. Philadelphia University is professionally oriented and offers undergraduate and graduate degree programs in the areas of architecture, business, design, fashion, general sciences, health sciences, and textile engineering and technology. The University's enrollment of approximately 2,300 undergraduates represents a diverse and talented group of students from forty-one states and forty-one countries. With an average class size of 18 and a 13:1 student-faculty ratio, students receive the personal attention so important to social and professional growth.

Through a unique blend of liberal and specialized education with an interdisciplinary focus, the University prepares students for today's complex, global workplace. Recognized as a premier professional university, Philadelphia University has established a phenomenal record of career success for its graduates. The University is committed to a technologically advanced approach to career planning and students have full access to the Career Services Center's Online Career Office, an Internet-based resume, interview, and job-listing management system that electronically stores, retrieves, and distributes resumes, job listings, and employer information. Nearly 2,000 job titles were posted in 2002. Students have access to the CareerSearch database of 1.5 million companies nationwide. Prospective employers utilize password-accessed Internet accounts to search the resume database, post positions, and schedule interviews. The University's innovative academic programs that meet emerging needs in the marketplace, extensive networking with prospective employers (connecting students with 150 employers on campus and 1,200 employers electronically last year), and extensive career and professional development opportunities for students all add up to a nearly 90 percent placement rate within just a few months of graduation.

Philadelphia University believes the college experience of every student should extend well beyond the classroom. The Student Life Program at Philadelphia University seeks to build bridges between the classroom (curricular) and out-of-class (cocurricular) experiences to create a dynamic learning community for students. Twelve varsity teams compose the intercollegiate athletics program. The men's soccer team competes in NCAA Division I, while the men's baseball, basketball, golf, and tennis teams and the women's basketball, field hockey, lacrosse, soccer, softball, tennis, and volleyball teams participate at the Division II level. An extensive intramural sports program is available to all students. Students are actively engaged in campus life, whether it is through one of the nationally ranked athletic teams, events sponsored by SGA and the Program Board, a wide array of community service opportunities, an extensive intramural program, or participation in the more than thirty student clubs and organizations.

More than 1,200 students live on campus in residence halls, apartments, and townhouses. Professional and paraprofessional staff members live within each residential area to assist students with daily concerns and program activities to enhance residential living.

The University holds accreditation from the Middle States Association of Colleges and Schools, the National Architectural Accrediting Board (NAAB), the Foundation for Interior Design Education and Research (FIDER), the American Chemical Society (ACS), the Commission for Accreditation of Allied Health Education Programs (CAAHEP), and the Engineering Accreditation Commission of the Accreditation Board for Engineering and Technology (ABET).

Location

The University's sprawling, 100-acre campus is adjacent to Fairmount Park, the largest urban park system in the country. Students enjoy the best of both worlds—a beautiful campus with tree-lined walkways, spacious lawns, and classical architecture, and easy access to Philadelphia (just minutes away) for entertainment, cultural events, great night spots, and more than 300 years of American history.

Philadelphia also serves as a "living lab" where students frequently interact with area professionals for class projects, internships, co-ops, and off-campus jobs.

Majors and Degrees

Philadelphia University offers the Bachelor of Science in more than thirty areas: accounting, architecture, architectural studies, biochemistry, biology, biopsychology, chemistry, computer information systems, digital design, e-commerce, environmental and conservation biology, fashion design, fashion industry management, fashion merchandising, finance, graphic design communication, industrial design, interior design, international business, landscape architecture (5-year B.L.A.), management, management information systems, marketing, physician assistant studies (5-year M.S.), premedical studies, psychology, science and business, textile design, textile engineering, textile management/marketing, and textile technology. The University also offers several five-year B.S./M.B.A. joint programs. The five-year architecture program leads to a Bachelor of Architecture (B.Arch.). For students wishing to keep their options open, an undeclared option offers an introduction to college courses in preparation for entering a specific major in the sophomore year.

Academic Program

Philadelphia University's commitment to quality professional education is realized in a curriculum that combines a solid foundation in liberal studies with career preparation. The curricula are designed to enhance students' ability and desire to learn; to ensure them an understanding of the ideas, traditions, and values of their own and other cultures; and to prepare them to apply the concepts and techniques of both general and specialized learning to their lives as citizens with productive careers. Degree requirements include successful completion of 121 to 138 credits (depending upon the major chosen), successful completion of both major and general education programs, and the satisfactory completion of at least 60 credits in residence at the University. All students have the option to participate in the University's Co-op Program, through which they earn both academic credit and a salary.

As a rule, the University grants credit to students who obtain satisfactory grades in subject examinations developed by the Advanced Placement Program, the College-Level Examination Program, and the Proficiency Examination Program. Students may, by invitation, participate in the Honors Program, which offers a number of courses expressly for honors students.

The University's academic calendar consists of two semesters and two summer sessions.

Off-Campus Programs

The University has a dynamic Study Abroad Program that includes a formal affiliation with the University of Rome, Italy. Students at the Philadelphia University, Center for Study Abroad study in areas such as architecture, fashion merchandising, fashion design, and apparel.

Studying abroad is an exciting way for students to see the world, experience other cultures, and learn about their field of study. Architecture students, for example, can travel to England to see firsthand the work of Christopher Wren; fashion design students can study in London, Paris, or Italy; and international business students can explore global trade in Spain or other overseas locations.

Cooperative education experiences are also available. Study-abroad options include Austria, Australia, England, France, Germany, Ireland, Italy, Japan, Mexico, Scotland, and Spain. The University's Co-op office has affiliations with such organizations as L. L. Bean, Isdaner and Co., the Hillier Group, Mellon Bank, Burlington Industries, J. Crew, and Federated Department Stores.

Academic Facilities

The Tuttleman Center at Philadelphia University, a 31,500-square-foot, high-tech academic building that opened in fall 2001, provides students and faculty members with access to the most sophisticated technologies for teaching and learning.

Many major labs and studios enable students to gain practical experience in art, design, textiles, apparel manufacturing, foreign language study, the sciences, computer technologies, and physician assistant studies. The University's Paul J. Gutman Library is a state-of-the-art information center. Through the contemporary information system, students can search the library's collections, as well as major indexes and full-text journals, from on or off campus. An international computer network links Philadelphia University to the resources of more than 14,000 libraries world-wide. With more than 400 study spaces and nine group study rooms, the library provides an ideal environment for reading and research. The Architecture and Design Center houses studio space, a photo lab, and computer-aided design labs. The Design Center at Philadelphia University houses an extensive collection of textile artifacts and hosts changing exhibits in its galleries.

General-purpose and departmental computing labs are updated using a multiyear migration strategy as changes in technology dictate. The labs are currently equipped with Pentium PCs and Macintoshes running at speeds from 1.0 to 1.8 MHz. The University operates a switched, 100-megabit network with building-to-building gigabit (1000-megabit) connections in high-traffic areas. The network provides students with access to the Internet, e-mail service, network storage (300 MB per student), digital library resources, online databases, and the Blackboard course management system.

Costs

The University's 2004–05 cost for regular tuition was $20,940. Room was $3834, and board was $3948.

Financial Aid

In 2003–04, Philadelphia University's total financial aid program amounted to more than $41.5 million; about $13.1 million came from the University itself and the remainder came from federal, state, and private sources. While 92 percent of the University's full-time day students receive direct institutional scholarship assistance, 95.5 percent receive some form of aid each year (e.g., other scholarships, loans, and job opportunities). The University attempts to meet the remainder of the financial need with University, state, and federal grants, scholarships, and loans. Candidates for aid should complete the Free Application for Federal Student Aid by April 15. The University offers a wide range of institutional scholarships and grants to incoming students each year. Award amounts vary according to the quality of each student's academic record. The University's scholarship program is available to all prospective students (freshmen and transfer students). Scholarships are awarded regardless of financial need. Students and parents are strongly encouraged to call the admissions or financial aid offices for further information.

Faculty

Primarily a teaching institution, the University encourages close connections between faculty members and students. Classes are intentionally kept small and faculty members make a practice of being available to students outside the classroom. Often, students can partner with faculty members to pursue joint research interests and gain career experience. The University's faculty is a diverse group of professionals who hold not only strong academic credentials, but also frequently possess impressive work experience. They are often sought out as consultants in their fields.

Student Government

The Student Government Association (SGA) is an independent, self-governing student group. In addition to the basic responsibility of protecting students' rights, SGA recommends students to University-wide committees, addresses student grievances, and sponsors campuswide events. The Programming Board is the major programming organization on campus. Its primary responsibility is to provide a wide variety of cultural, scholastic, social, educational, and recreational programs.

Admission Requirements

The University evaluates applicants on the basis of their high school record (including GPA and quality of courses taken), scores on either the SAT I or the ACT, and extracurricular activities. Normally, 15 units of secondary school preparation are required for admission. Three units of mathematics (including algebra II and geometry) are required for admission. Students who wish to enter a science curriculum are strongly encouraged to take 4 units of mathematics and 4 units of science. The University actively recruits qualified transfer students, who represent approximately one fifth of the incoming class each fall. The University also has a large international student population. These students must score at least 170 (computer-based) on the TOEFL in order to be considered for admission.

Application and Information

The University maintains a rolling admission plan. Applications are reviewed and decisions are made soon after an application, academic credentials, and standardized test scores are received. Students are encouraged to submit applications early in the senior year; applications received after March 1 are considered on a space-available basis. All applicants are encouraged to come to the campus for an interview with a member of the professional admission staff.

Christine E. Greb
Director of Admissions
Philadelphia University
School House Lane and Henry Avenue
Philadelphia, Pennsylvania 19144
Telephone: 215-951-2800
800-951-7287 (toll-free)
Fax: 215-951-2907
E-mail: admissions@PhilaU.edu
World Wide Web: http://www.PhilaU.edu

PINE MANOR COLLEGE

CHESTNUT HILL, MASSACHUSETTS

The College

Founded in 1911, Pine Manor College (PMC) is a small, private four-year liberal arts college that prepares women for roles of inclusive leadership and social responsibility. PMC enrolls approximately 500 students from a wide range of cultural, racial, educational, and socioeconomic backgrounds. Students come from twenty-seven countries and twenty-six states. Pine Manor provides an educational environment that supports individual growth and empowers young women for responsible leadership. The College's small size helps accomplish this, but so do interactive teaching, interdisciplinary study, and active learning techniques such as portfolio development and internships for all students. At Pine Manor, students learn to think critically, act cooperatively, and develop leadership skills in new ways, focusing on inclusiveness and responsibility for the common good. Pine Manor College is accredited by the New England Association of Schools and Colleges.

Student organizations provide many opportunities for cocurricular learning at PMC. Students are sure to find a club, athletic team, performance ensemble, affinity group, or service organization that provides a place to use their talents and expand their abilities. Fun activities abound on campus and there is always room for new groups to form with student interest. Intercollegiate athletics (NCAA Division III) are offered in basketball, cross-country, lacrosse, soccer, softball, tennis, and volleyball. Instruction is available in lifetime fitness activities and other areas of physical education. Members of the performing arts department and their students present musical, dramatic, and dance performances throughout the year. The visual arts department sponsors professional and student art exhibits throughout the year in the Hess Gallery.

There are three residential villages on campus, each of which includes five wired residence units, lounges, and computer facilities. All first-year students are encouraged to live on campus, and housing is guaranteed for students for four years. Housing is also available to all adult learners who wish to reside on campus. Meals are served in the dining center.

Location

Pine Manor College is located in the affluent Boston suburb of Chestnut Hill, Massachusetts, just 5 miles from the heart of the city and minutes away via public transportation. More than thirty buildings are nestled on the 60-acre wooded campus, which provides a safe environment for students. With more than fifty colleges and universities in the area and a wide array of intellectual, social, and cultural facilities, the range of activities offered is almost endless. Cape Cod, New England ski areas, and New York City are easily accessible.

Majors and Degrees

Pine Manor College offers a four-year liberal arts program leading to the Bachelor of Arts (B.A.) degree and a two-year program leading to an Associate in Arts (A.A.) or Associate in Science (A.S.) degree. B.A. majors are offered in biology, business administration, communication, English, history and culture, liberal studies, psychology, social and political systems, and visual arts. The College also offers a nursing program in which qualified students study two years at Pine Manor and complete a B.S.N. at the Boston College School of Nursing. Concentrations within these majors and associated minors include accounting, advertising and public relations, allied health, American political systems, art and museum studies, art history, biopsychology, child development, community systems, counseling, creative writing, criminal justice, dance, design, drama, electronic media programming and production, entrepreneurship, environmental studies, European studies, finance, French, global studies, graphic design, history, human resources management, human services, industrial/organizational psychology, international business, journalism, literature, management, marine biology, marketing, music, photography, political science, prelaw, premedical, sociology, sports management, studio arts, theater arts, and women's studies. Students majoring in liberal studies may elect to pursue teacher certification in elementary education (1–6). Students majoring in psychology may elect to pursue teacher certification in early childhood education (pre-K–2). Secondary certification is available in biology, English, and visual arts. Individualized and interdisciplinary majors may be arranged by the student in consultation with her adviser. A certificate program in community health-care outreach is also available.

Academic Programs

For the B.A. degree, students must complete thirty-two full-semester courses, or 132 semester credit hours. To receive the A.A. or A.S. degree, students must successfully complete sixteen full-semester courses, or 64 semester credit hours. Core curriculum requirements create a solid academic foundation for students by framing the major requirements with courses from the following: humanities, social sciences, natural and behavioral sciences, fine and performing arts, mathematics, and English composition.

Pine Manor College views education as a relationship between and among learners that requires the active engagement of students, faculty members, and others to be successful. These collaborative relationships provide a more focused method of teaching and learning. Classes are open discussions where everyone's contribution matters.

A student's learning portfolio forms the central focus of her educational experience at Pine Manor College. Presentation of a learning portfolio is a graduation requirement for all PMC students. The formal presentation of the portfolio takes place twice, ordinarily during the sophomore and senior years. The portfolio contains evidence of and reflections upon student learning related to the general education outcomes and accomplishments within the major. The portfolio approach promotes leadership skills by providing a holistic perspective on growth by requiring the student to take responsibility for her own learning. A key to leadership development is the ability to be reflective, to establish goals, and to assess progress toward them.

Portfolio Learning Seminars are led by a faculty member and a resource team of peer mentors and student life professionals. This program offers a comprehensive approach that is designed to help students become reflective, self-directed learners. The program offers opportunities to develop effective mentoring and leadership skills, which strengthen the students' capacity to work collaboratively and productively toward common goals.

Recognizing a fundamental link between a liberal arts education and the professional world, Pine Manor College integrates the required fourteen-week internship experience into the curriculum. The PMC internship combines students' academic knowledge with practical experience in the workplace, while students explore career options and develop the leadership skills that employers seek. Many PMC interns are offered permanent positions at their internship sites. After working with top professionals at Boston's best corporations, hospitals, museums, laboratories, publications, and social service agencies, PMC seniors are prepared to make informed career choices.

Adult learners may apply CLEP, transfer credits, or credits for prior learning toward their degrees and may take courses part-time or full-time. A certificate program is offered in community health-care outreach.

The English Language Institute at Pine Manor is a coed program designed for men and women whose native language is not English. Noncredit instruction in English is offered at the elementary and intermediate levels on a year-round basis. Sessions begin every two weeks and last anywhere from two to fifty weeks, depending on the individual needs of each student.

Off-Campus Programs

PMC participates in a program of cross-registration with Boston College, Babson College, and the Marine Studies Consortium. Study-abroad options are available throughout the world, along with the Washington Semester program for juniors sponsored by the American University in Washington, D.C.

Academic Facilities

The Ferry Administration Building accommodates most of the administrative offices and student services; Haldan Hall contains modern classrooms, faculty offices, and language laboratories; the recently renovated Dane Science Center has classrooms, laboratories for science courses, and computer laboratories; and Ellsworth Hall, the performing arts center, has a theater, classrooms, computer facilities, and listening and practice rooms. The Abercrombie Fine Arts Wing has studios for sculpture, printmaking, painting, design, and photography, as well as a state-of-the-art visual arts computer lab. The Annenberg Library and Communications Center houses the library, Learning Resource Center, Cherry Computer Center, radio and TV production studios, Hess Art Gallery, lecture halls, seminar rooms, and music-listening areas. The gymnasium includes basketball, volleyball, and badminton courts; a dance and exercise studio; and a fitness room with multistation exercise equipment. Other athletic facilities include new tennis courts, paddle tennis courts, softball fields, and the Hedley soccer/lacrosse field.

Costs

For 2004–05, tuition is $14,544. The cost of room and board (double-occupancy) is $9000, and the orientation fee for freshman students is $150. Private music lessons and student parking facilities are available for an extra charge.

Financial Aid

The College's financial aid resources include Pine Manor grants, merit grants, Federal Work-Study Program jobs, Federal Stafford Student Loans, Federal Supplemental Educational Opportunity Grants, Federal Pell Grants, and state scholarships.

To apply for aid, a copy of the Free Application for Federal Student Aid (FAFSA) must be submitted by April 30.

Faculty

Teaching is the number one priority of Pine Manor's faculty members. Eighty percent of Pine Manor's full-time professors hold terminal degrees, and 70 percent of faculty members are women. Part-time faculty members are professional practitioners in their fields of expertise. Seventy-five percent of classes have less than 20 students, and the low student-faculty ratio of 10:1 allows faculty members to take an active part in every phase of College life.

Student Government

Students participate in decision making at Pine Manor through the Student Government Association. In addition, student representatives sit on the Curriculum Committee, Library Committee, President's Leadership Group, Speakers and Programs Committee, and Academic Ethics Council.

Admission Requirements

Students are selected on the basis of an evaluation of their secondary school performance, SAT I or ACT scores, program of studies, school recommendations, and personal essay. While an interview is not required for admission, it is strongly recommended. SAT I scores are not required of international students; TOEFL scores, however, are required. Applicants are expected to have 16 academic credits, distributed among the following: English, social studies, mathematics, science, and foreign languages. Transfer students must submit transcripts of previous college courses completed. Accepted students may choose to enroll on a part-time basis.

The College considers applications from juniors in secondary school who have fulfilled the admission requirements (or who will have fulfilled them by September of the year they wish to enter).

Application and Information

All applications are handled on a rolling admission basis.

The College uses the College Board's Candidates Reply Date of May 1.

For further information, students should contact:

Dean of Admissions
Pine Manor College
400 Heath Street
Chestnut Hill, Massachusetts 02467
Telephone: 617-731-7104
800-PMC-1357 (toll-free)
Fax: 617-731-7102
E-mail: getinfo3@pmc.edu
World Wide Web: http://www.pmc.edu

Students in front of Dane Science Building.

PITZER COLLEGE

CLAREMONT, CALIFORNIA

The College

Pitzer is a nationally recognized independent, residential liberal arts and sciences college. The College's emphasis on interdisciplinary studies, intercultural understanding, and concern with social responsibility and the ethical implications of knowledge and action sets it apart from most other colleges in the country. The College believes that students should take an active part in formulating their individualized plans of study, bringing a spirit of inquiry and adventure to the process of planning. Because there are fewer required general education courses, Pitzer gives its students more freedom to choose the courses they want to take.

Pitzer offers the best of both worlds: membership in a small, closely knit academic community and access to the resources of a midsize university through Pitzer's partnership in the Claremont Colleges. The Claremont Colleges are a consortium of five distinct undergraduate colleges (Pitzer, Claremont McKenna, Harvey Mudd, Pomona, and Scripps) and two graduate institutions, the Claremont Graduate University and the Keck Institute for Applied Biological Sciences. Each school has its own academic focus and personality but all share major facilities, such as the main library, bookstore, campus security, health services, counseling center, ethnic study centers, and chaplains' offices. The total enrollment of all of the colleges is nearly 6,000 students. Students at Pitzer may enroll in courses offered by the other colleges and may consult with professors on all of the adjoining campuses.

The College was established in 1963. Historically, Pitzer was the Claremont College that focused on the behavioral and social sciences. Through the years, the curricular emphasis has expanded to include the arts, humanities, and sciences. Majors with the largest enrollments include anthropology, art, biology, economics, English, environmental studies, history, organizational studies, political studies, psychology, and sociology.

The 2003 first-year class of 241 students represented thirty different states and six other countries. About 45 percent of the first-year students came from outside of California.

Pitzer has had a deep commitment to welcoming members of underrepresented groups since its founding. In 2003, members of underrepresented groups made up about 33 percent of the total: 13 percent Asian American and Pacific Islander, 12 percent Chicano/Latino, 7 percent African American, and 1 percent Native American.

Residential life plays a significant role in the student's educational experience. Each of the three residence halls establishes its own Hall Council annually to serve as a forum for addressing and meeting the needs of the community. Pitzer students have a long tradition of arranging their living communities based on common interests. All rooms are wired for Internet access, television, and phone service.

Opportunities are abundant at Pitzer and throughout the other Claremont Colleges for students to participate in a wide variety of sports, clubs, community service programs, and social activities. Currently, more than seventy-five student organizations allow students to get involved in a wide variety of activities. Pitzer joins Pomona College to field NCAA Division III teams in baseball, basketball, cross-country, football, golf, soccer, softball, swimming and diving, tennis, track and field, volleyball, and water polo. Badminton, cycling, fencing, lacrosse, and rugby are offered as intramural sports.

Location

Pitzer is located in the city of Claremont (population 35,000) at the base of the San Gabriel Mountains, about 35 miles east of Los Angeles and 78 miles west of Palm Springs. Pitzer is within short driving distances of rock climbing at Joshua Tree National Park; the Getty, Norton Simon, and other Los Angeles County museums; skiing; and the beaches of southern California.

Majors and Degrees

Pitzer grants the Bachelor of Arts degree in more than forty fields of study. Majors are available in anthropology; art; Asian-American studies; Asian studies; biology; biology-chemistry; black studies; chemistry; Chicano studies; classics; creative writing; dance; economics; English and world literature; environmental science; environmental studies; European studies; French; gender and feminist studies; history; human biology; international and intercultural studies; Latin American and Caribbean studies; linguistics; mathematical economics; mathematics; media studies; music; neuroscience; organizational studies; philosophy; physics; political economy; political studies; psychology; religious studies; science and management; science, technology, and society; sociology; Spanish; theater; and Third World studies.

Academic Program

To earn the Bachelor of Arts degree, students are required to complete thirty-two courses, about one third of which are in the major. Students work with faculty advisers to organize a curriculum that meets the educational objectives of the College: breadth of knowledge, understanding in depth, written expression, interdisciplinary and intercultural exploration, and social responsibility and the ethical implications of knowledge and action. Specific course requirements depend upon the student's academic interests. Certain concentrations require a senior thesis.

The system of cross-registration at the Claremont Colleges provides Pitzer students with the opportunity to take advantage of the wide range of courses available at each of the other colleges. Advanced students may also enroll in certain courses at the Claremont Graduate University.

The College observes an early semester calendar; classes begin in early September and end in mid-May. There is a study break near the middle of each semester and another break between semesters from mid-December through mid-January.

Off-Campus Programs

About 60 percent of students participate in study-abroad programs at more than 100 sites throughout the world. Pitzer administers ten of its own language and culture programs in Botswana, China, Ecuador, Italy (Parma and Modena), Nepal, Turkey, Venezuela, and summer programs in Costa Rica and Japan.

The College also offers an innovative program in the city of Ontario, California. This program is modeled in part on the study sites abroad and emphasizes community involvement. The program features homestays with local families, internships with a wide range of city and nongovernmental agencies, and a program center in the community that serves as a base for classes and community service projects.

Academic Facilities

The central services of the Claremont Colleges include the Honnold-Mudd Library, which houses more than 1.4 million volumes, more than 4,000 periodicals, and nearly ninety newspaper subscriptions. Other shared facilities include theaters, music halls, music and dance studios, the Keck Joint Science Center, and a counseling/health center.

Specialized facilities at Pitzer include a television studio, film editing rooms, art galleries, social science laboratories, an arboretum, a reading library, and several computing facilities, including a computer center that is open 24 hours.

Costs

Expenses for 2003–04 were as follows: tuition and fees, $29,794; room and board, $7796; and books and personal expenses, $1900. Travel expenses vary. Costs are subject to change for 2004–05.

Financial Aid

Fifty-two percent of Pitzer's students receive aid in the forms of grants, loans, and work-study. To apply for aid, students must complete the Free Application for Federal Student Aid (FAFSA) and the Financial Aid PROFILE. California residents should also apply for California state grants. Students must reapply for aid each spring.

Faculty

Ninety-eight percent of Pitzer's faculty members hold a Ph.D. degree or the terminal degree in their field of expertise. Graduate students do not teach classes. The student-faculty ratio is 11:1, and faculty members are readily available for academic advising. Most faculty members are conversant with at least one other field of study in addition to the area of their degrees and may teach in more than one area.

Student Government

Pitzer's governmental structure is distinctive among American colleges. Instead of the traditional student government that restricts student participation to limited areas, students are represented on all of the standing committees of the College, including those that deal with the most vital and sensitive issues of the College community. Though it demands a serious commitment of time and energy from those who choose to participate, it offers interested students an active educational experience and the opportunity to make a genuine impact on the life of the College and its students, faculty, and staff.

Admission Requirements

Pitzer has developed a highly personalized admission process. Each applicant is considered on the basis of his or her own strengths. In general, the College seeks students who have performed well in high school, have shown a significant amount of involvement in activities outside of the classroom, are motivated to learn, and are interested in the opportunity to take an active role in planning their education in a liberal arts framework. The selection process is designed to help achieve a diverse and energetic entering class. Selection is based on high school transcripts, recommendations, essays, extracurricular activities, and special talents. Applicants are encouraged to visit the campus and arrange for an interview.

Application and Information

Pitzer College offers both early action and regular admission for prospective applicants. Students interested in applying early must submit a completed application by December 1 and will be notified by January 1. Regular admission candidates must submit their applications for admission by January 15 and will be notified by May 1. In addition, they should supply an official transcript of grades, two teacher recommendations, one counselor or school official recommendation, and the application fee of $50 by the necessary deadline. Pitzer accepts the Common Application as the only application for admission for first-year students. When submitting the Common Application, students must complete a supplemental form that is available on the Common Application Web site at http://www.commonapp.org.

For further information, students should contact:

Office of Admission
Pitzer College
1050 North Mills Avenue
Claremont, California 91711-6101
Telephone: 909-621-8129
800-PITZER1 (800-748-9371, toll-free)
Fax: 909-621-8770
E-mail: admission@pitzer.edu
World Wide Web: http://www.pitzer.edu

Students on the campus of Pitzer College.

PLYMOUTH STATE UNIVERSITY

PLYMOUTH, NEW HAMPSHIRE

The University

Plymouth State University (PSU) is a coeducational, residential university with an enrollment of approximately 3,500 full-time undergraduate students and 1,100 part-time and graduate students. Plymouth State was founded in 1871 and over the years has expanded to 170 acres and forty-six buildings. PSU preserves the brick-and-ivy look of its New England small-university heritage while integrating state-of-the-art technology and facilities into an attractive, contemporary campus design.

Plymouth's proud history has created a strong architectural identity, and successful renovations are part of a new, dynamic, and modern campus. Superb facilities have recently been added. The impressive physical facilities include living accommodations, which range from traditional residence halls to student apartments that are set in a wooded, landscaped section of the campus. All residences are wired for the Internet and cable television.

The student union, located in the center of the campus, is called the Hartman Union Building or, more popularly, the HUB. It houses a snack bar and café, the University bookstore, fitness and aerobics rooms, a gymnasium, a multipurpose room, administrative offices, and offices for student government, media, and activities. Nearly 2,500 meetings, receptions, programs, and conferences are held there annually.

Plymouth's athletic facilities and fields, supporting eighteen intercollegiate teams as well as numerous state and regional athletic contests, have long been recognized as being among the best in New England.

Students come to Plymouth State University for its caring academic community and friendly campus, the Main Street New England setting, and easy access to New Hampshire's great outdoors.

Student publications include *The Clock,* the weekly newspaper; *The Continuum,* the literary magazine; and *The Conning Tower,* the yearbook. An FM radio station, WPCR, regularly has 40 on-air disc jockeys and provides an eclectic range of musical programming seven days a week. Hundreds of activities and programs are sponsored each semester by Programming Activities in a Campus Environment (PACE) and other student organizations.

In addition to its undergraduate degrees, PSU offers the M.B.A., the M.Ed., and the Certificate of Advanced Graduate Studies.

Location

With the White Mountains to the north, the Lakes Region to the south, and the Pemigewasset River bordering the town to the east, Plymouth, New Hampshire, is home to some of the country's most spectacular wilderness. Plymouth State University students step outside every morning into a natural landscape that provides four seasons of recreational and educational adventure. Here, the outdoors offer a natural laboratory, a classroom, and a playground. Students in the arts and sciences sketch, describe, and study the area's distinctive seasonal landscapes. Meteorology students forecast the local weather and work in the surrounding areas on grant projects involving wind energy and climate changes. Geology students hike local trails and track the glacial migration of the last Ice Age. Archaeological field schools dig the land and dive the waters to discover lost pieces of America's heritage. During their free time, students cycle the area's back roads and highways; jog wooded paths; ski the slopes at Tenney, Cannon, Loon, Waterville Valley, and a number of other mountains; and snowshoe and hike dozens of trails within a short drive. Neighboring Rumney is famous for rock climbing. The Pemigewasset and Baker Rivers provide white water to kayakers and canoeists. The lakes—Little Squam, Big Squam, Newfound, and Winnipesaukee—are popular for sailing, flat-water paddling, water skiing, even scuba diving. The campus is nestled in the town of Plymouth, which has been ranked seventh in *The 100 Best Small Towns in America.* Plymouth is less than 2 hours' drive from Boston on Interstate 93. Two hours to the east is Portland, Maine; 2 hours northwest is Burlington, Vermont; and 3½ hours north is Montreal, Canada.

Majors and Degrees

Plymouth State University offers the B.A., B.F.A., and B.S. degrees in forty-seven undergraduate majors, with several options within each major. Some of these majors include accounting, adventure education, anthropology/sociology, applied computer science, applied economics, art, athletic training, biology, biotechnology, business administration, chemistry, childhood studies, communication studies, criminal justice, early childhood studies, English, environmental biology, environmental planning, French, geography, health education, history, humanities, information technology, interdisciplinary studies, management, marketing, mathematics, medieval studies, meteorology, music, philosophy, physical education, political science, psychology, public management, social science, social work, Spanish, and theater arts. Within these majors are sixteen state-approved and NCATE-accredited teacher certification programs. Individualized interdisciplinary majors may be arranged in consultation with an academic adviser.

Academic Program

Education in the liberal arts and sciences and in several professional fields is provided through associate and baccalaureate degree programs. The Plymouth State University curriculum provides the student with expertise in at least one area of knowledge and a broad background concerning the nature of humanity, the universe, and cultures of the world. If students are uncertain of the specific field of study they should follow, Plymouth allows them to consider a variety of programs in the first year of study while progressing toward a degree. In addition, a degree in interdisciplinary studies allows a student to concentrate in two or three areas. A wide variety of minors is also available, giving students an opportunity to study outside their chosen major and enhance their academic experience in other fields of interest.

Plymouth students usually enroll in five courses per semester. The school year consists of two 16-week semesters, a one-month optional January term (Winterim), and two optional summer sessions. In addition to the major courses, study in the humanities, social science, and mathematics and natural science is required.

Credit is granted for successful scores on Advanced Placement, DANTES, and CLEP examinations. Honors courses and independent study are also offered to Plymouth students.

Off-Campus Programs

Students are encouraged to broaden their academic experience by studying away for a semester or a year as part of a national or international student exchange program. Plymouth State participates in the National Student Exchange (NSE), a domestic parallel to study abroad, offering a diverse group of nearly 180 colleges and universities in forty-nine states, three U.S. territories, and four Canadian provinces. In addition to the New Hampshire College and University Council (NHCUC), PSU students can enroll at other NHCUC institutions for one or more courses during an academic semester. International study-away experiences are offered around the globe. PSU has exchange agreements and affiliations with schools in Australia, Canada, Cuba, England, France, Mexico, and Spain, although students study at many other institutions worldwide. Short-term study and field-based learning experiences are offered throughout the school year, and summer sessions are offered through individual departments. Internships, practicums, and field studies are all taken for credit and applied to the student's major. The Bagley Center for International Programs, National Student Exchange, Internship Partners, and Career Services are helpful in securing off-campus programs for credit, whether it be an internship at a design firm, a marketing internship at a ski resort, or a semester abroad studying in Australia.

Academic Facilities

The University's renovated and expanded Lamson Library provides more than 300,000 printed volumes, 700,000 microform and audiovisual items, 11,000 current periodical subscriptions, online facilities for database searches, a public-access catalog of its holdings, and an automated circulation system. The fully automated facility provides users with access to substantial electronic resources and includes forty workstations with Internet access for student use. The Silver Cultural Arts Center is home to the performing arts, with a 665-seat main-stage theater, a 174-seat recital hall, and a multipurpose black-box studio theater as well as classrooms and practice facilities for music, theater, and dance students. A $16.5-million renovation and construction has just been completed on the Boyd Hall science building, which houses the natural science department, the New England Weather Technology Evaluation Center, an observatory, an atrium, terraria, aquaria, and a planetarium that offers monthly programs to the public.

Older buildings on campus reflect Plymouth's historical importance to the region. The University has five sites that are listed on the New Hampshire Heritage Trail. Its landmark, Rounds Hall, is home to the education department and contains a bell in its clock tower that was cast by apprentices of Paul Revere. Poet Robert Frost taught education and psychology at Frost Cottage from 1911 to 1912. Holmes's Rock marks the site of Holmes Plymouth Academy, established in 1808, which was the first training school for teachers in New Hampshire. Holmes House is now home to the University's residential life offices. The Silver Cultural Arts Center showcases the department of music, theater, and dance, and it also hosts world-class performers year-round. The site of the building was formerly a stop on the Underground Railroad. The beautifully restored Draper & Maynard Building is home to the art department and the health, physical education, and recreation department. It also houses three floors of visual art studio space and the Karl Drerup Art Gallery.

Costs

For New Hampshire residents, tuition in 2002–03 was $4450; for out-of-state students, it was $10,110. Typical room and board costs for 2002–03 were $5768 for both New Hampshire residents and out-of-state students. Required fees totaled $1406.

Financial Aid

More than 80 percent of Plymouth's students receive some financial assistance from federal, state, University, and private sources. Scholarships, grants, loans, and work-study jobs are available for qualified students. Many students work at part-time jobs on campus and in or near Plymouth. Financial aid applicants should file the Free Application for Federal Student Aid (FAFSA) with the federal processor by March 1 for the following academic year.

Faculty

The resident faculty totals 170 full-time men and women who share a commitment to teaching and preparing students for careers in their field. Eighty-eight percent of the faculty members hold a doctoral or other terminal degree in their field. Faculty members are also active in their respective fields—attending conferences; presenting papers, workshops, and seminars; working as consultants; participating in exhibits; performing in concerts; and writing books and articles. The student-faculty ratio is 17:1. Each student has an academic adviser.

Student Government

The Student Senate provides a structure through which social, cultural, and recreational activities are organized and financed. Senators are elected to represent all four classes, residence halls, fraternities, sororities, nontraditional students, off-campus students, and graduate students.

Admission Requirements

A student is considered well prepared if the high school program has included English and literature, social sciences, natural sciences, foreign language, and three years of mathematics. Auditions are required for music, theater, and dance majors; an interview is required for criminal justice majors; and a portfolio is required for art majors. Official transcripts and SAT I or ACT scores are required. Home-schooled students should send an outline of their academic studies and subjects taken.

Plymouth welcomes applications from transfer candidates with proven academic ability. Transfer applicants must submit official transcripts from each college attended previously.

Application and Information

Applications are accepted for the fall or the spring semester. Application deadlines are April 1 for the fall semester and December 1 for the spring semester. Plymouth uses a system of rolling admissions, and students are notified of the admission decision after all materials have been received and evaluated. Applications received after the deadlines are considered on a space-available basis only. New students must attend student orientation in order to enroll for their first semester.

For more information about Plymouth State University, students should contact:

Admission Office
MSC #52
Plymouth State University
17 High Street
Plymouth, New Hampshire 03264-1595
Telephone: 603-535-2237
800-842-6900 (toll-free)
Fax: 603-535-2714
E-mail: pscadmit@mail.plymouth.edu
World Wide Web: http://www.plymouth.edu

Students and a faculty member at Plymouth State University.

POINT LOMA NAZARENE UNIVERSITY

SAN DIEGO, CALIFORNIA

The University

Point Loma Nazarene University celebrates more than 100 years of pursing excellence in Christian higher education. Founded as a small Bible college in 1901, the University has grown into a strong liberal arts institution. Still the tradition continues and the mission remains the same—Point Loma Nazarene University is an academically challenging environment and a community seeking to teach, shape, and send compassionate applied scholars.

Students attending Point Loma can expect Christianity to be incorporated into all aspects of their experience. Academically, three religion courses are integrated into the undergraduate curricula. Professors stimulate students' minds by teaching critical-thinking skills, combining faith into learning by encouraging students to ask tough questions. Within the community, students attend weekly chapel services, gathering together as a family for worship, praise, and teaching. Point Loma offers many exciting opportunities for students to take an active part in ministry. There are more than thirty student-led ministries, including accountability groups, Elderly Outreach, Homeless Outreach, Skaters and Surfers for Christ, Mexico Outreach, and international ministry teams.

Point Loma students can also find a wide variety of extracurricular activities in which to be involved, including student government, the yearbook, newspaper, literary magazine, fraternities and sororities, common interest clubs, professional organizations, forensics, theater, musical choirs and bands, intramural sports, and organized athletics. The University competes in National Association of Intercollegiate Athletics (NAIA) Division I and offers basketball, soccer, baseball, tennis, men's golf, cross-country, track and field, softball, and women's volleyball.

The University offers a personal approach to higher education and enrolls more than 2,300 undergraduate students and 500 graduate students. Sixty-seven percent of the undergraduate student body lives in technologically advanced on-campus dormitories, which range from energetic dorm rooms to apartment-style living spaces. The Church of the Nazarene is a large supporter of the University financially, yet more than two thirds of the student body represent various Protestant denominations.

Point Loma Nazarene University is accredited by the Western Association of School and Colleges and offers degree programs at the baccalaureate and graduate levels.

Location

Point Loma Nazarene University is located on a stunning 90-acre oceanfront property on the Point Loma peninsula between the San Diego Bay and the shore of the Pacific Ocean. It is 10 minutes from downtown San Diego and the airport, a half hour from Mexico, and 2 hours from Los Angeles. This ideal location in sunny, culturally rich Southern California provides students with countless internship and recreational opportunities.

Majors and Degrees

Point Loma Nazarene University offers the Bachelor of Arts and Bachelor of Science degrees in more than sixty-two majors and concentrations. Point Loma also offers the Bachelor of Science in Nursing degree. Undergraduate majors include accounting, art, athletic training, Bible and Christian ministries, biology, biology-chemistry, broadcast journalism, business administration, chemistry, child development, church music–youth ministries, computer science, consumer and environmental sciences, economic development, engineering physics, exercise science, family life services, graphic communications, history, industrial-organizational psychology, journalism, liberal studies, literature, managerial and organizational communication, management information systems, mathematics, media communication, music, music-business, nursing, nutrition and food, philosophy, philosophy and theology, physical education, physics, political science, psychology, romance languages, social science, social work, sociology, Spanish, and theater. Optional minors are offered in several departments. Preprofessional and cooperative programs are offered in engineering, prelaw, premedical/predental, pre–physical therapy, and allied health and in AFROTC, AROTC, and NROTC programs. Teaching and service credentials offered include Single Subject with CLAD emphasis (secondary and teacher education) and Multiple Subject with CLAD emphasis (elementary and teacher education).

Academic Program

Point Loma offers a strong Christian liberal arts education that develops character, commitment, reason, and faith. Educationally, Point Loma brings together opportunities for intellectual discourse, leadership development, and spiritual formation within a supportive faith community. The academic program is designed to balance a well-rounded general education program with the depth necessary to concentrate in one of the major programs. The curriculum broadens students' knowledge in the areas of scripture; Christian heritage; analytical, communication, and quantitative skills; natural and social sciences; literature and arts; and historical, cultural, linguistic, and philosophical perspectives. The University offers and encourages travel abroad, semester at sea, and internship programs.

Candidates for the baccalaureate degree are conferred upon successful completion of a total of 128 semester units, including a total of 44 upper-division units; satisfactory completion of the general education program; and completion of a major.

Students who have earned a satisfactory score on the Advanced Placement Examinations (AP), College-Level Examination Program (CLEP), or the International Baccalaureate (IB) exams are eligible to receive credit in applicable areas of the curriculum.

Integrated Semester for Freshmen is a fall semester program of four classes (14 units) for 48 freshmen. The program provides thematic studies and cross-disciplinary learning in a close-knit learning community, positioning students to achieve academic success in their first semester.

The academic year at Point Loma is divided into fall and spring semesters of sixteen weeks followed by two 5-week summer sessions and one 3-week session.

Academic Facilities

Point Loma's facilities are technologically developed to provide students with an excellent learning environment. Ryan Library and Learning Center contains more than 450,000 volumes, group study rooms, three computer labs, a language learning center, media center, and a full television production studio. In addition to these resources, the library also cooperates with the other universities in San Diego through online sharing of databases and interlibrary loan, giving students access to more than 8 million sources of information. The Bond Academic Center houses the Academic Support Center, Tutorial Center, and additional computer labs. Cooper Music Center provides rehearsal facilities for Point Loma music and instrumental groups and state-of-the-art recording and practice rooms. The Fermanian Business Center offers students professional development services and networking opportunities. All residence halls and classrooms are fully equipped with complete Internet access. Also located on campus are an art center and gallery, science research laboratories, a broadcast radio station, aerobic fitness center, and a weight room.

Costs

Tuition is $19,040 (12–17 units per semester). Room and board cost $6570, and fees are $500. Tuition and related expenses at Point Loma are among the lowest for private colleges and universities in Southern California.

Financial Aid

Financial assistance supports students who otherwise would be unable to attend Point Loma. The financial assistance program includes scholarships, grants, loans, part-time employment, and deferred payment programs. Point Loma understands the financial needs of its students and offers institutional financial aid in the form of Nazarene Church grants, need-based grants (ranging from $500 to $1000), diversity scholarships ($250,000 was awarded in 2001), multiple-child discounts, and departmental scholarships. Point Loma also awards students who demonstrate strength in music, theater, forensics, and athletics.

Institutional academic scholarships are available to eligible students. Five full-time and thirty-five half-tuition Honors Scholarships are awarded to first-time freshmen only. To be eligible, the applicant must have a 4.0 or above high school weighted grade point average (GPA) and a minimum 1200 SAT or 27 ACT composite score. The President's Scholarship of $3500 is available to all incoming students with a cumulative GPA of 3.7 or above and a minimum 1150 SAT or 26 ACT composite score. The Dean's Scholarship of $2250 is also available to all qualifying incoming students with a cumulative GPA of 3.5 to 3.69 and a minimum 1050 SAT or 23 ACT score.

All students who are residents of California are encouraged to apply for state and federal programs by submitting a completed Free Application for Federal Student Aid (FAFSA).

Faculty

Point Loma prides itself on the outstanding quality of its faculty. Composed of Christian teachers and scholars who are committed to the lives of students, the University has 140 full-time faculty members, 80 percent with an earned doctorate or the highest degree in their field. While teaching is their first priority, 60 percent of the faculty members pursue their own research through projects in which students have a vital role. Professors, not teacher's assistants, teach all classes. The average class size is 27 students; 85 percent of undergraduate classes enroll fewer than 50 students. With a student-faculty ratio of 15:1, professors at Point Loma are accessible, holding regular office hours to meet with students, and are dedicated to academic, professional, and Christian mentoring.

Student Government

The Associated Student Body (ASB) of Point Loma Nazarene University is composed of the entire student body and is managed by an elected student board of directors who sponsor events and organize activities for social, physical, personal, and spiritual growth.

Point Loma Nazarene University seeks to make a meaningful contribution to the religious life of its students. The University is committed, through positive teaching and spiritual guidance, to preserve the vitality of personal and spiritual experience in its campus community. Students joining the community embrace this spirit and contribute to the spiritual liveliness of Point Loma.

Admission Requirements

Point Loma Nazarene University offers admission to qualified applicants who demonstrate academic achievement, extracurricular and community involvement, and the potential to profit from and contribute to the Point Loma community. Transfer and international students and students who are members of underrepresented groups are welcome and encouraged to apply.

Prospective first-time college students are eligible for admission provided the following conditions are met: a minimum high school GPA of 2.8 with an SAT I combined minimum score of 860 or an ACT composite minimum score of 18. Transfer students may apply provided they have a minimum GPA of a 2.0 (a 2.8 GPA minimum is recommended). High school transcripts and SAT I or ACT scores for transfers must be submitted if the student has fewer than 24 completed college units. For fall 2001, Point Loma accepted 72 percent of the first-time college applicants and 58 percent of transfer applicants. The average GPA of an applicant was 3.65, and the average SAT I score was 1130.

A limited number of first-year students with a high school GPA or test scores below the University's minimums are considered for provisional standing. Provisional students are required to complete an accelerated college-preparatory summer program called Program Quick Start (PQS) before being considered for admission to the University in the fall.

The application for admission includes a formal application for admission, an application fee of $45, three essays, two recommendations, transcripts, official SAT I or ACT score reports, and an interview with an admissions counselor.

Application and Information

Students may apply as early as the fall semester of their senior year in high school or one year prior to transferring from another college or university. Applicants may apply for early action or regular admission. Early action is reserved for students who have made Point Loma Nazarene University one of their top choices, and it provides students with notification of their admission decision by January 15. Early action is not binding; students who are accepted during early action still have until May 1 to make their final college choice. The deadline to be considered for early action is December 1. The priority deadline for regular admission is March 1. Applicants for regular admission and those not offered admission through early action receive notification after February 1 or as admission files are completed. For more information, to arrange a campus visit, or to request more information or an application, students should contact:

Office of Admissions
Point Loma Nazarene University
3900 Lomaland Drive
San Diego, California 92106
Telephone: 619-849-2273
800-733-7770 (toll-free)
Fax: 619-849-2601
World Wide Web: http://www.ptloma.edu

POINT PARK UNIVERSITY

PITTSBURGH, PENNSYLVANIA

The University

Point Park University, founded in 1960, has undergone a vigorous development and is accredited by the Middle States Association of Colleges and Schools. Enrollment has grown to 3,100, and the number of majors available now totals more than fifty, including a Master of Arts in educational administration, Master of Arts degree programs in journalism and mass communications, a Master of Arts in curriculum and instruction, a Master of Science in criminal justice, a Master of Science in engineering management, an accelerated M.B.A., and an M.F.A. in theater arts.

Characterized by a willingness to innovate, the University has been active since its inception in establishing internship possibilities with the many resources for career preparation in Pittsburgh. In addition to those for the performing arts, internship programs have been developed with local broadcasting stations, area hospitals, and the management and technical training programs of such corporate giants as USX and PPG Industries. The University's numerous activities are designed to meet the needs of a diversified student body, representing more than forty-two states and thirty-nine countries. Clubs associated with specific majors, fraternities, sororities, the Point Park University Singers, and the Student Activities Center are a few of the organizations that students may join. Intramural sports include basketball, billiards, flag football, soccer, table tennis, tennis, volleyball, and weight lifting. The men's intercollegiate basketball and baseball teams are perennially included in the National Association of Intercollegiate Athletics (NAIA) national rankings and district and national playoffs. Point Park also has men's intercollegiate cross-country and soccer teams (NAIA). The women's basketball, cross-country, soccer, softball, and volleyball teams add another strong tradition to the Point Park University sports program. The University's teams compete in the American Mideast Conference (AMC).

Location

Metropolitan Pittsburgh has a population of more than 2 million. In the Golden Triangle, gleaming office towers loom high above landscaped plazas, fountains, and a 36-acre park fronting on Pittsburgh's three rivers. More than 100 major corporations have their headquarters in the city, making it the fifth-largest corporate center in the nation. Through its prominence as a corporate hub, a home for high-tech industries, and a major production center for steel, the city provides a vast array of career opportunities, as well as a distinctive population mix. Pittsburgh continues to be named one of the most livable cities in the United States in the *Rand McNally Places Rated Almanac.*

Through the philanthropic efforts of such financial entrepreneurs as Carnegie and Frick, Pittsburgh has had a long tradition as a cultural center. The city has an excellent symphony and ballet, and the Pittsburgh Opera gives performances regularly. Legitimate theater, ethnic festivals, and top nightclub attractions fill out the entertainment spectrum. In addition, the nation's first educational TV station, WQED, provides a wealth of stimulating offerings. PNC Park, Heinz Field, and the Mellon Arena, with its retractable dome, are sites of professional sporting events and frequent entertainment spectacles and are within walking distance of the University. A short bus ride away is the Oakland Civic Center, the location of several renowned museums. Close to Point Park's campus are the YMCA and YWCA, where a nominal fee entitles students to the use of extensive and varied facilities the year round.

Majors and Degrees

The Bachelor of Arts degree is offered in advertising/public relations, applied arts, applied history, behavioral sciences, broadcasting, dance, dance pedagogy, early childhood education, elementary education, English, film and electronic arts, general studies, journalism, legal studies, mass communication, photojournalism, political science, psychology, secondary education, and theater arts. The Bachelor of Fine Arts degree is conferred in dance, film and video production and photography (in conjunction with Pittsburgh Filmmakers), and theater arts. The Bachelor of Science degree is conferred in accounting, biological sciences, biotechnology, business management, civil engineering technology, criminal justice, electrical engineering technology, environmental health science and protection, general studies, health services, human resources management, information technology, management services, mathematics/secondary education, mechanical engineering technology, public administration, specialized professional studies–funeral service, and sport, arts, and entertainment management.

Preparation for teachers in secondary education is a cooperative effort of the Department of Education and the department of the student's major subject. Programs in predental, prelaw, and premedical studies are arranged within suitable majors.

Academic Program

Point Park is an innovative institution. Its philosophy is one of meeting and adapting to individual requirements within the framework of a sound humanistic education. This commitment is reflected in programs that, while providing for the expansion of mind and spirit that the liberal arts alone can give, places strong emphasis on developing career skills. Thus, all degree programs, with the exception of the B.F.A. programs, include a core curriculum requirement of 42 credit hours. The core curriculum includes choices in the humanities as well as in the social, behavioral, and natural sciences. Aside from completing the prerequisites for major offerings, students may elect to fulfill their core requirements on a schedule of their own choosing. At the same time, the student's introduction to specific career preparation can begin in the first semester. Indeed, this is typical for students majoring in computer science, dance, engineering technology, film production, journalism and communications, and theater arts. In order to encourage student experimentation, the University permits eight courses from the core curriculum to be taken under a pass/fail option.

With the approval of their guidance offices, high school students may take courses at Point Park for full college credit. The University grants advanced standing on the basis of the College Board's Advanced Placement tests, the CLEP examinations, and educational experiences in the armed forces. In addition, the University has long-standing experience in meeting the needs of transfer students.

The academic calendar consists of two semesters and a summer schedule offering two 6-week sessions and one 12-week session. This year-round utilization of facilities, combined with the University's extensive evening and Saturday programs, provides students with maximum flexibility in planning their schedules.

Off-Campus Programs

Point Park's membership in the Pittsburgh Council on Higher Education gives students the chance to cross-register at any of nine area institutions, including the University of Pittsburgh and Carnegie Mellon University.

Point Park University gives students the opportunity to earn a number of credits at various off-campus sites.

Academic Facilities

The Library Center of Point Park University, a joint operation with the Carnegie Library of Pittsburgh, opened in downtown Pittsburgh in May 1997. The Library Center houses the Point Park University Library and the Carnegie Library of Pittsburgh's Downtown and Business Information Center. Students have access to a 110,000-volume collection, 600 current periodicals and newspapers, and 100 computer terminals and are able to access online databases, CD-ROM, e-mail, and the Internet. This is the first collaborative effort between a private institution and a public library. A science and journalism laboratory complex, on-campus radio and television studios, ownership of the newspaper and magazine, an on-campus laboratory school, on-campus dance studios, numerous computer terminal rooms, a CADD lab, and other facilities and programs contribute to the University's philosophy of carefully balancing theory with practical experience. The University's location in the heart of Pittsburgh's business district opens numerous opportunities for practical learning. Point Park owns and operates the Pittsburgh Playhouse of Point Park University, which shows fifteen dance and theater performances per year.

Costs

For 2002–03, tuition and fees for full-time study totaled $7590 per semester. The charge for part-time study was $397 per credit hour. Room and board were $3230 per term for double occupancy. The majority of rooms are for double occupancy with private bath and phone.

Financial Aid

Point Park makes a sincere effort to ensure that each student who desires to attend is able to do so. Accordingly, the University administers a generous program of financial aid, including Federal Work-Study awards and Point Park, Federal Pell, and Federal Supplemental Educational Opportunity grants. The University administers loans under the Federal Perkins Loan Program and the Federal Stafford Student Loan Program. Academic, talent, and athletic scholarships are also available for all students, including transfer students.

Applicants for financial aid must demonstrate financial need and show evidence of academic promise or achievement. To apply, students must submit a completed University application form. All students must submit applications for federal, state, and Point Park financial aid through the Pennsylvania Higher Education Assistance Agency (PHEAA).

Faculty

Full- and part-time faculty members provide undergraduate instruction at an average faculty-student ratio of 1:15. Forty-four percent of full-time faculty members in the academic disciplines hold doctoral degrees. Faculty members in the performing arts and practical disciplines are involved in their professions outside of the University as well as in the classroom. The top priority among this faculty group is the instruction of undergraduate students rather than specialized research and publication. Students are advised throughout their college career by a designated faculty member in their major area.

Student Government

The United Student Government actively participates in the affairs of the University. The Student Affairs Committee acts in conjunction with the dean of students to coordinate social programs on the campus as well as to provide input for University policy.

Admission Requirements

Point Park University is very much concerned with the needs and interests of its students. This concern is extended not only to matriculated students but also to prospective students. For this reason, the admissions staff pursues a policy that is individualized, personal, and humanistic. Each student is viewed in terms of his or her own personal and academic potential. Recommendations from guidance counselors and teachers and an interview, while not required, are considered, along with motivational factors and relative maturity, in conjunction with the traditional objective criteria, such as class rank, high school record, and standardized test scores. All candidates are required to take either the SAT I or the ACT.

Application and Information

Applications for the fall semester are taken on a rolling basis; however, students are urged to apply early in their senior year of secondary school. Early application is particularly important for students desiring residence hall accommodations and financial aid. Applications from freshman and transfer candidates are also considered for the spring semester and should be filed by December 15. The University requires each freshman applicant to submit an application, a nonrefundable $20 fee, SAT I or ACT scores, and an official high school transcript. Transfer applicants must also submit official transcripts from all colleges and postsecondary schools attended.

Application forms and additional information may be obtained by writing to:

Office of Admission
Point Park University
201 Wood Street
Pittsburgh, Pennsylvania 15222-1984
Telephone: 412-392-3430
800-321-0129 (toll-free)
Fax: 412-392-3902
E-mail: enroll@ppc.edu
World Wide Web: http://www.ppc.edu

Point Park students enjoy the many social and sporting activities that Pittsburgh has to offer.

POLYTECHNIC UNIVERSITY

BROOKLYN, NEW YORK

The University

Long recognized as a leading technological university and research center, Polytechnic University offers fourteen majors leading to degrees in the arts and sciences, computer science, engineering, and information management. Founded in 1854 as Polytechnic Institute of Brooklyn (Brooklyn Poly), it is the second-oldest independent technological university in the United States. Polytechnic has a main campus in the MetroTech neighborhood of Brooklyn, New York, and graduate centers in Long Island, Manhattan, and Westchester. Polytechnic has an undergraduate student body of 1,525.

Polytechnic University is a microcosm of greater New York. Undergraduates come from nineteen states and nineteen countries. The students represent a mosaic of racial, ethnic, religious, and cultural backgrounds, all working together to achieve common goals. A student-faculty ratio of 12:1 enables students to work closely with professors in both the classroom and the research lab. Located at Polytechnic are a variety of research centers where students and world-renowned faculty members are involved in exciting and innovative fields of study, including telecommunications, electronic business, robotics, aerospace, digital systems, and wireless communications. Although it emphasizes science and engineering, the University has long recognized the importance of tempering technology with humanistic understanding.

The University offers a wide variety of student activities. The Student Council, a school newspaper and magazine, and a photography club are just a few of the options available. A number of academic organizations, many with national affiliations, host programs, lectures, and discussion groups for students majoring in the various disciplines. Athletics—from basketball to volleyball—are popular and widely available at Polytechnic on both intercollegiate and intramural levels.

The University offers on-campus housing in the new Othmer Residence Hall. Campus housing is available for matriculated, full-time, undergraduate, and graduate students. The residence hall is located across the street from the MetroTech campus in downtown Brooklyn. It features 4-student, two-bedroom suites for underclassmen and two-bedroom apartments for upperclassmen. Amenities include rooms that are fully wired for personal computers, laptops, cable TV, and telephone access; study rooms; student lounges; 24-hour security; a laundry room; and a modern dining hall.

Students can use the central computer labs and various specialized labs, connect wirelessly with a laptop, or dial in from home. The University was voted among the "100 Most Wired Colleges" by *Yahoo! Internet Life*.

Location

Polytechnic is located in the heart of historic downtown Brooklyn and in the middle of MetroTech Center, a 16-acre, $1-billion academic/professional park in New York City. Situated at the foot of the famous Brooklyn Bridge, just across from the tip of Manhattan, the campus is the gateway to such places as Wall Street, Broadway, and the South Street Seaport on one side of the river and the Brooklyn Museum and Prospect Park on the other. All of these attractions are readily accessible via public transportation and a network of modern highways.

Exceptional careers begin with exceptional locations, and Polytechnic has an unrivaled one in the greater New York area. Serving students with a dynamic range of experiences and powerful examples of excellence, New York City gives a unique context to their studies. In addition, it places them in the middle of an international capital with diverse surroundings, unique perspectives, vibrant cultures, and thriving enterprises. The career opportunities are virtually everywhere—from Wall Street to New York's new media industry, affectionately dubbed "Silicon Alley."

Majors and Degrees

Polytechnic University offers the Bachelor of Science degree. The undergraduate majors include biomedical sciences (premed), business and technology management, chemical engineering, chemistry, civil engineering, computer engineering, computer science, construction management, electrical engineering, liberal studies, mathematics, mechanical/aerospace engineering, physics, psychology, and technical and professional communication. Several five-year B.S./M.S. programs are also available.

Academic Programs

While requirements vary according to the major, students must complete an average of 128 credits with an average of at least 2.0 (on a 4.0 scale) to earn the Bachelor of Science degree. Science and engineering students begin fundamental courses in their specialties during their second year and concentrate on advanced courses in their last two years.

Recent academic initiatives include a newly established Honors College and an admission assurance program with the State University of New York Health Science Center at Brooklyn for outstanding premed students.

The unique Freshman Guarantee Program ensures that enrolled students will receive a career-related job offer within six months of graduation. If they do not, the University will award them a scholarship for up to 18 credits of graduate study at Polytechnic. Students in this program work closely with counselors from the Office of Career Services and are required to participate in internship programs throughout their studies.

Academic Facilities

The Bern Dibner Library of Science and Technology houses one of the finest collections of technical and scientific literature in the metropolitan area. In addition, the library hosts a massive collection of online reference databases to assist in classwork and scholarly research. A $130-million upgrade to the MetroTech campus is reflected in a newly constructed academic building, a modern residence hall, a new athletic facility, new labs, and a state-of-the-art computing infrastructure. Wireless networking is available, allowing students to connect to the University network and the Internet from virtually anywhere on campus. New computer labs feature high-end workstations for research, 3-D modeling, and dynamic simulation.

Well known for scientific and technological discovery, Polytechnic sponsors a number of important research centers that typically involve multidisciplinary teams of Polytechnic faculty members, research staff members, and students. Included among these centers are the Institute for Mathematics and Advanced Supercomputing, the Transportation Research Institute, the Othmer Institute for Interdisciplinary Studies, and the Polymer Research Institute, the oldest academic center of polymer (plastics) investigation in the United States. In 1983, the University was designated a Center for Advanced Technology in Telecommunications in New York State.

Costs

Tuition for 2003–04 was $24,800. Estimates of other expenses were $970 for fees, $600 for books, $1564 for personal expenses, and $8000 for room and board.

Financial Aid

Scholarships and loans are the principal sources of financial aid for full-time undergraduates. Federal sources of funds include Federal Pell Grants, Federal Supplemental Educational Opportunity Grants, Federal Stafford Student Loans, Federal Perkins Loans, and Federal Work-Study Program awards. New York State residents may be eligible for assistance under the New York State Tuition Assistance Program. In addition to the usual financial aid programs, Polytechnic offers a large number of scholarships, including several full-cost, four-year scholarships that are awarded to students admitted to the Honors College. The University offers a unique Poly-Loan-to-Grant program that offers students from $2000 to $5000 in loans each year. Under this program, loan recipients who maintain at least a 2.75 GPA while on a full-time track of study receive this money as a grant at the time of graduation—a potential tuition savings of $20,000. Approximately 98 percent of all undergraduates at the University receive some financial aid. Opportunities for student employment are good.

The average scholarship offer for 2003–04 was more than $9400, while the average financial aid package was more than $19,239.

Students desiring financial assistance should submit the Free Application for Federal Student Aid, preferably by March 1. For more detailed information about financial aid, students should contact the Office of Financial Aid at Polytechnic.

Faculty

Polytechnic has 160 full-time faculty members, 90 percent of whom have doctoral degrees. Most of the faculty members teach both graduate and undergraduate courses. The University's faculty is world renowned for the research and scholarly publications of its members. Several are members of the National Academy of Engineering, and many are frequent recipients of both national and international awards for excellence. Recent examples include the Institute of Electrical and Electronics Engineers' Educational Medal for Excellence, the President's Medal of Sciences, and the prestigious Humboldt Award. The American Society for Engineering Education recently ranked the graduate electrical engineering faculty among the top ten in the nation for scholarly activity; many of its members also teach on the undergraduate level.

Student Government

The Student Council is an important force on campus. They direct the activities of the undergraduate student body and speak for student interests. As the administrating agency for student fees, the councils allocate money to student organizations, publications, and activities. Student representatives serve on many faculty and administrative committees dealing with all phases of academic and student life.

Admission Requirements

Admission to Polytechnic is competitive. Candidates must submit a formal application for admission, a secondary school transcript, two academic recommendations, and standardized test scores (SAT I or ACT). The Committee on Admissions evaluates each applicant on an individual basis regardless of financial need and seeks students who rank in the top 25 percent of their graduating class, have taken three to four years of college-preparatory math and science, and have achieved a grade average of B+ or higher.

Students whose first language is not English are advised to submit scores on the Test of English as a Foreign Language (TOEFL). This test must be taken by all international applicants whose native language is not English regardless of whether or not their previous education was conducted in English. Students can also meet the language requirement by completing the Berlitz on Campus intensive language program. Polytechnic University is a host school for the Berlitz program. Advanced placement is awarded to students whose scores on the Advanced Placement tests indicate proficiency in a given subject.

Application and Information

A completed application form, $50 application fee, and supporting documents are required for evaluation of prospective students. Applications should be submitted as early as possible, preferably by February 1 for admission in the fall, and December 1 for admission in the spring. Admission decisions are made on a rolling basis. The deadline for early admission is at the end of the applicant's junior year in high school. Early Action candidates for freshman admission who submit their applications by November 1 receive an admission decision by December 1. Students participating in Early Action are not obliged to attend Polytechnic University.

For application forms and additional information, students should contact:

Office of Undergraduate Admissions
Polytechnic University
6 MetroTech Center
Brooklyn, New York 11201
Telephone: 718-260-3589
E-mail: admitme@poly.edu
World Wide Web: http://www.poly.edu/admissions

A view of the campus at Polytechnic University.

POMONA COLLEGE

CLAREMONT, CALIFORNIA

The College

An undergraduate residential college of 1,500 students, Pomona College is consistently recognized as one of the nation's finest colleges of the liberal arts and sciences. Pomona has been coeducational since its founding in 1887, and today it enrolls a student body whose diversity and talents are unmatched by those of similar institutions.

With complete devotion to undergraduate education and a student-faculty ratio of less than 9:1, the College enables students to interact closely with faculty members. As both researchers and teachers, Pomona's faculty provide students the opportunity to participate in research in almost every academic discipline, an experience that is unusual at institutions of any size.

Pomona's substantial endowment guarantees students access to resources and facilities rarely found at a college of this size. The endowment also supports a need-blind admissions program as well as a financial aid commitment to meeting each student's demonstrated need.

Pomona College is the founding member of the Claremont Colleges, five undergraduate colleges and two graduate schools that together constitute a major academic community of 5,000 students. Pomona students benefit from the additional resources of the consortium and share the academic and social opportunities available at a university without sacrificing the individual focus of a small college.

More than 95 percent of Pomona's students live on campus in the College's twelve dormitories. The campus is a center of social activities, including several film series, lectures and discussions, and student and professional music and theater productions, as well as a variety of more informal social events. Nineteen varsity and twelve club athletic teams compete intercollegiately, while intramural sports involve more than two thirds of the student body. The Liliore Green Rains Center for Sport and Recreation houses two gymnasiums, complete weight and training facilities, and six racquetball and squash courts. The facility is complemented by an all-weather track and field, fourteen lighted tennis courts, a 50-meter swimming pool, and renovated baseball, football, and soccer fields. The Smith Campus Center features a 200-seat movie theater, student organization offices and lounges, meeting rooms, the college store, the career development office, the multicultural center, game rooms, a snack bar, and dining facilities.

Location

A residential community of 35,000 near the foothills of the San Gabriel Mountains, Claremont offers a quiet environment and easy accessibility. The Pomona campus and the center of town are readily traveled on foot or by bicycle. Thirty-five miles to the west of Claremont lies Los Angeles, the commercial and cultural capital of the western United States. Students can take full advantage of one of the world's greatest cities, as well as of all of southern California's cultural, educational, and recreational opportunities.

Majors and Degrees

Pomona College grants the Bachelor of Arts degree in the fields of American studies, anthropology, art and art history, Asian studies, biology, Black studies, chemistry, Chinese, classics, computer science, economics, English, foreign languages, foreign literatures, French, geology, German, German studies, history, international relations, Japanese, linguistics, mathematics, media studies, molecular biology, music, neuroscience, philosophy, physics (astronomy option), politics, PPE (philosophy, politics, and economics), psychology, religious studies, Russian, sociology, Spanish, STS (science, technology, and society), theater/dance, and women's studies. Pomona sponsors 3-2 programs in engineering with the California Institute of Technology in Pasadena and with Washington University in St. Louis, Missouri. Students may also pursue independent study or design their own concentrations. Programs complementing the forty concentrations available include Chicano studies and public policy analysis.

Academic Program

To receive the Bachelor of Arts degree, Pomona College students take thirty-two courses. In 1994, the faculty developed and adopted an innovative general education program unique among college and university programs. The program is built around the development of perception, analysis, and communication skills in ten key areas: reading literature critically; using and understanding the scientific method; using and understanding formal reasoning; understanding and analyzing data; analyzing creative art critically; performing or producing creative art; exploring and understanding human behavior; exploring and understanding a historical culture; comparing and contrasting contemporary cultures; and thinking critically about values and rationality.

In addition to fulfilling the general education requirements, students must demonstrate proficiency in a foreign language and take writing-intensive and speaking-intensive classes. All freshmen enroll in Critical Inquiry, a writing-intensive, discussion-oriented seminar with enrollment limited to 15.

More than two thirds of the College's classes enroll fewer than 20 students; the average class size is 14 students. The seminar format promotes discussion and encourages students to challenge themselves, one another, and the faculty members and allows a variety of viewpoints to enhance the learning process. Pomona College offers 600 classes annually, and students can choose from more than 2,500 classes offered at the Claremont Colleges.

Credits may be awarded for Advanced Placement work and college-level courses taken in high school. The Claremont Colleges are on a semester calendar that begins in early September and ends in mid-May.

Off-Campus Programs

Pomona College encourages students to broaden their educational experiences with several programs that go beyond the traditional classroom setting. The Oldenborg Center for Modern Languages and International Relations is a dormitory for language study and the setting of the international relations colloquia. Almost half of the College's students study abroad, choosing from thirty-nine programs in thirty-five locations in twenty-two countries. Pomona students take internships in Washington, D.C., and participate in exchange programs with Colby, Smith, Spelman, and Swarthmore colleges.

A number of programs provide students practical experience while they are still undergraduates. The Office of Career Development arranges internships with more than 100 organizations in the Los Angeles area. The Claremont Colleges Liberal Arts Clinics allow students to use their knowledge and experience in solving immediate, real-world problems presented by industries and governments.

Academic Facilities

Pomona College students have access to facilities that are among the finest at any small liberal arts college. The renovations to the Seaver Science Center and the addition of a new life sciences building that is scheduled to include an array of conservation features is expected to become one of the nation's "greenest" laboratories. The 46,000-square-foot addition is scheduled to house the laboratories and offices of the biology department and the molecular biology program. The facilities house state-of-the-art laboratory equipment available for use by undergraduates. Brackett Observatory has two telescopes—one 12-inch and one 22-inch; the College operates a 40-inch telescope with the Jet Propulsion Laboratory at Table Mountain Observatory in the San Gabriel Mountains. With two microcomputer labs on campus, students have access to computers for unrestricted academic use. A teaching theater complex opened in 1990 and contains an auditorium seating 350, a 100-seat experimental "black box" theater, two studios, and costume and set shops.

In addition to the wealth of resources available at Pomona, students can take advantage of the facilities of the Claremont Colleges. These include a jointly held library system with holdings of more than 2 million volumes, two art galleries (Montgomery Gallery is at Pomona), a major bookstore, and a 2,500-seat performance hall.

Costs

Expenses for full-paying students in 2003–04 were tuition, $26,890; room and board, $9980; fees, $260; and books and personal expenses, approximately $1800.

Financial Aid

Pomona College guarantees to fund the full financial need of every enrolling student and admits students without regard to their ability to pay. The College awards aid on the basis of demonstrated financial need. More than 50 percent of the students receive some form of aid, which includes a combination of grants, loans, and part-time employment.

Faculty

All faculty members above the rank of lecturer hold a doctoral degree except in fields where a doctorate is not customary. As an undergraduate college, at Pomona all courses are taught by professors. The student-faculty ratio of less than 9:1 and the average class size of 14 ensure that students can work closely with their professors. The first priority of the faculty is to teach, but the College also recognizes that scholarship plays an essential role in the teaching process. In recent years, Pomona faculty have received grants in support of their research from such agencies as the National Science Foundation, the National Institutes of Health, the National Endowment for the Humanities, the Howard Hughes Medical Institute, and the Pew Charitable Trusts, and they publish annually more than 250 articles and reviews, many of which are coauthored by students.

Student Government

Officers of the Associated Students of Pomona College coordinate student activities and administer the affairs and properties of the Associated Students. Since most matters that affect the College are of concern to both faculty members and students, students also sit as voting members of policy-forming committees. Each residence hall is self-governing.

Admission Requirements

Admission to Pomona College is highly selective, based on a thorough review of each candidate's application materials. The Office of Admissions admits a freshman class whose members represent a broad range of interests, viewpoints, talents, and backgrounds. At Pomona, a diverse student body is considered an educational asset.

The primary criterion for admission is academic achievement. Eighty-five percent of the freshmen enrolled in 2003 were in the top 10 percent of their high school graduating class; their combined median SAT I scores were 1450.

Beyond academic achievement, Pomona seeks students who are aware of a broader world around them—locally, nationally, and internationally—students who have demonstrated a sense of responsibility and commitment to a larger community. The College enrolls students who have shown leadership or special talents in the sciences, communications, the arts, music, theater, athletics, government, or community service.

Early admission, deferred entrance, and transfer admission are available. Freshman candidates may apply under early decision or regular decision programs. The College admits first-year students for entrance in the fall semester only.

Students are strongly encouraged to visit the campus and arrange for an interview before applying. Information sessions and tours are offered daily and require no appointment. Freshman candidates outside of southern California who cannot visit Pomona may request an interview with an alumni volunteer.

Application and Information

Students applying to Pomona College are expected to furnish transcripts of all their academic work in high school and college; a school recommendation; two teacher references; and either ACT or SAT I and SAT II results. If students choose to take the SAT I, they must also take SAT II Subject Tests in writing and in two other subjects of their choice. Interviews are very strongly recommended but not required. All application materials must be received by November 15 for early decision I applicants, by December 28 for early decision II applicants, or by January 2 for regular decision applicants. The transfer application deadline is March 15 for fall admission.

For further information, students should contact:

Office of Admissions
Pomona College
333 North College Way
Claremont, California 91711-6312
Telephone: 909-621-8134
E-mail: admissions@pomona.edu
World Wide Web: http://www.pomona.edu

Carnegie Building, Pomona College.

PRAIRIE VIEW A&M UNIVERSITY

PRAIRIE VIEW, TEXAS

The University

The modern mission of Prairie View A&M University was most recently redefined by the people of Texas by an amendment to the state's constitution in 1984. Through that amendment, Prairie View A&M University joined the University of Texas at Austin and Texas A&M University as the state's only constitutionally designated "institutions of the first class." In support of that designation, in 1985, the Board of Regents of the Texas A&M University System expressed its intention that Prairie View A&M University become "an institution nationally recognized in its areas of education and research." Prairie View A&M University is a land-grant institution by federal statute. It is also a statewide special-purpose institution by state statute.

While striving to maintain excellent instruction and a strong curriculum, the University nurtures students' academic development and intellectual curiosity by providing a stimulating physical and cultural environment. As a special-purpose university, Prairie View A&M develops special programming to identify and assist talented students who may otherwise be overlooked. The University believes it can and should help students understand some of the possibilities of the mind and spirit so that they may be productive citizens and lead fulfilling lives.

The enrollment at Prairie View exceeds 7,600 students. Men account for 41 percent, while women account for 59 percent of the total enrollment. Approximately 95 percent of the students are state residents. Students from other countries account for 2 percent of the total enrollment. Approximately 70 percent of the students are between the ages of 18 and 24. On-campus housing consists of an ultramodern freshman residential complex and twenty-nine apartment buildings, which collectively accommodate 3,390 students. Each residence hall room is equipped with a direct-line telephone, cable television services, a microwave, and a freezer/refrigerator. The apartment buildings consist of suites with two or four private bedroom units, a community living room, and a kitchenette. A limited number (about 30 percent) of the apartments have full kitchens. All housing facilities have accommodations (per ADA requirements) for the physically challenged.

Student life programs are aimed at giving students an opportunity to achieve their educational and career goals without neglecting the support, encouragement, and sense of community that foster a feeling of belonging. The student development staff is committed to enriching the University environment so that students can establish personal value systems and refine interpersonal skills in support of their lifetime aims and objectives. Student organizations include sororities, fraternities, honor societies, the band, the choir, religious groups, special interest clubs, drama (Charles Gilpin Players), the forensic team, and social clubs. Students also have the opportunity to enhance their leadership skills. The University Marching and Symphonic Bands and the Percussion Ensemble develop students' musical talents. The Prairie View Panthers varsity sports teams for men and women compete in the Southwestern Athletic Conference and in NCAA baseball, basketball, bowling, football, golf, softball, tennis, track, and volleyball. Active intramural sports and recreational programs are provided.

Location

The main campus of Prairie View A&M University is situated on a 1,440-acre site in Waller County, approximately 40 miles northwest of Houston. It is accessible by major highways; bus service is available from Houston, Austin, and Dallas. Bush Intercontinental Airport and Hobby Airport provide air transportation. The University's location offers the advantages of a pleasant, semirural environment with convenient access to the excitement of a major American city. The city of Prairie View provides an opportunity to observe government at close range. There are a variety of restaurants, shopping facilities, rodeo events, and ethnic festivals, as well as access to lakes for water sports and facilities for horseback riding in the area.

Majors and Degrees

The University offers the following undergraduate degrees: Bachelor of Architecture, Bachelor of Arts, Bachelor of Arts in Social Work, Bachelor of Business Administration, Bachelor of Music, and Bachelor of Science. Undergraduate degree majors include accounting, accounting and information systems, agricultural engineering, agriculture, applied music, architecture, biology, chemical engineering, chemistry, civil engineering, communications, computer-aided drafting and design, computer engineering technology, computer science, criminal justice, dietetics, drama, electrical engineering, electrical engineering technology, English, family and community services, finance, health, history, human development and the family, human performance, human science, industrial technology, interdisciplinary studies, management, marketing, mathematics, mechanical engineering, mechanical engineering technology, merchandising and design, music, nursing, physics, political science, psychology, social work, sociology, and Spanish. Coordinate degrees are offered in biology, business, chemistry, education, engineering, human sciences, and sociology.

Academic Programs

The requirements for a bachelor's degree at Prairie View A&M University ensure that graduates have a well-rounded educational experience. Students must complete the University core course requirements in addition to the specific course and semester-hour requirements for the degree program selected. The University requires a minimum of 120 semester hours and at least a 2.0 cumulative grade point average for graduation. Specializations are offered within the major areas of study in some degree programs. The University awards credit for successful scores on the Advanced Placement examinations. Highly motivated students are rewarded with an opportunity to challenge themselves academically through the accelerated courses offered by the University Scholars Program. Military science programs include Army ROTC and Naval ROTC. Cooperative education programs are available in some departments. Support services, tutoring, assessment testing, career exploration, precollege programs, international-student advising, undecided-major advising, multicultural programs, crisis counseling, and placement counseling are offered through the Offices of Career Services, Cooperative Education, School Relations, and Developmental Studies; the Center for Academic Support; the Academic Advising Center; the Academy for Collegiate Excellence and Student Success (ACCESS); and University College.

The academic calendar is based on the semester system. In addition, three-, five-, eight-, and ten-week summer sessions are offered. The normal course load ranges from 12 semester hours to 18 semester hours during the regular academic year and up to a maximum of 12 semester hours during the summer terms.

Academic Facilities

Modern facilities include well-equipped classrooms and laboratories. Specially designed studios, theaters, and auditoriums are available for the visual and performing arts. The most modern facilities include a science building, a multimedia foreign language laboratory, an engineering technology building, a chemical engineering building, and the John B. Coleman Library, which features state-of-the-art equipment, an expanded Learning Resources Center, and a laboratory for computer-assisted instruction. The library contains more than 300,000 volumes, 618,663 microforms, and several special collections. More than 2,000 periodicals and other serials are currently received by the library. Nursing students who have fulfilled their foundation course work complete five semesters in the College of Nursing facility, located in the heart of the Houston medical complex. Other campus facilities include the Academic Computing Center and studios for Prairie View's radio station (KPVU) and cable television operations.

Costs

For 2003–04, students who are Texas residents paid $46 per semester hour but not less than $120 per academic semester. Out-of-state students paid $282 per semester hour. On-campus residence hall and University Village room rates vary according to the accommodations selected. All students who reside in University residence halls are required to participate in the University food service plan; students have the option of five, seven, ten, fourteen, or twenty-one cafeteria-style meals per week. The approximate total cost of room and board was $5510 per academic year. Annual costs of books and supplies vary according to major and class load but typically average $600. Additional fees vary, but the minimum full-time charge was $1832 per semester for a student enrolled for 15 semester hours.

Financial Aid

Prairie View A&M University administers a wide range of programs to help students meet the cost of attending the University. Various factors are considered in determining who qualifies for financial aid. Programs available to provide financial support include academic and need-based scholarships, state and federal loans and grants, and student employment. Students are required to complete a need analysis to determine their extent of need and eligibility for aid. Approximately 80 percent of the students at Prairie View receive some form of financial assistance. For more information, students should contact the Office of Student Financial Services at 936-857-2424.

Faculty

The University's faculty consists of 300 full-time faculty members, 73 percent of whom have earned doctoral degrees.

Student Government

All members of the student body are members of the Student Government Association (SGA). The SGA is the official voice through which students' opinions may be expressed. Its elected student members provide effective representation and responsible participation in the overall policymaking and decision-making processes of the University. While the SGA promotes academic excellence and quality education, its student members have the opportunity to obtain valuable leadership and management experience. The SGA also recommends students to serve on various committees and advisory boards of the University.

Admission Requirements

Admission to Prairie View A&M University is open to qualified individuals regardless of race, color, sex, creed, age, national origin, or educationally unrelated handicap. To apply for admission, students must provide a completed application and a $25 application fee, a certified high school transcript or a GED certificate (high school equivalency diploma), and SAT or ACT scores. In addition to the admission application, transfer applicants must submit transcripts from previous colleges attended and the confidential questionnaire. International students must also submit an Affidavit of Financial Support and Test of English as a Foreign Language (TOEFL) scores, along with supporting documents. Applicants should note that the Texas State Education Code requires that all students "who enter Texas public institutions of higher education in the fall of 1989 and thereafter must be tested for reading, writing, and mathematics skills." This includes all "full-time and part-time students enrolled in a certificate or degree program." Transfer students must provide Texas Higher Education Assessment (THEA) scores or proof of exemption or take the test. Students who plan to enroll must take the TASP test before enrolling in any college-level courses.

Application and Information

Office of Undergraduate Admissions
Telephone: 936-857-2626
Fax: 936-857-2699
E-mail: admissions@pvamu.edu
or
Office of Recruitment and Special Programs
Telephone: 936-857-3981
Fax: 936-857-2160
E-mail: recruitment@pvamu.edu
Prairie View A&M University
P.O. Box 3089
Prairie View, Texas 77446
World Wide Web: http://www.pvamu.edu

The Wilhelmina Fitzgerald Delco building.

PRATT INSTITUTE

BROOKLYN, NEW YORK

The Institute

Founded in 1887 on its present site in Brooklyn by industrialist and philanthropist Charles Pratt, the Institute educated on nonbaccalaureate levels for its first half-century. As the educational preparation necessary for various professions expanded, Pratt Institute moved with the times. It granted its first baccalaureate degree in 1938 and started its first graduate program in 1950. Pratt continues to add programs at all educational levels, including undergraduate and graduate programs in art history and graduate programs in art education and design management. Although the characteristics and educational requirements of the professions for which Pratt prepares people have changed over the course of a century, the Institute has succeeded in pursuing its abiding purpose—to blend theoretical learning with professional and humanistic development.

In educating more than four generations of students to be creative, technically skilled, and adaptable professionals as well as responsible citizens, Pratt has gained a national and international reputation that attracts undergraduate and graduate students from more than forty-six states, the District of Columbia, Puerto Rico, the Virgin Islands, and seventy countries. Unlike the typical American college student, most of those who choose Pratt already have career objectives, or at least they know they want to study art, design, architecture, or creative writing.

A short bus or subway ride from the museum, gallery, and design centers of both Manhattan and Brooklyn, Pratt Institute has twenty-four buildings of differing architectural styles spread about a 25-acre campus. Eighteen of the buildings house studios, classrooms, laboratories, administrative offices, auditoria, sports facilities, food services, and student centers. Six buildings are student residences, including the new Stabile Hall freshman residence, which provides studio space on each floor. There are adequate parking facilities for residents and commuters. Student services include career planning and placement, health and counseling, and student development. The more than sixty student organizations include fraternities and sororities, honorary societies, professional societies, and clubs.

Location

Pratt Institute, the country's premier college of art, design, writing, and architecture is located in the Clinton Hill section of Brooklyn, just minutes from downtown Manhattan. The majority of Pratt's freshmen live on the school's 25-acre, tree-lined campus. Pratt offers four-year bachelor's, two-year associate, and combined bachelor's and master's degrees.

Majors and Degrees

Pratt Institute offers the Bachelor of Architecture, Bachelor of Fine Arts, Bachelor of Art, Bachelor of Industrial Design, Bachelor of Professional Studies, Bachelor of Science, Associate of Occupational Studies, and Associate of Applied Science degrees.

The Bachelor of Architecture degree program is a five-year accredited program. For the Bachelor of Fine Arts degree, a candidate may choose to major in art and design education, art history, communications design (advertising, graphic design, illustration), computer graphics, fashion design, fashion merchandising and management, film/video, fine arts (ceramics, drawing, jewelry, painting, printmaking, sculpture), industrial design, interior design, photography, or writing for publication, performance, and media. The Bachelor of Art is in cultural studies and art history. In the Bachelor of Professional Studies degree program, the major is in construction management. Students seeking the Bachelor of Science degree can major in construction management. The two-year Associate of Occupational Studies degree is offered in digital design and interactive media, graphic design, and illustration. The Associate of Applied Science is offered in painting/drawing and graphic design/illustration. This two-year degree is transferable to a four-year program.

Students may also earn combined bachelor's/master's degrees. Programs include the B.F.A./M.S. in art history.

Academic Program

Educating artists and creative professionals to be responsible contributors to society has been the mission of Pratt Institute since it assembled its first group of students in 1887. Within the structure of that professional education, Pratt students are encouraged to acquire the diverse knowledge that is necessary for them to succeed in their chosen fields. In addition to the professional studies, the curriculum in each of Pratt's schools includes a broad range of liberal arts courses. Students from all schools take these courses together and have the opportunity to examine the interrelationships of art, science, technology, and human need.

At the time of graduation, students in the associate degree programs have completed 67 credit hours of course work. In the bachelor's programs, credit-hour requirements range from 132 to 135 credits, depending on the particular program. For the Bachelor of Architecture degree, 175 credits are required.

Pratt's academic calendar consists of two semesters plus optional summer terms that allows students to choose alternative courses or various options usually not offered during the fall or spring semester. A number of summer sessions are offered.

Off-Campus Programs

Pratt Institute offers credit for a wide variety of off-campus study programs. The Internship Program offers qualified students challenging on-the-job experience related to their major fields of interest; this extension of the classroom and laboratory into the professional world adds a practical dimension to periods of on-campus study.

International programs, available during all academic sessions, have included art and design offerings in the cities of Copenhagen and Rome and in the countries of England, France, and Italy. Architecture programs have been held in Venice, Italy, and in Finland and Japan. New programs are developed regularly in these and other countries.

Academic Facilities

Founded as the first free library in Brooklyn, the Pratt Institute Library now has more than 208,175 bound volumes, 540 periodical and newspaper subscriptions, 66,000 slides, 190,000 pictures, and 50,000 microforms the largest collection of any independent art school. Through the use of their ID cards, Pratt students also have access to numerous college libraries in the metropolitan area. The Multi-Media Center has been developed to facilitate and improve the educational communication process by providing materials in multimedia formats to support and enrich the Institute's curricula. These include slides, ¾-inch videotapes, 16-mm films, audiocassettes, and other formats appropriate for group use.

Extensive studio and state-of-the-art computer lab facilities are provided for all Pratt students. In the School of Art and Design, these include studio, shop, and technical facilities for work in all media, from the traditional to the most experimental. Graphics labs include color Macintosh IIs, Macintosh SEs, Cubicomps, Targa TIPS PCs with digitizer tablets, ALIAS labs, and a Quantel graphics system. Within the School of Architecture, students benefit not only from the design studios but also from the collective research facilities of the Institute. The School of Architecture uses SKOK CAD, Sun, and IRIS workstations. The School of Liberal Arts and Sciences maintains laboratory facilities for all science courses. Apple, AT&T, IBM, LSI-11, and TI microcomputers; a Burroughs batch-processing system; and an HP 100 computer are available to students in all majors. Pratt also has a DEC VAX 6210 minicomputer for Institute-wide integration of computer graphics and computer-aided design capabilities as well as AT&T 386 PCs and an extensive telecommunications laboratory. Gallery space, both on campus and at Pratt Manhattan, is extensive, showing the work of students, alumni, faculty members, staff members, and other well-known artists, architects, and designers. The Pratt Institute Center for Community and Environmental Development functions as a laboratory for the study of planning and advocacy issues in real-world situations.

Costs

Tuition for the 2004–05 academic year is $25,000. Room charges are $5000 per academic year. A meal plan is available and costs about $3100 per year. The fees are $670. The estimated cost of books and supplies is $3000 per academic year. Students should allow an additional $650 for transportation and personal expenses.

Financial Aid

Pratt Institute offers a large number of grants, scholarships, loans, and awards on the basis of academic achievement, financial need, or both. More than 75 percent of Pratt students receive aid in one or more of these forms. Through funds from the federal and state governments, contributions from Pratt alumni, and industry scholarships, Pratt is able to maintain an effective aid program in a time of escalating costs. Pratt attempts to ensure that no student is prevented by lack of funds from completing his or her education.

Faculty

The faculty at Pratt Institute is exceptional in that a large number of practicing professionals augment the regular full-time faculty. There are 98 full-time and 658 part-time faculty members; there are no graduate teaching assistants. In small classes and studios, students have easy access to professors whose natural environment is the design studio, the architectural office, or the industrial research department.

Student Government

The Student Government Association (SGA) maintains primary responsibility for all student interests and involvement at Pratt. The SGA structure includes the Executive Committee, Senate, Finance Committee, Buildings and Grounds Committee, Academic and Administrative Affairs Committee, and Program Board. Student representatives serve on the Board of Trustees and on its various committees. All undergraduate students are encouraged to become involved in the SGA, whose main functions are allocating and administering funds collected through the student activities fee, scheduling student activities, and representing the student viewpoint to the rest of the Pratt community.

Admission Requirements

Pratt Institute attracts and enrolls highly motivated and talented students from diverse backgrounds. Applications are welcome from all qualified students, regardless of age, sex, race, color, religion, national origin, or handicap. Admission standards at Pratt are high. One of the major components for admission consideration in art, design, or architecture is the evaluation of a student's portfolio by means of an interview, attendance at a Portfolio Day, or through the submission of work samples on slides.

All applicants must submit transcripts and letters of recommendation from any high schools and colleges attended. Additional professional requirements are requested by each department.

The admission committee bases its decisions on careful reviews of all credentials submitted by applicants in relation to the requirements of the program to which students seek admission. The SAT I or ACT and a strong college-preparatory background are required of all applicants for four-year programs. In certain cases an extraordinary talent may offset a low grade or a test score.

Application and Information

Pratt has three admissions deadlines: November 15 for early action and January 1 and February 1 for regular admissions. To receive full consideration, students must submit applications by February 1 for anticipated entrance in the fall semester and by October 15 for anticipated entrance in the spring semester.

For more information about Pratt Institute, students should contact:

Office of Admissions
Pratt Institute
200 Willoughby Avenue
Brooklyn, New York 11205
Telephone: 718-636-3669
800-331-0834 (toll-free)
E-mail: admissions@pratt.edu
World Wide Web: http://www.pratt.edu

PRESBYTERIAN COLLEGE

CLINTON, SOUTH CAROLINA

The College

Founded in 1880, Presbyterian College (PC) is a fully accredited, private four-year college of liberal arts and sciences. The College is widely known for its excellent academic program and congenial, friendly atmosphere. Twenty-eight states and nine countries are represented in the student body of 1,229 men and women. PC is associated with the Presbyterian Church USA, and approximately 30 percent of the students are members of the Presbyterian Church. The College welcomes students of all faiths.

Extracurricular activities are an extensive and vital part of the development of all students. There are intercollegiate athletic teams for men in baseball, basketball, cross-country, football, golf, soccer, and tennis and for women in basketball, cross-country, soccer, softball, tennis, and volleyball. The College also offers team handball, soccer, and lacrosse as club sports for men and women. Lacrosse is scheduled to become a varsity sport for men and women in fall 2005. An extensive intramural program provides exercise and entertainment in a variety of sports for both men and women. The Student Union Board provides a series of concerts, comedians, films, and special events. Students may also participate in a variety of fine arts, Greek, honorary, political, preprofessional, and religious organizations. Nearly 50 percent of PC students volunteer for community service. The College sponsors thirty-eight service projects, including tutoring, adult literacy, Big Brother/Big Sister, Habitat for Humanity, and Special Olympics.

The 240-acre campus has thirty major buildings of classical Jeffersonian architecture. These buildings are grouped around three plazas. Facilities include a 1,200-seat auditorium, a 342-seat recital hall, a science center, a library, an art gallery, a drama theater, eleven residence halls (including a newly constructed international house, an apartment complex, and a townhouse development), six major classroom buildings, a dining hall, a health center, a student center, a gymnasium, a six-house fraternity court, a Panhellenic house, and a 31-acre intramural park.

Students may keep automobiles on campus. Ninety-two percent of students live in a College residence hall. All single students are required to live on campus. Housing within the community is available for married students. All residence halls are wired for Internet access.

Location

Clinton, population 10,000, is located in the heart of the South Carolina Piedmont. Interstates 26 and 385 meet outside of Clinton and provide easy access from the metropolitan areas of Greenville, Spartanburg, and Columbia. It is a short drive from Clinton to the ski slopes of western North Carolina, the coast of South Carolina, and professional athletic events in Charlotte, North Carolina.

Majors and Degrees

Presbyterian College offers the Bachelor of Arts and the Bachelor of Science degrees, with majors in art history, biology, business/accounting, business/management, chemistry, computer science, early childhood education, economics, English, fine arts (concentrations in art, drama/speech, and music), French, German, history, mathematics, middle school education, modern foreign languages, music, music education, physics, political science, psychology, religion, religion–Christian education, religion–philosophy, sacred music, social science, sociology, Spanish, special education, theater arts, and visual arts.

Students may minor in African American studies, arts administration, athletic coaching, Christian youth work, international studies, journalism, Latin American studies, media studies, philosophy, physical education, prelaw studies, secondary education teacher certification, women's studies, and in each of the major areas.

Preprofessional programs are offered in Army ROTC, dentistry, law, medicine, ministry, pharmacy, and veterinary medicine. The College offers dual-degree programs in engineering with Auburn, Clemson, Mercer, and Vanderbilt Universities. A dual-degree program in forestry and environmental science is available with Duke University. With the Presbyterian School of Christian Education, students may receive a dual degree in Christian education.

Academic Program

All Presbyterian College students gain a comprehension of the liberal arts through a general education in English, fine arts, history, mathematics, modern foreign language, physical education, religion, science, and social science. To graduate, students must complete the required general education courses, fulfill the requirements of a major, attend forty cultural enrichment events, and pass 122 semester hours with a minimum cumulative average of 2.0.

The College operates on a semester system. The fall semester extends from late August to mid-December, and the spring semester runs from mid-January through early May. Classes meet Monday through Friday. An optional May fleximester enables students to travel and study with other PC students and staff. Two five-week summer sessions also are offered.

Directed study, honors seminars, honors research, internships, and independent research are offered through academic departments.

Students may earn credit by submitting scores from the College Board's Advanced Placement subject examinations. CLEP credit is granted for successful scores on the subject exams only. Credit is awarded to students in an International Baccalaureate program who have earned grades of 5 or better on higher-level subject tests.

An Army ROTC program is available.

Off-Campus Programs

Presbyterian College offers a variety of programs for students who are interested in spending a semester, summer, or academic year studying abroad. The College is associated with fifty programs in Australia, Austria, China, England, Finland, France, Honduras, Ireland, Italy, Japan, Korea, Mexico, the Netherlands, New Zealand, Scotland, Spain, and Wales. Students also may study for a semester in Washington, D.C. All credits that are earned through these programs count toward graduation from Presbyterian College. Other study-abroad programs may be developed by the student and his or her adviser to ensure credit toward graduation.

Special courses are available for students during PC's optional May fleximester. These for-credit courses provide students with off-campus educational experiences in Africa and Australia and such areas as the Caribbean, Europe, Galapagos Islands, and Southwestern United States.

Students have the opportunity to participate in a summer program at Oxford University's Corpus Christi College in England. This three-week course includes studies of two subjects in addition to travel and field trips in England.

Presbyterian College is affiliated with the Gulf Coast Research Laboratory and Duke University's marine research center. Students may enroll in marine science courses during the academic year or summer.

Academic Facilities

Harrington-Peachtree Hall, PC's mathematics and social science building, is the newest and largest academic building on the campus. The building contains psychology labs, classrooms with state-of-the-art audiovisual technology, and a computer lab. The Harper Center houses an art gallery and flexible theater. Other academic facilities include Richardson Science Hall, Neville Hall for the humanities, and Jacobs Hall for economics and military science. Thomason Library contains 165,000 volumes, provides extensive reference sources, and features a media learning center. Computer facilities are available in all major academic buildings, with more than 100 computer terminals available for students. Through the College, all students may have free access to the Internet and a Web-based e-mail system.

Costs

For the 2004–05 school year, the cost of tuition is $19,740. Fees are $1882. Room is $3028, and board is $3218 with the fifteen-meal plan. The cost of books, supplies, travel, and personal expenses is estimated at an additional $2500 per year.

Financial Aid

Presbyterian College endeavors to meet the financial need of all accepted students through scholarships, grants, loans, work-study, or a combination of these. The College may award academic, athletic, leadership, and music grants-in-aid to students with superior talent or achievement. Approximately 80 percent of the students receive some financial assistance each year. The Free Application for Federal Student Aid (FAFSA) and an institutional form are required of all financial aid applicants. For priority consideration, all financial aid information should be submitted by March 1 of a student's senior year. For further information, students should contact the Financial Aid Office at the College.

Faculty

Presbyterian College has a full-time faculty of 80 members. Ninety-five percent of the faculty members hold doctoral or terminal degrees in their field. The student-faculty ratio is 13:1. Students and instructors work closely together in both learning and counseling situations. All faculty members teach lower-division and freshman classes as well as upper-division courses. No graduate students serve as instructors at PC. Each student has an assigned faculty adviser for assistance in course selection and personal counseling.

Student Government

All Presbyterian College students are encouraged to fully participate in campus government. The Student Senate is composed of an executive council, the class representatives, and the organizational representatives. The duly elected Student Senate regulates the affairs of the student body, oversees the Student Union Board and student publications, and approves Honor Council membership.

The Honor Council enforces the College's Honor Code. All students pledge to enforce the honor system and to not lie, steal, cheat, or plagiarize. The honor system fosters a great deal of trust among students and faculty members. Professors may give unproctored exams; students may leave possessions unattended. Representatives from the student body serve on administrative, faculty, and trustee committees.

Admission Requirements

Presbyterian College normally requires for entrance the completion of a four-year high school course of study including 4 units of English, 3 units of math, and 2 or more units each of foreign language, history, laboratory science, and social science.

Admission is very selective. Once a student applies, the admissions committee carefully reviews the application, essay, high school transcript, recommendation from a high school official, and scores from the SAT I or the ACT. The College admits students based on the applicant's academic and personal qualifications. An interview is not required, but interested students are encouraged to visit the campus. An early decision plan is available. Presbyterian College strives to recruit a diverse student body. The College does not discriminate against applicants or students on the basis of handicap, national origin, race, religion, or sex.

Transfer students must submit a transfer application, essay, college and high school transcripts, board scores, and clearance forms. To be considered for admission, a transfer student must have a minimum overall C average in college work.

Application and Information

The application fee is $30 and is nonrefundable. Students may submit applications at any time during their senior year. If students wish to be considered for academic scholarships, they must apply before December 5 of their senior year.

Presbyterian College uses a rolling admissions process. Applicants are notified of the admission committee's decision shortly after the College receives the necessary credentials.

Students may apply electronically at the College's Web site.

For further information, students should contact:

Richard Dana Paul
Vice President for Enrollment and Dean of Admissions
Presbyterian College
503 South Broad Street
Clinton, South Carolina 29325
Telephone: 864-833-8230
800-960-7583 (toll-free)
Fax: 864-833-8195
E-mail: admissions@presby.edu
World Wide Web: http://www.presby.edu

The fountain plaza behind Neville Hall at dusk.

PRESCOTT COLLEGE
Resident Degree Program

PRESCOTT, ARIZONA

The College

Prescott College, an independent four-year liberal arts college, is committed to offering a personalized educational experience. Using nontraditional methods, Prescott College delivers a classical liberal arts education that focuses on communication, critical thinking, and problem solving. The educational philosophy stresses experiential learning and self-direction within an interdisciplinary curriculum. Respected for its environmental focus, Prescott College continually strives to expand and share its environmental mission by encouraging students to examine the relationship between human societies and the natural world.

Prescott College was established in 1966. Currently, there are three distinct programs: the Resident Degree Program (RDP), the Adult Degree Program (ADP), and the Master of Arts Program (MAP). This information focuses on the Resident Degree Program. The 2001–02 RDP enrollment was approximately 500 students.

Location

Located a mile above sea level in the forested mountains of central Arizona, Prescott has a moderate climate with four distinct seasons. Described by *Arizona Highways* magazine as "Everybody's Hometown," the community of Prescott is known for its fine quality of life, friendly atmosphere, and small-town charm. Because it has a growing spirit, the community strives to balance the needs of an environmentally conscious lifestyle with an expanding economy. The town offers facilities for racquetball, tennis, swimming, and horseback riding. Forests and wilderness areas are easily accessible for hiking, backpacking, biking, and mountain climbing, which are popular with students. Prescott is, in fact, the home of a lively and growing artistic community with many art fairs and gallery openings. Many people are active in photography, music, weaving, and dance. The Mountain Artists Guild and the Prescott Fine Arts Association make a substantial cultural impact. The Phoenix Symphony, visiting ballet and opera companies, and numerous art shows also provide regular programs.

Majors and Degrees

Individualized learning is possible because students design their own degrees. The Prescott College Resident Degree Program offers the Bachelor of Arts degree in a variety of areas. Under the general headings of adventure education, arts and letters, cultural and regional studies, education, environmental studies, and human growth and development, students create competence-based graduation plans in such topics as agroecology, conservation, counseling, ecological design, ecopsychology, education, environmental education, experiential education, field ecology, fine arts, holistic health, human ecology, literature, natural history, peace studies, philosophy, photography, psychology, religion, social and political studies, wilderness leadership, and writing.

Academic Programs

The College has created an innovative approach to higher education. It offers small classes (a student-faculty ratio of 10:1 in classrooms), extensive field work (a student-faculty ratio of 5:1 in the field), a close community atmosphere, and the opportunity for students to design their own educational paths. The philosophy of experiential education emphasizes the concept that learning is a lifelong process that helps students gain competence, creativity, and self-direction. In cooperation with an outstanding faculty, students are able to work in such special interdisciplinary fields as cultural and regional studies, ecopsychology, education and interpretation, human ecology, outdoor adventure education, social and political studies, and wilderness leadership.

Academic Facilities

The Prescott College Library has a collection of more than 28,000 volumes, 125 microforms, 1,200 audiocassettes and videocassettes, and 408 periodical titles, all of which relate specifically to the College's program offerings. The library is computer networked with all of the regional libraries in the area, including two other college libraries and the public libraries. If students are not able to locate necessary information from any of these sources, the College librarian borrows books through the interlibrary loan system. Because the College places great emphasis on student services, the faculty and staff members work diligently to assist each student in finding all information necessary for his or her pursuit of knowledge.

There are three fully equipped computer labs on campus, which are important resources for Prescott College students. All labs are staffed full-time by a competent team of computer professionals and College work-study students. Laser printers are available, and students have access to the Internet for research and e-mail. The largest lab houses IBM-compatible computers. The Geographic Information Science Lab has its own computer lab for conducting research in land-use planning and management. The College also offers a Mac lab for fine arts students who are interested in graphic manipulation and digital imaging.

Prescott College has surrounded itself with extracurricular facilities as well, offering a performing arts center and an organic café on campus where students can relax. Because the Southwest itself serves the College as a classroom, Prescott owns white-water rafts, kayaks, sea kayaks, cross-country skis, rock-climbing gear, camping equipment, and other gear that is important for the exploration and understanding of the southwestern United States and Mexico.

Two off-campus field sites complement the Prescott facilities: Wolfberry Farm and the Kino Bay Center for Cultural and Ecological Studies.

Located about 15 miles north of Prescott, Wolfberry Farm is a 30-acre farm dedicated to education, demonstration, and research in agroecology. Wolfberry Farm serves as the outdoor classroom for the summer program in agroecology and as a place where students can carry out independent studies and senior projects.

The Kino Bay Center for Cultural and Ecological Studies is located in Kino Bay, Mexico, on the Sea of Cortez. The Center is used by a variety of classes, such as Coastal and Cultural Ecology of Kino Bay, A Sense of Place, Field Methods for Intertidal Ecology, and Marine Conservation. It also serves as a launching point for sea kayaking courses and as a meeting place for many Mexican and American researchers.

Costs

Tuition for new and returning RDP students for 2004–05 is $16,320; tuition increases may occur in July of each year.

Financial Aid

The types of financial aid available are Federal Pell Grants, Prescott College grants, Arizona State Student Incentive Grants, Federal Supplemental Educational Opportunity Grants, student employment, Federal Stafford Student Loans, the Arizona Voucher Program, campus employment, and scholarships. More than 67 percent of the students at Prescott College receive financial aid.

Prescott College uses the Free Application for Federal Student Aid (FAFSA) to determine a student's financial need. Students wishing to apply for aid for the fall term should complete the financial aid form by April 15 for priority funding. Aid is awarded on a first-come, first-served basis until all available funds are used. FAFSA forms take four to six weeks to process, so students should submit them early, even if their plans are indefinite. Students who complete forms online may experience a quicker response than those who complete paper applications.

Faculty

Faculty members at Prescott College are devoted solely to the instruction of students. They are not burdened by the traditional "publish or perish" mandate faced by most educators but instead direct their energy toward being innovative instructors, positive role models, mentors, advisers, and friends. The faculty members are committed to the educational mission of Prescott College and thoroughly enjoy teaching, participating in College social activities, and working with individual students to help them comprehend challenging material.

Approximately 60 percent of the 45 full-time RDP faculty members hold doctorates or terminal degrees. The College recognizes the importance of individualized attention and small classes.

Student Government

Students participate in all levels of governance at Prescott College. Currently, 1 student is a full voting member of the Board of Trustees. Students are also represented on hiring committees. The Student Union is composed of all full-time students, each of whom has a vote.

Admission Requirements

In evaluating an applicant, the Admissions Committee seeks evidence of preparation for college-level academic work, a strong sense of community, and a desire to become a self-directed learner. The Admissions Committee looks for the ability to plan and make decisions and commitments and carry them out effectively. The applicant's essays, letters of recommendation, and transcripts are the strongest determining factors in the admission decision. Visits to the College and personal interviews are strongly recommended, and, in some cases, they are required. Students who consider applying to Prescott College should first attempt to gain a thorough understanding of the College's educational philosophy and practices.

Prescott College has created a special learning environment that requires motivation, maturity, and a desire to be actively involved in learning.

Application and Information

The Admissions Office strongly encourages applicants to submit all required application materials by the priority filing date. Complete files are then reviewed by the Admissions Committee, and admissions decisions are communicated by the notification date. Files that are received or completed after the priority filing date will still be considered on a rolling basis.

Once students are offered admission to an incoming class, they must submit a tuition deposit prior to the reply date to give evidence of intention to enroll and to reserve a space in that class. Tuition deposits are nonrefundable; applicants are advised to submit them only after determining that they are ready to commit to Prescott College. Tuition deposits received after the reply date are accepted on a first-come, first-served basis until the class has filled. Students whose deposits are received after the class is filled are placed on a wait list.

Applications for fall should be received by February 1; for spring, the priority filing date is September 1. The notification date for fall is March 15, for spring, October 15. The reply dates (deposit due dates) for fall and spring are, respectively, May 1 and November 1. Applications that are received or completed after the priority filing date will still be considered. These applications will be reviewed after those that were received and completed by the priority filing date.

For more information, students should contact:

Resident Degree Program–Admissions
Prescott College
220 Grove Avenue
Prescott, Arizona 86301
Telephone: 928-776-5180
800-628-6364 (toll-free)
E-mail: admissions@prescott.edu
World Wide Web: http://www.prescott.edu

Prescott College students experience active education in a Southwestern classroom.

PRINCETON UNIVERSITY

PRINCETON, NEW JERSEY

The University

The fourth-oldest college in the country, Princeton was chartered in 1746 and has roots that extend deep into America's past. Woodrow Wilson, a former president of Princeton (as well as a former governor of New Jersey and president of the United States), coined the phrase "Princeton in the Nation's Service" during his address at the University's 150th anniversary of its founding in 1896. It has served as Princeton's unofficial motto ever since, recently expanding to include "and in the Service of All Nations." It nicely summarizes the commitment of Princetonians to various kinds of public service around the nation and throughout the world.

Princeton owns more than 2,000 acres of land, of which 200 comprise the main campus. A wealth of architectural styles are displayed, ranging from the oldest Colonial buildings to the predominantly Gothic dormitories to modern structures by such eminent architects as Minoru Yamasaki, Edward Larrabee Barnes, Lew Davis, I. M. Pei, and Robert Venturi.

The total enrollment is about 6,300, of whom 4,600 men and women are undergraduates. In the three most recent entering classes, the ratio of men to women was about 52:48. Students at Princeton come from all fifty states, Puerto Rico, the Virgin Islands, Guam, and more than seventy countries. They come from a wide variety of ethnic and socioeconomic backgrounds. The University sponsors Third World, International, and Women's centers, which are open to all students. Interaction among students of different backgrounds is an important part of a Princeton education.

The Frist Campus Center, opened in fall 2000, is the hub of activity at Princeton. It offers the entire campus community a convenient place to eat, socialize, and connect with each other. Other services at Frist include theater and performance space, computer clusters, game rooms, and shopping. The Community Service Center (home of the Student Volunteers Council, Princeton's largest student organization) and Undergraduate Student Government are housed in Frist, as well as dining halls and restaurants, mail services, ATM machines, computer connection ports, and a convenience store. Frist also hosts film series, lectures, and special events. Princeton has more than 200 student clubs and organizations, including a radio station, daily newspaper and other publications, and numerous cultural, ethnic, political, religious, and service organizations. Performing arts facilities include McCarter Theatre (home to a professional company and performing arts center as well as Princeton's famed Triangle Club), Richardson Auditorium, Taplin Auditorium, and 185 Nassau Street, which is home to a variety of studios for the fine and performing arts, including the James Stewart Film Center.

Princeton has two gymnasiums. Jadwin Gym provides 250,000 square feet of indoor space for basketball, track, wrestling, fencing, squash, and tennis, in addition to large practice areas for outdoor field sports. Dillon Gym has facilities for swimming, diving, gymnastics, dance, weight training, and volleyball, plus additional space for basketball, wrestling, fencing, and squash. Other sports facilities include Princeton Stadium (multiuse), 1952 Stadium for lacrosse and field hockey, William Weaver Memorial Stadium for track and field, the DeNunzio Pool swimming and diving complex, Baker Rink for hockey and skating, Lake Carnegie's Olympic-quality racing course for crew and sailing, outdoor tennis courts, an eighteen-hole golf course, and numerous playing fields.

The University guarantees housing for all undergraduates. All freshmen and sophomores live and dine in five residential colleges. A small number of juniors and seniors live and eat in the residential colleges; but most live in the upperclass dorms, and more than half dine in the nonresidential independent eating clubs. The Center for Jewish Life offers a kosher dining facility open to all students and sponsors a wide array of social, educational, and religious programs.

Location

The town of Princeton, adjoining the University campus, has a population of 30,000. New York and Philadelphia are easily accessible by public transportation, and there are hourly departures throughout most of the day. The University regularly subsidizes and otherwise facilitates students' attendance at cultural, sports, and social events in both cities. Boston and Washington, D.C., are near enough for weekend visits by trains that stop in Princeton.

Majors and Degrees

Princeton University awards a Bachelor of Arts (A.B.) degree in anthropology, architecture, art and archaeology, astrophysical sciences, chemistry, classics, comparative literature, computer science, East Asian studies, ecology and evolutionary biology, economics, English, French and Italian, geosciences, Germanic languages and literatures, history, mathematics, molecular biology, music, Near Eastern studies, philosophy, physics, politics, psychology, religion, Slavic languages and literatures, sociology, and Spanish and Portuguese. An A.B. degree in public and international affairs is offered through the Woodrow Wilson School of Public and International Affairs. In addition, Princeton offers courses in more than thirty interdepartmental programs, many of which award a certificate of study. These programs include African-American studies, creative writing, environmental studies, musical performance, theater and dance, visual arts, and women's studies.

The Bachelor of Science in Engineering (B.S.E.) degree is awarded in chemical engineering, civil engineering, computer science, electrical engineering, mechanical and aerospace engineering, and operations research and financial engineering. Interdepartmental and topical programs are offered in areas such as engineering biology, engineering physics, geological engineering, materials science and engineering, and robotics and intelligent systems.

Academic Programs

Princeton endeavors to provide a broad education with emphasis in a particular field of study. Consequently, A.B. students are required to fulfill distribution, foreign language, and writing requirements, and every A.B. student is required to complete a total of thirty courses with at least eight in his or her concentration. In addition, students are expected to do independent research, which takes the form of junior papers and a senior thesis under the guidance of a departmental faculty adviser.

The School of Engineering and Applied Science requires thirty-six courses for graduation, and at least seven of these must be liberal arts electives. While specific prerequisites and requirements within each department may vary, all emphasize independent work during the junior and senior years.

Freshmen with scores of 4 or 5 on the Advanced Placement tests given by the College Board or scores of 6 or 7 on the International Baccalaureate Higher Level exams may, with the approval of the appropriate department, be granted advanced placement/standing.

Academic Facilities

The Princeton University library system consists of the Harvey S. Firestone Memorial Library, one of the country's major university libraries, which houses the largest portion of Princeton's collection, and eighteen special libraries, including fifteen academic department collections. Firestone Library's open-stack collections include more than 5 million books, records, and 3 million microforms. There are reading spaces for 2,000, study carrels for 500, and a number of offices and conference rooms.

The Engineering Quadrangle, home of the School of Engineering and Applied Science, contains numerous laboratories and classrooms, a library, a machine shop, a convocation room, more than 125 faculty offices and graduate-study spaces, and an energy-research facility.

The Art Museum has an extensive permanent collection that ranges from artifacts of the ancient world to paintings and sculpture of the Renaissance, modern Europe, and America.

Princeton students are given access to a varied and powerful computing environment. The cornerstone is DormNet, a fiber-optic-based network that brings a high-speed data connection to every dorm room on campus.

Costs

The basic 2003–04 academic-year expenses for all students were $28,540 for tuition and fees and $8120 for room and board.

Financial Aid

Admission decisions are need-blind. Princeton provides assistance to meet the full demonstrated financial need of all admitted students. Once admitted with aid, a student receives assistance for succeeding undergraduate years, as long as the family continues to demonstrate need and the student makes normal progress toward a degree. Financial aid packages consist of a combination of the University scholarship and federal assistance in the form of grant and work-study opportunities. Beginning in 2001, Princeton removed student loans from the award packages for aid students, replacing them with additional University scholarships.

Approximately 80 percent of the student body receives financial aid from outside sources and/or the University each year; about 46 percent receive financial aid from the University.

Faculty

One of Princeton's outstanding assets is its faculty. A single faculty teaches both undergraduate and graduate students, all of whom have close contact with scholars of national and international reputation. The current student-faculty ratio is 7:1.

Student Government

The Undergraduate Student Government (USG) is the undergraduate representative body that advocates students' interests to other groups. Other purposes of the USG include the exercise of leadership in undergraduate activities and the running of services for members of the University community.

Admission Requirements

Princeton does not require a specific set of secondary school courses for admission. It does, however, strongly recommend the following as a basic preparation for study at the University: 4 years each of English (including continued practice in writing), mathematics, and a single foreign language; 2 years each of laboratory science and history (including that of the United States and another country or area); some study of art or music; and, if possible, a second foreign language.

All candidates must submit the results of the SAT I and SAT II in three different subject areas of their own choice. (Candidates whose only other college choices require the ACT may substitute ACT results for the SAT I.) Students interested in pursuing a B.S.E. degree are expected to take SAT II Subject Tests in either Physics or Chemistry and in either Level I or Level II Mathematics.

Interviews on campus are not available. Applicants are encouraged to have an interview in their home area with a member of one of Princeton's Alumni Schools Committees and to visit the campus to attend group information sessions and take guided tours.

Application and Information

Students should apply to Princeton on an application form provided by the University. Those wishing to apply through the early decision program should submit materials by November 1; they are notified of the admission decision in early December. The deadline for regular decision application is January 2, and notification is in early April.

Requests for additional information and application forms should be sent to:

Admission Office
Princeton University
P.O. Box 430
Princeton, New Jersey 08544-0430
Telephone: 609-258-3060
World Wide Web: http://www.princeton.edu

Blair Hall, with its distinctive arch, is a landmark building at Princeton University.

PROVIDENCE COLLEGE

PROVIDENCE, RHODE ISLAND

The College

Conducted under the auspices of the Order of Preachers of the Province of St. Joseph, commonly known as the Dominicans, Providence College (PC) was established in 1917. Originally a college for men, it became coeducational in 1971. The College's full-time undergraduate enrollment is 3,700 students. Approximately 1,800 students live in nine residential halls, and an additional 900 upperclass students are housed in one of the five College apartment complexes. The remainder of the students live in apartments directly off campus or commute from home. At the graduate level, the College offers M.A., M.S., M.Ed., M.B.A., and Ph.D. degree programs.

The Slavin Center, as the nucleus of student, social, cultural, and recreational activity, provides numerous facilities. They include lounges; McPhail's Entertainment Facility; a newly renovated dining facility; club offices; an ATM machine; a bookstore/gift shop; the Student Activities, Involvement, and Leadership Office (SAIL); and offices for the Student Congress, the Board of Programmers, student publications, and the Career Services Office.

The Peterson Recreation Center is the site of intramural athletic activities on campus, in which more than 80 percent of the students participate. The center has five convertible basketball, tennis, and volleyball courts; a 220-yard track; three racquetball courts; a 25-meter pool; and an aerobics room. Providence College has a fine tradition of competition in intercollegiate athletics, and it continues to play an active role through its membership in the NCAA, RIRW, ECAC, Hockey East Conference, and Big East Conference. Additional on-campus sports facilities include Alumni Hall, Schneider Arena, and three large fields and recreational areas.

Location

The College is situated on a 105-acre campus in the city of Providence, Rhode Island. It has the advantages of an atmosphere far removed from the traffic and commerce of the metropolitan area but is also conveniently located near the many cultural attractions of a city that is not only the capital of a historic state but the center of a variety of institutions of higher learning. Providence College has an established relationship with the Tony Award–winning Trinity Square Repertory Company, located in downtown Providence. Trinity provides special discount rates for students for the full spectrum of its programs. The Providence Performing Arts Center, originally a movie palace, has been restored to its former baroque splendor and now serves as the site of symphony concerts, opera, ballet, and road shows of Broadway musicals. In addition, the Dunkin' Donuts Civic Center attracts well-known performers and rock groups, trade shows, and sports events. The center is also the home court of the Friars, PC's basketball team.

Majors and Degrees

Providence College offers the B.A. degree with major programs of study in American studies, art and art history, biology, business economics, chemistry, economics, education (elementary/special and secondary), English, history, humanities, mathematics, modern languages, music/music education (K–12), philosophy, political science, psychology, public and community service studies, social science, social work, sociology, theater arts, and theology. The B.S. degree is offered with major programs of study in accountancy, applied physics, biochemistry, biology, chemistry, combined biology/optometry (3-4 program), computer science, engineering (3-2 program), finance, health policy and management, management, and marketing. The College also offers a 4+1 B.A./B.S./M.B.A. program for qualified students.

Academic Programs

The primary objective of Providence College is to further the intellectual development of its students through the disciplines of the sciences and the humanities. The liberal education provided by the College gives students the chance to increase their ability to formulate their thoughts and communicate them to others, evaluate their varied experiences, and achieve insight into the past, present, and future of civilization. The College is concerned about preparing students to become intelligent, productive, and responsible citizens in a democratic society. To this end, it endeavors not only to develop the students' capacity for disciplined thinking and critical exactness but also to give them opportunities for healthy physical development and a wide range of activities that foster a sense of social responsibility. The College's programs are also designed to help students discover their particular aptitude and prepare them to undertake specialized studies leading to careers.

Students are required to complete a total of 116 credit hours in the core curriculum, in a selected major, and in electives. The core curriculum is built around a broad range of disciplines, and 20 semester hours are allotted to study of the development of Western civilization, 6 to social science, 6 to philosophy, 6 to religion, 6 to natural science, 3 to mathematics, and 3 to the fine arts. All undergraduates must demonstrate proficiency in writing by the end of the sophomore year as part of the College's core curriculum requirements. Special academic programs offered to enhance the educational experience and allow for a variety of interests, including double majors, individualized programs, nondepartmental courses, liberal arts honors, preprofessional medical and legal programs, the Early Identification Program (offered to Rhode Island residents in cooperation with Brown University Medical School), and Army ROTC.

The College participates in the Advanced Placement Program administered by the College Board. Students who demonstrate superior performance (a score of 4 or 5) on any of the Advanced Placement examinations are considered for advanced placement and standing in the area of study in which they qualify.

Providence College recognizes credit earned through the International Baccalaureate (I.B.), an internationally recognized curriculum and examination program. The College recognizes the Higher Level examinations when a score of 5, 6, or 7 has been achieved. Each examination that is successfully passed in the Higher Level of the I.B. program earns 3 credits.

PC operates on a two-semester calendar. Fall-semester classes begin in early September and spring-semester classes begin in mid-January.

Off-Campus Programs

For more than twenty-five years, Providence College has encouraged qualified students to consider the advantages of study abroad. Committed to offering students a comprehensive opportunity for a truly liberal education, the Study Abroad Office extends an invitation to all interested first-year and sophomore students to explore the possibilities for enriching their undergraduate education through a sojourn abroad. Providence College is one of the few institutions to have study-abroad arrangements with both Oxford University and Cambridge University in England. Students may also choose from the University of Glasgow in Scotland; Trinity College and University College in Dublin and National University of Ireland in Galway, Ireland; the University of Salamanca in Spain; and the University of Fribourg in Switzerland. In addition, the College offers a direct exchange program with Kansai-Gaidai University in Japan. The Study Abroad Office may be able to make other opportunities available for study abroad when the PC-sponsored programs are not suited to individual academic needs. In recent years, PC students have studied abroad in Rome, Florence, Salzburg, Madrid, Cannes, Paris, London, and Sydney. The Washington Semester is also an option for students, allowing them to enrich their education by spending one semester of academic study and experiential learning at American University in Washington, D.C.

Academic Facilities

The Phillips Memorial Library, which has received two national architectural awards for its design, is the center of intellectual activity at the College. PC's library is an electronic resource complete with radio frequency technology, a wireless network, electronic classrooms, and the second largest electronic database access in the state. The library has current holdings of 354,000 volumes in open stacks and seating accommodations for 750 students. Phillips Library also houses various faculty offices, reading and rare book rooms, archives, the Department of English, and the Office of Academic Services. The library is a member of the Consortium of Rhode Island Academic and Research Libraries, through which the resources of most of the libraries in the state are accessible to Providence College students. Located in Accino Hall and Koffler Hall are the College's academic microcomputer laboratories, which serve the computer instruction and research needs of faculty members and students. The College's state-of-the-art science laboratories, computer workstations, and research facilities are located in the Albertus Magnus-Sowa-Hickey Science Complex. The Feinstein Academic Center is a newly renovated academic facility that is the home of the Feinstein Institute for Public Service Program, the Liberal Arts Honors Program, and the Center for Teaching Excellence. The Blackfriars Theatre, located in Harkins Hall, provides versatile seating and staging for the performing arts.

Costs

The total costs for the 2004–05 academic year are tuition, $23,180; room, $4645; and board, $4250 (seven-day plan). Books, travel, and personal supplies are estimated to cost $1500.

Financial Aid

Providence College's financial aid is distributed on the basis of demonstrated need and the student's ability to benefit from the educational opportunity the assistance offers. To apply for financial aid, candidates who are applying for Early Action must submit a College Scholarship Service PROFILE application by December 1 and the Free Application for Federal Student Aid (FAFSA) by January 2. Students applying for Regular Decision must submit both the College Scholarship Service PROFILE application and the FAFSA by February 1. Upon final determination of students' need, the Office of Financial Aid constructs aid packages consisting of work, loan, and grant assistance in accordance with federal regulations, the availability of funds, and institutional policy as approved by the College's Financial Aid Advisory Committee. Sources of financial aid include Federal Work-Study awards, Federal Perkins Loans, Federal Pell Grants, Federal Supplemental Educational Opportunity Grants (FSEOG), Providence College grants-in-aid, Providence College Achievement Scholarships, and Merit Scholarships.

Faculty

The faculty consists of 262 full-time and 75 visiting and adjunct professors, approximately 10 percent of whom are Dominican fathers and sisters. The majority of PC instructors teach both undergraduate- and graduate-level courses; no graduate students or student assistants teach at either level. About 87 percent of the faculty members hold terminal degrees. All professors devote their time primarily to teaching and advising undergraduates; all students are assigned a faculty adviser in their major area. The student-faculty ratio is 12:1.

Student Government

The Student Congress represents the students in its emphasis upon lifestyles and student prerogatives. Its officers are elected annually by the entire student community, and representatives are elected by each class. The Student Congress has created the Providence College Bill of Rights, the most significant of its legislative actions. Student representatives are appointed annually by the Student Congress to all standing committees of the College. The Student Congress has primary responsibility for the allocation of $125,500 in student activity funds to support most student-run organizations.

Admission Requirements

The admission committee gives recognition to students with various talents, backgrounds, and geographic origins. Admission decisions are made without regard to race, color, sex, handicap, age, or national or ethnic origin. An estimate of the applicant's character and accomplishments by his or her college adviser in secondary school and an official transcript of the secondary school record should be sent to the College no later than November 1 for Early Action and January 15 for Regular Decision. The secondary school transcript should consist of courses of a substantially college-preparatory nature. Although individual cases may vary, the College recommends that a student complete 4 years of English, 4 years of mathematics, 3 of foreign language, at least 2 of laboratory sciences, and 2 of social sciences. Three additional units may be taken in any subjects that meet the secondary school's requirements for graduation. Applicants are encouraged to submit letters of recommendation and evaluation from their secondary school teachers, especially from English teachers. Letters of recommendation from people who know the applicant personally and who have been involved in his or her scholastic development are most valuable. Applicants are also required to submit their official scores on the College Board's Scholastic Assessment Test (SAT I). In addition, the admission committee recommends the submission of SAT II: Subject Test scores on the Writing Test and on two other tests of the applicant's choice (preferably in subject areas that the student plans to study in college). Information concerning these tests may be obtained from a high school guidance office; the College Board, Box 592, Princeton, New Jersey 08541, or by visiting the College Board's Web site at http://www.collegeboard.com. In lieu of SAT I scores, applicants may submit scores on the ACT Assessment of American College Testing. For more information about these tests, prospective students should contact American College Testing, P.O. Box 168, Iowa City, Iowa 52240.

Application and Information

Providence College accepts the Common Application. The deadlines for receiving applications for the September term are November 1 for Early Action and January 15 for Regular Decision. Transfer students must file an application by April 15. The deadlines for receiving applications for the January term are November 1 for freshmen applicants and December 1 for transfer students.

Further information may be obtained by contacting:

Office of Admission
Providence College
549 River Avenue
Providence, Rhode Island 02918-0001
Telephone: 401-865-2535
800-721-6444 (toll-free)
Fax: 401-865-2826
E-mail: pcadmiss@providence.edu
World Wide Web: http://www.providence.edu

Harkins Hall, the administration building at Providence College.

PURCHASE COLLEGE, STATE UNIVERSITY OF NEW YORK

PURCHASE, NEW YORK

The College

Purchase College is a selective public coeducational college that serves both residential and commuter students. It has an enrollment of 4,000. Founded in 1967, Purchase College is one of the first public institutions of higher learning to fuse the educational goals and traditions of a liberal arts college and an arts conservatory by combining the visual and performing arts and liberal arts and sciences on one campus. The combination of conservatory and liberal arts reflects the College's conviction that the artist and the scholar are both vital to an enlightened democratic society.

Representing a broad range of age groups and geographic, ethnic, and socioeconomic backgrounds, Purchase College students are characterized by individualism and creativity. The emphasis on individualized study—through tutorials, independent study, and the required senior project—encourages students to assume significant responsibility for their education. The intersection of the arts and liberal arts and sciences fosters an appreciation in students of the contribution of both scholarly and artistic achievement to a humane culture. An increasing number of students enter residential learning communities.

Although Purchase College is the youngest of the SUNY system's sixty-four campuses, it has rapidly emerged and is increasingly recognized as a distinguished, imaginative, and dynamic institution for the study of the liberal arts and sciences and the visual and performing arts and for its service to the region and the state.

Purchase is primarily a full-time undergraduate institution, but in fulfilling its role as a public institution, Purchase College welcomes the opportunity to promote lifelong learning for students of all ages, backgrounds, and incomes through its School of Liberal Studies and Continuing Education, which offers a Bachelor of Arts in liberal studies as well as many credit and noncredit courses, certificate programs, and part-time degree programs.

In addition to its baccalaureate degrees, Purchase College offers three postgraduate programs in music: Performers Certificate (one to two years postbaccalaureate), Master of Music, and Artist Diploma (one to two years post-master's). The College also offers an M.F.A. in theater arts/stage design, visual arts, and dance and an M.A. in art history.

Location

The Purchase campus, built on the 500-acre former Strathglass estate, combines the advantages of a semirural setting with proximity to the educational and cultural opportunities of New York City and Westchester County. As the only senior public institution in Westchester, Purchase College is a cultural resource for the entire community. Approximately 250,000 people visit the campus each year to take advantage of its many programs and activities, such as the President's Leadership Forum, the Purchase College Westchester School Partnership, exhibits at the Neuberger Museum, and the Performing Arts Center.

Majors and Degrees

Purchase College offers professional and conservatory training programs that lead to a Bachelor of Music degree and a Bachelor of Fine Arts (B.F.A.) degree in acting, dance, dramatic writing, film, stage design/technology, or visual arts.

Purchase College's liberal arts and sciences programs lead to Bachelor of Arts (B.A.) and Bachelor of Science (B.S.) degrees. The College offers a full range of disciplines through its two liberal arts schools: Humanities (art history, cinema studies, creative writing, drama studies, history, journalism, language and culture, literature, and philosophy) and Natural and Social Sciences (anthropology; biology; chemistry; economics; environmental science; mathematics; mathematics/computer science; media, society, and the arts; new media; political science; psychology; and sociology). Students may also study premedicine or prelaw. There are growing interdisciplinary programs in Afro-American and African (Black) studies, American studies, Asian studies, Latin-American studies, and women studies.

Academic Programs

Purchase College operates on a semester calendar. Students normally take 16 credits per semester so they can meet the minimum requirement of 120 hours for a bachelor's degree as well as the SUNY-mandated general education requirements. Most courses in liberal arts are 4 credits, as the College specializes in intensive study within the majors, and many courses include scheduled classwork in the arts, fieldwork, plenary sessions, and intensive tutorials.

Purchase has the only conservatory training programs for the arts within the State University of New York System. Professional training is provided by practicing professionals. Proximity to New York City gives access to these professionals and their respective art worlds, providing a network contacts developed during the undergraduate years. Placement in professional jobs begins at an early stage, with special assistance from the active career placement office. For example, some students occasionally interrupt their study program to work with a professional dance company or with a professional filmmaker.

Students in the liberal arts and sciences declare their major concentration by the junior year, electing intensive course work that builds toward their senior project. This project represents a culmination of their four years at Purchase and can take the form of a research paper, presentation, or original expression of thought and research (e.g., poem, artwork, multimedia presentation). The curriculum in each major is organized to build on disciplinary expertise and research and writing skills, starting with the freshman year and culminating in the senior project. Senior projects in natural sciences are often published or copublished with a faculty member.

For many Purchase students, internships in agencies, businesses, and corporations are also an important part of their educational experience and often lead to full-time employment.

Academic Facilities

The College's extraordinary facilities include the first building in the United States designed exclusively for the study and performance of dance; a large science research center; the Performing Arts Center, containing five theaters; the Neuberger Museum, which has an outstanding collection of modern American art. Both the center and the museum play central roles in the curriculum and the student experience. There is also an exceptionally well-equipped physical education building; an increasing number of multimedia and computer classrooms; and a 160,000-square-foot visual arts building.

Costs

For 2003–04, tuition for undergraduate in-state residents was $4350 for the academic year, $10,300 for nonresidents. Total room and board (dormitory double room and full meal plan) fees were $7122. Books and supplies were estimated at $1100. There is also an applied music fee of $1900 per year for music majors. Costs are subject to change for 2004–05.

Financial Aid

Purchase College participates in all federal and state financial aid programs. Approximately 68 percent of all matriculated undergraduate students apply for financial assistance. All students who complete the Free Application for Federal Student Aid (FAFSA) receive some form of financial assistance, which may include low-interest student loans. It is strongly recommended that students file the FAFSA prior to April 1 in order to receive the maximum amount of financial aid for which they are eligible.

Both merit-only and merit-and-need-based scholarships are available to qualified students.

Faculty

The Purchase College faculty is distinguished by depth of specialized knowledge as well as broad interdisciplinary interests, scholarly and professional activity, and dedication to undergraduate teaching. The liberal arts and sciences faculty includes prominent scholars in a variety of fields. More than 95 percent hold doctorates from prestigious schools and have won Guggenheim, Fulbright, NEH, and NEA awards, among others. The visual and performance arts faculty consists of leading teachers and practicing professionals in dance, film, music, theater, and visual arts.

Student Government

The Student Government Association, a campuswide organization, is made up of students elected by their peers. The organization is responsible for campus activities, sends representatives to faculty and administrative councils, and administers its own budget of approximately $240,000.

Admission Requirements

Applicants are considered by the Office of Admissions on an individual basis without regard to race, religion, geographic origin, or handicap. Major factors for admission consideration in the liberal arts and sciences programs are the high school and the academic records, including subjects studied, proficiency in English, test scores (SAT I or ACT), and recommendations. All students write an application essay to demonstrate an appropriate fit with Purchase. The liberal arts program has become increasingly selective, and early application is encouraged. A rolling admission system is used, with selective deadlines in some programs.

In the visual and performing arts, students must show proof of talent by means of an audition, interview, or portfolio review in addition to a review of their academic credentials. Entrance to these programs is very competitive. Therefore, the filing of an early application is encouraged for both freshmen and transfers. Typically, auditions of conservatory candidates are completed by the beginning of April.

Application and Information

Students are urged to visit the campus for information sessions. For further information, students should contact:

Betsy Immergut
Director of Admissions
Purchase College,
State University of New York
735 Anderson Hill Road
Purchase, New York 10577-1400
Telephone: 914-251-6300
Fax: 914-251-6314
E-mail: admissn@purchase.edu
World Wide Web: http://www.purchase.edu

A reason to cheer—graduation day at Purchase College.

QUEENS COLLEGE OF THE CITY UNIVERSITY OF NEW YORK

FLUSHING, NEW YORK

The College

Queens College, with more than 12,300 undergraduates, is one of the largest of the four-year colleges in the City University of New York (CUNY) system. The College opened its doors in 1937 with the goal of offering a first-rate education to talented people of all backgrounds and financial means. Often referred to as "the jewel of the CUNY system," Queens College enjoys a national reputation for its liberal arts and sciences and preprofessional programs. Like other CUNY colleges, Queens is a commuter school. Students come from 140 different nations; the result is an unusually rich education that gives Queens College graduates a competitive edge in today's global society.

The 77-acre campus is lined with trees surrounding grassy open spaces and a traditional quad. Some of the original Spanish-style stucco-and-tile buildings from the early 1900s still stand, including Jefferson Hall, which houses the beautiful new Welcome Center. The completely renovated Powdermaker Hall, the major classroom building, reopened in fall 2003 with state-of-the-art technology throughout. The College is also expanding its wireless capability, opening new cafés and dining areas, updating the spacious Student Union and several other buildings, and embarking on a variety of campus-beautification projects.

Since Queens is a commuter college, the administration is dedicated to making students feel that the College is their home away from home. A Child Development Center, staffed by professionals, offers inexpensive child-care services to students with children. There are more than 100 clubs on campus, from the Accounting Honors Society and Alliance of Latin American Students to clubs for theater, fencing, environmental science, salsa, and fine arts. Queens, the only CUNY college that participates in Division II sports, sponsors fifteen men's and women's teams and some of the finest athletics facilities in the metropolitan area. Ongoing cultural events include readings by renowned authors including Toni Morrison, Frank McCourt, and Norman Mailer; world-class concerts; and theater and dance performances. The College is home to the Godwin-Ternbach Museum, the only comprehensive museum in the borough of Queens, with art from antiquity to the present.

The College's centers and institutes also serve students and the larger urban community by addressing society's most important challenges, including cancer, AIDS, pollution, and racism; the changing workplace and workforce; and the heritages of the borough's many ethnic communities, including Asians, Greeks, Italians, and Jews.

Queens College has had a chapter of Phi Beta Kappa since 1950 (less than 10 percent of the nation's liberal arts colleges are members of Phi Beta Kappa, the nation's oldest and most respected undergraduate honors organization). In 1968, Queens College became a member of Sigma Xi, the national science honor society. The American Association of University Women includes Queens College in its list of approved colleges for membership.

Location

Queens College, located off Exit 24 of the Long Island Expressway, is in a residential area of Flushing. It is easily accessible by public transportation. The College is only 20 minutes from Manhattan, whose magnificent skyline overlooks the campus quad.

Majors and Degrees

The Bachelor of Arts degree is awarded in accounting, Africana studies, American studies, anthropology, art, art history, biology, Byzantine and modern Greek studies, chemistry, communication arts and media, communication sciences and disorders, comparative literature, computer science, drama and theater, East Asian studies, economics, education (early childhood and elementary), English, environmental sciences, environmental studies, film studies, French, geology, German, Greek, Hebrew, history, home economics, Italian, Jewish studies, labor studies, Latin, Latin American area studies, linguistics, mathematics, music, philosophy, physics, political science and government, psychology, Russian, sociology, Spanish, studio art, theater-dance, urban studies, and women's studies. The Bachelor of Arts program in secondary school teaching includes the following subject areas: Africana studies, anthropology, biology, chemistry, economics, English, French, geology, German, history, Italian, Latin American area studies, mathematics, physics, political science and government, sociology, Spanish, and urban studies. The College also awards the Bachelor of Arts in interdisciplinary studies; an individualized Bachelor of Arts program; the Bachelor of Business Administration; the Bachelor of Fine Arts in studio art; the Bachelor of Music in instrumental or vocal performance studies; and the Bachelor of Science in applied social science, computer science, environmental sciences, geology, nutrition and exercise sciences, and physical education.

The Departments of Chemistry, Computer Science, Philosophy, Physics, and Political Science and the Aaron Copland School of Music offer qualified undergraduates the opportunity to take combined bachelor's and master's degree programs.

Special interdisciplinary programs include Africana studies, American studies, business and liberal arts, business administration, Byzantine and modern Greek studies, Honors in Mathematical and Natural Sciences, Honors in the Humanities, Honors in the Social Sciences, Irish studies, Italian-American studies, Latin American and Latino studies, journalism, and religious studies. Special programs and advisement are also available in accounting, pre-engineering, prelaw, and the pre–health professions.

Academic Programs

Queens College prepares students to become leaders of today's global society by offering a rigorous education in the liberal arts and sciences under the guidance of a faculty dedicated to both teaching and research. Students graduate with the ability to think critically, address complex problems, explore various cultures, and use modern technologies and information resources.

The wide range of majors and interdisciplinary studies, combined with the award-winning Freshman Year Initiative Program, encourages students to explore their interests and abilities to the fullest. In most cases, degree programs require the completion of 120 credits.

The Bachelor of Business Administration (B.B.A.) degree provides a solid business education that responds to the demand of employers for specific quantitative and technological skills. Students may choose from three majors: finance, international business, and actuarial studies. The B.B.A. also has an investments/chartered financial analyst track to prepare students for the CFA examination, the only such undergraduate program in New York.

The business and liberal arts program is designed for students who want to study the theory and practice of business in a liberal arts context. Internships are sponsored by participating corporations.

The CUNY Honors Program includes unique interdisciplinary seminars, access to instructional technology, mentors, internships, and study abroad programs as well as a Cultural Passport that provides entry to the vast resources of New York City. Financial awards include full tuition and fees, an academic expense account of $7500 over four years, a textbook allowance, and a free laptop computer. The current profile for a Queens College honor student is a 95 average and 1320 combined SATs.

Honors in the Humanities includes a challenging curriculum based on the Great Books. Its facilities provide a quiet place for scholarly work and original research.

Honors in Mathematical and Natural Sciences is for students who have demonstrated exceptional ability in mathematics and science at the high school level.

The Honors in the Social Sciences program encourages students to gain an in-depth understanding of the traditions and methods of the social sciences.

The Adult Collegiate Education program, offered to students 25 and older, includes the option of obtaining college credit for life achievement. The Weekend College allows busy students to pursue their degrees by taking classes on Saturday and Sunday.

Academic Facilities

Among the many centers where research and creativity are joined in the pursuit of knowledge are the 2,200-seat Colden Center for the Performing Arts, which includes the Goldstein Theatre, designed especially for the staging of experimental student productions; the Aaron Copland School of Music facility, which includes thirty-five practice rooms and the 491-seat LeFrak Concert Hall; the Institute for Low-Temperature Physics; and the Speech and Hearing Center, which investigates communication disabilities and provides clinical experience for students of speech and hearing therapy.

Queens College Center for Environmental Teaching and Research, a "wilderness classroom" and research facility, is located at Caumsett State Park. At this lush, 1,600-acre site on Long Island's north shore, students come to study coastal and wetland ecology, botany, and environmental science. The College also administers the Louis Armstrong House, which in fall 2003 opened as a historic house museum. The Benjamin Rosenthal Library, with its soaring, light-filled atrium and art center, has more than 753,000 volumes. The Louis Armstrong Archives in the library, home to a vast personal collection of Armstrong's photographs, papers, recordings, and memorabilia, draws scholars and jazz fans alike from across America.

Costs

For New York State residents, undergraduate tuition for 2004–05 is $4000. For out-of-state and international students, undergraduate tuition is $360 per credit. There is a student activity and technology fee of $178 per semester for full-time undergraduate students and $110 per semester for part-time undergraduate students.

Financial Aid

More than 50 percent of Queens College students receive need-based financial aid. The aid may include state and federal loans and grants, Tuition Assistance Program awards, Regents Scholarships, Federal Direct Student Loans, Federal Pell Grants, State Aid for Native Americans, and Federal Work-Study awards.

The Queens College Scholars Program offers a variety of merit-based scholarships to full-time freshmen, with awards ranging from $2000 to $4500 per year. Selection is competitive, and scholarships are awarded on the basis of the high school record, test scores (SAT I and SAT II Subject Tests), writing ability, letters of recommendation, and extracurricular activities. Scholarships are renewable with continued high academic achievement. Applicants who rank in or near the top 10 percent of their class and have a rigorous academic program, excellent grades, and minimum combined SAT I scores of 1250 are encouraged to apply. The application deadline is February 1.

Faculty

The College's faculty consists of top scholars who are dedicated to teaching. There are 566 full-time faculty members; 95 percent have the terminal degree in their field and 80 percent have tenure. Many also teach in the doctoral programs at the CUNY Graduate Center. Faculty members have received numerous fellowships, awards, and research grants from such prestigious organizations as the National Science Foundation and the National Institutes of Health. In the past two years, faculty members received two Guggenheim awards and two Fulbright grants. CUNY has recognized the excellence of the faculty by honoring 10 members with the title of Distinguished Professor in fields as diverse as chemistry, economics, English, history, and physics. Among the more widely known faculty members are scientist Steven Markowitz; poets Nicole Cooley, Kimiko Hahn, and Yevgeny Yevtushenko; literary biographer Fred Kaplan; and Distinguished Professor Gregory Rabassa, renowned for his translation of writer Gabriel Garcia Marquez.

Student Government

Through the Student Association, students at Queens are able to run many services and activities that influence the daily operations of the College. Its elected officers and senators poll students regularly about relevant topics and sponsor such services as free legal advice, a typing center, apartment and tutor referral, and voter registration. In addition, students constitute one third of the College's Academic Senate.

Admission Requirements

Queens College seeks to admit freshmen who have completed a strong college-preparatory program in high school with at least a B+ average. Admission is based on a variety of factors, including the applicant's high school grades, academic program, and SAT or ACT scores. Successful candidates have chosen a well-rounded program of study that includes academic course work in English (4 years), foreign language (3 years), math (3 years), lab science (2 years), and social studies (4 years).

The Search for Education, Elevation & Knowledge Program (SEEK) offers academic support, counseling, and financial assistance to motivated students who would not otherwise qualify for admission. The SEEK Program has its own admissions criteria, including financial need.

For earliest consideration, students should apply by January 1 for fall admission and by October 15 for spring admission.

Application and Information

The staff of the Undergraduate Office of Admissions is available to answer questions and give more information. To make an appointment for a tour or to meet with a counselor, students should contact:

Office of Admissions
Jefferson Hall
Queens College of the City University of New York
65-30 Kissena Boulevard
Flushing, New York 11367-1597
Telephone: 718-997-5600
E-mail: admissions@qc.edu
World Wide Web: http://www.qc.cuny.edu

A view of the Queens College quad, part of a 77-acre campus in New York City, where students from 140 nations receive a solid education for today's global society.

QUEEN'S UNIVERSITY

KINGSTON, ONTARIO, CANADA

The University

Founded in 1841 by Royal Charter of Queen Victoria and named in honour of that monarch, Queen's University is the most exclusive university in Canada. Established as a Presbyterian seminary, Queen's has grown in a century and a half into an institution that offers undergraduate, graduate, and professional degrees in sixteen faculties, schools, and colleges and draws its faculty members and students from across Canada and throughout the world.

Queen's is recognized as a leader in postsecondary education. It was the first Canadian university to establish a scholarly journal, the *Queen's Quarterly*. Queen's was the first Canadian university to offer graduate programs and correspondence study and to establish programs in more than a dozen academic areas, including business and commerce, engineering physics, art conservation, policy studies, and industrial relations.

Queen's is host to fourteen federal and provincial research centres of excellence and the home of twenty-three research groups and institutes, including Canada's Cancer Clinical Trials Group and the Sudbury Neutrino Observatory. The University receives more than $70 million in research grants and contracts annually from federal and provincial governments and businesses, primarily in the fields of medicine, engineering, science, and social science.

National magazine polls of high school counsellors, academic administrators, and CEOs of major Canadian corporations consistently rank Queen's first in terms of its reputation for the quality of its programs, for its reputation for educating Canada's leaders of tomorrow, and for having the highest admission standards in the country.

Among the country's top research institutions, Queen's consistently attracts students from every Canadian province and more than seventy countries around the world. More than 15,000 students enrol annually, including 2,000 graduate students, medical residents, and interns. Another 3,000 students enrol in part-time and distance education programs. Undergraduate and professional enrolment is limited to approximately 12,000, and entrance requirements are the highest of all Ontario's universities.

Queen's has the oldest student association in Canada, the Alma Mater Society (AMS). The AMS oversees more than 200 student clubs, including the Debating Union, the Queen's Project on International Development, and CFRC-FM Radio. Apart from the Marconi companies, Queen's CFRC has the longest continuous history in radio of any institution in the world. When President Franklin Delano Roosevelt received his honourary degree from Queen's University in 1938 and used the occasion to make an important foreign policy speech, CFRC carried a feed to every radio network in North America.

Athletics and extracurricular activities are a long-standing tradition at Queen's. Nicknamed the Golden Gaels, the eleven men's and thirteen women's teams representing fourteen different interuniversity sports proudly wear the historic blue, gold, and red of the Tricolor. Along with the twenty-four interuniversity teams, Queen's athletics also supports six men's and five women's interuniversity clubs as well as three men's, two women's, and five coed competitive clubs. The combined number of forty-five interuniversity teams, clubs, and competitive clubs give the University's athletic program the distinction of being one of the largest of its kind in Canada. Queen's athletes are internationally competitive, having won Olympic, Commonwealth, and World University Games medals. Queen's crew is the most competitve Canadian team competing in the U.S. circuit. A team member won the U.S. College Singlehanded Championship in 1997 and earned Academic All-American status. The Queen's women's rowing team won the Club 8 Race at the 1997 Head of the Charles Regatta. In the past five years, Queen's varsity teams have won twenty-nine provincial and national titles.

Location

Queen's main campus is situated in the city of Kingston, Ontario, on the northeastern shore of Lake Ontario. It is halfway between Canada's two largest cities, Toronto and Montreal; a 2-hour drive from the nation's capital of Ottawa; and 90 miles north of Syracuse, New York. Founded in 1673, Kingston is one of Canada's oldest settlements and was the first capital of Canada. Kingston was originally settled by Europeans for its military value, and its strategic location and intellectual resources have made it home to international businesses such as Alcan, Bombardier, Bosal, Celanese, and DuPont. More than 1 million tourists visit the city annually to explore the museums and historic sites and enjoy the offerings of theatre troupes, classical concert groups, the Kingston Symphony, and art galleries and studios. Kingston is also a mecca for sailors, with some of the best freshwater sailing in the world. In 1976, the city hosted the sailing events of the XXI Olympiad.

Queen's also maintains a campus in the United Kingdom. Queen's International Study Centre (ISC) at Herstmonceux, East Sussex, is a modern educational facility housed within the walls of the fifteenth-century Herstmonceux Castle. The campus of the ISC is in a sheltered valley of gardens, walks, and groves in East Sussex, approximately 60 miles south of London.

Majors and Degrees

The Bachelor of Arts degree is offered in applied economics, art history, biology, Canadian studies, chemistry, classical studies, classics, computing and information science, developmental studies, drama, economics, English, environmental studies, film, French linguistics, French studies, geographic information management studies, geography, geological sciences, German, German studies, Greek, history, Italian, Jewish studies, language and linguistics, Latin, mathematics, mediaeval studies, music, philosophy, physics, political studies, psychology, religious studies, sociology, Spanish, Spanish and Latin American studies, stage and screen studies, statistics, and women's studies.

The Bachelor of Science degree is offered in astrophysics, biochemistry, biology, biomedical computing, chemical physics, chemistry, cognitive science, computing and information science, environmental science, geographic information management studies, geography, geological sciences, geological sciences with physics, life sciences, mathematical physics, mathematics, physics, psychology, respiratory therapy, software design, statistics, and X-ray technology.

The Bachelor of Science in Engineering degree is offered with the following specializations: chemical, civil, computer, electrical, geological, mechanical, mining, and engineering physics as well as two programs (engineering chemistry and mathematics and engineering) unique among Canadian universities. Five programs offer course patterns that lead to careers in environmental engineering.

The Bachelor of Commerce degree is offered with the following specializations: accounting, finance, industrial and human relations, international business, management information systems, marketing, operations, and quantitative methods.

Queen's offers a Bachelor of Education, a Bachelor of Fine Art, a Bachelor of Music, a Bachelor of Nursing Science, and a Bachelor of Physical and Health Education. Professional degrees are available in business administration, law, and medicine.

Academic Programs

The academic year runs from September through April and is divided into two 12-week terms. Spring and summer sessions are offered from May through August. Most undergraduate programs are of four years' duration.

Off-Campus Programs

Queen's International Study Centre at Herstmonceux, East Sussex, United Kingdom, offers students the opportunity to work toward their academic and professional goals with other university students from around the world. The ISC offers a number of programs, including the Canadian University Study Abroad Program (first-year and upper-year options), Visiting Upper Year Students Program, ESL Plus, and both spring and summer term programs. Programs permit students to choose from a series of courses that focus on the culture, history, and economics of Europe. The limited enrolment of the ISC helps create an enriched academic environment both inside and outside the classroom. Field studies are integrated into most courses to take advantage of the natural, historical, and cultural riches of Britain and Europe. In a typical term, art history students visit galleries, monuments, and buildings in and around London, and history students visit local sites of interest, such as Bath and Chichester. Major excursions to Brussels or Paris permit interdisciplinary visits to museums, embassies, international organizations, and agencies important to understanding the politics, economics, history, and culture of Europe. Regular excursions from the ISC to London also allow students to experience this major world capital both as students and as tourists. In addition to the established opportunities for participation in national and international exchanges, students may also arrange their own study-abroad term at any university in the world.

Queen's University also offers students the opportunity to participate in many exchange programs, including those in countries such as Australia, England, France, Germany, Scotland, and Sweden.

Academic Facilities

The Queen's Libraries, including the Stauffer Library, the Douglas Engineering and Science Library, four departmental libraries, and the faculty libraries of education, health sciences, and law, hold more than 5 million items, including books, journals, pamphlets, newspapers, audiovisual materials, and collections of microfilms, maps, aerial photographs, slides, and prints. The Queen's Libraries also provide access to hundreds of electronic resources and databases. The University Archives houses material of national, provincial, and regional significance. The Reading Room can accommodate laptop computers, allowing students to access materials relating to Canadian public affairs, business, literature, art, Kingston and the area, and the University itself.

The $56-million Biosciences Complex is home to the Biology Department, the School of Environmental Studies, three chemical engineering labs working on fermentation and bioremediation, the Kingston Technology Exchange Centre, a Molecular Evolution Laboratory, and a state-of-the-art Phytotron, including six research-quality greenhouses and twenty-five plant growth chambers. The recently completed Chernoff Hall is the largest chemistry complex of its kind in North America.

Queen's 5,000-acre biology station at Lake Opinicon is the largest research station of its kind in Canada. The station is internationally recognized for studies in freshwater biology. The Agnes Etherington Art Centre on Queen's campus is one of Canada's most attractive art galleries, the third largest among provincial galleries in Ontario, and Kingston's only art museum. Queen's Information Technology Services helps students and staff members to connect electronically with people and information across the campus and around the world. All Queen's students, whether they live in residence (where all 3,700 rooms have high-speed Ethernet connections) or off campus, have access to the Internet, unlimited e-mail, and personal space on the World Wide Web. Many professors now post lectures and other course materials on Web pages.

Costs

Queen's University is a publicly supported institution. There are significant financial advantages for American students who choose to attend Canada's most prestigious university. The fees charged to international students are very competitive when compared to those of programs of equivalent stature in the U.S. All fees are in U.S. dollars. Tuition fees for American and international students in the 2003–04 academic year were $7000 for arts and science students and $11,000 for engineering students. Room and board fees for students in on-campus residences were approximately $4000, regardless of citizenship. Health insurance, books, transportation, entertainment, and personal expenses are not included in the above fees.

Financial Aid

Four entrance scholarships are available to international students. After one year of study at Queen's, all students, regardless of citizenship, are eligible for all upper-year student awards and scholarships. U.S. students who qualify for the Federal Stafford Student Loan program may apply such funds to Queen's University fees. Queen's has been authorized by the U.S. Department of Education to administer Stafford Loans. Any student with Canadian citizenship, regardless of residency, is eligible for all entrance scholarships.

Faculty

Queen's faculty is drawn from leading institutions around the world. More than half of the teaching faculty members hold graduate degrees from universities outside of Canada, and nearly one third of the teaching faculty holds graduate degrees from U.S. colleges and universities, including Harvard, Princeton, MIT, Berkeley, and Cornell. More than 850 full-time faculty members are assisted by highly qualified adjunct faculty and staff members.

Student Government

The Alma Mater Society, the oldest student association in Canada, is the elected governing body of all Queen's students, except those in the School of Graduate Studies and Research, who elect their own Graduate Student Society. Students participate in all levels of decision making, with nearly one quarter of the seventy spaces on the University Senate devoted to elected students. The Board of Trustees also counts student representatives within its ranks.

Admission Requirements

Individual consideration is given to all candidates from an American school system. Students graduating from a university-preparatory program are considered for admission after providing midyear grade 12 marks (or final grade 12 marks if already graduated), SAT I scores (minimum combined score of 1200 and minimum scores of 580 verbal and 520 math), rank in class (if available), and a school profile. For programs in which mathematics is a requirement, four (preferably five) full-year credit courses in mathematics are required. For programs in which biology, physics, and/or chemistry are required, one (preferably two) full-credit courses in each are required. Advanced Placement (AP) courses in prerequisite subjects are highly recommended whenever possible. AP courses are considered excellent preparation for university courses. However, these courses do not carry degree credit.

Accommodation for first-year students is guaranteed in Queen's on-campus residences, provided the deadline for accepting the offer of admission is met.

Application and Information

Applications for full- or part-time studies must be submitted through the Ontario Universities' Application Centre (OUAC), Box 1328, Guelph, Ontario N1H 7P4, Canada; telephone: 519-823-1940. Online applications are available at http://www.ouac.on.ca.

For additional information, students should contact:

Admission Services
Queen's University
Kingston, Ontario K7L 3N6
Canada
Telephone: 613-533-2218
Fax: 613-533-6810
E-mail: admissn@post.queensu.ca
World Wide Web: http://www.queensu.ca

QUINCY UNIVERSITY

QUINCY, ILLINOIS

The University

Quincy University is a private Roman Catholic university of the liberal arts and sciences. It was founded in 1860 by the Franciscan Friars, who have influenced the world by caring about people as people and urging them to fulfill their potential. This spirit is still maintained at Quincy University today. The University prides itself on its personal approach to learning. Small classes, a dedicated faculty, close faculty-student relationships, and a comfortable atmosphere on campus all create an environment conducive to personal growth and development. The University offers courses on both its 52-acre main campus and the 23-acre North Campus, ten blocks away. Shuttle bus service moves students between these campuses regularly.

The 1,200 students come from diverse social and economic backgrounds. Although the majority are from the Midwest, twenty-four states and ten countries are represented in the student body. Quincy University is a residential campus with more than 70 percent of the students living on campus. Campus housing options are varied and include single-sex and coed residence halls, apartments, and houses. Numerous campus organizations offer unlimited opportunities for students to participate in both University and community activities. A National Public Radio station, music performance groups, publications, honor and service societies, a lecture series, and concerts are a few of the many extracurricular opportunities available to students. Eighty percent of the students participate in intramural sports. Quincy University also maintains membership in the NCAA and the Great Lakes Valley Conference. Intercollegiate sports for men are baseball, basketball, football, golf, soccer, tennis, and volleyball. Women's intercollegiate sports are basketball, golf, soccer, softball, tennis, and volleyball.

Career planning and placement counseling is available to students throughout their academic career. Quincy University has an outstanding placement record; more than 96 percent of graduates are placed in jobs or graduate schools within 180 days of graduation. Individual assistance with academic planning, study skills, and tutorial work, as well as personal and vocational counseling, is provided free of charge.

At the graduate level, Quincy University offers programs of study leading to the M.B.A. and M.S.Ed. degrees.

Location

The University is located in a residential section of Quincy, a city of 50,000 people, situated on the bluffs of the Mississippi River. It is within easy traveling time of St. Louis (2 hours), Kansas City (4 hours), and Chicago (4½ hours). Good highways and bus, train, and air service make the area easily accessible from any part of the nation. Quincy has a rich and distinguished tradition in the arts. It is noted for its fine architecture and extensive park system.

Majors and Degrees

Quincy University awards the Bachelor of Arts (B.A.), Bachelor of Fine Arts (B.F.A.), and Bachelor of Science (B.S.) degrees. Programs of study include accounting, art, aviation, aviation management, biology, biological sciences, biological sciences education, business administration, chemistry, clinical laboratory science, computer information systems, communication, computer science, criminal justice, elementary education, English, English education, finance, history, history education, humanities (interdisciplinary), human services, management, marketing, music, music education, nursing, physical education, political science, psychology, social work, special education–learning disabilities, sports management, theology, theology/Franciscan studies, and theology/pastoral ministry. A Bachelor of Science in Nursing (B.S.N.) is available through a cooperative program with Blessing-Riemann College of Nursing.

Minors are available in most programs; concentrations are offered in physics and reading. A certificate program in business and a coaching specialty in physical education are also available.

Preprofessional programs include dentistry, engineering, law, medicine, physical therapy, and veterinary medicine.

Academic Program

The academic program at Quincy University is based on the belief that liberal arts is the most functional and exciting tradition in education. The curriculum is designed to provide students with the fundamentals of a liberal arts education and at the same time prepare them for a rewarding professional and personal life. The flexible curriculum design allows for double majors or major-minor combinations, student-designed majors, and interdepartmental majors. An honors program, independent studies, special-topics courses, independent research, practicums, and internships are also available to meet the special needs of students.

To be eligible for a baccalaureate degree, a student must complete a minimum of 124 semester hours of university courses with at least a C average. The degree program requires 43 semester hours in general education and "tools" courses, 30–33 hours in a major, and at least 36 hours each in distributed electives and upper-level course work.

Quincy University accepts credit earned through the Advanced Placement Program, the College-Level Examination Program, challenge examinations, and, in some cases, academically related experience.

Off-Campus Programs

Arrangements are made with area schools, health facilities, businesses, and industries for such credit-bearing activities as student teaching, clinical training, internships, and practicums. The University also promotes the Early Exploratory Internship Program to its first- and second-year students, allowing them to gain preprofessional experience with area businesses and agencies. Study abroad is possible through many options, with the academic credit for this study preplanned and integrated into the degree program.

Academic Facilities

The Brenner Library, considered one of the top three private-college libraries in the state of Illinois, houses more than 260,000 volumes and 182,000 microtext items and subscribes to 725 periodicals. Among the outstanding holdings are a rare book collection, the 75,000-volume Bonaventure Collection of early Christian and medieval history and theology, and the 4,000-volume Fraborese Collection on Spanish-American history. Through the University's membership in the Online

Computer Library Center, Quincy University students have access to millions of books in libraries throughout the Midwest and the nation. The library is also equipped with a computerized reference service.

A modern academic complex located at North Campus houses laboratories for chemistry, physics, biology, engineering, and psychology as well as lecture halls and faculty offices. Six computer labs and more than 200 workstations are available for student use. Students also have unlimited access to personal computers, various networks, Internet, and UNIX. Additional special facilities are a radio station; a fully equipped television studio; the Ameritech Center for Communication, a state-of-the-art computer writing lab and classroom; and a newly opened Student Health and Fitness Center.

Costs

The costs for the 2003–04 academic year were $16,850 for tuition (12–18 credit hours), $450 for the student activity/computer fee, $3265 for room (double occupancy), and $2215 for board.

Financial Aid

More than 95 percent of the students at Quincy University receive some form of financial assistance. The University participates in the Federal Pell Grant, Federal Supplemental Educational Opportunity Grant (FSEOG), Federal Perkins Loan, Federal Work-Study (FWS), and Federal Stafford Student Loan programs. Illinois State Grants are available for qualified Illinois residents. Quincy University awards academic scholarships ranging from $500 to full tuition. Need-based grants are also available. Students who wish to apply for aid must complete the Free Application for Federal Student Aid (FAFSA) as well as the brief QU Application for Financial Aid. Notification of financial aid awards is made on a rolling basis. Early application is recommended, and priority is given to students who apply before February 15. Transfer applicants are required to submit a transcript from each college or university attended.

Faculty

The Quincy University faculty is composed of 102 professionals, highly qualified in their respective fields. Although many are engaged in research, teaching is the top priority at Quincy University. The University's favorable student-faculty ratio of 12:1 and its experienced faculty members, many of whom have had actual work experience in their field, bring an added dimension to the classroom. Eighty-six percent of the faculty members have the highest degree possible in their field.

Student Government

Students participate in University governance through representation on most University committees, including the Academic Affairs Committee, Athletic Advisory Committee, Student Life Committee, and University Judicial Board. The Student Senate provides for effective student participation in all aspects of University life.

Admission Requirements

Quincy University encourages applications from students who are serious about enrolling in a coeducational university of the liberal arts and sciences and who have demonstrated through their previous academic work an ability to profit from and contribute to the University. Each applicant for admission is evaluated individually. Primary consideration is given to the student's previous academic record. Quincy University recommends that prospective students take a strong college-preparatory program in high school. The Office of Admissions evaluates the prospective freshman's high school record in the following areas: number of academic courses taken, level of difficulty of courses attempted, type of high school attended, grade point average, standardized test scores, class rank, and extracurricular activities. All freshmen are required to submit SAT I or ACT scores.

Transfer students who have earned fewer than 24 semester hours must submit a high school transcript in addition to their college transcripts and should have maintained an overall grade point average of at least 2.0 (C) during their collegiate years. Transfer students may enter at three times during the year: August, January, or June.

International students must submit a transcript from each secondary and collegiate institution they have attended. All non-English transcripts must be translated into English before submission to the Office of Admissions. All international students must also submit TOEFL scores or demonstrate proficiency in the English language.

Application and Information

All students seeking admission are encouraged to apply early. Applications are evaluated after all required application materials have been received. Notification of admission decisions is made on a rolling basis.

Parents, students, and student groups are always welcome to visit the University. The Office of Admissions welcomes visitors from 8 a.m. to 5 p.m., Monday through Friday. Saturday visitors are welcome by appointment. If possible, campus visits should be scheduled during the academic year, when classes are in session. Accepted students may stay overnight in residence halls during the academic year.

For more information about the University's 143-year tradition of excellence, students should contact:

Director of Admissions
Quincy University
1800 College Avenue
Quincy, Illinois 62301-2699
Telephone: 217-228-5210
800-688-HAWK (4295) (toll-free)
E-mail: admissions@quincy.edu
World Wide Web: http://www.quincy.edu

Quincy University's new $12-million Student Health and Fitness Center.

QUINNIPIAC UNIVERSITY
HAMDEN, CONNECTICUT

The College

Quinnipiac offers four-year and graduate-level degree programs leading to careers in health sciences, business, communications, natural sciences, education, liberal arts, and law. A curriculum that combines a career focus with a globally oriented liberal arts background prepares graduates for the future, whether they start their careers right after commencement or opt to pursue advanced study.

Quinnipiac is coeducational and nonsectarian and currently enrolls 5,089 full-time undergraduates, 1,015 full-time graduates, and 1,017 part-time students in its undergraduate, graduate, professional, and continuing education programs. Less than 35 percent of the students are residents of Connecticut; the rest represent all regions of the United States and many other countries. The emphasis at Quinnipiac is on community. Students, faculty members, and staff members interact both in and out of the classroom and office. Quinnipiac is big enough to sustain a wide variety of people and programs but small enough to keep students from getting lost in the shuffle. Life on campus emphasizes students' personal, as well as academic, growth. The approximately sixty-five student organizations and extracurricular activities, including intramural and intercollegiate (NCAA Division I) athletics, give students a chance to exercise their talents, their muscles, and their leadership skills. The University has a student newspaper and an FM radio station (WQAQ) and intercollegiate teams in men's baseball, basketball, cross-country, golf, ice hockey, lacrosse, soccer, tennis, and track and in women's basketball, cross-country, field hockey, ice hockey, lacrosse, soccer, softball, tennis, track, and volleyball.

Quinnipiac's 400-acre main campus has fifty buildings. In addition to the academic facilities described in the section on the next page, the University has twenty-five residence halls of different styles, all with functional furnishings and decor. The residence halls house 3,500 men and women, about 70 percent of the undergraduate population. All students have in-room access to e-mail and Netscape. Housing on campus is guaranteed for three years. The Carl Hansen Student Center—containing recreational facilities, meeting rooms, and offices for student organizations—is adjacent to Alumni Hall, a large multipurpose auditorium used for theater productions, concerts, lectures, films, and various University and community events.

Facilities for athletic and fitness activities are found in and around the gymnasium and physical education building. The gymnasium seats 1,500 and includes two regulation-size basketball courts. Also available are a steam room, a sauna, and a 24,000-square-foot recreation/fitness center with a large free-weight room; an exercise machine center; aerobics studios; basketball, volleyball, and tennis courts; and a suspended indoor track. There are also lighted tennis courts, playing fields, and miles of scenic routes for running and biking.

Quinnipiac offers a full range of services to assist students in achieving personal and career goals. Individual career counseling is supplemented by a computerized guidance system that lets students enter information about their interests and skills and receive a printout with current data on professions, jobs, and graduate schools. Quinnipiac also has an active career and internship placement office that serves as a liaison between the corporate community and students, new graduates, and alumni.

Graduate programs lead to the Master of Science degree in advanced accounting, advanced practice or orthopedic physical therapy, computer information systems, e-media, journalism, and molecular and cell biology; the Master of Health Science in medical lab sciences, pathologist assistant studies, and physician assistant studies; the Master of Science in Nursing in nurse practitioner studies; the Master of Health Administration; the Master of Business Administration; and the Master of Arts in Teaching. A $22-million, on-campus facility houses the Quinnipiac University School of Law and its library. The School offers full-time and part-time programs leading to a J.D. degree or J.D./M.B.A. or J.D./M.H.A. degrees in combination with the School of Business.

Location

Situated at the foot of Sleeping Giant Mountain in the New Haven suburb of Hamden, Quinnipiac provides the best of the country and the city. The University is only 10 minutes from New Haven, 30 minutes from Hartford (the state capital), and less than 2 hours from New York City and Boston. The University shuttle bus provides easy access to area shopping and attractions. Bordering the campus is Sleeping Giant State Park, which also provides a range of recreational activities. In addition to adjacent towns such as Cheshire, Wallingford, and North Haven, a short trip by car or bus puts students in New Haven, where they can visit the acclaimed Yale Center for British Art, attend a performance at the Schubert or Long Wharf Theater, marvel at the dinosaurs in the Peabody Museum of Natural History, or dine in fine restaurants. Quinnipiac's New England location also makes it convenient to enjoy a day in the surf or on the slopes. The beaches on Long Island Sound are easy to reach, and major ski resorts are only an hour's drive from campus.

Majors and Degrees

The School of Health Sciences grants bachelor's degrees in athletic training/sports medicine, biochemistry, biology (with premedical options in chiropractic, dentistry, medicine, podiatry, and veterinary medicine), biomedical science, chemistry, diagnostic imaging, microbiology/molecular biology, nursing, occupational/physical therapy (5½-year entry-level master's), physician assistant studies (6-year freshman entry-level master's), respiratory care, and veterinary technology.

In the School of Business, bachelor's degree programs are offered in accounting, advertising, computer information systems, entrepreneurship, finance, international business, management, and marketing. The School also offers a five-year combined-degree program in which students may be awarded the B.S. degree in business and a graduate degree in accounting, business administration, computer information systems, or health administration (M.S., M.B.A., or M.H.A.).

The College of Liberal Arts offers bachelor's degree programs in computer science, criminal justice, English, gerontology, history, interactive digital design, legal studies (paralegal), liberal studies, mathematics, political science, psychology (with concentrations in child development, human services, and industrial psychology), social services, sociology, and Spanish. Students can also design their own majors. Certification for teaching elementary, intermediate, and secondary education is offered through a five-year program, resulting in a Master of Arts in Teaching. A bachelor's degree program in psychobiology is interdisciplinary in nature. Students can also continue their study in graduate programs in business, law, journalism, or e-media.

The School of Communications offers undergraduate majors in e-media, journalism, media studies, production, and public relations and graduate programs in journalism and e-media for writing and design in the journalistic community.

Academic Program

All degree programs at Quinnipiac University are offered through one of the five academic schools. The academic year consists of two 15-week fall and spring semesters and two summer sessions. All baccalaureate candidates are required to complete the

Core Curriculum, which consists of up to 50 of the 120 semester hours of credit generally needed for graduation at the bachelor's degree level. The Core Curriculum promotes the achievement of college-level competence in English, mathematics, and such specialized areas as foreign language or computer science. It requires study in the artistic tradition, behavioral and social sciences, humanities, and physical and biological sciences.

Advanced placement, credit, or both are given for appropriate scores on Advanced Placement tests and CLEP general and subject examinations as well as for International Baccalaureate higher-level subjects.

Off-Campus Programs

Students in any of the four undergraduate schools can get hands-on experience in their field through off-campus internships. The University is affiliated with outstanding health and scientific institutions—such as Children's Hospital (Boston), Yale–New Haven Hospital, Hartford Hospital, Gaylord Rehabilitation Hospital (Wallingford), and the University of Connecticut Health Center—throughout the state and the nation. Opportunities for internships also exist in industry, large and small businesses, media outlets, and social and governmental agencies. Academic credit is available for internships and affiliations, which are often part of degree requirements.

Academic Facilities

Academic life focuses on the Bernhard Library building, which recently underwent a $12-million renovation. Automated library systems and more than 150 personal computer workstations are located throughout the library and provide access to extensive electronic resources on CD and the Web, as well as the University's own print collections. The air-conditioned structure houses the library, with its extensive collection of books, periodicals, government documents, films, tapes, and microforms. Modern classrooms and laboratories are located in Tator Hall. The computing facilities include two Sun servers running Solaris and more than thirty Dell Windows 2000 servers. Five classrooms and four teaching laboratories contain approximately 200 computers. The multimedia and video laboratories in the Ed McMahon Mass Communication Center each have fourteen Apple MacIntosh G3 and G4 workstations.

The new Financial Technology Center at Quinnipiac University's School of Business is a high-tech, simulated trading floor providing students with the opportunity to access real-time financial data, conduct interactive trading simulations, and develop financial models in preparation for careers in finance.

All incoming students must purchase a University-recommended laptop that is supported by a campus wireless network, for classroom and residence hall use.

The Academic Center houses classrooms, laboratories, and an auditorium lecture hall. The Echlin Health Sciences Center houses physical and occupational therapy, nursing, and related fields of study. Buckman Center is where many of the science labs are located, including those for chemistry, respiratory care, and veterinary technology. A clinical skills lab, for use by nursing students and the physician assistant program, simulates a critical care hospital center. Also in the center is the Buckman Theatre, which holds plays, concerts, and lectures. The Lender School of Business Center has local area network classrooms, satellite capabilities, and the Ed McMahon Center for Mass Communications, containing state-of-the-art TV and radio broadcast studios, print journalism and desktop publishing laboratories, and a news technology center.

Costs

The basic 2003–04 cost was $30,570, of which tuition and fees were $21,120 and room and board were, on average, $9450. Other expenses, typically $1200 per year, include books, laboratory and course fees associated with specific courses, and travel costs.

Financial Aid

Quinnipiac designs financial aid packages to include grants and scholarships that do not have to be repaid, self-help financial aid programs such as federal and University-based work study, and loans. Quinnipiac uses the Free Application for Federal Student Aid (FAFSA) to determine need. Transfer students are eligible for the same need-based financial aid consideration as first-time freshmen. Quinnipiac also offers a number of renewable scholarships to new, full-time freshmen that are awarded partly or entirely on the basis of academic merit.

Faculty

The faculty is characterized by its teaching competence and outstanding academic qualifications. Of the 280 full-time faculty members, 70 percent have earned a Ph.D. or the appropriate terminal degree in their field. The faculty also includes a number of part-time teachers who are practicing professionals and experts in their fields. Classes are taught by these scholars and professionals and not by student instructors, and a low student-faculty ratio promotes close associations among faculty and students.

Student Government

The Student Government is the student legislative body of Quinnipiac. It represents student opinion, promotes student welfare, supervises student organizations, appropriates funds for student groups, and provides voting student representation on the Judicial Board, the College Senate, and the Board of Trustees.

Admission Requirements

Quinnipiac seeks students from a broad range of backgrounds. Candidates are evaluated on the basis of a completed application, as described below. Interviews are not always required, but visits to campus are strongly encouraged. Transfer students are welcome. Quinnipiac sponsors four open house programs during the year and several Saturday morning information sessions followed by a campus tour.

Application and Information

Quinnipiac has a rolling admission policy for its undergraduate programs but recommends that freshman applicants submit their application materials by February 1 and that students applying to the physical and occupational therapy and physician assistant studies programs submit their applications by December 31. Applications can be filed at any time beginning in the senior year of high school. Selection decisions are made as soon as applications are completed. For most programs, a completed application consists of a Quinnipiac application form; a transcript of completed high school courses, including grades for the first quarter of the senior year; a score report for either the SAT I or ACT; a personal statement (essay); and the application fee: $45, paper; $30 online at the University Web site. Students placed on a waiting list are notified of any openings by June 1. Transfer students are expected to forward a transcript of college course work undertaken. Quinnipiac subscribes to the May 1 Candidates Reply Date Agreement. For information regarding full-time undergraduate study, students should contact:

Office of Undergraduate Admissions
Quinnipiac University
Hamden, Connecticut 06518-1940
Telephone: 203-582-8600
800-462-1944 (toll-free)
Fax: 203-582-8906
E-mail: admissions@quinnipiac.edu
World Wide Web: http://www.quinnipiac.edu

For information regarding transfer and part-time study:

Office of Transfer and Part-time Admissions
Quinnipiac University
Hamden, Connecticut 06518-1940
Telephone: 203-582-8612
World Wide Web: http://www.quinnipiac.edu

RADFORD UNIVERSITY

RADFORD, VIRGINIA

The University

Radford University is a comprehensive, residential university committed to individualized instruction in medium-sized classes, high academic standards, and excellence in teaching. Established in 1910, Radford's enrollment has grown to more than 9,000, of whom 87 percent are undergraduates. The state-supported University offers 112 undergraduate and thirty-six graduate program options through the College of Arts and Sciences, the College of Business and Economics, the College of Education and Human Development, the College of Information Science and Technology, the College of Visual and Performing Arts, the Waldron College of Health and Human Services, and the College of Graduate and Extended Studies.

At the graduate level, Radford University awards M.S., M.A., M.B.A., M.F.A., M.S.N., M.S.W., and Ed.S. degrees.

Fifteen residence halls, housing from 120 to 950 students each, offer a variety of options to the 3,250 students who live on campus. All residence halls are in suite arrangements, with two rooms sharing one bathroom. Freshmen are required to live on campus and can choose one of several learning/residential communities. Most off-campus students reside in rental housing within four to five blocks of the campus. Members of the Radford community come from all over Virginia as well as from forty-five other states and forty-seven countries. Radford provides many opportunities for students to participate in exchange and study-abroad programs.

Radford University offers guest speakers, theater productions, concerts, films, social fraternities and sororities, student publications, WVRU radio station and television station, intramural sports, and other cultural, social, and leisure opportunities. In all, there are more than 200 clubs and organizations on campus. Heth Student Center has lounge, recreation, study, and meeting areas. Dalton Hall, the student services building, houses the food court, dining hall, bookstore, and post office. The Dedmon Center, a $10.8-million sports and recreation complex, provides complete sports and fitness facilities, including an Olympic-size swimming pool and Cupp Stadium, a new track and soccer complex. Radford University's teams participate in nineteen intercollegiate sports and are members of NCAA Division I.

Location

Radford, a city of 16,200 people, is located approximately 36 miles southwest of Roanoke in the Blue Ridge Mountains in scenic western Virginia. The Blue Ridge Parkway, Appalachian Trail, New River, and Claytor Lake, which has more than 100 miles of shoreline, offer many outdoor activities in a region noted for its natural beauty. Students can ski, hike, canoe, bicycle, and enjoy other seasonal activities.

The local community offers opportunities for dining, socializing, shopping, and off-campus living. The University's campus is near I-81 and is located about 45 minutes from the Roanoke airport.

Majors and Degrees

Radford University awards B.A., B.S., B.F.A., B.M., B.B.A., B.S.N., B.S.W., and B.G.S. degrees in the areas of accounting; anthropology; art; biology; chemistry; communication; communication sciences and disorders; computer science and technology; criminal justice; dance; economics; English; fashion; finance; foods and nutrition; foreign languages (French, German, Spanish); geography; geology; history; human development; information science and systems; interdisciplinary studies (education); interior design; liberal studies; management; marketing; mathematics and statistics; media studies; medical technology; music; music therapy; nursing; philosophy and religious studies; physical education; physical science; political science; psychology; recreation, parks, and tourism; social science; social work; sociology; and theater.

Academic Programs

To be eligible for an undergraduate degree, students must complete at least 120 semester hours of college-level academic work, including 50 semester hours of general education courses. Honors courses are available to students enrolled in the Highlander Scholars Program and to any qualified student. The Office of New Student Programs coordinates several programs designed to ease the transition from high school to college. The University 100 class and Success Starts Here are programs that help first-year students become active and successful college students. Quest, Radford's summer orientation program, allows incoming students to acclimate themselves to campus, receive advising, register for classes, and make friends before coming to school in the fall. An Army ROTC program is also available to interested and qualified students.

The University year consists of two semesters, August to December (fall) and January to May (spring), and summer sessions.

Academic Facilities

The McConnell Library offers students access to textual material, periodicals, and information recorded on film, microfilm, records, compact audio discs, and tapes. Services include interlibrary loans and computer-assisted bibliographical searches.

RU's newest academic facilities include Waldron Hall and a newly renovated Peters Hall. Completed in fall 2000, Waldron Hall serves as the home for the Waldron College of Health and Human Services and is one of the country's most comprehensive and technologically sophisticated educational environments. Academic divisions include the Schools of Nursing, Social Work, and Allied Health, which contains the departments of communication sciences and disorders, foods and nutrition, and recreation, parks, and tourism. An on-site interdisciplinary clinic, in which teams of students and faculty members treat and counsel underinsured and uninsured patients, provides students with hands-on experience in their chosen fields. Renovated in 2003, Peters Hall houses the entire College of Education and Human Development under one roof. This academic facility has numerous state-of-the-art classrooms with "smart boards," a Teaching Resource Center, and new studios for the Dance Department.

Costs

The basic expenses for the 2003–04 academic year (August–May) were $4140 for tuition and fees for in-state undergraduate students ($11,202 for out-of-state students), $5660 for room and board, and an average of $700 for books and supplies.

Financial Aid

The University provides financial aid awards, based on demonstrated financial need, and scholarships, based on leadership, character, and academic achievement. Financial aid at Radford University is provided through loans, work-study awards, and grants from the federal and state governments and from private funds established through the Radford University Foundation. In addition, some departments have special fellowship funds for undergraduates. Students seeking financial aid should submit the Free Application for Federal Student Aid (FAFSA) to Federal Student Aid Programs by March 1. Transfer students who have attended summer school or who transfer for the spring semester must also request a completed Financial Aid Transcript from colleges and universities previously attended, even if financial aid was not received.

The Radford University Foundation sponsors an annual scholarship competition for qualified freshman students. For students to be eligible to compete, completed admissions applications must be received by the Office of Admissions no later than December 15. Students chosen to compete for scholarships are those who have excelled academically during high school, and finalists are invited to campus for interviews with RU faculty and staff members and current scholarship recipients. Several full scholarships, which include the equivalent of in-state tuition and fees, room and board, and a book stipend, are available. Partial scholarships, which are applied to tuition and fees, are also available.

Faculty

Eighty-two percent of Radford University's faculty members hold terminal degrees in their fields of study. The faculty represents forty-five states and eleven countries. With a student-faculty ratio of 19:1, Radford is committed to interaction between faculty members and students both in and out of the classroom. In addition to their primary responsibilities of teaching and advising students, faculty members are engaged in research, publication, and other professional activities. Fewer than 5 percent of Radford's undergraduate classes are taught by graduate instructors.

Student Government

Radford University's Student Government Association enables students to participate in the administration of their own affairs and provides representation on the students' behalf. Every undergraduate student is automatically a member of the Student Government Association. The chief divisions of the association are the executive council, cabinet, senate, house of representatives, off-campus student council, graduate student council, class representatives council, black student affairs council, international student affairs council, and diversity promotions council.

Admission Requirements

Admission to Radford University is based on a review of each applicant's academic qualifications. The University admits students whose ability, preparation, and character indicate potential for success in the programs of study offered. Admission is not based on race, sex, handicap, age, veteran status, national origin, religious or political affiliation, or sexual preference. Applicants for admission are considered on the basis of high school records (course of study, grade point average, and rank in class), SAT I or ACT scores, and evidence of interest and motivation. Most successful applicants have taken 4 units of English, 4 units of college-preparatory math, 4 units of lab science, 4 units of social science (including American history), and 3–4 units of foreign language. Students planning to major in nursing should complete units in both biology and chemistry. Students who wish to visit the campus are encouraged to call for an appointment between 8 a.m. and 5 p.m., Monday through Friday. Tours of the campus are conducted at 10 a.m., noon, and 2 p.m., Monday and Friday; 10 a.m. and 2 p.m., Tuesday, Wednesday, and Thursday; and at 10 a.m., 11 a.m., and noon on most Saturdays during the academic year.

Application and Information

A complete application consists of an application form returned with a nonrefundable application fee, an official transcript of high school work completed, and official SAT I or ACT results. Students wishing to transfer to Radford University from an accredited college or university should send an application form and official transcripts of work attempted at all colleges attended. Applications for fall admission should be received by April 1 for new freshmen and June 1 for new transfer students. Applications received after these dates are reviewed on a space-available basis.

For more information, students should contact:

Office of Admissions
Radford University
Radford, Virginia 24142-6903
Telephone: 540-831-5371
540-831-5128 (V/TDD)
800-890-4265 (toll-free)
Fax: 540-831-5038
E-mail: ruadmiss@radford.edu
World Wide Web: http://www.radford.edu

Whitt Hall at Radford University.

RAMAPO COLLEGE OF NEW JERSEY

MAHWAH, NEW JERSEY

The College

Ramapo College of New Jersey has been recognized by the State General Assembly as New Jersey's "public liberal arts college." Offering a diverse student body the educational ambience associated with liberal arts colleges, Ramapo has fulfilled its promise as one of the more distinguished institutions of moderate size. In recognition of Ramapo College of New Jersey's strong commitment to character-building programs, The John Templeton Foundation, which publishes a reference guide for students, families, and high schools, named Ramapo to its Honor Roll. The Honor Roll program recognizes and promotes colleges and universities that emphasize character building as an integral part of the college experience.

Today, Ramapo is a coeducational college of liberal arts and professional studies that offers degree programs in the traditional arts and sciences, in interdisciplinary studies such as environmental science and law and society, and in the professions of business administration, education, nursing, and social work. The student body reflects the diversity of the regions served by the College, including more than twenty states and sixty countries. This diversity, the talents of the faculty, the expectations the College has of its students, and the proximity of the College to some of the world's major multinational organizations give Ramapo an edge in meeting its objective of preparing students of all ages for an increasingly interdependent and multicultural world. For these reasons, Ramapo is called "the college of choice for a global education."

Ramapo College takes pride in four distinctive features that enhance each student's education: concern for student development in and out of the classroom, an exemplary faculty committed to a curricular emphasis on the international and multicultural dimensions of all fields of study, an interdisciplinary orientation in its philosophy and programs, and a collaborative association with local corporations, communities, and educational institutions in the development of experiential educational opportunities and other new ventures both nationally and globally.

The current undergraduate enrollment is approximately 5,200 men and women. During the academic year, the campus is alive with exciting cultural events, such as music festivals, plays, art exhibits, and film and lecture series. The Student Center, with recreation rooms, lounges, and club offices, is the hub of on-campus activity. Students take an active part in planning the calendar of events for the College community. The campus contains attractive residential units housing approximately 2,300 students. An additional 300-bed residence hall opens in early 2004, along with a new 90,000-square-foot sports and recreation center. In addition, a sports complex has twelve lighted tennis courts; baseball, soccer, and softball fields; and a track. The gym is equipped with a full-size basketball court, an Olympic-size indoor pool, and a fitness center. At Ramapo, sports facilities are available for all students, not just the varsity athletes, who participate in fourteen intercollegiate sports in the most challenging NCAA Division III conference in the country. The College offers a rewarding blend of academic, social, and cultural experiences in the students' daily routine.

In addition to bachelor's degrees, the College offers the Master of Arts in Liberal Studies, the Master of Business Administration, the Master of Science in Educational Technology, and the Master of Science in Nursing.

Location

Ramapo College's barrier-free campus, more than 300 acres in size, is located in the foothills of the Ramapo Mountains in Mahwah, New Jersey, just 25 miles from New York City and all of its cultural advantages.

Majors and Degrees

Ramapo College offers programs of study leading to the Bachelor of Arts degree in American studies, communication arts, contemporary arts, economics, environmental studies, history, international business, international studies, law and society, literature, music, political science, psychology, social science, sociology, Spanish language studies, theater, and visual arts. The Bachelor of Science degree is awarded in accounting, allied health, biochemistry, bioinformatics, biology, biology/physical therapy track, biology/physician assistant track, business administration (including finance, management, and marketing), chemistry, clinical laboratory sciences, computer science, environmental science, information systems, integrated science studies, mathematics, physics, and psychology. The Bachelor of Social Work and Bachelor of Science in Nursing degrees are also offered.

Ramapo has offered state-approved teacher education programs to train and certify teachers. Students seeking teacher certification take a sequence of professional education courses in the following subjects relating to elementary, middle school, junior high, and senior high curricula: art, business, communications, elementary education, English, health, mathematics, psychology, science, social studies, and speech arts and dramatics.

Academic Program

Each course at Ramapo is offered through one of five academic units, called schools. These units are relatively small groupings of faculty members, organized around individual themes considered to be important and useful areas of study.

The five schools offer major programs and recommend students for degrees. These are the Schools of Administration/Business, American/International Studies, Contemporary Arts, Social Science/Human Services, and Theoretical/Applied Science. Each student is associated with one of these schools while at Ramapo. This association brings the student in contact with others who have the same or similar academic interests and provides the student with easy access to academic advisement and to most of the courses needed to satisfy degree requirements.

Academic Facilities

The campus houses a complex of award-winning academic buildings; state-of-the-art computer centers, telecommunications centers with satellite uplink and downlink capability, and TV centers; a four-story science building with modern facilities; an administration building; and the Angelica and Russ Berrie Center for Performing and Visual Arts. The College library is housed in a four-story building adjacent to the classroom buildings. The book collection contains approximately 145,000 volumes. In addition, the library has a collection of slides, films, records, cassettes, multimedia kits, and simulation games and maintains a collection of United States, New Jersey, and Bergen County government documents. It also contains all issues of *The New York Times* since it was first published in 1851.

Costs

Full-time tuition and fees in 2003–04 were $7411 for New Jersey residents and $11,666 for out-of-state students. The combined cost of tuition and fees was $232 per credit for New Jersey residents and $365 for out-of-state students. Other charges, depending upon circumstances, included $8000 per year for room and board and a parking fee of $75 per year for commuting students. Books and supplies cost about $700 per year.

Financial Aid

Most financial aid is awarded on the basis of a student's financial need. To qualify for aid at Ramapo, students must complete the Free Application for Federal Student Aid (FAFSA). A student should apply for financial aid prior to May 1 to receive preferential consideration. Federal Perkins Loans, Federal Pell Grants, and Federal Work-Study Program funds are vital parts of the College financial aid program. New Jersey residents should also apply for a state-supported tuition-aid grant. In addition, Ramapo College offers scholarships for high-achieving incoming freshmen students. These awards include tuition and fees, housing, or both. Merit awards are offered for eight semesters as long as the student maintains the required grade point average. New student applicants are automatically considered for these scholarships. Continuing students not receiving an initial scholarship award may apply for additional merit awards based on their academic achievement at the College.

Faculty

Ramapo College has 386 full- and part-time faculty members. Most have been at the College for a number of years and have played a significant role in shaping the College and building strong academic programs. Faculty members have been recruited principally for their effectiveness as teachers of undergraduate students. The College believes it has a distinguished faculty in this regard. Of the full-time faculty members teaching academic courses, 95 percent have a doctoral or equivalent final degree. Their graduate research training—from Ivy League institutions, from the great state universities of the nation, and from some universities abroad—as well as their professional experience—indicate that faculty members possess high quality and diverse experience in the subject matter of their courses.

Student Government

There is an active student government. Each spring, students are elected to this body. The group meets on a weekly basis to discuss any issues that it feels affect the welfare of the student body. Executive officers of the student government meet regularly with the College president and participate actively on committees of the Board of Trustees. Each year students elect a student trustee and student trustee alternate. A member of the Faculty Assembly is designated as liaison to the group so students and others are aware of issues being discussed by the faculty. The president of the Student Government Association makes presentations to both the Faculty Assembly and the trustees at their regular meetings. Students also participate actively in the governance of the College's schools as members of the unit councils. It is here that students have the greatest opportunity to influence decisions on personnel and academic programs.

Admission Requirements

High school seniors generally are expected to have completed a minimum of 16 academic units, distributed as follows: 4 units of English, 2 units of social studies, 3 units of mathematics (including algebra, algebra II, and geometry), 2 units of laboratory science, 2 units of a foreign language, and 3 units of academic electives. In addition, students applying from high school must take the SAT I or the ACT and have their test scores sent to Ramapo. If a prospective applicant has not been graduated from high school but holds a general equivalency diploma, an official copy of the scores of the tests taken for this diploma must be submitted to the admissions office.

Admission of candidates is made on the basis of the academic record, a school counselor's evaluation, evidence of motivation, community and school contributions, and SAT I or ACT scores. Rank in the top quarter of the student's secondary school class is expected. Transfer students are also admitted. Deferred admission is possible.

Immediate Decision Day, Ramapo College of New Jersey's antidote to the stress of the college selection and application process, is an opportunity to apply and receive a notice of acceptance in just one day. On the appointed day, high school seniors submit their applications and supporting materials, have an admissions interview, and receive a decision notice, all on the same day and before the start of the new year. In addition, students who are eligible for a scholarship are offered one at that time.

On the day of their visit, students and their families receive information about the College, tour the campus (including the residence halls), attend a class, and then have lunch in the student dining hall. They also meet individually with an admissions officer. At the end of the day, students receive the College's decision regarding their application. Immediate Decision Days are scheduled in August, October, November, and December.

The College hosts open house programs during the fall and spring that give students and their families the opportunity to learn about academic programs, admissions, and financial aid; to meet faculty and staff members and students; and to tour the campus. Students are encouraged to visit during these special events. Weekday tours of the campus are available as well and personal interviews are available during the Immediate Decision Days in the fall. Interested students should contact the Office of Admissions at 201-684-7300 or 7301 or visit Ramapo's Web site for further details about campus visits.

Application and Information

Students may enter in September or January. Freshmen are encouraged to apply during the fall of their senior year. Applications for the freshman year are accepted until March 1. Applications from transfer students are accepted until May 1. Applying for admission as a matriculating (degree-seeking) student involves completing an application, having the high school and college (if a transfer student) forward transcripts, and sending a $55 nonrefundable fee to the admissions office. Students may obtain the forms and instructions by visiting or contacting the admissions office or by visiting the Ramapo Web site. Admission decisions are made on a rolling basis. The College Board Candidates Reply Date of May 1 is used for confirming an offer of admission.

For a catalog, application forms, and additional information, including current costs, students should contact:

Director of Admissions
Ramapo College of New Jersey
505 Ramapo Valley Road
Mahwah, New Jersey 07430
Telephone: 201-684-7300 or 7301
E-mail: admissions@ramapo.edu
World Wide Web: http://www.ramapo.edu

The Russ and Angelica Berrie Center for the Performing and Visual Arts on the campus of Ramapo College of New Jersey.

RANDOLPH–MACON COLLEGE

ASHLAND, VIRGINIA

The College

Randolph-Macon is an independent liberal arts college for men and women founded in 1830. With 1,154 students, the College has deliberately maintained a limited enrollment so that it can give its students the opportunity for dialogue and more personal relationships that only a midsize college can provide. Randolph-Macon is fully accredited by the Southern Association of Colleges and Schools and is historically affiliated with the United Methodist Church.

Students come mostly from Virginia and nearby mid-Atlantic states, but usually about thirty-five states, the District of Columbia, and sixteen countries are represented in the student body. There is diversity among the students, and an atmosphere of informality and friendliness is evident. Students indicate that they are attracted to the College primarily because of its size, the quality of its academic program, the strong connections between students and faculty, and its supportive, unpretentious atmosphere.

The campus, situated on 110 wooded acres in the town of Ashland, is both convenient and spacious. Most students live in residence halls, fraternity houses, sorority houses, town-house apartments, and special interest houses. The Frank E. Brown Campus Center provides centralized facilities for a wide variety of student activities, including student government and the literary staffs, and also houses the bookstore, photography laboratory, game room, post office, and coffeehouse. Other noteworthy facilities include the McGraw-Page Library, the spacious Estes Dining Hall, the Crenshaw Gymnasium, the Center for Counseling and Career Planning, the Keeble Observatory with its 12-inch reflecting telescope, and several historic buildings, including the beautifully renovated Washington-Franklin Hall. The 73,000-square-foot Brock Sports and Recreation Center contains a field house for basketball, volleyball, badminton, and other activities; a six-lane, 25-yard pool; three racquetball courts; one squash court; a 4,000-square-foot fitness room; an indoor track; an aerobics room; a climbing wall; and a sauna and locker room for students and faculty members. A performing arts center was recently completed.

Location

Ashland, the home of Randolph-Macon for more than a century, is a pleasant residential town with a population of 6,000. Two shopping centers three blocks from campus offer a variety of stores. Daily Amtrak service is available just one block from the edge of campus. Ashland is 15 miles north of Richmond, the capital of Virginia, and 90 miles south of Washington, D.C. This proximity allows access to excellent facilities, such as the Smithsonian Institution, the Library of Congress, the Virginia Museum of Fine Arts, the Virginia State Library, and other educational resources. Shuttle service to downtown Richmond is available. These nearby cities are also popular sites for the College's fast-growing internship program. Midway between the Atlantic Ocean and the Blue Ridge Mountains, the College also provides students with diverse recreational opportunities.

Majors and Degrees

The B.A. and B.S. degrees are offered in the following fields: accounting, art history, arts management, biology, chemistry, classical studies (Greek and Latin), computer science, drama, economics, economics-business, English, environmental studies, French, German, Greek, history, international relations, international studies, Latin, mathematics, music, philosophy, physics, political science, psychology, religious studies, sociology, Spanish, studio art, and women's studies. In addition, students may formally select a minor field from the above areas. Additional minors are offered in Asian studies, black studies, astrophysics, elementary and secondary education, ethics, Irish studies, journalism, and speech communication.

The College offers preprofessional studies for such fields as business, dentistry, law, medicine, the ministry, and teaching, as well as preparation for graduate school in other major fields of study. A state-approved teacher education program leads to certification for teaching both in elementary and secondary schools. Dual-degree programs in engineering and forestry enable students to spend the first three years at Randolph-Macon and the final two years at a recognized college of engineering or forestry. In addition, students who follow a prescribed course of study at Randolph-Macon can obtain a master's degree in accounting at Virginia Commonwealth University in one year instead of the usual two years.

Academic Program

The College offers a liberal arts curriculum that is designed to allow students considerable freedom in planning their own program, while assuring them that they will acquire not only the breadth of knowledge traditionally emphasized in a liberal education but also a sound foundation in a particular field. There is a flexible system of collegiate requirements in English, mathematics, a foreign language, and physical education. In addition, all students take courses in literature, the natural sciences, the social sciences, the fine arts, philosophy or religion, history, computer literacy, and oral communication. The College offers the most comprehensive liberal arts core curriculum of any college in Virginia.

The academic calendar is on the 4-1-4 plan, featuring a one-course term in January. During the January term, students may take special-topic courses, traditional and interdisciplinary courses, and travel-study courses in the United States and abroad, or they may participate in off-campus internships and field-study programs. Internships and other field-study experiences enable students to test classroom theory in practical situations. Internships are offered in Richmond; Washington, D.C.; New York City (at the United Nations); and other locations both domestic and abroad. Independent study and senior project options are also available.

Off-Campus Programs

International study opportunities are offered through Randolph-Macon programs in France, Spain, England, Japan, Germany, Ireland, Italy, Korea, Mexico, Brazil, Greece, Northern Ireland, Australia, and New Zealand. Study abroad in other locations can be arranged through other institutions. The College is a member of a consortium composed of seven private colleges in Virginia. Students may apply to spend a term at one of the other participating institutions, taking advantage of special programs or courses offered at these colleges. The other colleges in the consortium are Washington and Lee, Hampden-Sydney, Mary Baldwin, Hollins, Sweet Briar, and Randolph-Macon Woman's College.

Academic Facilities

The multimillion-dollar Copley Science Center houses classrooms, study rooms, research and teaching laboratory facilities for all of the sciences, and an expanded computer center, including the technology hub for the College. Technology on campus is supported by a total of twenty servers. The network core includes four T-1s for Internet bandwidth, a Gateway firewall, Fortinet antivirus and intrusion prevention, 12 miles of fiber-optic cabling, and high-speed connections to all academic buildings, administrative facilities, and student residence halls on campus. In addition, students have access to more than 300 computers in computer centers throughout campus. The modern McGraw-Page Library, the College's main library and principal research center, has the capacity for 240,000 volumes and subscribes to more than 1,000 periodicals. Open stacks are maintained except in the special collections. The library also provides an audiovisual center, a personal computer lab, and access to computerized information sources, including the Virtual Library of Virginia.

Costs

College fees for 2003–04 totaled $27,190. This includes tuition, fees, and room and board. Approximately $600 pays for a student's books for a year if he or she buys them new. Transportation and personal expenses of up to $900 should also be anticipated. Members of fraternities and sororities must pay initiation fees as well as monthly dues.

Financial Aid

The College administers a diversified program of scholarships, grants, loans, student employment, and other forms of aid. Financial aid comes from a variety of sources, including federal (Federal Pell Grants, Federal Supplemental Educational Opportunity Grants, Federal Perkins Student Loans, and Federal Work-Study awards), state, College, and private funds. Academic scholarships (Randolph-Macon Presidential Scholarships) of $5000 to $15,000 are offered to outstanding students, and additional grants and scholarships are awarded on the basis of exceptional achievement and special talents. However, most financial aid is awarded on the basis of demonstrated need. Applicants should file the Free Application for Federal Student Aid no later than February 1. Virginia residents attending Randolph-Macon are eligible to receive the Virginia Tuition Assistance Grant (TAG). The College mails TAG applications to all Virginia residents who have been admitted. Most on-campus job opportunities are reserved for students in the Federal Work-Study program; however, a number of student assistantships are available through the various academic departments and other College offices. The Financial Aid Office also provides a student referral service for part-time jobs with employers within walking distance of the College. Inquiries regarding financial aid should be addressed to the director of financial aid.

Faculty

As an undergraduate institution, Randolph-Macon offers students full access to its teaching faculty. Ninety-three percent of the faculty members have earned the doctorate or highest appropriate degree in their field, The student-faculty ratio is 11:1. Almost all professors teach classes at all levels. Thus, a freshman is as likely as a senior to encounter the most distinguished and experienced members of the faculty.

Student Government

At Randolph-Macon the principal governing and coordinating agency for students is the Student Government Association (SGA). It represents student interests on College committees that deal with the curriculum, academic policies, orientation, and college life. In addition, the SGA charters and allocates funds for student organizations and activities. Together with the Committee on Assemblies and Special Events, SGA plans and sponsors social, cultural, and educational events throughout the year for the entire College community.

Admission Requirements

The Admissions Committee places primary emphasis on the applicant's secondary school record, scores on the SAT I or the ACT, the secondary school counselor's recommendation, personal characteristics, and evidence of leadership and involvement in extracurricular activities. The submission of SAT II: Subject Test scores for Writing, Mathematics, and a foreign language, although not required, is suggested.

The College does not discriminate on the basis of ethnicity, gender, disability, sexual orientation, or age in its admissions, financial aid, athletics, employment, or educational programs.

Applications should be received by March 1. Applications received after that date are considered as long as space is available. Students who have applied by March 1 are informed of the admission decision no later than April 1. The College also offers a first choice, early decision plan through which well-qualified applicants may apply for early notification of acceptance. Students may now apply online via the Internet.

Application and Information

For more information, prospective students should contact:

Dean of Admissions
Randolph-Macon College
P.O. Box 5005
Ashland, Virginia 23005-5005
Telephone: 804-752-7305
800-888-1762 (toll-free)
E-mail: admissions@rmc.edu
World Wide Web: http://www.rmc.edu

Randolph-Macon's 110-acre campus has been planned to complement the educational program and enhance student life.

RANDOLPH–MACON WOMAN'S COLLEGE

LYNCHBURG, VIRGINIA

The College

Randolph-Macon Woman's College (R-MWC) was the first women's college to be accredited by the Southern Association of Colleges and Schools and the first southern women's college to be granted a Phi Beta Kappa charter. Academic excellence through the liberal arts and an emphasis on individual learning continue to be Randolph-Macon's top priorities. The College's enduring commitment to women's education has fostered strong programs in career development and in alumnae networking.

The current enrollment is about 750 women. Students come from forty-three states and forty-six countries. Surveys show that many choose R-MWC for its academic reputation and for its warm, friendly atmosphere. There are six residence halls on the 100-acre campus, housing 90 percent of the students. The College's location near the Blue Ridge Mountains provides ample recreational opportunities, and proximity to neighboring men's colleges and major universities enhances the social life on and off campus. Most students are involved in at least one of the many clubs or organizations and activities, which include campus publications, Chorale and Songshine, the Dance Group, political organizations, language clubs, theater, religious and volunteer organizations, an outdoor club, and a nationally ranked riding program. Intercollegiate sports include basketball, field hockey, riding, soccer, softball, swimming, tennis, and volleyball. Courses are also offered in a variety of activities and sports, including aerobics, fitness walking, golf, kickboxing, weight training, and yoga.

The academic program is enhanced throughout the year by visiting speakers, performers, and artists. Recently, these have included Jehan Sadat of Egypt, advocate for women's rights and peace; Katha Pollitt, essayist and contributing editor of *The Nation;* Sister Helen Prejean, author of *Dead Man Walking;* and Barry Lopez, acclaimed naturalist writer and winner of the National Book Award. In addition, the College sponsors numerous plays, awards, and exhibitions.

Location

R-MWC is located in a beautiful residential area of Lynchburg, a city of 70,000 people in the foothills of the Blue Ridge Mountains. Shopping areas are convenient to the campus, and public transportation is readily available. Lynchburg is within easy driving distance of Washington, D.C., and Richmond, Virginia.

Majors and Degrees

Randolph-Macon Woman's College offers programs of study leading to the Bachelor of Arts (B.A.) degree in twenty-three fields: art (history, museum studies, and studio), American culture, biology (environmental, molecular and cell, and organismal), chemistry, classics (archaeology, classical civilization, and classical languages), communication, dance, economics, English (creative writing and literature), environmental studies, French, German studies, history, international studies, mathematics, music (history, performance, and theory), philosophy, physics, politics, psychology, religion, Russian studies, sociology-anthropology, Spanish, and theater. A Bachelor of Science (B.S.) degree may be elected by students majoring in biology, chemistry, engineering physics, mathematics, or physics. The double major is a popular option, and there is also the opportunity to devise a special major such as comparative literature or mathematical biology. In addition, there is the education program, which offers courses that meet the requirements for primary and secondary education certification. Travel/study opportunities and visiting scholar programs augment the international curriculum.

Every student has the option of selecting up to two concentrations in addition to her major. Concentrations are offered in all of the major fields as well as the interdisciplinary areas of American arts, Asian studies, British history and literature, the classical tradition, French civilization, French for commerce, human services, journalism, Renaissance studies, sport and exercise studies, symbol and myth, and women's studies. Students declare majors and concentrations in the spring of the sophomore year.

R-MWC has cooperative 3-2 programs in engineering and nursing and preprofessional programs in law, medicine, and veterinary studies.

Academic Programs

R-MWC's academic program is structured to develop the student as a whole person. The curriculum is designed to ensure that students acquire a broad range of knowledge and depth in their chosen field while they are prepared for meaningful careers. R-MWC trains students to think critically and independently and to speak and write effectively. The College's graduation requirement is 124 hours of credit with a quality point ratio of 2.0.

Students also use the Macon Plan, an individualized, systematic plan that helps them define their personal, educational, and professional goals. Working with faculty and staff members, students move through a series of steps to identify the many courses, internships, study-abroad opportunities, and clubs and activities that constitute a coherent plan to meet their goals.

The College operates on a traditional semester system, with self-scheduled exams given before the December vacation and at the end of the second semester in May. Most classes meet either two or three times a week. R-MWC provides maximum opportunity for independent study and research.

The Collegewide Writing Program includes formal evaluation of student writing skills in all courses at the end of every semester. There are elective courses in intermediate composition and in academic writing as well as writing-intensive sections across the curriculum. First-year students may be granted exemption from the English composition degree requirement on the basis of their entering record (usually Advanced Placement examination scores).

Sixty-five percent of R-MWC graduates continue their studies beyond the undergraduate level within five years of graduation. Special advisers at the College counsel students who are preparing for medical, veterinary, or law school or other specialized graduate study. Research is encouraged in the various areas of academic concentration, and in the senior year students may pursue honors work involving the presentation and defense of a thesis under the supervision of a faculty member. Sixty-seven percent of all seniors had their education broadened through internships or special summer experiences for academic credit.

Off-Campus Programs

Internships provide an exciting opportunity for students to gain valuable work experience in area hospitals, veterinary clinics, schools, law firms, industries, courts, social service agencies, and radio and television stations. The College maintains a listing of nearly 1,000 internship opportunities through which students may earn up to 6 hours of credit toward the R-MWC degree.

More than one fourth of the juniors study abroad. Approximately 40 juniors majoring in all fields participate in the College's Junior Year Abroad program at the University of Reading, England. In addition, students have studied recently in Argentina, Australia, the Czech Republic, France, Japan, Russia, Scotland, and Spain. Other students participate in programs sponsored by other colleges. Students of the classics may spend a summer working at an archaeological dig in Carthage, Tunisia. Other summer research and travel opportunities are available.

Programs in this country include the Washington Semester at American University. R-MWC participates in the seven-college consortium of colleges in Virginia, along with Hampden-Sydney College, Hollins College, Mary Baldwin College, Randolph-Macon College (in Ashland, Virginia), Sweet Briar College, and Washington and Lee University. The local Tri-College Consortium of R-MWC, Lynchburg College, and Sweet Briar College increases the diversity of courses open to students.

The College's spring semester American Culture Program offers a rigorous, interdisciplinary immersion into the study of American culture both on campus and at key locations in Virginia and across the nation. The program capitalizes on the College's central location in historic Virginia as well as its own outstanding Maier Museum of Art's collection of American art. This one-semester program is open to students from Randolph-Macon Woman's College as well as to undergraduate students, both men and women, from other institutions.

Academic Facilities

The Lipscomb Library contains more than 200,000 volumes, 860 current periodical titles, and more than 6,000 electronic periodical subscriptions. The Martin Science Building has been completely renovated to incorporate state-of-the-art laboratory design and instrumentation, enhanced facilities for student-faculty research, and multimedia instructional centers. Equipment and resources readily available for student use include an FT-NMR and computer-driven IR and UV spectrometers, exceptional herbarium and fossil collections, a greenhouse, and nature preserves. The Winfree Observatory houses a 14-inch pier-mounted telescope equipped with a computer-operated CCD camera for variable star research to support instruction in physics and astronomy. The Ethyl Science and Mathematics Resource Center in Martin offers a networked computer cluster with specific software for science and math applications and library, study, and lounge facilities. A satellite telecommunications program with the University of Virginia has been established to broaden learning opportunities.

The College's Maier Museum of Art houses an outstanding collection of nineteenth- and twentieth-century American paintings, while Presser Hall, the music building, has a concert auditorium, studios, and practice rooms. The Learning Resources Center and the Writing Lab offer academic support and tutorial services related to study skills, word processing, and the writing program.

Many facilities exist to integrate technology into teaching and learning. Virtually all of the classrooms on campus provide multimedia display capabilities, and several classrooms are equipped with student computer workstations for hands-on instruction in discipline-specific software and for general purpose technology workshops. The campus also has a number of rooms equipped with special purpose technology, including two rooms with Smartboards, a small theater with computer/video display and surround sound, a media center/language lab where students can work on language drills and exercises as well as edit digital video, and a digital darkroom for high-end digital, still picture editing.

Macintosh and PC-compatible computers are provided in numerous labs on campus for student use 24 hours a day, seven days a week. Laser printers and scanners are also available in all computer labs. Web-based information resources allow students to view their student records, class schedules, and grades.

All computer labs and residence hall rooms have access to the Internet and to the College's extensive Web site. The Web site provides comprehensive information about the College and a variety of services to prospective students and their parents. Students enjoy the campus portal system and the College's numerous locations for wireless connection to the network.

Costs

The 2003–04 comprehensive fee for room, board, and tuition was $28,430. The College recommends a budget of $1000 for books, supplies, fees, and personal expenses, excluding travel costs.

Financial Aid

R-MWC administers almost $14 million in aid each year through a comprehensive program of financial assistance, which includes merit-based scholarships, need-based grants, low-interest student loans, and campus employment. All students are encouraged to apply for financial aid, even those who assume that they are ineligible for assistance due to family income level. Merit scholarships, which range from $5000 per year to full comprehensive fees, are renewable for four years. The student's application for admission serves as her application for all merit scholarships, with the exception of the full-tuition Presidential Program Scholarships. More than 95 percent of R-MWC students receive financial assistance of some kind. The average need-based financial aid package is $19,000. To apply for need-based aid, students are encouraged to submit the Free Application for Federal Student Aid (FAFSA) by March 1. International students are eligible for merit scholarships, which range from $5000 to $13,000 per year.

Faculty

Approximately 92 percent of the full-time teaching faculty members hold a Ph.D. degree or terminal degree; about half of the faculty members are women. The faculty-student ratio of 1:9 encourages individual rapport between faculty members and students and contributes to the close community that typifies R-MWC. Faculty members are dedicated primarily to teaching, with secondary emphasis on research and publication.

Student Government

The honor system is a vital part of college life at R-MWC and allows students to live and study in an atmosphere of integrity and trust. Each student is a member of the Student Government, which voices student opinion, oversees student activities, and makes policy through the elected representatives. Students serve on almost all College committees.

Admission Requirements

A minimum of 16 academic high school units is recommended and should be distributed as follows: 4 units of English, 3 units of mathematics, 3–4 units of a foreign language, 2 units of laboratory science, 2 units of social studies, and sufficient electives from these areas to make up the recommended total. Because of the flexible nature of the College's curriculum, favorable consideration may be given to students whose high school preparation departs from the recommendations outlined above. Each applicant must have maintained a good academic record and must submit scores on the SAT I or ACT. R-MWC readily accepts the Common Application. An online application is available on the College's Web site.

Application and Information

Early decision candidates should apply by November 15 of the senior year in secondary school and will receive notification from the College about December 15. Candidates for general admission must apply by March 1 in order to receive preferential consideration; they will receive notification at the time their files are complete, beginning in late January. A $35 application fee must accompany the application for admission, but this fee may be waived in cases of hardship at the request of the student and the recommendation of her high school counselor. R-MWC also participates in the College Board test fee waiver program.

For more information, students should contact:

Director of Admissions
Randolph-Macon Woman's College
2500 Rivermont Avenue
Lynchburg, Virginia 24503
Telephone: 434-947-8100
800-745-7692 (toll-free)
E-mail: admissions@rmwc.edu
World Wide Web: http://www.rmwc.edu

REED COLLEGE

PORTLAND, OREGON

The College

For its 1,312 students and 133 faculty members, Reed College is foremost an intellectual community. Since its founding in 1909, Reed has attracted students with a high degree of self-discipline and a genuine enthusiasm for academic work and intellectual challenge. Reed attracts a geographically diversified student body: four fifths of Reed's students come from outside the Northwest, with more than 20 percent from the Northeast and 5 percent from outside the United States.

Campus social opportunities are open to all, with no closed clubs or organizations and no sororities or fraternities. Community life is full of activity and variety, with more than fifty student organizations. Club sports are competitive in a number of areas, but Reed is a college where varsity sports have always been viewed with skepticism. Fitness and development of lifelong skills take precedence over competition.

Location

Reed's 100-acre wooded campus is located in a quiet, suburban setting 5 miles from downtown Portland. The nearby ocean and mountains of the Pacific Northwest provide a balance to the social and cultural offerings of the greater Portland metropolitan area.

Majors and Degrees

Reed awards the Bachelor of Arts degree in a wide variety of fields, based on work in traditional departments or in interdisciplinary combinations. Students may select from the following: American studies, anthropology, art, biochemistry and molecular biology, biology, chemistry, chemistry-physics, Chinese, classics, classics-religion, dance-theater, economics, English literature, French literature, German literature, history, history-literature, international and comparative policy studies, linguistics, literature-philosophy, literature-theater, mathematics, mathematics-economics, mathematics-physics, music, philosophy, philosophy-mathematics, philosophy-religion, physics, political science, psychology, religion, Russian literature, sociology, Spanish literature, and theater.

Students may design interdisciplinary majors. The approval of special programs that link two or more disciplines is reviewed by the student's adviser and the departments concerned.

Reed offers several combined 3-2 programs, which allow the student to earn both a bachelor's degree from Reed and a professional degree from the cooperating institution. Science programs and institutions include applied physics and electronic science (Oregon Graduate Institute); engineering (California Institute of Technology, Columbia University, and Rensselaer Polytechnic Institute); computer science (University of Washington); and forestry and environmental sciences (Duke University). The College also has a combined program in fine arts (Pacific Northwest College of Art).

Academic Program

Hallmarks of academic life at Reed include the demanding, small group conference method of teaching and its reliance on active student participation, a de-emphasis of grades, a yearlong interdisciplinary humanities program, and an integrated academic program that balances the breadth of traditional course content and distribution requirements with flexibility in designing an in-depth senior thesis. Learning and the development of skills in preparation for a life of learning take precedence over the mere memorization of facts. In addition to fulfilling the requirements for the major, taking the humanities course, and writing the senior thesis, students must satisfy a distributional requirement, consisting of two core classes from each of the following academic divisions: literature, philosophy, and the arts; history, social sciences, and psychology; the natural sciences; and math, foreign language, logic, and linguistics.

Off-Campus Programs

Reed participates in domestic exchange programs with Howard University in Washington, D.C., Sarah Lawrence College in New York, and Sea Education Association in Massachusetts. In addition, Reed provides study-abroad opportunities for students at the University of East Anglia, University of Sussex, Oxford University, and the British Academy of Dramatic Arts in England; University of Rennes and University of Paris in France; Beijing Foreign Studies University, Capital Normal University, Fujian Normal University, and East China Normal University in China; Hebrew University of Jerusalem; University of Munich and Tübingen University in Germany; University of Florence; Trinity College Dublin; Universidad San Francisco de Quito and Universidad Catolica in Ecuador; Hertzen University, Irkutsk University, Moscow State University, and Smolny College in Russia; the University of Costa Rica; Budapest semester in mathematics in Hungary; universities in Getafe, Segovia, and La Rioja in Spain; and the Intercollegiate Center for Classical Studies in Rome. Students may also arrange independent study plans in consultation with appropriate faculty members, the director for off-campus studies, and the registrar.

Academic Facilities

Students have access to Reed's substantial library collection (512,000 volumes, 2,700 periodicals, and 340,000 government documents) by searching the online catalog in the library or from any computer on the campus network. Through its participation in PORTALS (Portland Area Library System) and Orbis, a union catalog of Oregon and Washington academic libraries, Reed provides online access to other library catalogs and databases. Students may borrow materials directly from academic libraries in the Portland area, and they have access to collections worldwide through interlibrary loan. In addition, the Reed library accommodates a first-rate art gallery, a language lab, and a music listening facility. The Reed library is open 18 hours most days (24 hours a day during examinations).

Computer technology is highly developed at Reed and widely used for instruction, research, and communication by all members of the College community. A state-of-the-art campus network links all residence halls, classrooms, laboratories, offices, and the library to one another and to the global Internet. The Educational Technology Center was completed in 2002; it houses more than 150 computers and a variety of other teaching and technology resources that are used by students and faculty and staff members. The science laboratories at Reed are among the best equipped of any undergraduate college in the United States. These include the A. A. Knowlton Laboratory of Physics, the Arthur F. Scott Laboratory of Chemistry, and the L. E. Griffin Memorial Biology Building, where a recent $10-million renovation includes improved student thesis space, a tiered-seating classroom, and new teaching labs. Reed's research nuclear reactor (the only reactor in the country that is staffed primarily by undergraduates) and radiochemistry lab are actively used for student research, instruction, and training. For those interested in the arts, the campus houses studio art facilities that recently saw a $2-million expansion, performing arts facilities, twenty instrumental practice rooms, a computer music laboratory, a recording system, and an 800-seat auditorium. Other popular facilities include a radio station and a modern sports center.

Costs

Tuition for 2003–04 was $29,000, and room and board were $7750. The student body fee was $200, bringing the yearly total cost to approximately $36,950. The cost of books and incidental expenses average $1500.

Financial Aid

Nearly half of Reed students receive financial assistance from the College. A full need-based financial aid program makes Reed accessible to students from a wide range of economic backgrounds. The College guarantees to meet the full demonstrated need of all continuing students in good academic standing and who file their financial aid applications on time. In addition, during their first two semesters, approximately 50 percent of the freshmen and transfer students receive financial assistance equal to their demonstrated need. Admission decisions are separate from financial aid procedures, and students are admitted regardless of ability to pay. Reed's own funds are the primary source of grants to students. The College budgeted more than $12 million for this purpose in 2003–04, with individual awards ranging from $1000 to $32,000. Reed also administers federal grants and a variety of other awards. Perkins Loans and other federally subsidized loans are available, along with campus employment and work-study programs. The size of a financial aid award is based upon analysis of the student's need. The financial aid program includes grants, loans, and work opportunities.

Faculty

All classes at Reed are taught by professors, 89 percent of whom hold the highest degree in their field. Reed students point to the opportunity to work closely with faculty members as one of the great benefits of a Reed education. Reed faculty members point to the opportunity to work with students who are serious scholars as one of the great benefits of teaching at Reed. Faculty members commit themselves primarily to teaching, with scholarly and scientific research furthering this primary goal; they view students as partners in learning, often serving as coauthors and coinvestigators on professional papers and research projects. This close association is due, in large part, to a 10:1 student-faculty ratio, and the one-on-one relationship between thesis adviser (a professor) and student during the senior year.

Student Government

The Student Senate is the central body in student governance. The Senate consists of the student body president, vice president, and 8 student representatives, all elected by the students. Its two primary functions are to allocate student body funds and to represent student interests and concerns to the faculty, administration, and the Board of Trustees. The Senate distributes approximately $80,000 each semester to the many student organizations on campus. As agreed under the community constitution, students participate fully in discussions and decisions on a wide variety of issues. The Student Committee on Academic Policy and Planning participates in debate about the curriculum at Reed; many other committees, from the Library Board to the Reactor Committee, have substantial student input. The Senate and student body president make all student appointments to such committees.

Admission Requirements

Reed welcomes applications from freshman and transfer candidates who are genuinely committed to the pursuit of a liberal arts education and a rigorous academic program. Those applicants are admitted who, in the view of the Committee on Admission, are most likely to become successful members of and contribute significantly to the Reed community. The College is committed to maintaining a student body distinguished by its intellectual passion, yet diversified in its range of backgrounds, interests, and talents.

Admission decisions are based on many integrated factors, but academic accomplishments and talents are given the greatest weight in the selection process. A strong secondary school preparation, including honors and advanced courses where available, will improve a student's chances for admission. Such a program usually would include 4 years of English, at least 3 years of a foreign or classical language, 3 to 4 years of mathematics, 3 to 4 years of science, and 3 to 4 years of history or social studies. Given the wide variation in high school programs and quality, however, there are no fixed requirements for secondary school courses. Applicants are expected to have obtained a secondary school diploma prior to enrollment, although exceptions are occasionally made. There are no "cutoff points" for high school or college grades or for examination scores.

Reed recognizes the qualities of character—in particular, motivation, intellectual curiosity, individual responsibility, and social consciousness—as important considerations in the selection process, beyond a demonstrated commitment to academic excellence. Thus, the Committee on Admission looks for students whose accomplishments and interests in various fields of endeavor will contribute to the overall liveliness of the Reed community. Personal interviews, either on campus or off campus, are not a requirement in the admission process but are strongly recommended whenever possible. Applications for early decision should be submitted by November 15 (Option I) or January 2 (Option II); regular freshman admission by January 15; and transfer candidates by March 1.

Application and Information

The Office of Admission is open Monday through Friday, from 8:30 a.m. until 5 p.m. (Pacific time) all year, except for major holidays. Students may apply online at http://web.reed.edu/apply/index.html. For further information or to arrange a campus tour, overnight stay, information session, or interview, students should call or write:

Office of Admission
Reed College
3203 Southeast Woodstock Boulevard
Portland, Oregon 97202-8199
Telephone: 503-777-7511
800-547-4750 (toll-free)
Fax: 503-777-7553
E-mail: admission@reed.edu
World Wide Web: http://web.reed.edu/

Reed College—where students enjoy their individuality as much as they do their academics.

REGIS COLLEGE

WESTON, MASSACHUSETTS

The College

Regis College is a leading Catholic liberal arts and sciences college for women prepared to excel. The College celebrates the rich diversity of its students as well as the many opportunities available in the Boston area and beyond. Innovative Academic Centers offer students the opportunity to take integrated and interdisciplinary courses, to interact with faculty members and students from different majors, and to participate in workshops, lectures, and cocurricular programs. In addition to rigorous and engaging academic programs, the College offers career-oriented internships in all disciplines, opportunities for developing leadership talents, and a social environment conducive to acquiring connections that can last a lifetime. The focus of Regis College is on the development of the whole person, enabling students to become educated in all aspects of human behavior: intellectual, spiritual, occupational, social, physical, and emotional. Consequently, Regis College students graduate prepared for life.

While many of the College's 850 undergraduates and 225 graduate students are New England residents, other students are from several different states, Puerto Rico, and seven other countries. Campus-based housing is guaranteed for all students. The multicultural student body offers a diversity that is shared and celebrated on the Regis College campus through programs and activities.

Twelve percent of the members of recent graduating classes have chosen to pursue graduate studies immediately. Among the career and employment fields recent graduates have entered are business (including banking, marketing, and sales), communications, counseling, graphic design, law, medical research, nursing, social work, and teaching.

A vital part of the Regis College experience is student involvement in activities outside the classroom. Cocurricular programs are offered for leadership development in more than thirty campus organizations. A variety of campus activities gives students the opportunity to explore their interests, make new acquaintances, and serve the community. Students with interests in specific areas may develop their talents and skills by becoming involved in such organizations as the Glee Club, AHANA, Dance Company, Board of Programmers, and student government. Students who want to enhance their literary, drawing, and photographic skills can contribute to the College publications, *Hemetera,* the literary magazine, and *Mount Regis,* the College yearbook. Regis students are engaged in a wide range of service activities through the Regis College Service Learning Project and volunteer activities through the Campus Ministry Program.

The outstanding Regis athletic program is a recent recipient of the NCAA award for sustaining academic achievement (a 100 percent graduation rate) among its students. The athletic programs are supported by a modern athletic/recreation facility that accommodates intercollegiate athletics, intramural activities, and physical and health education classes. This campus facility features a six-lane swimming pool; a sauna and Jacuzzi; an area that can be used interchangeably for two indoor tennis courts, a regulation basketball court, and volleyball courts; a training room; athletics offices; a dance studio; squash courts; and a state-of-the-art fitness center. Outdoor sports facilities include four tennis courts and an athletic field. Students at Regis College compete on an intercollegiate NCAA Division III level in basketball, cross-country, field hockey, soccer, softball, swimming and diving, tennis, track and field, and volleyball as well as in an intramural sports program.

In addition to the undergraduate degrees listed, Regis College offers the Master of Arts in Teaching, the Master of Science in Nursing, the Master of Science in Leadership and Organizational Change, the Master of Science in Organizational and Professional Communication, and the Master of Science in Health Product Regulation and Health Policy.

The College has modern residence halls: Angela Hall, Maria Hall, and College Hall. The student union building houses the residents' dining room, the commuters' café, the Tower Tavern, a campus radio station, a cyber café, the bookstore, numerous offices, and three multipurpose lounge areas for College meetings and lectures.

Location

Weston, Massachusetts, ideally located just 12 miles west of Boston, is a suburban town of 12,200 residents that has retained its New England charm. The campus is an 18-minute drive from downtown Boston and other towns such as Lexington, Concord, and Cambridge that have an abundance of cultural and historic sites. Regis operates its own hourly shuttle service, which provides quick and easy access to Boston and to the colleges in Regis's cross-registration program.

Majors and Degrees

Regis College grants a Bachelor of Arts or Bachelor of Science degree in the following subjects: biochemistry, biology, communication, computer studies, English, graphic design, history, management, mathematics education, museum studies, nursing, political science, psychology, sociology, social work, Spanish, and theater. In addition, a student may decide to complete an interdepartmental major or an individually designed major.

Qualified students can earn a bachelor's degree in three years in specific majors; the College also offers a four-year "3 Plus 1" combined bachelor's and master's degree program and 3-2 dual-degree programs in a variety of technical areas in cooperation with Worcester Polytechnic Institute. The College also offers preprofessional preparation in communications; computer science; graphic arts; legal studies; management studies; early childhood, elementary, and secondary teacher certification; and social work.

Academic Programs

Completion of thirty-six courses is required to earn the bachelor's degree. All bachelor's degree programs include an eleven-course liberal arts core curriculum, an academic major of concentrated study, and elective courses chosen according to the student's interests. The eleven-course core curriculum consists of courses in natural sciences, social sciences, English composition, mathematics, religious studies, and humanities as well as a first-year seminar. To fulfill departmental requirements, students must complete from eight to twelve courses in their major field of study. For graduation with Departmental Honors, students are required to complete a two-course sequence of independent study culminating in a written thesis, which must be orally defended, and to maintain averages of at least 3.0 overall and 3.5 in their major field.

Off-Campus Programs

Regis College participates in a cross-registration program with Babson College, Bentley College, and Boston College. Students may also study abroad in programs in many countries, including England, Ireland, Italy, Japan, and Spain. The Washington Semester, sponsored by the American University in Washington, D.C., provides students with an intensive program involving course work, research, seminars, and internships in government offices. The internship program and the Regis College Career Office provide Regis College students with professional experience in numerous agencies throughout the Boston area, across the U.S., and abroad.

Academic Facilities

The Regis Library's collection now stands at 131,749 volumes and 1,175 periodicals and serials. The library has a spacious reading room, extensive open stacks, private study carrels for concentrated research, seminar rooms for small classes and group study, and microfilm and microcard readers. Because of the College's proximity to Boston and its membership in the WEBnet Consortium, students also have access to many other libraries, including those of Babson, Bentley, and Pine Manor Colleges. The Watson-Hubbard Science Center has contemporary laboratory and lecture halls for biology, chemistry, physics, and psychology courses. The Fine Arts Center contains classrooms for the study of music, an art history lecture hall, graphic and fine art studios, the 650-seat Eleanor Welch Casey Theatre, and the Carney Art Gallery, in which artwork by faculty members, alumnae, and local artists is displayed.

Costs

For 2004–05, tuition for all students is $20,500, and room and board fees total $9360.

Financial Aid

Regis College endeavors to meet the need of every student through its financial aid program. Regis sponsors financial aid through federally funded grants, loans, and work-study awards and also provides scholarships from College operating funds. To apply for any scholarship or financial aid program, applicants should submit the Free Application for Federal Student Aid (FAFSA) and the Regis College Application for Financial Aid. All financial aid applicants are also required to forward a complete copy of their federal income tax return and a copy of their parents' federal income tax return. Students who apply for scholarships or other financial aid through Regis College are informed of the College's financial aid award decision after March 1. Approximately 85 percent of all Regis students receive scholarships and financial assistance through federal and College funds.

Regis College offers merit scholarships for first-year and transfer students in recognition of academic performance, community service, and leadership abilities. There are several levels of merit scholarships at the College: Presidential Scholar, $12,000 per year; Dean's Scholar, $9000 per year; Leadership and Service Award, in varying amounts; and Alumnae Sponsor Award, $2000 per year. These scholarships are awarded on a competitive basis. Information regarding the specifications for each of the merit scholarships can be obtained by contacting the Office of Admission.

Faculty

The Regis College faculty consists of 50 full-time members and 48 part-time members; 100 percent hold advanced degrees. In addition to carrying out research and publishing within their individual fields, faculty members at Regis possess a highly developed commitment to teaching. Each student has a faculty adviser to assist with course selection. A student-faculty ratio of 12:1 enables each student to receive personal attention, support, and academic advice.

Student Government

The Student Government is composed of elected representatives who administer the budget for all clubs and organizations. The representatives are involved with educational policy, social events, elections, and student publications.

Admission Requirements

Applicants for admission as first-year students are expected to complete a college-preparatory program at an accredited secondary school. The preparation for entrance should include 4 years of English, 2 years of foreign language, 3 years of mathematics, 2 years of laboratory science, 2 years of social science, and three or four electives. Consideration is given to applicants whose educational background varies from this profile. The Admission Committee places primary emphasis on the secondary school record (courses selected, grades received, and rank in class), two teacher recommendations, involvement in extracurricular activities, and SAT I or ACT scores. International students must submit the results of the Test of English as a Foreign Language (TOEFL) and a Declaration of Finance form. Interviews are not required but are strongly encouraged. The Admission Committee does not discriminate against applicants on the basis of race, color, religion, national origin, or handicap; in fact, Regis welcomes diversity among students. The Admission Committee considers applicants for rolling admission, delayed admission, and advanced placement. The College grants credit and advanced placement for scores of 3 or better on the Advanced Placement examinations sponsored by the College Board.

Transfer applicants for the fall or spring semester should be in good academic standing at the institution previously attended, have a quality point average of at least 2.0 on the Regis College scale, and not be on academic or disciplinary probation at the former institution. A maximum of twenty college-level courses are considered for transfer.

Application and Information

An applicant for admission registers by completing the application form, available upon request from the Office of Admission, and returning it with the $30 application fee. Regis College operates on a rolling admission basis; students hear from the Office of Admission regarding their status within seven to ten days of receipt of completed applications. Students are encouraged to visit the campus for interviews and guided tours. For more information and an application for admission, students should contact:

Director of Admission
Regis College
235 Wellesley Street
Weston, Massachusetts 02493
Telephone: 781-768-7100
866-438-7344 (toll-free)
E-mail: admission@regiscollege.edu
World Wide Web: http://www.regiscollege.edu

REGIS UNIVERSITY

DENVER, COLORADO

The University

In its 126th year, Regis University is the Rocky Mountain region's only Jesuit university and is well-known for innovation and educational leadership. Continuing a 450-year tradition of academic excellence, Regis is one of twenty-eight Jesuit colleges and universities located in the United States.

U.S. News & World Report named Regis University a "Top School" among colleges and universities in the western United States, marking the ninth consecutive year Regis has been in the publication's top tier. The University was also recognized as one of the top 100 universities and colleges for leadership in the field of student character development in *The Templeton Guide: Colleges That Encourage Character Development*. Regis University is ranked by *U.S. News & World Report* as the second-best university in the western United States for the highest proportion of classes with 20 students or fewer.

The University has an American Rhodes Scholar, 2 *USA Today* College All-Academic Team selectees (in 1993 and 2000), the top female collegiate athlete in NCAA Division II for 1998–99, 5 Fulbright professors, 2 Fuld Fellows, and a wealth of other national recognition of outstanding academic excellence. More than 90 percent of Regis's full-time faculty members have a Ph.D.

However, Regis University was not always Regis. The school was started in 1877 in Las Vegas, New Mexico, by a group of exiled Italian Jesuits. It was known as Las Vegas College. In 1884, a second venture, known as Sacred Heart College, was started at Morrison, Colorado.

In 1887, Las Vegas College and Sacred Heart College moved to North Denver, where the joint operation became known as the College of the Sacred Heart. The college was renamed Regis in 1921, in honor of St. John Francis Regis, an eighteenth-century Jesuit missionary and saint who was revered for his exemplary work with poor people in the mountains of France.

On July 1, 1991, Regis College became Regis University, with three constituent schools: Regis College, the School for Professional Studies, and the School for Health Care Professions. Regis College is the traditional residential school, with nearly 1,200 students, primarily in the 18- to 23-year-old range. The School for Professional Studies focuses on undergraduate and graduate adult higher education. The School for Health Care Professions educates men and women to be leaders who are committed to excellence within the health-care professions.

Regis College primarily serves traditional-aged, mostly residential undergraduate students. The college offers a full range of programs in the liberal arts, sciences, business, and education. Students may choose from twenty-four structured areas of study or design their own programs through the interdisciplinary and flexible major plans. A low student-faculty ratio permits small classes and learning formats that encourage critical thinking, thoughtful discussion, and well-developed communication skills. In the college, students receive highly personalized attention from more than 83 skilled professors and dedicated scholars.

Athletic opportunities are offered on all levels: recreational, intramural, and intercollegiate. Regis University is a member of NCAA Division II and the Rocky Mountain Athletic Conference and competes in twelve intercollegiate sports as well as a variety of intramural and club sport programs.

In addition to the undergraduate degree programs listed below, Regis offers a Master of Arts degree in education (learning and teaching).

Location

Regis University is located near the base of the Rocky Mountains in a residential suburban neighborhood of northwest Denver, just north of I-70 and 25 minutes from Denver International Airport. Within 15 minutes of the campus is one of the most exciting international downtowns in the world. Thirty minutes west of the campus are the snow-capped peaks of the Rocky Mountains. Denver is one of America's fastest-growing metropolitan regions, with an abundance of cultural and recreational opportunities; it is one of only a few American cities with seven professional sports franchises. Denver has low humidity, and the sun shines about 300 days a year. The metropolitan area averages only 15 inches of precipitation a year, about the same as Los Angeles. Midwinter temperatures of 60 degrees are common. Colorado ski country is nearby; the campus is just 2 hours from Breckenridge, Vail, and Winter Park.

Majors and Degrees

Undergraduate degree offerings include the Bachelor of Arts (B.A.), Bachelor of Science (B.S.), Bachelor of Arts and Science, Classical Bachelor of Arts, and Bachelor of Science in Nursing (B.S.N.), as well as special majors.

Business programs include accounting (major and minor); accounting/M.B.A. (major); business administration, with concentrations in finance, international business, management, management information systems, and marketing (major and minor); economics (major and minor); flexible major; and political economy (major and minor).

Programs in humanities include communication (major and minor), English (major and minor), fine arts: visual arts (major and minor), flexible major, French (major and minor), German (minor), Hispanic studies (minor), literature (minor), Spanish (major and minor), women's studies (major and minor), and writing (minor).

The University offers natural sciences and mathematics programs in biochemistry (major and minor), biology (B.A. and B.S., major and minor), chemistry (major and minor), computer science (major and minor), environmental studies/human ecology (major and minor), flexible major, kinesiology (minor), mathematics (major and minor), neuroscience (major and minor), and physics (minor).

Programs in philosophy and religious studies include Catholic studies (minor), Christian leadership (minor), flexible major, philosophy (major and minor), and religious studies (major and minor).

Social sciences programs include criminal justice (major and minor), education (minor), elementary education (minor), flexible major, history (major and minor), peace and justice studies (minor), physical education (minor), physical education: coaching/recreation (minor), political science (major and minor), psychology (major and minor), secondary education (minor), and sociology (major and minor).

Preprofessional programs are offered in dentistry, law, medicine, and physical therapy. A dual-degree engineering program is also offered.

Academic Program

Regis is part of a 450-year-old Jesuit tradition that provides a values-centered liberal arts education and is known for service to others. The Core Curriculum, designed to prepare students for life as well as a career, requires students to reflect on the purpose of human existence, to understand the roots of modern culture, to embrace philosophical and religious perspectives, and to think critically. These courses enrich perceptions, challenge assumptions, and broaden visions.

A total of 128 semester hours is required for a bachelor's degree. Regis chooses a select group of students for its honors program each year and offers a schedule of undergraduate courses in the summer session. The University's Center for Service Learning actively involves students in community service projects. Internships and study abroad are offered as well. Other academic programs include the writing program, teacher licensure, the Commitment Program, Air Force Reserve Officer Training Corps, Air Force University Scholarship Program, and the Army Reserve Officer Training Corps (military science).

Academic Facilities

Regis is committed to providing state-of-the-art facilities. The University offers students 24-hour access to personal computers, online service, and research tools in common lab facilities. In addition, labs are located in the three coeducational residence halls, in the town houses, and in specific departments. All students are offered full access to an e-mail account on the Internet.

The University has two libraries, housing more than 280,000 volumes, 2,100 periodical subscriptions, 150,000 microforms, and a 90,000-slide art history collection. Its CARL online catalog is a comprehensive index to the collections and provides 10,000 databases, document delivery options, and full-text online journals. The main library, which includes media services, provides network ports at every place that a student studies for ease of access to the Internet and the Regis database.

The Coors Life Direction Center houses the Office of Career Services and Personal Counseling as well as the Fitness Program and the Health Center.

Four modern residence halls—O'Connell, DeSmet, West, and the new townhouse complex—are fully staffed and offer computer labs, free cable TV, local phone service and voice mail, free laundry facilities, lounges, vending machines, and two phone and data lines in each room. More than 80 percent of freshmen live on campus.

Costs

Undergraduate tuition at Regis College for the 2003–04 academic year is $20,700. Room and board for the academic year cost $7600.

Financial Aid

In an effort to keep its high-quality Jesuit education affordable, Regis is committed to helping as many students as possible by continuing to increase scholarships and University grant funds. The student financial aid program invests more than $14 million in undergraduates. More than 90 percent of full-time Regis College students receive some financial assistance. Scholarships and grants are awarded on the basis of need, academic achievement, and leadership. The University participates in all federal and Colorado-supported programs. The Free Application for Federal Student Aid (FAFSA) or Renewal Application must be filed.

Faculty

Regis College has 83 full-time faculty members; 92 percent hold terminal degrees. Ten percent of the faculty members are Jesuit priests, and Regis has no graduate students/teaching assistants on its staff. The college has a 15:1 student-faculty ratio. Some professional staff members and Jesuit priests live and teach on Regis's campus. These committed adults are available for both academic and personal direction for Regis students. In addition, each undergraduate has an individual faculty adviser, who assists students in their academic choices.

Student Government

The Student Government at Regis is led by the Executive Board. The board is supported by the Senate, which comprises class representatives. The student leaders serve on University committees, plan entertainment, help determine student policy, and oversee more than thirty student organizations.

Admission Requirements

Regis College actively recruits students for equal opportunity and nondiscriminatory consideration of eligibility. In 2003, the average ACT composite score for incoming freshmen was 23, and the average SAT combined score was 1108. Admission is determined by a student's high school record, including grades, test scores, personal ability, and leadership qualities.

Requirements for freshman admission include high school graduation or its equivalent and evidence of college-level competency, as shown in high school courses, grades, ACT or SAT I test scores, a personal essay, and recommendations. Freshmen should present a minimum of 15 academic units. Successful candidates must have a satisfactory high school or college record in order to be admitted.

Application and Information

Completed applications for admission should be submitted to the Director of Admissions. Applications may be submitted any time after the beginning of the year. The Office of Admissions usually notifies each applicant regarding the decision within four weeks after the completed application and supporting documents have been received by the Office of Admissions. All requests for information or application forms should be addressed to:

Director of Admissions
Regis College Office of Admissions, A-12
Regis University
3333 Regis Boulevard
Denver, Colorado 80221-1099
Telephone: 303-458-4900
800-388-2366 Ext. 4900 (toll-free)
Fax: 303-964-5534
E-mail: regisadm@regis.edu
World Wide Web: http://www.regis.edu

The Regis University campus is located in a pleasant residential neighborhood with beautiful Rocky Mountain views, just a few minutes from downtown Denver.

RENSSELAER POLYTECHNIC INSTITUTE

TROY, NEW YORK

The Institute

The oldest degree-granting technological university in North America, Rensselaer Polytechnic Institute (RPI) was founded in 1824 "for the purpose of instructing persons in the application of science to the common purposes of life." Rensselaer has become one of the world's premier technological research universities, offering more than 100 programs and 1,000 courses lead to bachelor's, master's, and doctoral degrees. Undergraduates pursue their studies in the Schools of Architecture, Engineering, Humanities and Social Sciences, Management and Technology, and Science and in the multidisciplinary area of information technology (IT). As a pioneer in interactive learning, Rensselaer has a long tradition of providing real-world, hands-on educational experiences to its students. Many of the courses cut across academic disciplines. Students have ready access to laboratories and often work in teams on research projects. Classes involve lively discussion, problem solving, and faculty mentoring, which encourages students to formulate new ideas and new discoveries. Rensselaer's approach to education has created generations of graduates who are known for their ability to solve some of the world's most challenging technical problems.

Rensselaer's 5,100 undergraduate and 1,300 graduate students are a bright, ambitious, and technologically savvy group who come from all fifty states, the District of Columbia, Puerto Rico, the Virgin Islands, and seventy-two other countries. A wide variety of nonacademic activities, virtually all of which are run by the students, is available. There are thirty-three fraternities and sororities, a weekly newspaper, a progressive 10,000-watt FM stereo station, dramatics groups, musical ensembles, and more than 130 clubs, special-interest groups, professional societies, sports, and organizations. More than 5,000 students participate in nineteen intramural sports. Rensselaer is a member of the NCAA. Varsity sports include a Division I men's ice hockey team and twenty-two Division III men's and women's teams in thirteen sports. Women's ice hockey is on track to be elevated to Division I. Recreational facilities include the Mueller Fitness Center, an indoor track, all-weather track and field facilities, handball and squash courts, weight rooms, several indoor tennis courts, and two swimming pools. The Student Union, Chapel and Cultural Center, and Houston Field House bring many forms of entertainment and nationally known performing groups and lecturers to campus.

The Office of the First-Year Experience offers a comprehensive array of programs and initiatives for both students and their primary support team that begins before students arrive on campus and continues well beyond their first year. This office sponsors the Navigating Rensselaer orientation program, family programs, community service, and the Information and Personal Assistance Center (IPAC) along with many other programming initiatives for students and families.

Rensselaer recently completed renovations and upgrades of freshman residence halls and will finish work on upperclass halls in the fall of 2005. The Institute also is pursuing the development of several new athletics facilities, including a new field house, basketball arena, and natatorium as well as new administrative space, locker rooms, and weight rooms.

Location

Rensselaer is located in the northeastern United States in the heart of New York's Capital Region. The region, which includes the cities of Albany, Schenectady, and Troy and their suburbs, has a combined population of approximately 870,000 and is an important business, government, industrial, and academic hub. There are more than 40,000 college students at fourteen colleges and universities in the immediate area. Overlooking the city of Troy and the historic Hudson River, Rensselaer's 275-acre campus blends recently constructed facilities with a cluster of classical-style, ivy-covered brick buildings dating from the turn of the century. A program of extensive renovation has equipped the campus with ultramodern teaching facilities while preserving the traditional elegance of its historic buildings. Rensselaer retains the quiet and natural beauty of a parklike setting while offering many conveniences of an urban campus. Students enjoy easy access to Boston (3 hours away), New York City (2½ hours away), and Montreal (4 hours away). The Adirondacks, the Berkshires, and the Catskills, all within an hour of Troy, offer hundreds of areas for camping, hiking, and skiing. Many student clubs take full advantage of these natural resources.

Majors and Degrees

The Bachelor of Science is offered in aeronautical engineering; applied physics; biochemistry/biophysics; bioinformatics and molecular biology; biology; biomedical engineering; building sciences; chemical engineering; chemistry; civil engineering; communication; computer and systems engineering; computer science; economics; electrical engineering; electric power engineering; electronic arts; electronic media, arts, and communication; engineering physics; environmental engineering; environmental science; geology; hydrogeology; industrial and management engineering; information technology; interdisciplinary science; management; materials engineering; mathematics; mechanical engineering; nuclear engineering; philosophy; physics; psychology; and science, technology, and society.

Professionally accredited degree programs are offered in the fields of architecture and engineering. Architecture students may earn the Bachelor of Architecture after five years or the Master of Architecture after six. A five-year professional engineering curriculum can be accelerated to allow completion of both the Bachelor of Science and Master of Engineering degrees in four years. Rensselaer's professional program in engineering is one of the first of its type in the nation.

Accelerated physician-scientist students earn a B.S. degree in biology and an M.D. (from Albany Medical College) in seven years. Accelerated law programs allow management or science, technology, and society majors to earn a B.S. degree from Rensselaer and a J.D. from Albany Law School in six years. Other programs allow students to earn a B.S. in three years and a B.S./M.S. in four or five years.

Undergraduates at more than forty-four liberal arts colleges may transfer to Rensselaer and earn a B.A. from the first college and a B.S. or a master's degree from Rensselaer.

Academic Programs

While each of Rensselaer's schools has its own sequence requirements, the following minimums apply to all students: 124 credit hours and a 1.8 quality point average in total courses; 24 credit hours in physical, life, and engineering sciences; 24 in humanities and social sciences; 30 in a selected discipline; and 24 in electives. Students are strongly encouraged to learn outside of the classroom through independent projects, study abroad, cooperative education, internships, and partnering with faculty members on specific research projects. The Undergraduate Research Program offers hands-on experience to students in hundreds of areas where a full-time undergraduate may participate for credit or pay during the academic year or the summer. Co-op assignments give students the opportunity to add practical experience to their academic study. Air Force, Army, and Naval/Marine ROTC programs are available on an elective basis. Computing is integrated into the curriculum at Rensselaer, and all incoming undergraduates are required to have a laptop computer. Rensselaer's Mobile Computing Program provides students with the latest computing technology choices. Students may bring their own laptops to campus, but they must comply with Rensselaer's computing requirements.

Off-Campus Programs

Rensselaer has study-abroad programs in Australia, China, Denmark, England, France, Germany, India, Italy, Japan, Spain, Switzerland, and Turkey. Cooperative programs with 15 two- and four-year area institutions allow Rensselaer students to take courses for credit at no additional cost. More than 200 Rensselaer students use this cross-registration program each year. Rensselaer has transfer agreements with more than ninety institutions, including the 107 campuses of the California community college system.

Academic Facilities

Studio classrooms and laboratories across the campus use the latest educational technologies and encourage collaboration and team learning among students, having extensive wireless computing capabilities as well as more than 8,000 data ports on campus and specialized systems such as the visualization laboratory for high-performance computing.

Student research projects are supported by excellent facilities such as the Low Center for Industrial Innovation, the Darrin Fresh Water Institute at Lake George, the Center for Integrated Electronics, and the Lighting Research Center. One of the newest facilities, the Social Behavioral Research Lab (SBRL), provides a platform for research on the social, cognitive, and behavioral impact of IT on society. The Center for Biotechnology and Interdisciplinary Studies, opening in the fall of 2004, provides a fertile environment for student research and learning at the intersection of science and engineering. The Experimental Media and Performing Arts Center (EMPAC) plans to showcase Rensselaer's distinctive programs in the electronic arts while providing facilities to broaden campus discourse and allow students and artists-in-residence to fully engage the larger community in the performing arts.

The entrepreneurial spirit is infused throughout the curriculum at Rensselaer and supported by one of the first university-sponsored business incubators in the country. The Rensselaer Incubator Program harnesses academic, research, and community resources to assist technology-based start-up enterprises. Many Rensselaer students have created new companies, nurtured them in the incubator, and then moved them to Rensselaer Technology Park, which is owned and operated by the university.

Costs

Tuition for 2003–04 was $27,700. Fees were $796. Room and board costs averaged $9083. Books and miscellaneous personal expenses were $1621. A required laptop, offered through Rensselaer, costs about $2500. All incoming students are required to have a laptop computer that meets Rensselaer's specifications.

Financial Aid

Nearly all freshmen who have financial need are offered assistance under a comprehensive program of scholarships, loans, and part-time employment that provides annual assistance ranging from $100 up to full tuition, room, and board. Available federal funds include student loans, Federal Work-Study Program awards, and ROTC scholarships.

Faculty

Rensselaer has embarked on a program to hire the brightest faculty "stars" in selected fields and cluster them into constellations where they engage in innovative research to the benefit of the Institute's students as well as society. To date, Rensselaer's "constellation" initiative has met with great success in the areas of nanotechnology, biotechnology, and information technology. During the past three years, Rensselaer has welcomed 127 new faculty members. Approximately 400 tenured and tenure-track faculty members call Rensselaer home. Indicative of the talent of Rensselaer's young faculty, nearly 30 of them have won the prestigious National Science Foundation (NSF) Early Career Development (CAREER) Award. Faculty members are highly accessible to students, due to the university's internationally recognized studio-style classes, faculty-undergraduate research opportunities, and academic advising programs. While graduate students assist in some laboratory and recitation sessions, it is Rensselaer's policy to have professors teach undergraduate courses. Ninety-five percent of the faculty members have earned a Ph.D., First Professional, or other terminal degree in their fields.

Student Government

Students have an active voice in major university decisions through involvement in student government, a vital and influential force at Rensselaer. Elected student leaders include a Grand Marshal (student government president) and the President of the Student Union. The President of the Union and the Executive Board manage an $8.5 million budget to oversee more than 130 student clubs, intramural sports, and organizations.

Admission Requirements

Campus visits are strongly encouraged. Applications are reviewed individually by the admissions committee. It is important to note that some differences in preparation and academic background may be considered. In order to ensure success in Rensselaer's demanding curricula, an applicant's academic preparation should include 4 years of English, 4 years of mathematics through precalculus, 3 years of science (including physics and chemistry), and 2 years of social studies/history. The SAT I or ACT is required. Accelerated Program applicants must take the SAT II Subject Tests in math, writing, and a science or the ACT in lieu of the SAT I and SAT II. Electronic arts applicants are required to submit a creative portfolio; it is recommended that architecture applicants also prepare a portfolio.

International applicants' official transcripts must be translated into English, and the international financial statement should be completed and mailed with the application. International applicants who do not achieve a minimum SAT verbal score of 580 must take the TOEFL. The minimum scores are 570 for the paper-based exam and 230 for the computer-based exam. The closing date for September admission is January 1 of the student's senior year. January admission is offered to a limited number of freshman and transfer students. Rensselaer admits qualified students without regard to race, color, sexual orientation, national or ethnic origin, religion, gender, age, or disability.

Application and Information

Rensselaer Admissions
Undergraduate Programs
Rensselaer Polytechnic Institute
Troy, New York 12180-3590
Telephone: 518-276-6216
Fax: 518-276-4072
E-mail: admissions@rpi.edu
World Wide Web: http://admissions.rpi.edu

Many of Rensselaer's turn-of-the-century buildings house ultramodern classrooms and laboratories.

THE RESTAURANT SCHOOL AT WALNUT HILL COLLEGE

PHILADELPHIA, PENNSYLVANIA

The College

Walnut Hill College, home to the Restaurant School, was established in 1974 and is dedicated to inspiring the future of the restaurant and hotel industry through training that is dynamic, timely, and insightful, with a commitment of service to its students. Walnut Hill College combines both intensive classroom training and practical experience: students use their knowledge while they learn. Within thirty-four months, graduates are working in the field, earning an income, building a resume, and gaining practical and professional experience.

A student's education is cultivated by the College's philosophy that hands-on training is an essential part of education. This approach has multiple benefits—it enhances learning abilities, creates marketable skills and experience for a resume, brings education to life, and, most importantly, puts the student at the center of it all.

Walnut Hill College is licensed by the Pennsylvania Department of Education State Board of Private License Schools and is a member of the Pennsylvania Association of Private School Administrators. Accredited by the Accrediting Commission of Career Schools and Colleges of Technology, Walnut Hill College is certified for veteran's training by the Veterans Administration, is approved by the United States Department of Justice to grant student visas, and is recognized as a Professional Management Development Partner of the Educational Foundation of the National Restaurant Association.

There is a diverse population at Walnut Hill College, with students coming from throughout the United States and abroad and ranging in age from the high school graduate to the adult who wants to change careers.

Whether it is a celebrity chef's cooking demonstration, dinner and a tour at a notable restaurant or hotel, or a winery tour and tasting, students at the Restaurant School are exposed to the very best Philadelphia has to offer. There are activities and weekly special events that are sponsored by student clubs. The culinary salon team holds the title of 2002 Pennsylvania State Champions, and the Wine Club is undefeated in their scholastic debates. Activities are both educational and fun, combining opportunities to learn and to establish camaraderie and professional development. Events are listed in the student newsletter and monthly calendar.

Location

Philadelphia is a great place to live and learn. As the fourth-largest city in the United States, Philadelphia has much to offer and is a city of firsts—the first public library, the first college, and the first zoo—all in a first-class city.

Walnut Hill College is located in the University City section of Philadelphia, neighboring both the University of Pennsylvania and Drexel University. Located just across the Schuylkill River from Center City, University City has a wonderful college-town ambiance. Restaurants, museums, shops, and theaters abound, with local merchants offering discounts to students. The Amtrak train station is within walking distance of the campus, and the airport is 20 minutes away by car.

Center City is located just minutes from campus. Here, students find a bustling shopping and business district, complete with an award-winning restaurant row, luxury hotels, and exclusive boutiques.

Diversity abounds in this city of neighborhoods, including Chinatown, complete with exotic restaurants and shops; South Philadelphia, with its famed Italian market; and the ever-eclectic South Street, with blocks of restaurants, galleries, shops, and entertainment. Not to mention the Historic District, which was the birthplace of the nation, and a waterfront that features exciting nightlife.

Philadelphia is rich in culture and heritage. Students find world-class art and science museums, theaters that feature major Broadway shows and renowned regional production, and music, which includes everything from jazz to pop to the internationally acclaimed Philadelphia Orchestra.

Majors and Degrees

There are four Bachelor of Science degree program majors at The Restaurant School at Walnut Hill College: hotel management (133 credits), restaurant management (136 credits), culinary arts (133 credits), and pastry arts (123 credits). Each major provides the student with a broad-based knowledge of the overall workings of a fine restaurant or hotel. Beyond that, the programs prepares a student with the day-to-day skills and specific knowledge that are required as he or she develops a career as a restaurant manager, chef, pastry chef, hotel manager, or restaurateur. In partnership with the Educational Foundation of the National Restaurant Association, the College's curriculum includes up to twelve nationally recognized food service and hospitality management courses. Upon successful completion of the courses and the certification exam, students receive national certification.

Academic Programs

All students must successfully complete eight 15-week semesters to be awarded a Bachelor of Science degree in their field of study. Each academic year consists of two semesters, and summer semesters are available. A student must fulfill the required semester hours in a major as well as the basic requirements of the core curriculum. All students are required to participate in special service programs prior to graduating.

Off-Campus Programs

The Restaurant School at Walnut Hill College was the first school in the country to offer a travel experience as part of a curriculum. Culinary and pastry students participate in an eight-day tour of France, while hotel and restaurant management students participate in an eight-day Orlando resort and cruise tour. This travel experience enhances both training and resumes.

A study-abroad program to England is in place for all baccalaureate students. Students may contact the College for detailed information.

Academic Facilities

Recently completing a yearlong renovation, The Restaurant School at Walnut Hill College is poised to offer one of the most dynamic hands-on learning opportunities in the country. The dining experience, situated in the breathtakingly restored 1855

Allison Mansion, turns into a dining event with the addition of three theme restaurants, including Terraza di Italia, a casual Italian trattoria that features classic pasta presentations set amidst an Italian terrace. Guests are invited to sit inside the restaurant, where they can enjoy homemade pasta or dine amongst the twinkling lights in the European courtyard.

American cuisine is presented in an innovative new style in the American Heartland. Depicting a country farm with a painted blue sky and cornfields, this restaurant allows students to explore some of America's best cooking while guests enjoy the comfort of a country dining or veranda setting.

Most notable is the elegant Great Chefs of Philadelphia restaurant. Amidst glittering crystal chandeliers and a rich tapestry motif, guests enjoy wonderful cuisine and service designed by some of Philadelphia and America's top chefs.

Also in the mansion is the student resource center, featuring state-of-the-art computer lab stations as well as the Alumni Library, which encompasses thousands of books, magazines, and videotapes on cooking, management, and wine. The building also houses a student conference room and a wine lab.

The Pastry Shop and Café is filled each morning with buttery croissants, crisp French baguettes, and glistening pastries that are prepared by the pastry arts students. Also available is a selection of pastas, salads, soups, and entrees for an informal café lunch, prepared by the culinary arts students.

The education and the Center for Hospitality Studies buildings are the focal points of the student's training. They house six modern classroom kitchens, four lecture halls, and the College's purchasing center and school store.

Hunter Hall is a turn-of-the-century masterpiece that features magnificent carved mahogany, marble, and fireplaces. The College's Offices of Admissions, Financial Aid, and Independent Student Housing is located in this building.

Costs

Tuition for the four-year program for students starting September 13, 2004 is $12,100 per academic year. Equipment, books, activity fees, culinary, culinary whites, and management dining room attire cost approximately $1200. Students may contact the College for information regarding on-campus housing.

Financial Aid

Financial aid programs are available for those who qualify. It is recommended that students apply early. The College participates in the Federal Pell Grant, the Pennsylvania PHEAA State Grant, the subsidized Federal Stafford Student Loan, and the parents' Federal PLUS Loan, in addition to other alternative loans. The financial aid officers assist students and their families with the creation of a personal plan that outlines expenses and identifies financial resources that are available to incoming students. For more specific information, students may contact the College.

Faculty

Learning comes to life under the guiding hands and encouragement of the highly trained, technically skilled faculty. The Restaurant School at Walnut Hill College has on staff 1 of only 20 certified master pastry chefs in the country. The faculty members are seasoned professionals, having logged many years of experience in restaurants and food service. Through their instruction, students gain professional insight, which gives them a competitive edge upon entering the hospitality field. The chefs and instructors are committed to helping students achieve success. As professionals, they continuously keep pace with current trends in the hospitality industry and convey their professional dedication and work ethic to their students.

Admission Requirements

Typically, the admissions procedure begins with a visit to the College. At that time, prospective students and their families tour the campus, watch hands-on classes in action, and get a feel for campus life. Application for admission to the College is available to any individual with a high school diploma or its equivalent and an interest in developing a career or ownership options in the fine restaurant, food service, or hospitality field. Applicants are evaluated on their educational background and demonstrated or stated interest in their chosen field. Two references are required, as are high school transcripts.

Students may contact the College for information on the early decision program for high school juniors and seniors.

Application and Information

The Restaurant School at Walnut Hill College practices rolling admission; qualified applicants are accepted at any time. Applications for admission are submitted with a $50 application fee and a $150 registration fee. Prospective students should contact:

Office of Admissions
The Restaurant School at Walnut Hill College
4207 Walnut Street
Philadelphia, Pennsylvania 19104
Telephone: 215-222-4200 Ext. 3011
877-925-6884 Ext. 3011 (toll-free)
Fax: 215-222-4219
E-mail: info@walnuthillcollege.edu
World Wide Web: http://www.walnuthillcollege.edu

The Restaurant School at Walnut Hill College.

RHODES COLLEGE

MEMPHIS, TENNESSEE

RHODES

The College

Considered by many to be one of America's premier liberal arts colleges, Rhodes brings together three major purposes of learning seldom found at a single institution: intellectual growth that is fostered by intensive interaction between students and faculty members, preparation for professional life supported by a unique internship program that draws on the city's resources, and a development of values that is part of a diverse student body that adheres to a student-run honor code.

Rhodes is listed by *U.S. News & World Report* in the top tier of America's best national liberal arts colleges, is ranked as one of the top fifty institutions in terms of quality and cost by *Kiplinger's Magazine*, was selected as one of the top twelve hot colleges of 2004 by *Newsweek*, and is one of only forty schools listed in Loren Pope's *Colleges that Change Lives*. This recognition is primarily based on the College's long and steadfast commitment to providing its students with an education that challenges them to think critically, independently, and creatively; actively engages them in research and internships; and connects them in meaningful ways to one another and the larger Memphis community.

Rhodes is a private, coeducational college of liberal arts and sciences, founded in 1848 in Clarksville, Tennessee. The College moved to Memphis in 1925. The College is affiliated with the Presbyterian Church (U.S.A). In addition to the undergraduate degrees listed in this profile, Rhodes also awards the Master of Science degree in accounting.

Rhodes' 1,550 students represent forty-six states and ten countries. About 75 percent of them live on campus in fourteen ivy-covered residence halls. First- and second-year students must live on campus unless they live with their family in Memphis. The East Village, a new apartment-style residential complex, houses 200 juniors and seniors. Students, faculty members, and staff members enjoy the Bryan Campus Life Center, a multiuse campus gathering and recreational facility.

Residents and commuters enjoy the rich mix of extracurricular activities, from the internationally touring Rhodes Singers to the nationally ranked Mock Trial team to an active Black Student Association. Nearly 80 percent of Rhodes students are active in community service and numerous projects that help those in need. Rhodes sponsors more than eighty activities, clubs, and organizations—including seven national fraternities and seven national sororities. More than 250 events each year are sponsored by the College or student organizations, including films, dances, lectures, art exhibits, service projects, concerts, and theater productions. There are several campus publications, a weekly newspaper, a literary journal, the yearbook, and student home pages on the World Wide Web.

Rhodes is a member of Division III of the NCAA, and men's basketball and soccer and women's cross-country, golf, and tennis teams all have gone to national playoffs in recent years. More than 25 percent of the student body competes in varsity sports: baseball, basketball, cross-country, football, golf, soccer, swimming, tennis, and indoor and outdoor track for men and basketball, cross-country, field hockey, golf, soccer, softball, swimming, tennis, indoor and outdoor track, and volleyball for women. About 55 percent participate in the intramural and club sports programs that include basketball, equitation, lacrosse, rugby, softball, tae kwon do, and volleyball.

Location

Cited as one of America's most beautiful campuses, Rhodes' 100 acres are situated in an attractive residential section of midtown Memphis, just minutes from downtown and within walking distance of the Memphis Zoo and the Memphis Brooks Museum of Art. Memphis is America's eighteenth-largest city and the region's medical and business hub. The city offers many internships, research opportunities, and potential jobs. Sixty percent of students take part in local and international internships by the time they graduate. The birthplace of the blues and the home of international companies, including FedEx and International Paper, Memphis is a city of arts and culture, with ten local theaters, twelve museums and art galleries, three ballet companies, visiting Broadway shows, a symphony, and an opera company. Hundreds of restaurants, professional sports events, and good shopping facilities round out the entertainment package.

Majors and Degrees

Rhodes grants the Bachelor of Arts or Bachelor of Science degree in thirty-one departmental and interdisciplinary areas: anthropology/sociology, art, biology, business administration, chemistry, computer science, economics, economics and business administration, economics and international studies, English, French, French and international studies, German, German and international studies, Greek and Roman studies, history, history and international studies, international studies, Latin American studies, mathematics, music, philosophy, physics, political science, political science and international studies, psychology, religious studies, Russian studies, Spanish, theater, and urban studies. Students may also apply for interdisciplinary majors that reflect their own interests.

Academic Program

Rhodes students are required to take a representative group of courses from four major areas: humanities, social sciences, natural sciences, and fine arts. Students must fulfill the basic humanities requirement by taking a four-term, 12-credit-hour interdisciplinary course, Search for Values in the Light of Western History and Religion, or by taking four courses in religious studies and philosophy. The College requires one term of critical reading, thinking, and writing as well as one term of a foreign language at the intermediate level, but either can be waived by demonstrated proficiency. The academic year is divided into two semesters of fourteen weeks each, with an additional week for exams.

The acceptance rate to medical schools of Rhodes graduates is approximately twice the national average, according to American Medical College Application Service (AMCAS) data. Virtually all of Rhodes' graduates either secured jobs or were accepted into graduate schools last year. Typically, nearly 100 percent of applicants to business, law, and divinity schools are accepted.

Rhodes' strong career-counseling program provides advisers in law, business, international business, finance, museum careers, psychological and social services, medicine, accounting, church professions, foreign service, music, and teaching. A new research and teaching partnership with St. Jude Children's Research Hospital in Memphis allows for exciting exchanges between Rhodes students and St. Jude medical researchers. The College provides a fully staffed career development office. Students may gain additional knowledge and experience through independent research, internships, and honors programs.

Off-Campus Programs

Rhodes offers many off-campus credit-earning programs. Among them are a semester of study and travel in Europe focusing on literature, religion, art, and the humanities. Rhodes also has exchange programs at the University of Antwerp in Belgium; the University of Poitiers in France; Eberhard-Karls-Universitat Tubingen in Germany; the University of Lima in Peru; the University of Aberdeen in Scotland; Rhodes University in Grahamstown, South Africa; and the Universitas Nebrissensis in Madrid, Spain. Other Rhodes-sponsored programs are located in Buenos Aires, Argentina; Santiago, Chile; and Washington, D.C. Summer programs include British Studies at Oxford and language immersion programs in Spain, France, and Russia, as well as coral reef ecology and service-learning programs in Honduras. Domestic and international internships can be arranged through academic departments in conjunction with Career Services.

Academic Facilities

The stone and slate buildings on campus are constructed in collegiate Gothic style, and thirteen of them are listed on the National Register of Historic Places. The Burrow Library contains more than 260,000 bound volumes; 69,000 microform items; more than 9,600 records, tapes, and videos; and more than 1,200 periodicals. A citywide library consortium put more than 1.6 million volumes at the fingertips of Rhodes students. A new $40-million library is scheduled to open in 2005.

Excellent science facilities include physics laboratories equipped for sophisticated solar emissions research and biology and chemistry laboratories with an electron microscope, a cell culture lab, and a nuclear magnetic resonance instrument. The College's dual-platform computer network includes file, print, and e-mail servers and more than 200 microcomputers available primarily for student use. Rhodes is listed as one of the 100 Most Wired Colleges by *Yahoo! Internet Life* magazine. The Mathematics/Computer Science and Physics Departments are equipped with labs containing high-powered Sun Ultra workstations. Rhodes' campus network is connected to the Internet, with all residence hall rooms having an Ethernet connection for each resident.

Costs

Tuition at Rhodes for 2003–04 was $22,628, and room and board fees were $6692. There was a $200 student activity fee. Estimated expenses for books and supplies were $720. Transportation and personal expenses are additional.

Financial Aid

Rhodes invests considerable funds in need-based assistance to help make it possible for students who are admitted to the College to attend. The average need-based award for 2003–04 was more than $18,000. A large number of competitive scholarships are also available, ranging from $2000 to full tuition, fees, room, and board. Students interested in need-based financial aid must fill out the Free Application for Federal Student Aid (FAFSA) and the CSS PROFILE. Those interested in competitive scholarships must submit the application for admission by January 15. Notification of need-based awards occurs between April 1 and April 15.

Faculty

The College's 170 faculty members (129 full-time) are first and foremost teachers, but they also engage in research and creative activities, often working with students on scholarly projects. The student-faculty ratio is 11:1, and the average class size is 15. Ninety-four percent of full-time tenured or tenure-track faculty members hold the Ph.D. or other terminal degree in their discipline.

Student Government

Students govern their lives on campus through the Rhodes Student Government, the Honor Council, and the Social Regulations Council and through their participation on the Board of Trustees and various College committees. The honor system prevails at Rhodes; professors regularly leave the room when tests are administered.

Admission Requirements

Rhodes considers a number of criteria in the selection of its students: academic achievements, writing ability, letters of recommendation, standardized test scores, and extracurricular activities. The middle 50 percent of the freshman class who entered in fall 2003 had a combined SAT I score ranging from 1220 to 1370 and a composite ACT score ranging from 26 to 30, and 58 percent were in the top 10 percent of their high school class. Of the 457 first-year students, 34 were presidents of their class or student government and 49 were valedictorians or salutatorians. The College enthusiastically seeks geographic and racial diversity for its student body.

Applicants should have 16 or more high school academic units, with 4 of the units in English, 3 in mathematics (2 in algebra and 1 in geometry, or the equivalent), 2 in the same foreign language, two years of laboratory science, and two years of history or social science. Either the SAT I or ACT is required. In addition to submitting the same application materials and supporting documents as all other students, home-schooled students must submit the results of two SAT II Subject Tests from areas other than English or mathematics. Rhodes offers early decision, early admission, and deferred admission. Advanced Placement credit is normally given for scores of 4 or 5 on the Advanced Placement tests and 5, 6, or 7 on International Baccalaureate Diploma higher-level exams. An interview is not required but is strongly recommended for scholarship candidates. Appointments may be scheduled from 9 a.m. to 4 p.m. Central Time, Monday through Friday, and on Saturday morning from 9 to noon during the academic year. If they give notice, seniors in high school may spend the night in a residence hall between Sunday and Thursday, attend classes, and meet with faculty members and students during the week.

Application and Information

Priority is given to applications received by February 1 (January 15 for those applying for competitive scholarships). Students are notified of the admission decision by April 1. Early decision candidates must file by November 1 for decision notification by December 1 or by January 1 for decision by February 1. Accompanying the application must be a $45 fee, an official high school transcript, results of the SAT I or the ACT exam, a counselor's report, and a teacher's recommendation. Students may apply online free at http://apply.rhodes.edu. For further information, students should contact:

David J. Wottle, Dean of Admissions and Financial Aid
Rhodes College
2000 North Parkway
Memphis, Tennessee 38112-1690
Telephone: 901-843-3700
800-844-5969 (toll-free)
E-mail: adminfo@rhodes.edu
World Wide Web: http://www.rhodes.edu/admissions

Rhodes College has thirteen buildings named to the National Register of Historic Places for representing "one of the finest and most harmonious groupings of collegiate Gothic architecture in the nation."

RICE UNIVERSITY

HOUSTON, TEXAS

The University

Dedicated to the advancement of letters, science, and art, William Marsh Rice University offers undergraduate and graduate degrees in architecture, engineering, humanities, music, social sciences, and natural sciences. The faculty-student ratio is 1:5 and the median class size is 11 students. Undergraduates choose from more than fifty different majors and find research opportunities in more than thirty interdisciplinary research centers on campus.

Of the more than 4,000 students currently enrolled, 2,800 are undergraduates. The student body hails from all fifty states and thirty-seven other countries. Thirty-three percent are members of minority groups. More than 70 percent of the entering freshmen ranked in the top 5 percent of their high school class.

Perhaps the most distinctive feature of Rice's campus life is the residential college system. All new students are randomly assigned to one of nine residential colleges. The colleges serve not only as residence halls but also as primary centers for dining, studying, playing, networking, and developing leadership skills. The residential colleges facilitate a high degree of student-faculty interaction. A faculty master and his or her family live in a house adjacent to the college. The masters and several resident associates (faculty or staff members who live in the college) assist students in various ways, from enriching intellectual life to participating in cultural and service activities to cheering on intramural teams. Approximately 20 other professors per college are nonresident associates, eating lunch in the college, serving as academic advisers, and participating in a myriad of extracurricular activities organized by the students.

Rice undergraduates pursue the highest levels of athletic competition through NCAA Division I-A sports and through club sports. As members of the Western Athletic Conference, Rice athletes compete in baseball, basketball, cross-country, football, golf, soccer, swimming, tennis, track and field, and volleyball. Club sports include badminton, cricket, cycling, fencing, lacrosse, karate, rowing, rugby, sailing, soccer, Ultimate Frisbee, volleyball, and water polo.

Location

The fourth-largest city in the nation, Houston is a vibrant center for the arts and culture. The downtown Theater District, only 5 miles from the Rice campus, is host to permanent companies in ballet, opera, symphony, and theater. Just 3 blocks from campus is the Museum District, which is composed of eleven museums that feature outstanding collections and exhibitions of art, nature, science, medicine, and history. The district also encompasses Hermann Park, home to the Houston Zoo, an amphitheater, a public golf course, and a Japanese garden. The Texas Medical Center, the world's largest medical center, is adjacent to Hermann Park and across the street from Rice. The campus itself covers 300 acres, shaded by almost 4,000 trees and bordered by a 3-mile jogging trail. Rice is located on the edge of one of Houston's most beautiful residential areas and in one of the safest sections of the city.

Majors and Degrees

Students interested in architecture choose between the four-year B.A. program and the six-year Bachelor of Architecture (B.Arch.) degree. Those who have been admitted to the B.Arch. program spend their fifth year in a working preceptorship with an architectural firm, returning to Rice to complete a final year of architectural study for the degree. Among the approved preceptorships are Pei, Cobb, Freed & Partners, Cesar Pelli & Associates, Michael Graves, and Renzo Piano Building Shop.

The George R. Brown School of Engineering offers, through eight departments, majors in bioengineering, chemical engineering, civil engineering, computational and applied mathematics, computer science, electrical and computer engineering, mechanical engineering, materials science, and statistics. Environmental engineering is available as a double major with another science or engineering field. These programs lead to either the B.A. or the B.S. degree.

Through the School of Humanities, students may declare majors in art history, classical studies, English, French studies, German and Slavic studies, Hispanic studies, history, kinesiology, linguistics, philosophy, religious studies, and visual arts. Interdisciplinary majors are available in ancient Mediterranean civilizations, Asian studies, medieval studies, and the study of women and gender.

Music students may opt for either a B.A. or a Bachelor of Music (B.Mus.) degree in composition, music history, music theory, or performance. Students who pass the qualifying examination may elect an honors program that leads to the simultaneous awarding of the B.Mus. and the Master of Music (M.Mus.) degrees after five years of study, the final two years of which are devoted to the student's particular specialization.

The Wiess School of Natural Sciences awards the B.A. degree in the fields of biochemistry and cell biology, ecology and evolutionary biology, and mathematics. Students may elect either the B.A. or B.S. degree in chemistry, earth science, and physics and astronomy.

The School of Social Sciences offers majors in anthropology, economics, mathematical economic analysis, political science, psychology, and sociology.

Several interdepartmental majors are offered. The policy studies major includes six areas of specialization, ranging from environmental policy to international affairs, and a research project. The cognitive sciences degree provides a multidisciplinary study of the mind, and managerial studies is composed of course work in accounting, economics, political science, psychology, and statistics.

Students may pursue programs at Rice that satisfy the requirements for admission to graduate schools of business, dentistry, diplomacy, finance, health science, law, and medicine.

Academic Program

Because it believes that undergraduates should become acquainted with areas of study outside their specialization, Rice has implemented a set of distribution requirements. There is no core curriculum; rather, all students choose courses to fulfill the distribution requirements from a list that includes more than forty academic subject areas. The flexibility of the curriculum allows students the option of completing double or triple majors, interdepartmental majors, or area majors. Students are assisted in these choices by faculty advisers, who begin working with students as early as freshman orientation.

Classroom learning is enhanced by additional experiences. Each year, the number of internship opportunities posted by the Career Services Center exceeds the number of students looking for internships. In addition, a large number of undergraduates are conducting primary research. Since 1990, 224 undergraduates have earned graduate fellowships from the National Science Foundation.

Rice observes a two-semester calendar, and students enroll in an average of five courses per semester.

Off-Campus Programs

Recognizing the importance of a global perspective, Rice encourages students to enrich their academic experience with a summer, semester, or year of study abroad. The Office of International Programs and faculty members assist students in identifying the best programs for their individual interests and needs. Rice-affiliated programs allow students to study at nearly 400 sites around the world. Students can study on every continent—including Antarctica. Approximately 40 percent of Rice undergraduates study abroad. In the United States, Rice sponsors an exchange program with Swarthmore College in Pennsylvania and is affiliated with American University's Washington semester. Financial assistance is available for study-abroad and exchange programs.

Academic Facilities

The Fondren Library is accessible to students 24 hours a day and is a charter member of JSTOR, an electronic archive of important journals. The library contains more than 2.2 million volumes, 2.9 million microforms, and 33,200 current print and electronic journals. The library's holdings include extensive special collections, such as those in art and music and eighteenth-century British drama. Students have on-site and remote access to the library's online catalog, indexes, and full-text reference sources and direct access to the stacks, which are lined with private study carrels. Powerbooks and Macintosh and UNIX workstations are located throughout the building.

Rice students have access to some of the best computing facilities in the country. Owlnet is Rice's educational computing system, which includes computing tools on the UNIX, Macintosh, and PC computing platforms. All undergraduates are eligible for an Owlnet account, which gives them access to e-mail, word processing, spreadsheets, statistical and graphics software, and many other packages. Owlnet computing labs are located across the campus, including one in each residential college. Each residential college room is equipped with one network connection port for every student resident.

The Rice Media Center, which specializes in contemporary filmmaking and photography, is popular on campus. The Rice University Gallery functions principally as an extension of the teaching activities of the art and art history department and sponsors major exhibits regularly. Hamman Hall provides theater space for the student drama group. The Alice Pratt Brown Hall houses the Shepherd School of Music and provides concert facilities for the Shepherd School of Music series and for the Houston Friends of Music, the city's major sponsor of world-renowned chamber music ensembles. In addition, the University has extensive science and engineering laboratories, language laboratories, art studios, spacious architectural laboratories, and the Gardiner Symonds Teaching Laboratory, which facilitates interactive teaching through innovative architecture and computer technology.

Costs

Tuition at Rice is substantially less than that at comparable universities—$20,350 for the academic year 2004–05. The average cost, including tuition, room and board ($8380), fees ($854), books and supplies ($800), and personal expenses ($1550), totals $31,934.

Financial Aid

Rice offers need- and merit-based financial aid. To determine financial need, Rice requires the CSS Financial Aid PROFILE, the Free Application for Federal Student Aid (FAFSA), and a copy of the family's tax return. If need exists, Rice meets 100 percent of demonstrated need with a combination of grants, loans, and campus employment. The University also provides merit awards. All applicants are automatically considered regardless of financial status. Rice has been recognized consistently by *U.S. News & World Report, Time,* and *Money* magazine as one of the best values in higher education.

Faculty

Rice has a distinguished faculty that is devoted to teaching and research. In addition to the $48 million of sponsored research projects that are currently under way, one third of the faculty members edit or serve on editorial boards of scholarly research journals. Rice professors bring this excitement of discovery to the classroom. Ninety-one percent of undergraduate courses are taught by faculty members rather than lecturers or graduate students. Professors regularly interact with undergraduates in the classroom, as members of the residential colleges, and as academic advisers.

Student Government

All undergraduates are members of the Rice Student Association, which is governed through a Student Senate. Every student is also a member of one of nine residential colleges, each of which has its own government and judicial system. Rice also has an honor system, which is administered by an elected student Honor Council. All written examinations and assignments are conducted under the honor code.

Admission Requirements

The Admission Committee seeks students of keen intellect who will benefit from the Rice experience. Rice strives to create a rich learning environment in which all students will meet individuals whose life experiences differ significantly from their own. The Admission Committee evaluates course selection, grades, recommendations, personal qualities, essays, and standardized testing. All applicants are required to submit scores from the SAT I or the ACT and three subject tests from the SAT II. Interviews are optional.

Application and Information

Three application plans are available for freshmen. Early decision is binding; students apply by November 1 and are notified by December 15. Interim and regular decision are not binding; for interim, students apply by December 1 and are notified by February 10. Regular decision candidates apply by January 10 and are notified by April 1. Students who have completed two full semesters of college work may apply as transfers by October 15 for midyear (January) enrollment or by March 15 for fall-term (August) enrollment. There is a $40 application fee.

Office of Admission-MS 17
Rice University
P.O. Box 1892
Houston, Texas 77251-1892
Telephone: 713-348-RICE
800-527-OWLS (toll-free)
World Wide Web: http://futureowls.rice.edu

Lovett Hall, with its trademark Sallyport, is the oldest building on the Rice campus.

THE RICHARD STOCKTON COLLEGE OF NEW JERSEY

POMONA, NEW JERSEY

The College

The Richard Stockton College of New Jersey is an undergraduate college of arts, sciences, and professional studies within the New Jersey System of Higher Education. Named for Richard Stockton, one of the New Jersey signers of the Declaration of Independence, the College was authorized by the passage of the state's 1968 bond referendum for higher education and accepted its charter class in 1971.

More than 6,000 students are enrolled at the College, which provides distinctive traditional and alternative approaches to education. Stockton seeks to develop the analytic and creative capabilities of its students by encouraging them to undertake individually planned courses of study that promote self-reliance and an acceptance of and responsiveness to change.

The College's campus provides an excellent natural setting for a wide range of outdoor recreational activities, including sailing, canoeing, hiking, jogging, and fishing. Students and faculty and staff members take part together in an extensive intramural and club sports program that includes aikido, crew, flag football, golf, soccer, softball, street hockey, swimming, and volleyball. At the intercollegiate level, the College fields teams in men's baseball, basketball, lacrosse, and soccer; women's basketball, crew, field hockey, soccer, softball, tennis, and volleyball; and men's and women's cross-country and track and field. In addition, the College has a gymnasium with fitness facilities, a glass-enclosed indoor swimming pool, racquetball courts, weight rooms, and outdoor recreational facilities.

College Center I provides a focal point for social, recreational, cultural, and leisure activities. More than eighty clubs and organizations have their offices in the center: social clubs, such as the Film Committee, Concert Committee, and Performing Arts Committee; service clubs, including the Social Work Club, Speech and Hearing Association, and Unified Black Students' Society; special interest clubs, such as the Accounting and Finance Society, Dance Club, and Photography Club; and independent organizations, including the Jewish Student Union, New Life Christian Fellowship, and thirteen sororities and fraternities. Participation in cocurricular activities can be documented through the College's student development program, ULTRA (Undergraduate Learning, Training, and Awareness), and issuance of a Cocurricular Transcript to students.

College Center II, which is connected to the main academic complex, is a living room-type facility and features a cafeteria for on-campus students, a wide-screen television, a game room, lounge areas, and several conference rooms.

The Residential Life Center provides a curricular/cocurricular facility within the dormitory area. With its large and small meeting rooms, convenience store, and microcomputer room, the center permits the expansion of activities programs for both organized and informal student groups.

The Lakeside Center is located in the Housing I garden apartment area. The facility contains a convenience store, an outdoor concert area, a snack bar/pizza facility, a microcomputer lab, a multipurpose room for large programs, and a small meeting room for student groups.

On-campus housing for more than 2,000 students is available in the Housing I garden apartments, the Housing II and III residence halls, and the Housing IV complex, which opened in fall 1999. All types of units are fully furnished and air conditioned and are within easy walking distance of the College's main academic complex.

The College is accredited by the Commission on Higher Education of the Middle States Association of Colleges and Schools. As a college of the New Jersey System of Higher Education, Stockton offers programs that are approved by the State Board of Higher Education. The Environmental Health Program is accredited by the National Environmental Health Science and Protection Accreditation Council; the Social Work Program has been accredited by the Council on Social Work Education; the teacher education sequence has been approved by the New Jersey Department of Education and the National Association of State Directors of Teacher Education and Certification; the Nursing Program has been accredited by the National League for Nursing and is approved by the New Jersey Board of Nursing; and the Chemistry Program has been accredited by the American Chemical Society.

In addition to its bachelor's degrees, the College offers several graduate programs: a Master of Physical Therapy, a Master of Business Administration, a Master of Occupational Therapy, a Master of Instructional Technology; a Master of Nursing (speciality for adult health practitioner); and a Master of Arts in Holocaust and Genocide Studies.

Location

Stockton College is located in Pomona, New Jersey, and can be reached from Exit 44 South on the Garden State Parkway and Exit 12 of the Atlantic City Expressway. By car, the campus is approximately 1 hour from Philadelphia and 2½ hours from New York City.

The campus, which has lakes, forests, and hiking trails, is supplemented by nearby Brigantine Wildlife Refuge and the Bass River, Penn, and Wharton state forests. The active program of concerts, art exhibitions, lectures, recreation, and sports on campus is complemented by the nearby resort seashore. Within a 15-minute drive, students will find fishing, boating, swimming, and theatrical productions as well as the famous Atlantic City Boardwalk.

Majors and Degrees

The Bachelor of Arts degree is offered in applied physics, biology, business studies (corporate and public accounting, finance, international business, hospitality management, management, and marketing), chemistry, communication, criminal justice (forensic science), economics, environmental studies and geology, historical studies, information and computer sciences, liberal studies, literature and language, marine science, mathematics, philosophy and religion, political science, psychology, sociology and anthropology, and studies in the arts. The Bachelor of Science degree is offered in applied physics, biochemistry/molecular biology, biology, business studies (accounting, finance, hospitality management, international business, management, and marketing), chemistry, environmental studies and geology, information and computer sciences, marine science, mathematics, predentistry, pre-engineering, premedicine, pre–veterinary medicine, psychology, public health, social work, and speech pathology and audiology. The degree of Bachelor of Science in Nursing is offered to upper-division students.

The College has seven-year dual-degree programs with the University of Medicine and Dentistry of New Jersey, the Robert Wood Johnson Medical School, the Pennsylvania College of Podiatric Medicine, and the New York College of Podiatric Medicine, which guarantee Stockton students admission to medical and/or dental school. Students participating in the programs earn a Bachelor of Science degree from Stockton and an M.D. degree from the appropriate medical school. Stockton also has an articulation program with Cornell University for veterinary medicine as well as five-year, dual-degree programs with New Jersey Institute of Technology and Rutgers, The State University of New Jersey, for students interested in engineering. Students participating in the programs earn a Bachelor of Science degree in chemistry, physics, or math from Stockton and a Bachelor of Science degree in engineering from NJIT or Rutgers.

In addition, Stockton provides preparation for teacher certification in subject areas and elementary and other education programs.

Academic Programs

To earn a baccalaureate degree at Stockton, a student must satisfactorily complete a minimum of 128 semester credits. Degree programs include a combination of general studies and program (major field) studies. The Bachelor of Arts student must earn a total of 64 credits in general studies; the Bachelor of Science student must earn 48. General studies courses are broad cross-disciplinary courses designed to introduce students to all major areas of the curriculum and to the broadly applicable intellectual skills necessary for success in college. Students must select some courses from each major curricular area. The only specifically required courses within general studies are the basic studies courses (up to three), from which students may be exempted on the basis of diagnostic testing. The Bachelor of Arts student must earn a total of 64 credits in program studies; the Bachelor of Science student must earn 80. Program studies (major field) requirements are carefully structured and emphasize sequences of specific courses.

Students at Stockton have special opportunities to influence what and how they learn by participating in the major decisions that shape their academic lives. The main avenue of participation is the preceptorial system, which enables students to work, on a personalized basis, with an assigned faculty-staff preceptor in the planning and evaluation of individualized courses of study and in the exploration of various career alternatives. Stockton's academic programs emphasize curricular organization and methods of instruction that promote independent learning and research, cross-disciplinary study, problem solving, and decision making through analysis and synthesis.

Off-Campus Programs

Off-campus educational experiences for college credits are a central feature of most of the degree programs at Stockton. Internships, research projects, and field studies allow students to apply the principles and methods they have learned in their formal training. Opportunities for foreign study are also available.

The Washington, D.C., Internship Program gives Stockton students the opportunity to gain professional working experience. Stockton sends more students to the program than any other college or university outside the Washington area.

Coordination of off-campus internship programs is provided by the academic divisional offices; coordination of foreign study is provided by the coordinator of international education.

Academic Facilities

Situated on an attractive, heavily wooded 1,600-acre campus, Stockton's award-winning academic complex has been planned to serve as a living-learning center; academic, recreational, and living spaces are mixed to promote interaction among all students and faculty and staff members. The facilities, all constructed since 1971, include several large classroom-office buildings, a library, a lecture hall/auditorium, and a 550-seat Performing Arts Center. The new Multipurpose Recreational Center includes a gymnasium/field house, an outdoor NCAA track, field-event venues, and four playing fields for soccer and lacrosse.

The library contains more than 300,000 volumes, more than 2,600 current periodical subscriptions, 280,000 government documents, more than 19,000 reels of microfilm, and about 68,000 other units of microtext. The media collection includes films, slides, videotapes and audiotapes, compact discs, and phonographs. The library also houses a special collection on the New Jersey Pine Barrens and is a depository for federal, state, and Atlantic City documents.

Costs

Costs for the 2003–04 academic year were as follows: tuition and fees, based on 32 credits—$6224 for in-state students and $9168 for out-of-state students; on-campus housing—$4425; and board—$2379 for a fifteen-meal plan. Books, supplies, transportation, and personal items are extra. All costs are subject to change.

Financial Aid

Financial aid is available in the form of scholarships, grants, loans, and jobs. Aid is awarded both on a competitive (merit) basis and according to need. Students seeking financial aid should file the Free Application for Federal Student Aid (FAFSA) by March 1. This form is used by the College in evaluating all applications for financial aid.

Faculty

Stockton's faculty numbers 225 full-time and 112 part-time and adjunct members. They represent excellent and highly diversified academic backgrounds and training, with 95 percent holding a terminal degree in their field. Faculty members work closely with students through the College's preceptorial system and share with students and staff the initiative and responsibility for the College's social, recreational, athletics, and cultural programs and activities. This arrangement supports the exceptional rapport and communication that exist among students and faculty members.

Student Government

The Stockton College Student Senate consists of 25 student members. The advisory council is made up of 1 faculty member and 2 staff members. Student senators hold office for one year, and elections are held every spring. Among its other duties, the Student Senate reviews and makes recommendations on budgets of funded student organizations and acts as the official representative of the student body.

Admission Requirements

Stockton operates a continuous admission program. Students may apply for admission to the fall or spring term and are notified of the admission decision as soon as their application file has been completed. Applicants must submit ACT or SAT I scores. Admission is selective.

Stockton offers early acceptance programs for high school students in their junior year. Veterans and people who have been away from formal education for some time are also invited to apply for admission on an individual basis. Stockton makes no distinction between part- and full-time students in offering admission.

Stockton has a program that permits the admission on an individual basis of a limited number of students from educationally and financially disadvantaged backgrounds. Students who desire to explore this opportunity at the College should write expressing their interest in this program.

Transfer students are encouraged to apply for admission to either the fall or the spring semester.

Application and Information

For more information or application forms, students should contact:

Dean of Enrollment Management
The Richard Stockton College of New Jersey
P.O. Box 195
Pomona, New Jersey 08240-0195
Telephone: 609-652-4261
Fax: 609-748-5541
E-mail: admissions@stockton.edu
World Wide Web: http://www.stockton.edu

RICHMOND, THE AMERICAN INTERNATIONAL UNIVERSITY IN LONDON

LONDON, ENGLAND

The University

Richmond, The American International University in London, prepares men and women to serve with purpose and generosity in an interdependent and multicultural world. Richmond offers a strong academic program with many choices of fields of study, an exceptional faculty, superb campus life, and fellow students from all over the world. In the United States, Richmond is accredited by the Commission on Higher Education of the Middle States Association of Colleges and Schools, a regional accrediting body recognized by the U.S. Department of Education. Richmond is accredited in the United Kingdom by the Open University and holds related degree validation. The University's undergraduate and graduate degrees are designated by the United Kingdom's Department of Education and Employment. The University is a comprehensive American liberal arts and professional university. In addition to the undergraduate degree programs described below, Richmond offers a Master of Arts in art history and a Master of Business Administration (M.B.A.).

Freshmen and sophomores study and live at the Richmond campus, 7 miles from central London. Junior and senior years are spent at the Kensington campus in one of London's most beautiful residential and historic districts. As part of their four-year B.A. degree program, students may spend a semester or a year studying at one of the University's two international study centers in Florence and Rome, Italy. Richmond currently enrolls 1,000 students from more than 100 countries. Approximately 33 percent of the degree students are from Europe and the United Kingdom, 23 percent are from Pacific Rim countries, and 16 percent are from the Middle East. Nine percent of the student body represent the continent of Africa, and 2 percent are from Latin America. The remaining students are from North America. About 175 study-abroad U.S. students are enrolled for a semester or a year at the University.

Small classes, averaging 18 students, enable students to receive personal attention from professors in a supportive environment. The curriculum and academic advising system are structured to enable students to choose courses that provide broad knowledge, relevant skills, and an understanding of the world's many cultures and nations.

Richmond students supplement academic programs with activities that complement and balance the classroom experience. Many extracurricular and cocurricular programs are available to students, including Student Government, sports, and debate, drama, computer, Hellenic, Pan-African, and business clubs. There is also a University Honor Society.

Location

The lower campus in the London suburb of Richmond offers a variety of entertainment, shopping, cultural, and recreational opportunities. Only yards from the University campus is Richmond Park, more than 2,200 acres of rolling hills and lush woodland, where one can ride horses, jog, or simply relax. The journey from Richmond into Central London takes about 30 minutes.

The upper campus is located in the heart of London's Borough of Kensington, which has fine museums, libraries, theatres, concert halls, historic buildings, and well-known cultural and educational resources. The University takes full advantage of London's cultural and social resources through selected academic courses, work experience placements with multinational corporations, and special visits to museums, art galleries, theatres, and concert halls.

Majors and Degrees

Richmond operates its academic program on the American system. The University offers the four-year Bachelor of Arts (B.A.) and Bachelor of Science (B.S.) degrees in fourteen majors, with a further choice of seventeen minors, as well as the two-year Associate of Arts (A.A.) degree. Majors offered by the University are art, design, and media; business administration (finance, international business, marketing); communications; computing (computer systems engineering, information systems); economics; history; international relations; political science; psychology; and sociology. In addition, Richmond offers an engineering program jointly with George Washington University.

Academic Programs

In order to graduate with the dual-validated U.S. and U.K. degree [B.A./B.A. (Honors) or the B.S./B.Sc. (Honors)], students must earn a minimum of 120 credits. Usually, this means taking a full load for four years, or eight semesters. Within these 120 credits, students must complete all course requirements for their majors. Students must also meet the University's Language Proficiency and General Education requirements. In addition, valuable work experience for credit is offered through the International Internship and Career Apprenticeship programs. Recent placements have been at the International Herald Tribune, General Electric, The House of Commons, CNN, the United Nations, Lloyds Bank, the Museum of London, and Sony Music Corporation.

Credit is also awarded for Advanced Placement tests (6 credits for each subject grade of 3, 4, or 5); a grade of A, B, or C on the "A" Level exams is awarded 9 credits (6 for D or E). Credit is also awarded for the International Baccalaureate, the Baccalauréat de l'Enseignement du Second Degré (France), the Abitur/Reifzuegnis (Germany), the Diploma di Maturità (Italy), and the School Leaving Diploma (Denmark, Finland, Norway, and Sweden).

The fall semester begins in late August and ends in mid-December. The spring semester begins in mid-January and runs through mid-May. Two sessions of summer school run from mid-May to mid-June and mid-June to mid-July.

Off-Campus Programs

Students may complement their studies in London with a semester, year, or summer at one of two international study centers. The centers, each offering intensive study of the language and culture of the country, are in Florence and Rome, Italy. The Florence Study Center emphasizes studio and fine arts. The Rome Center offers study in the Italian language and culture, art history, economics, and political science.

Academic Facilities

Information technology is integrated into the curriculum in ways that are natural to the discipline under study. Supporting this are nine student computer laboratories with 300 PCs and Macintosh computers, which connect to the Internet and are networked for student, faculty, and administrative use. Wireless network access is also available.

Richmond's libraries support the courses taught at each campus. Students may use either campus library. The libraries house 75,000 volumes and add approximately 4,000 new titles each year. In addition, the libraries have subscriptions to approximately 250 periodicals. Computers are available in both libraries for CD-ROM data searches and access to online databases through the network. Richmond students also have access to thirty-seven of the best libraries in London.

Costs

Tuition for the 2004–05 academic year is $18,400. Room and board are $9200. Personal expenses, books and supplies, clothing, recreation, and travel costs also need to be factored in.

Financial Aid

Scholarships are awarded annually to students of high academic ability. Financial aid for U.S. citizens includes Federal Stafford Student Loans and Federal PLUS loans. All U.S. citizens must file the Free Application for Federal Student Aid (FAFSA) to qualify. Students should contact the admissions office for details regarding application procedures for scholarships and financial aid.

Faculty

The student-faculty ratio of 12:1 enables optimum interaction and individualized instructional assistance. The 105 faculty members (39 full-time, 66 part-time) have professional degrees from top European and American universities such as Harvard, Yale, the University of Michigan, Cambridge, Oxford, the London School of Economics, the Sorbonne, and the University of Bonn.

Student Government

The Student Government Association is a student-elected and student-run organization. Students are provided an opportunity to get directly involved with University governance and community life. The Student Government Association organizes social events and student activities and provides a forum for students' concerns.

Admission Requirements

Applicants are admitted on the basis of academic performance, references, intended major, and career interests. The required autobiographical essay is of paramount importance. Applicants to Richmond have usually completed a total of twelve years of primary and secondary school with a minimum grade of C+ (2.5 out of 4.0) in the American high school grading system, or its equivalent. British system students should have attained a minimum of five GCSE passes (grades of A, B, or C) in acceptable academic subjects, one of which must be mathematics or science. Equivalent qualifications gained under other educational systems are also considered for the purpose of admission.

Students must submit a completed application form, an essay, transcripts of all secondary and postsecondary school work, one letter of recommendation, and SAT I or ACT scores (applies only to students graduating from the American education system). The ATP code for Richmond is 0823L. The ACT code is 5244. Evidence of proficiency in the English language is required from students whose first language is not English or who did not attend English-speaking schools. Standardized test scores, such as the TOEFL or the ALIGU, or completion of recognized examinations, such as GCSE, Pitman, RSA, or lower Cambridge, are considered in assessing students' language capability.

Richmond admits students on a rolling basis, and applicants are encouraged to submit their application at the earliest opportunity. All documents in languages other than English must be accompanied by official translations. Applicants are usually notified of a decision within two to three weeks.

Application and Information

An application for admission and further information may be obtained by contacting the appropriate admissions office.

Applicants residing in the United States should contact:

Director of U.S. Admissions
U.S. Office of Admissions
Richmond, The American International University in London
343 Congress Street, Suite 3100
Boston, Massachusetts 02210-1214
Telephone: 617-450-5617
Fax: 617-450-5601
E-mail: us_admissions@richmond.ac.uk
World Wide Web: http://www.richmond.ac.uk

Applicants residing in all other countries should contact:

Director of Admissions
Office of Admissions
Richmond, The American International University in London
Queens Road, Richmond
Surrey TW10 6JP
England
Telephone: 44-20-8332-9000
Fax: 44-20-8332-1596
E-mail: enroll@richmond.ac.uk
World Wide Web: http://www.richmond.ac.uk

The Richmond Hill campus is situated near the River Thames in one of London's most attractive and secure areas. The impressive neo-Gothic structure was constructed in 1843.

RIDER UNIVERSITY

LAWRENCEVILLE, NEW JERSEY

The University

Founded in 1865, Rider University is an independent, coeducational, nonsectarian institution accredited by the Middle States Association of Colleges and Schools. Rider has two campuses, one in Lawrenceville, New Jersey, and one in Princeton, New Jersey.

Rider's four academic units include the College of Business Administration; the College of Liberal Arts, Education, and Sciences; the College of Continuing Studies; and Westminster Choir College, located in Princeton, New Jersey.

More than 95 percent of Rider's full-time faculty members hold a doctorate or other appropriate advanced degree. Primarily a teaching institution, Rider University selects instructors who are committed to imparting the knowledge and skills of a particular discipline. Full professors teach at all levels. There are no teaching assistants in the classrooms or laboratories.

Rider University is located on a 353-acre campus that contains large open areas and thirty-eight modern buildings constructed within the past thirty years. Approximately 70 percent of the 3,100 undergraduates live in University residence halls or in fraternities or sororities on the campus. Entering students and returning students are guaranteed housing on the campus provided that they meet the stated deadlines for submission of housing applications and deposits.

Rider participates in NCAA Division I in all of its intercollegiate sports. Women's sports are basketball, cross-country, field hockey, indoor track, soccer, softball, swimming and diving, tennis, track and field, and volleyball. Men's sports are basketball, cross-country, baseball, golf, indoor track, soccer, swimming and diving, tennis, track and field, and wrestling.

Location

Rider University is located in the suburban community of Lawrenceville, New Jersey, midway between Princeton and Trenton, New Jersey. It is approximately 35 miles northeast of Philadelphia and 65 miles southwest of New York City. The location combines the advantages of accessibility to the cultural and recreational facilities of major urban areas and to the peaceful surroundings of a suburban community.

Majors and Degrees

The College of Business Administration awards the Bachelor of Science in Business Administration (B.S.B.A.) degree in accounting, actuarial science, advertising, business administration, computer information systems, economics, finance, global business, human resource management, management and leadership, and marketing. The program is accredited by AACSB International–The Association to Advance Collegiate Schools of Business.

The College of Liberal Arts, Education, and Sciences (CLAES) awards the Bachelor of Arts (B.A.) degree in elementary education and secondary education and the Bachelor of Science (B.S.) degree in business education. Rider's education programs are recognized by the National Council for the Accreditation of Teacher Education (NCATE).

The CLAES also awards the B.A. degree in American studies, communications, economics, English, fine arts, French, German, global and multinational studies, history, journalism, mathematics, philosophy, physics, political science, psychology, Russian, sociology, and Spanish. It offers the B.S. degree in biochemistry, biology, biopsychology, chemistry, environmental sciences, geosciences, and marine sciences.

Preprofessional programs are available in allied health, dentistry, law, and medicine. Three out of four of Rider's premed graduates who apply to medical schools are accepted to medical school. Ninety-two percent of students who apply to law school are accepted.

Preparation for career success goes beyond the classroom at Rider. The Office of Career Placement and the Career Development Program help students prepare for their future with career counseling, resume writing, job search workshops, video interview sessions, and individualized counseling. Internships, on-campus recruiting by a wide variety of international, national, and regional companies, and an off-campus referral service helped more than 94 percent of Rider's graduates to successfully find employment or pursue advanced degree programs.

Academic Program

Rider University operates on the semester system. Each College requires a minimum of 120 semester hours of credit for graduation; the last 30 semester hours of credit must be earned at Rider University. The College of Business Administration requires that a student earn at least 45 semester hours, including the last 30, at Rider University.

The Baccalaureate Honors Program is available to students in all programs. To be considered for the program, incoming freshmen must be in the top 10 percent of their high school class and have a combined SAT I score of 1150 or higher. Students currently enrolled in the University and transfer students must have at least a 3.25 cumulative grade point average.

Rider University recognizes the Advanced Placement (AP) Program and offers credit and placement for scores of 3, 4, or 5 on most AP tests. Credit is awarded for the College-Level Examination Program (CLEP) tests provided that the minimum required score is obtained. The minimum score varies according to the specific area covered by the examination.

Off-Campus Programs

Rider University offers semester-long and academic-year programs at a variety of international sites.

Academic Facilities

The Franklin F. Moore Library contains 353,000 volumes, arranged in open stacks, and more than 1,500 periodicals and technical journals, magazines, and business services. The library is automated and has a computerized catalog and circulation system. To complement its on-campus holdings, the library offers online database searches of holdings of other libraries.

Students have direct access to a fiber-optic campus network linking approximately 300 terminals located in the Computer Center, Library, academic buildings, and residence halls. Students may use computing laboratories with multimedia workstations and comprehensive software libraries. Local area networks connect to the campus network to help students develop class projects and presentations. Digital VAX computer clusters in the central Computer Center provide students with network access, extensive software offerings, and compilation resources. E-mail, bulletin boards, Internet access, and other campus computer services are available via the University network.

Other academic facilities include well-equipped science laboratories for biochemistry, biology, biopsychology, chemistry, environmental sciences, geology, physics, and psychology and two 400-seat theaters.

Costs

The total annual tuition charge for new students who began their studies in 2003–04 was $20,590. Mandatory fees included a student activity fee of $200 and a one-time orientation fee of $200. Room (standard 2 to a room) and board charges totaled $8060 for the academic year. It is estimated that books and supplies, personal expenses, and transportation average $1900.

Financial Aid

Most financial aid is based upon demonstrated financial need. Students and their parents are required to file the Free Application for Federal Student Aid (FAFSA) prior to March 1 to be considered for financial assistance administered by Rider University. The University maintains a need-blind admission policy and attempts to meet the full financial need of all eligible applicants. Entering students are eligible for consideration for Federal Pell Grants, Federal Supplemental Educational Opportunity Grants, Federal Work-Study awards, Federal Perkins Loans, New Jersey Tuition Aid Grants, New Jersey Distinguished Scholar Scholarships, Rider University grants, Trustee Scholarships, Alumni Scholarships, and other forms of institutional aid. Rider University offers four merit-based scholarship programs for qualified applicants. These scholarships, the Presidential, Provost, Dean's, and Transfer scholarships, are for up to $16,000 and are renewable for up to four years of study if the student maintains the minimum grade point average specified by the Scholarship Committee. Rider also offers two full-tuition actors scholarships and a $7500 technical support scholarship in theater.

Faculty

There are 226 full-time and 187 part-time faculty members. Ninety-five percent of the faculty hold a doctorate or terminal degree in their field. The same faculty teaches both graduate and undergraduate courses; graduate assistants do not teach classes at Rider University. The student-faculty ratio is approximately 13:1. Faculty members serve on student affairs committees and as faculty advisers to all student organizations.

Student Government

There is an active Student Government Association (SGA) on the campus. The SGA sponsors concerts, lectures, plays, and other events. All social rules and regulations are made, enforced, and adjudicated by students. Each class, each residence hall, the Interfraternity Council, the Panhellenic Society, and commuting students are represented in the Student Government Association.

Admission Requirements

Students applying for admission to Rider University are expected to have completed a minimum of 16 acceptable college-preparatory units of study by the end of their senior year in high school. These 16 units must include 4 in English, and the other 12 units should be selected from traditional academic areas, including history, mathematics, science, social studies, foreign languages, and literature. Business or vocational courses completed in high school are not considered college-preparatory units. Students applying for admission to programs in premedicine, predentistry, science, business, and mathematics are expected to have completed 3 years of mathematics (algebra I, algebra II, and geometry). Students are required to submit official SAT I or ACT results and two letters of recommendation in support of their application. Most successful applicants rank in the upper half of their high school senior class.

Rider University seeks a diverse student body and encourages applications from students from varied ethnic, economic, and geographic backgrounds. Campus interviews are strongly recommended but not required for most candidates. There is an active Student Ambassador Program on campus, which consists of faculty-recommended student volunteers from each major area. These student ambassadors host prospective students individually, taking them to class and to lunch and seeing that they meet faculty members and other students. This allows the prospective student to experience life at Rider University for a day.

Application and Information

Rider University works on a rolling admissions basis, but it encourages applications for the fall semester to be submitted by January 15 if the student wishes to obtain housing on the campus. Applications for the spring semester should be submitted by December 15. An early action option is available. Students must submit all necessary documentation by November 15 and are notified of an admissions decision by December 15. The application fee of $40 should be included with the application. Students are notified of the admission decision in approximately three to four weeks, in accordance with the rolling admission policy. Transfer applicants receive the same priority for admission, housing, and financial aid as freshman applicants.

Interested students are encouraged to contact:

Director of Undergraduate Admissions
Rider University
2083 Lawrenceville Road
Lawrenceville, New Jersey 08648-3099
Telephone: 609-896-5042
800-257-9026 (toll-free)
E-mail: admissions@rider.edu
World Wide Web: http://www.rider.edu

Centennial Lake and Franklin F. Moore Library.

RIPON COLLEGE

RIPON, WISCONSIN

The College

One key reason why students choose Ripon College from among the more than 3,500 colleges and universities in the country is that Ripon offers an intensely personal undergraduate education. Since 1851, Ripon has provided a personal liberal arts education that makes a remarkable difference in the lives of students. In recent years, college guides such as *The Princeton Review*, *The Fiske Guide to Colleges*, and Kaplan's *328 Most Interesting Colleges* have noted that Ripon is among those national liberal arts colleges that offer high-quality education at a reasonable cost.

Companies look for college graduates who can adapt to change and who can write, use modern technology with confidence, communicate, and make a contribution to a team. These are the skills that a Ripon education offers students. In 2002, Ripon student Zach Morris became the College's third Rhodes Scholar, and in 2003, two students earned Fulbright Teaching Grants.

Ripon's curricular emphasis focuses on Communicating Plus. This program aims to assist students in the development of superior written and oral communication, critical-thinking, and problem-solving skills.

Ripon is a residential college; 90 percent of its 1,000 students live on campus, and because students remain on the campus after classes have ended, learning occurs around the clock. All students are encouraged to participate in Ripon's numerous extracurricular activities, including the campus radio station and the Student Senate.

Ripon College is fully accredited by the North Central Association of Colleges and Schools.

Location

Ripon College is situated on 250 tree-lined, rolling acres adjacent to downtown Ripon, Wisconsin, a charming turn-of-the-century community of 7,500 people. Ripon is a short drive from Green Bay, Madison, and Milwaukee. A variety of year-round recreational activities are available in Ripon and in Green Lake, a city just 6 miles from the campus.

Majors and Degrees

The Bachelor of Arts is offered in thirty majors: anthropology, art, biology, business administration, chemistry, chemistry-biology, computer science, economics, educational studies, English, environmental studies, exercise science, foreign languages, French, German, global studies, history, Latin American studies, mathematics, music, philosophy, physical science, politics and government, psychobiology, psychology, religion, sociology-anthropology, Spanish, communication, and theater. Self-designed majors and preprofessional programs are also available. Minors are available in most of the departments listed above and in leadership studies and women's studies. In addition, the educational studies department offers certification programs in elementary education, music, physical education, and secondary education.

Under a special program for engineers, a student may study for three years at Ripon and two at an engineering school, receiving a bachelor's degree from each institution. Ripon has formal cooperative engineering programs with Washington University in St. Louis and Rensselaer Polytechnic Institute. A student who desires to go into forestry may study for three years at Ripon and two years at Duke University, receiving both a bachelor's degree and a master's degree. In addition, Ripon College and Rush-Presbyterian-St. Luke's Medical Center in Chicago offer a cooperative program in nursing and allied health sciences in which students spend their first two years at Ripon and then transfer to Rush for their final two years.

Academic Program

Since its founding, Ripon has been a liberal arts college. Students have the opportunity to study all fields of human knowledge, including the social sciences, the natural sciences, the humanities, and the fine arts. While other colleges have become increasingly specialized, Ripon has remained steadfast in its belief that the liberal arts are the key for a life of both personal and professional success. Ripon operates on a schedule of two 15-week semesters and an optional 3-week "Maymester."

Off-Campus Programs

Ripon's off-campus studies program sends students to such places as Costa Rica, England, France, Germany, Italy, Japan, and Spain to study for a semester. In addition, students can select programs within the U.S., such as the Oak Ridge Laboratory Semester in Tennessee, the Newberry Library Seminar in the Humanities in Chicago, urban studies and urban teaching in Chicago, and study at the Marine Biological Laboratory at Wood's Hole Oceanographic Institution.

Academic Facilities

Ripon's campus combines the best of both historic and modern architecture. The College's three original buildings, constructed between 1851 and 1867, are still used for offices and classes. The Farr Hall of Science, which recently received a $4.4-million renovation and addition, holds a planetarium, a greenhouse, ample laboratory space, and state-of-the-art equipment. On the west side of campus, the C. J. Rodman Center for the Arts and the J. M. Storzer Physical Education Center house a recital hall, a theater, an art gallery, a sculpture garden, a multipurpose gymnasium, a pool, racquetball courts, free-weight and Nautilus rooms, and aerobics rooms. Adjacent to the Storzer Center is the Ceresco Prairie Conservancy, 3½ miles of recreational trails and 130 acres of restored native habitat. Ripon's student center, Harwood Memorial Union, holds a lecture hall, the Pub, a game room, the radio station, and student organization offices.

Costs

The costs for 2004–05 are as follows: tuition, $20,480; room, $2530; board, $2830; activity fee, $240; and additional fees, books, and miscellaneous personal expenses, $1000.

Financial Aid

Ninety percent of Ripon students receive financial assistance that meets 100 percent of their financial need. The average financial aid award equals 78 percent of a student's total costs. Ripon's extensive scholarship program is designed to recognize and reward applicants for their talents and abilities. Currently, seventeen types of scholarships that range from $1000 to full tuition annually are available.

Faculty

Ripon College's student-faculty ratio is 14:1, and the average class size is 20. Ninety-seven percent of the full-time faculty members have earned the highest degree in their fields, and, as a result of their hard work, Ripon has received ten National Science Foundation Grants since 1992 and six Fulbright Fellowships since 1989.

Student Government

The Student Senate, composed of representatives of all resident groups and campus organizations, is the main governing body and administers a budget of more than $100,000 for student organizations and activities. It is an active and influential means of bringing student opinion to bear on College affairs.

Admission Requirements

Important factors considered in the admission process include graduation from an accredited secondary school (or GED equivalent), the secondary school transcript, and results of standardized tests (SAT or ACT).

Application and Information

Prospective students who value a challenging liberal arts and sciences education in a small, caring community are invited to visit the campus, sit in on Ripon classes, and see firsthand how Ripon students and professors interact with one another.

Students who wish to apply to Ripon College should submit a completed application form, a secondary school transcript, results of standardized tests, and the $30 application fee. Ripon College application forms are available from the admission office and at the College's Web site (address below). Ripon participates in the Common Application Plan and accepts photocopies of the Common Application in place of the Ripon College application form. Common Application forms are available in many secondary school guidance offices. Ripon also accepts applications that are made through the Wisconsin Mentor site (http://www.wisconsinmentor.org/admissionapp).

Candidates for fall term consideration are encouraged to apply early. Notification of fall term admission occurs within two weeks of the completion of the student's application. Students applying for spring term consideration should submit applications by December 15. Notification occurs shortly thereafter.

For further information, students should contact:

Dean of Admission
Ripon College
300 Seward Street
P.O. Box 248
Ripon, Wisconsin 54971-0248
Telephone: 800-94-RIPON (toll-free)
E-mail: adminfo@ripon.edu
World Wide Web: http://www.ripon.edu
http://www.experience.ripon.edu

Ripon College students and their families celebrate commencement on the lawn of Harwood Memorial Union.

RIVIER COLLEGE

NASHUA, NEW HAMPSHIRE

The College

Rivier College, a private, Catholic college founded in 1933, has gained a reputation for academic excellence in more than forty programs. The College has adapted to changing needs by developing liberal arts/career-oriented programs designed to prepare graduates in many fields.

The undergraduate programs in the School of Undergraduate Studies enroll approximately 1,450 students, including 950 full-time day students. This results in an 18:1 student-faculty ratio, small classes, and the opportunity for students to become active members of the academic and social community. Rivier is growing, but it remains a small college, where an outstanding teaching faculty offers support and encouragement to its students.

Most full-time undergraduate day students are between 18 and 22 years old. The majority are residents of New England, although other states are represented, including Texas, Virginia, and others. International students represent countries in Africa, Asia, Europe, the Middle East, and South America. Students who live on campus reside in four modern residence halls. Most rooms are doubles and the newest hall offers apartment suites. The Dion Center houses the dining room, the commuter lounge, the mail room, a bookstore, student development offices, and meeting rooms. Students are permitted to have cars on campus.

Orientation sessions for new students are sponsored by the Office of Student Development. Assistance is offered throughout the year in academic and personal counseling. A full-time chaplain and Campus Ministry team coordinate spiritual activities. A comprehensive career development service helps students prepare for employment after graduation. Students' health needs are met by a Health Services Center. The Office of Student Development, the Student Government Association, and more than twenty-five student clubs and organizations provide a calendar of social, cultural, and recreational activities, including dances, live entertainment, films, and sports events. The College and student organizations frequently organize outings, including trips to Boston for shopping, dining, museums, concerts, or theater productions. Students also enjoy a variety of performances by the Rivier Theater Company. Rivier offers a wide range of team and individual sports, including NCAA Division III men's baseball, basketball, cross-country, soccer, and volleyball and women's basketball, cross-country, soccer, softball, and volleyball. The men's volleyball team has been nationally ranked every year since 2001. The Muldoon Health and Fitness Center is home to Rivier's varsity athletics and to many intramural sports and fitness activities, including volleyball, floor hockey, basketball, weight training, aerobics, self-defense, and more. The campus also has soccer and softball fields, as well as a beach volleyball court and campus cross-country trail. Student athletes and others can take advantage of an on-campus rehabilitation clinic offering free injury assessment, physical and occupational therapy, and athletic training.

Location

Nashua (population 84,000) is located in southern New Hampshire. The city of Boston lies within easy access 40 miles to the south. Local access to public transportation provides for easy travel to and from campus. Recreational activities abound year-round at nearby lakes and ski areas, in the White Mountains to the north, and at the seacoast, just an hour's drive to the east.

Majors and Degrees

Rivier College awards the Bachelor of Arts, the Bachelor of Fine Arts, and the Bachelor of Science degrees in the following areas of concentration: art (drawing and painting, graphic design, illustration, photography and digital imaging, and studio art); biology and biology education; business (administration, information technology management, and management); communications (advertising/public relations, journalism, photojournalism, scriptwriting, video production, and Web design/online publishing); computer science; education (early childhood/special education, elementary education/special education, human development/interdisciplinary); English and English education; history, law, and political science (criminal justice, history, political science, and social studies education); human development; liberal studies; mathematics and mathematics education; modern languages (modern language education and Spanish); nursing; psychology; and sociology. Preprofessional programs are offered in law, dentistry, medicine, and veterinary medicine. Associate degrees are offered in art, business, computer science, early childhood education, liberal studies, and nursing.

Academic Programs

Rivier College takes special pride in its curriculum, which offers both liberal arts and professional studies in order to prepare students for a fast-changing, highly technological society. The curriculum is broad-based, with emphasis on preparing students for challenging and rewarding careers and furthering their personal growth. Core curriculum requirements may vary slightly, depending on the degree to be obtained, but generally include courses in the areas of English, mathematics and/or natural sciences, modern language and literature, philosophy, religious studies, social science, and Western civilization. No fewer than ten courses must be taken in the major field. Electives may be chosen according to the student's interests. For the bachelor's degree, a minimum of 120 credits with a grade point average of at least 2.0 is required. For the associate degree, the student must complete a minimum of 60 credits with a grade point average of at least 2.0.

All departments encourage qualified students to pursue internships in their field of study during their junior or senior year. Education specialists student teach in local schools. Nursing majors complete clinical rotations in health-care facilities throughout southern New Hampshire and Boston. Law and government majors may work in a law office, business, legal-assistance agency, or government agency. Sociology and psychology majors work with local social service agencies. English and communications majors work in public relations, broadcasting, or corporate communications positions. Art majors work in advertising or graphic design or at local galleries.

Honors awards include placement on the dean's list, membership in Kappa Gamma Pi, listing in *Who's Who Among Students in American Universities and Colleges,* listing in *The National Dean's List,* and degrees with honors. Academically talented students may also apply to the four-year honors program.

The college year is divided into two 15-week semesters, with first-semester examinations held before Christmas recess. Students usually take five courses each semester. Academic credit may be granted to incoming freshmen on the basis of scores on Advanced Placement tests and CLEP examinations. Students may also "challenge" courses and receive credit by special examination.

Off-Campus Programs

Through Rivier College's membership in the New Hampshire College and University Council, a twelve-member consortium of senior colleges, Rivier students may register for courses at any of the member colleges and receive transfer credits.

Academic Facilities

Academic facilities include Memorial Hall, which houses fourteen classrooms, faculty offices, a lecture hall, a fully equipped digital imaging studio, a communications lab offering the most recent software and video/sound editing equipment, the studio of community television station Channel 13 (WYCN), and art department facilities that include a gallery, a slide library, and studios. The Academic Computer Center features up to sixty-eight workstations with a full range of cutting-edge software and Internet/e-mail access. Regina Library houses more than 100,000 volumes and provides access to more than 3 million volumes in twelve area libraries, as well as online access to licensed databases in virtually every academic subject. The Writing Center is staffed by professional writing consultants as well as student tutors. Other academic facilities include nursing and science laboratories; a physical assessment lab and model intensive care unit, which provide nursing students with practical experience using blood pressure cuffs, ophthalmoscopes, IV pumps, and more; electronic classrooms offering multimedia learning tools; and the Education Center, which houses an eight-classroom Early Childhood Center, observation rooms, and an educational resource center.

Costs

Tuition and fees for the academic year 2004–05 are $19,875; room and board, $7273; and books and supplies, approximately $700. Students should expect to pay a $100 activities fee and a $25 registration fee each semester.

Financial Aid

Financial aid is awarded on the basis of the financial need of the student and family. Approximately 80 percent of Rivier's students receive financial aid from the College or from government or private sources. Federal aid includes Federal Pell Grants, Federal Supplemental Educational Opportunity Grants, Federal Perkins Loans, Federal Stafford Student Loans, the Federal PLUS loan program, and the Federal Work-Study Program. To be considered for financial aid a student must file the Free Application for Federal Student Aid (FAFSA) with the federal government as soon as possible after January 1 for the coming year. FAFSA results should be on file with the College Financial Aid Office prior to March 1 for the following academic year. Each applicant is assessed individually to determine the best combination of grant, work, scholarship, and loan amounts to meet the need of the student. The College awards several merit-based scholarships and grants ranging in value from $1000 to full tuition. For more information students should contact the Director of Financial Aid.

Faculty

The College employs 80 full-time faculty members. The full-time student–faculty ratio is 13:1. Part-time instructors in specialized areas are working professionals who bring current knowledge and expertise in their field to their classes. All classes are taught by faculty members, and department chairs serve as academic advisers to students in their major programs.

Student Government

Every full-time day student automatically becomes a member of the Student Government Association (SGA) upon registration and payment of the student activity fee. The main goals of the SGA are to stimulate active participation in all College functions, to establish and maintain effective channels of communication among members of the College community and the community at large, and to foster a mutual trust, encourage a spirit of cooperation, and initiate new endeavors. The SGA also supervises student clubs and organizations and oversees their finances. The SGA Executive Board serves as the channel of communication through which the views of the students on institutional policies reach the College administration.

Admission Requirements

Applicants for admission should ordinarily have completed, in an accredited high school, a minimum of 16 academic units, including 4 in English, 2 in a modern foreign language, 3 in mathematics, 2 in social science, 2 in science, and 3 in electives. The most successful candidates are in the upper half of their class, with at least a B average. Combined SAT I scores average 950–1000. A personal interview is strongly recommended but not required.

Rivier welcomes applications from qualified transfer candidates from accredited institutions, as well as applications from international students. Transfer students must forward transcripts of all previous college work and a high school transcript. International students must fulfill the requirements for general admission, but they may be required to submit TOEFL (Test of English as a Foreign Language) scores. Deferred admission may be granted to students who wish to postpone entrance for up to one year, provided that they have not been enrolled full-time at some other postsecondary institution.

Application and Information

Applications must be accompanied by a nonrefundable $25 application fee, SAT I scores, one letter of recommendation, and a high school transcript. The School of Undergraduate Studies employs a system of rolling admission that allows qualified students to be admitted approximately one month after their application is completed. Transfers should apply by June 1 for fall admission and by December 1 for spring admission. Those applying for financial aid should observe the March 1 deadline. Prospective art majors must submit a portfolio of their work. Interviews are arranged through the Admissions Office.

More specific information and application forms can be obtained by contacting:

Director of Undergraduate Admissions
Rivier College
420 Main Street
Nashua, New Hampshire 03060
Telephone: 603-897-8507
800-44-RIVIER (toll-free)
Fax: 603-891-1799
E-mail: rivadmit@rivier.edu
World Wide Web: http://www.rivier.edu

The campus of Rivier College.

ROBERT MORRIS COLLEGE

CHICAGO, O'HARE, DUPAGE, ORLAND PARK, PEORIA, LAKE COUNTY, AND SPRINGFIELD, ILLINOIS

The College

Robert Morris College (RMC) is a private, not-for-profit, independent college dedicated to providing intensive career education and general education opportunities. Associate degrees, the Bachelor of Business Administration degree, the Bachelor of Applied Science degree in graphic design, and the Bachelor of Applied Science degree in computer studies are awarded. Robert Morris College is accredited by the Higher Learning Commission and is a member of the North Central Association of Colleges and Schools (30 North LaSalle Street, Suite 2400, Chicago, Illinois 60602; telephone: 312-263-0456; Web: http://www.ncahigherlearningcommission.org).

The history of Robert Morris College dates back to the founding of the Moser School, one of the outstanding independent business schools in Chicago, in 1913. Robert Morris College also has origins in Illinois at the site of the former Carthage College. Here, Robert Morris College was chartered and offered associate degrees in both liberal and vocational arts from 1965 to 1974. With the acquisition of the Moser School in 1975, RMC expanded to include business and allied health. The College now provides students with a choice of seven locations: Chicago, O'Hare, DuPage, Orland Park, Peoria, Lake County, and Springfield, Illinois.

RMC offers programs in the School of Business Administration, the School of Health Studies, the School of Computer Studies, the Institute of Culinary Arts, and the Institute of Art and Design. Each of these five divisions uses the most modern computer technology. Acquisition of such technology is imperative to providing real-world, educational experiences that are relevant to the evolving work place.

RMC's unique five-quarter system is designed for continuous learning. It enables students to accelerate their education, completing a bachelor's degreee in three years and an associate degreee in fifteen months.

The student body of approximately 6,000 is a cross-cultural, ethnic, and racial mix representative of the communities served. Each student works with a team of program directors, instructors, and placement specialists in an effort to achieve educational and career goals. The records of the College's students and graduates are the best indicators of what a prospective student can expect. Seventy percent of RMC students graduate from the programs they begin, compared to significantly lower percentages at other private and public colleges and universities.

The Placement Department, which has offices at each of the College's campuses, continuously cultivates employment opportunities for RMC graduates, with representatives in the business, allied health, art, and computer industries. Last year, 9 out of 10 RMC graduates who requested job placement assistance successfully secured employment in their chosen fields.

Robert Morris College is a member of the National Association of Intercollegiate Athletics (NAIA) and the Chicagoland Collegiate Athletic Conference (CCAC), Division II. The College offers men's and women's basketball, cross-country, golf, and soccer. It also offers men's baseball, men's and women's club hockey, and women's softball, volleyball, and tennis.

Location

Located in the heart of Chicago's bustling cultural and financial districts, the College's main campus is minutes from all that Chicago offers, including the Chicago Board of Trade, Art Institute, Field Museum, Merchandise Mart, lakefront, sports arenas, theaters, and all forms of public transportation. The Chicago campus is readily accessible from all parts of the city and suburbs by bus lines and trains. Parking is available in the immediate vicinity. Robert Morris Center is across the street from the renowned Harold Washington Public Library.

The O'Hare Campus opened to better serve the residents of western Cook and DuPage Counties and to meet the demands of employers in the area. The Springfield campus is located on Montvale Drive, just east of White Oaks Mall. The College is accessible by bus, and ample parking is also available. The recently expanded Orland Park campus now includes a technology center with the latest computer facilities available to industry and education. It is located adjacent to the Orland Square Mall, approximately 30 miles southwest of Chicago. It is accessible via public transportation and I-80 and I-55, which run parallel on the south and north ends of the campus, respectively. Orland Park is becoming a corporate center of the southwest Chicago suburbs, offering students ample opportunity for professional growth through internships and employment.

The DuPage campus opened on the border between Naperville and Aurora and serves students as well as employers along the East-West High Tech Corridor—the heart of rapid technological development and close to a wide range of employers. The Peoria campus in the busy downtown area of the city expands RMC's commitment to serving central Illinois. Beginning fall 2003, classes are available to Lake County area residents at a campus in Waukegan. Students in northern Illinois and southeastern Wisconsin can take advantage of RMC programs in this new setting.

All locations provide students with access to the unlimited variety of business services and enhance the students' understanding of the world of work and the employment process.

Majors and Degrees

The Bachelor of Business Administration degree at Robert Morris College offers concentrations in accounting, health-care management, hospitality management, and management. The Bachelor of Applied Science degree in graphic design offers concentrations in graphic arts and media arts. The Bachelor of Applied Science degree in computer studies offers concentrations in database management, networking, telecommunications management, and Web programming. RMC also awards associate degrees in accounting, business administration, CAD drafting (architectural/mechanical), computer networking, computer programming, culinary arts, fitness specialist, graphic arts, interior design, legal office assistant/paralegal studies, media arts, and medical assisting. More than twenty-six transfer agreements have been established between RMC and community colleges, allowing students who have earned associate degrees elsewhere to complete their bachelor's degrees at RMC by transferring in as a junior. Robert Morris College is the seventh-largest private college/university in Illinois; tuition is one of the lowest for Illinois private colleges/universities. RMC is the largest granter of baccalaureate degrees in business and awards more associate degrees (all disciplines combined) to members of minority groups than any institution in Illinois. RMC is the sixteenth-largest granter of Bachelor of Business Administration degrees to African Americans and the twenty-eighth to Hispanic Americans in the country.

Academic Program

The College's academic calendar consists of five quarters, each of which is ten weeks long. The program of study is designed so that students can complete their course work and enter their careers in the shortest time possible: in as little as three years for a bachelor's degree and fifteen months for an associate degree.

By concentrating on the specialized subjects related to the student's chosen career field, the College's curricula provide students with the skills and knowledge necessary to enter the job market. Each major consists of courses prescribed by the College to lead to this objective. An associate degree requires at least 92 quarter hours of credit with a minimum of 56 hours of credit in general education in the areas of communications, humanities, math and science, and social and behavioral science. A minimum of 52 quarter hours of credit are required in career courses, and the remaining hours are electives split between general education and career courses. A bachelor's degree requires a minimum of 188 quarter hours of credit. A minimum of 72 hours of credit are required in general education courses; 100 to 104 hours are required in major course work.

Robert Morris College offers students the opportunity to gain experience in their majors and improve their skills through internships and externships. Placement personnel work closely with students to secure positions related to their fields of study. Internships offer many educational and professional benefits and provide students with the opportunity to earn academic credit for participating in a career-specific work experience.

Off-Campus Programs

Robert Morris College offers students the opportunity to study abroad at the Institute of European Studies in Vienna, Austria; at Regent's College in London, England; and in Florence, Italy.

Academic Facilities

General purpose classrooms; high-tech equipment; specialized laboratories; study, practice, and leisure lounges; fitness centers; and cyber cafés are among the facilities the College provides at each campus. The technology-based library has online capabilities that connect the College's various campuses. Online Internet access offers students advanced research capabilities, sizable collections of reference and resource volumes, and periodical subscriptions. Vertical file information is available in addition to numerous computer and audio resources and a job search center.

Costs

Robert Morris College has one of the lowest tuition rates of any baccalaureate degree–granting private college in the state. Tuition for 2003–04 is $4500 per quarter. Book and supply costs vary by major from $300 to $500 per quarter.

Financial Aid

Robert Morris College participates in the following federal and state financial aid programs: the Federal Pell Grant, Illinois Monetary Award (SSIG/IMA), Federal Supplemental Educational Opportunity Grant (FSEOG), Federal Stafford Student Loan, Federal Perkins Loan, Federal PLUS Loan, and Federal Work-Study (FWS) programs. In addition, the College awards institutional grants on the basis of need, scholarship, residence, academic major, or a combination of these factors. All students must complete a financial planning interview with their admissions counselor, and all are urged to complete the Free Application for Federal Student Aid (FAFSA). Approximately 85 percent of the student body receive some financial assistance. In the 2001–02 academic year, the College awarded more than $12 million in institutional aid.

Faculty

The faculty members at Robert Morris College are selected on the basis of their academic credentials, career experiences in their field, and dedication to giving special attention to every student. All faculty members possess a master's degree in their chosen field, and many possess a Ph.D. in their area of specialization. In addition to teaching courses, faculty members promote the progress of their students through the individualized academic, employment, and personal development counseling they provide.

Student Government

Robert Morris College has no formal student government. Student representatives serve on committees that make recommendations about campus issues. Student organizations and activities are available.

Admission Requirements

All graduates of accredited high schools or the equivalent (GED) are eligible for admission to the College. All candidates are encouraged to have a personal interview with an admissions representative and to have a tour of the campus.

A variety of materials are considered for various applicants. Freshman applicants just graduating from high school must submit their high school record or GED score and test results from the ACT, SAT I, Applied Education Skills Assessment (AESA), Advanced Placement, and SAT II Subject Area tests.

Those enrolling as an adult (age 23 and above) must submit their high school record or GED score; test results from the ACT, SAT I, Applied Education Skills Assessment (AESA), College Level Examination Program (CLEP), and Dantes; and evidence of a successful employment experience.

Transfer students must present a minimum of 12 transferable credit hours from an accredited institution and their academic records from any high schools and colleges previously attended.

International students must forward their official education records, the results from either TOEFL or AESA, and an affidavit of financial support.

Home-schooled students must submit a complete transcript of all classes they have taken, curriculum documentation and its state certification, and results from any standardized examinations they have taken.

Application and Information

Applications can be obtained by contacting the Admissions Office at any of the College's campuses. The completed application and the $20 nonrefundable application fee ($100 nonrefundable application fee for international students) should be sent to the Admissions Office. The College operates on a rolling admissions basis, and students can enroll during any one of the five times offered during the year. For further information, prospective students should visit the Web site below or contact:

Admissions Office
Robert Morris College
401 South State Street
Chicago, Illinois 60605

Admissions Office
Robert Morris College
905 Meridian Lake Drive
Aurora, Illinois 60504

Admissions Office
Robert Morris College
43 Orland Square
Orland Park, Illinois 60462

Admissions Office
Robert Morris College
1000 Tower Lane
Bensenville, Illinois 60108

Admissions Office
Robert Morris College
211 Fulton Street
Peoria, Illinois 61602

Admissions Office
Robert Morris College
3101 Montvale Drive
Springfield, Illinois 62704

Admissions Office
Robert Morris College
Lake County
1507 South Waukegan Road
Lake County, Illinois 60085

Telephone: 800-RMC-5960 (toll-free)
World Wide Web: http://www.robertmorris.edu

ROBERT MORRIS UNIVERSITY

PITTSBURGH AND MOON TOWNSHIP, PENNSYLVANIA

The University

Robert Morris University (RMU), founded in 1921, is one of the leading universities in the Pittsburgh region and is now among the largest private institutions of higher learning in Pennsylvania. RMU built its reputation by offering strong academic programs in traditional business fields such as accounting, finance, economics, marketing, and management. To help prepare students for success in a changing and competitive workforce, the University has created programs in actuarial science, communication, elementary education, engineering, information systems, media arts, and nursing during the past decade. The University also offers students the opportunity to earn a global perspective by studying abroad.

Because Robert Morris University is a teaching-centered institution, classes are small and are taught by faculty members, not teaching assistants. The University employs more than 300 full-time and part-time faculty members; more than 80 percent of full-time members hold terminal degrees. The student-faculty ratio is 19:1.

The 78,000-square-foot Student Center, which opened in 1999, is located at the heart of the campus and provides a gathering place for students, alumni, and faculty and staff members. The Center is the hub for student activities and programs, and it houses a recreation room, a food court, a convenience store, a coffeehouse, a bookstore, an activities room, a TV and cyber lounge, a fitness center, and administrative offices.

Nearly fifty clubs and organizations help students develop leadership and management skills, network professionally, and meet new friends. Student activities include varsity and intramural sports, fraternities and sororities, professional clubs, and community service projects. RMU offers twenty-two NCAA Division I men's and women's varsity sports as well as an active intramural and club sports program. In 2003, the University purchased the Island Sports Center, a facility with four skating rinks, a golf structure, and land to build a track as well as fields for lacrosse and field hockey. Men's NCAA Division I ice hockey is scheduled to begin at RMU in 2004–05, and a women's team is scheduled to start in 2005–06. RMU is the only school in Pittsburgh to offer ice hockey at this level.

The Student Activities Office organizes dances, parties, movie screenings, comedy acts, health and wellness fairs, educational programs, and day trips. Business organizations, professional clubs, and honor societies provide students with career preparation opportunities. RMU students also get involved in the community, organizing Habitat for Humanity projects, coordinating blood drives, collecting food donations, and organizing holiday parties for needy youngsters.

Location

There are nearly 5,000 full- and part-time undergraduate and graduate students from thirty states and twenty countries enrolled at Robert Morris University. The 230-acre campus is located just 15 minutes from Pittsburgh International Airport and 17 miles from downtown Pittsburgh.

Majors and Degrees

Robert Morris University offers more than thirty undergraduate degree programs, many of which offer multiple specializations. Bachelor's degree programs include the Bachelor of Arts (B.A.) in applied mathematics, communication, English, media arts, and social science; the Bachelor of Science (B.S.) in actuarial science, applied mathematics, business education, economics, elementary education, engineering (logistics and software), hospitality administration, information sciences, information systems management, manufacturing engineering, nursing, social science, and tourism administration; and the Bachelor of Science in Business Administration (B.S.B.A.) in accounting, economics, finance, finance/economics, health services management, hospitality management, human resource management, logistics management, management, marketing, sport management, and tourism management. In addition, RMU offers preparation for state teacher certification in business, communication, English, social studies, and mathematics education.

Robert Morris University offers fourteen graduate degree programs, including the Master of Science (M.S.) in accounting, business education, communications and information systems, engineering management, finance, information systems management, instructional leadership, Internet information systems, nonprofit management, nursing, sport management, and taxation; the Master of Business Administration (M.B.A.); and the Doctor of Science (D.Sc.) in information systems and communications.

Academic Program

Robert Morris is on a two-semester schedule with various summer sessions. A total of 126 credits are required for the bachelor's degree. Internship or co-op credits of 3 to 12 hours may be used toward degree requirements. The University participates in a cross-registration program with nine local colleges through the Pittsburgh Council on Higher Education consortium.

Academic Facilities

Learning resources include a traditional library with 136,598 bound volumes, 358,760 items on microfilm and microfiche, and 853 current periodical subscriptions. The collection includes an extensive tax library and specializes in business information and materials made available to the professional and business community of the city.

The Academic Media Center, with full production facilities, provides students with opportunities to collaborate on projects in all areas of media, including television production, audio production, and photography.

Robert Morris University provides students with the opportunity for individualized study facilitated by audiotapes, videotapes, films, and slides. Also, a state-of-the-art laboratory and learning facility was recently opened to support the engineering, mathematics, and science programs.

Costs

Annual tuition for the 2003–04 year was a $13,484 flat rate based on a 36-credit, two-semester schedule. Resident facilities are available on campus.

Financial Aid

RMU has a comprehensive financial aid program that includes scholarships, grants, loans, and work-study programs. There are both need-based and achievement-based awards available. The Robert Morris University Merit and Honors Scholarship Awards are offered to freshman applicants who demonstrate high academic achievement and leadership qualities. Other endowed scholarships and grants are available to transfer and continuing students. All applicants must complete the admissions application, the Free Application for Federal Student Aid, and the grant forms from their own state.

Faculty

The University has 300 full- and part-time faculty members. The average class size is 23. Students may take advantage of the expertise offered by the faculty in academic advisement and counseling, as well as counseling from the staff at the Center for Student Success.

Student Government

The Student Government Association represents all student organizations, including fraternities and sororities. Members participate in the planning of all social and cultural events on campus.

Admission Requirements

Robert Morris University encourages students from other states to apply; the specialized business, communication, and engineering programs attract students from many areas of the country. Primary consideration is given to the applicant's performance in secondary school and scores on the SAT I or ACT.

Transfer students who have earned credits from another regionally accredited institution are evaluated for admission on the basis of their college performance.

Interviews are not required for admission except for students interested in the engineering, elementary education, and nursing programs. Students are encouraged to arrange for a campus visit with an enrollment manager.

Robert Morris University is committed to a policy of nondiscrimination on the basis of race, sex, color, religion, national origin, or handicap.

Application and Information

Students are encouraged to submit applications in the fall of their senior year of high school. Official transcripts and counselor recommendations should accompany the application; there is a $30 application processing fee that is waived for online applicants.

Robert Morris uses a rolling admission system; students are considered for acceptance as soon as all application materials have been received and evaluated.

For additional information and application materials, students should contact:

J. Donald Williams
Office of Enrollment Services
Robert Morris University
6001 University Boulevard
Moon Township, Pennsylvania 15108
Telephone: 412-262-8206
800-762-0097 (toll-free)
World Wide Web: http://www.rmu.edu

Students on the campus of Robert Morris University.

ROBERTS WESLEYAN COLLEGE

ROCHESTER, NEW YORK

The College

Roberts Wesleyan College (RWC) was founded in 1866 as the first Free Methodist academic institution in North America. Since then, the institution has continually adapted its programs to meet the current academic, professional, and personal needs of its students. The integration of broad-based intellectual thought with the Judeo-Christian heritage is and always has been the motivation for Roberts Wesleyan's existence. The College fosters wholesome principles by setting standards for student life, requiring regular chapel attendance, and maintaining a perspective rich in values within the classroom.

The current enrollment is 1,843: 1,250 women and 593 men. Although students come primarily from New York State, twenty-four other states and nineteen other countries are represented. The majority of students are between 18 and 25 years of age, but there is a growing population of married and older students. The traditional undergraduate population is primarily residential, and approximately 30 percent of those students commute.

RWC offers a broad selection of student activities. Student leaders plan a calendar of numerous events each year, including social, cultural, and religious programs. The College's suburban Rochester location also allows students to take advantage of cultural and academic opportunities within the community. The College's intramural program complements the intercollegiate sports program. There are six varsity sports for men: basketball, cross-country, golf, soccer, tennis, and track and field; there are seven varsity sports for women: basketball, cross-country, golf, soccer, tennis, track and field, and volleyball. Students may take advantage of the beautiful Voller Athletic Center, which includes a pool, four basketball courts, an indoor track, racquetball courts, a weight room, saunas, a student center, a snack bar, and a bookstore. The Career Services Office provides numerous services for students. Other College services available to students include academic advisement, counseling, and assistance from the Learning Center.

The College is a member of the Middle States Association of Colleges and Schools, the Association of Colleges and Universities of the State of New York, Rochester Area Colleges, the Association of Free Methodist Educational Institutions, the Council of Independent Colleges and Universities, and the Council for Christian Colleges and Universities. The programs in accounting, art, business, music, nursing, and social work are professionally accredited. The Art Department is accredited by the National Association of Schools of Art and Design. The Music Department is an accredited member of the National Association of Schools of Music. The Division of Nursing is accredited by the National League for Nursing Accrediting Commission, and the Social Work Department is accredited by the Council on Social Work Education. The Division of Business Administration and Management is accredited by the International Assembly for Collegiate Business Education.

In addition to its undergraduate programs, Roberts Wesleyan offers the Master of Education, Master of Social Work, Master of Science in Management, Master of Science in School Psychology, Master of Science in School Counseling, and Master of Arts: Counseling and Ministry degrees. Northeastern Seminary at Roberts Wesleyan College offers the Master of Divinity, Master of Arts in Theological Studies, Master of Divinity/Master of Social Work, and Doctor of Ministry degrees.

Location

Roberts Wesleyan College is located 8 miles southwest of Rochester, New York, in the suburb of North Chili. Rochester, with a metropolitan-area population of more than 1 million, is a thriving cultural and corporate area. Eastman School of Music, the Rochester Philharmonic Orchestra, and several of America's leading corporations, such as Eastman Kodak, Xerox, Paychex, and Bausch & Lomb, make their home there.

The College continues to develop a strong relationship with the community, and the resulting internships and opportunities for practical work are particularly advantageous for Roberts Wesleyan students. Current students and graduates enjoy the extensive employment opportunities that result from Rochester's healthy economy. Lake Ontario, Niagara Falls, Watkins Glen, Letchworth Park, and the Finger Lakes are all nearby.

Majors and Degrees

Baccalaureate degrees are offered in accounting and information management, adolescence education (biology, chemistry, English, mathematics, physics, and social studies), art, art education, art–graphic design, biochemistry, biology, business administration, chemistry, childhood education and special education (elementary education), communication, comprehensive science, comprehensive social studies, computer science, contemporary ministries, criminal justice, elementary education, English, fine arts–art, fine arts–music, history, humanities, information systems management, management, marketing, mathematics, middle childhood education and special education, music, music education, music performance (instrument, piano, and voice), nursing, physics, psychology, religion/philosophy, secondary education (see adolescence education), social work, sociology, and visual art education.

A 3-2 program in engineering is offered in cooperation with Clarkson University, Rensselaer Polytechnic Institute, and Rochester Institute of Technology. The program leads to a B.S. in mathematics, chemistry, or physics from RWC and a B.S. in engineering from Clarkson, Rensselaer, or Rochester Institute of Technology.

Secondary (grades 5–12) teaching certification may be earned in biology, chemistry, English, mathematics, physics, and social studies. Preprofessional programs include dentistry, law, medicine, pharmacy, and veterinary medicine.

Academic Programs

RWC endeavors to involve each student in learning experiences that promote commitment to Christian stewardship and service to society. Approximately 45 semester hours of core courses are required of each baccalaureate degree candidate. These liberal arts survey courses introduce four main fields of knowledge: biological science, physical science, and mathematics; history and the behavioral sciences; language, literature, and the fine arts; and biblical studies and philosophy. A total of 124 semester hours is required for graduation with a baccalaureate degree, including a minimum of 30 to 67 semester hours within the student's major discipline.

Many academic programs at Roberts Wesleyan include internships or practical work experiences. Independent study and cross-cultural study opportunities are also available. Students may receive credit through the Advanced Placement Program, the International Baccalaureate Program, Regents College Examinations, or the College-Level Examination Program. The Learning Center provides assistance for students possessing exceptional skills or a deficiency in any area.

The College calendar consists of two 15-week semesters scheduled from September to December and from January to May. Three sessions are held in the summer.

Off-Campus Programs

Various off-campus opportunities exist for which credit is awarded. These include the Appalachian Semester in Kentucky, Focus on the Family Institute in Colorado, EDUVenture in Irian Jaya, and a semester or full year of study at Richmond College in London, England. Under the direction of an RWC professor, students may also participate in a short-term exchange study program with Osaka Christian College and Seminary in Osaka, Japan. Opportunities for off-campus experiences also exist for Roberts Wesleyan students through the Council for Christian Colleges and Universities. These include the American Studies Program, China Studies Program, Contemporary Music Program, Honors Program in Oxford, Latin American Studies Program, Los Angeles Film Studies Center, Middle East Studies Program, Oxford Summer School, Russian Studies Program, and the Summer Institute of Journalism. The January Experience Program offers transcultural and enrichment courses in this country or abroad. In addition, through RWC's membership in the Rochester Area Colleges consortium, RWC students may cross-register to take courses at any of the other member institutions.

Academic Facilities

The Sprague Library, with 250 student stations, occupies a modern, air-conditioned building and holds over 120,000 volumes, 856 periodicals, more than 75 online databases (most with full text), Internet access, and more than 170,000 microforms, recordings, filmstrips, and slides. Also included in the library are the Information Literacy Center, the Learning Center, the Audio-Visual Center, the Historical Room, and the Rare Books Room. Through its participation in the Rochester Regional Research Library Council, the library provides access to extensive interlibrary loan resources. Well-equipped science laboratories, a lecture auditorium, and computer laboratories connected to the campus network are included in the Merlin G. Smith Science Center. Other facilities are the music studios, practice rooms, and recital auditorium of Cox Hall; the educational curriculum laboratory in Carpenter Hall; the Cultural Life Center, which houses Shewan Recital Hall, Hale Auditorium, and Davison Art Gallery; the new Rinker Community Service Center; and the new soccer stadium and Mondo track. High-speed Internet connections for each student are available in all residence halls.

Costs

For the 2004–05 academic year, tuition for full-time study is $17,183. Costs vary if a student's course load is fewer than 12 or more than 17 hours. Additional fees are charged for music and laboratory courses. Room is $4,707 and board is $1,896. Miscellaneous fees are $658. Book costs and personal expenses vary, depending on individual needs.

Financial Aid

Roberts Wesleyan College offers a complete financial aid program, consisting of grants, scholarships, loans, and employment. Filing the Free Application for Federal Student Aid (FAFSA) is a prerequisite for determining eligibility for most financial aid programs. Sources of aid include Federal Pell Grants, Federal Supplemental Educational Opportunity Grants, Federal Perkins Loans, and Federal Stafford Student Loans; New York State Tuition Assistance Program awards; and institutional resources. Numerous on-campus employment opportunities are available. Institutional aid is also available in recognition of academic, athletic, artistic, and musical achievement. More than 90 percent of the student body receives financial aid each year.

Faculty

The primary concern of the faculty at RWC is to provide an educational experience of high quality. Sixty-seven percent of the professors hold the doctoral or terminal degree, and all are well respected within their specific discipline. The 90 full-time and 106 part-time faculty members are committed to Christian higher education and are genuinely interested in each student's development. A 14:1 student-faculty ratio allows for much individualized attention, and most professors go well beyond their tasks of teaching and advising to participate in campus activities.

Student Government

All students belong to the Student Association and have the freedom to express their opinions to the staff, faculty, and administration. There are also elected senators and officers, under the direction of the Student Services Office, who act as liaisons between the student body and the administration in areas concerning academics and student activities.

Admission Requirements

Because the type of student a college enrolls significantly determines the personality of the institution, Roberts Wesleyan seeks students whose personal lives are characterized by honesty, integrity, and devotion to high moral and ethical standards. Admission consideration is given to applicants who rank in the upper third of their graduating class and have earned a minimum of 12 academic units of high school credit, with no fewer than 4 units in English, 2 units in algebra (or 1 in algebra and 1 in geometry), and 1 unit in biology, chemistry, or physics. Three years each of social studies, a foreign language, and science are strongly recommended. Further preparation in mathematics and science is required of applicants who wish to enter degree programs in nursing, mathematics, or science. Scores on the SAT I or ACT and a formal recommendation are required. Special talents are considered an asset for applicants but are not required. An on-campus admission interview is strongly recommended. In admitting students, the College does not discriminate on the basis of race, age, color, sex, handicap, creed, or national or ethnic origin. Children of alumni and staff are considered for admission on the same basis as all other applicants.

Transfer students must fulfill the same admission requirements as first-time students and must also have transcripts forwarded to the College from all the institutions they have attended. Credit is usually accepted for any course in which a grade of C– or above has been earned if the course parallels to some degree a course given at RWC or if the course fits into the student's total program.

Application and Information

Applicants should submit an application form, the $35 application fee, a completed recommendation form, SAT I or ACT scores, and transcripts from all schools previously attended. Art students should prepare a portfolio for review by the art faculty, and music students should schedule an audition with the Music Department. Students are encouraged to submit an application prior to the February 1 priority deadline. Admission decisions are made on a rolling basis, and students are notified of the admission decision as soon as all of their credentials have been received and evaluated.

For additional information and application forms, students should contact:

Kirk Kettinger
Director of Undergraduate Recruitment
Roberts Wesleyan College
2301 Westside Drive
Rochester, New York 14624-1997
Telephone: 585-594-6400
800-777-4RWC (toll-free)
Fax: 585-594-6371
E-mail: admissions@roberts.edu
World Wide Web: http://www.roberts.edu

Students are invited to join the Roberts Wesleyan community.

ROCHESTER INSTITUTE OF TECHNOLOGY

R·I·T

ROCHESTER, NEW YORK

The Institute

Rochester Institute of Technology (RIT) was founded in 1829 and has always had a strong focus on preparing students for sucessful careers and professional achievement. The more than 11,000 full-time undergraduates currently enrolled come from fifty states and ninety countries; 35 percent are women. The Institute is internationally known for its cooperative education work-study plan. A variety of graduate degree programs are offered, including the nation's only Ph.D. program in imaging science, and a new Ph.D. program in microsystems engineering.

In 1968, RIT moved to its present 1,300-acre campus in a suburban location. Unmarried freshmen not living with relatives are required to live in the residence halls or in fraternity or sorority houses and to participate in the board plan. A number of on-campus apartments are available for upperclass students, and more than 6,000 undergraduates live on campus. Besides the social fraternities and sororities, there are professional and honorary societies. A complete program of intercollegiate and intramural sports is offered, as are complementary activities for those with special interests.

Location

The greater Rochester area—the city and its immediate suburbs—has a population of about 700,000. Per capita income is among the highest for metropolitan centers in the nation. The area's many internationally known industries employ a high proportion of scientists, technologists, and skilled workers. Rochester is the world center of photography, the largest producer of optical goods in the United States, and among the leaders in graphic arts and reproduction and in production of electronic equipment and precision instruments. Rochester's industries have always been closely associated with RIT's programs and progress.

Majors and Degrees

The College of Applied Science and Technology offers the Bachelor of Science in environmental management, food management, food marketing, hotel/resort management, nutrition management, packaging science, safety technology, and travel management. It also grants the Bachelor of Science in civil, computer, electrical, manufacturing, mechanical, and telecommunications engineering technology.

The College of Business offers the B.S. in accounting, finance, graphic media marketing, international business, management, management information systems, and marketing. An accelerated B.S./M.B.A. option is available to outstanding students.

The Golisano College of Computing and Information Sciences offers the B.S. degree in computer science, information technology, networking and systems administration, and software engineering.

The Kate Gleason College of Engineering grants the B.S. in computer, electrical, electrical/biomedical, industrial, mechanical, mechanical/aerospace, mechanical/automotive, and microelectronic engineering. An undeclared engineering program is available for undecided freshmen. Accelerated B.S./M.S. programs are also offered.

The College of Imaging Arts and Sciences offers the B.F.A. in advertising photography; ceramics and ceramic sculpture; film, video, and animation; fine art photography; fine arts; glass; graphic design; illustration; industrial design; interior design; medical illustration; metalcrafts and jewelry; new media design; photojournalism; and woodworking and furniture design. The College also offers the B.S. in biomedical photographic communications, graphic media, imaging and photographic technology, imaging systems management, and new media publishing.

The College of Liberal Arts confers the B.S. in criminal justice, economics, professional and technical communication, psychology, public policy, and social work. The RIT Exploration Program is a one-year program option for undecided students.

The College of Science offers the B.S. in applied mathematics, applied statistics, biology, biochemistry, bioinformatics, biomedical computing, biotechnology, chemistry, computational mathematics, environmental science, imaging science, medical sonography (ultrasound), physician assistant studies, physics, and polymer chemistry.

The National Technical Institute for the Deaf, which has the only program of its kind in this country, provides certificate, diploma, and degree curricula for the hearing-impaired.

Academic Program

Students entering RIT enroll directly in the college and academic program of their choice; specialization is spread over the duration of their study. Approximately one third of the program of each professional curriculum consists of general education courses in the humanities, sciences, and social sciences.

The Colleges of Applied Science and Technology, Business, Computing, and Engineering require a cooperative education program for all undergraduate students. In this program, the student alternates periods of study on campus and paid work experience in business or industry during the upper-division years. This is not only invaluable experience but also a way of meeting the expenses of these years. The cooperative program is offered as an option in several other colleges and academic departments. Field experience is integrated with academic programs in the areas of criminal justice and social work.

A number of RIT's programs are unusual baccalaureate degree offerings. Among these are the programs of the School for American Crafts; programs in biotechnology, imaging science, international business, microelectronic engineering, new media, packaging, photography, physician assistant studies, printing, software engineering, and telecommunications; and the programs of the National Technical Institute for the Deaf.

Air Force and Army ROTC programs are available on campus. A Naval ROTC program is offered jointly with the University of Rochester.

Off-Campus Programs

The American College of Management and Technology is a branch campus of RIT located in Croatia, offering a summer study-abroad program. An off-campus program at the University of Strathclyde in Scotland is available to business students. RIT maintains an exchange agreement with Japan's Kanazawa Institute of Technology. Many additional opportunities for off-campus study abroad are provided through a partnership with Syracuse University.

Academic Facilities

Wallace Memorial Library is a true multimedia learning center. Its collections are exceptionally extensive in the areas of the arts, education for the deaf, photography, and printing.

RIT's modern campus provides maximum laboratory space for undergraduates to pursue their individual projects. The Institute's Center for Microelectronic and Computer Engineering and the Carlson Center for Imaging Science are recognized as the finest facilities of their kind in the United States. An addition to the College of Science opened in 1998, and new facilities housing the College of Computing and Information Sciences were completed in 2002. The $25-million Gordon Field House and Activities Center is scheduled to open in spring 2004, providing new recreational facilities with seating for 8,000 spectators.

Costs

For 2003–04, tuition for the normal academic year (three academic quarters) was $21,027. Students on the cooperative education plan pay tuition only for the quarters they are at RIT. Fees, including the activities and health fees, were $357 for the academic year. Room and board (twenty meals per week) cost $7833.

Financial Aid

Approximately 75 percent of the full-time undergraduates receive some form of financial aid: Institute scholarships; regional, alumni, or industry-supported scholarships; and state and federal government grants. A variety of loans and part-time work positions are also available. The FAFSA must be submitted by March 1. Giving full recognition to scholarship apart from financial need, RIT awards a number of academic scholarships based on grades, test scores, and activities. Freshmen applying by February 1 and transfers applying as juniors by April 1 are considered for these scholarships.

Faculty

There are 898 full-time faculty members, 445 part-time faculty members, and an administrative and supporting staff of more than 1,750. Approximately 80 percent of the faculty have earned a Ph.D. or the terminal degree in their field.

Student Government

The Student Government is the representative body for students. It works with RIT administration, faculty, and staff to communicate the needs and desires of the student body and to communicate the decisions of the administration to the students. Fraternity and sorority, off-campus, hearing-impaired, and minority students elect special representative bodies.

All full-time and part-time undergraduate and graduate students are members of the Student Government when they pay the student activities fee.

Admission Requirements

The general requirements for freshman entrance are graduation from high school (a high school equivalency diploma is considered), high school grades that give evidence of the ability to complete college work successfully, satisfactory scores on the SAT I or ACT, and completion of prerequisite high school level math and science courses indicated in the current undergraduate catalog. A very important factor for admission is the record of academic achievement in high school (or in another college in the case of transfer students). Transfer students are placed at the highest level possible at which success is predicted. The results of standardized tests, while important, are supplementary. Students applying for programs in the fine and applied arts must submit a portfolio of original artwork.

Rochester Institute of Technology admits qualified men and women of any race, color, national or ethnic origin, religion, sexual orientation, or marital status. RIT does not discriminate on the basis of handicap in the recruitment or admission of students or in the operation of any of its programs or activities, as specified by federal laws and regulations.

Application and Information

An application, a nonrefundable processing fee of $50 (payable to Rochester Institute of Technology), official transcripts of all high school or college records, and (for prospective freshmen) SAT I or ACT scores should be forwarded to RIT. Freshman applicants for entry in the fall quarter who provide all required materials by February 1 receive admission notification by March 15. Prospective freshmen who apply after February 1 and all transfer students are notified of the admission decision by mail on a rolling basis four to six weeks after their application is complete. RIT also offers an early decision plan, whereby prospective freshmen must have their completed application with all supporting credentials on file in the Admissions Office by December 15 to receive notification by January 15.

For application forms, students should contact:

Director of Admissions
Rochester Institute of Technology
60 Lomb Memorial Drive
Rochester, New York 14623-5604
Telephone: 585-475-6631
Fax: 585-475-7424
E-mail: admissions@rit.edu
World Wide Web: http://www.rit.edu

An aerial view of the campus.

ROCKFORD COLLEGE

ROCKFORD, ILLINOIS

The College

Rockford College challenges students to become leaders and make a significant difference in a world that faces incredible challenges. One of Rockford's most distinguished graduates was the prominent social reformer, Jane Addams, who, according to legendary FBI Director J. Edgar Hoover, was "the most dangerous woman in America." In 1931, Rockford's notable alumna was honored for her efforts to promote international peace and justice and became the first woman to win the Nobel Prize for Peace.

At Rockford, students find many of the same things that they can find at other colleges—great professors, wonderful students, and outstanding athletic teams. However, what sets Rockford apart from other schools is the spirit and legacy of Jane Addams. Through Addams' life work, students at Rockford become inspired to think big and to think independently about the important questions they face in this increasingly complex world. Students are inspired to act humanely by learning through service to their community, adapting and responding to both problems and opportunities while holding firm to such principles as integrity and democracy.

The Jane Addams Center for Civic Engagement at Rockford College brings students and faculty and staff members together to make the campus and local communities better places to live. All those working with the Center know that action has the potential to change lives, when what is learned in the classroom is connected to the community.

Interested students are encouraged to visit the campus in person and to check out the College's Web site at the address listed below to see what makes Rockford the special place it is.

Approximately 25 percent of all full-time students participate in the intercollegiate athletic program. The Rockford College Regents are a member of the NCAA Division III and compete in the Northern Illinois and Iowa Conference (NIIC). Women compete in basketball, soccer, softball, tennis, and volleyball. Men compete in baseball, basketball, football, golf, soccer, and tennis.

Location

Rockford is only 75 miles from both Chicago and Milwaukee and is easily accessible by car, bus, and plane. The College is located on a 130-acre wooded campus. The city of Rockford offers students all the advantages of a thriving community: off-campus entertainment includes more than 500 restaurants, concerts and attractions at the MetroCentre, the New American Theater, the Coronado Theater, the Rockford Dance Company, numerous malls and shopping centers, museums, riverside events, and an award-winning park district. Students benefit from volunteer, internship, and employment opportunities in the community. The involvement of students in the community provides unlimited experiences that enhance and complement their Rockford College education.

Majors and Degrees

The Bachelor of Arts degree is awarded in accounting, anthropology/sociology, art (with concentrations in ceramics, drawing, painting, photography, printmaking, and sculpture), art history, biology, business administration (with tracks in management and marketing), chemistry, classics, computer science (management information systems), criminal justice (program in anthropology/sociology), economics (with tracks in finance, international economics, and public policy), education, English, French, German, history, Latin, mathematics, music history and literature, philosophy, physical education (with tracks in business and teaching), political science, psychology, science and mathematics, social sciences, Spanish, theater arts, and urban studies.

The Bachelor of Fine Arts degree is awarded in art (with concentrations in ceramics, drawing, painting, photography, printmaking, and sculpture) and performing arts (musical theater performance).

The Bachelor of Science degree is awarded in accounting, anthropology/sociology, biochemistry, biology, business administration (with tracks in management and marketing), chemistry, computer science (management information systems), economics (with tracks in finance, international economics, and public policy), education, English, history, mathematics, physical education (with tracks in business and teaching), political science, pre–social work (program in anthropology/sociology), psychology, science and mathematics, social sciences, and urban studies.

A four-year NLNAC-accredited Bachelor of Science in Nursing program is offered. A B.S.N. completion program designed specifically for registered nurses is also available.

Preprofessional programs are carefully designed to meet the needs of students who plan to pursue careers in dentistry, engineering (3-2 program), health professions (optometry and physical therapy), law, medicine, pharmacy, and veterinary medicine.

In addition to the majors/programs/degrees listed above, Rockford College also offers minors in the following areas of study: British studies, communication, dance, Greek, human development, military science, peace and conflict studies, physics, and religious studies.

Academic Program

Education at Rockford College is intended to be both broad-based and preparatory. The liberal arts curriculum allows for a choice of course work with an emphasis on a major. To earn a degree from Rockford College, students must complete at least 124 credit hours. Courses are offered by semester; there are two semesters per year. Summer courses are also available. The Honors Program in Liberal Arts offers extensive study in the humanities, a challenging core curriculum, and rigorous distribution requirements. Entrance to this program is limited and available by application only. The Forum Series offers exposure to great scholars, artists, and ideas. Special features of the College's academic program include Phi Beta Kappa and other scholastic honor societies, the Archaeological Institute of America, faculty seminars, art exhibitions, independent study, academic internships, and an extensive study-abroad program. A freshman seminar program is required for new students.

Off-Campus Programs

Rockford College gives its students an opportunity to study for a semester or a year at Regent's College in London, England, for approximately the same cost as attending the Illinois campus. Regent's College, a residential campus located in Regent's Park, offers a wide variety of courses, including academic internships, in a fully accredited program. The campus is conveniently located close to museums, galleries, theaters, and other attractions. Residence at Regent's College makes travel throughout Britain and on the Continent possible.

Rockford College also participates in programs that allow students to study in Australia, France, Germany, Spain, and other countries.

In the United States, Rockford students may participate in the Washington and United Nations Semesters.

Academic Facilities

Among the major academic buildings on the Rockford College campus is the Howard Colman Library, which houses 170,000 volumes and more than 800 periodical subscriptions. CD-ROM computers provide easy access to library holdings and national indexes; the availability of resources is enhanced by the interlibrary loan system. Private study carrels are provided. The Starr Science Building houses the major science facilities, which include physics laboratories, chemistry teaching and research laboratories with a fully equipped instrumentation lab, biology and psychology teaching and research laboratories, and nursing laboratories. It also houses the student computer lab and language lab. Programs in fine and performing arts are housed in the Clark Arts Center, which has a 570-seat theater with computerized lighting and sound equipment; an experimental theater; an art gallery; a sculpture garden; studios for lithography/printmaking, drawing, painting, sculpting, and ceramics; a darkroom; and facilities for dance and music. The Seaver Physical Education Building is the campus sports complex. It includes locker rooms, a pool, a basketball court, a free-weight room, a fitness center, a training room, and classrooms. Dayton Hall houses the Learning Resources Center, which offers free tutoring. Scarborough Hall houses classrooms, faculty offices, and the writing center.

Costs

Costs for the 2003–04 academic year were $20,210 for tuition and $4034 for a double room. Several board plans were available, starting at $2547. Books are estimated to cost $900 per year. Miscellaneous expenses, including transportation, vary with individual needs but total approximately $2000 per year.

Financial Aid

Rockford wants to help those students who want to change the world with the cost of their college education. The College believes that a student who is like Jane Addams is an idealist and an activist, one who is willing to make sacrifices—not one who is asking for handouts. Rockford not only shares those values, but supports them with scholarships, grants, and a full array of financial aid programs. Every year, the College awards more than $4 million to students who make a difference.

Approximately 95 percent of students receive financial aid. Students may be considered for financial assistance if they are taking at least 6 credit hours per semester. Merit-based awards, including several full tuition scholarships, are available to full-time students. Need-based awards are determined by the results of the Free Application for Federal Student Aid (FAFSA). These awards include Rockford College grants and institutional loans as well as federal and state funds. Students are encouraged to file for financial aid by June 1. Rockford College students who attend Regent's College are eligible for the above awards.

Faculty

The student-faculty ratio at Rockford College is 12:1. The full-time faculty is composed of more than 80 men and women with outstanding academic backgrounds and varied international experience. Seventy percent hold terminal degrees in their respective fields. Some departments enlist part-time faculty members from the Rockford and Chicago professional communities to augment their programs. An extensive faculty development program helps ensure that the faculty members constantly update and improve their classroom teaching. Faculty members are involved in the lives of their students by serving as academic advisers, club and organization advisers, and mentors. A freshman advising program matches incoming freshmen with full-time faculty members who serve as advisers and mentors.

Student Government

The Rockford College Student Government serves its constituency in all areas of campus life. Students serve on College committees, judge their peers in student court, uphold the campus honor code, monitor campus media, and are consulted regarding changes in College policy. The Entertainment Council is responsible for organizing campus activities, including concerts, lectures, dances, and other social events.

Admission Requirements

Admission to Rockford College is based upon the applicant's potential for success as determined by prior academic preparation and personal achievement and is subject to satisfactory completion of academic work currently in progress. Students may apply upon completion of their junior year of high school. Admission is based on high school GPA, ACT or SAT test results, and class rank.

All applicants must submit an application and a nonrefundable $35 application fee. The fee is waived for students who visit the campus. On-campus interviews and personal statements are highly encouraged. Recommendations may be requested.

International students are welcome to apply; they should contact the Director of International Student Admission for specific application information.

Application and Information

Rockford College uses a rolling admission policy. Students can expect to be notified of decisions within two weeks of receipt of the completed application and all necessary documents.

For further information, students should contact:

Office of Admission
Nelson Hall
Rockford College
5050 East State Street
Rockford, Illinois 61108-2393
Telephone: 815-226-4050
800-892-2984 (toll-free in the U.S. and Canada)
Fax: 815-226-2822
E-mail: admission@rockford.edu
World Wide Web: http://www.rockford.edu

The accessibility of faculty members at Rockford College allows close interaction with students both in and out of the classroom.

ROCKHURST UNIVERSITY

KANSAS CITY, MISSOURI

The University

Rockhurst University believes in experience-based learning. The goal is to help students confront the challenges they will encounter in the real world by using the wide range of resources available in Kansas City as a learning laboratory. Through activities such as professional internships, research projects, and community service work throughout the city, students learn by doing. This approach to education helps students clarify their professional interests as well as acquire a deeper sense of confidence in themselves, their skills, and their life choices.

The intellectual community of 3,000 students encourages students to find their own capacity for original thinking and to approach new challenges as questioning, open-minded thinkers. This ability is one of the great gifts of a Jesuit education. Rockhurst is one of the most intimate, manageable, and affordable of the nation's twenty-eight Jesuit colleges and universities. It has been consistently ranked as one of the top fifteen universities in the Midwest by *U.S. News & World Report.*

Rockhurst enjoys an excellent reputation that translates into outstanding employment opportunities for graduates. About 1 in 10 graduates are presidents, chief executive officers, top leaders for not-for-profit organizations, or owners of their own companies.

Activities outside of class are a critical component of the Rockhurst experience. Rockhurst freshmen begin their college careers doing community service through the Finucane Service Project during orientation; seniors complete their education by participating in the Van Ackeren Service Project. In addition, many students spend spring break on a service project.

Classroom work is linked to service and extracurricular achievement. A few examples: one organizational behavior class studied a social service agency and eventually became the agency's consulting team; students have received National Science Foundation grants for undergraduate research; 2 students have been the only undergraduate presenters at the 7,000-person American Political Science Association convention; and students take leading roles in developing the campus master plan and the University's strategic plan.

Rockhurst recognizes that campus life involves more than academics and cocurricular activities. The Town House Village student residence complex provides an apartment-style residence experience for juniors and seniors. About half of Rockhurst's students live on the 55-acre main campus, located just a few blocks south of the famed Country Club Plaza.

Men's and women's basketball and soccer and women's volleyball teams have regularly participated in NCAA national tournaments. Men's baseball, women's softball, and men's and women's tennis and golf teams continue Rockhurst's strong athletic traditions at the NCAA Division II level. Construction is nearly complete on a new $5.5-million athletic complex named Loyola Park.

Students can also take advantage of the Rockhurst network in Kansas City's thriving business community. The Career Center offers the Cooperative Education program, placing students in full-time jobs for a semester, where they earn both pay and credit.

Rockhurst also provides opportunities for learning after students receive a bachelor's degree. Doctor of Physical Therapy, Master of Occupational Therapy, Master of Education, Master in Communication Sciences and Disorders, and traditional and executive Master of Business Administration degrees are offered. A postbaccalaureate premed program is also available.

Rockhurst's emphasis on values and lifelong learning leads students to new definitions of success. The process of being a successful person has been mastered by many famous "Rocks," as Rockhurst alumni are known. From space scientists to entrepreneurs to founders of a clinic for crack babies to college presidents, famous Rocks are found in nearly every state, making a difference in their fields and in their communities.

Location

The 55-acre Rockhurst campus is in the cultural heart of thriving Kansas City. Rustic stone classroom buildings surrounded by beautiful, shaded walkways provide the perfect atmosphere for study and relaxation. The campus is a short stroll from Kansas City's brightest cultural attractions, including the Nelson-Atkins Museum of Art and the Country Club Plaza. All of the metropolitan area's attractions, such as the Truman Sports Complex (home to the Chiefs and Royals), Crown Center, and jazz and rock concert halls, are easily accessible.

Majors and Degrees

Rockhurst University offers Bachelor of Arts, Bachelor of Science, Bachelor of Science in Business Administration, Bachelor of Liberal Studies, Bachelor of Professional Studies, and Bachelor of Science in Nursing degrees. Programs and majors in the College of Arts and Sciences include biology, business communication, chemistry, clinical laboratory sciences, communication, communication sciences and disorders, computer information systems, computer science, education, English, French, global studies, history, mathematics, philosophy, physics, political science, psychology, sociology, Spanish, theater arts, and theology. The Helzberg School of Management awards degrees in accounting, economics, finance/accounting, finance/economics, ISKM, international business, management, and marketing. The Research College of Nursing offers a degree in nursing. The Professional Studies Program offers degrees in accounting, business, computer technology, English, leadership of nonprofit organizations, organizational communication, and organizational leadership.

Preprofessional programs are available in dentistry, engineering, law, medicine, occupational therapy, optometry, osteopathic medicine, pharmacy, physical therapy, physician's assistant studies, and veterinary medicine. Areas of study include art, German, human service agency administration, medical sociology and healthcare adminstration, music, paralegal studies, women's studies, and writing.

Academic Program

Depending upon their intended major, beginning students are advised in the College of Arts and Sciences, the Helzberg School of Management, or the Research College of Nursing. Students eventually declare a major in one of these three schools. The Research College of Nursing provides an accelerated program for students with degrees in other fields. The Professional Studies Program offers opportunities for working adults to complete the bachelor's degree through part-time study. The University has an excellent honors program. A minimum of 128 credit hours is required for graduation; there are specific requirements for each degree area.

The University's programs in occupational therapy and physical therapy respond to the growing need for health-care professionals. Students entering Rockhurst as freshmen may pursue a program that leads to a bachelor's degree in a related field and a master's degree in occupational therapy after five years or a bachelor's degree in a related field and a doctorate of physical therapy after six years.

The Cooperative Education Program enables students to earn college credit while gaining valuable work experience in major companies. Cooperative education provides students with an opportunity to match academic learning with workplace experience, testing career choices and potential employers. By alternating semesters of study and work, students can complete course work in four years (including summers) and have a year's experience in real-world jobs. Many co-op students are offered permanent positions with firms for which they have worked in the program.

Off-Campus Programs

The study-abroad program coordinates course work in nine European cities: Madrid, Spain; Rome and Florence, Italy; Aix-en-Provence, Avignon, and Toulon, France; and Richmond, Surrey, and Kensington, England. In addition, scholarships have funded dozens of students on study trips to Russia, and a study in Mexico program is offered every summer in Xalapa, Mexico. Rockhurst students regularly find internships in government and in the nonprofit and private sectors through the Washington Center, in the nation's capital. Special scholarships have also provided internships in Congress for Rockhurst students. Students may also take courses at other local institutions, such as the Kansas City Art Institute and the Conservatory of Music of the University of Missouri at Kansas City, through an exchange program.

Academic Facilities

The Greenlease Library houses more than 100,000 volumes and is a repository for a variety of government documents, including the *Federal Register*, Congressional reports, Supreme Court decisions, and presidential papers. Rockhurst students also have access to the renowned Linda Hall Science Library, which is just a few blocks from campus. The Richardson Science Center houses science programs.

Costs

In 2003–04, the cost of tuition was $16,195; room and board costs averaged $5350.

Financial Aid

Rockhurst University arranges significant financial aid packages, which include scholarships, grants, loans, and part-time jobs, for eligible students. Nearly half of the entering freshman class receives partial to full scholarship awards based on academic, talent, service, and athletic achievements. Federal, state, Rockhurst University, and research grants are available. Low-interest student loans include the Federal Stafford Student and Federal Perkins loans; Federal PLUS loans are available for parents. The Federal Work-Study Program provides campus jobs. The Career Center helps students find part-time jobs throughout the Kansas City area. A monthly payment plan allows students to pay all or part of their fees in installments without interest. Students must file a Free Application for Federal Student Aid (FAFSA) to be considered for financial assistance.

Faculty

Rockhurst's outstanding faculty of 128 full-time and 88 part-time professors, including 8 Jesuits, staff day classes. Approximately 85 percent of full-time faculty members hold a Ph.D. or the terminal degree in their field. All classes and labs, including those on the freshman level, are taught by professors or instructors, not teaching assistants. Faculty members also act as academic advisers to students. Rockhurst's student-faculty ratio of 10:1 ensures close interaction between students, from freshmen to seniors, and faculty members.

Student Government

All full-time students can participate in the Student Senate. Students elect senate representatives and officers annually. The Student Activities Board, also elected, organizes social activities and allocates student activity fees. Resident students elect Residence Hall Councils to plan activities and help administer the residence halls. Students may also serve on tripartite committees that include students, faculty members, and administrators. These committees advise the President and others on policy issues. The Interfraternity Council and the Panhellenic Council provide leadership for the fraternities and sororities on campus.

Admission Requirements

Applicants must submit scores on the ACT or SAT I examination. Sixteen units of college-preparatory work are required, and an interview is recommended.

Application and Information

There is a $25 application fee. For further information, students should contact:

Office of Admission
Rockhurst University
1100 Rockhurst Road
Kansas City, Missouri 64110-2561
Telephone: 816-501-4100
800-842-6776 (toll-free)
Fax: 816-501-4241
E-mail: admission@rockhurst.edu
World Wide Web: http://www.rockhurst.edu

The distinctiveness of a Rockhurst University education stems from its Jesuit heritage, which calls for students to find their unique gifts and talents and become leaders in service to others.

ROGER WILLIAMS UNIVERSITY

BRISTOL, RHODE ISLAND

The University

Roger Williams University (RWU), ranked in the top tier of Best Comprehensive Colleges in its region and category by *U.S. News & World Report's America's Best Colleges,* has experienced tremendous growth with new facilities, record enrollment, and an increasingly diverse and vigorous academic curriculum. During the last decade, Roger Williams has moved ahead by expanding undergraduate programs and creating master's degree programs to meet students' needs.

As a leading liberal arts university, Roger Williams exemplifies core values that represent higher education at its best: a love for learning, preparation for the future, applied research, service, a global perspective, and respect for the individual. Accredited by the New England Association of Schools and Colleges and founded in 1956, Roger Williams University is an independent, coeducational university offering liberal arts and selected professional programs. The University enrolls approximately 3,400 full-time undergraduate students in more than thirty majors instructed by a full-time faculty of 173 in a residential campus setting. The School of Law, the first and only law school in Rhode Island, offers the Juris Doctor degree and enrolls approximately 500 students. Master's programs in criminal justice, teaching, and literacy education enroll approximately 200 students. RWU's strong teaching orientation and dedicated faculty members, who are noted experts in their fields, take a genuine interest in students, ensuring an engaging learning environment.

The main campus, overlooking beautiful Mt. Hope Bay in Bristol, Rhode Island, opened in 1969 and features modern academic and recreational facilities, including a waterfront Center for Environmental and Economic Development; the 150,000-square-foot School of Law and Law Library; an $8-million Main Library; the award-winning Architecture Building and Architecture Library; and the Performing Arts Center. In summer 2003, RWU opened a multimillion-dollar addition to the Campus Recreation Center. The addition includes an eight-lane swimming pool, racquetball courts, and a state-of-the-art workout facility. RWU values the importance of continuing to upgrade facilities for an ideal living, learning, and wellness environment for students.

Outdoor recreational facilities include softball and baseball diamonds, three rugby/lacrosse/soccer fields, six tennis courts, and a jogging track. RWU teams compete in Division III of the National Collegiate Athletic Association (NCAA), the Eastern College Athletic Conference (ECAC), and the Commonwealth Coast Conference (CCC); the University sponsors eighteen varsity sports for men and women as well as clubs in men's rugby, coed crew, and coed track and field. In addition, an extensive program of intramural and recreational activities is offered all year long, with drop-in recreational activities available to the student body.

Many student residences claim impressive sweeping, waterfront views of spectacular Mt. Hope Bay. One of the new residence halls, Stonewall Terrace, is a wonderful addition to students' housing options. The four 3-story complexes house approximately 400 upperclass residents in single and double rooms in a suite-style arrangement. Each room is carpeted and fully air-conditioned. Spacious common areas provide additional meeting, study, and programming space for residents. A variety of other comfortable residences located on the main campus offer students a choice of coeducational or single-sex residential living in facilities directly on Mt. Hope Bay. The Bayside Courts offers town-house-style accommodations overlooking the water. There also is an apartment complex, managed by the University, 2 miles from the campus. Residential units include 24-hour quiet areas for study and some specialized living/learning units grouped by major.

The hub of student activity on campus, the Student Union, is a two-level facility that houses the main dining hall, snack bar, game room, bookstore, and lounge. In summer 2002, a $1-million upgrade was made to the Student Union building. Among these exciting changes, the main dining hall was renovated to offer students a more pleasant atmosphere in which to enjoy their meals. All students residing on campus are required to participate in the board meal plan, with the exception of those students residing in the off-campus apartment complex, for whom the meal plan is optional. Students with special dietary needs may establish individual meal plans.

The University sponsors many athletic, social, cultural, and academic activities, and students may choose from a variety of structured and informal activities, including the Alive! Arts Series, Main Season theater and dance productions, Penny Arcade Film Series, visiting speakers forum, and lectures by visiting speakers, novelists, and poets. The student radio station, WQRI, provides opportunities to gain broadcasting experience; students gain journalism and publishing experience working on the yearbook, newspaper, and literary magazine. Additional opportunities include participation in campus and community choruses, service projects both on and off campus through the Volunteer Center and Community Service Association, numerous student clubs and organizations, and student government. Also of note are Alpha Chi (a national honor society), numerous departmental honor societies, continuing education opportunities, and a strong Career Services department.

In addition to its undergraduate degrees, the University awards the Master of Arts in Teaching (elementary education), Master of Arts in literacy education, Master of Science in criminal justice, and Master of Architecture.

Location

The University is located in Bristol, Rhode Island, a historic seacoast community with a small-town, residential character. A half-hour's drive from the campus, the Rhode Island cities of Newport, the city by the sea, and Providence, America's Renaissance City, feature restored historic buildings, shops, museums, theaters, and numerous cultural, educational, and recreational attractions. Boston is approximately 1 hour away by car or bus. A bus stop is located directly in front of the campus.

Majors and Degrees

At the undergraduate level, RWU awards the Bachelor of Science, Bachelor of Arts, Bachelor of Fine Arts, and Bachelor of Architecture degrees. In addition, the University also awards a combined Bachelor of Science/Master of Architecture degree. Academic programs are offered through one college and five professional schools that combine traditional liberal arts education with professional studies. Professional programs are offered through the School of Architecture, Art and Historic Preservation; the Gabelli School of Business; the School of Engineering, Computing and Construction Management; and the School of Justice Studies, and liberal arts majors are offered through the Feinstein College of Arts and Sciences and the School of Education. Continuing education is available through the University Colleges for Continuing Education.

All students complete an interdisciplinary core program, a major, and a core concentration or minor. Students select their majors and minors from the following disciplines: accounting, American studies, anthropology/sociology, architecture, art and architectural history, biology, business management, chemistry, communications, computer information systems, computer science, construction management, creative writing, criminal justice, dance performance studies, education (elementary and secondary education), engineering, English literature, environmental engineering, environmental science, financial services, foreign languages, historic preservation, history, international business, legal studies, marine biology, marketing, mathematics, philosophy, political science, psychology, theater, and visual arts studies. Other programs include an undergraduate Honors Program, prelaw, premedicine, pre–veterinary science, and a 3+3 program (bachelor's and Juris Doctor degrees). Students can also study English as a second language.

Academic Programs

The fall semester begins in September and ends in December; the spring semester begins in late January and ends in May. During the month of January, special on- and off-campus intersession programs, including opportunities for travel and service, are open to students at other institutions of higher learning. During the summer, undergraduate day and evening classes are available in Bristol, and evening classes are available at the University's Metropolitan Center for Education and Law in Providence. The University Honors Program is offered by invitation to high school students who have demonstrated academic excellence.

Off-Campus Programs

Honors, cooperative education, internships, study abroad, and community service programs enhance undergraduate studies. University career planning counselors work one-on-one with students and alumni, providing career development guidance, assessment, employment search skills, and placement assistance. Students are encouraged to participate in off-campus opportunities or study-abroad programs in Australia, Greece, Ireland, Italy, Mexico, and Scotland.

Academic Facilities

Two undergraduate libraries with a total of more than 168,000 volumes are open 92 hours a week to students, faculty members, and community residents. The 54,000-square-foot main library houses 1,225 periodical titles and seating and quiet study/reading areas for approximately 400 students, computerized databases, and an on-line catalog. The main library also houses special collections and the University archives. A computerized system allows students to utilize library services of four additional Rhode Island institutions.

The University maintains a fully staffed, state-of-the-art computer facility, where all students have access to Pentium-based Novell, Apple Macintosh, and DOS- or Windows-based servers and features such as the Internet, CD-ROM capability, color scanners, and laser printers.

The Marine and Natural Sciences Building, housing science and mathematics departments, features a wet laboratory with flowing seawater, research space, and modern physics, chemistry, and biology laboratories. The Engineering Building supports modern lab facilities equipped for computing, drafting, electronics, surveying, soil, fluid, and materials mechanics, and digital and environmental systems. Art and sculpting studios, an art gallery, photography labs, a theater, a dance studio, rehearsal rooms, and scene and costume shops support fine arts studies. The award-winning School of Architecture, Art, and Historic Preservation Building includes design studios, review and seminar rooms, a library, a photography studio and darkroom, a model shop, computer labs, and an exhibition gallery.

Costs

For the 2003–04 academic year, full-time tuition was $19,920 for 12 to 17 hours ($22,776 for architecture majors). Room and board charges for on-campus housing (double occupancy) averaged $9456 annually.

Financial Aid

The University offers merit scholarships, which are awarded regardless of financial need, to recognize students with superior academic achievement. Merit scholarship recipients are determined by high school or prior college record, class rank, grade point average (GPA), and SAT I scores. These scholarships are renewable yearly, provided that recipients maintain a designated GPA while enrolled full-time at the University. There is no separate application(s) for these scholarships. Each applicant's record is examined to determine eligibility as part of the routine admissions process.

The vast majority of the funds and programs administered by the Office of Student Financial Aid and Financial Planning at RWU require the demonstration of financial need as an essential consideration. Those not based on need determination include Federal Direct Unsubsidized Loan, PLUS loans, alternative loan programs, and various outside/external scholarships (where selection is made by the donor or organization). With few exceptions, all other programs require that need be evaluated and determined by the Office of Student Financial Aid and Financial Planning.

The University requires the submission of the Free Application for Federal Student Aid (FAFSA) and the CSS Financial Aid PROFILE to the respective processor by January 15. The Roger Williams University Title IV Federal Code Number is 003410. The FAFSA must be received at the federal processor no later than March 1 to be considered for maximum financial aid.

Faculty

The University's undergraduate program employs more than 173 full-time faculty members. Teaching is central to the undergraduate mission of the University, as is academic advisement. The University does not utilize teaching assistants, and all faculty members devote much time working with students both in and outside the classroom. The University faculty members also reflect distinguished scholarship and applied research.

Student Government

Leadership opportunities are available to students through the Student Government Association. Students may serve in elected positions on the Student Senate, which carries out the executive and legislative functions of the association.

Admission Requirements

The University encourages applications from motivated students who have completed college-preparatory courses. In determining admissibility, the Office of Admission considers the applicant's high school courses and grades, rank in class, SAT I scores, recommendation, and additional information (such as required audition or portfolio). Early decision is available for students who designate Roger Williams University as their first choice.

Application and Information

Applicants may submit applications and transcripts after September 1 for the following fall. The deadline for early decision is December 1. The deadline for the architecture program and merit scholarship consideration is February 1. A nonrefundable fee of $50 must accompany the application.

Application forms and admission information may be obtained by contacting:

Office of Undergraduate Admission
Roger Williams University
One Old Ferry Road
Bristol, Rhode Island 02809-2921
Telephone: 401-254-3500
800-458-7144 Ext. 3500 (toll-free outside Rhode Island)
E-mail: admit@rwu.edu
World Wide Web: http://www.rwu.edu

Roger Williams University is located on 140 scenic acres overlooking Mt. Hope Bay.

ROLLINS COLLEGE

WINTER PARK, FLORIDA

The College

Founded in 1885, Rollins College is Florida's oldest postsecondary institution. It is coeducational, nondenominational, and independently supported by income from tuition, gifts, and investments. Primarily a four-year undergraduate liberal arts college, Rollins offers graduate study in the Crummer Graduate School of Business and graduate studies in counseling, education, human resources, liberal studies, and corporate communication and technology. The undergraduate student body numbers approximately 1,730 and is international in scope. Most states of the Union, the District of Columbia, and fifty-one countries are represented.

The 67-acre campus is beautifully landscaped, and its buildings emphasize a traditional Spanish-Mediterranean architecture. The College campaign exceeded its target, securing approximately $200 million for financial aid, endowed faculty chairs, programming, and facilities, including the Harold and Ted Alfond Sports Center, the Cornell Campus Center, the Olin Electronic Research and Information Center, and the Marshall and Vera Lea Rinker Building.

Location

Winter Park is considered one of the nation's most beautiful residential communities. The town is adjacent to Orlando, one of the nation's fastest-growing and most popular metropolitan areas and an important center of business, science, and technology. Located 50 miles from the Atlantic Ocean and 90 miles from the Gulf of Mexico, the Rollins campus is bounded by Lake Virginia to the east and south.

Majors and Degrees

Rollins College confers the Bachelor of Arts degree in the following major areas: anthropology, art (studio and history), biochemistry/molecular biology, biology, chemistry, classical studies, computer science, economics, elementary education, English, environmental studies, European studies, French, history, international business, international relations, Latin American and Caribbean affairs, mathematics, music, philosophy, physics, political science, psychology, religious studies, sociology, Spanish, and theater. Minors are also offered in African and African-American studies, Archaeology, Asian studies, Australian studies, business, communications, dance, film studies, German, Jewish studies, Russian, sustainable development and the environment, women's studies, and writing. Course sequences can be arranged in predentistry, prelaw, premedicine, and pre–veterinary studies. Dual-degree (3-2) programs are available in pre-engineering in cooperation with Auburn University, Case Western Reserve University, Columbia University, and Washington University; in pre-environmental management and preforestry with Duke University; and in business management with the Crummer Graduate School of Business.

Academic Programs

The Rollins faculty has adopted a curriculum based upon a liberal arts pattern from the first year to graduation, designed to ensure that broadly educated graduates will be well prepared in a field of concentration. The student must complete the general education requirements, which are divided into three main areas: skills, cognitive courses, and affective courses. Self-designed majors are available to students who desire concentrations in more than one major field. The Honors Degree Program allows selected academically superior students to enter Rollins with full sophomore status and graduate with a special Honors B.A. degree in as few as three years by satisfying stringent criteria. All first-year students participate in the Rollins Conference, a fall semester seminar program taught by faculty members who also serve as the students' academic advisers.

The academic calendar consists of a fifteen-week fall semester and a fifteen-week spring semester.

Credit is awarded for appropriate Advanced Placement examination and CLEP scores, dual enrollment programs, and for achievement in the International Baccalaureate Program.

Off-Campus Programs

For approximately the same tuition and fees that they pay at Rollins, students may study abroad for a semester at Rollins-sponsored programs in Sydney, Australia; London, England; Muenster, Germany; and Asturias and Madrid, Spain. In addition to the traditional semester-long programs, Rollins offers dozens of study-abroad opportunities at various times of the year, in places such as Bali, China, Costa Rica, Dominican Republic, France, Greece, Hong Kong, Israel, Italy, Mexico, Namibia, and Turkey.

Academic Facilities

The College's academic facilities include the Knowles Memorial Chapel/Annie Russell Theatre complex, which through the years has become the traditional landmark of the College, and the Olin Library, which features reader stations, computer terminals, study areas, and faculty research offices. Other major academic facilities include the Bush Science Center, the Cornell Fine Arts Center, the Cornell Hall for the Social Sciences, the Johnson Center for Psychology, and the Olin Electronic Research and Information Center.

Costs

The basic academic-year expenses for 2004–05 are $26,910 for tuition and fees and $8570 for room and board, for a total of $35,480.

Financial Aid

Rollins seeks to help qualified students attend college regardless of their ability to meet the expenses. Funds are provided by Rollins College as well as by federal and state sources. Student aid consists of scholarships, grants, loans, and employment opportunities. Most students receiving aid are given a package consisting of two or three of these forms of aid. Aid is awarded on the basis of proven financial need and academic achievement. To apply for aid, a student must file the Free Application for Federal Student Aid and the Rollins College Undergraduate Financial Aid Application.

A number of renewable academic merit scholarships are available to entering first-year students, including Alonzo Rollins and Presidential Scholarships for overall academic excellence (up to $15,000 annually) and Donald Cram Scholarships for majors in mathematics and the sciences ($5000 annually). In addition, leadership awards are available to students with strong academic records who have demonstrated a significant contribution to school or community. All applicants are considered for these scholarships, and financial need is not a criterion. Scholarships are also awarded for artistic and athletic talent. More information may be obtained from the Offices of Admission and Financial Aid.

Due to the high number of student aid applicants and the limitation of funds, it is important that application for admission to the College be made no later than February 15 and preferably in the fall of the senior year of secondary school. Details and regulations regarding student aid are found in the College's *General Catalogue*.

Faculty

Ninety-four percent of the members of Rollins' teaching faculty hold doctoral degrees or the highest degree available in their field from distinguished universities in this country and abroad. The student-faculty ratio is 11:1. Students receive instruction from full-time faculty members, who also serve as academic advisers.

Student Government

The Student Government Association consists of a student senate elected from across the campus and an executive committee. The SGA is composed of executive, legislative, and judicial branches, each designed to provide a series of checks and balances in the administrative process. The SGA affords students participation in the decision-making process of college life and represents student opinion to the trustees, administration, alumni, faculty, and staff. It provides an avenue for student expression, social interaction, cultural awareness, and student services and publications.

Admission Requirements

Admission is competitive; approximately 2,700 applications are received annually for a first-year class of 460 and a transfer class of 60. More than 80 percent of the members of each entering first-year class rank in the top two fifths of their high school graduating class. The middle 50 percent of College Board SAT I combined verbal and math scores range from 1080 to 1260 and the middle 50 percent of ACT composite scores range from 24 to 28. Emphasis is placed on the student's high school record, including class standing, counselor's recommendation, the results of either the SAT I or ACT, and extracurricular involvement.

Application and Information

Candidates are encouraged to apply in the fall of their senior year. Applications should be submitted no later than February 15 of the senior year. Students are notified of a decision by April 1. The Candidates' Reply Date is May 1. Two early decision dates are available for 2004–05: applications must be received by November 15 for Round I applicants and by January 15 for Round II applicants. Candidates for early decision are notified by December 15 and February 1, respectively. A deposit of $500 ($300 tuition/$200 housing) is due and payable upon notification of acceptance.

Early admission candidates may be considered for entrance prior to secondary school graduation, usually for entrance following their junior year.

Application forms and additional information may be obtained by writing or calling:

Office of Admission
Rollins College
1000 Holt Avenue-2720
Winter Park, Florida 32789-4499
Telephone: 407-646-2161
Fax: 407-646-1502
E-mail: admission@rollins.edu
World Wide Web: http://www.rollins.edu

The Harold and Ted Alfond Sports Center, a 76,000-square-foot state-of-the-art facility, features a performance court, a recreation gym, and comprehensive aerobics and weight-training areas.

ROOSEVELT UNIVERSITY

CHICAGO AND SCHAUMBURG, ILLINOIS

The University

Roosevelt University was founded in 1945 to provide opportunities for learning and teaching in conditions of freedom and equality. Since 1947, the home of Roosevelt's Chicago Campus has been the famous Auditorium Building overlooking Grant Park and Lake Michigan. The University has restored to their original splendor various areas of this National Historic Landmark building. The Schaumburg Campus was established in 1978 and has become the largest and most comprehensive university in the northwest suburbs.

The University seeks to develop individuals who will be dedicated to the essential themes of a democratic society, who possess an understanding of human history and the basic ideas of the humanities and sciences, and who will accept their responsibilities as citizens of a vital nation and a changing world.

Involvement in the metropolitan experience is an integral part of the academic curriculum. The University is committed to serving the developing needs of Chicago as well as suburban communities.

Roosevelt serves more than 7,300 undergraduate and graduate students in the Colleges of Arts and Sciences, Business Administration, and Education; University College (adult degrees); and the Chicago College of Performing Arts.

Roosevelt schedules classes days, evenings, and weekends so that students may work while attending school. Approximately 85 percent of Roosevelt students are residents of the greater Chicago metropolitan area; the other 15 percent represent more than twenty states and sixty-three countries. The seventeen-story Herman Crown Center in Chicago provides housing for 300 students, with the new University Center residence hall scheduled to open in the fall of 2004.

Roosevelt University is accredited by the North Central Association of Colleges and Schools, and its programs are accredited by the American Chemical Society, the Association of Collegiate Business Schools and Programs, the Council for Accreditation of Counseling and Related Educational Programs, the National Association of Schools of Music, and the National Council for Accreditation of Teacher Education.

Location

Roosevelt University's Chicago Campus is conveniently located on Michigan Avenue in the heart of Chicago's cultural and political center, within easy commuting distance by car or public transportation. The Schaumburg Campus is located 30 miles northwest of downtown Chicago in Schaumburg, near O'Hare International Airport and numerous corporate headquarters.

Majors and Degrees

The Bachelor of Arts degree is awarded in African-American studies, art history, biology, chemistry, computer science, economics, English, environmental policy, history, integrated marketing communications/advertising, international studies, journalism, legal studies, mathematical sciences, media studies, metropolitan studies, music, philosophy, political science, professional communications, psychology, public administration, public relations, social justice, social science, sociology, Spanish, telecommunications, theater arts, and Web technology. The Bachelor of Science degree is awarded in actuarial science, allied health (medical technology, nuclear medicine technology, and radiation technology), biology, chemistry, computer science, electronics engineering technology, environmental science, hospitality and tourism management, mathematical science, premedical studies, pre–veterinary studies, psychology, telecommunications, and Web technology. The Bachelor of Fine Arts is awarded in music theater and theater. The Bachelor of Science in Business Administration is awarded in accounting, finance, human resource management, management, and marketing. The Bachelor of Music degree in performance is awarded in keyboard, composition, jazz studies, music history, music theory, performance (all instruments, orchestral/band, and voice), and piano pedagogy. The Bachelor of General Studies degree (B.G.S., for adults) is awarded with concentrations in communications, history, individualized programs, international studies, languages, liberal arts, literature, metropolitan studies, political science, psychology, sociology, and women's studies. The Bachelor of Professional Studies (B.P.S., for adults) is awarded with concentrations in administrative studies, business, computer science, early childhood teacher preparation, financial services, hospitality and tourism management, organizational communication, organizational leadership, paralegal studies, pre-biotechnology and chemical sciences, risk management and financial services, systems management, and telecommunications. The Bachelor of Arts in Education degree is awarded in early childhood, elementary, and special education. A sequence for secondary education certification is available in business-teacher education, English, general science, mathematics, social studies, Spanish, and theater.

Academic Programs

The requirements for the B.A., B.A.E., and B.S. degrees are completion of a minimum of 120 semester hours with at least a 2.0 average (2.5 in education), a major of no fewer than 24 semester hours, and at least 60 semester hours of work at the advanced level. The requirements for the B.S. degree in business mandates the completion of a minimum of 120 semester hours, a major of no fewer than 18 semester hours, at least 54 semester hours in business administration, and at least 57 semester hours in arts and sciences. The requirements for the B.M. in performance degree are completion of at least 120 semester hours with an average of 2.0 or better (2.3 in music education); participation in orchestra, band, chorus, or other related ensembles; completion of at least 27 semester hours of liberal arts courses; and a senior recital, thesis, or public performance of one original composition. The B.G.S./B.P.S. are special degree programs for adults (age 24 or over) and degree requirements vary according to the individual student's program.

Roosevelt University awards credit for successful completion of many CLEP examinations, as well as for satisfactory scores on Advanced Placement tests and International Baccalaureate course work.

Roosevelt Scholars is an honors experience that blends academic rigor with opportunities for developing metropolitan leadership abilities. Major scholarship support is available, along with mentoring relationships with Chicago's corporate, political, and social leaders.

Roosevelt University has a special cooperative arrangement with the School of the Art Institute of Chicago, in which Roosevelt students can apply courses taken in their major at the Art Institute to their Roosevelt degree.

A special support program is available for learning-disabled students.

Academic Facilities

The collections of the main library exceed 400,000 volumes, including 63,000 microforms. The Music Library houses an additional 40,000 books, 12,000 sound recordings, and 10,000 pieces of sheet music and is furnished with audio equipment for individual listening. Roosevelt students also have access to more than 25 million additional volumes through the University's membership in the Chicago Academic Library Council and the Illinois Library Network. Materials in libraries all over the country can be located quickly by means of the University's Online Computer Library Center (OCLC) computer terminals.

The University has IBM microcomputer laboratories, science laboratories, classrooms, and seminar rooms. Other University academic facilities include a language laboratory; a reading laboratory; Mildred Fagen Theatre of Art History, which has extensive collections of art slides; and a suite of thirty-five modern music practice rooms. Each year, music students and faculty members present more than 100 recitals and concerts in the renowned Rudolph Ganz Memorial Hall. Operatic and theatrical productions are staged in O'Malley Workshop Theatre.

The Schaumburg Campus is a 135,000-square-foot facility with more than sixty classrooms, an electronic library serving all research needs, computer classrooms and labs, and biology and research chemistry labs.

Costs

Undergraduate tuition for the 2003–04 academic year was $506 per semester hour or $15,180 (for 30 hours) per year. Room and board costs for the school year were $7150.

Financial Aid

Scholarships are awarded to entering freshmen and transfer students on the basis of academic ability. They award partial tuition, and many are renewable up to the completion of the bachelor's degree program. The University also has a limited number of Music Performance Awards and talent awards for theater majors through the Chicago College of Performing Arts.

Roosevelt's policy is to provide maximum financial assistance for students who demonstrate financial need. Students must submit the Free Application for Federal Student Aid (FAFSA). The priority deadline for applying for University financial aid is April 1 prior to the academic year for which aid is requested.

Faculty

The faculty includes 550 members, 189 of whom teach full-time. Although many faculty members conduct serious research and have numerous publications to their credit, they are primarily dedicated to classroom instruction. The student-faculty ratio is 16:1. Most faculty members serve as academic advisers and participate in University affairs through the Faculty Senate, the Board of Trustees, and major University committees.

Student Government

The student body has its own Student Senate, composed of students from the various colleges. Students also serve as voting members of the Faculty Senate and most major University committees and departmental groups.

Admission Requirements

Admission to Roosevelt University is determined on an individual basis. The student's academic ability, as demonstrated by grades, class rank, and test scores, are considered. Freshman applicants may submit either ACT or SAT I scores. Preference is given to applicants in the upper half of their class, with at least 16 units of high school work, a cumulative average of 2.0 or higher, and a minimum ACT composite score of 20 or SAT I scores of at least 520 verbal and 440 mathematics.

High school students may also attend Roosevelt University during the summer between their junior and senior years as well as evenings and weekends during the senior year. A discounted tuition rate is charged for University attendance concurrent with high school attendance. Regular freshman admission requirements must be met in order for students to attend.

Transfer students must have at least a 2.0 cumulative average (on a 4.0 scale). Upon admission, all degree-seeking undergraduate students, including all transfers and adult students, are required to take the Roosevelt University Assessment (RUA).

Application and Information

To complete the admission process, the student must submit an application, an official high school transcript (or GED test scores), official college transcript(s), either the ACT or other standardized test scores, and the nonrefundable $25 application fee. Admission decisions may be expected approximately two weeks after receipt of all necessary records.

For additional information, students should contact:

Office of Admission
Roosevelt University
Chicago Campus
430 South Michigan Avenue
Chicago, Illinois 60605-1395
Telephone: 877-APPLY-RU (toll-free)

Office of Admission
Roosevelt University
Schaumburg Campus
1400 North Roosevelt Boulevard
Schaumburg, Illinois 60173-4348
Telephone: 877-APPLY-RU (toll-free)
World Wide Web: http://www.roosevelt.edu

ROSEMONT COLLEGE

ROSEMONT, PENNSYLVANIA

The College

Founded in 1921, Rosemont College is an independent liberal arts institution in the Catholic tradition. Rosemont's reputation for academic excellence in an intimate setting is its hallmark. Rosemont College's community of students and faculty members are dedicated to developing the intellect and abilities of every student.

Rosemont College welcomes persons of all beliefs. It is committed to excellence and joy in teaching and learning. Rosemont seeks to develop open and critical minds and reasoned moral positions in all members of the community and to assist them in becoming persons capable of independent and reflective thought and action. It seeks also to prepare women and men for the world of work so that they can make a significant contribution.

Rosemont is consistently ranked by *U.S. News & World Report*. It has been named to the John Templeton Foundation Honor Roll for Character-Building Colleges, a designation that recognizes colleges and universities that emphasize character building as an integral part of the college experience.

Rosemont is one college with three schools: the Undergraduate Women's College, the School of Graduate Studies, and the School of Continuing Studies. The nationally acclaimed, traditional Undergraduate Women's College confers the Bachelor of Arts, the Bachelor of Fine Arts, and the Bachelor of Science degrees in twenty-two majors. Rosemont has approximately 6,300 living alumnae, many of whom have been in the vanguard of expanding career and professional opportunities for women. They can be found in high-ranking positions in science and medicine, law, business, education, the social sciences, publishing, and the arts.

Building on its historic commitment to the undergraduate education of women, Rosemont has expanded to include a School of Continuing Studies and a School of Graduate Studies, which are open to both women and men. The School of Continuing Studies offers seven undergraduate degrees and three graduate degrees, all in an accelerated format. Rosemont's School of Graduate Studies offers the Master of Education degree in curriculum and instruction and the Master of Arts in counseling psychology, English, and English and publishing. A Master of Fine Arts degree is offered in creative writing.

In the spirit of Cornelia Connelly, founder of the Society of the Holy Child Jesus, Rosemont is committed to preparing individuals to meet the challenges of the times and to act responsibly and effectively in an ever-changing world. Rosemont College looks forward to meeting the demands of the new century—and beyond.

Rosemont participates in NCAA Division III varsity teams of basketball, field hockey, lacrosse, softball, tennis, and volleyball.

Location

Rosemont's 56-acre campus is located in the town of Rosemont, a suburban historic community with many shops, movie theaters, restaurants, and bookstores. The city of Philadelphia is 11 miles east of Rosemont and just a 20-minute train ride from the campus. Rosemont's proximity to Philadelphia provides students with a vast array of cultural and social opportunities, such as the Philadelphia Museum of Art, the Philadelphia Orchestra, the Pennsylvania Ballet, and various professional sports events, including Phillies, Flyers, and Eagles games. Within the Philadelphia area there are approximately eighty other colleges and universities. Rosemont is ideally located for recreational activities; it is only a short distance from both the Pocono mountains and the New Jersey shore.

Majors and Degrees

Rosemont College awards the Bachelor of Arts, the Bachelor of Fine Arts, and the Bachelor of Science degrees. Majors are offered in the following fields: accounting, biochemistry, biology, business, chemistry, communication, economics, English, French, German, history, history of art, international business, mathematics, philosophy, political science, psychology, religious studies, sociology, Spanish, studio art, and women's studies. Interdisciplinary majors are offered in humanities, Italian studies, and social science. Prelaw and premedical programs and teacher certification for art, early childhood, elementary, secondary, and special education areas are available. Minors are available in most majors in addition to computer science and theater. Students may also choose to pursue a double major or create their own cross-disciplinary individualized major. Other special programs include a dual-degree program in chemical engineering and a transfer nursing program with nearby Villanova University and a cooperative program in information systems and technology with Drexel University.

In addition, Rosemont offers a combined B.A./M.A. in English and publishing and a combined B.A./M.A. in counseling psychology.

Academic Program

To earn a Rosemont undergraduate degree, each candidate must complete 128 credits. In addition to the requirements of a major concentration, all students must complete general requirements. An internship, service-learning, or study-abroad experience is required prior to graduation. During their senior year, all students must successfully complete a comprehensive exam exhibiting competency in their declared major.

Rosemont College offers a joint-admissions medical program with the Drexel University College of Medicine. This program is highly selective, and a December 31 deadline applies.

For students interested in a French and business major, Rosemont offers specialized courses in business French to prepare students for the examination of the Chambre de Commerce et d'Industrie de Paris. The Certificat Pratique de Français Commercial et Économique is awarded to students who successfully complete this exam.

Rosemont offers programs granting certification in the following teaching areas: art education, early childhood education/elementary education, elementary education, secondary education, and special education with a concentration in hearing impaired.

Off-Campus Programs

Through academic exchange programs that expand course offerings, students may take courses at neighboring Villanova University, Eastern University, Arcadia University, Cabrini College, Chestnut Hill College, Gwynedd-Mercy College, Holy Family College, Immaculata University, and Neumann College. The Art Institutes International Exchange Program, which allows studio art candidates to apply for admission into the commercial art program offered at any one of the eight Art Institute International Schools located in Atlanta, Dallas, Denver, Fort Lauderdale, Houston, Philadelphia, Pittsburgh, and Seattle, is also available.

Rosemont students may participate in any of a variety of study-abroad programs. These programs give students the opportunity to combine travel with academic and cultural study. Students receive full credit at Rosemont for course work successfully completed on an approved program. Rosemont, in cooperation with Villanova University, sponsors its own summer study-abroad program to Siena, Italy. This program focuses on course work in studio art, Italian Renaissance art history, and Italian language and literature.

There are many opportunities for full semester internships in various fields of study. Each candidate must be academically qualified and meet the approval of the appropriate faculty member. Fieldwork and practica, as well as summer internships, are also available.

Academic Facilities

The Gertrude Kistler Memorial Library creates a conducive setting for study and research. The library was the first academic building erected on the campus and was renovated in 1998. It houses more than 158,000 volumes, approximately 557 current periodicals, and numerous electronic indexes and databases as well as access to the Internet. The online catalog, the Rosemont Electronic Learning and Library System (TRELLIS), is the basic index to the library's collections. TRELLIS includes a number of computerized periodical indexes and encyclopedias and provides access to the Internet's World Wide Web.

The renovated science building is composed of the Dorothy McKenna Brown Science Building and the McShain Performing Arts Center. The Brown Science Building provides laboratory facilities and lecture rooms for the natural sciences. State-of-the-art equipment includes a phase microscope with video camera and color-TV monitor, physiographs, spectrophotometers, and an environment chamber. The building also houses three electronic classrooms equipped with the latest in Windows-PC and Macintosh technology. Students have access to laser and full-color printers, scanners, zip drives, and CD burners as well as numerous software resources for word processing, desktop publishing, indexing, and graphic arts. The McShain Performing Arts Center is a 413-seat auditorium used for special forums, theatrical performances, and ceremonies.

Costs

For 2003–04, costs for full-time students included tuition, $17,650; room and board, $8000; and general fees, $595.

Financial Aid

Approximately 90 percent of all Rosemont students receive some form of financial aid. Financial aid includes scholarships, grants, loans, and work-study awards. Most financial packages are a combination of various forms of aid. To apply for aid, students are required to submit the Free Application for Federal Student Aid (FAFSA) by March 1.

Faculty

The faculty is one of Rosemont's most important assets. The members are dedicated individuals who believe the student must be engaged to learn; therefore, all classes at Rosemont are small, which lends to the discussion or seminar format. Approximately ninety percent of the faculty members hold either the Ph.D or the highest degree in their field.

Student Government

The student government at Rosemont coordinates the ongoing governing processes to be responsive to the needs and opinions of students, to stimulate change as needed, to provide a range of programs and activities, and to represent students to Rosemont College as a whole.

Admission Requirements

Rosemont College seeks to enroll women interested in the liberal arts and who have the capacity and the desire to pursue a rigorous academic program. Students are considered without regard to race, religion, disability, or ethnic or national origin. A candidate for admission must present a satisfactory record of scholastic ability and personal integrity from an accredited high school as well as acceptable scores on the SAT I. Applicants' records are reviewed by the Admissions Committee. The student must have an official copy of her high school transcript sent to Rosemont's Office of Admissions. An applicant's secondary school preparation should include sixteen college-preparatory courses. For admission to the traditional college program, all applicants are advised to include in their high school program a minimum of 4 units of English, 2 units of foreign language, 2 units of social studies, 2 units of college-preparatory math, and 2 units of laboratory science. Prospective business majors must present additional units of college-preparatory math. Applicants are expected to carry a full academic program during their senior year of high school.

Two recommendations are required in support of the student's application. The applicant should ask her guidance counselor and a teacher to submit recommendations on her behalf and forward them to Rosemont's Office of Admissions. All applicants are required to submit results of the SAT I. The applicant may obtain the registration form for the test from her school or by writing to the College Board, Box 592, Princeton, New Jersey 08540. The code for Rosemont College is 2763. Puerto Rican students may submit scores from the Prueba de Aptitud Académica (PAA) in place of the SAT I. Students may also submit ACT scores. The code for Rosemont College is 3676. More information can be obtained by writing to ACT Registration–81, Box 414, Iowa City, Iowa 53343-0414. A personal interview with a member of the admissions staff is strongly recommended as an important part of the application process. Students who are seriously considering Rosemont should visit the campus to enhance their understanding of the academic and social atmosphere. Prospective students are also encouraged to make arrangements to visit classes, meet Rosemont students, and whenever possible, stay overnight. Arrangements can be made by calling the Office of Admissions.

Application and Information

Applications are accepted on a rolling basis. Those interested in scholarships should apply no later than February 15. To arrange for an interview and a tour, or to receive additional information, students should contact:

Rennie H. Andrews
Dean of Admissions
Rosemont College
1400 Montgomery Avenue
Rosemont, Pennsylvania 19010-1699
Telephone: 610-526-2966
800-331-0708 (toll-free)
E-mail: admissions@rosemont.edu
World Wide Web: http://www.rosemont.edu

Rosemont College—linking strong traditions with the future.

ROWAN UNIVERSITY

GLASSBORO, NEW JERSEY

The University

Rowan University is a selective New Jersey public institution that offers thirty-six undergraduate majors, plus graduate degrees and certificates. The 200-acre campus hosts approximately 6,500 undergraduates in Glassboro, New Jersey, just 17 miles from Philadelphia and central to the major urban areas of the East Coast, including New York City and Washington, D.C. Sixty-five percent of the full-time undergraduate students live on campus.

The University, established in 1923 for teacher training and later known as Glassboro State College, made philanthropic history with the 1992 Rowan $100-million donation. The University consists of six academic colleges—Business, Communication, Engineering, Fine and Performing Arts, Liberal Arts and Sciences, and Education.

The Wilson Music Building is the site of operas, plays, recitals, dance programs, and the Celebrity Concert Series each year. Varsity, intramural, and lifelong sports activities are also an important part of campus life.

Location

The University's main campus is located in the southern New Jersey town of Glassboro. It was because of the University's convenient location, halfway between New York and Washington, D.C., that it was chosen as the site of the historic conference in 1967 between President Johnson and Soviet Premier Kosygin. The town of Glassboro has been named "Summit City" because of that historic Hollybush Summit Conference. Facilities for all forms of surface and air transportation, including Philadelphia International Airport, are within minutes of the campus.

Just 20 minutes from the main campus, Rowan University Camden Campus serves the urban community with emphasis on nontraditional students in three degree programs, plus ESL studies and other services.

Majors and Degrees

The Bachelor of Arts degree is offered in art (areas of specialization in art education and fine arts), collaborative education, communication (areas of specialization in communication studies, journalism and creative writing, public relations, advertising, radio/TV/film, and writing arts), economics, elementary/early childhood education, English, environmental studies, geography, health and exercise science, history, law/justice, liberal studies (American studies and math/science options), mathematics, music, political science, psychology, school nursing, sociology, Spanish, special education, and theater. The Bachelor of Fine Arts degree is awarded in art (areas of specialization in ceramics, drawing, illustration/graphic design, jewelry/metalry, painting, photography, printmaking, puppetry, and sculpture). The Bachelor of Music degree is awarded in jazz studies, performance, theory and composition, and music education. The Bachelor of Science degree is awarded in accounting, biochemistry, biology, business administration (areas of specialization in entrepreneurship, finance, human resource management, management, management information systems, and marketing), chemistry, computer science, engineering (majors in chemical, civil, electrical and computer, and mechanical), mathematics, physical sciences, and physics.

Academic Program

Most degree programs include a 60-semester-hour general education requirement. Some degree programs require fewer semester hours. Students select their general education courses from the following areas of study: communications, science and mathematics, social and behavioral sciences, history, humanities and languages, and fine arts. In addition, most academic departments offering undergraduate majors have specified some general education courses that must be taken by students majoring in that academic area. Each degree program includes individual major requirements and free electives. A minimum of 30 semester hours is required in a major program, but many departments require more.

Students are encouraged to use free electives to establish a second major, a concentration, or a minor; strengthen their major program; or pursue personal interests.

Internships are available to juniors and seniors in most major programs. The University offers work-study opportunities through the academic departments and academic field experiences.

The University calendar is based on the two-semester system with summer sessions.

Off-Campus Programs

Rowan University offers a variety of travel/study programs in which students may participate for a year, a semester, or shorter periods of time. Among these are programs in Australia, the Commonwealth of Independent States, Denmark, England, France, Germany, Scotland, Spain, and Wales.

Academic Facilities

The new library houses more than 350,000 books, multimedia materials, microfiche, microfilm, and documents and subscribes to nearly 2,000 journals, newspapers, and indices. It also provides a selection of Internet-based subscription databases as well as intranetworked CD-ROM subscriptions and free Internet resources. Facilities include private seminar rooms, study carrels equipped for laptop access to the library's database and the Internet, electronic reference rooms, and computer labs. The library is also a repository of U.S. government documents and selected State of New Jersey documents.

Costs

In 2003–04, tuition and fees were $7258 for New Jersey residents and $12,654 for out-of-state students based on flat-rate tuition for full-time undergraduates taking 24 to 36 semester hours per year. Room and board costs for 2003–04 were $7248, based on housing in a double room and a primary meal plan. Apartment-style housing is available on campus for upperclass students in any one of the three University-owned complexes.

Financial Aid

In 2003–04, about 70 percent of all full-time undergraduate students received some form of financial aid. Federal aid is available in the form of Federal Direct Student Loans, Federal Pell Grants, Federal Supplemental Educational Opportunity Grants, and Federal Work-Study Program awards. State aid includes Garden State Scholarships, Educational Opportunity Fund awards, and Tuition Aid Grants. Students should submit a

Free Application for Federal Student Aid (FAFSA) and the Student Aid Report (SAR) by March 15 to be evaluated for the earliest consideration.

Faculty

Rowan University has 356 full-time faculty members. The faculty members' regularly scheduled office hours and participation in virtually all areas of campus governance and operations ensure that they have continual interaction with students. Part-time faculty members, including business leaders, industry representatives, and practicing professionals, provide valuable links with the community and offer knowledge of practical experiences to Rowan University students. The student-faculty ratio is approximately 14:1. All courses are taught by professors, not graduate assistants.

Student Government

The Student Government Association (SGA) is composed entirely of students chosen through campuswide elections. In 2003–04, student officers administered a budget of more than $700,000, derived from student activity fees and receipts. All students who have paid student activity fees are members of the SGA. Free legal advice, personal property insurance, and a tenants' association are some of the SGA's projects. The SGA oversees more than 150 chartered clubs on campus and sponsors intercollegiate athletics, social events, and service activities.

The University administration wholly supports the concept of student rights and student participation in all areas of campus governance.

Admission Requirements

Admission to Rowan University is based on a student's projected ability to complete a degree program, without regard to age, sex, race, color, creed, or national origin. SAT I scores and high school transcripts are required of all freshman applicants.

Applicants are also expected to have completed a minimum of 16 college-preparatory units: 4 units of English, 3 units of college-preparatory mathematics, 2 units of laboratory science, 2 units of social studies, and 5 units representing additional work in at least two of the following areas: history, languages (a minimum of two years), mathematics, and sciences. Exceptions to standards may be made in some individual cases. Highly qualified high school juniors may apply for early admission if they have a recommendation from their high school guidance counselor. Freshmen entering in 2003 ranked in the top 22 percent of their high school classes and attained an average combined SAT I score of 1160.

Admission for transfer students is competitive and offered on a space-available basis. Minimum grade point averages required for admission vary; for most programs, a 2.5 cumulative average is needed. If fewer than 24 college credits have been earned, a transfer applicant must meet freshman admission requirements and send a high school transcript and SAT I scores to Rowan University.

Application and Information

The University application, a $50 application fee, a high school or college transcript, and SAT I results should be forwarded to the Admissions Office. The application deadline for freshman and transfer applicants is March 15, except for transfer applicants to the elementary education program who must apply by February 15. The freshman enrollment deposit must be received by May 1. Students must also submit SAT II: Writing Test scores prior to enrollment. Campus visits are recommended.

For additional information and application forms, students should contact:

Marvin G. Sills
Director of Admissions
Rowan University
Glassboro, New Jersey 08028
Telephone: 856-256-4200
800-447-1165 (toll-free)
E-mail: admissions@rowan.edu
World Wide Web: http://www2.rowan.edu

Rowan Hall, home to the College of Engineering, features state-of-the-art classrooms, laboratories, and sophisticated technology that provides students with a flexible learning environment.

RUTGERS, THE STATE UNIVERSITY OF NEW JERSEY, CAMDEN

CAMDEN, NEW JERSEY

The University

Located in the heart of the University District on the exciting Camden Waterfront, Rutgers-Camden is a vibrant academic community of 5,800 undergraduate and graduate students who work closely with professors who are among the top scholars in their fields. These students enjoy strong success with national employers and in gaining admission to the nation's most prestigious graduate programs.

Rutgers-Camden is the southernmost of the three campuses that comprise New Jersey's flagship public research university: Rutgers, The State University. Faculty members at Rutgers-Camden are selected and promoted based on the same high standards as their peers across every Rutgers campus, and Camden students enjoy the same access to Rutgers' system-wide research library and state-of-the-art computing network.

Founded in 1926 as the South Jersey Law School and joined by the College of South Jersey in 1927, the Camden campus joined Rutgers in 1950. Today, Rutgers is a member of the prestigious Association of American Universities (a group comprising the top research universities in North America) and is accredited by the Middle States Association of Colleges and Schools. Rutgers-Camden is home to southern New Jersey's only law school and its first internationally accredited business school.

Students seeking the opportunity to work closely with world-class scholars select Rutgers-Camden for its unique combination of "small college" ambience, with day and evening classes offered during the traditional fall and spring semesters and a smaller schedule of offerings during abbreviated winter and summer sessions.

Located at the foot of the Benjamin Franklin Bridge, Rutgers-Camden is directly across the Delaware River from Philadelphia; in fact, Rutgers-Camden is the four-year college closest to the Liberty Bell. On-campus housing is available for 550 students on a first-come basis. Some students choose in live in the comfortable southern New Jersey communities located along the PATCO Speedline, which has a station located one block from campus and offers a very convenient option for commuting; the train also brings Philadelphia residents to campus. A light-rail system stops on campus and is an easy commuting option for residents of northern counties. The campus is accessible by all major regional transportation arteries.

A spacious Campus Center offers dining areas as well as offices for student organizations. A University District bookstore offers comprehensive service directly adjacent to the campus. The gymnasium offers a complete health club experience, including squash and racquetball courts, strength and cardio conditioning, and an Olympic-size swimming pool.

On-campus dining is available through a dining hall and the Courtyard Café restaurant. An on-campus Starbucks provides a relaxing gathering spot for students. In addition, a number of small eateries surround the campus.

The Rutgers-Camden Center for the Arts brings established and emerging performers to the campus and offers a series of intriguing exhibitions in the Stedman Gallery. The Office of Student Affairs works with students to provide a diverse schedule of activities throughout the year. The Rutgers-Camden Scarlet Raptors compete in NCAA Division III sports, with twelve competitive men's and women's teams.

Location

The metro Philadelphia/Delaware Valley region is a thriving area with many opportunities for careers, research, and social activities. The city of Camden is home to such notable attractions as the Tweeter Center, which books top headline performers on a regular basis; Campbell's Field, a Rutgers-owned stadium that is home to the Camden Riversharks minor league baseball team; and the New Jersey State Aquarium, just to name a few. Philadelphia is an easy commute by car, train, and ferry and offers world-class museums, cafés, restaurants, shops, clubs, theaters, and much more. Atlantic City and New Jersey's spectacular beaches are less than an hour away, and New York City and Washington, D.C., are both within a 3-hour drive. International travel is easy, courtesy of Philadelphia International Airport, which is located 15 minutes from campus.

Majors and Degrees

Rutgers-Camden awards the following baccalaureate degrees: Bachelor of Arts, Bachelor of Science, and Bachelor of Hospitality Management. First-year students also may apply to five-year programs leading to graduate degrees and programs that allow transition to Rutgers' College of Engineering or College of Pharmacy in the third year.

Majors are offered in accounting, African-American studies, American studies, anthropology, art, art history, biology, biomedical technology, chemistry, childhood studies, computer science, criminal justice, dance, economics, English, film studies, finance, fine arts, French, German, history, hospitality management, independent/individualized studies, Latin American studies, liberal studies, management, marketing, mathematics, music, nursing, philosophy, physics, political science, psychology, religion, general science, social work, sociology, Spanish, statistics, statistics/mathematics, theater arts, urban studies, visual arts, and women's and gender studies

Dual-degree programs include bachelor's/M.P.A, bachelor's/J.D., and bachelor's/M.A. in criminal justice.

Academic Programs

Each college or school establishes its own admission, scholastic standing, and graduation requirements, and each offers specific academic programs that reflect the mission and philosophy of the college or school. Special academic programs include honors courses, tracks, and programs; ROTC; national honors societies; undergraduate research; graduate course work; internships; cooperative education; and service learning. The academic year runs on a two-semester schedule, from September to December and from January to May. Limited class offerings are also available during summer and winter sessions.

Off-Campus Programs

Students can earn credit through the International Studies Program, which offers classes in numerous countries in Africa, Europe, Asia, and South America. The nationally recognized Citizenship and Service Education program offers a wide array of credit-bearing service learning experiences. Internships and other off-campus learning and research arrangements are routinely made between Rutgers and area businesses, nonprofits, and colleges and universities. The School of Business offers an aggressive internship program, while the Department of Nursing places students in clinical rotations at metro Philadelphia's top hospitals and health centers.

Academic Facilities

Rutgers-Camden is home to the Paul Robeson Library. It offers direct access to the Rutgers University Library system, which has holdings of more than 3 million volumes and is ranked among the nation's top research libraries. The library also offers online access to thousands of digital research resources. An on-campus Law Library serves the Rutgers-Camden School of Law. The RUNet communications infrastructure project continues to upgrade the University's communications network to support instruction, research, and outreach. Through RUNet, residence halls are wired for Internet, phone, and cable TV. Wireless service is available for students in the Campus Center, with plans to extend this service elsewhere on campus. Numerous student computing labs are located in virtually every academic building on campus.

Rutgers-Camden's outstanding academic facilities include an excellent performing arts theater; a state-of-the-art focus-group study facility; numerous technology-enhanced classrooms; computer graphic arts and animation labs; and a research facility in the heart of New Jersey's Pine Barrens. Technology available to assist undergraduate research includes a scanning electron microscope, a 300-MHz nuclear magnetic resonance spectrometer, and an upgraded fiber-optic network for student and faculty research.

Costs

Costs for the 2003–04 academic year included state resident annual tuition and fees of $7556. For nonresidents, annual tuition and fees were $15,474. Typical room and board charges were $6852. Part-time tuition (University College) was $208 per credit for residents and $423 per credit for nonresidents.

Financial Aid

A wide variety of merit and need-based financial aid is available to students at Rutgers. University-wide, undergraduate students received more than $235 million in federal and state grants and loans, work/study jobs, and university scholarships in 2002–03, with an average first-year award of $8658. More than 80 percent of Rutgers-Camden undergraduates receive financial assistance. Merit and need-based scholarships are offered by the University and by individual colleges and schools.

Faculty

There are a total of 260 full-time faculty members, 99 percent of whom hold terminal degrees. The student-faculty ratio is 14:1. Senior faculty members regularly teach undergraduate courses and include undergraduates in their research projects.

Student Government

The university-wide Rutgers University Senate is a deliberative body of faculty members, students, administrators, and alumni that meets seven or eight times during the academic year to consider matters of general University interest and make recommendations to the University administration. Student-run governing associations include Student Governing Association, Campus Activities Board, and School of Business Student Congress. Each has its own mission, goals, and operating procedures.

Admission Requirements

Admission to Rutgers' colleges and schools is competitive and selective, with primary emphasis on academic promise as demonstrated by grades; grade point average; rank in class; strength of the candidate's academic program as evidenced by the number of academic, honors, and Advanced Placement courses completed; and standardized test scores. High school course requirements vary by the individual college or school, but all require a combination of sixteen academic courses. In addition to SAT and/or ACT test scores, a completed undergraduate application form and official high school transcript are required. Advanced Placement and/or degree credit are awarded for AP grades of 5 and 4.

Application and Information

Candidates for admission submit a single application for consideration at any three Rutgers colleges or schools. Applying online to meet priority application dates is strongly urged. Priority dates are November 1 for spring admission for first-year and transfer students, December 1 for fall admission for first-year students, and January 15 for fall admission for transfer students. Letters of recommendation are not required. Personal interviews are not required and are not granted. Candidates may track the status of their applications and required credentials online.

Office of University Undergraduate Admissions
Rutgers, The State University of New Jersey
406 Penn Street
Camden, New Jersey 08102-1400
Telephone: 856-225-6133
World Wide Web: http://camden.rutgers.edu

RUTGERS, THE STATE UNIVERSITY OF NEW JERSEY, NEWARK

NEWARK, NEW JERSEY

The University

Newark, New Jersey's largest city, was a college town long before there was a Newark campus of Rutgers, the State University of New Jersey. It was the first home of the College of New Jersey, which later became Princeton University. Two law schools, a business school, and two colleges of arts and sciences called Newark home early in the 1900s. A series of mergers among these five institutions led to the creation of the University of Newark in the 1930s. Over the next decade, the college broadened its curriculum—including adding a nursing department—and was awarded a Phi Beta Kappa chapter. Then, in 1946, the University of Newark became the northern campus of Rutgers. Nearly sixty years later, Rutgers-Newark still reflects the academic depth and breadth of its founding schools and remains committed to its core mission of educational excellence with broad access, but it has also developed and changed a great deal since its founding.

Today, Rutgers-Newark provides a broad spectrum of undergraduate and graduate programs on a beautifully landscaped, 37-acre, fiber-optically wired urban campus in New Jersey's largest city. Its seven schools encompass the liberal arts as well as business, law, criminal justice, and nursing—many at both the undergraduate and graduate levels. This allows Rutgers-Newark to offer the best in undergraduate arts and science education as well as first-rate preprofessional and professional education to nearly 10,500 students. Most of these—approximately 6,756 students—are full-time and part-time undergraduates, including 3,854 women and 2,902 men, as of spring 2004. Sixty-seven percent of students are between the ages of 18 and 23, and 94 percent are New Jersey residents. Residents of twenty-eight states, the District of Columbia, the Commonwealth of Puerto Rico, and fifty-five other countries are enrolled in Rutgers-Newark. *U.S. News & World Report* consistently rates Rutgers-Newark as the nation's most diverse national university.

This combination of top-ranked academics and cultural diversity creates an academically challenging, rigorous learning environment that is also culturally stimulating, ensuring that students are well prepared for the demands of today's global society.

The modern campus has thirty-one buildings, including a state-of-the-art Center for Law and Justice, a Center for Molecular and Behavioral Neuroscience, the Management Education Center, the John Cotton Dana Library, the Paul Robeson Campus Center, and the Golden Dome Athletic Center. Most students still commute to campus, but more than 800 undergraduates expand their college experience by living in the on-campus residence halls, and many students live nearby in the University Heights district. The campus has a student center; an art gallery; a performance theater; two residence halls for undergraduates; dining facilities; two landscaped plazas where students can study, dine, or relax; an outdoor track and soccer/baseball field; and an athletic center with pool, racquetball and tennis courts, two gymnasiums, and workout rooms.

Location

Newark is, more than ever, a college town—home to three other major institutions of higher education. Rutgers and the other institutions enjoy close collaborative relationships, in some cases sharing academic programs and departments. Rutgers students and their counterparts at the New Jersey Institute of Technology can cross-register on both campuses, affording Rutgers students unique opportunities to broaden their studies through special courses not offered at this institution. All three institutions work together to ensure that their University Heights neighborhood is a vibrant community that contributes scientific, cultural, and educational resources to the city. Rutgers is actively working with the city and local organizations on exciting plans to bring more housing, stores, and restaurants to Newark.

Downtown Newark is New Jersey's legal, financial, and business center. It is home to major corporations, such as Prudential Financial, Verizon, IDT, and Public Service Electric & Gas, that work with the University to provide intern opportunities, as well as postgraduation employment possibilities, to Rutgers-Newark students.

Newark is enjoying an economic, cultural, and recreational upsurge, boasting attractions such as the Newark Museum, the New Jersey Performing Arts Center, the Newark Library, and the New Jersey Historical Society as well as the Newark Symphony Hall. Sports fans can take in a minor league baseball game, featuring Newark's own Bears team, at Riverfront Stadium or head over to the Meadowlands Sports Complex, which is home of the football Giants, the Stanley Cup–winning New Jersey Devils hockey team, and the New Jersey Nets basketball team.

The campus itself boasts an arts schedule that includes visual arts exhibitions; concerts of jazz, classical, folk, and contemporary music; theater productions; guest lecturers; films; and seminars. Campus life also includes intercollegiate sporting events and recreational activities such as barbecues and campus fairs, dances, and poetry slamdowns.

In Newark's famous Ironbound neighborhood, Portuguese culture flavors the neighborhoods and businesses, including outstanding Portuguese, Spanish, and Italian restaurants.

Since Newark is only a short train trip or drive to Manhattan, New York's nightlife and culture are less than 30 minutes away.

Majors and Degrees

Rutgers-Newark offers forty-seven majors and forty-four minors leading to Bachelor of Arts (B.A.), Bachelor of Fine Arts (B.F.A.), and Bachelor of Science (B.S.) degrees. Rutgers-Newark students also may apply for special dual-major programs with the New Jersey Institute of Technology (NJIT), special engineering programs with either Rutgers College of Engineering or NJIT, joint B.A./M.B.A. programs from the Rutgers Business School, and dual-admission programs with the New Jersey Medical School and the Rutgers School of Law-Newark. Detailed information is available in the Rutgers-Newark catalog or at http://ruweb.rutgers.edu/catalogs/.

Rutgers-Newark also offers both a summer program of studies and a winter (intersession) program. Separate catalogs for these programs are at http://ruweb.rutgers.edu/catalogs/.

Majors offered are accounting, African American and African studies, allied health technologies, American studies, ancient and medieval civilizations, anthropology, art, visual arts, biology, botany, Central and Eastern European studies, chemistry, clinical laboratory studies, computer science, criminal justice, economics, English, environmental sciences, finance, French, geology, geoscience engineering, German, history, human-computer interaction, information systems, interdisciplinary studies, journalism and media studies, management, marketing, mathematics, applied mathematics, music, philosophy, physics, applied physics, political science, Portuguese and Lusophone world studies, psychology, Puerto Rican studies, science, technology and society, social work, sociology, Spanish, theater arts and television, women's studies, and zoology.

Academic Programs

Each of the four undergraduate schools establishes its own degree requirements, course offerings, and admission requirements in accord with each school's mission and philosophy.

Special programs include the Honors College, the Educational Opportunity Fund, ROTC, the High School Scholars Program, joint-degree programs with New Jersey Institute of Technology and the University of Medicine and Dentistry, and five-year programs that allow students to earn both undergraduate and graduate degrees in specific disciplines, including criminal justice, business, public administration, and medicine.

The academic year consists of two semesters: September to December and January through May. Rutgers-Newark also offers both an extensive summer program of studies and a winter (intersession) program of studies. A separate catalog that lists these courses is available at http://ruweb.rutgers.edu/catalogs/.

Off-Campus Programs

Rutgers offers a program of junior-year studies in twelve foreign countries. Rutgers also participates in the Citizenship and Service Educational Program (CASE), which offers for-credit service learning opportunities. In addition, Newark and New York–area businesses, as well as nonprofit organizations, offer students a broad range of cooperative education and internship opportunities.

Academic Facilities

The campus's eleven academic buildings include the Center for Molecular and Behavioral Neuroscience, where internationally recognized research is conducted in brain functions; the Management Education Center; and the Center for Law and Justice. The John Cotton Dana Library offers state-of-the-art information access, extensive holdings, computer workstations, media stations, and the world's most extensive jazz archives. The campus is home to several centers for specialized scholarly studies, among them the Joseph C. Cornwall Center for Metropolitan Studies; the Center for Global Change and Governance; the Center for Integration Management, Integration and Connectivity; the Prudential Business Ethics Center; and the Center for Public Security.

Costs

For the 2003–04 academic year, state resident annual tuition and fees were approximately $7927, and nonresident annual tuition and fees were $14,441. Typical room and board costs were approximately $7711. Part-time tuition (University College) was $203 per credit for residents and $415 per credit for nonresidents.

Financial Aid

A wide variety of merit- and need-based financial aid is offered by the University and its individual colleges and schools. University-wide, undergraduate students received more than $235 million in federal and state grants and loans, work-study jobs, and University scholarships in 2002–03, with an average first-year award of $8658. More than 60 percent of Rutgers undergraduates receive financial assistance.

Faculty

Of the 449 faculty members, 99 percent are full-time. Faculty members are recruited based on both their scholarship and their commitment to teaching. Ninety-nine percent hold a Ph.D. or J.D. The student-faculty ratio is 14:1.

Student Government

The Newark College of Arts and Sciences, the College of Nursing, and University College-Newark each have a Student Governing Association (SGA) that serves as a liaison between the University administration and students. SGA members also serve as members of committees that deal with policies and procedures for each college and the University proper.

Admission Requirements

Admission to Rutgers' colleges and schools is competitive and selective, with primary emphasis on academic promise as demonstrated by grades; grade point average; rank in class; strength of the candidate's academic program as evidenced by the number of academic, honors, and Advanced Placement (AP) courses completed; and standardized test scores. High school course requirements vary by the individual college or school, but all require a combination of sixteen academic courses. In addition to SAT and/or ACT test scores, a completed undergraduate application form and official high school transcripts are required. Advanced Placement and/or degree credit are awarded for AP grades of 5 and 4.

Application and Information

Candidates for admission submit a single application for consideration at any three Rutgers colleges or schools. Applying online to meet priority application dates is strongly urged. Priority dates are November 1 for spring first-year and transfer students; December 1 for fall first-year students, and January 15 for fall transfer students. Letters of recommendation are not required. Personal interviews are not required and are not granted, except for Mason Gross School of the Arts, which requires a portfolio review or talent assessment. Candidates may track the status of their applications and required credentials online.

Office of Graduate and Undergraduate Admissions
Room 100
Rutgers, The State University of New Jersey
249 University Avenue
Newark, New Jersey 07102
Telephone: 973-353-5205
World Wide Web: http://admissions.rutgers.edu

RUTGERS, THE STATE UNIVERSITY OF NEW JERSEY, NEW BRUNSWICK/ PISCATAWAY

PISCATAWAY, NEW JERSEY

The University

Founded in 1766 as Queens College (later Rutgers College), the eighth college established in the American colonies, Rutgers has been preparing leaders of local, national, and international stature for more than two centuries. Rutgers today is New Jersey's flagship public research university, is a member of the prestigious Association of American Universities (a group comprising the top research universities in North America), and is accredited by the Middle States Association of Colleges and Schools.

With twelve schools offering more than ninety undergraduate majors, students choose Rutgers for all the advantages of a small school and all the resources of a leading research university. The liberal arts colleges are Rutgers College, Douglass College, Livingston College, and University College. The professional schools are Cook College, Mason Gross School of the Arts, Ernest Mario School of Pharmacy, Rutgers Business School, School of Engineering, Edward J. Bloustein School of Planning and Public Policy, School of Management and Labor Relations, and School of Communication, Information and Library Studies. Each has a unique culture, personality, and undergraduate enrollment that ranges from more than 10,000 at Rutgers College to about 600 at Mason Gross School of the Arts. Extensive graduate programs are also offered.

In fall 2002, 25,478 full time undergraduates were enrolled at the New Brunswick/Piscataway campus, including 13,460 women and 12,018 men, three quarters of whom were between the ages of 18 and 21. University-wide, 90 percent of Rutgers undergraduates are New Jersey residents. Residents of all twenty-one New Jersey counties, all fifty of the United States, and 124 nations of the world are enrolled at Rutgers.

Rutgers has an extensive network of housing, restaurants, museums, student centers, cultural centers, student clubs and publications, parks, hiking trails, recreational facilities, and more. The Division of Housing in New Brunswick houses approximately 13,000 undergraduate and graduate students on five residential campuses. Campus housing is allocated on a first-come, first-served basis and is generally assigned according to the undergraduate college in which one enrolls. On-campus housing is complemented by a lively fraternity and sorority scene and by off-campus housing in privately owned apartments and houses.

The campus offers a wide array of dining options that include meal-plan dining halls, food courts, snack bars, cafés, and concessions. Meal plan options include location, menu, and the number of meals. Take-out service is available. Valid meal cards may be used at any of the five dining halls on campus. Weekday hours of operation are from 7 a.m. to 8 p.m. Weekend hours vary.

The birthplace of college football, Rutgers has a proud past in producing outstanding scholar-athletes and is the alma mater of dozens of athletes who have distinguished themselves on America's national, Olympic, and professional sports teams. Recreational and athletic activities are available on every campus. Rutgers–New Brunswick/Piscataway participates in the NCAA Division I Big East Conference with twenty-five competitive men's and women's teams.

Rutgers offers numerous services to help students get the most out of their time spent "on the banks of the Old Raritan." Career counseling, learning resource centers, health services, academic advising, undergraduate research, and leadership training are just a small sampling of available services. Alumni say of Rutgers that its academic, cultural, recreational, and social opportunities are endless; students just have to jump in and take Rutgers for all they can.

Location

The greater New Brunswick/Piscataway area provides a perfect complement to Rutgers' academic environment. The city of New Brunswick, with its small-city feel, has fine restaurants, theaters, shops, clubs, taverns, cafés, and more, while many of Rutgers' academic, residential, and sports facilities are located just across the Raritan River in suburban Piscataway. New Brunswick is easily accessible by train to all eastern corridor cities, is 50 minutes by train from New York or Philadelphia, is less than an hour from the New Jersey shore, and is a short 40-minute trip from campus by train or car to Newark Liberty International Airport.

Majors and Degrees

Rutgers awards the following baccalaureate degrees: Bachelor of Arts, Bachelor of Fine Arts, Bachelor of Music, and Bachelor of Science.

Majors are offered in accounting; Africana studies; agricultural science; American studies; animal science; anthropology; applied sciences in engineering; art history; astrophysics; biochemistry; biological sciences; biomathematics; biotechnology; cell biology and neuroscience; chemistry; Chinese; classics; communication; comparative literature; computer science; criminal justice; dance; East Asian languages and area studies; economics; engineering (biomedical, bioresource, ceramic, chemical, civil, electrical and computer, industrial, and mechanical); English; environmental and business economics; environmental planning and design; environmental policy, institutions, and behavior; environmental sciences; evolutionary anthropology; exercise science and sport studies; finance; food science; French; genetics and microbiology; geography; geological sciences; German; history; history/French, history/political science; independent/individualized; information technology and informatics; Italian; Jewish studies; journalism and media studies; labor studies and employment relations; Latin American studies; linguistics; management; management science and information systems; marine sciences; marketing; mathematics; medical technology; medieval studies; meteorology; Middle Eastern studies; molecular biology and biochemistry; music; natural resource management; nursing; nutritional sciences; philosophy; physics; plant science; political science; Portuguese; psychology; public health; Puerto Rican and Hispanic Caribbean studies; religion; Russian; Russian and Central and East European studies; social work; sociology; Spanish; statistics; statistics/mathematics; theater arts; urban studies; visual arts; and women's and gender studies.

Certificate programs are offered in twenty-seven areas, ranging from behavioral pharmacology to international studies to urban planning. Dual-degree programs include bachelor's/M.D., bachelor's/M.B.A., bachelor's/M.Ed., bachelor's/M.P.A., bachelor's/M.P.H., bachelor's/M.P.P., B.A./B.S, B.A./B.S. (engineering), and bachelor's/M.A. in criminal justice.

Academic Programs

Each college or school establishes its own admission, scholastic standing, and graduation requirements, and each offers specific academic programs that reflect the mission and philosophy of the college or school. Special academic programs include honors courses, tracks, and programs; ROTC; national honors societies; undergraduate research; graduate course work; internships; cooperative education; and service learning. The academic year runs on a two-semester schedule, from September to December, and from January to May. Limited class offerings are also available during summer and winter sessions.

Off-Campus Arrangements

Students can earn credit during Study Abroad offered in eighteen countries. The nationally acclaimed Citizenship and Service Education program offers a wide array of credit-bearing service-learning experiences. Cooperative Education offers paid work experience that is also credit-bearing. Internships and other off-campus learning and research arrangements are routinely made between Rutgers and area businesses, nonprofit organizations, and colleges and universities.

Academic Facilities

Every Rutgers campus in New Brunswick/Piscataway has a library, a student center, a recreational center, a health center, computer labs, and dining halls. With holdings of more than 3 million volumes, the Rutgers University libraries rank among the nation's top research libraries. The system includes twenty-six libraries, centers, reading rooms, and RU-Online, a digital library. The RUNet communications infrastructure project continues to upgrade the University's communications network to support instruction, research, and outreach. Through RUNet, most residence halls are wired for Internet, phone, and cable TV. Rutgers' outstanding academic facilities run the gamut, from a state-of-the-art spinal cord injury research center to supercomputers to performing arts venues to experimental agricultural fields.

Costs

Costs for the 2003–04 academic year included state resident annual tuition and fees of $7927 (higher for Cook College and the Schools of Pharmacy and Engineering) and typical room and board of $7711. For nonresidents, annual tuition and fees were $14,441 (higher for Cook College and the Schools of Pharmacy and Engineering) and typical room and board was $7711. Part-time tuition (University College) was $203 per credit for residents and $415 per credit for nonresidents.

Financial Aid

A wide variety of merit and need-based financial aid is available to students at Rutgers, offered by the University and its individual colleges and schools. University-wide, undergraduate students received more than $235 million in federal and state grants and loans, work/study jobs, and University scholarships in 2002–03, with an average first-year award of $8658. More than 60 percent of Rutgers undergraduates receive financial assistance.

Faculty

There are 2,179 faculty members at Rutgers, 69 percent of whom are full-time and 99 percent with terminal degrees. The student-faculty ratio is 14:1. Senior faculty members regularly teach undergraduate courses and include undergraduates in their research projects.

Student Government

The University-wide Rutgers University Senate is a deliberative body of faculty members, students, administrators, and alumni that meets seven or eight times during the academic year to consider matters of general University interest and make recommendations to the University administration. Student-run governing associations include Cook College Council, Douglass College Governing Association, Engineering Governing Council, Livingston College Governing Association, Mason Gross School of the Arts Governing Association, Pharmacy Governing Council, Rutgers College Governing Association, and University College Governing Association. Each association has its own mission, goals, and operating procedures.

Admissions Requirements

Admission to Rutgers' colleges and schools is competitive and selective, with primary emphasis on academic promise as demonstrated by grades; grade point average; rank in class; strength of the candidate's academic program as evidenced by the number of academic, honors, and Advanced Placement (AP) courses completed; and standardized test scores. High school course requirements vary by the individual college or school but all require a combination of sixteen academic courses. In addition to SAT and/or ACT test scores, a completed undergraduate application form and official high school transcript are required. Advanced Placement and/or degree credit are awarded for AP grades of 5 and 4.

Application and Information

Candidates for admission submit a single application for consideration at any three Rutgers colleges or schools. Applying online to meet priority applications dates is strongly urged. Priority dates are November 1 for spring first-year and transfer students, December 1 for fall first-year students, and January 15 for fall transfer students. Letters of recommendation are not required. Personal interviews are not required and are not granted, except for Mason Gross School of the Arts, which requires a portfolio review or talent assessment. Candidates may apply online and track the status of their applications and required credentials online.

Office of University Undergraduate Admissions
Room 202
Rutgers, The State University of New Jersey
65 Davidson Road
Piscataway, New Jersey 08854-8097
Telephone: 732-932-INFO (Campus Information Services)
World Wide Web: http://admissions.rutgers.edu

SACRED HEART UNIVERSITY

FAIRFIELD, CONNECTICUT

The University

Sacred Heart University, established in 1963, is a coeducational independent institution of higher learning in the Catholic intellectual tradition whose primary objective is to prepare men and women to live in and make their contributions to the human community. The University aims to assist in the development of people who are knowledgeable of self, rooted in faith, educated in mind, compassionate in heart, responsive to social and civic obligations, and able to respond to an ever-changing world. Sacred Heart University is committed to combining education for life with preparation for professional excellence.

A ten-year strategic plan provides a road map for the University as it strives to meet the needs of today's students. The plan calls for the construction of new facilities as well as the implementation of new academic, athletic, and social programs. Seven residence halls have opened in the last ten years. Three new residence halls will open in fall 2004. A $17-million health and recreation complex opened in 1997. In addition, the University was one of the first Catholic colleges to introduce a student mobile computing program, providing new students with a wireless Dell notebook computer.

The current undergraduate enrollment includes approximately 3,100 full-time students. Extracurricular activities include fraternities, sororities, student government, the student newspaper, the student yearbook, a student radio station, academic clubs in almost every area of study, the debate club, the International Club, La Hispanidad, theater, dance, and intramural sports programs. Sacred Heart University offers men's and women's competition in NCAA Division I baseball, basketball, bowling, crew, cross-country, equestrian, fencing, field hockey, football, golf, ice hockey, lacrosse, soccer, softball, swimming and diving, tennis, track and field (indoor and outdoor), volleyball, and wrestling.

Sacred Heart University is committed to providing students with extensive services to complement their education. The University Learning Center offers tutoring and assistance.

In addition to its bachelor's degree programs, the University offers nine graduate degree programs: Master of Arts in Religious Studies (M.A.R.S.), Master of Arts in Teaching (M.A.T.), Master of Business Administration (M.B.A.), Master of Science in Nursing (M.S.N.), Master of Science (M.S.) in chemistry, Master of Science in computer science and information technology, Master of Science in occupational therapy, the Master of Science in geriatric rehabilitation and wellness, and the Doctor of Physical Therapy (D.P.T.).

Location

Ideally located in Fairfield County in southwestern Connecticut, Sacred Heart University is 1 hour northeast of New York City, 2½ hours southwest of Boston, and 1 hour southwest of Hartford. More than half of the 56-acre campus is surrounded by a thirty-six-hole golf course.

Opportunities for internships and co-op programs are extensive due to the number of corporate headquarters located throughout Fairfield County. Sacred Heart University's neighbors include the world headquarters for General Electric as well as the Discovery Museum of Science and Industry.

Majors and Degrees

Sacred Heart University offers Bachelor of Arts and Bachelor of Science degrees. Programs of study in allied health include athletic training, exercise science, nursing, occupational therapy, and physical therapy. The occupational therapy program and the physical therapy program are six-year B.S./M.S. programs. In the arts and sciences, the following areas of study are available: art, biology, chemistry, communications/media studies, communications technology, criminal justice, education, English, environmental science, French (minor only), global studies, history, Italian (minor only), mathematics, music (minor only), philosophy, political science, psychology, religious studies, social work, sociology, Spanish, and women's studies (minor only). In business, the University offers accounting, business administration, computer science, economics, finance, and sport management.

Preprofessional programs are available in dentistry, law, medicine, optometry, pharmacy, podiatry, and veterinary medicine.

Special programs include cooperative education, educational certification programs in elementary and secondary education, English as a second language, the Honors Program, internships, legislative internships, and study abroad.

Academic Program

A strong liberal arts core forms the basis for all curricula. Academic course work is divided into four colleges—the College of Arts and Sciences, the College of Business, the College of Education and Health Professions, and the University College. The academic year consists of two 15-week semesters. Both day and evening courses are available.

Candidates for the bachelor's degree must complete at least 120 credits, with a minimum of 30 credits taken at the University. The baccalaureate curriculum is made up of five components: the required core (18 credits), the elective core (30–32 credits), the B.A./B.S. requirements (6–8 credits), the major field (30–58 credits), and electives (4–36 credits).

Off-Campus Programs

Through the Internship Program, students combine employment in business, industry, government, or social service agencies with classroom work and receive academic credit for learning derived from the work experience. Cooperative education opportunities are also offered within various departments, such as accounting, communications/media studies, criminal justice, political science, psychology, social work, and sociology. Through a summer internship program, students may be employed in an area related to their major and their career goals. The Career Development Office places 95 percent of University students in a full-time job or graduate school.

Academic Facilities

The University's library contains more than 164,000 volumes, 716 periodical titles, and 110,000 nonprint items such as videotapes, audiocassettes, phonodiscs, microforms, filmstrips, and slide sets. It also provides on-line database searching services. The Art Department includes studios for painting, design, drawing, and illustration. Science facilities include four biology labs, a climate-controlled greenhouse, a microbiology preparation lab, and six chemistry labs. The modern foreign language laboratory is state-of-the-art. The campus also houses an 850-seat theater, an art gallery, and a professional radio station.

Sacred Heart University is in the seventh year of its Student Mobile Computing Program. Full-time students receive a Dell computer. The campus has been transformed into a fully networked environment. Sacred Heart University is one of the first higher educational institutions in the country to deploy a wireless computer network. The mission of the University calls people to combine education for life with preparation for professional excellence. Sacred Heart University believes that computer literacy is a necessary component of that preparation. Therefore, the University is committed to a system in which students can carry the laptop to class, to the library, and to their residence hall.

Costs

Costs for 2003–04 were $20,220 for full-time undergraduate tuition (includes laptop computer and fees), and $8910 for room and board. The cost of books is estimated to be $600 per year.

Financial Aid

Sacred Heart University maintains a strong commitment to provide higher education to as many students as possible by making available scholarships, grants, loans, and part-time employment. Financial aid packages are developed by combining Sacred Heart University's own resources with a variety of federal and state financial aid programs. Eighty-five percent of all students receive some form of financial assistance.

Any undergraduate or graduate student who is enrolled in the University on at least a part-time basis (6 credit hours per semester) is eligible for consideration. Emphasis is placed on students who are enrolled in a full-time degree program; part-time awards are limited. Applicants for aid must submit the Free Application for Federal Student Aid (FAFSA) and the CSS PROFILE to the College Scholarship Service on or before February 15.

The University offers several sources of financial aid, including academic scholarships, Connecticut Stafford Loans, and Federal Supplemental Educational Opportunity Grants. A Family Allowance is available when 2 or more members of the same family attend the University. Deferred-payment plans and endowed scholarships are also awarded. Employment within the University is awarded under the terms of the Federal Work-Study Program. The Office of Career Development maintains a list of part-time jobs in the local area. Further information can be obtained from the Dean of University Student Financial Assistance.

Faculty

The student-faculty ratio is 12:1. There are 392 faculty members, 162 of whom are full-time. Eighty-two percent have terminal degrees in their field, and 44 percent have tenure. Many faculty members are involved in research, writing, or production, yet their primary focus is on teaching. Close communication between students and faculty members is encouraged. All students are assigned faculty advisers within their major field.

Student Government

Students play a major role in planning and decision making. Student Government representatives and class officers are concerned with improving the University and working for the needs of their classmates. In addition to sponsoring many functions, the Student Government serves as a liaison between the administration/staff and the student body.

Admission Requirements

Sacred Heart University is small enough to work with each student individually throughout the admissions process. The University is committed to enrolling a diverse, highly qualified, and well-motivated student body. Candidates for admission must demonstrate their ability to perform academically and contribute significantly to the life of the University. High school seniors should submit an official high school transcript, SAT I or ACT scores, one letter of recommendation, an essay, and a completed application. Transfer students should submit an official transcript from all previously attended colleges, a high school transcript, two letters of recommendation, an essay, and a completed application.

Application and Information

Full-time students may enroll in either the fall or the spring semester. All applicants must submit a completed application, all necessary credentials, and an application fee of $50. Applications for the Early Decision Program must be received by October 1 for an October 15 notification date or December 1 for a December 15 notification date. Applications for Priority Admissions must be received by February 1 for an April 1 notification date. All other applications are considered on a rolling admission basis; candidates are notified of the admission decision as soon as all credentials have been received and reviewed.

Inquiries or application materials should be sent to:

Dean of Undergraduate Admissions
Sacred Heart University
5151 Park Avenue
Fairfield, Connecticut 06825-1000
Telephone: 203-371-7880
E-mail: guastellek@sacredheart.edu
World Wide Web: http://www.sacredheart.edu

ST. AMBROSE UNIVERSITY
DAVENPORT, IOWA

The University

St. Ambrose offers all of the advantages needed for a successful college experience and a bright future—a great selection of classes, top-of-the-line resources, professors who challenge and encourage, and the kind of people who will become friends for life. The student body comprises more than 3,400 (53 percent women, 47 percent men), all of whom acquire intellectual awareness for lifelong self-education.

St. Ambrose has been providing this style of education, one that nurtures the spirit while training the mind, for nearly 125 years. Founded in 1882, the University was named for St. Ambrose, the fourth-century saint and bishop of Milan, who was a doctor, scholar, author, orator, and teacher.

Today, the campus comprises more than 40 acres in a residential section of Davenport, with twenty-six buildings, including historic Ambrose Hall. Student housing at St. Ambrose, the best in the region, combines the comforts of home with the privileges of independence for more than 1,100 students who live on campus. Apartment-style residence halls have kitchen-equipped units for groups of 4 and 6 students and private bedrooms, and other halls provide extras such as semiprivate bathrooms and study rooms on each floor. A new residence hall for freshmen and sophomores is scheduled to open in fall 2004.

At the graduate level, the University offers master's degrees in accounting, business administration, business administration in health care, criminal justice, disability services, educational leadership, information technology management, juvenile justice education, occupational therapy, organizational leadership, pastoral studies, social work, and special education. Doctoral degrees are offered in business administration and physical therapy.

St. Ambrose has eighteen varsity sports for men and women in a widely varied athletic program. Five hundred undergraduate students, almost half of all campus residents, participate in NAIA Division II sports. Recreational facilities include a gymnasium, racquetball courts, an indoor track, weightlifting rooms, and a swimming pool. The University sponsors more than fifty clubs and organizations, and the student-run Campus Activities Board (CAB) plans events from major concerts such as Ben Folds and O.A.R. to family weekends to homecoming activities. Many students participate in intramural athletics, and Campus Ministry provides spiritual recreation through retreats, religious services, social justice activities, and volunteer opportunities, including annual trips to Chicago's inner city and Appalachia, Kentucky. In addition to the new residence hall, a new University Center is also scheduled to open in fall 2004, providing a new living room for the University's students.

Location

The Quad Cities, which includes Davenport, is a vibrant metropolitan area with a population of nearly 400,000. The Mississippi River joins the two-state (Iowa and Illinois) community, creating a very affordable, manageable urban setting distinguished by friendly people and unique river vistas. Whether students were born here or come here for the first time to begin their university studies, the Quad Cities is a great place to live and learn.

The area offers several first-class arts and entertainment venues and is host to many museums, theaters, and a symphony orchestra and ballet company. Throughout the year there are celebrations such as the Bix Beiderbecke Jazz Festival and Riverssance Fine Arts Festival. There is a range of lively nightspots in the area, and there are many fine restaurants. The shopping is great, too, whether it's in one of the many malls or the historic Village of East Davenport.

Students also find professional sports teams in hockey, baseball, and arena football, and major sporting events like the PGA's John Deere Classic and the Quad-City Times Bix 7 road race. The Great River Bike Trail runs along the Mississippi River, Snowstar ski area is nearby, and there are twenty-one public golf courses from which to choose.

Majors and Degrees

Programs are offered leading to bachelor's degrees in applied management technology, arts, arts in special studies, elected studies, music education, science, and science in industrial engineering. Undergraduate programs include accounting, applied management technology, art, biology, business, chemistry, communication, computer network administration, computer science, criminal justice, criminal justice and network security, economics, education (early childhood, elementary, and secondary), English, finance, fine arts, fitness and human performance, forensic psychology, French, German, graphic design, history, industrial engineering, international accounting and modern languages, Irish studies, journalism, management and organizations, marketing, mathematics, music, nursing, peace and justice, philosophy, physics, physical education, political science, pre-occupational therapy, prephysical therapy, psychology, public administration, public relations and marketing communication, radio and television, sociology, Spanish, special education, sports management, theater, theology, and women's studies.

Academic Programs

The best education combines courses that teach students how to think with those that help them apply that thinking to the real world. St. Ambrose has always emphasized liberal arts studies and career education enriched by a Catholic heritage of social justice and service.

Students must complete a minimum of 120 semester credits (usually forty courses). Some bachelor's programs have additional requirements. Ninety-eight percent of graduates are employed or in graduate school within six months of graduation.

Off-Campus Programs

St. Ambrose students may earn up to 44 credits in study-abroad programs around the world. University-sponsored experiential learning opportunities and internships are available in most departments, including business administration, communication, criminal justice, economics, education, industrial engineering, occupational therapy, physical therapy, political science, psychology, and sociology.

Academic Facilities

Studies at St. Ambrose are significantly enhanced by the high quality of the University's facilities and resources, including an impressive new library that houses an extensive collection of materials and the latest information technology. O'Keefe Library has more than 160,000 volumes, 700 journals, and 75 scholarly electronic databases and makes thousands of professional journals and archives available online.

Most of the academic buildings on campus have undergone complete or significant renovation within the past ten years to create comfortable seminar rooms, interactive classrooms, and modern labs. Although substantially modernized, these facilities have retained their wonderful architectural character. Depending on a student's area of study, he or she might take a class in stately Ambrose Hall, built in 1885, or in a lab in the Health Science annex, completed in 2001.

Costs

Costs for 2003–04 were $16,500 for tuition and $6500 for room and board.

Financial Aid

Federal, state, and University financial aid programs, scholarships, loans, grants, work-study and cooperative programs, and University employment opportunities are available. Federal programs include the Federal Pell Grant, Federal Supplemental Educational Opportunity Grant, Federal Work-Study, the Federal PLUS Loan, and Federal Stafford Loan Programs. State programs are the Iowa Scholarship and Iowa Tuition Grant programs. The priority deadline for financial aid applications is March 15 for the next fall semester. In addition to submitting an application for admission, applicants for financial aid must submit the Free Application for Federal Student Aid (FAFSA). This form is available in the offices of high school counselors or in the St. Ambrose University Financial Aid Office, or online at http://fafsa.ed.gov/.

Faculty

St. Ambrose's 309 distinguished faculty members are a diverse and talented group of individuals. More than 85 percent have earned the highest degree in their fields. Professors, not teaching assistants, teach all classes.

Student Government

All registered students are members of the St. Ambrose Student Government Association (SGA). Organized in 1925, the SGA served as one of the prototypes of such organizations among American colleges. Students are represented on virtually every committee of the University.

Admission Requirements

Admission to St. Ambrose is selective. Students who satisfy at least two of the following three requirements are encouraged to apply: a minimum 2.5 cumulative GPA, an ACT composite score of 20 or above or an SAT I combined score of 950 or higher, and/or ranking in the upper half of their graduating class. Prospective students must take the ACT or SAT I before being admitted. Placement tests in foreign languages, math, and writing are required of most students upon admission.

St. Ambrose's students come from a variety of religious and cultural backgrounds, but they share one thing in common: the desire to fulfill their potential. St. Ambrose welcomes students directly out of high school, transfer students, international students, and those who have postponed their education for various reasons, such as work or family responsibilities.

Application and Information

The completed application for admission, high school transcripts or equivalent credentials, and test scores should be sent to the Director of Admissions. Students also may apply online at the Web site listed below.

For more information or to arrange a campus visit, students should contact:

Meg Halligan
Director of Admissions
St. Ambrose University
518 West Locust Street
Davenport, Iowa 52803
Telephone: 563-333-6300
800-383-2627 (toll-free)
E-mail: admit@sau.edu
World Wide Web: http://www.sau.admissions

SAINT ANSELM COLLEGE

MANCHESTER, NEW HAMPSHIRE

The College

Founded in 1889 by the Order of Saint Benedict, Saint Anselm is the third-oldest Catholic college in New England. From its beginning, Saint Anselm has been, and desires to remain, a small college. With an enrollment of more than 1,900, the school continues to adhere to this decision not only because it wishes to accept only those students it can efficiently prepare for their life's work but also because it wishes to retain the family spirit that is characteristic of a Benedictine institution.

All students at Saint Anselm pursue specialized major courses of study in such areas as liberal arts, business, the sciences, nursing, and preprofessional preparation. The College's primary goal, however, is to provide educational opportunities that will endow students with a well-rounded, creative, and open-minded spirit. Saint Anselm prides itself on the ability to regard each student as a special individual with important personal goals.

Surrounded by the natural beauty of a scenic New Hampshire landscape, the campus blends both traditional and modern buildings to form a picturesque and striking academic setting. The College has students from twenty-eight states and thirteen countries. Approximately 87 percent of the students live on campus in traditional dormitories and modern apartments. There are more than eighty clubs and other organizations to satisfy students' diverse interests. Among these are the Abbey Players (theater group), a debate group, choral groups, a music society, a jazz band, a center for volunteers, a premed society, a prelaw society, an economics club, an outing club, and a local chapter of the Knights of Columbus. Intercollegiate sports are offered for men in baseball, basketball, cross-country, football, golf, hockey, lacrosse, skiing, soccer, and tennis and for women in basketball, cross-country, field hockey, lacrosse, skiing, soccer, softball, tennis, and volleyball. Intramural sports are basketball, ice hockey, indoor and outdoor soccer, racquetball, softball, tennis, touch football, and volleyball. There are club sports for men and women in both rugby and crew.

The John Maurus Carr Activities Center provides students with a multipurpose recreational facility that includes racquetball courts and a comprehensive fitness center. The Davison Hall dining commons, available throughout the day, is a beautiful, spacious addition to campus life. Other facilities include the Cushing Student Center, which houses academic and career counseling facilities, student organizations, health services, and the Academic Resource Center, and Stoutenburgh Gymnasium, home of Saint Anselm varsity athletics.

Location

Located on the outskirts of Manchester, the largest city in New Hampshire, Saint Anselm College offers the benefits of a primarily residential community in a suburban setting. The city has excellent restaurants, shopping malls, and movie theaters. Public transportation from the campus to the city is provided on an hourly basis.

Southern New Hampshire is an excellent setting for students who seek an active college lifestyle. For example, within less than an hour's drive are some of the finest mountains in America, the Atlantic Ocean, and the many cultural and recreational resources of the vibrant city of Boston.

Majors and Degrees

Saint Anselm College awards the Bachelor of Arts degree in accounting, biochemistry, biology, business, chemistry, classics, computer science, computer science with business, computer science with mathematics, criminal justice, economics, English, environmental science, financial economics, fine arts, French, history, liberal studies in the great books, mathematics, mathematics with economics, natural science, philosophy, politics, psychology, sociology, Spanish, and theology. It also offers a program leading to the Bachelor of Science in Nursing (B.S.N.) degree.

The College offers preprofessional programs in dentistry, education (secondary), law, medicine, and theology.

A 3-2 program in engineering is available in cooperation with the University of Notre Dame, Catholic University of America, Manhattan College, and the University of Massachusetts Lowell.

Academic Programs

Saint Anselm College provides students with a strong liberal arts background to complement their major area of study. Students generally take from ten to fifteen courses in their major, while the liberal arts core courses and a wide range of electives make up the remainder of the forty courses required for graduation. Honors Program participants distinguish themselves by taking additional courses in order to graduate with honors.

All Saint Anselm students participate in the College's nationally recognized humanities program during their freshman and sophomore years. This challenging program, entitled Portraits of Human Greatness, is centered on lectures and small-group seminars that explore Western civilization.

Saint Anselm College participates in the Advanced Placement Program of the College Board. Students who receive a score of 3 or better on the Advanced Placement examinations may obtain advanced placement and credit in the pertinent subject matter. Applicants who have completed examinations under the College-Level Examination Program may receive advanced placement and credit if the scores they receive are acceptable.

Off-Campus Programs

Most departments throughout the College offer a number of internship experiences related to the major fields of study. The internship program helps students to combine the theoretical experience gained in the classroom with a practical application to a specific area of study. Internships are generally taken in the junior or senior year. They are available either in southern New Hampshire or New York City or through American University in Washington, D.C.

The College also provides access to several study-abroad programs. These programs can be integrated into most majors and give students excellent opportunities to learn a foreign language and to study other cultures and civilizations.

Academic Facilities

The spacious, wooded 400-acre campus has fifty-one buildings. The six most recent facilities reflect the College's continued commitment to adapt to the needs of its students. Poisson Computer Science Center houses more than 200 microcomputers and a specially equipped computer classroom, as well as general-purpose classrooms and faculty offices. The Charles A. Dana Center houses a 700-seat theater and serves as the home of the humanities program. The College recently opened the New Hampshire Institute of Politics, a 20,000-square-foot facility that focuses on political and civic education. The Geisel Library, which holds 215,000 bound volumes and 18,000 microform titles and maintains a collection of 4,000 periodical titles and 1,100 video recordings, provides an excellent research base for Saint Anselm students and faculty. A major expansion and reconstruction project to enlarge the library to meet the expanding needs of the

College community has been completed, as has a $10-million expansion and renovation of the Goulet Science Center and student housing in the form of apartments and town houses.

Costs

Tuition for the 2003–04 school year was $21,410, and room and board charges were $8090, for a total of $29,500. Books and other miscellaneous fees cost approximately $1850.

Financial Aid

Saint Anselm College offers financial aid through various federal and private programs. Assistance is awarded as a supplement to the reasonable financial sacrifice that the College expects will be made by the interested student and his or her parents. Eighty-five percent of Saint Anselm's students are receiving some form of financial assistance to help defray the cost of their education. Financial aid packages consist of scholarships, grants, loans, and work opportunities. Merit awards (Presidential Scholarships) of up to $11,500 are awarded to outstanding students.

Two forms are required in applying for aid. The student must submit the CSS Financial Aid PROFILE and the Free Application for Federal Student Aid (FAFSA) to the College Scholarship Service by March 1.

Faculty

The College's faculty consists of 119 full-time and 56 part-time members. Ninety-six percent of the faculty members have earned doctorates or the appropriate terminal degrees in their fields. With a student-teacher ratio of 15:1, close interaction is possible between students and professors. In addition to their teaching responsibilities, faculty members serve as advisers to students enrolled in their department. No classes are taught by graduate students.

Student Government

Student government means students organizing themselves for a common purpose. At Saint Anselm, student government exists as the Student Senate, the Campus Activities Board, and the Class Councils. The aim of student government is to complement the essential aim of a college education: scholarship. Student government organizes and unifies social, intellectual, and cultural activities so that they become an important part of liberal education. Student government helps students develop such qualities as initiative, cooperation, and leadership.

Admission Requirements

In selecting a freshman class, the admission committee considers each candidate personally and thoroughly. The committee evaluates each student's high school record, scores on the SAT I, letters of recommendation, and written essay (part of the application). Of greatest importance is the student's high school transcript, in terms of both the quality of courses taken and the grades earned.

Transfer and international students are welcome to apply. The same general admission procedures are required, along with at least a C average in all transferable courses and, for international students, a satisfactory score on the TOEFL.

Application and Information

The College follows a rolling admission policy, with a priority date of March 1. The Admissions Office is open from 8:30 a.m. to 4:30 p.m. on weekdays and, during the fall, from 9 a.m. to 12:30 p.m. on Saturday. The College strongly recommends that students visit the campus and have an interview in order to discover the many benefits of Saint Anselm.

For more information, students should contact:

Director of Admission
Saint Anselm College
100 Saint Anselm Drive
Manchester, New Hampshire 03102
Telephone: 603-641-7500
888-426-7356 (toll-free)
Fax: 603-641-7550
E-mail: admission@anselm.edu
World Wide Web: http://www.anselm.edu

Saint Anselm College Alumni Hall.

SAINT AUGUSTINE'S COLLEGE

RALEIGH, NORTH CAROLINA

The College

Saint Augustine's College, founded in 1867 in Raleigh, North Carolina, is a private, urban, coeducational, undergraduate liberal arts institution with a core curriculum that includes rigorous, in-depth programs in adult education, business, communications, community development, computer science, interdisciplinary studies, mathematics, military science (a required course for all members of the College's notable Army ROTC battalion), natural sciences, social and behavioral sciences, teacher education, and theater and film. Accredited by the Commission on Colleges of the Southern Association of Colleges and Schools, the College awards the Bachelor of Arts and the Bachelor of Science.

With a student-faculty ratio of 16:1, Saint Augustine's provides an intimate educational setting where faculty members know students by name. The College enrolls more than 1,500 students; nearly half come from North Carolina, with the remainder from thirty states, the District of Columbia, the U.S. Virgin Islands, Jamaica, and twenty-two other countries. Its faculty consists of more than 100 dedicated members who are all skilled teachers and scholars.

Saint Augustine's College was the nation's first historically black college to have its own on-campus commercial radio and television stations (WAUG-AM 750, WAUG-TV 68, and cable channel 20) and is the only school in the Raleigh/Durham area to offer a degree in film production.

Location

Located in the state's capital, Raleigh, Saint Augustine's College has a beautiful 105-acre campus. The campus's thirty-seven historic and contemporary buildings are just minutes from downtown Raleigh's commercial, education, government, and entertainment centers. Located just 3 hours from the mountains and 2 hours from the coast, Raleigh has something for everyone. Its rich history and cultural sophistication are evident through an array of museums, art galleries, professional sports, and entertainment facilities.

With a comfortable climate, a great location, and a variety of resources, Raleigh is among the best places to live in the nation.

Majors and Degrees

The mission of Academic Affairs at Saint Augustine's College is to promote an educational environment that is conducive to lifelong learning across the broad spectrum of liberal arts. An important element of this mission is to prepare students for graduate and professional studies or employment in a complex, diverse, and rapidly changing world. The most popular majors at Saint Augustine's College are business administration, computer information systems, criminal justice, organizational management, and computer science.

Saint Augustine's College offers the Bachelor of Arts degree in communication, elementary education, English, English education, exceptional children's education, history, music, music education, political science, psychology, social studies education, sociology, theater/film production, and the visual arts.

The Bachelor of Science degree is offered in biology, biology education, business administration, business education, chemistry, community economic development, computer information systems, computer science, criminal justice, human performance and wellness, industrial hygiene and safety, industrial mathematics, international business, mathematics, mathematics education, organizational management, physical education (teaching), and premedical sciences.

Academic Program

The College is a member of the Cooperating Raleigh Colleges (CRC) consortium that enables students to cross-enroll in five colleges in the city of Raleigh.

A recently implemented program referred to as the Three-Tiered Approach to Learning (the TTAL Plan) applies a three-tier approach to education, allowing students to enroll in either a three-, four-, or five-year plan of study. Transitional students are those who fall short of the College's entrance standards but have demonstrated potential to succeed, both by attitude and by hard work. These students, enrolled in a five-year plan of study, spend their entire first year developing the skills and knowledge base to successfully transition into a regular four-year program. The unique aspect of this program is that it allows financial aid for participating students. The traditional four-year plan is targeted toward the college student who has the requisite skills to compete on the college level. This plan encompasses the majority of the student body. The accelerated three-year plan recruits high-achieving high school students who excel both academically and on the SAT and/or ACT examination. These students carry a minimum of 18 credit hours per semester and attend both summer sessions in order to complete their degree program in three years.

Some students may qualify for advanced placement (AP) or degree credits for certain college-level courses through the College Examination Board Advanced Placement Examinations. In addition, qualified high school students may dually enroll at Saint Augustine's for college credit. Other programs offered by the College for nontraditional students are the Gateway Adult Learner Program and the Second Chance Alternative Teacher's Certification Program, which allow professionals who are changing careers or teachers currently in the field to enhance their skills or to prepare for teacher certification.

The College also offers a Freshman Studies Initiative (FSI), which is a freshman-year academic advising and first-year enhancement program offered exclusively to first-time freshman enrollees. The Honors Program allows academically gifted students to pursue advanced-level courses in addition to participating in opportunities that enhance the student's educational experience.

The Student Development Center provides career services, internship opportunities, counseling, and job fair participation opportunities.

Academic Facilities

An Army ROTC program is housed in the Tuttle Building on the campus. The Prezell R. Robinson Library is a depository for African-American historical collections as well as the Delany sisters' (*Having Our Say*) papers and artifacts. The Seby B. Jones Fine Arts Center is home to art works produced by student art majors. The campus is home to radio and TV stations (WAUG) that offer internship opportunities to the College's communication majors. The College manages a

Community Development Facility, a small-business incubator sponsor. The Division of Education oversees the National Youth Sports Program on Saint Augustine's College campus. Equipped with an exercise and training room for its student athletes, the newly renovated Emery Gymnasium is the site of a variety of athletic competitions and also provides for noncompetitive student leisure sporting activities.

The Martin Luther King, Jr. Student Union serves as the hub of campus life, housing student activities, campus dining, and the campus bookstore. Students also have access to campus track-and-field facilities and a state-of-the-art Wellness Center.

Costs

For 2003–04, tuition, fees, room, and board totaled $13,490. Residence hall charges vary, depending on the facility.

Financial Aid

Saint Augustine's College offers financial aid through various federal and private programs. Students must complete the Free Application for Federal Student Aid (FAFSA) in order for the Department of Education to determine their expected family contribution (EFC), which is the amount the student and parents/spouse are expected to pay toward their estimated cost of attendance (COA). The cost of attendance at Saint Augustine's College consists of tuition and fees, room and board, books and supplies, transportation, and personal expenses. Ninety-five percent of Saint Augustine's College students are receiving some form of financial assistance to help defray the cost of their education. Financial aid packages consist of federal and state grants, loans, institutional scholarships (Presidential, Falcon Merit, Scholarship of Excellence, and Meritorious Achievement), United Negro College Fund (UNCF) scholarships, outside scholarships, and College work-study opportunities.

Two forms are required in order to apply for aid at Saint Augustine's College. Students must submit the Financial Aid Institutional Application and the FASFA to the Financial Aid Office no later than March 1 each year.

Faculty

The College has 118 faculty members, approximately 60 percent of whom hold terminal degrees. The student-faculty ratio is 16:1.

Student Government

The campus has a vibrant Student Government Association that is open to all students. There is also an at-large student representative to the Board of Trustees. Other opportunities for campus leadership include the Panhellenic Council and close to sixty student clubs and organizations.

Admission Requirements

Candidates for admission should be scheduled to graduate from an accredited high school. Students should have completed 20 units, consisting of at least 4 English, 2 math, 2 science, 2 social science, and 10 electives. The recommendations and reputation of the high school, the student's record in extracurricular activities and athletics, and International Baccalaureate program credit and Advanced Placement (AP) or honors courses are all factors that affect the admissions decision. Students are required to submit an official high school transcript (GED certificate and test scores, limited, are accepted), SAT or ACT scores, class rank, and two letters of recommendation. There is a $25 nonrefundable application fee.

Application and Information

The College adheres to a rolling admissions schedule, with priority given to those enrolling by June 1 for the fall semester and November 1 for the spring semester. The application deadline for international students is June 1 for fall and November 1 for the spring. A $125 nonrefundable room reservation fee is required for those living in campus housing. The deadline for payment is May 15 for the fall term and December 1 for the spring term.

For questions or assistance, students should contact:

Office of Admission
Saint Augustine's College
1315 Oakwood Avenue
Raleigh, North Carolina 27610
Telephone: 919-516-4016
800-948-1126 (toll-free)
E-mail: admissions@st-aug.edu

Students on the campus of Saint Augustine's College.

ST. BONAVENTURE UNIVERSITY

ST. BONAVENTURE, NEW YORK

The University

St. Bonaventure University provides a values-based, Franciscan liberal arts education with individual attention from professors, a beautiful residential setting, and a friendly, close-knit atmosphere. Of the 2,800 students enrolled, 2,200 are undergraduates. More than 74 percent of the undergraduates are full-time residents. Complementing St. Bonaventure's traditions are innovative degree programs, computerized career placement aids, comprehensive student life activities, and modern academic facilities. Among major campus events during the academic year are concerts and coffeehouse acts, indoor and outdoor recreational programs, current and classic film offerings, and dramatic and musical plays. Aspiring writers and broadcasters from all academic majors—Bonaventure has produced 5 Pulitzer Prize winners—find challenging and plentiful opportunities working with one of the four University media: WSBU-88.3 FM-The Buzz, the nationally ranked campus radio station; *The Bona Venture,* the award-winning weekly newspaper; *The Bonadieu,* the yearbook; and *The Laurel,* the nation's oldest student literary publication, which marked its 100th anniversary in 1999. Other organizations on campus include academic fraternities, academic honor societies, a variety of club and intramural sports, and arts organizations that include choral, instrumental, dance, and drama ensembles. The Thomas Merton Ministry Center is open 24 hours a day and aims to foster a community of friendship and mutual service. Many students take the opportunity to serve as Bona Buddies to area children or senior citizens; help with the national award–winning soup kitchen The Warming House, which is the oldest student-run soup kitchen in the nation; or volunteer in other service organizations. Volunteer opportunities expanded with the opening of St. Bonaventure's Franciscan Center for Social Concern, which offers immersion experiences and service opportunities with the poor.

St. Bonaventure University students enjoy three athletic facilities: the Reilly Center, housing a sports arena, swimming pool, and weight room; a fitness center, housing indoor tennis courts, racquetball courts, a volleyball court, a squash court, a multistation Universal Gym, free weights and Nautilus machines, an exercise room, and Lifecycles; and the recently renovated Butler Gym, which offers a basketball court and an indoor track. A new campus recreation facility is slated for completion in 2004. Also available are outdoor tennis and basketball courts, a nine-hole golf course, and a nearby ski resort and ice rink. NCAA Division I athletics for men are baseball, basketball, cross-country, golf, soccer, swimming, and tennis. Division I competition for women includes basketball, cross-country, lacrosse, soccer, softball, swimming, and tennis.

In addition to its undergraduate programs, St. Bonaventure offers the Master of Arts degree in English, Franciscan studies, history, psychology, and theology. A Master of Science is offered in professional leadership, while a Master of Science in Education program includes adolescence education, advanced inclusive processes, advanced teacher education, counselor education, educational administration, health education, reading, and supervision and curriculum. A Master of Business Administration degree program is available with concentrations in accounting/finance, general business, international business, and management/marketing, and a Master of Arts degree in integrated marketing communications was added in 2003.

Location

St. Bonaventure is located on Route 417 between Olean, a city of approximately 17,000 residents, and Allegany, a village with about 2,000 residents. Shops, restaurants, and theaters are all within walking distance. The campus is spread over 500 acres in a valley surrounded by the Allegheny Mountains. The free Bona Bus connects the campus with Olean and Allegany, carrying students to and from the area attractions. The region around St. Bonaventure provides a beautiful setting for many outdoor activities. A ski resort, ice rink, and snow-tubing resort attract students, and nearby Allegany State Park offers excellent facilities for swimming, boating, and hiking. St. Bonaventure is accessible by car, bus, and commercial air transportation, with Buffalo/Niagara International the nearest airport.

Majors and Degrees

St. Bonaventure University grants the Bachelor of Arts degree with majors in classical languages, English, history, interdisciplinary studies, journalism and mass communication, modern languages (French and Spanish), philosophy, political science, psychology, social sciences, sociology, theology, and visual arts. The Bachelor of Science is granted with majors in biochemistry, biology, chemistry, computer science, economics, elementary/special education (dual certification), environmental science, interdisciplinary studies, mathematics, physical education, physics, and psychology. The Bachelor of Business Administration is granted with majors in accounting, finance, management sciences, and marketing. Popular five-year programs are also available in business, English, physics, and psychology. Certification programs in business, education, and Franciscan and theological studies are also offered.

Academic Programs

Students in all majors begin their intellectual journey in Clare College, St. Bonaventure's nationally acclaimed core curriculum, which offers a values-based education grounded in the vision of St. Francis and St. Bonaventure. Composed of 49 credits, it begins with "The Intellectual Journey" and continues through courses in composition and critical thinking and various core areas, followed by a capstone University forum.

A candidate for a bachelor's degree must complete at least 120 credit hours, with a cumulative index of 2.0 or better in the major field and the overall program. A pass/fail grade option, available to all upperclass students, may be elected for one course per semester, but not for courses in a student's major field.

Advanced credit is granted for grades of C or better on either the College Proficiency Examination or the College-Level Examination Program (CLEP) tests. Advanced placement is granted on the basis of scores obtained on the College Board's Advanced Placement (AP) examinations.

Men and women may also elect to participate in the University's Army ROTC program, which earned the MacArthur Award as best small unit in the nation in 1998.

Off-Campus Programs

Through St. Bonaventure's membership in the College Consortium for International Studies (CCIS), St. Bonaventure students have access to six continents. More than sixty semester-long international study programs, including St. Bonaventure–sponsored study in Spain, Ireland, and Australia, are available to students in good academic standing in their junior year. Faculty-directed, short-term opportunities include a three-week intersession in China, the Francis E. Kelly Oxford summer program, and a three-week travel study program to Mexico. For further information, students should contact the Office of International Studies. Fieldwork or internships are available in several major programs.

Academic Facilities

Friedsam Memorial Library houses more than 250,000 volumes and includes a trilevel resource center with a curriculum center, the University archives, and digital media and conferencing centers, as well as world-class special collections. An automated online card catalog greatly improves research capabilities.

DeLaRoche Hall houses equipment for instruction and research in a variety of fields, including chemistry, geology, mathematics, microbiology, physics, and psychology. Research facilities include an atomic absorption spectrophotometer, a tissue-culture laboratory, a greenhouse, a radioactivity laboratory, equipment for research in the growth of microorganisms, and an extensive mammal collection.

The John J. Murphy Professional Building provides the most up-to-date equipment for the School of Business and the School of Journalism and Mass Communication. The Bob Koop Broadcast Journalism Laboratory features a television studio with an anchor desk, digital and videotape editing bays, while the building also houses offices, classrooms, and a 432-seat auditorium. A fiber-optic network connects microcomputers in academic and administrative areas. There are seven labs for student use containing more than 100 DOS and Macintosh systems. St. Bonaventure students also have access to the Internet via every residence hall.

An annex to Plassmann Hall houses computer-adaptable education classrooms, seminar rooms, and offices for the education faculty. An observatory allows students access to three compact telescopes, two 8-inch Celestron telescopes, and one 11-inch Schmidt-Cassegrain telescope, along with a heated classroom.

The Regina A. Quick Center for the Arts provides acoustically designed classroom space for music courses and painting and drawing studios for students enrolled in visual arts classes. The center also includes a musical instrument digital interface lab, a 325-seat theater, and an atrium that is often used for poetry readings and impromptu musical performances.

The F. Donald Kenney Museum and Art Study Wing, dedicated in 2001, includes four climate-controlled galleries offering nationally acclaimed traveling exhibits, works from the University's permanent collections, and student exhibits.

In 1999, St. Bonaventure completed the most comprehensive renovation project in its history, comprising $5 million in renovations to its residence halls and academic facilities and an additional $2 million to fund new apartment housing for 96 students.

Costs

For 2003–04, the annual costs were $17,190 for tuition and $735 for fees. Room and meal plans averaged $6594 per year.

Financial Aid

Students who qualify for financial aid normally receive a package consisting of a combination of scholarships, grants, loans, and work-study awards. Athletic Grants-in-Aid are available for men in baseball, basketball, golf, soccer, swimming, and tennis and for women in basketball, lacrosse, soccer, softball, swimming, and tennis. Music scholarships are also available. Students must file the Free Application for Federal Student Aid (FAFSA) in order to be considered for financial assistance. For more complete details, a student should contact the director of financial aid at the University.

Faculty

Like the student body, the 160 full-time and 67 part-time faculty members at St. Bonaventure come from a wide range of geographic, ethnic, and religious backgrounds. The student-faculty ratio of 15:1 allows faculty members the time to help each student to understand different modes of thinking, develop as a person, and lay a foundation for lifelong learning. Eighty-four percent of the faculty members hold the terminal degree in their field. Friars, many of whom teach, add to the unique atmosphere of St. Bonaventure.

Student Government

Life at St. Bonaventure is centered on the residence halls, and the foundation of student government begins in the dormitories with the Residence Hall Councils. The elected council members determine the norms by which the residents are guided in their daily lives. The Student Government, whose members are elected from the student body, serves as the general student-governing unit, and its members serve on every major University board and committee.

Admission Requirements

St. Bonaventure University welcomes applications for admission from all serious candidates from a variety of backgrounds. St. Bonaventure University provides equal opportunity without regard to race, creed, color, gender, age, national or ethnic origin, marital status, veteran status, or disability in admission, employment, and in all of its educational programs and activities. Applicants, who are welcome to apply online, must show evidence of academic achievement to be selected for admission. The criteria used in making admission decisions, in order of importance, are quality of the high school curriculum, grade point average in college-preparatory courses, ACT (preferred) or SAT I scores, class rank, recommendations from high school teachers and counselors, and extracurricular activities.

Application and Information

For more information about St. Bonaventure University, prospective students should contact:

Director of Admissions
St. Bonaventure University
P.O. Box D
St. Bonaventure, New York 14778
Telephone: 716-375-2400
800-462-5050 (toll-free)
E-mail: admissions@sbu.edu
World Wide Web: http://www.sbu.edu

Built in 1928 and renovated in 1999, Devereux Hall is an example of the beautiful Florentine architecture found at St. Bonaventure University.

ST. EDWARD'S UNIVERSITY

AUSTIN, TEXAS

The University

Students are the focus at St. Edward's University. Through innovative programs, committed faculty members and high-quality facilities, St. Edward's offers everything students need to create the kind of educational experience they desire. Students at St. Edward's learn to think in new ways. They have fun. They gain practical skills through internships, research, service projects, and study abroad. They are prepared for a life of discovery, leadership, and success.

St. Edward's is a close-knit, private, liberal arts university. It is also an energetic hub of activity for about 4,450 students. The individuals who choose St. Edward's are committed to learning. Independent, motivated, and diverse, these students represent thirty-one states, thirty-six countries, and all faiths and walks of life.

Founded by the Congregation of Holy Cross in 1885, the University provides a personalized education and an environment where freely chosen beliefs can be deepened and expressed. St. Edward's seeks to enable individuals to be independent and productive and to confront the critical issues of society with competence and conviction.

There are more than fifty student organizations at St. Edward's. Students explore their interests in everything from service to recreation and honor societies to politics. Along the way, students become leaders, develop communication skills, make friends, and have fun.

All entering students are paired with faculty advisers who assist them in planning degree programs and who provide academic counseling throughout the students' college careers.

An essential part of the academic experience at St. Edward's is preparing for life after earning an undergraduate degree. The Career Planning and Experiential Learning (CPEL) office helps students explore careers, secure internship opportunities, and prepare for graduate school and employment.

Students have many choices in on-campus housing, from apartments for upper-level students to traditional residence halls to house-style living in the Casitas. Freshmen are required to live in the residence halls unless they are living with their parents while attending the University.

St. Edward's is a member of the NCAA Division II. Men compete in baseball, basketball, cross-country, golf, soccer, and tennis. Women compete in basketball, golf, soccer, softball, tennis, and volleyball.

Location

St. Edward's University is located in Austin, the capital of Texas and one of the most vibrant educational and political centers in the United States. One in eight of its more than 657,000 residents is a college or university student. Along with its internationally known film festival and music scene, Austin also offers local theaters, galleries, and museums. Students at St. Edward's enjoy Austin's three major lakes and nearly 200 parks almost year-round, such as nearby Zilker Park with its natural, spring-fed swimming pool, canoe rentals for use on Town Lake, a hike-and-bike trail, a botanical garden, and playing fields.

Majors and Degrees

St. Edward's University confers five undergraduate degrees—Bachelor of Arts, Bachelor of Arts in Applied Science, Bachelor of Business Administration, Bachelor of Liberal Studies, and Bachelor of Science—and offers fifty-two areas of study through the schools of Behavioral and Social Sciences, Business Administration, Natural Sciences, Humanities, and Education. Majors offered are accounting, accounting information technology, art, biochemistry, bioinformatics, biology, business administration, chemistry, communication, computer information science, computer science, criminal justice, economics, English/language arts and reading, English literature, English writing and rhetoric, entrepreneurship, finance, forensic chemistry, graphic design, history, international business, international relations, kinesiology, language arts, Latin American studies, liberal studies, management, marketing, mathematics, philosophy, photocommunications, political science, psychology, religious studies, social studies, social work, sociology, Spanish, Spanish/bilingual education, Spanish/international business, and theater arts.

The School of Education also offers teacher certification programs for early childhood–grade 4, early childhood–grade 12, grades 4–8, grades 8–12, and secondary religious education.

Many students choose to pursue a preprofessional program in conjunction with their established majors. St. Edward's offers preprofessional programs in dentistry, engineering, law, medicine and physical therapy. In addition, St. Edward's offers seven master's degrees.

Academic Program

All students share an intensive general education requirement of 57 credit hours spanning all four years. The requirements are split into three areas: foundational skills (English writing, college math, computational skills, oral communication, and foreign language), cultural foundations (six courses including American Dilemmas, Identity of the West, and Contemporary World Issues), and foundations for values and decisions (five courses including Ethics and Science in Perspective). The general education curriculum culminates with Capstone, a writing course in which students investigate a controversial issue, analyze it, and propose a resolution, both orally and in a major paper. The reasoning and communication skills and the understanding of society that these general studies develop are reinforced in each student's in-depth study of a major discipline.

Graduation is based on the successful completion of 120 semester hours of study. St. Edward's observes a two-semester academic calendar, and the University's flexible summer course schedule offers day and evening classes.

Off-Campus Programs

Hands-on experiential learning is a central component of a St. Edward's University education. Students conduct research and complete internships on and off campus, including work for businesses, public and private organizations, or programs in Austin, across the country, and around the globe. In fact, students at St. Edward's have logged more than 58,000 hours at internships in Austin business and service organizations.

The University is a member of the International Student Exchange Program, which includes hundreds of programs and has reciprocal exchanges with universities in Germany, Mexico, and Australia. Students can also participate in exchange programs sponsored by other U.S. universities and in community service programs offered by the International Partnership for Service Learning.

Academic Facilities

St. Edward's provides facilities that support every aspect of the student experience—academic, residential, and social—because learning can happen in many places and situations. Main Building, named a Texas Historic Landmark for its architectural significance, is a focal point on the city of Austin's skyline. Trustee Hall, the award-winning academic building, enhances the University's outstanding record as a "wired" institution. In fact, a national consulting group recently described St. Edward's as one of "a very small group of schools that is doing instructional technology well."

The Robert and Pearle Ragsdale Center is home to everything from dining services and a coffeehouse to parties, concerts, lectures, and conferences. The Recreation and Convocation Center offers a fitness center, an indoor/outdoor swimming pool, and courts for basketball, racquetball/handball, and volleyball. Students also have access to on-campus 24-hour computer labs.

Costs

The 2003–04 fees for full-time undergraduate students were $14,710 for tuition and between $4640 and $7600 for room and board, depending on choice of residence hall and meal plan.

Financial Aid

St. Edward's has a strong track record of awarding financial assistance. In fall 2002, the average financial assistance package was $8015, and 82 percent of freshmen received merit or need-based financial assistance in 2002. St. Edward's University administers several financial assistance programs funded by federal, institutional, and state resources. These programs help students meet college expenses through grants, scholarships, low-interest loans, and work-study programs. To qualify for financial assistance, accepted students should submit, through the College Scholarship Service, the Free Application for Federal Student Aid (FAFSA).

All students are automatically reviewed for academic scholarships, including merit awards that consider leadership, involvement, and commitment as well as academic performance, when they apply for admission. The priority deadline for fall semester applications is February 1. The regular admission deadline for fall is July 1.

Faculty

Faculty members at St. Edward's do much more than teach students. From service projects to research projects, students get to know faculty members inside and outside the classroom, often forming lifelong friendships. The University's 14:1 student–faculty ratio fosters collaboration between students and faculty members.

Student Government

The Student Government Association (SGA), composed of elected student officers, has campuswide representation. The executive board and senate meet weekly to plan and direct activities that involve the entire St. Edward's community. In addition, the SGA president acts as the voice of the student body and regularly attends Board of Trustees meetings.

Admission Requirements

Students who apply for admission to St. Edward's are evaluated individually on the basis of their academic performance in high school, rank in class, SAT I or ACT scores, and level of high school curriculum. To be considered for admission, qualified applicants should rank in the top half of their class and have test scores at or above the national average for college-bound students.

Application and Information

St. Edward's University employs a rolling admission policy. The Admission Committee makes decisions on applications shortly after a student's file becomes complete. A completed file consists of an application, a $45 nonrefundable application fee, SAT I or ACT scores, and official high school transcripts.

All admission credentials should be mailed to:

Office of Undergraduate Admission
St. Edward's University
3001 South Congress Avenue
Austin, Texas 78704-6489
Telephone: 512-448-8500
800-555-0164 (toll-free)
Fax: 512-464-8877
E-mail: seu.admit@admin.stedwards.edu
World Wide Web: http://www.stedwards.edu

Main Building, designated a Texas Historic Landmark in 1973, is the center of the St. Edward's community.

SAINT FRANCIS UNIVERSITY

LORETTO, PENNSYLVANIA

The University

Saint Francis University is a small, coeducational, liberal arts university. The University was founded in 1847 and conducted under the tradition of the Franciscan Friars of the Third Order Regular. The University is concerned with the development of each student for the world of today. For more than 150 years, the University's philosophy of education and student life has continued to emphasize two values: instruction of high quality and respect for the student as an individual. The University believes that a liberal arts education, encompassing a major field of study, is the soundest kind of preparation a student can have for a productive life. The University is accredited by the Middle States Association of Colleges and Schools. The social work program is accredited by the Council on Social Work Education, and the programs in teacher education have been approved by the Pennsylvania State Department of Education. The physician assistant science program is accredited by the Accreditation Review Commission on Education for Physician Assistants. The nursing program has full approval by the Pennsylvania State Board of Nurse Examiners and is fully accredited by the National League for Nursing Accrediting Commission (NLNAC). The physical therapy program is fully accredited by the Commission on Accreditation in Physical Therapy Education.

Students at Saint Francis University can find a number of outlets for their talents, interests, and abilities. Departmental clubs; volunteer organizations; social, business, and service fraternities; social sororities; and a service sorority are part of campus life. Athletics have played a major role in the University's history, and the athletics program offers twenty-one NCAA Division I sports for men and women as well as intramural sports. The Student Activities Organization sponsors an impressive program of lectures, films, and concerts. The Southern Alleghenies Museum of Art, separately chartered, is located on the campus as well.

The full-time undergraduate enrollment is 530 men and 750 women; the University as a whole enrolls 2,000 students. Saint Francis University offers Associate of Science degrees in business administration, real estate, and religious education. On the graduate level, Saint Francis grants a Master of Arts degree in human resource management and industrial relations. The University also offers the Master of Business Administration, Master of Education, Master of Science in physician assistant sciences, Master of Science in Occupational Therapy, and Master of Science in Physical Therapy degrees.

Location

Saint Francis University is situated on 600 acres in the heart of the Allegheny Mountains. The campus is located in the borough of Loretto, which has a population of approximately 1,400. The campus is 6 miles from the county seat of Ebensburg, which has a population of 4,000. The cities of Johnstown and Altoona are within 25 miles of Loretto and have populations of 35,000 and 55,000, respectively. The University is a 90-minute drive east of Pittsburgh.

Majors and Degrees

Saint Francis University grants the Bachelor of Arts degree and offers majors in American studies, biology, computer science, engineering (3-2 program), English, English/communications, history, mathematics, philosophy, political science, psychology, public administration/government service, religious studies, and sociology. The Bachelor of Science degree is also granted, with majors in accounting, biology, chemistry, computer science, economics and finance, elementary education/special education, environmental management (3-2 program), information systems management, marketing, mathematics, medical technology, nursing, occupational therapy (five-year master's), physical therapy (six-year master's), physician assistant science (five-year master's), podiatric science, psychology, public administration/government service, social work, and sociology.

Areas of preprofessional study include dentistry, engineering (3-2 program), law, medicine, optometry, podiatry, and veterinary medicine. Areas of concentration within majors include anthropology, biochemistry, bioinformatics, communications, computer information systems, computer science, criminal justice, environmental politics, environmental science, forensics, international studies, marine and environmental education specialties, marine biology, molecular biology, political communications, public management, public relations, and systems/languages. The University also grants secondary education certification in the areas of biology, chemistry, English, general science, mathematics, and social studies. A 3-2 cooperative program with Duke University in forestry and environmental management, a 3+4 accelerated program in primary care, and a 3+4 accelerated program leading to the baccalaureate and Doctor of Dental Medicine degrees with Temple University are also offered.

It is possible for students to major in one area and minor in another or to have a double major. A self-designed major program is available as well. The University offers an honors program to challenge intellectually ambitious students from all disciplines. While pursuing their major field of study, students enroll in the full four-year curriculum, which allows in-depth, creative study in a variety of subject areas.

A continuing education program provides credit and noncredit courses on campus as well as in the communities surrounding Loretto. The Office of Continuing Education offers Associate of Science degrees in business administration and religious education and Bachelor of Science degrees in accounting and management.

Academic Program

The program of study leading to a bachelor's degree is usually completed in eight semesters. To qualify for graduation, a student must follow a program of study, approved by the Vice President for Academic Affairs, that totals at least 128 credits distributed among liberal arts courses, major requirements, collateral requirements, and general electives. All students, regardless of major, are required to complete the University's general education program of 58 credits.

The academic calendar is divided into two semesters and three summer sessions.

Electronic capabilities at Saint Francis University enable students to access library holdings and communicate with professors, fellow students, and the world through the use of personal computers via e-mail and the Internet. Every classroom and residence hall room is wired for Internet access. The University has several classrooms equipped with state-of-the-art equipment that allows videoconferencing. All incoming freshmen receive a laptop computer as part of their tuition. Saint Francis University is a wireless campus.

Off-Campus Programs

Students at Saint Francis University may, with permission of the University's administration, spend their junior year of study abroad or may earn credit for participation in summer programs conducted in Canada, France, Germany, Spain, and other countries by accredited American colleges and universities.

A number of departments offer students the opportunity for off-campus study. For some majors, such as nursing, physician assistant science, education, medical technology, and social work, off-campus study is required; in all other majors, an internship is available as an elective. Such an internship can be a meaningful experience and can significantly enhance a student's career preparation.

Academic Facilities

The six-story Pasquerilla Library contains more than 176,000 volumes, 582 periodicals, and a substantial microfilm collection. Other features of the library are typing areas, seminar rooms, reading rooms, microfilm reading rooms, several multimedia classrooms, technologically equipped study rooms, and a collection of study items and educational materials for elementary and secondary education majors. Special features of the library include a PC laboratory with printers, an automated card catalog, periodical search systems, and a satellite hookup.

Scotus and Padua halls contain modern classroom facilities, language laboratories, two computer laboratories, a recording studio for radio and television, and lecture facilities (halls and an amphitheater). Sullivan Science Hall contains twelve well-equipped biology, chemistry, and physics laboratories; fully equipped electronic classrooms; a greenhouse for botanical research; an examining room for use in the physician assistant science program; and other facilities.

Costs

For 2003–04, tuition was $18,292, room and board were $7346, and a laptop computer was $1050, for a total of $26,688.

Financial Aid

Approximately 90 percent of the Saint Francis University student body receive financial aid. In addition to participating in federal and state need-based student aid programs, Saint Francis University offers its own substantial grant program and a generous scholarship program that is based on SAT I or ACT scores, high school average, and class rank. Academic awards range from $1500 to full tuition.

Faculty

Faculty members are chosen for their knowledge of subject matter, as well as for their ability to communicate. Of the teaching faculty at Saint Francis University, 78 percent hold a doctorate or the highest degree attainable in their specific field of expertise. No graduate students teach classes at Saint Francis University.

Student Government

The Student Government Association's Steering Committee involves students who are interested in self-government. Students also serve on a number of committees in the Faculty Senate. The Student Government offices are located in the John F. Kennedy Student Center, which also houses a 600-seat auditorium, a campus bookstore and post office, a study lounge, a cafeteria, and the University dispensary.

Admission Requirements

The admission committee considers applicants and renders decisions on the basis of the secondary school record, the recommendation of the secondary school principal or counselor, and the results of the SAT I or ACT. Applicants should have a minimum of 16 academic units and are strongly encouraged to visit the University campus for an admission interview and tour. Interviews and campus tours are available Monday through Friday throughout the year and select Saturday mornings while classes are in session.

Transfer students must submit a formal transfer application and a college clearance form in addition to official transcripts from each high school and college previously attended. Transfer students receive an advanced standing evaluation after an offer of admission has been made.

Saint Francis University, an equal opportunity/affirmative action employer, complies with applicable federal and state laws regarding nondiscrimination and affirmative action, including Title IX of the Educational Amendments of 1972, Titles VI and VII of the Civil Rights Act of 1964, and Section 504 of the Rehabilitation Act of 1973. Saint Francis University is committed to a policy of nondiscrimination and equal opportunity in employment, education programs and activities, and admissions that includes all persons regardless of race, gender, color, religion, national origin or ancestry, age, marital status, disability, or Vietnam-era veteran status. Inquiries or complaints may be addressed to the University's Director of Human Resources/Affirmative Action/Title IX Coordinator, Saint Francis University, Loretto, Pennsylvania 15940; telephone: 814-472-3264. For other University information, students should call 814-472-3000.

Application and Information

The University operates under a rolling admission policy. The application deadline for the physical therapy, occupational therapy, and physician assistant programs is January 15. For further information about Saint Francis University, students should contact:

Evan Lipp
Dean for Enrollment Management
Saint Francis University
P.O. Box 600
Loretto, Pennsylvania 15940
Telephone: 814-472-3100
800-342-5738 (toll-free)
E-mail: admissions@francis.edu
World Wide Web: http://www.francis.edu

Christian Hall.

ST. FRANCIS XAVIER UNIVERSITY

ANTIGONISH, NOVA SCOTIA, CANADA

The University

Set in the breathtaking hills of Nova Scotia on a picturesque campus, St. Francis Xavier University (StFX) was founded in 1853. The University is renowned for its tradition of academic excellence, community service, loyal alumni, and strong athletics. StFX prides itself on a personalized learning experience, international outreach, and an innovative teaching and research environment.

StFX is ranked among the top universities in Canada with respect to its undergraduate programs, postgraduate scholarships, and research grants. Primarily an undergraduate university, StFX provides liberal arts, business, science, and applied studies programs to 4,000 students. Among its unique areas of study are Celtic studies, Catholic studies, jazz studies, and aquatic resources.

StFX has students from every county in Nova Scotia, with the remainder from every province and territory in Canada, the United States, and around the world.

Building on a tradition of academic excellence and a commitment to providing the best possible student experience, StFX has top professors and state-of-the-art classroom technology, taking tradition, teaching, and learning to new heights. Friendly, accessible faculty members; small classes; strong WebFX technology; and Excel, a first-year student support program, all reflect StFX's commitment to student success.

A hallmark of StFX is its service to the community. The Antigonish Movement, a self-help program for farmers and fisheries workers, was pioneered early in this century. It provided the foundation for the establishment of the University's Extension Department in 1928. This was augmented in 1959 by the establishment of the world-renowned Coady International Institute, which annually attracts more than 50 Third World leaders to its social development programs. The training on campus and through overseas programs empowers people of developing countries to reach their potential through economic and social action.

While maintaining a strong Catholic tradition, StFX welcomes students and faculty and staff members of all denominations. In 1897, degrees were granted to 4 women, making StFX the first coeducational Catholic institution in North America. Today, 57 percent of the students are women.

Location

St. Francis Xavier University is located in the dynamic coastal town of Antigonish, in the Canadian province of Nova Scotia. Known as the Highland Heart of Nova Scotia, Antigonish is a two-hour drive from the capital city, Halifax. The town is a service hub for 20,000 residents of surrounding areas with a full range of modern facilities, including a hospital, banks, a shopping mall, and numerous restaurants and food outlets. Vibrant Main Street is home to many shops, services, and entertainment venues. The cultural diversity of the area, populated by the descendants of the Mi'kmaq, Acadian, Scottish, Dutch, and black settlers, is reflected in most aspects of the community. The area is surrounded by picturesque beaches, highlands, hiking trails, and a wildlife sanctuary within walking distance. Antigonish, home to many artists, is a popular tourist attraction with the renowned Highland Games, Theatre Antigonish, lobster and salmon suppers, and the area's natural, unspoiled beauty.

Majors and Degrees

The Bachelor of Arts degree with major is offered in aquatic resources; Catholic studies; Celtic studies; economics; English; French; history; mathematics and statistics; computer science; music; philosophy; political science; psychology; religious studies; sociology/anthropology; women's studies; and development studies.

For the Bachelor of Business Administration, students may choose the general degree; the degree with aquatic resources; the major in accounting, economics, enterprise development, finance, information systems, leadership studies, and marketing; honours in accounting, enterprise development, finance, leadership studies, and marketing; or joint honours in business administration and economics.

The Bachelor of Information Systems is a major program designed to prepare graduates as systems analysts, applications programmers, and information systems specialists. Business administration and information systems students have the opportunity to enroll in the cooperative education stream. This initiative, called the Expanded Classroom, enables students to gain a year's worth of paid experience in their field while they are enrolled in university.

The Bachelor of Arts in human kinetics studies human movement from an arts (humanities/social sciences) perspective. It prepares students for careers in coaching, health and fitness, or sports-related media and for further studies in education, sport history, sport philosophy, sport psychology, or sport sociology.

The Bachelor of Arts in music is an advanced major or honours degree program in jazz performance. The Bachelor of Music in jazz studies combines composition, arranging, and performance. The diploma in jazz studies is designed for students who wish to enter the field of commercial music.

The Bachelor of Education is a professional degree program that prepares graduates to enter the school system as teachers at either the elementary or the secondary level.

The Bachelor of Science with major is offered in aquatic resources; biology; chemistry; earth science; mathematics, statistics, and computer science; and physics. The advanced major, joint advanced major, honours, or joint honours programs are available in the above subjects (except aquatic resources), economics, and psychology.

The Bachelor of Science in human kinetics focuses on the scientific study of human movement and prepares students for careers in the health and fitness sector; studies at the graduate level in biomechanics, motor control, or exercise physiology; and admission to programs such as education, physiotherapy, athletic/exercise therapy, or medicine.

The Bachelor of Science in human nutrition program is offered with a concentration in foods and/or nutrition. Graduates may qualify for entrance to the Dietitians of Canada dietetic internship programs.

The Bachelor of Science in Nursing focuses on a unique health profession that is both an art and a science. Nursing is the professional practice of caring. The emphasis of the program is on understanding the personal, family, group, and community dimensions of health and illness by blending biological and social sciences, humanities, and professional nursing courses.

The Bachelor of Engineering program consists of a two-year diploma at StFX, which is followed by two years of study at DalTech, Dalhousie University in Halifax, or a comparable university. A student entering the second year of the diploma must choose one of the following engineering disciplines: biological, chemical, civil, computer, electrical, environmental, industrial, mechanical, metallurgical, or mining engineering.

In association with DalTech, Dalhousie University, StFX offers the first two years of a minimum of four calendar years of study in architecture leading to a Bachelor of Environmental Design Studies degree.

Academic Program

All bachelor's degrees, except the two-year Bachelor of Education, are four years. The diploma in engineering and the diploma in jazz are two-year programs. In the four-year programs, students declare a major only in the second half of the second year, thus permitting students to sample a broad selection of courses. Over the next two years, students pursue courses in their major and minor subjects in greater depth. Where available, students may choose the advanced major or honours program during the second year of study. Many courses have a service learning component in which students have the opportunity to become involved in community-based issues and projects, thus making their classroom learning more relevant.

The academic year is from September to April. Because of the condensed year, students have four months (May to August) for employment, study, or travel. StFX has an intersession (May–June) and a summer session (July–August); each lasts six weeks.

StFx ranks second in students who complete their degrees in the primarily undergraduate universities in Canada.

Off-Campus Programs

StFX has exchange agreements with more than twenty-five colleges and universities in the United States, Mexico, and England for the junior year abroad. Students have also studied at universities in Russia, Scotland, Lesotho, and Israel. Students on an exchange pay tuition to StFX; room and board are paid at the host institution.

Academic Facilities

StFX consists of thirty buildings on 100 acres of land with fifteen residences. The campus has state-of-the-art classrooms, labs, offices, dining halls, playing fields, gyms, a swimming pool, an ice rink, a theatre, an auditorium, and chapels. The Angus L. Macdonald Library has more than 800,000 books, periodicals, newspapers, and government documents. It houses one of the largest collections of Scottish and Gaelic materials in North America. NOVANET allows students access to library holdings at most universities and colleges in the province. The campuswide WebFX technology systems allow all students and the faculty access to world-class software and systems that are designed to enhance teaching and learning. All residence rooms have access to telephone and cable television at no additional cost, and each student is also given a telephone voice-mailbox account. Rooms are also wired for computer access.

Costs

In 2003–04 undergraduate tuition was $5310 for students from Canada. Students from other countries paid $9210. The Students' Union fee was $147.50 for all full-time students, and the information and technology fee was $300. Room and board prices varied, depending on the type of room and meal plan chosen, but ranged from $5695 to $5995. Books cost up to $1200.

Financial Aid

Scholarships range from $500 to $8000 per year. Guaranteed entrance scholarships of $500 are awarded to students with an entering average between 85 and 90 percent. Students with an average greater than 90 percent receive a guaranteed minimum scholarship of $1000. All major scholarships are renewable for up to four years. Entrance scholarships are awarded on the basis of academic performance in high school. Students compete for in-course scholarships each year, with awards given to students who rank in the top 10 percent of their class.

Between $1.5 and $2 million is awarded to students annually in the form of scholarships, awards, and bursaries. In addition, StFX offers more than 1,000 on-campus student jobs.

Faculty

StFX has more than 200 full-time faculty members and 30 part-time faculty members. With a student-faculty ratio of 17:1, students receive personalized attention both inside and outside of the classroom. All new students are either assigned a faculty adviser or meet with the faculty of their departments prior to registration. Eighty-four percent of first-year classes are taught by tenured or tenure-track professors, and 90 percent of full-time faculty members have their Ph.D. degree. Most faculty members are actively engaged in primary research, and students have many opportunities to become involved.

Student Government

The St. Francis Xavier University Students' Union is the official representative organization of the students. There are more than forty clubs and societies, along with regular organized social activities such as concerts, dances, and intramural sports. The union employs nearly 40 students on a part-time basis. The activities of the executive are overseen by the Students' Council, which is made up of elected student representatives from the residences and off-campus constituencies.

Admission Requirements

Students are admitted upon the completion of Nova Scotia Grade XII or the equivalent. The minimum requirements are a combined average of 75 percent or the equivalent in Grade XI and Grade XII, to include English each year and credit for five university-preparatory courses in each of Grade XI and Grade XII.

Students from the United States must have completed sixteen academic subjects, with at least four English courses to be considered. Students from a British system of education must have a General Certificate of Education at the ordinary level, including English and four other academic subjects, with no mark below a C or equivalent. Other students are considered on an individual basis.

Students who have a grade 11 average of at least 80 percent may be considered for early fall admission before their first set of grade 12 marks is available. Students applying for early fall admission should include their final grade 11 marks and a school-approved list of courses they are taking in grade 12 (both semesters) with their application. Grade 12 courses must be consistent with the guidelines listed in the academic calendar.

Application and Information

StFX begins to process applications in October for September admission and employs a rolling admissions policy. However, since many programs have a limited enrollment, students are encouraged to apply as early in the new year as possible.

All applications are considered on an individual basis by using the quality of the high school record, recommendations, and any other information submitted. An audition, performed in person or submitted on a tape, is required for any music program.

Students may obtain an application from their high school guidance counsellor, the StFX Web site, or the address listed below. Applicants must request transcripts from high schools and any postsecondary schools attended. Students from the United States must submit ACT or SAT I results. Students for whom English is a second language are required to achieve a TOEFL score of at least 580 and a TWE score of at least 4. StFX may admit and grant advanced standing to a student who has attended another college or university.

StFX recognizes that some individuals have physical or learning disabilities. To assist individuals with disabilities, the University offers the services of a contact person. For further information, students should call 902-867-2281.

Students are encouraged to visit during the academic year. If visits are planned in advance, students may attend classes, meet with professors, talk with the admissions or high school liaison officer, visit a residence, and have a meal on campus. If students have to travel a long distance, complimentary accommodations on campus can be reserved when available.

For information on admissions or to schedule a campus visit, students should contact:

Admissions Office
St. Francis Xavier University
P.O. Box 5000
Antigonish, Nova Scotia B2G 2W5
Canada
Telephone: 902-867-2445
877-867-7839 (toll-free in Canada or the U.S.)
Fax: 902-867-2329
E-mail: admit@stfx.ca
World Wide Web: http://www.stfx.ca

ST. JOHN FISHER COLLEGE

ROCHESTER, NEW YORK

The College

Founded in 1948 by the Basilian fathers, St. John Fisher College is dedicated to serving the individual needs of its students. Originally a Catholic college for men, Fisher is now an independent, coeducational college with 57 percent women and 57 percent resident students. The College offers twenty-eight undergraduate programs in business, the humanities, nursing, sciences, and social sciences and is accredited by the Middle States Association of Colleges and Schools. The College also offers eleven graduate programs leading to the Master of Business Administration, the Master of Science, and the Master of Science in Education.

Fisher's unique First-Year Program reaches beyond the transition to college to focus on developing responsible campus citizens with independent learning skills, who fully explore educational and career aspirations. The Learning Communities Program gives first-year students the opportunity to take courses in clusters that focus on a central theme. Through this approach to learning, students and faculty members examine a complex topic from multiple perspectives and discover connections among various disciplines. Fisher's Learning Communities also enable students to learn cooperatively and develop close working relationships with other students and faculty members.

Fisher offers a full range of extracurricular activities designed to cater to the diverse interests of the 2,200 full-time and 900 part-time students. Such activities include a student newspaper, a campus radio station, a complete intramural program, and almost forty student organizations. In addition, the Student Activities Board sponsors appearances by on-campus lecturers and entertainers, often taking advantage of the FishBowl, the College's student union.

Fisher is a member of NCAA Division III, ECAC, the NYS Women's Collegiate Athletic Association, and the Empire 8. Men's intercollegiate sports are baseball, basketball, football, golf, lacrosse, soccer, and tennis. Women's intercollegiate sports are basketball, cheerleading, lacrosse, soccer, softball, tennis, and volleyball. Club sports include ice hockey and men's and women's rugby. The Student Life Center, which is the hub of the athletic activities, includes courts for basketball, racquetball, squash, tennis, and volleyball; a sauna; a whirlpool; a lounge; an exercise area; and game rooms. Growney Stadium, complete with 2,100 bleacher seats and a press box, is equipped with an all-weather synthetic playing field to allow for all-season and nighttime play. Other on-campus athletics facilities include a nine-hole golf course, a softball field, a baseball complex, four outdoor tennis courts, and three grass practice fields. In the summer, Fisher is proud to host the Buffalo Bills Training Camp on campus.

Location

Located on 140 parklike acres, Fisher offers a balance of city activity and suburban tranquility. Just 10 minutes from the Fisher campus, Rochester, the "World's Image Center," offers many cultural attractions, including the Eastman Theater, the Rochester Philharmonic Orchestra, the International Museum of Photography at George Eastman House, the Rochester Museum and Science Center, and the Strasenburgh Planetarium. Home to a number of Fortune 500 companies, such as Eastman Kodak Company, Xerox Corporation, and Bausch and Lomb, the city of Rochester offers Fisher students opportunities for internships and employment after graduation.

Majors and Degrees

St. John Fisher College offers courses leading to the Bachelor of Arts and Bachelor of Science degrees. Undergraduate majors are offered in accounting, American studies, anthropology, applied information technology, biology, chemistry, childhood education, communication/journalism, computer science, economics, English, French, history, interdisciplinary studies, international studies, management, mathematics, math/science/technology education, nursing, philosophy, physics, political science, psychology, religious studies, sociology, Spanish, special education, and sport studies. The areas of concentration available in the management major include finance, general business management, human resource management, and marketing.

Fisher offers a fast track to the B.S./M.S. in advanced practice nursing. The College also offers a cooperative 3+4 program with the Pennsylvania College of Optometry and a cooperative engineering program with the University of Detroit Mercy, Clarkson University, Manhattan College, Columbia University, and the University at Buffalo, The State University of New York.

Academic Programs

The bachelor's degree is conferred upon those who complete a minimum of 120 semester hours of credit with a cumulative GPA of at least 2.0. Thirty hours of credit and half of the requirements for the major must be earned at St. John Fisher College. Graduates of the accounting program are eligible to sit for the CPA and CMA examinations.

Off-Campus Programs

Fisher offers a multitude of special programs designed to complement its academic programs. Students in various disciplines can take advantage of an internship program, Albany and Washington Semesters, and cross-registration with fourteen member colleges of the Rochester Area College Consortium. Study-abroad opportunities throughout the world are also available to students.

Academic Facilities

Over the last five years, most of the academic and athletic facilities on campus have been upgraded and enhanced. Classrooms have been modernized and outfitted with state-of-the-art media facilities. Laboratory space has been upgraded with state-of-the-market educational technology. The Golisano Academic Gateway, complete with the Frontier Cyber Café and the learning resource center, opened in January 2001. The residence halls have been renovated, giving all students access to the Internet and cable TV in their rooms. The Ralph C. Wilson, Jr. Building opened in September 2003, expanding classroom capacity by 20 percent and providing additional faculty offices, seminar rooms, and meeting spaces.

The Charles J. Lavery Library is well positioned to meet the information needs of twenty-first-century students. A healthy blend of traditional and electronic resources, covering a broad range of subjects, is available to both the novice and experienced researcher. The library's automated catalog is supplemented by hundreds of electronic databases, and Internet access adds a whole new realm of information sources. Traditional resources in Lavery Library include 176,563 volumes; approximately 29,000 records, tapes, and CDs, and 1,133 periodical subscriptions. The library is open beyond regular academic hours for the convenience of students. Fisher's Career Services Department is also housed in the library.

Costs

Tuition for 2003–04 was $17,200. Room and board were $7450 with a fourteen-meal plan and a room in one of Fisher's residence halls.

Financial Aid

Committed to helping students meet the cost of their education, Fisher works to assess each individual's financial need. Financial aid is provided through scholarships, grants, loans, and work-study arrangements and is awarded by Fisher, the state, and the federal government. In 2003–04, the average financial aid package for Fisher students was $15,600.

St. John Fisher College offers a generous academic scholarship program that is based on high school average, class rank, and SAT or ACT results. Students eligible for academic scholarships are automatically notified by the Office of Undergraduate Admissions. Scholarship award amounts are $2500 to $9000 per year. The College also offers an honors program and a science scholars program. The award in each of these programs is $2500 in addition to an academic scholarship.

Eight years ago, the College introduced the Service Scholars Program. This program is designed to recognize and reward high school seniors who demonstrate an ongoing interest in serving the needs of others through a commitment to community service. Scholarship awards equal one third of the total yearly cost of tuition, fees, room, and board for four years. The Service Scholars Program recently won the President's Community Volunteer Award—the highest national honor for volunteering. The College was honored, along with 19 other winners from across the country, at a White House ceremony. Fisher was the only college or university and the only organization in New York State to be honored.

In 1998, the College announced the creation of the Fannie and Sam Constantino First Generation Scholarship Program, designed to provide financial assistance to students who are the first generation in their families to attend a postsecondary institution—much like the pioneer classes of St. John Fisher College. Recipients receive annual scholarships ranging from $4500 to one third of the total yearly cost of Fisher's tuition, fees, room, and board for four years.

Faculty

Fisher's 123 full-time faculty members are dedicated to helping students, both in and out of the classroom, as they strive to achieve their goals. Eighty-three percent of full-time faculty members hold doctoral or terminal degrees. The student-teacher ratio of 10:1 offers a personal approach to education; 75 percent of all classes have fewer than 30 students. Fisher's Office of Academic Affairs and an outstanding faculty share responsibility for academic advising, helping students to explore the twenty-eight majors that are available to them.

Student Government

Student leadership skills are developed through the Student Government Association, which is responsible for the social, cultural, and judicial areas of student life. Resident students elect a Resident Student Association, while commuting students elect a Commuter Council to represent them in planning special activities. The Student Activities Board is responsible for social activities and cultural events throughout the academic year.

Admission Requirements

Admission to St. John Fisher College is based primarily on the following: high school record, scores on standardized tests (SAT/ACT), extracurricular activities and/or work experience, and the high school's evaluation of the candidate. Interviews are also considered and strongly encouraged.

A candidate for admission to the freshman class must be a graduate of an approved secondary school and present a minimum of 16 units of college-preparatory course work in English, foreign languages, mathematics, and natural and social sciences. An applicant should present a secondary school average of 85 percent or above in these academic subjects.

Fisher welcomes qualified transfer students from two- and four-year colleges for both the fall and spring terms. To be considered for admission, transfer students must have a cumulative grade point average of 2.0 or better. If the student has obtained an A.A., A.S., or A.A.S. degree, 60 to 66 credit hours are transferred. All transfer applicants should consult the Undergraduate Bulletin for details.

The College has various special admission programs, including early decision, abbreviated procedures for veterans and other military personnel, and admission for nondegree and part-time study.

The College offers the New York State Higher Education Opportunity Program (NYS HEOP) for students who need special academic and financial assistance. The program provides academic support services, counseling, and financial aid for qualified students to help them achieve academic success.

Fisher grants college credit for satisfactory grades on the Advanced Placement test, the New York College Proficiency Examination, and the College-Level Examination Program (CLEP). Only students who receive a 3 or better in all AP subjects and a 4 or better on the AP science and language exams are granted advanced placement credit. CLEP scoring guidelines are available through the Office of Undergraduate Admissions.

Application and Information

Applications are accepted on a rolling basis. Early decision applications are due December 1. The priority deadline for freshman applications is March 1. A personal interview is not ordinarily required for admission; however, all applicants are encouraged to visit the College. Interviews and campus tours are available weekdays from 8:30 a.m. to 4:30 p.m. and on specified Saturdays from 9 a.m. to noon.

For additional information or an application, students should contact:

Office of Undergraduate Admissions
St. John Fisher College
3690 East Avenue
Rochester, New York 14618
Telephone: 585-385-8064
800-444-4640 (toll-free)
E-mail: admissions@sjfc.edu
World Wide Web: http://www.sjfc.edu

On the campus, with Kearney Tower rising in the background.

ST. JOHN'S COLLEGE

ANNAPOLIS, MARYLAND, AND SANTA FE, NEW MEXICO

The College

St. John's College maintains two widely separated campuses, one in Annapolis, Maryland, and another in Santa Fe, New Mexico. Each has its own admissions and financial aid offices. A common curriculum, however, enables students and faculty members to move from one campus to the other. Both campuses are cohesive intellectual communities in which students are eagerly responsive to one another. Students also pursue interests in such activities as publications, dance, dramatics, photography, art, wilderness exploration, and sailing. The social climate is informal and lively, and students enjoy many celebrations each year. Facilities are available for almost any intramural sport; most students participate. There is a bookstore on each campus. In fall 2003, opening enrollment at the Annapolis campus was 221 women and 259 men, for a total of 480 students. The opening enrollment of 444 at the Santa Fe campus consisted of 200 women and 244 men.

The students on both campuses are outstanding, yet they fit no pattern. Though their backgrounds are varied geographically, academically, and otherwise, they are, most typically, young people who habitually read books and value good conversation. Their commitment to ideas and their enthusiasm for the St. John's program are well illustrated by the fact that about one third of them on each campus have transferred to St. John's as freshmen after a year or more of college elsewhere.

Location

St. John's is the third-oldest college in the United States. It has been located since 1696 in the Colonial seaport city of Annapolis, the capital of Maryland, 30 miles from Washington, D.C. In 1964, a second campus was opened at the foot of the mountains surrounding Santa Fe, a cultural center and the capital of New Mexico. The campuses are alike in curriculum and methods, but their settings and moods are as different as sailing on the Chesapeake Bay and skiing in the Sangre de Cristo Mountains, as Georgian and Spanish Colonial architecture. St. John's students participate in a number of activities of benefit to their communities at large.

Majors and Degrees

St. John's College is committed to liberal education in the most traditional and yet radical way. It accomplishes this through direct engagement with the books in which the greatest minds of Western civilization have expressed themselves and through translation, mathematical demonstration, musical analysis, and laboratory experimentation. Whether in Annapolis or in Santa Fe, all St. John's students follow the same course of study leading to the B.A. degree. One of the purposes of this program is to emphasize the unity of knowledge; thus the faculty is not divided into departments and there are no majors.

Academic Program

The academic program is a unified, cohesive whole; instruction takes the form of annual sequences of related seminars, tutorials, and laboratories, in each of which the books that form the core of the curriculum are the basis of study and discussion. To ensure that the intellectual life of the College extends beyond the classroom and that students bring a common frame of reference to the continuing discussion, this academic program is required of everyone, but no two students are expected to approach any subject in the same way or to reach the same conclusions about it. A central purpose of the St. John's program is to give students both the opportunity and the obligation to think for themselves. The books at the heart of the program serve to foster that thinking. They not only illuminate the enduring questions of human existence but also have great relevance to contemporary problems. They can change minds, move hearts, and touch spirits. They help all students to arrive independently at rational opinions and conclusions of their own. From this common curriculum, about 35 percent of the students in each class go on to graduate and professional study in a wide range of fields.

There are two semesters a year. All classes are small discussion groups and range in size from between 12 and 16 students in tutorials to between 18 and 20 in seminars and laboratories. Final examinations are oral and individual. Students are not routinely informed of their grades. Instead, a student's tutors, as members of the faculty are called, evaluate the student's intellectual performance twice a year in his or her presence and with his or her help. St. John's students are participants in their own education. Annual essays and shorter papers, prepared by students without recourse to secondary sources, are based directly on the books of the program.

Seminars are devoted to reading works of the greatest minds and engaging in thoughtful discussion about them. The first-year seminar focuses on Greek authors; the second on the works of the Roman, medieval, and early Renaissance periods; the third on books of the seventeenth and eighteenth centuries; and the fourth on writings from the nineteenth and twentieth centuries. The seminar consists almost exclusively of student conversation. The aim of the discussions is to ascertain not how things were but how things are. Everyone's opinion must be heard and must also be supported by argument and evidence. The role of the tutors is not to give information or to produce the "right" interpretation; it is to guide the discussion, to aid in defining the issues, and to help the students to understand the authors, the issues, and themselves. If tutors do take a definite stand and enter the argument, they are expected to defend their positions just as students do. Reason is the only recognized authority.

Preceptorials replace seminars for eight weeks of the junior and senior years. In the preceptorial, students and tutors gather in groups of 8 or 9 to discuss, with more leisure than the pace and discipline of the seminar permit, books or topics of particular interest to them.

In the language tutorial, Greek is studied in the first two years and French in the last two. By translating works written in Greek and French into English and comparing those languages with each other as well as with English, the student gains an appreciation of all three and learns something of the nature of language in general.

The language of number and figure does not require a special aptitude. Rather, mathematics is an integral and necessary part of comprehending the world. The mathematics tutorial seeks to effect an understanding of the fundamental nature and intention of mathematics. Throughout the four years, the student is in contact not only with the pure science of mathematics but also with the foundations of mathematical physics and astronomy. The blackboard becomes an arena of logical struggle, which brings the imagination constantly into play.

The music tutorial aims at understanding music through study of musical theory and analysis of significant works. Students investigate rhythm, the diatonic system, the ratios of musical intervals, melody, counterpoint, and harmony.

In the modern world, the liberal arts are practiced at their best and fullest in the laboratory. This practice puts into serious question the common distinction between the "natural sciences" and the "humanities." The laboratory is a part of the program in all years but the second. It weaves together the main themes of physics, biology, and chemistry with careful scrutiny of the interplay of hypothesis, theory, and observed fact.

On Friday evenings, the College community assembles for a formal lecture or concert by a tutor or visitor. It is the only time the students are lectured to. Afterward, interested students and faculty members engage the speaker or performer in questions and discussion.

Academic Facilities

The library on each campus—about 100,000 volumes in Annapolis, nearly 60,000 in Santa Fe—emphasizes material appropriate to the nature of the academic program, supplemented by a more general collection and by a variety of special collections. Recordings and representative periodicals and newspapers are included. Academic facilities on each campus also include the resources and equipment necessary for study and experimentation in physics, chemistry, and biology (including a planetarium in Annapolis); for audition and performance of music; for display and studio work in art, photography, and other crafts; and for drama productions.

Costs

For 2003–04, annual tuition and fees totaled $28,840. Room and board were $7320. Books and supplies range in cost from $200 to $275. Personal expenses depend on the student's habits and tastes.

Financial Aid

The criterion for financial assistance is need. On both campuses the application for financial aid is the CSS PROFILE supplemented by the Free Application for Federal Student Aid (FAFSA) and an institutional aid application. More than half of all St. John's students receive aid, usually in a combination of grant, loan, and employment. Federal Perkins Loans, Federal Pell Grants, Federal Supplemental Educational Opportunity Grants, Federal Work-Study employment, and College grants and jobs are available.

Faculty

The faculty-student ratio is 1:8 on each campus. Faculty members all hold the same rank. Their intellectual range and vitality come from teaching throughout the curriculum. This breadth and tension and the fact that St. John's is an intellectual community in which all teach and all learn are distinctive characteristics of the St. John's faculty.

Student Government

Inside the classroom and out, the dignity of the students as adults is respected. On both campuses, student government is part of the general College pattern. A Delegate Council and Student Committee on Instruction work with the faculty and administrators on matters of mutual concern.

Admission Requirements

Criteria for admission to either campus are intellectual and academic, though any accomplishment showing initiative and drive may strengthen an application. The written application consists of a series of reflective essays. The academic record and recommendations are considered supplements to it. SAT I or ACT scores are optional but may prove helpful. There are no minimums for grades or test scores; both may be made irrelevant by what the candidate writes. On each campus, applicants are judged on their own merits. Each year a small percentage enter directly from the eleventh grade. Although interviews are not required except in special cases, interested students are urged to visit either campus for several days to sit in on seminars and tutorials.

Application and Information

Students may be admitted to either campus for the fall term or, if they are prepared to continue their studies through the following summer, in January. Application must be made to one campus or the other, not to both. Early application is advisable. Each campus seeks to complete its class by mid-May. All applications for admission and financial aid are acted on as soon as they are complete, and the candidate is notified of the decision within two weeks.

In response to inquiries, the College sends a catalog, information on financial aid, an application form, and forms for the school report and for recommendations. Students should contact:

John Christensen
Director of Admissions
St. John's College
Annapolis, Maryland 21404

Larry Clendenin
Director of Admissions
St. John's College
Santa Fe, New Mexico 87501

Annapolis campus.

Santa Fe campus.

ST. JOHN'S UNIVERSITY

JAMAICA, STATEN ISLAND, MANHATTAN, AND EASTERN LONG ISLAND, NEW YORK, AND ROME, ITALY

The University

Since its inception in 1870, St. John's University has excelled at preparing young people for personal and professional success. Founded by the Vincentian Community, St. John's is one of America's leading Catholic universities.

St. John's occupies five handsome sites: a tree-lined, 105-acre residential campus in Jamaica, Queens; a charming, 16.5-acre residential campus in Grymes Hill, Staten Island; an award-winning, ten-story residential campus in Manhattan's financial center; a 175-acre location in Oakdale, New York; and a Graduate Center in Rome, Italy. Chartered by the State Education Department of New York, St. John's is accredited by the Middle States Association of Colleges and Schools. Its varied programs are accredited by such organizations as AACSB International–The Association to Advance Collegiate Schools of Business, the American Association for Accreditation of Laboratory Animal Care, the American Bar Association, the American Chemical Society, the American Council on Pharmaceutical Education, the American Library Association, the American Psychological Association, the American Speech-Language-Hearing Association, and the Association of American Law Schools.

St. John's enrolls 11,602 full-time undergraduates, yet its low 18:1 student-faculty ratio ensures personal attention. Many of the University's 130,000 alumni hold top-level positions in government, industry, and the private sector. The Queens campus comprises St. John's College of Liberal Arts and Sciences, the Peter J. Tobin College of Business, the School of Education, the College of Pharmacy and Allied Health Professions, the College of Professional Studies, and the School of Law. The Staten Island campus includes St. John's College of Liberal Arts and Sciences, the Peter J. Tobin College of Business, the School of Education, and the College of Professional Studies. The Graduate Center in Rome, Italy, offers an M.A. in government and politics and an M.B.A. program.

Location

The Jamaica, Queens, campus is in a tree-lined, residential neighborhood that is just off the Grand Central Parkway. The Staten Island campus, on a hill that overlooks New York Harbor, is close to the Verrazano Narrows Bridge. By car, these two campuses are 40 minutes at most from the many attractions of midtown Manhattan. The Oakdale location is on Suffolk County's south shore. The Rome Graduate Center is located at the Pontificio Oratorio San Pietro, off Via Aurelia on Via Santa Maria Mediatrice.

Majors and Degrees

St. John's offers more than 100 academic majors. At the Queens campus, St. John's College of Liberal Arts and Sciences offers the B.A. in anthropology, Asian studies, economics, English, environmental studies, French, government and politics, history, Italian, mathematics, philosophy, psychology, public administration and public service, sociology, Spanish, speech (public address), speech pathology and audiology, and theology.

The Bachelor of Fine Arts is available in art (graphic design, illustration, painting, photography, and printing). The Bachelor of Science is available in biology, chemistry, environmental studies, mathematical physics, mathematics, physical science, and physics. St. John's College also offers a five-year B.A./M.A. program in English, government and politics, history, mathematics, sociology, Spanish, and theology. Students may also choose five-year B.S./M.S. programs in biology and chemistry, a B.A./J.D. or B.S./J.D. degree with St. John's School of Law, a B.S./D.D.S. degree that combines an undergraduate biology degree with a Doctor of Dental Surgery degree from Columbia University's School of Dental and Oral Medicine, a B.S./O.D. degree that combines undergraduate work in biology with a Doctor of Optometry degree from SUNY College of Optometry, and an early medical education program with SUNY Health Science Center at Brooklyn, guaranteeing admission after requirements are fulfilled. Bachelor's degree students in St. John's College are eligible for the pre-M.B.A. program. The Institute of Asian Studies, under the auspices of St. John's College, offers a B.A. in Asian studies and a five-year B.A./M.A. in East Asian studies. The Peter J. Tobin College of Business offers the B.S. in accounting, actuarial science, economics, finance, management, management information sciences, marketing, and risk management and insurance. A five-year B.S./M.S. in accounting is also available. In the School of Education, programs lead to the Bachelor of Science in Education (B.S.Ed.), including childhood education certification, grades 1–6, and childhood education/special education certification, grades 1–6. Also offered are the B.S. in human services and the B.S.Ed./M.S. in childhood education/special education certification. The School of Education also offers an adolescent education certification degree program in cooperation with St. John's College of Liberal Arts and Sciences. The College of Pharmacy and Allied Health Professions grants the Doctor of Pharmacy (Pharm.D., six years), the Bachelor of Science in cytotechnology, and the Bachelor of Science in Medical Technology. There is a five-year B.S./M.S. degree program in toxicology, along with programs leading to the B.S. in pathologist assistant studies, physician assistant studies, and toxicology. Programs in the College of Professional Studies lead to the B.S. in administrative studies, communication arts, computer science, criminal justice, funeral service administration, health services administration, hospitality management, journalism, legal studies, microcomputer systems, sport management, telecommunications, and television and film production. The B.A. is available with majors in literature and speech and in social science. Also offered are five-year B.S./M.A. programs in communication arts/government and politics, communication arts/sociology, criminal justice/government and politics, criminal justice/sociology, health services administration/government and politics, health services administration/sociology, journalism/government and politics, and paralegal studies/sociology.

Preprofessional programs include dentistry, engineering, law, medicine, osteopathy, social work, veterinary medicine, and other health-related fields. A combined B.A./J.D. or B.S./J.D. degree program is available with any undergraduate major.

Also, the College of Professional Studies offers an A.A. degree in liberal arts, as well as A.S. degrees in business (accounting and general business), criminal justice, electronic data processing, microcomputer technology, legal studies, paraprofessional school service, and telecommunications. Certificate programs are available in business administration, computer science, health services administration, international criminal justice, legal studies, sport management, and telecommunications. Most programs are also offered on evenings and weekends.

At Staten Island, St. John's College of Liberal Arts and Sciences offers the B.A. or B.S. in economics, English, government and politics, history, mathematics, philosophy, psychology, social studies, sociology, and speech (communication arts or language, pathology, and audiology). St. John's College also offers B.A. degrees in economics, philosophy, and theology, as well as a B.S. in computer science and speech-language pathology and audiology. Students may choose a five-year B.A./M.A. program in government and politics. Also available are a B.A./J.D. or B.S./J.D. degree that combines any undergraduate degree with a law degree from St. John's School of Law. Students pursuing a liberal arts degree may pursue a preprofessional concentration in business. The A.A. in liberal arts is also available.

The Peter J. Tobin College of Business at Staten Island offers the B.S. in accounting, actuarial science, finance, management, marketing, and risk management. Also offered is a five-year B.S./M.S. in accounting. In the School of Education, programs lead to the Bachelor of Science in Education, including childhood education certification, grades 1–6; childhood education/special education certification, grades 1–6; and the B.S./M.S. in childhood education/special education certification. The School of Education also offers an adolescent education certification degree program with St. John's College of Liberal Arts and Sciences.

The Staten Island campus also offers degree and certificate programs through the College of Professional Studies. Programs lead to the B.S. in administrative studies, communication arts, computer science, criminal justice, funeral service administration, hospitality management, legal studies, safety and corporate security administration, sports management, telecommunication, television and film production, and transportation and logistics. There are combined B.A./J.D. and B.S./J.D. programs. Also available are A.S. degree programs in business (accounting and general business), criminal justice, paralegal studies, and telecommunications. Preprofessional programs include dentistry, engineering, law, medicine, osteopathy, social work, veterinary medicine, and other health-related fields.

At the Manhattan campus, the Peter J. Tobin College of Business offers innovative degree programs in actuarial science, risk management, and insurance.

Academic Program

To graduate, students in St. John's College of Liberal Arts and Sciences are expected to complete a minimum of 126 semester hours for the B.A., 126 semester hours for the B.S., or 144 semester hours for the B.F.A. The School of Education requires completion of 126 to 139 semester hours.

The College of Professional Studies requires completion of 126 to 127 semester hours for the B.S. and B.A. degrees. Students in the Peter J. Tobin College of Business must complete 130 to 134 semester hours. In the College of Pharmacy and Allied Health Professions, students in the six-year pharmacy program are expected to complete a minimum of 201 semester hours. The B.S. program in cytotechnology requires 128 semester hours. For the physician assistant studies program, 134 semester hours must be completed; 133 semester hours in the toxicology or pathologist assistant studies program; and 132 semester hours in the medical technology program.

Students in associate degree programs are required to complete 60–63 semester hours. All students are expected to fulfill core requirements for their college, along with completing their major sequence and free-elective groupings.

Academic Facilities

The St. John's University Libraries comprise three major research libraries on three campuses. Their collections total more than 1.7 million volumes of books, periodicals, microfilm, microfiche, and audiovisual materials.

The Queens campus is home to the Main Library and the Law School Library. St. Augustine Hall houses the Main Library, including a selective depository for United States government documents. It also includes the Governor Hugh L. Carey Collection, the William M. Fischer Lawn Tennis Library, the Asian Collection, the Health Education Resource Center, an Instructional Materials Center, and a Media Center. At Staten Island, the Loretto Memorial Library includes a collection of literary masterpieces, a record collection of music and poetry readings, a language laboratory, and an audiovisual department. Both campuses feature state-of-the art computer laboratories. There are more than 100 high-tech classrooms and advanced laboratories for research in biology, chemistry, physics, pharmacy, and allied health. There is also a special laboratory that is specifically for students taking language majors. In addition, the Manhattan campus has one of the nation's largest collections of literature on insurance and actuarial science.

On the Queens campus, new residence halls offer students the best in on-campus living, including fully wired rooms, 24-hour security, a separate computer center, a fitness center, club space, and a spacious dining hall. On Staten Island, students can choose comfortable, apartment-style residences that are adjacent to the campus. Housing is also available at the Manhattan campus.

Costs

In the 2003–04 academic year, tuition for a full-time student (12 to 18 credits per semester) was $19,600 per academic year. Tuition may vary by program and class year. Mandatory fees totaled $480. St. John's offers a fixed rate tuition option for students who want to lock in at a set cost for all four years. Room and board were $10,100.

Financial Aid

During the 2003–04 academic year, approximately 90 percent of students at St. John's received some form of financial assistance. The University provided in excess of $242 million in aid through scholarships, loans, grants, and work-study programs. At St. John's, financial aid is awarded primarily on the basis of financial need. Students are encouraged to file the Free Application for Federal Student Aid (FAFSA) as their major financial aid application no later than February 1.

Faculty

Professors at St. John's enjoy international recognition for their scholarship and commitment to teaching. There are 1,111 faculty members (561 full-time, 550 part-time); 89 percent of full-time faculty members hold doctoral or other terminal degrees in their fields.

Student Government

At St. John's, the Student Government represents and serves the student body through effective and responsible leadership. Student Government funds and coordinates the more than 180 student organizations and clubs on both the Queens and Staten Island campuses.

Admission Requirements

Admission to St. John's is determined by the applicant's previous academic performance, satisfactory achievement on appropriate standardized tests, recommendations, and other factors that suggest academic potential and personal motivation.

A minimum of 16 academic units earned at an accredited secondary institution or an appropriate score on the GED test is required. The units should include 6 electives, of which at least 3 must be in academic subjects; 4 in English; 2 in mathematics (elementary algebra, plane geometry, or tenth-year mathematics); 2 in foreign language; 1 in history; and 1 in science. These requirements may vary, depending on the program.

Application and Information

Students may apply by submitting an official high school transcript, official scores on the SAT I or ACT, and a completed and signed application for admission along with a $30 processing fee. St. John's waives the processing fee for students who apply online via the University's Web site. Transfer students are encouraged to apply. St. John's advises transfer students to have all records of previous high school and college work forwarded to the Office of Admission. On-campus interviews are conducted through the Office of Admission. Students may apply anytime under St. John's rolling admission policy; this is true for all but the pharmacy degree program, which has a January 15 deadline.

For further information on the Queens and Manhattan campuses, students should contact:

Office of Admission
St. John's University
8000 Utopia Parkway
Jamaica, New York 11439
Telephone: 718-990-2000 (New York City area)
888-9STJOHNS (toll-free)
Fax: 718-990-2096

For further information on the Staten Island campus, students should contact:

Office of Admission
St. John's University
300 Howard Avenue
Staten Island, New York 10301
Telephone: 718-390-4500
Fax: 718-390-4298
E-mail: tolasb@stjohns.edu
World Wide Web: http://www.stjohns.edu

SAINT JOSEPH COLLEGE

WEST HARTFORD, CONNECTICUT

The College

For seventy years, Saint Joseph College has been combining excellence in liberal arts with professional education for women. Founded in 1932 by the Sisters of Mercy, the original Women's College has expanded to include a coeducational Graduate School and baccalaureate program for working professionals. In partnership with each other, these units of the College offer a diverse student population unmatched opportunities to excel—intellectually, socially, and ethically.

There are 1,287 undergraduates in the Women's College, where faculty members and students have high mutual expectations and strive to maximize each person's potential. The College is a community that promotes the growth of the whole person in a caring environment that encourages strong ethical values, personal integrity, and a sense of responsibility to the needs of society. Women lead every organization, from the Business Society and Student Government to Campus Ministry and Intercultural Affairs. They edit the journals; lead the choirs, dance, and drama groups; and captain every athletic team. Students also serve with faculty members and administrators on all major committees, from strategic planning to Web site development to the Administrative Council—a small group of top advisers to the President. In just nine years since the state-of-the-art athletic center was constructed, the College has become competitive in eight NCAA Division III sports: basketball, cross-country, lacrosse, softball, soccer, swimming/diving, tennis, and volleyball. The athletic center features a six-lane pool, gymnasium, suspended jogging track, dance studio, and fitness center.

Saint Joseph College has thirteen Georgian brick buildings, including five residence halls, which are arranged around two tree-lined quadrangles on an 84-acre campus. Approximately 75 percent of the full-time Women's College students live on campus. Special student services include career planning, alumnae mentors, internship placement, counseling, health services, academic advisement, and a campus ministry team. Most recently, the College constructed the new Carol Autorino Center to establish the arts and humanities as an integral part of the student psyche. The center celebrates and articulates the College's rich liberal arts tradition.

Saint Joseph College alumnae have considerable impact on the welfare of their communities. They are leaders in many fields, including aerospace research, business, medicine, education, social work, environmental science, law, and politics. Recent graduates enjoy successful careers in business, industry, government, nonprofit organizations, education, health care, human services, and the arts.

Saint Joseph College is accredited by the New England Association of Schools and Colleges. The chemistry program is approved by the American Chemical Society and the social work program, by the Council on Social Work Education. The Coordinated Undergraduate Program in Dietetics is accredited by the American Dietetic Association. The nursing program is accredited by the National League for Nursing Accrediting Commission.

Location

The College is located in suburban West Hartford, 4 miles from the state capital and the city of Hartford's arts and entertainment district. Among the nearby attractions are the Hartford Civic Center and Coliseum; Bushnell Memorial Hall, where the latest Broadway musicals are performed; and the Wadsworth Atheneum, the oldest public art gallery in the United States. Hartford is a cosmopolitan city with diverse ethnic flavors. It is also the home of the Tony Award–winning Hartford Stage Company; the Hartford Symphony Orchestra; the Connecticut Opera Company and the Hartford Ballet; the Meadows Music Theatre, which features indoor and outdoor concerts; and several shopping venues, coffee bars, and restaurants.

Majors and Degrees

Saint Joseph College has always enjoyed a strong academic reputation based on a combination of liberal arts and professional majors. The College awards the B.A. or B.S. in American studies, art history, biology, biology/chemistry, chemistry, child study, computer science, dietetics and nutrition, economics, English, environmental science, family studies, history, history/political science, international studies, management, mathematics, mathematics/economics, nursing, philosophy, psychology, religious studies, social work, sociology, Spanish, and special education.

Teaching certification is offered in five areas: early childhood education, elementary education, middle school education, secondary education, and special education.

Research, clinical, and work placements are factored into all majors as an important component of each student's program. For instance, nursing majors begin their clinical training early in the sophomore year.

Academic Programs

Each student must complete a minimum of 120 credits to obtain a baccalaureate degree, and 53 of those credits should be distributed among the general education/liberal arts courses at the College. Specifically, students must take courses in the humanities, social sciences, natural sciences, mathematics, religious studies, and physical education. The study of a foreign language is recommended. An academic adviser assists each student in planning her program of study.

An honors program is available. The Academic Resources Center provides tutoring and other academic support services. Students may design their own major or may develop an interdisciplinary major or minor around a particular theme or problem related to their special talents, personal interests, or career goals. An exciting component of most majors at Saint Joseph College is the internship. These supervised field placements provide on-the-job experience, introduce students to various career opportunities, and produce significant employment contacts. Students earn credit for internships at a variety of sites, including the state capital, the Bushnell Theatre, Aetna, Legislative Office, the Connecticut Department of Economic Development, WVIT-TV, Connecticut Children's Medical Center, and the Science Center of Connecticut.

Off-Campus Programs

Students at Saint Joseph College may take courses at cooperating institutions through the Hartford Consortium for Higher Education. This is a special arrangement among Hartford-area colleges—Saint Joseph College, Rensselaer at Hartford, Trinity College, Saint Thomas Seminary, and the University of Hartford—through which students are able to take courses not offered at their home institution. No additional tuition is charged, and all credits are transferable.

Students at Saint Joseph College may study abroad during their junior year, a winter recess, or a summer session. Certain majors have specific international-study recommendations and opportunities, and the student is assisted by the Director of International Study in planning for an international-study experience. Cultural exchange programs with institutions in Japan, England, and Denmark are also available.

Academic Facilities

The Pope Pius XII Library has a collection of more than 134,000 volumes, including computer databases, periodicals, microforms, audiovisuals, an OPAC, and a Web page. A collection of materials used in elementary and secondary education is featured in the Curriculum Materials Center.

The College has two laboratory schools. The renowned School for Young Children is located one block from campus. It is a preschool and prekindergarten/kindergarten that provides child study majors with training and experience. The Gengras Center is located on campus. It is a community resource serving children and young adults (ages 3–21). It provides for special education needs and also helps to prepare special education teachers.

The College's primary technology centers are located in McDonough Hall. World Wide Web and e-mail services are available throughout campus. Additional facilities and services include a media center that provides production materials, expertise, and equipment for making and using a number of media instructional aids; state-of-the-art science and nursing labs; the Academic Resources Center, which provides professional and peer tutoring; music and dance facilities; and an art study gallery that exhibits changing selections from the more than 500 prints and several hundred paintings that are part of the College's art collection. The College recently celebrated the grand opening of the Carol Autorino Center, which includes Lynch Hall and the Bruyette Athenaeum, featuring a 350-seat auditorium, five art galleries, print study room, large lecture hall, reception room, music practice rooms, and the Bistro. The building also houses the College's archives and art collections.

Costs

The tuition and fees for full-time freshmen entering in 2003 were $20,350. Room and board cost $8745. The cost per credit for part-time students was $515.

Financial Aid

The goal of the Saint Joseph College Financial Aid Program is to place a high-quality, private education within the reach of as many qualified students as possible. This goal is achieved by offering need- and merit-based financial aid awards that include a combination of grants, loans, and on-campus employment opportunities. More than 85 percent of full-time undergraduate students receive some form of financial assistance.

Faculty

Saint Joseph College's faculty consists of 78 full-time faculty members and 4 librarians. Of the total faculty, 68 percent are women. Of the full-time faculty, 90 percent have a doctorate or another terminal degree in their field. Small classes benefit both students and professors. The faculty-student ratio is 1:12. The faculty and all members of the College community promote the welfare of students and help them attain the objectives set forth by the College's mission. Faculty members also participate in many extracurricular activities, including sports, campus ministry, and community service; direct students in independent study; involve students in scholarly research; and act as mentors before and after graduation.

Student Government

The Student Government Association works for effective communication among students, faculty members, and administrators. Students are encouraged to voice their opinions and concerns to the association for consideration and action. In addition, student representatives sit as voting members with faculty members and administrators on major College-wide committees. The Student Government Association encourages the development of leadership skills and provides funds annually for several of its members to attend leadership workshops.

Admission Requirements

Saint Joseph College seeks women who are willing to accept the challenge of an excellent academic program while pursuing the interests and goals that will shape their future lives. Applications are encouraged from interested students of every race, age, and religious affiliation. In accordance with Section 504 of the Rehabilitation Act of 1973, which prohibits discrimination on the basis of disability, and the Americans with Disabilities Act of 1990, Saint Joseph College is committed to the goal of achieving equal educational opportunities and full participation for people with disabilities in higher education. Candidates for freshman admission should complete a four-year course of study in a regionally accredited secondary school. The program should include 16 academic units in college-preparatory courses distributed among the areas of English, mathematics, natural sciences, social studies, and foreign languages. Applicants are required to submit scores of the SAT I or ACT tests. A personal interview is a highly recommended part of the admission procedure, since it offers a mutual opportunity for the student and College personnel to discuss educational and professional goals. The Committee on Admissions operates on the principle that a student's ability, motivation, and maturity should be determined by a careful individual review of all the applicant's credentials, including the academic record, standardized test scores, written personal statement, and guidance counselor's evaluation. Special consideration may be given to some applicants whose preparation varies from the recommended pattern but whose record gives evidence of genuine intellectual ability and interest. International students should contact the director of admissions for further information. Saint Joseph College admits qualified students for transfer in both fall and spring semesters.

Application and Information

The Committee on Admissions recommends that application for freshman admission be made in the first semester of the senior year in secondary school. All applications should be completed by May 1. Students planning to apply for financial aid should do so at the same time they apply for admission. A nonrefundable $35 fee must be sent to the director of admissions with the application.

Transfer applicants for the spring semester should apply by December 1; applicants for the fall semester, by July 1. Students applying to the nursing program should contact the College to learn about special deadlines. Transfer candidates who wish to apply for financial aid should complete the admission procedure by June 1.

For further information about admission to Saint Joseph College, students should contact:

Mary E. Yuskis, Ed.D.
Director of Admissions
Saint Joseph College
1678 Asylum Avenue
West Hartford, Connecticut 06117
Telephone: 860-231-5216
Fax: 860-231-5744
E-mail: admissions@sjc.edu
World Wide Web: http://www.sjc.edu

Students at Saint Joseph College.

SAINT JOSEPH'S COLLEGE

RENSSELAER, INDIANA

The College

Saint Joseph's College (SJC), a private Catholic institution of higher education, was founded in 1889 by the Missionaries of the Precious Blood (C.PP.S.). Dedicated to individual learning, SJC prides itself on delivering academic excellence through the liberal arts and instilling in students the message of the Gospel for use in their personal lives and professional careers. The College's nationally recognized Core Program challenges each student to question his or her own values, as well as welcome the ideas and opinions of others.

Reaccredited by the Higher Learning Commission of the North Central Association of Colleges and Schools in 2002 and named as a "college that builds character" by *The Templeton Guide: Colleges That Encourage Character Development*, SJC has seventy-nine major, minor, and pre-professional programs, each with several tailored concentrations to meet the interests of every student. The College's enduring commitment to higher education has fostered strong programs in career development and alumni networking. The Career Development Center connects students with alumni who share similar career tracks, and many participate in internships as early as their sophomore year.

Approximately 1,000 men and women attend SJC, coming from twenty-seven states and seven countries.

A span of 180 acres, the campus can be grouped into four areas: academics, student activities, athletics, and housing. The center of academic activity is the Rev. Charles Banet, C.PP.S. Core Education Center. Dedicated in 1995, the facility includes state-of-the-art multimedia classrooms, computer and science laboratories, and faculty offices. The Arts and Science Building includes two newly remodeled science labs and the Robinson Memorial Library. Both buildings are handicapped accessible.

The Halleck Student Center is home to many of the College's student activities and social events. The center includes a dining facility, the College Store, a 300-seat ballroom, the student government offices, the student newspaper production center, a Counseling and Career Services Center, the Housing and Residence Life Office, the Office of Student Activities, a commuting-student lounge, and the Puma Marching Band headquarters. The Student Center also has a licensed private club, an after-hours snack bar, and a refurbished cafeteria.

The athletic complex contains a student/employee private fitness center, a three-court recreation center, and a weight-training facility. The housing facilities consist of renovated residence halls and newly built residential suites.

The College fosters opportunities for students to become actively involved in more than fifty academic and social clubs. An active social calendar is in force throughout the year and includes major weekend celebrations such as Homecoming, Little Sibs Weekend, "I Hate Winter" Week, "Little 500" Go-Kart Race, and Parents' Weekend. In addition, the Office of Student Activities sponsors several trips each semester to cultural, sporting, and recreational events in Indianapolis and Chicago.

The Pumas are members of the Great Lakes Valley Conference and are Division II members of the NCAA. The teams compete in a complete program of intercollegiate men's baseball, basketball, cross-country, football, golf, soccer, tennis, and track; women compete in basketball, cross-country, golf, soccer, softball, tennis, track, and volleyball. An active intramural sports program encourages students to keep fit and enjoy competition among the various residence halls in their leisure time.

There are nine residence halls on campus, housing 84 percent of the students. The residence hall program promotes a close living/learning community and has seniors, juniors, sophomores, and freshmen living on each floor. Students learn from their peers and pass on valuable traditions of school spirit, active participation, and academic integrity.

Saint Joseph's College also offers programs at the graduate level, including a master's degree in music with a concentration in church music and liturgy and courses in Gregorian Chant. These programs are only available during the summer months.

Location

The College is located in Rensselaer, Indiana. Rensselaer has a population of 5,500. It is 90 minutes southeast of Chicago, 90 minutes northwest of Indianapolis, 40 minutes northwest of Lafayette, and 40 minutes southeast of Merrillville.

Majors and Degrees

Saint Joseph's College offers programs leading to the Bachelor of Arts or the Bachelor of Science degree. Programs are offered in accounting, accounting/CPA track, art, art education, biology, biology-chemistry, business administration, chemistry, communication and theater arts, computer science, criminal justice, economics, elementary education, English, environmental science, history, international business, international studies, management information systems, mass communication, mathematics, mathematics–computer science, medical technology, music, music–business administration, nursing, philosophy, physical education, political science, psychology, religion/philosophy, social work, and sociology.

Pre-professional programs are offered in chiropractic, dentistry, law, medicine, occupational therapy, optometry, physical therapy, and veterinary medicine.

The College also offers a designer major, wherein qualified students can create individualized programs of study.

Associate degrees are offered in a number of areas, including biology-chemistry, business–computer science, church music, and humanities.

Academic Program

The general education requirements of the College are incorporated in a single four-year sequence common to all students and totaling 45 credit hours. This core curriculum comprises extensive reading, writing, and discussion, as well as lectures and other presentations focusing on the different aspects of the human condition in relation to various academic areas, including philosophy, history, science, and religion.

In addition to completing these 45 hours, a student must earn a minimum of 36 semester hours in a major and 18 semester hours in a minor. A minimum of 120 semester hours is required for graduation.

The College operates on a 4-4-1 academic calendar.

Off-Campus Programs

There are two types of programs available for students who wish to spend a semester or year abroad. An affiliation with Central University of Iowa allows students to study in Austria, England, France, Germany, Mexico, the Netherlands, Spain, and Wales. Also, students can attend Harlaxton College in England through an affiliation with the University of Evansville.

The College provides off-campus internship opportunities in all degree programs.

The Washington Semester program offers students the chance to live and learn in the nation's capital. On-the-job experience, through various private businesses, associations, government agencies, nonprofit organizations, and the U.S. Congress, is combined with academic study in Washington, D.C.

Academic Facilities

As the first college in Indiana on the World Wide Web, SJC has incorporated state-of-the-art technologies throughout the campus. These include personal computers, two Ethernet connections per residence hall room, five networked computer labs open to all students, nine networked computer labs open to students of particular departments, electronic and multimedia classrooms, Internet access and e-mail service, student home pages, and telephone systems with free voice mail.

The College library holds 156,931 books and bound periodicals and currently receives 416 periodicals. Microfilm material and an extensive audio library totaling more than 90,718 items are available for student use. The library is also a depository for a selected number of U.S. Government documents, which now number more than 158,000.

In addition, the library maintains a separate Curriculum Library of textbooks and other reading materials used in elementary and secondary schools to help students studying education prepare for their courses and practice teaching.

A collection of more than 33,000 maps is separately housed in the earth science department.

The biology laboratories provide equipment for courses in fundamental zoology and botany, microtechnique embryology, histology, comparative vertebrate anatomy, human anatomy, and physiology. There are also laboratories for general inorganic and organic chemistry, biochemistry, and quantitative and qualitative analysis. Geology laboratories serve the fields of physical geology, mineralogy, petrology, paleontology, subsurface geology, stratigraphy, and economic geology.

Costs

The costs for 2003–04 were $17,900 for tuition, $6190 for room and board, and $160 for fees.

Financial Aid

Financial aid is available in a variety of forms, including scholarships, grants, loans, and campus employment. More than 90 percent of the student body receives financial aid.

All candidates for financial aid must be accepted by the College and submit the Free Application for Federal Student Aid (FAFSA).

Academic merit scholarships are awarded in amounts varying from $5500 to full tuition, room, and board, based on academic record and talents. Performance Scholarships are available in band, cheerleading, choir, color guard, dance, radio, student athletic training, television, and theater. Other scholarships are awarded on the basis of need, and the financial aid program includes nationally funded grants, guaranteed loans, and Federal Work-Study awards.

Faculty

Of the 62 full-time-equivalent faculty members, 83 percent hold doctoral or terminal degrees. Most classes range in size from 10 to 19 students. No classes are taught by graduate students. The student-faculty ratio is 15:1.

Student Government

All full-time students are members of the Student Government Association and are governed by its constitution and bylaws. These students elect four officers of the Student Association, including a president who holds a seat on the College's Board of Trustees and appoints students to faculty and administrative committees. These officers, the four class presidents, and elected residence hall and commuting student representatives compose the Student Senate. This group provides a channel of communication among students, faculty, and administrators. Acting in concert, the Student Association officers and the Student Senate serve to propose policies and implement procedures to better the quality of life on the campus.

Admission Requirements

Candidates for freshman standing are selected from applicants who present the following academic credentials: a certificate of graduation from an approved high school or documentation of completion through home school; a minimum of 15 academic units, with a minimum C average; and SAT I or ACT scores, all to be forwarded to the Office of Admissions.

Transfer students, in addition to fulfilling these requirements, must be eligible to continue in the institution from which they wish to transfer, be entitled to honorable separation from the institution last attended, and present a minimum 2.0 (C) cumulative index for all completed work.

An early admission policy is followed for exceptionally well qualified students who have not graduated from high school.

Campus tours, conducted by SJC students, are highly recommended.

Application and Information

An application form must be filled out completely by the applicant and sent to the College along with a $25 nonrefundable fee. Official transcripts of credits from all high schools and colleges previously attended must be mailed directly from the schools to the Office of Admissions at SJC. Application postmark deadlines are October 1 for early decision, November 1 for early notification, and December 1 for standard notification. Candidates submitting applications postmarked after January 2 receive final notification based on space availability. Notification of admission decisions occurs approximately three weeks after the postmark deadline.

For further information, students should contact:

Office of Admissions
Saint Joseph's College
P.O. Box 890
Rensselaer, Indiana 47978
Telephone: 219-866-6170
800-447-8781 (toll-free)
Fax: 219-866-6122
E-mail: admissions@saintjoe.edu
World Wide Web: http://www.saintjoe.edu

Students unravel the mysteries of science.

ST. JOSEPH'S COLLEGE

BROOKLYN AND PATCHOGUE, NEW YORK

The College

St. Joseph's College, founded in 1916, is a private, coeducational institution specializing in the liberal arts and preprofessional programs. The College maintains separate campuses in Brooklyn and Patchogue, New York, and enrolls a total of 4,294 students in its School of Arts and Sciences and School of Adult and Professional Education.

The College seeks to create a free atmosphere in which students and faculty members together can investigate the major areas of human knowledge as the basis for a more effective participation in today's world. In support of this philosophy, the College pursues a number of specific objectives, including providing an atmosphere for open dialogue, individual attention, and innovative teaching; inspiring in students a spirit of inquiry and the joy of learning as an ongoing part of their lives; and preparing students for their lifework by providing the necessary professional and preprofessional training.

St. Joseph's College offers numerous extracurricular and cocurricular activities designed to help its students grow personally as well as academically. Each campus offers more than twenty clubs and activities, including intercollegiate basketball, women's softball, and volleyball. The Patchogue campus also offers men's soccer, a women's swim team, and a coed equestrian team. The social life is maintained through these clubs, which sponsor numerous dances, barbecues, intramural sports, screenings of current films, and vacation trips each year. Since all students live in the vicinity of their respective campuses, they often organize informal social events among themselves.

The ultramodern, 48,250-square-foot John A. Danzi Athletic Center houses a competition-sized basketball court, an elevated jogging and walking track, seating for 1,500 spectators, a 25-yard pool, and an aerobic and fitness center.

Location

The Brooklyn campus in the historic Clinton Hill section of Brooklyn is easily accessible by public transit lines and automobile. The convenient location, where undergraduates can enjoy the freedom of campus life while profiting from the many cultural advantages of the New York City area, attracts students from every part of the metropolitan region. The College is in the center of one of the nation's most diversified academic communities, with six colleges and universities within a 2-mile radius. St. Joseph's offers its students easy access to the other colleges and such cultural facilities as the Brooklyn Academy of Music, the Brooklyn Public Library, and the Brooklyn Museum.

The Patchogue campus, located on the beautiful south shore of Long Island, is easily accessible to its students from both Nassau and Suffolk Counties. Situated on the western rim of the Great Patchogue Lake, the 28-acre campus features comfortable classrooms and administrative and student facilities, surrounded by athletic fields and spacious lawns. The College and its students have established close ties with the neighboring communities and with the village of Patchogue itself.

Majors and Degrees

The Brooklyn campus offers four-year programs leading to B.A. and B.S. degrees, with majors in accounting, biology, business administration, chemistry, child study (a sequence in special education is optional), computer information systems, English, history, human relations, mathematics, psychology, social science (including economics, political science, and sociology), Spanish, and speech communication. Certificate programs are available in criminology/criminal justice, gerontology, information technology applications, leadership and supervision, management, and marketing, advertising, and public relations.

Through a partnership between St. Joseph's College and Polytechnic University, students at St. Joseph's now have the opportunity to earn a bachelor's degree in the field of their choice and a master's degree in computer science in a combined B.A./B.S. plus M.S. program. The bachelor's degree is issued from St. Joseph's, and the master's degree is issued from Polytechnic University.

The Brooklyn campus also offers an accelerated biomedical program in cooperation with the New York College of Podiatric Medicine (NYCPM). After two years at St. Joseph's, students spend four years at the NYCPM. At the end of the six years, students receive a B.S. in biology as well as the D.P.M. from NYCPM.

The Patchogue campus offers four-year programs leading to the B.A. degree, with majors in child study (including special education), English, history, human relations, mathematics, psychology, social sciences, and speech communication. The B.S. degree is available in accounting, biology, business administration, mathematics, mathematics/computers, and recreation. Certificate programs, which are registered with the New York State Education Department, are offered in applied sociology, criminology/criminal justice, gerontology, human resources, information technology applications, leadership and supervision, management, and marketing, advertising, and public relations.

Both campuses offer preprofessional programs in law, teaching, and numerous health fields, including dentistry, medicine, and optometry.

The School of Adult and Professional Education at each campus is designed especially for adults with nontraditional academic backgrounds or with professional training and experience. Bachelor of Science degrees are offered in community health, general studies, health administration, organizational management, and nursing.

Academic Program

The School of Arts and Sciences at each campus operates on the semester system, and there are limited course offerings during the summer and in January. Since students are expected to attain breadth and balance in their academic studies, a core curriculum is an integral part of the 128 credits required for graduation. However, a wide range of choices to satisfy the core curriculum requirements allows students to tailor their academic program in accordance with their personal and professional needs.

The College recognizes the Advanced Placement (AP) Program and offers credit and placement for scores of 3, 4, or 5 on the AP test. In each case, the score is reviewed by the registrar and/or department chairperson to determine credit and placement. Depending on the specific area covered by a College-Level Examination Program (CLEP) test, credit may be granted.

The School of Adult and Professional Education on each campus operates on numerous schedules. Courses are offered during the day, evenings, or weekends to best meet the needs of working students who are pursuing a degree. Some courses meet for a semester, some in six- or twelve-week sessions. An extensive summer program is offered.

Academic Facilities

The Brooklyn campus is composed of eight buildings. The Dillon Child Study Center, a laboratory preschool enrolling approximately a hundred 3-, 4-, and 5-year-olds, is used by child study students as a teaching and observation resource. McEntegart Hall, a modern five-level structure, houses the 122,563-volume library, audiovisual resource center, curriculum library, archives, and computer labs. Other academic facilities include fully equipped biology, chemistry, computer, physics, and psychology research laboratories.

At the Patchogue campus, the main building houses administrative and faculty offices; laboratories for biology, chemistry, physics, and psychology; the computer center; art and music studios; the Local History Center; and the Office of Counseling. A library building, with a capacity of 120,000 volumes, houses a curriculum library, seminar rooms, administrative offices, and two classrooms. The Clare Rose Playhouse, situated on the northeast corner of the campus, is an educational and cultural learning facility where students and local communities can explore the various aspects of theater from production to performance.

The College has constructed a high-speed fiber-optic intracampus network that connects all offices, institutional facilities, computer laboratories, and libraries on the Brooklyn and Patchogue campuses. Direct Internet access is available to all students and faculty and staff members through the College's server. The integrated online library system enables students to locate and check out books at either campus and also provides links to online databases and other electronic information sources.

Costs

In Brooklyn, the annual full-time undergraduate tuition for 2003–04 is $10,550. The cost for nonmatriculated or part-time students is $340 per credit. In Patchogue, the annual full-time undergraduate tuition for 2003–04 is $10,955. The cost for nonmatriculated or part-time students is $355 per credit. Mandatory fees are $322.

Financial Aid

Scholarships and grants-in-aid are available at St. Joseph's College. Students wishing to apply for either form of assistance must file the Free Application for Federal Student Aid (FAFSA), an institutional aid form, and a state aid form. After a student has been accepted to the College and all financial aid forms are properly processed, the Financial Aid Office will prepare packages of aid that usually consist of federal, state, and College funds. St. Joseph's is fully approved for veterans. Campus work-study programs are also available.

Faculty

The College's 16:1 student-faculty ratio ensures very close relationships between students and their professors. Faculty members serve as academic advisers, are active on student affairs committees, and act as moderators to student organizations.

Student Government

Student government on each campus is active in many facets of academic and student life and organizes social events such as mixers, film festivals, lectures, and off-campus trips.

Admission Requirements

St. Joseph's College seeks a diverse student body and welcomes applications from high school students, transfer students, and others who may have a nontraditional academic background. The College offers programs to serve all of these groups.

Students who wish to enter as freshmen are expected to have completed at least 18 units of college-preparatory work by the end of their senior year. This should include the following distribution: 4 years of English, 2 years of foreign language, 3 years of mathematics, 2 years of science, and 4 years of social studies. Applicants interested in accounting, allied health fields, biology, business administration, chemistry, or mathematics should have more extensive backgrounds in mathematics and science. The College will also consider students who have received a general equivalency diploma.

The School of Arts and Sciences requires the submission of official results from the SAT I.

St. Joseph's College will accept a block transfer of credits from students holding an A.A. or A.S. degree in certain majors from an accredited junior or community college. All other transfers are considered on an individual basis.

The Division of General Studies has more flexible admission requirements, reflecting its enrollment of adults with nontraditional academic backgrounds and work experience.

Application and Information

Admission is offered on a rolling basis. Applications and supporting documents should be submitted to the appropriate address below, along with a nonrefundable application fee of $25. Each application is reviewed very carefully, and a decision is usually sent within one month after receiving all necessary credentials. For more information, students can access the school's Web site at the address listed below.

Director of Admissions
St. Joseph's College
245 Clinton Avenue
Brooklyn, New York 11205
Telephone: 718-636-6868

Director of Admissions
St. Joseph's College
155 West Roe Boulevard
Patchogue, New York 11772
Telephone: 631-447-3219
World Wide Web: http://www.sjcny.edu

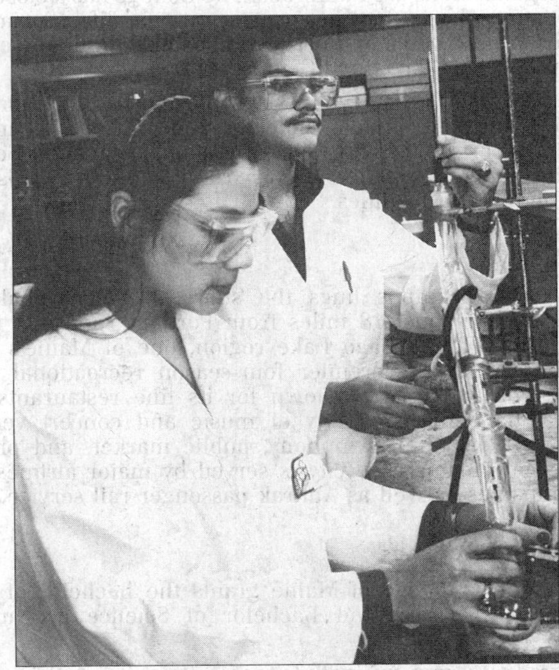

Both campuses of St. Joseph's College provide up-to-date science, computer, and psychology laboratories.

SAINT JOSEPH'S COLLEGE OF MAINE

STANDISH, MAINE

The College

Saint Joseph's College of Maine, the only Catholic college in Maine, offers a strong liberal arts education to men and women of all faiths. Founded in 1912 and sponsored by the Sisters of Mercy, the College's mission focuses on the intellectual, spiritual, and social growth of its students within a value-centered environment. Emphasis on service learning and internships complements the challenging curriculum.

A new four-story Academic Hall with sweeping views of Sebago Lake opened in fall 2004. The growth in student population has led to construction of two new residence halls each housing 120 students in suite-style accommodations, as well as expansion and renovation of the dining hall and a major academic building. The Harold Alfond Student Center opened in 1999 and houses a swimming pool, a gymnasium, an elevated jogging track, a rock-climbing wall, fitness rooms, and a dance/aerobics studio.

Full-time undergraduate enrollment is 1,000 students. The geographic distribution shows fifteen states and several foreign countries represented, with a majority of students coming from the Northeast. More than 80 percent of full-time students live on campus. The residence halls include a choice of single-sex, coed, and substance-free housing options. Off-campus housing is available in the local area. Bon Appetit, the campus food service, takes pride in its delicious and varied cuisine.

Saint Joseph's College of Maine looks to its students to take an active role in campus leadership. Opportunities to become involved in student government, athletics, and cultural and social organizations are numerous. The College has a close-knit family atmosphere that permeates campus life. Social life revolves around clubs and organizations and the many events held in the Chalet or Alfond Center.

The College sponsors eleven NCAA Division III intercollegiate athletic teams. Recreational choices include a strong intramural and club sports program, a private sandy beach on Sebago Lake, a skating pond, cross-country running and ski trails, and the Alfond Center facilities.

Location

The 331-acre campus hugs the shore of Sebago Lake in southern Maine, just 18 miles from Portland, and 125 miles from Boston. The Sebago Lake region, one of Maine's most beautiful spots, is a premier four-season recreational area. Greater Portland is well-known for its fine restaurants and shops along with its variety of music and concert venues, theater, art museum, symphony, public market, and professional sports teams. The city is served by major airlines and bus companies as well as Amtrak passenger rail service.

Majors and Degrees

Saint Joseph's College of Maine grants the Bachelor of Arts, Bachelor of Science, and Bachelor of Science in Nursing degrees.

Undergraduate majors include accounting, advertising, applied computer science, biology, business management, chemistry, communications, criminal justice, elementary education, environmental science and studies, exercise science, finance, history, international business, marine science, marketing, mathematics, nursing, philosophy, physical education, psychology, sociology, sports management, and theology. Secondary education preparation is also offered with the biology, English, history, mathematics, and physical education majors.

Academic Programs

The College follows a 4-credit, two-semester calendar, which runs from late August to mid-May. Candidates for a bachelor's degree must earn 128 semester hours and 256 quality points. An honors program for selected students has grown tremendously in recent years. Core curriculum requirements for all students include courses in English, fine arts, history, mathematics, philosophy, science, and theology. Credit by examination is available through CLEP, ACT-PEP, DANTES, and Advanced Placement examinations with scores of 4 or higher.

Off-Campus Programs

The College embraces both service learning and professional experience for its students. Internships and work experience are a vital part of the curriculum. Education majors begin classroom observation in their first year; nursing majors begin clinical training in their sophomore year; communications majors begin studio work as early as their first year; and business administration majors work for local companies. Comparable opportunities are available in all major fields of study. Another important way students enrich their education is through service learning, whereby they earn academic credit by applying what they learn in the classroom to a community service setting.

For those who want to study abroad, the College participates in ISEP, the International Student Exchange Program, in which students study for up to a year in one of more than thirty countries worldwide. The Nova Scotia Exchange Program allows students to study at one of several universities located in the Canadian maritime providence. Saint Joseph's also sponsors a summer study program at the Irish College for the Humanities in Tralee, County Kerry, Ireland.

Academic Facilities

The new Academic Hall features thirty-two modern classrooms with wireless technology, an auditorium, computer labs, and faculty offices. Mercy Hall houses classrooms, science laboratories, the computer center, and faculty offices. The College has renovated and added to Mercy Hall in the last two years, creating a physics lab, a business lab, an updated Nursing Resources Center, three new classrooms, and an atrium lounge overlooking the central quad. The Margaret H. Heffernan Center (1983) complements the distinguished original estate buildings and the other campus facilities that were added when the college moved to its present location in 1956. Located in the Heffernan Center are the Wellehan Library, Healy Chapel, and a large foyer for social gatherings. All student residence hall rooms are networked to accommodate e-mail and Internet access, cable television, and telephones.

Costs

For 2004–05, tuition for the regular campus-based programs is $19,615 and room and board are $8160, totaling $27,775. Students usually budget about $2455 for books, supplies, travel, and miscellaneous expenses.

Financial Aid

In the current year, the College awarded aid to more than 90 percent of full-time undergraduates in the form of grants, scholarships, work-study awards, and/or loans. Financial aid consideration includes federal and state aid programs as well as many grant and scholarship programs from the College itself. Scholarships are awarded on the basis of scholastic achievement, leadership skills, community service, and other talents as determined during the admission process.

Students who wish to apply for aid must file the Free Application for Federal Student Aid (FAFSA) and the College's financial aid application. The priority deadline for incoming students is March 1. Financial aid status does not affect admission decisions.

Faculty

A special feature of Saint Joseph's College of Maine is the care and concern given by the faculty members and the administration to each student in every aspect of his or her collegiate life. The faculty is an outstanding group of professional educators and 95 percent of faculty members have earned a doctorate or other terminal degree. The student-faculty ratio is 13:1 and average class size is 20 to 25. The faculty advising system is strong and faculty members are very accessible to students.

Student Government

An active Student Government Association manages a budget funded by student activity fees. A full slate of officers is elected annually. Students are represented in College committees and on all standing committees of the Faculty Senate.

Admission Requirements

Applicants to the first-year class are admitted on the strength of their secondary school curriculum, grade point average, and SAT I or ACT scores. About 80 percent of last year's freshman class ranked in the top half of their class. Their median SAT I verbal and mathematics scores were in line with the national averages. Counselor and teacher recommendations are required. Campus interviews are strongly recommended, and most prospective first-year students visit the College.

The College is a member of the Common Application Group, and students can apply online. Transfer students, a valuable addition to the student body, may be admitted in either the fall or spring semester.

Application and Information

Students are encouraged to call the Office of Admission in advance to schedule campus visits and interviews. Saint Joseph's sponsors visitation days throughout the year. Saint Joseph's offers an early admission option (Early Action) with a deadline of November 15. Saint Joseph's also has a rolling admission policy, and students using this option are notified of admission decisions beginning mid-December.

For students seeking admission for the 2005–06 academic year, a $40 application fee is required. However, for online applications, the application fee is waived. To obtain the College viewbook and information on each academic program, including the Graduate and Professional Studies program, prospective students should contact:

Office of Admission
Saint Joseph's College of Maine
278 Whites Bridge Road
Standish, Maine 04084-5263
Telephone: 207-893-7746
800-338-7057 (toll-free)
E-mail: admission@sjcme.edu
World Wide Web: http://www.sjcme.edu

Academic excellence in a magnificent setting at Saint Joseph's College.

SAINT JOSEPH'S UNIVERSITY

PHILADELPHIA, PENNSYLVANIA

The University

Saint Joseph's University, is a nationally recognized, Catholic, Jesuit university. For more than 150 years, Saint Joseph's has advanced the professional and personal ambitions of men and women by providing a rigorous Jesuit education—one that demands high achievement, expands knowledge, deepens understanding, stresses effective reasoning and communication, develops moral and spiritual character, and imparts enduring pride. One of only 137 schools with a Phi Beta Kappa chapter and business school accreditation by AACSB International–The Association to Advance Collegiate Schools of Business, Saint Joseph's is home to 3,900 full-time undergraduates and 3,400 graduate, part-time, and doctoral students.

As a Jesuit university, Saint Joseph's believes each student realizes his or her fullest potential through challenging classroom study, hands-on learning opportunities, and a commitment to excellence in all endeavors. The University also reinforces the individual's lifelong engagement with the wider world. Graduates of Saint Joseph's attain success in their careers with the help of an extensive network of alumni who have become leading figures in business, law, medicine, education, the arts, technology, government, and public service.

A Saint Joseph's education encompasses all aspects of personal growth and development, reflecting the Ignatian credo of *cura personalis*. Guided by a faculty that is committed to both teaching and scholarship, students develop intellectually through an intense liberal arts curriculum and advanced study in a chosen discipline. Students mature socially by participating in Saint Joseph's campus life, noted for its rich variety of activities, infectious enthusiasm, and mutual respect. Students grow ethically and spiritually by living their own values in the larger society beyond the campus.

Steeped in the Jesuit, Catholic tradition, Saint Joseph's provides a rigorous, intense education that both disciplines and expands the mind. Students develop a lifelong desire to learn and grow while also acquiring the skills and knowledge necessary for success in their professional lives. At the core of this education is a general education requirement, which exposes students to primary fields of inquiry and the cultural values that shape their world. A Jesuit emphasis on engaged teaching and mentoring permeates the university. Faculty members at Saint Joseph's, many of whom are leading scholars in their disciplines, expect students to perform at the highest level and set demanding standards in the classroom.

Saint Joseph's is at the forefront of utilizing innovative technologies to enhance and promote learning. These technologies are widely integrated into the educational process both in class and beyond, where they are also used for individual and collaborative research projects. By mastering these tools and achieving technological fluency, Saint Joseph's students gain a valuable edge in their careers.

Saint Joseph's students engage enthusiastically in all facets of campus life—academic, social, athletic, ethical, and spiritual. Their active participation creates a vibrant, dynamic campus community. In all their activities, students emphasize personal integrity as well as a respect and concern for others. This produces a mutually supportive, humane, and tolerant environment for individual success and service to others.

Location

Located on the edge of metropolitan Philadelphia, Saint Joseph's provides ready access to the vast career opportunities and cultural resources of America's fifth-largest city, while affording students a cohesive and intimate campus experience.

Because of its location, Saint Joseph's has close ties to the people, professional opportunities, and cultural life of Philadelphia. Students enjoy direct access to internships, cooperative programs, and positions in virtually all careers, most of which have a major presence in the Philadelphia area, the geographic hub of the Northeast corridor. Saint Joseph's location also offers ample outlets for community involvement and service, and students can easily partake of Philadelphia's big-time sports, entertainment, and cultural events.

Majors and Degrees

Saint Joseph's offers full-time baccalaureate degree programs in forty major fields of study and numerous specialty programs, which are administered by two separate colleges.

The College of Arts and Sciences awards the Bachelor of Arts degree in classics, economics, English, fine and performing arts, French, French studies, German, history, international relations, Latin, philosophy, political science, Spanish, and theology and the Bachelor of Science degree in biology, chemical biology, chemistry, computer science, criminal justice, education, environmental science, interdisciplinary health services, labor studies, mathematics, physics, psychology, and sociology.

The Erivan K. Haub School of Business awards the Bachelor of Science degree in accounting, finance, food marketing, information systems, international business, international marketing, management, marketing, and public administration. A co-op program is available for all business majors.

Five-year B.S./M.S. programs are offered in education, international marketing, and psychology. The University also offers special academic programs in aerospace studies (Air Force ROTC); allied health (diagnostic imaging, laboratory sciences, nursing, and occupational therapy); American, European, gender, Latin American, medieval, Renaissance, and Russian and East Central European studies; writing studies; and teacher certification at the elementary and secondary levels. Preprofessional study is available in most major fields.

Academic Program

At Saint Joseph's University, the aim of providing the student with the qualities of a liberally educated individual is pursued through a threefold plan encompassing 120 academic credits. The major concentration (30–45 credits) is intended to provide students with depth in a given field in order to prepare them for effective work in that field or for graduate study. The general education requirement (60 credits) is intended to ensure that students have mastered basic skills necessary for further work, have been exposed to the main divisions of learning, and have been introduced to several new fields of study. Languages and literature, mathematics, natural sciences, history, social sciences, philosophy, and theology are among the areas of study included in the general education requirement. Free electives (15–30 credits) are intended to provide flexibility by encouraging students to pursue studies in areas they have found interesting, to test their interest in an unexplored area, or to deepen their knowledge in the major field.

A competitive honors program is available for qualified students, as are independent and interdisciplinary study options. Claver House provides a place for honors students to have meetings, study, and relax.

Off-Campus Programs

Saint Joseph's offers to an increasing number of students the opportunity to study abroad and directly sponsors programs each year in London, England; Strasbourg, France; Marburg, Germany; Galway and Cork, Ireland; Tokyo, Japan; Mexico City, Mexico; Madrid, Spain; and three cities in Australia. International study tours have been made to Africa, Australia, Brazil, Canada, Greece, Ireland, Italy, Japan, Scotland, and Spain.

Students may take advantage of an arrangement with the Washington Center for Internships and Academic Seminars, which allows for a one-semester internship in the nation's capital.

Fieldwork experiences are required in several majors, and the University's location provides for internship opportunities to support virtually all other disciplines. The Career Services Center has a full-time internship coordinator and provides opportunities for on-campus interviews. The Alumni Mentor Alliance matches students with alumni in their fields of interest to gain real-world perspectives.

Academic Facilities

The facilities at Saint Joseph's are a blend of the old and the new. Barbelin/Lonergan Hall is a fine example of collegiate Gothic architecture. Its spired carillon tower rises above the campus and is easily the most recognizable landmark at Saint Joseph's. Mandeville Hall, a state-of-the-art international academic center, opened in fall 1998. Home of the Haub School of Business, Mandeville offers distance learning technology and unique learning environments. The Drexel Library has a collection of 335,000 volumes, 1,850 current periodical subscriptions, 800,000 microforms, and more than 4,000 titles that are available electronically.

Costs

For the 2003–04 academic year, tuition for majors in the humanities, politics, history, and economics was $23,990. Tuition in all other programs in the College of Arts and Sciences as well as the Erivan K. Haub School of Business was $24,195. Room fees ranged from $5800 to $6550 per year, and board fees cost $3410 per year.

Financial Aid

The majority of Saint Joseph's students receive merit and/or federal financial assistance. In the 2002–03 academic year, approximately 85 percent of the University's student body received assistance in the form of academic and athletic scholarships, grants, loans, and work-study funds, either singly or in combination.

To be considered for merit scholarships students should apply early in their senior year of high school. Students are automatically considered for scholarships upon application to the University.

Students who wish to be considered for federal financial assistance should submit the Free Application for Federal Student Aid (FAFSA). Residents from states other than Pennsylvania should file the FAFSA and the proper state grant application from the Education Assistance Agency of their resident state.

Faculty

Saint Joseph's possesses an esteemed research faculty that is committed to undergraduate teaching. A student-faculty ratio of 15:1 and an average class size of 25 offer excellent opportunities for student–faculty member exchange, both inside and outside the classroom. Approximately 98 percent of the full-time faculty members hold a doctorate or terminal degree in their field.

Student Government

The Office of Student Leadership and Activities is dedicated to enhancing the educational development of students by providing opportunities for involvement in co-curricular programs and services. These include leadership programs, student clubs and organizations, Greek life, event programming and planning, and the University Student Senate. Through innovative programming that complements academic and personal development, the University nurtures the mind, body, and spirit of each individual student while enhancing the Jesuit mission of the University.

The University Student Senate, the governing board for the student body, is dedicated to addressing student issues through advocacy and policy recommendations. The Senate consists of an executive board that includes the president, executive vice president, speaker of the Senate, vice president for financial affairs, vice president for student life, four elected representatives from each class, and five appointed at-large members. The Senate has four standing committees: Academic Affairs, Student Budget Allocations, Campus Life, and Administrative Services. Elections for the Senate take place in December. Freshman representatives are elected in September.

The Student Union Board, known as SUB, is a student-run organization that encourages the development of student leadership, responsibility, and social competency by planning and participating in campus programs. These activities are designed to enhance the educational, recreational, cultural, and social aspects of the collegiate experience. All registered undergraduate students are welcome to take part in the activities and to be a part of the standing committees that are responsible for the programming.

Admission Requirements

Candidates for admission to the freshman class are ordinarily expected to complete a secondary school program with a minimum of four academic subjects each year. Candidates must submit evidence of academic achievement in a college-preparatory program, which should emphasize study in English, mathematics, foreign languages (classical or modern), science, history, and social studies. Typical successful candidates have had a secondary school background that included the following: English, 4 units; foreign languages, 2 units; history and social studies, 3 units; mathematics, 3 units (4 units for students interested in the natural sciences or math); and science, 2 units. Applicants are required to submit scores on the SAT I or the ACT.

Application and Information

A completed application form may be submitted with the $45 application fee at any time after the student's junior year. The University adheres to a modified rolling admissions policy, with decisions being made approximately eight weeks after the applicant's file becomes complete. Students are encouraged to apply early in their senior year. The student should also see that the required test scores, a high school transcript, and one letter of recommendation are sent to the Admissions Office. This transcript should normally include grades from ninth grade through the first marking period of twelfth grade.

Susan P. Kassab
Director of Admission
Saint Joseph's University
5600 City Avenue
Philadelphia, Pennsylvania 19131-1395
Telephone: 610-660-1300
888-BE-A-HAWK (toll-free)
Fax: 610-660-1314
E-mail: admi@sju.edu
World Wide Web: http://www.sju.edu/admissions/

Mandeville Hall, Saint Joseph's international academic center and home of the Haub School of Business.

ST. LAWRENCE UNIVERSITY

CANTON, NEW YORK

The University

St. Lawrence University invites students to learn new ways of seeing the world, voicing ideas, and connecting with others. Graduates have the tools with which to think clearly, express themselves persuasively, and step into the world community with an understanding of their responsibility to all people and to the planet.

Founded in 1856, St. Lawrence is the oldest continuously coeducational degree-granting institution of higher learning in New York State. Initially established as a theology school for the Universalist Church, it quickly evolved into the liberal arts college that it is today. St. Lawrence is a private, nonsectarian university of approximately 2,100 undergraduate men and women, with a small graduate program in education. St. Lawrence is known for its residential/academic First-Year Program, its international study opportunities and area studies programs, its students' strong interest in the environment and the outdoors, and its friendliness.

St. Lawrence students are self-starters. The self-designed major is popular, intramural sports leagues are always full, and more than 90 student organizations serve broad interests from communication to community service and creativity to social action. The University routinely hosts well-known speakers, and concerts, plays, and films are regulars on the weekly events calendar. A new, 60,000-square-foot Student Center is planned to open in winter 2004.

St. Lawrence students have historically placed high value on athletic activity, and a large number participate in varsity, intramural, or club sports. The thirty-two varsity men's and women's teams compete at the Division III level of the NCAA, with the exception of men's and women's ice hockey, which compete in Division I. Recreational facilities include cross-country ski and running trails, a complete Nautilus facility, indoor and outdoor tennis courts, an athletic complex with a gymnasium, two field houses, a 133-station fitness center, a three-story climbing wall, a pool, a skating rink, an equestrian center, a golf course, a nine-lane all-weather track, an artificial turf field for lacrosse and field hockey, nine squash courts, and performance fields for soccer, football, baseball, and softball.

Residential life is an important aspect of the St. Lawrence experience. The University's innovative and highly regarded First-Year Program creates communities where groups of approximately 30–45 first-year students live and learn together. In the upperclass years, students can choose from traditional dormitories, Greek chapter houses, and suites and theme cottages that focus on student interests such as low-impact living and community service. New senior townhouses opened in fall 2003. St. Lawrence sponsors a full range of student services, from counseling to career planning.

Location

St. Lawrence is situated on a 1,000-acre campus on the edge of the village of Canton, New York (population 6,400), the seat of St. Lawrence County. Canton, with its Victorian homes, tree-lined streets, village green, and small shops, is typical of college towns throughout the Northeast. Students and residents often mix in stores, at athletic events, and in community projects. Ottawa, Canada's capital, is 75 minutes to the north, while Lake Placid, one of America's hiking and skiing meccas, is 90 minutes to the southeast.

Majors and Degrees

St. Lawrence offers the Bachelor of Arts and Bachelor of Science degrees; students can choose from thirty-five majors and have the option of picking one of thirty-seven minors. Combined five-year programs with other institutions are in place in engineering and management, and specialized advising is offered in preparation for postgraduate work in dentistry, law, medicine, and veterinary medicine.

Academic Program

St. Lawrence's foremost mission is to provide its students with a liberal arts education. Students complete requirements in six areas and concentrated work in a major field. Before graduating, students are expected to show competence in writing. Close faculty-student interaction is a hallmark of a St. Lawrence education, and every semester many students engage in independent or honors projects, often working with professors on joint research projects that lead to publication in leading scholarly journals. A senior project is required in certain majors and may be implemented campuswide.

Off-Campus Programs

More than one third of St. Lawrence students study in one of the University's international programs during their collegiate careers. St. Lawrence operates programs in Australia, Austria, Canada, China, Costa Rica, Denmark, England, France, India, Italy, Japan, Kenya, Spain, and Trinidad and Tobago. In addition, the University's membership in the International Student Exchange Program permits students to directly enroll in universities in more than twenty additional countries. St. Lawrence also operates programs at two other campuses in the U.S.: Fisk University in Nashville, Tennessee, and American University in Washington, D.C. St. Lawrence also administers its own Adirondack Semester Program.

Academic Facilities

Owen D. Young Library and Launders Science Library contain more than half a million volumes as well as electronic resources and ample space for reading and research. Griffiths Arts Center is home to the University's music, speech, and theater and fine arts programs, as well as two theaters and an art gallery in which selections from St. Lawrence's 7,000-piece collection are frequently shown. A unified science complex houses the Departments of Biology, Chemistry, Physics, Psychology, Geology, and Mathematics, Computer Science and Statistics and is connected via a covered hallway to the science library and computing center. Richardson Hall, St. Lawrence's oldest building and on the National Register of Historic Places, is home to the English and religious studies departments. Other departments can be found in various buildings, which are clustered on one part of the campus so as not to be a long walk apart. A summer 2004 groundbreaking is planned for new science facilities.

Costs

The comprehensive fee for 2003–04 was $35,940, including tuition, fees, and average room and board. Students should allow approximately $1450 for books and personal expenses.

Financial Aid

St. Lawrence awards both merit scholarships and need-based financial aid. More than 80 percent of the University's students receive some form of financial assistance, including scholarships, grants, student loans, and campus jobs. St. Lawrence is committed to assisting as many students as possible and will recognize academic and personal achievement in making financial aid decisions. To apply for need-based financial aid, students must file the Free Application for Federal Student Aid (FAFSA) between January 1 and February 15 and request that the results be sent directly to St. Lawrence. Submission of the Financial Aid PROFILE form is encouraged; completion of the St. Lawrence supplemental form is an acceptable alternative to the PROFILE.

Faculty

The 202 members of St. Lawrence's faculty are teachers and scholars. While teaching is their primary responsibility, they are also active researchers, artists, performers, and regular contributors in their academic disciplines. Faculty members teach all courses at St. Lawrence; no undergraduate courses are taught by graduate students. Active teaching assistant and tutoring programs, involving qualified upperclass students, are closely supervised by faculty members. The student-faculty ratio is about 12:1. Faculty members hold regular office hours, serve as academic advisers to students, and frequently take part in extracurricular activities on campus.

Student Government

The Thelomathesian Society, comprising all students on campus, is governed by a senate of elected representatives. The senate parcels out funds in support of student activities and provides two student delegates to the University's Board of Trustees.

Admission Requirements

St. Lawrence seeks students who can be successful in a demanding academic program and who can contribute to the quality of life of the community. The University is committed to enrolling students who represent the widest possible diversity of economic, social, ethnic, and geographic backgrounds. Academic preparation is, of course, important, but demonstrated ability in the creative arts, athletics, or social service is also a measure of a student's potential to benefit St. Lawrence. Scores on the SAT I or ACT are required for admission. A campus visit is strongly encouraged, and interviews may be scheduled on campus or off campus in certain areas.

Although there is no set distribution of high school courses, successful applicants typically show strong preparation in the humanities, the social sciences, mathematics, and the natural sciences. Honors work and Advanced Placement are opportunities for applicants to demonstrate intellectual maturity and curiosity, qualities highly valued in the admission process.

Application and Information

St. Lawrence uses the Common Application, with the St. Lawrence Supplement, as its sole application form. The application is available on the University's Web site. The application processing fee is $50. Regular decision applications should be submitted by February 15, with notification by late March. Students who decide that St. Lawrence is their first choice may apply under one of the early decision deadlines: November 15 or January 15. In each case, notification is one month after the deadline. Transfer candidates should submit applications no later than November 1 for the spring semester or April 1 for the fall semester.

To request an application or for more information, students should contact:

Office of Admissions and Financial Aid
St. Lawrence University
Canton, New York 13617
Telephone: 315-229-5261
800-285-1856 (toll-free)
E-mail: admissions@stlawu.edu
World Wide Web: http://www.stlawu.edu

SAINT LEO UNIVERSITY

SAINT LEO, FLORIDA

The University

Saint Leo University is a four-year, private, coeducational university affiliated with the Catholic Church. Founded in 1889 by the Order of Saint Benedict, Saint Leo has grown to an enrollment of 1,500 full- and part-time students on the main campus and 13,000 students in extension programs located on eleven military bases stretching from Virginia to Key West. The student body represents fifty states and forty countries; 60 percent are from Florida and 3 percent are international students. Of the students on the main campus, approximately 750 live on campus in the six residence halls.

Students can participate in the nationally recognized honors program and the more than forty different clubs and organizations on campus, including national fraternities and sororities.

Saint Leo competes in NCAA Division II sports for men in baseball, basketball, cross-country, golf, soccer, and tennis and for women in basketball, cross-country, golf, soccer, softball, tennis, and volleyball. Students can also participate in a variety of intramurals as well as men's and women's club lacrosse. On the campus there are lighted racquetball and tennis courts; soccer, baseball, and softball fields; a weight room; and an outdoor swimming pool. A 154-acre lake and an eighteen-hole golf course are adjacent to the campus. The University also hosts a variety of events that are open to the University community and residents of the surrounding area. There are art exhibits and musical concerts. In addition, the Student Government Union and various campus organizations sponsor movies, lectures, dances, and special events throughout the academic year.

Saint Leo is committed to giving its students an education that prepares them for the future. The goal of the University is to develop the whole person, both academically and personally, by providing a values-based education in the Benedictine tradition.

Saint Leo University is accredited by the Commission on Colleges of the Southern Association of Colleges and Schools to award the associate and bachelor's degrees. Saint Leo University's program in social work is accredited by the Commission on Accreditation of the Council on Social Work Education (B.S.W. level). Saint Leo University has Teacher Education Program approval by the state of Florida Department of Education. The School of Business is accredited by the International Assembly for Collegiate Business Education (IACBE).

In addition to associate and bachelor's degrees, Saint Leo University offers a Master of Business Administration (M.B.A.) degree, a Master of Education (M.Ed.) degree, and master's degrees in counseling psychology and criminal justice.

Location

Saint Leo is located 25 miles north of Tampa and 60 miles west of Orlando. The campus occupies 170 acres of rolling hills and wooded grounds. The rural setting is conducive to academic success, but the University is located near enough to metropolitan areas to give the students the advantage of a number of social and professional options.

Majors and Degrees

Saint Leo University offers nearly forty traditional majors, preprofessional programs, specializations, and career-oriented studies. Degrees offered are the Bachelor of Arts, Bachelor of Science, and Bachelor of Social Work.

The School of Business offers majors in accounting; business administration, with specializations in management, marketing, golf course management, hospitality and tourism, and international business; computer information systems; health-care administration; human resource administration; and sport management. The School of Arts and Sciences offers majors in biology, communications, English, environmental science, history, international studies, medical technology, political science, psychology, and religion. The School of Education and Social Services offers majors in criminal justice, elementary education, human services management, and social work. Preprofessional programs in dentistry, law, medicine, occupational therapy, physical therapy, and veterinary science are also offered, including 4+4 medical school and 3+4 dental school programs.

Academic Programs

The General Education curriculum ensures that all students have a solid grounding in theories, issues, and knowledge that prepares graduates for successful careers and graduate work. Students complete Foundation courses of core requirements (writing, computer literacy, math, and wellness), Perspectives courses (liberal arts, fine arts, humanities, and physical, social, and behavioral sciences), and a Senior Capstone course that connects all prior course work in the major and leads to research and independent projects demonstrating mastery of the field.

Most students at Saint Leo earn the 122 credits needed for their bachelor's degree through a four-year program of study. All major programs require a minimum grade point average of 2.0 (C) for graduation. Saint Leo has an academic skills program to assist first-year students in their adjustment to University life. Included in this program are freshman studies, tutoring, and advising. All first-year students at Saint Leo are assigned faculty advisers who act as mentors from the first day that the student arrives on campus through the time when the student selects a major.

Students have the opportunity to receive credit through examination. Students who demonstrate course mastery for any course listed in the catalog may earn up to 40 hours of credit through examination. Information about credit by examination is available through the Registrar's Office.

Off-Campus Programs

Saint Leo University is committed to helping students expand their horizons with study-abroad programs. Saint Leo currently has partnerships with schools in Rome, Italy; Paris, France; Leysin and Engelberg, Switzerland; London, England; and Ecuador. The University continues to add new programs and partnerships in order to provide students with a wide variety of experiences.

Academic Facilities

The Cannon Memorial Library contains more than 180,000 volumes, 743 current periodical and newspaper subscriptions, microforms, and a variety of media software. Also located in the library are the Hugh Culverhouse Computer Lab and an audiovisual lab that are available for student use. There is a biology lab on campus for research. Crawford Hall and the Julia Deal Lewis Hall of Science provide general classrooms.

Every student who resides in campus housing receives an IBM ThinkPad laptop computer. Saint Leo's campus is a totally wireless environment. For students who live off campus, laptops are available for use through the library.

Costs

For the 2004–05 school year, tuition is $13,650, room and board costs are $7260, and the student activity fee is $230. Estimated miscellaneous costs for the year total $1800.

Financial Aid

Financial aid is available in the form of scholarships, grants, and loans that are both federally funded and given through the University. Financial aid is allocated on the basis of academic performance and need, as determined by the federal government from the financial information provided on the Free Application for Federal Student Aid (FAFSA). On-campus jobs are available for students, with priority given to students with demonstrated financial need.

Faculty

Most courses are taught by full-time faculty members. In some cases, part-time faculty specialists are employed to provide students with real-world experience in their classes. Ninety-seven percent of all full-time faculty members hold a doctorate. The student-faculty ratio is 15:1.

Student Government

A significant contribution to the University comes from the activities initiated by the Student Government Union (SGU). The SGU is an annually elected body organized and conducted in accordance with democratic procedures. This organization strives to foster leadership and loyalty among the students, to formulate recommendations for student life, and to recognize all extracurricular activities.

Admission Requirements

All candidates for admission should be, or expect to be, graduates of secondary schools accredited by a regional or state accrediting agency. Applicants should show successful progress toward graduation with a minimum of 16 academic units of course work: 4 units of English, 3 units of mathematics (algebra I and II and geometry), 3 units of social studies, 2 units of science, and 4 units of electives. All applicants are required to take the SAT I or the ACT examination. A letter of recommendation from the student's guidance counselor and a student essay are also required. Preferred candidates are students with a B or better average grade and SAT I combined scores averaging 1010 (21 on the ACT). The records of students who do not meet these criteria are also reviewed by the Admissions Committee and considered for the Learning Enhancement for Academic Progress (LEAP) program, a preparatory program that has a summer attendance component.

Once the applicant has submitted the application with the $35 application fee, admission essay, high school transcripts, test scores, and letter of recommendation, the file is reviewed and a decision is rendered. Notification is on a rolling basis. The priority application deadline is March 1, but all applicants are encouraged to apply early.

Transfer and international students are also encouraged to apply. The same general admission procedures are required, along with at least a C average for all college work (for transfer students) and a score of at least 550 (paper-based test) or 213 (computer-based test) on the TOEFL (for international students).

Campus visits and interviews are recommended but not required. The Office of Admission schedules appointments Monday through Friday from 9 a.m. to 4 p.m. and on select Saturdays at 9:30 a.m. or 11 a.m.

Application and Information

Additional information and application forms can be obtained by contacting the Office of Admission.

Gary G. Bracken
Vice President for Enrollment
Office of Admission—MC2008
Saint Leo University
P.O. Box 6665
Saint Leo, Florida 33574-6665
Telephone: 352-588-8283
800-334-5532 (toll-free)
Fax: 352-588-8257
E-mail: admission@saintleo.edu
World Wide Web: http://www.saintleo.edu

The Saint Leo University campus.

ST. LOUIS COLLEGE OF PHARMACY

ST. LOUIS, MISSOURI

The College

Ranking among the top pharmacy colleges in the nation, St. Louis College of Pharmacy offers its students a strong liberal arts and professional degree program. Founded in 1864, St. Louis College of Pharmacy is the oldest and largest private independent college in the nation whose only degrees are in pharmacy. A recent $42-million, campuswide transformation makes it one of the most modern. Students can access the College's computer network wirelessly from virtually anywhere on campus. A new eight-story residence hall features suite and efficiency-style units and is connected to a spacious dining facility that serves both fast food and plate meals. Upper-level students may elect to live on campus in Rabe Hall, a fifty-seven-unit apartment building featuring studio and one-bedroom and two-bedroom units.

The total enrollment for 2002–03 was 549 women and 351 men. The students of the College maintain chapters of the Academy of Students in Pharmacy, the student National Community Pharmacy Association (NCPA), and the Student National Pharmaceutical Association. These chapters conduct programs of professional and general interest that are directed toward advancing pharmacy practice. The College recognizes five national professional fraternal organizations. These groups provide social activities in addition to their professional functions. All five groups are governed by an Interfraternity Council. A national honor pharmaceutical society, Rho Chi, is open to fourth- through sixth-year students who are both academically and professionally outstanding.

The Master of Science (M.S.) degree in managed-care pharmacy is offered as a part-time graduate program and provides upper-level management electives for fourth- through sixth-year students. A certificate in managed-care pharmacy is offered as well.

Extracurricular activities include the College band; chorus; theater and musical programs; dances; movies; lecture programs; the student newspaper, the *Pharmakon;* and the student yearbook, the *Prescripto.* Student ambassadors act as hosts at College functions.

St. Louis College of Pharmacy offers an athletic program for both varsity and intramural sports. The College is a member of NAIA Division III in men's and women's basketball, women's volleyball, and men's and women's cross-country. The College's student center has excellent facilities for weight training, aerobics, and body conditioning.

Location

Known for generations as the Gateway to the West, St. Louis is a center for cultural, educational, and industrial activities. It has many fine museums, a symphony orchestra, theaters, professional sports, historic landmarks, zoological and botanical gardens, and one of the nation's foremost medical centers. A number of these outstanding attractions are within a 2-mile radius of the College. St. Louis College of Pharmacy is located in the Washington University medical complex of St. Louis, one block from Forest Park and two blocks from Barnes Hospital.

Majors and Degrees

The College offers a six-year program leading to the Doctor of Pharmacy (Pharm.D.) degree.

Academic Program

The Doctor of Pharmacy program includes intensive, preprofessional courses in biology, chemistry, mathematics, and physics, as well as electives. Courses in literature, humanities, and social and behavioral sciences constitute a significant portion of the curriculum. Introductory practice experiences throughout the curriculum give students the opportunity to apply nearly all facets of their education and enable students to develop communicative and professional interactions with other health-care practitioners and with patients. The six-year Pharm.D. program comprises specialized didactic courses and includes a calendar year of clinical clerkship rotations.

Off-Campus Programs

The St. Louis College of Pharmacy offers clinical training in cooperation with the Washington University and Saint Louis University schools of medicine and in other facilities that include the Jewish, St. Louis Children's, St. John's Mercy, and St. Louis State hospitals. In addition, numerous clerkship rotations are available in a variety of community retail settings.

Academic Facilities

The O. J. Cloughly Alumni Library, located adjacent to the main academic building, is an integral supplement to the instructional program and contains a continually increasing number of volumes in the field of pharmacy, its allied sciences, and the liberal arts. It receives the leading pharmaceutical and scientific periodicals, journals, bulletins, and reports. The library is open throughout the day and most evenings and weekends under the administration of a professional librarian. The main academic building contains classrooms, lecture halls, laboratories, research laboratories, and faculty/administrative offices. Whelpley Hall contains a 300-seat auditorium in addition to small- and medium-size classrooms.

Costs

For 2003–04, tuition fees for students in the first and second years were $16,200; third through fifth years, $16,850; and sixth year, $19,000. Laboratory fees are included in tuition costs. Room and board costs were $6750 for the academic year. Additional costs, including books, vary each year but average $450 per semester.

Financial Aid

The awarding of financial aid is based on merit, need, and availability of funds. The College participates in all applicable federal and state financial aid programs, including the Missouri Advantage Program. Scholarships, grants, loans, and student employment are offered to help qualified students pay for their college expenses. Financial aid may be funded by the federal or state government, the College, benefactors and friends of the College, or other sponsoring organizations or agencies. Merit-based scholarships are offered to qualified students regardless of need.

Students planning to attend the College in the fall semester should submit the Free Application for Federal Student Aid (FAFSA) along with signed copies of student and parent federal tax returns as early as possible during the previous spring semester. The College begins awarding financial aid in

February and continues until all funds are exhausted. Further information on student financial aid may be obtained from the College's Financial Aid Office.

Faculty

An outstanding faculty teaches and counsels students at the College throughout their course of study. A favorable (1:13) faculty-student ratio ensures that there are no anonymous students. No classes are taught by graduate students. Sixty-two of the 65 full-time campus-based faculty members hold a doctoral degree. More than 200 registered pharmacists serve as adjunct instructors in the externship-clerkship program.

Student Government

The Student Council represents the interests of all students. It is composed of representatives elected by the various classes and is supervised by two faculty advisers. The council budgets and supervises the expenditure of funds provided by the student activities fee and sponsors numerous student activities and social events.

Admission Requirements

All students applying for admission must present evidence of the satisfactory completion of a four-year course of study in, and graduation from, a high school approved by a recognized accrediting body. A transcript of the high school record, including class standing, should be sent by the high school directly to the director of admissions. The high school course of study should include 4 units of English, 2 units of algebra, 1 unit of geometry, and at least 2 units of biology, chemistry, or physics. The College requires that the ACT examination be completed.

Transfer students must present transcripts of their college records and have taken the PCAT. Such records must demonstrate satisfactory academic status. Transfer students must apply for admission through Pharm CAS (www.pharmcas.org). Applications sent to St. Louis College of Pharmacy will not be accepted.

Advanced credit may be earned through Advanced Placement examinations. Further details are available from the Office of Admissions.

Application and Information

The College uses a system of rolling admission for freshman applicants. Students may apply at any time but should recognize that applications are no longer considered after the freshman class has been filled. Applicants are notified of an admission decision as soon as all of their materials have been received and reviewed. The priority deadline for applications is February 1.

The application deadline for transfer students is March 1. However, due to the large number of transfer applications in recent years, transfer students are encouraged to apply well in advance of this date.

For application forms or additional information, students should contact:

Registrar/Director of Admissions
St. Louis College of Pharmacy
4588 Parkview Place
St. Louis, Missouri 63110
Telephone: 314-367-8700, Ext. 1070
800-278-5267 (toll-free)
E-mail: pbryant@stlcop.edu
World Wide Web: http://www.stlcop.edu

SAINT LOUIS UNIVERSITY, MADRID CAMPUS

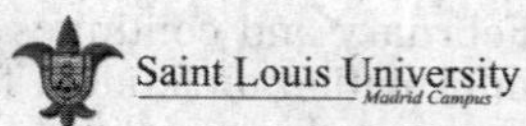

MADRID, SPAIN

The University

Founded in 1969, Saint Louis University, Madrid (SLU–Madrid), is the European campus of Saint Louis University in St. Louis, Missouri, United States, with an enrollment of approximately 600 undergraduate and 20 graduate students each academic semester. There are also about 200 undergraduate and 100 graduate students during the two summer sessions. About 25 percent of the University's students come from Spain, 40 percent from the U.S. (all fifty states), and the rest from sixty-five other countries.

Originally conceived as a home for study-abroad students, SLU–Madrid is now the only full-service American university in Spain. In addition to offering spaces to visiting students from all over the world, each year the University admits about 200 first-year students who begin their undergraduate careers on the Madrid campus. Students majoring in Spanish can do their entire four-year degree program in Madrid. Students studying in the dual-degree International Nursing Program spend the first, second, and fourth years in Madrid; the third year is spent at the School of Nursing on the home campus in Missouri. All other degree majors transfer after two or three years to either the University's home campus or elsewhere to finish their degrees.

In addition to offering undergraduate career options for students who begin their programs in Madrid, the University also offers a master's degree in English language and literature and another in Spanish language and literature. The master's in English is a dual-degree program offered year-round with the Universidad Autónoma de Madrid and requires one 6-week summer session on the home campus. The master's in Spanish, offered on both a year-round and summer-only basis, can be completed in its entirety on the campus in Madrid.

SLU–Madrid is accredited through the North Central Association of Colleges and Secondary Schools as an integral part of the St. Louis campus. Individual schools and programs on the home campus also maintain separate accreditations (e.g., business, engineering, nursing) with their respective professional organizations.

Academic and social orientation is held at the beginning of the fall semester for all new degree-seeking students. Five-day, orientation hiking trips in the Pyrenees and along the Camino de Santiago, the pilgrimage trail through northern Spain, give new students the opportunity to make friends and settle into life in Spain. A similar orientation program is offered at the beginning of each semester and summer session for visiting (study-abroad) students.

All new, first-year, degree-seeking students are required to live in University-approved housing. Students with extenuating circumstances may petition for independent housing arrangements prior to arriving in Spain. The University operates two full room and board residences on the campus and five apartment-based, half-room/half-board residences in surrounding neighborhoods. In addition, the housing department places students with Spanish host families—either single-stay or with other students. Second-, third-, and fourth-year continuing students can continue in the housing system or may make their own housing arrangements.

Visiting (study-abroad) students may choose to live with a Spanish host family or in the University-run residences, space permitting. Most years, about 90 percent of these students live within the housing system; the rest make their own housing arrangements.

Location

The Madrid campus was the first American university program in Spain and the first free-standing campus in Europe operated by a U.S.-based university. Madrid, Spain's capital, with a population of more than 3 million, is politically, culturally, and geographically the heart of Spain. From the Prado Museum to the Palacio Real, the city's spectacular cultural offerings are surpassed only by its vibrant nightlife.

The campus is located in the prestigious university quarter of Madrid, overlooking the Sierra de Guadarrama Mountains, yet it is only 20 minutes by metro from Puerta del Sol, the center of the city. Surrounded by other private Spanish universities, the campus' location facilitates interaction between the University's Spanish, international, and American students.

Majors and Degrees

SLU–Madrid offers the first two years of more than seventy undergraduate degree programs, all of which are fully integrated with programs at the Missouri campus. In fall 2003, the Madrid campus introduced its first four-year degree program, the Bachelor of Arts degree in Spanish. Spanish majors may choose to spend all four years of their degree program on the Madrid campus.

All students (permanent and visiting) are encouraged to participate in the Ibero-American Certificate Program. Over the course of two semesters (or one spring semester and one summer session) in residence in Madrid, the student takes courses on the arts, history, culture, economics, and politics of Iberia (Spain and Portugal) and Latin America. Participants can also opt to join a 7–8 day seminar trip to a major capital in South America during the spring semester.

SLU–Madrid places a strong emphasis on language acquisition and fluency. Portuguese, Italian, and Arabic are offered apart from the obvious offerings in English and Spanish.

Further, while most courses are offered in English, students can choose to take a number of selected courses across disciplines in Spanish, an exceptional opportunity to develop fluency.

SLU–Madrid, in conjunction with the Universidad Autónoma de Madrid, offers a four-year, dual-degree program in international nursing. Participants spend two years on the Madrid campus, the third year at the School of Nursing on the home campus in St. Louis, and the final year at the Universidad Autónoma campus in Madrid. Nursing students earn two degrees: the Bachelor of Nursing from Saint Louis University and *la Diplomatura en Enfermería* from la Universidad Autónoma.

Academic Program

The academic year consists of two semesters and two summer sessions. While the number of semester hours required for graduation varies with the program chosen, a minimum of 120 hours are required for a degree. A student must fulfill the required semester hours in a major as well as the basic requirements of the core curriculum. Students in most degree programs can complete 60–80 credits hours on the Madrid campus. The remainder must be completed on the home campus in St. Louis, or at any other American university. Students pursuing the Bachelor of Arts degree in Spanish can complete all 120 credits hours on the Madrid campus.

Off-Campus Programs

As an international campus of Saint Louis University, SLU–Madrid designs courses to take advantage of its location in Europe. Select classes in each of the disciplines include mandatory trips to destinations in Europe, the Middle-East, Africa, and/or South America.

In coordination with the Association of American International Colleges and Universities, students can pursue study-abroad opportunities at partner schools in Europe, Africa, and the Middle East.

Business and engineering students with the required level of Spanish language skills are encouraged to pursue internships in the offices of multinational corporations, such as Hewlett-Packard, Kodak, and John Deere, which are all located in Madrid.

Academic Facilities

The Madrid campus comprises four buildings: Padre Rubio Hall, Padre Arrupe Hall, and two single-sex dormitories. Padre Arrupe Hall, a restored eighteenth-century chalet, contains the library; three computer labs; the biology, chemistry and physics labs; and administrative and faculty offices. Padre Rubio Hall, also dating to the eighteenth-century, houses the student life offices, Campus Ministry, faculty offices, a snack bar, the bookstore and copy center, music practice rooms, a fourth computer lab, and air-conditioned classrooms.

Costs

Tuition and fees for U.S. permanent students at the Saint Louis University, Madrid campus, for 2003–04 were $7405 per semester. Non-U.S. students paid €5335 per semester. Non-U.S. status is determined by residency status outside the U.S. Room and board costs averaged €2145 per semester, depending on accommodations. Books and supplies cost approximately $500 per semester. Students should budget $500 per month for travel and activities.

Costs are subject to change.

Financial Aid

U.S. first-year, degree-seeking students who apply to the Madrid campus of Saint Louis University are automatically considered for the Madrid merit-based work-study scholarship. They are also considered through the home campus in Missouri for all federal, state, and privately funded student aid programs by submitting the Free Application for Federal Student Aid (FAFSA).

Non-U.S. students are automatically considered for Madrid-specific merit-based scholarships specifically designed for international students.

Faculty

The Madrid campus of Saint Louis University has approximately 90 full- and part-time faculty members, the majority of whom hold the highest degrees in their fields. The average class size is 20 students, and the student-to-teacher ratio is 8:1.

Admission Requirements

The programs of SLU–Madrid, are open to all without regard to race, color, sex, age, national origin, religion, sexual orientation, disability, or veteran status. All University policies, practices, and procedures are administrated in a manner consistent with its Catholic Jesuit identity. Students who have demonstrated past academic achievement and who show promise and aptitude for successful performance in an international-university environment are encouraged to apply for admission. SLU–Madrid welcomes students from diverse school systems around the world. This diversity of secondary school experience raises the academic level on the campus.

A student's potential for success in college studies on the Madrid campus is judged by the student's high school average, rank in class, aptitude test scores (ACT and SAT I), and recommendations.

Transfer students in good academic standing are invited to apply. Transfer students must submit transcripts from each high school and college attended.

Students from universities and colleges are invited to spend a semester, summer, or year on the Madrid campus. SLU–Madrid specializes in semester programs for students from academic disciplines, such as engineering and premedicine, who traditionally have a difficult time enrolling in a study-abroad program.

Admissions decisions are made on a rolling basis.

Application and Information

To be considered for admission, a student should complete the online application found at the Web site listed below. Paper applications are available upon request from the Admissions Department. The application deadline for the fall semester is May 30 for freshman enrollment.

Admissions Department
Saint Louis University, Madrid Campus
Avenida del Valle, 34
28003 Madrid, Spain

Telephone: 34-91-554-58-58
E-mail: madrid@madrid.sluiberica.slu.edu
World Wide Web: http://spain.slu.edu

SAINT MARTIN'S COLLEGE

LACEY, WASHINGTON

The College

Students choose Saint Martin's College for its intimate approach to academic excellence. Founded in 1895 by the Catholic Order of Saint Benedict, Saint Martin's College is the only Benedictine-Catholic college in the western United States. The academic and student life programs are influenced by the Benedictine values of hospitality, respect, and tolerance. Saint Martin's believes in the inherent value and worth of the individual and seeks to develop and nurture each student's unique gifts and talents to his or her full potential.

Students can anticipate lively class discussions and tolerance for their opinions, whether or not others agree with them. At a teaching institution like Saint Martin's College, the hallmark of a good professor is that his or her students are learning. An emphasis on critical thinking and thoughtful expression is a part of developing graduates recognized for their competency and work ethic. The College also stresses personal and spiritual growth through participation in community service.

More than 100 years since its inception, Saint Martin's enjoys the distinction of having one of the most successful placement rates in the state of Washington. The placement rate of students accepted to graduate school or finding employment within their field of study within six months of graduation has exceeded 96 percent for the past thirteen years.

Saint Martin's Institute of Pacific Rim Studies offers academic and cultural programs, opportunities for students to study abroad, an English as a second language (ESL) program, and a Semester-in-Residence Program, as well as summer cultural programs.

In addition to preparing undergraduate students for today's world, Saint Martin's offers the following graduate degrees: Master of Business Administration, Master of Civil Engineering, Master of Arts in Counseling Psychology, Master of Education, Master of Engineering Management, and Master in Teaching.

In a college where the students number approximately 1,000 it is easy to become involved in the educational process and campus community. In addition to Saint Martin's main campus in Lacey, Washington, two extension learning centers are located nearby at the Fort Lewis Army Post and McChord Air Force Base. Most students are from the Pacific Northwest, although seventeen other states and thirteen countries are currently represented. Another 30 percent describe themselves as minority students. Two distinguishing characteristics of Saint Martin's students are their friendliness and their active involvement in the campus community.

Student life offerings are varied and easy to participate in. Students can choose from social clubs, interest groups, cultural events, intramural sports, and student government, as well as sororities and fraternities. Many students participate in organizations that compliment their field of study. NCAA Division II intercollegiate athletic offerings for men include baseball, basketball, cross-country, golf, and track. NCAA Division II athletic offerings for women include basketball, cross-country, golf, softball, track, and volleyball.

Residence life is a valuable aspect of the student's educational experience. Thirty-one percent of Saint Martin's full-time undergraduate students make their home in the coed residence halls. A new residence hall is scheduled to open in 2005. Safety and respect for one's neighbor are two constants in residence life. The safety of Saint Martin's students is a top priority for security personnel and the campus community alike. Security personnel are available 24 hours a day, seven days a week. Security also offers a personal escort to and from any campus location. Cars are permitted for all students, and registered vehicles may park on campus at no charge.

Location

Saint Martin's College is located in Lacey, Washington, just minutes from the state capital of Olympia. The 280-acre wooded campus provides a peaceful and contemplative environment for students to focus on academic endeavors and career preparation.

Although the serenity of the campus would leave one to believe otherwise, it is easily accessible from I-5. Commercial train and bus stops are only 10 minutes away, and the SeaTac International Airport is only a 45-minute drive away.

Opportunities for outdoor activities are ample. The Pacific Ocean waters of Puget Sound are only a 15-minute drive from campus. The Cascade Mountain Range is 1 hour to the east, and the Olympics are 1 hour to the west. Students can enjoy beachcombing, mountain biking, camping, rock climbing, fishing, hiking, kayaking, mountain climbing, and snow and water skiing, all within an hour's drive of campus.

The greater Olympia area, which includes Lacey, has a population of 89,000 residents. Downtown Olympia provides an eclectic mix of coffee shops, restaurants, gift shops, theaters, and entertainment. People-watching opportunities abound, especially in the spring months at the local Farmer's Market.

Majors and Degrees

Saint Martin's College offers Bachelor of Arts and Bachelor of Science degrees in the following academic majors: accounting, biology, business administration (with areas of concentration in accounting, economics, finance, information systems management, management, and marketing), chemistry, civil engineering, community service, computer science, criminal justice, elementary education, English, history, humanities, mathematics, mechanical engineering, music, political science, psychology, religious studies, secondary education, social sciences, sociology and cultural anthropology, special education, and theatre arts. Preprofessional programs are offered in dentistry, law, medicine, pharmacy, and physical therapy.

Academic Programs

The academic program at Saint Martin's College is founded upon the belief that all academic preparation and professional development benefit from a grounding in the liberal arts. The curriculum allows double majors, independent studies, special-topic courses, practica, and internships designed to meet special student interests.

The College operates on a semester academic calendar, with fall semester beginning late in August and continuing through mid-December. Spring semester begins in mid-January and continues through mid-May. Two summer sessions are offered between mid-May and early August.

Academic Facilities

The state-of-the-art O'Grady Library opened in January 2001. The building, designed by Michael Graves, features two computer classrooms, an information commons, and more than 300 ports for connecting to the campus network and the internet. Current library holdings are supplemented by online automation for interlibrary loan.

The Saint Martin's Computer Resource Center is available for use by all students. Both Macintosh and IBM-compatible computers are available. Internet access and e-mail are provided at no charge to students.

Costs

Tuition and fees for 2004–05 are $18,950. Room and board costs (based upon double occupancy) are $5720 annually. Travel and personal expenses vary. Books and supplies are estimated at $740 per year.

Financial Aid

Saint Martin's College recognizes that financing a college education is an important factor in selecting a college. The selection of a particular college is also dependent upon the quality of education available for the tuition dollar. Saint Martin's has one of the lowest tuition costs of any independent college in the state of Washington. In 2002–03, the College distributed $13.7 million in financial aid, of which $4 million were institutional funds.

Saint Martin's College participates fully in all federal and state programs, including work-study, loan, and grant programs. Institutional scholarships and grants are awarded for academic achievement, community service, athletic participation, and demonstrated leadership. Some of the more distinctive scholarship programs at Saint Martin's are the Saint Benedict Award ($1000 to $4000), for students who have demonstrated involvement in community service and volunteer work; Returning Reward ($1000 to $4000), which encourages student retention by providing a "forgivable" loan during a student's freshman and sophomore years that is forgiven upon graduation from Saint Martin's; and a Valedictorian Scholarship (separate application required), which covers full tuition costs for four years. Academic scholarships range from $4500 to $12,500 for freshmen (based upon grade point average and SAT I or ACT scores) and $1500 to $3000 for transfer students (based upon college or university grade point average). Athletic talent awards range between $500 and full tuition and are determined by recommendations from Saint Martin's coaching staff.

Students applying for financial aid should complete the Free Application for Federal Student Aid (FAFSA). Students must be accepted by Saint Martin's before a financial award can be processed. A separate application is required for institutional financial aid. Students are encouraged to mail the FAFSA by February 15 in order to meet the priority deadline of March 1.

Faculty

Saint Martin's College has 57 full-time and 15 part-time faculty members. Eighty-four percent hold a Ph.D. or the terminal degree in their fields. All classes and lab sessions are taught by faculty members; graduate assistants do not teach classes. Faculty members are selected for their ability to teach, and classes are kept small so professors can know students not only by name but by personal interest, academic ability, and individual potential. SMC maintains a 14:1 student-faculty ratio. Ninety-nine percent of classes have less than 30 students. The average class size is 13.

Student Government

The Associated Students of Saint Martin's College (ASSMC) sponsors campuswide programming events and serves as a liaison between students and the administration. It includes the executive council, student senate, and club representatives. The ASSMC also supervises club activities and allocates student activity fees.

Admission Requirements

Saint Martin's College seeks to admit students who are comfortable with academic rigor, anticipate academic success, and look to become active members of the campus community. While admission to Saint Martin's is based primarily upon demonstrated academic ability, ACT or SAT I test scores and a personal essay are also required for consideration. A strong academic background including 4 years of English, 3 years of math, 2 years of science, and 2 years of social studies is preferred. Two years of foreign language is recommended. Extracurricular activities, leadership positions, and community involvement are looked upon favorably.

Freshman applicants should submit a completed Undergraduate Application for Admission, ACT or SAT I scores, an official high school transcript, and a personal essay. Upon graduation, a final official transcript must be submitted.

Transfer applicants should submit a completed Undergraduate Application for Admission, official transcripts from all colleges attended, and a personal essay.

Application and Information

Applications are accepted on a rolling basis, with priority deadlines of March 1 for the fall semester and November 1 for the spring semester. All students are encouraged to apply early, and high school seniors should aim to have applications submitted by late November. Students can expect to be notified within one week of the receipt of their completed application.

Additional information or application materials may be obtained by contacting:

Office of Admissions
Saint Martin's College
5300 Pacific Avenue, SE
Lacey, Washington 98503-1297
Telephone: 360-438-4311
800-368-8803 (toll-free)
Fax: 360-412-6189
E-mail: admissions@stmartin.edu
World Wide Web: http://www.stmartin.edu

Old Main at Saint Martin's College houses classrooms and administrative offices.

SAINT MARY'S COLLEGE

NOTRE DAME, INDIANA

The College

One of the oldest Catholic colleges for women in the United States, Saint Mary's College was founded and continues to be sponsored by the Sisters of the Holy Cross in 1844. The College has long been recognized as a pioneer in exploring with integrity and imagination the roles of women in society. Today, Saint Mary's enjoys a national reputation for academic excellence and vitality of campus life.

With more than 1,600 students from forty-nine states and twelve countries, Saint Mary's brings together women from a wide range of geographical areas, social backgrounds, and educational experiences. International and minority students comprise 8 percent of the student body.

Saint Mary's College's liberal arts emphasis enhances a comprehensive curriculum. Strong programs in the humanities and sciences are complemented by professional programs in business administration, education, nursing, and social work; majors in the fine and performing arts; and courses of preprofessional study that prepare students for law school, medical school, or advanced study in other health professions.

Small classes (median size: 16) and a low student-faculty ratio (12:1) encourage student participation in class discussions, collaboration with faculty members, and preparation for real-world challenges. The College enjoys a unique co-exchange program with the University of Notre Dame.

Approximately 80 percent of Saint Mary's students live on campus in four residence halls, each with its own distinctive character. Upperclass students may live off-campus. Residence halls offer a full calendar of activities, from twice-yearly dances to discussions with professors. The College has a student center, a dining hall, and a clubhouse for extracurricular activities. All residence halls have chapels, and the Church of Loretto is on campus.

As an NCAA Division III school and a member of the Michigan Intercollegiate Athletic Association, Saint Mary's sponsors varsity teams in basketball, cross-country, golf, soccer, softball, swimming and diving, tennis, and volleyball. Club sports, cosponsored with Notre Dame, include equestrian, gymnastics, lacrosse, sailing, skiing, and synchronized swimming. In addition, Saint Mary's offers many intramural sports.

The College's Angela Athletic Facility contains multipurpose courts for tennis, volleyball, and basketball; a training and fitness center; and racquetball courts. The campus has an indoor swimming pool, outdoor tennis courts, athletic fields, and a driving range for golf.

Location

Saint Mary's 275-acre campus, set alongside the Saint Joseph River, has great natural beauty. The College, located just across the street from the University of Notre Dame, just north of the city of South Bend, and just 90 miles from Chicago, is at the hub of much activity. Students from Saint Mary's and Notre Dame form a dynamic intercollegiate community. South Bend provides sites for internships and practicums and opportunities for volunteer service.

Majors and Degrees

Saint Mary's College offers programs leading to the Bachelor of Arts, Bachelor of Science, Bachelor of Fine Arts, Bachelor of Business Administration, and Bachelor of Music degrees.

For a Bachelor of Arts degree, students may choose majors in art, biology, chemistry, communication studies, economics, elementary education, English literature, English writing, French, history, humanistic studies, mathematics, music, philosophy, political science, psychology, religious studies, social work, sociology, Spanish, statistics and actuarial mathematics, and theater.

A Bachelor of Science degree may be obtained in biology, chemistry, computational mathematics, mathematics, medical technology, nursing, and statistics and actuarial mathematics.

The Bachelor of Music degree program, which is a member of the National Association of Schools of Music, offers concentrations in applied music and music education. For talented art students, Saint Mary's offers a Bachelor of Fine Arts degree.

The Bachelor of Business Administration degree program offers a major in business administration (with concentrations in accounting, finance, international business, management, and marketing) and a major in management information systems.

Superior students who are candidates for either a Bachelor of Arts or a Bachelor of Science degree may design a program of study outside of the traditional department structure.

For women interested in engineering fields, a five-year dual-degree program offered in cooperation with the University of Notre Dame leads to a bachelor's degree from Saint Mary's College and a Bachelor of Science in Engineering degree from Notre Dame in one of seven areas.

Saint Mary's education department, accredited by the National Council for Accreditation of Teacher Education, offers certification in elementary and secondary education.

In addition, the College offers more than forty minors in a variety of fields, including American studies, information science, justice studies, Latin American studies, urban studies, and women's studies.

Academic Program

Graduation from Saint Mary's College requires successful completion of at least 128 semester hours of credit with a minimum quality point average of 2.0. Every student must also complete a comprehensive examination in her major, which may take the form of a thesis, a research or creative project, or a written or oral examination, depending on the discipline. All students must demonstrate writing proficiency by satisfactorily completing a writing-intensive "W" course, usually in the first year, and an advanced portfolio of writings in the major discipline, usually as seniors.

Students spend approximately one third of their time in general education courses in humanities, fine arts, foreign language, natural and social sciences, theology, and philosophy. Remaining course hours are devoted to their major and electives or minors. The College assists those students interested in pursuing independent study or research and internships.

Off-Campus Programs

Through Saint Mary's international study programs, students can study with Irish students at the National University of Ireland Maynooth, just outside Dublin. They can absorb Italian art and culture on Saint Mary's campus in the center of Rome, or experience Southeast Asia and the Far East with the India-based Semester Around the World Program.

Students can spend a month during the summer based in London, earning credit hours while also traveling to other European countries.

Saint Mary's students may also enroll in the Spanish language programs of the Center for Cross-Cultural Study in Seville, Spain, or in the French language and culture study in Dijon, France. A new exchange program with the Australian University of Notre Dame has just begun.

Saint Mary's students may study in Austria, France, Japan, Mexico, and Toledo, Spain, as well as Jerusalem through a cooperative program with the University of Notre Dame.

A student majoring in political science has the opportunity to spend a semester at the American University in Washington, D.C. Saint Mary's also participates in student- and faculty-member exchange programs with the University of Notre Dame and members of the Northern Indiana Consortium for Education.

Academic Facilities

Students have abundant access to computers, the campus network, and the World Wide Web. Residence halls and classrooms are wired for network access. Computer labs for students are located in several campus buildings, and an expanding set of services and support is available. Many faculty members make use of information technology for teaching and research.

The modern Cushwa-Leighton Library houses a fine collection of 210,812 volumes. It includes offices, study areas, an after-hours study lounge, a media center, computer facilities, the College archives, and a rare book room.

In addition to extensive biology, chemistry, and physics lab facilities, laboratories for psychology research and for foreign language study and practice are available to students. Art studios, music practice rooms, the O'Laughlin Auditorium, and Moreau's Little Theatre provide ample space for arts creation, practice, and performance.

The professionally staffed Early Childhood Development Center on campus provides education and psychology majors with an unusual opportunity to work with young children. Other facilities include the Madeleva classroom building, Science Hall, Havican nursing facility, and Moreau Art Galleries.

Costs

The expenses for the 2003–04 academic year were tuition and fees, $21,624; room and board, $7289 (double occupancy); and miscellaneous expenses (books, transportation, and living costs), $2225.

Financial Aid

The College strives to make a Saint Mary's education available for every student by offering eligible students financial aid packages that may include grants, scholarships, work-study, and loans. Competitive scholarships, awarded solely on merit, as well as those determined by a combination of financial need and academic achievement are available. Last year, more than 87 percent of Saint Mary's students received more than $25 million in financial assistance, more than $9.7 million from the College alone.

All applicants for financial assistance must complete the Financial Aid PROFILE and the Free Application for Federal Student Aid (FAFSA) each year that they desire assistance. Applications for assistance must be received at the processing center by March 1 to be given priority consideration. Decisions concerning financial aid are made as soon as possible after a student has been accepted.

Faculty

Saint Mary's has 114 full-time and 75 part-time faculty members. About 96 percent of the faculty members hold earned doctorates or other terminal degrees; of these, most teach first-year students as well as upper-division students. Faculty members work with students in all phases of college life, including academic counseling.

Student Government

Students are active at every level of campus governance and share in community decision making. There are voting representatives on the president's two highest advisory boards, the Student Affairs Council and the Academic Affairs Council. A student is a voting member of the College Board of Trustees. Student government sponsors many extracurricular and cocurricular activities.

Admission Requirements

Applicants for admission to Saint Mary's College should be graduates of an accredited high school and should ordinarily have completed a four-year program of 16 or more academic units. They must include 4 units of English, 3 units of college-preparatory mathematics, 2 units of one foreign language, 2 units of social science, and 2 units of laboratory science. The remaining units should be in college-preparatory courses. An applicant's credentials should include an academic transcript showing current rank and senior-year subjects, a counselor/administrator recommendation, SAT I or ACT scores, and an essay.

Home-schooled students are encouraged to apply for admission and should contact the Admission Office for details.

An interview with an admission officer is recommended. Saint Mary's encourages students to visit the campus. The Admission Office can make arrangements for students who wish to attend classes or stay overnight.

Superior students who have studied for advanced placement may begin sophomore-level courses in their first year. Mature, well-qualified students who wish to enter college after three years of high school may apply for early admission. Saint Mary's College also grants deferred admission upon request to candidates who are accepted in the normal competition.

Application and Information

Saint Mary's has two application and notification programs: early decision and modified rolling admission. Highly qualified students who have selected Saint Mary's as their first choice for admission may apply under the early decision program. The application deadline is November 15, and the notification date is December 15. Students who apply for modified rolling admission and whose application files are complete on or before December 1 are notified of the admission decision in mid-January. Candidates are encouraged to apply by the end of their junior year of high school or in the fall of their senior year. Applications are accepted, however, as long as space is available.

Interested students are encouraged to contact:

Director of Admission
Saint Mary's College
Notre Dame, Indiana 46556-5001
Telephone: 574-284-4587
800-551-7621 (toll-free)
Fax: 574-284-4841
E-mail: admission@saintmarys.edu
World Wide Web: http://www.saintmarys.edu

SAINT MARY'S COLLEGE OF CALIFORNIA

MORAGA, CALIFORNIA

The College

Saint Mary's College, now in its second century of providing education in the liberal arts, the sciences, business administration, and economics, is one of the oldest colleges in the West. Founded in San Francisco in 1863, it survived the earthquake in 1906 and moved to the current campus in Moraga in 1928. The Christian Brothers, the largest order of Catholic religious devoted exclusively to teaching, assumed direction and ownership of the College in 1868 and have guided its destiny since.

By design, Saint Mary's has always been a small college. Today, the total undergraduate enrollment stands at about 2,500, and enrollment in the freshman class is limited to approximately 620 to maintain the close contact among the students, faculty, staff, and Christian Brothers that is a hallmark of the institution. Along with academic excellence, this personal feeling both inside the classroom and out is what draws students to Saint Mary's.

Since Saint Mary's is a residential college, there is a very strong on-campus life. The student government, clubs, and dorms sponsor parties, movie and comedy nights, dances, and dinners. There are a variety of clubs on campus, ranging from the Science, English, and Pre-Law clubs to the Black Student Union and MEChA to the Committee of Lectures, Arts, and Music to College Republicans and Young Democrats to Students for Peace and Justice to the Chess Club to the Women's Issues Group. Students may also participate in campus ministry; singing groups; *The Collegian,* the campus fortnightly newspaper; and KSMC, the campus radio station. Intercollegiate athletic teams include men's and women's basketball, cross-country, soccer, and tennis; men's baseball, football, and golf; and women's crew, lacrosse, softball, and volleyball. All teams compete at the NCAA Division I level. Club sports are available in men's and women's water polo and men's lacrosse, rugby, and volleyball.

Saint Mary's College is a member of the West Coast Conference (WCC), a Division I National Collegiate Athletic Association (NCAA) conference. In addition to intercollegiate sports, there are numerous intramural leagues for both men and women in the following sports: basketball, flag football, indoor soccer, softball, Ultimate Frisbee, volleyball, and others as announced during the academic year.

The red tile roofs and white stucco walls of the Spanish architectural style of the College's buildings blend with the rolling green hills to create a campus of almost indescribable beauty. The 420-acre campus, only 50 acres of which are covered by buildings, provides both the quiet necessary for academic pursuits and the space for athletics or hiking in the hills. More than half of the students live on campus in residence halls or town houses (apartment-type housing). There are also many off-campus housing facilities available in the nearby suburban communities of Orinda, Moraga, and Lafayette.

Location

Nestled in the rolling hills of the Moraga Valley, 20 miles east of San Francisco, the Saint Mary's campus has the dual benefits of a pastoral setting and proximity to a major metropolitan center. San Francisco and its rich cultural and social offerings are a half hour away by car or easily accessible by public transportation.

Majors and Degrees

The School of Liberal Arts at Saint Mary's College offers the Bachelor of Arts degree in the following departmental areas: anthropology; art; classical languages; communication; economics; English and drama; environmental studies; French; health, physical education, and recreation; history; integral program (Great Books); international area studies; liberal and civic studies; mathematics; performing arts; philosophy; politics; religious studies; sociology; and Spanish. Interdisciplinary majors are also available, as are alternative-plan majors in American studies, cross-cultural studies, European studies, and Latin American studies. Bachelor of Science degrees are offered in biology, chemistry, computer science, environmental science, mathematics, nursing, physics, and psychology through the following departmental areas: biology, chemistry, engineering (a 3+2 cooperative program with the University of Southern California and Washington University in St. Louis, Missouri), environmental science, health science, mathematics/computer science, nursing (a cooperative program with Samuel Merritt College in Oakland), physics, preprofessional curricula (dentistry, medicine, occupational therapy, pharmacy, and physical therapy), and psychology.

The School of Economics and Business Administration offers the Bachelor of Science in accounting, business administration, and economics. An honors program in financial management is also available.

Academic Programs

Saint Mary's College attempts to provide for both the academic and career needs of its students in all programs as far as that is compatible with the spirit of the liberal arts. Its goal is that most difficult liberation—liberation of mind. The favorable student-faculty ratio of 13:1 is conducive to the kind of dialogue necessary for intellectual, spiritual, and social growth among all members of the academic community.

The College's 4-1-4 calendar provides a framework for this faculty member–student interaction. During the fall and spring terms, students attend required seminars on the great books of the Western world and complete the specific core of study required by each of the major programs. Courses for the January Term vary from year to year and reflect the diversity of the Saint Mary's faculty. Besides providing an opportunity for students to focus all their energy on a single subject during one month, the January Term offers them the possibility of participating in various experimental courses, off-campus field study, travel courses in other countries, and special independent study projects.

To earn the bachelor's degree, students are required to complete at least thirty-six courses. Students must complete successfully both the general College requirements and the requirements of their major program.

Off-Campus Programs

Saint Mary's students are able to participate in study-abroad programs in Argentina, Australia, Belgium, China, England, France, Germany, Greece, Ireland, Italy, Mexico, Peru, Scotland, South Africa, and Spain. Internships in Sacramento and Washington, D.C., are available for politics majors. Students who wish to spend part or all of their junior year away from campus are able to receive academic credit directly from Saint Mary's College and to retain California State Grants. In addition, the College regularly conducts travel courses during the January Term.

Academic Facilities

Saint Albert Hall Library contains more than 190,000 volumes, receives 1,110 current periodical titles, and stocks newspapers, pamphlets, recordings, and audiovisual and microform materials. Saint Mary's has a 60,000-square-foot state-of-the-art science center, the J. C. Gatehouse Hall. The chemistry and physics collection is housed in Galileo Hall. Ferroggiaro Center houses LeFevre Theatre, the home of Saint Mary's drama and musical productions, which have been acclaimed throughout Contra Costa County and the greater Bay Area. The Hearst Art Gallery organizes four art exhibitions during each academic year. The shows cover a broad range of the visual arts, including painting, sculpture, crafts, graphics, and film. The gallery also maintains all of the College's extensive art collection, which is displayed in various places around the campus and occasionally highlighted in the gallery.

Costs

Tuition for full-time study for 2004–05 (including the January Term) is $25,000. Room and board (nineteen meals per week) are $9530. Required fees are $300. Town-house apartments with full living and kitchen facilities are available at $6200 per year.

Financial Aid

Seventy-one percent of the undergraduates at Saint Mary's College receive significant financial aid from a variety of sources. To apply for aid, applicants must file the Free Application for Federal Student Aid (FAFSA), which is distributed to high schools and colleges by the College Scholarship Service. Applicants who are residents of California and wish to apply for Cal Grants A and/or B must fill out the G.P.A. Verification Form in conjunction with the FAFSA. The financial aid deadline is March 2. Federal Pell Grants, Federal Supplemental Educational Opportunity Grants, Federal Perkins Loans, and Federal Stafford Student Loans are often part of an applicant's financial aid package.

Faculty

The undergraduate faculty at Saint Mary's consists of 185 full-time and 46 part-time members. Ninety-five percent hold Ph.D. degrees; but, regardless of the degree or professional status, the primary emphasis of the faculty is teaching. Department chairpersons and senior faculty members teach at least one freshman seminar or introductory major course each term. The Christian Brothers constitute one fifth of the faculty; the others are lay men and women. The student-faculty ratio is 13:1.

Student Government

The Associated Students of Saint Mary's College (ASSMC) is the governing body for all undergraduate students. The ASSMC president is an ad hoc member of the board of trustees, and the body as a whole administers significant funds to thirty-two clubs and organizations.

Admission Requirements

The chief qualities sought in a candidate for undergraduate admission are intellectual aptitude (as demonstrated by at least 16 units of college-preparatory courses completed with a minimum B average), seriousness of purpose, and moral integrity. The secondary school record is considered the most reliable measure of potential college ability. Scores on the SAT I of the College Board or on American College Testing's ACT and extracurricular accomplishments may strengthen an application insofar as they indicate special talents, maturity, and perseverance.

Application and Information

Applications must include SAT I or ACT scores, an essay, a completed secondary school recommendation form, and all academic transcripts. Applicants whose files are complete by November 30 receive early notification of the admission decision. The deadline for all other freshman applicants is February 1. The deadline for transfer applicants is July 1. Admission decisions for such applicants are made on a rolling admission basis, and students are notified of the admission decision as soon as all of their materials have been received and evaluated. Transfer students may apply for spring-term admission until January 1.

For additional information, a catalog, or an application form, students should contact:

Dorothy K. Jones
Dean of Admissions
Saint Mary's College of California
P.O. Box 4800
Moraga, California 94575-4800
Telephone: 925-631-4224 or 800-800-4SMC
Fax: 925-376-7193
E-mail: smcadmit@stmarys-ca.edu
World Wide Web: http://www.stmarys-ca.edu

The chapel of Saint Mary's College stands at the center of the 420-acre Moraga Valley campus.

ST. MARY'S COLLEGE OF MARYLAND

ST. MARY'S CITY, MARYLAND

The College

St. Mary's is a public, state-supported, coeducational college dedicated to providing an excellent liberal arts education. There are 1,648 full-time students: 671 men and 977 women. Seventy-nine percent of these students live on campus. Part-time enrollment is 148 students. St. Mary's combines the educational and personal advantages of a small private college with the affordability of a public institution. Active learning and the development of critical thinking are encouraged in the discussion-oriented format made possible by modest class size. Student leadership in academic, cultural, and social spheres is aided by the community atmosphere; opportunities are greater than at larger schools, and involvement is easier.

The College recently began construction on a new college entrance and a new athletic facility. A new apartment-style residence area was recently completed in August 2003.

The campus covers 313 acres, including riverfront, open space, and woodland. Among the waterfront facilities are a boat house, ocean kayaks, sailboards, and a fleet of sailboats. Other facilities include a field house, lighted tennis courts, a new baseball field, an outdoor track, and a stadium for field hockey, soccer, and lacrosse. Plans for the new athletic facility include an aquatic center with an Olympic-sized indoor pool, a new basketball stadium, a fitness center, an aerobic center, additional team rooms, and multipurpose racquetball courts. The College's teams compete in NCAA Division III and the Intercollegiate Sailing Association. Varsity sports for men are baseball, basketball, lacrosse, sailing, soccer, swimming, and tennis; for women, basketball, field hockey, lacrosse, sailing, soccer, swimming, tennis, and volleyball.

The College is accredited by the Middle States Association of Colleges and Schools and the National Association of Schools of Music.

Location

St. Mary's College of Maryland is situated in one of the most beautiful settings in the United States. It is tidewater country, still inhabited by people who make their living from the land and water. Rivermen take oysters and crabs from the Potomac and Patuxent rivers and the Chesapeake Bay; wild swans, ducks, and Canada geese winter in the creeks of St. Mary's County. The Patuxent River Naval Air Station, the county's largest employer, is a naval aircraft testing site, attracting many firms that supply technical support to the Navy and sponsor internships. It is an environment that is alive, providing fresh air and space. It is also convenient to the nation's capital, just 68 miles away.

Majors and Degrees

St. Mary's College offers the Bachelor of Arts degree in anthropology/sociology, art, biochemistry, biology, chemistry, computer science, dramatic arts, economics, English, history, human studies, international language and cultures, mathematics, music, natural science, philosophy, physics, political science, psychology, public policy, religious studies, and student-designed majors. Also available are elementary and secondary teacher education programs leading to certification in Maryland. Preprofessional sequences in dentistry, law, medicine, and veterinary medicine are available.

Academic Program

The course of study at the College provides both diversity and depth, leading to a broad understanding of the liberal arts and a specific competence in at least one major field. All students must complete requirements for one of the majors cited and the general education requirements. The general education requirements are designed to develop skills in communication and analysis, acquaint students with the legacy of the modern world, confront students with the forces and insights that are shaping the modern world, and promote the capacity for integration and synthesis of knowledge.

History, anthropology, and archeology students can take advantage of the College's location on the site of colonial St. Mary's City, Maryland's first state capital. Many experts consider this area to contain the most abundant and earliest undisturbed artifacts of any American seventeenth-century town.

St. Mary's College offers several courses in aquatic biology as an option within the major program in biology. The College's location on the St. Mary's River, a tributary of the Potomac near the mouth of the Chesapeake Bay, is ideal for the study of estuarine ecology.

A strong music program provides advanced training in composition and piano performance and the impetus for a jazz ensemble, percussion ensemble, choir, chamber vocal group, wind ensemble, and chamber orchestra for classical performances.

Students may receive credit for high scores on the Advanced Placement Program examinations. Independent study for credit is possible in every major, allowing students to investigate subjects not covered in normal course offerings. Also available is the opportunity for students to design their own majors.

Off-Campus Programs

An internship program for academic credit is available for junior- and senior-level students. Students find in these semester-long internships a way to test their career interests. In recent years, St. Mary's interns have worked in state and federal government offices and laboratories, in the news media, in museums and art galleries, in commercial organizations, and in positions abroad. In a number of cases, internships have led either to full-time employment after graduation or to graduate or professional study.

A semester or year of study abroad at the Centre for Medieval and Renaissance Studies at Oxford is available for qualified St. Mary's students. In addition, St. Mary's has an exchange program with Johns Hopkins University and offers qualified students a year's study at Fudan University in China, the University of Heidelberg in Germany, the University of The Gambia in The Gambia, and other international universities and colleges. St. Mary's also participates in the National Student Exchange Program with other colleges throughout the United States.

Academic Facilities

The College's laboratories are equipped for course work in anthropology, biology, chemistry, physics, and psychology. There are eleven computer laboratories on campus, including 24-hour labs in three of the residence halls. The College provides student accounts that include free e-mail and Internet access as well as access to the most up-to-date word processing and spreadsheet applications from anywhere on campus. St. Mary's also provides Macintosh laboratories on campus for students who are completing projects and for the arts and sciences. In the foreign language and music computer lab, PCs are equipped with specialized programs and equipment for these two disciplines. The biology and chemistry departments use Hewlett-Packard Kayak workstations, and physics primarily uses Macintosh. All residence hall rooms and town houses are wired with high-speed cable modems that allow students free Internet access and e-mail from their own computers.

The College library, which has a special research collection of early Maryland history, houses communication facilities with audiovisual aids and audio/video recording capability. Interlibrary loan and online database search services provide access to excellent resources at no cost to students.

The Montgomery Fine Arts Center includes facilities for performance in music and theater. It also contains an art gallery and facilities for the Division of Arts and Letters.

Students have access to a staffed writing clinic, which provides assistance in writing and researching papers.

Costs

Annual costs for 2003–04 included tuition and fees of $8803 for Maryland residents and $15,123 for nonresidents. Residence hall rooms were available for $3965 per year, and board was provided for an average cost of $3140 per year. Books and supplies are estimated at $1000 per year. Semester charges for tuition, room, board, and other fees are payable at or prior to registration in the fall and in the spring.

Financial Aid

The Office of Financial Aid provides advice and assistance to students in need of financial aid and joins other College offices in awarding scholarships and loans and in offering part-time employment under the work-study program. Several full scholarships are awarded to Maryland residents on a merit basis, and other scholarships, loans, and grants for students are awarded on the basis of ability and need as determined by the federal government's Free Application for Federal Student Aid, which should be filed no later than March 1.

Faculty

Faculty appointments and promotions are made on the basis of commitment to undergraduate teaching, an interest in new approaches to education, and academic and scholarly achievement. The faculty members have experience in a wide range of activities, including government, business, research, environmental studies, civil rights, the theater, musical performance, and writing. In recent years, 14 faculty members have been awarded Fulbright grants for study abroad. Ninety-four percent of the faculty members hold a doctorate or other terminal degree in their field. A student-faculty ratio of approximately 12:1, the relatively small size of the College, and the informal atmosphere encourage close and personal relationships between students and faculty. Faculty members serve as academic advisers and also provide much informal counseling and individual attention to students' academic and personal development outside of the formal structure.

Student Government

Student government is the center of many activities and sponsors a variety of social and cultural events, including campus movies, speakers, dances, concerts, and excursions to cultural centers such as Annapolis, Baltimore, and Washington, D.C. Opportunities exist for students to serve as voting members on various faculty committees.

Admission Requirements

Applicants for freshman admission are urged to apply before January 15. Strong high school preparation usually includes 4 units of English, 3 units of social science (including U.S. history), 3 units of laboratory science (exclusive of ninth-grade general courses in science), 3 units of mathematics, and 2 units of foreign language. Upon entrance, the student should have obtained a high school diploma with a minimum of 20 units or should present evidence of equivalent achievement (e.g., a passing score on the high school equivalency examination administered by the student's state department of education). The applicant must present scores on the SAT I and/or the ACT examination, which should be taken by the fall of the senior year. In addition, any student whose native language is not English must obtain a minimum score of 550 on the TOEFL. St. Mary's College is interested in evidence of talent and mature ability as demonstrated in a variety of ways by each student. Although admission is based primarily on the high school record and standardized test scores, recommendations and the essay on the application are also very important.

Transfer applicants with at least 24 semester hours of credit will be evaluated on the basis of their college transcripts. Students who have earned fewer than 24 semester hours of credit must submit their high school records and SAT I or ACT scores.

The College may grant credit toward a degree for satisfactory performance on the College Board's Advanced Placement tests or appropriate CLEP tests, for work completed in correspondence courses or at other two- or four-year colleges, or through DANTES.

St. Mary's College of Maryland does not discriminate for reasons of race, religion, ethnic origin, sex, or marital status in the admission of students. The College is in compliance with federal regulations prohibiting discrimination on the basis of age, conditions of handicap, or status as a veteran. The College complies with Title IX of the Education Amendments of 1972.

Application and Information

An application form, financial aid information, and other materials are available by contacting:

Director of Admission
St. Mary's College of Maryland
18952 East Fisher Road
St. Mary's City, Maryland 20686
Telephone: 240-895-5000
800-492-7181 (toll-free)
Fax: 240-895-5001
E-mail: admissions@smcm.edu
World Wide Web: http://www.smcm.edu

A waterfront location and a lengthy sailing season provide recreational opportunities at St. Mary's College of Maryland.

SAINT MARY'S UNIVERSITY OF MINNESOTA

WINONA, MINNESOTA

The University

Saint Mary's University of Minnesota (SMU), formerly Saint Mary's College, is a private, Catholic, liberal arts university. Founded in 1912 by Bishop Patrick Heffron, Saint Mary's University is sponsored by the De La Salle Christian Brothers, who trace their origins to a priest and educational innovator of seventeenth-century France, Saint John Baptist de La Salle. Saint Mary's University remains true to its Lasallian heritage by meeting the educational needs of people of the times while instilling a sense of community and Christian values. The liberal arts curriculum embraces a diverse mix of the arts and sciences, current technology, general education, and major studies while dealing with the personal, cultural, physical, and spiritual needs of students. The University is proud of its tradition of integrating educational excellence while attending to the overall needs of each individual.

Today, Saint Mary's enrolls approximately 1,400 undergraduates every year on the Winona campus; about 54 percent are women. About 90 percent hail from Minnesota, Wisconsin, or Illinois; approximately 80 international students enroll annually. Eighty-five percent of undergraduate students live in University residence halls. Ninety-six clubs and organizations thrive on campus. An active campus ministry program embraces and serves all members of the community and is integral in facilitating community service and outreach activities. An extensive intramural program and nineteen intercollegiate athletic teams provide opportunities for competition and recreation.

At the graduate level, Saint Mary's enrolls more than 4,000 students in twenty-four master's programs, an Education Specialist in educational administration, and a Doctor of Education in leadership; the University also offers several licensure programs. Saint Mary's residential campus in Winona offers the Bachelor of Arts degree, along with six graduate programs. Saint Mary's Bachelor of Science completion programs, twenty-one graduate programs, and the Education Specialist and doctoral programs are offered through its Twin Cities campus. Graduate courses are offered at instructional sites throughout the Minneapolis metropolitan area and in greater Minnesota; the Master of Arts in Education is offered in Wisconsin.

The University operates a number of institutes, including Christ the Teacher Institute of Education, the De La Salle Language Institute, the Hendrickson Institute for Ethical Leadership, and the Maryknoll Institute of African Studies.

Saint Mary's University is accredited by the Higher Learning Commission and is a member of the North Central Association of Colleges and Schools, 30 North LaSalle Street, Suite 2400, Chicago, Illinois 60602-2504 (telephone: 312-263-0456).

Location

Saint Mary's University's residential campus is located in Winona, among the scenic bluffs of the Mississippi River Valley. Students have the opportunity to hike and ski along 15 kilometers of cross-country trails or study by a stream on 400 acres of campus. Winona, a community of about 27,000, is a safe environment for students and provides a quaint atmosphere of small-town friendliness. Winona is located 30 miles from La Crosse, Wisconsin; 40 miles from Rochester, Minnesota; and 110 miles from Minneapolis, Minnesota. Saint Mary's University's Twin Cities campus is located in South Minneapolis, just minutes from the downtown area.

Majors and Degrees

Undergraduate Bachelor of Arts programs at Saint Mary's are organized into the School of the Arts, the School of Business and Computer Science, the School of Education, and the School of Humanities and Sciences, which include fifty-six majors divided into nineteen departments. The following undergraduate majors/programs are offered within these departments: art and design—art studio, graphic design; biology—biology, cytotechnology, environmental, life science education, medical technology, nuclear medicine technology, pre–physical therapy; business—accounting, international business, management, marketing; chemistry—chemistry, physical science education: chemistry; computer science—computer science, computer engineering, e-business technology, mathematical computer science; education—elementary education (grades K–6) with an early adolescence (grades 5–8) specialty, secondary education (with licensure in chemistry, communication arts and literature, life sciences, mathematics, modern/foreign languages, music, physics, social studies); English—communication arts and literature education, literature, literature: writing emphasis; history—history and history/social science; mathematics—mathematics, mathematics education; media communications—electronic publishing, public relations; modern/foreign language—French, modern/foreign language education, Spanish; music—music, music education: classroom and instrumental (grades K–12), music education: classroom and vocal (grades K–12), music industry: music business, music industry: music technology, music performance; philosophy; physics—biophysics, chemical physics, engineering physics, environmental engineering, physical science education: physics; political science—global studies, political science; pre–professional studies—predentistry, pre-engineering, prelaw, premedicine, preoptometry, pre–physical therapy, pretheology, pre–veterinary science; psychology; sociology—criminal justice, human services, social science, social science education, sociology; theater arts; and theology—theology, pastoral and youth ministries.

Academic Program

The Bachelor of Arts degree program requires completion of the general education program and a major field of study. Students must complete 122 credit hours, maintain a cumulative and major grade point average of at least 2.0, and complete 45 credit hours in upper-division courses. Full-time students carry a minimum of 12 credit hours per semester; the average semester load is 16 credits.

The general education program has three components: interdisciplinary studies, disciplinary studies, and skills. The interdisciplinary studies program offers a common experience which seeks to help students acquire and refine the knowledge and skills needed to describe, evaluate, and respond appropriately to humanity's current condition, both as an individual and as a society. The disciplinary studies program exposes students to artistic, social, historical, literary, mathematical, scientific, philosophical, and theological concepts which shape their future and provide a framework for lifelong learning and decision making rooted in the Christian tradition. In addition, students are required to satisfy written communication, oral communication, and critical thinking requirements.

The Lasallian Honors Program, an alternative general education program, provides an intensive interdisciplinary curriculum based on the great books of the Western and Eastern traditions. The program has a tradition of service learning, in which the practical dimensions of servant leadership are explored within the local community. Students are invited into the program based on demonstrated academic excellence in high school, scores on college entrance exams, and leadership in extracurricular activities.

The undergraduate Bachelor of Arts program operates on the semester system, with fifteen-week fall and spring semesters. Graduate and special programs operate on the semester system, with an additional summer session.

Off-Campus Programs

Study abroad programs are available through the Study Abroad Office and the Internship Office.

Saint Mary's offers semester-long study-abroad opportunities in Florence, Italy; London; and Mexico City. The Florence program is based in Fiesole, Italy, and offers courses in art, architecture, business, history, language and culture, politics, and theology. The program incorporates field trips to Assisi, Pisa, Siena, and Rome. The London program offers courses in art, theater, literature, theology, history, and culture. The Mexico program is based at LaSalle University in Mexico City. Classes range from Spanish and Mexican history to a cross-cultural field experience.

Student teaching abroad is available in English-speaking schools.

The Internship Office offers assistance in identifying appropriate internship options, including the Washington Center Internship Program in Washington, D.C., and the Dublin Program in Dublin, Ireland. The University is also a member of the Higher Education Consortium for Urban Affairs, which places students in individually designed internships abroad and at sites in the Minneapolis Metropolitan area.

Academic Facilities

Technology updates have been implemented in Winona Campus science laboratories and renovation of classrooms has included creating multimedia classrooms with network and Internet access. The Hendrickson Center houses the latest technology, including rooms with videoconferencing capabilities, and access to 130 computer terminals. In addition, fourteen residence halls each have a computer pod, and all rooms are wired for Internet connection and cable television. The library houses 175,000 volumes and more than a million volumes can be accessed through a consortium of Minnesota libraries via interlibrary loan. The state-of-the-art Performance Center allows students to perform on a Broadway-size stage. An indoor recreation/fitness center includes four multipurpose courts, a running tracking, pool, a workout center, weight room, and dance studio.

Costs

Undergraduate Bachelor of Arts tuition for the 2003–04 school year was $15,280 for students carrying 24 to 34 credits a year. The average room rate was $2900; the average board plan, $2300. Extra fees included a $150 activity fee, a $20 laundry fee, and a $275 technology fee.

Financial Aid

Federal, state, and institutional aid programs are available for students who demonstrate need. About 80 percent of all undergraduates receive nearly $14.5 million in some form of financial aid; approximately $5 million is provided by Saint Mary's as need-based or merit scholarships.

Faculty

Saint Mary's undergraduate Bachelor of Arts program has 99 full-time and 33 part-time faculty members. Seventy-seven percent of full-time faculty members hold the highest degree in their field. The student-faculty ratio is 12:1.

Student Government

The Student Senate is the representative voice of the student body and is responsible for communicating concerns of the student community to the administration. The senate oversees and distributes money to student groups, to specific capital improvement projects, and to residence hall activities. A House of Representatives is composed of one member of each student organization.

The Student Activities Committee is responsible for planning, organizing, and facilitating activities that are social, cultural, recreational, and educational in nature for the entire SMU community.

Admission Requirements

The pattern of high school college-preparatory courses and performance, while not the sole criterion for acceptance, is of primary importance. Rank in class, a personal essay, standardized test scores, activities, and school recommendations all provide additional data used in the evaluation of a student's academic potential for University success. The University processes admission applications throughout the year for fall or winter semester entrance.

Application and Information

A completed application, a $25 nonrefundable application fee, a personal statement or essay, an official high school transcript, and standardized test scores are required. Students may apply online. Rolling admission is offered for the application process, however, Saint Mary's University applies a priority deadline of May 1 for financial aid and housing. For information and an application, contact:

Admission Office
Saint Mary's University of Minnesota
700 Terrace Heights #2
Winona, Minnesota 55987
Telephone: 507-457-1700
800-635-5987 (toll-free)
Fax: 507-457-1722
E-mail: admissions@smumn.edu
World Wide Web: http://www.smumn.edu/admission/app.html

Saint Mary's University, nestled in the bluffs of the Mississippi River Valley.

ST. MARY'S UNIVERSITY OF SAN ANTONIO

SAN ANTONIO, TEXAS

The University

St. Mary's University is a 150-year-old, private, Catholic coeducational institution of higher education administered by the Society of Mary (Marianists). St. Mary's offers small classes and personal attention while integrating the core curriculum into each student's degree plan. Encompassing course work in the arts, humanities, social sciences, and natural sciences, the core helps develop creativity, analytical skills, and an understanding of the human condition. A St. Mary's education challenges students to academic excellence and personal integrity, preparing them for success in their careers and their lives. Founded in 1852, the University maintains a 135-acre campus in northwest San Antonio, 10 minutes from downtown. Modern and historic buildings combine to provide students with state-of-the-art learning facilities and comfortable living areas.

In fall 2002, St. Mary's enrolled 1,518 students in the Graduate School and School of Law, and 2,725 undergraduates in the Schools of Business and Administration; Humanities and Social Sciences; and Science, Engineering and Technology. The undergraduate population is comprised of 41 percent men and 59 percent women; 7 percent are out-of-state residents. Three percent of the student population includes international students who represent forty-one countries. Active student organizations include sororities and fraternities, the Student Government Association, a campus newspaper, honor societies, ethnic and cultural organizations, scientific clubs, and the International Student Association. There is an active University Ministry.

Beyond the undergraduate level, St. Mary's offers the Master of Arts degree in communication studies, counseling, economics, educational school leadership, English language and literature, history, international relations, justice administration, pastoral administration, political science, psychology, reading, and theology; the Master of Science in computer information systems, engineering (electrical and industrial), psychology, public administration, and systems administration; and the Master of Business Administration with concentrations in accounting, computer systems management, finance, international business, and management. St. Mary's also offers the Doctor of Philosophy in counseling and the Doctor of Jurisprudence.

St. Mary's is accredited by the Southern Association of Colleges and Schools, the Association of Texas Colleges and Universities, the Texas Education Agency, and the Accreditation Board for Engineering and Technology (ABET), Inc., and holds membership in the American Association of University Women, the National Catholic Educational Association, the Association of American Colleges, the American Council on Education, and the Association of American Law Schools. It is an associate member of the National Association of Schools of Music. The School of Business and Administration is accredited by AACSB International–The Association to Advance Collegiate Schools of Business. St. Mary's University is an equal opportunity institution and an Affirmative Action employer.

Location

Although it has grown to become America's eighth-largest city, San Antonio has retained its friendliness and charm amid the bustle of urban life. Located in southern Texas, just 150 miles from Mexico, the city is composed of a culturally diverse population. San Antonio's attractions include the historic Spanish missions (including the Alamo), art museums and galleries, Six Flags Fiesta Texas and Sea World of Texas theme parks, and the beautiful Paseo del Rio (River Walk)—a collection of shops, restaurants, and outdoor cafés along the San Antonio River. The city is also home to eleven colleges and universities, eight hospitals, biomedical research facilities, military bases, a symphony orchestra, an opera company, and numerous cultural festivals. The VIA Transit System provides St. Mary's students with access to all parts of San Antonio.

Majors and Degrees

A Bachelor of Arts degree is offered in computer information systems, criminal justice, criminology, economics, English, English communication arts, exercise and sports science, French, history, international relations, mathematics, multinational organization studies, music (vocal and instrumental), philosophy, physics, political science, psychology, sociology, Spanish, speech communication, and theology. Approved teacher preparation in elementary or secondary education leads to a Bachelor of Arts degree.

A Bachelor of Science degree is offered in applied physics, biochemistry, biology, biophysics, chemistry, computer engineering, computer science, earth sciences/geology, electrical engineering, engineering science, industrial engineering, mathematics, physics, and software engineering/computer applications. Approved teacher preparation in elementary or secondary education leads to a Bachelor of Arts degree.

A Bachelor of Business Administration degree is offered in accounting, corporate finance, entrepreneurial studies, financial services/risk management, general business, human resource management, information systems management, international business, and marketing.

Preprofessional preparation is offered in dentistry, law, medicine, pharmacy, nursing, and allied-health professions. Students may also obtain Texas elementary and secondary teacher certification or earn a commission through the Army ROTC program.

Academic Program

For the Bachelor of Arts degree, 128 hours of prescribed courses and electives must be completed. Requirements include English, natural science, mathematics, computer science, social science, theology, philosophy, foreign language, public speaking, and fine arts. Forty-five hours of study in residence are required, 12 of which should be in the major. Students seeking a Bachelor of Science degree are required to complete the same residence and core requirements as those for the Bachelor of Arts program, plus additional hours in their field of study. The Bachelor of Business Administration requires completion of 129 hours (132 hours for accounting); 45 hours must be completed in residence, and 12 of these must be in the major. Requirements include philosophy, English, social science, mathematics, natural science, economics, accounting, speech, fine arts, and theology. In addition to a liberal arts core of 66 hours, requirements for the Bachelor of Business Administration include 36 hours of a common body of business knowledge and 18–24 hours of upper-division course work in the major.

The University operates on a semester calendar. Advanced placement and/or credit may be granted to students who have scored 3 or higher on the appropriate College Board Advanced Placement examination. Up to 30 credit hours may be granted through the general examinations of the College-Level Examination Program (CLEP) or specific University-administered departmental exams.

Admission to an honors program is available for freshmen demonstrating high ability.

Off-Campus Programs

St. Mary's conducts a European Semester each year, the Washington Semester in cooperation with American University, and a summer program in Innsbruck, Austria. The Innsbruck program is limited to business and law students.

Academic Facilities

The Blume Academic Library and the Sarita Kenedy East Law Library house approximately 700,000 catalogued items, 175,000 U.S. government documents, the curriculum collection for teacher education, and an extensive collection of audiovisual aids. The Learning Resources Center contains fully equipped studios for audio, video, photographic, and graphic arts production. The Center for Legal and Social Justice provides a location for pro bono community service. St. Mary's has state-of-the-art laboratories for physics, engineering, biology, and geology that house equipment for X-ray diffraction and laser research, a metallurgical microscope, and a 150-keV accelerator. Computing facilities support Windows clients and Macintosh workstations are available campuswide. Students can run word processing, desktop publishing, spreadsheet, database, and mathematics application software packages and, through the Internet, can access computer sites throughout the world. Freshman students are provided with their own personal notebook computers as part of their tuition. Students receive St. Mary's e-mail accounts.

Costs

Tuition, fees, room, board, and books for the 2002–03 academic year were approximately $22,550—significantly less than the average for four-year private colleges.

Financial Aid

More than 80 percent of all St. Mary's students receive financial aid funds. A number of academic, music, and athletic scholarships are awarded on a non-need basis. All other financial aid awards are based solely on financial need, as determined by an analysis of the Free Application for Federal Student Aid (FAFSA), which is available online at http://www.fafsa.ed.gov or through the high school guidance counselor. Presidential Scholarships may be awarded to incoming freshmen who are in the top 10 percent of their high school class and have an ACT composite score of at least 26 or an SAT I combined score of at least 1150. All students who have applied by March 1 are considered for scholarships. Students should mail the FAFSA by February 15 so that the processed document is on file in the Office of Financial Assistance by April 1, the financial aid priority deadline.

St. Mary's undergraduates may qualify for the federally sponsored Federal Pell Grant, Federal Supplemental Educational Opportunity Grant, Federal Perkins Loan, Federal PLUS loan, Federal Stafford Student Loan, and Federal Work-Study programs. At the state level, students can apply for the Tuition Equalization Grant, State Incentive Grant, College Access Loan, and Texas College Work-Study programs. In addition, students may qualify for St. Mary's University grants and scholarships.

Faculty

St. Mary's student-faculty ratio of 15:1 and average class size of 20 enable the faculty to provide students with personal instruction and advisement. Faculty members take an active interest in students outside the classroom, with many serving as club moderators. Their concern for the individual student is matched by their professional accomplishment—more than 90 percent of the faculty members have earned the Ph.D. or the highest degree in their field. No courses are taught by graduate assistants.

Student Government

The University has increasingly allowed students to administer certain funds and to be represented on, or to advise, bodies governing all student and some University activities. The Student Government Association president sits on the Student Development Council, and students are represented on all University standing committees dealing with student personnel service areas (athletic, rules and discipline, religious activities, student financial aid, and publications). The bylaws of the Board of Trustees provide for representatives of the Student Government Association to sit on the committees of the board. Students are represented in some departmental staff meetings and sit on committees that prepare budgets and administer funds collected from the student activity fee.

Admission Requirements

For admission, students must have graduated from an accredited high school with 16 academic units, consisting of 4 in English, 3 in mathematics (including algebra II and geometry), 3 in social science, 3 in natural science, 2 in foreign language, and 1 additional academic unit. Applicants for engineering, biology, physics, chemistry, or mathematics must also have credits in solid geometry, trigonometry, and analysis. All freshman applicants are required to submit a high school transcript and to take either the ACT or SAT I. The General Educational Development (GED) test may serve as the high school transcript, provided that the total score is 45 or above and no area has a score lower than 40. International students must follow the same application process and must also submit a TOEFL score. A minimum score of 213 is required for admission. An intensive summer English program is available for applicants who meet all other admission requirements but score below the range on the TOEFL. Transfer students must have a 2.0 average on a 4.0 scale and be in good academic standing at their former college to be considered for admission. Transcripts must be submitted from every college previously attended. Transfer students who have completed fewer than 30 hours of college work must also submit high school transcripts and ACT or SAT I scores. Each application is considered in its entirety. Original transcripts become the property of St. Mary's University.

Application and Information

The application deadline is two weeks prior to registration; however, applicants interested in scholarship consideration must apply by March 1 of the year they intend to enroll. Students applying for financial aid and/or residence hall space on campus are strongly urged to submit all necessary forms and information prior to April 1. When all records are on file, the Admissions Committee will notify the student of its decision.

For application forms and more information, students should contact:

Office of Undergraduate Admissions
St. Mary's University of San Antonio
One Camino Santa Maria
San Antonio, Texas 78228-8503
Telephone: 210-436-3126
800-FOR-STMU (toll-free)
Fax: 210-431-6742
E-mail: uadm@stmarytx.edu
World Wide Web: http://www.stmarytx.edu

On campus at St. Mary's University of San Antonio.

SAINT MICHAEL'S COLLEGE

COLCHESTER, VERMONT

The College

Saint Michael's College is a residential, Catholic, liberal arts college in Vermont where 1,900 undergraduates from around the United States and the world take part in a fully engaging, total college life of the mind, body, and spirit.

Saint Michael's is among the elite ranks of only 270 colleges and universities nationwide allowed to host a prestigious Phi Beta Kappa chapter on campus. The superb faculty members are committed first and foremost to teaching and are known for challenging students to reach higher than they ever thought possible. With a student-faculty ratio of just 12:1, students are ensured personal attention from their professors both in class (lively First-Year Seminars set the interactive tone) and out of class. Because of the holistic approach, Saint Michael's graduates are the beneficiaries of an education that prepares them not only for their first jobs, but for entire careers.

For students who want to make the world a better place, Saint Michael's is the ideal environment. Service to the community and to all humankind is a vibrant part of student life, reflecting the heritage of service of the Edmundite priests who founded Saint Michael's—the one and only Edmundite College in the world—in 1904. Today, more than 70 percent of the student body actively pursues community service projects through Mobilization of Volunteer Efforts (M.O.V.E.), reflecting a unique passion for social justice issues on campus. In the classroom, ethical and moral considerations always complement intellectual discourse. Also, students can find spiritual engagement through the extensive programming offered by the Office of Edmundite Campus Ministry.

With nearly 90 percent of the students living on campus with guaranteed housing for four years, the "24/7" living and learning environment means that exceptional teaching extends beyond the classroom, building lifelong bonds among the College's students and faculty and staff members. The remarkable sense of community on campus is fueled by the size of the student body and the supportive learning environment, which compels students to get involved in campus organizations, take risks, and think differently. Global perspectives enrich the atmosphere through the thriving study-abroad programs and the presence of the School of International Studies, one of the nation's oldest English language institutes.

Location

Saint Michael's is situated just outside of Burlington, Vermont's largest city and a vibrant college town that is home to the 14,000 students enrolled in five local colleges and universities. In addition to the shops, restaurants, and cafés of the Church Street Marketplace and a lively local music scene, Burlington offers great opportunities for hands-on learning through internships. Vermont, known for its natural beauty, environmentalism, and year-round recreational activities, inspires many students to take advantage of some of the best skiing in the East through a new relationship with Smugglers' Notch ski resort—a program that provides an all-access season pass to any Saint Michael's student in good academic standing—and through the College's renowned Wilderness Program.

Saint Michael's enjoys a uniquely accessible location. Burlington International Airport is only a 10-minute drive from the campus. In addition, an Amtrak station is in nearby Essex Junction, and a Greyhound bus station is in Burlington; both are within a 15-minute drive of the campus.

Majors and Degrees

Saint Michael's College offers bachelor's degrees in the following areas: accounting, American studies, biochemistry, biology, business administration, chemistry, classics, computer science, economics, elementary education, engineering, English, environmental science, fine arts (art, music, and theater), French, history, information systems, journalism, mathematics, philosophy, physical science, physics, political science, psychology, religious studies, sociology, and Spanish. In addition, advising programs for premedicine, prelaw, predentistry, and pre–veterinary studies are available. Secondary education licensure is also available in several subject areas.

A special 3+2 engineering program is offered in conjunction with Clarkson University (Potsdam, New York) and University of Vermont (Burlington, Vermont) for students interested in combining a liberal arts background with engineering. A 4+1 M.B.A. program is offered in conjunction with Clarkson University. An English as a second language program is available for international students. Saint Michael's also offers minors in many subject areas.

Academic Program

Saint Michael's academic year consists of two semesters and a summer session. The College's focus is on undergraduate instruction, and its small classes generally support this primary emphasis. All students must complete a liberal studies core curriculum, which includes course work in the following areas: religious studies, philosophy, social sciences, organization studies, natural and mathematical sciences, humanities, and artistic experience. Students must also demonstrate writing and foreign language proficiency. In addition to fulfilling these requirements, students must complete the degree requirements for one of the majors listed above or for an approved combination of those majors.

Off-Campus Programs

Many students enhance their academic work with an internship related to their career goals and major. Internships are available both locally and in other selected areas around the country. Sites have included scientific research laboratories, brokerage houses, hospitals, schools, newspapers, and accounting firms.

Study-abroad programs are available to students in most majors. Programs and locations are selected by the student in consultation with the Director of Study Abroad.

Unique Saint Michael's programs include study-abroad experiences at University of the Americas, Mexico; College of Ripon and York St. John, England; Kansai Gaidai University, Japan; and a Washington, D.C., semester program.

Academic Facilities

The Jeremiah Durick Library holds more than 205,000 volumes, 100,000 microforms, 1,700 periodical subscriptions, and 10,000 maps, videos, and other items. Students in all majors are able to take short courses in computer applications. Although most students bring their own computers, students have access to more than 120 computers connected to the College's campuswide information technology network. This network provides access to PC applications, including Microsoft Office, the Internet, e-mail, and the College library. Computer hookups are available in all residence hall rooms.

Cheray Science Center has facilities for the study of biochemistry, biology, chemistry, environmental science, and physics. Generous grants in recent years have provided state-of-the-art research equipment that is always available to undergraduates.

Saint Edmund's Hall, an impressive academic complex, includes media labs, psychology labs, computer facilities, and language labs, in addition to traditional classroom and lecture hall space.

Costs

The 2004–05 tuition and residence fees are $31,785. The residence fee includes housing and meals and is based on a standard double room and a standard meal plan. Housing options on campus, which include traditional residence halls, apartment-style housing, theme housing, and suite-style housing, are available in three brand-new residence halls. Some science, journalism, language, and art courses require laboratory fees. Book, personal, and travel expenses vary according to course selection and individual needs.

Financial Aid

Financial aid at Saint Michael's is awarded primarily on the basis of financial need, as computed according to the FAFSA. In addition to need-based aid, the College offers a limited number of merit scholarships based upon achievement in high school and on standardized college entrance examinations. The deadline for financial aid applications is March 15 for fall semester enrollment.

Faculty

The undergraduate faculty at Saint Michael's consists of 144 full-time professors. Ninety-three percent of tenured and tenure-track faculty members have the doctoral or terminal degree in their field, and many have been recipients of grants, awards, and honors in recent years. While undergraduate instruction is the focus of the College, faculty members are encouraged to remain abreast of developments in their field through research and publication, often facilitated through sabbaticals.

Student Government

The Student Association (SA), an active and important part of campus life, is an elected body of students that authorizes and funds most other student activities and organizations. Representatives from the SA sit on many campuswide committees, including the Curriculum Committee and various committees of the Board of Trustees.

Admission Requirements

Successful applicants to Saint Michael's typically rank in the top 25 percent of their high school class and have a strong college-preparatory background. Students should have completed 16 units of courses in English, foreign language, mathematics, science, and social science. Candidates must also submit SAT I scores. (The range of SAT I scores for typical students at Saint Michael's is 1020 to 1210.) In addition, students should submit a counselor recommendation and any teacher recommendations they choose. An interview is not required but is strongly recommended. Alumni interviews are available in some locations. Transfer applicants must submit transcripts of all college work in addition to the information required of first-year applicants.

Application and Information

The application deadline for Early Action I is November 15. The Early Action II deadline is December 15. The regular application deadline is February 1. Candidates for the fall semester are notified of their admission decision on or before April 1. A limited number of students may be admitted to the spring semester and should have their applications in by November 1. The College adheres to the Candidates Reply Date of May 1 for the fall semester.

For further information, students should contact:

Office of Admission
Saint Michael's College
One Winooski Park
Colchester, Vermont 05439
Telephone: 800-762-8000 (toll-free)
Fax: 802-654-2591
E-mail: admission@smcvt.edu
World Wide Web: http://www.smcvt.edu

Students enjoy walking to and from class on a warm afternoon, with Saint Edmund's Hall in the background.

ST. NORBERT COLLEGE

DE PERE, WISCONSIN

The College

St. Norbert College (SNC) is the only college in the world sponsored by the Norbertines, a Catholic order devoted to community, education, and serving the needs of others. Father Bernard Pennings, a Norbertine priest, founded St. Norbert College in 1898 with the mission of providing a superior education for students that is personally, intellectually, and spiritually challenging. St. Norbert prides itself in sustaining an environment that encourages students from all religions to develop their full potential inside as well as outside the classroom.

The student body is made up of 2,100 students, hailing from twenty-eight states and thirty-one countries; more than half of the population come from distances of more than 100 miles. Nearly 90 percent of the students are between the ages of 18 and 22 years. Nearly all of the students live on or near the campus, which creates a strong sense of community and a wide range of opportunities for involvement.

About sixty student activities and organizations—academic honor societies, independent social organizations, academic clubs, local and national fraternities and sororities, and special-interest activities—await the St. Norbert student. The student who wants to write for a newspaper, get involved in community service, work for political candidates, or gain other leadership experiences find them at St. Norbert. Students who like physical activities should know that St. Norbert maintains membership in the Midwest Conference for men and women, offers NCAA Division III teams in twenty sports, and is a member of the Northern Collegiate Hockey Association. Successful men's and women's teams have acquired forty-eight conference championships since St. Norbert joined the Midwest Conference in 1983–84. An extensive intramural program complements the activities program and helps guarantee that St. Norbert does not become a suitcase college.

An innovative Career Services Office provides four years of service to help students toward a lifetime of productive, satisfying employment. Counseling, aptitude and interest assessments, career shadowing, career exploration workshops, resume writing workshops, on-campus recruitment interviews, and job-search strategies are among the services available. St. Norbert pioneered the Career Network, in which professionals—many of whom are alumni of the College—conduct interviews with St. Norbert students. Students learn about their chosen profession from people in the field and develop leads to future employment. Extensive on- and off-campus internships complement classroom learning and ease the transition to the professional world. The goal is to achieve near-perfect placement for St. Norbert graduates. Twenty-seven percent of a typical graduating class attends graduate or professional schools. Ninety-two percent of new graduates seeking employment or graduate school admission are successful.

Location

The St. Norbert campus—approximately 86 acres—is located on the banks of the Fox River in De Pere, Wisconsin, just minutes south of Green Bay, a metropolitan area of about 250,000 people and home to the world-famous Green Bay Packers football team. Wisconsin's oldest community, today De Pere is a charming blend of old and new. The community of 20,000 has recently redeveloped its business district, which is within walking distance of the campus. Motels of the major chains are within a few miles, and Door County, Wisconsin's favorite vacation spot, is less than an hour away. Greater Green Bay serves St. Norbert students as an internship laboratory. Students are found in financial, industrial, and retail organizations and as reporters and writers at newspapers and television stations.

Majors and Degrees

St. Norbert offers programs leading to the Bachelor of Arts, Bachelor of Science, Bachelor of Music, and Bachelor of Business Administration degrees. The Bachelor of Arts can be earned in art; communication, media, and theater; economics; education; English; graphic communication; history; international economics; international studies; mathematics; modern foreign languages (French, German, and Spanish); music education; philosophy; political science; psychology; religious studies; and sociology.

Bachelor of Science degrees are conferred in biology, chemistry, computer information systems, computer science, environmental policy, environmental science, geology, natural sciences, and physics. In addition, a Bachelor of Science in natural sciences is awarded to students bound for professional schools (dentistry, medicine, and veterinary medicine). The Bachelor of Music is awarded in applied music. The Bachelor of Business Administration degree is offered to majors in accounting, business administration, and international business and language area studies.

Academic Programs

Degrees are awarded upon the successful completion of thirty-two courses (128 semester hours) that include an approved major sequence, course work in general education, and either an academic minor or electives. Academic majors can be begun as early as the first semester of the freshman year. Early selection of a major is encouraged but not required in most majors.

The General Education Program spans nine areas. The goal is to educate students broadly, regardless of major. Competence in writing and quantitative skills is required of all graduates. Other areas include study of philosophy, religion, the sciences, fine arts, American heritage, foreign heritage, and social science areas, e.g., sociology and psychology. The academic minor option provides flexibility for students planning graduate or professional study or those who seek career-related course work prior to entering the job market. An Honors Program offers unusual challenge in areas of general education to those of superior ability, and an honors degree is awarded to those who successfully complete the program.

The accounting program is accredited by the Wisconsin Accounting Examination Board, and St. Norbert College is a member of the American Assembly of Collegiate Schools of Business. The education programs lead to certification at elementary and secondary levels. A nursery school option is included in the elementary program. Student teaching can be completed in the greater Green Bay area or in Australia, Belize, England, Kenya, New Zealand, Scotland, Ireland, the Virgin Islands, and Wales. A program leading to certification for K–12 teaching in music is available.

Army ROTC is available at St. Norbert through a collaborative program with the University of Wisconsin–Oshkosh. Several SNC students are recipients of full Army ROTC scholarships each year. Among the College's alumni are 10 Army generals who completed ROTC at the College.

Off-Campus Programs

St. Norbert students, regardless of major, can spend a summer, a semester, or a year abroad. Students completing liberal arts majors are encouraged to spend at least a semester abroad. A foreign study component is a part of majors in French, Spanish, and German and both the international business program and the international studies major. All approved foreign study carries regular academic credit. St. Norbert scholarship assistance and other financial aid are available to students studying overseas. Study-abroad opportunities include a Third World science field trip; exchange programs in Australia, France, Japan, Germany, the Philippines, Spain, and Ukraine; student teaching in Europe, Africa, Australia, and Latin America; and other study sites throughout Europe, South America, and Egypt. Programs from the International Center help students, faculty members, and others discover new and exciting ways to explore and broaden their global horizons. St. Norbert's international curriculum, taught by a faculty committed to global learning, prepares students to live in a global society. The international experience that St. Norbert considers vital to today's graduates is a key component of the College's educational mission. The Washington Semester is available through American University.

Academic Facilities

The John Minahan Science Hall houses the science programs and thirty-eight laboratories, including the Center for Adaptive Education. Austin E. Cofrin Hall houses the business administration, computer science, mathematics, and economics programs. It also contains computing resources for the campus, which include minicomputers and 350 microcomputers. The Todd Wehr Library's open concept provides easy access to the College's 274,000 books, periodicals, and manuscripts. The College's archives are located in the library. The College's art collection can be viewed throughout the campus. The F. K. Bemis International Center provides students with increased opportunities to prepare for careers with greater international emphasis. It is also a culture and language resource to K–12 schools and Wisconsin businesses. Campus improvements in the past six years include a $3.4-million renovation and expansion of the Abbot Pennings Hall of Fine Arts; a $3.1-million renovation of Main Hall; construction of the $6-million Austin E. Cofrin Hall; and the $9.2-million F. K. Bemis International Center. The $6.6-million Ray Van Den Heuvel Family Campus Center opened in September 2000. The $6.8-million Bush Family Art Center was dedicated in April 2002. Global links via multifaceted telecommunications technology, including compressed video, two-way interactive video, and satellite downlinks bring world news to student residence halls, classrooms, and conference and seminar rooms. Seven computer labs are available for student use at no charge.

Costs

For 2004–05, tuition and required fees for full-time students totaled $21,510. Room costs averaged $3000 per year, and the average meal plan for full-time students cost $2900 per year.

Financial Aid

Students share in more than $21 million of financial aid each year, including scholarships and grants, campus jobs, and educational loans. SNC awards $14 million of its own scholarships and grants annually. Awards are based on need and merit. No-need scholarships available for freshmen include the Trustees Distinguished Scholarship (special consideration for National Merit and National Achievement commended students, semifinalists, and winners), the Presidential Scholarship, and the John F. Kennedy Scholarship.

Wisconsin residents who show need can qualify for assistance provided by the state through the Wisconsin Tuition Grant Program, which pays up to $2300 of tuition each year. Students also utilize Federal Pell Grants and Federal Stafford Student Loans. The College participates in the Federal Supplemental Educational Opportunity Grant, Federal Perkins Loan, and Federal Work-Study programs. Each year, nearly 1,300 SNC students are employed on campus. The typical job involves about 10 hours of work per week and produces about $1600 in annual wages. A number of students are hired through the College's own $1.7-million-per-year employment program. Qualified students, regardless of financial need, fill positions.

Need-based awards are made on the basis of the Free Application for Federal Student Aid (FAFSA) and the St. Norbert College institutional application for financial aid. Freshman applicants should submit these forms by March of their senior year of high school.

Faculty

The St. Norbert faculty is composed of 170 men and women, 126 of whom are full-time. Ninety-two percent of the full-time faculty members hold the doctoral or other terminal degree in their field. The faculty-student ratio is approximately 1:14. Faculty members work closely with students in their major area of study, help students prepare for graduate school, and work with those who seek independent study and research opportunities. Faculty members also work with Career Services in its professional practice program.

Student Government

Leadership is a key component of community life at St. Norbert. As one of the few institutions to offer a leadership studies minor, St. Norbert includes cocurricular involvement in its description of a fulfilling college experience. Students may take advantage of numerous opportunities, including Emerging Leaders, a program providing guidance for students interested in leadership roles on campus.

The Office of Leadership, Services, and Involvement coordinates a variety of clubs and service organizations, adventure trip programming, and recreation tournaments. A student-elected Campus Ministry Council sponsors various community outreach activities, both local and in the inner-city areas of major cities. Other social action activities are offered through the Peace and Justice Center, and students with an interest in College government can contribute through such activities as serving on the student-run College Activities Board, being a student representative on College Committees, and taking a decision-making role on the Residence Hall Association.

Living and learning are linked at St. Norbert through programs in the residence halls. Some residence halls focus on community service or feature campus programs such as the Women's Center in Sensenbrenner Hall. Many halls have chapels for students to use to reflect and pray.

Admission Requirements

The student's high school record is the single most important element in the admission decision. Students who have taken an academic or college-preparatory program are considered best qualified. Nearly 80 percent of the freshman class ranked in the top two fifths of their high school senior class. The average composite ACT score is 24. Students with superior scores and grades may enroll in the honors program.

The College seeks a diversified student body. Because St. Norbert is residential in nature, great emphasis in admission decisions is placed on how a student used his or her spare time during the high school years. The College seeks students who have participated in, or are interested in participating in, a variety of athletic, social, cultural, and intellectual activities. Transfer students are encouraged to apply. The minimum acceptable GPA for transfers is 2.5 (C+) on a 4.0 scale.

Application and Information

Early applications for the freshman class are encouraged in order for students to benefit from the College's practice of registering students and assigning housing in the order in which they enroll. Notification of the admission decision is made on a rolling basis beginning in late September. A $350 deposit is required to confirm enrollment. For more information about St. Norbert, students should contact:

Dean of Admission
St. Norbert College
100 Grant Street
De Pere, Wisconsin 54115
Telephone: 920-403-3005
800-236-4878 (toll-free)
World Wide Web: http://www.snc.edu

SAINT PETER'S COLLEGE

JERSEY CITY, NEW JERSEY

The College

Saint Peter's College (SPC) offers a strong liberal arts education focused on the wholistic, personal development of the individual student; the advantages of its international, New York City metropolitan location; and affordable tuition. Located within minutes of New York City and the Statue of Liberty, the College has offered academic excellence in the Jesuit, Catholic tradition since its founding in 1872. Saint Peter's students can participate in class, internship, and cooperative education experiences in a variety of international, cultural, business, and communication institutions and corporations. Saint Peter's participates in NCAA Division I athletics with strongly competitive teams in both men's and women's sports. The diverse, international student body is composed of students from throughout the Northeast, America, and the world.

The College offers a curriculum based on students' developing a breadth of knowledge in the core curriculum of the liberal arts and sciences and depth of knowledge, skills, and proficiencies within the major area of study. The College seeks to develop graduates of competence and conscience by emphasizing ethical and moral decision making throughout the entire course of study. Students may choose to prepare for positions in professional fields such as business or education; preprofessional programs in fields such as medicine, law, and dentistry; or graduate study in many disciplines.

The goal of a Saint Peter's College education is to equip students to succeed in learning, leadership, and service. The *ethos* of the College is reflected in the motto of the twenty-eight American Jesuit colleges and universities, which is to develop "men and women for others." The College serves as a significant educational, religious, cultural, social, and economic resource for Jersey City and the surrounding area. Its main campus is located in Jersey City, New Jersey, with a branch campus in Englewood Cliffs, New Jersey. Total enrollment is 3,300, including 2,000 full-time undergraduates in the College of Arts and Sciences and the School of Business Administration, 600 adult undergraduates in the School for Professional and Continuing Studies, and 700 graduate students. SPC alumni, over 25,500 strong, are successful professionals in the arts, business, humanities, law, medicine, education, politics, public service, and the sciences.

The College offers more than thirty-five major programs leading to the baccalaureate degree as well as graduate programs in accountancy, business, education, and nursing.

Location

Saint Peter's College is easily accessible by all major forms of transportation. Midtown Manhattan is a short ride on the PATH subway system from Journal Square. Liberty International Airport is only 20 minutes away, and there are numerous trains (including Amtrak) and Greyhound buses leaving from Penn Station in Newark and New York City, the Erie-Lackawanna Railroad Terminal in Hoboken, and Port Authority and Grand Central Station in New York City. SPC is also accessible from the New Jersey Turnpike and other major highways.

Majors and Degrees

Saint Peter's College offers baccalaureate degrees in accountancy, American studies, art history, biological chemistry, biology, business management, chemistry, classical civilizations, classical languages, communications, computer science, computer science/CIS, computer science/MIS, criminal justice, economics, education, English literature, fine arts, history, humanities*, international business and trade, marketing management, mathematical economics, mathematics, modern languages and literature, natural science, nursing (RN required)*, philosophy, physics, political science, psychology, social sciences*, sociology, Spanish, theology, urban studies, and visual arts. Five-year bachelor's degree programs in cytotechnology, medical technology, and toxicology are offered in affiliation with the University of Medicine and Dentistry of New Jersey. Associate degrees are offered in banking*, business management, finance, humanities, information systems, international business and trade, marketing management, public policy*, and social sciences. (*School for Professional and Continuing Studies only.)

Academic Programs

The liberal arts core curriculum, required for all degrees, comprises 60 semester hours and includes study in composition and fine arts (a minimum of 3 semester hours each), history, literature, mathematics (6–8 semester hours), modern language, natural sciences (9 hours), philosophy, social sciences, theology (6 semester hours each), and a core elective in ethical values (3 hours). The baccalaureate degree requires the completion of 120 semester hours. Approximately half of the courses required for the degree are in the core curriculum, one quarter are in the major area of study, and one quarter are in elective courses. Students may complete majors in two areas by meeting all degree requirements or design a composite major to meet individual interests with consultation and approval from the academic dean. Summer sessions are available on both campuses. Sessions for full-time undergraduates are based on a semester system.

The honors program provides an opportunity for academically talented students to participate in challenging classes and to do research with a faculty mentor. Students who complete the entire Honors Program successfully are awarded degrees *in cursu honorum.* The College participates in both the Army and Air Force ROTC programs. The College recognizes the Advanced Placement (AP) Program as well as the College-Level Examination Program (CLEP).

Under the direction of the freshman dean, the College offers a number of summer and freshman-year programs in order to foster the successful transition of students to college life. All freshmen are assigned faculty advisers. SPC participates in the Educational Opportunity Fund (EOF) program in partnership with the State of New Jersey. This program offers a six-week summer study program and individual support and guidance throughout the entire college experience. The Summer Academy is offered to all students who would benefit from structure and directed study in order to successfully acclimate to the demands of college-level study. During the year, the Academic Success Program fosters student success through individual attention and mentoring. Additional resources are available to meet students' needs, such as the Tutoring Center, Counseling Center, Campus Ministry, Residence Life, and the Freshman Seminar.

Off-Campus Programs

Supervised, off-campus cooperative education opportunities and internships are available in all fields. Students in SPC's nationally ranked Cooperative Education Program may earn a maximum of 9 academic credits and up to $10,000. Up to 15 credits are awarded through the Washington Center Program in Washington, D.C., which provides experience working in the nation's capital in a wide range of internship positions. Study abroad is arranged through the International Student Exchange Program, which conducts programs in more than sixty universities in Europe, Asia, Africa, and Latin America.

Academic Facilities

The Edward and Theresa O'Toole Library houses a large collection of volumes, periodicals, and information databases. Students also benefit from interlibrary loan arrangements as well as access to the New Jersey state-supported university library system. Students may obtain referral cards to other metropolitan area libraries, including the New York Public Library and the Science, Industry, and Business Library, both located in midtown Manhattan, minutes from the campus.

Saint Peter's was one of the first colleges in the nation to adopt a wireless Ethernet throughout the campus. The College is also implementing a new information infrastructure that supports the Student Information System, instruction in the classrooms, student computer labs, and faculty and student research. Students are offered individual e-mail accounts and Internet connectivity through the campus local area network (LAN).

Costs

Annual tuition for 2002–03 was $16,908 for full-time study (12–18 semester hours each semester), and student fees were $450. Typical housing costs were $4610, and meal plan costs were an average of $2960. Personal expenses, books, supplies, and transportation were estimated to be $3450 for residential students and $1800 for commuter students.

Financial Aid

Saint Peter's College admits students without regard to financial status. Ninety percent of SPC students receive financial assistance, and for the 2002–03 academic year the average award was $16,000. The only form required is the Free Application for Federal Student Aid (FAFSA). It is recommended that students file the FAFSA by March 1 for full consideration of all federal, state, and institutional funds available.

Federal sources include Federal Pell Grants, Federal Supplemental Educational Opportunity Grants (FSEOG), the Federal Work-Study Program (FWS), Federal Stafford Student Loans, and Parent Loans for Undergraduate Students (PLUS). New Jersey state sources include Tuition Aid Grants (TAG) and the Educational Opportunity Fund (EOF). All applications for admission are reviewed for academic scholarships, grants, athletic scholarships, and need-based grants. Prospective students should call the Student Financial Aid Office at 201-915-9308 or 9309 for more information.

Faculty

All classes at Saint Peter's are taught by faculty members rather than graduate students or teaching assistants. Faculty members in every discipline are expected to meet high standards for teaching. Faculty members work with students as advisers, mentors in the classroom, and in supervised areas of study such as research or internships and cooperative education experiences. Faculty members are expected to maintain currency in their fields of instruction through a scholarly agenda of research and/or through continued development as active professionals. Saint Peter's offers small classes so that students can obtain the maximum benefit from their interaction with the faculty. The 115 full-time faculty members have completed advanced degrees at some of the nation's finest institutions of higher learning. All Saint Peter's faculty members are committed to *cura personalis*, or personal attention, to the success of each student individually.

Student Government

The Student Senate consists of an elected executive committee and 5 elected student senators from each class. The objectives of the Student Senate are to coordinate student activities, provide effective means of communication between the student body and the College administration, and strive to maintain and further the spirit and ideals of Saint Peter's College.

Admission Requirements

Admission to Saint Peter's College is based upon a student's demonstrated academic performance, academic preparation, and potential for success in college-level study. Each application is reviewed on an individual basis, and SAT scores, class rank, high school record, personal statement, letters of recommendation, part-time employment, leadership positions, athletics/extracurricular activities, and community service are all considered. Interviews are not required but are strongly recommended for all applicants. Students are expected to have a solid preparation for college. Saint Peter's requires a minimum of 16 units of high school academic courses for admission: 4 units in English, 2 units in history, 2 units in a modern language, 3 units of college-preparatory mathematics, and 2 units of science (including at least 1 unit of a laboratory science). In addition to these 13 basic units, students must have completed at least 3 more units in any combination of the subject areas listed above. One unit is the equivalent of one year of study in a high school subject.

Application and Information

Students are encouraged to submit their applications in the fall of their senior year of high school. Admission is on a rolling basis. Students who wish to be considered for an academic scholarship must apply by March 1. When a student's completed application and records are on file, they are reviewed by the committee. Students are ordinarily notified of the admission decision within two weeks of receipt of the complete admission file, which must include the completed application form, a personal statement, a high school transcript with official SAT scores, and recommendations. Transfer students must submit official copies of all college transcripts and their application fee by December 1 for admission to the spring semester and before August 1 for admission to the fall semester.

To complete their admission file, international students should submit the results of the Test of English as a Foreign Language (TOEFL) or the equivalent, all official documents of education, an affidavit of financial support, and the completed application form, including a personal statement and a $40 application fee. International students are encouraged to apply before March 1 for the fall term and before October 1 for the spring term.

For more information, students should contact:

Office of Admissions
Saint Peter's College
2641 Kennedy Boulevard
Jersey City, New Jersey 07306-5944
Telephone: 201-915-9213
888-SPC-9933 (toll-free)
Fax: 201-432-5860
E-mail: admissions@spc.edu
World Wide Web: http://www.spc.edu

ST. THOMAS AQUINAS COLLEGE
SPARKILL, NEW YORK

The College

St. Thomas Aquinas College (STAC) was founded in 1952 as a three-year teacher-training college with 30 students. Today, the College offers thirty-one majors and has a student body of 2,200. Much growth and development has taken place over the College's brief history. The College offers a Master of Science in Education with concentrations in elementary, reading, secondary, and special education as well as postgraduate certificate programs. The College also offers a quarterly weekend Master of Business Administration (M.B.A.) program with concentrations in finance, management, and marketing. St. Thomas also has a Master of Science in Teaching program for individuals without a background in teacher education who are seeking a career change. Certification is offered in childhood education, grades 1–6; childhood education and special education, grades 1–6; and adolescence education, grades 7–12.

The College's most dramatic growth has occurred to meet the challenges of the twenty-first century. Capital improvements were made and new facilities added, so that the main campus now consists of twenty-one buildings on 48 acres. The suburban campus includes two residential complexes: Aquinas Village, which consists of self-contained town-house units that house 150 students; and the McNelis Commons, which consists of town-house residential units that house 350 students and a common dining hall and laundry building. Approximately 35 percent of the College's full-time student population resides on campus.

Extracurricular activities are provided through some twenty-five different organizations, including the dramatic group (Laetare Players), a student-run radio station (WSTK), and the student-edited campus newspaper and yearbook. The College has excellent sports facilities, and several of its athletic teams have competed in national championships. The College fields NCAA Division II teams in men's and women's cross-country, golf, indoor track and field, and tennis; women's basketball, soccer, softball, and volleyball; and men's baseball, basketball, and soccer. Intramural athletics are also available.

The College has a campus ministry and health, housing, placement, and counseling services.

Location

The College is located in Sparkill, a hamlet in southern Rockland County, New York, 16 miles north of New York City and adjacent to Bergen County, New Jersey. Rockland County, a sprawling rural area of about 300,000 people, is rich in Revolutionary War history and convenient to the vast cultural and educational resources of New York City. Major arteries connect Sparkill to the tristate metropolitan area.

Majors and Degrees

St. Thomas Aquinas College's business administration division awards Bachelor of Science (B.S.) degrees in accounting (and accounting as a dual degree with a Master of Business Administration degree), business administration, finance, and marketing. Minors are offered in business administration, international business, and management information systems. Specializations are offered in management relations/industrial and organizational psychology. The humanities division awards Bachelor of Arts (B.A.) degrees in art therapy and fine arts, and a B.S. in graphic design, which are all also offered as minors. B.A. degrees include communication arts, English, philosophy and religious studies, romance languages, and Spanish. A journalism minor is also offered. The natural sciences and mathematics division offers B.S. degrees in applied mathematics, computer and information sciences, and mathematics. B.S. degrees are offered in biology, medical technology, and natural sciences. There are specializations in biology, chemistry, and physics. Dual-degree options are also offered and are described below. The social sciences division awards B.S. degrees in criminal justice, psychology, recreation and leisure studies, and social science, and a B.A. in history. The division of teacher education offers programs in grades 1–6 childhood education, the same plus special education, and grades 7–12 adolescence education, the latter offering certification in biology, English, mathematics, natural science with either biology or chemistry, social sciences, and Spanish.

The College offers a five-year dual-degree program in mathematics/engineering with the George Washington University (GWU) or Manhattan College. Students study at St. Thomas for three years. After completion of their final two years at either GWU or Manhattan, they earn a B.S. in mathematics from STAC and a B.S. in engineering from one of the latter two institutions. A dual degree is offered in biology (B.S. from STAC) and physical therapy (D.P.T. from New York Medical College). A dual degree is offered in biology (B.S. from STAC) and chiropractic (D.C. from New York Chiropractic College). A dual degree is offered in biology (B.S. from STAC) and podiatry (D.P.M. from New York College of Podiatric Medicine). St. Thomas offers a 63-credit prepharmacy program that enables a qualified student to transfer into the Arnold and Marie Schwartz College of Pharmacy and Health Sciences of Long Island University. There are several other strategic alliances, such as a guaranteed slot at the St. John's University School of Law in New York and a similar program with Barry University School of Law in Florida that includes scholarship funds. St. Thomas seeks out additional strategic opportunities for its undergraduate and graduate students on a regular basis; students should contact the College for information about new alliances.

Academic Programs

The College maintains academic flexibility and is committed to responding to the needs of individual students. The College strives to develop students who are not only generally educated but also possess advanced knowledge in specialized areas, are prepared for further study, and have the background to undertake fulfilling careers. To earn a bachelor's degree, students must complete a total of 120 semester hours, including a minimum of 51 credits in a core curriculum; complete all requirements for the specific major; and complete the final 30 hours at St. Thomas. The College awards up to 30 credits for life experience and up to 30 credits for achievement on the College-Level Examination Program (CLEP). The College operates on a semester calendar (trimester on the M.B.A. level). Students may enroll in classes in the fall, winter (a one-month session), spring, and summer (three separate sessions). Classes are scheduled during the day and evening, and students are permitted considerable academic flexibility in planning their programs.

Students can pursue independent study and internships, and many majors require a field practicum. The College maintains an active Academic Skills Center as a resource for developmental skills, and students are encouraged to meet regularly with faculty advisers for academic guidance and career direction.

Several unusual programs supplement the traditional academic areas. The College has a widely recognized program for college-age learning-disabled students called the STAC Exchange (at an additional cost). In addition, students may participate in Air Force ROTC programs through cooperative cross-enrollment with Manhattan College. The College also participates in the New York State Higher Education Opportunity Program for economically and academically disadvantaged students and provides an Honors Program for exceptionally qualified students.

Off-Campus Programs

The College offers a campus interchange program involving three other fully accredited colleges (Barry University in Miami Shores, Florida; Dominican College of San Rafael in San Rafael, California; and Aquinas College in Grand Rapids, Michigan) through which a student may attend a semester at one of the participating colleges during the junior year.

The College offers courses at local businesses and industries and an associate-degree program at West Point for eligible students at the United States Military Academy and Stewart Army Subpost.

A study-abroad program is offered through the College, providing students with the opportunity to study at colleges and universities in such places as Brazil, Canada, England, Hungary, Ireland, Italy, or Morocco. Several other locations are available.

Academic Facilities

The College's most dramatic growth occurred during the last decade as it modernized to meet the challenges of the twenty-first century. Costello Hall houses the science laboratories, technology theaters, and the Azarian-McCullough Art Gallery. Spellman Hall houses a multiroom technology corridor with state-of-the-art technology and language labs. Lougheed Library provides a variety of online research opportunities for students. Aquinas Hall houses athletic facilities and a new fitness center. Maguire Hall is home to classrooms and art studios, and Marian Hall houses accounting labs and a communications studio. Additional meeting areas are provided in the Romano Student-Alumni Center and in the two residence complexes, McNelis Commons and Aquinas Village.

Costs

For 2003–04, the tuition for full-time study (12 to 16 credits per semester) was $14,500. Room and board at the College Commons cost $8160. Certain studio, laboratory, and computer courses carry fees.

Financial Aid

The College is committed to providing competent but needy students with the resources necessary to continue their education. Students who lack adequate financial resources should submit the Financial Aid Form to the College Scholarship Service and to the College. Financial aid is usually granted in a package of awards. Financial aid programs include Presidential Grants, special scholarships, athletic grants, Federal Pell Grants, Federal Supplemental Educational Opportunity Grants, New York State Tuition Assistance Program (TAP) grants, Federal Perkins Loans, Federal Stafford Student Loans, Federal PLUS loans, and Federal Work-Study Program awards.

In 2002–03, 75 percent of the student body received financial aid. Athletic grants-in-aid are awarded to full-time students (men and women) in recognition of demonstrated athletic ability, academic achievement, and financial need.

Faculty

The faculty has 75 full-time and 55 part-time members; 75 percent have earned doctorates. The student-faculty ratio is 17:1. All faculty members participate in the academic advising of students and serve on College committees. Many serve as advisers to extracurricular activities.

Student Government

The Student Government consists of elected members who officially represent the student body, are responsible for planning and implementing student-originated programs, and coordinate and oversee all extracurricular organizations. Through its various offices, students play a vital part in offering consultation on new policies, planning social and cultural events, managing student funds, and operating the judicial system. In addition, the All-College Forum, composed of elected students, faculty members, alumni, administrators, and trustees, meets regularly to discuss policies, procedures, long-range plans, and any problems affecting the College.

Admission Requirements

All applicants must have successfully completed an approved secondary school program or the equivalent, including four years in English, two years in college-preparatory mathematics, at least two years in science, one year in a single foreign language, and at least one year in American history. Applicants whose high school background varies from the recommended pattern are considered if they demonstrate interest and ability. Freshman applicants must submit the application for admission, high school transcripts, SAT I scores, and their guidance counselor's recommendation. Transfer students must submit the application and official transcripts of all previous college work. All students are encouraged to visit the campus for an interview. An academic evaluation is prepared for every matriculant.

Application and Information

Candidates should submit completed application forms to the Admissions and Financial Aid Office and must request that their official transcripts be sent to the Admissions Office from their school. Students are notified of the admission decision on a rolling basis upon receipt of all the necessary credentials.

The College does not discriminate against students, faculty, staff, and other beneficiaries on the basis of race, color, national origin, gender, age, sexual orientation, disability, marital status, genetic predisposition, carrier status, veteran status, or religious affiliation in admission to, or in the provision of its programs and services. The Section 504 Coordinator, the Title IX Coordinator, and the Age Act Coordinator is the Executive Director of Human Resources, Marian Hall, 845-398-4038.

For more information or an application, students should contact:

Admissions and Financial Aid Office
St. Thomas Aquinas College
125 Route 340
Sparkill, New York 10976-1050
Telephone: 800-999-STAC (toll-free)
World Wide Web: http://www.stac.edu

STAC's McNelis Commons residence complex.

ST. THOMAS UNIVERSITY

MIAMI, FLORIDA

The University

Founded in 1961 by the Augustinian Order of Villanova, Pennsylvania, at the invitation of the late Most Reverend Coleman F. Carroll, the Archbishop of Miami, St. Thomas University has grown from an institution with an initial enrollment of 45 students to become one of Florida's most comprehensive Catholic coeducational universities, with more than 2,200 students in all programs of study. Founded originally as Biscayne College, the institution achieved university status in 1984 and changed its name to St. Thomas University. The University is sponsored by the Archdiocese of Miami and is accredited by the Southern Association of Colleges and Schools. At present, the undergraduate student population represents twenty-eight states, the District of Columbia, Puerto Rico, the Virgin Islands, and sixty-five countries. Fifty-nine percent of the undergraduates are women; 20 percent of the undergraduates reside on campus. The Office of Graduate Studies offers the Master of Business Administration (M.B.A.); Master of International Business; Master of Science (M.S.) in educational administration, guidance and counseling, management, marriage and family therapy, mental health counseling, special education, and sports administration; Master of Accounting (M.Acc.); and Master of Arts (M.A.) degrees in communication arts and pastoral ministry. The Ambassador Nicholas H. Morley Law Center was established in 1984 with a charter class of 160 students. St. Thomas University School of Law offers the Juris Doctor degree (J.D.) and is the only accredited Catholic law school south of Georgetown University's law school in Washington, D.C. The School of Law and the Graduate Studies Office offer four joint degree programs, including an M.B.A./J.D. in accounting and international business and an M.S./J.D. in marriage and family counseling and sports administration.

The University is located in northwest Miami on a 140-acre campus with fifteen major buildings. The Student Center contains a student lounge, a bookstore, the rathskeller, and other facilities. Adjacent to the University's two dormitories are the dining hall and the University Inn. Sports facilities include six tennis courts, a recreational swimming pool, two basketball courts, four baseball fields, a soccer field, and two football fields. As a member of the NAIA, St. Thomas supports men's varsity teams in baseball, golf, soccer, and tennis and women's varsity teams in fast-pitch softball, golf, soccer, tennis, and volleyball and men's and women's cross-country. The University offers a full range of cultural, governmental, and social activities, including publications and clubs. The Office of Campus Ministry provides liturgical celebrations in the University chapel and sponsors social justice and community service activities.

Location

Located midway between Fort Lauderdale and downtown Miami, the University is near numerous cultural and recreational facilities. In fact, St. Thomas is located approximately 1½ miles south of Pro Player Stadium, which is home to the Miami Dolphins. The area's subtropical climate allows students to enjoy the nearby Atlantic Ocean beaches and many other natural attractions, such as the Florida Keys, Everglades National Park, and state and county parks, throughout the year. A short drive from campus are Key Biscayne, Bal Harbour, Miami Beach, Fort Lauderdale, and other cities of Florida's Gold Coast. The city of Miami and surrounding Dade County, known as the "Gateway to South America," house an international banking and trade center and offer a truly cosmopolitan atmosphere.

Majors and Degrees

St. Thomas University awards the Bachelor of Arts (B.A.) or Bachelor of Business Administration (B.B.A.) degree through day and evening programs in twenty-five major fields of study: accounting, biology, business management, communication arts, computer information systems, computer science, criminal justice, elementary education, English, finance, global leadership, history, human services, international business, liberal studies, marketing, nursing (a 2+2 program with the University of Miami), political science/public administration, psychology, religious studies, secondary education (social studies), sports administration, and tourism and hospitality management. St. Thomas also offers a minor in environmental studies; preprofessional programs, which include dentistry, law, medicine, and veterinary studies; a joint B.A./J.D. program with the School of Law; and courses in French, humanities, Italian, philosophy, and South Florida regional studies.

Academic Programs

The University's academic calendar consists of two 15-week semesters, beginning in early September and in mid-January, along with two 6-week summer sessions. There are also three 1-week minimesters: one in January, one in May, and one in August.

To receive a bachelor's degree, students must complete at least 120 semester credits with a minimum grade point average of 2.0 overall and an average of at least 2.25 in their academic major; 30 of the last 36 semester credit hours must be earned and at least half of a student's academic major courses must be taken at St. Thomas University. All students must fulfill the general core education requirements of 42 semester credits, which include courses in English, humanities/foreign language, history, social science, mathematics/physical science, philosophy, and religious studies. An honors program is offered to qualified students to provide them with an interesting, stimulating, alternative way of fulfilling some or all of the University's general education requirements. The normal full-time academic load is 15 semester credit hours, but the load may range between 12 and 18 credit hours per semester. To graduate, all students must take an area of concentration or an academic major. A student may enter as an exploratory or undecided student but, with the assistance of a faculty adviser or a division chairperson, must declare his or her academic major by the second semester of the sophomore year.

Special academic features at the University include the Academic Support Center, Institute for Pastoral Ministries, summer school, and study abroad.

Off-Campus Programs

Internships are offered in nearly every academic major. A cooperative education program is also available. In addition, qualified students may participate in the Semester Abroad Program in Spain (El Escorial) and in Study Abroad for Earth (SAFE) in Italy.

Academic Facilities

The 50,000-square-foot library houses a 145,000-volume book collection, 850 periodicals, a reference room, a technical processing area, a convocation hall that seats 600 people, four seminar rooms for small classes and group study, and a Media Center with two screening rooms, a video studio, and an audiovisual laboratory with individually wired carrels. Kennedy Hall, the University's main academic center, includes administrative offices, classrooms, science laboratories, the Academic Support Center, the chapel, and a computer lab.

Costs

Tuition for the 2003–04 academic year was $16,200 ($540 per undergraduate semester credit hour), and room and board costs were $5200 for a double room and $7800 for a single room. Insurance, which is mandatory for all resident students, is estimated at $800 for the year. These costs do not include books, supplies, travel, and personal expenses and are subject to change.

Financial Aid

The University has established a financial aid program to assist as many students as possible. University scholarships and grants, along with federally funded scholarships, grants, loans, and work-study awards, are allocated in a financial aid package according to a student's financial need. Currently, about 92 percent of the University's students receive financial aid. Of all financial aid recipients, 90 percent receive University scholarships and grants. To be eligible for any scholarship or financial aid program, an applicant should complete a Free Application for Federal Student Aid (FAFSA) with the Department of Education. The filing deadline for University financial aid funds is April 1. Applicants should indicate affirmatively on the FAFSA that their information may be forwarded from the U.S. Department of Education in order to be considered for any state grants for which they may be eligible. The application deadline for need-based state financial aid programs is April 1.

Florida applicants who have resided in Florida for the prior twelve consecutive months are eligible to be awarded a Florida Resident Access Grant to attend a private four-year college or university in Florida. The funds for the Florida Resident Grant Program are dependent upon yearly appropriations from the Florida legislature. These funds are outright grants and are not based on financial need.

Faculty

The St. Thomas University faculty is a teaching faculty that is dedicated to furthering the academic and personal growth of students. The undergraduate student-faculty ratio is 18:1. Faculty-student interaction is a hallmark of the University because classes are small and because members of the faculty are available outside the classroom. Faculty members also participate in the academic advisement program to give students individual academic guidance, and they serve as advisers to student clubs and organizations.

Student Government

The Undergraduate Student Government Association, of which all full-time undergraduates are members, provides students with the opportunity to become involved in representative government. This democratic body is governed by elected student officers who serve on the Administrative Council and by representatives from each class who compose the Student Assembly. The association also assists in planning a varied program of social and cultural activities. In addition, students are represented on key committees throughout the University community. The Resident Council, consisting of representatives from each of the four dormitories, voices the concerns of residential students and is involved in the planning and implementation of University policies regarding residential life.

Admission Requirements

St. Thomas University seeks academically prepared students who are eager to improve themselves intellectually, socially, and spiritually within the University community. The Admissions Committee evaluates applicants individually in light of personal accomplishments, motivation, and the academic major selected. The committee places primary emphasis on the secondary school record, SAT I or ACT scores, class rank, a personal interview, a recommended 250- to 300-word personal essay, and a teacher's or guidance counselor's recommendation. The committee does not discriminate against applicants on the basis of race, sex, religion, or national origin; in fact, the University welcomes diversity. Applicants for most divisions must have earned 16 units from an accredited high school in a college-preparatory program that included 4 years of English, 2 years of mathematics, 2 years of social studies, 1 year of science, 1 year of a foreign language or computer elective, and six electives; applicants for the Division of Science must have earned 17 units, including 3 years of mathematics (including trigonometry) and 3 years of science, but they need have only four electives. All international applicants for either freshman or transfer entrance must also submit letters of financial guarantee.

The University offers early acceptance, deferred admission, dual enrollment, and early decision. It also gives credit and advanced placement for scores of 3 or better on the Advanced Placement examinations of the College Board. Credit is also awarded for successful scores on both the general and subject tests of the College Board's College-Level Examination Program.

Transfer applicants should be in good academic standing with a GPA of at least 2.0 and not be on disciplinary or academic probation at their former college. The University grants junior-year status to any admitted transfer student graduating from a Florida community college with an Associate of Arts degree. Transfer applicants must submit official transcripts from each of their previous colleges.

Application and Information

To facilitate the admission and financial aid processes, students should submit applications during the fall or winter of their senior year in high school and have all supporting material forwarded directly to the University's Undergraduate Admissions Office. Application for entrance as a resident student for the fall semester should be filed by May 15; for entrance as a commuting student, by August 1. Application for the spring semester should be made by December 15. The University operates with a policy of rolling admissions; beginning December 15, applicants for the fall semester are notified of the admission decision within a three-week period provided that all appropriate information has been received. The University adheres to the College Board's Candidates Reply Date of May 1 and does not require a tuition deposit or a room reservation deposit until May 1 in order to allow students ample opportunity to select the college or university of their choice. Dormitory space, however, is limited and is assigned in the order that room reservation deposits are received.

For further information, students should contact:

Office of Admissions
St. Thomas University
16401 Northwest 37th Avenue
Miami Gardens, Florida 33054
Telephone: 305-628-6546
800-367-9006 (toll-free in Florida)
800-367-9010 (toll-free outside Florida)
Fax: 305-628-6591
E-mail: signup@stu.edu
World Wide Web: http://www.stu.edu

SAINT VINCENT COLLEGE

LATROBE, PENNSYLVANIA

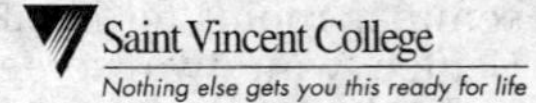

The College

Founded in 1846, Saint Vincent College is the first Benedictine college in the United States. It is an educational community rooted in the tradition of the Catholic faith, the heritage of Benedictine monasticism, and the love of values inherent in the liberal approach to life and learning. There are 1,107 full-time students and 115 part-time students, of whom approximately 73.7 percent reside on campus in five residence halls. The College has students from more than twenty-five states and fifteen countries. In addition to more than fifty programs in the liberal arts and sciences, the College offers a Master of Arts degree in accountancy through the Alex G. McKenna School of Business, Economics, and Government as well as a Master of Science degree in education curriculum and instruction. Student services include advising, athletics, career placement and planning, computer assistance, and a counseling center. Saint Vincent College is accredited by the Department of Education of the state of Pennsylvania, the Middle States Association of Colleges and Schools, and the Association of Collegiate Business Schools and Programs.

Location

Saint Vincent College is located on 200 acres in the Laurel Highlands of southwestern Pennsylvania. Noted for its beautiful countryside, the region offers abundant opportunities for outdoor recreation and adventure. Excellent sites for hiking, mountain biking, skiing, camping, and white-water rafting are less than half an hour from the campus in ten state forests. Pittsburgh, a regional center of culture and the arts, is only 35 miles to the west. The city offers music, museums, theater, shopping, nightlife, and sports.

Majors and Degrees

Saint Vincent College awards undergraduate Bachelor of Arts and Bachelor of Science degrees. In addition to majors offered by the Alex G. McKenna School of Business, Economics, and Government, students may select major courses of study in anthropology, art history, biochemistry, biology, Catholic theology, chemistry, communication, computing and information science, English, environmental chemistry, environmental science, fine arts, history, liberal arts, mathematics, music, music performance, philosophy, physics, physics education, psychology, psychology education, religious education, sociology, Spanish, and studio arts.

The Alex G. McKenna School of Business, Economics, and Government awards Bachelor of Arts and Bachelor of Science degrees in accounting, economics, environmental management, finance, international business, management, marketing, political science, and public policy analysis. In addition, the school offers minors in public administration and most of the fields listed above and certificates in business management and accounting. Plans are being developed to offer an additional major in management information systems.

Majors in theater and music education are offered in cooperation with Seton Hill University.

The College offers education certification in art, biology, business, chemistry, citizenship, computer and information science, early childhood, elementary, English, French, mathematics, physics, social studies, and Spanish.

The College offers a law school 3+3 program in cooperation with Duquesne University. Students complete the requirements of their majors at Saint Vincent College. At Saint Vincent, students major in English, history, political science, public policy analysis, or sociology. In addition, in conjunction with University Schools of Engineering, the College offers a five-year cooperative liberal arts and engineering program.

Saint Vincent offers prehealth training in accelerated osteopathic medicine, accelerated podiatric medicine, occupational therapy, pharmacy, physician assistant studies, and physical therapy in cooperation with various professional schools.

Various certificate programs are offered at the College, including accounting, addiction specialist training, business management, communication, and computing and information science.

Students may select minor areas of study in accounting, anthropology, art history, biochemistry, biology, chemistry, communication, computing and information science, economics, education, English, environmental affairs, environmental chemistry, fine arts, finance, French, general administration of justice, German, history, international studies, management, mathematics, music, music history, philosophy, physics, political science, public administration, psychology, religious studies, sociology, Spanish, and theater.

Academic Program

An academic year consists of two semesters, with the opportunity to earn credits in the summer. Saint Vincent College requires each student to complete a minimum of 124 credits, satisfy the requirements for the major(s) as specified by the department(s), achieve an overall grade point average of at least 2.0 as well as a grade point average of at least 2.0 in the major or at least a C in every course required for the major at Seton Hill University, and satisfy the capstone requirement as specified by the major department(s). Each student must complete a core curriculum. The core curriculum provides all students with a broadly based education that provides a general body of knowledge in the humanities, social sciences, natural sciences, and mathematics; an interdisciplinary view of that knowledge base; and the skills to increase that general body of knowledge throughout their lives. Special programs include national and international academic honor societies, a cooperative education and internship program, an interdisciplinary writing program, and an honors program.

Off-Campus Programs

Saint Vincent has a sister college relationship with Fu Jen Catholic University in Taiwan. The College is also a cooperating institution with Central College of Iowa, through which programs are offered in France, Germany, Austria, Spain, Mexico, Wales, England, and Holland. Students may enroll for summer study at Cuauhnahauc Institute of Language and Culture in Cuernavaca, Mexico. Each May and June, after the spring semester, Saint Vincent College students have the opportunity to participate in a three-week study tour of Taiwan and Japan. Students may also enroll in well-designed academic programs sponsored by recognized universities and institutes.

Academic Facilities

Saint Vincent College has coupled extensive renovation and new construction with the introduction of state-of-the-art technology in virtually every arena of College life. The result is a modern, student-friendly campus that features accessible computer laboratories and workstations, fiber-optic cabling among buildings, and specialized laboratories for the study of astronomy, ecology, genetics, geology, human anatomy, life sciences, microbiology, optics, organic chemistry, physiology, and other subjects.

Traditionally, Benedictine institutions have granted a place of honor to the library. A central reference room provides access to more than 3,500 resource titles, such as encyclopedias, abstracts, dictionaries, indexes, handbooks, atlases, concordances, and gazetteers. The periodical area displays some 811 current periodical subscriptions, and the adjoining stacks contain more than 263,000 volumes.

Prep Hall houses the Instructional Technology Resource Center, with an academic lounge for computer networking access, a reception area for the Small Business Development Center, smart classrooms, a multimedia laboratory, a media suite, a seminar room for videoconferencing, and the Barista Cafe coffee shop. In addition, the College features a science center with a planetarium, an amphitheater, and a life sciences research laboratory building. Kennedy Hall, covering more than an acre of ground, contains the Frank and Elizabeth Resnik Swimming Pool, the visitor center, a gymnasium, an auditorium, a wellness center, a book center, a snack bar, a student union, classrooms, a game room, a weight room, an art gallery, art studios, and music practice rooms.

Costs

Tuition and fees at Saint Vincent are $9650 per semester, while room and board costs average $3255 per semester, depending on accommodations. Books and supplies cost approximately $500 to $600 per year. Costs are subject to change.

Financial Aid

The financial aid program at Saint Vincent College offers a comprehensive program of financial aid in the form of scholarships, grants, loans, part-time employment, and deferred-payment schedules and coordinates programs from the federal and state financial aid program. In 2002–03, more than 90 percent of the students who applied for financial aid were offered assistance. The College annually awards qualified freshmen academic scholarships for excellence in academic achievement and grants in recognition of leadership abilities. In addition, the College offers athletic varsity grants, international student grants, Benedictine grants, and scholarships based on competitive examinations. Other financial aid opportunities include Federal Stafford Student Loans and Federal PLUS loans. Residents of Pennsylvania may be eligible for the Pennsylvania Higher Education Assistance Agency Grant program. In order to be considered for financial aid, students must complete the Free Application for Federal Student Aid (FAFSA).

Faculty

The faculty numbers 122 members, of whom 81 are ranked. Eighty-seven percent of the faculty members hold terminal degrees. Members of the faculty have earned doctorates or terminal degrees at such schools as Catholic University of America, Cornell, Ecole Biblique, Notre Dame, Stanford, the University of California, the University of Chicago, and Yale. Faculty members are engaged as principal investigators in research and other projects funded through government agencies such as the National Science Foundation and the U.S. Department of Education and private foundations. The student-faculty ratio is 14:1. Faculty members have chosen to teach at Saint Vincent in part because they value the quality of student-teacher interaction, specifically the emphasis on high standards, personalized learning, fieldwork, hands-on experience, and the high level of classroom participation.

Student Government

The Student Government Association (SGA) builds community at the College by providing opportunities for the students, faculty members, and administrators to share in their common interests. All class officers, senators, and representatives can vote in the unicameral senate that composes the student government. Each senator (every voting member of the SGA) has one vote and can vote for or against or abstain from voting on all issues brought before the senate. Students choose from more than fifty academic clubs and student organizations.

Admission Requirements

Saint Vincent College has a rolling admissions policy. Adequate preparation for college is an important determinant for a successful college education. Fifteen secondary school academic units are required for admission to Saint Vincent College. These 15 units must include 4 units of English, 3 or more units of college-preparatory mathematics, 1 unit of laboratory science, and 3 units of social science; 2 units of a foreign language are preferred among 5 elective units. Engineering students must have 1 unit in plane algebra, 1 unit in intermediate algebra, 1 unit in physics, and ½ unit in trigonometry in addition to those listed above. Music education and theater students must audition for acceptance to their respective departments at Seton Hill University. Art education majors must submit a portfolio for review. Music and music performance students must audition for acceptance, and studio arts students must submit a portfolio for acceptance to the Fine Arts Department.

Transfer students are invited to apply to Saint Vincent College. The applicant's academic achievement and personal history at the postsecondary schools previously attended are of primary importance in the decision for admission. The secondary school record is requested as background information for academic counseling.

Application and Information

To be considered for admission, a freshman applicant must submit a completed application form with the nonrefundable $25 application fee, an official transcript sent directly to Saint Vincent College from the guidance office at the secondary school of graduation, and an official copy of the test results from the SAT I or ACT.

To be considered for admission, a transfer applicant must submit a completed application form with the nonrefundable $25 application fee, an official transcript sent directly to Saint Vincent College from the postsecondary school(s) previously attended, and a secondary school transcript sent directly to Saint Vincent College from the secondary school of graduation.

Application and additional information may be obtained by contacting:

Office of Admission and Financial Aid
Saint Vincent College
300 Fraser Purchase Road
Latrobe, Pennsylvania 15650-2690
Telephone: 800-782-5549 (toll-free)
E-mail: admission@stvincent.edu
World Wide Web: http://www.stvincent.edu

An aerial view of the Saint Vincent College campus.

SAINT XAVIER UNIVERSITY

CHICAGO, ILLINOIS

The University

Saint Xavier University is one of the oldest institutions of higher learning in Illinois. Founded in 1846 and chartered in 1847 by the Sisters of Mercy, Saint Xavier continues its commitment to the pursuit of academic excellence within the context of respect, caring, and justice. The members of the University community affirm the rich tradition of Catholic higher education in America—one marked by spiritual development and intellectual vigor.

As a coeducational private Catholic university, Saint Xavier offers a solid liberal arts core and outstanding professional programs. The University serves a diverse student population of more than 5,600. Saint Xavier's students come from throughout the United States and the world, but the majority come from the Midwest region. The University offers a variety of housing options, including residence halls and on-campus apartment living. All campus housing has Internet access and cable television. There is plenty of on-campus parking available. Students enjoy easy access to Chicago by car and public transportation. Many college activities and a career program take advantage of the city of Chicago.

At Saint Xavier University, students are challenged to critically examine values that recognize individual dignity and worth and promote personal growth, professional integrity, and multicultural experiences. More than thirty clubs and organizations sponsor projects, dances, picnics, and lectures, so there are always activities going on outside of class. These clubs and organizations offer students social, cultural, professional, and athletic opportunities beyond the curriculum. As a member of the National Association of Intercollegiate Athletics, SXU's varsity athletic programs include intercollegiate baseball, basketball, football, and soccer for men and intercollegiate basketball, cross-country, soccer, softball, and volleyball for women. A variety of intramural programs are available to all students.

At the graduate level, master's degrees are offered in applied computer science, business, education, finance, health administration, management, nursing, public health, school counseling and community agency counseling, and speech-language pathology. A graduate certificate in pastoral ministry is also available.

Location

Saint Xavier University is located in a residential neighborhood on the city's southwest side, on 103rd Street and Central Park, between Pulaski Road and Kedzie Avenue. The campus is easily accessible by public transportation, major expressways, and through streets, including I-94, I-294, I-57, and Cicero Avenue. SXU is adjacent to the suburbs of Evergreen Park, and Oak Lawn and is 15 miles from the heart of Chicago's Loop, only 8 miles from Midway Airport and 35 miles from O'Hare International Airport.

Majors and Degrees

Saint Xavier University shares in the rich tradition of Catholic liberal arts higher education while offering flexibility in course scheduling and diversity of the degrees available. Saint Xavier University offers programs leading to a bachelor's degree in accounting, art, biology, botany, business administration, chemistry, communication, computer science, computer studies, criminal justice, education, English, history, international business, international studies, mathematics, mathematics education, music, natural science, nursing, philosophy, political science, psychology, religious studies, social science, sociology, Spanish, and speech-language pathology. Preprofessional programs include dentistry, law, medicine, optometry, pharmacy, podiatry, and veterinary medicine.

Minors are offered in most of the fields listed above as well as in anthropology, Catholic studies, pastoral ministry, speech communication, theater, women's studies, and writing.

Adult College is a specialized program offering majors in accounting, business administration, computer studies, English, industrial/organizational psychology, liberal studies, nursing, psychology, religious studies, RN completion, LPN completion, and sociology.

Academic Program

Saint Xavier University's core curriculum expresses the University's commitment to the values of a liberal education designed to be both foundational and exploratory. The curriculum develops the student's critical skills of writing, speaking, reading, and thinking as well as an understanding of the methods, approaches, and thought processes of the liberal arts disciplines. The core includes courses in natural science, mathematics, social sciences, history, literature, religious studies, philosophy, writing, and speech.

For graduation, a student must earn at least 120 semester hours, including completion of the University's specified curricular components. Transfer students must complete at least 30 semester hours and one third of the requirement in their major area at the University, including clinical or practicum experience in programs requiring such a component.

Academic Facilities

The academic facilities of the University's main campus include classrooms, labs, a library, Shannon Athletics and Convocation, an auditorium, conference center, residence halls, clinical facilities, and the McDonough Chapel and Mercy Ministry Center.

The University's computer equipment consists of thirteen computer labs. The University is connected to the Internet. Incoming students have the option of attending a workshop on computer literacy and word processing. Tutoring can be scheduled for assistance on several software packages. Advanced career planning software is utilized.

The Byrne Memorial Library at Saint Xavier University houses more than 170,000 volumes and an extensive microfiche and microfilm collection. With membership in three consortia, ILCSO, LIBRAS, and SMRHEC, students have access to the collections of more than 800 academic, public, and special libraries.

Saint Xavier University's interactive learning program uses the technology of live color compressed-video television, which has two-way full-motion video and audio capabilities to link SXU students with any of the nine other colleges and universities involved in this alternative learning program. Participants have the opportunity to speak with their instructor without ever leaving their designated sites.

Costs

Basic tuition for the 2003–04 academic year was $16,500. Basic room and board charges were $6464.

Financial Aid

Saint Xavier University's extensive financial aid program assists more than 80 percent of the student body. The Financial Aid Office participates in and coordinates aid from federal, state, University, and private sources. These funds help eligible students meet the cost of higher education. The University also offers academic and athletic scholarships to eligible students. Transfer students, new freshmen, and continuing studies students may be eligible for a no-need scholarship based on proven academic excellence. The scholarships and awards range is from $500 to $8000 for full- or part-time students. Any student interested in applying for aid must complete a Free Application for Federal Student Aid, which is used for federal, state, and Saint Xavier University aid programs. Students must file their financial aid application by March 1 to receive maximum consideration.

Faculty

Saint Xavier's 16:1 student-faculty ratio allows students accessibility to faculty members, who offer personal attention and act as both teacher and adviser. The University has 169 full-time faculty members, 82 percent of whom have terminal degrees. Nearly 80 percent of all classes are taught by full-time faculty members.

Student Government

Members of the Student Activities Board (SAB) apply and interview for paid positions in the following areas: finance, interclub council, intramurals, programming, and public relations. SAB offers students a wide variety of programs, such as dances, entertainment events, films, lectures, intramural sports, and parties. The University holds an election to choose the 8-member board who will serve as advisers on student life issues.

Admission Requirements

During the admission process, consideration is given to previous academic work, recommendations from counselors and teachers, and scores on the ACT or SAT I as well as the student's ability and desire to do college work. The Admission Committee is interested in the quality of a student's work and the kinds of courses taken in high school. Candidates should have a minimum of 16 units in English, math, natural and social sciences, foreign language, and academic electives. Applicants must submit an application for admission along with high school transcripts and test scores. Admission counselors are available to guide students through the application process.

Transfer students may be admitted to SXU if they present evidence of at least a 2.5 GPA in all college-level course work. For further information, students should contact the Office of Admission. All transfer credit is subject to validation by the academic departments. SXU will accept a maximum of 70 semester hours from a community college and 90 semester hours from a four-year college/university. Saint Xavier also has a number of transfer articulation agreements with area community colleges and is a participant in the Illinois Articulation Initiative.

Application and Information

Application forms for admission are available from the Office of Admission. Freshman applicants should submit an application for admission, ACT or SAT I scores, and high school transcripts or apply online at the Web site listed below. Transfer applicants are required to submit an admission application and a transcript from each institution where college-level work has been completed.

Office of Admission—Chicago Campus
Saint Xavier University
3700 West 103rd Street
Chicago, Illinois 60655
Telephone: 773-298-3050
800-GO 2 XAVU (toll-free)
Fax: 773-298-3076
E-mail: admission@sxu.edu
World Wide Web: http://www.sxu.edu

Office of Admission—Orland Park Campus
Saint Xavier University
18230 Orland Parkway
Orland Park, Illinois 60467
Telephone: 708-802-6200
E-mail: orlandparkcampusadmission@sxu.edu
World Wide Web: http://www.sxu.edu/orlandparkcampus

Saint Xavier University.

SALEM COLLEGE

WINSTON-SALEM, NORTH CAROLINA

The College

Since its founding in 1772, Salem College has been committed to preparing young women for productive lives and careers, increasing and adjusting its programs to educate women for roles in a continuously changing society. Of special interest to the 1,100 women at Salem today are the services of the Career Planning and Placement Office, which aids students in formulating career goals.

Students are encouraged to take advantage of the broad selection of extracurricular activities on campus, including intercollegiate and intramural athletics, publications, performing groups in the arts, academic organizations related to specific subjects, and social organizations.

The Center for Student Life and Fitness provides space for athletic, fitness, and recreational activities in the gymnasium and 25-meter competition indoor swimming pool. The Salem Commons is a four-level student center with lounges for dances and large social gatherings, the student grill and coffee house, meeting rooms, a dance studio, and performance space. Students enjoy the use of twelve tennis courts and playing fields for team sports such as soccer, softball, and field hockey.

Fully wired for cable and computers, seven residence halls blend well with their surroundings in atmosphere and style. For juniors and seniors, Fogle Flats offers apartment-style living on campus.

Location

The College's 67-acre campus is located in the nationally recognized Old Salem restoration area of Winston-Salem, only a 10-minute walk from the downtown area. Winston-Salem (population 187,500) is a recognized cultural center of the Southeast.

Winston-Salem is served by major airlines at Piedmont Triad International Airport near Greensboro and at Smith Reynolds Airport in Winston-Salem.

Majors and Degrees

The B.A., B.S., and B.M. degrees are conferred with majors in accounting, American studies, art history, arts management, biology, business administration, chemistry, communication, economics, English, French, German, history, interior design, international business, international relations, mathematics, medical technology, music, music education, music performance, philosophy, psychology, religion, sociology, Spanish, and studio art.

A careful selection of courses provides a foundation for a wide variety of professional careers, including business, communication, law, library work, medicine, and social service. Students may earn teacher licensure in elementary education, secondary school subjects, special education (general curriculum) and TESOL (Teaching English to Speakers of Other Languages).

Salem also offers a 3-2 program in engineering in cooperation with Duke University and Vanderbilt University.

Academic Program

Each degree program includes certain basic distribution requirements, the completion of a major, and a varying number of elective courses. The distribution requirements offer considerable latitude in the planning of individual programs. Independent study, planned jointly by students and faculty members, is encouraged. Minors in twenty-three areas may be taken in addition to a major to enhance and expand a student's academic experience. All students participate in the unique Salem Signature, a four-year leadership/development program. As part of the Salem Signature, each student completes 30 hours of community service and an internship in her field of interest before graduating.

Salem's 4-1-4 calendar gives students opportunities for preprofessional internships, in-depth courses, travel programs, and independent studies during the January term, either on campus or abroad.

Salem's Center for Women Writers provides opportunities for students who are interested in writing and in publishing their work. Through lectures and readings by acclaimed women writers as well as workshops and courses taught by experienced professionals, Salem students derive firsthand knowledge of the creative process, writing techniques, and the publication process.

The Women in Science and Mathematics program provides academic and career support for women planning to enter traditionally male-dominated fields. The program sponsors seminars, trips to conferences, and a mentoring program.

Off-Campus Programs

A qualifying full-time student may register at Wake Forest University for any course unavailable at Salem. Salem is affiliated with the Bowman Gray School of Medicine and Forsyth Memorial Hospital for professional training in medical technology.

Salem offers a variety of options for off-campus study. The College also participates in the American University Washington Semester and the Drew University United Nations Semester and has two summer study programs with St. Peter's College, University of Oxford, England. The six-week program in science and humanities allows students to study in the traditional tutorial setting. A three-week business program consists of in-depth study of cultural, ethical, and gender issues facing international business. Salem also offers study-travel opportunities to twenty locations in seventeen countries through Brethren Colleges Abroad.

Salem students have the opportunity to work closely with social and health agencies, public schools, the police department, business firms, and churches in Winston-Salem. Internships also provide opportunities in other cities nationwide and even abroad.

Academic Facilities

The Salem College libraries contain more than 128,000 print volumes and 10,000 sound recordings. The libraries are fully automated and share an online catalog with four other area colleges. An online request feature enables students to borrow circulating materials (exceeding 750,000 volumes) from all five institutions.

The Salem libraries offer users access to more than 100 databases, including LexisNexis Academic Universe, Historical Newspapers, and the full range of NC LIVE databases—

providing full-text articles published in thousands of scholarly journals, magazines, and reference resources. Salem faculty members and students have remote access to most of the databases accessible on campus. Public computers in the libraries, including wireless laptops, provide access to word processing, spreadsheet, and graphics software as well as to the Internet, catalog, and database services.

The Fine Arts Center houses a large auditorium, a smaller recital hall, a workshop theater, extensive gallery space, music teaching rooms, practice rooms, a library, four listening rooms, classrooms, a rehearsal-lecture hall, a videoconferencing room, and large art studios. The four-story Science Building has modern, fully equipped classrooms and laboratories for the teaching of biology, chemistry, physics, mathematics, and computer science.

Computer labs in the science building and learning center provide students with access to word processing, spreadsheet, database, graphics, and other software that is course specific. All campus computers and data ports in campus residence halls allow access to the Internet and the campus network for e-mail and an online library catalog.

Costs

The comprehensive fee in 2003–04 for traditional-age students who reside on campus was $24,370 (traditional-age students must reside on campus unless they reside with family in the immediate vicinity). Tuition was $15,500 and room and board cost $8870. Books and supplies are estimated at $500 to $600 per year. The student government fee of approximately $215 covers class dues, the yearbook, other student publications, and organizational dues. Students enrolled in the Adult Degree Program pay $830 per course.

Financial Aid

The College makes every effort to assist as many qualified students as funds permit. Approximately 80 percent of students receive assistance through scholarships, loans, employment, and grants-in-aid. The Free Application for Federal Student Aid and the Salem College application form are required.

Salem participates in the Federal Perkins Loan Program, the Federal Pell Grant Program, and the Federal Work-Study Program. The Federal Family Education Loan Programs, which include Federal Stafford Student Loans and Federal PLUS Loans for Parents, are also available. Competitive scholarships based on general academic excellence, as well as on talent in music, are available. Special application must be made for these Honor Awards.

Faculty

The Salem faculty numbers 98. Approximately 90 percent of the full-time faculty members hold Ph.D.'s or the equivalent. The emphasis at Salem is on teaching, and full professors teach freshmen and upperclass students. The student-faculty ratio is 13:1.

Student Government

The primary goals of the Student Government Association are to build a spirit of community and unity among students and to set and maintain standards for achievement and behavior in keeping with Salem's honor tradition. Students serve as consultants or voting members of faculty committees and the Board of Trustees.

Admission Requirements

Salem welcomes applicants whose school records give evidence of academic ability, personal integrity, and a desire for continuing growth and achievement. Students from all social, religious, geographical, racial, and ethnic backgrounds are encouraged to apply. The Admissions Committee recommends 16 academic units (4 in English, 3 in mathematics: 2 in algebra and 1 in geometry, 2 to 4 in foreign languages, 2 in history, 3 in science, and 4 academic electives), scores on the SAT I or ACT, and two recommendations. Applications are evaluated on the basis of individual merit; the selection of courses, grade point average, test scores, and recommendations receive major emphasis, and participation in extracurricular and community activities is also noted. Auditions are required of all prospective music majors. Interviews are recommended.

Application and Information

All students are urged to submit their applications in the fall of the year preceding proposed college entrance. The evaluation of applications is done on a rolling basis, beginning in the fall. Students may apply online at the Web address listed below or by using the Common Application. There is no deadline for transfer applicants, but it is suggested that their credentials be submitted by March 1. The College subscribes to the College Board's Candidates Reply Date of May 1.

Arrangements for an interview, a campus tour, or class visits may be made through the Admissions Office. An application form, a College catalog, and other informational brochures may be obtained by writing to:

Dean of Admissions
Salem College
Winston-Salem, North Carolina 27108
Telephone: 336-721-2621
800-32-SALEM (toll-free)
E-mail: admissions@salem.edu
World Wide Web: http://www.salem.edu

Main Hall of Salem College.

SALISBURY UNIVERSITY

SALISBURY, MARYLAND

The University

Salisbury University (SU) has gained a national reputation for excellence in undergraduate teaching and learning. It consistently ranks in the top 10 percent of public and private institutions in national guidebooks and magazines. A member of the University System of Maryland (USM), SU emphasizes undergraduate research, internships, community service, and study abroad as pillars of its academic programs.

The foundation of Salisbury's success is the relationship between students and professors. Some 6,200 undergraduates are taught by 299 full-time faculty members on a campus of 144 acres. Full professors serve as undergraduate advisers. They often teach freshman courses and routinely lead students on trips and retreats, from exploring the Chesapeake Bay to touring Europe and beyond. Their professional concern for educating the whole student has had measurable results: according to the latest figures, Salisbury freshmen have the highest graduation rates for colleges and universities in the USM. This success has not gone unnoticed. In *U.S. News & World Report*'s "America's Best Colleges" 2004 issue, SU earned top-tier status among its peers in the North, which included both public and private institutions. Similar kudos have come from the 2002 editions of *Kiplinger's Personal Finance Magazine,* Princeton Review's *The Best 351 Colleges,* and Kaplan's *Guide to the 328 Most Interesting Colleges.*

Salisbury students come from twenty-seven states, the District of Columbia, and thirty-six other countries. Some 53 percent are from Maryland's western shore (which contains the Metropolitan Baltimore-Washington corridor), 15 percent are from outside the state, and 42 percent live on campus and in University-affiliated housing. An International House allows students from other countries to study and socialize together in a residential environment.

All students, resident and commuter, are expected to contribute to University life. Many of the University's ninety-nine student organizations and clubs find a home in the Guerrieri University Center. Nearly half of the student body participates in a thirty-nine-sport intramural program and twenty additional sports clubs. SU is a member of NCAA Division III for intercollegiate athletics. Women's sports are basketball, cross-country, field hockey, indoor track and field, lacrosse, soccer, softball, swimming, tennis, track and field, and volleyball. Men's sports are baseball, basketball, cross-country, football, indoor track and field, lacrosse, soccer, swimming, tennis, and track and field.

The University has two art galleries; supports an International Film Series, distinguished lecture series, artist-in-residence programs, and a public access television station; maintains WSCL-FM, a national public radio affiliate, and WSUR-FM, a student-run radio station; offers performing arts disciplines in music, theater, and dance; and serves as home to the Salisbury Symphony. The Ward Museum of Wildfowl Art is considered one of the best folk art museums in the country. Beyond the campus are the scenic Eastern Shore, the pleasures of Ocean City, Maryland (a nearby popular beach resort), the activities of an energetic Outdoor Club, and University-sponsored bus trips to theaters and museums in New York and Washington, D.C. Faculty members lead trips abroad during winter and summer terms.

The University also offers eleven graduate programs.

Location

With a population of 85,000, metropolitan Salisbury is the cultural and economic hub of Delmarva (containing portions of Delaware, Maryland, and Virginia), a historically and ecologically rich peninsula located between the Atlantic Ocean and Chesapeake Bay. The city is ½ hour west of the white beaches of Assateague and Ocean City, Maryland; approximately 2 hours from Baltimore, Washington, D.C., Wilmington, and Norfolk; and 4½ hours from New York City.

Majors and Degrees

Three undergraduate degrees are offered in addition to the Bachelor of Arts and Bachelor of Science: the Bachelor of Arts in Social Work (B.A.S.W.), the Bachelor of Science in Nursing (B.S.N.), and the Bachelor of Fine Arts (B.F.A.) in art. B.A. degrees are awarded in art, communication arts, conflict analysis and dispute resolution, economics, English, French, history, interdisciplinary studies, international studies, music, philosophy, political science, psychology, sociology, Spanish, and theater. Bachelor of Science degrees are awarded in accounting, athletic training, biology, business administration, chemistry, clinical laboratory science/medical technology, computer science, early childhood education, electrical engineering, elementary education, environmental health science, environmental issues, environmental marine science, exercise science, finance, geography and geosciences, health education, interdisciplinary studies, management, management information systems, marketing, mathematics, nursing, physical education, physics, and respiratory therapy.

At Salisbury University, majors are designed to educate the whole student. No false distinctions are made between the liberal arts and the professions. While gaining a liberal education, for example, students in preprofessional programs prepare for careers in dentistry, law, medicine, optometry, pharmacy, physical therapy, podiatry, and veterinary science. Certification programs train educators for both elementary and secondary teaching. Dual-degree programs with the University of Maryland Eastern Shore (UMES) enable students to earn two bachelor's degrees in four years in social work/sociology and biology/environmental marine science. SU, UMES, and the University of Maryland College Park collaborate on an electrical engineering degree. Both the graduate and the undergraduate programs of SU's business school are nationally accredited by AACSB International. Other national accreditations are in chemistry, education, allied health, social work, clinical laboratory science, and nursing and through the Middle States Association of Colleges and Schools.

Academic Program

Four schools, the Franklin P. Perdue School of Business, the Samuel W. and Marilyn C. Seidel School of Education and Professional Studies, the Charles R. and Martha N. Fulton School of Liberal Arts, and the Richard A. Henson School of Science and Technology, administer the University's forty undergraduate majors. All four are endowed, a rarity among public institutions nationwide. These recent endowments have enriched the scholastic climate of the campus, providing expanded scholarships, resources, and opportunities for students.

University planning encourages interdisciplinary study. All students, whatever their major, must take 47 credits within three disciplines: the humanities, history and the social sciences, and the mathematical and general sciences. Nine credits must be taken in English composition and literature. All course syllabi, from science to music to business, require written assignments in analysis/criticism, research, or creative writing.

SU's advising system was recently praised by students in a Maryland Higher Education Commission survey as one of the best in the state. Exceptional orientation programs for students and their parents help freshmen make a successful transition from home to college. For example, SU offers a freshman orientation-in-the-wilderness experience, which won the Maryland Association for Higher Education Distinguished Program

Award. Other orientation options include community service with the University's award-winning Institute for Service Learning.

Incoming students may earn credit through Advanced Placement and departmental challenge examinations and the College-Level Examination Program (CLEP) for nontraditional educational experiences. Popular with students are internship programs, available in all four schools. Internships have included work abroad; legislative service in both Washington, D.C., and Annapolis; and media experience in fields ranging from fine arts to television. Students who relish intellectual challenge are invited to join the honors program housed in the Thomas E. Bellavance Honors Center. Each year, the University holds a campuswide conference on undergraduate research. Students also present research at national conferences and meetings. Travel and semester-abroad programs are popular. For example, Salisbury University students were recently studying simultaneously in Asia, Europe, and South America.

Academic Facilities

Blackwell Library, which has a number of computers available for research and more than a quarter of a million books and bound periodicals, is the main research center. In addition to an online catalog, library users have access to many other databases, including FirstSearch and the World Wide Web. Princeton Review recently ranked SU as one of the most connected campuses in Maryland. Seven computer labs are part of the campus Novell network, which connects students to various software applications, e-mail, and the Internet. Resident students also have network connections for the Internet and e-mail available in their rooms. Three theaters, including the acoustically lauded Holloway Hall Auditorium, are homes to the performing arts. Salisbury is the only institution in the USM with an endowed theater program. The Edward H. Nabb Research Center for Delmarva History and Culture is earning a national reputation for historical research of the Middle Atlantic area. The Communications Center has fully equipped television and recording studios. Fulton Hall is home to the fine and performing arts. In fall 2002, a $37-million state-of-the-art science education and research building opened. At 145,500 square feet, it is one of the largest in Maryland.

Costs

Maryland residents paid undergraduate tuition and fees of $5564 for the academic year 2003–04. Tuition for out-of-state undergraduates was $12,452. Students living on campus paid approximately $6900 for room and board; the figure varies, depending on the residence hall and meal plan.

Financial Aid

Financial assistance is available to students through loans, grants, scholarships, and on- and off-campus employment. The University participates in the Federal Perkins Loan, Federal Pell Grant, Federal Supplemental Educational Opportunity Grant, and Federal Work-Study and Direct Loan programs. Numerous other forms of financial aid are available on the state and local levels. These awards are based exclusively on demonstrated financial need. All students who wish to apply for financial assistance are required to complete the Free Application for Federal Student Aid (FAFSA) by February 15. Complete details are available through the University's Admissions and Financial Aid Offices.

Through the University's Work Experience Program, which has a budget in excess of $2 million and provides employment for one quarter of the student body, students may be assigned to jobs related to their academic interest. They can earn a minimum of $1500 to $2000 per academic year by working 10 to 15 hours a week. Non-need academic scholarships are available to incoming freshmen and are awarded on the basis of high school performance and SAT I scores. The application for admission to the University is the initial step in applying for these scholarships.

Faculty

Faculty members at Salisbury have won national teaching, research, and leadership awards. Ninety-one percent of the tenure-track faculty members, many of whom are National Endowment for the Humanities and Fulbright professors, have the Ph.D. or other highest degree in their field. Professors not only publish but donate countless hours to community service, thus teaching by deed as well as word. The student-professor ratio is 16:1, and smaller classes are not unusual.

Student Government

Shared governance is a hallmark of campus life, and students are actively involved in all aspects of it. The Student Government Association (SGA) serves as a liaison between faculty and administration and students. SGA officers serve on many University committees, both administrative and academic, including the President's Advisory Team. Students are also represented in the University Forum, which includes faculty and administration and meets regularly to discuss issues facing the University community. The all-student Appropriations Board budgets student activity fees to clubs and organizations. Students are encouraged to participate in a full complement of events, many sponsored by the Student Organization for Activity Planning.

Admission Requirements

The University seeks to admit outstanding students who can bring a diversity of talents, experiences, and points of view to the campus. Most successful candidates for admission have earned above-average high school grades in a strong academic program and a score above the national average on the SAT I or ACT. The high school record, test scores, essay, and recommendations of the high school principal and guidance counselors are considered. Interviews are not required, but applicants are encouraged to discuss programs and procedures for housing and financial aid with the staff of the Admissions and Financial Aid Offices.

Transfer students must have earned at least 24 semester hours at an accredited community college or four-year college or university and have a minimum 2.0 average (on a 4.0 scale). For transfer students who have attempted fewer than 24 hours at another institution, the University's admission policy for entering freshmen applies.

Application and Information

Applications are accepted beginning September 1 for the spring and fall semesters. Applications received by January 1 for the spring semester and by February 1 for the fall semester are given the fullest attention. The University reserves the right to close admissions when the projected enrollment is met.

For further information, students should contact:

Admissions Office
1101 Camden Avenue
Salisbury University
Salisbury, Maryland 21801-6862
Telephone: 888-543-0148 (toll-free)
410-543-6161
Fax: 410-546-6016
E-mail: admissions@salisbury.edu
World Wide Web: http://www.salisbury.edu

Salisbury University's Henson Science Hall was recently recognized by the Maryland Society Chapter of the American Institute of Architects as one of the state's best-designed new buildings.

SALVE REGINA UNIVERSITY

NEWPORT, RHODE ISLAND

The University

Salve Regina is a private, coeducational university of distinction that offers a comprehensive undergraduate program in the arts and sciences. The University is accredited by the New England Association of Schools and Colleges, and the Salve Regina campus is composed of a number of historic Newport estates that were built at the turn of the century against the backdrop of the Atlantic Ocean in the world-famous resort city of Newport. Chartered in 1934 by the state of Rhode Island and founded in 1947 by the Religious Sisters of Mercy, Salve Regina has positioned itself for academic excellence in the new millennium.

Today, more than 2,100 undergraduate and 500 graduate students from forty-six states and twenty-six other countries are enrolled in thirty undergraduate majors and twelve graduate programs, including a Ph.D. in humanities. Nearly 14,000 alumni have distinguished themselves in public service as health-care professionals and community leaders.

On-campus residence is an integral component of the Salve Regina educational experience—a living and learning environment that is like no other. Most of the University's residence halls are buildings of historical significance.

The University offers a wide spectrum of extracurricular activities, including student government, honor societies, art, theater and music programs, community outreach activities, and a full athletics program. A member of the Eastern Collegiate Athletic Conference and the Commonwealth Coast Conference, Salve Regina offers nineteen varsity sports at the Division III level for men and women. Varsity sports offered for both men and women are basketball, ice hockey, lacrosse, sailing, soccer, and tennis. Sports offered for women only are cross-country, field hockey, softball, track and field, and volleyball. Sports offered for men only are baseball and football. The new 69,000-square-foot recreation center meets the athletic and recreational needs of Salve Regina students and faculty and staff members. The Student Activities Program draws inspiration from the University's mission of service to others, and it includes many service clubs and organizations. Through the Feinstein Enriching America Program, students participate in an array of community enrichment projects and activities that broaden their classroom education. Students serve as volunteers and interns at local hospitals, schools, museums, libraries, human service agencies, and other institutions. The campus is also home to the Pell Center for International Relations and Public Policy, where international dialogue is enhanced in an effort to achieve world peace.

Location

With the good fortune to be located in the historic city of Newport, Rhode Island, Salve Regina has a unique campus situated in a recognized National Historic District, with a landscape befitting a national park. Against the backdrop of the Atlantic Ocean and Newport's famous Cliff Walk, the University campus contains twenty historic and significant buildings constructed at or near the turn of the century. These former "summer cottages" and estate buildings have been adapted by Salve Regina for academic, administrative, and residential uses. They have been augmented by the construction of modern residence halls and academic buildings that fit in with the historic flavor and distinctive landscape of the campus, which includes century-old shade trees imported from Europe and the Far East and beautifully sculpted gardens. Nearby Newport's world-famous harbor and beautifully preserved architecture reflect its colonial seaport heritage, yet the city maintains a modern resort personality. Cobbled streets and brick sidewalks in downtown Newport, just a short walk from the Salve Regina campus, connect historic homes to the city's museums, art galleries, quaint shops, world-class restaurants, and recreational areas. Just minutes from campus students can find beautiful beaches, nature trails, and the famous 10-mile Ocean Drive, ideal for hiking and biking. Newport is centrally located less than a 90-minute drive from Boston, 45 minutes from Providence, and 3½ hours from New York. Train and air connections are available less than an hour from the Salve Regina campus, and a University shuttle provides regular transportation between the campus and the surrounding community. Students receive a free statewide RIPTA bus pass.

Majors and Degrees

The University offers a selection of undergraduate degrees, including Associate of Arts (A.A.), Associate of Science (A.S.), Bachelor of Arts (B.A.), Bachelor of Science (B.S.), and Bachelor of Arts and Science (B.A.S.). Academic programs include accounting, administration of justice, American studies, anthropology, art, biology, ceramics, chemistry, communication media, cultural and historic preservation, cytotechnology, early childhood education, economics, elementary education, English, environmental science, finance, French, global studies (economics), graphic design, history, human resource management, information systems science, journalism, judicial administration, liberal studies, literature, management, marketing, mathematics, medical technology, microbiology, music, nursing, painting, philosophy, photography, politics, prelaw, premedicine, psychology, religious studies, secondary education, social work, sociology, Spanish, special education, and theater. Five-year programs offer students the opportunity to complete both a bachelor's and a master's degree within five academic years. Five-year combined degrees are offered in business administration and international relations.

Academic Programs

Students receiving an associate degree must complete a minimum of 64 semester hours. A bachelor's degree requires a minimum of 128 semester hours. Departments may require additional semester hours of course work in particular concentrations. General education requirements comprise approximately 40 percent of course work leading to a degree. Usually completed by the end of the sophomore year, the general education course work is linked to the theme of world citizenship. The undergraduate program operates on a two-semester calendar, with fall classes beginning in September and ending in December and spring classes beginning in mid-January and running through mid-May.

Off-Campus Programs

Salve Regina has built strong relationships with public and private agencies and businesses that provide numerous internship opportunities for students as well as expanded professional activities that enhance academic programs. Students in accounting, administration of justice, information systems science, management, medical technology, nursing, and social work all benefit from hands-on experience at professional agencies and organizations. Internships in all fields can be pursued both on and off campus to augment classroom learning with experience in a professional setting. Students seeking internships for academic credit must receive approval from the appropriate department chair and the academic dean. Salve Regina also offers students the opportunity to study abroad as a way of increasing global awareness. Programs are available in Australia, Mexico, the U.K., Japan, and Italy, among other locations. The University also encourages full-year and summer study-abroad programs in affiliation with other institutions. Several short-term study trips are available to destinations such as London, Cuba, Mexico, and France.

Academic Facilities

With a modern library serving as a hub of University academic activity, Salve Regina combines modern facilities with historic structures in its academic setting. The McKillop Library, in fact, was designed to reflect the architectural lines of nearby turn-of-the-century buildings, but its functional interior includes state-of-the-art information technology that provides educational resources to meet any research needs. Students and faculty members have direct access to an array of international research databases and other online tools from workstations throughout the building, and the library's circulation and internal procedures are fully automated. Salve Regina is a member of the Rhode Island HELIN library consortium. Salve Regina's academic facilities are informed by tradition and architectural history, with a number of nineteenth-century estate buildings serving as classrooms, visual and performing arts studio spaces, and faculty offices. Other academic facilities have been built to accommodate the specialized requirements of science laboratories, computer laboratories, and lecture halls for large audiences.

Costs

Tuition and fees for the 2003–04 academic year were $20,510. Room and board cost approximately $8700, depending on specific campus housing and dining arrangements.

Financial Aid

Salve Regina University is strongly committed to helping students obtain a private education. Approximately 70 percent of Salve Regina students receive financial aid through a combination of scholarships, loans, grants, and work-study employment. The University requires the Free Application for Federal Student Aid (FAFSA) and the College Scholarship Service PROFILE. A Salve Regina Financial Aid Institutional Form must also be submitted. These forms must be filed no later than March 1.

Faculty

During the 2002–03 academic year, there were 277 faculty members. Approximately 45 percent of the full-time faculty members are tenured. Approximately 75 percent have earned a doctoral or terminal degree. Faculty members are committed to excellence in teaching and to the development of the academic potential of each student.

Student Government

Students have the opportunity to offer input into University activities and policies by participating in Student Government and the Activities Funding Board. In addition, students serve as elected class officers.

Admission Requirements

The qualifications of each applicant are evaluated by a committee on admission, which focuses on academic ability, intellectual curiosity, strength of character, motivation, and promise for personal growth and development. The committee reviews applicants without regard to age, race, sex, creed, national or ethnic origin, or handicap. While secondary school preparation varies, the University strongly recommends that students accomplish the following 16 units: 4 in English, 3 in mathematics, 2 in laboratory science, 2 in foreign language, 1 in history, and 4 in electives. Salve Regina follows a rolling admissions policy but has a priority deadline of March 1. Transfer students should follow the procedure for regular application to the University. Applicants to the Nursing Program are also evaluated by a Nursing Review Committee. Students with superior academic credentials may be considered for a number of academic scholarship programs provided by the University.

Application and Information

Candidates for admission must furnish evidence of completion or anticipated completion of a level of education equivalent to four years of high school or submit results of the GED test. All candidates must furnish a completed application with a nonrefundable fee of $40 (unless a waiver is obtained from the dean of admissions), an official transcript of high school work and class rank, results of the SAT I or ACT, and two letters of recommendation. Early action candidates should file an application before November 15, and notification of acceptance under this plan is sent by December 15.

Applications for admission and further information may be obtained by contacting:

Admissions Office
Salve Regina University
100 Ochre Point Avenue
Newport, Rhode Island 02840-4192
Telephone: 401-341-2908
888-GO-SALVE (toll-free)
Fax: 401-848-2823
E-mail: sruadmis@salve.edu
World Wide Web: http://explore.salve.edu
http://www.salve.edu

Ochre Court is one of many historic buildings on campus that make the learning environment at Salve Regina like no other.

SAMFORD UNIVERSITY

BIRMINGHAM, ALABAMA

The University

Samford University is a private, liberal arts university with high academic standards. The University's academic reputation is due to well-prepared, accessible faculty members who take time to know and interact with students. Samford, which has some 4,500 students, offers a wide range of extracurricular activities diverse enough to satisfy the social, cultural, physical, and spiritual needs of all of its students. A lively Greek system; an honors program; men's and women's intramural and varsity athletics, including seventeen NCAA Division I sports; music and drama groups; an award-winning debate program; and other interest groups bond the students and the faculty members into a community of friends and scholars. Students come from forty-one states and fifteen countries. A large number of students live on campus, enhancing the sense of school spirit and involvement. Students enjoy modern recreational facilities, including a concert hall, a theater, an indoor pool, racquetball and tennis courts, and an indoor track. Comfortable housing, including modern apartment-style units and fraternity/sorority residence facilities, is available.

Samford University has ranked fifth among 130 regional universities in the South, as published by *U.S. News & World Report*; marked as "very competitive" by *Barron's Profiles of American Colleges*; and has been selected for *Peterson's Competitive Colleges*. Samford programs are included in *The Templeton Guide: Colleges that Encourage Character*.

Special student services include an active and successful Career Development Center, which offers guidance in career exploration as well as ample opportunities for placement interviews. Co-op programs add work experience and business contacts to the rewards of achievement and income for the participants. The co-op program is an excellent source of financial assistance that complements the significant scholarship and federal aid programs available to Samford students.

In addition to its extensive undergraduate program, Samford University grants the following graduate degrees: Doctor of Education in educational leadership, Doctor of Ministry, Doctor of Pharmacy, Educational Specialist, Juris Doctor, Master of Accountancy, Master of Business Administration, Master of Divinity, Master of Comparative Law, Master of Science in environmental management, Master of Music, Master of Music Education, Master of Science in Education, Master of Science in Nursing, and Master of Theological Studies.

Location

Samford's wooded 150-acre campus, with its Georgian architecture, is one of the most beautiful in the nation. Located in the picturesque, mountainous area of Shades Valley, the campus is less than 6 miles from the heart of Birmingham, Alabama's largest city and the state's industrial, business, and cultural center. Birmingham annually hosts the Bruno's Classic Professional Golf Association Seniors Tournament and other major sports events. The city attracts national entertainment acts to its Civic Center, historic Alabama Theater, and Oak Mountain Outdoor Amphitheater. Gulf Coast beaches to the south and ski slopes to the north can be reached within 4½ hours by car. The world's largest space and rocket museum, located in Huntsville, Alabama, is also only a short drive away. Alabama's abundant freshwater lakes and rivers are sites for enjoyable outings. One of the South's largest shopping centers, the Riverchase Galleria, is only 7 miles from the Samford campus. The Samford student enjoys the best of two worlds: a suburban setting for study, contemplation, and social enjoyment and easy access to the varied offerings of a metropolitan area.

Majors and Degrees

Samford University offers an Associate of Science (A.S.) degree in the following concentrations: administrative/community services, natural/environmental sciences, and social sciences.

The Bachelor of Arts (B.A.) degree is attained through the following majors: classics, communication studies, English, family studies, family studies (with a concentration in child life), fine arts, fine arts (with a concentration in graphic design), French, German, Greek, history, interior design, journalism and mass communication, Latin, music, musical theater, philosophy, philosophy and religion, physics, political science, psychology, religion, religion (with a concentration in congregational studies), sociology, Spanish, and theater. The interdisciplinary concentrations offered in the Bachelor of Arts degree are Asian studies, international relations, language and world trade (with a specialty in French, German, Spanish, or world languages), Latin American studies, and public administration.

The Samford University Metro College offers the Bachelor of General Studies (B.G.S.) degree in the following concentrations: administrative/community services, counseling foundations, human resource development, liberal studies, natural/environmental sciences, and police administration.

The Bachelor of Music (B.M.) degree is offered in the following majors: church music, music, music education (instrumental, vocal, and choral), music theory/composition, musical theater, and performance (instrumental, organ, piano, and voice).

Students can earn a Bachelor of Science (B.S.) degree through the following majors: biology, biology (with an emphasis in marine science), chemistry, computer science, engineering and mathematics (dual-degree), engineering and physics (dual-degree), engineering physics, environmental science, fine arts (with a concentration in graphic design), geography, mathematics, music, nutrition and dietetics, and physics. The interdisciplinary concentrations offered in the Bachelor of Science degree are biochemistry and environmental science/geographic information science.

The University offers the Bachelor of Science in Business Administration (B.S.B.A.) in the following majors: accounting, management, management (with a finance concentration), and management (with a marketing concentration).

The Bachelor of Science in Education (B.S.E.) is attained through the following majors: athletic training, biology/general science, early childhood/special education/elementary/collaborative teacher education, English/language arts, exercise science (pre–physical therapy), fitness and health promotion, fitness and health promotion and nutrition and dietetics (dual major), history/social science, physical education, P–12 education, secondary education, sports medicine (premedicine), and teacher education.

The University offers the Bachelor of Science in Nursing (B.S.N.) in the nursing major.

Various preprofessional programs are offered, including predental, pre-engineering, prelaw, premedicine, pre-optometry, prepharmacy, and pre–veterinary medicine.

The Degree with Honors is available to students whose academic achievement is remarkable.

Academic Programs

In order to graduate, students must complete a minimum of 128 semester credits with an average grade of C or better. The core curriculum consists of the following six courses: Cultural Perspectives I and II, Communication Arts I and II, Biblical Perspectives, and Concepts of Fitness and Health. The curriculum is designed to address ideas and issues that cross the usual disciplinary boundaries and to help students actively engage in learning rather than simply memorizing notes for an exam. The core is also designed to promote a global perspective, recognizing the influence and achievement of many cultures.

In addition, students complete several education courses designed to prepare them for work in a major field and/or to help them experience the sciences, the social sciences, the humanities, and the fine arts.

At least 40 credits must be earned in junior- and senior-level courses. The last 32 credits must be earned at Samford University. Between the end of the sophomore year and graduation, undergraduate students (including transfer students) must pass a writing proficiency test.

Off-Campus Programs

A semester-abroad program, headquartered in Samford's Daniel House Study Centre in London, England, offers opportunities to develop a broad worldview.

Academic Facilities

The Harwell Goodwin Davis Library furnishes the facilities and materials necessary for reference, research, and independent study. Its reading areas with individual carrels provide ideal working conditions for Samford students. The open-stack system allows students easy access to a collection of more than 961,000 volumes of books, periodicals, microfilm and microfiche, records, and tape. The library annually adds 7,000 volumes and 2,600 government documents. The library's Multimedia Collection houses the Religious Education Curriculum Laboratory and provides audiovisual aids and hardware, computers, and computer software. A staff of professional librarians guides students in the use of the fully equipped library. The Alabama Baptist Historical Commission's collection of Baptist church records and other important historical materials are located in the library and maintained by the Special Collection Department. Historical documents are also preserved through an active microfilming program. The Samford library system includes the L. R. Jordan Nursing Library; the Cordell Hull Law Library, which has more than 232,850 volumes; the Education Curriculum Laboratory; and the Music Library, which has more than 8,000 CDs, records, scores, and audiocassettes. University library holdings are accessed through a state-of-the-art library system. Other libraries in the Birmingham area cooperate with Samford on a reciprocal basis.

Costs

The cost of attending Samford is significantly lower than that of many institutions of comparable size and commitment to quality. The basic charge for 2003–04, including tuition ($13,154), room, and board, was $18,398. The typical student spends about $750 per year for books and supplies.

Financial Aid

At Samford University, a student's educational costs are frequently offset by scholarship and other financial assistance programs, which annually total more than $30 million. Applications for financial assistance are provided as students apply for admission. Awards are usually made by June. Most aid is need-based and is awarded according to the needs analysis report provided by the College Scholarship Service or American College Testing. In addition, non-need-based scholarship awards, usually based on academic merit, range from $500 to full tuition.

Faculty

Samford's faculty consists of 252 full-time and 160 part-time members who have earned academic degrees from universities throughout the world. All classes are taught by members of the faculty; the faculty-student ratio is 1:13. Faculty members serve as academic advisers and also serve on many University committees, including the Admission, Scholarship, and Honors Committees.

Student Government

The Student Government Association (SGA) provides an excellent opportunity for students to participate in and influence governance. The SGA has autonomy in many programs, activities, and budgetary decisions; through the Student Senate, proposals related to improvement of campus life are sent to the University administration for consideration. The largest SGA organization is the Student Entertainment Board. Through its committees a variety of activities are provided, including concerts, lectures, dances, and outdoor recreation. The largest student-run activity is Step Sing, an annual variety show involving several hundred students that fills the 2,700-seat concert hall for three consecutive nights. Students are also involved in disciplining students who do not live up to University values. Alcohol is not permitted on campus, and regular visitation by persons of the opposite sex in residence hall rooms is not allowed.

Admission Requirements

Samford University seeks to enroll students capable of success in a challenging academic environment. Every applicant is evaluated individually on the basis of academic preparedness and potential, as well as personal fit with the mission and purpose of the University. The Admission Committee considers factors such as the strength of the high school curriculum, grade point average, standardized test scores, demonstrated leadership skills, and recommendations. The freshman class that entered in 2003 possessed an ACT composite middle 50 percent range of 23 to 27; the SAT I middle 50 percent range was 1040 to 1240. The average high school grade point average of the entering class was 3.6. These statistics continue to demonstrate the competitive environment of Samford. International students must also demonstrate proficiency on the Test of English as a Foreign Language (TOEFL). Transfer students should have completed at least 24 semester hours or 36 quarter hours and maintained at least a 2.5 cumulative grade point average. Early admission is available to high school juniors who present an outstanding academic record and the recommendations of their parents and principal. Credit can be earned through CLEP and Advanced Placement tests. One school recommendation and an essay are required of every applicant. A campus visit is recommended.

Application and Information

Applications are received and processed on a monthly rolling basis. Students may also apply online by visiting the University's Web site. Applications are accepted until the class is filled. Notification is given on a rolling basis.

Application inquiries should be addressed to:

Phil Kimrey, Ed.D.
Dean of Admission and Financial Aid
Samford University
Birmingham, Alabama 35229
Telephone: 205-726-3673
800-888-7218 (toll-free)
World Wide Web: http://www.samford.edu

The Harwell G. Davis Library on the campus of Samford University.

SAN FRANCISCO ART INSTITUTE

SAN FRANCISCO, CALIFORNIA

The Institute

Founded in 1871, the San Francisco Art Institute (SFAI) is one of the oldest and most prestigious colleges of art in the United States. Among its alumni and faculty are many of the country's leading artists. The development of the individual artist is at the core of the San Francisco Art Institute's educational philosophy. Whether students choose to study painting, drawing, filmmaking, video, performance, sculpture, photography, digital media, or printmaking, their time here and the relationships they develop—with faculty members and fellow students—shape who they are as artists and as people. As artists become greater participants in all aspects of contemporary society, it is crucial that they acquire the tools, technical skills, and self-confidence to engage fully in these vital new roles. The Art Institute is committed to providing students with the best possible education by challenging them with a rigorous academic and studio program and by helping them meet the demands and expectations they will face as active community members and cultural contributors. The Institute is fully accredited by the Western Association of Schools and Colleges (WASC) and by the National Association of Schools of Art and Design (NASAD), and offers the Bachelor of Fine Arts, postbaccalaureate certificate, and Master of Fine Arts degrees. With 400 undergraduate and 250 graduate students, SFAI is small enough for students and faculty members to work closely together and develop important relationships, yet large enough so that students are exposed to a great variety of work and artists. SFAI emphasizes vision, skill, intellectual development, hands-on experience, and engagement with the world. At SFAI, art making is defined by a broad spectrum of forms, philosophies, and aesthetic approaches and does not presume separations between fine and applied arts or the arts and other disciplines. Inspiration can come from mass and popular culture, from contemporary politics, from cross-cultural experiences, or from community relationships. While studio practice and the critique process are at the core of the Institute's philosophy, courses in art history, liberal arts, and critical studies foster and challenge critical-thinking skills; strengthen students' abilities to speak and write confidently about their work; and help to place their work within the context of art history and contemporary culture. The faculty encourages students to be self-motivated and self-directed and provides the tools, knowledge, and resources to support students' work. At SFAI, artistic, personal, and intellectual development is fused so that the process of making work is a life-enriching experience and prepares students for lifelong learning and development

Location

The San Francisco Art Institute's main campus is located in San Francisco's Russian Hill neighborhood, within easy walking distance of historic North Beach and Chinatown. Extensive systems of public transportation link the Institute to the rest of the city and nearby communities.

The San Francisco Bay area is the country's sixth-largest metropolitan area and is home to an exciting art scene that includes community organizations, museums, galleries, and alternative spaces for performance and other work. The area also offers a wealth of cultural and educational resources—opera, dance, legitimate and experimental theater, symphony orchestras and new music, cinema, and libraries. Favored by a climate that is mild year-round, San Francisco is among the world's most livable cities. Physically beautiful with its hills, bay views, bridges, and eclectic architecture, the city is home to some 776,000 people representing distinct ethnic groups.

Majors and Degrees

The San Francisco Art Institute offers the Bachelor of Fine Arts degree in digital media/sound, filmmaking, interdisciplinary studies, painting/drawing, new genres/performance/video, photography, printmaking, and sculpture/ceramics. Students may major in more than one discipline or pursue an interdisciplinary curriculum.

Academic Programs

To earn the B.F.A. degree, students must complete a total of 120 semester units in studio art, art history, and liberal arts. The curriculum emphasizes studio work, which represents approximately two thirds of the degree requirements in each major. Courses in art history and the liberal arts are designed to support and complement students' studio work. Normally, a full-time undergraduate program consists of 15 units per semester.

Academic Facilities

The San Francisco Art Institute's main campus is located on Russian Hill, within walking distance of downtown galleries and the neighborhoods of North Beach and Chinatown. This 90,000-square-foot campus houses painting, drawing, and sculpture studios; printmaking areas for lithography, intaglio, and silkscreen as well as digital printmaking; photography studios and darkrooms; and black box studios for shooting film and video. Postproduction facilities include darkrooms, mural printing, and large-scale digital photo output; Super 8 and 16 mm editing; digital video and Avid editing; black-and-white and color film processing for photography and film; and sound studios. The Diego Rivera Gallery, an open-air amphitheater, and a 250-seat theater are available for use by students for exhibiting work. The Anne Bremer Memorial Library is a valuable resource for books and primary source material on California artists. The library's collection of more than 26,000 volumes emphasizes modern and contemporary art, art history, theory, and criticism. The Center for Digital Media (CDM) is an interdisciplinary campus resource facility available to all students for both static and time-based digital work. Equipment includes Dual Processor G4 Macs and SGI 3D workstations; scanners; digital video editing stations; a multiformat digital video suite; and an array of printers, including large-format, archival, photo-quality Epson printers. The CDM also provides free Internet access terminals located on campus in the Café, Career Resource Center, and library.

Costs

For the 2004–05 academic year, expenses for undergraduate students are $24,240 for full-time tuition, $1800 for supplies and books, about $3200 for personal expenses, and $405 for transportation. Housing and food for a single student cost about $9450 for the year. Most students live off campus in private apartments or studios. Freshmen may live in college-leased housing located at the San Francisco Presidio. The Institute also maintains a roommate referral service and housing bulletin boards. SFAI requires all full-time students to purchase health insurance. This requirement may be waived upon presentation of proof of other coverage. The 2004–05 insurance premium is $950.

Financial Aid

The San Francisco Art Institute administers four categories of aid: scholarships, loans, grants, and work-study opportunities. In addition to making awards solely on the basis of demonstrated financial need, the Institute has established Merit Scholarship competitions, which award merit-based scholarships each semester to students admitted for undergraduate study beginning in the subsequent semester.

Application for all types of need-based financial aid administered by the Institute requires a completed application for admission and the Free Application for Federal Student Aid (FAFSA). The FAFSA should be forwarded to the appropriate processing center. Students who apply by March 1 receive priority consideration for available financial aid funds.

Approximately 76 percent of the Institute's students receive some form of financial aid.

Faculty

The studio faculty is composed of professional artists, all of whom have exhibited widely and are recognized in their respective media of expression. Additional faculty members teach courses in liberal arts and art history. The current student-faculty ratio is slightly less than 12:1, conducive to close interaction between students and the faculty members with whom they choose to work. The Institute is committed to a personalized system of learning that emphasizes freedom and experimentation.

Student Government

The Student Senate is a forum for discussion and action concerning all matters of interest to students. Three Student Senate members are elected to the Institute's Board of Trustees and participate in all of its governing committees. Also under the jurisdiction of the Student Senate are the exhibitions program of the Diego Rivera Gallery, student publications, and various social functions.

Admission Requirements

All applicants are required to submit a portfolio of fifteen to twenty slides of original artwork. Official transcripts from all secondary and postsecondary institutions, SAT I or ACT scores, a statement of purpose, an application form, two letters of recommendation, and a $65 nonrefundable application fee are also required.

Admission decisions are made on an individual basis, taking into account artistic achievement, personal maturity, and dedication to fine art, as well as academic background.

Application and Information

All applicants must file a completed application form, letter of recommendation, statement of purpose, portfolio, test scores, and transcripts with the Office of Admissions. The Institute has a rolling admission policy; applicants are notified of the admission decision as soon as their file has been reviewed. For preferential consideration in the proposed major, applications should be received by March 1 for admission in the next fall semester and by October 1 for admission in the subsequent spring semester. International students are strongly encouraged to apply.

Application forms, a current college catalog, and additional information may be obtained by contacting:

Office of Admissions
San Francisco Art Institute
800 Chestnut Street
San Francisco, California 94133
Telephone: 800-345-SFAI (toll-free)
E-mail: admissions@sfai.edu
World Wide Web: http://www.sfai.edu

A student in one of the Art Institute's painting studios.

SANTA CLARA UNIVERSITY

SANTA CLARA, CALIFORNIA

The University

Located in the heart of California's Silicon Valley, Santa Clara University (SCU) offers a rigorous undergraduate curriculum in the arts and sciences, business, and engineering. It has nationally recognized graduate and professional schools in business, law, engineering, pastoral ministries, and counseling psychology and education.

The 8,047-student Jesuit university has a 153-year tradition of educating the whole person for a life of service and leadership. There are 4,551 undergraduate students and 3,496 graduate and law students. This diverse community of scholars, characterized by small classes and a values-oriented curriculum, is dedicated to educating students for competence, conscience, and compassion.

The University has three schools that offer undergraduate programs: the College of Arts and Sciences, the Leavey School of Business, and the School of Engineering. Graduate programs are offered by the engineering and business schools, the School of Law, and the divisions of Pastoral Studies and Counseling Psychology and Education.

SCU, founded in 1851 by the Society of Jesus, is California's oldest institution of higher learning. It was established on the site of the Mission Santa Clara de Asis, the eighth of the original twenty-one California missions. In 1928, the high school division was separated from the University and became Bellarmine College Preparatory, a private boys' high school. For 110 years, SCU was an all-male school. In 1961, the University admitted women students, making it the first coeducational Catholic university in California. In 2001, the American Association of Colleges and Universities awarded SCU a commendation for distinguished achievement in undergraduate education.

The Pat Malley Fitness and Recreation Center is open seven days a week and provides free use of more than thirty-five cardiovascular machines, saunas in locker rooms, three full basketball courts, a 2,100-square-foot multipurpose room, and indoor and outdoor lounge areas. The facility also has offices for expanded SCU recreation and wellness programs for students and faculty and staff members. The recreation programs include four interscholastic club sports and eight coeducational intramural programs. Bronco scholar-athletes distinguish themselves in seventeen intercollegiate sports. The school colors are Santa Clara red and white.

The University sponsors a wide variety of clubs and organizations to provide for academic and cultural enrichment, increased community involvement, and forums for special interest groups on campus. Among those offered are the Community Action Program, M.E.Ch.A.–El Frente, Black Student Union, and Asian/Pacific Union. Other special interests are served by the Campus Ministry and the student-run Multicultural Center.

SCU prides itself on its diversity. In fall 2003, the University enrolled 4,551 undergraduates and 3,496 graduate students, with male-female ratios at 43:57 (undergraduate) and 45:55 (graduate). In the same term, 32 percent of undergraduates and 43 percent of graduate students were members of minority groups. Sixty-four percent of SCU undergraduate students are from California; the others are from thirty-five states and twelve other countries.

SCU alumni live in all fifty states, although most—51 percent—live in the Bay Area, where many of them are leaders in business, law, engineering, academia, and public service. The University endowment reached $401 million in 2003.

Location

The 104-acre campus is located on El Camino Real in Santa Clara, near the southern end of San Francisco Bay. At the campus center is the Mission Church, restored in 1928 and surrounded by the roses and palm and olive trees of the historic Mission Gardens. It is located less than 2 miles from the San Jose Airport and 5 miles from downtown San Jose, the nation's eleventh-largest city. San Francisco is 45 miles away, conveniently reached by a CalTrain station that stops next to the campus. The campus is a half-hour drive from Pacific Ocean beaches and about 4 hours' drive from Yosemite National Park and the ski resorts of the Sierra Nevada.

Majors and Degrees

The College of Arts and Sciences offers B.A. degrees in ancient studies, art history, chemistry, classical studies, communication, English, environmental sciences, environmental studies, French and francophone studies, German studies, Greek, history, individual studies, Italian studies, Latin, liberal studies, music, philosophy, religious studies, Spanish studies, studio art, and theater arts and B.S. degrees in anthropology, biology, chemistry, combined sciences, computer science, economics, engineering physics, mathematics, physics, political science, psychology, and sociology. The Leavey School of Business offers the B.S. in Commerce degree in accounting, economics, finance, management, marketing, and operations and management information systems. The School of Engineering offers the B.S. degree in civil engineering, computer engineering, electrical engineering, general engineering, and mechanical engineering.

Academic Programs

SCU underscores its commitment to education with a strong undergraduate core curriculum. Opportunities for learning and personal development can be found in a wide variety of courses, interdisciplinary institutes, internships, an honors program, Army ROTC, undergraduate thesis projects and in the University's Office of Student Leadership. Also, students work with the Markkula Center for Applied Ethics in values education in local schools.

SCU's commitment to learning is expressed in the fact that 92 percent of freshmen advance to the sophomore year and 85 percent graduate in six years or less, among the highest percentages in the country. Undergraduate classes are small, averaging 25 students, with an overall faculty/student ratio of 12:1.

The academic year is divided into three 11-week terms. Students generally take four courses per quarter. Classes begin in late September and end in mid-June. Approximately 1,250 students participate in a summer school program.

Requirements for a degree vary according to the major program, but all degree candidates must spend at least one full year of study on the campus after achieving junior status.

Off-Campus Programs

Approximately 350 SCU students choose to study abroad during their junior or senior year, often at other Jesuit universities in Europe, Latin America, Asia, and Australia, for which academic credit is given. Students may also earn full academic credit for spending a semester in Washington, D.C., in internship programs.

The Pedro Arrupe, S.J. Center for Community-Based Learning is a center of distinction in which SCU students combine community service with the course work in a wide range of disciplines. Students can choose to work at a variety of nonprofit organizations that have established partnerships with SCU, including homeless shelters, multilingual/ESL educational programs, convalescent hospitals, immigrant service centers, and even a parish-based theater company. Each year, approximately 1,300 SCU students participate in the program in seventy-five different Arrupe Center classes. Law school students volunteer legal aid for indigent clients through the SCU School of Law's East San Jose Community Law Center.

Academic Facilities

The fifty-one buildings on campus include ten residence halls, two libraries, a student center, and extensive athletic facilities. In 2000, the University completed a $68-million construction program, including two science laboratory and classroom buildings, a performing arts center for music and dance, arts and sciences and communications classrooms, state-of-the-art television production facilities, a recreation and fitness center, an upperclass residence complex, and a parking structure.

The main library, Orradre Library, has 758,745 volumes, plus computer laboratories. The library's card catalog is accessible via computer. There are also 607,860 government documents and 780,895 microform units. Computer and telecommunications technology is an integral part of the life and learning at SCU. All residence hall rooms and approximately 90 percent of classrooms are connected to high-speed Internet access and campus e-mail; in addition, students use 766 computers in twenty-three computer laboratories.

The John B. Drahmann Undergraduate Advising and Learning Resource Center consolidates several historically separate programs into a single operation that seeks to promote the goal of student learning. Among its aims are connecting academic advising support and learning resources more effectively and efficiently; providing for more direct faculty involvement in key student learning areas, such as new student programs; and helping to promote the faculty-student interaction essential to a community of scholars by supporting residential learning communities and the peer educator program. The Drahmann Center provides academic advising in all undergraduate programs and also provides tutoring, learning resources, fellowship information, a disabilities resources program, and orientation programs for new students. In conjunction with the new Center for Multicultural Learning, the Drahmann Center also undertakes outreach to historically underserved students to ensure that they are connected to resources that will support their academic success.

Costs

The basic expenses for undergraduate students for the 2003–04 academic year were as follows: tuition, $25,365; room and board, $9336; and books and personal expenses, $3690.

Financial Aid

SCU administers four categories of financial aid: scholarships, loans, grants, and work-study awards. Sixty-nine percent of the student body receives some type of financial assistance. Awards are made on the basis of financial need and academic record. Students should contact the Financial Aid Office regarding application deadlines in order to receive full consideration for available funds. Students must also apply for the California State Grant program (Cal Grant A, B), when applicable, and for the Federal Pell Grant. Other supplementary aid opportunities are available through the Federal Perkins Loan, Ford Federal Direct Student Loan, and Federal PLUS loan programs and through Army ROTC. Further information may be obtained from the Financial Aid Office.

Faculty

The faculty at SCU is composed of Jesuit priests and lay teachers. Ninety-two percent of the full-time faculty members hold doctoral degrees. At SCU, there are no teaching assistants; all classes are taught by the professors of the University.

Student Government

The Associated Students for Santa Clara University (ASSCU) is the official organization for student government. Every student is automatically a member of ASSCU and participates through his or her elected representative in making policies that affect student life on campus. Student participation in University decision making is possible through student representation on the Board of Governors and other administration advisory committees.

Admission Requirements

Admission decisions are based on the overall quality of the applicant's high school and/or college courses, the cumulative academic GPA, the quality of the essay, SAT I or ACT scores, one recommendation from a teacher or counselor, and involvement with the school or community. Transfer students applying after completing 30 semester hours or 45 quarter units of college work are not required to submit SAT I or ACT scores.

Application and Information

Freshman candidates are welcome to apply to SCU's early action or regular decision programs during their senior year in high school. SCU's early action program is nonbinding. Applicants who wish to be considered for early action should submit the application by November 15; notifications are sent at the end of December. Applications for regular decision must be postmarked no later than January 15. Transfer candidates must submit applications by May 1 for the fall term and October 1 for the winter term. Prospective students may apply online at the Web site listed below.

Applications and additional information may be obtained by contacting:

Undergraduate Admissions
Santa Clara University
500 El Camino Real
Santa Clara, California 95053
Telephone: 408-554-4700
Fax: 408-554-5255
World Wide Web: http://www.scu.edu

The Mission Garden area of the campus at SCU.

SARAH LAWRENCE COLLEGE

BRONXVILLE, NEW YORK

The College

Sarah Lawrence College is a model for individualized education among leading liberal arts colleges. It offers an innovative program of study that encourages students to take intellectual risks and explore highly challenging topics as they take an active role in the planning and pursuit of their education.

Sarah Lawrence was named 2000 Liberal Arts College of the Year by *Time Magazine/Princeton Review* for its focus on writing.

The College's forty-six buildings are set on a 41-acre campus reminiscent of a rural English village. There are 1,292 undergraduates and 314 graduate students. Approximately 40 students attend the Center for Continuing Education, a flexible, supportive program for returning adult students. The College draws its students from across the country and around the world. Nearly 90 percent live on campus. Sarah Lawrence has an active campus, offering opportunities for involvement in clubs, student organizations, dramatic productions, literary societies, student publications, student government, and intramural athletics. There are no sororities or fraternities.

The College is accredited by the Middle States Association of Colleges and Schools and approved by the New York State Education Department.

On the graduate level, the College offers programs in women's history, human genetics, health advocacy, art of teaching, child development, dance, theater, and writing.

Location

Sarah Lawrence is located in southern Westchester County, 15 miles north of midtown Manhattan. Main roads and the railroad make it possible to reach the city in 30 minutes, enabling students to take advantage of a wide range of social and cultural riches as well as internship possibilities. Students obtain internships in the arts, business, communications, law, medicine, publishing, social services, and the theater.

Majors and Degree

Sarah Lawrence grants the Bachelor of Arts degree to undergraduate students. The academic program is divided into four divisions: history and the social sciences, consisting of anthropology, economics, history, political science, psychology, public policy, science technology and society, and sociology; humanities, consisting of art history, Asian studies, film history, languages, literature, music history, philosophy, and religion; natural sciences and mathematics, consisting of biology, chemistry, mathematics, and physics; and creative and performing arts, consisting of dance, music, theater, writing, and visual arts (ceramic sculpture, drawing, filmmaking, painting, photography, printmaking, and sculpture). There are no required courses or majors, but students are expected to work in at least three of the four divisions.

Academic Program

Each student works with his or her faculty adviser, called a don, in the Oxford and Cambridge tradition, to plan a course of study. Most courses consist of two parts: the seminar, limited to 15 students, and the conference, a private, biweekly meeting with the seminar professor. In conference, students create individual projects that extend the material assigned in the seminar and connect it to their academic and career goals. In the performing arts—dance, music, and theater—students participate in several components that together constitute a full course. While transcripts of official grades are available for graduate school, written evaluations that more clearly define strengths, weaknesses, and progress are provided to each student.

The College operates on the semester system, with terms beginning in early September and late January.

Off-Campus Programs

Sarah Lawrence College sponsors academic programs in Florence; Havana, Cuba; Oxford; and Paris, as well as a program in cooperation with the British American Drama Academy in London. Students may also study in other countries around the world. Students may also combine on-campus study with off-campus fieldwork and internships at a variety of places, including art museums, theaters, and hospitals and with orchestras, dance companies, publications, social action programs, government agencies, and businesses.

Academic Facilities

The College's facilities include classrooms, laboratories, and computer centers; a college-wide academic network to which all students' rooms are fully wired; a T-1 connection to the Internet; a library with 283,000 volumes and 916 periodicals, which is linked by computer to more than 6,000 other libraries; the Performing Arts Center, consisting of four theaters, a dance studio, and a concert hall; a music building, including a music library; a Sports Center with a competition pool, basketball and squash courts, a fitness center, an aerobics room, and a rowing tank; a laboratory preschool; a science center; the Center for Continuing Education; and the Ruth Leff Siegel Center, a student social space. A 60,000-square-foot visual arts center opens in fall 2004 and includes a 200-seat lecture hall/film theater, a café, a new media and sound stage, a darkroom, printmaking facilities, and eight ateliers—each with fifteen to thirty individual work areas.

Costs

Tuition for the 2003–04 academic year was $30,120. The costs of a room and the average meal plan were $10,394. The College fee was $704.

Financial Aid

All applicants with financial need are considered for Sarah Lawrence College aid programs and all federal campus-based programs. About 49 percent of the students receive financial aid. The awarding of institutional funds is based solely upon a determination of the student's financial need. Students are expected to apply for financial aid from the Federal Pell Grant Program and from their state scholarship and grant programs. Students must submit the Financial Aid PROFILE and the Free Application for Federal Student Aid (FAFSA) by February 1.

Faculty

Sarah Lawrence's student-faculty ratio is 6:1, one of the lowest in the country. Students work closely with an exceptional faculty of respected scholars, writers, artists, scientists, historians, and social scientists. Each faculty member is a committed teacher who attaches great importance to individual work with students. Ninety percent of Sarah Lawrence's faculty members in the sciences, social sciences, and the humanities hold a Ph.D. or terminal degree. Faculty members in the arts have achieved demonstrable excellence in the fields of music, dance, theater, the visual arts, and writing.

Student Government

The Sarah Lawrence College student body is self-governed by the Student Senate and the Student Life Committee. The Student Senate is the principal policymaking and legislative body for matters concerning student affairs.

Admission Requirements

Sarah Lawrence College accepts freshman and transfer applicants for both the fall and spring semesters. The College recognizes that intelligence and creative power can be expressed in many different ways and is willing to look at both traditional and nontraditional criteria in assessing applicants. The completion of 16 units of secondary school work or the equivalent is the standard academic requirement for freshman admission. The College does not specify these units but recommends the usual distribution of rigorous college-preparatory courses.

High school seniors who consider Sarah Lawrence their first-choice college and who wish to be informed of an admission decision early in their senior year may apply as early decision candidates. The Admission Committee will also consider as early admission applicants those students with very strong academic qualifications and personal maturity who have completed three years of high school.

The College welcomes transfer applications from students who have completed at least one full year of college and from students who expect, in qualifying for the Bachelor of Arts degree, to spend at least two consecutive years at Sarah Lawrence College. (Students with less than one full year of credits who have matriculated at another college may apply for freshman admission with possible advanced standing.) Approximately 50 transfers matriculate each year from a wide range of postsecondary institutions.

Sophomores, juniors, and seniors enrolled at other institutions may apply to the Sarah Lawrence Guest Year Program for one semester or a complete year of full-time study at the College. Guests attend Sarah Lawrence to concentrate in a particular discipline not offered at their home institution, to work with respected master teachers one-on-one in conferences, and to take advantage of the facilities of New York City in conjunction with rigorous academic study. Students who have not matriculated elsewhere but wish to enroll in one or two specific courses for credit may apply as special students.

The Test of English as a Foreign Language (TOEFL) must be taken by students who speak English as a second language. A personal interview on campus or with a local alumna/alumnus is strongly recommended for all applicants.

Sarah Lawrence College admits students regardless of race, color, sex, sexual orientation, handicap, or national origin and thereafter accords them all the rights and privileges generally made available to students at the College. The College is strongly committed to basing judgments about individuals upon their qualifications and abilities and to protecting individual rights of privacy, association, belief, and expression.

Application and Information

Students interested in attending Sarah Lawrence College should request application materials from the Office of Admission. The application deadline for freshmen for the fall semester is January 1. The notification date is early April, and the reply date is May 1. The College has two early decision programs. The fall early decision deadline is November 15, and notification is made on December 15. The winter early decision deadline is January 1, and notification is made on February 15.

The preferred filing date for transfer applicants for fall semester is March 1. Applications for transfer students are accepted and admission decisions are rendered on a rolling basis. The notification date is May 1, and the reply date is June 1. Applications for spring semester are accepted on a rolling basis. The preferred filing date is December 1. Application forms and additional information may be obtained by contacting:

Office of Admission
Sarah Lawrence College
Bronxville, New York 10708
Telephone: 914-395-2510
800-888-2858 (toll-free)
Fax: 914-395-2515
E-mail: slcadmit@sarahlawrence.edu
World Wide Web: http://www.sarahlawrence.edu

Students relax on Westland's lawn.

SAVANNAH COLLEGE OF ART AND DESIGN

SAVANNAH, GEORGIA

The College

The Savannah College of Art and Design (SCAD) is a private coeducational college that exists to prepare students for careers in the visual and performing arts, design, the building arts, and the history of art and architecture. Founded in 1978, the College offers a solid, innovative curriculum that attracts students from every state and more than 75 countries. Current enrollment is more than 6,200. The College awards Bachelor of Fine Arts (B.F.A.), Master of Fine Arts (M.F.A.), Master of Arts (M.A.), and Master of Architecture (M.Arch.) degrees. A postprofessional M.Arch. degree is also offered.

The College is accredited by the Commission on Colleges of the Southern Association of Colleges and Schools (1866 Southern Lane, Decatur, Georgia 30033-4097; telephone: 404-679-4500) to award bachelor's and master's degrees. The five-year professional M.Arch degree program is accredited by the National Architectural Accrediting Board (NAAB). The College has been recognized by the National Trust for Historic Preservation, the American Institute of Architects and the International Downtown Association, among others, for adaptive reuse of historic buildings.

SCAD competes in the National Association of Intercollegiate Athletics in men's and women's basketball, cross-country, equestrian, golf, rowing, soccer, swimming, and tennis; women's softball and volleyball; and men's baseball.

Location

SCAD is located in Savannah, Georgia, minutes from the Atlantic Ocean. Savannah's renowned National Historic Landmark district provides a culturally diverse, active, and inspiring urban environment for students. An international airport, as well as train and bus service, links the city to domestic and overseas destinations.

Majors and Degrees

Undergraduate and graduate degrees are offered in advertising design, animation, architectural history, architecture, art history, broadcast design, fashion, fibers, film and television, furniture design, graphic design, historic preservation, illustration, industrial design, interactive design and game development, interior design, media and performing arts, metals and jewelry, painting, photography, sequential art, sound design, and visual effects. Minors are offered in all major areas as well as in accessory design, cultural landscape, dance, decorative arts, drawing, electronic design, interaction design, marine design, museum studies, music performance, printmaking, sculpture, urban design and development, and writing. Certificate programs are offered in digital publishing, digital publishing management, historic preservation, and interactive design.

Academic Programs

The College operates on the quarter system. Fall, winter, and spring sessions extend from mid-September through May. Summer sessions in Savannah run from late June through August. Students may earn credits during all sessions.

A balanced curriculum offers a well-rounded liberal arts education, the traditional components of a fine arts education, the opportunity to acquire contemporary high-tech skills through the use of state-of-the-art facilities, and the option of pursuing double majors and multidisciplinary explorations. Total course of study for the B.F.A. degree consists of 180 quarter credit hours (36 courses). Of these, students take 30 to 50 hours in the foundation studies program, 55 to 65 hours in the liberal arts program (with a concentration on art history classes), 60 to 70 hours in the major area of study, and 10 to 20 hours in electives. The five-year professional M.Arch. degree requires 225 hours, which include 35 foundation hours, 65 hours of liberal arts study, 95 hours in the major program, and 30 hours of electives.

Off-Campus Programs

SCAD offers off-campus programs in Europe, Asia, and throughout the United States, emphasizing artistic, historical, and cultural experiences. At SCAD-Lacoste in Lacoste, France, students live, learn, and create in an environment rich in culture and history. Off-campus programs may combine independent study or internships with traditional course work. Some programs focus on specific academic and studio disciplines, while others feature a variety of study options.

Online distance learning programs are offered through SCAD e-learning at http://www.scad.edu/elearning.

Academic Facilities

College facilities include the latest industry-standard equipment. Architecture, interior design, and historic preservation facilities include an intranet of PCs that are configured with electronic design software, including AutoCAD, Bentley Microstation V8, Adobe Photoshop, 3D Studio VIZ, SURFCAM, and Alias/Wavefront Maya. A video microscope, architectural and metals conservation labs, and paint analysis labs are also available.

Art and architectural history students have access to resources, which include College galleries and the Earle W. Newton Center for British-American Studies. Internships with area heritage organizations or museums provide practical experience. Lectures and symposia offer opportunities to meet visiting scholars and professionals.

Animation, broadcast design, interactive design and game development, and visual effects facilities provide access to an intranet of Macintosh G4, Pentium IV, and SGI workstations that are configured with a diverse range of graphics software; high-end 2-D, 3-D, interactive, and compositing tools, including the Adobe product line; Alias/Wavefront Maya; Side Effects' Houdini products; Pixar's Renderman; Avid Softimage XSI, Symphony and Xpress DV; Discreet's 3d max, flame, flint, combustion, and smoke; Animo; and Shake. Other tools include Lightwave and Macromedia products.

Fashion and fibers students use computer-aided design workstations and scanners; Juki industrial sewing machines and sergers; a heat-transfer press; weaving facilities, including four- and eight-shaft floor looms, two AVL CompuDobby looms, and an AVL electronic Jacquard loom.

Furniture design and industrial design facilities include a woodworking and metals and plastics fabrication lab, bench rooms and design studios, a plastic working area, a welding facility, CNC milling, a Stratasys 3-D printer, spray booths, and a finishing room as well as an intranet of PCs configured with AutoCAD, MicroStation, SURFCAM, and Rhino, among other software.

Graphic design and illustration facilities include Macintosh computers with CD burners, scanners, and digital cameras. Adobe Illustrator, InDesign, and Photoshop; Macromedia Director, Dreamweaver, and Flash; Quark XPress; and other graphics packages are available.

Metals and jewelry studios include equipment for fabrication and stone setting, lapidary, precision casting, finishing, enameling, anodizing, CAD/CAM modeling, and forming and stone setting processes. Students also have access to a Stratasys FDM 3000 wax printer and use a network of PCs with a wide range of software, including Adobe Photoshop, Rhino, and SURFCAM.

Photography students utilize digital imaging labs, group and individual black-and-white darkrooms, individual color darkrooms, and graduate darkrooms. Macintosh digital imaging labs with peripherals, Imacon scanners, professional color print processing machines for both negative and reversal papers, E-6 and C-41 color film processing machines, an alternative processes lab, studios, lighting equipment, view camera systems and medium format camera systems, and digital backs also are available.

For film and television students, facilities include a Mark III Rank Cintel telecine and transfer suite; 16 mm, Super 16, and 35 mm film cameras; DV, DV200, and DVC Pro video cameras; a Sony High Definition television camera; Symphony workstations; an Avid Unity MediaNetwork; a mastering suite; Media Composer workstations with interactive CD-ROM/DVD technology; Avid Xpress DV editing stations; digital audio workstations; a Steadicam EFP and Super Panther Dolly; a chromakey/green screen studio; a sound stage; audio postproduction suites; an audio-for-video mixdown suite; a surround sound studio; a midi suite; and an audio production studio that supports a 16-track Pro Tools recording system fronted by a Control 24 digital control surface.

College galleries exhibit work by students, alumni, and faculty members. The College library contains approximately 320,000 slides, 113,000 volumes, 900 periodicals, 6,200 microform units, and 4,200 audiovisual materials. College facilities include a restored 1946 performing arts theater as well as a 150-seat, black-box theater and more than forty computer labs.

Costs

Undergraduate tuition for 2004–05 is $20,250. The housing fee for the academic year ranges from $5300 for dormitory-style to $5400 for apartment-style housing and includes a $250 nonrefundable deposit. Three dining plans offer a designated number of meals per week; the basic rate per quarter is $1010.

Financial Aid

Approximately 54 percent of undergraduates and 45 percent of freshmen receive financial assistance. The Savannah College of Art and Design has a number of financial aid programs, which may consist of scholarships, grants, loans, or any combination of these, from federal (including the Federal Direct Loan Program), state, and college sources. Application may be made at any time during the academic year; however, early application is advised. Students also help finance educational expenses by jobs secured through the Federal Work-Study Program and the College's Student Placement Service. A detailed listing of financial aid programs may be obtained from the admission office.

Faculty

The College maintains a low student-faculty ratio, with small classes taught by professors who hold terminal degrees and/or other outstanding credentials in their fields. Faculty members provide regularly scheduled conferences and extra help sessions.

Student Government

The United Student Forum is composed of representatives from various leadership groups on campus. The Inter-Club Council consists of delegates from the more than forty officially recognized student organizations.

Admission Requirements

Students may apply online at the College's Web site listed below. Undergraduate application requirements include SAT I or ACT scores, official transcripts from the last high school or college attended, a minimum of two recommendations, a statement of purpose, a completed application form, and a nonrefundable application fee of $50. Portfolio/auditions and interviews are encouraged but are not required for undergraduate admission. Home-schooled, transient, and non-degree-seeking applicants are welcome. A minimum SAT math score of 540 or ACT math score of 23 is required for regular acceptance into the architecture program.

A student may be admitted full-time at the end of the junior year in high school (omitting the senior year) or on a part-time basis during the senior year if he or she has a GPA of 3.5 (B+) or higher through the eleventh grade, if the SAT I or ACT scores are above the national average, and if the student's counselor and art teacher recommend early admission. The Rising Star program gives rising high school seniors the chance to experience college during a five-week summer program for college credit. Savannah Summer Seminars are one-week workshops open to high school students.

Transfer students may receive a maximum of 90 credit hours toward a B.F.A. degree. All students must complete in residence the final 45 hours of any degree earned at the College.

International students are encouraged to apply and must submit scores from the Test of English as a Foreign Language (TOEFL), and they must present proof of having adequate funds for one year. SAT I or ACT scores are not required for international students. Scholarships are available.

Exceptions to the general admission criteria may be made for applicants of unusual motivation and ability. The Savannah College of Art and Design admits students of any race, color, and national and ethnic origin to all the rights, privileges, programs, and activities generally accorded or made available to students at the College.

Application and Information

Applicants are encouraged to apply as early as possible. Files are reviewed as soon as they are complete, and applicants are notified immediately of their admission status. Only accepted students are eligible for scholarship consideration and federal/state aid.

For more information about the Savannah College of Art and Design, students should contact:

Admission Department
Savannah College of Art and Design
P.O. Box 2072
Savannah, Georgia 31402-2072
Telephone: 912-525-5100
800-869-7223 (toll-free)
Fax: 912-525-5986
E-mail: admission@scad.edu
World Wide Web: http://www.scad.edu

Poetter Hall.

SAVANNAH STATE UNIVERSITY

SAVANNAH, GEORGIA

The University

As the oldest public, historically black institution in Georgia, Savannah State University has been transforming the lives of generations of students in a nurturing learning environment since its founding in 1890. As a senior coeducational unit of the University System of Georgia, Savannah State continues that tradition in classrooms where cutting-edge instruction is complemented by one of the smallest student-faculty ratios in the region. The University is committed to serving students who are well prepared academically. Its programs are designed to provide opportunities for students to improve themselves, attain career objectives, and compete effectively in the job market. Savannah State offers undergraduate and graduate degrees in three colleges: the College of Business Administration, the College of Liberal Arts and Social Sciences, and the College of Sciences and Technology. Master's degrees are available in marine sciences, public administration, social work, and urban studies. All degree programs at Savannah State University are accredited by the Southern Association of Colleges and Schools. The programs in civil, electronics, and mechanical engineering technology are accredited by the Accreditation Board for Engineering and Technology and the social work programs by the Council on Social Work Education. The public administration program is accredited by the National Association of Schools of Public Affairs and Administration.

Most of the 2,800 undergraduate students enrolled at Savannah State University are Georgia residents, although eighteen states and seventeen other countries are represented. Students can participate in numerous social and academic organizations as well as in intercollegiate and intramural sports. Savannah State athletes compete in baseball, basketball, cross-country, football, tennis, track, volleyball, and more. Campus housing options include traditional residence halls and an apartment-style complex that features fully-furnished one-, two-, and four-bedroom apartments. A new Freshman Living Learning Center opened August 2003 to house new students in a state-of-the-art environment.

Location

The University is located in the Hostess City of the South, beautiful, historic Savannah, Georgia. The campus is a 10-minute drive from the Atlantic Ocean and the sandy beaches of Tybee Island. Students at Savannah State enjoy the best of two worlds—the cultural advantages of a metropolitan city and the sun and surf of the ocean and boating, fishing, and waterskiing on the many area rivers. The city also offers excellent golfing and tennis facilities.

Savannah offers exciting scientific resources like the Skidaway Marine Science Complex. Culturally, the city offers the Savannah Symphony Orchestra, ballet and theater groups, the Telfair Museum of Arts and Sciences, the King-Tisdell Black Heritage Museum, and special celebrations and festivals such as Night in Old Savannah. Savannah State University partners with the city to produce the annual Black Heritage Festival, a month-long heritage celebration that includes lectures, dance performances, concerts, and more.

Savannah has a population of approximately 250,000 and is famous for its Low Country cuisine, scenic boat tours, specialty shops, and riverfront activities. The international airport and extensive railway system make Savannah easily accessible to all of the Southeast and the nation.

Majors and Degrees

Savannah State University provides innovative instruction of high quality through the College of Business Administration, the College of Liberal Arts and Social Sciences, and the College of Sciences and Technology.

The College of Business Administration offers programs that lead to the Bachelor of Business Administration in accounting, computer information systems, management, and marketing.

The College of Liberal Arts and Social Sciences grants the Bachelor of Arts degree in Africana studies, English language and literature, history, and mass communication and the Bachelor of Science degree in criminal justice, political science, and sociology. The College offers a Bachelor of Social Work degree and a Bachelor of Fine Arts degree in visual and performing arts with concentrations in music, visual arts, theater, and dance. Minor areas include Africana studies, art, criminal justice, English language and literature, French, gerontology, history, mass communication, political science, psychology, religious and philosophical studies, sociology, Spanish, and theater.

The College of Sciences and Technology offers the Bachelor of Science degree in biology (premedicine or preprofessional), chemical engineering technology, chemistry, civil engineering technology, computer science technology, electronics engineering technology, environmental studies, marine sciences, mathematics, and mechanical engineering technology.

Academic Programs

The core curriculum of the University System of Georgia is the foundation upon which all degree programs are built. All candidates for a baccalaureate degree must complete a minimum of 125 semester hours, including health, physical education, and orientation; maintain a scholastic average of C or better; and satisfactorily complete the minimum requirements of the core curriculum and of the specific degree programs. Students must also satisfactorily complete the University System of Georgia Regents' Exam and the major comprehensive examinations as prescribed by their specific schools.

The University offers four-year Naval ROTC programs and two-year and three-year Army ROTC programs through either a scholarship or a regular University program. Graduates receive a commission as a second lieutenant in the U.S. Marine Corps, as an ensign in the U.S. Navy, or as a second lieutenant in the U.S. Army. The Army and Naval ROTC programs constitute academic minors in military science and naval science, respectively.

The University operates on the semester system, with each semester extending over a period of fifteen weeks. Normally, the baccalaureate degree is earned in eight semesters. A full course load is considered to be 12 hours, with the maximum load being 19 hours.

Savannah State may grant credit for satisfactory scores on selected tests of the College-Level Examination Program (CLEP), for satisfactory completion of appropriate courses and tests offered through DANTES (formerly the United States Armed Forces Institute), for work completed at military service schools, and for military experience as recommended by the Commission on Accreditation of Service Experiences of the American Council on Education. Such credits may not exceed more than one fourth of the work counted toward a degree. Advanced Placement scores are accepted from the College Board.

Off-Campus Programs

The cooperative education program provides an off-campus option that enables students to receive on-the-job training while earning money for their tuition. The University arranges and approves assignments with cooperating companies and agencies, and supervision is provided by representatives of the University as well as the employers.

Savannah State University students travel across the globe. The study-abroad program takes students and faculty members to universities in Ghana and the Republic of China and to the Caribbean. Exchange agreements with universities in Ghana, China, and the Virgin Islands provide faculty members and students with enriching experiences.

Academic Facilities

Gordon Library, a modern library with excellent facilities and a well-prepared staff, serves the University and the community. It houses more than 182,000 cataloged volumes, approximately 900 periodicals, more than 558,000 microfilms, and 25,000 bound periodicals. Approximately 8,000 volumes are added yearly to keep the collection up-to-date. There is an extensive collection of materials about African Americans. The library, which is the cultural and intellectual center of the University, can house 290,000 volumes. The building has many conference and individual study areas, an audiovisual department, two Distance Learning Centers, a Curriculum Materials Center, open stacks, classrooms, and computer stations. The library is easily distinguishable from the other buildings on campus because of its distinctive circular shape.

Other campus facilities include the College of Business building and the Marine Sciences Wet Laboratory.

Costs

In 2003–04, tuition and fees for students living on campus were $3664 per semester for Georgia residents and $6982 per semester for non-Georgia residents. The above costs include the matriculation fee, health fee, student activity fee, athletics fee, room, and board. Books cost approximately $300 per semester. The costs for housing varies, depending on the type of residence hall.

Financial Aid

Almost 90 percent of all Savannah State University students receive financial aid through federal and state grants, including Pell Grants, Supplemental Educational Opportunity Grants, Georgia Incentive Grants, Perkins Loans, College Work-Study Program awards, and work opportunities provided by the University. Students requesting financial aid are required to submit the Free Application for Federal Student Aid (FAFSA).

Faculty

Savannah State University has a full-time faculty of 157 members, with nearly 70 percent of them holding an earned doctorate. The full-time student-faculty ratio is 15:1.

Student Government

The Student Government Association serves the needs of the students; its members are elected by the student body. This organization is set up with executive, legislative, and judicial branches, and it is influential in campus affairs. The Student Government Association is the chief student organization on campus. It helps to govern the student body as well as to plan social events for the academic year. Students also serve on all major University committees.

Admission Requirements

Factors considered in assessing a student's readiness for admission to Savannah State University include the high school grade point average and curriculum, test scores, previous college work, and other qualifications. Each applicant for admission to the freshman class is required to take the SAT I or the ACT. Minimum scores on the SAT I are 430 verbal and 400 math. The minimum composite score on the ACT is 17; the minimum English and math scores are also 17. Completion of the College Preparatory Curriculum (CPC) is required. Transfers must have maintained a minimum 2.0 grade point average.

Application and Information

Application can be made anytime following completion of the junior year of high school. Students are notified of the admission decision soon after receipt of the completed application and supporting documents.

Office of Admissions
Savannah State University
P.O. Box 20209
Savannah, Georgia 31404
Telephone: 912-356-2181
800-788-0478 (toll-free)
Fax: 912-356-2256
World Wide Web: http://www.admissions.savstate.edu

SCHILLER INTERNATIONAL UNIVERSITY

DUNEDIN, FLORIDA

The University

Schiller International University (SIU) was founded in 1964. Although originally intended for American students, the University soon attracted men and women from other nations and is now an international, coeducational four-year institution with eight locations in six countries and alumni from more than 130 countries. SIU prepares students for careers in business and management, multinational organizations, government agencies, academic institutions, and the social services as well as for further study. Through enrollment in both practical and theoretical courses and through discussions with instructors and classmates with multicultural backgrounds, students gain firsthand knowledge of business and cultural relations among the peoples of the world. In addition, SIU students have the unique opportunity to transfer between SIU campuses, without losing any credits, while continuing their chosen program of study. The language of instruction at all campuses is English. The current enrollment is 1,500 students.

SIU students are housed in University residence halls, with selected host families, or in private rooms or apartments. On-campus residence is required at the Engelberg campus. Residence hall accommodations are also available at the London and Florida campuses and in Heidelberg, Strasbourg, and Leysin. At all campuses not requiring on-campus residence, or in the event that all residence halls are full, trained staff members assist students in securing housing in the private market or with families.

SIU offers the Master of Arts degree in international hotel and tourism management and in international relations and diplomacy with an optional specialization in international business or European studies; the Master of Business Administration degree in international business, IT management, hotel and tourism management, and international hotel and tourism management; and the Master of International Management in international business.

Schiller International University is an accredited member of the Accrediting Council for Independent Colleges and Schools, which is recognized by the United States Department of Education as a national institutional accrediting agency. SIU degrees correspond to the American system of university education and are authorized at the European campuses by the Delaware State Board of Education and at the Florida campus by the Florida State Board of Independent Colleges and Universities.

Location

Schiller International University has campuses in Dunedin, Florida; central London, England; Paris and Strasbourg, France; Heidelberg, Germany; Madrid, Spain; and Engelberg and Leysin, Switzerland. More detail about each campus location is offered below.

SIU–Florida (residential)—the main campus is in the city of Dunedin on the Gulf of Mexico, one of America's most beautiful coastal regions, near the Tampa–St. Petersburg metropolitan area. The campus facilities, a large former hotel and three additional buildings, face directly on the beach and include a large auditorium and swimming pool. The English Language Institute–Florida is on campus.

SIU–London—Waterloo (central London–residential) is in the magnificent Royal Waterloo House, centrally located near the Waterloo Bridge and the South Bank cultural center.

SIU–Paris (nonresidential) is centrally located in a modern building on the left bank of the Seine in the exciting Montparnasse area, with easy access to all of Paris.

SIU–Strasbourg (residential) occupies the Château de Pourtalès in Robertsau at the northern edge of the city. The Château offers classroom, dormitory, and dining facilities (two restaurants and a Salon de Thé) and access to the European Community's Parliament Building and Court of Justice in Strasbourg.

SIU–Heidelberg (residential) is located next to the Law School of the University of Heidelberg in the center of town. The Graduate Center and student residence are located just across the Neckar River in the beautiful Palais Friedrich.

SIU–Madrid (nonresidential) is located in a modern building in the Arguelles, one of the city's most attractive districts.

SIU–Engelberg (Switzerland-residential) is located in SIU's Hotel Europe, a large, well-known hotel of long tradition, and in the lovely Hotel Bellevue, both in the heart of the Swiss Alps, not far from Lucerne.

American College of Switzerland (residential) is a campus of SIU located above the eastern end of Lake Geneva in the French-speaking portion of Switzerland, near Geneva and the French and Italian borders. (A separate catalog is available.)

Majors and Degrees

Schiller International University offers the Bachelor of International Business Administration (B.B.A. in international business) degree, with concentrations in banking, financial management, management, and marketing. Schiller also offers the Bachelor of Business Administration degree in club management and in international hotel and tourism management, with concentrations in hotel management and tourism management.

The Bachelor of Arts (B.A.) degree is offered in interdepartmental studies, international economics, international relations and diplomacy, and psychology.

The Bachelor of Business Administration (B.B.A.) degree is offered in economics, IT management, and international business administration.

The associate degree in business administration (A.S.) is offered in club management and with an optional concentration in computer system management.

Schiller also offers the associate degree in business administration (A.S.) in international hotel and tourism management, with concentrations in hotel management and tourism management.

Associate of Science (A.S.) degrees are offered in premedicine and pre–veterinary medicine.

Associate of Arts (A.A.) degrees are offered in general studies, with a concentration in art and design.

Diplomas are available in hotel operational management and Swiss hotel management. The hotel operational management diploma requires two semesters of on-campus study and a six-month internship.

Certificates (awarded after completion of a one-year program) are offered in hotel operations.

Academic Program

The academic emphasis at Schiller International University is on international business, international relations and diplomacy, international hotel and tourism management, and languages.

The Collegium Palatinum, a division of the University, offers intensive language programs in German, French, and Spanish and in English as a foreign language (EFL) at the Language Institutes located on various campuses. EFL courses are offered at all SIU campuses. Regular University courses in German, French, Spanish, and English are also offered, although not all languages are available at every campus.

An associate degree program requires 62 credits; a bachelor's degree program requires 124 credits. An average grade of C (2.0) or higher is required for all programs. Each credit reflects 15 academic hours of classroom work; typical courses earn 3–4 credits.

Classes run during two 15-week semesters and a seven-week summer session in a manner similar to that at most universities in the United States.

Academic Facilities

Each campus includes classrooms, computer facilities, a library, and a student lounge. The University library holdings are about 92,000 volumes. In addition, students have access to extensive external libraries for original research.

Costs

For 2002–03, tuition and required fees at the Florida campus were $6780 per semester; room and board were $2850 per semester. Costs at the European campuses were $7280 per semester for tuition and required fees and $3600 per semester for room and board. Full room and board are available in London and Engelberg only; room without board is available in Heidelberg. The American College of Switzerland campus has a separate schedule of fees. Students are encouraged to see that school's statistical profile information at the front of this volume.

Financial Aid

SIU grants two kinds of financial aid: academic scholarships (for 200 students) and University service (work-study) grants. Total aid does not exceed one half of the tuition. Students are encouraged to seek assistance through private or government loan and scholarship programs before applying to the University. Eligible students may apply for a Federal Stafford Student Loan (U.S. citizens only) or a Canada Student Loan (Canadian citizens only). Applications for financial aid must be received by March 31 for the following academic year.

Faculty

The faculty consists of more than 280 men and women who are academically qualified and experienced in their fields. Extensive student-faculty interaction is encouraged; the student-faculty ratio is about 18:1.

Student Government

Each campus has an elected Student Council that acts as a liaison between the students and the administration and is involved in many areas of academic and social life.

Admission Requirements

Applicants must have completed the secondary level of education in a government-recognized educational system, generally of twelve years' duration, or have the equivalent of five GCE-O-level examinations (British school system). Students who have not completed the equivalent of high school studies or five GCE-O-level examinations may be eligible to apply for special University-preparatory programs.

All nonnative English speakers must take the SIU–English Placement Test when first enrolling. Those whose English language proficiency is not adequate for University-level studies are required to take additional English language courses.

Application and Information

Applications are handled individually and without regard to race, sex, religion, national or ethnic origin, or country of citizenship. Because SIU operates on a rolling admissions system, applicants are advised of their admission status soon after all application materials (a completed application form and official transcripts of all secondary-level education and, for transfer applicants, all college-level study) and the $50 application fee have been received. For application forms or further information, students should contact either admissions office listed below.

Admissions Office
Royal Waterloo House
Schiller International University
51-55 Waterloo Road
London, SE1 8TX
England
Telephone: 44-20-7928-8484
Fax: 44-20-7620 1226

Admissions Office
Schiller International University
453 Edgewater Drive
Dunedin, Florida 34698-7532
Telephone: 727-736-5082
800-336-4133 (toll-free within the U.S. only)
Fax: 727-734-0359
E-mail: admissions@schiller.edu
World Wide Web: http://www.schiller.edu/

The Dunedin, Florida, campus of Schiller International University.

SCHOOL OF THE ART INSTITUTE OF CHICAGO

CHICAGO, ILLINOIS

The School

Founded in 1866 as the Chicago Academy of Design, the School of the Art Institute of Chicago has been in continuous operation since then. The Michigan Avenue Museum building was originally constructed for the 1892 Columbian Exposition; in 1895, the Museum and the School acquired the structure. Expansion has continued through the years, and currently School facilities number five buildings. In 1997, the School purchased a 190-bed residence hall; in fall 2000, another 467-bed residence hall opened. The School now enrolls 1,707 full- and part-time undergraduate students representing forty-nine states and forty countries. Students are granted free entrance to the Art Institute of Chicago.

The School believes in facilitating the artist's imaginative depth and reach and seeks to promote the climate and base from which students can explore many artistic directions through a variety of media. No single aesthetic or style dominates the curriculum, the faculty, or the work of students. Every member of the faculty and staff and every student influences the School and helps determine its present and future directions.

The School offers a broad spectrum of services to accommodate its diverse population, including an international student office, multicultural affairs office, health and counseling services, and a learning center (offering one-on-one tutoring as well as support services for students with learning disabilities). Students may also take advantage of cooperative education opportunities throughout Chicago and the nation with individual artists, museums and galleries, multimedia firms, film and video production houses, interior architecture firms, fashion designers, and community service organizations. In addition, the Career Development Center recognizes the varied opportunities for employment in art-related fields and offers students assistance in developing skills, such as writing grants; preparing portfolios, artist statements, and teaching philosophies; exploring exhibition possibilities; and understanding the legal aspects of entrepreneurship. The center also maintains listings of many local and national positions, including freelance, part-time, and full-time employment.

Location

The School of the Art Institute of Chicago is located in the heart of downtown Chicago, the nation's third-largest city and home to the nation's second-largest art scene, including museums, more than 150 galleries, alternative spaces, and organizations supporting the arts. Students have a wide variety of cultural and recreational resources from which to choose: ballet, opera, theater, orchestra halls, cinemas, libraries, architecture, blues and jazz clubs, parks, ethnic restaurants, and street festivals. An extensive public transportation system allows students access to citywide events and to outlying communities.

Majors and Degrees

The School of the Art Institute of Chicago offers a four-year program leading to the Bachelor of Fine Arts degree, working in one or any combination of the following studio areas: art and technology, art education, ceramics, fashion design, fiber, filmmaking, interior architecture, painting and drawing, performance, photography, printmaking, sculpture, sound, video, and visual communication. The School also offers a Bachelor of Interior Architecture program, intended for students who plan to become registered professional interior designers. In addition, the School offers Illinois teacher certification (K–12) in art education, a Bachelor of Fine Arts degree with emphasis in art history, and a Bachelor of Arts in visual and critical studies.

Academic Program

Completion of 132 hours is required for the B.F.A. and B.A. degrees, approximately two thirds being in studio areas and one third in academic course work. All entering students who have completed fewer than 18 semester hours of college-level studio art must enroll in the First Year Program. Students in the First Year Program take two-, three-, and four-dimensional (performance, video, film, electronics, and kinetics) studio courses, art history, elective course work, and attend colloquium presentations that feature visiting artists and various School department heads. Majors are not required, and students develop their own areas of concentration with faculty and staff members' guidance. Courses are graded on a pass/fail basis.

Off-Campus Programs

Students attending the School of the Art Institute of Chicago can choose from a wide variety of off-campus programs. The Mobility program allows students to attend partner schools within the United States and Canada and includes the New York Studio semester. The School also maintains semester exchange agreements with more than twenty schools in Europe, Asia, and South America. The Off-Campus Programs office works closely with students to help them develop their individual programs. The School's faculty members also lead two- or three-week study trips during each summer and winter interim. In the past, groups have gone to China, England, France, Ireland, Italy, South Africa, and Vietnam.

Academic Facilities

The School of the Art Institute of Chicago's campus encompasses six buildings in downtown Chicago. There are fully equipped studios for each area of concentration, and the School's policy allows 24-hour access to facilities. In 1995, a 40,000-square-foot permanent exhibition space was added.

The painting and drawing department has many well-lit studios, individual space for select undergraduate and graduate students, and space for critiques. There are classes in particular disciplines, such as figure painting and drawing and materials and techniques as well as classes that encourage freely creative activity. Facilities in the sculpture department include a complete wood shop, a welding shop, a bronze and aluminum foundry, a plaster room, and an outdoor exhibition space. A well-equipped metals shop allows for forging, forming, joining, and casting of nonferrous metals. The printmaking department has five etching presses, six stone lithography presses, a Heidelberg Kord and Chief offset press, a process camera, a large-format camera, a professional photomechanical darkroom, bookbinding equipment, a Macintosh computer lab, and a Novajet printer.

The art and technology department supports several computer labs, including Macintosh-based labs and Silicon Graphics facilities equipped with ten Maya systems; in addition, an input-output room supports printing and scanning. All labs are networked together and are connected to the Internet via a high-speed link. The department also maintains a high-end video editing room, a multimedia authoring suite, an electronics construction shop, a microcontroller development and programming area, a kinetics shop, a fully equipped neon studio, a holography studio, dedicated installation space, and MIDI and digital sound systems. The film, video and new media department currently has a full range of video tools, ranging from a unique hand-built image processor to the latest industrial equipment. Editing systems support Hi-8, ¾-inch, S-VHS, and Beta SP, and there are AVID and MEDIA 100 digital editing suites. Equipment available to students includes Hi-8 and digital cameras, projectors, switchers, light kits, and microphones.

In addition, the department facilities also include a sixty-seat theater, a 25-foot shooting set, work studios for 3-D and 2-D animation, and a professional interlock sound suite. Equipment for students includes sync and nonsync cameras, sound equipment, optical printers, a wet lab for image processing, and an animation stand and camera. The photography department has three large printing labs, an alternative process darkroom, fourteen individual color exposing rooms, three mural printing rooms, 30 inch by 50 inch processors for color negative and positive printing, a computer classroom with thirteen stations, a computer peripheral with flatbed and a variety of film scanners, a 4 by 5 film recorder, various inkjet printers, and a 36-inch Novajet inkjet printer. Equipment checkout privileges give students access to photography equipment, supplies, and chemicals.

The ceramics department facilities include three clay mixers, an extruder, a slab roller, complete mold making and casting facilities, and several styles of wheels. Bulk materials (clay, slip, and glazes) are provided, and diverse firing options in various kiln styles include high- and low-fire oxidation and reduction, soda, and raku. The visual communication department facilities include a state-of-the-art computer lab with color scanners, a copy stand, and spacious studios. Fashion design students study design and construction in a spacious facility with industrial-grade equipment and a dedicated staff. The department houses a Fashion Resource Center with a collection of worldwide designer garments and a research library with rare books, videotapes, and international publications. The fiber and material studies department has thirty-two looms, a large area for hand construction, a computer lab with five stations, a computer loom, and a kitchen with industrial-sized washers and dryers used for the setting of dyes.

The John M. Flaxman Library collections include approximately 60,000 volumes on art and the liberal arts and sciences, 360 periodical subscriptions, and films, videos, audiotapes, CDs, microforms, and picture files. The Joan Flasch Artists' Book Collection contains more than 3,000 artists' books along with a research collection of exhibition catalogs and other related material. Students may also utilize the research collections of the Art Institute of Chicago's Ryerson and Burnham Libraries, one of the oldest, largest, and finest art museum libraries in the country. Its noncirculating, closed-stack collections include more than 300,000 volumes and 2,225 periodicals, constituting an invaluable resource for students of the history of art and architecture. The MacLean Visual Resource Center maintains a noncirculating collection of more than 500,000 slides.

The Video Data Bank houses more than 1,800 titles by and about contemporary artists, including experimental tapes spanning the history of video as an art form. The Film Center is a theater, research center, and archive, screening more than 500 films per year. The Poetry Center at the School provides a forum for public reading by local, national, and international poets and writers.

The School's exhibition spaces include the Betty Rymer Gallery, which highlights work from departments and presents special exhibitions, and Gallery 2, with exhibition space, a performance space, and a space designed for site-specific installations. In addition, Gallery X and the Lounge Gallery, sponsored by the Student Union Galleries, provide exhibition space for currently enrolled students.

Costs

Tuition for the 2003–04 academic year was $24,000 for full-time undergraduate students $800 per credit hour. For 2003–04, student housing facilities cost $8770 per academic year for a single room or $7300 per academic year for double occupancy. Unlike most schools, the School does not charge a lab or activities fee in addition to tuition. The estimated costs for books and supplies, room and board, travel, and personal expenses are between $12,000 and $14,000 per academic year, depending on individual need.

Financial Aid

The School makes every effort to assist students who need help in financing their education. Through an extensive financial aid program, $13.2 million in gift aid funding from private, institutional, state, and federal sources is distributed annually. In addition to scholarships and grants, the School grants merit scholarships and offers an extensive college work-study program. To apply for financial aid, students should complete the Free Application for Federal Student Aid (FAFSA), available online at http://www.fafsa.gov. To receive priority consideration, students should submit completed forms to the Financial Aid Office no later than March 1. All awards are made on a first-come, first-served basis to students in good standing who demonstrate need.

Faculty

Faculty members are selected for their effectiveness and dedication as teachers and for their professional activity and commitment as artists, designers, and scholars. There are currently 347 full- and part-time faculty members, among them 10 Guggenheim recipients and numerous NEA and NEH grant recipients. Each year, more than 100 well-known visiting artists, including poets and political activists, as well as visual artists, present workshops and provide individual student critiques.

Student Government

Student government officers are elected each spring, and their mission is to promote student interests and concerns to the broader School community. Student government representatives attend faculty department heads meetings and space-planning meetings and often sit on search committees for new faculty members. Open student government meetings are held weekly.

Admission Requirements

The School maintains a selective admission policy, favoring students who demonstrate an interest in producing work and exploring the possibilities of the visual arts in a professional setting. High school graduates, recipients of a high school equivalency certificate, and college transfer students are invited to apply. To be considered for the B.F.A. program, applicants are required to submit the admissions application; a nonrefundable application fee of $65; a portfolio of fifteen to twenty slides or original pieces showing a full range of the applicant's work; a statement of purpose; transcript(s) from high school(s) or an official copy of the high school equivalency certificate; transcripts from any college previously attended; one letter of recommendation; and, for all applicants who do not have two full years of college credit, SAT I or ACT scores and TOEFL scores for international students. Applicants with more than 18 semester hours of studio transfer credit must submit thirty slides of their art work, representing their current interest and educational experience. In addition to the above, the portfolio of Bachelor of Interior Architecture applicants should demonstrate understanding of and sensitivity to the built environment, including drawings from direct observation and a selection of plans, sections, and elevations.

Application and Information

Students may apply to the School by using the Immediate Decision Option (IDO) or the traditional admission procedure. The Immediate Decision Option allows those students who bring the required application materials listed above to visit the School on a designated day and have an admissions decision made at the end of that day. IDO applicants are encouraged to bring actual work with them rather than slides. During an IDO day, students tour the School facility, meet with currently enrolled students, and attend financial aid and career presentations.

Those students applying through the traditional admission procedure have their portfolio and academic credentials reviewed and evaluated by the Admissions Committee. Students are admitted on a rolling basis and are informed of the committee's decision by mail. Students who anticipate a need for financial assistance are urged to complete applications for admission and financial aid by March 1 in order to receive priority consideration. Students may apply online at http://www.artic.edu/saia/ugapp.

Office of Admissions
School of the Art Institute of Chicago
37 South Wabash
Chicago, Illinois 60603

Telephone: 312-899-5219
800-232-7242 (toll-free)
E-mail: admiss@artic.edu
World Wide Web: http://www.artic.edu/saic/

SCHOOL OF THE MUSEUM OF FINE ARTS

BOSTON, MASSACHUSETTS

The School

The School of the Museum of Fine Arts (SMFA) offers students the opportunity to design their own individualized course of study and to tailor a program that best suits their needs and goals. A division of the Museum of Fine Arts and in partnership with Tufts University, the Museum School offers a diverse curriculum with a full range of studio and academic resources. A large faculty of working artists and an intimate student-faculty ratio of 10:1 provide each student extensive opportunities for individual consultation and dialogue.

Similar to an artists' colony, the Museum School's focus is on creative investigation, risk-taking, and the exploration of individual vision. For artists working in the new millennium, individual vision may take many forms: private acts of object-making, performance, collaboration, electronic imaging, or computer networking.

In order to educate individuals who will become working artists of significance in local and global culture, the Museum School embraces a wide range of media and perspectives in the production of artwork. Similarly, the School makes available a number of different programs to accommodate the varied backgrounds and experiences of the individuals who attend.

The School's extensive interdisciplinary studio curriculum is developed continually in order to incorporate new media and new approaches, concepts, and theories. A rapidly changing and culturally diverse art world is further introduced through the School's dynamic exhibition and visiting artists programs.

Since the studio curriculum is entirely elective, the School requires only that students determine which faculty member, classroom, peer, and community resources are important for their development, and then pursue their work.

Students are free to work in a single medium or move across media, combining them according to their interests and inclinations. In this way, each student shapes a focus. Students may work in painting and video, in electronic imaging and stained glass, or in printmaking, film, and drawing—the combinations are endless, as are the results. To navigate such a liberal approach, students meet with faculty members and advisers for one full week prior to their first semester and then continuously throughout each semester.

Student Services has a knowledgeable staff that is available to assist students in finding living accommodations and to answer questions. Residence hall housing is available at a new state-of-the-art dormitory, built exclusively for artists, and at neighboring Simmons College (for women). The office also provides a comprehensive guide to housing in the city and listings of local realtors, studio contacts, and currently available apartments and roommates.

In addition to its undergraduate degree and diploma programs, the Museum School offers a postbaccalaureate certificate as well as a Master of Arts in Teaching and Master of Fine Arts in partnership with Tufts University.

Location

Boston is home to many educational and cultural institutions. The Museum School is a vital member of the art community, presenting a dynamic schedule of exhibitions, lectures, and panel discussions throughout the year. A variety of social events and activities are also presented, including frequent trips to New York City. An extensive public transportation system includes subways, buses, and commuter trains.

Majors and Degrees

The School of the Museum of Fine Arts offers the following programs: the all-studio diploma, the fifth-year certificate, and the post-baccalaureate certificate. In affiliation with Tufts University, it offers the following degree programs: B.F.A., B.F.A. in art education, and the five-year combined B.A./B.S. and B.F.A. The School offers courses in the following areas: art of Africa, artists' books and multiples, ceramics, computer arts, drawing, electronic arts, film and animation, glass, graphic design and illustration, metalsmithing, painting, papermaking, performance, photography, printmaking, sculpture, video, and visual and critical studies.

Academic Programs

Students design their own programs of study, with advice from teachers and members of the administration. The only limitations on this elective system in studio art are the prerequisites stipulated for some courses. The School recommends basic courses for students who need foundation work in any studio area.

Teaching methods range from structured classes, requiring regular attendance, to individual instruction for work done independently outside the School, with periodic visits by the teacher.

Students' studio art work is evaluated at the end of every semester by a review board made up of teachers and students; the student being reviewed participates in this evaluation. Letter grades are not given for studio courses. Students advance on an individual basis. In some cases, extra credits are granted for exceptional accomplishments, permitting a student to graduate in less than the usual four years. Academic courses are graded in the traditional manner.

The School's degree programs, offered in partnership with Tufts University, are variations on the diploma curriculum. Students in the degree programs take courses in studio art at the School and courses in academic areas of study at Tufts.

To earn a diploma, students must accumulate 120 studio credits. B.F.A. programs require a range of eighteen to twenty-four academic courses (depending on the program) and 90 semester-hour credits in studio art.

The Museum School also offers selective cross-registration with MIT and a dual-degree program with Wheaton College. The School is also a member of the Pro Arts Consortium, which allows students to take classes on a space-available basis at Berklee College of Music, the Boston Architectural Center, Emerson College, the Boston Conservatory, and Massachusetts College of Art.

Academic Facilities

The School is a division of the Museum of Fine Arts. Students and faculty members have special privileges of access to the museum's curatorial departments and library. The School also has its own library. The Exhibition Committee plans a program of shows covering work accomplished during the entire academic year. Work by students in each area of the School is represented on a rotating basis in the lobby, corridor, and student galleries.

Costs

For 2003–04, the full-year tuition for a diploma program was $21,320. Tuition for degree program students in any one semester varies individually with the ratio of academic to studio courses taken in that semester.

Financial Aid

Financial aid is awarded on the basis of demonstrated financial need; approximately 70 percent of the undergraduates apply for financial aid of which more than 80 percent are recipients. Merit scholarships range from advanced standing to full tuition scholarships. Students are eligible to apply for Federal Pell Grants, Federal Supplemental Educational Opportunity Grants, Federal Work-Study Program awards, Federal Stafford Student Loans, and SMFA Scholarships, which range from $200 to full tuition. The priority deadline for receipt of completed application forms is February 15. Students should contact the Financial Aid Office to request the necessary forms.

Faculty

All faculty members who teach studio courses are practicing professional artists who have regional, national, and international reputations in their fields. There are 50 full-time and 93 part-time faculty members. Selected members of the undergraduate faculty also work with graduate students. The student-faculty ratio is approximately 10:1.

Student Government

The standing committees of the School, made up of administrative staff members, students, and faculty members, meet regularly to review the School's goals, curriculum, and problems. Proposals voted on and approved by the School's Executive Committee become part of the School's program. Each student, teacher, or member of the administration has an equal opportunity to join committees and the Student Government Association.

Admission Requirements

The Admissions Committee endeavors to select for entrance those applicants who appear highly motivated and best suited by apparent creative potential and background to benefit from the professional education offered by the School.

Diploma evaluation criteria is based primarily on the strength of the applicant's portfolio. Degree program evaluation criteria consists of a review of the applicant's portfolio as well as the strength of his or her academic records. At the discretion of the committee, certain applicants may be invited to attend a six-week summer session before a final decision on acceptance is made. The School strongly recommends that prospective students arrange to tour the School or have an interview before a formal application is filed. Qualified secondary school students in their junior year are encouraged to apply at that time for early acceptance for the term beginning in the September following their senior year.

Because of the special structure of the School, the status of transfer students differs from that at other schools. Transfer students are placed at a studio level that the Admissions Committee deems appropriate, based on their portfolio presentation. Academic courses are transferable up to a maximum of eight courses for the B.F.A. and B.F.A. in art education programs and twelve courses for the combined B.F.A. with B.A./B.S. program.

Application and Information

Applicants should arrange for all of the following to be delivered to the School: transcripts from the secondary school and any institution of higher education attended, official SAT I or ACT scores, an application form and the $45 nonrefundable application fee, and a portfolio. The portfolio of work must be sent to the School to be reviewed by the Admissions Committee. The School intentionally does not designate any specific composition or number of pieces for the portfolio, yet a minimum of twenty pieces is recommended. Portfolios should be made up of what the applicant—rather than an art teacher, counselor, or relative—feels best shows a potential for development in visual art. Freehand drawing is often useful for the portfolio, but work in any technique may be submitted. A wide variety of techniques is not in itself considered a virtue. Original work is accepted, though slides are preferred.

The admission deadline for the diploma program is on a rolling basis. Portfolios received from September to May are reviewed within ten days, and diploma applicants are notified of the Admissions Committee's decision by mail within three weeks. Portfolios received from June through August are reviewed on a weekly basis. Students may be accepted to the diploma program for the second semester beginning in January. The regular procedure is followed, and all application materials should be delivered to the School by December 15. The deadlines for application to B.F.A. or B.F.A. in art education programs is February 1 for first-time freshmen and March 1 for transfer students for spring admission; the deadlines for spring admission are October 1 for first-time freshmen and November 15 for transfer students. The deadline for application to the combined B.A./B.S. and B.F.A. programs is January 1 for first-time freshmen and March 1 for transfer students for fall admission, and for spring admission, November 15 for both first-time freshmen and transfer students. Applicants to the degree programs will be notified of the Committee's decision by April 1 for fall admission and December 1 for spring admission.

Applications from international students are welcome. Applicants from countries other than the United States should offer documentary evidence of financial resources sufficient to satisfy all educational and living expenses for one year of study at the School. Applicants whose native language is not English should also submit scores on the Test of English as a Foreign Language (TOEFL).

For further information, students should contact:

Admissions Office
School of the Museum of Fine Arts
230 The Fenway
Boston, Massachusetts 02115
Telephone: 617-369-3626
800-643-6078 (toll-free)
E-mail: admissions@smfa.edu
World Wide Web: http://www.smfa.edu

The Review Board system, in which students are awarded credit based on a review of new and evolving artwork by a panel of faculty members and students, is a hallmark of the SMFA education.

SCHOOL OF VISUAL ARTS

NEW YORK, NEW YORK

The School

The School of Visual Arts (SVA) is currently the largest independent college of art in the country, with a full-time enrollment of approximately 3,000. Students who choose SVA are often attracted by the breadth and professional standing of the faculty members, the passion of the student body, the rigors of the curriculum, the industry standards within the studio facilities, and the energy and excitement that is New York City.

Location

Located in the heart of New York City, SVA offers students the opportunity to become involved in one of America's largest and most vibrant cities, the art capital of the world. The energy, the spirit, and the desire to be the best that characterize New York City—embodied in SVA's renowned professional faculty members—constantly challenge and inspire the students. The unparalleled leadership and accomplishment of the city's arts and design communities demand excellence, and the School of Visual Arts prepares students to compete successfully in this environment.

Majors and Degrees

SVA offers Bachelor of Fine Arts (B.F.A.) degrees in advertising, animation, cartooning, computer art, film and video, fine arts, graphic design, illustration, interior design, and photography.

Academic Program

The curriculum has been designed to prepare students to graduate as working professionals in the arts. Consequently, the four-year curriculum is designed to allow students greater freedom of choice in electives and requirements with each succeeding year. The first year of the program, a foundation year, ensures the mastery of basic skills in the chosen discipline as well as in writing and art history. After the first year, students choose their own area of concentration and, under the guidance of the academic advisers and faculty members, pursue their own individual goals. The B.F.A. degree programs require the completion of 120 credits, including 72 studio credits, 12 in art history, 6 in electives, and 30 in liberal arts.

Off-Campus Programs

Students have the opportunity to participate in art programs abroad during the summer semester in Barcelona, Florence, and Greece. SVA also offers third-year students in photography, graphic design, illustration, interior design, and fine arts the opportunity to study abroad at an AIAS (Association of Independent Art Schools) affiliate in Europe.

Academic Facilities

The Animation Department has fully equipped animation studios, a Stop Motion Control Studio, digital pencil test facilities, a Motion Control Pencil test stand and control tables, and a new, state-of-the-art Digital Compositing Ink and Paint facility. Film students use Bolex cameras, Arriflex S camera packages, and Arriflex BL camera packages. The department also houses a large inventory of lighting and grip equipment.

Sound inventory includes Fostex digital time code recorders, Sony D-10 Pro II DAT recorders, Nagra recorders, an audio transfer facility, and a large collection of specialized microphones and mixers. There is also a film library that houses more than 1,500 titles from a variety of film, video, DVD, laser, and tape formats. A 100-seat film theater is available for cinema studies classes.

Students utilize a variety of digital cameras: VX-1000, VX-2000, PD-100, and PD-150 digital video cameras and more than thirty Sony digital handycams. Thesis and third-year students have access to ENG-style professional camcorders, including UVW-100, DSR-370, and DXC-537 cameras and support accessories, including production monitors, remotes, follow focus units, and matte boxes.

Postproduction facilities include a state-of-the-art Avid nonlinear editing center containing Avid X-press DVs, a newly created Final Cut Pro facility, and a new digital postproduction audio facility complete with Pro Tools Mix24 suites. The department also supports multiplatform dub rooms with Beta SP, DVCAM, DVCPRO, S-VHS, DAT decks, and a telecine projection system.

In the Fine Arts Department, there are eleven large, well-ventilated studios with slop sinks and storage closets for foundation and second- and third-year drawing and painting workshops. Fourth-year students have their own studio spaces.

Printmaking studios are fully equipped for etching, lithography, silkscreen, papermaking, and woodcut/lino and mono print. The litho room has five lithography presses and a graining sink; etching has four etching presses, a rosin box, and hot plates; and silkscreen has a 48-inch by 48-inch exposure unit and screen darkroom and reclaiming facilities. There is a complete platemaking darkroom containing a flip top Nu Arc exposing unit for making photo lithography and etching plates, a developing sink, and a plate cutter. In addition to traditional hand-drawn separations, students can create digital color separations in the printmaking output facilities. The facilities contain four Power Macintosh G4 computers and one 7200 Macintosh used as a scanning station (8.5-inch by 14-inch maximum scanning area). Each computer has a Zip drive and Adobe Photoshop, Adobe Illustrator, and QuarkXPress installed. A large output laser printer (12-inch by 36-inch maximum) and a Toshiba photocopier (11-inch by 17-inch maximum) are available for creating separations.

The Sculpture Center has facilities for welding, woodworking, stone carving, ceramics, and performance and video art. The wood, metal, stone, and ceramic facilities are equipped with everything artists need for the physical construction of their work. The woodshop has a table saw, a sliding compound miter saw, a panel saw, a table sander, four band saws, and two drill presses. In the metalshop are three MIG welders, two ARC welders, one TIG welder, two plasma cutters, a horizontal and a vertical band saw, a sand blaster, and OXY-ACE torches. Stone facilities have air hammers and stone chisels. The ceramic studio has two electric kilns that fire up to cone 7, a clay extruder, six potter's wheels, and a slab roller. In addition to these facilities, there is a toolroom stocked with power hand tools and safety equipment. The Sculpture Center also has a performance area, a live-model area, and a slide room for presentations. The video computer lab has seven digital video cameras, three video projectors, and a postproduction facility consisting of three G3 and G4 iMacs and two G4 iMacs with Photoshop, Illustrator, Flash, Final Cut Pro, and DVD Pro software, which allows for professional editing and special effects. The center also manages an audiovisual facility with slide and video projectors, VCRs, DVDs, monitors, and audio equipment.

Fine Arts majors can choose to concentrate in traditional mediums of painting, drawing, sculpture, or printmaking; in recent trends in installation, computer art, or time-based media in computer, video, or performance art; in alternative media; or any combination of the above.

Graphic design and advertising students use the Digital Imaging Center, which houses 140 Power Macintosh G4 computers with CD/DVD burners. Peripheral drives include floppy drives, Zip drives, and Compact Flash/Smart Media card readers. There are sixteen high-definition flatbed scanners, a Polaroid film recorder, and a Polaroid slide scanner as well as nine high-quality laser printers, including two HP color printers and three Fuji dye-sub printers. The Broadcast Media room has Sony DV decks, JVC S-VHS VCRs, and Sony NTSC monitors. Students have access to Nikon digital cameras and Sony DV video cameras. Software includes Adobe Photoshop, Adobe Illustrator, Adobe Premiere, Adobe After Effects, QuarkXpress, Macromedia Director, Macromedia Dreamweaver, Macromedia

Flash, Apple Final Cut Pro, Cleaner, and other print media, Web design, and broadcast design applications. The equipment and software enables the students to produce and output work at a superior and highly professional quality. In addition, the Digital Imaging Center's workshop has twenty-two drafting tables for drawing, cutting, and mounting artwork for presentations. The workshop also provides the students with color copiers.

SVA's Computer Art Department continues to feature the finest and most powerful digital tools available. Currently, there are twenty-one SGI, twenty-one Intergraph, twenty-one Boxx, and 171 Apple Macintosh computers in fifteen instructional labs and DV editing facilities. The department features the latest software applications, including AliasWavefront Maya, SoftImage, Discreet Logic Flint, 3D Studio Max, Adobe AfterEffects, Adobe Photoshop, MacroMedia Director, and QuarkXPress. Computer art majors can choose to concentrate their studies in the fields of computer animation, interactive media, or dynamic media.

The Photography Department's black-and-white darkrooms are equipped with ninety omega D5XL enlargers for printing everything from Minox to 4-inch by 5-inch negatives. There is also an enlarger specifically designed to handle 8-inch by 10-inch negatives. Twenty-seven of these enlargers are equipped with dichroic color heads for making RA-4 prints. SVA also houses nine black-and-white film-processing workstations and two 30-inch Kreonite Promate RA4 processors. The color print viewing area is equipped with GTI 5000K viewing booths. The BFA Photo Department's two state-of-the-art digital labs contain a total of forty-three Macintosh G4 student workstations, and two instructor's G4s with projectors. All of these computers are loaded with digital-imaging software, including Photoshop 7, Illustrator 10, and Final Cut Pro and all of the necessary hardware and software to download images and video from digital cameras. All of the G4s are equipped with DVD/CD burners.

In addition, the labs contain six Nikon Coolscan film scanners capable of scanning 120mm and 35mm transparencies, four Epson Perfection flatbed scanners for reflective material up to 11-inch by 17-inch, and eight Epson Stylus Photo 870 printers. All of these workstations are networked together and provide Internet access for students. The seven shooting studios are included in the Photography Department's computer network, and each studio is set up with an iMac equipped with a CD burner, a Zip 250, and a Smart Card reader to allow the students to download and save digital images. Digital cameras available for student use include seventeen Canon D30 digital camera kits, twenty Nikon Coolpix 950, 990, and 4500 digital cameras, and thirty Sony digital video cameras. Students have access to a wide range of studio equipment, including Profoto strobes; Vivitar, Quantum, and Lumidyne portable flashes; Lowel quartz lights; Ari quartz lights; and an assortment of lighting accessories. SVA also provides large- and medium-format cameras for the students to use. SVA's stock includes twelve Hasselblad kits, seven Mamiya RZ67 kits, ten Mamiya 645 kits, six Mamiya M7 kits, four Contax 645 AF kits, Toyo 4x5 view and field cameras, a variety of Polaroid cameras, and 8x10 studio and field cameras.

The Interior Design program is FIDER-accredited. The curriculum integrates well-known professional faculty members and state-of-the-art technology with the traditions of drawing and drafting, with an emphasis on design. Classes are held in a studio environment. Each student has a personal 3-foot by 5-foot fully equipped drafting station and unlimited use of computers. Architectural Desktop, Form Z Radiosity, and 3D Studio VIZ software are in a 3D AutoCAD lab for exclusive use by interior design students. Output options include a large-format Hewlett Packard Designjet ColorPro CAD, a Hewlett-Packard Designjet 1055CM plotter, and an Epson Stylus Photo 2200.

SVA's library holdings include distinctive multimedia collections, more than 65,000 books, more than 260 current periodical subscriptions, and special collections of pictures, color slides, film scripts, comics, videotapes, exhibition catalogs, CD-ROMs, and recordings. The college has three campus galleries as well as a gallery at 137 Wooster Street, in the heart of SoHo.

Costs

Tuition for the 2003–04 academic year was $18,200. SVA offers dormitory space at costs that range from $7200 to $9800 per academic year. Other annual costs vary greatly, but it is estimated that supplies cost up to $3150 each year, depending on the department.

Financial Aid

During the 2002–03 academic year, SVA students received more than $40 million in scholarships, grants, loans, and work program funds provided by federal, state, private, and institutional sources to help families supplement their financial resources. Students interested in financial aid are required to file the 2003–04 Free Application for Federal Student Aid (FAFSA). Each year, SVA sets aside more than $1 million for Silas H. Rhodes Merit Scholarships, awarded annually to outstanding students with a minimum GPA of 3.0 who are accepted into the B.F.A. programs beginning in the fall semester.

Faculty

SVA is proud of having one of the largest faculties of art professionals in the world. The faculty at SVA is composed of more than 700 practicing artists and designers who represent an array of fields in the fine and applied arts. Each faculty member has chosen to commit to the professional art world as well as to teaching the next generation of artists. As a result of the college's policy of using working professionals to teach, the college has been able to attract to the faculty some of the most prominent artists in New York.

Student Government

The Visual Arts Student Association (VASA), the student government organization, represents the student point of view at SVA. The three officers elected to VASA each year serve as the liaisons between students and the administrators. VASA also supports more than twenty student clubs, such as Quest Anime, Inkstains, and the Sunday Painting Club.

Admission Requirements

In pursuing admission to the college, it is important that a student's passion, potential, and commitment be demonstrated in a variety of modes, including a portfolio of creative work, a record of academic success in a classroom environment, and an ability to express ideas in written and spoken terms. SVA is committed to identifying students who will benefit from enrollment at SVA and who will contribute to the creative and academic quality of the campus.

In making its decisions, the Committee on Admission considers information and materials that all applicants are required to submit. Admissions requirements are as follows: application for undergraduate admission form, a nonrefundable $50 application fee ($80 for international applicants), official transcripts from all high schools and colleges attended, results of the Scholastic Aptitude Test (SAT) or the American College Testing program (ACT), statement of intent, portfolio (two-part essay for film and video applicants), letters of recommendation (optional), interview (optional), demonstration of English proficiency (required of all applicants whose primary language is not English), and a declaration of finances form and bank statement and copy of Alien Registration Card, for international applicants only.

Application and Information

The recommended deadline for applicants to the departments of animation, computer art, film and video, and photography is March 15, 2004. Applications to all other departments are reviewed on a rolling-admission basis. First-time freshman applicants seeking scholarships must complete the application process by February 2, 2004. Transfer applicants seeking scholarships must complete the application process by March 1, 2004. Spring admission is also an option for all departments except animation, computer art, film and video, and interior design. The recommended deadline for spring admission is December 1, 2004.

For more information about SVA, students should contact:

Office of Admissions
School of Visual Arts
209 East 23rd Street
New York, New York 10010
Telephone: 212-592-2100
Fax: 212-592-2116
E-mail: admissions@sva.edu
World Wide Web: http://www.schoolofvisualarts.edu

SCRIPPS COLLEGE

CLAREMONT, CALIFORNIA

The College

Since its founding in 1926 as one of the few institutions in the West dedicated to educating women for professional careers as well as personal intellectual growth, Scripps College has championed the qualities of mind and spirit described by its founder, newspaper entrepreneur and philanthropist Ellen Browning Scripps. Scripps remains a women's college because it believes that having women at the core of its concerns provides the very best environment for intellectually ambitious women to learn from a distinguished teaching faculty and from each other. Scripps emphasizes a challenging core curriculum based on interdisciplinary humanistic studies, combined with rigorous training in the disciplines, and sees this as the best possible foundation for any goals a woman may pursue.

Scripps aspires to be a diverse community committed to the principles of free inquiry and free expression based on mutual respect. The College chooses to remain a largely residential college of fewer than 1,000 students, a scale that encourages women to participate actively in their community and to develop a sense of both personal ethics and social responsibility. Scripps cherishes its campus of uncommon beauty, a tribute to the founder's vision that the College's architecture and landscape should reflect and influence taste and judgment.

As full participants in the Claremont Colleges consortium, Scripps students are members of a small university community where they may enjoy academic and other educational opportunities throughout the coordinating colleges and the graduate school. As residents of southern California, Scripps women may explore varied cultural, ethnic, and geographical resources.

Scripps students have the opportunity to participate in a variety of activities on campus, or they may choose to get involved in any of more than 200 five-college clubs, eleven NCAA Division III sports teams, intramural and club sports teams, coffeehouses, and a multitude of five-college and Scripps campus events. In March 2000, Scripps dedicated the Elizabeth Hubert Malott Commons, which houses a large centralized dining facility, the student-run Motley Coffeehouse, a newly expanded Career Planning & Resource Center, a student activities office, the College mailroom, a student store, and a banquet facility that highlights a variety of speakers across many disciplines. In August 2000, a new residence hall opened, adding to the beauty of the campus.

Scripps emphasizes high aspirations, high achievement, and personal integrity in all pursuits, and it expects students, faculty members, staff, and alumnae to contribute to Scripps and to their own communities throughout their professional, social, and civic lives. Scripps believes that this form of challenging and individualized education will best prepare women for lives of confidence, courage, and hope.

Location

Listed on the National Register of Historic Places, Scripps is located in Claremont, California, a college town of 39,000 people. It is 35 miles east of Los Angeles and 25 miles east of Pasadena. The mountains, beaches, and deserts of southern California are easily accessible by car. The climate is cool and dry in the winter, warming in the late spring.

Majors and Degrees

Scripps College awards the Bachelor of Arts degree in accounting; American studies; anthropology; art history; Asian-American studies; Asian studies; biology; biology/chemistry; Black studies; chemistry; Chicano studies; Chinese; classics; computer science; dance; economics; English; environmental science; environment, economics, and politics; environmental studies; European studies; foreign languages and literature; French studies; geology; gender and women's studies; German literature/civilization; German studies; Hispanic studies; history; human biology; humanities; Italian literature/civilization; Japanese; Jewish studies; Latin American studies; legal studies; linguistics; management engineering; mathematical economics; mathematics; media studies; molecular biology; music; neuroscience; organizational studies; philosophy; physics; politics and international relations; psychology; public policy analysis; religious studies; Russian; science and management; science/technology and society; sociology; Spanish literature/civilization; studio arts; theater; and women's studies.

Scripps also cooperates in a dual bachelor's degree program in engineering with a large number of institutions, including Boston University, Columbia University, Rensselaer Polytechnic Institute, USC, and Washington University. Other joint programs offering a bachelor's and a master's degree are available with the Claremont Graduate University in American politics, business administration, economics, international studies, philosophy, public policy studies, and religious studies.

Academic Program

To graduate with a Bachelor of Arts degree from Scripps, students must successfully complete a minimum of thirty-two courses. Course work is divided into three parts: core curriculum requirements, major concentration course work, and elective or minor concentration course work. Core curriculum requirements provide a solid academic frame, while electives allow students significant flexibility in studying courses from the social sciences, humanities, fine arts, natural sciences, and mathematics. Scripps operates on a semester calendar, beginning in early September and ending in mid-May.

Off-Campus Programs

Local off-campus opportunities include internships with career professionals in a variety of fields: journalism, law, business, communications, medicine, and the arts. Examples of internship sites are the Getty Museum, the Walt Disney Company, Merrill Lynch, Warner Bros., the Minority Advertising Program, and INROADS. Students may also participate in political internships in Washington, D.C., and Sacramento, California, or in other internships in museums, biological field stations, and public policy organizations such as the United Nations.

Approximately 50 percent of Scripps students supplement their education and life experience by studying abroad or participating in domestic off-campus study programs. Students can select from more than fifty international options each year, including France, Germany, Ecuador, Zimbabwe, Greece, Nepal, China, and Japan. Students may also opt for domestic programs; going on exchange to Spelman, or combining classes at Drew University or George Washington University with an internship.

Academic Facilities

The Claremont Colleges library system holds more than 2 million volumes. The Denison Library at Scripps houses an impressive humanities and fine art collection and is renowned for its special and rare books. A cross-linked computer system affords access to off-campus libraries, including the University of California system.

The Performing Arts Center is the College's newest addition to its academic facilities. Formerly the Garrison Theater for the Claremont Colleges and newly renovated, the Performing Arts Center provides a new home for the College's Music Department and offers state-of-the-art acoustics and theatrical systems for both instruction and performance.

The Millard Sheets Art Center, a $4-million facility that opened in 1994, provides studio space for painting, drawing, printmaking, and ceramics and contains a state-of-the-art computer art and design laboratory and photography studio. The W. M. Keck Joint Science Center, a national model of undergraduate science facilities that opened in 1992, offers students of biology, chemistry, and physics top-grade facilities, research opportunities, and a biological field station. The Clark Humanities Museum and Ruth Chandler Williamson Art Gallery exhibit the work of professionals and students.

The Scripps Computer Facility, a well-equipped microcomputer laboratory, houses both Macintosh and IBM computers as well as laser printers. Scripps has opened a Multimedia Learning Center for faculty use in teaching and a Modern Language Laboratory/Technical Teaching Classroom. Seven "smart classrooms," each equipped with a new Macintosh G4 computer, an overhead projector, a laser disc player, and a VCR, are also available for instructional purposes. Users have access to a six-college network as well as the Internet. The Science Center and the Art Center have their own computer labs. The libraries and music studio also have computer facilities. All student rooms have access to the Scripps network and the Internet; all offer direct Ethernet access. Every residence hall offers computers with Pentium multimedia systems for student use.

Costs

For the 2003–04 academic year, tuition and fees were $29,964, room and board were $8600, and books and incidentals were approximately $1800.

Financial Aid

It is the goal of Scripps College to attract the best students, regardless of their ability to pay. Approximately 60 percent of Scripps students receive financial aid, usually in a combination of grants and scholarships, loans, and part-time student employment. Awards are based on the financial need of the student. The College also offers a variety of academic scholarships ranging from half tuition to full tuition, room, and board.

Faculty

With a student-faculty ratio of 11.5:1, the College is dedicated to a personalized education. Faculty members remain active in their fields, while making teaching Scripps students their first priority. Classes are taught by professors, not by graduate students. Of the full-time ongoing faculty members, 97 percent hold terminal degrees in their field; 59 percent are women; 100 percent participate in the faculty/student advising program.

Student Government

One of the most important aspects of life at Scripps is the governance system. Students participate in the curricular and policymaking functions of the College. The College Council is composed of student body officers elected each spring and is chaired by the president of the student body. Each of the eight residence halls is self-governing, and students serve on a variety of Board of Trustees committees. The College has a serious commitment to the concept of shared responsibility for governance among students, the faculty, and administrators.

Admission Requirements

Scripps College seeks energetic and intellectually curious students who are interested in pursuing a challenging liberal arts curriculum. In addition to high levels of academic and personal achievement, Scripps values demonstrated leadership, initiative, integrity, and creativity.

The Admission Committee gives careful consideration to every aspect of a student's application. Particular attention is given to the quality of an applicant's academic preparation. A recommended course of study consists of five academic subjects in each year of high school including 4 years of English, 3 years of mathematics, 3 years of social studies, 3 years of laboratory science (biology, chemistry, or physics), and either 3 years of a foreign language or 2 years each of two different languages. Applicants are encouraged to select Honors, Advanced Placement, or International Baccalaureate courses whenever available.

Application and Information

Students applying to Scripps College are expected to submit transcripts of all academic work in high school and college, a counselor recommendation, two teacher recommendations from teachers in different academic subject areas, a graded writing assignment, and SAT I or ACT results, along with the application and essay. Students are encouraged to take SAT II Subject Tests. The deadlines for application are November 1 or January 1 for early decision, November 1 for academic scholarships, and January 15 for regular decision.

Further information is available from:

Office of Admission
Scripps College
1030 Columbia Avenue
Claremont, California 91711-3948
Telephone: 909-621-8149
800-770-1333 (toll-free)
Fax: 909-607-7508
E-mail: admission@scrippscollege.edu
World Wide Web: http://www.scrippscollege.edu

Students relax amid the tree-lined terraces and Mediterranean buildings of the Scripps College campus.

SEATTLE PACIFIC UNIVERSITY

SEATTLE, WASHINGTON

The University

Seattle Pacific University (SPU) is a flourishing Christian university of the arts, sciences, and professions serving more than 3,700 students. Founded in 1891 by the Free Methodist Church of North America, it is recognized for both academic excellence and the efforts of its graduates to engage the culture in order to bring about positive change in the world. SPU has been designated one of "America's Best Colleges" by *U.S. News & World Report* and has been acknowledged as one of the country's character-building institutions.

Seattle Pacific University is fully accredited by the Washington State Board of Education and the Northwest Association of Schools and Colleges and is on the approved list of the American Council on Education and Board of Regents of the State of New York. SPU is a charter member of the Christian College Consortium and is also a member of the Council for Christian Colleges and Universities. Seattle Pacific meets the requirements of the Commission on Christian Education of the Free Methodist Church and those of other denominations for the collegiate preparation of ministers. The University's programs are accredited for business by the AACSB International–The Association to Advance Collegiate Schools of Business; for dietetics by the Commission on Accreditation/Approval for Dietetics Education of the American Dietetic Association; for education by the National Council for Accreditation of Teacher Education (NCATE) at both the graduate and undergraduate levels and the Association of American Colleges, the American Association of Colleges for Teacher Education, and the Washington State Board of Education for preparation of elementary and secondary school teachers; for electrical engineering by the Engineering Accreditation Commission of the Accreditation Board for Engineering and Technology Inc.; for music by the National Association of Schools of Music (NASM); and for nursing by the Commission on Collegiate Nursing Education (CCNE) for both undergraduate and graduate programs and the Washington State Nursing Care Quality Assurance Commission for the undergraduate nursing curriculum. The University also offers, as approved by the U.S. government, the education of veterans and their dependents under applicable public laws.

Students come to SPU from forty-four states and twenty-four countries, representing more than fifty different Christian denominations. More than half of Seattle Pacific's undergraduate students live on campus in four residence halls and several apartment complexes. All Seattle Pacific residence facilities are wired to allow students dedicated online connections to e-mail, the Internet, and the campus computer network.

Seattle Pacific's intercollegiate athletic program fields NCAA Division II teams in men's and women's basketball, crew, cross-country, soccer, and track and field, and women's gymnastics and volleyball. All students have access to thirty-five intramural sports as well as extramurals, special events, and health and fitness activities.

The University's unique leadership program encourages students to cultivate their individual talents by putting them to work in student government, ministries, performing groups, publications, clubs, and organizations.

In addition to its bachelor's degrees, SPU awards M.A., M.B.A., M.Ed., M.S., M.A. (TESOL), M.S.N., Ed.D., and Ph.D. degrees.

Location

Seattle Pacific's beautiful 45-acre, tree-lined city campus lies in a residential area just 10 minutes from downtown Seattle, the business and cultural heart of the Pacific Northwest. A gateway to Canada and the Pacific Rim, Seattle offers easy access to a wide variety of outdoor recreation such as sailing, skiing, hiking, and camping. The city also offers world-class fine arts, including opera, theater, symphony, and ballet. Seattle Pacific takes advantage of its urban setting by providing hundreds of internship and service experiences in the city's hospitals, schools, businesses, and churches.

Majors and Degrees

An array of academic options in the arts, sciences, and professions allows Seattle Pacific students to specialize in one discipline while exploring many others. The University awards B.A. and B.S. degrees and offers forty-eight undergraduate majors.

The College of Arts and Sciences offers the following undergraduate majors: art; biochemistry; biology; biology education; biotechnology; chemistry; classics; communication; computational mathematics; computer engineering; computer science; electrical engineering; engineering and applied science; English; European studies (Europe, French, German, Latin, Russian, and Spanish); exercise science; family and consumer sciences; fine and applied arts education; food and nutritional sciences; general studies; history; language arts education; Latin American studies (Spanish); mathematics; mathematics education; music; music education; philosophy; physical education; physics; political science; science education; social science education; sociology; textiles, clothing, and interiors; and theater.

The School of Business and Economics offers undergraduate majors in accounting, business administration, and economics. The School of Education offers elementary certification with any major of the University, secondary certification with endorsements in most Washington state–approved areas, and a major in special education. The School of Health Sciences offers an undergraduate nursing degree. The School of Psychology, Family and Community offers undergraduate majors in organizational behavior and psychology. The School of Theology offers undergraduate majors in Christian theology and educational ministries. Preprofessional programs are available in dentistry, law, medicine, optometry, and physical therapy.

Academic Program

Seattle Pacific's academic disciplines set high standards for students. Undergraduate students are taught not by graduate assistants but by experienced professors recognized locally and nationally for the quality of their scholarship. Small classes mean students actively participate in their own education, gaining the confidence to achieve their goals. In addition, SPU's clear Christian commitment gives depth and perspective to classroom learning, balancing knowledge with values.

The Common Curriculum, which includes seven required courses spread out over four years, is at the heart of an undergraduate liberal arts education at Seattle Pacific. Only 5 percent of four-year institutions in the United States, most of them very small and homogenous, offer such a curriculum. Until now, no comprehensive university in an urban setting with an equal mix of residential and commuter students requires participation in common learning over four years.

SPU students begin in the first quarter of their freshman year with University Seminar, a focused exploration of a special interdisciplinary topic. The fewer than 25 students enrolled in each course form a "cohort" and attend other freshman classes in the Common Curriculum together, with their University Seminar professor serving as their academic adviser. In their freshman, sophomore, and junior years, students participate in two parallel sequences of required courses that address key human questions from the perspective of various disciplines and the foundations of Christian faith. Cumulative and developmental in nature, these classes are designed to support and enhance students' learning in the majors.

Off-Campus Programs

Seattle Pacific students have many opportunities to enhance their education with off-campus study. The Pacific Northwest itself provides a living laboratory for academic pursuits in all disciplines. SPU's own campuses on Whidbey Island and Blakely Island in Puget Sound are ideal for research and field study in areas such as marine biology and environmental science.

Each year, approximately 65 Seattle Pacific students participate in overseas study programs: the European Quarter, the Normandy (France) Studies Program, and the Salamanca (Spain) Program. Biennially, 30 to 35 students travel and study in Britain during British Isles Quarter. During quarter and summer breaks, students have the opportunity to join Seattle Pacific Reachout International (SPRINT) teams that travel to countries like Northern Ireland, Russia, Nicaragua, Uganda, and Romania for a short-term mission experience.

The University maintains exchange agreements with institutions in Kenya, Japan, and Korea. Students may also apply to take one or two quarters of study at one of the twelve other Christian College Consortium campuses, or they may enroll in one of three programs sponsored by the Council for Christian Colleges and Universities: American Studies in Washington, D.C.; Latin American Studies in Costa Rica; Film Studies in Los Angeles. Programs in the Middle East and China are also available.

Academic Facilities

At the heart of the Seattle Pacific campus is the 62,000-square-foot library. This spacious, four-level facility serves as the center for academic endeavors outside the classroom. It provides learning resource services, the latest technology, space for study and research, and approximately 150,000 volumes arranged on open shelves for easy access. The library collection is accessible online in the library and through the campus computer network via its automated catalog. The library's Instructional Technology Services Department offers media production, satellite downlink, and duplication services.

Among the other educational facilities at SPU is the Otto M. Miller Hall, which houses electrical engineering and a ½-acre multidisciplinary laboratory. A $24-million science facility for biology, chemistry, and related sciences opened in fall 2003. The University's flexible-forestage performing arts facility, E. E. Bach Theatre, is one of the city's finest, and the Royal Brougham Pavilion is one of the premier sports and recreation arenas in the Puget Sound area.

Costs

Tuition for the 2003–04 academic year was $18,822; annual room and board were $7017 (based on 2 people in a room, full-meal plan). Individualized meal plans are available. Book costs and personal expenses vary, depending on personal needs.

Financial Aid

Seattle Pacific will award more than $34 million in scholarships and financial aid in 2004–05. Need-based financial aid is available in the form of scholarships, grants, loans, and employment. To be considered for maximum aid, students must submit the Free Application for Federal Student Aid (FAFSA) as soon as possible after January 1 and be admitted to the University by March 1. SPU participates in various federal aid programs, including the Federal Pell Grant, Federal Supplemental Educational Opportunity Grant, Federal Perkins Loan, Federal Work-Study, and Federal Stafford Student Loan programs.

Merit-based University scholarships are given annually to students who exhibit academic excellence and exemplify the ideals of the institution. Merit scholarships are available in amounts ranging from $1500 to $10,000. The Division of Fine Arts offers renewable scholarships (up to $3000) regardless of major. The Athletic Department awards scholarship aid to qualified athletes.

Faculty

The full-time faculty at Seattle Pacific is composed of 172 full-time faculty members who are committed to the highest academic standards. Eighty-four percent of SPU's full-time faculty members hold the Ph.D. or an equivalent terminal degree. Seattle Pacific professors are experts in their fields: they publish, speak, and conduct research throughout the world. Their first priority, however, is teaching. SPU faculty members also make themselves available to students outside the classroom and act as models of compassionate, educated Christians.

Student Government

All full-time students are members of the Associated Students of Seattle Pacific (ASSP). Each spring, students elect 5 ASSP executive officers along with representatives to the ASSP Senate, the student governing body. ASSP provides services to students in the areas of campus activities, campus ministries, leadership development, and student publications.

Admission Requirements

Admission to Seattle Pacific is offered on the basis of academic credentials and personal qualifications. SPU selects those students who will benefit most from a Christian university education. Factors in the admission decision include high school or college grades, academic and personal recommendations, the application essays, and scores on the SAT or the ACT. An applicant is also evaluated in terms of leadership potential, church and community activities, special talents, and personal responsibility. Prospective students are encouraged to visit the campus at any time.

Application and Information

Prospective students may write to the Seattle Pacific Office of Undergraduate Admissions to request application materials. High school students should request these materials early in the senior year. While applications for Autumn Quarter are accepted until June 1, prospective students must be admitted by March 1 in order to be considered for scholarships and the best financial aid, housing, and course registration opportunities.

Applications are reviewed in the order they are received in the Office of Undergraduate Admissions. Beginning December 1, decisions regarding admission are announced after all application materials have been received. If an interview is required, students are contacted by telephone.

For further details, students should contact:

Jennifer Kenney
Director of Undergraduate Admissions
Seattle Pacific University
3307 Third Avenue West, Suite 115
Seattle, Washington 98119-1922
Telephone: 206-281-2021
800-366-3344 (toll-free)
E-mail: admissions@spu.edu
World Wide Web: http://www.spu.edu/

SEATTLE UNIVERSITY

SEATTLE, WASHINGTON

The University

Seattle University (SU) provides an ideal environment for motivated students interested in self-reliance, awareness of different cultures, social justice, and the fulfillment that comes from making a difference. Its location in the center of one of the nation's most diverse and progressive cities attracts a varied student body, faculty, and staff. Its urban setting promotes the development of leadership skills and independence and provides a variety of opportunities for students to apply what they learn through internships, clinical experiences, and volunteer work. It is an environment that allows students to "connect the mind to what matters."

As a Jesuit institution, Seattle University is part of a network of twenty-eight colleges and universities and forty-six high schools noted for academic strength across the United States. Academic offerings are designed to provide leadership opportunities, develop global awareness, and enable graduates to serve society through a demanding liberal arts and sciences foundation. In the Jesuit educational tradition, students are taught how to think, not what to think. Professional undergraduate offerings include highly respected Schools of Business, Nursing, and Science and Engineering and career-oriented liberal arts programs such as communications, creative writing, criminal justice, and journalism. The University's Schools of Education, Law, and Theology and Ministry offer graduate-level opportunities.

Seattle University is noted for its focus on the individual through small, faculty-taught classes and excellent service. The result is mirrored by graduates who lead fulfilling and economically successful lives. SU leads the Pacific Northwest in producing Truman and Wilson scholars.

The fall quarter has a freshman class of 665, and 45 percent are from outside Washington State. The 3,765 undergraduate students represent forty-six states and seventy-six nations. Approximately 10 percent are international students. The ethnic breakdown for the fall 2003 freshman class was 56 percent white, 20 percent Asian American, and 18 percent African American, Latino, and American Indian.

The residential campus has undergone $157 million in recent improvements. Although it is in the center of Seattle, the campus has been designated by Washington State as an Official Backyard Sanctuary for its distinctive landscaping and environmentally conscious practices.

There is a wide variety of on-campus housing that accommodates 1,596 students, including a new apartment complex, and 85 percent of freshmen live on campus. There is a two-year on-campus residence requirement.

Seattle University has more than eighty-five extracurricular clubs and organizations and has five varsity teams for men (basketball, cross-country, soccer, swimming, and track) and seven for women (basketball, cross-country, soccer, softball, swimming, track, and volleyball). SU is in NCAA Division II. The student life program includes sixty extracurricular clubs and organizations, including the Hawaiian Club, Associated Students of African Descent, Hiyu Coulee Hiking Club, Beta Alpha Psi (national accounting honorary), and other professional honoraries and clubs.

The Connolly Athletic Center serves as the major facility for varsity and intramural athletics and recreation. It features two swimming pools, two full-size gymnasiums, and locker room saunas. A 6-acre complex provides fields for outdoor sports.

Seattle University receives the highest professional accreditation from the Accreditation Board for Engineering and Technology, Inc.; AACSB International–The Association to Advance Collegiate Schools of Business; the American Bar Association; the American Chemical Society; the Association of Theological Schools; the Commission on Accreditation of Allied Health Education Programs; the National Council for Accreditation of Teacher Education; the Commission on Collegiate Nursing Education; the Council on Social Work Education; and the Northwest Association of Schools and Colleges.

Location

Seattle University is located on First Hill in a port city of unsurpassed natural beauty. As the Pacific Northwest's largest city (and the fourteenth-largest metropolitan area in the U.S.), Seattle is a scenic and cultural center in a setting that includes breathtaking mountain views of the Cascades to the east and the Olympics to the west; skiing is within 60 minutes of campus. In addition to being situated along Puget Sound, Seattle also contains Lakes Union and Washington; both provide a wide variety of recreational opportunities. Seattle's residents love the outdoors, and areas for hiking, backpacking, and climbing are minutes from campus. Biking is also popular and special trails for cycling and running are located throughout the city.

Seattle's sights and sounds, rich ethnic diversity, celebrated restaurants, first-run entertainment, major-league athletics, theater, opera, and ballet are within walking distance and enhance campus life.

Majors and Degrees

Seattle University offers the following undergraduate degrees: Bachelor of Arts, Bachelor of Science, Bachelor of Science in nursing, Bachelor of Social Work, Bachelor of Criminal Justice, Bachelor of Public Affairs, and the Bachelor of Arts in business administration.

The University offers programs in six major academic units. The Albers School of Business and Economics awards degrees in accounting, business economics, e-commerce, finance, general business, international business, management, and marketing. The College of Arts and Sciences grants degrees in art, Asian studies, communication studies, criminal justice, drama, ecological studies, economics, English, fine arts, foreign languages, history, humanities, international studies, journalism, liberal studies, philosophy, political science, psychology, public affairs, social work, sociology, and theology and religious studies. The College of Nursing offers a Bachelor of Science in Nursing degree. The College of Science and Engineering offers degree programs in biochemistry, biology, chemistry, civil engineering, computer engineering, computer science, diagnostic ultrasound, electrical engineering, environmental engineering, general science, mechanical engineering, mathematics, medical technology, and physics. Preprofessional programs include dentistry, law, medicine, optometry, and veterinary medicine.

Academic Programs

The Core Curriculum is known for its strength and has several distinguishing characteristics in keeping with the Jesuit tradition: it provides an integrated freshman year; it gives order and sequence to student learning; it provides experience in the methods and content of the range of liberal arts, sciences, philosophy, and theology; it calls for active learning in all classes for practice in writing and thinking, and for an awareness of values; and it fosters a global perspective and a sense of social and personal responsibility.

Seattle University offers two honors program options for students seeking the greatest possible challenge. The University Honors Program is a small, select two-year-long learning community. It is humanities focused, and its fully integrated curriculum examines the most significant texts and ideas of Western culture. The Core Honors Program involves seminar sections of nine required courses in English, history, philosophy, social science, and theology/religious studies. This option is particularly suited to students in profession-oriented majors where participation in University Honors is less feasible due to specific major requirements and scheduling conflicts.

SU operates on a quarter calendar. The fall quarter begins in mid-September; the winter quarter in early January; the spring quarter in late March; and the summer quarter in mid-June. Undergraduates typically take 15 hours each during the fall, winter, and spring quarters.

Off-Campus Programs

SU offers international study programs—one for French in France, one for Latin American studies in Mexico, and two reciprocal exchange programs with the University of Graz in Austria and Sophia University in Japan. These are open to all students in all majors and emphasize appreciation of the language and culture. This is accomplished through the total immersion concept. Other programs include Campus Ministry missions in Nicaragua and Belize and Albers School of Business and Economics tours in Mexico, Italy, Hong Kong, and Vietnam. Seattle University maintains the only Calcutta Club in which students volunteer annually on behalf of Mother Teresa's ministry. Additional study-abroad programs in other nations, in conjunction with other colleges' overseas programs, are also offered. Arrangements are made through SU's Study Abroad Office.

Academic Facilities

The University is located on 45 acres in the First Hill neighborhood in the center of Seattle. There are twenty-eight buildings recently enhanced by $157 million in additions, renovations, and new construction.

Costs

In 2003–04, tuition was $20,070; room and meals were $6858. The estimate for books, fees, and personal expenses is an additional $2982. Travel costs varies among students. Costs are subject to change.

Financial Aid

Seattle University awarded $5.4 million in its own financial aid to fall 2003 freshmen, including 196 scholarships ranging from $6000 to $27,378. Sixty-nine percent of freshmen received University aid. Students are required to apply for financial aid by February 1 as awards are made early each spring for the following fall quarter. Applications that are received after this deadline will be evaluated in order received for any remaining aid. Students must submit the Free Application for Federal Student Aid (FAFSA) and be accepted for admission to be considered for financial assistance. There are also a number of scholarships for freshmen that are awarded on the basis of academic achievement, extracurricular involvement, and community service. Similar transfer scholarships are determined primarily on the basis of course selection and cumulative grade point average.

Faculty

There are 522 faculty members; 88 percent of full-time faculty members possess doctoral or terminal degrees. Like the University, the mission of faculty members who choose Seattle University is teaching. Most classes average 20; the faculty-student ratio is 1:14. All classes are taught by faculty members. The involvement of faculty members extends beyond the classroom. Faculty members are available to provide extra assistance, to help students with their research, and to assist in the arranging of internships. Faculty advisers provide guidance, direction, and encouragement throughout the year. New students are assigned faculty advisers according to major prior to registration.

Student Government

All undergraduates belong to the Associated Students of Seattle University (ASSU). This is the central student organization on campus. ASSU is organized around an elected president, an executive vice president, and an activities vice president. In addition, a 12-member representative council oversees every facet of the student body and is responsible for policymaking. Its primary responsibility is to provide a diverse activities program to meet the needs of SU's diverse student body. In addition, ASSU communicates student needs to the administration and faculty. ASSU oversees eighty-five clubs and organizations.

Admission Requirements

Freshman applicants are required to have a college-preparatory program, including 4 years of English, 3 years of social studies/history, 3 years of mathematics, 2 years of laboratory science, and 2 years of a foreign language. ACT or SAT scores, two recommendations, and an essay are also required. The middle 50 percent of freshman GPAs are between 3.3 and 3.8 on a 4.0 scale. The average score on the ACT is between 21 and 27, and the average SAT I scores are between 510 and 626 (verbal) and 510 and 620 (math). Seattle University accepts the Common Application, the Uniform Application, Peterson's Universal Application, the Catholic College Admissions Association Application, and its own admission application.

Essays or personal statements are required for admission and are carefully considered during application review.

College credit is awarded to those who have successfully completed Advanced Placement or International Baccalaureate examinations. Minimum scores can be obtained by contacting the Office of the Registrar.

Application and Information

Applications can be obtained by contacting the Admissions Office. Secondary school students who have completed at least six semesters are encouraged to apply by January of their senior year. Transfer students must submit official transcripts from all postsecondary institutions attended, regardless of whether course work was completed. For fall admission, freshmen should complete the process by February 1 to receive consideration for scholarships and other Seattle University financial aid; the recommended financial aid/admissions deadline for transfers is March 1. Please note that applications will usually be accepted after these dates but funds for financial aid may no longer be available. Campus visits can be scheduled Monday through Friday and most Saturdays. Guests can attend a class, meet with a faculty adviser, participate in a campus tour, and speak individually with representatives from admissions and financial aid.

For additional information students should contact:

Michael K. McKeon, Dean
Admissions Office
Seattle University
900 Broadway
Seattle, Washington 98122-4340
Telephone: 206-296-2000
800-426-7123 (toll-free)
E-mail: admissions@seattleu.edu
World Wide Web: http://www.seattleu.edu

SETON HALL UNIVERSITY

SOUTH ORANGE, NEW JERSEY

The University

Seton Hall University has been preparing students to assume leadership roles for nearly 150 years. A Catholic university founded with the purpose of "enriching the mind, the heart and the spirit," Seton Hall offers more than sixty majors and concentrations, as well as honors and leadership programs. With a 14:1 student-faculty ratio, and an average class size of 25, Seton Hall offers all the advantages of a big school, but, with just 4,900 undergraduate students, the University also provides the personal attention of a small college. Seton Hall's mission of "preparing student leaders for a global society" is evidenced through its high academic standards, values-centered curriculum, and cutting-edge technology. Recently cited by the Intercollegiate Studies Institute's critically acclaimed college guide *Choosing the Right College,* as "a Catholic university evolving from being a regional treasure to a national resource," Seton Hall was listed among 110 of the nation's top colleges.

The University comprises nine schools and colleges: the College of Arts and Sciences, the Stillman School of Business, the College of Education and Human Services, the College of Nursing, the John C. Whitehead School of Diplomacy and International Relations, the Immaculate Conception Seminary School of Theology, University College, and the School of Graduate Medical Education, all on the South Orange campus. The School of Law is in nearby Newark.

Emphasizing Judeo-Christian intellectual traditions and values, the University was founded by Bishop James Roosevelt Bayley, the first Catholic bishop of Newark. Seton Hall was named after Bishop Bayley's aunt, St. Elizabeth Ann Seton, the founder of the first American community of the Sisters of Charity. Established as the first diocesan college in the United States and organized into a University in 1950, Seton Hall continues to operate under the auspices of the Roman Catholic Diocese of Newark. As such, Seton Hall is both a Catholic university and a catholic university—meaning that the school fosters the values and traditions of the Catholic faith while also universally welcoming students of all denominations.

At Seton Hall, technology is integrated into the curriculum. Every undergraduate is issued a laptop computer to facilitate learning through technology both inside and outside the classroom. Seton Hall has integrated technology into course work by including the use of streaming video to increase learning, note-taking, and collaborative work online. The state-of-the-art laptop is upgraded after two years and students who graduate in four years keep their laptops after graduation. Students can plug in their laptops in residence halls, the cafeteria, the coffeehouse, the library, and even the park benches around campus. Seton Hall is also leading the way in wireless technology, allowing virtually limitless access to online learning.

Seton Hall's on-campus recruiting events and career fairs help students find paid internships at companies like CNN, Prudential, AT&T, Pfizer, Johnson & Johnson, the U.N., the FBI, ESPN, and the New Jersey Devils. More than 500 employers and alumni come to the campus each year to mentor and recruit students for internships and employment after graduation.

The relationships forged with these companies are so solid that more than 90 percent of the University's employers report that they would hire their Seton Hall interns after graduation if they had appropriate openings. Graduates of Seton Hall University join the ranks of 67,000 alumni who work in leadership positions in business, industry, law, health care, and education nationally and internationally.

Seton Hall graduates are successful doctors, dentists, optometrists, and veterinarians. Faculty members combine personal attention with strong academic advice to students wishing to enter medical and dental school, and, as a result, 78 percent of students gain entry to medical school and 100 percent into dental school. Unique opportunities with the Graduate School of Medical Education allow students to enter joint programs to earn advanced degrees in athletic training, physical therapy, occupational therapy, and physician's assistant studies.

Location

The suburban village of South Orange, New Jersey, is home to the University's 58-acre parklike campus. With the village center a short walk away, students find practically anything they need. Just beyond the border of the suburban residential community of South Orange is New York City—the Big Apple —the capital of finance, fashion, art, theater, and international relations. Travel to New York is convenient via a midtown direct train from the village center. Just 25 minutes away, New York provides students with opportunities for cultural exploration and internships. Career opportunities also abound throughout northern New Jersey, which is the site of an extensive pharmaceutical, chemical, and financial center. Social, cultural, and recreational opportunities are available throughout the area, with the New Jersey Performing Arts Center, the Meadowlands, numerous state parks, and the beautiful New Jersey shore all close by.

Majors and Degrees

The College of Arts and Sciences offers the Bachelor of Arts (B.A.) in African-American studies, anthropology, art, Asian studies, Catholic studies, classical studies, communication, criminal justice, economics, English, French, history, Italian, liberal studies, modern languages, music, philosophy, political science, social work, sociology, and Spanish. It offers the Bachelor of Science (B.S.) in biochemistry, biology, chemistry, computer science, mathematics, and physics. The John C. Whitehead School of Diplomacy and International Relations offers the B.S. in international relations. The Stillman School of Business offers the B.S. in accounting, economics, finance, management, management information systems, marketing, and sports management. It also offers the B.A. in business administration. The College of Education and Human Services offers the B.S. in early childhood education, elementary education, secondary education, and special education. The College of Nursing offers the Bachelor of Science in Nursing (B.S.N.).

Preprofessional programs are available in dentistry, law, medicine, optometry, and veterinary science. A dual-admission program with Seton Hall University School of Law is offered to qualified undergraduates. Engineering students participate in a five-year program (chemical, civil, computer, electrical, industrial, or mechanical) offered jointly with New Jersey Institute of Technology). Combination undergraduate and postgraduate programs in athletic training, occupational therapy, physical therapy, physician's assistant studies, and speech language pathology are also offered.

Academic Programs

The University uses a semester calendar. It also offers day and evening summer sessions.

The College of Arts and Sciences requires students to complete at least 130 credits. Select students are invited to participate in the Honors Program, which consists of four semester-long colloquia devoted to the history of civilization, from ancient through medieval and early modern cultures to contemporary civilization. Students interested in law can apply for the University's dual-admission program to Seton Hall Law School.

With the oldest college of nursing in New Jersey, Seton Hall provides nursing education that prepares its graduates for a variety of health-care settings. Clinical experience is provided in hospitals, public health agencies, schools, nursing homes, industrial organizations, and other community agencies. More than 97 percent of Seton Hall nursing students pass the national nursing exam. Graduates of Seton Hall hold leadership positions in nursing throughout the state.

Seton Hall's Stillman School of Business is accredited by AACSB International–The Association to Advance Collegiate Schools of Business, which puts it among the most rigorous business programs in the United States. Founded on a background of liberal arts courses, the Stillman School offers specialized programs in leadership studies, international business, and sports management.

The John C. Whitehead School of Diplomacy and International Relations is the only school affiliated with the United Nations Association and offers a Bachelor of Science degree in international relations. This program emphasizes ethnopolitical studies or world cultures and the development of management and leadership skills, as well as a high degree of competency in a second language. Requirements include study abroad.

The University offers an Army ROTC program on campus.

Off-Campus Programs

Seton Hall offers study-abroad programs in the People's Republic of China, Japan, Korea, the Dominican Republic, and Puerto Rico. Through the International Student Exchange Program, students may study at any of the 101 universities in thirty-five countries for one academic year. Students have several opportunities for cooperative learning and internships in the metropolitan area. Many co-op positions are with Fortune 500 companies, while others are with leading government, cultural, charitable, and scientific organizations. A semester in Washington, D.C., is also available for students to obtain internships and to take classes at exchange universities.

Academic Facilities

The University's Walsh library is a twenty-first-century research center with a computerized card catalog, four electronic multimedia rooms, ten CD-ROM information search and retrieval stations, 200 computer workstations for students, and nearly 1 million holdings. Fahy Hall contains classrooms and offices, a TV studio, two classroom amphitheaters, language and journalism laboratories, and the University Museum. In McNulty Hall, there are well-equipped laboratories for biology, chemistry, and physics. The Art Center (a registered National Historic landmark) houses an art gallery, studios, classrooms, and offices of the Department of Art and Music. The College of Nursing has multipurpose and audiovisual laboratories. Kozlowski Hall, completed in 1997, contains state-of-the-art lecture halls, computer rooms, faculty offices, a 300-seat auditorium, and conference rooms for several of the University's academic programs. There are also microcomputer laboratories in several locations on campus, and a large University-operated mainframe computer is located in the Computer Center. The University also has various centers and research institutes, including the Center for Catholic Studies, The G.K. Chesterton Institute, the Center for Jewish Christian Studies and the 50-year-old Asia Center.

Costs

For the 2003–04 academic year, tuition was $21,855 per year. This amount covers 30 credits and all fees, including a mobile-computing fee. The charge for room and board was $8550.

Financial Aid

The University offers federal, state, and institutional aid. Most aid is based on need, but many scholarships are based on outstanding scholastic ability and achievement. Athletic grants are also available. Currently, about 90 percent of the students receive financial aid, with 75 percent receiving aid directly from Seton Hall; 26 percent work part-time on campus. All applicants for aid are required to file the Free Application for Federal Student Aid (FAFSA) by April 1 for the fall semester and by October 1 for the spring semester.

Faculty

The University has about 400 full-time and more than 400 part-time faculty members. Eighty-seven percent of the full-time faculty members have doctoral degrees. The ratio of full-time students to full-time faculty members is 14:1. Faculty members serve as advisers to students in their respective departments.

Student Government

The Student Government Association consists of students who make up two legislative bodies that have the responsibility of representing their fellow students and providing programs of interest to the campus community. Students are elected to seats on the University Senate, which deals with all legislative matters pertinent to the University. In addition, the Resident Student Association represents the interests of resident students, and the Commuter Council represents the interests of commuter students.

Admission Requirements

Applicants are selected on the basis of their school achievement record, SAT I or ACT scores, personal essay, and teacher and counselor recommendations. Students must graduate from an accredited high school or have passing scores on the GED test. Sixteen high school units are required: 4 in English, 3 in mathematics, 2 in social studies, 2 in a foreign language, 1 in a laboratory science, and 4 in approved academic electives. Special admission policies exist for students who have been out of high school for an extended period of time. There is also a $45 application fee.

Transfer applicants must have a minimum 2.5 grade point average (a minimum 2.75 GPA for programs in science, business, math, and computer science) and must be in good standing at the last institution attended. Applicants must submit transcripts from all colleges and universities attended. Credit is usually given for grades of 2.0 or higher in University-equivalent courses taken at approved institutions; a maximum of 100 semester hours of transferable credit are allowed toward a bachelor's degree.

The application fee may be waived for applicants with financial need.

Application and Information

The University uses rolling admission. Admission decisions are announced on a rolling basis starting December 1. The preferred application deadlines are March 1 for freshman and June 1 for transfers.

Darryl E. Jones, Ph.D.
Director of Admissions
Seton Hall University
400 South Orange Avenue
South Orange, New Jersey 07079-2680
Telephone: 800-THE-HALL (toll-free)
E-mail: thehall@shu.edu
World Wide Web: http://www.shu.edu

SETON HILL UNIVERSITY
GREENSBURG, PENNSYLVANIA

The University

Seton Hill was founded by the Sisters of Charity in 1883 and chartered as a college by the commonwealth of Pennsylvania in 1918. In 2002, it became Seton Hill University.

Seton Hill, a liberal arts and sciences, coeducational institution, is situated in the Laurel Highlands, an area of southwestern Pennsylvania known for its beautiful scenery and wealth of outdoor activities such as skiing, cycling, hiking, and white-water rafting. Recreational opportunities include on-campus lectures, theater productions, a fitness center, and aerobics classes, as well as University-sponsored trips to Pittsburgh for cultural and sports events.

Seton Hill has varsity teams for women in basketball, cross-country, equestrian competition, field hockey, golf, soccer, softball, tennis, and volleyball and for men in baseball, basketball, cross-country, equestrian competition, football, golf, soccer, and tennis, as well as a variety of intramural teams.

At the graduate level, Seton Hill grants the Master of Arts degree in art therapy, elementary education, marriage and family therapy, special education, and writing popular fiction; a Master of Business Administration; and a Master of Education in technologies-enhanced learning.

Location

Seton Hill University's beautiful 200-acre campus is located in Greensburg, Pennsylvania. As a private university, Seton Hill is able to maintain a safe, secure environment that allows students to concentrate on academics.

Seton Hill is easily accessible by car, train, or plane. Just 35 miles east of Pittsburgh, Greensburg enjoys all the advantages of a large city while maintaining a small-town atmosphere. The seat of Westmoreland County, Greensburg is home to the Westmoreland Museum of Art, the Westmoreland Symphony Orchestra, a large mall, several shopping centers, and a hospital.

Majors and Degrees

The University grants the Bachelor of Arts, Bachelor of Fine Arts, Bachelor of Science, Bachelor of Music, and Bachelor of Social Work degrees.

Students choose from the following programs: accounting; art, including art and technology, art education, art history, art therapy, graphic design, studio art, and visual arts management; biology; chemistry, including biochemistry; communication; business, including entrepreneurial studies, human resources, information management, international organization, and marketing; computer science; dietetics; education, including early childhood, elementary, secondary, and special education; English, including creative writing, journalism, and literature; family and consumer sciences, including child care; history; hospitality and tourism; international studies; mathematics, including actuary science and a 3+2 engineering program; medical technology; music, including music education, music therapy, performance, and sacred music; a 2+2 nursing program; physician assistant studies; political science; psychology; religious studies/theology; social work; sociology; Spanish; and theater, including music theater, technical theater, theater arts, theater business, theater education, and theater performance.

The University offers preprofessional preparation for dentistry, law, medicine, occupational therapy, optometry, physical therapy, podiatry, and veterinary medicine.

Academic Program

Seton Hill offers five academic divisions, with the opportunity to self-design a major, all enhanced by the University's award-winning liberal arts core curriculum. Special programs are available for students who are undecided about their major.

The Seton Hill University Honors Program is available for students who have distinguished themselves academically in high school.

Prior to graduation, all undergraduate students complete a portfolio, a four-year compilation of their academic, professional, and personal achievements at Seton Hill. Portfolios allow students to showcase their learning and assist them in documenting their accomplishments as they transition from students to practicing professionals.

Students hoping to one day own a business may be interested in Seton Hill University's National Education Center for Women in Business. The center is the first organization of its kind in the United States to offer courses in business ownership and entrepreneurial activities to students in any major.

Off-Campus Programs

Seton Hill University recognizes that important learning experiences occur in nonacademic settings. For this reason, the University offers a variety of internships, fieldwork experiences, and cooperative education opportunities. The Office of Career Development and University faculty members assist students in finding an off-campus placement where practical experience related to the major and valuable job contacts for the future may be gained.

In addition, students may opt to spend a semester or year studying abroad.

Academic Facilities

At the center of the Seton Hill campus is Reeves Hall, housing a theater, art gallery, and spacious library that serves as the University's information center. Access to the library holdings is available via the library's online catalog which is also accessible through the Internet. Many online and CD-ROM research subscriptions are also available to students. In addition, students have access to six Pentium labs, a Power Mac lab, a multimedia lab, a Silicon Graphics lab, and clusters of computers in all residence halls. All students receive an Internet account for e-mail, navigating the Web, and conducting research. The on-campus Cyber Castle combines high technology with entertainment for all students.

In order to provide the maximum benefits possible, Seton Hill's nineteen academic and residence facilities have been specially designed with students' convenience in mind.

Costs

For the 2003–04 academic year, tuition for the full-time student was $18,930. Room and board fees were $6000. Books and personal expenses amounted to an additional $1000–$2000 per year.

Financial Aid

Seton Hill's Financial Aid Office works with each student to develop an aid package from the wide variety of scholarships, grants, loans, and work-study programs available.

Seton Hill offers Presidential Scholarships valued annually from $4732 to $9465, which are automatically awarded to students who rank in the top 10 percent, 20 percent, or 30 percent of their high school class and meet the admission criteria. In addition, valedictorian, leadership, community service, art, music, theater, biology, chemistry, math, and athletic scholarships are awarded based on merit.

Faculty

With a student-faculty ratio of 13:1, Seton Hill faculty members can explore the needs of each student and offer individual attention. The low student-faculty ratio allows each student to become personally acquainted with the instructor. In addition, Seton Hill faculty members understand the importance of being accessible to their students.

The Seton Hill faculty consists of 60 full-time professors, 81 percent of whom have doctoral or terminal degrees.

Student Government

Through the Seton Hill Government Association, students participate in the government of the University and enjoy voting representation on a number of faculty committees. Each residence hall floor is represented by a senator who acts as a liaison between the student senate and the student body. Participation in student government is a valuable experience that develops leadership skills and a working understanding of government.

In addition, the student government helps to sponsor numerous on-campus political, cultural, and social events. Off-campus activities include trips to Pittsburgh, New York City, and Washington, D.C.

Admission Requirements

Acceptance to the University is based on the successful completion of a college-preparatory curriculum in high school. Applicants should have completed at least 15 secondary school academic units. These units should include 4 units of English, 2 units of college-preparatory mathematics, 2 units of social science, 2 units of the same foreign language, 1 unit of laboratory science, and 4 academic electives.

Students who wish to transfer credits to Seton Hill from another college or university must present their transcripts for evaluation on a course-by-course basis. A transfer student will receive a credit evaluation upon admission to the University.

Application and Information

Seton Hill University has a rolling admissions policy. Decisions of the Admissions Committee are rendered shortly after all application materials have been submitted.

The first-time freshman applicant should submit a completed application form, a $30 nonrefundable application fee, an official secondary school transcript that includes the applicant's rank and cumulative grade point average, and official score reports from either the SAT or ACT.

Prospective students who do not have SAT or ACT scores may submit two graded written assignments from their junior or senior year for consideration.

For more information, students should contact:

Mary Kay Cooper
Director of Admissions and Adult Student Services
Seton Hill University
Seton Hill Drive
Greensburg, Pennsylvania 15601-1599
Telephone: 724-838-4255
800-826-6234 (toll-free)
Fax: 724-830-1294
E-mail: admit@setonhill.edu
World Wide Web: http://www.setonhill.edu

The Administration Building is a picturesque focal point on the Seton Hill campus.

SHAWNEE STATE UNIVERSITY

PORTSMOUTH, OHIO

The College

Shawnee State University (SSU), with 3,400 students, is Ohio's newest state university. Previously a community college, Shawnee State became the state's thirteenth university in 1986.

Although most students come from Ohio and contiguous states, Shawnee State encourages applications from other states and countries. Shawnee State is committed to the special educational value that is provided by a residential campus community. The University holds the belief that students who live on campus gain valuable life experience and form many lasting friendships. For that reason, freshmen who are single, under the age of 23, and live outside of a 50-mile radius of the University are required to live in campus housing and participate in a meal plan. Exceptions are made for those students who live with a direct relative within a 50-mile radius of campus or are single parents or military veterans. Shawnee State University Housing consists of town houses and apartments. There are no traditional-style dormitories.

To help new students through their first year on campus, Shawnee State's Student Success Center offers advising and scheduling of classes, counseling, and referral services to various support offices on campus.

The University's small-campus environment provides many opportunities for involvement and leadership in out-of-class activities, including Student Government Association, the student newspaper, athletics, intramurals, various clubs and organizations, and fraternities and sororities. The James A. Rhodes Athletic Center, which houses a junior Olympic-size pool, racquetball courts, tennis courts, a Nautilus room and free weights, fitness machines, a whirlpool, and saunas, is also open to Shawnee State students.

Location

Shawnee State's 50-acre campus is situated between the Ohio River and downtown Portsmouth, Ohio. A city of 23,000 people, Portsmouth provides the conveniences of life in a small town. With proximity to the larger cities of Columbus and Cincinnati, Ohio, and Huntington, West Virginia, SSU also offers the benefits of those metropolitan areas. Outdoor recreational opportunities are available at Shawnee State Park, which is located only a few miles from campus. This state facility provides nature trails and opportunities for hiking, boating, fishing, and golfing.

Majors and Degrees

Shawnee State University offers both baccalaureate and associate degrees. Bachelor of Arts (B.A.) programs include English/humanities; English/humanities, with an option in education licensure; history; social sciences, with integrated social studies licensure; and social sciences, with options in education licensure and legal assisting (2+2). Bachelor of Fine Arts (B.F.A.) degrees are offered with majors in ceramics, drawing, painting, studio arts with a multi-age visual arts licensure, and visualist digital design and interactive media. Majors offered for the Bachelor of Science (B.S.) degree include biology; biology, with an option in premedicine; business administration; business administration, with options in accounting, health management, management information systems, and legal assisting (2+2); chemistry; chemistry, with an option in premedicine; computer engineering technology; education, with licensure in early childhood, middle childhood, and intervention; environmental engineering technology; mathematical sciences; natural science; natural science, with options in applied mathematics, applied mathematics/education licensure, biology, biology/education licensure, biology/environmental science, chemistry, chemistry/education licensure, and chemistry/environmental science; occupational therapy; plastics engineering technology; and sports studies, with options in athletic training, fitness development, and sports management.

Associate of Applied Business degree programs include accounting, business information systems, business management, legal assisting, and office administration. Associate of Applied Science degree programs are offered in computer-aided drafting and design, dental hygiene, electromechanical engineering technology, instrumentation and control, medical laboratory studies, nursing, occupational therapy assistant studies, physical therapist assistant studies, plastics engineering technology, radiologic technology, and respiratory therapy. Associate of Arts degree programs include arts/humanities (with options in art, communications, English, and music) and social science. The Associate of Science degree is offered in mathematics and sciences.

Academic Program

Recognizing the importance of knowledge, values, and cultural enrichment, Shawnee State University is committed to providing an undergraduate education that fosters competence in oral and written communication, scientific and quantitative reasoning, and critical analysis/logical thinking. In addition to the course requirements in the academic major, all baccalaureate programs require the General Education Program (GEP), a combination of required and elective courses that contribute to the skills and knowledge characteristic of university graduates. All students also take Senior Seminar, which involves the research and writing of a major paper and an oral presentation of findings. Baccalaureate degree programs require a minimum of 186 quarter hours, including 48 credit hours in the General Education Program. Associate degrees generally require 90 quarter hours.

The Honors Program offers students the opportunity to interact more closely with motivated faculty members and other students in a learning community. Honors sections are typically smaller than normal classes and are more interactive in nature. Students in the Honors Program also have the opportunity to participate in special events and trips. Graduating with a honors degree signals potential employers or graduate schools that a student is the type of person likely to succeed. Students who successfully complete the Honors Program receive an honors certificate along with their diploma and special recognition at graduation. In addition, honors students receive preferential treatment for registration.

Off-Campus Programs

Some Shawnee State University students have participated in short-term exchange programs with Nizhny Novgorod State University in Russia; in cultural exchange programs with Zittau, Germany, and Orizaba, Mexico, sister cities of Portsmouth, Ohio; and with Universitat Jaume I in Castelló, Spain. Other off-campus opportunities include internships that are available through the Office of Career Services.

Academic Facilities

Shawnee State University is situated on a modern campus, with five major building projects completed since 1991. Among the newest buildings is the library, which houses more than 122,000 bound volumes and 1,000 periodical subscriptions, and provides 700 study stations and ten group study rooms. The Advanced Technology Center provides classrooms and computer laboratories for engineering technology students and houses a planetarium that features Digistar II, a computer that runs software of the heavens and the center of the earth.

Opened in 1995, the Vern Riffe Center for the Arts includes a 1,150-seat theater designed by George C. Izenour, a recital hall, a virtual-reality audio room, and art galleries. This state-of-the-art center also houses classrooms and studios for subjects that range from graphic studies and electronic graphics to printing, lithography, intaglio, painting, and sculpture.

Costs

Tuition and fees for Ohio residents in 2004–05 are $4905. Room and board costs range from $5583 to $6309, depending on the meal plan selected and place of residence. Out-of-state tuition and fees for the 2004–05 school year total $8001. Approximately $750 to $900 should be anticipated for books. Students from Boyd, Carter, Elliot, Fleming, Greenup, Lawrence, Lewis, Mason, and Rowan Counties in Kentucky are eligible to receive in-state tuition rates. Students should go to the University's Web site for more details.

Financial Aid

More than 80 percent of Shawnee students receive some form of financial aid, including more than 100 scholarships, grants, college work-study, and student loans. To apply for financial aid, students must file the Free Application for Federal Student Aid (FAFSA). Approximately $1.25 million in scholarship money is earmarked each year.

Faculty

While applied research and community service are respected and valued, Shawnee State University is first and foremost a teaching institution. All classes are taught by full-time or part-time faculty members, and all full-time faculty members serve as academic advisers. Classes are small, with a faculty-student ratio of 1:16. Fifty percent of full-time faculty members hold doctoral degrees.

Student Government

The Shawnee State University Student Government Association is composed of 25 students who are elected by the student body. The Student Government Association is the parent organization of the University's student clubs and organizations and provides an avenue to students to be represented on various university committees.

In addition to representation on the Student Government Association, 2 students, appointed by the Governor of Ohio, serve on the Shawnee State University Board of Trustees.

Admission Requirements

Admission to Shawnee State University is open and rolling. Applicants must be high school graduates or recipients of the GED. To be accepted without condition, applicants must file an application for admission and arrange for an official final transcript to be sent directly from the high school to Shawnee State. Transfer students must have official transcripts forwarded from all other colleges and universities previously attended.

The programs in health science are selective in admission and limited in enrollment. These may require specific academic preparation in high school and minimum high school GPA and ACT scores; some require specific volunteer experiences. All have deadlines by which all requirements must be met to be considered for program admission. There is a $20 application fee for health sciences programs.

Application and Information

The Office of Admission is open from 8 a.m. to 5 p.m. on weekdays. Saturday appointments are available. For further information about Shawnee State University, academic programs, and visitation days or to schedule a campus visit and tour, students should contact:

Office of Admission
Shawnee State University
940 Second Street
Portsmouth, Ohio 45662
Telephone: 740-351-4-SSU
800-959-2-SSU (toll-free)
Fax: 740-351-3111
E-mail: to_ssu@shawnee.edu
World Wide Web: http://www.shawnee.edu/

The courtyard in front of Massie Hall.

SHELDON JACKSON COLLEGE

SITKA, ALASKA

The College

As Alaska's oldest continuously operated institution, Sheldon Jackson College has had the privilege of serving the families of Alaska and the nation for 125 years. Since 1878, in historical covenant with the Presbyterian Church (USA), the mission of Sheldon Jackson College has been to teach and model the value of service through providing outstanding educational opportunities to the people of the region, state, nation, and world. Originally established by Presbyterian missionary Sheldon Jackson to provide for the education of Alaska's Native peoples, the College today enrolls students from approximately thirty states.

Sheldon Jackson College began as the Sitka Mission School. Since then, it has grown from an industrial trade school, boarding school, elementary school, high school, and junior college to a fully accredited, four-year liberal arts institution. In 1911, the main campus buildings were erected. Between 1971 and 1988, the campus flourished, and several new buildings were constructed, including the Rasmuson Student Center, the Metlakatla Apartments, the Caroline Yaw Chapel, the Brady Apartment Complex, the Lloyd F. Hames Physical Education Center, and the David Sweetland Hall.

Since its inception as a college, many degree programs have been added. The educational strengths of the College continue to be teacher education, environmental sciences, human services, outdoor leadership, business administration, liberal arts, and individual studies. All academic programs are fully accredited by the Northwest Association of Schools and Colleges. Sheldon Jackson College grants certificates and associate and bachelor's degrees.

Sheldon Jackson College is a residential campus, with nearly 65 percent of the students residing on campus. Students under the age of 21 are required to live in residence halls. Student residences are equipped with Internet access and are wired for phone and cable service. Students may choose from single or double rooms. Married students and students with children may live off campus or in the family housing apartments located on campus. Students who want family housing units are encouraged to apply early.

In addition to academic and residence buildings, the campus consists of the Hames Physical Education Center, with an indoor swimming pool, a climbing wall, racquetball courts, a full-size basketball court with seating for 600, and a weight room. The newly renovated Rasmuson Student Center offers a mini-theater, game room, bookstore, café, and many more student areas. Allen Memorial Hall, which is currently being renovated, will offer a 300-seat auditorium with a state-of-the-art sound system.

The Sheldon Jackson Child Care Center is currently located off campus. However, in 2004–05, a new child-care center is scheduled to be constructed on campus. The children of students have priority placement and receive a discount.

Location

The campus of Sheldon Jackson College and the city of Sitka, Alaska, are located on the western shore of Baranof Island in southeast Alaska. The campus setting provides a vista view of the North Pacific and is backed by part of the Tongass National Forest and an array of encompassing mountains. Because of its natural setting, Sitka is considered one of Alaska's most beautiful ports of call. Sheldon Jackson College is nestled within the largest temperate rain forest in the world. The island-studded waters of Sitka Sound provide shelter from the Pacific Ocean, and Mount Edgecumbe, an extinct volcano, rises majestically from nearby Kruzof Island, dominating the horizon. Warmed by the Japanese Current, Sitka enjoys a moderate climate, with cool summers (50 to 70 degrees Fahrenheit), mild winters (20 to 40 degrees Fahrenheit), and rainfall of nearly 90 inches per year.

Sitka, with a population of 8,500, is Alaska's fifth-largest city. It is a community of rich cultural heritage, and many reminders of Sitka's past are still visible today. Native totems in Sitka National Historical Park are silent testimony to Sitka's heritage as an Alaska Native settlement hundreds of years before the Russians arrived. The Russian Bishop's House and St. Michael's Russian Orthodox Cathedral are reminders that Sitka was the capital of Russian America and was once known as the "Paris of the Pacific." Sheldon Jackson plays a large part in the history of Sitka, and seventeen of the campus buildings have received Historic Landmark status.

While Sitka is firmly rooted in history, it is a vibrant and modern city. Since Sitka is located on an island, travel is by air, with daily flights by Alaska Airlines, or by sea, with the Alaska Marine Highway Ferry System.

Majors and Degrees

Sheldon Jackson College offers academic programs in business administration, elementary and secondary education, environmental sciences, human services, individualized studies, liberal arts, and outdoor leadership.

Academic Programs

The academic program at Sheldon Jackson College incorporates classroom instruction, hands-on education, wilderness experiences, Alaska Native perspectives, and active participation within a supportive community. It is the intention of the College that each student who graduates from Sheldon Jackson will have obtained not only intellectual competence and technical career skills but also wisdom, service leadership, and the personal character required to become a great leader.

Sheldon Jackson College uses a semester academic calendar. The fall semester runs from September through mid-December, and the spring semester runs from January through early May. A typical course load consists of five courses (15 credit hours) in the fall and spring semesters. A bachelor's degree requires the completion of 120 credit hours.

Academic Facilities

The 350-acre campus of Sheldon Jackson College is surrounded by thousands of acres of living laboratory. Temperate rain forests, muskeg, tidal zones, wetlands, mountains, and the Pacific Ocean are within walking distance of the campus. The College operates a full-production salmon hatchery, and the science building houses freshwater and saltwater aquariums with flow-through water systems.

Stratton Library houses more than 45,000 items in a variety of print and nonprint media. Because of the collection's historical breadth, it furnishes academic and research support about early

Alaska to the entire world as well as the Sheldon Jackson and Sitka communities. Noted author James Michener wrote his novel *Alaska* while in residence at Sheldon Jackson College. The Sheldon Jackson Museum, which contains the finest collection of Alaska Native artifacts in the world, is also located on campus.

Costs

Tuition and fees for 2004–05 are $10,600. Room and board costs (based upon a double-occupancy room and nineteen-meal plan) are $7300 for the year. Travel costs vary. Books and personal expenses are estimated at $1200.

Financial Aid

Sheldon Jackson College recognizes that financing a college education is a major factor in obtaining a college degree. In addition to federal financial aid, students may apply for a variety of institutional scholarships and awards. Priority scholarship consideration is given to students who apply and are admitted by February 28. All students are required to submit the Free Application for Federal Student Aid (FAFSA) along with the application for admission to Sheldon Jackson College.

Faculty

There are 20 full-time faculty members at Sheldon Jackson College. Faculty members are selected for their concern for students, their love of Alaska, and their commitment to the Sheldon Jackson College mission. The College has maintained a commitment to small classes in which professors come to know each student not only by name but also by background, potential, and personal interests. The student-teacher ratio is 13:1 and the average class size is 8.

Student Government

Students are elected to the Associated Student Body of Sheldon Jackson College (ASBSJC), which allocates budget expenditures for student clubs and organizations. The ASBSJC also acts as a student voice in policy matters and makes recommendations related to improvements in educational programs or campus facilities.

Admission Requirements

Sheldon Jackson College enjoys a flexible admittance policy. In order to be accepted, applicants must have graduated from an accredited high school (or present an equivalent credential) with a minimum 2.0 grade point average. Transfer students must have a minimum 2.0 grade point average to be admitted. Applicants who do not meet these requirements are considered for admission through the Sheldon Jackson College Achievement Program. It is recommended that students submit a letter of recommendation and a personal statement.

Application and Information

Application forms are accepted on a rolling basis. Priority scholarship consideration is given to students who apply and are admitted by February 28. Application materials may be obtained by contacting:

Office of Admissions
Sheldon Jackson College
801 Lincoln Street
Sitka, Alaska 99835
Telephone: 800-478-4556 (toll-free)
E-mail: admissions@sj-alaska.edu
World Wide Web: http://www.sj-alaska.edu

SHENANDOAH UNIVERSITY
WINCHESTER, VIRGINIA

The University

Shenandoah University was founded at Dayton, Virginia, in 1875. Although the institution was established to provide "classical" and music studies, by 1888 an unusual blend of educational opportunities had been formulated that included arts, sciences, music, medical arts, and business management. These programs, on a much more sophisticated basis, are found at Shenandoah today. In 1960, Shenandoah moved to a 62-acre campus in Winchester, Virginia. The main campus is now more than 100 acres with nineteen buildings, including six residence halls. Of these six facilities for boarding students, one is for women and five are coeducational. There are five additional buildings at off-campus locations. Shenandoah's historical relationship with the United Methodist Church does not place sectarian obligations on any student.

Shenandoah's students have the distinct advantage of being on a small campus near large metropolitan cultural centers. Such student organizations as academic fraternities, service and honor organizations, and various departmental clubs provide opportunities for leadership and recreation. Students come to Shenandoah because they want an educational experience of superior quality and believe that the facilities of a small campus, with a personal atmosphere, are the most conducive to achieving this experience. Fifty-seven percent of the 2,586 students are from Virginia; the remaining 43 percent represent forty-five states and forty-one countries.

Graduate study is also available at Shenandoah. Programs are offered in athletic training, business administration, dance, education, music, nursing, occupational therapy, pharmacy, physical therapy, and physician assistant studies. Further information about graduate study may be obtained by writing to the Director of Admissions.

Shenandoah University is accredited by the Commission on Colleges of the Southern Association of Colleges and Schools (1866 Southern Lane, Decatur, GA 30033-4097; telephone: 404-679-4501) to award associate, bachelor's, master's, and doctoral degrees. Shenandoah holds membership in a number of professional organizations.

Location

The Shenandoah campus, adjacent to Interstate 81, is located 72 miles west of Washington, D.C., in the historic Shenandoah Valley of Virginia. The University is located on the southeast edge of the city of Winchester, Virginia. Winchester/Frederick County, rich in history, is a vigorous community of approximately 70,000 people. The region has a moderate, healthful climate; cultural groups; park and recreation areas; resorts; fishing; hunting; winter sports; modern retail centers; and major medical facilities.

Majors and Degrees

Shenandoah University offers seven undergraduate degrees: the Bachelor of Arts, the Bachelor of Business Administration, the Bachelor of Fine Arts, the Bachelor of Music, the Bachelor of Music Therapy, the Bachelor of Science, the Associate in Science, and several certificate programs. Programs of study available include administration of justice, American studies, arts management (dance, music, and theater), arts studies, biology, business education, business administration (accounting, banking and finance, information systems and computer technology, international business, management, and marketing), business studies, chemistry, Christian leadership, church music, commercial music, composition, dance, dance education, educational psychology, elementary education, English, environmental studies, health-care management, history, information systems and computer technology, jazz studies, kinesiology (exercise science, physical education and health, and sports administration), mass communications, mathematics, middle school education, music education, music theater, music theater accompanying, music therapy, music with elective studies, nursing (LPN to B.S.N. and RN to B.S.N.), pedagogy (guitar or piano), performance (opera and pedagogy), piano accompanying, professional studies/teacher education, psychology, public administration/political science, purchasing management, religion, respiratory care (both two- and four-year degree programs), secondary education, sociology, Spanish, Spanish interpreting, teaching English to speakers of other languages, theater (acting, costume design, directing, and scenic and lighting design), theater for youth, and university studies. Selected programs of study may result in double majors for students who wish to concentrate on more than one area of study. Preprofessional programs of study are available in athletic training, dental, law, medicine, occupational therapy, pharmacy, physical therapy, physician assistant, and veterinary.

Academic Program

Shenandoah's academic calendar is divided into fall and spring semesters. Summer terms, ranging in length from two to eleven weeks, are also available. Each academic division (arts and sciences, business, conservatory, and health professions) offers diversified programs, with specific courses required by the various accreditation agencies. Credit is available through the tests of the College-Level Examination Program (CLEP), Proficiency Examination Program (PEP), and Advanced Placement (AP) Program and through various departmental challenge examinations.

Off-Campus Programs

Clinical practice, internships, and student-teaching opportunities are arranged with local businesses, hospitals, clinics, nursing homes, mental-health-care centers, and elementary, middle, and secondary schools in the Winchester area. Students are given the opportunity to enrich their educational experience through travel and study-abroad programs.

Academic Facilities

The Alson H. Smith, Jr. Library contains approximately 123,000 volumes, 134,169 microforms, 17,823 records and CDs, and 16,200 music scores and subscribes to 1,150 periodicals. The media center contains visual and audio materials and equipment and preview and listening rooms. The Gregory Building contains laboratories for biology, chemistry, environmental studies, modern languages, and physics; a digital radio station; and multimedia classrooms. A digital television station is on campus. Henkel Hall contains a 200-seat lecture hall, a student computer laboratory, and a teaching computer laboratory for business and arts and sciences students. The Health Professions Building contains a health professions library, computer laboratories, multimedia classrooms, research laboratories, and interactive video and computer laboratories that simulate clinical practice realities for nursing, pharmacy, and respiratory care students. Physician assistant program facilities include laboratories and multimedia classrooms. The Cork Street

Center contains multimedia classrooms, computer laboratories, the Center for Clinical Research, and the Clinical Skills Laboratory for occupational therapy and physical therapy students. Conservatory facilities include the Ohrstrom-Bryant Theatre, which seats 632 people and includes a scene shop, costume shop, and the Glaize Studio Theatre; Goodson Chapel–Recital Hall, with a Möller tracker-action organ; Ruebush Hall, with a fully equipped twenty-four-track professional recording studio, practice rooms, and music education and music therapy laboratories; the Shingleton Building, with two dance studios; and Armstrong Hall, with a 700-seat concert hall. The Shingleton Building contains a gymnasium, a fitness room, and athletic training laboratories. Athletic facilities include practice fields, Aikens Stadium, and the new 2,500-seat Shentel Stadium. The Athletic Center contains a weight room and athletic training laboratories.

The Shenandoah University Network (SUnet) structure provides a high-speed fiber backbone that supports numerous networked Windows and Macintosh workstations. The campus has four IBM-platform labs and a Macintosh-platform lab for general use. All workstations in the labs have full Internet and e-mail access, and all Shenandoah University students have Internet and e-mail accounts. Wireless internet access is available in some buildings and will be expanded to the entire campus. The campus is also equipped with e-mail stations. Remote access is available for faculty, staff, and student use.

Costs

The 2003–04 comprehensive annual fee (two semesters) for resident full-time undergraduate students was $25,110, which included tuition and room and board. The comprehensive annual tuition (two semesters) for commuting (day) full-time undergraduate students was $18,310. Undergraduate part-time tuition was $560 per credit hour. Private applied music lessons for music students cost an additional $500 per year for major study (1 hour per week) and $250 per year for minor study (1 half hour per week). Such incidentals as transportation, personal expenses, and laundry vary in cost; textbook costs, however, can be estimated at $1000 per year. There is no difference in the cost of tuition and fees for out-of-state students. The Board of Trustees reserves the right to alter charges at any time.

Financial Aid

Shenandoah makes every effort to assist students in finding resources to finance their education. Approximately 91 percent of the University's students receive some type of financial aid. Shenandoah annually awards more than $28 million in aid to students in the form of grants, loans, scholarships, and employment on the campus. Previous financial aid packages have averaged approximately $13,000 per undergraduate student per year. To qualify for scholarships and financial aid, students must submit the Free Application for Federal Student Aid (FAFSA). Aid is awarded on a first-come, first-served basis, as funds are available. A student must be accepted for admission to a degree program before a financial aid offer is made. Specific information regarding financial aid should be requested from the Director of Financial Aid.

Faculty

Shenandoah has 177 full-time faculty members and 152 part-time faculty members; 177 faculty members (136 full-time and 41 part-time) hold a Ph.D. or other terminal degree. The faculty-student ratio is approximately 1:8. The size of the student body encourages excellent communication and rapport among students and faculty members. Members of the faculty advise students and plan activities that concern the student body as a whole. Shenandoah faculty members have a strong commitment to teaching and counseling students.

Student Government

The Student Government Association (SGA) is the main student organization on campus. In addition to promoting activities of varied interest, the SGA provides a means of communication and understanding among students, faculty members, and administrators. Students are encouraged to participate in the governing of Shenandoah and are represented on all faculty and administrative committees.

Admission Requirements

Shenandoah seeks a diverse student body through the individualized admission processing of each applicant under a rolling admission program. Applicants are evaluated on the basis of their high school record and SAT I or ACT scores. Students applying for degree programs in music, dance, or theater must successfully complete an audition or portfolio interview. Shenandoah does not discriminate on the basis of sex, race, color, religion, national or ethnic origin, age, or physical disability. Although interviews are not required, students are encouraged to visit the campus.

Application and Information

To apply, a student must submit an application with a $20 nonrefundable application fee, SAT I or ACT scores, and an official high school transcript. Transfer students must submit an official college transcript for all postsecondary course work in addition to meeting the freshman score and transcript requirements. Applicants are notified of the admission decision after receipt of all credentials. An application, financial aid information, and other materials may be obtained by contacting:

Dean of Admissions
Shenandoah University
1460 University Drive
Winchester, Virginia 22601
Telephone: 540-665-4581
800-432-2266 (toll-free)
Fax: 540-665-4627
E-mail: admit@su.edu

SHEPHERD UNIVERSITY

SHEPHERDSTOWN, WEST VIRGINIA

The University

Shepherd University, founded in 1871, is a very competitive, four-year, state-supported institution offering more than seventy undergraduate fields of study in the liberal arts and sciences, business, and teacher education. Graduate programs are offered in ten fields. Shepherd is the fastest-growing institution in West Virginia. There are 4,800 students on the 323-acre campus; 60 percent come from West Virginia, and the remaining 40 percent represent forty-eight other states and twenty-four countries.

The University prides itself on its friendly and helpful atmosphere and the individual contact the students receive as a result of small classes. On campus there are fifty organizations, ranging from national fraternities and sororities to community service groups, from professional organizations to student government. Students are encouraged to join and interact with all of the groups that interest them.

Shepherd University also offers both men's and women's intercollegiate sports. The men's program consists of baseball, basketball, cross-country, football, golf, soccer, and tennis. The women's sports program consists of basketball, cheerleading, cross-country, soccer, softball, tennis, and volleyball. Men and women compete in the NCAA Division II program. An NCLC club lacrosse program is available for both men and women. For students not interested in playing intercollegiate sports, an extensive intramural and recreation program is also available.

Students are housed on campus in twelve residence halls. Seven offer suite arrangements with 4 students sharing two bedrooms, a living room, and bath. Five buildings house students in traditional 2-student dorm rooms. All buildings are coeducational. An apartment complex is being built for upperclass and graduate students.

Location

Shepherd University is located in historic Shepherdstown (founded in 1730), a small community on the banks of the Potomac River with a population of approximately 7,000. Shepherdstown is the oldest town in West Virginia and the site of the launching of the first successful steamboat in 1787 by James Rumsey. Shepherdstown hosted the Syrian-Israeli Peace Talks in January 2000. Other historic landmarks, located within 8 miles of campus, include the Antietam National Battlefield Park, Harpers Ferry National Historical Park, and the Chesapeake and Ohio Canal Historical Park and Trail. The area is rural, and hunting, fishing, horseback riding, waterskiing, and snow skiing are available for recreation. Communication and cooperation between the community and the University are very good, and many cultural events are sponsored jointly.

The University is a 10-minute drive from Martinsburg, West Virginia; 15 minutes from Charles Town and Harpers Ferry, West Virginia; 25 minutes from Hagerstown and Frederick, Maryland; and 90 minutes from Washington, D.C., and Baltimore, Maryland.

Majors and Degrees

Shepherd University offers the Bachelor of Arts, Bachelor of Fine Arts, and Bachelor of Science degrees in accounting, aquatic science, art and art education (graphic design, painting, photography, printmaking, and sculpture), athletic training, biochemistry, biology, broadcasting, business administration, business education, chemistry, Civil War and 19th-century American history, communications, computer science, computer programming and information systems, criminal justice, early childhood education, economics, elementary education, English, environmental chemistry, environmental engineering, environmental studies, exercise science/fitness, family and consumer sciences, finance, general science, health education, historic preservation, history, literature, management, marketing, mathematics, music and music education (musical theater, performance, piano pedagogy, and theory/composition), networking and data communication, physical education, physics, political science, psychology, recreation and leisure services (commercial and hospitality, sport communications, sport and event management, and therapeutic recreation), sociology, and theater; the Bachelor of Science in Nursing degree in nursing; and the Bachelor of Social Work degree in social work.

Shepherd University offers the Associate of Arts, Associate of Applied Science, and Associate of Science degrees in business, criminal justice, culinary arts, emergency medical services, engineering (2 + 2 program), fashion merchandising, fire service and safety technology, general studies, graphic design, information technology, nursing, office technology, photography, and studio art.

Preprofessional programs are available in the fields of dentistry, law, medicine, pharmacy, theology, and veterinary science.

An early acceptance to the medical school program with the West Virginia University School of Health Sciences is available to premedical students.

Academic Program

All candidates for the baccalaureate degree must complete a minimum of 128 semester hours of course work with a minimum 2.0 overall average and a minimum 2.0 average in their major. Students in teacher education must have a minimum 2.5 average in their elementary education or secondary education field. The 128 semester hours include a general studies core, consisting of 19 hours in the humanities, 11 hours in science and mathematics, 15 hours in social sciences, and 2 hours in physical education. To earn the associate degree, students must complete 64 to 73 semester hours, depending on the program of study.

Student internships and practicums are required or recommended in the following areas of study: education, fashion merchandising, graphic design, mass communications, nursing, photography, psychology, recreation and leisure services, and social work. Biology and chemistry majors may utilize such nearby research facilities as the U.S. Fish and Wildlife Service National Education Training Center, the National Cancer Research Center at Fort Dietrick, the National Fisheries Center at Leetown, and the Appalachian Fruit Research Center at Bardane for their directed research projects. CIS majors may do their internships with the IRS National Computer Center, ATF Firearms Identification Center, or the Coast Guard Vessel Identification Center located in Martinsburg. The Washington Gateway and Washington Semester programs provide formal internships in Washington, D.C. Co-op programs may be arranged in most major fields.

Academic Facilities

Academic facilities on the Shepherd University campus include an open-stack library with a collection of 500,000 materials; six academic buildings housing classrooms and laboratories; a Creative Arts Center housing the departments of art, music, and theater; and a comprehensive health, physical education, and athletic complex. The nearby libraries, museums, and cultural and research centers of the Washington, D.C., metropolitan area are also available for research and study.

Costs

For 2003–04, tuition and fees were $3270 per year for West Virginia residents and $8030 per year for out-of-state students. Average room and board charges were $5338 per year. Books and supplies were about $1000 a year. Additional expenses vary, depending on a student's personal tastes, but were estimated to be between $40 and $80 per week.

Financial Aid

The University offers financial aid through the Federal Pell Grant, Federal Supplemental Educational Opportunity Grant, Federal Perkins Loan, Federal Stafford Student Loan, and Federal Work-Study programs. Federally insured student loans (arranged in cooperation with the student's local bank) are also available. The University offers academic, athletic, and talent scholarships based on merit.

Faculty

Of the University's 120 full-time faculty members, 85 percent have earned doctorates or terminal degrees; all other faculty members have completed advanced work beyond the master's level, and many are doctoral candidates. All teaching is done by faculty members. The student-faculty ratio is 19:1. Faculty members serve as advisers to students in their respective disciplines, and they work with and participate in extracurricular organizations and activities on campus.

Student Government

The Shepherd University Student Government Association (SGA) consists of a policy-making body, the Executive Council, composed of the student body president and the cabinet, and an advisory and regulatory body, the Senate, composed of student representatives. Also affiliated with the SGA are 3 students who are elected to serve on the Student Affairs Committee, the central decision-making body on the campus concerned with student-life policies. The SGA sanctions student organizations and activities and controls the student activity fees and their disbursement among the various units of the University. Student representatives are members of all policy-making and program committees on campus.

Admission Requirements

Applicants must be graduates of accredited high schools and have at least 21 academic units of high school credit. Shepherd University requires that the 21 units be in the following areas: English, 4 units (years); mathematics, 3 units (algebra I and II and geometry); science, 3 units (biology, chemistry, and physics); social studies, 3 units (including American history); foreign language, 2 units; physical education, 2 units; and electives, at least 4 units (in such areas as music, art, drama, and computer science).

Applicants wishing full consideration for admission should have about a B average in high school, and they should have SAT I combined scores of about 1100 or ACT composite scores of about 21. Students are encouraged to take honors or advanced-placement courses in high school. College credit is given for most Advanced Placement test scores of 4 and 5 and in some cases for scores of 3. Written recommendations from high school guidance counselors are highly recommended for all freshman applicants. Admission interviews are not required, but campus visits are strongly advised.

Transfer students should have a minimum cumulative grade point average of 2.5 and a recommendation from the dean of students at their previous institution. Shepherd University does not admit transfer students who are on academic probation or suspension at any other institution. Transfer students majoring in any area of education must submit either SAT I or ACT scores for admission to the teacher education program.

Application and Information

The priority deadline for applications for the fall term is February 1, for the spring term it is November 1, and for the summer term it is February 1. Applications are accepted until June 15 if space remains in some academic programs. A separate departmental application must be filed along with the University application for entrance to the engineering and nursing programs (for fall term only). Art applicants must submit a portfolio, and music majors must audition for admission to the program. Teacher education majors must take and pass the PPST examination before enrollment in any Education Department courses. Early action applicants are notified of their admission status after December 15 of their senior year in high school. Students applying for regular admission are notified of their admission status on April 1. A nonrefundable enrollment deposit is due May 1, in compliance with the National Association for College Admission Counseling (NACAC) guidelines. Students are strongly encouraged to call the admissions office to schedule an admissions interview and a tour of campus.

For information about admission and programs, prospective students should contact:

Office of Admissions
P.O. Box 3210
Shepherd University
Shepherdstown, West Virginia 25443-3210
Telephone: 304-876-5212 or 5213
800-344-5231 (toll-free)
Fax: 304-876-5165
E-mail: kwolf@shepherd.edu
World Wide Web: http://www.shepherd.edu

McMurran Hall, built in 1859, houses the Office of Admissions.

SHIPPENSBURG UNIVERSITY OF PENNSYLVANIA

SHIPPENSBURG, PENNSYLVANIA

The University

Shippensburg University, founded in 1871, is a comprehensive public institution in south-central Pennsylvania enrolling more than 6,500 undergraduate students and approximately 1,000 graduate students. Of the undergraduates, 54 percent are women and 46 percent are men. The University is divided into the College of Arts and Sciences, the College of Education and Human Services, the John L. Grove College of Business, and the School of Graduate Studies. There is also a Division of Special Academic Programs, which includes the Division of Undeclared Majors.

Shippensburg University is a member of the Pennsylvania State System of Higher Education and is accredited by the Middle States Association of Colleges and Schools. Other accreditation is by the AACSB International–The International Association to Advance Collegiate Schools of Business, the American Chemical Society, the Council on Social Work Education, the Council for the Accreditation of Counseling and Related Educational Programs, the International Association of Counseling Services, the Council for Exceptional Children, the National Council for the Accreditation of Coaching Education, and the National Council for the Accreditation of Teachers. Shippensburg University is a member of the Council of Graduate Schools.

Graduate degrees conferred are the Master of Art, Master of Business Administration, Master of Education, Master of Science, and Master of Public Administration. Programs are as follows: Master of Art in applied history; Master of Science in administration of justice, applied gerontology, biology, communication studies, computer science, counseling (college, student personnel, community, mental health), geoenvironmental studies, information systems, organizational development and leadership, and psychology; Master of Science in business administration; Master of Public Administration in public administration; and Master of Education in counseling (elementary and secondary), curriculum and instruction, educational leadership and policy, reading, and special education (comprehensive, mental retardation, learning disabilities, behavior disorders). The School of Graduate Studies also offers post-master's degree curricula leading to various types of education certification, including supervisory certification, and is one of twenty-three national sites for a post-graduate academic training program in Reading Recovery.

More than 200 student clubs, organizations, and activity groups, resulting in nearly 600 leadership opportunities, are available. Organizations include academic clubs, community service groups, special interest organizations, media organizations, musical groups, performing arts troupes, and twenty national or local fraternities and sororities.

Student activities are complemented by programs that bring nationally and internationally known figures to campus. Coretta Scott King, widow of Dr. Martin Luther King Jr.; U.S. Supreme Court Justice Harry A. Blackmun; Nobel Peace Prize recipient Archbishop Desmond Tutu; Rev. Jesse Jackson; actor Danny Glover; actor Sidney Poitier; author and poet Maya Angelou; Vice President Dick Cheney; author Kurt Vonnegut Jr.; and Elizabeth Dole have all appeared on campus.

Each of the eight residence halls is equipped with lounges, exercise rooms, music practice rooms, study rooms, and computer connections to the online library catalog system. Each residence hall room has one cable television and two direct computer network connections. Most residence hall rooms are double occupancy; some single rooms are available. Seavers Complex houses six students in each unit. Student safety is emphasized through controlled access to the residence halls, trained supervisory personnel, and a keycard entry system. There is also an apartment-style student housing facility with one, two, or four bedrooms, living room, bathroom, and full kitchen.

The University offers a variety of athletic facilities for both intercollegiate and intramural sports. These include a 2,768-seat field house, an 8,000-seat stadium, a gymnasium, outdoor tennis courts, indoor and outdoor tracks, two indoor swimming pools, squash and handball courts, a physical fitness center, a rehabilitation center, and sand volleyball courts. The University is a member of the Pennsylvania State Athletic Conference and NCAA Division II. Men's intercollegiate sports include baseball, basketball, cross-country, football, soccer, swimming, track and field, and wrestling. Women's intercollegiate sports include basketball, cross-country, field hockey, lacrosse, soccer, softball, swimming, tennis, track and field, and volleyball. There are thirteen intramural sports, which include street hockey, and seventeen club sports, which include men's and women's rugby.

Etter Health Center provides 24-hour access to medical services. The eight-bed infirmary is staffed by a team of physicians and nurses. Chambersburg Hospital is only 20 minutes from campus.

Students have access to comprehensive counseling services on request in academic, career, psychological, social, personal growth, and religious areas. The Career Development Center offers career counseling, workshops in resume preparation, job interview techniques, and job search assistance.

Location

Shippensburg University is on 200 acres overlooking its namesake community, a borough of approximately 6,700 people in the Cumberland Valley. The University is about 40 minutes southwest of Harrisburg, 2 hours from both Baltimore and Washington, D.C., and 3 hours from Philadelphia. The campus is within easy walking distance of the center of town.

Majors and Degrees

Undergraduate degrees conferred are the Bachelor of Arts (B.A.), Bachelor of Science (B.S.), Bachelor of Science in Business Administration (B.S.B.A.), Bachelor of Science in Education (B.S.Ed.), and Bachelor of Social Work (B.S.W.). The College of Arts and Sciences awards the B.A. degree in art (computer graphics); communication/journalism (electronic media, print media, public relations); English (writing); French; geography (land use, regional development and tourism); history (public history); interdisciplinary arts; mathematics; political science; psychology; secondary certification (English, French, and Spanish); sociology; Spanish; and speech communications (African-American, applied, rhetoric/theory, women's). The B.S. degree is awarded in applied physics (nonfabrication); biology (biotechnology, ecology and environment, medical technology); chemistry (biochemistry, medical technology); computer science (computer graphics, information systems, scientific programming, software engineering, systems programming); geoenvironmental studies; geography (geographic information systems, land use, regional development and tourism); mathematics (applied, computer science, statistics); physics; public administration; and secondary education (biology, biology/environmental education, chemistry, mathematics). The B.S.Ed. degree is awarded in geography/citizenship, history/citizenship, political science/citizenship, earth science, elementary education, and physics.

The John L. Grove College of Business awards the B.S.B.A. degree in accounting, business administration general, economics, finance, information management and analysis, information technology for business education, and management (general, human resource, international), management information systems and marketing (supply chain operations and management); the B.S.Ed. degree in economics/citizenship; and the B.A. degree in economics.

The College of Education and Human Services awards the B.S. degree in criminal justice; the B.S.W. degree in social work; and the B.S.Ed. degree in elementary education (biology, chemistry, environmental education, mathematics, multicultural education, sociology, TESOL).

Preprofessional preparation is available for admission to schools of chiropractic, dentistry, engineering, law, medicine, optometry, pharmacy, physical therapy, podiatry, and veterinary medicine.

Shippensburg University offers 2+2, 3+3, and 4+3 transfer programs in the allied health fields of biotechnology, cytogenetic technology, cytotechnology, diagnostic imaging-multicompetency, nursing, occupational therapy, P.A.C.E. Program, and physical therapy.

Academic Program

The University is on the semester system with a fall semester beginning in late August and a spring semester beginning in mid-January. Three terms, one of three weeks and two of five weeks, comprise the summer program.

The general education program, which comprises one half of the credits required for graduation, is the core of the undergraduate curriculum. It includes courses to develop competence in writing, speaking, mathematics, and reading. The program ensures exposure to history; language and numbers; literary, artistic, and cultural traditions; laboratory science; biological and physical sciences; political, economic, and geographic sciences; and social and behavioral sciences. Ample elective opportunities are available.

The University requires students to take one approved diversity course for a total of 3 credit hours.

Academic options include an honors program, independent study and research, internships, field experience (mandatory in such areas as teacher education, social work, and medical technology), the Marine Science Consortium Program at Wallops Island, a 3+2 engineering program with several major schools of engineering, and Army ROTC.

Academic Facilities

Ezra Lehman Memorial Library has a computerized library system that includes access to full-text journal articles and electronic indexes to journal literature. The library also provides access to the Internet and many CD-ROM databases. The library's collection of more than 2 million items includes books, journals, government documents, maps, and audiovisual material. The library participates in several consortia that have reciprocal borrowing privileges for students.

Student instruction is supported by multiple computer systems for student e-mail and computer network connections to the Internet. Several hundred terminals or personal computers for student use are available in residence halls, the library, academic buildings, microcomputer labs, and the Computing Technologies Center. Students with their own computers also have access to the systems. All students can use the systems 24 hours a day and have unlimited computer time at no additional expense. Several buildings have wireless network capabilities and satellite capability for distance education. The University also has its own campuswide information system available on and off campus.

Costs

For Pennsylvania residents, the cost per semester in 2003–04 included tuition of $2299; housing, $1543; food service, $997; educational services fee, $229; student activities fee, $100; student union fee, $102; health services fee, $73; and recreation center fee, $20. Nonresidents paid tuition of $5748 per semester; the remaining fees were the same.

Financial Aid

The University's extensive financial aid program helps students who deserve a college education but who cannot afford to pay the full cost themselves. Shippensburg offers a wide range of aid in the form of grants, scholarships, loans, and campus employment. Most aid is awarded as a package consisting of all types for which the applicant is qualified. Nearly 80 percent of undergraduates receive some form of financial assistance.

Faculty

The University has 370 full- and part-time faculty members. The undergraduate student-faculty ratio is 19:1. Nearly 90 percent of the full-time instructional faculty members hold a doctorate or other terminal degree in their field. Each student has a faculty adviser.

Student Government

Shippensburg's strong Student Association, built around a Student Senate, standing committees, and an Activities Program Board, provides a highly diversified program of student activities. Students sit on many policymaking administration-faculty committees and administer their own budget for the Student Association.

Admission Requirements

Shippensburg University, in compliance with federal and state laws and University policy, provides equal educational, employment, and economic opportunities for all people without regard to race, color, gender, age, creed, national origin, religion, veteran status, or disability. A student's potential for success is judged by the high school average, rank in class, aptitude test scores (SAT I or ACT), and recommendations. The high school record is generally considered the most important factor. A college-preparatory program, consisting of 4 units of English, at least 3 units of math, 3 units in the sciences, 2 units of social studies, and 2 units in the same foreign language, is strongly recommended. A campus interview and visit are encouraged. Transfer students in good standing are welcome.

Application and Information

To be considered for admission, a student should submit the application form with a $30 application fee. The high school transcript, recommendations, and aptitude test results should be sent by the high school. Transfer students must submit college transcripts. The Admissions Office operates on a rolling basis.

Students can obtain application materials and information by contacting:

Dean of Admissions
1871 Old Main Drive
Shippensburg University of Pennsylvania
Shippensburg, Pennsylvania 17257
Telephone: 717-477-1231
800-822-8028 (toll-free)
Fax: 717-477-4016
E-mail: admiss@ship.edu
World Wide Web: http://www.ship.edu

The 200-acre Shippensburg University campus is located 40 miles southwest of Harrisburg, Pennsylvania.

SHORTER COLLEGE

ROME, GEORGIA

The College

Since 1873, Shorter College has been combining academic excellence with caring Christian commitment. The College was established through the generosity of a Baptist layman, Alfred Shorter, and the vision of his pastor. They led a group of northwestern Georgia Baptists in founding the school, originally named Cherokee Baptist Female College. The name was changed to Shorter Female College in 1878 and to Shorter College in 1923. The College became coeducational in 1951. Shorter's enrollment of 2,253 includes students in both traditional semester programs and in innovative continuous programs for working adults. Approximately 950 of these students are located on our main campus in Rome, Georgia. Students come from all parts of the United States and from other countries around the world. Shorter College has an overall graduate school acceptance rate of 80 percent and an impressive 87 percent acceptance rate to medical colleges over the past fifteen years. Shorter College is very committed to providing to providing a high-quality education in an intentionally Christian atmosphere. Each year the campus is visited by noted Christian leaders, scholars, and outstanding musical performers. The campus minister works with the director of religious activities to provide a wide range of opportunities for spiritual growth. The largest religious organization on campus is the Baptist Student Union (BSU), which includes Christians of many denominations. Student publications include a newspaper, a yearbook, and a literary magazine. Highly skilled music and drama groups include the Shorter Chorale, the Shorter Mixed Chorus, the Shorter Players, the Opera Workshop, and the Wind Ensemble. The Shorter Chorale was selected to represent the United States in choral festivals held in Yugoslavia, France, and Austria and represented the College in St. Petersburg, Russia. Shorter has also been the home of numerous National Metropolitan Opera Audition winners and finalists. The College has two local fraternities and three local sororities, as well as chapters of two national music fraternities and honor societies for majors in biology, English, music, religion, social sciences, and theater. Shorter College is a member of the Georgia Intercollegiate Athletic Conference of the NAIA. Varsity teams compete in men's baseball, basketball, golf, soccer, and tennis and in women's basketball, golf, tennis, softball, and soccer.

Location

The College is situated on 150 acres atop Shorter Hill, in Rome, Georgia (area population 85,000). Rome is located just 65 miles northwest of Atlanta and 65 miles south of Chattanooga, Tennessee, and cultural opportunities abound. In the city of Rome there are the Symphony Orchestra, Rome Little Theatre, Rome Area Council for the Arts events, popular concerts and attractions at the Roman Forum, and the 334,859-volume modern city library. The College sponsors numerous events, including faculty, alumni, student, and guest musical recitals; four guest-lecture series; speech festivals and recitals; drama and opera productions; art exhibits; and athletic events.

Majors and Degrees

Shorter College offers eight degrees: the Bachelor of Arts, the Bachelor of Science, the Bachelor of Business Administration, the Bachelor of Science in Education, the Bachelor of Fine Arts, the Bachelor of Music, the Bachelor of Music Education, and the Bachelor of Church Music. The Bachelor of Arts is offered in art, communication arts (with concentrations in electronic media and journalism), economics, English, French, history and political science, liberal arts, mathematics, music, psychology, public relations, religion, sociology, and Spanish. The Bachelor of Science is offered in biology, Christian ministry, communication leadership, economics, environmental science/conservation biology, general studies, mathematics, mathematics education, psychology, recreation management (with concentrations in public recreation and therapeutic recreation), and sociology. The Bachelor of Business Administration is offered in accounting (CPA track) and business administration. The Bachelor of Science in Education is offered in early childhood education (K–4) and middle grades (4–8). Programs leading to certification in secondary school teaching are available in English, general science, history, mathematics, and social science. Certification is also offered in music for grades K–12. The Bachelor of Fine Arts is offered in art, musical theater, and theater. The Bachelor of Music is offered in organ performance, piano pedagogy, piano performance, and voice performance. Preprofessional programs are available in allied health, dentistry, law, medicine, pharmacy, physical therapy, physician's assistant studies, and veterinary medicine. Courses are also available in German, health and physical education, and interdisciplinary studies.

Academic Program

Shorter is accredited by the Southern Association of Colleges and Schools and the National Association of Schools of Music, and strives to provide an academic environment of high quality. Teacher programs are approved by the Georgia Professional Standards Commission. Small classes (freshman lecture courses average 20 students) taught by dedicated and highly qualified professors (64 percent of freshman lecture courses are taught by full-time faculty members, 19 percent by full professors) ensure that each student receives an education that is both challenging and personally rewarding. For any degree, a candidate must have earned a minimum of 126 semester hours; some degrees require a greater number of hours. As part of the orientation program at the beginning of the fall semester, each new student is assigned to one of several small orientation groups that assists the student in adjusting to college life; the student is also assigned to an academic adviser who assists in the selection and scheduling of courses. Early registration sessions are available in the summer. Freshman advisers are specially trained faculty and staff members. The academic calendar is divided into two semesters from September to May, with two "mini" sessions offered during the summer. On-campus evening classes are available in selected disciplines. Shorter offers an honors program that spans all four years and provides students with learning opportunities not generally available to undergraduates.

Off-Campus Programs

The College conducts a program of extension courses in off-campus locations. A selection of courses is offered in the late afternoon and evening hours in nearby cities. Shorter's School of Professional Programs offers general education and degree-completion programs, specifically designed for working adults, on campus and in Lawrenceville, Riverdale, and Marietta, Georgia. Classes meet one evening or weekend per week, year-round, with a required weekly study group.

MAYTERM is the four-week period immediately following the end of the second semester in May. It is designed as a study-abroad program, in which students earn 9 semester hours of credit through travel, study, and classroom experiences. Students are housed in student residences or college dormitories, and the cost of most meals is usually included. The most likely location is the British Isles, but other sites are possible. Shorter College faculty members accompany the students and teach the courses that are offered. In cooperation with the American Institute for Foreign Study, Shorter is able to offer students the opportunity to study in London, England, at Richmond College. Since Richmond College is accredited by one of the recognized regional accrediting bodies in the United States, credits earned for a summer, a semester, or a year of study are readily transferable back to Shorter. MAYTERM is offered every other year. On alternate years, Shorter offers the China Educational Exchange, a four-week study-abroad program to Zhengzhou University in Henan Province, People's Republic of China. An agreement with Hong Kong Baptist University and Salzburg College allows students to study at those universities. Studies in other countries can be arranged on an individual basis through the Office of International Programs.

Academic Facilities

Livingston Library, dedicated in 1976 as a memorial to Ray Livingston, houses more than 82,597 books, 612 periodicals, 6,529 microform materials, 8,669 musical scores, and 10,788 audio/video items. The library also contains conference rooms (for both individual and group study), projection rooms, a graphics preparation room, computer terminals, typewriters, and music listening facilities for student use. The Alice Allgood Cooper Fine Arts Building and the Randall H. Minor Fine Arts Building are connected to form an outstanding fine arts complex, providing up-to-date facilities for the departments of music, communication arts, and art. The Cooper Building contains classrooms, music faculty offices, the art department's drawing and painting studio, and Brookes Chapel, the meeting place for convocations, concerts, recitals, and lectures. A renovated home adjacent to the campus houses expanded art facilities. The Minor Building contains classrooms, twenty-five music practice rooms (with a baby grand piano in each), a choral rehearsal room, a dance studio, faculty offices, photography facilities, a theater, a desktop publishing lab, a radio studio, and an art gallery. Rome Hall was named in honor of the citizens of Rome in appreciation of their generous support of the College. It contains classrooms, science laboratories (including the Stergus Collection of Internal Organs, one of the most complete pathology collections in the United States), faculty offices, lounges, and the Robert T. Connor exhibit of some 150 African and North American animals and skins. Alumni Hall houses the educational materials center and faculty offices. Construction of a $3.76-million gymnasium/athletic complex, the Winthrop-King Centre, was completed in 1994. Construction of a new $3-million Student Union was completed in 1998. Two computer labs are available for general student use. Computer labs for business and communication arts are also available. Smaller computer labs are available for art, music, and recreation. All residence halls have computer and Internet access.

Costs

Tuition for 2003–04 was $11,440. Room and board costs were $5665, fees were $265, and books and supplies were $750.

Financial Aid

Shorter College offers aid through each of the five federal programs: the Federal Pell Grant, Federal Supplemental Educational Opportunity Grant, Federal Work-Study, Federal Perkins Loan, and Federal Stafford Student Loan. Full-time students who are Georgia residents are eligible to receive the Georgia Tuition Equalization Grant and may be eligible to receive the HOPE Scholarship. Scholarships are offered for achievement in academics, music, art, theater, humanities, and athletics. Awards range from $500 to full tuition. Academic scholarships are renewable each year, provided the student maintains at least the required grade point average. Special grants and scholarships are available to students who plan to enter church-related vocations, who are members of churches in the Georgia Baptist Convention, or who are dependents of employees of a Southern Baptist church, institution, or agency. Small grants are also awarded to students recommended directly by alumni and when 2 or more students from the same family are enrolled at Shorter. One hundred percent of all full-time Shorter students receive some financial aid.

Faculty

The Shorter College faculty is composed of 68 full-time, highly qualified professors, of whom two thirds hold doctoral degrees. The College also employs 146 part-time faculty members, most of whom teach in the working adult program. A favorable student-teacher ratio of 12:1 in traditional programs ensures that each student receives individual attention.

Student Government

One of Shorter's truly distinctive features is that students may participate in a wide variety of significant extracurricular activities, each of which affords a chance to develop social and leadership skills that prepare a student to win in a competitive world. The Student Government Association (SGA) is the official voice of the students. Through SGA's Executive Council, Senate, judicial boards, and special committees, students are directly involved in the life of the College.

Admission Requirements

Students are admitted into the freshman class based on their academic grade point average and SAT I or ACT scores. A review of the student's goals and their compatibility with the purpose of the College are also determining factors. The College requires 4 years of English, 4 years of mathematics (including 2 years of algebra), 3 years of history/social science, 3 years of science, and 2 units of foreign language. In addition to the general requirements for admission to the College, students majoring in music must meet the following requirements: each student must perform in an audition of approximately 10 minutes in his or her major medium, and each student must take a series of music placement tests. Students must successfully fulfill these requirements prior to the beginning of classes in August of their freshman year, since the music curriculum requires at least four years for completion. An audition is also required for students majoring in theater, and an art portfolio review is required for students majoring in art. High school students who have completed their junior year, have an outstanding academic record, and have completed the units outlined above may be considered for early admission. High school seniors entering their senior year may be admitted on a joint enrollment basis. Such students should have above-average grades and SAT I or ACT scores. Transfer and international students are also welcome to apply. A minimum paper-based TOEFL score of 500 or a computer-based score of 173 is required for international students. Credit for college work below a C cannot be transferred. Homeschooled students should contact the Office of Admissions directly for requirements.

Application and Information

Shorter accepts students on a rolling basis. Campus visits are highly recommended through a personal campus tour or one of three Open Houses.

Director of Admissions
Shorter College
315 Shorter Avenue
Rome, Georgia 30165-4298
Telephone: 706-233-7319
800-868-6980 Ext. 7319 (toll-free)
Fax: 706-233-7224
E-mail: admissions@shorter.edu
World Wide Web: http://www.shorter.edu

SIENA COLLEGE

LOUDONVILLE, NEW YORK

The College

Siena College is a four-year, coeducational, independent liberal arts college with a Franciscan and Catholic tradition. It is a community of 2,900 full-time students that offers undergraduate degrees in business, the liberal arts, and sciences. Student-focused professors are at the heart of a supportive and challenging learning community that prepares students for careers, for an active role in their communities, and for the real world. Founded by the Franciscan Friars in 1937, Siena provides a personal, values-oriented education one student at a time. It welcomes all races and creeds and prides itself on the care and concern for the intellectual, personal, and social growth of all students that is the Franciscan trademark.

About 2,000 students live on campus in four housing options, including traditional residence halls, suites for 4 or 6 students, and town-house units for 7 or 8. When Siena students are not in class or in their residences, they have plenty to do. More than sixty teams, clubs, and committees are active each year. The Franciscan Center for Service and Advocacy places more than 300 students each week in some volunteer activity, including Habitat for Humanity, soup kitchens, and teaching in religious education programs. More than 75 percent of the student body is involved in some type of athletic program, from nineteen intercollegiate sports to club teams to intramurals. Siena also provides numerous student support services, including counseling, tutoring, health services, peer counseling, and a career center. Popular activities include the student theater company, the student newspaper, the radio station, the yearbook, the Karate Club, the Black and Latin Student Union, and the Model United Nations.

Siena provides additional learning and cultural experiences outside of its academic programs to both its students and the wider community. Examples of these efforts include the Martin Luther King Jr. Lecture Series, the Niebuhr Institute of Religion and Culture, the Jewish-Christian Institute, and the Women and Minorities Studies Committee, which plan programs to include the public on topics of current interest. The Greyfriar Living Literature Series (which features guest writers) and the Alternative Film Series are free to the public.

Siena has developed a number of cooperative and special programs. In addition to the college-wide honors program, Sienna offers a premed program with Albany Medical College; a five-year M.B.A. program with Clarkson University; a seven-year accelerated predental program with Boston University; a 3-2 engineering program in cooperation with Clarkson University, Catholic University, Rensselaer Polytechnic Institute, Manhattan College, SUNY Binghamton, and Western New England College; and the Washington Semester at American University.

Location

Siena's 155-acre campus is located in Loudonville, a suburban community 2 miles north of the New York State capital of Albany. With eighteen colleges in the area, there is a wide variety of activities on weekends. Regional theater, performances by major concert artists, and professional sports events compete with the activities on the campuses. Within 50 miles are the Adirondacks, the Berkshires, and the Catskills, providing outdoor recreation throughout the year. New York City and Boston are less than 3 hours away. With all of the professional, cultural, and recreational opportunities the Capital Region offers, many Siena graduates choose to begin their careers there.

Majors and Degrees

The College offers the Bachelor of Business Administration degree in accounting; the Bachelor of Arts in American studies, classics, creative arts, economics, English, environmental studies, French, history, mathematics, philosophy, political science, psychology, religious studies, social work, sociology, and Spanish; and the Bachelor of Science in biochemistry, biology, chemistry, computer science, economics, finance, marketing and management, mathematics, and physics. Certificate programs are available in computer science; environmental studies; health studies; international studies, foreign language, and business; peace studies; secondary education; and theater arts.

Academic Program

A strong liberal arts core forms the basis for all curricula. Course work is structured within the School of Business, School of Liberal Arts, and School of Science. All students take courses within a broad core requirement: 30 hours in the humanities and social sciences (including a 6-credit freshman foundations course), 9 hours in mathematics and science (with 3 of these in a natural science), and 3 hours in fine arts. Students must also maintain a minimum cumulative index of 2.0 and earn at least a C in every major field concentration course. Within the major, students must take a minimum of 30 credits, with no more than 39 credits counting toward the degree requirements. A total of 120 hours is required to qualify for a bachelor's degree.

Students may get credit for prior work by taking standardized college proficiency exams with the approval of the head of the department in the discipline to be examined. A total of 18 credits may be obtained this way. Siena offers honors courses in English and history. Many departments have seminars to cover current topics in the field. ROTC affiliation is available at Siena in a U.S. Army unit, and an Air Force ROTC unit is available at a nearby college through cross-registration.

Siena's academic year is two semesters. There are two summer sessions offered.

Off-Campus Programs

Siena students are encouraged to spend a semester or a year abroad. Programs directly affiliated with the College include Siena at Regent's College, London; the Siena in London Internship Experience; the Siena semester at the Centre d'Etudes Franco-Americain de Management in Lyon, France; and the Center for Cross-Cultural Studies in Seville, Spain. In addition, programs are available for all majors everywhere on the globe. International study is typically pursued during the junior year.

Locally, hundreds of internships are available through government, business, and nonprofit organizations on a two- or three-day-a-week basis, enabling students to continue with their course work at the same time. Many students are offered jobs by their internship organization upon graduation.

In addition, through the Hudson Mohawk Association of

Colleges and Universities (which comprises the eighteen colleges in the area), cross-registration is possible at such institutions as Union College, Skidmore College, Rensselaer Polytechnic Institute, and the University at Albany.

Academic Facilities

The mission of the Standish Library is to provide service and access to educational material and information to support the curricular and research needs of the students and faculty members. The library collection of more than 285,000 volumes consists of books, journals, microforms, compact discs, videocassettes, and a growing number of electronic information sources. More than 6,000 volumes are added annually, and 1,600 serial subscriptions are currently maintained, with electronic access to thousands of additional journals. During 2001, Siena opened the Sarazen Student Union (home to all student clubs and activities) and the Morelle Science Center (home to Siena's biology and chemistry departments). Siena also opened a new residence hall.

All academic and residential buildings are interconnected with a high-speed Ethernet network connected via fiber optics. This network backbone runs at 10 and 100 Mbps. Every student residence space includes a 10 Mbps connection point to access the College's network and the Internet. The network includes more than 2,500 ports. The computer facilities are accessible 24 hours a day, seven days a week. Numerous computers are available throughout the campus for student use.

Marcelle Athletic Complex features a natatorium, a field house with an elevated running track, racquetball and squash courts, an aerobics/dance studio, and an area with exercise and other weight-training equipment.

Costs

Tuition at Siena remains reasonable, helping the College to provide an education of fine quality at moderate cost. For 2003–04, tuition was $17,555; room, $4525; and board, $2680. There are lab fees for accounting, natural sciences, languages, and some fine arts and psychology courses. Miscellaneous fees may account for about $470 per year.

Financial Aid

Federal programs that Siena students may qualify for include Federal Pell Grants, Federal Supplemental Educational Opportunity Grants, Federal Perkins Loans, Federal Stafford Student Loans, and Federal PLUS loans. Residents of New York State may receive Tuition Assistance Program and Aid for Part-time Study awards. Financial need is determined by the Free Application for Federal Student Aid and, where applicable, the state version of the supplemental Financial Aid Form. Aid is usually awarded in a package combining scholarships or grants, loans, and a job. Students remaining in good academic standing will find their aid renewed.

Faculty

Siena's faculty is committed to teaching, and student concerns and development are at the heart of the curriculum. Eighty-three percent of the 171 full-time faculty members have terminal degrees. The student-faculty ratio of 14:1 helps to develop interaction with students, as does the fact that Siena professors even teach labs. Students are assigned a faculty adviser to help in the planning of their course of study.

Student Government

The Student Senate directs student involvement in academic and social life and interprets students' attitudes, opinions, and rights for the faculty and administration. It charters all student organizations and provides funds for many through fees collected by the College. The governing board is made up of officers and representatives of all four classes and of the commuting students. Elections are held in April for the following year, except for freshmen, who are elected in September.

Admission Requirements

Siena seeks bright, articulate young people who will blossom in the caring atmosphere that the College provides. The College is reaching out to more diverse geographical and ethnic groups. Academic standards are demanding without being threatening. Seventy percent of incoming freshmen have combined SAT I scores ranging from 1050 to 1200. School, grades, recommendations, and an interview all affect the final decision. Students seeking degrees in the science or business division should be well versed in mathematics. Those interested in American studies, English, history, or philosophy will find a working knowledge of a foreign language helpful.

Application and Information

The preferred deadline for the submission of a regular application is March 1 of a student's senior year in high school. Decisions are sent starting in mid-March. Siena also offers an early decision and an early action program. Early applications should be submitted before December 1. Candidates will be notified by January 1. Presidential scholar candidates must apply by January 15.

Transfer students must apply by December 1 for the spring semester or by June 1 for the fall semester. Generally, transfers are expected to have a cumulative average of at least 2.5. A minimum of 30 semester hours and half of the credits for the major must be earned at Siena. A maximum of 66 credits may be transferred from accredited two-year institutions. Credit will be given only for courses that are similar in content, level, and scope to those at Siena.

For more information, students should contact:

Admissions Office
Siena College
515 Loudon Road
Loudonville, New York 12211
Telephone: 518-783-2423
888-AT-SIENA (toll-free)
E-mail: admit@siena.edu
World Wide Web: http://www.siena.edu

SIENA HEIGHTS UNIVERSITY

ADRIAN, MICHIGAN

The University

Siena Heights University (SHU) was founded in 1919 by the Adrian Dominican Congregation as a Catholic liberal arts college. The name Siena honors Saint Catherine of Siena, a fourteenth-century Italian Dominican who dedicated her life to a quest for truth and social responsibility. Similarly, the mission of the University—to help students become more competent, purposeful, and ethical through a teaching and learning environment that respects the dignity of all—grows out of the philosophy of life exemplified in Saint Catherine of Siena.

Throughout its history, Siena Heights University has built a proud tradition of innovative response to challenging social needs. Originally a university for women who intended to become teachers, Siena broadened its offerings over the years and by the 1950s was recognized as one of the nation's ten best liberal arts colleges for women.

Today Siena Heights University continues its long tradition of integrating liberal arts and career education. A student's total development as an intellectually, socially, and spiritually responsible human being is the basis of Siena Heights University's education philosophy. The University provides an education that helps students create meaning in their lives and inspire others by their aspirations and achievements.

The mission of Siena Heights University is to assist students to become more competent, purposeful, and ethical through a teaching and learning environment that respects the dignity of all. The University therefore provides an educational process that challenges individuals to identify, to refine, and to achieve their personal goals. Through this process, Siena Heights University expects to engage each of its students in the development of a personal philosophy of life.

The University is accredited by the North Central Association of Colleges and Schools, the Department of Education of the state of Michigan, and the National Association of Schools of Art and Design and is organized into six departments: Art; Business and Management; Computing, Mathematics and the Sciences; Human Services; Humanities; and Performing Arts and Education.

More than 1,100 students (55 percent women, 45 percent men) study at Siena Heights University. Siena Heights students hail from twenty-eight states and eight countries.

Siena Heights University houses 380 students on campus. Hundreds of students live off campus within walking or biking distance. Students also commute from surrounding cities.

The University's Career Planning and Placement Center provides students with excellent placement services. Supported by state-of-the-art technology, the University has a 98 percent placement rate among its students within six months of graduation.

The Fieldhouse, home to the Saints' athletics programs, has five basketball courts, four volleyball courts, two indoor tennis courts, a 200-meter running track, and a training room. Outdoor facilities on campus include a soccer field, baseball fields, two tennis courts, a sand volleyball court, and a new softball complex.

Siena Heights University is proud of the accomplishments of its student athletes both in intercollegiate competition and in the classroom. The Saints have won three straight Wolverine-Hoosier Athletic Conference (WHAC) All-Sports competitions. Since 1985, Siena Heights athletic teams have won several conference, district, and regional championships, making SHU one of the finest athletic programs of its size in the nation.

The Saints have produced 62 NAIA All-Americans and 48 All-American Scholar-Athletes over the past two decades. The men's basketball team has advanced to the NAIA National Championship Tournament six times in the past eight years, and the 1997 team went 30-7 and was the national runner-up. In 1995, the men's baseball team became only the third NAIA institution in the state of Michigan to qualify for the NAIA World Series, and the women's soccer team has competed in three NAIA national championship tournaments in its twelve-year history.

More than thirty-five student clubs and organizations are available on the campus. They range from national social organizations to choirs, from Student Senate to intramural sports, and from international student organizations to various honor societies.

In addition to associate and bachelor's degree programs, Siena Heights offers later afternoon and evening graduate courses that lead to the Master of Arts degree.

Location

Siena Heights University is located in Adrian (population 22,000), which serves as the hub of the Lenawee County area. The campus is 75 miles from the Detroit metropolitan area, 30 miles from Ann Arbor, and 30 miles from Toledo, Ohio.

Majors and Degrees

Siena offers Associate of Art, Associate of Science, Bachelor of Arts, Bachelor of Fine Arts, Bachelor of Science, and Bachelor of Applied Science degrees.

Siena Heights has introduced a new major field of study, sport management. The curriculum combines a strong business foundation with a specialized knowledge in sport. Special emphasis is provided on all aspects of sport, including cultural, legal, ethical, economical, and philosophical components. The program provides students with career opportunities in facility management, professional sport management, sales, sport media, and athletic and recreational management.

The majors offered are accounting; art (ceramics, drawing, graphics, metalsmithing, painting, photography, printmaking, sculpture, watercolor); biology (premedical studies); business (business administration, hospitality management, management, marketing, retailing, retail merchandising); business education; chemistry; child development; computer and information systems; criminal justice; English (children's literature, communications, creative writing, English general); general studies; history; human services (gerontology, social work); humanities; language arts; mathematics (pre-actuarial studies); Montessori education; music (music business, electronic music synthesis, music general, music education); natural science; prelaw studies; philosophy; preprofessional science (dentistry, pharmacy, engineering, veterinary science); psychology; religious studies; social science; Spanish; sport management; teacher certification (nondegree program); theater/speech communications; and special majors such as contracted major, inverted major, and tri-major.

Academic Program

The academic calendar consists of two semesters; a summer session is available. In a typical baccalaureate program, 120 credit hours are required.

Off-Campus Programs

There are internships in all majors. The cooperative education program allows freshmen and sophomores to test potential career fields, while giving upperclass students on-the-job training. The foreign study program sends students to Florence, Italy; Paris, France; and Mexico.

Academic Facilities

The 140,000-volume library includes a computerized card catalog; automated circulation and book reserve functions; an expanded version of the academic index, INFOTRAC, to assist in retrieving recent periodical citations by subject; and Internet access. Information and research capabilities are available to students campuswide through the University's wireless computer network, which enables students to access the Internet and Siena Heights network files without plugging in to a hard-wired network connection.

Costs

For the academic year 2004–05, basic expenses are $15,520 for tuition and fees and $5455 for room and board, for a total of $20,975. There are no additional fees for out-of-state students. The average cost for books and supplies is approximately $300 per semester.

Financial Aid

Siena Heights University is committed to making an education affordable for every accepted student. Some form of financial assistance is given to nearly 86 percent of the University's full-time students. Need-based grants, loans, and work-study programs are available through the federal and state governments and the University itself. Siena Heights University also offers various academic scholarships. These awards are made on the basis of academic and leadership excellence, not necessarily because of need.

Students applying for financial aid should file the Free Application for Federal Student Aid (FAFSA) and have the results sent to Siena Heights. Applications are processed on a first-come, first-served basis only after a student has been accepted to the University.

Faculty

Siena Heights University employs more than 130 faculty members. Of the 65 full-time faculty members, more than 50 percent hold a doctorate or other terminal degree. Faculty members conduct recognized research and serve as advisers to aid in course selection and to offer career assistance.

Student Government

The Student Senate is involved with many topical issues touching all areas of University life. Students may serve in University government as elected senators or as volunteers on Student Senate committees. The Student Senate is open to all students of Siena Heights University.

Admission Requirements

Siena Heights admits students who are academically qualified, capable, enthusiastic, motivated, ready to be challenged, and ready to achieve. Admission decisions are based on high school academic performance, ACT or SAT I scores, extracurricular activities, leadership potential, class rank, and personal recommendations. The typical profile of a regularly admitted freshman reflects an average high school GPA of 3.3 on a 4.0 scale and an average composite ACT score of 21.2. Provisional admission is available to students who show academic potential.

Application and Information

Admission decisions are made on a rolling basis, and applicants are notified of an admission status within one week after receipt of all application materials. Tours and general information sessions are available Monday through Saturday; annual Campus Visit Days are also scheduled.

For further information, students should contact:

Office of Admissions
Siena Heights University
1247 East Siena Heights Drive
Adrian, Michigan 49221-1796
Telephone: 517-264-7180
800-521-0009 (toll-free)
Fax: 517-264-7745
E-mail: admissions@sienahts.edu
World Wide Web: http://www.sienahts.edu

Dominican Hall on the campus of Siena Heights University.

SIMMONS COLLEGE
BOSTON, MASSACHUSETTS

The College

Students who desire a small university with a confident, upbeat community of "sisters" combined with a world-class urban culture—from art, music, and Red Sox games to eclectic neighborhoods with distinct feels and flavors—find themselves in Boston, at Simmons College.

Simmons attracts high achievers, but it doesn't have a cutthroat environment. Small classes, close student-faculty relationships, and a collaborative community inspire personal and professional growth. Students choose from more than forty majors and programs, ranging from Africana studies to the Women in Materials physics research program. Simmons' most popular majors are biology, communications, education, English, nursing, physical therapy, premedicine, psychology, and sociology. Faculty advisers help students fulfill requirements while also addressing their aspirations.

Simmons places students first and encourages them to challenge themselves. Faculty members know students' names and look for them in class. Professors don't push students to major in their field; instead, they help students figure out what they want. Students explore different fields, discover their passion, and then go for it with gusto. As a result, nearly 30 percent declare a double major.

Career preparation is a big deal at Simmons. The College was established 100 years ago to educate young women so they could get jobs, a revolutionary concept at the time. To this day, Simmons delivers a strong liberal arts education for women, integrated with hands-on, professional experience. Simmons students do internships, independent study, and service learning at Boston's world-renowned hospitals, museums, law firms, and many other organizations. Some conduct research and copublish their findings with faculty members. Others explore the world through short-term and study-abroad programs. All gain valuable experience—including public speaking, negotiation, and critical-thinking skills—that help prepare them for successful, meaningful careers.

More than 80 percent of Simmons undergraduates live on the residential campus, two blocks from the academic campus. The "quintessential New England" residential campus has nine dormitories and a private, landscaped quadrangle. All dorm rooms are wired for high-speed Internet access and cable TV. The campus also houses a central dining hall, a student-run snack bar, an activities center, and a health center that offers services 24 hours a day. The award-winning Holmes Sports Center includes an indoor running track, swimming pool, weight room, and cardiovascular training facilities.

More than fifty student clubs and organizations—including student government, academic clubs, cultural organizations, honor societies, volunteer programs, eight NCAA Division III varsity teams, a literary magazine, and more—provide forums for students to get involved. Simmons' 1,500 undergraduates enjoy a safe, friendly campus with an upbeat attitude. They love Boston's rich social and cultural resources. Students walk to shops, cafés, clubs, and pubs or catch the T (Boston's public transportation) to anywhere they want to go.

Simmons is a women's college in a coed college town. More than 300,000 college students live in Boston, and there are lots of ways to meet them. Simmons is part of the Colleges of the Fenway consortium, which allows students to cross-register and participate in social activities with six coed colleges in the neighborhood. Simmons also shares greater Boston with Northeastern University, Boston University, MIT, Harvard, and more than a dozen other colleges.

In addition to its undergraduate programs, Simmons has nationally accredited, coed graduate programs in communications management, education, health studies, liberal arts, library and information science, and social work. Its M.B.A. program is designed specifically for women.

Location

Simmons' small-but-mighty community is located on the borders of Boston's lively Fenway neighborhood and the Longwood Medical Area, a world-renowned hub for research and health care. Simmons is literally surrounded by art and culture, music and history, and the resounding cheers of die-hard baseball fans at legendary Fenway Park. It shares the neighborhood with numerous other colleges and several world-class museums. It's a short walk from the campus to the Landmark Center's popular stores and Cineplex, as well as numerous other shopping areas, restaurants, and parks. Students hop aboard the T to head to Harvard Square, the Italian North End, funky Jamaica Plain, or any one of Boston's diverse neighborhoods.

Majors and Degrees

Undergraduates choose from more than forty majors and programs. Simmons grants the Bachelor of Arts degree in advertising, Africana studies, art, art administration, communications, East Asian studies, economics, education, English, finance, French, graphic design, history, information technology, international management, international relations, management, marketing, music, philosophy, physics, political science, psychology, public relations, public relations and market communications, retail management, sociology, Spanish, and women's studies. The Bachelor of Science degree is granted in biochemistry, biology, chemistry, chemistry management, computer science, dietetics, environmental science, management information systems, mathematics, nursing, nutrition, physical therapy, and psychobiology.

Simmons offers several undergraduate-to-graduate degree programs, including education, physical therapy, and science information technology. Simmons also offers dual-degree programs in physician's assistant studies and chemistry/pharmacy in collaboration with Massachusetts College of Pharmacy and Allied Health Sciences, as well as individually designed preprofessional programs for dentistry, medicine, veterinary medicine, and law.

Academic Program

Simmons offers a strong liberal arts education combined with professional preparation for undergraduate women. Simmons requires a minimum of 128 semester hours for graduation. Students must demonstrate competence in math and foreign language, complete a core curriculum in the liberal arts and sciences, complete the courses required for the selected major, fulfill an independent learning requirement, and round out their program with appropriate electives. The liberal arts and sciences requirement comprises 40 semester hours of course work; each major requires 20 to 40 semester hours, depending on the program. The independent learning requirement is 8 to 16 semester hours.

Independent learning is a key part of the Simmons education; Simmons believes it enhances student initiative and planning, develops leadership skills, and provides direct professional experience. The requirement may be fulfilled through internships, fieldwork, or an independent study.

Students may select interdepartmental programs, declare double majors, or participate in an undergraduate-to-graduate degree program. In addition, the OPEN program allows students to design their own program of study, combining courses from several fields. Other special academic opportunities include Simmons' outstanding honors program, service learning, and study-abroad programs.

Off-Campus Programs

Simmons is a member of the Colleges of the Fenway consortium, which allows students to cross-register with neighboring colleges, including the New England Conservatory of Music, Hebrew College, Massachusetts College of Art, Massachusetts College of Pharmacy and Allied Health Sciences, and Wentworth Institute of Technology. Simmons' domestic exchange program allows juniors to spend a semester at Mills College, Spelman College, or Fisk University. Qualified students, usually juniors, also may apply for the Washington Semester at American University in Washington, D.C. Students interested in international study may elect to spend one semester or one year at an approved university exchange. In addition, Simmons offers short-term study-abroad programs during the spring semester.

Academic Facilities

The historical Simmons campus is located in the heart of Boston, providing a small-college atmosphere enhanced by urban culture and conveniences. The Main College Building houses a dining and commons area, lecture halls and classrooms, administrative and faculty offices, the bookstore, the Student Activities Center, art studios, music practice rooms, and Trustman Art Gallery.

Park Science Center offers technologically advanced learning environments, including faculty and student research facilities, fully equipped science laboratories, environmental rooms, observation rooms for psychological testing, food science kitchens, and a human performance lab.

One Palace Road—a new state-of-the-art home for two of Simmons' graduate schools—includes electronic classrooms as well as centers for academic support, counseling, career education and resources, media, and technology. Beatley Library offers a wireless network, laptop loans, sophisticated online library service, and "Ask Now," an after-hours reference service.

Costs

Undergraduate tuition and fees for the 2003–04 academic year were $11,775 per semester; room and board charges were $4725 per semester. Total costs, not including books, supplies, and personal expenses, were $33,000.

Financial Aid

Approximately 75 percent of Simmons students receive financial aid. Scholarships, grants, loans, and federal work-study are determined by the Free Application for Federal Student Aid (FAFSA). Simmons also awards academic merit scholarships, ranging from $1000 to full tuition and renewable for four years.

Faculty

Simmons' professors are distinguished experts and practitioners who work closely with students and care about their success. Simmons has 109 full-time faculty members; 72 percent are women. The student-faculty ratio is 12:1, ensuring a strong tie between students and professors.

Student Government

Simmons has more than fifty student clubs and organizations. The Student Government Association (SGA) coordinates the policies and activities of various student organizations, allocates the student activities funds, and promotes the interests of the student body by working closely with the Simmons faculty and administration. In addition, every academic department has a student liaison who participates in department evaluations and helps promote educational and social activities for students, faculty members, and staff members.

Admission Requirements

There isn't one "type" of Simmons student, but there are common qualities. Simmons women are intellectually curious and open-minded. They are serious about their personal and professional goals, and they believe their college experience should be seriously fun. The admission team keeps this in mind as they review applications; they want to know not only what applicants have accomplished, but also who they are and what kind of person they hope to become.

The admission team evaluates high school performance, SAT I or ACT scores, recommendations, and the application essay. If English is not the applicant's first language, TOEFL or ELPT scores are required. Although it's not a requirement, Simmons highly recommends an interview. This gives Simmons a better perspective about an applicant's abilities and interests and, at the same time, gives the applicant the opportunity to evaluate Simmons and decide if it's the right place for her.

Simmons welcomes applications from prospective freshmen, transfer students, international students, and students who are beyond the traditional college age.

Application and Information

Students may apply online at the Web site listed below, use the Common Application, or submit a print application, along with the $35 fee and all supporting credentials. Simmons waives the application fee for students who use the online application. The early action deadline is December 1 and is a nonbinding deadline. The deadline for freshman applicants is February 1. Transfer students are evaluated on a continual basis; the preferred filing date for applications is April 1. Students applying for the semester beginning in January should apply by December 1.

Simmons encourages prospective students and their families to visit Simmons. They can attend an admission event or request an individual visit. They should check out Simmons' great Boston neighborhood, tour the campus, sit in on a class, talk to current students, and interview a professor, department chair, or program director.

For further information, interested students should contact:

Office of Undergraduate Admission
Simmons College
300 The Fenway
Boston, Massachusetts 02115
Telephone: 800-345-8468 (toll-free)
Fax: 617-521-3190
World Wide Web: http://www.simmons.edu

SIMON'S ROCK COLLEGE OF BARD

GREAT BARRINGTON, MASSACHUSETTS

The College

Simon's Rock College of Bard is the nation's only four-year college of liberal arts and sciences devoted solely to the acceleration and enrichment of younger scholars. The average age of an entering freshman is 16. Most candidates for admission enter after the tenth or eleventh grade of secondary school.

Simon's Rock challenges the traditional assumption that students must be 18 before they can be asked to seriously develop their intelligence, imagination, and self-discipline. Students at Simon's Rock pursue an academic program that enables them to fulfill their potential at an age when their interest, energy, and curiosity are at a peak. The College provides an academic and social structure for a distinctive peer group. Sixteen- and 17-year-old freshmen are the norm at Simon's Rock, not the exception.

The College was founded in 1964 by Elizabeth Blodgett Hall, former headmistress of Concord Academy, and first admitted students in 1966. Since its inception, Simon's Rock has based its program on a set of assumptions that thirty-eight years of experience have proved to be valid: that highly motivated students of high school age are fully capable of engaging in college work, that they are best able to develop in a small-college environment, that serving these students well requires a faculty committed to distinction in teaching and scholarship as well as active participation in the students' social and moral development, that a coherent general education in the liberal arts and sciences should be the foundation for such students, and that an early college founded on these assumptions should serve as a model for reform in American education.

In 1979, Simon's Rock became a part of Bard College, located 50 miles away at Annandale-on-Hudson, New York.

Location

The College is built on 200 rolling and wooded acres 1½ miles west of Great Barrington, a town of 8,500, in the Berkshire Hills of western Massachusetts. Boston and New York City are 140 miles away; Albany and Springfield are 40 miles away. The Berkshires' natural beauty and wide variety of cultural attractions make the area an unusually attractive place in which to live. Many artists, writers, and craftsmen live nearby; several contribute to the College's cultural and artistic programs. The countryside provides excellent terrain for hiking, bicycling, cross-country and Alpine skiing, canoeing, and climbing. The Tanglewood Music Festival, Jacob's Pillow Dance Festival, and numerous summer theaters are located in nearby towns. Great Barrington itself is a thriving business community with a variety of schools and service agencies in which Simon's Rock students work and volunteer.

Majors and Degrees

Simon's Rock offers programs leading to the A.A. and B.A. degrees in the liberal arts and sciences. Students may complete their B.A. studies with a concentration in most traditional disciplines such as biology, creative writing, humanities, mathematics, or choose one of several interdisciplinary concentrations such as gender studies, intellectual history, or Latin American studies. There is also a joint B.A. program with Bard College that allows students to take advanced courses and work closely with faculty members at both colleges in completing their degree requirements.

Academic Program

The academic program at Simon's Rock combines a substantial and coherent required core curriculum in the liberal arts and sciences with electives and extensive opportunities for students to pursue their own interests through advanced courses and independent study. The program is designed to engage students in the life of the mind by making them aware of their cultural heritage, introducing them to the spectrum of thought in the arts and sciences, and empowering them to satisfy their curiosity by thinking and learning independently.

Because Simon's Rock students begin college earlier than their peers, the College is particularly conscious of its responsibility to ensure that all students develop the skills and knowledge expected of an educated person. Consequently, during their first two years at Simon's Rock, all students are required to complete a core curriculum that comprises approximately half of their total academic load. The core curriculum includes a writing and thinking workshop (which new students attend during the week before the regular semester begins); first-year, sophomore, and cultural perspectives seminars and requirements in the arts, mathematics, natural science, and foreign language. The College also requires that students participate in a recreational athletics program and attend a series of health lectures.

All new students are assigned a faculty adviser, who meets with them weekly during their first semester and regularly throughout the rest of their career at Simon's Rock. Classes are small, faculty members are accessible, and the opportunities for students to pursue diverse interests are extensive.

The curriculum of the first two years at Simon's Rock leads to the A.A. in liberal arts. Students who successfully complete the A.A. requirements may continue at Simon's Rock for a B.A. or transfer to Bard College or another college or university to complete their baccalaureate degree. About one third of each class remains to complete a B.A. at Simon's Rock in one of thirty-four interdisciplinary concentrations; two thirds choose to transfer. The transfer record of Simon's Rock A.A. graduates is excellent.

Students wishing to stay at Simon's Rock for a B.A. must apply for admission to a major through a process called Moderation. At a formal conference, a faculty Moderation Committee and the student review the student's accomplishments and together plan the remainder of the student's education program. Students suggest and are advised of junior- and senior-year opportunities. These traditionally include advanced seminars, independent study involvement in faculty research projects, specialized tutorials, internships, courses at Bard, and a possible semester or full year of study abroad.

The senior thesis is the focus of each B.A. student's final year. A thesis project carries 8 credits and is expected to take a full academic year to complete. Drawing on the skills in analysis and synthesis acquired during the previous three years, students devote themselves wholeheartedly to the project and to learning, which has been personally defined and developed. Recent theses have taken many forms: critical studies in literature, sociological research, musical compositions, creative fiction, translations, scientific experiments, mathematical problem solving, artistic exhibitions and performances, and various combinations of these forms.

The regular academic program is supplemented by extensive cocurricular offerings, including annual poetry, fiction, concert, humanities, women's studies, and lecture series.

Off-Campus Programs

Juniors pursue a variety of study-abroad programs and options. In recent years, students have conducted extended campus field study projects in Ecuador, England, Honduras, Kenya, and Nepal. Through the School of International Training, Simon's Rock students have also participated in study programs at universities in England, India, Morocco, Nepal, and Israel. Others have studied at Oxford University in England, the University of Stirling in Scotland, Trinity College in Dublin, University of the Bosphorus in Turkey, and the University of Berlin in Germany. Students have also spent semesters away at a variety of colleges and universities throughout the United States and have participated in educational programs sponsored by the Washington Center for Learning Alternatives, the School for Field Studies, Global Roots, and the Semester at Sea program. Students have also earned credit for internship projects in journalism, government, business, and environmental policy.

Academic Facilities

The 16,000-square-foot Fisher Science and Academic Center was completed in January 1998. The center houses the College's biology, chemistry, ecology, and physics laboratories; research labs for faculty members and students; classrooms and tutorial rooms; a 60-seat lecture center; and faculty offices. There is also a public-access computer lab with Macintosh computers, and the library has several CD-ROM workstations and terminals dedicated to accessing the Internet. The mathematics department has a lab of IBM-clone computers and a NeXT cube workstation. The Arts Center incorporates a 200-seat theater; studios for painting, graphics, sculpture, photography, and ceramics; multimedia graphics workstations and scanning equipment; and an art gallery. The Liebowitz Arts and Humanities Building includes a dance studio and gallery, as well as classrooms, offices, and a slide library. A music hall, a recording studio, and music practice rooms are also available to students in the arts. The campus library houses 68,000 volumes and collections of recordings and periodicals, a listening room, and a language laboratory. Simon's Rock students also have access to the Bard College library. An interlibrary loan system provides access to other college and university collections. A 53,000-square-foot athletic complex with squash courts, a basketball court, an elevated track, and a swimming pool was completed in 1999.

Costs

For 2003–04, tuition was $24,280, room and board were $7100, and the student services fee was $2900, for a total of $34,340. The student services fee reflects the exceptional emphasis Simon's Rock, as an early college, places on student services. The fee provides funds for athletic programs, activities, health services, academic counseling, residence supervision, and security. For first-year students, there is also an orientation fee.

Financial Aid

Parents seeking consideration for financial aid should so indicate on the admission application. Simon's Rock promptly sends all the necessary forms and instructions. Upon completion of the Financial Aid PROFILE and the Free Application for Federal Student Aid (FAFSA), candidates are considered for all forms of financial aid available through Simon's Rock. Notification of awards is made as soon as possible after the decision regarding admission. Awards generally consist of several forms of government assistance combined with scholarships and campus employment opportunities.

Faculty

The College has 67 full-time faculty members, 87 percent of whom hold either an earned doctorate or an equivalent terminal degree in their field. Simon's Rock supplements this full-time faculty with visiting scholars, regular adjunct faculty members in music and studio arts, and part-time faculty members in other areas as needed. Faculty members are distinguished not only by their excellence in teaching and advising but also by their sensitivity to the particular developmental needs of the College's younger students.

Student Government

Students at Simon's Rock participate in the decision making and governance of the community through elected and appointed positions on House Councils, the Community Council, the Judicial Committee, and the Anti-Discrimination and Harassment Committee. Student representatives also serve on the College's Policy and Program and the Standards and Procedures faculty committees. The social life of the College is characterized by respect for individual rights and a strong sense of community.

Admission Requirements

Simon's Rock seeks students for early entrance who demonstrate the intellectual ability, motivation, and self-discipline to pursue college studies at a high school age. The admission staff recognizes its special responsibility to work closely with each prospective student and his or her parents to ensure that the decision to enter Simon's Rock is the right one. For this reason, a personal interview is required of each applicant. In addition to the interview, the College requires submission of written essays, two letters of recommendation, an official high school transcript, standardized test scores (PSAT, SAT I, ACT, or P-ACT), and a parent's statement. International students are required to submit TOEFL scores.

Application and Information

Candidates should submit their materials by May 30 for fall admission. Applications received after this date are considered if spaces are available. The application fee is $40.

To schedule an interview or request further information, students should contact:

Dean of Admission
Simon's Rock College of Bard
84 Alford Road
Great Barrington, Massachusetts 01230-2499
Telephone: 413-528-7312
800-235-7186 (toll-free)
Fax: 413-528-7334
E-mail: admit@simons-rock.edu
World Wide Web: http://www.simons-rock.edu

In the laboratory.

SIMPSON COLLEGE

INDIANOLA, IOWA

The College

Simpson College was founded in 1860. The institution was named Simpson College to honor Bishop Matthew Simpson (1811–1884), one of the best-known and most influential religious leaders of his day. The College is coeducational; although it is affiliated with the United Methodist Church, it is nonsectarian in spirit and accepts students without regard to race, color, creed, national origin, religion, sex, age, or disability.

For more than a century, Simpson has played a vital role in the educational, cultural, intellectual, political, and religious life of the nation. The College has thirty-two buildings on 73 acres of beautiful campus and enrolls more than 1,900 students.

Extracurricular activities at Simpson are designed to supplement and reinforce the academic program and contribute toward a total learning experience. Students may participate in student government, publications, music, theater, and social groups. Simpson competes in eighteen intercollegiate sports and has an extensive intramural program for both men and women. Men's and women's athletics at Simpson are governed by the NCAA. Simpson also has chapters of three national fraternities, one local fraternity, and four national sororities.

Location

Simpson is located in the city of Indianola, a residential community of 13,000 people. Indianola is 12 miles south of Des Moines, Iowa's capital city; 12 miles east of Interstate 35; and 15 miles south of Interstates 80 and 235. The Des Moines International Airport is 20 minutes from campus. Five miles south of Indianola is Lake Ahquabi State Park, where swimming and other recreational facilities are available. Every summer, Indianola is the home of the National Hot Air Balloon Classic and of the Des Moines Metropolitan Summer Opera Festival. The location of the residential campus provides the best of both metropolitan and suburban activities.

Majors and Degrees

Simpson College grants Bachelor of Arts and Bachelor of Music degrees in major and career programs, including accounting, art, athletic training, biochemistry, biology, chemistry, computer information systems, computer science, corporate communication, criminal justice, economics, education, English, environmental science, French, German, history, international management, international relations, journalism and mass communication, management, marketing, mathematics, music, music education, music performance, philosophy, physical education, physics, political science, psychology, religion, rhetoric and speech communication, sociology, Spanish, sports administration, and theater arts.

Simpson also offers preprofessional programs in dentistry, engineering, law, medicine, optometry, physical therapy, theology, and veterinary medicine.

Academic Program

Simpson College operates on a 4-4-1 academic calendar. The first semester starts in late August and ends in mid-December; the second semester starts in mid-January and ends in late April. A three-week session takes place during the month of May. During this period, students have the opportunity to take one class that focuses on a single subject, to study abroad, or to participate in a field experience or internship.

Students must participate in one May Term class or program for each year of full-time study at Simpson College. All students must complete the requirements of the cornerstone studies in liberal arts and competencies in foreign language, math, and writing. To earn the Bachelor of Arts degree, students may take no more than 42 hours in the major department, excluding May Term programs, and 84 hours in the division of the major, including May Term programs. In addition, at least 128 semester hours of course work must be accumulated with a grade point average of C (2.0) or better.

For a Bachelor of Music degree, the same requirements apply, except that 84 hours must be earned in the major, excluding May Terms, and the candidate is limited to 12 additional hours in the division of fine arts. In addition, a minimum of 132 hours of course work must be completed with a cumulative grade point average of C (2.0) or better.

The First Year Program is a broadly inclusive program of orientation, group-building, mentoring, community service, advising, and classroom work structured to help new students adapt to their first year of college. The program begins with summer orientation and extends throughout the full year.

The academic component of the First Year Program is the Liberal Arts Seminar, a joint classroom and advising concept that is unique among first-year programs. The seminars are small in size—no more than 18 first-year students each—and all are taught by students' faculty advisers.

Off-Campus Programs

A variety of programs are offered for off-campus study. Simpson offers semester-long study-abroad programs in London, England; Schorndorf, Germany; and Managua, Nicaragua. During May Term and an optional summer session in June, qualified students may study in Mérida, Mexico, in the Yucatán Peninsula. Students also may study in Paris and other cities in France for a semester or a year or during May Term.

Simpson is an affiliate of the American Institute for Foreign Study, which provides access to carefully planned semester or academic-year study programs in Austria, Britain, China, France, Germany, Italy, and Spain. Additional international travel programs are offered on a regular basis during the May Term as well.

The Washington Semester, offered in conjunction with the American University in Washington, D.C., permits a qualified student to study the political process in the nation's capital. Also available is the United Nations Semester with Drew University in Madison, New Jersey. Students undertake a course of study at Drew and at the United Nations in New York City. With both programs, students maintain enrollment at Simpson. In addition, the Washington Center Internships and Symposia Program consists of semester-long, full-time, supervised work experiences in the nation's capital, supplemented by weekly academic seminars.

Academic Facilities

The George Washington Carver Science Center provides state-of-the-art research facilities, computer labs, and classrooms. The computer labs contain Macintosh and IBM-compatible microcomputers. For academic computing, Simpson has a Compaq DS20E Alpha server computer and a campuswide Ethernet fiber-optic network.

The Henry H. and Thomas H. McNeill Hall houses classrooms for management, accounting, economics, and communication studies. In addition, the hall houses a seminar room and the Pioneer Hi-Bred International Conference Center.

The Amy Robertson Music Center houses the music department and contains the Sven and Mildred Lekberg Recital Hall, ten studios, twenty-two practice rooms, a music computer lab, and the band rehearsal room. A new wing includes a choral rehearsal room, a classroom, and studios.

Dunn Library, a contemporary learning resource center, contains approximately 155,133 volumes, 698 current periodicals, 2,075 DVDs and videotapes, 809 music CDs, and access to more than 6,769 e-books. Additional materials for research can be obtained through a national computer-based interlibrary loan network. The library also provides audiovisual equipment and services to the campus.

The A. H. and Theo Blank Performing Arts Center accommodates Simpson's well-known programs in theater arts and opera and includes the magnificent 500-seat Pote Theatre, with both proscenium and hydraulically controlled thrust stages; a studio theater; the Barborka Gallery; technical facilities and shops; and classrooms.

Wallace Hall reopened in 1996 after a complete internal renovation. Named to the National Register of Historic Places in 1991, Wallace Hall contains facilities for education, psychology, sociology, applied social science, and a biofeedback/psychology laboratory.

Costs

Tuition and fees for 2003–04 were $18,097, a room was $2669, and board was $2892. These figures did not include books, music fees, or personal expenses.

Financial Aid

Simpson College seeks to make it financially possible for qualified students to experience the advantages of a college education. Generous gifts from alumni, trustees, and friends of the College, in addition to state and federal student aid programs, make this opportunity possible. Simpson offers financial aid on both a need and non-need basis. Need is determined by filing the Free Application for Federal Student Aid.

Financial aid granted on a non-need basis includes academic scholarships, which are awarded on the basis of prior academic records, and talent scholarships, which are available in theater, music, and art. The talent scholarships are determined by audition/portfolio.

Faculty

Ninety-two percent of Simpson's 82 full-time faculty members have earned their terminal degrees. At Simpson, faculty members serve as academic advisers as well as teachers and often attend College plays, operas, and athletic events, reinforcing their sincere interest in students. The student-faculty ratio is 14:1.

Student Government

Student involvement in College governance is an integral part of the organization of the College. Students annually elect a president and vice president of the Student Government. The members of each housing unit and the off-campus students elect representatives to the Student Senate. The Student Senate appoints student members to all College committees in which students hold membership. The senate also appoints 4 students-at-large who attend plenary sessions of the Board of Trustees as members on the Student Affairs Committee.

Admission Requirements

Admission to Simpson College is selective and competitive. A strong academic record is essential. Applications are acted upon by an admissions committee, which is elected by the faculty and represents the five academic divisions of the College. These faculty members consider the college-preparatory courses taken, the grades received in those courses, rank in class, and standardized test scores (ACT and/or SAT I), including test subscores. A short time after all required credentials are received, the application is reviewed by the Admissions Committee. Transfer applicants are accepted on the basis of successful completion of academic work at an accredited college or university. In addition, transfer applicants are required to submit official high school transcripts and ACT/SAT I results.

Application and Information

Simpson's rolling admission policy allows flexibility; however, early application is recommended. Transfer and international students are welcome. Students are strongly encouraged to visit the campus.

For additional information or to obtain application materials, students should contact:

Office of Admissions
Simpson College
701 North "C" Street
Indianola, Iowa 50125
Telephone: 515-961-1624
800-362-2454 (toll-free)
E-mail: admiss@simpson.edu
World Wide Web: http://www.simpson.edu

The George Washington Carver Science Center provides Simpson students with state-of-the-art labs and research facilities.

SKIDMORE COLLEGE

SARATOGA SPRINGS, NEW YORK

The College

Skidmore College is an independent liberal arts college of 2,200 men and women. Founded as the Skidmore School of Arts in 1911, it became Skidmore College in 1922. In addition to being accredited by the Middle States Association of Colleges and Schools, the College has a chapter of Phi Beta Kappa and has program accreditation with the Council on Social Work Education and the National Association of Schools of Art and Design.

Throughout its history, Skidmore has steadily reflected a spirit of innovation and imagination in response to need. In the 1960s, the College decided to build an entirely new campus; in 1971, to become a coeducational college; in 1983, to completely revise its curriculum; and in 1993, to install a graduate program leading to the Master of Arts in Liberal Studies degree. Skidmore has welcomed change, seeing in it the opportunity to serve the needs and realize the potential of its students. By expanding its programs, the College has broadened its educational mission to reflect the evolving opportunities and challenges of a global society.

Students enjoy a full schedule of cultural, intellectual, and social activities, including lectures, art exhibits, concerts, opera, dance, and theater. There are more than ninety student organizations, such as a weekly newspaper, an FM stereo radio station, a TV station, an art and literary journal, a journal of social science and philosophy opinion, and the student-directed art gallery. There are no fraternities or sororities. A strong intercollegiate sports program for men and women includes baseball, basketball, field hockey, golf, ice hockey, lacrosse, riding, rowing, soccer, softball, swimming, tennis, and volleyball. The College has a vigorous intramural program and supports team activities of club status as well.

The modern campus of Skidmore College includes fifty buildings. The sports and recreation complex includes a pool, racquet-sport courts, basketball courts, a small stadium with artificial turf field and a 400-meter all-weather track, three dance studios, a weight room, a fitness center, and other recreational and competitive sport facilities. The $11-million Tang Teaching Museum and Art Gallery opened in fall 2000, and renovations to the student center have recently been completed.

Location

Set on 850 acres in historic Saratoga Springs, New York, the College offers students the advantage of a rural campus setting and the convenience of location in a city of 30,000 residents. Saratoga Springs has long been famous as a resort and as a horse-racing and cultural center. The city is located 30 miles north of Albany, the capital of New York State, and is cosmopolitan in character. Skidmore is within an hour of major ski areas, state parks, large lakes, and mountainous regions of eastern New York, Vermont, and western Massachusetts. During the summer, groups such as the New York City Ballet and the Philadelphia Orchestra are in residence at the Saratoga Performing Arts Center.

Bus service is available from Saratoga Springs to New York City, Montreal, Boston, and other major cities. There are daily trains to and from New York City and Montreal. Rental cars are available at the Albany International Airport, which is served by major airlines. The College is located near Exit 15 of I-87 (the Northway).

Majors and Degrees

Skidmore College grants a Bachelor of Arts degree in the following liberal arts subjects: American studies, anthropology, biology, chemistry, classical studies, computer science, economics, English, environmental studies, foreign languages and literatures (French, German, and Spanish), geology, government, history, history of art, mathematics, music, neuroscience, philosophy, physics, psychology, religion, and sociology. The Bachelor of Science degree is granted in areas of a more professional nature, including business, dance, education, exercise science, social work, studio art, and theater. There are thirty-three interdepartmental majors. Self-determined majors, double majors, and minors are also available.

The College offers 3-2 programs with the Thayer School of Engineering at Dartmouth College and with Clarkson University. Also available is a 4-1 M.B.A. program offered with the School of Management at Clarkson, a 3-2 M.B.A. program offered through Rensselaer Polytechnic Institute, and a 4-1 Master of Arts in Teaching program with Union College. Through a cooperative program with the Cardozo Law School, Skidmore students may obtain a bachelor's degree and a law degree in six years. In addition, Skidmore has certification programs in teaching and social work and preprofessional programs in law and medicine.

Academic Program

Skidmore College is known for its unusual blend of courses in the traditional liberal arts with opportunities in preprofessional disciplines. It is also recognized for its liberal studies core curriculum in which two interdisciplinary courses are required. Additional core requirements include two courses in science, two in the social sciences, one in the arts, one in a foreign language, and one in non-Western culture. All students choose a major at the end of their sophomore year from among sixty options, some of which include interdepartmental concentrations, self-determined majors, and minors.

The College operates on a two-semester system with opportunities for internships directly following the end of the second semester in May. Students normally carry four or five courses during each semester.

The College offers a six-week residential academic summer program (PASS) enabling high school students to take two courses for college credit.

University Without Walls (UWW) is the nontraditional, nonresidential baccalaureate degree program of Skidmore College. Students admitted to the program work individually with a faculty adviser to define the specific content of their degree programs. Skidmore UWW also encourages and helps the student to identify and use nontraditional means to acquire the requisite knowledge, including independent and self-directed study, as well as experiences gained in paid volunteer work. A similarly designed Master of Arts in Liberal Studies program was implemented in 1993.

Off-Campus Programs

Skidmore's membership in the Hudson-Mohawk Association of Colleges and Universities enables students to cross-register at any of fourteen other colleges and universities in the area. The Washington Semester, conducted through American University in Washington, D.C., offers an intensive workshop experience through course work, seminars, research projects, and internships with government committees. Skidmore's Study Abroad

Program enables students to study in China, England, France, India, and Spain. Skidmore is also affiliated with other study-abroad programs, facilitating study for a semester or a year in many locations in Asia, Australia, Europe, and Latin America.

Arrangements for student internships are made through academic departments or through the Office of Career Planning and Field Experience Programs. Internships are available in such diverse fields as government, social work, the arts (dance, theater, and museum work), business, scientific research, and medicine.

Academic Facilities

Scribner Library, housing approximately 500,000 volumes, has been designated a depository for U.S. government documents. Students have access to forty libraries in the region through the College's membership in an area council. Skidmore also participates in the Lockheed/Dialog system for information search and retrieval. Dana Science Center has laboratories and sophisticated equipment for the biology, chemistry, physics, and geology departments. The Filene Music Building contains a large recital hall, practice and listening rooms, and a music library. Other special facilities include a language laboratory in Bolton Hall; the Art Building, with studio space, numerous kilns, and ceramics, weaving, and jewelry-making studios; the Skidmore Theatre; and dance studios. Students have access to a computer center served by a cluster of nine SunSPARC-2 workstations. In fall 2000, Skidmore opened an $11-million art museum at the center of its campus.

Costs

Tuition in 2003–04 for all students was $29,350. Students living in dormitories paid a room and board fee of $8300. Additional fees were $280.

Financial Aid

Skidmore awards financial aid based on demonstrated need. The Free Application for Federal Student Aid (FAFSA), a copy of the federal income tax form, and the CSS PROFILE must be filed each year. The application date is January 15 for entering freshmen. The College hosts an annual Filene Music Scholarship Competition to award four $36,000 ($9000 per year) scholarships on the basis of musical ability without regard to financial need. Five $10,000 merit scholarships in math and science are also awarded annually. Detailed information concerning scholarships, grants, loans, and/or work awards can be obtained through the Office of Student Aid and Family Finance.

Faculty

Skidmore College has 189 full-time teaching faculty members and 10 part-time members, including those with special appointments. More than 90 percent of the liberal arts faculty members have doctoral degrees. The ratio of students to full-time faculty members is about 11:1, and the average class size is 16. Although actively engaged in research and publication in their individual fields, the Skidmore faculty members regard teaching as their primary commitment. All students have faculty advisers who assist them in selecting courses and in designing individual academic programs.

Student Government

Students at Skidmore play an active role in College governance. Through the Student Government Association (SGA) and by membership on a number of major College committees, they participate in all phases of academic and social life. The SGA operates under the authority granted by the Board of Trustees and is dedicated to the principles of democratic self-government and responsible citizenship. Within the association, elected faculty members and student representatives serve on the All-College Council, the Academic Integrity Board, and the Social Integrity Board. The broad concerns of the SGA include educational policy, elections, social and student events, freshman orientation, student publications, and student clubs and organizations.

Admission Requirements

Applicants for admission to the freshman class are expected to complete a secondary school program with a minimum of 16 college-preparatory credits. The Admissions Committee is also pleased to consider applications from qualified high school juniors who plan to accelerate and enter college early. Typical preparation for entrance includes 4 years of English, 4 years of a foreign language, 4 years of mathematics, 3 years of social studies, and 3 years of laboratory science. Among the required credentials are a secondary school transcript, a report from the school guidance counselor, and assessments from 2 teachers. Skidmore also requires applicants to take the SAT I or ACT examination and recommends that three SAT II Subject Tests, including the Writing Test, be taken. A campus interview is strongly recommended.

Through the Higher Education Opportunity Program (HEOP), Skidmore enrolls talented, energetic, and motivated students from New York State who would otherwise be unable to attend the College under traditional admission requirements because of academic and financial circumstances.

Application and Information

An applicant for admission registers by completing Skidmore's application form or the Common Application and returning it with a $50 fee. All information should be postmarked by January 15. Applications from early decision candidates may be submitted by December 1 for the Round I early decision plan or by January 15 for the Round II early decision plan. Transfer candidates are urged to apply by April 1 for the next fall term and by November 15 for the next spring term. Interested students are strongly urged to visit the campus for interviews and guided tours.

Mary Lou W. Bates
Dean of Admissions and Financial Aid
Skidmore College
Saratoga Springs, New York 12866
Telephone: 518-580-5570
800-867-6007 (toll-free)
E-mail: admissions@skidmore.edu
World Wide Web: http://www.skidmore.edu

Aerial view of the Skidmore College campus.

SLIPPERY ROCK UNIVERSITY OF PENNSYLVANIA

SLIPPERY ROCK, PENNSYLVANIA

The University

At Slippery Rock University, students receive a "rock solid" education: a classic residential campus in a safe, small-town setting; an affordable lifelong value; committed, caring faculty members; and a once-in-a-lifetime experience.

In 1889, the citizens of the borough of Slippery Rock founded the college and gave it the town's picturesque name. In 1983, the school became Slippery Rock University of Pennsylvania. Today, Slippery Rock University is a comprehensive university that comprises four colleges and is a member of the State System of Higher Education of Pennsylvania.

The colleges of Slippery Rock University are: Education; Humanities, Fine and Performing Arts; Business, Information, and Behavioral Sciences; Health, Environment, and Science; and Graduate Studies and Research. Most of the University's 7,800 students hail from Pennsylvania; they are joined by students from Ohio, New York, New Jersey, Maryland, and the rest of the nation. International students from more than seventy countries also call Slippery Rock home during the academic year. Residence life is popular, with close to half of the student population living on campus. Freshmen live on campus in University residence halls to facilitate their transition to college. Students also live off campus in fraternity and sorority residences, houses, and apartments, and a few students commute from their homes in neighboring cities and towns.

Students participate in more than 100 social, honorary, and special-interest clubs. Intercollegiate and intramural sports for both men and women are popular and played in the University's spacious indoor and outdoor facilities. Concerts, plays, lectures, and other cultural activities fill the University calendar to create an active tone in a congenial setting. Slippery Rock has a long and proud athletic tradition, with intercollegiate competition taking place on the NCAA Division II level in more than one dozen sports, and men's wrestling competing on the Division I level.

Academic support services and a well-structured set of learning communities are available to foster student success in a learner-centered environment. A technology-oriented career center allows students to explore interests and research job opportunities. An effective placement service provides assistance to students in their search for employment after graduation. Traditionally, more than 95 percent of graduates find employment in their respective fields or attend graduate or professional schools.

Location

The 600-acre Slippery Rock University campus is less than an hour north of Pittsburgh, 1½ hours south of Erie, and 45 minutes east of Youngstown, Ohio. The campus is in a safe, relaxed small-town community flanked by rolling farmlands, forests, and sparkling glacial lakes. Historic and modern buildings blend a sense of tradition with the latest technologies. Recreational opportunities abound both on and off campus in a variety of settings. Slippery Rock's ideal collegiate atmosphere provides the perfect setting as students make lifelong friends and enjoy a once-in-a-lifetime experience. Located in western Pennsylvania, the University is easily accessible from the Pittsburgh, Erie, and northeast Ohio regions. Two major interstate highways, I-79 and I-80, intersect within 7 miles of the University, conveniently linking Slippery Rock to the entire commonwealth of Pennsylvania and its contiguous region. Pittsburgh is one of the nation's great cities and a setting for major cultural and sporting events as well as internship opportunities. The University is located in a town of about 3,000 that resides in a population center of about 120,000.

Majors and Degrees

Slippery Rock University offers Bachelor of Arts, Bachelor of Fine Arts, Bachelor of Music, Bachelor of Science, Bachelor of Science in Business Administration, Bachelor of Science in Education, Master of Arts, Master of Education, Master of Science, and Doctor of Physical Therapy degrees as well as numerous majors, minors; and program tracks in a plethora of academic disciplines. Some of the program of study areas include: accounting; allied health; anthropology; art; art education; biology; chemistry; communication; community health; community programs for Americans with disabilities; dance; economics; elementary education; emerging technology and multimedia; English literature and writing; environmental education; environmental geoscience; exercise science; finance; French; geography; health services administration; history; human resources management; information systems; information technology; international business; journalism; management; marketing; mathematics; music; music therapy; music education; parks and recreation; philosophy; physical education; physical education: exercise science; physics; political science; psychology; public administration; safety and environmental management; secondary education in English, French, Spanish, social studies (science and mathematics secondary candidates complete bachelor's degrees in those areas and pursue graduate work for teacher certification); sociology; sociology-criminology; Spanish; special education; sport management; and theater. New for the 2004 academic year is a forensic track in chemistry.

In addition to having a history as a premier teacher education institution, Slippery Rock University offers programs that are not available everywhere and are areas of distinction. These include allied health and exercise and rehabilitative sciences, environmental studies and environmental education, parks and recreation, physical therapy (graduate program), special education, and sport management.

The University also offers special affiliation programs that lead to professional degrees at an accelerated pace. Students may enroll in one of several baccalaureate degree programs that precede Slippery Rock's Doctor of Physical Therapy program, including the 3+3 (three years of undergraduate work and three years of professional/graduate study) accelerated options in biology, exercise science, and other allied health and safety programs. New affiliation programs include a 3+4 track with the Lake Erie College of Medicine in Erie, Pennsylvania, for a Doctor of Osteopathy and 2+3 and 3+3 options for a Doctor of Pharmacy with the same institution. A 3+3⅓ affiliation program for students pursuing a Doctor of Chiropractic degree is available with the Logan College of Chiropractic in Chesterfield, Missouri. A dual-degree program in engineering is offered with Pennsylvania State University. The program involves three years of pre-engineering course work at Slippery Rock and two years of engineering study at Penn State. Students in this 3+2 program are awarded Bachelor of Science degrees from both institutions.

Academic Program

Two semesters make up the regular University calendar; the first semester ends before the Christmas break. The summer term is divided into two 5-week sessions, a three-week session, and a seven-week evening session. A minimum of 120 semester hours and a minimum grade point average of 2.0 are required for graduation. Higher grade and academic standards may apply for certain programs.

Through a continuing education program, the University offers credit and noncredit courses and workshops at on- and off-campus sites, including North Hills in suburban Pittsburgh.

Interested students may participate in the Army Reserve Officers' Training Corps (ROTC) program on campus. Completion of the ROTC program can result in a student's commissioning as an officer in the U.S. Army Reserve or National Guard upon graduation.

Off-Campus Programs

Internships and cocurricular experiences are recommended in most academic disciplines. Students in teacher education programs are required to take a semester of student teaching in their senior year. Student teaching experiences occur in many of the surrounding school districts and, in addition, the University offers student teaching experiences overseas and in high growth job markets in the United States. Students interested in marine sciences have the opportunity to participate in summer school sessions at Wallops Island Marine Science Center in Virginia and to utilize the instructional facilities at nearby Lake Arthur and the Jennings Environmental Education Center. The University's extensive and expanding international studies program offers educational opportunities for students in twenty-eight programs in nineteen countries: Austria, Bulgaria, Canada, China, England, France, Germany, Hungary, Ireland, Japan, Korea, Mexico, Poland, Russia, Slovakia, Scotland, Spain, Trinidad, and Wales. Scholarships are often available for students who want to study abroad for a year, a semester, or a summer. In addition, Slippery Rock offers extensive service learning and nonprofit opportunities in the community, including a center in nearby New Castle, Pennsylvania.

Academic Facilities

As a comprehensive university, Slippery Rock offers an extensive array of facilities. The following is but a partial listing. Bailey Library houses more than 850,000 volumes, subscribes to numerous journals and periodicals, maintains an extensive instructional materials center replete with numerous online research resources, and operates a media services center. The Physical Therapy Building, a recent addition to the campus, houses state-of-the-discipline labs and classrooms. Historic Carruth-Rizza Hall is undergoing a complete renovation and is designed to serve as the nexus of an extensive international initiatives program. Construction of a new Science and Information Technology Building began in the summer of 2003 and should offer numerous labs and "smart" classrooms. The Art Building is home to studios and gallery space. Swope Music Hall provides modern facilities for music and music therapy majors, including a concert hall with a pipe organ. Student computer labs are strategically located throughout the campus. Through the University's computing services, every residence hall room is connected with all classroom buildings, the library, and—via the Internet—to the world.

Costs

Tuition for the 2003–04 academic year at Slippery Rock University was $4598 for Pennsylvania residents and $11,496 for out-of-state students. Room and board were $4438 for the year, and other fees were $1202. The total tuition, fees, and room and board for Pennsylvania residents for 2003–04 amounted to $10,240. Total tuition, fees, and room and board for non-Pennsylvania residents were $17,288. Non-Pennsylvania residents who possess cumulative grade point averages of 3.0 (B) or better should contact the Office of Admissions for more information regarding nonresident tuition rates and options.

Financial Aid

About 80 percent of the University's students receive some form of financial aid. Slippery Rock participates in five college-based federal aid programs: the Federal Perkins Loan, Federal Stafford Student Loan, Federal PLUS, Federal Work-Study, and Federal Supplemental Educational Opportunity Grant programs. Federal Pell Grants are also available. Pennsylvania students may be eligible for Pennsylvania Higher Education Assistance Agency (PHEAA) grants and scholarships. Competitive University scholarships are also available. Job opportunities are available on campus and also in businesses in the surrounding area. Students interested in financial aid should contact the University's Office of Financial Aid.

Faculty

Slippery Rock University's faculty members excel as teachers, mentors, and scholars; however, teaching remains their priority. From the freshman year forward, it is the faculty member, not a graduate teaching assistant, whom students see in the classroom. To better serve students' interests, each faculty member also acts as an academic adviser to students. Many faculty members are involved in University activities; professional faculty-student relations are common, reflecting the friendly, personal character of the University.

Student Government

The Student Government Association (SGA), composed of elected student representatives from each class, is the primary student governing body at Slippery Rock University. The SGA regulates cocurricular activities, promotes spirit and unity, encourages student participation in University activities, and serves as an advocate for student interests. Students are active on all major University committees and on the Council of Trustees, one of the University's governing boards.

Admission Requirements

Students from all economic, geographical, cultural, and religious backgrounds are welcome at Slippery Rock University. Students are admitted to Slippery Rock on a rolling basis for all terms. Admission criteria usually include a student's previous academic record, standardized test scores, and rank in class. First-time, full-time freshman students who most often succeed at The Rock have a cumulative high school quality point average of 3.0 on a 4.0 scale and combined SAT scores of 950 or higher at the time of admission as well as demonstrated success in a college preparatory curriculum. However, grade point average and test scores do not always predict how students transition to college. Students who hold a 2.5 or greater QPA/GPA on a 4.0 scale or the equivalent are encouraged to apply.

Students who demonstrate their expertise in specific areas through testing may receive college credit and elect to substitute certain required courses through the Advanced Placement Program and the College-Level Examination Program. The University offers a dual enrollment admission program for outstanding local high school seniors. Students who plan to major in dance, music, music education, or music therapy are required to audition with the dance/music department prior to gaining full admission.

Application and Information

Students seeking admission must complete an application for admission form, submit a high school transcript, and have their scores from either the ACT or SAT I sent to the University. In addition to filing the application form, transfer students must submit transcripts of all previous college work. Students seeking fall semester admission as new freshmen are encouraged to apply during the fall and winter of their senior year of high school. Recently, interest in Slippery Rock has been so robust that freshmen admission has begun to be restricted during the spring preceding the fall semester. Other students, including transfer students, may have other options and should contact the Office of Admission for more information.

To obtain an application for admission, or for additional information on admission or any other aspect of the University, students should visit the Web site listed below.

Director of Admission
Slippery Rock University
Slippery Rock, Pennsylvania 16057-1326
Telephone: 724-738-2015
800-929-4778 (toll-free)
E-mail: apply@sru.edu
World Wide Web: http://www.sru.edu/

SMITH COLLEGE

NORTHAMPTON, MASSACHUSETTS

The College

Smith College was founded in 1871 as a liberal arts college for women and rapidly became one of the first such institutions to match the standards and facilities of the best colleges of the day. Today, with 2,560 undergraduates on campus, Smith is the largest privately endowed college for women in the country. Graduate degrees (master's, Ph.D.) are offered in a number of departments and in the Smith College School for Social Work. Currently, all fifty states and sixty countries are represented in the Smith student body. Approximately 85 percent of the members of each entering class were in the top fifth of their high school class; most chose Smith because of the excellence of its faculty and curriculum. Although most Smith students are between the ages of 18 and 22, Smith's Ada Comstock Scholars Program enables older women whose educations have been interrupted and who meet the College's admission standards to pursue an A.B. degree or one of several graduate degrees.

Smith's house system is unusual and highly regarded. Each of the College's thirty-five houses is home to between 15 and 100 women. Most houses have their own kitchens, dining rooms, living rooms, and study areas, and each building has a charm and character of its own. The house system stresses individual freedom, group autonomy, and mutual respect. Optional facilities, such as a cooperative house, a French house, and townhouse apartments, are available. Smith offers a wide variety of extracurricular possibilities, ranging from service organizations to musical groups and from student publications to fourteen intercollegiate sports teams. The already varied cultural and social opportunities—lectures, workshops, dance and theatrical performances, art exhibits, concerts, and social events—are increased by participation in Five Colleges, Inc., a consortium that opens to Smith students classes and activities at Amherst, Hampshire, and Mount Holyoke colleges and at the University of Massachusetts. Smith's athletic facilities include two gymnasiums, five squash courts, a 75-foot six-lane swimming pool with 1- and 3-meter diving boards, a human performance laboratory, climbing wall, fitness center, and an indoor track and tennis facility, which houses four tennis courts and a 200-meter track and accommodates all field events. Outside are 30 acres of athletic fields, a 400-meter track, a 5,000-meter cross-country course, and twelve lighted tennis courts. Smith also has indoor and outdoor Olympic-size riding rings and a forty-two-unit stable.

Location

Northampton, a cosmopolitan city with a population of more than 30,000, is in the Connecticut River valley of western Massachusetts. It is 93 miles west of Boston and 156 miles northeast of New York City. There are many shops and restaurants within walking distance of the campus and within the service area of a free Five College bus system. Buses run frequently to Boston and New York. Many students are involved in local organizations, and some intern in local city or county offices. Others participate on an extracurricular level in nonprofit agencies, day-care centers, or similar institutions.

Majors and Degrees

Smith College awards the Bachelor of Arts (A.B.) degree. Areas of major concentration include Afro-American studies, American studies, ancient studies, anthropology (anthropology, sociology and anthropology), art, astronomy, biochemistry, biological sciences, chemistry, classical languages and literatures (Greek, Latin, the classics, classical studies), comparative literature, computer science, dance, economics, education and child study, English language and literature, French language and literature (French language and literature, French studies), geology, German studies (German culture studies, German literature studies), government, history, Italian language and literature, Latin American studies, mathematics, medieval studies, music, philosophy, physics, psychology, religion and biblical literature, Russian language and literature (Russian literature, Russian civilization), sociology (sociology, sociology and anthropology), Spanish and Portuguese (peninsular Spanish literature, Latin American literature, Portuguese-Brazilian studies), theater, and women's studies. A Bachelor of Science (B.S.) degree in engineering science is also available. Interdepartmental majors and minors are offered in a variety of fields.

Academic Program

The academic year is divided into two semesters, the first ending before winter recess. Interterm courses, some for credit, are offered during January. Smith believes in the goals of a liberal arts education. Students have great freedom to design their own courses of study; the only requirement outside a student's field of concentration is one writing-intensive course. One hundred twenty-eight credits of academic work are required, with the normal course load consisting of 16 credits in each of eight semesters. There are no specific distribution requirements, but 64 credits must be taken outside the major field of study. If a student's educational needs cannot be met within any of the existing majors, she may design and undertake an interdepartmental major, subject to the approval of the Subcommittee on Honors and Independent Programs. A student may also complete the requirements of two departmental majors or of one departmental major and another departmental minor.

Through credit earned on Advanced Placement or International Baccalaureate Diploma examinations and by independent work and summer study, some students may be able to accelerate and complete degree requirements in six or seven semesters. The Departmental Honors Program enables a student with a strong academic background to study a particular topic in depth or undertake research in the field of her major. Through the Smith Scholars Program, some undergraduates can spend one or two years on projects they design, freed in varying degrees from normal College requirements.

Off-Campus Programs

Smith students may take academic courses and participate in social and cultural activities at any of the institutions participating in the Five College consortium, described above. Smith students may also spend a year at another member institution of the Twelve College Exchange Program (Amherst, Bowdoin, Connecticut, Dartmouth, Mount Holyoke, Trinity, Vassar, Wellesley, Wesleyan, Wheaton, and Williams) or spend a year at one of several historically black colleges in the South. Some students participate in the Jean Picker Semester-in-Washington Program in public policy, a fall internship program in Washington, D.C., sponsored by the College's Department of Government. The American Studies Program offers an internship at the Smithsonian Institution.

Smith offers Junior Year Abroad programs in Florence, Geneva, Hamburg, and Paris. Students may apply to affiliated programs in South India, Spain, Japan, and China, and some may study at the Intercollegiate Center for Classical Studies in Rome. Smith students may also participate in other programs arranged independently or by the College. Students eligible for financial aid are able to take that aid with them to any approved program.

Academic Facilities

The Smith College Library is the largest undergraduate library of any liberal arts college in this country. Its 1.3 million holdings are housed in the centrally located William Allan Neilson Library and in the libraries of the fine arts, performing arts, and science centers. The Neilson Library also houses a rare book room, the Nonprint Resource Center, the College archives, and the Sophia Smith Collection, a women's history archive. The Clark Science Center is a five-building complex that accommodates the nearly 30 percent of students who major in the sciences. The facilities include general laboratories, a molecular genetics facility, classrooms, a rooftop astronomy observatory, animal care facilities, scanning and transmission electron microscopes, an analytic ultracentrifuge, and a high-field nuclear magnetic resonance spectrometer. Academic computer facilities include more than 550 networked Windows and Macintosh computers in public labs, classrooms, the libraries, and the foreign language center. All buildings and student residences are networked to the academic UNIX systems, Novell file servers, and the Internet via a campus-wide fiber-optic network. These resources are available for student use without charge. Smith also has a digital design studio and several electronic classrooms. The Bass Science Building houses the psychology department, the scientific computing center, and Young Library, one of the largest undergraduate science libraries in the country. The Bass laboratories provide numerous facilities for research in neuroscience. The Mendenhall Center for the Performing Arts contains an experimental theater and a traditional theater, dance studios, and television and audio recording rooms. Sage Hall, the music building, includes an electronic music studio, a small recital hall, dozens of practice rooms, and a 750-seat concert hall. The Smith College Museum of Art houses one of the finest teaching collections in the country, and Hillyer Hall contains art studios as well as printmaking, darkroom, and sculpture facilities. Smith's Center for Foreign Languages and Cultures maintains a multimedia laboratory and classroom housing a network of student workstations with integrated and interactive computer, audio, and video components.

Costs

Tuition for 2003–04 was $27,330. The room and board charge for regular dormitories was $9490. Optional health insurance is estimated at $1120, the activity fee is approximately $215, and books, supplies, and personal expenses are estimated at $1500.

Financial Aid

Approximately 65 percent of all Smith students receive some form of financial assistance from grants, loans, and/or campus jobs. Aid is awarded on the basis of need, as determined by the College. Each applicant must submit the Free Application for Federal Student Aid (FAFSA), the PROFILE form from the College Scholarship Service, and a copy of her family's most recent federal income tax return. For all traditional-age admitted students, Smith makes every effort to fully meet documented need. The first portion of an aid award is an offer of a loan and campus employment; the remaining need is covered by grants from federal, state, and/or College funds.

Faculty

The teaching of undergraduate women is the priority of the Smith faculty. There are approximately 290 faculty members; most have earned a doctoral degree and are well-known in their professional field. Close ties between undergraduates and their teachers are forged through small classes (more than 70 percent have 20 or fewer students) and generous access to faculty members during and outside of regular office hours.

Student Government

Smith students assume much of the responsibility for their personal, social, and academic life at the College through the Student Government Association, which gives students representation on major College-policy committees and regulates the functioning of the house system.

Admission Requirements

Smith seeks students whose motivation, academic preparation, and diversity of interests will enable them to profit from and contribute to the varied possibilities of a liberal arts college. Smith is interested in the woman behind the record and the scores. However, as a highly competitive college, Smith gives primary consideration to the academic record of each candidate for admission. Strong high school programs usually have a basis of 4 years of English, at least 3 years in one foreign language or 2 years in each of two languages, 3 years of mathematics, 3 years of science, and 2 years of history. It is hoped that areas of special interest will have been pursued in depth. Students should submit ACT or SAT I scores. SAT II Subject Tests, especially the Writing Test, are strongly recommended but not required. An interview is strongly recommended. Either an on-campus interview or an interview with a local alumna can be arranged by calling the Office of Admission. A first-choice early decision plan is available.

Applications are also welcomed from students who wish to transfer from other college-level institutions or who wish to enter the Visiting Students Program or the Ada Comstock Scholars Program. Smith admits students of any race, color, creed, handicap, or national or ethnic origin.

Application and Information

A student interested in applying to Smith has three options: fall early decision, winter early decision, or regular decision. Applicants for fall early decision should apply by November 15 and receive a decision by December 15. Applicants for winter early decision should apply by January 1 and receive a decision in early February. Regular decision applicants should submit the Part I Application by January 15; all other parts of the application are due by February 1. These candidates receive their admission decision by April 1. Transfer applicants for January admission should apply by November 15 and receive an admission decision by mid-December. The preferred deadline for September transfer admission is February 1, with notification in early April. Applications are accepted until May 1, with decisions made on a rolling basis. Students applying to the Visiting Students Program should have a completed application in by July 1 and receive notification on a rolling basis.

For more information about Smith College, students should contact:

Director of Admission
Smith College
Northampton, Massachusetts 01063
Telephone: 413-585-2500
800-383-3232 (toll-free)
Fax: 413-585-2527
E-mail: admission@smith.edu
World Wide Web: http://www.smith.edu

Smith offers small classes and individual instruction.

SOUTHEASTERN UNIVERSITY

WASHINGTON, D.C.

The University

Southeastern University is a dynamic, small, business-oriented international university in Washington, D.C., with a declared mission as an academic innovator. The roots of the University reach back to 1879, when the Young Men's Christian Association (YMCA) organized business and liberal arts courses for residents of Washington, D.C. The University is chartered by an act of the Congress of the United States, is accredited by the Commission on Higher Education of the Middle States Association of Colleges and Schools, and is a full member of the prestigious Consortium of Universities of the Washington Metropolitan Area.

Although half of the students enrolled at the Washington campus are international (representing from forty to forty-five countries at any one time), traditionally, most students are adult workers who hold full- or part-time jobs. Some students come to the University directly from high school, while others—frequently, those who obtain jobs with the federal government and move to Washington—transfer credits previously earned from institutions of higher education.

The University has emerged in recent years as an intellectual, cultural, and economic force in the southwest quadrant of the city and as a leader in the attempt to organize Washington's institutions of higher education on behalf of businesses and economic development throughout the Potomac region.

The University offers Associate of Science, Bachelor of Science, and a wide variety of master's degrees. Majors include accounting, business administration, computer information systems, computer science, finance, government management, government program management, health services administration, information systems management, legal studies, and marketing. Many teachers in the D.C. Public School system take an exciting master's degree program that is offered in a compressed format as a result of a partnership between the University and the Washington Teachers Union. Southeastern offers a wide range of other instructional and in-service courses for D.C. teachers.

Over the past century, many of the city's leading professional practitioners have graduated from Southeastern. Also, the University has sponsored a widely commended and highly successful College Access Program for local high school graduates. Enrollment has tripled over the past several years, and more than 900 students currently enroll in Southeastern's programs each quadmester—quarter terms with full semester credits.

Southeastern University partners or joint ventures with a number of the most advanced professional associations and private industries on the Eastern Seaboard. These dynamic partnerships arise from the role played by the University's president, Dr. Charlene Drew Jarvis, a longtime District of Columbia Councilmember and distinguished expert on urban economic and community development.

The University partners with the Greater Washington Society of Certified Public Accountants, providing a wide range of programs jointly through the Washington School of Accountancy. CPAs from throughout the country may obtain a master's degree while satisfying their annual state continuing education requirements; courses have been specially designed with the working professional in mind.

The University cosponsors a Small Business Development Subcenter with nearby Friendship House. The subcenter, an affiliate of the federally funded Howard University Small Business Center, offers training and counseling throughout the year to many entrepreneurs and small-business owners. Southeastern is a partner and sponsor of Techworld Public Charter School, cosponsors the Certified Nurses Aide Program with Rosario Adult Charter School and Medlantic Hospital, and partners with groups such as the Marshall Heights Community Development Organization, the Potomac Regional Educational Partnership, and the Community Business Partnership of the Greater Washington Board of Trade.

The University's Student Government Association sponsors an active social and cultural program; prominent national and local leaders speak at colloquia, and access is facilitated to national institutions located on the Mall—"America's front yard"—just two blocks from the site of the main campus. A professional academic advising staff is available full-time, and there is a very active Student Services Office as well. Active student groups include Omega Psi Phi fraternity, Phi Chi Theta, the Chinese Students Association, and a variety of other political and social organizations.

In addition to the University's undergraduate programs, graduate degrees are available in accounting, business management, information system management, marketing, government management, health services administration, and nonprofit management. There is also a certificate program in computer information system. Graduate tuition fees cost $300 per credit.

Location

The University's main office is located in an attractive contemporary building close to the Maine Avenue waterfront in the redeveloped southwest section of Washington, D.C. The University is close to such well-known cultural institutions as the Arena Stage and L'Enfant Plaza and to the United States Capitol, the Supreme Court, the Smithsonian Institution, the Library of Congress, and many other significant political and aesthetic foci of American life. The proximity of most of Washington's federal agencies makes Southeastern especially convenient for many federal employees and others who live and work in Washington.

Majors and Degrees

Southeastern University awards the Associate of Science degree in business management (accounting, finance, and legal studies), computer information systems, computer science, government management, and health services administration.

The Bachelor of Science degree is granted in accounting, banking, business management, computer information systems, computer science, financial management, government management, health services administration, liberal studies, and marketing. In addition, a new Bachelor of Art is available in child development.

Academic Programs

The Associate of Science degree normally requires two years of study and 60 credit hours, of which at least 30 credit hours must be earned at the University.

The B.S. degree requires the completion of a minimum of 120 credit hours. At least 60 credit hours must be earned at the University. Baccalaureate candidates are required to complete 60 credit hours of general education course requirements; the remaining 60 credit hours consist of major courses or supplementary business courses.

A maximum of 30 credit hours may be awarded to undergraduates who earn successful scores on College-Level Examination

Program tests. Students may also seek credit by examination, and up to 25 percent of the total credit hours needed to complete the degree may be awarded for life/work experience in the undergraduate program. Southeastern University also recognizes the credit recommendations given in the *Guide to Evaluation of Educational Experience in the Armed Services,* published by the American Council on Education. Southeastern University also has a cooperative education program through which a student can earn up to 12 credit hours while working.

Southeastern University operates on a quadmester system, meaning that the academic year consists of four semesters per year. This is not a quarter system. Students receive full semester credits for each course. The four quadmesters—winter, spring, summer, and fall—begin, respectively, in early January, early April, late June, and late September. Under the quadmester system, students can conveniently take up to one third more courses during an academic year, flexibility in scheduling becomes greater, assistance is given to international students to facilitate the immigration requirements, slightly expanded class sessions provide innovative teaching approaches, and transfer students can enroll during any term. Undergraduate courses are taught on weekdays during day and evening hours as well as on weekends.

The English as a Second Language Program at Southeastern University is used by many international students in order to prepare themselves for successful academic endeavors at an American college. The program offers an intensive course that leads to a certificate in English communication skills and American cultural studies. Upon completion of the program, a student is prepared for admission to the undergraduate program of Southeastern University or to another college.

Academic Facilities

The University's facilities include an impressive library with audiovisual materials, several computerized classrooms, a computer center (equipped with the latest-model hardware and software), and many other innovations.

Costs

Undergraduate tuition for 2004–05 is $240 per credit hour. A full-time undergraduate taking 12 credit hours per term for four terms paid $11,425 in tuition and fees for the academic year. Book costs were estimated at $1000 per year, but the University is committed to working with students in order to facilitate their academic progress.

Financial Aid

Southeastern University participates in federally funded and subsidized student financial aid programs. Most financial aid awards are based on need, and eligible students are usually awarded a combination of grants and loans in a financial package. Federal Work-Study Program awards are available, as are a number of academic scholarships. Financial aid applications may be submitted at any time during the year, although the bulk of funds is committed to students who enter in the fall term. Grants constitute 40 percent of the financial aid awards, and 65 percent of the student body receives aid. A large and helpful staff is available to assist and guide each student through the financial aid process.

Faculty

There are 12 full-time and 82 part-time faculty members. Full-time faculty members are drawn from a national search process; they publish, teach, and perform community service in Washington. Part-time faculty members are outstanding professionals selected specifically for their special background and position; essentially all part-time faculty members are employed full-time in their disciplines and teach on the weekends or at night. Virtually every full-time faculty member holds a doctorate, as do most part-time members. The student-faculty ratio is 15:1. Faculty members act as academic and career advisers and are involved in many student organizations.

Student Government

The Student Government Association (SGA) works to promote and provide an organized program of student activities. The SGA is involved in developing new activities and organizations. Through the SGA and the representation of that body on the University's Board of Trustees, students have an active voice in University administration.

Admission Requirements

All entering students are required to take the University placement test (English and mathematics). Although SAT I or ACT scores are recommended, there is no minimum score requirement, nor are these tests mandated for students who desire to enter the University. Test scores are used for placement purposes only. International students, however, are required to submit TOEFL scores for determination of English proficiency; all courses are taught in English. Students who do not meet language or other standards and who do not qualify as degree candidates may be enrolled in either the English as a Foreign Language Program or in the widely acclaimed Developmental Studies Program. Then, when they achieve language or academic proficiency, they are automatically admitted into the regular program.

In addition, there are a number of programs the University offers for degree and nondegree students who are seeking job promotion and professional development. The University also partners with prominent businesses in the Washington area in an effort to place every graduate and those students who need ongoing job placement.

Application and Information

Southeastern University is a highly respected institution in Washington, D.C. To accommodate student interest, therefore, the University maintains a rolling admission plan. Applicants are notified of admissions decisions four to six weeks after receipt of all required documents. A nonrefundable $45 application fee is required of all applicants. Admission is granted to incoming students for any of the fours terms during the year.

For more information, students should contact:

Admissions Office
Southeastern University
501 I Street, SW
Washington, D.C. 20024
Telephone: 202-COLLEGE
World Wide Web: http://www.seu.edu

SOUTHERN CALIFORNIA INSTITUTE OF ARCHITECTURE

LOS ANGELES, CALIFORNIA

The Institute

Southern California Institute of Architecture (SCI-Arc) is a creative voice for evolving paradigms of culture and building, using Los Angeles as an experimental field, with a constantly renewed community of faculty members and students who continue to “make it new.” SCI-Arc’s new home in downtown Los Angeles allows students to experience firsthand the globalization of business, entertainment, media, and language, combined with the shifting boundaries of disciplines, cultures, and territories. The School stands at an urban pivot point on the east edge of downtown Los Angeles, at a confluence of races, politics, and urban tactics. The extreme social and natural conditions that make Los Angeles a focus of world attention serve as vantage points from which to debate the future of cities, the changing role of the architect, and the nature of architecture itself. As an independent degree-granting institution, the School tests the limits of architecture in order to transform existing conditions into the designs of the future. Its graduates meet the challenges of contemporary design practice by cultivating new visions that respond to the unfurling complexity of the contemporary urban environment. Using emerging technologies and tools, they develop new strategies for practice by uniting the conceptual and the technical. The curriculum tightly weaves the liberal arts and the disciplines of physical sciences, professional practice, and technology into architectural practice. This critical approach is manifested in building and object making, digital media, theoretical research, and creative design.

SCI-Arc began in 1972, when a small group of architects and students proposed a radical alternative to the conventional system of architectural education. United by their commitment to change, they established the school as a mechanism for invention, exploration, and criticism. The students and faculty members felt comfortable with uncertainty and risk, and relished independent thinking. Coexistence of diverse approaches and purposeful action generated a community. A passion for developing ideas and constructing them into buildings and cities drove the curriculum. Society and architecture were seen as inseparable.

In addition to its undergraduate programs, SCI-Arc offers three Master of Architecture programs, including a 3½-year program, a 2½-year program, and an intensive, three-term postgraduate course of research, analysis, and design.

Location

SCI-Arc’s new location in the heart of Los Angeles’ artist district, southeast of the downtown core, allows students and faculty members to participate fully in a vital urban environment. Adjacent to the toy and garment districts and just south of Little Tokyo, the school is close to museums, theaters, galleries, and many other cultural institutions. New neighbors include Gehry’s Concert Hall and Moneo’s Cathedral.

Majors and Degrees

The Bachelor of Architecture degree is awarded upon successful completion of a five-year program. Candidates must complete 186 credit units. The degree is accredited by the National Architecture Accrediting Board (NAAB) and the Western Association of Schools and Colleges (WASC).

Academic Programs

SCI-Arc’s undergraduate program educates students to become independent voices in leadership roles within the architectural profession. The program is recognized nationally and internationally for its fluid and experimental curriculum. In design studios and seminar courses, prevailing paradigms of design, production, representation, and technology are challenged.

At SCI-Arc, the undergraduate program consists of three sequential phases: foundation (first and second years), core (third year and first term of fourth year), and advanced (second term of fourth year and fifth year). Work in each of these phases in the design studio challenges and reflects course work in associated areas of study. The History, Theory, and Humanities program, the Technology and Professional Practice program, and the Soft Technology (visual studies) program are the underpinning disciplines that extend throughout the five-year course of academic studies. Students examine and develop approaches to the conventions of physical materials, intelligent and sustainable building practices, digital environments, and virtual sites. In the fifth year, prior to graduation, students work with an adviser and a faculty committee to develop an independent comprehensive project.

Undergraduate students transfer from two-year community college programs with majors in sciences and arts. Others are admitted after working for several years following high school. Previous studies or professional work in architectural design are not required to gain acceptance to the undergraduate program. Most students initiate a portion of core general studies prior to entering SCI-Arc and complete the sequence once enrolled. The diverse population includes students from Asia, Central and South America, Europe, Africa, and North America as well as from regional Los Angeles communities.

Making + Meaning, an intensive five-week summer foundation program, is open to nonmatriculating students who wish to learn more about the changing nature of the physical environment as well as the history, theory, and practice of architecture. Participants in this 14-year-old program come from the U.S., South and Central America, Europe, and Asia, and have ranged in age from 16 to 56.

Off-Campus Programs

SCI-Arc encourages educational experiences that expose the student to different cultures and allow direct contact with the great architecture of the past. Its campus in Vico Morcote, a medieval hill town above Lake Lugano in Switzerland, offers a travel/study program that focuses on modern and contemporary architecture. In addition, students participate in traveling studios every year and have recently studied in Spain, Japan, Holland, Mexico, China, Egypt, and Turkey. Exchange programs with schools in London, Melbourne, Tokyo, Frankfurt, Vienna, Jerusalem, Weimar, Venice, Delft, and Paris offer other study options.

Academic Facilities

In SCI-Arc’s renovation of the (1907) Freight Depot, a 1,250-foot-long industrial structure in Los Angeles’ artist loft district, lightweight steel structures were inserted inside a vast corridor of concrete and rebar to create a variety of work spaces. The on-campus community of 450 students and 80 faculty members engage this rich relationship between old and new, using the building as a laboratory for experimentation as they work together.

The Freight Depot, which houses all the school's facilities and is open to students 24 hours a day, includes individual studio spaces for each student; seminar and lecture rooms; the library; wood, metal, and CNC milling shops; computer labs; the service bureau; a darkroom; a gallery; and a supply store. The three computer labs are accessible 24 hours a day and house thirty MACs, including eleven G4s with superdrive DVD burners and flat screens; eight G4s with dual processors and 17-inch CRTs, and ten G3s. In the PC lab are ten new Dell dual processors. Each student has a free e-mail account, T1 Internet access from the studio desk, 10/100 network access, access to file/FTP/e-mail servers, black and white laser output, and large-format plotting at a nominal cost. Also available are large-format slide and flat art scanners and high-volume tabloid size laser printers. Up-to-date software includes MS Office 2001, I-Movie, I-View, Adobe Imageready, Adobe Photoshop, Adobe Pagemaker, Adobe Illustrator, Adobe Premiere, QuarkXpress, Electric Image, Macromedia Director, Form Z, Adobe After Effects, Macromedia Flash, Final Cut Pro, Acrobat Reader, AutoCAD 2000i, 3D Studio Viz, Form Z, Alias Wavefront Maya, Alias Wavefront Studio, MS Office 2000, Adaptec Easy CD Creator, and LSystem.

Costs

Tuition for the 2002–03 academic year was $16,740 ($8335 per term plus a $35 academic fee). The average cost for a shared apartment was $400–$500 a month. The cost of food, supplies, books, and incidentals ranged from $1000 to $1500 a month.

Financial Aid

Admission to SCI-Arc is determined without regard to a student's ability to pay the full cost of his or her education. The school's financial aid policy is designed to maximize assistance to all admitted students who demonstrate financial need.

U.S. citizens are eligible for Federal Pell Grants, Federal Supplemental Educational Opportunity Grants, Federal Stafford Student Loans, and Federal PLUS loans. The Federal Work-Study program involves part-time employment for U.S. citizens as well as international students. In addition, scholarships are awarded on the basis of merit and need.

Faculty

Students and faculty members work together in a fluid, nonhierarchical manner, exploring and testing new ideas. The student-faculty ratio is 16:1. The overlap of teaching and practice encourages the sharing of skills and knowledge. The faculty, directed by Eric Owen Moss and the Academic Council, represent a wide range of contemporary approaches to design, history, and urban theory. Among the faculty members are some of the leading practitioners of the discipline of architecture as well as renowned theorists, critics, and historians. These Los Angeles–based practitioners have devoted their careers to investigating how broad aesthetic, social, and cultural concerns can be integrated into an overall understanding of the built and natural environments. Their work has been widely published both nationally and internationally. To complement the richness of local talent and the regional urban experience, SCI-Arc offers studios, workshops, lectures, and seminars by international visiting faculty members.

Faculty members have been awarded numerous Fulbright Fellowships, Graham Foundation Grants, Progressive Architecture awards, AIA awards, Rome prizes, and a MacArthur grant. In addition, books by faculty members have been published by Verso, the University of Michigan Press, Routledge, Princeton Architectural Press, Monacelli Press, MIT Press, Rockport Editions, Rizzoli, Academy Editions, Rotovision, the University of California Press, and Artemis.

Student Government

The student union actively represents the students, who participate in all aspects of the operation of the school, including the lecture series, student journals and other publications, and exhibitions. Student representatives sit on the board of directors, academic council, curriculum committee, and other academic committees. Students organize and produce the lecture series and the graduation ceremony and run the lottery for vertical studio placement.

Admission Requirements

The Southern California Institute of Architecture seeks applicants who demonstrate interest, ability, and academic achievement that reveal potential for the study of architecture. Students who have completed high school are eligible for admission to the first professional degree program. One year of college-level work is recommended, and admission preference is given to students who have a balanced education in the arts, sciences, and humanities. Preparation in the visual arts is required; it may include drawing, sculpture, graphics, photography, video, or multimedia experience. International students are encouraged to apply and must submit TOEFL scores of at least 550.

Application and Information

Completed applications are due May 1 for fall entrance and October 1 for spring entrance. An interview is preferred. Late applications may be considered, but enrollment is generally filled early. Available spaces are limited for students applying for admission beyond the first-year, first-term program.

Inquiries and requests for application forms and a course catalog should be addressed to:

Director of Admissions
Southern California Institute of Architecture
Freight Depot
960 East Third Street
Los Angeles, California 90013
Telephone: 213-613-2200 Ext. 320
Fax: 213-613-2260
E-mail: admissions@sciarc.edu
World Wide Web: http://www.sciarc.edu

SOUTHERN CHRISTIAN UNIVERSITY

MONTGOMERY, ALABAMA

The University

Founded in 1967, Southern Christian University (SCU) is an independent, nonsectarian, coeducational institution dedicated to the spirit of its ideals and Christian heritage. All of SCU's programs are taught from a Christian perspective. SCU is the home of one of the nation's leading universities, offering distance learning programs and services to adults nationally. Adding to the prestige of the University is its recent designation as a Distance Education Demonstration Program Institution by the U.S. Department of Education. One of fifteen initial participants in the nation, SCU is partnering with the U.S. Department of Education to serve as a national model that will help chart the future of distance learning.

Accredited by the Southern Association of Colleges and Schools, SCU grants bachelor's, master's, and doctoral degrees, all available via a distance learning format. Graduate degrees are awarded in counseling/family therapy, organizational leadership, and religious studies. These degrees foster leadership counseling and family therapy skills, knowledge and skills, and biblical and Christian ministry skills. The counseling degrees are designed to help prepare students for licensure. Doctoral degrees include Doctor of Ministry and Doctor of Philosophy degrees. These are advanced professional degrees for community organization and church-related vocations, with a concentration designed to prepare participants to counsel families and individuals.

The policy of Southern Christian University is to provide reasonable accommodation for persons who are handicapped or disabled as designated in Section 504 of the Rehabilitation Act of 1973 and the Americans with Disabilities Act of 1990. Although the Morgan W. Brown building is not equipped with an elevator, the needs of the physically challenged can be met from the first floor. These include registration, counseling, library facilities, classroom facilities, rest rooms, break room facilities, and others. Ample parking is provided.

Location

Southern Christian University is located in Montgomery, Alabama, the capital city of the state. Strategically located in the central part of the state between Huntsville and Mobile and Atlanta, Georgia, Montgomery is one of the fastest-growing cities in the state and the region. The city is clean and modern, with beautiful residential areas, parks and playgrounds, and fine schools and universities. Students and families can also enjoy its museums, zoo, and capital facilities. Montgomery has two major U.S. Air Force installations: Maxwell Air Force Base and Gunter Annex. Maxwell is where the Air War College is located and is a strategic center for education. The city has a population of more than 245,000 citizens. There are many churches and educational institutions. The city has an abundance of good housing in addition to other advantages. Employment can be found easily in Montgomery.

Majors and Degrees

Undergraduate degrees are awarded in Bible studies, human development, human resource management, liberal studies, management communication, and public safety and human justice. These degrees promote biblical and Christian ministry skills, human development skills, knowledge in the arts, and management communication skills. SCU students are fully matriculated students of Southern Christian University with full student privileges, rights, and responsibilities.

Academic Programs

SCU is primarily a distance learning institution, although there are many classes offered on campus. The academic year consists of three semesters: fall, spring, and summer. A student must fulfill the required semester hours in a major as well as the basic requirements of the core curriculum. All core and major requirements can be received from the University. SCU programs have a traditional structure. Distance education is approved by the Southern Association of Colleges and Schools and the U.S. Department of Education, ensuring that distance education students receive the same high-quality education as on-campus students. Faculty and student services for online students are available to distance learners. SCU ensures that students have regular contact with faculty and staff members via e-mail and telephone. No residency is required for undergraduates. In addition to offering distance learning to a diverse array of individuals, SCU is participating in the expansion of eArmyU colleges and universities. eArmyU is the army's popular e-learning virtual university, offering more than 40,000 enrolled soldiers the opportunity to earn a college degree during their enlistment. With the flexibility of eArmyU, soldier-students continue their education uninterrupted, completing their degrees in a timely manner while they serve.

Academic Facilities

Southern Christian University sits stately on a 9-acre campus, adjoining Auburn University at Montgomery and Interstate 85. A beautiful building houses the administration offices, classrooms, and Library Resource Center.

Costs

Undergraduate tuition per semester hour is approximately $380. Full-time undergraduates receive a 50 percent scholarship. A comprehensive fee of $400 per semester is required of all students.

Financial Aid

Aid from institutionally generated funds is provided on the basis of academic merit, financial need, and other criteria. A limited number of scholarships are available. Priority is given to early applicants. Federal funding available for undergraduates includes Pell Grants, FSEOG, Federal Work-Study, and FFEL subsidized and unsubsidized loans. Eighty percent of students receive financial aid.

Faculty

The instructional faculty members total 65. Sixty-seven percent of the full-time faculty members hold doctoral degrees, 100 percent hold master's degrees, and 100 percent hold terminal degrees. Faculty members specialize in their areas and have exceptional training in distance learning delivery.

Student Government

All members of the student body belong to the Student Government Association. Officers and organizational representatives are elected annually. The University's organizational structure provides for and encourages democratic student involvement in the affairs of the University. Every student should feel at liberty to make suggestions to the Student Government Association, to any committee, or to any officer of the University administration.

Admission Requirements

Southern Christian University is open to all persons who are of good character and who are academically qualified. The University has developed a streamlined admissions process to help potential students complete the process in a timely manner so they can begin their studies. As new technologies and processes become available, SCU makes every effort to adopt and use the latest technologies to help the admissions process. Transfer students in good academic standing are invited to apply to SCU. Prospective students must submit a $50 nonrefundable fee along with the completed application for admission.

Application and Information

For further information, students may contact:

Rick Johnson
Southern Christian University
1200 Taylor Road
Montgomery, Alabama 36117
Telephone: 800-351-4040 Ext. 213 (toll-free)
E-mail: rickjohnson@southernchristian.edu
World Wide Web: http://www.southernchristian.edu

SOUTHERN CONNECTICUT STATE UNIVERSITY

NEW HAVEN, CONNECTICUT

The University

Southern Connecticut State University creates the kind of rich academic and social environment that encourages students to discover who they are, who they want to be, and how to make their dreams for the future come alive today. Founded in 1893, Southern is a public, multifaceted, coeducational university offering 116 undergraduate and graduate programs in the full range of academic and professional disciplines. It enriches those disciplines with fascinating internships, unique research opportunities, a challenging faculty, and a dynamic campus life. Southern is located in New Haven, the heart of "academic Connecticut," and students take full advantage of the city and its many beautiful communities.

Southern comprises seven academic schools: Arts and Sciences; Business; Education; Communication, Information, and Library Sciences; Health and Human Services, which includes programs in nursing, public health, recreation and leisure studies, and social work; Graduate Studies; and Extended Learning. For highly motivated students, Southern offers a number of honors programs, including the Honors College. Enrolling the most able and motivated members of the undergraduate student body, the Honors College is a four-year alternative program that features team-taught interdisciplinary courses and symposia and requires the writing of a thesis. Tutorial support for students in need of special academic assistance is provided through the Office of Student Supportive Services.

The student body represents the full spectrum of ethnic and socioeconomic groups. Although most students come from Connecticut, Southern students also represent more than thirty-four states and fifty-three countries. There are approximately 12,000 students enrolled, about 9,000 of whom are undergraduates. Of the 6,000 full-time undergraduates, 2,400 live on campus in twelve modern residence halls and town houses. The rest live at home or in off-campus housing in the Southern neighborhood.

The focal point of student life on campus is the University Student Center, which houses the student newspaper and radio station, a modern cafeteria, two game rooms, a TV lounge, a copy center, and other campus facilities. The University also supports more than sixty campus clubs and organizations, ranging from academic and career groups, such as the marketing club and the literary magazine, to religious, theatrical, and political clubs. Besides giving students a chance to meet others with similar interests and concerns, these groups sponsor a long list of extracurricular activities, including film festivals, concerts, dances, and art exhibits. Southern's intramural and intercollegiate sports programs provide year-round activities for seasoned athletes and eager amateurs alike. Intramural and club sports include badminton, basketball, cheerleading, golf, ice hockey, lacrosse, rugby, soccer, tennis, triathlon, touch football, volleyball, and weight lifting. The Owls, members of the Northeast-10 Conference and the National Collegiate Athletic Association, compete in numerous Division II programs for men and women. Men's programs are offered in baseball, basketball, cross-country, football, gymnastics, soccer, swimming, and indoor and outdoor track. Southern ranks among the top ten colleges and universities in NCAA Division II individual titles won. In addition, the Owls have won nine NCAA team titles, six in soccer and three in gymnastics. Southern offers intercollegiate programs for women in basketball, cross-country, field hockey, gymnastics, soccer, softball, swimming, indoor and outdoor track, and volleyball. All of Southern's athletes have access to outstanding facilities in Moore Fieldhouse, Pelz Gymnasium, and the Jess Dow Field outdoor sports complex.

Location

New Haven, Connecticut, is a sophisticated city of 130,000 people on picturesque Long Island Sound. The University is located in the Westville section of New Haven, near historic West Rock Park. Rich in history and tradition, New Haven is a classic college town; about 35,000 students are enrolled in its half-dozen fine universities and colleges. Just 75 miles from New York City and 3 hours from Boston, New Haven is an integral part of the economic, cultural, and social life of the Northeast. In addition to movies, restaurants, and concerts, students enjoy world-famous theaters—like the Yale Repertory, the Shubert, and Long Wharf—art and natural history museums, and a whole range of sports and seaside activities.

Majors and Degrees

Southern offers the Bachelor of Arts and the Bachelor of Science degrees. The Bachelor of Arts degree is awarded in anthropology, art history, biology, chemistry, communication, earth science, economics, English, French, geography, German, history, Italian, journalism, liberal studies, mathematics, philosophy, physics, political science, psychology, sociology, Spanish, studio art, and theater. The Bachelor of Science degree is awarded in accounting, anthropology, art education, biochemistry, biology, business economics, chemistry, computer science, corporate communication, early childhood education, earth science, elementary education, exercise science (including athletic training, human performance, and physical education), finance, French, geography, German, history, international business, Italian, journalism, liberal studies, library-information service, management, marketing, mathematics, media studies, music, nursing, physics, political science, psychology, public health, recreation and leisure studies, school health, social work, sociology, Spanish, special education, and studio art. Certification in secondary education is available in biology, chemistry, earth science, English, foreign languages, general science, geography, history, mathematics, physics, political science, social science, and sociology/anthropology. Southern also offers preprofessional study in dentistry, engineering, law, medicine, and veterinary science.

Academic Program

The University operates on a two-semester calendar. The fall semester usually begins the first week in September and ends before Christmas. The spring semester, which includes a one-week spring recess in March, runs from the third week of January to the middle of May. Southern also offers two 5-week sessions during the summer and a three-week intersession program each January.

Throughout its history, Southern has held fast to the conviction that the best education stresses the liberal arts and sciences. To ensure all students a chance to acquire such an education, Southern has designed a strong yet flexible program that underscores the basics while encouraging individual choice and self-expression. All baccalaureate degree candidates are required to complete a minimum of 122 hours of credit. Majors consist of at least 30 prescribed hours of credit in one specific, approved field. Degree candidates must also fulfill the All-University Requirements, a common core of courses ranging from 41 to 54 credits in liberal studies. In addition, candidates for the B.A. degree must meet a foreign language requirement and select 28 credits of electives from areas of interest. Candidates for the B.S. degree must also satisfy the foreign language requirement and meet certain distribution requirements. Some of the professional B.S. degree programs enable students to develop a minor or a concentration in addition to the major. Students in these programs are allowed a minimum of 12 credits in electives.

Off-Campus Programs

Southern's growing list of internships enables its students to use the city as a laboratory for learning. For Southern's social work students, New Haven's urban environment adds immediacy and relevance to their classroom study. Similarly, students enrolled in Southern's B.S. degree program in nursing acquire firsthand clinical experience at Yale–New Haven Hospital and the Hospital of Saint Raphael (and can complete course work at area hospitals through a distance learning program taught on video), while journalism students pound the keyboards in city newsrooms and cover late-breaking news at local TV stations.

Academic Facilities

The University's thirty-building campus provides students with a full range of learning facilities. The Hilton C. Buley Library maintains 470,000 bound volumes and 5,700 periodical subscriptions. There are also 23,000 microfilm reels, 677,000 microfiche pieces, and 287,000 government documents. The lower level of the library is the site of a modern Macintosh lab, where students have access to thirty-four Macintosh SE terminals with laser printers and dot-matrix printers. The library also houses the Learning Resources Center, which features an education curriculum laboratory, a growing collection of audiotapes and videotapes, and the equipment necessary for individual viewing and study. The newest academic building on campus is Manson Van B. Jennings Hall, the University's $13.1-million science center. Jennings Hall contains sixty-six laboratories, a large amphitheater, classrooms, and the University's Academic Computer Center, which houses more than 100 computer workstations for student and faculty research. Other campus facilities include a journalism lab with a satellite dish that picks up wire-service stories, a modern television studio in Ralph Earl Hall of Fine Arts, and the John Lyman Center for the Performing Arts, which contains a 1,650-seat theater for major productions and the Robert Kendall Drama Lab for experimental theater. The campus is now undergoing $230 million in renovations that include an expanded library, an upgrade of the science center, and a new state-of-the-art student center.

Costs

Annual tuition and fees for 2003–04 for Connecticut residents were $5360. Tuition and fees for out-of-state residents were $12,348. On-campus room and board fees for the year totaled $7100. Books, supplies, and personal expenses averaged $2000 a year. All costs are subject to change without notice. Students should check with the Financial Aid Office for the most current information.

Financial Aid

The Financial Aid Office coordinates a number of programs. These programs, which include grants and scholarships, long-term low-interest loans, and part-time student employment, are based on the demonstrated financial need of students and their families. The University offers the Federal Perkins Loan, the Federal Pell Grant, the Federal Supplemental Educational Opportunity Grant, the Federal Stafford Student Loan, the Federal PLUS loan, and the Federal Work-Study Program. Southern also provides assistance through alumni scholarships. More than 50 percent of Southern's undergraduates receive some form of financial aid. Students interested in applying for assistance must complete the Free Application for Federal Student Aid (FAFSA) and send it to the central processor so that it is received by March 18. Prospective students can either complete the FAFSA form on paper or file the FAFSA on the Web at http://www.fafsa.ed.gov.

Faculty

Like its student body, Southern's faculty represents a wide range of backgrounds, interests, and scholarly achievements. Faculty members have a deep commitment to teaching and a serious dedication to writing and research. More than 50 percent of the 700 full- and part-time faculty members hold Ph.D.'s from major colleges and universities around the world. All courses at the University are taught by faculty members, many of whom also serve as academic advisers. In addition, the University offers counseling services to help students with academic, personal, and career decisions. The student-faculty ratio is 15:1.

Student Government

The Student Government is the voice of the undergraduate student body on the Southern campus. Consisting of 24 voting members who meet eight times each semester, the Student Government provides a means through which individual students working together can influence a wide range of areas, from funding issues to academic policy. Student Government members also serve with faculty members and administrators on a number of key University committees. Resident students govern themselves through their own residence hall councils and, collectively, through the Inter-Residence Council.

Admission Requirements

Southern's admission policy is selective. The University considers each student on an individual basis, giving special consideration to personal accomplishments and motivation. Southern seeks a student body that reflects a wide range of cultural values and backgrounds; no applicant is accepted or rejected because of race, color, gender, sexual orientation, age, disability, religion, or national origin. Candidates must be high school graduates or have received an equivalency diploma. Their secondary school program should include at least 13 academic units of college-preparatory work, including 4 years of English, 3 years of mathematics, 2 years of foreign language, 2 years of science (including 1 year of laboratory science), and 2 years of social sciences (including U.S. history). Other factors include the student's general high school record, rank in class (preferably in the upper half of the high school graduating class), and competitive SAT I scores.

Application and Information

Candidates for admission should apply by May of their senior year in high school. The Admissions Office mails its first notice of acceptance on December 1, and early applicants have priority for housing and financial aid. Applicants must submit previous academic records, including a complete transcript of high school grades and rank in class; an admission application; a $40 nonrefundable fee; a written recommendation from the high school principal, a teacher, or a guidance counselor; and an official copy of the SAT I report. To request application forms and further information, students should contact:

Sharon Brennan
Director of Admissions and Enrollment Management
Admissions House
Southern Connecticut State University
131 Farnham Avenue
New Haven, Connecticut 06515-1355

Telephone: 203-392-SCSU
888-500-SCSU (toll-free)
World Wide Web: http://www.Southernct.edu

Southern's "Serie Metafisica XVIII" (1983), an outdoor sculpture by Herk Van Tongeren, provides the ideal setting for study in the sunshine.

SOUTHERN ILLINOIS UNIVERSITY CARBONDALE

CARBONDALE, ILLINOIS

The University

Southern Illinois University Carbondale (SIUC), chartered in 1869, is a comprehensive state-supported institution with nationally and internationally recognized instructional, research, and service programs. SIUC is fully accredited by the North Central Association of Colleges and Schools.

SIUC offers more than 150 undergraduate majors, specializations, and minors; four associate degree programs; more than ninety baccalaureate degree programs; more than sixty master's degree programs; thirty-two doctoral programs; and professional degrees in law and medicine. SIUC is a multicampus university and includes the Carbondale campus as well as the SIUC School of Medicine at Springfield and a branch campus in Nakajo, Japan.

During the 2003–04 academic year, SIUC's enrollment reached 21,387, which included 16,366 undergraduate students, 4,343 graduate students, and 678 professional students. The average age of undergraduates is 23. Seven percent of SIUC's enrolled students are international students. Of U.S. students, 13 percent are African American, .3 percent are American Indian/Alaskan, 2 percent are Asian or Pacific Islander, and 1 percent are Hispanic.

Students who are ready to start college but not ready to commit to a specific major can enroll in SIUC's Pre-Major Program. Premajor advisers and career counselors help premajor students plan their education and careers. SIUC faculty members, staff members, and alumni help students arrange internships, cooperative education programs, and work-study programs.

All single incoming freshmen under the age of 21 are required to live on campus their first year at SIUC unless they are living at home with a legal guardian or parent. SIUC has three on-campus residential areas for single students. Each area includes a cafeteria, a post office, laundry facilities, and computer labs. SIUC residence hall dining services provide nineteen meals per week with no limit on quantity at each meal. Optional meal plans are available. Meal hours are long enough to accommodate most schedules, but students with conflicts can arrange for take-out lunches or late plates. Dining services provide a variety of menus and a full-time dietitian to help students who have special dietary needs. Off-campus housing includes many types of privately owned units, including residence halls, apartments, and houses; many are within easy walking distance of the campus.

SIUC intercollegiate sports teams compete at the NCAA Division I level (football is Division I-AA). Conference affiliations include the Missouri Valley and Gateway Conferences. Intercollegiate sports teams include men's and women's basketball, cross-country, diving, golf, swimming, tennis, and track and field; men's baseball and football; and women's softball and volleyball. The campus holds various playfields, several tennis courts, and a campus lake with a beach and a boat dock. SIUC's Student Recreation Center houses an Olympic-size pool; indoor tracks; handball/racquetball and squash courts; a climbing wall; weight rooms; and basketball, volleyball, and tennis courts. It also offers outdoor equipment rental, an aerobic area, walleyball, martial arts, and dance and cardio studios.

The Student Center is one of the largest student centers in the U.S. without a hotel. It contains a bookstore, several restaurants, a craft shop, a bakery, and facilities for bowling and billiards. It is headquarters for 360 active student organizations and the student government office. It holds four ballrooms and an auditorium. On-campus events throughout the year include concerts, plays, festivals, guest speakers, and musicals.

Location

Carbondale is 6 hours south of Chicago, 2 hours southeast of St. Louis, and 3 hours north of Nashville. Four large recreational lakes, the two great rivers (the Mississippi and the Ohio), and the spectacular 270,000-acre Shawnee National Forest are within minutes of the campus. The mid-South climate is ideal for year-round outdoor activities.

Carbondale is a small city of 26,000 people that supports one large enclosed mall, several mini-malls, theaters, and restaurants. Students frequent the shops and restaurants that line Illinois and Grand Avenues.

Majors and Degrees

The University offers associate in applied science degree programs at the College of Applied Sciences and Arts in aviation flight, dental technology, physical therapist assistant studies, and respiratory therapy technology.

The College of Applied Sciences and Arts offers bachelor's degree programs in advanced technical studies, architectural studies, automotive technology, aviation management, aviation technologies, dental hygiene, electronics systems technologies, fire science management, health-care management, information systems technologies, interior design, mortuary science and funeral service, physician assistant studies, and radiologic sciences.

The College of Agriculture offers bachelor's degree programs in agribusiness economics, animal science, food and nutrition, forestry, general agriculture, and plant and soil science.

The College of Business and Administration offers bachelor's degree programs in accounting, business and administration, business economics, finance, management, and marketing.

The College of Education and Human Services offers bachelor's degree programs in communication disorders and sciences, early childhood education, elementary education, fashion design and merchandising, health education, physical education, recreation, rehabilitation services, social studies, social work, special education, and workforce education and development. Teacher preparation is available in art, biological sciences, English, French, German, health education, history, mathematics, music, physical education, secondary education, social studies, Spanish, and special education.

The College of Engineering offers bachelor's degree programs in civil engineering, computer engineering, electrical engineering, engineering technology, industrial technology, mechanical engineering, and mining engineering.

The College of Liberal Arts offers bachelor's degrees in administration of justice, anthropology, art, classics, design, economics, English, foreign language and international trade, French, geography, German, history, linguistics, mathematics, music, paralegal studies, philosophy, political science, psychology, Russian, sociology, Spanish, speech communication, theater, and university studies.

The College of Mass Communication and Media Arts offers bachelor's degrees in cinema and photography, journalism, and radio-television.

The College of Science offers bachelor's degree programs in biological sciences, chemistry, computer science, geology, mathematics, microbiology, physics, physiology, plant biology, zoology, and preprofessional programs in dentistry, medicine, nursing, optometry, osteopathy, pharmacy, physical therapy, physician assistant studies, podiatry, and veterinary medicine.

In addition to many majors offered at SIUC, specializations are offered in all colleges in many areas.

Academic Program

Each bachelor's degree candidate must earn a minimum of 120 semester hours of credit, including at least 60 at a senior-level institution and the last 30 at SIUC. Each student must maintain at least a C average in all course work at SIUC. Each student must fulfill the University core curriculum and the specific requirements of their degree programs. SIUC awards credit through qualifying extension and correspondence programs, military experience, the High School Advanced Placement Program, the College-Level Examination Program (CLEP), SIUC's proficiency examination program, and work experience.

SIUC offers honors course work and special recognition for students who demonstrate exceptional academic achievement. The Air Force and Army offer ROTC programs at SIUC. SIUC offers three semesters: fall, spring, and summer.

Off-Campus Programs

At Southern Illinois University Carbondale, distance education courses are offered in interactive, print-based and Web-based formats. Print-based (correspondence) and Web-based courses are offered by the Individualized Learning Program (ILP). Web-based courses and Two-Way Interactive Video courses are offered through the Office of Distance Education. Many of the courses offered through the ILP and other distance education courses can be taken to complete the University Studies Degree (B.A.) in the College of Liberal Arts.

Off-campus credit programs are designed to meet the educational needs of adults wishing to pursue a degree but who are unable to travel to the Carbondale campus. Faculty members who teach off-campus courses travel to distant sites to teach SIUC courses.

Contractual services are provided and include specialized educational services to groups, organizations, governmental agencies, and businesses on a cost-recovery basis. These services are provided regionally, nationally, and internationally.

All credit courses offered through these programs carry full SIUC academic credit and are taught by faculty members appointed by the academic departments of the University. Additional information can be found on the Web (http://www.dce.siu.edu/siuconnected).

Academic Facilities

In addition to the 2.4 million volumes, 3.5 million microfilms, and more than 11,000 periodicals currently available in Morris Library, students and faculty members have access to more than 10,000 full-text electronic journals. SIUC students have access to several computer learning centers that are equipped, in all, with more than 1,600 microcomputers. Additional information can be found on the Web (http://www.lib.siu.edu).

Students learn and practice in the Southern Illinois Airport, outdoor laboratories, the student-run *Daily Egyptian* newspaper, WSIU-TV, WSIU-FM, art and natural history museums, a literary magazine, McCleod Theater, Memorial Hospital, a vivarium, the plant biology greenhouses, the University Farms, and the Touch of Nature Environmental Center.

Costs

Tuition and fee charges for the 2003–04 academic year (fall and spring) for students enrolled in 15 or more semester hours were $4920 for Illinois residents and $12,300 for out-of-state residents, including international students. Room and board were $5200. All costs are subject to change. The cost of books and school supplies varies among programs. The average cost is $840 per academic year. Some courses require that students purchase special materials.

Financial Aid

More than $160 million in financial aid was distributed to more than 21,387 SIUC students in fiscal year 2003 through federal, state, and institutionally funded financial aid programs.

To apply for financial aid at SIUC, students should complete a Free Application for Federal Student Aid (FAFSA). Applications that are filed before April 1 receive priority consideration for campus-based aid. The FAFSA can be completed electronically at the U.S. Department of Education's Web site (http://www.fafsa.ed.gov). When completing the FAFSA, students should list Southern Illinois University Carbondale (Federal School Code 001758) as a school of choice.

SIUC has one of the largest student employment programs in the country, with approximately 6,000 students employed each year in a wide variety of job classifications. SIUC offers competitive scholarships based on talent and academic achievement.

Faculty

Faculty members are dedicated to excellence in teaching and to their advancement of knowledge in a wide variety of disciplines and professions. Many faculty members are well-known both nationally and internationally for their varied research contributions. The undergraduate student-faculty ratio is 17:1. There are 894 full-time and 218 part-time instructional faculty members.

Teaching assistants at SIUC are graduate students who assist faculty members in teaching. While some teach introductory undergraduate classes, others provide support to faculty members by assisting in laboratories, monitoring tests, and helping students.

Student Government

The undergraduate student government consists of a president, vice president, executive assistant, and chief of staff. Under the vice president, there are 58 senators: 1 senator per 300 students. Each student has at least 2 representatives: 1–6 for their residential area, and 1–6 for the college in which they are enrolled. Under the 6 commissioners are a list of committees on which a varying number of students sit to represent the student body. The student government writes and passes legislation on University policies, funding, student organizations, and other matters that affect the students and the University.

Admission Requirements

Freshman applicants whose ACT or SAT score is at or above the 50th percentile or whose ACT or SAT score is at or above the 33rd percentile and whose class rank is in the upper half are admitted. Admission standards are subject to change. Freshman applicants must meet course pattern requirements: 4 years of English, 3 years of mathematics, 3 years of laboratory science, 3 years of social science, and 2 years of electives.

Transfer applicants must have an overall grade point average of at least 2.0 on a 4.0 scale, based on work attempted at all institutions and calculated by SIUC grading policies. Transfer applicants must also be eligible to continue at the last institution attended.

Some programs have higher admission requirements or require additional screening for admission. Undergraduates can apply online (http://salukinet.siu.edu/admit/).

Application and Information

Admission is granted on a rolling basis. Application priority deadlines for freshmen are: June 1 for the Summer 2004 Term; April 30 for the Fall 2004 Term; and December 1, 2004 for the Spring 2005 Term. Application priority deadlines for transfer students are: June 1 for the Summer 2004 Term; July 1 for the Fall 2004 Term; and December 1, 2004 for the Fall 2005 Term. The application fee is $30.

Undergraduate Admissions MC 4710
425 Clocktower Drive
Southern Illinois University Carbondale
Carbondale, Illinois 62901
Telephone: 618-536-4405
Fax: 618-453-3250
E-mail: joinsiuc@siu.edu
World Wide Web: http://www.siuc.edu

SIUC's Pulliam Hall.

SOUTHERN METHODIST UNIVERSITY

DALLAS, TEXAS

The University

Southern Methodist University (SMU) is a small, caring academic community in the heart of a vibrant city, where excellence is the standard and the goal is helping students succeed. SMU prepares students for life and leadership in the twenty-first century by educating them to meet the challenges of a rapidly changing world, intellectually equipping them for lifelong learning, and preparing them for successful careers. The broad-based curriculum provides a strong foundation in the humanities and sciences. SMU's four undergraduate schools offer nearly eighty majors in business, engineering, the arts, and humanities and sciences. Learning at SMU includes opportunities for mentoring relationships, internships, leadership development, research experience, international study, and community service.

Founded in 1911, SMU welcomes students of every religion, race, color, ethnic origin, and economic status. Students come from all fifty states and more than 100 countries. Total University enrollment is 10,226; 5,836 are undergraduates. The undergraduate student-faculty ratio is 12:1, allowing students to interact closely with faculty members. Sixty percent of all undergraduate lecture sections have fewer than 25 students. Academically promising students are invited into the University Honors Program.

The life of a student's education is enriched at SMU, where there are nearly 200 student activities and organizations. From debate club to intramural sports, campus events to marching band, academic interests to community service, students have many options. There are also a large number of academic honorary societies.

SMU hosts more than 400 public arts events each year. The world-renowned Willis M. Tate Distinguished Lecture Series brings guests, such as Secretary of State Colin Powell, actor Julie Andrews, and former President George Bush to campus. SMU is a member of the National Collegiate Athletic Association and participates in the Western Athletic Conference, Division I-A. Nineteen Division I-A teams include basketball, cross-country, equestrian, football, golf, soccer, swimming/diving, tennis, track and field, and women's rowing and volleyball.

SMU offers fourteen residence halls and living communities, including an honors hall, a fine arts community, and a service-learning house. First-year students are required to live on campus, except in special circumstances. Residence halls have local phone service, voice-mail, Ethernet computer connections, Internet and e-mail, air conditioning, and community computer and lounge areas.

Location

SMU's park-like campus, located north of downtown Dallas in a traditional and upscale residential neighborhood, features Georgian-style architecture and enjoys a pleasant Sun Belt climate. Dallas, often ranked as one of the world's most livable cities, is home to more than 6,000 corporate headquarters and offers outstanding opportunities for internships and future employment. A convenient light rail and bus system is located near the campus.

Majors and Degrees

SMU offers nearly eighty degrees through its four undergraduate schools, with flexible options such as double majors, minors, and dual degrees. Dedman College offers a Bachelor of Arts (B.A.) degree with a major in a department of the College and a Bachelor of Science (B.S.) degree with a major in mathematics, a natural science, or selected social sciences. The College also offers two part-time multidisciplinary evening degrees: the Bachelor of Humanities (B.Hum.) and the Bachelor of Social Science (B.Soc.Sci). The Cox School of Business awards the Bachelor of Business Administration (B.B.A.) degree. The Meadows School of Arts awards the Bachelor of Fine Arts (B.F.A.) in art, art history, dance, and theater; the Bachelor of Arts (B.A.) in advertising, art history, cinema-television, journalism, music, corporate communications and public affairs; and the Bachelor of Music (B.M.) degrees. The School of Engineering offers the Bachelor of Arts (B.A.) degree in computer science and the Bachelor of Science (B.S.) degree in the fields of computer engineering, computer science, electrical engineering, environmental engineering, management science, and mechanical engineering, with specializations and biomedical and premed options.

Academic Programs

All undergraduates enter SMU through Dedman College. The College provides the University's general education curriculum, which is designed to help students develop analytical and communication skills, the ability to explore ethical issues, and a broad understanding of the world. The curriculum includes courses in such categories as cultural formation, perspectives, human diversity, and information technology. Students who know their career interest can select courses in their planned major while in Dedman College. Students majoring in the humanities, mathematics, the natural sciences, and the social or behavioral sciences remain in Dedman College. Requirements for graduation vary according to the major program.

SMU grants both credit and advanced placement for satisfactory completion of Advanced Placement (AP) courses in high school. Credit up to 6 semester hours is given for each course in which a score of 4 or 5 was earned; 12 to 14 hours of credit can be granted for foreign languages with a score of 4 or 5. SMU also gives credit for departmental examination. Credit also is awarded for scores from 5 to 7 on higher-level exams in transferable subjects for the International Baccalaureate. Credit is not awarded for subsidiary-level exams. High school students may earn dual credit by attending off-campus colleges. A maximum of 32 advanced credits can be awarded. The academic year at SMU is composed of two semesters, plus an optional summer session that comprises two 5-week terms. A May term is also available.

Off-Campus Programs

SMU Study Abroad offers eighteen programs in twelve countries: Australia, China, Denmark, France, Germany, Great Britain, Italy, Japan, Mexico, Russia, Spain, and Taiwan. SMU-in-Taos is the University's summer campus in northern New Mexico.

Academic Facilities

Newer facilities include the Meadows Museum of Art, which houses one of the world's largest collections of Spanish art; an addition to the Fondren Library Center; the Dedman Life Sciences Building; the Jerry R. Junkins Electrical Engineering Building; and the Gerald R. Ford Stadium and Paul B. Loyd Jr. All-Sports Center. The Laura Lee Blanton Student Services Building is under construction.

SMU libraries contain more than 3 million volumes. Fondren Library contains a catalog of all holdings and major works of a general nature. Other collections are located in the Science Information Center, the Underwood Law Library, the Bridwell Library (a component of Perkins School of Theology), Hamon Arts Library, DeGolyer Library, and the Business Information Center. The Altshuler Learning Enhancement Center, known as the A-LEC, offers students individual tutoring, study groups, and techniques to enhance study and time management skills and test-taking strategies.

SMU has high-quality facilities campuswide, including specialized laboratories in the Dallas Seismological Observatory and the electron microscopy laboratory. The Institute for the Study of Earth and Man houses specialized laboratories for archeology, ethnology, geology, and physical anthropology. The Dedman Life Sciences Building and the new Junkins Electrical Engineering Building feature state-of-the-art research, teaching, and computer labs.

Costs

The comprehensive fee for full-time undergraduate students for the 2003–04 academic year was $31,979. This amount included tuition and fees totaling $23,588 and a room and board charge of $8391. SMU offers a monthly payment plan and other resources and plans to help students manage their investment in a college education.

Financial Aid

About 79 percent of first-year students receive some form of financial assistance. The SMU financial aid program includes University, state, and federal scholarships; merit- and need-based scholarships; grants; part-time jobs; payment plans; and/or low-interest loans. Most students who demonstrate financial need are awarded an aid package that combines SMU funds with government resources. The University assists all qualified students who cannot afford an SMU education. Financial aid decisions are based on academic performance and financial need. Accepted students interested in federal or state financial aid must file the Free Application for Federal Student Aid (FAFSA). SMU's code is 003136. Students may file online at http://www.fafsa.ed.gov. Students should complete the FAFSA by February 15 to receive primary consideration.

Students who also wish to be considered for SMU need-based assistance must complete the College Scholarship Service Financial Aid PROFILE (CSS PROFILE) in addition to the FAFSA. The PROFILE is available online at http://profileonline.collegeboard.com.

Financial aid, such as grants, low-interest loans, and campus employment, is also available to transfer students who demonstrate financial need based on the FAFSA and the CSS PROFILE, both of which should be filed each year. SMU offers transfer students a range of merit scholarships. For details, students should contact a transfer admission counselor at the telephone number listed below.

SMU's merit-based scholarships have been named among the best in the United States by *America's Best College Scholarships 2001*. SMU's most prestigious scholarship programs include the President's Scholars, the Nancy Ann and Ray L. Hunt Leadership Scholars, Dean's Scholars, SMU Scholars, and University Scholars. National Merit Scholarships are available only to finalists who name SMU as their first college choice. Students must apply for merit scholarships by January 15.

Faculty

The undergraduate student-faculty ratio is 12:1, which allows students to interact closely with faculty members. Sixty percent of all undergraduate lecture sections have fewer than 25 students. Almost 90 percent of the full-time faculty members hold a Ph.D. or the highest degrees in their field. Regular, full-time faculty members teach most undergraduate classes (74 percent). SMU has more than 500 full-time faculty members.

Student Government

The SMU Student Senate is a comprehensive governing body that meets weekly to initiate and facilitate action on student affairs. The Senate is composed of 4 student body officers, 40 senators, and ten committees.

Admission Requirements

The Office of Admission bases selection of applicants on several criteria: the strength of the high school program and the grades received, SAT I or ACT scores, teacher and counselor recommendations, an essay, and optimal input from parents and peers. Applicants should present a college-preparatory program and are expected to complete a minimum of 4 years of English, 3 of mathematics (including algebra I and II and plane geometry), 3 of a natural science (including two lab sciences), 3 of social studies, and 2 of a foreign language. SMU places value on personal accomplishment, and an attempt is made to get to know the individual and the academic record beyond standardized scores.

Although the average GPA of successful transfer applicants who have completed 30 or more transferable hours is considerably higher than a 2.7 GPA (on a 4.0 scale), applicants with a GPA below this threshold are not typically successful in gaining admission. Candidates with a transferable GPA below 2.0 are not admitted to the University. For all candidates who have completed 30 or more college hours, the Admission Committee considers the rigorous nature of the courses attempted; in particular, applicants should have completed at least one course in English composition, a lab science, a math course beyond college algebra, and a course pertaining to the intended major. The committee weighs overall academic performance as well as evidence of recent improvement. For some applicants, the high school performance is also a factor. Candidates with fewer than 30 hours are considered on an individual basis and may be required to submit additional information, including high school records.

As a privately endowed institution, SMU has no limits on enrollment based solely on geography, and it makes no distinctions in tuition, fees, or other costs based on the home state of the student. Southern Methodist University does not discriminate on the basis of race, color, religion, national origin, sex, age, disability, or veteran status. SMU's commitment to equal opportunity includes nondiscrimination on the basis of sexual orientation.

Application and Information

Students should apply soon after completing the junior year of high school. Online applications are available at http://www.smu.edu/apply. The nonbinding early action deadline is November 1, with notification by December 30. For regular decision and priority merit scholarship application consideration, the deadline is January 15, with notification by March 15. SMU offers a spring decision deadline of March 15 on a space-available basis.

Transfer application deadlines are April 1 for the summer term entry, June 1 for fall term and merit scholarship consideration, and November 1 for spring term (including scholarship applicants).

For admission information, students should contact:

Division of Enrollment Services
Southern Methodist University
P.O. Box 750181
Dallas, Texas 75275-0181
Telephone: 214-768-2058
800-323-0672 (toll-free)
E-mail: ugadmission@smu.edu
World Wide Web: http://www.smu.edu/admission/

Dallas Hall is the landmark building of SMU, reflecting the neo-Georgian architecture of the campus.

SOUTHERN NEW HAMPSHIRE UNIVERSITY

MANCHESTER, NEW HAMPSHIRE

The University

Southern New Hampshire University, founded in 1932, is a private, accredited, nonprofit, coeducational, professional university, having changed its name from New Hampshire College in 2001. Southern New Hampshire University blends the best elements of its small college heritage with the power and prestige that come with university status. The University has a full-time day school enrollment of more than 1,700 students and a total enrollment of slightly more than 6,000 in the undergraduate, graduate, continuing education, doctoral, and distance education programs.

The campus, on 280 wooded acres, is located along the Merrimack River in Manchester, New Hampshire. A $13-million construction campaign was completed in 2001. New buildings include Newcastle Hall, a 200-bed residence hall, the 60,000-square-foot Robert Frost Academic Center, and a new fitness center. Campus facilities include twenty-six major buildings: classroom/administrative buildings, residence halls, a computer center, a library complex, a student center with dining facilities, and an athletic/recreational complex. The student body is varied in background and represents more than twenty-three states and thirty-five countries.

Student organizations range from social clubs, such as fraternities and sororities, to career-related associations, such as the Accounting Association. Athletic facilities include an indoor 25-meter competition-size swimming pool, a racquetball court, a dance studio, cardiovascular equipment, four outdoor lighted tennis courts, a soccer/lacross field with state-of-the-art field turf, two baseball diamonds, numerous practice fields, and two indoor gymnasiums with six full basketball courts, providing areas for indoor soccer, indoor tennis, volleyball, and many other activities. The new fitness center features 3,500 square feet of strength equipment and a 1,500-square-foot cardio deck. Fitness machines include selectorized and plate-loaded resistance equipment, free weights, and twenty cardio pieces, including treadmills, step mills, elliptical trainers, and bikes. The University supports an active athletic program, both intercollegiate and intramural, as an integral part of the educational process. At the intercollegiate level, teams are fielded in baseball, basketball, cross-country, golf, ice hockey, lacrosse, soccer, softball, tennis, and volleyball. Southern New Hampshire University is a member of the National Collegiate Athletic Association (Division II), the Eastern College Athletic Conference, and the Northeast Ten Conference. The Wellness Center provides short-term health care, health education, and counseling services for students, and the buildings and facilities are accessible to the physically handicapped. A well-qualified student-services staff provides personal, career, and academic counseling; counselors are available on campus. Lifetime job placement service is available to all current students and to alumni.

Southern New Hampshire University maintains continuing education centers in Laconia, Manchester, Nashua, Portsmouth, and Salem, New Hampshire; Brunswick, Maine; Dubai, United Arab Emirates; and Roosevelt Roads, Puerto Rico. Master of Business Administration and Master of Science programs are offered at the Manchester, Nashua, Portsmouth, Salem, Brunswick, Dubai, and Roosevelt Roads locations. Doctoral programs are offered at the Manchester campus in international business and community economic development.

Location

Manchester, New Hampshire, is the crossroads of northern New England. It is an hour's drive from the best skiing in the East, the beaches of New Hampshire and Maine, and the cultural activity of Boston. Manchester is home to some 115,000 residents and offers many social and cultural activities. Southern New Hampshire University students are very much involved in the Manchester community. In 1998, Manchester was ranked by *Money* magazine as the most livable city in the East.

Majors and Degrees

Southern New Hampshire University provides students with a solid educational foundation and professional training in business, education, hospitality, and liberal arts. Undergraduate degree programs available within the School of Business include accounting, accounting/finance, advertising, business administration, business studies, economics/finance, fashion merchandising, information technology, international business, management advisory services, marketing, retailing, sport management, and technical management. Degree programs offered by the School of Liberal Arts include advertising, communication, creative writing and English, digital media, English language and literature, graphic design, history, humanities, liberal arts, political science, psychology, public relations, and social science. Special programs are also available for prelaw and pre-M.B.A. Degree programs offered by the School of Hospitality, Tourism, and Culinary Management include an associate degree in culinary arts and bachelor's degrees in club management, convention and event management, destination management, food and beverage management, hotel and resort management, and tourism management. Education programs include early childhood education, elementary education/special education, and secondary education in business, English, marketing, and social studies.

The University offers an exciting nationally recognized Three-Year honors Program in Business Administration. This competency-based, technology-driven program allows select students to complete the equivalent of a four-year program in three years, and receive a Bachelors of Science degree in business administration.

A Bachelor of Applied Science in Hospitality Administration (B.A.S.H.A.) is designed for students who have already earned an associate degree in a hospitality field from an approved institution. The B.A.S.H.A. program allows students to complete a bachelor's degree in two years while they get firsthand experience with the hospitality industry.

Academic Program

Academic programs in the Schools of Business and Hospitality are career-oriented and designed to combine professional preparation in business, education, and the liberal arts. Students in these schools are required to take courses in accounting, business, information technology, and liberal arts in addition to those courses required in their major field of study. Education students complete course work that satisfies requirements for teacher certification in the state of New Hampshire. Academic programs in the School of Liberal Arts include a structured foundation of general knowledge, a focused in-depth study in the major area, and the flexibility to minor in another liberal arts or business area. Students choosing liberal arts majors may also select a business minor, a cooperative work experience, or a teacher certification program. The liberal arts curriculum affords flexibility and focus, allowing students to challenge themselves intellectually and experience the joy of learning while preparing for careers.

Off-Campus Programs

Cooperative education work experiences are available in all academic programs and range from 3 to 12 credits; all students have the opportunity to participate in work experiences. Selected students also have the opportunity to live and learn abroad through arrangements with London Metropolitan University in England.

Through the University's membership in the New Hampshire College and University Council, Southern New Hampshire University students may take advantage of academic facilities and course offerings at the ten other four-year colleges and universities in the consortium.

Academic Facilities

Webster Hall is a modern 50,000-square-foot facility that houses academic facilities for the School of Business. The 35,000-square-foot Hospitality Center has extensive facilities for culinary arts, including kitchens, bakeshops, a restaurant, and a retail bakery. The Robert Frost Academic Center features classrooms, technology labs, a Macintosh computer lab, a stock trading room, the Walker Auditorium, an audiovisual lecture hall, faculty offices, and the McIninch Art Gallery.

The Harry A. B. and Gertrude C. Shapiro Library has a networked computer center, a specialized career and placement area, student conference rooms, and a consistently expanding collection of bound volumes, microfilm, microfiche, and ultrafiche. Current holdings include more than 80,000 books, 600 paper periodical subscriptions, access to 12,000 proprietary online journals, and 12,000 company financial and annual reports. Audiovisual facilities include a videotape recording studio, an Internet-based radio station, a listening room, and a closed-circuit video network throughout the campus. The Computer Center is equipped with an NEC Powermate V166e computer and state-of-the-art equipment used in the most sophisticated corporate environments. All computers have Internet access. The system supports more than 250 direct-access computers on campus. The Center for Career, Learner, and Academic Support Services offers career counseling and academic advising to all students and coordinates support services free of charge. Academic support services include professional and peer tutoring and supplemental instruction labs.

Costs

The 2003–04 tuition for undergraduate day students was $18,264. Room and board costs were $7648. The student activity fee was $330 per year. Other expenses included books, supplies, and miscellaneous personal expenses.

Financial Aid

Approximately 90 percent of Southern New Hampshire University's full-time day undergraduates receive financial assistance, ranging from $250 to full cost. The average financial aid package, including gift, loan, and employment assistance, exceeds $14,000. The University participates in the Federal Pell Grant Program, the Federal Supplemental Educational Opportunity Grant Program, the Federal Perkins Loan Program, the Federal Work-Study Program, and the Federal Stafford Student Loan Program. The University requires that students submit the Free Application for Federal Student Aid (FAFSA). The University also allows students to submit an early financial aid estimator by December 15. The aid program is designed to assist deserving students who, without need-based assistance, would be unable to pursue or continue a program of study at Southern New Hampshire University. Academic, leadership, and athletic scholarships are also available for qualified students.

Faculty

Southern New Hampshire University employs 111 full-time and nearly 200 part-time faculty members. About 70 percent of the total faculty hold terminal degrees in their fields. The student-to-faculty ratio is 18:1. Some faculty members serve as consultants in the business world, and many have had prior industry-related job experience. Most accounting personnel are registered CPAs. Graduate students do not serve as instructors.

Student Government

The Student Government Association is led by 26 students, including 5 officers, who represent all the students at the University. Their primary function is to represent the student body in campus affairs and to dispense student activity funds. One student is appointed to represent the student body on the Board of Trustees. Students are also appointed to most other standing committees, including the Financial Aid Advisory Committee, the Curriculum Advisory Committee, the Library Committee, and judiciary committees.

Admission Requirements

Southern New Hampshire University seeks to attract students who are prepared to take full advantage of the academic and cocurricular opportunities offered. Candidates for admission are evaluated individually on the basis of academic credentials and personal characteristics. Separate consideration is given to admission decisions for freshmen, transfer, culinary arts, the Three-Year honors Program in Business Administration, nontraditional, and international applicants. Students may complete a paper application for admission or apply online.

Application and Information

Applicants for undergraduate day programs must submit a formal application for admission, an up-to-date official high school transcript, a personal essay, and high school recommendations. SAT I or ACT scores are required of freshman applicants. Three-year honors program candidates, in addition to the above, are required to have an interview. Transfer students must also submit official transcripts from all schools previously attended. International students whose native language is other than English must prove proficiency in the English language through the TOEFL examination. Admission decisions are based on the quality of academic performance, but a campus visit and interview are strongly recommended for all candidates. The University operates on a rolling admission basis, and applicants can expect a decision within one month of the receipt of their complete credentials. Applicants may also apply as early action candidates by submitting their application prior to November 15. There is a $35 application fee for students who complete the paper application. There is no fee required to apply online at the Web site listed below.

For further information about Southern New Hampshire University, students should contact:

Office of Admission
Southern New Hampshire University
2500 North River Road
Manchester, New Hampshire 03106-1045
Telephone: 603-645-9611
800-642-4968 (toll-free)
Fax: 603-645-9693
World Wide Web: http://www.snhu.edu

Students relaxing in front of Southern New Hampshire University's Washington Hall, a 250-bed dormitory.

SOUTHERN OREGON UNIVERSITY

ASHLAND, OREGON

The University

Southern Oregon University (SOU) is a contemporary public liberal arts and sciences university with a growing national reputation for excellence in teaching. It places student learning, inside and outside the classroom, at the heart of all programs and services. SOU is proud of its strengths in the sciences and humanities; its continuing tradition of preparing outstanding teachers, business leaders, and other select professionals; and its designation as Oregon's Center of Excellence in the Fine and Performing Arts. SOU was recently elected to the prestigious Council of Public Liberal Arts Colleges, recognizing the campus as a leader in providing a high-quality liberal arts education.

The University offers undergraduate majors in thirty-two areas of study, minors in fifty areas, and eleven graduate programs including management, applied psychology, and several areas of study in education. SOU also offers certificates in accounting, applied cultural anthropology, applied finance and economics, botany, business information systems, cultural resource management, interactive marketing and e-commerce, management of human resources, and Native American studies. Students may take preprofessional programs for entry into medicine, engineering, agriculture, law, and theology. The University offers nursing through its association with the nationally ranked nursing school at the Oregon Health Sciences University. SOU has an excellent Honors Program as well.

The combination of high-quality academics and a beautiful environment attracts approximately 5,500 students. SOU features small class sizes and a student-faculty ratio of 19:1. Students have special opportunities for research and internships with government agencies, such as the National Fish and Wildlife Forensics Lab on campus; businesses, such as the Bear Creek Corporation in Medford; media, such as Jefferson Public Radio; outstanding public schools; and arts organizations, such as the internationally renowned Oregon Shakespeare Festival. Students gain multicultural perspectives in classes, extracurricular activities, the International Student Exchange, and from 150 currently enrolled international students from thirty-three countries. SOU study-abroad programs span twenty countries.

SOU offers an impressive variety of extracurricular activities, clubs, and organizations. The University's newspaper, literary publication, honor societies, social issue groups, social clubs, and religious, preprofessional, international, and academic organizations provide students with multiple opportunities for involvement. Extreme sports, including sky diving, bungee jumping, rock climbing, kayaking, and mountain bike racing, are very popular. More than 65 percent of the student body participates in intramural sports and many compete in intercollegiate club sports, including skiing (Northern California Intercollegiate Conference); aikido, baseball, climbing, karate, rugby, soccer, swimming, tennis, and wrestling.

The University is a member of NAIA Division II. Women's varsity sports include basketball, cross-country, soccer, softball, tennis, track and field, and volleyball. Men's varsity sports include basketball, cross-country, football, track and field, and wrestling. The campus is a culturally dynamic and stimulating environment. Annual concerts bring world-class musicians and performers to the campus. The theater department has two seasons and performs before capacity crowds. Music groups include the concert and chamber choirs, vocal jazz ensemble, symphonic band, woodwind quintet, gamelan ensemble, saxophone quartets, clarinet ensemble, Rogue Valley symphony, and opera workshop. Five art galleries feature the work of students, faculty members, and locally, nationally, and internationally acclaimed artists. The International Writer Series attracts recognized writers, poets, and novelists from around the world.

Approximately 25 percent of the student body lives in one of thirteen residence halls or in family housing units. Freshmen are required to live on campus. The majority of students living off campus live in the immediate surrounding area. The track; the football field; volleyball, basketball, and tennis courts; climbing walls; a large swimming pool; dance studios; and the student fitness center are all nearby. The Cascade Food Court is open from 7 a.m. to 10 p.m. and offers a variety of food choices for every range of tastes.

The University's Student ACCESS Center houses student support services, including counseling services, academic advising, career advising, disabled student services, a learning center, testing center, and tutorial programs.

Location

The University's beautiful 175-acre campus is located in the idyllic community of Ashland. SOU was recently named by *Outside* magazine as one of the "coolest places to work, study, and live," recognizing Southern for its beautiful campus, incredible location, and abundant outdoor activities. Home of the Oregon Shakespeare Festival, the town of 20,000 draws 385,000 visitors each year to enjoy the lively downtown, exquisite Lithia Park, and abundant theater, music events, and other cultural happenings. The Ashland area has five fairs, thirteen festivals, twenty-five art galleries, and twenty-four museums. The town itself has sixty lodging facilities and eighty restaurants. Colorful flags and banners announcing events create a festive environment, and the many boutiques, cafés, coffee shops, movie theaters, and bookstores create an ideal environment for college students. Mt. Ashland and the Siskiyou Mountains serve as the town's backdrop and offer downhill skiing, cross-country skiing, hiking, and mountain biking. The Cascade Mountains, Rogue and Klamath Rivers, Crater Lake National Park, and numerous lakes offer world-class white water rafting, camping, hiking, sailing, kayaking, and rock climbing.

Majors and Degrees

The University is organized into four schools: Arts and Letters, Business, Sciences, and Social Science, Education, Health, and Physical Education. Bachelor of Arts (B.A.) and Bachelor of Science (B.S.) degrees are available in the following majors: anthropology, art, arts and letters, biology, business administration† (accounting; hotel, restaurant, and resort management; management; marketing; small business management), business-chemistry*, business-mathematics*, business-music*, business-physics*, chemistry, communication† (human communication, journalism, media studies), computer science† (computer information science, computer programming and software, computer science and multimedia, computer security and information assurance), criminology†, early childhood development, economics†, English and writing†, environmental studies*, geography†, geology, health and physical education† (athletic training, health promotion and fitness management), history†, human services, interdisciplinary studies, international studies*, language and culture† (French, Spanish, German), mathematics†, mathematics-computer science*, music, nursing (with Oregon Health Sciences University), physics†, political science†, psychology, science*, social science*, sociology, and theater arts. Bachelor of Fine Arts (B.F.A.) degrees are available in art and theater. (An * indicates interdisciplinary programs; majors with a † offer the accelerated-degree option.)

Preprofessional programs include agriculture, chiropractic medicine, dental hygiene, dentistry, engineering, law, medical technology, medicine, nursing, occupational therapy, optometry, pharmacy, physical therapy, physician's assistant studies, podiatry, resource management and conservation, theology, and veterinary medicine.

Minors include Africa-Middle East history; anthropology; applied multimedia; art history; biology; British literature; business administration; chemistry; communication; computer science; creative writing; criminology; economics; education; English education; European history; film studies; French; general studio art; geography; geology; German; hotel, restaurant, and resort management; human communication; interdisciplinary ethics; international peace studies; journalism; Latin American history; Latin American studies; media studies; mathematics; mathematics education; military science; music; Native American studies; philosophy; photography; physics; political science; psychology; public relations; Shakespeare studies; sociology; Spanish; theater arts; U.S. history; U.S. literature; video production; women's studies; and writing with professional applications.

Academic Program

Students are required to complete general education requirements in addition to the major requirements. The general education requirements provide students with skills in effective communication, critical judgment, and research, and cultivate an awareness of the social, artistic, cultural, and scientific traditions of civilization. The required freshman Colloquium provides a solid foundation in reading, writing, communication, and critical thinking. Class size is limited to 25 students, and the Colloquium professor also serves as an adviser. Students in a four-year bachelor's program must have a minimum of 180 quarter credits to graduate. Students admitted to the Accelerated Baccalaureate Degree Program complete between 135 and 150 quarter credits to graduate.

Off-Campus Programs

Southern Oregon University offers a wide variety of study-abroad and overseas internship opportunities. The University also participates in National Student Exchange, which allows students to attend any of 140 colleges and universities nationwide and pay resident tuition.

Academic Facilities

Recent developments on the SOU campus include the Center for Visual Arts, a 66,000-square-foot complex of modern glass and steel that serves as a showplace for art exhibition and education; a newly acquired biotechnology center featuring state of-the-art molecular biology instrumentation; and the acclaimed AuCoin Institute for Environmental, Economic and Civic Studies. Construction of a new library facility is expected to be completed in January 2005. The current library is open 69 hours a week each term and contains more than 300,000 volumes in the general collection. The University is a member of Orbis, a unified library catalog that provides students with access to 9 million books, sound recordings, films, video tapes, and more. Students have access to about 12,000 e-journals through the SOU database and electronic subscriptions.

SOU provides a strong information technology environment. Students have access to twenty-three computer labs on SOU's campus. The Main Computing Services Center lab is open more than 80 hours a week and houses more than 200 PCs and Macs, as well as printers and scanners. Other discipline-based and multimedia labs offer additional resources. Residence halls have labs, and student rooms are wired for computer access. Altogether, there are more than 600 workstations on the campus accessible to students. E-mail accounts, data storage, and access to the Internet are free of charge.

Costs

Resident tuition and fees for the 2003–04 academic year were $4152. As a member of the Western Undergraduate Exchange, SOU offers selected programs to residents of Alaska, Arizona, Colorado, Hawaii, Idaho, Montana, Nevada, New Mexico, North Dakota, South Dakota, Utah, Washington, and Wyoming for $5682 (150 percent of the cost of in-state tuition and fees). Other nonresidents' and international students' tuition and fees were $12,825. Room and board costs, including a double room and the maximum meal plan, were $6210.

Financial Aid

Financial aid is available in the form of grants, loans, and/or work-study. Sixty-five percent of freshmen who enrolled in fall 2003 received some form of financial aid. Students must file the Free Application for Federal Student Aid (FAFSA) to qualify. To be considered for financial aid at Southern Oregon University, students must have applied to the University for admission and have indicated the institution as one of their first six choices on the FAFSA. Students should mail the FAFSA by February 1 to receive maximum consideration for fall. The University offers merit and diversity scholarships to new freshmen and transfer students. Additional scholarships are available through departments and the Office of Financial Aid. For more information, students should contact the Financial Aid Office at 541-552-6161 or go online to http://www.sou.edu/finaid. For those seeking employment, the Student Employment Office lists the work-study and regular jobs available on and off campus.

Faculty

Ninety-three percent of the faculty members have Ph.D.s or the highest degree in their field. There are more than 200 full-time faculty members whose primary emphasis is on teaching and advising undergraduate students. Faculty members frequently include undergraduates in research projects, and many students have coauthored papers and made joint presentations at national conferences. Every student is assigned an adviser when they declare a major; freshmen have their Colloquium professor as their adviser.

Student Government

The Associated Students' governing body implements policies, makes budget recommendations, and participates in the allocation of more than $1.4 million each year to various clubs and organizations. They also work with the Oregon Student Association on issues important in higher education. Elected, appointed, and volunteer positions offer students valuable leadership experience.

Admission Requirements

Applicants for freshman admission must have achieved at least a 2.75 cumulative high school GPA, a minimum combined score of 1010 on the SAT I, or an ACT composite score of at least 21. In addition, applicants must have completed the following high school course requirements: 4 years of English, 3 years of mathematics (including geometry, algebra I, and algebra II), 3 years of social science, 2 years of science (one of which must have a lab), and 2 years of one foreign language. Students transferring from an accredited college or university must have earned at least 36 quarter credits of transfer-level credit with a minimum 2.25 GPA and, if a high school graduate of 1997 or later, meet the language requirement. Transfer applicants with fewer than 36 quarter credits must also meet the freshman admission requirements. Home-schooled students and graduates of nonstandard or unaccredited high schools are eligible for admission if they meet the following requirements: a minimum combined score of 1010 on the SAT I or a minimum score of 21 on the ACT, an average of 470 or above (1410 minimum total) on three SAT II Subject Tests (Writing, Math Level I or IIC, and a third test of the student's choice), and satisfaction of the second-language requirement.

Application and Information

Applicants must submit an application with a $50 nonrefundable application fee and official transcripts from each high school and/or university or college attended. Freshmen must submit official SAT I or ACT scores. Students may apply after September 1 for the following academic year. Admission is rolling, but the priority deadline for the fall is June 1. Students may apply using either the paper application or online at http://www.sou.edu/admissions.

A campus visit is encouraged. Tours are offered at the Office of Admissions, Monday through Friday at 10 a.m. and 2 p.m. and on select Saturdays at 11 a.m. by appointment. For a tour or more information, students should write or call:

Southern Oregon University
Office of Admissions
1250 Siskiyou Boulevard
Ashland, Oregon 97520
Telephone: 541-552-6411
800-482-7672 (toll-free in Oregon and from area codes 916, 707, and 530)
E-mail: admissions@sou.edu
World Wide Web: http://www.sou.edu

SOUTHERN VERMONT COLLEGE

BENNINGTON, VERMONT

The College

Southern Vermont College's philosophy begins with a deep belief in the potential of every individual. The College is committed to offering a career-oriented liberal arts education to a student body from diverse academic backgrounds. The College places an emphasis on serving students who have yet to fulfill their potential, ensuring accessibility to those with extra needs, financial and academic, who are serious about bettering their lives through higher education.

Southern Vermont College is located on a 371-acre campus at the base of Mount Anthony. The main College building, the former Everett mansion, is of English-Norman architecture and is patterned after mansions of the fourteenth century. The expansive twenty-seven-room building has been converted into classrooms, administrative offices, and the library. The five coed residence halls offer housing for all freshmen and other students who wish to live on campus. More than 500 students major in any of the bachelor's and associate degree programs listed below. A student-faculty ratio of 11:1 and small classes allow for maximum interaction. Special academic options include an honors program, internships, and independent studies. Opportunities for study abroad also exist. Southern Vermont College is accredited by the New England Association of Schools and Colleges.

Southern Vermont College has intercollegiate sports with teams competing at the NCAA Division III level. The College is also a member of the Great Northeast Athletic Conference (GNAC) and the Eastern Collegiate Athletic Conference (ECAC). Intercollegiate programs include men's and women's basketball, cross-country, and soccer as well as men's baseball and women's softball and volleyball. Many students participate in the numerous clubs, intramural sports, student government activities, publications, and theater programs available.

Location

Bennington, an historic New England town with a population of 19,000, is located in the heart of the Green Mountains in the southwest corner of the state. Bennington borders both New York and Massachusetts, and is a 1-hour drive from Albany and 3½ hours from Boston and New York City. The College is central to both prime ski country and the performing arts. Ten major ski resorts, along with the performing arts centers of Tanglewood, Saratoga, and Williamstown, are within 2 hours. Opportunities for hiking, cross-country skiing, and mountain biking are right outside one's campus room door.

Majors and Degrees

Southern Vermont College offers the Bachelor of Science (B.S.) degree, the Bachelor of Arts (B.A.) degree, the Associate in Science degree, and the Associate in Arts degree. Majors include business administration/management, communications, creative writing, criminal justice, English, environmental studies, human services, liberal arts, liberal arts/management, nursing, prelaw, psychology, and radiologic technology. The College also offers an individualized degree program.

Academic Program

Southern Vermont is a career-oriented, liberal arts college. The College values educating students for careers as strongly as it believes in educating them to be citizens who understand the complexities of today's world. Virtually every program requires an internship or practicum experience. Faculty members challenge students to think independently and creatively. They represent the best in their field and are often quoted in regional and national publications about current trends and popular events. With an average class size of 17, students receive the attention needed to achieve their personal best.

The ACTion program on campus provides academic, counseling, and tutoring support for students. The Career, Tutorial, and Writing Centers are places where students can receive professional and peer assistance with resume writing, job opportunities, and one-on-one tutoring. In addition, ACTion provides a counselor for students to ensure their personal well-being, and the Disabilities Support Program staff members offer those students with documented learning disabilities a supportive environment in which to achieve their academic goals.

Service-learning through the Community Action Office at Southern Vermont College offers students the opportunity to enhance what is taught in class by extending their involvement into the community. Students learn and develop through active participation in organized service experiences that meet actual community needs and course-learning objectives. The service-learning method is integrated into the student's academic curriculum and provides the student with opportunities to use newly acquired skills and knowledge in real-life situations. This successful program offers Southern Vermont College students the ability to grow as citizens—intellectually, socially, and personally—as well as enabling them to gain valuable career experiences.

Off campus, students are encouraged to participate in community activities and programs. The relationship between the town of Bennington and the College is a friendly and cooperative one, with students volunteering at many area organizations, including the rescue squad, the Big Brother/Big Sister program, and the Center for Restorative Justice. At the same time, Bennington welcomes students and offers them opportunities for employment and internships.

Academic Facilities

The library contains more than 25,000 volumes of reading and research material and 1,500 periodicals, newspapers, and government documents that have been carefully selected to support the academic programs. More than 2,000 full-text journals are available through Internet connection, which is networked through every computer on campus in both the labs and the residence hall rooms. The College laboratory provides the necessary facilities and support equipment for the study of the natural sciences. Two computer labs, one that is accessible 24 hours a day, provide up-to-date technological access for Southern Vermont's students.

Costs

Tuition for the 2004–05 academic year is $12,498. Room and board charges are $6432 for the academic year. Total tuition and room and board is $18,930. Southern Vermont College has the lowest comprehensive cost of all private, residential colleges in Vermont. There are no mandatory fees, but certain academic laboratory fees may apply. Students should budget approximately $1200 for books and supplies for the year.

Financial Aid

Southern Vermont College is able to offer generous financial aid packages to eligible students. In 2003–04, the College awarded nearly $1.4 million of its own funds to students. This program makes higher education available for many who otherwise could not afford to attend.

To be considered for financial aid, a student must file the Free Application for Federal Student Aid (FAFSA) and the Southern Vermont College Financial Aid Application. The College participates in a variety of federal, state, and local financial aid programs, including the Federal Pell Grant, Federal Supplemental Opportunity Educational Grant, and Federal Work-Study programs; various student loan programs, including the Stafford, and PLUS; state grant programs; and Southern Vermont College Opportunity Grants. Southern Vermont College also offers numerous scholarships to both new and returning students. Approximately 75 percent of the students enrolled receive some type of financial assistance.

Faculty

Southern Vermont College's faculty members enrich classes through their personal association with each student. They know many students on both an academic and personal level. The student-faculty ratio of 11:1 enables students to express their ideas, give feedback, and grow intellectually and socially within the academic environment. The exchange of thoughts and information continues even when the class period ends, taking place everywhere that students and faculty members interact. Currently, 21 full-time and 24 part-time dedicated faculty members provide hands-on professional experience and academic insight for Southern Vermont College students.

Admission Requirements

The Admissions Committee uses a portfolio approach to assess an applicant's file. The decision regarding admission to Southern Vermont College is based on the review of previous academic experience, the applicant's written statement of purpose, the admission interview (if requested), and any other relevant information. Applicants are evaluated not only on the basis of their academic performance, but also on potential for achievement in college. While test scores, grades, and rank in class all play an important part in the selection of the freshman class, other factors, such as teacher recommendations, leadership roles, volunteer and community service, and the personal essay are also very important in gauging a student's potential.

Southern Vermont College welcomes applications from students from diverse academic and social backgrounds.

Application and Information

Southern Vermont College follows a rolling admission policy. To be considered for admission, students must submit a completed application form with a $30 fee; scores on the ACT, the SAT I, or the Southern Vermont College Placement Tests; an official transcript from their high school and any colleges previously attended; at least two recommendations from teachers, guidance counselors, employers, or civic officials; and a 300-word essay. While a tour and interview are not required at Southern Vermont College, students are encouraged to visit the campus and meet with an admissions counselor.

For more information about Southern Vermont College, students should contact:

Admissions Office
Southern Vermont College
982 Mansion Road
Bennington, Vermont 05201
Telephone: 800-378-2782 (toll-free)
E-mail: admis@svc.edu
World Wide Web: http://www.svc.edu

The Everett mansion houses the main administrative offices, classrooms, and the library at Southern Vermont College.

SOUTHERN VIRGINIA UNIVERSITY

BUENA VISTA, VIRGINIA

The University

Southern Virginia University is a private, nonprofit, coeducational four-year university operated by a board of trustees predominately made up of members of the Church of Jesus Christ of Latter-day Saints (LDS). Although SVU is not owned or operated by the Church, its primary purpose is to provide a high-quality education in an environment supportive of LDS values and standards.

Southern Virginia University began as Bowling Green Female Seminary in 1867. At that time, "seminary" referred to a school for girls. In 1894, the school moved to a resort hotel in Buena Vista and changed its name to Southern Seminary. The hotel, built in 1890, is now Main Hall and is listed on the National Register as a National Historic Landmark. From 1922 to 1996, the school operated as a junior college, until declining enrollment and financial instability threatened to close its doors. In 1996, a group of Latter-day Saint educators and business leaders assumed responsibility for the college, converting it into a four-year liberal arts college. That fall, the "new" Southern Virginia College enrolled 74 students. It has since grown dramatically, enrolling 576 students in the fall of 2003. In 2001, the name was changed to Southern Virginia University to reflect growth of the curriculum and the rapidly increasing size of the student body.

Southern Virginia University (SVU) offers thirteen majors and seventeen minors and is fully accredited by the American Academy for Liberal Education. There are fourteen intercollegiate sports, a student government association, a student orchestra, chamber choir, theater guild, and other various campus groups and activities. SVU's intercollegiate sports include men's and women's basketball, cross-country, soccer, and track and field; men's baseball, football, and wrestling; women's softball and volleyball; and cheerleading. There are also several club sports, including lacrosse. The Church of Jesus Christ of Latter-day Saints offers an Institute of Religion on campus and four student wards.

Location

Buena Vista, Virginia, a town of just over 6,000 residents, is located by the scenic Blue Ridge Mountains in the heart of the Shenandoah Valley. Buena Vista is close to Interstate Highway 81 and is approximately 6 miles east of historic Lexington, a popular tourist destination. Nearby cities include Roanoke (50 miles south), Charlottesville (55 miles northeast), and Washington, D.C. (165 miles northeast). Air service to SVU is available from the Roanoke Airport, less than an hour's drive from Buena Vista.

The Blue Ridge Parkway, Appalachian Trail, and Blue Ridge Mountains offer many opportunities for hiking, skiing, biking, camping, and other outdoor activities. Many American historical sites are also nearby, including Monticello, Appomattox, Williamsburg, and Yorktown. The Virginia Military Institute and Washington and Lee University, located in the neighboring town of Lexington, offer many additional services to students.

Majors and Degrees

The State Council of Higher Education for Virginia (SCHEV) has granted Southern Virginia University approval to confer Bachelor of Arts degrees. SVU offers majors in the following areas: art, biology, business management and leadership, English, family life, history, information science and multimedia design, liberal arts, music, philosophy, physical education and recreation administration, Spanish, and theater.

Academic Programs

To be eligible for a baccalaureate degree, students must complete a minimum of 120 credit hours of study, at least 60 of which or at least the last two full-time semesters before graduation are at SVU. No more than 9 credit hours are granted for internship courses. In addition, students must complete all general education requirements (typically 61 hours), a minimum of 36 credit hours in upper-division (300- and 400-level) courses, and all the requirements of at least one major. Students must earn a minimum grade point average of 2.0 on all course work taken at the University, and they must comply with all University standards, regulations, and procedures, from the date of matriculation through the date of final graduation.

The academic year consists of three semesters: August to December (fall), January to April (spring), and May (summer) sessions.

Academic Facilities

The Von Canon Library offers students access to a collection of 107,630 titles, 37,000 periodicals, 4,299 reference materials, 4,350 audiovisual materials, and an on-campus computer lab. Durham Hall is the main academic building on campus, housing biology, chemistry, and geology lecture rooms and labs on the lower level. Classrooms for the social sciences, math, English, and business are located throughout the building, as are faculty offices. Other academic buildings include Landrum House, Chandler Hall, Tucson Art Building, the Knight Sports Arena, Main Hall, and the Student Union Building.

Costs

Southern Virginia University is a private, nonprofit institution. Tuition and other fees are maintained at a minimum consistent with high academic standards and efficiency of operation. The basic expenses for a full-time student for the 2004–05 academic year (excluding summer school) are $14,640 for tuition and fees and $5300 for room and board (breakfast, lunch, and dinner).

Financial Aid

Through its financial aid program, Southern Virginia University attempts to keep education costs as affordable as possible by providing assistance to many students through various scholarships and grants. SVU facilitates financing of educational expenses by offering financial aid from four general sources: federal, state, private, and institutional. A financial aid package often includes more than one type of aid.

To ensure that every student receives the maximum assistance for which they are eligible, every student is encouraged to complete the Free Application for Federal Student Aid (FAFSA) (http://www.fafsa.ed.gov). The U.S. Department of Education uses a standard formula, established by Congress, to evaluate the information reported on the FAFSA to determine a student's eligibility.

SVU offers a number of institutional scholarships, grants, and employment opportunities to both incoming and returning students. Scholarships and grants are awarded only to full-time students and, except for the Housing Grant, are applicable only to tuition. Students may receive additional funds from federal, state, and private sources other than SVU. Most SVU scholarships and grants are awarded for an academic year (meaning that they are good for both the fall and spring semesters) and are awarded half in the fall and half in the spring, unless otherwise stipulated. Institutional work-study and tuition installment plans are also offered by the University to assist in financing educational expenses.

Faculty

Seventy-four percent of all full-time faculty members at SVU hold terminal degrees in their fields of study. Including part-time professors, the SVU faculty is made up of 45 professors. With a student-faculty ratio of 12:1, SVU offers an interactive course setting where faculty members and students have a close mentor relationship. Faculty members also serve as academic advisers to all students enrolled.

Student Government

The SVU Student Association (SVUSA) provides students with a means to carry out programs, activities, and events that enhance student life and that promote within students the qualities of service, integrity, leadership, academic excellence, fellowship, and moral conduct. Student leaders are elected by students and are advised through the Office of the Dean of Students. SVUSA also acts as a mediator and advocate with the administration for student concerns and needs.

Admission Requirements

Each applicant is evaluated individually on academic performance, ACT or SAT I test scores, class rank, extracurricular activities, demonstrated leadership, exemplary standards of conduct, maturity, service, and a commitment to the pursuit of a college degree. An applicant's high school course of study should include at least 14 units of core academic classes in English, foreign language, mathematics, science, social science, and history and at least 4 units of elective classes. Although the University does not require specific courses for admission, successful applicants usually have completed at least 4 years of English, 2 years of foreign language, 2 years of college preparatory mathematics, 2 years of laboratory science, and elective credits in subjects such as art, music, drama, and physical education. Transfer students with fewer than 24 semester credit hours are evaluated according to the same admission criteria used for incoming freshmen, except that their college transcripts are also considered. Transfer students with 24 semester credit hours or more are evaluated academically according to their previous college work. Transfer students should have at least a 2.0 GPA for all previous college work.

Application and Information

A complete application consists of an official application form returned with a nonrefundable application fee of $35, official transcripts of completed high school course work, official SAT I or ACT results, and an ecclesiastical endorsement from a bishop or branch president for LDS applicants or a clergyman or other spiritual leader for applicants of other faiths. As part of the application, students must pledge to abide by the Principles of Honor and Conduct, which include standards of honesty, conduct, dress, and grooming. Visits to the campus are always welcomed.

For more information, students should contact:

Office of Admissions
Southern Virginia University
One University Hill Drive
Buena Vista, Virginia 24416
Telephone: 540-261-8421
800-229-8420 (toll-free)
Fax: 540-261-8559
E-mail: admissions@southernvirginia.edu
World Wide Web: http://www.southernvirginia.edu

SOUTH UNIVERSITY

MONTGOMERY, ALABAMA

The University

South University is a private academic institution dedicated to providing educational opportunities for the intellectual, social, and professional development of a diverse student population. To achieve this, the institution offers focused and balanced curricula at the associate and bachelor's degree levels in the areas of business, information technology, health professions, and legal studies.

South University traces its heritage back to 1899 when Dr. John Draughon established Draughon's Practical Business College in Savannah. The school's early years were marked by relocation and expansion, and in 1986 the institution changed its name to South College. In 2001, the college was approved to confer master's degrees and officially became South University. Today it has grown into a multicampus system with locations in Savannah, Georgia; West Palm Beach, Florida; Montgomery, Alabama; and Columbia, South Carolina. The Montgomery campus became part of South University in 1997 and has been part of the postsecondary education community in that city since 1887.

South University/Montgomery has a diverse student body enrolled in both day and evening classes. Like all of the University's campuses, the Montgomery campus is designed to accommodate the diverse needs of its student body. Students are primarily commuters who live within 50 miles of the city. They include men and women who have enrolled directly after completing high school, who have transferred from another college or university, or who have experience in the workforce and are pursing an education that will help them take a new professional direction.

In 2003, South University/Montgomery campus moved into a modern 26,000-square-foot building on a 3.75-acre campus. The two-story building houses computer and health professions labs, classrooms, a student center, bookstore, and faculty and administrative offices. The building is also equipped with advanced safety and security systems. Most students live within driving distance of the campus; therefore, the University does not offer or operate student housing. If housing is needed, students should contact the admissions department.

South University is accredited by the Commission on Colleges of the Southern Association of Colleges and Schools (SACS, 1866 Southern Lane, Decatur, Georgia 30033-4097; 404-679-4501) to award associate, bachelor's, master's, and doctoral degrees. South University/Montgomery is chartered as an educational institution in the state of Alabama and is authorized under Act No. 80-272, Regular Session, Alabama Legislature, 1980, to conduct programs within the state of Alabama. The institution is also authorized by the State Approving Agency for the training of veterans under chapters 31, 34, and 35.

Certain programs offered at South University/Montgomery campus have earned programmatic accreditation. The Associate of Science degree program in medical assisting is accredited by the Commission on Accreditation of Allied Health Education Programs (CAAHEP, 35 East Wacker Drive, Suite 1970, Chicago, Illinois 60601; 312-553-9355) on recommendation of the Committee on Accreditation for Medical Assisting Education. The Bachelor of Science in legal studies and Associate of Science in paralegal studies degree programs are approved by the American Bar Association (541 North Fairbanks Court, Chicago, Illinois 60611; 312-988-5616). The Associate of Science in physical therapist assisting degree program is an expansion program approved by the Commission on Accreditation in Physical Therapy Education of the American Physical Therapy Association (1111 North Fairfax Street, Alexandria, Virginia 22314; 703-684-2782).

Location

The campus is located on the rapidly growing east side of Alabama's capital city. As the state capital, Montgomery is a hub of government, banking, and law as well as a state center for culture and entertainment. Montgomery is situated in the middle of the southeastern U.S. and is less than a 3-hour drive from Atlanta and the Gulf of Mexico.

Majors and Degrees

South University/Montgomery awards the following two-year degrees: Associate of Science in accounting (92 credits), Associate of Science in business administration (92 credits), Associate of Science in information technology (92 credits), Associate of Science in paralegal studies (104 credits), Associate of Science in medical assisting (100 credits), and Associate of Science in physical therapist assisting (110 credits).

The following four-year bachelor's degrees are awarded: Bachelor of Business Administration (184 credits), Bachelor of Science in legal studies (180 credits), and Bachelor of Science in information technology (180 credits).

Academic Programs

South University/Montgomery offers degree programs that are designed to meet the needs and objectives of students. Each curriculum combines didactic and practical educational experiences that provide students with the academic background needed to pursue the professions of their choice. In addition, faculty members strive to instill the value not only of education and professionalism but also of contribution and commitment to the advancement of community.

Each university quarter comprises ten to twelve weeks. Associate degree programs require a minimum of eight quarters to complete, and bachelor's degree programs require a minimum of 12 quarters for completion. Programs are offered on a year-round basis, providing students with the ability to work uninterrupted toward their degrees. Classes on campus begin at 8:30 a.m., Monday through Thursday, and Saturday classes may be scheduled as necessary. Evening classes are in session from 6 to 9:30 p.m., Monday through Thursday.

Academic Facilities

The library has wireless technology throughout, comfortable seating, and quiet study space. Its collection includes books, print and online periodicals, CDs, videos, and numerous online proprietary databases. Materials are housed in circulating, reference, and reserve collections and have been selected to support the academic programs. Also for student use, the library has a modern computer lab with ten workstations, each with Internet access, online database services, an office suite, tutorials, and class-support software.

Costs

Tuition for most programs at South University/Montgomery for 2003–04 was $3395 per quarter for 10 to 18 credit hours, $2695 per quarter for 5 to 9 credit hours, and $1395 per quarter for 1 to 4 credit hours. Full-time students taking more than 18 credit hours per quarter were charged an additional $200 per credit hour beyond the 18 hours.

Financial Aid

South University's financial aid office helps eligible students secure financial assistance to complete their studies. The University participates in several student aid programs. Forms of financial aid available through federal resources include the Federal Pell Grant Program, Federal Supplemental Educational Opportunity Grant (FSEOG) Program, Federal Work-Study Program, Federal Perkins Loan Program, Federal Stafford Student Loan Program (subsidized and unsubsidized), and the Federal PLUS Loan Program. South University employs the Federal Methodology of Need Analysis, approved by the U.S. Department of Education, as a fair and equitable means of determining a family's ability to contribute to the student's educational expenses, as well as eligibility for other financial aid programs. Eligible students may apply for veterans educational benefits. Students also are encouraged to investigate the availability of grants and scholarships through community resources.

Faculty

The South University/Montgomery faculty includes individuals of high academic distinction. Out of 43 instructors, 26 percent hold terminal degrees within their fields of expertise. In addition to teaching, faculty members strive to help students develop the requisites to appreciate knowledge and understand how experiences in the classroom and laboratory relate to professional performance in the workplace. The average student-faculty ratio per class is 15:1. Each student is assigned a faculty adviser who oversees the student's progress and can answer questions about academic and career concerns. Students are encouraged to discuss program-related issues with and seek academic and career advice from their faculty advisers.

Admission Requirements

To be admitted to South University, a prospective student must be a high school graduate or hold a GED and submit a minimum combined SAT I score of 830, a combined ACT score of at least 17, or a satisfactory score on the University-administered admissions examination or meet the criteria established for acceptance as a transfer student. International students must show a sufficient knowledge of the English language as demonstrated by a minimum score of 550 on the TOEFL. South University does accept the International Baccalaureate Program diploma as meeting the requirement for high school graduation. Applicants not meeting the testing standards for general admission may be accepted under academic support admission by submitting a minimum combined SAT I score of 660, a combined ACT score of at least 14, or a satisfactory score on the University-administered admissions examination.

Application and Information

Applicants must complete and submit an application form along with the application fee and official transcripts from high school and all colleges attended. Faxed documents are not considered official. Applicants must also complete all tests administered by the University or submit their SAT or ACT scores to the registrar's office. Applications are accepted on a rolling basis and should be made as far in advance as possible. Admissions officers are available weekdays from 8:30 a.m. to 6 p.m. and on Saturdays from 9 a.m. to noon. An appointment for an admissions interview or tour of the campus should be made in advance.

For additional information, all prospective students should contact:

Director of Admissions
South University
5355 Vaughn Road
Montgomery, Alabama 36116-1120
Telephone: 334-395-8800
866-629-2962 (toll-free)
Fax: 334-395-8859
E-mail: mtgadmis@southuniversity.edu
World Wide Web: http://www.southuniversity.edu

South University in Montgomery, Alabama, has a diverse student body enrolled in both day and evening classes.

SOUTH UNIVERSITY

WEST PALM BEACH, FLORIDA

The University

South University is a private academic institution dedicated to providing educational opportunities for the intellectual, social, and professional development of a diverse student population. To achieve this, the West Palm Beach campus offers focused and balanced curricula at the associate and bachelor's degree levels in the areas of business, health sciences, information technology, and legal studies.

South University traces its heritage back to 1899 when Dr. John Draughon established Draughon's Practical Business College in Savannah. The school's early years were marked by relocation and expansion, and in 1986 the institution changed its name to South College. In 2001, the college was approved to confer master's degrees and officially became South University. Today it has grown into a multicampus system with locations in Savannah, Georgia; West Palm Beach, Florida; Montgomery, Alabama; and Columbia, South Carolina.

The West Palm Beach facility was established as a campus of South University in 1974. Since then, it has continued to seek new educational opportunities and has plans to offer new programs and services that will provide even more possibilities for its students and the greater West Palm Beach community. Despite these plans to grow, the University strives to maintain small class sizes that permit students to receive more individualized instruction and interaction with faculty and staff members.

The West Palm Beach campus of South University has a diverse student body enrolled in both day and evening classes. Students are primarily commuters who live within 50 miles of West Palm Beach County. They include men and women who have enrolled directly after completing high school, who have transferred from another college or university, or who have experience in the workforce and are pursing an education that will help them take a new professional direction.

In addition to classrooms and administrative offices, the campus includes a bookstore, student lounge, career services center, and ample parking. Since most students live within driving distance of the campus, the University does not offer or operate student housing. If housing is needed, students should contact the Admissions Department.

South University is accredited by the Commission on Colleges of the Southern Association of Colleges and Schools (SACS, 1866 Southern Lane, Decatur, Georgia 30033-4097; 404-679-4501) to award associate, bachelor's, master's, and doctoral degrees. The West Palm Beach campus specifically is licensed by the Commission for Independent Education, Florida Department of Education (2650 Apalachee Parkway, Tallahassee, Florida 32301; 850-245-3200) to confer Associate of Science and Bachelor of Science degrees. In addition, the campus is approved for training veterans and other individuals by the State of Florida Department of Veterans' Affairs, Division of Veterans' Benefits and Assistance, Bureau of State Approving for Veterans' Training.

Certain programs offered at the West Palm Beach campus have earned programmatic accreditation. The Associate of Science in medical assisting degree program is accredited by the Commission on Accreditation of Allied Health Education Programs (CAAHEP, 35 East Wacker Drive, Suite 1970, Chicago, Illinois 60601; 312-553-9355) on recommendation of the Committee on Accreditation for Medical Assisting Education. The Associate of Science in physical therapist assisting degree program is accredited by the Commission on Accreditation in Physical Therapy Education of the American Physical Therapy Association (1111 North Fairfax Street, Alexandria, Virginia 22314; 703-684-2782). The Bachelor of Science in legal studies and Associate of Science in paralegal studies degree programs are approved by the American Bar Association (541 North Fairbanks Court, Chicago, Illinois 60611; 312-988-5616). The Florida Board of Nursing has granted South University approval to accept a limited number of qualified applicants per year for admission into the nursing program.

Location

South University's West Palm Beach campus is centrally located near the heart of West Palm Beach County. Midway between Palm Beach International Airport and heavily traveled Okeechobee Boulevard, the campus is just minutes west of both Interstate 95 and downtown West Palm Beach.

Majors and Degrees

The West Palm Beach campus of South University awards the following two-year degrees: Associate of Science in accounting (92 credits), Associate of Science in allied health science (90 credits), Associate of Science in business administration (92 credits), Associate of Science in information technology (92 credits), Associate of Science in medical assisting (100 credits), Associate of Science in paralegal studies (104 credits), and Associate of Science in physical therapist assisting (110 credits). The following four-year bachelor's degrees are awarded: Bachelor of Business Administration (184 credits), Bachelor of Science in information technology (180 credits), Bachelor of Science in legal studies (180 credits), and Bachelor of Science in nursing (102 credits plus 90 prerequisite credits).

Academic Programs

The West Palm Beach campus of South University offers degree programs that are designed to meet the needs and objectives of students. Each curriculum combines didactic and practical educational experiences that provide students with the academic background needed to pursue the professions of their choice. In addition, faculty members strive to instill the value not only of education and professionalism but also of contribution and commitment to the advancement of community.

Each University quarter comprises ten to twelve weeks. Associate degree programs require a minimum of eight quarters to complete, and bachelor's degree programs require a minimum of twelve quarters for completion. Programs at the West Palm Beach campus are offered on a year-round basis, providing students with the ability to work uninterrupted toward their degrees. Classes on campus begin at 8:30 a.m., Monday through Friday, and Saturday classes may be scheduled as necessary. Evening classes are in session from 6 to 9:30 p.m., Monday through Thursday. Classes may be scheduled on Friday nights or Saturdays as necessary.

Academic Facilities

The 32,000-square-foot West Palm Beach campus is centrally located in two buildings on Florida's affluent Gold Coast. The campus is equipped with modern computer labs and field-related medical laboratories for use by students pursuing degrees in the allied health science, medical assisting, nursing, and physical therapist assisting programs.

The West Palm Beach campus library houses a large collection that includes extensive law resources. Students may retrieve periodicals in paper or electronic form. Library-based computers provide access to several commercial online services, including WESTLAW, the computerized legal research service, and the Southeastern Library Network (SOLINET). CD-ROM resources include the Grolier's Multimedia Encyclopedia and the EBSCO magazine full-text database. Internet access is available in the library.

Costs

Tuition for programs at South University's West Palm Beach campus for 2003–04 was $3695 per quarter full-time and $2995 per quarter part-time for the physical therapist assisting program, $5095 per quarter full-time for the nursing program, and $3395 per quarter full-time and $2695 per quarter part-time for most other programs. Full-time students taking more than 18 credit hours per quarter were charged an additional $200 per credit hour beyond the 18 hours.

Financial Aid

South University's Office of Student Finance helps eligible students secure financial assistance to complete their studies. The University participates in several student aid programs. Forms of financial aid available through federal resources include the Federal Pell Grant Program, Federal Supplemental Educational Opportunity Grant (FSEOG) Program, Federal Work-Study Program, Federal Perkins Loan Program, Federal Stafford Student Loan Program (subsidized and unsubsidized), and the Federal PLUS Loan Program. Eligible students may also apply for the Florida State Assistance Grant (FSAG), Florida Bright Futures Scholarship Program, and veterans' educational benefits. Students also are encouraged to investigate the availability of grants and scholarships through community resources.

Faculty

The South University faculty includes individuals of high academic distinction. Of the 60 instructors on the West Palm Beach campus, 32 percent hold terminal degrees in their fields of expertise. In addition to teaching, faculty members strive to help students develop the requisites to appreciate knowledge and understand how experiences in the classroom and laboratory relate to professional performance in the workplace. The average student-faculty ratio is 16:1. Each student is assigned a faculty adviser who oversees the student's progress and can answer questions about academic and career concerns. Students are encouraged to discuss program-related issues with and seek academic and career advice from their faculty advisers.

Admission Requirements

To be admitted to South University, a prospective student must be a high school graduate or hold a GED and submit a minimum combined SAT I score of 830, a composite ACT score of at least 17, or a satisfactory score on the University-administered admissions examination. Students who wish to transfer must meet the criteria established for acceptance as a transfer student. International students must show a sufficient knowledge of the English language as demonstrated by a minimum score of 550 on the TOEFL. South University does accept the International Baccalaureate Diploma as meeting the requirement for high school graduation. Applicants not meeting the testing standards for general admission may be accepted under academic support admission by submitting a combined SAT I score of 660, a composite ACT score of at least 14, or a satisfactory score on the University-administered admissions examination. General admission to the University does not guarantee admission to the nursing program; to obtain specific entrance requirements for this program, students should contact the campus Admissions Department or visit the South University Web site.

Application and Information

Applicants must complete and submit an application form, along with the general application fee, and official transcripts from all high schools and colleges attended. Faxed documents are not considered official. Applicants must also complete all tests administered by the University or submit their SAT or ACT scores to the registrar's office. Applications are accepted on a rolling basis and should be made as far in advance as possible.

Admissions officers are available weekdays from 9 a.m. to 6 p.m. and on Saturdays from 9 a.m. to noon. An appointment for an admissions interview or tour of the campus should be made in advance. For additional information, all prospective students should contact:

Director of Admissions
South University
1760 North Congress Avenue
West Palm Beach, Florida 33409-5178
Telephone: 561-697-9200
866-629-2902 (toll-free)
Fax: 516-697-9944
E-mail: wpbadmis@southuniversity.edu
World Wide Web: http://www.southuniversity.edu

South University serves the educational needs of students within and beyond Florida's West Palm Beach County.

SOUTH UNIVERSITY

SAVANNAH, GEORGIA

SouthUniversity℠

The University

South University is a private academic institution dedicated to providing educational opportunities for the intellectual, social, and professional development of a diverse student population. To achieve this, the Savannah campus offers focused and balanced curricula at the associate and bachelor's degree levels in the areas of business, health sciences, information technology, and legal studies. Master's degree programs are offered in clinical anesthesiology and physician assistant studies, and a Doctor of Pharmacy program was introduced in 2003.

South University traces its heritage back to 1899 when Dr. John Draughon established Draughon's Practical Business College in Savannah. The school's early years were marked by relocation and expansion, and in 1986 the institution changed its name to South College. In 2001, the college was approved to confer master's degrees and officially became South University. Today it has grown into a multicampus system with locations in Savannah, Georgia; West Palm Beach, Florida; Montgomery, Alabama; and Columbia, South Carolina.

In addition to classrooms and offices, the campus includes a bookstore, student lounge, career services center, and ample parking. Most students live within driving distance of the Savannah campus. Therefore, the University does not offer or operate student housing. If housing is needed, students should contact the Admissions Department.

The cornerstone of the Savannah campus is new School of Pharmacy building, which represents an addition to the University's current School of Business and School of Health Professions. South University is the first university or college in Savannah to offer a health professions doctoral degree program. The Savannah campus continues to seek new educational opportunities and has plans to offer new programs and services that will provide even more possibilities for its students and the greater Savannah community. Despite these plans to grow, the University strives to maintain small class sizes that permit students to receive much individualized instruction and interaction with faculty and staff members.

The Savannah campus of South University has a diverse student body enrolled in both day and evening classes. Students are primarily commuters who live within 50 miles of the city. They include men and women who have enrolled directly after completing high school, who have transferred from another college or university, or who have experience in the workforce and are pursing an education that will help them take a new professional direction.

South University is accredited by the Commission on Colleges of the Southern Association of Colleges and Schools (SACS, 1866 Southern Lane, Decatur, Georgia 30033-4097; 404-679-4501) to award associate, bachelor's, master's, and doctoral degrees. The Savannah campus is also authorized under the Georgia Non-public Postsecondary Educational Institutions Act of 1990 to confer those degrees. In addition, the campus is approved for training veterans and other individuals by the State of Georgia Department of Veterans' Services, State Approving Agency, in Atlanta, Georgia.

Certain programs offered at the Savannah campus have earned programmatic accreditation. The Associate of Science in medical assisting degree program is accredited by the Commission on Accreditation of Allied Health Education Programs (CAAHEP, 35 East Wacker Drive, Suite 1970, Chicago, Illinois 60601; 312-553-9355) on recommendation of the Committee on Accreditation for Medical Assisting Education. The Associate of Science in physical therapist assisting degree program is an expansion program approved by the Commission on Accreditation in Physical Therapy Education of the American Physical Therapy Association (1111 North Fairfax Street, Alexandria, Virginia 22314; 703-684-2782).

The physician assistant studies program is accredited by the Accreditation Review Commission on Education for the Physician Assistant (ARC-PA), an accreditation status that qualifies graduating students to take the national certifying examination administered by the National Commission on Certification of Physician Assistants (NCCPA). In addition, the South University physician assistant program is a member of the Association of Physician Assistant Programs, the national organization representing physician assistant education programs. The Bachelor of Science in legal studies and Associate of Science in paralegal studies degree programs are approved by the American Bar Association (541 North Fairbanks Court, Chicago, Illinois 60611; 312-988-5616).

Location

The Savannah campus, the largest among South University's four locations, is on the south side of this historic city. Surrounded by towering pines, the buildings are situated on 9 acres of land and are convenient to Savannah's bustling midtown section and a full range of educational and cultural activities.

Majors and Degrees

The Savannah campus of South University awards the following two-year degrees: Associate of Science in accounting (92 credits), Associate of Science in business administration (92 credits), Associate of Science in information technology (92 credits), Associate of Science in medical assisting (100 credits), Associate of Science in paralegal studies (104 credits), and Associate of Science in physical therapist assisting (110 credits).

Four-year degree programs are Bachelor of Business Administration (184 credits), Bachelor of Science in information technology (180 credits), Bachelor of Science in legal studies (180 credits), and Bachelor of Science in physician assistant studies (153 credits). No physician assistant studies credits from another institution may be transferred into the didactic or clinical year at South University. Students must complete the entire two-year program at South University.

Academic Programs

The Savannah campus of South University offers degree programs that are designed to meet the needs and objectives of students. Each curriculum combines didactic and practical educational experiences that provide students with the academic background needed to pursue the professions of their choice. In addition, faculty members strive to instill the value not only of education and professionalism but also of contribution and commitment to the advancement of community.

Each University quarter comprises ten to twelve weeks. Associate degree programs require a minimum of eight quarters to complete, and bachelor's degree programs require a minimum of twelve quarters for completion. Undergraduate programs are offered on a year-round basis, providing students with the ability to work uninterrupted toward their degrees. Classes on campus begin at 8:30 a.m., Monday through Friday, and Saturday classes may be scheduled as necessary. Evening classes are in session from 6 to 9:30 p.m., Monday through Thursday. Classes may be scheduled on Friday nights or Saturdays as necessary.

Academic Facilities

The Savannah campus library has a large collection that includes an extensive law library. Students may retrieve periodicals in paper or electronic form. Library-based computers provide access to several commercial online services, including WESTLAW, the computerized legal research service; GALILEO, the Georgia network of databases; and MEDLINE, for health sciences students. CD-ROM resources include the Encyclopedia Britannica, the Official Code of Georgia Annotated, ADAM, and the EBSCO magazine full-text database. Internet access is available on all computers throughout the campus.

Costs

Tuition for programs at South University's Savannah campus for 2003–04 was $5195 per quarter for the physician assistant studies bachelor's degree program and $3395 per quarter full-time and $2695 part-time for most other undergraduate programs. Full-time students taking more than 18 credit hours per quarter were charged an additional $200 per credit hour beyond the 18 hours.

Financial Aid

South University's Office of Student Finance helps eligible students secure financial assistance to complete their studies. The University participates in several student aid programs. Forms of financial aid available through federal resources include the Federal Pell Grant Program, Federal Supplemental Educational Opportunity Grant (FSEOG) Program, Federal Work-Study Program, Federal Perkins Loan Program, Federal Stafford Student Loan Program (subsidized and unsubsidized), and the Federal PLUS Loan Program. Eligible students may apply for the Georgia Tuition Equalization Grant, Georgia HOPE Scholarship, Georgia LEAP Grant Program, and veterans' educational benefits. Students are also encouraged to investigate the availability of grants and scholarships through community resources.

Faculty

The South University faculty includes individuals of high academic distinction. Of the 87 instructors on the Savannah campus, 40 percent hold terminal degrees within their field of expertise. In addition to teaching, faculty members strive to help students develop the requisites to appreciate knowledge and understand how experiences in the classroom and laboratory relate to professional performance in the workplace. The average student-faculty ratio is 15:1. Each student is assigned a faculty adviser who oversees the student's progress and can answer questions about academic and career concerns. Students are encouraged to discuss program-related issues with and seek academic and career advice from their faculty advisers.

Admission Requirements

To be admitted to South University, a prospective student must be a high school graduate or hold a GED and submit a minimum combined SAT I score of 830, a composite ACT score of at least 17, or a satisfactory score on the University-administered admissions examination. Students who wish to transfer must meet the criteria established for acceptance as a transfer student. International students must show a sufficient knowledge of the English language as demonstrated by a minimum score of 550 on the TOEFL. South University does accept the International Baccalaureate Diploma as meeting the requirement for high school graduation. Applicants not meeting the testing standards for general admission may be accepted under academic support admission by submitting a minimum combined SAT I score of 660, a composite ACT score of at least 14, or a satisfactory score on the University-administered admissions examination. General admission to the University does not guarantee admission to the physician assistant program; entrance into this program is gained through a formal application review and interview.

Application and Information

Applicants must complete and submit an application form, along with the general application fee, and official transcripts from all high schools and colleges attended. Faxed documents are not considered official. Applicants must also complete all tests administered by the University or submit their SAT or ACT scores to the registrar's office. Applications are accepted on a rolling basis and should be made as far in advance as possible. Application packets for the physician assistant program are available by contacting the South University Physician Assistant Department or visiting the University Web site.

Admissions officers are available weekdays from 9 a.m. to 6 p.m. and on Saturdays from 9 a.m. to noon. An appointment for an admissions interview or tour of the campus should be made in advance. For additional information, all prospective students should contact:

Director of Admissions
South University
709 Mall Boulevard
Savannah, Georgia 31406-4805
Telephone: 912-201-8000
866-629-2901 (toll-free)
Fax: 912-201-8070
E-mail: cshall@southuniversity.edu
World Wide Web: http://www.southuniversity.edu

South University is located on the south side of historic Savannah, Georgia.

SOUTH UNIVERSITY

COLUMBIA, SOUTH CAROLINA

SouthUniversity℠

The University

South University is a private academic institution dedicated to providing educational opportunities for the intellectual, social, and professional development of a diverse student population. To achieve this, the Columbia campus offers focused and balanced curricula at the associate and bachelor's degree levels in the areas of business, health sciences, information technology, and legal studies.

South University traces its heritage back to 1899 when Dr. John Draughon established Draughon's Practical Business College in Savannah. The school's early years were marked by relocation and expansion, and in 1986 the institution changed its name to South College. In 2001, the college was approved to confer master's degrees and officially became South University. Today it has grown into a multicampus system with locations in Savannah, Georgia; West Palm Beach, Florida; Montgomery, Alabama; and, most recently, Columbia, South Carolina.

The Columbia campus has a rich heritage in the Midlands area of South Carolina. Established in 1935, the institution was originally known as Columbia Commercial College and then Columbia Junior College. After becoming part of South University, program offerings were updated and expanded to meet the needs of the Columbia community. In recent years the campus has continued to grow through accreditation by the Southern Association of Colleges and Schools (SACS) and the addition of bachelor's degree programs. Enrollment has increased steadily, and graduates have been recruited by law firms, businesses, and medical institutions. The Columbia campus of South University has the only Bachelor of Science in legal studies program in the state of South Carolina, and program graduates are prepared to apply directly to law school.

In addition to classrooms and offices, the campus includes a bookstore, student lounge, career services center, and ample parking. Most students live within driving distance of the Columbia campus. Therefore, the University does not offer or operate student housing. If housing is needed, students should contact the Admissions Department.

The Columbia campus of South University has a diverse student body enrolled in both day and evening classes. Students are primarily commuters who live within 50 miles of the city. They include men and women who have enrolled directly after completing high school, who have transferred from another college or university, or who have experience in the workforce and are pursing an education that will help them take a new professional direction.

South University is accredited by the Commission on Colleges of the Southern Association of Colleges and Schools (SACS, 1866 Southern Lane, Decatur, Georgia 30033-4097; 404-679-4501) to award associate, bachelor's, master's, and doctoral degrees. The Columbia campus is licensed by the South Carolina Commission on Higher Education (1333 Main Street, Suite 200, Columbia, South Carolina 29201; 803-737-2260) to award associate and bachelor's degrees and certificates. The Columbia campus is also chartered by the state of South Carolina and approved by the South Carolina Commission on Higher Education (Veterans' Education Section) for the training of veterans and other eligible persons.

Certain programs offered at the Columbia campus have earned programmatic accreditation. The Associate in Medical Assisting degree program is accredited by the Commission on Accreditation of Allied Health Education Programs (CAAHEP, 35 East Wacker Drive, Suite 1970, Chicago, Illinois 60601; 312-553-9355) on recommendation of the Committee on Accreditation for Medical Assisting Education. The Bachelor of Science in legal studies and Associate in Paralegal Studies degree programs are approved by the American Bar Association (541 North Fairbanks Court, Chicago, Illinois 60611; 312-988-5616).

Location

Nestled in the historic district of Eau Claire, the campus is just north of downtown Columbia and the state capitol building. It is easily accessible from Interstates 20, 26, and 77, as well as the city bus route. In this urban setting, a landscaped courtyard surrounds the campus, and across the street is a city park.

Majors and Degrees

The Columbia campus of South University awards the following two-year degrees: Associate in Accounting (92 credits), Associate in Business Administration (92 credits), Associate in Computer Information Systems (92 credits), Associate in Medical Assisting (100 credits), and Associate in Paralegal Studies (104 credits).

The following four-year bachelor's degrees are awarded: Bachelor of Business Administration (184 credits) and Bachelor of Science in legal studies (180 credits).

Academic Programs

The Columbia campus of South University offers degree programs that are designed to meet the needs and objectives of students. Each curriculum combines didactic and practical educational experiences that provide students with the academic background needed to pursue the professions of their choice. In addition, faculty members strive to instill the value not only of education and professionalism but also of contribution and commitment to the advancement of community.

Each University quarter comprises ten to twelve weeks. Associate degree programs require a minimum of eight quarters to complete, and bachelor's degree programs require a minimum of twelve quarters for completion. Programs at the Columbia campus are offered on a year-round basis, providing students with the ability to work uninterrupted toward their degrees. Classes on campus begin at 8:30 a.m., Monday through Friday, and Saturday classes may be scheduled as necessary. Evening classes are in session from 6 to 9:30 p.m., Monday through Thursday. Classes may be scheduled on Friday nights or Saturdays as necessary.

Academic Facilities

South University's Columbia campus provides more than 21,000 square feet of classroom and student service areas on a 2.25-acre site. Facilities include field-related medical laboratories, new computer servers, a wireless network, two student computer labs with a total of thirty-five workstations, and both mobile and stationary LCD projectors with remote computer interaction. A well-appointed library houses a large collection that includes an extensive law library. Students may retrieve periodicals in paper or electronic form and access commercial online services, including WESTLAW, the computerized legal research service; LIRN; SearchBank; Infotract; UMI ProQuest; and the Electronic Library. Internet access is available on all computers throughout the campus.

Costs

Tuition for all programs at South University's Columbia campus for 2003–04 was $3395 per quarter for 10 to 18 credit hours, $2695 per quarter for 5 to 9 credit hours, and $1395 per quarter for 1 to 4 credit hours. Full-time students taking more than 18 credit hours per quarter were charged an additional $200 per credit hour beyond the 18 hours.

Financial Aid

South University's Office of Student Finance helps eligible students secure financial assistance to complete their studies. The University offers scholarships with awards ranging from $600 to $3000 for an academic year. Funds are limited, so students should apply as early as possible. The University also participates in several student aid programs. Forms of financial aid available through federal resources include the Federal Pell Grant Program, Federal Supplemental Educational Opportunity Grant (FSEOG) Program, Federal Work-Study Program, Federal Perkins Loan Program, Federal Stafford Student Loan Program (subsidized and unsubsidized), and the Federal PLUS Loan Program. South University employs the Federal Need Analysis Methodology, approved by the U.S. Department of Education, as a fair and equitable means of determining a family's ability to contribute to the student's educational expenses, as well as eligibility for other financial aid programs. Eligible students may apply for the South Carolina HOPE Scholarship and veterans' educational benefits. Students also are encouraged to investigate the availability of grants and scholarships through community resources.

Faculty

The South University faculty includes individuals of high academic distinction. Of the 46 instructors on the Columbia campus, 35 percent hold terminal degrees in their fields of expertise. In addition to teaching, faculty members strive to help students develop the requisites to appreciate knowledge and understand how experiences in the classroom and laboratory relate to professional performance in the workplace. The average student-faculty ratio per class is 14:1. Each student is assigned a faculty adviser who oversees the student's progress and can answer questions about academic and career concerns. Students are encouraged to discuss program-related issues with and seek academic and career advice from their faculty adviser.

Admission Requirements

To be admitted to South University, a prospective student must be a high school graduate or hold a GED and submit a minimum combined SAT I score of 830, a composite ACT score of at least 17, or a satisfactory score on the University-administered admissions examination. Students who wish to transfer must meet the criteria established for acceptance as a transfer student. International students must show a sufficient knowledge of the English language as demonstrated by a minimum score of 550 on the TOEFL. South University does accept the International Baccalaureate Diploma as meeting the requirement for high school graduation. Applicants not meeting the testing standards for general admission may be accepted under academic support admission by submitting a combined SAT I score of 660, a composite ACT score of at least 14, or a satisfactory score on the University-administered admissions examination.

Application and Information

Applicants must complete and submit an application form, along with the general application fee, and official transcripts from all high schools and colleges attended. Faxed documents are not considered official. Applicants must also complete all tests administered by the University or submit their SAT or ACT scores to the registrar's office. Applications are accepted on a rolling basis and should be made as far in advance as possible.

Admissions officers are available weekdays from 9 a.m. to 6 p.m. and on Saturdays from 9 a.m. to noon. An appointment for an admissions interview or tour of the campus should be made in advance. For additional information, all prospective students should contact:

Director of Admissions
South University
3810 Main Street
Columbia, South Carolina 29203-6443
Telephone: 803-799-9082
866-629-3031 (toll-free)
Fax: 803-799-9038
E-mail: vdebauche@southuniversity.edu
World Wide Web: http://www.southuniversity.edu

South University is located in the Eau Claire district of Columbia, South Carolina.

SOUTHWEST MISSOURI STATE UNIVERSITY

SPRINGFIELD, MISSOURI

The University

A short walk across the tree-covered Springfield campus of Southwest Missouri State University (SMSU) reveals high-tech classroom buildings, nationally acclaimed residence halls, and comfortable, quiet places to visit with friends and professors. Energetic students and friendly faculty members attest to the spirit and vitality of this major university.

More than 19,000 students, 57 percent women and 43 percent men, have come to SMSU from throughout Missouri, forty-eight other states, and more than eighty countries. Full-time students represent 85 percent of the total enrollment. Of the eight colleges within the University, the College of Business Administration enrolls the largest number of students, followed by the College of Health and Human Services, the College of Arts and Letters, the College of Education, the College of Natural and Applied Sciences, and the College of Humanities and Public Affairs.

The University's primary focus is on undergraduate education, and more than 80 percent of the students are seeking undergraduate degrees. Experienced faculty members teach courses at all levels. SMSU also offers graduate programs leading to a master's degree in forty fields as well as the Specialist in Education degree and the Doctorate of Audiology (Au.D.).

In 1995, SMSU was granted a statewide mission in public affairs by the Missouri legislature. Through this mission the University is committed to preparing students for success not only in their chosen career fields but also in their lifelong careers as citizens and leaders. This is accomplished through the curriculum, optional service-learning courses, special lectures and forums, and other opportunities to develop a greater understanding of the issues facing society. The John Templeton Foundation has named SMSU to its Honor Roll for Character-Building Colleges, a designation that recognizes colleges and universities that emphasize character building as an integral part of the college experience.

The University has more than 250 student organizations, including social, service, religious, political, and departmental organizations. There is an extensive intramural and recreational sports program. SMSU is a member of NCAA Division I and participates in men's intercollegiate baseball, basketball, cross-country, football (Division I-AA), golf, indoor and outdoor track, soccer, swimming, and tennis. NCAA Division I women's sports include basketball, cross-country, field hockey, golf, softball, swimming, tennis, track and field, and volleyball.

The University is accredited by the North Central Association of Colleges and Schools and has additional accreditation by AACSB International–The Association to Advance Collegiate Schools of Business; the National Association of Schools of Music; the National League for Nursing Accrediting Commission; the American Chemical Society; the Council on Social Work Education; the Computing Sciences Accreditation Board; the National Recreation and Park Association; the American Association for Leisure and Recreation; the American Home Economics Association; the National Athletic Trainers Association; the American Speech, Language, and Hearing Association; the National Council on Education for the Deaf; and the American Dietetics Association.

Location

Springfield, a city of 150,000, is Missouri's third-largest city and one of the fastest growing in the country. Located in Ozark Mountain country, one of the most popular entertainment, vacation, and resort areas in the nation, Springfield is within an hour's drive of several major lakes (Table Rock, Taneycomo, Stockton, Pomme de Terre, and Bull Shoals). SMSU students may take advantage of the cultural and career opportunities of the metropolitan area surrounding the University and still enjoy many outdoor recreational activities in the Ozarks.

Majors and Degrees

SMSU offers more than 140 programs of study in forty-two academic departments. Preprofessional programs in many fields are also available. The academic departments are accountancy; agriculture; antiquities; art and design; biology; biomedical sciences; chemistry; communication sciences and disorders; communications and mass media; computer information systems; computer science; consumer and family studies; defense and strategic studies; economics; English; finance and general business; geography, geology, and planning; gerontology; health, physical education, and recreation; history; library science; management; marketing and quantitative analysis; mathematics; military science; modern and classical languages; music; nursing; philosophy; physics, astronomy, and materials science; political science; psychology; reading and special education; religious studies; social work; sociology and anthropology; sports medicine and athletic training; teacher education; technology; and theater and dance. Individualized majors are available through the University College.

Academic Programs

A fall semester and a spring semester constitute the academic year; a summer session is also offered. All students take a base of 43 to 54 semester hours of general education courses in English, mathematics, speech, physical well-being, American studies, the natural world, culture and society, and self-understanding. A bachelor's degree requires 125 semester hours. Each degree program has specific course requirements and may require certain minimum grade point averages.

In addition to the traditional classroom experiences, SMSU offers one of the largest cooperative education programs in the Midwest, Army ROTC, practicums and internships, interactive video courses, and special-topics courses. A highly successful Honors College has attracted significant numbers of high-achieving students.

Students may receive credit by examination for selected subjects through the Advanced Placement (AP) Program, the International Baccalaureate (IB) Program, and the College-Level Examination Program (CLEP), as well as through departmental examinations.

Off-Campus Programs

SMSU is a member of the International Student Exchange Program (ISEP) and the National Student Exchange (NSE). A semester-abroad program, based in London, is offered to SMSU students for credit. Students may also take a great variety of short-term study tours for credit. In the past, these tours have visited China, England, Russia, and Spain.

Field studies are a required part of many academic programs. Students may take marine biology courses during the summer at the Gulf Coast Research Laboratory in Mississippi. Students in anthropology and antiquities can participate in archaeological research projects. Students majoring in consumer and family studies, recreation, social work, and many other academic programs participate in supervised internships or practicums. Geology students have a variety of field opportunities, including those offered at a permanent base camp in Colorado.

Academic Facilities

SMSU libraries, in Meyer Library and two branches, have more than 1.5 million items, including more than 640,000 cataloged items and approximately 4,800 periodicals. Meyer Library is a depository for federal and state government publications and is a full United Nations depository. The library has a map collection, a large reference collection, textbooks, curriculum guides, special learning materials, a curriculum library with a collection of children's literature, extensive back files of journals and newspapers, a variety of compact disc indexes, the online catalog and circulation systems, a Macintosh computer lab, and equipment adapted for students with disabilities. Meyer Library is open more than 100 hours per week.

Students in the sciences have access to 13-inch and 16-inch telescopes, an electron microscope, a thin-film polymer laboratory, a molecular beam epitaxy laboratory, and other well-equipped laboratories. Computer science and computer information systems students have the opportunity to work on the state-of-the-art, full-scale computer systems as well as minicomputer and microcomputer systems. Students may link to mainframe systems (IBM ES 9000 and several IBM RS 6000 units) with personal computers via modem. Each residence hall has computer facilities.

The Public Affairs Classroom Building, the University's $20.25-million classroom facility, houses twenty-one classrooms, seven laboratories, seven seminar rooms, 161 offices, and the College of Humanities and Public Affairs. Glass Hall is home for more than 3,100 business majors and is recognized as an outstanding teaching facility. Laboratories, studio facilities, and practice rooms are available for science, music, and art students. There are also excellent facilities for theater and dance. The University Childcare Center and Greenwood Laboratory School provide facilities for students in education, psychology, and other courses that require interaction with and observation of children. The University also has various research and service centers, such as the Sports Medicine Clinic, the Speech and Hearing Clinic, the Center for Gerontological Studies, the Center for Business Research and Development, the Archaeological Research Center, and the Center for Ozark Studies.

Costs

Fees are assessed based upon the number of hours for which a student enrolls. Most undergraduate students take 14–16 credit hours per semester. Fees can be found on the Web at http://www.smsu.edu/costs. Fees are subject to change by the University Board of Governors.

The University offers nine options for on-campus living. The average cost of room and board is approximately $4500 per year. The University estimates annual personal expenses (exclusive of automobile-related expenses) to be $800.

Financial Aid

Financial aid at SMSU consists of outstanding scholarship programs, Federal Pell Grants, Federal Stafford Student Loans, work-study programs, Federal Perkins Loans, Federal Supplemental Educational Opportunity Grants, Federal Parent Loans for Undergraduate Students, Missouri Student Grants, and SMSU short-term loans. Grants and other aid are provided for selected student athletes, and a student employment service is available for students seeking part-time work either on or off campus. March 31 is the priority date for scholarship and financial aid application. Contact the Financial Aid Office for information about scholarships that have earlier application deadlines.

A financial aid and scholarship booklet may be obtained by writing to the Student Financial Aid Office. The Free Application for Federal Student Aid (FAFSA) is the preferred application form; however, other financial aid assessment forms may be used.

Faculty

There are nearly 700 full-time faculty members; more than 80 percent hold doctorates or terminal degrees in their fields of study. Faculty members work closely with students as academic advisers in their area of specialization.

Student Government

The Student Government Association, the representative body of the student community, is composed of students who work toward problem solving, campus improvements, and meeting the needs of the SMSU student body. The association is organized into executive, legislative, and judicial branches.

Admission Requirements

For freshman applicants, requirements are based upon a combination of high school class rank or GPA and ACT composite scores. Students automatically qualify if they have a selection index (sum of class rank percentile and ACT percentile) of 106 or higher. These requirements are for the fall 2004 semester. In addition, students must meet the 16-unit core curriculum requirement. Transfer students must have at least a 2.0 (C) average in courses that are accepted in transfer to SMSU. International students must present evidence of an above-average record and are encouraged to write to the Office of International Student Services for specific admission information.

The application deadline for the University is one month before the start of each semester. Students are encouraged to apply early to receive preference in housing and registration.

Application and Information

For more information about undergraduate programs and admission to Southwest Missouri State University, students should contact:

Office of Admissions
Southwest Missouri State University
901 South National
Springfield, Missouri 65804
Telephone: 417-836-5517
800-492-7900 (toll-free)
800-836-4770 (TDD)
E-mail: smsuinfo@smsu.edu
World Wide Web: http://www.smsu.edu

A view of Carrington Hall—the SMSU administration building.

SPELMAN COLLEGE

ATLANTA, GEORGIA

The College

Spelman, a private, independent, historically black, four-year liberal arts college for women, was founded in 1881. The campus has grown from 9 acres of drill ground and five frame barracks used for federal troops after the Civil War to 32 acres and twenty-four buildings. As an integral part of the Atlanta University Center, Spelman benefits from proximity to and cooperation with the other member institutions, but it maintains its own identity nonetheless, thus offering outstanding opportunities for the education of women for leadership roles.

A focal point of campus activity for the 2,070 women enrolled is the Manley College Center, which houses the dining hall, a food court, faculty and student lounges, student government offices, and some administrative offices. There is a varied program of student and professional cultural activities on the campus. Many of the extracurricular activities are planned and sponsored by the Student Government Association. Others are presented by departmental honor societies and clubs, excellent dance groups, and both jazz and classical instrumental ensembles. The strong tradition in fine arts at Spelman gives students maximum cultural exposure through the renowned Spelman Glee Club, the Spelman-Morehouse Chorus, and the Spelman-Morehouse Players. Health and physical education facilities include a gymnasium, tennis courts, a swimming pool, bowling lanes, dance studios, and a weight room.

Student thought is expressed through several publications: *Reflections,* the yearbook; *Spotlight,* the newspaper; and *Focus,* the literary magazine. Religious life and services form an important part of campus life. Opportunities to experience fellowship in a meaningful fashion, special convocations, and counseling are provided.

Location

Spelman College is located in Atlanta, "The Gateway to the South," a city that is rapidly becoming one of the most dynamic and vital urban areas in the country. Proximity to other colleges and universities in the area provides additional educational, social, and cultural opportunities. Spelman College is one of six institutions that constitute the Atlanta University Center (AUC) consortium.

The city is one of the most exciting learning laboratories imaginable. Here, women can observe politics at work and can meet some of the world's leaders. As an urban center with crucial social problems, Atlanta challenges students to become involved in community programs. An extensive community services program coordinates the placement of students in community agencies.

Majors and Degrees

Spelman offers the Bachelor of Arts and the Bachelor of Science degrees. Majors are offered in art, biochemistry, biology, chemistry, child development, comparative women's studies, computer science, drama and dance, economics, engineering (through participating schools), English, environmental science, French, history, mathematics, music, philosophy, physics, political science, psychology, sociology/anthropology, and Spanish. An independent major option is also available. Special minors are available in dance, international studies, management and organization, teacher certification, women's studies, and writing. Premedical, predentistry, and prelaw sequences are offered.

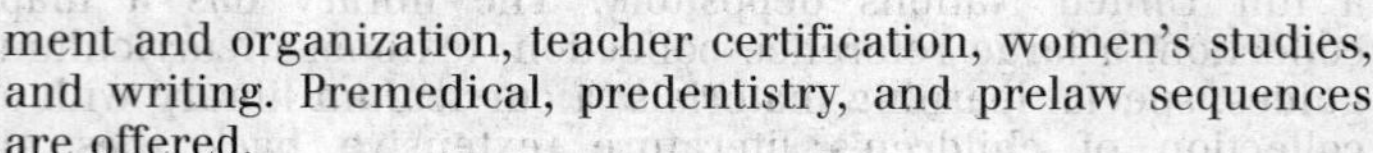

Spelman participates in a dual-degree engineering program through which students may combine three years of liberal arts courses at Spelman with two years of engineering studies at Georgia Institute of Technology, California Institute of Technology, Dartmouth College, University of Florida, Columbia University, Rochester Institute of Technology, Boston University, Rensselaer Polytechnic Institute, Auburn University, North Carolina A&T, and the University of Alabama in Huntsville. Students receive a bachelor's degree from each institution upon completing the program.

Academic Program

Spelman operates on a two-semester academic calendar. Through its core curriculum, the College introduces students to the principal branches of learning—languages and literature, natural sciences, mathematics, social sciences, fine arts, and humanities. All students are enrolled in courses designed to develop effective writing and reading skills and logical and imaginative thinking. An honors program is offered to academically outstanding students.

Credit-hour requirements vary with the major area. The core curriculum requirement includes a two-semester interdisciplinary survey course, the African Diaspora in the World, English composition, foreign language, health and physical education, history, literature, and mathematics. A minimum of 4 credits is also required in each of the following areas: fine arts, humanities, natural sciences, and social sciences.

Off-Campus Programs

Under the AUC consortium, four undergraduate colleges, one graduate and professional university, and one graduate theological seminary share facilities, resources, and activities. Through cross-registration, Spelman students may elect to take such courses as business administration, mass communication, and social welfare at the other undergraduate institutions.

Academic Facilities

The College's newest building, The Albro, Falconer, Manley Science Center, is state-of-the-art and was completed in 2000. It is a site for intellectual exchange and scientific creativity, accommodates current research and teaching practices, and supports the use of technology in teaching. The Camille O. Hanks Cosby Academic Center provides classrooms and laboratories for students studying in the humanities. It houses several interdisciplinary programs and departments and offices for faculty members in English, history, philosophy, religion, and modern foreign languages. The center also features an auditorium, an art museum, the Spelman College archives, the Ennis Cosby Reading Room, educational media, a writing center, and the Women's Research and Resource Center. The Fine Arts Building houses a small, up-to-date proscenium theater, music and art studios, and practice rooms. Spelman students are entitled to use the facilities of the Robert Woodruff Library of the Atlanta University Center, which has 500,000 volumes and a microfilm depository. Two living-learning centers house conference rooms and residence hall facilities. These provide space for work outside the classroom.

Costs

Tuition costs in 2003–04 were $11,950 per year; room and board were $7625 per year; fees were $2175. Total costs for students living on campus were $21,750; for students living off campus, costs were $14,125. Additional costs include transportation, $950; books, $750; and personal expenses, $1550. These costs are subject to change.

Financial Aid

The College makes every effort to assist students with financial need through scholarships, grants, loans, and work-study programs. The amount of aid is determined by need as indicated by the Free Application for Federal Student Aid (FAFSA). Although the Spelman Financial Aid Application deadline is April 1, applicants are advised to begin the process much earlier. Financial aid funds are limited and are awarded on a first-come, first-served basis. Spelman cannot meet the full documented need of every student who applies for financial aid. Those students whose financial aid files are complete by March 1 receive priority processing and consideration.

The Spelman scholarship program is meant to encourage academic excellence and to recognize outstanding achievement. Scholarships are awarded to entering first-year and continuing students on a competitive basis. Consideration is given to academic and personal achievement as evidenced by academic records, standardized test scores, leadership, special talent, character, community service, and, in some cases, financial need. Interested students must submit the Spelman College Application for Admission to be considered for Spelman scholarships. Additional application materials are required for the Women in Science and Engineering (WISE) Program Scholarship, and the Bonner Scholar Program.

Faculty

Spelman's full-time faculty numbers 156 members. More than 83 percent hold doctoral or other terminal degrees. The low student-faculty ratio (13:1) permits individualized instruction and small classes.

Student Government

Every student is a member of the Student Government Association (SGA). The SGA, with the approval of the administration, sets policies that govern student life. Meetings of the association are announced and held regularly, and all students are urged to attend.

Admission Requirements

Applicants for first-year admission are selected on the basis of their high school records, SAT I or ACT scores, recommendations, and personal information submitted in the application for admission. First-year students are admitted for the fall term only.

A limited number of spaces are available each term for transfer students. Applicants for transfer admission are selected based upon their complete academic records, recommendations, personal information submitted in the application for admission, and whether space is available in requested academic majors. In some instances, applicants who have achieved the equivalent of senior status are not considered.

The College selects qualified women candidates without regard to race; color; national, ethnic, or regional origin; physical challenge; or religious preference. The College seeks to admit students whose credentials give evidence of potential for academic success at Spelman and who demonstrate personal characteristics of high motivation, purpose, and integrity. Interviews are not required. Prospective applicants may request individual information sessions or tours through the Office of Admissions and Orientation Services.

Application and Information

Completed first-year applications for admission under the Early Action Plan must be postmarked and mailed by November 15 of the senior year. Notification of the admission decision is made by December 31. Completed regular first-year applications must be postmarked and mailed by February 1 of the senior year. Notification of the admission decision is April 1.

Completed transfer applications for the fall term must be postmarked and mailed by February 1. Notification of the admission decision is April 1. Completed transfer applications for the spring term must be postmarked and mailed by November 1. Notification of the admission decision is made by December 1. For application forms and additional information, contact:

Office of Admissions and Orientation Services
Box 277
Spelman College
Atlanta, Georgia 30314
Telephone: 404-681-3643
800-982-2411 (toll-free)
E-mail: admiss@spelman.edu
World Wide Web: http://www.spelman.edu

Sisters Chapel at Spelman College.

SPRINGFIELD COLLEGE

SPRINGFIELD, MASSACHUSETTS

The College

Ever since Professor James A. Naismith invented the game of basketball in 1891, Springfield College has enjoyed an international reputation as a pioneer in physical education and wellness. Founded in 1885 to train leaders for the YMCA, Springfield College has grown and expanded upon these fields and is known today for expertise in sports and movement activities, allied health sciences, human and social services, and the arts and sciences. Guiding all aspects of student-life is the distinctive "humanics" philosophy, which emphasizes education of the whole person—spirit, mind, and body—for leadership in service to others. Community service is encouraged, and many courses augment classroom learning with fieldwork in community programs that are related to studies. Springfield College is accredited by the New England Association of Schools and Colleges and serves more than 3,000 undergraduate and graduate students at its main campus. Another 1,900 students are enrolled in weekend or evening programs of its School of Human Services at eight satellite campuses around the country. At Springfield, cocurricular activities and athletics form an integral part of the undergraduate experience. There are more than 100 organizations and opportunities for involvement including drama, music, theater, dance, and other clubs. The College offers the largest undergraduate athletics program in the nation for an institution of its size. Ninety percent of undergraduates play intramural sports and more than 30 percent participate in intercollegiate athletics. There are men's and women's teams in basketball, cross-country, gymnastics, lacrosse, soccer, swimming, tennis, track, and volleyball. Women's teams also include field hockey and softball, and there are additional men's teams in baseball, football, golf, and wrestling.

Nine campus residence halls provide guaranteed on-campus housing for four years. Students may choose coeducational or single-sex accommodations, and seniors may elect to live off campus.

Location

Situated on Lake Massasoit in the Pioneer Valley of Western Massachusetts, Springfield College is located in Springfield, the fourth-largest city in the state. A wide range of social, cultural, and athletic activities enhance the valley, as well as twelve other colleges and universities. In Springfield, art, science, and historical museums surround the Quadrangle in the heart of downtown. Springfield Symphony Hall is the site of concerts, plays, musicals, and dance performances. The Springfield Civic Center is home to the American Hockey League's Springfield Falcons and host of the annual Tip-Off Classic, the official start of the college basketball season. The Basketball Hall of Fame is an international attraction.

Nearby cities and towns offer additional attractions. Northampton bustles with trendy shops, coffeehouses, galleries, theater productions, health food stores, nightclubs, and restaurants. The Holyoke Mall at Ingleside contains three floors of stores and restaurants. The Berkshire Hills offer hiking, skiing, biking, and other outdoor activities. Boston and New York City can be reached by car in 90 minutes and 3 hours, respectively. Vermont is less than 1 hour away.

Majors and Degrees

Springfield College offers Bachelor of Science or Bachelor of Arts degrees in the following programs: applied exercise science, applied sociology, art, art therapy, athletic training, biology, business management, communications/sports journalism, computer graphics, computer and information sciences, criminal justice, dance, early childhood education, elementary education, emergency medical services management, English, general studies, health services administration, health studies, mathematics, movement and sports studies, occupational therapy, physical education, physical therapy, physician assistant studies, psychology, recreation management, rehabilitation and disability studies, secondary education, sports biology, sports management, therapeutic recreation services, and undeclared major. Physical therapy is an entry-level 5½-year program culminating in a Master of Science degree. Physician assistant studies is an entry-level five-year program culminating in a Master of Science degree.

Academic Program

Consistent with Springfield College's humanics philosophy, undergraduate education is designed to promote an understanding of how the spirit, mind, and body work together in preparing students for a life of leadership in service to others. This approach combines theory and practice, augmenting classroom learning with extensive fieldwork opportunities.

The College has a two-semester academic calendar. To graduate, students must complete 130 credits including required courses for the major field of study, electives, and required courses for all students (English, philosophy, social science, health, history, mathematics, and natural science). Qualified students may also earn credit through the Advanced Placement Program and the College-Level Examination Program administered by the College Board.

Off-Campus Programs

Following the theory that the community is the best laboratory, Springfield College maintains relationships with businesses and human service agencies. Its fieldwork component is among the most extensive and challenging offered by institutions of higher learning. Fieldwork sites have included the Basketball Hall of Fame, the American Hockey League, the *Boston Globe,* YMCAs, the American Heart Association, MassMutual, Children's Hospital, the Hilton Head Crowne Plaza, the Reebok Health and Fitness Center, Baystate Medical Center, parks and recreation departments, and other venues.

The College's cooperative education program links students with work experience in their fields of studies, enhancing their learning and providing income to help finance their education. The program is open to second-, third-, and fourth-year students who average 15 to 20 hours per week of study-related work.

Study-abroad programs are available. Closer to home, students may enroll in courses at some of the other colleges in the Springfield area.

Academic Facilities

On Springfield College's 165-acre main campus, historic red brick campus buildings combine with such modern amenities as computer labs, a computer-based language laboratory, and a new human anatomy laboratory.

The Allied Health Science Center houses laboratories for performance assessment and exercise physiology/biomechanics, as well as an isokinetic muscle-testing device. The Physical Education Complex combines the Art Linkletter Natatorium;

Blake Arena, with seating for 2,000; Keith Locker Room and Training Facility; and Winston Paul Academic Center, with teaching gymnasiums and handball/racquetball courts. Other athletic facilities include Benedum Field with Astroturf, eight tennis courts, two baseball diamonds, one softball diamond, an eight-lane outdoor track, a weight room, and an indoor jogging track. The Wellness Center offers services and equipment for fitness testing and assessment, computerized check-in and tracking, exercise prescription, and personal training. The Strength and Conditioning Center is equipped with a wide selection of free weights and is designed as a classroom/laboratory.

The 20,000-square-foot Visual Arts Center includes airy, light-filled studios and an exhibition gallery. The multipurpose 300-seat Fuller Performing Arts Center features a proscenium theater and lecture hall.

The College's 52-acre East Campus, located 1 mile from the main campus, comprises a forest ecosystem with camping facilities, a picnic grove, and 2 miles of lake shoreline. It is a working laboratory and training ground for students in a variety of academic programs. The Springfield College Child Development Center, also located at East Campus, is licensed by the Massachusetts Office for Children and accredited by the National Association for the Education of Young Children. It provides an exceptional and convenient facility for teacher-supervised fieldwork for students concentrating in various education and psychology programs.

Babson Library is the College's major resource center with more than 650,000 microfilms, 170,000 books, 2,200 videos, 670 periodical subscriptions, 25,000 bound periodical volumes, and an archives collection. The library maintains complete files of the Education Resources Information Center, Human Relations Area Files, and the theses collections of the College's physical education and recreation and tourism management departments. Students have Web access to the library's research indexes and databases. The library also houses the Information and Technology Center, which features classrooms, a training/multimedia classroom, and an open computer laboratory.

Costs

For the 2003–04 academic year, tuition cost $19,210, required fees were $200, room was $3780, and board cost $3740. Costs for books and personal expenses vary depending upon the individual student and course of study.

Financial Aid

Students who feel they do not have sufficient funds to pay the costs of their educations are encouraged to apply for financial aid in the form of grants, loans, and student employment. Financial aid offered by Springfield College is based on need, intellectual promise, leadership, and character. The College gives full consideration to students who submit the Free Application for Federal Student Aid (FAFSA) and the College Scholarship Service Financial Aid PROFILE by March 15 for first-year students and May 1 for transfer students. Students not eligible for financial aid may still be considered for institutional employment.

Faculty

A committed group of 330 faculty members allows for a student-teacher ratio of 12:1. Small classes enable students to develop academic relationships with their professors, most of whom hold doctorates or other terminal degrees appropriate to their field. Springfield College's small-college environment attracts highly dedicated faculty members who share a commitment to students' whole development.

Student Government

Student government at Springfield College is best characterized as government by and for the students. The Student Association and the Board of Governors are responsible for planning and implementing student programs. The Beveridge Student Center houses the offices of these organizations, which are supervised by students under the guidance of the director of student activities.

Admission Requirements

In keeping with its humanics philosophy, Springfield College evaluates applicants on the basis of academic and personal factors. Applications for regular admission or early decision must be submitted to the Office of Undergraduate Admissions, including a completed application form, a high school transcript, one personal reference, and SAT I scores. Transfer students must also submit a transcript and a dean's report from each college attended. Springfield College's admissions staff is interested in getting to know each applicant and encourages candidates to get to know the College. Personal interviews, campus tours, and open-house programs provide opportunities to visit the College and experience campus life. The staff also facilitates contact with alumni and current students.

Application and Information

Springfield College's Admissions Committee reviews applications upon receiving them. For the 2004–05 academic year, applications are due April 1, 2004 for first-year students and August 1, 2004 for transfer students. For the 2005 athletic training and physical therapy programs, applications are due December 1, 2004. For the 2005 physician assistant and occupational therapy programs, applications are due January 15, 2005. Application forms (online applications are available from the Web site listed below) and information may be obtained from:

Office of Admissions
Springfield College
263 Alden Street
Box M
Springfield, Massachusetts 01109
Telephone: 413-748-3136
800-343-1257 (toll-free)
E-mail: admissions@spfldcol.edu
World Wide Web: http://www.springfieldcollege.edu

Students on the campus of Springfield College.

STANFORD UNIVERSITY

STANFORD, CALIFORNIA

The University

The Leland Stanford Junior University, referred to today simply as Stanford University, was founded in 1885 by Senator and Mrs. Leland Stanford, who devoted their entire fortune and their estate to its establishment in memory of their only child, Leland Jr., who died at an age when many young men and women are planning a college education. Leland Stanford, a distinguished businessman, governor of California, and U.S. senator, patterned the University after the great European universities. He set a pattern for students to receive a broad liberal education, as well as a practical one, that was remarkable for its time—one that would cultivate the imagination and develop character.

Although the University has grown and changed in many ways over the years, it is very much a product of its physical setting and of its early educational goals of practicality, humanism, and excellence. In terms of enrollment, Stanford is a medium-sized university, but its campus consists of more than 8,180 acres. Frederick Olmsted, the designer of New York's Central Park and America's foremost landscape architect of his day, was commissioned to locate the original central campus, indicate the layout and general character of the buildings, and plan the grounds. These original buildings with buff sandstone walls, red-tiled roofs, and long sandstone arcades still constitute the center of the campus today. Over the years, newer structures have been built to blend with the original architecture.

There are 14,454 students enrolled at the University; 6,654 are undergraduates. Undergraduate students come to Stanford from every state in the Union and about sixty other countries. Although they represent widely differing backgrounds and interests, all have displayed energy, intellectual curiosity, and commitment to their education both in and out of the classroom. Freshmen are required to live on campus. The undergraduate housing system includes seventy-six residential facilities, including academic, cross-cultural, Greek and language theme and focus houses; self-managed houses; apartments; suites; and traditional dormitories. Most students choose to live on campus all four years. Stanford supports a strong program of education in the residential setting to supplement students' classroom programs. Some faculty and staff members live in the residences; others come for meals and serve as guest speakers.

The scope of extracurricular activities reflects the diversity of backgrounds, interests, abilities, and experiences of the student body, and more than 500 organized student groups are available. These include a wide variety of academic, political, religious, social, and ethnic associations. In addition, students actively participate in music, drama, and journalism projects. The University's extensive athletic facilities include an 85,500-seat stadium, a 7,391-seat pavilion, a championship golf course, a fourteen-court tennis complex, and a three-pool swimming complex. Stanford fields men's varsity teams in baseball, basketball, crew, cross-country, fencing, football, golf, gymnastics, sailing, soccer, swimming and diving, tennis, track and field, volleyball, water polo, and wrestling. Women's varsity teams are fielded in basketball, crew, cross-country, fencing, field hockey, golf, gymnastics, lacrosse, sailing, soccer, softball, swimming and diving, synchronized swimming, tennis, track and field, volleyball, and water polo. About twenty additional club sports are available, and extensive intramural programs are also offered.

The University provides many student services, including academic advising, a health center, counseling and psychological services, and career development.

Location

Stanford is adjacent to the suburban communities of Palo Alto and Menlo Park, 30 miles south of San Francisco. Extensive cultural opportunities are available in the area. The famed Monterey Bay is 75 miles to the south; Sierra Nevada, where there is skiing in the winter, and Yosemite National Park are each 4 hours away.

Majors and Degrees

Stanford awards the Bachelor of Arts (B.A.), Bachelor of Science (B.S.), and Bachelor of Arts and Sciences (B.A.S.) degrees. Students may pursue the following major, minor, and honors areas of study: African and African-American studies; American studies; anthropological science; archaeology; art and art history; Asian-American studies; Asian languages (Chinese and Japanese); biological sciences; chemistry; Chicana/o studies; classics; communication; comparative literature; comparative studies in race and ethnicity; cultural and social anthropology; drama; East Asian studies; economics; education (honors only); English (creative writing interdisciplinary emphasis); English literature (minor only); ethics in society (honors only); feminist studies; French; German studies; history; human biology; individually designed majors; interdisciplinary studies in the humanities; international relations; Italian; Jewish studies (minor only); Latin American studies (honors only); linguistics; mathematical and computational science; mathematics; medieval studies; music; music, science, and technology; Native American studies; philosophy; philosophy and religious studies; physics; applied physics (minor only); political science; psychology; public policy; religious studies; science, technology, and society (major and honors); Slavic languages and literature; sociology; Spanish and Portuguese; statistics; symbolic systems; and urban studies.

Academic Programs

Stanford provides the means for undergraduates to acquire a liberal education—one that broadens their knowledge and awareness in each of the major areas of human knowledge, significantly deepens it in one or two, and prepares them for a lifetime of learning. The curriculum allows considerable flexibility. Individually designed majors, double majors that combine bachelor's and master's degrees, tutorials, and honors programs are all available for qualified students. A special emphasis is placed on encouraging close faculty and student interaction in the first two years through Stanford Introductory Studies, which includes freshman seminars. Students may declare a major at any time but must do so by the end of the sophomore year. Freshmen are assigned to general advisers upon entering; when they declare a major, they are assigned to an adviser from the faculty of the major department or program. To earn the B.A., B.S., or B.A.S. degree, students must complete 180 units; fulfill writing, general education, and foreign language requirements; and complete the requirements of at least one major department or program. All students take a three-quarter "Introduction to the Humanities" sequence as well as three courses (with at least one in each of the areas) in the humanities and social sciences. A requirement in natural sciences, applied science and technology, and mathematics may be fulfilled by three certified courses in these areas (no more than two in the same area). One certified course in at least two of the three areas of world cultures, American cultures, and gender studies is also required. Stanford's commitment to a broad liberal arts education is expressed through the yearlong course requirement "Introduction to the Humanities." The courses build an intellectual foundation in the study of human thought, values, beliefs, creativity, and culture. They also enhance students' skills in analysis, reasoning, argumentation, and oral and written expression. Students may select from a variety of courses that share these common goals. At least 45 units (including the last 18) must be completed at Stanford. With certain limited exceptions, no more than 90 quarter units of credit for work done elsewhere may be counted toward the bachelor's degree at Stanford.

Entering students may be allowed up to 45 units of credit on the basis of successful scores on the College Board's Advanced Placement tests or the International Baccalaureate examinations.

Off-Campus Programs

Stanford has overseas study programs in Australia, Beijing, Berlin, Florence, Kyoto, Oxford, Paris, and Santiago. Students may attend these centers for a three-, six-, or nine-month period, obtaining full academic credit. The teaching staff at each center consists of regular Stanford professors and resident academic staff members of the host country. Stanford also provides a special opportunity for students to study classics in Rome, Italy, through a consortium arrangement with other universities. About thirty percent of each graduating class participate in overseas programs.

Stanford students also have the opportunity to study in the nation's capital under the Stanford-in-Washington program. In addition, Stanford offers exchange programs with Dartmouth College, Howard University, Morehouse College, and Spelman College.

Academic Facilities

Stanford's library collection consists of more than 8 million books and journals and thousands of other materials spread among the main Green Library, the Meyer Undergraduate Library, and eighteen branch and department libraries. The undergraduate library serves as the hub of undergraduate resources and contains study carrels, classrooms, listening rooms, and a well-equipped language library with tapes and texts for nearly 100 languages. The Green Library houses the library system's central collections and also holds maps, microtexts, newspapers, government documents, rare books, and special collections, including writings of such notables as Sir Isaac Newton, Martin Luther, William Butler Yeats, and John Steinbeck. An added benefit for researchers is the cooperative link between Stanford's libraries and the University of California at Berkeley's library system.

Stanford's facilities are outstanding and include well-equipped classrooms, laboratories, computer facilities, and research centers. Among the University's many distinguished facilities are the Beckman Center for Molecular and Genetic Medicine; the John C. Blume Earthquake Engineering Center; the Remote Sensing Laboratory; the Stanford Linear Accelerator Center; the Hoover Institution on War, Revolution, and Peace; the Center for Economic Policy Research; the Institute for International Studies; and the Clark Center, housing the Bio-X Program for Bioengineering, Biomedics, and the Biosciences. In addition, the Jasper Ridge Biological Preserve constitutes a natural laboratory for biology and ecology students, and the Hopkins Marine Station in Pacific Grove, California, offers students an excellent opportunity to study marine biology in a natural habitat.

Costs

Tuition for 2004–05 is $29,847. Room and board costs average $9500. The cost of books is estimated at $1215 per year. Personal expenses are estimated at $1815 per year.

Financial Aid

Admission at Stanford is need blind. Nearly 75 percent of its undergraduates receive various types of financial assistance from Stanford and/or outside sources, totaling more than $101 million annually. Awards range in value depending on need and are renewable for each of the four undergraduate years on the basis of continuing need. Home value is capped at three times the annual parent income before home equity is determined in financial need calculations. There are also opportunities for students and their parents to secure long-term loans to help defray college costs. To apply for aid, applicants should complete the Free Application for Federal Student Aid (FAFSA) and the College Scholarship Service PROFILE. All financial aid applicants are expected to apply for Federal Pell Grants. California residents applying for financial aid must apply for Cal Grants, which require the FAFSA and the high school grade point average certification.

Many students work on campus during the academic year, and opportunities for off-campus part-time employment are numerous.

Faculty

Stanford has 1,749 faculty members. A high proportion of the full-time professors are involved in undergraduate teaching and advising. Stanford's current community of scholars includes 17 living Nobel laureates, 4 Pulitzer Prize winners, 1 winner of the Congressional Medal of Honor, 23 MacArthur Fellows, 21 recipients of the National Medal of Science, 4 National Medal of Technology recipients, 224 members of the American Academy of Arts and Sciences, 133 members of the National Academy of Sciences, 84 National Academy of Engineering members, 25 members of the National Academy of Education, 43 American Philosophical Society members, 6 Wolf Foundation Prize for Mathematics winners, 6 winners of the Koret Foundation Prize, and 3 Presidential Medal of Freedom winners. The student-faculty ratio is 7:1. All faculty members keep regular office hours, and students are encouraged to develop contacts with the faculty in and out of the classroom for advice and guidance.

Student Government

The Associated Students of Stanford University (ASSU) includes all registered students and serves as a forum for the expression of student opinion through its executive and legislative branches. The ASSU plans and executes numerous programs and activities. Students have many opportunities to become actively involved on councils, committees, and panels that offer interaction with professors and staff members. Many of the concrete and philosophical changes that have taken place at the University are attributable to student initiative, input, and interaction.

Admission Requirements

Admission is highly competitive, with 18,628 applications received for the 2003–04 entering class of 1,640 students. The University seeks an able and diverse student body, and no single criterion determines admission. Students are evaluated individually on the basis of their academic record, test scores, nonacademic achievements, and personal qualities. Because opportunities vary tremendously, students are judged on how well they have used the resources available to them. Every candidate for undergraduate admission must submit SAT I or ACT scores. College Board SAT II Subject Test scores are strongly recommended; Writing and Math IIC tests are preferred; any additional tests should be in the student's strongest subject areas. Transfer students, entering either the sophomore or the junior class, are admitted annually in the fall quarter only. The University does not use any racial, religious, ethnic, geographic, or sex-related quotas in admissions.

Application and Information

Application forms and other information about Stanford may be obtained from the Office of Admission. Detailed course descriptions and University policies can be accessed through the Stanford Bulletin via Stanford's Web pages. Copies can be purchased through the bookstore (telephone: 800-533-2670). Applications for the freshman class must be postmarked by December 15. Regular review applicants are notified around April 1. Stanford also offers a nonbinding, single-choice early action option, with a deadline of November 1. Early action applicants are notified approximately six weeks after the deadline. The deadline for the completion of transfer applications for autumn-quarter admission is March 15.

Office of Undergraduate Admission
520 Lasuen Mall
Room 232
Old Union
Stanford University
Stanford, California 94305-3005
Telephone: 650-723-2091
Fax: 650-723-6050
E-mail: admission@stanford.edu
World Wide Web: http://admission.stanford.edu

STATE UNIVERSITY OF NEW YORK AT BINGHAMTON

BINGHAMTON, NEW YORK

The University

In less than sixty years, Binghamton University has established itself as one of the best public universities in the nation, distinguished by its outstanding undergraduate programs, its vibrant campus culture, and its innovative and growing research initiatives. Recognized as "the premier public university of the northeast" and consistently ranked among the nation's top public universities by *U.S. News & World Report*, Binghamton offers an outstanding educational opportunity in a friendly, supportive environment.

As a medium-sized research university, Binghamton combines the best of the small college environment with the access to the academic choices and innovation of a research university. Undergraduates work alongside faculty members and graduate students in research laboratories and artistic pursuits. Much like the faculty members, students are encouraged to cross disciplinary boundaries to pursue their interests; chemistry majors are in the orchestra, art majors pursue computer studies, and math majors act in plays.

The students who enroll at Binghamton represent a wide range of socioeconomic, educational, and ethnic backgrounds. They are an academically motivated group who pride themselves on being individual thinkers and who are encouraged to broaden their educational and social experience. The campus embraces a student-centered philosophy that encourages students to pursue hands-on opportunities and to take charge of their learning with strong support from faculty members and peers. Graduates often comment that the strength of their Binghamton education is epitomized by strong writing and critical-thinking skills. Students like the accessibility of faculty members and their interest in students.

Binghamton is proud of its traditions of excellence and diversity. Almost one third of the undergraduates are members of minority groups, and many students come from homes where members speak languages other than English. Many students whose parents were educated in other nations bring a wealth of traditions to share with their campus friends and classmates. Binghamton has nurtured an international focus that encourages students to understand their role as citizens of the world by exploring it. Nearly one in five Binghamton students choose to study abroad in 350 programs in fifty-one countries. On campus, students pursue languages, area studies, and innovative programs such as Languages Across the Curriculum and the International Studies Certificate. International performers, ranging from the China Ballet and the Moscow State Symphony to Zulu Macbeth, regularly entertain in the performing arts center. In addition, students can explore their own heritage through a wide range of cultural groups.

More than 10,560 undergraduates enrolled in fall 2003, including 2,300 freshmen and 740 transfer students. Typically, 92 percent of the freshmen return as sophomores. With a graduation rate of nearly 80 percent after five years, two thirds of our graduates begin careers, while almost a third pursue graduate degrees. Of those, 16 percent choose law school and 12 percent go to medical school. Medical and law school acceptance rates are well above national averages. Binghamton graduates are recognized leaders in fields ranging from science to business and entertainment to education.

Binghamton University is a community of communities. The residence halls are clustered into close-knit colleges and communities, each with a dining center, recreation space, community government, theater companies, study lounges, and special interest housing. The traditional ceremonies and celebrations, including such whimsically titled events as Newing Navy, Hinman Hysteria, and Mutant Mania, bring students together to compete for prizes, socialize, and cheer each other on. The dining halls are complemented by such other eating options as a kosher kitchen, the mini-mall, and snack bars.

Students can participate in more than 200 student-run organizations. The focus of these organizations is as varied as the student body, including cultural and language groups, service clubs, religious organizations, musical and theatrical opportunities, an a cappella singing group, and outdoor pursuits. Students run their own on-campus radio and TV stations, numerous newspapers and magazines, ambulance corps, and a food coop. LateNite Binghamton offers music, movies, and activities throughout the weekend. More than 80 percent of the students take advantage of athletic opportunities through recreation programs, a wide range club and intramural sports, and twenty NCAA Division I varsity teams.

Students who come to Binghamton expect a high-quality education at an affordable cost. They expect openness and a generosity of spirit between students and faculty members. There is a great deal of mutual help among students as they compete against the standard of a class rather than against each other.

Location

The 887-acre Binghamton University campus is located in the scenic rolling hills of the Southern Tier of upstate New York. Located near the confluence of two major rivers, the suburban campus includes a 190-acre nature preserve and is within easy reach of hiking, biking, and boating opportunities. The Greater Binghamton area is a safe, family-oriented community with lots to do. The area is served by several major airlines and bus companies. Syracuse is 72 miles to the north, and Scranton, Pennsylvania, is equidistant to the south. New York's Finger Lakes are within an hour's drive.

Majors and Degrees

Binghamton offers baccalaureate degrees through its five schools: the Harpur College of Arts and Sciences, the Decker School of Nursing, the Watson School of Engineering and Applied Sciences, the School of Education and Human Development, and the School of Management. The areas of study are accounting; Africana studies; anthropology; Arabic; art; art history; Asian and Asian-American studies; biochemistry; bioengineering; biological sciences; chemistry; cinema; classical studies; comparative literature; computer engineering; computer science; economics; electrical engineering; English; environmental studies; French; geography; geological sciences; German; Hebrew; history; human development; industrial and systems engineering; Italian; Judaic studies; Latin American and Caribbean area studies; linguistics; management; mathematical sciences; mechanical engineering; medieval studies; music; nursing; philosophy; philosophy, politics, and law; physics; political science; psychobiology; psychology; sociology; Spanish; and theater. Students can also design their own majors.

Academic Programs

All students participate in the general education core curriculum while also selecting a major and elective courses from the school to which they are admitted. Students enter one of the five schools mentioned above, though they may take some courses offered by the other four schools, as appropriate. Students are encouraged to enhance their learning through real-world experiences through the Discovery Program.

There is a University-wide Scholars program as well as honors programs for several of the undergraduate schools. Binghamton students are eligible for more than eighteen honor societies, including Phi Beta Kappa, Tau Beta Pi, and Golden Key. More than 80 percent of all freshmen bring Advanced Placement credit, credit earned through Project Advance or the International Baccalaureate program, or credit from other colleges or universities.

Off-Campus Programs

In addition to 350 study-abroad options offered by Binghamton and other State University of New York (SUNY) campuses, there are hundreds of credit-bearing internships in local agencies, businesses, and health services. Binghamton participates in the National Student Exchange, which allows its students to spend a semester or year elsewhere, and students from other universities enroll at Binghamton.

Academic Facilities

The growing campus is home to high-tech teaching facilities, state-of-the-art laboratories, spacious residence halls, a world-class arts center, an art museum, a teaching greenhouse, and an array of social and recreational gathering places. Recent additions include a new University Union, a 6,000-seat Events Center, and a residential community. Work has begun on a 30-acre Innovative Technologies Complex adjacent to the campus. In addition to their own extensive collection, the University Libraries give students access to the resources of the sixty-four campuses that make up the SUNY system. The Anderson Center for the Performing Arts brings world-renowned artists to one of the most acoustically outstanding theaters in the country. Computing facilities provide broadband access to the Internet and convenient computer pods. The Center for Academic Excellence and Educational Opportunity Program offers tutorial and academic support.

Costs

In 2003–04, tuition and fees were $5690 for in-state students and $11,640 for out-of-state students. Room and board typically cost $7100.

Financial Aid

Binghamton's financial aid is designed to provide every student with options to make financing their education possible and affordable. Financial aid is awarded based on need calculated through completion of the FAFSA. Need- and academic-based scholarships, work-study, and loan programs are also available. Nearly 80 percent of incoming students receive some form of aid or scholarship. Binghamton ranks fourteenth in the country for the lowest loan indebtedness of its graduates.

Faculty

Faculty members include National Book Award and Pulitzer Prize winners, Guggenheim and Fulbright scholars, and members of the National Academy of Sciences and the American Academy of Arts and Science. Almost 70 percent of the classes have fewer than 30 students, and the student-faculty ratio is 19:1. More than 95 percent of the faculty members have the doctorate or appropriate terminal degree in their field. Faculty members conduct research and teach, and students are routinely able to participate in research, sometimes coauthoring publications.

Student Government

Extensive participatory democracy is a mark of the Binghamton experience. The Student Association is composed of campus-wide elected student representatives who allocate student activity funds to student organizations. In addition, each residential community elects it own hall officers.

Admission Requirements

Admission is highly selective. Students are admitted to one of the five schools. More than 19,000 freshmen apply for about 2,000 places, and about 40 percent are offered admission. SAT I or ACT scores are required. The middle 50 percent of freshmen score between 1160 and 1310 on the SAT I, with a mean score of 1236. The average freshman GPA is 92. Supplemental information is also taken into consideration. Transfer applications are encouraged, and students are admitted based on the strength of previous college work. The mean GPA of transfer students is 3.2, but the range varies by school and with personal circumstance.

Application and Information

Freshman applications for fall's nonbinding early action program must be submitted by November 1. Binghamton University operates on a rolling admission cycle; students are encouraged to apply before January 1. Transfer applications are received until spaces for programs fill, and transfer students should apply as early as possible. Some freshman and transfer students are also admitted for the spring semester, and applications should be in by November 1. Binghamton accepts the Common Application as well as the SUNY Common Application.

For more information, students should contact:

Office of Undergraduate Admissions
Binghamton University
P.O. Box 6001
Binghamton, New York 13902-6001
Telephone: 607-777-2171
E-mail: admit@binghamton.edu
World Wide Web: http://www.binghamton.edu

Binghamton's scenic campus.

STATE UNIVERSITY OF NEW YORK AT OSWEGO

OSWEGO, NEW YORK

The University

Founded in 1861, SUNY Oswego is well into its second century of meeting the needs of today's students. Although its origins were in teacher education, the curriculum expanded in 1962 to include the arts and sciences and professional studies.

Today, the University is a comprehensive college with an excellent academic reputation and commitment to undergraduate education. A wide array of liberal arts and career-oriented programs are offered through the College of Arts and Sciences, the School of Business, and the School of Education.

Located on 696 acres on the southern shore of Lake Ontario, the spacious tree-lined campus consists of forty-five buildings. Eleven residence halls offer on-campus housing opportunities to all degree-seeking students.

The campus is alive with more than 120 extracurricular organizations covering a wide range of social, academic, cultural, and intellectual interests. Theater, art, film, music, and dance events crowd the campus cultural calendar. SUNY Oswego also offers a full slate of intercollegiate and intramural sports for men and women. Approximately 2,926 men and 3,450 women are currently enrolled as full-time undergraduates.

Traditionally, the University receives among the largest number of applications of any similar-size college in the northeast. It is accredited by the Middle States Association of Colleges and Schools and has been recognized by a number of authoritative guides as a college with outstanding academic opportunities and high academic standards. In addition, Oswego is among a select few colleges or universities in New York State to offer both a nationally accredited school of business (AACSB International) and a nationally accredited school of education (NCATE).

During the last several years, SUNY Oswego has been cited in *The Princeton Review: Best Northeastern Colleges* and *U.S. News & World Report Best Colleges Guide.*

Location

With a population of nearly 20,000, the city of Oswego is a medium-sized upstate New York community. It is the country's oldest freshwater port and one of the leading ports on the Great Lakes/St. Lawrence Seaway. The city and its surrounding area are well known for all kinds of summer and winter recreation, including camping, boating, sailing, fishing, tennis, golf, and, in the winter months, ice-skating, cross-country skiing, and sledding. It is at the heart of the booming sports fishing industry, and tourism is on the upswing. The campus is conveniently located 35 miles northwest of Syracuse and 65 miles east of Rochester. Students traveling by rail or air may utilize bus service to Oswego through the Regional Transportation Center in Syracuse.

Majors and Degrees

SUNY Oswego awards the Bachelor of Arts, Bachelor of Science, and Bachelor of Fine Arts degrees for programs through its College of Arts and Sciences, School of Business, and School of Education.

Through the College of Arts and Sciences, students can earn a baccalaureate in American studies, anthropology, art, biology, broadcasting, chemistry, cognitive science, communication studies, computer science, economics, English, French, geochemistry, geology, German, global and international studies, graphic design, history, human development, information science, journalism, language and international trade, linguistics, math economics applied, mathematics, mathematics applied, meteorology, music, philosophy, philosophy-psychology, physics, political science, psychology, public justice, public relations, sociology, Spanish, theater, women's studies, zoology, and 3+2 zoo technology.

The School of Business offers Bachelor of Science degree programs in accounting, accounting management, business administration, finance, human resource management, management science, and marketing.

In addition, a five-year combined B.S. in accounting and M.B.A. in management is offered.

The School of Education offers Bachelor of Science degree programs in childhood education, industrial training and development, adolescent education, technology education, technology management, vocational-teacher preparation, teaching English to speakers of other languages (TESOL), and wellness management.

Special programs offered by SUNY Oswego include zoo technology, resulting in a bachelor's degree in zoology at Oswego and an associate degree in zoo technology from Santa Fe Community College (Florida); 3+2 engineering programs leading to a bachelor's degree from Oswego in chemistry or physics and a B.S. in engineering from the cooperating universities (Case Western Reserve, Clarkson, or SUNY Binghamton); 2+2 programs leading to a B.S. in cytotechnology, medical technology, respiratory care, or cardiovascular perfusion from SUNY Upstate Medical University (formerly SUNY Health Science Center) in Syracuse; a 2+3 program leading to a B.S./M.P.S. in physical therapy from SUNY Upstate Medical University; and a 3+4 pre-optometry program leading to a B.S. in chemistry from Oswego and an O.D. in optometry from SUNY College of Optometry.

Academic Programs

Because interest in obtaining marketable skills continues to increase, SUNY Oswego offers students a broad range of courses in the liberal arts and in preprofessional and professional studies.

In addition to core courses within a major, all students must satisfy general education requirements designed to strengthen basic writing and analytical proficiency, give students awareness of their cultural heritage, and provide them with a level of literacy in the social and behavioral sciences, natural sciences, and humanities.

By completing these general education requirements during their first two years of study, Oswego students are able to select a major with a sense of confidence and purpose. However, students who are certain of their academic interest may begin working on their major program in the first year.

Before arrival on campus, students are assigned an adviser from either their major area or the college's Student Advisement Center. Advisers assist students who have not declared a major; help students with their academic, personal, and career concerns; and collaborate in the scheduling of courses needed for graduation. In addition, most students are matched with a first-year peer adviser, an older student, to help them face the challenges of the first year.

Students may consider applying for the College Honors Program, which provides a challenging academic experience for high achievers regardless of major. Students also have the option of receiving credit through proficiency CLEP and Advanced Placement (AP) examinations.

Off-Campus Programs

Opportunities exist for students to broaden their knowledge of other countries by participating in one of the more than eighty overseas academic programs offered by the State University of New York. Programs are offered throughout the world, and costs are held as close as possible to the cost of an average semester on the Oswego campus. Through cooperative arrangements, Oswego participates in semester programs in Albany and Washington.

Internships and other field experiences are available for students from all disciplines through the Experience Based Education Office. Each year more than 800 Oswego students participate in internships on the Oswego campus, in the local area, and throughout the Northeast and beyond.

Academic Facilities

The Penfield library houses a collection of more than 2.7 million items, including 460,000 bound volumes, more than 1.8 million microforms, 180,000 government documents, and 42,000 nonprint media items. In addition, the library subscribes to more than 1,400 different journals and magazines and twenty-two newspapers. The library's listening area has more than 8,000 recordings, audiocassettes, and CDs, ranging from rock to classical. Additional facilities include an online catalog, periodical indexes and full-text databases on CD-ROM, access to 50 electronic databases, a 24-hour study room, study carrels, and a microcomputer laboratory utilized for word processing, Internet access, and classroom applications.

Campuswide computer technology services for student use include instructional and administrative technologies as well as network and telecommunications. The campus maintains several SUN servers providing e-mail, time sharing, and Web-publishing support. The time-sharing systems are networked to all locations on campus. In addition, the campus has more than 250 Macintosh and Windows-based computers and numerous SUN workstations for general student use and more than 500 computers in specialized departmental labs. Students are provided an account that can be activated online to use the time-sharing computers and to access e-mail, the Web, and other Internet services. Internet service is available from all residence hall rooms via Ethernet (fee required) or modem (free) connections. Wireless network access is available in Penfiels Library and Rich Hall, and additional wireless locations are being added.

Adjacent to the campus, the College maintains Rice Creek Field Station, including the 26-acre Rice Pond surrounded by 400 acres of natural habitat. The facility contains two lab/classrooms, a lecture room, and exhibit areas with an indoor viewing gallery providing a unique view of the creek and pond. Both College classes and community education programs are regularly held at the Field Station, which ranks among the five most extensively used facilities of their kind in the country.

Located in Tyler Hall, Oswego's fine arts center, are two art galleries that feature annual traveling exhibitions, locally produced theme exhibitions, and the best work of students and faculty members. Newly renovated Waterman Theatre, also located in Tyler Hall, has been cited as one of the fifty best theaters built in the United States since 1960.

WRVO, the College's 24,000-watt stereo public radio station, and two television studios are located in Lanigan Hall. In addition, a student-run TV station, radio station, and college newspaper and literary journal offices are located in the Media Center in the Hewitt Union.

Costs

Tuition for 2003–04 was $2175 per semester for New York State residents and $5150 per semester for nonresidents. Room and board charges were approximately $3370 per semester for entering students, depending on the meal plan selected. SUNY Oswego guarantees that a student's initial first-year costs for room and board will be frozen for up to four consecutive years. Books and supplies cost approximately $400 per semester, depending on the student's choice of major program. Although many activities on campus are free of charge, students will need to budget for personal expenses.

Financial Aid

Financial assistance, granted according to student need, consists of grants, loans, and part-time employment. Students interested in financial aid must file a Free Application for Federal Student Aid. New York State residents also need to file a TAP application for the state's Tuition Assistance Program. Priority is given to those applications on file by April 1 for the fall term and November 15 for the spring term.

Faculty

Oswego's faculty, consisting of more than 300 full-time educators, is dedicated to teaching undergraduate students. With 76 percent holding doctoral or other terminal degrees from many of the finest institutions in the country, students can be assured of the opportunity for an outstanding undergraduate education. The faculty-student ratio is approximately 1:19. While the Oswego faculty is first and foremost dedicated to teaching, faculty members are actively engaged in research, publication, and public service.

Student Government

Students at SUNY Oswego are represented by the Student Association, which has as its aim the efficient and intelligent governance of a democratic student body. The functions of the Student Association are divided among various committees that allocate funds to student organizations, intercollegiate and intramural athletics, the student newspaper, the yearbook, and the student literary magazine, along with various campus social, cultural, and intellectual activities.

Admission Requirements

Admission to Oswego is competitive, with high school average, academic program, and standardized test scores being the most important criteria for applicants. Special talents such as artistic, musical, athletic, and creative writing skills are also considered. The Committee on Admissions accepts results on either the ACT or the SAT I. Although not required, a campus admissions visit is encouraged.

Transfer students in good standing are encouraged to apply for admission through a specific program. Transfer admission to many programs is restricted and quite selective.

Application and Information

Application forms are available from New York State high school guidance offices and college transfer offices. Oswego evaluates applications as they are completed and as space remains available. Those applications completed by January 15 for the fall term or October 15 for the spring term are assured of equal consideration. Applications received after those dates will be considered as space remains available.

Prospective students and their parents are encouraged to visit the campus to participate in a student-guided tour and speak with an admissions counselor. Interested candidates should call the Office of Admissions at least one or two weeks in advance to schedule a visit.

For further information, students should contact:

Office of Admissions
SUNY Oswego
Oswego, New York 13126
Telephone: 315-312-2250
Fax: 315-312-3260
E-mail: admiss@oswego.edu
World Wide Web: http://www.oswego.edu

SUNY Oswego is located on 696 acres on the southern shore of Lake Ontario.

STATE UNIVERSITY OF NEW YORK AT PLATTSBURGH

PLATTSBURGH, NEW YORK

The University

Plattsburgh State is a comprehensive, coeducational college within the State University of New York (SUNY). Students benefit from an exceptional environment that enables them to stand out academically and achieve their highest potential. Academically, this environment is characterized by a curriculum that spans arts and science, professional studies, and business programs. Close interaction with faculty members—who teach, advise, and mentor undergraduates—further enhances student success. Plattsburgh's campus environment is rich in scenic beauty and is set in a small city on the shore of Lake Champlain between the Adirondack and Green Mountains. The college's cultural environment is characterized by a high degree of student involvement, an appreciation for diversity, and an exceptionally friendly and welcoming atmosphere. Plattsburgh State embraces a strong belief in the values of service and civic responsibility, offering service scholarships to both new and currently enrolled students.

A medium-sized college, Plattsburgh State places special focus on its 5,400 undergraduate students. Academic departments offer an excellent variety of programs and courses. About 600 students are enrolled in graduate programs leading to the M.A., M.S., M.S.T., and C.A.S. graduate degrees. The campus atmosphere is considered safe and strongly residential, with twelve residence halls located on an easy-to-walk campus. All dorm rooms come with high-speed computer access as well as telephone and cable television service. Approximately ninety Student Association clubs invite student participation. Fraternities and sororities comprise about 6 percent of the student population. Both club and intramural sports complement the extraordinary recreational opportunities that can be found in the region. Montreal, Lake Placid, and Burlington, Vermont, are popular nearby student destinations. Intercollegiate athletics are offered at the NCAA Division III level, with nine men's teams and ten women's teams.

Location

Plattsburgh State enjoys an outstanding location in upstate New York's scenic Champlain Valley. The campus is situated in a small city, with shopping malls, multiplex movie theaters, restaurants, and hotels all located near the campus. The surrounding region offers many recreational opportunities. Plattsburgh is easily accessible by Interstate, rail, and air, with a small local airport as well as three larger airports that are within an hour's drive.

Majors and Degrees

Plattsburgh State offers nearly sixty undergraduate degree programs (B.A., B.S., B.F.A., B.S.Ed.) in arts and science, business, and professional studies. Accounting, art, biology, communication, criminal justice, education, environmental science, hotel-restaurant-tourism management, journalism, nursing, and psychology are popular majors, in addition to premed and prelaw advisement. Many minor programs are also offered, including athletic coaching, gerontology, graphic design, health-care management, recreation, and more.

Academic Program

Plattsburgh State's programs provide students with the intellectual and experience-based preparation they need to become educated persons and successful professionals. Plattsburgh's academic approach helps students develop as thoughtful citizens, encouraging them to reach beyond the mere acquisition of knowledge. Many internships provide students with hands-on learning. Three academic divisions span Arts and Science, Professional Studies, and the School of Business and Economics, which is accredited by AACSB International–The Association to Advance Collegiate Schools of Business. A general education program provides students with a broad-based foundation of study. Baccalaureate degree programs require 120 credits for graduation. An exciting adventure-learning program called The Adirondack Experience makes the most of the region's outdoor possibilities. A high level of student-faculty interaction enhances the academic experience. Classes average 24 students and are taught by faculty members, not graduate teaching assistants. An active Honors Program provides students with small seminars, tutorials, mentoring, and opportunities to conduct advanced projects. Plattsburgh State hosts twenty-three honor societies. Classes are taught on a fall-spring calendar, with winter and summer terms available. Plattsburgh State accepts transfer credit from accredited institutions and awards nontraditional credit based on acceptable scores from the College-Level Examination Program (CLEP), Advanced Placement (AP), and the New York State College Proficiency Examination (CPE).

Off-Campus Programs

Plattsburgh State participates in the National Student Exchange as well as in an extensive SUNY network of more than 300 study-abroad programs. Programs carry credit and are offered year-round.

Academic Facilities

The facilities at Plattsburgh State are well supported by current technologies, including multimedia smart classrooms. The Feinberg Library and the computing environment offer a host of services, including electronic databases, high-speed Internet access, electronic mail, specialized software, instruction in information and computer literacy, document delivery, and an excellent book and periodical collection. The Division of Library and Information Services supports students in their learning needs with a help desk, walk-in and electronic reference services, residence hall support, microcomputer labs, wireless zones, and a convenient computer purchasing and service program.

Costs

State-subsidized costs help to make Plattsburgh an exceptional value. Annual billed costs for New York State residents are expected to total about $12,000 in 2004–05. Nonresident billed costs are expected to total about $18,000. Many renewable merit-based scholarships and other awards are available, including $2500 housing grants for international and out-of-state students living on campus.

Financial Aid

Plattsburgh State assists students with a variety of aid programs. Merit scholarships are awarded based on student credentials established in the regular admission process. To apply for need-based aid, students must file the Free Application for Federal Student Aid (FAFSA), which covers eligibility for the

Federal Pell Grant, Federal Supplemental Educational Opportunity Grant, Federal Work-Study Program, Federal Perkins Loan, Federal Nursing Loan, Federal Direct Student Loan Program, and need-based scholarships. New York State residents may also file a separate Tuition Assistance Program (TAP) application. Part-time on- and off-campus employment is available. For more information, prospective students should visit the Web site at http://www.plattsburgh.edu/financialaid.

Faculty

Plattsburgh's outstanding faculty members are a community of teachers, scholars, and artists. A high percentage of full-time faculty members hold the doctoral degree, and a number are recognized nationally and internationally on the merits of their scholarship, the importance of their published works, and the honors they have received. Faculty members regularly involve undergraduates in their research; this has led to a growing number of projects in which students are listed jointly with faculty members on publications, as participants in exhibitions and performances, and as presenters at conferences.

Student Government

The Student Association (SA) is a self-governing body that promotes the educational and general welfare of students. It acts as a unifying factor for the student voice and formulates, in conjunction with the faculty and administration, policies and procedures concerning overall aspects of college life. The SA sponsors many clubs and provides transportation as well as legal, financial, and recreational services for students.

Admission Requirements

Admission to Plattsburgh State is competitive and is based primarily on a review of academic credentials. An applicant's entire profile is considered in the admission review. Strength of program and grades are the most important considerations. Freshman applicants should have a college-preparatory program of study in high school with a minimum average of B in academic subjects. The SAT or the ACT is required. An SAT score of 1000 or better, or an ACT score of 22 or better, is recommended. Secondary review factors include activities, awards, the essay (required), and a personal interview (optional). Students holding a high school equivalency diploma are required to submit a high school transcript and SAT or ACT scores along with proof of high school equivalency. Transfer applicants are required to submit official transcripts from all colleges they have attended previously, with no more than one semester of course work undocumented at the time of application. A cumulative grade point average is calculated based on all course work. Students with GPAs of 2.0 are considered for admission; however, a higher GPA may be required in certain programs. Transfers with fewer than two full-time semesters of college course work completed at the time of application are required to submit an official high school transcript along with SAT or ACT scores. Plattsburgh State maintains an affirmative action policy and embraces the goal of increasing ethnic diversity on campus; therefore, the College encourages applicants to identify their ethnicity at the time of application. Applicants who are not residents of New York State are at no disadvantage in the admissions process.

Application and Information

Fall freshman applicants should apply before December 1 of their senior year in high school. Students requesting early decision need to apply by November 1. Spring applicants (freshman and transfer) should apply by November 1. Transfer applicants for fall should apply after they have completed the previous fall semester, so that no more than one semester (spring) is undocumented at the time of admission review.

Prospective students may apply online at http://www.applyweb.com/apply/suny44ud. For more information or to request a printed application, students should contact:

Richard Higgins, Director of Admissions
State University of New York at Plattsburgh
101 Broad Street
Plattsburgh, New York 12901
Telephone: 518-564-2040
888-673-0012 (toll-free)
E-mail: admissions@plattsburgh.edu
World Wide Web: http://www.plattsburgh.edu

Plattsburgh State's environment enables students to stand out.

STATE UNIVERSITY OF NEW YORK COLLEGE AT FREDONIA

FREDONIA, NEW YORK

The College

Founded as an academy in 1826, the College has a student body that reflects the great diversity of cultures in New York State. A public, coeducational institution, Fredonia has emerged as a highly respected liberal arts institution with recognized programs in business, communications, education, the fine and performing arts, science, and the social sciences. The College maintains a traditional small-college atmosphere, and students enjoy a variety of cultural and social activities. A high percentage of students participate actively in athletics and intramural sports.

The 240-acre campus has twenty-nine buildings. A modern field house provides facilities for ice hockey, swimming, diving, and indoor track and includes a large gymnasium to complement a second facility, which contains a fitness center, a dance studio, and two intramural gymnasiums. Thirteen residence halls house 2,400 students and offer accommodations to suit a variety of lifestyles, including traditional, coed, and apartment-style residence halls. On-campus housing is guaranteed for all undergraduates. The undergraduate enrollment at Fredonia is 4,900.

Location

The village of Fredonia has a population of 11,000 and is located 45 miles south of Buffalo near Lake Erie. The village has preserved its traditional small-town atmosphere. Tree-lined streets lead to a spacious downtown common surrounded by outstanding examples of nineteenth-century village architecture. Fredonia, essentially residential in nature, is surrounded by orchards and vineyards leading south to the Allegheny foothills. To the north lie the city of Dunkirk and Lake Erie. Summer and winter recreational facilities abound. The College benefits from its relative proximity to the cities of Buffalo, Niagara Falls, Toronto, Cleveland, and Pittsburgh.

Majors and Degrees

SUNY Fredonia degrees and program offerings include the Bachelor of Arts (B.A.) degree in applied music, art history, ceramics, criminal justice, drawing, earth science, economics, English, French, graphic design, history, illustration, interdisciplinary studies, painting, philosophy, photography, political science, psychology, sculpture, sociology, Spanish, and theater. A Bachelor of Fine Arts (B.F.A.) degree is awarded in acting, ceramics, drawing, graphic design, illustration, media arts, music/sound production, musical theater, painting, photography, production design, and sculpture. The Bachelor of Music (Mus.B.) degree is available in composition, music education, and performance. The Bachelor of Science (B.S.) degree is awarded in accounting, audio/radio production, biochemistry, biology, business administration–individual specialization, chemistry, communication disorders, communication studies, computer and information sciences, finance, geochemistry, geology, geophysics, industrial management, interdisciplinary studies, management, management information systems, marketing, mathematics, mathematics-physics, media management, medical technology, molecular genetics, music therapy, physics, public relations, social work, sound recording technology, and TV/digital film production. A Bachelor of Science in Education (B.S.Ed.) degree is offered with majors in childhood education, early childhood education, and speech and language disabilities. Adolescent education certification is available in biology, chemistry, earth science, English, French, mathematics, physics, social studies, and Spanish.

The Interdisciplinary Studies degree gives students the opportunity to design an individualized interdisciplinary major with guidance from experienced faculty members. Students in these programs work toward a Bachelor of Arts or Bachelor of Science degree. The Interdisciplinary Studies option also offers model majors or minors in such areas as African-American studies, American studies, arts administration, dance, environmental sciences, geographic information systems, gerontology, legal studies, multiethnic studies, music business, and women's studies.

The College is affiliated in a cooperative (3-2) engineering program with the following institutions: Alfred University, Case Western Reserve, Clarkson, Columbia, Cornell, Louisiana Tech, Ohio State, Penn State Behrend, Rensselaer Polytechnic Institute, Rochester Institute of Technology, SUNY at Binghamton, SUNY at Buffalo, Syracuse, and Tri-State University. The Department of Business Administration offers an accelerated M.B.A. program, including a 3-2 program with SUNY at Binghamton and SUNY at Buffalo and a 4-1 program with Clarkson and the University of Pittsburgh.

A complete listing of offerings is available on the SUNY Fredonia Web site at the address listed below.

Academic Programs

The bachelor's degree requires 120 credit hours, including a general education component, and there are opportunities for double majors, minors, and concentrations. The College offers an honors program for academically talented students. Up to 30 credits may be awarded through Advanced Placement, CLEP, and International Baccalaureate examinations.

Fredonia operates on a semester system with the fall term beginning in early September and ending in mid-December. The spring term begins the third week of January and continues into May. A summer program of two 5-week sessions is available.

Retention and graduation rates of entering freshmen at Fredonia are among the highest in the nation. To ensure continued success, the College has implemented "Fredonia in 4," a program for first-time freshmen that stipulates that the College pledges to adhere to a commonly understood agreement to provide the necessary courses and academic advising that guarantee that students finish in four years.

Off-Campus Programs

Fredonia students may participate in State University of New York overseas programs throughout the world and take part in the largest overseas study program in the nation. These programs provide educational opportunities in virtually every discipline. The College offers internships in courts and government agencies as well as in the areas of public relations, psychology, journalism, television production, radio, business, and the health sciences. Fredonia participates in the Washington Semester Program and in the Visiting Student Program, which enables students to study for a semester or a year at one of more than fifty participating colleges and universities. Credit is awarded on the basis of an academic contract.

Academic Facilities

Reed Library contains 391,000 bound volumes and 1,060,631 titles on microform, plus 1,983 professional and academic journals. There is seating for 1,054 students, including open study carrels. Open-stack privileges are available to all students, and separate areas are provided for special collections, a microtext room, and a music section consisting of 26,570 audio and video materials and 30,000 scores.

The College provides students and faculty members with extensive computing facilities. Campus computing facilities are used for instruction, research, and administrative projects by faculty members, students, and the staff. All students at Fredonia are assigned an access code and password that allow them to interact with the College computer network. Personal computers for student use are located in all academic buildings and various residence halls. Students living in residence halls have instant Internet connectivity in their rooms via an Ethernet connection to a T-100 line. Wireless connections are available in several campus locations, including the library and student union.

The Rockefeller Arts Center provides outstanding facilities for concert and theatrical productions and houses an art gallery, art studios, and classrooms.

Costs

Tuition and fees for 2003–04 were $5362 per year for state residents and $11,312 for non–New York state residents. Students living in College residence halls paid an additional fee of $3800 for room and $2550 for board.

Financial Aid

In 2002–03, 80 percent of Fredonia's students received financial assistance. The average award, consisting of grants, scholarships, loans, and campus jobs, was $7000. Students who are interested in applying for aid are encouraged to submit the Free Application for Federal Student Aid (FAFSA) by February 1. Sources of aid include Federal Pell Grants, Federal Supplemental Educational Opportunity Grants, Tuition Assistance Program awards, Educational Opportunity Grants, Federal Perkins Loans, New York State Stafford Student Loans, Federal Work-Study Program awards, on- and off-campus jobs, and Fredonia College Scholarships, including a freshman merit scholarship program.

Faculty

Fredonia's faculty consists of 253 full-time and 179 part-time instructional staff members. Ninety percent of faculty members have earned doctorates or a terminal degree in their field. All professors have weekly office hours, during which they are available to students. Faculty members are involved in instruction, research, publication, and academic advising. The small size of classes contributes to excellent faculty-student interaction.

Student Government

All students are members of the Student Association, which functions through elected officers and elected senators from the various College groups and organizations. Student representatives are voting members of the Faculty Council and are represented on most committees of the College. The Student Association provides funding for 120 campus organizations and clubs.

Admission Requirements

Admission to Fredonia is competitive. Particular attention is given to the quality of the academic program and the high school average. Other factors considered in the admissions process are the results of the SAT I or ACT, recommendations, rank in class, and extracurricular activities. Applicants should have completed at least 16 academic units of preparation. Those seeking admissions to math or science-related majors should include 4 units each of mathematics and science; those seeking admission to programs in business administration and accounting should include 4 units of college-preparatory mathematics. An audition is required for admission to programs in music, acting, musical theater, and production design. A portfolio is required for admission to visual arts and new media majors. A campus visit is recommended, but a personal interview is not required.

Application and Information

New York State residents may obtain application material from their high school guidance offices or any SUNY campus. Nonresidents should contact the Office of Admissions. An electronic application is available online at http://www.fredonia.edu/admissions/applying.html#online. Application review and notification are made on a rolling basis. Applicants may seek admission through the Early Decision Program. A deposit of $100, due May 1, is required to reserve a space in the entering class. Students interested in visiting the campus may obtain a visiting schedule and an appointment by calling the number below.

For further information, contact:

Office of Admissions
Fenner House
State University of New York at Fredonia
Fredonia, New York 14063
Telephone: 716-673-3251
800-252-1212
E-mail: admissions.office@fredonia.edu
World Wide Web: http://www.fredonia.edu

A view of Houghton Hall, a facility designed by I. M. Pei.

STATE UNIVERSITY OF NEW YORK COLLEGE AT OLD WESTBURY

OLD WESTBURY, NEW YORK

THE COLLEGE AT OLD WESTBURY STATE UNIVERSITY OF NEW YORK

The College

SUNY College at Old Westbury is a small, public college that teaches students to lead at work, in the community, and in life. In an environment that demands academic excellence and offers close interaction among students, faculty members, and staff members, Old Westbury weaves intercultural understanding into the very fabric of its liberal arts and professional programs. Old Westbury is a beautiful place to live, learn, and play. That is why F. Ambrose Clark built his estate on the 604 acres of rolling meadows and woods that are now the College's campus. Today, more than half of the campus has been preserved forever to maintain the quiet, sequestered setting for which Old Westbury has come to be known.

Most of the College's 3,300 students come from New York State, yet approximately twenty-two nations are represented within the student body. In fact, Old Westbury is among the most diverse student bodies within the State University system. Approximately 800 students currently live in five residence halls that were introduced to the campus in 2003. Each new hall features over-sized double-occupancy rooms with satellite television service, two DS-3 data ports, two telephone lines, and independent heating and air conditioning controls in each room. The remainder of the student body lives in private accommodations off campus or commutes from home.

Although the College was charted in 1965, the current hub of campus life is the Student Union Building, which opened in 2003 with a computer lab, two quiet study lounges, game rooms, and the Panther's Den—the gathering place where those on campus come together to discuss what is happening both on campus and around the world. The College's NCAA Division III athletic program is housed in the F. Ambrose Clark Physical Education and Recreation Center. Old Westbury fields ten successful men's and women's varsity programs that, since 2000, have earned conference championships in soccer and baseball; postseason tournament bids in baseball and men's and women's basketball; and all-star awards in baseball, basketball, cross-country, soccer, softball, and volleyball.

Location

Located on historic North Shore of Long Island, the nation's sixteenth largest population center, Old Westbury sits a short drive from the region's commercial centers and is less than 20 miles from the excitement, culture, and real-world educational opportunities of New York City. Local shopping malls and entertainment offerings, regional theaters and museums, the fine restaurants of Nassau County, and an array of outdoor activities—including South Shore beaches—are all just minutes away from the Old Westbury campus.

Majors and Degrees

Through twelve individual academic departments and a School of Business that houses three departments of its own, Old Westbury offers forty-five undergraduate degrees programs, enabling students to earn Bachelor of Arts, Bachelor of Science, and Bachelor of Professional Studies degrees. The undergraduate degrees include: accounting; American studies; biochemistry; biological sciences; business and management; chemistry; comparative humanities; computer information sciences; criminology; finance; health and society; industrial and labor relations; management information systems; marketing; mathematics; media and communications; philosophy and religion; politics, economics, and society; psychology; sociology; Spanish language and Hispanic literature and culture; teacher education (childhood, middle childhood, adolescence, and special); and visual arts. In 2004, Old Westbury introduced its first graduate degree, a Master of Science in accounting.

Academic Programs

The Old Westbury curriculum is carefully designed to enable students to compete in the global economy or to pursue further studies at the finest graduate and professional schools. Although all students focus on a major program of study, the College believes it is equally important for students to acquire a broad base of general knowledge and to develop strong analytical and creative skills.

The core of academic study at the College is a general education program that provides students with a broad multidisciplinary liberal arts education that serves as the intellectual foundation for further education, career preparation, and participation in an increasingly complex society. General education offerings are structured into seven domains (basic communication, creativity and the arts, the western tradition, the American experience, major cultures, foreign languages, natural sciences, and mathematics) and three knowledge areas (humanities, social science, and diversity).

All freshmen enroll in the First Year Experience program, which provides students with the academic and personal support needed to succeed as first-year students. All first-year students take a First-Year Seminar course that covers topics such as study skills, career planning, and time management and allows students to engage in an in-depth analysis of a selected academic topic. The program also includes an array of social events geared to ease the transition to college life of first-time students.

At Old Westbury, the cultivation of talents, acquisition of skills, and mastery of a robust core are central. With a guiding hand from a caring faculty, students pursue their studies within an atmosphere of trust and mutual respect, where each one is offered the challenge of high standards and is given the support to achieve them. It is in this environment that Old Westbury students are prepared to become the leaders of tomorrow in whatever pursuit they choose.

Off-Campus Programs

Along with learning in the classroom, Old Westbury offers a variety of ways for students to learn as they work in their chosen field. Formal internship and research opportunities are available in many academic departments. In addition, with Old Westbury's proximity to Long Island's commercial centers and metropolitan New York City, students have the advantage of selecting the experience that best suits them. A short list of some of the places where Old Westbury students have recently interned includes ABC News, Brookhaven National Laboratory, Grant Thornton, MTV, the New York Mets, USA Network, and the U.S. Senate Finance Committee.

Students can also experience the cultures of foreign lands through Old Westbury's overseas study opportunities. Old Westbury offers exchange and study abroad programs that offer travel to China, Puerto Rico, South Africa, South Korea, and Spain. Through the SUNY network, students can apply to one of the nearly 400 overseas studies programs offered in almost sixty different countries in North and South America, Africa, Asia, Eastern and Western Europe, Australia, and New Zealand.

Academic Facilities

In the Academic Village, the main center of the campus' academic life, students interact face-to-face with their professors in small, focused classes. Consisting of four academic buildings and nine residence halls, the Academic Village is also home to the Student Computing Center, which includes a discrete laboratory for language study and videoconferencing facilities used to enhance the offerings of the College's business and teacher education programs.

The Old Westbury Library today is a process as well as a place. The campus network and the Internet deliver library services far from the physical library, which is located in the L wing of Campus Center. The catalog to the College's nearly 400,000 volumes is available online. Links to libraries worldwide make it possible to locate and request material through interlibrary loan. The 900 periodical subscriptions are complemented by an even greater number of online, full-text periodicals that are accessible throughout the network. Online indexes direct the user to additional articles. The Media Services Department has 4,600 audiovisual items and private viewing booths.

With the second-highest level of scientific research funding among Long Island colleges and universities, Old Westbury features a Natural Science Building that offers essential laboratories both for classroom instruction and cutting-edge research. The facility also includes a lecture hall and greenhouse.

The College's new Graduate Studies Program is housed in newly renovated space within the Campus Center, which includes a graduate computer lab and smart classrooms. The Campus Center also includes the 400-seat John and Lillian Maguire Theater, the 330-seat Duane L. Jones Recital Hall, and the Amelie A. Wallace Art Gallery, which features rotating exhibitions of works by students and faculty members from the Visual Arts Department as well as work by area artists. The Campus Center also houses television studios that feature the latest in digital video production equipment.

Costs

For a New York State resident, full-time undergraduate tuition was $4350 in 2003–04, plus an annual college fee of $691 to cover such services as athletics, student activities, technology, and health care. Residential students paid $7749 for combined room and board (double-room, 19 meals) in 2003–04. Out-of-state students paid $10,300 annually in tuition. Part-time students who are residents of New York paid $181 per credit hour; nonresident part-time students paid $429 per credit hour. Full-time graduate tuition and fees for a New York State resident was $3695, while a non-resident paid $5495.

Financial Aid

Old Westbury participates in federal, state, and local aid programs that make the College's already affordable education even more so. The College also offers a variety of merit-based scholarships for students who are new to the College. Freshmen applicants may qualify for scholarships that reduce the cost of living (Residence Hall Scholarships) on campus or the cost of tuition (Tuition Scholarships) or both. Transfer students with outstanding academic achievement may qualify for full or partial-tuition awards made through the Presidential Scholarship program. The College's Office of Financial Aid assists students in applying for financial aid, maintains an extensive student aid resource center, and prepares estimated aid packages for all newly accepted students prior to enrollment.

Faculty

Old Westbury students experience a student-faculty ratio of 17:1. Of the College's 122 full-time professors, more than 100 hold the highest degree in their discipline. Seven members of the faculty have been named Distinguished Teaching Professors and another three have been named Distinguished Service Professors by the State University, which are among the highest ranks available in the University. While foremost among the goals of these outstanding researchers, writers, and teachers is the education of their students, Old Westbury faculty members are actively engaged in research, publication, and public service.

Student Government

Students at Old Westbury are represented by the Student Government Association (SGA), which serves as the parent organization for all student clubs and organizations. Officers of the organization are elected annually through campuswide voting. The SGA allocates student activity funds and helps to oversee the more than fifty student clubs and organizations on campus. The roster of clubs and organizations includes Greek organizations, a student newspaper, chorales, and academic, cultural, and professional societies. The offices of the SGA, along with most clubs and organizations, are housed in Old Westbury's state-of-the-art Student Union.

Admission Requirements

Freshman admission to Old Westbury is competitive; 57 percent of freshman applicants were accepted for fall 2003. A high school grade point average of at least 80 and an SAT 1 score of 1000 or a composite ACT score of 22 merits consideration. All qualified candidates are encouraged to apply for admission. Although not required, a campus admissions visit is encouraged. An interview is sometimes required to discuss specific concerns and program objectives. Students for whom an interview is required are notified by letter. Transfer applications are encouraged, and students with more than 24 credit hours of college work are evaluated based on their college achievement.

Application and Information

Students may apply for fall or spring admission on a rolling basis. SUNY application forms are available from the College's Office of Enrollment Services or from guidance offices in all New York State high schools. In addition, an Old Westbury Supplemental Application is required. To arrange a visit, make an appointment with an admissions counselor, or request an application, students should contact:

Office of Enrollment Services
State University of New York
College at Old Westbury
P.O. Box 307
Old Westbury, New York 11568-0307
Telephone: 516-876-3073
E-mail: enroll@oldwestbury.edu
World Wide Web: http://www.oldwestbury.edu

Students at SUNY College at Old Westbury take a breather between classes in front of the Student Union Building.

STATE UNIVERSITY OF NEW YORK COLLEGE AT ONEONTA

ONEONTA, NEW YORK

The College

A comprehensive college of arts and sciences in the SUNY system, the College at Oneonta strives to develop students to their full potential both academically and personally. The John Templeton Foundation twice named the College at Oneonta to its *Honor Roll of Character-Building Colleges.* Emphasizing excellence in classroom instruction, Oneonta's curriculum includes courses that broaden students' understanding of the human experience; sharpen writing, reasoning, and analytical skills; and offer in-depth, career-focused work in a broad range of major fields. With the second-largest library collection in its sector of SUNY, excellent computer facilities, and strong advisement and support programs, Oneonta provides students a solid academic foundation for careers or graduate study. Varied residence life programs and outstanding volunteer service and internship arrangements offer students vast opportunities for personal development. The College's Center for Social Responsibility and Community, established through a $500,000 Kellogg Foundation grant, actively develops and coordinates community service opportunities for students. Career planning and placement services assist students in preparing for careers and securing employment after graduation. A recent survey of graduates indicated that more than 80 percent were employed or enrolled in graduate study within six months.

Established as a state normal school in 1889, Oneonta was a founding college of the SUNY system in 1948. Ranked as one of *Money* magazine's 100 best buys in American higher education in its last three years of publication and named to *Yahoo! Internet Life*'s list of 100 Most Wired Colleges, the College is accredited by the Middle States Association of Colleges and Schools. Its programs in home economics are accredited by the American Home Economics Association, its programs in chemistry are accredited by the American Chemical Society, and its programs in education are accredited by the National Council for Accreditation of Teacher Education. The 250-acre campus has more than forty buildings. Off-campus facilities include the 672-acre Biological Field Station and research area on Otsego Lake and a History Museum Studies graduate program in nearby Cooperstown.

Though more than 90 percent of Oneonta students are state residents, the College attracts many out-of-state and international students. The College's 5,000 undergraduates represent a medley of cultures, backgrounds, ages, and experiences. Approximately half of Oneonta's students live in the seventeen on-campus residence halls, which have full-time professional directors and staffs of resident advisers. Residence life options include special interest areas. Residence halls are wired for telephone, cable television, and computer hook-ups. With keyed entry to residence halls, a campuswide emergency phone system, and other security measures, Oneonta has been cited as the safest campus setting in New York State for colleges of 5,000 or more students and the ninth-safest in the country. The Counseling, Health, and Wellness Center furnishes on-campus health care and confidential counseling. Three dining halls, a coffeehouse, snack bars, and a convenience store offer various dining options from early morning to late evening. Off-campus apartments and rooms are available in the community. A regular bus service, funded through activity fees, is provided free of additional charge.

More than seventy student organizations provide extracurricular cultural, social, athletic, and intellectual activities. A gymnasium, fitness center, and Alumni Field House provide recreational facilities. Eight varsity men's teams and nine women's teams compete in Division III intercollegiate sports, with the Division I men's soccer team recognized nationally. Nearby state parks, ski resorts, museums, and theaters enhance on-campus recreational and cultural opportunities.

Location

Located in the scenic, historic Susquehanna Valley in the western foothills of the Catskills, Oneonta (population 15,000) is midway between Albany and Binghamton on Interstate 88. A convenient 3-hour drive from the New York City area and accessible from anywhere in the state, the city provides an exceptional setting for college life. Downtown Oneonta, a short walk from campus, offers many restaurants and shops. The campus bus service provides transportation to and from downtown businesses, malls, and recreational facilities. Students are heavily involved in volunteer service and employment in the Oneonta community.

Majors and Degrees

The SUNY College at Oneonta offers a wide range of undergraduate programs leading to Bachelor of Arts and Bachelor of Science degrees. In the Division of Behavioral and Applied Science, majors are offered in accounting; adulthood and aging studies; business economics; child and family studies; dietetics; economics; food service and restaurant administration; human ecology, with options in child development and family studies, consumer studies, fashion merchandising and design, and general human ecology; home economics education; international studies; psychology; and sociology, with options in criminal justice, general sociology, and human services.

In the Division of Education, majors are offered in adolescence education (biology, chemistry, earth science, English, family and consumer sciences, French, math, physics, social studies, and Spanish), childhood education (1–6), early childhood education (B–2), and early childhood/childhood education (B–6).

In the Division of Humanities and Fine Arts, majors are offered in art history, art studio, computer art, English, French, interdisciplinary studies, mass communication, music, music industry, philosophy, Spanish, speech communication, studio art, and theater.

In the Division of Science and Social Science, majors are offered in Africana and Latino studies; anthropology; biology, with options in biochemistry, biotechnology, ecological science, general biology, and human biology; chemistry; computer science; earth science; environmental sciences, with options in biology, earth science, general environmental sciences, and planning; geography, with options in cartography, general geography, and urban and regional planning; geology; history; mathematics; meteorology; physics; political science; statistics; and water resources.

Preprofessional programs prepare students for advanced study in dentistry, law, medicine, and veterinary science.

Oneonta offers a variety of programs in conjunction with other institutions: 3 + 2 dual majors in accounting, management, and business economics; a 4 + 1 M.B.A. program; cooperative programs in engineering; 3 + 1 programs in advertising and communications, advertising design, fashion buying and merchandising, and fashion design; programs in cytotechnology, medical technology, nursing, physical therapy, and respiratory care; programs in pre–environmental science and forestry; and a program in hospitality management.

Academic Programs

Oneonta's academic program has three primary components: a general education requirement, specialized in-depth study in a major, and free electives. This combination helps students understand a plurality of perspectives, enables them to clarify their thought processes, and enhances their abilities to communicate effectively. The 36-hour general education requirement includes courses in American history, the arts, foreign language, humanities, mathematics, natural sciences, other world civilizations, social sciences, and Western civilization, as well as courses that develop thinking, problem-solving, and communication skills. In their major, students complete 30–60 hours of course work on their way to the 122 hours required for graduation. Transfer applications are encouraged, and students may transfer up to 66 credits from two-year colleges or 77 credits from four-year institutions. Degree credits may be earned through proficiency examinations, course challenges, and assessment of prior learning. Students must declare a major by their junior year. A strong academic advisement program provides assistance in choosing curricula and in planning the academic year, which is divided into two 15-week semesters with optional summer sessions.

The Oneonta honors program is designed for students with demonstrated high academic ability, a desire to succeed, and a willingness to seek out new challenges and experiences. It offers scholars all the benefits of an enriched undergraduate experience while emphasizing flexibility and choice.

Off-Campus Programs

Oneonta offers many opportunities to earn degree credits while studying abroad and to gain valuable employment experience through internships. The SUNY Study Abroad Program enables students to study throughout the world in nearly 100 programs. Oneonta offers programs with the University of Würzburg in Germany, the American Intercontinental University in London, and the University of Wales intersession programs in Europe; semester or academic-year programs in Ireland and England; direct exchange programs with Seinan Gakuin University in Japan and with the Siberian Aerospace Academy, the Higher Business Academy, and other academic institutions in Krasnoyarsk, Russia; fall semester programs in India; and summer programs in Israel. Credit-bearing internships are available through many academic departments and agencies. The Center for Social Responsibility and Community provides opportunities for noncredit community service, often in a field related to the student's major.

Academic Facilities

An exceptional library, excellent computer equipment, and several specialized facilities provide outstanding academic resources for students. The Milne Library houses more than 500,000 volumes of print material, offers an online catalog and computers with access to specialized CD-ROMs and the Internet, and provides study space for 900 students. The College's twenty computer labs, nine of which are open seven days a week, provide more than 400 computers. Students have free access to a powerful campuswide network and the Internet, with connections available in all academic buildings and in residence halls. Unique computer facilities include the nationally recognized Chemistry and Physics Multimedia Lab, the Computer Art Lab, and the Geographic Information Systems Lab. A "smart classroom" enables faculty members to incorporate multimedia presentations into their classes. Recently upgraded television, music, and video production equipment enables the campus to broadcast live events and the students to produce videos. The hands-on Science Discovery Center and the observatory and planetarium offer unique resources. Academic support services provide individualized self-instructional programs, tutorials, and skill-building classes.

Costs

Tuition for 2003–04 was $4350 per year for state residents and $10,300 for nonresidents. Fees were $933. Room and board were $6714. Costs for books, supplies, and personal expenses vary.

Financial Aid

Approximately 80 percent of Oneonta's full-time undergraduate students receive financial aid through federal, state, and local programs, including the Federal Pell Grant Program, Federal Supplemental Educational Opportunity Grants, Federal Perkins Loans, Federal Family Educational Loan Program, Federal Work-Study Program, on-campus part-time employment, and College scholarships. To be eligible for financial assistance, students must submit the Free Application for Federal Student Aid to the College as early as possible. Through a concerted effort to expand scholarship opportunities, the College now offers more than $500,000 in scholarship awards. Information about scholarships is available through the Admissions or Financial Aid Offices.

Faculty

Oneonta's 260 instructional faculty members, nearly all of whom hold doctoral degrees, are responsible for the development and implementation of the undergraduate programs. While many undertake research, their primary focus is on instruction, advisement, and counseling. A genuine sense of concern for the individual student's intellectual and personal development is the hallmark of Oneonta's faculty.

Student Government

Oneonta's Student Association, of which all registered students are members, is managed through democratically elected executive, legislative, and judicial branches. The Student Senate, composed of representatives of residence halls and off-campus residents, administers the student activity budget, which funds the campus organizations, athletics, entertainment activities, bus service, campus radio station, and student newspaper. Students are represented on the College Council, Alumni Association, College Senate, and many College-wide committees.

Admission Requirements

The College is strongly committed to academic excellence and the development of students to their full potential. Oneonta receives many more applications than there are available spaces, so admission is competitive. Applicants are evaluated on academic records, including their program of studies and results of standardized tests (ACT or SAT I), and on personal experiences, achievements, and talents. Each fall, the College enrolls some 1,000 freshmen and 700 transfer students. Approximately 250 additional students enter in the spring. The College welcomes applications from all candidates, including out-of-state and international students. On-campus interviews, tours, and information sessions are available but not required. Oneonta offers early action, admission through the Educational Opportunity Program, and admission to qualified high school students who graduate early. Freshman candidates should present a solid college-preparatory academic program, with at least 8 units of mathematics, science, and foreign language in addition to required social science and English courses. Accepted candidates generally rank in the top third of their class and have above-average test scores. Transfer students must present a minimum GPA of 2.3, although most accepted transfer students have GPAs of 2.5 or better; education majors must have a GPA of 2.8 or better.

Application and Information

The College at Oneonta uses the standard SUNY application, available in most New York State high school guidance offices or from the College's Admissions Office. Applications are accepted year-round and are evaluated on a rolling basis. For fall semester admission, freshman applicants should submit all materials by February 1; transfer applicants should submit materials by June 1. For more information, students should contact:

Director of Admissions
State University of New York College at Oneonta
Oneonta, New York 13820
Telephone: 607-436-2524
800-SUNY-123 (toll-free)
Fax: 607-436-3074
E-mail: admissions@oneonta.edu
World Wide Web: http://www.oneonta.edu

STATE UNIVERSITY OF NEW YORK COLLEGE OF TECHNOLOGY AT DELHI

Delhi
STATE UNIVERSITY OF NEW YORK
COLLEGE OF TECHNOLOGY

DELHI, NEW YORK

The College

The State University of New York (SUNY) College of Technology at Delhi is carving a unique niche in higher education by offering eleven specialized baccalaureate programs. Each builds on Delhi's long-standing position as a leader in providing a student-centered collegiate experience that emphasizes academic excellence, hands-on learning, and a residential experience in a spectacular natural environment.

Hands-on experience is the cornerstone of Delhi's academic programs. Bachelor's degree programs include extensive internships. Technical programs feature extensive, on-the-job experiences as well. It is a proven approach that gets results. More than 95 percent of Delhi students find jobs or continue their education within a year of graduating. Nearly 35 percent of Delhi students come from metropolitan New York and Long Island. Students of color make up 20 percent of the student body.

An on-campus Counseling and Health Center features professional counselors who can provide individual and group counseling to enhance the academic experience and personal growth of students. A medical clinic, staffed by registered nurses, nurse practitioners, and College physicians, provides a wide range of services. These services are complemented by a strong health education and outreach program.

Student life is a major part of a residential college experience; Delhi students have more than forty clubs and organizations from which to choose. Many are professional organizations, which give students an opportunity to network with professionals and learn more about the career fields they have chosen. Others, such as the photography club, drama club, outdoor club, ski club, and campus television and radio stations, give students the chance to pursue avocational interests. Thus, 65 percent of Delhi students are involved in community service, campus clubs, and student organizations.

Entertainment options are varied and have recently included headliners like Lit, MTV Campus Invasion Tour, Jay Mohr, Garbage, Carrot Top, Jim Breuer, the Harlem Globetrotters, and Rusted Root.

Intercollegiate athletics are also a major part of campus life. Delhi fields varsity teams in men's and women's basketball, cross-country, soccer, swimming, tennis, and indoor and outdoor track and field. Delhi also offers men's lacrosse and women's softball and volleyball. The men's and women's golf teams compete at the NAIA level. All other sports compete at the NJCAA Division III level. Delhi has won the Pepsi Cup, symbolic of the best men's and women's cross-country programs, for three consecutive years. Delhi has also served as host for the NJCAA Division III men's basketball finals since the tournament's inception in 1991.

Athletics facilities are modern and include a 50-meter indoor swimming pool, racquetball courts, a fitness center, an indoor track, indoor tennis courts, a gymnasium, a new outdoor track and tennis courts, an eighteen-hole golf course, and soccer, lacrosse, and softball fields.

Location

Located in the beautiful rolling foothills of the Catskill Mountains, Delhi is a residential college that attracts more than 2,200 students from New York and the surrounding states.

Majors and Degrees

SUNY Delhi awards Bachelor of Business Administration, Bachelor of Technology, Associate in Arts, Associate in Science, Associate in Applied Science, and Associate in Occupational Studies degrees and one-year certificates. Baccalaureate programs include applications software development, club manager studies, culinary arts, golf superintendent studies, hotel and resort management, network administration, professional golf management, restaurant and food service management, travel and tourism management, veterinary technology management, and Web development. Academic majors at the associate degree or certificate levels include accounting; architectural technology; automotive mechanics; building construction; business administration; business management; carpentry; computer-aided drafting and design; computer information systems; culinary arts; electrical construction and maintenance; electrical instrumentation and controls; engineering science; golf course operations; horticulture; hospitality management; hotel and resort management; humanities; HVAC; individual studies; landscape contracting technology; marketing; masonry; mathematics; nursing; park and recreation management; physical education studies; plumbing, heating, and pipefitting; pre–environmental science and forestry; refrigeration and air conditioning; restaurant and food service management; science; social science; travel and tourism; turf equipment management; turf management; veterinary science technology; and welding.

Academic Programs

SUNY Delhi has earned state and national reputations for excellence and innovation in several program areas.

Delhi's veterinary science technology program was the first of its type in the United States, and it continues to be a model for programs around the country. Program facilities are outstanding at the two-year level and include a surgical suite, radiography lab, and primate lab.

Delhi is a past recipient of the National Restaurant Association's award as having the best two-year hospitality program in New York State. Facilities are outstanding and include an on-campus hospitality and conference center that features guest suites furnished by Marriott and Sheraton, a beverage lab, a student-operated restaurant, banquet facilities, and multipurpose meeting rooms. Delhi's culinary team has been state champion for the last four years and a national competitor for the last two years.

Extensive industry support has made Delhi a nationally recognized leader in golf education. Delhi's is one of only two colleges in the United States to offer its unique bachelor's degree programs in golf education. The College's associate degree programs in golf course operations and turf equipment management are unique in the Northeast as well. In addition, Delhi owns its own golf course for educational use.

Delhi was a pioneer in educational programs for the construction industry and now offers comprehensive study in the field. The construction technology program is accredited by the American Association for Construction Education. Students in building trade programs complete both residential and commercial construction projects. The College's Applied Technologies Complex supports these and other programs, providing specialized laboratories for plumbing, heating, welding, refrigeration, air conditioning, and electrical studies.

Special programs include an Honors Option, which offers students challenging, seminar-style courses in the humanities. The courses emphasize critical thinking, writing skills, and independent research.

The Weekend College for Nurses gives career-minded adults the opportunity to pursue an associate degree in nursing. Classes are identical in content and level to those offered during the regular semester except that the schedule is accelerated to meet the needs of focused, mature students who are experienced LPNs.

Academic Facilities

Delhi's Academic Success Center is staffed by professionals who provide tutorial, study skills, English as a second language, and disabled student services.

The Sanford Hall Technology Center, which is open 100 hours per week and features 250 computer workstations loaded with industry-quality software. Wireless Internet access is available to students in residence halls, complementing the advanced-presentation-technology classrooms, a networked instructional lab, and electronic library resources.

The Career Services Center assists students and Delhi alumni with career decision making, career planning, job searches, and the selection of upper-division colleges and universities for transfer. Specialized services that are available include computer programs for and personal assistance with career/transfer planning; campus visits by business and industrial recruiters, as well as admissions representatives from four-year colleges and universities; internship information; a monthly job bulletin; and access to nationwide employment databases.

The Louis and Mildred Resnick Library features multimedia workstations, Internet access, CD-ROM and online databases, 40,000 books, 300 periodical titles, 5,000 reference courses, microforms, videos, and CD-ROMs. As Resnick Library is a member of the State University of New York, UCT, and regional and national library consortia, users have access to materials from across New York State and from around the world. The library is open seven days a week. Internet access is available at http://www.delhi.edu/page/lib/resnick.htm.

Costs

Tuition for New York State residents is $4350 per year. Tuition for out-of-state students is $7000 annually for associate students and $10,300 for bachelor's students. A double room in a residence hall is $3520 per year. Meal plan options vary between $2620 and $3080 per year.

Financial Aid

About 85 percent of Delhi's student body receives some form of financial aid. Delhi awards more than $100,000 each year in campus scholarships to students. The College also participates in all major federal financial aid programs and the New York State Tuition Assistance Program. Students should complete the Free Application for Federal Student Aid (FAFSA) and submit it by February 15. The FAFSA is available from high school guidance offices and from Delhi.

Faculty

Teaching is the top priority for the Delhi faculty. Faculty members are committed to helping students succeed both in and out of class. Small classes (a student-faculty ratio of 16:1) help students develop a close working relationship with faculty members. In addition, a large number of Delhi faculty members were employed in the field before joining the College staff, and their practical experience brings a realistic edge to classroom learning. Faculty members contribute to student advisement and participate in a wide range of cocurricular activities that also enhance the academic program.

Student Government

Delhi's Student Senate is the student governing body and takes an active leadership role as a voice of the students on major campus issues. The Senate is composed of representatives from all recognized clubs and organizations on campus, along with an Executive Board made up of 5 elected student officials. The Senate manages the student activity fund, which totals approximately $300,000 annually. The President of the Student Senate serves as a member of the College Council, the College Foundation, and the College's Auxiliary Services Corporation. In addition, the Senate elects 3 additional representatives to the Auxiliary Service Corporation Board.

Admission Requirements

Admission requirements vary according to the program selected. Candidates must submit the State University of New York application form, which is available from all high school guidance offices in New York State, or the SUNY Delhi application, which is available from the Office of Enrollment Services or via the Web site listed below. A personal interview is not required, but the College encourages students to make a campus visit. The Enrollment Services Office is glad to arrange a campus tour and on request personalizes each visit by setting up special activities and meetings with faculty members, staff members, and students.

Application and Information

Delhi operates on a rolling admission plan; applications are reviewed on a first-come, first-served basis. Applications are accepted until each curriculum is filled. Therefore, it is advisable to apply as early as possible. Decisions are released beginning November 1 of each year.

For more information, students should contact:

Enrollment Services Office
State University of New York at Delhi
2 Main Street
Delhi, New York 13753
Telephone: 607-746-4550
800-96-DELHI (toll-free)
Fax: 607-746-4104
E-mail: enroll@delhi.edu
World Wide Web: http://admissions.delhi.edu

Tree-lined mountains, beautiful streams, and picturesque views make SUNY Delhi's natural setting in the Catskill Mountains outstanding.

STATE UNIVERSITY OF NEW YORK EMPIRE STATE COLLEGE

SARATOGA SPRINGS, NEW YORK

The College

Empire State College was established as an arts and science college in 1971 to fill a unique and necessary role in the State University of New York (SUNY) system. Governor Nelson A. Rockefeller provided the first state funds to "create a new nonresidential college with a commitment to test new, flexible, and individualized modes of learning, including new approaches to the delivery of educational services." While the SUNY system had campuses throughout the state, a critical need existed to reach a substantial population who could not—due to location, schedule, family obligations, or limited course or program availability—participate in classroom-based study. Since that time, the College has pioneered new educational methods and technologies with programs and degrees designed specifically for adult learners. The College has continued to evolve and meet their varied and changing needs as it expands throughout New York State and internationally with more than 17,000 students and 40,000 alumni.

In addition to its undergraduate degrees, Empire State College offers four Master of Arts degrees (in business and policy studies, labor and policy studies, liberal studies, and social policy) and a competency-based Master of Business Administration.

Location

From the first locations established in Albany and New York City in 1971, Empire State College has continued to grow and today has more than thirty locations from the Canadian border to Long Island's eastern shore. Its seven primary centers are located in Albany, Buffalo, Hartsdale, New York City, Rochester, Syracuse, and Old Westbury on Long Island, with smaller units located in the surrounding communities. The coordinating center is located in historic Saratoga Springs, New York.

Majors and Degrees

Five undergraduate degrees are offered in eleven areas of study, from the arts to business, management, and economics. When student select the area of study they are interested in, they then choose a concentration—similar to a major—within this area. With the guidance of their professor—their faculty mentor—students have the opportunity to design their own degree program based on their goals and objectives. The faculty mentor is there to advise and assist every step of the way.

Degrees offered include the Associate in Arts (A.A.), Associate in Science (A.S.), Bachelor of Arts (B.A.), Bachelor of Science (B.S.), and Bachelor of Professional Studies (B.P.S.).

There is no hard and fast time frame for how long it takes to earn a degree, since it depends on how many courses a student takes at a time and how much credit they can include from other sources. However, approximately 40 percent of the students who enter at an advanced level complete their degrees within two to four years on a part-time basis; many take as little as a year. Students design individually tailored concentrations and earn degrees in the following areas of study: the arts; business, management, and economics; community and human services; cultural studies; educational studies; historical studies; human development; interdisciplinary studies; labor studies; science, mathematics, and technology; and social theory, social structure, and change.

Empire State College provides students with choices regarding how best to pursue their degree and offers a number of flexible education options. Guided independent study, where students complete course requirements on their own schedule and at times convenient to them, is one option. Instead of taking classes, a student and his or her mentor develop "a learning contract" specifying what is expected to be learned during a given term. After enrolling at an Empire State College location, a student works with a mentor to define a schedule to meet and evaluate progress.

If students need even more flexibility, live far from a regional center, or prefer Web-based courses, they may decide to enroll in the Center for Distance Learning. With more than 400 courses taught online, most students who choose to can complete their entire degree program via the Web. Others prefer a blend of print-based and Web courses. Students who take online courses enjoy the opportunity to interact through e-mail, not only with their professor, but with other students taking the same course.

Study groups are for students who study independently yet want to delve deeper into a subject through face-to-face interaction with others. Study groups allow students to discuss topics and assignments and share insights with other students.

Academic Programs

Most of the College's programs are not structured around the traditional college year or semesters, quarters, or summer sessions. Students are admitted and can begin their studies as resources are available to serve them either on a full-time (12–16 credits) or part-time (6–8 credits) basis. Each enrollment period is composed of sixteen calendar weeks. Enrollment occurs throughout the year except in the August reading period. Because the College does not have extended vacations or breaks, students may pursue studies continuously and make rapid progress toward their degree.

Empire State College also differs from some traditional colleges in recognizing the value of lifelong learning. Whether a student has attended other colleges, built a career, or simply pursued personal interests, odds are they've spent much of their life learning. Provided the life-learning experience is college level and relevant to their degree program, students can earn credits based on transcripts and evaluation.

The College also offers a number of specialized programs to serve various adult learners, such as the FORUM Management Education, a bachelor's degree program designed for experienced business professionals looking for an accelerated path to a college degree. The Harry Van Arsdale Jr. Center for Labor Studies offers members of unions and others interested in labor-related careers one of the most comprehensive labor programs in the nation. Although it specializes in labor issues, students can enroll in any of the areas of study offered by Empire State College. Many of the most prominent labor leaders across New York State can be counted among the center's graduates. The Center for Distance Learning is for students who prefer the flexibility of learning at a distance. The Center for Distance Learning offers all areas of study, but students complete their degrees through Web-based or print courses or other distance learning methods. The Center for

Workforce Advancement offers on-site and online workplace training primarily for corporate-sponsored employees.

Off-Campus Programs

The College offers other opportunities for learning. The SUNY Learning Network is a growing consortium of campuses in the SUNY system that have joined together to offer graduate and undergraduate online courses. The online courses are available to degree-seeking students and students who simply want to take courses for personal development.

Empire State College offers study-abroad opportunities to American students who wish to spend a summer, a semester, or even an academic year at Franklin College in Lugano, Switzerland. Students live in a beautiful campus community and choose from a broad selection of courses taught by a distinguished international faculty. As a member of the College Consortium for International Studies (CCIS), Empire State College coordinates the CCIS program in Lugano for students from Empire State College and other CCIS-member institutions.

Empire State College students may cross-register at other institutions to expand their course options, to get hands-on experience not readily available through independent study, or because a subject lends itself to classroom study. Empire State College grants credit toward a degree program for classes completed at other accredited institutions.

Academic Facilities

Empire State College is a college designed with the adult learner in mind, and students have access to many public and private library collections. As part of the State University system, the College participates in the SUNY Open Access library program, which allows students to use most services at participating SUNY libraries. Residents of the New York City metropolitan region benefit from a similar arrangement with the City of New York (CUNY) libraries.

Costs

Tuition and fees for the 2003–04 academic year were $4427 for in-state residents and $10,377 for out-of-state residents. Books and supplies cost approximately $500 per semester.

Financial Aid

Empire State College's Financial Aid Office administers funds from a variety of federal and state sources to students based on need. More than 40 percent of the students receive some kind of financial aid. There are three types of aid available at Empire State College: grants/scholarships, loans, and work-study. Other sources of financial assistance may be available from a wide variety of organizations, civic and cultural groups, and employers. Students are urged to explore these possibilities. In order to be considered for financial aid, students must complete the Free Application for Federal Student Aid (FAFSA). A time payment plan is also available whereby tuition and fees may be paid in three installments. For more specific information, students should visit http://www.esc.edu/financialservices.

Faculty

The 427 full- and part-time members of Empire State College's faculty come from a variety of backgrounds, including business, the arts, and traditional four-year colleges. More than 80 percent hold doctoral degrees in their area of expertise. What they all have in common is a passion for teaching adult students. Faculty members are called mentors because they are both partners and guides in students' education. They respect the years of experience and knowledge that adults bring to an academic program and are glad to share their own expertise. Students meet with their mentors on a regular basis to receive advice and to develop plans for carrying out their learning contracts. Students maintain contact with their mentors on an agreed-upon schedule, either face-to-face or by phone, mail, or e-mail. Most students value the personal attention, and when Empire State College students graduate, often it is their mentor whom they celebrate when they look back on their college years.

Admission Requirements

Decisions on admission to the College are made without regard to the race, sex, disability, religion, or national origin of the applicant. The two principal requirements for admission are (1) possession of a high school diploma or its equivalent or the ability to benefit from college study as demonstrated through means required by the College, and (2) the ability of an Empire State College learning location to meet the applicant's educational needs and objectives. Although the majority of applicants to the College are admitted, the College reserves the right to deny admission based on its ability to meet a student's needs. Standardized test scores are not used as part of the application process for admission.

Application and Information

Because the College's mode of education is unique, it is strongly recommended that students attend an information session at the nearest Empire State College location. Details regarding times and places of the information sessions are available on the College's Web site or by calling the phone number listed below.

Administrative Offices
Empire State College
One Union Avenue
Saratoga Springs, New York 12866
Telephone: 518-587-2100
World Wide Web: http://www.esc.edu

STATE UNIVERSITY OF NEW YORK INSTITUTE OF TECHNOLOGY AT UTICA/ROME

UTICA, NEW YORK

The Institute

As a unique member of the State University of New York family, SUNY Institute of Technology (SUNYIT) is the ideal choice for focused students interested in technology and professional studies. SUNYIT's broad curriculum also embraces the humanities, communications, math, and science. Students enjoy close contact with faculty members in small classes, most with fewer than 20 students.

Founded as an upper-division and graduate institution in 1966, SUNYIT now offers eleven bachelor's degree programs for freshmen, twenty bachelor's degree programs for transfer students, and eleven graduate degrees, including the Master of Business Administration in technology management.

SUNY Institute of Technology enrolled 2,046 undergraduate and 491 graduate students on both a full-time and part-time basis in 2002–03. The men-women ratio was approximately 1:1. Eleven percent of the student population was from minority groups; 4 percent were international students.

In addition to its academic facilities, SUNYIT provides student services through the Campus Life, Career Services, Health, and Counseling Center Offices. Townhouse-style residence halls provide on-campus housing to 584 students. The Campus Center provides health, physical education, and recreation facilities as well as a dining hall and student services offices. In addition to providing a wide variety of intramural sports for students, SUNYIT has competitive intercollegiate teams in men's and women's basketball, bowling, and soccer; men's baseball, golf, and lacrosse; and women's softball, cross-country, and volleyball.

Location

SUNYIT is located in Utica, New York. The city of Utica, which has a population of 60,000, is situated in the geographic center of New York State, approximately 220 miles from New York City and 190 miles from Buffalo on the New York State Thruway. Utica, a cultural and recreational center for this area of New York State, has a variety of recreational and educational opportunities. Museums, theaters, restaurants, and professional sports events are available either within walking distance of the campus or a short bus ride away. As a natural gateway to the Adirondack Mountains, Utica provides its residents with access to hiking, boating, skiing, and other outdoor activities. Served by buses, Amtrak, and airlines, the city is easily reached from locations throughout the eastern United States.

Majors and Degrees

SUNYIT awards the following baccalaureate degrees: Bachelor of Professional Studies (B.P.S.), Bachelor of Science (B.S.), Bachelor of Arts (B.A.), and Bachelor of Business Administration (B.B.A.).

Academic majors available to freshmen and transfer students include accounting, applied mathematics, business/public management, computer and information science, computer engineering technology, computer information systems, finance, health-information management, health-services management, industrial engineering technology, and mechanical engineering technology. Additional academic majors available to transfer students are civil engineering technology, electrical engineering, electrical engineering technology, general studies, nursing, professional and technical communication, psychology, sociology, and telecommunications.

A number of options and concentrations within specific curricula are also available, as well as minors in accounting; anthropology; computer science; economics; finance; gerontology; health-services management; manufacturing/quality assurance technology; mathematics; physics; professional and technical communication; psychology; science, technology, and society; and sociology.

Academic Program

SUNYIT's mission is to provide professionally oriented education in a variety of academic areas. The academic year is divided into two semesters and runs from September through May. Summer and Winterm sessions are also available.

Baccalaureate degree requirements vary from program to program but usually consist of a combination of specific major courses and liberal arts studies. Specializations and other options exist within the Schools of Arts and Sciences, Information Systems and Engineering Technology, Nursing and Health Systems, and Management. Specializations are developed through the use of electives and individual advisement.

Off-Campus Programs

Internship and cooperative education experiences are integral to effective career planning and job search strategies. These experiences can influence career plans by providing an opportunity for occupational exploration, developing marketable career-related skills and characteristics, and establishing a network of contacts that can provide relevant and timely information critical to the career decision-making process. In addition, employers are increasingly using internships and cooperative education programs as training opportunities leading to full-time permanent employment. All students, regardless of major, are encouraged to consider gaining experience in their chosen field that complements classroom learning. For additional information, students should contact the academic department or the Office of Career Services.

Academic Facilities

SUNYIT's academic facilities are located on its scenic 850-acre campus just north of the city of Utica and are easily accessible by municipal bus service. The campus consists of four building complexes, a facilities building, and residence halls. SUNYIT's newest addition is the Peter J. Cayan Library, a $14-million dollar project comprising 68,000 square feet of space, group and individual study rooms, and an advanced computerized library instruction room. Dedicated in May 2003, the state-of-the-art building houses library resources that include more than 170,000 bound volumes, 200,000 microforms, and an extensive collection of professional journals, newspapers, and other national publications. In addition, the library is a federal depository for government documents. Full-text databases and databases in FirstSearch are provided; all workstations have high-speed Internet access.

Kunsela Hall contains administrative offices, classrooms, and laboratories for the telecommunications, electrical engineering, electrical engineering technology, and computer science programs. Donovan Hall, the academic complex, houses classrooms, faculty offices, and laboratory facilities for all other programs, including business, industrial engineering technology, mechanical engineering technology, health-services management, nursing, and arts and sciences. A comprehensive student center contains a gymnasium, a swimming pool, recreational facilities, a cafeteria, a bookstore, student services offices, and meeting rooms for clubs, special activities, and student government.

Costs

Costs for the 2003–04 academic year included state resident tuition and fees of $5154 and out-of-state tuition and fees of $11,104. Room and board costs were $6800, and personal expenses, books, supplies, and travel cost approximately $2730. The total expenses were about $14,684 for New York State residents and $20,634 for out-of-state students. Costs may be subject to change.

Financial Aid

A wide variety of financial aid is available to students at SUNYIT. All financial aid is awarded on the basis of need, as determined by an assessment of the Free Application for Federal Student Aid. At present, approximately 85 percent of the students receive financial assistance. The forms of financial aid available include Tuition Assistance Program awards (for New York State residents only), Federal Supplemental Educational Opportunity Grants, Federal Pell Grants, Federal Work-Study Program employment, Federal Perkins Loans, federal Nursing Student Loans, Federal Direct Student Loans, a variety of state-sponsored loans, and a broad range of private scholarships and grants. Students with a GPA of 3.25 or better or a high school average of 90 are automatically considered for merit scholarships at the time of their application.

Faculty

SUNYIT faculty members come from all over the world and are committed to teaching, research, and service to the community. Among the faculty members are a Distinguished Service Professor, a Fulbright Scholar, and numerous recipients of the Chancellor's Award for Excellence in Teaching. Eighty percent of SUNYIT's full-time faculty members have doctoral or terminal degrees. The faculty members are fully engaged in academic orientation and advisement, individualized instruction, cooperative faculty-student efforts in research projects, and concern for students as individuals. In the classroom, the average student-faculty ratio is 18:1.

Student Government

All full-time undergraduates are members of the SUNYIT Student Association. Its primary functions are to develop and monitor the student-activity-fee budget, to approve and oversee all student organizations, to debate issues of concern to students and take action as needed, and to develop programs of interest to all students. Student government consists of a 7-person executive committee and 11 senators. Students are encouraged to take an active role in the governance process, and many opportunities for involvement, in addition to those listed above, are available for interested students.

Admission Requirements

Admission to SUNYIT as a freshman is competitive and selective. In order to be considered, students should have a minimum of a B+ average in a college-preparatory program, with approximate scores of at least 1140 on the SAT I or 25 on the ACT. In addition to the admission application, test scores, and high school transcripts, a supplemental application, and an essay are required as part of the process. Students who have completed Adavanced Placement course work in high school with a score of 3, 4, or 5 are considered for transfer credit.

Admission to SUNYIT as a transfer student is also competitive. Most programs require a minimum GPA of 2.5 for guaranteed admission. Transfer students below a 2.5 GPA but above a 2.0 GPA may be required to participate in an interview. Transfer students are required to furnish an official transcript from all previous colleges they attended.

Most programs are competitive, requiring a minimum GPA of 2.5 for guaranteed admission. Students with a cumulative GPA of at least 3.25 are automatically considered for merit and residential scholarships; no separate application is required.

Application and Information

Freshman applications are reviewed beginning January 15 and are considered on a rolling admissions basis thereafter. Freshman applicants may also apply for admission through the Early Decision program. Early Decision applicants must apply by November 15. A supplemental application, including an essay, is required for consideration.

Transfer applications are accepted on a rolling admissions basis. Prospective students are urged to apply early.

Students who wish to apply should obtain a copy of the State University of New York application booklet from a two-year college, a local high school, or the Admissions Office. In addition, students may apply online through the SUNYIT Web site listed below. Application forms for international students may also be obtained through the Admissions Office.

SUNY Institute of Technology adheres to the principle that all persons should have equal opportunity and access to its educational facilities without regard to race, creed, sex, or national origin.

Official transcripts from all previously attended high schools and colleges should be sent to the Director of Admissions at the address below. All communications and requests for additional information should also be directed to:

Director of Admissions
SUNY Institute of Technology
P.O. Box 3050
Utica, New York 13504-3050
Telephone: 315-792-7500
866-2SUNYIT (toll-free)
Fax: 315-792-7837
E-mail: admissions@sunyit.edu
World Wide Web: http://www.sunyit.edu

Townhouse-style residence halls afford students the opportunity to live and learn in a convenient, safe, and comfortable environment.

STATE UNIVERSITY OF NEW YORK MARITIME COLLEGE

FORT SCHUYLER, THROGGS NECK, NEW YORK

The College

Founded in 1874, the State University of New York Maritime College is the original, federally approved, commercial nautical institution in the United States. Maritime College has as its primary mission the preparation of men and women for a full spectrum of professional careers by providing high-quality undergraduate and graduate programs in international business, engineering, science, and technology, with particular emphasis on the marine industry. Most of the degree programs may be completed while concurrently preparing for the U.S. Merchant Marine officer's license as a third mate or third assistant engineer.

Maritime College graduates receive a well-rounded education that enables them to pursue career options in engineering or business, in private industry or government service, or at sea as civilian officers of merchant ships, research ships, and other U.S. vessels. In addition, commissioning options exist for those seeking careers as officers in the U.S. Navy, Marine Corps, Coast Guard, or Air Force or in the National Oceanographic and Atmospheric Administration (NOAA). Maritime College is the only college that hosts a Naval ROTC program in the greater New York metropolitan area. The College has a consistent record of 100 percent career placement upon graduation.

Maritime College fields sixteen varsity sports and is nationally known for its sailing and crew teams.

Location

The scenic 56-acre campus is located at historic Fort Schuyler on the Throggs Neck peninsula, where the East River meets Long Island Sound. The College campus has a suburban setting yet is a short bus ride from midtown Manhattan. The peninsula offers panoramic views of the East River and Long Island Sound, with impressive sights of coastal Connecticut, the North Shore of Long Island, and the Manhattan skyline.

The College's extensive waterfront property allows berthing of the College training ship, *Empire State VI*, several research craft, and a training coastal tanker as well as a waterfront activities center/boat house. The waterfront is home for its fleet of 420s, Lasers, FJ's, and offshore racing yachts.

Majors and Degrees

The College offers Bachelor of Engineering degrees in electrical, facilities, marine, and mechanical engineering; marine electrical and electronic systems; and naval architecture. It offers the Bachelor of Science degree in business administration/marine transportation, general business and commerce (with a humanities concentration), general engineering, international transportation and trade, marine environmental science (with a meteorology or oceanography concentration), and marine operations.

All degree programs may be combined with preparation for the professional license as a U.S. Merchant Marine Officer, except international transportation and trade, which is an upper-division transfer program.

Business administration/marine transportation couples the nautical education and training required of a ship's deck officer with the business administration academic core (liberal arts and sciences, accounting, economics, and marketing and management). Students may concentrate in the areas of management, logistics, international business, or vessel operations.

Graduates enrolled in this degree/license program are qualified to sail as third mates aboard oceangoing ships, on the Great Lakes, and on all types of inland and near-coastal vessels. In addition to careers at sea, the federal license enhances graduates' opportunities to find exciting positions in virtually all aspects of global transportation, from marine insurance to management of import/export industries and terminal operations. A related program, international transportation and trade, is designed for upper-division transfer students and does not require license preparation. Also available is a major in general business and commerce, which includes deck license preparation and a humanities study area concentration.

The College offers Accreditation Board for Engineering and Technology (ABET)-accredited programs in engineering and naval architecture. The marine engineering program at Maritime College provides graduates with a broad understanding of the energy and power industries and includes preparation for a third-assistant engineer's license. Electrical, facilities, and mechanical engineering programs offer specialization within some of the areas covered by the marine engineering discipline and may be pursued as license-option or intern-option students. Naval architecture, offered with a deck- or engine-license option or intern option, is a challenging enterprise, demanding imagination and technical expertise in the design of seaborne structures from ultralarge tankers to high-speed recreational craft. Engine-license candidates experience operating a live power plant aboard the training ship, while intern-option students utilize an industrial co-op experience to gain the hands-on component for which Maritime graduates are renown. A Bachelor of Science degree in marine operations combines a deck license with a technical background and a limited horsepower engineering license, and general engineering qualifies students for an engine license and offers a humanities study area concentration.

The marine environmental science (MES) program offers undergraduate study in the ocean and atmospheric sciences, including environmental chemistry, environmental protection, marine biology and ecology, and physical oceanography and meteorology. MES students have deck, engine, and nonlicense options.

A two-year associate degree program in marine technology/small vessel operations qualifies graduates for a 200-ton U.S. Coast Guard mate's license or a 1000-horsepower Designated Duty Engineer (DDE) license.

An important part of all Maritime College curricula is the annual Summer Sea Term aboard the 565-foot training ship, *Empire State VI*, the largest and best-equipped training ship in the United States. Summer Sea Term provides a leadership laboratory in which cadets assume responsibility for the operation of the ship under the supervision of licensed officers and staff. The *Empire State VI* visits nine European ports by the time the students graduate. Recent ports of call include Italy, Spain, Ireland, Bermuda, the Bahamas, and London.

Academic Program

Academic programs at the Maritime College lead to the Bachelor of Science or Bachelor of Engineering degree, and most include licensure as a commercial ship's officer (mate or engineer) as an option (license qualification is a requirement in some programs). These licenses, issued by the Coast Guard, qualify graduates to sail on oceangoing vessels engaged in international commerce or coastal, Great Lakes, or inland waterway shipping. License candidates are required to be members of the Regiment of Cadets. All programs include a hands-on, professional experience, either during summer sea terms aboard the training ship *Empire State* or through industrial co-ops/internships.

Academic Facilities

Pre–Civil War Fort Schuyler houses the Stephen B. Luce Library with its more than 80,000 volumes and 375 periodical subscriptions, accessed through an online catalog. Full-text CD-ROM databases and online searches are also available. A $1.5-million Center for Simulation and Marine Operations also resides in the Fort. It contains a state-of-the-art full bridge simulator, a liquid cargo simulator, an electronic navigation simulator, ten Automatic Radar Plotting Aid (ARPA)-equipped radar simulators, and Global Maritime Distress and Safety System (GMDSS) simulators.

The Science and Engineering Building contains a marine diesel simulator, a ship model basin (towing tank), and five computer classroom/laboratories as well as advanced electrical and mechanical engineering labs; physics, chemistry, and meteorology laboratories; and smart classrooms.

Floating laboratories include the training ship *Empire State VI*, a coastal tanker used for liquid cargo training, and several marine research craft, including a 147-foot buoy tender.

Costs

For 2003–04, tuition for New York State residents was $4350. Since the Maritime College has been designated as a regional maritime college, students from east and gulf coast states (Alabama, Connecticut, Delaware, Florida, Georgia, Louisiana, Maryland, Mississippi, New Jersey, North Carolina, Pennsylvania, Rhode Island, South Carolina, and Virginia) and the District of Columbia also pay the New York State tuition rate of $4350 per year.

In addition, students from any state who apply for and are qualified to enroll in the federally funded Student Incentive Program (SIP) are charged New York State tuition.

For students who did not participate in SIP and were not residents of New York or any of the regional states, tuition was $10,300 per year in 2003–04. This rate also applied to international students.

Additional costs in 2003–04 included fees averaging $500; room and board, including the two-month Summer Sea Term, at $9500 per year; and cadet uniforms at $2100 (first year only). Typically, books and supplies average $800 per year, and students should budget an additional amount for personal expenses.

Financial Aid

Maritime College students have access to several special forms of aid. Cadets who apply for and are selected for the federal Student Incentive Program receive $3000 per year. SIP participants pay New York State tuition rates regardless of residence and agree to complete one of the license programs at the College and serve in the U.S. Naval Reserve (inactive duty, including the Merchant Marine Reserve). Full-tuition scholarships are also available through Navy ROTC. Four-year NROTC scholarship winners are also offered free room at the College, and the Maritime Academy Reserve Training Program (MARTP), a Coast Guard Commissioning Program, provides generous compensation to select Maritime College cadets beginning their sophomore year.

A variety of privately funded scholarships, including a number of tuition Cadet Appointment Program Scholarships, are available to qualified students. Need-based aid, including Federal Pell Grants, TAP grants, Federal Perkins Loans, Federal Stafford Student Loans, and Federal Work-Study awards, is available and requires the Free Application for Federal Student Aid (FAFSA) as well as the Maritime College institutional form.

New York State residents who are in great financial need and who have not been able to achieve up to their academic potential because of factors beyond their control may apply for assistance through the Educational Opportunity Program when they apply for admission.

Faculty

Maritime College prides itself on an innovative, hands-on approach to instruction that is directed by a dedicated faculty composed of experts in their fields. The faculty members involved with license preparation course work have the appropriate United States Coast Guard licenses and professional credentials. Faculty members teaching in traditional academic disciplines possess appropriate credentials, with 35 holding the doctorate or other terminal degree in their field. Many faculty members, recognized as experts within the maritime industry, are involved with consulting work. A student-faculty ratio of 12:1 is maintained.

Student Government

The College has an active government association. It oversees College-wide activities, clubs and organizations, and a diverse athletic program. Students are also represented on various faculty committees.

Admission Requirements

Admission is competitive and is based strictly on the applicant's abilities. Political nomination is not required. Decisions are based on strength of academic preparation; grades, rank in class, and test scores; outside activities and achievements; and trends in performance. Transfer students are welcome. Math, through at least intermediate algebra and trigonometry, and a year of either chemistry or physics are required.

Application and Information

Applications (the SUNY Common Application for Admission form and College forms), catalogs, and additional information are available from the Office of Admissions. Prospective students are encouraged to schedule an interview and a student-guided tour (arranged with the admissions office). Students may apply online through the College's Web page.

Office of Admissions
State University of New York Maritime College
6 Pennyfield Avenue
Throggs Neck, New York 10465
Telephone: 718-409-7220
800-654-1874 (toll-free in New York State)
800-642-1874 (toll-free in the Northeast)
E-mail: admissions@sunymaritime.edu
World Wide Web: http://www.sunymaritime.edu

Maritime College—a degree and more!

STATE UNIVERSITY OF WEST GEORGIA

CARROLLTON, GEORGIA

The University

A coeducational, residential institution, the State University of West Georgia (UWG) is a charter member of the University System of Georgia. From its beginnings in 1906 as the Fourth District Agricultural and Mechanical School, West Georgia has grown into a leading comprehensive regional university that enrolled 10,255 students in fall 2003 from Georgia, forty-three other states, and forty-two other countries. About 64 percent of enrolled students are women, and 28 percent belong to minority groups. Today, UWG offers 113 programs of study through three colleges—the College of Arts and Sciences, the Richards College of Business, and the College of Education. Sixty programs are available at the bachelor's level, fifty-two at the master's and specialist levels, and one at the doctoral level. In addition, the Honors College, the only college of its kind in Georgia, offers an honors curriculum and the Advanced Academy of Georgia, one of fewer than twelve programs in the nation that allows gifted high school juniors and seniors to live and study full time at a university while completing high school graduation requirements in absentia. The Graduate School has one of the highest percentages of students enrolled in graduate classes in the University System.

UWG takes its motto of Educational Excellence in a Personal Environment seriously. Faculty members teach their own courses and take a personal interest in students. Undergraduates receive access to technology and research opportunities that are not usually available at other schools. In 2003, the Southern Association of Colleges and Schools (SACS) gave UWG a rare commendation for technology resources, equipment, and support, which a SACS visiting team called "far above that of similar institutions." Freshmen live on campus in one of eleven residence halls, and every residence hall has an Internet port for each occupant. If they wish, freshman can join a learning community of students who live in the same hall, share classes, and often earn higher grades as a result of this arrangement. Extracurricular activities are sponsored through more than 100 student organizations, which cover academics, professional and honor groups, politics, religion, service, recreation and sports, social fraternities and sororities, and a national champion debate team. The athletics program, one of the most varied among college-division schools, fields men's intercollegiate teams in baseball, basketball, cross-country, and football, and women's teams in basketball, cross-country, softball, and volleyball, with men's and women's golf and women's soccer to be added in 2004–05. All team are affiliated with Division II of the NCAA. West Georgia also has a nationally competitive cheerleading program, featuring the national champion coed team for 2002, 2003, and 2004; the 2004 national champion all-female squad; and a partner stunt team that ranks second in the U.S.

The State University of West Georgia is accredited by the Commission on Colleges of the Southern Association of Colleges and Schools (1866 Southern Lane, Decatur, Georgia 30033-4097; telephone: 404-679-4501) to award bachelor's, master's, and education specialist degrees and an education doctoral degree. All programs preparing teachers through the master's level are accredited by the National Council for Accreditation of Teacher Education, and the Georgia Professional Standards Commission approves UWG to recommend candidates for education certificates. The Georgia State Department of Education offers full recognition and accreditation as well. The undergraduate Bachelor of Business Administration and graduate Master of Business Administration and Master of Professional Accounting degrees in the Richards College of Business are accredited by AACSB International–The Association to Advance Collegiate Schools of Business. Only 7 percent of business schools across the nation—and only twelve other institutions in Georgia—hold this accreditation. Both the Bachelor and Master of Professional Accounting programs are accredited separately by AACSB International. The University's Department of Chemistry is accredited by the American Chemical Society, the Department of Psychology by the Consortium for Diversified Psychology Programs, and the computer science program by the Computing Accreditation Commission of the Accreditation Board for Engineering and Technology. The Master of Public Administration degree is accredited by the National Association of Schools of Public Affairs and Administration. Other programs are accredited by the National League for Nursing Accrediting Commission (61 Broadway, New York, New York 10006; telephone: 800-669-1656 (toll-free)), the National Association of Schools of Theatre, and the National Association of Schools of Music. All art programs are accredited by the National Association of Schools of Art and Design.

Location

Fifty miles west of Atlanta, the campus extends over approximately 400 wooded acres, and its picturesque blend of pre–Civil War and late-twentieth-century architecture complements the similar Southern style of surrounding Carrollton, Georgia. Named a City of Excellence in Georgia in 2002 and listed in *The Best Small Southern Towns* (Peachtree Publishers, 2001), Carrollton is the cultural, educational, health-care, and commercial center for the west Georgia region. A progressive city of about 20,000 with a diverse economic base, Carrollton offers a wide range of opportunities for professional work experiences as well as cultural activities and entertainment. Shops, galleries, and restaurants line the recently revitalized downtown square, and the city offers movies, dancing, theatrical productions, and dining that ranges from Southern to gourmet and international cuisine. A new $6-million Cultural Arts Center showcases the arts, and recreational activities abound through an award-winning parks and recreation program and the county's 33,421 acres of state, public, and private recreational parks and facilities.

Majors and Degrees

UWG offers twelve baccalaureate degrees as follows: Bachelor of Arts in anthropology, art, biology, chemistry, chemistry/secondary education, English, French, geography, German, global studies, history, international economic affairs, mass communications, mathematics, philosophy, political science, psychology, sociology, Spanish, and theater; Bachelor of Business Administration in accounting, economics, finance, management, management information systems, marketing, real estate, and technology support systems; Bachelor of Fine Arts in art and art education; Bachelor of Music in composition, music education, music with studies in business, performance, performance with emphasis in jazz studies, and performance with emphasis in piano pedagogy; Bachelor of Science in biology, biology/secondary education, computer science, criminology, economics, economics/secondary education, geography, geology, mathematics, physics, physics/secondary education, political science, and sociology; Bachelor of Science in Chemistry; Bachelor of Science in Earth Science; Bachelor of Science in Education in business education, early childhood education, middle grades education, physical education, special education in mental retardation, and speech-language pathology; Bachelor of Science in Environmental Science; Bachelor of Science in Environmental Studies; Bachelor of Science in Nursing; and Bachelor of Science in Recreation. Preprofessional programs are available in allied health, dental hygiene, dentistry, forestry, law, medicine, occupational therapy, pharmacy, physical therapy, physician assistant studies, and veterinary studies medicine. A dual-degree program in engineering is offered with Georgia Institute of Technology, Auburn University, and Mercer University.

Academic Program

The academic year consists of two 15-week semesters that begin in August and January, a three-week miniterm in May, and summer semesters of about four or eight weeks. During the freshman and sophomore years, students complete the core curriculum, 60 semester hours of general education courses designed by the faculty to provide a foundation for all degree programs. Included in the core are courses in written and oral communication, mathematics, natural science, technology, social science, and the humanities and fine arts as well as courses designed to lead to one's chosen major. Undergraduates have nationally acclaimed access to research opportunities, and instruction is enhanced by faculty member research that is supported by more than $2.2 million in grants.

Off-Campus Programs

Off-campus classes are offered in Newnan, Georgia, (at the University's Newnan Center) and in Dalton, Georgia (through the cooperative External Degree Program with Dalton College). Courses are offered to students at remote locations through the Distance Education Program, which conducts classes both on line and through two-way live videoconferencing. Some degrees may be earned by attending only evening and weekend classes. Study-abroad programs for credit are offered in art (Bayeux and Paris), culture (Cuba), economics and finance (Atlanta, New York, and London), French language and civilization (Tours, Paris, and Sainte Maxime), geography (Canada), management and marketing (Atlanta and London), Spanish language and culture (Cuernavaca), and internships are available in Germany. Students may also participate in multidisciplinary summer programs in Athens, Germany, Italy, London, Paris, and St. Petersburg, or semester-long programs throughout the world.

Academic Facilities

The new $19.5-million Technology-enhanced Learning Center (TLC) is a three-building complex that occupies more than 1 acre and houses laboratories, lecture halls, classrooms, and offices. The center features pioneering classroom and laboratory technology, and approximately 2,600 computer network connections provide Internet access from virtually anywhere in the complex. In the TLC's studio laboratories, students have access to computers and tabletop labs for conducting hands-on experiments while receiving instruction.

One of the most modern library facilities in Georgia, Ingram Library, participates in Georgia Library Learning Online (GALILEO), an award-winning Web-based virtual library that offers access to Internet databases, full-text journals, electronic books, newspaper and magazine articles, and countless research tools. Local resources, GALILEO, and the new Georgia Interconnected Libraries (GIL) project give students complete access to local, state, regional, and international library collections.

The Townsend Center for the Performing Arts presents a number of special performances and concerts annually by local, regional, and national entertainers and personalities and is available for performances of theatrical and musical events by both student and community groups. The center features a 455-seat proscenium theater, a 155-seat experimental theater, a rehearsal room, dressing rooms, a costume shop, and a set design center. In addition, the Townsend Center houses two Bösendorfer Imperial Grand pianos, one of which is one of only four 290SE player pianos in the United States.

Costs

Based on a 12-hour or more on-campus semester, tuition and fees for the 2003–04 school year were $1387 for Georgia residents and $4705 for nonresidents. Room charges were $1210 per semester, and board cost $993 per semester. Books totaled approximately $600 per semester, and other expenses vary by major. Part-time students are charged tuition and fees on a prorated basis.

Financial Aid

All applicants interested in federal and state financial aid programs must submit a Free Application for Federal Student Aid (FAFSA) and any required documents regarding their own and their family's financial resources. In order to receive financial aid at the State University of West Georgia, students must be in good academic standing and they must be accepted for admission. The state of Georgia provides the HOPE Scholarship to eligible students who are Georgia residents. In addition, UWG offers outstanding students a variety of academic and performing arts scholarships. Some academic scholarships are available to students regardless of their major, and others are for students majoring in particular fields. Still others are designed to encourage students from a specific county or minority group to attend the University. Work programs that are open to students include the Federal Work-Study Program, student assistantships, internships, and cooperative work situations.

Faculty

UWG has 373 full-time faculty members, 82 percent of whom hold the terminal degree in their associated field. The student-to-faculty ratio is approximately 20:1.

Student Government

The Student Government Association deals with matters of student affairs, sets forth general principles of governance of the student body, and approves mandatory student fees. Any enrolled undergraduate or graduate student is eligible to participate in student government.

Admission Requirements

To ensure admission as a freshman, it is desirable for applicants to have a combined SAT I score in the range of 900 or higher or an ACT composite score of 18 or higher as well as a high school grade point average in academic courses of 2.4 or higher. In fall 2003, entering freshmen had a mean SAT I score of 1008 (506 verbal, 502 math) and a mean GPA of 2.98. In addition, all freshman/freshman transfer applicants must complete 16 high school college preparatory units (including a math course higher than Algebra II/geometry), according to standards approved by the University System of Georgia for admission to a four-year state university. Transfer students are considered for admission on the basis of their previous college records and such additional information as is pertinent to their academic abilities. A minimum college cumulative GPA of 2.0 is required for transfer admission.

Application and Information

Every undergraduate applicant must submit a formal application to the Admissions Office along with a $20 nonrefundable application processing fee. July 1 is the deadline for application and document submissions for fall semester, including final high school/college transcripts. Spring and summer semester deadlines are approximately December 1 for spring and May 1 for summer. Prospective students should visit the University's Web site at the address below for specific dates. Beginning freshmen are encouraged to complete the application procedures during the first half of their senior year in high school. For further information, contact:

Director of Admissions
State University of West Georgia
Carrollton, Georgia 30118
Telephone: 770-836-6416
E-mail: admiss@westga.edu
World Wide Web: http://www.westga.edu/prospective/admissions

Classes at the State University of West Georgia are small and dynamic, and faculty members take a personal interest in students.

STEPHENS COLLEGE
COLUMBIA, MISSOURI

The College

Stephens College, founded in 1833 as the nation's second-oldest women's college, is a premier national liberal arts college for women in the Midwest. Stephens is ranked nationally in *U.S. News & World Report* and has repeatedly been selected to the *Princeton Review*'s list of the best colleges in the country. Students from around the globe enrich Stephens with their varied talents, interests, and backgrounds. Stephens students may choose to join one of twelve honorary societies on campus, including Psi Chi, Alpha Epsilon Rho, and Mortar Board, or become involved in student government. Leadership experience is emphasized in all aspects of life at Stephens. Stephens' residence halls provide much of the focus for campus activity. The Searcy House Plan offers a living/learning environment in the humanities to a select group of freshmen each year. Since it began in the 1960s as an experiment funded by the Ford Foundation, the Searcy program has served as a model for similar living/learning communities in colleges and universities across the nation.

In addition to undergraduate degrees, Stephens offers Master's degrees.

Location

Stephens College is located in Columbia, Missouri. Situated halfway between Kansas City and St. Louis, Columbia is the cultural, medical, and business center of mid-Missouri. Often called "College Town, USA," Columbia is also the home of Columbia College and the University of Missouri. Stephens students have easy access to Columbia's shopping, dining, and entertainment offerings.

Majors and Degrees

Stephens College awards the Associate in Arts, Bachelor of Arts, Bachelor of Fine Arts, and Bachelor of Science. Majors include accounting; biology; business administration; creative writing; dance; digital filmmaking; early childhood education; elementary education; English; equestrian business management; equestrian science; fashion communication; fashion design and product development; fashion marketing and management; graphic design/multimedia; health sciences; liberal studies; marketing: public relations and advertising; mass communication (electronic media, journalism, or public relations); psychology; student-initiated majors; and theater arts. The B.F.A. program includes professional-level work in the fine or performing arts plus a strong component in liberal studies.

Academic Programs

The B.A. degree is generally completed in four years. Students pursue depth of study in an academic area, breadth in liberal arts study, and elective course work with guidance from faculty advisers. Academic departments require relevant internships and often provide opportunities for research projects in field settings.

Stephens has introduced many innovative educational concepts into its programs. Stephens emphasizes personalized teaching and development of the individual. Small classes are offered, and most departments offer tutorial projects and readings.

Students in the bachelor's degree programs, either B.A., B.F.A., or B.S., must complete the residence requirement of seven semesters. Students must demonstrate the ability to write proper English or pass two courses in English composition, and must complete at least twelve courses at an advanced level (including five in the major). All degree candidates take eight courses selected from seven areas: natural sciences, social and behavioral sciences, languages and literature, fine arts, history, humanities/religion/philosophy, and mathematics and analytical reasoning. In addition, all degree candidates complete one upper-level liberal arts requirement in each of the following areas: cross-cultural studies, interdisciplinary studies, and moral and ethical issues.

Degree requirements for the Bachelor of Arts include completion of at least eight courses in a department. At least five of these courses must be at or above the 300 level. As many as fifteen courses may be required in the major, but no more than fifteen may count toward a forty-course degree program. Students also may elect to design an interdisciplinary student-initiated Bachelor of Arts major.

The Bachelor of Science degree program requires completion of fifteen to nineteen courses, including a minimum of five courses at or above the 300 level. Bachelor of Science candidates may elect additional courses in the major, but no more than twenty courses may count toward a forty-course degree program. Students also may elect to design an interdisciplinary student-initiated Bachelor of Science major.

Degree requirements for the Bachelor of Fine Arts include completion of twenty to twenty-five courses, including at least five courses at or above the 300 level. B.F.A. candidates may elect additional courses in their major, up to a maximum of twenty-six within a forty-course degree program. The B.F.A. in theater and in dance are completed in three years and two summers.

Through Stephens College School of Graduate and Continuing Education, nontraditional students throughout the country have the opportunity to complete an online program that builds on past learning. Most of Stephens' programs, including courses of study leading to the B.A. degree, are open to Stephens College School of Graduate and Continuing Education students. In addition, the School of Graduate and Continuing Education has programs in business administration; English; health care and a second area; health information administration (the first accredited external degree program in medical record administration in the country); health science and a second area; law, philosophy, and rhetoric; psychology; and student-initiated majors. In addition, Stephens offers graduate degrees in business (through an Internet-based program) and education. Undergraduates in business, fashion marketing/management, and equestrian business management can complete the online M.B.A. through a tuition-paid fellowship, provided they meet certain stipulations.

Stephens also offers numerous partnerships with other institutions wherein students may earn a bachelor's degree from Stephens in three years and a master's degree from another college or university after two additional years. Partnerships currently exist in occupational therapy, physical therapy, physician assistant studies, and accounting.

Off-Campus Programs

Stephens sponsors summer seminars in several countries, including France, Italy, and Japan, as extensions of courses that are regularly offered at the College. Summer-study programs include drama and musical theater at Lake Okoboji, Spirit Lake, Iowa. Stephens also offers study opportunities in Sweden, Ecuador, Korea, and Cambridge, England.

Many other study opportunities are available through global partnerships with other universities.

Academic Facilities

The Hugh Stephens Resources Library contains more than 120,000 volumes. The library is the central building of a quadrangle that includes the Helis Communication Center and the Patricia Barry Television Studio. The E. S. Pillsbury Science Center houses science and mathematics classrooms and laboratories, and the Ellis Learning Laboratories provide modern equipment for individual and group study of foreign languages. Other working laboratories include the student-run Warehouse Theatre, the Johnson Plant Laboratory, and the Audrey Webb Child Study Center, which has an enrollment of approximately 100 children in preschool through third grade.

Costs

For 2004–05, tuition is $18,230, and room costs for single occupancy are $4210. Costs for room and board are subject to change. Additional costs for books, supplies, and personal expenses range between $750 and $1000. The enrollment deposit is $100.

Financial Aid

More than 80 percent of the student body receive some form of assistance through scholarships, grants, loans, or employment. Stephens participates in the Federal Pell Grant, Federal Supplemental Educational Opportunity Grant, Federal Perkins Loan, Federal Stafford Student Loan, and Federal Work-Study programs. Missouri residents are encouraged to apply for aid under the Missouri Student Grant Program. The Free Application for Federal Student Aid (FAFSA) is required for financial aid consideration. Applications for financial aid should be received by March 15. Stephens also offers an early financial aid estimate service.

Faculty

Though most faculty members have come to college teaching via the recognized route of graduate study and scholarship, some have prepared for teaching through work experience, particularly those in applied and performing arts with careers as actors, dancers, musicians, and artists. The faculty is primarily a teaching faculty, and many of the instructors include students in independent scholarly research. Men and women join the Stephens faculty with a commitment to individualized education. They are actively engaged in academic advising and tutorial relationships and frequently spend many more hours working with students outside the classroom than in formal teaching situations. The student-faculty ratio is 10:1.

Student Government

Each student is a member of the Student Government Association (SGA). Working in the SGA provides women with experience in planning and administering cultural, social, and recreational activities and in dealing with academic, residential, and community concerns. The association has executive and legislative powers to govern student activities and to develop and maintain group-living standards. Students also serve as voting members of established faculty committees and in advisory capacities to committees of the Board of Trustees. Stephens has been nationally recognized for the many leadership opportunities it provides for students.

Admission Requirements

Applicants are considered by the Director of Admission and the Admission Committee on an individual basis without regard to race, religion, geographic origin, or handicap. Major factors for admission consideration are the recommendations and academic record, including rank in class, subjects studied, grade point average, proficiency in English, and test scores (SAT I and ACT).

Application and Information

Candidates for admission should submit the application with the $25 application fee and arrange to have transcripts and recommendations mailed to the Office of Admission. Upon receipt of the application, any additional material is mailed to the student. Qualified students are accepted on a rolling admission basis upon receipt of all necessary credentials.

Office of Admission
Campus Box 2121
Stephens College
Columbia, Missouri 65215
Telephone: 573-876-7207
800-876-7207 (toll-free)
Fax: 573-876-7237
E-mail: apply@stephens.edu
World Wide Web: http://www.stephens.edu

On the Stephens College campus.

STERLING COLLEGE

CRAFTSBURY COMMON, VERMONT

The College

Sterling was founded in 1958 as a boys' preparatory school, with an educational philosophy rooted in the precepts developed by Kurt Hahn, the founder of Outward Bound. His four compelling educational pillars included academics, physical challenge, craftsmanship, and service to others. Never losing sight of its educational philosophy, Sterling grew from a secondary school to a postsecondary institution, and awarded its first Associate of Arts degree in 1982. Accreditation by the New England Association of Schools and Colleges was granted to Sterling College in 1987.

In 1997, the College received approval for an accredited Bachelor of Arts degree. Sterling's environmentally based, integrated liberal arts curriculum continues to embody the special distinctions that set a Sterling College education apart: traditional academics, experiential learning, work experiences, challenge activities, and living and working in a community.

In 1996, Sterling College joined the federally funded Work College Consortium, which allows a student to earn a $1300 tuition and books credit in exchange for work. Sterling College believes that by directly involving students in the work that maintains their environment, they develop a greater sense of responsibility toward the environment and others.

Students share a desire for a meaningful education that is relevant to their lives and they appreciate Sterling's small community and commitment to minimizing its impact on the environment. With a projected enrollment of 130, Sterling College remains one of the smallest private coeducational colleges in the country.

Twenty-one percent of Sterling's students are Vermont residents, 41 percent come from the remaining New England states, and 38 percent come from thirteen states outside of New England. International students are welcome. Most of the College's students completed a traditional college-preparatory program at either a private or public high school. Others attended high school in an alternative setting, were home-schooled, took time off for travel and work before attending college, or transferred from another college. The average age of an entering Sterling College student is 19. Generally, 75 percent of the students live on campus in four residence halls, with the remainder commuting from nearby towns.

Location

Sterling College's campus is very much a part of life in Craftsbury Common, a community of classic New England beauty that sits on a ridgetop overlooking the forested sweep of northern Vermont's hills and mountains. The setting is no mere scenic backdrop. Students engage in it—from local craftspeople, creative artists, and other community members to the rivers, woods, and mountains all around—as part of a living laboratory for Sterling's approach to learning. Craftsbury Common was first settled in 1789, and the local economy has always been based on forestry, farming, and education.

Sixty-five miles from Burlington, Vermont's largest city; 120 miles from Montreal; and 200 miles from Boston, Sterling College is close to dozens of beautiful rivers, lakes, and streams, as well as mountains for hiking, several nearby Alpine ski resorts (approximately 30 miles to Stowe, Jay Peak, and Smugglers' Notch), and hundreds of kilometers of cross-country skiing trails. Locally, the Craftsbury Outdoor Center is a popular training and competition facility for world-class Nordic skiers, scullers, runners, mountain bikers, and soccer players.

Majors and Degrees

Sterling College offers the Bachelor of Arts degree in northern studies, outdoor education and leadership, sustainable agriculture, and wildlands ecology and management. Sterling also offers the Associate of Arts degree in resource management.

Students may also choose to design a major that explores an area outside the scope of existing programs. After completion of the second year, all students earn an Associate of Arts degree in resource management.

Academic Program

The Sterling College curriculum combines academic study, to provide a theoretical foundation; laboratory exercises and fieldwork experiences, to develop specific skills; practical experience, to foster a responsible work ethic; and challenge activities, to enhance the student's self-confidence and ability to work effectively in groups. Optional international field-study programs focusing on social ecology expose students to environmental issues in other cultures and help students develop a global perspective.

In the first two years of study, the College guides each student through a trio of linked experiences: academic studies that examine humankind's relationship with the environment; hands-on skills development in the realms of agriculture, forestry, wildlife, and outdoor leadership; and a program of outdoor challenge activities that can include backcountry travel, rock climbing, white-water canoeing, winter expeditions, hiking, and cross-country skiing.

Highlights of the second year include a ten-week, 6-credit internship anywhere in the world. Internships in agriculture, cross-cultural education, ecotourism, environmental education, hydrology, land and resource management, outdoor education and leadership, and wildlife rehabilitation and research are popular. Throughout the internship process, students are supported by the College's comprehensive Career Resource Center.

The third year focuses on the student's chosen major and offers an opportunity for the student to design a semester. Options include domestic or international exchanges with another college or university, in-depth independent study, a second internship, or participation in the Mountain Cultures Semester, where students travel through another country, are immersed in its culture, and learn about social ecology through trekking, homestays, service work, and an optional high-altitude ascent. The Solu Khumbu region of Nepal and Sikkim, India, are two recent destinations.

The culmination of the Sterling College experience is the Senior Applied Research Project (SARP)—an integrated learning experience that applies the student's education and skills to the study of a real-world problem. Research, data collection, implementation, a written thesis, and an oral presentation are required.

Throughout the curriculum, students complete a combination of core and elective courses. First-year and second-year core courses total 44 credits, including a 6-credit off-campus internship. Students choose elective courses to earn a minimum of 60 credits before the end of their second year of study. Third-year core courses carry 5 credits. Fourth-year core courses consist of 19.5 credits, 15 of which apply to the student's SARP. Required core courses total 68.5 credits. Academic major requirements range from 24 to 29 credits.

Academic Facilities

There are fourteen residential, administrative, and classroom buildings on campus. Facilities include a woodshop, a darkroom, two computer rooms, two greenhouses, and the Brown Library. Outdoor teaching facilities include a challenge course with a 30-foot climbing tower, a managed wood lot, recreation and nature trails, an acre of organic gardens, and a small livestock farm with solar- and wind-powered barns. In addition, Vermont's variety of wetlands, woods, and mountaintops provides students with an engaging learning environment. Students spend about 40 percent of their time outside the traditional classroom setting.

Costs

Tuition for the 2003–04 academic year was $15,080, fees were $250, and room and board were $5784. Some field courses require additional lab fees. In 2003–04, all residential students received a $1300 tuition and books credit in exchange for work completed through the College Work Program.

Financial Aid

Sterling College uses the Free Application for Federal Student Aid (FAFSA) and the Sterling College Application for Financial Aid to determine a student's financial need and to measure the student's ability to pay. Students are eligible for up to six federal aid programs, including Pell Grants, Supplemental Educational Opportunity Grants, Stafford Student Loans (subsidized or unsubsidized), PLUS Loans, Work-Study, and Work College. Students may also be eligible for state grants, Vocational Rehabilitation or Veteran's Administration Benefits, or Sterling College grants and scholarships.

One hundred percent of the College's students are eligible to receive financial assistance through the Work College Program. The average undergraduate need-based gift award for 2002–03 was $7300. For the 2002–03 academic year, 101 enrolled students received a total of $756,450 in aid.

Faculty

Sterling's faculty is composed of 17 full-time members and the full-time equivalent of 5 part-time members; 76 percent of the faculty members hold an advanced degree. In a continuous attempt to bring learning to life, faculty members teach in both traditional and experiential ways. With a student-faculty ratio of 10:1, faculty members are accessible and students get to know them in diverse contexts, from classroom to dining room. They are united by an affinity for small-town life, the Earth and its people, a strong interest in relating human experience to natural resources, and a determination to work with students as whole people.

Student Government

Extracurricular events, entertainment, and community issues are defined and discussed at weekly Student Life Committee meetings and Community Meetings. Community Meeting serves as a forum to resolve community issues, make announcements, discuss College policy, and share experiences.

Admission Requirements

Sterling's programs are designed for students who are academically prepared for college studies, eager to embrace the demands of Sterling College, and able to participate in all aspects of the curriculum.

The Admissions Committee evaluates each applicant on an individual basis and assesses a range of academic and personal information. Previous academic records play an important role in the admissions process, but equally important are academic potential, life experience, and readiness to commit to Sterling College. Three references are required. Standardized tests, such as the SAT and ACT, are optional. An interview is required and a campus visit is highly recommended.

Transfer, home-schooled, and international students are also encouraged to apply. In the case of home-schooled students, a portfolio of educational and life experiences may be submitted in lieu of a diploma or its equivalent. International students should submit the TOEFL score in addition to other application materials.

Application and Information

Sterling College operates on a rolling admissions basis. Although applications are accepted throughout the year, it is recommended that students submit their application before March 1. Once an application is complete, the Admissions Committee reviews the information and notifies the applicant of a decision, usually within two weeks.

Students should contact:

John Zaber, Director of Admissions
Sterling College
P.O. Box 72
Craftsbury Common, Vermont 05827
Telephone: 800-648-3591 (toll-free)
802-586-7711
Fax: 802-586-2596
E-mail: admissions@sterlingcollege.edu
World Wide Web: http://www.sterlingcollege.edu

Sterling College combines structured academic study with experiential challenges and plain hard work to help students become problem solvers and stewards of the environment.

STETSON UNIVERSITY

DELAND, FLORIDA

The University

Stetson University, with its curriculum breadth, small classes, many nationally recognized programs, and commitment to values and social responsibility, offers students an educational experience that is unique in the Southeast. At Florida's first private university, Stetson students encounter the "feel" of a small college—close interaction with professors who teach all undergraduates, concern for the individual, and opportunities to learn and test leadership skills and to form lifelong friendships. Stetson's university-class curriculum offers students a broad foundation of knowledge in the context of contemporary issues and needs.

Stetson is committed to undergraduate education that is enriched by selected high-quality graduate programs. The College of Arts and Sciences, the School of Business Administration, and the School of Music are located on the DeLand campus. The Stetson University College of Law has its own campus in St. Petersburg. A second College of Law campus opened in January 2004 in Tampa. The Stetson University Center at Celebration, Florida, opened a $7.2-million facility in fall 2001. Master's degrees are awarded in accounting, business administration, counseling, education, and English on the DeLand campus; the College of Law awards the Juris Doctorate and the Master of Laws. The Stetson University Center offers graduate programs in business, counseling, and education, along with professional development programs for educators.

Stetson's diverse campus community enables students to see the world from many points of view. The University's 2,161 undergraduates are from forty states and thirty-seven other countries. The student population is 57 percent women and 43 percent men. Twelve percent are members of minority groups, and 77 percent of students are Florida residents. The most prestigious accrediting groups recognize Stetson's quality, including the AACSB International–The Association to Advance Collegiate Schools of Business, the American Bar Association, the National Association of Schools of Music, the National Council for Accreditation of Teacher Education, the American Chemical Society, and the Council for Accreditation of Counseling and Related Educational Programs. Stetson also is accredited by the Commission on Colleges of the Southern Association of Colleges and Schools to award the Bachelor, Master, and Specialist in Education degrees in the College of Arts and Sciences; bachelor's degrees in the School of Music; bachelor's and master's degrees in the School of Business Administration; and the Juris Doctor and Master of Laws degrees and a joint J.D./M.B.A. degree in the College of Law. The College of Arts and Sciences was awarded the first private-university Phi Beta Kappa chapter in Florida.

Campus living is important at Stetson. Sharing experiences, having fun, learning to live in a community, and taking responsibility for shaping residence hall life are part of the self-discovery process that makes Stetson so rewarding. Sixty-five percent of all Stetson students choose to live in on-campus housing; all single undergraduate students who are younger than 21 and who do not reside with immediate family are expected to live on campus. Stetson is a caring community that encourages students to make a difference, both on campus and in their future lives. Stetson students are known for their volunteerism and social responsibility. Through the Hollis Leadership Program, the Program in Religion and Ethics, and a range of campus organizations, most students participate in volunteer projects such as recycling, building housing for the disadvantaged, and tutoring at-risk high school students. The School of Music enriches the cultural life of the campus. Performances are given in Elizabeth Hall Chapel by the all-student Stetson Symphonic Orchestra, choir, and band, and faculty members and students give recitals. Musical theater presentations are also performed. The Duncan Gallery of Art exhibits both professional and student work. Stover Theatre regularly hosts student drama productions. Stetson's athletic membership in NCAA Division I provides a wide range of intercollegiate sports for both spectators and participants. Junior varsity opportunities and an extensive intramural program offer team and individual sports competition. A completed $9.5-million campus expansion program to increase learning and recreational opportunities for students includes the Hollis Center, a recreation and wellness center adjacent to the present outdoor pool and Carlton Student Union; the addition of a 13,400-square-foot wing to the duPont-Ball Library and renovations that have significantly increased its technological capabilities; a new tennis center; and expanded classroom and lab space for allied health programs in the Integrative Health Science and Sports Management Department. The heart of the campus is the Carlton Student Union, which has dining facilities; offices for the student newspaper, student organizations, and Residential Life staff; a night club; the Stetson Bookstore; and the post office. Several meal plan options are available in The Commons cafeteria and The Hat Rack sandwich shop. Behind the Student Union are Student Health Services, the Counseling Center, and the Center for International Education.

Location

Stetson's hometown, DeLand, is a charming central Florida city of 30,000 with unique shops, unusual restaurants, and many cultural and recreational opportunities. Because of its location in central Florida, the University is less than an hour away from Daytona Beach and Orlando. The nearby St. Johns River and numerous lakes offer water sports opportunities. The cooperative relationship between Stetson and the city of DeLand enhances the student experience. A wide variety of internships are available in the central Florida area.

Academic Program

Stetson students participate in a wide range of educational experiences. They can research the habits of pygmy rattlesnakes at a national wildlife preserve minutes from campus, develop software programs for an international firm, or develop a marketing plan for a classical music ensemble. These diverse opportunities flow from the University's breadth of curriculum. Bachelor of Arts degrees are offered in American studies, art, biology, communication studies, digital arts, economics, elementary education, English, English–secondary education, environmental science, French, geography, German, history, humanities, international studies, Latin American studies, mathematics, music (liberal arts), philosophy, political science, psychology, religious studies, Russian studies, social science and social science–education, sociology, Spanish, sports management, and theater arts. Bachelor of Business Administration degrees are offered in accounting, accounting information systems, e-business technology, economics, finance, general business administration, international business, management, and marketing. Bachelor of Music degree programs are available in digital arts, guitar, orchestral instrument, piano/organ, theory and composition, and voice. Bachelor of Music Education degrees are offered in instrumental/general studies and vocal/general studies. Bachelor of Science degrees are offered in aquatic and marine biology, biochemistry, biology, chemistry, computer science, economics, elementary education, environmental science, geography, integrative health science (health science or rehabilitative studies), mathematics, medical technology, molecular biology, physics, political science, psychology, secondary education, and sociology. Students' choices are further broadened by other multidisciplinary programs such as Africana Studies, applied ethics, the Family Business Center, health-care issues, the Hollis Leadership Development Program, journalism, and women and gender studies and by strong preprofessional and cooperative programs in dentistry, engineering, forestry, law, medicine, and veterinary medicine. DeLand campus students who meet rigorous academic requirements are guaranteed admission to the College of Law on a regular or accelerated schedule. The Discovery Program assists undecided students in choosing a major. The University Experience Program quickly integrates newcomers into the campus community. Degree sequences "in honors" are offered through the Honors Program in arts, science, music, and business. A growing Army ROTC program provides scholarship assistance for students interested in careers with the nation's armed forces. A developing Africana Studies program focuses on the development and spread of the heritage of Sub-Saharan Africa. Stetson's year-round academic calendar includes 15-week fall and spring terms and an 8-week summer term. Degrees are conferred at the end of each academic term. Most undergraduate degrees require completion of 120 semester hours of work that are distributed among core requirements, the major field, and electives. Students must maintain a C average or better.

Off-Campus Programs

Through programs such as Russian Studies, Latin American Studies, International Studies, the Washington Semester, and the Summer Business Program, Stetson students prepare to succeed in the global marketplace. With the Institute for Christian Ethics, these programs bring to Stetson political and cultural leaders from around the world, including scientist and conservationist Jane Goodall, former president Jimmy Carter, South African Archbishop Desmond Tutu, Nobel Peace Laureate Elie Wiesel, and journalist and author Bill Moyers, to lecture and meet informally with students. During the Washington Seminar, students intern in the nation's capital and at the United Nations. Stetson students can study for a semester or a full year at universities in Avignon, France; Freiburg, Germany; Madrid, Spain; Nottingham, England; Oxford, England; Guanajuato, Mexico; Hong Kong, China; and Moscow, Russia. Through a linkage program with the American Graduate School of International Management, Stetson also has relationships with institutions in the Republic of Korea and Latin America.

Academic Facilities

Stetson's campus is a charming mix of historical and contemporary buildings among green lawns, palms, and oaks. The heart of the campus is in the Stetson University National Historic District, while the five-floor Lynn Business Center houses the School of Business Administration. A $13-million renovation to the center was completed in fall 2002. The duPont-Ball Library, which includes the new North Wing, provides students access to more than 26 million cataloging records in libraries worldwide through its advanced computer retrieval system. The Gillespie Museum of Minerals boasts the largest private mineral collection outside the Smithsonian Institution. The Edmunds Center, a 5,000-seat gymnasium-field house, hosts intercollegiate athletic events, contemporary concerts, and special events such as commencement. Other facilities include the Sage Hall Science Center, which houses highly advanced equipment and individual research areas; computer labs with Internet access for student use in each school; and Presser Hall, home of the School of Music, which has a variety of individual and ensemble practice halls.

Costs

Tuition and fees (two semesters) for new students in 2003–04 were $22,640. Room and board averaged $6855 for the academic year.

Financial Aid

Financial aid needs have no bearing on the admission process. To reward outstanding academic achievement and special talents and to assure access for qualified students, Stetson made nearly $18.6 million ($41 million overall) available from University funds in 2003–04. Assistance is offered through academic merit and music talent scholarships, athletic grants-in-aid, a monthly payment plan, and low- and no-interest loans. Stetson participates in federal and state need-based programs. Help from other external sources, such as line of credit programs, also is available. The amount of aid awarded to students is determined by an analysis of their financial need through the Free Application for Federal Student Aid (FAFSA). Financial aid forms should be submitted as soon as possible after January 1 and before March 1 of the year in which admitted students plan to enter Stetson. Stetson encourages families to utilize the financial aid estimator as early as the summer prior to the student's senior year.

Faculty

Stetson's 195 faculty members have many individual interests, but they are united by their desire to help undergraduates achieve a broad understanding of the world in which they will live and work. Ninety-five percent of full-time faculty members hold Ph.D.'s or equivalent degrees. Seminar-size classes and personal attention from professors are hallmarks of an education at Stetson. The low student-faculty ratio of 11:1 means that classes are small enough for personal interaction. Professors are accessible, and high-quality advising is a faculty priority. In satisfaction surveys, Stetson students rate class size, faculty quality, and student–faculty member interaction very high.

Student Government

Stetson emphasizes individual growth and the development of leadership skills. Students participate directly in forming campuswide policy through such groups as the Student Government Association and the Council for Student Activities. The Student Strategic Planning Council advises the president on policy and long-range planning issues. More than 100 student organizations encourage diverse interests. Included are service and special interest organizations; seventeen scholastic and honorary societies, including Phi Beta Kappa; and fourteen national sororities and fraternities (six sororities and eight fraternities).

Admission Requirements

All new students at Stetson have completed a college-preparatory program, and most rank in the top 30 percent of their high school class. High school preparation should include four years of English, three of mathematics and laboratory science, and two years of foreign language and social sciences, plus college-preparatory electives. Admission to Stetson is based on academic course selection, grade achievement, involvement in school and community, leadership potential, and achievement on standardized tests. Prospective music students are required to audition. Transfer students must be in good standing at their former institution and must have achieved a cumulative grade point average of at least 3.0 on a 4.0 scale. Early admission is offered to promising high school juniors who have completed their required course work. A student may earn credit and advanced standing through the Advanced Placement Program, the International Baccalaureate, and department exams.

Application and Information

The application priority deadline for the fall semester is March 15; for spring, January 1; and for summer, May 1. Regular decision candidates for fall admission receive notification by April 1. Under an early notification policy, candidates with the strongest credentials are notified after December 1, as soon as their applications are processed. An early decision option is for exceptionally qualified students who are certain Stetson is their first choice. Candidates should apply before November 1. A complimentary loan video on Stetson University is available through VIDEC INC. To receive a copy, students should call 800-255-0384. For more information, students can contact:

Office of Admissions
Stetson University
421 North Woodland Boulevard, Unit 8378
DeLand, Florida 32723
Telephone: 386-822-7100
800-688-0101 (toll-free)
Fax: 386-822-7112
E-mail: admissions@stetson.edu
World Wide Web: http://www.stetson.edu

STEVENS INSTITUTE OF TECHNOLOGY

HOBOKEN, NEW JERSEY

The Institute

Founded in 1870, Stevens Institute of Technology declares its mission is to educate and inspire students to acquire the knowledge needed to lead in the creation, application, and management of technology and to excel in solving problems in any profession. Approximately 130 years later, Stevens upholds its purpose and has become a leader in technology.

Twenty-first-century careers will be increasingly rooted in ever-changing technologies. In order to meet this need, Stevens undergraduates have a strong and versatile background in business, engineering, the sciences, computer science, management, and the humanities. A broad-based education, intertwined with hands-on experience in research and with industry, is the cornerstone.

Stevens holds general accreditation in engineering and specialized accreditation in all engineering disciplines from the Accreditation Board for Engineering and Technology, Inc., as well as general accreditation from the Middle States Association of Colleges and Schools. It is also included in the first group of colleges to receive accreditation in computer science from the Computer Science Accreditation Board, and the chemistry program is accredited by the American Chemical Society.

The Institute encompasses three schools: the Schaefer School of Engineering, the Imperatore School of Sciences and Arts, and the Howe School of Technology Management. Bachelor's degrees are awarded in various areas within the sciences, business, computer science, engineering, and the humanities. Master's and doctoral degrees are also awarded in a multitude of similar areas.

Stevens has long-standing ties with industry leaders, including AT&T, Becton Dickinson, ExxonMobil, Johnson & Johnson, Lockheed Martin, Merck, and Verizon, among others.

Overlooking the Hudson River and New York City from Castle Point in Hoboken, New Jersey, the 55-acre, parklike Stevens campus encompasses more than thirty buildings, including classroom, residence, departmental, administrative, and research facilities. Approximately 80 percent of all undergraduate students live on campus, and they originate from more than thirty states and international countries.

There are more than seventy student activities and organizations, including *The Stute,* the weekly campus newspaper; *Link,* the yearbook; WCPR, the radio station; the Glee Club; brass and jazz ensembles; the Drama Society; ethnic and religious organizations; and national honor and professional societies. Eight national fraternities and three sororities have chapters on campus, and most maintain houses where members live. Approximately 35 percent of the 1,700 undergraduates join a fraternity or sorority. The state-of-the-art Charles V. Schaefer, Jr. '36 Athletic and Recreation Center houses an NCAA Olympic-sized swimming pool and Jacuzzi, basketball courts, racquetball courts, and a fitness room with Stairmasters and Universal weight equipment. Other features include Walker Gym, Davis Field, a climbing wall, and four tennis courts. NCAA Division III sports include men's baseball, basketball, cross-country, fencing, indoor/outdoor track and field, lacrosse, soccer, swimming, tennis, volleyball, and wrestling and women's basketball, cross-country, equestrian, fencing, field hockey, indoor/outdoor track and field, lacrosse, soccer, swimming, tennis, and volleyball. Students may also play a club sport or intramurals.

Location

The city of Hoboken is contemporary with a small-town aura. Due to its waterfront location, the mile-square city, with its charming old brownstones and dozens of shops and restaurants, welcomes a diversity of new residents and is the focus of an urban renaissance. A project is under way to turn the waterfront's old ferry slips and empty piers into a $500-million complex of housing units, office space for high-tech businesses, parks, marina and hotel facilities, and biking/jogging paths. Located on a high bank of the Hudson River, the Stevens campus, with red brick buildings and old maple and elm trees, is just minutes from Manhattan and the educational, cultural, and social opportunities available there.

Majors and Degrees

Stevens Institute of Technology awards the degrees of Bachelor of Engineering (B.E.), Bachelor of Science (B.S.), and Bachelor of Arts (B.A.). Majors in engineering include biomedical, chemical, civil, computer, electrical, environmental, mechanical, systems, and engineering management. Science majors include bioinformatics, chemical biology, chemistry, computational science, information systems, mathematical sciences, and physics. Computer science features a selection of concentrated courses in computer theory and applications, database management, game design, and management information systems. The business program enables students to create a comprehensive business plan and to concentrate in an area such as health-care management or entrepreneurship. Humanities specialties are English and American literature, history, philosophy, and science and technology studies. New humanities majors added in 2004 include art and technology, music and technology, and Turkish, Central Asian, and Middle Eastern studies. There are preprofessional programs in medicine and dentistry (seven years) and law (five years); there are accelerated scholars programs (four years) in these three areas as well. Stevens Scholars may also earn their bachelor's and master's degrees simultaneously in four years.

Academic Program

The undergraduate division is concerned with the intellectual enrichment and education of the student as a whole person in preparation for a satisfying, productive, and successful future in a technological world. Computer fluency and usage are essential; therefore, freshmen are given a personal notebook computer. The learning process is fulfilled by having students solve real-world problems, undertake internship projects, and participate in simulations and faculty research investigations. The rigorous education in technical, scientific, and management subjects is carefully balanced by eight humanities courses (for technology students) and six physical education courses. In the typical baccalaureate program, 156 credit hours are earned. The academic calendar consists of two semesters and a summer session.

Stevens offers a number of special programs. The Stevens Scholars Program, for truly talented students, provides the challenge of accelerated course work as well as the opportunity to earn the master's degree in addition to the bachelor's degree within four years at no additional cost. The Personalized Self-Paced Instruction program (PSI) provides an alternative to the conventional lecture-recitation method of instruction, enabling students to work with self-instruction materials at their own pace in selective courses. The Lore-El Center for Women offers a variety of mentoring and networking programs. The Stevens Technical Enrichment Program (STEP), a precollege and in-college program, broadens the access of minority and economically disadvantaged students to careers in technology. Undergraduate Projects in Technology and Medicine (UPTAM), conducted in cooperation with the University of Medicine and Dentistry of New Jersey and other area medical facilities, is a summer program for selected students interested in medical engineering or biomedical sciences. The Freshmen Summer Internship Program enables new students to obtain hands-on experience immediately. The Cooperative Education Program is available for any undergraduate wanting to alternate semesters of classroom study with semesters of paid, professional work experience over a five-year period. The Academic Support Center also offers free and confidential academic tutoring and other resources.

Off-Campus Programs

Through the International Scholars Program, students can spend their junior year abroad at the University of Dundee in Scotland, or in one of many other countries on an individual basis.

Academic Facilities

Rated in 2003 as the nation's "most connected campus," the environment of Stevens is highly computer intensive. More than 2,100 systems are distributed throughout the campus, and each of the 1,700 undergraduates has a personal computer. Notebooks lead in popularity as a way to enable students to plug into their residence hall rooms, networked SMART classrooms, and even Café on the Hudson, the cyber café. The computer center has a multitude of high-capacity UNIX servers and various workstations and personal computers. Department labs for student use are distributed throughout campus, and T1 lines connect the campus network to the Internet. All residence halls and academic buildings are wired to the fastest gigabit networking to enable additional resources for networked notebook access as well as for delivery of additional distance learning instruction. In addition, most of the Stevens campus has wireless capabilities.

Among the specialized laboratory facilities used for academic and research functions are Davidson Laboratory, a center for the study of marine hydrodynamics and coastal engineering; the Keck Geoenvironmental Laboratory; the Nicoll Environmental Laboratory; the Design and Manufacturing Institute; the Highly Filled Materials Institute; the Wireless Network Security Center; the Center for Maritime Systems; the Plasma and Surface Physics Laboratory; the High Sensitivity Laser Spectroscopy Laboratory; the Clean Air Vehicle Center; the Robotics Laboratory; the Center for Improved Engineering and Science Education; the Center for Product Lifecycle Management; the Noise and Vibration Control Lab; the Optical Communications Lab; the Polymer Processing Institute; the Technology Ventures Incubator; and the Schacht Management Lab. Stevens is also an institutional member of the New Jersey Space Grant Consortium and the Hazardous Substance Management Research Consortium. The Samuel C. Williams Library has been recognized as one of the top twenty providing just-in-time delivery and access to 30 million volumes. The DeBaun Auditorium, a New York metro area cultural and educational facility, provides the technology infrastructure for distance learning programs, teleconferencing, and, like other campus facilities, Internet and intranet connections.

Costs

Tuition for the 2003–04 year was $26,000. The cost of room and board were $8400. Other estimated costs include $900 for books and supplies, $750 for personal/miscellaneous expenses, and $525 for first-year fees.

Financial Aid

Stevens offers a variety of both need- and merit-based institutional aid programs in addition to all federal and New Jersey state assistance. (New Jersey programs are for state residents only.) Merit scholarships range from $1000 to full tuition annually and are renewable for up to four years. Specific grade point averages are required for renewal. Need-based grants range from approximately $100 to $12,000 annually and are renewable for four years based on financial eligibility. All incoming students should submit the Free Application for Federal Student Aid (FAFSA) no later than February 15. Matriculated students electing to extend their undergraduate course of study to five years (a total of ten semesters) will not be charged tuition during their fifth year as long as arrangements are made during their first semester of enrollment at Stevens.

Faculty

The full-time faculty is composed of 170 men and women, 95 percent of whom hold doctoral degrees. Most faculty members are engaged in specific research projects. Special faculty and research staffs number an additional 110 people. The student-faculty ratio is approximately 9:1.

Student Government

The Undergraduate Student Government Association (SGA) directs and funds all student clubs and activities. Other governing bodies include the Student Review Board and the Commuter, Ethnic Student, Co-op Student, Interfraternity, Interdormitory, Panhellenic, and Athletic Councils. The Stevens Honor System, in existence since 1907, is directed by the Honor Board, a group of students elected by their peers to investigate any students violating this pledge.

Admission Requirements

Admission is very selective. Each year, fewer than 50 percent of the applicants are accepted, and 35 percent enroll. Strength in mathematics and science is essential. The high school record should include English (4 years); standard college-preparatory mathematics (4 years), including algebra, geometry/trigonometry, and precalculus/calculus; biology (1 year); chemistry (1 year); and physics (1 year). Applicants are required to submit scores on the SAT I or ACT. SAT II Subject Tests in mathematics, science, and English are highly recommended. Recommendations, a personal statement, extracurricular activities, leadership positions, and other nonacademic factors are considered of major importance in the admission decision and are required for consideration for the accelerated programs. An on-campus interview is required for all students who live within a 250-mile radius. Freshmen earned an average GPA of 3.8, and their SAT I scores ranged from the 25th to the 75th percentiles, between 1200 and 1370.

Advanced placement credit is given to students who have taken Advanced Placement (AP) courses in high school and have earned a 4 or more on the College Board's AP exams in biology, calculus AB or BC, chemistry, economics, English, government and politics, history, physics, psychology, and statistics.

Stevens Institute of Technology does not discriminate against any person because of race, creed, color, national origin, sex, age, marital status, handicap, liability for service in the armed forces, or status as a disabled or Vietnam-era veteran.

Application and Information

Applications may be submitted after completion of the junior year of high school. The application deadline is February 15. Early decision and early admission programs are available. The deadline is November 15. Transfer students should apply by July 1 for the fall semester and December 1 for the spring semester. All decisions are made on a rolling basis once a student's file is complete. All students must apply either by using the traditional paper application or electronically via the admissions Web page. Students with requests for further information should contact:

Office of Undergraduate Admissions
Stevens Institute of Technology
Castle Point on Hudson
Hoboken, New Jersey 07030
Telephone: 800-458-5323 (toll-free)
201-216-5194
Fax: 201-216-8348
E-mail: admissions@stevens.edu
World Wide Web: http://www.stevens.edu

STONEHILL COLLEGE

EASTON, MASSACHUSETTS

The College

Stonehill is a competitive, coeducational, Catholic college located just south of Boston. Established in 1948 by the Congregation of Holy Cross (founders of the University of Notre Dame, Indiana), Stonehill continues the rich Holy Cross tradition of a rigorous liberal education. As a comprehensive undergraduate college of 2,200 full-time degree students, Stonehill offers thirty major programs in the liberal arts, natural sciences, and business. The College's programs, through an involved and engaging faculty and a commitment to hands-on learning, aim to foster effective communication, critical-thinking, and problem-solving skills in all students.

Stonehill provides its students with a powerful environment for learning where students are safe, known, and valued. The College has a beautiful campus, an enviable location, and state-of-the-art facilities. Stonehill fields varsity teams (NCAA Division II) in twenty sports, in addition to a vibrant intercollegiate club and intramural sports program. More than 85 percent of the students live in first-rate on-campus housing and take advantage of the wide range of social and cultural activities offered on campus or in nearby Boston. Housing is guaranteed for four years.

In addition to the undergraduate programs listed below, the College offers a Master of Science in Accountancy degree.

Location

Just 20 miles south of Boston, Stonehill is located in the town of Easton (population 23,329). Featuring stunning Georgian-style architecture, the College's twenty-six main buildings are set among a beautifully landscaped 375-acre campus of ponds, rolling fields, and wooded glens. The beaches of Cape Cod and the mansions and history of Newport and Providence, Rhode Island, are within 45 minutes of the campus, as are major concert (the Tweeter Center for Performing Arts) and sports (Gillette Stadium) venues. The most popular off-campus destination is Boston. Students from more than sixty area colleges and universities converge on Boston to experience its museums, art galleries, theaters, sporting events, and other exciting nightlife offerings. During the week, Stonehill students enhance their academic experience through internships with the city's plethora of high-tech, medical, and financial institutions.

The College provides a shuttle service that connects to Boston's subway system and area shopping. Stonehill's student government organization also has vans that student clubs can reserve for trips to sporting events, concerts, skiing, and other activities.

Majors and Degrees

The College offers Bachelor of Arts degrees in American studies, chemistry, communication, criminal justice, economics, education studies (early childhood, elementary and secondary), English, fine arts, French, foreign languages, health-care administration, history, international studies, mathematics, multidisciplinary studies, philosophy, political science, psychology, public administration, religious studies, sociology, and Spanish. Bachelor of Science degrees are offered in biochemistry, biology, chemistry, computer engineering, and computer science. Bachelor of Science in Business Administration degrees are offered in accounting, finance, management, and marketing.

Preprofessional programs are offered in dentistry, education, law, medicine, and theology. Students interested in the field of education can receive early childhood, elementary, middle, and secondary school teacher certification. Students may also design their own majors by combining various departmental courses into a comprehensive multidisciplinary program.

Academic Program

Stonehill's primary mission is to provide a challenging program of academic studies in the liberal arts tradition that engages students in a lifelong quest for intellectual excellence and dedication to service. All students receive a strong foundation in the liberal arts in addition to expertise in one or more fields. The liberal arts courses in the core curriculum are designed to help students understand their culture, find and analyze information, develop critical-thinking skills, and become effective communicators. Developing writing proficiency is a central objective of the core curriculum and is emphasized in all classes.

Interaction with faculty members and academic advisers is a vital part of a Stonehill education. At freshman orientation, each student is assigned an academic adviser. Students who declare a major are assigned a faculty mentor from within their major; students who do not declare a major receive assistance from an adviser who specializes in helping undecided students. Advisers help students choose their major, approve course selections, and give advice on study-abroad, internship, and graduate school opportunities.

Students are encouraged to explore various fields of interest in their first two years, but they must choose a major by the middle of their junior year. They take five courses a semester and must complete forty courses to receive a bachelor's degree.

Off-Campus Programs

In addition to the tremendous on-campus opportunities at Stonehill, the College offers an abundance of domestic and international programs to enhance a student's learning experience. One of the most exciting opportunities at Stonehill is internships, which are offered in every major. Internships give students hands-on experience in their chosen field, help them focus their career objectives, and afford them opportunities to network with professionals.

Within the United States, students have the opportunity to participate in internship programs in Boston; Providence, Rhode Island; and Washington, D.C. Stonehill participates in the Washington Center in Washington, D.C., and the Marine Studies Consortium in Boston. Students can also choose to take classes at eight nearby colleges through a specially designed consortium to which Stonehill belongs.

Stonehill students have the option of interning or studying in virtually any country. Students can earn a full semester of credit participating in a full-time international internship in cities such as Dublin, London, and Zaragoza. Examples of domestic and international internship sites include Children's Hospital, PriceWaterhouseCoopers, Gillette, Massachusetts General Hospital, Fidelity Investments, Reebok International, Eli Lilly Pharmaceuticals, and the *Boston Globe*.

Academic Facilities

Stonehill's outstanding facilities include state-of-the-art technologies incorporated into architecturally stunning buildings. Students have access to the Internet and the College's intranet from virtually any building on campus, including their rooms in the residence halls. The newest addition to Stonehill's impressive array of Georgian-influenced buildings is the MacPhaidin Library. The library provides access to the Internet, College intranet, electronic journals, multimedia computer clusters, and an extensive collection of texts, novels, and publications. The Joseph W. Martin, Jr. Institute for Law and Society is a regional center for education, research, and public service. It houses an archival research library, the Center for Regional and Policy Analysis, and the Stonehill Educational Project. Housed in the institute are the papers of former Speaker of the U.S. House of Representatives Joseph Martin and Templeton Award winner Michael Novak. The Lockary Computer Center supports Windows-based computers and provides students with access to the College's computer network.

Costs

For the 2003–04 academic year, Stonehill's tuition for full-time students was $20,432. Room and board charges were $9450. These figures do not include a comprehensive fee of $870, health insurance (optional), books, supplies, or travel and personal expenses.

Financial Aid

Financial aid is awarded on the basis of financial need and academic performance, as well as for merit only. Financial aid is packaged in a combination of scholarships, grants, loans, and/or campus employment. Stonehill uses the Federal Methodology to determine student eligibility for federal and state government funds. The information is obtained from the student's Free Application for Federal Student Aid (FAFSA). An Institutional Methodology (used by most private colleges and universities) is used to assess a student's eligibility for College awards. The College Scholarship Service's PROFILE form is the vehicle used to determine a family's "Expected Family Contribution," which is subtracted from Stonehill's total educational costs to determine a family's level of financial need. In addition to scholarships that are awarded on the basis of need or a combination of merit and need, there are also scholarships available on a non-need basis, which are awarded as a result of a student's academic performance. Special forms are not required, as all applicants are considered for non-need-based merit scholarships.

Faculty

Stonehill's faculty is committed to teaching, advising, and working closely with students. At Stonehill, every professor is not only directly engaged with students in class, but is also involved beyond the classroom as well. Many students are involved in faculty members' research, which sometimes leads to joint publications and/or presentations at professional conferences. The faculty-student ratio is 1:15; classes are small enough to ensure that students receive the individual attention they need. At Stonehill, there are no teaching assistants, and the majority of the faculty members hold terminal degrees in their respective fields.

Student Government

The Student Government Association (SGA) is the most influential student organization on campus, and its goal is to improve the quality of student life at Stonehill. SGA members participate in academic and strategic planning, sit with the Board of Trustees, plan and organize campus social and cultural events, and help ensure that Stonehill remains a vibrant and fun community. In addition to SGA, students can get involved in more than sixty active clubs and organizations, ranging from volunteer groups to political activism, to recreational clubs. Stonehill offers something for all of its students.

Admission Requirements

With approximately 5,000 applicants for 560 places, admission to Stonehill is selective. The College actively seeks an academically strong, geographically, culturally, and ethnically diverse student body. In the admissions process, all information on each applicant is carefully considered, but academic performance and curriculum in high school are given the greatest weight. The Admissions Committee evaluates the depth and strength of each applicant's course selection and the consistency of their grades. Competitive students should have completed a strong academic program from among their high school's most challenging offerings. Students must submit scores from either the SAT I or ACT, which should be taken no later than January of the senior year. The committee also evaluates extracurricular activities, work, volunteer and community activities, recommendations, and writing samples. In 2003, 49 percent of the incoming freshmen were in the top 10 percent of their class and 86 percent were in the top 25 percent of their class. The College awards credit for strong scores on Advanced Placement, CLEP, and higher-level International Baccalaureate exams.

Application and Information

Stonehill uses the Common Application (CA) as its application for freshman, transfer, and international students. The College prefers that students apply online using the CA and Stonehill Supplemental Form via the Web sites at http://www.princetonreview.com or http://www.commonapp.org, and the application will be electronically transferred to Stonehill. The CA and the Stonehill Supplemental Form are also available as fill-in forms at Stonehill's Web site listed below, and the CA is available in paper form in high school guidance offices. For September admission, the deadline for applying through the freshman early decision process is November 1. The freshman regular decision and the international freshman deadlines are January 15 for September admission. For January admission, the freshman regular decision deadline is November 1. Serious candidates are strongly encouraged to attend a Group Information Session (GIS) and a student-led campus tour, which are both offered on a regular basis throughout the year. In addition, an award-winning virtual tour may be accessed via the Web site listed below. Students should contact the Admissions Office to arrange a campus visit. For further information, students should contact:

Dean of Admissions and Enrollment
Stonehill College
320 Washington Street
Easton, Massachusetts 02357-5610
Telephone: 508-565-1373
Fax: 508-565-1545
E-mail: admissions@stonehill.edu
World Wide Web: http://www.stonehill.edu

The MacPhaidin Library is a high-tech learning center, with fully networked seating areas for individual and collaborative study.

STONY BROOK UNIVERSITY, STATE UNIVERSITY OF NEW YORK

STONY BROOK, LONG ISLAND, NEW YORK

The University

Stony Brook University was founded in 1957. In the forty-eight years since its founding, the University has grown tremendously and is now recognized as one of the nation's leading centers of learning and scholarship, fulfilling the mandate given by the State Board of Regents in 1960 to become a university that would "stand with the finest in the country."

Stony Brook is at the forefront of integrating research and education at the undergraduate level; it was recently selected by the National Science Foundation as one of only ten universities in the nation to receive a special recognition for this based on educational vision, a significant record of accomplishments, and leadership in the field of higher education. A member of the highly selective Association of American Universities, Stony Brook is one of only eighty-eight public and private colleges and universities nationwide to be classified a Research I institute by the Carnegie Foundation. With seventy academic departments, Stony Brook is among the top twenty-five institutions funded by the National Science Foundation, and external support for research has grown to an annual sum of more than $125 million.

Stony Brook enrolls approximately 21,989 full- and part-time students—14,224 undergraduates and 7,765 graduate and professional students. Students hail from all fifty states and fifty-four other countries. More than 16,000 students are enrolled full-time. More than half of Stony Brook's undergraduates live in campus residence halls, which are organized as small residential colleges in order to foster social, intellectual, and cultural interaction.

The Stony Brook Seawolves' twenty varsity teams compete in NCAA Division I and include men's baseball and football; women's softball and volleyball; and men's and women's basketball, cross-country, lacrosse, soccer, swimming, tennis, and indoor and outdoor track and field. Athletic facilities are extensive and include the Indoor Sports Complex, which seats up to 5,000; a multipurpose outdoor stadium with seating for 8,500; and several outdoor athletic fields, tennis courts, bicycle and jogging paths, handball courts, and a track.

Location

Situated on 1,100 wooded acres, Stony Brook is located midway between New York City and the resort area of the Hamptons on Long Island's East End, a setting rich in both natural and architectural beauty. Students find large wooded areas on and around campus, sandy beaches are a comfortable bicycle ride away, a working harbor and tourist area are nearby, and a historic hamlet that was once home to George Washington's Revolutionary War spy ring is within walking distance. A train station on the University's perimeter offers students easy access to New York City.

Majors and Degrees

Stony Brook has exceptional strength in the sciences, mathematics, humanities, fine arts, social sciences, engineering, and health professions. Major academic units of the University include the College of Arts and Sciences, the College of Engineering and Applied Sciences, the W. Averell Harriman School for Management and Policy, the Marine Sciences Research Center, and the Health Sciences Center, which is made up of the Schools of Medicine, Health Technology and Management, Dental Medicine, Nursing, and Social Welfare.

The University offers undergraduate majors leading to Bachelor of Arts (B.A.), Bachelor of Science (B.S.), and Bachelor of Engineering (B.E.) degrees in Africana studies, American studies, anthropology, applied mathematics and statistics, art history and criticism, astronomy and planetary sciences, athletic training, atmospheric and oceanic sciences, biochemistry, biomedical engineering, biology, business management, chemical and molecular engineering, chemistry, cinema and cultural studies, clinical laboratory sciences, comparative literature, computer engineering, computer science, cytotechnology, earth and space sciences, economics, electrical engineering, engineering chemistry, engineering science, English, environmental studies, French, geology, German, health science, history, humanities, information systems, Italian, linguistics, mathematics, mechanical engineering, multidisciplinary studies, music, nursing, pharmacology, philosophy, physician assistant studies, physics, political science, psychology, religious studies, respiratory care, social work, sociology, Spanish, studio art, theater arts, and women's studies. The University also offers nearly sixty minors.

Students may earn New York State provisional certification for secondary school teaching in biology, chemistry, earth science, English, French, German, Italian, mathematics, physics, Russian, social studies, Spanish, and K–12 in teaching English as a second language. Dual bachelor's/master's degree programs are available in all of the engineering departments, applied mathematics and statistics, computer science, health sciences/occupational therapy, nursing, and political science/public affairs.

Academic Programs

Six different undergraduate colleges at Stony Brook provide freshmen with a small-college environment along with all the advantages of a major research university. Living/Learning Centers are designed to enable students with common interests to live and learn together.

Stony Brook accepts up to 30 credits by examination toward the bachelor's degree, through such means as AP, CLEP, CPE, higher-level International Baccalaureate subjects, and Stony Brook's own Challenge Program. Students need a minimum of 120 credits for the B.A. or B.S. degree and 128 credits for the B.E. degree; 39 of these credits must be earned at the upper-division level. All students must satisfy general education requirements and maintain at least a 2.0 cumulative grade point average. Grading is traditional; a pass/no-credit option is available for some elective courses. Stony Brook's academic year starts in early September and ends in mid-May, with the exception of some Health Sciences Center programs that begin in June or July.

Off-Campus Programs

Students have the opportunity to enrich their education by pursuing their academic interests in an overseas location for a summer, semester, or academic year. Stony Brook sponsors programs in England, France, Germany, Italy, Japan, Korea, Madagascar, and Spain; students may also participate in programs sponsored by the State University of New York system in Western Europe, the Middle East, the Far East, Canada, and Latin America.

Statewide and national exchanges enable students to study for up to a year at one of more than fifty colleges and universities in New York and eight institutions elsewhere in the United States.

Opportunities also exist for students to earn academic credit and gain valuable experience while participating in internships and field research. Placements include government agencies and laboratories, hospitals and clinics, businesses and industries, and legal and social agencies on Long Island and in New York City, Albany, and Washington, D.C.

Academic Facilities

Stony Brook's major academic facilities include the Frank Melville, Jr. Memorial Library, one of the nation's largest academic libraries, with holdings of more than 1.9 million volumes and 3 million publications in microformat; the University Teaching Hospital, which is ranked among the top fifteen in the nation; and the five-theater Staller Center for the Arts. The Centers for Molecular Medicine, the Biology Learning Laboratories, and the Asian-American Center were recently completed. Stony Brook is also home to a myriad of centers, laboratories, and institutes. Some of these include the Institute for Theoretical Physics, Institute for Mathematical Sciences, Institute for Pattern Recognition, Institute for Terrestrial and Planetary Atmospheres, Center for High Pressure Geophysics, Center for Biotechnology, Howard Hughes Medical Institute, and Center for Regional Policy Studies.

Costs

For 2004–05, the annual tuition and fees for New York State residents are $5306. Nonresident tuition and fees are $11,256. Room and board costs are $7457. Books and supplies are estimated at $750.

Financial Aid

The Office of Financial Aid and Student Employment administers several federal and state programs, including the Federal Perkins Loan, Federal Supplemental Educational Opportunity Grant, Federal Work-Study Program, New York State Higher Education Tuition Assistance Program (TAP), and Federal Stafford Student Loan. To apply for these programs, a student must complete the Free Application for Federal Student Aid (FAFSA). The FAFSA is available at all high schools and colleges. The University's scholarship program includes more than $5 million in scholarship offers to new students each year, based on meritorious academic performance.

Faculty

Stony Brook's faculty members are intellectual leaders in their disciplines and include a Nobel laureate; a Pulitzer Prize winner; 5 MacArthur Fellows; a Fields prize winner; recipients of the National Medal of Technology, the National Medal of Science, and the Benjamin Franklin Medal; 16 members of the National Academy of Sciences; 14 members of the American Academy of Arts and Sciences; and 3 members of the National Academy of Engineering. They are also dedicated teachers and include 105 recipients of the Chancellor's Awards for Excellence in Teaching.

With 1,902 faculty members, the faculty-student ratio is about 1:14. All of Stony Brook's full-time faculty members hold either doctoral or terminal degrees in their fields, and more than 90 percent are engaged in active research that leads to publication. In fact, Stony Brook's faculty is ranked second in the nation in articles published in prestigious journals.

Student Government

Undergraduates are represented by Polity, the student government, whose members are elected by the students. Student representatives help shape University policy and advise fellow students as members of the University Senate and other organizations. Polity administers an annual budget of more than $1 million, which it uses to sponsor more than 100 student interest clubs and organizations. Varied student interests are represented by groups as diverse as the Pre-Med Society, the Commuter Student Association, Stony Brook at Law, the Cycling Club, the Committee on Cinematic Arts (COCA), the Chess Masters, the Science Fiction Forum, and several cultural clubs that include the Caribbean Students Organization, Asian Students' Alliance, Club India, African Student Union, and Latin American Student Organization.

Admission Requirements

Stony Brook is a selective institution and evaluates applicants on an individual basis. There is no automatic cutoff in the admission process, either in grade point average, rank, or test scores. The Admissions Committee seeks to enroll the strongest and most diverse class possible. Stony Brook welcomes applications from those with special talent or exceptional ability in a particular area. Freshman admission is based primarily upon the strength and breadth of the student's academic preparatory program, grade point average, and standardized test scores. Additional criteria include class rank, extracurricular activities, and letters of recommendation, if requested. The University accepts a limited number of high school students for early admission. Students who have attended college or university after graduating from high school are eligible to apply as transfers. Transfer applicants are expected to have performed well in a strong academic program. Transfer students applying to the upper-division programs in the Health Sciences Center must have completed at least 57 credits in liberal arts and sciences and some specific course requirements. If fewer than 24 credits were earned, the student's high school record will be requested for review.

Application and Information

Students are encouraged to submit applications for admission by December 1. The deadline for filing early action applications for fall admission is November 15; students receive notification of the early action by January 1. Although interviews are not mandatory, they are recommended as a useful part of the application process. Admission counselors are available to meet with prospective students and their families by appointment throughout the year. Campus tours with knowledgeable student guides are also available throughout the year; interested students should call ahead for a schedule. To request an application form, schedule an interview, sign up for a campus tour, or obtain additional information, students should contact:

Office of Undergraduate Admissions
Stony Brook University
Stony Brook, New York 11794-1901
Telephone: 631-632-6868
631-632-6859 (TDD)
Fax: 631-632-9898
E-mail: enroll@stonybrook.edu
World Wide Web: http://www.stonybrook.edu/admissions

Stony Brook combines a small-college environment with all the advantages of a major research university.

STRATFORD UNIVERSITY

FALLS CHURCH AND WOODBRIDGE, VIRGINIA

The University

Stratford University was founded in 1976 and has undergone constant changes as it has continued to expand and adapt to changing employer demands. Stratford is a small, private institution with a personalized approach to student needs. The Stratford community includes two campuses in northern Virginia just a short distance from Washington, D.C. The Stratford philosophy is to provide professional competencies that satisfy employer needs, utilizing a teaching method that accommodates a variety of different learning styles.

Stratford enrolls more than 800 students in its programs, offering small classes to ensure personal attention to each student. Stratford students represent a diverse population, from recent high school graduates to adult learners seeking to make a career change. The friendly and supportive environment at Stratford University ensures that students feel comfortable and well supported.

The University offers programs in technology, business, hospitality, and culinary arts at both the undergraduate and graduate levels. The University is located in the heart of Fairfax County, Virginia, home of the Internet and numerous businesses that support the Internet, telecommunications, and information. User groups, national societies, and various technology councils provide networking avenues for Stratford students. Hospitality-related businesses abound in the Washington area, from world-class restaurants to boutique hotels; career opportunities are numerous. In addition, the business of government provides varied career paths for Stratford graduates.

The University provides a full array of career development and placement services. Students attend workshops on academic planning, resume writing, and effective interviewing skills. Career Services strives to help students make the contacts that lead to internships or permanent positions.

Stratford University partners with Collegiate Housing Services to offer comfortable and affordable dormitory-style apartments near both campuses. The typical housing configuration is a furnished, two-bedroom, two-bathroom apartment shared by up to 4 Stratford students of the same gender.

Location

Stratford University has two campuses in the greater Washington, D.C., region. Washington has much to offer. From politics to urban events, culture to recreation, the capital region is a great place to live, work, and study. Local sights include Mount Vernon, Old Town Alexandria, the White House, Capitol Hill, the Mall, and the Smithsonian Institute. Most of the sights are easily accessible by public transportation.

The prosperous D.C. job market is a draw for Stratford students. For both working students looking to upgrade skills and full-time students concerned with finding a job quickly after graduation, the region offers a wealth of jobs for graduates of all of Stratford's programs. As the nation's capital and a major tourist center, the metropolitan Washington area is a center for business, finance, industry, and entertainment.

Majors and Degrees

The School of Business Administration offers Associate of Applied Science (A.A.S.) and Bachelor of Science (B.S.) degrees in business administration. The School of Computer Information Systems offers A.A.S. degrees in digital design and animation and network design and security and a B.S. degree in information technology as well as diplomas in network management and security and digital design and animation. The School of Culinary Arts and Hospitality confers A.A.S. degrees in advanced culinary arts, baking and pastry arts, and hotel and restaurant management; a B.S. degree in hospitality management; and an advanced culinary arts professional diploma. The business administration, hotel and restaurant management, and information technology programs are also offered online.

Academic Programs

Stratford University delivers competency-based educational programs that prepare individuals for employment in specific career areas. These competencies are employer centered. The curriculum in each program is designed to ensure that students have the required competencies demanded in their fields of endeavor. The instructional techniques at Stratford are student centered. At the beginning of each program, students are tested for both learning styles and learning modes, and instruction in all classes is individualized based on the results of this assessment. This dual emphasis results in student academic success, without lowering required employer-based standards. As a result, students who graduate enjoy a high placement rate.

The A.A.S. and the B.S. degree programs include core requirements, elective requirements, and general education requirements. The total requirement is 90 quarter credits for the A.A.S. programs, and they normally take sixty weeks to complete. The total requirement for the B.S. degree programs is 180 quarter credits. The first 90 quarter credits are completed prior to beginning the 90 credits of junior- or senior-level courses. The B.S. programs take 120 weeks to complete.

The diploma programs include core and elective requirements. The total requirement for these programs is 60 quarter credits, and they normally take fifty weeks to complete.

Students may receive transfer credit for courses transferred from regionally accredited institutions. Also, certain training received from prior military schools, military service, or prior work experiences may be awarded as transfer credit. Stratford is approved for the training of veterans.

The course calendar is divided into five sessions, each of which is ten weeks in length. With start dates in January, March, May, August, and October, Stratford's flexible scheduling accommodates its busy students.

Academic Facilities

Stratford's library is located at the Falls Church campus, but all 2,400 titles are available online. In addition, the library subscribes to OCLC FirstSearch, a collection of more than 50 databases.

The campus has state-of-the-art facilities equipped with the latest technology and resources. All information systems classrooms are equipped with one computer for every student, and Stratford's networking students work with state-of-the-art Cisco routers and switches. Students may also access one of several computers for general use in the library. Culinary arts students are trained in one of six fully equipped professional kitchens.

Costs

Tuition is $275 per credit hour. Laboratory fees are $50 for each class that utilizes computer laboratories. The online technology fee is $120 per class. A one-time supply fee of $2560 for culinary students in the associate and diploma programs defrays the cost of food, uniforms, cutlery, and consumable goods used throughout the program. Upper-level hospitality kitchen classes have a $165 fee per class.

Financial Aid

Financial aid officers at Stratford are trained to guide students through the financial aid process to ensure that all available financial aid has been explored. Federal loans and grants (including PLUS, PELL, FSEOG, FWS) are applicable toward tuition at Stratford. The University is also approved for Veterans Association benefits, Vocational Rehabilitation benefits, and private institutional financing.

Stratford offers the Graduating High School Senior Scholarship Program and the Culinary Scholarship Programs. Stratford University also accepts private scholarships from foundations, service clubs, and other organizations.

Faculty

Stratford University's faculty members have been hand-chosen for their teaching ability, personality traits, and experience in their fields. The entire Stratford University staff works as a team to help students succeed.

Admission Requirements

Graduation from a secondary school or equivalent education as certified by the state department of education is normally required for admission. In addition, all students must pass the CPAt examination prior to acceptance by the University or provide SAT scores of 1000 or higher or ACT scores of 21 or higher.

Stratford is approved to offer I-20 certification for F1 visas for international students. Students for whom English is a second language are required to demonstrate English proficiency through a TOEFL or CPAt score. Qualifying scores vary by program as follows: information systems, 150; culinary arts, 130; hotel and event management, 130; and business administration, 140.

Application and Information

Students must submit a completed application for admission and a $50 nonrefundable application fee. Applicants must also schedule an interview with admissions to complete the assessment instrument. Students may bring or have the registrar from their high school, college, or state GED office forward a copy of their transcripts to Stratford University. Student-issued copies of transcripts or diplomas can be submitted directly to the University.

Students interested in applying should contact:

Stratford University
7777 Leesburg Pike
Falls Church, Virginia 22043
Telephone: 703-821-8570
800-444-0804 (toll-free)
Fax: 703-734-5339

Stratford University
13576 Minnieville Road
Woodbridge, Virginia 22192
Telephone: 703-897-1982
888-546-1250 (toll-free)

E-mail: admissions@stratford.edu
World Wide Web: http://www.stratford.edu

SULLIVAN UNIVERSITY
LOUISVILLE, KENTUCKY

The University

In 1962, A. O. Sullivan, a postsecondary educator since 1926, and his son, A. R. Sullivan, decided to form a higher education institution founded on the highest ideals and standards to prepare students for successful careers. Since that time, the University has earned a reputation as one of the leading career institutions in the nation. Accredited by the Commission on Colleges of the Southern Association of Colleges and Schools, Sullivan offers master's, baccalaureate, associate, and diploma programs. Since achieving Level III accreditation in December 1996 and baccalaureate accreditation in January 1992, Sullivan has grown to become both Kentucky's newest four-year university and its largest independent college or university. The University also has a branch in Lexington, Kentucky, and an extension at Fort Knox, Kentucky.

With a current enrollment of more than 4,900 men and women, Sullivan is a nationally recognized leader in career training. For students with special physical needs, the University is equipped with special parking facilities, ramped entrances, elevator services, and handicapped-accessible rest-room facilities.

At Sullivan, students gain not only a valuable education but access to a variety of helpful services. All Sullivan graduates have access to the Graduate Employment Service, which provides lifetime, nationwide assistance and has a 99 percent graduate employment rate. In order for students to get hands-on experience in their chosen field from the very first day, the University also offers a special "inverted curriculum" in which students take skills courses in their particular field first and general education courses later in their course of study. To whet the student's appetite, the University's award-winning National Center for Hospitality Studies provides delicious meals at the Culinary Food Service Center on campus.

The Dean of Students coordinates a variety of activities in conjunction with the Assistant Dean of Students, such as academic advisement; clubs and organizations, including Phi Beta Lambda, Student Government Association, the Baptist Student Union, Summit Club, and Travel Club; and clubs related to several academic disciplines. Annual events that bring excitement to the University are the cruise down the Ohio River on the Belle of Louisville Riverboat, the Spring Jam Festival, the annual summer picnic, and special camping and ski trips. Available to students under 21 are spacious apartments near campus furnished with modern furniture.

Sullivan students have won the NSCAA National Bowling Championships for both men and women in recent years.

In addition to undergraduate degrees, Sullivan University also offers the Master of Business Administration (M.B.A.) degree, the executive M.B.A. degree, the Master of Science in managing information technology degree, the Master of Science in dispute resolution degree, and the dual M.B.A./MSMIT degree.

Location

Only minutes from downtown Louisville, Kentucky, Sullivan is conveniently located within a block of one of Louisville's major interstate highways. Students can enjoy the metropolitan environment of Louisville by attending the symphony, ballet, opera, art museums, theaters, the Museum of History and Science with its IMAX theater, the Louisville Zoo, the Louisville Slugger Museum, historic sites, quaint restaurants, multiple shopping centers, or a professional ice hockey game. With the flowering of spring comes the thundering excitement of the Kentucky Derby. For nature lovers, the Ohio River as well as nearby lakes and parks provide leisurely activities after a day of studies.

Majors and Degrees

Sullivan University confers the Bachelor of Science degree in business administration (with concentrations in accounting, computer systems, construction management, finance, healthcare management, hospitality management, logistics and distribution management, management, and marketing), the Bachelor of Science degree in human resource leadership, the Bachelor of Science degree in information technology, and the Bachelor of Science degree in paralegal studies. The Associate of Science degree is offered in baking and pastry arts, business administration (with options in accounting, business management, and marketing and sales management), computer science (with concentrations in computer programming, information technology, Internet/Intranet programming, and PC support specialist studies), culinary arts, hotel/restaurant management, office administration (with options in executive professional studies, legal professional studies, medical office management, and office administration specialist studies), paralegal studies, professional catering, and travel and tourism. Sullivan also offers diplomas in business administration, early childhood education, legal nurse consultant studies, office administration, professional baker studies, professional cook studies, professional nanny studies, and travel and tourism as well as Microsoft certificate programs in MCSE and MCSD.

Academic Program

All Sullivan students study practical courses designed to build a foundation for their careers. Just the opposite of most colleges and universities, Sullivan students begin by concentrating specifically on their areas of interest; then, their general and advanced education courses are taken within the final few months, or quarters, of the degree program. The University operates on a quarter-hour system of four 11-week sessions, which allows baccalaureate students to finish their degrees in as little as thirty-six months. Credits are awarded on a credit-hour basis. Day classes are offered every day of the week except Friday. "Plus Friday" is a free day when students may utilize the facilities and equipment for individual study and practice and faculty members are available to give students special assistance.

To qualify for graduation in the Bachelor of Science program, students must complete a minimum of 180 credit hours. In addition, all students must attain a minimum cumulative grade point average of 2.0 on a 4.0 scale. The curriculum includes 60 credit hours of core business requirements, 28 credit hours of business support requirements, 16 credit hours of classes in the student's option, 48 hours of general studies, and 60 hours of electives.

Sullivan University offers a number of courses and programs on line, with nearly 40 databases available through its participation in the Kentucky Commonwealth Virtual University. This exciting method of delivery is rapidly becoming very popular with Sullivan's busy student population. To learn more about this option, students should consult the University's Web site listed in the Application and Information section.

Students may earn credit for certain requirements by taking the College-Level Examination Program (CLEP) subject examinations. Students may also receive credit for courses by taking the University bypass examinations.

Academic Facilities

Sullivan University's multimillion-dollar complex is climate-controlled and houses a variety of training equipment. From the state-of-the-art AS-400 and numerous personal computer labs utilizing the latest in software packages to the WorldSpan computerized travel reservation system, Sullivan students have outstanding technology right at their fingertips. A multimillion-dollar, state-of-the-art Sullivan University Library opened in January 1999. The library contains a diversity of current reference and circulating materials as well as a high-speed computer network that provides access to the Sullivan University virtual library's (http://www.sullivan.edu/library) latest full-text and full-image electronic databases, such as ABI/Inform, LEXIS-NEXIS, and WESTLAW. Sullivan University also has resource sharing agreements with six other area libraries.

Costs

Expenses for the 2003–04 academic year ranged from $12,240 to $16,320 for tuition and $300 to $450 for first-quarter books. Housing cost was $3690, the general fee was $415, and there was a $72 fee for parking. An additional comprehensive fee is applied for some hospitality programs.

Financial Aid

Students attending Sullivan have access to numerous federal and state financial aid programs, such as all Title IV programs as well as Job Training Partnership Act (JTPA) funds. Many loans, grants, work-study programs, academic scholarships, and private scholarships are also available. As directed by the Department of Education, federal funds are allotted to the lowest-income families first, but funds are also available for middle- and upper-income families.

Faculty

Sullivan's 89 full-time and 125 part-time faculty members share years of education and experience with their students. Faculty members are available daily for student assistance. With a 19:1 student-faculty ratio, the faculty can provide students with the academic guidance that they deserve.

Student Government

The Student Government Activities Council is responsible for coordinating most student activities and social affairs. Officers serve for a term of two quarters. In addition, representatives and alternates are elected from each class to serve for one quarter. The Student Government Activities Council offers an excellent opportunity for involvement in the very heart of most student social events and fosters cooperation among the student body, administration, and the faculty of Sullivan University.

Admission Requirements

To be considered for admission to Sullivan University, a student is required to demonstrate the appropriate aptitude and background for his or her anticipated field of study by successful completion of an entrance test and/or submission of ACT or SAT I test scores. Students also must have a high school diploma or its equivalent, such as a General Educational Development (GED) certificate. Sullivan has a rolling admissions policy; those who apply first are accepted first. The University individually interviews and advises each person seeking admission either at the University or at the student's home. Students from other regions of the United States and international students may complete the application by mail. A University preview video is available for review if a visit is impossible prior to entry. New classes normally begin the first week of January, April, July, and October of each year.

Application and Information

Students considering applying to the University are strongly encouraged to visit the campus. Included in a weekday visit are an interview with an admissions officer, a tour of the campus, an opportunity to observe classes, and discussions with professors and students. A Sullivan representative assists out-of-town visitors in finding accommodations. Approximately six open houses per year allow prospective students and their families an opportunity to visit the campus and participate in campus activities.

For more information and application materials, prospective students should contact the appropriate campus:

Director of Admissions
Sullivan University
P.O. Box 33-308
Louisville, Kentucky 40232-9733
Telephone: 502-456-6505
800-844-1354 (toll-free)
World Wide Web: http://www.sullivan.edu

Director of Admissions
Sullivan University, Lexington
2355 Harrodsburg Road
Lexington, Kentucky 40504
Telephone: 859-276-4357
800-467-6281 (toll-free)

Director of Admissions
Sullivan University, Ft. Knox
P.O. Box 998
Fort Knox, Kentucky 40121
Telephone: 502-942-8500
800-562-6713 (toll-free)

Greek revival–style architecture and picturesque grounds characterize Sullivan University.

SUSQUEHANNA UNIVERSITY

SELINSGROVE, PENNSYLVANIA

The University

Susquehanna is a national liberal arts university enrolling approximately 1,900 undergraduates in its three schools: the School of Arts, Humanities, and Communications; the Sigmund Weis School of Business; and the School of Natural and Social Sciences. The University offers the best qualities of a residential college and a challenging university. Distinctive liberal arts programs such as biology and writing are enhanced by equally strong professional programs in areas like music and business. A Susquehanna education builds the broad base of knowledge to help students become educated citizens of the world while offering the in-depth preparation needed to succeed in graduate or professional school or in a job after graduation. Susquehanna is affiliated with the Evangelical Lutheran Church in America, and since its founding in 1858 the University has welcomed students and faculty and staff members from all racial, ethnic, and religious backgrounds.

As a residential university, Susquehanna believes that extracurricular activities should be an integral part of each student's experience. There are twenty-three varsity sports teams as well as an extensive intramural program, numerous academic clubs, one of the most powerful student-run radio stations in Pennsylvania, a host of musical activities, and many other organizations, ranging from the Marketing Club to the Student Association for Cultural Awareness. Approximately 80 percent of the students live on campus in seven residence halls, six apartment-style units, several academic or volunteer student project suites and houses, a scholars' house, four fraternity houses, and four sorority houses.

Location

Selinsgrove is a town of about 6,000 inhabitants. It is approximately 90 minutes west of the Pocono Mountain resort areas; about an hour from State College and Harrisburg; about a 3-hour drive from Philadelphia, New York City, and Washington, D.C.; and about a 4-hour drive from Pittsburgh. Located on U.S. Routes 11 and 15 and near I-80, the area is readily accessible, and public transportation is available. Cultural, dining, recreational, and shopping opportunities abound. Susquehanna has close ties with the community, where a number of students participate in internships and many take part in the University's extensive, award-winning volunteer program. Susquehanna is one of three universities in the area.

Majors and Degrees

Susquehanna University offers the Bachelor of Science degree with majors in biochemistry, biology, chemistry, computer science, ecology, education, geological and environmental science, and physics and the Bachelor of Arts degree with majors in art, art history, chemistry, communications and theater arts, computer science, economics, English, French, geological and environmental science, German, graphic design, history, information systems, international studies, mathematics, music, philosophy, physics, political science, psychology, religion, sociology, Spanish, and writing. The Bachelor of Music is offered in church music, music education, and performance. The Bachelor of Science in Business is offered in accounting, business administration (with emphases in finance, global or human resource management, information systems, or marketing), and economics. There are also a number of program options with interdisciplinary and self-designed majors.

Two dual-degree programs are available: a joint-degree program with Temple University's School of Dentistry and a 3-2 program in forestry or environmental management with Duke University. A 2+2 program in allied health is offered with Thomas Jefferson University.

Academic Programs

Susquehanna's core curriculum, which provides the breadth of knowledge needed for graduate school or a career, includes traditional and contemporary components. The traditional courses offer exposure to the humanities, social sciences, and natural sciences. Contemporary courses help students understand relationships among individuals, organizations, and the natural world. Susquehanna's core curriculum also has an extensive personal development sequence, which includes the nation's first required course on career planning.

Susquehanna offers a competitive four-year interdisciplinary Honors Program affiliated with the National Collegiate Honors Council. Preprofessional studies may be pursued in law, medicine and allied health fields, and the ministry. Teaching certification is offered at the elementary and secondary levels in all the usual subjects. Teachers are certified for grades K–12 in music and modern foreign languages (French, German, and Spanish). Nearly fifty academic minors, including programs in diversity studies, film, health-care studies, Jewish studies, and journalism, are available. Army ROTC is available under a cross-enrollment program with Bucknell University.

Off-Campus Programs

Susquehanna students may participate in a variety of off-campus programs, including the Washington Center in the nation's capital, the Washington Semester of American University, the United Nations Semester of Drew University, and the Philadelphia Center Program. Each semester, the University approves numerous off-campus departmental internships, some of which are in other countries. Students are encouraged to study abroad, and Susquehanna is a participating member of the Institute of European Studies. The University is a coordinating institution with Senshu University in Japan and offers a semester in London for juniors majoring in business. Susquehanna-designed Focus programs complement special groups of courses with travel to the country being studied. Recent trips included southern Africa, Australia, Ecuador, and Martinique. All of these programs carry academic credit.

Academic Facilities

Susquehanna is an undergraduate university. All facilities and equipment are for the exclusive use of undergraduate students. The Blough-Weis Library houses Susquehanna's language lab, music and sound media, and the Film Institute. The library collection numbers about 280,000 volumes and other items, including microforms and records. About 2,400 periodicals are received, and 350 individual study spaces are maintained. Fisher Science Hall provides facilities for all the sciences, including experimental psychology. General classrooms are in Steele and Bogar Halls. The Center for Music and Art, completed in 2002, includes music and art studios and a performance hall. Seibert Hall houses the University Computer

Center. Apfelbaum Hall, opened in fall 1999, provides the business and communications programs with multimedia computer labs, video studios, offices, and conference, presentation, and seminar rooms. The Charles B. Degenstein Campus Center houses the Lore Degenstein Gallery and a state-of-the-art 450-seat teaching theater. The James W. Garrett Sports Complex, completed in 2001, includes a 51,000-square-foot field house, a fitness center, racqetball courts, and a football and track stadium.

Costs

Tuition and fees for 2004–05 are $24,810. Room and board costs are $6840. A student's personal expenses, including books, travel, and other costs, are estimated at $1600 to $1900 per year.

Financial Aid

Susquehanna University offers renewable academic and music scholarships, which are awarded on a competitive basis without regard to financial need. In addition, need-based financial aid is awarded to permit attendance by full-time students whose personal and family resources are not sufficient to meet the costs. The amount of financial aid is based on need, not on family income alone. The level of need is determined annually by information provided on the PROFILE and the Free Application for Federal Student Aid (FAFSA). More than half of all students receive financial assistance that ranges from $1000 to full need. Aid is provided in packages that may include grants, scholarships, loans, and jobs. The various state and federal assistance programs are also taken into consideration when aid packages are created. International applicants may be considered for merit-based scholarships but are not eligible for financial aid based on need.

Faculty

Susquehanna's teaching faculty members help students develop their views of themselves and of the world and play an important part in preparing them for life after college. The faculty-student ratio is about 1:14, and 92 percent of the 108 full-time faculty members hold an earned doctorate. Most faculty members serve as student advisers, and full-time counseling services are also available. There are no graduate assistants at Susquehanna.

Student Government

The Student Government Association provides a representative student organization to assure students of a voice in University governance. The Student Senate, the legislative branch, provides a forum for student opinion, deals with issues of concern to the entire student body, and seeks solutions to campus problems. The senate is responsible for the allocation of funds collected through the student activity fee and is the body that designates student representatives for University committees and the Board of Directors, of which 2 students are voting members.

Admission Requirements

Susquehanna admits students without regard to race, color, religion, national or ethnic origin, age, sex, sexual orientation, or handicap. Students who gain admission are those whom the Admissions Committee deems able to profit from and contribute to the Susquehanna experience. Graduation from an accredited secondary school or a high school equivalency certificate is required. Experience has shown that the best preparation includes at least 4 years of English, 4 years of mathematics, 3 years of social science, 2 or 3 years of one foreign language, 2 or 3 years of laboratory science, and 3 or more units of electives. In evaluating a candidate, the committee considers academic performance, major interests, test scores, recommendations, extracurricular activities, and demonstrated interest in the University. In addition to the application and secondary school records, the candidate must submit scores from either the SAT I or the ACT, unless he or she chooses the Write Option. An applicant with a cumulative ranking in the top 20 percent of the high school class may submit two graded writing samples instead of standardized test scores. Students for whom English is not their native language must submit official score reports of the TOEFL or the ELPT. Although SAT II Subject Tests are not required for admission to Susquehanna, it is strongly recommended that the candidate take the Writing Test and one other test of his or her choice. Subject Test scores assist in placement as well as admission decisions. Applications for early decision are encouraged, and deferred admission is available. Interviews are strongly suggested for early decision and transfer candidates, although all candidates are encouraged to arrange a visit to the campus. Applicants to the Bachelor of Music program and to the Bachelor of Arts program in music must audition. Applicants to the Bachelor of Arts in writing program must also submit a portfolio. Transfer candidates can be considered for either semester, and the University recognizes the Advanced Placement and CLEP programs of the College Board and the International Baccalaureate program.

Application and Information

Application materials and introductory and departmental information may be obtained by contacting the Office of Admissions. All interview appointments should be made two weeks in advance to allow time for faculty contact and the scheduling of student-conducted tours. The priority application deadline is March 1 (for early decision I, November 15; for early decision II, January 1). The University adheres to the Candidates Reply Date of May 1 and is a Common Application participant.

Office of Admissions
Susquehanna University
514 University Avenue
Selinsgrove, Pennsylvania 17870-1040
Telephone: 570-372-4260
800-326-9672 (toll-free)
Fax: 570-372-2722
E-mail: suadmiss@susqu.edu
World Wide Web: http://www.susqu.edu

Graceful Seibert Hall at Susquehanna University.

SWARTHMORE COLLEGE

SWARTHMORE, PENNSYLVANIA

The College

Swarthmore, regularly ranked among the top three liberal arts colleges in the country, is well known as an academic powerhouse. But, while intellectual, Swarthmore is also alive with passions. The College is made up of students and faculty members who are both brilliant and adventurous; thinkers who live vigorously. Everyone spends a substantial amount of time in classes and at the library, but most students spend a great deal more time engaged in philosophy debates with friends at dinner, working in soup kitchens, doing soccer drills, partying, playing music, tutoring children, and walking in the woods. The trick is to fit it all into a 24-hour day.

At the College, twenty-one varsity sports teams compete in Division III. There are 120 student organizations, including the African American, Asian American, Latino, multicultural, Native American, and international student organizations; music ensembles; the Outing Club; the student newspaper; the radio station; the yearbook; a lesbian/bisexual/gay group; religious organizations; a wide range of community service programs; and several political organizations. In addition, students are welcome to start new groups with support from the activities fund. All campus events are free as part of Swarthmore's commitment to equality of opportunity.

Swarthmore is rooted in the ideals of its Quaker founders: social action, pacifism, and respect for the "inner light" of each person. Professors and administrators encourage students to follow their own passions. There are even funds to support student-run projects. Faculty members use their great expertise to help with student projects, and students also take responsibility for helping each other. As a result, Swarthmoreans can take tremendous personal and intellectual risks in safety—and grow enormously in the process.

Almost all of Swarthmore's 1,400 students live in the College's residence halls, which range from tiny Woolman (originally a private Victorian house) to the Elizabethan-style Worth to the more traditional Mertz. Most dorms are coed, but single-sex housing is available too. Everyone eats together in a central dining hall, thus ideas and friendships spread rapidly around the campus.

Swarthmore actively welcomes and knits together people of widely diverse backgrounds. Students come from fifty states and sixty other countries, and the College's policy of admitting students without regard to financial need means that students' economic and social circumstances vary widely too.

Location

Swarthmore's campus is a 357-acre arboretum and its beauty defies description. A gorgeous, 50-acre carpet of emerald lawn at the center of the campus invites reading, studying, playing, and napping outdoors in fall and spring. The wooded creek, with an amphitheater terraced into its hillside, makes a wonderful refuge for walks, conversations, and contemplation.

At the same time, all the excitement, history, and culture of downtown Philadelphia is less than half an hour away by a train that leaves from the foot of the campus. Philadelphia's many and diverse restaurants are renowned, and a walk around the city offers a primer in the history of American government and architecture since 1600. Music, dance, and theater events are plentiful each week.

Majors and Degrees

Swarthmore offers undergraduate education only, with programs leading to B.A. or B.S. degrees. Courses of study include art, art history, Asian studies, astronomy, astrophysics, bioanthropology, biochemistry, biology, black studies, chemical physics, chemistry, classics (ancient history, Greek, Latin), cognitive science, comparative literature, computer science, dance, economics, education, engineering, English literature, environmental studies, film and media studies, Francophone studies, German studies, history, interpretation theory, linguistics, literature, mathematics, medieval studies, modern languages and literatures (Chinese, French, German, Russian, Spanish), music, peace and conflict studies, philosophy, physics, political science, psychobiology, psychology, public policy, religion, sociology and anthropology, statistics, theater studies, and women's studies. Students can also design an interdepartmental special major.

Swarthmore's strong engineering program is one of the few in the country that offers students a chance to acquire both a top-notch engineering education and an extraordinary liberal arts background.

Academic Program

Swarthmore's Honors Program (which is almost impossible to explain on paper, although it is fairly simple in practice) offers a rare opportunity to do graduate-style work as an undergraduate.

Students choose to follow either the Course or Honors Program starting in their junior year. Course students continue to take an average of four classes each semester, generally selecting courses from among a number of departments. The Course Program offers the chance to investigate a wide range of disciplines.

Honors students, on the other hand, take four "preparations" over the course of their junior and senior years—three in the major and one in a minor. Like graduate seminars, these involve a tremendous amount of individual study and collegial relationships with faculty members. The preparations may take the form of seminars, independent reading, thesis work, or other projects designed by the student and the department. These preparations comprise half of the student's course load in the junior and senior years.

Perhaps the most striking feature of the Honors Program is that final examinations are given by external examiners—distinguished faculty members from other colleges—rather than by the professors with whom the student has been working.

Off-Campus Programs

Swarthmore actively encourages students to study abroad as an excellent way to enrich study in any field and to discover broad perspectives.

In recent years, Swarthmore students have completed international study programs in Australia, Brazil, Cameroon, Chile, China, Colombia, Ecuador, Egypt, England, France, Germany, Ghana, Greece, Hungary, India, Ireland, Italy, Japan, Kenya, Mexico, Nepal, Nigeria, Russia, Scotland, Spain, Sri Lanka, Sweden, Taiwan, and Thailand.

A special Office for Foreign Study offers support and guidance, and financial aid is normally applicable to international study.

Students can also spend a semester at Tufts University, Rice University, Pomona College, Mills College, Middlebury College, and Harvey Mudd College, with which Swarthmore has exchange arrangements. While at Swarthmore, it's also possible to take courses at nearby Haverford College, Bryn Mawr College, and the University of Pennsylvania.

Academic Facilities

There are approximately 1,117,499 books, periodicals, collections, and recordings housed in McCabe Library, Cornell Science Library, and Underhill Music Library. In addition, the campus has a computer center; an observatory; engineering and science laboratories, including a new science center that opened in 2003; a greenhouse; a music building with a 420-seat concert hall and eleven practice rooms; a theater complex with a flexible stage/seating arena; and large, light-washed dance and art studios.

Swarthmore's wonderful, airy student center, built inside the Gothic shell of a stone-and-stained-glass theater, is a splendid spot to meet friends and members of the faculty over a snack any time of year.

Costs

For 2003–04, fees were $37,716, which included tuition of $28,500. Room was approximately $4572, board was $4342, and the activities fee totaled $290. Additional costs families should consider when budgeting include books, supplies, and travel.

Financial Aid

The College is committed to a long-standing policy of meeting 100 percent of admitted students' demonstrated financial need. A very high percentage—approximately half—of Swarthmore students receive substantial financial aid. The average award, including work, loan, and grant, was approximately $23,965 last year.

Faculty

There are just 8 students per faculty member at Swarthmore. All professors dedicate their time and attention exclusively to teaching undergraduates. There are no teaching assistants, and students work directly with the most expert minds on campus.

Student Government

The 20-member Student Council is elected by the student body to represent student opinion to faculty and administration and encourage discussion of important community issues. The Council's Budget Committee controls and allocates the multithousand dollar student fund, and its Appointment Committee places students on committees of administration and faculty, alumni/alumnae committees, and the board of managers.

Admission Requirements

Admission to Swarthmore is highly competitive. A strong academic record is essential. In addition, the College looks for students who have far-ranging interests and abilities, especially an interest in social action and service. Swarthmore encourages all students to visit the campus and, if possible, to have an interview on campus or close to where they live.

Applications must include SAT I or ACT scores; scores in three SAT II Subject Tests, one of which must be the writing test; a high school transcript; a brief personal essay on a meaningful interest or activity; and a longer essay on a topic specified by the College. Swarthmore is also interested in applicants' reading, research, work, and travel experience both in and out of school.

Application and Information

The deadline for fall early decision is November 15 and for winter early decision, January 1. The deadline for regular decision is also January 1. April 1 is the date for fall transfer applications. For more information or an application, students should contact:

Admissions Office
Swarthmore College
500 College Avenue
Swarthmore, Pennsylvania 19081-1390
Telephone: 610-328-8300
800-667-3110 (toll-free)
E-mail: admissions@swarthmore.edu

Tree-lined Magill Walk, Swarthmore College.

SWEET BRIAR COLLEGE

SWEET BRIAR, VIRGINIA

The College

Deeply committed to the education of women since its founding in 1901, Sweet Briar College is consistently ranked as one of the top national liberal arts and sciences colleges in the country. Recently, Sweet Briar was chosen by the National Survey of Student Engagement as one of the four liberal arts colleges who best engage students both in and out of the classroom. Its excellent academic reputation, beautiful campus, and attention to the individual attract smart, confident women who want to excel. Students can expect that their Sweet Briar experience—connecting academic work to the wider world—will allow them to fulfill their promise as scholars and leaders, while enjoying the close-knit friendships and camaraderie that come with a small, residential community.

A Sweet Briar education sets in motion the conviction that any goal is achievable. Classes average 12 students, and a student to faculty ratio of 8:1 ensures academic interaction and personal attention. Students work one-on-one with faculty members and visiting scholars and artists to engage in meaningful creative activity, scholarship, and research. A four-year career planning program develops worldwide career opportunities, capitalizing on an international network of successful Sweet Briar alumnae. The College has a wide geographic, ethnic, and socioeconomic representation. About 600 women from more than forty states and thirteen countries are enrolled at Sweet Briar's Virginia campus; another 100 students are enrolled in Sweet Briar's coed Junior Year in France and Junior Year in Spain.

Students who derive the most from the Sweet Briar experience are those who contribute the most, striking a good balance between academic work and the rest of life. A majority of students enter Sweet Briar having already been involved extensively in extracurricular activities; they recognize that one of the advantages of the College is the unlimited opportunities for women to participate and assume leadership roles in many types of organizations and activities. More than sixty-two campus organizations are available, including honor societies, a literary journal, community service groups, a multicultural club, political groups, a student newspaper, drama and dance clubs, a radio station, and singing groups. Students plan and participate in an extensive array of concerts, films, and dance and theater productions as well as workshops and master classes by visiting scholars and performers. Recent visitors include the author Salman Rushdie, writer and missionary Elisabeth Elliot, Olympic swimmer Maddy Crippen, and civil rights pioneer Elaine Jones.

Beginning May 2004, Sweet Briar will enroll its first graduate students. The College has started the only graduate education program in the country that focuses on differentiated curriculum and instruction and will be offering the Master of Arts in Teaching and the Master of Education degree.

Varsity athletes compete in NCAA Division III field hockey, lacrosse, soccer, swimming, tennis, and volleyball. Club sports include fencing, riding, and softball. Sweet Briar's equestrian program, both competitive and instructional, has consistently garnered national recognition.

Location

Sweet Briar's natural 3,300-acre campus in the foothills of the Blue Ridge Mountains is crisscrossed with hiking, biking, and riding trails through woodlands and dells and around small lakes that provide spectacular outdoor recreational activities. The magnificent campus, the Georgian masterpiece of renowned American architect Ralph Adams Cram, is on the National Register of Historic Places. Recent additions to the campus include a state-of-the-art conference center and a beautiful student center that opened in 2002. Sweet Briar is also the only college in the United States with a residential artists' colony on its campus, the Virginia Center for the Creative Arts. The on-campus equestrian center, one of the largest and best-designed college facilities in the country, attracts both competitive and recreational riders. The College is centrally located on the outskirts of Lynchburg, Virginia, southwest of Washington, D.C., and Charlottesville. Students also enjoy activities in nearby Roanoke and Richmond.

Majors and Degrees

Sweet Briar awards the Bachelor of Arts, Bachelor of Science, or Bachelor of Fine Arts degree in forty majors: anthropology, art history, biochemistry and molecular biology, biology, business management, chemistry, classical studies: civilization, classical studies: Greek and Latin languages, computer science, dance, economics, engineering (3-2 dual degree), engineering science, English, English and creative writing, environmental science, environmental studies, fine arts, French, German, German studies, government, history, integrated engineering and management, international affairs, Italian studies, liberal studies, mathematical physics, mathematics, modern languages and literatures, music, philosophy, physics, psychology, religion, sociology, Spanish, Spanish/business, studio art, and theater arts.

Additional area studies, minors, and certificate programs include: archaeology, arts management, equine management, film studies, Italian, law and society, musical theater, prelaw, premed, and pre–veterinary. Students may design an interdisciplinary major focused on a topic of special interest or may construct individualized majors.

Academic Program

Sweet Briar's nationally celebrated academic program supports its mission to prepare women to be active, responsible members of a world community by integrating the liberal arts and sciences with opportunities for internships, research, campus and community leadership, and career planning. Underscoring every one of the forty major fields of study is the idea that the best way to learn about the world is to experience it. The curriculum emphasizes comprehensive understanding, analysis, reflection, creation, and communication across disciplines. The general education requirements include composition, oral communication, quantitative reasoning, Western and non-Western culture, literature, modern language, value assessment, creative artistic expression, world systems, scientific theory and experimentation, research, self-assessment, and physical activity. Independent studies and seminars are included in most majors, with a culminating senior course or exercise required in most majors. Sweet Briar has a chapter of Phi Beta Kappa and was the first women's college to establish a chapter of the prelaw honorary society Phi Alpha Delta. The four-year Honors Program is nationally recognized for its innovative partnering of interdisciplinary academic and cocurricular programs. Honors students may take special tutorials and seminars as well as complete a yearlong research project culminating in an honors thesis on an original topic.

Sweet Briar's two-semester calendar allows students to participate in intensive courses, independent research projects, or internships on campus or throughout the world.

Off-Campus Programs

Sweet Briar participates in the Tri College Consortium, which also includes Randolph-Macon Woman's College and Lynchburg

College. In addition to taking courses at the other colleges, students can participate in combined social and cultural activities. More than a third of Sweet Briar's junior class studies abroad. The Sweet Briar Junior Year in France, the first program in Paris for American students, is considered the most academically rigorous program available today. Students from 258 colleges and universities have participated in the coed program. The successful Junior Year in Spain is recognized as the premier program in Seville. The College has special relationships with the University of St. Andrews in Scotland, Heidelberg University in Germany, Doshisha Women's College in Japan, and the University of Urbino in Italy. Sweet Briar students have chosen the following destinations for study abroad: Australia, Austria, Bermuda, Canada, China, the Czech Republic, Cuba, Denmark, England, Germany, Greece, Guam, Holland, Ireland, Jamaica, Korea, Mongolia, Morocco, New Zealand, and Thailand. Students have also gained valuable experience by participating in internships abroad. Off-campus study may also include an Environmental Junior Year, the Washington Term at American University, and summer programs at St. Anne's College, Oxford; in Münster, Germany; in Rome or Urbino, Italy; Central America; Nepal; Spain; Australia; and Costa Rica.

Academic Facilities

Sweet Briar has the largest private undergraduate library collection in the state of Virginia with resources of more than 240,000 volumes, 1,000 journal subscriptions, 430,000 microforms, 6,800 audiovisual materials, and special libraries in art, music, and the sciences. Some of the notable special holdings include Virginia Woolf, T. E. Lawrence, George Meredith, W. H. Auden, and a rare collection of twentieth-century Chinese works. A fiber-optic backbone allows high-speed Ethernet communication among all academic and administrative buildings, as well as in residence hall rooms, with more than 1,000 terminal and network connections campuswide. Three computer labs with Macintosh and Windows/Intel Pentium computers are open free of charge 24 hours a day. The student-to-computer ratio is 6:1. Students studying science use state-of-the-art equipment that enhances faculty-student collaborative research. Biology equipment includes a scanning electron microscope with digital imaging system, equipment for plant and animal tissue culture, DNA sequencing equipment, and advanced video production facilities; chemistry students have access to two nuclear magnetic resonance spectrometers (NMR; 400 MHz and 60 MHz), an atomic absorption spectrometer (AAS), a diode array UV/Vis spectrometer, a Fourier transform-infrared spectrometer (FT-IR), a modular LASER laboratory, a gas chromatograph/mass spectrograph (GC/MS), a high-pressure liquid chromatograph (HPLC), and a differential scanning calorimeter (DSC); mathematics facilities include a calculus computer lab. Physics equipment includes a scanning tunneling microscope, an X-ray crystallography system, a 10-inch diameter reflecting telescope, and holographic instrumentation. The Academic Resource Center provides assistance to students in writing, reading, study skills, time management, stress management, and peer tutoring. The Babcock Fine Arts Center includes individual practice rooms, an electronic piano lab, art studios, a photography lab, and computer graphics facilities.

Costs

For 2004–05, tuition is $20,880 and room and board charges total $8520. Books, supplies, and fees cost about $750. Personal expenses averaged $750. All students may have cars.

Financial Aid

A family's financial circumstance does not limit a student's choices at Sweet Briar because of the College's generous financial aid program. More than 90 percent of enrolling students receive financial assistance from the College, including merit scholarships, need-based grants, loans, and work-study awards. Scholarships for international students are also available on a competitive basis.

Faculty

Sweet Briar's faculty members have been commended by numerous regional and national educational groups for their excellence in teaching. Faculty members are actively engaged in teaching, research, publication, and other forms of creative activity. More than 95 percent of full-time faculty members have a doctorate or the highest professional degree in their fields. About one half are women.

Student Government

The Student Government Association is founded upon a highly developed concept of honor, which through the Honor System applies to all phases of academic and social life. Each entering student becomes a full member of the Student Government Association upon taking the Honor Pledge, which states that Sweet Briar women do not lie, cheat, steal, or violate the rights of others. Students participate in the governance of the College through the many offices and committee positions of the Student Government Association (SGA). SGA and its committees are largely responsible for the self-governance of the student body.

Admission Requirements

Sweet Briar seeks talented women who are adventurous, enthusiastic about learning, and want to take an active part in their education. The Admissions Committee looks for qualities such as independent thinking, ethical principles, assertiveness, and an appreciation of diversity. Sweet Briar welcomes students of all economic, ethnic, geographic, religious, and social backgrounds.

Requirements normally include a minimum of 4 units in English, 3 in mathematics, 3 in social studies, 2 sequential years in a foreign language, and 3 units in science, as well as additional units in these subjects to total 16. Most candidates have 20 such academic units. Special attention is given to the difficulty of the applicant's curriculum, her class rank, and the school attended; scores on the SAT I or on the ACT are required. An interview at the College is strongly encouraged but not required. Candidates who are unable to visit the campus are urged to meet with staff members, to talk with alumnae in their home towns, or to request the Sweet Briar CD-ROM.

Application and Information

Candidates should apply by February 1 of the senior year. Early decision applications are due by December 1 of the senior year, and notifications are sent December 15; the enrollment deposit is due January 15. Transfer applications are due by July 1. A completed application includes a transcript of the candidate's academic work, scores on the required tests, recommendations from the guidance counselor and a teacher, and an essay written by the candidate. There is a $25 application fee, but it may be waived at the request of the student's guidance counselor if it is deemed to be a financial burden. Sweet Briar also accepts the Common Application and online applications. All materials should be sent to the address given below; information may be requested from the same office.

Dean of Admissions
Sweet Briar College
Sweet Briar, Virginia 24595
Telephone: 434-381-6142
800-381-6142 (toll-free)
Fax: 434-381-6152
E-mail: admissions@sbc.edu
World Wide Web: http://www.sbc.edu

SYRACUSE UNIVERSITY

SYRACUSE, NEW YORK

The University

Syracuse University, founded in 1870, is an independent, privately endowed university with an international reputation. Students attend from all over the United States and from more than ninety other countries. There are about 15,500 students enrolled; 10,700 are undergraduates. Approximately 70 percent of the students live in University housing, which includes modern residence halls, apartments, and fraternity and sorority houses. The 200-acre campus features a main grassy quadrangle surrounded by academic buildings, with residential facilities nearby. The campus is situated on a hill overlooking the downtown area of Syracuse. Social life is centered on the campus, and there are innumerable recreational, athletic, and academic activities. The 50,000-seat Carrier Dome is the site of concerts, sports events, and commencement. The residence halls are wired for direct connections from student rooms to the campus computer network.

Location

The city of Syracuse (metropolitan area population of 500,000) is the business, educational, and cultural hub of central New York. The city offers professional theater and opera, as well as visiting artists and performers. Highlights of the downtown area include the Everson Museum of Art, the impressive Civic Center, and the Armory Square shopping area. Central New York has many lakes, parks, mountains, and outstanding recreational opportunities.

Majors and Degrees

Syracuse University awards B.A., B.S., B.Arch., B.I.D., B.Mus., and B.F.A. degrees.

The School of Architecture offers a five-year baccalaureate program leading to the first professional degree of B.Arch.

Departmental and interdisciplinary majors in the College of Arts and Sciences are African-American studies, American studies, anthropology, biochemistry, biology, chemistry, classical civilization, classics (Greek and Latin), communication sciences and disorders, earth sciences, economics, English and textual studies, European literature, fine arts, French, geography, German, history, history of architecture, international relations, Italian, Latin, Latino-American studies, linguistic studies, mathematics, medieval and Renaissance studies, modern foreign languages, philosophy, physics, policy studies, political philosophy, political science, psychology, religion, Russian, Russian studies, sociology, Spanish, and women's studies.

The School of Education offers majors in art education, elementary education (inclusive with special education), health and exercise science, music education, physical education, secondary education, and special education (inclusive with elementary education).

The L. C. Smith College of Engineering and Computer Science majors include aerospace, chemical, civil, computer, electrical, environmental, and mechanical engineering; bioengineering; computer science; engineering physics; and systems and information science.

The College of Human Services and Health Professions majors include child and family studies, hospitality and food service management, nursing, nutrition/dietetics, nutrition science, selected studies (undecided), and social work.

The School of Information Studies offers a four-year baccalaureate program in information management and technology.

The School of Management majors include accounting, entrepreneurship and emerging enterprises, finance, general studies in management, marketing management, and supply chain management.

The S. I. Newhouse School of Public Communications majors are in the following areas: advertising, broadcast journalism, graphic arts, magazine, newspaper, photography, public relations, and television/radio/film.

The College of Visual and Performing Arts majors are in the following areas: art and design, drama, music, retail management and consumer studies, and communication and rhetorical studies. Art majors offered are advertising design, art photography, art video, ceramics, communications design, computer graphics, environmental design (interiors), fashion design, fiber arts, film, history of art, illustration, industrial design, interior design, metalsmithing, painting, printmaking, sculpture, surface pattern design, and textile design. Drama majors include design/technical theater, drama, and musical theater. Music majors include music composition, music industry, organ, percussion, piano, string instruments, voice, and wind instruments. The Department of Retail Management and Consumer Studies majors include retailing and consumer studies. Speech communication is the major in the Department of Communication and Rhetorical Studies.

Academic Programs

The University operates on a two-semester calendar with two 6-week summer sessions. Students generally take five 3-credit-hour courses each semester. A minimum of 120 credit hours is required for graduation. Special programs include dual, combined, and accelerated enrollment; selected studies; internships; an honors program; ROTC; and preprofessional advising for students going on to study dentistry, law, medicine, or veterinary science.

Off-Campus Programs

Through the University's Division of International Programs Abroad, students may study in Australia, Belgium, Chile, China, Czech Republic, France, Germany, Hungary, Ireland, Israel, Italy, Japan, Poland, Russia, Spain, and United Kingdom.

Academic Facilities

The academic buildings at Syracuse University span the century, with fifteen listed in the National Register of Historic Places and others representative of some of the most modern and technologically sophisticated architecture in the country. The Ernest Stevenson Bird Library houses approximately 2.8 million volumes; 18,000 journals and serials; 7 million microforms; 36,000 online and electronic resources; rare books; and archives. The University has computer facilities with laboratories and a data communications network that links computers to hundreds of terminals. The Newhouse Communications Center has some of the finest facilities available for journalism and telecommunications. The Center for Science and Technology is a state-of-the-art facility uniting research and academic programs in computer science and technology. It also houses the CASE Center for research in computer applications and software engineering. The high-tech Melvin A. Eggers Hall offers superior facilities for the University's social science programs.

Costs

Tuition for 2004–05 is $25,720, room and board are $9960, and fees are $1014. The total cost of attendance is $39,520, including estimates for the cost of books, supplies, and personal and travel expenses.

Financial Aid

About 75 percent of all entering freshmen and transfers receive some form of financial aid. By filing the Free Application for Federal Student Aid (FAFSA) and the College Scholarship Source (CSS) profile, students are automatically considered for all financial aid programs administered by Syracuse University, including federal financial aid, Syracuse University grants, and Federal Work-Study awards. Merit-based scholarships are available to both freshmen and transfer students, based solely on their academic record. Syracuse University evaluates candidates for admission without respect to financial need. Information on financial aid policies, procedures, and deadlines can be obtained from the Office of Financial Aid and Scholarship Programs.

Faculty

The majority of faculty members hold the highest degree in their professional field. There are more than 800 full-time faculty members, including recognized experts in their fields who teach at both the graduate and undergraduate levels.

Student Government

The Syracuse University Student Association works to protect students' rights and offers services through its three branches—the executive, the legislative, and the judicial.

Admission Requirements

Syracuse University seeks a diverse student body from all social, cultural, and educational backgrounds. Each candidate is evaluated individually, based on the requirements of the college of the University to which he or she has applied. Emphasis is placed on students' high school performance, standardized test scores (SAT I or ACT), an essay, recommendations, extracurricular activities, and portfolios or auditions when required. Special admission requirements and deadlines for some programs are described in the *Undergraduate Application for Admission* and on the Web site listed below.

Syracuse University is an Equal Opportunity/Affirmative Action institution and does not discriminate on the basis of race, creed, color, gender, national origin, religion, marital status, age, disability, or sexual orientation.

Application and Information

Regular decision applicants for the fall semester should submit their completed application along with transcripts, standardized test scores, the essay, teacher recommendations, and the counselor evaluation by January 1 (postmarked deadline). Notification begins in March.

Completed applications for early decision applicants must be postmarked by November 15. Notification begins in late December.

Detailed information and application forms may be obtained by contacting:

Office of Admissions
201 Tolley Administration Building
Syracuse University
Syracuse, New York 13244
Telephone: 315-443-3611
World Wide Web: http://admissions.syr.edu

The main quadrangle reflects the architectural span of the century, from the 50,000-seat Carrier Dome (left) to the classic Hendricks Chapel (center) and Crouse College spires (right).

TALLADEGA COLLEGE

TALLADEGA, ALABAMA

The College

Talladega College is a private, four-year liberal arts college founded in 1867 by former slaves Thomas Tarrant and William Savery. Tarrant and Savery met in Mobile, Alabama, with a group of newly freed men in 1865. The commitment and pledge written from this meeting, "we regard the education of our children and youth as vital to the preservation of our liberties, and true religion as the foundation of all real virtue, and shall use our utmost endeavors to promote these blessings in our common country," was the beginning of Tarrant's and Savery's ambition to provide a school for the children of former slaves. With the help of the American Missionary Association and General Wager Swayne of the Freedman's Bureau, they were able to purchase a three-story brick high school building and 34 acres. This building was built by slave labor and was originally used to educate young white men.

Talladega College provides a culturally rich education in a nurturing environment. The beautiful tree-lined campus is comprised of forty-two buildings on 50 acres located in the heart of a fertile valley in the foothills of the Blue Ridge Mountains. Swayne Hall, the College's oldest building, is a national historic landmark. DeForest Chapel is used for religious services and convocations. Callanan Union Building is the center of recreational activities. It houses a swimming pool, a gymnasium, a bookstore, a student lounge, and a snack bar and offers after-hours recreational activities. Silsby Athletic Field, which is about 15 acres in size, is an enclosed field used for touch football, baseball, softball, and track. Four outdoor tennis courts provide additional recreational amenities. The Golf Driving Range is open to the public and serves as a practice tee for the Talladega College golf team.

The Student Government Association and the Office of Student Activities consistently plan extracurricular activities. Eight fraternities and sororities and several social, civic, professional, and academic organizations operate on campus. Students are exposed to a variety of outstanding artists and scientists and political, business, and civic leaders throughout the year.

Location

Talladega College is located in the historic district of Talladega, Alabama. Talladega is about 50 miles east of Birmingham, 25 miles south of Anniston, 85 miles north of Montgomery, and 115 miles west of Atlanta, Georgia. The city is also home to the International Motorsports Hall of Fame Museum and the Talladega Superspeedway, which hosts the Winston Select 500, the International Race of Champions, and ARCA's Mountain Dew 500K.

Majors and Degrees

The Bachelor of Arts degree is awarded in various majors by the Divisions of Business and Administration, Natural Sciences and Mathematics, Social Sciences and Education, and Humanities and Fine Arts. Majors offered are art, biology, business administration (accounting, economics, or management emphasis), chemistry, computer science, English, finance and banking, French, history, marketing, mass media studies, mathematics, music performance (piano or voice emphasis), physics, psychology, public administration, secondary education, social work, and sociology. Programs are also provided for students with career interests in computational sciences, languages and literature, pre-engineering and pre–allied health, and prelegal and pre-medical-professional studies.

A dual-degree program is offered for students who wish to pursue careers in allied health, engineering, geology, and veterinary medicine. Students may remain at Talladega College to receive a degree in one of the sciences or transfer to a cooperating professional institution after two or three years to complete the professional phase of the program. Upon completion of the transfer program, an undergraduate degree from Talladega College and a professional degree, certificate, or diploma is awarded from the professional school.

Academic Program

Talladega is a college where fostering leadership is a tradition. Since its founding, it has sought to instill in its graduates the values of morality, intellectual excellence, and hard work. Peterson's has identified Talladega as one of approximately 200 colleges and universities in the United States that offers an outstanding undergraduate program in science and mathematics. The College seeks to nurture the whole person through close, personal relations between faculty members and students and by providing experiences that develop a strong personal value system. Talladega College believes that an essential part of leadership is skill in communications. Thus, it places special emphasis on the ability to listen and to read critically, to write and to speak with clarity, and to think analytically and strategically. The College is also mindful that it is part of a larger universe of nations, cultures, races, and religions and seeks to instill an understanding and appreciation of those differences through its curriculum and multicultural faculty. The College maintains its tradition of preparing students thoroughly—not only for the world of work but also for advanced graduate education. According to the National Science Foundation, Talladega ranks second in the United States in graduating Black students who receive terminal degrees. Talladega College prepares students to be well-rounded individuals who are articulate, view the world with an international perspective, possess confidence in themselves, have strong ethical and moral values, and are dedicated to serving their community.

The academic year is divided into fall and spring semesters. During the summer, many students participate in internship programs, some of which are recorded on the official transcript. Course credit is earned in semester hours. Credit-hour requirements vary with the major area.

Course work is divided into two phases: the General Education Requirements and the Major Program Requirements. The required courses in General Education are intended to establish a strong base for a liberal arts education. The Major Program courses afford the student in-depth study to the field of interest and professional plans.

Incoming students take examinations for course-level placement. Students showing exceptional skills in mathematics or communications may be exempted from one or both semesters of the regular first-year courses. The innovative Student Support Program is designed to enhance academic success through skill development and individualized tutoring in academic areas.

Several programs expand career opportunities and allow students to enhance basic major programs. Among these programs are Army Reserve Officers' Training Corps, the Kennon Investment Group, the Black Executive Exchange Program, Project Reachout: Family Life Center, and the Ronald E. McNair Post-Baccalaureate Achievement Program. Talladega College is one of two colleges in the state of Alabama that has a human cadaver for anatomy instruction. The College is accredited by the Southern Association of Colleges and Schools.

Academic Facilities

Academic buildings include Andrews Hall, Callanan Union Building, Goodnow Fine Arts Center, Silsby Science Hall, Swayne Hall, and Drewry Hall. Savery Library houses the Science Drop-In Center, and the Computer Assisted Instruction/ Curriculum Learning Laboratories, and the Amistad murals. DeForest Chapel also contains classrooms.

Costs

There is no out-of-state fee for attending Talladega College. Tuition and fees for each semester are $3313.50. Room, board, telephone, and cable total $1881 per semester. Off-campus yearly costs (tuition and fees) total $6627, and on-campus yearly costs (room, board, tuition, and fees) total $10,389.

Financial Aid

The financing of a college education may well be one of the largest investments students and their families will make in a lifetime. Through a comprehensive financial aid program administered and coordinated by the Office of Student Financial Aid, Talladega College is committed to assisting all students who demonstrate financial need and have a strong desire for education.

In order to be considered for financial aid, candidates must complete the Free Application for Federal Student Aid (FAFSA). This application must be filed with the director of financial aid. Four types of financial assistance are available: scholarships, grants, part-time employment, and loans.

Faculty

Talladega College has 42 full-time instructors and 3 adjunct instructors. Students receive personal attention at Talladega College from instructors and College staff members. The student-teacher ratio is 13:1. Sixty-two percent of full-time faculty members have terminal degrees. Talladega College instructors are at the top of their field and have a special blend of dedication and teaching commitment to students.

Student Government

Each student enrolled at the College is a member of the Student Government Association (SGA). The governing body is patterned after the national government with a Senate, House of Representatives, Executive Cabinet, and class officers. SGA meetings are held monthly. The SGA president meets weekly with the Office of Student Affairs to discuss concerns of the student body. The SGA sponsors an annual spring carnival.

Admission Requirements

Talladega College welcomes students of all races, creeds, and national origins. SAT I or ACT scores are required, as is an official high school transcript. Students for whom English is not the first language should submit Test of English as a Foreign Language (TOEFL) scores. College-preparatory courses should include 3 years of math and 3 years of science. Talladega also requests one letter of recommendation, a personal essay, and a completed medical record form.

Transfer students are required to have a minimum GPA of 2.9 and to submit an official transcript from all accredited colleges or universities, a personal essay, and a letter of recommendation.

Application and Information

Application for admission should be made as soon as possible before the beginning of the school year. The College uses the rolling admission plan and therefore can accept students until registration for the semester. It is highly advisable for students to apply early in order to be considered for scholarship opportunities.

Applications are available from the Office of Admissions, to which all applications and inquiries should be addressed.

Office of Admissions
Talladega College
627 West Battle Street
Talladega, Alabama 35160
Telephone: 256-761-6235
800-762-2468 (toll-free in Alabama)
800-633-2440 (toll-free outside Alabama)
World Wide Web: http://www.talladega.edu

Swayne Hall, listed on the National Register of Historic Places, contains classrooms, a hearing and vision laboratory, and a writing laboratory.

TAYLOR UNIVERSITY

UPLAND, INDIANA

The University

Founded in 1846, Taylor University was named for the missionary statesman Bishop William Taylor and is one of America's oldest evangelical Christian liberal arts colleges. The University offers residential living in an environment conducive to Christian growth. There is a strong community of faith, where the love of God becomes real intellectually as well as spiritually. As a Christian college, Taylor recognizes that all truth has its source in God. The quest for truth begins with this conviction and relates to all aspects of education. Academic pursuits are intensive and demand imagination, dedication, and integrity from students and faculty members alike. The students value the "whole person" educational adventure for which Taylor is well-known. The University prepares young people for meaningful careers and educates them for effective Christian living.

Student activities, which are coordinated by the Student Activities Council, are appreciated by Taylor students for both the quantity and high-quality of the programs. Intercollegiate athletics are offered in eight sports for men and seven for women. There is also an outstanding intramural program. Cocurricular activities include student publications, musical organizations, a University radio station, a TV studio, clubs in nearly every field, and various cultural events. Numerous ministry opportunities are also available. Student services include a counseling center, a career development program, and a student orientation program, which carries credit.

The current enrollment at Taylor is approximately 1,850 students. Eighty-one percent live in residence halls and approximately 67 percent of Taylor's students are from out of state.

Location

Taylor University's campus, located in Upland, Indiana, covers 250 acres and is situated 1 hour north of Indianapolis and 45 minutes south of Fort Wayne. Taylor students enjoy the community life inspired by the University's rural setting, while also taking advantage of the opportunities available from Indiana's two largest cities.

Majors and Degrees

Baccalaureate majors are offered in the following areas: accounting, art, art education, biblical literature, biology, biology science education, chemistry, chemistry–environmental science, Christian educational ministries, communication studies, computer engineering, computer graphic arts, computer science (business information systems, graphics, integrated program, intelligent systems, and scientific computing), economics, elementary education, engineering physics, English, English education, environmental biology, environmental engineering, environmental geography, exercise science, finance, French, geography, geology, history, international business, international studies, management, marketing, mass communication/journalism, mathematics, mathematics education, mathematics–environmental science, math science education, music, music education, natural science, philosophy, physical education, physics, physics science education, political science, psychology, social studies, social work, sociology, Spanish, sport management, and theater arts. Preprofessional programs include law, medical technology, and medicine. Associate of Arts degrees are offered in business administration, early childhood education, liberal arts, and management information systems. Certificates may be earned in the areas of coaching and missions.

Academic Programs

Taylor University offers programs leading to the Bachelor of Arts degree, Bachelor of Science degree, Bachelor of Music degree, Associate of Arts degree, preprofessional training, and a Master of Environmental Science. Each student selects a major and meets the requirements for the chosen course of study. In addition, every student meets general requirements and may select from electives to complete his or her studies. A foreign language is required of students pursuing the Bachelor of Arts degree. The Bachelor of Arts degree may be combined with education, environmental science, or systems analysis. Most Bachelor of Science degree programs are only available when combined with education or systems analysis. Only one degree is awarded for each major. A minimum of 128 hours is required for a baccalaureate degree. The Associate of Arts degree requires a minimum of 64 hours, with at least 22 of the last 30 hours taken in residence at Taylor.

In 2004, Taylor University unveiled the creation of the Center for Research and Innovation (CR&I). The Center is involved in three primary activities: the long-standing Research Training Program (RTP), the Internship Pathways Program (IPP), and the Interdisciplinary Enterprises Program (IEP). RTP is being strengthened through an integrated approach uniting science and the humanities. This is designed to encourage increased faculty member and student research. Plans for the new RTP should provide additional research staff members in science and the humanities, offer more research stimulation grants, appoint faculty mentors to assist with research efforts, and provide specialized training. The IPP links students with employment and internships through an expanded Alumni Career Network and the establishment of a Career Calling initiative. The IEP specializes in early-stage development, encouraging students to generate ideas and mentoring them to create vibrant ventures. The IEP director teaches the Innovation and Entrepreneur class in which students from different disciplines transform an idea into a new product and company. For more information on the Center for Research and Innovation, students should e-mail CRI@taylor.edu.

Taylor's Master of Environmental Science (M.E.S.) program provides a unique opportunity for incoming environmental science majors. Known around Taylor as the 6-5-4 plan, students are able to obtain six years of education (B.S. and M.E.S. degrees) in five years for the cost of four years through a generous private grant that pays tuition costs for students enrolled in the M.E.S. program. Taylor's undergraduate program provides master's-level training, enabling students to finish the M.E.S. program in one year.

The University awards credit for acceptable scores on Advanced Placement, CLEP, college proficiency examinations, and International Baccalaureate programs. Students may use a limited number of these credits to complete their college degree in 3 to 3½ years.

The University operates on a 4-1-4 academic calendar. A January interterm that lasts 3½ weeks features experimental and conventional courses. In addition, two summer sessions are offered for a total of nine weeks.

Off-Campus Programs

Opportunities for travel and course study are regularly available for students who wish to accompany professors going to Asia, Europe, Israel, Greece, Albania, Latin America, Ireland, India, Zimbabwe, and the Bahamas. Taylor University is affiliated with AuSable Institute of Environmental Studies in Mancelona, Michigan, where students may take summer courses for credit. Taylor is also affiliated with the Christian Center for Urban Studies (CCUS) located in Chicago. Through its affiliation with the Council of Christian Colleges and Universities, Taylor provides an opportunity for students to study in the following areas: American Studies Program, Washington, D.C.; Latin American Studies Program, San Jose, Costa Rica;

Summer Institute of Journalism; Middle East Studies Program, Cairo, Egypt; the Russian Studies Program, Moscow, St. Petersburg, and Nizhni Novgorod; China Studies Program, Beijing; Oxford Honours Programme, Keble College of the University of Oxford; or the Los Angeles Film Studies Center. In addition, students may spend one semester on the campus of another coalition college without formally transferring. Taylor maintains an affiliation with Jerusalem University College in Israel. Taylor has also established an exchange program with Lithuania Christian College. There is a consortium agreement between Hong Kong Baptist University and Taylor University providing fall and spring semester study opportunities. There is an exchange program with Daystar University in Nairobi, Kenya, through the Christian College Consortium. Taylor students participate in study during January interterm at the HEART Institute in Lake Wales, Florida, and at Oak Ridge Institute for Science and Education in Oak Ridge, Tennessee.

Academic Facilities

Taylor operates an extensive computing network utilizing Windows XP, Windows 95–2000, Digital's Open/VMS running on a series of Intel-based servers, and DEC's Alpha hardware platform. Each residence hall on the campus has been wired so that the Taylor network and Internet access is available from each student's room. In addition, extensive networking to all academic and administrative buildings provides full network access across the campus. Wireless access continues to expand aggressively throughout the campus.

The opening of the new Kesler Student Activity Center is planned for October 2004. This facility includes a field house with four playing courts, a fitness/wellness center, a 200-meter track, an aerobics room, and support areas such as locker rooms, storage, and general circulation.

Professional quality radio and T.V. facilities are enhanced by digital media production, editing, and distribution facilities for audio, video, broadcast, Web, and interactive media. The science center, which contains laboratories, a greenhouse, and the computing center, serves students majoring in biology, chemistry, computer science, mathematics, and physics. The liberal arts building houses an Educational Technology Center. The University library has more than 188,925 volumes, 725 print and 6,100 online current periodicals, and twelve newspapers and houses the Learning Support Center. In addition, Taylor's library belongs to national networks and features an online catalog for electronic searching for all private colleges and universities in Indiana. Taylor also provides online access to thousands of databases, including major library holdings around the world. The music center has a recital hall, practice rooms, and a band rehearsal room. The state-of-the-art Randall Center for Environmental Studies, located on Taylor's 65-acre arboretum, houses fully equipped labs in hydrologic, biotic, and spatial analysis for classroom and field instruction and research.

Costs

Ranked as a best buy in *Barron's Best Buys in College Education* and as one of Kiplinger's "100 Best Private Colleges" for academic excellence and lower total costs, Taylor's tuition and fees for 2004–05 are $19,674. Room and board are $5452 with indirect costs estimated at $2200.

Financial Aid

Scholarships, grants, loans, work-study, and church matching grants are available for students who need assistance in meeting college expenses. Merit scholarships are available to incoming freshmen. In addition, nearly 600 employment opportunities are available through the University. Nearly 84 percent of Taylor's students receive some form of financial aid.

Faculty

The faculty consists of 118 full-time and 39 part-time professors; 77 percent have earned a terminal degree. Faculty members are academically recognized, personally committed to the authority of Scripture, and available to and involved with students. The student-faculty ratio is 15:1.

Student Government

The Taylor Student Organization (TSO) has several branches: the Student Senate, the Student Activities Council, the Multicultural Council, the Interclass Council, Press Services, and the Leadership Council.

Admission Requirements

Taylor is committed to enrolling students with high academic motivation, and it continues to honor classroom achievements of applicants in its selection process. However, Taylor also believes that other factors beyond a student's intellectual gifts must guide admission decisions. Leadership skills, extracurricular activities, spiritual motivations, character, and personal aspirations are also considered. While academic preparedness and achievement are key issues (recent freshmen classes average a 3.6 GPA, with average SAT test scores of 1200 or ACT scores of 26), Taylor believes the complete answer includes more factors and looks at the thoughtfully completed personal essays as well as recommendations. In addition, the required interview offers admissions officials an opportunity to get to know students better while providing meaningful counsel as students search for the right fit in a college.

Application and Information

Prospective students are encouraged to start the application process early. Students may apply after completing their junior year of high school.

For further information or to apply online, students should contact:

Director of Admissions
Taylor University
236 West Reade Avenue
Upland, Indiana 46989-1001
Telephone: 765-998-5511
800-882-3456 (toll-free)
E-mail: admissions_u@taylor.edu
World Wide Web: http://www.taylor.edu

The Taylor tradition: scholarship, leadership, and Christian commitment.

TEIKYO POST UNIVERSITY

WATERBURY, CONNECTICUT

The University

Founded in 1890, Teikyo Post University is a globally focused, private, coeducational, residential institution. The University is accredited by the New England Association of Schools and Colleges. The diversity of the student body makes this school a particularly attractive choice for those seeking a good education and a place to grow and interact with a small yet unique group of people. Teikyo Post University's mission centers around four fundamental themes: globalization, restructuring the economy around information and knowledge, technology, and collaboration.

As a small, private university, Teikyo Post has the dedication, commitment, and resources to take a personal interest in every student. The University is dedicated to providing a cohesive global environment in which more than 1,300 students from the United States and twenty-five countries learn to become knowledgeable participants in the global marketplace. While engaging in a close and caring University community, students learn to appreciate other attitudes and cultures through classes, course offerings, activities, and one-on-one relationships with faculty members and peers. Approximately half of Teikyo Post University's students live on campus in one of the six residence halls. Seventeen percent of the student body are international students.

The 70-acre campus is a safe, comfortable, and convenient location for learning. The Leever Student Center houses a dining facility, student service offices, and a student lounge. The Teikyo Post student activities calendar is filled with a variety of options and opportunities. Local civic, religious, and professional organizations bring forums, seminars, lectures, exhibits, shows, and other events to the University. Clubs and activities abound, including the International Club, the Care Bears, the Creative Elevations Outdoor Club, the Science Club, and the Step Squad. Day trips are often scheduled to New York City and Boston.

Teikyo Post students participate in a year-round schedule of intercollegiate and intramural athletic activities. The Teikyo Post University Eagles are members of the National Collegiate Athletic Association (NCAA) Division II and the New England Collegiate Conference (NECC). Men's intercollegiate sports teams include baseball, basketball, cross-country, and soccer. Women's athletics include basketball, cross-country, soccer, softball, and volleyball. The University also sponsors an active, coeducational equestrian team. Men's golf was added in 2003–04. Intramural sports are diverse, ranging from softball and volleyball to basketball and flag football. Students enjoy the facilities of the Drubner Conference and Fitness Center, including a gymnasium, a swimming pool, tennis and racquetball courts, a fitness club, and weight training rooms. The Drubner Conference and Fitness Center also houses the campus bookstore.

Location

Located midway between New York City and Boston, Teikyo Post University's 70-acre campus in the hills outside suburban Waterbury, Connecticut, offers a variety of opportunities for social, cultural, and recreational activities with its proximity to the Yale museums and theater and the Connecticut shoreline.

Majors and Degrees

Teikyo Post offers four undergraduate degrees: the Bachelor of Arts, the Bachelor of Science, the Associate in Arts, and the Associate in Science.

The Division of Business Administration offers the Bachelor of Science degree with majors in accounting, computer information systems, criminal justice, equine management, integrated business, international business, legal studies, management, and marketing. The Associate in Science degree is offered with majors in accounting, equine studies, legal studies, management, and marketing. The School of Arts and Sciences offers the Bachelor of Science in biology, environmental science, general studies, and human services and the Bachelor of Arts with majors in English, environmental studies, history, psychology, and sociology; and the Associate in Science with majors in early childhood education, equine studies, and general studies. Advising in course selection for a prelaw concentration is also available.

Academic Program

For the bachelor's degree, students must complete a minimum of 120 credit hours. To receive an associate degree from Teikyo Post, students must complete a minimum of 60 credit hours.

All programs offer opportunities for internships and cooperative education. For students seeking additional academic challenges, the Teikyo Post University Honors Program offers the opportunity to pursue independent research and special projects under the guidance of a faculty member.

The University has a two-semester calendar.

Off-Campus Programs

Teikyo Post University, as a member of the Teikyo University Group, offers several study-abroad programs for interested students, including a semester abroad in either Berlin, Germany; Cracow, Poland; or Maastricht, the Netherlands. Students also participate in a summer-study program in Tokyo, Japan. The equine management program offers a study-abroad option in England. Through these programs, students have an opportunity to broaden their perspective and experience. Courses taken abroad are accepted for degree credit at Teikyo Post University.

To qualify for study abroad, a student must have a cumulative grade point average of 2.0 or better at the time of attendance.

Academic Facilities

All classroom buildings are equipped with the facilities necessary for the applied arts and sciences, business, and liberal arts curricula. The Academic Computer Center houses microcomputers to serve all components of the academic curriculum. The Center is open to all students who use the facility for course assignments, simulations, and special projects. The Harold Leever Center provides learning systems structured to meet the needs of individual students. A media-equipped Programmed Auto Learning Systems Laboratory (PALS Lab) is an integral part of this program. The PALS Lab is a unique, self-paced, and widely diverse facility giving instructional support to the center's program by providing supplementary and review materials through the use of audiovisual software, media equipment, and innovative use of computer-assisted instruction. A new Writing Center is staffed by 5 experienced writing coaches, who work with students at all levels of ability. The Traurig Library and Learning Resource Center has a capacity of more then 45,000 volumes and a growing media collection. As a government document depository, the library houses an extensive government publications collection. University-wide Internet access is available. Students majoring in the equine area use several nearby facilities.

Costs

For 2003–04, full-time resident students paid a comprehensive fee of $24,875, covering tuition, most fees, and room and board. For commuting students, this comprehensive fee was $16,950 per year. Equine and laboratory fees, the $40 application fee, and an estimated $500 per year for books and supplies are not included in this basic comprehensive fee.

Financial Aid

Teikyo Post offers financial assistance through the Federal Work-Study, Federal Supplemental Educational Opportunity Grant, Federal Stafford Student Loan, and Federal Perkins Loan programs. Aid is awarded upon evidence of financial need, as determined by the Free Application for Federal Student Aid (FAFSA). In addition, the University has its own scholarship and grant-in-aid programs, both academic and athletic, and participates in all state programs that are applicable. In order to apply for financial assistance, a student must apply for admission and be accepted to Teikyo Post and then submit the FAFSA. An institutional application for financial aid must also be submitted. A student may apply for the Federal Pell Grant by submitting the application directly to the federal government or by submitting the FAFSA.

Faculty

The Teikyo Post faculty has 29 full-time and many part-time members, the majority of whom hold advanced degrees in their respective fields. Faculty members focus on instruction and are involved in all facets of student life. All full-time faculty members serve as academic advisers and maintain weekly office hours for student consultation. The student-faculty ratio is 14:1.

Student Government

Students actively participate in the operation of the University. The Student Government Association (SGA) is the official vehicle for student advocacy at Teikyo Post University. SGA formulates major recommendations regarding student life on campus, oversees all student organizations, and provides funding for all active clubs. The Programming Board plays an active role in programming and calendar planning. Students are represented on many of the University's standing committees.

Admission Requirements

Teikyo Post University seeks students who are likely to benefit from the University's multicultural atmosphere and welcomes applications from individuals interested in pursuing academic studies. A decision with respect to a candidate's admission is made by the Admissions Committee and is based upon careful evaluation of the student's qualifications. A student who wishes to be considered for admission should provide Teikyo Post with an official copy of the secondary school transcript, a written recommendation from a counselor or teacher, and SAT I or ACT scores. If the candidate holds an equivalency diploma (GED), a copy must be submitted in lieu of a secondary school transcript. International students must submit a minimum TOEFL score of 500 in addition to the requirements listed above. Teikyo Post offers English as a second language to those students who do not meet the minimum TOEFL score requirement. If possible, an interview with an admissions counselor is strongly recommended.

Students interested in transferring to Teikyo Post must submit transcripts from all colleges previously attended. A GPA of at least 2.0 (on a 4.0 scale) is required. Credit may be awarded for grades of C or better. Teikyo Post University accepts a maximum of 90 credits toward the baccalaureate degree and a maximum of 30 credits toward an associate degree.

Application and Information

Students should send an application for admission, accompanied by a nonrefundable application fee of $40. Teikyo Post University accommodates candidates by processing applications on a rolling basis. It is advantageous to file an application as early as possible. This allows the Admissions Committee to give an application the attention it deserves and enables the applicant to prepare for college life. An application is reviewed when all the necessary credentials have been received. Applications are available online at the Web site listed below.

Further information may be obtained by contacting:

Office of Admission
Teikyo Post University
800 Country Club Road
P.O. Box 2540
Waterbury, Connecticut 06723-2540
Telephone 203-596-4520
800-345-2562 (toll-free)
Fax: 203-756-5810
E-mail: tpuadmis@teikyopost.edu
World Wide Web: http://www.teikyopost.edu

The Teikyo Post University campus is lovely year-round.

TEMPLE UNIVERSITY

PHILADELPHIA, PENNSYLVANIA

The University

Students come to Temple University to build their futures. Temple, a state-related institution, is located in Philadelphia. Its reputation for excellence in teaching and research, however, stretches around the world. Temple offers 133 undergraduate, 125 master's, and sixty-four doctoral and professional programs of study on five regional campuses as well as international campuses in Rome and Tokyo.

Temple's Philadelphia-area campuses include the 100-acre main campus, located 2 miles from the city's center. This is where nine of the eleven undergraduate schools and colleges are headquartered. It is also home to performance spaces for theater, music, dance, and film; a large indoor-outdoor athletic complex; the Liacouras Center; and the Learning Center. The Liacouras Center is a recreation, entertainment, and convocation center featuring space for sports, cultural, and educational events. Across the campus is the Learning Center, a four-story hub of computer labs, lounges, smart classrooms, and distance learning sites linking students to educational resources on Temple's campuses, across the country, and around the world.

Temple University–Ambler is Temple's 187-acre suburban home; all undergraduate programs can be started there, and twenty-two can be taken there in their entirety. Ambler features its own science labs, library and computing center, bookstore, fitness center, pool, and athletic courts, all in a spacious natural setting of woodlands, meadows, formal gardens, and greenhouses. These amenities are integral to the programs in landscape architecture and horticulture, which reside at Ambler. Temple's other local campuses include Tyler, just outside Philadelphia, home to the Tyler School of Art, and the Health Sciences Center, where the College of Allied Health Professions, Temple University Hospital, Temple University School of Medicine, and Temple Dental School are located.

Temple's campuses offer lots to do. On the main campus the calendar is crammed with theater, dance, and music performances as well as movies, guest speakers, and the activities of more than 100 clubs and groups. Sports are available on the individual, intramural, and intercollegiate levels. About 5,000 Temple students live on campus, mostly on the main campus, but at Ambler and Tyler too. Accommodations on the main campus include high-rise residence halls and apartments, and students can choose among coed or single-sex floors. Wellness floors, where residents pledge to follow a healthy lifestyle, have proven very popular.

Location

Philadelphia enhances the Temple experience in many ways. The cultural, commercial, and intellectual life of America's fifth-largest city touches every academic program, providing real-world reference points, internships, and co-ops. The region offers a wealth of activities, from the nightlife of Penn's Landing to the enthusiasm of the sports complex in South Philadelphia to the quieter pleasures of the renowned Philadelphia Museum of Art.

Majors and Degrees

The College of Health Professions offers the Bachelor of Science in communication sciences, health information management, nursing, public health, and therapeutic recreation.

The Fox School of Business and Management offers the Bachelor of Business Administration in accounting, actuarial science, business management, economics, entrepreneurship, e-marketing, finance, human resource administration, international business administration, legal studies, management, management information systems, marketing, real estate, and risk management and insurance.

The School of Communications and Theater offers the Bachelor of Arts in advertising; American culture and media arts; broadcasting–telecommunications and mass media; communications; film and media arts; journalism; speech communication; strategic and organizational communication; and theater.

The College of Education offers the Bachelor of Science in career and technical education in business education, distributive education, and industrial education; early childhood education and elementary education; secondary education in English/communications, foreign languages, mathematics, science, social studies; and kinesiology.

The College of Engineering offers the Bachelor of Science in Engineering in civil engineering, electrical engineering, and mechanical engineering. The Bachelor of Science is offered in civil engineering/construction technology, environmental engineering technology, general engineering technology, and materials science.

The College of Liberal Arts offers the Bachelor of Arts in African American studies, American studies, anthropology, Asian studies, classics, criminal justice, economics, English, French, geography and urban studies, German, Hebrew, history, Italian, linguistics, philosophy, political science, Portuguese, psychology, religion, Russian, sociology, Spanish, and women's studies.

The Esther Boyer College of Music offers the Bachelor of Music in composition, dance, jazz studies, music history, music therapy, performance (specific instrument or voice), and theory; the Bachelor of Music Education is offered in music education.

The College of Science and Technology offers the Bachelor of Science in biochemistry, biology, biophysics, chemistry, computer and information sciences, environmental studies, geology, mathematical economics, mathematics, physics, and prepharmacy.

The School of Social Administration offers the Bachelor of Social Work degree.

The School of Tourism and Hospitality Management offers the Bachelor of Science in sport and recreation management and in tourism and hospitality management.

The Tyler School of Art offers the Bachelor of Fine Arts with concentrations in ceramics/glass, fibers, graphic design, metalsmithing, painting, photography, printmaking, and sculpture; the Bachelor of Arts in art history and studio art; and the Bachelor of Science in art education.

Tyler's Architecture Program confers the Bachelor of Architecture and the Bachelor of Science in architecture.

In addition, Ambler College offers Bachelor of Science degree programs in horticulture and landscape architecture, and community and regional planning.

Academic Programs

Temple provides an excellent and affordable education which not only prepares the student for the specific demands of a career, but also enhances understanding of the world and ability to continue learning throughout life.

All students are required to complete the core curriculum, a cross-section of liberal arts courses that form the intellectual foundation of a Temple education. Many first-year students take advantage of Learning Communities—groups of 20 to 30 participants who pursue common studies under the direction of a faculty team. They spend a semester together, taking a few common courses, participating in faculty-led discussion groups, studying together, and taking field trips related to their studies. University Studies is a home for the many students who have not declared a major and for students interested in graduate or professional programs in health fields. Academically qualified students may seek extra intellectual challenge through the Honors Program, taking about a quarter of their course work in the program's smaller, more demanding classes. The TempleMed Scholars Program offers exceptional students provisional admission to Temple University School of Medicine at the same time they are admitted as undergraduates, contingent on their academic performance in college.

Temple has an active Career Development Services office. Career Development Services arranges cooperative education assignments, schedules on-campus interviews with employers and graduate schools, offers employment skills workshops, provides career and graduate school advisement, and maintains a network of thousands of successful Temple alumni.

Off-Campus Programs

Temple offers many ways for students to combine travel with study. On the Rome campus, students can take courses in architecture, business, liberal arts, and visual arts, while Temple University Japan, in Tokyo, instructs Japanese and American students in the Japanese language and Asian studies. The Temple Overseas study-abroad program enables students to spend a summer in Paris studying French literature and civilization, in London examining British mass media, or in Ghana learning about West African civilization. The University also participates in exchange programs with the University of Puerto Rico, the University of Hamburg (Germany), the Institut Franco-Americain de Management (Paris), and others.

Academic Facilities

Learning requires lots of information, and Temple has information both on shelves and online. With more than fifty computer labs and a growing number of wireless zones on campus, information is more accessible than ever. The University's Learning Center is a state-of-the-art classroom and laboratory complex. Built on 2.3 acres, the Learning Center has twenty high-tech classrooms containing the latest, most sophisticated equipment and technology for the twenty-first century. The Learning Center is connected to the Samuel Paley library, home to 1.8 million volumes and 11,000 periodicals.

Costs

Tuition and fees for the 2003–04 academic year were $8594 for Pennsylvania residents and $13,856 for out-of-state residents. Room and board for the academic year were $6800.

Financial Aid

Scholarships, grants, loans, and work-study programs are available; 2 out of every 3 Temple students receive financial aid. Four-year academic merit scholarships for talented entering freshman range from $2000 to full tuition. Students need only apply for admission to be eligible for these scholarships. Applicants for need-based aid must file the Free Application for Federal Student Aid (FAFSA). Transfer students must file a financial aid transcript, even if they have received no aid from their previous school.

Faculty

At Temple, faculty members are valued not only for their ability to pursue knowledge, but also to share that knowledge with students. Full-time faculty members teach many introductory courses, and often act as academic advisers; from their first semester students can expect to have contact with the people at the forefront of their fields, winners of prestigious teaching and research awards such as the Lindback, the Golden Apple, the Sowell, the Fulbright, the Guggenheim, the Carnegie, and the National Endowment.

In addition to being superlative teachers and researchers, Temple faculty members are also known for their practical experience. For example, a marketing class may be led by a successful entrepreneur, or music lessons given by a member of the Philadelphia Orchestra. Marine biologists, newspaper editors, published authors, practicing architects, and health-care professionals all bring their expertise to the classroom to enhance students' education.

Student Government

Temple Student Government advocates students' views to faculty members and the administration regarding University policies and programs through its members' participation in various University committees, both on a voting and nonvoting basis.

Application Requirements

Admissions decisions are based on evidence that applicants have the necessary qualifications for successful work at Temple. An applicant should be a graduate of an accredited secondary school or hold an equivalent diploma earned by completion of the General Educational Development (GED) test. Applicants should also have completed the following distribution of high school credits: 4 years of English, 2 years of mathematics, 2 years of the same foreign language, 1 year of history, 1 year of a laboratory science, and 6 additional academic credits in mathematics, science, history, or a foreign language. Scores on the SAT I or ACT are required. The Tyler School of Art, the Department of Dance, and the Esther Boyer College of Music have additional requirements. Transfer students must submit official copies of high school and college transcripts.

Application and Information

A completed file should contain an application form accompanied by a nonrefundable $35 fee, a secondary school transcript (sent by the student's school), and SAT I or ACT scores. The University has a rolling admission policy; applicants will be notified of the admission decision as soon as possible after all credentials have been received and reviewed.

For additional information, students may contact:

Office of Undergraduate Admissions
Temple University (041-09)
Philadelphia, Pennsylvania 19122-1803
Telephone: 215-204-7200
888-340-2222 (toll-free)
E-mail: tuadm@temple.edu
World Wide Web: http://www.temple.edu

TENNESSEE STATE UNIVERSITY

NASHVILLE, TENNESSEE

The University

Tennessee State University (TSU), founded in 1912, is a multiracial, urban, land-grant university that fulfills its mission of providing education, research, and public service for residents of central Tennessee through myriad academic, cultural, research, service, and professional activities. Students can pursue degrees during the day or in evening courses. The Center for Extended Education and Public Service offers a wide variety of off-campus credit programs, contract credit classes with local employers, noncredit courses, and seminars to serve the expanding educational needs of local business and the professional community. The University also offers graduate programs and is dedicated to providing all students with a strong academic background. The Graduate School offers programs leading to the master's, Educational Specialist, and doctoral degrees. (Information on graduate programs is available from Graduate Admissions at the address given at the end of this description.) It is hoped that students will take full advantage of the University's offerings, use the experiences to serve themselves and society, and continue the institution's tradition of excellence.

The 9,024 students (7,118 undergraduates) currently enrolled at Tennessee State University come from a variety of cultural backgrounds and geographical areas. Although there are seven dormitories (four for women, three for men), a large percentage of students live off campus. Easily accessible public transportation facilitates the commute to either campus. Extracurricular activities include Greek fraternities and sororities, academic societies, drama and dance groups, a concert choir, and marching, jazz, and concert bands. The University has competitive intercollegiate athletic programs in football as well as men's and women's basketball, cross-country, golf, track, and tennis. There are women's programs in softball, track, and volleyball. Intramural sports are also offered. An athletic and convocation complex seats 10,000 for basketball games and assemblies; it also contains a 220-yard indoor track, dance studios, racquetball courts, and a 35-meter swimming pool. The football team won the Ohio Valley Conference Championships two consecutive years, in 1998 and 1999. In addition, the women's track team won the Ohio Valley Conference Championship in 2001–02 and 2002–03.

Special student services are offered through such resources as a counseling center, reading center, health service center, and career placement center. Tennessee State University is in the midst of a $112-million capital improvement project. The capital project includes seven new buildings and a completely landscaped campus with courtyards, plazas, and a state-of-the-art utility tunnel. The three-story campus center houses student services facilities, including offices for student organizations, admissions and records, and financial aid, and a bookstore and additional recreational facilities.

Location

Nashville is the state capital and the second-largest city in Tennessee. More than 600,000 people live in this thriving center of government, business, industry, and education. Known internationally as "Music City USA," it is the hub of the nation's country music industry. The entertainment and cultural scene does not stop there, however. A performing arts center offers an active schedule of Broadway plays, community theater, films, and performances by professional dance troupes, the Nashville Symphony, and a variety of vocal and instrumental musicians. Nashville also has three professional sports teams. Night spots and restaurants cater to a variety of cultural and ethnic tastes. Nashville's 6,000 acres of public parks and recreational facilities allow for the pursuit of many sports and leisure activities. As the city's only public four-year institution, Tennessee State University occupies an important place in Nashville. Its Main Campus is located in a residential area of the city, providing students with the atmosphere of a neighborly community. The Avon Williams Campus is located in the heart of downtown Nashville, within walking distance of the capitol and the central business district. TSU students and graduates are involved in a wide variety of academic and employment activities throughout the city.

Majors and Degrees

The College of Arts and Sciences offers majors in Africana studies, art, biological sciences, chemistry, criminal justice, English, foreign languages (French and Spanish), history, mathematics, music, physics, political science, social work, sociology, and speech communications and theater. The College also offers an interdisciplinary degree with concentrations in the humanities, the sciences, and the social sciences. Teacher certification in art, biological sciences, chemistry, elementary education, English, foreign languages, history, mathematics, music, political science, and speech communications and theater is also available. The College awards both the Bachelor of Arts and the Bachelor of Science degrees.

The College of Business offers majors in accounting, business administration, business information systems, and economics and finance and grants the Bachelor of Business Administration degree.

The College of Education certifies students in elementary, special, and secondary education and awards the Bachelor of Science degree to students majoring in health, physical, and recreational education. The Bachelor of Arts degree is also awarded to students who major in psychology.

The College of Engineering and Technology offers Bachelor of Science degree programs in aeronautical and industrial technology, architectural engineering, civil engineering, computer science, electrical engineering, and mechanical engineering.

The School of Nursing grants the two-year Associate of Science and four-year Bachelor of Science degrees in nursing. The School of Allied Health Professions offers an Associate of Applied Science degree in dental hygiene and a Bachelor of Science degree to students who major in cardiorespiratory therapy, dental hygiene, health information management, health-care administration and planning, medical technology, occupational therapy, or speech pathology and audiology. The School of Agriculture and Home Economics offers undergraduate programs leading to the Bachelor of Science degree in agricultural sciences, early childhood education, family and consumer sciences, and hospitality and tourism administration. The Department of Agricultural Sciences offers a bachelor's degree in agricultural sciences with options in agribusiness, agricultural education, agricultural statistics, agronomy, animal science and pre–veterinary medicine, food technology, ornamental horticulture, and resource economics. The Department of Family and Consumer Sciences offers bachelor's degrees in early childhood education and family and consumer sciences, with options in child development and family relationships, clothing and textiles, design, fashion merchandising, foods and nutrition, and food service management. The Department of Hospitality and Tourism Administration offers a curriculum that prepares graduates for career management positions in the hotel, restaurant, and tourism industries.

Academic Program

Tennessee State University operates on a semester calendar and conducts two sessions during the summer. A minimum of 130 credit hours and a 2.0 or higher cumulative GPA are required for graduation. Individual departments may have additional requirements. An honors program, independent study, cooperative education, teacher certification, and the Air Force ROTC program are available. Early admission and advanced standing are offered to qualified students, and credit is given for satisfactory scores on the College-Level Examination Program tests.

The University honors program is designed to provide the challenge and opportunity for the academically superior student to achieve academic excellence. Honors courses require a higher level of achievement than those in the regular curriculum and are restricted to students in the honors program and to those with a B average who are recommended by an adviser or a teacher. Other courses from the regular curriculum may be taken for honors credit.

Off-Campus Programs

So that students can receive the practical training necessary for some professions, Tennessee State University has affiliations with several public and private institutions and agencies. The opportunities include a joint-degree program in allied health with Meharry Medical College, clinical training for nursing students through contractual arrangements with local hospitals, student teaching programs with the Metropolitan-Davidson County Public Schools, and field training programs with government agencies for students in social welfare and criminal justice. Students who participate in these programs earn credit toward their degree. The College of Arts and Sciences offers a dual degree in chemistry and pharmacy with Howard University and a dual degree in biology and medicine with Meharry Medical College, as well as co-op and internship experiences.

Academic Facilities

Tennessee State University has two campuses, the Main Campus and the Avon Williams Campus. The Main Campus, located on 450 acres, consists of sixty-five buildings, farmlands, and pastures. The Tennessee State University libraries house 463,621 volumes, 1,446 current periodical subscriptions, 78,185 bound periodicals, 816,934 microfiche, and 14,748 microfilm reels. A CD-ROM LAN serves both libraries with eleven CD databases; additional CD-ROM databases and Dialog services are also available. The Avon Williams Campus is housed in a large, modern building containing a library, a cafeteria, and ample meeting rooms. Parking facilities are adjacent to the building. A full curriculum is offered at this campus during evening hours.

A Learning Resource Center provides multimedia support for both campuses. Students pursuing programs in agriculture, engineering, biological sciences, chemistry, physics, dental hygiene, and nursing have access to fully equipped laboratories. Students also have access to advanced computer equipment and software.

Costs

Costs fall into four areas—maintenance, tuition, room and board, and special fees. In 2003–04, the maintenance fee for in-state students was $1566 (12 hours). Board plans range from $370 to $905 per semester, and room rental costs range from $800 to $1830 per semester. The average total cost for a full-time, in-state undergraduate is $1909 per semester ($3818 per year). Out-of-state undergraduates pay tuition of $5875 per semester (including maintenance and special fees) in addition to room and board. Out-of-state students pay an average tuition of $11,750 per year. Average expenses for books, supplies, and personal items are $900 per semester ($1800 per year) for most students.

Financial Aid

The University has a strong commitment to assist students seeking financial aid. The types of aid available include grants, scholarships, loans, and employment. The University participates in the Federal Pell Grant, FSEOG, Federal Perkins Loan, Federal Stafford Student Loan, Federal PLUS loan, Federal Work-Study, and Tennessee Student Assistance Grant programs. Presidential Scholarships, Academic Work Scholarships, University Scholarships, Departmental Scholarships, and several private scholarship programs are also available. The minimum financial aid award is about $200, the average is about $4500, and the maximum is about $10,000. Approximately 80 percent of freshmen receive some type of financial assistance. Students who have a high school GPA of 3.0 or above (on a 4.0 scale) and an ACT score of 21 or above may apply for scholarships.

Prospective students must file the Free Application for Federal Student Aid by April 1 in order to be considered for financial aid. Students are also required to submit a processed Student Aid Report to the Financial Aid Office. All students are urged to apply early.

Faculty

Tennessee State University has a 338-member full-time faculty and a part-time faculty of 154, some of whom teach at both the undergraduate and graduate levels. Eighty percent of the faculty members hold doctoral degrees. The student-faculty ratio is 17:1. Some faculty members, particularly in the areas of agriculture, biological sciences, history, and psychology, are actively involved in research. Faculty members serve as advisers for students majoring in their discipline, and some also serve as advisers for student organizations.

Student Government

The Student Government Association consists of a president, a vice president, class officers, representatives-at-large, and organization representatives, all elected by student vote. The association operates under a formal constitution and is recognized by University administrators as the official voice of students.

Admission Requirements

In-state residents must pass the High School Proficiency Exam and have a high school GPA of 2.25 or better, an ACT score of at least 19, or a minimum SAT I score of 900. Out-of-state residents must have a GPA of 2.5 or better, an ACT score of at least 19, or an SAT I score of at least 900. In addition, students must pass fourteen State Board of Regents high school unit requirements. Scores on the TOEFL are required of international students.

Transfer applicants must submit a transcript from every college attended and must present a minimum grade point average of 2.0. Transfer students usually receive credit for grades of 2.0 and higher in Tennessee State University-equivalent courses taken at approved institutions. At least 30 hours must be completed in residence at Tennessee State University.

Application and Information

Applications should be received by August 1; the fee is $15. Late applications are accepted. Additional information is available from:

Office of Admissions and Records
Tennessee State University
3500 John A. Merritt Boulevard
P.O. Box 9609
Nashville, Tennessee 37209-1561
Telephone: 615-963-5052
888-463-6878 (toll-free)
World Wide Web: http://www.tnstate.edu

TENNESSEE TECHNOLOGICAL UNIVERSITY

COOKEVILLE, TENNESSEE

The University

Tennessee Technological University (TTU) has no typical students, for the present student body is diverse, representing many different backgrounds and groups. The current enrollment consists of 8,890 men and women from Tennessee as well as forty other states and fifty-six other countries. Tennessee Tech students are often characterized as friendly and outgoing; they are confident and excited about their future and involved in their education at TTU. They want to be—among other things—doctors, lawyers, sales representatives, teachers, engineers, and scientists. They want to be helpful to society and successful in their chosen fields.

From its early beginnings in 1911 as Dixie College, TTU has continued to serve students who are focused on a high-quality education and to provide the state with its only technological university. Students at TTU can participate in a variety of more than 190 clubs and organizations, including religious organizations, major-related clubs, and Greek life.

The Graduate School offers programs leading to a master's degree in biology, chemistry, education, engineering, English, and mathematics. In addition, the Education Specialist degree is awarded in education and the Doctor of Philosophy in engineering, education, and environmental science. The M.B.A. degree is also available. Admission to graduate study at Tennessee Tech is on a merit basis and is limited to applicants whose previous study is of sufficient quality and scope to indicate promise of high success as a graduate student. Interested students should write to the dean of the Graduate School for specific information.

Location

Tennessee Tech is located in Cookeville, Tennessee, on the Eastern Highland Rim. The city of Cookeville, with a metropolitan population of about 26,000, offers a cordial welcome to Tennessee Tech students. Churches, theaters, banks, and shopping facilities are easily accessible from the campus, and students are welcome to share in the civic and cultural events of the community.

Situated in one of the most picturesque sections of the southeastern United States, the area abounds in the scenic beauty of hills, lakes, and waterfalls. Several state parks are within a short driving distance. An elevation of 1,140 feet provides a favorable climate the year round.

The Tennessee Tech campus is located on Interstate 40, Highway 111, and Highway 70 North. Nashville is only 1¼ hours away by interstate highway; Knoxville is less than 2 hours away. Major airline service is available from Nashville, Knoxville, and Chattanooga.

Majors and Degrees

Tennessee Technological University offers the Bachelor of Science degree in accounting, agribusiness management, agricultural engineering technology, agricultural environmental agriscience, agriculture education, agronomy and soils, animal science, art education, biochemistry, biology, business management (management information systems, personnel and labor relations, and production and operations management), chemical engineering, chemistry, civil and environmental engineering, computer engineering, computer science (information and systems emphasis and software and scientific applications), early childhood education, economics (through the College of Business or the College of Arts and Sciences), electrical engineering, elementary education, finance, health and physical education, history, human ecology (child and family science; consumer homemaking education; foods, nutrition, dietetics, and food service administration; and merchandising/fashion and design), horticulture, industrial engineering, industrial technology, journalism, marketing, mathematics, mechanical engineering, music education, nursery and landscape management, nursing, physics (applied and traditional), political science, psychology, secondary education (biology, chemistry, communications, earth and space science, English, French, German, history, mathematics, physics, professional communications, social science, Spanish, and speech), sociology, special education, turfgrass management, Web design, and wildlife and fisheries science. Tennessee Tech also offers the Bachelor of Arts in English, foreign language (French, German, and Spanish), and history; the Bachelor of Science in world cultures and business; and the Bachelor of Fine Arts.

Strong preprofessional programs in medicine, dental hygiene, dentistry, health information management, medical technology, optometry, pharmacy, and physical therapy are offered through the College of Arts and Sciences. The College of Agriculture offers pre–veterinary medicine and preforestry.

Academic Program

Tennessee Tech continues to demonstrate that values are relevant, that humanity's accumulated knowledge is useful, and that broad, general study can be combined effectively with either specialized preparation for a profession or intensive pursuit of a discipline.

The general requirements for a baccalaureate degree include a major as outlined under the curriculum chosen, a first minor of 18 semester hours, and a second minor of 12 semester hours; a minimum of 120 semester hours, including 36 of junior and senior rank, in approved courses; and a minimum general grade point average of 2.0 (C) and a minimum general average of 2.0 in the courses offered in the major subject. Special course requirements in the humanities and sciences differ according to the degree sought.

The University offers an Army ROTC program on campus. Air Force ROTC is offered in affiliation with Tennessee State University in Nashville.

Off-Campus Programs

The voluntary cooperative education program integrates formal class work with practical off-campus experience in all fields. Campus studies and industrial or business assignments are alternated on an annual basis: the first, third, and fifth years involve eight semesters of resident academic study, and the second and fourth years are spent off campus in employment. This program gives students the opportunity early in their educational experience to become involved in work that directly relates to a chosen professional career. The cooperative program normally involves students after the completion of three semesters of academic work; however, upperclass students and transfer students may also apply.

Tennessee Tech is affiliated with the Gulf Coast Research Laboratory in Ocean Springs, Mississippi. This affiliation permits students to enroll in marine biology courses that otherwise would be unavailable so far inland.

Academic Facilities

The Tennessee Tech Library contains 328,000 bound volumes well as more than a million microform items. The twenty-eight computer labs on campus, with more than 800 computers, are available for student use throughout the day and on weekends. Excellent laboratories are furnished for modern languages and for each of the physical sciences. The Learning Resources Center provides students in the College of Education with the best in teaching materials, including microteaching facilities and closed-circuit television. The College of Business Administration houses the Fleetguard Cummins Computer Center and offers training in systems analysis and computer applications in business. The Business Media Center in the College of Business Administration provides the community with cutting-edge technology that would otherwise be unavailable. The School of Human Ecology has a home management laboratory, an arts and crafts laboratory, and a nursery school. A 300-acre farm, including an agricultural pavilion, provides practical training for agriculture majors. The engineering laboratories support instruction and research within the Departments of Chemical, Civil, Electrical, Industrial, and Mechanical Engineering and Industrial Technology. There are individual practice rooms and auditoriums for the Department of Music as well as special facilities for physical education, drama, and Army ROTC. The Appalachian Center for Crafts offers courses and experience in such craft areas as wood, clay, fibers, metals, and glass.

Costs

For Tennessee residents, 2003–04 fees were $1889 per semester, room and board were $2446 per semester, and books and supplies cost approximately $350 per semester. Out-of-state residents paid an additional $3966 per semester. The total costs were $4685 per semester ($9370 per year) for Tennessee residents and $8651 per semester ($17,302 per year) for out-of-state students. These costs are subject to change for 2004–05.

Financial Aid

Financial aid includes grants, scholarships, loans, and work-study opportunities. The University participates in the Federal Pell Grant, Federal Work-Study, Federal Perkins Loan, and Tennessee Student Assistance Corporation programs and also offers a variety of private agency scholarships. The average financial aid award is $4969, and the maximum is $11,800. Of the full-time enrolled students, 67 percent receive some type of financial aid. Applicants for aid are required to file the Free Application for Federal Student Aid (FAFSA). The priority deadline for application is March 15; notification is on a rolling basis after April 1. Student employment opportunities are available. Financial aid brochures, application forms, and other relevant information may be obtained from the Office of Student Financial Aid.

Faculty

The student-faculty ratio is about 18:1. There are 371 full-time and 163 part-time faculty members, and more than 78 percent hold doctoral degrees from diverse institutions throughout the nation. The graduate faculty also serves at the undergraduate level. The faculty is reasonably active in research and public service, although most members are also active in academic advising, freshman orientation, and student organizations. Limited use is made of well-qualified part-time faculty members, and approximately 15 carefully selected graduate teaching assistants have direct teaching assignments.

Student Government

The Student Government Association (SGA) is composed of all regularly enrolled students at Tennessee Tech. Its purposes are to promote student participation in the affairs of the University, to serve as a channel for the expression of student opinion, to coordinate student activities on campus, to uphold the constitutional liberties and rights and promote the general welfare of all segments of the University community, and to encourage the development of student responsibility, character, leadership, scholarship, and citizenship. The student government organization is composed of the Executive Council, made up of the SGA executive officers and the President's Cabinet; the Student Senate; and the SGA Student Supreme Court. The SGA officers are elected by the entire student population, while members of the senate are elected by the students from the University's various colleges and schools. A monthly luncheon forum, open to every student, offers a lively interchange of ideas among administrators, faculty members, and students. Every standing committee of the faculty includes student representatives.

Admission Requirements

Scores on the ACT are required for admission. Applicants must also present a high school transcript showing graduation, or the GED equivalent. Transfer students are welcome. To find out how many previously earned credits can be transferred, the transfer applicant should apply for admission to Tennessee Tech in the regular fashion and have an official transcript of previous college work mailed to the Admissions Office. The official evaluation should be received within two weeks. A student must have a high school academic average of at least 2.35 on a 4.0 scale or have an ACT composite score of 19.

A prefreshman summer program is offered in which high-achieving high school juniors can earn college credit and return to their high schools to graduate. Such students must have the approval of their high school principal and guidance counselor and must have completed 12 or more academic units with at least a B (3.2) average.

Application and Information

Transcripts and test scores must be submitted. The application fee is $15. Students are notified of the admission decision within a few days of the receipt of all materials.

For more information, students should contact:

Office of Admissions
Tennessee Technological University
P.O. Box 5006
Cookeville, Tennessee 38505
Telephone: 931-372-3888
800-255-8881 (toll-free)
World Wide Web: http://www.tntech.edu

On the campus of Tennessee Technological University.

TEXAS CHRISTIAN UNIVERSITY

FORT WORTH, TEXAS

The University

The mission of Texas Christian University (TCU) is to educate individuals to think and act as ethical leaders and responsible citizens in the global community, an idea that influences every area of the University.

Founded in 1873, TCU defied the American frontier status quo and offered an education grounded in values, innovation, and creativity. It was the first college in the Southwest to educate both men and women.

Today, TCU is a major teaching and research institution balanced by student-centered warmth typical of a smaller liberal arts college. The University rolls across some 260 picturesque tree-lined acres and within sixty buildings, from the traditional yellow-bricked neo-Georgians to a few angular ultramodern creations. Students find a diverse learning community offering nearly 100 undergraduate majors across seven colleges: business, communication, education, fine arts, health and human sciences, humanities and social sciences, and science and engineering. Ninety-one percent of TCU's professors hold the highest degrees in their fields. It is also common to find qualified undergraduates assisting professors in the latest research activities.

TCU enrolls about 6,900 full-time undergraduate men and women from every state and seventy countries. The University competes in the nation's top collegiate athletics tier, Division I-A, offering nineteen sports. TCU is also a member of leading education organizations such as Phi Beta Kappa, Sigma Xi, and Mortar Board. Research-oriented Ph.D. programs are offered in chemistry, divinity, English, history, physics, and psychology. Facilities and services include sixteen residence halls, each with telephone, cable, and high-speed Internet connections. Upperclassmen have the option of living in fully furnished apartments complete with full kitchens. Other campus amenities include three campus cafeterias, a sub shop in the business school, a bistro in the library, a coffee shop in the humanities building, a campus store, a post office, thirty-one tennis courts, and a new University Recreation Center with five basketball courts, a climbing wall, six racquetball courts, an elevated running track, pool and game tables, video arcade, outdoor pool and patio, and a floor full of the latest in cardio-fitness equipment. Students publish an award-winning newspaper and magazine and operate a top Dallas–Fort Worth radio station featuring alternative music and campus sports coverage.

Location

Fort Worth is home to one of the finest museums in the Southwest, the Kimbell Art Museum. In fact, its cultural district includes Casa Mañana, the Amon Carter Museum, the Modern Art Museum of Fort Worth, and the Fort Worth Museum of Science and Natural History. Downtown, one finds the Texas Ballet, the Fort Worth Opera, the Fort Worth Symphony and the world-class Bass Performance Hall, called one of the top ten opera houses in the world by *Travel and Leisure* magazine.

While the TCU Horned Frogs are considered the home team of Fort Worth, other nearby sports teams include the Texas Rangers, Dallas Cowboys, Dallas Stars, and Dallas Mavericks, and north of Fort Worth, the Texas Motor Speedway. Those looking for other entertainment won't be disappointed, either. The Fort Worth Zoo is 1 minute from campus, and the world-famous stockyards just a bit farther. Six Flags Over Texas is only a short drive away, as is Hurricane Harbor.

Fort Worth is also home to some of America's greatest corporations, including Radio Shack, Bell Helicopter-Textron, American Airlines, Pier 1 Imports, and Lockheed Martin. Other companies that look to TCU for employees are BankOne, Arthur Andersen, Intel, Frito-Lay, and Electronic Data Systems.

Majors and Degrees

Programs lead to fourteen bachelor's degrees in more than eighty major areas: advertising/public relations, allied-health professions (athletic training, pre–occupational therapy*, pre–physical therapy*, and pre–physician assistant studies*), anthropology, art (art education, art history, and studio, with concentrations in ceramics, painting, photography, and sculpture), astronomy, ballet, biology, broadcast journalism, business (with concentrations in accounting, electronic business, finance, management, and marketing, all of which are available with an international emphasis), chemistry, communication sciences and disorders (speech-language pathology and habilitation of the deaf), computer information science, computer science, criminal justice, design, dietetics, economics, education (early childhood, exceptional children, middle school, secondary, all-level certification, and endorsement in English as a second language), engineering (electrical and mechanical), English, environmental earth resources, environmental sciences, fashion merchandising (fashion merchandising, merchandising and textiles), food management, foreign languages, general studies, geology, graphic design, health and fitness, history, international communications (emphasizing advertising/public relations and news), journalism (broadcast and news-editorial), Latin American studies, liberal studies, lighting (minor), mathematics, modern dance, modern languages and literature (majors in French and Spanish and minors in German and Japanese), movement science, music (church music, music education, music history, performance, piano pedagogy, and theory/composition), neuroscience, nursing, nutritional sciences, philosophy, physical education, physics, political science and international relations), pre–health professions (dentistry, medicine, optometry, podiatry, and veterinary), prelaw, psychology, radio-TV-film (criticism, industry, and production), ranch management, religion, Reserve Officers' Training Corps (ROTC) (aerospace studies or military science), social work, sociology, Spanish (fluency and teaching), speech communications (communication in human relations and communication studies), sports and recreation, theater (performance, production, and theater and television), and women's studies (minor). Programs that are indicated by an asterisk (*) begin at TCU and finish elsewhere.

Preprofessional programs are available in dentistry, law, and medicine. A certificate in ranch management is available; other certificate programs are offered by the Office of Extended Education.

Academic Programs

TCU specializes in a liberal arts and sciences education that strives to expose students to the world around them. Within the University core curriculum requirements, students have wide choices in the humanities, natural sciences, social sciences, fine arts, religion, and physical education. Emphasis is placed on writing skills and critical and evaluative thinking. Freshmen are also given the opportunity to take part in Freshman Seminars, which are small classes taught by top professors.

The Center for Academic Services provides full-time advisers for students who choose to postpone the choice of a major. During the first four semesters of study, such students can satisfy University requirements while investigating potential majors. The Writing Center, also provided by the Center for Academic Services, is available to all students and faculty members who wish to refine or improve their writing skills. A full-time professional writing staff conducts individual consultation and group workshops.

Most TCU programs include internships, practicums, or other field experiences with organizations in the Dallas–Fort Worth area. Such local off-campus learning experience is required of all students in nursing, medical technology, and education.

In addition, TCU's honors program challenges students to pursue high intellectual goals. It joins interdisciplinary colloquia and independent research with dedicated faculty and motivated students in all fields of study.

Off-Campus Programs

Nationally recognized for the international experiences available to students, TCU's offerings include the TCU London Centre, which offers fall, spring, and summer courses in a variety of disciplines. Other study abroad programs include those in Germany, Hungary, Japan, Mexico, Spain, and the United Kingdom. In addition, annual summer-study tours with faculty-led seminars are conducted in a variety of fields, such as language, art, and international business.

Academic Facilities

The library houses more than 1.8 million volumes, not to mention an Internet collection that links students to hundreds of thousands of other periodicals and resources. It also has special collections in music, theology, government documents, and rare books. More than fifteen spacious computer labs are open to fit students' schedules, with a few open 24 hours a day. Of two concert halls, one is rated among the nation's best acoustically. The M. J. Neeley School of Business, geared toward e-business and entrepreneurship, is equipped with a trading room with stock market quote machines and newswire services, presentation rooms with videotape equipment, board rooms, a staffed computer resource center, and classrooms with a computer at every desk. Theater students enjoy the Walsh Center for Performing Arts, which includes the Pepsico Recital Hall, a theater, an all-Steinway piano wing, and two large rehearsal rooms.

Costs

For 2003–04, tuition and fees were $8815 per semester, or $17,630 per academic year. Residence hall costs averaged $3780 per academic year. Board fees, which averaged $2000 per academic year, cover the cost of most meals in campus cafeterias or snack bars. Books and supplies averaged $720 per year. Total annual costs for resident students were about $24,130.

Financial Aid

Approximately 70 percent of last year's freshman class received aid. Academic scholarships are based on the student's SAT I or ACT scores, rank in class, and overall application. Awards range from $1000 to full tuition and include the Chancellor, Dean, Faculty, and TCU scholarships. National Merit Finalists who name TCU as their first choice receive a basic scholarship of $4000 and may be eligible for higher awards. Students with demonstrated financial need are eligible for federal-, state-, and University-funded awards, which include grants, loans, and work-study programs.

Faculty

The 420 full-time faculty members hold their highest degrees from 125 different institutions; more than 90 percent have the Ph.D. or other appropriate terminal degree. The University has kept classes comparatively small, with less than 4 percent of all classes having more than 50 students. Most instructors have an open-door policy for students, and all instructors post regular office hours. Some departments enlist part-time faculty members from the Dallas–Fort Worth professional community to augment their programs.

Student Government

The Student Government Association, composed of elected members, serves as the basis for student government. Its officers and programming council direct a varied program of entertainment, speakers, films, and social and cultural events. The Student House makes many of its own policies within broad University guidelines. Residence halls form student councils to recommend policies and to provide activities for the hall. Students are voting members of all University-wide committees that recommend policy changes.

Admission Requirements

TCU evaluates applications by using broad criteria. Emphasis is placed on both test scores and on individual character. While academic credentials are most important, TCU also looks for talent, leadership potential, and personal determination to make a difference. Admitted students show above-average academic ability. Applicants are expected to have completed a college-preparatory curriculum during high school. A campus visit and interview are recommended before a decision is reached; admitted students are required to take part in an orientation session on campus before enrolling officially. Qualified students are admitted without regard to race, color, creed, age, sex, or ethnic or national origin, in accordance with Title IX and other government regulations.

Application and Information

Information about application deadlines and notification dates may be obtained from:

Raymond A. Brown
Dean of Admission
TCU Box 297013
Texas Christian University
2800 South University Drive
Fort Worth, Texas 76129
Telephone: 817-257-7490
800-TCU-FROG (toll-free)
Fax: 817-257-7268
E-mail: frogmail@tcu.edu
World Wide Web: http://www.tcu.edu

TCU graduates earn more than degrees that will improve their lives. They learn to change their world.

TEXAS LUTHERAN UNIVERSITY

SEGUIN, TEXAS

The University

Texas Lutheran University is a fully accredited coeducational liberal arts college supported by the Evangelical Lutheran Church in America. Texas Lutheran traces its roots back to 1891, when the first Evangelical Lutheran Synod of Texas founded a college in Brenham. The University moved to Seguin in 1912. The Seguin campus has grown from an original 15 acres to its present 196 acres.

Approximately 6 percent of the University's 1,400 students come from outside the state of Texas. Lutherans constitute 28 percent of the student body. Students may participate in more than sixty campus organizations, including nine academic honor societies, nine local social sororities and fraternities, various student volunteer groups, the Concert Band, the Concert Choir, the Chapel Choir, a newspaper, a yearbook, the Black Student Union, and the Mexican-American Student Association. There are fourteen intramural sports. Intercollegiate sports are baseball, basketball, football, golf, soccer, and tennis for men and basketball, cross-country, golf, soccer, softball, tennis, and volleyball for women.

The 20,000-square-foot Hein Dining Hall was dedicated in 1993. With four separate dining/meeting areas, this facility serves as the gathering place for students during meal time, as well as the site for Language Tables, faculty lunches, special event meals, and other college functions. The Alumni Student Center, totally refurbished in 1995, is the center of activity and has a large snack bar, enclosed game room, three computer labs, a "great lounge," the University bookstore, the post office, student government office, student publication office, multipurpose room for student organizations, a counseling center, and office space.

Location

Seguin, a city of 23,000 people, is 35 miles east of San Antonio. This proximity makes it easy for students to take advantage of that historic city's cultural, social, and artistic attractions. Facilities for such outdoor sports as fishing, waterskiing, scuba diving, rafting, and sailing are readily available on the rivers and lakes of the surrounding Texas hill country. In addition, the sun, sand, and surf of the Texas Gulf Coast are only a 2-hour drive away.

Majors and Degrees

Texas Lutheran University grants the Bachelor of Arts (B.A.), Bachelor of Science (B.S.), Bachelor of Music, and Bachelor of Business Administration (B.B.A) degrees. Bachelor of Arts degrees are offered in biology, business administration, chemistry, communication studies, computer science, computer systems management, dramatic media, economics, English studies, history, kinesiology, mathematics, multidisciplinary studies, music, philosophy, physics, political science, psychology, sociology, Spanish, theology, and visual arts. Bachelor of Science degrees are available in biology, chemistry, and mathematics. A collateral major is offered in international studies. Concentrations are also available in certain majors: accounting, applied music, athletic training, environmental biology, exercise science, finance, international business, management, marketing, molecular biology, music history/literature, public history, and sport and fitness management. Thirty minors are also offered. The Bachelor of Business Administration degree is offered in accounting as a concurrent degree with the B.A. for professional concentration in accounting.

Professional preparation is offered in education and sports medicine.

Preprofessional preparation is available in dentistry, law, medicine, nursing, occupational therapy, pharmacy, physical therapy, theology, and veterinary science. A dual engineering program is also available.

Academic Programs

The academic program at Texas Lutheran University is designed to provide an education in the liberal arts that makes life more exciting and satisfying. TLU students pursue a broad and general education while following programs of study that prepare them for employment directly after graduation or for further academic work at graduate or specialized professional schools.

Texas Lutheran uses a 4-4 academic calendar. The fall semester of four months begins in late August, and final examinations are completed before the Christmas vacation begins. The spring semester of four months starts in mid-January and ends in May.

Special academic programs offered include international studies, the Scholars program, independent study, off-campus semester programs, Mexican-American studies, the International Student Exchange Program, the Center for Women's Studies, and the KROST Life Enrichment Program. The KROST Symposium annually brings scholars, journalists, and government officials to campus to discuss issues of relevance and importance to the community at large. Emphasis is placed on the TLU Internship Program. These valuable career experiences, in conjunction with the efforts of the Career Services Center, have resulted in 95 percent of the alumni being placed in graduate school or professional careers within six months of graduation.

To graduate with a bachelor's degree, students must complete a minimum of 124 semester hours with a cumulative grade point average of at least 2.0. Each student attending TLU is required to complete a general education curriculum in addition to a major area of study.

Off-Campus Programs

Students may participate in a variety of off-campus programs, all of which carry academic credit. The Washington Semester Program allows students to enroll in a 12-semester-hour curriculum at the American University in Washington, D.C. The curriculum involves research, seminars, and lectures and is open to juniors and seniors who have taken a basic course in American government. Study-abroad opportunities are available through the International Student Exchange Program. This exchange brings students from various countries to Texas Lutheran as well as placing TLU students in universities across the globe.

Academic Facilities

The O. G. Beck College Center houses administrative offices, a classroom, and meeting rooms. The Jesse H. Jones Physical Education Complex incorporates a 2,200-seat gym, fitness center, auxiliary activity center, faculty offices, a classroom, handball/racquetball courts, and an eight-lane heated aquatic center. The Blumberg Memorial Library houses more than 260,000 items of library materials and subscribes to 720 journal titles. The Yolanda Schuech Fine Arts Center is a multipurpose facility that includes a little theater, recital hall, music studios, band hall, art labs, and art gallery. Chapel of the Abiding Presence, Weinert Memorial is the campus worship center, seating 500 and containing a tracker-action Schlicker organ. Moody Science Building provides classrooms, laboratories, and student research space. In 1995, an additional 10,000-square-foot KROST Center was added to include seminar rooms, classrooms, student labs, offices, and equipment for the KROST fitness tests. The 1,100-seat John and Katie Jackson auditorium is the sight for student productions, fine art presentations, and major lectures and serves as home for the Mid-Texas Symphony. A building immediately adjacent to the campus has been converted into the psychology building with classroom space, numerous experimentation labs, a lounge, and study space. Langner and Weeber Halls contain various size and style classrooms and professor offices.

Costs

For 2003–04, the comprehensive fee was $20,370, which included room, board, tuition, phone service, and the activities fee. Health insurance is available to students at additional cost. Parking fees are $50 per year. Private music lessons (one lesson per week) cost $210 per semester. Most students spend $2400 for books, entertainment, travel, clothing, and other expenses.

Financial Aid

More than 90 percent of the students at Texas Lutheran University receive some type of need-based or merit-based financial support. In 2003–04, more than $20 million in financial aid was given to TLU students; the average financial aid package was $14,700. Campus employment and work-study awards are readily available. A variety of merit and competitive scholarships are also offered.

Faculty

In 2003–04, Texas Lutheran employed 67 full-time and 51 part-time faculty members. Eighty-five percent of the faculty members have doctorates or terminal degrees in their fields. The student-faculty ratio is 15:1, which allows the students' names to be known, their faces recognized, and their futures brought into focus with the professors' supportive guidance.

Student Government

All full-time students are members of the Student Government Association, a comprehensive student government structure. The president and vice president of the student body, together with a representative Student Government Association, work with the faculty and staff in achieving University goals and in providing an open forum for student opinion and action. Students appointed by the student-body president represent student opinion on most faculty committees that are concerned with academic matters as well as with certain aspects of the cocurricular program.

Admission Requirements

Each candidate is considered individually by the Admissions Committee, which evaluates the student's probable success at TLU based on courses taken in secondary school, test scores (either ACT or SAT I), grade point average, essay, and activities. Although not required, a personal interview is recommended. Seventy-eight percent of the freshmen rank in the top half of their high school graduating class. Fifty-four percent of the freshmen have a minimum SAT I verbal score of 500, and 58 percent have a minimum SAT I math score of 500. Sixty-five percent of the freshmen have a minimum ACT score of 21.

Transfer applicants must submit a transcript from each college previously attended and may be asked to submit their high school records. A minimum 2.25 grade point average on previous college work is required for admission consideration.

Application and Information

A completed application form, SAT I or ACT scores, and an official transcript are required for admission. Admission decisions are announced on a rolling basis.

For more information about TLU, students should contact:

Norm Jones
Vice President for Enrollment Services
Texas Lutheran University
1000 West Court Street
Seguin, Texas 78155
Telephone: 830-372-8050
800-771-8521 (toll-free)
E-mail: admissions@tlu.edu
World Wide Web: http://www.tlu.edu

A view across the center of the campus as seen from the front doors of Blumberg Memorial Library.

TEXAS TECH UNIVERSITY

LUBBOCK, TEXAS

The University

Texas Tech University, founded in 1923, is a residential state university with a population of 28,500 students who come from all fifty states and ninety-nine countries. Students at Texas Tech have the opportunity to study from more than 300 graduate and undergraduate degree programs. Academics are the top priority at Texas Tech, and students find admission standards comparable to other state institutions.

Texas Tech is one of the country's top universities to offer such diverse academic programs on one campus. The University is built around nine colleges: Agricultural Sciences and Natural Resources, Architecture, Arts and Sciences, Business Administration, Education, Engineering, Honors, Human Sciences, and Visual and Performing Arts. A law school, which has one of the highest number of students passing the bar exam in Texas, is conveniently located on the main campus. Also present is the Texas Tech University Health Sciences Center with its Schools of Medicine, Nursing, Pharmacy, and Allied Health.

Texas Tech has become a leader in academic programs ranging from pioneering research with the U.S. Department of Agriculture to improving alternative fuel capabilities for the nation's leading automakers. Wind engineering research has led to the creation of shelters that withstand some of the nation's most deadly tornadoes. Students also find opportunities to master the arts with instruction from classically trained musicians. Unique study abroad programs are also available. The creation of the Institute for Environmental and Human Health provides a new addition to the academic program. The institute offers graduate and undergraduate education in environmental science, toxicology, and environmental health.

The University joined the Big XII Conference for intercollegiate athletics in 1996. Women participate in basketball, golf, soccer, softball, tennis, track and field, and volleyball while men participate in baseball, basketball, football, golf, tennis, and track and field. In addition, the University offers club sports such as lacrosse, polo, swimming, rugby, men's soccer, and ice hockey.

Location

The 1,850-acre campus is located in Lubbock, which is a west Texas city of more than 200,000 people. Within a few hours' drive, students can find skiing in the mountains of northern New Mexico, the lush scenery of the Texas Hill Country, and the vast canyons of Palo Duro and Big Bend. Temperatures are mild in the winter and warm in the summer, with an average of 267 days of sunshine each year.

Majors and Degrees

Texas Tech University, through the College of Agricultural Sciences and Natural Resources, offers majors in the following areas: agribusiness, agricultural and applied economics, agricultural and applied economics/general business, agricultural communications, agriculture undeclared, agronomy, animal science, environmental conservation of natural resources, food technology, horticulture, integrated pest management, interdisciplinary agriculture, landscape architecture, pre–veterinary medicine, range management, and wildlife and fisheries management. The College of Architecture offers majors in architecture (Bachelor of Science), architecture/business administration (dual), architecture/civil engineering (dual), and architecture/Master of Business Administration (dual). The College of Arts and Sciences offers majors in advertising, anthropology, arts and sciences undeclared, biochemistry, biology, cell and molecular biology, chemistry, classics, communication studies, economics, English, exercise and sport sciences, French, general studies, geography, geology, geophysics, geosciences, German, health, history, international economics, journalism, Latin, Latin American/Iberian studies, mass communications, mathematics, mathematics and computer science (dual), microbiology, philosophy, photocommunications, physics, political science, pre–communication disorders, predental, prelaw, pre-medical technology, premedicine, prenursing, pre–occupational therapy, pre-optometry, prepharmacy, pre–physical therapy, psychology, public relations, Russian language and area studies, social work, sociology, Spanish, telecommunications, and zoology. The College of Business Administration offers majors in accounting, business economics, finance, finance/real estate emphasis, general business, general business/international emphasis, honors program in management, international business, management, management information systems, management/lead, marketing, and petroleum land management. The College of Education offers majors in early childhood–grade 4, grades 4–8, and grades 8–12 teacher certification programs; multidisciplinary science; multidisciplinary studies; and special education and bilingual education teaching fields. The College of Engineering offers majors in architecture/civil engineering (dual), chemical engineering, chemical engineering/computer science (dual), civil engineering, computer enginerring, computer science, construction technology, electrical electronics technology, electrical engineering, electrical engineering/computer science (dual), engineering physics, engineering technology, engineering undeclared, environmental engineering, industrial engineering, mechanical engineering, mechanical technology, and petroleum engineering. The College of Human Sciences offers majors in apparel design and manufacturing; early childhood education (pre-K–4); family and consumer sciences; food and nutrition (dietetics); human development and family studies; interior design; personal financial planning; restaurant, hotel, and institutional management; retailing; and substance abuse studies. The College of Visual and Performing Arts offers majors in art, art history (Bachelor of Arts), dance, design communications, fine art photography, music (Bachelor of Arts), music composition, music performance, music (teacher certification), music theory, music undeclared, studio art, theater–acting and directing, theater arts (Bachelor of Arts), theater–design technology, theater–management, and visual studies (teacher certification). The Honors College offers majors in honors natural history and humanities and an honors high-performance management major.

Academic Program

Texas Tech's undergraduate curriculum provides courses in more than 150 programs of study. Recently, students at Texas Tech have seen an increase in competitive scholarships and the creation of the University's Honor's College. Students accepted into the college find unparalleled undergraduate research opportunities for students in all major disciplines. As a result, students are consistently awarded the prestigious Barry M. Goldwater Scholarship for science, engineering, and mathematics. Since 1995, 19 students have received the Goldwater Scholarship. In 2001, a Texas Tech student was recognized as a Truman Scholar. The latest accomplishment is a Gates-Cambridge scholarship awarded in 2002 for study at Cambridge in 2003–04.

Off-Campus Programs

Texas Tech University operates a 400-acre south Texas center in Junction where summer classes and May intersessions are held. The latest addition to the University is the Texas Tech Hill Country University Consortium, which is a collaboration of universities and community colleges that bring four-year, public higher education services to the Hill Country Region. Classes are offered in person and via distance education to academic centers at the Texas Tech Junction Campus, in Fredricksburg, and in Marble

Falls. For more information, students should visit the Web site at http://www.hillcountry.ttu.edu. Just minutes from the main campus, the Lubbock Lake Landmark Historical Park is an excavation site where Texas Tech researchers have documented a 12,000-year record of continuous human habitation. In addition, numerous study-abroad opportunities are available for college credit in many countries.

Academic Facilities

The University Library, the Medical Library, the Southwest Collection Archival library, the Law Library, and the Architectural Library are linked by a common online catalog, TechPAC. Additional access is provided to numerous bibliographic and full-text databases as well as catalogs from libraries throughout the nation. The University Library collection includes 1.3 million volumes, 15,000 subscriptions, and nearly 1 million microforms. The library is one of only two regional depositories in the state for more than 1.4 million U.S. government documents. The library also houses the Advanced Technology Learning Center, which is a multiroom lab with a wide variety of computers and programs. There are also computer facilities located in each college and residence halls throughout campus.

Costs

Texas Tech is listed in *The 100 Best College Buys for 2003–2004*, which is a directory of the top colleges and universities in the country whose costs are below the national average, but whose academics are above the national average. In 2003–04, the estimated average cost for 30 undergraduate credit hours, including books and nine-month room and board, was $12,451 for Texas residents. Residents of Arkansas, New Mexico, and Oklahoma living in bordering counties to Texas paid in-state tuition; residents of nonbordering counties paid an additional $900 per year. Students from other states paid an additional $7080 per year for out-of-state tuition. It is important to note that students who receive a $1000 academic scholarship from Texas Tech are exempt from out-of-state tuition. Costs are subject to change.

Financial Aid

A variety of financial aid is offered to students via scholarships, grants, and loans. Competitive scholarships are awarded on academic merit, SAT I or ACT scores, and class rank. More than 300 Presidential Endowed Scholarships are awarded to students each year. Need-based assistance is also available in the form of scholarships, government and private loans, grants, and work-study. Students' need for assistance is determined from the Free Application for Federal Student Aid (FAFSA). For more information about scholarships and deadlines, students should contact the Office of Student Financial Aid (telephone: 806-742-3681; Web site: http://www.fina.ttu.edu).

Faculty

Full-time faculty members number approximately 1,041. There are 1,001 part-time faculty members and teaching assistants. Among faculty members are distinguished professionals serving as visiting and adjunct professors. Faculty members' research has gained international attention and has been published in leading academic journals. The University's average student-faculty ratio is 20:1.

Student Government

The Texas Tech Student Government Association includes a student senate whose elected members serve as official student representatives and act as liaisons to the Lubbock community and the University administration. In addition, a freshman council of first-year students works specifically on issues relating to the freshman experience.

Admission Requirements

Admission criteria for all students are designed to ensure academic success. For freshmen, admission decisions are based primarily on test scores and class rank. Additional factors such as leadership experience and extracurricular activities, community or volunteer service, talents and special honors, awards and achievements, and employment and internships are considered.

Students in the top 10 percent of their graduating class are guaranteed admission to the University. For assured admission, students who rank in the first quarter of their class must score at least 1140 on the SAT I or 25 on the ACT. Students who rank in the second quarter must score a minimum of 1230 on the SAT I and 28 on the ACT. Applicants in the lower half must score a minimum of 1270 on the SAT I and 29 on the ACT.

Those students who are not admitted with a favorable review are eligible to participate in one of the alternative admissions programs and must complete a prescribed number of college hours and earn a prescribed grade point average.

Admission requirements for transfer students differ, depending on the number of college hours a student has earned. Transfer students are admitted to Texas Tech by transferring 24 or more hours from an accredited institution with a minimum cumulative 2.25 grade point average or by transferring 12 to 23 hours with a minimum cumulative 2.5 grade point average and at least 12 hours of required basic courses. Students with less than 12 transfer hours must meet freshman requirements and have a minimum 2.0 grade point average. All students must be eligible to return to the institution from which they are transferring.

The University admits all students who hold scholarships awarded by an official Texas Tech scholarship committee.

Application and Information

All students should submit the State of Texas Common Application, a high school transcript, SAT I or ACT test scores, and a $50 application fee. Applications can be accessed via the Web site at http://www.applytexas.org.

Requests for information should be directed to:

Office of Admissions
Texas Tech University
Box 45005
Lubbock, Texas 79409-5005
Telephone: 806-742-1480
Fax: 806-742-0062
E-mail: admissions@ttu.edu
World Wide Web: http://www.ttu.edu
http://www.admissions.ttu.edu

Students receive support and encouragement to achieve academic and personal goals at Texas Tech University.

TEXAS WOMAN'S UNIVERSITY

DENTON, TEXAS

The University

Texas Woman's University (TWU) is a public university offering bachelor's, master's, and doctoral degree programs. A teaching and research institution, TWU emphasizes the health sciences, education, and the liberal arts. With an enrollment of approximately 9,700 students (fall 2003), the University enrolls 10 percent men and welcomes all qualified students.

Established in 1901 by the Texas Legislature, Texas Woman's University is organized into three major academic divisions: the University General Divisions, the Institute of Health Sciences, and the Graduate School. Included in the University General Divisions are the College of Arts and Sciences, College of Professional Education, and School of Library and Information Studies. The Institute of Health Sciences includes the College of Health Sciences, College of Nursing, School of Occupational Therapy, and School of Physical Therapy. The Graduate School coordinates advanced degree programs across the University.

Old Main, the University's first building, still stands amid high-rise buildings and other modern facilities that distinguish the beautiful 270-acre wooded campus in Denton. Residence halls, recreational facilities, the conference center, the library, and classroom buildings are conveniently located throughout the campus. Special campus landmarks include the statue of the Pioneer Woman and the historic Little Chapel-in-the-Woods.

Location

TWU's main campus is in Denton, Texas (population 79,000), just 35 miles north of Dallas and Fort Worth—the nation's ninth-largest urban center. Clinical centers, offering upper-level and graduate studies in the health sciences, are located in Dallas (near the Parkland and Presbyterian hospitals) and in Houston (in the Texas Medical Center).

Majors and Degrees

Undergraduate programs lead to the Bachelor of Arts, Bachelor of Business Administration, Bachelor of Fine Arts, Bachelor of Science, and Bachelor of Social Work degrees. Baccalaureate degrees are offered in art (with concentrations in art history, ceramics, painting, photography, and sculpture), biology (with a concentration in human biology), business administration (with concentrations in accounting, management, and marketing), chemistry, child development, communication science, community health, computer science, criminal justice, dance, dental hygiene, dietetics, drama, English, family studies, fashion design, fashion merchandising, government (with concentrations in government service and paralegal studies), history, kinesiology, library science, mass communications, mathematics, medical technology, music, music therapy, nursing, nutrition, predental science, prelaw, premedicine, preoccupational therapy, prephysical therapy, psychology, social work, sociology, and teacher preparation for elementary, reading and bilingual, secondary, and special education.

Academic Program

TWU is accredited by the Commission on Colleges of the Southern Association of Colleges and Schools to award bachelor's, master's, and doctoral degrees. Various programs are also accredited by appropriate state, regional, and national agencies. The University emphasizes the importance of a liberal arts education and specialized or professional study, especially in the health sciences.

The University's requirement for all bachelor's degrees comprises the successful completion of a minimum of 124 credit hours, including at least 42 semester credit hours of core curriculum requirements, plus additional hours specified for each degree. The University calendar consists of two semesters of approximately four months each, one minimester, two summer terms of five weeks each, and one summer session of ten weeks. Most degree programs are designed to allow students who carry a normal course load to complete degree requirements in eight semesters.

Any full- or part-time student who has not earned at least 3 semester credit hours prior to fall 1989 must be tested for reading, writing, and mathematics skills under the Texas Academic Skills Program (TASP). No student may graduate from a baccalaureate degree program without passing all sections of the examination, unless she or he meets specific requirements for exemption. (That exemption does not apply to students entering teacher education.)

Off-Campus Programs

Programs in each of the University's colleges and schools include clinical and practicum experiences that give students access to outstanding facilities of major health-care, business, and other institutions located in major metropolitan centers. Programs are offered annually to provide study-travel opportunities in the United States and abroad. A diverse cooperative education program integrates classroom study with planned and supervised work experience in educational activities outside the formal classroom.

Academic Facilities

The University library has holdings of 549,116 print volumes and 10,000 e-book volumes, 8,287 current periodical and serial publications, 1,532,563 microforms, and 84,120 audiovisual materials to support all major areas of study at TWU. In addition to the standard printed bibliographies, indexes, and abstracts, the library offers Web-based and local access to literature searches from 90 computer databases. Special resources include the Woman's Collection, the largest depository in the South and Southwest of research materials about women. Other materials include a rare book collection as well as a departmental children's library in the School of Library and Information Studies. Students have access to Texas academic and public library collections through TexShare, and, through membership in Amigos Library Services (the OCLC regional network) the TWU Library has access to collections in libraries throughout the United States. The Dallas Center maintains a special collection for students in the health sciences. Through a consortia membership, the students at the Houston Center have access to printed and online database collections and full library services in the Houston Academy of Medicine–Texas Medical Center Library as well as to an in-house TWU librarian for assistance with accessing and using all TWU Library resources.

Numerous classroom and laboratory buildings, including an

undergraduate science laboratory building, are conveniently located on the Denton campus to meet specific needs of the individual components of the University. Special facilities on the Denton campus include honors and international programs with special housing facilities; Margo Jones Performance Hall, a theater, an auditorium, and four dance studios; television studios; numerous art and music studios and practice rooms; science laboratories; a computer center and computer center learning laboratory; a writing laboratory; woodworking, weaving, and other laboratory facilities for programs related to therapy; and the Institute for Women's Health. Clinics are provided for speech and hearing, dental hygiene, occupational therapy, and reading. A nursery school serves as a laboratory for students majoring in child-development programs. Also included are tennis courts, a golf course, an indoor track, indoor and outdoor pools, a Wellness Center and fitness room, and other facilities that support programs in physical education and human movement. Residence hall rooms are linked to the campus computer network.

The Dallas Center includes a campus in the Parkland Memorial Hospital complex and a campus adjacent to Presbyterian Hospital of Dallas. The Houston Center is located in the heart of the Texas Medical Center. Both centers offer outstanding instructional facilities, including excellent library holdings, clinical learning resources, simulation and research laboratories, laboratories for occupational and physical therapy, and anatomy laboratories. The Dallas and Houston Centers also have renovated nursing skills laboratories, and the Houston Center has research laboratories in biochemistry and nutrition.

Costs

The average cost for in-state resident students in 2004–05 for one semester of 15 semester hours is $1605 plus course fees and $450 for books and supplies. For out-of-state residents, the average cost of tuition for 15 semester hours is $4455. Residence hall rates, meals, and personal expenses vary. All rates are subject to change. Scholarship programs for honors students, class valedictorians from Texas, new freshmen, new transfer students, and international students are available.

Financial Aid

More than 60 percent of TWU's students receive financial aid in the form of scholarships, grants, loans, or on-campus employment. In addition to offering numerous scholarships and grants funded by the state and by friends of the University, TWU participates in many federally funded programs. Federal Pell Grants, Federal Supplemental Educational Opportunity Grants, Federal Perkins Loans, Federal Nursing Student Loans, Federal Stafford Loans, Federal Parent Loans, and Federal Work-Study Program awards are available. Suggested filing dates for financial aid applicants are April 1 for the fall and spring terms and March 1 for summer sessions. Applications for academic scholarships for both the fall and spring semesters should be made by March 1.

Faculty

A faculty of approximately 500 guides the academic program at TWU and gives careful attention to student needs. Faculty members hold the doctoral degree or another terminal or graduate degree in their field.

Student Government

All students are members of the United Student Association, which enables them to participate in a wide variety of activities. Students work with the faculty and administrators to develop University policies and programs of special interest and concern to the student body. Students also serve on various University committees. Leadership development is a special focus.

Admission Requirements

First-time freshman applicants are assured admission to Texas Woman's University if they have graduated from a regionally accredited high school in Texas within the last two years and have a class ranking that places them in the top 25 percent of their high school graduating class. Regular admission to the University is based on graduation from an accredited high school, a grade point average of at least 2.0 on a 4.0 scale, a score of at least 950 (verbal and math combined) on the SAT I or a composite score of at least 20 on the ACT, and completion of at least 22 academic credits of the new recommended Texas high school graduation program. Transfer students must submit an official transcript from each college previously attended. They must have obtained a GPA of 2.0 or higher on a 4.0 scale when transferring to the University. Students holding an Associate of Arts or Associate of Science degree are assured admission.

Application and Information

Applicants should submit a completed application for admission and their official transcripts to the Office of Admissions. The fall and spring priority deadlines are June 30 and November 1, respectively. There is a $30 application fee for all new students.

Additional information about the University and its programs is available from:

Office of Admissions
Texas Woman's University
P.O. Box 425589
Denton, Texas 76204-5589
Telephone: 940-898-3188
866-809-6130
E-mail: admissions@twu.edu
World Wide Web: http://www.twu.edu

TWU welcomes women and men and traditional and nontraditional students to its campuses in Denton, Dallas, and Houston. TWU offers more than 100 degree programs and awards bachelor's, master's, and doctoral degrees.

THIEL COLLEGE

GREENVILLE, PENNSYLVANIA

The College

Thiel College was founded in 1866 as one of the first coeducational institutions of higher education in the United States. Located in Greenville, Pennsylvania, in the northwestern corner of the commonwealth, Thiel has become known for the quality of its educational offerings and its blending of liberal arts cutting-edge technology and experiential learning through extensive cooperative education and internship opportunities. *U.S. News & World Report* has ranked Thiel College among the top ten Best Value Colleges among northern comprehensive colleges in its *America's Best Colleges 2004* guide. In addition, Thiel has also been ranked in the "top tier" of northern liberal arts colleges by the same publication. The College's sciences and mathematics programs are rated "among the 200 best in the United States" by *Peterson's Guide to the Sciences*. Thiel was also included in the 2003 edition of Princeton Review's *Best Mid-Atlantic Colleges: 98 Great Schools to Consider.*

Affiliated with the Evangelical Lutheran Church in America, the College enrolls more than 1,260 women and men. Most students come from Pennsylvania, Ohio, and the Middle Atlantic States. Nine percent of the students are members of minority groups, and 5 percent are from seventeen other countries.

Social life at Thiel is based on involvement as part of a holistic approach to education. Students are encouraged to participate in activities and sports programs that are of interest to them. Cocurricular activities and sports programs are viewed as an important complement to the academic life of the College community and to the individual.

Thiel College competes in the Presidents' Athletic Conference and the NCAA Division III. The athletic team nicknames are Tomcats and Lady Cats. Intercollegiate sports include basketball, competitive cheerleading and dance, cross-country, golf, soccer, tennis, and track and field; men's baseball, football, and wrestling; and women's softball and volleyball. Intramural competition is available in a variety of sports for men and women. Outstanding fitness and recreation includes downhill and cross-country skiing, hiking, boating, hunting, and fishing.

Fraternities and sororities add to the mix of college organizations, but student life includes all students whether they are Greeks or non-Greeks. The fraternities include Alpha Chi Rho, Delta Sigma Phi, Kappa Sigma, and Sigma Phi Epsilon. The sororities include Alpha Xi Delta, Chi Omega, Sigma Kappa, and Zeta Tau Alpha.

Most students at Thiel live on campus and can choose from a variety of housing options. During the first year, students reside with members of the Residential Learning Community in a first-year residence hall. In their sophmore year, students may choose from the following three options: coed residence halls, theme housing, or college apartments and town houses.

Thiel offers its students several dining choices: the Dining Place student dining hall, the Rotunda Bistro, the Grab-n-Go Kiosk, and the Convenience store.

The College Counseling Center is located in the Howard Miller Student Center, Thiel's student union, and is affiliated with the Sharon Regional Health System. Counseling services are available on a variety of topics. The Thiel College Pastor can also provide pastoral assistance and spiritual guidance.

Location

Thiel College is located in Greenville, a small town of about 7,000 people in the northwestern corner of the commonwealth. The 135-acre campus is an attractive combination of wooded walkways and academic, residential, and recreational use facilities. Students find ample shopping, dining, and entertainment options in the Greenville area. Thiel College and Greenville have a mutually supportive relationship.

Because of their proximity, the Cleveland, Pittsburgh, Erie, and Youngstown metro areas are used by Thiel students and faculty members for additional cultural, shopping, and recreational experiences.

Majors and Degrees

Thiel College awards the Associate of Arts and the Bachelor of Arts degrees. Bachelor's degrees are awarded in accounting, actuarial studies, animation/multimedia, art, bioforestry, biology, biology/conservation, business administration, business administration/culinary arts, business communication, chemistry, communication, computer science, criminal justice, cytotechnology, elementary education, English, environmental chemistry, environmental science, French, gerontology, history, international business, management information science, mathematics, medical illustration, medical technology, mortuary science, parish education, philosophy, physics, political science, psychology, religion, sociology, Spanish, speech and hearing science, and exploratory (undeclared major). Preprofessional programs are offered in the areas of dentistry, engineering 3-2, law, medicine, ministry, pharmacy, physical therapy, and veterinary medicine. Teacher certification is available in secondary education. Thiel awards Associate of Arts degrees in general studies, accounting, and management information science.

Academic Program

Thiel College provides students with a liberal arts education that increases general and special knowledge of the world, promotes creative and critical thinking, and strengthens communication skills. Each of the majors and degree programs combines liberal arts instruction and values with cutting-edge technology and hands-on learning through internships and co-ops.

The Bachelor of Arts degree program requires a minimum of 124 credits for graduation. The Associate of Arts degree programs require a minimum of 64 credits for graduation. All majors must complete liberal arts integrative requirements as well as core and elective courses.

Advanced Placement (AP) and CLEP examination scores are welcome from students entering Thiel. Courses taken at other colleges while students are still in high school are accepted for consideration provided that the grade earned is a C or better (on a 4.0 scale).

The Honors Program is offered to outstanding students and provides students with the opportunity to develop special projects, interests, and activities; to meet with visiting artists, scholars, and public figures; and to work closely with professors and other members of the College community.

Thiel College follows a two-semester system. Classes typically start near Labor Day in August or September and end in mid-December. Second-term classes begin in mid-January and continue through mid-May. Summer session classes are also offered.

Off-Campus Programs

Students at Thiel are encouraged to broaden their horizons, to take advantage of off-campus learning experiences, and to integrate a world community approach to their studies.

Cooperative learning (co-op) experiences are available to students in industry, government agencies, and educational institutions and with nonprofit and charitable organizations. The co-op enhances professional development through planned supervised work experiences.

The Haller Enterprise Institute at Thiel is an innovative concept that encourages students to pursue their business ideas while they continue their education. The Institute is a support system through which students with entrepreneurial ideas can receive advice, training, and encouragement in starting their own businesses.

Additional options for students include Thiel's Center for Women's Leadership; junior year study-abroad programs in the country or countries of the student's choice; the Semester in Washington program, which focuses on ethical issues and public affairs; the United Nations Semester; the Washington Semester, open to any major; the Appalachian Semester; Argonne National Laboratories Semester; EWHA Woman's University Semester in Seoul, Korea; the Drew University Art Semester; and the Saltillo Experience in Mexico.

A cooperative degree program with the Art Institute of Pittsburgh allows Thiel students to earn a baccalaureate degree in art with commercial art emphasis. Another cooperative program with the Art Institute in Pittsburgh allows Thiel students to earn a Bachelor of Arts degree in business administration from Thiel with a certificate in culinary arts from the Art Institute. Thiel College and the Pittsburgh Institute of Mortuary Science offer a cooperative program leading to a Bachelor of Arts degree in business administration and a diploma in funeral directing/embalming.

Academic Facilities

Thiel College is set on a parklike 135-acre campus. Greenville Hall, the oldest building at the College, was constructed in 1872 and houses classrooms as well as offices for humanities faculty members. The Beeghly-Rissell Gymnasia house the basketball, wrestling, and volleyball arenas; a fitness center; weight-lifting center; team locker rooms; and coaches' offices. Roth Memorial Hall is home to administrative offices and the auditorium for the Thiel Players, the college theater company. Alumni Stadium, a 1,400-seat multisports complex featuring synthetic turf, was completed in 2001.

Langenheim Memorial Library houses study carrels for 600 students and contains a computer center for instruction or Internet access. The library collection includes 151,000 books, 213,000 government documents, 921 periodicals, and more than 22,000 microfiche/microfilm items.

The Academic Center/Science Hall is an integrated five-level complex, which includes classrooms, laboratories, art studios, a rooftop greenhouse, specialized teaching facilities, faculty offices, lecture halls, and computer centers.

The William Passavant Memorial Center, a multiuse conference and convocation center, contains a 2,000-seat auditorium, which is also home to the Greenville Symphony.

The Brucker Great Blue Heron Sanctuary and the East Acres complex provide natural outdoor laboratories for wildlife and biological observation and environmental and geological study.

Costs

Tuition for the 2003–04 year was $13,500. Room and board charges were a minimum of $6584. Books, fees, and personal expenses average an additional $1800 to $2300 per year.

Financial Aid

Thiel College participates in all federal financial aid programs. Students are encouraged to check with state agencies as well as with local, community, civic, industrial, and church-related groups for additional funding sources. Students are encouraged to file the Free Application for Federal Student Aid (FAFSA) as early as possible after January 1 of their senior year. Award notifications are mailed beginning in late January and continue until funding is exhausted. Admission decisions are non-need-based.

Thiel College awards its institutional funds after consideration of academic achievement, special talents and skills, and financial need. Thiel maintains an extensive grant, loan, scholarship, and college work program. In 2002–03, more than $6 million was awarded to students from institutional resources, and 96 percent of students received funding through a combination of federal, state, local, and Thiel resources.

Faculty

Fifty-nine full-time faculty members and 30 adjunct/part-time faculty members are responsible for instruction. Most faculty members serve as advisers to students, and 75 percent hold advanced degrees. Faculty members are very involved in the life of the Thiel community and work with students on campus media, theater, music, student government, special interest clubs, and organizations and with fraternities and sororities. No graduate students or teaching assistants/fellows are employed by Thiel College. The student-faculty ratio is 15:1.

Student Government

Students have many options for involvement and governance at Thiel. Elections are held each spring to elect a collegewide Student Government Association. In addition, each class elects its own officers. The Student Government Association works with the administration on matters of concern and supervises the various clubs, organizations, and student activities at the College. The Greeks are served as well by Panhellenic and intrafraternity advisory boards.

Admission Requirements

Thiel College seeks students who are interested in taking an active part in their education. The College is committed to diversity and, as part of its world view, encourages international applicants and transfer students to complete degree studies at Thiel.

Applicants to Thiel directly from high school are expected to have completed or be nearing completion of a college-prep curriculum that is strong in English, social sciences, mathematics, natural and laboratory sciences, a second language, and academic electives. Applicants should have a minimum of 16 academic units. Average SAT I scores are 950; average ACT scores are 21. Most applicants have earned a B average (on a 4.0 scale) and are in the top two fifths of their high school class. The Admissions Committee considers special talents and encourages students to submit an essay as well as letters of recommendation. Interviews prior to application are highly recommended.

Application and Information

Thiel begins to consider applicants in September each year for the following fall. Decisions are made on a rolling basis, and applicants are notified within ten days of the completion of an application packet. Applications should be received no later than August 1 for the fall term and December 1 for the spring term.

For inquiries and requests for information, students should contact:

Thiel College Admissions Office
75 College Avenue
Greenville, Pennsylvania 16125
Telephone: 724-589-2345
800-248-4435 (toll-free)
Fax: 724-589-2013
E-mail: admissio@thiel.edu
World Wide Web: http://www.thiel.edu

THOMAS EDISON STATE COLLEGE

TRENTON, NEW JERSEY

The College

Thomas Edison State College specializes in providing flexible, high-quality educational opportunities for adults. Identified by *Forbes* magazine as one of the top twenty colleges and universities in the nation in the use of technology to create learning opportunities for adults, Thomas Edison State College provides high-quality higher education to adults wherever they live and work. Founded in 1972, Thomas Edison State College enables adults to complete associate, baccalaureate, and master's degrees through distance learning and the assessment of knowledge they already have.

The College's convenient programs are designed to help students pursue their educational goals while attending to the challenges and priorities of adult life. Accredited by the Commission on Higher Education of the Middle States Association of Colleges and Schools, Thomas Edison State College offers a distinguished academic program for the self-motivated adult learner. The College has more than 21,480 alumni worldwide.

Academic advisement is provided to enrolled students by the College's Advisement Center, which assists students in integrating their learning style, background, and educational goals with the credit-earning methods and programs available. Students may access advisement through telephone and in-person appointments through the Advisement Phone Center, and they have 24-hour-a-day access through fax and e-mail.

In addition to the undergraduate programs described below, the College offers three online master's programs. The Master of Science in Human Resources Management (M.S.H.R.M.) degree serves human resources professionals who wish to become strategic partners in their organizations. This online program uses a cohort model and is designed to position human resources professionals as leaders within their organizations. The 36-semester hour program provides practitioners with technical human resources skills in staffing, providing professional development, managing organizational culture, and measuring and rewarding performance. The Master of Science in Management (M.S.M.) degree serves employed adults who have had professional experience in the management field. The M.S.M. program, which has two brief residency requirements, integrates the theory and practice of management as it applies to diverse organizations, educational institutions, and nonprofit agencies. The emphasis is on theory and practice in the management of organizations. The Master of Arts in Professional Studies (M.A.P.S.) degree enables students to study and apply the liberal arts to their professional lives. The M.A.P.S. program serves practitioners interested in broadening and deepening their professional skills, knowledge, and competencies through an intensive exposure to the liberal arts. The focus is on a deeper appreciation of the value and relevance of the arts, sciences, and humanities to the practical concerns of the workplace. These degrees are designed to have broad appeal for those not served by conventional programs.

Location

Thomas Edison State College is located in Trenton, New Jersey.

Majors and Degrees

Thomas Edison State College offers fourteen associate, baccalaureate, and master's degree programs in more than 100 areas of study. Undergraduate degrees offered include Associate in Applied Science, Associate in Science in Management, Associate in Science in Applied Science and Technology, Associate in Arts, Associate in Science in Natural Sciences and Mathematics, Associate in Science in Public and Social Services, Bachelor of Arts, Bachelor of Science in Applied Science and Technology, Bachelor of Science in Business Administration, Bachelor of Science in Health Sciences [a joint-degree program with the University of Medicine and Dentistry of New Jersey (UMDNJ) School of Health Related Professions (SHRP)], Bachelor of Science in Human Services, and Bachelor of Science in Nursing. The College's Undergraduate Prospectus contains a list of the more than 100 areas of study available within these degrees. To obtain the Undergraduate Prospectus, students should contact the College at its toll-free number or by e-mail (both listed below).

Academic Program

At Thomas Edison State College, students have the opportunity to earn degrees through traditional and nontraditional methods. These methods take into consideration personal needs and interests while ensuring both breadth and depth of knowledge within the degree program. Thomas Edison State College offers one of the most highly regarded, comprehensive distance learning programs in the United States. Students at Thomas Edison State College may use several convenient methods of meeting degree requirements, depending upon their individual learning styles and preferences. Thomas Edison State College courses, examinations, prior learning assessment, corporate or military education, and credits earned at other accredited colleges may be combined in a number of ways to earn credits toward an undergraduate degree.

Each undergraduate degree requires work in general education, a major area of study, and elective subjects. Students are encouraged to familiarize themselves with the requirements of their chosen degree and work in conjunction with one of the College's knowledgeable program advisers to develop a program plan that best meets their individual needs, goals, and interests.

Thomas Edison State College's Military Degree Completion Program (MDCP) serves military personnel worldwide. The MDCP was developed to accommodate the special needs of military personnel whose location, relocation, and time constraints make traditional college attendance difficult, if not impossible. The program allows students to engage in a degree program wherever they may be stationed. The program allows maximum credit for military training and education. As a result of its long-standing commitment of providing access to educational options for military personnel, Thomas Edison State College has been chosen as a partner college for the U.S. Navy's Navy College Program Distance Learning Partnership (NCPDLP) and is a participant in the U.S. Army's eArmyU program.

In addition, the College has an exceptional program designed specifically for community and county college students and graduates. The Degree Pathways Program allows community college students and graduates to complete a baccalaureate degree at home, in the workplace, or at their local two-year college.

The Degree Pathways Program lets community college students and graduates make a smooth transition directly into a Thomas Edison State College baccalaureate degree program by transferring up to 80 credits from a community or county college toward the 120 credits needed for a baccalaureate degree. The program was developed to help students make a seamless transition by providing coordinated support in admissions, academic programming, advisement, registration, and the sharing of technologies.

Students who have earned an associate degree within the past five years or are six months from completing an associate degree are eligible for the Degree Pathways Program. Students may continue to take classes and use technologies available at their community or county college as they move closer to the 80-credit limit of the 120 credits required for a baccalaureate degree.

In addition, students are able to take distance learning courses through Thomas Edison State College, and they may earn credit for what they already know through testing, prior learning assessment, and other methods of earning credit available through the College.

Thomas Edison State College also provides services for individuals not seeking a degree. These are credit-earning options for non-degree-seeking students, credit banking, and credit for licenses and certificate.

Credit-earning options for non-degree-seeking students benefit individuals who would like to earn credits through examinations, prior learning assessment, guided study, and online courses. They may do so by paying the appropriate fee for these programs. An application to Thomas Edison State College is not required to take advantage of these credit-earning options.

Credit Banking is for students who wish to document college-level learning gained through military experience, professional licenses, college proficiency examinations, college-level corporate training programs, or American Council on Education (ACE) recommendations. Thomas Edison State College offers a Credit Banking service for individuals who wish to consolidate college-level work into a Thomas Edison State College transcript. Credits transcripted under the Credit Banking program may or may not apply to a degree program at Thomas Edison State College.

Thomas Edison State College grants credit for current professional licenses or certificates that have been approved for credit by ACE and the College's Academic Council. Students who have earned one of the licenses or certificates approved for credit must submit notarized copies of the license or certificate and a current renewal card, if appropriate, to receive credit. A list of licenses and certificates approved for credit may be found in the College's Undergraduate Prospectus.

Academic Facilities

Distance education courses are provided through several venues, including guided study at home or work and online courses. Interactive television classrooms with satellite downlinks and cable access are also utilized. The College's distance learning program is administered through its Center for Distance & Independent Adult Learning (DIAL).

Costs

Tuition is payment for all costs directly associated with the academic delivery of a Thomas Edison State College education to registered students. Fees are designated as payment for administrative services associated with other activities in support of that educational process and for materials used by students for courses and other activities undertaken by them. Thomas Edison State College offers one annual tuition plan, the Comprehensive Tuition Plan, for students who want access to all components of the tuition package. Students who determine that they require only components of the Comprehensive Tuition Plan are offered the Enrolled Options Plan. A complete listing of tuition and fees is included in the College's information packet, which may be obtained by calling the toll-free number or visiting the College Web site, both listed below.

Financial Aid

Thomas Edison State College participates in a number of federal and state aid programs. Eligible students may receive Federal Pell Grants or federal education loans, such as the Federal Stafford Loan (subsidized and unsubsidized), for courses offered by the College. Eligible New Jersey residents may also tap a variety of state grant and loan programs. Students may use state aid to meet all or part of their College costs, provided they are taking at least 12 credits per semester. Students interested in using financial assistance, including student loans, should file an application as well as the Free Application for Federal Student Aid (FAFSA) and submit all required documentation at least two months prior to the start of the first semester for which they plan to enroll at the College. Once a student's financial aid file is complete, a letter is sent to the student indicating what aid has been awarded.

Detailed information about the financial aid process may be found in the financial aid packet, which is available from the Office of Financial Aid & Veterans' Affairs. To receive this information, students should call the toll-free number listed below or e-mail finaid@tesc.edu.

Faculty

There are more than 300 mentors at Thomas Edison State College. Drawn from other highly regarded colleges and universities, mentors provide many services to Thomas Edison State College, including assessment of knowledge adults already have, advisement, and other special assignments.

Admission Requirements

Adults seeking an associate, baccalaureate, or master's degree who are high school graduates and at least 21 years of age are eligible to become Thomas Edison State College students. Because Thomas Edison State College delivers high-quality education directly to students wherever they live or work, students may complete degree requirements at their convenience. There are two brief residency requirements for the Master of Science in Management degree. A computer is required to complete graduate degrees and to take online courses. Once a student is enrolled in a specific degree program, an evaluator determines the number of credits the student has already earned and fits those into the degree program requirements.

Application and Information

Students may apply to Thomas Edison State College any day of the year by mail or fax or through the College Web site. The Office of Admissions assists potential applicants in determining whether Thomas Edison State College suits their particular academic goals. For more information, students should contact:

Director of Admissions
Thomas Edison State College
101 West State Street
Trenton, New Jersey 08608-1176
Telephone: 888-442-8372 (toll-free)
Fax: 609-984-8447
E-mail: info@tesc.edu
World Wide Web: http://www.tesc.edu

THOMAS JEFFERSON UNIVERSITY
Jefferson College of Health Professions

PHILADELPHIA, PENNSYLVANIA

The University and The College

Thomas Jefferson University is one of the oldest and largest academic health centers in the United States. The University is made up of Jefferson Medical College, one of the largest private medical schools in the country; Jefferson College of Graduate Studies, for advanced study in the basic medical sciences; and Jefferson College of Health Professions (JCHP). The University shares its campus with Thomas Jefferson University Hospital, one of the nation's premier health-care facilities, and is a member of Jefferson Health System, a regional, integrated health-care delivery system. Jefferson College of Health Professions provides innovative academic programs for a highly qualified, culturally diverse student population. An integral component of the College is the generation of new health-care knowledge through scholarship and applied, collaborative, and interdisciplinary research.

The student body is heterogeneous, with the majority of students coming from the Middle Atlantic states. Twenty-five percent are members of minority groups. The current undergraduate enrollment in the College of Health Professions is 770 (147 men and 623 women). Student activities include lectures, musical programs, social activities, and intramural sports. Professional counseling services are available for all students who need assistance in resolving academic, vocational, and personal concerns.

Dormitory space is available in the James R. Martin Residence Hall. Additional on-campus housing is available in Orlowitz Residence Hall, a modern twenty-story apartment building; Barringer Hall, a ten-story apartment building; and the newly renovated Victory Building. Information about other housing facilities in the community may be obtained from the Housing Office. Food services are available on campus.

Master's degrees are offered in nursing (M.S.N.), occupational therapy (combined B.S./M.S.), and bioscience technologies (M.S.B.T.). A doctoral degree (D.P.T.) in physical therapy is also offered.

Location

The University is located in downtown Philadelphia, within walking distance of many places of cultural interest, including theaters, museums, art galleries, and historic sites. Many intercollegiate and professional athletic events take place nearby. Convenient bus, rail, and subway lines offer transportation to a variety of interesting attractions. The nearby New Jersey shore and Pennsylvania mountains offer year-round recreational opportunities, and New York City and Washington, D.C., are just a few hours away.

Majors and Degrees

Jefferson College of Health Professions is an upper-division college (junior and senior years only) that provides undergraduate education in the health-related professions. Approximately two years of college credit are required for admission; students enter in their junior or senior year. Baccalaureate degree programs are offered in biotechnology, cytotechnology, diagnostic imaging (radiography/ultrasound/computed tomography/magnetic resonance imaging, nuclear medicine technology, cardiovascular technology, cardiac sonography, computer tomography, general sonography, invasive cardiovascular technology, magnetic resonance and imaging, nuclear medicine, radiography, and vascular technology), medical technology, nursing, and occupational therapy. The College offers a three-year combined Bachelor of Science and Master of Science degree program in occupational therapy, also beginning in the junior year. The Doctor of Physical Therapy program is a three-year program for students with a bachelor's degree and appropriate prerequisites.

Advanced placement programs are available in computed tomography, diagnostic medical sonography, magnetic resonance imaging, nuclear medicine technology, and nursing for credentialed professionals in these areas who wish to pursue the Bachelor of Science degree in their field. Postbaccalaureate certificate programs are available in biotechnology, cytotechnology, and medical technology.

In addition, the College houses the Department of General Studies, which offers general courses in arts, humanities, and sciences as well as associate degrees and certificate programs. Associate degrees are available in emergency medical services, business, and medical practice management. Bachelor's degrees are offered in health services management and health services management information systems.

Academic Programs

The biotechnology/molecular sciences program is designed to educate students for health-care-related laboratory careers in the development of products using biologic and engineering principles. Through a combination of classroom and laboratory experience, students are prepared to work with DNA, molecular modeling, and related areas.

In the cytotechnology/cell sciences program, students learn the specific microscopy skills necessary to study slides for evidence of normality or disease. The interpretation of microscopic findings, as well as of clinical information, is facilitated by study of normal body functions and disease processes. Electron microscopy, cytogenetics, and the preparation and study of tissues add to the student's educational background with possibilities for further study, research, or teaching.

The medical technology/clinical laboratory sciences curriculum provides a thorough background in the physical and biological sciences, culminating in the application of research, theory, and principles to the performance of clinical laboratory procedures. Intensified theoretical science preparation in automation and computer technology is provided in the junior year. The senior year prepares the student for a high level of proficiency in the clinical laboratory, with emphasis on laboratory technique, professional practice, quality control, and administrative functions. The curriculum provides a firm foundation for teaching, supervisory functions, or graduate study.

The program in diagnostic imaging prepares students to function competently in the expanding and multifaceted role of diagnostic imager, thereby meeting the challenges of the present and the future in health care and society. Recent trends and advances in the delivery of health care indicate that the diagnostic imaging curriculum must provide the student with expanded opportunities to develop skills in more than one imaging modality. Of equal importance is the need for the graduate to understand the relationships of each of the imaging specialties to the overall pattern of patient care. Graduates of the Multicompetency Program and the Advanced Placement Program are eligible to take the examinations of the American Registry of Radiologic Technologists and American Registry of Diagnostic Medical Sonographers. Students who pass these examinations receive national certification.

The baccalaureate nursing program prepares men and women to become effective professional nurses with the background necessary to be responsible, self-directed practitioners of nursing. This educational program is designed to provide students with the knowledge and clinical skills necessary to plan, implement, and evaluate nursing care for individuals, families, and communities. Emphasis is placed on health promotion, prevention and control of disease and disability, and rehabilitation. Both part-time and full-time programs are available.

The program in occupational therapy provides students with an understanding of the development of human occupation and the application of purposeful activity to facilitate a client's achievement of good health. Emphasis is placed on a bio-psycho-social approach to health care that concentrates on an individual's ability to perform daily-living activities, including self-care, work, and leisure. Course work is supplemented by six to nine months of supervised fieldwork. The program gives students the foundation necessary to successfully complete the national certification examination after graduation and to develop skills in the areas of clinical practice, teaching, administration, or research.

The physical therapy program emphasizes course work in the physical and biological sciences and physical therapy theory and practice. The curriculum integrates lecture and laboratory classwork related to clinical skills with carefully supervised clinical practice. The program prepares graduates to meet the challenging responsibilities of diagnostic evaluation, treatment implementation, and ongoing assessment. It also provides a firm foundation in the areas of administration, research, consultation, planning, and education, as well as in clinical practice.

Academic Facilities

The Edison Building houses various Jefferson College of Health Professions administrative and departmental offices, classrooms, laboratories, and a Learning Resource Center, which includes a computer laboratory. Jefferson Alumni Hall, a basic medical science/student commons building, houses Jefferson College of Graduate Studies, basic science departments, classrooms, and research laboratories. The Scott Building houses University administrative offices and the University library. Clinical experience is acquired at Thomas Jefferson University Hospital or at more than 1,500 clinical affiliate sites.

Costs

Tuition for 2003–04 was $19,824 for full-time undergraduate students. Full-time graduate tuition was $21,866. Housing costs ranged from $762 to $1664 per month for one-, two-, and three-bedroom accommodations. Meal plans are not offered. Fees for advanced-placement/postcertificate programs vary, depending on the type of credits completed.

Financial Aid

Aid includes Federal Pell Grants, Federal Perkins Loans, Federal Work-Study Program awards, Air Force ROTC scholarships, Nursing Scholarships, Nursing Loans, state grants or scholarships, and state-guaranteed loans. About 76 percent of the current students receive financial assistance. To apply for aid, students must submit the Free Application for Federal Student Aid (FAFSA) as well as a Thomas Jefferson University application. Completed applications must be received by the Financial Aid Office not later than May 1.

JCHP also offers graduate research assistantship programs in physical therapy, occupational therapy, and bioscience technologies to qualified graduate students who have demonstrated financial need. Students must qualify through the Office of Financial Aid to be eligible for the award. Students should apply by August 1 (spring term) or May 1 (fall term) for consideration.

Faculty

Jefferson College of Health Professions has 50 full-time and more than 100 part-time faculty members; most of the part-time faculty members serve in clinical teaching positions. The student-faculty ratio for the entire college is 11:1.

Student Government

Students are free to express their views on issues of institutional policy and on matters of student interest. Active membership on faculty and administrative committees enables students to participate in the formulation and application of University and College policy.

Admission Requirements

Admission for high school students is available through the Plan A College Education (PACE) Program based on a student's academic record, scores on the SAT, recommendations, an interview, extracurricular activities, and possible work experience. Students admitted through PACE attend another college for at least two years to complete prerequisite courses. Approximately two years of college-level course work (39–59 semester credits, depending on the program) are required for transfer admission. For a list of specific prerequisite courses and application deadlines for each program, prospective students should contact the Office of Admissions.

Jefferson College of Health Professions offers an equal opportunity for admission to all candidates who meet the admission requirements, without regard to race, color, national and ethnic origin, age, religion, sex, sexual orientation, disability, or veteran status.

Interviews are recommended after all credentials have been received. The nonrefundable application fee is $45.

Application and Information

Admission and financial aid application forms and further information can be obtained by contacting:

Director of Admissions
Jefferson College of Health Professions
Thomas Jefferson University
Edison Building, Suite 1610
130 South 9th Street
Philadelphia, Pennsylvania 19107-5233
Telephone: 215-503-8890
800-JEFF-CHP (toll-free)
World Wide Web: http://www.jefferson.edu/jchp

Thomas Jefferson University is located within walking distance of many places of cultural interest.

THOMAS MORE COLLEGE

CRESTVIEW HILLS, KENTUCKY

The College

Thomas More College is a small, private, Catholic liberal arts college affiliated with the Diocese of Covington, Kentucky. The College was ranked in the top tier of Southern liberal arts colleges by *U.S. News & World Report* in their 2003 "America's Best Colleges" issue. Thomas More College fulfills its liberal arts commitment by maintaining an atmosphere and curriculum that give students the opportunity to grow academically, spiritually, and professionally.

Of the diverse student population of 1,446, there are 776 attending classes full-time; 240 are resident students. A new residence hall opened in fall 2002, adding 160 spaces to the College's expanding student life program. The student body is drawn primarily from the states of Kentucky, Ohio, and Indiana, but many other states and a number of countries are also represented. Students who choose to live on campus reside in one of three town-house-style residence halls. All residence halls offer comfortable, air-conditioned rooms; Internet and cable TV access; and free laundry facilities. The new 27,000-square-foot Holbrook Student Center contains a spacious bookstore, computer and study lounges, student activity offices, a TV and game room, food court, and dance rehearsal studio.

The students' college experience is enhanced through their participation in many academic, social, and sports organizations. Intercollegiate athletics are governed by NCAA Division III. Thomas More College competes in men's baseball, basketball, football, golf, soccer, and tennis and women's basketball, fast-pitch softball, soccer, tennis, and volleyball. Intramural sports offered include, among others, coed flag football, basketball, and volleyball. The campus contains a new on-campus football stadium; baseball, soccer, and softball fields; and volleyball and basketball courts as well as training and health facilities. Students can also enjoy world-class facilities for swimming, tennis, racquetball, and basketball and a complete fitness area at the Four Seasons Sports Club, adjacent to the campus.

Location

Thomas More College is located 10 minutes south of Cincinnati, Ohio, in Crestview Hills, Kentucky. The campus is convenient to major highways. The Greater Cincinnati/Northern Kentucky International Airport is just 10 minutes away. All students are permitted to have cars on campus.

The Greater Cincinnati area offers a wide array of cultural and sporting events. Local attractions include the Broadway Series, the Cincinnati Pops, the Riverbend Music Center, and the Cincinnati Reds and Bengals. Numerous shopping areas and restaurants are also available.

Majors and Degrees

Thomas More College offers bachelor's degrees in accounting, art, biology, business administration, chemistry, computer information systems, criminal justice, drama, economics, education, English, history, international studies, mathematics, medical technology, nursing, philosophy, physics, psychology, sociology, speech communication, and theology.

Preprofessional programs are available in dentistry, law, medicine, occupational therapy, optometry, pharmacy, physical therapy, and veterinary science. There is a 3-2 program in engineering.

The Associate of Arts degree is available in accounting, art, art history, biology, business administration, chemistry, computer information systems, criminal justice, drama, economics, English, exercise science, French, gerontology, history, international studies, math, philosophy, physics, political science, pre–legal studies, psychology, sociology, Spanish, speech communication, and theology.

Academic Programs

To earn the Bachelor of Arts, Bachelor of Science, or Bachelor of Science in Nursing degree, a student must complete 128 credit hours, including 61 credit hours in liberal arts courses. The Associate of Arts degree requires the completion of 64 credit hours, including a liberal arts component.

The academic calendar is composed of a fall and a spring semester and two summer sessions. The Office of Continuing Education offers a full schedule of evening and Saturday classes.

The Cooperative Education program enables students to gain hands-on professional experience in their field of interest. All students are eligible for this program after the completion of their freshman year. Cooperative Air Force and Army ROTC programs are available in conjunction with nearby universities.

Off-Campus Programs

Thirteen area colleges, including Thomas More College, form the Greater Cincinnati Consortium of Colleges and Universities through which all students at the local member colleges may take courses not available at their home institution. Thomas More encourages full-time students to take advantage of this opportunity for curriculum enrichment through cross-registration. In addition, students who wish to study abroad as part of their undergraduate education have a number of possibilities open to them.

Academic Facilities

The library has a collection of more than 130,000 volumes of books, periodicals, and audiovisual materials, and as a selective depository it houses more than 12,000 volumes of U.S. government documents. In addition, the library's membership in the Greater Cincinnati Library Consortium gives Thomas More students access to more than 10.6 million books and more than 50,000 periodicals held by forty-four other libraries in the region.

Thomas More's computer facilities include a PC classroom and three labs containing Pentium 350 PCs for student use. Student computers are also available in some academic departments and in the library. All PCs are connected to a campuswide Novell network, with access to e-mail, the Internet, and an on-campus Intranet server. There is a laser printer in each lab and a color laser printer and scanner in the PC lab in the main computer center. Software includes Microsoft Windows 98, Office 97, and Visual Studio; Adobe PageMaker and Illustrator; MicroFocus COBOL; and additional software used for departmental instruction.

Students in the science programs receive hands-on experience through the use of the advanced biology, chemistry, and physics laboratories. The facilities include an environmental chamber, an aquatic research station, research and measurement labs, a synthesis lab, a light-sensitive project room, and a machine and electronics shop.

The nursing and sociology departments have excellent working relationships with nearby hospitals and social service agencies.

Costs

The 2002–03 annual costs for Thomas More College were $14,200 for tuition and $5300 for room (double occupancy) and board. There was a differential fee of $30 per semester hour for all nursing courses. The Student Government fee was $50 per semester and the computer fee was $100 per semester for full-time students. The cost of books was estimated at $600 per year.

Financial Aid

Thomas More College assists approximately 90 percent of its full-time students in meeting college costs. Awards are determined on a rolling basis, with priority consideration given to applications filed by March 1. Financial aid awards are based on economic need, merit, scholastic achievement, and extracurricular activities. ROTC scholarships are also available. The filing of the Free Application for Federal Student Aid (FAFSA) and the Thomas More College Application for Financial Aid and Scholarship is required before any awards are determined. Other Thomas More College awards may require additional applications.

An extensive Federal Work-Study Program is in place, and there are excellent opportunities for outside employment in the immediate area.

Faculty

The faculty is committed to the ideals of a Catholic liberal arts education with the main focus on teaching. The faculty has 174 members, of whom 30 percent hold tenure and 62 percent hold doctoral or other terminal degrees. Faculty members serve as academic advisers to students in their disciplines. The student-faculty ratio is 14:1.

Student Government

The purpose of the Student Government Association is to serve as the official representative organization of the Thomas More College student body; to serve as the liaison between the student body and the faculty, administration, and Board of Trustees; to promote student projects and activities and improve the quality of student life; to assist the Dean of Students in supervising student organizations and student activities on campus; to protect the rights of the individual; and to preserve the general welfare of the student body of Thomas More College.

Admission Requirements

The admission criteria are as follows: an applicant should have a high school grade point average (based on college-preparatory courses) of 80 percent or better; a high school rank in the top half of the graduating class; and a minimum composite score of 20 on the ACT Assessment, with a minimum of 20 in English, or a minimum combined score of 1010 on the SAT I, with a minimum of 530 on the verbal portion. If the applicant does not meet all the admission criteria, the file is forwarded to the Admissions Committee for individual consideration.

Transfer students with 24 or more semester hours of transferable credit and an overall grade point average of at least 2.0 on a 4.0 scale are automatically accepted. Transfer students with fewer than 24 transferable hours must meet the general admission criteria.

The applicant must provide a completed application with a nonrefundable $25 fee (waived for online applicants), high school transcripts, college transcripts (if applicable), and ACT or SAT I score reports.

Application and Information

Thomas More College operates under a rolling admission policy, with a final application deadline of August 15. Admission decisions are usually made within two weeks of receiving all application materials. Students can apply online at the Web site listed below. The $25 application fee is waived for online applications.

For further information or to schedule a campus visit, students should contact:

Bob McDermott
Director of Admissions
Thomas More College
333 Thomas More Parkway
Crestview Hills, Kentucky 41017
Telephone: 859-344-3332
800-825-4557 (toll-free)
E-mail: bob.mcdermott@thomasmore.edu
World Wide Web: http://www.thomasmore.edu

Residence life on the Thomas More College campus.

TIFFIN UNIVERSITY

TIFFIN, OHIO

The University

Tiffin University, established in 1888, is an independent, coeducational institution with no religious affiliation. The University is accredited by the Commission on Institutions of Higher Education of the North Central Association of Colleges and Schools.

The programs of emphasis at Tiffin University are accounting, forensic psychology, management, law enforcement, psychology, and communication, which draw students from all over Ohio, eighteen states, and twenty countries.

Tiffin University also grants the Master of Business Administration and Master of Criminal Justice degrees.

Tiffin University provides a variety of living arrangements for students interested in on-campus housing. These students enjoy both the traditional residence-hall environment as well as small-group living on Tiffin's 103-acre campus. Living options include coed and single-sex residence halls and fraternity and sorority houses. All of the units are in proximity to the academic buildings, recreational and laundry facilities, and the dining hall. Students residing in University housing are required to participate in the University board plan, which offers three options in dining.

There are two sororities and two fraternities on campus. The Delta Beta Chapters of the Alpha Iota sorority and the Phi Theta Pi fraternity are international groups concerned with commerce and business. The Sigma Delta Sigma sorority and Sigma Omega Sigma fraternity sponsor a variety of events for the University community. There are also two honor societies on campus. Other student organizations include the student government, the World Student Association, the Black United Students, the Intervarsity Christian Fellowship Club, the school newspaper, and departmental clubs.

Tiffin University is a member of the NCAA, the NAIA, and the American Mid-Eastern Conference. The University offers intercollegiate athletics for men in baseball, basketball, cross-country, football, golf, soccer, tennis, and track and field. Women's varsity athletics include basketball, cross-country, golf, soccer, softball, tennis, track and field, and volleyball. The University also sponsors coed intramural sports events and club sports such as bowling, lacrosse, rugby, men's volleyball, and x-treme outdoors. The Gillmor Student Center houses a basketball gymnasium, an activities room, offices, and a bookstore. Student services include career and placement counseling, academic tutoring, and personal counseling. Construction was completed on a 78-acre multifield athletic complex.

Location

Tiffin University is located on Ohio Route 53 in Tiffin, which is 50 miles south of Toledo, 90 miles southwest of Cleveland, and 90 miles north of Columbus. The city of Tiffin, with a population of approximately 22,000, is the center of an area rich in college tradition. Within a 70-mile radius are located fourteen private colleges and universities, two state universities and several two-year branch campuses, and community colleges. Tiffin is located on the green banks of the Sandusky River in north-central Ohio, and offers residents and visitors a variety of fine restaurants, shopping, a museum, historic sites, and numerous recreational opportunities. Tiffin is the home of the historic Ritz Theatre, which offers a wide selection of cultural events throughout the year.

Majors and Degrees

Tiffin University grants the Bachelor of Arts degree, the Bachelor of Business Administration degree, the Bachelor of Criminal Justice degree, the Associate of Business Administration degree, and the Associate of Science in Business Technology degree.

The Bachelor of Arts degree is granted in communications, English, human services, international security studies, law and society, and psychology.

Majors in the business administration program are accounting, finance, information technology, management (arts, hospitality and tourism, information systems, human resource management, international business, managerial studies, operations management, and sports management), and marketing.

The Bachelor of Criminal Justice degree is granted in corrections, forensic psychology, and law enforcement.

The Associate of Business Administration degree is granted in accounting, business administration, computer programming, and hospitality management.

The Associate of Criminal Justice degree is granted in law enforcement.

Academic Program

Tiffin University operates on a semester system. Students must complete at least 130 semester hours with a minimum grade point average of 2.5 in their major and 2.0 overall to earn a bachelor's degree. Students work with academic advisers to organize a schedule that meets the requirements of the University.

Along with their regular course work, students must also participate in Tiffin University's cocurricular program. This program provides students with the opportunity to develop an interest in such areas as health and personal fitness, recreation, the arts, and community service. Students are required to participate in 26 clock hours (2 units) of cocurricular activity to graduate.

Off-Campus Programs

Tiffin University has established a junior-year study-abroad semester in cooperation with Webster College. The courses are taught at one of four European campuses located in London, England; Leiden, the Netherlands; Geneva, Switzerland; and Vienna, Austria. All locations draw upon the academic traditions and resources of both the resident campus and the United States. The university-level courses are taught in English by an international faculty. All courses are accredited in the U.S.

Tiffin University's agreement with Webster College permits students to study overseas and receive academic credit for all course work completed. The credit is transferred directly to the student's file at Tiffin University.

Academic Facilities

Tiffin University's campus is small, and the academic buildings are within a short walking distance of the residence halls.

The focal point of the Tiffin campus is the classroom building, which was built in 1884 and is now listed on the National Register of Historic Places. The classroom building houses classrooms, faculty and administrative offices, a computer center, and graduate offices. The computer center has sixty IBM-compatible PCs available for student use.

The Richard C. Pfeiffer Library has 255 subscriptions to magazines and newspapers, 27,500 books, 32,000 microfiche units, and several other computers for online searching. The library is a member of OhioLink and Online Computer Library Center (OCLC). The Pfeiffer Library also has classrooms in the lower level. Construction of a classroom building and residence hall was completed in fall 1994, and a library expansion was completed in early 1996, doubling the size of the facility.

Costs

For 2003–04, tuition was approximately $13,590, and average room and board charges were $5900, for a total of $19,490. Books and supplies are approximately $1000. Travel costs vary.

Financial Aid

Ninety percent of all students at Tiffin University receive some type of financial aid. The average award is $9770. Aid is available in the form of scholarships, grants and loans given by the University, and state and federal loans. A complete Free Application for Federal Student Aid (FAFSA) is required for financial aid consideration. Some scholarships and grants require special applications, tests, or recommendations from counselors, teachers, and coaches. Additional information can be obtained from the Financial Aid Office.

Faculty

The Tiffin University faculty is composed of 81 dedicated individuals serving in either a full-time or adjunct capacity. Of the full-time faculty, 83 percent hold doctorates or the highest certification in their field. Many faculty members are involved in the business community in either a research or consulting capacity. Members of the faculty also serve as officers in regional and national academic organizations. Faculty members are accessible to students and show genuine interest in their academic and personal concerns.

Student Government

Tiffin University's student government is one of the most active organizations on campus. It is responsible for planning, organizing, and executing social, cultural, and educational programs and activities. With representatives from all facets of the student body, along with 5 officers, the group serves as a voice for student concerns and needs. The student government fosters a sense of community among faculty, administrators, and students. In addition, the group offers students the opportunity to obtain and utilize valuable leadership skills necessary for today's business world.

Admission Requirements

Individuals wishing to further their education are invited to apply to Tiffin. Admission policies are moderately selective, applicants must be graduates of secondary schools with a 2.5 grade point average, must report a minimum score on the ACT or SAT, and must meet specific entrance requirements. Applications may be submitted anytime after students complete their junior year in high school. It is recommended that a student's high school transcript show credit for at least the following: 4 units of English, 3 units of mathematics, 2 units of science, and 2 units of social studies, as well as 3 units of electives from academic or commercial subjects and 2 other units of electives.

Applicants are considered for admission according to their potential to benefit from instruction at Tiffin University. Students with less than a 2.5 grade point average college preparatory classes may be admitted through the Learning Assistance Program.

Application and Information

Students must submit a completed application to Tiffin University's admission office. In addition to the application, they should supply ACT or SAT scores, an official transcript of grades, and a $20 application fee. The application fee will be waived for students who apply online at http://www.tiffin.edu.

For further information, students should contact:

Office of Admission
Tiffin University
155 Miami Street
Tiffin, Ohio 44883
Telephone: 419-447-6443
800-968-OHIO (toll-free)
Fax: 419-443-5006
E-mail: admiss@tiffin.edu
World Wide Web: http://www.tiffin.edu

Franks Hall.

TOCCOA FALLS COLLEGE

TOCCOA FALLS, GEORGIA

The College

Toccoa Falls College (TFC) provides both the strengths of a Bible college and the strengths of a Christian liberal arts college offered in a nourishing evangelical Christian environment. TFC was founded in 1907 and moved to its current main campus location in 1911 for the uneducated young people of the South who had no access to a Christian education to prepare them for Christian service. Despite seemingly impossible obstacles, God has led and sustained the College through severe testing—including fire and flood. Throughout its history, the College has consistently transmitted to its students, along with their other studies, a practical knowledge of the Word of God. TFC is now a four-year, independent, interdenominational Christian college affiliated with the Christian and Missionary Alliance. TFC offers a wide array of four-year ministry-related, liberal arts, and professional majors at its main campus in Toccoa Falls, Georgia. TFC also offers a two-year Associate of Arts (A.A.) program at both its main campus and at its branch campus in Epworth, Georgia.

TFC remains committed to the challenge of preparing men and women to proclaim the gospel of Jesus Christ around the world. Along with their studies, students attend chapel four days per week, participate in student ministry assignments, and enjoy other spiritual formation opportunities as part of the extracurricular program.

TFC is committed to maintaining the highest standards of Christian scholarship. The College is accredited to award associate and bachelor's degrees by the Commission on Colleges of the Southern Association of Colleges and Schools (1866 Southern Lane, Decatur, Georgia 30033-4097; 404-679-4501) and by the Accrediting Association of Bible Colleges (5575 South Semoran Boulevard, Suite 26, Orlando, Florida 32822-1781; 407-207-0808). TFC holds teacher education approval by the Professional Standards Commission of the state of Georgia (1452 Twin Towers East, Atlanta, Georgia 30334; 404-657-9000) and membership in the National Association of Schools of Music (11250 Roger Bacon Drive, Suite 21, Reston, Virginia 22090; 703-437-0700).

Toccoa Falls College enrolls about 850 students each year who are serious about impacting the world with the love and message of Jesus Christ. The majority of the student body consists of traditional residential students. Students at the College come from thirty-eight states and twelve countries and represent twenty-eight evangelical denominations. On-campus housing is required for single students through their junior year. TFC does not offer mixed-gender housing options. Single-gender housing options include residence halls, cottages, mobile housing, and apartments. Married students (13 percent of the TFC student population) can rent apartments from TFC or in the community. Forty percent of the student body lives off campus. Campus dining facilities include a cafeteria, a casual restaurant, a coffee shop, and a formal restaurant. A virtual tour of the campus is available on the College Web site.

Information about student activities can also be found online. Each weekend, the social calendar has something enjoyable to offer, including formal and informal dinners, social events, musical performances, and athletic events. Varsity sports include men's baseball, basketball, and soccer, and women's basketball, soccer, and volleyball. Intramural sports offer TFC students and staff the chance to enjoy additional sports, such as coed soccer, volleyball, flag football, Ultimate Frisbee, men's and women's basketball, indoor soccer, and softball.

Location

The Toccoa Falls College campus is located on a 1,000-acre tract holding natural forest, mountain streams, and a breathtaking 186-foot waterfall. The thirty-six major campus buildings currently utilize only about 100 acres, leaving the other 900 acres for outdoor recreation and future development.

In northeast Georgia, students have immediate access to lakes, rivers, caving, hiking, fishing, waterskiing, boating, river rafting, rappelling, golf, and camping. The city of Toccoa offers a variety of choices for dining, entertainment, and employment for TFC students. The cities of Athens and Gainesville, Georgia, and Seneca, South Carolina, are within an hour's drive of the campus. The Atlanta metropolitan area is 90 miles from TFC, and the Atlanta airport is about 104 miles away. Atlanta offers a full range of cultural opportunities, including entertainment of all kinds, restaurants, parks, professional athletics (Atlanta Braves, Atlanta Falcons, Atlanta Hawks, and Atlanta Thrashers), shopping, and various other historic charms of the state capital. Students at Toccoa Falls College enjoy big-city advantages and small-town hospitality.

Majors and Degrees

Toccoa Falls College offers students the Bachelor of Science and Bachelor of Arts degrees in the following majors: biblical studies, broadcasting–radio, broadcasting–TV, business administration–management, Christian education, church music, counseling psychology, cross-cultural studies, early childhood education, English, family ministries, interpersonal communication, middle grades education, music education, music performance, pastoral ministries, philosophy and religion, secondary education (English), secondary education (history), and youth ministries. Toccoa Falls College offers an Associate of Arts degree in general studies.

Academic Programs

Toccoa Falls College operates under a semester calendar with two summer sessions. A minimum of 126 credit hours is required for the bachelor's degree. Core courses in humanities, social sciences, computers/mathematics, and general education are required as well as 42 major-specific credit hours. Students are encouraged to take advantage of CLEP tests and AP courses. Toccoa Falls College recognizes that complete academic preparation for the Christian comes through advanced knowledge of a specific field of study and the integration of faith in learning. Every major includes a minimum of 30 hours of Bible credit to provide a biblical understanding and stimulate spiritual growth along with academic and professional development. Also required is the satisfactory completion of four semesters of student ministry, which gives students the opportunity for a practical ministry outlet.

Academic Facilities

Academic life centers around the Seby Jones Library, which currently houses a total of more than 139,790 holdings, including books, bound volumes, scores, vertical files, audiovisuals, and microfiche, with 300 periodical subscriptions in print and thousands of full-text journals available online. The Seby Jones Library also contains a full-service media center and curriculum labs for the School of Teacher Education. Other resources include the Interlibrary Loan Service, GALILEO (Georgia's statewide resource-sharing project), and direct access to the Internet. Other academic facilities include the computer lab, the Clary Science Building (including chemistry and biology labs), McCarthy Hall (home of the School of Teacher Education), the Woerner World Missions Building, and the White Memorial Photo Lab, complete with photo labs and curriculum labs for the School of Christian Education. The Grace Chapel and Performing Arts Center is used for artists' series and concerts, while also providing classroom space and practice rooms for the School of Music.

Costs

Tuition for 2004–05 full-time students (12 or more semester hours) is $11,450. Students are charged $4450 for room, meals, and health fees. A one-time matriculation fee of $450 is charged to the student upon initial enrollment. Students should estimate $800 per year for books.

Financial Aid

Toccoa Falls College seeks to assist every qualified student who demonstrates financial need with one or more of the following types of aid: grants, loans, scholarships, work-study programs, and on- or off-campus employment. Funds come from federal, state, private, and school resources. Currently, 93 percent of Toccoa Falls College students receive some type of aid. All students must submit the Free Application for Federal Student Aid (FAFSA) to apply for specific programs. To receive priority consideration for maximum financial aid, students must submit all paperwork by May 1 for the fall semester and November 1 for the spring semester.

Faculty

Students at Toccoa Falls College benefit from professors who are academically qualified, experienced in their field, and take a personal interest in their students. While their main responsibility is teaching students, many faculty members are recognized nationally and publish books, write for major magazines, serve in national organizations, or are featured guest speakers and lecturers. Their primary role on campus is active involvement in the interests of the students and as faculty advisers to assist in the course selection and academic counseling needs of the students. All courses at TFC are taught by degree-holding faculty members, not student-aide teachers. Fifty percent of full-time teaching faculty members hold earned doctoral degrees or the highest degree in their field. There are 68 faculty members; 45 are full-time and 23 are part-time. The student-faculty ratio is 15:1.

Student Government

The Student Government Association (SGA) acts as the umbrella organization over all student groups at Toccoa Falls College. SGA is the legislative and governing organization of the student body and the official representative of the student body to the TFC administration. The purpose of the SGA is to serve the student body, promote unity and spiritual growth, and control the student activity budget. SGA plays a vital role in organizing social events, activities, and spiritual meetings. SGA also stimulates communication between faculty and staff members and students and represents the needs of students to various official administrative committees.

Admission Requirements

TFC encourages applications from students interested in studying in an evangelical Christian environment. In selecting students for admission, Toccoa Falls College seeks evidence of Christian commitment and character as well as the capacity and desire to learn. The Office of Admissions considers applications for admission after the applicant file is complete. A completed admissions file includes a completed and signed application, a $20 nonrefundable application fee, an official high school or GED transcript, official transcripts from all colleges attended, an official SAT or ACT score report, a 250-word testimony, and a pastoral reference. In addition, Toccoa Falls College has the following spiritual requirements: students must have accepted the Lord Jesus Christ as Savior at least six months prior to enrollment; have evidence of good Christian character; have abstained from the use of tobacco, alcohol, and illegal drugs for at least six months prior to enrollment; have regular attendance in an evangelical church; and be in agreement with the College's doctrinal statement and policies, as printed in the current catalog and student handbook. All new freshman, transfer, international, former, joint-enrolled, transient, and audit-only students from both in and out of state are considered on an equal basis. Campus visits and personal interviews with admissions counselors are highly encouraged. Toccoa Falls College reserves the right to examine further an applicant by psychological, achievement, and aptitude tests or by personal interview. Toccoa Falls College admits qualified students without regard to race, age, creed, color, gender, physical handicap, or national or ethnic origin.

Application and Information

Qualified students are encouraged to apply as early as possible after the final semester of their junior year in high school. Toccoa Falls College makes admissions decisions on a rolling basis and notifies applicants of their admission status by e-mail, mail, and phone within one week after all materials are received.

For more information, students should contact:

Office of Admissions
Toccoa Falls College
P.O. Box 800–899
Toccoa Falls, Georgia 30598
Telephone: 706-886-6831 Ext. 5380
Fax: 706-282-6012
E-mail: admissions@tfc.edu
World Wide Web: http://www.tfc.edu

The Toccoa Falls College campus has a beautiful 186-foot waterfall.

TOWSON UNIVERSITY

TOWSON, MARYLAND

The University

Established in 1866, Towson University (TU) is a regional comprehensive university that offers degree programs in the liberal arts and sciences and preprofessional and professional areas of study. As Maryland's metropolitan university, Towson provides innovative solutions to the region's educational, economic, and societal needs through business outreach and community partnerships. The University's beautiful 328-acre campus is located in the suburban community of Towson, Maryland, just 8 miles north of downtown Baltimore. Towson is nationally recognized for its programs in business, communications, computer information systems, education, fine arts, health professions, and women's studies. The University offers sixty-four bachelor's degree programs, thirty-five master's degree programs, and four applied doctoral programs and emphasizes excellence in teaching and continued scholarly growth by faculty members.

Towson University is composed of seven colleges: the College of Business and Economics, the College of Education, the College of Fine Arts and Communication, the College of Health Professions, the College of Liberal Arts, the College of Science and Mathematics, and the College of Graduate Education and Research.

The University enrolls more than 17,000 full- and part-time students, including more than 800 international students from 100 countries. More than 14,000 TU students are undergraduates, and about 13 percent of the student body are members of minority groups. More than 3,900 students (almost 77 percent of the freshman class) live on campus at TU. There are twelve University residence halls, including modern high-rise towers, apartment complexes, and two- and three-story traditional buildings. Student life on campus offers exciting academic, social, cultural, and athletic opportunities. At Towson, there are more than 100 student clubs and campus organizations, including fraternities, sororities, and social and professional clubs. The University Union is a popular gathering place, housing the campus bookstore; the post office; dining facilities; ATM machines; a new student center with billiards, food, entertainment, music, and a cyber café; and more. Also available to students are the services of the University's health center, counseling center, academic advising center, and career center.

A Division I member of the NCAA since 1979, Towson University fields intercollegiate athletic teams in twenty-three sports. The Tigers have twelve sports for women and eleven sports for men. The Tigers compete in the Colonial Athletic Associate (CAA) in twenty-one of those sports, joining CAA rivals Delaware, Drexel, Hofstra, George Mason, James Madison, North Carolina at Wilmington, Old Dominion, Virginia Commonwealth, and the College of William and Mary. In addition, the nationally recognized Tiger gymnastics team competes in the East Atlantic Gymnastics League; the Tiger football squad plans to join the Atlantic 10 Conference in fall 2004. The University's 24-acre sports complex includes the recently dedicated Johnny Unitas Stadium, home of the Tiger football, field hockey, track, and lacrosse teams. With a seating capacity of 5,000, the Towson Center is the home of the Tiger basketball teams and the volleyball and gymnastics squads. The University's athletic facilities at Burdick Hall include three gymnasiums, a fitness center, a climbing gym, a 25-yard swimming pool, locker rooms, and playing fields. Additional sports facilities available at the Towson Center include tennis courts, playing fields, handball/squash courts, and locker rooms. Towson also offers a comprehensive intramural program for men and women.

Location

Towson University is located in Baltimore County, in the suburban community of Towson. The campus is 10 minutes from Towson Town Center, a large upscale shopping mall, and within walking distance of restaurants, bookstores, movie theaters, and the public library. The University is 20 minutes from the cultural and educational resources of downtown Baltimore, home of the National Aquarium, the Maryland Science Center, Oriole Park at Camden Yards, the Walters Art Museum, and Federal Hill. Towson is also centrally located in the mid-Atlantic region, convenient to the Atlantic beaches; the Appalachian Mountains; Washington, D.C.; Philadelphia; and New York City.

Majors and Degrees

The Bachelor of Arts or Bachelor of Science degree is offered in accounting; art; art education; athletic training; biology; business administration; chemistry; communication studies; computer information systems; computer science; cultural studies; dance performance and education; deaf studies; early childhood education; earth-space science; economics; electronic business; electronic media and film; elementary education; English; environmental science and studies; exercise science; family studies; forensic chemistry; French; geography and environmental planning; geography and land surveying; geology; German; gerontology; health-care management; health science; history; integrated elementary education–special education; interdisciplinary studies; international studies; law and American civilization; mass communication; mathematics; medicinal chemistry; metropolitan studies; molecular biology, biochemistry, and bioinformatics; music; music education; nursing; occupational therapy; philosophy; physical education; physics; political science; psychology; religious studies; secondary education certification; social science; sociology-anthropology; Spanish; special education; speech-language pathology and audiology; sport management; sport studies; theater; and women's studies. The Bachelor of Fine Arts degree is offered in dance. The Bachelor of Technical and Professional Studies is offered in chemical dependency counseling and education, allied health, and information technology.

Academic Programs

The University follows the semester system, with spring and fall semesters, an optional January minimester, three 5-week summer sessions, and one 7-week summer session.

The University's goal is to enrich lives by providing a strong liberal arts and sciences education for all students. The General Education Program (46 semester hours) is structured to develop intellectual skills that advance lifelong learning and to help students understand how the chief branches of knowledge investigate, present findings, and form conclusions about human experience and the natural world. The academic majors, whether in the arts and sciences, interdisciplinary fields, or applied and professional practices, are structured to promote liberal learning and explore the continuity and connectedness of experience as well as its factual specificity. In addition, TU takes pride in maintaining in its curriculum a high percentage of small-enrollment sections, which help promote student-centered learning, collaborative exchange, and individualized attention from the instructor. Faculty members offer extensive academic advising both to students in general education and to those enrolled within an academic major. The baccalaureate degree is earned by completing general education and major field requirements and earning a minimum of 120 semester hours of credit.

Students in the Honors College may major in any academic discipline offered by the University. To be eligible, students must first be admitted to Towson University. If they meet the requirements for the Honors College, they are invited to apply. In addition to taking Honors courses and seminars, Honors College students can pursue research, leadership, and service opportunities designed to enhance their college experience. Other benefits of membership include priority scheduling, eligibility for Honors College scholarships, honors housing, honors study-abroad programs, and Excelsior, the Honors Student Council.

Towson University offers more than 900 courses during the spring and fall semesters and the summer sessions. Students can attend full-time or part-time, and classes are offered during the day, in the evening, and on Saturday.

Off-Campus Programs

The University offers opportunities for study in more than forty countries in Central and South America, Asia, Europe, Australia, Canada, and the Middle East. More than 250 students from a variety of disciplines participate in study-abroad and exchange programs each year. TU's Internship Program offers students opportunities to earn college credit, gain work experience, and explore career choices. Each year, Towson places more than 700 students in internships around the country.

Academic Facilities

The Albert S. Cook Library, located near the center of the campus, contains more than 580,000 books, more than 2,180 periodicals, and a variety of other media, including microforms, audiocassettes, videos, and DVDs. In addition to Towson's library, the online catalog gives TU students access to the collections of all of the other University System of Maryland campus libraries. The more than 75 online databases and 400 electronic journals provide indexing to thousands of periodical articles, many of which are in a full-text format. The Center for the Arts houses the Departments of Art, Dance, Music, and Theatre Arts; a 346-seat main stage theater; a 520-seat concert hall; and two art galleries. Van Bokkelen Hall, which houses the Department of Audiology, Speech-Language Pathology, and Deaf Studies and the Department of Mass Communication and Communication Studies, contains modern communication equipment and a clinic that offers services to people with hearing and speech disorders. Smith Hall, home to the science departments, contains modern laboratory facilities and a planetarium. Historic Stephens Hall houses the College of Business and Economics and the 700-seat Stephens Hall Theatre. TU's Media Center houses the student-run television station (WMJF-TV) and the campus radio stations.

Costs

Anticipated 2004–05 tuition and fees are $3336 per semester for Maryland residents and $7676 per semester for out-of-state students. The estimated cost for room and board is approximately $3535 per semester.

Financial Aid

Approximately 66 percent of the full-time undergraduates at Towson University receive financial assistance of some kind. Assistance is available to eligible students through loans and grants from major federal and state programs, scholarships, and on- and off-campus employment. In addition, the University offers non-need scholarships based on merit or academic performance.

Faculty

Towson offers many opportunities for close student-faculty contact and promotes a supportive environment designed to meet the professional and personal goals of students. A student-faculty ratio of 17:1 and small classes, which average 25 to 35 students, allow students to interact closely with their professors.

Nearly 90 percent of the full-time faculty members have earned the highest degree of academic preparation in their fields of specialization from some of the finest colleges and universities in the world. Many of the 601 full-time instructors are recognized nationally and internationally for their published works and honors.

Student Government

The Student Government Association (SGA) officially represents all students on campus. The SGA plans, organizes, and directs student organizations and programs on campus and works with the faculty and administration in certain areas of University governance.

Admission Requirements

Towson considers applicants who have taken college-preparatory courses in high school; the Admissions Committee looks at the applicant's high school grade point average in academic courses, standardized test scores (SAT I or ACT), letters of recommendation from appropriate academic officials, and other indications of the applicant's ability to succeed at the college level. All entering freshmen must take placement exams in mathematics, reading, and writing, unless SAT I scores allow an exemption.

Priority admission is reserved for transfer students from a Maryland community college, who have earned at least 56 transferable credits, are in good academic standing, and have maintained a GPA that meets the policies set by the Maryland Higher Education Commission and University System of Maryland. Students who have earned fewer than 56 transferable credits or who are transferring from an institution other than a Maryland community college are admitted based upon combined cumulative GPA of transferable credits and space availability. Transfer applicants must have completed a minimum of 30 transferable college course work hours in which they have achieved a minimum 2.25 cumulative GPA. Transfer students who have earned a minimum of 56 transferable credits and achieved a 2.0 cumulative GPA may receive priority admission. Students wishing to transfer must provide transcripts from all previously attended colleges. Transfer students with fewer than 30 transferable credits must take assessment tests in basic skill areas before commencing study at the University. International applicants who are not native English speakers must provide an official report of Test of English as a Foreign Language (TOEFL) scores. Applicants must earn a minimum score of 500 on the paper-based TOEFL; a score of 173 is required for those taking the computer-based TOEFL. Towson is a selective undergraduate institution. Fifty-eight percent of all freshman applicants for fall 2003 were offered admission. The middle 50th percentile of students admitted scored between 560 and 600 in Verbal and 580 and 620 in Math on the SAT I. The mean high school GPA for this group was 3.66.

Application and Information

Towson admits applicants on a continuous basis (rolling admissions). Applicants seeking fall admission should submit all required application materials and academic credentials by February 15; those seeking spring admission must submit application by November 15. However, the University reserves the right to close applications when space is no longer available.

Each applicant is responsible for submitting all required materials (application forms, recommendations, test scores, and transcripts) to the Admissions Office in compliance with official deadlines. Applications that are incomplete or improperly filled out may be cancelled. A nonrefundable $35 application fee or an authorized form granting fee deferment must accompany all applications. Students may apply electronically by downloading a PDF file, by requesting an application from the Web site at the address listed below, or by contacting the Admissions Office.

Admissions Office
Towson University
8000 York Road
Towson, Maryland 21252-0001
Telephone: 410-704-2113
888-4TOWSON (toll-free)
World Wide Web: http://www.discover.towson.edu

Students relax on the Towson University campus.

TRANSYLVANIA UNIVERSITY

LEXINGTON, KENTUCKY

The University

Transylvania, a small, private liberal arts college of about 1,075 men and women, is consistently ranked among the best of its kind in the nation. The name—from the Latin that means across the woods—refers to the heavily forested Transylvania settlement in which the University was founded in 1780. Transylvania was the first college west of the Allegheny Mountains and the sixteenth in the nation. The University established the first schools of medicine and law in what was then the West and educated the doctors, lawyers, ministers, political leaders, and others who helped shape the young nation. Transylvania also founded the first college literary magazine in the West, *The Transylvanian*, still published by students today. Transylvania's link with early Lexington is symbolized by its administration building, Old Morrison, a registered National Historic Landmark and the central feature on the official seal of the city of Lexington.

After more than 220 years of academic excellence, Transylvania continues as a pioneer in higher education, preparing future leaders in business, government, education, the sciences, and the arts. Students work closely with professors in small classes, many with fewer than 10 students. The student body represents twenty-eight states and eleven countries. A high percentage of graduates attend selective medical, law, and other professional programs.

Transylvania offers more than fifty cocurricular activities, and most students participate in several of these. The Lampas Circle of the national leadership honorary society Omicron Delta Kappa recognizes students for academic excellence and campus leadership. The athletics program includes seven varsity sports for men, eight for women, and more than a dozen intramural sports. Transylvania also has four national sororities and four national fraternities.

Location

Transylvania is located in Lexington, Kentucky, a city of 242,000 and a growing center of commerce, culture, research, and education. Known as the horse capital of the world, Lexington is surrounded by the rolling green pastures of the famous Bluegrass region of central Kentucky. The area is also home to nearly 30,000 college students. Transylvania's parklike campus is just a 5-minute walk from downtown, with easy access to restaurants, shops, and entertainment. The proximity to downtown is also an advantage for students who want convenient part-time jobs and internship opportunities in law offices, accounting firms, hospitals, and other organizations. Transylvania offers its students a shuttle service between the modern Transylvania library and the University of Kentucky libraries every day, and the Lexington Public Library is a few blocks from the campus. Lexington is served by major airlines, and Louisville and Cincinnati are only 80 miles away.

Majors and Degrees

The Bachelor of Arts degree is awarded in the following majors: accounting, art, biology, business administration (specializations in finance; hotel, restaurant, and tourism administration; management; and marketing), chemistry, computer science, drama, economics, education, English, exercise science, French, history, mathematics, music, philosophy, physical education, physics, political science, psychology, religion, sociology, sociology/anthropology, and Spanish. Individually designed majors also may be arranged. Minors are available in most majors and in anthropology; classical studies; communication; European studies; German; hotel, restaurant, and tourism administration; international affairs; multicultural studies; and women's studies. Advising and undergraduate preparation are provided for dentistry, engineering, law, medicine, ministry, pharmacy, physical therapy, and veterinary medicine. A cooperative program in engineering allows students to earn a B.A. in physics or liberal studies from Transylvania in three years and a B.S. in engineering from the University of Kentucky, Vanderbilt University, or Washington University in two years. A cooperative program in accounting allows students to earn a B.A. in accounting from Transylvania in four years and an M.S. in accounting from the University of Kentucky in one year; graduates qualify to take the CPA exam.

Academic Program

The academic year is based on a 4-4-1 academic calendar, with two 14-week terms (fall and winter) and a one-month May term. The fall term begins in early September and ends in mid-December. The winter term begins in mid-January and ends in late April. During the May term, students may participate in a variety of programs on or off campus. Students normally take four courses in each of the fall and winter terms and one course in the May term. Thirty-six courses are required to graduate. Freshmen participate in a two-term program called Foundations of the Liberal Arts, which features small-group discussions with a faculty leader; lectures, films, concerts, and other presentations; and a tutorial program in basic communication, critical thinking, and study skills. Special study-skills clinics and workshops are offered on an optional basis. Students must complete requirements designed to ensure broad familiarity with the major areas of learning and human endeavor in the humanities and fine arts, social sciences, natural sciences and mathematics, logic, and languages.

Transylvania grants credit for scores of 4 or 5 on the Advanced Placement examinations of the College Board and at least 5 on the International Baccalaureate program. Detailed information may be obtained from the Office of the Registrar.

Off-Campus Programs

Experiencing diverse cultures through international study is a vital part of a Transylvania education. It is common for Transylvania students to study abroad for a summer, a term, or a year. A program at Regent's College, London, allows students to study there for the same cost and course credit as a semester at Transylvania. Scholarships are available for both semester-long and summer study abroad. Summer study programs, including those in Austria, Brazil, China, Costa Rica, Ecuador, France, Germany, Italy, Japan, Mexico, and Spain, are available through Transylvania's affiliation with the Kentucky Institute for International Studies. Transylvania also cooperates with the English-Speaking Union to offer advanced students scholarships for summer study at Cambridge and Oxford Universities. Students may participate in seminars or internships in Washington, D.C., through the Washington Center. Internships with congressional offices, Kentucky state government, city government, and local firms are easily arranged. Participation in Reserve Officers' Training Corps (Air Force and Army ROTC) is offered in cooperation with the University of Kentucky.

Academic Facilities

Two new Georgian-style buildings combine elegance with high-tech facilities to offer the latest advances in teaching and learning. The Cowgill Center for Business, Economics, and Education includes a multimedia classroom where professors from any discipline can use a large display screen to show the entire class information from one of the twenty-five networked student computers or from a TV, video, CD-ROM, or satellite. A specialized area for education majors includes a laboratory classroom for teacher training. The new Lucille C. Little Theater, used for faculty- and student-directed productions and drama classes, is a technically innovative facility that includes computerized lighting and sound, flexible staging options, and movable seating.

The Frances Carrick Thomas/J. Douglas Gay, Jr. Library offers sophisticated computerized databases, which are invaluable for research and can be accessed from any computer connected to Transylvania's server, including PCs in dorm rooms. The Mitchell Fine Arts Center provides music program facilities, including practice rooms, a recital hall, and an auditorium. It also houses the Career Development Center, which provides free interest testing and helps students research careers, improve job search skills, arrange internships and part-time jobs, and apply to graduate schools. Mitchell also houses a teaching laboratory for the hotel, restaurant, and tourism administration program. A newly acquired building is dedicated to art classes, studios, and a student gallery. Other modern facilities include the L. A. Brown Science Center and the Haupt Humanities Building. The Clive M. Beck Athletic and Recreation Center opened in January 2002.

About 80 percent of students live on campus in six residence halls—two for men, one for women, and three for men and women. These include apartment-style living for upperclass students and suite-style rooms. All rooms are air-conditioned and completely furnished and offer private telephone service with voice mail, access to cable television and Transylvania's computer network, ample lounge and study areas, computer labs, and recreational facilities. The dining hall is in the women's residence hall. The William T. Young Campus Center offers a competition-size indoor pool, a gymnasium, a fitness center, and other facilities.

Costs

Transylvania charges an annual tuition that covers fall, winter, and May terms for a normal full-time schedule of courses. Special instruction fees are charged in addition for certain designated courses, such as applied music. For 2002–03, tuition was $16,170, the room and board (double occupancy) cost was $5940, and the general fee was $620.

Financial Aid

Transylvania is committed to providing financial aid to students and their families. Four types of financial assistance are available: scholarships, which are based on academic performance, leadership, and citizenship, and grants, loans, and campus work, which are based on financial need. About 90 percent of Transylvania students receive some form of financial assistance and many receive more than one type of aid. Outstanding entering freshmen may qualify for one of twenty-five William T. Young Scholarships—each worth more than $55,000 over four years—which cover tuition and fees. Submission of Transylvania's Application for Admission and Scholarships by the appropriate deadline is all that is necessary to be considered for all scholarships at Transylvania. Students who are interested in need-based aid must file the Free Application for Federal Student Aid (FAFSA).

Faculty

Transylvania's relatively small size and low student-faculty ratio of 13:1 allow for close, personal attention in teaching and advising. Ninety-seven percent of full-time faculty members hold a doctorate or the highest degree in their field and have come to Transylvania from a variety of graduate and professional schools. Many faculty members are recognized for their scholarship and professional activities, but their central concern is teaching and advising students. Transylvania's commitment to outstanding teaching is reflected in its nationally recognized Bingham Program for Excellence in Teaching. The program seeks to attract and retain gifted teachers through an evaluation process and financial incentives.

Student Government

Students at Transylvania have a high degree of access to the administration and governing board of the University. The Student Government Association serves as a representative government, and students also hold positions on standing committees of the faculty and the Board of Trustees.

Admission Requirements

Each applicant is considered individually on the basis of academic records, SAT I scores and/or ACT scores, activities, interests, essays, and recommendations. Admission is also offered to transfer students, international students (through the SAT I, ACT, or Test of English as a Foreign Language), and nontraditional students. High school students who graduate at the end of their junior year may also be considered for admission.

Transylvania enrolled 330 new students for the 2001–02 academic year. The middle 50 percent composite ACT score for the freshman class was 24 to 29; the middle 50 percent combined SAT I score was 1100 to 1290. Sixty percent were in the top 10 percent of their high school class.

Application and Information

Submission of a Transylvania Application for Admission and Scholarships or the common application is all that is necessary to be considered for admission and most merit scholarships at Transylvania. Application deadlines vary with particular scholarships and types of financial aid.

The priority admission and scholarships deadline is December 1 for applicants who wish to learn of their acceptance by January 1 and who want to be considered for all Transylvania scholarships. February 1 is the general admission and scholarships deadline for applicants who wish to be considered for all Transylvania scholarships except the William T. Young Scholarship. Applicants who apply after the December 1 priority deadline and by February 1 are considered for admission and scholarships on a rolling basis. Applicants who apply after February 1 are considered on a space-available basis. The deadline for applications for the winter term, which begins in January, is December 5. The same deadlines apply to electronic applications, which may be submitted on the Internet at the Web address listed below.

Students considering Transylvania are urged to visit the campus. High school seniors are encouraged to stay overnight in a dorm with a student admissions assistant. Weekday visits may include a customized campus tour and an opportunity to attend classes; talk with professors, students, and admissions and financial aid counselors; and enjoy meals on campus. Visits should be arranged with the Office of Admissions, preferably one to two weeks in advance. Open houses are held in the fall and winter, and a college planning workshop for high school juniors and sophomores is held in the spring.

For more information and application materials, students should contact:

Office of Admissions
Transylvania University
300 North Broadway
Lexington, Kentucky 40508-1797
Telephone: 859-233-8242
800-872-6798 (toll-free)
E-mail: admissions@transy.edu
World Wide Web: http://www.transy.edu

Small class sizes at Transylvania give professors and students the opportunity to work closely together, and many are directly involved in student research projects.

TRENT UNIVERSITY

PETERBOROUGH, ONTARIO, CANADA

The University

Trent University has long been recognized as one of Canada's outstanding small universities. As a primarily undergraduate university committed to excellence in the humanities, social sciences, and natural sciences, Trent places great value on personal care and attention and remains committed to its low student-faculty ratio and its emphasis on interdisciplinary research. A vibrant international program draws gifted students from more than 110 countries around the globe. All Trent students find a welcoming community and a safe, diverse environment in which to learn.

Trent University was formally created as an independent university with full degree-granting powers by the Ontario Legislature in 1963. It is a member of the Association of Universities and Colleges of Canada and the Association of Commonwealth Universities. Trent graduates have received prestigious graduate scholarships and have assumed leadership roles in the public and private sectors.

With 7,000 full-time students, the University has chosen to remain small and concentrate on undergraduate studies while gradually expanding its interdisciplinary graduate programs. More than 75 percent of first- and second-year classes have fewer than 25 students. In Trent's graduate programs—anthropology, watershed ecosystems, Canadian heritage and development studies, methodologies for the study of Western history and culture, and applications of modeling in the natural and social sciences—there are presently about 200 students.

Trent's 1,400-acre Symons campus, situated on the banks of the Otonabee River amid forests, lakes, and gently rolling hills, features award-winning modern architecture. On this campus, 3 miles north of Peterborough's downtown core, are located the administrative offices, library, athletics facilities, Science Complex, Environmental Sciences Centre, and three of the five residential colleges. The other two colleges, in residential areas of Peterborough, are housed in Victorian buildings with stained-glass windows and hardwood floors. A new college is currently under construction on the Symons campus and is planned to be fully operational by September 2004. A shuttle bus makes the 10- to 20-minute trip between the Symons campus and the downtown colleges throughout the day.

The colleges combine residential and teaching space, allowing students to live and learn in a friendly, close-knit environment. All colleges have common areas, a dining hall, study and recreation areas, and laundry facilities, as well as academic, social, and athletic activities. Early application is strongly encouraged to all international students intending to stay in residence.

Trent provides students with the support services they need to succeed, from finding a part-time job or seeing a doctor to coping with family or personal relationships. For international students, Trent's International Program Office offers counselling in areas such as health insurance, immigration information, and academic programs. To ease the transition to university, the office also publishes the *International Students Handbook* and organizes a three-day orientation camp in September and January. After the camp, all new students starting in September take part in Introductory Seminar Week. "Intro Week" provides social activities and an opportunity for students to choose their courses. Academic departments give introductory lectures to provide a better understanding of course content and workload, and each student is assigned an academic adviser.

With a variety of facilities, student clubs, and organizations, Trent offers diverse ways to spend time outside the classroom. Athletics facilities include a 25-metre pool, a gymnasium, squash courts, a floodlit playing field, tennis courts, a rowing course, and cross-country trails for skiing, running, and biking. The University hosts the largest timed rowing regatta in Canada each fall and a triathlon each March.

Location

Trent's Symons campus lies 3 miles north of downtown Peterborough, a city of 80,000 that blends all the comforts of small-town living with the cultural amenities of a larger center. The city's strategic location in the Kawartha Lake district—with proximity to lakes, beaches, hiking/ski trails, and conservation areas—allows for ample recreational opportunities. Students are just 90 minutes by car from Toronto, Canada's largest city; 3½ hours from Ottawa, the nation's capital city; and a quick 1-hour flight from New York, Boston, and Washington, D.C.

The city of Peterborough offers a wide range of restaurants, shops, cafés, bookstores, galleries, cinemas, and museums, as well as a comprehensive performing arts center. Trent students, faculty members, and staff members play an important role in the city's political and cultural life and are active in such projects as the Peterborough Symphony, the Peterborough Theatre Guild, and the Kawartha World Issues Center.

Majors and Degrees

The majority of Trent students pursue honours degrees, the normal prerequisite for graduate studies. Honours and General Bachelor of Arts degrees are available in ancient history and classics, anthropology, Canadian studies, computer studies, cultural studies, economics, education, English literature, environmental and resource studies, French studies, geography, global studies, German studies, Hispanic studies, history, indigenous environmental studies, international development studies, modern languages and literatures, museum studies, Native management and economic development, Native studies, philosophy, political studies, psychology, sociology, and women's studies.

There are Honours and General Bachelor of Science degrees in anthropology, biochemistry and molecular biology, biology, chemical physics, chemistry, computer science, computing and physics, economics, environmental and resource science, environmental chemistry, forensics, geographical information systems (GIS), geography, mathematics, nursing, physics, and psychology.

Trent also offers an Honours Bachelor of Business Administration.

Students may use the Special Emphasis option to create an integrating theme to govern their choice of courses if their academic needs cannot be met by any of the existing majors.

In the concurrent teacher education program, cosponsored by Queen's University in Kingston, Trent students graduate with a Bachelor of Arts or a Bachelor of Science from Trent and a Bachelor of Education from Queen's. Students may also choose a one-year Consecutive Bachelor of Education degree at Trent after the successful completion of an undergraduate degree.

In affiliation with Sir Sandford Fleming College, Peterborough's community college, Trent offers degree programs in geographical information systems, museum studies, nursing, and forensic science.

The University also offers diplomas in the Canadian Studies, Indigenous Environmental Studies, Native Management and Economic Development, and Native Studies Programs.

Academic Program

The academic year consists of three sessions. The fall session is a twelve-week term that runs from September to December. The winter session is a twelve-week term that runs from January to April. The summer session runs from May to August and is made up of twelve-, eight-, and six-week terms. September and January are entry points for full-time studies. Four-year honours degrees require successful completion of 20 course credits. Three-year general degrees consist of 15 course credits. All degrees require completion of University and program requirements.

The Academic Skills Centre offers assistance in writing, reading, and study techniques. It also offers tutoring in mathematics and French and additional help for students for whom English is a second language. The Special Needs Office assists students with physical, sensory, or learning disabilities.

Off-Campus Programs

Trent students are encouraged to spend one year of their undergraduate programs studying in another country. The Trent International Study and Exchange Program (TISEP) offers exchange and study abroad opportunities in many countries, including Australia, England, Finland, France, Germany, Iceland, Japan, Korea, Malaysia, Mauritius, Mexico, Scotland, South Africa, Spain, the United States, and Wales. The International Development Studies programs in Ecuador and Ghana and the Native Studies Program in Thailand combine academic courses with work-placement experience. Students receive full credit for all courses successfully completed while abroad.

Academic Facilities

The bright and spacious Bata Library is electronically connected to the two in-town college libraries and the Peterborough Public Library. An extensive interlibrary loan network enables students to borrow material from all parts of North America. Three hundred fifty computers are available for general student use in the computer centre, library, classrooms, residences, and labs. They provide access to the Internet, Gopher, e-mail, Microsoft programs, and library catalogues.

Costs

Tuition fees (including ancillary fees) for Canadian citizens and permanent residents for the 2003–04 academic year were CAD$5200; they were CAD$13,000 for international students. A single room in residence, including various meal plans, costs between CAD$6000 and CAD$7600.

Financial Aid

All students are considered for entrance scholarships when admitted. Exceptional students are invited to apply for the Board of Governor's Scholarship and the two Champlain Scholarships, prestigious renewable scholarships. Upperclass students are automatically considered for in-course scholarships. Among primarily undergraduate institutions in Canada, according to the 2003 *Maclean's* magazine annual ranking, Trent has one of the highest scholarships and bursaries (percentage of budget). Bursary funds, primarily to assist in emergency situations, are available. There are scholarships and bursaries specifically for international students. International students also are allowed to work on campus part-time and up to one year after graduation.

Faculty

Much of the teaching at Trent takes place in seminars and labs that provide an interactive learning environment. Because these are generally led by professors rather than teaching assistants, students have ample opportunity to get to know their instructors. Trent has the highest proportion of faculty members who have received national awards, as well as research grants from Canadian government funding agencies, among primarily undergraduate institutions in Canada, according to the 2003 *Maclean's* magazine annual ranking.

Student Government

There is active involvement in student politics through such groups as the Trent Central Student Association and the five residential College Cabinets. Students have a voice in the administrative affairs of the University through membership in the University Senate and the Board of Governors.

Admission Requirements

For Ontario residents, an Ontario Secondary School Diploma (OSSD); ENGL1 or ENG4U, with a grade of 70 percent or higher; and five additional OAC, Gr 12U, or Gr 12M courses are required. For Quebec residents studying CEGEP, a minimum of twelve academic courses is required. Other Canadian residents are required to have a grade 12 diploma.

Advanced credit is granted for select Advanced Placement programs with examination grades of 4 or better.

For students from the United States, a high school diploma, with a minimum average of B (3.0 GPA on a 4.0 scale) is required. An overall SAT I score of at least 1100 or a composite ACT score of 24 is preferred. Senior students should send their mid-term grades. A minimum of 70 percent in grade 12 English is required.

General Certificate of Education requirements include passes in at least five subjects, two at the advanced level with grades of C or better, or passes in four subjects, three at the advanced level with grades of C or better. Two advanced supplementary courses may be substituted for one advanced-level course. Advanced credit may be granted for A levels with a grade of C or better.

International Baccalaureate requires a minimum of 28 points. Advanced credit may be granted for higher-level subjects with a score of 5 or higher.

Students who believe that their marks do not accurately reflect their ability to succeed at university may send supporting documentation, such as references from teachers or guidance counsellors, to the Registrar's Office.

The language of instruction at Trent is English. All students must be proficient at speaking, reading, writing, and understanding English. Candidates from areas where English is not the language of instruction must provide evidence of language proficiency. Trent accepts results from a variety of tests. The more commonly used services and minimum required scores are as follows: Test of English as a Foreign Language (TOEFL), 580 on the paper-based test or 237 on the computer-based test, with a minimum TWE score of 4.5; Michigan English Language Assessment Battery (MELAB), 85, with no part below 80; International English Language Testing System (IELTS), overall band of 6.5, with no band below 6.0; and Canadian Academic English Language Assessment (CAEL), 60. Results from Canadian university English language testing services are also accepted. International students who meet all criteria for admission except the language requirements may be admitted to the TRENT-ESL, English for University program. Upon successful completion of this program, students continue regular degree programs.

Application and Information

Applications for admission for the 2004–05 academic year must be received by the Office of the Registrar no later than June 1, 2004. The deadline to apply for residence is June 16, 2004. Early application is strongly encouraged. Complete applications should include official transcripts, language test scores (if needed), and notarized translation of material not in English. For information on admission and programs and for application forms, students should contact:

Office of the Registrar
Trent University
1600 West Bank Drive
Peterborough, Ontario K9J 7B8
Canada
E-mail: tip@trentu.ca
World Wide Web: http://www.trentu.ca
http://www.trentu.ca/tip

One of the residential colleges at Trent University.

TREVECCA NAZARENE UNIVERSITY

NASHVILLE, TENNESSEE

The University

Trevecca Nazarene University is a private, coeducational, four-year accredited liberal arts university. Founded in 1901 and affiliated with the Church of the Nazarene, its academic programs are based on Christian values that promote scholarship, critical thinking, and meaningful worship for students in preparation for lives of leadership and service to the church, the community, and the world. More than 1,900 students from thirty-five states and seven countries are enrolled at Trevecca. They represent nineteen different denominations. Students who are members of minority groups make up 14 percent of the population. Trevecca places distinct emphasis on its community, with 84 percent of the undergraduate student body living on campus. Trevecca is situated atop one of the only hills in the lively city of Nashville, with a view of beautiful Music City, USA. Campus life reflects the vibrancy of Nashville. A variety of extracurricular clubs and ministry opportunities are available. Student government, the campus newspaper and yearbook, special interest and discussion groups, drama productions, and two radio stations provide additional opportunities for involvement.

The University is a member of the NAIA Division I and participates in the highly competitive TranSouth Athletic Conference. Men compete in baseball, basketball, golf, and soccer, while women compete in basketball, golf, soccer, softball, and volleyball. An excellent intramural program includes basketball, football, and volleyball. In addition, tennis tournaments, racquetball tournaments, golf tournaments, table tennis, and aerobics are available. Athletic facilities include a gymnasium, tennis courts, racquetball courts, a 25-meter indoor pool, a state-of-the-art wellness center, a walking track, a baseball diamond, a soccer field, and a softball field.

Location

Trevecca is located on a beautiful 68-acre campus near downtown Nashville in the heart of middle Tennessee. It is 10 minutes from the award-winning Nashville International Airport. The cities of Knoxville, Memphis, and Chattanooga are no more than 3 hours away. The Cumberland River, Old Hickory Lake, and the Great Smoky Mountains provide beauty and opportunities for leisure. The city of Nashville is a center for internship and service opportunities.

Majors and Degrees

Trevecca offers fifty-one baccalaureate and six associate degrees through eleven academic departments and four schools. Undergraduate majors include accounting, allied health, biology, broadcast technology, business administration, chemistry, communication studies, computer information systems, criminology, dramatic arts, economics, education, English, general science, history, management and human relations, marketing, mathematics, medical technology, music, music business, physical education, physics, political science, psychology, religion, social and behavioral sciences, social science, speech, sports and exercise science, and sports management.

Trevecca also offers nine preprofessional programs: dentistry, engineering, law, medicine, nursing, pharmacy, physical therapy, physician assistant studies, and veterinary science.

Academic Program

Trevecca's academic degrees are conferred upon successful completion of a major, at least one minor, and 59 (or an appropriate variation) credit hours of general education courses to meet the 128-credit-hour requirement for graduation. These general education core courses have been selected to provide broad liberal arts training as a foundation for students majoring in any field.

The University's academic year consists of two semesters (fall and spring) and several summer sessions. Orientation of new students is prior to each semester, with a special summer orientation program for first-time college freshmen.

Career internship elective courses are offered for credit to upperclass students. The student is in a professional setting in his or her field under contract supervision for one semester. Two career internships are recommended prior to graduation.

Academic Facilities

Trevecca recently opened a state-of-the-art library and technology center, which houses more than 447,000 items (from traditional and electronic sources) and nineteen group study rooms. Academic computer labs include thirteen fully networked labs, which provide full Internet and LAN access. All undergraduate residence halls provide complete Internet and LAN connection capabilities, including a minilab and laser printer in each building. Also located on campus are a fine arts center, a sports center, a hall of science, and an education center.

Costs

Tuition for 2004–05 is $12,797 (13–18 hours) and room and board are $5867. The estimated cost of books is $1200, travel costs about $960, and personal expenses are estimated at $1180.

Financial Aid

The purpose of the student aid program at Trevecca is to provide financial assistance to qualified students who, without such aid, would be unable to attend. Tuition, room, and board costs are consistently lower than the average cost of attending most private four-year colleges and universities.

Nearly $12 million was awarded last year through institutional merit scholarships and need-based aid, federal and state grants, loans, and on-campus employment programs. Approximately 91 percent of students received financial aid, with an average annual award per recipient of $15,000, including loans. The deadline to apply for institutional aid is March 1 for the following fall semester.

Students at Trevecca can divide charges into three equal payments during the semester or, through special arrangement, spread payment over ten months.

Faculty

Trevecca is a learning-oriented institution whose mission is to prepare graduates of all degree programs to develop a depth of understanding in their major field and to prepare them for a career or graduate school following graduation. Faculty members must have a clear commitment to academic excellence and Christian values. There are 92 full-time teaching faculty members, of whom 65 percent hold earned doctorates. All faculty members serve as student advisers. The student-faculty ratio is 16:1.

Student Government

The Student Government Assembly (SGA) is composed of elected representatives of the associated student body of Trevecca Nazarene University. It is self-governing and controls its own budget. Its purpose is to promote the best interests of all students. The SGA serves as a liaison between the faculty, the administration, and student groups. It plans programs and activities for the school year. Student representatives serve on all University committees and are nominated by the SGA. Each year, the SGA assists in the sponsorship of the Staley Lecture Series, which features outstanding Christian leaders.

Admission Requirements

As a private Christian university, Trevecca is open to any qualified student without regard to race, color, sex, age, creed, national or ethnic origin, or physical disability. Transfer and international students and students who are members of minority groups are welcome and encouraged to apply.

Trevecca is selective in its admission policy. A freshman applicant is admitted provided one of the following conditions is met: they must have a high school grade point average of 2.5 or above on a 4.0 scale, an ACT composite score of 18 or above, or an SAT I combined score of 860 or above. If none of the admission requirements is met, a freshman applicant who has an ACT composite score of 15 to 17 or an SAT I combined score of 720 to 850 and a minimum high school grade point average of 2.0 on a 4.0 scale is granted admission on academic restriction.

For the best preparation for college, Trevecca recommends that secondary school credits include 4 units of English, 2 units of mathematics, 2 units of foreign language, 2 units of social science, and 1 unit of natural science. SAT I scores (code 1809) are acceptable, although ACT scores (code 4016) are preferred. Transfer applicants should request that an official transcript be forwarded directly to Trevecca from each college or university previously attended. Trevecca provides all applicants with an official evaluation of their transfer credit.

Application and Information

Trevecca has a rolling admission policy: applications are reviewed and acted upon as they are received. Application priority deadlines are July 1 for fall semester and December 1 for spring semester. The housing deposit priority deadline for fall semester is May 1. The Office of Enrollment Management is open from 8 a.m. to 4:30 p.m. on weekdays. For more information, to arrange a campus visit, or to request a catalog and application, students should contact:

Enrollment Management
Trevecca Nazarene University
333 Murfreesboro Road
Nashville, Tennessee 37210
Telephone: 615-248-1320
888-210-4TNU (toll-free in the U.S.)
Fax: 615-248-7406
E-mail: admissions_und@trevecca.edu
World Wide Web: http://www.trevecca.edu

Built in 1984, Jernigan Student Center houses the student dining room, a bookstore, a post office, student government and class offices, a snack shop, and several classrooms.

TRINITY CHRISTIAN COLLEGE

TRINITY CHRISTIAN COLLEGE Palos Heights, Illinois

PALOS HEIGHTS, ILLINOIS

The College

In 1952, a group of 10 professionals and business leaders began to study the feasibility of establishing a two-year junior college in the Chicago area that would uphold higher education from a Christian worldview and lifeview. By April 1956, this visionary group had drafted a constitution and incorporated as the Trinity Christian College Association. The first Board of Trustees was elected to oversee the fledgling College's operation, and in 1959, they purchased the Navajo Hills Golf Course in suburban Palos Heights, Illinois, for its campus. After remodeling the former clubhouse and pro shop, the College opened that fall with a class of 37 students taught by 5 full-time faculty members. The liberal arts program led to a two-year certificate, enabling students to transfer to a four-year institution.

As the response of the community grew and students embraced the College's unique perspective, it became evident that Trinity Christian College was fulfilling a greater need beyond providing a solid liberal arts basis for two-year students. In 1966, the board initiated the process for the College to become a four-year, degree-granting institution. A third year of courses was introduced in 1969, with the fourth year offered in 1970. The College's first baccalaureate degrees were awarded in May 1971.

Trinity Christian College developed a cohesive approach to its core curriculum of philosophy, history, English, and theology. In the years since its original vision was conceived, the College has kept pace with the changing educational landscape by offering a broader scope of courses and programs. The curriculum has expanded to include business, education, and nursing in addition to its traditional liberal arts focus. Today, there are adult learners seeking to complete their undergraduate degrees alongside recent high school graduates exploring a future in information technology, graphic design, and social work.

The student body has swelled to more than 1,100 undergraduates, taught by a dedicated faculty of more than 45 full-time and 51 part-time instructors, of whom more than 62 percent have terminal degrees in their disciplines. All faculty members teach classes and advise students. With the average class size at 25 and a student-faculty ratio of 13:1, Trinity students receive individual attention that affirms their spiritual and academic experience. Although students are drawn from predominantly Reformed and Presbyterian church backgrounds, there is also a diversity of traditions represented including Baptist, Lutheran, Methodist, and Roman Catholic.

With more than thirty majors, Trinity offers a variety of educational and ministerial experiences including studies abroad; interim trips to the Philippines, South Africa, Jamaica, Italy, China, and France; and hands-on internships with corporations and nonprofit organizations. The College's proximity to the resources of metropolitan Chicago offers students an exceptional "classroom" that provides experiential learning opportunities. Intercollegiate sports for men and women, student-run ministry programs, and a full scope of creative expression in fine arts and student publications complete the Trinity experience on the tree-lined campus tucked away in a quiet suburban neighborhood.

In February 2001, the College dedicated the Martin and Janet Ozinga Chapel. This facility serves as a cultural and spiritual focal point for the entire student body, as well as the greater community. The building provides the music program with practice and rehearsal rooms and houses the campus ministries department, under the direction of Chaplain Tim Hoekstra. One of two pipe organs has been installed in the recital hall; the larger organ has been installed in the 1,200-seat auditorium, adding a fantastic new dimension to an already beautiful building. The Grand Lobby has hosted a variety of meetings and banquets beneath a striking stained-glass window, one of a quartet of windows throughout the building designed to celebrate Trinity's mission in Reformed higher education. The new worship space has seen an increase in participation and enthusiasm among students at chapel serves held three times a week and at weekly praise and worship services. In the past year, *River*, a multigenerational, interdenominational worship service, has drawn the campus community and area residents together on the first Sunday night of each month.

In spring 2002, the new Heritage Science Center opened, which is a 38,000-square-foot, state-of-the-art facility that provides classroom and lab space for chemistry, biology, and physics programs, as well as additional classrooms and a lecture hall for technology and computer science studies. A new residence hall, aptly named Alumni Hall to honor Trinity graduates, is being constructed to meet the increased demand for more on-campus housing. It is expected to be ready for occupancy in fall of 2004.

Location

The College's proximity to metropolitan Chicago appeals to students everywhere. The 50-acre campus is surrounded by forest preserves in Palos Heights, Illinois, a community of 12,000 residents that combines the safety of a small town with the excitement of a big city nearby. Hiking, biking, and tobogganing are popular recreational options, and the shops and restaurants of the local business district are within walking distance. Just a few miles south are the shopping malls of Orland Park, which also offer a wide selection of dining and entertainment choices. The College is easily accessible from I-294, with a variety of hotel accommodations located within 2 miles of the campus.

Majors and Degrees

With more than thirty majors, Trinity grants Bachelor of Arts, Bachelor of Science, and Bachelor of Science in Nursing degrees. The College's location extends the classroom in ways that provide experiential learning opportunities for students. Majors include accounting, art, biology, business, business communication, business education, chemistry, church education, communication arts, computer science, elementary and secondary education, English, exercise science, history, information systems, mathematics, music, nursing, philosophy, physical education, political science, psychology, science education, social work, sociology, Spanish, special education, and theology. Preprofessional programs in dentistry, law, medicine, physical therapy, and seminary are also available.

Academic Programs

Depending upon the goal, each student is able to create a unique set of courses to meet the particular needs and interests. A faculty adviser is assigned to provide encouragement and guidance throughout the student's college career. Opportunities are available for faculty mentoring in which students and professors work together on research projects, presentations, and papers, often leading to national recognition. A minimum of 125 total semester hours of credit is required to earn a degree in each of more than thirty majors.

Designed to help new students gain an understanding of Trinity's transformational vision for education, the First-Year Forum explores the ways Christianity impacts their encounters with the world during the course of their studies. The program focuses on three objectives from the College's mission statement: enfold students initially into a community of scholarship; introduce them to Trinity's vision of God's world and their role in it; and challenge students to use their years at Trinity in service to God and His world.

The Honors Program provides a community of challenge and support for academically gifted students who take delight in learning and discovery both inside and outside of the classroom. Because Trinity's Honors Program is based upon the principle that effective education involves the whole person, the program combines its academic, curricular components with a rich offering of cocurricular opportunities. These opportunities include exploring and enjoying the cultural resources of Chicago and cultivating friendships with fellow students and professors through social interaction, spiritual growth, and service in projects on Trinity's campus and the surrounding community.

Off-Campus Programs

Trinity students are required to complete a field education course in at least one major program with the objective of introducing students to a professional application of their chosen major in an actual work environment. This experience brings the student into direct contact with the challenges and realities that await after graduation, while providing opportunity to discuss questions and problems encountered in the real world with professors.

Field experience is available in a variety of settings depending upon the major program. For example, nursing students gain exposure to different departments of a hospital; education students take responsibility for a classroom or subject; business majors provide consulting services for area businesses and firms. Credit hours earned are determined by the student's adviser, following the typical guideline of 40 hours of experience per credit. A maximum of 12 semester hours for field education or internships can be earned; students are permitted to accept compensation for their work.

Trinity's Chicago Metropolitan Studies program offers the opportunity for a full semester of working and living off-campus. Offered to upperclass students, the Metro program focuses on leadership training by challenging undergraduates to integrate their classroom theory with professional work experience. Features of the curriculum include internships related to students' professional interests, seminars on the urban phenomenon, extensive cultural exposure through scheduled fine-arts activities, and a complete orientation process that familiarizes each student with the Metro program, the city of Chicago, and the world of work.

Based in Seville, the Semester in Spain program is designed to provide a rich academic and cultural experience as well as foster lasting relationships between students and their host families. The entire teaching faculty are native Spaniards and hold advanced degrees in Spanish studies. Since all classes are conducted in Spanish, students gain proficiency in the language within a context of spiritual growth and critical reflection. The curriculum takes a global approach, concentrating on developing and enhancing listening, speaking, reading, and writing skills. Classes are held in Trinity's own classroom building in Seville, consisting of eight classrooms, a study room, a media room, and administrative offices.

As a member of the Council for Christian Colleges and Universities, Trinity students can also pursue a variety of semester programs ranging from film studies in Hollywood, California, to study-abroad opportunities in Oxford, England; Costa Rica; Russia; and Egypt.

Costs

Trinity Christian College's tuition and fees were $15,490 for the academic year 2003–04 ($520 per semester hour). Room and board costs amounted to $5790. The comprehensive fee was $21,280.

Financial Aid

More than 90 percent of Trinity Christian College students receive financial aid to help meet the costs of their education. Eligible students may be awarded scholarships, grants, work opportunities, educational loans, or any combination of these.

The College offers a variety of scholarships, including merit-based awards for honor students, leadership scholarships for participation in extracurricular activities, and special scholarships. All entering students are automatically considered for honors scholarship when their applications are reviewed.

Each year, two incoming freshmen are awarded a renewable Founders' Scholarship, which provides full tuition for four years. The scholarship recognizes Christian scholars who have demonstrated consistently high academic achievement and exemplify the mission of Trinity Christian College. Each year, more than 30 candidates who meet the criteria of a minimum 3.8 GPA and a composite score of 30 on the ACT are considered for the Founders' Scholarship. To apply for need-based federal or state financial aid, students must submit the Free Application for Federal Student Aid (FAFSA) and the Trinity Christian College financial aid form.

Faculty

Trinity Christian College has 45 full-time faculty members. All faculty members teach classes and advise students. The average class size is fewer than 25 students. Small class sizes allow students to receive individual attention and spiritual experience at Trinity Christian College. The faculty-student ratio is 1:13.

Admission Requirements

Applicants must demonstrate academic potential as reflected in their official high school transcripts and scores from either the SAT I or ACT Assessment. Transfer students must provide official transcripts from every college attended; transferees with fewer than 24 credit hours must also submit high school transcripts. Students who have earned an associate degree from an accredited community college can be accepted into Trinity with junior status.

Application and Information

For more information, students should contact:

Pete Hamstra
Vice President of Admissions
Trinity Christian College
6601 West College Drive
Palos Heights, Illinois 60463
Telephone: 708-239-4708
866-TRIN-4-ME (toll-free)
Fax: 609-896-4531
World Wide Web: http://www.trnty.edu

Trinity Christian College students enjoy the "incredible classroom" experience of downtown Chicago.

TRINITY COLLEGE

HARTFORD, CONNECTICUT

The College

Since its founding in 1823, Trinity has provided an undergraduate education of uncommon quality. Widely acknowledged as one of the top liberal arts colleges in the country, Trinity has been recognized by a panel of national education editors for its "bold and innovative ideas" to advance the cause of higher education and ensure greater access.

In its commitment to the rigorous pursuit of the liberal arts and to instruction that is personal and conversational, Trinity is an ideal college. At the same time, Trinity is in close touch with the world beyond its campus. In that respect and in terms of the outstanding opportunities Trinity's capital city location offers students, a Trinity education is indeed a real education.

While remaining faithful to the classic liberal arts tradition, Trinity offers a distinctive educational experience that prepares students for the challenges and opportunities of the twenty-first century. Building on its traditional strengths in arts and humanities and exceptional offerings in science and engineering, Trinity engages students in a conversation with the world through its study-abroad programs, interdisciplinary programs, and innovative, rigorous programs that draw on the rich cultural, educational, and professional assets of Hartford. State-of-the-art electronic facilities support Trinity's pioneering use of information technology in classrooms. The heart of a Trinity education, however, remains the personal encounter between professor and student, the intellectual partnership that discovers a world of ideas and ignites a passion for learning.

Trinity's students come from forty-four states and twenty-eight countries. The College believes that a diverse community makes learning flourish. Trinity's undergraduate enrollment of more than 2,000 students is about equally composed of men and women. More than 90 percent of undergraduates live on campus in College housing. Trinity is engaged in continuing campus revitalization programs that preserve its impressive Gothic buildings as it also develops a campus for the twenty-first century.

Trinity offers a rich array of extracurricular activities—films, plays, concerts, musical theater, sports, academic symposia, and visits by nationally and internationally known writers, speakers, and performers. Participation is an important word on campus, and Trinity students have abundant opportunities to lead and to be involved in numerous student clubs; special interest groups; theater, dance, and music groups; debate; academic programs; campus cinema; Trinity's radio station; and many student publications. With 19 acres of playing fields, Trinity also offers an extensive athletic program. More than half of the student body participates on twenty-nine men's and women's varsity teams (Division III) and in twelve intramural sports. The Ferris Athletic Center features a swimming pool, a fully equipped fitness center, crew tanks, eight international-size squash courts, basketball courts, and an indoor track.

Location

Situated on a beautiful 100-acre campus in the center of Hartford, the capital of Connecticut, Trinity offers the best of both worlds—a supportive and active campus community located in a city that provides students with myriad opportunities for internships, community service, and cultural exploration. Hartford's businesses, governmental agencies, cultural organizations, and nonprofit institutions offer Trinity students hundreds of opportunities to explore future careers through the College's extensive internship program. Hartford is also host to a number of cultural institutions, including the Wadsworth Atheneum (the oldest public art museum in the nation), Mark Twain House, Harriet Beecher Stowe Center, Connecticut Opera, Hartford Ballet, Hartford Symphony, Hartford Stage, and a number of smaller theaters and clubs that provide a cultural stew of dance, theater, and music. The shopping districts of Hartford and the surrounding suburbs are nearby. The impressive Connecticut coast is easily accessible, and Boston and New York are each about 2 hours from campus. Off campus, the 256-acre Trinity College Field Station at Church Farm in Ashford, Connecticut, is dedicated to research in the natural sciences and a wide range of environmental educational endeavors. Plans are being developed for use of Church Farm buildings to support programs in the arts.

Majors and Degrees

The College offers a Bachelor of Arts degree and a Bachelor of Science degree. Majors offered include American studies; anthropology; art history; biochemistry; biology; chemistry; classical civilization; classics; computer science; economics; educational studies; engineering; English; environmental science; history; international studies; Jewish studies; mathematics; modern languages: Chinese, French, German, Italian, Japanese, Russian, and Spanish; music; neuroscience; philosophy; physics; political science; psychology; public policy and law; religion; sociology; studio arts; theater and dance; and women, gender, and sexuality. Trinity also offers a computer coordinate major, and interdisciplinary majors may be individually constructed. Trinity offers a five-year program in engineering and computer science, which leads to a bachelor's degree from Trinity and a master's degree from Rensselaer Polytechnic Institute through Rensselaer at Hartford.

Academic Programs

Featuring more than 970 courses, Trinity's curriculum provides a framework within which students may explore the many dimensions of an undergraduate education. At the same time, the curriculum offers each student flexibility to experiment, to deepen old interests and develop new ones, and to acquire specialized training in a major field. Students must demonstrate proficiency in writing and mathematics and fulfill a five-part distribution requirement that comprises at least one course in each of the following categories: arts, humanities, natural sciences, numerical and symbolic reasoning, and social sciences.

Off-Campus Programs

More than 50 percent of Trinity students study abroad for a semester or a year at Trinity's Rome Campus, at Trinity in Spain, or in other approved study programs in more than forty countries on five continents. Several Trinity-sponsored global learning sites operate in Chile, China, Nepal, Russia, South Africa (Cape Town), Trinidad, and Turkey. Through the theater and dance department, Trinity offers the Trinity/LaMaMa Performing Arts Program in New York City, an extraordinary program that provides intensive study in theater, dance, and performance.

Academic Facilities

The Raether Library and Information Technology Center is home to the College and Watkinson Libraries, as well as the Computing Center. It is a place where students and faculty members come together for the serious work of scholarship, where researchers can pore over a book or conduct investigations through a wide selection of online databases. The College Library, one of New England's largest collegiate libraries, houses nearly 1 million print volumes and approximately 700,000 nonprint materials, including slides, microforms, sound recordings, and other materials in audiovisual and electronic formats. In addition, an online catalog linked with Wesleyan University and Connecticut College provides access to more than 2 million titles. The Watkinson Library, with its impressive collection of rare books, manuscripts, and other unique resources, supports a broad range of research interests.

The campus is fully wired, with every student room connected to the College network and the Web. Public access computers are also available 24 hours a day in select facilities.

Costs

Costs for the 2003–04 academic year were $28,740 for tuition, $5020 for room, $2790 for board, and $1490 for fees.

Financial Aid

The College meets 100 percent of the need of all students who are offered admission and demonstrate financial need. While need status is occasionally a factor, the vast majority of admissions decisions are made on a need-blind basis. Students must file the Free Application for Federal Student Aid (FAFSA) as well as the Financial Aid PROFILE of the College Scholarship Service. Admissions applications are due by January 15; FAFSA and PROFILE applications are due by February 1. Students are notified of admission and aid decisions by the first week of April. Normally, need is met with a financial aid package that includes grant assistance, work-study, and federal student loans. Federal funds for which accepted students are eligible include Pell Grants, Federal Supplemental Educational Opportunity Grants (FSEOG), Perkins Loans, Stafford Loans, and PLUS Loans. Most students who demonstrate need are granted an on-campus job as part of their financial aid package. Approximately 50 percent of all students have a job; about 40 percent of all students have employment based on need. The ratio of grant assistance to loans and work-study aid is sometimes affected by the academic strength of the student's record. Trinity continues to expand its aid budget to keep pace with the College's goal to increase the socioeconomic and ethnic diversity on campus. Forty percent of the students receive financial aid, and the average award was $25,650 in 2002–03.

Faculty

The distinctive strength of a Trinity education has always been the close interaction between students and a faculty of devoted teacher-scholars. A student-faculty ratio of 10:1 enables supportive yet challenging educational experiences that establish a foundation for lifetime learning and enables students to pursue academic interests with passion. Nearly 30 percent of recent graduating classes collaborated with faculty members in conducting research; many students have made joint presentations at international, national, or local symposia or have published jointly prepared papers. All courses are taught by Trinity faculty members and not by graduate assistants.

While the first calling of Trinity's professors is teaching, they are active publishing scholars of national and international distinction. History professor Joan Hedrick, for example, won the Pulitzer Prize for her biography of Harriet Beecher Stowe. Other notable professors include Henry DePhillips, distinguished chemist and researcher on art restoration; Dan Lloyd, acclaimed philosopher and author of *Radiant Cool;* Lesley Farlow, accomplished dancer and choreographer; Fred Pfeil, prizewinning writer and English professor; Samuel Kassow, distinguished historian; and Joseph Bronzino, an authority on biomedical engineering. Trinity professors pride themselves on their accessibility and keen interest in helping students.

Student Government

Trinity fosters the growth of future leaders by providing students with many opportunities to exercise and test their leadership skills. The Student Government Association (SGA), for example, provides students a strong voice in social, cultural, and—through membership on faculty committees—academic matters. Composed of elected class representatives, the SGA constantly seeks the expertise and insights of all interested students, and its committees offer enterprising students many chances to participate and to develop leadership skills.

Admission Requirements

Trinity seeks an ethnically and geographically diverse group of highly motivated students who have completed a rigorous course of study in secondary school and have demonstrated energy, talent, and leadership in a variety of extracurricular activities. Trinity has no specific GPA minimums or test-score cutoffs. The College is highly selective, and its candidates typically have an A– high school average. At least 16 academic units of college-preparatory course work are recommended, including a minimum of 4 years of English, 2 years of foreign language, 2 years of laboratory science, 2 years of algebra, 1 year of geometry, and 2 years of history. Last year, 5,500 men and women from all over the nation and world applied for admission to the College, which enrolls an entering class of 550 students. Transfer students with a 3.0 GPA in a strong course of study at another accredited college or university are considered for admission to the sophomore or junior classes.

Admissions officers review each application individually; decisions are based on each candidate's academic record (course of study and GPA), recommendations from secondary school teachers and counselors, test scores, personal strengths, talents, activities, and application essay.

Application and Information

Students must submit completed applications to the Admissions Office. Application deadlines are November 15 for early decision I applicants (with notification by December 15), January 15 for early decision II applicants (with notification by February 15), and January 15 for regular decision applicants (with notification by April 1). Transfer applicants must submit applications by April 1 for admission in the following fall semester (with notification by early June) and by November 15 for admission in the following spring semester (with notification by early January). Students may download an electronic Common Application from Trinity's Admissions Web site address below.

Inquiries should be made to:

Larry Dow
Dean of Admissions and Financial Aid
Admissions Office
Trinity College
Hartford, Connecticut 06106-3100
Telephone: 860-297-2180
Fax: 860-297-2287
E-mail: admissions.office@trincoll.edu
World Wide Web: http://www.trincoll.edu/admissions

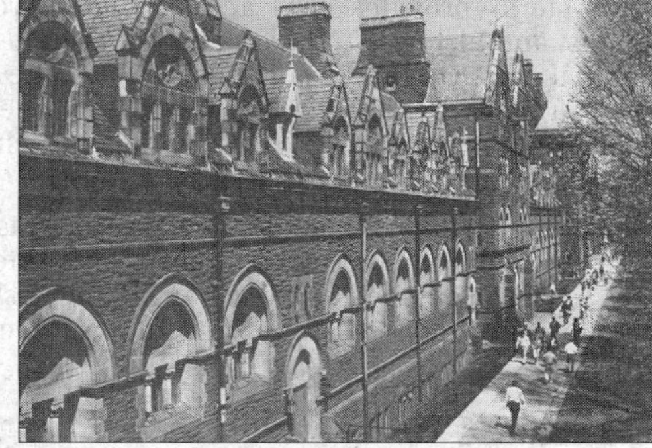

The Long Walk at Trinity College.

TRINITY COLLEGE

WASHINGTON, D.C.

The College

Trinity College is one of the nation's first Catholic women's colleges. Founded in 1897 by the Sisters of Notre Dame de Namur, Trinity has maintained its commitment to provide an excellent, value-centered education to women in a personalized atmosphere. Today, Trinity offers the best of all possible worlds—a tradition of academic excellence, a high-quality liberal arts program, a prestigious faculty, unlimited internship and career opportunities, and an exciting location in the nation's capital. Trinity's commitment to excellence has earned the College top ratings in *U.S. News & World Report's* guides to "America's Best Colleges" and "America's Best College Values."

Trinity enrolls more than 1,500 full-time and part-time undergraduate and graduate students representing thirty-two states and forty-two countries. Sixty percent of the full-time students reside on campus.

Trinity's Honor Agreement is a vital part of the College's academic and social environment. The Honor Agreement expresses a way of life rooted in personal integrity and founded on mutual respect and cooperation. Each student signs the agreement that confirms her understanding and acceptance of the responsibility that is hers as a member of the Trinity community.

A member of the Atlantic Women's Colleges Conference (AWCC), Trinity has ten NCAA Division III athletic programs: basketball, crew, field hockey, lacrosse, tennis, track, soccer, softball, swimming, and volleyball. The Trinity Center for Women and Girls in Sports—the College's 85,000-square-foot fitness complex—is the nation's largest athletic facility designed especially for women's sports. The Trinity Center houses a competition swimming pool, a spa, a basketball and volleyball arena, a weight room, a dance studio, a fitness center, a walking track, and locker rooms. Other new athletic facilities include tennis courts and a field for soccer, field hockey, and lacrosse.

Location

Located on a 26-acre campus just 2½ miles from the U.S. Capitol, Trinity offers all the advantages of living in one of the world's most powerful cities, while maintaining the serenity and beauty of a suburban campus. Metro—Washington's bus and subway system—provides easy access to numerous theaters, museums, and historic landmarks in and around the city. Reagan National and Dulles airports as well as the famous Union Station are nearby and Trinity provides a free shuttle service to and from the nearest Metro station, which is also within walking distance from the College.

Often referred to as Trinity's extended classroom, Washington offers access to endless political, cultural, and intellectual opportunities. Trinity offers a wide array of internships for academic credit that draws on the abundant resources of the capital area.

Majors and Degrees

Trinity's College of Arts and Sciences and School of Professional Studies offer the Bachelor of Arts (B.A.) and Bachelor of Science (B.S.) degrees in the following areas: accounting, art history, biochemistry, biology, business administration, business economics, chemistry, computer science, economics, education, engineering, English, entrepreneurship and small business management, environmental science, fine arts, history, human relations, information systems, international affairs, language and cultural studies, liberal arts studies, mathematics, physical science, political science, psychology, public affairs, social science, and sociology. Concentrations are available in twenty-nine areas.

Academic Program

The Trinity Foundation for Leadership Curriculum is an innovative interdisciplinary program designed to provide students with the knowledge, skills, and values to meet the challenges and opportunities of the twenty-first century. Trinity's curriculum and major programs offer a contemporary approach to education by combining the liberal arts with practical experience and a professional focus. Internships and selected career-related courses are available within the curriculum. Advising and career development programs assist in integrating academic success with personal career goals. The Academic Support and Career Services Center provides personal, academic, and career counseling. The on-campus Writing and Math Centers provide students with additional resources for strengthening individual skills in these areas.

Trinity is one of only ten Catholic colleges and universities in the country with an active Phi Beta Kappa chapter, the oldest honor society in the nation.

Off-Campus Programs

Trinity is a member of the Consortium of Universities of the Washington Metropolitan Area, a cooperative arrangement among the major institutions of higher learning in and around the District of Columbia. Member schools share their facilities, and give students the opportunity to take courses not offered by their own institution. Other member institutions include: American University, Catholic University of America, Gallaudet University, George Mason University, Georgetown University, George Washington University, Howard University, Marymount University, the University of the District of Columbia, and the University of Maryland, College Park.

Academic Facilities

Trinity's Sister Helen Sheehan Library is affiliated with the Washington Research Library Consortium (WRLC), which provides access to a catalog of more than 5 million volumes in the libraries of American, Catholic, Gallaudet, George Mason, George Washington, and Marymount Universities, and the University of the District of Columbia. The library also enjoys reciprocity agreements with the libraries at Georgetown University and Howard University. Trinity also has wireless Internet capability across much of the campus, and many of its classrooms are equipped with computers connected to the Internet, digital projectors, and smart boards in order to integrate technology into every aspect of the curriculum.

Costs

In 2003–04, full-time tuition was $16,222. Room and board were $7170.

Financial Aid

Financial assistance is available through grants, campus employment, loans, and scholarships. Nearly 80 percent of students receive some form of financial assistance. Trinity's priority deadline for submitting the Free Application for Federal Student Aid (FAFSA) to the Federal Processing Center is February 1. Trinity's code is 001460. Students should apply for financial aid as early as possible.

Faculty

There are 91 faculty members, 51 of whom are full-time. Ninety-five percent of the full-time faculty members hold doctoral degrees or the professional equivalent. Trinity's low student-faculty ratio makes it possible for students and faculty members to develop meaningful, lifelong relationships.

Student Government

The Student Government Association (SGA) at Trinity carries on an eighty-year tradition of responsible student participation in College governance and academic and social affairs. In addition to representing students and voicing their concerns to the entire Trinity community, the SGA also coordinates student activities and supervises the functions of all committees and organizations, which fall under the Association. The judicial branch of the Student Government Association is responsible for upholding the College's Honor Agreement.

Admission Requirements

Trinity College seeks women who have demonstrated academic achievement and potential and who will bring varied interests, talents, and experiences to the community. Applicants are encouraged to complete a four-year secondary school program, including a total of 16 credits in English, foreign languages, history, mathematics, science, and social science. Trinity's admissions counselors review each candidate's cumulative grade point average, SAT and/or ACT scores, and personal statement. Trinity also considers extracurricular activities, community service, and work experience. Students are encouraged to research each of Trinity's programs in order to determine which best meets their academic goals.

Advanced Placement course work may be considered for credit and advanced standing. Early entrance is available for mature and well-qualified students who wish to enter Trinity after their junior year of high school. Early entrance candidates are required to have an interview with a member of the admissions staff. Transfer students are also encouraged to apply. Credit is given for all course work completed at an accredited college or university in which a grade of C or higher was earned. Trinity's SAT code is 5796 and its ACT code is 0696. All international students for whom English is not the first language are required to submit TOEFL scores.

All applicants are invited to arrange a personal interview with an admissions counselor, attend class, and tour the campus. The Office of Admissions is open Monday through Friday from 9 a.m. to 7 p.m. and on Saturday from 8 a.m. to 2 p.m.

Application and Information

Trinity College offers admission to qualified students in both the fall and spring. Applications are considered on a rolling basis, and decisions are rendered upon receipt of a completed application and all required supporting credentials. Students wishing to be considered for early action and scholarships are asked to submit an application by December 1. Candidates for financial aid are asked to submit the FAFSA to the Federal Processing Center by March 1.

For additional information and/or to receive an application, students should contact:

Office of Admissions
Trinity College
125 Michigan Avenue, NE
Washington, D.C. 20017-1094
Telephone: 202-884-9422
800-492-6882 (toll-free)
Fax: 202-884-9403
E-mail: admissions@trinitydc.edu
World Wide Web: http://www.trinitydc.edu

The Trinity Center for Women and Girls in Sports is the nation's largest athletic facility designed especially for women's sports.

TRINITY UNIVERSITY

SAN ANTONIO, TEXAS

The University

More than anything else, Trinity University is about achievement. Since its founding in 1869 this private, coeducational institution has been dedicated to helping capable, motivated students hone their talents, define their goals, and pursue their dreams. The academic program—rigorous enough to challenge and enhance every student's abilities, flexible enough to be tailored to an individual's personal and professional needs—is designed to teach students how to be critical and creative thinkers and clear and persuasive communicators and prepares them for a lifetime of success in any endeavor.

Today Trinity is a nationally recognized institution characterized by a demanding curriculum, distinguished faculty members, exceptionally bright and diverse students, and a campus that is among the most modern and beautiful in the country. The size, character, and quality of the institution overall most closely resemble the nation's elite liberal arts colleges, but Trinity University's unique curriculum extends beyond the scope of the traditional liberal arts and sciences education to offer practical expertise for the challenges of the twenty-first century. The breadth of professional, preprofessional, study-abroad, and internship programs Trinity offers is rare within the liberal arts and sciences context and in a school with a personalized and intimate learning environment. Conversely, Trinity is unique among comprehensive institutions in that it focuses its extraordinary resources almost wholly on undergraduates and provides an unusually large number of undergraduate research opportunities, even at the first-year and sophomore levels.

Trinity students intensify their educational experience through interaction with diverse and talented students, rich cultural experiences, exposure to world leaders and newsmakers, and close contact with a distinguished faculty. Several annual endowed lecture series bring to campus such noted figures as Secretary of State Colin Powell, authors John Updike and Joyce Carol Oates, Madeleine Albright, Rudy Giuliani, and John Glenn. Scientists, artists, and scholars from a range of disciplines visit classes and give free lectures every month at Trinity.

More than 75 percent of students live in sixteen modern and spacious residence halls. The primarily residential campus provides ample opportunities to become involved in the university's thriving cocurricular life. More than 130 student-run social, political, creative, and service organizations sponsor countless social activities, lectures, discussions, and other events both on and off campus. The 185,215-square-foot William H. Bell Athletic Center's recreational resources include a performance gymnasium, a natatorium, six racquetball courts, a squash court, a modern fitness center, a sports forum, an aerobics and dance studio and an athletic training facility. Trinity fields nine men's and nine women's varsity teams, which compete in the NCAA Division III Southern Collegiate Athletic Conference. More than 70 percent of the students participate in the popular intramural program.

Trinity University is able to offer an exceptional and affordable educational experience, largely based on its endowment of more than $600 million, which subsidizes nearly one third of the cost of a Trinity education.

U.S. News & World Report has ranked Trinity University the top comprehensive university in the West for the last eleven years, and *Money* magazine included Trinity in its ten "best buys" among America's most selective colleges and universities.

Location

Trinity's hilltop campus commands a magnificent view of San Antonio, the ninth-largest city in the U.S. The city brims with cultural and economic opportunities, offering a rich and diverse university setting. The Paseo del Rio, or River Walk, features cobblestone paths lined with cafés, clubs, restaurants, and speciality shops. San Antonio's cultural attractions include the San Antonio Museum of Art, home to the Nelson A. Rockefeller Center for Latin American Art, as well as numerous art galleries and theaters. Trinity students have free access to San Antonio Symphony performances in the historic Majestic Theater. In addition to great culture, San Antonio has a great climate, with more than 300 days of sunshine annually and an average temperature of 68.8 degrees. The surrounding Texas hill country provides hiking, fishing, boating, and horseback riding. Spectator sports include the American Hockey League's San Antonio Rampage, the San Antonio Missions minor league baseball team, and the San Antonio Spurs. An international airport located within a 5-minute drive of the campus provides millions of annual tourist visitors easy access to the city.

Majors and Degrees

Trinity offers majors and degrees in anthropology, art, art history, biochemistry, biochemistry and molecular biology, biology, business administration, chemistry, Chinese, classical studies, communication, computer science, drama, economics, engineering science, English, French, geosciences, German, Greek, history, international studies, Latin, mathematics, music, philosophy, physics, political science, psychology, religion, Russian, sociology, Spanish, speech, and urban studies.

Preprofessional programs are offered in health professions and law. Five-year programs in education and accounting lead to the bachelor's and master's degrees.

Interdisciplinary minors are offered in African-American studies, American intercultural studies, astronomy, cognitive science, communication management, comparative literature, environmental studies, linguistics, medieval and Renaissance studies, new media, and women's studies.

Academic Programs

Trinity's curriculum is designed to allow students to broaden their horizons and test their limits. At the heart of this rigorous academic program is the Common Curriculum, a series of seminars, workshops, and courses designed to give students a thorough grounding in the world's scientific, political, philosophical, and artistic traditions. These courses provide context for learning within a chosen major and may also introduce students to new interests and enthusiasms. For many Trinity students, a class taken to fill the Common Curriculum requirement becomes the seed of a second major. The First Year Seminar and Writing Workshop gives first-year students a taste of college-level debate and discussion as well as helping to refine their critical reading, writing, and research skills.

To receive an undergraduate degree from Trinity University, students must successfully complete at least 124 semester hours (129 semester hours for a Bachelor of Science in engineering science, 132 hours for a Bachelor of Music in choral or instrumental music, and 141 hours for a Bachelor of Music in performance or composition), with 60 hours outside the major.

Off-Campus Programs

Trinity has been ahead of the international trend for more than twenty years, carefully designing a study-abroad program that meets each student's academic and professional needs through advising and placement. This very flexible program has allowed

Trinity students from every discipline to study in forty-five countries and on every continent (except Antarctica) in the last three years alone. Nearly half of graduating students spend some time abroad. Students are placed in a variety of programs ranging from direct university enrollments to field study and academic internships.

Academic Facilities

The Coates Library, with more than a million volumes and vast resources in microform, is one of the leading undergraduate libraries in the country and has an acquisition budget of more than $1 million. The recently expanded Multimedia Development Center offers students and faculty members the flexibility to develop multimedia presentations, reports, and projects with state-of-the-art computer workstations, scanners, color printers, audio and video digitizers, film recorders, and synthesizers. In 2003, the library's Information Commons opened as a space for research and collaboration that rethinks the conventional library for the twenty-first century.

The Richardson Communications Center offers two television studios with control rooms, remote and cable television news feed and production services, an interactive multimedia lab, a popular radio station, and a live newsroom with regional news services. The three-building Ruth Taylor Center for the fine arts houses studios, practice rooms, and performance facilities. The art, music, and theater facilities, which are scheduled for renovation in 2004, also include painting and sculpture studios, a concert hall, a 2,500-seat auditorium, and three theaters, one of which is the 500-seat Stieren Theater.

Trinity's modern, spacious science laboratories are equipped with sophisticated instrumentation and provide hands-on experience generally found only at the graduate level. The greenhouse, animal research facilities, and walk-in environmental chambers of the Cowles Life Science Building support teaching and research in everything from botany and biochemistry to ecology and physiology. Engineering and computer science majors use the Keck Design Center's powerful UNIX workstations for complex analysis, design, and simulation projects. The physics and astronomy students have access to an observatory, an atmospheric physics lab, an astrophysics imaging lab, and a laser lab.

Costs

Tuition for the 2004–05 academic year is $19,860. Fees are $775 and room and board are $7580.

Financial Aid

More than 85 percent of Trinity students receive merit or need-based financial aid. Students receiving need-based aid must submit the Free Application for Federal Student Aid (FAFSA) each year. Awards are renewable, provided students maintain satisfactory progress toward their degree and family financial circumstances continue to demonstrate need. Need-based packages include a variety of federal, state, and Trinity grants, loans, and work-study. Academic scholarships are based solely on academic achievement.

Faculty

The Trinity faculty members, 99 percent of whom hold terminal degrees in their fields, are internationally recognized, accomplished scholars dually committed to undergraduate teaching and research. Close personal attention from professors is a significant and treasured part of the Trinity experience; all classes are taught by professors, and the student-faculty ratio of 11:1 ensures access. Of the 218 full-time faculty members, 21 hold endowed Distinguished Professorships.

In addition to being deeply committed teachers and mentors, Trinity's professors are accomplished writers, scholars, scientists, and artists. In the past year, faculty members have received grants to support their work from organizations that include the National Science Foundation, the National Endowment for the Humanities, the American Chemical Society, the Freeman Foundation, the Welch Foundation, the Woodrow Wilson National Fellowship Foundation, and the Merck Corporation/American Association for the Advancement of Science.

Student Government

All full-time undergraduate students are members of the Association of Student Representatives, which is governed by a Student Senate elected by the student body. The University also encourages students to hold seats on administrative committees in order to represent student interests. The Student Court and the appellate University Court deal with infractions of campus rules and regulations.

Admission Requirements

Trinity University seeks to enroll a highly motivated, talented, and diverse population. Admission is selective and based on a thorough assessment of each application. The Admissions Committee reviews not only academic performance as measured by GPA and standardized test scores, but also the difficulty of courses taken, cocurricular commitments, writing ability, and teacher recommendations. Upon high school graduation, applicants are expected to have completed 4 years of English; 3 or more years of college-preparatory mathematics, including trigonometry or precalculus; 3 years of social studies; 3 years of science; and 2 years of the same foreign language. A campus visit is recommended.

The students who enrolled in fall 2003 had a mean SAT I score of almost 1300 and an average ACT composite score of 29. Their average high school GPA, recalculated and based on academic solids, was 3.5.

Trinity does not discriminate on the basis of sex, race, ethnic background, age, or physical disability.

Application and Information

The deadline for binding early decision and nonbinding early action I is November 1, with notification by December 15. The deadline for nonbinding early action II is December 15, with notification by February 1. The regular admission deadline is February 1, with notification by April 1. Transfer students must apply by March 1, with notification by April 1. A $40 application fee must accompany all paper applications. The application fee is waived for first-year applicants who apply online at http://www.commonapp.org. All required tests must be completed by the application deadline.

For more information, students should contact:

Office of Admissions
One Trinity Place
San Antonio, Texas 78212-7200
Telephone: 210-999-7207
800-TRINITY (toll-free outside San Antonio)
E-mail: admissions@trinity.edu
World Wide Web: http://www.trinity.edu

Trinity's famed skyline campus overlooks the San Antonio skyline.

TRI–STATE UNIVERSITY

ANGOLA, INDIANA

The University

Tri-State University (TSU) is a private, independent, coeducational institution offering associate and baccalaureate degrees in more than programs to students in engineering, mathematics, science, computer science, business administration, teacher education, communications, criminal justice, and social sciences. In the fall of 2002, TSU was elevated to a graduate degree-granting institution and began its first graduate degree program, the Master of Science in engineering technology.

Since its founding in 1884, Tri-State's emphasis has been on providing an affordable, comprehensive, career-oriented, hands-on education. With a worldwide reputation for being "job-ready," Tri-State graduates are in demand. That is why each year, an average of 90 percent of Tri-State graduates are employed in major-related positions within six months of graduation.

Tri-State's current undergraduate enrollment is nearly 1,400. Approximately 500 of these students live on campus in one of six residence halls. The University's 485-acre campus includes an 18-hole, championship golf course.

The University's campus offers an informal and friendly atmosphere, which complements the seriousness and determination with which Tri-State students pursue their academic goals. While focused on pursuing their goals, Tri-State students enjoy many opportunities to develop friendships and to build leadership and teamwork skills through their participation in athletics and a range of campus organizations.

Men's intercollegiate sports include baseball, basketball, cross-country, football, golf, soccer, tennis, and track. Women's sports include basketball, cross-country, golf, soccer, softball, tennis, track, and volleyball. Intramural sports are also a big part of recreational life at Tri-State.

Student organizations that offer opportunities for participation include the student senate, honor societies, professional organizations, the campus newspaper, the FM radio station, the yearbook, the drama club, and more. In addition, there are a total of twelve social fraternities and sororities on campus, in which approximately 20 percent of the student body participate after their freshman year.

Tri-State University is accredited by the Higher Learning Commission and a member of the North Central Association of Colleges and Schools, (Web site: http://www.ncahigherlearningcommission.org; telephone: 312-263-0456). Tri-State University's programs in chemical engineering, civil engineering, electrical engineering, and mechanical engineering are accredited by the Engineering Accreditation Commission of the Accreditation Board for Engineering and Technology (ABET). ABET's national office is located at 111 Market Place, Suite 1050, Baltimore, Maryland, 21202-4012; telephone: 410-347-7700. All teacher preparation programs are accredited by the Indiana Professional Standards Board.

Location

Tri-State University is located in Angola, Indiana, which is in the heart of northeast Indiana's scenic lake resort region and about halfway between the metropolitan areas of Chicago, Illinois, and Cleveland, Ohio. Just a 45-minute drive from Fort Wayne, Indiana, Tri-State offers the safety and ease of a small-town environment while being close to some of the nation's most vital cities. Pokagon State Park provides year-round recreational opportunities for the community and is just 5 miles from Tri-State's campus.

Majors and Degrees

The Allen School of Engineering and Technology awards Bachelor of Science degrees in chemical, civil, computer, electrical, and mechanical engineering; computer-aided drafting and design technology; and engineering administration. It awards associate degrees in construction management technology, drafting and design technology, and manufacturing technology.

The Ketner School of Business awards the following degrees: Bachelor of Science in Business Administration in accounting, business/arts and sciences, finance, management, management information systems, marketing, production and operations management, and technical sales and marketing; a Bachelor of Science degree in golf management; and a Bachelor of Applied Management. Associate degrees are awarded in accounting, business administration, and turf grass management.

The School of Education awards Bachelor of Science degrees in elementary education, physical education, and secondary education. Secondary education majors can specialize in English, mathematics, science, and social studies.

The School of Arts and Sciences awards Bachelor of Arts degrees in communication, psychology, and social sciences. Bachelor of Science degrees are awarded in biology, chemistry, English education, environmental science, forensic science, health education (K–12), health education (9–12), health promotion and recreational programming, mathematics, mathematics education, physical education (K–12), physical education (5–12), physical education (9–12), physical science, premed, science education, social studies education, and sport management; a Bachelor of Science in computer science; and a Bachelor of Science in criminal justice. Associate degrees are awarded in arts, computer technology, criminal justice, and science.

Academic Programs

The graduation requirements for a bachelor's degree are a cumulative grade point average of not less than 2.0 (on a 4.0 scale) and the completion of 120 to 132 semester hours, depending upon the major.

Tri-State's engineering programs concentrate on providing a fundamental, application-oriented engineering education. In addition to concentrating in a specialized area, students are required to successfully complete courses in communication skills, sociohumanistic studies, and analysis and design.

The University's business programs include a broad range of hands-on practical experience that acquaints the student with the practices, procedures, and problems of the contemporary business professional. Guest lecturers are frequent visitors to the campus, and field trips are considered vital to the total educational experience.

Off-Campus Programs

Co-op and internship opportunities are available. Semesters of classroom study are alternated with professional work experience, giving students the opportunity to integrate theory with practice and gain a competitive edge in the job market. The length of a co-op program depends upon the student's class status when entering the program. Work-study schedules require from three to six semesters on work assignments. During the semesters worked, students are paid directly by the employer.

Academic Facilities

Named in honor of a former chair of the Board of Trustees, the Perry T. Ford Memorial Library is a three-level building with reading and study areas, library offices, work and exhibit areas, the University archives, and the Hershey Museum. The library's physical collection includes books, videos, microfilm, journals, and newspapers as well as kits, models, maps, and globes. The catalog of the entire collection is Web based and available via the Internet. Materials not available in the TSU collection are easily accessed via interlibrary loan. In addition, TSU students receive reciprocal borrowing privileges with a number of private Indiana colleges and universities.

The library also offers a strong collection of electronic resources, including scholarly and technical indexes, databases with full-text articles, and online resources with a range of technical, statistical, legal, and political information. These resources may be accessed by PC workstations in the library or by any computer on the Tri-State network.

Fawick Hall of Engineering reopened in 1997 after a year-long $5-million complete interior demolition to load-bearing walls and then full reconstruction to house the University's Departments of Chemical Engineering, Civil and Environmental Engineering, Electrical and Computer Engineering, Mechanical and Aerospace Engineering, and Technology. Because of the University's commitment to a high-quality education, Tri-State's students use sophisticated equipment such as a scanning electron microscope in their cast metals laboratories and in projects related to industrial consulting. Each department has a computer lab with pertinent software for their students.

Named in honor of John G. Best, a distinguished alumnus and former member of the Board of Trustees, the John G. Best Hall of Science contains classrooms and science laboratories. Best Hall also houses the Fairfield Lecture Room; the Department of Mathematics and Computer Science; the Department of Science; the science laboratories; the Computer Center; the telephone services; and the Department of Criminal Justice, Psychology, and Social Sciences.

The University Computer Center houses an academic computer system that consists of Pentium microcomputers running Windows NT Workstation and Windows 2000. The academic system is an Internet site supporting Telnet, the World Wide Web, and e-mail to other Internet sites. A Microsoft Exchange server handles the e-mail. There are more than 200 computers dedicated to student access in labs across campus. Every room in each dorm is wired to the University network and the Internet.

Costs

Tuition for the academic year (two semesters) in 2004–05 is $19,260. Room and board for the academic year is $5700.

Financial Aid

Financial aid may be awarded in the form of scholarships, grants, loans, or employment. Any of these aids or any combination may be necessary to supplement family and student resources to meet basic educational expenses.

Tri-State requires the use of the Free Application for Federal Student Aid (FAFSA) and recommends its submission by March 1. Admitted students who qualify for academic merit awards must complete the TSU Application for Scholarship form.

Faculty

Tri-State University has a full-time faculty of 65 members, most of whom have doctoral degrees and/or are registered professional engineers. The central mission of the faculty members is teaching. The student-faculty ratio is 15:1.

Student Government

The student senate is organized for the purpose of promoting and coordinating campus activities for students. Representatives elected from campus organizations form the senate, which sponsors social activities and campus projects and aids in formulating policies for student organizations.

Admission Requirements

Graduation from an approved high school or equivalent preparation is required for admission. Tri-State gives careful consideration to the caliber of the academic records. Selection is made without regard to race, religion, or color. The University requires that applicants for admission arrange to take American College Testing's examination (ACT) or the SAT prior to approval for admission.

Admission requirements for engineering include 4 years of English, 1 year of chemistry, 1 year of physics, 1 year of social studies, 2 years of algebra, 1 year of geometry, and ½ year of trigonometry. Preparatory courses are available for students who have not completed all the high school subjects normally required for admission.

Students who wish to enroll in business must have completed 4 years of English, 2 years of algebra, and 1 year of social studies.

All other applicants must have the following high school credits: 4 years of English, 2 years of mathematics (3 years for computer science majors), 2 years of science, and 2 years of social studies.

Tri-State's associate degree programs require 3 years of English, 2 years of algebra, and 1 year of social studies for entry into the computer technology program and 3 years of English, 1 year of algebra, and 1 year of geometry for drafting and design technology.

Graduates of preprofessional or college-parallel programs at approved community or junior colleges are eligible for transfer into Tri-State's baccalaureate programs. Qualified graduates of these programs may be granted junior standing upon transfer. In general, credit may be allowed for subjects equivalent to those in the program at Tri-State University provided that the student earned a C or better in the course.

Application and Information

Tri-State University operates on a semester schedule. Admission decisions are made on a rolling basis. Applicants are notified of their status within three weeks after the application and high school record have been received. Transfer students must also submit an official copy of their college transcript(s).

Interested students and their parents are encouraged to visit the campus. Arrangements can be made by writing or calling the Office of Admission.

For additional information, students should call or write:

Office of Admission
Tri-State University
1 University Avenue
Angola, Indiana 46703-1764
Telephone: 260-665-4132
800-347-4TSU (toll-free within continental U.S.)
E-mail: admit@tristate.edu
World Wide Web: http://www.tristate.edu

TROY STATE UNIVERSITY
TROY, ALABAMA

The University

Troy State University was founded in 1887 as a Troy State Normal School. The name was changed to Troy State Teachers College in 1929, to Troy State College in 1957, and to Troy State University in 1967, when it was granted university status. Founded as a teacher-training institution more than 100 years ago, the University now offers arts and sciences, business and commerce, education, fine arts, health and human services, journalism and communications, applied science, and preprofessional programs. The University System operates four campuses in Alabama and more than fifty sites on military bases in twelve states and eight other countries. The availability of programs on these branch campuses may vary.

Students come from throughout the United States and several other countries. The total University enrollment is more than 17,000. There are 5,000 undergraduates enrolled at the main campus in Troy. Approximately half live on campus in men's, women's, or coeducational residence halls or in sorority or fraternity housing. Noncommuting students who are under 19 at the time of registration are required to live in University housing for one academic year. All students who live in the residence halls must choose from one of four meal plans. The Adams University Center provides areas for student services, dining, recreation, and quiet study. The University post office, store, and recreation room offer additional services. The offices of Placement, Student Activities, Student Government, the Union Board, *The Palladium* (yearbook), and the Interfraternity and Panhellenic Councils are all located in the University Center, and a performing arts theater, food court, and fitness center have recently been added.

The Ralph Wyatt Adams Administration Building contains the business office and University College in addition to the offices of enrollment management, financial aid, University records, public affairs, alumni affairs, development, institutional research and planning, student affairs, financial affairs, academic affairs, and the chancellor of The TSU System. Students may conduct most of their collegiate business within this one building.

Students participate in the Sound of the South Marching Band, Collegiate Singers, weekly newspaper, yearbook, radio and television stations, University Dancers, debate and forensics, musical theater productions, pageants, foreign language clubs, religious organizations, intramural sports, service clubs, honor societies, ethnic and political organizations, Trojan Ambassadors, social fraternities and sororities, and special interest clubs. A championship golf course is located on campus. The natatorium building houses an Olympic-size swimming pool, a sauna, a weight room, and a gymnasium. Lighted tennis and handball courts, a 30,000-seat football stadium, a 3,000-seat gymnasium, a baseball complex, a modern field house, intramural fields, an outdoor pool, sand volleyball courts, a state-of-the-art track, and a press box with VIP seating are among the athletic facilities. Troy State University is affiliated with the NCAA and fields fifteen intercollegiate sports. The Trojans play at the Division I-A level in all sports, as well as men's and women's rodeo teams, which are part of the National Intercollegiate Rodeo Association.

Location

The University's beautifully landscaped 577-acre campus is situated in a residential area of Troy. The city offers numerous cultural resources. The State Theater, home of the Alabama Shakespeare Festival, is less than an hour's drive from the campus. Rivers, lakes, streams, and farmland surround Troy. Birmingham, Atlanta, and Mobile are a few hours away and the Gulf of Mexico is only 2 hours away.

Majors and Degrees

Troy State University awards a Bachelor of Arts (B.A.) or a Bachelor of Science (B.S.) degree in accounting, art, art history, athletic training, biology, broadcast journalism, business administration, chemistry, collaborative K–6 education, computer science, criminal justice, dramatic arts, economics, English, environmental science, finance, general science, geomatics, graphic design, health education, history, journalism, management, marine biology, marketing, mathematics, medical technology, music education, nursing, physical education, physical science, political science, psychology, rehabilitation, risk management and insurance, secondary education, social work, sociology, speech communication, and sports and fitness management. Preprofessional concentrations are available in agriculture, dentistry, engineering, forestry, law, medicine, optometry, pharmacy, physical therapy, and veterinary medicine.

Academic Program

The general studies curriculum, consisting of 60 semester hours, is required of all students pursuing a bachelor's degree. It provides work in English grammar and composition, biology, algebra or general mathematics, music, literature, and visual arts. In addition to this, the student must select one series of courses in U.S. history or history of Western civilization; three courses chosen from anthropology, economics, ethics, geography, mythology, philosophy, political science, psychology, religion, or sociology; one course in earth or physical science; one course in microcomputing; and one course in speech in order to complete the general studies requirements. Ten hours in a foreign language will satisfy an elective portion of the general studies requirements.

Most degrees require 120 semester hours, 60 of which consist of major and/or minor courses. Double majors are available in various combinations. Besides meeting the requirements of a specific degree program, the student may choose courses from the general curriculum to satisfy elective requirements. Proficiency in English and mathematics is emphasized. The B.A. is awarded to students who enroll in at least 12 semester hours of a foreign language (French, German, Spanish, or Latin); other students are awarded the B.S. The average course load per term is 15 semester hours, or five classes carrying 3 semester hours of credit each. Students are encouraged to enroll in general studies and major courses simultaneously.

Academic Facilities

The University Library contains 247,761 volumes, more than 500 maps, 500,000 units of microtext, 47,000 government documents, and subscriptions to 1,500 periodicals and more than seventy newspapers. The library is part of an ultramodern Educational Resources Center, designed for comprehensive study and research, and includes a complete audiovisual facility. The Hall School of Journalism within this center features a 100,000-watt FM radio station affiliated with National Public Radio and a cablevision-affiliated television studio. The Office of Communications Services includes a photography laboratory and studios, a printing and quick copy facility, and a graphics design studio.

The Claudia Crosby Theater is a complete theater facility that is used for plays, pageants, ceremonies, and commencement exercises. It also provides a facility for students enrolled in the Department of Speech and Theatre. John Maloy Long Hall contains an acoustically perfect recording studio for the symphonic and concert bands and the collegiate and madrigal singers. McCartha Hall, housing the School of Education, contains a reading laboratory and an all-purpose lecture hall. A computer center is located in Bibb Graves Hall, along with offices and classrooms for the Sorrell College of Business and the Department of History and Social Sciences. The Center for Business and Economic Services, an office for research and information, is also located in Bibb Graves Hall. McCall and Sorrell halls contain laboratories and classrooms for science and mathematics. Smith Hall houses classrooms, offices, and lecture halls for the Department of English and studios for the Department of Music. *The Alabama Literary Review* operates from offices in Smith Hall. The Writing Center, staffed by permanent faculty members and student tutors, provides free services for students who are having difficulty with writing assignments. A similar facility, the Mathematics and Natural Science Laboratory, is designed to foster proficiency in those areas. A Fine Arts Center contains classrooms, studios, galleries, and a complete library to meet the needs of art, art history, and foreign language students.

Costs

Approximate annual full-time student expenses for the 2003–04 academic year for fall through spring are as follows: in-state tuition, $3530, out-of-state tuition, $7060; on-campus housing (room rent), $2440; meal plan, $2635; and books and expenses, $500.

Financial Aid

The University encourages all students to apply for admission regardless of their financial status. Scholarships, grants, loans, and work-study awards are given on the basis of priority and need analysis. For each academic year, beginning in September, the priority deadline is May 1. Approximately 70 percent of the current students are receiving financial assistance.

The University has an extensive scholarship program, which is based upon academic achievement and demonstration of leadership or particular talents. The following Troy State University Academic and Leadership Scholarships are awarded: Scholar's Award, a four-year full tuition, room, and board award; Chancellor's Award, a four-year full tuition award; and Leadership Award, for varied amounts. Other scholarships include athletic grants-in-aid and departmental and organizational awards.

Faculty

Individualized instruction and friendly student-teacher rapport are the keynotes of education at Troy State University. Even tenured full professors teach introductory-level courses. The number of courses taught by graduate teaching assistants is kept at a minimum. The visiting professor program has featured such dignitaries as Dr. Edward Teller, the nuclear physicist; Patrick Buchanan, syndicated columnist and former Presidential candidate; and Cyril Northcote Parkinson, the author of *Parkinson's Law*.

Student Government

The University's Student Government Association (SGA) consists of the president, vice president, secretary, and clerk who are elected by the student body to one-year terms. Senators are elected from each residence hall and from commuter seats. Senators may be chosen to serve on committees concerning academic affairs, publications, public relations, the Union Board, the Judicial Board, and curriculum revision. The SGA president is the only student member of the University's Board of Trustees.

Admission Requirements

Admission is based on the grade point average in high school or in previous college work, along with acceptable ACT or SAT I scores. Students are given placement examinations in mathematics and English before registering for classes in their first term of enrollment. Transfer students with fewer than 20 semester hours of college work are treated as beginning freshmen. Visits to the campus are recommended but are not required. Upon tentative acceptance of the application, the applicant is required to attend Pre-College Orientation, which takes place during the summer before the fall term. Similar shorter sessions are presented prior to each term. A student may enroll for any term, fall through summer. Prospective students are encouraged to visit the admissions office and make application well in advance of the term in which they wish to enroll.

Application and Information

There is no application deadline, but high school seniors are encouraged to apply as soon as possible during their senior year; housing assignments are made in the early spring. The application fee is $20.

Admissions Office
111 Adams Administration Building
Troy State University
Troy, Alabama 36082
Telephone: 334-670-3179
800-551-9716 (toll-free)
World Wide Web: http://www.troyst.edu

TRUMAN STATE UNIVERSITY

KIRKSVILLE, MISSOURI

The University

Truman State University has forged a national reputation for offering an exceptionally high-quality undergraduate education at a competitive price. For the seventh consecutive year, *U.S. News & World Report* has ranked Truman State University as the number one master's-level public institution in the Midwest. In addition, Kaplan's 2004 National Survey of High School Guidance Counselors describes Truman as a "hidden treasure" and one of only fifty-nine universities that offer the best value when weighing the quality of education versus the cost. A commitment to student achievement and learning is at the core of everything the University does. This commitment is evidenced by faculty and staff members who recognize the importance of providing students with the opportunity to interact with their professors both in and out of the classroom. With class sizes averaging only 22 students and 95 percent of freshman courses being taught by full-time faculty members, students find ample opportunity to ask questions of professors as well as interact with their multitalented peers. Truman's academic environment is enhanced by a student body that achieves at remarkable levels. The 2003 freshman class had an ACT midrange of 25 to 30 and an average GPA of 3.75 on a 4.00 scale. In addition, numerous opportunities exist for students to engage in undergraduate research. Each year, approximately 1,000 students work side by side with professors on University research projects, gaining greater confidence, knowledge, and skill in their chosen disciplines. The University offers these students the opportunity to present the results of their research at the annual Undergraduate Research Symposium. In addition, selected students travel to the National Undergraduate Research Symposium to present their research findings. Undergraduate research stipends are also available.

The teaching degree at Truman is the Master of Arts in Education. Students wishing to pursue a teaching career first complete a bachelor's degree in an academic discipline and then apply for admission into professional study at the master's level. Master's programs in special education, elementary education, and secondary education are available.

With more than 200 University organizations available to students, encompassing service, Greek, honorary, professional, religious, social, political, and recreational influences, Truman students have tremendous opportunities to become involved while enrolled at the University. Truman's Student Activities Board provides popular culture entertainment such as current box office films like *Two Weeks Notice, Old School,* and *The Recruit;* special events like MTV's "Campus Invasion;" comedians such as Jimmy Fallon, David Chapelle, and Bill Bellamy; and musical artists like Jimmy Eat World and Lifehouse. In addition, admission to all varsity athletic events, Truman threater productions, and Lyceum Series events is free to Truman students. Recent theater productions have included *Arcadia, A Christmas Carol, Cat on a Hot Tin Roof,* and *Lysistrata.*

Location

Truman State University is located in Kirksville, a town of approximately 17,000, nestled in the northeast corner of Missouri. The town square, located within walking distance of the Truman campus, provides a connection to Kirksville's past. A multiplex movie theater opened on the town square in 2001. Local merchants operate specialized gift, book, and clothing stores, and several restaurants offer a wide selection of American and international cuisine.

The Kirksville Aquatic Center is a great place to have fun and get fit. An indoor/outdoor pool complex, the Aquatic Center, offers a variety of activities, classes, and programs designed to appeal to people of all ages. Inside the complex is a six-lane indoor swimming pool, perfect for swimming, relaxing, or playing a game of water-basketball. The outdoor pool is designed with a zero-depth entry, a 1-meter diving board, and four 25-yard outdoor lap lanes as well as a 20-foot water slide.

The northeast region of Missouri is also home to Thousand Hills State Park. A 3,252-acre state park and 573-acre lake for camping, hiking, biking, fishing, swimming, boating, and water skiing is located within 10 minutes of the Truman campus.

Majors and Degrees

Undergraduate degrees offered by Truman include the Bachelor of Arts (B.A.), Bachelor of Science (B.S.), Bachelor of Music: Performance (B.M.), Bachelor of Fine Arts (B.F.A.), and Bachelor of Science in Nursing (B.S.N.). Truman offers more than forty areas of study in the following disciplines: accounting, agricultural science, art, art history, biology, business administration, chemistry, classics, communication, communication disorders, computer science, economics, English, exercise science, French, German, health science, history, justice systems, mathematics, music, music: performance, nursing, philosophy and religion, physics, political science, psychology, Russian, sociology/anthropology, Spanish, and theater.

Professional paths include but are not limited to dentistry, engineering, law, medicine, optometry, pharmacy, physical therapy, and veterinary medicine.

Academic Program

Truman is Missouri's premier liberal arts and sciences university and the only highly selective public institution in the state. The Liberal Studies Program is the heart of Truman's curriculum and is intended to serve as a foundation for all major programs of study offered by the University. Truman's mission is to "offer an exemplary undergraduate education, grounded in the liberal arts and sciences, in the context of a public institution of higher learning." Therefore, Truman is providing the kind of education in the liberal arts and sciences that has historically been offered only at private colleges. The program is a blend of two intellectual traditions in higher education, one that emphasizes the traditional thought and learning of the culture as reflected in the classical works produced by it, and the other that emphasizes personal investigation and freedom of discovery. The philosophy behind the Liberal Studies Program is based upon a commitment that Truman has made to provide students with essential skills needed for lifelong learning, breadth across the traditional liberal arts and sciences through exposure to various discipline-based modes of inquiry, and interconnecting perspectives that stress interdisciplinary thinking and integration as well as linkage to other cultures and experiences. All students graduating from Truman must complete 63 or more credit hours in liberal arts and sciences courses.

Truman's Residential College Program brings the University learning community inside the student residence halls. Historically, residential colleges have been places where faculty members and students join together as "friends of learning." At Truman, this living/learning tradition is honored as one means of furthering its specific goals as a public liberal arts university. The Residential College Program seeks to make liberal arts education personally vital and engaging to the whole person.

Truman also offers an especially challenging General Honors Program. This program provides students with the opportunity to select the most rigorous honors courses to satisfy the liberal arts component of their respective programs. Students who successfully complete this program not only benefit from an even richer academic experience at Truman but also receive special recognition at graduation. Departmental honors are also available in several disciplines.

Off-Campus Programs

Each year, more than 300 Truman students participate in enriching and life-changing study-abroad experiences. Truman's own study-abroad programs, combined with programs offered through Truman's membership in the College Consortium for International Studies, International Student Exchange Program, Australearn, and the Council on International Educational Exchange, provide students with study-abroad opportunities in more than thirty-five countries worldwide, including Australia, England, France, Hong Kong, Italy, Russia, Spain, Thailand, and Wales.

In addition, there are several cooperative programs affiliated with biology. Students interested in medical technology may complete classes at one of several medical technology schools in Iowa, Illinois, or Missouri. Truman is also affiliated with the Gulf Coast Research Laboratory at Ocean Springs, Mississippi. Marine biology courses may be taken at the laboratory during the summer with credit awarded at Truman. In-depth study of the Ozark habitats is also available through Truman's affiliation with Reis Biological Station located near Steelville, Missouri.

In cooperation with the Washington Center for Internships and Academic Seminars, Truman offers a wide variety of experiential internships in Washington, D.C. Included are work-experience opportunities in such areas as public administration, the fine and performing arts, foreign affairs/diplomacy, government affairs, criminal justice, international relations, health and human services, environmental policy, business administration, and communications as well as other areas. Placement sites include non-profit groups, media organizations, Congress, museums, and much more.

Truman requires internships in education, health science, and exercise science and annually offers internship opportunities with the Missouri State Legislature. In recent years, students have completed internships with United States senators, the governor of Missouri, business and industry managers, zoos, broadcast and print media professionals, accountants, advertising agencies, physical therapists, musicians, artists, and the United States Supreme Court.

Academic Facilities

The Truman campus contains forty buildings in an expanse of 140 acres. Featured among these facilities is Pickler Memorial Library. This 449,275-volume facility provides a state-of-the-art library resource for students and faculty members alike. Materials not available in Pickler Memorial Library can be obtained through the Interlibrary Loan Office and MOBIUS.

Improvement to campus facilities have recently included the construction of a $750,000, eight-lane, all-weather track as well as construction of the $8-million Student Recreation Center complete with four athletic courts, an aerobic room, a weight room, an indoor track, and a lounge. In addition, the $7-million renovation to Violette Hall incorporated technologically advanced classrooms, two 100-seat auditoriums, and several student meeting rooms as well as faculty and division offices. The $20-million renovation and 80,000-square-foot addition to Ophelia Parrish Building was completed in summer 2002 and has transformed this facility into the new Fine Arts Center housing art studios, practice facilities, a performing arts center, and a black box theater. The $20-million renovation and expansion of Truman's science facility, Magruder Hall is under way.

Additional facilities include a student media center with a TV studio, a radio station, and print media production facilities, a biofeedback laboratory, an organic chemistry lab, an analytical chemistry lab, an independent learning center for nursing students, an observatory, a greenhouse, a 5,000-seat football stadium, a soccer field, tennis and racquetball courts, a softball diamond, a 3,000-seat arena with three basketball courts and an Olympic-size swimming pool, a multicultural affairs center, a writing center, and a career center.

Costs

Tuition for Missouri residents for the 2003–04 academic year was $4600; out-of-state tuition was $8400. Room and board totals for both Missouri residents and nonresidents were $5072. Additional fees included a $150 freshman orientation fee, an annual $56 activities fee, a $50 parking fee for those with a vehicle, and the costs of books and personal expenses.

Financial Aid

Truman offers automatic scholarships ranging from $1000 to $2000. Competitive scholarship awards vary from $500 up to full tuition, room, and board, plus a $4000 study-abroad stipend. The application for admission also serves as the application for the automatic and competitive scholarship programs.

Several scholarships are awarded to students for excellence in music, theater, or art. These scholarships are available for instrumental, strings, or vocal music; acting or dramatic production; and studio art or art history. Of special interest to piano students is the Truman Piano Fellowship Competition.

The National Collegiate Athletic Association and the University authorize a limited number of grants to outstanding athletes. The value of this aid may vary with each individual recipient.

Truman accepts the Free Application for Federal Student Aid (FAFSA) and participates in all Federal Title IV financial aid programs. Financial aid estimates are available upon request.

Faculty

Truman State University is committed to teaching the academically talented undergraduate student. The University has 381 full-time faculty members and 23 part-time faculty members. Of these, 98 percent teach undergraduates and 85 percent hold a doctoral degree or the highest terminal degree in their discipline. Most major graduate institutions are represented among the Truman faculty, including Harvard, Princeton, Yale, Berkeley, Oxford, and the Sorbonne. The student-faculty ratio at Truman is 15:1.

Student Government

Student Senate is the official elected governing body of the Student Association representing approximately 6,000 students. Its mission is to represent the views of the Student Association in the formulation of the University policy through legislation and membership on all University committees; to facilitate communication and mutual understanding among the Student Association, faculty and staff members, and administration; to maintain a cohesive vision for the future of the University; and to actively participate in the fulfillment of the University's mission as an exemplary public liberal arts and sciences university.

Admission Requirements

Admission to Truman is competitive. Each applicant is evaluated for admission based upon academic and cocurricular record, ACT or SAT results, and the admission essay. Truman requires the following high school core: 4 units of English, 3 units of mathematics (4 recommended), 3 units of social studies/history, 3 units of natural science, 1 unit of fine arts, and 2 units of the same foreign language.

Application and Information

Students interested in early admission must submit an application by November 15. Notification of acceptance is mailed after December 15. Applications received after November 15 are processed on a rolling basis. The recommended final deadline to apply for the fall semester is March 1. There is no application fee. Students may apply online at the Web site listed below. For further information or to schedule a campus visit, students should contact:

Admission Office
Truman State University
205 McClain Hall
100 East Normal
Kirksville, Missouri 63501
Telephone: 660-785-4114
800-892-7792 (toll-free, Missouri only)
Fax: 660-785-7456
E-mail: admissions@truman.edu
World Wide Web: http://www.truman.edu

TULANE UNIVERSITY

NEW ORLEANS, LOUISIANA

Tulane

The University

Tulane University in New Orleans is known nationally and internationally for its teaching and research. At Tulane a student can get an international education in a European city without leaving America. One of a handful of national independent universities in the South, Tulane was founded in 1834 as the Medical College of Louisiana and reorganized as Tulane in 1884. The University is comprehensive by nature, with more than 11,000 students enrolled in eleven schools and colleges ranging from the liberal arts and sciences through a full spectrum of professional schools: law, medicine, business, engineering, architecture, social work, and public health and tropical medicine. Tulane's 5,600 full-time undergraduates choose from seventy majors in colleges of liberal arts and sciences, engineering, architecture, and business and may opt for joint-degree programs in Tulane's professional schools to earn undergraduate and graduate degrees in a shorter period of time. Tulane's distinctive arrangement of undergraduate schools gives every student the personal attention and teaching excellence of a small college while providing the interdisciplinary opportunities and research resources of a university that *U.S. News & World Report* ranks in the nation's top quartile. The average class size is 22. Senior faculty members are in the classroom at all levels, and the 12:1 student-teacher ratio ensures individual attention.

On its residential campus about 4 miles from downtown New Orleans, Tulane requires housing for freshmen. Students may choose from several special interest floors in the residence halls, with areas for honors students, those interested in international and urban affairs, and women science majors, among others. Students participate in more than 200 campus organizations. About 1 student in 3 joins a fraternity or sorority; 2 in 3 play intramural or intercollegiate club sports, and more than 500 participate in Tulane's community volunteer organization. Tulane fields sixteen NCAA Division I sports, competing in Conference USA.

More than 80 percent of Tulane students plan to go on eventually to graduate or professional school. Shortly after graduation, 10 percent enter medical school; 16 percent, law school; and 32 percent, other graduate study. Just over one third accept jobs. Tulane students are among the country's most likely to be selected for several prestigious fellowships, including the Fulbright, Marshall, Rhodes, Truman, and Watson scholarships, that support postgraduate study.

Recent additions to Tulane's campus have included a state-of-the-art student recreation center, a center for engineering and biotechnology, a law school building, a fine arts complex, a residence hall, and a new science facility.

Location

The University is in a historic New Orleans residential area next to renowned Audubon Park, which offers 440 acres of recreational facilities. While the 110-acre campus maintains a traditional collegiate atmosphere, with Gothic stone and red brick amid blooming azaleas and lawns that are green year-round, new buildings are going up at the rate of one a year. The only remaining streetcar line in the country clatters by the campus, connecting students with downtown New Orleans. Tulane students find enrichment through entertainment, education, and community service.

Majors and Degrees

The B.A., B.S., B.F.A., B.S.E, and B/M.Arch. degrees are offered. Programs are for four years with the exception of the five-year architecture program. Students interested in business spend two years in the liberal arts and sciences before enrolling in the A. B. Freeman School of Business in the junior year. Students may major in seventy departmental and interdisciplinary areas, including accounting; American studies; anthropology; architecture; art and biology; art history; art studio; Asian studies; biological chemistry; biomedical engineering; business; cell and molecular biology; chemical engineering; chemistry; civil engineering; classical studies; cognitive studies; communication; computer engineering; computer science; earth sciences; ecology, evolution, and organismal biology; economics; electrical engineering; engineering science; English; environmental engineering; environmental studies; exercise science; finance; French; geology; German; Greek; history; international relations; Italian; Jewish studies; Latin; Latin American studies; linguistics; management; marketing; mathematical economics; mathematics; mechanical engineering; medieval studies; music history or theory; music performance or composition; philosophy; physics; political economy; political science; Portuguese; psychology; religious traditions of the West; Russian; Russian studies; sociology; Spanish; theater; and women's studies. Talented students may also design their own majors, and those who meet requirements may begin professional study in law, medicine, or other professional schools in the senior year, reducing by a year the time spent earning undergraduate and graduate degrees.

Academic Programs

Most freshmen enroll in one of five undergraduate schools and colleges profiled below. Tulane has a two-semester calendar, with first-semester exams held before the holiday break. Faculty advisers assist in course selection and in planning major requirements.

The Paul Tulane College (for men) and Sophie Newcomb College (for women) offer programs leading to the B.A., B.S., and B.F.A. degrees. In Tulane's coordinate college structure, men and women attend classes together, Newcomb and Tulane share a faculty and a curriculum, and most residence halls are coeducational. The two-college model, however, gives men and women the opportunities for student government leadership, the personalized advising, and the sense of belonging that comes from affiliation with their own colleges. The liberal arts and sciences curriculum has proficiency requirements in English, a foreign language, and mathematics. Each student must also complete courses distributed across the disciplines—humanities and fine arts, social sciences, and sciences—in a nine-course requirement that gives each student a common basis of knowledge. Proficiency in writing is also required.

The School of Engineering emphasizes design, research, and laboratory experimentation for its Bachelor of Science degree programs in biomedical, chemical, civil, computer, electrical, environmental, and mechanical engineering as well as computer science. The modern laboratories in the engineering complex, including the $12-million Boggs Center for Energy and Biotechnology, support courses and studies in subjects as varied as robotics, environmental clean-up, the design of artificial joints, laser fabrication, and drug purification.

The School of Architecture takes advantage of its location in New Orleans, a fascinating living architecture laboratory, where about 300 students are enrolled in the five-year Bachelor/Master of Architecture program. Students graduate fully prepared to become licensed architects with no further study. The faculty members, nationally known for their scholarship and art as well as their teaching, often involve students in real-world architectural concerns.

The A. B. Freeman School of Business offers majors in accounting, business, finance, management, and marketing, leading to the Bachelor of Science in Management degree. The curriculum emphasizes ethics, entrepreneurship, international business, leadership, and communication skills as well as the major areas.

The honors program, with approximately 600 academically outstanding students, emphasizes small seminars during the first three college years and a research-based honors thesis the senior year. More than 100 students choose honors floors in the residence halls. The English as a Second Language/Bachelor of General Studies program, offered through University College, is specifically designed for international students who are academically qualified for Tulane but must improve their skills in English.

Off-Campus Programs

With more than 900 students from more than 100 other countries at Tulane, undergraduates don't have to go abroad for an international experience. But many of them choose to take advantage of one of the University's programs for a summer, a semester, or a year of study abroad. Each year, approximately 100 academically talented Tulane students participate in the Tulane/Newcomb Junior Year Abroad (JYA) program, attending universities in France, Germany, Great Britain (including Scotland and Wales), Ireland, Israel, Italy, and Spain. Most scholarships and loans may be applied to JYA costs. Others opt for internships in New Orleans or Washington, D.C. or places as far afield as London and Cambridge, England.

Academic Facilities

Tulane's library system is ranked among the nation's top 100 research collections. University library holdings total more than 2 million volumes, with several special research collections among the best in America: the William Ransom Hogan Jazz Archive; the Newcomb College Center for Research on Women; and the Amistad Research Center, with its collection of primary source materials on the history of America's ethnic minorities, race relations, and civil rights. Other research facilities include the Roger Thayer Stone Center for Latin American Studies and the Murphy Institute for Political Economy. The Newcomb Gallery exhibits a wide range of art work, including shows by students and faculty members. State-of-the-art computing facilities include dozens of public terminals and a fiber-optic network connecting all campus buildings to the Internet.

Costs

In 2003–04, the cost for a year at Tulane was $37,451. Of this amount, tuition and fees were $29,810 and room and board were $7641 for a typical double room and an all-you-can-eat twenty-three-meal plan (cost may vary for upperclass students).

Financial Aid

The University operates a comprehensive aid program; more than half of the students receive some form of financial aid. The average financial aid package (through scholarships, federal grants, loans, and work-study jobs) was nearly $23,000 for 2001–02. Need, determined by family financial information on the Free Application for Federal Student Aid and the PROFILE from the College Scholarship Service, establishes the appropriate amount of assistance. Merit, based on academic record, determines the proportion of Tulane-funded scholarships in the aid package. The University offers assistance to applicants who demonstrate financial need, and 90 percent of freshmen offered aid had their full need met. If financial need continues and the student has an acceptable academic record, aid extends through the normal period of undergraduate study. Notification of the financial aid award follows admission notification. Deans' Honor Scholarships are offered each year to approximately 100 freshmen and cover tuition for the undergraduate career; other merit scholarships, including those for middle-income students, are also available. Tulane also gives at least thirty National Merit Scholarships to National Merit Finalists who have named Tulane as their first-choice college. Tulane offers creative financing options for families that do not qualify for traditional aid but need assistance in meeting costs.

Faculty

The small, personal settings of Tulane classes give students immediate contact with their professors. Some of Tulane's most seasoned faculty members teach introductory and lower-level courses. About 98 percent of the 676 faculty members hold the highest academic degrees in their field, and there are broad opportunities for students, from the freshman year to graduation, to work closely with the faculty on research. Endowed chairs bring distinguished visiting lecturers to the campus every semester. Students have access to faculty members and counselors in the Career Services Center, the Newcomb College Center for Research on Women, and the Educational Resources and Counseling Center as well as in their own colleges and departments.

Student Government

Open communication between elected student representatives and the University's administrators makes Tulane responsive to students' needs. All students are members of the Associated Student Body of Tulane University and participate in University-wide elections. They can hold office and serve on a variety of student-faculty administrative committees. Students are also members of student government associations in each University college or division and can participate on a class level within those divisions.

Admission Requirements

Tulane seeks students who have proven academic capabilities combined with talents or achievements that would enrich the quality of life on campus. All applicants are considered without regard to race, sex, color, religion, sexual orientation, national origin, or physical handicap. Secondary school preparation consisting of 16 or more academic units is expected. In general, quality of achievement is more important than the number of units completed. Applicants to the School of Architecture are encouraged to submit evidence of creative interests with their application. Official SAT I or ACT scores are required. Three SAT II Subject Tests are strongly recommended for course placement and four SAT IIs are required of home-schooled applicants. Interviews are not required, but applicants are encouraged to visit the campus. The admission office is open year-round, except on holidays, from 8:30 a.m. to 5 p.m. central time, Monday through Friday.

Application and Information

Regular decision applications should be submitted by January 15 for admission to the fall semester; admission notification is made no later than April 1, with a May 1 deposit deadline. Deans' Honor Scholarship applicants must apply by December 15 and are notified by February 20. Early decision/early action candidates should have all credentials on file by November 1 for notification by December 15. The application fee is $55.

Richard Whiteside
Vice President for Enrollment Management
Tulane University
210 Gibson Hall
6823 St. Charles Avenue
New Orleans, Louisiana 70118-5680
Telephone: 504-865-5731
800-873-9283 (toll-free)
Fax: 504-862-8715
E-mail: undergrad.admission@tulane.edu
World Wide Web: http://www.tulane.edu/Admission

TUSCULUM COLLEGE

GREENEVILLE, TENNESSEE

The College

Founded in 1794, Tusculum is one of the most innovative institutions in the nation. Not only is Tusculum the oldest college in Tennessee and the twenty-eighth oldest college in the country, it is the oldest coeducational institution affiliated with the Presbyterian Church (U.S.A.). Tusculum is one of the few colleges in the nation to offer students the opportunity to take one course at a time; this is called the focused calendar. The result is an accelerated academic schedule that encourages mastery and retention of subject matter over memorization. It also allows close daily interaction with instructors and classmates, building a community of learning through strong personal bonds. The calendar is an integral part of the College's civic arts mission: to build character and active citizenship through education.

Facilities on the wooded, 140-acre campus comprise nineteen buildings, eight of which are listed on the National Register of Historic Places. A new multipurpose facility, known as the Alpine Arena and the Niswonger commons, has recently been completed. The complex contains a gymnasium, training facilities, classrooms, and offices. The College's residence halls are single-sex. Due to Tusculum College's expansive growth, four new apartment-style residence halls were completed in spring 2002. Each residence hall is within easy access of the classrooms, gymnasium, pool, student union, and tennis courts. Tusculum is a member of Division II of the NCAA. It fields teams in the following varsity sports: men's baseball and football, women's softball and volleyball, and men's and women's basketball, cheerleading, cross-country, golf, soccer, and tennis. Many other intramural sports, student organizations, and social events are sponsored by the College.

Location

Located in Greeneville, Tennessee, Tusculum is surrounded by mountains and beautiful rivers, streams, and lakes. The Great Smoky Mountains National Park and Cherokee National Forest are both within an hour's drive. It is an ideal area for many recreational activities, including hiking, camping, backpacking, white-water rafting, fishing, hunting, and skiing.

The city of Greeneville has been listed as number 38 in *The 100 Best Small Towns in America*. Greeneville, combined with Greene County, has a population of approximately 65,000. The region is rich in the history of east Tennessee, going back to pre–Revolutionary War times. With an elevation of about 1,500 feet, Greeneville has a moderate climate with four distinct seasons. In addition to providing recreational activities, the surrounding mountains offer cooling breezes in the summer and protective barriers from large snow storms in winter, although two or three light snows a year are not uncommon. Knoxville and the Tri-Cities—Kingsport, Johnson City, and Bristol—are all within an hour's drive, offering a wide variety of entertainment, shopping, and cultural activities. Off-campus employment opportunities are readily available within the Greeneville community.

Majors and Degrees

Tusculum College awards the Bachelor of Arts degree in athletic training, biology, business, computer information systems, computer science, education (early childhood, elementary, middle school, secondary, and special education), English, environmental science, graphic arts, history, management (accounting, general management, small business organization, and sports management), mass media, mathematics, museum studies, naturalist field guide, physical education, psychology, and visual arts.

Special programs are offered in medical technology, predentistry, prelaw, premedicine, pre-optometry, pre-pharmacy, pre-physical therapy, and pre–veterinary studies. Teacher certification/licensure is awarded for secondary education in biology, science, English, history, and history with psychology. Teacher certification/licensure is also awarded for K–12 in physical education and visual arts. Students can choose to minor in chemistry, journalism, political science, or religion in addition to any of the preceding areas of study.

Academic Programs

Students generally complete course requirements for the baccalaureate degree in four calendar years. The College divides the academic year into two semesters. Each semester consists of four courses or blocks, where the students study the same subject for approximately 3½ weeks straight. When one course ends, students get a four-day break before the next one begins. Each course is worth 4 semester hours, resulting in 32 semester hours per year. A minimum of 128 credit hours is required for graduation. Within the 128 hours, students fulfill requirements not only in their chosen major but also in the College's core curriculum, called the Commons. The Commons is a combination of interdisciplinary courses and disciplinary courses in writing, mathematics, history, and environmental science. Tusculum also prepares students for a professional and productive life by guaranteeing graduates the skills necessary to succeed in life.

The focused calendar and Commons courses enable students to experience the world for themselves and not just in a textbook. They also allow Tusculum graduates to become positive role models for the next generation.

Students have the option of pursuing internships in conjunction with almost every major. They can also pursue an independent study project. Tusculum requires all students to complete a Service Learning Project before graduation. Credit is granted to students for AP exams and CLEP tests.

Off-Campus Programs

Tusculum College offers a 3-1 medical technology major. For the first three years the student must satisfy the fundamental course requirements. The program is completed in the fourth year by attending an approved hospital for clinical study and fieldwork. In addition, Tusculum has a 3-2 pharmacy program in conjunction with Campbell University. Tusculum College affords students the opportunity to study abroad in such places as Costa Rica, England, Mexico, Scotland, and Spain.

Academic Facilities

The Albert Columbus Tate Library, built in 1910 and a National Historic Site, houses more than 185,000 books and microform texts; 600 periodical titles, records, films, audiotapes, and videotapes; ERIC and Infotrac computerized databases; and Internet capability.

The College is also the site for the President Andrew Johnson Museum and Library, which houses the collection of the seventeenth president's private and family papers, donated to the College by Margaret Johnson Patterson Bartlett, Johnson's great-granddaughter. The library also holds the Charles C. Coffin Rare Book Collection, the original Tusculum College library, which is the largest extant library dating before 1807 in the Southeast. Named after an early president of the College, it contains books from the collections of Thomas Jefferson, Jonathan Edwards, John Hopkins, and the Mathers, with imprints back to the fifteenth century. The library is also a valuable resource for scholars interested in frontier education in the late eighteenth and early nineteenth centuries.

Costs

Tuition and fees for the 2004–05 academic year are $14,810, and room and board cost $5955. Textbooks and supplies average $300 per semester. Personal expenses and travel costs vary with the individual student.

Financial Aid

Tusculum College offers a wide range of financial aid programs, and approximately 90 percent of all students receive some type of assistance. The forms of aid available include grants, loans, work-study, and scholarships. The Federal Pell Grant, Federal Supplemental Educational Opportunity Grant, and Tennessee Student Assistance Award are nonrepayable and funded by federal and state programs. Loans offered by Tusculum are repayable either by the student or parents and include the Federal Perkins Loan, Federal Stafford Student Loan, and Federal Parent Loan for Undergraduate Students (FPLUS). Most grants and loans are awarded on the basis of need, while most scholarships are awarded on a non-need, merit basis to students with exceptional academic or athletic talents. All applicants interested in receiving financial aid should check the appropriate box on the admission application, and a financial aid application packet will be sent; the student should return the appropriate materials to the College as soon as possible to be considered for all available programs. Priority is given to applications processed before April 1.

Faculty

The student-faculty ratio is 12:1. More than 80 percent of the full-time faculty members hold the Ph.D. or appropriate terminal degree. The primary responsibilities of the faculty are teaching and academic advising. Because of the focused calendar, the relationships between faculty members and students are strong and involved.

Student Government

As an institution dedicated to preparing people for effective participation in a democratic society, Tusculum offers many avenues for authentic deliberation, collaboration, and decision making. A set of committees composed of students, faculty members, and staff members, all voting members, oversees the academic and student life functions of the College. In addition to this participation in general campus governance, the Student Government Association is constituted entirely of students and serves to provide a democratic means for distributing student activity and organization funds and as a forum for presenting student concerns to faculty and administration.

Admission Requirements

Candidates for admission to Tusculum College must have graduated from an approved or accredited secondary school or have a general equivalency diploma. The College expects students to demonstrate their preparedness for college with a minimum 2.0 GPA in academic core courses. Students must have at least twelve academic core courses, including English, math (algebra I or higher), science, and social studies. Students must also have taken the SAT or the ACT. The curriculum at Tusculum places strong emphasis on writing, analytical reading, and critical analysis. A demonstration of personal commitment and motivation is also taken into consideration. Although a personal interview is not required for admission, prospective students are encouraged to visit the Tusculum campus.

Application and Information

Tusculum College has a rolling admission policy. Applicants are reviewed for admission once the application is completed. A one-time application fee of $20 is required. Interviews and campus tours are available through the Admissions Office.

For additional information, students should contact:

Admissions Office
Tusculum College
P.O. Box 5051
Greeneville, Tennessee 37743
Telephone: 423-636-7312
800-729-0256 (toll-free)
E-mail: admissions@tusculum.edu
World Wide Web: http://www.tusculum.edu

The main entrance to Tusculum College and the Annie Hogan Byrd Fine Arts Building.

UNION COLLEGE

BARBOURVILLE, KENTUCKY

The College

Union College is a small, spirited, independent liberal arts college in the Appalachian Mountain range. The College, affiliated with the United Methodist Church, was founded in 1879, a time when simple survival, not higher education, was the top priority of most of the country. However, for the citizens of Barbourville, a town of 450 people and three brick buildings, establishing a college for their children was essential. The name they chose reflected the unity of purpose they felt; they believed education was the path to leadership.

Union's nearly 600 undergraduates and 316 graduate students represent twenty-four states and several countries. The College's academic program fulfills the goal of a liberal arts education. It also provides students with the skills necessary to compete in a diverse job market. The undergraduate liberal arts curriculum makes available a body of knowledge drawn from the applied sciences, humanities, natural sciences, and social sciences. Majors and areas of study in preprofessional, technical, and skills-oriented fields enhance postgraduate employment opportunities.

Union's 100-acre campus is on the edge of the beautiful Appalachian Mountains in southeastern Kentucky. Approximately 44 percent of the students live in three dormitories or apartments on campus, all of which provide Internet, e-mail, and cable access. Dozens of student organizations offer many opportunities for participation in a wide range of extracurricular activities. Union's full-time campus minister organizes various religious activities, including weekly voluntary chapel services and monthly convocations.

Intercollegiate sports include basketball, cross-country, golf, mountain biking, soccer, and tennis for men and women; softball and volleyball for women; and baseball and football for men. Intramural sports vary according to student request. The College recently completed a new softball field and refurbished the baseball, soccer, and football fields.

Location

Just 17 miles east of Interstate 75 and about an hour south of Lexington, the town of Barbourville sits in the Appalachian Mountains and is surrounded by four state parks filled with waterfalls, lakes, and streams. While it has the typical warmth and charm of a small community, Barbourville has also been designated as one of America's best-wired small towns by *Yahoo! Internet Life* magazine. The campus itself includes more than 100 gently rolling acres that are covered in overhanging elms, mountain laurel, and Georgian architecture. The famous Wilderness Road spans the east side of the campus, and Cumberland Gap National Historic Park is just 30 miles away. The air is clean and fresh, and the people are friendly and down to earth.

Majors and Degrees

Union College offers Bachelor of Arts and Bachelor of Science degrees. Majors are available in accounting, biology, business administration, chemistry, Christian ministries, criminal justice, education (elementary, middle grades, music, physical, secondary, and special), English/communications, health, history, history and political science, mathematics, psychology, recreation management, religious studies, sociology, and sports management.

In addition to programs in the pure disciplines of biology, chemistry, mathematics, and physics and their education counterparts, Union has programs in place for professional and health science careers. These programs combine the advantages of the small private college and those of the large university and include dentistry, engineering, medical technology, medicine, optometry, pharmacy, physical therapy, and veterinary medicine. Some of the programs have cooperative agreements; some are based on competition, while others give preference to Union students.

Academic Programs

Union College helps students make learning connections. Students are given opportunities for practical applications through an academically rigorous liberal arts curriculum. Upon admission to the College, students begin a process whereby career counselors and academic advisers help them articulate career goals, select academic courses of study appropriate to those goals, and achieve suitable placement upon completion of their studies.

The College operates on a two-semester calendar, with a May interim session and two summer terms. Students must successfully complete a total of 128 semester hours to earn a bachelor's degree. This includes up to 50 semester hours of required core classes. Union's Liberal Education Core, nicknamed UCore, represents a complete break from outmoded models of learning where professors simply disperse information. In contrast, the College strives for a more interdisciplinary, integrated approach to creating an environment where student learning is modeled, facilitated, and enhanced.

The cornerstone of UCore is a course entitled Critical Dialogues: Western Cultures in World Contexts. Critical Dialogues is a civilization course expanded to examine history, literature, philosophy, religion, and the fine arts simultaneously from both a chronological and a thematic approach. Teams of faculty members share lecture responsibility, while each faculty member also leads a discussion-oriented group of approximately 12 students.

Another unique feature of Union's academic program is its recognition of its connection to Appalachia. Through Appalachian Explorations, an integrated introduction to culture, service learning, and wilderness experiences, students begin to explore the Appalachian region. UCore also includes an interdisciplinary social and behavioral sciences sequence, which consists of a foundations course and an applications course. The first explores the theoretical and methodological foundations of sociology, psychology, and anthropology, as well as political science, economics, and geography.

UCore's 8-semester hour general sciences sequence (GSS) is an interdisciplinary natural sciences option for non-science majors. One half of the GSS stresses the life sciences, while the other emphasizes the physical sciences.

Added to these opportunities is a Life Choices course. Rather than being simply a physical education activity option, Life Choices provides an opportunity for students to gain the knowledge and insight to develop and implement a positive personal lifestyle plan.

One-hour reading courses taken in the junior year help students remain focused on the issues raised in UCore as they work toward completion of their majors. In the senior year, Union students also participate in a capstone course in their majors, where they work toward the formation and written expression of a personal life philosophy.

Off-Campus Programs

Union College is a cooperating member of the Kentucky Institute of International Studies (KIIS). The College joins with a number of other Kentucky colleges and universities to provide summer study opportunities in ten different locations. The programs in France, Spain, Mexico, Germany, Austria, Italy, and Ecuador are open to all Union College students, who may earn credits toward their degree at Union.

Academic Facilities

The Weeks-Townsend Memorial Library, with seating for 300, contains more than 150,000 books, bound periodicals, government documents, microforms, and media materials. Numerous online reference and full-text periodical databases enhance student research capabilities. Special collections include the Lincoln-Civil War Collection, the Kentucky Collection, and the Curriculum Collection of teaching materials. Library functions, including the public access catalog, circulation, and academic reserves, are fully automated. The main campus computer lab in the library and two additional computer labs in the Centennial Hall classroom building are open a variety of hours each week to support the academic programs of the College and to provide access, through the campus network, to e-mail and the Internet.

The Sharp Academic Center, a teaching and administrative facility completed in 2000, includes a video conference room available for use by students, faculty, and the surrounding community. Union's newest facility, the Edward H. Black Technology Center opened in spring 2003. The two-story tech center includes a training/computer lab and a state-of-the-art audio/video studio, which will house a College-operated cable channel as well as extensive multimedia hardware and software.

The Academic Resource Center (ARC) provides free services to Union College students in several academic support areas. Individual tutoring is available in a variety of subject areas in both upper- and lower-division classes. Students may work with a tutor to review for classes, refresh study skills, or prepare for professional examinations such as GMAT, LSAT, MCAT, GRE, and NTE. Each semester, courses that have been deemed academically challenging are selected for supplemental instruction (SI). Students attend group study sessions, which are held a minimum of three times a week, with a student leader who has already excelled in that particular course. The SI leaders model good study strategies and encourage collaborative learning.

Costs

Tuition for the 2004–05 academic year was $13,550, and room and board were $4400, for a total of $17,950. Books were estimated at $600 per year. Personal expenses were estimated at $500 per year, depending upon the individual.

Financial Aid

In 2004–05, 97 percent of Union's undergraduate students received financial assistance. Students wishing to be considered for aid must file the Free Application for Federal Student Aid (FAFSA) by March 15. The Federal Pell Grant, Federal Supplemental Educational Opportunity Grant, and Federal Work-Study programs are sources of aid. Kentucky residents may apply for the Kentucky State Tuition Grant.

Faculty

Union's faculty members are intensely committed to the adventure of learning as well as the greater adventure of life. One faculty member had the adventure of a lifetime on a trek in the Amazon, and another is one of today's foremost authorities on one of the richer cultures in America, Appalachia. The faculty-student ratio is 1:13.

Student Government

Union College Community Government provides an opportunity to examine and seek solutions for quality-of-life issues of the campus. The Campus Activities Board seeks to design, sponsor, and produce a broad range of activities on campus. The Commuter Council seeks to examine the needs and interests of nonresidential students and to provide programs to meet those needs.

Admission Requirements

To be considered for admission, a student must submit a completed application, a $10 application fee, ACT or SAT I scores, and official high school transcripts. The following high school academic units are required: 4 in English, 3 in mathematics, 2 in social studies, and 2 in science. Foreign language study is recommended but not required. Applicants must have maintained a minimum average of C in their secondary school work. References and student activities are also considered.

Transfer students must submit a completed application, a $20 application fee, and official transcripts from any college or university previously attended. Official high school transcripts are required if the student is transferring fewer than 31 semester hours. Transfer students must be eligible to return to the institution last attended and may be admitted to Union in any semester or summer session.

At Union, the doors are open to anyone who wants a more fulfilling life, regardless of race, color, sex, disability, or national or ethnic origin.

Application and Information

Application forms may be obtained by writing to the Admission Office or may be completed online. Applications are processed on a rolling admission basis. Students must present ACT or SAT I scores and official high school transcripts. Upon acceptance, students must complete the health form provided by the College.

Additional information may be obtained by contacting:

Admission Office
Union College
310 College Street
Barbourville, Kentucky 40906
Telephone: 606-546-4151 Ext. 1657
800-489-8646 (toll-free)
E-mail: enroll@unionky.edu
World Wide Web: http://www.unionky.edu

Union's "Get Outside Yourself" experience is multifaceted: from the classroom to the athletic fields, from community service to the great outdoors, students learn how to explore, stretch, grow—and make life an adventure.

UNION COLLEGE
LINCOLN, NEBRASKA

The College

Union College, established in 1891, is a Christian liberal arts institution offering four-year postsecondary degrees and a limited number of two-year degrees. Graduate programs in education and nursing are offered on campus through cooperating institutions.

Union's population exhibits a diverse international flavor. Students bring varied experiences and backgrounds from throughout the United States and forty other countries. One in 6 students is an international student. The student body of approximately 900 makes the College small enough for each student to receive individual attention and to form lifelong friendships.

Union is renowned for the humanitarian service of its graduates. Each year for more than ninety years, an average of 20 students and alumni have begun international humanitarian, medical, and/or educational services.

A multimillion-dollar capital campaign of renovations and additional campus facilities is nearly complete. Residence halls, new classrooms, and laboratory and performance centers are included in the proposed facilities/renovations. Union's percentage of alumni contribution is among the highest in the nation and allows for major campus improvements.

Location

Union is perched on the highest point in Lincoln, the capital of Nebraska. The 110-year-old campus features more than 100 species of trees in a beautiful parklike setting. The 50 surrounding acres of property are a part of the statewide arboretum system. The College is an eclectic blend of ivy-covered neo-Greco brick buildings, brick walkways, and modern academic and student service structures. Near the campus are connections to more than 80 miles of scenic biking and walking trails within the city and the surrounding area.

Lincoln is the forty-fifth largest city in the United States and among the most rapidly growing. It is small enough to have a sense of community yet large enough to have its own culture. The historic Haymarket district offers shopping, bistros, galleries, boutiques, and ethnic restaurants. The downtown contains galleries, museums, playhouses, state and federal offices, gardens, fountains, banking centers, the Lied Center for the Performing Arts, and one of two sprawling Lincoln campuses of the University of Nebraska, with its Devany Sports Complex, and more.

Majors and Degrees

Union College offers majors, emphases, and minors (* denotes example of twenty-six minors) in academic disciplines leading to the following 7 four-year degrees: Bachelor of Arts, Bachelor of Science, Bachelor of Science in Nursing, Bachelor of Technology, Bachelor of Social Work, Bachelor of Music, and Bachelor of Arts in Theology. Nine two-year associate degrees are offered. Union offers programs of study in art (graphic design and studio art), behavioral science (psychology, social work, and sociology*), biology (biology and marine biology), business (accounting, administration, finance, institutional development, international business, international studies, management, marketing, science, small-business management, and technology), chemistry (biochemistry, chemistry, and general chemistry), communication (communication, drama*, journalism, and public relations), computer science (computer information systems and computer science), education (elementary and secondary), English (English literature/drama, speaking, and writing), general studies, global relief, health and human performance (business/sport management and fitness/cardiac rehabilitation), health science (clinical laboratory medical technology, and nursing), history, mathematics (mathematics and statistics), modern language (French, German, and Spanish), music education (instrumental, keyboard, and vocal), music performance (conducting, instrumental, keyboard, and vocal), physics, religion (missions and evangelism, pastoral care, religion, theology, and youth ministry*), and social science*.

Preprofessional programs are offered in architecture, dental assisting, dental hygiene, dentistry, dietetics, engineering, law, medical records, medicine, occupational therapy, optometry, osteopathy, pharmacy, physical therapy, public health, radiologic technology, respiratory therapy, speech-language pathology and audiology, and veterinary medicine.

National Council for the Accreditation of Teacher Education (NCATE)–approved teaching degrees and endorsements are offered in art, biology, business, chemistry, computer science, English, history, language arts, mathematics, music, physical education, physics, religious education, and social science. A limited number of technical degrees are also available.

Union offers nine Associate of Arts and Associate of Science degrees in accounting, art, business administration, computer information systems, engineering, graphic design, music pedagogy, office management (some courses are taken at affiliated local colleges), and pre–allied health.

Academic Programs

Baccalaureate degrees are awarded after students complete requirements. Degree requirements include general education, the major, contextual requirements, and electives, totaling a minimum of 128 semester hours. At least 40 of these 128 semester hours must be in courses numbered at the 300 level or above. A minimum of 56 semester hours must be completed in four-year colleges or universities. Three writing-designated (WR) courses are required after satisfactory completion of ENGL 111 and ENGL 112. A minimum grade point average (GPA) of 2.0 in all course work attempted at Union College and all transferred credits is required. (Students should consult the Academic Bulletin for further details.)

Union Scholars, the College's honors program, offers an enriched academic experience and substantial annual scholarship awards.

In addition to traditional liberal arts education, Union offers practical experiences such as internships, career counseling, and study abroad.

The Teaching Learning Center offers such services as instruction, bypass strategies, note takers, and tutors for students with learning differences such as dyslexia.

Four levels of English as a second language (ESL) offer beginning conversation to university-level preparation. Students with TOEFL scores between 450 and 549 may take select university-level courses. Dual-enrollment tuition rates vary based on the number of ESL and non-ESL courses. All levels offer reduced tuition. Four hours of ESL classes may count toward a degree. The TOEFL is required of all non-native English speakers upon arrival. Completion of the ESL program occurs when the student is able to score at least 550 on the TOEFL.

Academic Facilities

The Engel Hall fine arts complex houses both visual and musical arts programs. The Everett Dick Building includes the divisions of humanities, business and computer science, human development, and religion. Microcomputer labs use cutting-edge software and hardware and provide access to the Internet and advanced business, art, and desktop publishing programs. Jorgensen Hall houses engineering, chemistry, biology, and mathematics. Science students use an in-house HP 5890 capillary gas chromatography unit and other advanced analytical equipment. The Ella Johnson Crandall Memorial Library has more than 130,000 volumes of print and nonprint media. In addition to physician assistant studies, nursing, health, and exercise science classrooms, offices, and labs, the Larson Lifestyle Center houses an Olympic-size pool, weight rooms, a Jacuzzi, tennis courts, and sand volleyball courts. Classroom buildings contain PC and scientific/health science laboratories.

The Career Center offers resources to assist students in making career decisions, writing resumes and cover letters, conducting job searches, perfecting interview techniques, and arranging career shadowing and internships.

Each residence hall room's computer terminal provides free access to the Internet, WordPerfect, Quattro Pro, library card catalogs, e-mail, and more.

Costs

Annual estimated expenses for 2004–05 total $19,146 (tuition, $13,380; room, $2576; estimated cafeteria expenses, $1790; technology fee and miscellaneous expenses, $500; and textbooks, $900). Tuition is based on 12 to 17.5 credit hours.

Financial Aid

Union College tailors financial aid packages to fit individual student needs. Proceeds from more than $7.7 million in endowments (145 endowed scholarship funds), federal and institutional scholarships, student loans, grants, and work-study programs are available to qualified students. On- and off-campus employment may also defray costs and provide career experience. Grants and loans are available from federal and state agencies.

Students who have finished a four-year degree at Union and later decide to change careers may return for another degree, tuition free. (Interested students should consult the Academic Bulletin for details of the Guaranteed Degree Program.)

Students apply for financial aid by completing the Free Application for Federal Student Aid (FAFSA), which is available at any local college, many libraries, the Internet, and high school guidance counselors' offices.

Faculty

The Union College faculty includes 55 full-time faculty members and additional part-time faculty members. Over forty percent of the full-time faculty members hold terminal degrees.

In addition to being qualified professionals, Union's professors are Christian role models who portray their values through their actions and speech. They are committed to the art of teaching and to caring for each student. Professors, not graduate assistants, teach classes and supervise labs.

Student Government

Students participate in College governance through elected positions in the Associated Student Body (ASB). Students are also members of most campus committees. Regularly scheduled town hall assemblies are held to allow students direct interaction with administrators. In addition to the ASB, other recognized campus clubs and organizations meet regularly.

Admission Requirements

Specific admission requirements include at least a 2.5 GPA (applicants with a GPA between 2.0 and 2.5 are accepted into A.S.A.P.—Academic Success and Advising Program—only); an ACT score for entering freshmen; three references; high school transcripts, home school transcripts, or GED; and transcripts from other colleges (if applicable). Special assistance and admission is available to students with certified learning differences (interested students should see the Teaching Learning Center in the College bulletin for details).

Union College does not discriminate on the basis of race, religion, disability, age, or gender and is affiliated with the Adventist Church.

Application and Information

Applications may be submitted year-round. Notification of acceptance occurs approximately two weeks after all requirements are met. Prospective applicants should contact:

Office of Admissions
Union College
3800 South 48th Street
Lincoln, Nebraska 68506
Telephone: 402-486-2504 (outside North America)
800-228-4600 (toll-free inside North America)
Fax: 402-486-2566
E-mail: ucenroll@ucollege.edu
World Wide Web: http://www.ucollege.edu

The Everett Dick Administration Building is one of six classroom buildings at Union College.

UNION COLLEGE

SCHENECTADY, NEW YORK

The College

Union College is an independent, undergraduate, residential college for men and women of high academic promise and strong personal motivation. Founded in 1795, it was the first college chartered by the Regents of the State of New York and is one of the oldest nondenominational colleges in the country. The first college in America with a unified campus plan, Union was the first liberal arts college to offer engineering (in 1845). It has more than 20,000 alumni and an endowment of approximately $246 million. The College seeks a geographically and socially diverse student body; at this time, the 2,100 undergraduates represent thirty-seven states and several countries. Approximately one-third of each graduating class continues directly on to graduate or professional school, and Union has earned an excellent reputation for the placement of its graduates in medical, law, and business schools.

Union believes that a student's life outside the classroom is a vital part of his or her total education and therefore encourages a variety of student organizations—approximately 100 at last count—and a rich cultural and social life. Union also offers an extensive program of intercollegiate, intramural, club, and recreational sports. Highlights among the athletic facilities are the Alumni Gymnasium with an eight-lane swimming/diving pool and squash and racquetball courts; a 3,000-seat ice rink; an Astroturf field; and an all-weather track. The Reamer Campus Center provides space for social and community activities and services for the entire campus. Dining facilities, a pub, an auditorium, a radio station, and multiple student activities spaces are important parts of the building. The historic Nott Memorial has been renovated into a discussion and display center for students and alumni.

Students are expected to live on campus during their undergraduate years. Union's innovative new House System is designed to provide additional social, academic, and residential opportunities for students; it joins a residence life program that includes student-initiated theme houses, traditional residence halls, apartments, co-ops, theme houses, and fraternities and sororities.

Location

Union is located in the the small upstate New York city of Schenectady, part of a metropolitan area based on Albany, the capital of New York. The Capital District's population of nearly 900,000 includes more than 55,000 college and university students. Schenectady is 3 hours from New York City and Boston and 4 hours from Montreal. Wilderness camping, white-water canoeing, skiing, and cross-country ski touring are available in the nearby Catskills, Adirondacks, Green Mountains, and Massachusetts Berkshires. A great number of volunteer opportunities are available within the Schenectady community.

Majors and Degrees

Union offers the Bachelor of Arts (B.A.)degree in anthropology, art (art history, music, theater arts, and visual arts), classics, economics, English, history, modern languages, philosophy, political science, and sociology. The Bachelor of Science (B.S.) degree is awarded in biochemistry, biology, chemistry, computer science, computer engineering, electrical engineering, geology, mathematics, mechanical engineering, neuroscience, physics, and psychology. Formal interdepartmental work is offered in Africana studies, American studies, East Asian studies, industrial economics, Latin American and Caribbean studies, managerial economics, Russia and Eastern European studies, and women's studies. Transdisciplinary studies, individually designed majors, and concentrations within departments are also available. Programs in which a student may earn two baccalaureate degrees are available in the following combinations: engineering and bachelor of science or bachelor of arts, or two engineering degrees. Students may also declare up to two academic minors in any of twenty-five disciplines. In addition, Union offers programs that lead to a B.A. degree from Union and a law degree from Albany Law School or to a B.S. from Union and an M.S. or M.B.A. from the Graduate College of Union University and an M.D. from Albany Medical College. Union also offers a variety of programs that combine a Union College degree with an advanced degree from the Graduate College of Union University.

Academic Program

As a college committed to the liberal arts ideal, Union prepares students for roles as useful, informed citizens and leaders as well as jobholders. Students are encouraged to strive for a breadth of learning to complement the expertise acquired through studies in their major. In its General Education program, for example, Union ensures that its students are exposed to important areas of knowledge in history, literature, science, mathematics, and social science and offers strong incentives to study other cultures. In its Converging Technologies programs, faculty members from engineering and the liberal arts work together to create courses that cross traditional disciplinary boundaries. Students may explore such areas as bioengineering, mechatronics, nanotechnology, neuroscience, and pervasive computing. Independent study and undergraduate research are strongly encouraged. To foster initiative in educational programs and individual academic exploration, Union's own Internal Education Foundation makes grants for special projects to students, faculty members, and administrators. The College annually sends one of the largest delegations to the National Conference on Undergraduate Research. Degree requirements include successful completion of 36 courses in all programs except engineering, which may require up to 40, and the successful completion of the requirements in the major and the general education program. Students who pass examinations taken under the College Board's Advanced Placement Program with a score of 4 or higher (except in calculus, for which a score of 3 is acceptable) are typically given college course credit and are exempted from any requirement to take the equivalent college courses. Union's calendar consists of three 10-week terms, and students normally take three courses each term. The academic year begins in early September and ends in early June.

Off-Campus Programs

Union participates in programs of cross-registration that enable students to take courses at fourteen consortium colleges and universities in the Capital District, including Reserve Officers' Training Corps (ROTC). Union's own international resident-study programs are among the most extensive of any American college. Terms abroad are available in Austria, Barbados, Brazil, China, England, Fiji, France, Germany, Greece, Israel, Italy, Japan, Mexico, and Spain. There is a term of marine studies in Bermuda and Newfoundland and at the Woods Hole Oceanographic Institution in Massachusetts as well as a summer program in which students examine the national health programs of England, Holland, and Hungary. Union, in conjunction with Hobart and William Smith Colleges, also offers programs in Australia, Ireland, Vietnam, and Central Europe (Germany, Hungary, and Romania). The College has eight formal exchange programs: full-year exchanges in Japan and Wales and one-term exchanges in Barbados, Belgium, Bulgaria, the Czech Republic, India, and Korea. Political science internships are available in the New York State legislature and in Washington, D.C.

Academic Facilities

The F. W. Olin Center, a high-technology classroom and laboratory building, contains a multimedia auditorium, collaborative computer classrooms, and a 20-inch remote-controlled telescope. Available for student use in the nearby Science and Engineering Center are such research tools as a nuclear magnetic resonance spectrometer, a Pelletron accelerator, X-ray diffraction equipment, a centrifuge, and a scanning electron microscope. The Arts Center has been extensively renovated and the Yulman Theatre greatly enhances the arts program.

Housed in the Stanley G. Peschel Center for Computer Science and Information Systems, Union's central computer facility consists of several multiuser servers on a campuswide fiber-optic-based network. Included in the network are UNIX, Windows, and Apple Macintosh servers. Connected to the network are more than 1,400 College-owned personal computers and workstations. More than twenty electronic classrooms are used to enhance the integration of technology and academic studies through the use of the Internet and multimedia materials. Each residence hall room is wired with one Ethernet network connection per resident, providing access to the College's computing resources and the Internet. Wireless network connections are available in selected locations on the campus. Personal computer laboratories with Windows, Apple Macintosh, and UNIX workstations are available for student use. Departmental computer labs provide access to specialized computing needs. Access to the Internet, personal Web page space, and e-mail is provided for all Union students and faculty and staff members. Scanners, digital cameras, and other equipment are also available for student use.

A major renovation and expansion of Schaffer Library was completed in 1998. The library houses more than 500,000 volumes and approximately 2,000 current serials, a periodicals reading room, faculty studies, and more than 500 individual study spaces. The library operates on the open-stack plan and offers bibliographic instruction, interlibrary loans, online bibliographic retrieval services, electronic document delivery, and Internet workstations for access to indexes, abstracts, full-text journals online, automated circulation of books, and other library materials as well as the online catalog. Professional reference service is offered during nearly all the hours that the library is open.

Costs

Charges for 2003–04 included tuition, $28,608; average room and board, $7077; and an activities fee, $320.

Financial Aid

Union has a strong philosophical and financial commitment to ensure the affordability of a high-quality education for its students and recognizes students' outstanding academic performance with scholarship assistance. Scholarship awards are based on academic performance and financial need. In 2003–04, Union's total financial aid program amounted to approximately $27.4 million; about $17.8 million came from the College itself and the rest from federal, state, and private sources. More than 55 percent of Union's students receive some form of aid each year (e.g., scholarships, guaranteed loans, and job opportunities) and the average aid package is $22,000. Union strives to keep students' total debt as low as possible. Candidates for aid should complete the Free Application for Federal Student Aid (FAFSA) and the College Scholarship Service's PROFILE form and mail them directly to the appropriate agencies by February 1.

Faculty

Union believes that the close relationship between its students and faculty members motivates students to learn through inquiry and discourse. Its 190 full-time faculty members were chosen with specific reference to their capabilities as teachers. Excluding the library staff, 94 percent of the faculty members hold the doctorate, and faculty salaries are above the national averages for colleges of comparable size. Union does not determine the functions of faculty members on the basis of rank; full professors often teach introductory courses. Class size generally is small; many upper-level courses function as seminars.

Student Government

Students have full voting rights on the two councils that recommend educational policy and student life policy to the president. Students also have seats in groups that advise the president on such matters as budgetary planning and long-range needs.

Admission Requirements

The College considers four factors in evaluating each application: the secondary school record, including rank in class and the quality of courses taken; the recommendations of secondary school teachers; the personal qualities and extracurricular record of the applicant; and scores on the tests given by the College Board (SAT I) or ACT. Students are required to submit one of the following: the SAT I or three SAT II Subject Tests (Writing, Mathematics, and Science are required for the eight-year leadership in medicine program and preferred for engineering and science program candidates; all other students should submit scores on the Writing Test and two others) or the ACT. Those interested in accelerated programs must submit the SAT I and three SAT II Subject Tests. Normally, 16 units of secondary school preparation are required for admission. These should include credits in certain fundamental subjects, such as English, a foreign language, mathematics, social studies, and science. It is strongly recommended that students visit Union for an admission interview and a student-guided tour. Alumni interviews may be arranged for students by calling the Admissions Office.

Application and Information

Early decision candidates have two options. The application deadline for Option I is November 15, with notification by December 15. Option II has a January 15 deadline and February 1 notification. All supporting credentials are due November 15 for Option I and January 15 for Option II. Applications for regular admission should be filed by January 15, with the exception of the accelerated programs. Applications to the eight-year leadership in medicine program must be filed no later than December 15, and applications for the six-year law and public policy and the five-year B.A./B.S. and Master of Business Administration programs must be filed no later than January 1. Those deferred under early decision and all regular applicants are given a final decision by early April. Union adheres to the Candidates Reply Date of May 1.

Office of Admissions
Grant Hall
Union College
Schenectady, New York 12308
Telephone: 518-388-6112
888-843-6688 (toll-free)
Fax: 518-388-6986
E-mail: admissions@union.edu
World Wide Web: http://www.union.edu

The sixteen-sided Nott Memorial is Union College's centerpiece.

UNION UNIVERSITY

JACKSON, TENNESSEE

The University

Union University is committed to equipping persons to think Christianly and serve faithfully in ways consistent with its core values of being Christ centered, people focused, excellence driven, and future directed. These values shape its identity as a learner-centered institution that prioritizes liberal arts–based undergraduate education enhanced by professional and graduate programs. The academic community is composed of high-quality faculty members, staff members, and students working together in a caring, grace-filled environment conducive to the development of character, servant leadership, and cultural engagement.

Union University is the oldest Southern Baptist–related college or university. For more than 180 years, Union has prepared students for the future. Union has consistently received national recognition for academic excellence and value. *U.S. News & World Report* ranked Union in the top tier of "Best Universities–Master's." *Time* and *The Princeton Review* recognized Union as one of only five "highly selective" private universities in Tennessee.

More than 2,800 students enjoy a rich, quality-oriented educational experience in a place where Christian faith and academics complement one another. The average high school GPA is 3.52. The average ACT score is 24. Forty-four states and thirty-six countries are represented in the student body. Fifteen national merit finalists currently attend Union. The University offers more than 100 majors and programs of study in the arts, sciences, humanities, social sciences, business, education, and nursing.

College is more than just classes. At Union, students have the opportunity to enjoy a lively and active social life in addition to academic pursuits. Campus organizations offer opportunities to get involved in a host of possibilities, from drama and music to journalism and ministry. The campus also hosts six Greek fraternal organizations—three for men and three for women. Intramural sports involve a large number of students each year. Union is a major force in the National Association of Intercollegiate Athletics (NAIA). Several men's and women's sports are usually nationally ranked.

On its residential campus, the University provides housing in apartment suites. More than 95 percent of freshmen live on campus. Each resident has a private bedroom with an Internet port. Each suite has four or five bedrooms sharing a common living room and bathroom. Some units have kitchens. Each complex includes a commons building with gathering areas, laundry facilities, and other services. A full-time Residence Director and student Resident Assistants serve each complex.

In addition to residential facilities, Union has excellent academic and student service facilities. At one end of the campus is Penick Academic Complex, with a 1,200-seat chapel, a theater, and administrative center. At the other end is the recreation center, complete with two gyms, a wellness center, racquetball courts, and an indoor pool. In between are classrooms, faculty offices, high-tech computer and natural science labs, and the Emma Waters Summar Library. The Student Union Building houses the cafeteria, snack bar, post office, and the student lounge with a game room. The Blasingame Academic Complex features microcomputer and education labs and state-of-the-art lecture rooms. Hammons Hall is home to the University bookstore, classrooms, and offices. Newly built Jennings Hall features the Biblical studies library and language lab, digital media labs, a broadcast studio, music practice labs and the performance hall, as well as classrooms and faculty offices. Groundbreaking has occurred for a new state-of-the-art science building.

Location

The 290-acre campus is located in suburban Jackson, Tennessee. Jackson is a growing community of 92,000 located just 80 miles from Memphis and 120 miles from Nashville. Students find convenient access to entertainment, shopping, and many other services. Jackson has something to offer everyone through many cultural, recreational, or sports events. The city is served by McKellar-Sipes Regional Airport, which features daily flights via AmericanConnection. Major airports in Memphis and Nashville provide worldwide service via most major airlines.

Majors and Degrees

The associate, Bachelor of Science, Bachelor of Arts, and graduate degrees are offered. Union has more than 100 majors and programs of study. Majors offered in the College of Arts and Sciences include art, biblical studies, biblical studies/languages, biology, broadcasting, ceramics/sculpting, chemical physics, chemistry, Christian ethics, Christian ministries, Christian studies, church music, computer information systems, computer science, digital media studies, drawing/painting, engineering, English, French (languages and culture or literature), graphic design, Greek, history, honors studies, international studies, journalism, mathematics, mechanical engineering, medical technology, music, music education, music management, music marketing, music performance, music theory and literature, philosophy and Christian theology, physical science, physics, political science, politics/philosophy/economics, public relations/advertising, Spanish (languages and culture or literature), teaching English as a second language, theater/speech, writing, and youth ministry. Majors offered in the McAfee School of Business Administration include accounting, business administration, economics/finance, international business, management, management information, and marketing. In addition, the McAfee School also offers a Bachelor of Science in organizational leadership. Majors offered in the School of Education and Human Studies include athletic coaching, athletic training, Christian ministry/recreation, family studies, health education/teacher licensure, human studies, learning foundations (K–8 or early childhood), liberal studies (middle grades 5–8), physical education/teacher licensure, psychology, secondary education (7–12), social work, sociology, special education (K–12), sport management/communication, sport management/marketing, sports medicine/exercise wellness, and sport ministry. The School of Nursing offers a Bachelor of Science in Nursing and the RN–B.S.N. completion program.

Preprofessional programs include chiropractic, cytotechnology, dental hygiene, dentistry, health information management, medicine, occupational therapy, optometry, pharmacy, physical therapy, physician assistant studies, podiatry, and veterinary medicine.

Academic Programs

Union University offers a unique opportunity to study in a context of both academic excellence and deep Christian commitment. Union offers seven traditional undergraduate degrees and five graduate degrees. The requirements of each undergraduate degree include one major and one minor unless otherwise specified in the *Union University Academic Catalogue*. A student may have two baccalaureate degrees conferred when the requirements of both have been met.

The requirements of each bachelor's degree awarded by Union University include 46 hours of general core curriculum, 18 to 21 hours of specific core curriculum, a minimum of 30 hours in the major academic program, and 18 hours in the minor academic program. The completion of the required 128 hours usually requires four years with 32 hours per year.

For each undergraduate degree granted by Union University, at least 25 percent of the semester hours required for the degree must be earned through instruction at Union University. The last 56 semester hours of credit for a bachelor's degree must be earned at an accredited senior college.

The Dean's List recognizes students enrolled for 12 or more hours and that attain an average of 3.5 or above each semester. The President's List recognizes students with a semester average of 4.0. Students making an average of 3.5 or above in courses taken at Union can graduate with cum laude, magna cum laude, or summa cum laude honors.

The academic calendar is divided into fall semester from August to December, winter term during January, spring semester from February to May, and three summer terms. In addition, evening accelerated courses are available each term.

Off-Campus Programs

The University offers several opportunities to study off campus and abroad. Students should refer to the online catalog at the Web site listed below for updated information. Union also participates with four Southern Baptist seminaries in a program designed to allow qualified Christian studies majors to enter a Master of Divinity degree track with advanced studies.

Academic Facilities

Keeping pace with technological demands, Union provides more than 200 computers for student use with full access to e-mail and the Internet. In addition, each residential student has a port for the campus network and Internet access in the private bedroom.

The Emma Waters Summar Library provides resources for students. The library has entered several formal agreements with other libraries and library organizations to further extend its service base. These services enhance students' access to materials through a full range of resources.

Other academic facilities include top-quality lecture facilities, laboratories, and fine and performing arts theaters and practice rooms.

Costs

The cost for a typical student for the 2003–04 academic year (two semesters) was $13,950 in tuition (15 hours), $2730 for housing in an apartment-style residence hall, $1910 for meals (twelve per week), and $500 for a student services fee. The total cost, excluding books, was $19,090 per academic year.

Financial Aid

More than 80 percent of Union students receive some financial aid based on need or merit. Union commits very competitive scholarships and grants to qualified students. In addition, the University helps connect students with other financial resources such as loans, student work programs, privately funded scholarships, and a host of state and federal assistance programs.

For best consideration, the Free Application for Federal Student Aid (FAFSA) should be filed with the Federal Processing Center before February 15 using Union's federal code. In addition, applicants must complete the Union University traditional undergraduate application for financial assistance by February 15. Students who have been accepted for admission and have completed the financial aid process are mailed an award letter on March 15. Students who apply after February 15 are awarded on a rolling basis as funds are available.

Faculty

Union's faculty members are selected based on their academic qualifications. The faculty is teaching focused, with nearly 80 percent holding doctorates or the highest degree offered in their field of study from many of the world's premier graduate programs. Classes at Union are small, with a student-faculty ratio of 12:1.

Faculty members also serve as student advisers. Advisers are assigned within the department of the student's major. Faculty advisers assist students in planning schedules and defining educational and career goals. The student and adviser meet at least once each semester.

Student Government

Union's Student Government Association (SGA), composed of all students enrolled in Union University, functions through its executive, legislative, and judicial branches. Its elected officers and representatives serve as the official voice of the students in institutional affairs. The SGA seeks to foster University unity, promote student welfare, and provide students with programs, activities, and services designed to meet the needs and interests of students.

Admission Requirements

Union University accepts students on a rolling admission basis, but since a limited number of spaces may be available for a class, early application is strongly recommended. Applicants must graduate from an accredited high school with at least 20 units in the areas of English, foreign language, mathematics, social and natural sciences, and approved electives. A state high school equivalency diploma is accepted in lieu of a high school diploma. Union also actively admits home-schooled students. Transfer students who have completed more than 12 semester hours of transferable credit at an accredited college may also apply.

Applicants must complete and return the Union University application for undergraduate admission along with the $25 application fee. All official transcripts must be requested and mailed directly to the Office of Enrollment Services. Results of either the ACT or SAT must also be sent. For detailed admission requirements, students should call the Office of Enrollment Services at the telephone number listed below.

Application and Information

For more information or to request an application, students should contact:

Office of Enrollment Services
Union University
1050 Union University Drive
Jackson, Tennessee 38305-3697
Telephone: 800-33-UNION (toll-free)
E-mail: info@uu.edu
World Wide Web: http://www.uu.edu

UNITED STATES AIR FORCE ACADEMY

COLORADO SPRINGS, COLORADO

The Academy

Established in 1954, the Air Force Academy prepares and motivates cadets for careers as Air Force officers. The Academy stresses character development, military training, and physical fitness as well as academics, emphasizing leadership in all areas.

The total enrollment is approximately 4,000; nearly 1,200 fourth class (freshman) students enter each year. The composition of the student body mirrors that of the Air Force officer corps: about 17 percent women and 18 percent minorities. Students come from all fifty states and several other countries. Their common bond is the desire to be military officers. All cadets must live in on-campus dormitories and wear uniforms.

The Academy is accredited by the North Central Association of Colleges and Schools. Its engineering programs are approved by the Engineering Accreditation Commission of the Accreditation Board for Engineering and Technology, and its computer courses are approved by the Computing Sciences Accreditation Board. The chemistry and biochemistry majors fulfill the requirements of the Commission on Professional Training of the American Chemical Society.

All cadets must participate in intramural, club, or intercollegiate athletics every semester. The intramural sports include basketball, cross-country, flag football, flickerball, men's boxing, mountain biking, racquetball, rugby, soccer, softball, team handball, tennis, Ultimate Frisbee, volleyball, and wallyball. The intercollegiate teams compete in Division I of the NCAA regionally and nationally. The men's teams include baseball, basketball, cross-country, diving, fencing, football, golf, gymnastics, hockey, indoor and outdoor track, lacrosse, riflery, soccer, swimming, tennis, water polo, and wrestling. The women's teams include basketball, cross-country, diving, fencing, gymnastics, indoor and outdoor track, riflery, soccer, swimming, tennis, and volleyball. Cadets may also choose from nearly 100 extracurricular activities, which include professional organizations, mission support, competitive and recreational clubs, sports groups, and hobby clubs.

Qualified Academy graduates may enter flight training upon graduation, and approximately 75 percent of the students in each graduating class pursue graduate education at other institutions within ten years of their graduation. Each year, numerous Academy graduates receive graduate scholarships and fellowships, such as the Marshall, Rhodes, National Science Foundation, National Collegiate Athletic Association, and Guggenheim awards.

Location

The Academy campus sits in the foothills of the Rampart Range of the Rocky Mountains in a setting of natural beauty. Built on a mesa at 7,000 feet, it is one of Colorado's top tourist attractions. The Cadet Chapel, with its seventeen aluminum spires towering 150 feet into the air, highlights the contemporary architecture of the buildings in the cadet area. The space-age effect reflects the Academy's mission of preparing cadets to become officers and leaders in the Air Force of the future. The Academy borders the northern edge of Colorado Springs, which lies at the foot of the famous 14,100-foot Pikes Peak. Colorado Springs has a metropolitan population of more than 300,000. Denver, the state's capital, has a population of almost 2 million in its greater metropolitan area and is located 55 miles north of the Academy. In addition to the social, sports, and cultural activities available in these cities, cadets enjoy skiing, hunting, horseback riding, white-water rafting, and other activities in the Colorado Rocky Mountains and nearby resorts.

Majors and Degrees

Graduates of the four-year service academy receive the Bachelor of Science degree and a commission as a second lieutenant in the Air Force. The B.S. is granted in thirty-two majors: aeronautical engineering; astronautical engineering; basic sciences; behavioral sciences and leadership; biology; chemistry; civil engineering; computer engineering; computer science; economics; electrical engineering; engineering mechanics; English; environmental engineering; foreign area studies; general engineering; geography; history; humanities; legal studies; management; mathematical sciences; mechanical engineering; meteorology; military strategic studies; operations research; physics; political science; social sciences; space operations; systems engineering; and systems engineering management. The Academy also offers minors in foreign languages and philosophy.

Academic Program

A class enters the Academy during the last week in June or the first week in July. Incoming cadets undergo a strenuous six-week summer training program that tests both their mental and physical abilities. Upperclass cadets conduct basic cadet training; commissioned officers serve as advisers. Basic cadets who complete this program are accepted into the Cadet Wing as fourth-class cadets. The academic year starts in early August and continues through May. During the first two years, cadets concentrate on core courses in engineering, humanities, science, and social science. During the last two years, they specialize in an academic major.

The required core courses prepare cadets for a broad scope of activity as Air Force officers. The core curriculum embraces courses in academic subjects, leadership and military training, and physical education and athletics. In addition, cadets complete the requirements for any of the thirty-two academic majors. To be eligible for graduation, cadets must also demonstrate an aptitude for commissioned service and leadership, demonstrate character consistent with professional military service, maintain a minimum cumulative grade point average and core grade point average of 2.0, and complete a minimum of 148 credit hours. The curriculum includes many elective courses.

All students must begin as freshmen; however, cadets who have taken some of the core course material prior to entry into the Academy may receive transfer or validation credit for this work. They may then substitute other courses for those granted transfer credit. Cadets who maintain the required grade point average may take advanced study classes.

The Academy aviation program familiarizes all cadets with operational activities of the Air Force. Optional courses provide instruction in soaring, parachuting, navigation, and basic flying. Those who take these courses may fulfill the requirements for Federal Aviation Administration pilot or glider certificates. Cadets who qualify and are selected for pilot or navigator training may enter Air Education and Training Command flight programs following graduation from the Academy. Diversified summer programs in aviation and military training prepare cadets for officer responsibilities in the Air Force. Cadets may select their programs from several optional assignments at the Air Force Academy and other military installations.

Off-Campus Programs

Selected cadets may exchange visits with cadets from the Military Academy, Naval Academy, Coast Guard Academy, or one of fifteen international Air Force academies. The exchange program varies from one to two weeks for most of the international programs to a semester for the other U.S. service academies and the Canadian, Chilean, French, German, and Spanish Air Force academies.

Academic Facilities

The Air Force Academy's excellent facilities support the academic, military, and athletics programs. Most classrooms accommodate small class sessions, averaging 17 students. Several classes and assemblies meet in larger lecture halls. Well-equipped laboratories supplement classroom instruction. Cadets conduct experiments using the Aeronautics Laboratory's wind tunnels, shock tubes, and rocket engines. A local network connects every dorm room, faculty and staff office, classroom, and laboratory at the Academy, and all entering cadets purchase a laptop computer for academic and personal use. The Academy planetarium is a multimedia education and research facility used for cadet instruction in astronomy and navigation. The Academy library, with more than 600,000 volumes, supports all educational programs and maintains a collection of historical materials concerning aeronautics.

Costs

There are no tuition charges; the cost, including room, board, and medical and dental care, is borne entirely by the U.S. government. In addition, cadets receive a monthly salary to pay for supplies, clothing, and personal expenses. Careful management of the money covers obligations, with a small amount remaining for personal use.

Financial Aid

All cadets are on full scholarship at the Air Force Academy, as described above.

Faculty

The Academy's faculty is composed of Air Force officers and civilian professors. A few officers from other branches of the U.S. Armed Forces from allied nations and distinguished civilian visiting professors supplement the faculty. There are no graduate student instructors. Faculty members must have a master's degree, and many have earned doctorates. Their educational backgrounds represent many outstanding colleges and universities in the United States, as well as some international institutions of higher education. Faculty members sponsor, coach, and referee extracurricular activities and athletics; adopt squadrons and attend their special events; and provide academic, career, and personal counseling.

Student Government

The Air Force Academy trains cadets for future leadership by allowing them to hold positions of responsibility in the Cadet Wing, the organization to which all cadets are assigned. The wing is under the operational supervision of first-class cadets (seniors). They hold cadet officer rank and command the wing and the subordinate units of groups, squadrons, flights, and elements. Through this organization, the upperclass cadets are responsible for military training of the underclasses, the honor education and honor system, character development, and ethics and human relations programs.

Admission Requirements

Each year, young men and women who are U.S. citizens may be appointed from all states and territories of the nation. Citizens of other countries are admitted in limited numbers. Applicants must be at least 17 and not yet 23 years of age on July 1 of the year in which they desire to be admitted. They must be unmarried, have no dependents, be of high moral character, and in good physical health.

Applicants must receive an official nomination. Members of Congress make the majority of the nominations for residents of their states and districts. Senators and representatives nominate young men and women who have excelled academically in high school, have demonstrated leadership potential through school activities, are physically fit, are respected by associates, and want to pursue military careers. Applicants need not know their member of Congress personally. Students may be eligible in nomination categories other than congressional. Students should ask high school counselors or Air Force Admissions Liaison Officers about other categories and apply for nominations in all categories for which they are eligible.

To enter the Academy upon graduation from high school, students should apply as soon as possible after January 31 of their junior year. If successful in receiving a nomination, they must take a physical fitness test, a medical exam, and either the SAT I or the ACT.

Application and Information

High school juniors may obtain application forms by writing to the address below. Applicants should study the instructions included in the application package and follow the proper application procedures. The package also includes sample letters for requesting nominations. Air Force Admissions Liaison Officers, located in all states, assist students and counselors with the application and testing requirements.

HQ USAFA/RRS
2304 Cadet Drive, Suite 200
USAF Academy, Colorado 80840-5025

Telephone: 719-333-2520
800-443-9266 (toll-free)

World Wide Web: http://academyadmissions.com

The Cadet Color Guard is the centerpiece of a Cadet Parade.

UNITED STATES COAST GUARD ACADEMY

NEW LONDON, CONNECTICUT

The Academy

Founded in 1876, the United States Coast Guard Academy has a proud tradition as one of the finest and most selective colleges in America. The smallest of the five federal service academies, the Coast Guard provides a four-year Bachelor of Science program with a full scholarship for each individual. Unlike the other federal service academies, however, there are no congressional appointments.

The mission of the United States Coast Guard Academy goes well beyond academics: "To graduate young men and women with sound bodies, stout hearts, and alert minds, with a liking for the sea and its lore, with that high sense of honor, loyalty, and obedience which goes with trained initiative and leadership; well grounded in seamanship, the sciences, and amenities, and strong in the resolve to be worthy of the traditions of commissioned officers in the United States Coast Guard in the service of their country and humanity."

Students come to the Academy to be challenged academically, physically, and professionally. By providing excellent academic programs, a structured military regimen, and competitive athletics, the Academy graduates competent and professional military officers to serve the country. The Academy's four primary objectives are to provide by precept and example an environment that encourages a high sense of honor, loyalty, and obedience; to provide a sound undergraduate education in a field of interest to the Coast Guard; to provide a living laboratory for leadership education; and to provide training that enables graduates to assume their immediate duties as junior officers.

After successfully completing the Academy program, each graduate receives a Bachelor of Science degree in one of eight majors and a commission as an Ensign in the U.S. Coast Guard. Each graduate is required to serve a minimum of five years of active duty upon graduation.

Admission to the Academy is based on nationwide competition. An average of 300 students enter the Academy each year out of approximately 3,000 applicants. Midyear students are not accepted. The student body, known as the Corps of Cadets, consists of approximately 1,000 cadets made up of approximately 30 percent women and 20 percent members of minority groups, plus international students representing various countries.

The Academy experience goes far beyond an ordinary classroom curriculum. Freshman year begins in July, seven weeks prior to the academic school year. The first seven weeks, known as "Swab Summer," are an invigorating period of physical, military, and leadership training. The last week is spent sailing aboard America's only active duty square rigger, the *CGC Eagle*—America's Tall Ship.

Summer is devoted to professional and military training except for three weeks of vacation. Cadets spend five weeks of their sophomore summer sailing on board the training tall ship *CGC Eagle* and five weeks at a Coast Guard ship. Junior summer involves one week of leadership training, three weeks training the incoming freshmen, one week of specialized shipboard training, one week qualifying in rifle and pistol, and two weeks of aviation training. In preparation for shipboard life after graduation, seniors spend ten weeks aboard a Coast Guard cutter learning the roles they will be responsible for as junior officers. In addition, academic internships are available on Capitol Hill, Washington, D.C., and in Coast Guard specialty fields such as mechanical and civil engineering.

The athletic facilities include two pools, four basketball courts, two gyms, baseball and softball fields, a football/soccer stadium, an indoor and outdoor track, five racquetball courts, volleyball courts, eight outdoor and two indoor tennis courts, a rifle/pistol range, a fully equipped Rowing Center, and a Seamanship-Sailing Center. The waterfront facilities are among the finest in the nation. Athletic participation in at least two of the three seasons at the intramural, club, or intercollegiate level is mandatory. Academy intercollegiate sports for men (m) and women (w) include baseball (m), basketball (m,w), crew (m,w), cross-country (m,w), football (m), indoor/outdoor track (m,w), pistol (m,w), rifle (m,w), sailing (m,w), soccer (m,w), softball (w), swimming/diving (m,w), tennis (m), volleyball (w), and wrestling (m). The Academy is a member of the National Collegiate Athletic Association (NCAA) Division III.

In addition to an extensive athletic program, there are various extracurricular activities. The music department has a variety of programs to offer, including the Regimental Band, CGA choir groups known as the Idlers and Icebreakers, Windjammer Drum and Bugle Corps, Bagpipe Band, Glee Club, Dixie Band, Protestant and Catholic choirs, a jazz band, a concert band, a pep band, an annual cadet musical, and various ensembles. The Academy's cadet yearbook staff produces the Academy's annual yearbook, *Tide Rips*. Various athletic clubs include hockey, marathon/road runner club, tae kwon do/martial arts, water polo, lacrosse, bowling, women's tennis, men's volleyball, and the spirit team. Academy-sponsored clubs include outdoor sports (hiking/camping), paintball, scuba, snowboard, downhill skiing, dance, golf, fencing, international, and the Genesis Club. Additional extracurricular activities include the Political Affairs Association (PAA), Officer Christian Fellowship (OCF), American Society of Mechanical Engineering (ASME), Society of Women Engineering (SWE), Fellowship of Christian Athletes (FCA), Scoutmaster Council, Drill Team, and Big Brothers/Big Sisters.

Location

The campus is in New London, Connecticut, on the western shore of the Thames River. It has twenty-six buildings on 120 acres of land. Halfway between New York City and Boston, the Academy is easily accessible by plane, train, bus, or car.

Majors and Degrees

Each student graduates with a Bachelor of Science degree in one of the Academy's eight majors: civil engineering, computer analysis, electrical engineering, government, management, marine and environmental sciences, mechanical engineering, naval architecture and marine engineering, and operations research.

Academic Programs

The Coast Guard Academy program is designed to provide a superb academic foundation in a military environment designed to produce future leaders of America. No one teaching method or forum is given precedence. Academic work is interactive and a joint effort of faculty members and students.

The Academy is fully accredited by the New England Association of Schools and Colleges (NEASC). Engineering majors are accredited by the Engineering Accreditation Commission of the Accreditation Board for Engineering and Technology (ABET). The core curriculum encompasses chemistry I and II; physics I and II; calculus I and II; introduction to engineering and design; introduction to electrical engineering; nautical science I, II, III, and IV; economics; American government; English composition and speech; criminal justice; maritime law enforcement; leaders in

U.S. history; morals and ethics; literature of leadership; organizational behavior and leadership; oceanography; leadership and organizational development; and probability and statistics. Upon graduating, the student will have completed a minimum of 126 credit hours to earn a Bachelor of Science degree.

The typical Academy class size is small, resulting in an average instructor-student ratio of 1:8. Only a few of the lower-level classes are taught in large group/lecture format. Additional instruction and tutoring outside of the classroom is always available through a strong academic support program.

The Academy offers an Honors Program to combine a technical education with liberal arts and cultural awareness through a series of cultural events and seminars. The Honors Program can also lead to in-depth research projects and internships in Washington, D.C.

Upperclass students who have demonstrated a high level of academic performance may also take elective courses at Connecticut College in New London.

Academic Facilities

All academic buildings conveniently surround the living quarters and are well within walking distance. All students are required to live in CG Academy living quarters.

The Coast Guard Academy library houses 150,000 volumes, 600 periodicals, interlibrary loan/document delivery, and an Online Public Access Catalog (OPAC). The library provides a Cadet Writing Center for individual instruction in writing, reading, and comprehension.

Laboratories are maintained for physics, chemistry, computers, oceanography, electronics, navigation, and engineering experimentation and analysis. The Academy also has a Bridge/Combat Information Center simulator, a radar trainer, 65-foot training vessels, and the 295-foot sailing ship, the *CGC Eagle*.

Costs

There is no fee to apply. All candidates who are offered and accept an appointment to the Academy must pay an entrance fee of $3000. Other than this initial cost, there are no additional fees. Students receive a full four-year scholarship with a monthly stipend of about $700, which covers the cost of uniforms, textbooks, a brand new computer, and any other expenses. Each student receives a monthly allowance for personal expenses.

Upon graduating from the CG Academy, there is a five-year commitment to serve as a commissioned CG officer.

Financial Aid

All cadets receive pay exceeding $7200 per year. Cadets' pay is not a wage or salary; it is money furnished by the government for uniforms, equipment, textbooks, and other expenses incidental to training. These funds cover all the cadets' expenses and are disbursed and expended only as directed by the Academy's superintendent. Each cadet receives a portion of his or her monthly stipend as an allowance for personal expenses. Any funds remaining in cadets' accounts are given to them upon graduation.

Faculty

The Academic Division consists of five departments under the direction and supervision of the Dean of Academics. These departments are completely staffed by Coast Guard officers and permanent professors, both civilian and military. Faculty members are invariably available for additional instruction as desired by the student. The amount of personal attention given to students by the faculty is one of the Academy's major strengths.

Each student is assigned an academic adviser to assist in choosing courses and to aid with any issues of concern.

Student Government

The students are known as cadets and organized as a regiment. This military organization of the student body is known as the Corps of Cadets. Within the regiment is a chain of command requiring compliance with military orders, rules, and regulations. Leadership and military discipline are required of each cadet. The discipline of the Academy teaches how to respond to authority and how to be an effective leader by providing each person the opportunity to be a follower as well as a leader.

On a day-to-day basis, each cadet participates in routine regimental formations, watches, and military appearance inspections. Cadets' responsibility and authority increases as they advance through the four years, and individuals that excel are rewarded with special privileges and honors.

Admission Requirements

Competition is open to any young American across the country who meets the basic eligibility requirements. The U.S. Coast Guard Academy is unique from the other four federal service academies in that there is no congressional nomination involved. The individual must be a U.S. citizen (U.S. born or naturalized), unmarried, no dependents, 17–22 years of age (cannot be 23 prior to July 1 of the year of entrance into the Academy), a high school graduate, and have competed either the SAT I or ACT timed test. In addition, a medical exam must be passed.

Over the past four years, 90 percent of entering students have been in the top 25 percent of their high school class and 62 percent in the top 10 percent of their high school class. Average SAT I scores in math were 652 and in verbal were 621. Average ACT scores in math were 28 and in English were 28.

Application and Information

Applications must be received by January 31 of the year of entrance into the Academy. Students may apply online at the Web site listed below. Those accepted into the Academy receive appointments between November and April of each year. The Academy participates in an early action program allowing student who submit their entire packet of forms by November 1 a guaranteed notification of application results by December 15. Whether an applicant receives an appointment through the early action program or by meeting the standard deadlines, the student is required either to notify the Academy of acceptance or to decline by May 1 of the entering year.

A viewbook or CD-ROM and application may be obtained by contacting:

Director of Admissions
USCG Academy
31 Mohegan Avenue
New London, Connecticut 06320-8103
Telephone: 860-444-8501
800-883-8724 (toll-free)
E-mail: admissions@cga.uscg.mil
World Wide Web: http://www.cga.edu

The United States Coast Guard Academy is located on the Thames River in New London, Connecticut.

UNITED STATES MERCHANT MARINE ACADEMY

KINGS POINT, NEW YORK

The Academy

The United States Merchant Marine Academy is a four-year, tuition-free federal service academy founded in 1943 to educate and train merchant marine officers, officers on active duty in the armed forces, and leaders in the maritime and intermodal transportation industry. It is an accredited, degree-granting college whose students are commissioned as ensigns in the Navy upon graduation. The Academy is one of the world's foremost institutions in the field of maritime education and is operated under the Maritime Administration of the Department of Transportation.

There are 950 men and women enrolled as midshipmen at the Academy. Their daily routine at Kings Point is very demanding. The academic day begins at 8 a.m. and concludes at 5 p.m. After classes, midshipmen are free to participate in recreational activities until dinnertime. After dinner, they are required to devote their time to study and academic preparation.

The extracurricular program is broad and varied. In addition to varsity athletics in eighteen intercollegiate sports, the Academy has an extensive intramural program that permits all students to enjoy physical activity and competition.

The nonathletic activities are also wide ranging and abundant, falling into as many categories as there are individual interests. Publications and the Debate Council, Glee Club, Regimental Band, Scuba-Diving Club, International Relations Club, and Broadcast Unit are but a few of the pursuits available to the midshipmen. Regimental and class dances and informal mixers provide the midshipmen with an interesting social program.

Midshipmen are granted liberty on weekends and leave at Thanksgiving, Christmas, and fall and spring trimester breaks as well as annual leave during July. Perhaps the most unusual and exciting part of the Academy curriculum is the Shipboard Training Program. Each midshipman, during three trimesters of the sophomore and the junior years, serves 300–360 days at sea aboard commercially operated American-flag merchant ships. This exceptional work-study program takes the midshipmen to many parts of the world and provides them with practical experience on several different types of vessels. It can be said that the world is their campus during their three trimesters of sea service.

Location

The Academy is located on 80.5 acres of land at Kings Point, on the North Shore of Long Island. Kings Point is a suburban residential community only 20 miles east of midtown New York City, close to various cultural and recreational facilities.

Majors and Degrees

A graduate of the U.S. Merchant Marine Academy receives a Bachelor of Science degree, a merchant marine license as a third mate or third assistant engineer, and a commission as an ensign in the U.S. Naval Reserve. Graduates may apply to the Army, Navy, Air Force, Marine Corps, Coast Guard, or NOAA (National Oceanic and Atmospheric Administration) to serve on active duty. Six major programs are offered: marine transportation for the preparation of deck officers; maritime operations and technology (a marine transportation program enhanced with marine engineering studies); marine engineering for students interested in becoming engineering officers; marine engineering systems, which, in addition to leading to a license as a third assistant engineer, is accredited by the Accreditation Board for Engineering and Technology (ABET) and includes a curriculum with greater depth in mathematics and a significant component of engineering design, as compared to the marine engineering curriculum; shipyard and engineering management, which is also accredited by ABET; and Logistics and Intermodal Transportation, a marine transportation program focusing on logistics and intermodal systems management.

Academic Program

During the first trimester of the plebe (or freshman) year, all students take a common program of mathematics, science, English, and professional courses. This background enables midshipmen to determine intelligently the area of their special interest. After the first trimester, midshipmen select their major and from then on concentrate on a program aligned with their career choice. The professional majors each consist of required core courses in technical and general education areas as well as selected electives. The option program consists of six courses for marine transportation and marine engineering majors, who have a choice of taking a series of related elective courses in a specific area of concentration or any individual elective course for which they qualify. These courses include such specialized fields as nuclear engineering, management science, computer science, mathematics, chemistry, and naval architecture. By choosing to take the series of related courses, midshipmen can develop a proficiency in a subspecialty, supplementing their major field of study. Students in the marine engineering systems majors are not offered the choice of electives because of the required course load in their programs. General education courses make up about one third of each of the professional curriculums, and all midshipmen are required to take naval science courses prescribed by the Department of the Navy.

Thus, the Academy provides a balanced program of theoretical and practical study designed to provide the undergraduate with technical competence, leadership skills, and the well-rounded general education so essential for responsible citizenship in contemporary society.

Exemption credit may be awarded for college-level work completed at an accredited college if the course is equivalent to a course offered at the Academy.

Academic Facilities

With the exception of Wiley Hall, the former residence of Walter P. Chrysler and now the Administration Building, all the buildings of the Academy have been constructed since 1942. The Inter-Faith Chapel was dedicated in 1961, a three-story library was completed in 1968, and an indoor swimming pool and an engineering and science wing have been added since 1972. A modernization of all other academic buildings was completed in 1982. Upgrades to the dormitories and other facilities are currently underway.

Costs

Tuition, room and board, and medical and dental care are provided by the U.S. government. Each midshipman also receives $700 per month while assigned aboard ship for training. Entering plebes are required to pay a little more than $6000 to cover the initial cost of lab fees, equipment, and a laptop computer.

Financial Aid

In effect, each midshipman receives a four-year scholarship from the U.S. government. Financial assistance is also available through the Federal Pell Grant Program, Federal Stafford Student Loans Program, and the Federal PLUS Program. A very limited number of need-based scholarships are also offered, and students may use outside scholarships to defray their costs.

Faculty

The Academy has 84 full-time faculty members and a student-faculty ratio of approximately 9:1. One third of the faculty are licensed deck or engineering officers. Most hold advanced degrees in an academic discipline: 90 percent of the total faculty hold master's degrees or higher; 50 percent have earned doctorates.

Student Government

The student body at the Academy is organized along military lines as a regiment, consisting of two battalions. Regimental life at the Academy is a form of student government and is an important part of the midshipman's total educational experience. The first classmen, or seniors, under the direction of the Commandant of Midshipmen, are responsible for exercising military command of the regiment and for administering the daily routine of the midshipmen. The military program is designed to develop leadership ability, self-discipline, and a sense of responsibility—attributes that are essential for effective citizenship as well as for a successful career as an officer.

Admission Requirements

Candidates for admission must be American citizens, be at least 17 years of age and must not have passed their twenty-fifth birthday by July 1 of the year of entry into the Academy, and be of good moral character. Candidates must be nominated by a U.S. representative or senator and must compete for vacancies allocated to their state in proportion to its representation in Congress. Candidates must achieve qualifying scores on the standard administration (timed) SAT or ACT. Candidates must have successfully completed chemistry or physics (including lab), as well as mathematics up to and including one semester of trigonometry or precalculus. Candidates' competitive standing is determined by their College Board score, their high school academic record and extracurricular participation, and their overall leadership potential. All candidates must meet the physical requirements for appointment as a midshipman in the Naval Reserve. Although not required, all applicants are strongly encouraged to perform a day or overnight visit to learn firsthand about midshipman life and academics. Visits are arranged through the Admissions Office when classes are in session, which is from mid-August to May.

Application and Information

Prospective candidates should write to the Admissions Office. They will be sent detailed information on the nomination procedure, required tests, application procedures, and specific requirements. It is advisable to apply for a nomination during the spring of the junior year in high school.

Further information may be obtained by contacting:

Director of Admissions
U.S. Merchant Marine Academy
300 Steamboat Road, Wiley Hall
Kings Point, New York 11024-1699
Telephone: 516-773-5391
866-546-4778 (toll-free)
Fax: 516-773-5390
E-mail: admissions@usmma.edu
World Wide Web: http://www.usmma.edu

An aerial view of the 80.5-acre "sea campus" of the U.S. Merchant Marine Academy at Kings Point, Long Island, on the shores of Long Island Sound.

UNITED STATES MILITARY ACADEMY

WEST POINT, NEW YORK

The Academy

The United States Military Academy, the nation's oldest service academy, offers young men and women one of the premier education and leadership development programs in the nation. West Point advocates the "whole person" concept. The Military Academy has, since its founding in 1802, provided a broadly structured undergraduate curriculum that balances the physical sciences and engineering with the behavioral and social sciences.

West Point's mission is to educate, train, and inspire the Corps of Cadets so that each graduate is a commissioned leader of character committed to the values of duty, honor, and country; professional growth throughout a career as an officer in the United States Army; and a lifetime of selfless service to the nation. The Military Academy provides its graduates with a solid foundation for intellectual and moral/ethical growth that is essential for successfully handling high-level responsibilities in national service. When students enter West Point, they are also beginning a profession. Upon graduation, cadets are commissioned as second lieutenants in the U.S. Army and are normally required to serve on active duty for at least five years.

There are more than 4,000 men and women enrolled at West Point. Cadets compete for Rhodes, Olmsted, Gates Cambridge, George Mitchell, Hertz, National Science Foundation, Rotary Foundation, Truman, East-West Center, and Marshall scholarships. West Pointers who remain in the Army are normally selected to attend civilian graduate schools in the United States or abroad between their fourth and tenth years of service.

The Academy develops the nation's future Army leaders by immersing cadets in programs of academic, military, and physical development. Each of these programs is rooted in principles of ethical-moral development, epitomized by the Academy motto, "Duty, Honor, Country." The Academy provides cadets with opportunities to observe and practice leadership and to develop vital intellectual and interpersonal skills through formal instruction. The honor code simply states: "A cadet will not lie, cheat, steal, or tolerate those who do." The code is a source of pride and mutual trust essential in the profession of arms.

In addition to academic and military education, cadets participate in athletic and extracurricular activities. Cadets have distinguished themselves in twenty-five intercollegiate varsity sports: baseball, basketball, cross-country, football, golf, gymnastics, hockey, indoor track, lacrosse, outdoor track, soccer, sprint football, swimming, tennis, and wrestling for men and basketball, cross-country, indoor track, outdoor track, rifle, soccer, softball, swimming, tennis, and volleyball for women.

West Point's modern academic facilities are matched by its athletic facilities. Michie Stadium, home of the Army football team, attracts crowds in excess of 39,000 during picturesque fall football weekends. The Kimsey Athletic Center and the Hoffman Press Box are completed, and Randolph Hall is expected to be completed in 2004. The Gross Center is used as a gymnastics and multisport practice and competition facility. Adjacent to Michie Stadium is the Holleder Athletic Center, a multisport complex housing a hockey rink with seating for 2,746 and a basketball arena with a 5,045-seat capacity. The huge Arvin Cadet Physical Development Center is under major reconstruction and renovation. West Point has a track stadium, a baseball stadium, an indoor tennis facility, and numerous athletic fields, outdoor tennis courts, and outdoor swimming facilities. Victor Constant Ski Slope is used for instructional and recreational skiing. A redesigned 18-hole golf course is also located on the Academy grounds.

There are more than 100 organized extracurricular activities, including mountaineering, hunting, fishing, scuba diving, archery, team handball, and orienteering clubs as well as clubs that compete on a national or intercollegiate level in crew, orienteering, power lifting, handball, rugby, sport parachuting, triathlon, horseback riding, sailing, judo, karate, bowling, and marathon running. There are academic clubs, including mathematics, language, and electronics clubs; the Cadet Fine Arts Forum; Model United Nations; and the Debate Council. The Student Conference on United States Affairs has met for more than thirty years.

Location

The military reservation, consisting of more than 16,000 acres, overlooks the Hudson River, 50 miles north of New York City.

Majors and Degrees

Cadets may choose an academic concentration from twenty-four majors. A cadet may study applied science and engineering; art, philosophy, and literature; basic sciences; behavioral sciences; chemistry and life science; civil engineering; computer science; economics; electrical engineering; engineering management; environmental engineering; environmental science; foreign area studies (Latin American, Western Europe, Middle East, Eastern Europe, and East Asia); foreign languages (Arabic, Chinese, French, German, Portuguese, Russian, or Spanish or any two); geography; history; law and legal studies; management; mathematical sciences; mechanical engineering; military art and science; nuclear engineering; operations research; physics; political science; social sciences; and systems engineering.

Academic Programs

The academic program at the United States Military Academy provides cadets with a broad background in the arts and sciences and prepares them for future graduate study. The total curriculum is designed to develop essential character, competence, and intellectual ability in an officer. The core curriculum is the cornerstone of the academic program and provides a foundation in mathematics, basic sciences, engineering sciences, information technology, humanities, behavior sciences, and social sciences. The core curriculum, ranging in size from twenty-six to thirty courses, depending on the major, represents the essential broad base of knowledge necessary for success as a commissioned officer while also supporting each cadet's choice of academic specialization.

Classes at West Point are small, averaging 12 to 18 cadets per section. Cadets receive individual attention, and tutorial sessions are available upon request. Advanced and honors courses are available to cadets having exceptional ability.

All cadets study military science and receive classroom instruction in the principles of small-unit tactics and leadership in eight semester courses. Concentrated summer field training provides each cadet with the opportunity to learn and practice individual military skills and to apply the principles of tactics and leadership studied in the classroom.

Off-Campus Programs

During the summer before their first (freshman) academic year, cadets are initiated into the Military Academy through a Cadet Basic Training program. Uniforms, room inspections, military drill, parades, and physical exercise become part of everyday life, and extensive demands are made upon new cadets to foster maturity, perseverance, and ability to succeed when challenged. All cadets complete Cadet Field Training (CFT) during their second summer at West Point. The emphasis in Cadet Field Training is on the close, combined fight, both light and mechanized. Extensive training on infantry operations, artillery firing, weapons training, Army aviation, military engineering, and land navigation make up most of this training experience. CFT also provides a powerful leadership experience that develops the leadership skills and abilities of the first and second class cadets. Operation Highland Warrior, a ten-day tactical field exercise that focuses on the combined arms close fight, is the capstone event of Cadet Field Training. During Operation Highland Warrior, cadets execute air assault raids and lead fire ambushes and defensive operations. Cadets are also exposed to the heavy forces of the Army (armor, artillery, air defense, and aviation) when they deploy to Fort Knox, Kentucky, for a week of Mounted Maneuver Training. The highlights of this training event are a Combined Arms Live Fire Exercise, which allows the cadets to see all of the Army's most lethal fighting systems operating as a team on the battlefield, and Operation Thunderbolt Strike, a mounted "force-on-force" battle where cadet companies engage each other in M1A2 tanks.

All cadets complete Cadet Advanced Training during their last two summers at West Point. Cadet Advanced Training consists of three parts: attendance at a military school, serving in a field Army unit, and serving in a leadership position at West Point during Cadet Basic Training or Cadet Field Training. Cadets can attend one of many United States Army military schools, which include Airborne School, Air Assault School, the Sapper Leader's Course, and the Combat Diver Qualification Course. First class cadets also participate in Cadet Troop Leading Training (CTLT). CTLT is a thirty-day troop-leading experience during which cadets go to a field Army unit and perform the day-to-day functions of a platoon leader. Each summer, more than 1,000 cadets participate in CTLT at more than twenty-seven locations worldwide. Selected second class cadets may participate in the Drill Cadet Leader Program (DCLT) instead of CTLT. During DCLT, second class cadets serve as company executive officers and platoon trainers in basic training units. DCLT is conducted at major training installations such as Fort Benning, Georgia; Fort Sill, Oklahoma; Fort Leonard Wood, Missouri; and Fort Jackson, South Carolina. Each summer, approximately 40 second class cadets participate in DCLT. During one of their last two summers at West Point, second and first class cadets are also required to serve in various leadership positions, from platoon leader to Regimental Commander, in Cadet Basic Training or Cadet Field Training. Here, they further develop their leadership skills while teaching, training, and leading new cadets or third class cadets in a demanding, fast-paced environment.

Academic Facilities

West Point maintains some of the finest facilities and equipment in the world. There is a personal computer at every desk, and everyone is connected to a large array of powerful academic computing services at West Point, with unlimited access to the Internet. West Point has carefully crafted an electronic environment in which virtually every course offered has integrated computer use. This developmental "computer thread" fosters cadet use of personal computers in the barracks. Computer-aided math, design, and simulation; dynamic news sources; worldwide e-mail; spreadsheets; statistical analysis; database access; library bibliographic research; and electronic bulletin boards; document preparation, and printing, among other resources, all contribute to an academic environment rich with information resources and electronic media tools. Among the research facilities are general and physical chemistry laboratories and engineering, analog computer, digital computer, electromagnetic energy, electronics, physics, solid-state, hydraulic turbine, thermodynamics, fluid mechanics, nuclear science, free flight, rocket testing, land locomotion, and wind tunnel laboratories. The modern 600,000-volume library contains reading rooms, seminar rooms, and microfilm and audiovisual facilities.

Costs

The cost of the four-year West Point experience, including tuition, room, board, and medical and dental expenses, is paid by the U.S. government. Cadets, as members of the Army, receive an annual salary of approximately $9200, which helps to pay for uniforms, books, a personal computer, supplies, and incidental living expenses. A deposit of $2400 to $3000 is required to cover the initial uniform costs, a personal computer, and other incidental services (haircuts, laundry, etc.) during the first year.

Financial Aid

There are no financial aid programs because expenses are paid by the U.S. government. Scholarship awards may be used by candidates to offset the cost of the initial deposit.

Faculty

Most faculty members are Army officers who hold advanced degrees from civilian colleges and universities; approximately 30 percent have earned doctorates. The teaching faculty numbers nearly 500 and includes civilian professors and several visiting professors from civilian academic institutions. Because many of the faculty members are Academy alumni and most are Army officers, the faculty has unusual rapport with the cadets. The student-faculty ratio is 8:1. Typical class size is 16.

Student Government

All cadets are strongly encouraged to serve in positions of student leadership and to seek responsibility as a means of enhancing their effectiveness as leaders. Cadets manage the social program, the Cadet Honor System, the intramural athletic program, and a wide range of extracurricular activities.

Admission Requirements

Admission is open to all unmarried U.S. citizens who are at least 17 and have not yet had their 23rd birthday on July 1 of the desired year of admission. They must have no legal responsibility to support a dependent (e.g., a child). West Point offers equal admission opportunities for all qualified applicants. Candidates for West Point must seek a nomination from a legal authority (usually a member of Congress), preferably in the spring of the junior year in high school. All candidates must take either the standardized timed ACT or the SAT. Applicants must also pass a Qualifying Medical Examination and a Physical Aptitude Examination.

The Directorate of Admissions has a rolling admissions process. The sooner a candidate's admissions file is complete, it is evaluated by the admissions committee. All applicants must complete their admissions file by the first Monday in March.

Application and Information

Prospective candidates should write to Admissions, stating their interest in the Military Academy. Each applicant will be sent a Precandidate Questionnaire and prospectus, which outlines the West Point entrance requirements. All applicants are encouraged to start a candidate file at West Point at the end of their junior year or as soon thereafter as possible. This allows for early completion of all candidate file requirements. The easiest way to open an admissions file is to visit the Web site at the address below and fill out a candidate questionnaire online. There is also additional information on the admissions process to answer most candidate questions.

Director of Admissions
United States Military Academy
646 Swift Road
West Point, New York 10996-1905
Telephone: 845-938-4041
E-mail: admissions@www.usma.edu
World Wide Web: http://www.usma.edu/admissions

Students examine soil properties during a civil engineering lab.

UNIVERSITÉ LAVAL

QUÉBEC CITY, QUÉBEC, CANADA

The University

The first French-speaking university in North America, Laval traces its origins to 1663 when Mgr. François de Laval, the first Bishop of New France, founded Le Séminaire de Québec. In 1852, Queen Victoria granted Le Séminaire de Québec a Royal Charter, thus creating Université Laval.

Université Laval was, until 1920, the only French-speaking university in Canada. Through the years, it has contributed to the education of the French-speaking intellectual elite of Québec and Canada, giving the country several Prime Ministers, artists, writers, business leaders, scientists, and musicians. Considered a leading university since its founding, Laval is today a member of the "Group of Ten," a designation of the ten top-ranked Canadian universities (in terms of research). The University's well-established reputation extends beyond Québec and Canada. Laval attracts students from more than 86 countries who enroll at Laval to obtain a diploma recognized throughout the world.

Université Laval offers some 530 programs to more than 36,000 students at both undergraduate and graduate levels. It is the only North American university to offer full programs in forestry and geomatics as well as agriculture and food sciences, with French as the language of instruction. Throughout Canada and the United States, Laval is particularly renowned for its teaching of French as a second language.

Laval is well known for its PEPS, a French acronym that refers to its Pavilion of Physical Education and Sports. The PEPS is considered one of the best-equipped university athletic centres in Canada. Some students even choose Laval for its PEPS. The PEPS is used for teaching physical education sciences, but all full-time students may use it. Its facilities include an Olympic-size swimming pool, an Olympic-size diving tower, an arena that houses two skating rinks, an interior track-and-field area, five gymnasiums, a tennis court, a football field, and more.

The Housing Service operates four residences, allowing 2,400 students to live on-campus. All residences are linked to the rest of the campus by underground walkways. Two of the four residences are coed. All rooms are single and the price includes cable television and a telephone with voice mail. All rooms are wired for Internet access for a competitive monthly fee. Cooking facilities are offered in every residence. Students who prefer to live off campus can easily find an apartment through the Off-Campus Housing Service.

Because Laval is a comprehensive university, many services and attractions can be found on campus, including a Career and Placement Centre, a Financial Aid Service, a Medical Centre with a sports medicine division, a Psychology and Counselling Service, a Concert Hall, a theatre, a botanical garden, museums, a bookstore, a bank, a hairdresser, restaurants and fast-food counters, and more. International students are encouraged to visit the International Student Welcome Centre when they arrive on campus to learn more about the different services available.

Location

Choosing Laval is also choosing Québec City, the capital city of the province of Québec and the oldest city in North America. In this historic city, designated by the United Nations Educational, Scientific, and Cultural Organization (UNESCO) as a World's Heritage city, one can still feel the soul of the French period. Old Québec's steep, winding, narrow streets give the city a European look and charm that makes it unique and unforgettable. Québec City is one of the most visited cities in North America.

Outside the strong walls of its eighteenth-century fortifications, Québec presents itself as a modern and dynamic city where one can find everything that makes life pleasant. Well known for its Winter Carnival, the largest event of its kind in the world, Québec offers a variety of cultural riches and activities throughout the year that suit many tastes, including numerous festivals, museums, movies, restaurants, theaters, art galleries, and more. The sports fan can ski, skate, play golf, and go swimming, rafting, or bicycling, thanks to Laval's position on the St. Lawrence Seaway and its proximity to the Laurentian Mountains.

Université Laval's campus, straddling Sainte-Foy and Sillery, is one of the most striking in the province of Québec. It covers 1.2 square kilometers (300 acres) and includes more than thirty buildings, all linked by 10 kilometers (6 miles) of underground walkways. Université Laval also maintains a presence in Old Québec and the nearby downtown area, where its Faculty of Architecture, Planning and Visual Arts occupies a wing of the Vieux-Séminaire and part of the "La Fabrique" building.

Majors and Degrees

Laval offers some 530 programs at both undergraduate and graduate levels. Students may pursue a bachelor's degree in almost every field of study.

The Bachelor of Arts (B.A.) degree is offered in ancient civilizations, anthropology, anthropology and ethnology, archaeology, art history, consumer studies, economics, economics and politics, English as a second language, English studies, French as a second language, French language and professional writing, geography, Hispanic studies, historical sciences and patrimonial sciences, history, industrial relations, insurance and financial products, international studies and modern language, jazz and pop music, Jewish theology, linguistics, literary studies, mass communication, mathematical economics, music education, pastoral studies, philosophy, political science, psychology, Québec folklore, sociology, theater, and translation.

The Bachelor of Teaching (B.Ens.) is offered in music education, physical education, plastic arts, preschool and elementary, professional and technical, secondary, and second-language teaching.

The Bachelor of Science (B.Sc.) degree is offered in actuarial science, athletic studies, biochemistry, biology, chemistry, geology, health sciences, kinesiology, mathematics, microbiology, nursing, nutrition, occupational therapy, physical education, physical therapy, physics, secondary teaching, and statistics.

The Bachelor of Applied Science (B.Sc.A.) is offered in agri-food economics and management, agronomy, computer science, environmental and forest management, food sciences and technology, forest operations, geomatics, mathematics and computer science, and wood processing engineering.

The Bachelor of Engineering (B.Ing.) degree is offered in agri-environmental, chemical, civil, computer, electrical, food, geological, geomatics, mechanical, metallurgical, mining and mineral, physics, and software engineering.

The University also offers a Bachelor of Architecture (B.Sc.Arch.), a Bachelor of Business Administration (B.A.A.), a Bachelor of Education (B.Ed.) in counselling and guidance, a Bachelor of Law (LL.B.), a Bachelor of Music (B.Mus.), a Bachelor of Pharmacy (B.Pharm.), a Bachelor of Social Work (B.Serv.Soc.), a Bachelor of Theology, (B.Th.), and a Bachelor of Visual Arts and Graphic Arts (B.A.V.).

The University offers a four-year program in dentistry (D.M.D.) and a five-year program in medicine (M.D.).

In most of these fields of study, Laval also offers diplomas (60 credits) or certificates (30 credits). It is also possible to obtain a 90-credit bachelor's degree by combining a diploma with a certificate or combining three certificates.

Academic Program

The academic year is composed of two regular semesters (September through December and January through April) and one summer semester, which is divided into two parts (May through June and July through August).

To meet the admission requirements, applicants must have completed a pre-university diploma totalling thirteen years of schooling. High school graduates who have completed a pre-university diploma totalling 12 years of schooling may be admitted to a four- or five-year program.

All degrees at Laval have specific requirements that students must meet in order to graduate. Teachers combine theory and practice, including internships, in their regular curriculum. Laval has also adopted a Policy on Internationalisation according to which all programs must prepare students to face the globalisation of markets. To meet that policy, students are required to learn a second language.

Off-Campus Programs

Laval puts a special emphasis on establishing relations with universities and research centers inside and outside of Canada. It offers numerous exchange and study-abroad programs through partnering and institutional agreements with establishments on all continents. Moreover, Laval's membership in the "Group of Ten" allows Laval to offer its students specific exchange opportunities with other member universities. Laval has more international agreements than any other Canadian university.

In addition to regular programs, self-organised year-abroad projects are also possible for students who wish to make their own arrangements. Academic credits may be earned for all of these programs.

Academic Facilities

The library offers more than 3.4 million documents, 17,625 periodical titles, and 585,000 audiovisual items (slides, microfiches, films, videos, discs, aerial photographs, and maps). Students may use the Internet to borrow books from the University Library as well as from most university libraries around the world.

The Computing and Telecommunication Service provides services to the entire University community. Numerous computers are available for student use in every teaching pavilion, and all students owning a home computer have free access to the Internet through the University network.

Costs

Full-time tuition fees range from Can$1008 a session for Québec residents and French citizens to Can$2260 for Canadians and permanent residents of Canada. For international students, tuition ranges from Can$4908 to Can$5433. For students enrolled in French-related programs and students from countries that have signed an agreement with the Québec government, the fees may be similar to those of Québec residents. International students must also buy health insurance, which costs Can$588. Housing on campus costs Can$222 a month. Travel expenses, books, food, clothes, and other personal expenses are not included in these figures.

Financial Aid

Several kinds of scholarship awards are offered to Laval students. Awards for academic merit are given by Université Laval as well as by external organisations. The Financial Aid Office issues a list of these awards each year. This list is also available on the Financial Aid Office's Web site (http://www.bbaf.ulaval.ca). Laval also offers a Work-Study Program that allows students with financial needs to work on campus.

Faculty

The faculty is composed of more than 1,440 professors. Almost 95 percent hold a Ph.D., which is a particularly high percentage compared to other universities. In addition, some 665 assistant lecturers are hired every trimester.

Developing research is a strategic priority for Université Laval, and research is an important part of the mission of every faculty member and school. More than 1,200 professors receive research grants. They work in the 35 accredited research centres and institutes or in the almost 100 other research groups, centres, or laboratories. Université Laval is also very active on the international scene. It has set up eighteen projects involving developing countries with funding assistance from AUPELF-UREF, an international organisation of partly or entirely French-language universities.

Student Government

The partnership between the University governance and its student population is of key importance; therefore, students participate in all levels of University government, be it consultative or governing. In addition, undergraduate students can join a University student union called CADEUL (Confédération des associations d'étudiantes et d'étudiants de l'Université Laval). Each Faculty and department also has one or more student associations. Many other clubs, groups, and associations exist that bring together students who share similar interests (social, ethnic, religious, and others).

Admission Requirements

A pre-university diploma totalling 13 years of schooling is the normal basis for admission. Graduates of secondary or high schools who have had a total of 12 years of schooling may be admitted to a freshman program individually adjusted to allow them to complete different courses relevant to their intended area of study. In addition, all students must demonstrate proficiency in written and spoken French. Letters of recommendation and SAT I scores are not required. In some programs, applicants may be required to pass different tests (auditions, interviews, letters of intent, appreciation by simulation, or others). The Admission Guide provides full details on all admission requirements.

Application and Information

The admission deadline for the semester beginning in September is March 1; for the January semester, it is September 1 for students living outside of Canada and November 1 for students living in Canada; for the summer semester, it is February 1 for students living outside of Canada and April 1 for students living in Canada. Late applications can be considered in programs in which places are still available. Application fees are Can$30. Application forms may be submitted through the Internet. All documents submitted with an application must be official and translated into French or English.

For further information (in French) on programs and admission requirements or to obtain the application kit, please write to:

Bureau d'information et de promotion
2435 Pavillon Jean-Charles-Bonenfant
Université Laval
Québec City, Québec G1K 7P4
Canada
Telephone: 418-656-2764
877-785-2825 (toll-free in Canada and the U.S.)
E-mail: info@vrd.ulaval.ca
World Wide Web: http://www.ulaval.ca

A modern university in the oldest city in North America.

UNIVERSITY AT ALBANY, STATE UNIVERSITY OF NEW YORK

ALBANY, NEW YORK

The University

A University Center of the State University of New York (SUNY), the University at Albany offers a broad spectrum of academic programs for undergraduate and graduate students while fulfilling the missions of research and service. More than 17,000 students, including 11,900 undergraduates, are enrolled in the University's nine schools and colleges: arts and sciences, business, education, criminal justice, public affairs, information science and policy, social welfare, and public health. The University has also established the School of Nanosciences and Nanoengineering, one of the first of its kind in the country.

Albany is distinguished by the high quality of its academic programs, many of which are consistently ranked among the best in the nation. These include atmospheric science, management information systems, criminal justice, public administration and policy, social welfare, psychology, and sociology. More than 900 faculty members jointly offer Albany's graduate and undergraduate programs, thus giving all students access to leading researchers in an environment that emphasizes active learning, inquiry, and discovery. Throughout their undergraduate education, students are encouraged to pursue the intellectual goals of breadth and coherence while acquiring the skills of critical inquiry and public responsibility.

Freshmen are invited to participate in Project Renaissance, a distinctive general education program. Project Renaissance offers an integrated introduction to the University through a yearlong 12-credit interdisciplinary course that is team taught by several faculty members. The course includes inquiry projects, which grow out of students' community action work and require them to become researchers, inquiring into the meaning of events that surround them. Thus, students learn how the larger issues of research are often tied to everyday life and how systematic inquiry helps address these questions. Students create a true living-learning community by also sharing a residence hall.

Since the University is located in New York State's capital, Albany students have access to a wide range of internship opportunities, including a full-semester, 15-credit internship with the New York State Legislature.

Albany's Presidential Scholars Program considers only the top students admitted to the freshman class. The fourfold increase in the number of Presidential Scholars since the program was established in 1993 attests to the outstanding quality of incoming freshman classes. Frederick Douglass Scholars, selected from Presidential Scholars, have demonstrated high academic achievement and are from underrepresented groups. Honors programs are also available in the following majors and departments: anthropology, art, art history, atmospheric science, biology, chemistry, Chinese studies, computer science, East Asian studies, economics, English, geography, geology, Greek and Roman civilization, history, Italian, Japanese, Judaic studies, Latin American studies, linguistics, mathematics, philosophy, physics, political science, psychology, public policy, Puerto Rican studies, rhetoric and communication, Russian, sociology, Spanish, theater, and women's studies.

About 40 percent of Albany graduates go directly on to graduate or professional school. More than 80 percent of the qualified medical school applicants educated at Albany are accepted, while more than 70 percent of law school applicants from Albany are accepted. Albany's graduation rate is 20 points higher than the national average. A network of more than 100,000 Albany alumni throughout the nation and the world provide an important link to business, education, law, medicine, and state, national, and international government as well as other related fields.

Six residential quadrangles uptown and one quad downtown house 7,000 Albany students. Most residential facilities are organized in suite arrangements, and each resident student has access to an individual phone line and voice mail, cable television hookup, and a high-speed Ethernet connection to the Internet. There are fifteen special-interest housing options. In fall 2002, Empire commons opened, providing new single-room apartment-style living for 1,200 students.

Campus life is sustained by the activities of the nearly 200 University-recognized social and professional clubs, which offer numerous opportunities for leadership development. The University competes at the Division I level and is affiliated with the America East Conference and the Northeast Conference in football. Men's varsity sports are baseball, basketball, cross-country, football, indoor track, lacrosse, outdoor track, and soccer. Women's varsity sports are basketball, cross-country, field hockey, golf, indoor track, lacrosse, outdoor track, soccer, softball, tennis, and volleyball. In addition, Albany offers a wide range of intramural opportunities, and more than 5,000 Albany students participate in intramural sports each year. The Recreation and Convocation Center (RACC) offers students the latest in sports facilities, including three full basketball courts, racquetball and squash courts, a main arena with an indoor track, and a fitness center with Nautilus equipment. The RACC's 4,800-seat arena is also used for concerts and other events.

Location

Albany, the hub of the lively Capital Region, offers students a host of internship and work opportunities in government, finance, education, high technology, business, and the arts as well as the cultural and social environment of a major city. The climate is milder than elsewhere in upstate New York and New England, with stunning natural beauty. Albany's historic Hudson Valley location is convenient to recreation areas in Vermont's Green Mountains, the Berkshires of Massachusetts, the Catskills, and the Adirondacks, site of two Winter Olympics. Boston, Hartford, New York City, Montreal, and Philadelphia are also within a convenient distance. Two major interstates, I-87 and I-90, serve the campus, and airline, train, and bus terminals are just minutes away.

Majors and Degrees

Undergraduates may choose from more than 100 degree programs. SUNY at Albany offers the bachelor's degree in accounting, actuarial and mathematical sciences, Africana studies, anthropology, art, atmospheric science, biology, business administration, chemistry, Chinese studies, computer science, computer science and applied mathematics, criminal justice, economics, English, environmental science, French, geography, geology, Greek and Roman civilization, history, information science, Italian, Judaic studies, Latin American and Caribbean studies, linguistics, mathematics, music, philosophy, physics, political science, psychology, public policy, Puerto Rican studies, rhetoric and communication, Russian, Russian and East European studies, social welfare, sociology, Spanish, theater, and women's studies. Interdisciplinary majors are offered in art history, Asian studies, biochemistry and molecular biology, broadcast meteorology, East Asian studies, human biology, Japanese studies, medieval and Renaissance studies, Mediterranean archaeology, and religious studies. Student-designed interdisciplinary majors are available with the guidance of a faculty member. The University has implemented a bachelor's/master's degree (4 + 1) program for students interested in secondary education. Students complete an undergraduate degree in the area they wish to teach and a master's degree in basic classroom teaching in five years or less. This program assures that Albany graduates are prepared to meet new certification requirements being developed in New York State and throughout the country.

Academic Programs

To earn the bachelor's degree, a student must complete a minimum of 120 credits (including general education requirements), satisfy major requirements, and complete a minor or a second major. Students are admitted to the University as open majors and are encouraged to use their general education requirements to explore a variety of disciplinary interests. General education requirements specify that students complete 6 credits of approved course work in each of three categories: humanities and the arts, natural sciences, and social sciences. In addition, students must satisfactorily complete two writing-intensive courses, a 3-credit course in cultural and historical perspectives, and a 3-credit course in human diversity. Students may elect a double major or create their own interdisciplinary major if no existing program suits their particular interests. Prehealth, predental, and prelaw preparation is available through selected course work with any of the major programs. Special advisement for these programs is also available. Admission to most programs occurs at the end of the student's sophomore year.

The University also offers many combined bachelor's/master's degree programs that allow students to complete the requirements of both degrees at an accelerated pace. A host of combined degree options is available, including the option of combining a bachelor's degree in an area of the liberal arts and sciences with the M.B.A. degree. Albany's 3-3 program with Albany Law School allows students to earn a bachelor's degree and a law degree in a total of six years rather than seven. Students apply for this program as freshmen. The 3-2 engineering program allows Albany students to study physics on the Albany campus for three years and then complete an engineering degree through Clarkson University, Rensselaer Polytechnic Institute, SUNY at Binghamton, or SUNY at New Paltz.

Albany also offers three special admissions programs for prehealth students: the Early Assurance of Admission to Albany Medical College; the Joint Seven-Year Biology/Optometry Program, in conjunction with the SUNY College of Optometry in New York City; and a seven-year dental program with Boston University's Goldman School of Dental Medicine.

Off-Campus Programs

For juniors and seniors, Albany offers study-abroad programs in Brazil, China, Costa Rica, Denmark, France, Germany, Great Britain, Hungary, Israel, Japan, the Netherlands, Russia, Singapore, and Spain. Albany students may also participate in any of the more than 300 study-abroad programs offered through the State University of New York. The University also offers summer archaeological dig programs, performance experiences in music and theater, and opportunities for independent study and projects.

The school's location in the state's capital has created exciting career-preparation opportunities for students. A wide range of internships are available, including those in agencies, accounting firms, high-technology facilities, a major medical facility, local and national television stations, and various corporations. In addition, students may participate in an internship through the Washington Center or elect the Washington Semester at American University in Washington, D.C. They can also earn academic credit for approved volunteer work through the Community and Public Service Program.

Academic Facilities

SUNY at Albany's main campus, designed by the noted architect Edward Durrell Stone, is a unique architectural structure. Its thirteen academic buildings rest on a common "Academic Podium" of classrooms, laboratories, and offices. The University also has a large computing center, a nuclear-particle accelerator, and the largest fine arts museum in the SUNY system. The University maintains three libraries that contain more than 2 million volumes. They include the University Library and the new Science Library located on the main campus and the Dewey Graduate Library located on the downtown campus.

Costs

For 2003–04, the annual undergraduate tuition was $4350 for New York State residents and $10,300 for out-of-state students. Mandatory fees totaled $1420. Room cost $4417 and board cost $2796.

Financial Aid

Merit scholarships are available to Presidential Scholars and other exceptional students. The Office of Financial Aid administers all undergraduate need-based financial assistance, including Federal Work-Study Program employment, Federal Perkins Loans, Federal Supplemental Educational Opportunity Grants, New York Equality of Opportunity Grants, Alumni Scholarships, Federal Pell Grants, Federal Stafford Student Loans, New York Tuition Assistance Program awards, and New York Regents Scholarships. General part-time employment is available both on and off the campus. Aid awarded to students through the Office of Financial Aid is based on demonstrated financial need as determined by the Free Application for Federal Student Aid (FAFSA).

Faculty

At SUNY at Albany, the faculty is fully engaged in teaching undergraduates. There are 585 full-time faculty members, 99 percent of whom have earned a Ph.D. Undergraduates have the opportunity to conduct supervised research with Albany faculty members, who are known for their expertise in a wide variety of fields. The University is also the home of the New York State Writers Institute, headed by Pulitzer Prize–winning author William Kennedy. The Institute affords students access to lectures and readings by acclaimed authors and poets. Residential quads include a faculty member in residence. The student-faculty ratio is 19:1.

Student Government

Students are represented on the University Senate and its committees and have their own governing organization, the Student Association (SA). The Central Council, the SA's legislative body, deals with internal policy and administers more than $1 million from student activity fees.

Admission Requirements

Applicants are evaluated on the basis of their three-year high school average, class ranking, and SAT I and/or ACT scores. Students should generally have grades of at least B+ and rank within the top quarter of their class in order to be competitive. All applicants must complete a minimum of 18 credits in high school, including 2 units of academic mathematics, 1 unit of which must be in elementary algebra. The University also actively seeks transfer students; competition for admission varies, depending on the program sought. The average grade point average for an admitted transfer student is 3.2. (Applicants for the Schools of Business, Criminal Justice, and Social Welfare are expected to achieve a cumulative average above 3.0.) The University also welcomes applications from educationally and financially disadvantaged students (Educational Opportunity Program), multicultural students, and international students. Recommendations are not required but are welcome, especially when they can help the University to assess the validity of the credentials being reviewed. Interviews are generally not required. The Admissions Office conducts information sessions, and student-led tours are available seven days a week when classes are in session. Students should call for an appointment.

Application and Information

Students may apply for fall, spring, or summer admission. SUNY Common Application forms are available in New York State high schools and all SUNY two- and four-year colleges. To receive full consideration, students should apply by March 1 for the fall term and by December 1 for the spring. Transfer students are encouraged to apply as early as possible and no later than July 1 for fall admission and December 15 for spring admission. Notification is on a rolling basis.

For further information, students should contact:

Director of Admissions
University at Albany,
State University of New York
1400 Washington Avenue
Albany, New York 12222
Telephone: 518-442-5435
E-mail: ugadmissions@albany.edu
World Wide Web: http://www.albany.edu/

UNIVERSITY AT BUFFALO, THE STATE UNIVERSITY OF NEW YORK

BUFFALO, NEW YORK

The University

The University at Buffalo (UB) is a major public research university where undergraduate education is enriched and intensified by its close association with graduate programs and cutting-edge scholarship. With more than 100 bachelor's degree programs and more than seventy undergraduate minors, 179 master's and eighty-seven doctoral degree programs, and more than 3,000 courses, UB offers more academic choices than any other public university in New York and New England. In addition to twenty-eight departments in the College of Arts and Sciences, UB has schools of architecture, dental medicine, education (graduate, with a provisional teacher certification program for undergraduates), engineering, informatics, law, management, medicine, nursing, pharmacy, public health and health professions, and social work.

Because UB is a research-intensive university, undergraduates study and work with faculty members who are leaders in their fields in academic and research facilities that support work at the most advanced levels of knowledge. This environment involves students in the discovery process and encourages them to develop the kind of critical thinking required in the creation of new knowledge. UB undergraduates have an opportunity to combine elements from several fields of knowledge or to design their own bachelor's degree programs. UB's University Honors Program enrolls more than 200 freshmen every year, with SAT I scores ranging from 1300 to 1600. Graduates of UB's Honors Program have won Fulbright, Marshall, Guggenheim, and other distinguished awards.

As a large university with approximately 27,000 students, of whom some 17,000 are undergraduates, UB can sustain a rich and varied student life. The University has men's and women's sports programs at both the intramural and NCAA Division I levels, extensive recreational and entertainment facilities, more than 250 student organizations, and a busy calendar of general interest lectures, concerts, and films.

The University at Buffalo has two campuses. Its North Campus, the seat of most of the undergraduate academic programs, occupies 2 square miles in suburban Amherst. It is one of the most modern university campuses in the nation. More than 5 million square feet of academic space, laboratories, libraries, residence halls, and recreation facilities have been built there since 1972. A Center for the Arts, an expanded athletics stadium, a Natural Sciences Complex, and a new mathematics building were completed in the past decade. The University's commitment to adding apartment-style living space has resulted in five new apartment complexes on or adjacent to campus, providing new and attractive living options for more than 1,900 students. Flickinger Court, Flint Village, Hadley Village, and South Lake Village apartments opened during the past six years.

The South Campus, 3 miles away in the residential northeast corner of Buffalo, is largely devoted to the health sciences and architecture. Buffalo's rapid transit line connects that campus with the city center and the waterfront. The South Campus also has residence halls for undergraduates. Many students who live off campus find rooms and apartments in the surrounding area.

Location

Buffalo is a Great Lakes city on an international border with a metropolitan area population of more than 1 million. It is a city of friendly neighborhoods with big-city recreation for all tastes: professional sports teams, the Buffalo Philharmonic Orchestra, the renowned twentieth-century art collection in the Albright-Knox Art Gallery, and a lively club scene. It also has a dramatic setting on Lake Erie and the Niagara River. Buffalo has abundant outdoor recreation in all four seasons. Skiing, hiking, camping, Lake Erie beaches, and the natural wonder of Niagara Falls are all nearby.

Majors and Degrees

UB is organized into one college and seven schools that serve undergraduates. The College of Arts and Sciences offers academic majors in African-American studies, American studies, anthropology, art, art history, Asian studies, bioinformatics and computational biology, biological sciences, chemistry, classics, computational physics, dance, economics, English, fine arts, geography, geological sciences, history, linguistics, mathematical physics, mathematics, mathematics-economics, media study, medicinal chemistry, modern languages and literatures (French, German, Italian, and Spanish), music, music performance, music theater, philosophy, physics, political science, psychology, sociology, speech and hearing science, studio art, theater, and women's studies. An interdisciplinary degree program in the social sciences, with concentrations in cognitive science, environmental studies, health and human services, international studies, legal studies, and urban and public policy studies, is offered. The School of Architecture and Planning offers majors in architecture and environmental design. The School of Engineering and Applied Sciences offers academic majors in computer science and engineering physics and in aerospace, chemical, civil, computer, electrical, environmental, industrial, and mechanical engineering. The School of Informatics offers a major in communication. The School of Management offers a major in business administration, with concentrations in accounting, financial analysis, human resources management, internal auditing, international business, management information systems, and marketing. The School of Medicine and Biomedical Sciences offers academic majors in biochemical pharmacology, biochemistry, biophysics, biotechnology, medical technology, and nuclear medicine technology. The School of Nursing offers an academic major in nursing. The School of Pharmacy and Pharmaceutical Sciences offers academic majors in pharmaceutical sciences and a six-year Pharm.D. pharmacy program. The School of Public Health and Health Professions offers academic majors in exercise science and occupational therapy. Physical therapy is now offered as a six-year doctorate; undergraduates major in exercise science. UB also offers an undergraduate certification program for secondary education. UB has thirty-five combined-degree programs (B.A./M.A. and B.S./M.B.A., for example) that can be completed in five years. Students whose objectives cannot be met through existing programs can formulate their own degree programs through double-degree or double-, joint-, or special-major options and an extensive minors program.

Academic Program

Candidates for a baccalaureate degree are required to complete a minimum of 120 semester hours, 30 of which must be completed in residence, and earn a minimum grade point average of 2.0. Students have great flexibility in planning their academic programs. All students must fulfill a University general education requirement. They must also complete an academic major, which is selected, with the advice of an academic adviser, usually by the end of the sophomore year. Students also have ample opportunity for independent study under departmental or faculty auspices. Placement and credit are granted on the basis of Advanced Placement or College-Level Examination Program scores. The academic year has two semesters, one beginning in late August, the other in late January. An extensive summer session is also offered.

Off-Campus Programs

Full-time undergraduates may cross-register for a maximum of two courses per term at other colleges in western New York. Many students take advantage of study-abroad programs. UB administers overseas programs in nearly thirty countries for full academic years or fall, spring, or summer sessions. Students who wish to study abroad in locations not offered by UB may take advantage of nearly 300 programs offered by other colleges in the SUNY system.

Academic Facilities

The University at Buffalo's academic library collections are the largest in the SUNY System; in addition to more than 3.2 million bound volumes, they include more then 25,000 serials and periodicals, 5 million microforms, specialized holdings including one of the world's largest collections of James Joyce manuscripts, and a renowned collection of twentieth-century poetry in manuscript. All library holdings are digitally cataloged and accessible from terminals and computers on and off campus. UB is among the first to have software that makes the entire SUNY library system—more than 18 million volumes—available to students. State-of-the-art computer workstations for student use are located at public sites in UB's libraries.

The University's varied computational facilities, including three supercomputer configurations at the Center for Computational Research, can support learning, instruction, and research on any scale. Undergraduates are exposed to the latest in educational technology innovation at every level of the University, from lightning-fast Internet access and Web-based course materials to online "chat" with tutors. For everyday use, UB has more than 100 public and departmental labs with nearly 2,500 workstations for students. Many labs are available 24 hours a day, seven days a week. All students receive free UB IT accounts, which provide access to the Internet and to UB services. Residence halls and University apartments are all wired with high-speed (Ethernet) data connections.

Costs

In 2003–04, tuition for New York State residents was $4350 and for out-of-state residents, $10,300. For all students, fees were $1500, and room and board were $6736. Students should expect additional expenses for books and supplies, transportation, and personal expenses. (Costs are subject to change.)

Financial Aid

The University participates in all New York State and federal financial aid programs, including the Tuition Assistance Program (available only to New York State residents) and the Federal Pell Grant, Federal Work-Study, Federal Direct Student Loan, and Federal Perkins Loan programs. Interested students must complete the Free Application for Federal Student Aid in early March for fall semester entry. All inquiries concerning financial aid should be addressed to the Student Response Center, 252 Capen Hall (telephone: 866-838-7257). UB awards more merit-based scholarships than any other public university in New York State. In fall 2003, 1 in 3 incoming freshmen received merit scholarship support, with more than $2.5 million awarded in all. Honors Scholars receive scholarships that range from $2500 up to the full cost of attendance as well as benefits such as faculty mentors, priority registration, and special seminars. The UB Scholars Program awards scholarships of $1500 to $5000 per year and offers a number of enhanced benefits. The Daniel Acker Scholars Program provides support services and activities for talented African-American, Latino, and Native American students. Acker Scholars usually receive scholarships starting at $4350 per year. Athletic grants-in-aid are awarded to students recruited to participate in UB's NCAA Division I athletics program.

Faculty

UB's nationally renowned faculty includes National Medal of Science, Nobel, Pulitzer, and other award winners. Of the 1,932 faculty members, 98 percent hold the doctorate or another terminal degree. A large number have published books or scholarly articles. Many have held major national or international fellowships; conducted research funded by government agencies or national foundations; served as consultants to business, education, and government; or otherwise demonstrated professional expertise. More than 100 have won the SUNY Chancellor's Award for Excellence in Teaching, the largest number of recipients on any SUNY campus.

Student Government

All daytime undergraduate students are members of the Student Association and are entitled to participate in its activities. The Student Association is involved at every level of student life, from freshman orientation to commencement. By their membership on many University-wide policy committees, representatives of the association are given a legitimate, permanent voice in the policies and direction of the University.

Admission Requirements

Applicants are required to submit their high school record and the results of the SAT I or ACT. Applicants should plan to take the SAT I or ACT no later than November. Application review and notification begins in mid-January and continues until the freshman class is filled. Most freshmen admitted to the University make application to the major of their choice during the sophomore year. However, architecture, engineering, health-related professions, management, music, nursing, and public health and health professions offer departmental admission to freshman applicants.

Admission is competitive. Most successful students at the University have come to it with a strong level of academic preparation in basic academic areas. In recent years, nearly two thirds of accepted freshmen had high school averages of 90 or higher, and 79 percent had combined SAT I scores of 1100 or higher.

The University provides an opportunity to enroll a limited number of freshmen who demonstrate academic potential through means other than quantitative measures. Creative talent, athletics, special academic achievement, demonstrated leadership, community service, and personal circumstances are examples of areas that the University may consider. Students admitted through this process will receive specialized advisement and support.

Transfer applicants must have completed a minimum of 12 semester hours at a regionally accredited college prior to application. Students with fewer than 24 semester hours are evaluated on the basis of their college and high school credentials in combination with standardized test score results. Admission of transfer students is based on the quality of previous academic performance and space availability. Students should present a minimum grade point average of 2.5 (calculated according to UB grading policy) to be considered for admission to the University. It should be noted, however, that requirements may vary depending on the academic program. Admission to an academic department may occur concurrently with University admission if the applicant has fulfilled prerequisite requirements. These requirements include completed courses, but may also comprise essay, portfolio, exam, or audition requirements. Some departments have significantly higher GPA standards and early deadlines for application.

Application and Information

Applications are available in New York State high schools or by contacting:

Office of Admissions
15 Capen Hall
University at Buffalo, The State University of New York
Buffalo, New York 14260-1660
Telephone: 716-645-6900
888-UB-ADMIT (toll-free)
E-mail: ub-admissions@buffalo.edu
World Wide Web: http://www.buffalo.edu/admissions

UNIVERSITY OF ADVANCING TECHNOLOGY

TEMPE, ARIZONA

The University

The University of Advancing Technology (UAT) is a prestigious private university with a dynamic and innovative campus culture. UAT offers unique bachelor's and master's computer technical degrees. Programs include digital animation, digital video production, Web design, game design, computer programming, database programming, game programming, Internet development and administration, network engineering, network security, e-commerce marketing, technology management, and Web site production.

UAT was founded in 1983 and has grown from a small computer manufacturer and corporate training center to today's modern University, located in the Phoenix metropolitan area. The school has close ties to industry through technology forums, a corporate training program, and an industry advisory board. These industry leaders provide input into the curriculum and insight into computer technologies needed in the workforce. This constant two-way communication between UAT and industry means that the University is on the leading edge of technology education and careers.

Classes are small, and students attend a full-time accelerated program in three 15-week semesters each year. Bachelor's degree programs are completed in fewer than three years and associate degrees in sixteen months. There are three regular start dates in January, May, and August/September and three early-entry start dates in March, July, and November.

Programs utilize a cutting-edge educational model called *Year-Round Balanced Learning*. Students are expected to attend lectures, participate in hands-on computer labs, and work on projects emphasizing teamwork and individual study. There is a focus on teaching and collaboration with emphasis placed on problem-solving skills. The Balanced Learning teaching method employs lecture, instructor or self-directed tutorial teaching, group recollection, and student teachback models.

UAT students graduate with not only expertise in today's latest technologies, but also with the framework and foundation needed to continue to be a leader as technology changes in the future. To provide the hands-on skills necessary to succeed today and also immerse students in theory and background so they may grow with technology, Balanced Learning uses a unique three-tiered approach of educational delivery. First, conceptual foundations give students an understanding of the intellectual and systemic underpinnings of their technology discipline. Then skills development trains them in the latest technologies, from software packages and applications to networking hardware, communication, and writing within the discipline. Finally, synthesis has the students utilize the conceptual foundations and their skills as they create and produce complete, complex projects representative of their discipline. Past works have included the creation of a Governor's Award-winning Web site for an Arizona nonprofit organization; completed game mods, for titles like Battlefield 1942 and Starcraft, that have received interest from studios and design companies; and development of new software and database applications.

The UAT campus is designed to enhance Balanced Learning techniques as well as to develop the creative skills needed in the new technologies. There are drawing and art studios, digital media production studios, computer classrooms, computer commons, a technology laboratory to explore the latest in hardware and software, and an output lab with a variety of plotters and printers. The computer commons can be viewed through the UAT Web Cam at http://www.uat.edu.

The student body is composed of students from all fifty states and twenty countries. They are a variety of ages, ranging from recent high school graduates to individuals working on their second career. Students live off campus in surrounding neighborhoods accessible by public transportation or bicycle as well as automobile. The University is close to major freeways and an international airport located in the Phoenix metropolitan area.

Higher education is all about opportunities for growth, self-expression, and interaction. Students at the University of Advancing Technology have a wide range of choices for academic, personal, and professional growth both inside and outside the classroom. They are a part of a rich learning environment where students and faculty have a passion for learning and playing with computers, while relentlessly pursuing technology.

Students are surrounded by the technology they come to study. They gather at Cuban Pete's for cappuccino or to watch UATv. Students play computer games at the Computer Gaming Center or work on projects in the New Technologies Lab. Students are encouraged to join local computer user groups or campus-based clubs and/or the national student Siggraph Chapter. There are organized trips to regional conferences, including Siggraph, E3, and other large industry trade shows. UAT plays a key role in facilitating communication between technology professionals and students.

The University hosts several technology forums annually to bring industry experts on campus for presentations and conversation with UAT students. The campus environment promotes awareness and involvement in the latest computer applications in modern industry. UAT students work with a community of passionate professionals and peers, and they have access to tutors and lab monitors to help them master the wide variety of software they are exposed to in the curriculum.

The Center for Learning Research (CLR) is under the auspices of the Graduate College. The CLR centralizes and supports research and development efforts by faculty members and students as well as select industry groups. The CLR is intended as a catalyst between technology in industry and higher education. It also is the mechanism through which more theoretical questions about educational processes can be explored. The Balanced Learning teaching method was developed by a team of faculty members within the CLR, where their research into learning methods continues.

A Master of Science in technology degree program is offered, with a thesis option or a capstone project option.

Location

Arizona is a land of incredible beauty, contrast, and opportunity. The Grand Canyon, as well as snow-covered mountains and forest streams, is a short drive from the exquisite Sonoran Desert surrounding metropolitan Phoenix.

The Phoenix metropolitan area, which includes Tempe, is a cosmopolitan Southwestern center nestled in a beautiful desert valley. There are more than 3 million people who live, work, and play in this modern financial and commercial hub. The weather is dry, the temperature is mild, and there are more than 300 days of sunshine a year.

The University is strategically located near the center of the Valley of the Sun, as the area is known. Students are minutes from the airport, Arizona State University, shops, restaurants and nightclubs, sports arenas, theaters, concert halls, and many culturally diverse activities. The school is within easy reach of Old Mexico, with its culture and beautiful beaches; Los Angeles and Disneyland; Las Vegas; and San Diego and Sea World. It's a short flight to skiing in Vail, Aspen, and Utah.

There are year-round outdoor activities, such as hiking, camping, horseback riding, snow skiing, hunting, tennis, and golf. Numerous lakes offer boating, swimming, fishing, and water skiing.

Majors and Degrees

UAT offers Associate of Arts and Bachelor's of Arts degrees in digital animation, digital art and design, digital video production, game design, and Web design.

Associate of Science and Bachelor's of Sciences degrees are offered in entrepreneurship, game programming, network administration and architecture, network security administration and architecture, software and database development, system administration and architecture, technology management, and Web programming.

UAT-Online offers today's most sought-after technology degrees in a success-oriented, proven, and totally online format. Accredited academic associate degrees are available in such exciting fields as digital animation, game design, and network defense (with a bachelor's in game programming and a master's in technology coming). Classes are highly interactive and faculty members are responsive, and these factors build upon each other progressively, with technology courses up front. Students take one course every five weeks and utilize the software currently used by industry—plus students complete portfolio-quality work as part of the program.

Academic Program

The Bachelor of Arts in multimedia is a 120-week program that requires a minimum of 120 semester credits, 84 area-of-concentration credits, 40 300- and 400-level credits, and 36 general-studies credits. The Associate of Arts in multimedia is a sixty-week program that requires a minimum of 60 semester credits, 45 area-of-concentration credits, and 15 general-studies credits. The Bachelor of Science in software engineering is a 120-week program that requires a minimum of 120 semester credits, 84 area-of-concentration credits, 40 300-and 400-level credits, and 36 general-studies credits. The Associate of Science in software engineering is a sixty-week program that requires a minimum of 60 semester credits, 45 area-of-concentration credits, and 15 general-studies credits. The Bachelor of Science in technology commerce is a 120-week program that requires a minimum of 120 semester credits, 84 area-of-concentration credits, 40 300- and 400-level credits, and 36 general-studies credits. The Associate of Science in technology commerce is a sixty-week program that requires a minimum of 60 semester credits, 45 area-of-concentration credits, and 15 general-studies credits.

Academic Facilities

The UAT campus was completed in 1998. The entire facility is designed for networked workstations connected by fiber-optic cable throughout the facility. There are a digital media theater, projection systems in the classrooms, a video and digital effects production studio, artists' studios, electronic classrooms, a technology laboratory, and a large computer commons area that looks out on the desert mountain landscape.

Costs

There is a processing fee, upon enrollment, of $100 for U.S. residents and $250 for non-U.S. residents. For 2004–05, tuition is $6800 per full time semester (12 or more credits).

Financial Aid

The professionals in the UAT Financial Aid Department work closely with each student to develop specific programs for obtaining funding for his or her education. The University of Advancing Technology is approved for the training of veterans, and the University was among the first in the country to participate in the Direct Student Loan Program. For information about scholarships awarded through the University, students should contact the Admissions Department. Financial aid and scholarship applications are available online at http://www.uat.edu.

Faculty

There are approximately 50 full-time faculty members. Technical instructors have experience in industry and often utilize real-world examples in their classes. Faculty members are committed to helping students achieve their educational goals.

Student Government

There is no formal student government. Student feedback is achieved through meetings, surveys, focus groups, a volunteer student mentor program, and other campus community-based informal groups.

Admission Requirements

University of Advancing Technology programs are open to all persons who have a high school diploma or hold the educational equivalent and display a serious intent toward their education. Applicants under the age of 18 must have a legal guardian sign all admission agreements and a financial responsibility statement.

Prospective students must provide evidence of the required SAT I or ACT scores, proof of a cumulative high school grade point average of 2.5 or better, the required GED composite score, or a college credential from an accredited institution. An ACT minimum score of 21 meets the minimal requirement for admission. An SAT I minimum score of 500 in the verbal and 520 in the math or a combined minimum score of 1020 meets the minimal requirement for admission. A college credential at the associate or bachelor's level meets the requirement for admission in place of a cumulative high school GPA of 2.5 or GED average scores. A personality profile that is used only for retention studies may be administered.

In addition to the standard admission requirements, non-U.S. citizens applying for admission to the University of Advancing Technology must provide proof of English proficiency if English is not the native language in one of the following ways: the Test of English as a Foreign Language (TOEFL) with a score of 500 or higher (Test of Written English must be included), successful completion of Level 108 from an ESL Center, completion of the ASPECT English Language Proficiency Level 5, or attendance for at least one year at a regionally accredited U.S. college or university and completion of English 101 and 102 (or equivalent) with grades of C or better. International students are not required to provide ACT or SAT I scores if they are high school graduates in their country of origin.

Transcripts must be submitted with an English translation and be evaluated for educational credentials (must show U.S. high school equivalent) by the Educational Credential Evaluators, Inc., P.O. Box 17499, Milwaukee, Wisconsin 53217-0499, U.S.A.

Application and Information

Applications are accepted throughout the year, and students may choose one of six start dates. Students may request an application from the address below.

UAT Admissions
2625 West Baseline Road
Tempe, Arizona 85283
Telephone: 602-383-8228
800-658-5744 (toll-free)
E-mail: admission@uat.edu
World Wide Web: http://www.uat.edu

THE UNIVERSITY OF ALABAMA AT BIRMINGHAM

BIRMINGHAM, ALABAMA

UAB

The University

The University of Alabama at Birmingham (UAB) is a fully accredited research university and academic health center with an annual enrollment of more than 16,000 students. In a short time, UAB has established outstanding programs through six liberal arts and professional schools, six health professional schools, and graduate programs serving all major units. As the University has grown, so have its contributions to the state, the nation, and the world. UAB is committed to education, research, and service programs of excellent quality and far-reaching scope. In terms of research and development funding, UAB ranks twenty-sixth nationally and first in the state of Alabama, receiving more funding than all Alabama universities combined. In such an environment, undergraduate students can pursue a wide array of research opportunities and gain valuable experience that pays off later in graduate studies or career development.

As an autonomous campus of the University of Alabama System, the University of Alabama at Birmingham resides in the largest metropolitan area in the state and offers unique educational opportunities with day and evening classes. Both commuting and residential students learn in an environment supportive of the needs of the individual.

Part of the UAB experience is student life, consisting of a rich mix of academic organizations, honor clubs, social fraternities and sororities, volunteer groups, and activities ranging from sports to performing arts. With more than 200 campus organizations to keep students involved, UAB offers the chance to make lifelong friendships while assisting in the development of skills essential to leadership and teamwork. The South is the place for sports year-round, and UAB is no exception. The athletic program is a Division I member of the NCAA and a founding member of Conference USA, which includes twelve universities. UAB athletes participate in seventeen intercollegiate sports, including men's and women's basketball, golf, rifle, soccer, and tennis; men's baseball and football; and women's cross-country, track, softball, synchronized swimming, and volleyball. Intramural sports, aerobics, and outdoor recreation are also available. Student housing is limited and is available on a priority basis; early application is encouraged.

Location

Birmingham earned the name "The Magic City" during its first boom days. The expression still rings true as the metropolitan area continues to mirror UAB's phenomenal growth and reflects the many cultural opportunities available within the city. With a budget of more than $1 billion, UAB is the city's largest employer and the second largest in the state. Birmingham is easily reached by automobile from major national routes (Interstates 20, 59, and 65), and UAB is only minutes away from the Birmingham International Airport.

Majors and Degrees

UAB's degree programs offer strong career preparation. With fifty-one majors from which to choose, UAB's broad curriculum allows students to explore new interests while receiving specialized training. Students may also integrate different areas of knowledge by choosing a minor in an additional field of study or by exploring the possibilities for developing an individually designed major.

The School of Arts and Humanities offers the Bachelor of Arts degree in African-American studies, communication studies (concentrations in broadcasting, communication arts, journalism, mass communication, and public relations), English, French, music (concentration in music technology and music education), philosophy, Spanish, studio art, (concentrations in art education, art history, ceramic sculpture, drawing, graphic design, painting, photography, printmaking, and sculpture), and theater.

The School of Business offers the Bachelor of Science degree in accounting, economics (concentrations in economic analysis and policy and quantitative methods), finance (concentrations in financial management, investments and institutions, and real estate), industrial distribution, management (concentrations in general management, human resource management, management information systems, and operations management), and marketing.

The School of Education offers the Bachelor of Science degree in early childhood education, elementary education, health education, high school education, physical education, and special education.

The School of Engineering offers the Bachelor of Science degree in biomedical engineering, civil engineering, electrical engineering, materials engineering, and mechanical engineering.

The School of Health Related Professions offers the Bachelor of Science degree in health sciences, cytotechnology, health information management, medical technology, nuclear medicine technology, radiologic sciences (concentrations in advanced imaging, radiation therapy, and radiographer studies), respiratory therapy, and surgical physician assistant studies.

The School of Natural Sciences and Mathematics offers the Bachelor of Science degree in biology, chemistry, computer and information sciences, mathematics, natural science, and physics.

The School of Nursing awards the Bachelor of Science degree. Students interested in pursuing the nursing degree and who meet the University's admission requirements are admitted to UAB as prenursing students. To be eligible for admission in good standing to the School of Nursing, students must successfully complete a prescribed set of courses with an acceptable grade point average.

The School of Social and Behavioral Sciences offers the Bachelor of Arts degree in anthropology, economics, history, international studies, political science, and sociology and the Bachelor of Science degree in criminal justice, psychology, and social work.

Academic Program

UAB's undergraduate instructional programs are broad based and designed to serve the needs of its diverse student body while providing a strong general education foundation. All programs of study leading to the baccalaureate degree have as an essential component a common core curriculum. The minimum total credit hours required for a baccalaureate degree are 120 semester hours with a cumulative grade point average of at least 2.0 (C) in all credit hours attempted. A student may obtain a certain number of semester hours of academic credit for knowledge acquired independently through Advanced Placement (AP), International Baccalaureate (I.B.), College-Level Examination Program (CLEP), Credit by Examination (CBE), evaluation of noncollegiate-sponsored courses, armed services courses, and prior learning.

There are two academic semesters and a summer term during a calendar year. The fall and spring semesters each consist of approximately sixteen weeks of classes. Summer term offers several options, including twelve-week, nine-week, three-week, and 4½-week terms.

Academic Facilities

The UAB campus occupies more than 100 major buildings, more than 10 million gross square feet, and 75 square blocks near downtown Birmingham. The undergraduate area of campus is concentrated wit hin a five-square-block area, however, giving students the convenience and togetherness that is so important to the college experience.

The Mervyn H. Sterne Library houses a collection of more than a million items selected to support teaching and research at UAB. In addition to books and subscriptions to more than 2,000 periodicals, the collection consists of microforms and other print and nonprint materials. Study areas and photocopying machines for the convenience of patrons are located throughout the library. The online catalog provides rapid access to the collection and to other major library collections in Alabama. The Educational Technology Services Department (ETS) includes dozens of microcomputers and is available to anyone with a valid UAB ID card. In addition to Sterne Library, the Lister Hill Library of the Health Sciences provides a comprehensive collection of materials for medical study and research.

In 1996, UAB unveiled the Alys Robinson Stephens Performing Arts Center, with state-of-the-art concert halls and practice facilities. This beautiful facility draws national and international performers, enhancing the strong cultural opportunities in Birmingham.

Costs

For the 2003–04 academic year, tuition was $116 per semester hour for in-state students and $290 per semester hour for out-of-state students. Based on a full load of course work for the academic year, tuition and fees for Alabama residents is estimated at $4274 and $9494 for nonresidents. A typical amount for books and supplies total approximately $900 per academic year. A shared room in a residence hall ranges from $1732 to $3316 per academic year.

Financial Aid

UAB's financial aid package consists of loans, employment, and grants and scholarships, enabling students from all economic backgrounds to attend UAB. UAB offers a growing number of scholarships to provide support for eligible students who attend UAB. Newly admitted students are considered for all academic scholarships for which they are qualified. Awards are distributed on a first-come, first-served basis; students are encouraged to apply as early as possible. Financial aid applications are available in early January for the following academic year, with a priority packaging deadline of April 1.

Faculty

UAB has approximately 1,817 full-time faculty members, with 91 percent holding doctoral degrees. The student-faculty ratio is 18:1, with the vast majority of freshman- and sophomore-level courses taught by full-time faculty members.

Student Government

In addition to eight student government associations, the Office of Student Life offers many student-run committees and programs that are open to all students. These committees provide entertainment through comedy, music, movies, lectures, and multicultural programming. Other opportunities to lead and serve include social fraternities and sororities, a student leadership program, an ambassador program, a volunteer program, a scholarship pageant, and three award-winning student publications.

Admission Requirements

UAB is an equal educational opportunity institution. The requirements for regular admission for entering freshmen include a minimum high school GPA of 2.0 on a 4.0 scale in academic subjects and a minimum ACT score of 20 or SAT I score of 950. For tentative action, a transcript may be sent during the student's senior year in high school. A final transcript must be sent upon graduation.

Transfer students must have a minimum cumulative GPA of 2.0 on a 4.0 scale after completing 24 semester hours (or 36 quarter hours) of college-level work. Students with previous college work must submit an official transcript from each institution attended and must be eligible to enroll at the last institution attended. UAB also encourages international students who have academic, linguistic, and financial capabilities to apply for admission.

Application and Information

All students who wish to attend UAB must complete an application for admission and submit proof of immunization against measles. An application may be submitted as early as one year prior to admission. A completed application, a nonrefundable $25 application fee ($30 for international students), and all supporting documentation must be received by the Office of Undergraduate Admissions by the priority deadline for the term for which admission is requested. The application deadline for fall term is March 1, 2004. For an application and further information, students should contact:

UAB Undergraduate Admissions
Hill University Center, Room 260
1530 3rd Avenue, South
Birmingham, Alabama 35294-1150
Telephone: 205-934-8221
800-421-8473 (toll-free)
E-mail: undergradadmit@uab.edu
World Wide Web: http://Students.uab.edu

THE UNIVERSITY OF ALABAMA IN HUNTSVILLE

HUNTSVILLE, ALABAMA

The University

The University of Alabama in Huntsville (UAH) is a public, four-year, coeducational institution and is a member of the University of Alabama System. UAH was founded in 1950 as an extension center of the University of Alabama and became an autonomous campus in 1969. UAH has earned national recognition in engineering and the sciences, and its programs in the humanities, fine arts, social sciences, business, and nursing are outstanding. Students interact with some of the most productive researchers in their respective disciplines. Close ties with business, industry, and government give students real-world opportunities and experience. UAH is a partner with more than 100 high-tech industries as well as major federal laboratories such as NASA's Marshall Space Flight Center and the U.S. Army. Its unique location makes possible many co-op opportunities for students to earn much of their college costs and to maximize their employment potential. Students have many opportunities to work with some of the top scientists in the country. UAH is accredited by the Southern Association of Colleges and Schools' Commission on Colleges. In addition, UAH holds professional accreditation from the American Chemical Society; the Computing Sciences Accreditation Board; the Accreditation Board for Engineering and Technology, Inc.; the National League for Nursing Accrediting Commission; the National Association of Schools of Music; and AACSB–The International Association for Management Education.

The fall 2003 enrollment consisted of 5,481 undergraduate and 1,570 graduate students. Seventy-eight percent are from Alabama, 7 percent are from other countries, 52 percent are men, and 48 percent are women. UAH students represent forty-five states and more than eighty-six countries. Of the total undergraduate enrollment, 24 percent are members of ethnic minority groups. The median ACT composite range for entering students was 22-27; the median GPA was 3.4.

UAH has more than 115 active student groups and organizations, including national fraternities and sororities, honor societies, special interest groups, religious organizations, the Student Government Association (SGA), the student-run newspaper, the student-run literary magazine, minority student organizations, international student organizations, the choir, the chorus, a film and lecture series, service organizations, professional interest groups, and intramural athletics. The University is a member of the NCAA Division II and the Gulf South Conference and competes in the following intercollegiate sports: men's baseball, basketball, cross-country, soccer, and tennis and women's basketball, cross-country, soccer, softball, tennis, and volleyball. In addition, UAH competes at the NCAA Division I level in men's ice hockey.

On-campus housing is available for undergraduate and graduate students. The new North Campus Residence Hall opened in fall 2002. The Central Campus Residence Hall is a seven-story residence hall that offers private bedrooms, is located in the center of campus, and is connected to the University Center by an enclosed walkway. Student apartments in Southeast Housing are reserved for upperclassmen and graduate students. Private apartments are available for married students and students with children. Handicapped-accessible apartments are available. Meals are available in the University Center cafeteria.

The Colleges of Administrative Science, Engineering, Liberal Arts, Nursing, and Science and the School of Graduate Studies administer the degree programs of the University. Through the School of Graduate Studies, students may earn the master's degree in accounting, atmospheric science, biological science, chemical engineering, chemistry, civil engineering, computer engineering, computer science, electrical engineering, English, history, industrial and systems engineering, management, management information systems, management of technology, materials science, mathematics, mechanical engineering, nursing, operations research, physics, psychology, public affairs, and software engineering. The Ph.D. degree is awarded in applied mathematics, atmospheric science, biotechnology, civil engineering, computer engineering, computer science, electrical engineering, industrial and systems engineering, materials science, mechanical engineering, optical science and engineering, and physics.

Location

The University of Alabama in Huntsville is located in the Tennessee River Valley of north-central Alabama, 100 miles north of Birmingham and 100 miles south of Nashville, Tennessee. Huntsville is home to more than fifty Fortune 500 companies that specialize in high technology, including aerospace engineering, rocket propulsion, computer technology, weapons systems, telecommunications, software engineering, information systems design, and engineering services. Most of these companies are located in one of the top ten research parks in the world and the second-largest research park in the U.S., Cummings Research Park, which is adjacent to the UAH campus.

Majors and Degrees

The College of Administrative Science awards the Bachelor of Science in Business Administration (B.S.B.A.) degree in the fields of accounting, finance, management, management information systems, and marketing. The College of Engineering awards the Bachelor of Science in Engineering (B.S.E.) degree in the following engineering disciplines: chemical, civil, computer, electrical, industrial and systems, mechanical, and optical. The College of Nursing awards the Bachelor of Science in Nursing (B.S.N.) degree. The Bachelor of Arts (B.A.) degree is awarded by the College of Liberal Arts in the fields of art, communication arts, education, English, foreign languages and international trade, history, music, philosophy, political science, psychology, and sociology. In the College of Science, the Bachelor of Science (B.S.) degree is available in biological science, chemistry, computer science, mathematics, and physics. A Bachelor of Arts degree is available in biological science and mathematics.

Fifth-year certificates are available in accounting, education, and human resource management for individuals who already hold a bachelor's degree in another field. Undergraduate teacher certification programs are offered in the following areas: art education (N–12), elementary education (K–6), and music education (N–12) and in secondary/high school education (4–8 or 7–12), with majors in biology, chemistry, English, French, general science, German, history, language arts, mathematics, physics, Russian, social science, and Spanish.

Academic Programs

The general education course work is designed to broaden intellectual awareness and enhance cultural literacy and analytical thinking. All undergraduates are required to complete course work in English composition, humanities and fine arts, history, social and behavioral sciences, natural and physical sciences, and mathematics. B.A., B.S., B.S.B.A., and B.S.N. degrees require the completion of at least 128 total semester hours; B.S.E. degrees in electrical and industrial and systems engineering require 131; B.S.E. degrees in chemical and civil engineering, 132; B.S.E. degrees in mechanical and optical engineering, 134; and the B.S.E. in computer engineering, 135. A variety of special academic programs and options are available, including academic remediation, accelerated degree completion, cooperative education, cross-registration with other institutions, distance learning, double majors, dual enrollment, English as a second language, an honors program, independent study, internships, and learning disabilities services. Credit is awarded for appropriate scores on CLEP and AP examinations. UAH offers Army ROTC at a participating institution off campus. Special services are available for handicapped students, including note-taking services, readers, tape recorders, tutors, interpreters for the hearing impaired, special transportation, special housing, adaptive equipment, and Braille services. The fall 2004 semester begins August 30 and ends December 16; spring semester 2005 begins January 10 and ends May 3. Two summer sessions are offered and begin May 31 and July 5, 2005.

Academic Facilities

The 376-acre campus is in northwest Huntsville. All academic buildings have been constructed since 1960 and exemplify modern functional design. The UAH library houses more than 300,000 books, serial backfiles, and government documents; more than 1,000 current serials; and more than 550,000 microforms. The UAH Art Gallery hosts art exhibits by local, regional, and national artists as well as by students and faculty members. More than 900 personal computers are available across the campus for student use. Computer labs, one of which is open 24 hours a day, are located in several buildings and are staffed to provide assistance. Access to the University fiber-optic network is available in all buildings, including the Central Campus Residence Hall. Internet access and e-mail are available to all students. UAH has a number of state-of-the-art research labs that are accessible to undergraduates.

Costs

In 2003–04, tuition for undergraduate Alabama residents was $4126 (15 credits each semester) for the academic year. Out-of-state students paid $8702 (15 credits each semester) for the academic year. Undergraduates can expect to spend approximately $720 on books and supplies for the academic year. Undergraduate students pay an estimated $3400 for room, $1600 for board, $1080 for transportation, and $1200 for personal and miscellaneous expenses per year.

Financial Aid

UAH awards nearly $20 million annually in need-based and non-need-based financial aid in the form of scholarships, grants, loans, and campus jobs. The following financial aid programs are available: Federal Stafford Student Loans (subsidized and unsubsidized), Federal PLUS Loans, Consolidation Loans, Federal Pell Grants, Federal Supplemental Educational Opportunity Grants (FSEOG), state scholarships and grants, private scholarships, and institutional scholarships. Non-need-based scholarships are available for athletics, ROTC, academic merit, creative and performing arts, special achievement, leadership skills, and minority status. Students should submit the Free Application for Federal Student Aid (FAFSA) and the UAH financial aid form before April 1 for priority consideration and no later than the final closing date of July 31. Award notifications are made on a rolling basis. The priority date for scholarship application is February 1.

Faculty

Of the 277 full-time instructional faculty members, 87 percent hold the Ph.D. or other terminal degree in their field. The student-faculty ratio is 16:1. Graduate students teach 5 percent of introductory undergraduate courses. The average introductory lecture class size is 29.

Student Government

The primary purpose of the Student Government Association is to help improve the educational environment and promote the welfare of students in all areas of University life. The SGA is responsible for developing and sponsoring programs that enrich the students' cultural, intellectual, and social life. An executive branch, a 15-member legislature, and a 5-member arbitration board are responsible for carrying out the official business of the organization. The SGA sponsors more than 110 clubs and organizations in addition to providing many student services, such as health insurance, special rates for community cultural events, and a student directory.

Admission Requirements

High school graduates may be admitted as regular freshmen based on acceptable high school achievement and standardized test scores (SAT I or ACT), which are considered together. A higher result in one area offsets a lower performance in the other. For example, a minimum high school GPA of 3.0 is required if the ACT composite score is 18 or the combined SAT I score is 850. A high school GPA of 2.0 requires an ACT composite score of 23 or higher or a combined SAT I score of 1050 or higher. Applicants should present a minimum of 20 Carnegie high school units, including 4 units of English, 3 of social studies, 1 of algebra, 1 of geometry, 1 of biology (recommended), 1 of chemistry/physics (required by the Colleges of Engineering and Science and recommended by all other Colleges), 1 of algebra II/trigonometry (one each required by the College of Engineering and recommended by all other Colleges), and sufficient academic electives to meet the required 20 units. First-time freshmen and transfer students are admitted for every academic term. Transfer students with fewer than 18 hours of earned college credit are admitted based on high school transcripts, test scores, and college course work. Transfer students are required to submit transcripts of all university work and have at least a 2.0 average on all work attempted to qualify for regular admission.

Application and Information

Completed applications and a nonrefundable $20 application fee should be sent by August 1 for admission in the fall semester and by December 15 for admission in the spring semester. Admission notifications are sent on a rolling basis.

For an application form and more information, students should contact:

Office of Admissions
The University of Alabama in Huntsville
301 Sparkman Drive
Huntsville, Alabama 35899
Telephone: 256-824-6070
800-UAH-CALL (toll-free)
Fax: 256-824-6073
E-mail: admitme@uah.edu
World Wide Web: http://www.uah.edu

UNIVERSITY OF ALASKA ANCHORAGE

ANCHORAGE, ALASKA

The University

The University of Alaska Anchorage (UAA) is a public institution accredited by the Commission on Colleges of the Northwest Association of Schools and Colleges. Since its creation, UAA has established a record of continuing growth and development in its academic, vocational, and public-service activities. The University of Alaska Anchorage promotes student success by maintaining a strong emphasis on faculty excellence and student services. Programs are focused on student needs and support the development of students by contributing to their cultural, social, intellectual, physical, and emotional growth. UAA also provides support services for students with special needs. UAA offers a broad range of certificate programs, associate degree programs, bachelor's degree programs, and master's degree programs. Programs span the social sciences, English literature and creative writing, foreign languages and cultures, the natural sciences, mathematics and engineering, and the fine arts, providing students with the opportunity to pursue interests beyond their selected academic fields and explore a variety of subjects. UAA also offers a statewide distance education and independent learning program with multimedia distribution.

The academic units on the Anchorage campus are the College of Arts and Sciences, the College of Business and Public Policy, the College of Education, the College of Health and Social Welfare, the Community and Technical College, the School of Engineering, and the School of Nursing. Research units include the Alaska Center for Rural Health, the American Russian Center, the Biomedical Program, the Center for Alcohol and Addiction Studies, the Center for Economic Development, the Center for Economic Education, the Center for Human Development University Affiliated Program, the Environmental and Natural Resources Institute (the Alaska Natural Heritage Program, the Alaska State Climate Center, the Arctic Environmental and Information Data Center, and Resources Solutions), the Institute for Circumpolar Health Studies, the Institute of Social and Economic Research, the Justice Center, the Psychological Services Center, and the Small Business Development Center (Procurement Technical Assistance Center, BUY ALASKA, and Alaska Technology Transfer Center).

The University offers a wide range of programs at the graduate level: the Alaska State Teacher Certificate/Endorsement; the Master of Arts (M.A.) in anthropology, English, and interdisciplinary studies; the Master of Business Administration (M.B.A.); the Master of Civil Engineering (M.C.E.); the Master of Education (M.Ed.) in adult education, counseling and guidance, educational leadership, master teacher, and special education; the Master of Fine Arts (M.F.A.) in creative writing and literary arts; the Master of Public Administration (M.P.A.); the Master of Public Health (M.P.H.); the Master of Science (M.S.) in arctic engineering, biological sciences, civil engineering, clinical psychology, engineering management, environmental quality engineering, environmental quality science, global supply chain management, interdisciplinary studies, nursing science, science management, and vocational education; and the Master of Social Work (M.S.W.).

Location

The University of Alaska campus is nestled in a lush greenbelt filled with ponds, lakes, and spruce forests, surrounded by the mountains and glaciers of Chugach State Park and the beautiful Cook Inlet. Student housing and classrooms are within easy walking distance. An extensive system of trails provides opportunities for running, cross-country skiing, inline skating, and biking. The geographical features in the Anchorage area provide world-class climbing, downhill skiing, and snowboarding. Cook Inlet and nearby Prince William Sound offer an amazingly rich and diverse marine environment supporting a host of marine mammals and legendary salmon runs. These waters contribute to the area's relatively mild weather and are well known among the world's windsurfers and sea kayakers. Summertime temperatures range between 60 and 70 degrees. Winters include snow from October to April but are less severe in Anchorage than in many other U.S. cities. Anchorage, a city of 260,000 people, is the chief business, professional, international, transportation, and entertainment center of the state.

Majors and Degrees

The Bachelor of Arts degree (B.A.) is awarded in anthropology, art, biological sciences, computer science, economics, early childhood education, education, elementary education, English, history, hospitality and restaurant management, interdisciplinary studies, journalism and public communication, justice, languages, mathematics, music, political science, psychology, sociology, and theater. The Bachelor of Business Administration degree (B.B.A.) is awarded in accounting, economics, finance, global logistics management, management, management information systems, and marketing. The Bachelor of Fine Arts degree (B.F.A.) is awarded in art. The Bachelor of Human Services degree (B.H.S.) is awarded in human services. The Bachelor of Liberal Studies degree (B.L.S.) is awarded in liberal studies. The Bachelor of Music degree (B.M.) is awarded in music (music education emphasis) and performance. The Bachelor of Science degree (B.S.) is awarded in anthropology, aviation technology, biological science, chemistry, civil engineering, computer science, geomatics, health sciences, interdisciplinary studies, mathematics, medical technology, natural science, nursing science, psychology, sociology, and technology. The Bachelor of Social Work degree (B.S.W.) is offered in social work.

The Associate of Arts degree (A.A.) is awarded with a general studies program. The Associate of Applied Science degree (A.A.S.) is awarded in accounting; air traffic control; apprenticeship technologies; architectural and engineering technology; automotive technology; aviation administration; aviation maintenance technology; business computer information systems; culinary arts; dental assisting; dental hygiene; early childhood development; fire service administration; geomatics; heavy duty transportation and equipment; human services; logistics operations; medical assisting; medical laboratory technology; nursing; occupational safety and health; office management and technology; paramedical technology; professional piloting; radiologic technology; refrigeration and heating technology; small business administration; telecommunications, electronics, and computer technology; and welding technology.

Certificate programs designed to meet the needs of students who wish to attain a high level of proficiency in specific career areas are offered in applied ethics, architectural drafting, automotive technology, aviation maintenance technology, civil drafting, computer and networking technology, dental assisting, early childhood development, geographic information systems, heavy duty transportation and equipment, logistics, massage therapy, mechanical and electrical drafting, mechanical/electrical draft, office technology, paralegal studies, pharmacy technology, practical nursing, structural drafting, and telecommunications and electronic systems.

Academic Program

UAA's fall semester begins in August, the spring semester in January, and the summer session in May. An undergraduate student who registers for 12 or more credits is considered to be full-time. The minimum number of credits that must be earned for a baccalaureate degree, including those accepted by transfer, is 120. A minimum of 60 semester credits is required to complete the Associate of Arts and Associate of Applied Science degree programs. Completion requirements vary from one discipline to another. All degree programs offered by UAA require students to maintain a GPA of at least 2.0; some programs require a higher GPA.

Degree-seeking students with experience acquired outside the conventional college classroom have an opportunity to demonstrate college-level achievement. UAA grants Advanced Placement credit for satisfactory performance (scores of 3 or higher) on the College Board Advanced Placement tests. UAA's credit-by-examination program rewards students who do well on either the College-Level Examination Program (CLEP) or the challenge examinations, the latter of which are locally developed comprehensive exams covering specific subject areas. Credit may be granted for military service. Details on eligibility, restrictions, and procedures are in the course catalog.

Academic Facilities

The Consortium Library, located on the Anchorage campus, serves the academic clientele of the University and that of its nearby neighbor, Alaska Pacific University. The Anchorage campus consists of twenty academic, administrative, and laboratory structures. These include specially equipped buildings for the arts, culinary arts, allied health science, automotive and diesel, business, and engineering programs. The Merrill Aviation Complex houses the aviation program. In Anchorage, courses are also taught at Elmendorf Air Force Base, Fort Richardson, and Chugiak–Eagle River.

Costs

In 2004–05, Alaska residents pay $90 per credit hour. Nonresident students pay $281 per credit hour. Students enrolled under the Western Undergraduate Exchange pay $135 per credit hour. On-campus apartments and residence halls with meals range from $3115 to $3615. Extra funds are needed for student activity fees, textbooks, and miscellaneous expenses.

Financial Aid

The Office of Student Financial Aid assists students and prospective students in securing the funds needed to begin or continue studies at the University. The state and federal government make available financial assistance in the form of grants, loans, and employment opportunities for students who demonstrate the need for such assistance. The amount and type of award may vary depending upon state and federal guidelines, student need, and availability of funds. Applications for aid should be received by April 1 of the year the student plans to enroll. In addition to government funds, the University and many private organizations offer scholarships, tuition waivers, and veteran benefits.

Faculty

A high percentage of UAA faculty members have doctoral degrees. Students find their introductory classes taught by highly qualified and experienced faculty members. The student-faculty ratio on the Anchorage campus is 14:1, and the average class size is 19. Faculty members in the academic units also serve students as academic advisers.

Student Government

The Union of Students of the University of Alaska Anchorage (USUAA) is the sole official representative for students on campus. This body is duly recognized by the Board of Regents. USUAA administers funds for various student organizations, programs, and activities, such as movie tickets, concerts, dances, special events, lectures, legal services, the Club Council, the student radio station, and the student newspaper.

Admission Requirements

Most certificate and associate degree programs operate under an admission policy that allows any student who has earned a high school diploma or the equivalent (GED), or is 18 years of age or older and has participated in UAA's Assessment and Advisement process, to apply for admission. First-time degree-seeking freshmen and those degree-seeking applicants with fewer than 60 college-level semester credits must submit official high school transcripts (or GED scores) and official copies of ACT, SAT, or ASSET test scores along with the application for admission. Freshmen applying to associate or certificate programs must take an approved placement test. In addition, freshmen who have earned credits at other regionally accredited colleges and universities must submit official transcripts from all institutions previously attended. To qualify for baccalaureate degree admission, students must also have maintained a high school GPA of at least 2.5; a GPA of 2.0 or higher is required for transfer students.

Application and Information

Prospective baccalaureate degree, associate degree, and certificate students must submit the application for admission and a nonrefundable $40 application fee. Deadlines for receipt of the application and all supporting documents are July 1 for the fall semester and November 1 for the spring semester.

For more information concerning admission or the general curriculum, students should contact:

Cecile Mitchell
Director, Enrollment Services
University of Alaska Anchorage
P.O. Box 141629
Anchorage, Alaska 99514-1629
Telephone: 907-786-1480
World Wide Web: http://www.uaa.alaska.edu/

UNIVERSITY OF ALASKA FAIRBANKS

FAIRBANKS, ALASKA

The University

Founded in 1917, the University provides education, research, and service in the "last frontier." The Fairbanks campus, one of three in the statewide system of higher education, is the primary administrative and research center and has branches in Bethel, Dillingham, Kotzebue, and Nome, along with Rural Centers throughout the state.

The total University of Alaska Fairbanks (UAF) enrollment in fall 2002 was 9,390. Eighty-five percent of the students have Alaskan residency, although nearly half of the students graduated from high schools in forty-nine states and thirty-eight other countries. The nine residence halls on campus are renovated and are capable of lodging 1,322 students. The Student Apartment Complex has sixty furnished two-bedroom units reserved for sophomore and upperclass students. The Eileen Panigeo MacLean House, housing for rural students, holds 22 students. The University also manages 153 furnished apartments for students with families.

The large campus contains a core of academic buildings and residences, as well as miles of ski trails, two lakes, and an arboretum. Most of the University's research institutes, including the noted Geophysical Institute and the new International Arctic Research Center, are clustered on the West Ridge. The University's Agricultural Experiment Station farm is on campus, as are a Cooperative Fish and Wildlife Research Unit and various state and federal agencies and laboratories. The University awards graduate degrees in many of the same areas as the undergraduate studies, often in conjunction with one of its research institutes. A natural science facility, housing chemistry, physics, geology, and earth sciences, was completed in 1995.

Intercollegiate athletics include men's and women's basketball, cross-country running and skiing, and riflery and a women's volleyball team. The University sponsors an outstanding men's intercollegiate ice hockey team, which plays at the 4,665-seat Carlson Center. The UAF hockey team is a member of the Central Collegiate Hockey Association (CCHA). The Student Recreation Complex houses a variety of sports and physical activities facilities, including multipurpose areas for basketball, volleyball, badminton, tennis, calisthenics, dance, gymnastics, judo, and karate; a rifle and pistol range; courts for handball, racquetball, and squash; an elevated 200-meter, three-lane jogging track; a swimming pool; weight-training and modern fitness equipment areas; an ice arena for recreational skating and hockey; a special aerobics area; and a three-story climbing wall. The cheery and roomy student union, the William Ransom Wood Center, is the focus of various out-of-class activities for students and faculty members. The center houses meeting and exhibit rooms, lounges and television areas, the student government offices, campus information, a pub, a bowling alley, a games room, a cafeteria, a snack bar, an espresso bar, and a photography darkroom.

Location

The campus of the University of Alaska Fairbanks is situated on a ridge overlooking the valley of the Tanana River and the city of Fairbanks. Serving a population of more than 85,000 within the 7,561-square-mile North Star Borough, Fairbanks is a major trade center for outlying villages in Interior Alaska. The city is connected with the rest of the state and the lower forty-eight states by air and highway. Municipal bus service is available between downtown Fairbanks, the surrounding area, and the campus. Shuttle bus service is available around the UAF campus at no cost. Fairbanks offers the sophistication of larger cities through such luxuries as first-run movies and fine restaurants while maintaining the atmosphere of smaller, more personal towns. Denali National Park and other vast wilderness areas are close at hand, and Anchorage is 350 miles south via the Parks Highway. Members of the Fairbanks community and the University join together in the University-Fairbanks Symphony Orchestra and in many other musical and theatrical enterprises.

Majors and Degrees

The University of Alaska Fairbanks awards certificates, A.A. and A.A.S. degrees, and B.A., B.S., B.T., B.B.A., B.Ed., B.M., and B.F.A. degrees in accounting, airframe studies, Alaska Native studies, anthropology, applied accounting, applied business, applied physics, apprenticeship technology, art, arts and sciences, aviation maintenance technology, aviation technology, biochemistry, biological sciences, business administration, chemistry, civil engineering, communication, community health, computer science, culinary arts, dental assistant studies, drafting technology, early childhood, earth science, economics, electrical engineering, elementary education, emergency medical services, emergency services, English, Eskimo, fisheries, foreign languages, general science, geography (environmental studies), geological engineering, geology, ground vehicle maintenance technology, health-care reimbursement, health technology, history, human services, Japanese studies, journalism, justice, linguistics, maintenance technology, mathematics, mechanical engineering, medical assistant studies, microcomputer support specialist studies, mining engineering, molecular biology, music, Native language education, natural resources management (including forestry), Northern studies, office management and technology, paralegal studies, petroleum engineering, philosophy, phlebotomy, physics, political science, powerplant studies, process technology, psychology, renewable resources, rural development, rural human services, Russian studies, social work, sociology, statistics, technology, theater, tribal management, and wildlife biology. Preprofessional advising is available in dentistry, law, library science, medicine, physical therapy, and veterinary medicine.

Academic Program

The academic year is divided into two semesters; registration is in early April for the fall semester and in November for the spring semester. Preregistration is available for returning students. In addition, there are three-week, six-week, and twelve-week summer sessions. UAF offers an early orientation for new students in the fall and spring semesters. The University is organized into three colleges and five professional schools: the College of Liberal Arts; the College of Science, Engineering and Mathematics; the College of Rural Alaska; and the Schools of Agricultural and Land Resources Management, Education, Fisheries and Ocean Sciences, Management, and Mineral Engineering. A minimum of 120 semester credits must be completed for the four-year baccalaureate degree programs.

Students who receive scores of 3 or higher on the College Board's Advanced Placement tests may be awarded advanced-placement credit by the University. Currently enrolled students may challenge courses for credit by successfully completing College-Level Examination Program examinations or by completing locally prepared examinations. Requests for advanced-placement credit and credit by examination are coordinated through the Office of Admissions.

The honors program is designed for highly motivated undergraduate students who wish to acquire a superior understanding of the natural and social sciences, the arts, and the humanities. Prospective honors students need a minimum ACT composite score of 28 or a combined SAT I score of approximately 1270 with a minimum 3.6 high school GPA.

Off-Campus Programs

The University maintains exchange programs with McGill University in Canada and with universities in Australia, Denmark, Ecuador, England, Finland, Japan, Mexico, Norway, Russia, and Taiwan. The University also participates in the Northwest Interinstitutional Council for Study Abroad, providing students with an opportunity to enroll in liberal arts programs in Austria, England, France, Greece, Italy, and Spain. UAF is also a member of the National Student Exchange, participating with 177 colleges and universities throughout the United States and in U.S. territories and at five locations in Canada.

Academic Facilities

The Fine Arts Complex features a 480-seat theater, a 1,072-seat concert hall, FM public radio (KUAC) and educational-television (PBS) studios, an art gallery, and the Elmer E. Rasmuson Library. The library collection contains more than 1.75 million volumes, including the prestigious Alaska and Polar Regions Collection. Electronic catalogs provide access to collections in 11,000 libraries nationwide.

Students have free use of the University's academic computing facilities (Aurora), which are accessible from Windows and Macintosh computer labs and by remote access. Various schools and colleges have their own special-purpose computer labs.

The University Museum attracts more than 100,000 visitors a year to Interior Alaska and is located on the UAF campus. The museum collects, preserves, and exhibits materials from Alaska and the North.

Costs

In 2003–04, tuition and fees were $1705 per semester for full-time (12 credits) students. Nonresident students paid an additional $2292 for 12 credits of tuition each semester. Residents of Alaska, the Yukon Territory, British Columbia, and the Northwest Territories are exempt from the nonresident tuition fee. Students must live in Alaska for twelve months to qualify as residents. The approximate cost per semester for books and supplies is $500 and for personal items and recreation, $450. A double-occupancy residence hall room on campus costs $1255 per semester. Meals, which all residence hall occupants are required to purchase, cost approximately $1220 per semester. (These costs are subject to change.) Married student housing on campus is also available.

Financial Aid

A large portion of financial aid is derived from the Alaska Supplemental Education Loan Program, which is available to all students attending UAF, regardless of residency. Three kinds of aid are available: grants and scholarships (which need not be repaid), loans, and part-time employment. Students seeking financial assistance for the fall term should submit applications by March 15. Inquiries should be addressed to the Financial Aid Office, University of Alaska Fairbanks, P.O. Box 756560, Fairbanks, Alaska 99775-6560.

The Chancellor's Scholarship, a one-year tuition waiver, is available to entering freshmen with a minimum 3.0 GPA and 1150 SAT I combined score or 25 ACT composite score. To apply, students should submit an application for admission, a high school transcript, a tuition waiver application, and test scores for review. the deadline for scholarships is February 15. National Merit Finalists qualify for a four-year tuition waiver plus a $10,000 scholarship.

Faculty

Sixty-six percent of the 784 faculty members hold doctoral degrees, and many are actively engaged in research. In keeping with University policy, faculty members provide academic counseling for students. The combination of a student-faculty ratio of 12:1 and easy access to instructors for help outside of class produces a maximum educational benefit for students.

Student Government

The Associated Students of the University of Alaska Fairbanks (ASUAF) protects students' rights through its various governmental functions and also offers educational, social, recreational, and service activities. The school newspaper, *Sun Star,* is published weekly with the sponsorship of ASUAF, which also supports KSUA, the campus radio station; the international cinema and weekly movie series; and dances, concerts, and other entertainment. ASUAF publishes the results of its faculty evaluations and sends several student lobbyists to the Alaska state legislature in Juneau each spring. A student member sits on the Board of Regents of the University.

Admission Requirements

For admission to a baccalaureate program, applicants must be high school graduates with a cumulative grade point average of at least 2.0 and have earned a GPA of at least 2.5 in a high school core curriculum of 16 credits. Transfer students must also have a minimum grade point average of 2.0 in all previous college work. Applicants for a major in a scientific or technical field may be required to present a higher grade point average and to have completed specific background courses before being accepted into the major department. All entering freshmen are required to submit the results of either an ACT or SAT I examination prior to registration for placement in English and math courses.

Application and Information

The application deadlines are August 1 for the fall semester (April 1 for nonresident freshmen) and December 1 for the spring semester. Applications are processed after the deadlines only as long as space is available. Applicants are notified of the admission decision as soon as all application material has been received. Only accepted students are allowed to apply for campus housing. Students desiring campus housing should apply for admission as early as possible prior to the start of the semester to increase their chances of obtaining residence hall accommodations.

For further information, applicants should contact:

Office of Admissions
University of Alaska Fairbanks
P.O. Box 757480
Fairbanks, Alaska 99775-7480
Telephone: 907-474-7500
800-478-1UAF (toll-free)
World Wide Web: http://www.uaf.edu

The Plaza outside the classroom buildings at the University of Alaska Fairbanks. The flags represent the fifty states of the United States.

UNIVERSITY OF ALASKA SOUTHEAST

JUNEAU, KETCHIKAN, AND SITKA, ALASKA

The University

The University of Alaska Southeast (UAS) is a growing university with the main campus located in Juneau, Alaska's capital city, and branch campuses located in Ketchikan and Sitka. UAS is part of the University of Alaska system of higher education.

Enrollment at the main campus is about 700 full-time and 1,900 part-time students. About 60 percent of students are women and 40 percent are men. About 20 percent of the students are Alaska Natives, Asian, African American, and Hispanic. UAS offers a rich cultural environment plus varied activities and special events at both indoor and outdoor locations. Students may take part in intramural sports such as basketball, softball, and volleyball. Other activities include rock climbing, dances, swimming and local racquet club use in Juneau, and a variety of special-interest clubs.

More than a million people visit Juneau each year to enjoy its abundant forests and beautiful waterways. Ample opportunities exist for activities such as rock and ice climbing, kayaking, canoeing, camping, fishing, hiking, snowboarding, scuba diving, and skiing. Few areas in the world offer Juneau's world-class wilderness access combined with its big city amenities, such as shopping and restaurants.

Master's degrees include a Master of Arts in Teaching, with an emphasis in elementary education, early childhood education, or secondary education; a Master of Education with an emphasis in early childhood education, reading education, or educational technology; a Master of Business Administration; and a Master of Public Administration.

Professional development programs include post-baccalaureate endorsements in early childhood education, educational technology, reading, or special education; and post-baccalaureate credentials in early childhood or elementary education.

Location

Juneau is small by "Lower 48" standards, but with a population of 32,000 it is the third-largest city in the state and the largest in Southeast Alaska. Located along the shores of the Inside Passage, Juneau is surrounded by the world's largest expanse of an ancient temperate rainforest. The rainforest provides a surprisingly mild climate. The January mean temperature is 26 degrees. During the summer months, the normal high temperature is in the upper 60s. The area around the UAS campus averages 56 inches of annual precipitation.

Juneau is accessible by plane and ferry but not by road. Jet service from Seattle and Anchorage is offered daily. The state runs a year-round ferry service between Bellingham, Washington, and Southeast Alaskan cities. Those who bring cars must use the barge service from Seattle or the Alaska Marine Highway System. The ferries provide a spectacular cruise through the breathtakingly beautiful Inside Passage.

Majors and Degrees

One of the many advantages to the University's small campus is the ability of faculty and staff members to work with individual students to meet their educational goals. UAS offers a Bachelor of Arts in elementary education, with a special education endorsement; a Bachelor of Arts in English; a Bachelor of Arts in social science with an emphasis in anthropology, economics, government/political science, history, psychology, or sociology; a Bachelor of Business Administration with an emphasis in accounting, general business, management, or marketing; a Bachelor of Liberal Arts with an emphasis in art, communications, general studies, government, human communication, or mathematics; a Bachelor of Science in biology with an emphasis in general biology or marine biology; a Bachelor of Science in environmental science; and a Bachelor of Science in information systems with an emphasis in e-commerce, networking, or programming.

UAS also offers an Associate of Arts degree and Associate of Applied Science degrees in apprenticeship technology, business administration, computer information office systems, construction technology, early childhood education, environmental technology, health information management, paralegal studies, power technology–automotive, or power technology–diesel. In addition, certificate programs are available in subjects such as accounting technician studies, automotive technology, computer information and office systems, early childhood education, environmental technology, health information management coding specialist studies, law enforcement, outdoor skills and leadership, residential building science, or small business management.

Academic Program

UAS operates on the semester system. Fall semester begins in early September and spring semester begins in mid-January. The summer semester begins in May with courses offered through June and July.

A minimum of 120 semester credits is required to complete a baccalaureate degree program, a minimum of 60 semester credits to complete an associate degree program, and a minimum of 30 semester credits to complete a certificate program.

For all programs, students must maintain a minimum 2.0 GPA; in some core program areas, the minimum GPA requirement is higher.

Advanced placement credit is given to high school students who achieve scores of 3 or higher on the College Board's Advanced Placement tests. Scores above 620 on the SAT verbal or 30 on the ACT English qualify new students for advanced UAS class placement.

Students who are currently enrolled may challenge courses for credit through either the College-Level Examination Program (CLEP) or University challenge examinations. Requests by students for Advanced Placement credit and credit by examination are coordinated through the Office of Records and Registration.

Academic Facilities

The main campus is located 11 miles from downtown Juneau, between the shores of Auke Lake and Auke Bay. The campus faces the Mendenhall Glacier and is often referred to as the most beautiful place in Juneau. Located across from the spectacular Auke Bay, the Student Activity Center houses a climbing wall, the Outdoor Recreation Center, a big-screen TV, a movie screen with a surround-sound system, exercise facilities, and a student lounge with computers, pool tables, and other games. The Technical Education Center is located in downtown Juneau, on the waterfront. It serves as the base for the vocational/technical programs such as auto, construction, power, and welding.

The Egan Library contains more than 420,000 volumes. This award-winning facility offers seating for more than 200 users, the most current computer technology for access to information, and extended hours for student study. The Learning Center and Media Services are also housed in the Egan library, as is a representative collection of southeastern Alaskan Native art.

The campus operates on a state-of-the-art wireless network that students may access with the addition of a wireless Internet card. The card allows students access to the network, Internet, and e-mail from virtually anywhere on the campus.

Costs

For purposes of tuition costs, a resident is any person who has been physically present in Alaska for one year and who declares their intention to remain in Alaska indefinitely. In most instances, students may establish residency in Alaska after one year. Others exempt from nonresident fees are residents of British Columbia, Yukon, Northwest and Nunavut Territories, military personnel stationed in Alaska and their dependents, and residents of several foreign sister cities. UAS also participates in the Western Undergraduate Exchange (WUE) program for all degree programs. Students from the fourteen member states are eligible for WUE tuition rates.

For 2004–05, in-state full-time tuition, which is 12 or more credit hours, costs from $1188 to $1485 a semester. Lower division 100- and 200-level courses are $99 per credit hour; upper division 300- and 400-level courses are $112 per credit hour. Full-time non-resident students can expect to pay between $4116 and $5145 a semester, depending on the level of classes. Western Undergraduate Exchange students can expect to pay between $1782 and $2227 a semester, depending on the level of classes. In addition, all students must pay a mandatory $3 per-credit-hour (not to exceed $45) student government fee, a $5 per-credit-hour (not to exceed $60) technology fee, a $4 newspaper fee, and a $100 student-activity fee each semester.

Campus housing is available in Juneau. Freshman housing at Banfield Hall is $1675 per semester per person. Residents of Banfield Hall are required to have a roommate and purchase the meal plan at an additional cost of $985 per semester. Banfield Hall is reserved for freshmen, but on-campus housing, including apartment-style housing, is available to all students. Apartment-style housing with private rooms is available at a cost of $1840 per person per semester and family housing is available at a cost of $4400 per semester.

Financial Aid

UAS participates in the Federal Pell Grant, Federal Supplemental Educational Opportunity Grant, Federal Stafford Student Loan, and Federal Work-Study programs in addition to state student loan, family loan, and grant programs. Most aid is awarded on the basis of financial need. Some scholarships, however, are based on academic potential and performance. The deadline for merit-based UAS scholarships is early February. To apply for need-based programs, students should request a packet from the financial aid office.

Faculty

Classes are taught by highly qualified and experienced faculty members. Classes vary in size but are typically much smaller than at larger institutions; the average class size is approximately 15 students. The size of UAS contributes to a high degree of personal interaction between students and faculty members. In addition to their primary teaching responsibilities, some faculty members also serve as advisers for undergraduate students as well as on advisory committees for graduate students.

Student Government

The student government plays an important role in the development of UAS policies and activities. Students serve on a number of important committees and participate in lobbying the state legislature on behalf of students' interests.

Admission Requirements

Students are qualified for admission as an undergraduate if they are a high school graduate with a minimum high school GPA of 2.0 and can supply all the required documentation. Successful completion of the GED test is accepted as an equivalency of high school graduation. Official transcripts from all regionally accredited colleges and universities are also required if applicable. ACT and/or SAT I test scores are also required.

Admission is on a rolling basis; applications are processed in the order they are received. Applicants generally receive an initial response within two weeks of receipt of the completed application packet.

Application and Information

To apply, students must complete an application form and send it with the required $40 application processing fee to the Office of Admissions on the campus of intended enrollment. Students can mail or fax applications or apply online. Official high school transcripts showing graduation or a GED credential are required of applicants seeking bachelor degees, as are official transcripts from all regionally accredited colleges and universities attended, if applicable.

For further information, application forms, or any other materials, prospective applicants can use the inquiry form on the UAS Website or contact:

Admissions Office
University of Alaska Southeast
11120 Glacier Highway
Juneau, Alaska 99801
Telephone: 907-465-6350
877-465-4827 (toll-free)
Fax: 907-465-6365
E-mail: admissions@uas.alaska.edu
World Wide Web: http://www.uas.alaska.edu

Environmental science students at UAS have measured the face of the LeConte Glacier near Petersburg.

UNIVERSITY OF ARKANSAS

FAYETTEVILLE, ARKANSAS

The University

Established in 1874, the University of Arkansas (U of A) is the flagship campus of the University of Arkansas System. The University offers more than 215 undergraduate and graduate degrees in more than 180 fields of study in agricultural, food, and life sciences; architecture; the arts and sciences; business; education and health professions; engineering; human environmental sciences, law, nursing, and social work. The University is also recognized as the only comprehensive doctoral degree–granting institution in the state. Fayetteville's 345-acre campus is home to students from all counties in Arkansas, every state in the U.S., and more than 100 countries throughout the world. The enrollment for fall 2003 was 16,449 students (13,125 in undergraduate programs) and included a diverse student population, with 886 international students representing 109 countries.

Students choosing to live on campus may select from a diverse array of residential experiences. The First Year Experience program, which is designed to support students academically, culturally, and socially, is a popular choice among entering freshmen. The Honors Quarters are also among the more popular residences, featuring specialized floors for specific academic fields and reduced-noise floors. In fall 2004, the University is scheduled to unveil its newest addition, the Northwest Quad—the latest in apartment-style living.

The University's drive to emerge as one of the top fifty public research universities in America got a tremendous boost in April 2002 when the University received a $300-million gift from the Walton Family Charitable Support Foundation. The gift—the largest ever made to a public university—established and endowed the undergraduate Honors College, providing academic research and study-abroad opportunities, a challenging curriculum, and financial support to high-achieving students.

Among the more than 180 fields of study offered at the University, graduate degrees are offered in ninety-six fields. The School of Law offers a skilled and scholarly faculty of teaching and practicing lawyers. The National Center for Agricultural Law Research and Information has been praised for its research and publications and makes possible the law school's unique degree offering in agricultural law.

Location

The city of Fayetteville is a community of more than 60,000 people. *Money* magazine has rated it as one of the top ten most desirable places in the nation to live. Fayetteville is nestled in the Ozark Mountains near lakes and rivers but is accessible to major metropolitan amenities, making it an excellent place for a well-balanced college experience.

Majors and Degrees

Named for Senator J. William Fulbright, the Fulbright College of Arts and Sciences is the largest of the U of A colleges, with seventeen departments offering concentrations in an extended range of fields. The Dale Bumpers College of Agricultural, Food and Life Sciences offers more than twenty-five majors that give students the ability to improve agriculture and the family environment. The School of Architecture offers majors in architecture and landscape architecture. The Sam M. Walton College of Business offers programs that parallel real business processes and allow students to look across a broad spectrum of disciplines. Preparing professionals for research, teaching, and service-oriented positions, the College of Education and Health Professions offers a variety of majors in education, recreation, and health sciences as well as a Bachelor of Science (B.S.) degree in nursing. The College of Engineering offers top-tier undergraduate and graduate engineering programs.

A complete listing of current degrees and programs offered by the University of Arkansas can be found on the Web site at http://admissions.uark.edu/majors/majors/shtml.

Academic Programs

The U of A operates on a traditional two-semester academic year schedule, with additional summer sessions. Requirements for graduation include a minimum University-wide core along with core requirements in each college. The majority of undergraduate degree offerings follow a four-year plan requiring from 124 to 156 credit hours for graduation. There are some exceptions to this requirement, such as the five-year, design-oriented architecture program, which requires 165 hours.

A course in English as a second language is offered in five 9-week sessions throughout the year. Classes focus on all language skills: grammar, reading, writing, and listening/speaking.

Off-Campus Programs

The University conducts extensive cooperative education programs through several colleges that offer off-campus opportunities for work or learning in other cities and countries. The University offers a broad range of independent study opportunities for both credit courses and noncredit programs.

Academic Facilities

The University library contains nearly 1.5 million volumes, approximately 14,168 subscriptions to periodicals and journals, 3.2 million titles on microform, and more than 19,400 recordings. The Enhanced Learning Center facilitates student learning by promoting a rigorous academic process that fosters student participation—encouraging students to ask questions, develop their skills, and apply those skills independently to their own work. The University of Arkansas also provides multiplatform computer labs. Students can connect to the campus wireless network or check out laptops in the student union and the library. Recent renovations in the fine arts center provide theater facilities and a stunning gallery. The state-of-the-art Bell Engineering Center offers the optimum in computer capabilities and laboratory research. The Center of Excellence for Poultry Science is a $22-million facility offering the finest training for poultry scientists in the United States. The High Density Electronics Center (HiDEC) has established itself as one of the top electronics packaging research and education facilities in the world. HiDEC has executed contracts from the government and industry totaling more than $30 million. Projects have ranged from multichip module (MCM) design to the development and evaluation of new technologies and electronic products. The Arkansas-Oklahoma Center for Space and Planetary Sciences houses a large stainless steel vacuum chamber donated to the University of Arkansas by the Jet Propulsion Laboratory (JPL) in Pasadena. The chamber was constructed for comet simulations and had recently been used for simulating surface processes on Mars.

Costs

For the 2003–04 school year, the average full-time tuition rate for in-state students (Arkansas residents) was $3810 per semester; nonresidents paid $10,560. Students from neighboring states with a minimum ACT score of 24 and a 3.0 GPA may be eligible to pay in-state rates. Native Americans belonging to tribes that lived in Arkansas before relocation may be eligible for in-state residency.

Students age 60 and older may have the fees waived for credit courses on a space-available basis. Room and board costs for students on campus averaged $5087 per year. For international students, the annual nine-month academic year costs totaled $18,890 and included tuition, fees, housing, health insurance, books and supplies, equipment fees, and personal expenses.

Financial Aid

A completed application for admission is required for students wishing to receive institutional, federal, or scholarship aid. Students are encouraged to visit the University of Arkansas' scholarship Web site at http://scholarships.uark.edu to review the various scholarship programs available to new and returning students. A Free Application for Federal Student Aid (FAFSA) is required of all students requesting federal assistance such as student loans, Federal Pell Grants, and Work-Study. Some loans and campus employment opportunities do not require these forms. To receive priority consideration for scholarships, a student enrolling for the fall semester must submit an application for admission by February 15. The fall scholarship deadline for international and transfer students is March 15.

Faculty

The University has 792 full-time faculty members, the majority of whom hold the highest degree in their field. There are 47 part-time faculty members as well as 3,616 staff members, including 1,185 graduate assistants. For international students, an international student adviser and a fully staffed International Programs Office are available to assist with orientation sessions, immigration counseling, and activities programming.

Student Government

The University of Arkansas offers students the opportunity to participate in various forms of campus government. The Associated Student Government, the Off-Campus Student Government, Residents' Interhall Congress, the Interfraternity Council, and the Panhellenic Council are the main governing bodies that aid students in expressing their opinions or interests to the faculty, administration, and community.

Admission Requirements

Entering freshmen are advised to prepare for admission to the U of A while in high school by taking 4 years each of English and math, 3 years each of social studies and natural sciences, and two academic electives. Though not required, the University recommends that a student takes 2 years of foreign language. For the best possible chance of being admitted to the University of Arkansas, students should have a minimum average of a B (3.0) and score a minimum of 20 on the ACT or 930 on the SAT I. The ACT code for the U of A is 0144, and the SAT I code is 6866. Transfer students must have an overall GPA of at least 2.0 on all college course work attempted. Any transfer student with fewer than 24 hours must also meet the requirements for entering freshmen.

International students must have above-average secondary school records, and those who are not native speakers of English must submit a minimum TOEFL score of 550 (paper) or 213 (computer). The University of Arkansas offers qualified applicants conditional admission to the Spring International Language Center, with academic admission granted upon reaching a satisfactory English language level.

Application and Information

To enroll in the University, students must submit a completed Application for Undergraduate Admission and an application fee of $30. An online admission form can be found at the University's Web site listed below. The priority application consideration date for the fall semester is February 15 for freshman enrollment. Transfer students are advised to apply by March 15. The spring preferred completion date is January 1. The student must also request that official transcripts be mailed to the Office of Admissions. A preliminary admission is provided for those high school seniors who have a transcript of six or seven semesters, but a final transcript is needed to certify high school graduation. SAT I or ACT scores, no more than 5 years old, must be submitted by all entering freshmen and transfer students with fewer than 24 transferable hours. These scores must be sent directly to the Office of Admissions from the testing agency or appear on an official high school transcript.

International students must submit an application for admission with a $50 application fee. A financial statement, TOEFL score, and official secondary and postsecondary academic records are also required. For the fall term, the application priority date is May 1; the summer term priority date is March 1; and the spring term priority date is October 1. International students can download the undergraduate application at the Web site listed below.

For further information, students should contact:

Dawn S. Medley
Office of Admissions
232 Silas H. Hunt Hall
University of Arkansas
Fayetteville, Arkansas 72701
Telephone: 479-575-5346
800-377-UOFA (toll-free)
479-575-6246 (international)
Fax: 479-575-7515
E-mail: uofa@uark.edu
iao@uark.edu (international)
World Wide Web: http://www.uark.edu
http://apply.uark.edu (online application)

A friendly campus, the University of Arkansas offers a wide range of academic majors and campus activities for student involvement.

UNIVERSITY OF BALTIMORE

BALTIMORE, MARYLAND

The University

The University of Baltimore (UB) serves a unique role in the University System of Maryland. It is the state's only upper-division (transfer) and graduate institution, offering a diversity of bachelor's, master's, and first-professional degrees in liberal arts and business. UB operates a law school and a number of professionally oriented combined-degree programs with other Maryland colleges and universities. The University also offers a limited number of sophomore opportunities.

Founded in 1925, UB has a very clear mission: to provide flexible educational programs to professionally oriented students. Approximately 4,700 students study in the University's three schools—the Yale Gordon College of Liberal Arts, the Robert S. Merrick School of Business, and the School of Law. UB traditionally attracts students with strong career ambitions and provides them with the latest skills and techniques in their chosen fields.

UB students can choose from more than fifty active clubs and organizations, which range from the Student Government Association to discipline-specific clubs.

Location

The University of Baltimore is located in the cultural corridor of Baltimore, a thriving city with cultural, athletic, educational, and recreational opportunities that has received national recognition for its recent renaissance. The Meyerhoff Symphony Hall; the Lyric Opera House; Maryland Institute, College of Art; and the Baltimore Museum of Art are located within one mile of UB. Oriole Park at Camden Yards, M&T Bank (Ravens) Stadium, and Harborplace are approximately three miles south of campus. Annapolis, on the beautiful Chesapeake Bay, is a 45-minute drive away, and Washington, D.C., is a 1-hour commute from the University.

Majors and Degrees

Bachelor of Arts and Bachelor of Science degrees are offered in accounting, applied information technology, business administration, business operations, computer information systems, corporate communication, criminal justice, economics, English, entrepreneurship, finance, forensic studies, government and public policy, health systems management, history, human resource management, human services administration, interdisciplinary studies, international business, jurisprudence, management, management information systems, marketing, and psychology. Specializations are offered in language, technology, and culture; literature; public history; and women's studies. A Bachelor of Technical and Professional Studies in simulation and digital entertainment is also offered, as is a certificate in computer information systems.

Academic Program

The University follows a semester system, with fall and spring semesters, a minimester in January, and a summer session. The University offers several special degree programs that follow four 10-week sessions in an academic year. The University offers more than 600 courses during the fall, spring, and summer semesters. Students can attend full time or part time during the day or evening, on Saturdays, and on the Web.

A humanities-centered, interdisciplinary core curriculum is required of all undergraduate students. In these core courses, students examine the relationship between ethics and values while exploring business and public policy, and they trace major themes and ideas in philosophy and the arts. Throughout the core, students are assisted in refining their skills in critical thinking and oral and written communication. To be awarded a bachelor's degree, students must satisfactorily complete a minimum of 120 hours of college credit and have satisfactorily completed a specific curriculum with a grade point average of at least 2.0.

The University's Helen P. Denit honors program offers honors-level versions of the core curriculum courses. Students who transfer to UB with a grade point average of 3.5 or higher are invited to apply to the program. Other students may be nominated by a UB professor.

Off-Campus Programs

Several off-campus sites are available for students who desire to take courses closer to home. UB also offers online (Internet) courses and programs in various disciplines. The University offers students opportunities to participate in professional internships, and students from certain majors may also participate in study-abroad opportunities.

Academic Facilities

Located on the corner of Mt. Royal and Charles Streets, the University of Baltimore offers a variety of campus facilities. The Academic Center houses many of the administration offices as well as classrooms, a fitness center, faculty offices, and the dean's offices of the Yale Gordon College of Liberal Arts. Connected to the center is Charles Hall, which features the president's suite and a student lounge as well as business, registrar, and student affairs offices and classrooms. The Thumel Center houses the Merrick School of Business, with computer laboratories and state-of-the-art communication and computer-capable classrooms, and features a six-story atrium. UB's Langsdale Library compares favorably with those of its peer institutions in Maryland, both in breadth and quantity of holdings. The Charles Royal Building is home to the School of Communications Design, and the Schaefer Center Building is the location for the School of Public Affairs. The John and Frances Angelos Law Center houses the law library, classrooms, and administrative offices of the School of Law as well as Poe's House, the University's dining facility.

Costs

Anticipated in-state full-time tuition for the 2003–04 academic year was $2306.50 per semester, plus fees. Part-time in-state tuition was $211 per credit, plus fees. Out-of-state full-time tuition was $7509.50 per semester, plus fees, and out-of-state part-time tuition was $626 per credit, plus fees. Tuition and fees are subject to change.

Financial Aid

Students at the University of Baltimore are eligible to participate in all regular federal financial aid programs, including the Pell Grant, the Supplemental Educational Opportunity Grant, the Perkins Loan, the Stafford Loan, the PLUS Loan, and the Work-Study programs. Applications for federal aid should be submitted by April 1 for fall and November 1 for spring.

In addition, the University offers an extensive scholarship program for transfer students. Students who transfer with 56 or more credits and at least a 3.25 cumulative transfer GPA are eligible for a Dean's Scholarship (50 percent of full-time in-state tuition); students with a cumulative transfer of at least 3.5 and who are members of Phi Theta Kappa at their community college are eligible for a Phi Theta Kappa Scholarship (75 percent of full-time in-state tuition); and students with a cumulative transfer GPA of at least 3.5 are eligible for Wilson Scholarships (100 percent of full-time in-state tuition.) Scholarship recipients who are not residents of Maryland receive an additional $1500 above the amounts noted. The deadline for scholarship applications is March 1 for fall and November 1 for spring.

Faculty

With a student-faculty ratio of 15:1 and a personalized system of student advising, UB programs emphasize one-on-one interaction and individual attention for all students. The University of Baltimore employs 166 full-time and 176 part-time faculty members. Ninety-two percent of the full-time faculty members hold terminal degrees. All full-time faculty members teach at both the undergraduate and graduate levels and have responsibilities in research and public service. UB does not utilize graduate teaching assistants. Part-time faculty members are expert practitioners who are employed full time in business, industry, and government.

Student Government

The student government consists of three branches serving as representative bodies for all students at the University of Baltimore. The Undergraduate Student Senate, the Graduate Student Senate, and the Student Bar Association oversee the allotment and expenditure of funds to more than 50 student organizations and are responsible for issues of governance and a variety of programming.

Admission Requirements

The University of Baltimore is an upper-division university that offers the junior and senior years of undergraduate study leading to a Bachelor of Arts, Bachelor of Science, or Bachelor of Technical and Professional Studies degree. The University also admits a limited number of sophomores each academic year. Admission to a baccalaureate or certificate program is open to students who hold an associate's degree or who have at least 56 transferable credits with a GPA of at least 2.0, 42 transferable credits with a GPA of at least 2.3, or 24 transferable credits with at least a 2.5 GPA. Specific programs may have more restrictive admissions criteria. Applicants who are nonnative speakers of English must demonstrate a satisfactory level of English proficiency. A minimum score of 550 on the paper-based version or 213 on the computer-based version of the Test of English as a Foreign Language (TOEFL) is required of both degree and nondegree applicants regardless of citizenship or visa status. Applicants with international transcripts must arrange to have their academic records evaluated by a U.S. credential evaluation service.

Application and Information

The University of Baltimore has a rolling admissions policy, and applications are accepted until the last day of registration each semester, space permitting. However, the earlier an application and credentials are received, the earlier an admission decision can be made. It is recommended that students file an application by August 1 for the fall semester, December 1 for the spring semester, and May 1 for the summer session. A nonrefundable application fee is required at time of application. An online application is available on the Web (http://www.ubalt.edu/admissions), or students may request an application by calling or writing the Admissions Office:

Admissions Office
University of Baltimore
1420 North Charles Street
Baltimore, Maryland 21201-5779
Telephone: 410-837-4777
877-ApplyUB (toll-free)
World Wide Web: http://www.ubalt.edu

On the campus of the University of Baltimore.

UNIVERSITY OF BRITISH COLUMBIA

VANCOUVER, BRITISH COLUMBIA, CANADA

The University

The University of British Columbia (UBC) is one of Canada's leading universities, with an international reputation for excellence in teaching and learning. UBC was incorporated in 1908 and admitted its first students in 1915. The University's 1,000-acre campus atop a forested peninsula enjoys spectacular views of the Pacific Ocean, the Vancouver skyline, and the snowcapped peaks of the surrounding Coastal Mountains.

Through its twelve faculties and eleven schools, UBC provides a wide range of bachelor's degree programs as well as graduate and professional programs. The number of students currently registered in degree programs is 39,224 (32,214 undergraduates). A majority of students are from Canada, with more than 3,000 (8 percent) from the United States and 126 other countries. UBC's International House offers a full range of reception, advising, and social services to international students. The University strives to be accessible to all, and special-needs provision is made through the Disability Resource Centre, the Equity Office, the First Nations House of Learning, and the Women Students' Office.

On-campus University residences accommodate more than 6,000 students in single-student coed, shared, and family housing units. Most students live off campus. The University is served by reliable public transport, and a local transit pass is included in student fees. UBC's athletics and sport services administer one of Canada's most successful interuniversity athletic programs, and the Alma Mater Society maintains more than 200 clubs that cater to a wide variety of academic and social interests. Other important facilities include the Asian Centre, the Liu Centre for Global Studies, the Museum of Anthropology, the Botanical Gardens, a conference centre, the aquatic centre, a fitness centre and gymnasium, tennis courts, and a sports stadium.

Location

The University of British Columbia is located a few miles from downtown Vancouver, Canada's third-largest city with 2 million inhabitants. Its vibrant urban community, thriving cultural life, and ethnic diversity is reflected in world-class art galleries, conference centres, hotels and restaurants, major sports, film, theatre, music, and several international festivals held throughout the year. In 2010, Vancouver and neighbouring Whistler are scheduled to host the Winter Olympic Games. The proximity of mountains, forest, and public beaches provides outdoor recreational opportunities year-round. Warm Pacific currents give Vancouver mild winters, with plenteous rains from fall to spring, and pleasant dry summers.

Majors and Degrees

The Faculty of Agricultural Sciences offers a Bachelor of Science (B.Sc.) for programs in animal studies; dietetics; food and nutritional science; food, nutrition, and health; global resource systems; horticulture; human ecology; pre–veterinary studies; resource economics; and soils and environment. The Bachelor of Environmental Design (B.En.D.) is offered jointly with the School of Architecture.

The Faculty of Applied Sciences offers programs of study leading to the Bachelor of Applied Sciences (B.A.Sc.) in the following fields: chemical and biological engineering, civil engineering, computer engineering, electrical engineering, engineering physics, environmental engineering, geological engineering, integrated engineering, mechanical engineering, metals and materials engineering, and mining engineering.

The Faculty of Arts offers a wide range of undergraduate programs leading to bachelor degrees. The Bachelor of Arts (B.A.) is offered in anthropology; archaeology; art history; Asian area studies; Canadian studies; Chinese; classical studies; classics; cognitive systems; critical studies in sexuality (minor); drama; economics; English; family studies; film; First Nations languages; First Nations studies; French; geography; German; Greek (minor), health and society, Hispanic studies; history; interdisciplinary studies, international relations; Italian and Italian studies; Japanese; Korean (minor); Latin (minor); Latin American studies; linguistics; mathematics; medieval studies; modern European studies; music; myth and literature in Greece, Rome, and the Near East; nineteenth-century studies (minor); philosophy; political science; psychology; religion, literature, and the arts; religious studies; Romance studies; Russian (minor); science studies (minor); sociology; South Asian languages; Spanish; speech sciences; and women's studies. The Bachelor of Fine Arts (B.F.A.) is offered in creative writing, fine arts, and theatre. The Bachelor of Social Work (B.S.W.) is offered jointly with the School of Social Work for the family studies program.

The Sauder School of Business (formerly the Faculty of Commerce and Business Administration) offers undergraduate programs leading to the Bachelor of Commerce (B.Comm.), with specializations in accounting, commerce and economics, finance, general business management, human resources management, international business, management information systems, marketing, real estate, and transportation and logistics.

The Faculty of Dentistry offers the Bachelor of Dental Science (B.D.Sc.) in dental hygiene, which is competitively open to all applicants. Admission to the Doctor of Dental Medicine degree program is restricted to Canadian citizens and permanent residents, meeting minimum requirements of previous study at UBC or equivalent.

The Faculty of Education offers initial teacher education leading to the Bachelor of Education (B.Ed.) in elementary teacher education, elementary native Indian teacher education, middle-years teacher education, and secondary teacher education. The latter provides a wide range of teaching concentrations, from arts and science to computer science and technology education.

The Faculty of Forestry offers the following four-year programs: a Bachelor of Science in Forestry (B.S.F.) in forest operations and forest resources management, and a B.Sc. in forest science, natural resources conservation, and wood products processing.

The School of Human Kinetics within the Faculty of Education offers a Bachelor of Human Kinetics (B.H.K.) for four-year programs in exercise science, health and fitness, leisure and sports management, and physical education.

The Faculty of Law offers a Bachelor of Laws (LL.B.), a three-year course that prepares students for practice in law. Applicants for admission must have obtained an undergraduate degree in an approved course of study or have successfully completed the first two years of an approved course at UBC (or other approved college or university), and be enrolled in the third year.

The Faculty of Medicine offers undergraduate programs of study that lead to the Doctor of Medicine (M.D.). Preference is currently given to well-qualified Canadian citizens and permanent residents residing in British Columbia. Degree programs competitively open to all applicants are the four-year program for the Bachelor of Midwifery (B.Mw.) and the two-year program of medical laboratory theory and practice leading to the Bachelor of Medical Laboratory Science (B.L.Sc.).

The School of Music within the Faculty of Arts offers programs of study in performance and composition leading to the

Bachelor of Music (B.Mus.) as well as programs in musical scholarship and programs designed for prospective school teachers.

The School of Nursing (Faculty of Applied Science) offers a four-year program of study leading to the Bachelor of Science in Nursing (B.S.N.).

The Faculty of Pharmaceutical Sciences offers courses that lead to the Bachelor of Science in Pharmacy (B.Sc.Pharm.). For admission to the Faculty, students are required to complete the first year in the Faculty of Science in required courses.

The Faculty of Science offers major and honours undergraduate programs leading to the B.Sc. in animal biology, astronomy, atmospheric science, biochemistry, biology, biophysics, biotechnology, chemistry, cognitive systems, computer science, earth and ocean sciences, environmental sciences, general science, geography, geological sciences, geophysics, integrated sciences, mathematics, mathematical sciences, mathematics and economics, microbiology and immunology, oceanography, pharmacology, physics, physiology, psychology, and statistics.

Academic Program

The academic year runs from September to August. Winter Session consists of Term 1, from early September to late December, and Term 2, from early January to the end of April. Summer Session runs for two terms, May through August, but not all programs are offered during the Summer Session. In general, major or general programs require a minimum of 120 credits to obtain a bachelor's degree; honours programs may require 132 credits. Programs allowing a cooperative education work term may take longer to complete.

Off-Campus Programs

The University offers 150 exchange programs with universities in more than forty countries. Co-op (work-study) programs are available in selected programs in the Faculties of Applied Sciences, Arts, Forestry, and Science, and the Sauder School of Business.

Academic Facilities

With twenty-one branches, the University of British Columbia's library is one of the largest research libraries in Canada. The central libraries at UBC include the Walter C. Koerner Library (social sciences and humanities) and the Main Library (physical sciences and engineering). Students have ready access to the Internet and free e-mail. Most residences have high-speed Internet access, and wireless connectivity is virtually campus-wide. A number of industry-related research centres and organizations are located on campus, including Tri-University Meson Facility (TRIUMF), one of the world's largest national particle-accelerator facilities for research in subatomic physics.

Costs

For U.S. and international students undergraduate program tuition for the 2004–05 academic year is Can$542 per credit. A typical first-year course load costs Can$16,260, plus applicable student fees (typically about Can$600). For Canadian citizens and permanent residents, undergraduate program tuition for 2004–05 is Can$115.30 per credit, with higher fees in business, dentistry, law, and medicine. A typical first-year course load of 30 credits costs Can$3459 plus student fees. Room and board costs, plus related living expenses, books, and health insurance, are approximately Can$10,000.

Financial Aid

The University administers a number of merit-based awards for undergraduates. Students should contact UBC's Office of Student Financial Assistance and Awards for more information about eligibility, application deadlines, and student loans and bursaries (http://students.ubc.ca/welcome/finance.cfm).

For U.S. citizens applying for Stafford Loans, the UBC Title IV code is G08369. More information about the Free Application for Federal Student Aid (FAFSA) is available on the Web at http://www.fafsa.ed.gov.

Faculty

UBC's full-time faculty number 1,740, more than 98 percent of whom hold a Ph.D. degree. Faculty members are regularly recognized with national awards for outstanding teaching and achievement. Innovations in teaching and learning include UBC's pioneer interdisciplinary first-year programs, such as Arts Foundations, Arts One, Science One, and the Integrated Science option. Each of the faculties provides academic advising and mentoring programs to support undergraduate student achievement.

Student Government

Originally established in 1908, the Alma Mater Society (AMS) of UBC represents more than 30,000 students. The AMS is governed by a 45-member Student Council, which ensures student participation at all levels of student government, administers clubs, and represents student interests to the University and the provincial government of British Columbia.

Admission Requirements

Admission to UBC is competitive and is based on a strong academic background. The minimum academic qualification for undergraduate admission is graduation from an accredited secondary school having an acceptable university preparatory curriculum with applicable program prerequisites. General admission for students from an American school system is based on 4 years of English and 3 years of math, with an admission average based on eight full-year academic courses (four from junior year and four from senior year). International Baccalaureate (I.B.) students require a completed I.B. diploma, with admission average calculated on three standard levels (including English) and three higher levels. Admission for I.B. Certificate course students is based on high school curriculum. Students applying to science-based programs must meet specific program requirements in math, chemistry, physics, and/or biology. All students must demonstrate competence in written and spoken English. SAT/ACT scores are not required, but can strengthen an application if submitted. Generous course credits are allowed for students achieving specified grades in enriched curriculums, such as I.B., A-levels, or Advanced Placement. For further information, prospective students should visit the Web at http://www.welcome.ubc.ca/transfer.cfm. Well-qualified students at recognized universities and colleges may apply to transfer to UBC. Completion of the equivalent of 30 UBC credits is normally required to gain admission to UBC second year. All applicants to UBC must complete the application for admission, accompanied by a nonrefundable application fee. A separate application and supplemental fee is required for the Sauder School of Business. Early admission is possible for students with strong academic standing enrolled in their final year of secondary school.

Application and Information

Early application is encouraged and should be made online at http://www.welcome.ubc.ca/apply.cfm. The application deadline for undergraduate programs is February 28.

International Student Recruitment and Reception
Room 1206, 1874 East Mall (Brock Hall)
University of British Columbia
Vancouver, British Columbia V6T 1Z1
Canada
Telephone: 604-822-8999
877-272-1422 (toll-free in the U.S. and Canada)
Fax: 604-822-9888
E-mail: international.reception@ubc.ca
World Wide Web: http://www.welcome.ubc.ca

UNIVERSITY OF CENTRAL FLORIDA

ORLANDO, FLORIDA

The University

The University of Central Florida (UCF) is a comprehensive, metropolitan university with approximately 42,000 students. As one of the nation's fastest-growing universities, UCF enrolls a diverse student body representing fifty states and more than 120 countries. The University offers educational and research programs that complement the economy, with strong components in aerospace engineering, business, education, film, health, nursing, social sciences, and tourism. UCF's programs in communication and the fine arts help to meet the cultural and recreational needs of a growing metropolitan area. The University also offers many graduate programs leading to master's and doctoral degrees.

UCF is accredited by the Commission on Colleges of the Southern Association of Colleges and Schools. In addition, a number of scientific, professional, and academic bodies confer accreditation in specific disciplines and groups of disciplines. In the College of Arts and Sciences, accreditation is conferred in chemistry by the American Chemical Society and in music by the National Association of Schools of Music. The programs of the International Association for Management Education and the College of Business Administration are accredited at the undergraduate and graduate levels by AACSB International–The Association to Advance Collegiate Schools of Business. In the College of Engineering and Computer Science, programs are accredited by the Engineering Accreditation Commission of the Accreditation Board for Engineering and Technology, Inc. (ABET). Also, engineering technology programs in design, electronics, and operations engineering technology are accredited by the Technology Accreditation Commission of ABET. In the College of Health and Public Affairs, programs have been approved by the following agencies: health information management by the American Medical Record Association; medical records administration, medical technology, and radiologic technology by the Committee on Allied Health Education and Accreditation and the National Accrediting Agency for Clinical Laboratory Services; nursing by the National League for Nursing Accrediting Commission and the Florida Board of Nursing; cardiopulmonary sciences by the American Registry of Respiratory Therapists; speech pathology and audiology by the American Speech-Language and Hearing Association; and social work by the Council of Social Work Education. All teacher education programs are fully accredited by the Florida State Department of Education and the National Council for Accreditation of Teacher Education.

UCF has established extensive partnerships with business and industry in the central Florida area that provide students with exceptional research and learning experiences. These partnerships bring practical learning environments to UCF students through co-op and internship programs. Joint curriculum development strategies include BE2010, which is a widely modeled business curriculum incorporating classes taught by local business and industry executives.

The on-campus and campus-affiliated housing facilities include traditional residence halls, apartment-style options, and Greek housing that accommodates approximately 8,000 students. Construction of new residential facilities that are designed as academic villages is complete, accommodating 1,600 students. Several thousand students live in apartments located within walking distance of the campus. Approximately 400 students live in on-campus Greek housing.

Students participate in more than 300 organizations, including special interest clubs, multicultural associations, fraternities and sororities, honor societies, and academic and preprofessional organizations. The offices of student life and student activities schedule a wide array of extracurricular programs, including concerts, movies, and guest speakers.

The University of Central Florida is a member of the NCAA, the Mid-American Conference (MAC), and the Atlantic Sun Conference. All teams compete on the NCAA Division I level. UCF's men's teams compete in intercollegiate baseball, basketball, cross-country, football, golf, soccer, tennis, and track. Women's teams compete in basketball, cross-country, golf, soccer, softball, tennis, track, and volleyball. Intercollegiate coed club activities include championship cheerleading, crew, and waterskiing teams. The University intramural sports program offers disc golf, flag football, floor hockey, racquetball, soccer, softball, tennis, and volleyball.

Location

The University of Central Florida is located on approximately 1,415 acres 13 miles east of downtown Orlando. Regional campuses are located in Daytona Beach, Cocoa, and South Lake.

Majors and Degrees

The University awards the degrees of Bachelor of Arts, Bachelor of Fine Arts, Bachelor of Science, Bachelor of Science in Business Administration, Bachelor of Science in Aerospace Engineering, Bachelor of Science in Civil Engineering, Bachelor of Science in Computer Engineering, Bachelor of Science in Environmental Engineering, Bachelor of Science in Industrial Engineering, Bachelor of Science in Mechanical Engineering, Bachelor of Science in Engineering Technology, Bachelor of Science in Nursing, and Bachelor of Social Work. These degrees are available in the colleges listed below, with majors or areas of specialization as indicated.

The College of Arts and Sciences offers degrees in actuarial science, advertising, animation, anthropology, art, art history, biological science, chemistry, cinema studies, communication, digital media, economics, English, film, foreign language combination, forensic science, French, history, humanities, journalism, liberal arts, liberal studies, mathematics, music, music education, music performance, philosophy, physics, political science, psychology, public relations, radio-television, social science (interdisciplinary), sociology, Spanish, speech, statistics, and theater. Preprofessional programs in biology and law are also offered.

The College of Business Administration offers degrees in accounting, economics, finance, general business administration, management, management information systems, and marketing. The College also offers a minor in international business.

The College of Education offers degrees in art education, early childhood education, elementary education, English language arts education, exceptional education, foreign language education, mathematics education, physical education, science education, social science education, sports and fitness, and vocational training and industry training.

The College of Engineering and Computer Science offers degrees in aerospace, civil, computer, electrical, environmental, industrial, and mechanical engineering and in computer science. The Bachelor of Science in Engineering Technology is awarded in computer, design, electronics, information systems, operations engineering, and space science technology.

The College of Health and Public Affairs offers degrees in athletic training, biomolecular sciences, cardiopulmonary sciences, communicative disorders, criminal justice, health information management, health sciences, health services administration, legal studies, medical laboratory sciences, molecular biology, microbiology, nursing, physical therapy (five-year master's program), public administration, radiological sciences, and social work. Preprofessional programs are offered in chiropractic, medicine, optometry, osteopathy, pharmacy, podiatry, and veterinary medicine.

The Rosen School of Hospitality Management offers specializations in convention and conference management, financial management and technology, food service and restaurant operations management, lodging management, theme park and attraction management, tourism management, and vacation ownership resort management.

Academic Programs

UCF provides a total education through a core curriculum of 36 hours of general education courses. In addition to fulfilling the general education requirement, each student must complete the necessary major and/or minor requirements to reach the minimum of 120 semester hours necessary for graduation.

Several special programs help students reach their academic and leadership potential. The Burnett Honors College at UCF encourages students to achieve academic excellence through small classes and interactive symposiums. The innovative Leadership Enrichment and Academic Development (LEAD) Scholars Program fosters leadership and service commitment through a comprehensive student development program for freshmen. The Academic Exploration Program (AEP) helps entering freshmen define their career goals and develop an academic strategy to reach those goals. The University also offers an increasing number of Web-based courses and degree programs.

In addition, UCF offers Air Force and Army ROTC programs.

Off-Campus Programs

A cooperative education program is offered, in which students alternate semesters of classroom study with equal periods of paid employment in government, industry, or business. The Department of Foreign Languages offers summer-study programs in Canada, Eastern Europe, France, Germany, Italy, Japan, Poland, Spain, Sweden, and Russia. Courses are available in the subject areas of language (all levels), art, and civilization. UCF is also a participant in the National Student Exchange Consortium.

Academic Facilities

In addition to the academic programs offered on the Orlando campus, students can work toward a degree at campuses located in South Lake, Cocoa, and Daytona Beach. These regional campuses work cooperatively with local community colleges to provide all four years of course work in many academic areas. The library houses nearly 1.4 million volumes and subscribes to more than 10,000 periodicals and journals. In addition, students have access to an online computer catalog that provides information on the collections of the State University System libraries. An extensive online network of more than 500 computer terminals and a network of nearly 1,000 IBM PCs cover the campus. The Institute for Simulation and Training gives students the opportunity to pursue undergraduate research. The School of Optics allows faculty members and students to work directly with industrial personnel in conducting basic and applied research at the regional and national levels. The Central Florida Research Park, located next to the UCF campus, houses more than ninety important high-technology firms and agencies. This proximity fosters relationships between industry and the University, which strengthens the academic programs at UCF.

Costs

For Florida residents, the cost of tuition and fees in 2003–04, based on a full-time course load, was $3000 for the year; for out-of-state residents, the cost was $14,000. Room and board were approximately $6600 per year, and costs for books and supplies were approximately $800.

Financial Aid

Financial aid is awarded according to each student's demonstrated need in relation to college costs and may include grants, loans, scholarships, and part-time employment. Programs based on need include the Federal Perkins Loan, Federal Pell Grant, Florida Student Assistance Grant, Federal Work-Study Program, Florida College Career Work-Study Program, and Federal Stafford Student Loan. To qualify for these programs, students must complete the Free Application for Federal Student Aid (FAFSA). The priority application deadline is March 1. Approximately 66 percent of UCF students receive some form of financial aid.

Faculty

The University's faculty consists of more than 1,000 full-time members and 330 adjunct members. More than 70 percent of the full-time faculty members hold a doctoral degree. Undergraduate instruction is given primarily by the full-time and adjunct faculty members; graduate students play a very minor role in undergraduate instruction. Students are assigned a faculty adviser in their area of specialization for assistance in academic matters. The student-faculty ratio is 18:1.

Student Government

UCF's Student Government Association, voted the best in Florida for three of the last four years by *Florida Leader Magazine*, provides an opportunity for students to become involved at UCF. Every UCF student is encouraged to voice his or her opinion through senate representatives. Student Government is divided into three branches—the student-elected executive branch, the student-elected legislative branch, and the appointed judicial branch. Student Government is responsible for allocation of all activity and service fees paid by students as part of their tuition. This money goes toward student services, including the online Macintosh lab, homecoming activities, the campus activities board, legal services, and funding for clubs and organizations. Admission is free to all events directly sponsored by the Student Government.

Admission Requirements

A freshman applicant is a student with fewer than 12 hours of college course work after high school graduation. The most important criterion in the admission decision for these applicants is the high school academic record: quality and level of difficulty of courses, grade point average, grade trends, and SAT I or ACT test scores. UCF operates on a rolling admission basis. Students are generally notified of their admission decision within two to four weeks after receipt of the application and all supporting documents. If the number of qualified applicants exceeds the number the University is permitted to enroll, a waiting list is established.

All applicants must have earned a minimum of 19 high school academic units (yearlong courses that are not remedial in nature). These include 4 units of English (3 must include substantial writing), 3 units of mathematics at or above the algebra I level, 3 units of natural science (2 must include a laboratory), 3 units of social science, 2 units of one foreign language, and 4 units of academic electives. Grades in honors, International Baccalaureate, and Advanced Placement courses are given additional weight in the GPA computation. Students must meet the Division of Colleges and Universities minimum eligibility to be considered for admission. Applicants should understand that the satisfaction of minimum requirements does not automatically guarantee admission to UCF.

Transfer applicants with fewer than 60 semester hours of college course work must submit official high school transcripts, SAT I or ACT test scores, and all official college transcripts. Transfer students with more than 60 semester hours or who have earned an Associate in Arts or one of the seven statewide articulated Associate in Science degrees from a Florida public community college need only submit all official college transcripts. A transfer credit summary evaluation is provided to students once they are offered admission to UCF.

Application and Information

Students are encouraged to apply several months in advance and may apply online at the Web site listed below. It is recommended that freshmen apply early during the fall semester of their senior year. Applications are accepted up to a year prior to the start of the term for which entry is desired. Priority application deadlines are May 1 for the fall semester, November 1 for the spring semester, and March 1 for the summer term. Campus tours are given Monday through Friday at 10 a.m. and 2 p.m. (except holidays).

For additional information, students should contact Undergraduate Admissions at the number listed below, which also serves as a 24-hour application request line.

Office of Undergraduate Admissions
University of Central Florida
P.O. Box 160111
Orlando, Florida 32816-0111
Telephone: 407-823-3000
E-mail: admission@mail.ucf.edu
World Wide Web: http://www.ucf.edu

UNIVERSITY OF CHARLESTON

CHARLESTON, WEST VIRGINIA

The University

The University of Charleston strives to educate each student for a life of productive work, enlightened living, and community involvement. Therefore, the University takes very seriously its responsibility to provide students with the knowledge, abilities, and character necessary for them to have successful careers and to be active citizens.

Founded in 1888 and formerly known as Morris Harvey College, the University acquired its new name in 1979 when it began offering several graduate degrees. Today, 1,200 students representing forty states and twenty-four countries enjoy the University's 40-acre riverfront campus overlooking the State Capitol Complex and the beautiful city of Charleston.

Education at the University of Charleston focuses on "learning your way" and asks students to demonstrate what they have learned in order to earn the credits necessary for graduation. Demonstrable knowledge and skills in the areas of communication, critical thinking, citizenship, ethical practice, and creative responsiveness are integrated with knowledge and skills in a field of study. Future employers and graduate schools consistently recruit college graduates with these abilities. The University of Charleston has designed a program to help students master the knowledge and skills that are necessary for success. Students are encouraged to demonstrate mastery and earn credits at their own pace. Many students earn more than the traditional 15–18 credits per semester and graduate within three years, double major, or earn a master's degree in four years.

Because the University believes that students learn from their involvement in community and campus activities, students are strongly encouraged to participate in one or more of the forty cocurricular organizations found at the University. There are academic clubs, publications, fraternities, sororities, religious organizations, intramural sports, honorary societies, drama clubs, cheerleading, chorus and music ensembles, and many student leadership organizations. The University's Colleague program integrates student involvement, the academic curriculum, community service, and leadership. The Community Service program provides opportunities for students to participate both on campus and in the Charleston area. In addition, there are numerous civic, political, social, and charitable organizations easily accessible in the community.

The varsity sports program for men and women has become one of the University's most valuable assets. Men and women may participate in basketball, cheerleading, crew, soccer, swimming, tennis, track, and cross-country. Men may also participate in baseball, football, and golf, and women in softball and volleyball. The University's varsity athletic teams compete in Division II of the NCAA. In recent years, men's and women's teams have been contenders in the WVIAC tournaments, with some teams winning conference championships and attending national championship tournaments.

The University of Charleston is accredited by the North Central Association of Colleges and Schools, National Council for Accreditation of Teacher Education, National Athletic Trainers Association, Committee on Allied Health Education and Accreditation of the American Medical Association in cooperation with the Joint Review Committees for Respiratory Therapy Education and Radiological Technology Education, and the Commission on Accreditation for the National League for Nursing. The University holds a variety of professional recognition, approvals, and memberships, including the AACSB International–The Association to Advance Collegiate Schools of Business.

Master's degrees are offered in business administration and human resource management. The University also offers an Executive M.B.A. and a plus-one M.B.A. for full-time study one year beyond the bachelor's degree.

Location

Charleston, the state capital, is the cultural, social, political, and economic hub of West Virginia. Located in the Kanawha Valley near the foothills of the Appalachian Mountains, it offers scenic tranquility as well as the convenience and excitement of a modern city. With a metropolitan population of 250,000, Charleston has grown to be West Virginia's finest city. Accessibility to the city is quite easy via bus, car, plane, and train. A large civic center, historic sites, libraries, movie theaters, shopping malls, and a symphony orchestra are all highlights of the Charleston business district. The rapport between the University and the community is excellent, and many events are cosponsored annually. Downtown Charleston, just a 10-minute ride from the campus by campus shuttle or city bus, offers the kind of social and cultural opportunities that can be found only in a large city. In addition, fishing, hunting, horseback riding, water-skiing, snow-skiing, mountain biking, and white-water rafting are just a few of the many recreational activities to be found within a short distance of the campus.

Majors and Degrees

The University of Charleston offers undergraduate degree programs through its various divisions: the Morris Harvey Division of Arts and Sciences, the Jones Division of Business, and the Division of Health Sciences.

The Morris Harvey Division of Arts and Sciences offers the Bachelor of Arts degree with the following majors: art, education (various certifications), English, general studies, history, interior design, mass communications, music, music administration, political science, and psychology. The Bachelor of Science degree is offered with majors in biology, chemistry, and environmental science.

The Jones Division of Business offers Bachelor of Science degree programs in accounting, athletic administration, business administration (with concentrations in finance, management, and marketing), computer information systems, and information technology. Associate of Science degree programs are offered in accounting, business administration, and computer information systems.

The Division of Health Sciences offers the Bachelor of Science degree in athletic training education, nursing, and radiological science and also offers an Associate of Arts degree in nursing.

Academic Programs

Candidates for a bachelor's degree from the University of Charleston are required to complete a minimum of 120 semester hours and have a cumulative grade point average of at least 2.0 on all college work attempted. This must include 30 hours in upper division courses; demonstration of learning in the required outcomes of communication, critical thinking, ethical practice, creativity, science, and society; and advanced work leading to a major in a department or a division. The minimum requirement for an associate degree is 60 semester hours and a cumulative grade point average of at least a 2.0 on all college work attempted, including completion of a prescribed program of general education and specialized work in a department.

Students may pursue directed independent study and internships in most majors. ROTC is offered to interested men and women. The Byrd Institute of Government Studies offers special opportunities to work with state and local governments.

The University follows a semester academic calendar and offers summer terms for students who wish to accelerate their college program. Students may enroll in as many credit hours per academic semester as they wish.

Academic Facilities

A large number of support facilities and programs supplement the various academic offerings at the University of Charleston. The Schoenbaum Library serves as the center of the learning experience. Located in the Clay Tower Building, it has a collection of more than 120,000 books, 200,000 microforms, and 3,600 audiovisual items. More than 8,000 journal titles are available either in print or electronically and are accessible from any Web-enabled computer, on or off campus. In addition, numerous specialized collections, CD-ROM-based electronic indexes, and online electronic search services are at the students' disposal for specialized research and study.

The University has several computer labs for student and faculty use: the Cabot Apple Lab, the IBM-PC combination classroom labs, an IBM-PC network lab, and an IBM-PC open lab. The Learning Support Office provides a variety of services and classes to help students achieve academic, personal, and professional success. The Communication Resource Center provides support for faculty members and students through consultation services, workshops, and electronic access to a variety of writing resources.

The Clay Tower Building, which opened in 1997, houses state-of-the-art science, technology, and information resource facilities. Riggleman Hall, the main college building, houses classrooms, a 976-seat auditorium and stage, education and language laboratories, the Carleton Varney Department of Art and Design, and administrative offices. Housing facilities for residential students include a recently renovated hall housing approximately 100 students; and Brotherton Hall, housing 230 students; and a recently constructed new hall, housing approximately 180 students, with primarily apartment-style residences.

Costs

For the academic year 2004–05, tuition costs $19,400 and remains frozen at that rate for students who remain enrolled full-time for eight semesters, room (double occupancy) and board cost $7200 for a total of $26,600. This does not include costs of books or insurance.

Financial Aid

The University of Charleston provides financial assistance that may include a combination of scholarships, grants, loans, and work-study. In 2003–04, 90 percent of full-time students and 80 percent of part-time students received some form of financial aid. Special academic scholarships and grants are awarded to outstanding full-time students. The University also offers grants to qualified athletes and to students who are involved in leadership, community service, or vocal music.

Faculty

The University has 61 full-time and 38 part-time undergraduate faculty members. At the University of Charleston, faculty members provide academic, career, and in some cases, personal advice to students. They encourage active learning, including collaborative projects and faculty/student research.

Student Government

The Student Government Association is a policy-making body composed of students representing most campus organizations and student classes. Both the Student Government Association and the University believe that students should have the privilege, along with the faculty and administration, of participating in the governance of the University.

Admission Requirements

Admission to the University of Charleston is based on the academic records, potential for leadership and involvement, and personal qualities of the applicant. A qualified applicant's credentials must strongly suggest ability and motivation to succeed in higher education and in the University community. Candidates for admission must present a transcript of work from an accredited secondary school showing 16 academic units and grades indicating intellectual ability and promise. The pattern of courses must show purpose and continuity and furnish a background for the liberal learning outcomes curriculum offered by the University. Since this curriculum emphasizes communication, critical thinking, and citizenship, the secondary school courses most acceptable would emphasize courses in English, mathematics, sciences, and social sciences. Candidates are also required to submit scores on the ACT or SAT I. Students must have an above-average academic profile that includes a minimum 2.25 academic grade point average and a minimum ACT composite score of 19 or SAT I score of 900. Applicants for admission are considered on an individual basis without regard to race, religion, geographic origin, or handicap. Recommendations and a personal visit to the campus scheduled with the Admissions Office are highly recommended.

Application and Information

For more information, interested students should contact:

Director of Admissions
University of Charleston
2300 MacCorkle Avenue, SE
Charleston, West Virginia 25304
Telephone: 304-357-4750
800-995-GO UC (toll-free)
Fax: 304-357-4781
E-mail: admissions@ucwv.edu
World Wide Web: http://www.ucwv.edu

The Clay Tower Building houses state-of-the-art science facilities and a library with lounges overlooking the river.

UNIVERSITY OF CHICAGO
CHICAGO, ILLINOIS

The University

With its Gothic quadrangles, dynamic faculty and student body, exciting research, and seminar-style classes that emphasize critical thinking and interdisciplinary scholarship, the University of Chicago stands as one of the world's great intellectual communities and centers of learning. Founded in 1891 by John D. Rockefeller, who called it "the best investment I ever made," the University is private, nondenominational, and coeducational. Through the years, it has played a leading role in providing equal opportunity for women and minorities in higher education. The strength and distinction of its faculty is reflected in the 75 Nobel laureates who have been associated with Chicago, including 7 current faculty members. In addition to the undergraduate liberal arts college, the University of Chicago is composed of four graduate divisions, six graduate professional schools, the extensive library system, the Graham School of General Studies, the Laboratory Schools, and the University of Chicago Press. In more than a century of challenging existing educational traditions, Chicago has established new ones such as a coherent program of general education for undergraduates, the four-quarter system, and the "Chicago School" of thought in economics, sociology, and literary criticism.

The University of Chicago stands at the forefront of academic discovery. Some of the innovations and groundbreaking studies of Chicago scholars include Carbon-14 dating, REM sleep, urban sociology, classical literary criticism, the first controlled nuclear chain reaction, the F-scale for measuring tornado severity, pioneering scientific archaeology of the ancient Near East, the nation's first living-donor liver transplant, and discovery of three new prehistoric creatures from the dinosaur era in the last three years. Chicago undergraduates are often involved in academic exploration with graduate students and faculty members. In addition, they take graduate-level courses, travel and study abroad, and participate in internships in Chicago and beyond. Indeed, Chicago shows a dedication to the undergraduate college experience that is rare among research universities.

Currently enrolling 4,300 students, the undergraduate college is the largest division of the University of Chicago. Students come from all parts of the United States and forty-nine countries. Most undergraduates live on campus in the unique House System that includes graduate students and faculty members in housing that is guaranteed for all four years. Ninety percent of arts and sciences faculty members teach undergraduates. Eighty-eight percent of classes have fewer than 30 students, with most classes based in discussion and the free exchange of ideas and numbering fewer than 15. Arts and sciences faculty members total 982, and the student-faculty ratio is 4:1.

Students pursue every aspect of life—athletic, academic, social, cultural—enthusiastically and with a distinctly Chicago style. They are involved in more than 300 student organizations, including numerous groups for community service, academic interests, publications, cultural awareness, music, and theater. Some popular activities are University Theater, Model UN, Quiz Bowl, DOC Films, Jazz X-Tet, and the *Chicago Maroon* newspaper. A member of the Division III University Athletic Association, Chicago is a great place to play athletics, with nineteen varsity sports for men and women and more than 70 percent of the student body participating in intramural sports. In 2003, the new Gerald Ratner Athletics Center opened, providing new athletic facilities to the entire Chicago community.

Location

Located approximately 7 miles from the center of the city, the University of Chicago's dramatic Gothic buildings frame tree-shaded quadrangles and occupy a 204-acre campus. Recently, the campus was designated a botanic garden, and, with such architectural landmarks as Rockefeller Chapel and Frank Lloyd Wright's Robie House, it is listed on the National Register of Historic Places. The University's neighborhood, Hyde Park, is a residential community of 43,000 situated on the banks of Lake Michigan. Home to more than 60 percent of the faculty who walk or bike to campus, the neighborhood is often cited as a model of cosmopolitan and multiethnic city living. Other Chicago neighborhoods are accessible by commuter trains, University-operated express buses, and elevated trains. As the largest city in the Midwest and the third-largest in the nation, Chicago offers abundant cultural and entertainment opportunities, including the Lyric Opera, the Chicago Symphony Orchestra, the Art Institute of Chicago, Comiskey Park and Wrigley Field, the Field Museum of Natural History, Steppenwolf Theatre, and the city's myriad ethnic neighborhoods.

Majors and Degrees

The College of the University of Chicago grants Bachelor of Arts and Bachelor of Science degrees in more than fifty concentrations in the biological, physical, and social sciences, as well as in the humanities and interdisciplinary areas. A concentration may provide a comprehensive understanding of a well-defined field, such as anthropology or mathematics, or it may be an interdisciplinary program such as African and African-American studies, environmental studies, biological chemistry, or cinema and media studies. Joint B.A./M.A. and B.S./M.S. programs are offered in a number of disciplines. Degrees are awarded in the following majors: African and African-American studies; ancient studies; anthropology; art history; astronomy and astrophysics; biological chemistry; biological sciences; chemistry; cinema and media studies; classical studies; comparative literature; computer science; early Christian literature; East Asian languages and civilizations; economics; English language and literature; environmental studies; fundamentals: issues and texts; gender studies; general studies in the humanities; geography; geophysical sciences; Germanic studies; history; history, philosophy, and social studies of science and medicine (HiPSS); human development; international studies; Jewish studies; Latin American studies; law, letters, and society; linguistics; mathematics; medieval studies; music; Near Eastern languages and civilizations; philosophy; physics; political science; psychology; public policy studies; religion and the humanities; religious studies; Romance languages and literatures; Russian civilization; Slavic languages and literatures; sociology; South Asian languages and civilizations; South Asian studies; statistics; tutorial studies; and visual arts.

Academic Program

Chicago's undergraduate curriculum is designed to give students the opportunity to fully participate in the intellectual life of a world-renowned research university. The curriculum became famous in American higher education during the 1930s when it challenged the prevailing model of elective-based programs by introducing a coherent core of general education courses. These courses made it possible, then and now, for college students to share certain kinds of crucial intellectual experiences, to create a community of young scholars who can talk across disciplines, and to form habits of mind necessary for advanced study, for successful careers, and for a productive life. One third of the courses taken for graduation are modern descendants of that first revolutionary general education core. They include courses in social and natural sciences, humanities, mathematics, Western or non-Western civilization, and art or music. These small, faculty-taught courses, taken in the first two years, lead naturally to the next stages of the curriculum, which is equally divided between courses in the concentration and elective courses. The total program may also include research projects, honors projects, foreign travel and study, and internships. The eventual shape of the individual Chicago experience is determined by the student, in consultations with an academic adviser, departmental adviser, and faculty mentors.

Off-Campus Programs

Students in the College of the University of Chicago are encouraged to study abroad and can take part in programs in many countries. Programs range in length from a summer or a single academic quarter to a full academic year and include course work and other experiences that can be tailored to fit degree programs in any discipline, whether humanities, social sciences, or natural sciences. Most important, all programs provide the opportunity to live among people whose ways of living and thinking challenge students to look at their own lives with a fresh perspective.

These programs are sponsored by the University of Chicago, either alone or in cooperation with other universities and with two groups to which the University belongs: the Associated Colleges of the Midwest (ACM) and the Committee on Institutional Cooperation (CIC). For most programs, participants receive full credit for courses and are eligible for University of Chicago financial aid.

Academic Facilities

One of the strengths of the University of Chicago is that the campus maintains excellent academic facilities that serve the community as a whole. The University library system holds more than 6 million volumes and 7 million manuscripts and archival materials. Regenstein Library for humanities and social sciences is one of the nation's largest academic libraries, and John Crerar Library is recognized as one of the best libraries in the country for research and teaching in the sciences, medicine, and technology. Joining Crerar Library to form a science quadrangle is the Kersten Physics Teaching Center, the most advanced facility in the U.S. for the teaching of undergraduate physics. Students in the College have access to all the University's special libraries, including the D'Angelo Law Library, Yerkes Observatory Library for astronomy and astrophysics (home of the world's largest refracting telescope), the Social Service Administration Library, and the Eckhart Library for mathematics and computer science.

Other facilities providing Chicago students with research and internship opportunities are the recently renovated Oriental Institute Museum, a showcase of the history, art, and archaeology of the ancient Near East; the Smart Museum, which houses a collection of more than 7,000 works of art, spanning five centuries of both Western and Eastern civilizations; the Enrico Fermi Institute, which has played a central role in nuclear physics and nuclear chemistry research, elementary particle physics, and astrophysics; Midway Studios, where art students enjoy studio space; and the University of Chicago Medical Center, which includes five major hospitals and 125 specialty outpatient clinics that work to advance biomedical innovation, serve the health needs of the community, and further the knowledge of medical students, physicians, and others dedicated to medicine.

Costs

Tuition for the 2003–04 school year was $28,689, and room and board charges were $9165. Fees for other services, including health insurance, orientation, and activities, totaled $3586.

Financial Aid

Chicago is committed to helping students from all economic backgrounds attend the University and makes admissions decisions on a need-blind basis. Furthermore, the University meets 100 percent of students' demonstrated financial need. More than 65 percent of Chicago students receive some form of financial assistance. Students wishing to apply for financial aid should submit the University of Chicago financial aid application along with the Free Application for Federal Student Aid and the Financial Aid PROFILE of the College Scholarship Service. Merit scholarships are also available.

Faculty

The instructional faculty of the University of Chicago and is composed of distinguished scholars and teachers. Faculty members typically teach both undergraduate and graduate courses, and senior professors often teach undergraduate general education courses. Because classes are small and discussion is the preferred mode of instruction, faculty members often become mentors and partners in inquiry with students.

Student Government

Student Government is composed of students in the College and other graduate and professional schools. Student government assists student organizations, sponsors events, and deals with the academic, social, and economic issues of University life. The Student Assembly, the legislative branch, is the only organization on campus that represents all students. Members of the Assembly are elected in the autumn quarter. Student Government also supports a number of committees that focus on issues ranging from student affairs to community relations to student services. The Inter-House Council serves as an advisory body for the House System and allocates money for Inter-House activities.

Admission Requirements

The Office of College Admissions doesn't have a rigid formula for the successful applicant and considers a candidate's entire application: academic and extracurricular records, essays, letters of recommendation, and SAT or ACT scores. A personal interview is optional and can provide prospective students with a chance to learn more about the College. The essay is an opportunity to show individuality, in addition to clear and effective writing ability.

Though no specific secondary school courses are prescribed, a standard college-preparatory program is recommended: 4 years of English, 3 to 4 years of math and laboratory sciences, 3 or more years of social sciences, and a foreign language. The University of Chicago does not employ numerical cut-offs when evaluating applications for admission. Of the 1,180 students in the class of 2007, 79 percent graduated in the top 10 percent of their high school classes. The middle 50 percent of admitted students scored between 1330 and 1480 on the SAT or between 27 and 32 on the ACT.

Application and Information

The University of Chicago offers students two application plans. Early action is for candidates who seek an admission decision in mid-December and a provisional financial aid assessment by early January. Candidates must complete their applications by November 1 and may apply to other schools if they wish. Chicago's early action program is nonbinding; admitted students need not reply to the Office of Admissions until May 1. Regular notification is for candidates who prefer an admission and financial aid decision by early April. Candidates must complete their application by January 1 and must reply to the offer by May 1. Students who have completed one or two years of course work at another college are welcome to apply for transfer admission.

For further information students should contact:

Office of College Admissions
University of Chicago
1116 East 59th Street
Chicago, Illinois 60637
Telephone: 773-702-8650
World Wide Web: http://collegeadmissions.uchicago.edu
http://collegeadmissions.uchicago.edu/answers

UNIVERSITY OF CINCINNATI

CINCINNATI, OHIO

The University

The University of Cincinnati (UC), which traces its roots to 1819, is a multifaceted academic institution. The metropolitan campus offers programs in allied health sciences; applied science; business administration; design, architecture, art, and planning; education; engineering; liberal arts; nursing; performing arts; and social work. Many of its programs are nationally ranked. Its design programs are rated in the top five, the interior design program is ranked first, the architecture program is ranked third in the nation, and the engineering program is ranked in the top ten. The Cincinnati Initiative for Teacher Education Program is a national leader, and the College-Conservatory of Music (CCM) is internationally renowned. Cincinnati has three 2-year colleges that provide a general education, a high-quality technical education, and transition programs that enable students to enroll successfully into bachelor programs at UC's main campus.

Both alumni and faculty members have made outstanding social contributions; UC is credited with the development of the first oral polio vaccine, the first antihistamine, the first electronic organ, the first steam fire engine and, more recently, performance of the first brain operation—by employing a YAG laser—and the first inner-ear implant.

There are more than 33,000 students, of whom more than 18,000 are full-time undergraduates. Eighty-eight percent of the students are from Ohio, and 78 percent are graduates of public schools. The ethnic population is made up of 6,714 students while 1,837 international students are working toward undergraduate and graduate degrees. Of the baccalaureate freshman students, 13.4 percent ranked in the top tenth of their high school graduating class, and 34 percent ranked in the top quarter.

At UC, education is more than academics. The University believes that a significant part of a student's personal growth and development is learning to cooperate with others. Living on campus provides immediate access to academic and recreational facilities, helps a student establish meaningful social relationships, and promotes involvement in campus life. Residence halls accommodate 3,500 undergraduates, and there are 300 graduate family units. Each of the six halls is unique, with special features ranging from balconies and sun decks to computer facilities. Students can request coed or non-coed accommodations and arrange for such amenities as telephone voice mail, microwave ovens, and cable TV. Many students live in the surrounding neighborhoods of Clifton, which offer many apartment complexes, restaurants, and specialty shops as well as an active nightlife.

Student involvement is important at the University of Cincinnati. More than 275 student organizations are available, including 33 social fraternities and sororities and a broad variety of special interest groups. Bearcat basketball is played in the Shoemaker Center and UC football in the recently renovated Nippert Stadium. The University of Cincinnati competes at the NCAA Division I level, fielding varsity teams for men in baseball, basketball, cross-country, football, soccer, swimming and diving, and outdoor track and field and for women in basketball, cross-country, golf, rowing, soccer, softball, tennis, and volleyball. Athletic clubs provide opportunities for participation in ice hockey, lacrosse, mountaineering, rugby, sailing, and skiing. Students also enjoy free fitness facilities, including racquetball, track, swimming, and Nautilus weight lifting. Counseling services include STEPS (Steps Toward Educational Progress and Success), educational advising and orientation, career development and placement, and tutorial and referral services.

Location

Cincinnati was cited by *Places Rated Almanac* as the most livable city in the United States. The University of Cincinnati has made major contributions to the city's environment. The College-Conservatory of Music, for instance, provides more than 1,000 different entertainments each year, including concerts, Broadway musicals, ballet, drama, and opera. The cultural resources of the city complement those of the University. Jazz concerts, the circus, rock concerts, and art exhibits all contribute to the rich atmosphere. Sports enthusiasts can watch the Reds or the Bengals or participate in a number of outdoor activities. Though Cincinnati offers all the amenities of a major city, it is within an hour's drive of several state parks.

Majors and Degrees

The University of Cincinnati offers a wide range of opportunities through forty certificate programs, eighty-six associate degree programs, and more than 200 bachelor's degree programs. The associate degree is offered through departments in the College of Applied Science, Clermont College, Raymond Walters College, and University College. A bachelor's degree is available through departments in the College of Allied Health Sciences; College of Applied Science; the McMicken College of Arts and Sciences; the College of Business Administration; the College-Conservatory of Music; the College of Design, Architecture, Art, and Planning; the College of Education; the College of Engineering; the College of Nursing; and the School of Social Work. Certificate programs are available through many colleges and vary from computer technology to historic preservation. More than twenty preprofessional programs are available, including those in education, law, medicine, nursing, and social work. The College of Pharmacy offers a Pharm.D. program.

Academic Programs

The University of Cincinnati is unified in its basic academic values but highly diverse in its educational offerings. Credit hours required for graduation vary from college to college and from department to department; associate degree programs generally require at least 95 quarter credit hours and bachelor's degree programs generally require a minimum of 186 quarter credit hours. Most of the colleges on campus participate in the University Honors Scholars Program. The honors program is highly flexible, broad in scope, and designed to provide students with the personal attention of a small college as well as the wide range of intellectual activity of a major university. ROTC programs are available in air science (Air Force ROTC) and military science (Army ROTC).

The academic calendar consists of three 10-week quarters and a summer session. The summer session offers three 3-week terms, each equivalent to a regular quarter; a ten-week term; and many shorter sessions, institutes, and workshops. The traditional academic year begins in late September and ends in early June.

Off-Campus Programs

Cooperative education, founded at the University in 1906, is one of the best programs in the country and serves as a model for colleges worldwide. This program integrates on-the-job experience with the student's academic program by alternating quarters of work in the student's field. More than 4,100 students from forty disciplines gain professional experience in more than 1,400 organizations in thirty-six states and eleven other countries.

Academic Facilities

The main campus sits on 392 acres and consists of 108 buildings, including state-of-the art facilities such as the Engineering Research Center, the Aronoff Center, the CCM Village, the Vontz Center for Molecular Studies, and the anticipated Main Street.

The University libraries contain more than 1.6 million books and more than 20,000 journal and serial publications. In addition to a modern central library featuring an online catalog system, the University library network includes a health sciences library, a law library, and nine college and department libraries. Media facilities and services include audiovisual equipment, photographic services, and a curriculum resource center.

Students in the College-Conservatory of Music, one of the premier performing arts schools in the country, have several theaters on and off campus at their disposal.

As a major research institution, the University of Cincinnati offers many modern computer facilities and innovative applications. Nine PC labs house hundreds of personal computers for student use. A student access system for interactive computing is provided by VAX computers and by other terminal systems using the MVS operation. A number of electronic classrooms, which allow for a high degree of interaction between students and faculty members, are located throughout the University.

Costs

For 2003–04, the central campus instructional and general fee was $7623 per year for Ohio residents and $19,230 per year for out-of-state students. For Clermont College, the instructional and general fee was $3765 per year for Ohio residents and $9537 for out-of-state students. The instructional and general fee for Raymond Walters College was $4335 for Ohio residents and $11,331 for out-of-state students. Parking fees were included in the instructional and general fees of these two Colleges. On the main campus, room and board costs began at $6840 per year. The application fee is $35, and the matriculation fee is $50; both are nonrefundable. Books and supplies are estimated at $815 per year but may be greater for students in special programs. Costs for a 24-hour-parking decal begin at $82 per quarter. Students in the Professional Practice Program pay a $100 registration fee for the quarters they are working but pay one third less in annual student fees in their last two years.

Financial Aid

Financial aid is awarded on the basis of need through grants, loans, and work-study opportunities and/or on the basis of scholastic accomplishment through a variety of scholarships. Federal Pell Grants, Ohio Instructional Grants, and Federal Supplemental Educational Opportunity Grants are given to approximately 13,000 students each year. To apply for aid, students must file the Free Application for Federal Student Aid (FAFSA) after January 1. This form is available at the University's Student Financial Aid Office and at all colleges and high schools. Major loans are available through the Federal Perkins Loan, Federal Stafford Student Loan, and Federal PLUS loan programs. Short-term loans are provided by the University of Cincinnati for unexpected college-related expenses. The Federal Work-Study Program provides part-time work for students on the basis of financial need. The University awards scholarships for outstanding freshmen through a competition called the Cincinnatus Scholarship Competition. Each participant receives at least a $1500 renewable scholarship.

Faculty

The University of Cincinnati faculty consists of 2,621 full-time members and 2,386 part-time members. Approximately 72 percent have doctorates. Research and scholarship are emphasized but not to the exclusion of teaching and counseling. The ratio of undergraduate students to full-time faculty members is 18:1. The average class size is 18.

Student Government

Cabinet, senate, and executive branches make up the Student Government, which directs all student organizations and administers funds to student groups. Members of the Student Government serve on University committees and represent the student body at meetings of the Board of Trustees.

Admission Requirements

Freshman candidates may be admitted directly into baccalaureate programs. Each individual college has specific high school unit entrance requirements and class rank requirements. The minimum high school unit requirements for the baccalaureate colleges are 4 in English, 3 in mathematics, 2 in science, 2 in social science, 2 in foreign language, and 2 additional college-preparatory subjects in the aforementioned areas. An average letter grade of C must be earned across courses in these areas. ACT or SAT I scores must be submitted for consideration for admission to a baccalaureate college. The University of Cincinnati also operates several "open admission" colleges for students who wish to earn an associate degree or for students who wish to gain access later to a baccalaureate college after satisfying admission requirement deficiencies. Candidates for admission must be graduates of accredited high schools or, in the case of the "open admission" colleges, must possess a General Educational Development equivalency diploma.

Application and Information

To be assured of consideration, candidates for admission should submit an application between October 1 and January 15 of their senior year of high school. For highly competitive programs, it is recommended to apply by November 15. Notification is made on a rolling basis beginning November 1. Transfer applications generally are processed on the same basis as freshman applications. The UC *Viewbook* is available in many guidance libraries or upon request from the Office of Admissions.

University of Cincinnati
P.O. Box 210091
Cincinnati, Ohio 45221-0091
Telephone: 513-556-1100
Fax: 513-556-1105
E-mail: admissions@uc.edu
World Wide Web: http://www.admissions.uc.edu

A view of the University of Cincinnati's main campus.

UNIVERSITY OF COLORADO AT BOULDER

BOULDER, COLORADO

The University

The University of Colorado (CU) was founded in 1876, the same year that Colorado became the Centennial State. Today the University system, governed by a 9-member Board of Regents, includes the main campus at Boulder, campuses at Colorado Springs and Denver, and the Health Sciences Center in Denver. The University of Colorado is one of thirty-four U.S. public institutions belonging to the prestigious Association of American Universities (AAU) and the only member in the Rocky Mountain region. CU-Boulder ranked tenth among public research universities and third among rising research universities in the public sector in a study called *The Rise of American Research Universities: Elites and Challengers in the Postwar Era*, published in 1997.

The Boulder campus, the largest in the CU system, offers more than 3,400 courses each year in approximately 150 areas of study. Outstanding academic departments and academic programs include astrophysical and planetary sciences, biochemistry, biology, chemistry, engineering, English, entrepreneurial business, geography, music, physics, and psychology. There are fifty-eight academic programs available at the bachelor's level, forty-eight at the master's level, and forty-four at the doctoral level. Talented undergraduate students may participate in honors programs, the Undergraduate Research Opportunities Program, and several residential academic programs featuring small-class environments.

Total enrollment for fall 2003 at the Boulder campus was 29,151, including 24,540 undergraduate students. The student population comes from every state in the nation and more than 100 countries. Approximately two thirds of the students come from Colorado. Many ethnic, religious, academic, and social backgrounds are represented, fostering the development of a multicultural community that enriches each student's educational experience.

Undergraduate students may apply to the following colleges and schools: Architecture and Planning, Arts and Sciences, Leeds School of Business, Engineering and Applied Science, Journalism and Mass Communication, and Education. Students are admitted to Journalism and Mass Communication and Education only after completing one or two years of study at CU-Boulder.

CU-Boulder offers a wide variety of campus activities. Students may participate in student government; clubs and organizations; intramural, club, and intercollegiate sports; and fraternities and sororities. An extensive calendar of cultural events is available.

Location

CU-Boulder is located in a scenic valley at the foot of the Rocky Mountains, 1 mile above sea level. With a population of just under 97,000, Boulder is among the most dynamic, progressive, and attractive cities of its size in the United States. The Colorado state capital, Denver, is a 30-mile drive or bus ride (free for students) from Boulder. Boulder is surrounded by a greenbelt of more than 20,000 acres of open space. Much of the open space is crisscrossed by an extensive system of hiking, biking, and riding trails, as are the nearby mountains. Many CU-Boulder students enjoy skiing, hiking, backpacking, rock climbing, white-water rafting, or mountain biking. Boulder was ranked first by Norman Ford in *The 50 Healthiest Places to Live and Retire in the United States.*

CU-Boulder has been rated as one of the "most artistically successful campuses in the country" in *The Campus as a Work of Art* by Thomas Gaines. The 600-acre main campus, in the heart of the city of Boulder, is distinguished by buildings featuring native sandstone walls and dramatic red-tiled roofs.

Majors and Degrees

CU-Boulder offers the following undergraduate majors: accounting; aerospace engineering; anthropology; applied mathematics; architectural engineering; Asian studies; astronomy, biochemistry; chemical engineering; chemistry; Chinese; civil engineering; classics; communication; computer science; dance; distributed studies; economics; electrical and computer engineering; electrical engineering; engineering physics; English; environmental design-architecture; environmental design-design studies; environmental design-planning; environmental engineering; environmental, population, and organismic biology; environmental studies; ethnic studies; film studies; finance; fine arts–art history; fine arts–studio arts; French; geography; geology; Germanic studies; history; humanities; information systems; international affairs; Italian; Japanese; journalism–advertising; journalism–broadcast news; journalism–broadcast production management; journalism–media studies; kinesiology; linguistics; management; marketing; mathematics; mechanical engineering; molecular, cellular, developmental biology; music; music–arts in music; music education; philosophy; physics; political science; predentistry sequence; premedicine sequence; pre–veterinary medicine sequence; psychology; religious studies; Russian studies; sociology; Spanish; speech, language, and hearing sciences; theater; and women's studies.

The following bachelor's degrees are offered: B.A., B.Envd., B.F.A., B.Mus., B.Mus.Ed., and B.S.

Concurrent bachelor's and master's degree programs are available in the following departments: applied mathematics, business (accounting, finance, information systems), cognitive psychology, East Asian languages and cultures, economics, environmental population and organismic biology, French, Germanic studies, kinesiology and applied physiology, linguistics, mathematics, and all engineering departments, including aerospace, architectural, chemical, civil, computer science, electrical, mechanical, and telecommunications.

Academic Program

CU-Boulder operates on a two-semester academic calendar. The fall semester begins in late August and the spring semester begins in early January. Summer Session lasts ten weeks; courses meeting for shorter periods (one to four, five, or eight weeks) are scheduled during the ten-week session.

The mission of the University of Colorado at Boulder is to educate undergraduate and graduate students in the accumulated knowledge of humankind, discover new knowledge through research and creative work, and foster critical thought, artistic creativity, professional competence, and responsible citizenship. Depending on their degree program, students may be required to complete 120, 124, or 128 semester hours for graduation. CU-Boulder offers a very flexible curriculum. Students may graduate with more than one major and with two different degrees from different colleges. Minors also are offered in arts and sciences, business, and engineering. The College of Arts and Sciences and the College of Engineering and Applied Science offer a four-year graduation guarantee, providing specific requirements are met.

Off-Campus Programs

CU-Boulder sponsors more than 150 study-abroad programs each year. Programs are offered in sixty countries on six continents, including Australia, Canada, Costa Rica, Cuba, Denmark, Egypt, England, France, Germany, Hungary, Japan, and Mexico. CU-Boulder is ranked tenth among all institutions of higher education in the nation for number of students studying abroad.

Academic Facilities

The University library system consists of more than 3 million volumes, 6 million titles on microform, more than 25,000 periodical subscriptions, and more than 60,000 video and audio titles. The libraries system includes a main library and five branch libraries: Business, Earth Sciences, Engineering, Math-Physics, and Music. There is also a law library. Other facilities and resources aiding students in their studies include a planetarium and observatory, a natural history museum, extensive computing resources, a state-of-the-art foreign language technology center, a concert hall, and three theaters. The Integrated Teaching and Learning Laboratory and the Discovery Learning Center provide hands-on, real-world experience to engineering undergraduates. One of the most recent additions to the campus is a new humanities building, equipped with smart classrooms.

Costs

For 2003–04, annual expenses for undergraduate students who are Colorado residents totaled $15,177 ($4020 for tuition and fees as well as an estimated $1163 for books and supplies, $6754 for room and board, and $3240 for transportation, medical, and personal expenses). Nonresident tuition and fees were $19,508.

Financial Aid

Slightly more than half of Boulder students receive some type of financial assistance, totaling more than $120 million in awards. Students receive aid in the form of grants, loans, work-study awards, and scholarships. Funding is provided from federal, state, University, and private sources. All students applying for need-based financial aid are required to submit the Free Application for Federal Student Aid (FAFSA). Application forms are available from high school and community college counselors as well as from the CU-Boulder Office of Financial Aid. The priority processing deadline is April 1. Students may apply for CU-Boulder scholarships online beginning November 1. Students may also obtain loans directly from the Office of Financial Aid rather than from a private lender.

Faculty

Approximately 1,200 full-time instructional faculty members teach undergraduate and graduate courses. The faculty includes nationally and internationally recognized scholars with many academic honors and awards. Tom Cech, former professor of chemistry and biochemistry and now Director of the Howard Hughes Medical Institute, shared the 1989 Nobel Prize in chemistry with Sidney Altman of Yale University. Carl Wieman and Eric Cornell won the 2001 Nobel Prize in Physics for their creation of a new state of matter, just above absolute zero. Kristi Anseth was named among the top 100 young innovators for developing materials that aid in the healing of bones and cartilage. Seven faculty members have received MacArthur Fellowships, knows as the "genius grant," the most recent two being in linguistics (2002) and physics (2003).

Student Government

One of the most influential student governments in the nation, the University of Colorado Student Union (UCSU) administers an operating budget of more than $27 million. UCSU student leaders and volunteers, working with the University staff, make policy decisions concerning the operation of the University Memorial Center, Student Recreation Center, Wardenburg Student Health Center, cultural events, the campus radio station, and other programs. Student fees and student-generated revenue support all of these activities. The student government also takes an active role in advocating student concerns.

Admission Requirements

Many factors are considered by the University in making admission decisions. Previous academic achievement, the quality of courses taken, GPA, college entrance test scores, the trend in grades and the extent to which the applicant has completed the recommended high school curriculum, and letters of recommendation are considered. Because CU-Boulder practices competitive admission, not all qualified applicants can be admitted. About one third of the freshman class typically ranks in the top 10 percent of their high school graduating class. In fall 2003, 56 percent of the freshman class were Colorado residents. The University seeks to enroll students from a wide range of ethnic, cultural, economic, geographic, and educational backgrounds. Applications are available in Colorado high school guidance offices, community college counseling centers, or from the CU-Boulder Office of Admissions.

Application and Information

Students are considered for admission for fall, spring, and summer terms. Each year, the Office of Admissions begins notifying applicants of admission decisions in October. Summer and fall application deadlines are January 15 for freshmen and April 1 for transfers. The spring application deadline for freshmen and transfers is October 1. After these dates, applications are considered only if space is available. An online electronic application for admission is now available through the University's home page, listed below.

For information and applications, students should contact:

Office of Admissions
552 UCB
University of Colorado at Boulder
Boulder, Colorado 80309-0552
Telephone: 303-492-6301
303-492-5998 (TTY)
World Wide Web: http://www.colorado.edu

The University of Colorado at Boulder is a major research and teaching university located in one of the most spectacular environments in the country, at the foot of the Rocky Mountains.

UNIVERSITY OF COLORADO AT DENVER

DENVER, COLORADO

The University

Set against the majestic backdrop of the Rocky Mountains, the University of Colorado at Denver (CU-Denver) serves as the intellectual and technological centerpiece of one of America's most flourishing cities. As the only comprehensive public university in Denver, the school's commitment to research and its dedication to adult learners has benefited the Denver community as well as the lives of its students. Founded in 1912 as the University of Colorado's Department of Correspondence and Extension, the downtown campus was established to meet the needs of the city's rapidly expanding population. By 1969, the school offered thirty-four programs at the undergraduate and graduate levels. In 1974, the University of Colorado at Denver was formed, eventually sharing space within the Auraria Higher Education Center. CU-Denver is one of four campuses that comprise the University of Colorado System, which also includes campuses at Boulder and Colorado Springs as well as a Health Sciences Center, also in Denver.

CU-Denver provides students, whatever their age or circumstances, with opportunities to enhance their lives and careers. Graduates are highly sought after by area businesses and organizations. In addition, the school is committed to research, technology, and creative scholarship and to providing an institutional culture that reflects the plurality, collegiality, and integration of an increasingly diverse global workplace.

More than eighty programs at the undergraduate and graduate levels span a wide range of fields and disciplines, each of which is recognized nationally for producing leaders in business, industry, and government. Programs are offered through the University's seven distinct academic units, which include the College of Architecture and Planning, the College of Arts and Media, the Business School, the School of Education, the College of Engineering and Applied Science, the College of Liberal Arts and Sciences, and the Graduate School of Public Affairs. The University is accredited by the Higher Learning Commission of the North Central Association of Colleges and Schools.

CU-Denver's 12,200 students are a diverse mix of ages, ethnicities, and backgrounds. Ages range from 17 to 75 years, with an average undergraduate age of 24, and one out of every five students represents an ethnic minority. Although their ages, countries of origin, backgrounds, and beliefs may vary greatly, all students at CU-Denver share the desire to succeed and to broaden their appreciation of the world around them. Students take advantage of course offerings that are scheduled at times that meet their needs and match their lifestyles; they can also participate in nearly sixty student clubs and organizations.

The University works hand-in-hand with businesses, community organizations, and neighborhoods in the greater Denver area to ensure that the school's top-quality education meets the needs of the ever-changing job market. Courses are designed to best equip CU-Denver graduates with the essential skills and knowledge they need to compete successfully across the state, within the region, throughout the nation, and around the world.

Location

The University's campus is located in the heart of downtown Denver, surrounded by an abundance of recreational, cultural, academic, and professional outlets. The campus provides a unique blend of metropolitan buzz, set against the peaceful and majestic backdrop of the Rocky Mountains. CU-Denver is within walking distance of the Pepsi Center, Invesco Field, Coors Field, the Denver Center for Performing Arts, parks, museums, theaters, and an eclectic assortment of restaurants, coffeehouses, and shops. At the same time, it is less than an hour away from some of the best skiing, snowboarding, camping, hiking, whitewater rafting, and rock-climbing in the world.

Majors and Degrees

Students can earn a Bachelor of Arts (B.A.) degree in anthropology, communications, economics, English, English writing, fine arts, French, history, philosophy, political science, psychology, sociology, Spanish, and theater. The Bachelor of Science (B.S.) degree is offered in biology, business administration, chemistry, civil engineering, computer science and engineering, electrical engineering, geography, mathematics, mechanical engineering, music, and physics. Students can earn a Bachelor of Fine Arts (B.F.A.) degree in drawing, 3-D graphics and animation, multimedia studies, painting, photography, sculpture, and theater, film, and television. Preprofessional programs are available in health careers, law, and teacher education. Minor and certificate programs are also available in these areas.

Academic Programs

Although CU-Denver is devoted to the needs of Denver and its residents, an increasing number of students from across the nation and overseas also pursue their studies at the University. The undergraduate Colleges of Arts & Media, Engineering, and Liberal Arts and Sciences, and the Business School offer programs leading to the baccalaureate degree in the arts, business, engineering, humanities, and sciences. A solid education is assured through a comprehensive core curriculum. Preprofessional training in the fields of education, the health careers, and law also are available. Telecommunications and other electronic media make instruction more stimulating and more widely available, connecting faculty, students, and alumni as well as state, regional, national, and international leaders. Many programs emphasize practical, businessworld applications, and specific computer-oriented academic programs are offered in applied mathematics, computer science, and information systems. To graduate, students must complete 120 credit hours and maintain a minimum 2.0 GPA. Courses must include 45 hours of upper division course work and 30 hours of course work within the chosen major. Courses are offered during the spring, summer, and fall semesters.

Off-Campus Programs

The Office of International Education offers countless study-abroad options in more than twenty countries throughout the world, including Australia, China, England, Mongolia, and Russia. Students can earn credit participating in yearlong, semester, summer, or winter-break programs. Financial aid may be used for a study-abroad program. The University is a participating institution of the Western Undergraduate Exchange (WUE). Through WUE, students in western states may enroll in many two-year and four-year college programs at a reduced tuition level.

Academic Facilities

The Auraria Library serves the largest campus student population in Colorado. The collection contains more than 600,000 books, microforms, and bound periodicals, and more than 3,300 current journals and newspaper subscriptions are located in the Periodicals Reading Room. As a member of the Colorado Alliance of Research Libraries, the library has access to an additional 6 million volumes through interlibrary loans. Services include an online public access catalog, computerized literature searches, CD-ROMs, a depository of U.S. and Colorado government publications, and media listening and viewing facilities. The Center for Learning Assistance promotes student success, retention, and graduation in the academic setting. Services include English as a second language study skills courses, tutoring, study strategies seminars, peer advocacy, a test file, and a minority resource library.

Costs

For spring 2004, tuition was $161 per credit for Colorado residents and $880 per credit for out-of-state residents. Tuition for 12–15 credits was $1514 for in-state residents and $7328 for out-of-state residents. Other fees included a student activity fee of $11, an information technology fee of $5 per credit hour, and a student services fee of $36. The University does not provide campus housing, but students can find off-campus housing at affordable rates.

Financial Aid

Financial aid is available to CU-Denver students through scholarships, loans, and work-study opportunities. Colorado residents are eligible for a Colorado Student Grant or a LEAP Grant of up to $3000 per year each. Federal Perkins Loans are awarded in amounts of up to $3000 annually, and students may earn up to $5000 a year through work-study. Scholarships for Colorado residents include the Academic Achievement Award, the Pinnacle Scholarship, and the Regents Scholarship; however awards from individual schools within CU-Denver and outside sources are also available. Students should complete the Free Application for Federal Student Aid (FAFSA) and the University Financial Aid Application (UAPP). For more information, prospective students should visit the financial aid page of CU-Denver's Web site at the address below.

Faculty

CU-Denver employs more than 460 regular instructional faculty members who are renowned educators and experts in their fields. They incorporate both novel and traditional methods of instruction. Four out of five faculty members hold the highest degree within their fields, earned from some of the finest institutions in the world. Faculty members bring with them recognized scholarly achievements; a deep appreciation for technology in the classroom; an emphasis on practical, hands-on learning; and a very real passion for teaching.

Student Government

The Executive Board members are elected in the spring of the previous year in the University's general election. The president runs the executive meetings according to parliamentary procedure. The vice president serves as a liaison between the various committees and meets with the Chancellor on a regular basis. The legislative committee establishes bylaws, rules, and procedures for the Executive Council, including all senators. This committee is responsible for proposing policies that are presented to the Executive Council and must be approved in order to be implemented. The finance board and Student Government support cocurricular activities, and funds are set aside for educational and social activities.

Admission Requirements

Admission is based on several factors, including the student's GPA, high school rank, scores on the ACT or SAT, and classes taken. In recent years, most freshmen have been in the top 25 percent of their classes, had at least a 3.3 GPA, and scored approximately 23 on the ACT or 1060 on the SAT. Based on the Colorado Commission on Higher Education (CCHE) Admissions Standards (Index), the College of Arts and Media and the College of Liberal Arts and Sciences require an Index score of 93, while the Business School and the College of Engineering require an Index score of 103. The Index is the starting point in the admissions process and is calculated from a student's high school grades and standardized test scores. Applicants with an Index score of less than 93 are considered on an individual basis. All music applicants, except those entering the Music Industry Studies Program, must pass an entrance audition before being accepted into the program.

Students are required to meet the following minimum academic preparation standards: 4 years of English, 3 years of college-preparatory mathematics, 3 years of natural science, 2 years of social science, 2 years of a single foreign language, and 1 year of the arts.

Transfer students must have attained a minimum 2.0 GPA in all completed course work and be eligible to return to all prior institutions. Requirements for Business and Engineering are higher. The admission decision for transfer applicants with 12 or more semester credits is based on college transcripts. Students with fewer than 12 semester credits of college work need to submit high school transcripts and test scores as well as their college transcript.

International students seeking admission must meet the specific program requirements. In addition, all international students whose first language is not English must have a minimum score of 525 (197 computer-based) on the Test of English as a Foreign Language (TOEFL). International students must also demonstrate adequate funds or financial support to attend the University.

Application and Information

Each application must include a completed application form; a $50 nonrefundable application fee; an official transcript of high school grades, including class rank; and an official copy of SAT or ACT scores. The deadline to apply is July 22 for fall, December 1 for spring, and May 1 for summer.

For more information, prospective students should contact:

Office of Admissions
University of Colorado at Denver
Campus Box 167, P.O. Box 173364
Denver, Colorado 80217-3364
Telephone: 303-556-2704
Fax: 303-556-4838
E-mail: admissions@cudenver.edu
World Wide Web: http://www.cudenver.edu

UNIVERSITY OF CONNECTICUT

STORRS, CONNECTICUT

The University

The University of Connecticut (UConn) is a premier public research university in the United States. Established in 1881 with a class of 12 students, UConn has grown into a nationally ranked university with more than 16,000 undergraduate students, 7,000 graduate and professional students, 1,500 faculty members, and 140,000 alumni. The University has been recognized in numerous college guides for its excellent academic programs, knowledgeable professors, and top-notch athletics. It has also been called a top value and a best buy.

UConn encompasses seventeen schools and colleges that offer eight undergraduate degrees in ninety-eight majors, twelve graduate degrees in eighty fields of study, and graduate professional programs in law, medicine, and dental medicine. The University consistently attracts and accepts some of the nation's most talented students. The University's faculty members are among the most impressive scholars in the U.S. and are recognized throughout the world as leaders in education, research, and scholarship. Ninety-one percent have a Ph.D. or the highest degree in their field.

The University's research activities advance knowledge in a range of academic disciplines. UConn stands among the country's leading institutions in the breadth and contribution of its research. The Carnegie Foundation classifies UConn as a Research I University; it is one of only two public universities in New England to hold this distinction. In terms of research funding, UConn is ranked in the top thirty-five public universities by the National Science Foundation.

UConn's library system maintains the largest publicly supported collection of research materials in Connecticut. The Homer Babbidge Library on the main campus in Storrs contains 2.1 million volumes and is among the top thirty major research libraries nationally in terms of total holdings and funding. The University is home to the Roper Center for Public Opinion Research, the world's most comprehensive library of public opinion and survey data, and the Thomas Dodd Research Center, which maintains an international collection of historical manuscripts and archives, including an agreement between the African National Congress (ANC) and UConn to form a partnership to achieve and share with scholars material from the ANC's struggle for human rights in South Africa.

UConn's flagship campus is located on a beautiful 4,000-acre setting in Storrs, Connecticut. The University also offers the convenience and accessibility of campuses in Stamford, West Hartford, and Waterbury as well as the natural splendor of its Torrington and Avery Point facilities. The University's school of law is located in Hartford, while its schools of medicine and dental medicine are located at the University of Connecticut Health Center in Farmington. A graduate school of social work is in West Hartford. Through UCONN 2000, a landmark ten-year, $1-billion plan to renew, rebuild, and enhance UConn's campuses, the University is building and maintaining superior academic facilities throughout the state and creating state-of-the-art residential and recreational facilities at its main campus in Storrs.

The University of Connecticut maintains a strong tradition of student involvement. More than 250 clubs and organizations offer students access to everything from academic discussion groups to a vast assortment of intramural recreational programs offered in state-of-the-art facilities. UConn's athletic programs perennially rank among the best in the country. UConn offers twenty-two men's and women's varsity sports, most competing at the highest level. The Storrs campus also has student-run media, including radio station WHUS, *The Daily Campus* newspaper, and cable television station UCTV.

Location

The University is located in Storrs, Connecticut, midway between New York and Boston, each of which is about 1½ to 2½ hours away. The most used route to the University is exit 68 off I-84. The University's property to the east of the highway on the knoll where the campus begins includes pastures, hilltop cornfields, and picturesque barns, charming reminders of the area's agricultural origins of more than a century ago. Connecticut's capital city, Hartford, is only a half hour away. UConn is a cultural and recreational focal point in Connecticut.

Majors and Degrees

Undergraduates at the University of Connecticut may major in any of the more than ninety-eight different fields. The College of Liberal Arts and Sciences offers the Bachelor of Arts and Bachelor of Science degrees in approximately thirty-nine academic areas, ranging from anthropology to statistics and including coastal studies, ecology and evolutionary biology, and journalism. The College of Agriculture and Natural Resources offers the Bachelor of Science in ten special areas, including natural resources and environmental science. The School of Allied Health offers the Bachelor of Science in dietetics and medical laboratory sciences and the integrated Bachelor of Science/Master of Science in physical therapy. The School of Business Administration offers the Bachelor of Science in nine areas, including accounting, finance, and management information systems. The School of Education offers the five-year integrated bachelor's/master's teacher education program as well as the Bachelor of Arts and Bachelor of Science degrees in the Department of Kinesiology including athletic training, fitness management, exercise physiology, sports marketing, and park and recreational management. The School of Engineering offers the Bachelor of Science in Engineering degree and has programs in biomedical, chemical, civil, computer engineering, computer science, electrical, environmental, materials, mechanical, and metallurgy and materials engineering and management and engineering for manufacturing (in conjunction with the School of Business Administration). The School of Family Studies offers the Bachelor of Science with a major in human development and family relations. The School of Fine Arts offers the Bachelor of Fine Arts and Bachelor of Music degrees with majors in art, dramatic arts, music, and puppetry. The School of Nursing offers the Bachelor of Science in nursing. The School of Pharmacy offers a four-year Bachelor of Science program in pharmacy studies and a six-year Doctor of Pharmacy program.

The University offers an individualized major to meet the needs of students whose academic interests encompass two or more of the academic departments. The University also offers a Bachelor of General Studies degree program at the junior-senior level for nontraditional part-time students. A two-year associate degree is available through the Ratcliffe Hicks School of Agriculture.

Academic Programs

Most bachelor's degree programs require the successful completion of 120 semester hours. The exceptions are nursing, which requires 131 semester hours; engineering, which requires 134; pharmacy studies, which requires 125, the Doctor of Pharmacy, which requires 196; physical therapy (an integrated Bachelor of Science/Master of Science program), which requires 153; and education (an integrated bachelor's and master's degree program), which requires 150 semester hours. All programs require the completion of courses in eight core areas in addition to the work required for the major. UConn follows a two-semester system. Shorter sessions are offered for summer study and during the intersession between the fall and spring semesters.

Entering freshmen at Storrs may be selected for admission to the Honors Scholar Program, a nationally competitive academic program for outstanding students. Admission to the program at a later time, but before the junior year, is open to students who have done exceptional work at the University.

A cooperative education program for students in most majors integrates classroom learning and work experience in business, industry, and public service. The University offers interdisciplinary majors in Latin American, Slavic, and East European language and area studies; urban and women's studies; environmental science; and mathematical actuarial science. Individualized majors are available in Judaic, Asian, European, Native American, medieval, and peace studies, as well as in public relations, international studies, and criminology. Intensive study of critical languages such as Arabic, Chinese, or Japanese is also offered. Army and Air Force ROTC programs are available.

Off-Campus Programs

The University grants credit for programs and courses taken abroad through programs sponsored by the University as well as other institutions and agencies in Argentina, Australia, Austria, Brazil, Canada, Chile, China, Costa Rica, Czech Republic, Denmark, Dominican Republic, England, France, Germany, Ghana, Hungary, Ireland, Israel, Italy, Japan, Mexico, the Netherlands, Poland, Portugal, Russia, Spain, Sweden, and Switzerland. The Semester-at-Sea Program is also offered. Since 1968, through the Urban Semester Program, the University has given students a special educational opportunity to live, learn, and work in Hartford, Connecticut. The University also participates in the National Student Exchange Program, which allows students to spend a year of study at another university.

Academic Facilities

The University's facilities are undergoing a huge transformation, thanks to a ten-year, $1-billion commitment from Connecticut's state legislature. Now in its seventh year, the program already has resulted in a completely renovated Student Recreational Facility, four multilevel buildings that comprise the South Campus residence halls, a 220,000-square-foot chemistry building, a biotechnology building, six additional student residence halls, more than forty classrooms that have been renovated, and the University's first parking garage. In addition, construction is complete on a new physics/biology building, the Avery Point Marine Sciences Building, a new School of Business Administration, a second parking garage/bookstore, and two new residential complexes. The University's academic core has been transformed into a pedestrian campus. At least a dozen more buildings, including a huge addition to the Student Union, are scheduled for completion in the next three years. The Homer Babbidge Library at Storrs houses more than 2 million volumes, more than 3.1 million units of microtext, 603,790 government documents, and 7,867 current periodical subscriptions. It is one of the most technologically sophisticated research libraries in the United States. Specialized libraries in music and pharmacy are housed separately in those schools and raise the library systems total holdings to approximately 2.1 million volumes, including the regional campuses and law school. The art department has spacious, well-lighted studios and galleries. Other academic facilities provide specialized classroom and laboratory space for psychology, communication sciences, pathobiology, material sciences, physics, computer science, and human development and family relations, to name but a few. Computer facilities and laboratories are located in libraries, academic buildings, and residential facilities. There are 1,800 computers on campus in approximately ninety computer labs. The University also has an art museum, the William Benton Museum of Art, and the State Museum of Natural History. Theatrical, musical, and speaker programs take place in the Harriet S. Jorgensen Theatre, the Albert N. Jorgensen Auditorium, and the von der Mehden Recital Hall.

Costs

For students attending the Storrs campus, tuition and University and student fees are $7338 for state residents and $19,066 for out-of-state students in 2004–05. The average residence hall cost is $3872 and the seven-day University meal plan costs $3428. For students attending the University at a regional campus, in-state tuition and University and student fees total $6140 in 2004–05.

Financial Aid

Financial assistance in the form of grants, low-interest loans, and part-time employment is administered by the Student Financial Aid Office. All financial aid applications must be submitted by March 1 for both the fall and spring semesters. The assessment of need is based on the ability of the student's family to contribute, the amount of the student's savings for college, and other financial resources that may be available. To be considered for financial aid, all applicants must submit the Free Application for Federal Student Aid (FAFSA). Applicants for the Federal Stafford Student Loan must also file the FAFSA. The University awards a number of renewable merit-based scholarships to students with outstanding academic credentials, as well as to Finalists and Semifinalists in the National Merit Scholarship, National Achievement, and Hispanic Scholars programs.

Faculty

Nearly 91 percent of the University's 1,096 full-time faculty members hold a doctorate or another terminal degree in their field. The student-faculty ratio is 17:1. Faculty members at all levels teach undergraduate courses, including freshman courses. Faculty members engage in a wide variety of research, which in recent years has been sponsored by grants totaling about $110 million for the University and its Health Center schools.

Student Government

All undergraduates are members of the Undergraduate Student Government, the principal and officially recognized organization representing the undergraduate student body. The units of governance and service formed by this body reflect the major areas of interest and need among the students.

Admission Requirements

Applicants must be graduates of an approved secondary school and have completed at least 16 units of work. At least 15 of the secondary school units must consist of college-preparatory work, including 4 years of English, 2 years of a single foreign language (3 years strongly recommended), 3 years of mathematics (2 years of algebra and 1 year of geometry or the equivalent), 2 years of a laboratory science, and 2 years of social science, including at least 1 year of U.S. history. Several of the undergraduate schools and colleges of the University have additional course prerequisites for admission. Applicants should be in the upper range of their high school graduating class and must submit satisfactory scores on the SAT I or ACT. SAT II Subject Tests are not required for admission. The University is committed to ensuring access to higher education for students from minority groups. Transfer students are also encouraged to apply; their admission depends primarily upon the quality of the college record, the quantity and character of courses completed, and the intended field of study at the University. Advanced standing or course credit may be given to students on the basis of Advanced Placement examinations or through successful completion of regular University courses sponsored by the University at selected Connecticut secondary schools. Campus visits and interviews are encouraged although not required.

Application and Information

The application form, available from the University's Admissions Office or from the guidance offices of all Connecticut high schools, should be submitted early in the senior year of high school or no later than February 1 for freshmen; the application deadline for transfer students is April 1. For all students, the financial aid application deadline is March 1.

For more information, students should contact:

Office of Undergraduate Admissions
University of Connecticut
2131 Hillside Road, Box Unit 3088
Storrs, Connecticut 06269-3088
Telephone: 860-486-3137 (freshmen and transfers)
860-486-4900 (Lodewick Visitors Center)
E-mail: beahusky@uconn.edu
World Wide Web: http://www.uconn.edu/

UNIVERSITY OF DALLAS

IRVING, TEXAS, AND ROME, ITALY

The University

In 1955, the Roman Catholic Diocese of Dallas/Fort Worth purchased land for a university on a 1,000-acre tract of rolling hills northwest of Dallas, and in 1956 the University of Dallas (UD) opened. His Excellency Bishop Thomas K. Gorman, Chancellor of the new university, announced that it would be a coeducational institution welcoming students of all faiths and ethnic backgrounds. Headed by a lay president and a lay academic dean, the faculty was composed of laymen, diocesan and Cistercian priests, and sisters of the Order of St. Mary of Namur.

Current undergraduate enrollment is about 1,250 men and women. Undergraduates come from all fifty states and thirty-three other countries. Although approximately 75 percent are Catholic, twenty faiths are represented on campus.

The University of Dallas was the first Catholic institution to have a board of trustees made up of both lay and religious members. Since its founding, many other universities and colleges have followed its example. The first class, a group of individuals who won significant honors, such as Fulbright and Woodrow Wilson fellowships, was graduated in 1960. There is a Phi Beta Kappa chapter on campus.

Through a $6-million endowment provided by the Blakley-Braniff Foundation, the Braniff Graduate School was established in 1966. Twelve graduate programs are now in existence, including doctoral programs in philosophy, politics, and literature and the M.F.A. program in art. The College of Business houses the Graduate School of Management, which is distinguished by its practice-oriented education, close ties with leading companies and professionals, and a global student body. In addition to its undergraduate programs, the College of Business offers Master of Business Administration and Master of Management degrees. The M.B.A. includes sixteen concentrations in the areas of finance, health care, information technology, management, marketing, and telecommunications.

The University of Dallas is a center of learning, and the experience on campus is intensive and highly directed. People choose to come to the University because they are serious students, and, while they engage in a full complement of extracurricular activities and independent study, it is the act of learning in association with their professors that shapes their college years. Because the undergraduate college is small and largely residential, it forms a close-knit community. The University sponsors a number of lectures, concerts, and art exhibits, ranging from the old masters to the UD international printmaking invitational. The Student Government sponsors weekly events and current and classic films. The *University News* has consistently won awards for excellence in writing and design. Collegium Cantorum, the a cappella liturgical choir, performs both nationally and internationally. Intercollegiate NCAA Division III sports include baseball, basketball, cross-country, golf, lacrosse, soccer, softball, tennis, track, and volleyball. Rugby and sailing are enjoyed at the club level. Eighty-five percent of the on-campus students are involved in intramurals: basketball, flag football, soccer, softball, paintball, and other sports. Traditional events include coffee houses featuring student entertainment, Charity Week, Mallapalooza, Oktoberfest, Spring Olympics, and Groundhog.

For Catholic students, daily and weekly Mass, Reconciliation, and rosary are held in the 500-seat Church of the Incarnation. Transportation is arranged for students of other faiths to attend services nearby. Campus Ministry provides numerous volunteer opportunities, including annual service projects in Appalachia and Ecuador.

Location

Irving, Texas, a city of 195,000 on the northwest side of the city of Dallas, is about 15 minutes from downtown Dallas, 10 minutes from Love Field airport, and 15 minutes from DFW airport. The Dallas–Fort Worth Metroplex offers a diverse mix of cultural and entertainment attractions, including the Dallas Museum of Modern Art, the new Nasher Sculpture Center and the Kimbell Museum in Fort Worth. The Dallas Theater Center and Stage One have built reputations as top-notch theaters and as proving grounds for Broadway-bound productions. Texas Stadium, home of the Dallas Cowboys, is just three blocks from the University. Dallas is home to professional sports teams in hockey, soccer, and basketball. Nearby Arlington is home to the Texas Rangers.

Majors and Degrees

The Constantin College of Liberal Arts offers programs leading to the Bachelor of Arts degree in art and art history, biology, business, chemistry, classics, computer science, drama, economics, economics and finance, education, English, history, mathematics, modern languages (French, German, and Spanish), philosophy, physics, politics, psychology, and theology. The Bachelor of Science degree is awarded in biochemistry, biology, chemistry, mathematics, and physics.

The College of Business offers Bachelor of Arts degrees in business leadership.

The University offers 27-credit concentrations, including applied math, applied physics, art history, business, Christian contemplative studies, computer science, entrepreneurship, environmental science, international studies, journalism, math, medieval and Renaissance studies, modern language, music, and pure math.

Preprofessional programs in architecture, business, dentistry, engineering, law, medicine, and physical therapy are carefully integrated with the Core Curriculum of the Constantin College. The rate of acceptance and enrollment of the college's students by professional schools is exceptional. More than 60 percent go on to graduate school, and the rate of acceptance for medical and law school applicants is more than 90 percent.

A five-year, dual-degree program allows students to combine any undergraduate major with the graduate program in business management. Upon completion of the program, a student will have earned both the B.A. and M.B.A. degrees.

Academic Programs

The Core Curriculum is a shared series of specific courses that outline the development of Western thought and culture from classical to modern times. Every student becomes familiar with the same works of literature and the same great books and concepts, fostering a natural understanding and exchange of ideas. All students then go on to pursue their chosen major discipline, reaching a level of maturity and competence in the discipline that they could not have attained in the absence of a broad general foundation. The student body has an active and personal involvement with the Core Curriculum.

The University observes a two-semester calendar, with the semester examinations occurring before the monthlong Christmas break. An interterm session and three summer sessions are also offered.

Off-Campus Programs

All undergraduates, regardless of major, are encouraged to spend one semester on the University's campus in Rome. While not compulsory, the Rome experience is an important part of the undergraduate education; to seek one's heritage in the liberal arts and to be a student of the Western world is, in a sense, to be a citizen of Rome. Courses offered in Rome are from the Core Curriculum and are taught by professors from the Texas campus. The Rome campus is located just outside of downtown Rome. Transfer students who need courses offered on the Rome campus may participate after one semester on the main campus. The cost for tuition, room, and board for all participants is roughly equivalent to that on the main campus. More than 80 percent of University of Dallas graduates have participated in the Rome program.

Academic Facilities

The Science Center, a $6-million state-of-the-art facility, houses some of the most advanced tools for scientific research available, including a working observatory. The Haggerty Arts Village has established the University as a leading center for ceramics and fine arts in the Southwest. Drama productions are staged in the Margaret Jonsson Theater. Blakely Library holds more than 275,000 volumes, including the personal library of the late political philosopher Wilmoore Kendall.

Costs

The cost of tuition and fees for 2003–04 was $18,104; room and board costs averaged $6100. Costs were the same for in-state and out-of-state students.

Financial Aid

Tuition, fees, room, and board are substantially lower at the University of Dallas than at many other nationally recognized universities. In addition, all high school seniors who apply for admission by the freshman scholarship priority deadline of January 15 receive priority consideration for all of the University's achievement-based awards. The University currently offers four types of achievement-based awards: academic achievements, community achievements, leadership achievements, and special talents. Talent areas currently recognized include art, business, chemistry, classics (Latin and Greek), German, French, math, physics, and Spanish. Students who apply for admission between January 16 and March 1 receive regular consideration for achievement-based awards. Those who apply for admission after March 1 are considered for achievement-based awards dependent on the availability of funding.

All students who submit a Free Application for Federal Student Aid (FAFSA) are considered for all forms of financial assistance based on their family's finances. These forms of assistance include scholarships, grants, loans, and work-study programs. Priority is given to applicants whose FAFSA is received by the University of Dallas on or before March 1. The school code for sending a FAFSA to the University of Dallas is 003651.

Faculty

The University prides itself on its teaching faculty. Ninety-two percent hold terminal degrees. There are no graduate assistants. With a faculty-student ratio of 1:12, extensive consultation and direction are possible. The average class size is 19. The faculty is characterized by authority in the various disciplines, and its members have published more than a thousand books and articles and secured major research grants.

Student Government

The Student Government Association and various departmental and special clubs, such as the social, film, lecture, and fine arts committees, encourage an extracurricular life created by the students themselves.

Admission Requirements

Although no rigid cutoff point is adhered to in admission, 52 percent of the students who enter as freshmen rank in the top 10 percent of their high school class. General admission requirements include SAT I or ACT scores, rank in upper third of the high school class, and 16 college-preparatory units, including 4 in English, 3 in mathematics, 2 in the same foreign language, 2 in social science, and 2 in a laboratory science. Interviews are not required but are strongly recommended. Through the Office of Undergraduate Admission, counseling appointments, tours, and overnight accommodations on campus may be arranged. Transfer students are welcome.

Application and Information

A transcript, official rank in class, and SAT I or ACT scores must be submitted along with a letter of recommendation and a completed application form, obtainable online or via mail or telephone from the Office of Admission. Transfer students should submit all transcripts from colleges previously attended. A $50 application fee should accompany the application; the other material may follow as ready. Early action deadline is December 1. Freshman priority scholarship deadline is January 15. Regular admission deadline is March 1. Rolling admission is March 2–August 1.

For applications or further information, students should contact:

Office of Undergraduate Admission and Financial Aid
University of Dallas
1845 East Northgate Drive
Irving, Texas 75062
Telephone: 972-721-5266
800-628-6999 (toll-free)
World Wide Web: http://www.udallas.edu

The University of Dallas campus.

UNIVERSITY OF DAYTON

DAYTON, OHIO

The University

Established in 1850 by the Marianists, the University of Dayton (UD) is a Catholic leader in higher education, committed to educating students as value-centered leaders in their chosen professions and in society. More than 10,000 students attend UD, including 6,500 full-time undergraduate students. Students attracted to the University come from most states and many countries. More than 95 percent of full-time undergraduates live on campus. The technology-enhanced learning and student computer initiative provides every student living in a UD residence with high-speed data access to learning resources and collaboration tools. Extensive programs of study are offered in the College of Arts and Sciences and in the Schools of Business Administration, Education and Allied Professions, Engineering, and Law.

The residential nature of the campus encourages active extracurricular involvement. More than 190 clubs and organizations exist on campus, including more than thirty service organizations, forty professional clubs, fourteen honor societies, recreation/sports clubs, theatrical and musical performance groups, and fraternities and sororities. NCAA Division I intercollegiate athletics as well as intramural sports are also prevalent. Men's intercollegiate teams include baseball, basketball, cross-country, football, golf, soccer, and tennis. Women's intercollegiate sports include basketball, crew, cross-country, golf, indoor and outdoor track, soccer, softball, tennis, and volleyball. Club sports such as archery, lacrosse, rugby, and soccer are also popular. A variety of special events include everything from symposia and concerts to parents' weekends and a huge Christmas on Campus celebration each December 8.

The John F. Kennedy Memorial Union offers a variety of services for the University community, including numerous cultural, educational, social, and recreational activities. The facility includes a theater; an art gallery; a food court containing a pizzeria, a bakery, a grill, a delicatessen, and a candy counter; WGXM, a student-operated FM radio station; Flyer TV, a student-run television station; and the commuter lounge. A $1 million renovation to the Kennedy Union games room provides bowling lanes, billiards, a cyber café, games, a lounge, and performance space.

Location

The campus is located on a 123-acre hilltop, 2 miles from the city of Dayton. The Dayton metropolitan area is a vibrant, growing community of approximately 950,000 people in southwestern Ohio. Top cultural, recreational, and entertainment programs are available during the year. Varied business, industrial, research, and educational enterprises provide students with extensive work opportunities related to their academic disciplines.

Majors and Degrees

The College of Arts and Sciences offers the Bachelor of Arts degree in American studies, art history, chemistry, communication (electronic media, journalism, communication management, public relations, and theater), criminal justice studies, economics, English, fine arts, geology, history, international studies and human rights, languages (French, German, and Spanish), mathematics, music, philosophy, photography, political science, psychology, religious studies, sociology, theater, and visual communication design.

The Bachelor of Science is awarded in applied mathematical economics, biochemistry, biology, chemistry, computer information systems, computer science, environmental biology, environmental geology, geology, mathematics, physical science, physics, physics–computer science, predentistry, premedicine, and psychology.

The School of Business Administration offers the Bachelor of Science degree in accounting, business economics, finance, international business, management information systems, management (leadership), marketing, and operations management.

The Bachelor of Science in Education is awarded in the ADA didactic program in dietetics, exercise science/fitness management, exercise science/fitness and nutrition, exercise science/pre-physical therapy, physical education, and sport management through the Department of Health and Sport Science. Through the Department of Teacher Education, a Bachelor of Science degree is awarded in early childhood education, intervention specialist (special education), middle childhood education, and adolescent to young adult education.

The School of Engineering awards the Bachelor of Chemical Engineering, Bachelor of Civil Engineering, Bachelor of Science in Computer Engineering, Bachelor of Electrical Engineering, and Bachelor of Mechanical Engineering. The School of Engineering also offers a Bachelor of Science in engineering technology, one of the few four-year programs available in the country. Programs include computer engineering technology, electronic engineering technology, industrial engineering technology, manufacturing engineering technology, and mechanical engineering technology.

The University also offers the Bachelor of Fine Arts (art education, fine arts, photography, and visual communication design), Bachelor of Music (music composition, music education, music performance, and music therapy), and Bachelor of General Studies. Undeclared admission options are offered in the College of Arts and Sciences and the Schools of Business Administration, Education and Allied Professions, and Engineering. A prelaw program (including advising and assistance in course selection) is available to students in all degree programs.

Academic Programs

The academic year consists of two semesters, with two 6-week sessions available during the summer. While graduation requirements vary according to academic majors, a minimum of 120 semester credit hours is required of all bachelor's degree programs. Students following four-year programs must successfully complete requirements in communication, English, mathematics, and philosophy and/or religious studies. Likewise, the University has instituted a program of study for all students that provides a general education in the humanities, arts, and social and natural sciences. This program develops students' abilities to integrate their knowledge and express themselves effectively. The University offers two distinct honors programs for its most academically accomplished students. Both the University Honors Program and the John W. Berry Sr. Scholars Program provide UD students with an enhanced undergraduate education. The programs' academic benefits and privileges are numerous and multifaceted but are unified by the distinctive qualities of undergraduate research, international experience, and service and leadership. Several opportunities also exist for students to integrate traditional academic majors with many progressive, innovative programs. These programs include study abroad, cooperative education and internship programs, the ability to earn the B.A. or B.S. degree with teacher certification, and multidisciplinary programs.

Academic Facilities

ArtStreet, an innovative living and learning complex, combines student residence quarters with performance and visual arts spaces, a recording studio, a radio station, and a café. Construction is scheduled to be completed in fall 2004. At the Arena Sports Complex, a practice track and football practice field were completed in fall 2003. Additional construction, to be completed in fall 2004, includes a baseball facility, an area for long jumping and pole vault, a softball field, and track throwing fields. Construction is scheduled for completion in fall 2004 for a new residence hall on Founder's Field for student housing, a book store, a post office, a credit union, a food emporium, worship space, and a learning center. The student housing component consists of three 4-story residential wings with a total of 400 beds.

Construction began in spring 2004 on a new fitness and recreation complex, Rec Plex. The facility will include four courts for basketball and volleyball; three racquetball courts; two courts for aerobics, basketball, floor hockey, inline hockey, lacrosse, a rope course, soccer, tennis and volleyball; two aerobics/multipurpose rooms; sixty cardiovascular machines; sixty weight machines; a free-weight area; a ⅛-mile track; administrative offices; classrooms; a climbing wall; a juice bar; a lounge; men's and women's locker rooms; an eight-lane natatorium; an outdoor deck; a sand volleyball court; and a whirlpool.

Other recently completed campus construction projects include the Science Center, a 44,000-square-foot facility that connects Sherman and Wohlleben Halls. New construction and renovations provide for new laboratories, classrooms, offices, and gathering spaces. The first phase of the central mall project, which provides green space adjacent to Kennedy Union, was completed in fall 2003. In addition, University-owned houses in the student neighborhood have been and continue to be rebuilt or renovated.

Existing campus facilities include the recently renovated Miriam Hall, home of the School of Business Administration, the Davis Center for Portfolio Management, and the Crotty Center for Entrepreneurial Leadership. Opened in 2000, the Ryan C. Harris Learning-Teaching Center is technologically ahead of its time with a wireless network installed throughout the center. This high-tech, experimental learning space includes a meeting room with groupware capability and an adaptive computer lab to help students with physical or learning disabilities. Roesch Library, an eight-story facility with more than 1.2 million volumes, provides exceptional resources for research and scholarship. The Anderson Information Sciences Center, a $3.5-million complex donated to the University by NCR Corporation, contains state-of-the-art undergraduate computer laboratories and classrooms. Kettering Laboratories, location of the School of Engineering, also houses part of the University of Dayton Research Institute, which performs more than $40 million annually in research. The University's nationally famous general education program is housed in the Jesse Philips Center for the Humanities, which opened in fall 1993. The $4.3-million Donoher Basketball Center, a 23,000-square-foot, NBA-quality facility, opened in fall 1998.

Costs

Tuition, including the University fee, for 2004–05 is $10,125 per semester. The cost of a double room in a residence hall is $1800 per semester. Private and University-owned accommodations are available off campus for upperclass students. Three types of meal plan contracts are available, beginning at $1350 per term. To cover weekend meals and other food expenses, students may open a debit account, Flyer Express, which is accepted at most on-campus locations as well as select vendors.

Financial Aid

Each year, more than 90 percent of first-year UD students receive financial aid. Assistance is available in the form of nonrepayable grants, educational loans, and part-time employment. A parent loan program and a University-sponsored payment plan are available. Students applying for federal, state, and University-sponsored financial aid must complete the Free Application for Federal Student Aid (FAFSA). Priority is given to students whose completed applications are received by the office of scholarships and financial aid by March 31.

UD has an extensive academic scholarship program. Scholarships are based on academic achievement, demonstrated leadership, and athletic and artistic talent. Students must complete the Application for Undergraduate Admission and Scholarship. UD prefers early submission; the application priority date is January 1, but students are strongly encouraged to apply before the Christmas holiday. Athletic scholarships are available in men's intercollegiate basketball, baseball, soccer, golf, tennis, and cross-country, as well as women's intercollegiate basketball, volleyball, soccer, softball, golf, tennis, indoor/outdoor track, and cross-country. Athletic scholarship eligibility is determined by the Department of Intercollegiate Athletics. Music awards are available for both music majors and nonmajors who distinguish themselves as outstanding performers at their admission audition. Scholarships for musical or visual art talents are determined by the faculties of the appropriate academic departments.

A financial aid counselor is available to meet with interested students and their parents to review information pertaining to financial aid eligibility. High school seniors and their parents who are interested in receiving an estimate of financial aid eligibility are encouraged to request an appointment when scheduling a campus visit and should complete the free Financial Need Estimator at http://admission.udayton.edu/finaid/estimator.asp prior to their visit or bring along a copy of their completed FAFSA form so that their eligibility for aid can be discussed in detail.

Faculty

There are 401 full-time faculty members, 94 percent of whom hold a Ph.D. or terminal degree. UD faculty members have been recognized for their excellence by several organizations, including General Motors Corporation, the National Institute of Education, and the National Endowment for the Humanities. Professors are actively engaged in research and scholarship, often involving undergraduate students, but their primary focus is teaching. Classes are generally small enough for close personal contact. Faculty members act as advisers to students and are frequently accessible in and out of the classroom.

Student Government

The Student Government Association (SGA) is an autonomous association that concerns itself with the academic, recreational, and cultural welfare of UD students. SGA support prompted the opening of UD's first student-owned and -operated convenience store. The organization's efforts were instrumental in creating the National Association for Students at Catholic Colleges and Universities, which addresses the specific concerns of Catholic campuses. SGA-sponsored activities include a speaker series, Little Siblings' Weekend, and the annual Dayton-to-Daytona trip.

Admission Requirements

The University of Dayton admits qualified students regardless of sex, race, color, creed, national or ethnic origin, age, or handicap. Students possessing the aptitude and motivation to succeed at UD are encouraged to apply for admission. Balanced consideration is given to all aspects of students' demonstrated preparation, including selection of college-preparatory courses, grade point average and grade pattern throughout high school, class rank, standardized test scores (SAT I or ACT), and record of leadership and service. A personal statement and guidance counselor recommendation are strongly recommended. In recent years, more than 75 percent of entering students graduated in the top half of their high school class.

Applicants should present 16 core units from an accredited high school. The minimum core includes 4 units in English, 4 electives, 3 in math, 3 in social studies, and 2 in science. Some programs may require more extensive preparation in specific subject areas. Two units of a foreign language are required for admission to the College of Arts and Sciences. Students who plan to major in a natural science, mathematics, computer science, engineering, or business will find a strong mathematics background necessary.

Application and Information

There is only one way to apply to the University of Dayton—online. Students must submit their Application for Undergraduate Admission and Scholarship electronically at the Web site listed below. Applicants must also submit a satisfactory high school record and results of the SAT I or ACT examination. The University operates on a rolling admission policy; however, there is a priority deadline of January 1. The first notifications of acceptance are mailed in October. Some academic programs close new student enrollment before others, so it is recommended that students apply as early as possible.

The UD admission Web site allows students to apply for admission and scholarship, use a free financial need estimator service, check the status of their application, and take a virtual tour.

Office of Admission
University of Dayton
300 College Park
Dayton, Ohio 45469-1300
Telephone: 937-229-4411
800-837-7433 (toll-free)
E-mail: admission@udayton.edu
World Wide Web: http://admission.udayton.edu/

UNIVERSITY OF DAYTON
School of Engineering
DAYTON, OHIO

The University

The University of Dayton was founded in 1850 and the School of Engineering in 1910. The total undergraduate enrollment in engineering and engineering technology is approximately 1,131, of whom 867 are in the undergraduate engineering programs and 264 are in the engineering technology programs. States with the largest enrollments are New York, New Jersey, Pennsylvania, Indiana, Illinois, and Ohio. Twenty-nine countries are represented. The total University undergraduate enrollment is approximately 7,103.

The University engages in intercollegiate competition in baseball, basketball, cross-country, football, golf, soccer, and tennis. Top-ranked basketball teams meet the University team in a modern arena that seats 13,409. The Kennedy Union is a center for social life.

Location

With its suburbs, Dayton has a metropolitan population of nearly 951,200. The area offers the recreational, cultural, social, and educational facilities that are usually found in communities of this size. It is within commuting distance of Cincinnati (60 minutes), and Indianapolis and Columbus are nearby.

Ohio ranks high among the states in the number of engineers and technologists who live within its boundaries. There is a heavy concentration of technology in the area, which is an excellent setting for a school of engineering and technology. Many engineering and engineering technology students either work part-time or serve summer internships in local industry.

Majors and Degrees

The School of Engineering offers four-year curricula leading to the degrees of Bachelor of Chemical Engineering, Bachelor of Civil Engineering, Bachelor of Electrical Engineering, Bachelor of Mechanical Engineering, Bachelor of Science in computer engineering, and Bachelor of Science in engineering technology. Engineering Technology curricula are offered in computer engineering technology, electronic engineering technology, industrial engineering technology, manufacturing engineering technology, and mechanical engineering technology.

Academic Program

The engineering program in each of the fields is designed to lead to a bachelor's degree in a four-year period. For the bachelor's degrees in engineering, the number of semester hours required varies from 130 to 136; for the Bachelor of Science in technology, from 129 to 131. For graduation, the cumulative grade point average must be 2.0 or higher. Each engineering program is flexible and permits additional minors in such areas as industrial, environmental, aerospace, and materials engineering, as well as mathematics, music, and languages. Students who major in any engineering technology program may earn a minor in another engineering technology program by completing 12 approved semester hours of work in the second discipline. In addition, the Department of Mechanical and Aerospace Engineering offers students the opportunity to pursue a concentration in aerospace engineering.

As the first-year curriculum is the same for all branches of engineering, students may choose to wait until they have completed the first year before deciding on their special field.

As an educational unit within a private university, the School places strong emphasis on the individualized faculty/student advising program that begins before the start of the student's formal course work at the University. The advising program is designed to ensure that each student is challenged and meets his or her educational objectives within the School's program by being paired with a faculty member. Advanced placement is granted to those students who qualify under certain AP testing programs.

At the end of the junior year in engineering, students qualified for graduate study may arrange their senior year to include some courses for graduate credit.

Students may participate in the cooperative education, internship, and summer employment programs. These programs offer the student the opportunity to put classroom work into practical use while still in school, resulting in early career identification and greater motivation as well as providing a source of income.

Academic Facilities

The Eugene W. Kettering Engineering and Research Laboratories houses nearly all of the engineering, technology, and Research Institute activities. The six-floor structure is air conditioned and contains 88 laboratories, 3 computer classrooms, 11 classrooms, 115 faculty offices, and 8 seminar rooms in 211,000 square feet of space. All departments in the school are directly connected with the facilities of the University computer center.

The University engages in approximately $50 million worth of research each year. Several research projects at the University of Dayton are attracting international attention.

Costs

Tuition and University fees for 2004–05 are $19,570 for two terms. The engineering surcharge is $600 per term. Room and board on campus is approximately $5890 for two terms. Books and supplies cost approximately $600 to $650 per term.

Financial Aid

The University of Dayton attempts to help all qualified students in obtaining financial assistance to continue their education. The University has established a comprehensive program of student aid that includes loans, grants, scholarships, tuition reductions, and part-time employment. Approximately 90 percent of the students receive financial aid, primarily in the form of scholarships, grants, work-study, and loans. For a detailed description, interested students may write for a financial aid brochure.

Faculty

The School of Engineering has 71 full-time and 51 part-time faculty members, most of whom have doctoral degrees. Graduate assistants are employed in laboratory and research work, but classroom instruction is always conducted by regular faculty members. All faculty members serve as advisers to the students.

Student Government

The Student Government is the major vehicle for student opinion at the University of Dayton. Other student groups abound, including special interest clubs, service organizations, the Interfraternity Council, and the Panhellenic Council. There are twenty-one student organizations related to engineering and engineering technology.

Admission Requirements

Applicants for the first-year class must have graduated from a high school accredited by a regional accrediting association or by a state department of education. The following units are recommended for entrance into the engineering program: English, 4; algebra, 1; geometry, 1; trigonometry/algebra II, 1; math IV, 1; chemistry, 1; physics, 1; and foreign language, 2–4. For the engineering technology program, it is recommended that students have 4 units of English, 2 units of algebra, and 1 unit in another mathematics area.

To apply for entrance into the first-year class, candidates must submit an online application, a transcript of their high school record, and scores from the SAT I or ACT.

The School of Engineering welcomes transfer students from both community and senior colleges and works closely with many schools to facilitate transfers from pre-engineering programs. Students may complete the first two years of study in other accredited institutions and transfer to the University of Dayton with little or no loss of credit provided they follow a program similar to that prescribed by the University of Dayton School of Engineering.

Application and Information

Students must submit the admission application electronically via the World Wide Web. Students may visit the University's admission page at http://admission.udayton.edu or go directly to the application at http://admission.udayton.edu/apply/application_login.asp. Applications are accepted throughout the year and reviewed on a rolling basis. Due to an increase in applications, some academic programs close new student enrollment early. The Office of Admission has implemented a priority application deadline of January 1. Students are encouraged to apply well in advance of the term in which they would like to enter the University.

For further information, students should contact:

Mr. Rob Durkle, Director of Admission
University of Dayton
300 College Park
Dayton, Ohio 45469-1300
Telephone: 937-229-4411
800-837-7433 (toll-free)
Fax: 937-229-4729
E-mail: admission@udayton.edu

Dean
School of Engineering
University of Dayton
300 College Park
Dayton, Ohio 45469-0228
Telephone: 937-229-2736
E-mail: udsoe@udayton.edu

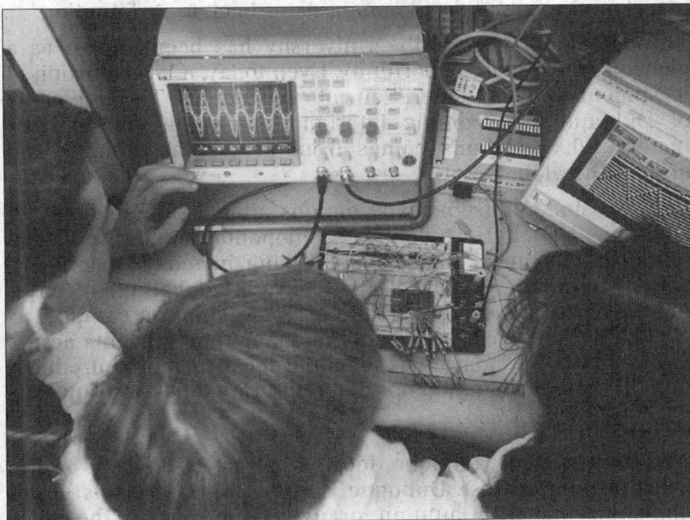

Students at the University of Dayton School of Engineering.

UNIVERSITY OF DUBUQUE

DUBUQUE, IOWA

The University

The University of Dubuque (UD) is a private, Presbyterian, professional university with a focus in the liberal arts, as well as a theological seminary in Iowa's first city—Dubuque. The Key City is on the Mississippi River at the point where the borders of Wisconsin, Illinois, and Iowa meet. Founded in 1852, the University is an institution in three parts: the undergraduate college, the graduate theological seminary, and the graduate institute. The University's mission of encouraging intellectual, moral, and spiritual development dates back to its founding.

Throughout its history, the University has been known as a place of educational opportunity. Even today, a large portion of its students are first generation college students. The University of Dubuque's welcoming interfaith community of approximately 1,000 students comes from across the country and around the globe.

Because students from many nations attend the University of Dubuque, UD offers students a cosmopolitan atmosphere. The school is convinced that students living in today's world are better prepared for life if they have a global perspective. American and international student interaction on campus, as well as the movement of faculty members and students across international boundaries, is essential for a meaningful education, human enrichment, and intercultural global awareness.

Location

The University of Dubuque, located in eastern Iowa, is in the heart of the Midwest. Dubuque is a city for all seasons. From bluffs blazing with autumn oranges and reds to the river sparkling with summer's blues and greens, the area scenery is spectacular year-round. Dubuque, the oldest city in Iowa, is a dynamic community built along the majestic Mississippi River and surrounded by dramatic bluffs. The setting is ideal for outdoor enthusiasts, with four seasons of ample outlets for recreation, including hiking, biking, boating, skiing, camping, golfing, climbing, and caving.

Dubuque offers the amenities of a larger city with the security and comfort of a smaller town. A lively cultural scene includes the Grand Opera House, the Dubuque Symphony Orchestra, and the Dubuque Museum of Art. The National Farm Toy Museum and the Mississippi River Museum provide glimpses of the area's past. The city's theater productions, boutiques, and restaurants are wonderful ways to take a study break.

Nearby are some of the Midwest's most interesting cities, an easy drive for a weekend road trip. Historic Galena offers quaint shops and period architecture, while vibrant Chicago is famous for its museums and night life. Madison, Milwaukee, and Minneapolis–St. Paul are only hours away.

Majors and Degrees

With seventeen undergraduate majors, the University prepares students for careers in a variety of fields. From future teachers to corporate leaders to aspiring pilots, the University of Dubuque helps students achieve their career goals. The University's education department has the most majors, and its future teachers graduate with twice as many field-experience hours as required by the state of Iowa.

The University plans the reinstatement of its Nursing Program in the fall 2004 semester. The program will offer a Bachelor of Science in Nursing (BSN) degree. Nursing began at University of Dubuque in 1976 and, until 1997, the program offered fully accredited RN-to-B.S.N., B.S.N., and M.S.N. nursing preparation. As early as possible, the University will move to renew the program's national accreditation.

Academic departments encourage internships as an experiential component to complement classroom learning. For example, environmental science majors take advantage of the natural classroom of the Mississippi River, where students study the interaction between people and the environment. Aviation majors complete internships at the Dubuque Regional Airport or major airlines in addition to flying state-of-the-art equipment from UD's Garlick Flight Operations Center.

Academic Program

The University of Dubuque education aims at helping students develop patterns of scholarship that make them effective learners throughout life. UD students are nurtured in the virtues of scholarship: the desire for understanding different peoples and cultures, an interest in learning, the skills to use multiple resources to explore ideas and find answers for life's questions, an understanding of conceptual connections, and the ability to reason and communicate effectively. Each graduate develops depth of knowledge in a particular field of study based on an integration of this field, the liberal arts, and his or her values.

University of Dubuque students begin to understand their chosen field of study by experiencing how it relates to other areas of knowledge. The process of exploring a variety of interests and possibilities in course work and in University activities results in the choice of a major. Current trends indicate that today's graduates change jobs and/or careers several times during their lifetimes. Therefore, professional preparation is more than a narrow, vocationally oriented process through which students prepare for one specific job. Rather, it is the development of transferable skills and attributes that allow students to succeed in a changing job market.

In the University of Dubuque community, the arts foster intellectual, emotional, and spiritual development. In literature, the visual arts, dance, drama, and music, students not only find aesthetic pleasure but also learn about other people's ideas, beliefs, and experiences and come to deeper understandings of their own.

Because of the University's location near the Mississippi—one of the world's great river systems—students have an appreciation of environmental issues. Through academic endeavors involving formal and experiential learning, students develop an understanding of the basic processes that underpin various ecological communities and of the complex interaction of human activities on the environment. The University of Dubuque encourages individuals to integrate their knowledge of the environment into personal, ethical, and spiritual guidelines, which can be used to improve their lives, their communities, and society.

Off-Campus Programs

As a member of the Dubuque Tri-College Cooperative Effort, the University of Dubuque offers its students the opportunity to attend and receive credit for courses at Clarke College and

Loras College, also in the city, thus providing access to the many different faculty members, professional societies, educational opportunities, and social activities of combined campuses of more than 3,500 students.

The University of Dubuque affirms the value of an international/intercultural experience and considers it to be an important component of any student's education. Overseas travel, exchanges, and study programs are available to help increase the global perspective of the students and to promote cross-cultural education.

Academic Facilities

In December 2002, just 2½ years after the original structure was completed, the University's Myers Library expansion welcomed students with additional classroom space, individual and group study rooms, and a cozy fireplace lounge where students can curl up with a good book. The original structure, completed in August 2000, substantially increased the floor space available in the previous facility. Students now have more access to books, periodicals, and special collections. With large glass windows and skylights along the south side of the building, students and faculty members enjoy a bright, open atmosphere that is aesthetically pleasing and conducive to study and research. Other features of the new library include a twenty-nine-station computer center, a multimedia laboratory, individual and small-group study areas, an Academic Support Center with the latest technology, and a coffee shop/café. Students and faculty members are able to employ the finest available technology in order to access information from around the country and across the globe.

An addition to and renovation of Goldthorp Science Hall is in the active-planning stage. The renovation and new construction brings state-of-the-art lab and research facilities to the campus.

Costs

Tuition costs for the 2003–04 academic year were $16,100. Average room and board costs were $5430. These costs do not include books, supplies, personal expenses, and travel.

Financial Aid

Eighty-five percent of the University of Dubuque's students receive financial assistance through scholarships, awards and grants, loans, or work-study programs. The average financial assistance package is $16,694. All levels of household incomes receive financial assistance.

To apply for financial assistance, applicants must submit a completed application package for admission to the University of Dubuque, file a FAFSA after January 1 and before April 1 (the priority deadline), and send or fax a copy of the completed FAFSA to the University of Dubuque Office of Student Financial Planning. Institutional, federal, state, and alternative loan programs are all available as forms of financial assistance.

Faculty

Seventy percent of University of Dubuque faculty members have earned a Ph.D. or terminal degree. The student-faculty ratio is 15:1.

Student Government

The Student Government Association (SGA) represents the student body through general election of individual student representatives. The SGA sponsors four campus organizations, the University Program Council (UPC), the Spartan Spirit Club, *Under the Bell Tower* (student newspaper), and *The Key* (student yearbook). SGA provides student representatives for a number of key administrative committees.

Admission Requirements

An applicant for admission to the University of Dubuque undergraduate program is a graduate of a high school or equivalent (GED) and presents a minimum of 15 high school units, of which 10 are from academic fields (English, social studies, natural science, mathematics, foreign language). Either ACT or SAT scores are required. The admission committee looks at the application and transcript for indications of school achievement as well as aspiration, creativity, and adventurousness. Applicants to the University are usually active in cocurricular activities and these, as well as leadership qualities and character, are considered. An on-campus visit is encouraged. Two recommendations and an essay are requested and read with care.

Application and Information

First-year students are admitted to the University on a rolling basis. When the application and all supporting materials (e.g., transcripts, teacher and counselor recommendations) have been received, admission decisions are made by the admission committee and students are advised of the University's decision.

Transfer students who are enrolled or who were previously enrolled at another college or university may apply for transfer to the University of Dubuque. The University considers transfer applications for fall and spring semesters.

In addition to completing the application materials required for first-year applicants, transfer applicants must submit a complete official transcript for all college courses taken and grades received and a complete official transcript for all secondary school courses taken and grades received.

For further information, students should contact:

Office of Admission
University of Dubuque
2000 University Avenue
Dubuque, Iowa 52001
Telephone: 563-589-3000
800-722-5583 (toll-free)
E-mail: admssns@dbq.edu
World Wide Web: http://www.dbq.edu

The newly expanded Myers Library.

UNIVERSITY OF EVANSVILLE

EVANSVILLE, INDIANA

The University

The University of Evansville (UE), established in 1854, is a private, coeducational university affiliated with the United Methodist Church. It offers a curriculum deeply entrenched in the traditional arts and sciences, while emphasizing skills essential to personal and professional success. Also inherent in the University of Evansville's educational mission is the enhancement of a student's view of the world. Students have the unique opportunity to experience study abroad at the University's own British campus, Harlaxton College, located in Grantham, England, or through a host of other international study opportunities made available to UE students. Approximately 43 percent of UE students study abroad, compared to 6 percent nationally.

The student body of 2,200 undergraduates is diverse; students come from forty-five states and forty-four countries. Students participate in more than 140 social and academic organizations and more than forty intercollegiate and intramural sports.

In addition to regional accreditation, the University has program accreditation with the American Bar Association, the Accreditation Board for Engineering and Technology, the American Chemical Society, the American Physical Therapy Association, the National Association of Schools of Music, the National Association for Music Therapy, the National Council for Accreditation of Teacher Education, and the National League for Nursing. Among the graduate degrees offered at the University is the Master of Science degree in health services administration, Master of Public Service Administration, and the entry-level Master of Science degree in physical therapy.

Location

With a population of 122,000, Evansville, Indiana, is the third-largest city in the state. It is situated at the southwestern corner of Indiana on the banks of the Ohio River in proximity to Indianapolis, Indiana; St. Louis, Missouri; Nashville, Tennessee; and Louisville, Kentucky. The city has a variety of cultural outlets, such as museums, galleries, theaters, and orchestras, as well as numerous outdoor recreation adventures such as hiking in the nearby Hoosier National Forest, boating on the Ohio River, and snow skiing at Paoli Peaks, to name a few.

Students gain valuable real-world experience from cooperative relationships between the University and tri-state area businesses and industries via cooperative work programs, internships, and externships.

Majors and Degrees

Within the College of Arts and Sciences, degrees are awarded with majors in archaeology, athletic training, biochemistry, biology, chemistry, classical and biblical studies, creative writing, economics, English, English literature, environmental administration, environmental studies, exercise science, French, German, health and physical education, history, international studies, interpersonal communication, legal studies, mass communication, mathematics, philosophy, physics, political science, psychobiology, psychology, religion, sociology, Spanish, sports medicine, and visual communication. Preprofessional programs are available in dentistry, law, medicine, optometry, pharmacy, social work, theology, and veterinary science. Minors are offered in anthropology, criminal justice, English as a new language, geography, and women's studies.

The School of Business Administration confers the Bachelor of Science in Business Administration, with concentrations in finance, global studies, management, and marketing; the Bachelor of Science in Accounting; and the Bachelor of Science in Economics.

The School of Education and Health Sciences confers the Bachelor of Science degree with majors in clinical special education, elementary education, physical education, and secondary education. Special education endorsements are available in education of the mildly disabled, seriously emotionally handicapped, and severely disabled. The School of Education participates in an Activity-Based Learning Experience program in elementary education, which enables students to take part in classroom experiences throughout their program. A Bachelor of Science degree in nursing, a master's degree, and an Associate of Science degree in physical therapist assistant studies are available, as is a certificate of specialization in gerontology.

The College of Engineering and Computer Science grants the Bachelor of Science degree in civil, computer, electrical, and mechanical engineering, as well as in computer science, engineering management, and Internet technology. Degree programs in civil, computer, electrical, and mechanical engineering are accredited by the Engineering Accreditation Commission of the Accreditation Board for Engineering and Technology (ABET). A cooperative education program combining study with practical work experience is also available.

The Bachelor of Fine Arts is available in art, theater design and technology, and theater performance; the Bachelor of Music in music education, music performance, and music therapy; the Bachelor of Science in art, art and associated studies, graphic design, music, music management, theater, and theater management; and the Bachelor of Arts in art, art education, art history, music, and theater. The art and associated studies program is sound preparation for students seeking a graduate degree in art therapy.

Academic Program

Forty credit hours must be completed in general education for the bachelor's degree. General education is based on a world cultures theme. The requirement consists of a two-course sequence in world cultures; courses in humanities, fine arts, natural science, social science, mathematics, and foreign language; and a senior capstone course, all integrated into the theme. The University follows a semester calendar. Fall classes begin in late August, and the second semester begins in mid-January. Summer session course work is also offered.

Credit by examination may be granted to an incoming student who demonstrates a superior level of achievement in a particular subject. The University of Evansville participates in the College Board's Advanced Placement Program and College-Level Examination Program. For entering freshmen and transfer students, the University also conducts its own testing program during orientation through which a student may demonstrate proficiency or place out of course requirements.

Off-Campus Programs

Harlaxton College, the British campus of the University of Evansville, is located in Grantham, Lincolnshire, England—22 miles east of Nottingham and 110 miles north of London. Established by the University in 1971, Harlaxton College provides fully accredited course work in a variety of disciplines for 180 students each semester. This unusual study-abroad program offers students the opportunity to experience a culture different from their own while strengthening their understanding of our Western society. Study on the campus in England is open to all upperclass UE students and students from other colleges and universities who are currently in good academic standing. All financial assistance awarded at the Evansville campus may also be utilized at the Harlaxton campus.

Academic Facilities

The Bower-Suhrheinrich Library houses 275,000 bound volumes and journals, 1,350 current titles, 454,088 microforms, and 10,094 video and audio titles. The University also maintains more than 100 online databases and a music listening library.

All University buildings, thirteen computer labs, and residence halls are connected with the Internet.

The newly renovated and expanded Koch Center for Engineering and Sciences houses offices, classrooms, and laboratories for the College of Engineering and Computing Sciences as well as for the departments of biology, chemistry, mathematics, and physics.

The Krannert Hall of Fine Arts includes music listening and practice rooms, the Wheeler Concert Hall, an art exhibit gallery, studios, and art laboratories.

The University has an award-winning student-operated radio station with a Foreign Correspondent Program that is available through UE's Harlaxton College, located in Grantham, England. A TV production studio on campus also offers students hands-on experience.

Costs

Tuition for 2003–04 was $18,900; campus room and board were $5630. The required full-time registration and activity fees were $330, and the average cost of books and supplies was $700.

Financial Aid

The University's comprehensive financial aid program, through which 90 percent of the students receive assistance, consists of scholarships, grants, loans, and on-campus employment. UE participates in the Federal Pell Grant and Federal Work-Study programs. Federal Perkins Loans and Federal Stafford Student Loans are also available. Merit scholarships are also available and consist of Academic Departmental Scholarships, which are awarded by all academic departments to outstanding students displaying high academic achievement; the Leadership Activity Award for students who have been active in multiple school, church, or community organizations; the Trustee Scholarship, for students who are ranked number one in their high school class at the time of application; the Multicultural Scholars Award for students of various ethnicities; the Legacy Award for children or grandchildren of University of Evansville graduates; United Methodist Scholarships for students who are active in a United Methodist Church. Special scholarships are available to Indiana Honors Diploma graduates and valedictorians from Indiana high schools. Phi Theta Kappa Scholarships are available for transfer students who are members in good standing.

Students applying for aid must file the Free Application for Federal Student Aid (FAFSA).

Faculty

Serious students require an excellent faculty, and the faculty of the University of Evansville is composed of 177 men and women who are outstanding in their respective fields of study. Eighty-seven percent hold earned doctorates or other terminal degrees. Students are able to develop close personal relationships and to freely exchange ideas with faculty members because of the student-faculty ratio of 13:1 and because no classes are taught by graduate students.

Student Government

The Student Congress of the University is elected by the students and has representation in the University Senate and on the University Judicial Board. The Student Association includes every enrolled student and, through its executive offices, is responsible for providing effective representative student government. The Student Activities Board is a student organization responsible for arranging social events for the campus community.

Admission Requirements

Factors considered in evaluating a student's readiness for admission to the University of Evansville include high school rank and strength of the curriculum, test scores, previous college work, and other qualifications. Recommendations from high school officials are also considered.

Each applicant for admission to the freshman class is required to take the SAT I or the ACT and should rank in the upper half of his or her high school class. A strong college-preparatory curriculum is necessary. Transfer students must have maintained a minimum 2.0 grade point average.

Application and Information

The University employs two selective deadline dates: an early notification deadline of December 1 and a regular decision deadline of February 1. Admission is on a rolling basis after February 1 as space in the freshman class is available. Transfer admission deadlines are on a rolling basis.

For additional information and application materials, students should contact:

Office of Admission
University of Evansville
1800 Lincoln Avenue
Evansville, Indiana 47722
Telephone: 812-479-2468
800-423-8633 (toll-free)
E-mail: admission@evansville.edu
World Wide Web: http://www.evansville.edu

The University of Evansville's Olmsted Administration Hall.

THE UNIVERSITY OF FINDLAY

FINDLAY, OHIO

The University

The University of Findlay is a private coeducational institution with 4,711 full- and part-time students. Founded in 1882 by the Churches of God, General Conference, it emphasizes preparation for careers and professions in an educational program that blends liberal arts and career education. Students of many denominations attend Findlay, and religious participation is a matter of personal choice.

Bachelor of Arts degree programs are available in sixty different majors. The Associate of Arts degree is awarded in nearly twenty areas. Master's degrees are offered in athletic training, business administration, education, environmental management, liberal studies, occupational therapy, physical therapy, and teaching English to speakers of other languages (TESOL).

The largest programs at Findlay are in business, education, and health professions. Majors in the sciences and health professions include athletic training, computer science, equestrian studies (English, Western, and equine management), nuclear medicine, occupational therapy, physical therapy, physician assistant studies, premedicine, pre–veterinary medicine, and technology management. Business degrees are founded in a comprehensive core program with eleven different majors, including an individualized major option.

Opportunities for internships and work-related experiences are available in most major fields through the Professional Experiences Program (PEP).

Most of Findlay's students come from Ohio and the surrounding states of Michigan, Indiana, and Pennsylvania. More than thirty other states are also represented. Because of the Intensive English Language Institute located on the campus, many international students are part of the total student body.

Resident students live in eight modern residence halls and several town-house-style apartments. All students eat their meals in an attractive, newly renovated dining hall. Social life at Findlay centers on student organizations, fraternities, and sororities. Findlay has three officially recognized fraternities: Alpha Sigma Phi, Tau Kappa Epsilon, and Theta Chi; there are two sororities: Phi Sigma Sigma and Sigma Kappa. Organizations include department and special interest clubs, the newspaper, musical groups, a radio and T.V. station, Circle K, and Aristos Eklektos (honors).

Athletic programs are affiliated with NCAA Division II and the Great Lakes Intercollegiate Athletic Conference. Findlay offers thirteen intercollegiate sports for men: baseball, basketball, cross-country, equestrian, football, golf, indoor track and field, outdoor track and field, soccer, swimming and diving, tennis, volleyball, and wrestling. It has eleven varsity sports for women: basketball, cross-country, equestrian, golf, indoor track and field, outdoor track and field, soccer, softball, swimming and diving, tennis, track, and volleyball. Club sport teams include the equestrian and ice hockey teams. Athletic scholarships are available.

Croy Physical Education Center has a 25-meter swimming pool, exercise areas, a gymnasium, offices, and classrooms. The Gardner Fitness Center is a state-of-the-art facility. The 130,000-square-foot Koehler Recreation and Fitness Complex, opened in 1999, contains the Malcolm Athletic Center, with a six-lane, NCAA regulation track and four multipurpose courts; the Clauss Ice Arena; locker rooms; and offices for the athletic department.

Student services include career and placement counseling, the Cosiano Health Center, academic tutoring and personal counseling, and study skills assistance through the Academic Support Center.

Location

Findlay was voted the most livable micropolitan city in Ohio and scored among the top twelve in the United States. It is within easy driving distance of Toledo, Columbus, Detroit, and Fort Wayne. Interstate 75 and the Ohio Turnpike (Interstates 80 and 90) are major highways serving the area. Airports in Toledo, Columbus, and Detroit are convenient. The town of Findlay has 39,000 residents and is home to Marathon Oil Corporation and Cooper Tire and Rubber Company. The Findlay campus consists of more than 200 acres on several sites. A 72-acre campus-owned farm houses pre–veterinary medicine and English equestrian studies. A second 32-acre facility houses the English riding program. Many opportunities exist for students who want business-related and social service agency experience. The University has established strong relationships with the community, which supports athletic and cultural events on the campus. Besides the full program of on-campus activities, off-campus trips to cultural and entertainment events are scheduled. The city of Findlay, which has an excellent business climate, offers part-time job opportunities, volunteer service organizations, and the chance to be involved with the larger civic community. Findlay's campus is attractive, safe, comfortable, and friendly.

Majors and Degrees

The Bachelor of Arts (B.A.) degree is awarded in the following majors: adolescent/young adult/integrated English/language arts, adolescent/young adult/integrated social studies, art, children's book illustration, communication (broadcast journalism emphasis), communication (broadcast telecommunication emphasis), communication (journalism emphasis), communication (organizational communication emphasis), communication (public relations emphasis), criminal justice administration, English, English as an international language, general social studies, graphic communication, health communication, history, interpersonal and public communication, Japanese, law and the liberal arts, middle childhood/language arts and social studies, multi-age/drama/theater, multi-age/Japanese, multi-age/Spanish, multi-age/visual arts, philosophy/applied philosophy, political science, psychology, religious studies, social work, sociology, Spanish, studio art, teaching English to speakers of other languages, technical communication, and theater. Minors are offered in numerous areas.

The Bachelor of Science (B.S.) degree is granted in accounting; adolescent/young adult/earth science; adolescent/young adult/integrated mathematics; adolescent/young adult/life science; athletic training; biology; business administration; business management; computer science; early childhood; economics; environmental, safety, and occupational health management; equestrian studies (English and Western emphases); equine business management; finance; health education; health studies; hospitality management; human resource management; international business; intervention specialist/mild to moderate disabilities; language and international business; marketing; mathematics; medical technology; middle childhood/language arts/math; middle childhood/language arts/science; middle childhood/math/science; middle childhood/math/social studies; middle childhood/science/social studies; multi-age/health education; multi-age/physical education; nuclear medicine technology; occupational therapy; operations and logistics; physical education; physician assistant; physical therapy; premedicine; prenursing; pre–veterinary medicine; recreation therapy; small business/entrepreneurship; strength and conditioning; and technology management.

The Associate of Arts degree is available in accounting, computer science, criminal justice administration (corrections or law enforcement emphases), English as an international language, equestrian studies, financial management, general social studies, human resource management, humanities, management information systems, massage therapy, nuclear medicine technology, office administration, personal training, religious studies, sales/retail management, small business/entrepreneurship, and technology management. Certificate programs are available in a variety of areas.

Academic Programs

Findlay operates on the semester system. Students must complete at least 124 semester hours with a minimum overall grade point average of 2.0 to earn a bachelor's degree. General education requirements and competency requirements in English, reading, computer literacy, speech, and library use must be fulfilled. The First Year Seminar introduces students to living and learning at Findlay and gives them the opportunity to work with the same teachers and student group in two related courses. The Foundations Program offers students the chance to develop those skills in writing, reading, and thinking needed for their success as college students. Study skills, time management, and academic advising are included. Students are selected for this program at the time of admission. The Honors Program provides additional challenge to those students who qualify on the basis of academic credentials. Study- and travel-abroad programs are offered by various departments. Credit and/or placement can be earned through Advanced Placement (AP) exams.

The Equestrian Program is a well-recognized program of its kind and serves approximately 250 students from throughout the United States and abroad. Majors in equine business management and in English and Western riding are offered. The instruction, both in the classroom and on horseback, makes use of the expertise of recognized national equestrian champions. The pre–veterinary medicine program, using the farm facilities, offers the advantages of hands-on experience with livestock and an internship program in a distinctive curriculum. The pre–veterinary medicine program has a placement rate into veterinary schools that is much higher than the national average.

The Nuclear Medicine Institute provides the training necessary to qualify students for careers in nuclear medicine technology, a growing health-related career field.

The Health Professions Program provides eleven majors, including athletic training, nuclear medicine technology, strength and conditioning, recreation therapy, occupational therapy, physical therapy, and physician assistant studies.

Academic Facilities

The focal point of the Findlay campus is Old Main, which houses classrooms, faculty and administrative offices, the computer center, facilities for various student activities, and the Ritz Auditorium. Shafer Library is a member of a consortium that provides extensive resources to students. The Gardner Fine Arts Pavilion, dedicated in 1994, houses the Mazza Museum of original art from children's books. The University has numerous computer labs. Other academic buildings include the Frost Science Center, with a greenhouse and the Newhard Planetarium, and the Egner Center for the Performing Arts, which houses a 200-seat theater and the student-operated radio and television stations. A 101,000-square-foot athletic complex was completed in January 1999. This facility houses a six-lane indoor track, sand pits for long jump, a state-of-the-art timing system, and a wrestling room. Also under the same roof is an ice arena with a seating capacity of 1,200. Approximately 450 horses are stabled and trained at the equestrian facilities, which offer barns and indoor and outdoor riding arenas.

Costs

Tuition for the 2003–04 academic year totaled $19,052 for most programs, $22,402 for the equestrian programs, and $20,322 for the pre–veterinary medicine program. Room and board cost $7062. The estimated cost for transportation, books, and supplies is $1500.

Financial Aid

Ninety percent of Findlay students receive financial aid. Assistance is based on need as well as scholastic achievement. Factors used in determining aid are the Free Application for Federal Student Aid (FAFSA), grade point average, and ACT or SAT results. Federal and state programs are used with institution grants and scholarships, including sibling grants. The FAFSA must be filed. Notification of aid awards is made on a rolling basis. Work-study jobs are available. Scholarships for high-achieving students and student athletes are offered.

Faculty

The 16:1 student-faculty ratio results in small classes—usually fewer than 30 students. Professors know their students, and every student has a faculty adviser.

Student Government

The Student Government Association (SGA) and the Campus Program Board are involved in planning and implementing student activities. SGA provides leadership experience for students and enhances cooperation among faculty members, the administration, and students. A representative from SGA sits on the Board of Trustees. The Campus Program Board plans activities for recreation and cultural enrichment.

Admission Requirements

Applicants to Findlay should have a college-preparatory high school background, including 4 years of English, 2 to 3 years of mathematics, 2 to 3 years of social studies, and 2 years of sciences. A foreign language is recommended but not required. Results of the ACT or SAT and high school transcripts should be submitted with the application for admission. Transfer students must be eligible to return to the institution last attended and must submit transcripts of all college work. Decisions are made on a rolling basis. Application deadlines are August 1 for fall semester and December 15 for spring semester. A campus visit is strongly recommended. For students not meeting regular minimum admission requirements, Findlay has a Foundations Program, which provides skill building and academic support during the first semester of the freshman year. Findlay is an equal opportunity institution in admission and employment.

Application and Information

For application forms and other information, students may contact:

Office of Undergraduate Admissions
The University of Findlay
1000 North Main Street
Findlay, Ohio 45840
Telephone: 419-434-4732
800-548-0932 (toll-free)
E-mail: admissions@findlay.edu
World Wide Web: http://www.findlay.edu

Old Main.

UNIVERSITY OF GEORGIA

ATHENS, GEORGIA

The University

Chartered in 1785, the University of Georgia (UGA) is the oldest state-chartered public university in the United States. Approximately 25,000 undergraduate students attend the University, which has a total enrollment of 32,800 students. The University attracts students from all fifty states and the District of Columbia as well as more than 130 countries. Undergraduates may choose from more than 170 majors and programs of study in ten colleges. UGA, a land-grant and sea-grant university with statewide commitments and responsibilities, is the state's flagship institution of higher education. It is also the state's most comprehensive and most diversified institution of higher education. Its motto, "To teach, to serve, and to inquire into the nature of things," reflects the University's integral and unique role in the conservation and enhancement of the state's and nation's intellectual, cultural, and environmental heritage. As a public research institution, the University of Georgia offers numerous opportunities for academic research, study abroad, and interdisciplinary study.

Location

The University's main campus, in Athens, Georgia, covers 706 acres and includes 367 buildings. To its north, the campus adjoins historic downtown Athens, which features many boutiques, restaurants, entertainment options, and service businesses. The University covers 4,308 acres in Clarke County and owns a total of 42,064 acres throughout the state. Athens, considered one of the nation's best college towns, is home to a vibrant and popular music scene, earning recognition by *Rolling Stone* magazine in 2003 as the number one music city in the U.S. In proximity to the foothills of the Blue Ridge Mountains, Athens is approximately 70 miles northeast of Atlanta, making it easily accessible by most modes of travel. In addition, the proximity to a large metropolitan area provides students opportunities for internships and externships, research opportunities, and careers after graduation.

Majors and Degrees

The University of Georgia's Franklin College of Arts and Sciences offers degrees in a broad spectrum of disciplines, including, but not limited to, anthropology, art, biological sciences, chemistry, classics, comparative literature, computer science, dance, drama, English, genetics, geology, history, marine sciences, music, philosophy, physics and astronomy, psychology, religion, Romance languages, sociology, speech communication, and statistics. Students are also able to participate in preprofessional advisory programs in dentistry, law, medicine, nursing, optometry, pharmacy, theology, and veterinary medicine, in which preprofessional advisers assist students in course selection and graduate/professional school preparation. Advanced undergraduates participating in pre-veterinary medicine and prepharmacy are also afforded the opportunity to matriculate early in the Colleges of Veterinary Medicine and Pharmacy upon successful completion of required course work and appropriate standardized tests.

Two of the most popular undergraduate schools are the Grady College of Journalism and Mass Communication and the Terry College of Business. Grady, sponsor of the prestigious Peabody Awards, offers degrees in advertising, broadcast news, magazines, newspapers, publication management, public relations, and telecommunication arts. Terry offers degrees in accounting, banking and finance management, economics, general business, international business, management, management information systems, marketing and distribution, real estate, and risk management and insurance. Students enter the Grady College or the Terry College in their third year after successfully completing prejournalism or prebusiness requirements in the Franklin College of Arts and Sciences.

Other schools and colleges offering undergraduate programs of study include the College of Education, the College of Agricultural and Environmental Sciences, the College of Environment and Design, the College of Family and Consumer Sciences, the Warnell School of Forest Resources, the School of Public and International Affairs, and the School of Social Work.

Academic Program

The academic year at the University of Georgia consists of two semesters, two short summer terms, and a May term. Although major requirements vary from program to program, a minimum of 120 credit hours are required for graduation. Undergraduate students are required to complete a core curriculum of broad-based liberal arts course work as well as major requirements. With the University of Georgia's broad array of programs of study, such as animal health, agricultural engineering, genetics, magazines, music therapy, and social work, students are provided ample course selections to fulfill their requirements. Students normally take four or five classes per semester and must be enrolled in at least 12 credit hours to be considered full-time students.

The University's nationally recognized Honors Program affords superior students opportunities for undergraduate research as well as increased access to distinguished faculty members. Independent study and interdisciplinary majors are permitted, and many students take advantage of the opportunity to pursue a dual or double major to create a course of study that is specific to their career and academic goals. Advanced honors students may be permitted to take graduate-level course work.

All of UGA's schools and colleges offer internship and externship opportunities for students to enhance classroom learning with real-world experience. The Career Center also works with students in obtaining internships and externships and, eventually, jobs to link their classroom knowledge with their career aspirations.

First-year students are able to participate in first-year seminars. These seminars provide an opportunity for new students to become acquainted with a senior faculty member and to learn about the excitement of study and research in a specific discipline and the intellectual challenge of academic life at the University of Georgia. First-year seminars are taught by the most distinguished members of the University faculty, who focus on topics of special interest to their research and teaching. In addition, first-year students are invited to participate in the Freshman Summer College Experience, in which students take two courses during the summer before their first year and live with fellow first-year students in the residence halls. This unique opportunity allows them an enhanced transition to their collegiate experience.

Off-Campus Programs

The University of Georgia participates in the Atlanta Regional Consortium for Higher Education (ARCHE), a consortium of nineteen public and private institutions of higher learning in the Atlanta/Athens area. Students enrolled at any ARCHE participating school may take classes at any other member institution. UGA also participates in the Academic Common Market, which allows students from the Southeast to major in specialized areas not offered in their home state at the tuition rate for Georgia students.

The University of Georgia offers study-abroad programs in more than thirty different countries. Students participating in study abroad receive resident credit for their international course work. In addition, with approval, students may participate in exchange opportunities with other accredited study-abroad programs and transfer credits back to UGA. Programs are offered for varied lengths during the summer, one semester, or the full year. More than 20 percent of UGA students spend some time studying abroad during their undergraduate career.

Academic Facilities

At the heart of the University, the state-of-the-art Student Learning Center contains 200,000 square feet of digital classroom and study space, providing students and faculty members with a place to gather. The Paul D. Coverdell Building for Biomedical and Health Sciences houses the UGA Biomedical and Health Sciences Institute, which combines interdisciplinary programs in public health, infectious disease and immunity, and molecular medicine. Home to the School of Health and Human Performance, the 430,000-square-foot Ramsey Student Center for Physical Activities has been recognized twice by *Sports Illustrated* as the best student recreational facility of its kind. Moore College, on UGA's historic North Campus, serves as home to the nationally recognized Honors and Foundation Fellows Program and includes twenty-four Internet-wired workstations, a thirty-station computer lab, and seminar rooms. The Performing and Visual Arts Complex provides a home for the music department as well as the Georgia Museum of Art.

Costs

Estimated total costs for the 2003–04 academic year, including tuition and fees, residence hall, meal plan, books and supplies, and personal expenses, were $12,274 for Georgia residents and $23,050 for non-Georgia residents.

Financial Aid

Approximately 34 percent of students received need-based financial aid in 2003–04. Students seeking need-based aid should submit the Free Application for Federal Student Aid (FAFSA) by March 1. Students are awarded scholarships, grants, loans, and Federal Work-Study Program positions through the Office of Student Financial Aid.

The Foundation Fellowship and Bernard Ramsey Honors Scholarship are the premier scholarships available for first-year students and require a separate application. The fellowship covers nearly the full cost of attendance for four years of study as well as numerous opportunities for study and travel abroad, while the Ramsey awards $4000 for an in-state student and $6500 for an out-of-state student plus a Regents Waiver for nonresident tuition. Approximately 25 Fellows and 45 Ramsey Honors Scholars are selected each year.

The Office of Admissions also awards merit-based scholarships to first-year students based on their academic merit, leadership capabilities, and outstanding accomplishments outside the classroom. Approximately 5 percent of the entering first-year class is awarded a UGA merit scholarship. The Charter Scholarship includes $1000 per year and a Regents Waiver for nonresident tuition for out-of-state students. No additional application is needed for Charter Scholarship consideration.

Faculty

Along with teaching in the classroom, UGA faculty members are also researchers. The faculty of the University of Georgia includes numerous leading researchers and scholars in various fields: 1 MacArthur Foundation Fellowship recipient, 2 Pulitzer Prize recipients, 6 members of the National Academy of Sciences, 2 members of the National Academy of Engineering, and 6 members of the American Academy of Arts and Sciences. More than 80 percent of undergraduate classes are taught by 1,800 full-time faculty members, 96 percent of whom hold terminal degrees. The student-faculty ratio is 14:1, and the average class size is 33.

Student Government

UGA students are afforded the opportunity to become involved in more than 500 student organizations, allowing them to shape student life at the University as well as develop leadership and interpersonal skills that carry over into their professional lives. The representative Student Government Association serves every facet of the University, from administrators and faculty members to the community and beyond. The purpose of the Student Government Association is to serve the students through student rights advocacy as well as programmatic offerings. Students serve on committees and as representatives of their school or college.

Admission Requirements

Demonstrated academic achievement is the primary factor in first-year admission decisions at the University of Georgia. The academic review of first-year applications centers on three criteria: the students' grade point average (GPA) in core academic courses, the rigor of their curriculum, and their best combination of scores on the SAT or ACT. Additional factors that may be considered in admission decisions include intellectual pursuits and creative endeavors; an understanding of and respect for intellectual, social, and cultural differences; significant commitment to citizenship through public service, school activities, community involvement, leadership, and/or family; evidence of integrity and personal maturity; and the ability to benefit from a culturally and intellectually diverse community of scholar-citizens. Advanced standing is available for students pursuing Advanced Placement and International Baccalaureate programs. The University of Georgia does not take race, color, national origin, sex, age, veteran status, or disability into consideration when making admission decisions.

Application and Information

All applicants must complete the application for first-year admission, including an essay, and submit it along with an official high school transcript, the counselor/school evaluation, official SAT I and/or ACT scores, and teacher recommendation form in order to receive a final admission decision. The nonbinding Early Action deadline is November 1, with notification in mid-December. The Regular Decision deadline is February 1, with notification by early April. Admitted students are required to submit a commitment deposit by May 1 to secure their place in the first-year class. An application and additional information may be obtained by contacting:

Office of Undergraduate Admissions
Terrell Hall
University of Georgia
Athens, Georgia 30602-1633
Telephone: 706-542-8776
Fax: 706-542-1466
E-mail: undergrad@admissions.uga.edu
World Wide Web: http://www.admissions.uga.edu

UNIVERSITY OF GREAT FALLS

GREAT FALLS, MONTANA

The University

The University of Great Falls (UGF) is a private, independent Catholic university sponsored by the Sisters of Providence within the jurisdiction of the Catholic Bishop of Great Falls–Billings. It is open to qualified men and women of every race and creed. Its academic programs are designed to educate students through curricula featuring liberal arts courses combined with career and professional preparation. The University's mission is to provide students with the opportunity to obtain a liberal arts education for lifelong learning and a successful career or profession. The faculty and staff members of the University join with students in a cooperative and enthusiastic search for truth, meaning, and the analytical skills to resolve moral and ethical dilemmas. Although faculty members participate in applied research, the focus is on teaching. Because teaching students is the primary concern of faculty members, they combine traditional classroom instruction with education using multimedia computer technology and learning through internships, field experiences, and community service.

The University was founded in 1932 by Bishop Edwin V. O'Hara to fill the need for an institution of higher education in Great Falls and the central Montana area. The present campus opened in 1960. Providence Tower, the main campus landmark, was constructed in 1964, and McLaughlin Memorial Center, a spacious physical education and recreation facility, was added in 1965. The campus consists of more than a dozen buildings, including Sullivan Hall, Emilie Hall, the DiRocco-Peressini Science Center, a theater/music building, an art building, the Galerie Trinitas, the Trinitas Chapel, and the library. The library, which expanded in 1999, doubled its size and provides additional study room for students. The University of Great Falls has been accredited by the Northwest Association of Schools and Colleges since 1935.

In addition to its programs at the undergraduate level, the University also offers the following graduate degrees: the Master of Arts in addiction counseling, the Master of Human Services Administration, the Master of Science in counseling, the Master of Education, the Master of Science in school psychology, the Master of Arts in secondary teaching, the Master of Science in criminal justice administration, the Master of Information Systems, and a certification in elementary school administration.

The University's athletic programs include men's and women's basketball and women's volleyball. Playing in the Frontier Conference, the Argonauts are an exciting enhancement to the community's quality of life and offer student athletes opportunities to be a part of a highly competitive, nationally recognized program. "Jason the Argonaut" has been the school's mascot since UGF started athletic programs in 1967. UGF's chosen mascot stems from Greek mythology and the story of Jason and his band of courageous men, called the Argonauts, in their quest for the Golden Fleece.

Location

The city of Great Falls is located in north central Montana. Situated next to the five waterfalls of the Missouri River at an elevation of 3,300 feet, the city lies between the Rocky Mountains and Great Plains. The river, a historically significant waterway explored by the Lewis and Clark Expedition in 1805, provides abundant recreational opportunities such as boating, canoeing, and fishing its blue-ribbon trout waters. Great Falls is also home to the Lewis and Clark National Historic Trail Interpretive Center and the Charlie Russell Museum, which showcases the treasured works of the famous western artist Charles M. Russell. On the museum grounds sits the Russell home and the artist's log studio. Great Falls exemplifies the Western heritage and ethos of the Big Sky Country of Montana.

Nestled near the Big Belt, Little Belt, and Highwood Mountain Ranges, Great Falls is centrally located in one of the nation's most scenic regions. For skiing enthusiasts, the Little Belt Mountains, an hour south of Great Falls, offer excellent downhill skiing and 17 miles of groomed cross-country trails at Silver Crest. In addition to skiing, the surrounding area provides extensive outdoor recreational activities, including biking, hiking, camping, technical rock climbing, white-water rafting, archeological exploration, fishing, and hunting. About an hour west of the city lies the Rocky Mountain Front Range, which extends northward to one of the country's crown jewels, Glacier National Park. The majestic peaks of this area provide outdoor enthusiasts with hundreds of miles of trails and pristine lakes and streams. Four hours to the south of Great Falls is Yellowstone National Park, where abundant herds of bison and elk roam the vast spaces. Many other species of wildlife call Yellowstone home, including the reintroduced wolf.

Majors and Degrees

At the undergraduate level, the University of Great Falls offers curricular programs in forty-five areas, including bachelor's degrees in twenty-three majors and associate degrees in four majors. Through the integration of liberal arts and professional preparation, the University helps students prepare for lifelong learning and rewarding careers.

Academic Program

The University develops professional/career programs and continuing education courses designed to meet society's present and future needs, as well as traditional academic degrees in appropriate fields. As part of the undergraduate core curriculum, students acquire fundamental skills and experiences that facilitate comprehension, information processing, and communication within particular disciplines. Beyond the learning required for their chosen majors, students embark on a path of self-discovery and learn to apply meaning to the world around them from historical, contemporary, and future perspectives. All students are required to complete courses in communications, composition, computer science, fine arts, history, literature, mathematics, natural science, social sciences, and theology and religion.

The University serves students of all beliefs, while offering a foundation for actively implementing spiritual values and a variety of religious teachings, especially in the Catholic tradition. Students are strongly encouraged to complement classroom learning with nonacademic learning in the areas of community service, wellness activities, and cultural arts.

Off-Campus Programs

The Distance Learning Program provides instruction to students throughout the country and around the world, enabling them to complete four undergraduate degrees and one master's degree from their home or work. Many students choose to begin their lower-division course work at home and then move to the campus to complete their degree. The UGF Distance Learning Program offers high-quality educational opportunities to students who would not otherwise have access to the campus. Distance learning students receive instruction through a variety of media technologies, such as videotapes, e-mail, and Internet conferencing.

Academic Facilities

The University library provides informational resources for students and faculty and staff members. The collection contains more than 106,000 books and 400 journal subscriptions. Services include access to reference materials, interlibrary loan, and more than 50 online databases from InfoTrac, ProQuest, OCLC First Search, and LEXIS. In addition, fax services, copiers, and workstations for the disabled are available for student use. Special collections include the McDonald Collection of Business Resources, the Bertsche Collection of Montana History, and the Korontzos Law Library. An audiovisual collection with videocassettes, records, CDs, scores, and other media can be checked out or used in the library.

The main computer lab, centrally located in Sullivan Hall, houses more than forty personal computers, while other labs on campus house more than thirty-five additional personal computers. These computers are upgraded yearly and are available for use by all students. Students can access the Internet and e-mail through the UGFNET from on-campus residence halls. The lab supports one of the most widely used Windows-based software suites, and peripheral equipment is always available.

The Center for Academic Excellence serves first-generation students, students with limited income, and students with disabilities and is strongly committed to both their academic success and personal growth. To accomplish this goal, the center provides a wide range of services and activities to all eligible students, including academic support, personal counseling, minority student support, and support for students with disabilities.

The McLaughlin Memorial Center is a site used for health and physical education classes, as well as athletic competition. Facilities include a large gymnasium, swimming pool, wellness exercise center, a large conference room, and academic classrooms. A high- and low-element ropes course, known as Adventure Quest, is located in the building and in the surrounding grounds.

With seating for 357 people, the University Theater is used frequently by the campus and the community. Theater students produce one play per semester as part of their course requirement. Musicians, comedians, and local groups also perform regularly in the building.

Costs

Undergraduate tuition for the 2004–05 school year is $5750 per semester. Room and board for students living in University housing is $2250 per semester. Books and supplies are estimated to cost $750 per year. Emilie Hall, a newly renovated residence hall on campus, is designated for students under 21 years old. The Villa, an off-campus apartment complex, is designated for students age 21 and older, married students, or students with children.

Financial Aid

Approximately 90 percent of the University of Great Falls's students receive some form of student financial assistance. The assistance includes funding from the U.S. Department of Education, Department of Veterans Affairs, various state agencies, University-managed resources, and private donors. The University offers Federal Pell Grants, Federal Supplemental Educational Opportunity Grants, State Student Incentive Grants, Federal Perkins Loans, federal- and University-supported student employment, and Federal PLUS Loans. In addition, the University offers merit-based scholarships to new and continuing students. Information on need-based financial aid assistance programs is available from the Financial Aid Office. Scholarship information for new students is available from the Admissions Office. To be considered for financial aid, students should submit a Free Application for Federal Student Aid (FAFSA) form electronically at http://www.fafsa.ed.gov with UGF's school code of 002527. To be considered for scholarships, students should submit an application for admission along with academic transcripts.

Faculty

The University of Great Falls features faculty members who possess personal philosophies compatible with a Catholic learning environment. These experienced teachers, of whom 57 percent possess terminal degrees, are not only highly competent in their academic fields, but are also persons of integrity to whom students can look to for example, inspiration, and information. Since a faculty member's influence is of paramount significance in education, ability and willingness to counsel students about classroom concerns are traits that are expected of each teacher. A 14:1 student-faculty ratio boosts this influence.

Student Government

University of Great Falls's students are represented by the Associated Students of the University of Great Falls. The governing body is an elected Student Senate. The University student government was the first in Montana to eliminate the class structure in favor of giving greater representation to all students. One student is a full voting member of the Board of Trustees. Students are represented in each academic school and serve on the Curriculum Committee, the Scholarship and Financial Aid Committee, the Student Rights and Responsibilities Committee, and the Library Committee.

Admission Requirements

The University of Great Falls's Admissions Office accepts applicants on a rolling basis. Applicants may apply for admission at any time; however, all applicants are strongly urged to apply at least one month prior to the first day of classes of the term for which they intend to enter the University. Students are encouraged to submit their test scores from the ACT or the SAT I whenever possible. The scores from these tests are used in scholarship consideration, academic counseling, and course placement. The University also has an early admission program for students in high school. The University of Great Falls grants advanced standing credit for AP, CLEP, and ACE military programs.

Application and Information

The University of Great Falls is committed to a program of equal opportunity for education, employment, and participation in University activities without regard to race, color, gender, age, religion, marital status, sexual orientation, physical handicap, national origin, or mental handicap. For additional information about the University of Great Falls, including an admission packet, students should contact:

Office of Admissions
University of Great Falls
1301 20th Street South
Great Falls, Montana 59405
Telephone: 406-791-5200
800-856-9544 (toll-free)
Fax: 406-791-5209
E-mail: enroll@ugf.edu
World Wide Web: http://www.ugf.edu

Trinitas Chapel on the University of Great Falls campus.

UNIVERSITY OF GUELPH

GUELPH, ONTARIO, CANADA

The University

The University of Guelph is a high-quality, student-focused, residential college that is committed to innovative programs, dynamic student-faculty interaction, and an integration of learning and research. It offers a wide range of undergraduate and graduate programs in the arts, humanities, social sciences, and natural sciences. Building on these core disciplines, Guelph also has a strong commitment to interdisciplinary programs, to a selected range of professional and applied programs, and to agriculture and veterinary medicine as areas of special responsibility.

Established in 1964 when three century-old founding colleges joined with a new college of arts and science, the University of Guelph is a vital community of more than 17,000 students on a campus of historical and modern buildings and red brick walkways. By Canadian standards Guelph is of medium size, offering a wide range of academic programs while providing a safe, accommodating environment for learning. On-campus living is available for more than 5,200 students, with all new first-semester students guaranteed on-campus housing if they apply by the deadline.

Guelph features state-of-the-art athletic facilities that include a double arena with an Olympic-size ice surface, two pools, and a fieldhouse. Guelph offers thirty varsity sports teams and in recent years has fielded national and provincial championship football, hockey, and rugby teams.

With more than 78 percent of Guelph's undergraduate classes consisting of fewer than 50 students, Guelph ensures a personal approach to learning with a 1:22 faculty-student ratio. Canada's first Office of First-Year Studies assists new students with the transition from secondary school to university, which gives Guelph an 88 percent student retention and graduation rate, the highest among Canadian comprehensive universities.

The University of Guelph offers a Doctor of Veterinary Medicine degree as well as several diploma programs and more than seventy-five master's and doctoral degree programs. The graduate calendar is available on the World Wide Web at http://www.uoguelph.ca/GraduateStudies/calendar.

Location

Guelph is located in the southwestern Ontario region the *New York Times* calls "Canada's Technology Triangle," a locale known for its high-caliber educational institutions and its innovative companies. This city of more than 100,000 features internationally recognized folk, jazz, and writers' festivals as well as a new multipurpose performing arts center and a new sports and entertainment center. Positioned within an hour's drive of Toronto, Canada's largest city and airline hub, Guelph offers the comfort of small-community living with the excitement of an international metropolis at its doorstep.

Majors and Degrees

The University of Guelph offers a number of undergraduate degree programs. Programs followed by * indicate co-op programs, which are not normally available to international students.

The University of Guelph offers Bachelor of Arts degrees in agricultural economics, anthropology, art history, classical languages, classical studies, computing and information science*, criminal justice and public policy, drama, economics*, English, European studies, French, geography, history, information systems and human behaviour, international development, applied economics, mathematical economics, mathematics, music, philosophy, political science, psychology*, rural development sociology, sociology, Spanish, statistics, studio art, and women's studies. In addition, a Bachelor of Arts and Sciences degree is available to students who excel in both arts/social sciences and sciences.

Bachelor of Applied Science degrees are available in applied human nutrition; child, youth and family; and gerontology*. Bachelor of Commerce degrees are available in agricultural business*, hotel and food administration*, housing and real estate management*, human resources management, management economics (industry and finance)*, marketing management*, public management, and tourism management. Bachelor of Computing degrees with various areas of application are available.

Bachelor of Science degrees are available in animal biology, applied mathematics and statistics*, biological chemistry, biomedical science, biomedical toxicology*, biochemistry*, biological science, biophysics*, chemical physics*, chemistry*, computing and information science*, earth surface science, ecology, environmental biology, environmental toxicology*, food science*, human kinetics, marine and freshwater biology, mathematics, microbiology*, molecular biology and genetics, nutritional and nutraceutical sciences, physical sciences, physics*, plant biology, plant biotechnology, psychology, statistics, theoretical physics, wildlife biology, and zoology.

Bachelor of Science, Agriculture degrees are available in agricultural economics, agroecosystem management, agronomy, animal science, and horticultural science. Bachelor of Science, Environmental Sciences degrees are available in earth and atmospheric science*, ecology*, environmental economics and policy*, environmental monitoring and analysis*, environmental protection*, environmetrics*, environmental geography*, and natural resources management*. Bachelor of Science, Engineering degrees are available in biological engineering*, engineering systems and computing*, environmental engineering*, and water resources engineering*. Bachelor of Science, Technology degrees are available in applied pharmaceutical chemistry* and physics and technology*. The University of Guelph also offers a Doctor of Veterinary Medicine degree, a Bachelor of Landscape Architecture degree, and a Bachelor of Bio-Resource Management in horticulture management degree.

Academic Program

The academic year is divided into three semesters: fall (September through December), winter (January through April), and summer (May through August), with the majority of students in attendance during the fall and winter semesters. Fall is the normal entry point for all students.

Four-year honors degrees require the completion of eight semesters. Three-year general degrees require the completion of six semesters. A typical full-time semester totals 2.5 credits.

Off-Campus Programs

An important part of Guelph's mission is to attract students from around the world and to develop a global perspective in its students. The campus attracts more than 540 international students from more than 100 countries and maintains fifty-seven exchange programs with twenty-nine countries. In addition, approximately 350 Guelph students study overseas each year in programs in Africa, Australia, Europe, and South and Central America.

Thirty-four of the programs offered at the University of Guelph include co-op work semesters, with 90 percent of the students in these programs finding work. Guelph also offers more than 100 distance degree credit courses to nearly 8,000 Open Learning course registrants.

Academic Facilities

Guelph's two libraries are linked with libraries at two other universities in the region, providing students with access to 7.5 million items through a new, state-of-the-art automated library system. Guelph's library holdings include Canada's largest collection of theater archives, extensive Scottish study materials, and one of the best collections of postcolonial African literature in Canada.

A 30-acre research park adjacent to the campus is home to a growing number of research-intensive industries. Industry and government trust Guelph's faculty members to meet their research needs, offering approximately Can$100 million annually for research that ranges from workplace efficiency to developing better approaches to food packaging and marketing to ensuring the availability of clean water.

All students receive free central computing accounts, which allow access to the University's integrated electronic services from on or off campus. These services include e-mail, access to the World Wide Web, computer-assisted instruction, conferencing, course selection, and high-quality laser printing. All student residences are directly connected to the Internet via the campus high-speed network. Off-campus students have dial-up access to both free and chargeable modems.

The campus also features two art galleries, a Sculpture Park, two performance stages, and a new covered field house. The 408-acre Arboretum has nearly 5 miles of jogging trails and nature paths.

Costs

Full-time tuition for the 2003 academic year ranged from Can$2053 to Can$2230 per semester for Canadian residents and from Can$4678 to Can$6725 per semester for international students. Mandatory fees total approximately Can$200 per semester, with slight variations according to each college. Student health/dental fees are Can$180 per year. International students are obliged to purchase health-care coverage through the University. The cost for international students to attend Guelph for two semesters, including tuition and academic fees, housing, clothing, food, and books, totals between Can$19,000 and Can$27,000.

Financial Aid

The University of Guelph is committed to ensuring that a university education remains an attainable goal. In total, Can$10 million in annual student financial aid is given in the form of scholarships, awards, bursaries, and work-study opportunities. There are scholarships (ranging from Can$250 to Can$6000) and bursaries specifically designed for international students who are also allowed to work on campus.

Faculty

More than 96 percent of Guelph's 760 full-time professors hold the Ph.D. degree or its equivalent, and all strive to bring the excitement and process of research into the learning environment. More than 100 professors have been recognized for their excellence in teaching by external agencies, their peers, and students. No comparably sized university in the country has garnered more 3M awards, Canada's most prestigious university teaching honour. Guelph numbers 19 Fellows of the Royal Society of Canada among its researchers.

Student Government

Students are involved at all levels of University government, from the residence council to the Senate and the Board of Governors. The Central Student Association (CSA), which represents all undergraduate students, oversees more than fifty student clubs that range from political to recreational. In addition, there are more than fifty academic and other student-government organizations located on campus. Students also have access to a number of service groups on campus, which range from the Ontario Public Interest Research Group to a community radio station.

Admission Requirements

Ontario applicants must present the Ontario Secondary School Diploma (OSSD), with a minimum of 6 Ontario Academic Credits (OAC) and specific subject requirements for the degree program desired. OAC English 1 is required for all degree programs. For those outside the Ontario secondary school system, the secondary graduation certificate that would admit a student to a university in his or her home country is normally acceptable. Applicants must also satisfy the specific subject requirements for the program desired. Students admitted on the basis of having completed the International Baccalaureate (I.B.) are granted credit for higher-level courses with grades of 5 or better. Applicants who have completed Advanced Placement (AP) exams with a minimum grade of 4 are eligible to receive University credit to a maximum of 2 credits, which is subject to the discretion of the appropriate faculty. United States applicants are required to have a minimum grade point average of 3.0 and a combined SAT I score of 1100 or an ACT score of 24. Applicants should include specific subject requirements at the highest secondary school level offered.

Interested students should call Admission Services or refer to its Web site for application and deadline dates, detailed admission information, and downloadable application forms.

Application and Information

For additional information about admissions, academic programs, or University visits and tours, students should contact:

Admission Services
Office of Registrarial Services
Third Floor, University Centre
University of Guelph
Guelph, Ontario N1G 2W1
Canada
Telephone: 519-821-2130 or 519-824-4120 Ext. 56070
Fax: 519-766-9481
E-mail: internat@registrar.uoguelph.ca
World Wide Web: http://www.uoguelph.ca/liaison/

Students on the campus of the University of Guelph.

UNIVERSITY OF HARTFORD

WEST HARTFORD, CONNECTICUT

The University

The University of Hartford is a fully accredited, independent, nonsectarian institution. The University is composed of eight schools and colleges: the Colleges of Arts and Sciences, Engineering and Technology, and Education, Nursing, and Health Professions; Hillyer College; the Barney School of Business and Public Administration; the Hartford Art School; The Hartt School; and Hartford College for Women.

The current full-time undergraduate enrollment is about 4,400 men and women. A wide range of interests, goals, and backgrounds is found among the students, who represent most of the states in the nation and sixty-two countries. There are about 100 organized student groups, including clubs devoted to special interests or to political, professional, religious, or civic activities. Intercollegiate (NCAA Division I) and intramural athletics, student publications, and AM and FM radio stations provide further opportunities for extracurricular involvement. In addition, The Hartt School, the Hartford Art School, and the University Players present a variety of concerts, exhibitions, and theatrical productions each year. Recreational and fitness needs of the University community as well as intramural and intercollegiate sports are served by a modern 130,000-square-foot Sports Center.

The University maintains a Career Development and Placement Center that provides vocational counseling and information on occupations, employers, testing, and graduate schools; serves as a reference and credential source; and provides an on-campus recruiting program for graduating students. The Division of University College addresses the needs of the part-time adult learner through courses, programs, and educational counseling. A trained counseling staff is available to assist part-time students in planning their education and resolving some of their special concerns and needs.

More than 77 percent of all full-time undergraduates reside on campus. The University offers a wide array of types of residence halls, from traditional dormitory-style to fully equipped town house–style apartments.

Location

The University maintains two campuses, which are located in the residential suburb of West Hartford. The area provides an environment conducive to the development of the student's cultural and intellectual pursuits. The many facilities include libraries, museums, theaters, the Hartford Civic Center and Coliseum, a symphony orchestra, several other colleges, modern shopping centers, fine restaurants, an international airport, surface transportation, and intercity highway systems.

Majors and Degrees

The Bachelor of Arts is offered with majors in art history, biology, chemistry, communication, criminal justice, drama, economics, English, foreign languages and literatures, history, interactive information technology, international studies, mathematics, music, philosophy, physics, political economy, politics and government, professional and technical writing, psychology, and sociology. A Bachelor of Arts in secondary education with a major in English is offered in the College of Education, Nursing, and Health Professions. The Bachelor of Fine Arts is offered in actor theater training, ceramics, dance, design, drawing, experimental studio, illustration, music theater, painting, photography, printmaking, sculpture, and video.

The Bachelor of Music is offered at The Hartt School, with majors in applied music (guitar, orchestral instrument, organ, piano, and voice), composition, jazz studies, music education, music history, music management, music production and technology, opera, piano accompanying and ensemble, and theory. A five-year music education program is also offered, as are five-year double-major programs. Two interdisciplinary music programs are available: the Bachelor of Music with an emphasis in management, offered by The Hartt School in conjunction with the Barney School of Business and Public Administration, and the Bachelor of Science in Engineering with a music-acoustics major, offered by the College of Engineering and Technology.

The Bachelor of Science is awarded with majors in biology, chemistry, chemistry-biology, computer science, early childhood education, elementary education, health science, human services, mathematics, mathematics–management science, medical technology, nursing (for registered nurses only), occupational therapy, physics, radiologic technology, respiratory therapy, and integrated special education/elementary education, offering dual certification and covering emotional disabilities, learning disabilities, and mental retardation. Majors for the Bachelor of Science in Business Administration (B.S.B.A.) degree are accounting, economics and finance, entrepreneurial studies, finance and insurance, insurance, management, and marketing. A combined B.S. in health science and M.S. in physical therapy (B.S./M.S.T.) program is also available.

Additional B.S. programs, offered by the College of Engineering and Technology, include ABET-accredited B.S.E.E., B.S.M.E., and B.S.C.E. as well as B.S.Comp.E. and interdisciplinary B.S.E. options. The most popular B.S.E. options are acoustics/music, biomedical engineering, and environmental engineering. The School of Technology offers the Bachelor of Science in architectural engineering technology, audio engineering technology, chemical engineering technology, computer engineering technology, electronic engineering technology, and mechanical engineering technology as well as the Associate in Applied Science in electronic engineering technology (A.S.) and the Associate in Applied Science in computer engineering technology (A.S.). Also available is a fall-semester noncredit pretechnology program designed to prepare students for the degree program.

Hillyer College offers the Associate of Arts and provides the general education course work required to complete most of the University's baccalaureate programs. Particular emphasis is placed on the development of academic skills through small classes and close faculty-student interaction. Hartford College for Women offers four degree programs: Associate of Arts, Associate of Science in Legal Assistance, Bachelor of Arts in Women's Studies, and Bachelor of Science in Legal Assistance.

The new Bachelor of University Studies is a B.A. degree program created for the part-time adult student who typically has previous college experience.

Academic Program

The University of Hartford enjoys a national reputation for the breadth and depth of its program. More than seventy undergraduate majors are offered through nine schools and colleges. Students are encouraged to sample a variety of academic areas and can enroll in courses in any of the colleges on campus. Those who have special interests can develop interdisciplinary majors that combine courses from the different schools within the University. Academic advisers are assigned to all students to help guide them in curriculum choices, career exploration, and the transition to University life. In order to help students learn more about how different academic disciplines approach related problems, the All-University Curriculum was developed. Each course is team taught from different fields of expertise, and topics are examined from the perspective of several academic disciplines. The University also has a special program to assist students who may be undecided about a major. A reading and writing center, where students on an individual basis are helped to increase their proficiency in writing, research, reading comprehension, and speed as well as study and test-taking skills, is available to the entire student body. Further help in math is given through the Math Tutoring Lab, which is staffed by full-time faculty members and math majors. Selected students are encouraged to participate in the Honors Program. Honors students have the opportunity to graduate with an Honors Degree.

Off-Campus Programs

Intercampus registration through the Hartford Consortium for Higher Education permits University of Hartford students to take certain courses at the School of the Hartford Ballet, Saint Joseph College, and Trinity College. Teaching and human services majors in the College of Education, Nursing, and Health Professions have opportunities for field and/or clinical experiences where applicable. A central cooperative education office is available to custom-tailor work experiences within many of the University's programs.

Academic Facilities

Eight colleges and schools are housed on the main campus. The Harry Jack Gray Center houses the William H. Mortensen Library; the Mildred P. Allen Memorial Library; the Museum of American Political Life; the Harry J. Gray Conference Center; the Joseloff Gallery; the University Bookstore; studios for art, radio, and television; and the Communication Department. The library has approximately 583,000 items, including books, musical scores, recordings, periodicals, journals, and microfilm units. Extensive resources are also available through the Hartford Consortium for Higher Education, the Hartford Library, and the Inter-Library-Loan systems.

Hartford College for Women's 13-acre wooded campus is listed on the National Register of Historic Places. The campus is a blend of traditional ivy-covered Georgian buildings and modern classroom and laboratory buildings.

The University of Hartford Computer Center houses the central computer systems and operates a high-performance campus-wide network, which connects all student residential housing, all academic buildings on campus, and the University's remote locations. The University's network is connected via a high-speed telecommunication link to the Internet and the World Wide Web. The residential network gives each student resident his or her own Ethernet connection to the campus network and the Internet. The library is connected to the campus network and provides network access in study carrels and study rooms. The online systems of the library include the online catalog for book, audio, and video collections; CD-ROM databases; and certain Internet resources (e.g., 1,000 electronic journals). Ongoing improvements at the library include easy-to-use Web access for many of the library's online resources and electronic reserves. All of the University network resources may be accessed on campus at University facilities and off campus by using computers with modems.

Computing labs, used by all students of the University, are provided at six locations around the campus. The labs are equipped with microcomputers (both PCs and iMacs) and are connected to the campus network and the Internet. Typical microcomputer software includes word processing, spreadsheet, database management, and graphics programs; HyperCard; programming languages; and Web browsers for accessing the Internet. Help is available from on-duty lab assistants. In addition to these computer labs, there are specialized computer facilities for instruction and learning. Some examples of these specialized facilities are the Gilman Center for Communication Technology for English and journalism instruction; Information Technology Center for MIS and quantitative methods; the Computer Learning Center; the Center for Computer and Electronic Music; the Computer Aided Design/Computer Aided Manufacturing Laboratory; the Sun Workstation Laboratory for Computer Science; and the Electronic Learning Laboratory (Instructional Media Services). Additional facilities and advanced equipment for the study of earth sciences are available at the nearby Talcott Mountain Science Center.

Costs

Tuition for incoming students was $21,330 for the 2003–04 academic year; student service fees, $1140; on-campus room costs, $5310; and board, $3300. A variety of on-campus housing accommodates about 3,500 students.

Financial Aid

The University's financial aid program totals approximately $74 million annually, including student loans. Scholarships, grants, loans, and work-study opportunities are provided through the federal government, private agencies, interested individuals, and University funds. University funds are disbursed based upon the college or school in which the student is enrolled, availability of funds, applicant pool, and competition for funds. More than 90 percent of all full-time undergraduate students receive some type of University assistance; the average amount is $16,420 per year. Partial-tuition scholarships are awarded to entering students who have demonstrated outstanding academic achievement.

Faculty

There are 739 full-time and adjunct faculty members. The undergraduate and graduate faculties are essentially the same group, and 78 percent of the members hold the terminal degree in their field. Academic and personal advisory service is readily available. Each new student is assigned to a faculty adviser during summer orientation.

Student Government

The student governing body that represents all full-time students is the Student Government Association, through which students and faculty join in developing and coordinating the cocurricular activities of the University. Students are also represented on all major administrative committees, including the Board of Regents.

Admission Requirements

The Committee on Admission considers the quality of the secondary school curriculum, academic performance in secondary school, recommendations of the secondary school principal or guidance counselor, ACT or SAT I results, evidence of a desire to succeed, and leadership qualities shown by academic and extracurricular activities. Auditions, portfolios, and other tests are required of music and art applicants.

Application and Information

The University employs a rolling admission policy. For further information, students should contact:

Richard A. Zeiser
Dean of Admission
University of Hartford
West Hartford, Connecticut 06117-0395
Telephone: 860-768-4296
800-947-4303 (toll-free)
Fax: 860-768-4961
E-mail: admission@mail.hartford.edu
World Wide Web: http://www.hartford.edu/admission

UNIVERSITY OF HAWAII AT HILO

HILO, HAWAII

The University

Students who step into University of Hawaii at Hilo (UH Hilo) find that they have stepped into one of the world's best-kept secrets for a high-quality college education. With the Spirit of Aloha deeply embedded in the culture that exists within the University and the surrounding community of the Big Island of Hawaii, students and graduates alike often attribute their successful college experiences to the safe, friendly, and caring environment; the one-on-one interaction with faculty and staff members; and the valuable hands-on learning and leadership opportunities. These are the very qualities that have made UH Hilo an increasingly attractive campus for college-seeking students.

UH Hilo is a comprehensive regional institution offering a residential campus experience. As a state university, UH Hilo functions within the University of Hawaii system, serving students from the state of Hawaii, from the U.S. mainland, and from many countries in Europe, Asia, and Pacific regions.

Over the past five years, overall enrollment has increased 15 percent. The number of international students has also increased to more than 300 international students on campus, with a total student population of more than 3,000. Recently, *U.S. News & World Report* ranked UH Hilo number one in diversity for public universities and sixth among both private and public universities in the United States.

UH Hilo is accredited by the Accrediting Commission for Senior Colleges and Universities of the Western Association of Schools and Colleges (WASC). Education program majors are accredited by the National Association of State Directors of Teacher Education Certification. The nursing program is accredited by the National League for Nursing Accrediting Commission (NLNAC). The business administration (B.B.A.) program has been accepted for candidacy for accreditation by AACSB International–The Association to Advance Collegiate Schools of Business.

With the pristine blue waters of the Pacific Ocean, the majestic mountains of Mauna Kea and Mauna Loa, the captivating volcanoes, and the various distinctive types of climatic zones and ecosystems, UH Hilo is fully equipped with natural, living laboratories to command some of the world's best programs in marine science, vulcanology, astronomy, and conservation biology. The rich heritage of the Hawaiian culture has also paved the way for a strong program in Hawaiian studies at both the undergraduate and graduate levels. The M.A. in Hawaiian language and literature is UH Hilo's first graduate program and the first in the United States focusing on a Native American language. UH Hilo also offers a Master of Education degree (M.Ed.) and is working on adding more graduate programs, including counseling psychology and China-U.S. relations.

The University offers a wide range of activities and services to meet its students' social, cultural, and recreational needs. From canoe club and international student association to mountain biking and surfing, there are numerous on-campus and off-campus activities for students to participate in, come rain or shine. The athletic department offers various intercollegiate and intramural sports. The Vulcans are members of the National Collegiate Athletic Association (NCAA) Division II in men's basketball, cross-country, golf, and tennis as well as women's cross-country, softball, tennis, and volleyball. The men's baseball team competes on the NCAA Division I level as an independent.

Students can choose to live on or off campus. Currently, more than 600 students are housed in four coeducational residence halls on the UH Hilo campus—two are traditional, one is suite-style, and one is apartment-style. Residents in the traditional- and suite-style halls must participate in a board program, with meals served at the residence-hall dining room. Off-campus housing includes privately owned apartments, homes, or rooms in the Hilo community. The housing office provides assistance in finding off-campus accommodations.

Location

The University is located in the city of Hilo, on the east side of the Hawaii island, about 200 air miles from Honolulu, the state's capital. The peaceful city of Hilo offers a moderate cost of living, clean air, and a low-density population of about 50,000. Within 10 minutes of campus are shopping malls, theaters, restaurants, grocery stores, and a post office as well as a major harbor and international airport. Some of the world's best beaches and golf courses are only a few hours' drive away. Throughout the winter months, the island of Hawaii is also a popular destination for whales that come to indulge themselves in the lavishness of the warm Hawaiian waters.

Majors and Degrees

More than thirty-five majors are offered through four main colleges. The College of Arts and Science, the largest of the colleges, offers undergraduate degrees in administration of justice, anthropology, art, astronomy, biology (with a premed option), business administration, chemistry, communication, computer science, drama, economics, English, geography, geology, health and physical education, history, Japanese studies, linguistics, marine science, mathematics, music, natural sciences, nursing, performing arts, philosophy, physics, political science, psychology, recreational management, religious studies, and sociology. Certificates offered within this college include environmental studies, international studies with emphasis in international relations and tourism, marine science option, Pacific Island studies, planning (under the geography program), systems modeling (under the mathematics program), and women's studies.

The College of Agriculture, Forestry, and Natural Resource Management offers the Bachelor of Science degree in seven areas of specialization: agribusiness, agroecology and environmental quality, animal science (options in production and pre–veterinary studies), aquaculture, crop protection, general agriculture, and tropical horticulture.

The College of Hawaiian Language offers the Bachelor of Arts in Hawaiian studies and certificates in Hawaiian language or culture.

The College of Continuing Education and Community Service offers an exciting array of credit, noncredit, professional, and personal-development courses and a customized English as a second language program designed for foreign students who seek to increase their command of English prior to starting their undergraduate studies.

Of particular interest to many students is UH Hilo's Marine Science Summer Program (MSSP). It has received the Excellence of Program Award from the Western Association of Summer Session Administrators, which represents some eighty colleges and universities in the western United States, Canada, and Mexico. The MSSP provides several introductory-level courses, including oceanography, marine biology, and the Hawaii marine field experience.

The QUEST (Quantitative Underwater Ecological Surveying Techniques) is a popular one-of-a-kind, two-week-long, full-time course in which students learn underwater ecological surveying methodologies.

Academic Programs

UH Hilo stresses rigorous education in a caring, personalized atmosphere; encourages student-faculty interaction and collaboration on research projects; and offers hands-on learning and leadership opportunities by utilizing the natural settings of the location as well as by partnering with the business community and various state agencies.

The honors program is designed to motivate, challenge, and enrich students in order to promote their intellectual curiosity, nurture their intellectual independence, and deepen their sense of scholarship.

Baccalaureate degrees are granted only to those students who have satisfactorily completed the program of courses prescribed for their majors, earned at least a 2.0 cumulative GPA as well as a 2.0 GPA in courses required for the major and minor (if any), earned a minimum of 30 semester hours in the college from which a degree is sought, were registered and in attendance at the University during the semester or summer session in which the degree is granted, and met all requirements of their respective colleges and departments.

Off-Campus Programs

The University of Hawaii at Hilo is a member of the National Student Exchange Program (NSE) in the United States. Each year, selected students attend one of the more than 170 colleges and universities in forty-eight states. The study-abroad program allows students to enjoy first-hand experiences of other cultures and provides for the acquisition of valuable skills and expertise for an increasingly internationalized and interdependent world. In addition, students are eligible to participate in study-abroad programs sponsored by participating universities in the National Student Exchange Consortium.

Academic Facilities

Most of the learning facilities are located on the main campus, which spreads across 115 acres. To serve the needs of the University, there are more than eighty classrooms, a library and media center, faculty and staff buildings, a student services building, a fully-equipped theater complex, a campus center for student activities, an athletic complex, tennis courts, and a playing field.

Adjoining the main campus is a 163-acre University Park, which is home to an impressive array of world-class multinational tenants representing science, technology, and agricultural biotechnology. This research park has allowed faculty and staff members to interact with a distinguished community of scientists and technicians from around the world.

Within a 10-minute drive from the main campus is a 110-acre University Agricultural Farm Laboratory, which provides valuable hands-on learning opportunities.

Costs

For 2004–05, work is in progress to implement a one-level undergraduate tuition per year for full-time students: $2424 for Hawaii residents, $7992 for international students and U.S. students from non-WUE (Western Undergraduate Exchange) states, and $3636 for students from WUE states (Alaska, Arizona, California, Colorado, Hawaii, Idaho, Montana, Nevada, New Mexico, North Dakota, South Dakota, Oregon, Utah, Washington, and Wyoming).

Room and board costs per year are estimated to be $4840; books and supplies, approximately $985; and student fees, about $50.

Financial Aid

The financial aid program at UH Hilo is designed to provide financial assistance to students who would not be able to attend college without such assistance. Need-based and non-need-based financial assistance is available to students in numerous forms: federal student aid; Hawaii State Tuition Waivers; loans, grants, and scholarships from state and federal agencies; and a range of scholarships from private sponsors/donors.

Federal (Federal Work-Study) and state (general) funds are provided for the employment of students under the Student Employment Program. The priority processing deadline is March 1.

Faculty

The faculty members are highly qualified and recognized in their fields of expertise. They hold advanced degrees and are committed to high-quality teaching by incorporating the surrounding natural environment as a leading-edge learning laboratory. Hands-on experience as part of the learning process in the personal settings of UH Hilo's campus invariably broadens students' horizons, thus preparing them to better handle graduate school or the working world.

Student Government

Major student organizations include the UH Hilo Student Association, the Student Activities Council, and the Board of Student Publications. These organizations provide opportunities for students to acquire leadership and social skills.

Admission Requirements

All interested students need to submit their completed application forms, including a $40 application fee, to the Admissions Office. They must also have official high school transcripts sent directly from their high school and have their SAT I/ACT (and GED, if applicable) scores sent directly from the testing agencies to the Admissions Office. International students need to complete and submit all required documents as outlined in the application form.

Application and Information

Applications and all supporting documents noted in the application form, including the $40 application fee, must be received by July 1 for fall semester and December 1 for spring semester. For application materials or for more information, students should contact:

Admissions Office
Student Services Building
University of Hawaii at Hilo
200 West Kawili Street
Hilo, Hawaii 96720-4091
Telephone: 808-974-7414
800-897-4456 (toll-free, United States only)
Fax: 808-933-0861
E-mail: uhhadm@hawaii.edu
World Wide Web: http://www.uhh.hawaii.edu

On the campus of University of Hawaii at Hilo.

UNIVERSITY OF HOUSTON

HOUSTON, TEXAS

The University

The University of Houston's (UH) main campus, a leading institution in the state-assisted system of higher education in Texas, stands on the forefront of education, research, and service. The largest and most comprehensive component of the University of Houston System, the UH main campus serves more than 35,000 students in thirteen colleges and a host of schools and programs offering more than 300 undergraduate, graduate, and special professional degrees.

UH conducts basic research in each academic department and operates more than forty research centers and institutes on campus. Through these facilities the University maintains creative partnerships with government and private industry, and the research conducted breaks new ground in such vital areas as superconductivity, space commercialization, chemical engineering, economics, and education. The Conrad N. Hilton College of Hotel and Restaurant Management attracts students from all over the country. The University's advanced professional programs include architecture, law, pharmacy, and optometry.

Sponsored research was at $72 million for fiscal year 2003. Considering its commitment to excellence, the University anticipates continued support and growth in the amount of grants and awards.

Outstanding faculty members and facilities draw students from across the country and around the world. As a result, UH is characterized by a rich mix of cultural backgrounds in a student body that is 40.5 percent white, 18.4 percent Asian/Pacific Islander, 17.8 percent Hispanic, 13.5 percent African American, 7 percent international students who represent countries across the globe, and .4 percent Native American.

University of Houston public service and community activities, such as cultural offerings, clinical services, policy studies, and small-business initiatives, serve a diverse metropolitan population. Likewise, the resources of the Gulf Coast region complement and enrich the University's academic programs, providing students with professional expertise, practical experience, and career opportunities and allowing them to secure career-level jobs soon after graduation.

Location

Located just minutes from downtown Houston on Interstate 45, the University is set on 557 acres of parks, fountains, plazas, sculptures, and recreational fields surrounding more than ninety modern facilities. This offers students a comfortable and well-equipped setting for academic pursuits and proximity to the resources of the nation's fourth-largest city. Gulf Coast beaches, Texas hill country, and piney woods are equally accessible from Houston, and a warm climate permits outdoor activity throughout the year.

Majors and Degrees

UH awards Bachelor of Arts and Bachelor of Science degrees, with majors in accounting, accountancy, anthropology, applied music, architecture, art, art history, biochemical/biophysical sciences, biology, biomedical technology, chemical engineering, chemistry, civil engineering, civil technology, classical studies, communication disorders, computer drafting design, computer engineering technology, computer science, computer science–business, computer science–systems, construction management and technologies, consumer science and merchandising, creative writing, earth science, economics, education, electrical engineering, electrical technology, electrical technology–control systems, electrical technology–electrical power, English, entrepreneurship, environmental design, exercise science, finance, French, geology, geology-geophysics, German, graphic communications, health, history, hotel and restaurant management, human development and family studies, human nutrition and foods, industrial distribution, industrial engineering, industrial supervision, information systems technology, interdisciplinary studies, interior design, interpersonal communication, Italian studies, journalism, kinesiology, management, management information systems, manufacturing systems technology, marketing, mathematics–applied analysis, mechanical and related technology, mechanical engineering, media policy/studies, media production, merchandising and industrial distribution, movement and sports studies, music, music composition, music theory, occupational technology and industrial studies, operations management, optometry, organizational/corporate communication, painting, pharmacy, philosophy, photography, physics, physics-geophysics, political science, preprofessional English studies, printmaking, psychology, Russian studies, sculpture, sociology, Spanish, sports administration, statistics and operations research, studio art, theater, and training/human resources.

Academic Program

UH offers an undergraduate curriculum that provides students with a broad base in the liberal arts complemented by in-depth studies in disciplines of their choice, affording students a foundation for lifelong learning. UH enrolls a substantial number of National Merit Scholars each year, and the quality of UH students is further reflected in the growing enrollment in the Honors College. Created to serve the intellectual needs of gifted undergraduates in more than 100 fields of study, the Honors College provides the careful guidance, flexibility, and personal instruction that nurture individual excellence. The Honors College offers all the advantages of a small college without sacrificing the wealth of resources and the rich diversity of a large university.

Off-Campus Programs

The College of Humanities, Fine Arts, and Communication and the College of Business Administration offer fall and spring semesters in London, during which students can earn 15 hours of credit. Courses are taught by UH professors, faculty members from other Texas universities, and the University of London faculty. The Department of Modern and Classical Languages sponsors two summer programs in Puebla, Mexico, and Madrid, Spain. The Department of French has a summer program in Bourges, France, and the College of Architecture sponsors two summer programs in Saintes and Paris, France. In addition, UH has a wide variety of courses and programs that are offered through distance education and study abroad.

Academic Facilities

Libraries at UH provide abundant resources for research, with total collective holdings of more than 2 million volumes, 3.8 million microfilm units, 15,152 research journal subscriptions, and various other research materials. A computerized catalog system links all four UH System libraries and the specialized libraries in architecture, law, music, optometry, and pharmacy at UH. The University's computer-intensive environment enhances both teaching and research. A computer network links more than 4,000 workstations across the campus, and UH is connected to several wide area networks, providing access to more than 1,100 universities, research institutions, and corporations worldwide.

Costs

The estimated average total cost for 15 units for the fall 2003 semester was $1749 for Texas residents and $5019 for nonresidents. Costs are subject to change. Prospective students should visit the Student Financial Services Web site at http://www.uh.edu/sfs/ for updated tuition information.

Financial Aid

Several types of student financial assistance are offered, including scholarships, which are generally based on measures of academic performance such as GPA, class rank, and SAT I or ACT scores, and need-based (as determined from the Free Application for Federal Student Aid) assistance, which includes loans, grants, and part-time employment. Applicants are encouraged to apply online at http://www.fafsa.ed.gov/. For additional information, students should write directly to Office of Scholarships and Financial Aid, Room 26 E. Cullen Building, University of Houston, Houston, Texas 77204-2010.

Faculty

Ranked faculty members number more than 850. The number of lecturers, teaching fellows, and visiting and adjunct faculty members is more than 900. Faculty members are published in the most prestigious journals, and their research garners national and international acclaim. Students also benefit from instruction at an urban institution where more than 1,000 business and community leaders bring their expertise and experience to the classroom.

Student Government

The Students' Association is the University's student government and official student representative organization. It works to improve the quality of education and campus life and participates in policymaking decisions. The association participates in student disciplinary cases and works to preserve student rights.

Admission Requirements

Freshmen should submit their high school transcript, including class rank and GPA plus SAT I or ACT test scores. Applicants should have taken 4 years of English and 3 years each of math and science in high school; 2 years of foreign language are recommended. Transfers should have 15 or more hours of transferable college credit and a minimum GPA of 2.5; some majors require a higher GPA. The TOEFL is required for international students.

Application and Information

Notifications of acceptance are based on a review of an applicant's complete file and continue on a rolling admission basis. An application fee of $40 is required. Students are urged to apply early. Deadlines for summer and fall are April 2 for freshmen and May 1 for transfer/postbaccalaureate students; for spring, applications should be received by December 1 for both freshman and transfer/postbaccalaureate students.

Applicants are strongly encouraged to apply for admission using the Internet at the address listed below and are reminded to select the University of Houston main campus as the receiving institution.

For additional information, students should contact:

Office of Admissions
122 E. Cullen Building
University of Houston
Houston, Texas 77204-2023
Telephone: 713-743-1010 Option 2
World Wide Web: http://www.uh.edu

Houston: The city and its university.

UNIVERSITY OF IDAHO

MOSCOW, IDAHO

The University

The University of Idaho (UI) was established in 1889 and is a publicly supported, land-grant, Doctoral/Research University–Extensive. There are 12,894 students enrolled at the UI; 8,727 are undergraduate students at the Moscow campus. UI students come from eighty countries around the world and all fifty states. The University is a member of the National Association of State Universities and Land-Grant Colleges and is accredited by the Northwest Association of Schools and Colleges. UI offers more than 150 degree programs in nine colleges. Bachelor's, master's, doctoral, and specialist degrees are offered, as are certificates of completion in sixteen areas of study. The Moscow campus and adjacent farms cover nearly 800 acres. Other University lands, including the nearby University farms and experimental forests, exceed 10,000 acres. The UI is a residential campus. More than 90 percent of UI freshmen live on campus. Housing options include the Living and Learning Community suites that offer single rooms and a shared full kitchen, den with fireplace, and study areas; five residence halls with themed communities; four apartment complexes; and nineteen fraternities and nine sororities. UI has more than 100 student organizations and nearly as many intramural sports. Men and women compete in NCAA Division I-A in the Big West Conference except for football, which is played in the Sun Belt Conference.

Location

The University of Idaho is located in Moscow, Idaho (population about 21,000). A small but vibrant community, Moscow offers many amenities for students and is very rich in cultural events—having been ranked thirty-eighth in "The Best 100 Small Art Towns in America." The surrounding Palouse hills and the mountains and lakes of the northern Idaho panhandle provide a scenic background for many activities within easy driving distance, such as white-water rafting, snowboarding and skiing, biking, climbing, and camping. *Outdoor* magazine recently ranked UI as one of the top fifty schools for a great education and outdoor experience. Moscow is 90 miles south of Spokane, Washington, and is served by the Spokane International Airport and the Pullman-Moscow Regional Airport.

Majors and Degrees

In the College of Agricultural and Life Sciences, students learn to use science and the latest technologies to help meet today's challenges facing families, the food supply, and the environment. Majors include agribusiness; agricultural economics; agricultural education; agricultural science and technology; agricultural systems management; animal science; child, family, and consumer studies; clothing, textiles, and design; early childhood development and education; entomology; food and nutrition; food science; horticultural and crop science; medical technology; microbiology; molecular biology and biochemistry; range livestock management; science/preveterinary; and soil and land resources.

The College of Business and Economics (CBE) is one of only 25 percent of the business colleges across the country to be accredited by the AACSB International–The Association to Advance Collegiate Schools of Business. CBE's Integrated Business Curriculum (IBC) positions UI as a national leader in the business and industry-inspired curriculum movement. Upper-division IBC students are issued laptop computers. Students have many majors to select from, including innovative new programs like the professional golf management program that prepares students for careers in the fast-growing golf industry. Majors include accounting, business economics, economics, finance, information systems, management and human resources, marketing, and production/operations management.

With the most comprehensive programs in Idaho, the College of Education offers seven undergraduate degrees with fifteen academic majors and thirty-five secondary teaching majors and minors. Graduates teach in K–12 school settings; work in public, private, and community agencies; manage recreational and sports programs; and work as athletic trainers. Some students continue in graduate programs in specialized areas such as counseling, physical therapy, and technology. Majors include athletic training, business education, dance, elementary education, industrial technology, marketing education, office administration, physical education, professional/technical education, recreation, school and community health education, secondary education, special education, sport science, and technology education.

The College of Engineering attracts some of the best and brightest students in the University, judging from GPA and test scores, and its graduates are highly sought. Majors include agricultural engineering, biological systems engineering, chemical engineering, civil engineering, computer engineering, computer science, electrical engineering, geological engineering, materials science and engineering, mechanical engineering, metallurgical engineering, and mining engineering.

The College of Letters, Arts and Social Sciences provides a solid liberal and professional education in the humanities, studio and performing arts, architecture disciplines, languages and literatures, and the social sciences. Outstanding among the college's many excellent programs are architecture, with the field's only accredited master's degree in Idaho; the Lionel Hampton School of Music and its world-renowned jazz festival; and one of the oldest and best repertory theater groups in the Northwest. Majors include advertising, American studies, anthropology, architecture, art, art education, communication studies, crime and justice studies, English, environmental science, foreign language, general studies, history, interdisciplinary studies, interior design, international studies, journalism, landscape architecture, Latin American studies, music, music education, naval science, philosophy, political science, psychology, public relations, radio/TV/digital media production, sociology, studio art, theater arts, and virtual technology and design.

The College of Natural Resources' nationally accredited programs, excellent professors, and field experience is a potent combination that gives graduates a competitive edge in the job market. The field campuses and research areas provide students with a diverse sampling of Idaho's plant and wildlife habitat, including rangelands, forests, and aquatic environments. Majors include fishery resources, forest products, forest resources, natural resources ecology and conservation biology, range livestock management, rangeland ecology and management, resource recreation and tourism, and wildlife resources.

The College of Science includes biological sciences, chemistry, geography, geological sciences, mathematics, physics, and the division of statistics. The college offers many valuable hands-on learning and research opportunities to undergraduates and is committed to excellence in teaching. Many faculty members are nationally and internationally recognized experts in their fields. Majors include biology, chemistry, geography, geological sciences, mathematics, and physics.

Academic Programs

The academic year consists of two semesters, with winter intersession and summer session available. The number of credit hours required for graduation varies with the program selected, but a minimum of 128 is required for a bachelor's degree. Students must fulfill the required credit hours in a major and the requirements of the core curriculum. The University has long possessed nationally recognized marks of excellence, including chapters of national honorary and scholarship societies in practically every specialized field and chapters of the following general honorary societies: Phi Beta Kappa, Phi Kappa Phi, Sigma Xi, and Golden Key. In addition, the University Honors Program features a diverse curriculum and extracurricular opportunities that offer cultural enrichment, friendship, and learning. Classes are small and faculty members work to foster and stimulate intellectual growth, which significantly contributes to the academic success of students. Special academic programs include the Washington, Wyoming, Alaska, Montana, and Idaho (WWAMI) medical education program; the Washington, Oregon, and Idaho (WOI) veterinary medicine program; and ROTC.

Off-Campus Programs

The UI offers academic learning centers in Coeur d'Alene, Boise, Idaho Falls, and Twin Falls. Engineering Outreach provides distance learning for UI engineering programs. National Student Exchange and International Study Abroad programs are available.

Academic Facilities

The University Library and the Law Library contain more than 2 million items of books, bound periodicals, microforms, and U.S. government publications. Students receive free e-mail and unlimited high-speed Internet service and have access to more than 900 computers in twenty-two computer labs across the campus. Courtesy laptops are available for student use, and more than forty campus buildings offer wireless Internet connectivity.

Costs

Tuition and fees for full-time students (12 or more credits) for the 2003–04 academic year were $3348 for Idaho residents and $10,740 for nonresident students. Room and board costs averaged $4868 per year and books and supplies cost approximately $1250. (Costs are subject to change.)

Financial Aid

The University of Idaho has more than $60 million in scholarships, grants, low-interest student loans, work-study, and internship opportunities available to students. Included are merit-based tuition waiver programs, such as the Western Undergraduate Exchange (WUE) and the Idaho Tuition Scholarship. Other merit scholarships include UI Scholars, Presidential Academic, Presidential Achievement, Presidential Leadership, Alumni Scholarship, and Idaho Promise Scholarship. Many academic colleges and departments offer a variety of scholarships to top students in their major field of study. General UI scholarships are available to students in any area of study. Some of these general awards require students to show financial need through a processed Free Application for Federal Student Aid (FAFSA). Grant and loan programs include the Federal Pell Grant, Federal Supplemental Educational Opportunity Grant (FSEOG), LEAPP State Grant, College Assistance Migrant Program (CAMP), Federal Perkins Loan, Federal Ford Direct Stafford Student Loan, Federal Parent Loan (PLUS), and loans from private lenders. Federal and Idaho work-study programs and on- and off-campus employment are available. To receive priority consideration for all financial aid, the FAFSA must be completed and sent by February 15. Applicants should visit http://www.students.uidaho.edu for a complete list of available scholarships and financial aid information.

Faculty

The UI faculty totals 874 members who engage in teaching and scholarly research; 85 percent are full-time and 15 percent are part-time employees. Nearly 70 percent have earned their terminal degree. Members of the undergraduate faculty are selected to present graduate-level courses. Faculty members also serve as academic advisers for students. There are 724 teaching and research assistants; the teaching assistants serve as undergraduate instructors. The student-faculty ratio at UI is 20:1.

Student Government

All enrolled undergraduate students are members of the Associated Students of the University of Idaho (ASUI). The 15-member ASUI Senate is the legislative body, with the purpose to initiate and coordinate student activities; promote and represent student interests, needs, and welfare within the University community; provide for the expression of student opinion and interests to the community at large on issues affecting student life; develop in students an understanding and appreciation of their personal, social, and vocational relationship to society; and provide a physical and social environment in which to achieve these objectives.

Admission Requirements

Students who graduate from an accredited high school must submit an admissions application and a $40 nonrefundable application fee and have their transcripts sent to the UI. Students must have completed the high school core curriculum requirements with a GPA of 2.0 or better, including English, 8 semester credits; math, 6 semester credits (algebra 1 or more); humanities/foreign languages, 2 semester credits; natural science, 6 semester credits; social science, 5 semester credits; and other college-preparation courses, 3 semester credits. Students must have a combined GPA and minimum ACT or SAT score as follows: GPA 3.0–4.0, with any ACT or SAT score; GPA 2.6–2.99, with minimum ACT 15 or SAT 790; GPA 2.5–2.59, with minimum ACT 17 or SAT 870; GPA 2.4–2.49, with minimum ACT 19 or SAT 930; GPA 2.3–2.39, with minimum ACT 21 or SAT 1000; or GPA 2.2–2.29, with minimum ACT 23 or SAT 1070.

Students who graduate from a nonaccredited high school, are home-schooled, or otherwise do not meet the above criteria are considered for admission. Transfer students are selected from applicants with at least 14 transferable credits who present a cumulative GPA of at least 2.0 on all college-level study attempted in all accredited colleges attended. International students are invited and encouraged to apply. Early admission may be granted based on a sixth or seventh semester high school transcript if it appears that the student meets admission requirements. Applicants should visit http://www.students.uidaho.edu for complete admission requirements for all types of undergraduate students.

Application and Information

Students must have the University of Idaho Admissions Application Form to the Admissions Office by February 15. Students may apply online by visiting http://www.students.uidaho.edu or by contacting Undergraduate Admissions.

Carolyn Lazzarini
Admission Services Representative
Undergraduate Admissions
University of Idaho
P.O. Box 444264
Moscow, Idaho 83844-4264
Telephone: 208-885-6326
Fax: 208-885-9119
E-mail: carolynl@uidaho.edu
World Wide Web: http://www.students.uidaho.edu
http://www.uidaho.edu

Student on campus at the University of Idaho.

UNIVERSITY OF INDIANAPOLIS

INDIANAPOLIS, INDIANA

The University

The University of Indianapolis is a private residential institution of higher learning. Established in 1902 and now an integral part of the educational and cultural life of Indianapolis, the University maintains a moderate size and a diverse student body, and it provides a comprehensive set of general, preprofessional, and professional programs, grounded in the liberal arts.

Students indicate that they choose the University because of its challenging, yet supportive, atmosphere and relatively small size, combined with the advantages of its location in the southern suburbs of a thriving state capital. As a result, there is a great sense of community and pride on the campus. The University helps students to determine and achieve their individual academic goals. The University has experienced much growth and has instituted many enhancements recently, having followed the redesign and landscaping of the campus with a new health science building, new facilities for the communications department, a major renovation to the student center, and a fifth residence hall.

More than 2,000 Day Division students are enrolled. There are students from sixty countries and twenty states. Approximately 75 percent of the students live in on-campus housing. The warmth and sensitivity of the faculty and staff members and students alike enable those who are a part of the campus to feel a strong sense of community.

In addition to the undergraduate division, the University is composed of the Graduate and Doctoral Division, including the nationally recognized Krannert School of Physical Therapy. The most popular programs in the undergraduate division include pre–physical therapy, business, athletic training, communication, nursing, education, premedicine, psychology, music, and art. Social life is organized through the Campus Program Board, Indianapolis Student Government, and the Residence Hall Association, student organizations that plan weekly activities for all students. There are numerous social clubs and interest groups available for students who wish to become involved in extracurricular activities. Five residence halls house students; four house both men and women, and one is only for women. Students must be admitted on a full-time basis in order to be assigned housing. NCAA Division II sports for men include baseball, basketball, cross-country, football, golf, soccer, swimming and diving, tennis, track and field (indoor and outdoor), and wrestling. NCAA Division II sports for women include basketball, cross-country, fast-pitch softball, golf, soccer, swimming and diving, tennis, track and field (indoor and outdoor), and volleyball. There are eight intramural sports open to all students.

Location

The University is located in the southern neighborhoods of Indianapolis, the nation's third-largest capital city. Indianapolis and the surrounding area constitute a metropolitan area of more than 1 million people. As a result, the city offers students valuable internship and service learning experiences as well as recreational and cultural opportunities too numerous to mention. The campus is extremely accessible, just a few blocks from two major interstate highways (I-65 and I-465). The campus is served by Metro bus, and Amtrak trains arrive daily at historic Union Station, just 10 minutes from the campus. Indianapolis International Airport is about 15 minutes away.

Majors and Degrees

The undergraduate programs are offered through the College of Arts and Sciences, the School of Business, the School of Nursing, the School of Education, the Krannert School of Physical Therapy, and the School of Psychological Sciences. The degrees awarded are the Associate in Arts, Associate in Science, Associate in Science in Nursing, Bachelor of Arts, Bachelor of Science, and Bachelor of Science in Nursing. Baccalaureate and preprofessional fields of study include accounting (CMA/CPA), anthropology, archeology, art, art therapy, athletic training, biology, business administration, chemistry, communication studies, computer science, corporate communication, corrections, earth-space sciences, economics and finance, electrical engineering (dual degree), electronic media, elementary education, English, environmental science, financial services, French, German, history, human biology, human communication, human resource management, information systems, international business, journalism, law enforcement, marketing, mathematics, mechanical engineering (dual degree), medical technology, music, music performance, nursing, philosophy, physical education, physics, political science, predentistry, prelaw, premedicine, pre–occupational therapy, pre–physical therapy, pretheology, pre–veterinary science, production and operations management, psychology, public relations, religion, secondary education, social work, sociology, Spanish, speech communication, sports information, theater, and visual communication design. Teaching majors are offered in business education, English, French, mathematics, music (all grades), physical education (all grades), science (five primary areas), social studies (six primary areas), Spanish, speech communication and theater, and visual arts (all grades).

Associate degrees are awarded in business administration, chemistry, computer programming/ASI 400, corrections, industrial chemistry, financial services, information systems, law enforcement, liberal arts, nursing, and physical therapist assistant studies.

Academic Programs

The goal of the University is most accurately reflected in its motto, "Education for Service." Associate degrees require 62 semester hours of credit; baccalaureate degrees require 124 semester hours of credit. All students are required to complete the general education core curriculum. A complete testing program is in place that awards credit by examination through CLEP, PEP, DANTES, Advanced Placement examinations, University examinations, and other tests. In addition to credit, these may be for exemption or placement, depending upon the particular examination. The testing program is administered through the Office of the University Registrar.

Students are selected to participate in the honors program by invitation only, based upon their high school record. Students who complete three of five offered honors courses with a B– or higher and who satisfactorily complete a senior honors project receive the designation "Graduation with Distinction" at commencement. Through the Consortium for Urban Education, the University has a cross-registration program with six other area colleges. The academic calendar is composed of two 15-week semesters (the last week is finals week), a three-week Spring Term beginning in May, and two 6-week summer sessions (with limited course offerings).

Off-Campus Programs

The University operates two fully accredited branch campuses in Cyprus in the eastern Mediterranean Sea and in Greece that offer students a unique exchange program. Other off-campus study opportunities take place during the Spring Term, including assorted overseas travel openings. The University has an Office of Career Services, which arranges off-campus internships related to one's field of study.

Academic Facilities

Krannert Memorial Library, which operates an online card catalog, houses more than 170,000 volumes, more than 1,000 periodicals, and more than 19,000 microfilm/microform/microfiche records. The library is home to a full media center as well as the communications department with new state-of-the-art equipment for its radio station and television studio. Recently built Martin Hall contains outstanding resources for the Schools of Nursing, Physical Therapy, and Occupational Therapy and is connected to Lilly Science Hall, which recently underwent a major upgrade to all its science labs. Access to computers is available in all of the academic buildings and residence halls. Students have access to the campuswide information system from their rooms in the residence halls. Ransburg Auditorium, with seating for nearly 800, is the setting for concerts, recitals, and theatrical productions. The $10-million Christel DeHaan Fine Arts Center features state-of-the-art music and art facilities, an art gallery, and a 450-seat, Viennese-style concert hall.

Costs

Directly billed expenses for the 2004–05 academic year are $17,200 for tuition and $6150 for room and board. Nonbilled indirect expenses are estimated at $640 for books and supplies, an average of $590 for transportation, and $1170 for miscellaneous and personal expenses.

Financial Aid

All applicants for admission are eligible to apply for financial aid. Indiana residents should file the Free Application for Federal Student Aid (FAFSA) by March 1 to qualify for state of Indiana financial aid programs. All students should file the FAFSA along with the University of Indianapolis Application for Financial Aid by March 1 for priority consideration. For the 2003–04 academic year, about 82 percent of the enrolled full-time students received more than $37 million from all sources.

Faculty

All Day Division faculty members are assigned teaching (not research) duties, including many administrators and some professional staff personnel. Graduate students do not teach any undergraduate classes. Over the past five years, the student-faculty ratio has been 14:1, and the average class size has ranged from 17 to 20.

Student Government

The Indianapolis Student Government (ISG) consists of students elected to officer positions plus student representatives from each class, chosen for a one-year term in an annual student body election. ISG's main focus is to pass resolutions regarding student concerns.

Admission Requirements

Applicants for admission must be high school graduates or have a GED certificate and are expected to have taken a college-preparatory curriculum in high school. Applicants for regular admission should have completed a minimum of 4 years of English, 3 years of mathematics, 3 years of laboratory science, 2 years of social science (U.S. history, government, and economics), and 2 years of any foreign language. In addition, applicants for full-time admission without restrictions should rank in the upper half of their class and have either a combined SAT I score of at least 920 or an ACT composite score of at least 20. Essays are not required for admission. For immediate consideration, transfer applicants should be in good academic standing at their original college and maintain a cumulative GPA of at least 2.0. An on-campus interview is recommended, anytime after the junior year of high school. To apply for admission, the Application for Admission, official high school transcript, official college transcript (if applicable), and official SAT I or ACT scores should be forwarded to the Office of Admissions.

Application and Information

All applications are reviewed on a rolling basis—an admission decision is made as soon as all documents are received, and notifications are mailed immediately thereafter. The deadline for applications is August 15 every year, but high school seniors should apply during the fall semester of their senior year for priority consideration.

Requests for appointments and information about the University should be directed to:

Director of Admissions
University of Indianapolis
1400 East Hanna Avenue
Indianapolis, Indiana 46227-3697
Telephone: 317-STUDENT
317-788-3216
800-232-8634 (toll-free)
Fax: 317-788-3300
E-mail: admissions@uindy.edu
World Wide Web: http://www.uindy.edu/

Smith Mall, the centerpiece of the University of Indianapolis campus, features a beautifully landscaped water garden canal.

UNIVERSITY OF JUDAISM
College of Arts and Sciences
BEL AIR, CALIFORNIA

The University

The University of Judaism's (UJ) College of Arts and Sciences offers a thorough and traditional liberal arts education with a Jewish perspective. The unique balance of a pluralistic Jewish environment and rigorous nonsectarian academics has proven to be a highly successful combination, as evidenced by a ten-year placement rate into graduate schools that exceeds 95 percent. This success is due largely to the UJ's caring and accessible faculty of distinguished scholars who teach classes of typically 12–15 students and who emphasize interactive seminars more than impersonal lectures. Frequently, a spirited classroom discussion continues in the hallways or cafeteria.

Accredited by the Western Association of Schools and Colleges, the school began in 1982 as Lee College at the University of Judaism. The University itself was founded in 1947 and also offers graduate degree programs in business, Jewish communal service, education, and rabbinics. The central institutional mission is to develop the future volunteer and professional leadership of the community, both Jewish and at large, and to do so in an atmosphere of academic openness and intellectual excellence.

What particularly sets UJ apart from other small, private, coed, liberal arts colleges is the Jewish life that flourishes on campus. Not only does UJ have a kosher cafeteria and no classes on Jewish holidays, but its celebration of holidays and its weekly Shabbat activities foster a lively community environment that invites, but does not demand, participation.

Most undergraduates live on campus, enjoying spacious residence hall rooms, each with air conditioning, cable, phone jacks, wireless Internet access, and a large private full bathroom. Residential-life features include a brand new, state-of-the-art student center with a big screen TV, fitness center, athletic facilities, and coffee and juice bar. Activities range from a campus newspaper, choir, and national literary magazine to political clubs, theater productions, musical ensembles, a radio station, and less structured favorites like mud football and midnight deli runs. The UJ also regularly hosts wider community events such as regional Hillel dances attended by hundreds of students from other Southern California colleges and universities.

A select fall entering class of about 60 students is drawn from thousands of inquiries representing every region and social segment of the U.S. and from numerous countries. When assessing applicants, the UJ values diversity, intellect, achievement, self-motivation, respect for Judeo-Christian values, and the eagerness to fully participate in a close campus community.

Location

Bel Air is one of the most desirable residential communities in Los Angeles. The University of Judaism is set on a 27-acre campus adjacent to both a quiet residential neighborhood and a rustic area that is great for hiking. Located on a hilltop, the setting offers panoramic views of the Santa Monica Mountains and San Fernando Valley. Within a 30-minute driving radius are the major resources of Southern California, from Hollywood and beaches to L.A.'s governmental, business, and religious centers. Within 10 minutes are such attractions as the Getty Museum, the Skirball Cultural Center, and UCLA. Accordingly, UJ students access internships and community service projects just as readily as they venture to concerts, plays, movies, cafés, and sporting events. The campus itself is characterized by contemporary open-air architecture and grassy, tree-lined walkways.

Majors and Degrees

The College of Arts and Sciences confers the Bachelor of Arts degree. Standard academic majors include bioethics (premedicine), business, Jewish studies, journalism, law and society (prelaw), liberal studies, literature and communications, political science, psychology, and U.S. public policy. Students may also design individualized majors or undertake a program that extends the Bachelor of Arts into a Master of Business Administration focused on nonprofit management or a master's in Jewish education.

Academic Program

The 70-credit general education program blends Jewish, Western, and other world civilizations; communication; and distribution requirements in math, science, arts, and computer study. The core curriculum is distinctive for its multidisciplinary approach, which draws on history, literature, philosophy, political science, and religion in its objective study of culture and civilization. There is no religious instruction required or expected.

Close faculty advisers assure graduation in four years for nearly every UJ undergraduate. The B.A. requires completion of 120 semester credits, including fulfillment of residency, general education, and major requirements. The number and pattern of major requirements vary by department. Fifteen elective credits must be taken outside the major. If concentrated in one field of upper-division study, elective courses may count as an academic minor. Residency requirements consist of 34 credits completed at the UJ, at least 15 of which are in the major.

Off-Campus Programs

Arranged individually to accommodate each UJ student's specific goal, study-abroad opportunities are abundant, typically occurring in the junior year. There is also a unique Freshman Year Abroad option for high school graduates who want a rich Israel immersion experience without delaying the start of their college education. This is done through Hadassah's Young Judaea Year Course in Israel, with academic oversight by the University of Judaism.

Those pursuing medically related studies through the innovative bioethics major regularly utilize the laboratories, staff, and other resources at nearby Cedars Sinai Medical Center. This partnership gives undergraduates an exceedingly rare opportunity for hands-on learning in a professional environment, using state-of-the-art equipment and techniques. It is an opportunity that also bolsters preparation for medical or other competitive graduate schools.

Academic Facilities

The campus library serves the University's wide range of academic disciplines with more than 100,000 volumes. Some highlight collections include microfilm manuscripts of the Jewish Theological Seminary, all dissertations on Jewish subjects published in the U.S., and 5,000 rare Bibles, dating back as far as the sixteenth century. In addition, the Documentation Center houses archives of more than 1.5 million topically arranged articles relating to topics such as contemporary Jewish issues, Israel, the Middle East, Diaspora communities, and international affairs.

Adjacent to both the library and Documentation Center is the main Computer Center. In 1997, the University significantly upgraded and enlarged the Center to meet the curricular, research, creative, and recreational needs of UJ students, including Internet and e-mail access. Both PC and Macintosh stations are abundant.

Campus arts facilities include studios for dance, music, and the visual arts. There is also a luxurious 475-seat theater, with superb acoustics for plays, concerts, and speakers. Also notable is a scenic, terraced sculpture garden and a campus art gallery that offers exhibits by artists of local, national, and international renown as well as work by the University's own art students.

Costs

For the 2003–04 academic year, full-time tuition (12–18 units per semester) was $16,700. Room and board rates depend on the housing and meal plan selected; a double room and standard nineteen-meal-per-week plan cost $4790 per semester. Required student fees (registration, health services, etc.) amount to approximately $700 per year. Incidental expenses, such as books, transportation, and personal expenses, vary from student to student but average $2000 per year.

Financial Aid

The aforementioned costs are eligible for coverage in a need-based financial aid package from the University of Judaism. Even those with low need or no need, but who are particularly strong candidates, may be awarded merit-based scholarships, that range in value, through the UJ President's Scholars Program, the JEWELS Scholarship, or the Transfer Excellence Award.

The University of Judaism believes in need-blind admissions and commits major resources to seeing that genuine financial need is no barrier to attending. Therefore, any student who applies within deadlines (March 1 for the following fall) and who earns admission to the UJ receives an aid package that covers 100 percent of his or her federally established need eligibility.

A financial aid package may include a mixture of University tuition and housing grant allocations, external scholarships, Federal Pell Grants, Cal Grants, Federal Stafford Loans (subsidized and unsubsidized), Federal Parent Loans for Undergraduate Students (PLUS), alternative loan programs, and the Federal Work-Study Program (for campus jobs). Approval for federal Stafford subsidized and unsubsidized loans is assured for qualified applicants. Federal PLUS and alternative (not federally guaranteed) bank loans may be included in some financial aid packages. These are credit-based loans; applicants are advised that approval is at the sole discretion of the lender. Eligibility is determined by the nationally centralized needs analysis that is generated after the student submits a Free Application for Federal Student Aid (FAFSA). A brief supplemental UJ financial aid application is also required. Financial aid packages are offered within days of receiving all requested documentation. More than 80 percent of UJ students receive financial aid.

Faculty

Nearly every full-time faculty member at the University of Judaism holds a doctorate degree from a highly esteemed university. Most are widely published and have received prestigious academic awards, yet their priority at the UJ is classroom teaching and personalized student advisement, much more so than outside research.

Student Government

Through elected officers and volunteer committees, student government at the UJ plays a meaningful and frequently decisive role in everything from programming campus social activities to revising academic policies. Participation is open to all students regardless of major or class standing.

Admission Requirements

Admission to the College of Arts and Sciences at the University of Judaism is selective and individualized. Applicants are evaluated based on a combination of factors, including quality of preparatory curriculum, grades, SAT I or ACT scores, writing ability, academic references, quality of activities, character, and potential. An interview is recommended but not usually required. Freshman and transfer applications are welcome regardless of a candidate's religion, race, color, nationality, handicap, sex, or age. Applicants whose primary language is not English must submit a TOEFL. Students with 30 transferable college units may petition for a waiver of the SAT or ACT. Official transcripts of the entire secondary school and college record (if any) are mandatory.

A profile of a typical freshman is a B+ student who took a demanding preparatory track and scored in the mid-1100s on the SAT or mid-20s on the ACT while also exerting energy and leadership in significant outside activities, such as youth groups, school publications, performing arts, or student government. Involvement in Jewish life is also common for most UJ students butp not required or expected.

Application and Information

Early decision candidates must apply by November 15 and are notified by December 15. For regular fall admission, the priority application deadline for freshmen is January 31 (January 10 for President's Scholars Program applicants); for transfer students, it is April 15. Applications are accepted thereafter only if spaces are available. For spring admission, all candidates should apply by November 1. Regular fall admission notifications are issued as files are completed, starting in January.

For more information or other requests, students should contact:

Office of Admissions
University of Judaism
15600 Mulholland Drive
Bel Air, California 90077
Telephone: 310-476-9777
888-UJ-FOR-ME (toll-free)
Fax: 310-471-3657
E-mail: admissions@uj.edu
World Wide Web: http://www.uj.edu

A study break on the sunny UJ campus.

UNIVERSITY OF LA VERNE

LA VERNE, CALIFORNIA

The University

Founded in 1891, the University of La Verne (ULV) is an independent university that emphasizes the liberal arts, the sciences, and career preparation. Faculty members and students are drawn from all segments of life and are reflective of the diverse nature of contemporary society. The current undergraduate enrollment is approximately 1,400, and there are more than 200 faculty members. The University of La Verne prides itself on offering personalized education to students in small classes and excellent academic resources such as the Wilson Library. Approximately one half of the students live on the campus in residence halls, and nearly 85 percent receive some form of financial assistance. The University of La Verne is also proud of its generous merit scholarship program.

ULV students are encouraged to think seriously about the world and its people through a core curriculum that promotes values, community service, lifelong learning, and diversity. The University also offers study through graduate and professional studies programs, the School of Continuing Education, and the College of Law. Bachelor's, master's, and doctoral degrees are offered in a variety of fields, including forty-eight liberal arts fields, educational leadership, jurisprudence, public administration, and psychology. The University is accredited by the Western Association of Schools and Colleges.

Students are motivated to involve themselves in the many athletic events, plays, concerts, art exhibitions, and student life activities on campus. Students are also involved in the campus newspaper, *La Verne Magazine*, the yearbook, literary publications, and the campus radio and television stations. ULV teams participate in eleven intercollegiate men's sports and nine intercollegiate women's sports. Men's sports are baseball, basketball, cross-country, football, golf, soccer, swimming and diving, tennis, track and field, volleyball, and water polo. Women's sports are basketball, cross-country, soccer, softball, swimming and diving, tennis, track and field, volleyball, and water polo.

Location

The city of La Verne, located 35 miles east of Los Angeles, is a small residential community (population 32,000) in the heart of what was once a center of citrus culture. La Verne has become a city of change as the population in this and other Los Angeles suburbs has skyrocketed in the past few years. The city is close to all of southern California's cultural and entertainment centers and is only a short ride from beaches, mountains, and deserts.

Majors and Degrees

The University of La Verne offers the Bachelor of Arts and/or Bachelor of Science degree in accounting, anthropology, art, art history, behavioral science, biology, broadcasting, business administration, business economics, business management, chemistry, child development, communications, comparative literature, computer science/computer engineering, criminology, economics, English, environmental biology, environmental management, executive management, French, German, health services management, history, international business and languages, international studies, journalism, legal studies, liberal studies (education), marketing, mathematics, movement and sports science/athletic training, music, music education, organizational management, philosophy, physics, political science, psychology, public administration, religion, social science, sociology, Spanish, speech and debate, and theater arts.

Academic Program

The University of La Verne provides breadth and depth in academic exploration. All students complete the ULV Core, an interdisciplinary program in the humanities, social sciences, and natural sciences leading to majors/concentrations in fields such as business, broadcast journalism, communications, education, prelaw, and premedicine. Students are admitted to ULV rather than to a major and typically select a major at the close of the sophomore year.

The 4-1-4 academic calendar, paired with enrollment held at 300 freshmen per year, translates into flexible scheduling, generous access to course work, and faculty focus on individual student success. The January interterm allows for interesting additional course work at no additional tuition rate. Many faculty members take advantage of this opportunity to offer special internships or study-abroad classes.

All undergraduate students must complete at least 128 semester hours to qualify for graduation. The residence requirement is 32 semester hours. Each student must complete a minimum of 44 upper-division semester hours, with at least 24 upper-division hours being taken in the major field.

Off-Campus Programs

As a member of worldwide associations, ULV offers students the opportunity to participate in a variety of structured programs abroad for the January interterm, a semester, or a full year. In the study-abroad program, students may study in Germany, France, England, Spain, Ecuador, China, or Japan. Faculty member–led excursions are offered to such places as Greece, the Pacific Rim countries, Italy, Australia, Hawaii, and many other areas of the world.

Academic Facilities

Besides classrooms and administrative offices, the La Verne campus has laboratories for the physical and natural sciences, with instrumentation available to undergraduates that many universities are unable to offer even to graduate students. Language laboratories and a writing center provide assistance for students. ULV also provides students with tutoring services through the Learning Enhancement Center and an Honors Program for academically advanced students. A communications center houses radio and television equipment.

Costs

For the 2004–05 academic year, the cost of tuition and fees for a full-time student is $21,500. Room and board are approximately $8140 per year. The total costs per year vary according to the room and meal plan chosen.

Financial Aid

In an attempt to bring a liberal arts education within the reach of qualified students, ULV makes financial assistance available through many sources. The primary consideration when awarding financial aid is the need of the student. The University provides aid through major federal and state financial aid programs as well as through ULV grants and scholarships. Academic scholarships that are unrelated to financial need are also offered. The University of La Verne provides financial assistance to approximately 85 percent of its undergraduate student body.

Faculty

The faculty is composed of nearly 200 men and women of high academic distinction, more than 80 percent of whom have earned the highest degree in their field. The faculty members at ULV are committed to teaching as their primary focus. The student-faculty ratio of 14:1 allows for personalized treatment of students. Upon enrollment, each student is assigned an adviser from his or her academic field to assist in scheduling classes and ensuring a positive academic experience.

Student Government

The Associated Students Federation (ASF) is headed by student leaders in a 12-person forum. The ASF forum establishes activities and maintains school policies. The ASF coordinates on-campus events, movies, concerts, presentations by guest performers, and other student activities.

Admission Requirements

Admission to the traditional undergraduate program for high school seniors and transfer students with fewer than 32 semester units is based on the application along with a personal essay, curriculum, academic record, SAT I or ACT scores, and two letters of recommendation.

Transfer students with 32 or more semester units must submit the application with a personal essay, transcripts from all colleges attended, and two letters of recommendation.

Admission decisions are made without regard to race, national background, religion, or sex.

Application and Information

The priority deadline for freshman applications is February 1 for the fall semester and December 1 for spring entry.

For application forms or further information, students should contact:

Office of Admissions
University of La Verne
1950 Third Street
La Verne, California 91750
Telephone: 909-392-2800
800-876-4858 (toll-free)
Fax: 909-392-2714
E-mail: admissions@ulv.edu
World Wide Web: http://www.ulv.edu

UNIVERSITY OF LOUISIANA AT LAFAYETTE

LAFAYETTE, LOUISIANA

The University

Founded in 1898, the University of Louisiana at Lafayette (UL Lafayette), once a fundamentally undergraduate institution, has rapidly expanded its role in research and graduate education. The University now awards the Ph.D. in applied language and speech sciences, cognitive science, computer engineering, computer science, English, environmental and evolutionary biology, Francophone studies, and mathematics. UL Lafayette also offers twenty-seven master's degrees.

The current enrollment is 16,208 men and women. The University has students from fifty U.S. states and possessions and from 102 countries; 666 international students are enrolled. Twenty-six percent of the students are 25 years of age or older.

Campus housing and off-campus apartments are available. Dormitory rooms and on-campus apartment-style housing are assigned on a first-come, first-served basis. It is suggested that an application for University housing be sent to the director of housing by March 1.

More than 150 different campus organizations, including eight sororities and twelve fraternities, give students a range of extracurricular opportunities. UL Lafayette competes at the Division I-A level of NCAA athletics.

Location

The University of Louisiana at Lafayette is the largest of eight publicly supported state institutions governed by the University of Lousiana system. The Carnegie Foundation has classified UL Lafayette as a Doctoral/Research-Intensive institution. Located midway between New Orleans and Houston, Lafayette is the heart of Louisiana's Acadian-Creole region, commonly known as Cajun country. It was originally settled in the eighteenth century by French exiles from Nova Scotia. The city of 120,000 is one of Louisiana's fastest growing and is the hub of numerous cultural festivals and celebrations.

Majors and Degrees

The University of Louisiana at Lafayette offers sixty bachelor's degree programs through its nine undergraduate colleges. In addition to regional institutional accreditation, 100 percent of UL Lafayette's eligible undergraduate programs have achieved professional accreditation. The colleges and their programs are as follows: College of the Arts: architecture, interior design, industrial design, music (performance, piano pedagogy, jazz studies, music media, and theory-composition), performing arts (theater and choreography/dance), and visual arts (drawing, painting, sculpture, printmaking, media-film/video/animation, advertising design, ceramics, metal jewelry, photography, electronic art, and computer animation); College of Applied Life Sciences: apparel design and merchandising, child and family studies, dietetics, environmental/sustainable resources, hospitality management, pre–veterinary studies, and sustainable agriculture; College of Business Administration: accounting, business systems analysis and technology, economics, finance, insurance and risk management, management, marketing, and professional land and resource management; College of Education: elementary education, kinesiology (including concentrations in athletic training, exercise science, health promotion and wellness, sports administration, and sports medicine), music education (instrumental and vocal), secondary education (art, English, French, mathematics, general science/biology, social studies, Spanish, and speech), special education (mild/moderate elementary, mild/moderate secondary, and early intervention), and vocational education (agriculture, general business, business, industrial arts, and family and consumer science); College of Engineering: chemical engineering, civil engineering, electrical engineering (computer engineering and telecommunications), industrial technology, mechanical engineering (CAD/CAM option), and petroleum engineering; College of Nursing and Allied Health Professions: nursing and dental hygiene; College of Liberal Arts: anthropology, criminal justice, English, history, interpersonal/public communication, mass communication (broadcasting, journalism, and media advertising), modern languages (French, Francophone studies, and Spanish), philosophy, political science (prelaw option), psychology, public relations, sociology, and speech pathology/audiology; College of Sciences: biology, chemistry, cognitive science, computer science, geology, health information management, mathematics and statistics, microbiology, physics, resource biology and biodiversity, and preprofessional programs in dentistry, medicine, optometry, medical technology, pharmacy, and physical therapy; and College of General Studies: Bachelor of General Studies.

Academic Program

Bachelor's degree programs generally require the completion of at least 124 semester hours. That requirement includes a 42-hour core curriculum, which incorporates classes in English, communication, mathematics, science, literature, history, behavioral science, arts, computer literacy, and humanities. An active honors program offers advanced courses in many departments as well as special interdisciplinary honors courses. Highly motivated students can earn an honors degree by completing a quota of honors courses and by producing an honors thesis. Advanced placement is available through the College Board's Advanced Placement Examinations Program and by examinations given on campus in about a dozen subject areas shortly before classes begin.

Off-Campus Programs

Study abroad for degree credit is available through UL Lafayette exchange agreements with the University of Guadalajara, Mexico; through the Université Sainte-Anne, Nova Scotia; and through the UL Lafayette Summer Schools in France, England, and Mexico. Students may take a variety of undergraduate and graduate courses, which are taught by UL Lafayette faculty members and geared to the surroundings. UL Lafayette is a member of the Codofil Consortium of Colleges and Universities, which sponsors an academic-year program at the Université d'Aix-Marseille in Aix-en-Provence, France, and the Université de l'État à Mons in Mons, Belgium. Financial aid is available. In addition, the French government offers teaching assistantships through which UL Lafayette students can teach English in France to finance their study at the Université du Maine le Mans.

UL Lafayette students can take graduate or undergraduate courses in marine biology through a summer field program sponsored by the Louisiana Universities Marine Consortium. Classes are held at field stations along the Louisiana coast.

Academic Facilities

Dupre Library houses more than 956,562 volumes, 4,637 periodicals, more than 2 million microforms, more than 6,129 recordings, and special photography and archive collections. Among these are the world's largest collection of French, Spanish, and British colonial records of Louisiana; the Women in Louisiana Collection; more than 1,500 photographs of the sugar industry; archives of Acadian and Creole folklore and folklife; and an expanding collection of Cajun and Creole music.

Free e-mail, a personal Web page, and Internet access are provided for students both from campus residence halls and from home. There are more than 700 PCs in open-access labs across the campus providing students with standard applications such as word processing. Many academic departments also provide computer labs for use by their students. UL Lafayette utilizes both telephone and Web course registration.

UL Lafayette is well provided with modern engineering equipment, including a highly sophisticated computer-aided design/manufacturing laboratory. The University's 600-acre farm laboratory includes a 30-acre pond for crawfish and catfish culture. Other facilities include two Van de Graaff accelerators, a modern electron microscopy laboratory, a television production laboratory with state-of-the-art digital sound and video recording equipment, the Center for Greenhouse Research, an extensive herbarium, and two federal research facilities, the National Wetlands Research Center and the National Oceanic and Atmospheric Administration.

Costs

Tuition in 2003–04 for full-time undergraduate students who are Louisiana residents was $1495.75 per semester (for 12 hours). Out-of-state undergraduates paid costs of $4585.75 per semester. Books cost an estimated $400 per semester. A dormitory room and meals were about $1563 per semester. Other fees included occasional laboratory fees ($10–$50), a technology fee ($5 per credit, up to $100 per semester), the admissions fee ($20), and car registration. Children of alumni are granted in-state residency for fee purposes. All fees are subject to change and can be confirmed by the Registrar's Office.

Financial Aid

About 65 percent of UL Lafayette students receive some type of financial aid. UL Lafayette participates in federal and state financial aid programs, including the Federal Pell Grant, Federal Supplemental Educational Opportunity Grant (FSEOG), Leveraging Educational Assistance Partnership (LEAP), Tuition Opportunity Program for Students (TOPS), Federal Perkins Student Loan, Federal Work-Study, and Federal Stafford Student Loan programs. Financial need is assessed through the Free Application for Federal Student Aid (FAFSA), which is available through high school counselors, the UL Lafayette Financial Aid Office, and online at http://www.fafsa.ed.gov. On-campus jobs are based on financial need, and the community has many off-campus job opportunities. Assistance in securing an off-campus job is available through Career Services.

The University also has an excellent scholarship program. The application deadline is in January, but students are encouraged to apply earlier. UL Lafayette annually awards about $3 million in scholarships to academically gifted students, including transfer students. Out-of-state fee waivers may be available for freshmen with a minimum ACT score of 23 or a minimum SAT score of 1060 who also have a minimum GPA of 2.5 and do not need any developmental courses. Out-of-state transfers with at least a 2.75 GPA on all college work are also considered for fee waivers. Fee waivers may also be granted to out-of-state students on the basis of special talents.

Faculty

UL Lafayette places a high premium on its nationally competitive faculty. Its faculty includes MacArthur and McDonnell Fellowship winners, 20 endowed chairs, and 173 endowed professorships. This teaching-research–balanced faculty invites undergraduate students to participate in research projects. Students consistently rate faculty members as highly caring.

The faculty numbers 550 members, with 79 percent holding the terminal degree. Virtually all graduate faculty members also teach undergraduate courses; graduate assistants teach freshman-level classes in some departments.

Student Government

An elected Student Government Association (SGA) represents student interests on campus and controls the disbursement of more than $4.5 million in self-assessed student fees and oversees the allocation of almost $70,000 for student activities. An SGA-appointed technology committee allocates $1.9 million annually to enhance technological capabilities on campus. SGA provides legal consulting for students and funds a child development center and other services, including various special events. It also disburses about $40,000 annually in scholarships.

UL Lafayette students are represented on almost all University committees. The UL Lafayette president makes himself available at a regular Monday afternoon meeting to answer students' questions and listen to problems. Student publications are independent of direct University control, although UL Lafayette provides an adviser for them.

Admission Requirements

UL Lafayette seeks a culturally, racially, and geographically diverse student body and currently enrolls students from throughout the United States and more than 100 nations.

Freshman applicants are required to have completed the high school core curriculum established by the Louisiana Board of Regents and may be admitted on the basis of several possible combinations of standardized test scores (ACT or SAT), high school GPA, and/or high school class rank. Out-of-state students who do not meet the core curriculum requirement may be admitted on the basis of more stringent test scores, high school GPA, and class rank.

Transfer applicants must have a cumulative college GPA of at least 2.25 and must be eligible to return to the last institution they attended. In addition, their readiness for college-level English and mathematics must be demonstrated by standardized test scores (ACT or SAT) or the successful completion of appropriate college-level course work in English and mathematics.

International students are admitted on the basis of prior course work, GPA, and standardized test scores (ACT, SAT, or TOEFL). International students who satisfy all other requirements, but have not achieved college-level English proficiency, may enroll in the UL Lafayette English as a Second Language (ESL) program.

Students who do not fully meet the University's admissions criteria may be offered admission by exception. The University may admit by exception up to 15 percent of each incoming class.

Application and Information

U.S. citizens should apply for admission at least thirty days prior to the beginning of classes, but earlier application is strongly recommended. International students should apply at least ninety days before classes begin. The application fee is $20 for U.S. citizens and $30 for international students.

For more information, prospective students should contact:

Enrollment Services
University of Louisiana at Lafayette
P.O. Box 44652
Lafayette, Louisiana 70504
Telephone: 800-752-6553 (toll-free)
E-mail: enroll@louisiana.edu
World Wide Web: http://www.louisiana.edu

UNIVERSITY OF MAINE

ORONO, MAINE

The University

The University of Maine, the land-grant university and sea-grant college of the state of Maine, has a mission to provide teaching and public service and to carry out research for the state of Maine and the country. The University was established in 1865 as the Maine State College of Agriculture and the Mechanic Arts. When the institution opened its doors in 1868, it had 12 students and 2 faculty members. Today, as the University of Maine, it has 679 faculty members and 11,135 students who represent forty-nine states and seventy-four countries. The University of Maine is a participant in the New England Regional Program sponsored by the New England Board of Higher Education.

The University of Maine is the flagship institution of the seven-member University of Maine System. Two hundred four buildings sit on the University of Maine's 660-acre central campus. Forests, botanical gardens, and other "green" spaces make up the rest of the 5,500-acre campus, overlooking the Stillwater River. Ivy-covered buildings and pathways shaded by evergreens create a campus that is inviting and picturesque during all four seasons. Students living on campus may select from a variety of housing options, from residence halls to apartment-style complexes to fraternity and sorority houses.

The University has more than 225 student organizations, including honor and professional societies, fraternities, and sororities. Ten women's and nine men's intercollegiate NCAA Division I athletic programs are part of the campus community. Numerous intramural club sports give all students an opportunity to be physically active. Two gymnasiums, a field house, an indoor pool, a sports arena, a fitness center, a climbing wall, and a 10,000-seat athletic stadium are used for both NCAA Division I athletics and recreational sports. For students' creative interests, there are two theaters, excellent music facilities, recital halls, and studios for dance and the visual arts. Community services include a newspaper, a radio station, a police and safety department, and a health facility.

Location

The town of Orono is situated in central Maine, 8 miles north of Bangor, Maine's third-largest city. The University of Maine is 240 miles north of Boston and 306 miles from Montreal. The Bangor area is served by daily air and bus transportation. The local area offers many opportunities for a wide range of recreational activities. Within an easy drive of the campus are many sites of great natural beauty, such as Acadia National Park, Mount Katahdin, and Baxter State Park, as well as several ski resorts, including Sugarloaf/USA and Sunday River.

Majors and Degrees

The University of Maine offers more than seventy 4-year baccalaureate degree programs through five colleges: the College of Business, Public Policy, and Health; the College of Education and Human Development; the College of Engineering; the College of Liberal Arts and Sciences; and the College of Natural Sciences, Forestry, and Agriculture. The Division of Lifelong Learning also offers a Bachelor of University Studies degree for part-time evening adult learners.

Academic Programs

The University of Maine is a year-round educational institution. The academic year is divided into two 15-week semesters, from early September to mid-May; a 3-week May term; a summer session with 2- to 8-week sessions; and a summer field session. The University offers day as well as evening classes.

All students in baccalaureate degree programs must meet the University's general education requirements. In addition, each academic college sets its own requirements in terms of grades and the number of credits required for graduation. Information concerning specific graduation requirements can be found in the undergraduate catalog. Academic advisers assist all students with completing their degree requirements and fulfilling their personal educational objectives.

The University of Maine provides many opportunities to encourage intellectual curiosity and recognize exceptional achievement. Outstanding entering first-year students are offered the opportunity to participate in one of the country's oldest honors programs. Those who successfully complete the program graduate with Honors, High Honors, or Highest Honors. In addition, many academic colleges and majors also offer membership in various honor societies. Students and faculty members on campus are members of thirty-nine such societies, including Phi Beta Kappa, Phi Kappa Phi, Tau Beta Pi, Xi Sigma Pi, Kappa Delta Pi, Beta Gamma Sigma, and Alpha Zeta. The University also recognizes top graduates as cum laude, magna cum laude, or summa cum laude.

ROTC programs are available in Army and Navy/Marine Corps.

Off-Campus Programs

At least forty departments of the University offer field-based learning programs, including internships, practicum, cooperative education programs, and field experience. Students are given academic credit and/or compensation for on-the-job experience in their major field.

The University of Maine offers a variety of national and international student exchanges through the National Student Exchange (NSE), the Council on International Education Exchange (CIEE), the College Consortium for International Studies (CCIS), and the International Student Exchange Program (ISEP). The University also sponsors reciprocal exchanges between the University of Maine and such countries as Australia, France, Germany, and Japan.

The University sponsors a Junior Year Abroad Program in Salzburg, Austria, and administers an exchange program with University College, Galway, Ireland. The Canada Year program, coordinated by the University's Canadian-American Center, offers students the opportunity to study at various Canadian universities.

Academic Facilities

Fogler Library, located at the center of campus, was built in 1942, and an addition was completed in 1976. It is Maine's largest library collection and the eighteenth-largest library in New England. It contains 1,261,243 volumes and more than 2.4 million microforms, subscribes to 13,041 periodicals, and is a regional depository for more than 2 million government documents. Its departments include Reference Services, the Science and Engineering Center, Special Collections, the Learning Materials Center, Government Documents, and the Listening Center.

All departments on campus have the necessary laboratories and equipment to support student research. The most widely used facility is the Computer Center, which houses IBM, Digital, and Macintosh computers. Undergraduates have access to computer facilities through computers located throughout the campus. All residence halls are connected to the University's computer system, which provides access to a variety of software programs and network services.

Among the other facilities on campus are the Maine Center for the Arts, which includes the Hutchins Concert Hall (seating capacity of 1,628) and the Hudson Museum, an ethnographic and archeological museum with a permanent collection of 8,000 pieces of pre-Hispanic Mexican, Central American, and Native American artifacts. The University of Maine Museum of Art (UMMA), located in downtown Bangor, is the only museum owned by the citizens of the state of Maine to house a permanent fine arts collection (more than 5,700 works of art), Art Department Galleries, a public observatory (the only one in the state), and a planetarium. Recently completed or renovated buildings include the Advanced Engineered Wood Composites Building, the Buchanan Alumni House, the expanded Memorial Union (student union), the remodeled and expanded Hitchner Hall (lab science building), and the remodeled Maine Bound Barn (outdoor recreation and climbing wall).

Costs

Costs are adjusted annually by the University of Maine Board of Trustees. For the 2003–04 academic year, tuition for state residents was $157 per credit hour; for nonresident students, it was $447 per credit hour. (The average credit load for full-time students is 15 credit hours per semester or 30 credit hours for the academic year.) Nonresident students who qualify for the New England Regional Program pay the state resident tuition plus 50 percent. Required University fees ($1204 per year for a full-time student) include the Comprehensive Fee, which provides a variety of health-care services and admission to cultural and recreational events. Books and supplies cost about $720 for the academic year. Room and board (nineteen meals per week) charges for the academic year were $6166. These costs are subject to change by legislative action.

Financial Aid

The University requires all financial aid applicants to file the Free Application for Federal Student Aid (FAFSA) with the College Scholarship Service. The form may be obtained from high school guidance offices or online. The deadline to apply for aid is March 1. The University believes awards of financial aid should be based upon financial need. Awards usually consist of a combination of several types of aid ranging from grants and scholarships to work-study jobs and student loans.

Faculty

The University of Maine has 679 full- and part-time faculty members and a student-faculty ratio of 17:1. A number of faculty members teach both undergraduate and graduate courses. Graduate students serve as teaching assistants in some departments. Faculty members are involved in both teaching and research and also serve as academic advisers to undergraduate students. In addition, the faculty takes an active part in the education of students outside of the classroom through seminars, workshops, and discussion groups and by serving as advisers to student organizations. Many faculty members also serve on the Student Advisory Committee, the Student Conduct Committee, and other organizations on campus that serve the needs of students.

Student Government

An elected president, vice president, and vice president of financial affairs direct and coordinate Student Government programs at the University of Maine. Student Government works closely with the Office of the Vice President for Student Affairs and appoints 200 student representatives to the various University committees. These committees are involved with residence hall programs, student discipline, athletics, and cultural activities on campus. The work of the executive budgetary committee of Student Government includes the budgeting of approximately $400,000 in student activity fees. Student Government comprises five governing boards and the General Student Senate.

Admission Requirements

Admission to the University of Maine is a selective process. Successful applicants are those whose scholastic achievement, intellectual curiosity, and established study habits promise success in a comprehensive university environment. The admissions committee reviews the strength of the high school curriculum, the grades received, the counselor recommendation, and either SAT I or ACT scores as the primary criteria for admission. Additional information regarding the applicant's school and community activities provides information that may help the committee evaluate potential for success.

The University recognizes advanced work completed in secondary schools by means of Advanced Placement tests. Also, students who demonstrate advanced knowledge may be exempted from certain courses and requirements if they pass examinations specially developed by the University's academic departments.

Application and Information

An application form, available from the Admissions Office, any Maine high school guidance office, or online, should be submitted with the nonrefundable application fee. In addition, candidates are requested to submit official transcripts of their high school records along with counselor recommendations. Traditional age applicants are required to submit scores on either the SAT I or ACT.

To be considered for full financial aid, students are encouraged to submit their applications by February 1. Students applying for the spring semester are encouraged to submit applications by December 1. All applications must be filed no later than two weeks prior to the start of classes for any semester. Nonrefundable admission deposits are due May 1.

University of Maine
Office of Admission
5713 Chadbourne Hall
Orono, Maine 04469-5713
Telephone: 207-581-1561
Fax: 207-581-1213
E-mail: um-admit@maine.edu
World Wide Web: http://www.go.umaine.edu/

UNIVERSITY OF MAINE AT FARMINGTON

FARMINGTON, MAINE

The University

The University of Maine at Farmington (UMaine Farmington) is a public baccalaureate institution committed to quality programs in arts and sciences, teacher education, and human services. Its primary mission is to offer its students opportunities for intellectual and personal growth in a challenging academic environment. In order to accomplish this, UMaine Farmington remains an undergraduate institution, limits its enrollment by means of selective admissions, and provides a supportive atmosphere that fosters close student-faculty interaction.

Founded in 1864, UMaine Farmington is Maine's first public institution of higher education and continues its long tradition of integrating liberal arts and professional studies. The University prepares its graduates to excel in their chosen fields and become responsible citizens in the global community. The University's aim is to educate people for life by encouraging intellectual curiosity, critical thinking, aesthetic appreciation, respect for cultural differences, and a concern for the environment.

The University gives first priority to excellence in teaching, but also encourages and supports research, other creative and scholarly activity, and public service by its faculty. The University takes pride in being an intellectual and cultural center for the members of the campus community, the region, and the state, which it serves in cooperation with the other campuses of the University of Maine system.

An enrollment cap of 2000 full-time students creates a student-faculty ratio of 16:1 and an average class size of 19. About 20 percent of the student population comes from outside the state of Maine. Approximately 1,000 students are in the College of Arts and Sciences and 1,000 students are in the College of Education, Health and Rehabilitation. The small campus environment provides opportunities for students to work collaboratively with faculty members and become involved in exciting projects in addition to their course work.

The seven residence halls provide opportunities for students to get to know each other and participate in the life of the institution. There are more than forty-five different clubs and organizations on campus as well as eleven intercollegiate sports, including baseball, basketball, cross-country, soccer, and golf for men and basketball, cross-country, field hockey, soccer, softball, and volleyball for women. Club sports include rugby, ice hockey, and Ultimate Frisbee. The student-run Program Board regularly sponsors campus activities. The art gallery, theater, dance company, chorus, band, and orchestra provide cultural activities. The Health and Fitness Center features a six-lane indoor pool, a fully equipped weight-training room, a cardiovascular fitness area, an indoor jogging/walking track, and multipurpose courts for tennis, basketball and volleyball.

Location

Surrounded by the mountains, lakes, and rolling countryside of western Maine, the University provides the setting and friendly atmosphere of a small New England college. Located near world-class skiing at Sugarloaf/USA and Sunday River, the campus is a few hours drive from Boston, Massachusetts, and Quebec City, Canada. The area is known for its skiing, hiking, camping, mountain biking, fly-fishing, kayaking, and white-water rafting. Downtown Farmington, with its shops, restaurants, banks, and movie theater, is a three-minute walk from the campus.

Majors and Degrees

Programs leading to Bachelor of Arts, Bachelor of Fine Arts, Bachelor of General Studies, and Bachelor of Science degrees include art, art administration/art history, art administration/music, art administration/theater, biology, business economics, community health/school health education, computer science, creative writing, early childhood education, early childhood special education, elementary education, English, environmental planning and policy, environmental science, geography, geology/chemistry, geology/geography, history, international studies, mathematics, music/arts, philosophy/religion, political science/social science, psychology, rehabilitation, secondary education (with concentrations in biology, English, language arts, mathematics, mathematics/computer science, physical science, science and social science), sociology/anthropology, special education (with concentrations in emotional disturbance, learning disabilities, and mental retardation), theater/arts, and women's studies. Students may also design their own interdisciplinary or individualized majors with the approval of the Arts and Sciences Committee.

Academic minors are available in art, athletic coaching, biology, business, chemistry, computer science, economics, English, exercise science, French, geography, geology, history, mathematics, music, nutrition, philosophy, physics, political science, psychology, rehabilitation services, religion, sociology, theater, and women's studies.

Preprofessional advising is available for students planning to enter postbaccalaureate programs in allied health, dental, medical, optometry, veterinary, and law programs.

A certificate program is offered in ski industries.

Academic Program

As Maine's most selective public liberal arts college, UMaine Farmington focuses exclusively on undergraduates and offers quality academic programs in a challenging, supportive educational environment. All degree programs are built on a strong interdisciplinary, liberal arts foundation. Students complete a total of between 120 and 122 credit hours to earn their degree, including a mixture of general education, major requirements, and elective courses. Many students are able to earn college credit through the College Board's AP (Advanced Placement) program or through the CLEP (College-Level Examination Program).

Students are encouraged to connect classroom study with career opportunities by incorporating practical experience into their college experience. More than 70 percent participate in some kind of hands-on experience, including internships, academic practicums, service-learning opportunities, and the Campus Work Initiative program. Past participants in such hands-on experiences have taught French in local elementary schools; evaluated wetlands research data for the Maine Department of Environmental Protection; served internships at the White House fitness center, the Portland International Trade port, and with Alice James Books (an award-winning poetry publishing house); worked with the U.S. Ski Association; created Web pages for the University's Public Relations office; and worked as software troubleshooters at the UMaine Farmington Computer Center Help Desk.

The Honors Program creates a focused community of students and faculty members who are committed to inquiry and discussion. The program, designed for highly motivated, intellectually curious students in any major, combines interdisciplinary seminars with an opportunity for a senior thesis or creative project. Honors students have access to the seminar rooms, kitchen, and quiet-study and meeting rooms of the Honors Center, 24 hours a day.

The University operates on a semester schedule and offers a May term and summer courses.

Off-Campus Programs

Students can take advantage of opportunities to travel while they learn. Academic departments offer field trips and research opportunities that have included travel to the American Southwest, Iceland, Ireland, Italy, and Newfoundland. The University also operates international exchange programs in China, England, France, and Russia. Through the National Student Exchange (NSE), students can attend any of more than 150 public institutions in the U.S. or institutions in more than fifty countries through NSE-partner international exchange programs.

Academic Facilities

The Mantor Library has the technology necessary for advanced bibliographic research and gives students access to numerous electronic database resources. In addition to more than 100,000 volumes and 700 journals, the library provides a gateway to the University of Maine system libraries, a collection of more than 2 million volumes. UMaine Farmington's cutting-edge technology resources include wireless and wired networks, smart classrooms, numerous labs, specialized equipment, and extensive user services. The University makes wireless laptop packages available to students for purchase at attractive prices to facilitate anytime-anywhere campus access to computing resources. The Computer Center supports more than 120 networked computers, many of which are available 24 hours a day, seven days a week for students who choose not to bring a computer to campus. Specialty computer labs are available for education, music, art, foreign languages, geography, geology, and natural sciences. The residence halls provide free Internet access through the Ethernet connection in each room or through wireless connections. All students receive free e-mail accounts. The Instructional Media Center provides support services including multimedia computing, black and white photographic processing and printing, television recording, and analog and digital video and sound editing equipment. The Learning Assistance Center provides free tutoring for all students in any class, upon request.

Costs

For the 2003–04 academic year, full-time tuition and fees (based on 30 credits per year) were $4880 for Maine residents, $7040 for Canadian residents and New England residents admitted into a program that qualified for the New England Regional tuition, and $11,060 for nonresidents of Maine. Average room and board costs (based on a double room and nineteen meals per week) were approximately $5318 for the academic year.

Financial Aid

In 2002–03, students received more than $16.5 million in financial aid, with aid packages averaging $6957 per student. To apply for need-based financial aid or an unsubsidized Federal Stafford Loan, students are required to complete the Free Application for Federal Student Aid (FAFSA) or the Renewal FAFSA. Priority consideration for funds is given to students whose FAFSA arrives at the federal processor by March 1 preceding the award year. The University also offers several merit scholarship awards based on academic talent, demonstrated leadership, community service, and contribution to diversity. Priority for some merit scholarships is given to those who have completed an admission application by December 1. The campus work initiative program is open to all students regardless of financial need.

Faculty

At UMaine Farmington, the priority for the more than 150 faculty members is teaching. All of the University's full-time faculty members teach and advise students. Seventy-nine percent of the full-time faculty members hold terminal degrees. Faculty members and students work together closely to help students meet their individual educational goals.

Student Government

The student governing body at the University of Maine at Farmington is the Student Senate. The Student Senate is made up of six resident senators, six commuter senators, three at-large senators, and five executive members. All senators are elected by the student body. The senate represents all student affairs, allocates students funds, oversees student clubs and organizations, and works directly with the student body on issues of concern. Senators represent the student body to the University administration, faculty senate, student service providers, and the University of Maine System.

Admission Requirements

The University seeks to enroll students who demonstrate the potential for academic success. Admission is competitive and space is limited. Applicants are encouraged to apply early in the admission cycle, especially for education and creative writing programs. General admission criteria include a college preparatory program in high school, an official high school recommendation (not required for transfer applicants), extracurricular activities, work experience, and a student essay. SAT scores are optional but will influence the admission decision and academic placement, if submitted. Transfer students must submit official college transcripts. International applicants must submit evidence of English proficiency and documentation of finances.

Application and Information

Early Action (nonbinding) applications for fall are due by December 1. After January 1, regular first-year fall admission is done on a rolling basis; some programs fill early. Materials for transfer applicants to the College of Education are due March 1 for fall admission and October 1 for spring admission.

For applications and information about the University of Maine at Farmington, students should contact:

Office of Admission
University of Maine at Farmington
246 Main Street
Farmington, Maine 04938
Telephone: 207-778-7050
Fax: 1-207-778-8182
E-mail: umfadmit@mmaine.edu
World Wide Web: http://www.umaine.farmington.edu

UMaine Farmington students participating in the orientation training for their new wireless laptops.

UNIVERSITY OF MAINE AT FORT KENT

FORT KENT, MAINE

The University

The University of Maine at Fort Kent (UMFK) offers the combination of high-quality education and personalized attention today's students are looking for. The small campus population of 850 assures professors know their students by name. The favorable student-faculty ratio of 15:1 provides many opportunities for interaction. At the same time, the University is large enough to offer a wide variety of academic and extracurricular opportunities. The University's diverse student body includes individuals from small towns and big cities across the United States and Canada, as well as from Europe, Africa, South America, and Asia.

UMFK was founded in 1878 as the Madawaska Training School to educate teachers for what was known as the Madawaska Territory. Over the next century, the school evolved and refined its program into a comprehensive liberal–arts based institution. In 1970, it became part of the seven-campus University of Maine System.

The University's two residence halls, Crocker and Powell Hall, offer housing, and the dining facility, Nowland Hall, provides meal service for the student body. Computer, cable TV, and phone hookups are provided in every room, and the halls also have lounges, game rooms, and free laundry facilities. Resident students and commuters alike participate in a variety of campus activities, including theatrical and musical performances, intercollegiate and intramural athletics, and numerous student organizations.

Location

The town of Fort Kent is situated on the banks of the Fish and St. John Rivers in an area originally settled by French-speaking Acadians from Maritime Canada. The St. John Valley community is noted as one of the country's few truly international, bilingual-bicultural regions, and the University of Maine at Fort Kent is known as a great place to learn and grow within that community.

The campus has convenient access to numerous areas of scenic natural beauty, as well as recreational opportunities, including ski areas and resorts, Baxter State Park, the Allagash Wilderness Waterway, and the Gaspé Peninsula in Canada's Quebec Province.

The University of Maine at Fort Kent is in proximity to the newly built Maine Winter Sports Center, which is the home to Olympic biathlon training. The facility typically offers on-snow training from Thanksgiving to Easter, and also offers summer training on its paved rollerski training and advanced training loops and cross-country running trails. Mountain biking trails are also available at the site. The center boasts a new three-story lodge with showers, locker rooms, and waxing facilities. Former Olympians provide world-class coaching in cross-country skiing and biathlon.

Majors and Degrees

The University of Maine at Fort Kent is a four-year baccalaureate-granting institution that offers the Bachelor of Arts in English and French; the Bachelor of Science in behavioral science, biology, business management, computer applications, e-commerce, education (K–12), environmental studies, nursing, public safety, social sciences, teacher certification (both elementary and secondary education), and University studies; the Associate of Arts in business, computer science, criminal justice, general studies, and human services; and the Associate of Science in forest technology.

Academic Program

Dedicated to providing a solid liberal arts education within programs designed to equip students for the twenty-first century, the University of Maine at Fort Kent divides the academic year into two 16-week semesters. Both day and evening classes run from early September through early May. Summer classes and workshops are also offered, beginning in May and usually ending in late July. All students, regardless of degree program and major, are required to complete a general education core curriculum and meet certain requirements for graduation. Each degree program and major also has a number of specific requirements that are described in the University catalog.

Entering freshmen are assigned an adviser who is a member of a special advising team devoted to ensuring the success of every student's first year at UMFK.

After the first year, students choose a faculty academic adviser in their field of study, who guides them toward completion of their program requirements.

Off-Campus Programs

UMFK offers opportunities for students to study abroad, including exchange programs with Canadian and European universities. A cooperative agreement between the University of Maine at Fort Kent and Université de Moncton-Edmundston Campus provides students with a unique opportunity for cross-registration at either campus. The French branch of the University of Moncton, is located only 22 miles from Fort Kent in Edmundston, New Brunswick. The universities celebrate the heritage of the original settlers of the Upper St. John River Valley.

Along with approximately 130 other public universities across the United States, the University of Maine at Fort Kent is a member of the National Student Exchange Program as well as the New England–Quebec and the New England–Nova Scotia Student Exchange Programs. These programs allow full-time students to pursue course work at other universities in the United States, Quebec, or Nova Scotia to satisfy part of the credit requirements for a degree at UMFK.

Bachelor of Science in environmental studies students also benefit from a cooperative program that allows them to spend a semester or a year studying at either the University of Maine at Presque Isle or the University of Maine at Machias. In addition, practical field experience is available to UMFK environmental studies students through an agreement with the National Audubon Expedition Institute. Through this program, students in good standing can spend a year on an excursion that takes them across the country and requires that they encounter and deal with an array of environmental issues.

Academic Facilities

UMFK is home to the newly constructed, state-of-the-art Northern Maine Center for Rural Health Sciences and Northern Aroostook Technology Center. The facilities serve as a home for the University's nursing program and also house the most modern classrooms and teleconferencing center in northern Maine.

Additional buildings on UMFK's 52-acre campus include the Cyr Hall classroom complex and computer laboratory, Fox Auditorium, the Sportscenter, Nowland Dining Hall, Crocker and Powell residence halls, the Old Model School, the Computer Center, and Nadeau Hall, which houses an e-commerce lab, faculty offices, a nursing lab, a music lab, an on-campus health clinic, and a satellite conference center. In addition to its own collections, Blake Library provides students with a variety of available databases and electronic access to more than a million volumes in libraries of the University of Maine System. New construction and renovation projects for additional facilities are in the works. One new construction project is the Acadian Archives building, which will preserve, celebrate, and disseminate information about the region's history and will house documents and artifacts. These archives will contain a conference room, reading room, work room, reference desk, a bank of computers, and research materials stacks as well as personnel space, a collections area, and an accessioning room.

The University also owns or has access to a number of off-campus facilities that are available to students, and enhance academic programs by providing opportunity for hands-on study. The Elmer Violette Wilderness Camp, located on the Allagash Wilderness Waterway in the famed North Maine Woods, is frequently used by the Environmental Studies and Forestry Programs to conduct fieldwork. The wilderness camp includes housing and classroom facilities. Other academic programs also use the camp at various times throughout the year.

Other off-campus UMFK facilities include a 1,000-acre wooded lot bordering St. Froid Lake, a biological park near the campus, and access points to the Fish and St. John Rivers.

Costs

In 2003–04, tuition was $3690 per year for Maine residents and $8940 per year for out-of-state students. Nonresident students who qualify for the New England Regional Program paid $5550 per year for tuition. Room and board costs for 2003–04 were $4880. Required University fees for new students were $500, which include application, matriculation, orientation, student activity, and technology fees. Tuition and fee figures listed are based on 15 credit hours per semester.

Financial Aid

The University of Maine at Fort Kent Office of Financial Aid administers scholarships, grants, loans, and work assistance to more than 80 percent of enrolled students. The University requires all applicants for financial aid to file the Free Application for Federal Student Aid (FAFSA), which is available from the UMFK Office of Financial Aid, from high school guidance offices, and online at http://www.fafsa.cd.gov. UMFK has a preferred filing date of March 15. Consideration is given at any time during the year; however, early application is recommended because awards depend on the availability of funds.

Faculty

Excellence has always been the goal of the 36-member UMFK faculty. Its members include accomplished scholars who hold the highest degree in their professional field. Faculty members are active in professional activities, research, and continuing education. Their top priority, however, is always teaching. Classes are generally small, and every faculty member teaches and advises students.

Student Government

UMFK has a long tradition of strong student government. The Student Senate, which represents all students, is a member of the University of Maine Organization of Student Governments.

Admission Requirements

The UMFK Office of Admissions considers each applicant on an individual basis. Consideration is given to academic preparation, maturity, personal motivation, and goals. Particular attention is given to secondary school performance, especially in the junior and senior years. SAT I scores or ACT results are strongly recommended but not required.

Application and Information

Application for admission is made by completing a University of Maine System application form or by applying online at http://www.umfk.maine.edu. A nonrefundable fee of $25 must be submitted to the UMFK Office of Admissions. The University follows a rolling admissions schedule and accepts applications at any time during the year. Students are usually accepted for entry in either September or January.

Applications and additional information are available from:

Office of Admissions
23 University Drive
Fort Kent, Maine 04743
Telephone: 207-834-7600
888-TRY-UMFK (879-8635, toll-free)
Fax: 207-834-7609
E-mail: umfkadm@maine.edu
World Wide Web: http://www.umfk.maine.edu

Students enjoy the close, family-like atmosphere that the University of Maine at Fort Kent provides. The low student-teacher ratio, personalized attention, and numerous campus events and activities all create the ideal setting for a top-quality learning and life experience.

UNIVERSITY OF MAINE AT MACHIAS

MACHIAS, MAINE

The University

Located on the spectacular coast of Downeast Maine, the University of Maine at Machias (UMM) is a small, residential, undergraduate liberal college of more than 1,200 students. The college was incorporated in 1909 and is a member of the University of Maine system. Small classes (the average is 16 students) and a faculty-student ratio of 1:14 contribute to an academic atmosphere which is intimate, intense, and where independent thinking is encouraged.

Although many UMM students are from the state of Maine, the University's distinctive programs and location attract many others from the New England, the mid-Atlantic, and the Midwest regions of the country.

Location

Machias, Maine, is a classic small New England town located on the tidal Machias River, with a town center that includes a number of retail stores, restaurants (including fast-food), a supermarket, a natural foods store, as well as churches of various denominations. The greater Machias area population is 5,000 and the region is a popular outdoor recreation destination, with ocean beaches, inland lakes and streams, and miles of mountains, forests, and trails.

Downeast Maine has been a source of inspiration for generations of artists, outdoorsmen, mariners, and environmentalists. UMM's coastal location provides a unique learning environment, with unparalleled opportunities for fieldwork, hands-on learning, and cooperative education and internship experiences.

Majors and Degrees

The University of Maine at Machias awards Bachelor of Arts and Bachelor of Science degrees in behavioral science (concentrations in human services and psychology), biology (concentrations in dentistry, field biology, medicine, opthamology, pharmacy, and veterinary), business administration (concentrations in accounting, business technology and teacher education, marketing/management, medical office management, and public administration), college studies (secondary mathematics education and self-designed program option), elementary teacher education, environmental studies (self-designed concentration), English (concentrations in literary studies and creative writing), history, interdisciplinary fine arts (concentrations in creative writing, music, theater, and visual arts), marine biology (concentrations in mariculture, biological science, marine ecology, and self-designed), and recreation management (concentrations in park management, adventure recreation, sports and fitness management, and self-designed concentration).

Academic Programs

Bachelor's degree candidates must complete at least 120 credit hours with a minimum cumulative grade point average of 2.0 and must also complete the core requirements in business studies, fine arts, humanities, science/mathematics, physical education, and social sciences.

Academic Facilities

All of the University's academic buildings are of modern construction and include a well-equipped science building with laboratories, a greenhouse, marine science aquariums and a GPS computer laboratory. Computer labs, some of which are open 24 hours a day, seven days a week, for student use, house the latest in technology hardware and software.

Merrill Library provides a 24-hour study center with computer workstations for students, houses a collection of more than 100,000 volumes, and is linked to other libraries and educational resources throughout the state. A computer center with cross-campus networking and multiple computer labs enhances all of UMM's programs and provides access to the Internet and the Web. Individual computer access is also available in every residence hall room. The University of Maine at Machias Student Support Center provides faculty, peer, and professional assistance as well as computer and audiovisual aids for all students. A new residence facility with contemporary suites and single rooms was completed in 2003.

The Center for Lifelong Learning (CLL) includes a large gymnasium, an aquatics center with a competition-size pool, a state-of-the-art fitness center, racquetball/handball courts, and a recreational equipment center, in which students may check out canoes, kayaks, snowshoes, cross-country skis, bicycles, and camping equipment. The Early Care and Education Center provides child-care facilities for the community and the University; it also provides an on-campus site for UMM elementary teacher education students to participate in field studies.

A wide variety of student activities, from meetings to coffee houses and other social events, are accommodated in the Student Center. Located in the same building, the campus radio station, WUMM, is run entirely by students. The Performing Arts Center, a 358-seat amphitheater auditorium, is host to numerous campus and community meetings, seminars, festivals, as well as performing arts and theatrical presentations.

Costs

The basic expenses for the 2003–04 academic year (based on a 15-credit-hour load per semester) were $3690 per year for in-state tuition and $9630 per year for out-of-state tuition. The University of Maine at Machias participates in the New England Board of Higher Education Regional Student program that allows reduced tuition ($5130 per year) for students from the other New England states enrolled in specific academic programs.

Financial Aid

The University of Maine at Machias administers scholarships, loans, grants, and work-study awards. UMM has a Presidential Scholarship Program, a Leadership Scholarship Program, and a Distinguished Scholar Program for students who have excelled in academics and leadership. Financial aid awards are made on the basis of need, and students must submit the Free Application for Federal Student Aid (FAFSA) to the College Scholarship Service. March 15 is the University's financial aid priority deadline.

Faculty

Nearly all of the University of Maine at Machias faculty members hold the highest degree in their professional field. The faculty-student ratio is 1:14. All faculty members work as advisers and mentors to students within their areas of academic expertise. Usually on a first-name basis, faculty members develop a close relationship with students during their years of study at UMM and beyond.

Student Government

The University of Maine at Machias is a member of the University of Maine Organization of Student Governments and operates its own Student Senate. Students are encouraged to become involved and participate.

Admission Requirements

Graduation from secondary school or a high school equivalency diploma is the basic requirement for admission. Applicants to the University should have followed a college-preparatory high school program with 4 years of English, 3 years of math, 3 lab sciences, 2 social sciences, a foreign language, and computer utilization. If a student is entering one of the business programs, consideration is given to business courses taken in high school. However, college-preparatory English, math, science, and social science courses are still necessary. Scores from the SAT I or ACT are also required. Applicants should rank in the top half of their high school class and have an overall grade average of B or better.

The University of Maine at Machias does not discriminate on the basis of race, creed, color, sex, or national origin and is an Equal Opportunity/Affirmative Action Employer.

Application and Information

The University of Maine at Machias operates on a rolling admission system. Candidates should complete their applications as early as possible. Students may apply for early admission, through which they may be admitted directly into the University after completing three years of secondary school. Candidates for this program must have recommendations of support from their guidance counselor, principal, superintendent, and/or school board. Their high school grades should place them in the top 15 percent of their class. UMM accepts applications from transfer students. Transfer applicants should complete their applications by June 1 for the fall term or by December 1 for the spring term.

Application materials and additional information may be obtained by contacting:

Director of Admissions
University of Maine at Machias
9 O'Brien Avenue
Machias, Maine 04654
Telephone: 207-255-1318
888-468-6866 (toll-free)
Fax: 207-255-1363
E-mail: ummadmissions@maine.edu
World Wide Web: http://www.umm.maine.edu

The University of Maine at Machias is located on the spectacular coast of Downeast Maine.

UNIVERSITY OF MARYLAND, BALTIMORE COUNTY

UMBC
AN HONORS UNIVERSITY IN MARYLAND

BALTIMORE, MARYLAND

The University

At the University of Maryland, Baltimore County (UMBC), students find out quickly that learning at an honors university takes place in many different ways and in a variety of settings. Students discover an environment with a strong undergraduate liberal arts and sciences focus. A medium-sized public research university, UMBC provides students with opportunities to get hands-on research experience working with professors at the top of their fields. The University has been recognized by *Kaplan/Newsweek's* "How to Get Into College" guide as one of the twelve hottest schools in the country. The Carnegie Foundation ranks UMBC in the category of Doctoral/Research Universities–Extensive, the top tier of the nation's research universities. The University is also a two-time winner of the U.S. Presidential Award for Excellence in Science, Mathematics and Engineering Mentoring. UMBC's academic reputation and industry partnerships help to place students in promising careers and leading graduate programs. One third of UMBC students immediately go on to leading graduate or professional schools such as Harvard, Johns Hopkins, Stanford, and Yale.

Few universities can match UMBC for commitment to undergraduate education or for undergraduate participation in real problem solving. Undergraduate students have access to the latest technology in areas from geography to art history to chemistry. The International Media Center offers students multilingual word processing, worldwide databases, and satellite feeds from the International Channel, Deutsche Welle, and French, Russian, and Spanish stations. The Goddard Earth Science and Technology Center brings NASA scientists and UMBC professors and students together to study the earth's surface, atmosphere, and oceans. Students in UMBC's Imaging Research Center (IRC) gain professional experience with companies such as the Discovery Channel, CNN, and PBS; students use the IRC's high-end equipment for applications such as molecular imaging and three-dimensional cartography. UMBC is also home to the prestigious Howard Hughes Medical Institute, a privately sponsored research facility dedicated to the study of the structural building blocks of the AIDS virus.

The campus climate is friendly and energetic. UMBC's more than 9,600 undergraduates have enough ideas and interests to support more than 180 student groups, including Greek organizations; recreational sports clubs, such as skydiving and crew; community outreach efforts, such as Habitat for Humanity; and campus events, including lectures, films, concerts, and plays. Students enthusiastically follow UMBC NCAA Division I athletic teams, such as basketball, lacrosse, and soccer, attending games in the UMBC Stadium and Retriever Activities Center, which includes a multipurpose gym, auxiliary gym, weight room, and classrooms.

UMBC students are from forty-eight states and 108 countries. More than 75 percent of freshman students live on campus, with close to 20 percent come from out of state. UMBC's diverse undergraduate community includes 50 percent women, 66 percent Caucasians, 16 percent Asian Americans, 15 percent African Americans, and 3 percent Native Americans and Hispanic Americans. In the past four years, two new residence halls and two apartment complexes have been constructed; these house 1,250 students. Room layouts are based on a suite concept, with a shared living room. Residential communities feature living-learning programs and special living options for students. More than one third of UMBC undergraduates live on campus.

Location

Located a few miles south of Baltimore, UMBC is 15 minutes from downtown Baltimore and 45 minutes from Washington, D.C. Surrounded by business, government, and metropolitan centers, UMBC places students in co-ops and internships in more than 210 organizations each year in the Baltimore-Washington area and abroad. UMBC matches students with employers such as IBM, Northrop Grumman, Centers for Medicare and Medicaid, Bank of America, Silicon Graphics, MBNA, the Smithsonian Institution, NASA, and the National Aquarium. The Baltimore-Washington area is known for its music, sports, museums, restaurants, and historical traditions. Favorite student haunts include Fells Point, the Inner Harbor, Oriole Park at Camden Yards, M&T Bank Stadium, Patapsco State Park, Annapolis, and Georgetown.

UMBC's 530-acre campus includes more than thirty buildings accessed by a 2-mile elliptical drive, with housing and dining facilities on one side and core facilities (classroom/lab buildings, a library, galleries, a student union, a bookstore, a gymnasium, an Olympic-size pool, and tennis courts) surrounding a central walkway. bwtech@UMBC Research and Technology Park, on the campus of UMBC, focuses on attracting firms in the high-technology fields, including engineering, information technology, and the life sciences. Adjacent to the campus, techcenter@UMBC is a magnet for high-technology business development and offers a dynamic, fully equipped facility for start-up and emerging companies.

Majors and Degrees

UMBC offers programs leading to Bachelor of Arts, Bachelor of Fine Arts, and Bachelor of Science degrees in the following areas: Africana studies, American studies, ancient studies, biochemistry and molecular biology, bioinformatics and computational biology, biological sciences, chemical engineering, chemistry and biochemistry, computer engineering and computer science, dance, economics and financial economics, emergency health services, English, environmental science and environmental studies, geography and environmental systems, health administration and policy, history, information systems, interdisciplinary studies, mathematics and statistics, mechanical engineering, modern languages and linguistics, music, philosophy, physics, political science, psychology, social work, sociology and anthropology, theater, visual and performing arts, visual arts, and women's studies. Students in the interdisciplinary studies program, working with faculty members, design their own course of study according to their specific educational and career goals. UMBC offers preprofessional studies programs, including two- and four-year advisement programs to prepare students for clinical training in dental hygiene, medical and research technology, medicine, nursing, pharmacy, physical therapy, and veterinary medicine. Minor programs include Africana studies, American studies, ancient studies, anthropology, applied politics, art history and theory, biological sciences, computer science, dance, East Asian history, economics, emergency health services, environmental geography, geography, history, international affairs, international economics, Judaic studies, legal policy, literature, mathematics, modern languages and linguistics, music, philosophy, physics, political science, political thought, psychology, public administration, religious studies, social welfare, sociology, statistics, theater, women's studies, and writing.

Academic Programs

UMBC's academic calendar consists of fall and spring semesters, a four-week mini session in January, and summer sessions ranging from six to eight weeks. To receive a UMBC degree, students complete 120 to 128 credits plus two physical education courses. In addition to the requirements for the chosen major, a core of courses, called the general foundation requirements (GFR), provides a solid basis for a lifetime of learning. The GFR courses encompass four broad areas: humanities and fine arts, mathematics and natural sciences, social sciences, and languages and culture.

The UMBC Honors College is a special option for students seeking a community of like-minded people for whom the quest for knowledge is its own reward. Honors College students gain the enlightened perspective that comes with immersion in the liberal arts. Innovative approaches to study, unique internship options, a living-learning community, and emphasis on independent research are among the hallmarks of the program. All Honors College students must take at least one honors course per semester. Students choose from honors versions of core courses, special honors seminars, and plenty of other honors courses.

The Shriver Center links the resources of the campus to urgent social problems, particularly in the areas of education, criminal justice, health, the environment, and jobs, with special priority given to the needs of citizens with mental retardation. The Shriver Center places students in co-ops and internships at hundreds of businesses and organizations, organizes and manages community service projects, and connects students to a wide range of social service projects.

Academic Facilities

UMBC's landmark building, the Albin O. Kuhn Library and Gallery, rises seven stories over the UMBC campus. The library contains 938,653 books and bound volumes of journals, an extensive reference collection, 4,302 current journal subscriptions, wired communication jacks to the Internet, and more than 3 million other items, including slides, photographs, maps, musical scores, recordings, and microforms. The Commons, UMBC's state-of-the-art community center, is the hub of campus life. The Commons includes a food court, general lounges, the University bookstore, meeting spaces, a student recreation center, a full-service bank, student organization offices, administrative offices, and other retail-type spaces. It also features wireless computer connectivity and Web-accessible kiosks.

UMBC students have access to research opportunities and equipment that students at other schools do not have until they enter graduate school. The Physics Building houses a telescope for atmospheric research and astronomical observation. New facilities for fall 2004 include a new Public Policy Building and a modern Information Technology/Engineering Building. UMBC's Engineering Building contains several general-access computer labs, which offer 360 PC workstations running Windows NT, 120 Silicon Graphics workstations, and 200 Power Macintosh workstations. The University computer services include a high-speed campus network, remote-access capabilities, powerful networked multiprocessor systems for research, online information, e-mail accounts for all students, and directory services.

Costs

Tuition and fees for 2003–04 were $7388 for Maryland residents and $14,240 for nonresidents. Room and board costs vary but average $7007. Miscellaneous expenses, books, and transportation cost about $1000 per year.

Financial Aid

Approximately 55 percent of undergraduate students receive some financial aid in the form of grants, work-study, or loans. UMBC uses the Free Application for Federal Student Aid (FAFSA) to help determine a student's financial need. Aid is awarded to qualified applicants on a first-come, first-served basis. In order for the applicant to be considered on time, the FAFSA report and all supporting documents must reach the UMBC Financial Aid Office by March 1. Since aid is awarded only to admitted students, early application for admission is also important. A wide range of merit scholarships, ranging from $500 to a fixed-dollar, four-year award covering incoming tuition, mandatory fees, and room and board costs, are awarded to students on the basis of academic or artistic merit. Well-qualified freshmen are automatically considered for general merit scholarships once they are admitted to the University. The Scholars programs at UMBC provide special opportunities for outstanding entering freshmen who want to focus their education through intense study in their major. Scholars programs at UMBC include the Humanities Scholars, the Linehan Artist Scholars, the Sondheim Public Affairs Scholars, Meyerhoff Scholarship, and Center for Women and Information Technology Scholars. Students in the Scholars programs participate in a wide range of academic and cultural enrichment activities, extracurricular travel, or summer-study. The selection process for specialty scholarships includes application, an interview, and, in some cases, nomination from a high school official.

Faculty

Many UMBC faculty members work at the frontiers of their disciplines, and they are eager to share their expertise with undergraduates. Students have opportunities for research experience, instruction in state-of-the-art techniques, and introductions to prospective employers who partner with UMBC faculty members in research. Leading faculty members, including deans and award-winning professors, teach entry-level classes. The student-faculty ratio is 17:1.

Student Government

Elections are held each year for officers in UMBC's Student Government Association (SGA). The SGA represents the student body on a number of administrative committees.

Admission Requirements

In fall 2003, the average incoming freshman had a 3.5 cumulative GPA, ranked in the top quarter of his or her senior class, and had a combined SAT I score approaching 1220. Approximately 65 percent of freshman applicants are admitted each year. More than 20 percent enter with advanced credit, either through AP, I.B., or other college courses. Academic performance and curriculum strength play an important part in the decision. An essay is required, and a letter of recommendation is strongly encouraged. Transfer students who present at least 30 semester hours of college-level work are admitted based on the strength of college success. A minimum 2.5 cumulative average is recommended for full consideration.

Application and Information

Prospective freshmen are encouraged to submit applications by the early action deadline of November 1 for full consideration for admission, campus housing, financial aid, and scholarships; the final deadline is February 1. The priority deadline for transfer students is March 15 for fall admission and November 1 for spring admission for students seeking admission to special programs or wishing to be considered for campus housing, financial aid, or scholarships. The final deadline for applications is May 31 for fall and December 15 for spring.

Yvette Mozie-Ross, Director of Admissions
Office of Admissions
University of Maryland, Baltimore County
1000 Hilltop Circle
Baltimore, Maryland 21250
Telephone: 410-455-2291
800-UMBC-4U2 (toll-free)
Fax: 410-455-1094
World Wide Web: http://www.umbc.edu

UMBC's chess team has won the Pan-American Intercollegiate Team Chess Championship—the "World Series" of college chess—six times in the past seven years.

UNIVERSITY OF MARYLAND, COLLEGE PARK

COLLEGE PARK, MARYLAND

The University

Throughout its 148-year history, the University of Maryland has served as a premier public research university while dedicating itself to providing the highest quality undergraduate education. Designated as the state's flagship university, Maryland attracts the best students and faculty members from across the nation and around the world. Students enroll at Maryland for the reputation and quality of its academic programs, the outstanding and diverse opportunities both in and outside the classroom, and the success of its alumni.

Choosing from among more than 100 academic programs, 23,016 full-time and 2,430 part-time undergraduates are taught by a faculty of more than 3,500. Approximately 9,560 master's- and doctoral-level students are enrolled in the graduate school. About 75 percent of Maryland's undergraduates are state residents, with the remaining quarter coming from all fifty states, the District of Columbia, three territories, and 110 other countries. Maryland's diversity is one of its strongest assets, with 35 percent of students belonging to minority groups.

More than 10,000 undergraduates live on-campus. From traditional halls to apartments with kitchens and from single rooms to special-interest housing, students individualize their housing experience. Many students live near the campus in fraternity and sorority houses, apartments, and private homes. An extensive University shuttle bus system provides free transportation to neighboring communities in ten directions, allowing commuting students easy access to campus. Parking is readily available for both resident and commuter students.

The University sponsors more than 300 student clubs and organizations and hosts dozens of social, athletic, academic, and recreational activities each week. About 10 percent of students are members of twenty-five fraternities and twenty sororities. A full range of intramural and club sports use the University's campus recreation center, which houses indoor and outdoor swimming pools, free weights, fitness machines, courts, and a running track. Outdoor athletic facilities include an eighteen-hole golf course, a soccer/track complex, a 55-foot climbing wall, a ropes course, and playing fields. In addition, Maryland hosts teams in twenty-seven NCAA sports for both men and women, which compete in the Atlantic Coast Conference.

Location

Maryland students step off the campus and into one of the world's most vibrant centers of government, business, research, and culture. The University is located just minutes from the heart of Washington, D.C., and within half an hour of both Baltimore and Annapolis. Maryland's dynamic relationship with these cities gives students access to hands-on experience with government agencies, international corporations, trade associations, and foreign embassies. The Kennedy Center, NASA, the Smithsonian, the NIH, the Environmental Protection Agency, CNN, the National Archives, the FBI, and the *Washington Post* are just a few of the hundreds of places where Maryland students find opportunities for internships, research projects, and jobs. A Metrorail and MARC train station (easily accessible via the ShuttleUM) provide quick and easy public transportation to the entire Washington-Baltimore region. In addition, the city of College Park is a true college town, with dozens of restaurants, clubs, shops, and recreational activities designed for students.

Majors and Degrees

The University of Maryland offers one of the most comprehensive course selections available at any public or private institution.

Programs leading to Bachelor of Arts and Bachelor of Science degrees include accounting; aerospace engineering; Afro-American studies; agricultural and resource economics; agricultural and veterinary medicine; agricultural sciences; American studies; animal management and industry; animal preprofessional/science; animal sciences; anthropology; architecture; art education; art history and archaeology; art studio; astronomy; avian business; behavior evolution, ecology, and systematics; biochemistry; biological resources engineering; biological sciences; business and management; cell and molecular biology and genetics; chemical engineering; chemistry; Chinese; civil and environmental engineering; classical languages and literature; communication; computer engineering; computer science; criminology and criminal justice; dance; dietetics; early childhood education; economics; electrical engineering; elementary education; English; English education; environmental resources and park management; environmental science and policy; equine studies; family studies; finance; fire protection engineering; food science; foreign language education; French language and literature; geography; geology; German language and literature; government and politics; hearing and speech sciences; history; horticulture and crop production; human resources management; international business; Italian language and literature; Japanese; Jewish studies; journalism; kinesiology; laboratory animal management; land and water resource management; landscape architecture; linguistics; logistics and transportation; marine biology; marketing; materials sciences and engineering; mathematics; mathematics education; mechanical engineering; microbiology; music; music education; natural resource science (conservation of soil, water, and the environment; landscape management; plant science; turf and golf course management; and urban forestry); natural resources management; nuclear engineering; nutritional science; operations and quality management; philosophy; physical education; physical sciences; physics; physiology and neurobiology; plant and wildlife resource management; plant biology; psychology; Romance languages; Russian area studies; Russian language and literature; science education; social studies education; sociology; Spanish language and literature; special education; speech education; theater; theater and English education; women's studies; and zoology.

Preprofessional programs are also available in allied health, dental hygiene, dentistry, law, medical technology, medicine, nursing, occupational therapy, optometry, osteopathic medicine, pharmacy, physical therapy, and podiatry.

Academic Program

Undergraduate education at Maryland aims to provide students with a sense of identity and purpose, a concern for others, a sense of responsibility for the quality of life around them, a continuing eagerness for knowledge and understanding, and a foundation for a lifetime of personal enrichment and success. Within a research setting such as Maryland's, undergraduate students take strong, interdisciplinary courses taught by renowned researchers and scholars.

Every undergraduate completes at least 120 credit hours to earn a degree, 46 of which are general education or CORE courses. The purpose of CORE is to help students achieve the intellectual integration and awareness they need to meet challenges in their personal, social, political, and professional lives. Although each program is unique, generally 30 to 36 credit hours are earned in the major field. Students may earn a double major, earn a certificate in a second area of study, and use AP and IB credit toward a degree.

University Honors offers the most academically talented students the opportunity to join a close-knit community of students and faculty members in small, challenging seminar courses and residential communities. College Park Scholars, an innovative living/learning program that is also designed for academically talented students, encourages students who share common intellectual interests to study and live together. Other special academic opportunities for undergraduates include First Year Learning Communities, Gemstone, Honors Humanities, CIVICUS, Global Communities, Jiménez-Porter Writers' House, Air Force ROTC, and a research assistant program.

The University operates on a semester system and offers two 6-week summer sessions and a three-week winter term. More than 3,000 undergraduate courses are taught at the University of Maryland.

Off-Campus Programs

Students at Maryland have the opportunity to formally study abroad for credit in Amsterdam; Argentina; Austria; Belgium; Belize; Brazil; China; Costa Rica; Cuba; Denmark; France, including Paris; Germany, including Tübingen; Ghana; Great Britain, including England (London, Oxford, and York); India; Israel; Italy; Japan; Korea; Mexico; Spain; and Sweden. The National Student Exchange program allows students to study at one of more than 140 different U.S. colleges and universities for a semester or a year. Internships and cooperative education opportunities are plentiful in and around the nation's capital.

Academic Facilities

Encompassing more than 300 buildings on 1,500 acres, the University of Maryland houses dozens of research laboratories, performance venues, art galleries, and centers of study. Major academic and research facilities include the National Archives II, the Academy of Leadership, the Center for Agricultural Biotechnology, the Astronomy Observatory, the Center for Young Children, the Center of Entrepreneurship, the Engineering Wind Tunnel, the Fire and Rescue Institute, the Institute for Systems Research, a Performing Arts Center, the Space Systems Laboratory, and the Superconductivity Research Center.

A state-of-the-art computer science center and dozens of laboratories across the campus hold more than 800 computer terminals for student use. All residence hall rooms have high-speed (10 MB) Ethernet connections to the Campus Data Network and to the Internet, World Wide Web, and e-mail. Seven campus libraries contain 2.8 million books, 5.4 million microfilm units, 166,000 audiovisual materials, and subscriptions to 30,000 periodicals.

Costs

For the 2003–04 academic year, undergraduate tuition and fees were $6759 for Maryland residents and $17,433 for out-of-state residents. Room and board costs were approximately $7240 for an academic year.

Financial Aid

An array of financial aid programs, including scholarships, grants, loans, and student employment opportunities, are available to undergraduates. To be considered for maximum need-based financial aid, students must submit the completed FAFSA to the FAFSA processor in time for receipt and acceptance by the University's February 15 priority financial aid deadline. The University proudly offers several merit scholarships for academically and creatively talented students; approximately $4 million per year is awarded. To be considered for most merit scholarships, an application for admission must be submitted by December 1. Last year, 68 percent of full-time students who applied for financial aid received it and were awarded an average of $7300.

Faculty

Maryland has a full-time teaching faculty of 2,766 and a part-time teaching faculty of 825 members. Ninety percent hold a Ph.D. or terminal degree in their fields. Faculty honors recipients include Fulbright Scholars, Guggenheim Fellows, NSF Presidential Young Investigators, Sloan Fellows, and members of the National Academy of Sciences and the American Academy of Arts and Sciences. The average class size is 31; the student-faculty ratio is 14:1.

Student Government

Maryland students constitute a self-governing student body, of which every undergraduate is a member. The Student Government Association (SGA) is an integral part of the University's shared governance and regularly provides input and feedback to the University president, campus senate, and state legislature. Student leaders—both executive and legislative—are elected each fall in a multiparty election and are responsible for allocating more than $1 million to student organizations. The SGA also provides funding to a student legal aid office and student entertainment productions. In addition, the students are represented on the University System of Maryland Board of Regents by a student member.

Admission Requirements

The University of Maryland seeks to enroll students who demonstrate that they have potential for academic success and who, the University believes, will help build a talented, diverse, and interesting entering class. Admission to the University of Maryland is competitive. Each year nearly 25,000 applications are received for a fall freshman class of approximately 4,100. Transfer applications are received from approximately 7,500 students, of whom Maryland enrolls 2,100 per year.

Academic potential of freshmen is assessed primarily by examination of high school course work and SAT I or ACT scores. All entering freshmen must have completed a minimum of 4 years of English; 3 years of social studies or history; 3 years of mathematics courses (4 years is recommended), including 2 years of algebra and 1 year of geometry; 2 years of a foreign language; and 2 years of science that involves laboratory work. Most successful applicants have also completed several honors and advanced courses during high school. Additional criteria reviewed include an essay, leadership and extracurricular activities, honors and awards, and counselor and teacher recommendations. Transfer students are assessed primarily by examination of previously completed college-level work.

According to the most recent profile of the enrolled freshmen class, the middle 50 percent have a combined SAT I score between 1200 and 1350, with an average high school GPA of 3.87.

Application and Information

Applications for fall freshman admission are due by January 20. Students are encouraged to apply by Maryland's priority application deadline of December 1 for best consideration for admission, merit-based scholarships, and invitation to University Honors or College Park Scholars. The spring freshman application deadline is December 15. Applications for fall transfer admission are due by July 1; for the spring semester, December 1. International students and students with any foreign academic records have earlier deadlines.

For application forms and further information about the University of Maryland, students should contact:

Office of Undergraduate Admissions
University of Maryland
College Park, Maryland 20742-5235
Telephone: 301-314-8385
800-422-5867 (toll-free)
301-314-9197 (TTY)
Fax: 301-314-9693
E-mail: um-admit@uga.umd.edu
World Wide Web: http://www.umd.edu

UNIVERSITY OF MARYLAND EASTERN SHORE

PRINCESS ANNE, MARYLAND

The University

The University of Maryland Eastern Shore (UMES) is a land-grant, historically black college founded in 1886 as the Delaware Conference Academy. Since its beginning, the institution has had several name changes and governing bodies. It was Maryland State College from 1948 until 1970, when it became one of the five campuses that formed the University of Maryland. In 1988, it became a member of the eleven-campus University of Maryland System. UMES is approved by the state of Maryland and fully accredited by the Middle States Association of Colleges and Schools.

The campus is located on 700 acres of land. There are approximately 3,600 students enrolled; 93 percent are undergraduates. Students have various backgrounds and come from thirty states and a number of other countries. Fifty-five percent of the students live in on-campus housing. All students may keep cars on campus.

Graduate degree programs offered are as follows: Master of Arts in Teaching (M.A.T.); Master of Education (M.Ed.) in career and technology education, guidance and counseling, and special education; Master of Science (M.S.) in applied computer science, criminology and criminal justice, food and agricultural sciences, marine-estuarine-environmental sciences, rehabilitation counseling, and toxicology; Doctor of Physical Therapy (D.P.T.) in physical therapy; Doctor of Philosophy (Ph.D.) in food science and technology, marine-estuarine-environmental sciences, organizational leadership, and toxicology; and Doctor of Education (Ed.D.) in education leadership.

Location

UMES is located in the small town of Princess Anne on the Eastern Shore of Maryland. The town dates back to 1733 and has many buildings and landmarks of historic interest. The quiet community environment is excellent for learning, yet it is only 3 hours by car from the abundant cultural and recreational facilities of Washington, D.C., and Baltimore, Maryland. The state's famous seaside resort, Ocean City, is only 1 hour from the campus. The campus is located 13 miles south of the town of Salisbury, which provides shopping and recreational facilities.

Majors and Degrees

The University of Maryland Eastern Shore awards the Bachelor of Arts (B.A.) and Bachelor of Science (B.S.) degrees in teaching and nonteaching programs in the following areas: accounting, agribusiness, agriculture, applied design, aviation sciences, art education, biology, business administration, chemistry, computer science, construction management technology, criminal justice, education, engineering technology, English, environmental science, exercise science, general studies, human ecology, hotel and restaurant management, mathematics, music education, physician's assistant studies, rehabilitation services, and sociology. UMES offers teacher education programs in the following areas: specialty programs in art and music for grades K–12 and special education for grades 1–8 and 6–12; secondary/middle school programs (grades 5–12) in biology, chemistry, English, mathematics, social science, and technology education; and secondary school programs (grades 7–12) in agriculture and business education. UMES offers a dual-degree program in sociology/social work in conjunction with Salisbury State University.

Teaching certification is offered in a number of the above areas at the secondary level.

UMES offers an engineering program in cooperation with the College of Engineering of the University of Maryland College Park and Salisbury State University.

UMES also offers two-year and four-year preprofessional programs in biology/dentistry, biology/medicine, biology/physical therapy, chemistry/medicine, dental hygiene, engineering, law, nursing, pharmacy, radiologic technology, and rehabilitation services.

Academic Program

The Bachelor of Arts or Bachelor of Science degree is awarded upon the completion of 120 hours of work. These credit hours are divided among general education requirements, core courses for the selected major, and electives. Students may receive credit by examination or through Advanced Placement tests.

UMES, in cooperation with the professional schools of the University of Maryland at Baltimore and the Virginia-Maryland Regional College of Veterinary Medicine, offers an honors program for students of promise and ability who can meet rigorous standards. The program includes preprofessional tracks in dental hygiene, dentistry, medicine, nursing, pharmacy, radiologic technology, social work, and veterinary medicine.

The University also offers a cooperative education program that gives students the opportunity to gain practical work experience in their major area while earning academic credit. Employment opportunities are located off campus.

An Individualized Admissions Program is available to a limited number of students who do not meet the requirements for regular admission. Students who are selected are required to enroll in the University's precollege summer program (PACE).

UMES operates on a semester system and offers a five-week winter session and three summer sessions.

Academic Facilities

The UMES Frederick Douglass Library houses more than 177,000 books and periodicals, approximately 6,005 microforms, CD-ROMs, and other media within its expanded facility. It also has access to worldwide information via OCLC and Carl Systems Incorporated. The campus has a Student Development Center, which houses the Support Center, the Counseling Center, and various other student-centered operations.

A newly constructed student center houses a six-lane bowling alley, a grand ballroom, a movie theater, dining services, student government offices, and other areas designed to enhance on-campus student life.

Other facilities include the Ella Fitzgerald Performing Arts Center; the Richard A. Henson Education Center; the Art and Technology Center; a computer center; a number of laboratories in such areas as agriculture, biology, business education, chemistry, construction management, home economics, industrial arts, and physics; and the William P. Hytche Athletic Center.

Costs

For the 2003–04 academic year, tuition for Maryland residents was $5105. For out-of-state residents, tuition was $10,541. Room and board costs were estimated at $5380. These costs do not include books, laboratory fees, or personal budgets.

Financial Aid

Financial aid consists of both federal and institutional programs. Federal programs consist of the Federal Pell Grant, Federal Supplemental Educational Opportunity Grant, and Federal Work-Study programs. Institutional programs consist of scholarships and departmental assistantships. To be considered for financial aid, students should apply as early in the year as possible since financial aid is generally awarded on the basis of need and in the order of application. The Free Application for Federal Student Aid (FAFSA) is required in addition to the institutional financial aid form. Merit scholarships are available.

Faculty

UMES has a faculty of 200 members (133 full-time and 67 part-time). Of tenured and tenure-track faculty members, 94 percent have terminal degrees. The average class size is 30 students. Students are assigned faculty advisers who help them to achieve degree goals by aiding in course selection and other academic matters.

Student Government

The University of Maryland believes strongly in student participation in its decision-making bodies. Two students from the eleven-campus system serve on the University's Board of Regents. The Student Government Association is the student-governing body on the UMES campus through which students promote the interests and welfare of the University community. Students are represented on the UMES Senate and all its committees and on the Student Judiciary Council, the Student Life Committee, and other student organizations through which students provide leadership.

Admission Requirements

Freshman applicants must have graduated from an accredited secondary school with a minimum 2.5 grade point average. Competitive scores must be earned on the SAT I or ACT. Students who did not graduate from a secondary school may be admitted on the basis of their GED test scores. Out-of-state students are admitted on a competitive basis.

Honors applicants, in addition to fulfilling regular admission requirements, must have an A average or better in academic subjects and three letters of recommendation and must have a special interview with the Honors Committee. Successful completion of the honors program facilitates admission to the professional schools of the University of Maryland in the city of Baltimore.

Transfer students must have maintained a C average or better in all previous college work and must be in good academic standing.

Application and Information

To be considered for admission, all students must submit an application with a $25 nonrefundable application fee and SAT I or ACT scores. Applicants should request that their high school forward an official copy of their transcript directly to the Office of Admissions. Transfer students should submit official transcripts of all college work completed at all other institutions. Transfer students who have earned fewer than 12 credits of work at other colleges must submit their high school transcript as well.

Application material may be obtained by contacting:

Office of Admissions and Recruitment
University of Maryland Eastern Shore
Princess Anne, Maryland 21853
Telephone: 410-651-6410 (Admissions Office)
410-651-2200 (general information)
410-651-6178 (Recruitment Office)
World Wide Web: http://www.umes.edu

UNIVERSITY OF MASSACHUSETTS AMHERST

AMHERST, MASSACHUSETTS

The University

One of today's leading centers of public higher education in the Northeast, the University of Massachusetts Amherst is a major Carnegie I research university, enrolling more than 18,600 undergraduates (about equally divided between genders). The University offers ninety bachelor's degree programs and six associate degree programs at the undergraduate level as well as sixty-eight master's programs and fifty doctoral programs. The University's size offers a great diversity and choice of academic programs, housing arrangements, and extracurricular involvements. In addition, students can enroll with no extra charge in courses at Amherst, Hampshire, Mount Holyoke, and Smith Colleges through the Five College Consortium.

While many of the undergraduates are Massachusetts residents, students hail from fifty-two states and territories and seventy countries. Nearly 11,000 students reside (in either coed or single-sex accommodations) in forty-one residence halls in five different areas, each with its own unique atmosphere. Residence hall living is required in the freshman and sophomore years. Many students choose to live in residence halls their entire four years. Meal plans are available to fit student lifestyles, including quantity of meals, types of meals (kosher, vegetarian, ethnic offerings), and dining facilities (dining halls, on-campus locations, and even off-campus locations). To ensure a smooth transition to college life, the University has a first-year experience program that welcomes new students to life at UMass Amherst. The University also knows that parents are a key component of a student's success and offers a parent program that supplies parents with timely University information and runs parent and family special events, such as Family Weekend.

The New Students Program (NSP) welcomes all first-year students to UMass Amherst for an all-encompassing orientation. Incoming students come to campus during the summer and meet new classmates, decide where to live, discuss academic paths with a faculty adviser, select fall semester courses, and take placement exams. New students participate in workshops, learn about extracurricular activities, and listen as students and faculty and staff members discuss both opportunity and responsibility at the University of Massachusetts Amherst. NSP orientation covers all the details and signifies the transition in becoming a member of the UMass Amherst community.

Campus social life revolves around the Five College area, the residence halls, student organizations, sports (intercollegiate and intramural), religious and cultural activities, and a Greek organization of fraternities and sororities. Many social-action, professional, and special interest groups are active in the community. The Student Activities Center (SAC) brings writers, nationally recognized comedians, musicians, and other celebrities to campus. It provides support to more than 200 registered student organizations, including student government and cultural and religious groups. The SAC also supports student-run businesses. About 150 students manage and operate these businesses, which provide vital services to the campus.

The University participates in ten men's and eleven women's NCAA Division I intercollegiate varsity sports as a member of the Atlantic 10 Conference for basketball, football, ice hockey, and other sports. The 9,000-seat Mullins Center, home of UMass Amherst basketball and ice hockey, is a state-of-the-art facility with an Olympic-size ice surface. The arena also has an adjoining practice ice rink and seven racquetball courts. The intramural program, one of the largest in the East, draws more than 11,000 participants annually and runs more than 335 hours a week of recreational programming.

Students are welcome to join the Minuteman Marching Band, which has long been a source of great pride for the University and the surrounding region. At home football games, the "Power and Class" performs its traditional postgame show for its enthusiastic, dedicated fans. In 1998, the Minuteman Marching Band received the Louis C. Sudler Trophy, the highest honor awarded to a collegiate marching band.

Location

Situated on the Connecticut River in the Pioneer Valley of western Massachusetts, 20 miles north of Springfield, the campus of the University of Massachusetts Amherst consists of 1,430 acres of land and buildings. The *New York Times* calls Amherst one of the country's "Ten Best College Towns." The area offers the cultural and educational advantages of an urban environment while also enjoying a rural setting. Amherst is less than 100 miles from Boston, 175 miles from New York City, and only 30 miles from Vermont and New Hampshire. The Five College area in and around Amherst and Northampton offers an impressive array of cultural activity (film, dance, theater, music, and art) while also facilitating outdoor recreation, such as hiking, skiing, and camping in the Berkshire Hills and Vermont's Green Mountains. An extensive, free Five College bus service makes it easy for students to take advantage of academic and extracurricular activities at all five campuses.

Majors and Degrees

A two-year associate degree is offered in six majors in the Stockbridge School of Agriculture. A four-year bachelor's degree is offered in ten colleges or schools: Education, Engineering, Natural Resources and the Environment, Humanities and Fine Arts, Management, Natural Sciences and Mathematics, Nursing, Public Health and Health Sciences, Social and Behavioral Sciences, and Commonwealth Honors College. Within many of these majors, a number of different programs, options, and concentrations are possible. A bachelor's degree with an individualized concentration (BDIC) is also available for upper-division students who wish to create their own faculty-advised major.

Academic Programs

The traditional academic calendar includes a fall and a spring semester. The winter break gives students the opportunity to enroll in a unique four-week winter session program. Two summer sessions are also available. Students seeking a bachelor's degree must successfully complete a minimum of 120 credit hours (128 to 136 for engineering majors), including a core of required courses. In addition to the student's main course of study, there are more than twenty nonmajor curricular programs (e.g., aerospace studies, African studies, film studies, military science, and statistics) and an array of minors to choose from to enhance an academic portfolio. A variety of special academic programs are also offered: the Commonwealth College Honors Program, community service, legal studies, and women's studies as well as Learning Support Services, residential academic programs (RAP) for first-year students, and advising for undeclared majors. Options are available for honors study, independent study, credit by examination, and advanced placement. The Division of Continuing Education serves nonmatriculated students.

The University has programs designed especially for the enrollment, retention, and graduation of African, Latino/a, Asian/Pacific Islander, and Native American (ALANA) students: the Committee for the Collegiate Education of Black and Other Minority Students (CCEBMS), the Bilingual Collegiate Program (BCP), the United Asia Learning Resource Center (UALRC), and the Native American Student Support Services Program (NASSS). The Diversity in Management Education Services for business majors and the Minority Engineering Program provide other special academic opportunities.

Off-Campus Programs

The Five College Consortium (Amherst, Hampshire, Mount Holyoke, and Smith Colleges and the University of Massachusetts Amherst) permits students from the University of Massachusetts Amherst to study at and use the resources of any of the four other colleges in the area. A number of academic and cultural cooperative programs are also offered through the Five College Consortium.

A variety of programs facilitate study off campus. The Field Experiences Office is the source for internships and cooperative educational experiences, where students gain firsthand knowledge of their intended industry before graduation. The National Student Exchange Program offers students the opportunity to explore other geographical and cultural environments within the U.S. at one of more than 170 state colleges and universities for one or two semesters, earning transferable credits. The International Programs Office assists students in arranging international exchange and overseas study experiences in more than twenty countries. The University Without Walls features off-campus study arrangements for returning adult students. In addition, specific departments sponsor clinical programs, international study, and internships as part of their individual curricular requirements or offerings.

Academic Facilities

The library system of the University of Massachusetts Amherst is composed of the twenty-six-story W. E. B. Du Bois Library and several branch libraries. With more than 5 million books, periodicals, and government documents, UMass Amherst has the largest library system at any state-supported institution in New England. The Fine Arts Center, a working sculpture in itself, houses the fine arts departments (music, dance, art, and theater), several performance areas (including the main Concert Hall), galleries, and other fine arts facilities. Morrill Science Center, the Graduate Research Center, the computer science complex, and several laboratories serve the sciences and applied sciences.

The University's computing center is one of the largest university-based systems in the Northeast. Students register for classes online and receive free UMass Amherst e-mail accounts. Internet and e-mail access is available from campus terminals in the library, various computer labs, and academic buildings as well as in each residence hall.

Costs

Tuition and fees for 2003–04 were $8232 for in-state students and $17,085 for nonresident students. Room and board cost about $5748, depending on a student's choice of three meal plans. Students must be covered by health insurance either through the University's Student Health Insurance Plan or from an outside source, which must be of comparable coverage.

Financial Aid

Financial aid is offered to students who cannot, through their own and/or their parents' reasonable efforts, meet the full cost of a UMass Amherst college education. Aid consists of scholarships and grants, loans, and work-study employment. Students applying for financial aid are automatically considered for every University-administered program for which they are eligible. The basic financial aid application form required of all applicants is the Free Application for Federal Student Aid (FAFSA). The financial aid resources available total more than $140 million for all types of aid. More than half of the students receive some support from the Financial Aid Office. Students should check with their guidance counselor for the most current financial aid information.

Faculty

More than 1,075 full-time, teaching faculty members compose a distinguished group committed to excellence in both teaching and scholarly research. More than 93 percent of the full-time members hold the highest degree in their fields. Most faculty members not only teach and conduct research in their disciplines but also assist in the advising of students. Close interaction between students and faculty, both in and out of the classroom, is highly encouraged.

Student Government

Most University and student organizations rely on student participation in their decision-making processes. Selected in yearly campuswide elections, student government leaders and representatives participate in the decisions that shape students' educations and futures. The Student Senate is the legislative arm of the Student Government Association, and there is a Student Judiciary whose judges are appointed through the Student Senate and Area Governments. These area residential governments represent students regarding housing, social, cultural, and educational programs and issues. Students are also represented on many of the administrative decision-making bodies of the University, including the Board of Trustees.

Admission Requirements

All applicants must have a diploma from an accredited high school or a general equivalency diploma by the time they enroll at the University. A college-preparatory high school background is required for entering freshmen. The SAT I or ACT is also required, as is an essay. In fall 2003, 44 percent of entering freshmen averaged in the top 25 percent of their class. The middle 50 percent of their SAT I scores were 520 to 630 verbal and 510 to 610 math. Transfer students are considered after they have completed at least 12 credits of college work, although the most common entry level is after two years of satisfactory community or junior college study. The most important criterion in the freshman admissions decision is the high school academic record: SAT or ACT scores, quality and level of courses, grade point average, and grade trends. Achievement tests and letters of recommendation are not required but can strengthen an application. A personal statement, special talents, work experience, and extracurricular activities are also considered.

Application and Information

For application forms and further information, students should contact:

Office of Undergraduate Admissions
University Admissions Center
University of Massachusetts Amherst
37 Mather Drive
Amherst, Massachusetts 01003-9291
Telephone: 413-545-0222
Fax: 413-545-4312
World Wide Web: http://www.umass.edu

The University of Massachusetts Amherst offers academic challenge, choice, and diversity in a quintessential New England college town.

UNIVERSITY OF MASSACHUSETTS BOSTON

BOSTON, MASSACHUSETTS

The University

The University of Massachusetts (UMass) Boston was founded in 1964 by the state legislature to provide the opportunity for superior undergraduate and graduate education at a moderate cost at an urban campus located in the capital city of Boston. With nearly 13,000 commuting students in its undergraduate, graduate, and continuing education programs, UMass Boston is the second-largest campus of the University of Massachusetts system. The University of Massachusetts Boston is a community of scholars who take pride in academic excellence, diversity, research, and service. The fabric of academic research and scholarship is tightly woven into the public and community service needs of Boston and the modern metropolitan center.

UMass Boston enrolls a diverse student body that is representative of a wide variety of ages, ethnicities, academic interests, and life backgrounds. The median age of incoming freshmen is 19. Three out of every 4 students are transfers. African- and Asian-American students make up about 24 percent of the total enrollment; another 7 percent are Hispanic.

More than seventy-five student organizations provide opportunities for cocurricular and extracurricular activities. University institutes provide scholarly research and public-service activities that focus on environmental issues, labor studies, gerontology, international programs, women in politics, the study of war and social consequences, and public policy. Further research is conducted on African-American, Asian, and Latino community issues, along with other concerns of the public interest that are particularly indigenous to metropolitan areas.

The student body is composed of young, mature, and working adults, all of whom share a strong motivation to succeed academically and relate their classroom pursuits to their career aspirations. The University Advising Center provides comprehensive academic support, planning, and career advising services. A team of professional counselors provides personalized assistance to students in designing their course of study, utilizing tutorial and mentoring services, choosing a major and career path, and developing interviewing, resume writing, and job search skills.

Location

The University is located on a beautiful landscaped peninsula on Boston Harbor, just south of downtown Boston, overlooking the bay and harbor islands. The University's neighbors are the John F. Kennedy Presidential Library and the Massachusetts State Archives and Commonwealth Museum.

Located just a half mile off the Southeast Expressway (Interstate 93), the campus is easily accessible by motor vehicle and public transportation. The entrance to the campus is a seaside promenade drive. Two levels of underground parking are available at reasonable short- and long-term rates. A free shuttle bus runs every few minutes for the half-mile ride from the Metropolitan Boston Transit Authority's (MBTA) JFK/UMass "T" stop on the Red Line to the front door of the campus. Student discount "T" passes are available for frequent users.

The University wants students to be at home at UMass Boston. Many students commute from their home communities, while others utilize the free computerized Housing Referral Service for assistance with finding rental property and/or roommates. Construction of on-campus housing is planned within the next four years.

Boston itself, with its worldwide standing as a cultural center and its well-earned reputation as America's favorite college town, offers UMass Boston students a wealth of resources for exploration and entertainment. Everything from Fenway Park and the FleetCenter to the Museum of Fine Arts is easily accessible from UMass Boston.

Majors and Degrees

Five undergraduate colleges award bachelor's degrees: the College of Liberal Arts and the College of Science and Mathematics (with thirty-seven majors, twenty-one programs of study, and eight special course groupings between them), the College of Management (with seven concentrations), the College of Nursing and Health Sciences (with both a B.S.N. and an R.N.-to-B.S.N. accelerated program as well as a program in exercise science and physical education), and the College of Public and Community Service (with six majors and six career concentrations). Premed, prelaw, and teacher-preparation programs are also offered, along with programs for honors study, credit by examination, and advanced placement. Students are encouraged to participate fully in designing their academic plan.

A joint Bachelor of Arts or Science/master's degree in business program is available for high academic achievers as well as a liberal arts or science degree with a minor in management and an engineering program.

Academic Program

The academic calendar runs from early September through the end of May. There are also a one-month optional winter session in January and summer school in June, July, and August. Matriculating students may choose to attend on a full- or part-time basis and may adjust their schedules from semester to semester. A minimum of 30 credits must be earned at UMass Boston as a residency requirement for graduation.

For the College of Liberal Arts and the College of Science and Mathematics, 120 credits are required to graduate. The general education curriculum comprises three elements: the distribution requirement, the core curriculum requirement, and the writing requirement. In addition, requirements of the major must be fulfilled. The Colleges both offer an Honors Program and an individual major option.

For the College of Management, the 120-credit undergraduate program leads to a B.S. degree in management. By fulfilling the general education, management, and elective course work requirements, graduates receive a liberal arts foundation and the theoretical, technical, and functional training to succeed in the business world. An Honors program is also offered.

The College of Nursing and Health Science's B.S. program in nursing requires 123 credits with a liberal arts foundation and intensive study of 63 credits in the principles and practices of nursing. The program in exercise science and physical education prepares graduates for the technical aspects of a professional discipline with a foundation in liberal arts and an optional teacher training component. Students may also elect to enter an Honors program in nursing.

The College of Public and Community Service is a nationally acclaimed model for competency-based education. It offers an innovative curriculum with a strong emphasis on social justice. The completion of a total of 40 competencies is required for graduation. Students may draw upon a variety of learning options, including classroom study, self-directed study, project-based learning, and the demonstration of competence gained through relevant prior experience in completing their degree.

Off-Campus Programs

The National Student Exchange Program offers UMass Boston students the opportunity to study at one of more than seventy participating colleges and universities in forty states at a cost comparable to what they pay to attend UMass Boston. The study-abroad program is available for students with a 3.0 GPA or better who seek international travel and academic experiences as well as summer and winter session programs. UMass Boston also participates in the New England Regional Student Program and the Boston Five-College Exchange Program.

Cooperative Education and Internship Programs place students in work assignments related directly to their fields of study so that they may apply what they learn in the classroom to practical work settings. Under the Co-Op Program, students are placed in full-time paid positions for six-month work periods. Under the Internship Program, students are placed on a part-time basis, usually 15–20 hours per week, for the length of the semester or the summer months. Some internships are paid and some are on a volunteer basis. Both co-op and internship placements benefit students by combining relevant practical learning, valuable work experience, career awareness, resume enhancement, personal and professional growth, and, in many instances, opportunities for academic credit, good pay, and a permanent job after graduation.

Academic Facilities

The University's Healey Library holds a collection of more than 575,000 volumes and subscribes to more than 3,120 domestic and international journals and newspapers. UMass Boston is a member of the Boston Library Consortium.

The University's Computing Services provides students with seven-day-a-week access to desktop labs, with some 250 Dell Pentium III and Apple Macintosh G4 computers, as well as to other specialized, course-related facilities. A wide variety of information technology and data communications resources are available, with network connections in every office and classroom. The campus network is fiber-optic based, with ATM protocol. Computing Services houses equipment from Data General, Dell, Compaq, Sun, and Apple, and operating systems include NT, UNIX, Linux, Apple OS, and VMS.

The Kennedy Presidential Library is linked to the University by a variety of educational programs, enabling students to conduct research utilizing the more than 28 million pages of documents, 6.5 million feet of film, and more than 100,000 still photographs in the library's archives. Next door, the Archives of the Commonwealth of Massachusetts are a rich depository, covering more than 5½ centuries of Massachusetts history.

Major new construction is being planned for a $50-million Campus Center that is designed to centralize student services at the University.

Costs

Tuition and fees for the spring 2004 semester were $3861 for Massachusetts residents studying full-time (12 or more credits) or $9191 for out-of-state students. Students enrolling part-time were charged tuition according to the number of credits taken, with Massachusetts residents paying tuition of $71.50 per credit; out-of-state residents paid tuition of $406.50 per credit. Annual mandatory fees for in-state residents ranged up to $3003 and up to $4313 for out-of-state students.

Financial Aid

Financial aid is based on need and/or merit. Applicants complete the Free Application for Federal Student Aid (FAFSA), keeping in mind the priority deadline of March 1 for fall entrants and November 1 for spring entrants. Need-based aid is awarded to students who demonstrate financial need, as determined by federal methodology. Aid consists of grants, waivers, and self-help in the form of loans and work-study employment. An on-time applicant is automatically considered for every University-administered program for which they are eligible. Fifty percent of the student body receives some form of financial aid, which last year totaled nearly $40 million.

Faculty

UMass Boston is proud of its distinguished faculty of 850 members, some 90 percent of whom have doctoral degrees. UMass Boston also has a student-faculty ratio of 15:1 and a small class size that averages 28 students. The faculty's top priority is teaching and advising students. Many of the faculty members also conduct research, publish materials, and participate in grant activities and professional organizations. Faculty members maintain office hours for students and make themselves accessible as mentors. The Faculty Council is the faculty governance body.

Student Government

The Undergraduate Student Senate is composed of elected members from the undergraduate colleges and programs and participates fully in matters related to the quality of student life and the allocation of the student activities trust fund. Students are also represented on numerous University- and college-based committees and councils that initiate major policy and procedural recommendations, forwarding those recommendations to governance bodies and the administration for enactment.

Admission Requirements

All applicants must demonstrate that they have earned a diploma from an accredited high school or a general equivalency diploma by the time they matriculate at the University.

For freshman applicants, an official copy of the high school transcript is required, and a minimum of 16 college-preparatory academic units must have been taken (4 English, 3 mathematics, 2 social studies, 2 foreign languages, 3 sciences (2 with labs), and 2 electives). If the applicant has graduated from high school within the last three years, an official report of the SAT I or ACT score is also required. The mean SAT I score for recent freshman applicants was 1042. Non-native English-speaking students who have been in the U.S. for fewer than four years may also submit the TOEFL score report. For GED applicants, an official copy of the GED score report is required. All freshmen are required to submit an essay. Letters of recommendation are encouraged but not required.

All transfer applicants must also submit an essay. Letters of recommendation are encouraged but not required. Transfer applicants are required to have at least a 2.5 GPA for admission, although some programs require a 2.75 minimum GPA. While the student's high school academic record remains the primary criterion, all applications are evaluated on an individual basis, and all aspects of the application package are considered in making the admission decision.

Application and Information

For an undergraduate viewbook and application for admission, students should contact:

Enrollment Information Service
University of Massachusetts Boston
100 Morrissey Boulevard
Boston, Massachusetts 02125-3393
Telephone: 617-287-6000
617-287-6010 (TTY/TDD)
Fax: 617-287-5999
World Wide Web: http://www.umb.edu

UMass Boston is located on an easily accessible, picturesque peninsula just south of downtown Boston.

UNIVERSITY OF MASSACHUSETTS DARTMOUTH

NORTH DARTMOUTH, MASSACHUSETTS

The University

The University of Massachusetts Dartmouth traces its roots to 1895 when the Massachusetts legislature chartered the New Bedford Textile School and the Bradford Durfee Textile School in Fall River. As the region's economic base shifted from textiles to more diverse manufacturing and service industries, the program of the colleges changed. Courses were developed to respond to the needs of new generations of students, stimulated by the clear economic and social advantages of a well-educated citizenry. In 1962 Southeastern Massachusetts Technological Institute (SMTI) was created, and in 1969, out of a need and a clear demand for a comprehensive public university, SMTI became Southeastern Massachusetts University. Then, in 1988, the Swain School of Design was merged with the University's College of Visual and Performing Arts.

In 1991, a new University of Massachusetts system was created, which combined the Amherst and Boston campuses with the University of Lowell, Southeastern Massachusetts University, and the Medical Center in Worcester. Today, UMass Dartmouth provides educational programs, research, extension, and continuing education and cyber education in the liberal and creative arts and sciences and in the professions. A broad range of bachelor's and master's degrees and one program leading to a doctorate are offered. Graduate programs lead to the Master of Arts, Master of Business Administration, Master of Arts in Teaching, Master of Fine Arts, Master of Art Education, and Master of Science. A Ph.D. is offered in electrical engineering, chemical engineering, biomedical engineering, marine science, and physics.

UMass Dartmouth enrolls approximately 8,500 students; 90 percent are from Massachusetts, with a growing number from other states and countries outside the United States. A residential campus with a variety of student organizations, athletic programs, cultural opportunities, and interest groups, the University fosters personal development, diversity, and responsible citizenship.

Location

Located in historic and scenic southeastern Massachusetts, which includes the nearby cities of Fall River and New Bedford and the Cape Cod region to the east, the campus is situated on 710 acres. The dramatic campus is the work of architect Paul Rudolph, former dean of the Yale University School of Art and Architecture. Metropolitan areas, with libraries, museums, theaters, and numerous educational institutions, are within an hour's drive: Boston to the north and Providence, Rhode Island, to the west. Recreational sites are minutes away and include beaches, hiking, and cultural and nightlife opportunities. New York City is four hours by car; the mountains of New Hampshire and Vermont are three to four hours away. Students can walk to homes and shops in the immediate area of the campus, while public transportation is available to nearby communities.

Majors and Degrees

There are five colleges within the University: College of Arts and Sciences (sixteen majors); Charlton College of Business (five majors); Engineering (eight majors); Nursing (one major); and Visual and Performing Arts (twelve majors). In addition, honors programs, interdisciplinary studies, prelaw, premedical advising, and a number of different minors and options are available within various departments. The University offers the Bachelor of Arts, Bachelor of Fine Arts, Bachelor of Science, and Bachelor of Science in Nursing degrees at the undergraduate level.

Academic Programs

The University operates on a two-semester calendar with the fall semester beginning the first week of September and concluding in mid-December and the spring semester beginning in late January and concluding in late May. A five-week intersession is offered between semesters. Summer term courses are offered in June, July, and early August. Undergraduate students usually enroll in four or five courses each semester, and a typical course earns 3 credits. An undergraduate degree requires a minimum of 120 credits (there are a few majors which require 135 credits); a student can complete degree requirements for a specified major within a department or an approved interdepartmental major (30 credits). Students must also complete requirements according to the degree being sought.

Other learning opportunities include independent study, contract learning, and directed study; study abroad; study at a nearby university through cross-registration; and credit by examination. UMass Dartmouth is a member of SACHEM (Southeastern Association for Cooperation in Higher Education in Massachusetts), allowing for cross-registration at Bridgewater State College, Bristol Community College, Cape Cod Community College, Dean College, Massachusetts Maritime Academy, Massasoit Community College, Stonehill College, and Wheaton College. The University has formal exchange agreements with the University of Grenoble (France), the Lycée du Grésivaudan at Meylan and the Lycée Aristide Berges, Nottingham Trent University (England), the Baden-Württemberg Universities (Germany), Centro de Arte e Comunicação (Portugal), Nova Scotia College of Art and Design, the École Nationale Supérieure des Industries Textiles, Université de Haute Alsace (France), and Minho University (Portugal). Students may also take initiative in finding other programs in addition to the exchange-agreement institutions.

The College of Engineering provides majors in any of the engineering fields to gain work experience through cooperative education or internships.

Academic Facilities

Computing is an integral part of the curriculum. All academic buildings, including student residences, are connected to a campuswide network. Computing clusters, located in the library and in most classroom buildings, support the classwork of students. More than 200 microcomputers (Apple Macintosh and IBM) or terminals are readily available. The University library supports all programs of instruction and research with 455,323 volumes and 2,925 periodicals. A large interlibrary loan network and delivery system makes millions of volumes available to the students. Each of the five colleges within the University is housed in academic facilities designed for its purposes with classrooms, laboratories, studies, galleries, faculty offices, and lounges.

Costs

In-state tuition and fees for 2003–04 were $6904; non-Massachusetts resident tuition and fees were $16,404. Room and board expenses range from $6756 to $7099, depending on the meal plan chosen. Books and supplies cost approximately $900 a year depending on a student's courses. Specific fees may be assessed, depending on a student's course of study.

Financial Aid

Nearly all students are eligible for some type of financial aid. UMass Dartmouth awards financial aid based on federal, state, and institutional guidelines; students must submit the Free Application for Federal Student Aid (FAFSA). In determining need, the Financial Aid Services Office considers the total costs of attending the University (tuition, fees, books, room and board, the cost of commuting, and an allowance for living and personal expenses). The difference between total University cost and the estimate of expected family contribution is the amount that the financial aid staff considers to be financial need.

Faculty

The faculty, numbering 350 full-time members, is distributed over twenty-nine departments in the five colleges. More than two thirds of the faculty members have a Ph.D., with a significant number holding the terminal degree in their chosen discipline (e.g., business, fine arts, education). A student-faculty ratio of 16:1 ensures that classes are reasonably sized, with an average class size of 30 students. Faculty members are actively engaged in advising students, providing guidance throughout a student's academic career.

Student Government

The Student Senate is the governing body offering a forum for debate on matters of importance to the student body. The Student Judiciary, a system of courts or judicial agencies, provides students and organizations with the protection of due process in all disciplinary matters. A student is also elected to the University of Massachusetts Board of Trustees. Students serve on the Board of Governors, policy makers for the Campus Center; the Resident Hall Congress; and the Student Activities Board. Students are active, voting participants on policy-making committees that regulate both academic as well as social aspects of the University.

Admission Requirements

Admission is selective. Applicants are evaluated by both the general standards of the University and by the special standards of the academic areas that they request. In addition, the Board of Higher Education sets guidelines governing admissions standards for the University. Admission to some colleges or majors may be limited by spaces available. Students are admitted on a rolling basis with no set deadline. Qualified candidates are accepted until the capacity has been reached in the program of choice. Each applicant's record is assessed on the basis of the depth and rigor of the secondary school program, rank in class and grade point average, SAT I or ACT results, college-level records for transfer applicants, and other appropriate measures. Students are invited to visit the University for a campus tour and a meeting with an admissions officer; interviews are not required.

The University realizes its commitment to equal access through standard, as well as alternative, admission programs. For College Now, the alternative program, applicants must meet at least one of three eligibility criteria: low income status, limited English background, or ethnic student of color status.

All applicants for freshman admission to the University are required to submit an application form with appropriate fee ($35 in-state and $55 out-of-state), a transcript of the secondary school record, SAT I or ACT results, and any other information that candidates consider important for the admissions committee to review. Transfer students, who comprise approximately one third of the new student population every year, are required to submit records for all college-level work completed in addition to the application form. The admission process is virtually the same for transfer candidates with primary emphasis on the student's previous college/university record.

Application and Information

Admissions is rolling except for early decision (freshman). The early decision deadline is November 15, with notification by December 15. All other decisions are made within three weeks of the completion of an application. For application forms and related information, students may call, write, or e-mail the admissions office.

Office of Admissions
UMass Dartmouth
285 Old Westport Road
North Dartmouth, Massachusetts 02747-2300
Telephone: 508-999-8605
Fax: 508-999-8755
E-mail: admissions@umassd.edu
World Wide Web: http://explore.umassd.edu/

The size of UMass Dartmouth appeals to many students.

UNIVERSITY OF MASSACHUSETTS LOWELL

LOWELL, MASSACHUSETTS

The University

Throughout its 100-year history, the University of Massachusetts Lowell has excelled at providing innovative, responsive programs that meet both the needs of its students for a quality education and the needs of regional industry for skilled leadership. Formed through the merger of a technical institute and a teacher's college, the University is part of the five-campus University of Massachusetts system. UMass Lowell students look at the world and society through a wide lens. While they learn the specifics of a major, they also explore its context so they understand how the economy, the environment, and society connect. Courses typically involve a practical component that can range from the political science team that competed nationally in a United Nations Model Assembly to the music business majors who went to a recording industry conference in California to the civil engineering students who helped the city of Lowell inventory and replace all its street signs. Faculty members are respected researchers who value their commitment to teaching and extend the learning experience beyond the classroom. Undergraduates participate in funded research and college policy committees, and senior faculty members are involved in student projects such as building and racing a solar-powered car. Strong links with local businesses, educational systems, and health-care providers benefit students through an increasing number of internships, part-time jobs, and grants. In short, students graduate with the hands-on experience and practical problem-solving skills employers are looking for.

The University campus covers 100 acres on both sides of the Merrimack River, and includes classroom and laboratory buildings, two libraries, a student center, two gymnasiums, two dining halls, a Center for the Performing Arts, an art gallery, and numerous residence halls. A new campus center provides additional social and recreational facilities. State-of-the-art laboratories include such special interest facilities as the six Sound Recording Technology Program studios, an interactive video lab that enables nursing students to simulate medical emergencies, and a manufacturing lab where engineering and management students team up to produce microelectronic components. The University's collaborative relationship with the city of Lowell has resulted in the completion of a nearby hockey arena and a baseball stadium on campus, both shared by UMass Lowell and professional teams.

UMass Lowell's 6,000 undergraduate students are ethnically, culturally, and economically diverse. Students are active in a wide variety of community service activities, including athletics-based programs for local high school students, the Adaptive Technology Program in which students create modified devices for the disabled, and volunteer work at local shelters and community programs. There are more than 100 campus organizations to choose from: academic, recreational, and special interest groups; the women's center; marching band; the student newspaper; an FM radio station; and the Off-Broadway Players. Campuswide events include University Week and Spring Carnival, and resident hall associations sponsor social and recreational events. The University sponsors fifteen intercollegiate sports teams, including the nationally ranked Division I hockey team and an active recreational sports program. In conjunction with the five colleges, the Graduate School enrolls nearly 3,000 students in twenty-nine master's degree and twelve doctoral programs.

Location

The University is located in Lowell, a city of 110,000 that has gained national attention by successfully leveraging its history, ethnic diversity, and entrepreneurial spirit to create a vital urban center. The site of a National Historical Park that honors the city as the birthplace of the industrial revolution, Lowell is also home to an acclaimed professional theater company, annual Kerouac and folk festivals, and museums that include the Museum of American Textile History and the Whistler House Museum. Located 26 miles from the cultural and educational riches of Boston and Cambridge, Lowell is also within an hour of ocean beaches and the lakes and mountains of New Hampshire via major highways and regional train and bus service.

Majors and Degrees

The College of Arts and Sciences offers baccalaureate programs in American studies, art, biological sciences, chemistry, computer science, criminal justice, design, economics, English, environmental studies, history, liberal arts, mathematics, modern languages, music, music business, philosophy, physics, political science, psychology, sociology, and sound recording technology. Dual majors are permitted. Dual B.A./B.S. and B.S./M.S. degree programs are available in liberal arts, science, and engineering fields. Predental and premedical programs are available. The James B. Francis College of Engineering offers baccalaureate day programs in chemical, civil, electrical, mechanical, and plastics engineering. Engineering programs are accredited by the Engineering Accreditation Commission (EAC) of the Accreditation Board for Engineering and Technology (ABET). Combined bachelor's/master's programs, internships, and co-op opportunities are available in the College of Engineering. The School of Health and Environment offers baccalaureate day programs in clinical laboratory sciences, accredited by the NAACLS (National Accrediting Agency for Clinical Laboratory Sciences); medical technology; nutritional science; exercise physiology; community health education; and nursing, accredited by the NLNAC (National League for Nursing Accrediting Commission). The College of Management offers baccalaureate day programs, all accredited by AACSB International–The Association to Advance Collegiate Schools of Business in business administration (B.S.B.A.), with concentrations in accounting, finance, management, management information systems, and marketing.

The University's Division of Continuing Studies and Corporate Education offers evening programs through the various colleges. Through the College of Arts and Sciences, baccalaureate programs in applied mathematics, criminal justice, information technology, and liberal arts are offered. Through the College of Engineering, associate and baccalaureate degrees are offered in civil engineering technology, electronic engineering technology, and mechanical engineering technology. Through the College of Management, an associate degree program in accounting and a baccalaureate degree in business administration are available. Certificate programs are offered in accounting, computer-assisted manufacturing, computer engineering technology, data/telecommunications, electrooptics, environmental technology, graphic design and digital imagery, hazardous waste management, Internet technology, land surveying, manufacturing technology, multimedia applications, nutrition, paralegal studies, plastics engineering technology, quality assurance, Spanish, technical writing, UNIX, wastewater treatment, water treatment, and Web site design and development.

Academic Program

The University operates on a calendar of two semesters, a condensed two-week intersession in January, and a summer term (with two sessions). Full-time undergraduates generally take five courses each semester. A minimum of 120 credits is required for baccalaureate degrees; the minimum credits required for professional degree programs are generally higher. A University general education requirement is imposed for all baccalaureate curriculums. Majors require 30–60 credits. Elective course options vary widely according to the degree program and major area. Professional degree program options and requirements follow specific accreditation guidelines. Maximum curricular freedom is permitted in B.A. programs. The academic climate is serious and competitive and requires self-motivation. Approximately 50 percent of the undergraduates complete graduation requirements in four years.

Academic Facilities

The University has two comprehensive libraries with online capabilities that can be accessed from networked computers across the campus and from all dormitory rooms.

The University operates a state-of-the-art network facility that includes an OC-3 ATM backbone and 10/100 mbps switched technology to all desktops. Remote access via PPP or ISDN is also available. Clients to the network include more than 4,000 desktop and laboratory PCs with more than 100 servers. Applications on the network include e-mail, groupware, Microsoft Office products, cybereducation, interactive video, and numerous academic programming applications.

Costs

In 2003–04, full-time undergraduate day tuition and fees for residents of Massachusetts were $6963 per year; for nonresidents of Massachusetts, $17,401 per year. Residence hall charges were $3486 per year. A full meal plan was $2238 per year. Accident insurance is covered by fees; major medical insurance is optional. Books and supplies are estimated at $400 to $600, depending upon the program. Undergraduate continuing education tuition was $235 per credit for on-campus courses and $265 per credit for off-campus and distance learning courses. Quoted rates are subject to change.

Financial Aid

The University is committed to making higher education accessible to all qualified students. The University participates in federal and state programs, assisting students through grants-in-aid, loans, employment opportunities, and scholarships. The amount of an award is determined by need, as indicated by the Free Application for Federal Student Aid (FAFSA), which should be filed by March 1. The University awards a growing number of merit-based scholarships.

Faculty

The full-time resident faculty members number 359. The part-time day faculty members number 235. In addition, 175 part-time faculty members are employed in continuing education programs. Most faculty members teach and conduct research in their disciplines. Graduate teaching assistants also hold part-time instructional positions, particularly as discussion section leaders and laboratory teaching assistants.

Student Government

The Student Government Association and the Residence Hall Association provide opportunities in student government at the all-campus level. Leadership opportunities are provided in residence halls and student organizations. Students also participate in the disciplinary system and in most University committees.

Admission Requirements

All undergraduate day applicants must have a high school diploma or a general equivalency diploma and satisfactory SAT I scores. A minimum recalculated high school grade point average of 2.5 (on a 4.0 scale) is recommended, and the University places primary emphasis upon the high school record. Students whose high school average is below the required minimum may be considered for admission if they present SAT I verbal and mathematics scores that are higher than those specified for the admission of degree candidates by the college or program to which they wish to apply.

Transfer students are considered for fall- or spring-semester admissions. Transcripts of completed work must be on file prior to acceptance. Depending on the number of transfer credits and college GPA, transfer students who seek admission as matriculating day students may be asked to provide a high school record and SAT I scores.

Application and Information

For day programs, the University practices rolling admissions, which means that applications are evaluated as soon as they are complete. Entering freshmen are admitted for the fall or spring semester. Deadlines for freshman applications are July 1 for the fall semester and December 1 for the spring semester. Deadlines for transfer applications are August 15 for the fall semester and January 7 for the spring semester. For application forms and further information, students should contact the address listed below.

Office of Undergraduate Admissions
University of Massachusetts Lowell
883 Broadway Street
Suite 110
Lowell, Massachusetts 01854-5104
Telephone: 978-934-3931
800-410-4607 (toll-free)
World Wide Web: http://www.uml.edu

The main administration building makes a convenient gathering spot between classes.

The University of Massachusetts Lowell is an Equal Opportunity/Affirmative Action, Title IX, employer.

THE UNIVERSITY OF MEMPHIS

MEMPHIS, TENNESSEE

The University

Located on a beautifully landscaped campus in the heart of one of the South's largest and most progressive cities, the University of Memphis (U of M) is the flagship institution of the Tennessee Board of Regents System. Since its beginning in 1912, the University of Memphis has matured into a major public, metropolitan university recognized regionally and nationally for its academic, research, and athletic programs. The University offers more than 129 areas of study from which to choose.

The University campus comprises 1,160 acres at four sites. In addition to the main campus, the South Campus contains spacious living accommodations for married students, a research park, and outstanding varsity athletic training facilities. The University of Memphis also owns the Meeman Biological Field Station, a 623-acre tract used for biological and ecological studies. The Chucalissa Archaeological Museum in southwest Memphis is frequently used as a research and training facility in archaeology and anthropology.

The University of Memphis is an Equal Opportunity/Affirmative Action institution committed to the education of a diverse student body. It has a total enrollment of 19,911 students, including 15,209 undergraduates, from almost every state and many other countries. Approximately 46 percent of University of Memphis students are between the ages of 18 and 22, and members of minority groups account for 42 percent of the enrollment.

Location

The greater Memphis area has a population of approximately 1 million, which makes the city the eighteenth largest in the country. Centrally located on the Mississippi River, Memphis is an active hub for business, agriculture, and the transportation industry. The city has the mid-South's largest medical center and offers many cultural and entertainment opportunities. Major museum exhibits, sporting events, concerts, art shows, lectures, and even barbecue contests take place throughout the year. The AAA baseball team, the Redbirds, and the NBA team, the Grizzlies, both make their homes in Memphis. With its many businesses, industries, and schools, Memphis provides students with employment opportunities in a variety of fields during and after their college careers.

Majors and Degrees

The College of Arts and Sciences offers twenty-one undergraduate majors organized into three concentration groups: the humanities, the natural and mathematical sciences, and the social sciences. Three degree programs are offered: the Bachelor of Arts, the Bachelor of Science, and the Bachelor of Science in Chemistry. Majors include African and African-American studies, anthropology, biology, chemistry, computer science, criminology and criminal justice, economics, English, foreign languages and literatures, geography, geological sciences, history, international studies, mathematical sciences, microbiology and molecular cell sciences, philosophy, physics, political science, psychology, social work, and sociology.

The Fogelman College of Business and Economics offers programs of study leading to the Bachelor of Business Administration degree. Majors include accounting, business economics, finance, hospitality and resort management, international business, management, management information systems, marketing management, sales, and supply chain management. The programs of the College of Business and Economics are fully accredited by AACSB International–The Association to Advance Collegiate Schools of Business.

The College of Communication and Fine Arts is made up of the Departments of Art, Communication, Journalism, Theatre and Dance, and the Rudi E. Scheidt School of Music. Majors include architecture, art, art history, communication, journalism, music, music industry, and theater. The College offers three undergraduate degrees: the Bachelor of Arts, the Bachelor of Fine Arts, and the Bachelor of Music.

The College of Education offers programs leading to the degree of Bachelor of Science in Education. The college is fully accredited by NCATE, the National Council for Accreditation of Teacher Education, and offers teacher licensure programs in early childhood education, elementary education, physical education, and special education. Secondary school teacher licensure programs are offered in nineteen subject areas and require the baccalaureate degree in the chosen teaching field, followed by graduate study that culminates in the Master of Arts in Teaching (M.A.T.) degree. The College also offers nationally accredited programs in dietetics, exercise and sport science, food systems management, and sports management.

The Herff College of Engineering offers undergraduate programs in civil, computer, electrical, and mechanical engineering and in computer, electronics, and manufacturing engineering technology. College of Engineering courses can be used in other individual programs of undergraduate study, such as for biomedical engineering in the degree offered through the University College.

The University College offers two nontraditional degrees: the Bachelor of Liberal Studies and the Bachelor of Professional Studies, for students with experience, talents, and interests served through personally designed or multidisciplinary programs. Examples of programs that have been developed include aviation administration, biomedical engineering, biomedical illustration, family and consumer science, fashion merchandising, fire administration and fire prevention technology, health services administration, home merchandising, human services, information technology, organizational leadership, paralegal studies, preschool and child-care administration, religion in society, and services for the aging.

The University of Memphis also offers specialized degree programs. The Loewenberg School of Nursing offers a professionally accredited Bachelor of Science in Nursing degree. Preprofessional training is offered for students who intend to enter law school or a college of dentistry, medicine, nursing, optometry, pharmacy, physical therapy, or veterinary medicine. The University also offers Air Force, Army, and Navy ROTC programs.

The University of Memphis has joined forty-five Tennessee Board of Regents institutions in offering Regents Online Degree Programs. The U of M offers two degree programs: the Bachelor of Professional Studies in information technology or organizational leadership and the Bachelor of Liberal Studies in interdisciplinary studies. These degree programs are entirely online and are transferable among the participating institutions.

Academic Program

Many freshmen are advised through the Academic Counseling Unit of the Center for Student Development in preparation for formal enrollment in one of the degree-granting colleges. In addition to meeting the requirements for a specific degree, as established by the appropriate college or department, each student initially selects courses from broad offerings in the areas of communication skills, sciences, humanities, and social sciences, thereby ensuring the acquisition of breadth as well as depth of knowledge in various fields. A University-wide honors program is available for academically talented students. Student services that are normally available for day students are provided for evening and Saturday students through the Office of Student Information Services. Some entering freshmen are assigned to their degree-granting college immediately for academic advising.

The academic year begins in late August and is divided into two semesters and a summer session. The fall semester ends in mid-December, and the spring semester begins in mid-January. There are also courses offered during shorter sessions within the semesters.

Off-Campus Programs

The University of Memphis participates in both the International and National Student Exchange Programs, allowing students to study in other countries as well as in other states in the continental United States. The University also offers credit and noncredit courses at various locations throughout west Tennessee.

Academic Facilities

The University of Memphis' Ned R. McWherter Library provides one of the most electronically up-to-date information repositories within hundreds of miles. Students are able to tap into information stored in libraries around the world. Library collections contain more than 13 million items, which include monographs, periodical volumes, federal and state documents, maps, and manuscripts. The University also provides state-of-the-art computing facilities for student and faculty use, including two TigerLAN labs that are open 24 hours a day. Seventy-three additional labs with more than 1200 PC and Mac workstations and fifty-six "smart" classrooms complement the University's teaching and research activities. The Department of Theatre and Dance and the Rudi E. Scheidt School of Music, in their adjoining facilities, make an appreciable contribution to campus activities with live drama and concert series, films, and programming over WUMR, the campus radio station.

Included among the many research facilities at the University of Memphis are the Center for Earthquake Research and Information, the Integrated Microscopy Center, the FedEx Center for Supply Chain Management, the Ground Water Institute, and the Barbara K. Lipman Early Childhood School and Research Institute. The FedEx Institute of Technology opened in the fall of 2003. This cutting-edge facility brings together students, professors, researchers, and the global business community to formulate the ideas and products of tomorrow.

The state of Tennessee has designated five Centers of Excellence at the University: the Center for Applied Psychological Research, the Center for Research Initiatives and Strategies for the Communicatively Impaired, the Center for Research in Educational Policy, the Center for Egyptian Art and Archaeology, and the Center for Earthquake Research and Information. In addition, the University houses 25 endowed Chairs of Excellence.

Costs

In 2003–04, in-state students paid a maintenance fee of $2117 per semester for full-time study or $199 per semester hour for part-time study. Out-of-state students were assessed fees of $6149 per semester (full-time) or $539 per semester hour (part-time). On-campus residence hall rates ranged from $2250 to $4350 for an academic year. Full-time students paid an activity fee of $44 per semester, which is included in the above cost information.

Financial Aid

Financial assistance is provided through four basic sources: scholarships, grants, loans, and employment. Scholarships are offered through the Scholarship Office as well as through various academic, performance, and athletic departments. An application for admission is required to be considered for general and distinguished academic scholarship programs. Applicants for financial aid must submit the completed Free Application for Federal Student Aid (FAFSA) to the Financial Aid Office, which places the student under consideration for all financial aid programs. More than $70 million is awarded annually. The University operates two programs of student employment: the Federal Work-Study Program and a regular work program.

Faculty

The University of Memphis has approximately 800 ranked faculty members. In addition, many adjunct professors are hired from the community to teach in their fields of expertise.

Student Government

The Student Government Association consists of officers, a senate, a cabinet, and a judiciary elected annually by the student body. Its goals are to present the opinions of the student body to the administration, to enact legislation beneficial to the students, and to promote a broad range of student activities.

Admission Requirements

The admission of entering freshmen is based on the transcript of a four-year course of study at an approved or accredited high school that includes prescribed units of English, mathematics, natural/physical sciences, U.S. history, social studies, foreign language, and visual/performing arts. The General Educational Development test and high school equivalency diploma are accepted when applicable. An Admission Index is calculated by first multiplying the cumulative high school GPA by 30 and then adding the ACT composite score. Applicants under 21 years of age who meet all other requirements, including high school graduation and the mandated curriculum, and whose Admission Index is 95 or greater are granted admission. Applicants who do not meet the Admission Index requirement but provide an ACT score of 26 or greater or a cumulative GPA of 3.0 or greater are also admitted. Those applicants whose Admission Index is at least 80 but less than 95 are considered for acceptance by the Admission Committee. The admission of transfer students is based on the applicant's quality point average, academic standing at a former institution, and scores on the approved admission tests.

Application and Information

Inquiries about admission and requests for information about any undergraduate college of the University should be addressed to the Office of Admissions. Applications and supporting credentials must be submitted to the Office of Admissions at least thirty days before the beginning of the intended term of entry. While the established application deadlines are August 1 for the fall semester, December 1 for the spring semester, and May 1 for the summer session, early application is strongly encouraged to be considered for scholarship opportunities and to take advantage of early registration. Registration for fall classes occurs at New Student Orientation, which begins in June. Prospective students are encouraged to visit the University for a campus tour, which can be arranged by contacting the Office of Admissions.

Office of Admissions
Recruitment and Orientation Services
101 John Wilder Tower
The University of Memphis
Memphis, Tennessee 38152-3520
Telephone: 901-678-2169
800-669-2678 (toll-free)
World Wide Web: http://www.memphis.edu

The McWherter Library.

UNIVERSITY OF MINNESOTA, CROOKSTON

CROOKSTON, MINNESOTA

The University

Nationally recognized as a leader in information technology education, the University of Minnesota, Crookston (UMC), is part of the world-renowned University of Minnesota System. Founded in the late 1800s as a research station and then as a school of agriculture, UMC became a part of the University of Minnesota in 1965. Today, UMC is a four-year, public coeducational institution of 1,650 full- and part-time students.

Its focus on polytechnic education, commitment to technology, and overall high-quality programs have captured national attention. UMC earned a ranking in *U.S. News & World Report*'s 2000 listing of America's Best Colleges and received other national notice in publications such as the *Washington Post* and the *Atlanta Journal-Constitution.*

UMC is continuing to evolve to meet the educational demands of Minnesota and the world by developing a technology-rich, interactive living and learning community. In 1993, UMC was one of the first campuses in the nation to begin issuing notebook computers to all full-time students. In addition, the entire campus is fully wired to the World Wide Web, with an Internet connection available at every classroom seat and in the library, the cafeteria, every study room, and every residence hall room. Students use their personal computers to gain access to and send information worldwide, write reports, analyze data, develop and deliver multimedia presentations, complete and turn in assignments, receive grade reports, and communicate with faculty members, friends, and family. UMC has become known nationally as the "ThinkPad University" and has emerged as one of the most technologically advanced campuses in the country.

UMC's mission of research and discovery, teaching and learning, and outreach and public service encompasses applied undergraduate instruction and research in agriculture; aviation; business; education management; environmental and natural resources; equine industries; health management; hotel, restaurant, and institutional management; information networking management; scientific and technical communication; sport and recreation management; and appropriate interdisciplinary studies (a complete program list can be found in the Majors and Degrees section).

UMC also is responding to the demands of life in the information age by offering a technologically advanced curriculum that prepares students for today's careers and also promotes an understanding of and appreciation for lifelong learning that prepares them for the careers of tomorrow.

UMC continues to keep its link to agriculture by offering several programs that reflect the technological advances of modern agriculture. Agriculture used to mean only animals and tractors, but the precision agriculture of today involves chemistry, biology, electronics, and business sciences.

Location

UMC's 237-acre scenic campus on the northern edge of Crookston combines the best of both worlds when it comes to location. It is situated in a small, safe community in the middle of one of the richest and most diversified agricultural regions in the world, the Red River Valley. At the same time, Crookston is a short drive away from a number of urban centers, such as Minneapolis–St. Paul, Duluth, Fargo, Grand Forks, and Winnipeg, Canada.

In addition, students live in a community that celebrates its diversity. Several years ago, a colorful mural was painted on a wall of a building near downtown that, according to newspaper accounts, "stands for the colors of life—the variety of people who live and work together in Crookston."

Majors and Degrees

A wide range of specialty programs are offered at UMC, many of which are available only at UMC and a handful of other institutions nationally.

Students can obtain a Bachelor of Science degree in accounting; agricultural business; agricultural education; agricultural systems management (farm and ranch management, power and machinery, and precision agriculture); animal industries management; applied studies; aviation (agricultural, law enforcement, business, and natural resources); business management (management, marketing and entrepreneurship, and small business management); early childhood education (primary education and program management); equine industries management; golf facilities and turf systems management; health management; hotel, restaurant, and institutional management (food service administration, hotel/restaurant management and resort/spa management); information technology management (application development, e-learning technology, and systems administration); natural resources (natural resources management, law enforcement, park management, water resource management, and wildlife management); plant industries management (agronomy and horticulture); and sport and recreation management. Minors in applied ethics, business management, coaching, information technology management, music, and technical communication are also available.

Students can obtain a Bachelor of Applied Health or Bachelor of Manufacturing degree.

Two-year options are also available. Students can enroll in Associate in Applied Science degree programs in agriculture; dietetic technician studies; hotel, restaurant, and institutional management; information management; and marketing and management. An Associate in Science degree program is also available in business. Certificate programs are available in applied ethics; hotel, restaurant, and institutional management; and manufacturing management.

Academic Program

Students benefit from a personalized learning approach that centers on practical, direct applications for the real world. The curriculum is learner driven, interactive, and supported with technology and involves collaboration among students, faculty members, and prospective employers. Students now enroll in classes at UMC on a semester calendar system.

With UMC's emphasis on technology, teaching methods are dramatically different. Students find a classroom environment that is completely connected to technology, allowing students and instructors to gain access to information and exchange information more effectively. That classroom environment also includes the latest in computer- and video-presentation technology that is available to instructors.

Communication between faculty members and students now includes the use of e-mail and the World Wide Web for such tasks as distributing a course syllabus, sending out assignments or worksheets that had previously been distributed as printed handouts, and turning in assignments to faculty members. In addition, students have 24-hour access to UMC's library holdings as well as to all of the information available on the World Wide Web through the personal computer each student is issued.

Off-Campus Programs

Through a number of programs available at other University of Minnesota campuses, UMC students can travel and study overseas. Students have the opportunity to study at sites around the world in such countries as Costa Rica, England, Japan, Sweden, and other European countries. Through the University of Minnesota System, students can take advantage of more than 170 study-abroad programs in sixty countries.

Academic Facilities

UMC is one of the most technologically advanced campuses in the country. Nearly 100 percent of campus classrooms have advanced faculty workstations, featuring overhead projection graphics cameras for still, video, and computer display.

The University's attractive grounds include thirty buildings, flower gardens that border a spacious mall, and a natural history area that contains virgin prairie land. UMC has many well-equipped special-purpose laboratories; an indoor animal science arena and equine stable; an enlarged library and learning resource center; a food service and hotel, restaurant, and institutional management building; a large indoor physical education and intercollegiate athletic facility; an outdoor recreational and athletic complex; an expanded student center; a $2.2-million environmental science facility that enables students to conduct undergraduate research in the areas of horticulture, botany, and agronomy; and a student housing apartment complex.

Costs

Tuition for 2003–04 was $4871 for residents. Room and board costs were $4684. Minnesota has a reciprocal agreement with South Dakota, North Dakota, and Wisconsin that allows students from those states to pay Minnesota resident tuition. Beyond these agreements, all U.S. and Canada residents pay UMC's in-state rate.

Financial Aid

Removing financial barriers to students' enrollment and success is the ultimate goal of UMC's financial aid program. UMC wishes to ensure that any qualified student who desires to pursue an education at UMC can obtain sufficient resources to do so. Accordingly, the University's Office of Admissions and Financial Aid administers a number of financial aid programs.

A number of need-based funding sources are available for new, incoming freshman students as well as for transfer students—whether part-time or full-time. UMC also offers a variety of merit-based scholarships.

For the need-based funding sources, a formula is used that factors the difference between UMC's estimate of what it will cost to attend UMC and the amount the federal and state governments expect students and their families to contribute to their education, based on information provided on the Free Application for Federal Student Aid (FAFSA).

The specialty merit-based scholarships range in awards from $300 to a maximum of full tuition. Many are renewable.

Faculty

UMC's faculty members bring a wide range of teaching and research expertise to the classroom. Faculty members are dedicated to teaching and also encourage students' involvement in undergraduate research, internships, and other out-of-classroom learning experiences. Students find a professor at the head of the class, not a teaching assistant.

Faculty members also pride themselves on building a true scholarly community at UMC. Because of the small class sizes, faculty-student interaction, both in and out of the classroom, is common. With a student-faculty ratio of 15:1, students are not anonymous at UMC.

Student Government

The Student Forum is the student government body that represents the interests of students at the University of Minnesota, Crookston. The Forum is the major source for expressing student opinion and initiating legislative action to promote and protect student interests. In addition, UMC's Office of Student Activities coordinates more than thirty student organizations that provide students with a chance to pursue their special interests, meet new people, and develop their potential for leadership, organization, and creativity.

Admission Requirements

Freshman students are eligible for traditional admission if they are in the upper half of their graduating class. Students may also be admitted with a composite score of 21 or above on the ACT. Students who do not meet either of these requirements are considered using a combination of high school rank, GPA, test scores, high school curriculum, and other indicators of academic potential.

Transfer students should consult with the transfer specialist in admissions for specific information.

UMC recommends a college-preparatory program that includes 4 years of English, 3 years of natural sciences, 3 years of mathematics, 2 years of social science, and 2 years of a second language.

Application and Information

Applying for admission to the University of Minnesota, Crookston, involves some important preliminary steps. Freshman students should send high school transcripts, submit an application fee and a completed application form, and submit results from the ACT. Transfer students must send college transcripts and submit an application fee and completed application form. The application priority deadline is December 15.

UMC has developed a helpful application guide called *Getting Started At UMC: Admissions Application Guide,* which is available for free by calling UMC's Office of Admissions and Financial Aid at the toll-free number listed below. Students can also visit UMC on the World Wide Web. Campus tours are available each weekday at 10 a.m. and 2 p.m. Students are encouraged to call two days before a planned visit.

For more information, students should contact:

Office of Admissions and Financial Aid
170 Owen Hall
University of Minnesota, Crookston
2900 University Avenue
Crookston, Minnesota 56716-5001
Telephone: 218-281-8569
800-862-6466 (toll-free)
World Wide Web: http://www.umcrookston.edu

UMC is known nationally as the "ThinkPad University."

UNIVERSITY OF MISSOURI–KANSAS CITY

KANSAS CITY, MISSOURI

The University

The University of Missouri–Kansas City (UMKC) is a comprehensive, public, coed university. Beginning as the private University of Kansas City in 1933, the institution became part of the four-campus University of Missouri System in 1963. UMKC's vision is manifested through four mission areas: life and health sciences, visual and performing arts, urban issues and education, and a vibrant learning and campus life experience.

UMKC's fall 2003 student population was more than 14,200, with undergraduates making up 64 percent of the total. Student diversity is a reality at UMKC. Thirty-two percent of on-campus students are international, are members of a minority group, or have a special cultural/ethnic heritage.

UMKC offers more than 200 student organizations, including student government, academic societies, and fraternities and sororities.

Students may choose to live on campus in the residence halls, including the new Oak St. Hall or in UMKC's Twin Oaks apartments. However, many choose among the plentiful apartment complexes or areas that are within a 5- to 20-minute drive of the campus.

UMKC offers graduate degrees in nearly all of the undergraduate areas that are in the Majors and Degrees section listed below.

Location

UMKC is located in a vibrant area of Kansas City, one that encompasses the arts, residential neighborhoods, major shopping/entertainment areas and businesses, along with plenty of green space and tree-lined boulevards.

The University's Volker (main) campus is located on a 93-acre site lush with mature trees, gentle hills, and plenty of green space. UMKC also has a Hospital Hill campus located north of the main campus. UMKC's bus service connects the two campuses. Easy access is a Kansas City hallmark: in addition to a well-developed interstate highway system, Kansas City features more miles of tree-lined boulevards than Paris. There are also more fountains than in any city outside of Rome.

Majors and Degrees

The University of Missouri–Kansas City offers nationally accredited programs of study over a broad range of selected academic disciplines that lead to the Bachelor of Arts (B.A.); Bachelor of Science (B.S.); Bachelor of Business Administration (B.B.A.); Bachelor of Fine Arts (B.F.A.); Bachelor of Information Technology (B.I.T.); Bachelor of Music (B.M.); Bachelor of Liberal Arts (B.L.A.); Bachelor of Science in Nursing (B.S.N.); accelerated degree programs, such as the Fast Track bachelor's in nursing; and combined baccalaureate/professional degrees, such as the six-year B.A./M.D.

Degree programs and areas of emphasis within those programs are as follows: accounting (B.S.); American studies (B.A.); art (B.A.); architectural and environmental studies (cooperative degree); art history (B.A.); biology (B.A., B.S.); business administration (B.B.A.); chemistry (B.A., B.S.); civil engineering (B.S.Ci.E.); communications studies (B.A.); computer science (B.A., B.S.), with emphases in software architecture (B.S.) and telecommunications networking (B.S.); criminal justice and criminology (B.A., B.S.); dance (B.F.A.); dental hygiene (B.S.D.H.), general and with emphases in clinical and classroom teaching; early childhood education (B.A.); earth sciences (B.S.); economics (B.A.); electrical engineering (B.S.E.E.); elementary education (B.A.); English (B.A.), with emphases in journalism and creative writing and secondary English education; environmental studies (B.A., B.S.), with emphases in chemistry (B.S.) or geosciences (B.S.); French (B.A.); geography (B.A., B.S.); geology (B.S.); German (B.A.); history (B.A.); information technology (B.I.T.); interdisciplinary studies (B.A., B.S.); Judaic studies (B.A.); liberal arts (B.L.A.); mathematics and statistics (B.A., B.S.); mechanical engineering (B.S.M.E.); medical technology (B.S.); middle school education (B.A.); music (B.A.), with an emphasis in music therapy; music composition (B.M.), music education (B.M.E.), with emphases in choral, instrumental, and music therapy; music theory (B.M.); nursing (B.S.N.); performance (B.M.), general and with emphases in accordion, bassoon, cello, clarinet, flute, guitar, harpsichord, horn, jazz and studio music, oboe, organ, percussion, piano, piano pedagogy, saxophone, string bass, trombone, trumpet, tuba, viola, violin, and voice; philosophy (B.A.); physical education (B.A.), with emphases in teaching and nonteaching; physics (B.A., B.S.); political science (B.A.); psychology (B.A.); secondary education (B.A.), with emphases in art, English, foreign languages, general, mathematics, music, natural science, and social science; sociology (B.A.), with emphases in anthropology, deviant behavior, life course, and urban sociology; Spanish (B.A.); studio art (B.A.), with an emphasis in graphic design/photography; theater (B.A.); urban affairs (B.A.), and urban planning and design (B.A.).

Academic Programs

Baccalaureate degrees require a minimum of 120 course credits and a common core of lower-division general education courses that may be selected from among several options in the arts, humanities, and social sciences and from the mathematical, physical, natural, and computer sciences. Baccalaureate degree requirements are designed by the faculty for students seeking a broad background in either specific academic disciplines, the liberal arts, or interdisciplinary studies.

In many disciplines, individual programs of study can be designed for the student seeking employment immediately following graduation or for those preparing for graduate or professional education. In particular, the baccalaureate degree provides UMKC graduates a base of understanding across many disciplines.

The College of Arts and Sciences offers an honors program that admits students who rank in the top 10 percent of their high school class and place in the top 10 percent on the ACT.

Students ranking in the top 10 percent of their graduating class are graduated "with distinction." Students who complete the honors program receive their degrees with the designation "with honors."

UMKC's academic calendar offers fall semesters from August to December and winter semesters are from January to May. A summer session is also available.

Off-Campus Programs

Study-abroad programs for students are available through numerous sources, including People to People International, the Missouri-London Program, Summer Study programs through the College of Arts and Sciences, and a variety of exchange agreements.

Academic Facilities

The UMKC library system, which includes its main library and libraries at the schools of dentistry, medicine, and law, holds more than 1.6 million volumes, more than 6,800 current serial subscriptions, and substantial collections of government documents, microfilms, sound recordings, and musical scores.

In addition to participating in a variety of local, state, and national library organizations, UMKC has close ties with the Linda Hall Library of Science and Technology, which is adjacent to UMKC's main campus.

Extensive academic computing facilities include a COMPAQ/DEC Alpha Cluster running OpenVMS, one of the highest performance superminicomputer installations in Missouri. A high-speed Internet connection gives users easy access to the World Wide Web, e-mail, library systems, data archives, bulletin boards, listservs, chats, and digests. Software provided free of charge connects home computers and student dormitory rooms to e-mail and the Internet. Students have an account as long as they are enrolled in for-credit courses. Computer labs with networked Macintosh and PC workstations, adaptive workstations, laser printers, and scanners are located throughout campus. UMKC staff members support each lab. The labs include a wide variety of popular software as well as specialized software for the academic disciplines.

Costs

For fall 2004, the UMKC educational fees are estimated to be $194.50 per credit hour; other fees bring the estimated typical total cost per hour to $219.55. On-campus room and board expenses average $5595 for 2004–05 for a double occupancy room and the University's Meal Plan A (average). Off-campus expenses are room and board, $6890; transportation, $2880; and medical insurance and personal expenses, $2910, for a total of $12,600.

The UMKC Metro Rate is a plan that provides in-state fees for undergraduate degree-seeking residents from the following neighboring Kansas counties: Miami, Leavenworth, Johnson, and Wyandotte.

Financial Aid

In 2003, UMKC arranged for more than $95 million in financial assistance to more than 10,500 students, representing nearly 88 percent of the on-campus student population. The Financial Aid Office administers some 500 aid sources. These include federal aid programs and academic scholarships, as well as benefit programs for veterans and their dependents.

There are two kinds of assistance offered: need-based (determined by family income and ability to pay according to a federal formula) and merit-based (determined by academic achievement, leadership, and special talents). Need-based programs include Federal Pell Grants, Federal Supplemental Educational Opportunity Grants, Federal Perkins Loans, Federal Direct Loans, and Federal Work-Study.

UMKC has extensive merit-based scholarship resources. Eligible freshmen can qualify for renewable scholarships of up to $12,000 per year. Merit-based scholarship programs also are available for transfer, minority, and nonresident students. No separate application is usually required; applications for admission are reviewed for eligibility.

To apply for financial aid, students must first apply for admission or readmission to UMKC. Students also must submit the Free Application for Federal Student Aid (FAFSA) to the federal processor, preferably by March 1 of the year they intend to apply.

Faculty

UMKC has a faculty of 1,111, including 48 endowed chairs and professorships. More than 83 percent of full-time faculty members have a Ph.D. or the terminal degree in their field. Many have received designations of distinction or awards for teaching and scholarship. Fifteen have been named Curators' Professors or Distinguished Teaching Professors, the UM System's top faculty honors. More than 20 have received Fulbright scholarships. UMKC's student-teacher ratio is 10:1.

Student Government

The student governing body at UMKC is the Student Government Association (SGA) and comprises representatives from all academic units. In addition, each academic unit has a council to serve the needs of its students. Council and SGA elections are held annually.

Admission Requirements

UMKC is considered a selective institution, which means certain academic criteria must be met before official admission. Basic criteria for admission direct from high school include 4 units of English, 4 units of math (algebra I or higher), 3 units of science (including one lab class), 3 units of social studies, 1 unit of fine arts, and 2 units of a single foreign language. Previous academic success, extracurricular activity, and a specific talent or ability are other factors that are considered. Many new students transfer to UMKC. Special policies are in place to ensure their success, including full transfer of course work from any other university in the UM System and articulation agreements with area community colleges.

Application and Information

A formal application for admission includes a complete application for admission, with nonrefundable application fee; high school class rank; official transcripts from previous higher education institutions, if any; and ACT scores, if fewer than 24 transferable college hours.

The ideal application deadlines for admission directly from high school are fall semester, April 1; winter semester, November 1; and summer session, May 1. Some UMKC academic units have earlier deadlines. Students are notified in writing regarding the status of their admission. For an application, information, or to arrange a campus visit, students should contact:

Office of Admissions
120 Administrative Center
University of Missouri–Kansas City
5100 Rockhill Road
Kansas City, Missouri 64110-2499
Telephone: 816-235-1111
800-775-8652 (toll-free)
800-735-2966 (TT) (toll-free)
800-735-2466 (voice) (toll-free)
Fax: 816-235-5544
E-mail: admit@umkc.edu
World Wide Web: http://www.umkc.edu

UMKC's campus is a tree-lined site of gently rolling hills located adjacent to Kansas City's Country Club Plaza district.

UNIVERSITY OF MISSOURI–ST. LOUIS

ST. LOUIS, MISSOURI

The University

Helping students succeed is the mission of the University of Missouri–St. Louis (UM–St. Louis). An exciting atmosphere of living and learning is apparent the moment people step foot on the University's beautifully landscaped, 300-acre campus in suburban St. Louis. More than 15,000 students, including 12,630 undergraduates, come to UM–St. Louis from forty states and more than eighty other countries.

Founded in 1963 as one of the four campuses of the University of Missouri, UM–St. Louis quickly grew to be the largest university in St. Louis and the third-largest in Missouri. UM–St. Louis offers students all the educational advantages and resources of a major urban research university with the personal attention of a small college; the average class size is 20 students.

Faculty members are nationally recognized experts in their fields, with 96 percent of tenured faculty members holding a Ph.D. Classes are taught by professors, not graduate students or teaching assistants, to give students the utmost experience and knowledge.

UM–St. Louis offers eighty-nine graduate and undergraduate degree programs in more than 100 instructional areas. Chemistry and political science are internationally recognized departments of eminence. Graduate and undergraduate degree programs are offered through the College of Arts and Sciences, the College of Business Administration, the Barnes College of Nursing and Health Studies, the College of Education, the College of Fine Arts and Communication, the Evening College, the Graduate School, the School of Optometry, and the Pierre Laclede Honors College. The Honors College is one of the fastest growing honors programs in the country and the only one with its own separate campus. UM–St. Louis also offers an innovative joint undergraduate degree in civil, electrical, and mechanical engineering in partnership with Washington University. A Bachelor of Fine Arts degree program started in 1996 in partnership with St. Louis Community College. The flexible curriculum offers numerous independent study options, certificate programs, and interdisciplinary studies.

Students get valuable real-world experience and a head start on their careers through internships and cooperative education programs with more than 400 St. Louis companies and organizations. Eighty percent of students graduating in the class of 2002 received job offers within three months of graduation.

UM–St. Louis has made a major investment in technology to provide some of the most technologically sophisticated classroom facilities in the U.S. Students are speeding through cyberspace with a new generation of computers, interactive media, and worldwide teleconferencing. This technology is integrated throughout the curriculum so all students, regardless of major, are on the cutting edge of advanced technology.

UM–St. Louis has on-campus residence halls totaling 334 spaces. Student rooms are linked to the campus computer network, e-mail, the Internet, and the World Wide Web. University Meadows student apartments provide a choice of efficiency and two- and four-bedroom units that house a total of 504 students. Amenities include a clubhouse and pool. Mansion Hill Condominiums, located on a wooded estate next to campus, offers additional housing for 164 students.

UM–St. Louis is fully accredited by the North Central Association of Colleges and Schools. Additional accreditations include AACSB International–The Association to Advance Collegiate Schools of Business, the National Council for Accreditation of Teacher Education, and the Missouri Department of Elementary and Secondary Education. The degrees offered through the UM–St. Louis/ Washington University Joint Engineering Program are accredited by the Accreditation Board for Engineering Technology (ABET).

Location

UM–St. Louis occupies a beautiful suburban campus within easy reach of all the attractions of St. Louis, Missouri, a thriving metropolitan area with 2.6 million residents. The campus is served by two MetroLink stations, St. Louis's newest form of rapid transit, to provide direct access to Lambert St. Louis International Airport and the region's major cultural, sports, and entertainment attractions such as Cardinals baseball, Blues hockey, the St. Louis Rams, St. Louis Art Museum, St. Louis Zoo, St. Louis Symphony, Union Station, Laclede's Landing, and Forest Park. UM–St. Louis is the largest supplier of university-educated employees in the region, which ranks fifth nationally in the number of Fortune 100 headquarters.

Majors and Degrees

Undergraduate majors include accounting; anthropology; applied mathematics; art history and fine arts; behavioral sciences; biochemistry; biological sciences; biology; biotechnology; business administration, with areas of emphasis in finance, international business, logistics and operations management, management and organizational behavior, and marketing; chemistry; civil engineering; communication; community education; computer science; criminology and criminal justice; early childhood education; economics; educational studies; electrical engineering; elementary education; English; French; general studies; health sciences; history; management information systems; mathematics; mechanical engineering; music; music education; nursing; optometry; philosophy; physical education; physics; political science; prelaw; premedicine; prepharmacy; preveterinary; psychology; public administration; secondary education; social work; sociology; Spanish; special education; studio art; and theater and dance.

Academic Programs

The University offers courses during fall and spring semesters, two 8-week summer sessions, three 4-week summer sessions, and one 12-week session. All undergraduates take 42 semester hours of general education courses in English, mathematics, humanities, natural sciences, and social sciences. The bachelor's degree for most majors requires 120 credit hours. The bachelor's degree in electrical engineering requires 131 credit hours, and the bachelor's degree for civil and mechanical engineering requires 137 credit hours. Each degree program at UM–St. Louis has specific course requirements and may require a minimum grade point average.

Students enjoy a variety of educational experiences outside the classroom, including internships, cooperative education programs, study abroad and international exchange programs, and ROTC. Other opportunities include independent study options, accelerated-degree programs, advanced placement, English as a second language programs, tutorials and mentoring programs, organizations for African-American and international students, and specialized services for LCD students.

Off-Campus Programs

UM–St. Louis offers students extensive opportunities for study abroad through exchange programs in thirty-three countries worldwide. In the London Business Internship Program, for example, students spend a semester learning and working in London, one of the world's foremost financial centers. In addition, students may spend a year or a semester at one of 125 universities in the U.S. through the National Student Exchange Program.

Academic Facilities

UM–St. Louis debuted its newest addition to the campus September 2003—the Blanche M. Touhill Performing Arts Center. The

$52-million performance venue opened on the north campus and is the only one of its size in the St. Louis area. It offers two theaters—a performance auditorium with a warm European-opera-house feel that seats up to 1,625 patrons and a smaller black-box-like theater space that seats 300. The flexibility of the two theaters allows the University to bring a wide range of performing arts to the facility and make it the ultimate teaching and learning experience for students, faculty members, and the community. Since the doors to the University first opened in 1963 on the grounds of the former Bellerive Country Club, UM–St. Louis has grown to include forty-four modern classroom buildings, research facilities, residence halls, student apartments, and an athletic complex. The $10-million computer center is one of the most technologically sophisticated classroom facilities in the U.S. The $10-million Molecular Electronics Center opened in 1996 to house expanded research and teaching in chemistry, physics, engineering, and physical sciences. The Anheuser-Busch Ecology Complex augments research activities of the biology department and the University's renowned International Center for Tropical Ecology in partnership with the Missouri Botanical Garden. In addition to spacious lecture halls and a 435-seat theater, the campus features extensive computer labs, multimedia facilities, a radio station, a child care center, and a community optometry clinic. The Millennium Student Center opened in October 2000 and provides many conveniences to students. The center is designed to offer many frequently used services under one roof. Inside, students find Admissions, Financial Aid, Academic Advising, Registration, Cashiers, Career Services, and Student Activities offices; the bookstore; the copy center; and the United Missouri Bank. If students wish to relax or study, the center offers television lounges, a cyberlab chat room, a game room, quiet lounges, and three food venues.

The Mark Twain Athletic Complex features a state-of-the-art fitness center, weight room, indoor track, swimming pool, and basketball, volleyball, handball, and racquetball courts.

UM–St. Louis has three libraries: the main Thomas Jefferson Library, the Ward E. Barnes Education Library, and the Health Sciences Library. Library collections consist of 743,097 books, approximately 1.5 million microfilm titles, 3,922 periodicals, and extensive automated databases in both online and CD-ROM formats. In addition, the Western Historical Manuscript Collection contains primary source materials for research in history, the environment, politics, and social issues.

Costs

UM–St. Louis is a publicly supported, land-grant institution. The 2003–04 educational fee for full-time, undergraduate Missouri residents was $5838 per year. The annual educational fee for full-time nonresident undergraduate students was $15,285.

Financial Aid

The primary function of the Student Financial Aid Office is to provide financial assistance to students who would otherwise be unable to attend UM–St. Louis. More than 66 percent of students receive some form of financial aid or scholarships. In the 2002–03 academic year, this aid exceeded $55 million. UM–St. Louis was one of the first universities nationally to participate in the Federal Direct Loan Program. Financial aid consists of a variety of scholarships, Federal Pell Grants, Federal Stafford Student Loans, work-study programs, Federal Perkins Loans, Federal Supplemental Educational Opportunity Grants, Federal Parent Loans for Undergraduate Students, and Missouri Student Grants. Some aid is available to qualified nonresident students through the National Access Award. Additional information may be obtained by contacting the Office of Financial Aid at 314-516-5526; e-mail: sfinaid@umslvma.umsl.edu; or World Wide Web at http://www.umsl.edu/services/finaid/.

Faculty

UM–St. Louis has 682 faculty members, including 11 Fulbright scholars. Ninety-six percent of tenured professors have a Ph.D. The student-faculty ratio is 20:1. Faculty members are noted researchers, scholars, authors, educators, and sought-after consultants to business, industry, government, and nonprofit groups. However, their principal mission is to teach. The vast majority of classes are taught by professors, not graduate students or teaching assistants.

Student Government

The Student Government Association welcomes participation by students. Additional student organizations include the Evening College Council, Panhellenic Council, University Program Board, and Residence Hall Council and the *Current* newspaper.

Admission Requirements

For first-time freshmen, selection for regular admission is based on high school class rank; ACT or SAT I scores; and required high school units. Applicants should submit an application, an official high school transcript, and appropriate test scores.

Students applying as transfer students who have fewer than 24 hours of college-level work should follow procedures for entering freshmen. Selection of students for regular admission is based on a minimum overall 2.0 grade point average (4.0 system) in all college-level courses at previous institutions. Students should submit an application and official transcripts from all colleges and universities attended.

Application and Information

The University of Missouri–St. Louis employs a rolling admission policy enabling students to start in any semester. A nonrefundable fee of $35 ($40 for international students) by check or money order made payable to University of Missouri must accompany all first-time applications for graduate and undergraduate student classifications.

Application forms and additional information are available by contacting:

Melissa Hattman
Director of Admissions
Office of Admissions
351 Millennium Student Center
University of Missouri–St. Louis
8001 Natural Bridge Road
St. Louis, Missouri 63121-4499
Telephone: 314-516-5451
888-GO-2-UMSL (toll-free in Missouri and in 618 area code in Illinois)
Fax: 314-516-5310
E-mail: admissions@umsl.edu
World Wide Web: http://www.umsl.edu

Students enjoy exciting opportunities for living and learning at UM–St. Louis.

UNIVERSITY OF MONTEVALLO

MONTEVALLO, ALABAMA

The University

The University was founded in 1896 and served as the state college for women. Known as Alabama College, the school first admitted men in 1956. In 1969, the name was changed to the University of Montevallo (UM) to reflect the growth in both enrollment and academic programs.

Montevallo's "small college" experience features classes of reasonable size and an individual advising system, enhanced by an active Career Center. In addition, the University's emphasis on liberal arts is supported by a core curriculum with a comprehensive writing component. In order to achieve and maintain high-quality programs, UM is committed to the maintenance of national accreditation for all of its undergraduate programs where such recognition is available and appropriate. Montevallo is accredited by the Commission on Colleges of the Southern Association of Colleges and Schools.

Located on a 160-acre campus, the University has redbrick walkways and tree-shaded lawns, with central portions of the campus designated as a National Historic District. The Olmsted brothers, landscape architects famous for designing New York's Central Park, Atlanta's Ponce de Leon Avenue Parks, and the Biltmore Estate near Asheville, North Carolina, also developed the first plan for the Montevallo campus. Their basic design ideas are still followed.

The University of Montevallo is a member of the Council of Public Liberal Arts Colleges (COPLAC). Montevallo is one of nineteen public liberal arts colleges and universities in the United States that are members of this alliance. As a member, Montevallo is dedicated to the education of undergraduates in the liberal arts tradition, the creation of teaching and learning communities, and the experience of access to undergraduate liberal arts education. The University has recently been recognized as a "Best Value" among southern universities by *U.S. News & World Report* in its "America's Best Colleges" publication and as a public institution that "has the advantage of a good private college at a fraction of the cost" in *Looking Beyond the Ivy League* by Loren Pope.

A variety of social and recreational opportunities are available. Campus activities, such as Greek-sponsored events, movies, theater productions, concerts, and athletic and other events, are regularly scheduled. Students may also participate in more than seventy campus organizations, including national fraternities and sororities, intramural athletics, clubs, and service and religious organizations. The University fields nine intercollegiate teams that compete in the Gulf South Conference and the NCAA Division II.

In fall 2003, the enrollment was 3,124, representing seventeen states and twenty-two countries. The enrollment is approximately 65 percent women and 14 percent members of minority groups. In 2002, 76 percent of the freshmen returned for the sophomore year. Of those who returned for the sophomore year, 64 percent graduated within five years.

Location

Located approximately 25 miles south of the metropolitan Birmingham area and with a population of 5,000, Montevallo offers students the advantage of living within walking distance of shops, restaurants, and banks. The location provides students with easy access to Birmingham, the state's largest metropolitan area, which offers many cultural, recreational, retail, and employment opportunities.

Majors and Degrees

UM's academic programs reflect its evolution from a school into a college and finally into a university with four colleges: the College of Arts & Sciences, Michael E. Stephens College of Business, College of Education, and College of Fine Arts. The following undergraduate degrees are granted: Bachelor of Arts, Bachelor of Business Administration, Bachelor of Fine Arts, Bachelor of Music, and Bachelor of Science.

The University offers programs in accounting, art, biology, chemistry, child and family studies, communication studies, dietetics, early childhood education, education of the deaf and hard of hearing, elementary education, English, family and consumer sciences, finance, foreign language (French, German, and Spanish), history, interior design merchandising, kinesiology, language arts, management information systems, marketing, mass communication, mathematics, music, political science, psychology, retail merchandising, social sciences, social work, sociology, speech language pathology, and theater. Middle school endorsements and secondary education certifications are available in most areas.

The five largest degree programs are business (B.B.A.), education (B.A., B.S.), art (B.A., B.F.A., B.S.), biology (B.A., B.S.), and family and consumer sciences (B.A., B.S.). Also popular are English (B.A.), communication science and disorders (B.S.), history (B.A., B.S.)., mass communication (B.A., B.S.), and psychology (B.A., B.S.). Preprofessional studies in dentistry, engineering, law, medicine, nursing, pharmacy, and veterinary medicine are available. Air Force and Army ROTC programs are also available.

Academic Program

Montevallo's academic calendar consists of a fall semester, a spring semester, a May term, and a summer session with two 5-week terms. Students fulfill the core requirements in general education to qualify for undergraduate degrees. Courses in English, science, mathematics, the arts, and languages introduce students to a broad spectrum of knowledge and experiences designed to develop the mind, emotions, spirit, and body. The purposes of the programs are to enable students to participate as responsible and informed citizens, to become self-educating individuals, to work creatively and effectively, and to lead satisfying personal lives. A candidate for a degree must have a minimum of 130 semester hours of credit distributed according to curriculum requirements, 260 grade points, and a minimum cumulative grade point average of 2.0 (on a 4.0 scale) on all study attempted. Students can earn a bachelor's degree in three years by attending six semesters and three summer sessions.

The popular University Honors Program is designed to provide intellectually talented students with specifically designed academic offerings, cocurricular activities, and recognition. CLEP, AP, IB, and military credit may be applied toward a degree.

Off-Campus Programs

The University's Stephens College of Business has sponsored student travel to Quebec City, Canada, New York City, and Europe for seminars and cultural activities. In addition, business majors may take advantage of student exchange agreements to study in Amsterdam, the Netherlands; Brussels, Belgium; Donetsk, the Ukraine; or Quebec City, Canada.

The University has offered international travel and summer-study programs each year since 1959 via group study and travel experiences developed by the UM faculty. Students earn up to 8 semester hours for group study and travel experiences developed by the UM faculty. Montevallo is a member of the Marine Environmental Sciences Consortium, a public, nonprofit corporation dedicated to providing marine education, research, and service. Biology students with an emphasis in marine biology take courses at the Dauphin Island Sea Laboratory, Dauphin Island, Alabama.

There are 3-2 engineering programs with Auburn University, the University of Alabama, and the University of Alabama at Birmingham. These five-year dual-degree programs enable students to enroll at Montevallo for three years, then transfer to the School of Engineering of their choice. Upon successful completion of two years of engineering study, the student receives a Bachelor of Science in a specific area of engineering and a Bachelor of Science in mathematics from Montevallo.

The UM Career Center provides students and alumni with a wide range of programs and services related to career development issues and prepares candidates for entry into the world of work. Career counseling, career testing, employability training, posting of full-time and part-time jobs, job market information, internship information, graduate school information, employer files, on-campus interviews, and career fairs are offered by the UM Career Center. A career resource library is located on the premises.

Academic Facilities

The library has a collection that includes more than 250,000 books and subscribes to more than 2,400 journals in print, microform, and electronic versions. The library provides access to a wide variety of electronic databases, more than 20 of which are provided through the Alabama Virtual Library. Many of these databases include the full text of the materials retrieved. Other academic facilities available to students include computer labs in several programs, the Harbert Writing Center, and the Speech and Hearing Center, which provides assistance to students and the general public with hearing, language, or speech problems. Because Montevallo expects its students to graduate, not just enroll, many services are available to help them. One example is Student Support Services, a program funded by the U.S. Department of Education, which offers tutoring assistance in core curriculum courses, including mathematics. Another is Counseling Services, which provides individual counseling to any student.

Costs

For the 2003–04 academic year, tuition was approximately $4000 for full-time, in-state students. Out-of-state tuition was approximately $8000 per year. Room and board charges were approximately $3500, the Student Government Association fee was $70, and the technology (computer services) fee was $70. Additional fees were charged for vehicle registration ($15) and music lessons ($50 for private lessons and $42 for group lessons), and an optional health/wellness fee was $90.

Financial Aid

The University administers a comprehensive program of financial assistance. Federal, state, and University funds are combined to provide students with the scholarship, student employment, loan, and grant aid for which they qualify. Financial aid is meant to supplement students' resources and is not intended to be their only support. In 2003–04, 72 percent of undergraduate students received some form of financial aid. The awarding of need-based financial aid usually begins in May. The priority deadline is April 15. Students applying for federal financial aid or need-based scholarships should complete the Free Application for Federal Student Aid (FAFSA).

Every fall, the University publishes a brochure that includes information regarding available financial aid and scholarships. To request the brochure, students should contact the Student Financial Services Office, Station 6050, University of Montevallo, Montevallo, Alabama 35115-6000.

Faculty

Faculty members are committed to teaching, advising, research, and service. In 2003–04, there were 136 full-time and 76 part-time members of the faculty. Of these, approximately 90 percent held terminal degrees in their respective fields. The student-faculty ratio is 16:1. Several campus surveys have revealed that students have found the faculty to be accessible and willing to help them succeed both inside and outside the classroom.

Student Government

Since 1916, the president and faculty have encouraged students to govern themselves in important areas of student life. The Student Government Association (SGA), whose motto is "students serving students," consists of an Executive Cabinet and Senate, elected annually by the student body. Each class and college, as well as commuters, adult returning students, graduate students, and international students, maintains representation in the Senate. In representing student interests and concerns, the SGA appoints students to various University interest committees and the Justice Council and publishes the *Fledgling,* a student handbook that contains pertinent information regarding student life. The SGA is also responsible for sponsoring the University Program Council (UPC), the Miss University of Montevallo Scholarship Pageant, College Night, and student publications.

Admission Requirements

Montevallo welcomes applications from those whose academic preparation, experience, and interests indicate a reasonable chance for success in a degree program. Applications are reviewed on an individual basis, and the University considers information from a variety of sources regarding a candidate's qualifications. Satisfactory scores on the ACT or the SAT I are required. International applicants are required to submit the results of the Test of English as a Foreign Language (TOEFL).

A freshman applicant must present a satisfactory high school transcript with a minimum of 16 academic credits from ninth grade through twelfth grade. The credits must include 4 in English, 4 in social studies, 2 in mathematics, 2 in science, and 4 in academic electives. A minimum grade point average of 2.0 on a 4.0 scale is required for regular admission. The University offers summer conditional admission for those who present marginal credentials, allowing limited numbers of students to enroll for the University's summer session(s) and to continue in the fall semester if summer grade point average requirements are met. Early admission and advanced placement are also available.

Students applying for transfer admission from accredited colleges and universities must have a minimum cumulative GPA of 2.0 on previous study attempted. A transfer student must be in good standing at the current or previous college.

Prospective students are encouraged to visit the campus. The Admissions Office is open on Monday, Wednesday, and Friday for interviews and tours by appointment at 10 a.m. and 1 p.m. Campus tours are available on Saturday at 10 a.m., with no appointment necessary.

Application and Information

The application deadline is August 1. All applications must be accompanied by the required $25 processing fee. Prospective students are encouraged to apply early to take advantage of scholarship and housing options. Once an applicant has submitted all required information, an admissions decision is made and notification is forwarded immediately.

For more information or an application packet, students should contact:

Lynn Gurganus
Director of Admissions
Station 6030 Palmer Hall
University of Montevallo
Montevallo, Alabama 35115-6000
Telephone: 205-665-6030
800-292-4349 (toll-free)
E-mail: admissions@montevallo.edu
World Wide Web: http://www.montevallo.edu/

UNIVERSITY OF NEBRASKA–LINCOLN

LINCOLN, NEBRASKA

The University

The University of Nebraska–Lincoln is one of today's most dynamic universities. Over the past decade, the University has developed a national reputation for undergraduate education grounded in technology, research, innovation, and student engagement. Undergraduates have the opportunity to work with world-renowned researchers, dedicated professors, and accomplished peers.

Established in 1869, the University of Nebraska–Lincoln has a rich tradition of excellence. Students join more than 200,000 alumni who have made their mark as industry leaders in business, engineering, the arts, journalism, education, and the sciences. A degree from Nebraska opens doors. Nebraska graduates recently interviewed on campus with major national companies such as Abercrombie & Fitch, the Central Intelligence Agency (CIA), IBM, Microsoft, Sprint, Target, and the *Washington Post.* While attending Nebraska, students have built-in connections with 116 graduate degree programs, including those in the University of Nebraska law, dental, and medical centers located either on campus or 50 miles east in Omaha.

The University of Nebraska–Lincoln is a major research university. Nebraska is one of sixteen schools nationwide to be recognized as innovators in undergraduate education and one of only five major research universities to be named to the "first tier" for its innovative programs for students. Nebraska has also been a member of the Association of American Universities since 1909; it is one of only sixty-two universities to claim this prestigious membership. This gives students an advantage. Classes are taught by faculty members who are experts in their fields, and students find a diverse variety of academic choices.

At Nebraska, technology is invented, and real-world problems are solved. Researchers and students at Nebraska have developed everything from turfgrass that can survive with very little water to eggs that contain less cholesterol to a highway guard rail that helps stop the impact of a car crash.

Nebraska's community is local and global. More than 18,000 undergraduate students from a wide range of ethnic, cultural, and economic backgrounds make their college home at Nebraska. Many students choose to live in one of Nebraska's fifteen residence halls, which include the new apartment-style Husker Courtyards, scheduled for completion in August 2004. Each residence hall has high-speed Internet access, cable television, air conditioning, and local phone service in every room and a resident assistant and health aid on every floor. Greek organizations at Nebraska offer social, academic, community-service, and campus-living opportunities. Nebraska has twenty-one fraternities, fourteen sororities, four National Pan-Hellenic Council fraternities, two National Pan-Hellenic Council sororities, one Multicultural Greek Council fraternity, and two Multicultural Greek Council sororities. Greek recruitment information is mailed to students in the spring prior to enrollment.

Location

The University is located in the capital city of Lincoln, a community of 230,000 that combines a friendly college-town atmosphere with the cultural and employment opportunities of a larger city. Students looking for cultural experiences and internship possibilities find art, music, theater, state government, and industry all within walking distance of the campus. On campus, students receive ticket discounts for major Broadway performances such as *Riverdance, Les Misérables,* and Disney's *Beauty and the Beast* at one of the Midwest's premier venues, the Lied Center for Performing Arts. Lincoln has more parks per capita than any other city in the U.S. and a growing network of bike paths that extends far beyond the city limits. There are sixteen golf courses, hundreds of restaurants, more than thirty movie screens, major shopping malls, and a restored downtown historic district complete with specialty shops, coffeehouses, and a dinner theater. Major metropolitan cities—such as Kansas City, Chicago, Minneapolis–St. Paul, and Denver—are within a day's drive, and Lincoln is easily accessible by plane, train, and bus.

Majors and Degrees

The University of Nebraska–Lincoln offers 140 undergraduate majors, providing students with the opportunity to choose a challenging course of study and gain a solid background of fundamentals, critical thinking, and experience. With more than 87 percent of the classes under 50 students, there is a balance between lecture and lab and practice and theory, and the classes are taught by faculty members who are highly respected in their fields. Degree programs are distributed over eight Colleges: Agricultural Sciences and Natural Resources, Architecture, Arts and Sciences, Business Administration, Education and Human Sciences, Engineering and Technology, Fine and Performing Arts, and Journalism and Mass Communications.

Academic Programs

Nebraska offers classes during the fall and spring semesters and during the summer sessions, which consist of a three-week presession, two 5-week sessions, and one 8-week session. Undergraduates must take a minimum of 12 hours to be full-time. Most undergraduate degree programs require 120 to 130 credit hours for graduation. Each degree program at Nebraska has specific course requirements, and some require a minimum grade point average.

The University Honors Program provides motivated students with academic challenges, opportunities to learn from and do research with top faculty members, and a community of supportive peers. Students admitted to the highly selective J. D. Edwards Honors Program in Computer Science and Management become tomorrow's leaders in technology applications and solutions. Outside the classroom, students can participate in various experiences, including study abroad, internships, cooperative educational programs, ROTC, and research opportunities with faculty members. Students may also participate in tutoring and mentoring programs such as supplemental instruction, the Husker Teammates program, and the English conversation program.

Off-Campus Programs

Students gain professional experience through an extensive internship and cooperative education program, connecting them to industry leaders in the U.S. government, NASA, General Motors, Microsoft, Gannett Newspapers, and Gallup. Through Nebraska's study-abroad programs, students can choose to study in one of more than fifty countries and at 140 universities. Financial aid often applies to study-abroad programs. Field courses are held at on-site locations to give students hands-on experience. Examples of popular courses include excavation of earth lodges at Fontenelle Forest and the study of parasitology specimens at Cedar Point Biological Station in western Nebraska.

Academic Facilities

The University is housed on 616 acres of land across two campuses, City Campus and East Campus. One of the University's newest facilities is the George W. Beadle Center for Genetics and Biomaterials Research. City Campus is also home to the nationally renowned Sheldon Memorial Art Gallery and Sculpture Garden, the Christlieb Collection of Western Art, and several other galleries. The Lied Center for Performing Arts draws big-name acts in contemporary entertainment, and the University of Nebraska State Museum boasts a world-class fossil collection. A number of specialized centers offer assistance to the state's citizens, including the Bureau of Business Research, the Food Processing Center, and the Technology Transfer Office, which expedites the movement of University-developed knowledge into real-world products and processes.

Nebraska also offers students a variety of research libraries. Love Library is the main library located on City Campus and contains about half of the University's collection of 2.5 million volumes. C. Y. Thompson Library on East Campus and the various departmental libraries offer students excellent research facilities.

Costs

For the 2003–04 academic year, in-state tuition and fees were approximately $4400 and out-of-state tuition and fees were approximately $12,400 (based on a single undergraduate student taking 15 credit hours per semester for two semesters). Room and board were approximately $5200 for a double room for two semesters. Books and supplies are estimated at $720.

Financial Aid

The University of Nebraska offers one of the most affordable high-quality educations in the country. It has one of the lowest total costs among Big 12, Big 10, and AAU institutions. In addition, about 76 percent of full-time undergraduate students at the University receive some type of scholarship or financial aid. During the 2003–04 school year, 2,795 full-time freshman students received $20,892,480 in financial assistance of some kind. Nebraska offers a wide range of scholarships based on academic achievement, leadership and involvement, and specific academic interests such as engineering, mathematics, computer science, business, and agricultural sciences. While scholarship awards are made on a rolling basis, full consideration for freshman scholarships is given to students whose admissions application materials are complete and on file in the Office of Admissions by January 15 (March 15 for transfer students).

Faculty

Nebraska has a strong reputation for excellence in teaching. Highly respected in their fields, Nebraska faculty members conduct research that leads to new discoveries and pass on their new knowledge to the students. Some of the recent achievements by Nebraska faculty members include being named as Outstanding Science Teacher Educator of the Year by the Association for the Education of Teachers of Science; being elected to the National Academy of Sciences, one of the highest honors for a U.S. scientist; earning a $5-million children and family education grant; and earning a $6.5-million botulism grant to help the fight against bioterrorism.

Student Government

The Association for Students at the University of Nebraska (ASUN) serves as the representative voice for Nebraska students by gathering input from all students, advocating student concerns to the administration, and providing essential student services, ultimately working to improve the campus and enhance student life. The functions of ASUN are carried out by elected student senators representing each of the nine academic colleges, the divisions of general studies and graduate studies, and the professional schools.

Admission Requirements

In order to be eligible for assured admission to the University of Nebraska–Lincoln, students who graduated from high school after 1997 must have completed a set of 16 units of core courses, including 4 units of English, 4 of math, 3 of natural science, 3 of social science, and 2 of foreign language (1 unit = 1 high school year). In addition, students must have graduated in the upper half of their graduating class or earned a combined score of 950 or higher on the SAT I or a composite of 20 or higher on the ACT. Transfer students must also have a minimum 2.0 cumulative grade point average and at least a 2.0 GPA in their final semester of attendance at another postsecondary institution. Some academic programs may require higher test scores and class ranks than these minimums. Students are encouraged to apply for admission even if they do not meet one or more of the above requirements.

Application and Information

Students interested in applying for the fall semester should apply by the May 1 deadline, and those interested in applying for the spring semester should apply by December 1. While scholarship awards are made on a rolling basis, full consideration for freshman scholarships is given to students whose admissions application materials are complete and on file in the Office of Admissions by January 15 (March 15 for transfer students). A $45 application fee is required as are official transcripts from the student's high school and/or postsecondary institution and official ACT or SAT I scores. Students whose first language is not English should also send official TOEFL scores.

To make arrangements to visit the University or to receive an application and admissions information, students should contact:

Office of Admissions
University of Nebraska–Lincoln
313 North 13th Street
Lincoln, Nebraska 68588-0256
Telephone: 402-472-2023
800-742-8800 (toll-free)
Fax: 402-472-0670
E-mail: admissions@unl.edu
World Wide Web: http://www.unl.edu/
http://www.admissions.unl.edu

Students participating in the J. D. Edwards Honors Program live in the Kauffman Center, one of the many living and learning communities offered at Nebraska. Opened in 2001, the center contains 82,500 square feet of classrooms, living space, and social areas.

UNIVERSITY OF NEVADA, LAS VEGAS

LAS VEGAS, NEVADA

The University

The University of Nevada, Las Vegas (UNLV), is recognized nationally as a comprehensive teaching and research university that provides students with an excellent education at a reasonable cost. UNLV has established an agenda for the next decade to become a premier urban university. All UNLV programs are accredited by the Northwest Association of Schools and Colleges. Individual programs have further accreditation from professional accrediting organizations.

Since its founding in 1957, UNLV has seen dramatic growth in both its academic programs and its facilities. There are 180 undergraduate, master's, and doctoral degree programs offered to more than 26,000 students. Of UNLV's students, 79 percent are undergraduates, 76 percent are Nevada residents, 29 percent are members of minority groups, and 4 percent are international students. The average class size is 30.

The University is located on a beautifully landscaped 337-acre campus. Classes are held in comfortable, well-equipped buildings that are showcases of modern architecture. Classroom, physics, and student services buildings opened in 1994, and an architecture building opened in 1997. The $57-million Lied Library, one of the most technologically advanced libraries in the Southwest, opened in spring 2001, while the Beam Music Center, with a music library, opened in fall 2001.

UNLV's residential life program provides students with a secure, convenient place to live on the University campus. The modern residence halls are organized into suites of two rooms joined by a bathroom. Four students share a suite, with 2 per room. UNLV's dining facilities are excellent, providing students with quality, quantity, and choice.

More than 150 groups offer students an active social life, including intramural sports, Greek organizations, ethnic and religious clubs, a student newspaper, and campus radio and television stations. UNLV's Division of Student Life provides an array of advising, tutorial, and counseling services. Learning Enhancement Center provides textbooks on tape, interpreters for the deaf, lab assistants, and other services to students with disabilities.

Numerous concerts are performed throughout the year by UNLV's student music groups, choirs, dance companies, and ensembles. The Department of Theatre Arts also offers an excellent season of comedies, dramas, and musicals performed by students and community members, as well as performances by national professional touring companies. The student government sponsors lectures, films, concerts, and entertainment throughout the year.

Location

Las Vegas, touted by historian Hal Rothman as the First City of the Twenty-First Century, is located at the southern tip of Nevada in a desert valley surrounded by mountains. The Las Vegas metropolitan area is a rapidly growing community of more than 1 million residents with a strong sense of family and community pride. The surrounding area is one of the Southwest's most picturesque, offering residents outdoor recreation year-round. Within a 50-mile radius lie the shores of Lake Mead, Hoover Dam, and the Colorado River recreation area; the snow-skiing and hiking trails of 12,000-foot Mount Charleston; and a panoramic view of rugged rock mountains. Las Vegas has an average of 320 days of sunshine per year. The average daytime winter temperature is 60 degrees Fahrenheit. Summer daytime temperatures are usually more than 100 degrees Fahrenheit.

Majors and Degrees

Undergraduate programs are offered by the Colleges of Business, Honors, Education, Fine Arts, Health Sciences, Liberal Arts, and Sciences; the Greenspun College of Urban Affairs; the Howard R. Hughes College of Engineering; and the William F. Harrah College of Hotel Administration.

Majors include accounting, Afro-American studies, anthropology, applied physics, architecture, art, art history, Asian studies, athletic training, beverage management, biochemistry, biological sciences (including preprofessional), chemistry, civil and environmental engineering, clinical lab sciences, communications studies, comprehensive medical imaging, computational physics, computer engineering, computer science, construction management, criminal justice, culinary arts management, dance, early childhood education, earth science, economics, electrical engineering, elementary education, English, environmental studies, film, finance, fitness and sports management, French, geoscience, German, gerontology, health-care administration, health education, health physics, health sciences, history, hotel administration, human resources management, interior architecture and design, international business, jazz studies, kinesiological sciences, landscape architecture, Latin American studies, liberal studies, library science, linguistic studies, management, management information systems, marketing, mathematics, mechanical engineering, multidisciplinary studies, music, musical theater, nuclear medicine, nursing, nutritional sciences, philosophy, physical education, physics, political science, psychology, radiography, real estate, recreation, Romance languages, secondary education, senior adult theater, social science studies, social work, sociology, Spanish, special education, theater arts, urban and regional planning, women's studies, and workforce education.

Academic Programs

The UNLV General Education Core requirement, which must be completed by all baccalaureate degree candidates, consists of courses in English composition and literature, international and multicultural studies, logic, mathematics, computer science or statistics, U.S. and Nevada constitutions, social sciences, natural sciences, fine arts, and humanities. The balance of baccalaureate degree programs consists of college and departmental requirements. The number of credit hours required for baccalaureate degrees varies between 124 and 136, depending on the program of study. Numerous special academic opportunities are available, such as dual majors, dual baccalaureates, approved minors, internships, international studies, interdisciplinary programs, honors programs, and nontraditional credit (military credits, Advanced Placement, College-Level Examination Program, and correspondence credits).

The UNLV academic calendar has two semesters (fall and spring), each lasting approximately sixteen weeks. Three summer sessions are held from mid-May through August.

Off-Campus Programs

International study-abroad programs are available throughout the year, with opportunities to spend one semester, one academic year, or a summer abroad. Academic credits earned in UNLV study-abroad programs are part of regular authorized course offerings. Students can make normal progress toward their UNLV degree while utilizing international resources and experiencing a different culture.

Academic Facilities

The campus has an excellent Curriculum Materials Library, which is used extensively by local school teachers and University students. The National Supercomputing Center for Energy and the Environment facilitates study of the engineering, socioeconomic, transportation, and social impacts of energy and hazardous waste management along with other appropriate studies. The center includes a Cray YMP 2/215 supercomputer and a Sun 4/490 front-end computer, ten color graphics workstations, and a Silicon Graphics workstation. There are seven public computer labs on the UNLV campus with various types of equipment, including IBM PCs, Spool Printers, Gateways, NEC machines, Macintoshes, Image Writers, letter quality and laser printers, Apple II's, and DEC workstations.

Costs

For the 2003–04 academic year, average room and board costs were $7706 per year. Nonresident tuition was $11,039 per year (12 credits per semester), and in-state tuition was $2352 per year (12 credits per semester). UNLV has a Good Neighbor Policy for the following counties in California: Alpine, El Dorado, Inyo, Lassen, Modoc, Mono, Nevada, Placer, Plumas, San Bernadino, and Sierra. High school graduates in these counties may be eligible for reduced tuition. Residents of thirteen states (Alaska, Arizona, Colorado, Hawaii, Idaho, Montana, New Mexico, North Dakota, Oregon, South Dakota, Utah, Washington, and Wyoming) may enroll at reduced tuition rates through the Western Undergraduate Exchange Program (WUE). Children of alumni (bachelor's degree graduates only) may qualify for a reduction in nonresident tuition.

Financial Aid

UNLV provides a variety of financial assistance to qualified students. Loans, grants, scholarships, and employment are all awarded to help students meet their educational expenses while attending UNLV. All students should explore every possible resource. A student's eligibility may be determined by financial need, scholastic achievement, special skills, or service. Prospective students may complete a scholarship application prior to or at the same time as the application for admission. The priority deadline for applying for scholarships is February 1. All paperwork for other forms of financial aid (loans, grants, and work-study) should also be submitted by February 1, but later submissions are processed.

Faculty

More than 800 full-time instructional faculty members are involved in teaching, research, and community service. The scholars and scientists at UNLV are warm, caring people committed as much to excellence in teaching as they are to their research. In most colleges, a faculty adviser is assigned to each student to provide academic counseling through the undergraduate years. All levels of faculty are involved in undergraduate education. Graduate assistants have limited teaching and laboratory assignments. About 500 professional staff members and 700 state employees also serve students.

Student Government

All undergraduate students are automatically members of the Consolidated Students of the University of Nevada, Las Vegas (CSUN). CSUN is a self-governing body and is recognized by UNLV's faculty and the University and Community College System of Nevada. All officers are elected by the student body. CSUN has many boards and committees in which students are encouraged to get involved. CSUN provides students an opportunity to practice their communication skills and enrich their education both socially and academically.

Admission Requirements

Regular admission to UNLV is objectively based on a student's academic record and placement examination scores. The University does not limit the number of students that can be regularly admitted for any semester. An admitted student is placed in introductory English and mathematics according to his or her SAT I, SAT II, or ACT scores. The minimum grade point average (GPA) requirement for incoming freshmen from high school is 2.5. Completion of the following precollege curriculum in high school is also required: 4 years of English; 3 years of algebra or higher-level mathematics, such as algebra II, geometry, precalculus, or calculus; 3 years of natural science, with at least 2 years in a lab science; and 3 years of social studies. A student's cumulative GPA is used for admission. Transfer admission is granted to a student who completes a minimum of 12 or more semester credits in transferable courses and earns a recalculated GPA of 2.0 or higher from a regionally accredited university or college. The applicant must be in good standing and eligible to return to the educational institution last attended.

Application and Information

Application deadlines are April 2 for the fall semester and November 1 for the spring semester. The nonrefundable application fee of $60 for domestic students and $95 for international students cannot be waived.

Prospective students may access the UNLV applications and catalog online by clicking the Rebel Express icon at the Web site listed below or by going to http://www.unlv.edu/admissions/.

For further assistance, students may contact:

Office of Undergraduate Recruitment
University of Nevada, Las Vegas
Box 451021
4505 Maryland Parkway
Las Vegas, Nevada 89154-1021
Telephone: 702-774-UNLV
702-774-TOUR
Orientation: 702-895-2970
Main University number: 702-895-3011
Financial aid: 702-895-3424
UNLV events: 702-895-3131
Fax: 702-895-1200
World Wide Web: http://www.unlv.edu

UNIVERSITY OF NEVADA, RENO

RENO, NEVADA

The University

For the fourteenth straight year, the University of Nevada, Reno has been named to the honor roll of "America's Best Colleges" by *U.S. News & World Report*. Nevada was the state's only university named in the top three tiers of the 2004 "National Universities" category—a superior group of 248 schools including Harvard, Princeton, and Yale. This is further evidence of Nevada's growing reputation as one of the nation's best universities. The American Association of University Professors has given Nevada a Class 1 rating as a research institution. The Carnegie Classification of Institutions of Higher Education lists Nevada as a Doctoral/Research Universities–Extensive institution. Funds for sponsored research, training, and public service totaled more than $106 million during the fiscal year 2003. Nevada's Reynolds School of Journalism has produced six Pulitzer Prize winners. Fortune 500 companies rate the University's supply chain management program in the College of Business Administration among the nation's top ten. The Chemistry Department was ranked "very best" for its size in the U.S. and Canada by the National Science Foundation; the Geography Department, fifth in the U.S. for its size for undergraduate teaching; the Honors Program among the fifty-five best nationally in "a state's major university" category; and the hydrologic sciences program, eighth nationally.

Accredited by the Northwest Association of Schools, Colleges and Universities, the University has 12,500 acres of field laboratories and research areas statewide. Nevada is internationally known for its research in earthquakes, fetal transplants, heap leach mining, Basque studies, remote sensing, watershed preservation, and structural engineering. The University's Center for Environmental Sciences and Engineering prepares students for the growing demand for environmental scientists. Nevada is also known for having strong programs in agriculture, biochemistry, geriatrics, heart disease, theoretical chemistry, and speech pathology and audiology.

Within the past three years, the 255-acre campus has opened an $8 million Student Services Building and a $17-million residence hall with a parking garage and a full-service dining center. Students and visitors enjoy the University's historic brick buildings and tree-lined walkways. Students at Nevada may live in one of seven residence halls on the campus or at one of fourteen fraternity and sorority houses nearby. They come from all seventeen Nevada counties, from all fifty states, and from more than eighty countries. For extracurricular activities, students may participate in more than 120 student organizations recognized by the Associated Students of the University of Nevada (ASUN). Support services include intensive orientation sessions for new students, a freshman and sophomore success center, academic advisement, counseling, tutoring, financial aid, health services, and special programs. Mackay Stadium is home to the Wolf Pack football and soccer teams. Nevada, a member of the Western Athletic Conference, has seven men's and twelve women's varsity sports teams.

A land-grant university that opened in 1874, Nevada has an enrollment of 15,534 students. Approximately 11,000 are undergraduates. Degree programs at the University include seventy-seven majors for an undergraduate degree and seventy-six master's, thirty-four Ph.D., three Ed.D., and the M.D. and M.D./Ph.D. programs.

Location

The University is four blocks from downtown Reno and serves as both an educational and cultural resource for the community. It is easily accessible from Interstate 80.

Reno itself has one of the most attractive locations in the country. Situated in northern Nevada's Truckee Meadows at an elevation of 4,600 feet, it is on the eastern slope of the Sierra Nevada Mountains. The climate is cool and dry, and there are four distinct seasons. The six counties of northwestern Nevada have a population of 526,000. Reno is only a 45-minute drive from scenic Lake Tahoe with its world-class skiing and limitless summer recreation, a 2-hour drive from Sacramento, and a 4-hour drive from San Francisco. Reno offers cultural events, including the symphony, ballet, theater, and opera. Many University facilities, such as the Fleischmann Planetarium and Science Center and the Sheppard Fine Arts Gallery, are open to the public. The University also sponsors concerts, lectures, films, plays, and many other events for the community.

Majors and Degrees

Undergraduate degrees are awarded in the following academic units and majors: College of Agriculture, Biotechnology, and Natural Resources: agricultural and applied economics, agricultural education, animal science, biochemistry, biotechnology (cooperative program), environmental and natural resource science, environmental policy analysis, and pre–veterinary science; College of Business Administration: accounting, computer information systems, economics, finance, gaming management, international business, management, marketing, and supply chain management; College of Education: early childhood education (cooperative program), elementary education, elementary/special education, secondary education, and special education; College of Engineering: civil engineering, computer science, electrical engineering, engineering physics, environmental engineering, materials science and engineering, and mechanical engineering; College of Extended Studies: construction sciences (cooperative program) and general studies (cooperative program); College of Human and Community Sciences: criminal justice, health ecology, human development and family studies, nursing, nutrition, and social work; Reynolds School of Journalism: journalism; College of Liberal Arts: anthropology, art, English, French, German, history, interior design, international affairs, music, music (applied), philosophy, political science, psychology, sociology, Spanish, speech communication, theater, and women's studies; School of Medicine: speech pathology and audiology; and Mackay School of Earth Science and Engineering: chemical engineering, geological engineering, geology, geophysics, hydrogeology, and mining engineering; and College of Science: biology, chemistry, geography, mathematics, physics. The University also offers preparatory programs for law, medicine, dentistry, and several other health-related fields.

Academic Program

Students must complete a core curriculum of English, mathematics, natural sciences, social sciences, fine arts, core humanities, capstone courses, and diversity, in addition to completing specific requirements for their degree. The number of credit hours required for graduation is typically 128–134. Credit by examination is available. The University also offers an honors program for exceptional students and an active Army ROTC program. The school calendar includes two 15-week semesters, beginning in August for the fall and January for the spring; an early summer minisession; and two 5-week summer sessions.

Off-Campus Programs

The University offers a number of study-abroad programs for credit in twenty countries, including Australia, the Basque Country in Spain, Chile, Costa Rica, Israel, Malta, New Zealand, Thailand, and several European sites. The University is also a member of the National Student Exchange Program, which gives undergraduates from Nevada an opportunity to study in other parts of the country. Similarly, the Western Interstate Commission for Higher Education (WICHE) provides grants to Nevada scholars to pursue disciplines not available in Nevada.

Academic Facilities

The Getchell Library is one of the largest libraries in Nevada. It contains more than 1 million books and bound periodicals and offers access to government documents, patents, microforms, newspapers, online databases, full-text electronic journals, and e-books. There are a main library facility and four branch libraries that are located near the academic units they serve.

Costs

The per-credit cost for Nevada residents is $95 for 2004–05. Thus, the total estimated cost for a student taking an average 15-credit load for two semesters is $2850. Out-of-state students pay $4337 per semester in addition to per-credit fees. Students from certain California counties, however, are eligible for a reduction in out-of-state tuition under the University's "Good Neighbor" policy. The University of Nevada, Reno also participates in the Western Undergraduate Exchange (WUE) program that allows students from thirteen western states (Alaska, Arizona, Colorado, Hawaii, Idaho, Montana, New Mexico, North Dakota, Oregon, South Dakota, Utah, Washington, and Wyoming) to pay a reduced nonresident tuition. Fall 2004 WUE students pay $142.50 per credit and do not pay any additional out-of-state tuition. This reduced nonresident tuition is available for all programs of study. More information on these policies can be obtained by contacting the Office for Prospective Students. Though residence hall and meal plan fees vary, new students should budget about $6500 a year for room and board. Books and supplies are approximately $1000 per year. Students should also budget extra money for personal needs and expenses.

Financial Aid

The University administers more than $43 million annually in grants, scholarships, student employment, and loans. To be eligible for financial aid, a student must be admitted into a degree program at the University.

To access all need-based programs, the Free Application for Federal Student Aid (FAFSA) must be filed with the federal processor as soon as possible after January 1 for the upcoming academic year. Early filers with the greatest financial need have the best opportunity for grant and work-study programs. The FAFSA can be filed on the Internet or in a paper format.

Students should apply for admission early in the fall to maximize the opportunity for University scholarships. The University of Nevada awards merit scholarships to incoming freshmen based upon grade point average (GPA) and ACT or SAT test scores. New transfer students are evaluated by college GPA. For priority consideration for scholarships, students must be admitted by February 1; awards are made based upon available funds. Students admitted by November 15 are considered for early awarding of merit scholarships.

Faculty

In 2002–03, the University had a total of 900 full-time-equivalent faculty members. Students benefit from studying at a school where approximately 87 percent of tenured faculty members and 79 percent of full-time faculty members hold the highest degrees attainable in their fields. Since the University of Nevada, Reno is a land-grant institution, faculty members are expected to teach, conduct research, and provide public service to the state. The student-faculty ratio is 17:1.

Student Government

The ASUN government represents students in all University affairs. The ASUN Senate is composed of students from every school and college on campus. Students appointed by the ASUN president serve on University-wide committees and represent the students' viewpoints on all issues. ASUN recognizes more than 120 organizations ranging from the advertising and international clubs to the peace and human rights group and wildlife organizations. It also provides the financial support for concerts, lecture series, and dining events. Students participate in annual major events, such as Homecoming, Mackay Days, and Winter Carnival, sponsored by ASUN and the Greek organizations. ASUN also operates the campus bookstore.

Admission Requirements

To be admitted as a freshman, a potential student must be a graduate of an accredited high school and have an overall GPA of 2.5 or above. Prospective freshmen may submit college entrance examination (ACT/SAT) scores. The state of Nevada also requires that all applicants have had a diphtheria-tetanus shot in the last ten years and two doses of measles-mumps-rubella vaccine prior to admittance.

High school students should have taken a minimum of 4 years of English; 3 years of mathematics; 3 years of natural science, including 2 years of laboratory sciences; and 3 years of social studies. Requirements are changing for fall 2006; students should contact the Office for Prospective Students for more information.

International students must have a minimum 3.0 GPA (B average) and a minimum score of 500 on the Test of English as a Foreign Language (TOEFL) or a recommendation from the Intensive English Language Center (IELC). They must also provide financial verification equivalent to tuition, fees, and living expenses for one academic year. For more information, students should contact International Application Services/074, University of Nevada, Reno, Reno, Nevada 89557 U.S.A. or call 775-784-6318 or visit the University's Web site at http://www.unr.edu/oiss.

Application and Information

Application for admission can be made at any time but should be completed no later than March 1 for the fall semester and November 1 for the spring semester. To apply, individuals must submit a completed application form, a nonrefundable $60 application fee, immunization records, an official transcript sent directly from the high school or each college the student attended, and ACT or SAT scores. Online applications are available via the University's Web site at http://www.unr.edu/oiss.

For a campus tour and other information, students should contact:

Office for Prospective Students/110
University of Nevada, Reno
Reno, Nevada 89557-0002
Telephone: 775-784-4700
866-2NEVADA (toll-free)
E-mail: asknevada@unr.edu
World Wide Web: http://www.unr.edu

UNIVERSITY OF NEW ENGLAND

BIDDEFORD AND PORTLAND, MAINE

The University

The University of New England (UNE) is a small, independent, coeducational university that offers a personalized education. It is composed of the College of Arts and Sciences, the College of Osteopathic Medicine, and the College of Health Professions. The College of Osteopathic Medicine grants the Doctor of Osteopathic Medicine degree. At the graduate level, the University confers the Master of Social Work, Master of Science in nurse anesthesia, Master of Science in Education, and Master of Science in physician assistant studies degrees.

The University has chosen as its primary fields of education business management, education, health sciences (both mental and physical), the humanities, the natural sciences, and social sciences. The University of New England's philosophy of education and student life places emphasis on the quality of instruction and the practical application of academic material.

Each program includes the opportunity for learning in a community-based setting. Internships, co-ops, clinicals, and student teaching add up to the practical experience that allows students at UNE to apply the skills learned in the classroom to real job situations.

The University of New England has two campuses. The University Campus is located on the southern coast of Maine, in Biddeford, 90 miles north of Boston and 20 miles south of Portland, Maine's largest city. UNE's Westbrook College Campus is located in Portland, Maine. As both campuses are geographically placed in areas that afford a high-quality lifestyle, it is only natural that the University of New England consistently engages itself in providing its students with high-quality programming and high-quality education.

The men and women who teach at the University of New England are an experienced group of people whose average age is 40. More than 85 percent have earned the highest degree in their field, and they bring to the University varied backgrounds as teachers and practitioners of their disciplines. They are highly competent, demanding, concerned, accessible, and willing to give individual attention to students. Most important, they have come to the University for many of the same reasons that prompt their students to attend. The match between what the faculty has to offer and what the students need and expect is the key to the rare educational environment at the University of New England.

The University encourages students to become involved in activities, clubs, and sports. Popular interests include scuba diving, skiing, hiking, biking, swimming, and photography. The University of New England offers a wide range of services on both campuses. Special features include a full health clinic, a dental hygiene clinic, career counseling, personal counseling, learning support services, and an extensive student leadership development program.

Both campuses offer a variety of cultural and social events. The Campus Center at the University Campus and the Finley Recreation Center on the Westbrook College Campus provide a setting for many recreational and sports activities. The University of New England Athletic Department operates an NCAA Division III varsity athletics program. Varsity sports for men are basketball, cross-country, golf, lacrosse, and soccer; varsity sports for women are basketball, cross-country, field hockey, lacrosse, soccer, softball, and volleyball. Intramural teams in basketball, floor hockey, softball, skiing, and volleyball are popular.

On the University Campus in Biddeford, Decary Hall houses a cafeteria, classrooms, meeting rooms, and faculty and administrative offices. The University Health Center houses classrooms and the physical therapy clinic and also operates a community health clinic and the University's Sports Medicine Clinic. The Campus Center contains a fitness center, bookstore, gym, pool, student union, racquetball courts, an indoor track, a variety of multipurpose rooms, and administrative offices. The University maintains seven dormitories on campus. Marcil Hall houses a variety of classrooms, faculty offices, and a facility for the physical therapy program. The Harold Alfond Center for Health Sciences houses biology and chemistry labs as well as lecture halls, classrooms, a gross anatomy lab, and UNE's medical school facilities. The new $7.5-million Marine Science Education and Research Center has classrooms, wet labs, aquaculture labs, and a marine mammal rehabilitation wing.

On the University of New England's Westbrook College Campus, there are three residence halls and the Alexander Hall Student Union, which houses the dining hall, bookstore, the Wing Lounge, and a variety of meeting rooms. The Finley Recreation Center has a full gym and fitness facilities. Ludcke Auditorium, whose main structure was built in 1887, is home to concerts, plays, and a number of workshops and meetings.

Location

The University of New England's Westbrook College Campus is located in a quiet residential area just outside Portland, Maine. Portland is a vibrant city offering a great variety of entertainment options for the students. Portland's International Jetport allows easy access to the city, which is only a 2-hour drive north of Boston, Massachusetts. The University Campus is located on the banks of the Saco River and the shores of the Atlantic Ocean in Biddeford, Maine. This 540-acre campus is situated between the towns of Old Orchard Beach and Kennebunkport, 20 miles south of Portland, Maine, and 90 miles north of Boston, Massachusetts.

Majors and Degrees

The University Campus in Biddeford grants B.A. and B.S. degrees in the following programs: American studies, aquaculture and aquarium science, art education, athletic training, biochemistry, biological sciences, business, chemistry, elementary education, English, environmental science, environmental studies, exercise and health promotion, history, liberal studies (including a prelaw curriculum), marine biology, mathematics, medical biology (predental, premedicine, and pre-veterinary), political science, a 3+2 pre–physician assistant accelerated program, psychobiology, psychology, psychology and social relations, secondary education, sociology, and sport management. There is a five-year entry-level master's degree program in occupational therapy and a graduate physical therapy program with an undergraduate track. A certification program in education is offered. Individualized majors are also available.

The University of New England's Westbrook College Campus grants A.S., B.A., and B.S. degrees in dental hygiene (A.S. and B.S.) and nursing (A.D.N. and B.S.N.).

Academic Programs

The University has chosen as its primary fields of education the areas of business management, education, health sciences, the humanities, the natural sciences, and social sciences. The core curriculum is so designed that all students are effectively exposed to the liberal arts, natural sciences, social sciences, and business, while concentrating on the development of their chosen career program.

A bachelor's degree is awarded upon successful completion of 120 credit hours and fulfillment of specific program and University requirements.

The University calendar consists of two semesters.

Off-Campus Programs

The University is committed to supplementing the traditional learning process with practical applications. All students are encouraged to participate in cooperative education programs, field placements, and practicums. These programs provide valuable learning situations and increase a student's exposure to job-related opportunities. These experiences are required by most majors for graduation.

Academic Facilities

On the University Campus, Decary Hall houses classrooms, laboratories, and faculty and administrative offices. The Sanford E. Petts Health Center is home to the physical therapy clinic and the campus and community health clinic. The library (which has 143,927 books and print journals, 17,334 journal subscriptions, and 4,667 electronic books) has been expanded to provide more library and classroom space. Marcil Hall houses classrooms, faculty offices, and the facility for the physical therapy program. The Harold Alfond Center for Health Sciences houses labs and classrooms for the medical school, undergraduate health and life science programs, and graduate health programs. The Marine Science Education and Research Center is a new $7.5-million facility featuring a marine mammal rehab center as well as classrooms, wet and dry laboratories, and research areas.

On the University's Westbrook College Campus, Ludcke Auditorium is used for a variety of academic programs. Coleman Dental Hygiene Building houses classroom, clinic, and faculty space. The Blewett Science Center, home of UNE nursing programs, consists of science labs and classrooms, and Alumni Hall is a classroom facility. Proctor Hall is also a classroom building and is home to the Proctor Learning and Career Center. Josephine S. Abplanalp Library houses study space and computer terminals, along with an outstanding collection of books and periodicals and the Maine Women Writers Collection.

Costs

The costs per academic year in 2003–04 were tuition, $18,990; room and board, $7560; and fees, $630.

Financial Aid

In 2003–04, approximately 90 percent of all full-time freshmen received some form of financial assistance. The average package was $12,200. Financial award packages include scholarships, grants, loans, and employment.

Faculty

The University has 100 full-time undergraduate faculty members, 85 percent of whom have the terminal degree in their field, and 40 part-time members, a number of whom have doctoral degrees and hold administrative positions.

Student Government

The Student Senate is a vital part of the student life at both campuses of the University of New England. The student government has its own funds, derived from the student fees. The organization covers student services and public relations.

Admission Requirements

The University welcomes applications from students who are seriously pursuing an education of high quality. Candidates can file their admission application after the completion of their junior year of high school. All applicants are considered on an individual basis.

Students applying for admission are expected to submit a completed application, a $40 nonrefundable application fee, transcripts of all academic work (high school and college), and scores on either the ACT or SAT I. Students applying for admission should have completed a curriculum that includes English, mathematics, science, and social sciences. Those considering majors in the life or health sciences should show strength and preparation in mathematics and science. All prospective students are strongly encouraged to visit the campuses of the University of New England for an interview and tour. Interviews are held weekdays from 10 a.m. to 4 p.m. An appointment should be requested by letter or telephone.

Application and Information

Applications for the fall term are accepted until registration closes in September; those for the spring term are accepted through December.

For application information, students should contact:

Office of Admissions
University of New England
University Campus
Hills Beach Road
Biddeford, Maine 04005
Telephone: 207-283-0171
800-477-4863 Ext. 2297 (toll-free)
Fax: 207-294-5900
E-mail: admissions@une.edu
World Wide Web: http://www.une.edu/

UNIVERSITY OF NEW HAMPSHIRE

DURHAM, NEW HAMPSHIRE

The University

The University of New Hampshire (UNH) is a rising star among American research universities, a community of exceptional faculty members and talented and energetic students from forty-five states and twenty-eight countries. The University has a sizeable undergraduate population of nearly 11,000 but still feels cozy and intimate. This is due in part to a campus layout that is manageable and beautiful—with college greens, water, and a pleasing mix of classic and modern buildings that gradually give way to 2,600 acres of woods, fields, and farms. It's also due to the school's traditions of strong student-faculty interaction and active student culture. As one student put it, "It's easy to meet people and get involved in campus activities here. You need to have some initiative, but student leaders, residence hall staff, and others also seek you out."

The University offers students a variety of housing options, including halls of 100 to 600 students and two on-campus apartment complexes. Special-interest housing is offered in the minidorms (each focuses on a theme) and in Smith Hall, where the focus is on international and intercultural activities. Mills Hall, a new 360-bed residence hall, opened in fall 2002, and Holloway Commons, a spectacular dining and conferencing facility, with seating for 850 and an after-hours café, opened in fall 2003.

The Memorial Union Building (MUB) is the University's community center. Headquartered in the MUB are two movie theaters, the UNH Copy Center, the UNH Bookstore, the Ticket Office, specific lounge/study space for both nontraditional and graduate students, and Granite Square Station, the undergraduate mail center. Computing and Information Services provides a computer cluster and a help desk with walk-in service. The MUB Food Court offers expanded dining options, and food service is also available in the Coffee Office. The Student Senate Office; the Office of Multicultural Student Affairs; WUNH-radio; the *New Hampshire,* the student newspaper; and nearly sixty other student organizations have office space in the MUB. Students at the University can participate in a rich cultural life. Numerous lectures, films, concerts, exhibitions, meet-the-artist receptions, master classes, dance performances, and theatrical productions are offered throughout the year. The UNH Celebrity Series, the Art Gallery, and the Departments of Music, Theater and Dance, and Art and Art History bring artists of international stature to campus. Most events are free for students.

Many opportunities for leisure activities, regardless of skill or ability, are offered through Campus Recreation. The Hamel Student Recreation Center is available to all full-time matriculating students and Rec Pass holders. The center offers participants two multipurpose courts, a group exercise studio, a club/martial art studio, an 8,000-square-foot fitness center with more than 100 exercise stations, three basketball/volleyball courts, an indoor track, a lounge, several classrooms, locker rooms, towel and lock service at the equipment room, and saunas. Campus Recreation offers a variety of activities designed to make it easier to reach personal fitness goals and have fun. Participants may take part in one of the many group exercise classes, such as step aerobics, Reebok cycling, or cardio kickboxing. Other opportunities include Pilates, yoga, tai chi, racquetball, personal training, or massage therapy. Noncredit courses are also offered, including CPR and first aid. The intramural sports program consists of twenty-three different sports and activities offered to co-rec and men's and women's teams. Campus Recreation forms and assists special interest groups or sport club teams to reflect the varied recreation and cultural preferences of campus community members. Some clubs are intensely competitive, requiring a daily commitment to workouts and conditioning. They compete either on an intercollegiate basis with New England teams or sponsor University tournaments. Other clubs meet on a casual "come when you can" basis. In addition, Campus Recreation offers ice skating, manages a large outdoor recreation facility with its own sailing and canoe center, runs a children's camp (Camp Wildcat) in the summer, and supports the men's sport club crew boat house.

Location

Nestled in New Hampshire's seacoast region, the town of Durham is an outdoor-lover's dream, with ocean, ski mountains, and charming working-port cities nearby. Popular road trips for students include Boston (about an hour), Portsmouth (about 20 minutes), and the White Mountains (about an hour). With a non-student population of 8,000, Durham is a classic college town that caters to the student clientele. Main Street includes restaurants, coffeehouses, a bookstore, an ice cream parlor, and other student hangouts.

Majors and Degrees

The University of New Hampshire comprises seven colleges: College of Liberal Arts; College of Life Sciences and Agriculture; Whittemore School of Business and Economics; School of Health and Human Services; College of Engineering and Physical Sciences; Thompson School of Applied Science; and the University of New Hampshire at Manchester, the University's urban campus. The University offers more than 100 majors through these fully accredited academic divisions. New Hampshire enjoys a strong reputation in a wide range of academic fields, with history, creative writing, journalism, performing arts, hospitality management, occupational therapy, child and family studies, engineering, marine and animal sciences, and environmental studies among those topping the list. The business school offers several options under the business administration major that include entrepreneurial venture creation, information systems, international business and economics, management, accounting, and a student-designed track. First-year students take introduction to business and introduction to information systems, which blend classroom theory with direct industry exposure.

Academic Program

The University's general education requirements provide students with a broad foundation in the liberal arts and an introduction to the methods of inquiry needed for academic success. All students must complete ten courses from eight categories: writing skills; quantitative reasoning; biological, physical, and technological sciences; historical perspectives; foreign culture; fine arts; social science; and works of philosophy, literature, and ideas. Depending on their academic program, students may begin course work in their major as early as their first year.

A major research university, UNH prides itself on producing students who have had meaningful research experiences with a world-class faculty. Programs such as the Undergraduate

Research Opportunities Program and International Research Opportunities Program provide research grants each year for undergraduates to work closely with faculty members, on campus or abroad, on original projects. Students majoring in a wide range of subjects can access a wealth of research centers and facilities, some on the campus itself, others in surrounding towns. As New Hampshire's major public institution, the University is involved in a wide range of outreach programs with state and industry groups. These partnerships provide abundant opportunities for students interested in internships.

Academic Facilities

The Dimond Library is the state's only public university research library. The library offers three grand reading rooms, seating for 1,200 students, and state-of-the-art technology. The Parker Adaptive Technology Room provides an array of technological options for patrons who have learning, mobility, or vision disabilities. Through ResNet, students who live on-campus have high-speed Internet access to UNH library resources, class software and information, e-mail, and other services. The Environmental Technology Building is a multidisciplinary science and engineering research facility with a focus on environmental technology development. Most all of the University's cultural events take place in the Paul Creative Arts Center, which houses two theaters, dressing rooms, a well-equipped scene shop, a costume shop, a green room, storage facilities, classrooms, and the faculty and staff offices. New Hampshire Hall contains the Newman Dance Studio and a smaller "stage" studio.

Costs

The 2003–04 tuition and fees for undergraduate in-state students was $8664. Room (double) and board (19-meal plan) costs were $6234.

Financial Aid

Approximately 75 percent of students receive some form of financial assistance from UNH. University scholarships ranging from $500 to $8000 are awarded automatically to qualified students who apply for admission. Amounts are subject to change. Other scholarships are awarded by individual academic departments. The average first-year student's financial aid package, including gift, loan, and employment assistance, is $13,855. The University participates in the Federal Pell Grant Program, the Federal Supplemental Educational Opportunity Grant Program, the Federal Perkins Loan Program, the Federal Work-Study Program, and the Federal Stafford Student Loan Program. Students are required to submit the Free Application for Federal Student Aid (FAFSA) by March 1.

Faculty

The University of New Hampshire has 596 full-time and 121 part-time faculty members, 90 percent of whom hold doctoral degrees, with 7 percent at the master's level. The student-faculty ratio is 14:1. The UNH faculty includes winners of the Pulitzer, Guggenheim, and many other prestigious awards and honors, while the University ranks among the top campuses in the nation in the percentage of faculty members who have won Fulbright scholarships. This research productivity has a powerful effect on students, who can share the experience of discovery.

Student Government

The Student Senate comprises a governing body of student officers and senators. They are the voice of the student body, representing student opinion to members of the faculty, staff, and administration as well as the University community and the state legislature. The Senate believes that all students have the right to participate in University decisions and policy making. Committees of the Senate include areas in academics, residential life, commuters, health and human services, judicial affairs, and community change. They also approve and monitor the rates and uses of all mandatory student fees.

Admission Requirements

Admission to a bachelor's degree program is based upon successful completion of a strong secondary school program of college-preparatory course work. Primary consideration is given to the academic record, as demonstrated by the quality of the candidates' secondary school course selection and achievement, recommendations, and SAT I or ACT results. Consideration is also given to character, initiative, leadership, and special talents. Most successful candidates present at least four years of English and mathematics and three or more years of laboratory science, social science, and foreign language. Recommended mathematics preparation includes the equivalent of algebra I, geometry, algebra II, and trigonometry or advanced math. Students who plan to specialize in engineering, biological/physical science, mathematics, or forestry should present at least four years of mathematics including trigonometry as well as laboratory course work in chemistry and/or physics. Students pursuing business-related studies should also have completed four years of mathematics including trigonometry. For students planning to major in health-related disciplines, four years of math as well as laboratory courses in biology and chemistry are strongly recommended.

All candidates for admission to bachelor's degree programs are required to submit SAT I or ACT results. SAT II tests are not required. A foreign language Subject Test may satisfy the foreign language requirement of the Bachelor of Arts degree programs. Required scores vary by test. International students whose primary language is not English must submit TOEFL results. The recommended minimum TOEFL score is 213 (computer-based) or 550 (paper-based).

Candidates applying to a program within the Department of the Arts (except art history) are required to submit a portfolio to the department chairperson (603-862-2190). Candidates applying for programs in the Department of Music must make arrangements with the department chairperson for an audition (603-862-2404).

Application and Information

High school students who seek fall-semester admission may apply anytime after the start of the senior year and before the February 1 priority deadline. Admission notifications are provided on a continuous basis through April 15. Admitted first-year student have until May 1 to confirm their intent to enroll at the University. The review of candidates begins with the receipt of all review application materials. The Early Action Program allows candidates to receive a response by mid-January of their senior year; candidates are encouraged to submit admission applications by December 1. In some cases, the Admission Committee requests senior mid-year grade reports in order to make a final admission decision. All positive admission decisions made prior to the completion of a candidate's course work in progress are considered "provisional" and are subject to the verification of satisfactory senior-year achievement when final high school transcripts are reviewed.

Office of Admissions
University of New Hampshire
4 Garrison Avenue
Durham, New Hampshire 03801
Telephone: 603-862-1360
Fax: 603-862-0077
World Wide Web: http://www.unh.edu/admissions

UNIVERSITY OF NEW HAVEN

WEST HAVEN, CONNECTICUT

The University

The University of New Haven's mission is to prepare career-ready graduates for meaningful roles in today's global economy and to nurture pursuit of lifelong learning. Founded in 1920, the University of New Haven (UNH) is a private, independent, coeducational institution focused on combining professional education with liberal arts and sciences. UNH is committed to educational innovation, to continuous improvement in career and professional education, and to support of scholarship and professional development. UNH became a four-year college in 1958. Moving to its present location in West Haven in 1960, UNH rapidly expanded its programs, facilities, and faculty, attracting a student body that now stands at nearly 4,500—including the current enrollment of 1,950 full-time day students among its undergraduates.

The University is fully accredited by the New England Association of Schools and Colleges (NEASC). Individual programs, departments, and schools hold various forms of national professional accreditation. Five of the University of New Haven's bachelor's degree programs—chemical, civil, electrical, industrial, and mechanical engineering—are fully accredited by the Engineering Accreditation Commission of the Accreditation Board for Engineering and Technology (EAC/ABET). The computer science program is fully accredited by the Computer Science Accreditation Commission of the Computing Sciences Accreditation Board (CSC/CSAB). The UNH School of Business has been admitted to candidacy status for accreditation by the American Assembly of Collegiate Schools of Business.

Despite a broad academic program, UNH is small enough to accommodate individualized educational needs. Programs evolve and adapt to meet changing career interests as well as the requirements of business, industry, and professional fields. Small classes foster close student-faculty relationships. Accelerated weekend and evening programs in business and convenient evening hours provide access for part-time students in engineering, computers, public safety, and the arts and sciences.

The main campus is in West Haven, Connecticut, on a hillside close to Long Island Sound. UNH also operates a satellite branch in New London. Main campus administrative and classroom buildings support the University's five academic schools—the College of Arts and Sciences, the School of Business, the School of Engineering and Applied Science, the School of Hospitality and Tourism, and the School of Public Safety and Professional Studies. Following the addition of the Graduate School in 1969, New Haven College was designated a university. Twenty-eight master's degrees attract full- and part-time graduate students, while some eighty associate and bachelor's degree programs are available to entering freshmen and transfer students in a great variety of academic disciplines.

Other main campus buildings include the Peterson Library, Echlin Hall Computer Center, Bayer Hall admissions building, the Campus Book Store, new residence halls and apartments, and the Campus Center, which houses dining facilities and student activities. The Charger Gymnasium and athletic fields are located on the North Campus, just two short blocks from Maxcy Hall, the main administration building.

UNH is an NCAA Division II school and offers twenty intercollegiate varsity athletic programs as well as an extensive intramural program for both men and women. Varsity teams for men include football, cross-country, soccer, basketball, indoor track, baseball, volleyball, golf, and outdoor track and field. Women's varsity sports are cross-country, soccer, tennis, volleyball, basketball, indoor track, softball, golf, lacrosse, and outdoor track and field. UNH Charger teams have earned national top-20 ranking in a variety of sports.

Of the undergraduate day students, approximately 65 percent live on campus in the five residence halls. Three coed apartment complexes house primarily upperclass students. Apartments range from one to three bedrooms and hold 2 to 6 students. Approximately fifty clubs and organizations are open to students. Included are student chapters of professional societies, religious organizations, social groups, special interest clubs, student councils, cultural groups, and fraternities and sororities.

Location

West Haven is contiguous to New Haven. There are theaters, a coliseum that attracts star performers from the entertainment and sports worlds, a deepwater harbor and beaches, fine restaurants, museums, and galleries in the area. Numerous social and cultural programs are presented by the six colleges and universities in the area. New Haven is served by a local airport and major railroads, and its location at the junction of two interstate highways places the University of New Haven within easy driving distance of New York, Boston, Cape Cod, and the ski areas of New England.

Majors and Degrees

The College of Arts and Sciences offers the Bachelor of Arts degree in art, chemistry, communication, English, graphic design, history, interior design, liberal studies, mathematics, music, music and sound recording, music industry, political science, and psychology; the Bachelor of Science degree in biology, biotechnology, dental hygiene, environmental science, general dietetics, marine biology, and music and sound recording; and the Associate in Science degree in dental hygiene, general studies, graphic design, and interior design. The School of Business offers the Bachelor of Science degree in accounting, business administration, business economics, communication, finance, international business, management of sports industries, and marketing and electronic commerce as well as the Associate in Science degree in business administration and communication. The School of Hospitality and Tourism offers the Bachelor of Science in hotel and restaurant management and in tourism administration. An Associate in Science degree is available in hotel and restaurant management. The School of Engineering and Applied Science offers the Bachelor of Science degree in chemical engineering, chemistry, civil engineering, computer engineering, computer science, electrical engineering, general engineering, industrial engineering, and mechanical engineering and the Associate in Science degree in chemistry, chemical engineering, civil engineering, computer engineering, computer science, electrical engineering, industrial engineering, and mechanical engineering. The School of Public Safety and Professional Studies offers the Bachelor of Science degree in air transportation management, criminal justice, fire protection engineering, fire science, forensic science, legal studies, occupational safety and health administration, and occupational safety and health technology and the Associate in Science degree in aviation science, criminal justice, fire and occupational safety, legal studies, occupational safety and health administration, and occupational safety and health technology.

Academic Program

The University of New Haven offers a broad range of programs in both liberal arts and professional areas. Professionalism is emphasized, and there are diverse opportunities for career-oriented internships, cooperative education, independent study, and industrial projects. Certain types of professional experience are required in a number of degree programs. The Center for Learning Resources offers a tutoring service that is open to all students.

The undergraduate division operates on a 4-1-4 calendar. Credit is given for successful scores on the CLEP and Advanced Placement examinations. A University honors program provides outstanding study opportunities in most undergraduate disciplines. The residence requirement for all degrees is 30 credit hours.

UNH believes that all students studying for a bachelor's degree should develop a common set of skills; the University's goal is to prepare all graduates for the complex lives they will lead in a changing world. This can best be done through the University core curriculum, which consists of a minimum of eleven courses totaling 34 credits.

An available option at the University is cooperative education, an academic program that offers students the opportunity to combine career-oriented, paid, full-time work with education.

Academic Facilities

The Marvin K. Peterson Library contains more than 300,000 volumes and is a U.S. government documents depository library. Information is accessible through manual as well as electronic retrieval methods. Internet access, online databases, and an online catalog are available. The library subscribes to hundreds of journals and has a CD-ROM collection for accessing materials published in a wide variety of subjects. Through interlibrary loan services, UNH has access to holdings of more than 8,650 libraries. Communication majors participate in workshops along with studying sound, film production, and radio broadcasting techniques in well-equipped radio/television laboratories and studios. The School of Engineering and Applied Science has modern laboratories and equipment to support its programs. The College of Arts and Sciences maintains art studios, music practice rooms, a state-of-the-art sound recording studio, and science, psychology, and language labs. There are more than a dozen computer labs for student use and teaching on campus. One of these is devoted to forensic computing instruction for the School of Public Safety and Professional Studies. Hands-on instruction and demonstrations are available in kitchen facilities for the School of Hospitality and Tourism and for the students in dietetics. Dental hygiene students gain experience in the Dental Hygiene Clinic.

Costs

Full-time undergraduate tuition for the 2002–03 academic year, including the activity and health fees, was $17,480; room and board were $7960.

Financial Aid

UNH offers a comprehensive financial aid program that includes University resources as well as state, federal, and private aid programs. Approximately 80 percent of full-time undergraduate students receive some form of assistance. Students receive federal aid through the Federal Pell Grant, Federal Supplemental Educational Opportunity Grant, Federal Work-Study, Federal Perkins Loan, Federal Stafford Student Loan, and Federal PLUS loan programs. The University also administers programs sponsored by the state of Connecticut for Connecticut residents attending the University. Some students also qualify for financial aid from other states and from private companies, organizations, and foundations.

Faculty

It is a long-standing University policy that the faculty members teach a mix of undergraduate and graduate courses in order to preserve academic quality at all levels. Faculty members are selected and promoted primarily on the basis of teaching effectiveness, professional qualifications and performance, and contributions to the academic community. No classes are taught by teaching assistants. Some faculty members hold administrative positions and continue to teach. There are 185 full-time and more than 200 part-time faculty members, making the student-faculty ratio 10:1. More than 90 percent of the faculty members hold terminal degrees in their disciplines.

Student Government

The Day Student Government and Evening Student Council supervise annual expenditures by undergraduate clubs and organizations, direct liaison committees, support student publications and the student-operated FM radio station, and schedule cultural and social events. Students are elected annually to the University's Board of Governors.

Admission Requirements

To be eligible for admission, one must be a high school graduate or present evidence of equivalent preparation. Scores from the SAT I or the ACT are required. The admission decision is based on the student's overall high school record, class rank, SAT I or ACT results, letters of recommendation, and personal essay.

Prospective students are encouraged to visit the campus for a personal interview and tour. Outstanding athletes with satisfactory academic qualifications are referred to members of the coaching staff for interviews. Out-of-state residents are considered for admission on the same basis as state residents.

Application and Information

To apply to the University, a student must submit the completed application form, a nonrefundable $50 fee, official records of all academic work completed, SAT I or ACT results, letters of recommendation, and a personal essay. International students are required to demonstrate proficiency in English as well as provide documentation of financial support. The University of New Haven does not discriminate on the basis of age, color, sex, religion, race, sexual orientation, national origin, or disability in admission or treatment of students, in administration or distribution of financial aid, or in recruitment or treatment of employees. The University is authorized under federal law to enroll nonimmigrant alien students who meet the University's academic and English proficiency standards. The admissions office employs a rolling admissions system.

Undergraduate Admissions
University of New Haven
300 Orange Avenue
West Haven, Connecticut 06516
Telephone: 203-932-7319
800-DIAL-UNH Ext. 7319 (toll-free)
E-mail: adminfo@newhaven.edu
World Wide Web: http://www.newhaven.edu

UNIVERSITY OF NEW ORLEANS

NEW ORLEANS, LOUISIANA

The University

The University of New Orleans (UNO) is part of the rich cultural tapestry of its hometown, which is one of the most extraordinary cities in the world. Established in 1956 to bring publicly supported higher education to the New Orleans area, UNO is fully accredited by the Commission on Colleges of the Southern Association of Colleges and Schools. With an enrollment of 17,360 (13,338 undergraduates and 4,022 graduate students) in fall 2003, UNO offers both undergraduate and graduate degrees through the doctoral level. UNO derives its strength from its urban setting and strives to enhance the economic, social, and cultural amenities of New Orleans through its numerous research projects, outreach programs, and special cooperative agreements. The University of New Orleans attracts students from forty-five states (5.3 percent) and eighty-eight countries, with a majority of the students Louisiana residents (94.7 percent). The diverse student population (35.4 percent of students are members of ethnic minorities) provides an excellent opportunity for personal growth and understanding.

For students who are interested in on-campus housing, UNO offers three unique styles living. Privateer Place overlooks beautiful Lake Pontchartrain and includes a swimming pool and Jacuzzi. Privateer Place contains seventy-two 2-person unfurnished efficiency apartments, 216 furnished two-bedroom apartments, and sixty furnished four-bedroom apartments. Bienville Hall is a coeducational dormitory for single students and has 306 two-person rooms, seventy-eight of which have been recently remodeled. Lafitte Village is married student housing, with 48 one-bedroom apartments and 72 two-bedroom apartments. Waiting lists for Lafitte can be up to a year, so students who are interested in these units should apply early. All complexes have disability-accessible rooms available. Campus dining facilities are conveniently located near all on-campus housing facilities and heavily populated student areas, with various hours of operation. Other student services include six on-campus computer labs that provide free Internet access, a learning resource center that offers additional tutoring services, student counseling services, an on-campus medical office and pharmacy, student legal counseling, and religious centers.

UNO has more than 100 active student organizations on campus, including academic, professional, Greek, social, political, and religious organizations. UNO's newest addition is the University pep band, the UNO Blue Zoo, which performs at all UNO home basketball games and other University-related events. The *Driftwood,* UNO's student newspaper, is published weekly, and the *Ellipsis,* a literary magazine, is published annually.

As a Division I member of the National Collegiate Athletic Association (NCAA), UNO fields men's teams in basketball, baseball, cross-country, golf, tennis, and track and field (indoor and outdoor) and women's teams in basketball, volleyball, cross-country, golf, tennis, and track and field (indoor and outdoor). UNO students can also participate in several recreational and intramural sports. Students have access to a new 85,000-square-foot Wellness Center, which features a 12,000-square-foot cardiovascular, circuit, and free weight training room; an indoor jogging track; racquetball courts; outdoor sundeck; juice bar; and social lounge.

Location

The University's 195-acre main campus is set in one of the most beautiful residential areas on the south shore of Lake Pontchartrain, only minutes from the fun and excitement of downtown New Orleans and the French Quarter. New Orleans is a cosmopolitan city, known for its great Southern hospitality and its unique tourist attractions. Renowned for its Creole and Cajun cuisine, Mardi Gras, and jazz music festivals, New Orleans culture offers a unique environment for students to grow, both socially and academically. Whether exploring the artsy Warehouse District or strolling down stately St. Charles Avenue, New Orleans has something for everyone, and the University of New Orleans is a part of it all.

Many of UNO's hotel, restaurant, and tourism administration majors find internships in the city's best hotels and restaurants. Naval architecture students have access to the nation's largest undergraduate program in naval architecture and marine engineering as well as to the UNO–Avondale Maritime Center. As New Orleans continues to attract computer technology–based businesses to what has been called "the Silicon Bayou," the UNO Research and Technology Park continues to expand, producing more than 8,000 new jobs. Computer science majors are able to network with potential employers in one of the fastest-growing computer technology markets in the country.

Majors and Degrees

Bachelor of Science degrees are offered in accounting; biological sciences; chemistry; civil and environmental engineering; computer science; economics; electrical engineering; environmental science and policy; finance; general business administration; general science; geology; geophysics; hotel, restaurant, and tourism administration; management; marketing; mathematics; mathematics education; mechanical engineering; naval architecture and marine engineering; physics; preprofessional programs; predentistry; premedicine (with biology, chemistry, and psychology tracks); prenursing; pre–occupational therapy studies; pre-pharmacy; pre-physical therapy studies; pre–rehabilitation counseling; pre-respiratory therapy studies; pre–veterinary medicine; psychology; science education; and urban studies and planning.

Bachelor of Arts degrees are offered in anthropology; drama and communications, with drama options including acting, directing, and design and communications options including film, message design, radio, television, and video; economics; elementary education; English; English education; fine arts–history; fine arts–studio (with options that include painting, photography, and sculpture); foreign language education; French; geography; history; human performance and health promotion education; international studies; mathematics education; music (with options including instrumental, jazz studies, theory and composition, and vocal); music education; philosophy; political science; secondary education; social science education; sociology; Spanish; urban and public administration; and women's studies.

A four-year Bachelor of General Studies degree program is available for students who wish to design individual curricula. Credit programs in paralegal studies and medical coding are also offered. Additional interdisciplinary minors are offered in interdisciplinary studies in Africana studies, Asian studies, entrepreneurship, environmental economics, environmental studies, Latin American studies, medical coding, Native American studies, paralegal studies, and print journalism.

Academic Program

All baccalaureate degree programs require a minimum of 128 semester hours with a minimum grade point average of 2.0 (C) in all work attempted in the college major. Also, all students must successfully complete an approved course demonstrating computer literacy. Other course requirements vary according to program. Programs leading to degrees with honors are offered in most academic majors. Credit for selected courses may be earned either through advanced-standing exams administered by the academic departments or through the College Board's Advanced Placement and College-Level Examination Program tests. College credit may also be gained for certain armed services and other nonacademic training. The academic year is composed of sixteen-week fall and spring semesters and three summer sessions.

Off-Campus Programs

The University of New Orleans Metropolitan College coordinates international study programs in Austria, Costa Rica, the Czech Republic, Ecuador, France, Greece, Honduras, and Italy. UNO's partnership with the University of Innsbruck, Austria, affords students an opportunity to participate in the largest international summer school of any American university in Europe. UNO offers college-credit exchange programs in Brazil and Canada. Students may also attend another school within the continental United States via the National Student Exchange (NSE) for one semester or one year.

UNO offers several off-campus facilities throughout the metropolitan New Orleans area, demonstrating UNO's commitment to community outreach. Off-campus locations offer both credit and noncredit courses, with hours varying from sunrise to evening and weekend classes.

Academic Facilities

The Earl K. Long Library's 1.5-million-volume collection includes approximately 12,000 journals, of which 3,800 are current subscriptions. Microform holdings include microfilm, microcard, and microfiche formats; microtext readers and reader-printers are also available. Other facilities include individual study carrels, a music listening room, computer terminals connected to the Computer Research Center, a Kurzweil reader for the visually impaired, and photocopy services. The Office of Educational Support Services includes a media resources center, which provides important media aids for the instructional staff in classroom presentations, and Television Resources, which coordinates a closed-circuit cable system and TV production studio. WWNO, the first public radio station in Louisiana, is located on the UNO campus.

All enrolled students and faculty and staff members receive a LAN and e-mail account. The University's computer network provides connections to approximately 5,000 locations campus-wide. High-speed ResNet service is available to students living in Privateer Place, and a free dial-up Internet modem pool provides access for all off-campus enrolled students and faculty and staff members.

The UNO Lee Circle Centre for the Arts includes the Ogden Museum, which houses the largest collection of Southern art in the world. The center also houses the National D-Day Museum, which includes the world's largest collection of World War II color film. The 70,000-square-foot UNO Studio Center, located 20 minutes from the main campus, houses a professional-quality sound stage, including a 10,000-square-foot studio for University film projects. The UNO Studio Center is also available for professional film projects.

Costs

In 2003–04, combined undergraduate fees for full-time students for the fall and spring semesters were $3084 for Louisiana residents and $10,128 for nonresidents; summer session fees for full-time students were $795 for Louisiana residents and $1345 for nonresidents. Residence hall and board fees totaled $3520 (double occupancy) for the fall and spring semesters. Costs of books and supplies totaled $825 per year. Additional charges include a $20 application fee, a $10 registration fee, field service and laboratory fees (usually $10 to $35) for some courses, a $50 car registration fee, a $30 late application fee, a $30 late registration fee, a $5 per-credit-hour (maximum $75) technology fee, and a $10 per-credit-hour (maximum $120) academic enhancement fee. All fees are subject to change and can be confirmed by calling the Office of Admissions.

Financial Aid

The Office of Student Financial Aid develops financial aid packages to assist students with their educational expenses. This package is usually a combination of grants, loans, student employment, and/or scholarships, which, along with family contribution, help to finance the student's education. To be eligible for most federal financial aid programs, students must enroll for at least 6 credit hours (half-time) in an eligible program (one that leads to a degree or certificate). Approximately 90 percent of all freshmen in fall 2002 who showed financial need and took at least 6 credit hours were offered some form of financial aid. The priority date for the financial aid application is May 1. All applications postmarked on or before January 15 are considered for UNO's numerous academic scholarships. The University of New Orleans also offers scholarships in jazz studies, classical music, fine arts, drama and communications, and creative writing. These scholarships require either an audition or the submission of a portfolio or manuscript along with the scholarship application.

Faculty

UNO has 577 full-time and 267 part-time faculty members, most of whom participate in both graduate and undergraduate instruction and research activity. Graduate students serve as teaching assistants in laboratory courses under the close supervision of the faculty. Approximately 80 percent of the faculty members hold doctorates. Most full-time faculty members devote themselves exclusively to University-related pursuits and are integrally involved in student affairs through counseling, teaching, research, and social activities. The student-faculty ratio is 24:1.

Student Government

Every student enrolled at UNO is a member of the Student Government (SG). SG offers students a way to create effective change, express opinions and concerns, and utilize resources to enhance their educational experiences. Some of the programs SG currently offers and/or sponsors are Student Legal Services, the Academic Travel Fund, 24-hour study hall during finals week, UNO pep band (The Blue Zoo), UNO Soccer Club, Mini Baja, UNO Jazz Night at the UC, musical excursions, UNO Ambassadors Fishing Rodeo, the UNO student literary magazine (*Ellipsis*), recreation and intramural sports, cheerleaders, and Starlettes.

Admission Requirements

Students seeking admission to the University of New Orleans should submit their application as early as possible in their senior year. Admission requirements for fall 2004 include either a composite score of at least 20 on the ACT (950 on the SAT I) or a grade point average (GPA) of at least 2.0 on a 4.0 scale for 17½ specific core courses. Out-of-state students who satisfy the GPA core must also have a minimum composite score of 17 on the ACT or 820 on the SAT I. Transfer students are required to submit official transcripts from each institution previously attended and must have a minimum cumulative 2.0 GPA to be considered for admission. Students with fewer than 24 credit hours must satisfy both freshman and transfer requirements.

Beginning in fall 2005, entering freshmen must meet new admission requirements, including the completion of the Board of Regents core curriculum. Prospective students must also have either a high school cumulative GPA of at least 2.5 (students with less than a 2.0 GPA cannot be admitted) or an ACT composite score of at least 23 (1060 SAT I) or rank in the top 25 percent of their high school graduating class, and students must not have taken more than one developmental/remedial course. Transfer requirements beginning in fall 2005 include the completion of 18 semester hours of nondevelopmental work, a minimum 2.25 cumulative GPA, and completion of all developmental course work before transferring. Students with fewer than 18 semester hours must meet both freshman and transfer requirements.

Application and Information

The University of New Orleans has a rolling admissions policy. The application fee is $20. Priority deadlines for application are as follows: July 1 for the fall semester, November 15 for the spring semester, and May 1 for the summer semester. Deadlines for international students are June 1, October 1, and March 1, respectively.

Office of Admissions
University of New Orleans
Lakefront 103 Administration Building
New Orleans, Louisiana 70148
Telephone: 504-280-6595
800-256-5-UNO (toll-free)
Fax: 504-280-5522
World Wide Web: http://www.uno.edu/~admi

UNIVERSITY OF NORTH CAROLINA AT ASHEVILLE

ASHEVILLE, NORTH CAROLINA

The University

An outstanding learning community, the University of North Carolina at Asheville (UNCA) focuses on undergraduates, with a core curriculum covering humanities, language and culture, arts and ideas, and health and fitness. Students thrive in small classes with faculty members dedicated first of all to teaching. The liberal arts emphasis develops discriminating thinkers and expert and creative communicators with a passion for learning. These are qualities needed for today's challenges and the changes of tomorrow. UNCA is advancing as the premier public liberal arts university in the country and is pursuing new initiatives that emphasize academic excellence, service-learning, diversity, and community partnerships.

UNC Asheville opened in 1927 as Buncombe County Junior College for area residents interested in pursuing higher education. The school underwent several name changes, mergers, and moves before relocating in 1961 to its present campus in north Asheville. Asheville-Biltmore College joined the University of North Carolina system in 1969 as the University of North Carolina at Asheville, with the distinct mission of offering an undergraduate liberal arts education of superior quality. Today, UNC Asheville is the only designated, undergraduate, public liberal arts university in the state of North Carolina and one of only twenty-six such universities in the country.

UNC Asheville enrolls 3,200 students pursuing bachelor's degrees in about thirty majors in the natural and social sciences, humanities, preprofessional, and professional areas, as well as the Master of Liberal Arts. Students represent nearly all North Carolina counties, all regions of the United States, and more than twenty-five countries.

With an average class size of 18, UNC Asheville emphasizes a personalized education characterized by close faculty-student interactions, challenging academic programs, and service-learning activities. The University has received national recognition for its interdisciplinary approach to undergraduate liberal arts education.

Location

UNC Asheville's scenic 265-acre campus is 1 mile north of downtown Asheville, the population center (286,000 in the metropolitan area) of western North Carolina, in the heart of the Blue Ridge Mountains. Asheville rates high in cultural, recreational, and educational opportunities. An All-America city, Asheville is described as one of the country's most livable cities. More than 1 million acres of national parks and forests are close by, including the Blue Ridge Parkway, the Great Smoky Mountains National Park, Mount Mitchell State Park, and several national forests. Asheville's revitalized downtown mixes mountain culture and modern life. Coffee houses and ethnic restaurants, clubs and night spots, shopping malls and crafts shops, art galleries and museums all make Asheville a place where diverse interests and activities thrive. A regional airport is only minutes away, and the campus is only 2 to 4 hours from Atlanta, Chapel Hill, Charlotte, Raleigh, and Knoxville, Tennessee.

Majors and Degrees

UNC Asheville grants the Bachelor of Arts in art, biology, chemistry, classics, drama, economics, French, German, history, interdisciplinary studies, literature, mass communication, mathematics, multimedia arts and sciences, music, philosophy, political science, psychology, sociology, and Spanish. Programs in mechatronics, forestry, and textile chemistry are offered in a partnership with North Carolina State University. A Bachelor of Fine Arts is offered. UNC Asheville also grants the Bachelor of Science in accounting, atmospheric sciences, chemistry, computer science, environmental studies, industrial and engineering management, interdisciplinary studies, management, music technology, and physics. Teacher licensure is available for K–12 and is available in a variety of subject areas. Minors are offered in all major departments as well as in art history, creative writing, dance, health promotion, Africana studies, humanities, international studies, religious studies, and women's studies. A 2+2 program in engineering with North Carolina State University and a nursing program in conjunction with Western Carolina University are also available. Preprofessional programs in dentistry, law, medicine, pharmacy, and veterinary medicine further expand UNC Asheville's offerings.

Academic Program

The University is committed to a liberating education emphasizing the central role of human values in thought and action, the free and rigorous pursuit of truth, and a respect for differing points of view and heritage. It aims to develop men and women of broad perspective who think critically and creatively and who communicate effectively. All students must complete a minimum of 120 semester hours of credit, which includes approximately 56 hours of general education courses (the arts, English, foreign language, health and fitness, the four-course humanities sequence, library research, mathematics, and natural and social sciences). The humanities sequence, which has been used as a national model, serves as the core of the UNC Asheville experience and provides students with an interdisciplinary approach to recorded history. The University operates on a semester schedule, with a fall (August until December) and spring (January until May) semester, plus two shorter summer terms.

Off-Campus Programs

Students may participate in numerous study-abroad opportunities. Summer programs are offered in Oxford and Cambridge, England; Dijon, France; Cuenca, Ecuador; Granada, Spain; Greece; and Italy. Semester or yearlong programs are available in some thirty-five countries through various UNCA-sponsored or affiliated programs. Academic credit may be earned, allowing students to progress toward their liberal arts degree. In addition, UNCA is a member of the National Student Exchange, which allows a student to study at more than 175 other U.S. institutions for either a semester or year exchange.

Academic Facilities

UNC Asheville's campus comprises about thirty buildings for classrooms, administration, residence, and recreation, with a new Master Plan in place for expansion over twenty years. The newest buildings on the campus are two residence halls, a state-of-the-art health and fitness center, and a dining hall. New residence halls, an expanded student center, and a state-of-the-art math and science building are scheduled to be constructed over the next few years.

All academic buildings and residence halls have Macintosh and PC computer lab facilities. Each student has access to these labs, some open 24 hours, as well as to high-speed Internet connections in each residence hall room.

Ramsey Library and the Media Center house 3,334 current journal subscriptions; 378,000 books, bound periodicals, and government documents; and 9,300 audiovisuals, in addition to a special archives collection. The online library system connects students to the combined holdings of the libraries at UNCA, Western Carolina University, and Appalachian State University. The Media Center includes the Square D Teleconference Center, allowing for distance learning.

Robinson and Rhoades Halls house several laboratories, a mathematics assistance center, a computer center, Steelcase Teleconference Center, a meteorology lab, and other research facilities. Carol Belk Theatre is a 200-seat arena theater that hosts the four main-stage productions each year in addition to student-directed forum plays. Owen Hall is home to a conference center, art gallery space, and numerous indoor and outdoor art studios. Karpen Hall features the Writing Center and the Honors Program.

Other buildings include Lipinsky Hall, Phillips Hall, Weizenblatt Hall, and Zageir and Carmichael Halls.

Costs

For 2003–04, tuition and fees for North Carolina residents are $3100 per year. For out-of-state students, tuition and fees are $11,984 annually. Room and board costs for all on-campus students are $4600 per year. Books average $700 per year.

Financial Aid

Both merit- and need-based financial assistance are available to students. Nearly all merit-based scholarships for incoming freshmen are part of the University Laurels Scholarship program. Students must submit an application for admission and the separate scholarship application and essays by December. To be considered competitive, students must have at least two of the following: 3.5 GPA, top 10 percent of high school graduating class, 1250 SAT I, or 28 ACT. Western North Carolina Leadership Scholarships are available to students living in the western North Carolina region and showing promise in community service and student leadership. These scholarships require a separate application, and the deadline is December. North Carolina Teaching Fellowships are also available to North Carolina students interested in teaching.

Need-based assistance is available and may include grants, loans, Federal Work-Study, and/or scholarships. The Free Application for Federal Student Aid should be filed by March 1 for the upcoming academic year. Applications received after March 1 are given consideration on a fund-available basis.

In addition, numerous on-campus jobs are available to students, permitting flexible scheduling around classes and providing competitive wages.

Faculty

UNC Asheville is focused on undergraduate education. Its 290 faculty members, 88 percent with the highest degrees in their fields, make excellence in teaching their highest priority. All courses are taught by faculty members, including introductory courses. The student-faculty ratio is 13:1. Students attending UNC Asheville work one-on-one with faculty members in both classes and collaborative research projects. Faculty members serve as general academic advisers and as advisers in specific departments in addition to serving as mentors to students engaged in research.

Student Government

An active Student Government Association is elected annually by the student body. Students may participate in more than eighty student organizations, spanning a wide variety of interest areas, from religious to academic to social. Greek fraternities and sororities, honor societies, a student newspaper, academic clubs, activist groups, religious organizations, student activities, and ethnic and cultural groups are just a few. An extensive outdoor program sponsors activities ranging from white-water rafting and kayaking to backpacking and rock climbing. Intramural and club sports are also popular. Volunteer and community service, while a part of UNC Asheville's service-learning curriculum, are popular with students outside the classroom.

Admission Requirements

Admission to UNC Asheville is competitive. Applicants are reviewed individually to evaluate how well their goals and strengths match the University's educational mission. UNCA does not discriminate based on race, color, national origin, religion, gender, age, sexual orientation, gender expression, or disability. The majority of the decision is based on the high school record. Close attention is paid to college-preparatory course work, including honors and other advanced work, grade trend, overall grade point average, and rank in class. SAT I and/or ACT scores, extracurricular activities, and special interests and talents are also considered. Financial need is not a factor in the admission decision. TOEFL scores are required of students whose native language is not English.

Students must complete the Minimum Course Requirements for the UNC system, which include a high school diploma from an accredited secondary school; 4 units of English; 3 units of math (including algebra I and II and geometry); 3 units of science (including physical science, biological science, and a laboratory science); 2 units of social studies, including U.S. history; and 2 units of a foreign language. Additional math and science courses are strongly recommended.

Transfer students must maintain a minimum 2.5 GPA on all transfer work. A maximum of 18 percent of the incoming class is from out-of-state (including international students).

Application and Information

Freshman applications are due by mid-March. Transfer students should submit applications by April 1 for fall semester and December 1 for spring semester. Notification of decisions is by letter and usually follows two weeks after all application materials are received. Applications and all credentials should be submitted along with the application fee to:

Office of Admissions
Lipinsky Hall 117, CPO #2210
University of North Carolina at Asheville
One University Heights
Asheville, North Carolina 28804-8510
Telephone: 828-251-6481
800-531-9842 (toll-free)
Fax: 828-251-6482
E-mail: admissions@unca.edu
World Wide Web: http://www.unca.edu

THE UNIVERSITY OF NORTH CAROLINA AT PEMBROKE

PEMBROKE, NORTH CAROLINA

The University

The University of North Carolina at Pembroke (UNCP), a constituent institution of the University of North Carolina, serves as a comprehensive university committed to academic excellence in a balanced program of teaching, research, and service. Combining the opportunities available at a large university with the personal attention characteristic of a small college, the University provides an intellectually challenging environment created by a faculty that is dedicated to effective teaching, to interactions with students, and to scholarship. Graduates are academically and personally prepared for rewarding careers, postgraduate education, and community leadership.

UNC Pembroke is a coeducational institution that enrolls approximately 4,700 students in undergraduate and graduate programs. Class size ranges from 25 to 40, and the student-faculty ratio is 16:1. Freshmen are guaranteed housing in one of the five residence halls on campus. UNC Pembroke offers approximately eighty clubs and organizations, including fraternities and sororities, professional honor societies, and ethnic and religious groups. UNCP offers special programs, such as the North Carolina Teaching Fellows, Honors College, and Health Careers Programs, as well as various research and internship opportunities. UNCP students have the unique opportunity to work for the University's public television facility, WNCP-TV. Among the many programs broadcast to more than 660,000 homes is Action News 31, the only live, student-produced television news program in the state and one of only three in the nation. UNC Pembroke also has strong student ensembles in the performing and dramatic arts.

UNCP is a member of the Peach Belt Athletic Conference of the National Collegiate Athletic Association Division II and fields teams in men's and women's basketball, cross-country, soccer, and track; men's baseball, golf, and wrestling; and women's softball, tennis, and volleyball. The University also offers a full range of intramural sports programs.

Founded in 1887 to educate Native Americans, the University now serves a student body reflective of the rich cultural diversity of American society. *U.S. News & World Report* ranks UNCP second in campus diversity among Southern regional universities. As it stimulates interaction within and among its cultural groups, the University enables students to become informed, principled, and tolerant citizens with a global perspective. Drawing strength from its heritage, UNCP continues to expand its leadership role in enriching the intellectual, economic, social, and cultural life of the region, the state, and the nation.

Location

UNCP is located in the sandhills of North Carolina, an area famous for its temperate climate, natural scenic beauty, golf resorts, and Southern hospitality, in the historic town of Pembroke. Easily accessible from Interstate 95 and U.S. 74, North and South Carolina beaches are within a 1½-hour drive, and campus is within a 2-hour drive of the cities of the Research Triangle Park, Fayetteville, and Charlotte.

Majors and Degrees

UNC Pembroke offers a broad range of degrees and nationally accredited professional programs at the bachelor's and master's levels. The University is organized into the College of Arts and Sciences, School of Mass Communications and Business, School of Education, and School of Graduate Studies. UNCP confers five undergraduate degrees: the Bachelor of Arts, Bachelor of Music, Bachelor of Science, Bachelor of Science in Nursing, and Bachelor of Social Work. Majors, minors, and/or concentrations are offered in African-American studies; American Indian studies; art (art education, arts management, studio art); biology (biology education, biomedical emphasis, botany, medical technology, molecular biology, zoology); business administration (accounting, applied science, economics, management); chemistry (physical science, science education); communicative arts (English, English education, theater arts); computer science; education (birth–kindergarten, elementary, middle grades, special education–learning disabilities and mental retardation); health, physical education, and recreation (community health education, health and physical education, physical education, recreational management/administration); history (American studies, social studies education); mass communications (broadcasting, journalism, public relations); mathematics (mathematics education, mathematics–computer science); music (elective studies in business/music industry option, music education); nursing (for registered nurses); philosophy and religion; political science (gerontology, international studies, prelaw, public policy and administration); psychology; social work and criminal justice; and sociology.

Preprofessional programs are offered in dentistry, law, medicine, optometry, pharmacy, public health, and veterinary medicine. A candidate for a degree in medical technology completes a three-year program at UNC Pembroke and an additional year at one of several cooperating hospitals. The student receives a Bachelor of Science in either biology or chemistry upon completion of the year's hospital work.

Academic Program

UNC Pembroke seeks to poduce graduates with broad vision, who are sensitive to values, who recognize the complexity of social problems, and who will be contributing citizens with an international perspective and an appreciation for the achievements of diverse civilizations. To earn a degree, students must earn at least 120–128 semester hours of credit in a program of study. In addition to meeting all major program requirements, students seeking baccalaureate degrees are required to complete a 44-hour General Education program, which provides students with an understanding of the fundamental principles and contributions of a variety of disciplines. Moreover, the program fosters the ability to analyze and weigh evidence, exercise quantitative and scientific skills, make informed decisions, write and speak clearly, and think critically and creatively.

Academic Facilities

The Sampson-Livermore Library houses more than 200,000 books, 1,300 periodicals, and local historical materials and serves as the depository for selected state and federal documents. The School of Education's Education Center maintains a curriculum laboratory and test review resource center. The Department of English, Theatre, and Languages maintains a library of books, journals, and media resources for English education and foreign languages. Moreover, the

Department of Music's library is home to various recordings and music scores by regional artists.

The Native American Resource Center offers a rich collection of authentic American Indian artifacts, handicrafts, and art as well as books, cassettes, record albums, and filmstrips about Native Americans, with emphasis on the Lumbee Indians of Robeson County. The center's exhibits include prehistoric tools and weapons, nineteenth-century household and farm equipment, and contemporary Indian art. Artifacts from Indian cultures of Canada and Central and South America as well as from other sections of the United States are also on display.

Each academic building houses at least one microcomputer laboratory. Additional computers are located in the Computer Center, the D. F. Lowry Building, and the Sampson-Livermore Library. The University's computer network is connected to LINC NET, a statewide data network, and the Internet, which provides worldwide computer access.

Costs

The 2002–03 estimated cost, including tuition, for in-state students residing on campus was $7245, and out-of-state students residing on campus paid $16,609. In-state students not living on campus paid $1440, while out-of-state students not living on campus paid $6122. Costs are subject to change by the state legislature.

Financial Aid

U.S. News & World Report listed UNC Pembroke as one of the most affordable universities in the South. UNC Pembroke makes every effort to assist students in securing the financial means necessary to attend the University. Aid is available to eligible students through scholarships, state and federal grants, loans, and college work-study. To apply for financial aid, students must complete the Free Application for Federal Student Aid (FAFSA), which is available from high school guidance offices. A variety of scholarships are available to students who demonstrate superior academic ability. Scholarships are awarded on the basis of personal and academic merit; some, however, are also based on financial need. The deadline for scholarship applications is December 1 if a student is applying for the spring and March 1 for the fall. Students applying for financial aid should complete the FAFSA by March 15.

Faculty

UNC Pembroke's teaching faculty numbers 186 full-time members, 80 percent of whom have doctoral or terminal degrees. The University has long valued personal attention within the classroom. With that in mind, all classes are taught by faculty members, not graduate assistants.

Student Government

The Student Government Association represents and safeguards the interests of the student body. Once a student enrolls at UNCP, he or she becomes a member of the SGA. Officers and class representatives are elected by the student body each spring. The Student Senate is the legislative branch and policymaking body of the SGA. The senate recommends policies and regulations necessary for the general welfare of the student body.

Admission Requirements

Applicants for freshman admission must provide evidence (high school transcript) of graduation from high school, satisfactory class rank and GPA, and scores from either the SAT I or the ACT. Students who graduated from high school in 1990 and after must present the following courses: 4 course units in English (the courses should emphasize grammar, composition, and literature); 3 course units in mathematics, including algebra I, algebra II, and geometry or a higher-level mathematics course for which algebra II is a prerequisite; 3 course units in science, including a life or biological science, a physical science, and a laboratory science; and 2 course units in social studies, including 1 unit in United States history. Students who graduate from 2004 onwards must complete 2 course units in a foreign language. It is recommended that students take mathematics in their senior year. If more than 24 transferable semester credit hours are presented, transfer students are evaluated for admission based on college work. Moreover, students must have at least a C average. For those students who have fewer than 24 semester credit hours, admissions decisions may be based on freshman criteria.

Application and Information

Applications should be submitted by December 1 for the spring semester and by July 15 for the fall semester. Students are encouraged to apply earlier if they wish to be considered for financial aid and scholarships. In addition, applications are accepted for both summer sessions. The deadlines are May 15 for summer session I and June 15 for summer session II. Applications and additional information are available from:

Director of Admissions
The University of North Carolina at Pembroke
One University Drive
P.O. Box 1510
Pembroke, North Carolina 28372-1510
Telephone: 910-521-6262
800-949-UNCP (toll-free)
Fax: 910-521-6497
E-mail: admissions@uncp.edu
World Wide Web: http://www.uncp.edu/admissions

UNIVERSITY OF NORTHWESTERN OHIO

LIMA, OHIO

The University

In 2004 the University of Northwestern Ohio celebrated its eighty-fourth anniversary. Founded in 1920, it is a private, not-for-profit institution. The University of Northwestern Ohio is a coeducational institution authorized by the Ohio Board of Regents to grant baccalaureate degrees (Bachelor of Science) and associate degrees in applied business (A.A.B.) in the College of Business and associate degrees in applied science (A.A.S.) in the College of Technologies. Diplomas are also granted in both colleges.

The University of Northwestern Ohio's enrollment averages 3,000; approximately 1,180 students live in on-campus residence halls. A gymnasium, restaurant, student lounges, and picnic areas are available for student enjoyment.

The University is accredited by the Higher Learning Commission of the North Central Association of Colleges and Schools. The Association of Collegiate Business Schools and Programs has accredited the University's accounting, administrative assistant, business administration, business computer applications, legal secretarial, marketing, medical secretarial, and word processing/administrative support associate degree programs. The American Association of Medical Assistance (AAMA) has accredited the medical assistant technology and medical assistant programs. In addition, the College of Technologies is certified by the National Automotive Technicians Education Foundation. The Ohio Board of Regents provides authorization for the degrees.

The University of Northwestern Ohio realizes that student activities are an important part of the University experience. To provide the activities required by ever-expanding enrollments, the University has a gymnasium and recreational center. To serve all students' schedules, the recreational center remains open from 9 a.m. to 12:30 a.m., Monday through Thursday, and from 5 p.m. to 11 p.m. on Sunday.

The recreational center is available for intramural sports, aerobic dancing, basketball, entertainment groups, visiting lectures, and special programs. Intramural sports programs have been expanded to provide a softball diamond and an indoor/outdoor volleyball court. These facilities provide excellent opportunities for activities that develop skills in leadership and responsibility and activities that are necessary for success in the business world. They provide the necessary cultural, social, and recreational events for a productive life. A travel agency and a restaurant are also located on campus.

The University of Northwestern Ohio has on-campus housing available to students. Students are not required to live in campus housing, but new students are advised to reside in University housing for at least six weeks for proper adjustment to campus life. Married students must reside off campus and can obtain a list of apartment complexes in the area at the housing office.

Location

The University of Northwestern Ohio is located at 1441 North Cable Road in Lima, Ohio, midway between Dayton and Toledo. The University sits on a 35-acre campus surrounded by a residential area that offers opportunities for shopping and entertainment.

Majors and Degrees

The business department offers baccalaureate degrees in accounting, business administration, specialized studies, and in business administration with an agribusiness management option, a marketing option, and an automotive management/automotive aftermarket option. The health technology department offers a bachelor's degree in health-care administration.

In the College of Business, programs offered in the evening are designed to serve the needs of the students interested in furthering their education in accounting, business administration, and marketing.

Classes for the degree programs meet Monday through Thursday evenings beginning at 5:45 p.m.

Two accelerated on-campus programs are available: the business administration associate degree program and the Bachelor of Science degree in business administration. These programs meet one night a week from 6 to 10 p.m.

The students in the accelerated business administration associate degree program must be professionally employed and be at least 22 years of age. The program, if taken as designed, can be completed in twenty-four months.

Majors in the College of Business are offered through the Virtual College (VC) and the College Without Walls (CWW) programs. Working adults may apply for admission to this unique program, which provides the opportunity for nontraditional students to study independently. These prospective students must be self-motivated, since the program is rigorous and self-directed. Faculty members are available for personal consultation through a variety of media, including e-mail. Virtual College students must take UN071 as their orientation. All course work must be completed within each quarter. Faculty members may be reached by chat, e-mail, fax, and phone.

Accelerated baccalaureate degree–completion programs are available through distance learning. Students who have earned associate degrees in a health-related field may complete a Bachelor of Science degree in health-care administration in as little as fifteen months if all course requirements are met satisfactorily.

Beginning in the fall quarter 2001, students may complete an accelerated Bachelor of Science degree in business administration through the distance learning options.

Academic Programs

Each department has identified Program/Major Competencies that are developed during the required courses in that program or major. These competencies are measured during the program/major course work, and statistics are compiled and distributed to faculty members in the department. Faculty members then make adjustments to the course work, lesson plans, textbooks, assignments, etc., in order to increase the students' level of understanding of the Program/Major Competencies. These changes are documented and maintained by the Assessment Coordinator. The Program/Major Competencies for each department are listed in the course catalog with the curriculum for that program/major.

Academic Facilities

The University offers spacious classroom and lab facilities that complement the library, recreation center, and student services center.

Costs

Tuition and fees for the University of Northwestern Ohio for 2004–05 average $2550 per quarter, while room costs are $800 per quarter. Books, lab fees, and supplies vary with each major.

Financial Aid

Grants are financial aid awards that do not require repayment. They are available to eligible students usually based upon financial need. The Federal Pell Grant can provide financial support to students who have the highest financial need. Students can apply for the Federal Pell Grant by completing the Free Application for Federal Student Aid (FAFSA). Federal Supplemental Educational Opportunity Grants (FSEOG) are another aid source for students with high need who are eligible for the Pell Grant. Students can apply for the FSEOG by completing the FAFSA. Priority is given to those students who apply by April 1. The Ohio Instructional Grant (OIG) is a state-funded grant available to eligible Ohio residents who demonstrate financial need. Students must be enrolled in an associate or baccalaureate degree program to receive the Ohio Instructional Grant. Students can apply for the OIG by completing the FAFSA. The Ohio Choice Grant is available for an Ohio resident who meets the following requirements: is a resident of Ohio, enrolled full-time, enrolled in a course of study leading to a baccalaureate degree, and has not enrolled as a full-time student in an institution of higher education on or prior to July 1, 1984. Students who meet these requirements can receive the Ohio Choice Grant automatically. There is no formal application for the Ohio Choice Grant, as the financial aid office verifies enrollment. Renewal of this award is based upon maintaining satisfactory academic progress and continuance by the Ohio Board of Regents.

Loans are available to eligible students or their parents through a variety of need-based and non-need-based programs. Typically, student loans are offered at low interest rates and need not be repaid while the student is enrolled at least half-time. Interest rates and repayment varies according to the terms of the individual programs. Most loans require the student to complete the FAFSA. The Federal Stafford Student Loan Program (subsidized) is a federal program that allows freshmen to borrow up to $2625 per year, sophomores up to $3500 per year, and juniors and seniors up to $5500 per year. Under this program, students are not charged any interest as long as they meet enrollment requirements (enrolled on at least a part-time basis). The interest rate is variable but is capped at 8.25 percent. Federal Unsubsidized Stafford Student Loans (dependent) are available to students who were either limited or determined to be ineligible for the Federal Subsidized Stafford Loan. The amounts per grade level are the same as for the Federal Subsidized Stafford Loan; however, the student is responsible for the interest charges while in school. Federal Unsubsidized Stafford Student Loans (independent) are the same as for dependent students. The amounts are up to $4000 for freshmen and sophomores and $5000 for juniors and seniors.

Federal PLUS loans (parent loans) are available to parents of dependent students to meet any costs that other financial aid does not cover. Repayment of PLUS loans usually begins within thirty days after the loan is fully disbursed by the lender. Family income is not a criterion in obtaining parental loans; a good credit history is required.

Admission Requirements

Applicants are interviewed by an Admissions Representative. During this interview, the representative explains the programs in detail, answers questions regarding the University, and discusses career opportunities.

Visitors to the University are welcome. General offices are open Monday through Friday from 8 a.m. to 5 p.m.; the admissions office is open also on Saturday from 9 a.m. to 2 p.m. or by appointment from September (Labor Day) through May (Memorial Day).

Applications for enrollment are completed by the applicants and forwarded to the administrative staff for review. After applicants go through the selection process, they are notified of acceptance or refusal within four weeks. If accepted, this notification indicates a conditional acceptance contingent upon final transcripts after graduation from high school. At the time of application, a $50 application fee must be paid. ACT scores are recommended but not required.

Students are accepted at the University on one of two levels. The first is full acceptance, which means that no restrictions are placed upon the students. The second is conditional, which means that students are being accepted for one academic quarter/session on the condition that normal scholastic progress is achieved.

Students are admitted at the beginning of each term, according to the dates in the catalog. Students may not begin after the first week of classes. Only students who are graduates of an accredited high school or its equivalent are eligible to be awarded a diploma or degree by the University. Students must have a high school diploma or a GED before they may begin classes, unless they are in an early admissions or postsecondary options program. Students who have been home-schooled must also present proof of graduation and other appropriate documentation.

Application and Information

To be considered for admission to the University of Northwestern Ohio, a prospective student must submit an application along with a $50 application fee. The prospective student must also submit a signed transcript release form.

For more information, students should contact:

Office of Admissions
University of Northwestern Ohio
1441 North Cable Road
Lima, Ohio 45808
Telephone: 419-998-3120
E-mail: Info@unoh.edu
World Wide Web: http://www.unoh.edu

UNIVERSITY OF OREGON

EUGENE, OREGON

The University

The University of Oregon (UO), an internationally recognized research university committed to liberal arts and sciences education and career preparation, is known as a rising star in the academic world. The UO is among the smallest public universities in the Association of American Universities—one of the most prestigious associations of colleges and universities in the world. Five generations of teachers have studied at the University of Oregon since its founding more than 125 years ago. Today's students have access to a broad curriculum and internationally recognized researchers and scholars. The 295-acre campus is large enough for students to experience a comprehensive research university yet small enough to foster personal interaction with the faculty. The University of Oregon provides a rich and unique environment for discovery.

In fall 2002, approximately 20,044 undergraduates enrolled at the UO. Almost one fourth of the student body is from outside the state of Oregon. Of the total number of students, 13 percent are members of minority groups, and 7 percent (nearly 1,400 students) are international students from seventy-eight countries.

The UO offers students more than 250 different student organizations, including political and environmental groups, professional organizations, cultural heritage organizations, religious groups, and service programs. Intercollegiate athletics, club sports, and intramurals offer students several levels at which to participate in athletics. The University is a member of the PAC-10 Conference (NCAA Division I) and sponsors ten women's teams, including basketball, volleyball, and soccer, and seven men's teams, including football, tennis, and golf. The Outdoor Program takes advantage of the University's unique location and offers a host of wilderness adventures to students. *Sports Afield* rated the UO the nation's best university for all-around outdoor activities. The University's School of Music hosts the internationally acclaimed Oregon Bach Festival and presents more than 250 concerts and recitals by visiting artists, faculty members, and students each year. Three theaters on campus offer a full range of productions produced by both faculty members and students. The University of Oregon is also home to a Museum of Natural History and a Museum of Art (UOMA). Recognized for its collections of Asian and Pacific Northwest art, UOMA is the largest art museum between Portland and Sacramento and is an educational resource to the University, the Willamette Valley, and the state of Oregon.

Location

The 295-acre campus is located in the center of Eugene (population 136,490), a city known for its commitment to individuality, in the heart of the Willamette Valley. Both the Willamette and McKenzie Rivers run right through town, bordered by more than 250 miles of running trails and paved bike paths. Campus buildings date from 1876, when Deady Hall opened, to 1999, when renovation of the Recreation and Fitness Center and construction of the new William Knight School of Law building were completed. The Pacific Ocean is a 1-hour drive west of Eugene, and the Cascade Mountains are a 1-hour drive east. Eugene is served by several major airlines and is on the main north-south Amtrak line, which runs between Seattle and San Diego.

Majors and Degrees

The University is organized into the College of Arts and Sciences and six professional schools and colleges (School of Architecture and Allied Arts, Lundquist College of Business, School of Law, College of Education, School of Journalism and Communication, and School of Music). The College of Arts and Sciences serves as a base for a liberal arts education and offers undergraduate majors in anthropology, Asian studies, biochemistry, biology (with concentrations including marine biology), chemistry, Chinese, classical civilization, classics, comparative literature, computer and information science, computer and information technology, dental hygiene*, dentistry*, East Asian studies, economics (with concentrations including business economics), engineering*, English, environmental sciences, environmental studies, ethnic studies, European studies, exercise and movement science, film studies, folklore, forensic science*, French, general science, geography, geological sciences, German, Greek, health sciences*, history, humanities, independent study, international studies, Italian, Japanese, Judaic studies, Latin, Latin American studies, law*, linguistics, mathematics, mathematics and computer science, medical technology*, medicine*, medieval studies, nursing*, occupational therapy*, optometry*, peace studies, pharmacy*, philosophy, physical therapy*, physician assistant studies*, physics (emphasis in astronomy), podiatry*, political science, psychology, religious studies, Romance languages, Russian, Russian and East European studies, Scandinavian studies, second-language acquisition and teaching*, social work*, sociology, Southeast Asian studies, Spanish, theater arts, veterinary medicine*, and women's and gender studies. Preparatory programs in the College of Arts and Sciences include business administration, dentistry, engineering, forensic science, health sciences, law, library science, medical technology, medicine, nursing, occupational therapy, optometry, pharmacy, physical therapy, physician assistant studies, podiatry, social work, teacher education, and veterinary medicine.

The School of Architecture and Allied Arts offers degree programs in architecture, art, art history, community arts, ceramics, fibers, historic preservation, interior architecture, landscape architecture, metalsmithing and jewelry, multimedia, multimedia design, painting, photography, planning, public policy and management, printmaking, sculpture, and visual design. The Lundquist College of Business undergraduate program ranks in the top 2 percent of all public universities in the United States, offering a major in business administration with concentrations in corporate accounting, entrepreneurship and small business, finance, management, marketing, and sports marketing. The School of Journalism and Communication is nationally accredited and offers journalism majors in advertising, electronic media, communication studies, magazine journalism, news-editorial journalism, and public relations. The School of Education offers majors in communication disorders and sciences, educational studies, family and human services, special education, and teacher education*. The School of Music offers degrees in dance, jazz studies, and music (with concentrations in music composition, music education, music education: elementary education, music performance, and music theory). An * denotes preparatory programs.

Academic Program

Regardless of their major, students are required to complete general requirements. Students spend about one third of their academic careers on each of three areas of course work: the general requirements, requirements for their major, and their electives or the requirements for completing a minor or a second major. The University is on a quarter system.

Small learning communities are available for new students: Freshman Interest Groups (FIGs) allow a small group of freshmen interested in the same academic area to share enrollment in three related courses. Freshman Seminars are small-group discussion courses taught by some of the University's most outstanding faculty members. Pathways are carefully designed one- or two-year groups of integrated courses that satisfy general education requirements, develop academic skills, and emulate a small-college experience.

Off-Campus Programs

The UO offers students eighty different overseas opportunities in fifty countries that include Australia, Austria, Belize, Botswana, Cameroon, China, Costa Rica, Cote d'Ivoire, Cuba, the Czech Republic, Denmark, Ecuador, England, Finland, France, Germany, Ghana, Greece, Hungary, India, Israel, Italy, Jamaica, Japan, Jordan, Kenya, Madagascar, Mali, Mexico, Morocco, New Zealand, Norway, Poland, Russia, Scotland, Senegal, South Africa, South Korea, Spain, Sweden, Tanzania, Thailand, Turkey, Uganda, Vietnam, Zimbabwe, and the newly independent states of the former USSR. Students may study for a maximum of one year at a university overseas, earning UO course credit. The University also participates in the National Student Exchange program, through which students may attend any of 173 colleges or universities in another state and pay that state's resident tuition.

Academic Facilities

The University of Oregon library system consists of the Knight Library, law library, and four branch libraries (science, mathematics, architecture and allied arts, and map and aerial photography). The library system has more than 2 million volumes and subscribes to more than 17,000 journals.

University Computing provides central computing facilities and services, including the VMS cluster for interactive research and several instructional and open-access laboratories that provide connection to network resources. The Yamada Language Center is equipped with state-of-the-art computer-aided audio-visual equipment.

Costs

Resident undergraduate tuition for the 2003–04 academic year was $4527 and nonresident undergraduate tuition was $15,961. On-campus residence halls, including room and board, cost $6875 per academic year for multiple housing.

Financial Aid

Financial aid is available in the form of grants, loans, and/or work-study. To qualify, students must file the Free Application for Federal Student Aid (FAFSA). To be considered for financial aid at the UO, students must have applied for admission to the University and should indicate the UO as one of their first six choices. The UO awards financial aid based on individual need. Scholarships are awarded through the University, academic departments, and private sources. The general University scholarship application is due by January 15. For information on financial aid or scholarships and for applications, students should contact the Office of Student Financial Aid, 1278 University of Oregon, or call 800-760-6955 (toll-free).

For those seeking employment on or off campus, the Office of Student Employment provides several services, both for students who qualify for work-study and for those who do not qualify.

Faculty

At the UO, the student-teacher ratio is 18:1 and the median class size is 23 students.

Students have access to teachers recognized for their outstanding teaching skills and who are renowned for original research. Among them are winners of every major UO teaching award and every major recognition given for research and scholarship, including the Fulbright, Woodrow Wilson, Guggenheim, National Science Foundation, American Council of Learned Societies, and National Endowment for the Humanities awards, as well as membership in the National Academy of Sciences.

Student Government

The Associated Students of the University of Oregon (ASUO) administers a budget of $8.2 million, financing a broad range of academic, political, ethnic, religious, and recreational programs. The ASUO is part of the governing body of the University and also works as a lobbying organization at the state and national levels.

Admission Requirements

To be considered for admission, students must have a minimum high school GPA of 3.0, be a graduate of a standard or accredited high school, and submit SAT I or ACT scores. For guaranteed admission, applicants must have a minimum high school GPA of 3.25, have at least sixteen total college-preparatory units, and meet the other admission requirements.

Required college-preparatory courses include English, four years (English language, literature, speaking and listening, writing); mathematics, three years (first-year algebra, two additional years of college-preparatory mathematics); science, two years; social science, three years (one year of U.S. history, one year of global studies such as world history or geography, one elective); and a second language (two years in one language).

For students who meet the minimum admission standards, UO next looks at such factors as the quality of course work, grade trend, class rank, and senior-year course work. Academic potential and special talents are also considered.

Students with a GPA below 3.0 or less than 16 total academic units must submit a one-page personal statement with their application.

To be considered as a transfer student, a student must have earned 36 or more quarter hours (24 semester hours) of college transfer credit and have a minimum GPA of 2.25 if an Oregon resident, or 2.5 if a nonresident. Transfer students must have completed one college-level English composition course and one college-level math course (with a prerequisite of intermediate algebra or above) with a grade of C or better. Transfer applicants who do not meet regular admission requirements may be admitted on a special basis and should contact the Office of Admissions for information.

Applicants must submit an application with a $50 nonrefundable application fee, transcripts from each high school and/or college or university attended, and, for freshmen, SAT I or ACT scores.

A campus visit is the best way to decide whether the University of Oregon is right for a student.

Application and Information

Students may apply any time after September 1 for the following academic year. The freshman application deadline is January 15. The transfer application deadline is May 15. Students planning to enter programs in architecture, fine and applied arts, interior architecture, landscape architecture, music, or the Clark Honors College should inquire directly to the appropriate department or to the Office of Admissions for early deadlines.

For information and an application, students should contact:

Office of Admissions
1217 University of Oregon
Eugene, Oregon 97403-1217
Telephone: 541-346-3201
800-BE-A-DUCK (toll-free)
E-mail: uoadmit@uoregon.edu
World Wide Web: http://admissions.uoregon.edu

UNIVERSITY OF PITTSBURGH AT BRADFORD

BRADFORD, PENNSYLVANIA

The University

The University of Pittsburgh at Bradford (Pitt-Bradford) was founded in 1963. It is dedicated to providing students with a high-quality undergraduate education. Pitt-Bradford students enjoy the best of both worlds—a personalized undergraduate experience in a liberal arts college setting, coupled with the prestigious Pitt degree and the affiliation with an internationally recognized university. The University of Pittsburgh at Bradford is committed to preparing professionals in the liberal arts tradition.

Pitt-Bradford is noted for its dedicated and highly qualified faculty and staff, its strong academic and professional programs, and the attention it pays to students' individual needs. All of this leads to a prevailing sense of community. State-of-the-art computer equipment and modern facilities highlight the safe and friendly campus. In addition, the 1,200 Pitt-Bradford students have the distinct advantage of earning nationally recognized degrees at a cost that is less than that of 90 percent of private colleges nationwide.

Active learning is fostered through students' involvement in debates, discussions, individual and group research projects, computer-aided learning projects, art, field trips, drama, music, and a host of internships and independent study projects. On-campus apartment and town-house living provides a unique experience for students. Both types of living arrangements are complete with furnished rooms. Campus residents are required to participate in a board plan at the University dining hall. All students are guaranteed housing, and students are permitted to have cars on campus.

The Pitt-Bradford Sport and Fitness Center provides facilities for intercollegiate and intramural athletics as well as for a variety of recreational activities. A $9.3-million renovation and addition opened in 2002. Pitt-Bradford fields five men's and six women's NCAA Division III intercollegiate teams.

Location

The University of Pittsburgh at Bradford is located near the Allegheny National Forest in northwestern Pennsylvania. The 125-acre campus is 80 miles south of Buffalo and 160 miles northeast of Pittsburgh. The population of the Bradford region is approximately 22,000. Many national and international firms are located in Bradford, including Zippo Manufacturing and Dresser Manufacturing. Outdoor recreational opportunities such as hiking, camping, hunting, boating, fishing, and downhill and cross-country skiing are abundant. Pitt-Bradford is easily accessible by both air and ground transportation.

Majors and Degrees

Pitt-Bradford offers four-year majors in administration of justice, athletic training, biology, business management, chemistry, communications (radio and television), computer science, economics, education, English, environmental studies, geology and environmental science, history/political science, human relations, mathematics, nursing, physical sciences, psychology, public relations, radiological sciences, social sciences, sociology, sport and recreation management, sports medicine, and writing. Many of these majors prepare students for graduate study in dental medicine, law, medicine, optometry, physical therapy, and veterinary medicine. Students in a variety of majors can also choose to earn elementary or secondary education certification or school nursing certification.

Engineering (chemical, civil, computer, electrical, industrial, manufacturing, mechanical, and petroleum) are available at Pitt-Bradford for the first two years of study. The remainder of the program must be completed at the Pittsburgh campus.

Associate degrees are available in information systems and nursing (RN).

Pitt-Bradford offers a 3-4 program with the University of Pittsburgh School of Dental Medicine and the Pennsylvania College of Optometry, where students spend their first three years at Pitt-Bradford and spend the remaining four years at the appropriate graduate school.

Pitt-Bradford offers the first two years of preprofessional study for the doctorate in pharmacy. The final four years are completed at the Pittsburgh campus, where admission is competitive. Qualified high school seniors may be guaranteed admission to Pittsburgh's School of Pharmacy following successful completion of the preprofessional years at Pitt-Bradford.

Academic Program

Pitt-Bradford's academic programs are designed to prepare students for rewarding careers. The programs emphasize communications and critical-thinking skills and promote active learning through internships, field experiences, and collaborative faculty-student research. To earn a bachelor's degree, students must complete between 120 and 128 credit hours, depending on the program. To earn the associate degree, students must complete 60 to 70 credit hours.

In the business management program there is a strong teaching emphasis on real-world applications, and courses frequently involve cases drawn from actual business situations. Students may select a concentration in accounting, finance, international business, management information systems, or marketing. A new specialization in information technology is also available.

In the communication arts and humanities, Pitt-Bradford students in the communications, English, public relations, and writing programs gain experience by working on the staff of *The Source*, the student newspaper; participating in WDRQ, the college radio station; and publishing their works in *Baily's Beads*, the student literary magazine. Communication arts students utilize other excellent facilities on campus, including a television studio, an electronic newsroom, a radio room, and a video editing room with analog and digital technology, which are all located in the new, state-of-the-art Blaisdell Hall.

Students interested in education may choose between elementary education and secondary education certification. Secondary education certification is available in biology, business, chemistry, citizenship education, communication, Earth and space science, English, environmental education, general science, mathematics, and social science.

The mathematics, computer science, and engineering department provides numerous opportunities for Pitt-Bradford students. Students interested in mathematics may choose from secondary education, applied mathematics, and concentrations in actuarial science and physics. Computer science offers a variety of two-year and four-year programs, which are supported by the Pitt network and the computer science lab.

In the natural sciences, students may major in biology, chemistry, environmental studies, geology and environmental science, physical sciences, psychology, sport and recreation management, and sports medicine. These programs have outstanding success rates for students pursuing postgraduate studies in the medical, dental, and other health-related fields. Pitt-Bradford is also the home of the Allegheny Institute of Natural History.

Pitt-Bradford offers a variety of educational programs in nursing. The Associate of Science in Nursing (A.S.N.) is a two-year program. The Bachelor of Science in Nursing (RN-B.S.N. completion) is an additional two-year program that builds directly upon the A.S.N. degree. The School Nurse Certification is also available for registered nurses interested in caring for children of all ages in the school setting.

In the social sciences, students have a wide range of academic opportunities. The social science programs prepare students for careers in government and nonprofit organizations or, alternatively, for graduate study or law school. The administration of justice major allows students to pursue their interests in the American justice system, law, corrections, and the court system. The human relations program teaches behavioral sciences by combining course work in anthropology, psychology, and sociology.

Students who wish to pursue academic programs not completed at Pitt-Bradford may earn a maximum of 70 credits before relocating to another campus of the University. Students in arts and sciences have the opportunity to relocate if they are in good academic standing. Engineering students must maintain a minimum quality point average of 2.5.

Academic Facilities

In addition to the T. Edward and Tullah Hanley Library on campus, Pitt-Bradford students have online access to the entire University of Pittsburgh library system, which includes nearly 4 million bound volumes, 3.8 million microform holdings, and 24,000 periodical subscriptions. Swarts Hall houses Pitt-Bradford's modern nursing laboratory, a writing lab, and O'Kain Auditorium, which is a 300-seat center for plays, concerts, and lectures. Fisher Hall, the science and computer science building, contains modern lab equipment and computer-aided learning centers. Blaisdell Hall, the fine arts center, houses television, radio, and art studios.

Costs

For 2003–04, tuition for full-time students is $4307 per semester for Pennsylvania residents and $8963 for out-of-state students. Nursing tuition is $5542 per semester for Pennsylvania residents and $11,455 for out-of-state students. Room and board expenses are $6030 per year. Other costs include fees of $650 per year. Books and supplies cost approximately $400 per term.

Financial Aid

Ninety-three percent of all Pitt-Bradford students receive some form of financial aid. A variety of loans, grants, scholarships, and work-study opportunities are awarded through the University. Applicants for all types of need-based financial aid must submit the Free Application for Federal Student Aid (FAFSA) by the March 1 priority deadline preceding the academic year for which assistance is requested. All Pennsylvania residents seeking aid will be considered for Pennsylvania Higher Education Assistance Agency (PHEAA) grants by completing the FAFSA. Out-of-state residents should check with their state agency for state grant requirements. Merit-based scholarships, awarded at entry, are based on academic achievement. Financial aid is also available through the University ROTC program. Veterans are encouraged to utilize VA educational benefits.

Faculty

Pitt-Bradford's 75 full-time faculty members hold doctorates and master's degrees from some of the most prestigious universities in the nation, including Cornell, Harvard, Stanford, and the University of Pittsburgh. Teaching is the primary activity of the faculty, and personal attention is emphasized in the classroom. Faculty members welcome the chance to meet with their students and know them by name. The student-faculty ratio is 13:1.

Student Government

The Student Government Association (SGA) plays an important role in college life. The SGA is responsible for chartering and funding more than thirty college clubs and organizations. The Student Activities Council branch of the SGA is responsible for scheduling diversified entertainment for Pitt-Bradford students throughout the year.

Admission Requirements

In reviewing applications, the Admissions Committee considers three primary factors in evaluating an applicant's ability to succeed in college work: the high school record, the results of standardized tests, and the high school's recommendations. In addition, personal qualifications, extracurricular activities, and potential to contribute to the college community may be taken into consideration.

Application and Information

Pitt-Bradford has a rolling admissions program, and students may apply at any time. All candidates are notified as soon as action is taken on their application.

Candidates for admission should complete and return the application with a nonrefundable $35 fee. Students must also submit an official copy of their high school record and scores from either the Scholastic Assessment Test (SAT I) or American College Testing's examination (ACT). In addition to fulfilling the above requirements, transfer applicants must submit all official college transcripts and must have a minimum cumulative grade point average of 2.0. The admissions office welcomes campus visits by students and their families; such visits help students arrive at a final decision about Pitt-Bradford. Interviews and tours are scheduled Monday through Friday, 9 a.m. to 4 p.m., and on selected Saturdays. Arrangements for these visits can be made by contacting the Office of Admissions.

For more information on the financial aid programs available, students should visit the Pitt-Bradford financial aid Web site, listed below, or contact the Financial Aid Office.

For application forms, catalogs, and further information, students should contact:

Office of Admissions
University of Pittsburgh at Bradford
300 Campus Drive
Bradford, Pennsylvania 16701-2898
Telephone: 814-362-7555
800-872-1787 (toll-free)
World Wide Web: http://www.upb.pitt.edu

The University of Pittsburgh at Bradford.

UNIVERSITY OF PITTSBURGH AT GREENSBURG

GREENSBURG, PENNSYLVANIA

The University

Established in 1963, the present campus is now home to a four-year, degree-granting, residential undergraduate college of the University of Pittsburgh. Accredited by the Middle States Association of Colleges and Schools, the University of Pittsburgh at Greensburg (UPG) offers twenty baccalaureate degrees in both liberal arts and career-oriented programs. In addition to its bachelor's degree programs, UPG offers relocation options in baccalaureate programs that may be completed at other Pitt campuses after an initial year or two at Greensburg. The beautiful 217-acre streamside campus is situated in a wooded suburban location, once the setting of a private estate.

There are 1,915 students currently enrolled. The majority are Pennsylvania residents, but eight other states and several countries are also represented. There are more than 600 students living on campus.

In 1982, UPG acquired University Court (three apartment buildings) to house students on campus; each apartment in the complex accommodates 4 students. A Faculty Office Building was constructed in 1987. Both Chambers Hall (with a gymnasium, an indoor track, racquetball courts, dining facilities, offices, and a bookstore) and Robertshaw Hall (a residence hall) were completed in 1989. The McKenna Computer Center was doubled in size when it underwent major rebuilding in both 1989 and 1997. Millstein Library, a library and administration building, was completed in 1995. College Hall (a residence hall) opened in 1996.

Terra Rossetti House, a residence for internationally minded students, and three newly constructed garden-style apartment buildings were first occupied in August 1999. Three additional garden-style apartment buildings were completed for occupancy in August 2001. Campus housing standards encompass private or semiprivate rooms and private or semiprivate baths. All residence facilities come equipped with basic cable service for television, microwave ovens (along with full-size ranges in all apartment units), refrigerators, local telephone service, and computers, each connected through a high-speed Ethernet port to both the Internet and the University-wide network (Pittnet).

Location

UPG is located a little more than 2 miles southeast of the city of Greensburg (population 23,000) and about 35 miles southeast of Pittsburgh. Greensburg is the home of the Westmoreland Museum of Art, the Westmoreland Symphony Orchestra, and the Westmoreland Choral Society. Nearby recreational facilities include the Kirk Nevin Recreation Center (ice-skating, tennis, and swimming), Mt. Odin Park (golf), and Laurel Mountain, Seven Springs, and Hidden Valley (ski resorts).

Majors and Degrees

Four-year offerings include the following: the Bachelor of Arts degree in administration of justice (corrections and law enforcement options available), American studies, anthropology, communication, English literature, English writing (including creative writing, journalism, and public relations/advertising options), history, a humanities concentration, interdisciplinary arts, political science, a self-designed major, and a social science concentration; the Bachelor of Science degree in biological sciences (environmental science and preprofessional options available), business management (a management/information systems option is available), management/accounting, mathematics (applied), a natural science concentration, psychology, and a self-designed major. Four years of preparation are offered in such preprofessional areas as chiropractic, dental medicine, education, law, medicine, occupational therapy, optometry, physical therapy, physician assistant studies, podiatry, and veterinary medicine. Two years of preparation for the University of Pittsburgh's upper-division programs in child development and child care, clinical dietetics and nutrition, health information management, pharmacy, and social work are also available. Guaranteed/conditional admission is available to qualified students in selected areas. The first year for all of the University of Pittsburgh School of Engineering programs can be completed at Greensburg. In addition, all four years of the Bachelor of Science in Information Science degree program may be completed under the auspices of the Pittsburgh campus–based School of Information Sciences.

Academic Program

The entire degree program is designed to provide students with a sound program of general education, give them the breadth of learning necessary in the modern world of specialized education, and give them the depth of learning required for a vocation.

In addition to completing specific courses in their major, students must also complete general requirements. The total number of credits required for UPG's baccalaureate degree programs is 120 (126 for accounting and business management, 123 for management/information systems).

The University of Pittsburgh at Greensburg, with the diversified backgrounds of its student population, utilizes the general examinations of CLEP as a means of evaluating adult candidates for advanced placement after admission to the college. The general examinations consist of five areas: English composition, humanities, social sciences, natural sciences, and mathematics.

Students who have participated in the Advanced Placement (AP) Program of the College Board may request consideration for college credit from UPG by having the Educational Testing Service forward their AP scores to the Office of Admissions.

The University calendar consists of three terms that run from August to December (fall term), January to April (spring term), and May to August (summer term). The fall and spring terms comprise the typical academic year. A number of shorter summer sessions run concurrently with the summer term.

Off-Campus Programs

Study abroad and Pitt's Semester at Sea programs afford interested students a wealth of educational and experiential possibilities. A wide range of local internships are designed to meld traditional academics with practical experience.

Academic Facilities

The campus evolved around Lynch Hall, now an administration building but formerly the Tudor mansion of the original estate. Powers Hall, the second home of the library, was built in 1974 and underwent major reconstruction, enlargement, and conversion to classrooms in 1996.

The McKenna Computer Center provides all students with easy access to a wide range of local Windows 2000, Windows XP, and UNIX applications through the high-speed University-wide Pittnet, through which students may also access the Internet and remote VMS and UNIX applications. Software packages include graphical Internet access tools, word processing, database, spreadsheet, graphics, statistics, CAD, communications, and courseware applications. The center also provides high-quality laser printing and color-scanning services.

The Millstein Library houses an expanding collection of more than 75,000 items, including books, microfilm, videotapes, records, and compact discs and subscribes to more than 400 periodicals. Students are able to search PittCat, the University's online catalog, which has access to more than 3 million titles, and the University of Pittsburgh's Digital Library, which contains hundreds of databases on a variety of subjects. Access to the Internet is provided on all library devices through the University's computer system. Interlibrary loan service with other Pitt campuses is also available.

Smith Hall was added in 1976 and underwent major renovations and enlargement in 1997. The building contains classrooms, the 270-seat Ferguson Theater, faculty offices, and labs for anthropology, biology, chemistry, physics, and engineering. The Natural Sciences and New Technologies (NSNT) Academic Village has a separate common facility, the Lyceum, where commuters and residents can met and participate in various activities.

Additional building and renovations are planned for the future.

Costs

For the 2003–04 academic year (two terms), full-time students who are Pennsylvania residents paid $9214 for tuition and general required fees; out-of-state residents paid $18,526. The 2003–04 academic-year room and board charges ranged from $6780 to $8790.

In 2003–04, part-time students who were Pennsylvania residents paid $296 per credit; out-of-state students paid $610 per credit. General required fees for part-time students were $110 for each term of enrollment.

Financial Aid

About 67 percent of UPG's students receive some form of financial aid, including Federal Pell Grants, Federal Supplemental Educational Opportunity Grants, Federal Work-Study, Federal Perkins Loans, Federal Stafford Loans, Federal PLUS Loans, and Pennsylvania Higher Education Assistance Agency Grants. University Scholarships based on academic achievement are also available.

All applicants for financial aid must complete the Free Application for Federal Student Aid (FAFSA) and the UPG Financial Aid Application Supplement. They should also apply for a state grant according to the procedures established by their own state of residence.

Faculty

The faculty includes 136 members, 53 of whom teach part-time. Eleven of the full-time faculty members are winners of the prestigious Chancellor's Outstanding Teaching Award. Most have earned their doctorate at one of a number of distinguished colleges and universities. They continue to author books, publish their work in journals, and present papers at national and international conferences.

Student Government

The Student Government Association (SGA) is composed of elected representatives from each class and provides students with an opportunity to participate in University planning and decision making. The SGA also serves as the principal forum for student views. The Activities Board similarly provides an opportunity for students to plan, promote, and produce a variety of educational, social, and recreational programs.

Admission Requirements

Applicants for full-time admission should have completed at least 15 units of credit in college-preparatory courses, taken in grades 9 through 12, including English, 4 units; algebra I; algebra II or geometry; history, 1 unit; laboratory science, 1 unit; and 7 additional units in any combination of those subject areas or a foreign language. Some students who have not completed 3 years of the same foreign language in high school may be required to take 1 year of a foreign language at UPG.

Students interested in engineering should have taken 2 years of algebra; ½ year of trigonometry; and 1 year each of plane geometry, chemistry, and physics.

Applicants for full-time admission must also submit the results of the SAT I or ACT.

Part-time admission is open to high school graduates or those who hold recognized equivalency certificates such as the GED.

Application and Information

An application fee of $35 must accompany the application. High school transcripts (as well as college transcripts for those who previously attended another postsecondary institution) must also be submitted. Full- or part-time admission is offered for the fall term (September through December), spring term (January through April), and summer term (May through August).

To obtain application materials or further information, students should call 724-836-9880. To arrange a meeting with an admissions officer and/or a tour appointment, students should call 724-836-9881.

For more information, students should contact:

Office of Admissions and Financial Aid
University of Pittsburgh at Greensburg
1150 Mt. Pleasant Road
Greensburg, Pennsylvania 15601-5860
Telephone: 724-836-9880
E-mail: upgadmit@pitt.edu
World Wide Web: http://www.upg.pitt.edu

View from center campus toward Millstein Library, one of the newest additions to the growing campus.

UNIVERSITY OF PITTSBURGH AT JOHNSTOWN

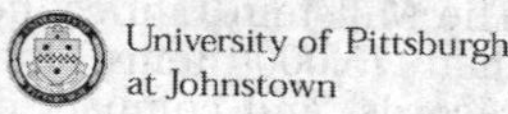

JOHNSTOWN, PENNSYLVANIA

The University

Founded in 1927 as one of the first regional campuses of a major university in the United States, the University of Pittsburgh at Johnstown (Pitt-Johnstown) is a four-year, degree-granting, fully accredited, coeducational, residential undergraduate college of the University of Pittsburgh. With 2,800 well-qualified full-time students and a suburban campus of striking beauty, Pitt-Johnstown combines the strong academic reputation and outstanding resources of a major research university with the personal appeal of a smaller college.

There are thirty-one campus buildings, including a library, student union, sports center, performing arts center, and chapel, in addition to a 40-acre nature preserve and outdoor recreation areas. The college has five different styles of housing, including residence halls, small-group lodges, apartments, and a new state-of-the-art living/learning center. An aquatic center includes a weight room and exercise rooms.

In addition to the undergraduate degrees listed below, the University also offers postbaccalaureate nondegree teaching certificates.

Location

Located in a suburb of Johnstown, a city of 40,000 only 70 miles east of Pittsburgh, the spacious 650-acre campus is the third-largest in Pennsylvania and is recognized as one of the most attractive in the eastern states. The University's facilities blend easily with the rustic wooded setting, creating a campus of distinctive natural beauty. Shops, entertainment, and cultural activities are conveniently available, and the city is in the heart of Pennsylvania ski country.

Majors and Degrees

Pitt-Johnstown offers the Bachelor of Arts (B.A.) degree in American studies, business (accounting, economics, finance, and management), communication, composite writing, creative writing, economics, English literature, environmental studies, geography, history, humanities, journalism, secondary education (citizenship education with several social science strands, communication, and English), social sciences, sociology, and theater arts. The Bachelor of Science (B.S.) degree is awarded in biology, chemistry, civil engineering technology, computer science, ecology, electrical engineering technology, elementary education, geology, mathematics, mechanical engineering technology, natural sciences, psychology, and secondary education (biology, chemistry, earth and space science, general science, mathematics, and physics).

An Associate of Science (A.S.) degree is available in emergency medical services, respiratory care, and surgical technology.

Dual teaching certification and dual education degree programs are offered. A cooperative program with a local hospital allows students to combine a B.S. in biology with a certificate in medical technology. A certificate in international studies can be earned in conjunction with any major.

With the assistance of academic advisers, Pitt-Johnstown students can construct interdisciplinary majors, double majors, and self-designed majors. They can also develop their specific fields of study with preprofessional preparation for advanced study in such areas as dental medicine, law, medicine, optometry, physical therapy, and veterinary medicine.

Academic Program

Pitt-Johnstown seeks to provide contemporary, innovative academic programs that combine the practical concerns of career orientation with the spirit of inquiry and the traditional goals of higher education. Practical experience of all types is encouraged, including campus activities, community service, media work, and research projects. The Freshman Seminar series introduces freshmen to rigorous intellectual work through small-group elective seminars. Students who show extra potential receive special advising, registration privileges, and scholarships through the President's Scholars Program. Students may complete preliminary requirements for upper-division programs that require relocation to the Pittsburgh campus, including requirements for programs in pharmacy and other health-related areas. In some programs, guaranteed admission is offered to qualified students.

Off-Campus Programs

The Semester-at-Sea allows students to pursue course work while traveling the world on an ocean liner. The study-abroad program, in conjunction with the University Center for International Studies (UCIS), is a program that promotes the integration and synthesis of international knowledge. A wide range of internship projects on campus and at nearby sites is also offered.

Academic Facilities

In addition to the more than 145,500 volumes housed in the Pitt-Johnstown library, students have direct request and retrieval access to the 3 million volumes contained in the University Libraries system. The college maintains several computer classrooms and laboratories equipped with more than 150 computers, including Windows-based PC's, Macintosh computers, and powerful UNIX-based workstations. Computer classrooms offer projection facilities, and laboratories provide access to laser printers and state-of-the-art color scanners. All computers at Pitt-Johnstown are connected to the Internet, allowing students access to information from around the world and to a large suite of software shared with the University's other campuses. In addition to microcomputer facilities, which include both UNIX and VMS time-sharing systems, Pitt-Johnstown maintains a pool of high-speed modems that support off-campus access to the network. To ensure compatibility with the latest technology, computers are replaced on a four-year cycle.

Costs

For full-time students in arts and sciences and education programs, 2003–04 tuition was $4307 per fifteen-week term for Pennsylvania residents and $8963 for nonresidents. For full-time students in engineering programs, tuition was $4625 per fifteen-week term for Pennsylvania residents and $9816 for nonresidents. Room and board expenses were $2880 per term. Other costs included an activities and facilities fee of $158 per term and a $130 per term computing service fee. A $10 fee was charged for each physical education course. Books and supplies were estimated at $400 each term. All costs are subject to change.

Financial Aid

Nearly 80 percent of all Pitt-Johnstown students receive some form of financial assistance. In addition to the Pennsylvania Higher Education Assistance Agency (PHEAA) state grant, the Federal Pell Grant, and the Federal Stafford Student Loan, a variety of loans, grants, scholarships, and student-employment positions are awarded through the University. Applicants for all types of financial aid must submit the Free Application for Federal Student Aid (FAFSA) by April 1 prior to the academic year for which assistance is requested.

Faculty

Holding degrees from more than 100 distinguished American and international universities, the 136 full-time members of the Johnstown faculty represent a broad diversity in background and experience. Personally committed to undergraduate teaching, each faculty member is actively involved in a full range of intellectual activities as well as student advising, curriculum development, and the extracurricular and cultural life of the University community. Classes at Pitt-Johnstown are small, and opportunities for faculty-student interaction outside of the classroom are plentiful. Personalized instruction is emphasized. Full-time faculty members teach almost all courses. The student-faculty ratio is 19:1, and the typical class size is 25–30.

Student Government

The Student Senate plays a significant role in building cooperation among all members of the University community. It deals with matters affecting the entire student body and formally represents students in relations with the administration, faculty, and other nonstudent groups. The Programming Board, an administrative branch of the senate, schedules diversified entertainment.

Admission Requirements

All applicants for full-time study must have completed, or be in the process of completing, at least 15 units of work in an accredited secondary school. In addition, candidates must take either the SAT I or the ACT. Admission decisions are made after careful study of each applicant's high school record, performance on college entrance examinations, high school recommendations, and personal qualifications. Of the 2002–03 freshmen, more than 80 percent ranked in the top half of their high school class. Interviews are not required; however, applicants are encouraged to arrange a visit to the campus by phoning or writing the Office of Admissions.

About 250 transfer students apply annually, and approximately 68 percent are accepted. Application requirements for transfer students include high school and college transcripts. Transfer students should have a minimum quality point average of 2.0.

High school graduates and transfer students must file an application, with a $35 fee, on forms provided by the school.

Application and Information

The candidate is notified as soon as action is taken on the application.

For more information about University of Pittsburgh at Johnstown, students should contact:

Office of Admissions
157 Blackington Hall
University of Pittsburgh at Johnstown
Johnstown, Pennsylvania 15904
Telephone: 814-269-7050
800-765-4875 (toll-free)
World Wide Web: http://www.upj.pitt.edu

UNIVERSITY OF PUGET SOUND

TACOMA, WASHINGTON

The University

Founded in 1888, the University of Puget Sound is an independent university committed to the liberal arts and sciences, superb teaching, and the recognition of each student as an individual. A nationally acclaimed teaching faculty, well-planned facilities, and a limited enrollment ensure excellence in education.

Puget Sound, the only national liberal arts college in western Washington, is one of only two independent colleges in Washington State to be granted a chapter by Phi Beta Kappa. A record number of Puget Sound graduates have received undergraduate and postgraduate honors, including Rhodes, National Science Foundation, Fulbright, Rotary, Watson, Phi Kappa Phi, Truman, Goldwater, Hertz, and National Endowment for the Humanities fellowships and scholarships.

In the fall of 2003, the University enrolled 2,600 students, with 75 percent of the freshman class coming from outside the state of Washington. In addition, forty-six states and sixteen other countries were represented in the student body. Puget Sound is a 24-hour-a-day, seven-day-a-week residential community. Students live in eleven residence halls, eight Greek-letter-society residences, and more than fifty University-owned houses on campus. Special theme houses and halls are available for students with common interests. The neighboring residential community provides many facilities for those who wish to live off campus. Nearly 30 percent of students belong to Greek letter organizations. State-of-the-art athletic facilities include Memorial Fieldhouse and Pamplin Fitness Center, Wallace Pool, Baker Stadium, an indoor climbing wall, and numerous varsity and intramural athletic fields.

Location

The campus is located in a quiet residential neighborhood in the historic North End of Tacoma. Thirty-five miles south of Seattle and easily accessible from Interstate 5, Tacoma is a dynamic city of 200,000 people. The University occupies thirty-nine buildings on a 97-acre parklike campus. The architecture is Tudor Gothic, with its distinctive red-brick pattern arches and porticoes. Located close to the shores of Puget Sound and a short distance from ski slopes and the Pacific Ocean, the University is also the center of much of Tacoma's cultural life. Tacoma also features Point Defiance Zoo and Aquarium, many parks, a public library system, museums, and hospitals.

Majors and Degrees

The University of Puget Sound offers more than fifty majors leading to the Bachelor of Arts, Bachelor of Science, and Bachelor of Music degrees. Academic programs are art, Asian studies (interdisciplinary emphasis), biology, business, chemistry, classics, communication, comparative sociology, computer science, computer science in business, economics, English, exercise science, foreign languages and literature (majors in French, German, international affairs, and Spanish; course offerings in Chinese, Greek, Japanese, and Latin), geology, history, international political economy, mathematics, music, natural science, philosophy, physics, politics and government, psychology, religion, and theater arts. Latin American studies, African-American studies, environmental studies, and women studies are minor-only programs. The introduction of a special interdisciplinary major allows exceptional students the opportunity to pursue a degree in a recognized interdisciplinary or emergent field.

The University offers a dual-degree program in engineering, leading to a joint Bachelor of Arts/Bachelor of Science degree in engineering. A Bachelor of Engineering degree may also be earned. Students in this program complete prerequisites in chemistry, mathematics/computer science, and physics, then transfer to an accredited engineering school for course work in chemical, civil, electrical, environmental, mechanical, or petroleum engineering, among others. Affiliated schools are Washington University in St. Louis, Columbia University, Duke University, and the University of Southern California. Graduate degrees offered include the Master of Occupational Therapy, Doctor of Physical Therapy, Master of Arts in Teaching, and Master of Education.

Academic Program

At the heart of the academic program is the core curriculum—eight course groupings around which major and elective studies are arranged over a four-year period. The emphasis throughout a student's undergraduate education is on the acquisition of intellectual skills: the ability to express oneself clearly, both orally and in writing; the ability to reason quantitatively; and the ability to think logically, critically, and independently. By mastering the literature and techniques of a specific academic major, the student learns to cultivate the unique power of his or her own mind and to respond vigorously, but humanely, to important social, moral, and intellectual challenges.

A particularly well-designed curriculum for the freshman year and a model program of academic advising and career counseling enable each student to develop his or her own skills and interests in preparation for a lifetime of creative work and leisure. The highly successful and award-winning student orientation process—Prelude, Passages and Perspectives—is a nine-day program that allows new students to become involved in writing and thinking seminars, academic workshops, community service, and a three-day excursion to the nearby Olympic Peninsula.

The academic year is divided into two semesters, beginning in late August and mid-January, and a thirteen-week summer session (two miniterms). A normal academic load is 4 units (typically four courses) per semester. Each unit of credit is equivalent to 6 quarter hours or 4 semester hours. Thirty-two units are required for graduation.

Off-Campus Programs

The University of Puget Sound offers an outstanding selection of international opportunities for its students and operates or offers programs in nearly sixty countries, including Australia, England, Scotland, Spain, France, Germany, Italy, Austria, China, Japan, Taiwan, Argentina, and Chile, among others. The Pacific Rim/Asia Study-Travel Program offers students an intense year of study and travel in six to eight Asian countries. A summer archaeological excavation in Greece rounds out the international opportunities at Puget Sound.

Puget Sound's location in one of the fastest-growing regions of the country places its internship program at the forefront of national liberal arts colleges. Opportunities for student research abound, as students may apply for summer research grants in the sciences, social sciences, humanities, and the arts.

Academic Facilities

Collins Memorial Library contains more than 544,528 volumes of books and periodicals plus a sizable collection of federal and

Washington State government publications, maps, microforms, videotapes, cassettes, compact discs, and other media materials. These resources are strengthened through participation in the Orbis Cascade Alliance, a consortium of twenty-seven public and private institutions of higher education in Oregon and Washington, with combined holdings of more than 22 million volumes. Among the other major academic facilities are Thompson Science Complex, Kittredge Art Gallery, the Concert Hall, Norton Clapp Theatre, Gordon D. Alcorn Arboretum, Lowry Wyatt Hall (completed in May 2000), and Slater Museum of Natural History.

Puget Sound, as a natural resource, provides students of environmental science and marine biology with a superb outdoor laboratory. A working relationship with Point Defiance Zoo and Aquarium, just minutes north of the campus, offers teaching and research opportunities in marine and biological sciences. Equipment and facilities in the Thompson Science Complex include a modern greenhouse; an observatory; an aquarium with a tidal cycle; a state-of-the-art genetics laboratory; a scanning electron microscope and a transmission electron microscope; ultraviolet, visible, fluorescence, infrared, and nuclear magnetic resonance spectrophotometric equipment; and a seismograph. Students also have access to human cadavers as learning tools. The University has special facilities for students of occupational and physical therapy, education, counseling, foreign languages, and psychology. The music building has twenty-two individual practice rooms.

All University residence halls and Greek houses are wired to provide students with instant access to the Internet and e-mail accounts. In addition, on-campus computer labs offer 24-hour access to these services.

Costs

Tuition and required student fees were $25,190 and $170, respectively, for the 2003–04 academic year. Room and board were $6400. It is estimated that an additional $3300 per year is adequate for books, laundry, and other essentials, including travel to and from home.

Financial Aid

Eighty-five percent of the University's students receive financial aid in one or a combination of the following forms: scholarships, grants, low-interest loans, and part-time employment. Most financial aid is awarded on the basis of demonstrated financial need, as determined through analysis of the Free Application for Federal Student Aid (FAFSA). In addition, the University's Financial Aid Office administers a scholarship program based solely on academic merit: the Wyatt ($9000), the Trustee ($8000), President's ($6000), and Dean's ($3000) Scholarships. Each award is renewable annually. Many other talent awards are available in the arts, selected academic areas, forensics, and leadership. Admission decisions are made independent of financial need, and all students, regardless of family income, are encouraged to apply for financial aid.

Faculty

Members of the faculty work closely with individual students both in the classroom and in student-originated research projects within and across the disciplines. Ninety-three percent of the faculty members teach full-time. Ninety-eight percent of tenured faculty members hold a Ph.D. or an equivalent terminal degree. In agreement with Ted Taranovski, professor of history, the faculty feels that the University of Puget Sound is "an institution geared to human beings—small enough to give one a sense of community and yet large enough to provide an excellent academic curriculum; it is not an impersonal machine where people become cogs." In recent years, professors at the University have been recognized for their academic and teaching achievements through awards and distinctions, including the Graves Award in the Humanities and fellowships from various organizations, including the National Endowment for the Humanities, the American Council of Learned Societies, and the Danforth Foundation. Recently, the Carnegie Foundation for the Advancement of Teaching named history professor Suzanne Barnett the Washington State Professor of the Year. Perhaps the best indicator of the faculty's expertise, however, lies in the comment made by a Puget Sound student: "The chance to get to know my professors has been one of the best experiences of my college education."

Student Government

Students find that participating in activities sponsored by the student government is an excellent way to learn outside the classroom and improve leadership abilities. Athletics include twenty-three varsity, various club, and numerous intramural teams. In addition, students are involved in numerous clubs and associations, such as forensics, theater, music, FM radio station, art and literary magazine, weekly newspaper, yearbook, Student Senate, religious groups, a variety of faculty and trustee committees, Black Student Union, Hui-O-Hawaii, Earth Activists, B-GLAD (Bisexuals, Gays, Lesbians, and Allies for Diversity), Asian Pacific American Student Union, Community for Hispanic Awareness, and Habitat for Humanity. Seventy-five percent of students participate in community service activities, one of the highest participation rates in the country.

Admission Requirements

Each applicant to the University of Puget Sound is considered individually and is admitted on the basis of his or her qualifications and achievements. In considering applicants for freshman admission, the Admission Committee evaluates the following: high school course selection, high school grade point average, rank in graduating class (if available), SAT I or ACT scores, a counselor's and an academic teacher's recommendations, an essay, a recommended interview, and extracurricular activities. College credit is awarded to students who have earned scores of 4 or higher on Advanced Placement examinations. Credit for a score of 3 is available for selected examinations only. Credit is also available for the International Baccalaureate examinations.

Application and Information

Prospective freshmen may apply for admission anytime after the beginning of the senior year in high school. An admission decision is generally made on or before March 15. The application preference deadline is February 1. Students who have decided that Puget Sound is their first-choice college may choose one of two early decision plans. Early Decision I has a November 15 application deadline, with admission and tentative financial aid notification by December 15. Early Decision II has a December 15 application deadline, with admission and tentative financial aid notification by January 15. Transfer students are admitted in both semesters and for the summer session as well. Students applying for transfer admission should request the *Application for Advanced Standing/Transfer Students*.

For more information about the University or for application materials, students should contact:

George H. Mills
Vice President for Enrollment
University of Puget Sound
1500 North Warner Street, #1062
Tacoma, Washington 98416-1062
Telephone: 253-879-3211
800-396-7191 (toll-free)
E-mail: admission@ups.edu
World Wide Web: http://www.ups.edu

UNIVERSITY OF REDLANDS
REDLANDS, CALIFORNIA

The University

The University of Redlands has, for more than ninety years, offered its select student body a tradition of superior liberal arts education. While students may select from a variety of programs that prepare them for professional or graduate school, the heart and foundation of Redlands is in liberal studies. Its outstanding faculty, educated in the world's finest colleges and universities, provides students with extraordinary opportunities for learning and growth through excellent teaching and close, informal interaction. Intense intellectual activity is balanced by opportunities for quiet reflection, fun, and recreation.

The University enrolls more than 2,000 students. Sixty-five percent of the freshman class comes from California and the remainder from forty-five other states and eighteen countries. In addition to a strong academic program in the liberal arts, the sciences, preprofessional programs, and the arts, many extracurricular programs are available to the student, including forensics, music, drama, dance, and athletics. Internships are available for students in many academic programs. The School of Music and the Glenn Wallichs Theatre provide a rich selection of cultural events throughout the year. Prominent speakers are invited to the campus each year to give major addresses and participate in classes and public discussion groups, and many social functions are organized by the Student Life Office and individual residence halls. Additional social opportunities are provided for interested students by local nonresidential fraternities and sororities. A special counseling center provides services in the area of career and personal counseling.

Eighty percent of the students live on campus in residence halls that offer a variety of accommodations, including single sex, coed by separate wings, and coed by alternate suites.

The University of Redlands is one of a select number of schools that have a chapter of Phi Beta Kappa, the nation's oldest and most prestigious academic honor society.

Master's programs are available at the University of Redlands in the fields of business, communicative disorders, education, geographic information systems, and music.

Location

The University is located in the city of Redlands within the San Bernardino Valley. Overlooking the 140-acre campus are the two highest mountains in southern California, Mt. San Gorgonio and Mt. San Bernardino, each more than 10,000 feet high. Redlands has a population of 64,000 and is situated at an elevation of 1,500 feet. Metropolitan Los Angeles to the west and Palm Springs to the east are both about an hour's drive away by freeway.

Majors and Degrees

The B.A. degree is offered in the academic areas of art history, Asian studies, biology, business administration, communicative disorders, creative writing, economics, English literature, environmental studies, French, German, government, history, international relations, music, philosophy, professional writing, psychology, religion, sociology/anthropology, Spanish, studio art, and theater arts. The B.S. degree is offered in accounting, biology, business administration, chemistry, computer science, economics, environmental management, environmental science, mathematics, and physics. The professional degree of Bachelor of Music (B.M.) is offered by the School of Music. Primary and secondary credentials are granted by the School of Education. Strong interdisciplinary programs in Latin American studies, prelaw, premedicine, race and ethnic studies, and women's studies are also available.

Academic Program

Academic majors are offered in the spirit of a liberal arts program with emphasis on developing the whole student. In addition to the standard academic program, international study programs, independent study, and an honors program are offered to provide greater diversity.

A liberal arts education, by definition, is an exposure to a wide variety of academic disciplines. Typically, such exposure carries no underlying theme but is distributed among broad categories such as the humanities, arts, social sciences, and natural sciences. The University of Redlands has never considered itself typical and, as a result, has developed an unusual approach to the implementation of its liberal arts philosophy by restructuring the general education requirements to provide a contemporary curriculum. This common experience emphasizes competence in writing, computing, problem solving, and creative skills, all of which are fundamental to a lifetime of learning and career development. In addition, the requirements include a first-year seminar that integrates the academic program and close personal relationships between students and faculty members. The overriding emphasis of this innovative curriculum is on a thorough investigation of human values as they affect the individual and society. An examination of the worth of the individual, respect for nature and life, free inquiry, and the understanding of other cultures are a few of the topics covered through various courses. It is hoped that this experience will broaden each student's understanding and will better equip the student to deal with our dynamic society.

The Johnston Center for Integrative Studies provides a nontraditional structure for a select group of highly motivated students. Johnston Center students are exempted from most of the academic structure of Redlands and instead negotiate their entire course of study with a faculty/peer committee. Drawing from the Redlands curriculum as well as from courses created each semester by the Johnston community, each student proposes an individually-designed general studies program and an area of concentration. Their course performance is evaluated in a narrative format rather than with letter grades. Johnston students live in the Johnston Complex, a living/learning community that includes student rooms, faculty offices, classrooms, and space for weekly community meetings. Students enrolled in the Johnston Center are expected to contribute to the life of the center's community.

The academic calendar divides the school year into a 4-4-1 plan, providing a fall semester, spring semester, and a May term. The four classes taken in the fall semester are completed prior to the third Friday in December. The spring semester begins in January and runs through April. The four-week May term offers students the chance to pursue one subject in depth. Extensive off-campus opportunities, including internships, international study, and on-campus independent study are available.

Academic Facilities

The institution has extensive facilities for student use, including a modern library with 400,000 publications, Internet access, and online databases such as Dialog, ABI/Inform, PsychLit, ERIC Wilson Indecis, and Music Index. Additional facilities include the Glenn Wallichs Theatre, the Fletcher Jones Academic Computing Center, the Hunsaker University Center, the Peppers Art Center, and the Stauffer Center for Science and Mathematics. There are forty-two buildings on the 160-acre campus.

Costs

Tuition for 2003–04 was $23,796, and room and board costs were $8478.

Financial Aid

Recognizing that some worthy and capable students find it impossible to obtain a college education without financial assistance, the University has established a program of aid. Most aid is need-based, but no-need scholarships based on academic achievement in high school and/or college are available. Presidential Scholarships are also available, based on grades and test scores, as are Achievement Awards. Talent Awards, ranging from $500 to $6000 each, are available in art, creative writing, debate, and music.

Students seeking financial assistance should inquire through the Office of Admissions when applying for admission. The Free Application for Federal Student Aid (FAFSA) should be submitted by February 15. FAFSA forms received after this date are evaluated subject to the availability of funding. Forms may be obtained most conveniently from high school counselors' offices and college financial aid offices, as well as online at http://www.fafsa.ed.gov.

Faculty

The highly qualified full-time faculty numbers 171 men and women, 90 percent of whom hold doctorates or other terminal degrees in their field. The wide variety of academic backgrounds represented in the faculty provides students with an excellent opportunity to live and work in an atmosphere of intellectual inquiry. Academic advising is handled by faculty members, and all students are assigned an adviser in the area of their major interest.

Student Government

Authority and responsibility for student government is delegated to the Associated Students of the University by the president and the faculty to make possible genuine participation by students in the governance of the University. The organization is composed of all students in the college, and its officers are chosen by the student body. More than sixty positions of representation are open to students on faculty, administrative, trustee, and alumni committees. Among other activities and responsibilities, the student government finances and operates a student-union complex, on-campus bus system, information center, vending program, convocation series, and weekly newspaper.

Admission Requirements

Graduation from an accredited high school, or the equivalent, is necessary for admission. No set pattern of courses in high school is required, but applicants should have had 4 years of work in English and should have completed an academic program strongly emphasizing such studies as foreign language, science, mathematics (including algebra II), and social science. An average grade of at least B should have been maintained in the high school program. Applicants are requested to submit the results of the SAT I or the ACT. Standardized test scores are not required of transfers who bring 24 transferable units to the University.

Transfer students should have maintained a minimum 2.8 grade point average and may transfer up to 66 units of credit from a community college. There is a 30-unit residence requirement for transfers from other four-year institutions.

Application and Information

Applications are processed on a rolling basis. Those wishing to be considered for an academic or merit scholarship should apply by December 15. Those applying for need-based financial aid should apply by February 1. Transfer and late applicants should apply by March 1. Applications made after this date are considered on a space-available basis.

Further inquiry should be addressed to:

Dean of Admissions
University of Redlands
P.O. Box 3080
Redlands, California 92373-0999
Telephone: 800-455-5064 (toll-free)
Fax: 909-335-4089
E-mail: admissions@redlands.edu
World Wide Web: http://www.redlands.edu

The University of Redlands stands out brilliantly against the majestic San Bernardino Mountains.

UNIVERSITY OF RHODE ISLAND

KINGSTON, RHODE ISLAND

The University

As a land-grant college since its founding in 1892, the University of Rhode Island emphasizes preparation for earning a living and for responsible citizenship, fosters research, and takes its expertise to the community in extension programs. The current undergraduate enrollment is about 11,000 men and women. The center of the spacious country campus is a quadrangle of handsome old granite buildings surrounded by other, newer academic buildings, student residence halls, and fraternity and sorority houses. On the plain below Kingston Hill are gymnasiums, athletic fields, tennis courts, a freshwater pond, agricultural fields, and greenhouses. There are nineteen residence halls on campus that offer a variety of living accommodations, including several theme residence halls and a "wellness dorm." Freshmen are guaranteed dormitory space if they meet the February 1 application deadline and send in their housing deposit by May 1. Three dining centers are operated by the University for the convenience of resident students. There are approximately 1,000 fraternity and sorority members living in nationally affiliated houses that are privately owned by alumni corporations. Some students commute from home, and about 2,000 students commute from houses or apartments in the beach areas known as "down-the-line." Approximately 45 percent of the undergraduate students come from outside Rhode Island.

Lectures, art programs, music and dance concerts, film programs, and theater presentations are available. An extensive program of intercollegiate and intramural athletics is offered and is sufficiently varied to provide an opportunity for every student to participate. The Tootell Physical Education Center and the Keaney Gymnasium provide excellent facilities, including three pools, three gymnasiums, three weight-training rooms, five handball courts, and a modern athletic training room. The Mackal Fieldhouse provides gymnasium space for a variety of recreational uses as well as an indoor track. In addition to a football stadium, there are twelve tennis courts, two softball diamonds, a baseball field, a lighted lacrosse/soccer field, a hockey field, and numerous practice fields for recreation and competition. The 8,000-seat Ryan Center opened in 2002 and houses the men's and women's basketball programs. The Boss Ice Rink opened in fall 2002. A sailing pavilion and rowing facility are located off campus. The Memorial Union Building houses a wide variety of educational, social, cultural, and recreational services, including lounges, browsing rooms, study rooms, darkrooms, a student video center, a radio station, the campus newspaper, a games room, a craft center, a cafeteria, a snack bar, a restaurant, a ballroom, and a special events room.

Location

The University's 1,200-acre campus is located in the historic village of Kingston, 30 miles south of Providence in the northeastern metropolitan corridor between New York and Boston. Bus transportation is available from the campus to most locations in the area, including Wakefield, where the nearest shopping facilities are located. The Kingston Amtrak train station is 1 mile from campus, and the T. F. Greene Airport in Warwick, Rhode Island, is only about 25 miles from campus. The campus is only 6 miles from the ocean, and weekend ski trips are easily managed in the winter season.

Majors and Degrees

The College of Arts and Sciences offers the Bachelor of Arts, Bachelor of Science, Bachelor of Fine Arts, and Bachelor of Music degrees. The Bachelor of Arts degree is offered in African and African-American studies, anthropology, art history, art studio, biology, chemistry, classical studies, communication studies, comparative literature, economics, English, French, German, history, Italian, journalism, Latin American studies, mathematics, music, philosophy, physics, political science, psychology, public relations, sociology, Spanish, and women's studies. The Bachelor of Science degree is available in applied sociology, biological sciences, chemistry, chemistry and chemical oceanography, computer science, economics, environmental plant biology, marine biology, mathematics, physics, and physics and physical oceanography. The Bachelor of Fine Arts degree is offered in art and theater, and the Bachelor of Music degree is available in music education and music theory and composition.

The College of Business Administration offers the Bachelor of Science degree in accounting, finance, financial services, general business administration, international business, management, management information systems, and marketing.

The College of Engineering makes the Bachelor of Science degree available in biomedical, chemical, chemical and ocean, civil, computer, electrical, industrial, mechanical, and ocean engineering.

The College of the Environment and Life Sciences offers the Bachelor of Science degree in animal science and technology, aquaculture and fishery technology, clinical laboratory science, coastal and marine policy and management, environmental economics and management, environmental management, environmental plant biology, geology and geological oceanography, geosciences, marine resource development, microbiology, nutrition and dietetics, resource economics and commerce, urban horticulture and turf management, water and soil science, and wildlife biology and management. The Bachelor of Landscape Architecture degree is awarded in landscape architecture.

The College of Human Science and Services offers the Bachelor of Science degree in communicative disorders, elementary and secondary education, human development and family studies, physical education, textile marketing, and textiles, fashion merchandising, and design.

The College of Nursing offers the Bachelor of Science degree in nursing.

The College of Pharmacy offers a six-year Doctor of Pharmacy degree.

Preprofessional preparation is available in dentistry, law, medicine, physical therapy, and veterinary studies.

Academic Program

All programs of study aim for a balance of the natural and social sciences, the humanities, and professional subjects. The courses and programs of study have been approved by national accrediting agencies and are accepted for credit by other approved institutions of higher education. All freshmen who enter the University to earn a bachelor's degree are first enrolled in University College; its advising program helps students choose a concentration and appropriate courses. A student must meet the curricular requirements of the college in which the degree is to be earned. As a general rule, 120 credits are required for a Bachelor of Arts degree and 130 for a Bachelor of Science degree, including the specified general education requirements. The University of Rhode Island operates on a two-semester calendar, with semesters beginning in September and January. Two 5-week summer sessions are also available. Advanced placement is granted to students who have passed a College Board Advanced Placement examination with a grade of 3 or better. In addition, credit may be given for satisfactory scores on departmental proficiency examinations or College-Level Examination Program (CLEP) subject examinations. The University Honors Program offers bright and motivated students opportunities to broaden their intellectual development and to strengthen their preparation in their major fields of study.

Off-Campus Programs

The University Year for Action provides a full-time one- or two-semester internship for students interested in public service careers. The University has exchange agreements with universities in England, France, Germany, Japan, and Spain. Other off-campus study and exchange programs are also available.

Academic Facilities

The University library has more than 1 million bound volumes and 1.5 million titles on microform. Active research programs are carried on in all seven colleges, and many laboratories are available. The Graduate School of Oceanography, located on the Narragansett Bay Campus, provides undergraduates with a living research lab for science-related courses. The University houses a large collection of American historic textiles, a center for robotics research, a planetarium, the Watson House Museum, and an animal science farm.

Costs

The comprehensive cost for 2003–04 was estimated at $25,024 for out-of-state students and $14,892 for Rhode Islanders. This covered tuition, fees, and room and board. Books, travel, and personal expenses are not included in these figures. Laboratory fees are extra. The University participates in the cooperative plan of the New England Board of Higher Education, whereby students from other New England states are admitted to certain curricula at the University that are not offered in their own states. These students are charged in-state tuition plus a surcharge of 50 percent.

Financial Aid

To be considered for financial aid at the University, students must submit the Free Application for Federal Student Aid (FAFSA). The University's financial aid application must also be submitted. Although there is no deadline for applying, priority is given to applications received by March 1. Most students receive notification of decisions on or about April 1. Academic scholarships are available to incoming freshmen with superior academic credentials. Consideration for these scholarships is given to freshmen who apply by the December 15 early action deadline. For 2002–03, 67 percent of new students who completed applications were awarded some form of aid. In addition, students have opportunities for employment through work-study programs that use federal, state, and institutional funds.

Faculty

The faculty consists of 648 full-time and 17 part-time members, or 1 professor for every 18 students. Eighty-eight percent of the full-time faculty members hold doctoral degrees. Faculty members serve both the graduate and undergraduate populations and have wide-ranging interests and responsibilities. In addition to teaching and research, they serve as advisers to the students in the University College and at the departmental and college levels.

Student Government

The Student Senate is a legislative body that represents the students to the administration and faculty and supervises extracurricular activities. It also distributes the activities tax funds among the various student organizations through its tax committee. Individual residence halls form their own governments. The Interfraternity Council supervises fraternity affairs, and the Panhellenic Association governs sorority life. The Commuter Association provides social and other assistance to commuter students.

Admission Requirements

Ideally, admission is a mutual selection process. It is hoped that those who seek admission will also be the kind of students sought by the University. Applicants are given individual consideration, but it is expected that all candidates will have completed at least 18 units of college-preparatory work; specific unit requirements vary for each of the seven colleges of the University. Academic achievement in a challenging high school program receives the strongest consideration in the review of an applicant's credentials. An audition is required to register for work toward the Bachelor of Music degree. All freshman candidates must submit a high school transcript and scores on the SAT I or the ACT examination, which should be taken no later than January 1 of the senior year. International students who are not immigrants must also complete an English proficiency test, administered by the U.S. Consulate, or the Test of English as a Foreign Language (TOEFL). Scores on equivalency examinations may be presented by applicants who have not been able to complete formal high school studies. Transfer students may enter in either semester and must submit transcripts of all previous work at both the high school and college levels. Early admission is available to high school juniors with superior records.

Students are selected primarily on the basis of academic competence and without regard to age, race, religion, color, sex, creed, national origin, handicap, or sexual orientation.

Visits to campus are encouraged. Question-and-answer sessions are scheduled daily during the week during the fall and winter. Students and parents are invited to participate in these meetings, which include a campus tour. Daily tours are provided for visitors, Monday to Saturday, while classes are in session. The Office of Admissions sends representatives to college fairs in Rhode Island and neighboring states throughout the year.

Application and Information

High school students are encouraged to submit applications early in their final year of preparatory study, as the University subscribes to a rolling admissions policy and reviews folders as soon as complete credentials have been submitted. The closing date for fall term freshman applications is February 1, and the deadline for transfer applications is May 1. Most decisions are reported in February, March, and April. The closing date for spring term applications is November 1. The early action deadline is December 15, and students receive notification by January 15. Requests for application forms and further information should be directed to:

Office of Admissions
14 Upper College Road
University of Rhode Island
Kingston, Rhode Island 02881
Telephone: 401-874-7000
E-mail: uriadmit@etal.uri.edu
World Wide Web: http://www.uri.edu/admissions

UNIVERSITY OF RIO GRANDE

RIO GRANDE, OHIO

The University

The University of Rio Grande, founded in 1876, is a private four-year institution in partnership with Rio Grande Community College, a two-year college supported by the state of Ohio. It is the only Ohio institution with a combined two- and four-year mission in higher education. Accredited by the North Central Association of Colleges and Schools, Rio Grande has a diverse population of approximately 2,600 students with an average age of 25 years.

Vibrant, progressive, and developing, the University of Rio Grande and Rio Grande Community College offer a stimulating learning environment combining the advantages of a small, rural community college with the colorful, challenging atmosphere of a university.

Rio students are diverse; they include traditional students in residence on a 170-acre campus as well as a growing population of nontraditional students who commute from Ohio and the contiguous states of West Virginia and Kentucky.

Rio Grande has created a student base that can be described as multicultural: some students travel from all over the nation and the world to study in one of the few fine woodworking programs in the nation. Rio Grande is particularly strong academically in education, business, and nursing programs. From two-year programs to four-year degrees and a unique master's program in classroom teaching, Rio Grande offers a comprehensive array of technical, professional, and liberal arts preparation.

A variety of student activities, from Student Senate and fraternal life to a student-run newspaper, *Signals,* offer students a diverse out-of-classroom experience in the heart of Appalachia.

The University is a member of the American Mideast Conference and competes in men's baseball, basketball, cross-country, and soccer and women's basketball, softball, track, and volleyball. A women's soccer program is scheduled to begin in 2004–05. The University also has a complete intramural program. Athletic facilities include a sports center with an indoor pool, a fitness center, four racquetball courts, and varsity and multipurpose gymnasiums; baseball, softball, and soccer fields; a resilient all-weather track; sand volleyball courts; and four lighted tennis courts.

A graduate program is offered in the area of professional education with Master of Education degrees granted in the following areas of classroom teaching: fine arts, reading education K–12, intervention specialist, and mathematics. Other concentrations are currently being added.

Location

Rio Grande is located in southeastern Ohio, 12 miles from Gallipolis, a town along the Ohio River, and 75 miles from Columbus. The major airports that serve the area are in Columbus; Charleston, West Virginia (65 miles away); and Huntington, West Virginia (60 miles away). Canoeing and horseback riding in connection with the nearby Bob Evans Farms are recreational activities for many Rio students.

Majors and Degrees

The University of Rio Grande grants bachelor degrees with majors in accounting, adolescent to young adult education, American studies, art education, behavioral and social science comprehensive, biology, business administration, business economics, chemistry/physics, clinical laboratory sciences, communications, computer science, early childhood education, economics, English, entrepreneurship, environmental science, finance, fine and performing arts, health-care administration, health education, history, humanities, human resource management, industrial management, industrial technology, information technology, international business, intervention specialist, liberal studies, management, marketing, mathematics, music, music education, nursing, physical education, preprofessional studies (engineering, dentistry, law, medicine, ministry, pharmacy, veterinary medicine), psychology, public administration, real estate, social work, and sports and exercise studies.

The University also grants associate degrees in accounting, art, biology, business management, career-technical education, chemistry, communications, computer-aided design and drafting, early childhood, electronics technology, fine woodworking technology, general studies, health, history, information technology, manufacturing technology, mathematics, medical laboratory technology, nursing, office technology, plant maintenance, political science, psychology, social services, sociology, and technical theater.

Academic Programs

In addition to the specific curriculum required for their major or minor, candidates for the bachelor's degree are required to complete a core of general studies courses designed to expose students to the vast body of knowledge that exists beyond the declared major. This core covers communication, arts, sciences, mathematics, history, philosophy, and social sciences and provides students with a basic foundation of human learning.

Individualized majors are available for those students whose plans and goals differ from the University's established degree programs. These unique degree programs are individually designed through existing course work.

Many degrees require that students participate in extensive internships and practicum situations throughout the length of their program. The University believes that practical application is a major part of the learning process.

The University Honors Program offers talented and motivated students challenging opportunities for intellectual, academic, social, and ethical growth on both personal and societal levels. Freshman and sophomore students enroll in honors classes for general studies, while upperclass students focus on projects related to their field of study.

The University is set up on a semester calendar, offering two full semesters (fall and spring) and a Summer Term that consists of two 5-week terms.

The University awards credit to students who have successfully completed the College-Level Examination Program, the Advanced Placement Program of the College Board, the ACT Proficiency Examination Program, Life Experience Credit, or locally administered proficiency tests, as well as credit for military service.

Academic Facilities

The University library currently contains 70,000 books, 784 periodicals, 1,750 recordings and other media, microcomputers for student use, tape recorders, and microfilm and microfiche and conducts an active interlibrary loan program. There are special collections in business management, art, science fiction, curriculum, juvenile literature, and government documents.

All classrooms and laboratories have been built or renovated in the last ten years.

Costs

The University of Rio Grande is one of the most distinctive institutions in America because it is the only private university that is subsidized by the state for a student's first two years of study. In addition, because of its dual role of private and public educational interests, tuition costs are lower than those at other private institutions. In-state students, therefore, enjoy an extremely low tuition rate for each of the first two years or until they complete 64 credit hours. Out-of-state students also benefit from this arrangement in that the University is able to keep their private rates extremely competitive because of this special contract with the state of Ohio. In 2003–04, tuition rates for in-state entering students were approximately $3000, and out-of-state students paid $10,532. Room and board were set at $5768, but charges vary, depending on the board option selected by the student. These are annual rates; one half is due each semester.

Financial Aid

The financial aid program combines merit-based assistance with traditional need-based assistance to further make the Rio experience an affordable one. More than 80 percent of all applicants for financial aid receive some form of assistance. The University administers federal and state programs, including the Federal Pell Grant, Federal Stafford Student Loan, Federal Perkins Loan, Federal PLUS loan, Federal Supplemental Educational Opportunity Grant, and the Ohio Instructional Grants programs. Campus employment is available, and a monthly payment plan is available. To apply for assistance, students must complete the Free Application for Federal Student Aid (FAFSA) along with the institutional application for aid.

Faculty

Currently, the University has a full-time teaching faculty of 82 members. Approximately 60 percent of the full-time faculty members have doctoral or terminal degrees in their fields. All classes and labs are taught by faculty members, not by graduate students. Faculty members also serve as academic advisers to students and are involved in a variety of student activities. The student-faculty ratio is about 18:1, which fosters an excellent rapport between professors and students.

Student Government

Through various committees and organizations, particularly student senate, students have the opportunity to take part in determining scholastic, intellectual, recreational, social, and cultural activities. They have a voice and vote on every standing committee on campus.

Admission Requirements

The admission policy is formulated to implement the philosophy of the University, which implies that all who may profit from college-level education will be admitted. Admission is determined without regard to race, color, age, marital status, national or ethnic origin, socioeconomic status, political affiliation, religion, gender, or disability.

Applicants for admission are required to submit the following: an official secondary school record documenting satisfactory completion, official postsecondary transcripts, the official Admission Application, the application fee of $15, and the official medical record form. Other documentation and credentials, such as ACT scores, may be required in certain admission categories. Students should consult the catalog.

Transfer students are evaluated with regard to the college-level work they have completed.

Application and Information

For more information, students should contact:

Director of Admissions
University of Rio Grande
Rio Grande, Ohio 45674
Telephone: 740-245-7208
800-282-7201 (toll-free in Ohio, West Virginia, and Kentucky)
Fax: 740-245-7260
E-mail: elambert@rio.edu
World Wide Web: http://www.rio.edu

Students on their way to class at the University of Rio Grande.

UNIVERSITY OF ROCHESTER

ROCHESTER, NEW YORK

The University

Founded in 1850, Rochester is one of the leading private universities in the country, one of sixty-three members of the prestigious Association of American Universities, and one of eight members of the University Athletic Association, which is made up of national research institutions with similar academic and athletic philosophies. Including the University's Eastman School of Music, the University has a full-time enrollment of 4,448 undergraduates and 2,336 graduate students. Rochester's personal scale and the breadth of its research and academic programs permit both attention to the individual and unusual flexibility in planning undergraduate studies. Along with the distinctive Rochester Curriculum to help make the most of the undergraduate years, students in the college (arts, sciences, and engineering) also find ready resources through the Eastman School of Music, the Simon Graduate School of Business Administration, the Warner Graduate School of Education and Human Development, the School of Medicine and Dentistry, and the School of Nursing. Special opportunities include the Take Five program, which allows selected undergraduates a tuition-free fifth year of courses; REMS, an eight-year combined B.A./B.S.-M.D. program; study abroad; Quest courses; seven certificate programs; Senior Scholars Program; and employment programs that offer a national summer jobs program and paid internship experiences.

Located on a bend in the Genesee River, the River Campus is home to most undergraduates, who live in a variety of residence halls, fraternity houses, and special interest housing. Most of the original buildings have been recently renovated, and all residence halls are fully wired for computer access and cable television. Among the facilities are Wilson Commons, the student union; the multipurpose Robert B. Goergen Athletic Center; the Computer Studies Building; and Gleason Hall (Business School). Students participate in more than 200 student organizations, including twenty-two varsity teams, thirty-six intramural and club sports, eighteen fraternities and ten sororities, performing arts groups, musical ensembles, a radio station, and a newspaper.

Location

With Lake Ontario on its northern border and the scenic Finger Lakes to the south, the Rochester area of more than a million people is located in an attractive setting that has been rated among the most livable in the United States. It offers a wide range of cultural and recreational opportunities through its museums, parks, orchestras, planetarium, theater companies, and professional sports teams.

Majors and Degrees

The University of Rochester offers a Bachelor of Arts program through the college, with majors in African and African-American studies, American Sign Language, anthropology, art history, biology, brain and cognitive sciences, chemistry, classics, comparative literature, computer science, economics, English, environmental studies, film and media studies, French, geological sciences, German, health and society, history, interdepartmental studies, Japanese, linguistics, mathematics, mathematics/statistics, music, philosophy, physics, physics and astronomy, political science, psychology, religion, Russian, Russian studies, Spanish, statistics, studio arts, and women's studies. Bachelor of Science programs are offered in the college, with majors in applied mathematics, biological sciences (biochemistry, cell and developmental biology, ecology and evolutionary biology, microbiology, molecular genetics, or neuroscience), chemistry, computer science, environmental science, geological sciences, geomechanics, physics, and physics and astronomy. The college also offers certificate programs in actuarial studies, Asian studies, biotechnology, international relations, management studies, mathematical modeling in political science and economics, and Polish and Central European studies. The School of Engineering and Applied Sciences—part of the college—offers Bachelor of Science programs in biomedical, chemical, electrical and computer, and mechanical engineering; geomechanics; optics; and engineering and applied sciences, an interdepartmental program with specializations in a variety of areas. A B.A. program in engineering science is also offered. In addition to the college's B.A. in music, a Bachelor of Music degree is offered through the Eastman School, with majors in applied music, composition, jazz studies and contemporary media, music education, musical arts, and music theory. A B.S. degree is offered through the School of Nursing for those who already have their RN certification.

Additional opportunities include a 3-2 program offered through the William E. Simon Graduate School of Business Administration in which students earn both a B.A. or B.S. from the college and an M.B.A. from the Simon School in five years; 3-2 B.S./M.S. programs in biological sciences—biomedical engineering, chemical engineering, electrical and computer engineering, mechanical engineering, neuroscience, and optics; a program leading to a B.A. or B.S. and a master's in public health; a 3-2 program leading to a B.A. in music and an M.A. in music education; and a 3-2 program in human development leading to a B.A. or B.S. in an undergraduate major and an M.S. in human development from the Warner School. Transfer students can pursue a 3-2 program that combines a B.A. and a B.S. in an engineering concentration.

Academic Programs

To receive a bachelor's degree, students should maintain a minimum average of C and complete thirty-two courses (thirty-two to thirty-six for the Bachelor of Science).

The distinctive Rochester Curriculum allows students to select their major from one of the three branches of learning (the humanities, the natural sciences, and the social sciences). In each of the two branches outside their major, students choose a "cluster" of three courses that allows them to dig deeply in an area that particularly interests them. For most students, there are no other distribution requirements, except a freshman-year writing class.

The Take Five program offers selected students the opportunity to take a tuition-free fifth year in order to pursue their varied interests.

The Quest program offers first-year students the advantages of small classes, student/teacher collaboration, and original research. As a result, Quest courses teach students how to learn, both as undergraduates and beyond.

Students may arrange independent study courses or pursue research in most departments. Those whose interests may not be fully realized through a traditional major, double major, or major/minor, may work with faculty advisers to design an interdepartmental concentration.

Undergraduates from any academic discipline may devote their senior year to a self-designed creative project in the form of scholarly research, a scientific experiment, or a literary or artistic work through the Senior Scholars Program.

Undergraduates enrolled in the college may take private instruction at the Eastman School of Music. A double-degree program leading to the Bachelor of Music degree from Eastman and a bachelor's degree from the college is also available.

The Rochester Early Medical Scholars (REMS) program is an eight-year B.A./B.S.-M.D. program for exceptionally talented undergraduates. Students enrolled in this program enter the University of Rochester with assurance of admission to the University's medical school upon successful completion of their undergraduate degree program.

The University's research centers include the Frederick Douglass Institute for African and African-American Studies, the Susan B. Anthony Institute for Gender and Women's Studies, the Center for Future Health, the Center for Judaic Studies, the W. Allen Wallis Institute of Political Economy, the Center for Visual Science, the Sign Language Research Center, the Skalny Center for Polish and Central European Studies, the Center for Optics Manufacturing, the Center for Electronic Imaging Systems, and the Center for Biomedical Ultrasound.

The University's calendar includes two regular semesters.

Off-Campus Programs

Rochester offers full-year and semester-long study-abroad opportunities, as well as special summer and winter trips, through fifty different study-abroad programs. Semester and full-year destinations include Argentina, Australia, Austria, Belgium, Chile, China, Czech Republic, Egypt, France, Germany, Ghana, Hungary, Ireland, Italy, Japan, Jordan, Mexico, Netherlands, Poland, Russia, Senegal, Spain, Sweden, and Taiwan. International internships are offered in Berlin, Bonn, Brussels, London, Madrid, and Paris.

Academic Facilities

As one of the smallest of the 151 American universities classified by the Carnegie Foundation for the Advancement of Teaching as offering an extensive range of doctoral programs, Rochester offers an environment that combines the vast learning resources of a national university with the intensive personalized attention of a private college. Research opportunities for undergraduates are available in every field. Major research facilities include a comprehensive Medical Center; an extensive on-campus computer system; direct access to the CYBER 205 Supercomputer in Princeton, New Jersey; fifteen electron microscopes; a 12-trillion watt, 24-beam laser fusion laboratory; and a 3-million-volume library system, including the Eastman School's Sibley Music Library, the largest collection of any music school in the Western Hemisphere. The University is widely known as the nation's premier institution for the study of optics and is home to the Omega, the world's most powerful ultraviolet laser.

Costs

The costs for 2003–04 were tuition and fees, $27,573; average room and board costs, $8770; and average books, transportation, and other expenses, $2422. Part-time study is offered on a per-course basis.

Financial Aid

The University offers a strong program of financial assistance, including academic merit scholarships, grants, loans, tuition payment plans, and part-time jobs. Applicants for financial aid should submit the CSS PROFILE application and the Free Application for Federal Student Aid (FAFSA). Special awards include full tuition Renaissance Scholarships, Bausch & Lomb Honorary Science Scholarships, the University of Rochester Humanities and Social Sciences Scholarships, Kodak Young Leaders Scholarships, Rush Rhees Scholarships, National Merit Scholarships, National Achievement Scholarships, Urban League Scholarships, and AHORA Scholarships. The University also awards grants to children of alumni, room and board grants to selected Naval ROTC scholars, and Phi Theta Kappa Scholarships for transfer students. Special applications are not required for consideration for merit scholarships.

Faculty

Students work closely with a stimulating faculty of internationally renowned scholars, all of whom engage both in advanced research and in teaching at the undergraduate level. The University's faculty is held in particularly high regard by colleagues at sister institutions, and many of its departments are widely recognized as among the best in the country.

Student Government

All undergraduates are members of the Students' Association, which has an annually elected president and a student Senate; there is also a Judicial Council, whose members are appointed by the Senate. The Students' Association in the college strives to coordinate student activities; protect academic freedom; improve students' cultural, social, and physical welfare; develop educational standards and facilities; and provide a forum for the expression of student views and interests.

Admission Requirements

The University of Rochester seeks to admit students who will take advantage of its resources, be strongly motivated to do their best, and contribute to the life of the University community. An applicant's character, extracurricular activities, job experience, academic accomplishments, and career goals are considered. More than half of last year's enrolled students ranked in the top tenth of their secondary school classes. The middle 50 percent of enrolled freshmen scored between 1250 and 1440 on the SAT I and between 27 and 32 on the ACT.

The recommended application filing date for freshman applicants is January 5 for fall admission and October 1 for spring admission. An early decision plan is available. Transfer students are welcome for entrance in the fall and spring semesters, and applications are reviewed on a rolling basis. The University accepts the Common Application in addition to its own school application. An electronic online application is available from the University's Web site. Applicants for freshman admission are required to submit scores from either the SAT I or the ACT. SAT II examination results are reviewed but are not required. Candidates for admission from lower-income groups are encouraged to investigate the Higher Education Opportunity Program (New York State residents only), which provides supportive services and financial aid.

The University of Rochester values diversity and is committed to equal opportunity for all persons regardless of age, color, disability, ethnicity, marital status, national origin, race, religion, sex, sexual orientation, or veteran status. Further, the University complies with all applicable nondiscrimination laws in the administration of its policies, programs, and activities.

Application and Information

To obtain application forms and further information on admission and financial aid, students should contact:

Director of Admissions
University of Rochester
P.O. Box 270251
Rochester, New York 14627-0251
Telephone: 585-275-3221
888-822-2256 (toll-free)
World Wide Web: http://www.rochester.edu/admissions

Director of Admissions
Eastman School of Music
Rochester, New York 14604
Telephone: 585-274-1060
World Wide Web: http://www.rochester.edu/eastman

Rush Rhees Library on the University of Rochester's Eastman Quadrangle.

UNIVERSITY OF ST. FRANCIS

JOLIET, ILLINOIS

The University

Committed to the success of its students, the University of St. Francis (USF) offers a global perspective to its students, with strong career preparation, a liberal arts base, and the self-confidence to take on the world. About 85 percent of USF graduates find employment or enter graduate school within six months of graduation.

The University of St. Francis offers an intimate, personalized college experience, and students—residents, commuters, adult learners, and graduate students—benefit from an innovative student-centered approach. The University serves some 1,500 students at its Joliet campus. More than 2,800 students throughout the nation are served by programs offered at off-site locations and online.

Some interesting facts about The University of St. Francis include the following: 75 percent of the University's science graduates are women; nearly 25 percent of all students are involved in volunteer programs; 76 percent of students are transfer students; the University has provided Illinois schools with more than 1,000 teachers; the average undergraduate class size is 16; the University offers more than thirty student organizations; and prominent Chicago-based and national companies recruit on the campus each year.

More than sixty areas of undergraduate study are offered in the arts and sciences, business, computer science, education, and nursing. The University also offers undergraduate programs designed for adult learners, such as the Bachelor of Science in professional arts/applied organizational management, the RN-B.S.N. Fast Track program for registered nurses, and the health arts program.

Nine graduate programs are offered: the M.S. in health services administration, M.B.A., M.S. in management, M.S. in training and development, M.S. in nursing, M.S. in physician assistant studies, M.S. in educational leadership, M.S. in teaching and learning, and M.Ed. in education with certification.

USF offers programming nationwide at on-site locations, online, and through faculty-directed distance tutorials. USF is committed to teaching and to providing students with the challenges and support essential to meeting their potential. Small class sizes ensure that students get the individual attention and focus they need. The University's writing and math centers and tutoring programs provide an important support network. Programs for scholars, such as the Biology Fellows Program and various honor societies, provide challenging and relevant educational experiences beyond classroom learning. USF is at the forefront of technology, providing a variety of online research work and experiences to its students.

USF is committed to educating the student as a whole. A variety of student clubs and organizations are available, as are volunteer activities. Student Affairs sponsors many entertainment events as well as the Student Government Association. Schola, the student choir, and *Loquitur*, the University's literary magazine, are popular activities. The University is also host to the annual Undergraduate Conference on English Language and Literature, which draws student presenters from prestigious colleges and universities throughout the nation. Cultural musical events, which bring internationally and nationally acclaimed performers to the University, are sponsored through the Featured Performances series. Exhibits that bring the works of regionally recognized artists to the campus are planned.

During the past twenty years, USF teams have won sixty conference championships, have had sixty-two national tournament appearances, and have won one national championship. USF has six sports programs for men and eight programs for women, as well as ten intramural programs.

Location

USF's main campus is on 16 acres in the midst of a historic residential area known as Joliet's Cathedral area. The University is 35 miles southwest of Chicago (about 45 minutes) and is easily accessible by major roadways and trains. USF is also conveniently located between Argonne National Laboratory and Midewin National Tallgrass Prairie. Both sites provide excellent opportunities for research, internships, and paid cooperative job programs with professionals in many disciplines, including math, natural sciences, education, computer science, and mass communication.

The University's College of Nursing and Allied Health is located 5 minutes from the main campus, adjacent to Provena Saint Joseph Medical Center. The University also holds classes at a variety of health-care facilities throughout the nation and maintains a regional center in Albuquerque, New Mexico, where the M.S. in physician assistant studies and the Master of Science in Nursing with a family nurse practitioner track are offered.

The Regional Education Academy for Leadership (REAL), an initiative of the College of Education, is housed on Jefferson Street in the Twin Oaks office center, approximately 10 minutes from the campus. In partnership with area school districts, REAL offers educational opportunities for area educators at convenient locations throughout the region.

Majors and Degrees

Undergraduate programs of study include accounting, actuarial science, advertising/public relations, American politics, applied organizational management, art, arts–management, arts–marketing, biology, broadcasting/audio-video, commercial/public recreation, computer science, computer science/electronics, elementary education, English, environmental science, finance, general management, health arts, history, human resource management, information technology, management, marketing, mass communications, mathematics, media arts, medical technology, music, nuclear medicine technology, nursing, pastoral ministry, political science, predental, premedical, prepharmacy, pre–physical therapy, preveterinary medicine, professional arts/applied organizational management, psychology, public policy, radiation therapy, radiography, recreation administration, secondary education (science, language arts/English, social science, mathematics), social work, special education, studio art, teaching ministry, theology, therapeutic recreation, visual arts, visual arts/graphic design, and Web application development.

Academic Programs

The University of St. Francis offers a comprehensive education designed to introduce the student to various modes and areas of inquiry. The core curriculum includes interdisciplinary courses taken in the freshman through junior years. The relationship of the major to the liberal education courses is addressed in a senior capstone experience in the major. For a baccalaureate degree, a student must earn 128 semester hours. Thirty-two semester hours must be earned at USF. In addition to the overall requirement of at least a 2.0 GPA, a student must achieve a grade of C or better in every course required for the major program. The University also offers Prior Learning Assessment (PLAP), College-Level Examination Program (CLEP), and advanced placement opportunities. Various honors and internship programs are available.

Academic Facilities

The University's oldest building, Tower Hall, is the focal point of activities, housing interactive learning classrooms, state-of-the-art laboratories, offices, two residence wings, dining facilities, the chapel, the bookstore, and the radio and television stations. St. Albert Hall is home to the Natural Science Learning Center and the University's main computing lab. Marian Hall is a residence hall housing 225 students, a residence wing for science students, lounges, a game room, computing lab, and Information Services offices.

The main campus also includes the three-story library, which offers Internet access and houses the distance learning classroom. Online and off-campus students may fully utilize USF library services through the University's Web site. The recreation center, with seating for 1,500, is a three-level facility that includes basketball, volleyball, and racquetball courts; a Nautilus training and exercise room; a conference room; and a classroom. The Moser Performing Arts Center houses an auditorium, art gallery, studio theater, and music and choir practice rooms. The College of Nursing and Allied Health is housed at a medical center complex about 5 minutes from the Wilcox Street campus.

Costs

In 2003–04, tuition and fees for full-time undergraduates were $16,480 per year; room and board were $6030 per year. Tuition for part-time students was $480 per credit hour; RN-B.S.N. Fast Track, $345 per credit hour; professional arts/applied organizational management, $450 per credit hour; and health arts, $305 per credit hour.

Financial Aid

USF is committed to assisting students in obtaining a high-quality private education. The University spends more than $5 million in institutional aid and scholarships, in addition to nearly $6 million in federal and state assistance, to enable students to attend USF. In order to apply for all forms of federal, state, and USF assistance, students must complete a financial aid application form. USF prefers that students complete the Free Application for Federal Student Aid (FAFSA).

Faculty

The University of St. Francis faculty is committed to teaching. The University has 76 full-time faculty members, more than half of whom have terminal degrees. Forty adjunct faculty members bring a variety of academic and professional experience to the classroom. Faculty advisers are an integral part of the USF experience.

The USF faculty is invested in the success of its students, both academically and personally. Nursing faculty members are strong clinicians. Their intense commitment to health care and to patients ensures that students are challenged academically and offered a personal, caring support system.

Admission Requirements

Although each applicant is considered individually, there are four general requirements for admission to the University of St. Francis as an incoming freshman: satisfactory ACT or SAT I scores; rank in the upper half of their graduating class; at least 16 high school units in academic subjects, or the equivalent of a high school diploma, including 4 units of English, 2 units of mathematics (algebra and geometry), 2 units of social studies, 2 units of science (one with lab), 3 units total with courses from two of three areas (foreign language, computer science, or music/art), and 3 units of electives; and satisfactory scores on the TOEFL from applicants for whom English is a second language.

A $100 registration deposit is required thirty days after acceptance. This deposit is credited to the applicant's bill and is fully refundable until May 1 for students entering in the fall semester or January 1 for students entering in the spring semester.

Students attending other colleges may transfer to the University of St. Francis at any time during their academic careers. A minimum 2.0 GPA and demonstration of college-ready proficiency in math and English are required of transfer students for admission. Students attending community colleges are not required to earn an associate degree to enter. The University has outstanding services for transfer students. Articulation agreements with community colleges ensure a smooth transition to USF.

Application and Information

Freshmen are admitted in the fall and spring. Students should take the ACT or SAT I and visit the campus for an interview by April 1. Entrance exams should be taken in the spring of the junior year or the fall of the senior year in high school. Applications, including a high school transcript and an application fee, should be filed by July 15 for fall entry and December 1 for spring entry. Notification is on a rolling basis. Students transferring from a community college or another senior college or university may seek admission for either the fall or spring semester. Transfer students anticipating enrollment as nursing majors should submit an application for admission and have transcripts forwarded to the Admissions Office from one year to one semester before their projected entry date.

Registered nurses seeking admission to the RN-B.S.N. Fast Track degree completion program must submit the application for admission with the fee, official transcripts from each school attended, a copy of current licensure as an RN, and two letters of reference. Specific prerequisite and major supportive courses are also required.

Health-care professionals (dental hygienists, radiologic technologists, registered nurses, respiratory therapists, and other qualified health-care professionals) seeking admission as a health arts major must submit an application; transcripts of academic credit from all colleges, universities, or diploma programs; proof of current licensure; prior learning documentation of appropriate work experience, as specified; and applicable fees.

For information about admissions:
University of St. Francis
500 Wilcox Street
Joliet, Illinois 60435
Telephone: 815-740-3400
800-735-7500 (toll-free)
E-mail: admissions@stfrancis.edu
World Wide Web: http://www.stfrancis.edu

Tower Hall, on the campus of the University of St. Francis.

UNIVERSITY OF ST. THOMAS

ST. PAUL, MINNESOTA

The University

The University of St. Thomas, founded in 1885, is a Catholic, independent, liberal arts university that emphasizes values-centered and career-oriented education. With 11,084 students, it is Minnesota's largest independent college or university. St. Thomas ranked fifth (and highest among schools) in a newspaper-sponsored survey on "Which Minnesota nonprofit organizations have the most respected reputations?" St. Thomas has been coeducational at the undergraduate level since 1977; today 51 percent of its 5,241 undergraduates and 51 percent of its 5,843 graduate students are women. St. Thomas welcomes students of all ages, nations, and religions and from a broad range of racial and socio-economic backgrounds. While 87 percent of St. Thomas students hail from Minnesota, the University enrolls students from forty-seven states and sixty-one countries. Overall, 7 percent are international students (3 percent of undergraduate and 11 percent of graduate students). Eight percent are U.S. students who are members of minority groups.

St. Thomas has both undergraduate and graduate seminaries and its Center for Catholic Studies is home to the nation's oldest and largest undergraduate program in Catholic studies. Of students who report their religion, 42 percent are Catholic (52 percent of undergraduate and 33 percent of graduate students). At the graduate level, St. Thomas offers fifty degree programs: forty-two master's, two education specialist, one juris doctor, and five doctorates. It also offers five joint- or dual-degree programs that combine a degree in law with degrees in business, psychology, education, or social work. The University consists of nine divisions: College of Arts and Sciences, College of Business, Graduate School of Professional Psychology, Graduate Programs in Software Engineering, Programs in Engineering and Technology Management, St. Paul Seminary School of Divinity, School of Education, School of Law, and School of Social Work.

Entrepreneurship programs at the University of St. Thomas' College of Business are ranked among the top fifty in the nation, according to a survey published in *Entrepreneur* magazine. In addition to the main ranking, programs also were ranked by alumni, faculty members, and entrepreneurship-program directors. In those rankings, St. Thomas is rated seventh-best in the country. St. Thomas has won both the National Model Undergraduate Program of the Year and the National Model M.B.A. Program of the Year awards by the U.S. Association for Small Business and Entrepreneurship. St. Thomas is one of only two U.S. universities to receive the distinction at both the graduate and undergraduate levels.

Murray-Herrick Campus Center, the center of student life, contains the University's post office, bookstore, and dining facilities; student-life offices, such as Campus Ministry, Multicultural Student Services, the Career Development Center, and Personal Counseling and Testing; and the student government, newspaper, yearbook, and club and student organization offices. More than seventy clubs, sororities, fraternities, and professional and social groups thrive on campus. Students produce a weekly newspaper, *The Aquin*; the *Aquinas* yearbook; a literary magazine, *Summit Avenue Review*; and on-campus television and radio programs. Students with musical talent choose from about twenty vocal and instrumental groups. Numerous events, such as homecoming, keep the campus calendar full.

St. Thomas' extensive intramural sports program is home to eleven men's and eleven women's varsity teams that compete in the Minnesota Intercollegiate Athletic Conference and the National Collegiate Athletic Association (NCAA) Division III. St. Thomas men have won the conference all-sports trophy for eighteen of the last twenty-three years, while the women have won that honor fourteen of the last eighteen years. In the last two seasons, St. Thomas was the only school in its conference to qualify in all six sports that sponsored post-season tournaments. St. Thomas teams have won nine national championships over the past twenty years. The centerpiece of St. Thomas' sports facilities is a physical education, athletic, and activities complex that includes the 2,200-seat Schoenecker Arena and Coughlan Field House, with an indoor track and basketball, racquetball, tennis, and volleyball courts. Two swimming pools, a 5,000-seat stadium, fitness and weight-room facilities, and an Olympic-caliber track are among the facilities.

The historic Chapel of St. Thomas Aquinas houses the magnificent 2,787-pipe Gabriel Kney organ, a gift to the University in 1987. The Chapel of St. Thomas Aquinas and the St. Mary's Chapel on the School of Divinity campus are the University's main worship centers. Masses are celebrated daily during the academic year; ecumenical prayer services also are offered.

Ninety-three percent of freshmen and 40 percent of undergraduates reside in nine campus residence halls. The date of application and class year are among the criteria considered for on-campus housing. Handicapped-accessible facilities are available.

Location

St. Thomas' main campus is located in St. Paul, where the city's historic Summit Avenue meets the Mississippi River. While situated in a quiet, residential neighborhood, the 78-acre parklike campus is only minutes from the downtowns of Minnesota's Twin Cities, St. Paul and Minneapolis. Its three-block downtown Minneapolis campus is home to the University's business law, psychology, and education divisions. St. Thomas' Gainey Conference Center is located in Owatonna, Minnesota. The Bernardi Campus in Rome, Italy, is located on the Tiber River. The Twin Cities are known for a high quality of life. St. Paul is a winner of a "Most Livable City" award and is the home of the acclaimed Ordway Music Center for the Performing Arts and the Science Museum of Minnesota. Minneapolis, the "City of Lakes," has the renowned Guthrie Theater, Walker Art Center, and Nicollet Mall. The cities are also home to scores of lakes, professional sports teams, and companies with worldwide reputations, such as 3M, Pillsbury, General Mills, and Medtronic.

Majors and Degrees

St. Thomas awards the Bachelor of Arts degree in seventy-eight major fields, the Bachelor of Science degree in eight majors, the Bachelor of Science in Mechanical Engineering (B.S.M.E.) degree, and the Bachelor of Science in Electrical Engineering (B.S.E.E.) degree. The majors available are actuarial science, art history, biochemistry, biology, business administration (accounting, communication, entrepreneurship, financial management, general business management, human resources management, international business, leadership and management, legal studies in business, marketing management, operations management, and real estate studies), Catholic studies, chemical dependency counseling, chemistry, classical civilization, classical languages, communication studies, communication arts and literature (for grades 5-12 teacher licensure), community health education, criminal justice, dance and theater arts (for grades K–12 teacher licensure), East Asian studies, economics, electrical engineering, elementary education, English, English-writing, environmental studies, French, geographic information studies, geography, geology, German, health education (for nonlicensure and for grades 5–12 teacher licensure), history, international business (in French, German, and Spanish intensive), international studies, journalism and mass communication (in the fields of advertising, broadcast journalism, media studies, print journalism, and public relations), justice and peace studies, Latin, literary studies, mathematics, mathematics (for grades K–12 teacher licensure), mechanical engineering, music, music business, music education (for grades K–12 teacher licensure), music-liturgical music, philosophy, physical education, physical education (for grades K–12 teacher licensure), physical education health promotion, physical education health promotion-science emphasis, physics, political science, psychology, psychology-behavioral neuroscience, quantitative methods and computer science, Russian, Russian and Central and East European studies, science and mathematics for elementary education, science-chemistry (for grades 5–12 teacher licensure), science-earth and space science (for grades 5–12 teacher licensure), science-life science (for grades 5–12 teacher licensure), science-physics (for grades 5–12 teacher licensure), secondary education, social sciences, social studies (for grades 5–12 teacher licensure), social work, sociology, Spanish, theater, theology, and women's studies.

Students may take courses or choose a major field (if it is not offered by St. Thomas) through the Associated Colleges of the Twin Cities, a consortium of St. Thomas and four other nearby private colleges and universities. Free intercampus bus transportation and a common class schedule make access to other colleges convenient.

St. Thomas undergraduates may elect minors from fifty-nine fields of study. Additional study and licensure programs are offered in Air Force, Army, and Navy ROTC; elementary and secondary school teacher licensure programs; individualized majors; predentistry; pre-engineering; prelaw; premedicine; prepharmacy; pre–physical therapy; pre–veterinary medicine; social work licensure; and school social worker licensure programs.

Academic Program

The undergraduate program has two components: general education requirements (in literature and writing, fine arts, social analysis, human diversity, historical studies, moral and philosophical reasoning, faith and the Catholic tradition, natural science and mathematical and quantitative reasoning, language and culture, health and fitness, and computer competency) and course requirements, for completion of a major concentration. A total of 33 semester courses (132 semester credits) is required for a degree. The University operates on a 4-1-4 calendar, with spring and fall semesters and a four-week January Term. St. Thomas also offers summer sessions.

Special programs include the Freshman Year Program, designed to promote student achievement in college; the Aquinas Scholars Honors Program; study-abroad programs; internships; and the Renaissance Program, which blends a liberal arts major with a business-related minor. In most academic areas, credit is granted to students who have a score of 3 or higher on Advanced Placement examinations sponsored by the College Board. Students also may receive credit, with qualifying scores, through the College-Level Examination Program (CLEP). It is possible to earn credit for scores of 4 or higher on the International Baccalaureate Diploma examination in subjects included in the St. Thomas curriculum.

Off-Campus Programs

In 2003, St. Thomas was ranked first nationally (in the master's institution category) for the number of students who study abroad. In May 2003, 52 percent of graduating seniors had studied abroad during their years at St. Thomas. Students have access to more than ninety semester or yearlong study-abroad programs and another forty-two short-term programs, in more than forty countries. About 650 students studied abroad under these programs in 2003. St. Thomas sponsors six international semester programs in London, Paris, Glasgow, and Rome as well as twenty international short-term programs.

Academic Facilities

The University has eighty-four buildings on four campuses, with seventy-six on its main campus. The value of St. Thomas' physical plant is $409 million. Its newest building, for the School of Law, opened in Minneapolis in the summer of 2003.

St. Thomas is home to four libraries. Three of them—the O'Shaughnessy-Frey Library Center on the main campus, John Ireland Memorial Library on the St. Paul "south" campus, and the Charles J. Keffer Library on the Minneapolis campus—collectively house 466,493 volumes and have seating for 1,900 readers. The new School of Law library has room for 250,000 books and 250,000 volumes on microfiche. Library users have access to hundreds of electronic databases and online resources, including electronic collections of books, newspapers, and journals. CLICNet, the libraries' online catalog, is searchable via the Internet. It serves as the catalog of the holdings of the St. Thomas libraries as well as the collections of an eight-library consortium in the Twin Cities, with a combined collection of 2 million volumes.

Three auditoriums and the Foley Theater provide facilities for student theatrical performances as well as speakers, forums, and concerts. State-of-the-art equipment in the Frey Science and Engineering Center includes a Fourier-transform infrared spectrometer. Students also have access to 1,249 computer terminals throughout the campus in the Learning Center, residence halls, departmental labs, and other locations. Students have access to the Internet and the campus e-mail network.

Costs

Tuition for the 2003–04 academic year was $20,240 for full-time students carrying 32 credits a year. The average combined room and board rate was $6310. Student fees (student activities and technology) were $368.

Financial Aid

Federal, state, and institutional aid programs are available for students who demonstrate need. St. Thomas is committed to students who demonstrate academic achievement and who have contributed to their community, school, or church. The University makes that commitment by offering merit scholarships to outstanding students. St. Thomas awards more than $20 million annually in both need- and non-need-based institutional scholarships and grants. More than $1 million is awarded annually in University-endowed scholarships from private foundations, individuals, alumni, families, and friends of the University. In 2003–04, more than 75 percent of all St. Thomas undergraduates received financial aid. All freshmen received some form of financial aid. For freshmen who applied, the average award was about $13,000.

Faculty

St. Thomas' 677 faculty members make teaching their highest priority. Many involve students in their research efforts as well. Eighty-five percent of full-time St. Thomas faculty members have the highest degree in their field. An undergraduate student-faculty ratio of 17:1 allows for personal interaction between professors and students both inside and outside the classroom. All classes are taught by professors, not by teaching assistants.

Student Government

The All College Council (ACC) is the main student government board at St. Thomas. It represents student views and interests in academic, financial, and social affairs. The ACC plans numerous campus events, provides a variety of student services, and communicates regularly with the University's administrators and faculty members. The ACC holds regular office hours and maintains an open-door policy.

Admission Requirements

Incoming freshmen should be in the top 40 percent of their high school class and have earned an ACT composite score of 20 or higher or an SAT I combined math and verbal score of 970 or higher. A GPA of 2.3 or better in transferable credits is required of transfer students. A rolling-admission system, which begins October 1, enables applicants to learn of their admission status within three weeks after their completed applications are reviewed.

Application and Information

A completed application (including a writing sample), an official high school transcript, and standardized test scores are required. The application fee is waived. Students may download an application from the Web site (listed below) or submit one electronically. High school seniors are encouraged to apply by the end of December. Transfer students are encouraged to contact the Office of Admissions for details.

For information and application forms, students should contact:

Office of Admissions
University of St. Thomas
Mail #32F-1
2115 Summit Avenue
St. Paul, Minnesota 55105-1096
Telephone: 651-962-6150
800-328-6819 Ext. 2-6150 (toll-free)
Fax: 651-962-6160
E-mail: admissions@stthomas.edu
World Wide Web: http://www.stthomas.edu/undergraduate

UNIVERSITY OF SAN DIEGO

SAN DIEGO, CALIFORNIA

The University

Known for its commitment to Catholic tradition and the liberal arts, the University of San Diego (USD) has created academic programs providing students with the skills necessary to grow and advance personally and professionally. Beyond the traditional arts, sciences, and humanities, USD has developed exceptional programs in business, engineering, marine science, international relations, and the health sciences. With a holistic philosophy, USD seeks to foster competence, international and cultural sensitivity, professional responsibility, and a spirit of volunteerism in each student.

The students who share in the life at USD and contribute to its growth are a diverse group representing all fifty states and more than sixty countries. There are currently 4,800 undergraduates out of a total University enrollment of 7,200 students. Fifty percent of USD's undergraduate students reside on campus, many in recently constructed facilities. The residence halls consist of traditional dormitories, suites, and apartment-style buildings. Several meal plans accommodate different schedules and tastes in food.

A friendly campus atmosphere, the opportunity for close rapport between faculty members and students, and small classes that facilitate personal attention and faculty accessibility characterize the educational environment at the University of San Diego. Numerous campus activities are available to students, including social and cultural events, informal parties, special-interest groups and clubs, and intercollegiate and intramural sports. The Office of Campus Recreation complements the academic experience at the University by offering students many opportunities to use their leisure time constructively and enjoyably. The Shiley Theatre is the center of many cultural activities on campus, including concerts, lectures, plays, and recitals. There are also more than seventy student-controlled clubs and organizations, including nationally affiliated fraternities and sororities, national honor societies, and service organizations.

Location

The 180-acre campus sits on a mesa commanding inspiring views of the Pacific Ocean, Mission Bay, and San Diego harbor. USD is conveniently located minutes away from the cultural, recreational, business, and residential areas of San Diego, California's birthplace and second-largest city.

Located on the southern tip of California, San Diego offers a wide variety of recreational, business, science, art, and cultural activities. With an average daily temperature of 66 degrees in February and 78 degrees in August, the area is perfect for biking, jogging, tennis, softball, and all aquatic sports. In addition, San Diego is noted for an outstanding zoo, museums, Spanish missions, Sea World, and major sports programs. The proximity to Mexico provides an excellent opportunity for gaining firsthand insights into Mexican culture. The city of San Diego also offers educational advantages to students in the fields of social services, education, environmental and marine science, art, music, and archaeology. The International Airport, downtown, Mission Bay, and the Aquatic Center are just a few minutes from the campus.

Majors and Degrees

The University confers the Bachelor of Arts, Bachelor of Science, Bachelor of Business Administration, and Bachelor of Accountancy degrees. Undergraduate major programs are offered in accountancy, anthropology, art history, biology, business administration (with areas of concentration in finance, information systems, management, marketing, procurement, and real estate), business economics, chemistry, communication studies, computer science, economics, electrical engineering, English, ethnic studies, environmental studies, ethnic studies, French, history, interdisciplinary humanities, industrial and systems engineering, international relations, liberal studies, marine science, mathematics, mechanical engineering, music, nursing (post-RN only) philosophy, physics, political science, psychology, sociology, Spanish, theater arts, theology and religious studies, urban studies, and visual arts.

Advanced degree and teaching credential programs are available in bilingual/cross-cultural studies, counselor education, educational administration, elementary and secondary education, pupil personnel services, and special education.

Academic Programs

The Freshman Preceptorial program begins each USD student's academic career with a combination of advising, orientation, and an introduction to college-level scholarship. The preceptor, instructing in a supportive, small-group environment, has frequent contact with each advisee and continues advising throughout the student's general education program. Once students declare a major, the responsibility of advising shifts to the department chairman, who provides guidance in regard to specialized and professional study. Several programs, such as those in marine science and international relations, combine multiple disciplines, and special advisers are assigned to these areas. All of USD's programs are built solidly on the liberal arts, developing critical thinking skills through an emphasis on fundamental disciplines, written and oral communication, and an understanding of the past. USD gives special attention to the exploration of human and spiritual values, the interrelations of knowledge, and the development of an international perspective.

The University operates on a 4-1-4 academic calendar. Normally, the student is in residence for eight semesters and completes approximately forty-four courses, completing a minimum of 124 units.

The honors program at the University gives promising students the opportunity for both independent academic research and intensive exchange of ideas with other honors students. Selection of students to the program is made primarily on the basis of past academic achievement. The program accepts 45 students per class and offers preceptorial and seminar course work.

College credit may be granted for Advanced Placement courses taken in secondary schools when the classes are completed with scores of 3, 4, or 5 on the appropriate Advanced Placement tests given by the College Board (a score of 4 or 5 must be attained for English credit).

A number of subject examinations of the College-Level Examination Program (CLEP) have been approved by the

University faculty, and in certain specified areas students may qualify for college credit by satisfactory performance on the CLEP tests.

Off-Campus Programs

University of San Diego undergraduate students can live and study in Austria, England, France, Germany, Ireland, Italy, Japan, Mexico, or Spain while earning credit at USD. Additional science programs are also offered in Australia, Canada, Costa Rica, England, Kenya, Mexico, and the West Indies for students majoring in environmental and marine sciences or in a related field.

USD conducts a five-week summer session in Guadalajara, Mexico, in cooperation with several other American universities. The summer's experiences include concerts, lectures, and planned tours and excursions.

Academic Facilities

Named Alcalá Park after the Spanish university city of Alcalá de Henares, the campus is built in the style of the sixteenth-century Spanish Renaissance. Five important academic buildings have been constructed in recent years.

Opened in 2003, the 150,000-square-foot Donald Shiley Center for Science and Technology contains seventy-three state-of-the-art laboratory facilities for biology, chemistry, physics, environmental studies, and marine science. In addition, the center features aquariums, an astronomy deck, and a greenhouse.

Through the Joan Kroc Institute for Peace and Justice, the students and faculty members of the University of San Diego have stepped into an active role in the worldwide quest for human dignity and hope. The Institute is a magnet for political leaders and distinguished academics. Students may participate in both undergraduate and graduate programs of study.

The University Center, a two-story, 78,000-square-foot facility, serves as the hub of student life on campus. It offers students and faculty the use of music and study lounges, student organization offices, and a choice of five dining areas, including a grill, a deli, and a bakery.

Camino Hall is home to Shiley Theatre and also holds offices of the Fine Arts Department, soundproof practice rooms for music students, and foreign language laboratories. Founders Hall includes Founders Chapel and the Founders Art Gallery, which features exhibits by both professional and student artists.

Costs

Tuition was $23,410 for the 2003–04 academic year. Estimated residence costs, including room and board, average $9000 per year, depending on accommodations. Personal expenses, including books, are estimated at $3000.

Financial Aid

In order to be considered for need-based financial assistance, students must complete the Free Application for Federal Student Aid (FAFSA). During the 2002–03 academic year, more than 70 percent of undergraduate students received some form of financial assistance. Financial assistance can be in the form of loans, grants, scholarships, and student employment. In addition, the University offers academic, athletic, and leadership scholarships that are not dependent on financial need.

Faculty

The University of San Diego has a faculty of 341 full-time members and 339 part-time members. More than 97 percent of the faculty members hold earned doctorates or the terminal degree, and all are committed to teaching as their primary responsibility. Only faculty members teach classes, and the members of the undergraduate and graduate faculty are the same. The undergraduate student–faculty ratio of 14:1 fosters small classes, personal instruction, and individual attention, as well as faculty involvement in academic advising and University activities.

Student Government

The officers of USD's Associated Students and the class senators, who together make up the central representative group of the undergraduate students, are responsible for overseeing campus activities and the distribution of student funds.

Admission Requirements

Admission is based upon evidence of the applicant's ability to achieve success—academically, socially, and personally—at the University of San Diego. The admission criteria are highly selective. Decisions are based on the following items: the student's high school record, satisfactory SAT I or ACT scores, a letter of academic recommendation, and an essay. Decisions are made by an admission committee, which reviews each application individually.

Applicants are expected to present a well-balanced secondary school program comprising at least four academic subjects each year. Both the content of the program and the quality of the student's performance are considered.

Transfer students are considered for admission after the successful completion of 24 semester units of academic course work at an accredited college or university, with a GPA of 3.0 or better. Students who have not completed the requisite 24 units must apply for freshman admission.

The University welcomes international students who can demonstrate an ability to undertake college work with success in the United States. TOEFL and SAT I scores are required for their admission. There is no financial assistance available for international students.

Arrangements for an admission informational seminar and a campus tour may be made through the Admissions Office. Students are selected without regard to race, religion, handicap, or national or ethnic origin.

Application and Information

Application for admission is made through the Admissions Office. Forms should be completed and filed, together with a transcript of credits, as early as possible and no later than January 5 for freshmen and March 1 for transfers. Upon receipt of all necessary materials, each application is reviewed. Candidates are notified of acceptance by April 15. USD observes the Candidates Reply Date (May 1) set by the College Board and requests accepted applicants to notify the University of their intentions by that date.

For additional information about the University of San Diego, students should contact:

Director of Admissions
University of San Diego
5998 Alcalá Park
San Diego, California 92110
Telephone: 619-260-4506
800-248-4873 (toll-free)
Fax: 619-260-6836
World Wide Web: http://www.sandiego.edu

UNIVERSITY OF SAN FRANCISCO

SAN FRANCISCO, CALIFORNIA

The University

From its beginnings as a one-room schoolhouse, founded in 1855 by the Jesuits, the University of San Francisco has developed into one of the largest Catholic universities on the West Coast. Throughout its growth, the University has maintained its small class size and low student-faculty ratio. For 148 years, USF has been committed to preparing students to improve the world in which they live. Jesuit education at USF focuses on individual attention to each student. Its programs in the arts, the sciences, business, education, nursing, and the law foster a love of learning grounded by the challenge to serve society.

The city of San Francisco is the USF student's laboratory. The histories of the city and its university are intertwined. A dynamic partnership between the city and the University creates countless opportunities for students to relate classroom theory to the realities of life now and into the twenty-first century. The 57-acre residential campus has 3,800 undergraduates. The student body consists of students from all fifty states and seventy-six countries. All freshman and sophomore students are required to live on campus, unless living with parents. Students have access not only to the University's facilities, such as libraries, gymnasiums, a health and recreation center with an Olympic-size swimming pool, a pub, a coffeehouse, and a games room, but also to all that the city of San Francisco has to offer, including the ballet, opera, museum exhibits, concerts, theater, and sports events. The University is located in a beautiful residential neighborhood.

Residence hall life is an opportunity for students to live with their peers in a safe, relaxed environment. The University of San Francisco has six residence halls and six off-campus, apartment-style residences. Gillson Hall and Hayes-Healy Hall house mainly freshmen and are coed. Xavier Hall is all women. Phelan Hall is for upperclassmen and is coed. The Lone Mountain Hall is for students who are over 21 and is also coed. Loyola Village is a student residential community that features new apartment-style living with Internet access and lofty ceilings. The Village is for students who are 21 or over or who have reached their junior year. Most rooms in residence halls are doubles; however, some single rooms are available for upperclassmen. Each residence hall has laundry facilities, study/computer rooms, and television lounges.

There are many places to eat on campus and all are within easy walking distance of the residence halls and classrooms. The World Fare offers a food court–type dining environment. There is also a coffeehouse, a Mexican-style fast-food restaurant, an ice cream shop, a Jamba Juice, and a bookstore.

USF undergraduates participate in more than eighty student-run associations, fraternities and sororities, honor societies, and clubs such as the USF Rugby Club and the USF Dons Club. Among these are the oldest continuously performing theater group west of the Mississippi River, an award-winning FM radio station, a weekly newspaper, and a literary magazine. One of the most active offices on campus is the Career Services Center, which helps students to select career fields and to learn about the work opportunities available to them as both students and graduates. The Koret Health and Recreation Center is an exciting complex that provides facilities for exercise, racquetball, swimming, court games, and socializing.

Graduate programs are available in the arts and sciences, business, education, law, and nursing.

Location

The University of San Francisco is located on a beautiful 57-acre campus in a residential neighborhood. It is minutes from downtown San Francisco and the Pacific Ocean and just one block from the 1,000-acre Golden Gate Park. The advantages of an urban campus are numerous. Because of the diversity and geographical compactness of San Francisco, students find research facilities, opportunities for community involvement, and employment experiences that few cities can match.

Majors and Degrees

The University of San Francisco grants both B.A. and B.S. degrees. Majors available within the College of Arts and Sciences are biology, chemistry, communication studies, computer science, economics, English, environmental science, environmental studies, exercise and sports science, fine arts, French, graphic design, history, Latin American studies, mathematics, media studies, performing arts, philosophy, physics, physics/engineering, politics, psychological services, psychology, sociology, Spanish, theology/religious studies, undeclared arts/science, and visual arts. The McLaren College of Business offers degrees in accounting, business administration, finance, hospitality management, international business, and marketing. The School of Nursing offers a four-year baccalaureate program in nursing for qualified high school graduates and for second-baccalaureate candidates. Teacher certification is available at the elementary or secondary level with the addition of a fifth year of study.

The USF Pre-Professional Health Committee serves to guide and recommend students to medical and dental professional health schools, as well as to schools for pharmacy, optometry, veterinary medicine, and podiatry. A student may complete the premedical or other prehealth science requirements as part of, or in addition to, the requirements of an academic major. The Pre-Professional Health Committee assists students with the application process, develops a professional file for each student, collects and mails recommendations to professional schools, conducts interviews in preparation for application, and endorses approved candidates via a committee letter of recommendation sent to all professional schools selected by the student.

Academic Program

The University of San Francisco is committed to providing students with the essentials of a well-rounded education. A baccalaureate degree is issued upon the successful completion of a 128-unit curriculum. The curriculum consists of 44 units of courses in the core, chosen from six specified categories of knowledge, and 80–83 units that are divided between departmental major requirements and electives. An honors program is available for selected superior students seeking a strong academic challenge.

In an effort to encourage able high school students to move rapidly into the study of subjects now customarily reserved for colleges, the University of San Francisco honors the advanced placement of students, as certified by the College Board's Advanced Placement Program tests. The University also cooperates with the College-Level Examination Program (CLEP). Students intending to earn such credit must take CLEP examinations prior to their freshman course registration at the University.

The University of San Francisco offers a special program through the St. Ignatius Institute, which has an integrated core curriculum based on the great books of Western civilization and an emphasis upon the great works of Christianity. Any undergraduate student at the University, regardless of major, may take courses through the institute to meet general education requirements. The University offers Army ROTC. ROTC scholarships are available for qualified applicants as well as continuing students.

The academic year is based on the two-semester system. Summer sessions and a January intersession are also available.

Off-Campus Programs

The University of San Francisco sponsors numerous study-abroad programs including ones to Sophia University (Tokyo), Oxford (England), and Innsbruck (Austria), through USF's St. Ignatius Institute, a program at Universidad Iberoamericana in Mexico City, and a joint program with Hungary's Péter Pázmány Catholic University in Budapest. USF is affiliated with Gonzaga University's study-abroad program in Florence (Italy) and with Loyola University of Chicago's program in Rome. USF is also an associate member of the Institute of European and Asian Studies, which offers programs in Durham and London, England; Paris, Dijon, and Nantes, France; Berlin and Freiburg, Germany; Vienna, Austria; Madrid and Salamanca, Spain; Milan, Italy; Tokyo and Nagoya, Japan; Moscow, Russia; Adelaide and Canberra, Australia; Beijing, China; and Singapore. Numerous other study-abroad opportunities are also available. USF assists students in selecting a location, applying to programs, making financial arrangements, registering for academic credit, securing a passport and visa, and making travel plans.

A domestic student exchange program is also available with American University in Washington, D.C., Jackson State University in Mississippi, and Xavier University in Louisiana.

Academic Facilities

University of San Francisco students have access to Gleeson Library and its more than 700,000 volumes and to Harney Science Center, which houses the Computer Center, the Applied Math Laboratory, the Institute of Chemical Biology, and the Physics Research Laboratories. Cowell Hall, in addition to being the base for nursing classes and the Nursing Skills Laboratory, houses the Instructional Media Center, and Phelan Hall is the home of KDNS and KUSF, the University's AM and FM radio stations. McLaren Center, headquarters for the McLaren College of Business, houses an additional computer laboratory and special seminar rooms.

Costs

Tuition for the 2003–04 school year was $23,220. Room and board were $9790 for the academic year. Books, fees, travel, and other expenses are about $3200 per year.

Financial Aid

A wide variety of scholarships, grants, loans, and work-study programs are available at the University. All students must submit the Free Application for Federal Student Aid (FAFSA). More than two thirds of all University students receive some type of financial aid. There are many on- and off-campus jobs available.

The University Scholars Program is available to new freshman applicants who have an exceptional cumulative grade point average, SAT I score, or ACT composite score. Scholars are awarded a non-need-based scholarship that pays a significant percentage of the cost of tuition for four years of undergraduate study. To remain eligible, University Scholars are expected to maintain a GPA of 3.25. Eligible students are identified during the admission process and must apply under Early Action, which has a deadline of November 15.

Faculty

The University has a faculty of nearly 240 full-time and 350 part-time members; 91 percent of the full-time faculty members hold a doctoral degree. Approximately 250 faculty members are employed in the undergraduate divisions. The University of San Francisco tradition involves a close relationship between students and faculty members. This is reflected in the small size of classes, the low student-faculty ratio, and the faculty members' availability for counseling. Classes are not taught by student teachers or teachers' assistants.

Student Government

All undergraduates are members of the Associated Students of the University of San Francisco (ASUSF). The ASUSF government has three functions: to represent the official student viewpoint, to recommend policies, and to fund activities and services. It consists of three branches: the executive branch, the Student Senate, and the Student Court. The Senate is the central representative body of the undergraduate day students and oversees the spending of the $200,000-plus student budget.

Admission Requirements

The University seeks students who are sincerely interested in pursuing a well-rounded education. The admission process is selective, and each application is reviewed individually. To enhance the quality and diversity of its student body, the University of San Francisco encourages men and women of all races, nationalities, and religious beliefs to apply. Eligibility is based on the high school grade point average, the application essay, a personal recommendation, and satisfactory test scores. All applicants are required to take the SAT I or the ACT, and international applicants are required to take the TOEFL. Students are encouraged to take the SAT II writing exam. It is not used to evaluate admission, but is used by academic advisers to place students in the correct English course upon arrival.

Application and Information

A completed application file consists of the application form, an essay, all academic transcripts, SAT I or ACT scores, and one letter of recommendation. For the fall semester, the application deadlines are November 15 for early action and February 1 for regular action.

Inquiries should be addressed to:

Office of Admission
University of San Francisco
2130 Fulton Street
San Francisco, California 94117-1046
Telephone: 415-422-6563
800-CALL-USF (toll-free outside California)
Fax: 415-422-2217
E-mail: admission@usfca.edu
World Wide Web: http://www.usfca.edu

Students gather on the Harney Plaza lawn between classes for further discussion and socializing.

UNIVERSITY OF SCRANTON

SCRANTON, PENNSYLVANIA

The University

At The University of Scranton, all of the programs and services provided are developed with the student in mind. The faculty, staff members, and advisers are committed to offering students the best possible educational experience and opportunities both inside and outside the classroom. This balanced focus helps give students all of the tools and training necessary for a successful career and a lifetime of learning. It has also gained the University national recognition. For ten consecutive years, *U.S. News & World Report* has ranked Scranton among the ten finest master's universities in the North, ranking it sixth in the 2004 edition. For three consecutive years, *Yahoo! Internet Life* magazine ranked Scranton among the nation's 100 Most Wired Colleges, ranking it thirty-ninth in the 2001 edition. In addition, Scranton is one of only 100 schools in the nation on Templeton's Honor Roll of Character-Building Colleges.

The University proudly shares in the 450-year-old tradition of Jesuit education, which is renowned for unparalleled quality and prepares young men and women to make a difference in their fields and in the world. The University educates the whole person intellectually, socially, physically, and spiritually.

The University historically has achieved both a high graduation rate and a high retention rate. Graduation rates are tracked at four- and six-year intervals. Scranton's graduation rate is 66 percent for four years (38 percent above national averages) and 78 percent for six years (24 percent above national averages). The University's retention rate, the percentage of students continuing their education after the first year of college, is 90 percent. Employment outcomes for Scranton graduates are equally strong. On average, 98 percent are either employed, volunteering full-time, or pursuing additional education within six months of graduation. The University consistently places an average of 50 students per year into American schools of medicine, dentistry, optometry, podiatry, and veterinary medicine. Throughout the past five years, the acceptance rate of Scranton applicants into medical and related schools has ranged from 80 to 100 percent, which is twice the national average. Law schools accept an average of 40 Scranton students per year, with an acceptance rate of more than 75 percent of Scranton's applying graduates.

There is yet another success story at Scranton—the Fulbright story. Since 1972, 111 Scranton graduates, including 6 students from the class of 2001, have received prestigious Fulbright or other international fellowships to pursue advanced study and research abroad. These numbers are unparalleled among universities of similar size. Many other Scranton students have also received scholarships and fellowships. In 2002, one Scranton student was among 300 graduates in the nation to be awarded a Goldwater Scholarship for 2003; another Scranton student was one of 43 recipients of the Jack Kent Cooke Graduate Scholarships, which are awarded nationally; and a third Scranton student was one of only 76 students from sixty-three colleges in the nation to be selected as a 2003 Truman Scholar.

University of Scranton students can choose from more than eighty social, academic, religious, volunteer, and honorary organizations and activities. Through Collegiate Volunteers, students can participate in a wide range of community service activities. In the 2001–02 academic year alone, Scranton students volunteered more than 155,000 hours of time.

The University of Scranton is a campus with culture. Students can perform with the University Players or the University Band, Singers, and String Ensemble. There are exhibitions and lectures at the University Art Gallery. Students can become involved in *The Aquinas* (Scranton's weekly student newspaper), *Windhover* (the yearbook), *Esprit* (the literary magazine), *Retrospect* (the student history journal), WUSR-FM, or *Royal Network News* (the student-operated news telecast).

The University of Scranton continues a long and storied history of success in NCAA Division III athletics. Both the men's and women's basketball teams have won national championships. Ten men's and nine women's teams regularly compete for and win Middle Atlantic Conference (MAC) titles. In addition, the University offers numerous strong intramurals, recreational sports, and club sports that include crew, equestrian, rugby, skiing, track, and men's volleyball.

Location

The University's 50-acre hillside campus is nestled in the heart of Scranton, a community of 70,000 within a greater metropolitan area of 750,000 people. Its location in Pennsylvania's Pocono Northeast places it in one of the East Coast's premier vacation spots and a growing center for major corporations looking for locations outside—but still comfortably close to—major metropolitan areas. The University is just 2 hours from New York City, Philadelphia, Syracuse, and Danbury, Connecticut. The campus is easily accessible by a network of interstate highways and a local airport. Nearby historical and cultural attractions include the Scranton Cultural Center, Steamtown Mall, Steamtown National Historic Site, and the Lackawanna Coal Mine Tour. Just a 10-minute drive away is Montage Mountain with its winter ski area, summer water slides, and concert amphitheater. Other local attractions include baseball, professional ice hockey, the Pocono Motor Speedway, several state parks, and three museums.

Majors and Degrees

The University of Scranton offers fifty-seven bachelor's degree programs and twenty-three master's degree programs through five colleges and schools. There are forty-four undergraduate minors and thirty-one undergraduate concentrations or tracks.

Bachelor of Arts degrees are available in classical languages, communications, English, French, German, history, interdisciplinary studies, international language–business, philosophy, Spanish, theater, and theology and religious studies.

Bachelor of Science degrees are offered in accounting, accounting information systems, biochemistry, biology, biomathematics, biophysics, chemistry, chemistry-business, chemistry-computers, computer engineering, computer information systems, computer science, criminal justice, early childhood education, economics, electrical engineering, electronic commerce, electronics-business, elementary education, enterprise management technology, environmental science, exercise science, finance, gerontology, health administration, human resources studies, human services/counseling, international business, international studies, management, marketing, mathematics, media and information technology, medical technology, military science, neuroscience, nursing, occupational therapy, operations management, physical therapy, physics, political science, psychology, secondary education, sociology, and special education.

Academic Program

In addition to the traditional academic areas, students can enhance their study through special-concentration minors, double majors, bachelor's/master's degree combinations, ROTC, international study, internships, clinicals, and research. Highly motivated students can take advantage of honors programs that provide an interdisciplinary approach as well as a greater depth and breadth in a subject area through special courses, seminars, and independent work. The Special Jesuit Liberal Arts Program (SJLA), available to incoming freshmen by invitation, fulfills general education requirements in a distinctive way with a focus on critical thinking and key liberal arts subjects. The Business Leadership Program helps students hone the talents and skills needed in leadership settings, with special emphasis on the corporate world. The Faculty/Student Research Program provides opportunities to be involved in faculty research in fields as diverse as the natural sciences, humanities, social sciences, and business. In 2002–03, 73 students and 40 faculty members participated in this program.

Academic Facilities

In the last two years, The University of Scranton has spent more than $6 million on computers and scientific equipment. The campus has sixty-five computer laboratories for instruction and student use, with a total of 817 computer stations. The Weinberg Memorial Library has more than 120 workstations with Internet access. In the last twenty years, the University has constructed twenty-five new buildings and renovated twenty-four others. Recent additions to the campus include Brennan Hall, a five-story, 71,000-square-foot home for the Kania School of Management; McGurrin Hall, a four-story, 65,000-square-foot home for the Panuska College of Professional Studies; and Madison Square, a four-building, 40,000-square-foot town-house complex.

Costs

Annual tuition for the 2003–04 academic year was $21,208. Room and board charges were approximately $9400. Expenses for books, travel, and personal supplies are estimated at about $2000 for the year.

Financial Aid

A comprehensive financial aid and scholarship program assists approximately 80 percent of the full-time undergraduate body in the form of scholarships, grants, loans, and work-study opportunities. An aid package may consist of any or all of these sources. The average financial aid package for 2002–03, exclusive of parent loans, was $15,700. Both full and partial tuition academic scholarships are available and are awarded on the basis of strong academic achievement, with extracurricular activities also being considered. To be considered for academic scholarships, students need only to apply for admission; scholarships are need-blind and do not require any separate applications or interviews. The University also offers two special awards for minority students: the Claver Award for students demonstrating financial need and the Arrupe Award for high-achieving minority students. Freshman and transfer applicants who wish to be considered must complete the Free Application for Federal Student Aid (FAFSA). The preferred filing deadline is February 15.

Faculty

University of Scranton professors are known for their excellence in teaching and for the personal attention they give to students. Approximately 84 percent of the University's 252 full-time faculty members hold doctoral or other terminal degrees in their field. With a student-faculty ratio of 13:1 and an average class size of 23, students have ample opportunity to ask questions, participate in research, and meet with faculty members.

Student Government

Student government gives students a chance to put their ideas into action, from sponsoring speakers' visits and other campus events to working side-by-side with administrators. Students are elected by the student body and serve on the Student Life Board and University Council and sit on important committees where they represent the entire student body. Student government plans student activities and entertainment by working with class officers, club presidents, and the director of student activities and represents student opinion on various campus and community issues.

Admission Requirements

The University welcomes men and women of all races, national origins, and religious beliefs. It seeks students who have demonstrated the readiness and ability to enter a challenging college program through a strong curriculum and high grades, class rank, and SAT/ACT scores. It is recommended that a student complete a minimum of 4 years each of English and history/social sciences, 3 years each of mathematics and laboratory science, and 2 years of a foreign language. A minimum of 18 academic units is required for admission. Candidates for mathematics and science programs should have 4 units in both of these areas. Physical therapy students are required to submit documentation of experience in their field. The University also pays special attention to students' involvement in activities, athletics, and service and their work experience. Students are strongly encouraged to visit the campus for a small-group presentation or a personal appointment.

The University of Scranton welcomes transfer students from accredited two- and four-year colleges and universities. Transfer students are considered for physical therapy and occupational therapy programs only on a space-available basis. As a guideline for admission, transfer applicants must have a minimum grade point average of 2.5 (on a 4.0 scale) for consideration. No transfer credit is given for grades below 2.0. Early action, advanced standing (through AP, CLEP, and college transfer credit), and deferred entrance are available.

Application and Information

Students seeking freshman admission must complete the application form and have an official copy of their high school transcript sent to the admissions office. Scores from the SAT or ACT are also required. The Test of English as a Foreign Language (TOEFL) is a prerequisite for international students. International students seeking scholarships need to submit SAT scores in order to be considered. There is an early action program with a November 15 deadline; students who apply by this date receive early notification by December 15. Students who submit the common application must include a statement specifying early action intent. For students who choose not to apply for early action, the University operates on a rolling admissions basis, with an application deadline of March 1. The application deadline for the physical therapy program is January 15, with notification by February 15. The deadline for submission of class confirmation fees is May 1. Students may also apply online, with no application fee, at http://www.scranton.edu/apply. Transfer students should follow the same procedures as freshman applicants and submit an official transcript from all colleges previously attended. The preferred deadline for transfer students is August 1 for the fall semester and December 15 for the spring semester.

For further information, students should contact:

Office of Admissions
The University of Scranton
800 Linden Street
Scranton, Pennsylvania 18510-4699
Telephone: 570-941-7540
888-SCRANTON (toll-free)
Fax: 570-941-5928
E-mail: admissions@scranton.edu
World Wide Web: http://www.scranton.edu

UNIVERSITY OF SOUTH CAROLINA

COLUMBIA, SOUTH CAROLINA

The University

For more than 200 years, the University of South Carolina (USC) has been in the business of providing high-quality education for its students. Today, with more than 25,000 students enrolled on the Columbia campus, USC has grown to meet the needs of an increasingly diverse population, while facing the demands of a burgeoning global marketplace. A major research university offering both undergraduate and graduate degrees, the University of South Carolina is a state-funded coeducational institution. Situated in the state's capital city, the location of the campus is ideal for students participating in internships related to their majors or seeking part-time employment in the area. In addition, Columbia offers a wide variety of restaurants, entertainment, and shopping, all within walking distance of the campus. Columbia also is home to a philharmonic orchestra, a symphony, ballet and dance companies, and theaters and galleries. Described as one of the most beautiful college campuses in America, the historic original campus is surrounded by restored nineteenth-century buildings and shaded by ancient oaks. Spreading out from the Horseshoe for more than thirty-five city blocks, the rest of the campus is composed of contemporary facilities in landscaped settings. Regularly scheduled or self-guided campus tours may be arranged through the University's Visitor Center (http://www.sc.edu/visitor).

South Carolina is a comprehensive university that offers students nearly eighty undergraduate majors ranging from traditional disciplines to technical and professional areas of study. USC also has a graduate school, schools of law and medicine, and advanced professional degree programs. The University is fully accredited by the Southern Association of Colleges and Schools to award baccalaureate, master's, and doctoral degrees. Though the campus is a major research institution, it manages to keep its class sizes surprisingly small. The average class size for introductory lecture courses is fewer than 30 students, 63 percent of courses taken by freshmen have 25 or fewer students, and only 1.2 percent of courses taken by freshmen have more than 100 students.

While about 78 percent of USC students are South Carolinians, 22 percent come from forty-nine states and more than 100 other countries. USC provides an abundance of amenities to enhance the living and learning environment for this diverse student body. On-campus housing offers a variety of residence halls, including honors housing, health and wellness-focused housing, international housing, and a residential college with live-in faculty members. There are more than twenty places to eat on campus, ranging from full-service cafeterias to salad bars and sandwich shops. Recent on-campus additions include Cinnabon, Pandini's, and Zia Juice. A variety of meal plans may be purchased. All students are encouraged to participate in at least one of the nearly 300 student organizations on campus. On the recreational side, there also are 120 intramural sports teams from which to choose. The University's varsity athletic teams, the Gamecocks and Lady Gamecocks, compete in Division I of the NCAA and play national schedules as part of the Southeastern Conference (SEC).

Location

The University's main campus is located in downtown Columbia, a Sun Belt city with a metropolitan population of about 500,000. Columbia is in the center of the state, a 3-hour drive from the scenic Blue Ridge Mountains or Myrtle Beach and the Grand Strand.

Majors and Degrees

Of the University of South Carolina's seventeen colleges and schools, twelve offer the undergraduate degree.

The Moore School of Business awards the Bachelor of Science in Business Administration degree in accounting, business economics, finance, insurance and risk management, international business, management, management science, marketing, and real estate.

The College of Education's undergraduate program awards the Bachelor of Arts degree in early childhood education, elementary education, and middle-level education; the Bachelor of Science degree in physical education is also offered. All other teacher-preparation degrees are a combination of the baccalaureate and master's degrees, culminating in teacher certification.

The College of Engineering and Information Technology offers the Bachelor of Science degree in chemical engineering, civil engineering, computer engineering, computer information systems, computer science, electrical engineering, and mechanical engineering.

The School of the Environment provides an interdisciplinary curriculum and offers the environmental studies minor.

The College of Hospitality, Retail, and Sport Management offers the Bachelor of Science degree in administrative information management; hotel, restaurant, and tourism management; retailing; and sport and entertainment management. It offers the Bachelor of Arts degree or the Bachelor of Science degree with a major in interdisciplinary studies.

The College of Mass Communications and Information Studies awards the Bachelor of Arts degree in journalism and mass communications in advertising, broadcast journalism, print journalism, and public relations.

The College of Liberal Arts offers the Bachelor of Arts degree or, in some instances, the Bachelor of Science degree in African-American studies, anthropology, art education, art history, art studio, classical studies, contemporary European studies, criminology and criminal justice, economics, English, film studies, French, geography, German, history, international studies, Italian, Latin American studies, media arts, philosophy, political science, psychology, religious studies, Russian, sociology, Spanish, theater, and women's studies.

The School of Music awards the Bachelor of Arts degree and the Bachelor of Music degree in music performance, pedagogy, and composition; music theory and history; and music education.

The College of Nursing offers the Bachelor of Science in Nursing degree.

The College of Pharmacy offers a six-year program to undergraduates that culminates in the Doctor of Pharmacy (Pharm.D.) degree.

The Arnold School of Public Health offers an undergraduate program leading to the Bachelor of Science degree in exercise science.

The College of Science and Mathematics awards the Bachelor of Science degree in biological sciences, cardiovascular technology, chemistry, geology, geophysics, marine science, mathematics, physics, and statistics.

The South Carolina Honors College awards the *Baccalaureus Artium et Scientiae* degree, which allows honors students to pursue advanced study in several disciplines rather than in a single major. Students completing the Honors College's requirements, regardless of degree earned, are awarded that degree "with honors from South Carolina Honors College."

Academic Programs

Many of USC's academic programs are ranked in the top twenty-five nationally. Highly motivated exceptional students find a distinctive educational niche in the University's South Carolina Honors College—rated one of the best in the United States. Also of note is the University 101 program, which is designed to acquaint new students with the University and its academic resources. South Carolina's program is recognized as a model for other colleges and universities both in the United States and abroad. In fact, it was recently ranked number one for "Programs That Really Work" by *U.S. News & World Report.* The periodical also ranks USC number one for its undergraduate international business education, number eight for marine science, and numbers twelve and thirteen respectively, for its public relations and advertising programs.

Off-Campus Programs

The University has study-abroad programs with more than fifty institutions in Europe, Africa, the Middle East, South America, and the Far East. Study for a semester or a year at another American university is also available. The National Student Exchange program allows students to study at any one of more than seventy-five U.S. college campuses for up to two semesters.

Academic Facilities

Each of the University's colleges and schools has its own computer laboratories, computerized learning centers, and/or research laboratories. Classroom and computer lab space is located on-site in some of the newer residence halls. Every residence hall is equipped with Internet access. Thomas Cooper Library, the University's largest library (ranked in the top fifty in the country), has holdings in excess of 8 million titles. The card catalog is accessible on the Internet. A new $40-million, 192,000-square-foot fitness center features indoor and outdoor pools, an indoor track, ball courts, a 52-foot climbing wall, an 18,000-square-foot strength and conditioning area, food service, wireless Internet access, a pro shop, and a whirlpool sauna. Another new facility, Carolina Center, USC's 18,000-seat arena, features nationally touring concerts and family shows and also serves as home to USC men's and women's SEC basketball teams. Other campus facilities include two theater stages, Williams-Brice Stadium, and Carolina Coliseum (home of the city of Columbia's hockey team). The University's Koger Center for the Arts attracts nationally and internationally known performing artists.

Costs

For 2004–05, in-state expenses, including tuition, fees, room and board, and books and supplies, total approximately $13,095, while out-of-state expenses total approximately $23,935. All full-time students living on campus incur these expenses. Students have additional expenses for personal and miscellaneous items. Tuition and fees are determined annually by the University Board of Trustees and are subject to change at any time.

Financial Aid

Nearly 80 percent of the University's students receive some type of financial assistance, including financial aid, loans, work-study opportunities, and/or scholarships. Applicants must complete the Free Application for Federal Student Aid (FAFSA) before they may be considered for financial aid. The priority deadline for submitting the FAFSA is April 1. Generally, students considered for scholarships have excellent grades and score 1300 or better on the SAT I. Scholarships based upon merit and strong academic potential are available, with awards ranging from $500 to $12,000 per year. Several of the University's departments also award scholarships to outstanding entering freshmen.

Faculty

There are 1,416 full-time faculty members at the University, all of whom hold a Ph.D. or other terminal degree. Faculty members are engaged in teaching, research, student advising, and working with student organizations.

Student Government

The University's Student Government Association is large, with more than 500 students currently holding positions. There are 5 executive officers, an executive staff, a legislative branch, and a judicial system.

Admission Requirements

A combination of high school records and SAT I or ACT scores determine freshman admission. The following college-preparatory high school courses are required for admission to the University: 4 units of English (at least 2 with strong grammar and composition components, at least 1 in English literature, and at least 1 in American literature, but completion of college-preparatory English I, II, III, and IV meets this criterion); 3 units of mathematics (including algebra I and II and geometry, but applied mathematics I and II may count together as a substitute for algebra I if a student successfully completes algebra II), and a higher-level mathematics course is strongly recommended (e.g., algebra III, trigonometry, precalculus, or calculus); 3 units of laboratory science (2 units must be taken in two different fields, selected from among biology, chemistry, or physics, and the third unit may be from the same field as 1 of the first 2 units or from any laboratory science for which biology and/or chemistry is a prerequisite); 3 units of social studies (including 1 unit of U.S. history, although ½ unit of economics and ½ unit of government are strongly recommended); 2 units of the same foreign language; 4 units of academic electives (at least three different fields, selected from computer science, English, fine arts, foreign languages, humanities, laboratory science, mathematics above algebra II, or social sciences, with 1 unit in computer science, including programming, and 1 in the fine arts suggested); and 1 unit of physical education or ROTC. Courses in earth science, general environmental science, general physical science, or other introductory science courses for which biology and/or chemistry are not prerequisites do not meet the laboratory science or academic electives requirements. Furthermore, it is strongly recommended that students take physical science as a prerequisite to the 3 required units of laboratory science.

Application and Information

High school seniors applying for admission should do so during the fall of their senior year. Transfer students are advised to apply at least three months prior to the semester in which they plan to enter. The application fee is $40.

For additional information about the University, students may contact:

Office of Undergraduate Admissions
University of South Carolina
Columbia, South Carolina 29208
Telephone: 803-777-7700
800-868-5USC (toll-free)
E-mail: admissions-ugrad@sc.edu
World Wide Web: http://www.sc.edu/admissions

UNIVERSITY OF SOUTHERN CALIFORNIA

LOS ANGELES, CALIFORNIA

The University

The second-largest private university in the country, the University of Southern California (USC) is an international center of learning, enrolling more than 29,000 students, about half of which are undergraduates. USC's educational mission is to develop students as leaders of the twenty-first century. Toward this end, the University stresses the blending of theory and practice in undergraduate education. Students can select courses, majors, and minors from the liberal arts offerings of the College of Letters, Arts and Sciences as well as the curricula of seventeen professional schools. The combination of breadth and depth that USC offers is unsurpassed in American higher education.

In addition to academic major and minor programs, USC offers undergraduates an academic life full of opportunities—to conduct research with faculty members, to study abroad, to learn by serving the community, to pursue a variety of internships, and much more.

USC was chosen as College of the Year by the 2000 edition of the *Time/Princeton Review College Guide*, largely because of the remarkable bonds the University has forged with local schools, community residents, police, businesses, and community organizations. More than half of all undergraduates volunteer their services to the surrounding community.

More than two thirds of the students, including 90 percent of the freshmen, live on or near the campus. Three major theaters on campus offer a regular series of concerts, operas, plays, and other events. The more than 450 clubs and organizations include chapters of more than thirty honor societies, more than fifty academic organizations, twenty-six fraternities, twelve sororities, and more than thirty-five ethnic/cultural groups.

USC's intercollegiate athletics program has won more NCAA men's team championships, produced more Olympic athletes, and had more members receive NCAA postgraduate scholarships and fellowships than the intercollegiate sports program at any other school. The proud Trojan tradition also extends to intramural competition in twenty-eight sports.

USC is among the nation's most diverse campuses. Students come from all fifty states and more than 100 countries.

Location

USC's location in the heart of Los Angeles exposes undergraduates to one of the world's great cosmopolitan centers. USC students take advantage of this setting through internships with major corporations, new technology ventures, the entertainment industry, museums and galleries, nonprofit organizations, and government agencies.

Across the street from USC in Exposition Park are museums, gardens, and the Memorial Coliseum. The nearby Figueroa Boulevard Sports and Entertainment Corridor includes the Shrine Auditorium, frequent host to the Grammy event; the enormous Los Angeles Convention Center; the new Disney Concert Hall; and the Staples Center, which hosts the Lakers, Kings, and Clippers.

USC is minutes away from the beaches of Santa Monica and Venice and also offers easy access to the hiking and bike trails of the Santa Mountain Mountains. Local ski resorts are about a 90-minute drive from the campus.

Majors and Degrees

With the unique combination of a strong liberal arts college and outstanding professional schools, USC offers bachelor's degrees in more than eighty undergraduate majors and more than 100 minors. Many freshmen select majors within the College of Letters, Arts and Sciences. Among the more popular choices are biochemistry, economics, English, international relations, and psychology. Students can also select majors such as American studies and ethnicity, biophysics, East Asian languages and culture, or environmental studies.

Many USC undergraduates also select majors or minors in USC's professional schools, including the Leventhal School of Accounting; the School of Architecture; the Marshall School of Business; the School of Cinema-Television; the Annenberg School for Communication; the School of Engineering; the School of Fine Arts; the Leonard Davis School of Gerontology; the Keck School of Medicine; the Thornton School of Music; the School of Policy, Planning, and Development; and the School of Theatre.

Perhaps what distinguishes USC most is the breadth of disciplines that undergraduates can pursue. For example, USC students can major in business and minor in bioethics, major in political science and minor in international urban development, double major in biomedical engineering and Russian, major in cinema-television and minor in music industry, or double major in psychology and art history.

The USC Renaissance Scholar program recognizes students who achieve academic excellence in two or more disparate fields of study. In addition to the academic honor, graduating seniors who meet the USC Renaissance Scholar eligibility criteria may compete for a select number of $10,000 prizes.

Academic Programs

With an 11:1 student-faculty ratio and an average class size of 26, USC has succeeded in creating within a large research university the intimacy typically associated with smaller colleges.

The distinctive USC Core is designed to help students acquire the analytical tools to question things often taken for granted and to understand the values at issue in contemporary society. The core sharpens students' skills in critical thinking, learning to weigh competing theories, evaluating new evidence, and articulating an informed, individual point of view.

USC's Learning Communities help students make informed choices about a major. Learning Communities are groups of up to 20 students who take two courses together. Students select the Learning Community that best fits their interests. Learning Communities have a variety of themes, such as "Media and Culture," "Medicine, Science, and Technology" or "Law and Society." Each group shares a faculty mentor and a staff adviser. Whether students are considering a health profession, law school, journalism, or a business career, there is a Learning Community to suit their interests and help organize their options.

The Freshman Seminar Program was created to ensure that incoming freshmen would have opportunities to work closely with faculty members. Students learn the excitement of intellectual inquiry by participating once a week in a 2-hour seminar limited to 18 freshmen. Past topics include political cartooning, the Internet, Israel, psychoanalysis, ecological issues, the arts, science fiction, issues in law and medicine, international terrorism, and the value of a college education.

Students can participate in laboratory research as early as their freshman year, and all USC undergraduates are encouraged to engage in research or scholarship with faculty members and graduate students. USC also offers extensive opportunities to study abroad, pursue internships, and integrate service to community with academic study.

The fall semester runs from late August to December, and the spring semester runs from January to late April. Students normally enroll for four classes per semester. A maximum of 32 units of credit may be earned by examination.

Academic Facilities

The USC libraries house nearly 3 million volumes and more than 20,000 current journal subscriptions. Designed to support undergraduate learning, the Thomas and Dorothy Leavey Library is one of the most technologically sophisticated libraries in the world, featuring a core collection of books and journals, two electronic information commons with nearly 200 computer workstations, more than fifty collaborative workspaces, a hands-on learning classroom, a multimedia auditorium, and more than 1,400 reader seats.

All of USC's freshman housing facilities have at least one Ethernet connection per student. Computer labs throughout campus provide hundreds of workstations, each offering access to USC hosts, library resources, and the Internet. The campus has a variety of computer classrooms and multimedia-equipped auditoriums. Other USC facilities range from highly sophisticated laboratories in engineering and the natural sciences to state-of-the-art production facilities in the School of Cinema-Television.

Costs

For 2003–04, the estimated cost of attendance for undergraduates was $28,692 for tuition and fees, $8632 for room and board, and $650 per year for books and supplies.

Financial Aid

USC attempts to meet the full USC-determined financial need of all undergraduates who meet the established deadlines and requirements. More than 60 percent of undergraduates receive some form of need-based assistance. The University annually administers more than $250 million in undergraduate financial aid. Students interested in receiving financial aid must submit the Free Application for Federal Student Aid (FAFSA) and the Financial Aid PROFILE by January 20 to receive priority consideration for available funds. California residents must apply for Cal Grants when submitting the FAFSA. Those who submit their FAFSA and Financial Aid PROFILE forms by January 20 receive notification of their financial aid eligibility by April 1. Students may be asked to submit additional materials in support of their financial aid applications. USC offers scholarships ranging from several hundred dollars up to the full cost of tuition; many are based on academic performance, and some require students to submit separate scholarship applications.

Faculty

USC has approximately 3,800 faculty members. The ratio of instructional faculty members to undergraduate students is approximately 1:11. USC is one of a small number of academic institutions in which research and teaching are inextricably intertwined. Faculty members are not simply teachers of the works of others, but active contributors to what is taught, thought, and practiced throughout the world.

Student Government

Recognized by the administration as the official voice of the student body, the Student Senate is a student-elected representative body of 32 senators that provides a forum for the expression and advocacy of student concerns and is responsible for planning many of the events and programs held on campus.

Admission Requirements

USC is a highly selective institution. The University admits students of diverse backgrounds, seeking a broad geographical and ethnic representation. All students must meet a set of basic requirements and standards; in addition, some professional schools and majors are more competitive or require special attributes.

Freshman admission is based on the high school record, class rank, SAT I or ACT scores, the secondary school report, the trend in grades and the strength of the academic program, and the quality of the writing samples. Letters of recommendation and interviews are also welcomed. Sixteen yearlong courses, including at least thirteen in academic solids, are required of entering freshmen. The recommended pattern of academic course work for entrance is 4 years of English, 3 years of mathematics, 2 years of a single foreign language, 2 years of laboratory science, and 2 years of social science, plus 3 years of further study in any of the above areas or in acceptable electives. Students planning to study business, engineering, or any of the natural sciences or health professions should have taken 4 years of mathematics and as many science courses as possible. Transfer applicants with fewer than 30 semester units, or 45 quarter units, of satisfactory course work from a fully accredited college or university are evaluated on the basis of both high school and college work. Transfer applicants with more than 30 semester units, or 45 quarter units, of satisfactory course work from a fully accredited college or university are evaluated primarily on their college work but still must present high school records. Students may enter with advanced standing as the result of credit earned through the Advanced Placement or International Baccalaureate Higher Level examinations. USC is an Equal Opportunity/Affirmative Action institution.

Application and Information

Students must apply by December 10 to be considered for available scholarships. The freshman application deadline is January 10, with notification by April 1. The deadline for transfer students who wish to enter in the fall is February 1. However several schools and departments have different deadlines, and applicants should refer to the USC Undergraduate Application for Admission. For more information, application materials, and complete instructions, students should contact:

Office of Undergraduate Admission
University of Southern California
University Park
Los Angeles, California 90089-0911
Telephone: 213-740-1111
E-mail: admitusc@usc.edu
World Wide Web: http://www.usc.edu/admission

UNIVERSITY OF SOUTHERN MAINE

PORTLAND, MAINE

The University

Since its founding in 1878 as the Western Maine Normal School, the University of Southern Maine (USM) has evolved into a selective, comprehensive, regional, residential public university. USM undergraduates learn from exceptional professors who give personal attention to students. The average class size at USM is 22 students. Students can enjoy the friendly atmosphere of a small residential New England college campus combined with many opportunities typically available only at large, national, urban universities.

The University of Southern Maine offers students a unique blend of academic and residential life opportunities on two campuses only 8 miles apart in Portland and Gorham. USM's third campus, Lewiston-Auburn College, serves the educational needs for this growing region of the state. The Portland and Gorham campuses enjoy full classroom facilities, library services, athletic facilities, and student centers. The Portland campus is the site of the Southworth Planetarium, which is ranked among the top ten small planetariums in the United States. On the Gorham campus there are seven residence halls, cross-country ski trails, an art gallery, a campus center, a theater, and a concert hall. The sports complex features an Olympic-size ice arena and a field house that features a six-lane, 200-meter track; four tennis courts; basketball courts; and baseball and softball practice areas. The diverse student body of 4,500 full-time undergraduates representing students from thirty-five states and thirty-seven countries includes accomplished artists, musicians, writers, actors, and numerous all-American athletes. Approximately 1,700 students reside in University-owned housing.

The athletic program is a vital part of the USM community and the greater Portland area. In addition to a full intramural program, USM currently fields intercollegiate athletic teams (NCAA Division III) for men in baseball, basketball, cross-country, ice hockey, indoor and outdoor track, lacrosse, soccer, tennis, and wrestling and for women in basketball, cross-country, field hockey, ice hockey, indoor and outdoor track, lacrosse, soccer, softball, tennis, and volleyball. Cheerleading, golf, and sailing are coeducational offerings.

USM offers master's degrees in the areas of adult education, American and New England studies, applied immunology, business administration (M.B.A.), community planning and development, computer science, counselor education, educational administration, educational leadership, English as a second language, health policy and management, industrial education, literacy education, nursing, occupational therapy, public policy and management, school psychology, social work, special education, and statistics; doctoral degrees are offered in law and public policy. The College of Education and Human Development also offers a postbaccalaureate fifth-year program leading to either elementary or secondary teacher certification.

Location

USM's location in southern Maine is an ideal place to be a college student. Students have access to a rich array of social, cultural, and athletic activities in Portland, as well as the endless opportunities provided by proximity to the Atlantic Ocean, mountains, lakes, and woods. Therefore, it is no surprise that Portland is continuously recognized as one of the best cities in the country for outdoor recreation. The coast of Maine, one of the most spectacular scenic regions in the country, offers many fine beaches for relaxing and islands for exploring, while nearby mountains and forests offer skiing and hiking. The city of Portland is a haven for the nearly 35,000 college students from the twelve colleges and universities that are within an hour's drive of USM.

Majors and Degrees

USM offers forty-seven bachelor's degrees, two associate degrees, twenty-one master's degrees, and two doctoral degrees through its College of Arts and Sciences, Lewiston-Auburn College, and six professional schools: the College of Education and Human Development; the School of Business; the School of Applied Science, Engineering and Technology; the College of Nursing and Health Professions; the Muskie School of Public Service; and the School of Law.

The College of Arts and Sciences is the heart of USM, comprising twenty-three academic departments. The College offers an associate degree in liberal arts and the following baccalaureate degrees (Bachelor of Arts degrees, except as noted): art (B.A. or B.F.A.), biology, chemistry/applied chemistry, communication, criminology, economics, English, environmental science and policy, French, geography-anthropology, geosciences, history, linguistics, mathematics, media studies, music, music education, music performance (B.M.), philosophy, physics, political science, psychology, social work, sociology, and theater. Self-designed majors include classical studies, foreign languages, French studies, German studies, Hispanic studies, international studies, Russian studies, and social science. In addition, preprofessional study is offered in dentistry, law, medicine, and veterinary science. The College of Education and Human Development offers an undergraduate teacher certification program, Teachers for Elementary and Middle Schools (TEAMS). It includes course work in an academic major that leads to a degree in a liberal arts field and a professional program of elementary teacher certification (K–8). The School of Business offers Bachelor of Science (B.S.) degree programs in accounting and finance and business administration. These degrees provide the basis for careers in accounting, finance, banking, industry, government, and organizational management. The School of Applied Science, Engineering and Technology offers B.S. degrees in applied technical leadership, computer science, electrical engineering, environmental safety and health, and industrial technology. The pre-engineering program provides introductory courses suitable for transfer elsewhere in any engineering discipline. B.S. degrees and teacher certification in technology education and applied technical education are also offered. The College of Nursing and Health Professions offers B.S. degrees in health sciences, nursing, radiation therapy, sports medicine, and therapeutic recreation. An associate degree is also offered in therapeutic recreation. The sports medicine program includes three majors: athletic training, exercise physiology, and health fitness. The health sciences and radiation therapy degrees are available to those who have completed a two-year degree in a health field.

Academic Program

USM's educational programs are designed to meet the needs of a changing society. The curriculum offers a variety of courses in liberal arts that foster creative thinking and communication skills. Undergraduate education at USM is built around a strong, three-component core curriculum. The Basic Competence component develops a foundation of skills necessary for academic success, including the ability to write clearly, the ability to use quantitative information, and the ability to reason effectively. The Methods of Inquiry/Ways of Knowing component introduces the student to different disciplines: their subject matter, methods, and broader purposes. These include the fine arts, humanities, social sciences, and the natural sciences. The Interdisciplinary component seeks to counteract the fragmentation that results from academic specialization.

Examples of interdisciplinary courses include Global Enlightenment; the Illuminated Autobiography; and Old and in the Way: Aging in America.

The honors program provides an enriched undergraduate education to students who are outstanding in their ability, curiosity, creativity, and motivation. Approximately 30 to 40 students are admitted to the honors program each year. Students work closely with faculty members in a series of small seminar-type courses. Later, honors students participate in an advanced seminar and undertake a major independent research project under the direction of a faculty member. All honors program work stresses independent learning, original thinking, and the development of skills in research, writing, and oral expression. Speakers, seminars, discussion groups, artistic presentations, and social events are scheduled regularly at Honors House.

The Russell Scholars Program, an innovative living and learning community, features collaborative teaching and learning, interdisciplinary courses, and a residential component. It includes a mentoring program, community service projects, and internships. In addition to the traditional and self-designed majors that are currently offered, motivated students may choose to design an academic program that is specifically suited to their personal career goals. In conjunction with a faculty committee, students have self-designed majors in many areas, including organizational behavior, public relations, and medical technology. USM's Cooperative Education Program provides students with opportunities to apply the knowledge they gain in the classroom.

Off-Campus Programs

USM offers study-abroad programs in cooperation with institutions in Austria, Canada, England, France, Ireland, Italy, the Netherlands, Scotland, Russia, China, and Japan. USM also participates in the National Student Exchange.

Academic Facilities

USM comprises more than 140 acres in Gorham, Portland, and Lewiston. The campus facilities include seventy-eight buildings with more than ninety classrooms and seventy-four laboratories. The library's collection includes more than a million books, documents, journals, and microforms. Full reference, circulation, and interlibrary loan services are available at each location. An online catalog provides access to and remote borrowing from all University of Maine System libraries. Access to the Internet and other computerized indexes and databases is available at workstations in the library and remotely to authorized users. Special collections include the Jean Byers Sampson Center for Diversity in Maine and the renowned Osher Map Library. USM has a variety of computer resources available for student use. Networked microcomputers are available on the Portland, Gorham, and Lewiston-Auburn campuses. Internet access and e-mail services are available from any of the networked computers. Students who own computers can connect from their residence hall rooms. The computer science department offers UNIX on Digital/Compaq Alpha systems and Windows NT. Specialized Windows NT labs are also available for students in electrical engineering, environmental science and policy, geography, and geosciences. Music and foreign language departments have specialized Macintosh labs. Student microlab centers, staffed by student assistants, have been established on all three campuses. The labs have Windows- and Macintosh-compatible computers with many general purpose and course-specific software packages, including software for work processing, spreadsheets, mathematics/statistics, and databases.

Costs

Expenses for the 2002–03 academic year were $134 per credit hour for in-state tuition and $5958 for room and board. Out-of-state tuition was $373 per credit hour. USM also participates in the New England Regional Program, which allows reduced tuition for some out-of-state New England students. Tuition and fees are set annually.

Financial Aid

Lack of funds should not deter students from applying for admission to USM. During 2002–03, more than $43 million was awarded to students through various financial aid programs, including grants, loans, and employment opportunities. More than 8,000 students received an average of $7663 in financial aid. USM also helped more than 4,700 students borrow more than $24 million in low-interest loans from commercial banks. The average loan was $4500. The Office of Student Financial Aid is available to help students explore funding sources outside USM. All students must complete the Free Application for Federal Student Aid (FAFSA). These forms are available from most high school guidance offices. For priority consideration, students are encouraged to apply by February 15.

Faculty

USM's dedicated faculty members represent a wide range of knowledge and expertise. They include Fulbright Fellows and authors of national note in every academic discipline. In the last ten years, more than 100 faculty members—all with doctoral degrees or the most advanced degrees appropriate to their disciplines—have been recruited from major institutions throughout the country. Faculty members are teachers who can communicate the excitement of learning and the joy of discovery to their students. USM does not employ graduate teaching assistants for undergraduate classes; labs and discussion groups are taught by faculty members themselves. The student-faculty ratio is approximately 13:1.

Student Government

A 21-member Senate, elected by undergraduates, is the principal governing body for student life. Students having problems in any aspect of university life have recourse through the Senate and the Student Grievance Committee.

Admission Requirements

Admission to USM is competitive and based primarily on the applicant's academic background, rigor of the high school program, and grades achieved. USM also considers SAT I or ACT scores, individual talents, and activities. Evaluations of transfer students emphasize their most recent college grades. USM recognizes that prospective students may come from differing academic backgrounds, some far removed from high school; therefore, USM has established different admission categories to accommodate the needs of various students. The admission staff can arrange tours of the campuses, provide information about academic programs, and discuss admission requirements. Industrial technology, technology education, environmental safety and health, and applied technical education/leadership programs require interviews prior to admission; music programs require an audition.

Application and Information

To apply to USM, students should submit a completed University of Maine System Application, online application, or the Common Application and a nonrefundable fee of $40. The application asks for details of their academic, extracurricular, and personal background and an essay on their interest in USM and the degree program to which they are applying. Admission is on a rolling basis. Priority deadlines for admission are February 15 for the fall semester and December 1 for the spring semester. For more information, students should contact:

Director of Admission
University of Southern Maine
37 College Avenue
Gorham, Maine 04038
Telephone: 207-780-5670
207-780-5646 (TTY)
800-800-4USM (toll-free)
Fax: 207-780-5640
E-mail: usmadm@usm.maine.edu
World Wide Web: http://www.usm.maine.edu

UNIVERSITY OF SOUTH FLORIDA

TAMPA, FLORIDA

The University

The University of South Florida (USF) is among America's largest and most dynamic national research universities. Founded in 1956, USF opened in 1960 with an enrollment of nearly 2,000 and now has more than 41,000 students in almost 200 degree programs at all levels. As the principal university for the Tampa Bay region, USF serves the community and offers degrees at several campuses: Tampa, St. Petersburg, Lakeland, and Sarasota/Manatee, with additional centers in Pinellas, Pasco, and Hernando counties and downtown Tampa.

USF's national stature as an academic institution was acknowledged by the Carnegie Foundation for the Advancement of Teaching, which ranked the University in the top tier of American colleges and universities as Doctoral/Research-Extensive. USF is among the top three tier-one universities in the state of Florida. In 2002–03, USF researchers generated more than $250 million in research awards. USF's libraries include more than 1.6 million titles and provide access to hundreds of databases worldwide.

USF's student body is as diverse as its academic program profile. Students come from fifty-two states and territories and 116 other countries. African Americans, Hispanics, and students from other minority groups comprise 27 percent of the student body. Nearly 60 percent of the students are women.

USF is accredited by the Commission on Colleges of the Southern Association of Colleges and Schools. In addition, a number of scientific, professional, and academic bodies confer accreditation in specific disciplines and groups of disciplines.

The Office of Career Services works with more than 800 companies to provide internships and cooperative education programs for students. The office also provides an online and on-campus referral service and interview program. Classes for students are available in resume writing, interviewing, and etiquette. The University hosts both full- and part-time career fairs each semester.

Thirteen percent of the students on the Tampa campus live in traditional housing, suites, apartments, fraternities and sororities, and married and family student housing. Several thousand students live in apartments located within walking distance of the campus. All residence halls are wired and furnished and include all utilities. Special-interest and honors housing is also available to students who qualify.

There are more than 300 student clubs and organizations at USF. The University also has seventeen national fraternities and thirteen national sororities. The Campus Activities Board and the Offices of Student Activities and Residence Services schedule a wide array of extracurricular programs including concerts, movies, and a lecture series. USF is a member of the NCAA and Conference USA (Big East, 2005). All teams compete on the NCAA Division I level. USF's men's teams compete in intercollegiate baseball, basketball, cross-country, football, golf, soccer, tennis, and track. The USF women's teams compete in intercollegiate basketball, cross-country, golf, sailing, soccer, softball, tennis, track, and volleyball. Campus Recreation also offers club sports, intramural sports, and outdoor adventures. On the Tampa campus, there is an 18-hole championship golf course, four swimming pools, sand volleyball courts, tennis courts, a state-of-the-art recreation center, indoor and outdoor racquetball courts, and a private riverfront park.

Location

USF is located on 1,700 acres in north Tampa, near the Busch Gardens Theme Park. Regional campuses are located in St. Petersburg, Lakeland, and Sarasota/Manatee.

Majors and Degrees

The University awards the Bachelor of Arts and Bachelor of Sciences degrees and a variety of graduate and doctoral degrees through the Colleges of Architecture, Arts and Sciences, Business, Education, Engineering, Marine Science, Medicine, Nursing, Public Health, and Visual and Performing Arts.

At the undergraduate level, USF offers the following degree programs: accounting; Africana studies; American studies; anthropology; applied science; architecture; art history; art studio; biology; business administration; business and office education; chemical engineering; chemistry; civil and environmental engineering; classics: Latin and Greek; communication; communication sciences and disorders (deaf studies, interpreter training, language/speech/hearing) computer engineering; computer science; criminology; dance studies (ballet, modern); distributive education; early childhood education; economics; electrical engineering; elementary education; engineering; English (literature, creative writing, professional and technical writing) English education; environmental science and policy; finance; foreign language education (French, German, Italian, Russian, Spanish); French; geography; geology; German; gerontology; history; hospitality management; humanities; industrial and management systems engineering; information systems; information technology; interdisciplinary natural sciences–clinical lab sciences; interdisciplinary social sciences–urban studies; international business; international studies; Italian; liberal studies–community design (pre-architecture); liberal studies–community planning (pre-architecture); management; management information systems; marketing; mass communications (advertising, broadcasting news, broadcasting program and production, journalism magazine, journalism news editorial, public relations); mathematics; mathematics education; mechanical engineering; medical technology; microbiology; music (performance, education); music studies; nursing; philosophy; physical education (athletic training elementary/secondary; wellness, nonteaching); physics; political science; preprofessional programs in dentistry, law, medicine, osteopathic medicine, optometry, physical therapy, podiatric medicine, public health, and veterinary medicine; psychology; religious studies; Russian; science education (biology, chemistry, physics); social science education; social work; sociology; Spanish; special education (behavior disorders, mental retardation, specific learning disabilities); theater; theater arts; and women's studies.

Academic Programs

USF offers students a well-rounded education through a core curriculum of general education and liberal arts requirements. In addition to fulfilling the general education requirements, each student must complete the necessary major and/or minor requirements to reach the minimum of 120 hours for graduation. USF also requires students to complete 9 hours of exit requirements; these courses complement the overall curriculum of all degree programs.

The University Honors College and University Experience are programs that help students broaden their horizons and expand their critical thinking skills. The University also offers Army, Air Force, and Naval ROTC leadership courses and off-campus courses for those students who prefer to study independently.

Off-Campus Programs

A cooperative education program is offered through the Office of Career Services. Students may either alternate semesters between school and work experience or choose to do a parallel program. USF also offers an internship program for local, state, and national government. The Office of Study Abroad and Exchange offers one-on-one exchanges and group trips and is a member of the College Consortium for International Study. Students are able to take courses for credit or complete an internship overseas. The University is a member of the National Student Exchange program. This consortium of 170 schools allows students to study at other member institutions throughout the country.

Academic Facilities

In addition to the programs offered on the main campus in Tampa, USF offers degree programs in St. Petersburg, Lakeland, and Sarasota/Manatee. The St. Petersburg campus is located on the Bayboro Harbor and is an ideal place for its 4,400 students to study. The campus offers small class sizes with a diverse student body. Unique to the St. Petersburg campus is the nationally respected College of Marine Science, which allows graduate students to research the sea's effect on the world.

USF Sarasota/Manatee offers junior, senior, and master's course work in arts and sciences, business administration, education, and nursing. The campus is located on 140 acres in Manatee and Sarasota counties. The West campus touches the shoreline of Sarasota Bay, while the East campus is situated near the Sarasota/Bradenton International Airport.

USF Lakeland is a community university, delivering top-quality professional programs to students throughout Polk, Highlands, Hardee, and Eastern Hillsborough counties. A joint-use facility, USF Lakeland shares the campus with Polk Community College. This collaborative campus makes transferring easy for upper-level students. USF Lakeland is an upper-division campus, serving students entering at the junior level and up. In addition to conventional classroom learning, USF Lakeland is wired with the latest in distance learning technology, including the Florida Education Engineering Delivery System (FEEDS). FEEDS is a statewide program that offers undergraduate and graduate engineering telecourses at USF Lakeland.

Costs

For 2003–04, tuition costs were as follows: $2900 for state residents attending full-time ($14,000 for nonresidents) and $96.95 per credit hour for residents ($464.56 per credit hour for nonresidents). Full- and part-time tuition and fees vary according to class time, course load, and location. Room and board costs were $6200. Room and board charges vary according to board plan, housing facility, and location. Costs are subject to change each academic year.

Financial Aid

The University of South Florida awards $138 million in aid to assist students in reaching their educational goals. Financial aid is awarded according to each student's need, academic standing, and/or talents in relation to college costs and may include grants, loans, scholarships, and/or part-time employment. The priority application deadline is December 31 for academic scholarships and March 1 for federal and institutional aid. Programs based on need include Federal programs such as Pell Grant, Work-Study, and Stafford and Perkins Loans. State aid includes programs such as the Florida Student Assistance Grant, Florida College Career Work-Study Program, and the Florida Bright Futures Scholarship program. To qualify for federal and state aid, students should submit the Free Application for Federal Student Aid (FAFSA).

Faculty

The University has 1,611 faculty members; there are 42 endowed chairs and more than 75 Fulbright Scholars. Approximately 61 percent are full-time and more than 80 percent of faculty members hold a terminal degree in their field. Each student is assigned an academic adviser and all faculty members are required to hold office hours to meet with students in groups or on an individual basis. The student-faculty ratio 17:1.

Student Government

USF's Student Government is open to all students. Each College within the University and each regional campus elects its own Student Government representatives. The Student Government is divided into three branches: the executive, the legislative, and the judicial. Student Government is responsible for the allocation of all activity and service fees paid by student tuition. Student Government-sponsored events and services are free to students.

Admissions Requirements

For admissions purposes, USF computes a high school GPA based on grades earned in all college-prep academic courses. In computing a GPA, USF assigns additional weight to grades earned in honors, Advanced Placement, Advanced Certificate of Education (AICE), and International Baccalaureate courses. The most important factors in determining admission to USF are the quality of the high school record and the performance on either the SAT I or ACT.

To be considered for admission, freshman applicants must submit an application for admission, a nonrefundable $30 application fee, an official high school transcript, official SAT I or ACT scores, and official GED or TOEFL scores (if applicable).

Transfer applicants with fewer than 60 transferable semester credit hours are considered lower-level transfers. These students must meet all freshman and transfer requirements and submit an application for admissions, a nonrefundable $30 application fee, an official transcript from each college or university they have attended, an official high school transcript, and SAT I or ACT scores. Upper-level transfer students are those with 60 or more transferable semester credit hours. These students must submit an application for admission, a nonrefundable $30 application fee, and an official transcript from each college or university they have attended.

USF accepts transfer credits from institutions that are accredited by one of the regional accrediting agencies/commissions recognized by USF at the time the credits are earned. Students with an Associate of Arts (A.A.) degree from a Florida public community college are automatically admitted into the University of South Florida. Students must have the A.A. prior to enrolling at USF, and there are not guarantees of admission into limited-access majors. All students must have at least a 2.0 GPA and be in good academic standing from the last college or university they attended.

Application and Information

Students are encouraged to apply at least two semesters prior to the term in which they wish to enter USF. All admitted freshman students are required to attend an orientation program prior to registering for classes. Freshman admission deadlines are May 1 for the fall semester, October 1 for the spring semester, and March 1 for the summer semester. Transfer admissions deadlines are July 1 for the fall semester, November 1 for the spring semester, and April 1 for the summer semester.

Information sessions, student-guided campus tours, and tours of the residence halls are available Monday through Friday at 10 a.m. and 1 p.m., excluding University holidays. USF also hosts First Saturday each month. Appointments can be made online at http://www.usf.edu/campusvisit.

For more information, students should contact:

Mr. Dewey E. Holleman, Director of Admissions
University of South Florida
4202 East Fowler Avenue, SVC-1036
Tampa, Florida 33620-9951
United States
Telephone: 813-974-3350
877-USF-BULL (873-2855, toll-free)
Fax: 813-974-9689
E-mail: http://www.usf.edu/askrocky
World Wide Web: http://www.usf.edu/admissions

THE UNIVERSITY OF TAMPA

TAMPA, FLORIDA

The University

The University of Tampa is a private comprehensive university that offers challenging learning experiences in two colleges: the College of Liberal Arts and Sciences and the John H. Sykes College of Business. Together, they offer hundreds of courses in more than sixty fields of study. In both colleges, students work with experts in their fields, and there is a shared belief in the value of a liberal arts–centered education, practical work experience, and the ability to communicate effectively, all of which are trademarks of a University of Tampa education.

Situated on a beautiful, parklike campus on the Hillsborough River, the University is just two blocks from downtown Tampa. At the center of campus is Plant Hall, once a luxurious 511-room hotel for the rich and famous. Its ornate Victorian gingerbread and Moorish minarets, domes, and cupolas still remain a symbol of the city and one of the finest examples of Moorish architecture in the Western Hemisphere. Although Plant Hall receives most of the attention, the campus has forty-five other buildings, including a new student center, a library, modern art galleries and studios, state-of-the-art science labs, a computer resource center, a television studio, a theater, six residence halls, and complete athletic facilities. Eighty percent of all residence hall space is new and built within the last six years. Representing fifty states and more than eighty countries, 4,500 students, including 3,700 full-time undergraduates, are enrolled.

The environment outside the classroom is supportive, stimulating, and fun. Students choose from more than 100 student organizations, including honor societies, social clubs, fraternities, and sororities. The University of Tampa has one of the best NCAA Division II sports programs in the nation. Spartan athletes have won nine national championships, including three in baseball and three in men's soccer. Intercollegiate sports for men and women include basketball, cross-country, soccer, and swimming. Men's baseball and golf and women's crew and softball, tennis, and volleyball are also offered. All students may have cars on campus.

The University is accredited by the Southern Association of Colleges and Schools (SACS). The John H. Sykes College of Business is accredited by AACSB International–The Association to Advance Collegiate Schools of Business. The music program is accredited by the National Association of Schools of Music, and the RN to B.S.N. and M.S.N. nursing programs are accredited by the National League for Nursing. In addition, the University is accredited for teacher education by the Florida State Board of Education.

Location

There is much more to Tampa's location than beautiful beaches and pleasant year-round temperatures. Home to 2.3 million people, Tampa Bay is one of the fastest-growing areas in the United States. The city is the commercial and cultural center of Florida's west coast.

Students attend concerts, art exhibitions, theater productions, dance performances, and special lectures on campus and nearby. Just across the river are the Museum of Art, the St. Pete Times Forum, the Performing Arts Center, the Convention Center, the Aquarium, and a public library. Busch Gardens is just a few miles from campus. Within one hour are Disney World and Universal Studios in Orlando. Tampa International Airport, which is just 15 minutes from campus, conveniently connects students with every major city in the United States and around the globe.

Majors and Degrees

The University of Tampa offers bachelor's degrees in accounting, art, athletics training, biochemistry, biology, chemistry, communication, computer graphics, computer information systems, criminology, digital arts, economics, education, English, environmental science, exercise science and sport studies, finance, government and world affairs, graphic design, history, international business, liberal studies, management, marine science (biology and chemistry), marketing, mathematical programming, mathematics, music, nursing, performing arts, psychology, social sciences, sociology, Spanish, sports management, and writing. Certificate programs include art therapy, European studies, gerontology, and Latin American studies. Preprofessional programs include Allied Health, dentistry, law, medicine, and veterinary science. Minors and concentrations are offered in accounting, advertising, adult fitness, aerospace studies, arts administration and management, business administration, computer information systems, dance/theater, economics, English, environmental science, exercise science and sports studies, finance, French, humanities, international studies, law and justice, marketing, military science, molecular biology, music, philosophy, physical education, recreation, sports medicine, theater and speech, urban studies, and women's studies.

On the graduate level, the University offers the Master of Business Administration degree, the Master of Science in Technology and Innovation Management degree, and the Master of Science in Nursing degree.

Academic Program

The curriculum is designed to give students a broad academic and cultural background as well as concentrated study in a major. Hundreds of internships are available in many areas of study. The Baccalaureate Experience begins with a special freshman seminar program designed to help students assess their skills and research their interests. Students participate in a special Gateways orientation program during the freshman year. During the first two years, students pursue an integrated core program of thirteen courses consisting of two in English, one in math, one in computer science, two in natural sciences, three in social science, and three in humanities. Prior to graduation, students are also required to take three writing-intensive courses, one course that deals with non-Western/Third World concerns, and an international/global awareness course.

Transfer students who have an associate degree may be given full junior status. Students receive advanced placement by earning acceptable scores on Advanced Placement exams, the College-Level Examination Program tests, or by completing the International Baccalaureate Diploma. As much as one year's credit may be awarded.

For qualifying students, the University offers an Honors Program of expanded instruction and student research. The program features honors classes, honors floors in residence halls, a senior thesis, and study in London or at Oxford University.

From basic tutoring to graduate school placement test practice, the Academic Center for Excellence helps students stay on track academically. The Center is one of the few facilities internationally certified by the College Reading and Learning Association. The Saunders Writing Center also offers free tutorial assistance to students working on writing projects. Other academic support offices include the Academic Advising and Career Services Offices.

Army and Air Force ROTC programs are offered.

Off-Campus Programs

One-year study-abroad programs are available during the sophomore and junior years. Programs of shorter duration are also offered such as the Oxford Program in England; the Washington Center in Washington, D.C.; and the Model United Nations Program in Cambridge, Massachusetts.

Academic Facilities

The University has recently undertaken $110 million in construction and technology improvements. These include four new residence halls, a new student center, and the John H. Sykes College of Business building. A high-speed computer network connects the entire campus. Every student has free access to the Internet and e-mail, either from their residence hall room or from one of the convenient computer labs located on campus.

The library is computerized and well equipped to meet the diversified needs of the students. It is also a depository for United States and state government publications.

The University has a fully equipped marine science research center and three boats located on Tampa Bay, which is near the Gulf of Mexico and numerous freshwater lakes, rivers, and cypress swamps. Other facilities include the Ferman Music Center, the Jaeb Computer Center, the R.K. Bailey art studios, Falk Theatre, and the Walker Hall science wing. There are also a public-access cable television station and a radio station on campus.

Costs

The total estimated cost for the 2003–04 academic year, excluding summer sessions, was $23,982. This cost includes tuition and fees of $17,572 and average room and board costs of $6410. There is also a $35 application fee.

Financial Aid

A high-quality, private education at the University of Tampa is not as difficult to finance as students may think. Each family's situation is evaluated individually for need-based assistance. Academic achievements, leadership potential, athletic skills, and other special talents are recognized, regardless of need. Army and Air Force ROTC scholarships are also available. The Free Application for Federal Student Aid (FAFSA) is required to determine eligibility for need-based funds. Early estimates of aid are available October through January.

Faculty

UT faculty members hold degrees from the most prestigious universities. Ninety-five percent have Ph.D.'s, and many are Fulbright Scholars and recipients of teaching awards. All classes are taught by professors, not by graduate assistants. Faculty members prize the relationships they are able to fashion with students in classes where enrollment averages 20. The student-faculty ratio is 17:1. Faculty members also pursue scores of research projects each year, often with students as assistants. The College of Business provides cutting-edge opportunities for practical experience through its Strategic Analysis Program.

Student Government

Student Government is the principal avenue for student participation in campus governance. It also provides leadership and serves as the major coordinating body for more than 100 recognized student organizations, interest groups, fraternities and sororities, residence halls, and student productions.

Admission Requirements

Fifteen high school units are recommended from the following areas: 4 units in English, 2 units in college-preparatory mathematics, 2 units in science, 2 units in social studies, and 5 units of academic electives. A foreign language is not required, but 2 units are recommended. The results of the SAT I or the ACT are required. A personal essay and at least one recommendation from a high school counselor are requested.

Early admission may be granted to students who have completed 14 academic units by the end of their junior year and who have a minimum 3.0 average (on a 4.0 scale), good SAT I or ACT scores, and their counselor's or principal's recommendation. Transfer students should have an overall 2.5 average or better (on a 4.0 scale) for college or university work attempted.

All international students for whom English is not a native or first language should take the Test of English as a Foreign Language (TOEFL).

Application and Information

For more information or to apply online, students may contact:

University of Tampa
Office of Admissions
401 West Kennedy Boulevard
Tampa, Florida 33606-1490
Telephone: 813-253-6211
888-MINARET (toll-free)
Fax: 813-254-4955
E-mail: admissions@ut.edu
World Wide Web: http://www.ut.edu

The University of Tampa's Plant Hall was once a luxury hotel.

THE UNIVERSITY OF TEXAS AT DALLAS

RICHARDSON, TEXAS

The University

The University of Texas at Dallas (UTD) is one of the fastest-growing and most selective public universities in the nation. Enrollment has increased 42 percent during the past four years and now stands at 14,000 students.

UTD provides a high-quality education at a relatively low price. Students at the University of Texas at Dallas enjoy many benefits, from apartment-style living to easy access to the members of a first-rate faculty and research team. The large concentration of high-tech companies nearby and the cultural and recreational opportunities of the Dallas metropolitan area provide additional advantages. Students have a sense of community and an opportunity to shape the traditions at a relatively young university.

The University of Texas at Dallas is considered a highly selective university, with average SAT scores above 1200. It also ranks second among public universities in Texas in the percentage of National Merit Scholars in its freshman class.

UTD students excel in national and international competitions of the mind. Its chess team won the Final Four of Chess in both 2001 and 2002, and its debate and creative problem solving (formerly Odyssey of the Mind) teams have done well in numerous competitions. Other mind-game endeavors include moot court, legal mediation, model United Nations, and college bowl.

The emphasis on academics at UTD dates back to the University's founding in 1969, when civic and industrial leaders Cecil Green, Erik Jonsson, and Eugene McDermott, the founders of Texas Instruments, gave the Southwest Center for Advanced Studies (a private research center) to the State of Texas. For the first six years, UTD offered only master's and doctoral degrees. Junior and senior undergraduate students were admitted in 1975, but UTD did not enroll its first freshman class until 1990.

Today, the University of Texas at Dallas has more than 100 degree programs and has developed a national, and in some cases an international, reputation in such areas as audiology, telecommunications, brain health, digital forensics and cybercrime prevention, nanotechnology, sickle-cell disease research, and space science. UTD launched the first accredited telecommunications engineering degree of any university in the United States, and it is one of only a handful of institutions with a software engineering degree.

Exciting research in next-generation technology and biotechnology is at the crux of many collaborative efforts at such UTD centers as NanoTech Institute, Digital Forensics and Emergency Preparedness Institute, Callier Center for Communications Disorders, and Institute of Biomedical Sciences and Technology. The University provides outstanding education and research programs from the freshman through Ph.D. level. Qualified undergraduates benefit from having access to research opportunities with faculty members, employment at the many nearby high-tech companies, and participation in academic programs offering fast-track master's degrees.

Beyond the classroom, students at the University of Texas at Dallas find an outstanding quality of life. Students live in convenient apartments (featuring wireless access to the Internet) that are competitively priced to dormitories on other campuses. The apartments provide students with their own living areas, kitchens, swimming pools, volleyball courts, and clubhouses. The Activities Center houses basketball courts, a 25-meter pool, a fitness/weight room, racquetball and squash courts, locker rooms, and an auxiliary gym for indoor soccer. With more than 100 organizations on campus, students can pursue a wide range of personal interests, such as educational, departmental, ethnic, honor, Greek, political, professional, recreational, religious, service, special interest, and student governance. Students also have opportunities to pursue music, theater, debate, and varsity sports, and they have a strong tradition in creating new organizations to meet their needs.

Location

UTD is located on 500 acres in the Dallas suburb of Richardson and sits among the second-largest concentration of high-tech companies in the nation (about 900 such companies are within a 5 mile radius). The University actively maintains a synergy with its locale and has developed partnerships with those companies—and many others—to provide employment opportunities and co-op programs for UTD students.

While the suburban environment offers a quieter setting for studying, the Dallas–Fort Worth area also provides all the excitement and advantages of a major metropolitan city, including movies, restaurants, the arts district, theater productions, museums, the symphony, theme parks, and professional sports teams.

Majors and Degrees

The University of Texas at Dallas offers Bachelor of Arts and Bachelor of Science degrees in a wide range of academic programs. Majors include accounting and information management, American studies, applied mathematics, arts and humanities, arts and performance, arts and technology, biochemistry, biology, biology–premedicine, business administration, chemistry, cognitive science, computer science, crime and justice studies, economics/finance, electrical engineering, gender studies, geography, geosciences, government/politics, historical studies, interdisciplinary studies, literary studies, mathematical sciences, molecular biology, neuroscience, physics, pre-health programs, psychology, public administration, sociology, software engineering, speech-language pathology and audiology, statistics, teacher certification (secondary and elementary), and telecommunications engineering.

Academic Program

Undergraduate education at UTD is designed to acquaint students with knowledge of natural sciences, mathematics, arts, humanities, and social and behavioral sciences through a general education core of 42 semester credit hours; to provide depth in a major field of study; and to enhance depth of knowledge through courses outside students' majors and beyond the general education core. A total of at least 120 semester credit hours are required for graduation, with at least 51 junior- and senior-level semester credit hours.

Outstanding freshmen are eligible for admission to Collegium V, the UTD honors program, featuring an enriched curriculum, special seminars, and research opportunities with faculty members.

Academic Facilities

The University of Texas at Dallas has a well-equipped, modern campus with extensive research facilities, including student labs in natural sciences, engineering, computer science, and rhetoric. Students have access to Internet accounts and e-mail.

The Eugene McDermott Library houses a collection of 750,000 volumes and 1.65 million units of microform and provides access to a wide range of journals and newspapers through its Electronic Reference Center.

Costs

The cost of college varies from student to student, even at the same university. The following costs are what students might expect to pay for one year at UTD, taking 15 semester credit hours in fall and spring semesters for a total of 30 semester credit hours. Texas residents can expect total costs of $14,250, including $7000 for tuition and fees, $1000 for books, $3750 for housing, and $2500 for meals. Oklahoma residents can expect to pay $15,150, while other nonresidents would pay approximately $21,250. Personal and transportation costs vary, but a typical student can expect $1700 in miscellaneous expenses and $2000 in transportation costs. Nonresidents who earn a competitive scholarship of $1000 or more are eligible to pay the Texas-resident tuition rate.

Financial Aid

The Academic Excellence Scholarship (AES) program offers a variety of generous awards to outstanding students. Scholarship programs range from $1000 per semester (for eight semesters) to cash awards, tuition, fees, and housing allowance for up to four years. Last year, approximately 40 percent of the freshman class received these scholarships. In addition, UTD is a sponsor of the National Merit Scholarship program.

The Financial Aid Office provides a comprehensive program of need-based grants and scholarships, loans, and job opportunities. To apply for need-based financial aid, students should complete the Free Application for Federal Student Aid (FAFSA). The FAFSA is available from high school counselors and via the World Wide Web. Students can visit the Financial Aid Office Web site at http://financial-aid.utdallas.edu, select the Applications option, and access the FAFSA. To receive priority consideration for the fall semester, students should submit all financial aid application materials prior to April 15.

Faculty

The University of Texas at Dallas has a world-class faculty that includes 2 Nobel laureates. With renowned experts in all of the University's schools, UTD has one of the best research faculties in the Southwest. Since most of the undergraduate courses are taught by full-time faculty members, students learn from leaders in their fields. Students regularly praise the availability of faculty members to answer questions, give advice, and provide mentoring. Students can also easily access the top administrators on campus. UTD President Franklyn Jenifer holds office hours for students on Friday afternoons.

Student Government

Students play a critical role in shaping UTD. Student Government Association leaders are instrumental in advocacy for policy changes and facility expansion. The University administration seeks student input on a wide range of issues, including fee structure, sports, recreation, entertainment, and other University programs affecting students.

Admission Requirements

The curriculum and the expectations of student performance at the University of Texas at Dallas assume that entering freshmen have successfully completed a full, college-track high school curriculum, including language arts (4 units), mathematics (3.5 units), science (3 units of laboratory science, excluding physical science), social sciences (3 units), foreign language (2 units in a single foreign language), and fine arts (.5 unit in music, art, or drama). In addition, students must demonstrate strong general verbal/quantitative aptitudes as measured on national standardized tests (ACT or SAT I).

Students are automatically admitted to the University as first-time freshmen if they graduate in the top 10 percent of their class from an accredited Texas high school. Applications from all students not graduating from Texas high schools in the top 10 percent of their class are reviewed by the UTD Admissions Committee, chaired by the Dean of Undergraduate Studies. These reviews give primary consideration to the applicant's scores on standardized tests and high school scholastic records, regarding both the type and nature of courses taken and the grades achieved in specific courses. Applicants may submit additional materials for the Admissions Committee to consider in evaluating their prospective success with a rigorous college curriculum in a challenging environment. Such material can document the applicant's achievements in work experiences, community service, extracurricular activities, and surmounting obstacles to pursue higher education. Letters of reference from high school teachers, counselors, supervisors, and activity leaders are appropriate in such instances. Students should refer to the UTD catalog on the Web at http://www.utdallas.edu/student/catalog/ for further clarification.

Application and Information

To apply for admission to the University of Texas of Dallas, students should submit a completed application; two current high school transcripts sent directly from each school (two final high school transcripts that reflect graduation date, class rank, and national test scores must be sent upon graduation from high school); SAT I or ACT scores (if test scores are not on the high school transcript, they must be submitted by the testing agency); and a $50 nonrefundable application fee. Although paper applications for admission are acceptable, the University prefers the electronic application available at http://www.applytexas.org.

Permanent residents and U.S. citizens should submit applications, including all necessary supporting documents, prior to the following dates to ensure timely processing: fall semester, July 1; spring semester, November 1; and summer semester, April 1. Application deadlines for international students are: fall semester, May 1; spring semester, September 1; and summer semester, March 1. International applicants must also submit a financial affidavit of support, TOEFL scores (550 paper-based test or 213 computer-based test), and an additional $50 fee for evaluation of international documents.

For further information, students should contact:

Barry Samsula
Director of Enrollment Services
The University of Texas at Dallas
P.O. Box 830688, HH10
Richardson, Texas 75083-0688
Telephone: 972-883-2270
800-889-2443 (toll-free)
E-mail: interest@utdallas.edu
World Wide Web: http://www.utdallas.edu/

University of Texas at Dallas students enjoy apartment-style living.

UNIVERSITY OF THE ARTS

College of Art and Design
College of Performing Arts
College of Media and Communication

PHILADELPHIA, PENNSYLVANIA

UArts
The University of the Arts

The University

The only university in the nation devoted exclusively to education and training in design and the visual, media, and performing arts, the University of the Arts (UArts) is located in the heart of Philadelphia's professional arts community. More than 2,000 students from forty states and thirty countries are enrolled in the undergraduate and graduate programs. Composed of the College of Art and Design, the College of Performing Arts, and the College of Media and Communication, the University offers intensive concentration within a major field as well as creative challenges in multidisciplinary exploration. Founded in 1876, the Philadelphia College of Art and Design is one of the country's leading art colleges, with nationally renowned design, fine arts, and crafts departments. Since its founding in 1870 as the Philadelphia Musical Academy, the Philadelphia College of Performing Arts has expanded to include a School of Dance, with programs in ballet, modern, jazz, and tap, as well as a School of Theater Arts, with acting and musical theater. In 1996, the University inaugurated the College of Media and Communication to prepare students for new careers in emerging interdisciplinary fields, such as multimedia design, electronic communication, information architecture, computer-generated design, electronic arts and performance, and writing for film/TV.

The University sponsors a variety of activities and regular gallery and museum trips to New York City and Washington, D.C. One fourth of the students live in University housing, which provides coed apartment-style accommodations with complete kitchen and bath facilities and laundry rooms on the premises. Resident advisers live on each floor, and there is 24-hour security. Out-of-town freshmen are guaranteed housing if their contracts are received by June 1. The University also assists students in finding off-campus residences.

Location

With the acquisition and renovation of a seventeen-story, 220,000-square-foot building, the University campus now spans the Avenue of the Arts from South Street to Walnut Street, the business and cultural nerve center of Center City Philadelphia. Next door to the University's historic Hamilton Hall is the city's magnificent Kimmel Regional Performing Art Center; in the adjacent blocks are the famous Academy of Music, the Wilma Theater, and the University's own Merriam Theater, which books touring Broadway shows for the general public and hosts UArts student performances. The area also has world-class museums (notably the Philadelphia Museum of Art and the Barnes Museum), galleries, music and dance facilities, superb restaurants, and retail stores. Of historic importance, but also modern and sophisticated, the city is at the same time a series of small, close-knit neighborhoods with verdant squares. Fairmount Park, the largest city park in the world, provides facilities for sports activities and picnicking. UArts has the reputation of being the safest campus in the city.

Majors and Degrees

In the art and design fields, the University confers the B.F.A. degree in animation, crafts, film, graphic design, illustration, painting and drawing, photography, printmaking, and sculpture and the B.S. degree in industrial design. It also offers a certificate program in art education and a concentration in art therapy. In the School of Music, the University confers the B.M. degree in composition, instrumental performance (with a jazz/contemporary focus), and vocal performance. The School of Dance offers B.F.A. degree programs in dance and dance education, and the School of Theater Arts offers B.F.A. degree programs in acting, applied theater arts, design technical theater, and musical theater, plus a concentration in stage combat. A two-year certificate is available in dance and music. The University also confers the B.F.A. degree in writing for film and television, a B.F.A. in multimedia, and a B.S. degree program in communication.

Academic Programs

Students are attracted to UArts because of its dynamic, creative atmosphere. Whether majoring in dance, sculpture, graphic design, or multimedia, they enjoy interacting with their talented peers in other disciplines. The Freshman Project, the culmination of the required first-year writing course in liberal arts, provides the first opportunity for freshmen to work with students in other majors on a cross-disciplinary creative project. Students are further encouraged, to the extent that their busy schedules allow, to take free elective courses outside their chosen major. All students take a total of 42 credits in liberal arts, which gives them substantial exposure to humanities, social science, and science and provides them with the historical and theoretical framework of their major field.

The freshman year in the College of Art and Design is devoted to the Foundation Program and is exploratory, allowing students to investigate various disciplines before deciding on a specific major. Students are assigned to small sections, each with a team of 3 instructors. In the fall, students take two-dimensional design, three-dimensional design, and drawing; in the spring, they may substitute a Time and Motion course for one of these. General program requirements vary from department to department. At the end of the freshman year, students select a major in animation, crafts, film/TV, fine arts, graphic design, illustration, or photography, and they may add a concentration in art education or art therapy. A wide variety of internship experiences is available to qualified students. A minimum of 123 credits is required for graduation, including 18 credits in the Foundation Program, 42 credits in the major, 42 credits in liberal arts, 15 credits in electives (9 credits of which must be taken in a department other than the major), and 6 credits in other areas outside the major. Students may request credit by examination in liberal arts subjects and by portfolio examination in studio art subjects.

In the College of Performing Arts, the School of Music program stresses individualized training, with a performance emphasis. Students undergo intensive training in theory and musicianship. Private lessons are supplemented by master classes and ensemble work. In the School of Dance, two years of ballet, modern, and jazz dance are required before students choose a major in the junior year. Electives include improvisation, repertory, partnering, Spanish dance, ethnic dance, character, and mime. The School of Theater Arts concentrates on developing the student's skill as an actor. In addition to the acting studio, requirements include courses in movement, stage combat, mime, and modern dance. In the College of Performing Arts, a minimum of 126 to 130 credits is required for graduation, 42 of which must be in liberal arts. Participation in the 17-credit MATPREP Program enables students to complete bachelor's and master's degrees in teaching music in five years. The University has close working relationships, including internships, with professional theater, dance, and music groups in Philadelphia and elsewhere. Students are also encouraged to seek professional roles.

The College of Media and Communication was inaugurated in 1996 in recognition of new artistic opportunities that have arisen due to advances in digital technology. In the College's first B.F.A. program, Writing for Film and Television, students learn to create original narrative prose and to adapt stories to different media through intensive creative writing experiences as well as through the study of mainstream and experimental literature, emphasizing the art of storytelling. The B.F.A. program in multimedia is designed to prepare students to work in fields in which close interaction among arts disciplines, digital fluency, collaboration, and effective communication are key components. Students learn to combine text, image, video, animation, and sound to educate, entertain, and communicate and explore concepts of interaction and communication design. The B.S. program in communication enables students to develop, in the first two years of this major, the conceptual understanding, creative problem-solving and technical skills, and storytelling ability required for effective communication in all media. After selecting a concentration in digital journalism, documentary media production, or advertising and social marketing, students work in the studio and on location, both collaboratively and individually, on creative projects using primarily digital media. Internships in professional settings provide students with real-life experience in the field.

Academic Facilities

The University facilities are composed of numerous buildings, with studios, classrooms, galleries, theaters, lounges, cafes, dormitories, and administrative offices. The Terra Building considerably augments the University's academic space, providing seventeen floors of studios, computer labs, classrooms, performing spaces, and TV and video production and recording studios. All design departments provide individual workstations for seniors and exhibition spaces that feature student and faculty work throughout the year. The University also maintains several public galleries, where students may exhibit their work along with curator-managed exhibitions of the work of distinguished guest artists. These include the Rosenwald-Wolf Gallery, the Arronson and Great Hall Galleries, and the Mednick Gallery. Student performances are held in the University's formal theaters, such as the 200-seat Dance Theater, the historic 1,668-seat Merriam Theater, the black box theater, the music recital hall, the Arts Bank, and a 239-seat state-of-the-art theater and rehearsal hall, and in the many informal spaces on campus.

As part of a multimillion-dollar telecommunications project, the campus has installed a multifunctional telephone system and a campuswide data network, which provides Internet access for every computer attached to the network. Academic computing resources include more than twenty labs on Macintosh and PC platforms that are used for special applications, such as animation, digital imaging, 3-D modeling, multimedia, music, CAD, Web page design, and more, as well as some for word processing and general purposes. Several "smart" classrooms enable faculty members to use computer applications and Internet access in their presentations; smart studios allow students to function as they would in the professional world, with a computer in the studio or office.

Students work in a large number and variety of specialized facilities—both high and low technology—throughout the campus that support the learning of their craft. Among these are the Typography Lab, the Borowsky Center for Publication Arts, digital video editing suites, photo/film/animation labs and darkrooms, a scanner lab, an SGI lab, a bronze foundry and plaster workshop, and crafts studios and workshops for ceramics, metals, wood, glassblowing, papermaking, and fibers. The performing arts facilities include a recording studio; music technology (MIDI) studios; editing suites; chamber music studios and practice rooms; computer labs; dance and movement studios, with barres, mirrors, and resilient floors; and acting studios.

The University's library facilities include the Albert M. Greenfield Library, which contains an extensive collection of books, journals, photographs, and videotapes devoted to the arts; a Picture Resource File; Special Collections, with special strengths in book arts and textiles; a slide library that has a collection of more than 140,000 slides of art works and historical images; and a music library that contains manuscripts, journals, scores, and listening and viewing facilities. The holdings include books and periodicals, music scores, mounted pictures, slides, music recorded in LP and CD formats, videocassettes, videodiscs, and multimedia formats.

Costs

Tuition for the 2004–05 academic year is $22,060 plus a general student fee of $850. Accommodations in 3- or 4-person apartment-style dormitory units range from $4850 to $6200.

Financial Aid

More than 75 percent of the University's students received more than $26.5 million in scholarships and other financial aid in 2003–04. The University funds presidential scholarships based on artistic potential and academic achievement. Financial aid is also available on the basis of the applicant's demonstrated financial need. Applicants must submit the Free Application for Federal Student Aid (FAFSA). March 1 is the suggested filing date. The University administers the following federal, campus-based student assistance programs: Federal Perkins Loans, Federal Work-Study, and Federal Supplemental Educational Opportunity Grants. Applicants who wish to be considered for scholarships should complete applications for admission and financial aid prior to March 31. Families from many different income levels can qualify for some type of financial assistance. In addition, the University's location in a large, active city provides students with diverse opportunities for part-time employment.

Faculty

University faculty members are practicing professionals who are deeply committed to the development of their students. As active participants in the arts, they have successfully achieved recognition in their specific fields of study. It is this real-world experience that gives them the knowledge and understanding that are so vital in the training of young, emerging artists—not just professionally, but also in terms of personal growth. The faculty consists of 325 full- and part-time members; the majority hold advanced degrees. The faculty-student ratio is approximately 1:9.

Student Government

The Student Congress is composed of representatives of the entire student body. Regulations governing student conduct (nonacademic) have been developed to maintain a viable and orderly institutional society, to protect and safeguard the common welfare of the student body, to provide leadership training, and to promote the best possible environment for professional growth and study.

Admission Requirements

Freshman applicants must be graduates of an accredited high school. In addition to submitting a portfolio or auditioning, applicants should submit their high school transcript, SAT I or ACT scores, one letter of recommendation, and a personal statement of purpose.

The placement of transfer students is made after an evaluation of their portfolio or audition and a determination of their approved credits. Transfer students may be given advanced standing.

International applicants are required to submit scores on the Test of English as a Foreign Language (TOEFL); a minimum score of 500 on the paper-based TOEFL or 173 on the computer-based TOEFL is required. Early entrance and deferred entrance are possible.

Application and Information

The University of the Arts follows a system of rolling admission. All students are notified within two weeks of the receipt of all required materials. Students are encouraged to submit applications by March 15 for fall admission and December 1 for spring admission. For additional information, students should contact:

Office of Admission
University of the Arts
320 South Broad Street
Philadelphia, Pennsylvania 19102
Telephone: 215-717-6030
800-616-ARTS (toll-free)
Fax: 215-717-6045
World Wide Web: http://www.uarts.edu

UNIVERSITY OF THE DISTRICT OF COLUMBIA

WASHINGTON, D.C.

The University

The University of the District of Columbia (UDC) is the only public institution of higher education in Washington, D.C. UDC was established in 1976 through the merger of Federal City College, Washington Technical Institute, and District of Columbia Teachers College. The University, through its predecessor institutions, has antecedents dating back more than 100 years. The University of the District of Columbia is the nation's first exclusively urban land-grant university. Certificate programs and associate, baccalaureate, and graduate degree programs are offered in academic, vocational, and technical areas.

The Van Ness Campus, located in the upper-northwest section of the city of Washington, D.C., accommodates facilities for University programs. The modern 21-acre campus includes a media center with the latest automated equipment; a 1,000-seat auditorium; an outdoor amphitheater; a physical activities center, which features a regulation-size swimming pool and a diving pool; outdoor tennis courts; handball courts; and an athletic field.

The University of the District of Columbia is fully accredited by the Middle States Association of Colleges and Schools. The UDC David A. Clarke School of Law, which offers rigorous and community-focused legal training for the Juris Doctor degree, is provisionally accredited by the American Bar Association.

The College of Arts and Sciences offers the following graduate degrees: Master of Arts in early childhood education, elementary education, special education, and English composition and rhetoric; Master of Science in counseling, clinical psychology, and speech and language pathology; and Master of Science in Teaching in mathematics.

The School of Business and Public Administration offers the following graduate degrees: M.B.A. with concentrations in accounting, computer information systems science, finance, management, marketing, and international business and M.P.A. in public administration.

Location

Located in the capital of the United States, the University of the District of Columbia gives its students the opportunity to partake of the cultural, political, economic, and intellectual diversity that such a location provides. As an urban land-grant institution, the University takes an active part in the life of the Washington, D.C., community through outreach programs such as the Institute of Gerontology and the Cooperative Extension Service. It also operates the Agricultural Experiment Station and the District of Columbia Water Resources Research Center as part of its land-grant mission.

Majors and Degrees

The University of the District of Columbia offers undergraduate degrees in its College of Arts and Sciences, School of Business and Public Administration, and School of Engineering and Applied Sciences.

In the College of Arts and Sciences, the following degrees are offered: Bachelor of Arts in administration of justice, art, early childhood education, elementary education, English, French, history, mass media, music education, political science, sociology, Spanish, special education, and theater arts; Bachelor of Music; Bachelor of Science in biology and biology education, chemistry, environmental sciences, health education, mathematics, nutrition and food science, physics, psychology, and speech and language pathology; Bachelor of Social Work; Associate of Arts in child development and nursery school education; Associate of Music in music and music education; and Associate of Arts and Sciences in corrections administration, law enforcement, and water quality and marine science. There are certificate programs in education, gerontology, and nonprofit leadership as well. For further information, students should visit http://www.udc.edu/cas.

The following degrees are offered in the School of Business and Public Administration: Associate of Applied Science in administrative office management, business technology, computer accounting technology, hospitality management and tourism, and legal assistant studies; Bachelor of Arts in economics; Bachelor of Business Administration in accounting, business management, computer information systems science, finance, marketing, and procurement and public contracting; and Bachelor of Science in office administration. Additional academic offerings include certificate programs in entrepreneurship, office technology, and procurement. For further information, students should visit http://www.udc.edu/sbpa.

The School of Engineering and Applied Sciences offers the following degrees: Associate of Applied Science in architectural engineering technology, aviation maintenance technology, computer technology, electronics engineering technology, fire science, medical radiography, mortuary science, nursing, and respiratory therapy and Bachelor of Science in airway science, architecture, civil engineering, computer science, electrical engineering, fire science administration, mechanical engineering, and nursing. The School of Engineering also offers the Bachelor of Arts in computer science with an emphasis on applications. The Bachelor of Science in Engineering is also offered for disciplines in construction and public works. For further information, students should visit http://www.udc.edu/seas.

Academic Programs

The requirement for a baccalaureate degree is the completion of a minimum of 120 semester hours, depending upon the academic program. A minimum of 60 semester hours is required for an associate degree. A minimum of 30 semester hours is required for the master's degree.

Off-Campus Programs

Through its Division of Continuing Education, the University provides opportunities for federal and District of Columbia government employees to enroll in classes at their work sites. Under the terms of contracts and special arrangements with government agencies, the University provides opportunities for government employees to take undergraduate courses and participate in credit and noncredit short courses, workshops, and seminars.

Through its Servicemembers Opportunity College Program, the University gives members of the armed forces the opportunity to pursue educational goals and to receive maximum credit for educational experiences obtained in the military services.

Academic Facilities

The University offers students an opportunity for hands-on experience in a wide variety of disciplines, using modern, up-to-date equipment in many fields, including a printing laboratory equipped with computerized typesetting equipment and offset presses, computer laboratories, laboratories for the physical and life sciences, fine arts studios, music practice rooms, and media learning laboratories.

The University library collection consists of more than 500,000 books, approximately 19,000 audiovisual items, more than 600,000 volumes in microform, and more than 1,400 periodical subscriptions. The collection provides the latest technology, with Internet access for students' study, research, and enrichment.

Costs

The tuition for undergraduate residents of the District of Columbia is $75 per semester hour. For undergraduate nonresidents and international students, the tuition is $185 per semester hour. All students are charged the following mandatory fees: a $75 athletics fee, a $15 student activity fee, a $15 health service fee, and a $30 technology fee. There is a $35 fee for each laboratory course. Students without private health insurance are required to purchase health insurance through a group plan provided by contract to the University.

Financial Aid

The University's student aid program is designed to meet the needs of eligible students by providing grants, part-time employment, and loans. The amount of assistance awarded is governed by the availability of funds, a student's academic progress, and the amount of financial need. Generally, awards are made for the fall and spring terms; summer-session awards are made separately. Students can complete the Free Application for Federal Student Aid (FAFSA) to determine eligibility for all federal and institutional aid programs administered by the University's Office of Financial Aid. The application deadline is March 15.

Faculty

The University's faculty comprises nine departments in the College of Arts and Sciences, two departments in the School of Business and Public Administration, four departments in the School of Engineering and Applied Sciences, and the Learning Resources Division. There is no separate graduate faculty. Most faculty members who teach graduate courses also teach undergraduate courses. All faculty members serve as advisers or academic counselors.

Student Government

The Undergraduate Student Government Association, whose representatives are elected by the entire undergraduate student body, is responsible for planning, budgeting, and implementing all student activities except for intercollegiate athletics. The entire University student body also elects a voting member to the University's Board of Trustees each year.

Admission Requirements

The University of the District of Columbia exercises an open admissions policy. Proof of high school graduation or satisfactory completion of the General Educational Development (GED) test is required for admission. Because the University is a commuter institution, its student population is drawn mainly from the Washington metropolitan area. International applicants are considered on a competitive basis.

Applicants to the School of Law must take the Law School Admissions (LSAT) exam, complete applications for LSDAS and the School of Law, and submit two letters of recommendation. The law student population reflects undergraduate and graduate credentials from UDC and a variety of national institutions of higher learning. Transfer and visiting students are accepted each semester. First-year students commence study during the fall semester only.

Transfer applicants are admitted each semester. Admission is dependent upon the student's academic standing at the previous institution attended and high school record, if applicable.

Application and Information

The application deadlines for U.S. citizens are June 15 for fall admission, November 1 for spring admission, and April 1 for summer admission. International students should apply by May 1 for fall admission and by September 15 for spring admission.

April 1 is the deadline for law school applications. Applications for financial aid may be filed upon admission to the School of Law. For additional information, students should contact the Office of Recruitment and Admissions at 202-274-6110 or on the Web at http://www.law.udc.edu.

For further information, students should contact:

Office of the Registrar
University of the District of Columbia
4200 Connecticut Avenue, NW
Washington, D.C. 20008
Telephone: 202-274-6200
World Wide Web: http://www.udc.edu

UNIVERSITY OF THE INCARNATE WORD

SAN ANTONIO, TEXAS

The University

Consistently rated among the top liberal arts universities in the Southwest, the University of the Incarnate Word (UIW) welcomes the interest of prospective students seeking a challenging and diverse small Catholic university atmosphere. The University seeks students who value small classes, interaction with faculty members, and dynamic learning experiences. Founded in 1881 as Incarnate Word College by the Sisters of Charity of the Incarnate Word, the school achieved university status in 1996. The University has a population of 4,200 students, with more than 3,500 students seeking baccalaureate degrees in more than forty undergraduate programs and more than 700 students seeking degrees in more than ten graduate programs. Men represent 40 percent of the student population. The student body at the University of the Incarnate Word reflects the rich cultural diversity of south Texas—52 percent of students are Hispanic American, 33 percent are European American, 6 percent are African American, and 9 percent are international. Students at the University come from twenty-nine states and Puerto Rico as well as twenty-six other countries. More than thirty percent of students reside on campus with housing options that include traditional dormitories, suites, and apartments. There are two dining facilities on campus, one of which is a full-service cafeteria, as well as a Chick-fil-A and a Starbucks. There are more than thirty different clubs and organizations on campus, including fraternities and sororities, honors organizations, *The Logos* campus newspaper, and theater and musical ensembles.

The School of Graduate Studies offers a Master of Arts (M.A.) in biology, communication arts, education, English, multidisciplinary studies, and religious studies; the Master of Arts in Administration (M.A.A.); the Master of Education (M.Ed.) in physical education; the Master of Science in Nursing (M.S.N.); and the Master of Science (M.S.) in mathematics and nutrition. The Graduate School also offers a joint master's program in nursing and business (M.S.N./M.B.A.). In 1998, the University initiated its first doctoral programs, with concentrations in the three areas of organizational leadership, mathematics education, and international education and entrepreneurship. A Doctor of Pharmacy (Pharm.D.) program will be launched in 2006.

The University of the Incarnate Word is fully accredited by the Southern Association of Colleges and Schools, Texas Education Agency, Council of Baccalaureate and Higher Degree Programs of the National League for Nursing, Committee on Accreditation of Allied Health Education (CAAHE), American Dietetic Association, and Joint Review Committee on Educational Programs in Nuclear Medicine. The University is affiliated with the American Association of Colleges for Teacher Education, Association of Collegiate Business Schools and Programs, Association of Texas Colleges and Universities, Association of Texas Graduate Schools, and National Catholic Education Association.

The University of the Incarnate Word is an equal opportunity institution and an Affirmative Action employer.

Location

The University of the Incarnate Word is located in the Alamo Heights area of San Antonio—an area replete with artisans, studios, specialty shops, cafés, and coffeehouses. The 115-acre campus of rolling hills is filled with live oak and pecan trees and many varieties of blooming trees and flowers. In addition, the waters of the San Antonio River flow through the campus, originating from natural springs located nearby. Within easy walking distance are the Witte Museum, San Antonio Zoo, Brackenridge Park, Sunken Garden Theatre, and San Antonio Botanical Gardens. San Antonio, the "City of Fiesta" and America's eighth-largest city, boasts an international reputation for beauty and excitement—the Alamo, Paseo de Rio (Riverwalk), historic missions, Market Square, Institute of Texan Cultures, Sea World of Texas, and Six Flags Fiesta Texas are among its largest attractions. San Antonio is also home to four military bases, numerous cultural and civic groups, a symphony orchestra, the San Antonio Spurs (NBA), major concerts, and many festivals and celebrations. San Antonio International Airport and downtown San Antonio are just 10 minutes from the University and easily accessed via public transportation.

Majors and Degrees

The Bachelor of Arts (B.A.) degree is offered in art, communications arts, computer graphic arts, English, fashion management and design, fashion merchandising, history, interdisciplinary studies, interior environmental design, mathematics, music, music industry studies, Native American studies, philosophy, political science, psychology, religious studies, sociology, Spanish, and theater arts.

The Bachelor of Business Administration (B.B.A.) degree is offered in accounting, banking and finance, computer graphic design, fashion design, general business, international business, management, marketing, and sports management.

The Bachelor of Music (B.M.) is offered in accompanying, applied music, music education, music therapy, and performance.

The Bachelor of Science (B.S.) is offered in athletic training, biology, chemistry, environmental science, nuclear medicine science, nutrition, and physical education. The Bachelor of Science in Nursing (B.S.N.) is also offered.

The University now offers a complete program in engineering management. It also offers teacher certification and preprofessional programs, including a new prepharmacy track.

Academic Programs

To receive any degree from the University of the Incarnate Word, a student must fulfill the requirements of the University's core curriculum in addition to course work specific to the major. The University of the Incarnate Word recognizes the core curriculum as the heart of the institution. Its mission of producing critical thinkers, effective communicators, ethical leaders, responsible citizens, and caring individuals is well demonstrated in the many successful graduates of the University. The core is composed of approximately 53 hours of course work in rhetoric, literature and arts, foreign language, wellness development, mathematics and natural science, and computer literacy. Students must complete 45 hours of community service to receive their diploma.

The Bachelor of Arts degree entails 128 hours of specified course work; the Bachelor of Business Administration requires 133 hours; the Bachelor of Music specifies 137 hours; the Bachelor of Science in Nursing requires 136 hours; and the Bachelor of Science specifies 133 hours. Individual programs may vary in graduation requirements depending on the minor sought, teacher certification requirements, clinical requirements, and credits transferred.

Academic credit is granted to students who achieve a score of 3 or higher on the College Board Advanced Placement examination. The University routinely administers examinations in the College-Level Examination Program (CLEP) for credit purposes. The University operates on semester calendar with two summer sessions.

Off-Campus Programs

The School of Extended Studies operates education sites at four locations: Alamo Heights, Northeast, Villa Rosa, and Del Mar College in Corpus Christi. The School's burgeoning Adult Degree Completion Program (ADCaP) assists working adults with college credit who seek to complete their bachelor's degree. Consortium agreements allow UIW students access to libraries at eight local colleges and universities. In addition, students may cross-register with three of these institutions for course work if necessary. The University of the Incarnate Word recognizes the importance of providing opportunities for students to gain employment experience in their major field before graduation. As a result UIW students are involved in numerous challenging and rewarding internship and cooperative education ventures. With a diverse student body, UIW is a leader in international education with more than sixty sister schools around the world. UIW is also the first North American university with a campus in the People's Republic of China.

Academic Facilities

The library at the University houses 235,000 volumes and 3,048 periodical titles. Information systems currently available to students include CINAHL and HaPI for nursing majors; ERIC for education students; ABI/INFORM for business majors; and OCLC online system, Info Trac, National Newspaper and Dissertation Abstract, Books in Print, Dynix, and the Internet for general student use. All housing units are computer accessible. The Learning Assistance Center (LAC) underscores the University's commitment to student achievement. Study groups, tutors, and special services are coordinated through the LAC as well. The University's fine arts complex is among the most impressive in south Texas; it includes three theaters (including a downstage), art and music studios, and the Semmes Art Gallery. The commitment to technology extends beyond classrooms and dormitories. UIW, the largest ThinkPad University in the southern United States, offers IBM ThinkPad laptops to all students. The laptop charge varies.

Costs

For the 2002–03 academic year, full-time resident students paid $20,638 for tuition, room and board, books, and fees. Full-time students who commute to campus paid $15,128 for tuition.

Financial Aid

More than 80 percent of all students at the University receive some type of financial assistance, and more than $37 million is spent annually in scholarships, work-study, loans, and grants. The University awards Presidential/Academic, performance/visual arts, and athletic scholarships, none of which are need-based. Presidential/Academic scholarships are awarded based on high school grade point average and SAT/ACT test scores. All other forms of financial assistance are awarded based on financial need as determined by the Free Application for Federal Student Aid (FAFSA). Other federal/state/institutional financial assistance awarded includes the Federal Pell Grant, Federal Supplemental Educational Opportunity Grant, Texas Equalization Grant, UIW Grant, Federal Perkins Loan, Federal Subsidized and Unsubsidized Stafford Loans, Federal Parent Loan, Texas College Access Loan, Federal Work-Study, Texas Work-Study, and Institutional Employment.

Faculty

The University of the Incarnate Word prides itself on its more than 120-year tradition of teaching excellence. The University's 341 faculty members (131 full-time and 210 part-time) include scholars with a variety of backgrounds and experiences. Seventy-nine percent of the full-time faculty members possess either a doctorate or terminal degree. Faculty members at the University insist on playing an active role in the students' learning process. Small class sizes facilitate the dialogue and interaction that faculty members and students enjoy most.

Student Government

The Student Government Association has a long and productive history at the University. Student representatives are included on every policymaking body, including the Board of Trustees. SGA initiatives include a number of forums each year on issues of student concern and workshops/seminars on events of significance (Black History Month, Women's History Month, Earth Day, and the annual Golden Harvest). SGA also approves funding allocations for student clubs and organizations. Elections are held in April of each year for president and executive officers and in September for individual representatives.

Admission Requirements

The University of the Incarnate Word actively recruits students who can enrich and be enriched by a small private selective Catholic liberal arts atmosphere. Applicants are evaluated using a number of criteria—GPA, course difficulty, class rank, SAT and/or ACT scores, letters of recommendation, and extracurricular activities (including part-time work). Prospective students are strongly encouraged to visit the campus and interview with the Office of Admissions. Applicants with nontraditional or disadvantaged backgrounds are encouraged to apply. Prospective freshmen are advised to complete a minimum of 16 Carnegie units of work in high school, including 4 units of English, 2 units of mathematics, 2 units of natural science, 2 units of language, and 1 unit of the fine arts. Favorable consideration is given to students who enroll in courses at the honors or advanced placement (AP) level. High school graduates within less than two years of the entrance date must submit either SAT I or ACT test scores. Applicants must submit an official transcript of high school work completed or General Educational Development (GED) test scores. Transfer students must submit official transcripts of all college-level work completed. Those with fewer than 24 college credits attempted must submit official high school transcripts and ACT or SAT I scores as well. The University requires a minimum 2.5 cumulative GPA for consideration as a transfer student. It is recommended that international students apply no later than three months prior to the beginning of the intended semester of attendance. The Test of English as a Foreign Language (TOEFL) is required of international students. UIW offers an intensive summer English as a second language (ESL) institute.

Application and Information

Applications for admission are accepted on a rolling basis, but April 1 is the priority deadline for financial assistance. A complete application file is processed within one week.

Office of Admissions
University of the Incarnate Word
4301 Broadway
San Antonio, Texas 78209
Telephone: 210-829-6005
800-749-WORD (toll-free)
Fax: 210-829-3921
E-mail: admis@universe.uiwtx.edu
World Wide Web: http://www.uiw.edu

Blue skies and warm temperatures make for the ideal college campus.

UNIVERSITY OF THE PACIFIC

STOCKTON, CALIFORNIA

The University

The University of the Pacific was established in 1851 as California's first chartered institution of higher education. The University's classic college environment combined with modern facilities provides students with the best of both worlds. An independent university known for the diversity of its academic programs and outstanding teaching faculty, Pacific has also acquired a reputation for educational innovation, as demonstrated by the development of its cooperative engineering program and its three-year professional programs in pharmacy and dentistry. The University, which draws its 3,100 undergraduate students from more than forty states and fifty countries, is located in a residential area of Stockton, and the architecture and landscaping of the 175-acre main campus provide an Ivy League type of setting.

The University of the Pacific is a residential university, offering on-campus housing in twelve residence halls, six fraternities, four sororities, and four apartment complexes (including a married student apartment complex). Approximately 62 percent of the undergraduate students live in these facilities. Excellent support services are available to Pacific students to enhance their academic and personal development; these are offered through the Career and Internship Center, the Health Center, and the Counseling Center. Extracurricular activities include plays, concerts, speakers, and movies in one of four theater/auditoriums on campus; excellent athletic programs at the intercollegiate, intramural, and physical education levels; broadcasting (on KUOP-FM), journalism, and forensics; professional organizations and honor societies; and more than seventy special interest clubs. The McCaffrey Center (student union) houses a grocery store, a bookstore, a movie theater, a games area, two additional dining areas, and the Associated Students of the University of the Pacific (ASUOP) offices. Recreation and athletic facilities include three gyms; playing fields; tennis, volleyball, basketball, and racquetball courts; a 28,000-seat stadium; the 6,000-seat Spanos Center; an Olympic-size swimming pool; and a student fitness center.

The University's School of Dentistry is located in San Francisco, and Pacific's McGeorge School of Law is in Sacramento. Professional and graduate programs on the Stockton campus include the Doctor of Pharmacy (Pharm.D.) degree; master's and doctoral programs in a variety of areas in education; Master of Arts programs in communication, music therapy, psychology, and sport sciences; Master of Business Administration; Master of Science programs in biological sciences, chemistry, pharmaceutical sciences, and speech-language pathology; and Doctor of Philosophy programs in chemistry and pharmaceutical sciences. A Doctor of Physical Therapy program is also available.

Location

Stockton (population 250,000) is California's largest inland port. Situated between San Francisco and the Sierra Nevada, the area provides unlimited cultural and recreational opportunities within a short drive, including entertainment in San Francisco; skiing, camping, and backpacking in the Sierra Nevada; and waterskiing and boating in the California Delta area. Stockton is served by Amtrak, bus lines, and three major freeways. Sacramento and Oakland International Airports are both within an hour drive from campus. The climate during the school year is pleasantly warm, with the rainy season generally restricted to the period between December and March. Summer temperatures are in the 80- and 90-degree ranges. Stockton has a diverse ethnic and economic background, offering opportunities for cultural enrichment and community service.

Majors and Degrees

The University of the Pacific offers the undergraduate degrees of Bachelor of Arts, Bachelor of Arts in Liberal Studies, Bachelor of Fine Arts, Bachelor of Music, Bachelor of Science, and Bachelor of Science in Engineering. Major areas are accounting, art, arts and entertainment management, athletic training, biochemistry, biological sciences, business administration, chemistry, chemistry-biology, classics, communication, computer science, dental hygiene, economics, education, engineering (bio, civil, computer, electrical, management, and mechanical), engineering physics, English, entrepreneurship, finance, French, geology, geophysics, German, global economic relations, graphic design, history, international environmental policy, international management, international relations, international studies, Japanese, liberal studies, marketing, mathematics, music (composition, education, history, management, performance, and therapy), philosophy, physical sciences, physics, political science, psychology, religious studies, social science, sociology, Spanish, speech-language pathology, sport management, sports medicine, studio art, and theater arts. For a complete listing of majors, prospective students should visit the University's Web site at http://www.pacific.edu/majors.

Special programs include a five-year bachelor's/M.B.A. option; a six-year bachelor's/J.D. option; several predental/D.D.S. accelerated programs; a five-year engineering program, which incorporates twelve months of mandatory cooperative education work experience; a three-year professional pharmacy program leading to the Doctor of Pharmacy; a preliminary-teaching-credential program; an optional cooperative education program in the liberal arts; and preprofessional studies in dentistry, law, medicine, pharmacy, physical therapy, and other fields.

Academic Program

The University emphasizes a personal approach to education, featuring small classes and close working relationships between students and faculty members. The undergraduate academic programs are arranged through seven schools and colleges, each having its own distinctive features. Students enroll in one division but can take classes in the others and share common facilities. The College of the Pacific is a departmentally arranged liberal arts and sciences college, offering more than forty majors and preprofessional programs. Undergraduate professional divisions include the Conservatory of Music, the Eberhardt School of Business, the Benerd School of Education, the School of Engineering, and the School of International Studies. The Thomas J. Long School of Pharmacy and Health Sciences includes both undergraduate and first professional degree students. The Center for Professional and Continuing Education also offers special academic opportunities.

Each of the University's undergraduate divisions has its own academic requirements. However, the University emphasizes a commitment to the liberal arts and requires all students to have some exposure to the humanities, behavioral sciences, natural sciences, and social sciences through a University-wide general education program. Many freshmen enter the University without having decided on a major area of study, and they work extensively with their academic advisers before selecting a major. The liberal arts college allows a considerable amount of flexibility in the academic program, but the professional schools are more structured in their academic requirements. All divisions on the Stockton campus follow a semester calendar; however, the professional pharmacy program has three terms per year.

Off-Campus Programs

The University of the Pacific currently participates in more than 200 programs in seventy countries in Africa, Asia, Central and South America, the Middle East, North America and the Caribbean, Oceania, and Western and Eastern Europe. Students may pursue interests as varied as art, business, or chemistry and may be allowed independent study, travel, and homestay opportunities. Pacific has arrangements for participation in study abroad through the Institute of European Studies, the International Student Exchange Program, and the School of International Training as well as through special arrangements with individual universities.

Cooperative education and internships play important roles at the University. All School of Engineering students spend two 6-month periods off campus working in full-time paid co-op positions. Students enrolled in all other University divisions have the option of participating in part-time or full-time internships, arranged through the Career and Internship Center.

Academic Facilities

Excellent equipment and facilities are available to assist students in their academic work outside the classroom. The Stockton campus of the University of the Pacific maintains a main library with 400,000 volumes, 2,700 periodicals, 595,000 microform items, and 7,900 video and audio units. In addition, a science library is maintained by the School of Pharmacy and Health Sciences. Students have access to extensive computer facilities. Also available for students are the Educational Resource Center, language laboratories, the drama studio, music practice rooms, the music laboratory, and the student advising center.

Costs

For 2003–04, tuition and fees were $23,700, and room and board were $7490.

Financial Aid

The University of the Pacific encourages students to apply for financial aid from all sources, including local clubs and organizations, state and federal programs, and the University. It is the intention of the University, within the limits of its resources, to provide assistance to promising students who would not otherwise be able to attend. To this end, the University has developed a financial aid program that includes scholarships, grants, loans, and job opportunities. Financial aid awards from Pacific are based on a combination of financial need and/or academic achievement. In recent years, Pacific has significantly increased its merit-based scholarship programs and, in 1997, became the first institution to provide matching scholarships to new students who receive a Cal Grant (California state gift aid). More than 75 percent of the student body receive some type of financial aid, and on-campus jobs are available through the Career and Internship Center. The priority date to apply for financial aid is February 15 for the fall semester.

Faculty

Of the 370 full-time faculty members on the Stockton campus, 86 percent have earned doctoral degrees or the highest degree in their field. The priority of Pacific's faculty is the education of individual students rather than research. The faculty members are actively engaged in classroom teaching and academic advising and also participate in numerous student social activities on campus. The faculty-student ratio is 1:13.

Student Government

The ASUOP, the student government organization, provides many services to the campus. The ASUOP president and Senate express the students' views as they work with the University administration. ASUOP operates a 200-seat movie theater, a grocery store, and an equipment-loan store. ASUOP Presents brings nationally known speakers to the campus, and a very active social commission plans an extensive activities calendar that includes films, dances, and concerts on campus. Each school and college also has its own student association, and all are concerned with both academic and social activities. Students are included on committees reviewing academic affairs and the curriculum structure, evaluating courses and faculty members, and planning future facilities and programs.

Admission Requirements

The University of the Pacific seeks freshman applicants who have had strong college-preparatory backgrounds of four academic subjects each semester. A challenging secondary school program of 4 years of English, 4 years of social studies, 3 years of mathematics, 2 years of laboratory sciences, and 2 or more years of foreign language is highly recommended. Science students should include chemistry, physics, and higher mathematics. The University requires an official high school transcript, a counselor or teacher recommendation, SAT I or ACT scores, and a personal essay.

Application and Information

Out-of-state and international students are encouraged to apply, and approximately 250 transfer students and 750 freshmen enroll each year. Early Action (non-binding admission) is available for outstanding students who apply by December 1. Applications are accepted on a rolling basis, but applicants are encouraged to meet a January 15 priority date. All interested students are encouraged to arrange with the Office of Admissions to visit the campus. Further information may be obtained by contacting:

Office of Admissions
University of the Pacific
Stockton, California 95211
Telephone: 209-946-2211
E-mail: admissions@uop.edu
World Wide Web: http://www.pacific.edu/admission

These students are meeting outside the Holt Memorial Library with the Robert Burns Tower in the background.

UNIVERSITY OF THE SCIENCES IN PHILADELPHIA

PHILADELPHIA, PENNSYLVANIA

The University

The University of the Sciences in Philadelphia (USP), formerly the Philadelphia College of Pharmacy and Science, was founded in 1821 as the Philadelphia College of Pharmacy, America's first college of pharmacy. The University of the Sciences in Philadelphia is located on a 25-acre campus in the academic section of historic Philadelphia known as University City. Besides USP, the University of Pennsylvania and Drexel University also call University City home. USP currently enrolls more than 2,300 undergraduate students in twenty majors and 200 students in twelve graduate programs. The campus consists of fifteen buildings, with a major campus expansion project currently underway. The University offers a wide variety of cocurricular activities that include intercollegiate and intramural athletics; literary publications; social, professional, religious, and honors organizations; and musical and drama groups. USP competes athletically at the NCAA Division II levels, with men's teams in baseball, basketball, cross-country, golf, tennis, and rifle. Women's teams are available in basketball, cross-country, golf, softball, tennis, rifle, and volleyball.

Location

USP's location in the University City section of Philadelphia offers considerable advantage and appeal. It not only offers a wide variety of educational opportunities, but it also is a culturally, architecturally, and socially diverse community that caters to the local college student population. The University of the Sciences in Philadelphia is also actively involved with a number of local community organizations that are designed to foster improvement, development, and unity in the University City community. The Philadelphia metropolitan area is the home of more than forty other colleges and universities. USP students realize that Philadelphia and its immediate region provide unmatched levels of off-campus clinical and scientific opportunities, which are required in a number of programs. Within a short 20-minute trolley ride to the Center City area are the vast cultural, historical, and shopping attractions of the fifth-largest city in the United States.

Majors and Degrees

The University of the Sciences in Philadelphia includes three undergraduate colleges: the Philadelphia College of Pharmacy, which offers programs in pharmacy, pharmacology and toxicology, pharmaceutical sciences, and pharmaceutical marketing and management; the College of Health Sciences, which offers programs in physical therapy, occupational therapy, physician assistant studies, health science, and medical technology; and the Misher College of Arts and Sciences, which offers majors in biochemistry, bioinformatics, biology, computer science, chemistry, environmental science, health psychology, microbiology, pharmaceutical chemistry, and psychology. Students with strong academic interests in multiple areas may pursue double degrees, including two B.S. degrees or one B.S. degree and one entry-level professional degree.

Academic Program

Four majors are offered in the Philadelphia College of Pharmacy: a six-year Doctor of Pharmacy (Pharm.D.) program and four-year B.S. degree programs in pharmacy and toxicology, pharmaceutical technology, and pharmaceutical marketing and management. In the Doctor of Pharmacy program, students are guaranteed a seat in the professional phase (years 3–6) as long as the preprofessional phase (years 1–2) is successfully completed and an acceptable academic record is maintained. The pharmacy program at USP is recognized worldwide and prepares students for the increasingly clinical nature of pharmacy practice.

Pharmacology and toxicology, pharmaceutical sciences, and pharmaceutical marketing and management are unique B.S. degree programs that provide excellent career opportunities and address specific manpower needs within the pharmaceutical industry.

Five programs of study are available in the College of Health Sciences: physical therapy, occupational therapy, physician assistant, health science, and medical technology. Both physical therapy and occupational therapy programs are direct-entry, integrated undergraduate/professional degree programs that lead to the Doctor of Physical Therapy (D.P.T.) and Master of Occupational Therapy (M.O.T.), respectively. The physical therapy program recently became one of America's first programs to receive approval to offer the six-year, direct-entry D.P.T. In both the physical therapy and occupational therapy programs, students are admitted as first-year students and are guaranteed a professional phase seat, provided an acceptable academic record is maintained.

The physician assistant studies program at the University of the Sciences in Philadelphia is a five-year program that leads to the Bachelor of Science and Master of Science degrees in health science and is in partnership with the Philadelphia College of Osteopathic Medicine (PCOM). Students enrolled in the physician assistant studies program complete their preprofessional component (years 1–3) in the natural sciences, social sciences, and humanities at USP. The professional component of the program (years 4–5) is completed at PCOM. A four-year B.S. degree in health science for students who want to focus on general health care and community service is also available.

Medical technology students at the University of the Sciences in Philadelphia receive an excellent three-year academic foundation in preparation for their fourth year, which is spent in a clinical setting at an approved hospital school of medical technology.

Ten different four-year Bachelor of Science degree programs are offered in the Misher College of Arts and Sciences. They include biochemistry, bioinformatics, biology, computer science, chemistry, environmental science, health psychology, microbiology, and pharmaceutical chemistry. Psychology and health psychology B.S. students may elect to remain at USP for an additional year and qualify for the M.S. in health psychology program. The College of Arts and Sciences combines the expertise of an outstanding group of scientists, researchers, and educators with academic facilities not often found at an institution the size of USP. This combination creates an academic atmosphere of especially high quality.

The University of the Sciences in Philadelphia's strong tradition of excellence prepares graduates to enter postbaccalaureate degrees in medicine, dentistry, veterinary medicine, and other health professions. Traditionally, premed students choose to major in chemistry, biochemistry, biology, microbiology, or pharmacology and toxicology. The curricula in these and most of the other programs include the basic courses required for admission to medical school. Beginning with the first year, premed students receive individualized counseling by the Pre-Professional Advisor and their faculty adviser in selecting courses to meet their career goals.

An innovative Science Teacher Certification program is available for those students who are majoring in biology or chemistry and wish to pursue teaching careers. The areas of certification include biology, chemistry, general science, and environmental science.

Students may enroll at the University of the Sciences in the one-year Undeclared program. Through a special orientation program, undeclared students are introduced to the various academic disciplines and career opportunities available to them. Undeclared students formally declare a major during the spring semester of the first year.

Academic Facilities

Classes and laboratory course work are conducted in seven academic buildings on the University of the Sciences in Philadelphia's campus, while the remaining buildings serve as residence halls or support-service facilities. USP houses more than eighty scientific laboratories and a sufficient number of computer terminals for student use. The Joseph W. England Library contains more than 84,000 volumes and 8,400 periodicals in addition to numerous electronic information programs.

Costs

Tuition for the 2003–04 academic year is $19,800; room and board are anticipated to be $8800. Costs are subject to change.

Financial Aid

Currently, 95 percent of the undergraduates at USP receive financial assistance, amounting in the aggregate to more than $7 million. Types and sources of aid include Federal Perkins Loans; Health Professions Loans; Federal Work-Study Program; USP Merit Scholarships and Grants, student employment, and institutional loan funds; deferred tuition payment plans; student loans; and scholarships received from states, municipalities, and service clubs or other organizations. All applicants who seek financial assistance must complete the Free Application for Federal Student Aid (FAFSA). A greatly increased merit scholarship and grant program has been developed, which provides awards for both first-year and transfer candidates.

Faculty

There are 152 full-time faculty members. Of these, over 100 have doctoral degrees. All full-time faculty members teach undergraduates, and many also teach graduate students and conduct research. A total of 40 graduate assistants serve as laboratory aides.

Student Government

Student government is composed of representatives from all undergraduate classes and class officers. It takes an active part in governance through participation in faculty and administrative committees and sponsors a number of campus activities and functions.

Admission Requirements

The University of the Sciences in Philadelphia seeks students whose aptitudes and achievements are in the areas of science, mathematics, and humanities. Sixteen total high school credits are required and must include English (4 credits), mathematics (3 credits, including algebra I and II and plane geometry), and science (3 credits of laboratory science, including at least two of the following: biology, chemistry, and physics). Class rank, if provided by the applicant's high school, and grade point average are also considered in the admission decision process. Candidates are required to submit the results of their SAT and/or ACT examinations. Supplemental testing or an interview may be requested to clarify a specific aspect of a candidate's record. For students whose first language is not English, it is strongly recommended that the SAT II–English Language Proficiency Test (ELPT) or the Test of English as a Foreign Language (TOEFL) are completed. Applications for transfer are welcome, although the number of seats available each year are less than that for first-year students, since all students admitted to USP are admitted for the entire program length.

The University of the Sciences in Philadelphia does not discriminate in the administration of its educational policies, admission policies, scholarship and loan programs, or athletic and other University-administered programs on the basis of sex, age, handicap, race, creed, color, or national origin. All students are entitled to all of the rights, privileges, programs, and activities generally accorded or made available to students at the University. This institutional policy complies with the requirements of Title IX of the Education Amendments of 1972 (45 CRF 86), Section 504 of the Rehabilitation Act of 1973, and other applicable statutes and regulations.

Application and Information

An Admission Application Booklet may be obtained by calling the Admission Office. Applicants may submit an online application at http://www.usip.edu/applying. Each application must be accompanied by a nonrefundable $45 application fee. First-year applications for admission are considered until the entering class roster has been completed. USP follows a rolling admission policy, and applicants are notified of the admission decision after the University has received all required data. Students accepted into any of the programs have until May 1 to submit a nonrefundable deposit of $150 to hold a place in the class, although tuition deposits may be accepted in most programs after May 1. Applicants accepted after May 1 have two weeks to submit a tuition deposit.

Applicants for transfer to the professional programs should submit completed applications no later than the following dates: physical therapy (January 1), pharmacy (January 15), occupational therapy (March 1), and physician assistant (March 15). Applications for transfer may be submitted after the priority filings deadlines. However, they will be considered only after those received by the priority filing deadlines are reviewed. All transfer applications are reviewed on a rolling basis except for physical therapy and pharmacy, which are reviewed during the spring semester.

Director of Admission
University of the Sciences in Philadelphia
600 South 43rd Street
Philadelphia, Pennsylvania 19104-4495
Telephone: 215-596-8810
888-996-8747 (toll-free)
Fax: 215-596-8821
E-mail: admit@usip.edu
World Wide Web: http://www.usip.edu

UNIVERSITY OF THE VIRGIN ISLANDS

ST. THOMAS, U.S. VIRGIN ISLANDS

The University

The University of the Virgin Islands (UVI) was established by an act of the Virgin Islands legislature in 1962. UVI is the publicly supported university system of the U.S. Virgin Islands, serving the territory and the Caribbean. Originally the College of the Virgin Islands, the name was changed to University of the Virgin Islands in 1986 to better reflect the growth and diversification of its academic programs, community and regional service, and research.

The University is a comprehensive institution offering degrees in liberal arts and in professional programs to meet the higher education needs of the people of the Virgin Islands, the wider Caribbean, and the United States mainland. It is a major provider of the intellectual capital for development of the region through the integration of its teaching, research, and public service activities. The University offers undergraduate, graduate, and continuing education programs for responsible citizenship and productive, fulfilling careers. The University is a land-grant institution and a historically black university; therefore, it is committed to advancing knowledge through instruction, research, and public service, particularly in areas that contribute to understanding and resolving issues and problems unique to the Virgin Islands and the Caribbean.

The University's two campuses, on the islands of St. Croix and St. Thomas, are separated by 40 miles of Caribbean sea. The St. Croix campus has beautiful new residential facilities that provide housing for 102 students. The St. Thomas campus residence halls house 250 students.

UVI's 2,500 full-time, part-time, and graduate students come from the U.S. Virgin Islands, twenty-one states, and approximately fifteen other countries (mainly the nearby Caribbean island nations). As a small institution, UVI is able to ensure close contact among student, professors, and faculty advisers.

The University offers a wide range of extracurricular activities and events. Student publications include a literary magazine, a newspaper, and a yearbook. Musically talented students may be members of the Concert Band, the Jazz Ensemble, and the Concert Choir. Basketball, cricket, netball, soccer, tennis, and volleyball are included in the sports program. The University is acclaimed for the excellence of its dramatic productions.

Location

The Virgin Islands are located about 1,600 miles southeast of New York City and 1,200 miles east-southeast of Miami. The St. Thomas campus occupies 175 acres overlooking the Caribbean Sea and has its own beach and golf course. The St. Croix campus comprises 130 acres and includes the Virgin Islands Agricultural Experiment Station and Cooperative Extension Service. Both campuses have playing fields and outdoor athletic and recreational facilities, including basketball, volleyball, and tennis courts.

Majors and Degrees

UVI offers undergraduate degrees at the associate and baccalaureate levels. On the St. Thomas campus, B.A. degrees are offered in accounting, biology, business administration, elementary education, English, humanities, marine biology, mathematics, music education, psychology, social sciences, and vocational education. B.S. degrees may be earned in biology, chemistry, computer science, marine biology, mathematics, and nursing. A.A. degrees are awarded in accounting, business management, computer information systems, hotel/restaurant management, and police science and administration. The A.S. degree is awarded in physics.

On the St. Croix campus, B.A. programs are offered in accounting, business administration, and elementary education. B.S. degrees in computer science and mathematics are also available. The A.A. majors are accounting, business management, computer information systems, office systems, and police science and administration. The A.S. degree is awarded in nursing.

Academic Programs

The University was founded as a liberal arts institution. For baccalaureate degrees, a minimum of 120 credits is required. An associate degree requires a minimum of 62 credits. To ensure a strong liberal arts background, all students must complete general education requirements. The successful completion of an English proficiency examination and a computer literacy examination are required for all degrees. The University operates on a semester system, with a six-week summer session.

University credit may be given for certain College Board Advanced Placement tests, the College-Level Examination Program, and the Proficiency Examination Program of American College Testing, Inc. Credit may be given for General Certificate of Education subjects passed at "A" level for students from British-oriented education systems.

Students have the opportunity to explore career options, serve as research assistants, and volunteer in the many research projects and public service activities conducted by professors and the research faculty. Areas of ongoing research related to small tropical island issues include marine biology, aquaculture, demography, hydrology, and geographic information systems.

Off-Campus Programs

The University is a member of the National Student Exchange (NSE) consortium. NSE enables students from member institutions to spend a year studying at UVI, and qualified UVI students may spend up to one year at one of the 161 institutions that participate in the NSE consortium. UVI also participates in the Caribbean Intercollegiate Exchange program, faculty and student exchanges with Emory University, a 3-2 engineering degree program with Columbia and Washington Universities, and a cooperative early medical school admissions program with Boston University. Qualified UVI students may be accepted provisionally into Boston University's medical school on completion of their sophomore year. Students attend Boston University during summer sessions and for their final year of undergraduate education, which is combined with the first year of medical school.

Academic Facilities

The collections of the University libraries total some 126,000 volumes and are developed collaboratively between campuses in support of academic programs. In addition, through membership in the Southeastern Library Network for interlibrary lending and through subscriptions to a variety of online databases, the libraries provide access to digital and traditional library resources worldwide. An extensive Caribbean collection is included among the libraries' holdings. Interested students can visit the libraries' Web page (http://libraries.uvi.edu) to review other resources and collections.

Telecommunications equipment facilitates communication between the two campuses and connects the University to the Internet. Voice mail, e-mail, audio, and video teleconferencing are utilized to bridge the distance between the islands and link the two campuses; distance-learning technology allows classes to be taught simultaneously on both campuses by video. Computers are available for students' use in the Freshman Center and in microcomputer laboratories on both campuses.

Facilities for laboratory courses in the sciences are available, as is a language laboratory. The Reichhold Center on the St. Thomas campus includes a 1,200-seat amphitheater and other facilities for the performing and visual arts. The new UVI Music Education Center houses music suites and a small theater.

Costs

Tuition for the 2002–03 academic year was $1365 per semester for residents of the Virgin Islands; for nonresidents, the equivalent figure was $4095. Students paid $128 for medical insurance, health service, student activity, and technology fees. Rooms on both campuses were $1250 per semester (single occupancy) and $1000 per semester (double occupancy). Board on the St. Thomas campus was $1915 per semester; on St. Croix, meals are purchased from the snack bar.

Financial Aid

Approximately 70 percent of the full-time undergraduate students receive financial aid. Available programs include federal and institutional scholarships, grants, loans, and work-study jobs. The Free Application for Federal Student Aid (FAFSA) is used to evaluate need. Financial aid applications should be submitted prior to March 1 for priority consideration. For further information, students should contact the Financial Aid Office.

Faculty

The University's teaching faculty is composed of 180 highly qualified full-time and part-time members. Of the full-time members, 60 percent hold doctoral degrees in their disciplines. Faculty members come from diverse ethnic and cultural backgrounds, from the United States, the Virgin Islands, and a number of countries around the world. The faculty elects a member to the Board of Trustees annually.

Student Government

All members of the full-time student body are members of the Student Government Association. Officers elected by the student body serve as its voice within the University community. Students elect a representative to the Board of Trustees, alternating each year between the two campuses. In addition, students are members of most University standing committees, including the committees for academic standards, programs, and commencement.

Admission Requirements

A candidate for admission to the University must have earned a high school diploma or have achieved the equivalent of high school graduation (GED). The minimum acceptable high school grade point average is 2.0 on a 4.0 scale. All applicants must submit scores on either the SAT I or ACT. Transfer applicants must be in good academic and social standing and must have a minimum grade point average of 2.0 at previously attended institutions.

Application and Information

To complete the admission process, a student must submit a completed application form, a nonrefundable $20 application fee, high school and/or college transcripts, and SAT I or ACT scores. Students are admitted in both the fall and spring semesters. The application deadline for the fall semester is April 30 and for the spring semester, October 30. All required documents must be received by the deadline. Application forms and more detailed information can be obtained on line or from the Admissions Office.

Students should direct inquiries and applications to the St. Thomas campus to:

Director of Admissions and New Student Services
Admissions Office
University of the Virgin Islands
#2 John Brewers Bay
Charlotte Amalie, Virgin Islands 00802-9990
Telephone: 340-693-1150
E-mail: admissions@uvi.edu
World Wide Web: http://www.uvi.edu

For inquiries and applications to the St. Croix campus, students should contact:

Director of Admissions and Academic Services
Academic Services Office
University of the Virgin Islands
RR02, Box 10,000 Kingshill
St. Croix, Virgin Islands 00850
Telephone: 340-692-4158
World Wide Web: http://www.uvi.edu

The dormitories, viewed from the golf course, on the St. Thomas campus.

UNIVERSITY OF THE WEST

ROSEMEAD, CALIFORNIA

The University

The University of the West (UWest), formerly Hsi Lai University, is a multidisciplinary institution committed to providing a comprehensive student-centered educational experience of the highest quality that integrates the finest of liberal arts traditions with a global perspective. Founded in 1991 by Master Hsing Yun of Fo Guang Shan, the campus features a uniquely multicultural faculty and student body complemented by an equally diverse curriculum that is deeply committed to the interaction of Western and Asian cultures and the comparative teaching of international perspectives. As a physical and intellectual meeting place between East and West, the University welcomes people of all beliefs and world views. Students and faculty members come together as a community of scholars to participate in an ongoing dialogue to advance knowledge, address societal and cultural issues, and promote education and understanding across cultures. At UWest, creativity, adaptability, and leadership are fostered together with tolerance, ethical commitment, and social consciousness.

A range of activities that enhance learning and physical and mental well-being are available to students outside of the classroom. These include lectures, concerts, seminars, noncredit classes, and religious celebrations, observances, and Dharma (doctrine) classes at Hsi Lai Temple.

The Student Recreation Center is equipped with fitness and weight-training equipment, table tennis, billiards, and a student lounge with a kitchen. The two residential halls each have a 24-hour study room, a multipurpose student lounge on each floor, a laundromat, and a kitchen. Each room is furnished and has its own air-conditioning unit, private bathroom, and telephone and high-speed Internet access. Recreational facilities include a swimming pool, spa, and exercise and game rooms.

UWest is a member of NAFSA, the Association of International Educators, and the American Association of Collegiate Registrars and Admissions Officers.

Location

UWest is located in the City of Rosemead in Los Angeles County. It occupies 10 acres of beautifully landscaped grounds and has modern, well-equipped facilities.

Majors and Degrees

The University offers Bachelor of Arts (B.A.) degrees in business administration, with majors in accounting, marketing, information technologies and management, and international business; Chinese; English literary studies; history, with tracks in Asian history and Western history; philosophy, with tracks in Eastern philosophy and Western philosophy; humanistic psychology, which integrates Western and Eastern psychology; and religious studies, with majors in Buddhist studies and comparative religious studies. There is also a dual-degree program in religious studies (B.A./M.A.). Several English as a second language (ESL) programs are offered, and there is a Three-in-One education plan that combines English as a second language studies and a B.A./M.A. in religious studies or a B.A./M.A. in business administration.

Academic Program

The Department of Religious Studies' majors in Buddhist studies and comparative religious studies offer students the unique opportunity to study religion in a setting that is informed by Buddhist wisdom and values and dedicated to furthering religious and cultural understanding between East and West. All Buddhist traditions are covered, and students can choose to study any of the Buddhist canonical languages, i.e., Canonical Chinese, Pali, Sanskrit. or Tibetan. The library contains one of the best American collections of writing from all the major Buddhist traditions.

The business administration majors in accounting, marketing, information technologies and management, and international business address the issues of business and management from the particular perspective of Eastern and Western cultural interaction. Students are educated in small, interactive classes where they can learn, acquire skills, and form attitudes and values appropriate for leading and serving in a global society. The campus' Eastern and Western cultural environment furthers students' appreciation and understanding of the intercultural issues that shape business on the Pacific Rim.

The major in Chinese offers students a unique environment for learning the language. UWest's close connections with Asia and its large number of Chinese-speaking students and staff members give students the opportunity to immerse themselves in the Chinese language and to practice and develop their Chinese language skills almost anywhere on campus at any time. The major is designed to educate students in modern and classical Chinese. In addition, courses are available in Chinese culture.

The major in English literary studies is dedicated to the study of the literature and cultures of Great Britain and the U.S., with attention also given to influential writers and literary movements from other countries such as Australia, Canada, India, and Ireland. The goal of this major is to provide the guidance, instruction, and intellectual environment for each student to develop the skills that would enable the student to make the balanced critical judgments necessary for textual analysis and the practice of interpretation. UWest's role as a meeting place between East and West is reflected in course offerings devoted to the Asian-American literary experience.

The major in history provides students with the unique opportunity to appreciate the interaction between East and West. After a general overview of both Eastern and Western history, students can choose from two tracks: Western history, which covers American and European history, or Eastern history, which covers South, East, and Southeast Asian history. While the major covers religious, political, social, and cultural history, some emphasis is also given to the history of arts and philosophy.

The major in philosophy is unique in requiring students to be exposed to philosophical thinking from both Eastern and Western perspectives. Students can then specialize in either the Eastern or Western philosophy track. This study of Eastern and Western philosophy is further enhanced by the East/West cultural environment of the campus. Students can interact on a formal and informal basis with many faculty members and students of diverse cultural and philosophical backgrounds. This ensures that philosophical inquiry extends well beyond the classroom and the library.

UWest's major in humanistic psychology adds the dimension of human interests, values, dignity, and life goals to the traditional study of the human mind and behavior. Course offerings include instruction in the major Eastern and Western psychological theories and applications that have developed in human history. Students are able to focus their study on both of these systems as well as to the integration of the two into a new theory of humanistic Buddhist and Western psychology.

All of the bachelor's programs require the completion of a minimum of 120 semester units.

The ESL program provides a variety of instructional formats to improve students' command of the English language and familiarize them with American life and culture, including a residential English program and short-term English Immersion Programs.

Academic Facilities

The library provides access to the University's collection as well as electronic access to the collections of many other public and university libraries. The library also offers Internet access and services and subscribes to several major databases, including LexisNexis and ProQuest. The University's Computer Lab is equipped with Windows-based PCs and provides computer technology for students and faculty members, including Internet access. The Language Lab, equipped with the latest audio learning technology, is available for language instruction for both class and self-study uses.

Three research centers are located on campus. The International Academy of Buddhism is designed as an international Buddhist research and publications center. It also serves as a forum for consultation and exchange of information and experience for scholars and students specializing in various aspects of Buddhist studies. The Buddhist Psychology and Counseling Research Center develops a theoretical foundation and practical methodology for integrating Buddhist psychology with modern modalities of counseling so that appropriate therapy can be provided to designated individuals and groups. The Center for the Study of Minority and Small Business helps the Department of Business Administration reach out to minority and small-business sectors for potential resources and support, so that the students at UWest can be exposed to and become familiar with business realities and the existing business environment.

Costs

In 2004–05, tuition for business administration courses is $250 per unit; all other courses are $200 per unit. Other fees also apply. Room and board range from $2400 (double occupancy) to $4800 (single occupancy) per fall and spring semester and from $1200 to $2400 per summer semester.

Financial Aid

Financial aid is available in the form of a work-study program, private scholarships and grants (both need- and merit-based), and a limited number of partial tuition waivers.

Faculty

There are approximately 70 faculty members, and they represent a wide range of ethnic and cultural backgrounds. Many are internationally renowned, and all have excellent qualifications in their subjects.

Student Government

The UWest Student Association acts as a liaison between the University and the students to provide services, programs, and facilities that enhance the quality of education by extending the learning environment beyond the classroom into the extracurricular lives of UWest students. It also provides a forum for student expression and interests. All students enrolled at the University are included as members of the Student Association.

Admission Requirements

Applicants are required to supply accurate and complete information on the application for admission form and to submit official transcripts from each school or college attended. Other application requirements and documentation can be found on the University's Web site (address below). Student selection is based on academic achievement and potential, irrespective of ethnicity, gender, disability, or religion.

Application and Information

Application deadlines for domestic applicants are August 15 for fall, December 15 for spring semester, and May 15 for summer. International applicants (F-1) should apply by July 31 for fall, December 1 for spring, and April 30 for summer. ESL applications are accepted on an on-going basis. There is a $50 nonrefundable application fee for domestic applicants and a $100 nonrefundable application fee for international applicants ($50 for all ESL applicants).

Ms. Grace Hsiao
Registrar and Admissions Officer
University of the West
1409 North Walnut Grove Avenue
Rosemead, California 91770
Telephone : 626-571-8811 Ext. 120
Fax: 626-571-1413
E-mail: info@uwest.edu
World Wide Web: http://www.uwest.edu

A panoramic view of UWest campus.

UNIVERSITY OF TULSA

TULSA, OKLAHOMA

The University

The University of Tulsa (TU) is a midsized, four-year, private, liberal arts university featuring highly personalized study in the humanities, computer sciences, engineering, natural sciences, business, health professions, and fine and performing arts. TU features three undergraduate colleges: the Henry Kendall College of Arts and Sciences, the College of Business Administration, and the College of Engineering and Natural Sciences.

TU also has a College of Law and master's and Ph.D. programs in select disciplines. The University is fully accredited by the North Central Association of Colleges and Universities, and is an NCAA Division I participant in the Western Athletic Conference. TU maintains an affiliation with the Presbyterian Church (USA).

A customizable array of majors, minors, concentrations within majors, and certificate programs allows undergraduates to put together a personalized education, which can include a self-designed major. TU's low 11:1 student-faculty ratio, average class size of 19, and emphasis on individual attention anchor an educational culture where students are rigorously challenged and comprehensively supported.

Long regarded for programs that include accounting; MIS; petroleum, mechanical, and chemical engineering; English; environmental law; and psychology, TU is also emerging as a leader in computer science and information security. TU is one of six pioneer institutions selected by the National Science Foundation for the Federal Cyber Service Initiative (Cyber Corps). The University's strength in computer science extends to its graduate program, which regularly graduates Ph.D.'s in computer security.

Students targeting careers in information technology, fine and performing arts, law and government, or health and sports sciences may be especially well served by TU's programs. Joint bachelors and M.B.A. programs are available, as well as a highly selective six-year joint bachelor's and J.D. (law degree) program.

The University's new 34-acre sports and recreation complex features a student fitness facility, competition-grade tennis complex, NCAA soccer and softball fields, multiuse recreational fields, and a student apartment complex. An NCAA track and field are scheduled. TU offers ample extracurricular opportunities, including intramural sports, special interest clubs, preprofessional organizations, fraternities and sororities, and campus ministry groups.

Total fall 2002 enrollment was 4,049, with 2,691 undergraduates and 1,358 graduate and law students. There is a 51:49 ratio of men and women. International and multicultural students make up about 30 percent of the student population, with seventy-one countries represented.

Based on academic reputation and other factors, *U.S. News & World Report* ranks TU among the top 130 national universities of the 1,400 colleges and universities it surveys. *Princeton Review* ranks TU eleventh in the nation for student happiness.

Location

University of Tulsa features a residential campus in midtown Tulsa, Oklahoma. Tulsa's prominent industries include energy, telecommunications and data, finance, medicine, aerospace, transportation, and education—all of which present rich internship opportunities for students and employment opportunities for graduates. *Newsweek* has named Tulsa one of ten "New Frontier" technology cities, and the *New York Times* declared Tulsa "a new economy hotbed." *Southern Living* magazine named Tulsa one of its five favorite Southern cities. Tulsa has more than 550,000 residents and features cultural assets including the Performing Arts Center, ballet theater, symphony, opera, two nationally renowned museums, and cultural festivals such as Jazzfest, Mayfest, and Octoberfest. Professional sports in Tulsa include baseball, golf, hockey, arena football, and horse racing. The extensive River Parks development, 3 miles from the campus, has facilities for outdoor activities, jogging and bicycle trails, and an outdoor floating amphitheater.

Majors and Degrees

The Henry Kendall College of Arts and Sciences grants the Bachelor of Arts or Bachelor of Science degree in anthropology, art, art history, arts management, communication, deaf education, economics, education, English, environmental policy, film studies, French, German, history, law and society (an accelerated B.A./J.D. program), music, musical theater, philosophy, political science, psychology, religion, sociology, Spanish, speech/language pathology, and theater. Students also have the opportunity to create their own designated area of concentration with the approval of the dean of the college. Teacher certification at the elementary and secondary levels is available through the college.

The College of Business Administration awards the following degrees: Bachelor of Science in business administration (majors in accounting, economics, finance, management, management information systems, and marketing); Bachelor of Science in international business and language (with emphases in French, German, Spanish, and Russian); Bachelor of Science in athletic training; Bachelor of Science in exercise and sports science; and Bachelor of Science in nursing. The college offers minors in accounting, business administration, coaching, finance, international business studies, management information systems, and marketing communication. Management majors may choose concentrations in business law, entrepreneurship and family business management, and human resource management. Marketing majors may choose an emphasis in integrated marketing communication. The college is home to several specialized centers, including the Family Owned Business Institute, the Genave King Rogers Center for Business Law, and the Williams Risk Management Center.

The College of Engineering and Natural Sciences offers the Bachelor of Science degree in applied mathematics, biochemistry, biology, chemical engineering, chemistry, computer information systems, computer science, earth and environmental science, electrical engineering, engineering physics, geology, geosciences, mathematics, mechanical engineering, petroleum engineering, and physics. The college also offers a B.A. in chemistry, earth and environmental science, and geology. The college features state-of-the-art research facilities, including the Center for Information Security and the Williams Communications Fiber Optic Networking Laboratory. From 1995 to 2003, 30 TU engineering students were named recipients of the prestigious Barry M. Goldwater Scholarship, the nation's premier award for undergraduate students studying engineering, math, or science.

Academic Program

The TU education links a broad, humanities-based core curriculum for all majors and a highly flexible group of majors, minors, concentrations, and certificate programs. With so many program options and a high level of faculty support, TU students can receive an education that is well-rounded, in-depth, and uniquely personalized. Candidates for graduation must complete at least 124 semester hours of course work, with more hours required of students majoring in engineering and business administration.

The University offers a number of special academic programs. The Honors Program engages students in intensive multidisciplinary work and in specialized study culminating in a major research or creative project during the senior year. Honors freshmen may live in the Honors House. The Tulsa Undergraduate Research Challenge program (TURC) combines advanced research, scholarship, and community service. The Federal Cyber Service Initiative (Cyber Corps) prepares students for advanced federal careers in computer security. Other special programs include internships, study abroad, Air Force ROTC, and an honors program.

Qualified students may receive advanced standing or credit for scores on the tests of the Advanced Placement and College-Level Examination programs. Students who complete the International Baccalaureate diploma with a score of 28 or above receive at least 30 college credits, the equivalent of one year in college.

The University of Tulsa operates on a semester calendar. The fall term begins in late August, the spring term in early January, and the summer session in mid-May.

Off-Campus Programs

The University of Tulsa administers its own study-abroad programs in Argentina, Canada, France, Germany, Ireland, Italy, Russia, Spain, Switzerland, and the United Kingdom. Tulsa is also affiliated with the University Studies Abroad Consortium. Select individual programs, including some in art and business, incorporate international experiences.

Academic Facilities

The University of Tulsa's libraries (McFarlin Library and the Mabee Legal Information Center) house more than 3.6 million items, including periodical subscriptions to scholarly and popular journals. McFarlin holdings include 825,000 print volumes, 19,700 electronic book titles, and 11,000 journal titles. McFarlin's special collections are internationally recognized, particularly for holdings in Native American history and nineteenth- and twentieth-century Irish, English, and American literature. McFarlin is home to the papers of Nobel Laureate V. S. Naipaul. McFarlin is also developing a specialization in World War I literature, correspondence, and artifacts. Special Collections rare book holdings currently number about 125,000 volumes.

Keplinger Hall is the $15-million home to the College of Engineering and Applied Sciences. An array of equipment complements this facility, including a comprehensive multimillion-dollar telecommunications networking laboratory developed with Williams Communications and other industry partners.

The TU Center for Information Security is developing defenses against cyberterrorist attacks and information warfare. The center also supports the University's National Security Agency (NSA)–accredited certificate program in information assurance, a curriculum that integrates information security with computer law and policy issues. TU has been designated a Center of Excellence in Information Assurance by the NSA and is one of six pioneer institutions selected by the National Science Foundation for the Federal Cyber Service Initiative (Cyber Corps).

The Mary K. Chapman Center for Communicative Disorders links the University to the community with its clinical facility and its curricula in education of the deaf and speech/language pathology. The Tulsa Center for the Study of Women's Literature offers concentrated studies in women's literature and in feminist literary critical theory. The National Energy Law and Policy Institute researches energy law and policy development. The Petroleum and Energy Research Institute offers students the opportunity to participate in funded research projects. The Family-Owned Business Institute provides a forum for the development and dissemination of information relevant to the succession and stability of the family business. The TU Innovation Institute combines research and interdisciplinary programs in innovation, product development, and entrepreneurship.

Other facilities include the Genave King Rogers Center for Business Law, which supports the business law specialization within the management major; the Williams Risk Management Center in the College of Business Administration, an advanced learning environment combining the latest in trading floor technology and advanced study in risk-management theories and techniques; the Chapman Theatre, home to TU's symphony orchestra, concert band, wind ensemble, jazz workshop, modern choir, theater, and opera productions; the Allen Chapman Activity Center, which is the University's student union, featuring student organization offices, the Great Hall for lectures and entertainment, a food court, and the University bookstore; and the Donald W. Reynolds Center, the campus arena and convocation center. This $28-million facility is the home for several intercollegiate athletic programs, cutting-edge facilities for video editing and strength training, and the state's only accredited academic program in athletic/sports medicine.

Costs

In 2003–04, the typical cost for students living on campus was $22,443, including $16,400 for tuition and $5610 for room and board, a one-time fee of $325, and $110 in recurring fees. Expenses for books average about $1200 per year.

Financial Aid

In 2002, nearly 90 percent of entering students received some form of financial aid (including grants, scholarships, work-study, and loans). Academic, athletic, and performance scholarships are available, as well as federally funded grants, loans, and Federal Work-Study awards. The University of Tulsa participates in the National Merit and National Achievement Scholarship Corporation's Finalist program, and the National Hispanic Scholar program. TU offers full tuition, room, and board scholarships for National Merit Finalists and full tuition scholarships for National Achievement Finalists and National Hispanic Scholars. Presidential and University Scholarships are also awarded to qualified students. Performance scholarships are available in music and theater. Applicants for aid should submit the Free Application for Federal Student Aid (FAFSA) and the TU Financial Aid Application by March 1 for priority consideration.

Faculty

The University has 308 full-time faculty members, with 90 percent having earned the highest degree in their field of study. The faculty is primarily a teaching faculty, although most of its members are also involved in funded research or publishing activities. Many faculty members serve as student advisers and work collaboratively with students in and outside the classroom. The faculty includes a number of distinguished scholars, with eighteen endowed chairs and seven endowed professorships.

Student Government

All full-time students are members of the Student Association, which consists of legislative, executive, and judicial branches. Regular elections are held for representatives from each college, who appropriate nearly $400,000 annually for student organizations and special events. The executive cabinet's main function is to arrange the programs of the speakers, artists, and events on campus that are sponsored by the Student Association.

Admission Requirements

The University of Tulsa seeks students whose academic background indicates potential for success in the University's competitive environment. Performance in high school college-preparatory subjects and scores on the SAT I or ACT are the primary criteria considered in the admission evaluation. The counselor recommendation and information about applicants' extracurricular activities and job experience are also considered. Campus visits and interviews are highly recommended but not required.

Application and Information

Students are encouraged to complete an application for admission as early as possible during their senior year. The admission process is rolling, and applicants are reviewed and notified as their admission files are completed. The reply date for students is May 1. An application, accompanied by a six-semester secondary school transcript, ACT or SAT I scores, and a guidance counselor's recommendation are required when applying for admission. Completed applications should be sent to the Office of Admission. For additional information, students should view the online tour (http://www.utulsa.edu/virtualtour) or contact:

John C. Corso
Associate Vice President for Enrollment and Student
Services and Dean of Admission
University of Tulsa
600 South College Avenue
Tulsa, Oklahoma 74104-3189
Telephone: 918-631-2307 (in Tulsa)
800-331-3050 (toll-free)
Fax: 918-631-5003
E-mail: admission@utulsa.edu
World Wide Web: http://www.utulsa.edu

UNIVERSITY OF VERMONT

BURLINGTON, VERMONT

The University

The University of Vermont, or UVM (from the Latin name Universitas Viridis Montis, which means University of the Green Mountains), is in its third century of educational excellence.

Founded in 1791, the University of Vermont is the fifth-oldest university in New England (after Harvard, Yale, Dartmouth, and Brown) and among the twenty oldest institutions of higher learning in the nation. UVM was one of the first universities to earn a chapter of Phi Beta Kappa and, in 1875 and 1877, became the first to admit women and African Americans, respectively, to this national honor society.

A doctorate-granting research university, UVM enrolls students from a variety of geographical, social, economic, ethnic, and personal backgrounds. The University of Vermont deliberately seeks students with such diverse backgrounds, with approximately 40 percent of the student population coming from Vermont and 60 percent drawn from throughout the United States and around the world. Each of the 7,600 undergraduate students contributes his or her unique experiences to enrich this diverse campus community.

UVM is composed of seven undergraduate colleges and schools: the College of Agriculture and Life Sciences, the College of Arts and Sciences, the College of Education and Social Services, the College of Engineering and Mathematics, the College of Nursing and Health Sciences, the School of Business Administration, and the School of Natural Resources.

In addition there are the Graduate College and the College of Medicine. The Graduate College offers seventy-two master's degree programs and twenty doctoral programs in a variety of fields, including agriculture, business, education, engineering, foreign languages, health sciences, natural resources, physical and biological sciences, psychology, and social sciences. A Master of Physical Therapy program is also offered.

In the first two years, students are required to live in one of the twenty-nine residence halls, with options including small and large housing complexes, and historic older buildings as well as modern residence halls. Many students opt for theme-based housing.

Nearly 100 student organizations are currently recognized by the Student Government Association. These include a broad range of academic, media-based, and recreational options, as well as arts, religious, cultural, and political organizations.

UVM fields ten men's and twelve women's NCAA Division I athletic teams. More than twenty-seven intramural and club sports are available to all UVM undergraduates.

Location

UVM is located in Burlington, Vermont, a city of approximately 40,000. The University's main campus sits on a hill nestled between Lake Champlain and the Green Mountains. Because of the natural beauty of its surrounding area and its many sporting and entertainment opportunities, Burlington has been named one of the nation's "Big Ten" college towns by Edward B. Fiske in his book *The Best Buys in College Education.*

Majors and Degrees

The University of Vermont offers more than ninety undergraduate majors leading to Bachelor of Arts and Bachelor of Science degrees.

The College of Agriculture and Life Sciences offers the following majors: agricultural and resource entrepreneurship, animal science, biochemistry, biological sciences, botany, community and international development, dietetics, environmental science, environmental studies, microbiology, molecular genetics, nutrition and food sciences, plant and soil science, self-designed, sustainable landscape horticulture, and undeclared.

The College of Arts and Sciences offers the following majors: anthropology, art history, art studio, biology (B.A. and B.S. options), biochemistry, botany, chemistry (B.A. and B.S. options), classical civilization, communication science, computer science, economics, English, environmental sciences, environmental studies, French, geography, geology (B.A. and B.S. options), German, Greek, history, individually designed, international studies (Asian studies, Canadian studies, European studies, Italian studies, Latin America, and Russia/Eastern Europe options), Latin, mathematics, music (B.A. and B.Mus. options), philosophy, physics (B.A. and B.S. options), political science, psychology (B.A. and B.S. options), religion, Russian, sociology, Spanish, theater, undeclared, women's studies, and zoology (B.A. and B.S. options).

The College of Education and Social Services offers the following majors: art (B.S.A.E), early childhood education (P–3 and preschool; P–3 leads to the B.S.E.D.), elementary education (K–6 and reading options leading to the B.S.E.D), family and consumer sciences, human development and family studies, middle-level education, music education (B.S.M.S), physical education, secondary education (English, language, mathematics, science, and social science options leading to the B.S.E.D.), self-designed majors, social work, and undeclared.

The College of Engineering and Mathematics offers the following majors: civil engineering (B.S.C.E.), computer science (B.S.C.S.), computer science information systems (B.S.), electrical engineering (B.S.E.E.), engineering management (B.S.E.M.), environmental engineering (B.S.), mathematics (B.S.M.), mechanical engineering (B.S.M.E.), statistics (B.S.M.), and undeclared.

The School of Business Administration offers the business administration major (B.S.B.A.). During their senior year, business administration majors must complete one of the following concentrations: accounting, entrepreneurship, finance, human resource management, international management, management and the environment, management information systems, marketing, production and operations management, or a self-designed concentration.

The School of Natural Resources offers the following majors leading to the B.S. degree: environmental science, environmental studies, forestry, natural resources, recreation management, undeclared, and wildlife and fisheries biology.

The College of Nursing and Health Sciences offers the following Bachelor of Science degree majors: biomedical technology, medical laboratory science, nuclear medicine technology, nursing, and radiation therapy. Graduates of this Bachelor of Science degree program are eligible for registered nurse (RN) licensure.

An accelerated B.S./D.V.M. program with Tufts School of Veterinary Medicine and a B.A./J.D. program with Vermont Law School are available. A 3 + 3 guaranteed admission to the Master of Physical Therapy program is available to a limited number of entering first-year students. The University also offers curricula and advising for predental, prelaw, premedical, and pre–veterinary students.

Academic Program

The University's academic calendar consists of two semesters (fall and spring), with extensive summer courses also available. Students are classified based on progress toward meeting degree requirements in terms of credit hours earned as follows: first year, fewer than 27 credit hours; sophomore, 27 to fewer than 57 credit hours; junior, 57 to fewer than 87 credit hours; senior, 87 or more credit hours. A total of 122 credit hours are needed for graduation for most bachelor's programs at UVM. The number varies, however; some programs, such as those in the College of Engineering and Mathematics, require as many as 130 credit hours.

General requirements are designed by the specific departments within the colleges and schools. In addition to the course requirements of the particular curriculum, students must also fulfill the general requirements in physical education and complete a course in race and culture. Academic advising is facilitated through faculty members who are assigned to incoming students. These faculty members assist the student with academic planning and course registration. A student remains under the guidance of this adviser until a major has been selected, at which time a department adviser is assigned.

Off-Campus Programs

The University offers an array of study-abroad programs in Africa, Asia, Canada, Central and South America, Eastern and Western Europe, the Middle East, and Oceania through its Office of International Education as well as in conjunction with other colleges and universities.

Academic Facilities

Facilities at the University of Vermont include state-of-the-art laboratories, computer services, and other educational resources. Main Campus, with its red brick buildings and classic architecture, has the stately look of an historic university, while Redstone and East campuses have a more contemporary feel, with modern buildings and views of the mountains and of Lake Champlain.

UVM libraries include Bailey/Howe, the largest library in Vermont; Dana Medical Library; and Cook Physical Sciences Library. Holdings include more than 1.3 million books and bound serial files, 1.1 million government documents, 20,000 serial subscriptions, 1.8 million microforms, significant manuscripts and archival materials, and graphic, cartographic, audio, and film materials. Library users also have access to 240 online databases and full-text resources and access to more than 800 e-journals.

University computing facilities are accessible to all students and include microcomputer labs housing Macintosh and DOS/ Windows systems. All labs are networked, allowing access to UVM's host systems as well as national and international resources on the Internet. Network connections are also available in all residence hall rooms.

Costs

Tuition and fees for the 2003–04 school year are $22,688 for out-of-state students and $9636 for Vermont residents. Room and board were $6680. Miscellaneous personal expenses, including books and supplies, are in addition to these costs.

Financial Aid

More than half of UVM's students receive financial aid. Awards are based on need as determined by the Free Application for Federal Student Aid (FAFSA). An applicant's financial aid award may include University and federal grant funds, on-campus employment, and student loans. More than one third of admitted students are offered non-need-based scholarship assistance. Financial assistance has no bearing on admission to the University.

Faculty

The University's student-faculty ratio of 15:1 enables faculty members to be accessible to students. UVM's faculty is composed of very distinguished scholars, 88 percent of whom hold a terminal degree in their specific field of interest.

Student Government

The Student Government Association, the primary student governing organization, assumes responsibility for voicing student concerns and interest in the political activities of the University community. It recognizes and funds more than 100 student organizations.

Admission Requirements

Prospective first-year students must present at least 16 high school units, including a minimum of 4 years of English, 3 years of mathematics up to Algebra 2, 3 years of social sciences, 2 years of the same foreign language, and 2 years of natural or physical science, including at least 1 year of lab science. Some areas of study have additional requirements. In addition to the required and recommended courses, the overall strength and challenge of a student's course load is important.

Qualification for admission is determined on the basis of secondary school record, rank in graduating class, recommendations, writing ability, strength of preparation in the area chosen as a major, and scores on the SAT I. The ACT examination may be submitted in place of the SAT I.

Admission is competitive. Twenty-seven percent of admitted students rank in the top 10 percent of their graduating class; 62 percent rank in the top quarter.

Transfer students must meet all entrance requirements mentioned above. Candidates must send an official transcript from each postsecondary school attended. SAT I and ACT results are not required for transfers.

Application and Information

Applications and supporting materials for first-year fall admission should be completed and on file by January 15 (November 1 for early action and early decision). Transfer students seeking fall admission should apply by April 1. First-year and transfer students seeking admission for spring semester should apply by November 1. The nonrefundable application fee is $45. The Common Application is accepted.

The University welcomes applications from all interested students regardless of race, color, religion, sexual orientation, age, disability, nationality, or sex. Prospective first-year and transfer students interested in applying for admission in either January or September can receive application forms by contacting:

Admissions Office
The University of Vermont
194 South Prospect Street
Burlington, Vermont 05401-3596
Telephone: 802-656-3370
Fax: 802-656-8611
E-mail: admissions@uvm.edu
World Wide Web: http://www.uvm.edu

UNIVERSITY OF WEST FLORIDA

PENSACOLA, FLORIDA

The University

One of the eleven state universities of Florida, the University of West Florida (UWF) enrolls approximately 9,200 students in its Colleges of Arts and Sciences, Business, and Professional Studies. The University of West Florida, which opened in fall 1967, is located on a 1,600-acre nature preserve 10 miles north of downtown Pensacola. The University's facilities, valued at more than $81 million, have been designed to complement the natural beauty of the site.

The University currently enrolls students from forty-seven states and sixty countries. Students and professors enjoy a relationship that is more common at a small, private college. Approximately 940 freshmen began their studies at UWF last year. The middle 50 percent statistics for the class are as follows: high school grade point average ranged from 3.1 to 3.9; SAT I total score ranged from 1010 to 1210; and ACT composite ranged from 21 to 26.

In addition to its undergraduate programs, UWF also offers the master's degree in twenty-nine areas of study and specialist and Ed.D. degrees in education.

UWF operates centers in downtown Pensacola and at Eglin Air Force Base, a branch campus in Fort Walton Beach (in conjunction with a local community college), and a Navy program office at Naval Air Station Pensacola. In addition, UWF owns 152 acres of beachfront property on nearby Santa Rosa Island, adjacent to the Gulf Islands National Seashore. Available for both recreation and research, this property provides special opportunities for students pursuing degrees in marine biology, maritime studies, and coastal zone studies.

The University of West Florida is a member of the NCAA Division II. Men's sports include baseball, basketball, cross-country, golf, soccer, and tennis. Women's sports include basketball, cross-country, golf, soccer, softball, tennis, and volleyball. Students also participate in more than nineteen intramural sports and twenty club sports. The Program Council and the Residence Hall Advisory Council provide activities and events open to the entire campus community. UWF hosts six national sororities and five national fraternities; 110 professional, academic, and religious organizations are open to UWF students.

A natatorium housing an Olympic-size pool adjoins the Field House, center for indoor sports and large-group activities and events. Varsity soccer fields, tennis courts, handball and racquetball courts, jogging trails, picnic areas, and sites for canoeing are available on campus. Varsity baseball and softball fields and a lighted track complete the UWF sports complex. Sailing and waterskiing facilities are nearby, and campus nature trails attract thousands of visitors annually.

Students may choose to live on or off campus. The Office of Housing oversees 1,250 total residence hall spaces that include low-rise residence halls, two- or four-bedroom residence hall apartments that are equipped with modern conveniences, and three new residence halls, one with 300 spaces and the other two with 200 spaces.

There are also various apartment complexes conveniently located just beyond the campus.

Location

Students and visitors alike delight in the beauty of the campus, which is nestled in the rolling hills outside Pensacola, Florida. Wide verandas, massive moss-draped oaks, and spacious lawns capture the traditional charm and grace of the South, while modern architecture and state-of-the-art facilities blend in naturally among loblolly pines and meandering walkways.

Only minutes from the campus gate are the emerald waters and white beaches of the Gulf of Mexico and the Gulf Islands National Seashore, one of the nation's most beautiful beaches. The Pensacola area attracts vacationers from all around the country to its historic Seville Square, golf tournaments, sailing regattas, restaurants on the bay, and a variety of art and music festivals. WUWF, the University's public radio station, produces a monthly live program, Gulf Coast RadioLive. UWF is 3½ hours from New Orleans, 1 hour from Mobile, 3 hours from Tallahassee, and 5 hours from Atlanta.

Majors and Degrees

The University of West Florida awards the bachelor's degree in forty-four undergraduate programs with many areas of specialization. Undergraduate majors are available in the College of Arts and Sciences in anthropology, art, biology, chemistry, communication arts, computer information systems, computer science, English, environmental studies, fine arts, history, interdisciplinary humanities studies, interdisciplinary information technology, interdisciplinary science, international studies, leisure studies, marine biology, mathematics, medical technology, music, nursing, philosophy, physics, pre-engineering, preprofessional studies, psychology, social sciences (interdisciplinary), studio art, and theater as well as joint computer engineering, electrical engineering, and seven-year predental B.S./D.M.D. programs with the University of Florida.

Undergraduate majors in the College of Business include accounting, economics, finance, management, management information systems, and marketing. The College of Business is accredited by AACSB International–The Association to Advance Collegiate Schools of Business.

The College of Professional Studies, which includes education programs that are accredited by the National Council for Accreditation of Teacher Education (NCATE), offers professional training and majors leading to bachelor's degrees in the following areas: criminal justice; elementary education; engineering technology; health education; health, leisure, and science; legal administration; middle school education; political science; prekindergarten/primary education; prelaw; social work; special education (emotionally handicapped, learning-disabled, mentally handicapped); sports science; and vocational education. There are specialist programs in educational leadership and in curriculum and instruction and a doctoral program in curriculum and instruction.

Academic Programs

A general curriculum is required for entering freshmen and for transfer students without an Associate in Arts degree from a Florida public community college. General studies provide students with a broad foundation in the liberal arts, science, and career and life planning. The academic skills of reading, writing, discourse, critical inquiry, logical thinking, and mathematical reasoning are central elements of the general studies curriculum.

Students of high ability may enter an honors program offering intensive instruction in a more individualized setting. Cooperative education programs are available in nearly every field, allowing UWF students to get a head start on their careers while paying for their education. Army and Air Force ROTC programs and scholarships are also available.

Off-Campus Programs

The Office of International Education and Programs arranges more than twenty study-abroad and student exchange programs on every continent except Antarctica. Participants may study in Austria, Canada, England, Finland, France, Germany, Japan, Mexico, the Netherlands, and Portugal.

Academic Facilities

The main campus consists of more than 100 buildings. One of the most prominent of these is the five-floor John C. Pace Library, which houses a collection of more than 2.3 million bound volumes and micropieces. Interconnected through computer linkages with state and national libraries for research purposes, the UWF library contains one of the finest special collections about the Gulf Coast area. Some of the items in this collection date back to the fourteenth century, and there are also a manuscript letter signed by Thomas Jefferson, books autographed by Albert Einstein, and materials carried aboard the space shuttle by UWF alumni.

Excellent science and technology laboratories for preprofessional majors, extensive video and film equipment, desktop publishing labs, an AP wire service, and an impressive computer science facility also support students' scholarly endeavors. Microcomputers, minicomputers, a diverse inventory of software, a real-time laboratory, modem linkages to residence halls, and 24-hour-a-day access to the computer center all are available to students in every field of study. Other major facilities include a Center for Fine and Performing Arts, a College of Professional Studies Complex, a Student Services Complex, and a renovated Commons.

Expansion and renovation continue to enhance the main campus. Ongoing renovations of the Commons feature a bookstore, post office, and snack bar. An archaeology building and museum opened in 1999. An expansion and renovation of the student sports and recreation facility is planned for the next few years.

Costs

For fall 2004, tuition is $95.19 per credit for Florida residents and $462.79 per credit for out-of-state students. Room and board costs total $6000. The cost of books is estimated at $800. Transportation and personal expenses vary according to students' individual needs.

Financial Aid

About 60 percent of UWF students receive some form of financial aid and scholarships. UWF is committed to meeting a student's financial need. Aid is awarded on a first-come, first-served basis.

The Scholarship Program for outstanding freshmen allows students to receive early scholarship commitments as soon as they have decided to enroll in UWF. The John C. Pace Jr. scholarships are awarded to meritorious freshmen, transfers with A.A. degrees from Florida's community colleges, and minority students who are Florida residents. Awards are $1000 per year. Special scholarships for National Achievement Scholars and students with talent in the arts are awarded through this program. Non-Florida tuition grants are awarded to outstanding freshmen and transfer students. These awards reduce the amount of out-of-state fees.

Faculty

Faculty members at the University of West Florida include published authors, scientists engaged in a wide range of research projects, and journalists skilled in advertising and filmmaking. Eighty percent of the faculty members hold doctoral degrees from major institutions throughout the United States.

Student Government

The Student Government Association is authorized to represent the student body in all matters concerning student life. The basic purposes of the student government are to provide students with an opportunity to participate in the decision-making process of the University; to review, evaluate, and allocate all student activity and service fee monies as allowed by state law (annually, some $1 million is allocated by students); to consider and make recommendations on all phases of student life; and to serve as the principal forum for discussion of matters of broad concern to the students.

Admission Requirements

The University of West Florida admits freshman applicants based on high school GPA, completion of college-preparatory courses, and test scores (either the ACT or the SAT I is accepted). Special consideration is given to applicants with special talents. College-preparatory courses should include 4 years of English; 3 each of math, social science, and natural science; 2 of the same foreign language; and 4 academic electives.

Transfer applicants with fewer than 60 hours are required to submit SAT I or ACT test scores and official transcripts from both the college(s) and the high school attended. Students transferring with 60 hours or more must submit their college transcript(s) only.

Application and Information

Students are encouraged to apply early in order to allow time for receipt of transcripts and to receive full consideration for financial aid and scholarships. Admissions decisions are made on a rolling basis. The University encourages visits to its beautiful campus and offers riding tours Monday through Friday at 10 a.m. and 1 p.m. central standard time. Students can visit the University of West Florida's home page via the Internet at the World Wide Web address listed below. Among the available features are the catalog, Saturday Open House dates, applications for admission, and the course guide for the current term. The Lighthouse Information System allows applicants to view their admission and financial aid status via the Internet.

Additional information and application materials may be obtained by writing or calling:

Office of Admissions
University of West Florida
11000 University Parkway
Pensacola, Florida 32514-5750
Telephone: 850-474-2230
800-263-1074 (toll-free)
E-mail: admissions@uwf.edu
World Wide Web: http://uwf.edu

The UWF Sailing Club goes out for a day of sun and recreation on Pensacola Bay.

UNIVERSITY OF WEST LOS ANGELES
School of Paralegal Studies
LOS ANGELES, CALIFORNIA

The University and The School

Since 1971, men and women seeking a high-quality education in paralegal studies have made the University of West Los Angeles's (UWLA's) School of Paralegal Studies their first choice. Not only is UWLA accredited by the Western Association of Schools and Colleges (WASC), but the School of Paralegal Studies has also been approved since 1975 by the American Bar Association (ABA) as a paralegal school that meets the ABA's rigorous standards. The School of Paralegal Studies is one of two schools that constitute the University of West Los Angeles; the School of Law (which offers the J.D. degree) is fully accredited by the Committee of Bar Examiners of the State Bar of California.

The philosophy and purpose that led to UWLA's founding in 1966 as a nonprofit private educational institution remain the essence of its mission today: to offer quality programs in legal education to men and women from diverse backgrounds, especially those who must study part-time. At UWLA's School of Paralegal Studies, students may earn their Bachelor of Science degree with a major in paralegal studies by completing a variety of challenging and interesting courses that are offered on a flexible schedule of evening classes.

For people who have already earned their baccalaureate or associate degree or at least 60 college semester units, the School offers the Paralegal Specialist Certificate Program, which enables students to obtain career training in as little as 1½ years. For people who have earned at least 30 transferable college semester units of general education, the School offers a 51-unit Legal Assistant Certificate Program. UWLA is not a traditional four-year collegiate institution; all entering students in the B.S. degree/Legal Assistant Certificate program are college sophomores or juniors who have earned transferable credits elsewhere. The School prides itself on offering working adults an excellent opportunity to conveniently complete their college degrees in a field of study that is not only academically enriching but also career-relevant. As part of the B.S. degree program, students may earn the Legal Assistant Certificate, which is awarded upon completion of the courses required in the major, along with two paralegal specialist certificates.

Students at UWLA come from a variety of backgrounds and commute to campus from throughout the southern California area. Since UWLA's campus serves a small student population, students can expect and receive personal attention from academic counselors, registrars, internship coordinators, faculty members, and deans. Study skills workshops, student tutoring, and other academic support programs are part of the regular student services offered by the School, all of which are designed to help students achieve their fullest potential.

The School of Paralegal Studies has been on the cutting edge of paralegal education for several decades. The School offers specializations in such diverse areas as litigation, corporations, criminal law, real estate law, probate law, and family law.

The School has an active placement service, which assists students and alumni with finding employment in the legal community. The career development counselor continually seeks new job source contacts.

The School remains committed to its goal of offering quality paralegal education to those men and women who know the value of an academically rewarding yet practical education, and it remains equally committed to helping its alumni—who are employed as paralegals/legal assistants, staff advocates, legal managers, and mediators—meet their personal and career goals.

The School has, at present, a student body composed of about 75 percent women and 25 percent men. Many students are in their thirties, but ages range from 22 to 62. The student body has students from various racial and ethnic backgrounds, including African American, Asian–Pacific Islander, Latino/Latina, Caucasian, and Native American.

Graduates are eligible to join the Paralegal Alumni Association (PAA), which is one of the strongest and most active paralegal alumni groups in the country; it offers annual continuing education seminars and other social events.

Location

The University of West Los Angeles has two campuses. The West Los Angeles campus is located on 4.5-acres near the Los Angeles International Airport. The campus is situated approximately 3 miles from the Pacific Ocean to the west and 1 mile from the San Diego Freeway to the east. The San Fernando Valley campus is located at the Warner Center in Woodland Hills. Both campuses have convenient access to freeways, making the University attractive to students from all areas of greater Los Angeles and from Ventura to Orange County. Ample free parking for all students adds to UWLA's convenience and accessibility. The University's long-standing reputation as an excellent paralegal training institution makes it possible for students to consider internship and employment opportunities throughout the entire southern California legal community and beyond.

Majors and Degrees

The School of Paralegal Studies offers the B.S. degree in one major, paralegal studies, along with the opportunity to specialize in one of several areas, including litigation, corporations, criminal law, real estate law, probate law, and family law. The School also offers certificate programs leading to the Paralegal Specialist Certificate and the Legal Assistant Certificate. Exceptional students may earn such commendations as Dean's List or graduation with honors.

Academic Program

Almost all courses are 3-credit units, with a total of 27 to 51 units required for a certificate in paralegal studies. For the Bachelor of Science degree, 6 additional units of upper-division general education are required at UWLA, for a total of 57 units. All students must complete a required set of core courses, including legal theory and ethics, legal research and writing, and selected areas of substantive law. Students are given a choice of specialization courses such as real estate law and litigation, which cover both substantive and procedural law. Students are able to choose several courses from a variety of electives, including entertainment law, bankruptcy, family law, immigration, juvenile law, and computers and the law.

Substantive classes, such as contracts and torts, provide students with a strong foundation in the principles of common law and positive law. Students learn legal concepts through a combination of learning methods, including class discussions, case briefing exercises, research projects, and lectures. Each course is designed to give students the opportunity to integrate theoretical legal concepts with practical legal experience. As students progress in their course of study, they have a chance to research and write everything from legal memoranda to corporate resolutions to motions to the court. With the thorough education that UWLA provides, students complete their degrees and/or certificates at UWLA with a high degree of conceptual and practical legal knowledge that enables them to successfully compete in the workplace.

So that students can reach their educational goals as quickly as they wish, the School's academic calendar is offered on a trimester basis, with a flexible schedule of evening classes offered each term. The fall trimester is from September to December, the winter trimester is from January to mid-April, and the spring trimester is from May to early August.

Academic Facilities

The University is proud of its Kelton Law Library, a full-service law library with a collection of federal and state materials in addition to access to computerized legal research databases, including LEXIS and WESTLAW. The library offers materials on CD-ROM, videotape, and microfiche and includes a Computer Learning Lab with learning tutorials and various software used in legal work. Students have access to word processing computers and printers in the library. Study group meeting rooms and a periodical reading room are available to students as needed. A fully equipped computer lab provides students with access to the legal software commonly found in law offices today.

Costs

In the 2003-04 academic year, tuition was $255 per unit. Fees include computer use and library use. Costs of books and materials range from approximately $25 to $250 per course. UWLA does not provide housing for students.

Financial Aid

The Financial Aid Office assists students in finding resources to finance their education at UWLA. The governmental financial aid programs available to students attending UWLA's School of Paralegal Studies include Federal Pell Grants, Federal Supplemental Educational Opportunity Grants (FSEOG), Federal Work-Study (FWS), the Bureau of Indian Affairs Grant (BIA), Federal Stafford Student Loans, and benefits available through government sources to veterans of the U.S. armed forces. To apply for financial assistance, applicants must file a Free Application for Federal Student Aid (FAFSA), which is available from UWLA's Financial Aid Office, any college financial aid office, or any high school guidance office. Although applications are accepted throughout the year, students are encouraged to apply by March 2 of the calendar year for which aid is being requested if they want consideration for California State Grants/Fellowships for the academic year beginning in July or September.

A number of scholarships, some funded by alumni of the School, are available to students. Each year the School offers a program of scholarships (covering tuition for one or more courses) to qualified students. Specific information about scholarship criteria is available from the School.

Faculty

The School prides itself on its faculty, which includes a full-time professor as well as about 20 adjunct professors who are lawyers or paralegals bringing the "real world" of current legal practice into the classroom. Since class size is often small, teachers need not rely solely on lecture methods to convey information. Teachers are committed to sharing with students the academic challenges found in learning the law and the practical necessities found in the daily legal work faced by most paralegals. The faculty reflects the same diverse communities as the student body; teachers come from different age groups, racial and ethnic backgrounds, and from colleges and law schools throughout the country. The School is a member of the American Association for Paralegal Education (AAfPE), which helps to keep the faculty apprised of national trends in paralegal education and practice.

Student Government

All enrolled students are members of the Paralegal Student Body Association (PSBA), which is the student government for the School of Paralegal Studies. It is administered by its Executive Board, which consists of representatives elected by the student body each fall term. The board acts as the student voice in University affairs, including representation at meetings of the University's Board of Trustees. The PSBA occasionally engages in cooperative efforts with the Student Bar Association of UWLA's School of Law.

Admission Requirements

Admission to the various programs is based on educational level and a minimum GPA of 2.0. A student may be admitted with as few as 21 semester units of college-level general education, 60 semester units of college-level courses, and an A.A./A.S. degree and/or a B.A./B.S.degree. The School's admissions policy is designed to enable all qualified applicants to meet their educational goals.

Application and Information

Applicants must complete an application (which includes a short writing sample) and submit that application, along with the $55 application fee, to the School's Admissions Office. Official academic transcripts of all college work completed prior to application must be sent directly to UWLA from every institution that the applicant has attended. No letters of recommendation are required.

Applications are accepted on a rolling basis and may be submitted at any time throughout the calendar year; accepted students may enroll in the next available term. Applications for the fall trimester should be submitted by August; for the winter trimester, by December; and for the spring trimester, by early April. Students are notified of admissions decisions promptly once all official transcripts have been received. Applicants are encouraged to make an appointment to meet with the Admissions Counselor (telephone: 310-342-5287) to discuss their individual questions and concerns.

Interested students may request an application and information from:

The School of Paralegal Studies
The University of West Los Angeles
1155 West Arbor Vitae Street
Inglewood, California 90301-2902
Telephone: 310-342-5208
Fax: 310-342-5296
World Wide Web: http://www.uwla.edu

The School of Paralegal Studies
The University of West Los Angeles
21300 Oxnard Street
Woodland Hills, California 91367
Telephone: 818-883-0529
Fax: 818-883-8142
World Wide Web: http://www.uwla.edu

The Kelton Law Library.

UNIVERSITY OF WISCONSIN–GREEN BAY

GREEN BAY, WISCONSIN

The University

The University of Wisconsin–Green Bay (UW–Green Bay) is a comprehensive university with exceptional new facilities, a dynamic atmosphere, and a fresh approach to student learning.

UW–Green Bay is a midsize public university with 5,500 students. About one third of the student body resides on campus. Most students are from Wisconsin and other Midwest states, but the University enrolls individuals from twenty-five states and about three dozen other countries.

Founded in 1965, the campus is among the most modern and attractive in the highly respected, tradition-rich University of Wisconsin System. The setting is safe, scenic, and comfortable, with wooded trails, a nine-hole golf course, and a million-dollar view of the bay.

UW–Green Bay is heavily invested in state-of-the-art academic facilities and special amenities for students. A high-tech classroom building opened in 2002, and a multimillion-dollar makeover of the laboratory sciences building was completed in 2004. The David A. Cofrin Library at the center of campus is regarded among the finest in the state. Other notable facilities include attractive on-campus housing (with single rooms, private baths, and apartment-style options) and newly dedicated student space in the University's Weidner Center—a major performing arts center described as one of the Midwest's best concert halls. Students find a rich array of clubs, organizations, and leisure-time options, including a highly successful NCAA Division I sports program and performances by big-name entertainers at the Weidner Center.

The University prides itself on "Connecting Learning to Life." Students connect what happens in the classroom to real needs in the community. They examine issues from multiple perspectives and make connections to unravel complex problems. Senior faculty members lead advanced and entry-level courses, emphasizing critical thinking and problem solving as essential skills for a lifetime of learning.

Location

UW–Green Bay is located on the suburban, northeast edge of Green Bay, Wisconsin. Famous for the Packers and NFL football, the city is also known as a center of industry and commerce, with manufacturing, transportation, health care, communication, and insurance as the most important sectors of the economy. With a metropolitan population of about 250,000, Green Bay is home to a developing entertainment district and excellent museums, parks, theaters, and sports-related facilities. It is the gateway to a favorite vacation destination in the scenic Door Peninsula, with its forested bluffs, historic harbors, and Lake Michigan beaches.

The campus is less than 2 hours north of Milwaukee and about 5 hours east of Minnesota's Twin Cities via interstate highway. Green Bay's airport provides direct service to Chicago, Minneapolis, Detroit, and other major cities.

Majors and Degrees

UW–Green Bay grants Bachelor of Arts and Bachelor of Science degrees in seventeen interdisciplinary majors and eighteen disciplinary majors. Professional programs in nursing completion and social work award the B.S.N. and B.S.W., respectively. The disciplinary program in music awards the B.M. degree. A two-year associate degree is available. Undergraduate certificate programs are offered in athletic coaching, English as a second language, international studies, and military science. The University has preprofessional programs in nearly twenty fields, including dentistry, engineering, law, medicine, and pharmacy.

Interdisciplinary majors are as follows: business administration, with emphases in finance, management, and marketing; communication and the arts, with emphases in communication arts and environmental design; communication processes, with emphases in electronic media, journalism, linguistics/teaching ESL, organizational communication, photography, and public relations; education, with preparation in early childhood/elementary through secondary teaching; environmental policy and planning, with emphases in public policy and planning; environmental science, with emphases in ecology and biological resources management and in physical systems: technology and management; human biology, with emphases in cytotechnology, exercise science, general human biology, health science, and nutritional science/dietetics; human development; humanistic studies, with emphases in American Indian studies, religious studies, and Western cultures; individual major; information sciences; interdisciplinary studies; nursing; public administration; social change and development, with emphases in American social issues, global studies, law and justice studies, and women's studies; social work; and urban and regional studies, with emphases in environmental design and general program.

Disciplinary majors are as follows: accounting; art, with emphases in art education, gallery/museum practices, and studio art; biology, with emphases in animal biology, cell/molecular biology, field biology and ecology, and plant biology; chemistry, with general and environmental American Chemical Society programs; computer science; earth science; economics; English, with emphases in creative writing, English education, and literature; French; German; history; mathematics, with emphases in math and statistics; music, with emphases in applied music, jazz studies, music education, music history and literature, and performance; philosophy; political science; psychology; Spanish; and theater, with emphases in design/technical theater, musical theater, performance, and theater studies.

The following areas are only available as minors: American Indian studies, anthropology, corporate communications, geography, physics, sociology, and women's studies.

Academic Programs

The most notable component of a UW–Green Bay education is an emphasis on interdisciplinary—or multiple-subject—fields of study. These majors apply knowledge from several subject areas to one broad field of study. As an example, an environmental science major applies biology, chemistry, mathematics, botany, and other disciplines to the larger study of environmental issues. Every student completes either an interdisciplinary major or a disciplinary major coupled with an interdisciplinary minor. The general education program includes course work in the natural sciences, social sciences, humanities, fine arts, and other cultures.

The interdisciplinary approach demands that students learn to examine things from many perspectives and work effectively with those from other fields. Students then pursue hands-on learning through internships, citizenship, research, and team projects.

Off-Campus Programs

Formal exchange agreements exist with several universities abroad, and UW–Green Bay students have participated recently in formal exchange and language-immersion programs in Chile, Denmark, Germany, Mexico, the Netherlands, and Spain. Students can arrange to study almost anywhere through the University's links to international exchange networks. Those interested in two- to four-week excursions can join study tours of countries such as Australia, Costa Rica, India, and Switzerland. UW–Green Bay participates in the National Student Exchange, which facilitates out-of-state study for a semester or year at universities and colleges across the United States.

Academic Facilities

The eight-story David A. Cofrin Library remains the landmark building at the physical and symbolic heart of the modern campus, but new facilities are gaining renown. UW–Green Bay has a newly opened state-of-the-art classroom facility in Mary Ann Cofrin Hall and just unveiled another with the modernization of the laboratory sciences building. Central computing laboratories for students are located near the library and are open nearly 100 hours per week. A reconfigured information technology network positions the University among the state's leaders in terms of access and capabilities for student and faculty users. Special computer labs serve academic programs such as business, graphic arts, geography, music, and psychology. The Weidner Center for the Performing Arts hosts major Broadway musicals, large-scale orchestras, dance companies, and pop performers. The center features academic studios and provides master classes with acclaimed visiting artists as well as opportunities for internships and paid employment in the entertainment field. Students use the 2,000-seat hall for music, theater, and dance performances. Outdoors, science students enjoy field experience on the 270-acre campus arboretum and University-managed nature preserves along the Lake Michigan shoreline.

Costs

In 2003–04, tuition and fees for full-time students were $4654 for Wisconsin residents and $14,701 for nonresidents. By reciprocal agreement, Minnesota residents pay University of Minnesota tuition rates. Room and board averages $4000 for the academic year. Estimated expenses for books and supplies are $750 per year.

Financial Aid

Financial aid awards are based on need and use the Free Application for Federal Student Aid (FAFSA), with an April 15 priority date. Academic and athletic scholarships are available. Using all typical aid programs, the University provides more than $17 million to more than 60 percent of its enrolling students. More than 1,000 students typically find part-time employment on campus. The community offers a wide variety of work opportunities for students.

Faculty

UW–Green Bay has about 175 full-time faculty members. Ad hoc, or part-time, instructors push the full-time-equivalent count to nearly 200. There are few, if any, teaching assistants. Senior professors teach courses for freshmen and sophomores as well as upper-level courses. They engage in interesting and varied research but have teaching and advising students as their primary focus. Of full-time tenured and tenure-track faculty members, 97 percent hold the Ph.D. or other terminal degrees.

Student Government

Elected and volunteer leadership opportunities exist through the Student Government Association (SGA). Members of the SGA leadership team serve as liaisons to the administration, serve on campuswide committees, and advise on issues of student concern. The Good Times Programming Board arranges social, cultural, recreational, and educational programming for students, with recent Hollywood blockbusters and college classics in the popular film series, and acts including comedians, hypnotists, and up-and-coming bands on the events calendar. More than ninety clubs and organizations focus on special interests. These range from the weekly student newspaper to environmental, service, sports, and cultural groups.

Admission Requirements

Prospective students must have completed high school and have finished 17 prescribed academic high school units. Admission to UW–Green Bay is based on a comprehensive evaluation of factors such as grade point average, ACT/SAT I scores, and other relevant factors. Admission for transfer students depends on the completion of at least 15 applicable credits with a minimum GPA of 2.50. ACT and SAT I scores are both accepted. (Note: The minimum requirements for both class rank and GPA may change since they are determined by enrollment-management needs.) Both paper and electronic applications are accepted. Electronic applications are available on the Web at http://apply.wisconsin.edu/.

Application and Information

Admission decisions are made on a rolling basis and early application is recommended.

For more information, students should contact:

Pam Harvey-Jacobs
Office of Admissions and Orientation
University of Wisconsin–Green Bay
2420 Nicolet Drive
Green Bay, Wisconsin 54311-7001
Telephone: 920-465-2111
Fax: 920-465-5754
E-mail: uwgb@uwgb.edu
World Wide Web: http://www.uwgb.edu

Comfortable and new on-campus housing, every room with a private bath, is a popular feature of UW–Green Bay.

UNIVERSITY OF WYOMING

LARAMIE, WYOMING

The University

The University of Wyoming (UW), a public land-grant institution founded in 1886, is a reflection of the global community it serves. The extensive range of academic programs offered at UW inspires the development of "new thinking" and promotes fulfilling careers in the rapidly evolving world.

As a Carnegie Research University–Extensive, UW's research goals are continually being pushed to the boundaries and beyond by its professors and students. It is this academic ambition that has allowed UW to provide high-quality undergraduate and graduate education, research, and service since 1886.

Wyoming, unique among the fifty states, has only one university. UW enjoys tremendous support from within its state as well as from an alumni network that spans the globe. More than 11,900 students from all parts of the U.S. and sixty other countries attend UW classes in Laramie and at outreach sites around the state. The variety of students at UW enriches the educational experience for all by fostering a multicultural environment that encourages sharing and learning about those with different heritages and cultural backgrounds. It is this dialogue that continues to promote respect and appreciation for diversity.

UW offers bachelor's degree programs in six undergraduate colleges: the Colleges of Agriculture, Arts and Sciences, Business, Education, Engineering, and Health Sciences. Undergraduate education is a high priority at UW. More than 88 percent of the undergraduate courses are taught by professors, and the average class size is 24 students. UW also offers eighty-five graduate and professional programs, including the Doctor of Pharmacy, the Juris Doctor, and the new master's program in e-business.

There are more than 180 recognized campus clubs and organizations, including fourteen national fraternities and sororities, honor and professional societies, political and religious organizations, and special-interest groups. Students have the opportunity to participate in more than sixty different intramural and club sports. UW is a Division I member of the NCAA and competes in the Mountain West Conference in seventeen men's and women's sports. Campus recreational facilities include the Wyoming Union, which recently underwent a $10-million renovation and includes the UW bookstore, eating establishments, student computers, study areas, and a variety of services and resources for students. Additional facilities on campus include Half Acre Gym, an indoor climbing wall, an 18-hole golf course, tennis and racquetball courts, weight rooms, two swimming pools, rifle and archery ranges, indoor and outdoor tracks, softball and baseball fields, and a hockey rink.

UW houses 2,400 students in six residence halls, and freshmen are required to live on campus during their first year. While primarily coed, the residence halls offer a number of unique living environments, including quiet/study floors, special-interest floors, honors floors, single-sex floors, and other academic living environments. UW also offers fourteen different Freshman Interest Groups (FIGS), which are learning communities that offer common living areas and clustered classes to students with similar academic areas of interest.

Location

UW's 785-acre campus is located at the foot of the Rocky Mountains in Laramie, a scenic town of 30,000 people in southeastern Wyoming. Many UW students enjoy the easy access to Alpine and Nordic skiing, snowboarding, snowmobiling, hiking, backpacking, camping, hunting, fishing, rock climbing, and mountain biking. Laramie—with its blue skies, clean air, and 320 days of sunshine a year—is a friendly and supportive university town, conveniently located 45 miles west of Wyoming's capital, Cheyenne, and only 130 miles northwest of Denver, Colorado.

Majors and Degrees

UW offers seventy-seven undergraduate programs within its six colleges, leading to B.A., B.S., B.F.A., and B.S.N. degrees.

The College of Agriculture offers majors in agricultural business (with options in agribusiness management, farm and ranch management, and international agriculture), agricultural communications, agroecology, animal and veterinary sciences (with options in animal biology, business, communication, meat science and food technology, pre–veterinary science, production, and range livestock), family and consumer science (with options in child development, dietetics, family services, human nutrition and food, and textiles and merchandising), microbiology, molecular biology, and rangeland ecology and watershed management.

The College of Arts and Sciences offers majors in American studies, anthropology, art, astronomy/astrophysics, biology, botany, chemistry, communication, criminal justice, English, French, geography and recreation, geology (with options in earth science and environment/natural resources), German, history, humanities/fine arts, international studies, journalism, management, mathematical sciences, mathematics, music (with options in education, performance, and theory and composition), philosophy, physics, political science, psychology, recreation and park administration, Russian, social science, sociology, Spanish, statistics, theater and dance, wildlife/fisheries, women's studies, and zoology and physiology as well as the option of a self-designed major.

The College of Business offers majors in accounting, business administration, business economics, economics, finance, management, and marketing.

The College of Education offers majors in elementary and special education, elementary education, industrial technology education, secondary education (with options in agriculture, art, biology, business, chemistry, earth/space science, English, family and consumer sciences, French, German, industrial technology, mathematics, physics, Russian, social studies, and Spanish), special education, trades and industrial education, and vocational homemaking.

The College of Engineering offers majors in architectural engineering, chemical engineering (with environmental and petroleum options), civil engineering, computer engineering, computer science, electrical engineering (with bioengineering and computer engineering options), management information systems (with accounting, business, and computer science options), and mechanical engineering.

The College of Health Sciences offers majors in dental hygiene, exercise and sports science, health education, health sciences, nursing, pharmacy, physical education teaching, social work, and speech-language and hearing sciences.

UW offers preprofessional programs in dentistry, forestry, law, medicine, nursing, occupational therapy, optometry, pharmacy, physical therapy, and veterinary medicine. The School of Environment and Natural Resources also offers interdisciplinary studies that can be combined with course work in seven other fields of study, including the humanities, physical sciences, and social sciences.

Academic Program

The UW academic calendar consists of two semesters and a complete summer session. Depending on their degree program, students are required to complete 120 to 164 credit hours for graduation. Undergraduate programs for most majors can be completed in four years. Students may choose to double major within the same college, or they may pursue majors in two separate colleges for a cross-college major. Minors are also available in many areas. All students are required to complete the University Studies Program, which is a core curriculum that assists students in developing their skills and/or knowledge in oral and written communication, mathematics, science, diversity, global awareness, government, and culture. The University Honors Program provides academically ambitious undergraduates innovative and intellectual learning opportunities. Award-winning faculty members, unique and challenging course work, and senior research projects are the hallmarks of this program.

Off-Campus Programs

UW has approximately 350 international students and close to 100 international researchers/scholars during any given academic year. This diverse community represents some sixty-five countries. International Students Services provides support to this population through an extensive orientation program, the Friendship Families program, the International Neighbors program, and the International Resource Center.

International Student Services coordinates the National Student Exchange (NSE), which is a domestic student exchange consortium of more than 180 colleges and universities throughout the U.S. In addition, NSE host sites are available in Canada, Puerto Rico, the Virgin Islands, and Guam. Membership in the NSE provides UW students with access to thousands of unique academic programs, classes, and faculty members on host campuses for either a semester or an academic year.

The UW Outreach School extends the university learning experience to Wyoming and the nation through credit and noncredit programs, University of Wyoming Television, Wyoming Public Radio, and the UW/Casper College Center. Credit programs are delivered via Internet/Web-based instruction, compressed video, audio teleconferencing, flexible enrollment (correspondence study), and onsite instruction. Select programs are offered, and degree availability may be limited.

Academic Facilities

The University libraries' collections number nearly 1.3 million volumes and offer links to a variety of library service collections. The William Robertson Coe Library houses materials in the social sciences, humanities, visual and performing arts, business, education, and health sciences as well as more than 2 million federal publications and the Audio Visual Library, a collection of 4,000 video and film titles. Other libraries include the Science Library, the Brinkerhoff Earth Resources Information Center (geology library), and the Rocky Mountain Herbarium Research Collection. Additional collections are housed in the American Heritage Center and the George W. Hooper Law Library. A branch library is located at the National Park Service Research Center in Jackson, Wyoming. UW libraries participate in the Colorado Alliance of Research Libraries and in Region Four of the National Network of Libraries of Medicine. In addition, FERRET provides high-speed access to UW's online library catalogs.

Costs

UW tuition and fees for full-time undergraduates in the 2003–04 academic year were $3090 for Wyoming residents and $8940 for nonresidents. Room and board (double occupancy, unlimited meal plan) were $5546. Estimated expenses include $1000 for books and $2000 for personal expenses.

Financial Aid

Nearly 80 percent of all UW students receive financial assistance. More than $48 million is available in the form of scholarships, loans, grants, and work-study opportunities. The Free Application for Federal Student Aid (FAFSA) is required for need-based assistance (loans, grants, work-study) and for many scholarships. Most scholarships at UW are based on academic merit. UW participates in the Western Undergraduate Exchange (WUE) program and offers the Nebraska Good Neighbor Scholarship. UW also offers the Western Heritage Scholarship Package to qualified students from non-WUE states. The priority deadline for financial aid is March 1.

Faculty

More than 650 professors from the world's most respected colleges and universities have come to teach at UW. Recognized nationally and internationally as experts, 87 percent of the professors hold the highest degrees in their fields. UW professors are deeply committed to the success of their students. Only a small number of undergraduate courses are taught by graduate assistants, and many of the most distinguished and accomplished professors at UW teach first-year courses. UW maintains a low student-faculty ratio (16:1), which allows for individualized attention, instruction, and academic advising, as well as the inclusion of undergraduates in cutting-edge research projects.

Student Government

The Associated Students of the University of Wyoming (ASUW) comprises all students at UW. ASUW serves as the voice of the students, and its legislation has impact on many aspects of student life. The ASUW Senate acts as a liaison between the student body and the administration as well as the UW Board of Trustees and local and state governments. The student body president also sits as an *ex officio* member of the UW Board of Trustees. UW encourages all students to get involved and actively participate in ASUW.

Admission Requirements

To be admitted, high school graduates and new first-year students with fewer than 30 transferable college credit hours should have a cumulative high school GPA of 2.75 or above (Wyoming residents) or 3.0 or above (nonresidents) and a composite ACT score of 20 or above or an SAT I composite score of 960 or above and completed 13 high school units that include 4 units of English, 3 units of mathematics, 3 units of science (including a physical science), and 3 units of cultural context courses (behavioral or social sciences, visual or performing arts, humanities or foreign languages). Admission with conditions can be granted to students who do not meet these standards but have a minimum 2.5 GPA or a 2.25 GPA with a composite ACT score of at least 20 or an SAT I score of at least 960. Transfer students with 30 or more transferable semester credit hours must have a minimum cumulative GPA of 2.0.

Application and Information

Students must submit a completed UW Application for Admission, official high school/college transcripts, ACT or SAT I scores, and a $30 nonrefundable application fee. Students may apply and pay the application fee online at the Web address below. UW strongly encourages all prospective students and their parents to visit the campus.

Admission Office
University of Wyoming
P.O. Box 3435
Laramie, Wyoming 82071-3435
Telephone: 307-766-5160
800-DIAL-WYO (342-5996) (toll-free)
E-mail: why-wyo@uwyo.edu
World Wide Web: http://www.uwyo.edu/

Historic Old Main was built in 1886.

URSINUS COLLEGE
COLLEGEVILLE, PENNSYLVANIA

The College

The cornerstones of the Ursinus College liberal arts program are self-reliance and responsibility, developed through an emphasis on independent achievement. The program is coherent, cumulative, and comprehensive, as all students are required to complete an Independent Learning Experience, which includes an internship, independent research, study abroad, or student teaching. Ursinus distributes laptop computers to all entering students, so all students have 24-hour access to the full range of computer applications, e-mail, and the Internet. All student residences are fully networked for computers, cable television, and personal telephones. Thus, the Ursinus program does not stop at the classroom door, but touches every area of students' lives.

As one of 240 colleges granted a chapter of the national academic ghonor society Phi Beta Kappa, Ursinus College joins together some of the very best students and professors in the nation in a safe, beautiful setting that features outstanding facilities. Three out of 4 students go on to graduate study at some point after graduating from Ursinus. Students develop the habits of mind to become doctors, attorneys, college professors, high school teachers, artists, scientific researchers, writers, and corporate leaders. The College ranks seventeenth in the nation in the percentage of its graduates who have attended medical school. Historically, 90 percent of those who apply to medical, dental, and veterinary schools gain acceptance. College graduates also have a law school admissions record better than 90 percent. Among Ursinus' 11,000 living alumni are 1972 Nobel laureate, Gerald Edelman; NASA Magellan Mission Director, James F. Scott III; Chancellor of the Jewish Theological Seminary of New York, Ismar Schorsch; Ambassador and architect of the Camp David Peace Accord, Hermann F. Eilts; Sam Keen, author of *Fire in the Belly: On Being a Man* and other major books; United States Ambassador to Sierra Leone, Joseph H. Melrose Jr.; Geoff Bloom, president and CEO of Wolverine Worldwide Incorporated; and pediatric AIDS researcher Loretta P. Finnegan.

Since its founding in 1869, Ursinus has combined a residential experience with an uncompromising drive toward academic quality. Ursinus students are intelligent, motivated, and academically curious, as demonstrated by their excellence in advanced college-preparatory high school programs and cocurricular activities. The student body at Ursinus numbers approximately 1,450, with equal numbers of men and women. Ursinus receives 2,000 applications each year and enrolls 400 students each fall. Forty percent of those enrolled in fall 2003 were ranked in the top 10 percent in their high schools, 176 were elected to the National Honor Society, 91 were captains of varsity sports, 17 were valedictorians or salutatorians, and 4 were National Merit Scholars. Thirteen percent of the entering class is composed of members of minority groups, and 5 percent of the class is composed of international students. The student body comes from thirty-one states and sixteen other countries.

The Ursinus College graduating class of 2003 achieved exceptional results. Thirty-nine students published research papers, 127 gave presentations of their research and internship results via conferences, and 25 received grants and fellowships to graduate schools. Graduates of the class of 2003 attend thirty-six graduate schools, seven law schools, fourteen medical schools, three dental schools, three veterinary schools, and four graduate schools of physical therapy.

Ursinus provides a variety of cocurricular outlets for students. The nationally recognized Berman Museum of Art, which features the collection of Philip and Muriel Berman, is open to the public. Their collection of American art is one of the finest in the world. Changing exhibits range from sixth-century B.C. excavations from Jerusalem to the hyperrealistic contemporary sculpture of Marc Sijan. Zack's Snack Bar is located in the recently renovated Wismer Center, which also houses the Ursinus Book Store, game room, television lounge, dance and movie facilities, and the Student Activities, Student Government Association (SGA), and Campus Activities Board (CAB) offices. The Residential Village, comprised of twenty-five renovated Victorian homes, complements the campus culture.

Ursinus students may live in these houses or in one of the residence halls. Six of the homes are special interest houses: Unity House, Musser International House, Service Learning House, Wellness House, the Java Trench (coffeehouse), and Biology House. Ursinus students, 93 percent of whom live on campus, enjoy their involvement in College activities. Willing to assume leadership roles, all students participate in at least one of the seventy-five special interest clubs and organizations, honorary academic societies, theater and musical programs, service opportunities, and preprofessional advisory groups. Publications include the weekly *Grizzly* newspaper and the *Lantern* literary magazine. The Literary Society meets weekly. The College offers fraternities and sororities and an extensive athletic program, including Division III intercollegiate varsity sports, Division I women's field hockey, junior varsity sports, and club and intramural activities.

Location

Ursinus is located in the town of Collegeville, which lies 25 miles northwest of Philadelphia along the Route 422 corridor. Its location offers both the charm of a small-town community surrounded by farmland and the convenience of restaurants, theaters, shops, and cultural and sports events in Philadelphia and nearby communities. Interests of all kinds can be explored within a 50-mile radius of the College. There are opportunities to ski in the mountains of the Poconos, hike and camp in French Creek State Park, shop in the famous King of Prussia malls, and relive history in Valley Forge National Park and the historic district of Philadelphia. The College is situated 100 miles from New York City. The recent relocation of three major pharmaceutical companies to the immediate area provides research opportunities for students.

Majors and Degrees

Ursinus offers undergraduate degrees in arts and sciences. The Bachelor of Arts (B.A.) is awarded to students with majors in anthropology/sociology, business and economics, classical studies, communication arts, English, environmental studies, French, German, history, international relations, philosophy and religion, politics, and Spanish. The Bachelor of Science (B.S.) is awarded to students with majors in biochemistry, biology, chemistry, computer science, exercise and sports science, mathematics, physics, and psychology. In addition, interdisciplinary majors may be arranged. The College offers a cooperative 3-2 engineering program. Secondary teaching certification is offered in many areas.

Academic Programs

Ursinus is committed to undergraduate liberal education and requires students to select among choices in a core curriculum, with a minimum of 128 credits for the bachelor's degree. While completing departmental requirements in one of the major fields, students may add one or more minors. All students are required to complete an internship, an independent research project, a study-abroad program, or a student teaching experience. The College operates on a semester calendar. The fall term begins in late January and ends in mid-May. The College offers funded summer research opportunities with its aggressive undergraduate research scholars program.

Off-Campus Programs

Ursinus believes that students in all fields can be transformed by contact with other cultures, so it has created both national and international academic, research, and volunteered internship programs that turn the College into a global gateway. Ursinus offers a broad and diverse set of opportunities for off-campus study. Examples of national programs are the Howard University Semester and the Washington, D.C., Semester. Ursinus also sponsors international study programs to Australia, Costa Rica, England, France, Germany, Ireland, Japan, Mexico, New Zealand, Scotland and Senegal. Ursinus works with the Council on International Education Exchange to provide international experiences to various sites, including Argentina, Belgium, the Czech Republic, Ghana, Hungary, Indonesia, the Netherlands, Poland, Russia, and Tunisia.

Academic Facilities

Myrin Library's open-stack structure houses 185,000 volumes, 155,000 microforms, 17,500 audiovisual materials, and 900 current periodical subscriptions and is a selective depository for U.S. and Pennsylvania state government documents. All materials are accessible through a state-of-the-art Windows-based online computer catalog. Students also have access to more than 3.7 million volumes through the Tri-State College Library Cooperative. Pfhaler Hall of Science has recently reopened after a $15-million renovation and addition. Within Pfhaler Hall, the Musser Lecture Hall features the latest in videoconferencing and audiovisual technology, the observatory features excellent high-resolution telescopes, and the laboratories are designed for faculty and student collaborative research. The F. W. Olin Academic Building is the home of all departments in the humanities and contains a 320-seat lecture hall, classrooms, seminar rooms, two microcomputer centers, the Writing Center, and faculty offices and research space. The International Learning Center, also in Olin Hall, provides computer, video, and satellite technology to practice languages. Bomberger Hall provides classrooms for many courses in the social sciences. Thomas Hall houses the psychology and biology departments and provides recently renovated facilities for independent student laboratory research as well as regular course work. Major pieces of scientific instrumentation include infrared spectrometers, a flow cytometer, liquid chromatographs, and a scanning electron microscope. Ritter Center for the Dramatic Arts houses a 260-seat theater with flexible staging, a television studio, and various auxiliary rooms. Helfferich Hall offers a swimming pool, studio, and a fully mirrored weight room with hydra equipment. The Lewes Field House features a four-lane indoor track, indoor tennis courts, and a fully equipped recreation and weight room. Outdoor sports facilities include eight tennis courts, an all-weather track and steeplechase pit, and nine oversized athletics fields for intramural and intercollegiate sports.

Costs

The comprehensive cost for the 2003–04 academic year for entering first-year students was $34,400. The cost includes $27,500 for tuition, which includes a laptop computer, and $6900 for room and board.

Financial Aid

Approximately 85 percent of Ursinus students receive financial aid in the form of scholarships, grants, loans, campus employment, and state or federal aid. Eligibility for need-based financial aid is determined by the Ursinus Office of Financial Services using the Free Application for Federal Student Aid (FAFSA) and the CSS PROFILE. Approximately half of the College's students work part-time on campus each year. Merit- and talent-based scholarships, which are awarded regardless of need, include a number of awards of up to $13,500. The FAFSA and PROFILE should reach the College Scholarship Service by February 15, which is the College's preferred filing date. No student is denied admission because of financial need. Ursinus College guarantees to meet the CSS PROFILE need of early decision admitted students.

Faculty

The focus of the College's 147 full- and part-time professors and instructors is on teaching students. All faculty members are also involved in research and writing. Ninety percent of the full-time faculty members have earned doctorates or the highest degree in their fields, and all members are encouraged to explore their fields of study through faculty development grants, leaves, and sabbaticals. The student-faculty ratio is 11:1. Most faculty members serve as academic advisers, and many serve as advisers to academically oriented clubs and interest groups.

Student Government

Through the Ursinus Student Government Association (USGA), students have responsibility in all essential areas of campus governance. Through the USGA committees, students may participate in the development of the academic, residential, and extracurricular life of the College. Great emphasis is placed on fostering responsibility in campus life.

Admissions Requirements

Applicants for admission to Ursinus must be graduates of an accredited high school and present a minimum of 16 academic credits starting in the ninth grade. Candidates for admission are required to submit SAT I or ACT scores. Students who have achieved top 10 percent ranking in their high schools or who have achieved a GPA of 3.5 or better at high schools that do not rank have the option of waiving their standardized test scores. For fall 2003, the middle 50 percent of combined SAT I scores earned by students entering Ursinus ranged from 1150 to 1350. SAT II Subject Tests are recommended but not required. Ursinus also recognizes the Advanced Placement Program of the College Board for college credit. All applicants are encouraged to arrange for a personal interview on campus, and merit scholarship applicants are required to have an on-campus interview.

Application and Information

Ursinus College accepts the Common Application. Candidates are asked to send a completed application accompanied by the nonrefundable $45 application fee no later than February 15. Candidates who wish to be considered for early decision must submit an application and complete their credentials prior to January 15. Ursinus College also has an early admission program for outstanding high school juniors; such students should contact the Office of Admissions for further information. Academic program brochures and application forms may be obtained by contacting:

Office of Admissions
Ursinus College
P.O. Box 1000
Collegeville, Pennsylvania 19426
Telephone: 610-409-3200
Fax: 610-409-3662
World Wide Web: http://www.ursinus.edu

UTICA COLLEGE

UTICA, NEW YORK

The College

Founded in 1946 as a college of Syracuse University, Utica College has a liberal educational philosophy and an informal, personal atmosphere. On the modern 128-acre campus on the southwestern edge of the medium-sized city of Utica, New York, students enjoy a close personal relationship with the faculty and staff. The student body (with a full-time enrollment in fall 2003 of 774 men and 1,095 women) is diverse, made up of men and women from many socioeconomic backgrounds. They represent a wide variety of ethnic groups, older students, veterans, and handicapped persons. Most students live on campus in six residence hall complexes and in one apartment-style complex. While students come from all parts of the United States and several other countries, most come from New York, New England, and the Middle Atlantic States.

The College is accredited by the Middle States Association of Colleges and Schools, and, where appropriate, certain programs are accredited by specific discipline-oriented accrediting organizations. Special student services are offered by the College in the areas of academic, personal, and career counseling, health, and international-student advising. There are more than eighty campus organizations devoted to individual interests, from service and social fraternities and sororities to cultural activities; from major-related clubs to sports groups; from student government to professional group affiliations. The Department of Athletics offers one coed, eight men's, and ten women's intercollegiate sports programs and four club sports. In addition, there is a complete system of intramural and recreational sports.

Strebel Student Center is the social and recreational center of the campus. It houses Strebel Auditorium, the site of theatrical presentations; the Student Health Center; the bookstore; the Student Activities Office; a computer lounge; the dining hall; the Pioneer Cafe, a meeting and eating place; and offices for student clubs, the student newspaper, and the student radio station. Burrstone House and Conference Center contains meeting rooms, banquet halls, and entertainment space for the College community. The physical education complex includes a 1,400-seat stadium with all-weather turf field, a gymnasium, a minigym, racquetball courts, outdoor multipurpose fields, fitness and dance rooms, and a swimming pool. Other facilities include the Newman Center (for religious activities).

Location

Utica, with a population of 70,000, is the major city of the western Mohawk River valley. It is located 90 miles west of Albany and 50 miles east of Syracuse. The Munson-Williams-Proctor Institute, just a few minutes from campus, is an internationally known arts center, featuring an extraordinary museum of art and a school of art as well as a performing arts program. The Stanley Performing Arts Center in downtown Utica is home to the Broadway Theatre League, the Great Artists Series, the Utica Symphony Orchestra, and other major theatrical and musical productions. Other attractions include the F. X. Matt Brewery and the Utica Zoo. The city's park system includes the Val Bialas municipal ski slopes just a mile from the campus, public tennis courts, swimming pools, and public athletic fields. Excellent golfing, swimming, boating, fishing, hiking, camping, and shopping facilities surround the city. Utica is served by a major airport, a train station, and bus lines. City buses make regular stops on campus, providing easy access to the Utica area.

Majors and Degrees

Utica College offers the B.A. degree from Syracuse University in communication arts, economics, English, government and politics, history, international studies, mathematics, philosophy, and sociology and anthropology. The Syracuse University B.S. degree is offered in accounting (private and CPA), biology, business economics, chemistry, computer science, criminal justice, criminal justice–economic crime investigation, health studies, health studies–human behavior, health studies–management, health studies/occupational therapy, health studies/physical therapy, journalism studies, liberal studies, management, nursing, psychology–child life, public relations, public relations/journalism studies, and therapeutic recreation. The B.A. or the B.S. degree may be earned in physics.

Preprofessional programs include dentistry, law, medicine, pharmacy, and veterinary medicine. Special programs are available in teacher education, gerontology, liberal arts–engineering, and a joint health professions program. Students may minor in anthropology, chemistry, communication arts, computer science, English language, film studies, French, gender studies, gerontology, government, history, human rights advocacy, literature, management, mathematics, philosophy, psychology, sociology, Spanish, theater, and writing. Graduate degrees are available in economic crime management, education, liberal studies, occupational therapy, and physical therapy.

Academic Programs

Students may either enter the College without a declared major or enter directly into one of thirty-one degree programs. To assist students in planning their programs of study and declaring a major, the Office of Academic Support assigns a faculty adviser to each student. In many instances, it is possible for a student to elect a dual major. Students who have not decided on a major are assigned special advisers. Accelerated programs, independent study, cooperative education, field placements, and internships are offered.

To earn a bachelor's degree, a student must complete a minimum of 120 to 128 credits, satisfy major and major-related requirements, and complete any special program requirements. All Utica College students, regardless of their major, must complete a liberal arts core program as part of the degree requirements and submit a satisfactory writing portfolio.

Utica College operates on a semester system, with the day and evening fall term beginning in late August and ending shortly before Christmas and the day and evening spring term beginning in late January and continuing until early May. A summer program also offers both day and evening sessions. Utica College offers the Higher Education Opportunity Program (HEOP), the Collegiate Science and Technology Entry Program (CSTEP), and a Summer Institute, which serves as an academic bridge between high school and college. Students enrolled in the fall Freshman Year Initiative receive guidance in the transition to college life while earning academic credit.

Off-Campus Programs

Utica College students are eligible to participate in the Division of International Programs offered through Syracuse University. This arrangement allows Utica College students to study abroad in France, Italy, and Spain, among other countries. Students are encouraged to complete internships and field placements to gain professional experience with businesses and organizations as well as College credit. Utica College's Cooperative Education Program allows students to earn money while gaining professional experience.

Academic Facilities

The Frank E. Gannett Memorial Library collection consists of 181,050 volumes, 1,303 serial subscriptions, and a microfilm collection of 64,031 units. The library is fully automated and shares a local system with Mid-York Library System. It also is a member of OCLC, a bibliographic database through which it is possible to locate and borrow interlibrary loan items from local, regional, national, and international libraries. The lower level of the building houses a Media Center, computer labs, and rooms for music and fine arts. Utica College hosts musical recitals, receptions, and special events in the Library Concourse, which contains the Edith Barrett Art Gallery and an atrium. Four buildings house classrooms, laboratories, and faculty offices: Hubbard Hall, the Administration Building, Gordon Science Center, and Rocco F. DePerno Hall. The academic buildings house eight computer laboratories for student use, including IBM-compatible and Apple Macintosh computers, as well as an Academic Support Services Center, Mathematics and Science Center, and Writing Center.

Costs

For 2003–04, tuition was $19,980. Room and board costs, based on a double room and four meal plans, were $8070 annually. There were a student activities fee of $110 and a technology fee of $180. Books and supplies average $680 per year.

Financial Aid

The College is recognized as a best buy in education and works to control costs and keep its education affordable. The average financial aid package for 2003–04 freshmen was $21,071. About two thirds of that aid came from grants and a third from loans and/or jobs. Approximately 90 percent of the freshmen received a financial aid package. At the same time, the College awarded numerous merit scholarships to students with outstanding grades and test scores.

Almost every federal and state financial aid program is available through Utica College. Students apply for institutional and governmental financial aid by filing the required financial aid forms by February 15. In addition, Utica College offers three different deferred-payment programs that spread out payments over the academic year.

Faculty

The faculty is a diverse group of academicians who can best be described as energetic and accomplished. While most of the 113 full-time faculty members hold advanced degrees, 94 percent have the terminal degree in their field—usually the Ph.D. While many faculty members are involved in research, the primary concern of the faculty is undergraduate education. All faculty members teach classes, providing constant direct contact between faculty and students. Class sizes average 15 to 20, and the student-faculty ratio is 17:1. All faculty members are involved in assisting students with their major areas of academic planning.

Student Government

One of the strongest traditions of the College is student participation in all of the College's affairs. Students participate in campus governing bodies and policymaking groups, extending the learning experience beyond the classroom. Students, faculty, and staff participate in the College Council, which gives each group a representative voice in governance of all College affairs—academic, social, cultural, administrative, and regulatory. Students also serve on all standing committees of the College.

Admission Requirements

Utica College admits students who can best benefit from the educational opportunities the College offers. The Admission Committee gives each application individual attention, and the prospect of a student's success at Utica College is measured primarily by an evaluation of past academic performance, scholastic ability, and personal characteristics. Freshman applicants must have completed 16 academic units, including four years of English. Students should follow a college-preparatory program, including 3 units of mathematics, 3 units of science, 2 units of foreign language, and 3 units of social studies.

Application and Information

Students may apply for fall, spring, or summer admission. Materials required include a completed Utica College application form, official high school or college transcripts, and a $35 application fee. Utica College prefers, but does not require, SAT I or ACT scores. A personal interview for all applicants is strongly suggested. Occupational therapy, physical therapy, and joint health professions program applicants must submit SAT I or ACT scores, a preferred letter of clinical recommendation, and a personal statement. International students must complete the international student application form. The application fee is waived for students who apply to HEOP or CSTEP. The College conducts a rolling admissions program (except for those applying for occupational therapy, physical therapy, the joint health professions program, or for academic achievement awards, for whom the application deadline is January 15).

Inquiries should be sent to:

Director of Admissions
Utica College
1600 Burrstone Road
Utica, New York 13502-4892
Telephone: 315-792-3006
800-782-8884 (toll-free)
E-mail: admiss@ucsu.edu
World Wide Web: http://www.utica.edu

The Frank E. Gannett Memorial Library on the campus of Utica College.

VALPARAISO UNIVERSITY
VALPARAISO, INDIANA

The University

Valparaiso University was founded in 1859 by citizens of Valparaiso, Indiana, but its recent history dates from 1925, when it was purchased by the Lutheran University Association. Valpo is one of the nation's largest Lutheran-affiliated universities, yet it remains independent and is open to individuals of all faiths. The University's 3,700 students represent most states and more than forty countries; 66 percent come from outside of Indiana. Valparaiso University is a residential community in which activities outside the classroom form an important part of campus life; more than 66 percent of its students live on campus. Approximately 100 extracurricular and cocurricular programs are open to all, including various NCAA Division I intercollegiate and intramural sports teams for men and women. Approximately 30 percent of the students are members of the eight national fraternities and seven national sororities at the University. Both in and out of the classroom, students and professors operate under a student-initiated honor code in which integrity is assumed to be the norm. When violations do occur, they are handled by peers through a student-composed Honor Council. Because of these structures and the whole philosophy of the University, relationships among students, the faculty, and the administration can be unusually free and open.

Major divisions at Valpo are the Colleges of Arts and Sciences, Business Administration, Engineering, and Nursing; Christ College (the honors college); the School of Law; and the Graduate Division. Graduates have enjoyed a 93 percent placement rate over the past five years.

Location

The University is located in Valparaiso, a safe community of 26,000 in northwest Indiana. Only one hour west, Chicago and its theaters, museums, restaurants, and cultural and sports offerings are accessible by auto, train, or bus. The campus is within walking distance of a vibrant town square and of a commercial/entertainment center with national chain stores and restaurants. Just 15 miles north is the Indiana Dunes National Lakeshore on Lake Michigan, a famous recreational area and perhaps the finest ecological laboratory in the nation. Air service is available from Chicago's O'Hare and Midway International Airports and South Bend's Michiana Regional Airport.

Majors and Degrees

Valparaiso University offers the following undergraduate degrees: Associate in Science, Bachelor of Arts, Bachelor of Music, Bachelor of Music Education, Bachelor of Science, Bachelor of Science in Accounting, Bachelor of Science in Business Administration, Bachelor of Science in Civil Engineering, Bachelor of Science in Computer Engineering, Bachelor of Science in Education, Bachelor of Science in Electrical Engineering, Bachelor of Science in Fine Arts, Bachelor of Science in Mechanical Engineering, Bachelor of Science in Nursing, Bachelor of Science in Physical Education, and Bachelor of Social Work. The B.A. or B.S. degree may be earned in actuarial science, American studies, art, astronomy, biochemistry, biology, broadcast meteorology, chemistry, Chinese and Japanese studies, classics, communication (5 areas), computer science, criminology, economics, English, environmental science, exercise science, French, geography, geology, German, history, humanities, international economics and cultural affairs, international service, mathematics, meteorology, modern European studies, music, music enterprises, music performance, philosophy, physics, political science, pre-medical arts, psychology, sociology, Spanish, sports management, theater, theology, and youth, family, and education ministry.

Academic Program

Valparaiso University has a long tradition of combining professional colleges with a strong commitment to the values and broadening experiences of the liberal arts. The University helps students of varied interests and objectives to clarify their goals and explore new possibilities. Connections between students' lives and the classroom are encouraged through an emphasis on hands-on learning and programs like the Valpo Core. Programs are structured to provide a solid base for exploration in various fields, while offering students the freedom to develop depth in a specific interest. This philosophy is extended through the upper division, where students have three options in completing a degree: an individual plan of study involving the major and complementary courses from related fields of study, the election of a second academic major in addition to the first, or a special minor in connection with the major. Career planning is aided through the professional programs and the University's Career Center. Many students also gain professional work experience in their chosen field before graduation by participating in the cooperative education program and internships.

Valparaiso operates on the semester system; the fall semester begins in late August and ends before Christmas, and the spring semester starts in early January and ends during the second week in May. Valpo also has two summer terms that further extend opportunities for study on campus or at various off-campus locations.

The University participates in the Advanced Placement Program, the College-Level Examination Program, and the International Baccalaureate Program. In addition, Valparaiso provides its own placement testing in several academic areas.

All departments of the University offer opportunities for honors work through independent study, seminars, and research. Christ College, the honors college of Valparaiso, has a well-established but continuously evolving program designed to challenge gifted students. Christ College students enroll concurrently in any other Valpo college.

Off-Campus Programs

Valparaiso University sponsors study-abroad programs in Reutlingen and Tübingen, Germany; Puebla, Mexico; Paris, France; Hangzhou, China; Granada, Spain; and London and Cambridge, England. Valparaiso also sponsors semester-long study opportunities at two universities in Japan, one in Namibia, and another in Greece. Valpo students may study at other overseas locations through Valparaiso's membership in the Central States College Association. In addition, Valpo grants credit for the following cooperative programs: Urban Studies Semester (Chicago), Urban Affairs Semester and Washington Semester (Washington, D.C.), and United Nations Semester (New York City).

Academic Facilities

The Henry F. Moellering Memorial Library contains more than 568,949 volumes and more than 1.6 million microforms and receives 13,984 subscriptions. Moellering and the School of Law's library operate with open stacks and are available to undergraduate and graduate students. A 16,830-square-foot building addition with Doppler radar and Weather Channel access opens in spring 2005. In addition, the high-tech, 115,000-square-foot Christopher Center for Library and Information Services is scheduled for completion in fall 2004. The Neils Science Center houses an astronomical observatory, a greenhouse, a subcritical nuclear reactor, and other facilities that have earned the University a citation from the Atomic Energy Commission for having a model undergraduate physics laboratory. The Kade-Duesenberg German House, the Virtual Nursing Learning Center, weather station, Center for the Arts, and nonlinear (digital) editing lab are state-of-the-art facilities.

Costs

Tuition for the 2003–04 academic year at Valparaiso University is $20,000, room is $3480, and board is $2000. General fees are $638. The total cost of tuition, room, board, and fees is $26,118. Students spend $1700 per year for books, supplies, and such miscellaneous expenses as laundry and travel.

Financial Aid

Ninety percent of Valparaiso's undergraduate students receive financial aid totaling more than $42 million. Many scholarships and awards are determined by the admissions application. Students are also encouraged to file the Free Application for Federal Student Aid (FAFSA) to apply for need-based grants, loans, and employment. Valpo awards federal, state, and university need-based aid based on FAFSA results, attempting to make up the difference between the cost of attending Valpo and the amount a family can afford. Early application is recommended for Valpo assistance, since the awarding of aid begins in February of the year of enrollment.

Faculty

Valparaiso's 378 faculty members share a common interest—teaching in ways that encourage students and faculty members to get to know one another. The majority are full-time, and a considerable number serve as advisers to the various academic and social organizations on campus. There are no graduate teaching assistants at Valpo. Almost 90 percent of the full-time professors have terminal degrees, and this figure reaches 100 percent in some departments. Each department has a full advising system to help students in course and program selection.

Student Government

Students and faculty members alike are involved in the internal governance of the institution. House Councils in each of the residence halls are composed of representatives elected by the residents. Each council makes decisions and sets standards within the rules established by the University. Students in the living units and off-campus students elect representatives to the Student Senate (composed entirely of students) and the University Senate (made up of an equal number of representatives from the student body, faculty, and administration). The functions of these two separate bodies cover most phases of student life.

Admission Requirements

Valparaiso admits candidates who exhibit the potential for academic success at the University. The freshman retention rate is 88 percent, reflecting in part the high quality of the admission program. Qualified students are admitted without regard to race, color, gender, disability, national origin, or ancestry. The credentials of each applicant are individually and personally evaluated, and consideration is given not only to ACT or SAT I scores, grade point average, and rank in class but also to grades and trends in the student's record, the nature of the high school and the program followed, outside interests, and recommendations. A campus visit and an interview with an admission counselor are recommended but not required. Students who have taken the ACT or SAT I in their junior year and have submitted their high school transcripts, complete through the eleventh grade, may be considered for admission.

Application and Information

An applicant must complete a formal University admission application or the Common Application to be considered for admission. In addition, Valpo requires a high school transcript (complete through the junior year), ACT or SAT I scores, and college transcripts (when applicable). Valpo's nonbinding early action option requires applicants to submit their applications no later than November 1. Regular admission notification begins on a rolling basis after December 1. First priority for scholarship consideration is given to those who apply for admission by the early action deadline; preference is then given to those who apply by January 15.

Information and application forms for admission and financial aid may be obtained from:

Office of Admissions
Valparaiso University
Valparaiso, Indiana 46383-6493
Telephone: 219-464-5011
888-GO-VALPO (toll-free)
Fax: 219-464-6898
E-mail: undergrad.admissions@valpo.edu
World Wide Web: http://www.valpo.edu

Students on the campus of Valparaiso University.

VANDERBILT UNIVERSITY

NASHVILLE, TENNESSEE

The University

When Commodore Cornelius Vanderbilt gave a million dollars to build and endow Vanderbilt University in 1873, he did so with the wish that it would "contribute to strengthening the ties which should exist between all sections of our common country." Today, Vanderbilt enrolls America's most talented students and challenges them daily to expand their intellectual horizons and to free their imaginations. Dialogue, service, the Honor Code, the search for knowledge, and personal fulfillment are all hallmarks of a Vanderbilt education.

Vanderbilt is a medium-sized university that includes four undergraduate schools and six graduate and professional schools. Each year, 1,500 freshmen join the University, bringing the total undergraduate population to approximately 6,300 students. The total enrollment at Vanderbilt is 10,300.

Known for the Southern splendor of its residential 300-acre campus, Vanderbilt provides a variety of housing options for its undergraduates, 87 percent of whom live on campus all four years. One of its unique housing options is the McTyeire International House, designed for students interested in a range of foreign languages, such as Chinese, French, German, Japanese, and Spanish. Other options include traditional dormitories, apartments, and suites. Only six officers are allowed to live in each of the fraternity and sorority houses.

The Sarratt Student Center houses a cinema, a pub, game and music-listening rooms, meeting rooms, an art gallery, craft and darkroom facilities, and an FM radio station. Facilities at the Student Recreation Center include gymnasiums, handball courts, an indoor swimming pool, racquetball courts, a climbing wall, an indoor suspended track, and a weight room. Other facilities include indoor and outdoor tennis courts, baseball and softball diamonds, and a sand volleyball court.

Location

Vanderbilt University is located approximately 3 miles west of downtown Nashville, the capital of Tennessee. As the music industry's "third coast," Nashville is a vibrant, growing city of more than 1 million residents. The greater Nashville area is also home to eighty-one parks and more than 30,000 acres of lakes. Three interstate highways intersect the city, and its international airport is served by eighteen airlines.

Majors and Degrees

The B.A., B.S., B.E., or B.M. degree is offered in African-American studies; American and Southern studies; ancient Mediterranean studies; anthropology; art and art history; biological sciences; biomedical engineering; chemical engineering; chemistry; child development; child studies; civil engineering; classical languages; classics; cognitive studies; communication studies; comparative literature; computer engineering; computer science; early childhood education; East Asian studies; ecology, evolution, and organismal biology; economics; economics and history; electrical engineering; elementary education; engineering science; English; English and history; European studies; French; French and European studies; geology; German; German studies; history; human and organizational development; Latin American and Iberian studies; mathematics; mechanical engineering; molecular and cellular biology; musical arts; musical arts/teacher education track; music composition/theory; music performance; neuroscience; philosophy; physics; physics-astronomy; political science; psychology; public policy studies; religious studies; Russian; Russian and European studies; secondary education; sociology; Spanish; Spanish and European studies; Spanish and Portuguese; Spanish, Portuguese, and European studies; special education; theater; and women's studies.

Academic Programs

Students apply directly to one of the four schools that offer undergraduate programs: the College of Arts and Science, the School of Engineering, Peabody College (education and human development), or the Blair School of Music. In all four schools, advanced placement and opportunities for independent study and internships are available. Vanderbilt University operates on a two-semester calendar, and classes begin in late August. First-semester examinations take place prior to the winter holidays, and the second semester ends in early May. A variety of courses are offered during Maymester and two summer sessions.

The College of Arts and Science provides many opportunities to experience a wide range of academic disciplines and subjects. Within the requirements of the College Program in Liberal Education (CPLE), students refine their skills in writing, mathematics, foreign language, the humanities, natural sciences, social sciences, history, and culture.

The Blair School of Music offers the Bachelor of Music in composition/theory, musical arts, musical arts/teacher education, and performance. Instruction is available in every instrument of the orchestra as well as piano, organ, saxophone, guitar, and voice. The curriculum combines intensive musical training with liberal arts studies. Approximately one third of a student's work is outside of music. The school also offers a liberal arts major, two minors, and a wide variety of courses, private instruction, and performing organizations for nonmajors.

The School of Engineering offers a century-long tradition of educating engineers for practice in industry, government, consulting, teaching, and research. In addition to technical courses, each student's program must include course work in English, the humanities, and the social sciences.

Peabody College offers degree programs leading to teacher certification and to careers in other areas of education, child development, cognitive studies, and human and organizational development. The degree reflects a strong liberal arts foundation on which is built a solid program of professional courses. All undergraduates must complete requirements in communication, the humanities, mathematics, the natural sciences, and the social sciences. Students have many field experiences throughout the four years.

Off-Campus Programs

Overseas study programs allow students to immerse themselves in the languages and cultures of other countries. Programs are offered in Argentina, Australia, Brazil, Chile, China, the Dominican Republic, England, France, Germany, Israel, Italy, Japan, Russia, and Spain. There is a variety of programs in which students can participate without extending the time it takes to get their degree. Vanderbilt students receive direct credit for their courses, and the cost of tuition for most of the programs is the same as for study on campus in Nashville.

Academic Facilities

Students and faculty members take advantage of Vanderbilt's extensive library resources, obtaining easy access to books, periodicals, documents, microforms, and reference materials. The Jean and Alexander Heard Library is supported by nine major resource centers, which include special collections, University Archives, and more than 2.3 million volumes.

Costs

The costs for 2004–05 are as follows: tuition, $29,250; room and board, $9735 (average); books and supplies, $1030 (average); and the student activities and recreation fee, $750. All costs are subject to change. They are slightly higher for School of Engineering students.

Financial Aid

About 55 percent of the University's undergraduate students receive some type of financial aid. Need-based aid is awarded according to the evaluation of the College Scholarship Service's PROFILE and the FAFSA. Vanderbilt provides assistance through Federal Pell Grants, Federal Supplemental Educational Opportunity Grants, state grants, University scholarships, Federal Stafford Student Loans, institutional loans, Federal Perkins Loans, and Federal Work-Study employment. Information on these and other programs can be obtained from the Office of Student Financial Aid, 2309 West End Avenue, Vanderbilt University, Nashville, Tennessee 37203-1725. Approximately 200 honor scholarships based on academic merit are available.

Faculty

Vanderbilt has a full-time faculty of 1,944 and a part-time faculty of 292. All undergraduate faculty members, many of whom hold awards for distinguished scholarship, are required to teach undergraduates. A low student-faculty ratio of 9:1 provides for close working relationships between students and professors who are recognized nationally and worldwide for their research. The average class size is 19.

Student Government

The SGA provides students with an opportunity to participate actively in maintaining the high quality of life on campus. It works with many of the more than 250 student organizations to bring nationally prominent speakers to campus. A vital part of life at Vanderbilt is the honor system, which is governed entirely by students through representatives on the Honor Council. Each year a senior is selected as a Young Alumni Trustee of the University's Board of Trust.

Admission Requirements

Vanderbilt seeks students with high standards of scholarship and character. Admission is based on a thorough review of academic and personal credentials.

Students must submit a minimum of 15 academic units at the secondary level, although most admitted students present 20 or more academic units. Applicants to the College of Arts and Science and the Blair School of Music must present a minimum of 2 years of a foreign language and applicants to the School of Engineering, a minimum of 4 units of mathematics. The Admissions Committee evaluates each student's secondary school academic record, extracurricular involvement, counselor and teacher recommendations, and personal characteristics. Students must also submit scores from either the SAT I or ACT. Applicants are encouraged to submit scores from three SAT II Subject Tests (including Writing and Math I, IC, or IIC) for class placement. Applicants to the Blair School of Music must also audition on their primary instrument. A personal audition is preferred. Applicants for the musical arts program may audition by tape.

Campus visits are strongly recommended. Prospective students should call in advance of their visit for information about group information sessions, campus tours, overnight accommodations, and opportunities to attend classes.

Application and Information

Students whose first choice is Vanderbilt may apply under the early decision plan. Applications and all supporting materials must be submitted by November 1 for Early Decision I and by January 2 for Early Decision II; notification is made by December 15 for Early Decision I and by February 15 for Early Decision II. The deadline for applying under the regular decision plan is January 2. Personal auditions are scheduled in December, January, and February at the Blair School of Music. Students are informed of the admission decision by April 1. Students seeking transfer admission must submit an application and all supporting materials no later than February 1 for fall semester admission and no later than November 15 for spring semester admission.

Office of Undergraduate Admissions
Vanderbilt University
2305 West End Avenue
Nashville, Tennessee 37203-1727
Telephone: 615-322-2561
800-288-0432 (toll-free)
E-mail: admissions@vanderbilt.edu
World Wide Web: http://www.vanderbilt.edu/Admissions

VANDERCOOK COLLEGE OF MUSIC

CHICAGO, ILLINOIS

The College

VanderCook College of Music traces it's roots back to the early 1900s when Hale A. VanderCook opened his downtown studio. By the late 1920s, the studio had developed into what would become one of the first three institutions to offer a degree in instrumental music education. The development of music education in the United States is closely linked to VanderCook's development as an institution.

VanderCook's hands-on curriculum is a practical and fundamental approach to learning. Having only one major, music education, VanderCook students are allowed a greater opportunity to focus on their education. The success of the College is determined by both the advancement of its students and the success of its graduates.

While students are taught all aspects of music, the main focus remains on music education. This is the point at which VanderCook students excel above all others. Their dedication to both education and performance helps make them aware of all areas of music. More than 95 percent of the graduates make their career in the field of music education. VanderCook continues to have a 95 to 100 percent job placement rate.

VanderCook College of Music is accredited by the National Association of Schools of Music, the North Central Association of Colleges and Schools, and the Illinois Board of Higher Education.

VanderCook also offers a Master of Music Education degree and a Master of Music Education degree with teaching certification.

Location

The College is in the South Loop area of Chicago on the campus of the Illinois Institute of Technology, close to the heart of the city's magnificent musical and cultural centers. VanderCook students have the opportunity to hear the world-renowned Chicago Symphony Orchestra, the Lyric Opera, and many other musical performers. Transportation to and from campus is readily accessible with public transportation stops located on campus and a shuttle bus, which runs between campus and the train stations. The city of Chicago is an important extension of the VanderCook campus.

Majors and Degrees

VanderCook College of Music offers one major at the undergraduate level, music education. Upon completing the appropriate course of study, vocal or instrumental, undergraduate students are awarded the Bachelor of Music Education degree.

Academic Program

VanderCook College of Music trains students in both a musical course of study and in general academic areas. The curriculum is practical, emphasizing the proven fundamentals of music education developed by founder H. A. VanderCook. In addition to studying voice, all students learn to perform and teach seventeen different types of instruments and upon graduation are prepared to teach band, choir, and classroom music.

The academic year, which begins in the fall, is based on a semester system. Students may enter in either fall or spring. (Summer terms are for graduate students only.)

Academic Facilities

The College is housed in a two-story building located on the campus of the Illinois Institute of Technology. The building contains classrooms, an academic library, a music library, a listening laboratory, practice rooms, a recital hall, a conference room, an instrument repair laboratory, and various offices. VanderCook's newly renovated Electronic Music Center contains computer workstations and MIDI hardware that use the latest in computer technology and music software. In addition, VanderCook students have complete access to the student services provided by the Illinois Institute of Technology such as dormitories, the library, the gymnasium, and the recreation center.

Costs

Tuition in 2003–04 was $15,290. Room and board, provided by the Illinois Institute of Technology, totaled $6200, and fees were $370.

Financial Aid

Each student is considered on an individual basis for financial aid. Merit-based scholarships are given for musical talent and are based on competitive auditions. Academic scholarships are also available to qualified students. Scholarships are renewable based on musical growth and participation and also cumulative grade point average. Illinois residents may apply for the Monetary Award Program and Federal Stafford Student Loans are also available.

Faculty

At VanderCook College of Music, all undergraduate classes are taught by either full-time or part-time faculty members who have many years of in-depth, practical experience in the field of music education to share with their students. Faculty members are dedicated to giving individual instruction, made possible by a 6:1 student-teacher ratio.

Admission Requirements

VanderCook College of Music seeks musically proficient students who have demonstrated talent and who desire to become the finest music educators.

Candidates for admission must submit an application and essay along with high school transcripts, ACT or SAT I scores, and three letters of recommendation. Following the application, students should schedule and audition and interview with the Director of Admission.

Transfer students must submit both high school and college transcripts. VanderCook is authorized under federal law to enroll international students. These students must submit TOEFL scores and the I-20 form.

Application and Information

Applications are accepted up to four weeks prior to the beginning of a term, subject to the availability of space.

Information or an application may be obtained by contacting:

Tamara V. Trutwin
Director of Student Recruitment
VanderCook College of Music
3140 South Federal Street
Chicago, Illinois 60616-3731
Telephone: 312-225-6288
800-448-2655 (toll-free)
Fax: 312-225-5211
World Wide Web: http://www.vandercook.edu

VASSAR COLLEGE

POUGHKEEPSIE, NEW YORK

The College

Vassar is a coeducational, independent, residential undergraduate college of liberal arts and sciences. Founded in 1861, Vassar's original purpose was to provide for women the same high-quality education afforded only to men at the leading institutions of the day. Since its founding, Vassar has been both a pioneer and a leader in American higher education. Becoming fully coeducational in 1969, Vassar today offers its students a distinctive education that features a high level of academic rigor, a strong sense of equality between the sexes, a willingness to experiment, a dedication to the values of the liberal arts and sciences, and a commitment to the development of leadership.

Vassar's 2,400 students come from all fifty states and forty countries. Vassar seeks a high level of ethnic, geographic, religious, and socioeconomic diversity in its student body, believing strongly that students with different backgrounds and experiences can play an important role in the overall educational purpose of the College. Students of color make up approximately 22 percent of the student body, while about 6 percent are international students. Firmly convinced of the advantages of a residential college setting, Vassar provides a variety of housing options to its students, and 98 percent of students live on campus. Housing is guaranteed for all students.

Students enjoy an active extracurricular, social, and cultural life at Vassar. There are more than 100 student clubs and organizations, including a weekly newspaper and nearly a dozen other student publications; political, religious, and personal affinity groups; a student-run FM radio station; theater, music, and dance performance groups; a volunteer network; debate; student government; an outing club; and dozens of other such activities. There are no fraternities or sororities. A pub and nonalcoholic café showcases local talent, while nationally known speakers, writers, and performers appear on campus throughout the year. A strong Division III athletic program features twenty-three varsity teams, twelve for men and twelve for women. Baseball is exclusive to men, as are field hockey and golf to women; both sexes compete in basketball, crew, cross-country, fencing, lacrosse, soccer, squash, swimming and diving, tennis, and volleyball. Club sports include riding, rugby, sailing, skiing, and track. The College also supports a vigorous and popular intramural program.

Maintained as an arboretum with more than 200 varieties of trees, Vassar's landscaped 1,000-acre campus contains more than 100 buildings, including the College Center, the libraries, three theaters, a music recital hall, studio art facilities, two observatories, three science buildings, the computer center, the Frances Lehman Loeb Art Center, an environmental station, three athletic facilities, residence halls, and extensive classroom space.

Location

Vassar is located in a residential area 3 miles from the center of Poughkeepsie, New York, a city with an area population of approximately 100,000 people. Situated in the historic and beautiful mid-Hudson River Valley, the College offers its students easy access to New York City, about 75 miles to the south and served by extensive commuter rail connections, and to nearby outdoor recreational opportunities, including climbing, hiking, skiing, and camping at the region's many state parks, lakes, and mountainous regions. Students make extensive use of the city of Poughkeepsie and surrounding communities for internship and volunteer options in business, the arts, social service agencies, health facilities, and legal or political organizations.

Majors and Degrees

Vassar College grants the Bachelor of Arts degree to undergraduates. Departmental programs include anthropology, art, biology, chemistry, classics, computer science, drama and film, economics, education, English, French, geology and geography, German, Hispanic studies (Spanish), history, Italian, mathematics, music, philosophy, physical education and dance, physics and astronomy, political science, psychology, religion, Russian, and sociology. Interdepartmental programs include biochemistry, biopsychology, geography-anthropology, Latin American studies, medieval and Renaissance studies, and Victorian studies. Multidisciplinary programs include Africana studies; American culture; Asian studies; cognitive science; environmental studies; international studies; Jewish studies; science, technology, and society; urban studies; and women's studies. Students interested in engineering can complete a five-year dual-degree program with Dartmouth College.

Academic Program

Vassar's academic program is notable for its flexibility and breadth. No core curriculum exists, and students are given both great freedom and significant responsibility in shaping their own education. Students must select a major by the end of the sophomore year, but beyond the major they must fulfill only three additional specific requirements: a freshman course, a quantitative course, and a foreign language sequence. Freshman courses, offered across the curriculum, feature small, discussion-based classes, which usually serve as introductions to their disciplines and stress the effective expression of ideas in both written and oral work. By the end of the second year, all students must take one course that demands a significant amount of quantitative analysis, chosen from a broad array of options in the sciences, mathematics, computing, and the social sciences. Finally, all students must demonstrate intermediate proficiency in a foreign language, either by completing course work in one of the many languages taught at the College or by achieving sufficiently high scores on Advanced Placement or SAT II language tests.

Off-Campus Programs

Thirty-seven percent of Vassar's students spend at least one semester studying away from campus and earn full academic credit. Many students choose to study at one of the programs sponsored by Vassar in England, France, Germany, Ireland, Italy, Morocco, or Spain. Those meeting major and GPA requirements may also join approved programs offered by other colleges in additional countries. Vassar students have studied at more than 100 sites in Africa, Asia, Australia, Europe, and the Americas, usually during their junior year. Domestically, students may elect to study at another institution through the Twelve College Exchange, a consortium of Northeastern liberal arts colleges, or through a variety of other exchange arrangements.

Academic Facilities

The libraries at Vassar offer holdings of almost 1 million volumes, 4,000 periodicals, and 350,000 microforms, as well as access to sophisticated databases and research networks. Extensive special collections are also offered by the art and music departments. These resources are augmented by an extensive campuswide computing network linking all student rooms and faculty offices via a fiber-optic network and providing access to the Internet. Computer clusters, strictly for student use, are located in every residence hall, the College Center, the library, the computer center, and most academic buildings. Three theaters, a concert hall, and extensive practice facilities provide space for performance opportunities in drama, music, and dance. The Frances Lehman Loeb Art Center, completed in 1993, houses one of the oldest and most extensive college art collections in the country, including more than 12,500 paintings, sculptures, prints, drawings, and photographs. Each of the physical science departments (biology, chemistry, geology, and physics-astronomy) has its own building with classrooms, offices, laboratory space, and modern equipment for study and research. The adjacent Vassar farm provides a 550-acre ecological field station for use by students in related disciplines. In astronomy, students use the campus observatory, completed in 1996, which houses three telescopes, including a 32-inch instrument, which is the largest at any college in the Northeast.

Costs

In 2003–04, costs included $29,095 for tuition, $445 for required fees, and $7490 for room and board. Books and personal expenses generally range from $1200 to $1500, and travel expenses vary.

Financial Aid

Bright and academically talented students are encouraged to apply to Vassar regardless of their personal financial circumstances. The College awards financial assistance to nearly 60 percent of the student body, and all aid is awarded solely on the basis of demonstrated financial need. In 2002–03, students received nearly $27 million in assistance, including Vassar College scholarships, federal and state funds, student loans, and campus employment.

To apply for financial aid, students should submit Vassar's Preliminary Application for Financial Aid and also must register during the fall of their senior year with the College Scholarship Service Financial Aid PROFILE service to obtain the appropriate forms. Both the PROFILE and the Free Application for Federal Student Aid (FAFSA) must be filed according to the schedule annually distributed with Vassar's application for admission. Financial aid award letters are sent within several days of admission decisions.

Faculty

More than 225 men and women comprise Vassar's outstanding faculty. More than 95 percent hold the doctorate or equivalent terminal degree in their fields. All faculty members teach undergraduates, and all are required to meet high standards for excellence in both teaching and research. The student-faculty ratio is 9:1, and the average class size is 16. Vassar professors have won virtually every external prize and grant for teaching and research, and many are nationally recognized as authorities in their disciplines. A majority of the faculty members live on campus or in the immediate neighborhood; 1 or 2 faculty members, often with their families, live in each residence hall as house fellows.

Student Government

Much of the on-campus cultural and social environment at Vassar is student-created. The Vassar Student Association (VSA) oversees the allocation of operating funds for campus organizations and events, sponsors elections for student leadership positions, and maintains standing committees for governance activities. Students serve on important campus committees with faculty members and contribute to the formation of college priorities.

Admission Requirements

Admission to Vassar is highly selective: in 2002–03, 6,200 students applied for 640 places in the entering class. The primary criterion is academic ability, as evidenced by both high achievement in a demanding secondary school program and demonstrated intellectual curiosity. Standardized test results are also considered, and all candidates must submit results of the SAT I and three SAT II Subject Tests or the ACT. Nonnative speakers of English should also submit results of the TOEFL.

The Admission Committee also seeks evidence of leadership and talent, as demonstrated through participation in activities in the candidate's school, community, or personal endeavors. Motivation, potential, and personal strengths—as revealed primarily in essays and recommendations—are also weighed in the admission process.

Candidates are encouraged to visit the Vassar campus for a tour and group information session, which are offered weekdays year-round and on most Saturday mornings in the fall. Personal interviews are not required, but applicants may usually arrange an interview with alumni representatives by checking the appropriate space on the application form.

Application and Information

Applications for regular decision admission are due by January 1. Applicants are notified by April 1, and candidates must respond by May 1. Early decision, intended for those students who have concluded that Vassar is a clear first choice, has two possible submission deadlines: November 15 or January 1. Candidates who use the first deadline are notified by December 15, and those electing the second option hear from the College by early February. If accepted, early decision candidates must withdraw all other applications and submit the enrollment deposit to Vassar.

Transfer applications are accepted for both the fall and spring terms. The deadline for submission of transfer applications for midyear admission is November 15, with notification by mid-December. Candidates for transfer admission for the fall term must apply by April 1, with notification usually coming in early May.

Students should direct requests for additional information to:

Office of Admission
Vassar College
124 Raymond Avenue, Box 10
Poughkeepsie, New York 12604-0010
Telephone: 845-437-7300
800-827-7270 (toll-free)
Fax: 845-437-7063
E-mail: admissions@vassar.edu
World Wide Web: http://www.vassar.edu

VERMONT TECHNICAL COLLEGE

RANDOLPH CENTER, VERMONT

The College

Founded in 1866 and situated in a hilltop village near the heart of the Green Mountains, Vermont Technical College (VTC) is the only technical college in the Vermont State Colleges system. Most of the 1,250 students enrolled come from Vermont and the other New England states.

Through its bachelor, associate, and certificate programs, the College provides students with a broad-based practical education. As a result, Vermont Tech graduates are prepared to work effectively in a variety of positions that support the activities of engineers, scientists, and other professionals. A major advantage of the Vermont Tech education is that it gives students the skills and knowledge to go right into their careers or continue their education. For students interested in pursuing the bachelor's degree, VTC offers "two-plus-two" programs leading to the Bachelor of Science. The College also has articulation agreements with a number of top four-year institutions, including the University of Vermont, Northeastern University, Norwich University, Rochester Institute of Technology, SUNY Institute of Technology, the University of New Hampshire, and the College of Agriculture and Life Sciences at Cornell University. Since 1982, 98 percent of each year's graduates have been placed in jobs or continued their education within six months of graduation. Of those taking jobs, 95 percent were working in fields directly related to their VTC degree.

There are twenty-two major buildings on the 544-acre campus, including a Student Health and Physical Education facility with a double-court gymnasium, a six-lane indoor pool, and two racquetball courts. The four residence halls can house 567 students. Every student room has connections for direct access to the campuswide computer network, telephone service, and cable TV lines.

Campus life at Vermont Tech includes sports, recreation, social events, and community-service learning opportunities. The Student Life Office arranges weekly activities and social events and provides students with support and counseling. There are more than thirty student clubs, from radio station WVTC-FM to the yearbook and student chapters of professional organizations. There is also an on-campus ski hill and a fitness center. Students enthusiastically participate in the College's six varsity and twenty-five intramural sports for men and women. The men's basketball and volleyball teams won the Northern New England Small College Conference championship tournament in 1995 and 2000; the men's soccer team won in 1999, 2000, 2001, and 2002; and the men's baseball team won in 1996, 1998, and 1999. VTC also competes in the U.S. College Athletic Association and has advanced to its national men's soccer tournament in each of the last five years. The women's volleyball team were NNESCC champions in 1999 and 2000.

Location

Vermont Tech's location is rural but far from isolated—exit 4 of Interstate 89 is just a mile away. For day-to-day needs, the nearby village of Randolph offers a variety of shops and restaurants as well as a movie theater, a bowling alley, and the Chandler Music Hall. For special shopping and events, Burlington and Montpelier, Vermont, and Hanover, New Hampshire, are within an hour's drive. Boston and Montreal are just 3 hours away. There is convenient bus service from Randolph, and Amtrak's "Vermonter" stops in Randolph twice daily.

Students enjoy the variety of recreational activities available to them in Vermont. Some of the top ski resorts in the East are less than an hour from the campus. Students can also hike on the Appalachian Trail, canoe on numerous lakes and rivers, camp in the Green Mountain National Forest, and bike on the miles of country roads.

Majors and Degrees

Vermont Technical College offers the Bachelor of Science in architectural engineering technology, computer engineering technology, electromechanical engineering technology, and management of technology.

VTC offers four programs leading to the Associate in Engineering degree: civil and environmental engineering technology, computer engineering technology, electrical engineering technology, and mechanical engineering technology.

Programs leading to the Associate in Applied Science degree are agribusiness management technology, architectural and building engineering technology, automotive technology, biotechnology, business technology and management, construction practice and management, dairy farm management technology, e-commerce technology, general engineering technology, landscape development and ornamental horticulture, small-business management, and veterinary technology.

Vermont Tech offers certificate programs in practical nursing and pharmacy technology. The certificate in practical nursing program leads to the Associate in Science in Nursing degree.

Programs leading to the Associate in Science are dental hygiene, nursing, and pharmacy technology. The nursing programs (certificate and associate degree) offered by Vermont Tech are located in Bennington, Brattleboro, or Colchester, Vermont, and on the College's residential main campus in Randolph Center. Other locations are available for part-time study in collaboration with the Community College of Vermont.

VTC also offers three-year options in selected associate degree programs for those students whose math, science, or English skills need some strengthening.

Academic Program

Whether preparing for an associate or a bachelor's degree, Vermont Tech students receive a rigorous broad-based education centered on a core curriculum that includes both technical and general education electives. The number of credits required for graduation ranges from 65 to 72 for the associate degree and from 130 to 139 for the bachelor's degree, depending on the program. Honors courses are offered in all engineering technology programs. Most degree programs also offer project courses in which students work as teams on real-world applications in their fields of study.

The College is accredited by the New England Association of Schools and Colleges. In addition, the following degree programs are accredited by the Technology Accreditation Commission of the Accreditation Board for Engineering and Technology, Inc. (TAC of ABET): architectural and building engineering technology, architectural engineering technology, civil and environmental engineering technology, computer engineering technology, electrical engineering technology, and mechanical engineering technology. The veterinary technology program is accredited by the American Veterinary Medical Association as a program for educating veterinary technicians. Practical nursing programs are approved by the Vermont Board of Nursing and accredited by the National League for Nursing Accrediting Commission (NLNAC). The associate degree program in nursing is approved by the Vermont Board of Nursing.

Academic Facilities

Vermont Tech students learn in modern laboratories with state-of-the-art equipment. Hartness Library is the on-campus library for the Vermont Community & Technical Colleges (VCTC) Library, serving about 3,000 on-campus, extended-campus, and distance education students of VTC and the Community College of Vermont. Hartness houses most of the combined collection of more than 57,000 books, 9,000 reels of microfilm, 300 periodical subscriptions, and thousands of audiocassettes and videocassettes. A Web page (http://www.vtc.vsc.edu/library) gives access to library catalogs and databases. Facilities housed in the major academic buildings include four computer-aided drafting and design labs (one 13-station, one 19-station, and two 21-station); four 21-station general academic computing labs; an eight-station electrical/electronics lab; recently renovated mechanical labs that include computer-numerically-controlled equipment and computer-aided manufacturing software; state-of-the-art veterinary technology facilities, including a twelve-station lab area, a radiography suite and darkroom, and a surgery suite; a biotechnology lab with instrumentation typical of the most modern research labs; a nursing lab with a dedicated computer room and nursing station; two civil engineering labs; architectural drafting studios; a campuswide microcomputer network with Internet access; four instrumented electronics labs; and a fully equipped automotive technology center with the latest in computerized diagnostics.

Agriculture students gain practical experience at the College's dairy facility, where a main free-stall barn houses a milking herd of 80 registered Holsteins. Students have the opportunity to participate in all aspects of the farm's management. Veterinary technology students work with several species of domestic animals in the livestock facility on the farm. The Judd Support Center houses most of the College's academic support services. Students visit Judd to sign up for tutoring, meet with counselors to discuss personal or academic issues, or visit the career/transfer center to update their resumes and explore career options and internship opportunities. Disabilities Services, where students with a disability can find out about classroom accommodations or assistive technology, is also located in Judd. In Conant Hall are the Learning Center, which offers drop-in and scheduled tutoring, supplemental instruction, study groups, and review sessions; and the General Education Department's Writing and Communication Center, which provides help with reading, writing, oral presentations, study skills, and assistive-technology training.

Costs

Tuition for 2003–04 is $6684 per year for Vermont residents and $12,716 for out-of-state students. The yearly room rate is $3518, and the meal plan was $2496 per year. Other required annual fees total $160. An additional $826 health insurance fee is required of students not covered by another medical plan. Many of VTC's programs are available at reduced tuition to New England students through the New England Regional Student Program, sponsored by the New England Board of Higher Education.

Financial Aid

About 80 percent of Vermont Tech students receive financial aid from federal, state, and campus-based sources. There are a growing number of institutional scholarships available, including the VTC Scholars Program as well as work-study opportunities. Prospective students seeking aid must file the Free Application for Federal Student Aid (FAFSA). Some state agencies may require additional information. Students are urged to apply for financial aid by the March 1 priority deadline so awards can be announced by May. However, applications are reviewed on a rolling basis after March 1 until available funds are exhausted. The Vermont Tech Web site provides more financial aid information.

Faculty

The College's excellence in instruction is a direct result of the quality of the faculty at VTC. The 65 full-time faculty members bring to the College a special blend of industrial experience and teaching expertise. Almost all have advanced degrees. Students are assured individual attention as a result of the 12:1 student-faculty ratio.

Student Government

The Associated Students of Vermont Technical College (ASVTC) is composed of elected student officers and volunteers representing residence halls and commuting students. ASVTC acts as liaison between the students and administration, advances students' interests, and promotes social activities.

Admission Requirements

Each applicant receives individual consideration for admission based on receipt and review of the official secondary school transcript, letters of recommendation, proof of high school graduation or a high school equivalency diploma, and SAT I scores. A personal interview is required only in the veterinary technology program, although an interview and campus visit are strongly recommended for all applicants. Because of the technical nature of the curriculum, applicants should have a strong math and science aptitude.

Application and Information

Vermont Technical College follows a rolling admission policy, but timely application is recommended. Applicants are notified of their status within two weeks of receipt of their completed application and supporting documents. For more information on Vermont Technical College, students should contact:

Director of Admissions
Vermont Technical College
Randolph Center, Vermont 05061
Telephone: 802-728-1000
800-442-VTC-1 (admissions; toll-free)
E-mail: admissions@vtc.edu
World Wide Web: http://www.vtc.edu

The high-tech campus of Vermont Technical College is situated in a scenic New England village in the heart of Vermont.

VILLA JULIE COLLEGE

STEVENSON, MARYLAND

The College

Villa Julie College is a private institution dedicated to educating its 2,500 students in a personal atmosphere using state-of-the-art technology while being mindful of the significance of a strong liberal arts education. Individual attention by faculty members, extensive career preparation gained through real-world training, and an ideal location just north of Baltimore, Maryland, make the College truly unique. At Villa Julie, professors are more than just instructors; they are friends who promote intellectual growth and curiosity. By bringing years of professional experience into the classroom, the faculty members truly enhance the quality of learning. With a student-faculty ratio of 12:1, it is easy to understand why students often site the congenial rapport with faculty members as one of the College's strong points.

Villa Julie College has developed a unique adjunct to its liberal arts, technology, and science programs, an approach known as Career Architecture. The process begins in freshman year with each student developing a vision of personal success. Students define what they value and determine where they are going and how they will get there. In essence, they develop an individual career strategic plan. There is support campuswide from the Career Services (Career HQ) team and faculty and staff members who collaborate and care about each student's growth and accomplishments.

Some of the elements of the Career Architecture experience are individual sessions/individual opportunities; group presentations, activities, and seminars; self-paced learning in the Career HQ resource area; learning through Cooperative Education—paid career positions; and through the College's Web-based comprehensive information center, 24 hours a day, 365 days a year.

A general freshman seminar includes an introduction to Career Architecture and Values Exploration. In 2002, Villa Julie science majors started on a comprehensive program to investigate career options in the evolving area of science. Students identify their interests, skills, and abilities; define their personal and professional values; and use in the Predictive Index as a professional career tool. Furthermore, they develop a personal portfolio and learn how they make decisions and solve problems—important elements of choosing a values-based career. Thanks to a grant from the Verizon Foundation, the science majors also participate in a Science Portfolio and Research Showcase, a Science Symposium with visiting professionals from diverse fields of science, and participate in Career Exploration Science tours to a variety of science-focused employers. Those majoring in other career areas are also involved in portfolio development and career exploration, including a planned nonprofit and government exploration fair. There are building steps for the Career Architecture process throughout the freshman to senior years.

Underscoring the College's theme, "Imagine your future. Design your career," the concept of Career Architecture starts with the process of students' understanding of themselves while the Imagine theme then encourages the students to think about their future in the world of jobs and work. Ultimately, Career Architecture is the process that helps students get to their carefully thought out career path and allows them to realize how values play into their long-term career choices and satisfaction.

Villa Julie's students are afforded the opportunity to reside in a college-supervised off-campus apartment complex 4½ miles from the main campus. This refreshing alternative to the traditionally crowded college-dormitory lifestyle places 4 students together in a spacious, fully furnished apartment. A free shuttle is provided to transport students between the apartments and the college campus. The cocurricular education gained by Villa Julie students through involvement in more than forty clubs and organizations, multiple honor societies, intramural sports, and NCAA Division III athletics is often as fulfilling as their classroom experiences. A few of the College's more popular organizations include the Student Government Association, the Drama Society, the Environmental Club, the Wilderness Leadership Society, the Community Service Corps, and *The Villager*, the campus newspaper. The Villa Julie Mustangs compete at the NCAA Division III level. The following sports are offered: men's and women's basketball, cross-country, golf, lacrosse, soccer, tennis, and track and field; men's baseball and club volleyball; and women's field hockey, softball, and volleyball. Cheerleading, dance, and intramural sports are also available.

Villa Julie College's Master of Science degrees in advanced information technologies, business and technology management, and e-commerce provide students with the technical knowledge required to help organizations achieve a competitive advantage in an increasingly global, technology-driven, and information-rich marketplace. The degree programs accomplish this by providing students not only with the knowledge about a wide variety of technologies and their architectures, but also with an understanding of how technologies can be integrated. Unlike other programs that focus on learning one or more specific technologies, these programs address the most important business issue—the integration of the full range of information technologies within an organization from both the strategic and operational perspective.

Location

Villa Julie's 60-acre wooded campus lies in one of Baltimore's upscale neighborhoods, Greenspring Valley. While being surrounded by horse farms and estate homes, the College is just 12 miles from downtown Baltimore. This location offers the student body the advantages of a quiet and peaceful learning atmosphere with the immediate availability of urban life. A variety of museums, theaters, historical sites of interest, and professional, semiprofessional, and intercollegiate sporting events are offered in the metropolitan area. A number of neighboring colleges and universities help round out the students' social opportunities.

Majors and Degrees

Villa Julie College awards master's, bachelor's, and associate degrees. The following undergraduate areas of study are offered: accounting, applied mathematics, art, biology, biotechnology, business administration, business communication, business information systems, chemistry, computer information systems, early childhood education, early childhood leadership, economics, elementary education, English language and literature, family studies, film, financial management, general studies, graphic design, history, human resources, information systems, interdisciplinary studies, international business, liberal arts and technology, marketing, medical laboratory technology, microbiology, military science (Army ROTC), nurse paralegal studies, nursing, paralegal studies, predentistry, prelaw, premedicine, prepharmacy, pre–physical therapy, preveterinary science, psychology, RN to B.S., science, theater, video, visual communication design, and writing.

Academic Program

The College is committed to providing a solid basis in the liberal arts within every curriculum. Therefore, all students are required to complete courses that help them develop an understanding of their cultural heritage, an appreciation of the arts and the humanities, the ability to easily and effectively communicate orally and in writing, an understanding of society and how it functions, a knowledge of scientific methods and an interpretation of the natural world, and the ability to reflect, to reason, and to handle quantitative knowledge.

Through courses in the major fields, students gain knowledge and a greater understanding of the subject area while gaining competency in applying the content and methods of inquiry to daily life. Students in all academic disciplines are also required to study subjects that enhance the knowledge acquired in their major and that relate technology to their field. The College's goal is to offer a synthesis of the liberal arts, current technology, and a major field that provides an education that prepares the student for gainful employment, successful graduate study, and productive involvement in today's world.

Academic Facilities

A recent expansion allows the College to utilize more than 100,000 square feet of new facilities, which include a 400-seat theater, multiple state-of-the-art computer labs and classrooms, video and graphic studios and suites, a student union, and an athletic complex. In addition, Knott Hall, one of the College's primary academic facilities, houses a number of multidimensional classrooms, computer labs, science labs, a lecture auditorium, faculty offices, and small study areas. Renovations include a new science wing that houses classrooms, laboratories, cold-storage facilities, a greenhouse, and independent research sites. Each classroom and laboratory throughout the campus is capable of state-of-the-art multimedia projection and computer-assisted learning. In the College's learning center, the Academic Link, students of all academic capabilities can gain educational assistance and advice from faculty members.

The College's library boasts an extensive collection of more than 100,000 printed volumes, periodicals, video and audio tapes, CD's, microfilm and microfiche selections, and an interlibrary loan consortium. Complementing this collection is a highly automated system, which provides the library's catalog and the full-text editions of a number of periodicals and newspapers on CD-ROM. In addition to the electronic databases it owns, the library has access to thousands of outside databases such as LexisNexis Academic Universe, WESTLAW, Dialog, Dow Jones News Retrieval, and the Internet. Through these databases, individuals can access information immediately from anywhere in the world. The theater is home to the College's drama and video departments.

Costs

Villa Julie's cost is very reasonable. For the 2003–04 academic year, tuition and fees for full-time students were $13,693. Part-time tuition and fees were $365 per credit hour, plus a $70 registration and technology fee per semester. The expense for off-campus housing was $4700 per year; shuttle service included.

Financial Aid

Villa Julie College offers financial assistance to qualified students in the form of scholarships, grants, loans, student employment, and a special payment plan. Villa Julie prides itself on the variety of scholarships it offers to incoming freshmen. In fall 2003, approximately 80 percent of the College's students received some financial assistance, and 45 percent of the freshmen entering the College received a Villa Julie Scholarship. Villa Julie College participates in all major federal aid programs as well as all Maryland state programs. Student applicants are required to file the Free Application for Federal Student Aid (FAFSA). The priority deadline for filing is March 1.

Faculty

The faculty at Villa Julie College, which numbers more than 280, is first and foremost a teaching faculty. The College's 12:1 student-teacher ratio demonstrates the institutional emphasis on a personalized education. A majority of the faculty members have the doctoral or terminal degree offered in their field and a significant number are widely published. In addition, the majority are concurrently employed as professional specialists in their fields.

Student Government

The Student Government Association (SGA) facilitates an environment that encourages students to express their thoughts and opinions concerning Villa Julie College, its policies, and sponsored activities. The SGA serves as the principal governing body of all campus clubs and activities. Through SGA events, students develop and learn the importance of time management skills and interpersonal relations. In conjunction with the Office of Campus Life, the SGA organizes an array of campuswide events that promote the social aspects of college life such as cookouts, bonfires, flag and powderpuff football games, movie nights, and formal dances. Each student at Villa Julie is welcome and encouraged to participate in all SGA functions.

Admission Requirements

Applications for admission to Villa Julie College are reviewed on a rolling basis. Candidates are evaluated according to their academic qualifications and personal character. The successful completion of a four-year college-preparatory program is the basis for success at Villa Julie. Therefore, a candidate's high school record receives the greatest weight in the Admissions Committee's decision. Other important factors include performance on standardized tests (SAT I or ACT), feedback provided on the Secondary School Report and Recommendation Form, student-produced writing samples, and the optional admissions interview. Admission to the College is determined without regard for race, color, sex, religion, national or ethnic origin, or handicap. The College complies with all applicable laws and federal regulations regarding discrimination and accessibility on the condition of handicap, age, veteran status, or otherwise.

Application and Information

Applications for admission should be received by March 1 for fall semester entry and December 1 for spring semester entry. Scholarship consideration adheres to earlier deadlines. Applications received after these dates are reviewed on a space-available basis. Students applying to the College as freshmen must submit official high school transcripts, standardized test scores, the Secondary School Report and Recommendation Form, a writing sample, and a $25 nonrefundable application fee. In addition, each applicant is encouraged to complete an admissions interview. Transfer students must submit official transcripts from all colleges or universities they have attended and should contact the Transfer Coordinator to discuss additional credential requirements.

For further information, scholarship deadlines, and application forms, students should contact:

Office of Admissions
Villa Julie College
1525 Greenspring Valley Road
Stevenson, Maryland 21153-0641
Telephone: 410-486-7001
877-GO-TO-VJC (877-468-6852) (toll-free)
Fax: 410-602-6600
E-mail: admissions@mail.vjc.edu
World Wide Web: http://www.vjc.edu

VILLANOVA UNIVERSITY

VILLANOVA, PENNSYLVANIA

The University

Since 1842, Villanova University has been under the direction of the Order of St. Augustine, better known as the "Augustinians," one of the oldest religious teaching orders of the Roman Catholic Church. The University's 254-acre campus is located 12 miles west of downtown Philadelphia in an attractive residential area. There are approximately 10,000 men and women currently enrolled; 6,300 are undergraduates.

Campus life encompasses a wide range of activities and groups. The Campus Activities Team provides a full schedule of films, concerts, and social events throughout the year. Special interest organizations are available in many areas; these include publications, music, theater, professional societies, fraternities and sororities, cultural and political groups, and volunteer organizations.

Location

Philadelphia, America's fifth-largest city, offers unparalleled opportunities to supplement campus life with cultural, recreational, and social service activities. The city offers professional sports in the form of basketball's 76ers, football's Eagles, hockey's Flyers, and baseball's Phillies. Philadelphia is the home of the world-renowned Philadelphia Orchestra and also the location of a wealth of museums, theaters, galleries, and historic attractions.

Majors and Degrees

Villanova University grants the Bachelor of Arts degree in the following majors: art history, classical studies, communication, economics, English, French, general arts (concentrations in Africana studies, Arab and Islamic studies, cognitive science, criminal justice, elementary education in cooperation with Rosemont College, ethics, Honors Program Sequence, Irish studies, Latin American studies, peace and justice, Russian area studies, and women's studies), geography, German, history, honors, human services, philosophy, political science, psychology, sociology, Spanish, and theology and religious studies. Instruction in Arabic, Chinese, Italian, Japanese, and Russian is also available. The Bachelor of Science is awarded in the following majors: astronomy and astrophysics, biology, chemistry (concentration in biochemistry), comprehensive science (concentrations in biological chemistry and geography), computer science, honors, information science, mathematics, physics, and secondary education. Also offered are the following professional degrees: D.M.D. (seven-year Doctor of Medical Dentistry program in conjunction with Drexel University School of Medicine), M.D. (seven-year Doctor of Medicine program in conjunction with MCP Hahnemann University), optometry (seven-year Doctor of Optometry program in conjunction with the Philadelphia College of Optometry), and allied health (six-year Master of Science program in conjunction with Thomas Jefferson University College of Health Professions). The College of Commerce and Finance grants the Bachelor of Science degree in accountancy, business administration, and economics. The degree program in business administration has majors in finance, information systems, management, and marketing. The College of Engineering offers degrees in chemical, civil, computer, electrical, and mechanical engineering. The College of Engineering offers a concentration in business and a dual degree with liberal arts. The College of Nursing grants a Bachelor of Science in Nursing degree. The Honors Program Sequence in Liberal Studies is available to students in all four colleges.

Academic Program

The principal aim of the College of Liberal Arts and Sciences is to assist persons in educating themselves. To achieve this, the College offers a traditional liberal arts and sciences curriculum with a great deal of flexibility built into it, including a Humanities Core Seminar Program with class sizes of 10 to 15 students. Both general and specialized courses are provided. Stress is laid on critical thinking and effective communication. Accordingly, hundreds of theoretical and practical courses are offered in the arts, the humanities, and the physical and social sciences. Required components of the curriculum include ethics, fine arts, and courses designed to develop students' writing abilities.

Emphasizing the analytical approach to business, the curriculum in the College of Commerce and Finance combines broad educational foundation courses with in-depth study of major functional fields of business and business processes, such as accounting information systems, financial flows and markets, management, and the impact of economic variables upon business and social issues. Foundation courses aim at developing proficiency in oral and written communications, the ability to apply the tools of quantitative analysis to the solution of business problems, and awareness of and sensitivity to moral values and law, the need for social responsibility, and the exercise of conscience.

In the first two years of the College of Engineering curriculum, work concentrates on such basic areas as chemistry, engineering science, mathematics, and physics, while in the last two years engineering analysis and design are stressed. Courses in the humanities are included in each engineering curriculum to make the young engineer more fully aware of social responsibilities and better able to consider nontechnical factors in the engineering decision-making process. Students learn the theoretical foundations of the engineering field through lectures and discussions, which are integrated with extensive hands-on laboratory and computer experience. Individual and group design projects utilize state-of-the-art equipment and instrumentation.

The College of Nursing curriculum consists of academic and professional study, including laboratory and health-agency experience under the guidance of qualified faculty members. Clinical facilities are selected on the basis of the educational objectives of the curriculum. The program provides clinical experiences beginning in the sophomore year in a variety of settings, including medical centers, community hospitals, and community health agencies. The curriculum builds upon a strong foundation of liberal arts and physical and behavioral sciences.

Naval and Marine ROTC programs are available for men and women on campus, Air Force ROTC through St. Joseph's University, and Army ROTC through Widener University on campus.

Off-Campus Programs

The Office of International Studies assists undergraduates in studying overseas in Africa, Asia, Europe, Latin America, and the Middle East for a summer, semester, or full academic year. All overseas programs must be affiliated with an overseas four-year college or university, have overseas faculty members, and provide bicultural experiences such as homestays. Students usually study overseas in their sophomore or junior year. Villanova's summer programs support language studies and area studies at such sites as Athens-Corinth (Greece), Bethlehem (Palestine), Cádiz (Spain), Dijon (France), Edinburgh (U.K.), Galway (Ireland), Megiddo (Israel), London (U.K.), Mafraq (Jordan), Nizhni Novgorod (Russia), Rome (Italy), Shanghai (China), Tübingen (Germany), Siena (Italy), Urbino (Italy), and Valparaíso (Chile). Villanova also has special relations with Bethlehem University and Birzeit University (Palestine), University of Cádiz (Spain), University College of Galway (Ireland), University of Glasgow (Scotland), University of Urbino (Italy), and Victoria University of Manchester (England). Nursing majors may complete a year at King's College, London. College of Commerce and Finance students can spend a year at European School of Business (Germany), University of Lille-Nice ESPEME (France), or University of Maastricht (Netherlands). College of Liberal Arts and Sciences students may spend a year studying at National University of Ireland-Galway (Ireland); Queens University, Belfast (U.K.); Sophia University (Japan); Universidad Popular Autonóma del Estado de Puebla (Mexico); Universita degli Studi Urbino (Italy); University Colleges Cork and Dublin (Ireland); Trinity College, Dublin (Ireland); and Westfield College, London (U.K.).

The College of Liberal Arts and Sciences offers an Internship Program in which students work during the summer, fall, or spring terms of the junior or senior year. The internships are departmentally related, and students obtain from 3 to 15 credits for the experience. Part-time and full-time work experience is available in the Delaware Valley as well as New York City and Washington, D.C., which offers access to business, political, professional, and media leaders. The Colleges of Engineering and of Commerce and Finance also offer internship programs.

Academic Facilities

The Falvey Memorial Library provides resources and facilities for study and research by undergraduate students, graduate students, faculty members, and visiting scholars. The library's total seating capacity is 1,200. Its holdings include more than 800,000 volumes, 5,400 serial subscriptions, and more than a million microform items.

Costs

Tuition costs, including fees, averaged $26,890 for the 2003–04 academic year. Room and board costs for the full academic year averaged $8775. Expenses for books, travel, and personal supplies are estimated at $1000 for the year.

Financial Aid

Financial assistance is granted on the basis of need. The aid applicant must file the Free Application for Federal Student Aid (FAFSA) no later than February 15, with the request that the results be sent to the Villanova University Office of Financial Assistance. The family's income tax return for the previous year and Villanova's institutional financial aid application should be sent to Villanova's Office of Financial Assistance by March 15. Academic and athletic merit scholarships are also available.

Faculty

Villanova has 499 full-time and 309 part-time faculty members. The undergraduate and graduate faculty are the same. Of the faculty members, 90 percent hold doctorates or the equivalent. The student-faculty ratio is 12:1.

Student Government

The Student Government of Villanova is a representative body of all students. Its purpose is to provide a channel of communication between students and the University, to promote student legislation, and to assist in concerns involving students and the Villanova community. The Student Government performs the double role of providing student representation in the formulation of University policies and of expanding student services. Student senators provide input on matters of policy as voting members of the University Senate and its committees.

Admission Requirements

The basic criteria for admission are the applicant's high school record and class standing, scores on the SAT I or ACT, an essay, guidance counselor recommendation, and extracurricular activities. Applicants must be graduates of approved secondary schools and must present units of study as prescribed for the various curricula of the University.

Application and Information

The deadline for receipt of the application by the Office of University Admission is January 7. The deadline for Early Action, Presidential Scholarship consideration, and Health Affiliation programs is November 1. Applications should be sent to:

Office of University Admission
Villanova University
800 Lancaster Avenue
Villanova, Pennsylvania 19085-1672
Telephone: 610-519-4000
Fax: 610-519-6450
E-mail: gotovu@villanova.edu
World Wide Web: http://www.admission.villanova.edu

St. Thomas of Villanova Church

VIRGINIA COMMONWEALTH UNIVERSITY

RICHMOND, VIRGINIA

The University

Virginia Commonwealth University (VCU) was created in 1968 by an act of the General Assembly that combined the Richmond Professional Institute and the Medical College of Virginia (MCV). However, VCU uses the founding date of 1838, the year in which the Medical College of Virginia was created. VCU is one of three comprehensive universities in Virginia. On the graduate level, the University offers the M.A., M.Acc., M.B.A., M.F.A., M.A.E., M.Ed., M.H.A., M.M., M.M.Ed., M.P.A., M.P.H., M.S., M.S.N.A., M.S.O.T., M.S.W., M.T., M.Tax., M.I.S., M.U.R.P., D.D.S., M.D., Pharm.D., D.M.D., D.H.A., D.B.A., D.P.T., and Ph.D. degrees. Undergraduate and graduate programs are offered in more than 175 fields.

VCU is a diverse metropolitan university that has a major educational, cultural, and economic impact on the Richmond community. VCU is administratively and structurally composed of two campuses, the Academic Campus (west) and the VCU Medical Center (east), operating as one institution. The two campuses provide distinct locations for learning. The Academic Campus, located in the historic Fan District, combines hand-paved streets and Victorian town houses with spacious, contemporary classroom facilities. It houses the following colleges and schools: Arts, Business, Education, Engineering, Government and Public Affairs, Humanities and Sciences, Mass Communications, Social Work, World Studies, the School of Graduate Studies, and the Division of External Relations. The VCU Medical Center is located in the business section of Richmond, 1½ miles east of the Academic Campus. At this campus are the Schools of Allied Health Professions, Dentistry, Medicine, Nursing, and Pharmacy. Each campus has several buildings listed on either the Virginia or National Historic Landmarks registers. Free shuttle service between the campuses is provided by the University.

Of the 26,770 men and women at VCU, 16,504 are undergraduates. Sixty-eight percent of the 3,326 freshmen reside in University residence facilities, which include modern high-rise buildings and stylish town houses. Approximately 150 student organizations exist on campus, reflecting the diverse social, political, religious, and academic interests of the student body. Campus life is active, and there are numerous social and athletic events scheduled through these groups. VCU also has one of the largest evening schools in the nation.

VCU offers postbaccalaureate certificate programs in accounting, aging studies, applied social research, computer science, criminal justice, environmental studies, human resource management, information systems, international management studies, marketing, mathematical sciences, patient counseling, planning information systems, premedical basic health sciences (anatomy, biochemistry and molecular biophysics, human genetics, microbiology and immunology, pharmacology and toxicology, and physiology), public management, real estate and urban land development, statistics, teaching, and urban revitalization.

Location

VCU is located in the city of Richmond, the state capital and focal point for Virginia's political, cultural, and social events. It is within a 1-hour drive of Williamsburg and within a 2-hour drive of the Blue Ridge Mountains, Virginia Beach, and Washington, D.C. Founded in 1607, Richmond is home to many historic sites. It also offers theater, concerts, symphony performances, ballet, art museums, shopping, athletics, and recreational opportunities. The University extends into the life of the city, and students participate in many activities in the University and Richmond communities.

Majors and Degrees

Virginia Commonwealth University awards B.A., B.F.A., B.I.S., B.M., B.M.Ed., B.S., and B.S.W. degrees. The undergraduate majors are accounting; advertising (business and creative); African-American studies; art; art education; art history; athletic training; biology; broadcast journalism; business administration and management; business law and marketing; chemistry; clinical laboratory sciences; clinical radiation sciences; communication arts and design; computer science; crafts (ceramics, fabric design, fiberwork, furniture design, glassworking, jewelry, metalsmithing, and woodworking); criminal justice (corrections, juvenile justice, law enforcement, and legal studies); dance and choreography; dental hygiene; economics; education (art, early childhood, elementary, health and physical, middle school, music, secondary, special, and theater); engineering (biomedical, chemical, computer, electrical, and mechanical); English; exercise science (applied health science, athletic training, clinical exercise science, and community health education); fashion design; fashion merchandising; finance; finance/insurance and risk management; financial technology; forensic science; French; German; history; home fashions merchandising; human resource management/industrial relations; information systems; interior design; interdisciplinary studies; international studies; journalism (broadcast and print); management; marketing; mass communications (advertising, journalism, and public relations); mathematical sciences (applied mathematics, computing science, mathematics, operations research, and statistics); music (performance/jazz studies and composition); nontraditional studies; nursing; occupational therapy; painting and printmaking; pharmacy; philosophy; photography and film; physical education; physical therapy; physics; political science; predentistry studies; prelaw studies; premedicine studies; preoptometry studies; preveterinary studies; print journalism; psychology; public relations; radiological sciences (nuclear medicine, radiation therapy, and radiological technology); real estate and urban land development; recreation, parks, and sport management (recreation and park management, sport management, and therapeutic recreation); religious studies; science; sculpture; social work; sociology and anthropology; Spanish; theater (performance and design/technical); urban and regional planning; urban studies and geography; and women's studies. Selected study plans resulting in double majors and/or minors are available to students who wish to intensify their academic backgrounds in more than one area of study. A number of major programs offers students an opportunity to specialize within their major. Extensive pre–health sciences programs are also offered.

Several undergraduate programs serve as preparatory programs for graduate and professional programs. Undergraduate studies in early childhood/elementary, middle, secondary, and special education are part of a five-year program culminating in a B.A. or B.S. and a Master of Teaching. Students must apply to the upper-division graduate program once they have junior status. Undergraduate study in the pre–health sciences prepares students to apply for the professional or graduate portion of the program. Acceptance to a preparatory program does not guarantee admission to the professional or graduate program.

Academic Programs

The numerous schools that exist within the University allow students to take courses in many different disciplines. The requirements for a bachelor's degree vary from 120 to 135 semester hours, according to the major program. Advanced placement, early admission, early decision, honors programs, and credit by examination are available. An eight-year medical program, an eight-year dental program, and guaranteed admission to graduate and professional programs in basic health sciences and programs in business (four-year programs leading to the master's degree) are available to superior freshmen. VCU operates on a traditional semester calendar with a winter intersession and numerous summer sessions. Cooperative education and internships are available in most majors.

Off-Campus Programs

VCU sponsors various travel/study-abroad programs for students interested in gaining exposure to other cultures and languages.

Academic Facilities

A large number of support facilities and programs supplements the various academic offerings at VCU. These include animal laboratories and a workshop, a greenhouse and aquatics laboratory, math tutorial labs, well-equipped labs for the sciences, language labs, the Foreign Language Bank for those needing translating services, the Psychological Services Center, the Management Center, the Computer Center, the Center for Public Affairs, the Correctional Training and Evaluation Center, the Reading Center, the Teachers' Media Workshop, the University Child Study Center, the Cancer Center, the Poison Control Center, four teaching hospitals, two theaters, a music center, a ceramics and sculpture workshop, art studios, a graphics lab, an audiovisual lab, and a photography studio with complete darkroom facilities. The Anderson Gallery, a University-owned art museum, is located on the Academic Campus. The University is also the location of Virginia's Highway Safety Training Center and a Biotechnology Research Park.

Costs

Academic-year expenses for undergraduate students in 2003–04 were $4869 for in-state tuition and fees and $17,213 for nonresident tuition and fees. Room and board were estimated at $6591.

Financial Aid

University financial aid programs serve approximately 64 percent of the student body. The University participates in all federal and state grant, loan, and work-study programs. The University also sponsors a major academic scholarship program whose awards are based upon academic merit rather than need. Normally, students encounter few problems finding part-time employment on campus or in the community. To apply for assistance, students are required to complete the Free Application for Federal Student Aid (FAFSA). The FAFSA must be mailed before March 15 to meet the University deadline. Further information may be obtained by contacting the Financial Aid Department at 901 West Franklin Street, P.O. Box 843537, Richmond, Virginia 23284-2527.

Faculty

Eighty-nine percent of VCU faculty members hold the highest degree in their professional field. Faculty members work with students in developing academic programs, supervise independent study programs, and assist with academic advising.

Student Government

The student government at Virginia Commonwealth University consists of a body of 33 senators representing both schools. Each of the senators serves on at least one of seven subcommittees. Elections are held during spring preregistration. The student government provides programs and services to the University community and gives students the opportunity to get involved with the governance of the institution.

Admission Requirements

Admission to programs on the Academic Campus requires graduation from an accredited secondary school (or a high school equivalency diploma) with a minimum of 20 units, which must include 4 units in English; 3 units in history, social sciences, or government; 3 units in mathematics (including at least 2 units in algebra I, geometry, and algebra II); and 2 units in science (including 1 unit in a laboratory science). Two units of foreign language are strongly recommended. Additional units in mathematics and other academically challenging areas of study are also recommended. The Advanced Studies diploma is preferred. Applicants are evaluated on the basis of their academic record in high school, class standing, SAT I or ACT scores, extracurricular activities, and suitability of preparation for the intended major. Transfer students with at least 30 semester hours or 45 quarter hours of undergraduate credit are admitted on the basis of their accumulated college credits.

Admission to programs at the VCU Medical Center requires from two to four years of undergraduate study. Each school and program has specified academic requirements.

VCU is an Equal Opportunity/Affirmative Action institution providing access to education and employment without regard to age, race, color, national origin, gender, religion, sexual orientation, veteran's status, political affiliation, or disability.

Application and Information

The processing of applications for the spring and fall semesters begins in October. Applicants are considered when all necessary documents have been received, and applicants are notified by April 1 if the application file is complete by February 1. Applicants interested in being considered under the early decision plan must apply before November 1 and are notified by December 1. Applicants interested in the School of Medicine's Guaranteed Admission Program must apply by December 15. The necessary materials include the official application form; a $30 nonrefundable application fee; official high school transcripts, indicating class rank and grade point average; and scores on the SAT I (the VCU code number is 475570) or ACT (the VCU code number is 474379). Those applying to visual arts programs in the School of the Arts must submit a portfolio, and those intending to major in theater, dance, or music must audition or interview. Transfer applicants who have earned fewer than 30 semester hours or 45 quarter hours of credit must also meet freshman guidelines and submit those documents required of freshmen (including SAT I or ACT scores if the candidates are under 22 years of age) in addition to official transcripts from all institutions attended. The transfer application deadline is June 1 but may vary for health science programs.

Applications and additional information may be obtained by contacting:

Office of Undergraduate Admissions
Virginia Commonwealth University
821 West Franklin Street
P.O. Box 842526
Richmond, Virginia 23284-2526
Telephone: 804-828-1222
800-841-3638 (toll-free)
E-mail: ugrad@vcu.edu
World Wide Web: http://www.vcu.edu

VCU offers many excellent academic programs and a diverse faculty and student body.

VIRGINIA INTERMONT COLLEGE

BRISTOL, VIRGINIA

The College

Virginia Intermont College (VIC) was founded in 1884 and is a four-year, liberal arts–based, private institution for men and women. There are 1,147 students currently enrolled. Virginia Intermont is affiliated with the Baptist General Association of Virginia, but it is open to any qualified applicant regardless of sex, creed, race, handicap, or national origin. Students represent more than thirty-eight states, more than thirty countries, and some twenty-three religious faiths.

The Fine Arts and Humanities programs at the College offer opportunities to see and hear renowned lecturers, poets, musicians, writers, artists, and performing groups. These cultural activities are offered for inspiration, education, and entertainment.

The student activities program provides a wide variety of activities that includes dances, intramurals, theme weeks, ski trips, concerts, and modern and classic films. There are five colleges within a 25-mile radius, and students from area colleges participate in many of these events.

The nationally recognized equestrian program leads a quality list of successful athletic offerings at VIC. As a member of the Appalachian Athletic Conference (AAC), which is affiliated with the National Association of Intercollegiate Athletics (NAIA), the athletic programs include men's and women's basketball, cross-country, soccer, tennis, and track; men's baseball and golf; and women's softball and volleyball. Student-athletes are seen on campus as an integral part of the community. VIC is extremely proud of its student–athlete's accomplishments in the classroom as well as in athletic competition.

Location

The name Intermont, meaning "between the mountains," is descriptive of the setting of the College. Virginia Intermont is located in Bristol, Virginia, one of the Tri-Cities, the other two of which are Johnson City and Kingsport, Tennessee. The campus is located on I-81 between Roanoke and Knoxville, only eight blocks from the heart of downtown Bristol.

Majors and Degrees

The Bachelor of Arts degree is offered in art, business (international business, management, and marketing), culinary arts (pastry arts and restaurant management), dance, English, equine studies, history, interdisciplinary studies, legal studies, liberal arts, management and leadership, performing arts (dance, music, and theater), photography and digital imaging, political science, religion, social work (B.S.W. degree), teacher education (art K–12, biology 6–12, business 6–12, English 6–12, history/political science 6–12, interdisciplinary K–6, and physical education K–12), and theater (B.F.A.).

The Bachelor of Science degree is offered in biology (environmental science, general biology, premedicine, and pre-veterinary medicine), business, computer information management, criminal justice, management and leadership, physical education, psychology, and sport management.

The Associate of Arts degree is offered in allied health, culinary arts, general studies, and graphic design.

Minors are offered in art, biology, business administration, chemistry, computer applications/technology, dance, English, environmental management, equine studies, equine-assisted growth and development, gerontology, history, mathematics, photography, political science, psychology, religion, sociology, sports medicine, and theater.

Academic Program

The academic year is divided into two semesters, running from late August through December and from January through May. There are a three-week May term and a six-week summer term available.

The core curriculum is made up of visual and performing arts, English, literature, math, biology or physical science, world civilization, computer fundamentals, economics or political science, psychology or sociology, philosophy or religion, physical education, and public speaking. All first-time freshmen are required to take core studies, a semester-long orientation course.

Many departments offer minicourses on weekends. These allow students the opportunity to learn new techniques in horsemanship, art, or photography as well as meet writers of national prominence.

Academic Facilities

Virginia Intermont's campus has a blend of modern and historic buildings. In addition to the traditional labs and classrooms there are ballet studios, the Trayer Theatre, the Fine Arts Gallery, art studios, and photography labs, all available for instruction and student use, as are the indoor swimming pool, the Smith-Canter Gymnasium, the Fitness Center, and the tennis courts. Equine courses are taught at the Riding Center, which is made up of two indoor rings, one outdoor ring, and stables for 80 horses, located 10 minutes from campus on 136 acres. A recent addition to the Virginia Intermont campus is the Virginia Hutton Blevins Art Complex, which houses sculpture, drawing, and painting studios; classrooms and offices; and gallery and storage space.

Harrison-Jones Memorial Hall contains a 1,000-person capacity auditorium and chapel, dressing rooms, and reception areas.

Costs

Tuition for the 2003–04 year was $13,900. For the residential student, room and board were $5470. There were technology and services fees of $500. Additional fees are charged for riding classes, ballet classes, science laboratories, and other special classes.

Financial Aid

Ninety percent of all students attending the College receive financial aid. Virginia Intermont makes aid available through the Federal Pell Grant, Federal Supplemental Educational Opportunity Grant, Federal Perkins Loan, and Federal Work-Study programs. All Virginia residents are eligible to receive a VTAG grant. Residents of Georgia, Rhode Island, Vermont, Pennsylvania, and Washington, D.C., should also apply for state-based aid. A number of scholarships are available for those who do not qualify for federal aid, such as honor scholarships, the Tri-Cities Scholarship, and the Whitehead Award. Loans at low interest rates are available from the Virginia Intermont College Loan Association, the Federal Stafford Student Loan Program, the Keesee Educational Loan

Fund, and the Pickett and Hatcher Loan Fund. Benefits are available for veterans and veterans' dependents.

An academic scholarship program has been implemented for students with grade point averages from 2.5 to 4.0. Scholarships range from $2500 to full tuition, based on the student's qualifications.

Faculty

The student-faculty ratio at Virginia Intermont is 12:1. There are 84 full-time and regular part-time faculty members, who play an active part in advising students regarding scheduling and campus activities. The close student-faculty relationship allowed by the small size of the campus fosters interaction between the two groups.

Student Government

The Student Government Association (SGA) is the organization chiefly responsible for formulating and enforcing the regulations governing student life. The SGA has as its stated purpose "to represent and to further the best interests of the student body, to secure cooperation between different organizations, and to promote responsibility, leadership, and community among the students."

Admission Requirements

Applicants must be graduates of an accredited high school, with at least a C average, who have taken a minimum of 15 units (4 units of English, 2 units of college-preparatory math, 2 units of social science, 1 unit of laboratory science, and 6 units of other electives). Students may also be admitted under the early admission plan after their junior year in high school. Applicants who have a GED diploma, those who have satisfactorily completed 24 semester hours of college work, or those seeking admission as special (non-degree-seeking) students are also considered.

Transfer students are welcome. Transfer credit is subject to approval by the academic dean before the student's acceptance by the College, and a cumulative grade average of C or better must be attained before admission to the upper division. Virginia Intermont requires that the final 30 semester hours toward degree requirements be earned at the College.

Application and Information

Applicants should submit an application, a high school transcript, SAT I or ACT scores, transcripts of previous college work (if applicable), and the nonrefundable $15 application fee.

For an application and financial aid information, students should contact:

Office of Admissions
Box D-460
Virginia Intermont College
1013 Moore Street
Bristol, Virginia 24201-4298
Telephone: 276-669-6101
800-451-1-VIC (toll-free)
World Wide Web: http://www.vic.edu

Virginia Intermont College's close-knit community is a great place to make friends.

VIRGINIA MILITARY INSTITUTE

LEXINGTON, VIRGINIA

The Institute

The Virginia Military Institute (VMI) is the nation's oldest state-supported military college, founded in 1839 in Lexington, Virginia and located at the southern end of the Shenandoah Valley. VMI offers qualified young men and women a demanding combination of academic study and rigorous military training that exists nowhere else, and grants B.A. and B.S. degrees in fourteen disciplines within the general fields of engineering, science, and liberal arts. The Institute's emphasis on qualities of honor, integrity, and responsibility contributes to its unique educational philosophy. Professional leadership training is provided to all cadets through the Reserve Officers' Training Corps (ROTC) programs, maintained at VMI by the Department of Defense. Cadets may pursue commissions in the U.S. Army, Air Force, Navy, or Marine Corps.

In every field of endeavor, whether it's leadership in business, industry, public service, education, the professions, or careers in the military, success comes early to a high number of VMI graduates. In an independent survey of college graduates seeking employment, armed forces commission, or admission to graduate or professional school following graduation, 95 percent of VMI graduates met their goal by the following October.

VMI's academic breadth is diverse, and curricula for the selected major begins the first year. About 30 percent of cadets major in civil, electrical, or mechanical engineering; more than 40 percent of VMI graduates major in liberal arts fields; and the two most popular majors are economics/business and history.

In the 2002 edition of *U.S. News & World Report,* "America's Best Colleges," VMI claims the number one spot as the nation's "top public liberal arts college," and its engineering program remains in the top one third of "best undergraduate" accredited programs at schools offering only bachelor's and master's degrees. In separate rankings for engineering "specialities," VMI's civil engineering program ranks sixth, and its mechanical engineering program, seventeenth.

VMI's alumni support is unparalleled in many ways, especially in their financial support. In a 1999 survey by the National Association of College and University Business Officers, VMI's $280-million endowment was the largest per student of any public institution. The VMI Foundation launched a five-year capital campaign for $175 million in 2000, and most of the goal was met by 2001, well ahead of schedule.

VMI alumni include Nobel Prize winner George C. Marshall; 9 Rhodes scholars, VMI's thirteenth Superintendent, Josiah Bunting III ('63), being one; and 39 college presidents. VMI alumni have distinguished themselves in every American conflict since the Mexican War, among them 7 Medal of Honor recipients and 265 general and flag officers. Some 500 alumni served in Gulf War operations Desert Storm and Desert Shield, and VMI graduates participated in special operations in Afghanistan in the aftermath of the September 11 terrorist attack. General John P. Jumper, Chief of Staff of the U.S. Air Force, and General Robert B. Flowers, Chief of Engineers for the U.S. Army, continue a long line of VMI graduates in the highest positions of military leadership.

After nearly 160 years of preparing young men for distinguished leadership roles, VMI made the transition to coeducation in 1997, successfully assimilating women into the Corps of Cadets. The Institute graduated its first women cadets in May 1999.

Today, 1,300 young men and women in the VMI Corps of Cadets represent forty-six states and twenty other countries. More than 100 cadets study abroad each year, one third compete in athletics, and all have significant leadership opportunities.

All cadets reside in "Barracks," at the centerpiece of the VMI "Post." The original structure was built in 1850 and is a National Historic Landmark. An additional wing was added in 1949. All cadet rooms are equipped for computer technology. Adjoining Barracks are offices and meeting areas for dozens of VMI clubs and organizations, the cadet visitors center and lounge, a snack bar, and a Barnes & Noble–operated bookstore.

VMI cadets uphold an honor system as old as the Institute. An oath of honor is taken by each cadet, "not to lie, cheat, or steal, nor tolerate those who do," and the oath is practiced in daily life. As it is basic to cadet life, it is ingrained, and builds strong character. Honor is at the cornerstone of every cadet's lifelong commitment to integrity, duty, self-discipline, and self-reliance.

One of the oldest VMI traditions is the orientation and instruction provided to new cadets by old cadets. Regardless of background or prior training, every cadet in his or her first year at VMI is a "Rat," and each is a "Brother Rat" to the other. They live under the "Rat System" until "Break Out" in late winter, and their bonds formed by this experience are lifelong.

VMI places great emphasis on physical fitness and training programs, whether cadets participate in athletics, ROTC training, or physical education programs. VMI offers seventeen intercollegiate athletics programs at the NCAA Division I level, and supports several club sports and intramural activities. The VMI "Keydet" Club is one of the oldest and most productive athletic foundations in the country, raising more than $1 million annually for athletic scholarships and grants-in-aid to 185 cadets in all sixteen sports. Athletic grounds and facilities are within easy access to the Post.

A member of the Southern Conference since 1924, VMI recently made the decision to move to the Big South conference.

Location

Lexington is in Rockbridge County, Virginia, an area rich in history and natural beauty. VMI adjoins the campus of Washington and Lee University, the nation's ninth-oldest institution of higher learning. Both colleges are within walking distance to historic downtown Lexington, a popular tourism destination. Interstate Highways 81 and 64 intersect only minutes from VMI, north of Lexington's downtown area. U.S. Highways 11 (north-south) and 60 (east-west), the area's crossroads for two centuries, intersect in downtown Lexington. Air service to VMI is available from Roanoke Regional Airport, less than an hour's drive from Lexington.

Majors and Degrees

VMI offers the baccalaureate degree in fourteen curricula. The B.S. is awarded in chemistry, civil engineering, computer science, electrical engineering, mechanical engineering, and physics. The B.A. is conferred in economics and business, English, history, international studies, modern languages, and psychology. A B.S. or B.A. can be earned in biology and mathematics. A course of study leading to a B.S. or B.A. is chosen upon entering VMI, but a transfer from one major field of study to another is permitted.

Academic Programs

VMI's demanding academic program reflects established needs and emerging trends of an ever-changing, global society. A newly funded undergraduate research initiative extends through summer, affording cadets and faculty members financial incentives and continuous support for a wide range of investigative projects. The Institute's international programs include faculty and student exchanges with more than a dozen international academies and universities, seven international internships, and numerous study-abroad programs each semester and during the summer.

VMI is accredited by the Southern Association of Colleges and Schools, is a member of American Council on Education, the Association of American Colleges, the College Entrance Examination Board, and the Association of Virginia Colleges. VMI's engineering programs are ABET accredited; the chemistry program is accredited by ACS.

Academic Facilities

The VMI Post covers 134 acres, of which 12 acres is designated a National Historic District. VMI's academic facilities, Superintendent's quarters, library, alumni hall, and other administrative buildings, along with Barracks, encircle a 12-acre parade ground used for marching drills, weekly parades, training exercises, and social gatherings. The physics department has X-ray and nuclear physics laboratories, and operates both an observatory and planetarium. The George C. Marshall Research Museum and the VMI Museum are located on Post.

Costs

Charges at VMI are based on a cadet's classification as a Virginia or out-of-state resident. Total charges cover most direct expenses, including tuition, room, board (twenty-one meals per week), fees, uniforms, laundry, routine medical care, and barber services. As an example, in 2001–02 total costs were $9968 for Virginia residents and $21,036 for non-Virginia residents. (Books and transportation are additional.) ROTC pay and allowances to qualified cadets total up to $10,000 over four years, and should be considered in "net costs" at VMI.

Financial Aid

Although aid is generally awarded on the basis of financial need, numerous scholarships are awarded for academic and athletic excellence and as room and board supplements to ROTC scholarship recipients. Persons interested in financial assistance should write to VMI's Director of Financial Aid.

Faculty

All VMI faculty members teach in the classroom, and 97 percent hold doctoral or terminal degrees. The cadet-faculty ratio is 12:1, permitting a close, "mentor" relationship between a cadet and instructor, and faculty research is conducted in partnership with cadets. ROTC instructors are experienced military officers and make an outstanding contribution to cadet leadership training.

Student Government

VMI has two systems of student government. The "regimental system" oversees cadet accountability for conduct, appearance, military training, and all ceremonial functions. The regiment of the Corps is divided into two battalions of four companies each, plus a band company.

Although Institute regulations govern the discipline of cadets, a large measure of supervision resides in each of the four closely knit classes within the Corps. The "class system" administers the Corps' standards and privileges accorded each class, and governs with the regimental system to oversee cadet appearance and conduct.

Representatives to the Honor Court are elected from the Corps, by the Corps, to enforce the rules of the honor system and prosecute Honor Court cases.

Admission Requirements

Applicants must be unmarried, 16 to 22 years of age (a one-year age waiver may be granted for an applicant who has served in active duty in the armed forces, or in certain other circumstances), physically fit for enrollment in ROTC, and graduated from an accredited secondary school with 16 or more academic units. Recommended course credits include 4 English, 3 social studies, 3 laboratory sciences, 3 foreign language, 3 mathematics (including 2 years of algebra and 1 of geometry), and 2 electives. The average GPA of incoming freshmen is approximately 3.1. Other qualifications include rank in the upper 50 percent of the senior class (significance of rank depends on class size and other factors), above-average scores on SAT I or ACT, and satisfactory character recommendations. Extracurricular activities are viewed as favorable indicators of leadership and character traits. Transfer students are accepted, but two years of residency at VMI are required. Admissions standards are applied without regard to gender, race, nationality, or religion, and all factors are weighed in the final determination of the applicant's qualifications.

Application and Information

An application may be submitted anytime between September 1 and February 15 of the senior year in high school and should be accompanied by a nonrefundable $35 application fee, a transcript of the school record for grade 9 through the last completed semester, and SAT I or ACT scores. Visits to the Institute are highly recommended. Open House visits are held throughout the academic year.

Interested students should contact:

Director of Admissions
Virginia Military Institute
Lexington, Virginia 24450
Telephone: 540-464-7211
800-767-4207 (toll-free)
Fax: 540-464-7746
E-mail: admissions@vmi.edu
World Wide Web: http://www.vmi.edu

VMI Barracks, a National Historic Landmark and home to the VMI Corps of Cadets.

VIRGINIA STATE UNIVERSITY

PETERSBURG, VIRGINIA

The University

Founded in 1882, Virginia State University (VSU) is the nation's first fully state-assisted four-year, historically black college or university. Located in historic Chesterfield County on a bluff overlooking the Appomattox River, VSU sits upon 236 acres of history and tradition. A comprehensive university encompassing both undergraduate and graduate divisions, VSU is one of two land-grant institutions in the commonwealth of Virginia. With a mission emphasizing the integration of academic instruction, research, and public service, Virginia State welcomes students of any race, religion, or ethnic heritage.

VSU offers forty-six programs leading to a bachelor's degree, a master's degree, or a doctoral degree. What sets this University apart from all others is its family structure, which is emphasized in its small class sizes that give individualized academic instruction.

Going to class, studying for exams, and writing papers are essential tasks for the student's academic success. However, they are still only a part of college life. Another substantial portion of the student's education consists of the formal and informal activities that are pursued beyond the classroom. A comprehensive cocurricular environment developed and maintained by the University's Student Activities Department offsets VSU's rigorous academic curriculum. Through its student union, educational, cultural, social, and recreational programs are developed and implemented to enrich student's academic experiences, individual social competencies, leadership skills, and group effectiveness.

VSU students take full advantage of the extracurricular activities offered throughout the school year. There are more than 125 student organizations and clubs, including nine Greek organizations. VSU also has the region's top NCAA Division II athletic program, in which teams compete in the Central Intercollegiate Athletic Association (CIAA). They offer fifteen athletic sports including men's baseball, basketball, cross-country, football, golf, indoor and outdoor track, and tennis and women's basketball, bowling, cross-country, golf, indoor and outdoor track, softball, tennis, and volleyball.

The University is a member institution of several consortia, including the National Student Exchange, a consortium of twenty-two state colleges and universities across the country.

Location

The University is situated in Chesterfield County at Ettrick on a bluff across the Appomattox River from the city of Petersburg. It is accessible via Interstate 95 and 85, which meet in Petersburg. The University is only 2½ hours away from Washington, D.C., to the north; the Raleigh-Durham-Chapel Hill area to the southwest; and Charlottesville to the northwest.

Majors and Degrees

VSU offers thirty-two programs leading to a bachelor's degree. Four schools make up the University's undergraduate division: the School of Agriculture; the School of Business; the School of Engineering, Science, and Technology; and the School of Liberal Arts and Education. The Bachelor of Arts degree is offered in criminal justice, English, fine art, history, mass communications, music education, music performing arts, philosophy, political science, and sociology. The Bachelor of Science degree is offered in the fields of accounting; biology; business administration; chemistry; computer science; drafting technology; economics and finance; elementary education; engineering (mechanical, electrical, computer, industrial, and manufacturing); family and consumer science; food and nutrition; health education; health, physical education, and recreation; hospitality management; information systems and decision science; management; marketing; mathematics; physics; premed biology; psychology; and social work.

Academic Programs

Students admitted to Virginia State to study for a Bachelor of Arts or Bachelor of Science degree are generally expected to adhere to the accepted standards of higher education. Honors programs, independent study, and cooperative education programs are available in most areas. For those students who require special placement and/or special assistance, support services and programs are provided.

To earn a bachelor's degree, students must generally complete a minimum of 120 semester hours, depending on the program of study. Engineering students should expect to earn 128 semester hours to qualify for the degree. Through the Continuing Education and Outreach Program, students can pursue an education outside traditional daytime classwork. Participants in the program include part-time students, as well as many full-time students who have been away from a formal educational experience for two or more years and want to pursue courses for personal fulfillment or career advancement. The Continuing Education Program includes summer school, weekend classes, intersession, and extension programs.

Academic Facilities

In the first academic year, 1883–84, the University had 126 students and 7 faculty members, one building, 33 acres, a 200-book library, and a $20,000 budget. By the centennial year of 1982, the University was fully integrated, with a student body of nearly 5,000; a full-time faculty of about 250 members; a library containing more than 200,000 books and 360,000 microform and nonprint items; a 236-acre campus and 416-acre farm with research and testing facilities; more than fifty buildings, including fifteen dormitories and sixteen classroom buildings; and a state-of-the-art corporate extension building. Virginia State's radio and television stations, WVST-91.3 FM and VSUN, are great resources for mass communication students.

Costs

In 2003–04, tuition and fees were $4350 for residents of Virginia and $11,260 for nonresidents. Room and board were $6008 for all students. Costs are subject to change without prior notice.

Financial Aid

VSU assists students in gaining an education by providing the most comprehensive financial assistance possible to current and prospective students. The Financial Aid Office is dedicated to maintaining accurate records and complying with federal, state, and University regulations. Through a partnership with students, parents, and numerous offices and organizations, the Financial Aid Office is committed to timely communication and high-quality customer service. Scholarships, loans, and campus employment are available, and awards are made on the basis of student merit and financial need. Information on these as well as on Federal Pell Grants, other federal grants, and Federal Work-Study awards may be obtained by writing to the Financial Aid Office.

Faculty

Virginia State University has a long history of outstanding faculty and administration members. The first person to bear the title of President, John Mercer Langston, was one of the best-known African Americans of his day. Until 1992, he was the only African American ever elected to the United States Congress from Virginia (elected in 1888), and he was the great-uncle of the famed writer Langston Hughes. A large majority of the University's 250 faculty members hold doctoral degrees and are recognized nationally and internationally for their published works and honors.

Virginia State University offers many opportunities for close student-faculty contact and promotes a supportive environment designed to meet the professional and personal goals of students. A student-faculty ratio of 19:1 and small classes, which range from 25 to 35 students, allow students to interact closely with their professors.

Student Government

Student government at Virginia State University is part of the student activities program, which is considered a vital element of the total educational program. VSU believes in the education of the complete individual.

Admission Requirements

To experience education at VSU, applicants must complete a college-preparatory program in high school, which includes 4 years of English, 3 years of mathematics, and 2 years each of science and social studies. Two units of a foreign language are strongly recommended. A student must also have two letters of recommendation, SAT or ACT test scores, and a personal statement.

Application and Information

Applications for August entrance should be submitted no later than May 1; those for January entrance should be submitted no later than December 1. Applications to Virginia State University are accepted as far as classroom space permits. Transfer students must submit a transcript from every college previously attended. All application forms must be accompanied by a $25 application fee and should be forwarded to:

The Office of Admissions
Virginia State University
P.O. Box 9018
1 Hayden Drive
Petersburg, Virginia 23806
Telephone: 804-524-5901
E-mail: admiss@vsu.edu
World Wide Web: http://www.vsu.edu/

VOORHEES COLLEGE

DENMARK, SOUTH CAROLINA

The College

Voorhees College was established in 1897 by a young black woman, Elizabeth Evelyn Wright. A former student of Booker T. Washington, Miss Wright, at 23, dreamed the seemingly impossible dream of starting a school for African American youth in Denmark, South Carolina. The College's historic mission was to provide educational opportunities for young blacks in rural Bamberg County.

Today, Voorhees College, with an enrollment of almost 800 students, has evolved into a four-year liberal arts college with full accreditation by the Southern Association of Colleges and Schools. It is affiliated with the Episcopal Church and the College Fund/UNCF. The mission of the College remains the same—to educate the minds, hearts, and spirits of young African American men and women.

Voorhees students participate in a variety of College-sponsored activities, including four national fraternities and four national sororities; two campus publications; theater and drama productions; intramural sports; ethnic, political, and religious organizations; honor, service, and leadership societies; the Voorhees College Concert Choir; the Student Government Association; and special interest groups.

The Voorhees College Tigers participate in the Eastern Intercollegiate Athletic Conference of the NAIA Division I in men's baseball, women's softball and volleyball, and men's and women's basketball and cross-country.

The College's buildings represent a pleasant combination of turn-of-the-century and contemporary architecture. Eight of the campus buildings make up a Historic District and are listed on the National Register of Historic Places. The significance of the district lies not only in the building styles but also in the fact that many of the buildings were built solely by students at the school. The most recent addition to the campus is the Leonard E. Dawson Health and Human Resources Center, which houses a 2,200-seat arena, a student center, a snack bar, a swimming pool, a weight room, a dance studio, classrooms, and offices. In addition, a Humanities, Education, and Fine Arts Center housing an art studio, a music hall, practice rooms, classrooms, and faculty offices. A track and field complex has also been completed, along with baseball and softball fields.

Location

Situated in the midlands of South Carolina, Voorhees is located 1½ miles from the town of Denmark, South Carolina, on a well-landscaped 350-acre campus. Denmark is the home of approximately 4,500 residents. The campus is accessible by bus, train, and airline. The College's closest metropolitan neighbor is Columbia, the state's capital and largest city, which is approximately 50 miles north. The historic seaport of Charleston is 86 miles to the east of the campus.

Majors and Degrees

The Bachelor of Science (B.S.) and Bachelor of Arts (B.A.) degrees are awarded in accounting, biology, business administration, computer science, criminal justice, health and recreation, mass communications, mathematics, organizational management, and sociology.

Preprofessional programs that prepare students for degrees in medicine and nursing are also available.

Academic Programs

A student must satisfactorily complete a minimum of 124 semester hours of course work with a minimum cumulative grade point average of 2.0 (on a 4.0 scale) to be eligible for a Voorhees College bachelor's degree. Fifty semester hours of General Education Requirements are required of all students, regardless of their major(s). The College does not require a minor for graduation.

The College has established special programs to meet the academic needs and interests of its students: the Honors Program, the Academic Achievement Center, the Cooperative Education Program, and an ROTC program held in cooperation with South Carolina State University.

The College operates on a two-semester calendar consisting of a fall semester and a spring semester, each lasting fifteen weeks. The fall semester begins in August and ends in mid-December; the spring semester begins in early January and ends in early May, with a nine-day spring break at Easter. The College's summer session consists of one 6-week term. During the fall and spring semesters, the normal class load ranges from 12 to 16 hours. A minimum of 12 hours are required for full-time enrollment; for the summer session, 6 hours are required.

Academic Facilities

Twenty-three buildings are located on the campus and are used for classrooms, faculty offices, administrative offices, student services, academic support programs, and cultural, recreational, and religious activities as well as residential living.

The Wright-Potts Library is a contemporary two-story facility located in the center of the campus. It contains more than 100,000 volumes supplemented by 431 periodicals. The collection also includes newspaper subscriptions, phonograph records, microfiche, tape cassettes, filmstrips, and video tapes.

The Academic Computing Center consists of three computer laboratories, including two PC labs. The College is fully networked and online.

Costs

For the 2003–04 academic year, tuition was $7106, room charges were $1904, and board charges were $2668. The total cost for a full-time residential student was $11,678 plus additional fees for telephone and technology. Charges are subject to change.

A minimum fee of $350 must be paid by all students at the time of registration (per semester), with the exception of Presidential Scholars. Students who have paid their accounts in full and have a credit balance will be given a refund.

Financial Aid

Voorhees College's financial aid program includes College grants-in-aid, state and federal grants, employment, scholarships, and loans. Students eligible for financial aid must be accepted for admission to Voorhees College and complete the appropriate financial aid application in a timely manner.

Parents are urged to file the appropriate tax forms early and complete the Free Application for Federal Student Aid (FAFSA) as soon after January 1 as possible. Applicants must include the

Voorhees College code (003455) to ensure that the Office of Student Financial Aid receives the processed FAFSA. A financial aid award cannot be made without this document. Residents of the state of South Carolina are encouraged to file early for the South Carolina Tuition Grant. The application for fall enrollment is April 15. Approximately 94 percent of Voorhees students receive some form of financial assistance.

Faculty

The College's faculty is composed of 37 full-time faculty members and 27 part-time and adjunct faculty members. Fifty percent of the faculty members have earned doctorates. The faculty is in compliance with the accrediting body's criteria for scholarly preparation. The student-faculty ratio is 20:1.

Student Government

The Student Government Association is the official governing body of the Voorhees College student body. It is organized and operates under a constitution and bylaws outlined in the *Student Handbook*. Student representation is included on many standing committees of the College.

Admission Requirements

Voorhees College values diversity within its student body and encourages applications from qualified students who come from a wide variety of cultural and socioeconomic backgrounds. The College accepts students who have graduated from accredited high schools with at least a 2.0 GPA or have earned the GED. Transfer students are accepted if they are in good academic standing with the last college in which they were enrolled. All students must take the SAT or ACT and have scores submitted to the Admissions Office.

Qualified applicants are admitted without regard to race, color, creed, national origin, sex, or physical handicap.

Application and Information

Voorhees College operates on a rolling admissions policy. The application for admission, along with a $25 nonrefundable fee, should be accompanied by official high school and/or college transcripts, SAT or ACT scores, the official high school evaluation and recommendation form, a transfer confidential form (transfer students only), and a medical form.

For additional information, prospective students are encouraged to contact:

Director of Admissions
Halmi Hall
Voorhees College
P.O. Box 678
Denmark, South Carolina 29042-0678
Telephone: 803-703-7112
800-446-6250 (toll-free)
Fax: 803-793-1117
E-mail: bwaston@voorhees.edu
World Wide Web: http://www.voorhees.edu

WABASH COLLEGE

CRAWFORDSVILLE, INDIANA

The College

Founded in 1832, Wabash has remained a small liberal arts college for men, dedicated to academic excellence and to "the development, right direction, and permanent discipline" of all the powers of the mind. A common reaction of freshmen to the first semester was expressed in a recent course evaluation: "It's a lot harder than I thought it would be, but I've done a lot better than I expected to." Academic challenges, ample extracurricular activities, and maximum personal autonomy foster independence and versatility in Wabash graduates. Of graduating seniors in the class of 2002, 37 percent entered private industry, 40 percent pursued further study, 18 percent went to graduate school in the arts and sciences, and 10 percent went to law school. Approximately 74 percent of the 863 students are from Indiana; the remaining 25 percent come from thirty-five states and thirteen countries.

Outside the classroom, Wabash students have a rich choice of activities to explore. There are workshops, seminars, visiting artists and lecturers, films, music, theater and forensic events, special interest clubs, and intramural sports. Varsity sports are baseball, basketball, cross-country, football, golf, soccer, swimming, tennis, track, and wrestling. Wabash belongs to Division III of the NCAA. Past championships prove that athletic achievement can accompany academic excellence.

Housing is guaranteed to all entering students, and all students are required to live on campus for their freshman and sophomore years. There are ten national fraternities and four residence halls. The single-sex environment fosters a serious academic routine during the week. Fraternities and other social organizations help to organize communication with women at coed institutions in the area. Purdue University, the University of Illinois, Indiana University, DePauw University, and other fine colleges and universities are within easy driving distance.

Although there are strong academic pressures at Wabash, most students find a Wabash education highly rewarding. Of colleges in the Great Lakes Colleges Association, Wabash has one of the highest rates of student retention.

Location

Crawfordsville, a town of approximately 14,000, is 45 miles northwest of Indianapolis. Chicago and Cincinnati are each within a 3-hour drive, and it is a 4-hour drive to St. Louis. Relations between townspeople and the College are excellent. Crawfordsville is a safe and quiet town and was recently listed among the 100 best small towns in America.

Majors and Degrees

Wabash College awards the Bachelor of Arts degree. Students may major in art, biology, chemistry, classical languages and literature, economics, English, history, mathematics, modern languages (French, German, and Spanish), music, philosophy, physics, political science, psychology, religion, speech, or theater. Double majors are permitted. Students may minor in one of the departments listed above or an area concentration in two or more departments. There are 3-2 programs in engineering, offered in cooperation with Columbia University (New York) and Washington University (St. Louis), and a 3-3 program in law, offered with Columbia University.

Academic Program

To graduate, Wabash students must complete thirty-four courses, including the freshman tutorial and the sophomore-level course on cultures and traditions; demonstrate proficiency in English composition and in a foreign language; and pass the senior oral and written comprehensive examinations. With the help of a faculty adviser, students choose courses from the offerings of the many College departments. The curriculum seeks to allow maximum flexibility as well as provide the broad base of understanding that is at the core of the liberal arts concept. In coordination with an adviser, students may arrange special courses of study. Faculty committees and advisers and the Office of Career Services assist students who are interested in careers in business, engineering, law, and medicine in planning a major program appropriate to their needs.

Wabash measures credits in semester-course units. The academic calendar consists of a fall semester, beginning in August and ending before Christmas, and a spring semester, beginning in January and ending in May.

Off-Campus Programs

Approximately 1 of every 4 Wabash students takes advantage of the opportunity to study off campus. In addition to the thirteen programs around the world sponsored by the Great Lakes Colleges Association, students are encouraged to consider independently planned programs and to write directly to universities abroad that interest them.

For most students, the cost of studying off campus is no greater than the cost of on-campus study. All financial aid extends to approved off-campus programs. Students receive credit, but not grades, for work done in approved programs.

Academic Facilities

In 2002–03, the open-stack library collection had 420,406 books and bound periodicals, 1,634 serial and periodical titles, a 153,562-item government documents section, and 10,557 phonograph records, videos, and CDs. The 10-person staff provides students and faculty with reference assistance, information database searching, and computerized interlibrary loan access to more than 25 million volumes in more than 5,000 libraries worldwide. Students are free to use the microform facilities and campus computer terminals in the building.

All students have full and free access to computing facilities, including a DEC Sable Alpha VMS server and five classrooms equipped either with Macintoshes or Power PCs, including Pentium microcomputers. In all, there are more than 160 computers or terminals available for students. All of these systems are linked together with an Ethernet WAN with a connection to the Internet so that faculty and students have access to the same programs and files from any computer classroom, residence hall room, or fraternity room on campus. In most English and speech courses, students use Microsoft Word or WordPerfect to create and subsequently edit documents. Students either electronically transfer documents to faculty members or use laser-jet printers to obtain high-quality copies. Spreadsheet, paint, and drawing programs are also available. On the DEC Sable Alpha VMS server, students have access to SAS, a statistics program, and a wide-area network linking campuses throughout the world.

The chemistry department has infrared spectrophotometers, an atomic absorption spectrophotometer, and two nuclear magnetic resonance spectrometers. Special equipment and facilities for the biology department include an electron microscope, ultramicrotomes, fluorescence and phase microscopes, scintillation counters, a Beowulf-style supercomputer for use with biochemistry courses, gamma counters, electrophoresis apparatus, physiographs, a 180-acre field station with living facilities and laboratory space, and an experimental greenhouse. Special physics department equipment includes an X-ray diffraction machine, a neutron source available for use in the atomic and nuclear physics labs, a multichannel analyzer, a photography darkroom, Mössbauer-effect equipment, a special electronics laboratory, and three Macintosh IIci computers for advanced labs.

Since 1995, Wabash students have had the opportunity to study in the Detchon Center for Modern Languages and International Studies, a completely renovated and expanded facility. With a computerized classroom providing the most modern technical equipment to make the study of language interesting, an electronic classroom, small rooms for tutorial discussions, and lounge areas where international publications are available, the Detchon Center is an integral part of preparation for life in an ever smaller world. The Detchon Center rivals the recently expanded Fine Arts Center with its two art galleries; photography, sculpture, ceramic, painting, and drawing studios; and for music students a MIDI lab, a concert hall, and a practice room. Theater patrons and students continue to benefit from the 370-seat proscenium house, scene shop, and 150-seat experimental theater.

Costs

Tuition for 2003–04 was $20,829. Room and board cost $6717, and there was an activity fee of $386. Most Wabash students spend approximately $1700 per year on books and personal expenses.

Financial Aid

Wabash College is independent of any direct government funding and has a substantial endowment of nearly $300 million. Cutbacks in government-sponsored financial aid have had no effect on Wabash's generous financial aid and scholarship programs. To apply for financial aid, students must file the Free Application for Federal Student Aid (FAFSA) and the College Scholarship Service (CSS) PROFILE. Students are expected to file the FAFSA by February 15. Wabash College assists families with a combination of scholarships, grants, the Federal Stafford Student Loan, and campus employment.

The Wabash scholarship program is one of the best in the nation. Scholarships are worth up to full cost for each of four years. Wabash sponsors awards in three general categories: Lilly Awards, Honor Scholarships, and President's Scholarships. The Lilly Awards are valued at full cost and are given annually to students who excel in the areas of character, creativity, leadership, and academic achievement. Honor Scholarships that are worth up to $15,000 per year are awarded based on competitive examinations administered on campus in March.

Faculty

Ninety-seven percent of Wabash faculty members hold doctorates or other terminal degrees in their fields. While the College encourages faculty research, Wabash is primarily a teaching institution for undergraduates. The faculty-student ratio is 1:10. In addition to serving as advisers, faculty members have frequent informal contacts with students. Most faculty members live close to campus. The average class size is 13.

Student Government

Wabash has only one rule: Wabash men will behave as gentlemen and responsible citizens at all times. Beyond diplomatic enforcement of that rule, the College does not undertake to regulate student life. Consequently, Wabash students have a great deal of autonomy. The Student Senate manages and allocates the more than $300,000 collected each year in activity fees. Communication among students, faculty members, and administrators is open and congenial.

Admission Requirements

Wabash seeks academically well-qualified young men from all parts of the United States. The Admissions Committee recommends the following high school courses: 4 years of English, 3 to 4 years of college-preparatory mathematics, 2 years of a foreign language, 2 to 3 years of laboratory science, and 2 years of social studies. In recent years, 75 percent of Wabash's students have ranked in the top quarter of their high school class. The strength of the high school preparation is the most important factor in admission decisions. SAT I or ACT scores, counselors' recommendations, and the essay portion of the application form are also important. Personal interviews are not required, but prospective students are strongly encouraged to visit the Wabash campus.

Wabash admits students and gives equal access to its programs and facilities without regard to race, color, national or ethnic origin, or physical or other disabilities.

Application and Information

Students seeking admission to Wabash must submit the Wabash application form, a nonrefundable $30 application fee, and a secondary school report that includes a transcript of grades, SAT I or ACT scores, a list of senior-year courses, and the counselor's recommendation. Transfer students must submit transcripts of college courses as well. The application deadline for priority consideration for Wabash merit scholarships and aid is December 15. The final deadline for fall enrollment is March 15. Applicants who are accepted are asked to submit a $150 deposit by May 1.

Application forms and other information may be obtained from:

Steven J. Klein
Dean of Admissions
Wabash College
P.O. Box 352
Crawfordsville, Indiana 47933-0352
Telephone: 765-361-6225
800-345-5385 (toll-free)
World Wide Web: http://www.wabash.edu

The heart of the Wabash College campus, the chapel is the site of student gatherings ranging from football rallies to weddings.

WAGNER COLLEGE

STATEN ISLAND, NEW YORK

The College

Founded in 1883, Wagner College is a four-year, private residential college with a strong tradition in the liberal arts. Located in New York City's borough of Staten Island, the campus is situated atop Grymes Hill on the nineteenth-century estate of the Cunard family, founders of the famous shipping line. Wagner's 105-acre campus provides a setting that feels far away from the city; yet, Manhattan is just a free 25-minute ferry ride away. Recently, the College received attention for its nationally recognized curriculum, the Wagner Plan for the Practical Liberal Arts, which integrates courses across disciplines and directly connects course work to field experiences and internships. Wagner was ranked "top tier" by *U.S. News & World Report* in their "America's Best Colleges" 2004 issue. *TIME* magazine, in their "Colleges of the Year" 2001 issue, cited Wagner as one of only four liberal arts colleges nationwide for its outstanding First Year Program.

Wagner enrolls approximately 1750 undergraduate and 350 graduate students. About 82 percent of Wagner undergraduates live on campus in three residence halls that offer spectacular views of the New York Harbor, Manhattan, and the Atlantic Ocean. Students come from thirty-seven U.S. states and eighteen foreign countries. Students choose Wagner because it offers excellent academic preparation, superb access to professional and cultural opportunities, and a traditional college campus setting. Students gain access to exceptional professional opportunities within the curriculum and through the College's large and supportive alumni base in the New York City area and beyond. Wagner strongly believes that career development is an integral part of a student's education—one that begins in a student's first year at Wagner and culminates in a senior year practicum in a specific field of study.

Student life is active on the campus with more than sixty different clubs and organizations, including both national and local fraternities and sororities. Wagner offers a full array of activities and social events, many of which are planned by the student life staff. Wagner expands students' experiences beyond the campus with trips around New York City to museums, concerts, professional sporting events, Broadway shows, and many other attractions.

The College offers outstanding athletics programs, which include NCAA Division I standing in twenty-two areas, many intramurals, and an excellent coaching staff. Athletic teams offered are: men's baseball, basketball, football (IAA), golf, lacrosse, tennis, track/cross-country, and wrestling; and women's basketball, golf, lacrosse, soccer, softball, swimming, tennis, track/cross-country, volleyball, and water polo; club sports are cheerleading and men's ice hockey.

In addition to undergraduate programs, Wagner offers master's degree programs in business administration (M.B.A.), education, microbiology, nursing, and physician assistant studies.

Location

Wagner's location offers students the best of both worlds. Living on a wooded campus 35 minutes from Manhattan has distinct advantages. The 105-acre campus overlooks New York Harbor and Manhattan. Students enjoy living in the beautiful Grymes Hill section of Staten Island and the proximity to the resources of Manhattan, which are easily accessible by bus, ferry, or car. Wagner has much to offer students who want the benefits of an education in New York City but who also wish to pursue their studies in a classic suburban college setting.

Majors and Degrees

Wagner College offers the Bachelor of Arts, Bachelor of Science, and Bachelor of Science in Education. Undergraduate majors and fields of concentration are in accounting, anthropology, art, art history, arts administration, biology, biopsychology, business administration, chemistry, computer science, dance, economics, education, English, foreign languages (French, German, and Spanish), gender studies, history, international affairs, Italian studies, journalism, mathematics, microbiology, music, nursing, philosophy, physician assistant studies, physics, political science, psychology, public policy and administration, religious studies, sociology, and theater. A seven-year dentistry program with NYU is also offered.

Academic Program

Wagner's undergraduate program, the Wagner Plan, is designed to provide a broad education in the liberal arts and in-depth study in a major. Wagner also believes that students learn best by "reading, writing, and doing," and therefore incorporates field experiences directly into the curriculum. As part of the graduation requirements, students must complete three Learning Communities (LCs)—one in the first year, one in either sophomore or junior year, and one in the senior year in the major area of study. At Wagner, LCs consist of three courses that are linked by a single theme and share a common set of students. They are also directly connected to field experience based on the theme of the LC. Throughout the first semester, first-year students spend time at the designated site observing the organization, its practices, and its dynamics. Seniors are involved in a practicum connected to their major field of study.

Each candidate is required to complete 36 units for the baccalaureate degree. Students must elect a major as part of their studies, and may select from more than sixty different majors, minors, and/or concentrations. Majors must be selected by the end of the sophomore year, with the exception of physician assistant studies, theater, and music students, who must apply directly to the respective program. The academic year is divided into the fall semester (September–December) and spring semester (January–May). Students may also enroll in one of several summer sessions.

Off-Campus Programs

Wagner College is a member of the prestigious Institute for the International Education of Students program (IES), which is the nation's oldest and most selective study-abroad program. Interested and qualified Wagner students may choose among semester, summer, and vacation study-abroad programs in such diverse urban-based centers as Beijing, Berlin, Canberra, Dublin, LaPlata, London, Madrid, Paris, Tokyo, and Vienna. Classes are taught through a combination approach in which U.S. students take classes designed expressly for them as well as classes run by universities located within the host city, thereby integrating the U.S. students with students from that nation.

Academic Facilities

College facilities include twenty-three buildings for academic, recreational, and residential use. Wagner's recently updated science buildings house two electron microscopes and a fully functioning planetarium. Other facilities include a theater, a studio theater, an art gallery, a new sports and fitness facility, an indoor pool, and a new football stadium. All of Wagner's classrooms have been recently renovated.

Computer facilities at Wagner are abundant and accessible. The Spiro Computer Technology Center features Pentium III PCs, while Novell network servers provide numerous application software programs for word processing, spreadsheet, graphics, statistical analysis, and programming languages. Additionally, Wagner provides a Mac lab for graphics applications and a UNIX lab. The three residence halls are fully wired for free Internet and e-mail access in each room along with a new voice-mail system and free cable.

The Horrmann Library houses approximately 310,000 volumes as well as 1,000 titles in its periodical collection. The library is a member of the New York Metropolitan Reference and Research Agency, which provides access to more than 25 million volumes in the area.

Costs

Tuition for the 2003–04 academic year was $22,600. Room and board for the academic year were $7300.

Financial Aid

More than 70 percent of Wagner students receive some kind of financial aid. In addition to the availability of state and federal aid programs, the College itself is a source of more than $8 million in student aid each year. Counselors are available to assist in completing the Financial Aid Form.

Faculty

Because of its commitment to academic excellence, Wagner has always drawn a gifted faculty. Ninety-five percent of the 95 full-time faculty members hold a doctoral degree or the equivalent in their field. Many have published books and articles, and a large number have a combination of in-depth experience and academic qualifications. Wagner is strongly committed to keeping classes small and maintaining close relationships between faculty members and students; the student-faculty ratio is 16:1. Teaching is the first priority at Wagner, and all classes are taught by professors. Because faculty members are concerned about their students' intellectual and personal growth, they participate in all areas of College life. Faculty members regard New York City as an incomparable resource for course work and field experience.

Student Government

The Wagner College Student Government is democratically elected by the undergraduate student body. The government has legislative and judicial responsibilities. Students have numerous opportunities for involvement in organizations, special interest groups, and committees. Activities and events are planned by students with the assistance of the director of student activities.

Admission Requirements

Admission to Wagner is based primarily on academic ability. The admission committee also considers personal qualities that, in the College's view, enable a student to take maximum advantage of what Wagner has to offer and to contribute to the quality of campus life.

The applicant is assessed on the basis of high school achievement, class rank, recommendations of the guidance counselor or academic teacher, standardized test scores (SAT or ACT), and an essay. In addition, the student's citizenship record (participation in extracurricular, community, or religious activities) and character record (including information derived from the recommendations) are reviewed. A personal interview is optional but recommended. Scores on the SAT I or ACT are required, and SAT II: Subject Tests are recommended. None of these factors is considered in isolation; all are weighed together so that a clear picture of the applicant and his or her chances for success at Wagner emerge.

Students considering Wagner should have completed a minimum of 18 units in the following academic areas: English, 4; history, 3; mathematics, 3; foreign language, 2; and science, 2. Four additional units from the following list of electives are recommended: art, 1; computer science, 1; foreign language, 2–4; history, 1–3; mathematics, 1–3; music, 1–2; natural sciences, 1–3; religion, 1; and social studies, 1–2.

Application and Information

Application should be made early in the senior year of high school. In addition to the completed application form and the nonrefundable fee, students are responsible for forwarding a secondary school transcript, two letters of recommendation, their personal essay, and SAT I or ACT scores to the Admissions Office. The early decision application deadline is December 1. The physician assistant studies and theater deadlines are January 1. The general application deadline is February 15, and there is a final application deadline of March 15.

Candidates are urged, whenever possible, to make an appointment with the Admissions Office to visit the campus and discuss their plans and goals with a member of the admission staff. They are also encouraged to talk with currently enrolled Wagner students. Arrangements can be made for candidates to meet with faculty members in departments of particular interest.

Further information may be obtained by contacting:

Admissions Office
Wagner College
1 Campus Road
Staten Island, New York 10301
Telephone: 718-390-3411
800-221-1010 (toll-free outside New York)
Fax: 718-390-3105
E-mail: admissions@wagner.edu
World Wide Web: http://www.wagner.edu

Wagner students in front of Main Hall.

WALSH UNIVERSITY

NORTH CANTON, OHIO

The University

Walsh University, founded in 1958 by the Brothers of Christian Instruction, is one of northeast Ohio's finest liberal arts and sciences universities. As a coeducational Catholic institution, Walsh provides a values-based education with an international perspective in the Judeo-Christian tradition. With more than 1,600 students and a 15:1 student-faculty ratio, the University promotes academic excellence, a diverse community, and close student-faculty interaction. Its curriculum fosters critical thinking and strong communication skills and encourages students to pursue opportunities and interests that allow for the development of their personal, spiritual, and professional growth.

Students at Walsh pursue studies in more than forty academic majors and four graduate degree programs. More than 1,100 students attend Walsh as full-time undergraduates. Other students attend Walsh as part-time undergraduates, as graduate students, or as students in the Intensive Degree Experience for Adult Learners (IDEAL) program, an accelerated degree completion program for working adults.

Walsh's tree-lined campus encompasses thirteen separate buildings on 100 acres. Most full-time undergraduate students reside in one of seven modern residence halls that include three apartment-style complexes.

Active and involved in campus and community life, Walsh students participate in a number of extracurricular programs. Organizations, academic clubs, and social events provide opportunities for students to work and relax together on and off campus. Student-run outreach projects help students serve the community while developing their leadership skills.

Students also enjoy intramural and intercollegiate athletic activities. Walsh's Division II NAIA athletic teams compete in the American Mideast Conference and in the Mid-States Football Association.

Walsh University is accredited by the North Central Association of Colleges and Schools, the National League for Nursing Accrediting Commission, and the Commission on Accreditation in Physical Therapy Education. Walsh is a member of the Ohio College Association, the National Association of Independent Colleges and Universities, and the Association of Catholic Colleges and Universities.

Location

Walsh University is conveniently located 3 miles east of I-77 in North Canton, a safe, pleasant residential suburban community. Canton, which is about 5 miles south of the Walsh campus, is a city of 84,000 that offers a wide array of cultural, recreational, and athletic activities. Home of the Professional Football Hall of Fame, the President McKinley National Memorial, and the National First Ladies Library, the city also hosts a symphony orchestra, an art museum, and a civic opera, theater guild, and ballet. A number of major companies are headquartered in Stark County, including the Hoover Company, the Timken Company, and Diebold, Inc.

Majors and Degrees

Through a liberal arts curriculum emphasizing the integration of the humanities and natural and social sciences with knowledge in a chosen major or area of preprofessional study, Walsh prepares its graduates to move into the current job market as well as graduate and professional schools. It awards the Bachelor of Arts and Bachelor of Science degrees in the following majors: accounting (general and specialized CPA tracks), biology, chemistry, clinical laboratory science, communication, computer science, corporate communication, education (early childhood, middle childhood, adolescence to young adulthood, integrated language arts, integrated mathematics teacher licensure, integrated science teacher licensure, integrated social studies teacher, intervention specialist, life science/biology teacher licensure, life science/biology and chemistry teacher licensure, and multiage physical education), English, finance, French, general business, history, international studies, Latin American business studies, management, management information systems, marketing, mathematics, nursing, philosophy/theology, physical education, political science, psychology, sociology, and Spanish.

Walsh offers preprofessional programs in dentistry, law, medicine, natural resources, optometry, physical therapy, podiatry, and veterinary science. Each is developed within the context of a regular academic major. Students enrolled in the University's B.A./M.A. program can earn a bachelor's degree in behavioral science and a master's degree in counseling and human development in 5½ years. An affiliation with Case Western Reserve University's (CWRU) program in dentistry leads to a B.S. from Walsh and ultimately a D.D.S. from CWRU.

In addition, Walsh offers the Associate of Arts degree in accounting, finance, human services, liberal arts management, and marketing.

Academic Programs

The University promotes six basic values through its academic program: respect for self, others, and the environment; hospitality; service; integrity; an ethical approach to decisionmaking; and excellence in the teaching-learning process.

Designed for the academically gifted, the honors program offers challenges that lead students to achieve academic excellence. Honors students take advantage of such offerings as special seminars, independent studies, internships, and research projects.

The University's broad liberal arts base supports all its academic programs. Forty percent of a student's program of study is within the liberal arts. The University's core curriculum is composed of interdisciplinary foundation courses and thematic clusters of courses. In foundation courses, students learn the rigors of interdisciplinary study by examining different topics from a range of perspectives, such as art, literature, science, and technology. Cluster courses include five coordinated electives that center on such themes as shaping civilization or the environment. These courses help students examine how issues are shaped by many factors.

The rest of a student's academic program comprises courses within a major field of study and elective courses. Major course work, constituting one fourth or more of a student's program of studies, is designed to help students prepare for their careers. Elective courses, which constitute the remaining portion of a student's program of studies, enable students to develop personal interests, take more courses within their major field, or enroll in additional core courses. The University encourages students to give careful thought to selecting a program of study and a major. While many students select double majors as a way to improve their career opportunities, the design of individual programs requires consultation with a faculty adviser and a division chair. To earn a bachelor's degree, students must successfully complete 130 semester hours.

The University's Intensive Degree Experience for Adult Learners program is an academic program targeted at working adults who have earned college credits and who wish to earn their bachelor's degree in an accelerated format. Classes are scheduled on nights and weekends to accommodate busy schedules. By taking these classes and earning credits for both past college work and for life experiences, IDEAL students complete work for a bachelor's degree at a quicker pace than students in traditionally designed college programs.

Academic Facilities

The Walsh Library contains 130,000 volumes, 630 current periodical subscriptions on paper, thousands of online periodicals, a curriculum library, and an audiovisual collection. Databases bring many full-text articles immediately for download or print, and information technology systems enable online requests for physical delivery of material, often via rapid courier. Library staff members give introductory lectures on research techniques. The library has a quiet study room, a snack lounge, and a mini-theater.

Faculty

Walsh University fosters close working relationships between faculty members and students. Beyond classroom teaching, faculty members serve as student counselors and tutors and take on roles as advisers for student organizations. The Walsh faculty is composed of full-time, part-time, and adjunct members. The student-faculty ratio is 15:1. The majority of full-time faculty members hold Ph.D.'s or terminal degrees in their respective fields.

Student Government

Walsh University Student Government provides capable, responsible student governance. Through its executive, legislative, and judicial branches, it fosters student involvement in the governance of the University, serves as a forum for student opinion, and functions as a liaison between students, faculty and staff members, and the administration. Along with the Student Affairs staff, it plans student activities and community projects.

Costs

Tuition and fees for the academic year are $15,650 ($495 per credit hour) plus a $17 per-credit-hour general fee. Room and board charges are $6650 per year. Books and personal expenses cost an estimated $700–$900 for the year. The University reserves the right to change the cost structure without notice.

Financial Aid

Walsh is dedicated to providing outstanding liberal arts education at an affordable price. The primary purpose of Walsh University's financial aid program is to assist deserving students who cannot otherwise meet the costs of a college education. Financial aid takes the form of scholarships, work-study awards, grants, or loans, depending upon the resources available. The University offers a number of scholarships in amounts from $1500 to full tuition, in addition to institutional need-based grants. The Alumni Association offers scholarships as well. State and federal grants and loans are available to students along with the University's work-study program which provides work compatible with a student's academic schedule. Financial aid is awarded for one year and is renewable in subsequent years if the student shows a continuing need and maintains an appropriate academic record.

Applicants for admission may apply for financial aid by submitting the Free Application for Federal Student Aid (FAFSA) and the University's financial aid form. To allow for timely notification of financial awards, the University recommends that the FAFSA be mailed by March 15 in order to receive full analysis by May 1. Prospective students may obtain a FAFSA from their high school guidance counselor or from the University's financial aid office. The Walsh financial aid form is available from the financial aid and admissions offices of the University.

Admissions Requirements

Every student seeking admission to Walsh University is reviewed individually to asses the student's ability to meet the rigors of the University's curriculum. A minimum cumulative grade point average of 2.1 and ACT of 17 or SAT of 830 must be attained to be considered for admission, but does not guarantee a favorable admission decision. The composition of high school classes, grades achieved, class rank, and standardized test scores are all taken into consideration before an admission decision is rendered. Essays and interviews are highly recommended but not required.

Walsh grants credit for college-level work completed in high school and for credits earned through the College Level Examination Program. Qualified high school juniors and seniors may enroll for college credit under the University's postsecondary enrollment program. The University seeks a diverse student body.

Application and Information

Early application is recommended. Walsh University operates under a rolling admissions policy. The completed admission application, $25 application fee, ACT or SAT I scores, and a high school transcript are required for a student's application to be considered for admission. Transfer students must also submit transcripts from all colleges and universities attended.

Interested students are encouraged to contact:

Brett Freshour
Dean of Enrollment Management
Walsh University
2020 Easton Street NW
North Canton, Ohio 44720-3396
Telephone: 330-492-7172
800-362-9846 (toll-free)
Fax: 330-490-7165
E-mail: admissions@walsh.edu
World Wide Web: http://www.walsh.edu

Walsh University bases its education on three core values: excellence, integrity, and service.

WARNER PACIFIC COLLEGE

PORTLAND, OREGON

The College

Warner Pacific College promotes excellence in its students and offers them an individualized education in a Christian context. To uphold this mission, the academic program provides experiences that integrate knowledge, attitude, and faith with meaningful relationships. The concept of a Christian liberal arts education does not discount the importance of practical experience or the need to translate theory into practice. In fact, as a Christ-centered college, Warner Pacific emphasizes careers and lifelong learning with faculty and staff members and administrators who seek to prepare men and women for Kingdom service in the next millennium. And unlike many colleges, Warner Pacific's graduates are distinguished not only by their academic prowess but also by their exemplary character, a quality much sought after by prospective employers.

Since its founding in 1937, Warner Pacific has developed a full range of liberal arts curricula. Today, more than twenty-three fields of undergraduate study are offered as well as a certificate in family life education and a Master of Religion degree program.

Students are challenged in the classroom and encouraged to develop leadership skills by participating in on-campus activities and completing internships with organizations scattered throughout the Portland metropolitan area. Applying theory to real life maximizes the learning experience. Stemming from the College's belief in the value of hands-on application and accountability, Warner Pacific impresses upon students the importance of a lifelong commitment to service, which is modeled after the life and teachings of Jesus Christ. Consequently, Warner students tutor young children, visit the elderly, work with the homeless, and participate in many other worthwhile projects. In addition, numerous study-abroad opportunities are available through Warner Pacific and the Coalition for Christian Colleges and Universities.

Life on the Warner Pacific campus reverberates with activity, including residence life events aimed at building community, intramurals, drama, the yearbook, online student newspaper, and music. Warner Pacific is a member of the National Association of Intercollegiate Athletics and the Cascade Collegiate Conference as well as the National Christian College Athletic Association. Women's sports include basketball, cross-country, soccer, track and field, and volleyball. Men compete in basketball, cross-country, soccer, and track and field. By becoming involved in the Warner Pacific community, students develop friendships that often last a lifetime.

Traditional residence hall and apartment living provide an incomparable experience to 272 students. Total enrollment exceeds 600 students, representing seventeen states, eight nations, and twenty-seven denominations.

Location

Warner Pacific's central location in the Pacific Northwest provides students with access to impressive natural wonders. Snow-capped mountains, rugged coastlines, and vast wilderness and park areas offer ample opportunities for skiing, biking, hiking, rock climbing, and walking. Besides the attraction of the surrounding scenery, Warner Pacific's prime location, just 15 minutes outside of the thriving Portland metropolitan area, affords students the opportunity to partake of flourishing centers of technology, commerce, and the arts. As a result, exciting internships abound. In addition, students enjoy gallery openings, the theater, dining in unusual restaurants, and attending concerts. Reliable bus and light-rail systems allow students to take full advantage of all the Pacific Northwest has to offer.

Majors and Degrees

Warner Pacific offers two associate degrees and two bachelor's degrees. The Associate of Arts (A.A.) degree is offered in Christian education, general studies, and youth ministries. The Associate of Science (A.S.) degree is offered in business administration, health sciences, and social sciences. The Bachelor of Arts (B.A.) degree is offered in American studies, English, history, liberal studies, music and youth ministries, and religion and Christian ministries. The Bachelor of Science (B.S.) degree is offered in biological science (preprofessional), business administration, developmental psychology, health and human kinetics, human development, human development and family studies, music/business, music education, physical science, social science, and social work. A 2-2 degree program in nursing (guaranteed admittance) is offered in conjunction with Walla Walla College's Portland Adventist Hospital School of Nursing. Individualized majors, double majors, and several minor concentrations are also available.

Warner Pacific is accredited for teacher education and training through the Oregon State Teachers Standards and Practices Commission. The curriculum builds up a broad liberal arts foundation toward specialization in a chosen field while serving the Christian mission of the College. Extended field-based practicums are an integral part of the program. Education certification programs that prepare teachers for careers in public and private schools are available in the following areas: biology, grades 5–12; early childhood/elementary education (age 3–grade 8); elementary/middle school education, grades 3–10; language arts, grades 5–12; math, grades 5–9; music, grades K–12; physical education, grades K–12; reading, grades K–12; and social studies, grades 5–12. A cooperative program with the University of Portland leads to certification in handicapped learner studies.

Academic Program

In order to promote Christian excellence and an individualized education, students take courses in three categories: core studies, a major area of study, and elective credits. In general, each of these categories requires a third of a student's total program. A minor may be chosen as part of the elective program.

Course work to complete a bachelor's degree is available during the summer semester. In addition, the Degree Completion Program makes it possible for qualified adult learners to earn a Bachelor of Science in business administration or human development within a nontraditional course design and evening schedule.

The College operates on a semester calendar. The core studies requirement includes a minimum of 42 semester hours in communications, humanities, religion, mathematics, laboratory science, social science, the fine arts, and physical education/health. The major area of study requires completion of certain courses as specified in the College catalog. The remainder of the 124 semester hours may be earned through elective course work and/or a minor concentration.

Off-Campus Programs

Through the Oregon Independent Colleges Association, Warner Pacific has cooperative relationships with all of the private colleges and universities in the state. In addition, Warner accepts the completed Oregon Transfer Degree and the Clark

College (Vancouver, Washington) A.A. degree as fulfillment of general education core requirements, with the exception of two religion and two upper-division humanities courses. ROTC programs are available in cooperation with the University of Portland; study opportunities and laboratory access at the Oregon Health Sciences University in Portland are readily available. The College participates in a consortium of colleges that maintains the Malheur (eastern Oregon) High Desert Study Center and is a member of the Coalition for Christian Colleges and Universities, which provides study opportunities in Oxford, England; Cairo, Egypt; Israel; Russia; Latin America; Los Angeles, California; Washington, D.C.; Au Sable, Michigan; and Colorado Springs, Colorado.

Academic Facilities

The Otto F. Linn Library provides study areas and housing for a collection of nearly 53,000 books and 450 periodicals. Access to a much larger collection is obtained through OPALL, a computer network that links the College with major public and university collections in Oregon and across the United States. Two biology, one physics, and two chemistry labs and an electron microscope are available. A performing arts auditorium and a small lecture/performance hall feature concerts and dramatic productions. There is a student computer lab as well as modem access in every student residence.

Costs

Annual costs for the 2003–04 academic year are $16,510 for tuition (12 to 18 credits per semester) and $4990 for room and board (double room, 255-meal block per semester).

Financial Aid

Warner Pacific believes that any student who demonstrates the ability and motivation to learn should have access to Christian higher education; therefore, the staff is committed to helping parents and students find the necessary financial resources through federal and state assistance, personal and federally insured loans, private scholarships and programs, institutional assistance, and parental and student contributions. More than 90 percent of Warner students receive some type of aid, whether institutional or otherwise. In order to determine the amount of assistance a student qualifies for, the Financial Aid Office should receive a completed Free Application for Federal Student Aid (FAFSA) by April 15. The College manages nearly $2 million in institutional assistance each year in the form of competitive academic merit scholarships and fellowships, talent grants in music, international student fellowships, assistance designed to enhance ethnic diversity on campus, various types of church-related assistance (including a $2500 tuition discount to members of the Church of God, which is headquartered in Anderson, Indiana), and awards for dependents of alumni. The scholarship/fellowship priority application deadline is March 15. Students may be eligible to work on campus and are assisted in locating employment off campus.

Faculty

The 40 full-time and 20 part-time faculty members are solid academicians who are committed to excellence. These scholars bring their expertise, seasoned professional records, and commitment to the art of teaching at Warner Pacific. Students thrive under the tutelage of these ardent supporters. The student-faculty ratio is 14:1. All faculty members and most administrators teach; the undergraduate and graduate religion faculties teach in both programs. Faculty members also serve as academic advisers, and many are advisers to student organizations and clubs.

Student Government

Democratic self-government is seen as essential to the development of maturity and is a strategic part of the educational mission of the College; for this reason, student life is largely self-governed. The Student Council is the executive body of the Associated Students of Warner Pacific College; it operates under its own grant of powers from the Board of Trustees and creates policy that contributes to the governance of student life and activities. The council develops and coordinates an active social and spiritual agenda to meet the needs of all students.

Admission Requirements

Each applicant is considered on the basis of standard admission factors with an emphasis on the personal references submitted. The College seeks students who have the ability to pursue a course of study that emphasizes academic achievement, an openness to learning and teaching that is integrated with the Christian faith, and a willingness to live a disciplined life in accord with Christian principles and community practice (this includes agreeing to live within a Lifestyle Agreement that governs the social and ethical life of the campus). Graduation from an accredited high school (or the test equivalent) is required for admission to Warner Pacific College. A strong college-preparatory program is recommended. A minimum GPA of 2.5 in academic subjects, along with a combined SAT I score of at least 910, or ACT composite score of at least 19, is required. The GPA of first-year students averages 3.3. The average combined SAT I score is 1010, and the average composite ACT score is 22. Students graduating from high school with a GPA of less than 2.5 may be considered for provisional admission. Transfer students make up a significant percentage of new students. Warner has transfer agreements with many community colleges, including all public two-year institutions in Oregon.

Application and Information

The College has a rolling admission policy; May 1 is the priority date for fall freshman applications. The following must be supplied in order for a student to be considered for admission: the application (including the application form, the Lifestyle Agreement, the personal essay, and a $25 nonrefundable fee), two references, an official transcript from high school and each college/university attended, and official scores on the SAT I, ACT, or other tests. Applicants can expect official notification of acceptance status within ten days of receipt of all required materials. Requests for further information and all forms should be addressed to:

Dean of Enrollment Management
Warner Pacific College
2219 Southeast 68th Avenue
Portland, Oregon 97215

Telephone: 503-517-1020
800-804-1510 (toll-free)
Fax: 503-517-1352
E-mail: admissions@warnerpacific.edu
World Wide Web: http://www.warnerpacific.edu

WARREN WILSON COLLEGE

ASHEVILLE, NORTH CAROLINA

The College

Since its founding in 1894, Warren Wilson College has educated students with a unique triad of a strong liberal arts program, work for the College, and service to those in need, which makes Warren Wilson unlike any other college. Its 800 students come from forty-two states and twenty-five countries, creating a diverse and vibrant academic community.

The academic program features a first-rate faculty that does all of the teaching and frequently participates in research with students. The average class size is small, and discussion is an important part of teaching. Fifteen majors are offered, with a commitment to quality in each program. Art, English, economics and business administration, education, biology, the nationally recognized environmental studies program, and outdoor leadership are the most popular majors.

Students at Warren Wilson are integral to the day-to-day operation of the College. Each student works 15 hours a week at a job that is essential to running the school. This experience helps build student confidence (students learn that there is no job they cannot learn to do) and a strong sense of community at the College. Many juniors and seniors have work assignments that coincide with their major. Students receive a work fellowship in the amount of $2472 each year for the work they do.

Service is also integral to the College's way of thinking. Warren Wilson is one of only a few colleges in the country that require student participation in community service for graduation. Service is offered to a wide range of individuals and agencies, nationally and abroad. Students must provide at least 20 hours of service each year to someone off campus.

The 1,100-acre campus includes a 300-acre working farm, 600 acres of forest, 25 miles of hiking trails, and a white-water kayaking course. The campus and the area are havens for outdoor activities, such as white-water sports, hiking, camping, mountain biking, and rock climbing.

Ninety-three percent of the students and 60 percent of the faculty and staff members live on campus. The College offers intercollegiate basketball, cross-country, soccer, and swimming for men and women. White-water sports, softball, and cross-country are offered as club sports. The College also offers intramural sports, a wellness program, and a wide range of other activities.

Location

Warren Wilson, on the edge of the city of Asheville, North Carolina, is in the heart of the Blue Ridge Mountains. Asheville, a city of nearly 100,000 people, is considered one of the most livable cities in the United States and was selected by the National League of Cities as the All-America City for 1998.

Surrounded by more than 1 million acres of national forest, Asheville is located in an ideal setting, presenting views of outstanding beauty throughout all four seasons. In the spring and summer, variations in altitude together with warm southern sun favor native vegetation: dogwood, wildflowers, rhododendron, mountain laurel, and azaleas cover the mountains. The arresting beauty of the autumn colors attracts photographers, artists, and sports enthusiasts from the world over. During the winter, natural snow is enhanced by machine-made snow, producing excellent downhill skiing.

A short drive from the Warren Wilson College campus are Great Smoky Mountains National Park, Pisgah National Forest, and the Blue Ridge Parkway, offering panoramic views, excellent camping facilities, and a perfect setting for class field trips.

Majors and Degrees

The bachelor's degree is awarded in art, biology, chemistry, creative writing, economics and business administration, education (K–6 and secondary), English, environmental studies, history and political science, humanities, global services, integrative studies, mathematics and computer science, outdoor leadership, psychology, social work, and sociology/anthropology.

Academic Programs

The goal of the degree program at Warren Wilson College is the completion of three well-designed areas of study. First, students are expected to complete a core of required courses based on the theme "ways of knowing." A student earns 4 credits in each of the ten core areas. Second, students must develop a strength in one or more disciplines. A minimum of 128 semester hours is required for the baccalaureate degree, including the core plus major hours. Finally, a student must demonstrate the ability to work effectively with others by participation in a work-and-service program.

There is a required freshman seminar designed to provide new students the opportunity to explore various fields. A senior seminar, designed as a capstone experience, is required, as is a senior letter to evaluate the student's college experiences.

All Warren Wilson students must demonstrate competence in writing and mathematics either through testing or by completing core courses.

Each semester in the academic calendar is broken into two 8-week terms. A student traditionally takes only two courses per term (3 or 4 credit hours per course).

There are two honors programs at Warren Wilson. One is in English and the other is in the Division of Natural Sciences, where honors can be earned in biology, chemistry, environmental studies, and mathematics.

Off-Campus Programs

In addition to academics, work, and service, all qualified students are afforded the opportunity to study abroad. The College heavily subsidizes the cost for a cross-cultural international experience taken during the junior year or summer.

Academic Facilities

The Martha Ellison Library houses a collection of 100,000 books and 450 periodicals. It provides written records in all areas of the college curriculum and contributes to the cultural enrichment of students. The library is open and served by librarians and student assistants 75 hours each week. The building provides open access to books and periodicals during these hours. Individual carrels, lounge areas, and microfilm readers and printers are available, and there are IBM and Macintosh computers that students may use as word processors or for other prescribed purposes, including access to the Internet.

Computerized literature searching is available. The Martha Ellison Library is a teaching library, providing extensive and continuing bibliographic services, including courses, for the entire student body. Any resource materials not owned by the library may be acquired through interlibrary loan.

The campus arts complex includes the modern Kittredge Theatre; the Kittredge Music Wing, housing classrooms, studios, and a performance area; the Holden Arts Center, with a gallery, classrooms, studios, and a lecture hall; and an outdoor amphitheater. Instruction and performance events also take place in the chapel and the Craftshop/Ceramics Studio.

Costs

Total costs for the 2004–05 school year are $23,016. From this amount, the student's Work Program Fellowship of $2472 is deducted, leaving an actual cost of $20,544 for each student before any other aid.

Financial Aid

Warren Wilson offers a comprehensive financial aid program that seeks to enroll students from all economic backgrounds. This is accomplished through a combination of work, loans, grants, entitlements, and scholarships to students who complete their file prior to May. Students and their families should file the FAFSA and the Warren Wilson Financial Aid Application to be considered for all possible funds.

Faculty

The teaching faculty consists of 63 full-time members. Of these, 91 percent hold doctoral degrees. All classes and labs are taught by faculty members, not graduate students. Faculty members—1 for every 13 students—are available after class, during regular office hours, and often in their homes.

Student Government

The student body is involved in the democratic decision-making process of the College. A wide variety of leadership positions, elected and appointed, are open to students. Campuswide elections provide opportunities for student involvement in Student Caucus, Judicial Board, Social Regulations Committee, other College advisory committees, and the Cabinet. Student Caucus, the representative voice of the student body, is also responsible for appointing students to positions on approximately fifteen other campus committees ranging from Admissions to Library to Buildings and Grounds.

Admission Requirements

Admission to Warren Wilson College is based on both the personal and the academic qualifications of the applicant.

The selection criteria are devised to choose a student body with high standards of scholarship and personal goals and a willingness to provide community service.

Each candidate for admission must present an academic transcript from a secondary school. The transcript must show at least 12 academic units (a unit is one year's study in one subject). At least 4 years of English, 2 years of algebra, 1 year of geometry, 2 years of laboratory science, and 1 year of history are recommended for admission. Performance during high school is the best predictor of success in college. Therefore, great emphasis is placed upon the high school record. Grade trends can be very important.

Applicants must submit a recommendation from their high school counselor and scores from the SAT I or ACT. Students are also required to submit a personal essay.

Transfer students must present both high school and college transcripts. Transfer applicants must be in good standing with the college last attended and should also have a minimum 2.75 cumulative grade point average. At least one school year in residence at Warren Wilson is required for a transfer student to be eligible for a degree from Warren Wilson College.

There is no fee to apply for admission to Warren Wilson College.

Application and Information

An application form and further information may be obtained by contacting:

Office of Admission
Warren Wilson College
701 Warren Wilson Road
Asheville, North Carolina 28815-9000
Telephone: 800-934-3536 (toll-free)
E-mail: admit@warren-wilson.edu
World Wide Web: http://www.warren-wilson.edu

Warren Wilson College's Valley Home.

WARTBURG COLLEGE

WAVERLY, IOWA

The College

Founded in 1852 by German Lutheran immigrants, Wartburg is a college of the Evangelical Lutheran Church in America. Wartburg challenges and nurtures students for lives of leadership and service as a spirited expression of their faith and learning. The College's name honors the Wartburg Castle, a landmark in Eisenach, Germany, where Martin Luther sought refuge during the stormy days of the Reformation. The College and the castle have close ties, and the communities of Waverly and Eisenach are sister cities.

Wartburg enrolls 1,775 students from twenty-three states and thirty-two countries. Eighty-five percent of Wartburg's first-year students graduated in the top half of their high school class. The average ACT score for first-year students is 23.7. The campus is 85 percent residential. Living accommodations include traditional residence halls; small manor units; 4-, 6-, and 8-person suites; and town house–style apartments for senior students.

Wartburg students are active in more than 100 campus organizations, including honor societies, interest groups, and department-related clubs. The Wartburg Choir, Castle Singers, and Wind Ensemble make annual concert tours in the United States and travel abroad every third year during the College's one-month May Term. The annual Christmas with Wartburg production attracts more than 6,500 people to performances in Waverly, Cedar Falls, and Des Moines, Iowa. The Wartburg Community Symphony presents a five-concert season. Student publications include a weekly newspaper, a daily information bulletin, a yearbook, and a literary magazine. Students also manage a campus radio station, operate and produce programs for the College's local cable television access channel, and manage the city of Waverly's local channel. The Artist Series brings renowned performing artists to the campus, and a convocation series presents lectures by nationally and internationally recognized speakers. The Art Gallery features touring exhibitions and the work of prominent regional artists. Wartburg is a member of Division III of the National Collegiate Athletic Association. Its nineteen (ten men's, nine women's) athletic teams compete in the Iowa Intercollegiate Athletic Conference and regularly earn conference championships and national rankings. The Physical Education Center provides recreational facilities that include an indoor track, handball and racquetball courts, a weight room, a sauna, a cardiovascular room, and an area that accommodates four basketball courts or five tennis courts. Walston-Hoover Stadium opened in 2001 with seating for 4,000 fans, a lighted FieldTurf football field, and an eight-lane all-weather track. Athletic facilities also include two new soccer fields and a throwing venue for track and field.

Wartburg welcomes students of all faiths and offers many avenues for worship, study, fellowship, service, and outreach. A chapel serves as a center for worship and a home for the College's active campus ministry program. Chapel services are scheduled three times a week, and a midweek Eucharist and Sunday morning service provide a variety of worship formats.

The College is accredited by the Higher Learning Commission of the North Central Association of Colleges and Schools. Individual programs are accredited by the National Council for the Accreditation of Teacher Education, the Council on Social Work Education, the National Association of Schools of Music, and the American Music Therapy Association.

Location

Waverly, a northeast Iowa community of 10,000 residents, is recognized statewide for its progressive businesses and industries. Its quiet neighborhoods, low crime rate, clean air, and friendly atmosphere contribute to a high quality of life. Scenic parks along the Cedar River, shopping areas, restaurants, a hospital, medical clinics, dental offices, and many churches are within walking distance. Students find part-time jobs and internships in Waverly, and local residents attend campus events and support College programs. The Waterloo–Cedar Falls metropolitan area (population 128,000) is 20 minutes from Waverly.

Majors and Degrees

The heart of education at Wartburg College is a four-year liberal arts curriculum. The Bachelor of Arts degree signifies study in the liberal arts with a concentration of courses in a major. The Bachelor of Music degree adds an extended concentration of work in musical performance. The Bachelor of Music Education degree prepares students to teach music or major in music therapy.

Departmental majors are offered in accounting, applied music, art, biochemistry, biology, business administration (finance, international business, management, marketing, and sports management), chemistry, church music, communication arts (electronic media, print media, public relations), communication design, communication studies (speech and theater), computer information systems, computer science, economics, education (Christian day school, early childhood, elementary, and secondary), engineering science, English, fitness management, French, French studies, German, German studies, history, international relations, mathematics, music education (instrumental or vocal), music performance, music therapy, philosophy, physical education, physics, political science, psychology, religion (camping ministry, parish education, urban ministry, and youth and family ministry), social work, sociology, Spanish, Spanish studies, and writing.

Minors are offered in most academic departments and in four interdisciplinary programs: environmental studies, intercultural certification, leadership certification, and women's studies.

Wartburg offers cooperative programs and preprofessional advisement in dentistry, engineering, law, medical technology, medicine, nursing, occupational therapy, optometry, pharmacy, physical therapy, and veterinary medicine.

Wartburg is the only private college in Iowa offering a major in music therapy.

Academic Programs

Academic studies are divided into three relatively equal parts. The Wartburg Plan of Essential Education comprises one third of the classwork and is designed to create liberally educated, ethically minded citizens for the twenty-first century. Essential Education courses emphasize thinking strategies, reasoning skills, fundamental literacies, faith and reflection, health and wellness, and a capstone course that addresses ethical issues in the student's academic major. The second third of work is devoted to a major field of study, consisting of a prescribed group of courses that offer depth of knowledge in a discipline. The final third consists of elective courses, which students may choose from any academic area.

The College's 4-4-1 calendar culminates in the one-month May Term, when students concentrate on one course. May Term classes travel within Iowa, across the country, and abroad.

The Pathways Center coordinates academic advising and support services, providing a one-stop resource for guiding students through college and beyond. Services include academic advising, career services, counseling services, first-year programming, senior-year experience, supplemental instruction, testing services, and the writing/reading/speaking laboratory. A special Exploring Majors program is available to students who have not settled on a major. Wartburg consistently places 95 percent or more of each year's graduating class in jobs or graduate school within seven months of graduation.

Wartburg encourages and fosters academic excellence through close faculty-student relationships and an integrated approach that combines the liberal arts with leadership education, global and multicultural studies, a focus on ethics, and opportunities for service and hands-on learning. The student-faculty ratio is 14:1.

The College recognizes credit through Advanced Placement examinations, the College-Level Examination Program, DANTES, Departmental Challenge Examinations, and work at other institutions. It also awards credit for experiential learning.

Off-Campus Programs

Wartburg West in Denver, Colorado, places students in internships or field experiences related to their majors or in community service organizations. They also take academic courses dealing with religion and urban issues. The Washington Center Program allows students to participate in an academic internship program in Washington, D.C. International exchange programs with Bonn University and Jena University in Germany and International Christian University in Japan enable students to study abroad. French, German, and Spanish majors spend significant time studying abroad. Through the Venture Education Program, cultural immersion experiences are available in Australia, China, England, France, Germany, Ghana, Guyana, Israel/Palestine, Jamaica, Mexico, Spain, and Tanzania. Academic travel and on-site course work are offered each May Term, and students may enroll in internships during any term.

Academic Facilities

Wartburg doubled its science facilities in 2004 with the opening of a new Science Center that houses outstanding science, mathematics, and physics programs. An expansive new Student Center provides facilities for campus dining, student organizations, and student services, as well as a multipurpose performance space for campus programming. The Vogel Library is designed to accommodate all types of learning from individual research to group projects and faculty-student interaction. It houses books, periodicals, and reference materials as well as extensive electronic resources. Librarians teach courses in information literacy as part of the Wartburg Plan of Essential Education. The Classroom Technology Center is the home for the social sciences department and several technology-enhanced classrooms. Students have access to more than 400 Macintosh and PC-compatible microcomputers in open-access and departmental computing clusters throughout the campus. Classrooms and residence halls are connected to the campuswide computer network. The Fine Arts Center provides spacious rehearsal and recital halls, music studios, practice rooms, a music therapy suite, art studios, and an art gallery. Its twenty-one-workstation Presser Music Technology Classroom is equipped with keyboard/synthesizers and Macintosh computers for music theory, composition, and ear training classes. McElroy Communication Arts Center includes a journalism laboratory with Macintosh computers, a television studio with video capabilities, and a television control room equipped with TV production and digital editing equipment. The College radio station has two on-air production studios, digital audio editing, and computer-controlled programming, and broadcasts over the Internet. Whitehouse Business Center has specially designed rooms for accounting, business, marketing, and economics classes.

Costs

For the 2004–05 academic year, tuition is $18,150, room is $2430, board is $2650, and fees are $400, for a total cost of $23,630.

Financial Aid

Wartburg supports the concept of a socially, culturally, and economically diverse student body, believing that contact with others from various backgrounds better prepares students for contemporary life. The College admits applicants on the basis of academic and personal promise, not the ability to pay. More than 97 percent of students receive financial aid in the form of scholarships, grants, loans, and employment. Merit-based academic and music scholarships are awarded to qualified students. The College allocates more than $11 million annually from its own resources for student aid. The application deadline for financial aid is May 1.

Faculty

The 103 full-time and 59 part-time faculty members form a close living-learning community with students and serve as academic advisers. Eighty-three percent of the full-time faculty members hold an earned doctoral degree or the highest degree in their discipline. Wartburg emphasizes good teaching and also provides faculty research and development opportunities. Many faculty members involve students in their research projects. A sabbatical program permits professors to spend a term or a year on a growth project. Endowments support academic chairs in banking and monetary economics, biology, chaplaincy, choral conducting, communication arts, ethics, global and multicultural studies, and leadership.

Student Government

The Student Senate provides a student voice on campus issues. Its 35 members are selected annually. The Senate selects students to serve on a number of faculty-student committees dealing with all aspects of campus life. Senate members represent student interests to the faculty, administration, and Board of Regents.

Admission Requirements

Applicants are considered according to their potential for academic success, based upon high school rank, breadth and depth of previous study, test scores on the ACT or SAT I, an academic recommendation, and a personal interview with an admission representative. The recommended high school background is 4 years of English, 3 years of mathematics (advanced courses preferred), 3 years of science, 2 years of social science, 2 years of foreign language, and 1 year of computer study. Transfer students and international students should contact the Admissions Office to determine any special admission requirements.

Application and Information

A rolling admission policy is used, and applicants may apply at any time. The Wartburg College application for admission, the $20 application fee, one academic recommendation from a teacher, ACT or SAT I scores, and official copies of high school and college transcripts should be sent to the Admissions Office. The application fee is waived for students who make an official campus visit.

Doug Bowman, Dean of Admissions and Financial Aid
Wartburg College
100 Wartburg Boulevard
P.O. Box 1003
Waverly, Iowa 50677-0903
Telephone: 319-352-8264
800-772-2085 (toll-free)
Fax: 319-352-8579

The Vogel Library is designed as a learner's library. The library's espresso coffee shop is a popular gathering spot for students and faculty members.

WASHINGTON & JEFFERSON COLLEGE

WASHINGTON, PENNSYLVANIA

The College

Founded in 1781, Washington & Jefferson College (W&J) is an independent, coeducational, liberal arts college, located in Washington, Pennsylvania. The current enrollment is 1,249 (696 men and 603 women), including representatives from thirty-one states, the District of Columbia, and seven other countries. As the student body is relatively small, students and faculty members are able to maintain close personal relationships both inside and outside the classroom. All students, except married students and those within commuting distance, live in campus housing. W&J is concerned with the full development of each student. Academic pursuits are considered most important, but opportunities to develop socially, culturally, and physically are also abundant.

The College is accredited by the Middle States Association of Colleges and Schools, and its chemistry program is approved by the American Chemical Society. W&J received its Phi Beta Kappa charter in 1937.

Location

Washington, Pennsylvania, is a small, safe, and charming city 30 minutes south of Pittsburgh, a major metropolitan area that offers a wide range of cultural, social, and religious options. Hiking, skiing, camping, kayaking, climbing, and other forms of outdoor recreation are also within easy reach.

Majors and Degrees

Washington & Jefferson College offers the Bachelor of Arts degree in accounting, art, art education, biochemistry, biology, business administration, chemistry, childhood development and education, economics, English, French, German, history, industrial chemistry and management, information technology leadership, international business, mathematics, music, philosophy, physics, political science, psychology, sociology, Spanish, theater, and a thematic (self-designed) degree. Cooperative programs are offered in engineering (3-2) with Case Western Reserve University or Washington University; in law (3-3) with Duquesne University and the University of Pittsburgh; in optometry (3-4) with the Pennsylvania College of Optometry; in podiatric medicine (3-4) with the Pennsylvania College of Podiatry or the Ohio College of Podiatric Medicine; and in pre–physical therapy (3-4) with the Medical College of Pennsylvania and Hahnemann University. Medical Scholars and Early Assurance programs with Temple University School of Medicine and Western Pennsylvania Hospital are also available.

Preprofessional programs are offered in dentistry, elementary and secondary education, entrepreneurial studies, environmental studies, human resource management, law, medicine, optometry, osteopathy, physical therapy, podiatry, and veterinary medicine. Courses leading to secondary school teaching certification are offered in combination with a number of major areas.

Academic Program

The College utilizes a 4-1-4 academic calendar, with the year divided into three distinct terms: fall (September through December), intersession (January), and spring (February through May). During the January Intersession, students may elect to remain on campus and take a course, attend another college, study abroad, develop an independent study project, or intern in a career area. The 4-1-4 also denotes the number of courses that a student carries throughout the year: four courses are taken in both the fall and spring terms, and one is taken during intersession.

Academic freedom and individual consideration characterize the curriculum at W&J. Students have time to explore new fields and interests before declaring their major, which they must do by their junior year. Students must complete a core curriculum and take freshman English, two courses in physical education, and the Freshman Forum. To satisfy major requirements, a minimum of eight to ten courses must be taken in the major field. Students may double major.

Advising is an important component of a W&J education. Faculty advisers and student mentors are assigned to all entering freshmen. Later, students select their academic advisers from the faculty members in their major departments. Advising is available for those who are undecided about a major. Those with a preprofessional interest receive guidance through the various committees and faculty members who are able to provide information concerning career possibilities, graduate school, and academic course work.

Off-Campus Programs

Students may take advantage of the Junior Year Abroad program, or they may study in another country during the January intersession. Recently, W&J students have studied in London, Paris, Australia, Egypt, Germany, Greece, Holland, Italy, Japan, Kenya, Mexico, the People's Republic of China, Russia, and Spain. W&J also has cooperative arrangements with institutions in Colombia, Germany, and Russia. The College sponsors courses in the United States in such diverse areas as New York City, Hawaii, Texas, and the Florida Everglades. Qualified students may participate in the Washington Semester at American University in Washington, D.C., during which they work with students from across the country, interview experts in shaping legislative policy, and attend seminars with top government officials.

Academic Facilities

Washington & Jefferson College contains a blend of historic and modern buildings. John McMillan Hall is one of the nation's oldest educational buildings, and the newest buildings incorporate state-of-the-art technology. Well-lit and safe, the campus is designed so that all facilities are within easy walking distance. The library, dining halls, and athletic facilities have been recently renovated. Approximately 350 computers reside in academic areas around campus, with a student-to-computer ratio of 3:1. The $30-million Vilar Technology Center, scheduled to open in fall 2003, will bring 200 additional computers to campus. The campus network is accessible from students' rooms and off campus. In addition, a 54-acre biological field station, containing more than 100 different tree species, is available for research and course instruction.

Research facilities and equipment include a computer-based language laboratory, a full range of spectrometers, an isolator laboratory, an X-ray diffraction unit, a digital calorimeter, gas chromatography equipment, a neutron howitzer, an analog computer, a differential thermoanalyzer, an atomic absorption unit, a Gauss polygraph, a refrigerated centrifuge, a UV-visible flame spectrophotometer, Kirlian photography equipment used in the study of ESP, and a neuropsychology laboratory with stereotaxic equipment and a polygraph.

Costs

For 2003–04, the total cost of an academic year at W&J was $29,570, with $22,860 allotted for tuition, $3440 for room, $2870 for board, and a $400 student service and activity fee. All fees are subject to change annually.

Financial Aid

Approximately 70 percent of W&J's student body receives some type of aid, such as a grant, loan, or work-study award. Aid is based on financial need, demonstrated ability, and the contribution the student will be able to make to the College community. Federal funds are available through the Federal Pell Grant, Federal Perkins Loan, Federal Stafford Student Loan, and Federal Work-Study programs. College funds awarded can include grants, GATE loans, and non-need-based employment. Aid is offered for a one-year period but is renewable as long as the student meets annual application deadlines, maintains good academic standing, and demonstrates financial need. Veterans are eligible for assistance under the G.I. bill. A tuition payment plan is available through American Management Services (AMS).

Each year, the College rewards distinguished academic performance by offering merit scholarships to selected full-time members of the entering freshman class. Scholarships vary, based on the candidate's level of achievement. Merit awards typically range from $10,000 to $80,000 over four years and are renewed annually, subject to academic performance. In addition, Alumni Awards are made to the sons or daughters of W&J graduates. Eagle Scholarships are given to selected participants in the Entreprenuerial Studies Program. Recipients must possess strong entrepreneurial abilities and vision as well as academic excellence. Students who are qualified for two merit scholarships receive the higher of the two awards.

All applicants for financial aid must file a Free Application for Federal Student Aid (FAFSA). The priority filing date for prospective freshmen is February 15. For further information, students should contact the Office of Financial Aid.

Faculty

W&J has 100 full-time faculty members; the student-faculty ratio is 12:1. Ninety-three percent of the full-time faculty members hold a doctorate or appropriate terminal degrees, and their primary concerns are their students and teaching.

Student Government

Student government is a strong and vigorous organization at W&J. Students are regarded as mature individuals capable of governing themselves while furthering the best interests of the College community. Elected officials lead the student body in campus life programs, including the coordination of activities, legislation, student regulations, and distribution of funds to the various student groups.

Admission Requirements

The breadth and depth of academic background, extracurricular interests and achievements, personal character, and recommendations are evaluated together with standardized test scores to determine a student's qualifications for admission. Applicants must complete at least 15 units of college-preparatory courses at an accredited secondary school, including 3 units of college-preparatory English, 3 units of college-preparatory mathematics, 2 units of the same foreign language, and 1 unit of history, social science, or natural science.

Early admission is available for qualified high school students who wish to begin college after their junior year. Academically qualified international students are encouraged to apply and should submit TOEFL scores if English is not their native language.

A personal interview, while not required, is strongly recommended. Applicants should contact the Office of Admission to schedule an interview or campus visit. Students who are unable to visit the College may arrange an interview with a traveling College representative or an alumni admission representative in their area.

Washington & Jefferson College does not discriminate in its educational programs, activities, or employment on the basis of race, color, religion, sex, age, disability, national origin, or any other legally protected status. Inquiries may be directed to the Affirmative Action Officer, Washington & Jefferson College, 60 South Lincoln Street, Washington, Pennsylvania 15301.

Application and Information

For application materials and additional information about W&J, students should contact the Office of Admission or go to the College's Web site (listed below). W&J also accepts the Common Application. In addition, applicants should request that their SAT I or ACT scores, high school transcripts, and letters of recommendation be sent to the College. Transfer students are required to submit an official high school transcript, official transcripts from all colleges previously attended, and a Transfer Student Clearance Form. A nonrefundable application fee of $25 must accompany the application for admission. The fee is waived for students who visit the campus or apply online. Students should apply by December 1 for early decision, January 15 for early action, or March 1 for regular decision.

For further information, students should contact:

Office of Admission
Washington & Jefferson College
60 South Lincoln Street
Washington, Pennsylvania 15301
Telephone: 724-223-6025
888-W-AND-JAY (toll-free)
Fax: 724-223-6534
E-mail: admission@washjeff.edu
World Wide Web: http://www.washjeff.edu

WASHINGTON COLLEGE

CHESTERTOWN, MARYLAND

The College

Founded in 1782, Washington College is the tenth-oldest college in the United States. George Washington, for whom the College was named, was an early benefactor and member of the College's Board of Visitors and Governors. Today, the College is one of the few nationally recognized selective liberal arts institutions with an enrollment of fewer than 1,300 students. The intimacy of a small-college environment, the tradition of a challenging liberal arts curriculum, and the relaxed informality characteristic of the Chesapeake Bay region continue to exert their influence on the College and all who come to it.

The current enrollment is 1,300 men and women. Although most students come from the Northeast, international students and students from other regions of the country are enrolled in numbers sufficient to add geographic diversity to the student body. Eighty percent of all students live in residences located on the 120-acre campus; special interest housing is available for students interested in science, foreign languages, international studies, creative arts, and Greek organizations.

The College enjoys a high participation rate in intramural sports, in the performing arts, and in student publications, community service clubs, recreational activities, and social organizations. The Division III intercollegiate program offers fifteen varsity sports, including baseball, basketball, lacrosse, rowing, soccer, swimming, and tennis for men and basketball, field hockey, lacrosse, rowing, sailing, softball, swimming, tennis, and volleyball for women.

Location

Chestertown, a community of 4,000 people, is a popular port-of-call for Chesapeake Bay boaters, outdoors enthusiasts, and tourists on day trips from nearby Philadelphia, Baltimore, and Washington, D.C. The center of this eighteenth-century river town, with its historic district, shops, and restaurants, is a 5-minute walk from campus. The "town-gown" relationship is excellent.

Majors and Degrees

The Bachelor of Arts is awarded in American studies, anthropology, art, business management, drama, economics, English, environmental studies, French, German, history, humanities, international studies, mathematics, music, philosophy, political science, psychology, sociology, and Spanish. The Bachelor of Science is awarded in biology, chemistry, physics, and psychology.

Washington College also offers certification programs in elementary and secondary education. Preprofessional programs in dentistry, medicine, or veterinary medicine may be developed within a major in the natural sciences; a preprofessional program in law is also available. A 3-2 dual-degree program in engineering with the University of Maryland and a 3-2 dual-degree program in nursing with Johns Hopkins University are also offered.

Academic Program

The College's four-course plan is intended to broaden and deepen a student's education by providing for the intensive study of a limited number of subjects and by encouraging individual responsibility for learning. General education requirements include two freshman seminars and ten semester courses chosen from the following categories: social science, natural science, humanities, fine arts, quantitative studies, and foreign language. Candidates for a degree must satisfactorily complete thirty-two semester courses and must fulfill the senior obligation (for example, a comprehensive examination or thesis).

Washington College offers a nationally renowned creative writing program and awards the prestigious Sophie Kerr Prize every year to the graduating senior who shows the most promise for a career in literary endeavors.

Successful scores (4 or 5) on Advanced Placement examinations can provide exemption from distribution requirements. With the aid of a faculty adviser, students can construct their own major fields of study in some areas or pursue independent study for course credit.

Off-Campus Programs

Students receive academic credit for a variety of off-campus programs. A study abroad program is offered at twenty-five sites worldwide, including sites in England, France, Spain, Germany, Scotland, Mexico, and Japan. In addition, subject to faculty approval, students can spend a year abroad at a university of their choice. The College participates in the Washington Semester at American University. Political science majors can also intern with the Maryland State Legislature in Annapolis, the state's capital. A clinical practicum in psychology and field experience in social work are also available.

Academic Facilities

The library, which has 200,000 volumes, more than 800 current periodical subscriptions, and extensive microfilm holdings, benefits from an efficient interlibrary loan system and an online card catalog. Well-equipped science laboratories allow for independent research, and an extensive microcomputer network are readily available to interested students. The Gibson Fine Arts Center houses a 600-seat theater/auditorium that has complete facilities for study and performance in music and drama. Full facilities for art majors are located in the Constance S. Larrabee Creative Art Center.

Costs

Tuition for 2003–04 was $24,240 and room and board were $5740, making a total of $29,980. Expenses, including books and transportation, usually range from $600 to $1000 annually.

Financial Aid

Washington College offers financial assistance to approximately 85 percent of its student body. Awards are based on need and academic performance. Financial aid includes scholarships, grants, loans, and jobs. The College participates in the Federal Perkins Loan Program, the Federal Stafford Student Loan Program, and the Federal Work-Study program. Federal Pell Grants and Federal Supplemental Educational Opportunity Grants are applicable to Washington College. In addition, financial assistance from the Maryland scholarship program and other state programs can be applied to expenses at the College.

Members of the National Honor Society and Cum Laude Society who are admitted to Washington College are awarded $40,000 academic scholarships ($10,000 annually for four years). Other academic scholarships ranging in value from $5000 to $17,500 are offered without regard to financial need.

To be eligible for financial assistance, applicants should file the FAFSA by February 15. An application for admission, with all supporting credentials, should be received by February 15 to establish eligibility. Students interested in Federal Pell Grant assistance or in-state scholarship programs must apply directly to the program concerned.

Faculty

Ninety-five percent of the more than 90 full-time faculty members hold either a doctoral degree or a terminal degree in their discipline. Faculty members engage in professional research and publication but emphasize teaching. Along with performing their classroom duties, faculty members serve as advisers to individuals and student groups. No classes are taught by graduate assistants. Faculty participation in student and College affairs reflects the strong sense of community that characterizes Washington College.

Student Government

The Student Government Association (SGA) is a significant part of the College community. In addition to coordinating social activities, the SGA plays an active role in academic affairs. Students elected by the SGA are voting members of College committees and attend faculty and board meetings.

Admission Requirements

High school students should complete a college-preparatory program, including a minimum of 4 years of English, 4 of social studies, 3 of mathematics, 3 of science, and 2 of a foreign language. SAT I or ACT scores and one teacher recommendation are also required. While interviews are not usually required for admission, interested students are strongly encouraged to visit the campus. Both interviews and campus tours are available by appointment on weekdays throughout the year and on selected Saturdays during the fall semester.

Members of the College admission staff visit high schools throughout the United States, seeking above-average students with solid academic backgrounds. There are no quotas based on sex, and there are no religious, geographic, or ethnic restrictions. Indeed, the College seeks the most diverse student body possible, realizing that such diversity is an important aspect of the academic community.

Transfer students are accepted with or without the A.A. degree, and applicants with above-average records are encouraged to apply.

Application and Information

The application, a $40 fee, the high school transcript (and college transcript, for transfer applicants), scores on the SAT I or ACT, and two teacher recommendations are required. Applications for early decision must be received by November 15, and candidates are notified of the admission decision by December 15. For regular admission, forms must be submitted prior to February 15. Regular-decision candidates are notified of the admission decision on a rolling basis between January 15 and April 1. Applicants for financial assistance must complete the procedures outlined under Financial Aid.

Further information and application forms are available from:

Office of Admissions
Washington College
300 Washington Avenue
Chestertown, Maryland 21620-1197
Telephone: 410-778-7700
800-422-1782 (toll-free)
E-mail: adm.off@washcoll.edu
World Wide Web: http://www.washcoll.edu

Casey Academic Center at Washington College.

WAYNESBURG COLLEGE

WAYNESBURG, PENNSYLVANIA

The College

Waynesburg is a private, liberal arts, Christian college affiliated with the Presbyterian Church (U.S.A.) and a member of the Council for Christian Colleges and Universities. The coeducational College serves more than 1,200 undergraduate students on a picturesque campus 1 hour south of the city of Pittsburgh. The College also serves about 800 adult students in a graduate and professional studies program. The College's adult centers are located throughout the Pittsburgh region in Monroeville, Southpointe, and Wexford. Waynesburg College offers students the broad knowledge that is required for global citizenship, a structured approach to personal and social development, and leadership opportunities in service to others.

The College's Service Learning Project allows students to earn college credit and experience relationships with others beyond the classroom as they develop a sense of social responsibility and community service. Waynesburg College is the only institution in Pennsylvania to host the Bonner Scholars Program (http://www.bonner.org/campus/bonnerscholars.htm), a leadership-through-service opportunity funded by the Bonner Foundation of Princeton, New Jersey. High schools students who are actively involved in community service are able to apply for the Bonner Scholars Program, which provides scholarship aid to students who commit to weekly volunteer service. The Service Learning Project also offers students many opportunities to participate in intensive mission experiences both in the United States and around the world. Recent international service projects have taken place in Australia, Austria, Haiti, Singapore, and South Africa.

Other specialized programs at the College include the Mentor Program, which provides students the opportunity to connect with alumni who work in a student's major, and the Electronic Portfolio, which is a personal electronic chronicle of students' College experiences that are shared with employers.

The Waynesburg College campus features such buildings as the Stover Campus Center for student activities, a Fine Arts Center, a Performing Arts Center, Marisa Fieldhouse, and new residence halls that have private baths. Student publications, such as the newspaper, yearbook, and poetry magazine, provide outlets for aspiring writers, journalists, and those planning futures in the communications industry. Student groups include a Christian drama troupe, Student Senate, intramurals, a marching band, cheerleaders, a pep band, an ensemble, a drama group, and the Lamplighters (a mixed chorus). Special campus events are planned through the Guest Lecture Series, the Christ and Culture Lecture Series, the Performing Arts Series, the Benedum Fine Arts Center Gallery, and Celebrating the Arts. The Student Activities Board sponsors concerts, dances, comedy clubs, and various regional excursions. In addition, students may become involved in organizations such as Leadership Scholars, the Black Student Union, the Commuting Student, the student chapter of Habitat for Humanity, the Christian Fellowship, the Newman Club, the Fellowship of Christian Athletes, and countless departmental clubs and honorary/professional societies.

For students interested in media, the College communication department operates a community-access television channel where students, no matter what their major, can hold staff positions. Additionally, the remote television production operation recently went state of the art with the purchase of a custom-built television production truck. The truck is a 24-foot box with countertops, carpeting, air conditioning, and new equipment, which allows students to learn television production in a professional environment. Other media opportunities are available at the student-operated radio station.

Students who want to participate in sports find that the College offers intercollegiate varsity sports for men and women. Men compete in baseball, basketball, cross-country, football, golf, soccer, tennis, and wrestling. Women compete in basketball, cross-country, golf, soccer, softball, tennis, and volleyball. Club sports are offered in men's volleyball and track and women's track. In addition, Waynesburg offers an extensive intramural program. Skiing and snowboarding are popular winter sports, and seven resorts are within an hour of Waynesburg. Students may also take an active part in Southwestern Pennsylvania's hiking, bicycling, and canoeing opportunities.

At the graduate level, the College offers degree programs such as Master of Business Administration (M.B.A.), Master of Education (M.Ed.), Master of Science in Nursing (M.S.N.), a combined M.S.N./M.B.A., and other programs.

Location

The College's main campus is 50 miles south of Pittsburgh, in the community of Waynesburg, which has a population of 12,000. The campus, just two blocks from the Waynesburg business district, is adjacent to a park with more than 12 acres of lawn and trees. The adult learning centers are located throughout the Pittsburgh area in Monroeville, Southpointe, and Wexford.

Majors and Degrees

Students can choose their major from more than forty areas of study, and preprofessional training is given in dentistry, law, medicine, ministerial studies, physical therapy, professional psychology, and veterinary medicine. The Bachelor of Arts (B.A.) degree is offered in the arts, art administration, communication (advertising, digital media, electronic media, journalism, and sports broadcasting/sports information), criminal justice administration, education, English (literature, professional writing), forensic accounting, history, human services, international studies, psychology, and social science. The Bachelor of Science (B.S.) degree is available in athletic training, biology, business information science, chemistry, computer forensics, computer science, environmental science, exercise science, forensic chemistry, forensic science, human services, information technology, marine biology (3-1 program with Florida Institute of Technology), and mathematics. The Bachelor of Science in Nursing (B.S.N.) degree is offered in nursing. The Bachelor of Science in Business Administration (B.S.B.A.) degree is offered in accounting, finance, management, marketing, small business management, and sports management. Through the B.S. in education, students may earn certification in secondary and elementary education or special education. The prelaw program is a 3-3 program in conjunction with Duquesne University School of Law.

Waynesburg College, in conjunction with several cooperating university schools of engineering, offers various 3-2 engineering programs. Upon successful completion of a five-year program, the student receives a B.S. in engineering from the cooperating university and a B.S. from Waynesburg College.

The Associate in Science (A.S.) degree in business administration is offered in a two-year course of study with concentrations in accounting, finance, management, and marketing. An Associate in Arts (A.A.) degree in general studies and an A.S. in information technology are also offered.

The College offers accelerated programs in nursing (an RN to B.S.N. program and an eighteen-month second-degree B.S.N.). An accelerated business degree program is also offered, leading to the B.S. in Business Administration. The programs are designed for adult students with previous college credit and work experience.

Academic Programs

All candidates for a baccalaureate degree complete a core of liberal arts courses, which provides them with a broad background in the sciences, humanities, and arts. This core curriculum offers students a general approach, flexibility in terms of course selection, and time for the pursuit of special interests. In all major fields, at least 124 semester hours of work are required to obtain a baccalaureate degree. In addition, students are required to complete 30 hours of volunteer service before graduation. All candidates for the associate degree must complete a total of 60 semester hours of work.

Students may elect to take a total of 12 semester hours on a pass/fail basis in areas other than their major or a correlated field.

The College offers students the opportunity to earn undergraduate credit through the College Level Examination Program (CLEP). In addition, the College grants academic credit and/or advanced placement to students who have scored 3 or above on the Advanced Placement tests of the College Board.

Waynesburg College offers several summer sessions, as well as evening and summer-evening classes. The regular academic year is divided into two semesters, with a four-week break (mid-December to January) between terms.

Off-Campus Programs

Internships are available in the areas of accounting, art, biology, business, chemistry, child development, communications, computer science, criminal justice, economics, English, finance, history, mathematics, music, philosophy, political science, psychology, religion, sociology, and theater.

Several opportunities for study abroad in Austria, China, Costa Rica, Egypt, England, Ireland, Israel, Kenya, Korea, Russia, Singapore, and the Ukraine are available for interested students. One such opportunity, the Vira I. Heinz Study Travel Award, is awarded annually for summer travel and study to a woman who has completed her junior year at the College.

Academic Facilities

The 100,000-volume Eberly Library provides online access to major university and public libraries, in addition to electronic cataloging of its own collection. Online access is also provided to abstracts and full-text versions of many periodicals. Every student receives an e-mail account to access the resources of both the campus network and the Internet in classrooms, labs, and resident halls. All students are encouraged to develop an electronic portfolio containing the best "artifacts" from their college experience. Labs are open during convenient hours in all classroom buildings. Lab assistants are available to help students with a variety of software applications for PCs or Macintoshes. As a leader in distance learning, the College maintains several videoconference rooms that connect classes on campus to classes around the region.

Costs

For the 2004–05 academic year, tuition is $14,200. The activity fee for student organizations, publications, and athletic events is $340. The estimated annual cost for students who do not live on campus is $14,540. Room and board costs are $5800 per year. The estimated cost for resident students who live on campus is $20,340. These figures do not include travel, books, and incidental expenses.

Financial Aid

Waynesburg College strives to make its education affordable for all students. More than 89 percent of the students attending the College during the 2003-04 academic year received some form of financial assistance. All students are encouraged to apply for financial aid even if they feel they may be ineligible. The College offers assistance/awards from federal, state, private, and College sources. Assistance may include scholarships, grants, work-study employment, and/or loans. Most financial aid awards are based upon financial need, which is calculated by subtracting the expected family contribution (EFC) from the cost of education. The EFC is calculated by the U.S. Department of Education, which uses the information that the family provides on the federal need-analysis application. To apply for any form of aid, students must complete the Free Application for Federal Student Aid (FAFSA). For financial aid forms and information, students should contact the Financial Aid Office at 724-852-3208.

The College awards several honor scholarships for achievement and potential. The Waynesburg College Ohio Honors Scholarship, which pays full-tuition, room, and board, is given annually to two Ohio high school students interested in a career in the sciences or mathematics. The A.B. Miller Scholarship is awarded to students with a minimum 3.75 cumulative high school GPA and with 1200 or higher on the SAT I or 27 or higher on the ACT. This scholarship may also be awarded to class valedictorians or salutatorians. The Presidential Honor Scholarship is a $4500 annual award. This award requires a high school GPA of 3.75. The Waynesburg Honor Scholarship is a $3000 annual award, and it requires an overall average of 3.5. All honor scholarships are renewable for up to four years if the student maintains the required grade point average. The Waynesburg College Alumni Council Scholarship is a $1000 annual award, and the Waynesburg College Leadership Award is a $1000 to $2000 annual award. The Bonner Scholars Program, which is supported by the Corella and Bertram F. Bonner Foundation, Inc., provides annual awards of $2100 to students who have demonstrated a previous commitment and indicate a future commitment to community service. Many departments offer $2000 merit scholarships.

Faculty

More than 60 percent of the faculty have earned doctoral degrees. Each faculty member has demonstrated that teaching is his or her primary concern. At the same time, many faculty members have written scholarly articles and taken part in research and study projects. The student-faculty ratio is 16:1.

Student Government

The Student Senate consists of 7 officers elected by the student body. The president of the Student Senate also appoints student representatives to all major College committees, including a representative to the monthly faculty meetings.

Admission Requirements

In judging the qualifications of applicants, the Committee on Admissions adheres to the following requirements: graduation from an accredited high school, satisfactory grade point average and class rank in high school, and ACT or SAT I scores.

Students desiring to transfer to Waynesburg College should submit a formal application for admission and official high school and college transcripts to the Director of Admissions. Waynesburg welcomes transfer applications, and the evaluation program is flexible. Each course is evaluated individually, and all courses for which students have earned a grade of C or above may be accepted for transfer from a regionally accredited institution if they are similar to those courses offered at Waynesburg. Each year, transfer applicants are accepted from community and junior colleges, as well as from other four-year institutions.

Waynesburg College admits students of any race, color, sex, religion, or national or ethnic origin, does not discriminate on the basis of sex in the educational programs or activities that it operates, and is in compliance with Title IX of the Education Amendments of 1972. In compliance with Section 504 of the Rehabilitation Act of 1973, Waynesburg College does not discriminate on the basis of handicap in admission or access to its programs or activities.

Application and Information

Waynesburg operates on a rolling admission program and admits qualified applicants as soon as their application is complete. An enrollment deposit ($150 for resident students, $75 for commuting students) is required on the date stipulated in the acceptance letter. One half of this deposit is refunded if the College is notified of withdrawal according to the schedule published in the *Waynesburg College Catalogue.*

The Admissions Office welcomes telephone calls and campus visits from 8:30 a.m. to 4:30 p.m., Monday through Friday. Saturday morning interviews are available by appointment. College literature, such as catalogs, application forms, and financial aid information, may be obtained by contacting:

Director of Admissions
Waynesburg College
Waynesburg, Pennsylvania 15370
Telephone: 724-852-3248
800-225-7393 (toll-free)
E-mail: admissions@waynesburg.edu
World Wide Web: http://waynesburg.edu/

WEBBER INTERNATIONAL UNIVERSITY

BABSON PARK, FLORIDA

The University

Webber International University was founded in 1927 by Roger Babson, who was an internationally known economist in the early 1900s. The four-year independent coeducational university is located on a beautiful 110-acre campus along the shoreline of Lake Caloosa, 45 minutes from Disney World, Cypress Gardens, and many other attractions. Webber is accredited by the Southern Association of Colleges and Schools. Built on a strong tradition that sets it apart, the University exemplifies integrity, high standards, and achievement. Webber International University provides an environment that encourages success through academic excellence and hard work. About 313 men and 213 women are enrolled as undergraduates at Webber. Seventy percent of them are from Florida; the other 30 percent represent twenty-one states and twenty-eight different countries.

Webber International University's off-campus internship programs provide a real-world business environment for Webber students. Field trips also supplement students' business education.

Webber International University also offers a Master of Business Administration (M.B.A.) program with options in management, accounting, and sport management.

The University offers intercollegiate sports in baseball, basketball, cross-country, football, golf, soccer, tennis, and track and field for men and in basketball, cheerleading, cross-country, golf, soccer, softball, tennis, track and field, and volleyball for women. Intramural athletics are also available for all students. The University's physical education complex includes two gymnasiums, a fitness room, racquetball courts, a soccer field, a junior Olympic-size swimming pool, beach volleyball court, and tennis courts. Webber students also enjoy lakeside activities such as beach volleyball, canoeing, fishing, and kayaking. Among the wide variety of social organizations and clubs are Phi Beta Lambda, a student government association, an international club, Webber ambassadors, Eta Sigma Delta and the Society of Hosteurs, a marketing club, a tourism society, FCA, a sport management club, SIFE, and athletic boosters. These groups and others help to sponsor the various social functions at Webber. The University also offers a Bachelor of Science degree in general business studies.

Location

The town of Babson Park, a very small rural residential community, is located in the heart of Florida's citrus country near a chain of freshwater lakes. The area has a relaxed and friendly atmosphere. Babson Park is conveniently near many major recreational facilities and national tourist attractions in central Florida.

Majors and Degrees

Webber International University offers bachelor's and associate degrees in business administration, with nine different majors: accounting, computer information systems management, finance, global business, hospitality business management, management, marketing, pre-law, and sport management. The University also offers a bachelor of science degree in general business studies.

Academic Program

The school operates on the semester system with two 15-week semesters, a six-week Summer Term A, and a six-week Summer Term B. The University requires the completion of 60 credit hours for the Associate of Science degree and 120 credit hours for the Bachelor of Science degree with a minimum grade point average of 2.0. The average course load is 15 hours per semester. Students in the Bachelor of Science degree program are required to complete approximately 30 hours in the major, 36 hours in the business core, 36 hours in the general education core, and 18 hours of tailored electives. Students in the Associate of Science degree program are required to complete 27 hours in the business core, 18 hours in the general education core, and 15 hours in the major and tailored elective.

The Bachelor of Science degree in general business studies requires the completion of 45 hours in the general business studies core, 39 hours in the general education core, and 36 hours of tailored electives.

All students must complete 30 of the last 33 hours at Webber International University to receive a degree. Credit is awarded for successful scores on Advanced Placement (AP) and College-Level Examination Program (CLEP) general tests.

Off-Campus Programs

A study-abroad program for students working toward a bachelor's degree is offered for one or two semesters in Barcelona, Spain, or Paris, France.

The hospitality and marketing departments have arrangements for internship programs with major hotels and restaurants in the Orlando area and major retail stores, both in-state and out-of-state.

The finance department places student interns in various financial institutions and financial departments of local corporations.

Other off-campus experiences include elective courses in which students observe and analyze business operations and functions of local companies and present their findings in a project format comparable to a professional business consultant's.

The departmental field trip is an opportunity for students in all ten majors to travel abroad during a summer semester and to discover business techniques in an international environment.

Academic Facilities

The Roger Babson Learning Center, located in the central part of the campus, is a modern and comprehensive business library facility. The collection currently contains about 35,500 volumes, an assortment of audiovisual materials, and a CD-ROM computer program for reference materials. The library houses computers for student use. Several research databases are available for student access.

The computer resources centers are data processing centers and teaching facilities whose microcomputers offer the latest modern technology for developing student excellence in business, communication, and creativity.

Costs

In 2003–04, the annual fee, which includes tuition, room and board, and the student activities fee, was $17,220. For commuting students, the annual fee was $11,500. These figures are subject to change. The University estimates that $1200 is adequate for books and supplies. Laboratory fees are additional.

Financial Aid

The Student Financial Aid Department offers students its counsel and assistance in meeting their educational expenses.

Aid is awarded on the basis of an applicant's need, academic performance, and promise. Approximately 80 percent of the students at Webber International University receive financial assistance. To demonstrate need, applicants are required to file the Free Application for Federal Student Aid (FAFSA). Various types of aid, such as scholarships, grants, loans, and Federal Work-Study awards, are used to meet student needs. A limited number of no-need scholarships are available; these awards are based on academic performance, on community and college service, or on athletic ability in basketball, tennis, volleyball, golf, soccer, softball, cross-country, and track and field. Applicants for aid must reapply each year. Webber participates in the Federal Perkins Loan, Federal Supplemental Educational Opportunity Grant, and Federal Work-Study programs. All applicants are expected to apply for any entitlement grant for which they are eligible, such as the Federal Pell Grant; Florida residents must apply for a Florida Student Assistance Grant and the Florida Tuition Voucher Program. Federal Stafford Student Loans are also available. Financial aid applicants should submit their requests and forms before April 1 in order to be eligible for certain financial aid programs.

Faculty

More than 60 percent of Webber's full-time faculty members hold doctoral degrees. The faculty-student ratio is 1:21, and all students are assigned a faculty adviser. All faculty members have posted office hours and are available for consultation and advising. Many of Webber's faculty members have a minimum of five years' actual professional work experience in their area of specialization in addition to their years of classroom teaching. This combination of applied and classroom work experience gives them an unusual ability to relate to the needs and concerns of their students.

Student Government

The Student Government Association, the chief governing body on Webber's campus, is composed of elected student representatives and a faculty adviser and deals with nonacademic areas of student life. The association serves as an advisory and coordinating body for student organizations and involves students in campus policy and actions. Representatives from various student organizations serve on the Student Government Association, as do members elected from the University community.

Admission Requirements

Applicants must have graduated from high school with a recommended minimum of 4 years of English and 2 to 3 years of mathematics and preparation in seven other academic subjects. Most accepted candidates rank in the top 50 percent of their high school class. Scores on the SAT I or ACT are required for admission. International applicants must submit scores on the Test of English as a Foreign Language (TOEFL).

Early admission is possible for promising high school juniors who have test scores near the top 15th percentile statewide or nationally, a minimum 3.0 grade point average (on a 4.0 scale), a strong recommendation from their counselor or principal, and a letter of permission from their parents or guardian. A campus interview with the Dean of Student Development is required.

Applications from transfer students are welcome, as are those from students resuming their education or adult students who have delayed their entrance to college. Transfer students must be in good standing at their former institution.

Applicants who fail to meet regular admission requirements may be considered on an individual basis for the Fresh Start program by the Fresh Start admissions committee. An interview is required for all Fresh Start applicants.

Application and Information

An application is ready for consideration by the Admissions Committee when it has been received with a $35 application fee for domestic students and $75 for international students, the required test scores and references, and transcripts from each school attended. The University uses a system of rolling admissions. It is recommended that applications be submitted as early as possible, since on-campus housing is limited. Freshmen are required to live in the dormitory unless they reside with a parent, guardian, or spouse.

For application forms, catalogs, and additional information, students should contact:

Webber International University
1201 North Scenic Highway
P.O. Box 96
Babson Park, Florida 33827-9990

Telephone: 863-638-2910
E-mail: admissions@webber.edu
World Wide Web: http://www.webber.edu

Students take a break between classes at Webber International University.

WEBB INSTITUTE

GLEN COVE, NEW YORK

The Institute

Webb Institute was founded in 1889 to provide an opportunity for worthy young students to obtain an education in the "art and science of designing ships and their propulsion systems." The Institute has followed this basic objective to the present, and its graduates are active throughout the United States in the ship design, ship construction, yacht design, and marine operations industries and in appropriate government offices.

The 26-acre campus is the former estate of Herbert L. Pratt and is located on Long Island Sound. Because of the Institute's small size and intensive academic program, varsity sports are limited. However, Webb participates in intercollegiate basketball, cross-country, sailing, soccer, tennis, and volleyball, for which ample facilities are provided. The campus has a gymnasium, tennis courts, playing fields, and a beach. Golf and swimming facilities are available nearby.

Webb Institute maintains an enrollment that ranges from 70 to 90 students, all of whom live on campus. Webb students must be U.S. citizens.

Location

Glen Cove is a city of more than 25,000 residents and is located on Long Island's North Shore, which is nearly an hour from New York City. Convenient train service from Glen Cove to New York brings the variety of cultural, educational, and recreational activities available in the city within easy reach of Webb students.

Majors and Degrees

Webb Institute offers an engineering program in ship design, which involves both naval architecture and marine engineering. The undergraduate degree awarded is the Bachelor of Science in naval architecture and marine engineering.

Academic Programs

The engineering program in ship design consists of fundamental foundation courses in mathematics, science, and engineering sciences, capped by extensive professional design courses. A coherent program in humanities supplements the technical program to round out undergraduate education.

In addition, students have a two-month, cooperative-job experience each year in the U.S. marine and maritime industry. During this period, freshmen work as helper mechanics in shipyards, sophomores obtain seagoing experience aboard ship, and juniors and seniors work as engineering assistants in design and technical offices of various marine firms. This important part of the program provides excellent articulation of the educational and career experiences. Innovative engineering ideas are encouraged in the thesis required during the last year. The program is fully accredited. Graduates are well equipped to pursue postgraduate studies.

Semesters run from late August to mid-December and from late February to late June. January and February are winter work periods, and the period from late June to late August is designated for vacation.

Academic Facilities

Full laboratory support is provided for chemistry, physics, metallurgy, and various engineering courses. A ship-model testing tank is available for ship and boat hull studies. Computer facilities are provided on campus. The Livingston Library contains extensive holdings in naval architecture, marine engineering, and general engineering, as well as collections in literature, arts, social sciences, and music.

Costs

All students admitted to Webb are accepted on a tuition- and fee-free basis (full scholarship). Room and board costs are approximately $7550 in 2004–05. Nearly $800 per year is required for books and supplies. A $150 room deposit fee is payable on entry and refunded, less any breakage costs, on departure. The Student Organization requires a $40 deposit on entry, also refundable on departure.

Financial Aid

As stated, a full scholarship that covers tuition and fees is awarded to all accepted candidates. The winter work co-op in industry provides income for students that significantly assists in other expenses. Supplementary aid opportunities are available through the Federal Pell Grant, Federal Stafford Student Loans, and in-house grant programs. Students requiring financial assistance must submit the Free Application for Federal Student Aid (FAFSA) after March 31 but not later than July 1 of the year of entry.

Faculty

Webb Institute has a highly qualified faculty. Many members possess engineering licenses and engage in sponsored research programs, consult for commercial firms, and research and write technical papers. Classes are limited to 25 students, and the student-faculty ratio is 7:1. Each student is assigned a faculty adviser, and consultation with individual faculty members is encouraged.

Student Government

The Student Organization is highly active in student administrative, social, and educational affairs. It is supplemented by an Honor Council and honor system. Together, these entities provide students with a high degree of responsibility for ordering and conducting student life.

Admission Requirements

Admission to Webb is highly competitive. The qualifying requirements for admission are graduation from high school with a B+ (87) or better average in 16 credits of basic high school subjects. Admission selections are based on high school standing (generally in the upper 10 percent) and scores on the College Board's SAT I and Subject Tests in Mathematics (Level I or II), Physics or Chemistry, and the Writing Test. The final selection follows a personal interview conducted at Webb or at a location convenient to the applicant. The entering class is usually restricted to 25 freshmen.

All application papers must be submitted by February 15, and all required College Board tests must be taken before that date. Advanced Placement is not given in any of the course offerings. Campus visits by interested students are strongly recommended; prior appointments must be made. An early-decision plan is available for qualified candidates.

Webb Institute does not discriminate in admission in the areas of gender, race, or religion. Academic qualities and career motivation are the only criteria.

Application and Information

For a catalog and application forms, students may contact:

William G. Murray
Director of Admissions
Webb Institute
Glen Cove, New York 11542

Telephone: 516-671-2213
E-mail: admissions@webb-institute.edu
World Wide Web: http://www.webb-institute.edu

The academic facilities of Webb Institute are located on Long Island Sound in the former residence of Herbert L. Pratt.

WELLESLEY COLLEGE

WELLESLEY, MASSACHUSETTS

The College

Wellesley College is an independent, residential liberal arts college for women with an enrollment of 2,300 students. Situated on a 500-acre campus 12 miles west of Boston, Wellesley is a college for the serious student with high expectations for her personal and professional life. Students at the College come from across the U.S., from around the world, and from many different cultures and backgrounds. They have prepared for Wellesley at hundreds of different secondary schools.

Most students live in residence halls on campus—each hall is its own community within the larger Wellesley community. Residents may gather for informal talks over dinner. Residences also sponsor social events, guest lecturers, dinners with faculty members, and guests-in-residence.

Wellesley's Sports Center includes an eight-lane, 25-meter/25-yard swimming pool and separate diving well; a volleyball arena; badminton, squash, and racquetball courts; fencing/dance/exercise studios; weight machine and free-weights rooms; and an athletic training area. The field house has a basketball arena, indoor tennis courts, a 200-meter track, and a cardiovascular machine area. Outdoor sports facilities include a boathouse for canoes, sailboats, and crew shells and a swimming beach, both located on the campus's Lake Waban. Wellesley also maintains a nine-hole golf course, and twelve tennis courts. In 2002, the College added new soccer, lacrosse, and field hockey fields, a softball diamond, and an outdoor track.

Many extracurricular activities are often held in the Schneider Student Center, which is used by all members of the College community. Throughout the year, distinguished artists, musicians, lecturers, and public figures are invited to the campus, and their presentations are free of charge. There are no sororities, but there are several academic societies, including two historically black public service organizations. Ethos, the black student association on campus, is housed in Harambee House and brings speakers as well as artistic and cultural events to the College throughout the year. Alianza, the organization primarily for international Hispanic and Latin American students, and Mezcla, the organization for Hispanic/Latina students, were formed by students from these groups at Wellesley to promote their feelings of solidarity and to enrich the College community through cultural offerings. These two groups collaborate closely. Members of Alianza and Mezcla are also involved in communities off campus, especially in the Spanish-speaking communities of Greater Boston. The Asian Student Union, an umbrella organization for many clubs, sponsors films, seminars, and workshops on campus as well as social and cultural events with other colleges in the Boston area. The Slater International Center provides a meeting place where international students at Wellesley can relax and share common experiences.

Location

The College is located in the town of Wellesley, a suburban community of more than 27,000 people, with many shops, restaurants, and bookstores. Its proximity to Boston allows students to take advantage of the vast array of opportunities there, which include volunteer work and internships in government or social agencies; performances given by the Boston Ballet or the Boston Symphony; sports events, such as Boston Celtics, Bruins, and Red Sox games; and visits to the Museum of Fine Arts, the Museum of Science, or the many historic sites. Within metropolitan Boston, there are approximately 250,000 college and university students and many major educational institutions. The campus is only a short distance from New England winter sports areas as well as from the Atlantic coast and Cape Cod beaches.

Majors and Degrees

Wellesley College grants the B.A. and offers majors in humanities: art history, Chinese, English, French, German, Greek, Italian studies, Japanese, Latin, music, Russian, Spanish, and studio art; in social sciences: Africana studies, anthropology, economics, history, philosophy, political science, psychology, religion, sociology, and women's studies; and in science and mathematics: astronomy, biological sciences, chemistry, computer science, geology, mathematics, and physics. The twenty-three interdepartmental majors are American studies, architecture, astrophysics, biological chemistry, Chinese studies, cinema and media studies, classical and Near Eastern archaeology, classical civilization, cognitive and linguistic sciences, comparative literature, environmental studies, French cultural studies, German studies, international relations, Japanese studies, Jewish studies, Latin American studies, medieval/Renaissance studies, Middle Eastern studies, neuroscience, peace and justice studies, Russian area studies, and theater studies. Students may also design individual majors, such as media arts and sciences and Islamic studies.

Academic Program

Each candidate is required to complete 32 credits of academic work with a C average or better. Nine credits must be taken in the following general areas: language and literature; visual arts, music, video, film, and theater; social and behavioral analysis; epistemology and cognition; ethics, religion, and moral philosophy; historical studies; natural and physical science; and mathematical modeling and problem solving in the natural sciences, mathematics, and computer science. Proficiency in one foreign language is required, as are courses in writing and quantitative reasoning. Students must also complete a one-course multicultural requirement designed to allow the student to see a people, culture, or society through its own eyes. Wellesley offers a thorough background for students preparing to attend medical school or law school. The medical school acceptance rate is generally more than 70 percent; acceptance to law school is approximately 80 percent. Between 25 and 30 percent of Wellesley's graduates continue directly on to graduate school.

The Elisabeth Kaiser Davis Degree Program at Wellesley welcomes women who are beyond the traditional undergraduate age to complete a B.A. degree on a part-time or full-time basis. The program takes into account the special needs of adult students regarding admission, advising, orientation, housing, and financial aid. Postbaccalaureate study at Wellesley is for men and women who have a bachelor's degree and wish to complete further undergraduate work for a specific purpose. Many students take courses to prepare for medical school or other graduate programs. Those interested in these programs should contact the Board of Admission.

Off-Campus Programs

Wellesley has cross-registration programs with MIT, Babson, Brandeis, and Olin College of Engineering. Through the Twelve College Exchange program, students may live and study for a semester or a full academic year at any of the member institutions (Amherst, Bowdoin, Connecticut College, Dartmouth, Mount Holyoke, Smith, Trinity, Vassar, Wesleyan, Wheaton, and Williams). Students may also attend the National Theater Institute at the Eugene O'Neill Theater Center, which is accredited by Connecticut College, and the Williams–Mystic Seaport Program in Maritime Studies. In addition, there are exchanges with Spelman College, a predominantly black liberal arts college for women in Atlanta, Georgia, and with Mills College in Oakland, California.

Approximately 30 percent of the junior class studies abroad each year for either a semester or a year. Students attend programs sponsored by other colleges and universities or those sponsored by Wellesley. At present, Wellesley runs programs in Aix-en-Provence, France; Vienna, Austria; and Oaxaca, Mexico. Wellesley is a consortium member for programs in Spain, Italy, and Japan and offers exchange programs with institutions in the United Kingdom, Japan, Argentina, and Korea. The Washington Internship Program provides 18 to 20 juniors with an opportunity to spend the summer in Washington, D.C., working within the federal government, within Congress, at public interest organizations, and at cultural and scientific institutions.

Academic Facilities

The College library contains more than 1.3 million volumes and more than 2,500 periodical subscriptions, government documents, and audiovisual holdings. Special collections include rare books and manuscripts, book arts, and English and American poetry. Departmental libraries focus on art, astronomy, music, and science. Access to a broad range of electronic reference and full-text resources is provided through the library's World Wide Web site. Wellesley is the only undergraduate institution in the Boston Library Consortium, an association of major research and academic libraries devoted to sharing resources. The Knapp Media and Technology Center consolidates course support services, media services, and language laboratory facilities. Providing access to the most current instructional technology, the center is a facility where students, the faculty, and staff members can collaborate in interactive learning and on creating multimedia projects. Technology is an integral part of every student's life at Wellesley. The campus network provides a wealth of research opportunities on campus and through the Internet. E-mail and electronic bulletin boards are important extensions of both social and academic communication. Courses use technology for activities as diverse as reviewing art history slides and interacting with animated simulations of biological and chemical processes. Every student has network access in her dorm room. In addition, there are shared clusters of PCs and Macintoshes in every residence and areas throughout campus for wireless connections.

The Jewett Arts Center houses extensive facilities for the art and music departments, including a concert hall, student galleries, two libraries, and art studios and music practice rooms. The Davis Museum and Cultural Center, located in a separate building, houses exhibition galleries, an art collection of 5,000 works, a print room, a study gallery/seminar room, a café, and a cinema. The Science Center houses laboratories, classrooms, and offices for eight scientific disciplines; a vivarium; a science library of more than 105,000 volumes; and shared support facilities. The completely up-to-date instrumentation available for undergraduate use includes an X-ray diffractometer, spectrometers (nuclear magnetic resonance, mass, Mössbauer, UV, and IR), electron microscopes, and argon and dye lasers. An expansion and renovation project of the Science Center made available several laboratories (molecular biology, cognitive learning, laser, electronics, and optics) and other facilities. The Whitin Observatory includes 24-inch, 12-inch, and 6-inch telescopes, as well as a library, classrooms, and auxiliary instruments. The greenhouses contain two research houses and one of the largest teaching collections of plants in the Northeast, including specimens that range from temperate to tropical species. Botanical facilities include growth chambers with temperature, light, and humidity control as well as extensive botanical gardens and an arboretum.

Costs

For 2003–04, costs were $27,314 for tuition and $8612 for room and board. The student activity and the facilities fee is $590. Wellesley estimates that an additional $1800 per year is adequate for books, laundry, and other essentials, exclusive of travel to and from home.

Financial Aid

Approximately 50 percent of Wellesley students receive financial aid through the College. The decision to admit a student is made independently of her financial need. Full need, as determined by Wellesley's standards and policies, is met through the financial aid package. Usually aid consists of a combination of grants and loans, as well as student employment during the academic year. In addition, other students receive outside scholarships and grants, and many work on or off campus through the Student Employment Office.

Faculty

Instruction by faculty members of all ranks is available to all students. Currently, there are 235 full-time and 102 part-time faculty members; 98 percent of full-time tenure-track faculty members hold the doctoral degree or final degree in their field, and 58 percent of tenured faculty members are women. The faculty consists of scholars actively involved in research and writing; however, teaching is a major priority, and students find their professors to be easily accessible.

Student Government

Students, through election to the College Government Senate and through voting representation on College committees, share responsibility in the decision-making processes of the College. Students serve on committees of the Board of Trustees, on the Board of Admission, and on important departmental committees. Students regulate their lives in the residence halls through House Council and manage student activity funds used to support more than 160 student organizations. The honor system is a strong tradition at Wellesley, permitting self-scheduled examinations, take-home tests, and a lack of stringent social regulations.

Admission Requirements

Admission to Wellesley is competitive. Prospective applicants should have a strong secondary school record and are advised to take the most academically challenging course of study available to them. Students entering Wellesley normally have completed four years of college-preparatory studies in secondary school. However, Wellesley also considers applications from students who plan to complete only three years of high school and who demonstrate academic strength and social and personal maturity. Good preparation includes training in clear and coherent writing and in interpreting literature, in the principles of mathematics, and in history; experience in at least two laboratory sciences; and competence in at least one foreign language—ancient or modern—usually achieved through four years of study. College credit may be given to students who have taken Advanced Placement examinations. Wellesley participates in an early decision plan. Transfer students are admitted in both semesters. The ACT or SAT I and three SAT II Subject Tests, one of which must be the Writing Test, are required for admission. An interview is strongly recommended. The Test of English as a Foreign Language (TOEFL) or the Advanced Placement International English Language Exam (APIEL) is highly recommended of all international students when English is not their first language.

Application and Information

For more information about Wellesley College, students should contact:

Dean of Admission
Wellesley College
106 Central Street
Wellesley, Massachusetts 02481
Telephone: 781-283-2270
Fax: 781-283-3678
World Wide Web: http://www.wellesley.edu/Admission/

WELLS COLLEGE

AURORA, NEW YORK

The College

Wells College, founded in 1868, is proud to be the second institution in the country to award the baccalaureate degree to women. Its founder, Henry Wells, who built his fortune with the creation of the Wells Fargo Express, believed that women would play a vital role in the future of America.

What truly distinguishes Wells from other colleges and universities is that it dares to be small. With an enrollment of 450 students, Wells students do not sit quietly among rows of neatly lined desks; instead, they join their classmates and professors around seminar tables where they are expected to contribute their ideas. Wells faculty members are widely published and respected in their fields, but teaching is their first priority.

Academic opportunities include independent and interdisciplinary study, internships, and study-abroad programs. In addition, a campus newspaper, several musical and drama groups, a literary magazine and book arts center, environmental and political organizations, and other organizations provide important opportunities for student involvement. A full program of cultural events, symposia, and lectures enhances the academic and social life of the College.

Students interested in athletics may participate on intercollegiate teams in field hockey, lacrosse, soccer, softball, swimming, and tennis. There are also a number of intramural opportunities, including basketball, soccer, swimming, tennis, and volleyball. Athletic facilities include indoor and outdoor tennis courts, a gymnasium, a weight room, a nine-hole golf course, and a campus boathouse and dock used in teaching sailing, canoeing, lifeguarding, and outdoor survival skills.

Location

The village of Aurora is located on the eastern shore of Cayuga Lake in the Finger Lakes resort region of upstate New York. Aurora is in the center of an area well-known for its concentration of prestigious private colleges, including Cornell University, Ithaca College, Hobart and William Smith College, Colgate University, Hamilton College, and Syracuse University. Wells College is within a 60-mile radius of five colleges and universities with a total enrollment of more than 50,000 students. Aurora is 25 miles from Ithaca, 60 miles from Syracuse, and 60 miles from Rochester.

Majors and Degrees

Wells College offers the Bachelor of Arts degree with concentrations in African-American studies, American cultures, anthropology/cross-cultural studies, art history, biochemistry and molecular biology, biology, chemistry, computer science, creative writing, economics, English, environmental policies and values, environmental sciences, ethics and philosophy, French, government and politics, history, human nature and values, international studies, literature, management, mathematics, music, physics, psychology, religious studies, sociology, Spanish, studio art, theater and dance, and women's studies. In consultation with the dean and faculty, students may design their own concentrations and majors. In addition, Wells offers programs that lead to provisional certification in elementary and secondary education, as well as preprofessional programs in business, engineering, law, medicine, and veterinary science.

The College offers dual-degree programs in engineering with Case Western Reserve University, Clarkson University, Columbia University, Cornell University, and Washington University, as well as dual-degree M.B.A. and M.P.H. programs with the University of Rochester. Wells also offers a dual-degree 3-4 program with the College of Veterinary Medicine of Cornell University, which leads to the D.V.M. degree. In the dual-degree programs, the student earns both her B.A. from Wells College and the professional degree from the affiliated university within five years, with the exception of the D.V.M. program, which takes seven years.

Academic Programs

The academic philosophy at Wells is firmly rooted in the liberal arts. The College is organized into four academic divisions: the humanities, natural and mathematical sciences, social sciences, and the arts, but faculty members in all divisions work together to produce a curriculum that recognizes connections between subject areas and fits many pieces together, just as they fit together in life.

Students take two multidisciplinary courses during their first year that have an emphasis on the scope and breadth of human inquiry and creative synthesis necessary for leadership in a wide range of areas. Wells 101, Approaches to the Liberal Arts, is a shared experience for first-year students in the fall that incorporates a multidisciplinary approach to familiarize students with the liberal arts. Writing, critical thinking, discussion, collaborative learning, respect for diversity, and attendance at campus cultural events are integral to the course. Wells 102, the first-year seminar, consists of various topics that continue to develop writing and other skills that are important to students in their academic careers.

Wells students are traditionally required to complete a thesis or project during their senior year. While the core curriculum provides a shared academic experience for students, the senior thesis provides a student with the opportunity to complete a thoughtful, in-depth analysis of a topic of the student's choosing.

Off-Campus Programs

Wells College students may spend January intersession, a semester, or even a year in another setting abroad or in the United States. Wells sponsors or is affiliated with programs in the following cities and countries: Copenhagen, Denmark; Paris, Grenoble, and St. Victor Lacoste, France; Berlin, Bonn, and Heidelberg, Germany; Cork, Ireland; Florence and Rome, Italy; Puebla, Mexico; Dakar, Senegal; Seville, Spain; and London, Bath, and York, United Kingdom. Students may pursue global study in science through the School for Field Studies in Africa, Australia, the Caribbean, and Hawaii. The Washington Semester at American University in Washington, D.C., is a popular option for those students interested in communication, economics, or government. Wells also offers an independent cross-registration with Cornell University and Ithaca College.

Academic Facilities

The Louis Jefferson Long Library has received numerous awards for its architectural design. It has an open-stack collection of 220,189 volumes, 402 periodicals, and 14,773 microfilms. The library is a member of the South Central

Research Library Council and the New York State Interlibrary Loan Network. Facilities include an online computer center, individual study carrels, seminar and group-study rooms, and an art gallery. There are department libraries in art, economics, English, mathematics, music, philosophy, and the sciences located throughout campus. The Barler Hall of Music houses a recital hall with superb acoustics, vocal and instrumental practice rooms, a music library, and a listening laboratory. Facilities for printmaking, painting, ceramics, sculpture, and photography are located in the Campbell Arts Building. The Cleveland Hall of Languages contains modern equipment for learning foreign languages. The Zabriskie Science Building houses modern laboratories for chemistry, biology, and physics, as well as a computer laboratory, library, darkroom, and greenhouse. The art history and history departments are located in Morgan Hall. In addition to the seminar rooms and art history library, Morgan has an extensive slide library and small art gallery. Macmillan Hall has classrooms, faculty and administrative offices, several computer laboratories, and department libraries. The east wing of Macmillan houses the Margaret Phipps Auditorium, a theater facility used for theater arts instruction, concerts, lectures, and dramatic productions.

Costs

Tuition fees for the students in 2003–04 were $13,592; room and board were $6830, and fees were $700.

Financial Aid

Approximately 85 percent of Wells students receive financial aid packaged in the form of grants, scholarships, and loans.

Faculty

Wells College has 66 faculty members. Fifty-three percent of the faculty members are women. Ninety-four percent of the Wells College faculty members hold a Ph.D. The first priority of the faculty members is teaching, although they do receive recognition for scholarship in their respective fields.

Student Government

The student body is self-governing through the Collegiate Association. The three main governing bodies of the association are the Student-Faculty Administration Board, the Collegiate Council, and the Community Court. Students serve on faculty committees that make decisions concerning administrative and curricular matters.

Admission Requirements

Wells College students come from diverse geographic and socioeconomic backgrounds. To provide the foundation for study at Wells, each candidate for admission is expected to complete a solid college-preparatory program during her four years of secondary school. The College recommends a program of study that includes 4 years of English grammar, composition, and literature; 2 years of history/social science; 2 years of a foreign language; 3 years of mathematics, with emphasis on basic algebraic, geometric, and trigonometric concepts and deductive reasoning; and 2 years of laboratory science. Scores from the SAT I or the ACT are required, and a personal interview is strongly encouraged.

Application and Information

Applications should be received early in the senior year of high school and not later than March 1 of the year in which entrance is desired. Applications from early decision and early action candidates must be received by December 15.

Transfer applications are reviewed on a rolling basis. Transfer students are eligible for merit scholarships and financial aid.

A campus visit is highly recommended for prospective students. Typically, the visit includes a guided tour of the Wells College campus and facilities, overnight accommodations in the residence halls, a personal interview, and the option of attending classes. Appointments with faculty members and financial aid representatives are also available.

For more information about Wells College or to schedule a campus visit, students should contact:

Admissions Office
Wells College
Aurora, New York 13026
Telephone: 800-952-9355 (toll-free)
E-mail: admissions@wells.edu
World Wide Web: http://www.wells.edu

Students enjoy a close-knit college environment at Wells.

WENTWORTH INSTITUTE OF TECHNOLOGY

BOSTON, MASSACHUSETTS

The Institute

Wentworth Institute of Technology was founded in 1904 to provide education in the mechanical arts. Today, it is one of the nation's leading technical institutes, offering study in a variety of disciplines. Wentworth has a current undergraduate day enrollment of approximately 3,200 men and women (2,400 full-time) and graduates more engineering technicians and technologists each year than any other college in the United States. The technical education acquired at Wentworth enables graduates to assume creative and responsible careers in business and industry. Wentworth is located on a 35-acre campus on Huntington Avenue in Boston.

Wentworth provides dormitory and suite-style residence halls on campus for men and women. Students residing in the residence halls are on a full meal plan. Upperclass students have the option of living in on-campus apartments. Students residing in the apartments may prepare their own meals. A cafeteria, snack bar, and new convenience store are available for those wishing to purchase their meals.

Career counseling and placement assistance are available to all alumni and to students who have completed at least one semester of study at the Institute. While many graduates of Wentworth are employed in the Boston area, alumni have secured positions throughout the United States and abroad.

Location

Boston is the educational center of New England. It is a city of charm, tradition, and elegance—a major center of art, science, music, history, medicine, and education. Wentworth is situated near the heart of Boston and is surrounded by institutions that provide the cultural advantages for which the city is famous. The Museum of Fine Arts, with its store of art treasures, is diagonally across the street, and admission is free to any student with a Wentworth ID card. Symphony Hall is just a few blocks away. The Harvard Medical School, the New England Conservatory of Music, Emmanuel College, Simmons College, Massachusetts College of Pharmacy and Allied Health Sciences, the Massachusetts College of Art, Roxbury Community College, and Northeastern University are among the many educational institutions within a few blocks of the campus.

Majors and Degrees

Wentworth Institute of Technology is a technical college of great diversity. Degree programs are offered in the fields of architecture, computer science, design, engineering, engineering technology, and management of technology.

Specifically, bachelor's degrees are awarded in the following majors: the Bachelor of Architecture; the Bachelor of Science in architectural engineering technology, civil engineering technology, computer engineering technology, computer network and information systems, computer science, construction engineering technology, construction management, electromechanical engineering, electronic engineering technology, facilities planning and management, industrial design, interior design, management of technology, and mechanical engineering technology. Baccalaureate degrees in architecture and interior design are designated as first professional degrees. Completion of a Wentworth baccalaureate degree requires four or five years, depending on the program.

Associate in Applied Science degrees can be earned in most majors that grant bachelor's degrees at Wentworth. Although students must apply and be admitted to a four- or five-year bachelor's degree program, they may elect to leave with an associate degree after two years.

Academic Program

At Wentworth Institute of Technology, college-level study in technological fundamentals and principles is combined with appropriate laboratory, field, and studio experience. Students apply theory to practical problems, and they acquire skills and techniques by using, operating, and controlling equipment and instruments particular to their area of specialization. In addition, study in the social sciences and humanities provides a balanced understanding of the world in which graduates work. Wentworth's programs of study are more practical than theoretical in approach, and the Institute's academic requirements demand extensive time and effort.

During the first two years of study in a degree program at Wentworth, students lay the foundation for more advanced study in the third and fourth (and fifth, where applicable) years. While nearly all majors allow continuous study from the freshman through the senior year, the architecture major requires a petition for acceptance to the baccalaureate program during the sophomore year.

All bachelor's degree programs are conducted as cooperative (co-op) education programs: upon entering their third year, students alternate semesters of academic study at Wentworth with semester-long periods of employment in industry. Two semesters of co-op employment are required; one additional (summer) semester of co-op is optional. Both students and the companies that hire them are enthusiastic about the co-op program and agree that it is a mutually valuable experience.

Academic Facilities

Wentworth's twenty-seven buildings house classrooms, laboratories, studios, administrative offices, and other facilities. Beatty Hall houses the Alumni Library, computer center, classrooms, dining areas, and office space. State-of-the-art laboratories, such as the Richard H. Lufkin Technology Center and the Davis Center for Advanced Graphics and Interactive Learning, are situated throughout the campus.

Costs

For 2003–04, tuition was $15,000, books and supplies were approximately $1000, and room and board were about $8200 (this figure varies according to accommodation).

Financial Aid

Scholarships are available to students who demonstrate need and academic promise. Merit-based scholarships are also available. Wentworth also provides federal and state financial assistance, such as Federal Pell and Federal Supplemental Educational Opportunity Grants, Federal Perkins Loans, Federal Work-Study awards, Gilbert Matching Grants, and Massachusetts No-Interest Loans to students with financial need in accordance with federal and state guidelines.

Wentworth participates in the Federal Direct Lending program. As a result, students are eligible to borrow under the Federal Direct Stafford Loan program and parents may borrow under the Federal Direct PLUS program. Individuals participating in these programs borrow money directly from the federal government rather than through lending institutions.

In addition to these need-based programs, Wentworth also participates in the MEFA loan program sponsored by the Massachusetts Educational Financing Authority. Wentworth offers several payment options through payment plans and alternative loan financing.

To apply for financial aid, new students should complete the Free Application for Federal Student Aid (FAFSA) by March 1. Applications received after this date are considered as funds allow.

Faculty

Wentworth's faculty includes 121 full-time and 89 part-time members. The primary responsibility of every faculty member is teaching. Although professors may engage in some research and related work, student development remains the central mission of Wentworth's faculty. Upon entering Wentworth, every student is assigned a faculty adviser.

Student Government

Wentworth's Student Government performs an essential function as the official representative of the student body. Its purposes are to receive and express student opinion, to advance the best interests of the student body with the administration and faculty and with other institutions and associations, to support all extracurricular activities of the student body, and to serve as a bond between the student body and the faculty to foster mutual cooperation and understanding. The Student Government is made up of elected representatives from each class section and the officers elected by the student body at large. The Student Government sponsors social functions and student organizations and serves as an advocate for student concerns.

Admission Requirements

Applicants must be graduates of secondary schools (or have passed the GED test) and must meet specific entrance requirements. All programs require four years of English, a laboratory science, and mathematics through algebra II in a college-preparatory program. Both the electromechanical engineering and the computer science programs require a background in precalculus or trigonometry. All programs require the submission of SAT I scores. International students and transfers are welcome.

Application and Information

Students are admitted to Wentworth for September and January enrollment. The priority application deadline for the fall semester is May 1; for the spring, the deadline is December 1. Notification of admission is made on a rolling basis. An application form, an application fee of $30, transcripts from the secondary school and any colleges previously attended, and SAT I scores should be sent to:

Admissions Office
Wentworth Institute of Technology
550 Huntington Avenue
Boston, Massachusetts 02115
Telephone: 617-989-4000
800-556-0610 (toll-free)
Fax: 617-989-4010
E-mail: admissions@wit.edu
World Wide Web: http://www.wit.edu

Wentworth Hall.

WESLEYAN COLLEGE

MACON, GEORGIA

The College

Wesleyan College, chartered in 1836, has the distinction of being the world's first college chartered to grant degrees to women. Today, Wesleyan is regarded as one of the nation's finest colleges and remains dedicated to the education of women.

Wesleyan is a four-year, Methodist-related, liberal arts college. Enrollment is limited to fewer than 1,000 students. This is done primarily to support a learner-based curriculum that limits classes to no more than 20 students and to provide opportunities for meaningful participation in the life of the college community. Wesleyan's student body has been cited among the nation's most diverse and includes students from twenty-five states and thirty other countries.

The College is located on a beautiful 200-acre wooded campus. The Georgian-style brick buildings include two student apartment buildings. All residential halls have been recently renovated and offer single rooms and suites. Approximately 70 percent of students reside on campus. A multipurpose athletic facility includes a fitness center, an equestrian center, tennis courts, and soccer and softball fields. Among other recreational facilities are a gymnasium with a heated pool and a lake with a jogging trail.

Most of the extracurricular activities of Wesleyan's students are coordinated through Activity Councils. The Campus Activities Board plans concert-dance weekends, events with nearby colleges, international fashion shows, holiday trips, and special dinners. The Student Recreation Council coordinates competitive activities in basketball, soccer, softball, swimming, and individual sports. Wesleyan is a member of the National Collegiate Athletic Association (NCAA) Division III. There are intercollegiate basketball, equestrian, soccer, softball, tennis, and volleyball teams. The Council on Religious Concerns encourages religious life on campus and sponsors activities that involve students with community life. Students volunteer at local institutions such as the Georgia Academy for the Blind, the Methodist Children's Home, and neighborhood schools and churches. They also participate in interest clubs, student publications, performing arts groups, honor societies, and professional fraternities. A number of College traditions are perpetuated by spirited but friendly competition among the four classes.

Wesleyan also offers the Master of Arts degree in middle-level science and middle-level mathematics and in early childhood education. Open to women and men is the College's new Executive Master of Business Administration program.

Location

Wesleyan is located in a suburb of the beautiful, historic city of Macon, Georgia, the third-largest city in the state. Macon is the cultural, educational, medical, and economic leader of middle Georgia and is located about an hour's drive south of Atlanta. The city of Macon offers varied entertainment and many cultural opportunities, including the Georgia Music and Sports Halls of Fame. Visits by nationally and internationally acclaimed speakers and a series of popular and classical concerts are held on the Wesleyan campus each year, as are special events associated with Macon's renowned Cherry Blossom Festival.

Majors and Degrees

Wesleyan College offers thirty-two majors, twenty-four minors and five preprofessional programs. The Bachelor of Arts (A.B.) is offered in advertising and marketing communication, American studies, art history, biology, business administration (concentration in accounting or management), chemistry, communication, education (early childhood, middle grades, and secondary), English, French, history, history/political science, humanities, international business, international relations, mathematics, music (performance emphasis—piano, organ, and voice), philosophy, psychology, religion, sociology, Spanish, and studio art. In addition to these majors, the following academic concentrations are offered as minors: African studies, computer science, economics, French, neuroscience, physics, theater, and women's studies. Self-designed interdisciplinary majors are also available

There are preprofessional programs in dentistry, engineering, law, medicine, and veterinary medicine. Students may elect to pursue their academic or professional interests through a double major, a major in combination with a minor program of studies, an interdisciplinary major, or an independently developed program of studies.

Wesleyan offers a dual-degree program in engineering in cooperation with Georgia Institute of Technology, Auburn University, and Mercer University. Three years of study at Wesleyan and two years of study at Georgia Tech, Auburn, or Mercer lead to an A.B. degree from Wesleyan and a B.S. degree from the other institution.

Academic Programs

The College's goal is to prepare students for a lifetime of learning and change. Each major program contains general education requirements for breadth of learning and major field requirements for career and/or graduate school preparation. All degree programs require the completion of 120 semester hours with a cumulative average of C (2.0) or better.

Wesleyan provides a challenging academic environment coupled with individualized attention. Each student is assisted by a faculty adviser, a preprofessional or career adviser, and a peer counselor in the selection of academic and internship experiences that lead to intellectual and career fulfillment. All classes are offered in a seminar style, with an emphasis on interactive or participatory learning. Each student has a research or internship experience.

Each entering full-time student is required to purchase a personal computer, for which the College offers special financing options. The ability to utilize information technology toward the enhancement of learning and career preparation is central to the academic program. The networked campus is connected to the Internet, which gives each student access to a world of information from her residence hall.

Credit by examination and exemption from required courses are possible with acceptable scores on the Advanced Placement (AP), International Baccalaureate (I.B.), and College-Level Examination Program (CLEP) tests or acceptable grades in high school–college joint enrollment courses. Students may also exempt courses by taking departmental examinations. Thirty semester hours of credit is the maximum a student can receive by exemption through AP, I.B., CLEP, or departmental exams.

The College operates on an early semester plan. First-semester classes begin in late August and end in early December. The second semester begins in the beginning of January and ends with graduation in early May. Wesleyan College offers an optional May term as well as two summer school sessions.

Off-Campus Programs

Through Wesleyan's International Study Abroad and Exchange Program, students can study abroad for one full year, one semester, a May term, or a summer session. Through cooperative agreements with the Institute for the International Education of Students (IES) and National Student Exchange (NSE), students may study abroad in Australia, China, France, Germany, Great Britain, Japan, Russia, Spain, and other countries. In addition, Wesleyan has direct exchange agreements with Sofia University (Bulgaria), Sookmyung Women's University (South Korea), International Christian University (Japan), Osaka University (Japan), Westminster College (England), and Ulyanovsk State University (Russia).

Off-campus opportunities in Macon are available through the Internship Program, which places students with area businesses, community agencies, health organizations, arts groups, and the media. Summer internships can be arranged through the Governor's Intern Program, in a student's hometown, and in other locations. Academic credit given for off-campus experiences varies.

Academic Facilities

Willet Memorial Library has 141,818 volumes and subscribes to 630 periodicals. There are 33,216 items in microform and 6,500 tapes and records. Through the library's participation in GALILEO, students have access to more than 100 bibliographic and full-text databases. The library has informal study areas, individual carrels, a language lab, seminar rooms, and a listening room. The Georgia Room houses 4,500 rare volumes and treasures of Americana. The Porter Fine Arts Building serves as a cultural center for the campus and community. It houses the music and theater departments, and, in addition to classrooms, offices, and studios, it contains two art galleries and a studio theater. Its Porter Auditorium has a seating capacity of 1,200 and contains one of the largest pipe organs in the Southeast. Taylor Hall houses laboratories and classrooms for science and math. This building includes state-of-the-art laboratory equipment, a computer lab, and an electronic classroom. Tate Hall contains classrooms for the Humanities, Social Science, and Education divisions. The art department is located in a 10,000-square-foot building designed exclusively for teaching the studio arts.

Costs

Tuition for 2004–05 is $10,050. Room and board cost $7450. There are $850 in fees. Students should also keep in mind the additional cost of books, supplies, travel, and personal expenses.

Financial Aid

Students seeking financial assistance are required to submit the Free Application for Federal Student Aid (FAFSA). This form may be obtained from a high school counselor or from Wesleyan. Any student who demonstrates financial need is qualified for some type of assistance.

Wesleyan offers scholarships to incoming first-year students on the basis of academic ability, leadership, or special talents. Transfer scholarships are available based on cumulative grade point average and hours earned. Minimum requirements are a 3.0 GPA and 30 semester hours or 45 quarter hours.

Wesleyan participates in the Federal Perkins Loan, Federal Pell Grant, Federal Supplemental Educational Opportunity Grant, Federal Work-Study, and Federal Family Education Loan programs. Any resident of Georgia who wishes to attend a private college in the state and has at least a B average may apply for the Georgia State Tuition Equalization Grant and Hope Grant. Georgia Student Incentive Grants are also available, as are certain loans, other scholarships, and part-time employment. Approximately 90 percent of Wesleyan's students receive financial assistance.

Faculty

The academic program at Wesleyan is guided by an exceptionally able, dedicated, and caring faculty. There are 48 full-time faculty members; 44 have earned doctoral or terminal degrees. The student-faculty ratio is 11:1. No courses are taught by graduate assistants. Faculty members serve as academic advisers and help students plan their academic program. Many professors participate in extracurricular activities with students on campus.

Student Government

Wesleyan's Student Government Association, through an agreement with the president and faculty of the College, governs the student body with emphasis on responsibility and freedom. An honor tradition, based upon the concept that individual freedom is a right founded on responsibility, is inherent in campus life. Violations of student government regulations are handled through a system of judicial processes with a system for appeals.

Admission Requirements

Applicants to Wesleyan must submit a completed application with a $30 application fee, official academic transcripts, official SAT I or ACT scores, an evaluation written by a teacher, a recommendation from a guidance counselor or principal, and an essay. The completion of a minimum of 16 academic course units in a secondary school is required. Wesleyan feels that a campus visit is extremely beneficial, and visitors can be full participants in campus activities. An interview is strongly recommended. Applications from transfer and international students are welcome. Credit for work below a grade of C cannot be transferred, and a minimum score of 550 on the Test of English as Foreign Language (TOEFL) is required of international students. Wesleyan accepts qualified students without regard to race, religion, national or ethnic origin, age, or handicap.

Application and Information

Admission to Wesleyan is selective. For additional information or to request an application form, students should contact:

Vice President for Enrollment Services and Student Affairs
Wesleyan College
4760 Forsyth Road
Macon, Georgia 31210-4462
Telephone: 478-757-5206
800-447-6610 (toll-free)
World Wide Web: http://www.wesleyancollege.edu

Wesleyan has the distinction of being the world's first college chartered to grant degrees to women.

WESLEY COLLEGE

DOVER, DELAWARE

The College

Wesley College, the oldest private college in Delaware, is a fully accredited, coeducational, comprehensive liberal arts institution.

Nestled in a quiet, historic residential community, Wesley College is United Methodist Church–affiliated with an enrollment of 2,300 full- and part-time students, mostly representing the Mid-Atlantic region. The average class size is 20 students.

The Wesley residence community is made up of six buildings. Each building has special characteristics that make it unique. The facilities are all air conditioned, and all rooms offer Internet access. The newest is an apartment-style facility. The purpose of the Residence Program is to enhance the academic mission of Wesley by providing educational and social experiences outside the classroom to help develop contributing members of society.

Each building has a Resident Director and assistant. Student staff members are selected and trained and live on each floor to provide additional resources to their peers. The living arrangement in each hall enables students to get to know one another well and to develop close-knit relationships. Students come from all over the United States and overseas, providing the opportunity to meet and live with people from many diverse backgrounds.

Wesley has many special interest groups in which students are involved. These include environmental education, drama, music, business activities, the Christian Unity Association, student government, black student union, dance team, the College newspaper, the TV station, cultural lecture series, and many other College-sponsored activities.

A well-organized intramural program offers a wide variety of athletics competitions, including, but not limited to, basketball, flag football, soccer, and volleyball. Wesley is a member of NCAA Division III intercollegiate athletics and the Pennsylvania Athletic Conference. Men have teams in baseball, basketball, cross-country, football, golf, lacrosse, soccer, and tennis. Women compete in basketball, cross-country, field hockey, golf, lacrosse, soccer, softball, and tennis. There is also a cheerleading squad.

The mission of the College is to be the premier institution for helping students gain the knowledge, skills, and moral and ethical attitudes necessary to achieve their personal goals and contribute to the welfare of their communities in a global society. The College endeavors to impart a desire for lifelong learning and an enhanced capacity for critical and creative thinking, so that students can reap the rewards of intellectual growth and professional effectiveness. As a college in a covenant relationship with the United Methodist Church and founded upon Christian principles, Wesley strives to realize a holistic campus environment of common purpose, caring, tolerance, inclusiveness, responsibility, and service that is the heart of community.

In addition to its undergraduate degrees, Wesley College awards the Master of Science in Nursing (M.S.N.) degree, two Master of Education degrees, and the Master of Business Administration (M.B.A.) degree.

Location

Dover is the capital of the country's first state and has approximately 35,000 residents. New York City, Baltimore, Philadelphia, and Washington, D.C. are within a 2- to 3-hour drive of the campus. The College is located within Dover's major residential community, with stores and banks within easy walking distance and malls a short commute. Seafood is a specialty in Dover because of the city's proximity to the Delaware and Chesapeake Bays and to the Atlantic Ocean. Delaware Transit Corporation (DART) provides bus service throughout the city of Dover. Daily bus service is available to and from the campus. In addition, Delaware's famous beaches are within driving distance of the campus.

Many students become involved in local activities, including volunteer work at private and public agencies. On-campus volunteer activities include a unique three-way partnership between a state-funded charter school (Campus Community School), the Wesley Boys and Girls Club, and the College. The area churches welcome Wesley students. Students are employed in many community businesses through the cooperative-education program at Wesley or simply work in part-time jobs to earn extra money. Many Dover residents attend Wesley as part-time students and use the College's facilities on a regular basis.

Majors and Degrees

Bachelor of Arts and Bachelor of Science degrees are awarded in accounting, American studies, biology, business administration (international business, management, and marketing), education (elementary K–8 and physical education K–12), English, environmental studies (environmental policy and environmental science), history, international studies, liberal studies, media arts, medical technology, nursing, paralegal studies, physical education (exercise science and sports management), political science, and psychology.

Academic Program

The comprehensive academic calendar year consists of two semesters and a double summer session. Winter sessions are available in England and France, offering unique opportunities for travel and study.

Bachelor's degree candidates begin with the foundation core curriculum, which emphasizes an overarching theme of the individual in a global community. Interdisciplinary threads bind the core curriculum and the major programs into a purposeful design. These threads are critical thinking, communication across disciplines, technological literacy, multicultural awareness, aesthetic appreciation, and ethical sensibility. The core provides a distinctive undergraduate experience for students, establishes coherent links between the curricular and cocurricular programs, and provides community service options beyond the College campus.

Academic Facilities

The Robert H. Parker Library is the College's library and resources center, with a collection of hardbound volumes, academic journals, and periodicals. In addition, Wesley is part of KentNet, a consortium of Dover-area libraries. Through the consortium, more than 500,000 volumes are accessible to Wesley students at facilities within a mile of the campus. Computers located in the library are connected to the College's campuswide network and have the capability to access the library's CD-ROM network. Individual and group instruction on the use of information resources, including the World Wide Web, is provided by the library staff. The library also carries a collection of videotape titles that are available for individual and group viewing.

Access to new communications technology is provided through facilities equipped for production of on-campus broadcasts or taped distribution. The multimedia lab allows students to create and print electronic messages.

Costs

For 2004–05, Wesley's tuition and fees are $14,290 per year. Room and board costs range from $6480 to $9940 per year. Books and supplies total approximately $600 per year.

Financial Aid

Financial aid is available in the form of endowed scholarships, federal scholarships, grants, work-study programs, and loans. Approximately 85 percent of Wesley students receive financial aid. Wesley uses the Free Application for Federal Student Aid (FAFSA). Students and their families are urged to complete and send their FAFSA as early as possible. Financial aid awards must be confirmed by the student within fifteen days of notification.

Wesley College provides numerous academic scholarships to its top undergraduate students. Applications for these awards are not required. Interested seniors should contact the Office of Admissions.

Faculty

Wesley College emphasizes teaching. More than 80 percent of faculty members hold a doctoral or other terminal degree in their subject area and attend workshops and conferences to keep abreast of current activities in their fields. Most faculty members serve as academic advisers to students. All have regularly scheduled office hours and are available for student conferences on a regular basis.

Student Government

Student leadership develops through various aspects of College governance. Student representatives work in close cooperation with faculty members and administrators.

Admission Requirements

Many factors are considered in the selection of a Wesley student. The most important are the applicant's secondary school courses and grades, along with the required SAT I or ACT scores. On-campus interviews are strongly recommended. Secondary school recommendations are also important. International students are welcome and are encouraged to apply by February 1 for the following fall semester. Admission decisions are made without regard to race, religion, color, age, gender, handicap, or national origin. Applicants should have 16 secondary school units in English, social studies, laboratory science, mathematics, and electives.

Wesley offers an early decision plan for qualified candidates who have completed their junior year of secondary school. Early acceptance and deferred entrance are also available. Students, parents, and counselors are welcome to contact the Office of Admissions for information.

Wesley College reserves the right to change some or all rates, policies, or courses when necessary, without prior notice.

Application and Information

Secondary school records should be attached to the Wesley College application form.

To schedule an admission interview and campus tour, students should call the Office of Admissions. A College prospectus, application form, and financial aid information are available by contacting:

Arthur T. Jacobs
Director of Admissions
Wesley College
120 North State Street
Dover, Delaware 19901
Telephone: 302-736-2400
800-937-5398 Ext. 2400 (toll-free)
Fax: 302-736-2382
E-mail: admissions@wesley.edu
World Wide Web: http://www.wesley.edu

A student relaxes in the beautiful surroundings of Wesley College.

WEST CHESTER UNIVERSITY OF PENNSYLVANIA

WEST CHESTER, PENNSYLVANIA

The University

West Chester University (WCU) is the second largest of the fourteen institutions in the Pennsylvania State System of Higher Education and the fourth-largest university in the Philadelphia metropolitan area. Officially founded in 1871, the University traces its heritage to the West Chester Academy, which existed from 1812 to 1869. The University's 388-acre campus has well-maintained facilities, including eight modern residence halls and garden-style apartments. In keeping with West Chester's rich heritage, the University's Quadrangle buildings, part of the original campus, are on the National Register of Historic Places.

While the University attracts the majority of its students from Pennsylvania, New Jersey, and Delaware, it also enrolls many students from other areas across the United States and from more than fifty countries. The undergraduate enrollment is approximately 9,077 women and men full time and 1,390 part time.

Each year, the University community schedules an impressive series of events, including programs with well-known musicians, authors, political figures, and others. Numerous campus groups in music, theater, athletics, and other activities, as well as clubs, fraternities, sororities, service organizations, and honor societies, provide students with the opportunity to participate in a full range of programs. The University offers twenty-three intercollegiate sports and eleven club sports for men and women. In addition to the facilities in the health and physical education complex, the University has a field house and a gymnasium for varsity sports.

Location

The University is located in West Chester, a community in southeastern Pennsylvania that is strategically located at the center of the mid-Atlantic corridor. The seat of Chester County government for almost two centuries, West Chester retains much of its historical charm in its buildings and unspoiled countryside, yet it offers the twenty-first-century advantages of a town in the heart of a thriving suburban area. West Chester is just 25 miles west of Philadelphia and 17 miles north of Wilmington, Delaware, putting the libraries, museums, cultural resources, entertainment, and historical sites of both cities within easy reach. It is also only 2 hours from New York City and 3 hours from Washington, D.C.

Majors and Degrees

The Bachelor of Arts is offered in American studies, anthropology, art, biology, communication studies, communicative disorders, comparative literature, English, French, geography, German, history, Latin, liberal studies, literature, mathematics, philosophy, philosophy–religious studies, political science, political science–international relations, political science–applied public policy, psychology, Russian, social work, sociology, Spanish, theater arts, and women's studies.

The Bachelor of Science is offered in accounting, athletic training, biology, biology–cell and molecular biology, biology-ecology, biology–medical technology, biology-microbiology, biochemistry, chemistry, chemistry–biology (pre-medical), computer and information sciences, criminal justice, forensic chemistry, geoscience–earth systems, geoscience–environmental geosciences, geoscience–geology, health and physical education, health science–general, health science–respiratory care, liberal studies–science and mathematics, liberal studies–professional studies, prebusiness-economics, prebusiness-finance, prebusiness-management, prebusiness-marketing, pharmaceutical product development, physics, physics-engineering, public health–environmental, public health–health promotion, and public health–nutrition.

The Bachelor of Science in Nursing, the Bachelor of Fine Arts (studio arts), and the Bachelor of Music (general, instrumental, keyboard, music education, and vocal) degrees are also offered.

The Bachelor of Science in Education degree is offered in biology, chemistry, citizenship education, communication, early childhood education, earth-space science–astronomy, earth-space science–geology, elementary education, English, French, German, Latin, mathematics, physics, Russian, social studies, Spanish, and special education.

Paraprofessional studies are available in law, medicine, and theology. In cooperation with the Pennsylvania State University, West Chester University offers a 3-2 dual-degree program combining liberal arts, physics, and engineering. Also available are early admission assurance programs with Drexel School of Medicine, Pennsylvania State University College of Medicine, Philadelphia College of Osteopathic Medicine, and Temple University School of Medicine. The University provides special admission opportunities and scholarships to the Widener School of Law–Harrisburg Campus.

Certification programs are available in health and physical education teacher certification, driver education and safe living, and outdoor recreation.

Interdisciplinary areas of study with transcript recognition include ethnic studies, Latin American studies, Russian studies, and women's studies. Minors are available in most majors and in several interdisciplinary areas.

Academic Program

West Chester University is a comprehensive, multipurpose institution now in its second century. The University comprises the College of Arts and Sciences, the School of Business and Public Affairs, the School of Education, the School of Health Sciences, and the School of Music. It operates on a two-semester basis; summer sessions are available.

An honors program is available to qualified students for both upper and lower division study; internships and field experiences, self-designed majors, and independent study are also offered. A variety of credit-by-examination programs are available.

Off-Campus Programs

Through the Junior-Year-Abroad program, students may spend one or more semesters at the University of Ghana, Ghana; University of Edinburgh, Scotland; University of Wales, Swansea; Leeds University, England; and Paul Valery University, France. West Chester also sponsors a number of annual courses, which include study abroad during spring, summer, and winter breaks.

West Chester University participates in the National Student Exchange Program, in which students spend up to a year at any one of seventy member schools across the United States, broadening their cultural and academic horizons. Automatic transfer of credit is arranged.

Academic Facilities

The Francis Harvey Green Library houses more than 500,000 volumes, more than 2,500 periodicals, and a micromedia collection with more than 350,000 titles. Services include interlibrary loans, reference advice, computerized online literature searching, and the availability of CD-ROM databases.

The University's extensive state-of-the-art computer facilities include more than 700 IBM and Apple workstations that are available to students and Internet access from residence halls and computer labs. The University has Braille printers, translators, and speech synthesizers for its visually impaired students. Students can use the computing facilities 16 hours a day.

The Boucher Science Center offers modern multimedia lecture halls, extensive laboratories, and study areas where students can work together. Boucher Science Center is connected to the Schmucker Science Center, which houses a fully equipped observatory and planetarium. The center's extensive laboratories have such instrumentation as automated spectrophotometers, electron analytical equipment, atomic absorption spectrometers, and a variety of chromatographs, including gas chromatographs–mass spectrometers.

The campus includes a 100-acre natural area for environmental studies; speech and hearing and reading clinics; two theaters; music facilities with practice, rehearsal, and listening rooms; and a large, modern health and physical education complex that houses a gymnasium, a natatorium with two pool areas and a diving well; dance studios; research laboratories; physical therapy rooms; saunas; and a health resource center.

West Chester University is committed to providing barrier-free facilities for persons with impaired mobility.

Costs

West Chester University provides a quality education at an affordable cost. Full-time undergraduate students who are legal residents of Pennsylvania paid $4598 per year for tuition for 12 to 18 semester hours in 2003–04. For semester hours more than 18 or fewer than 12, the cost was $192 per semester hour. Out-of-state students were charged $11,496 per year for 12–18 semester hours and $479 per semester hour for hours more than 18 or fewer than 12. Room and board were $5146 per year for on-campus residents. Student fees were $990 per year, plus a technology fee of $100 for in-state students and $150 for out-of-state students. Tuition is determined by the state. Fees are subject to change without notice.

Financial Aid

The financial aid available to students includes work-study programs, grants, loans, special awards, and scholarships. A limited number of Merit Scholarships are awarded based on the student's academic standing and accomplishments in high school. Students who qualify are invited to apply. About 69 percent of all full-time undergraduate students receive some form of aid.

Faculty

West Chester University has a faculty of nearly 800 members. The majority hold doctoral degrees, and many are engaged in research and serve as consultants in their field of expertise. The student-faculty ratio is 17:1.

Student Government

The Student Governmental Association represents all students on the West Chester campus. In addition, the Residence Hall Association represents resident students, and the Off Campus Student Association represents commuting students.

Admission Requirements

Applicants to West Chester University are evaluated on the basis of scholarship, character, and potential for achievement. The requirements for freshman admissions consideration include graduation from an approved secondary school or a General Educational Development (GED) certificate from an approved agency, as well as satisfactory scores on either the SAT I, ACT, or TOEFL (for international applicants). Transfer applicants must have a minimum cumulative grade point average of 2.0 for admissions consideration. Certain academic programs may require an interview or specific course prerequisites. The University does have several other admissions options such as early admission and special admissions programs, including ACT 101. Based on the scores received on Advanced Placement (AP) tests and subject examinations administered through the College-Level Examination Program (CLEP), students may receive advanced placement or credit.

Application and Information

Students are admitted for the fall or spring semester. Freshman applicants for the fall semester are urged to begin the application procedure at the start of their senior year in high school. Transfers should begin the process beginning in January for a fall semester. Applicants for a spring semester should apply by December 1. International students must apply by May 1 for the fall semester and August 1 for the spring semester. The University operates on a modified rolling admission policy; applicants with the strongest qualifications are given priority, and their applications are processed expeditiously. Students are encouraged to visit WCU's campus. To arrange a visit or to attend an information session, students may call the Office of Admissions. For updated information or directions, they may visit the University's Web site listed below.

For additional information and required forms, students may contact:

Office of Admissions
Emil J. Messikomer Hall
West Chester University of Pennsylvania
100 West Rosedale Avenue
West Chester, Pennsylvania 19383
Telephone: 610-436-3411
877-315-2165 (toll-free)
E-mail: ugadmiss@wcupa.edu
World Wide Web: http://www.wcupa.edu

Class is held on the academic quad during a beautiful spring day.

WESTERN CAROLINA UNIVERSITY

CULLOWHEE, NORTH CAROLINA

The University

Excellent teaching is a strength and personal touch makes a difference at Western Carolina University (WCU), the first public university in North Carolina to require that freshmen bring computers to campus. WCU prepares students well for careers and lives in the technological age. Equally committed to providing personal attention and guidance to each student, WCU places strong emphasis on teaching and creating a learning environment in which students are central. Founded in 1889, WCU is a campus of the University of North Carolina, one of the strongest academic university systems in the nation. Support for master's degrees in accounting, nursing, and physical therapy; funding for an intercollegiate women's soccer team; preparation for a $28-million fine and performing arts center; a campuswide computer network; and millions of dollars in renovation funds are some of the recent benefits of WCU's affiliation. While most classes are held at the main campus in Cullowhee, WCU conducts a variety of programs at western North Carolina sites, including the University of North Carolina Center in Asheville and the Cherokee Center in Cherokee. A distance learning and teleconference center provides non-credit, continuing education, and other programs to hundreds of participants each year. The Research and Graduate School offers twelve master's degrees in more than fifty areas, the doctorate in educational leadership, and the educational specialist degree.

Location

WCU is located in Cullowhee, North Carolina, 52 miles west of Asheville. Scenic vistas, clear white-water streams, and dense forests abound in the southern Appalachian Mountain region. The climate is mild, with four distinct seasons. The nearby Blue Ridge and Great Smoky Mountains attract millions of tourists each year to take part in recreational activities, including snow skiing, white-water rafting, canoeing, kayaking, mountain biking, camping, and hiking. Major southeast cities such as Charlotte, North Carolina; Knoxville, Tennessee; Atlanta, Georgia; and Greenville, South Carolina, are within a 2- to 3-hour drive of the campus. WCU's 265-acre campus offers all the amenities of a small town: classroom buildings, eleven residence halls, two full-service cafeterias, two food courts, fast-food restaurants, health services, a bank, a computer store, a bookstore, a library, a fitness center, two indoor swimming pools, tennis courts, a golf driving range, a jogging trail, a quarter-mile track, intramural fields, a dance club, and ample parking that allows freshmen to bring cars to campus.

Majors and Degrees

WCU offers 120 majors and areas of concentration to undergraduates through four colleges: Applied Sciences, Arts and Sciences, Business, and Education and Allied Professions. The Honors College offers extra academic challenge and social opportunities in an optional residential setting for high-achieving, qualified students. For undergraduates, WCU offers the Bachelor of Arts (B.A.), Bachelor of Science (B.S.), Bachelor of Science in Education, Bachelor of Fine Arts (B.F.A.), Bachelor of Science in Business Administration, and Bachelor of Science in Nursing (B.S.N.) degrees in the following majors: accounting, anthropology, art, art education, athletic training, biology, birth–kindergarten, business administration and law, chemistry, clinical laboratory sciences, communication, communication disorders, computer information systems, computer science, construction management, criminal justice, electrical and computer engineering technology, electrical engineering, elementary education, emergency management, emergency medical care, English, English education, entrepreneurship, environmental health, finance, geology, health information management, history, hospitality and tourism, interior design, international business, management, marketing, mathematics, mathematics education, middle grades education, music, music education, natural resources management, nursing, nutrition and dietetics, parks and recreation management, philosophy, physical education, political science, psychology, recreational therapy, science education, social sciences, social sciences education, social work, sociology, Spanish, Spanish education, special education, special studies, speech and theater arts, sport management, telecommunications engineering technology, and theater. WCU's preprofessional programs (pre-engineering, preforestry, prelaw, premedicine, prepharmacy, and pre–veterinary medicine) prepare students well for admission to professional schools with tailor-made academic programs, small classes, undergraduate research, internships, and individual counseling. Students who participate in the International Baccalaureate (I.B.) or Advanced Placement (AP) programs in high school may receive college credit from WCU in as many as thirty areas.

Academic Programs

WCU is one of North Carolina's five National Merit Universities, authorized to grant scholarships to students who qualify as National Merit finalists. The Western Meritorious Award for finalists provides a four-year scholarship, which covers the equivalent amount of in-state tuition, fees, room, and board, to National Merit finalists, who also receive a computer. The Honors College offers extra academic and social opportunities for qualified students who want to make the best of their college experience. One of the few honors programs in the state to offer students a residential option, the college is among the few nationwide to award graduates with a special honors diploma. Each spring, students are invited to present research findings in the WCU Undergraduate Research Symposium. The best projects proceed to national conventions, where WCU students consistently win top honors. At Western Carolina University, all bachelor's degree programs include courses in liberal studies designed to provide each student with the knowledge, skills, and attitudes of an educated person. These include the ability to think critically, to communicate effectively, to identify and solve problems reflectively, to use information and technology responsibly, to appreciate the creative and performing arts, and to seek personal development and lifelong learning. To earn a bachelor's degree, students must successfully complete between 120 and 128 semester hours of credit, or about forty courses. Students are encouraged to select a major—an academic area of focus—by their second year, which determines course selections for the junior and senior years and often a career path. Students who are undecided about a major can get help from a variety of sources, including professors, personal academic advisers, and career counselors.

Off-Campus Programs

WCU offers a wide array of study-abroad experiences. Students take advantage of opportunities such as studying the criminal justice and education systems in England, international business law in the Netherlands, hospitality management in China, and language and culture in Mexico. WCU is a member of the National Student Exchange, and students can pay WCU tuition to take courses on other U.S. and international campuses. Closer to home, WCU students in natural resources management and the sciences routinely conduct field work at off-campus field stations in the nearby Pisgah and Nantahala National Forests and in the Great Smoky Mountains National Park, where WCU students are participating in a vast scientific inventory of all the park's living organisms. Education, nursing, geography, and other fields offer off-campus internships and opportunities for hands-on learning as well.

Academic Facilities

WCU lends its resources—cultural, financial, and informational—to the western North Carolina region, sustaining and enhancing the lives and livelihoods of businesses, families, individuals, schools, and local governments. WCU fulfills part of this commitment through galleries, museums, theaters, music halls, and centers such as the Center for Mathematics and Science Education, Computer Center, Coulter Faculty Center, Developmental Evaluation Center, Highlands Biological Station, International Programs and Services, Mountain Aquacultural Research Center, Mountain Heritage Museum, Mountain Resource Center, North Carolina Center for the Advancement of Teaching, Hunter Library's Special Collections, Reading Center, Speech and Hearing Center, and the Distance Learning and Teleconference Center. WCU is home to two of the largest facilities in western North Carolina. The 8,000-seat Ramsey Regional Activity Center attracts nationally known speakers, major concerts, theater and television productions, banquets, receptions, and conferences, as well as WCU athletic events. A major research facility, Hunter Library, contains more than 500,000 books and bound periodicals and provides access to 90 databases and the Internet.

Costs

The projected undergraduate costs for the 2004–05 academic year (fall and spring semesters), including tuition and fees, room, the standard meal option, and a cost-saving book rental program, are $6929 for North Carolina residents and $16,290 for out-of-state residents and international students. All undergraduate students are required to have an appropriate, networkable computer.

Financial Aid

Nearly two thirds of Western's freshmen receive some form of financial assistance, which includes grants, loans, scholarships, and student employment. Entering students who are interested in applying for financial aid must complete the Free Application for Federal Student Aid (FAFSA) as soon as possible after January 1. Since the most attractive sources of assistance are limited, applicants are encouraged to complete the FAFSA by the University priority deadline of March 31. WCU awards three types of financial aid: scholarships and grants, which do not have to be repaid; long-term and low-interest loans; and employment. University and departmental merit scholarships, such as the Achievement Award, Excellence Award, Founder's Scholarship, Computer Scholarship, WCU Meritorious Award, and Valedictorian Scholarship, are also available to qualified students. The North Carolina Teaching Fellows Program at WCU provides full tuition and other expenses for eight semesters to qualified North Carolina residents who agree to teach in the state for a specified period upon graduation. Students who complete the application for admission, submit supporting documentation, and gain admittance receive automatic consideration for University merit-based awards for which they may be eligible.

Faculty

There are approximately 331 full-time faculty members who hold degrees from major colleges and universities. Eighty percent have doctoral or terminal degrees. The student-faculty ratio is 16:1. As a result, WCU faculty members know their students as well as they do their subjects. They spend time with students outside of class, meeting for informal study groups, organized trips, and individual counseling sessions. While they conduct research, write books, publish in professional journals, and belong to state and national professional organizations, WCU faculty members love to teach.

Student Government

WCU strongly supports active student participation in campus leadership through groups such as the Student Government Association (SGA), Resident Student Association, Student Media Board, fraternities and sororities, and student advisory councils. The SGA promotes students' interests while serving as a liaison between students and the administration. The SGA governs through the executive, legislative, and judicial branches. The SGA president is an ex officio member of the WCU Board of Trustees and a member of the Association of Student Governments, which serves the sixteen campuses of the University of North Carolina. The SGA coordinates the disbursement of student activity fees to some sixty campus organizations. Each year, WCU students receive a copy of the Student Handbook, which lists student organizations and includes the Student Bill of Rights and Code of Conduct. The recently adopted *Greek Life: A Plan for Excellence* was written by a committee of students, faculty members, and administrators; it defines the relationship between WCU and its fraternities and sororities.

Admission Requirements

Western Carolina University seeks students with proven academic performance and solid academic potential. National Merit finalists, high school valedictorians, and students in the top 10 percent of their high school classes are strongly encouraged to apply for merit scholarships. Admission decisions for incoming freshmen are based on the strength of the applicants' credentials, including high school course work, grades, class rank, and standardized test scores (SAT or ACT). Required courses include 4 units of English; algebra I, algebra II, and geometry or an advanced math course for which algebra II is a prerequisite; one physical science, one biological science, and a third laboratory science; and U.S. history and one additional social science course. Two units of one foreign language are required. On-campus interviews and letters of recommendation are not required but are useful for students who wish to appeal an admission decision. College courses and grades are used to determine the eligibility of transfer students and freshmen with dual enrollment credit.

Application and Information

Western accepts students on a rolling admission basis, which means that the earlier students apply, the better their chances for admission and the sooner they are notified of a decision. Students are usually notified of a decision within three to four weeks of submitting all required admissions materials. All required materials must be received no later than thirty days prior to the term for which a student is making application. The application for admission and supporting documentation also serve as a student's merit-based scholarship application. For more information, application forms, and additional information, students may contact:

Philip Cauley, Director of Admissions
242 H. F. Robinson Building
Western Carolina University
Cullowhee, North Carolina 28723

Telephone: 828-227-7317
877-WCU4YOU (toll-free)
Fax: 828-227-7319
E-mail: admiss@wcu.edu
World Wide Web: http://www.poweryourmind.com

An opening celebration welcomes students each fall to Western Carolina University in the Great Smoky Mountains of North Carolina.

WESTERN CONNECTICUT STATE UNIVERSITY

DANBURY, CONNECTICUT

The University

Founded in 1903, Western Connecticut State University (WestConn) is dedicated to providing both a high-quality university education and a memorable campus experience at an affordable cost. With programs in the arts and sciences, business, and professional studies, WestConn takes pride in providing an outstanding education to more than 3,800 full-time undergraduates and nearly 2,300 graduate or part-time students.

WestConn offers excellent educational programs through five academic units: the Ancell School of Business, the School of Arts and Sciences, the School of Professional Studies, the Division of Graduate Studies and External Programs, and the University Center for Adult Education. The most popular majors include communications and theater arts, education, business, justice and law administration, and nursing.

In addition to the University's full menu of undergraduate degrees, the Ancell School of Business offers the Master of Business Administration, Master of Health Administration, and Master of Science in justice administration degrees. The School of Arts and Sciences offers the Master of Arts degree in biology and environmental sciences, earth and planetary sciences, English, history, and mathematics. The Master of Fine Arts is offered in visual arts. The School of Professional Studies offers the Master of Science degree in elementary education, secondary education, counselor education, and nursing. WestConn launched its applied doctoral program in education during fall 2003. Prelaw and pre–health professions programs also are available.

The University also is rich with a number of learning and social activities beyond the classroom. Students run academic and fraternal organizations, publish an award-winning newspaper and yearbook, and run a radio station. They stage theater and musical productions, participate in cooperative education and internship programs, and administer their own campus government association.

The University provides services for learning-disabled students, study abroad, a University Scholars program, precollegiate and access initiatives, international student services, and community service learning opportunities. There are a variety of NCAA Division III men's and women's sports, intramural sports, and a premier recreation center that includes a swimming pool, indoor track, and weight-lifting machines. The campus also features a child-care center, counseling center, health services office, career development center, and campus ministries.

WestConn is accredited by the New England Association of Schools and Colleges, Inc.; the Board of Governors for Higher Education, State of Connecticut; the Connecticut State Department of Education; the American Chemical Society; the National League for Nursing Accrediting Commission; the Council on Social Work Education (baccalaureate level); the Council for Accreditation of Counseling and Related Educational Programs; and the National Association of Schools of Music.

Location

WestConn offers two campuses in Danbury, in the heart of western Connecticut, as well as a satellite campus in Waterbury. Danbury is a major city in Fairfield County in the foothills of the Berkshire Mountains, just 65 miles north of Manhattan and 50 miles west of Hartford.

In Danbury, the Midtown campus is a 34-acre, fifteen-building campus with an interesting mix of old and new architecture, and it offers easy access to downtown entertainment, restaurants, and shopping. The 364-acre Westside campus is ideal for hikers and nature buffs who want to discover its woodland wonders while enjoying state-of-the-art facilities. The WestConn at Waterbury campus offers a convenient location closer to the center of the state, with the same level of excellent service.

Majors and Degrees

The Ancell School of Business offers the Bachelor of Business Administration degree in accounting, finance, management, management information systems, and marketing, as well as the Bachelor of Science degree in justice and law administration.

The School of Arts and Sciences offers the Associate of Arts, Bachelor of Arts, and Bachelor of Science degrees. The Associate of Arts is offered in American studies–liberal arts. The Bachelor of Arts is offered in American studies, anthropology/sociology, art, biology, chemistry, communications, computer science, earth and planetary sciences–astronomy, economics, English, English–professional writing, history, mathematics, music, political science, psychology, social sciences, and Spanish. The Bachelor of Science is offered in medical technology and meteorology.

The School of Professional Studies offers the Bachelor of Arts and Bachelor of Science degrees. The Bachelor of Arts is offered in social work. The Bachelor of Science is offered in elementary education, secondary education, health science, music education, and nursing.

Academic Programs

The University offers a diverse mix of programs designed to inspire students. From the enlightening category of the arts to specialized fields such as meteorology, the emphasis is on the individual student's learning experience.

Special offerings at WestConn include the nation's first program in computer information security management, a cutting-edge direct/interactive marketing certification program, and the only licensed meteorology program in Connecticut.

Academic Facilities

A number of facilities contribute to academic life on campus. The newly renovated and expanded library holds 142,698 volumes and nearly 1,000 periodicals. Students are encouraged to make use of the campus's cutting-edge computer and laboratory facilities, and they are invited to hone their craft in superior theater and musical facilities. Students, as well as the greater Danbury community, benefit from the offerings of the WestConn International Center, German Studies Center, Institute for Holistic Health Studies, Weather Center, Jane Goodall Center for Excellence in Environmental Studies, Center for Collaboration, Center for Business Research, and Westside Observatory and Planetarium.

Costs

As part of the Connecticut State System of Higher Education, WestConn offers a high-quality educational program at a reasonable cost. It is estimated that a full-time, in-state undergraduate student who lives and eats on campus pays $12,746 for 2004–05. This estimate of annual costs includes tuition, fees, and room and board. Books, laboratory fees, health insurance, and personal expenses are not included in the estimate.

WestConn participates in the New England Regional Student Program of the New England Board of Higher Education. This program offers residents of other New England states the opportunity to enroll at WestConn at Connecticut resident tuition rates, plus an additional fee, in courses not available in their home states. Details about the regional program can be obtained through the Office of University Admissions at the telephone number listed below.

Financial Aid

Any student matriculated at WestConn and registering for at least 6 credits per semester may apply for student aid, which includes federal, state, and institutional funding. Students must complete the Free Application for Federal Student Aid (FAFSA) and be sure to list WestConn's school code of 001380 in the college release section. Students also need to submit appropriate signed copies of federal income tax returns. Academic scholarships are available to students with superior academic credentials. Students with demonstrated financial need also have the opportunity to participate in work-study programs. For more information, students should contact the Financial Aid Office at 203-837-8580 or financialaid@wcsu.edu.

Faculty

Nationally respected, WestConn's faculty members and administrators are continually cited for scholarly achievement. The faculty has 428 members, or 1 professor for every 16 students. Ninety percent of the University's full-time faculty members have doctoral, terminal, or master's degrees.

Admission Requirements

WestConn welcomes applications from all qualified individuals. Admission to the three undergraduate schools is competitive. University admissions criteria include grade point average, types of courses taken, extracurricular activities, and standardized test results. Applications are reviewed by admissions professionals. If an applicant feels that individual circumstances warrant special consideration, a personal letter explaining those circumstances may be submitted with the application.

Academic preparation is the most important factor in determining admission. Freshman candidates for admission must have a high school diploma from an accredited secondary school or an equivalency diploma. General Educational Development (GED) test scores must be converted into a State of Connecticut Equivalency Diploma.

WestConn applicants should present evidence of successful completion of the following academic units in high school with a cumulative grade point average of B- (80) or higher: 4 years of English, including writing skills and literature; 3 years of mathematics, including algebra I, geometry, and algebra II; 2 years of social sciences, including U.S. history; 2 years of laboratory sciences; and 2 to 3 years of a single foreign language (3 years are recommended). Academic course work in computer science, visual arts, theater, music, or dance may be substituted for one of the areas above.

Those applicants who do not meet these guidelines may be considered under the Educational Achievement and Access Program. For more information about the program, students should call the Office of University Admissions (number below).

For specific information about transfer student admission, early admission, freshman entrance with advanced standing, special transfer arrangements for associate degree recipients, guest student admission, readmit admission, fresh start admission, and international student admission, students should call the Office of University Admissions.

Interviews are not required, but candidates are encouraged to attend an information session before they enroll. These sessions provide students with information about the University and the admissions process and offer an important opportunity to assess how the University can help students meet their long-term educational goals. They also afford students the opportunity to meet with professors, other potential students, and current students. Student-guided tours are available. While on tour, students are able to visit the library, the residence halls, science and computer laboratories, the student center, and the recreation center. For information about appointments and campus visits, students should call the Office of University Admissions.

Application and Information

WestConn seeks to enroll students who will benefit from and contribute to the University. Rolling admissions for the fall semester begin December 1, with class spaces filled on a first-come basis. Rolling admissions for the spring semester begin October 1, with class spaces filled on a first-come basis. To apply, students should obtain an application from the Office of University Admissions or from a secondary school or community college guidance office. WestConn welcomes transfer and international student applications.

For application forms and more information, students should contact:

William Hawkins
Enrollment Management Officer
Office of University Admissions
Western Connecticut State University
181 White Street
Danbury, Connecticut 06810
Telephone: 203-837-9000
877-837-WCSU (toll-free)
E-mail: hawkinsw@wcsu.edu
World Wide Web: http://www.wcsu.edu

A view of the Western Connecticut State University Midtown campus.

WESTERN ILLINOIS UNIVERSITY

MACOMB, ILLINOIS

The University

The campus of Western Illinois University (WIU) extends more than 1,464 acres and includes fifty-two buildings. The residence halls on campus provide for a variety of lifestyles and house more than half of the 13,461 students at the University. Single and double rooms, study floors, and academic major areas are just a few examples of residence options. The University Union is the center of campus activities and includes a food court, a bookstore, bowling alleys, an ice-cream parlor, meeting rooms, an area for billiards, and lounge areas. More than 250 student organizations offer a variety of cocurricular activities to supplement formal classroom education. Cultural programs reflecting both local and national interests are on the calendar several evenings each week.

Intercollegiate and intramural athletic programs are available for both women and men. The campus has three swimming pools, an eighteen-hole golf course, tennis courts, assorted activity fields, and a Campus Recreation Center, which is open evenings and weekends for student enjoyment.

There are 11,033 undergraduate students currently enrolled. Although the majority of students are from Illinois, forty-six other states and fifty-four countries are represented in the student body.

Career placement services are offered to graduating students and graduates. Nearly 93 percent of the graduates who register with the job placement office are placed in desirable positions. Health services are available through the Beu Health Center, which is located in the center of the campus and is staffed and in operation at all times when the University is in regular session.

Location

Macomb, a community of 19,000 people, is located in the heart of the western Illinois farmland about 240 miles southwest of Chicago. Amtrak offers daily service to and from Chicago. Bus service is available, and the Macomb Municipal Airport provides facilities and services for charter and private planes. The community serves a large rural area as a center for shopping, health services, industry and employment, and recreation. Most religions are represented in the immediate area. Argyle Lake State Park, which is located about 9 miles from the campus, provides opportunities for boating, fishing, camping, and other outside activities.

Majors and Degrees

Western Illinois University offers the following undergraduate degree programs: Bachelor of Arts, Bachelor of Business, Bachelor of Fine Arts, Bachelor of Science, Bachelor of Science in Education, and Bachelor of Social Work. Major programs of study include accountancy, African American studies, agriculture (agricultural business, agricultural science),* art,* bilingual/bicultural education,* biology (botany, microbiology, zoology),* board of trustees, broadcasting, chemistry,* clinical laboratory science, communication, communication sciences and disorders, community health, computer science (business), economics, elementary education (early childhood education),* English (literature and language),* family and consumer sciences (dietetics, fashion merchandising, hotel/restaurant management), finance, French,* geography,* geology, graphic communication, health services management, history,* human resource management, individual studies, information management, instructional technology and telecommunications, journalism, law enforcement and justice administration, management, manufacturing engineering technology, marketing (marketing management, supply chain management), mathematics,* music (applied music, musical theater, music business, music therapy),* philosophy, physical education (athletic training, exercise science and fitness),* physics,* political science (American government, international relations/comparative politics, public policy/public service), psychology, recreation/park/tourism administration, social work, sociology, Spanish,* special education,* theater, and women's studies. Those programs followed by * offer teacher certification.

Thirteen preprofessional programs are offered to prepare students for professional study at other universities: agricultural engineering, architecture, chemical engineering, dentistry, engineering, forestry, law, medicine, nursing, optometry, pharmacy, physical therapy, and veterinary medicine. The majority of students in the premedicine program have attended medical school at Southern Illinois University, the University of Illinois, and Loyola University. In addition, dual programs are available in engineering and clinical laboratory science in cooperation with the University of Illinois at Urbana-Champaign and approved schools of medical technology.

Academic Program

It is the philosophy of the University that a broad general education should be an integral part of every degree program. Thus, approximately one third of the degree requirements involve study and the development of fundamental skills in the arts and sciences. The remainder of the program is devoted to either a comprehensive major or a major/minor plus general electives. Credit is awarded for acceptable scores on CLEP general and subject examinations and on the College Board's Advanced Placement examinations in English, foreign languages, history, and mathematics. Proficiency examinations are administered on campus through specific departments. Special educational opportunities for students with high aptitude and superior ability are offered through the honors college. Western Illinois University is on the semester system; the fall semester closes before the winter holidays and the spring semester closes in mid-May. Two 4-week summer sessions run concurrently with one 8-week summer session from mid-June to early August.

Western offers a four-year and a two-year program in the study of military science through Army ROTC. Successful completion of the program and requirements for the baccalaureate degree leads to a commission as a second lieutenant in the Army.

Off-Campus Programs

WIU's program in clinical laboratory science includes three years of study on campus followed by twelve months at an approved school of medical technology. Students enrolled in a teacher education program spend one term off campus as supervised student teachers in cooperating public schools. Off-campus internships or field experiences are available.

One-year and one-semester study-abroad programs are available in Australia, Canada, England, France, Germany, Japan, Mexico, Spain, and any one of a hundred other locations worldwide. Students electing to participate in a study-abroad program earn credit toward their undergraduate degree program while enrolled in a university abroad.

Academic Facilities

Western's Leslie F. Malpass Library has six floors of library materials, with shelving space for 1 million volumes and seating for 2,500 readers. It has a regional research center in special collections, four on-campus specialized branch libraries, an extensive legal reference collection, depository status with the Illinois and U.S. governments, and access to the

ILLINET Online, which provides a catalog of WIU's library holdings and those of the University of Illinois and forty-four other academic libraries throughout the state.

Major computer facilities staffed by trained personnel are strategically located across the campus in residence halls and academic buildings. Laboratory facilities containing state-of-the-art equipment provide students with current technological hands-on experience in their discipline of study. A research station west of campus on the Mississippi River, a field campus south of campus, and a 300-acre farm north of campus provide nearby instructional facilities for students enrolled in agriculture, biology, and recreation, park, and tourism administration courses. Three theaters, a recital hall, and an art gallery provide performing arts students with a rich variety of local, regional, national, and international cultural and artistic opportunities. WIU's off-campus undergraduate center in Moline, Illinois, offers area residents and placebound students the opportunity to enroll in undergraduate course work in several disciplines and complete degree requirements in ten different majors.

Costs

Western ensures that a student's college years are a good investment with its guaranteed four-year rate for tuition, fees, and room and board. All new undergraduate students entering the University are automatically included in the plan, which freezes the per-hour rate that a student pays for a four-year period, so costs stay the same each year as long as the student maintains continuous enrollment at Western.

New students enrolling for the 2002–03 academic year paid the following annual guaranteed rates (based on an average class load of 15 semester hours): $3465 for tuition ($115.50 per credit hour), $1033 for fees, $3032 for a double room, and $2030 for the basic a la carte board rate. Out-of-state tuition is assessed at two times the rate of in-state tuition.

Financial Aid

During the 2002–03 academic year, 11,513 WIU students received financial aid from funds totaling $70 million. Financial aid is available through state and federal programs for full- or part-time WIU students. Students should use the Free Application for Federal Student Aid (FAFSA) to apply for the following state and federal programs: Federal Pell Grant, Federal Supplemental Educational Opportunity Grant, Federal Perkins Loan, Federal Stafford Student Loan, Federal Work-Study Program, and Illinois Monetary Award Program (MAP). Students should begin the process by completing their federal income tax return as early as possible to provide accurate information on the FAFSA and then filing the FAFSA as soon as possible after January 1. Many student jobs are available in areas such as secretarial work, food service, and building and grounds maintenance. WIU also awards talent grants and academic scholarships. Talent grants are offered in men's and women's athletics, music, art, theater, agriculture, student services, and debate. More than 1,700 scholarships are awarded annually through the WIU Foundation. The majority of scholarships reward high academic potential and achievement, while others consider hometown, academic interest, or financial need. To receive an application for WIU scholarship opportunities, students should contact the WIU Scholarship Office.

Faculty

Sixty-two percent of the 429 faculty members have doctorates or the highest degree in their fields. The student-faculty ratio is 17:1, and the average class has 25 students. The faculty is responsible for 95 percent of the total student credit hours earned at the undergraduate level, with graduate teaching assistants contributing the remaining 5 percent. As a group, full professors devote approximately 90 percent of their professional responsibilities to undergraduate instruction. Publication and research are encouraged, and many of the faculty members have received federal and other grants, fellowships, and awards.

Student Government

Students are actively involved in University affairs through elected representatives to the Student Government Association. As students at a public institution, these representatives also frequently become involved in the legislative process through lobbying efforts in the state capital.

Admission Requirements

Students who apply as freshmen are admitted if they have a minimum ACT composite score of 22 (or an equivalent SAT I score) and a minimum of a 2.2 GPA (on a 4.0 scale) or if they rank in the upper 40 percent of their high school graduating class and achieve a minimum ACT composite score of 18 (or an equivalent SAT I score) and a minimum of a 2.2 GPA (on a 4.0 scale). Students must also have completed 4 years of English; 3 years each of math, science, and social sciences; and 2 years of electives. Transfer students who have earned 24 semester hours of college credit are considered on the basis of college performance only. These students must have a cumulative average of at least C for all hours attempted and must have been in good standing at the last school attended. Students who have earned fewer than 24 semester hours of college credit must meet the freshman admission requirements, have a cumulative average of at least C in all college hours attempted, and be in good standing at the last college attended. All documents required for admission must be sent directly from the reporting institution to the Admissions Office at Western. There is a nonrefundable application fee of $30 for a traditional paper application and $25 for an electronic application.

Application and Information

Application forms and admission materials may be secured by contacting:

Undergraduate Admissions
Sherman Hall 115
Western Illinois University
1 University Circle
Macomb, Illinois 61455-1390
Telephone: 309-298-3157
877-PICKWIU (toll-free)
World Wide Web: http://www.wiu.edu

Sherman Hall, the main administration building.

WESTERN MICHIGAN UNIVERSITY

KALAMAZOO, MICHIGAN

The University

Western Michigan University (WMU) has emerged as one of the nation's top public universities and enjoys an international reputation in fields as varied as medieval studies, blind rehabilitation, jazz studies, aviation, paper science, graph theory, and evaluation.

The University is one of only 102 public universities in the nation placed by the Carnegie Foundation for the Advancement of Teaching in its top classification of Doctoral/Research–Universities–Extensive. It also is one of only ninety-seven public universities in the United States to have its own chapter of Phi Beta Kappa, the nation's premier honor society. In addition, *U.S. News & World Report* has ranked WMU as one of America's top 100 public universities for the past five years.

With 29,178 students, WMU is Michigan's fourth-largest university and is among the nation's fifty largest institutions of higher education. Despite its size, complexity, and variety of offerings, WMU is committed to its mission of being a student-centered research university and has worked to maintain a comfortable student-faculty ratio of 16:1. Because of its relatively low tuition and required fees, the University is often listed as one of the country's best buys in higher education.

Founded in 1903, WMU has seven degree-granting colleges: Arts and Sciences, Aviation, the Haworth College of Business, Education, Engineering and Applied Sciences, Fine Arts, and Health and Human Services as well as the Graduate College and Lee Honors College, which is one of the oldest honors programs in the nation. The University offers 254 academic programs, 152 of them at the undergraduate level. Because it has a vibrant graduate component that includes thirty doctoral degree programs, the University attracts faculty members who have been trained at the world's leading universities and who have well-established research and teaching careers.

Over the past decade, WMU has focused on enhancing its out-of-class learning opportunities by expanding its study-abroad programs, internships with organizations around the nation, and regional and national business partnerships. Its on-campus learning environment is bolstered by some of the best instructional, cultural, and recreational facilities in the Midwest. In recent years, more than half a billion dollars in new construction and equipment has transformed the campus, giving students access to acclaimed performance spaces; a state-of-the-art science pavilion; a world-class aviation college; a large, well-equipped student recreation center; and a cutting-edge engineering campus adjacent to a new Business Technology and Research Park.

The University is home to a diverse student body that includes students from all fifty states as well as an international enrollment of more than 1,700 students representing 110 nations. Minority students also are well represented and typically make up about 9 percent of the student body. The University's on-campus enrollment of more than 27,000 includes about 6,200 students who live in twenty-two campus residence halls that offer a variety of living arrangements.

There are more than 375 registered student organizations, including a wide range of Greek, academic honorary, and professional organizations. In addition, the University has nationally recognized arts programs, a lively cultural calendar, and NCAA Division I-A Mid-American and Central Collegiate Hockey Association sports teams. It's nine men's and eleven women's varsity sports, intramural teams, and club sports add vitality to campus life.

Location

Kalamazoo, one of Michigan's larger cities, is at the center of a county whose population exceeds 280,000 residents. The campus is located midway between Detroit and Chicago, about 2 1/2 hours from each city. Commercial transportation includes train, bus, and airline services. The Kalamazoo community offers a wide array of lively entertainment: sports, such as professional baseball, hockey, and soccer; music, from jazz to heavy metal; intimate comedy clubs; and dining, from fast food to international cuisine. West Michigan is also home to numerous thriving businesses, industries, and Fortune 500 companies, including Haworth Inc., the Whirlpool Corp., and the Kellogg Co., and many of these organizations offer internships to WMU students. Kalamazoo is just 45 minutes from Lake Michigan beaches and only 3 to 4 hours from northern Michigan's ski country. Excellent local skiing is only 30 minutes from the campus.

Majors and Degrees

WMU offers bachelor's degree programs in these fields: accountancy; administrative systems; advertising and promotion; aeronautical engineering; Africana studies; American studies; anthropology; art; art education; art history; athletic training; aviation flight science; aviation maintenance technology; aviation science and administration; biochemistry; biology; biomedical sciences; broadcast and cable production; business-oriented chemistry; chemical engineering; chemistry; civil engineering; communication studies; community health education; computer engineering; computer information systems; computer science; computer science–theory and analysis; construction engineering; criminal justice; dance; dietetics; earth science; economics; electrical engineering; elementary education–art, elementary group minors, music, physical education, speech pathology and audiology; engineering graphics and design technology; engineering management technology; English; environmental studies; exercise science; family studies; family studies–child development; finance; food marketing; food service administration; French; general business; geochemistry; geography; geology; geophysics; German; gerontology; global and international studies; graphic design; health education; history; human resource management; hydrogeology; imaging; industrial design; industrial engineering; industrial technology; integrated supply matrix management; interdisciplinary health services; interior design; interpersonal communication; journalism; Latin; management; manufacturing engineering; manufacturing engineering technology; marketing; mathematics; mechanical engineering; media studies; music; music composition; music education; music history; music–jazz studies; music performance; music theater performance; music theory; music therapy; nursing; nursing RN completion; occupational education studies; occupational therapy; organizational communication; paper engineering; paper science; personal financial planning; philosophy; physics; political science; predentistry; prelaw; premedicine; professional studies; psychology; public administration; public history; public relations; recreation; religion; sales and business marketing; school health education; secondary education–art education, biology, chemistry, dietitics, earth science, English, family and consumer sciences, French, geography, German, health education, history, industrial technology, Latin, mathematics, music education, physical education–teacher/coach, physics, political science, secondary education in business, secondary education in marketing, Spanish, technology and design; social work, sociology, Spanish, technology design; special education–emotionally impaired; special education–mentally impaired; speech pathology and audiology; statistics; student-integrated curriculum; student-planned curriculum; student-planned major; technology and design; telecommunications management; textile and apparel studies; theater; theater–design and technical production; theater–performance; theater–theater studies; tourism and travel; travel instruction; and women's studies.

Academic Program

WMU offers undergraduate students a rich blend of academic majors and minors, as well as its comprehensive general education program and an honors college. These programs ensure that students graduate with the proficiencies and perspectives they need to succeed. The University Curriculum Program is available to students who are undecided about a major and wish to explore WMU's academic offerings. Last fall, more than 2,000 students enrolled in the program, which won a national award for outstanding academic advising. The Lee Honors College provides undergraduates with a unique living/learning environment, offering the intimacy of a small college with the resources of a major university.

Off-Campus Programs

A host of U.S. business-industry partnerships as well as exchange agreements with universities around the world provide numerous training and research opportunities for graduate and undergraduate students alike. The University provides assistance to students seeking internships in their chosen fields of study.

Academic Facilities

The University Libraries, with the fourth-largest holdings in Michigan, and the University Computing Center together provide campuswide access to worldwide information resources, comparable to other top universities in the Midwest. Computer labs are available across the campus, many in residence halls. In addition, WMU is a completely wireless campus.

Costs

WMU is committed to keeping costs as low as possible to ensure that all qualified students have access to the University. WMU's tuition and fees are among the lowest in the state. Costs for 2003–04 were tuition and fees, $5535, and room and board, $6496. Books and supplies and personal and travel expenses vary based on individual factors.

Financial Aid

Last year, more than 24,000 students received financial assistance totaling nearly $175 million. There are three basic types of financial aid: merit-based programs, need-based programs, and student employment.

Merit-based programs include the Medallion Scholarships, which are valued at $32,000 over four years and are the University's most prestigious award for entering freshmen. Other financial aid includes the Army ROTC awards, Michigan National Guard awards, the National Merit Scholarships Award, and numerous sponsored and departmental scholarships for new and currently enrolled students. Merit-based scholarships, ranging in value from $2000 to $6000, also are available to community college transfer students.

Need-based loans, grants, college work-study, and other aid options are provided for students who demonstrate particular financial need. To be considered, students should complete the Free Application for Federal Student Aid (FAFSA).

The student employment option reflects research indicating that students who work part time are more likely to graduate than students who do not work at all. About 40 percent of WMU's students work while in school, and more than 700 jobs are offered through the college work-study program.

WMU provides a tuition payment plan through Academic Management Services (AMS) and Tuition Management Systems (TMS). This allows parents and students to pay college costs in monthly installments. No interest is charged for these services, which may be renewed annually for $55. Students should contact AMS at 800-556-6684 or TMS at 800-722-4867 for more information.

Faculty

WMU's commitment to academic excellence means that many of its 986 full-time and 203 part-time faculty members conduct research. Tenured professors teach freshman-level courses, and full-time faculty members teach three quarters of all classes. Almost 93 percent of WMU faculty members have earned a doctorate or other terminal degree in their fields.

Student Government

Governance structures include the Western Student Association and its Student Senate and the Residence Hall Association. Each provides students with a wide variety of opportunities for leadership.

Admission Requirements

Admission to the University is based on a combination of factors, including grade point average, ACT scores, number and kinds of college-prep courses, and trend of grades. In addition, students must meet specific course requirements that include 4 years of English; 3 years of mathematics, including intermediate algebra; 3 years of social sciences; and 2 years of biological/physical sciences. Students who do not meet these requirements but are otherwise admissible may still be admitted to WMU and take the necessary courses as University-level work for credit during their first year.

Transfer students with a minimum of 26 transferable hours (39 quarter hours) at the time of application and a GPA of at least 2.0 (C average) are considered for admission. The trend of the most recent grades is also taken into account. Applicants with fewer than 26 transferable hours (39 quarter hours) at the time of application also must submit a high school transcript. In such cases, admission is based on both college and high school records. For more information, students can request a transfer brochure from the Office of Admissions and Orientation.

Application and Information

For an application or additional information, students should contact:

Office of Admissions and Orientation
Western Michigan University
1903 West Michigan Avenue
Kalamazoo, Michigan 49008-5720
Telephone: 269-387-2000
800-400-4WMU (toll-free)
World Wide Web:
http://www.wmich.edu/admi/undergradapp/

This imposing clock tower joins Waldo Library, on the right, with the University Computing Center.

WESTERN NEW ENGLAND COLLEGE

SPRINGFIELD, MASSACHUSETTS

The College

Western New England College, founded in 1919, is a private, independent coeducational institution offering more than thirty undergraduate majors at the baccalaureate level in the Schools of Arts and Sciences, Business, and Engineering. The College offers a unique combined Bachelor of Arts and Juris Doctor program and seven graduate degrees. The American Bar Association–accredited School of Law provides full- and-part-time programs leading to Juris Doctor degrees. Western New England College also serves part-time working professionals through its continuing education programs offered in Springfield and at fourteen sites throughout the commonwealth.

Western New England College began as a satellite campus of Northeastern University in rented rooms located in the downtown Springfield YMCA. Its mission was to provide a college education for working people who could not afford the time to attend college classes full-time during the day. The high-quality instruction gave "The Springfield Division," as the College was known, a growing reputation, and by 1951, when Northeastern elected to end its satellite program, there was a demand for the institution to continue. That year, Western New England College was incorporated by the Massachusetts Board of Collegiate Authority.

Western New England College is known for providing strong professionally based programs with a solid liberal arts background to prepare students for entry into professional careers or graduate school. There are approximately 2,250 full-time undergraduates, while the total enrollment, including part-time undergraduates and graduate students, is about 4,500. Approximately 56 percent of the full-time undergraduates are men, and about 79 percent of the students live on campus. The College annually enrolls students from about twenty-six states and eight countries; 58 percent come from out of state.

The College has developed a unique Wholistic Student Development Program that provides a comprehensive educational experience to the student inside and outside of the classroom. In addition to the academic component, other aspects of Learning Beyond the Classroom include personal and social development, career planning, multicultural awareness, physical fitness and health, and artistic and cultural appreciation. The Campus Activities Board is primarily responsible for coordinating a student activities calendar. The Western New England College Career Center is staffed with professional career counselors who provide students with the tools they need to succeed professionally, from mock, taped interviews to challenging employment opportunities. The College currently offers students nineteen varsity sports (NCAA Division III) in which to become involved. Men's sports include baseball, basketball, cross-country, football, golf, ice hockey, lacrosse, soccer, tennis, and wrestling. Women's sports include basketball, cross-country, field hockey, lacrosse, soccer, softball, swimming, tennis, and volleyball. Non–NCAA participation sports include men's and women's bowling and martial arts.

Location

Western New England College's 215-acre campus was developed in a residential section of Springfield, Massachusetts. It is located about 4 miles from downtown Springfield, which is serviced by Greyhound and Peter Pan bus lines, Amtrak, and Bradley International Airport in Windsor Locks, Connecticut. Hartford is just 30 minutes away; Albany, Boston, and Providence are less than 100 miles from campus; and New York City is a 3-hour drive.

Majors and Degrees

Undergraduate programs offered by the School of Arts and Sciences are majors in biology, chemistry, communication, computer science (concentrations in information technology and software development), criminal justice, economics, education (elementary and secondary), English, history, international studies, liberal studies, mathematical sciences, philosophy, political science, political studies, prepharmacy, pre–physician assistant studies, psychology, social work, and sociology. The School of Business offers degrees in accounting, computer information systems, finance, general business, management, marketing, marketing communication/advertising, and sport management. The School of Engineering offers majors in biomedical engineering (concentrations in bioinstrumentation, biomechanics, and cell and tissue), electrical engineering (concentrations in computer and electrical), industrial engineering, and mechanical engineering (concentrations in mechanical and manufacturing). The prepharmacy and pre–physician assistant programs are affiliated with the Massachusetts College of Pharmacy and Health Sciences in Boston. Specialized programs include secondary teacher certification (biology, business, chemistry, English, history, and mathematics), elementary education certification (English, history, psychology, or sociology can be completed in four years; math takes longer to complete), and premed and prelaw programs. The College's 3+3 Law Program offers eligible students the opportunity to earn their bachelor's and Juris Doctor degrees from Western New England College School of Law in just six years instead of seven. The College is accredited by the New England Association of Schools and Colleges, and the School of Business is fully accredited by AACSB International. Various programs have additional accreditation from specific agencies.

Academic Programs

The College operates on a two-semester calendar and has a limited summer school program. Students normally take five courses each semester. Specific information on the various academic programs is available from the Office of Admissions.

Western New England College participates in the College Board's Advanced Placement (AP) Program and College-Level Examination Program (CLEP). Successful completion of these programs may result in the earning of academic credit and the waiving of certain courses.

Academic Facilities

The Western New England campus contains twenty major buildings and is situated on 215 acres. Classes are held in five classroom-laboratory buildings, which contain more than sixty-five classrooms. The D'Amour Library contains 119,000 volumes and is currently receiving 266 periodicals, with access to more than 5,000 titles via the Internet. The College is committed to providing students with access to a wide range of computing hardware and software. The College has a campus-wide network linking all buildings to hundreds of PCs in public areas, including the Churchill Hall Lab, the D'Amour Library, the Writing and Math Centers, the Accounting Lab, the School of Law, and the Engineering Labs. In addition, the School of Engineering has a large number of microcomputers, graphic plotters, and other peripherals used to support the laboratory programs. All College residence hall rooms are wired for Internet access, and all registered students have Internet e-mail accounts. In addition, each semester more than 20 faculty members and several hundred students use a special software package, customized for Western New England College, to provide safe and secure file transport between faculty members, students, campus organizations, and informal groups.

Costs

Tuition and fees for the 2004–05 academic year are $22,914 for engineering students who are commuters and $31,438 for engineering students who are residents. For students in the Schools of Business and Arts and Science, they are $21,986 for commuters and $30,510 for residents.

Financial Aid

Western New England College offers comprehensive programs of financial assistance to students who demonstrate financial need. The programs include merit- and need-based scholarships, grants, loans, and on-campus employment. Students seeking financial aid must submit the Free Application for Federal Student Aid (FAFSA) and a copy of the federal income tax return and W2. Approximately 90 percent of Western New England College students annually receive assistance.

Faculty

Western New England College has a faculty of 157 full-time instructors of whom 90 percent have received their terminal degrees. The College also has 222 adjunct instructors who share important specialized information with the students. The Western New England College School of Law has a distinguished legal faculty numbering 34 full-time instructors and 30 adjunct instructors.

The ratio of students to faculty members is 17:1. The average class size is 21, and students have ample opportunity to meet with faculty members outside of class.

Admission Requirements

Applicants must have graduated from an approved secondary school or have obtained a General Educational Development (GED) credential. The minimum units of high school preparation units should include 4 units of English, 2 units of mathematics, 1 unit of laboratory science, and 1 unit of U.S. history. Applicants to the School of Business and those who wish to major in chemistry, computer science, or mathematics are required to present 3 units of mathematics. Prospective engineering students must present 1 unit of physics or 1 unit of chemistry as well as 4 units of mathematics. Prospective majors in prepharmacy and pre–physician assistant studies are required to present 3 units of mathematics, including algebra I and II and geometry. These students are also required to present 2 units of laboratory science, including biology and chemistry; physics with a laboratory and precalculus are both recommended. Freshman applicants are required to submit scores on the SAT I or ACT. International applicants should take the Test of English as a Foreign Language (TOEFL) and have their scores forwarded to the Admissions Office.

Application and Information

Admission is offered to students on a rolling basis for all programs. However, students are encouraged to apply early in order to receive complete consideration for admission, financial aid, and housing. Students must submit the Western New England College application, SAT I or ACT scores, an official secondary school transcript, and a recommendation from a guidance counselor or teacher. International students can substitute the Test of English as a Foreign Language (TOEFL) for the SAT or ACT. American students for whom English is not the first language are encouraged to submit TOEFL scores. Transfer students must also submit official transcripts for any collegiate work. An essay is not required, but essays and personal statements are welcome. Notification of acceptance begins in late fall.

For further information, students should contact:

Office of Admission
Western New England College
1215 Wilbraham Road
Springfield, Massachusetts 01119-2684
Telephone: 413-782-1321
800-325-1122 Ext. 1321 (toll-free)
Fax: 413-782-1777
E-mail: ugradmis@wnec.edu
World Wide Web: http://www.wnec.edu

Students enjoy the beautiful and spacious Western New England College campus.

WESTERN STATE COLLEGE OF COLORADO

GUNNISON, COLORADO

The College

Western State College of Colorado (WSC) is a more than just a college—it's a destination. WSC students come from all fifty states, several countries, and all sixty-four Colorado counties. They are adventurous individuals who have chosen to study in a beautiful mountain setting where the academic experience extends beyond the classroom. The College's highly qualified professors are accessible and committed to undergraduate teaching and learning. Small classes, personalized attention, and enriching cocurricular and extracurricular activities result in an outstanding college experience. Students interested in experiencing a private-college atmosphere at a public college usually find Western State College appealing to them.

Western offers twenty-two majors leading to a bachelor's degree as well as supporting minors and teacher licensure programs. Many of the academic programs take advantage of WSC's remarkable mountain setting and rich natural resources and incorporate the environment into the learning experience.

At Western, students have many opportunities to become involved in life outside the classroom. Western's staff members and student leaders develop programming each year to support the academic, cultural, and diversity-related interests of the students. Some of the opportunities for students include Wilderness Pursuits, the fitness and health centers, student government, and the WSC Mountain Rescue Team. Students are also welcome to participate in music ensembles, vocal groups, theatrical productions, and student-run media. Western promotes an active and healthy lifestyle and provides many opportunities for athletic participation. Western's intercollegiate athletic teams compete in the Rocky Mountain Athletic Conference (NCAA Division II). Students have organized a number of club sports, with many of the teams also participating in intercollegiate competition. The intramural sports program provides competitive opportunities in several sports.

Location

Western State College of Colorado is in Gunnison, Colorado. What makes everything about the towns of Gunnison and neighboring Crested Butte so special is the area's unmatched Colorado Rocky Mountain beauty. With the Gunnison Valley lying between them, these authentic, unspoiled towns have many buildings dating back to the 1800s. Beyond its rich history, virtually the entire area is protected by national and state parks and forests, securing a sense of how an unspoiled Colorado must have appeared to brave adventurers centuries ago. Students can immerse themselves in a Colorado that no longer exists elsewhere in the state. They understand why Gunnison and Crested Butte are considered to be the pure and simple Colorado.

Majors and Degrees

Western State College of Colorado offers the Bachelor of Arts degree in accounting, anthropology, art, biology, business administration, chemistry, communication and theater, computer information systems, economics, education, English, environmental studies, geology, history, kinesiology, mathematics, music, political science, psychology, recreation, sociology, and Spanish. Minors are offered in all of these disciplines and in computer science, environmental studies, geography, headwaters regional studies, journalism, prelaw, and small business.

Students desiring certification as teachers or school administrators at the elementary or secondary level pursue academic majors in other disciplines while taking the required courses in professional education.

Western State College also confers the Bachelor of Fine Arts degree in art.

Within the academic majors, students may gain preprofessional preparation for dentistry, engineering, law, law enforcement, medicine, nursing, optometry, osteopathy, pharmacy, physical therapy, theology, veterinary medicine, and other professions.

Academic Program

The faculty of Western is committed to the delivery of a curriculum that requires students to (1) demonstrate mastery of basic skills; (2) engage in breadth of study, integrate knowledge from a variety of fields, and apply what is studied to life; (3) study one discipline or group of disciplines deeply enough to prepare for professional employment and/or future study; and (4) demonstrate leadership and self-discipline. To graduate, students must complete a minimum of 120 semester hours of credit. Successful completion of a core curriculum of interdisciplinary studies and of a concentrated course of study in a selected academic major are also required.

Academic Facilities

Academic facilities at the College include well-equipped classrooms, three auditoriums (a traditional theater, a theater-in-the-round, and a recital hall), an art gallery, television and radio studios, laboratories for the natural sciences, botany laboratories, a biofeedback laboratory for psychology, and a darkroom.

Western State College maintains outstanding computer laboratory facilities that are available in each academic building, the student center, and in every residence hall. Students have high-speed Internet access as part of their computer and e-mail accounts.

The spacious library contains more than 110,000 volumes; more than half a million government documents, microforms, and audiovisual materials; and more than 825 carefully selected periodicals. Computerized access to all local and regional library holdings is available. The library also provides a supervised place for late-evening study and has a staff that is professionally and personally committed to providing the best possible service.

Costs

Tuition for the 2003–2004 academic year was $1783 for residents of Colorado. Nonresident tuition was $8965. Fees totaled $781. Room and board costs were about $6300. The College maintains an excellent accident-and-health insurance plan. The plan covers the expense of illness and injury, subject to certain exclusions. The cost of the insurance for one calendar year was $650. The average cost of books and supplies was $500 per year. Students involved in classes that require auxiliary supplies and equipment were charged a fee that usually averaged $14 per class. (These figures are subject to change.)

Financial Aid

Sufficient financial assistance is available to enable diligent and deserving students to complete their education. At Western, this assistance takes many forms, including state, federal, and institutional scholarships; grants; loans; and opportunities for employment on campus. Interested students should write to the Office of Financial Aid for a booklet that provides essential and up-to-date information. An extraordinary opportunity for qualified students comes through the Foundation Scholarship program funded by the Western State College Foundation.

Faculty

The faculty of Western comprises 120 full-time and 18 part-time teachers. While many do independent research in support of their teaching and some publish the results of their work, the primary basis of their employment is teaching and advising students and assisting with extracurricular student activities. Approximately 85 percent of the faculty members hold doctorates in their fields.

Student Government

The Student Government Association assumes responsibility through its Student Senate for representing student interests in numerous ways. The Senate assigns student members to important College committees; organizes most extracurricular activities, such as concerts, speakers, movies, club programs, and student media; and participates directly in the processes of budgeting and administering almost half a million dollars in student fees. The students also elect a Student Trustee, who sits as a member of the Board of Trustees for the Consortium of State Colleges.

Admission Requirements

Each prospective student at Western is considered individually. Admission is based on both academic and personal attributes that match the outstanding opportunities for study, recreation, and personal involvement at Western. Applicants for admission to the College should have graduated from an accredited high school. The successful applicant has completed 4 years of English; 3 years of mathematics, including 2 years of algebra; 3 years of natural and laboratory sciences; 3 years of social studies; and 2 years of academic electives. In addition, students should have a GPA of at least 2.5, rank in the upper two thirds of their high school graduating class, and earn a combined score of 950 or higher on the SAT I or a composite score of 20 or higher on the ACT. Prospective transfer students must have earned a minimum 2.0 GPA in at least 12 academic credit hours. Those not meeting this criteria are considered on an individual basis.

Application and Information

Applications for admission to Western may be submitted after the student has completed his or her junior year. The application form should be submitted with previous college and/or high school transcripts, SAT I or ACT scores, and a $40 fee. Transfer students with 30 undergraduate credit hours need only submit their college transcripts, the application, and the fee. While not required, a campus visit is strongly recommended. The application form identifies the required information and materials.

Timothy Albers
Director of Admissions
Western State College of Colorado
Gunnison, Colorado 81231
Telephone: 800-876-5309 (toll-free)
E-mail: admiss@western.edu
World Wide Web: http://www.western.edu

WESTMINSTER CHOIR COLLEGE OF RIDER UNIVERSITY

PRINCETON, NEW JERSEY

The College

Home of the famous Westminster Symphonic Choir, Westminster Choir College integrates music study with professional choral performances conducted in concert with major symphony orchestras. Westminster Choir College offers outstanding music training in a stimulating yet friendly learning environment. Westminster appeals to students who seek excellent musical training and substantial performance experience to become well-rounded career musicians. The College attracts talented musicians from around the world for superb training and practical experience as performers, composers, conductors, teachers, and church musicians.

As a world-renowned music conservatory within Rider University, Westminster provides the advantages of a small, private college with the breadth of curriculum and recreational opportunities of a comprehensive liberal arts university. The Westminster student body is diverse and multicultural (approximately 20 percent are members of minority groups and 15 percent are international students) yet totals more than 400 students.

All Westminster students perform in professional concerts each year. The 200-voice Westminster Symphonic Choir sings and records on a regular basis with the New York Philharmonic under world-class conductors in Lincoln Center and Carnegie Hall. The Westminster Symphonic Choir has performed and recorded with conductors, including Bernstein, Ormandy, Masur, Toscanini, Walter, Leinsdorf, Mehta, Ozawa, and Muti. Students may also perform in six additional choirs, including the Westminster Choir (Choir-in-Residence at the Spoleto Festival U.S.A.), the Westminster Singers, Chapel Choir, Westminster Concert Bell Choir, Jubilee Singers (performing music of the African-American heritage), and Schola Cantorum. The Westminster choirs tour nationally and internationally. Westminster also offers students opportunities to perform in ensembles with pianists, organists, and the Westminster Conservatory Community Orchestra. Young composers' works are showcased on campus and in community concerts.

All Westminster classes are taught by faculty members; no classes are taught by graduate students. The student-faculty ratio of 6:1 creates an intimate and supportive learning environment.

Westminster's distinguished alumni include the winner of the 1994 Metropolitan Opera National Competition; professors at Rice, Notre Dame, Manhattan School of Music, and the Cincinnati Conservatory of Music; performers with the Metropolitan Opera, the New York City Opera, and the Chicago Lyric Opera; and leading music ministers and teachers worldwide.

Westminster's scenic 23-acre campus, ideally situated in picturesque Princeton within walking distance of Princeton's Palmer Square, is an outstanding atmosphere for living, performing, and learning. Westminster's campus centers around elegant Williamson Hall in the original Georgian quadrangle, providing an intimate setting for recitals and chamber ensembles. The College also has a Student Activities Center that houses the student newspaper, other organizations, the dining commons, and the College bookstore.

Rider University offers all of its students many extracurricular activities, including opportunities to participate in theatrical productions, intramural athletics, and intercollegiate athletic teams in several sports. NCAA Division I sports include baseball, basketball, lacrosse, soccer, swimming, volleyball, and wrestling.

At the graduate level, Westminster offers programs leading to the Master of Music degree in choral conducting, composition, music education, organ performance, piano accompanying and vocal coaching, piano performance and pedagogy, sacred music, and voice performance and pedagogy.

Westminster is accredited by the National Association of Schools of Music (NASM) and the Middle States Association of Colleges and Schools. Its undergraduate music education program is accredited by the National Association of State Directors of Teacher Education and Certification (NASDTEC), which facilitates transferring teaching certificates from participating states.

Location

Located in the culturally rich town of Princeton, New Jersey, Westminster is a 40-minute train ride from the cosmopolitan cultural centers of New York City and Philadelphia, offering Westminster students a wealth of educational and recreational activities. Princeton University, a short walk from Westminster, offers lectures, art exhibits, recitals, and concerts. Through a cooperative agreement, Westminster students may enroll in courses at Princeton University and use the University's athletic and recreational facilities. Near the Westminster campus, the Tony Award–winning McCarter Theatre stages several major productions each year and hosts guest artists and musical performers.

Majors and Degrees

Westminster grants the Bachelor of Music degree, with majors in music education, music theater, organ performance, piano (with emphases in accompanying, pedagogy, and performance), sacred music, theory and composition, and voice performance, and the Bachelor of Arts degree in music, with concentrations in organ, piano, and voice. A minor in music theater may be combined with any of the undergraduate programs. Cross-registration with Princeton University, Princeton Theological Seminary, Princeton Ballet School, and Rider University further enhances academic offerings for Westminster undergraduates. Rider University offers a full spectrum of liberal arts and science degrees.

Academic Programs

In addition to course work in their major and minor areas, students take courses in arts and sciences, including foreign languages, English, mathematics, computer science, and world cultures. Course work may be supplemented by internships, fieldwork, and independent study. Approximately 80 percent of Westminster students are employed in sacred music positions in the region as choir directors, organists, pianists, and soloists. The Westminster Career Development Office provides specialized career services for musicians.

Westminster Choir College follows a two-semester calendar. Academic courses and music workshops are also available in the summer session and in special weekend workshops throughout the year.

Off-Campus Programs

Internships are available in theater, arts administration, sacred music, and piano pedagogy. Students may also teach music lessons at the Westminster Conservatory and teach music in public and private schools through the music education fieldwork program. Qualified students may apply for a semester or year abroad.

Academic Facilities

Westminster Choir College performance facilities include the Fine Arts Theatre (550 seats), Bristol Hall (350 seats), Williamson Hall (100 seats), Scheide Hall (100 seats), and the Playhouse/Opera Theatre (300 seats). Stately Bristol Hall, housing a 50-rank Aeolian-Skinner organ, a 16-rank Fisk organ, a 14-rank Noack organ, and a 9-foot Steinway grand piano, is a large recital facility for student, faculty, and guest performers. Nestled among the trees, the Playhouse/Opera Theatre offers a stage and two Steinway grand pianos. Beyond Bristol Chapel, Scheide Recital Hall showcases a 44-rank Casavant organ. Westminster offers practice rooms in each of its three residence halls and has more than 120 pianos and 21 pipe organs, including practice organs by Flentrop, Holtkamp, Schantz, Moller, and Noack.

Talbott Library/Learning Center houses 55,000 books and microforms, plus 23,000 music scores and 160 periodical titles. The Performance Collection contains 6,000 titles in multiple copies for student study, class assignments, student teaching, and church choirs. A single-copy reference file of 45,000 individual octavos is the largest collection of its type in the United States. Voice students use a state-of-the-art voice laboratory, an invaluable resource for vocal pedagogy, for the scientific study of the vocal mechanism and singing. The Piano Department has a fully equipped piano laboratory in which an entire class of students can be instructed simultaneously. The Media Center contains more than 9,000 recordings and videos, with facilities for student playback. The Music Education Resource Collection contains 1,000 textbooks, recordings, filmstrips, charts, and resource materials in addition to listening equipment and an electronic piano. The library also houses a state-of-the-art electronic music computer laboratory with fifteen Kurzweil synthesizers, sixteen Macintosh Power PCs running Finale and Performer, a multimedia center with CD-ROM and laser disc, computers customized for music theory and sight-singing programs, and 100 music fundamental programs.

Westminster students may also consult the comprehensive collections of the Rider and Princeton University libraries. Westminster students use the campus academic computing laboratory, containing a combination of Macintosh and IBM computers, printers, and scanners for word processing, spreadsheets, database, draw and paint, desktop publishing, and multimedia applications and general academic computing needs. Additional computer laboratories at Rider with connections to the University mainframe are also available.

Costs

Westminster's tuition and fees are $20,590 per academic year. The complete cost of tuition and room and board in a campus residence hall (double occupancy) is $28,960. Tuition for part-time students is $780 per credit. Special program-related fees include $245 for senior student teaching.

Financial Aid

Westminster provides substantial financial aid awards to its students. All accepted students who complete the Free Application for Federal Student Aid (FAFSA) are automatically evaluated for financial aid. Students who have been accepted and have submitted the FAFSA before March 1 receive priority consideration for financial aid awards. Those accepted and applying for aid after the March priority deadline are considered for the remaining funds. Financial aid awards include scholarships for talent and academic merit plus state scholarships, Federal Pell Grants, Tuition Aid Grants, Federal Supplemental Educational Opportunity Grants, Distinguished and Garden State Scholars Program, and Educational Opportunity Program awards.

Faculty

Westminster has a teaching faculty of 85. Faculty members are all distinguished performers and scholars. Leonard Bernstein described Joseph Flummerfelt, Principal Conductor and Artistic Director, as the "greatest choral conductor in the world." Composers-in-Residence include Daniel Pinkham, Morten Lauridsen, and Libby Larson. Master classes have included such noted artists as Marilyn Horne and Claude Frank.

Student Government

Through student government, Westminster students have the opportunity to participate in determining cultural, recreational, and policy issues. The Joint Committee on Academic and Student Life, consisting of students, faculty members, and administrators, makes policy recommendations about academic and student life.

Admission Requirements

Westminster accepts applicants based on indicators of musical talent and academic achievement. Audition scores, high school grade point average, SAT I or ACT test scores, and recommendations are all considered in determining the applicant's potential for academic and musical achievement at the college level. Early admission is available for outstanding students after completion of the junior year.

Transfer students are evaluated on the basis of their audition score and their academic record in college in addition to the above criteria. Transfer credits are evaluated after enrollment. Freshmen and transfer applicants are considered on a continuous basis. An audition, high school transcripts, two letters of recommendation, SAT I or ACT test scores (for first-time freshmen who are not international students), and an interview (for some majors) are required. An essay, a minimum 3.0 grade point average, 3 years of high school math and science, and 3 years of high school foreign language are recommended. Auditions are held several times per year on campus. Taped auditions are permitted when distance is prohibitive. All international students are required to submit TOEFL scores with their application, in addition to the criteria listed within the application packet.

Application and Information

For admissions information, students should contact:

Monica Thomas Tritto
Director of Admissions
Westminster Choir College
101 Walnut Lane
Princeton, New Jersey 08542-3899
Telephone: 609-921-7144
800-96-CHOIR (toll-free)
Fax: 609-921-2538
E-mail: wccadmission@rider.edu
World Wide Web: http://westminster.rider.edu

Students on the campus of Westminster Choir College.

WESTMINSTER COLLEGE

FULTON, MISSOURI

The College

Founded in 1851, Westminster is a private, coeducational, liberal arts and sciences college that has a proven record of preparing its graduates for promising careers in business, public service, and in the professional area. Westminster College currently enrolls 850 students, and 35 percent of these students come from outside Missouri. States strongly represented are Oklahoma, Arkansas, Texas, Kansas, and Illinois. Six percent of Westminster's students are international.

Facilities include the Hunter Activity Center, which houses a gymnasium, an indoor running track, racquetball courts, student mailboxes, a recreation room, student activity offices, and the campus grill. The expanded Priest Athletic Complex includes varsity and practice facilities for soccer, softball, baseball, and football, including new lights for night events. The Wetterau Field Sports Facility includes athletic offices, varsity locker rooms, training rooms, and a varsity weight room. The Mueller Student Center is a popular place for student parties, special College events, and athletic practices.

Westminster's Center for Leadership and Service promotes leadership development, character development and community service on the campus and in the community. The Center for Leadership and Service works closely with the Center for Teaching Excellence to promote service-learning opportunities and excellent teaching throughout the Westminster campus.

Whether students plan to enter the professional world immediately or pursue a graduate program, they are given encouragement, advice, and guidance in preparing for life after Westminster. Included in the placement effort is an important linking of current students with graduates who are now in influential positions in society. In addition, Westminster's formalized internship program is designed to extend the student's learning opportunities beyond the traditional classroom setting into professional work environments.

The Green Lecture Series, a distinguished series on economic, social, and international affairs, was established in 1936 as a memorial to John Findley Green, an 1884 Westminster graduate. The roster of past speakers includes former Presidents Bush, Reagan, and Truman; former British Prime Minister Edward Heath; former CIA Director William Casey; former U.S. Ambassador to Russia Robert S. Strauss; former President of the Soviet Union Mikhail Gorbachev; and Nobel laureate Lech Walesa, former President of Poland. The 1996 Green Lecture, presented by Lady Margaret Thatcher, commemorated the fiftieth anniversary of Winston Churchill's "Iron Curtain" address held in the historic Westminster Gym.

Westminster College uses as its chapel a seventeenth-century English Church, which was dismantled in London and rebuilt on the campus. The lower level of the church houses the Winston Churchill Memorial and Library, which contains memorabilia of Sir Winston Churchill and World War II. The church, originally designed by Sir Christopher Wren, is a national landmark that attracts 30,000 visitors annually.

Westminster College is a member of the National Collegiate Athletic Association (Division III) and the St. Louis Intercollegiate Athletic Conference. Westminster fields teams for men in baseball, basketball, golf, soccer, and tennis and for women in basketball, golf, soccer, softball, tennis, and volleyball. Westminster's football team plays in the Upper Midwest Athletic Conference; it won the conference championship in 2003.

Location

Fulton is a safe, historic community of more than 12,000 people, situated in the rolling hills and trees of central Missouri. Nearly 15 percent of Fulton's population are college students. Westminster is located a little more than an hour north of the Lake of the Ozarks, a beautiful recreational area. Within 25 minutes to the west is Columbia, a college town of more than 80,000 people. Just to the south of Fulton is Jefferson City, Missouri's state capital. Kansas City is 2½ hours west, and St. Louis is located 2 hours east on Interstate 70.

Majors and Degrees

Westminster grants the Bachelor of Arts degree in the following major fields: accounting; anthropology; biology; business administration; chemistry; computer science; economics; elementary, middle school, and secondary education; English; environmental studies; French; history; international business; international studies/sciences; management information systems; mathematics; philosophy; physical education; physics; political science; psychology; religious studies; sociology; and Spanish.

Preprofessional tracks are offered in the health professions and law. An individualized five/six-year engineering program is available to Westminster students in cooperation with Washington University in St. Louis.

Students who wish to design their own academic majors may do so through the self-designed major, which brings together an interdisciplinary committee of faculty members to serve as advisers. Examples include advertising, communications, hospital management, public administration, and sports management.

Academic Programs

Westminster is a selective college with an innovative curriculum based on the liberal arts that emphasizes breadth as well as depth. The College's general education program reflects a commitment to liberal learning in the arts and sciences and to providing its students with opportunities to explore the aesthetic, cultural, ethical, historical, scientific, and social contexts in which they will live, work, and learn in the twenty-first century. Requirements for the baccalaureate degree are usually completed in four years. Students must satisfy general course requirements as well as departmental requirements in courses outside of their major. Academic advisers guide all students through the four years of their enrollment.

The Westminster Seminar Program is designed to bridge the gap between high school and college and introduce students to campus facilities, resources, faculty members, and other students. The program begins prior to the start of classes and continues for the remainder of the semester for all first-year students. The professor of this class is the students' faculty adviser until the student declares a major.

Westminster operates on a traditional two-semester calendar. A three-week term is available after the spring semester for special travel and field study courses or internships.

Off-Campus Programs

The College's Center for Off-Campus and International Programs assists students seeking overseas study opportunities or pursuing exchange opportunities with sister institutions. Westminster participates in the Institutes of European and Asian Studies, which provide twenty campuses throughout the world for Westminster students to spend a semester or a year studying abroad. The College's strong historical relationship with England has led to several educational opportunities, including exchange programs with Queen Mary and Westfield College and the University of East Anglia School of English and American Studies, which allows study in Norwich, located 2 hours from London. Other overseas exchange programs are available at Kansai Gaidai University (Osaka, Japan) and with L'Ecole Supérieure des Sciences Commerciales (ESSCA: School for Business Study) in Angers, France; the latter allows French majors the opportunity to study abroad in a French-speaking environment. Other off-campus programs include the United Nations Semester, the Washington Semester, and the Chicago Urban Studies Semester.

Academic Facilities

The new 80,000-square-foot Coulter Science Center provides space for modern classrooms and laboratories for biology, chemistry, computer science, mathematics, physics, and psychology. Most other classes meet in Newnham Hall and Westminster Hall. Reeves Library includes ample space for study and research, with four computer classrooms, a language lab, multimedia classrooms and facilities, additional computers, and student workstations. Students also have computer connections available in all residence halls and fraternity rooms, allowing 24-hour access to computers and the Internet.

Costs

The basic cost for the 2004–05 academic year is $18,880 for tuition, room, board, and the student activity fee. The College estimates that students should allow $2400 annually for books, supplies, and personal expenses.

Financial Aid

More than 98 percent of the College's students receive assistance through scholarships, grants, loans, or employment. Federal aid programs include the Federal Pell Grant, Federal Supplemental Educational Opportunity Grant, Federal Perkins Loan, and Federal Work-Study programs. To determine eligibility for need-based aid, students should complete the Free Application for Federal Student Aid (FAFSA) after January 1.

A merit-based aid program recognizes and rewards outstanding students. Academic scholarships and leadership awards, ranging from $1000 to full tuition, are awarded based on grades, test scores, and leadership activities.

Faculty

The 57 faculty members are part of a unique learning environment where students and teachers work together to discover answers to the complex problems faced in and out of the classroom and, in the process, establish lifelong relationships. Approximately 75 percent of the distinguished faculty members hold the doctorate or equivalent terminal degree, many are published authors, and others are engaged in advanced research and scholarly study. Although faculty members are involved in research and writing, they primarily constitute a teaching faculty whose main concern is the education of the undergraduate student.

Student Government

The Westminster College Student Government Association is composed of all students of the College. Its officers are elected by the entire student body. The Student Government Association serves the interests of the individual student and student groups and sponsors and supports activities and events on their behalf. The activity fee charged each student gives the Student Government Association a sizable budget ($200,000) to carry out such programs as intramurals, community relations, publications, entertainment, and other special events.

Admission Requirements

Each application is considered individually by the Enrollment Services staff and the Admissions Committee, who evaluate a number of factors, including courses taken in secondary school, a counselor's recommendation, test scores (either ACT or SAT I), grade point average, and activities. Transfer students must submit a transcript from each college previously attended. International students must submit the TOEFL score report.

Application and Information

To apply to Westminster College a student should submit the application for admission along with an official copy of the secondary school transcript, test scores on either the ACT or SAT I, and a recommendation from a high school official. The College operates on a rolling admissions calendar. While there is no application deadline, students are encouraged to apply by February 1 of their senior year.

Westminster College does not discriminate on the basis of race, sex, color, national or ethnic origin, sexual orientation, or physical handicap in the administration of its educational policies, admissions policies, scholarship and loan programs, or other school-administered programs.

For further information regarding admissions, financial assistance, academic programs, and campus visits, students should write or call:

Office of Enrollment Services (Admissions
and Financial Aid)
Westminster College
501 Westminster Avenue
Fulton, Missouri 65251-1299
Telephone: 573-592-5251
800-475-3361 (toll-free)
Fax: 573-592-5255
E-mail: admissions@jaynet.wcmo.edu
World Wide Web: http://www.westminster-mo.edu

The monumental sculpture "Breakthrough" incorporates eight sections of the Berlin Wall and commemorates the collapse of the Iron Curtain and the end of the Cold War.

WESTMINSTER COLLEGE

NEW WILMINGTON, PENNSYLVANIA

The College

Westminster College, an independent, coeducational liberal arts college related to the Presbyterian Church (U.S.A.), was founded in 1852. Westminster's liberal arts foundation thrives in a caring environment supported by an integrative curriculum featuring state-of-the-art technology and opportunities for involvement to prepare students for a diverse world. Westminster College is annually recognized among the nation's best liberal arts colleges by *U.S. News & World Report* and as one of the nation's best college buys by *Money*. Nearly 1,400 students benefit from individualized attention from dedicated faculty members while choosing from more than forty majors and nearly 100 campus organizations on the New Wilmington, Pennsylvania, campus. The College provides many programs to augment the academic and social life of the academic community, including lectures, dramatic productions, art exhibitions, concerts, symposia, dances, films, and other activities. Students may choose to participate in a wide variety of groups and activities, such as dramatics, publications, volunteer and social service teams, athletics, religious groups, musical groups, radio and television stations, fraternities and sororities, honoraries, and special interest groups.

A natatorium and physical education and fitness center are included among Westminster's major buildings, and athletics are carefully integrated into the overall educational program. A full range of intercollegiate and intramural sports for men and women gives each student the opportunity to participate at the level of his or her interest and ability. Westminster students compete in twenty varsity sports as Division III members of the NCAA. Westminster has been called the most successful football program at any level, based on its six national championships and eleven undefeated seasons, and the men's basketball team has had more wins than any other program in NAIA history. Nearly 99 percent of student athletes who letter in a varsity sport graduate.

Location

Westminster is located in New Wilmington, a small residential town in western Pennsylvania. The campus is surrounded by wooded hills, Amish farmlands, scenic country roads, and streams. The town is not far from several large cities. It is 60 miles north of Pittsburgh, 80 miles south of Erie, and 85 miles southeast of Cleveland. New Castle is 9 miles to the south, and Youngstown, Ohio, is 17 miles to the west. The College is within a few miles of I-79, I-80, and the Ohio and Pennsylvania turnpikes. Nearby cities provide transportation to all points by bus, and transportation is available from the Pittsburgh and Youngstown airports.

Majors and Degrees

Westminster College grants three undergraduate degrees: the Bachelor of Arts, the Bachelor of Science, and the Bachelor of Music. The choice of major field can be made from the following: accounting, art, biology, broadcast communications, business administration (finance, health administration, human resource management, and marketing), chemistry, Christian education, computer information systems, computer science, economics, elementary education, English, French, German, history, Latin, mathematics, molecular biology, music, music education, music performance, philosophy, physics, political science, psychology, public relations, religion, sacred music, sociology (criminal justice), Spanish, speech communications, and theater. Interdisciplinary majors are available in environmental science, financial economics, intercultural studies, international business, international politics, and neuroscience. Preprofessional programs are offered in dentistry, environmental science, health management systems, law, medicine, the ministry, occupational therapy, and veterinary medicine. A 3-2 engineering program is offered in cooperation with Pennsylvania State University, Case Western Reserve University, and Washington University in St. Louis.

Secondary education certification with a major in an academic discipline is offered.

Academic Program

The liberal arts degree offered by Westminster College reflects the diversity and depth of the classical education and the practicality of its application. Good writing and speaking skills are emphasized, and science and philosophy become a part of life at Westminster.

Course requirements for graduation vary according to the major fields, but all-College requirements include courses in writing, oral communication, religion, computer science, foreign language, and physical education as well as courses from categories covering the humanities, fine arts, social sciences, natural sciences, and literature. Double majors, minors, and individual interdisciplinary programs are possible.

Westminster operates on a two-term academic year. The fall term runs from September through December, and the spring term runs from January through May.

Every four years since 1936, in conjunction with the Presidential election year, Westminster has held a Mock National Political Convention (for the party out of office) in which more than three fourths of the students have participated, naming their own "candidate."

Off-Campus Programs

Westminster engages in several cooperative programs with other colleges and institutions to provide students with opportunities for in-depth study off campus. Among these is a program at Berea College in Kentucky, in which students study the culture of southern Appalachia. Westminster also offers a Washington Semester in the nation's capital and a Sea Semester in conjunction with Boston University. In addition, it is possible to spend a semester or year studying in France, Germany, Spain, and other countries.

Academic Facilities

McGill Library and the J. S. Mack Science Library contain more than 220,000 volumes and receive about 970 periodicals per year. These library collections are supplemented through the College's membership in the Library Consortium and two computerized networks (one regional and the other national), which provide the best services possible through interlibrary loans and other library activities.

Westminster's campus extends more than 300 rolling acres and has more than twenty major buildings. The facilities include classrooms, a 300-seat theater, a 1,750-seat auditorium, radio and TV stations, and an outdoor environmental-science field laboratory. The Hoyt Science Resource Center contains modern science areas, including electron microscopes and an X-ray defractor, expanded computer science facilities, and a planetarium.

Costs

Westminster College is one of the most affordable national liberal arts colleges in Pennsylvania and is annually listed as one of America's best college buys. For the academic year 2003–04, tuition and fees are $20,270, and room and board are $5990, bringing the total cost for the year to $26,260.

Financial Aid

About 96 percent of Westminster's students receive some sort of financial aid. Scholarships, Federal Stafford Student Loans, grants, and campus employment are offered to students who have financial need. The student's eligibility for financial aid is determined by the Free Application for Federal Student Aid (FAFSA) form. Also, non-need scholarships of up to more than 50 percent of tuition are awarded to students of high academic ability; these are renewable each year if the student maintains good academic standing. Activity grants in music and theater are also available. Information is available through the Dean of Admissions or Director of Financial Aid.

Faculty

There are 105 full-time faculty members at Westminster College, 91 percent of whom hold earned doctorates or the highest terminal degree in their field. The student-faculty ratio is 11:1. The faculty members are characterized by their interest in and concern for their students.

Student Government

All students, by virtue of their undergraduate registration and payment of fees, are members of the Student Government Association. The Student Senate, the central representative and legislative organization of the Student Government Association, recognizes student organizations, allocates money appropriated by the Board of Trustees, and carries out other responsibilities. In cooperation with the staff of the Dean of Student Affairs, the student senators, through the Campus Programming Committee, plan an extensive student activities program.

Admission Requirements

Students admitted to the College should have received a high school diploma and should have completed a college-preparatory program of study in secondary school, consisting of a minimum of 16 units (including at least 4 units of English, 2 units of a foreign language, 3 units of mathematics, and 2 units each of lab science and social studies). Each new applicant is required to take the SAT I or the ACT, preferably during the junior year of high school or early in the senior year.

Application and Information

A completed application with the $35 application fee may be submitted anytime after the student's junior year in secondary school. The student should also see that the required SAT I or ACT scores and a high school transcript are sent to the College. The transcript should include grades from the ninth grade through the eleventh grade.

For application forms and further information, students should contact:

Dean of Admissions
Westminster College
New Wilmington, Pennsylvania 16172
Telephone: 800-942-8033 (toll-free)
E-mail: admis@westminster.edu
World Wide Web: http://www.westminster.edu

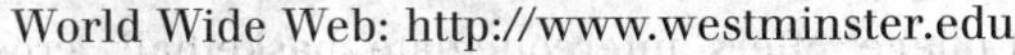

A student takes a break from studying and gets her feet wet at Westminster College.

WESTMINSTER COLLEGE

SALT LAKE CITY, UTAH

The College

Westminster College is the only independent, private, comprehensive liberal arts college in Utah. Westminster has been a vital part of the Intermountain West's history and educational heritage since 1875.

The current student body of 2,500 is characterized by diversity as well as a spirit of community. Students come from twenty-eight states and twenty countries. Most are attracted to the College because of its small size and the personal attention students receive, its prime location in a moderately large urban area close to mountain skiing and recreation areas, and its relatively modest tuition and fees.

The College is located in a quiet residential area about 10 minutes southeast of downtown Salt Lake City. On-campus housing consists of residence halls for both men and women, which can accommodate 500 students. Off-campus rental housing (apartments and homes) is readily available in the neighborhood.

Student activities include student government, campus publications, choir, intramural sports, honorary societies, the campus ministry council, the ski club, and a variety of special interest groups, including aviation, nursing, science, education, premed, and computer science.

Westminster College offers intercollegiate basketball, cross-country, golf, and soccer for men and basketball, cross-country, golf, and volleyball for women.

Student services include academic advising, career planning and placement, internships, personal counseling, tutoring, and testing.

Location

Salt Lake City, home of the 2002 Winter Olympics and the Sundance Film Festival, is a metropolitan area of approximately 1.3 million people. It is located in a valley (elevation 4,700 feet) between two rugged mountain ranges. Salt Lake City has an international airport and good rail service. Downtown Salt Lake City is easily accessible to students by bus, car, or bicycle. Attractions in the downtown area include professional sports events, ballet, theater, concerts, and shopping to suit all tastes.

The area has four pleasant seasons, with limited amounts of rain and snow in the valley and moderate temperatures. The Wasatch Mountains, bordering the Salt Lake Valley on the east, have what has been called "the greatest snow on earth." These mountains are ideal for the winter sports enthusiast as well as those who enjoy hiking, biking, and camping.

Majors and Degrees

Westminster College offers Bachelor of Arts and Bachelor of Science degrees in the following areas: accounting, art, aviation, biology, chemistry, communication, computer science, economics, education (early childhood, elementary, secondary, and special education), English, finance, history, human resource management, information resource management, international business, justice studies, management (business), marketing, mathematics, nursing, philosophy, physics, political studies, preprofessional programs (dentistry, law, medicine, veterinary medicine, and 3-2 engineering), psychology, social science, and sociology.

Course work leading to an academic minor is available in the following additional areas: environmental studies, gender studies, French, music, religion, Spanish, and speech and theater arts.

Academic Program

Each student must complete at least 124 semester hours to receive a bachelor's degree. Of this amount, approximately 40 hours consist of liberal arts education core requirements common to all students regardless of major. Semester-hour requirements vary widely among majors, but all students are exposed to liberal arts concepts as well as practical, career-oriented experiences.

Credit is awarded for successful scores on Advanced Placement and CLEP examinations.

Students can participate in the Reserve Officers' Training Corps programs of the U.S. Air Force, U.S. Army, and U.S. Navy through cooperative programs at the University of Utah.

The College has a 4-4-1 calendar, consisting of two 15-week semesters followed by a one-month May Term. There is also a summer session.

Off-Campus Programs

Westminster students may participate in travel/study trips (for credit) during May Term and the summer session. Students can also make individual arrangements for international study by advisement from the College's International Studies Chair and the Career Resource Center and through a cooperative agreement with the Foreign Study Office at the University of Utah.

Academic Facilities

Westminster's campus has six major classroom buildings, a science laboratory building, six computer classrooms, thirty-six presentation classrooms, a fine arts building, a nursing laboratory, and a separate building for classes in wheel-thrown and hand-built pottery. A multilevel, 47,000-square-foot, $15-million library opened in fall 1997. A recent $8-million addition to the business building includes the center for financial analysis and a behavioral simulation lab, along with a flight simulation and testing center that features the latest industry ground training equipment, including a jet simulator. Westminster's 22,500-square-foot hangar houses fifteen new planes, including complex multiengine and spins/upset recovery trainers. A $7-million renovation to the performing arts center is scheduled for completion in 2004.

Costs

Tuition and fees for 2003–04 were $16,994 for the academic year for a full-time student (registering for 12 to 16 semester hours). This figure includes costs for the fall semester, spring semester, and May Term. Room and board were $5300 for the same period. Books and supplies are estimated at $900 per year.

Financial Aid

Ninety-six percent of freshmen at Westminster receive financial aid, averaging approximately $13,270 each year per student. Aid programs include need-based institutional grants and need-based federal aid programs, such as grants, loans, and employment (Federal Work-Study Program). The Free Application for Federal Student Aid is the only form required for new students. Students wishing to apply for federal aid programs should plan to submit applications by early April, although there is no set deadline for federal aid applications.

Merit-based scholarships are available to incoming freshmen and transfer students as well as to continuing students, thanks to a generous endowment program and institutional aid program. Every full-time student admitted to Westminster is automatically considered for merit-based scholarships awarded by the College, which are based on GPA from previous academic (high school or college) course work. More than $9.8 million was awarded in institutional scholarships and grants in 2001–02.

Faculty

With 100 full-time and a number of part-time faculty members, the student-faculty ratio is 11:1. All faculty members teach; no research faculty positions exist. Graduate students do not teach. Many full-time faculty members are actively involved as advisers and sponsors of campus-based student activities. Approximately 80 percent of the faculty members hold terminal degrees.

Student Government

The official student governing body is the Associated Students of Westminster College (ASWC), which controls all student activities and organizations and provides funding and authorization for them. The ASWC is made up of three branches: the Executive Cabinet, the Legislative Assembly, and the Judiciary Branch. The three branches function in similar fashion to the federal government system. The president of the ASWC is considered chief spokesperson for the student body and has access to all chief administrators of the College.

Admission Requirements

Individual applications are reviewed on the basis of a student's potential for success at Westminster. Academic preparation, which includes both course work and grades, is most important. Also important to the review committee are items such as entrance exams (ACT or SAT I), recommendations, and extracurricular activities. A campus visit to meet with an academic counselor is recommended, as it helps complete the picture for both the prospective student and the college.

Transfer students must have earned at least a 2.5 cumulative GPA in previous college work.

International students must have at least a 3.0 GPA in non–U.S. high school or college work and a TOEFL score of at least 550 (or equivalent).

Application and Information

To apply for admission, a student must submit an application for admission, application fee, and official transcripts of previous high school and/or college classwork. Freshman applicants must submit ACT or SAT I scores. Applicants are notified of their admission status within two weeks of receipt of all required materials. All admission decisions are made on a rolling basis, and applications are processed until the date of class registration. New applicants are accepted for the start of all sessions.

For application forms and additional information, students should contact:

Office of Admissions
Westminster College
1840 South 1300 East
Salt Lake City, Utah 84105
Telephone: 801-832-2200
800-748-4753 (toll-free)
World Wide Web: http://www.westminstercollege.edu

Westminster College blends educational tradition with the spirit of the West.

WESTMONT COLLEGE

SANTA BARBARA, CALIFORNIA

The College

Westmont, a nationally ranked liberal arts college, offers an exclusively undergraduate, rigorous, academic education rooted in the Christian faith. Students develop a heightened appreciation for their cultural and religious heritage, the ability to direct their continuing self-development and learning, the competence to function as leaders and servants in society, a foundation for entering or receiving advanced training in a profession or career, and confidence in the authority of Scripture. Residence life, athletics, off-campus programs, and opportunities for local and international Christian service also contribute to balanced personal and spiritual development. Alumni enter a wide variety of professions and vocations and pursue professional-, master's-, and doctoral-level programs at the world's finest research universities, including UCLA, Stanford, Harvard, Yale, Princeton, the University of Chicago, Cambridge, and many others.

Although its 1,200 students come to Westmont from the majority of states and many countries throughout the world, the highest percentage come from California. Approximately 60 percent are women, 40 percent are men, 16 percent are from minority groups, and 1 percent are international students. More than eighty percent of the students live in the five residence halls on campus or the apartment complex off campus.

As a member of the National Association of Intercollegiate Athletics and the Golden State Athletic Conference, Westmont provides intercollegiate sports for men and women in basketball, cross-country, soccer (NAIA champions), tennis, and track and field. Men also compete in baseball, club polo, club rugby, club soccer, and club volleyball, and women also compete in volleyball and club polo. The intramural program offers a wide variety of activities as well. There are numerous clubs and organizations, including a student newspaper, literary magazine, yearbook, radio station, choral and music ensembles, a multicultural club, political organizations, theater productions, community service organizations, and Christian service, mission, and outreach programs. The Ruth Kerr Memorial Student Center (1983) houses the main campus dining facilities. Two integral components of the Westmont experience are the Chapel-Convocation Program and the Leadership Program. The Chapel Program, which students are required to attend three days a week, provides speakers and programs to inspire and challenge students to continue growing in their relationship with Christ. The Leadership Program is committed to training leaders to facilitate positive global changes.

Location

Ruth Kerr, president of the Kerr Manufacturing Company, was one of the founders of Westmont College. She was instrumental in opening the first campus in Los Angeles in 1937 and in moving the College to Santa Barbara in 1945. Westmont is located on a 111-acre campus, rich with pine, oak, and eucalyptus trees, in Montecito, an estate area of Santa Barbara between the Pacific Ocean and the Santa Ynez Mountains. Students enjoy the beach and mountain trails year-round. Santa Barbara has a wealth of history and culture, and theaters, libraries, community concerts, and other civic offerings are just minutes from the campus.

Majors and Degrees

Westmont awards Bachelor of Arts (B.A.) and Bachelor of Science (B.S.) degrees in twenty-seven liberal arts majors. These include alternative major, art, biology, chemistry, communication studies, computer science, economics and business, education, engineering physics, English, English and modern languages, French, history, kinesiology and physical education, mathematics, music, neuroscience, philosophy, physics, political science, psychology, religious studies, social science, sociology and anthropology, Spanish, and theater arts. The College offers a teacher-preparation program, which is approved by the California Commission for Teacher Preparation and Licensing, enabling students to qualify for either the single-subject or the multiple-subject credential. Preprofessional programs include architecture, athletic training, dentistry, engineering, film studies, law, medicine, ministry and missionary studies, optometry, pharmacy, physical therapy, and veterinary studies. A 3-2 program combining liberal arts and engineering is offered in cooperation with Stanford University; the University of Southern California; the University of California, Santa Barbara; Boston University; Washington University (St. Louis); and other institutions having accredited schools of engineering.

Academic Programs

Westmont offers majors in dozens of exciting fields and disciplines, from neuroscience to European studies and from theater arts to dance. All majors and programs of study feature thought-provoking and inspiring ways to integrate belief, thought, and action and to come to a deeper, more accurate understanding of the world.

Westmont's commitment to academic freedom is clear, not only in courses that demand students' best critical thinking, but also through a wide range of opportunities and organizations that explore the world of ideas. Students consider issues of science and religion through the Pascal Society and attend lectures in the humanities sponsored by the Erasmus Society. They discover room for all of their ideas and beliefs.

As an exclusively undergraduate college, Westmont has a deep understanding of the ideas and issues that absorb students. From its faculty and staff members to its alumni, Westmont is committed to helping students grow through their questions toward ever-deeper faith. Ministries such as Periago, which works with new students to ease their transition to college, are great tools for spiritual growth.

Off-Campus Programs

Off-campus programs include the Europe Semester, which is offered each fall and provides the broadest geographical scope, with extended stays in Athens, Florence, Jerusalem, London, Paris, and Rome. The England Semester, offered every other year, combines travel and residential study in the British Isles for students of literature. Semesters in France and Spain offer French and Spanish majors the opportunity to study these languages in their home countries, as does the Latin American Studies Program, which combines the study of Spanish culture and language in Belize, Chile, Costa Rica, and Honduras. Similar programs are offered at Jerusalem University College in Israel; Daystar University in Nairobi, Kenya; the Middle East Studies Program at the American University in Cairo, Egypt; and in the Russian Studies Program in Moscow, Nizhni Novgorod, and St. Petersburg (through Westmont's membership in the Coalition for Christian Colleges and Universities). Participants in the International Business Institute program visit the major economic and political capitals of Europe and Asia. The Westmont Economics/Business Program in Asia introduces students to the diverse economic growth in the Pacific Rim. The East Asia Program addresses contemporary world issues in China, Japan, and Taiwan. An additional summer program in Asia offers students an opportunity to study life and culture in Sri Lanka.

Domestic off-campus programs include the San Francisco Urban Program, which studies modern American urban society and offers urban internships; the Washington Semester, highlighting national political processes and incorporating internships in national, international, and economic policy, justice, and journalism; a semester at Bethune-Cookman, a historically black college in Florida; the Consortium Visitor Program, enabling students to study at any of the Christian College Consortium's twelve other member colleges; and other programs sponsored by the Coalition for Christian Colleges and Universities.

Academic Facilities

The trilevel Roger John Voskuyl Library is the academic center of Westmont. The library holds 150,385 catalogued items (35,000 bound periodicals, 121,329 reference and general items, and 7,945 media items), 465 print periodical subscriptions, and 2,494 online periodical subscriptions as well as seven classrooms; audiovisual equipment; math, language, and computer laboratories; and three IBM RS-6000 computers, which are used for instructional purposes. Forty-seven lab computers are connected to the mainframe for student use. Westmont has a 100Base-TX Ethernet network with a fiber-optic backbone, operating at 10 MB/second. There are Ethernet connections in every office and dorm room and in many classrooms. The entire network has access to e-mail and the Internet through a T3 line. A total of 100 terminals are available throughout the College for student use. The network accommodates IBM-compatible, Macintosh, and RISC/UNIX microcomputers. The library features an after-hours study room, a rare book archives room, and dozens of individual carrels and lockable study cubicles for faculty members and students. It also houses the Writer's Corner and offices for the Director of First-Year Students and the Career and Life Planning department.

The Reynolds Art Gallery features art studios and a classroom. Students and professional artists exhibit their work year-round in the gallery. Porter Theatre contains state-of-the-art equipment for dramatic productions and concerts.

The George Carroll Observatory contains a 16½-inch reflecting telescope, the largest in Santa Barbara. The Mericos H. Whittier Science Building houses the College's science program and equipment, including an ultracentrifuge, a liquid scintillation counter for measuring radioactivity, physiographic units and other equipment for advanced physiological studies, low-pressure liquid chromatography equipment, sophisticated environmental instrumentation, atomic absorption spectrophotometers, Fourier-transform NMR spectrometers, infrared and ultraviolet-visible spectrophotometers, gas and high-performance liquid chromatographs, and gamma-ray spectrometers.

Costs

Tuition and fees for 2004–05 are $25,544, and room and board for the academic year are $8610. The cost of books, personal expenses, and transportation is estimated at $3690.

Financial Aid

Westmont has a strong financial aid program, so no student should hesitate to apply for lack of financial resources. Ninety percent of Westmont's students receive some form of financial assistance; the average amount of aid awarded exceeds $16,500 per year. Westmont offers full tuition scholarships, which are available only to first-year applicants who apply via the early action (nonbinding) process. A select group of these applicants are invited to the campus to participate in a formal competition process. Students should contact the Admissions Office for further details. Other merit awards in the financial aid program are the President's, Provost's, and Dean's Scholarships, which range from $3500 to $9500. These merit scholarships are awarded to students who have demonstrated impressive academic achievement. Westmont also gives awards to students who demonstrate strength in art, music, theater arts, dance, and athletics. After submitting the Free Application for Federal Student Aid (FAFSA), students may be eligible for generous state grants, aid from federal programs, institutional grants, loans, and work-study programs, based on financial needs.

Faculty

One of the highest priorities at Westmont is the attraction and retention of outstanding Christian teachers and scholars. The College's professors are dedicated to the integration of faith and learning, while also being actively involved in the lives of students. There are 83 full-time and 56 part-time faculty members. The student-faculty ratio is 13:1; the average class size is 20. Eighty-seven percent of the full-time faculty members have their doctoral degree. Westmont's faculty members are committed to teaching at the undergraduate level, and they have additional advising responsibilities with either incoming first-year students or students in their major. A director of first-year programs is responsible for the advising and orientation of new students. Although teaching is their primary scholarly activity, many faculty members engage in research, write books, and publish articles in leading journals and periodicals.

Student Government

The Westmont College Student Association (WCSA) is an entirely self-governing body. Students elect their own WCSA representatives, who are then responsible for organizing social, cultural, and educational activities. They actively participate in and are voting members on almost all faculty committees, while also allocating the student budget to various clubs and organizations. Westmont Student Ministries, another student-managed organization, is responsible for organizing on- and off-campus ministries and mission opportunities.

Admission Requirements

Westmont selects candidates for admission from those prospective students who produce evidence that they are prepared for the academic stimulation and spiritual vitality that are central to the character of Westmont. For example, students should place a high priority on undergraduate education, and living and learning in a classic liberal arts environment should be valued. Applicants must have a clear understanding of the Christian mission of the College as well as an explicit desire to benefit from being in this environment. In addition, applicants should possess the strong moral character, values, personal integrity, and social concern that would be in accord with the Westmont community.

All applicants must submit two academic letters of recommendation, official high school or college transcripts, and official SAT I or ACT scores. A pastoral/character reference is optional. An interview is strongly encouraged.

For transfer students from an accredited two- or four-year college or university or a Bible college or university that is accredited by the American Association of Bible Colleges, the evaluation is based on achievement in solid, transferable course work; an assessment of the personal areas covered by the application (as stated above); and the quality of the written responses. High school records must be submitted if the applicant has completed fewer than 24 college-level credits at the time of application.

Application and Information

Entrance to Westmont is possible at the beginning of either the fall or spring semester. Westmont offers an early action plan. High school seniors interested in applying for early action must submit the application by November 1; notifications are mailed on January 15. The priority deadline for regular decision is February 1 for first-year applicants and March 15 for transfers; notifications are mailed beginning April 1. Applications may be submitted online via Westmont's Web site (listed below) with an application fee of $40. The fee for Westmont's paper application and all other online versions is $50. The Admissions Office encourages applicants to complete the application process as early as possible.

Visitors are welcome at any time. Campus visitors can stay overnight in the residence halls, attend classes and chapel, speak with professors or coaches, have a music audition, share a portfolio with the art department, and have meals with Westmont students. Several Preview Day events are planned each semester.

Westmont desires to enroll a well-rounded and balanced first-year class. Every year brings a new and exciting group of applicants. Due to the College's limited enrollment requirement, there are always more capable applicants than are able to be admitted. A goal of Westmont is to create a dynamic as well as culturally and traditionally diverse community of learners who bring with them a variety of attributes, accomplishments, backgrounds, and interests.

For further information regarding admissions, students should contact:

Director of Admissions
Westmont College
955 La Paz Road
Santa Barbara, California 93108

Telephone: 800-777-9011 (toll-free)
Fax: 805-565-6234
E-mail: admissions@westmont.edu
World Wide Web: http://www.westmont.edu/

WEST VIRGINIA UNIVERSITY INSTITUTE OF TECHNOLOGY

MONTGOMERY, WEST VIRGINIA

The University and the Institute

West Virginia University Institute of Technology has experienced a number of significant changes since it began as a preparatory school extension of West Virginia University in 1895. It began offering bachelor's degrees in engineering in 1952. Since 1961, the number of students has tripled to the current enrollment of more than 2,400, and the number of academic buildings has similarly increased from six to twenty. Students from more than twenty states and fifteen countries create a cosmopolitan population. Approximately one third of the full-time students live in the three dormitories on the 200-acre campus, which is located in the mountains of West Virginia. There are numerous social, athletic, and cultural activities on campus through which students can satisfy personal interests. Five national social fraternities and two sororities have chapters at Tech.

Location

Montgomery, West Virginia, is a small town of about 2,500 residents, just 28 miles southeast of Charleston, the state capital. Interstate Highways 64, 77, and 79 all run within 30 miles of the campus, and U.S. Route 60, a major east-west artery, runs immediately adjacent to the campus. Hawks Nest State Park, with its aerial tram to the bottom of the New River canyon, is located 30 miles from the campus. The New River, considered by many authoritative geologists to be the second-oldest river in the world, is a challenge to enthusiasts of white-water rafting, and the New River Gorge Bridge is the largest arch bridge east of the Mississippi. Tech is also conveniently located near Snowshoe Mountain, Silver Creek, and Winter Place Ski Lodge, three popular skiing areas.

Majors and Degrees

Tech offers the Bachelor of Arts, Bachelor of Science, Associate in Science, and Associate of Applied Science degrees. The Bachelor of Arts degree is available in history and government. Bachelor of Science degrees are offered in accounting; athletic coaching education; biology; business management; chemical, civil, electrical, and mechanical engineering; chemistry; computer science; electronic, industrial, and engineering technology; health services administration; history and government; industrial relations and human resources; interdisciplinary studies; management information systems; mathematics; nursing; printing management; public service administration; and technology management. Two-year Associate in Science degrees are offered in business technology (emphases in accounting, banking, business supervision, computer information systems, and restaurant management) computer and information technology, dental hygiene, engineering technologies (civil, drafting and design, electrical, and mechanical), general studies, office technology management (emphases in computer applications specialist, legal, and medical studies), printing, respiratory care technology, and surgical technology. A two-year Associate of Applied Science degree is offered in automotive service technology and technical studies in information technology. A one-year certificate program is offered in office technology, prepress technology, and press technology.

Academic Programs

Tech is organized into three major divisions: the Leonard C. Nelson College of Engineering; the College of Business, Humanities, and Sciences; and the Community and Technical College. The baccalaureate and associate degrees offered by Tech prepare students for careers in areas where today's job market has many openings. Although it is the only institute of technology in West Virginia, Tech realizes that leaders in all fields should have training in the liberal arts, and it has programs in business, the humanities, and the social sciences as well as two-year programs in several engineering technologies and other career-oriented areas. All students are required to take core courses in the liberal arts and sciences.

In addition to being earned in a traditional program, the Bachelor of Arts degree may also be earned through the Regents Program, which has been designed for adults who wish to complete their college studies. This program offers them an opportunity to gain credits toward the degree for work and life experience.

To earn a bachelor's degree, students must complete a minimum of 128 semester hours. To earn an associate degree, students must complete a minimum of 64 semester hours.

Tech has a two-semester calendar. The first semester begins in August and ends in December; the second begins in January and ends in May. Limited summer course offerings are available.

Off-Campus Programs

An optional five-year cooperative education program is open to students majoring in several fields. More than 100 students are placed each year in approximately fifty private and public businesses. The co-op student's second, third, and fourth years provide four semesters of study and five periods of work, while the freshman and senior years are spent on campus.

Academic Facilities

Tech's twenty academic buildings range from Old Main, built in 1896 and renovated in 1958, to Orndorff Hall, which houses modern science laboratories, classrooms, and offices. The $5-million Vining Library holds more than 520,000 volumes, including microtext, and houses the Center for Instructional Technology, which provides the latest in teaching innovations and instructional methodologies for use by both faculty and students.

Costs

For 2003–04, costs for tuition and fees per semester were $1690 for West Virginia residents and $4219 for out-of-state students plus an additional $600 for engineering students. Room costs are $1130 per semester; board costs total $1075 for a fifteen-meal plan and $1250 for a nineteen-meal plan. Students should expect to spend approximately $300 each semester for books.

Financial Aid

Tech offers a wide range of financial aid resources, including privately and federally funded loans, Federal Pell Grants, Federal Supplemental Educational Opportunity Grants, Federal Work-Study Program awards, privately funded scholarships for both academic and special talent, and West Virginia Higher Education Grant Program awards. The student's parents or guardians are required to submit the Free Application for Federal Student Aid (FAFSA) to the Pennsylvania Higher Education Assistance Agency for processing and eventual receipt of the need analysis report by Tech for determination of eligibility. Applications for financial aid, both from incoming freshmen and from enrolled students, should be submitted to

WVU Tech's Office of Student Financial Aid by April 1 in order to receive consideration for the next academic year.

Faculty

Faculty members at Tech are well prepared both academically and professionally to teach the institution's career-oriented curricula. Faculty members come from all over the United States and from several other countries, and most have had considerable practical experience in their field. In the Leonard C. Nelson College of Engineering alone, nearly 90 percent of the faculty have earned doctorates. The student-faculty ratio is 16:1. Faculty members work with students in developing academic programs, and they assist in personal counseling, although Tech also has professional counselors on the staff to help students with their problems.

Student Government

The Student Government Association (SGA) at Tech consists of students elected in campuswide referendums that are held each fall and spring. One of the SGA's most important functions is to develop a budget on which to base the student activity fees that fund the many diverse student activities and organizations on campus.

Admission Requirements

Applicants who are residents of West Virginia must graduate from an accredited high school or pass the GED test and must take the ACT and have test scores sent to the Institute directly from American College Testing, Inc. Out-of-state residents must graduate from an accredited high school or pass the GED test, rank in the upper three fourths of their graduating class or attain a standard composite score of at least 17 on the ACT (SAT I combined score of at least 820), and have their scores sent to the Institute directly from American College Testing, Inc., or the Educational Testing Service. Scores are used for placement and counseling purposes, and no other test may be substituted.

Admission to the college does not necessarily admit a student to all programs. Prerequisites apply for admission to certain curricula, as follows: for engineering, 2 units of algebra, 1 unit of plane geometry, 1 unit of advanced math, a minimum 3.0 GPA, and a math ACT score of at least 19; for engineering technology, 1 unit of algebra, 1 unit of plane geometry, and ½ unit of trigonometry. If a student lacks one or more of these prerequisites, he or she will be given an opportunity to enroll in pretechnology mathematics courses. Allied health–nursing candidates need 2 units of algebra and 2 units of laboratory science, 1 unit of which must be in chemistry. Dental hygiene candidates need 1 unit of algebra, 1 unit of biology, and 1 unit of chemistry. Because of the limited enrollment in allied health programs, candidates for these areas are selected by a special committee. Students with high school averages of B or better and/or ACT composite scores of 20 (SAT I combined score of 950) or higher are given priority by the admission committee.

Application and Information

Students are encouraged to apply by January. Applications are processed on a rolling decision basis. Students with a B average or better are notified of the admission decision upon receipt of their sixth-semester high school transcript and ACT or SAT I scores. All other students are notified upon receipt of their seventh-semester or final transcript and ACT or SAT I scores.

Applications for admission and requests for further information should be addressed to:

Director of Admissions
West Virginia University Institute of Technology
Montgomery, West Virginia 25136
Telephone: 888-554-TECH (toll-free)
E-mail: admissions@wvutech.edu

Old Main.

WEST VIRGINIA WESLEYAN COLLEGE

BUCKHANNON, WEST VIRGINIA

The College

Founded by the United Methodist Church in 1890, West Virginia Wesleyan is a coeducational, residential, liberal arts college. The College has an enrollment of 1,530 undergraduate students from thirty-five states and twenty-three countries. The average class size is 19 and the student-faculty ratio is 15:1. Nearly 80 percent of the faculty members hold the highest degree in their respective teaching field. Each fall, West Virginia Wesleyan enrolls approximately 425 freshmen and 45 transfers. Forty-five percent of the students originate from West Virginia, and the male-female ratio is 1:1. Approximately 10 percent of the students are minority or international students. Nearly 90 percent of the students live on campus, and housing is guaranteed for all four years of study. Housing options include residence halls, suites, on-campus apartments, and campus-adjacent residence units.

Wesleyan participates in the IBM ThinkPad University program. All students are provided a laptop computer for all four years of undergraduate study. This allows students to communicate with faculty members, do research, complete essays, and e-mail family and friends from the privacy of their residence hall rooms. With more than 2,500 Ethernet connection points, in addition to wireless Internet access, logging on is never a problem.

Wesleyan students are encouraged to pursue international travel and career-related internship opportunities. The international experience is available to students during the fall and spring semesters and during the three-week optional May Term. Wesleyan students also pursue a variety of semester-long internship programs, including the Washington Center for Internships.

Among the many services available to students is an Advising and Career Center that helps students with job placement, class scheduling, selection of a major program of study, internship opportunities, and international travel. The center also provides special tests, such as the LSAT, GRE, or GMAT to prepare graduates for professional schools. A Counseling and Wellness Center allows students to receive personal and educational guidance, as well as health services, through the Health Center. The Student Academic Support Services provides learning resources for all students, as well as specific services for students with diagnosed learning differences.

In addition to a challenging academic curriculum and innovative technology, Wesleyan offers a balanced and comprehensive student life program. Cocurricular activities include seventeen NCAA II sports, intramurals, outdoor recreation adventures, vocal and instrumental musical ensembles, theater arts, dance, community service, religious life programs, and fraternities and sororities. There are more than seventy campus organizations, including a radio station, student newspaper, and yearbook. The Campus Activities Board schedules a variety of cultural and social entertainment every week during the academic year.

Location

Situated in the foothills of the Allegheny Mountains, Wesleyan's 100-acre park-like campus is located in the historic town of Buckhannon, West Virginia. Buckhannon is 2 ¼ hours south of Pittsburgh, Pennsylvania, and 1 ¾ hours north of Charleston, West Virginia. It is easily accessible by interstate highways. Buckhannon has been included in Norman Crampton's book, *The Top 100 Best Small Towns in America*, a Random House publication. Students are drawn to this picturesque and friendly setting and the many restaurants, social events, and outdoor adventures available within a short distance from campus.

Majors and Degrees

The College awards a Master of Business Administration (M.B.A.) degree and has a five-year undergraduate Master of Business Administration (M.B.A.) program in accounting, business administration (M.B.A.), economics, finance, international business, management, and marketing. Wesleyan also offers four undergraduate degrees: the Bachelor of Arts in art (ceramics, painting and drawing, graphic design, and intermedia), arts administration (art, music, and theater arts), chemistry, Christian education and church leadership, communication studies, criminal justice, education (elementary, secondary, and combined elementary/secondary), English (literature, teaching, and writing), environmental science, history, human services, international studies, music (applied and theory), musical theater, philosophy, physics, political science, psychology, public relations, religion, sociology, and theater arts; the Bachelor of Fine Arts in musical theater, theater performance, and technical theater design; the Bachelor of Music Education; the Bachelor of Science in accounting, athletic training, biology, business administration, chemistry, computer information science, computer science, economics, engineering physics, environmental science, finance, international business, management, marketing, mathematics, and physical education (health promotion and fitness management); and the Bachelor of Science in Nursing.

Preprofessional programs are offered in dentistry, law, medicine, ministry, optometry, pharmacy, physical therapy, and veterinary medicine. The degrees are determined by the content of the student's program.

Academic Program

Students are required to complete 120 credit hours of course work to become eligible for graduation. Approximately one third of those hours are taken in a student's major, one third in the general studies curriculum requirement, and one third in electives. The general studies and elective courses are taken to develop and enhance a student's world view. These classes range from contemporary issues to humanities and can be taken along with courses within the individual's major concentration throughout the four years.

Wesleyan operates on a traditional semester system. The optional May Term is a three-week intensive period of study giving students the opportunity to earn 3 credit hours.

The honors program is offered for superior students who meet the specific requirements and are willing to commit themselves to a rigorous and enriching curriculum that affirms the highest ideals of a liberal arts institution. Challenging classes and cultural outings are an integral part of the honors program and are offered throughout the academic year.

Advanced credit is available for students who achieve required scores on Advanced Placement exams, International Baccalaureate exams, and CLEP tests.

New students are assigned a faculty adviser who assists with course selection and student concerns. All first-year students are required to successfully complete the one-hour Freshman Seminar course. This course eases the transition from high school to college by providing faculty advising and student mentoring for the first semester. The program begins at orientation and helps students become acclimated to the Wesleyan community.

Off-Campus Programs

Study abroad is highly encouraged and is an important part of the Wesleyan student's experience. In the past, students have studied in such countries as Australia, Austria, Bulgaria, England, Ireland, Italy, Korea, Spain, and Wales, but there are a number of other countries in which students may study. Internships are required for many majors and highly encouraged for others. They are available locally, as well as in such cities as Pittsburgh, New York City, Washington, D.C., and other cities around the globe. These off-campus opportunities can be taken for a complete semester or during the May Term.

Academic Facilities

Wesleyan's twenty-three buildings, including ten modern residence hall units, house some of the most impressive facilities in the region. The Annie Merner Pfeiffer Library is a spacious facility housing more than 105,000 volumes, 700 periodicals, and 10,000 media materials. With its wireless environment, more than 220 million additional resources worldwide can be accessed online or through a number of CD-ROM databases. Located in the center of the campus is Wesley Chapel, the largest sanctuary in West Virginia, and the Martin Religious Center. The Benedum Campus and Community Center houses a convenience store, bookstore, swimming pool, the Cat's Claw restaurant, the campus radio station, and student services offices. The Rockefeller Health and Physical Education Center includes a main gymnasium that seats 3,700 spectators, an intramural gymnasium, Nautilus and weight-training rooms, and an indoor Astroturf training and recreational area. Other vital buildings include Christopher Hall of Science, which houses well-equipped laboratories that complement the building's planetarium, herbarium, and greenhouse; the Loar Memorial Building, which includes a 165-seat recital hall and a state-of-the-art computer music lab; Middleton Hall, which houses admission and financial planning offices as well as the Nursing Department; Haymond Hall of Science; and the Lynch-Raine Administration Building.

Costs

The 2003–04 costs at Wesleyan were $18,250 for tuition, $5200 for room and board, and $1400 for fees. Students should allow $700 for books per year. Wesleyan offers an interest-free monthly payment plan during the academic year.

Financial Aid

Wesleyan allocates nearly $15 million each year to help supplement the financial needs of students and their families. Merit scholarships are available for students who demonstrate excellence in the classroom, as well as those who demonstrate talent in the arts and athletics. Scholarship opportunities are available for students who have a strong commitment to community service and for those who have a comprehensive cocurricular resume. A variety of need-based programs are also available, including government grants and loans, institutional grants, and student employment. Students and their parents should file the Free Application for Federal Student Aid by February 15. The institutional code number is 003830.

Faculty

The faculty at Wesleyan has a primary goal of teaching and advising. Nearly 80 percent of the full-time faculty members hold the highest degree in their respective fields. With a 15:1 student-faculty ratio, classes are small, and personal attention is evident in all departments. Not only are faculty members teachers and advisers, but they are also mentors and friends.

Student Government

The Community Council, one of the first college-based community governing bodies in the country, is structured to encourage and promote student participation. The four peer-elected officers are elected by their respective classes or representative student organizations. The Community Council meets weekly, along with faculty members, administration, and staff members, and is recognized as the driving force behind many issues on campus.

Admission Requirements

Wesleyan seeks students who have proven academic credentials, combined with achievements and talents that enhance the quality of life on campus. Students are selected by the Office of Admission on the basis of their high school transcripts, college entrance exam results, letters of recommendation, campus interviews, and other supportive information. All applicants must take the SAT or ACT and submit secondary school transcripts from all schools attended, along with the application for admission. Candidates are considered on an individual basis without regard to race, religion, geographic origin, or handicap. Essays and campus interviews are strongly encouraged and may be required in some instances.

Transfer students from accredited institutions are considered for admission. All official college transcripts must be submitted, along with high school transcripts and college entrance exam results.

Applicants who complete their secondary education through an alternative program (e.g., home schooling) must present evidence that they have been adequately prepared for college work to be considered for admission. SAT or ACT results are also required.

Application and Information

Applicants must submit an application for admission, official transcripts, and ACT or SAT scores. While applying online is free of charge, a $25 nonrefundable fee for paper applications is required. Early decision applicants must have their completed application submitted by December 1. Admission decisions are made on a rolling basis, and students are notified within three weeks of receipt of all required documents. The preferred application deadline for the fall semester is March 1, and December 1 for the spring semester. Applicants who wish to be considered for merit scholarships must apply before March 1. Interviews, campus tours, faculty and staff appointments, and class visits are encouraged and may be arranged through the Office of Admission.

For additional information, students should contact:

Office of Admission
West Virginia Wesleyan College
59 College Avenue
Buckhannon, West Virginia 26201
Telephone: 304-473-8510
800-722-9933 (toll-free)
E-mail: admission@wvwc.edu
World Wide Web: http://www.wvwc.edu

The Benedum Campus and Community Center is the hub of student life—both inside and out.

WHEATON COLLEGE

WHEATON, ILLINOIS

The College

Wheaton College's 140-year history demonstrates the benefits of stable leadership in private Christian higher education: it has had only 7 presidents since it was founded in 1860. Interdenominational and international in constituency, the student body of about 2,300 undergraduates (including 220 students in the Conservatory of Music) and 450 graduate students represents all fifty states, some forty countries, and about forty Christian denominations. Eighty percent of the students come from outside Illinois.

In addition to its undergraduate programs, Wheaton College offers the Master of Arts in Teaching (M.A.T.) degree and the Master of Arts (M.A.) degree in clinical psychology, educational ministries, evangelism, missions/intercultural studies, and theological studies, as well as a Doctor of Psychology degree and a Ph.D in biblical studies. Two certificate programs—Advanced Biblical Studies and Teaching English as a Second Language—are available.

The student activity calendar includes concerts of all kinds, Chicago outings, films, theater productions, athletic contests, and banquets. The Office of Christian Outreach provides opportunities for student ministry through the Student Missionary Project, Christian Service Council, and World Christian Fellowship. The Men's Glee Club, the Women's Chorale, the Concert Choir, the Symphony Orchestra, the Wind Ensemble, and the Gospel Choir, open by audition to all Wheaton students, give concerts throughout the Chicago area and make annual tours to other sections of the United States and to Canada. Radio broadcasting experience is provided by WETN, the campus FM radio station.

Wheaton is a member of NCAA Division III. Intercollegiate sports include baseball, basketball, cross-country, football, golf, soccer, softball, swimming, tennis, track, volleyball, wrestling, and women's water polo. In addition, the College has a well-developed club sports program, including crew, drill team, ice hockey, lacrosse, and tae kwon do as well as fifteen intramural sports. The Sports and Recreation Complex, which opened in 2000, comprises a newly constructed Eckert Recreation Center, a renovated King Arena, and the Chrouser Fitness Center. In addition to housing academic offices and classrooms, the complex's amenities include multiple baksetball courts, an 8,000-square-foot weight and fitness area, an elevated running track, an indoor climbing wall, and a glassed-in upper walkway above the fitness center's 35-meter pool.

Through efforts of the student body, the College publishes *The Record,* a weekly newspaper; *Kodon,* the College literary magazine; and *The Tower* yearbook. An additional thirty clubs and organizations round out the cocurricular offerings.

Location

Wheaton's 80-acre campus is located in a residential suburb (population 50,000) 25 miles west of Chicago. The educational and cultural features of the Chicago metropolitan area are easily accessible by train and regularly visited by students. The Wheaton area is the home of more than forty Christian organizations.

Majors and Degrees

Wheaton grants the Bachelor of Arts and Bachelor of Science degrees and, through the Wheaton Conservatory of Music, the Bachelor of Music and Bachelor of Music Education degrees.

The following majors are available in the arts and sciences: ancient languages, anthropology, archaeology, art, biblical studies, biology, business/economics, chemistry, Christian education, communications, computer science/math, economics, education, English, environmental science, geological studies, history, interdisciplinary studies, international relations, kinesiology, mathematics, modern languages (French, German, and Spanish), music, philosophy, physical science, physics, political science, psychology, religious studies, social science, and sociology. Also, 3-2 programs are available in engineering and nursing, as is a five-year cooperative engineering program with Illinois Institute of Technology.

The Wheaton Conservatory of Music offers majors in music composition, music education, music history–literature, music performance, and music with elective studies in an outside field. Students seeking these professional music degrees normally begin their programs as freshmen.

An on-campus program in military science leads to a commission in the U.S. Army at graduation. In addition to the majors offered, Wheaton has programs leading to teacher certification and to athletic training certification as well as programs preparing students for careers in business, health professions, law, and ministry.

Academic Program

Wheaton is a distinctively Christian college at which faculty and students work together, both inside and outside the classroom, to apply Christian principles and values to the needs and problems of the individual and society. The vigorous search for knowledge and wisdom in any area of human activity is based on the belief that all truth is God's truth. The academic curriculum combines with the extensive cocurriculum of artistic, athletic, religious, service, and social activities to achieve a lively interaction of Christian faith, learning, and living. Because of the College's strong commitment to developing effective servant/leaders for the church and society worldwide, there is a particularly strong integration of faith and learning in all degree programs.

To meet the requirements of all baccalaureate degrees, students must complete a minimum of 124 semester hours, 36 of which must be in the upper division, and have at least a C (2.0) average overall.

The major field is selected during the second semester of general education courses taken to meet competency and area requirements. Students must demonstrate competence (either by examination or by taking prescribed courses) in foreign language, mathematics, speech, and writing. All students must complete area requirements in art, biblical studies, history, kinesiology, literature, music, natural science, philosophy, and social science. A student may be granted advanced placement or college credit on the basis of examination (SAT II or AP). The number of credits granted and the level of placement are determined by the registrar and the chairman of the department in which the course is taught.

The College operates on a semester academic calendar, beginning in late August and ending in early May. An eight-week summer term is also offered.

Off-Campus Programs

Wheaton College offers a variety of off-campus opportunities to enhance students' programs of study. The High Road program is a rugged wilderness education experience available to new students at the College's Honey Rock Camp in northern Wisconsin. The Human Needs and Global Resources (HNGR) Program focuses on responses to human needs from a multidisciplinary perspective. It offers a concentration of courses leading to a six-month internship overseas, followed by a seminar on campus. By participating in this program, students can earn up to 24 hours of credit. A similar program in urban studies is focused on U.S. cities.

Other special summer programs for credit include field study at the Wheaton College Science Station in the Black Hills of South Dakota; working with youth at Honey Rock Camp; interdisciplinary study in East Asia; the study of English literature in England; language study in France, Germany, and Spain; the Wheaton-in-the-Holy-Lands Program, involving biblical and archaeological studies; and an international study program based in England and the Netherlands, offering courses in economics, political science, and psychology.

Wheaton is a member of the Council of Christian Colleges and Universites, based in Washington, D.C. The council's activities increase students' learning opportunities by bringing special programs to campus and by providing off-campus study. Off-campus programs include American Studies in Washington, D.C., Latin American Studies in Costa Rica, Middle East Studies in Cairo, and the Los Angeles Film Studies Center. In addition, Wheaton's membership in the Christian College Consortium allows students a semester of study at one of the other twelve consortium colleges.

Cooperative programs in social science are available at American and Drew universities, and students may participate in a European seminar conducted by Gordon College.

Academic Facilities

Wheaton's combined libraries have a collection of more than 1 million items and belong to LIBRAS, an association of fourteen suburban liberal arts college libraries, and the Chicago Area Theological Library Association. The Peter Stam Music Library holds more than 9,500 recordings, 8,000 scores, and 425 titles in music education. The Wade Center is a special collection of the books and papers of 7 British authors, including C. S. Lewis and J. R. R. Tolkien.

The Billy Graham Center, a research and study center, houses a museum, a library, and archives, all focused on evangelism and world missions.

Adams Hall houses an art gallery and studios, and Arena Theater is home to several theater productions each year.

Specialized laboratory facilities and modern equipment are available for general and advanced work in various science departments and for individual student research projects. Numerous microcomputers, as well as larger types of data processing equipment, are readily available for student use.

Costs

Tuition for the 2003–04 year was $18,500; room and board for the year were $6100.

Financial Aid

Most Wheaton College financial aid is allocated on the basis of need as demonstrated by information supplied on the Free Application for Federal Student Aid (FAFSA) and the CSS Profile. Students from Alaska, Illinois, Pennsylvania, Rhode Island, and Vermont are expected to apply for state grants or scholarships along with their application for Wheaton College aid.

Substantial student aid is available in the form of grants, loans, and work-study opportunities provided by government and College resources. The average aid package is more than $15,000. The Career Development Center provides free service to help students secure part-time jobs.

Faculty

The 183 Wheaton faculty members, of whom nearly 91 percent hold earned doctorates, come from a variety of colleges and universities in the United States and abroad. As active Christians, they are interested in the spiritual and intellectual development of their students. The faculty members' primary commitment as educators and advisers is enriched by their considerable research, publishing, and artistic performance activities. All undergraduate courses are taught by faculty members.

To ensure a rich range of perspectives and expertise, every department at Wheaton has at least 3 full-time professors, and most have 5 to 10. The student-faculty ratio is 12:1.

Student Government

Student Government ensures a student voice in institutional affairs and provides a wide range of opportunities to develop leadership abilities. Student Leadership Workshops, the apportionment of student fees, and the official representation of the student body are some of the activities under the direction of the Student Government. The College Union, an all-student organization, plans and directs cultural, social, and recreational activities.

Admission Requirements

Wheaton is a selective college that seeks to enroll students who evidence a vital Christian experience, high moral character, personal integrity, social concern, strong academic ability and motivation, and the desire to pursue Christian higher education as defined in the aims and objectives of the College. These qualities are evaluated by consideration of each applicant's academic record, autobiographical essays, test scores, recommendations, optional interview, and participation in extracurricular activities. For students applying to the Conservatory of Music, strong consideration is given to the evaluation of the required audition.

Applicants must have a high school diploma or the equivalent and, at the time of graduation, should have completed a college-preparatory curriculum with a minimum of 18 acceptable units. Of the 18 units, 15 must be in English, foreign language, mathematics, science, and social studies. No units are granted for health, band, choir, driver's education, or physical education, but a maximum of 3 units for vocational subjects is allowed.

Satisfactory scores on the SAT I or on the ACT examination are required of all applicants to the freshman class. The middle 50 percent range of scores for those admitted is 26–31 (ACT) and 1250–1400 (SAT I).

Application and Information

An application packet, complete with detailed instructions and requirements, can be obtained from the Admissions Office. For early action (non-binding), students seeking admission in the fall term should apply to the College by November 1. All other applications for undergraduate admission in the fall should be received by January 15. The final deadline for Conservatory of Music and transfer applications is March 1.

Further information is available from:

Admissions Office
Wheaton College
Wheaton, Illinois 60187
Telephone: 630-752-5005
800-222-2419 (toll-free)
E-mail: admissions@wheaton.edu
music@wheaton.edu
World Wide Web: http://www.wheaton.edu

WHEATON COLLEGE

NORTON, MASSACHUSETTS

The College

Wheaton College is an independent liberal arts college of approximately 1,500 women and men. Founded as a seminary for women in 1834, Wheaton was chartered as a college in 1912 and enrolled its first coeducational class in 1988. Students come from forty-two states and thirty-two countries. Nearly all students live on campus in both single-sex and coed student-run dormitories.

The vitality of this classic liberal arts college grows out of each student's involvement in the social and academic life of the campus. There are many extracurricular activities and organizations, including intercollegiate and intramural sports such as baseball, basketball, cross-country, field hockey, lacrosse, soccer, softball, synchronized swimming, tennis, and track; musical groups such as the Whims, Wheatones, Gentleman Callers, and chamber music ensembles; the Modern Dance Group; the Black Students Association; the Student Government Association; the Christian Fellowship; Hillel; the International Students Association; the Latino Students Association; the Asian Student Association; and the newspaper, yearbook, campus radio station, and literary magazine. Wheaton also has a chapter of Phi Beta Kappa. A number of lecture series are offered, and concerts, plays, films, colloquia, art exhibits, and social events are scheduled regularly. Through the Filene Center for Work and Learning, hundreds of students annually undertake career exploration internships, field placements, and community service positions in local towns as well as in Boston, Providence, and overseas. The Filene Center also provides a full range of career services, graduate and professional school counseling, alumnae networks, and databases of part-time and summer job opportunities.

Location

The 385-acre campus with its eighty-seven buildings is in the countrylike surroundings of Norton. The newest additions to the campus include a $20-million arts complex with a state-of-the-art studio arts building; 100-bed Beard Hall; two 50-person residence halls; a multipurpose athletics facility, which includes a field house, a pool, and a gymnasium; and Sidell Baseball Stadium. Norton is located 30 minutes from Providence and 45 minutes from Boston. Public buses connect the campus to nearby commuter rail stations serving Boston, Providence, and numerous points in between. The College provides individuals with transportation for academic and internship activities as well as direct service to Boston's center and Providence, Rhode Island on weekends. The College is also situated within an hour's drive of the beautiful beaches of Cape Cod, Massachusetts and Newport, Rhode Island. The Tweeter Center for Performing Arts is located 2½ miles away.

Majors and Degrees

Wheaton College grants the Bachelor of Arts degree with formal majors in American studies, ancient studies, anthropology, art (history and studio), Asian studies, biochemistry, biology, chemistry, classical civilization, classics (Greek and Latin), computer science, economics, economics-mathematics, English (literature and writing), English dramatic literature, environmental science, French, German, Hispanic studies, history, international relations, Italian studies, mathematics, mathematics and computer science, music, philosophy, physics, physics and astronomy, political science, psychobiology, psychology, religion, religion and history, religion and philosophy, Russian, Russian studies, sociology, theater, and women's studies. Students may also create their own interdepartmental majors.

Five-year dual-degree programs are available in engineering with Thayer School of Engineering (Dartmouth), George Washington University, and Worcester Polytechnic Institute; in business and management with Clark University and the University of Rochester; in religion with Andover-Newton Theological School; in optometry with the New England School of Optometry; in communications with Emerson College; and in fine arts with the School of the Museum of Fine Arts in Boston.

Academic Programs

Wheaton's programs reflect the traditional depth and breadth of the liberal arts while going beyond prescribed boundaries. The College's new curriculum helps students push past one-dimensional views of the world to acquire a deeper understanding of the topics that interest them. Through a series of linked courses, Wheaton students approach the same topic from two or more academic perspectives. Thus, students who examine public policy and politics may also choose to explore environmental management. An art class in figure drawing may be paired with study of human anatomy. Or students investigating evolutionary theory may survey the literature of the Victorian society from which Darwin and his work sprung. This approach helps students discover doorways to new insights and possibilities.

Course credit is granted through the Advanced Placement Program on an individual basis. Independent studies, research, and fieldwork are available to students for academic credit.

In addition to major department offerings, courses may be taken in education, family studies, film, geology, and linguistics.

Off-Campus Programs

Wheaton participates in the Twelve-College Exchange Program, whose other members include Amherst, Bowdoin, Connecticut College, Dartmouth, Mount Holyoke, Smith, Trinity, Vassar, Wellesley, Wesleyan, and Williams. Locally, Wheaton students may cross-register for courses at Brown University and other colleges in the Southeastern Association for Cooperation in Higher Education in Massachusetts (SACHEM).

Wheaton students may study government or economics during a semester in Washington, D.C., sponsored by American University, explore marine ecology at the Marine Biological Laboratory at Woods Hole, or participate in a semester-long program in American maritime studies, sponsored by Williams College at Mystic Seaport. The National Theater Institute Program offers selected students the opportunity to spend a semester at the Eugene O'Neill Theater Center in Waterford, Connecticut. Students may also participate in the Salt Center for Documentary Field Studies in Portland, Maine.

International study is available through any one of several approved Junior Year Abroad programs, for which the College grants credit. Wheaton sponsors its own programs as part of a consortium in Cordoba, Spain and Rehovot, Israel. Part or all of the junior year may also be spent at universities in Belgium, China, France, Germany, Great Britain, Greece, India, Israel, Italy, Japan, Kenya, Spain, Switzerland, Thailand, and the Latin American republics. Through a program affiliation, many of the College's study-abroad opportunities include the opportunity to combine university study with related internships with multinational corporations, foreign governments, art galleries, museums, advertising agencies, and much more. In addition, the College sponsors faculty-led summer and January-term programs in Belize, Ecuador, Kenya, and Thailand.

A Career Exploration Internship Program allows students to work from one to four weeks in a professional field of interest during the January break. More than 600 internship positions are listed with the Filene Center for Work and Learning; housing is often provided in various locations by Wheaton graduates.

Academic Facilities

Wheaton's library has 373,659 volumes, 3,186 current periodicals and newspapers, 84,124 microfilm units, and 13,306 audiovisual items; a College Archives/Special Collections area; and a College Learning Center. Wheaton participates in library consortia, which provides direct access to three other local college libraries and computer and interlibrary loan access to libraries around the country. Automated services include online searching of remote databases, full-text electronic journals, and a fully integrated system containing the Wheaton Library catalog and acquisitions and circulation information. The Library also supports the academic program through bibliographic instruction sessions, including participation in the First-Year Seminars and individual consultations.

The Science Center has fully equipped laboratories for both faculty and student research and two greenhouses. Other facilities include a new studio arts building with public exhibition space and private studio studies for students; the Balfour-Hood Student Center; the Watson Fine Arts Center with a proscenium theater, a black box theater, art studios, and a gallery; a laboratory nursery school; and the Academic Computing Center. The Academic Computing Center offers students access to more than sixty-five Macintosh computers and PCs as well as multimedia equipment, digital cameras and camcorders, scanners, and laser printers. The center also supports twenty-five classrooms on campus, with permanently installed computers, digital projectors and sound systems, and nine computer labs with 130 computers dedicated to specific academic courses and programs, e.g., Geographic Information Systems, Graphic Lab Design, Astronomy, and Language Lab. All academic and administrative buildings and all dormitories are part of a campuswide network. Students are offered accounts for e-mail and Internet access.

Costs

The comprehensive fee for 2003–04 was $36,330, which consisted of tuition, $28,675; room, $3920; board, $3510; and a student activities fee, $225.

Financial Aid

Students who demonstrate financial need normally receive a combination of grants, loans, and opportunities for employment on campus. The decision to award financial aid is made independently of the admission decision. Students applying for financial aid must complete the Free Application for Federal Student Aid (FAFSA) and the CSS PROFILE by January 15. Fifty-eight percent of Wheaton's students receive some form of financial aid.

Faculty

The student-faculty ratio is 11:1. Ninety-seven percent of the full-time faculty members hold the Ph.D. degree. Professors are very accessible to students, act as academic advisers, and often become involved with student activities.

Student Government

The Student Government Association, an active and influential organization, includes all members of the Wheaton community. Students are invited to attend faculty meetings and serve as voting members on most faculty committees. Rules are minimal, based on student self-government and an honor system stressing individual honor and responsibility.

Admission Requirements

Wheaton does not prescribe rigid entrance requirements, but most entering students have had 4 years of English, 3 years of mathematics, 4 years of one or two languages, 2 years of social studies, and 3 years of science. However, these guidelines are not to be taken as requirements. Applications are reviewed on an individual basis, and the academic achievement, the challenge of the curriculum, evaluations by teachers and counselors, and the extracurricular contributions of each candidate are all taken into account.

The submission of standardized test results is optional for the purposes of admission. Those who wish their scores to be considered should arrange for official score reports to be sent from the appropriate testing agency directly to the Wheaton Office of Admission. Reports must be received no later than the application deadline for the corresponding decision plan. Unofficial test scores (i.e., those reported on high school transcripts) are not considered. A personal interview is expected for all applicants.

Transfer students are admitted to the sophomore and junior classes each year. Transfer applicants must have maintained a promising record and must be eligible for honorable dismissal from the college they are attending. A transfer student must attend Wheaton at least two years in order to receive a degree from the College. Students who wish to enter in the spring semester must apply by November 15. The regular decision deadline for transfer students is April 1.

Application and Information

Students who consider Wheaton their first choice may apply for Early Decision by November 15 or Early Decision 2 by January 15. Decisions are mailed by December 15 and February 15, respectively. The deadline for regular-decision applicants is January 15; notification for these students is made during the first week of April.

For more information, students are encouraged to contact:

Dean of Admission and Student Aid
Wheaton College
Norton, Massachusetts 02766

Telephone: 508-286-8251
800-394-6003 (toll-free)
E-mail: admission@wheatoncollege.edu
World Wide Web: http://www.wheatoncollege.edu

Park Hall, the administration building (left), and Mary Lyon Hall, a classroom building (right), are among the handsome facilities on Wheaton College's extensive 385-acre campus.

WHEELING JESUIT UNIVERSITY

WHEELING, WEST VIRGINIA

The University

Wheeling Jesuit University (WJU), founded in 1954, is the youngest of America's twenty-eight Jesuit colleges and the only one that has been coeducational from the beginning. The University aims to develop men and women who think clearly and act wisely, with courage, competence, and compassion. Students have the advantage of a world-recognized Jesuit education on a scale where personal student-faculty interaction occurs daily. Although Catholic in affiliation, Wheeling Jesuit University welcomes students of all faiths. Of the 1,228 undergraduate students, approximately 66 percent are Catholic. Students come from thirty-two states, with the majority from the East and Midwest. International students come from twenty-three different countries.

Wheeling Jesuit University is accredited by the North Central Association of Colleges and Schools, and its programs in the respective areas are accredited by the National League for Nursing and the AMA Committee on Allied Health Education and Accreditation.

The campus has fifteen modern buildings spread out over 65 acres of rolling hillside. Residential housing is available to all students who wish to live on campus, and 75 percent of the students enrolled take advantage of this. The dining hall and snack bar are operated by Parkhurst Dining Services, and a rathskeller is operated by the students. Student organizations and clubs offer an array of cultural and social activities, including dramatics, a University newspaper and magazine, cinema, concerts, and community services. Intercollegiate sports include men's and women's basketball, cross-country, golf, soccer, swimming, and track and field; men's lacrosse; and women's volleyball and softball. Club and intramural sports include basketball, football, ice hockey, lacrosse, rugby, softball, tennis, and volleyball. The Health and Recreation Center features a 2,200-seat gymnasium, a jogging track, racquetball courts, and a six-lane swimming pool.

In addition to the undergraduate degree programs shown below, the University offers a six-year program leading to a doctoral degree in physical therapy.

Location

Wheeling, one of the country's most livable and safe small cities, has a population of approximately 50,000 and is easily accessible by interstate highways. The University is a 1-hour drive from the international airport in Pittsburgh, Pennsylvania, and a 2-hour drive from Columbus, Ohio. Many recreational and cultural facilities are available, including 1,500-acre Oglebay Park and 250-acre Wheeling Park. Excellent local recreational areas provide opportunities for camping, golf, hiking, skiing, swimming, and other activities.

Majors and Degrees

The Bachelor of Arts degree is granted in criminal justice, French, history, international studies, liberal studies (elementary, secondary, and special education), English, philosophy, political and economic philosophy, political science, professional communications, psychology, Romance languages, Spanish, and theology. The Bachelor of Science degree is awarded in accounting, biology, business (with concentrations in international business, management, and marketing), chemistry, computer science, environmental studies, mathematics, nuclear medicine technology, nursing, physics, and respiratory therapy. Independent majors may be arranged. Preprofessional programs in dentistry, law, medicine, physical therapy, and veterinary medicine are also available. A teacher preparation program provides teaching certification in many subjects. This program prepares students to teach grades kindergarten through 12. A learning disabilities special endorsement, at grade level K–6 or 5–12, may be added, if desired.

A 3-2 engineering program is offered in conjunction with Case Western Reserve University.

A special program called "Hunting for a Future" (HUNT) is available to help entering students who are undecided about a major.

Master's degrees are also offered in accountancy, applied theology, business administration, nursing, and physical therapy.

Academic Programs

Wheeling Jesuit University combines preprofessional majors with those in traditional arts and sciences. A strong background in the liberal arts is provided to all students through a required general studies core curriculum. A minimum of 120 credit hours completed with an average of 2.0 or better is required for graduation. The Laut Honors Program for students of exceptional ability is a sequence of honors courses, an independent project or thesis, a special senior seminar, and a January cross-cultural experience.

Off-Campus Programs

Wheeling Jesuit University students have a wide range of study-abroad opportunities, ranging from short study tours to semester or year-long programs overseas. WJU offers semester and year-long programs in London, England; Macerata, Italy; Vienna, Austria; Segovia, Spain; and Beijing, China. Summer programs are available in London, Segovia, and Dublin, Ireland. Students can also participate in a number of short study trips led by WJU faculty members to such locations as Vietnam, Dominica, France, and Ireland. In addition to the programs outlined above, students can avail themselves to a host of other programs throughout the world through WJU's membership in various consortia and ties with other Jesuit universities.

Academic Facilities

Wheeling Jesuit University's campus has recently undergone an eleven-year $53-million renovation and expansion, resulting in a quality and depth of facilities unprecedented for an institution its size. There are fifteen modern and spacious buildings, including an $8.5 million science center, a state-of-the-art health and recreation facility, a $1.5-million soccer and track complex, new and renovated residence halls, and a 142,000-volume library with 28 online databases. The campus is linked by a fiber-optic network, and both students and faculty members have unlimited access to the resources at the Robert C. Byrd National Technology Transfer Center. The Erma Ora Byrd Center for Educational Technologies is a NASA building that houses the Classroom of the Future Program, with its high-tech teaching and research rooms that serve as the cornerstone for the teacher education programs.

Costs

Tuition and fees in 2003–04 were $19,280. Room and board costs were $6000. Books and supplies cost approximately $300 to $600, and personal expenses average $600 per year.

Financial Aid

Wheeling Jesuit University assists students who have financial need with financial award packages that include loans, grants, work-study jobs, and scholarships. In 2003–04, 95 percent of full-day students received some form of aid. The average assistance level to those receiving aid was nearly $18,000, including working loans. Federal aid includes Federal Perkins Loans, Federal Pell Grants, Federal Work-Study awards, Federal Supplemental Educational Opportunity Grants, and Federal Direct Student Loans. West Virginia, Pennsylvania, Rhode Island, and Vermont state grants can be used at Wheeling Jesuit University by eligible students. The University also provides need-based grants from institutional funds.

Scholarships based solely on academic ability are also awarded by the University. These scholarships range from $500 to $11,000 per year. Two full-tuition scholarships are awarded on a competitive basis to entering Laut Honors Program students. All academic scholarships are renewable for four years if the specified cumulative grade average point is maintained. Athletic scholarships are awarded to men and women in various intercollegiate sports. Athletic awards are determined by the Athletic Department.

For further information on scholarships or financial aid, applicants should contact the Financial Aid Office (telephone: 800-624-6992; e-mail: finaid@wju.edu). The FAFSA should be filed before March 1.

Faculty

An energetic, diversified faculty (84 percent of whose members have doctoral or other terminal degrees) has a strong voice in the policies of the institution through a faculty council and other standing committees. All 83 full-time faculty members are professional teachers; no teaching is done by graduate assistants. About 10 percent of the faculty members are Jesuits. Faculty members and students interact outside the classroom through activities, dining, intramural sports, and informal gatherings. The student-faculty ratio is 14:1. Academic advising is done by the faculty.

Student Government

Students participate fully in formulating the policies of the University through the Student Government and residence hall governments and as voting or auditing participants on virtually all faculty-administration committees of the University. Students plan and control the entire student activity budget.

Admission Requirements

Wheeling Jesuit University is a democratic institution where all students are accepted on the same basis regardless of sex, race, creed, or color. The Committee on Admissions selects students best qualified to complete the required program of studies. Applicants are considered for admission if they have successfully completed a high school course of study and have achieved reasonable success on either the SAT I or the ACT. For transfer students, transcripts are required from colleges previously attended.

Application and Information

There is a rolling admissions policy. Students receive notification of the admissions decision shortly after all their academic credentials have been received by the Admissions Office.

For more information, students should contact:

Office of Admissions
Wheeling Jesuit University
Wheeling, West Virginia 26003
Telephone: 304-243-2359
800-624-6992 (toll-free)
Fax: 304-243-2397
E-mail: admiss@wju.edu
World Wide Web: http://www.wju.edu

Wheeling Jesuit University's main classroom building, Donahue Hall.

WHEELOCK COLLEGE

BOSTON, MASSACHUSETTS

The College

Wheelock College prepares students for careers that enrich the lives of children and families. Founded in 1888, Wheelock has consistently produced progressive and highly respected professionals for such fields as elementary education, preschool and kindergarten teaching, special education, day care, social work, juvenile justice, and child life work. The 600 undergraduate women and men at Wheelock come from throughout the United States and from several countries. Beginning in their freshman year, students benefit from close contact with outstanding faculty and from direct fieldwork with children and families.

Wheelock's campus is beautifully kept, and the atmosphere is warm and friendly. Classes are small, and professors are known by their first names. Comfortable dormitories provide housing and many social activities for those who wish to live on campus. The Student Center, with its wide-screen TV, snack bar, and often-used dance floor, is an attraction for the entire Wheelock community and for many students from neighboring schools. Wheelock students enjoy more than twenty-five clubs and organizations and actively participate in a variety of varsity and intramural sports. The College sponsors many cultural and theatrical events as well as such traditional activities as Family Weekend, the Sophomore-Senior Banquet, and Black History Month.

Location

Bordering Boston and suburban Brookline, Wheelock is ideally located across from Longwood Park and only a few blocks from the Museum of Fine Arts, several world-renowned hospitals, and many other institutions of higher learning. Students can walk to the shops and restaurants in Coolidge Corner or cheer for the Red Sox in nearby Fenway Park. They can discover the unmatched cultural and historical richness of downtown Boston, only a short subway ride away. They can walk the Freedom Trail, attend concerts and plays, or meet friends from other colleges for a day of fun at Faneuil Hall. The entire Boston area provides Wheelock students with exciting opportunities for extracurricular enjoyment and for their practical fieldwork with children and families.

Majors and Degrees

At Wheelock, students pursue one of four professional directions: teaching, child life, juvenile justice, or social work. Within teaching, there are two separate areas of concentration: early childhood care and education focuses on the comprehensive care and education of children from birth to 8 years old; elementary education prepares students to become teachers of children in grades 1–6. The child life program explores the emotional and psychological needs of hospitalized children and their families and prepares students to work as child life specialists with medical teams in hospitals or clinics. The juvenile justice program prepares students to work with youth and their families in a range of settings including preventative programs, advocacy programs, and programs for juvenile offenders. Students interested in teaching, juvenile justice, or child life major in one of five liberal arts areas: American studies, human development, the arts, the humanities, or mathematics/science. These multidisciplinary majors are designed to form a strong foundation for professional studies and for lifelong learning. Social work majors prepare to work in social service agencies, state agencies, and schools to advocate for and support children and their families. Graduates of Wheelock receive the Bachelor of Arts, the Bachelor of Science, or the Bachelor of Social Work degree.

Academic Programs

The focus of study at Wheelock is education and human services. Faculty members stress the importance of combining liberal arts, professional studies, and hands-on experience. Students begin work with children and families in their freshman year as part of a required course entitled Human Growth and Development. Practical work continues in the sophomore year. Juniors and seniors participate in supervised field experiences and student teaching in a variety of settings—elementary schools, day-care centers, nursery schools, museums, hospitals, social service agencies, and clinics—in urban and suburban locations. Professional courses provide preparation for field experience and support to students during their fieldwork. By combining the appropriate courses and field experience, Wheelock graduates are eligible for certification as early childhood or elementary school teachers.

Off-Campus Programs

Students are encouraged to engage in independent study in an area of specific academic interest. In some academic programs, students may elect to study off campus.

Wheelock College is a member of the Colleges of the Fenway, a collaboration among Emmanuel College, Massachusetts College of Art, Massachusetts College of Pharmacy and Health Sciences, Simmons College, Wentworth Institute of Technology, and Wheelock College. Each college maintains its unique identity, while providing students with access to academic programs and student services on all six campuses. Wheelock students can cross-register for courses and participate in social and extracurricular activities at any of the other institutions.

Academic Facilities

Wheelock's innovative Resource Center has a fully equipped workshop and holds a large collection of commercially manufactured scrap and natural materials for students to use in the creation of projects and original curriculum tools. Wheelock's library contains 92,000 volumes, providing reference and study facilities, collections in liberal arts areas, and extensive resources in children's literature and curriculum materials. The College also has extensive art studios with facilities for work in ceramics, weaving, and photography. One of the largest and best-equipped stages in Boston is found in the Lucy Wheelock Auditorium and Activities Building. The Activities Building also houses science and music classrooms, a 700-seat auditorium, the Little Theatre, a music listening room, and an art gallery. All classrooms at Wheelock are equipped with dataports for Internet access and teacher workstations for integrating technology into the classroom. In addition, all students have Internet capabilities in their rooms.

Costs

In 2003–04, tuition was $20,400, and room and board were $8600, for a total of $29,000. A reasonable estimate for books and supplies is $500 per year and for personal expenses, $800, exclusive of travel to and from school.

Financial Aid

Wheelock provides financial aid for all applicants who demonstrate need. Currently, about 80 percent of the student body receives financial aid, usually in a combination of grants, loans, and work. Wheelock participates in the Federal Stafford Student Loan, Federal Perkins Loan, Federal Supplemental Educational Opportunity Grant, Federal Pell Grant, and Federal Work-Study programs. The College uses its own funds to provide additional grants, loans, and employment. The Financial Aid Office must receive the Free Application for Federal Student Aid (FAFSA) and the Wheelock College Application for Financial Aid by February 15 for students who plan to enter in September or by October 15 for midyear students.

Faculty

All of Wheelock's faculty members, many of whom are nationally recognized for their research, are actively engaged in classroom teaching. Faculty members also serve as academic advisers, as fieldwork supervisors, and, often, as advisers for student organizations. A student-faculty ratio of only 11:1 allows Wheelock professors to work closely with students both in and out of the classroom.

Student Government

The student government organization is the principal undergraduate governing body on campus. Its members are elected in the spring from the resident and day student population. The board meets weekly, often with the vice president for student development and the president of the College, to discuss issues of concern to the student body. In addition, each residence hall has its own governing body and makes its own policies and regulations. Through the Commuter Organization, commuting students participate in most aspects of student life. Students sit on many of the administrative committees of the College.

Admission Requirements

Wheelock seeks and admits women and men of all ages, from a variety of racial, geographic, ethnic, and economic backgrounds, who have the potential for creative, effective work with young children. Each admission decision is made after careful consideration of an applicant's academic record, interview, SAT I scores, written essay, recommendations, and work experience and involvement with children. On-campus interviews are highly recommended and can be arranged by mail or telephone. A telephone interview can be arranged for those students who are unable to visit the campus. The College has Open Houses in October and November for prospective students.

Application and Information

A complete Wheelock application consists of the Wheelock application form with a writing sample, one work and one academic recommendation, the school transcript, SAT I scores, and an application fee. The Admissions Committee is glad to review additional information that the candidate feels would be helpful to the committee in making the admission decision. Early decision applications are due on December 1, regular freshman applications on March 1, and transfer applications on April 15. Applicants can expect to hear from the Admissions Office by January 1 for early decision and within one month after regular applications are completed.

For more information about Wheelock, students should contact:

Lynne D. Harding
Dean of Admissions
Wheelock College
200 The Riverway
Boston, Massachusetts 02215-4176
Telephone: 617-879-2206
800-734-5212 (toll-free)
E-mail: undergrad@wheelock.edu
World Wide Web: http://www.wheelock.edu

Fieldwork in schools, hospitals, and social services settings is one of the focal points of education at Wheelock.

WHITMAN COLLEGE

WALLA WALLA, WASHINGTON

The College

Challenging its students to excel in the sciences, the humanities, the arts, and the social sciences, Whitman College is one of the nation's leading liberal arts colleges. It combines the educational values of the best liberal arts colleges of the East with the outdoor frankness and vigor of the Pacific Northwest. Since 1859, men and women have chosen this private, independent college because of its commitment to undergraduate education. With just 1,400 students and an average class size of 14, Whitman encourages students to be active participants in their own education. In 1913, the College led the nation by requiring all undergraduates to successfully complete a comprehensive examination in the major field of study. The installation of a chapter of Phi Beta Kappa in 1919 marked the general recognition of the high quality of Whitman's curriculum and the standards of teaching and learning that distinguish the College. More than 60 percent of Whitman's students enroll in a graduate program of some type within five years of earning their undergraduate degree.

The current enrollment includes students from forty-three states and thirty countries. A residential college, Whitman has approximately 75 percent of its students residing on campus. A variety of residence hall living options are available, including coeducational housing, apartment-style housing, eleven special interest houses, four fraternity houses, and an all-women's residence hall that houses, among others, the members of four sororities. Freshmen and sophomores must live on campus and may indicate a preference for a particular residence hall. Whitman has an intensely active student body. The College offers more than 100 interest groups and clubs and has a nationally recognized debate team, a highly acclaimed theater program, and a music department that includes twenty-four music groups on campus. The College fields eighteen varsity teams (nine for men and nine for women) and offers ten club sports and twelve intramural activities.

Location

Whitman is located in Walla Walla, a historic community of 30,000, nestled in the foothills of the Blue Mountains of southeastern Washington. The Walla Walla Valley has four distinct seasons and a dry, sunny climate. With rich natural terrain at its doorstep, outdoor activities abound. These include cross-country and downhill skiing, backpacking, hiking, kayaking, rafting, and rock-climbing. Whitman imports a wide array of cultural activities to campus, including concerts, art exhibits, forums, internationally renowned speakers and performers, and cinema arts films. Students also perform with the community symphony, browse in the area's seventeen art galleries, and act in the community theater.

Majors and Degrees

Whitman College confers the B.A. degree with departmental majors in anthropology; art (history and studio); biochemistry, biophysics, and molecular biology (BBMB); biology; chemistry; classics; economics; English; foreign languages and literatures (French, German literature, German studies, or Spanish); geology; history; mathematics; music; philosophy; physics; politics; psychology; religion; rhetoric and film studies; sociology; and theater. Combined or interdepartmental major study programs are offered in Asian studies; astronomy-geology; biology-geology; chemistry-geology; economics-mathematics; environmental studies (emphasis in biology, chemistry, economics, geology, physics, politics, or sociology); geology-physics; mathematics-physics; and physics-astronomy. Minor study options are available in each of the departmental programs, as well as American ethnic studies, astronomy, Chinese, computer science, education, environmental studies, gender studies, Japanese, Latin American studies, sports studies/recreation and athletics, and world literature. Students with special interests may develop combined or interdepartmental major programs, subject to faculty approval. Whitman offers outstanding cooperative programs in engineering with Caltech, Columbia, Duke, University of Washington, and Washington University in St. Louis; in environmental management or forestry with Duke; in law with Columbia School of Law; in international studies and international business with the Monterey Institute of International Studies; in education with the Bank Street College of Education; and in computer science and oceanography with the University of Washington.

Academic Programs

Whitman's primary goal is to provide an atmosphere in which students can learn how to learn. At the heart of Whitman's academic curriculum is the general studies program, through which students learn how to develop intellectual skills, reason, read critically and write effectively, understand humanity's cultural and historical roots, fashion standards for judgment of basic values, and lead others. The required general studies program consists of a freshman core and distribution requirements. The freshman core is an interdisciplinary seminar with extensive reading, writing, and discussion. To satisfy the distribution requirement, students must complete at least 6 semester credits in fine arts, humanities, science, and social sciences; take two courses dealing with alternative voices; and take at least one course in quantitative analysis. Every candidate for a bachelor's degree must complete at least 124 credits in appropriate courses with acceptable grades. Honors programs are available for qualified students. Whitman helps fund student research, and approximately 125 students present professional-level research at the College's Annual Undergraduate Conference. Advanced placement and a maximum of 8 semester credits in each subject area are allowed for scores of 5 and 4 on the College Board's Advanced Placement tests. (The economics, English, and history departments accept only a score of 5.) Whitman observes a two-semester calendar with a three-day student-run interim program in early January.

Off-Campus Programs

Whitman is noted for its strong study-abroad and domestic off-campus study programs. Each year, approximately 40 percent of the junior class studies in programs in more than thirty overseas locations. In addition to academic course work, many students pursue internships for credit or research opportunities. The College is formally affiliated with the Institute for the International Education of Students, which has programs in Australia, Austria, China, England, France, Germany, Italy, and Spain. The School for Field Studies has opportunities in Australia, Canada, the Caribbean, Costa Rica, Kenya, and Mexico. Students may also study at the Universities of East Anglia, Manchester, and York in England; St. Andrews University in Scotland; Doshisha University in Kyoto, Japan; and the University of Otago in Dunedin, New Zealand and at programs in Argentina, China, Costa Rica, Greece, Hungary, Ireland, Italy, Japan, Mexico, Spain, Sri Lanka, Taiwan, and Zimbabwe. Each year, 4 Whitman students or graduates are selected to teach English to university students in Kunming or Xi'an in the People's Republic of China. The College offers urban-semester study and internships in Chicago, Philadelphia, and Washington, D.C. Students may participate in one of more than 300 science research internships available through the College.

Academic Facilities

To enhance Whitman's learning environment, students have access to exceptional facilities and technological and cultural resources. The recently expanded 24-hour Penrose Memorial Library houses more than 350,000 volumes, 550,000 government documents, and 2,000 subscriptions. In addition, the ORBIS Cascade Alliance provides access to approximately 3.5 million volumes that can be delivered to Whitman in three or fewer days. A $13-million, 51,000-square-foot campus center, featuring a ballroom, a cyberlounge, and flexible dining and meeting facilities opened in January 2002. Olin Hall of Humanities and Fine Arts features an audiovisual center, extensive art studios, foreign language labs, and the Donald Sheehan Art Gallery; another addition houses the computing equipment and is the center for the campuswide fiber-optic network. The student-computer ratio is 14:1. Maxey Hall, the center for the social sciences, includes a natural history and anthropology laboratory, a 350-seat auditorium, and animal demonstration labs. The Hall of Science houses a sophisticated physics lecture-demonstration hall and laboratory and support facilities for two electron microscopes. The hall also contains laboratories for botany, ecology, vertebrate biology, physiology and developmental biology, and biochemistry and genetics; preparation and display areas for the herbarium and the preserved animal collections; a planetarium; a seismograph; and large, well-equipped student research laboratories. In 2002, a new $13-million science building that features chemistry and geology labs, a computer lab, and a new greenhouse was completed. After an additional $6.4-million renovation of the existing science building, the 105,000-square-foot Hall of Science will have a wireless network for Internet access, more student/faculty research labs, and enhanced classroom space. The Frances Geiger Hunter Conservatory, which houses communication arts and technology facilities, includes videoconferencing facilities and multimedia labs. Whitman operates an observatory located several miles from campus as well as a 27-acre mountain property serving as an environmental studies field station. The Hall of Music houses an acoustically perfect performance hall and more than twenty-five practice rooms. Other major facilities are the Harper Joy Theatre, a 315-seat drama center, and Cordiner Hall, a 1,400-seat concert auditorium that features a 3,000-pipe Holtkamp organ.

Costs

Tuition and fees for 2004–05 are $26,870. Room and board are $7180. The estimated cost of books, supplies, and incidentals is $1250. Associated student body fees are $250.

Financial Aid

Financial aid offers are usually a combination of scholarship and grant aid, low-interest loans, and employment opportunities. In 2003–04, Whitman provided more than $12 million in scholarships to 85 percent of its students. Fifty percent of Whitman students qualified for need-based aid. About half of the students are employed part-time on campus. Whitman also has an extensive achievement scholarship program that rewards students with exceptional academic records. Awards range from $6000 to $9500 and are renewable for four years. Special awards are also available for students with exceptional academic achievement or talent in art, music, debate, theater, and leadership. To apply for financial aid, students must submit the Free Application for Federal Student Aid (FAFSA) and the CSS PROFILE form. Early decision candidates should apply for financial aid by January 5; regular admission and transfer admission candidates must apply by February 1. Spring semester candidates must apply by December 1.

Faculty

Whitman College's faculty is composed of men and women selected, retained, and promoted chiefly for their demonstrated effectiveness as teachers as well as for their leadership in their fields. Ninety-eight percent of the faculty members hold a doctorate degree or terminal degree in their field, and virtually all serve as academic advisers. The student-faculty ratio is 10:1. Recognized nationally for faculty accessibility, Whitman offers personal attention outside the classroom that differentiates its education from others. At Whitman, students collaborate with professors on research projects, compete with them on the athletics field, serve with them on College committees, and dine with them in their homes. In the past five years, Whitman faculty members have distinguished themselves by receiving awards, honors, and fellowships from the National Institute of Mental Health, National Endowment for the Humanities, Battelle Research Institute, Washington State Arts Commission, Burlington Northern Foundation, Department of Health and Human Services, and Department of Energy.

Student Government

The College encourages students to participate and to take leadership roles in self-governing campus organizations. The largest of these is the Associated Students of Whitman College (ASWC), of which every student is a member. The ASWC acts through an elected student congress and executive council and is responsible for the *Pioneer* (the weekly student newspaper), choral contest, homecoming, Renaissance Faire, radio station KWCW-FM, Interim, and many concerts, presenters, and social events.

Admission Requirements

Whitman is a highly selective college that seeks academic excellence and diversity within its student body. Competition for admission is keen; more than 60 percent of entering freshmen rank in the top 10 percent of their high school class. The Admission Committee looks for evidence of demonstrated intellectual achievement, motivation, creativity, responsibility, and maturity. The middle 50 percent of the class that entered Whitman in 2003 scored in the following ranges on the SAT I: 620–730 verbal and 610–700 math. The minimum TOEFL scores for international students are 220 on the computer-based test and 560 on the paper test; the minimum ELPT score was 960. The following pattern of high school subjects is recommended: 4 years of English, 4 of mathematics, 3 of laboratory science, 2 of history or social science, and 2 of foreign language. Students who have decided early in their senior year that Whitman is their first choice are encouraged to apply for admission under the early decision plan.

Application and Information

The application deadlines and notification dates for admission to Whitman are as follows: early decision candidates apply by November 15 or January 1 and receive notification of admission in December or January; regular admission and transfer candidates for the fall semester apply by January 15 and receive notification by April 1; spring semester candidates apply by November 15 and receive notification by December 15. Freshman candidates are required to submit the following credentials: the Common Application (for selective colleges), School Report Form, secondary school transcript, test scores (SAT I or ACT), Personal Supplement (Whitman's own form), a teacher recommendation, and an application fee of $45. International applicants must also submit a TOEFL, ELPT, or APIEL score and the College Board's International Student Financial Aid Application and Certification. For more information, students should contact:

Office of Admission
Whitman College
515 Boyer Avenue
Walla Walla, Washington 99362-2046
Telephone: 509-527-5176
877-462-9448 (toll-free)
Fax: 509-527-4967
E-mail: admission@whitman.edu
World Wide Web: http://www.whitman.edu

Students on the Whitman College campus.

WHITWORTH COLLEGE

SPOKANE, WASHINGTON

The College

Whitworth, founded in 1890, is among a select group of educational institutions known for both academic rigor and Christian commitment. The Whitworth faculty is committed to encouraging open intellectual inquiry as well as respect for diverse points of view. The College's community of scholars is also dedicated to the challenging task of integrating faith perspectives into all aspects of life and learning. This dual commitment distinguishes Whitworth among Christian colleges and universities.

The campus has thirty-eight buildings, mostly of red brick, which border the parklike Loop, including the Harriet Cheney Cowles Memorial Library, Cowles Memorial Auditorium, Hixson Union Building, and Dixon Hall. The Seeley Mudd Chapel, located at the heart of the campus, has an expanded worship area, seminar rooms, and staff offices. The Whitworth Fieldhouse is home to the Scotford Fitness and Aquatic Center, which has a 25-meter, six-lane pool with a movable bulkhead and a 15-foot diving pool. The Hixson Union Building houses the bookstore, post office, snack bar, and student media, student government offices, and a 450-seat dining hall.

The College's 1,700 full-time undergraduate students come from thirty-one states and twenty-five countries. Nearly 65 percent of the full-time undergraduate students live on campus in nine residential areas that range from traditional dormitory buildings to cottage-size apartments and theme houses. Residence life is considered an essential part of a student's growth process, and living groups are encouraged, with the help of trained residence staff, to design their own living environments. Peer leaders in each residence hall include resident assistants, health coordinators, ministry coordinators, and cultural diversity advocates.

Also serving the personal development of each student are the Office of the Chaplain and Student Life Department. Religious life on campus is centered on midweek chapel; and Hosanna, a student-led praise service. Bible studies, discussion groups, and opportunities for service also originate in the Office of the Chaplain. The Student Life Program assists all students in adjusting to college life and defining individual goals by providing counseling, tutoring, services for international students and members of minority groups, job placement, career planning, and aptitude testing.

Whitworth College holds membership in the NCAA Division III and is a member of the Northwest Conference. Varsity teams for men compete in baseball, basketball, cross-country, football, golf, soccer, swimming, tennis, and track and field. Women's teams compete in basketball, cross-country, golf, soccer, softball, swimming, tennis, track and field, and volleyball. Nine Whitworth teams have won conference championships in the past three years, and four teams have led the nation in team GPA for their sports in NCAA Division III. A broad intramural program, as well as club sports, offers athletic competition to everyone on campus, including faculty and staff members, and fitness evaluation services in the Scotford Fitness Center are available to all. Whitworth believes that physical development is an essential element in each student's pursuit of personal wholeness.

Location

Whitworth College is located just 15 minutes from downtown Spokane on a scenic, wooded 200-acre site, surrounded by quiet suburban residential areas. Spokane, a metropolitan area with a population of 414,500, is surrounded by an extraordinary outdoor recreation area, containing thousands of acres of state and national forests, four major ski resorts, and more than seventy-five lakes within an hour's drive. The city is the commercial and cultural center for more than a million people, and the size of this market area is reflected in the excellence of Spokane's many cultural and entertainment opportunities, restaurants, shopping centers, and transportation.

Majors and Degrees

Whitworth awards Bachelor of Arts and Bachelor of Science degrees. Programs and majors are available in accounting, American studies, art, arts administration, athletic training, biology, business management, chemistry, communication, computer science, cross-cultural studies, economics, education (elementary and secondary certification programs, with academic department emphases), English, environmental studies, French, German, history, international business, international studies, journalism and mass communications, kinesiology, leadership studies, liberal studies, marketing, mathematics, modern languages, music, organizational management, peace studies, philosophy, physical education, physics, political studies, pre-ministry, psychology, quantitative analysis, religion, sociology, Spanish, speech communication, theater, and women's studies.

Preprofessional programs are offered in dentistry, engineering (3-2), law, medical technology, medicine, occupational therapy, pharmacy, physical therapy, and veterinary medicine.

Academic Program

The College is dedicated to academic excellence as expressed through its core of liberal arts and sciences and through rigorous disciplinary and interdisciplinary study. A Whitworth education is designed to broaden students' understanding of their cultural heritage, to promote critical thinking, to prepare students for productive work, and to stimulate creativity in responding to the challenges of life. As a Christian institution, Whitworth takes seriously its responsibility to help students understand and respond compassionately to the needs of the world. Recognizing that contemporary society is globally interdependent and increasingly multicultural, Whitworth seeks to foster in its students an attitude of curiosity and respect for diverse cultures.

The College's 4-1-4 calendar provides time for intensive study in a single subject during the month of January, often in an off-campus setting.

Off-Campus Programs

January terms and full semesters of off-campus study are available to encourage students to relate their education to real-life environments. Urban studies in San Francisco; international studies in Europe, Latin America, South Africa, Thailand, and the Middle East; music studies in Rome and Munich; and rural studies in various locales are offered to augment classroom learning. Students are not traveling as tourists; they are accompanied by faculty members who guide their research and studies and join them in experiencing the culture to the greatest degree possible.

Exchange-student arrangements are available through the International Student Exchange Program (ISEP). This program offers placements in any of the 150 member universities in Africa, Asia, Australia, Canada, Europe, or Latin America.

Cooperative education/internship opportunities are available for Whitworth students in Spokane or in almost any area of the country. For instance, political studies majors routinely intern in Washington, D.C. The co-op/internship program enables students to gain actual experience and build contacts in a chosen field prior to graduation. A January-term internship often leads to declaring a major, a modification of a career goal, or, just as often, a job opportunity.

Academic Facilities

With its state-of-the-art information retrieval technology and a capacity exceeding 250,000 volumes, the Harriet Cheney Cowles Memorial Library provides students and faculty members with a superb research facility. The library's computerized card catalogs and databases also provide access to the holdings of other libraries in the region and across the country. In addition, the library is home to three computer labs, six group study rooms, climate-controlled archives, a music library, a curriculum lab for teacher education, audiovisual services, and a Writing Center.

The Whitworth Music Building has the most advanced facilities available for music education. Laboratories for chemistry, physics, and biology are maintained in the Eric Johnston Science Center. A generous grant from the National Science Foundation provided funds to upgrade these laboratories. The Fine Arts Building contains studios for drawing, painting, and pottery and houses the John Koehler Gallery, which is used for student shows. The Dr. James P. Evans Sports Medicine Center includes a complete hydrotherapy center, ultrasound equipment, and a variety of ergometers and isokinetic machines.

Costs

For the 2004–05 academic year, tuition is $20,980 and room and board are $6500. Additional costs for books, fees, and personal expenses vary.

Financial Aid

More than 90 percent of Whitworth's students receive financial aid, with the average freshman scholarship and grant award exceeding $8500. The Free Application for Federal Student Aid (FAFSA) is used to determine a student's financial need for awarding grants, scholarships, loans, and work-study. Academic scholarships and fine arts, pre-engineering, and science and journalism talent awards are available to exceptional students regardless of their demonstrated need. Student employment, under the Federal Work-Study Program, is available on campus for up to 20 hours per week through the Student Employment Office, which provides placement assistance for off-campus jobs as well. The following non-need-based federal loan programs are available to Whitworth students and their families: the Federal Unsubsidized Stafford Loan and the Federal PLUS loan for parents. Whitworth also recently joined The Tuition Plan program, offering tuition discounts and prepayment options to lock in tuition costs.

Faculty

The Whitworth faculty is made up of 112 full-time professors, most of whom have earned either a Ph.D. or the terminal degree in their field. These dedicated Christian scholars conduct important research, perform in demanding musical venues, write critically acclaimed books, and earn recognition in their fields. But their primary commitment is to teaching—sharing their knowledge, their faith journeys, and their friendship with students inside and outside the classroom.

Student Government

A full-time student activities coordinator works with the elected members of the Associated Students of Whitworth College (ASWC) and the appointed student managers to plan and carry out College activities, which range from Homecoming festivities to mountain climbs to political lobbying. Student government is responsible for the continuing involvement of students in the community, organizing outreach ministry opportunities on- and off-campus, and meeting the academic, social, and spiritual needs of the campus community. Individual students are full-fledged members, along with faculty members, of various councils that formulate major campus policies.

Admission Requirements

Whitworth selects its students from those applicants who, by reason of their academic achievement, measured aptitudes, and academic interests, demonstrate their ability to succeed at a rigorous Christian liberal arts college. Generally, 4 years of English; 3 years each of history, science (including lab science), and mathematics; and 2 years of a foreign language constitute a competitive college-preparatory program for a high school applicant. Transfer students are also welcome to apply; Whitworth grants junior standing and a waiver of most general graduation requirements to students who have earned an approved Associate of Arts degree at any Washington community college as well as North Idaho College.

Application and Information

High-achieving students who have decided that Whitworth College is their first or second choice are eligible to apply for early action. The early action application deadline is November 30. For regular admission, the deadline is March 1. Campus visits are recommended from September through May while classes are in session.

Application for admission may be made by submitting a completed Whitworth application form, a personal statement, an evaluation by the student's high school counselor or principal, a current transcript of high school work, and ACT or SAT I scores.

For information and application forms, students should contact:

Office of Admissions
Whitworth College
West 300 Hawthorne Road
Spokane, Washington 99251-0106
Telephone: 509-777-3212
800-533-4668 (toll-free)
E-mail: admission@whitworth.edu
World Wide Web: http://www.whitworth.edu

Whitworth students represent thirty-one states and twenty-five countries.

WIDENER UNIVERSITY

CHESTER, PENNSYLVANIA

The University

Widener University is a multicampus, independent, metropolitan institution located in and accredited by the commonwealth of Pennsylvania and the state of Delaware. The University distinguishes itself by connecting curricula to societal issues through civic engagement, inspiring its students to be citizens of character as well as professional and civic leaders.

Widener provides a unique combination of liberal arts and professional education in a challenging, scholarly, and culturally diverse learning environment. More than 100 programs of study leading to associate, baccalaureate, master's, and doctoral degrees are available. Currently, there are 6,608 students, including 1,778 graduate students and 2,327 full-time undergraduate students. Wilmington, Delaware, and Harrisburg, Pennsylvania, are the sites for the Widener University School of Law, where 1,862 students are enrolled.

Widener offers both diversity and excellent quality in its extracurricular activities. More than eighty student organizations are recognized on the Widener campus, including student government, musical groups, honor societies, fraternities, sororities, academic and professional associations, publications, social and recreational clubs, and an FM radio station, recording studio, and TV production studio. Widener offers eleven intercollegiate sports for women and eleven for men, as well as several intramural sports. Traditional residence halls, apartments, and theme houses are available. Housing is guaranteed for all four years of undergraduate study.

Location

Located in Delaware County, Pennsylvania, Widener's Main Campus is easily accessible from I-95, I-476, and the Philadelphia Airport and is an easy commute from southern New Jersey and Delaware. The University is only 15 minutes from historic Philadelphia, approximately 2 hours from either New York City or Washington, D.C., and 1½ hours from Baltimore or the New Jersey beaches.

Majors and Degrees

Widener offers the degrees of Bachelor of Arts and Bachelor of Science in the following fields: accounting, anthropology, behavioral science, biochemistry, biology, chemical engineering, chemistry, civil engineering, communication studies, computer information systems, computer science, creative writing, criminal justice, early childhood education, economics, electrical engineering, elementary education, English, environmental science, fine arts, French, government and politics, history, hospitality management, humanities, international business, international relations, management, mathematics, mechanical engineering, nursing, physics, political economy, psychology, science administration, science education, social work, sociology, Spanish, and special education.

Dual majors may also be taken in many areas, and a multidisciplinary (open) major may be created by any degree-seeking candidate in consultation with a faculty adviser. Freshmen who are undecided about a major may elect the Exploratory Studies program during the first year. In addition, options exist in the School of Business Administration and the Center for Education for accelerated programs leading to combined undergraduate and M.B.A., Master of Science, or Master of Education degrees.

The Center for Education offers two options for students seeking certification in elementary and/or early childhood education: the bachelor's degree in elementary and/or early childhood education or the bachelor's degree in an academic major with certification. Students can also choose the bachelor's degree in special education. Multiple secondary certifications include bilingual education, biology, chemistry, earth and space science, English, French, general science, math, physics, social studies, Spanish, and special education.

Academic Programs

The distribution of required courses and the quantitative requirements are set by the various undergraduate units (the College of Arts and Sciences, the School of Engineering, the School of Human Service Professions, the School of Business Administration, the School of Hospitality Management, and the School of Nursing). All students are required to complete a minimum of 12 semester hours in each of the three areas of humanities, social science, and science/mathematics. (A semester hour consists of 1 hour per week in the classroom each semester or 2 to 3 hours per week in laboratory or fieldwork each semester.) An overall academic average of at least 2.0 is required for graduation. In addition to satisfying all other requirements for any degree, a candidate must complete in residence at Widener the final 45 semester hours required for that degree.

High school students who participate in the Advanced Placement (AP) Program of the College Board and earn scores of 3 or better receive degree credit for the subjects concerned upon submission of the examination results.

Widener operates on a two-semester calendar. The first semester begins in early September and ends before Christmas; the second semester runs from mid-January to mid-May. The summer sessions include one presession of three weeks and two regular sessions of five weeks each, providing fully accredited courses in economics and management, engineering, the humanities, the physical sciences, and the social sciences.

Off-Campus Programs

Four-year cooperative education programs are offered to computer science majors and students in the Schools of Engineering and Business Administration. These programs are designed to augment the curricula with two periods of full-time, off-campus work experience (totaling twelve months of employment), while enabling the student to earn a bachelor's degree within the normal four-year period. Field experience is also offered in education, psychology, and social work.

Academic Facilities

The academic buildings on Widener's Main Campus provide an eclectic mix of tradition and cutting-edge technology. A 50,000-square-foot addition to Kirkbride Hall, the University's science and engineering building, is scheduled to open in December 2004. The addition is anticipated to provide new classrooms, state-of-the-art teaching and research laboratories for biology and engineering, and a rooftop astronomical observatory. The Leslie C. Quick Jr. Center, which opened in the fall of 2002, is home to the School of Business Administration and houses offices, multimedia classrooms, an information systems lab, and a simulated Wall Street trading room. Beautiful

Old Main, built in 1867 and featured on the National Register of Historic Places, houses the School of Nursing as well as a variety of administrative offices. Other academic buildings include the Robert J. Bruce Graduate Center, home to the School of Human Service Professions; Academic Center North, which houses the School of Hospitality Management; and Kapelski Learning Center, a modern classroom facility. At the center of the campus is the Wolfgram Memorial Library, which currently houses more than 240,000 volumes and 175,000 microforms. Through interlibrary loan, students also have access to resources of the School of Law library, which holds an additional 575,000 volumes.

University Center is the hub of campus activity, with student and faculty dining rooms, a convenience store, coffee shop, TV lounge, post office, bookstore, bank branch, and fitness center. Alumni Auditorium—built with funds donated by the Alumni Association—houses the Burt Mustin Memorial Theatre, a 400-seat auditorium for dramatics, lectures, movies, and mass meetings. The University also has a modern, all-weather sports facility, the Schwartz Athletic Center, which features a track and a 3,000-seat athletic stadium.

Costs

Tuition for the 2004–05 academic year for most students is $22,800. The cost of room and board ranges from $8100 to $10,700, depending on the accommodations selected.

Families who wish to spread the payment of tuition over several months each semester or year may take advantage of the payment plan that Widener offers in conjunction with CampusMate.

Financial Aid

The goal of Widener's financial aid program is to make sure that every qualified student who wants to attend the University has the financial resources to do so. Widener University offers both need-based and merit-based financial aid, and currently 90 percent of the student body receives some form of financial assistance. Financial aid consists of scholarships, grants, loans, and employment, which may be offered to students singly or in various combinations. Special merit scholarships are available to incoming students of exceptional academic ability or achievement. Scholarships are also awarded to students with talent in music or student leadership. Awards range from $3000 per year to full tuition.

Students who submit an application for financial aid are considered under all programs for which they are eligible. Financial aid applicants are notified of their aid in the spring prior to their enrollment at the University. Students are required to file either the Free Application for Federal Student Aid (FAFSA) or the Pennsylvania Higher Education Assistance Agency form. The priority deadline for new students is February 15.

Faculty

The University faculty of 334 members is drawn from leading national and international graduate schools. Doctoral and terminal degrees are held by 94 percent of the faculty members. The student-faculty ratio is 12:1, and the average class size is 24.

Student Government

The Student Government Association (SGA) coordinates student activities and exercises legislative, executive, and judicial authority. Participation benefits the students' total collegiate experience, and students are encouraged to become active in the SGA.

Admission Requirements

Admission to Widener is competitive and is based primarily upon the quality of the high school record. Recommendations, extracurricular involvement, the personal essay, and the pattern of test scores are also weighed in the decision.

To apply for admission, students should submit a completed application with the $35 application fee, have their current high school forward a transcript of their academic records, send a copy of their SAT I or ACT scores, and ask their high school counselor to complete and return the high school recommendation form. Scores on SAT II Subject Tests are recommended but not required. An interview is highly recommended but not required.

Students from twenty-three states and fifteen other countries are attending Widener; 50 percent ranked in the top quarter of their high school graduating class, 80 percent in the top half. Their mean combined SAT I score was 1040, and 80 percent scored between 940 and 1060.

Application and Information

The University offers a nonbinding early action program and has a priority application deadline of February 15 for fall admission. Qualified students applying after March 1 are offered admission on a space-available basis.

Transfer applicants are encouraged to apply and are also admitted on a rolling basis.

For further information or an appointment, students should contact:

Widener University
Office of Admissions
One University Place
Chester, Pennsylvania 19013-5792
Telephone: 610-499-4126
E-mail: admissions.office@widener.edu
World Wide Web: http://www.widener.edu

WILBERFORCE UNIVERSITY

WILBERFORCE, OHIO

The University

Currently, more than 800 students are enrolled at Wilberforce University, allowing for a 14:1 student-teacher ratio. The student body is diverse, with a number of students coming from Ohio, Michigan, Illinois, Indiana, New York, Pennsylvania, California, and Georgia. International students come from Africa, Canada, the Caribbean, and the British West Indies.

The experiences that students have outside the classroom are important elements of campus life. Wilberforce University is committed to the development of students. Social life and academic achievement are integral aspects of the educational experience. Activities include scholarly forums, service learning/volunteering, poetry readings, travel to nearby colleges and communities, plays, movies, and local sporting events.

Departmental clubs and social organizations enable students to concentrate on particular areas of study, career fields, and academic honors. Eight chapters of national Greek-letter fraternities and sororities offer service, social activities, and opportunities for lasting friendship. Other outlets include the Student Government Association, national honor societies, the campus newspaper, the yearbook staff, the campus radio station, the Debate Club, the Engineering and Computer Science Club, the Business and Economics Club, Students in Free Enterprise, the National Association of Black Accountants, the National Student Business League, the University Concert Choir, the Gospel Chorus, the Jazz Band, the Black Male Coalition, the International Student Club, the University Jazzers and Cheerleaders, and Black Women United.

Wilberforce University's athletic programs (NAIA Division I) include men's and women's basketball, cross-country, golf, and track and field. Wilberforce University is a member of the American MidEast Conference. The intramural program offers basketball, flag football, soccer, softball, and tennis.

The North Central Association of Colleges and Universities accredits Wilberforce University.

Location

The University is situated in southwestern Ohio in the city of Wilberforce, offering tranquility and proximity to major urban areas and their cultural opportunities. Dayton is just 20 miles away; Cincinnati and Columbus are within an hour's drive. Xenia, with a population of 25,000, is 3 miles from campus, and Springfield, a metropolitan area of 100,000, is 15 miles away. Southwestern Ohio is a region that has major cultural attractions, ballets, theaters, and museums. The National Afro-American Museum is located on the old campus of Wilberforce University. Near the campus are John Bryan State Park, the Clarence Brown Reservoir, and the Glen Helen wilderness area. The famed King's Island Amusement Park is less than an hour's drive from campus.

Majors and Degrees

Wilberforce University awards the Bachelor of Arts and Bachelor of Science degrees. Majors are offered in accounting, art, biology/premed, business economics, chemistry, communications, economics, finance, health-services administration, humanities, liberal studies, literature, management, marketing, mass media, mathematics, music (composition, piano, theory, and voice), philosophy and religion, political science/prelaw, psychology, rehabilitation services, social science, social work, sociology (applied and criminal justice), and sport management. Bachelor of Science degrees in engineering or computer science can be earned in computer engineering, computer information systems, computer information systems (graphic design), computer science, electrical engineering, engineering management, and mechanical engineering. Wilberforce University also offers dual-degree programs (3-2) in aerospace, architectural, and nuclear engineering in conjunction with the University of Cincinnati and in chemical, civil, electrical, and mechanical engineering in cooperation with the University of Dayton. Upon completion, students receive degrees in comprehensive science or mathematics and engineering or computer science. Additional courses are offered in Caribbean studies and the Black Heritage Series.

Academic Programs

To receive a bachelor's degree, students must complete at least 128 semester hours with an overall grade point average of no less than 2.0. At least 30 semester hours must be completed in residence during the senior year. Graduation prerequisites also include the satisfactory completion of a program of core requirements. Advanced standing may be granted through successful scores on College-Level Examination Program (CLEP) general and subject tests and Advanced Placement (AP) examinations. All students must demonstrate competence in writing by passing the Junior Level Competency Test, become computer literate by enrolling in a required computer literacy course, and successfully complete two cooperative education experiences. Army and Air Force ROTC programs are offered through nearby Central State and Wright State universities.

Wilberforce follows a semester schedule. The fall semester begins in mid-August and ends in mid-December. The spring semester begins in mid-January and ends in mid-May. There are no summer sessions.

Off-Campus Programs

Wilberforce University is a member of the Southwestern Ohio Council of Higher Education (SOCHE), an eighteen-college consortium. Membership enables Wilberforce students to cross-register for courses and use the library facilities of any of the other seventeen institutions.

Academic Facilities

The University library, with more than 63,000 volumes, 350 periodicals, and 300 microfilm titles, operates seven days a week. The modern classroom building, like all of the facilities on the main campus, is air conditioned. It contains a radio station, a state-of-the-art computer center, numerous classrooms, and the reading, writing, math, and speech laboratories.

Costs

Wilberforce University is a competitively priced, private liberal arts university. Students are able to gain all the benefits of a high-quality liberal arts education at an affordable cost. Wilberforce University is affiliated and supported by grants the African Methodist Episcopal Church. The University is also a member institution of the United Negro College Fund (UNCF). Grants from the government, foundations, corporations, alumni, and other friends of the University help to keep the cost affordable. Student living on campus find each room equipped with a Pentium computer, which provides each student with online access, e-mail, research, and the Internet. Provisions for this service are included in the general fees.

Student dormitories and housing have been renovated and new buildings were built in 2000. Students who live on campus must apply for housing upon being admitted. Admitted students planning to attend the University must submit a $225 enrollment fee by June 1 for the fall semester and December 15 for the spring semester.

Financial Aid

Loans, grants, and scholarships are available and are awarded on the basis of need. Ninety-five percent of the enrolled students receive some form of financial assistance. Eligible students can receive federal funds, such as Federal Pell Grants, Federal Supplemental Educational Opportunity Grants, Federal Work-Study employment, Federal Perkins Loans, and Federal Stafford Student Loans. State grants are also available for residents of Ohio, Pennsylvania, and Washington, D.C.

The priority deadline to file for financial aid for the fall semester is April 30; the final deadline is June 1. The deadline for the spring semester is November 15. All students should use the Free Application for Federal Student Aid (FAFSA) in applying for aid. The University also requires the completion of its financial aid application. All students must provide proof of income through copies of income tax returns or related documents. All financial aid is awarded on a rolling basis.

Faculty

There are 55 full-time and 20 part-time faculty members at Wilberforce University. All have advanced degrees, and 53 percent have a Ph.D. or the terminal degree in their field. The student-faculty ratio is 14:1. Since the University has primarily a teaching faculty, each student is ensured personalized attention.

Student Government

Leadership opportunities are provided through the Student Government Association (SGA), class offices, committees, and residence halls. The SGA is the main voice and political force of the student body. The members are elected by students to serve as student representatives to the Board of Trustees or as officers in their respective classes. Student representation on faculty-staff committees ensures vital input regarding recommendations and changes in academic, student life, and University-wide policies.

Admission Requirements

Wilberforce University is a selective university that operates on a rolling admissions basis. Students applying for admission must have at least a 2.0 (C) grade point average with a strong showing in the college-preparatory areas and must have completed 15 acceptable units of study, including 4 units of English, 2 to 3 units of mathematics (including algebra), 2 to 3 units of science (including one laboratory science), and 2 units of social studies (including U.S. history). ACT or SAT scores are required for evaluation purposes. An interview is not required but is helpful, and it can be conducted either in person or by telephone. Early decision and early admission are also available.

Wilberforce actively recruits students from throughout the continental United States and other countries, as well as those who want to transfer from community and junior colleges or other four-year institutions. Wilberforce University has articulation agreements with several community colleges throughout the United States. Students are able to transfer credits from associate degree programs to the University and continue pursuing their bachelor's degree. Additional information can be requested from the Office of Admissions.

Applicants should arrange to have an official copy of their high school transcript or evidence of an equivalent level of academic attainment, such as the GED, sent to the admissions office. Ohio students must show proof of passing the Ninth Grade Proficiency Test. Applicants must also submit two recommendations (one from a counselor and one from a teacher) and an essay. In addition to high school transcripts, transfer students should provide copies of transcripts from any college or university attended.

Application and Information

New students are accepted for each semester. Applications for admission in the fall semester must be submitted by July 1. The application deadline for the spring semester is November 15. Applications are accepted anytime after the junior year is completed in high school.

For additional information or application materials, students should contact:

Office of Admissions
Wilberforce University
Wilberforce, Ohio 45384
Telephone: 937-376-2911
800-367-8568 (toll-free)
800-367-8565 (toll-free, Student Financial Services and Scholarships)
World Wide Web: http://www.wilberforce.edu

WILKES UNIVERSITY

WILKES-BARRE, PENNSYLVANIA

The University

Located at the foothills of the Pocono Mountains, along the shore of the Susquehanna River and within walking distance of downtown Wilkes-Barre, Pennsylvania, Wilkes University is a private, comprehensive institution with more than 2,100 undergraduate students. The University is structured into the College of Arts, Humanities, and Social Sciences; the College of Science and Engineering; the Nesbitt School of Pharmacy and Nursing; and University College (for undecided students). Wilkes offers a broad range of bachelor's and master's degree programs in the humanities, social and natural sciences, business administration, nursing, and education as well as the Doctor of Pharmacy degree.

The Wilkes campus features a parklike quadrangle surrounded by modern classroom buildings and historic nineteenth-century mansions that have been restored as student residences and academic buildings. Campus facilities include a sports and conference center, an outdoor athletic complex and field house, a state-of-the-art science classroom building, a modern academic classroom/office building, a performing arts center, and a student center with a food court, bookstore, entertainment rooms, post office, and ballroom.

Hands-on learning, small classes, and strong student-professor relationships are the hallmarks of the Wilkes experience. Programs are designed to prepare students with a well-rounded liberal arts foundation that cultivates independent thinking and gives students the credentials necessary for entrance into graduate and professional schools and professional life. Academic advising integrated with career planning is stressed, and hands-on experiences are provided in laboratory, internship, and cooperative education settings. Free tutorial services are available to all students as well.

The University is accredited by the Middle States Association of Colleges and Schools and has specialized accreditation in the sciences, engineering, nursing, education, and business. The Nesbitt School of Pharmacy was granted full accreditation by the American Council on Pharmaceutical Education. Wilkes students graduate with the confidence and competence they need to succeed professionally and with the knowledge required to participate as enlightened members of society. More than 99 percent are employed or attending graduate/professional school within six months of receiving their degrees.

Residential alternatives range from traditional single-sex residence halls to coeducational facilities in nineteenth-century mansions. First-year students applying prior to May 1 are guaranteed housing. Campus housing is available for all four years. Architecturally, residence halls vary from modern, multifloor buildings to mansions listed on the National Register of Historic Places. Medical and dental care, department stores, specialty shops, and other services are available within three blocks of campus. A large number of nearby churches and synagogues welcome students' participation in worship.

At Wilkes University, student activities complement academic life. Intercollegiate athletics encompass fourteen Division III sports, and an active and varied intramural program is offered. Nearly seventy clubs and organizations recognize student achievement and provide opportunities for leadership development, professional growth, and community service. The student-run Programming Board schedules movies and performances by comedians, musicians, and other entertainers, while other organizations sponsor dinner dances, block parties, and special events. Wilkes students are active community volunteers, participating in numerous local and national service projects each year.

Master's degrees are awarded in business administration, creative writing, education, electrical engineering, and nursing. The University also offers a six-year program leading to the Doctor of Pharmacy degree. Wilkes is the first school in Pennsylvania to offer a dual Doctor of Pharmacy and Master of Business Administration degree. A Master of Science degree is also offered.

Location

The county seat of Luzerne County, Wilkes-Barre is a medium-sized city of 50,000 in the midst of a metropolitan area of 400,000. A wide range of recreational facilities are minutes away, including the Lackawanna County Multi-Purpose Stadium (home of the Wilkes-Barre/Scranton Red Barons Triple A baseball team); the new Wachovia Arena, which serves as home for the Wilkes-Barre/Scranton Penguins hockey team; the Pocono Mountain ski resorts; numerous golf courses; state parks; outdoor tennis courts; and Pocono Downs harness racing.

Located in downtown Wilkes-Barre, the F. M. Kirby Center of Performing Arts features symphony, ballet, theatrical, and musical performances. Other area cultural offerings include art galleries, ethnic and community festivals, and numerous libraries and museums. The city is also approximately 2 hours from the cultural resources of both New York City and Philadelphia.

The area's economic strength derives in part from its transportation resources. Wilkes-Barre is in proximity to the intersection of Interstates 80, 81, and 476 and within 3 to 6 hours of major markets such as Washington, D.C.; Baltimore; and Boston. The Wilkes-Barre/Scranton International Airport enables travelers to arrive at most domestic destinations via one-stop or nonstop flights.

Majors and Degrees

Wilkes University offers Bachelor of Arts, Bachelor of Business Administration, Bachelor of Science, Bachelor of Fine Arts, and Bachelor of Music degrees. Majors include accounting; applied and engineering sciences; biochemistry; biology; business administration (concentrations in finance, international business, and management); chemistry; communications (concentrations in journalism, organizational communications, public relations, rhetoric and public communications, and telecommunications); computer information systems; computer science; criminology; earth and environmental sciences; e-business; electrical engineering; elementary, secondary, and special education (all with certification); engineering management; English (concentrations in literature and writing); entrepreneurship; environmental engineering; history; integrative media; international studies; mathematics; mechanical engineering; medical technology; music education; musical theater; nursing; pharmaceutical science; philosophy; political science; psychology; sociology; and theater arts. Individualized studies are also available, and students may participate in the Air Force ROTC program.

Premedical and prelaw preparation are particularly strong programs. In addition to the University's prepharmacy program, other preprofessional programs are available in dentistry, optometry, and veterinary science. The University offers affiliated programs in medicine with the Philadelphia College of Osteopathic Medicine; in optometry with the Pennsylvania

College of Optometry and the State University of New York (SUNY) College of Optometry; in podiatry with Temple University School of Podiatric Medicine; in occupational therapy with Temple University; in physical therapy with Drexel University, Temple University, and Widener University; in medical technology with Robert Packer Hospital; and in psychology with Widener University.

Academic Program

Through a rigorous curriculum that emphasizes hands-on experience and training, Wilkes helps students to prepare in all majors to adapt to a technologically and socially evolving world. To graduate, students are required to complete a core curriculum and must complete from 120 to 136 credits, depending upon their major field. Graduates demonstrate mastery of the fundamental intellectual skills as well as the essential concepts and techniques of their field. Wilkes also teaches students responsibility and independence by expecting and encouraging active participation in the classroom and laboratory.

The University operates on a dual-semester calendar, with optional summer sessions and a January intersession. Advanced Placement test credits are accepted.

Off-Campus Programs

An extensive cooperative education program is available to all students, with credit applicable in most major fields. Many government offices and private businesses in northeastern Pennsylvania, as well as in New York City, Philadelphia, Harrisburg, and Washington, D.C., employ Wilkes students. The study-abroad adviser works with interested students, placing them in the situation best suited to their academic pursuits. Most recently, students have attended programs in Austria, England, the Dominican Republic, France, and Germany.

Academic Facilities

The Eugene S. Farley Library has more than 220,000 volumes of books and bound journals, 857 current print journal and newspaper subscriptions, hundreds of database searches, and 800,000 microforms. Complete laboratory facilities are available for biology, chemistry, earth and environmental sciences, engineering, nursing, pharmacy, and psychology. Student-produced programming is broadcast from WCLH-FM, the University's 2,000-watt radio station, and transmitted from a professional-quality television studio via a local cable provider. More than 650 PC and Macintosh microcomputers are available for student use. The Sordoni Art Gallery is professionally equipped and staffed and produces exhibits each year by regionally, nationally, and internationally known artists. The Dorothy Dickson Darte Center for the Performing Arts contains a fully equipped 500-seat theater for the presentation of plays, concerts, ballet, and other performances and lectures. Adjoining the center are studios, practice and rehearsal rooms, and faculty offices for the Department of Visual and Performing Arts. Breiseth Hall accommodates extensive computer facilities, psychology research laboratories, and modern classrooms with the newest audiovisual equipment. The University also operates a state-of-the-art distance learning facility that allows global conferencing and study using Internet and videoconferencing technology.

Costs

For the 2003–04 academic year, tuition and fees were $19,630 per year, and room and board were $8200. Books cost approximately $700 per year.

Financial Aid

Financial aid is available to those students who demonstrate quality academic ability and/or financial need, as verified by the Free Application for Federal Student Aid (FAFSA). Merit-based and need-based aid is available from Wilkes University for qualified students. Scholarships beginning at $6000 per year are available to students solely on the basis of academic ability. Approximately 90 percent of the student body receive some type of financial assistance, including scholarships, grants, loans, and work-study awards.

Faculty

Wilkes University has a nationally recruited full-time faculty of 115 members, approximately 91 percent of whom have earned Ph.D.'s or terminal degrees in their chosen field. Faculty evaluation criteria emphasize teaching excellence and effective advising, while recognizing continued scholarly activities. The student-faculty ratio is 14:1.

Student Government

An active student government provides a structure for student participation in University governance and student discipline. The Inter-Residence Council and Commuter Council coordinate extracurricular activities for on-campus and commuter students.

Admission Requirements

Admission to Wilkes University is traditional. SAT I and/or ACT scores are required. In cases where a student has taken the examination more than once, scores from the highest testing in each category are used in the evaluation process. Applicants for the freshman class should either have completed or be in the process of completing a college-preparatory course of study, including 3 to 4 years of mathematics, social studies, science, and English. Additional courses should be elected in academic subjects according to individual interests. Acceptable electives include foreign language and computing, among others. Students who have not followed this pattern may still qualify for admission if there is other strong evidence of preparation for college work. Letters of recommendation and SAT II Subject Test scores are not required but may be submitted. Students intending to major in engineering, mathematics, or medical technology should have completed algebra I and II, geometry, and trigonometry prior to enrollment. Students intending to major in nursing should have completed courses in biology and chemistry. An audition is required for all prospective music and theater arts students. Transfer students must submit a transcript from every college previously attended. All students are admitted to the University and not to specific departments, with the exception of the professional Nesbitt School of Pharmacy and the Department of Visual and Performing Arts. Students individually receive academic advisement at the time of registration and throughout their enrollment.

Wilkes University is an Equal Opportunity/Affirmative Action institution. No applicant shall be denied admission to the University because of race, color, gender, religion, national or ethnic origin, sexual orientation, or handicap.

Application and Information

Applications for admission should be completed early in the senior year of secondary school and sent to the Admissions Office. Applications are reviewed after all of the student's credentials have been received. The review of applications generally begins on September 1, and notification of the University's decision reaches the student two to four weeks after the application file is complete.

Admissions Office
Wilkes University
P.O. Box 111
Wilkes-Barre, Pennsylvania 18766
Telephone: 800-945-5378 Ext. 4400 (toll-free)
570-408-4400
World Wide Web: http://www.wilkes.edu

WILLAMETTE UNIVERSITY

SALEM, OREGON

The University

As the first university in the West, Willamette has a history of scholarship, leadership, and innovation. Willamette offers serious students a place to be serious that is not elitist or quirky. The campus ethos embodies the ideal that leadership is founded on lives lived with meaning and purpose. The University motto, "Not unto ourselves alone are we born," further reinforces the expectation that Willamette graduates can make a difference in the world.

Students who enroll at Willamette can expect to be challenged academically by accessible faculty members and to be engaged in their education. In the 2003 National Survey of Student Engagement, Willamette students reported on average that they were more likely than their peers at other liberal arts colleges to have an internship/practicum experience, conduct research with a faculty member, and take a class that incorporated service learning (community service). According to the same survey, they were also more likely to have contributed to class discussions, discussed ideas from readings and classes outside of the formal classroom experience, and to have had serious conversations with students whose religious beliefs, political opinions, or personal values were unlike their own.

Currently, the student body comprises 1,750 undergraduates from thirty-six states and twelve countries; 17 percent identify themselves as multicultural students. The sense of community is very strong, bolstered by the fact that nearly three-quarters of the students live on campus. There are more than 100 student-run clubs and organizations, thirteen music ensembles, award-winning theater productions, a lively intramural program, NCAA Division III varsity teams for women and men (ten sports each), and an extensive outdoors program.

The University's Atkinson Graduate School of Management, College of Law, and School of Education provide tremendous opportunities for graduate studies. Willamette is accredited by the Northwest Association for Schools and Colleges and is a charter member of the National Commission on Accrediting.

Location

In the heart of Oregon's lush Willamette Valley, the 135,000 residents of Oregon's capital city enjoy one of the nation's most balanced and hospitable communities. Known for its quality of life, the natural beauty of the surrounding area, and the activism of its residents, Salem has twice been recognized as an All-America City. Just one block from campus, students can access the Oregon State Capitol, Salem's busy downtown, or the serene 87-acre Bush Pasture Park. The Pacific Ocean, the world-class city of Portland, and the breathtaking Cascade Mountain range are each within an hour's drive of the campus.

Majors and Degrees

The College of Liberal Arts awards the Bachelor of Arts and Bachelor of Music degrees. Majors are offered in American studies, anthropology, art history, art studio, biology, chemistry, Chinese studies, classical studies, comparative literature, computer science, economics, English, environmental science, exercise science, French, German, history, humanities, international studies, Japanese studies, Latin American studies, mathematics, music, philosophy, physics, politics, psychology, religious studies, rhetoric and media studies, sociology, Spanish, and theater. Minors are available in anthropology, art history, art studio, biology, chemistry, Chinese studies, classical studies, computer science, economics, English, environmental science, film studies, French, geography, German, history, Japanese, Latin American studies, mathematics, music, philosophy, physics, politics, psychology, religious studies, rhetoric and media studies, Russian, sociology, Spanish, theater, and women's studies. Combined degrees are offered in business (B.A./M.B.A. with Willamette's Atkinson School of Management), engineering (B.A./B.S. with Columbia University, the University of Southern California, and Washington University), and forestry (B.A./M.S. with the Duke University School of Forestry).

Academic Programs

The goal of Willamette is to prepare students to lead rich and rewarding lives, rejoicing in the diversity of the world and contributing to its welfare. Willamette operates on a semester system and students are required to complete 31 credits (equivalent to 124 semester hours or 186 quarter hours) to graduate. Students must also complete a major and the General Education Program, designed by the faculty to provide the breadth characteristic of a liberal arts education. Credit may be earned with scores of 4 or 5 on an Advanced Placement test or 5, 6, or 7 on International Baccalaureate higher-level examinations. The internship program and undergraduate research grants provide exceptional opportunities for students to augment their classroom work in various valuable ways.

Off-Campus Programs

More than half of Willamette's undergraduates study abroad in credit-granting academic programs, either through Willamette's own programs or through Willamette's arrangements with the International Student Exchange Program (ISEP), the School for International Training, the School for Field Studies, the Council for International Exchange Programs, and a variety of other consortia and institutions.

Placements are available on every continent except Antarctica, and for 2003–04, placements included Australia, Chile, China, Costa Rica, Cuba, Denmark, Ecuador, England, Finland, France, Germany, Greece, Ireland, Italy, Japan, Kenya, Korea, Mexico, Namibia, New Zealand, South Africa, Spain, Sweden, Thailand, Ukraine (Crimea), and Wales.

Academic Facilities

The Mark O. Hatfield Library houses more than 300,000 volumes and more than 243,000 titles in addition to 1,400 current journal subscriptions. Willamette is a member of the ORBIS exchange program, allowing students to request materials from eighteen other universities in the region at no charge. Research librarians work one-on-one with students to ensure they are well versed in the most current research methods and materials. The Hallie Ford Museum of Art showcases the University's growing collection of Northwest and Native American works. Art students are able to focus their studies through use of the museum's Print Study Room and the four distinct art galleries. The Rogers Music Center features an intimate and acoustically superior 420-seat recital hall, a music technology lab, soundproof faculty offices and practice rooms, and a full rehearsal hall. The Olin Science Center houses six biology and five chemistry teaching labs, research facilities, a large greenhouse, an electron microscopy suite, a herbarium, lecture and seminar rooms, and student research labs. Chemistry and biology majors enjoy their own computer lab in Olin as well as a comfortable hearth area for study. In addition to the computers available to students in every residence hall and academic facility on campus, Willamette has two 24-hour computer labs for student use. Students also have Internet access in their residence hall rooms, with a T-1 connection port available to every resident.

Costs

For the 2003–04 academic year, tuition was $25,300; room and board charges were $6600. Books, personal and travel expenses, and fees are estimated at $1920.

Financial Aid

Both merit- and need-based financial assistance is available for qualified applicants. Four out of 5 Willamette undergraduates receive an award from the University. For 2003–04, the total need-based package for entering students averaged more than $20,000, including state and federal assistance. Federal Work-Study is commonly a part of aid packages, and at least half of all students work part-time on campus. No athletic scholarships are offered at Willamette; however, Talent Awards are available in music, theater, and forensics. Students interested in need-based financial assistance are required to submit the Free Application for Federal Student Aid (FAFSA) by February 1. Consideration for merit-based awards is automatic for all applicants with two exceptions: the prestigious Mark O. Hatfield Public Service Scholarship and the Talent Awards.

Faculty

The 293 members of the University faculty have a reputation for dedication to their students. With an undergraduate student-faculty ratio of 10:1, it is not difficult to see why Willamette's academic community is recognized for outstanding student-faculty interaction and collaboration. Nearly all (95 percent) of the faculty members hold the terminal degree (Ph.D. or equivalent) in their field and all teach; there are no teaching assistants at Willamette. In addition, each faculty member serves as an academic adviser to ensure that students are afforded full advantage of Willamette's rich academic environment. Willamette faculty members have been frequently recognized for their scholarship and their dedication to teaching.

Student Government

The Associated Students of Willamette University (ASWU) is the representative body dedicated to enriching the Willamette community for all students. Membership is automatic to all who enroll in more than 1.5 credits, and participation is encouraged for all students who take particular interest in the social and academic communities at Willamette. ASWU governs the hundreds of thousands of dollars available to the more than 100 clubs on campus and organizes numerous events for student entertainment, relaxation, education, and political activism.

Admission Requirements

Admission to Willamette University is competitive. Each application is reviewed for its individual merits, with consideration for a balance of academic and personal strengths. In keeping with Willamette's academic focus, evidence of previous strong academic achievement receives the greatest consideration in the admission decisions. Preference for admission is given to those first-year candidates who have completed four-years of rigorous course work in English, mathematics, foreign languages, laboratory sciences, and social studies/history, including honors, Advanced Placement, International Baccalaureate, or accelerated courses, if available. Transfer applicants are expected to present evidence of appropriate college-level course work and achievement. Other factors such as creativity, leadership, work experience, study abroad, and exceptional talent in a particular field are also weighed in the admission decisions. Interviews are not required; however, they are strongly encouraged for all applicants.

Applications and Information

Candidates for undergraduate admission should submit the Willamette University Application for Admission or the Common Application, including the accompanying essays, official high school and/or college transcripts, the School Report Form (recommendation), SAT or ACT scores, and the $50 application fee (waived for applications submitted online). Application forms and instructions for applicants, including slightly varied application requirements for transfers, home-schooled students, and international students, are available on the Web at http://www.willamette.edu/admission/application.

Willamette offers two nonbinding early action options (postmark deadlines of November 1 and December 1) or a regular decision option (postmark deadline of February 1). For Early Action I, notification is made by December 15; for Early Action II, applicants are notified by January 15. Regular decision candidates are notified by April 1. All applicants for need-based aid are required to file the FAFSA by February 1; in addition, all early action applicants for need-based aid must submit the CSS Financial Aid PROFILE by December 1. All undergraduate application materials as well as questions about the University or the application should be directed to:

Office of Admission
Willamette University
900 State Street
Salem, Oregon 97301
Telephone: 877-LIBARTS (toll-free)
Fax: 503-375-5363
E-mail: libarts@willamette.edu
World Wide Web: http://www.willamette.edu/admission

Students on the campus of Willamette University.

WILLIAM JESSUP UNIVERSITY

ROCKLIN, CALIFORNIA

The University

Founded in 1939 by William Jessup, San Jose Christian College has undergone many changes. The latest change will take effect in fall 2004 when the school is renamed William Jessup University and moves to its new home in Rocklin, California. The school will continue to be a Christ-centered, Bible-based institution preparing young people to be world changers through the Church. The name William Jessup University will be used in conjunction with San Jose Christian College for the 2003–04 academic year and will become the official name of the institution in the fall of 2004.

In partnership with the Church, the purpose of William Jessup University (WJU) is to prepare Christians for leadership and service in the Church and society through Christian higher education, spiritual formation, and directed experiences. This mission mandates a curriculum that prepares persons who are thoughtful, compassionate, culturally sensitive, and capable of integrating personal faith and vocation in all avenues of society.

The primary goal of education at WJU is the integration of faith and learning. In pursuing this goal, WJU accepts the unity of all knowledge under God and perceives no contradiction between the truth of the Christian revelation and that of scholarly investigation. The University offers both general education courses that provide the broad scope of human knowledge and a biblical/theological core that establishes a perspective that gives coherence and purpose to that knowledge.

The University has two residence halls, one for men and one for women.

Location

William Jessup University is located just minutes from the heart of Sacramento. The area offers a wide variety of exciting cultural, recreational, educational, and entertainment opportunities, including amusement parks, professional sports teams, outdoor activities, and museums.

Majors and Degrees

William Jessup University offers four-year baccalaureate degree programs as well as two-year associate degree programs and one-year certificate programs.

Bachelor of Arts degrees are offered in Christian education, Christian leadership, counseling psychology, management/ethics, missions and intercultural studies, music and worship, pastoral ministry, and youth ministry. There is also a one-year program for students who already have a bachelor's degree to gain a second bachelor's degree. WJU also offers two-year Associate of Arts degree programs.

The one-year programs award certificates in Bible, children's ministry, counseling, family ministry, missions, music and worship, pastoral ministry, sports ministry, and youth ministry.

Academic Program

All students in the baccalaureate programs complete the general education curriculum, which develops the whole person by developing skills in communication, quantitative reasoning, and critical thinking and by exposing students to a broad cross section of knowledge in science, social science, and the humanities. General education provides context for the major, a foundation for lifelong autonomous learning, and the skills and broad worldview needed for effective service and leadership, both in the Church and in an increasingly multicultural society. The remainder of the baccalaureate curriculum consists of 48 units of Bible and theology courses and the Ministry Core, which is 12 units. At least two courses that promote cross-cultural understanding must be taken within a student's general education or ministry degree program.

Academic Facilities

In addition to classrooms and the chapel, the University has an impressive library. The WJU Memorial Library is one of the best theological libraries in Placer County. The library has more than 34,000 volumes and a complete collection of more than 62,000 items including magazines, journals, CDs, and audiotapes and videotapes. Recent upgrades to the library include an Internet-accessible library catalog, reference works on CD-ROMs, computer search stations with Internet access, an ESL/language lab, and music listening stations. There is also a computer lab for student use.

Costs

Tuition is $425 per semester-hour unit. Room and board cost $2000 per quarter.

Financial Aid

WJU offers a wide variety of tuition scholarships to new and returning students. Application information for each scholarship is provided in the WJU Financial Aid Application. Some scholarships require a specific application. Applications for all institutional aid must be made by the priority deadline of August 1, unless otherwise specified.

Faculty

The faculty members at WJU are committed to God, the mission of the College, academic excellence, and the students. Excellence in teaching and personal interaction with the students are the two main priorities of the faculty. The student-teacher ratio at WJU is 9:1, which allows professors the opportunity to know their students on a personal level. Interaction with students outside of the classroom is not something that just happens to occur, but is purposefully initiated and enjoyed. There are 14 full-time and 21 part-time faculty members.

Student Government

Student government at WJU is composed of an 8-member council of a president, vice president, business manager, student activities coordinator, and representatives from each class. Officers are elected by the student body in May of the preceding year, while class representatives are elected by each class in the fall quarter. The student government president appoints committee chairpersons to oversee social events, academic affairs, and social publications.

Admission Requirements

William Jessup University practices selective admission. An applicant's academic records, supporting documents, moral character, and willingness to comply with the standards and values of the College are considered before a final decision about admission is made. The University reserves the right to reject any applicant or any request for readmission for any reason it may consider valid.

A minimum high school cumulative GPA of 2.0 is required. It is recommended that a high school student follow the college preparatory plan that most high schools have established. SAT or ACT scores are required for all first-time freshmen and for transfer students with fewer than 24 semester or 36 quarter units. A minimum composite score of 17 on the ACT or 830 on the SAT is required. If ACT or SAT scores fall below these minimums, applicants may be accepted probationally at the discretion of the Admissions Committee.

Application and Information

Applicants must submit a formal application; a nonrefundable application fee of $35; the personal recommendation form filled out by a friend, pastor, or mentor; an Academic Recommendation form completed by a teacher; and a personal letter of introduction that addresses how the applicant became a Christian, his or her life goals, and the applicant's reasons for wanting to attend William Jessup University. This letter must be typed and have a minimum of 300 words. Applicants must also submit an official high school transcript showing graduation (or its equivalent), official transcripts from all colleges attended, and official SAT or ACT score reports.

The admission deadlines are August 1 for the fall quarter, November 1 for the winter quarter, and February 1 for the spring quarter. Application forms, letters, and fees are to be received and admission procedures completed by these dates.

Admissions Office
William Jessup University
333 Sunset Boulevard
Rocklin, California 95765
Telephone: 916-577-1800
800-355-7522 (toll-free)
Fax: 408-293-7352
World Wide Web: http://www.jessup.edu

Students on the campus of William Jessup University.

WILLIAM JEWELL COLLEGE

LIBERTY, MISSOURI

The College

The architecture of the William Jewell College campus has a classic Colonial American style, with a collection of red brick, ivy-covered, hilltop buildings overlooking the Kansas City skyline 12 miles away. Founded in 1849 in cooperation with the Baptists of Missouri, William Jewell was among the first four-year men's colleges west of the Mississippi River. In 1921, it became coeducational. The College prepares students for leadership by challenging them to achieve their highest level of excellence and to embrace a spirit of service. The quadrangle of six buildings located "on the hill" forms the nucleus of campus life. The Mabee Center for Physical Education, Greene Stadium, Brown Hall, and the Pillsbury Music Center are adjacent. The White Science Center provides state-of-the-art facilities for the departments of biology, chemistry, computer studies, mathematics, and physics. Seven modern residence halls are all within walking distance of the quadrangle. The 1,200 men and women attending William Jewell College are drawn from thirty-one states and twelve countries. More than fifteen denominations are represented. Most students live on campus. Participation in extracurricular activities is encouraged as a valuable extension of academic work. Students may choose to involve themselves in music, forensics, religious programs, athletics, departmental honoraries, sororities and fraternities, and many other activities and groups. The nationally recognized Harriman Arts Program provides opportunities for students to enjoy such performers as Luciano Pavarotti, Kiri Te Kanawa, and Marilyn Horne or to attend performances by such professional companies as the Houston Ballet, the Royal Shakespeare Company, and the Alvin Ailey Dance Theatre.

Location

Liberty, Missouri, is located 15 minutes north of downtown Kansas City, Missouri. The College's location provides a quiet campus of surpassing beauty, ideal for study and contemplation, and easy access to the social and cultural advantages of a city of 1.6 million people. Liberty, which has a population of 25,000, is near the Kansas City International Airport (20 minutes), an Amtrak station (20 minutes), and bus stations (15 minutes).

Majors and Degrees

William Jewell College offers four-year programs that lead to Bachelor of Arts and Bachelor of Science degrees. The Bachelor of Arts degree is granted in art, biochemistry, biology, business administration, chemistry, communication, computer science, economics, education, engineering, English, French, history, international business and language, international relations, Japanese area studies, mathematics, music, philosophy, physics, political science, psychology, religion, and Spanish. The Bachelor of Science degree is conferred in accounting, business administration, clinical laboratory science, education, information systems, mathematics (with data processing emphasis), music, and nursing. In addition, there are opportunities for preprofessional study in dentistry, engineering, environmental management, forestry, journalism, law, medicine, ministry, and occupational therapy.

Academic Programs

Named *Time* magazine's "Liberal Arts College of the Year" for 2001–02, William Jewell College is an institution dedicated to preparing a new generation of leaders through a distinctive liberal arts curriculum that embraces the whole individual. The Jewell curriculum allows students to make connections between liberal arts and the professions, service and career accomplishments, and the campus and the complex world beyond. Under College guidelines, students may choose or design their area of concentration (major) in accordance with their own interests, abilities, and objectives. The area of concentration is worked out in consultation with each student's personal adviser and normally consists of six to ten courses (24 to 40 semester hours). Students who want an added challenge of academic excellence may do independent study in the honors program and seek graduation with honors or achievement. A small number of highly motivated students may plan from one to four semesters of their college career in unconventional patterns that will help them meet their educational goals. William Jewell College's commitment to liberal arts education is expressed in degree requirements that guarantee breadth of education as well as specialization in a major. A general education curriculum aims to prepare students to be vital, contributing, and successful citizens of a global community. Students study the traditional disciplines as they arise from and are relevant to the search to understand the meaning of "the responsible self" in modern society. The curriculum offers students a learning experience that builds through three stages: an introductory/skills level, an intermediate interdisciplinary level, and an advanced capstone level. A small number of intellectually outstanding students are admitted each year to the Oxbridge Honors Program, which is supported by a multimillion-dollar gift from the Hall Family Foundation. An Oxbridge student may pursue a major in English language and literature, history, history of ideas (an interdisciplinary major in the great books of the Western intellectual tradition), institutions and policy (philosophy, economics, and political science), music, or science (molecular biology or ecology and systematics) under a tutorial system of directed study and examinations adapted from the traditional method of the Universities of Oxford and Cambridge. Oxbridge tutorial majors spend the junior year in either Oxford or Cambridge. William Jewell supports several unique programs designed to train future leaders, including the Emerging Leaders, American Humanics, and the Pryor Leadership Programs. All three programs give students an opportunity to explore the theory and practice of leadership in the liberal arts setting. Emerging Leaders is available for first-year students to study the nature and practice of leadership at an annual conference. American Humanics' mission is to prepare and certify nonprofit professionals to work with America's youth and families through meetings, internships, and conferences. The Pryor Leadership Studies Program gives selected students from all academic majors the opportunity to participate in an Outward Bound course in the Florida Everglades, a vocational internship, a volunteer internship, and a Leadership Legacy project that benefits the entire William Jewell campus or the surrounding area. Students at William Jewell College may be granted advanced placement with or without credit through the Advanced Placement Program and College-Level Examination Program tests of the College Board, through the International Baccalaureate Program, and through departmental examinations.

Off-Campus Programs

Each student is encouraged to pursue an off-campus field experience. Advisers assist students in developing a program that relates to their educational goals. Typical programs involve study-abroad programs, work-study programs in the inner city, social or religious service, vocational internships, or study at another college. Programs may be formally structured classwork or independent study. In addition, students may participate in the United Nations Semester of Drew University and the Washington Semester of American University. Nearly 30 percent of the students participate in an overseas study opportunity. William Jewell has relationships with universities and study programs around the world and is distinguished by its ties to England. The College offers three programs in Oxford and Cambridge for honors students: a year of study at Homerton College (Cambridge) or at the Centre for Medieval and Renaissance Studies (affiliated with Keble College, Oxford) or either a semester or a year of study with the Oxford Overseas Study Course in Oxford. Harlaxton College, near Grantham, England, offers a full academic program for one semester of study, including an interdisciplinary course in British studies, which is required of all students. Two specialized programs of study in England connect overseas study with William Jewell's elementary education program. The British Teacher Education Program affords elementary education majors the chance to observe interdisciplinary, thematic teaching in British primary schools. The College also has strong ties to Asia. An exchange program with Seinan Gakuin University in Fukuoka, Japan, allows William Jewell students to earn a Japanese area studies major for their year of study. Each year, several William Jewell students may enroll at Hong Kong Baptist University, an English-language university with strong programs in business and many other academic areas. Other English-language programs are located in Australia; Vienna, Austria; Freiburg, Germany; and Milan, Italy. Foreign language programs are offered in France, Germany, Mexico, and Spain, including a summer program in Córdoba led by William Jewell faculty members.

Academic Facilities

The Charles F. Curry Library houses more than 255,000 volumes, with more than 10,000 items added annually. The library also has several special collections. The Learning Resource Center provides audiovisual services for the entire campus. William Jewell is a member of MOBIUS, a statewide shared computerized library system that includes fifty private, public, two-year and four-year institutions. When completely implemented, more than 14 million volumes will be accessible. Jewell Hall, which is listed on the National Register of Historic Places, served as a hospital for Union soldiers during the Civil War. Construction began on the building in 1849 and was completed in 1853. Jewell Hall has been completely renovated and remains one of the College's primary classroom buildings.

Costs

For the 2003–04 academic year, tuition and fees were $16,500, and room and board were $4820.

Financial Aid

Academic scholarships ranging from $500 to full tuition are awarded annually to qualified students. Activity and athletic scholarships are also available. William Jewell College participates in the Missouri Student Grant Program and in the Federal Pell Grant, Federal Supplemental Educational Opportunity Grant, Federal Work-Study, and Federal Perkins Loan programs. Students seeking financial assistance are encouraged to submit the Free Application for Federal Student Aid (FAFSA), designating William Jewell as a school choice. Applicants must apply for assistance before March 15 and must be accepted for admission before assistance can be awarded. Awards are often in the form of a package, which may include a combination of federal, state, and College funds.

Faculty

The faculty is a group of professionals highly qualified in their respective academic disciplines. All hold master's degrees; 4 of every 5 hold doctoral degrees. It is a teaching faculty; the entire energy of the faculty is spent in undergraduate instruction rather than in graduate teaching or research. From their freshman year, students are under the instruction of full professors, never under the instruction of graduate students or graduate assistants. All faculty members are designated "teacher-adviser," because the personal advisory relationship with students is an important part of the educational experience at William Jewell College. Each student is assigned an academic adviser who takes a personal interest in assisting the student to plan an academic program to meet specific goals. The majority of the faculty are full-time members who are totally committed to the academic and personal growth of students. Most faculty members live close to campus, and many are closely involved with student activities and cocurricular programs.

Student Government

The Student Senate provides a forum for student opinion on many diverse issues and serves as a working link among the students, faculty, administration, and Board of Trustees. The College is receptive to student ideas, and dialogue is encouraged.

Admission Requirements

Admission to William Jewell College is competitive. The College encourages applications from students who are serious about enrolling in a coeducational liberal arts college and who have indicated through their secondary school record that they are sufficiently mature to profit from and contribute to the College. William Jewell actively encourages geographic and cultural diversity on the campus. To be considered for admission, students are asked to submit ACT or SAT I scores; a copy of the secondary school record; one recommendation, preferably academic; and a personal essay. Preference is given to graduates of an accredited high school who have had 20 units of high school credits, as follows: English, 4; mathematics, 3; science, 3; social studies, 3; foreign language, 2; fine arts, 1; and 4 additional units in the areas above. Transfer students are welcome, and credit is granted for work comparable to that offered at William Jewell College. Each candidate for admission should have a personal interview with a member of the admission staff when visiting the College.

Application and Information

An applicant for admission may complete the William Jewell application form or the Common Application form. William Jewell processes applications for the fall semester under three plans. For early action, the application deadline is November 15 and the notification date is December 1. For scholarship priority, the application deadline is January 31 and the notification date is February 15. For regular decision, the application deadline is March 15 and the notification date is April 1. All applications received and completed after March 15 are reviewed on a space-available basis; notification begins after April 1. The application fee is $25.

For additional information, interested students should contact:

Dean of Enrollment
William Jewell College
500 College Hill
Liberty, Missouri 64068
Telephone: 816-781-7700 Ext. 5137
800-753-7009 (toll-free)
Fax: 816-415-5040
E-mail: admission@william.jewell.edu
World Wide Web: http://www.jewell.edu

White Science Center (on the left) stands near the gateway to William Jewell College in Liberty, Missouri. The $7.5-million structure houses laboratories and classroom facilities for biology, chemistry, physics, and computer sciences.

WILLIAM PATERSON UNIVERSITY OF NEW JERSEY

WAYNE, NEW JERSEY

WILLIAM PATERSON UNIVERSITY

The University

Since its founding in 1855, William Paterson University has grown into a comprehensive state institution whose programs reflect the area's need for challenging, affordable educational options. Ideally midsized (the total enrollment is 11,210, of whom 9,302 are degree-seeking undergraduates), William Paterson offers a wider variety of academic programs than smaller universities, yet provides students with a more personalized atmosphere than larger institutions. Once the site of the family estate of Garret Hobart, the twenty-fourth vice president of the United States, William Paterson's 370-acre spacious campus, which has wooded areas and waterfalls, offers an environment in which students may develop both intellectually and socially. Although the majority of the University's students come from the New Jersey and New York vicinity, some international and out-of-state students enroll each year. Twenty-five percent of the undergraduates reside on campus in residence halls or apartment-style facilities, which accommodate nearly 2,300 students. In general, on-campus housing is offered on a first-come, first-served basis.

Social, cultural, and recreational activities complement the academic programs. Cultural events take place throughout the year, featuring both William Paterson's own talent and renowned professional artists. Among the programs are concerts presenting jazz, classical, and contemporary music; theater productions; gallery exhibits; and a distinguished-lecturer series. The most popular spot for social activities is the Student Center, which contains an art gallery, a performing arts lounge, a game room, an ATM, a bookstore, and several auxiliary dining areas. The Student Activities Programming Board helps the more than fifty clubs and organizations to develop diverse activities for the entire student body. William Paterson has twenty-two social fraternities and sororities and twenty-one honor societies. Students staff the campus radio station (WPSC) and the television station (WPC-TV), which develops a number of widely distributed television programs for local and statewide cable networks. The Rec Center serves as the focal point for physical recreation. In addition to the main courts, which accommodate badminton, basketball, indoor tennis, and volleyball, the 4,000-seat facility has racquetball courts, an exercise room, saunas, and Jacuzzis. The University has fifteen intercollegiate sports teams, seven for men and eight for women, including successful NCAA teams in men's baseball and women's softball. In 2002, the Pioneers won the coed cheerleading and dance team national championship. In addition, bowling, dance, horseback riding, and ice hockey are organized as club sports. The University has a competition-sized indoor pool, outdoor tennis courts, and a lighted athletics field complex.

Location

William Paterson University is located in northern New Jersey in the busy suburban town of Wayne. Several major recreational and cultural centers are nearby. New York City is just 20 miles to the east, the seacoast is an hour's drive south, skiing is 30 miles north, and the Meadowlands Sports Complex is a half-hour drive away.

Majors and Degrees

William Paterson University grants four undergraduate degrees—the B.A., B.S., B.F.A., and B.M.—and offers degree programs through its five colleges: Arts and Communication, the Christos M. Cotsakos College of Business, Education, Humanities and Social Sciences, and Science and Health.

The Bachelor of Arts degree is awarded in African, African-American, and Caribbean studies; anthropology; art; communication; English; French and Francophone studies; geography; history; Latin American studies; mathematics; music; philosophy; political science; psychology; sociology; Spanish; special education; and women's studies. The Bachelor of Science degree is conferred in accounting, applied chemistry, biology, biotechnology, business administration, community health/school health education, computer science, environmental science, nursing, and physical education. The Bachelor of Fine Arts degree in fine arts and the Bachelor of Music degree in music are also offered. Asian studies and urban studies, two cross-disciplinary minors, are part of the curriculum as well.

Certification is available in early childhood, elementary, secondary, and special education. Preprofessional programs in dentistry, engineering, law, medicine, pharmacy, physical therapy, speech-language pathology, and veterinary medicine are arranged at the request of students.

Academic Programs

Students must complete a minimum of 128 credits to earn a baccalaureate degree. Degree programs include a 60-credit general education requirement, 30–60 credits in a major, and 20–40 credits in elective courses. (In specialized degree programs, such as the B.F.A. and the B.M., general education and major course requirements may differ.) Students uncertain of which career path to follow may take advantage of advisement and counseling programs. In addition, the general education requirements enable students to take up to 60 credits before declaring a major, so that they can acquire a basic understanding of all major fields of knowledge before having to choose a specific area. Diagnostic testing and career seminars, provided by the Career Development Office, also ensure that students receive the guidance necessary to make wise course selections and career decisions.

William Paterson offers a variety of special programs. Honors programs are designed for those ambitious and well-qualified students who want to add a challenging dimension to their major. Currently, there are eight honors programs—in biopsychology, cognitive science, humanities, life science and environmental ethics, music, nursing, performing and literary arts, and social science. Students who have completed the premedical program in the College of Science and Health have consistently been accepted by American medical schools during the last eleven years.

Students who successfully complete Advanced Placement tests and/or College-Level Examination Program tests may receive credit for acceptable scores. Credit may also be awarded for military training and experience. William Paterson University operates on a two-semester and two-summer-session system.

Off-Campus Programs

William Paterson offers a special opportunity for off-campus study. Semester Abroad, a 15-credit program, is open to sophomores and juniors who wish to study for a semester at selected institutions in Australia, Denmark, Great Britain, Greece, Israel, Spain, and other countries around the world.

Distance learning opportunities are available through the Center for Continuing Education and Distance Learning. The University also has regional centers in association with several New Jersey community colleges.

Academic Facilities

Situated on a 370-acre campus set in the hills of suburban Wayne, New Jersey, William Paterson's facilities are easily accessible, promote interaction among students, and encourage participation by all students in the various academic, cultural, and recreational programs. The University has recently expanded the David and Lorraine Cheng Library's bound collection area by 33 percent and increased the seating capacity by 100 percent. The library contains a collection of more than 350,000 volumes, 18,000 audiovisual items, and 1,500 print subscriptions. A special-collections room houses rare and out-of-print items on New Jersey and valuable editions of literary works. Media services, group studies, carrels, and computer labs provide space for a variety of student uses. An extensive collection of online journals and resources is accessible campuswide from the library Web site. Supporting William Paterson's varied cultural and artistic offerings are the Power Arts Center, an extensive facility accomodating an array of studio arts; the Ben Shahn Center for Visual Arts, which contains art galleries, studios, and classrooms; and the Shea Center for Performing Arts, which contains a 940-seat theater as well as band, choral, and orchestra practice rooms and classrooms.

Hobart Hall, a state-of-the-art communication facility, is designed to educate communication majors in the most contemporary communication technology, including teleconferences. The facility houses two broadcast-quality TV studios, a multipurpose computer lab, a film studio, an FCC-licensed FM radio station, an uplink and four downlink satellite dishes, audio and video digital nonlinear editing systems, a cable system linking 95 percent of the buildings on campus, and a computerized telephone system for voice and data transmission. Also, William Paterson is finalizing the process of creating fiber-optic links throughout the campus.

A two-story academic building, the Atrium, which contains a writing center, multimedia language lab, tutorial center, and computing support facilities, was completed in 1996.

Among the other academic resources are extensive computer facilities, a filmmaking laboratory, a professionally equipped television production truck, a child-care center, a nursing instructional center, a language lab, and a speech and hearing clinic. William Paterson University has dual accreditation from the American Speech-Language-Hearing Association for its speech and hearing clinic and its graduate program in communication disorders. The science research facilities contain two electron microscopes and various specialized labs.

Costs

Annual tuition (including fees) for the 2004–05 academic year is $7120 for full-time (12 credits or more) students who are New Jersey residents and $11,500 for full-time nonresident students. Room and board cost approximately $7130 per year. All charges are subject to change per the Board of Trustees.

Financial Aid

Financial aid is available through a number of federal and state grant, loan, scholarship, and work-study programs. To apply for need-based aid, students must file the Free Application for Federal Student Aid (FAFSA) with the United States Department of Education by the priority date of April 1.

Both the University and the Alumni Association award a number of competitive scholarships, based solely on academic merit, to entering freshmen. They are the Scholarships for Academic Excellence, Scholarships for African-American and Hispanic Students, and Trustee and Presidential Scholarships. Academic Achievement Scholarships are awarded only on a competitive basis to continuing students.

Faculty

William Paterson's 354 full-time and 618 part-time faculty members bring to the classroom a valuable blend of accomplished scholarship and practical, applied experience. Faculty members assist students with curriculum and career planning, which engenders open, personal communication between the students and faculty.

Through a formal reciprocal exchange relationship with various institutions worldwide, and through the Fulbright Scholarship Program, William Paterson University often receives visiting international scholars.

Student Government

The Student Government Association (SGA), of which all full-time and part-time students are automatically members, has become an influential voice in University decision making. Elected officers and various committees convey students' perspectives to the administration and advance their causes. The SGA is also responsible for chartering more than fifty campus organizations and allocating student activity fees among them.

Admission Requirements

Admission to William Paterson University is competitive. Admissions decisions for entering freshmen are based on a complete review of the students' academic record (course of study, grades, and rank) as well as the results of the SAT I or ACT. Applicants are considered eligible if they have taken a minimum of 16 Carnegie units and have demonstrated strong academic ability. The students' secondary school record must show the following courses: English, 4 years (composition and literature); mathematics, 3 years (algebra I and II and geometry); laboratory science, 2 years (biology, chemistry, or physics); social science, 2 years (American history, world history, or political science); and additional college-preparatory subjects, 5 units (advanced mathematics, literature, foreign language, or social sciences). In addition, students selecting a major in art or music (except musical studies) must submit a portfolio for review by the Art Department or must audition for the Music Department.

Transfer students must present at least 12 college-level credits with a minimum 2.0 GPA; science and nursing majors must have a minimum 2.5 GPA; and special education majors, as well as teacher certification program applicants, must have a minimum 2.75 GPA. Applicants with fewer than 12 college credits must submit a high school transcript. Application review will be completed only upon receipt of official transcripts from high schools and especially colleges and universities. Unofficial transcripts or transcripts sent by students will not be used for admissions.

Application and Information

Application forms and transcripts from candidates for freshman status must be received by May 1 for fall admission and November 1 for spring admission. Transfer students, readmitted students, and students seeking a second bachelor's degree must submit their materials by May 1 and November 1 for fall and spring entry, respectively. However, the University closes the application process earlier when the number of new and continuing students strains its ability to provide effective programs and services. A $50 application fee is required. Applications are reviewed on a rolling basis. Campus tours are available during the fall and spring semesters on weekdays by appointment when classes are in session.

For additional information and to apply online, students should go to the undergraduate admissions site at the address listed below or contact:

Office of Admissions
William Paterson University of New Jersey
Wayne, New Jersey 07470
Telephone: 973-720-2125
877-WPU-EXCEL (toll-free)
E-mail: admissions@wpunj.edu
World Wide Web: http://www.wpunj.edu

William Paterson University's hilltop suburban campus offers an environment where students may develop both intellectually and socially.

WILLIAM PENN UNIVERSITY

OSKALOOSA, IOWA

The University

A world of opportunities is available at William Penn University in Oskaloosa, Iowa. From excellent academic programs and a caring faculty to extracurricular activities and athletics to internships and exciting career prospects, William Penn University challenges students to explore it all.

One hundred thirty-two years ago, members of the Society of Friends (Quakers) established William Penn University with a vision for the future. The Quaker values of integrity, simplicity, compassion, ethical practice, acceptance, tolerance, and service continue to be the framework for the quality of education that William Penn University provides to students today.

The University is organized into two colleges: the College of Arts, Sciences, and Professional Studies and the College for Working Adults, which is also located in Ames and West Des Moines, Iowa. More than 1,400 students are enrolled at William Penn University on the three campuses, with forty-one states and twelve countries represented. Twenty-three undergraduate majors with forty-one areas of emphasis and thirty-three education endorsements are offered.

Twelve major buildings, including a women's residence hall, a men's hall, one coed hall, and a town-house residence facility for upperclassmen, are centered on the 60-acre campus. One- and two-bedroom apartments are also available for upperclassmen and married students. Many student activities are held in Atkins Memorial Union and the gymnasium. The George Daily Auditorium, a community auditorium two blocks from the campus, is a 700-seat, state-of-the-art facility that is the site of many University functions.

Opportunities abound for students to get involved at William Penn University, including student government, campus ministries, departmental clubs and organizations, intramural athletics, and fine arts activities. After-class activities include regular movie nights, organized dormitory events, performances by professional entertainers, late-night bowling, and snow-skiing trips. Special events and guest speakers provide students with study breaks.

William Penn University has a strong tradition of excellence in college athletics, having won national, regional, and conference championships in both men's and women's athletics. Men compete in baseball, basketball, cross-country, football, golf, soccer, track, and wrestling. Women compete in basketball, cross-country, soccer, softball, track, and volleyball. William Penn is a member of the National Association of Intercollegiate Athletics (NAIA).

Location

Located in the rolling hills of southeast Iowa, William Penn University lies on the north edge of Oskaloosa, Iowa. Oskaloosa was established as a small mining center in the early 1800s. It has since grown to more than 11,000 people but still retains a small-town atmosphere.

In the summer, a community band performs weekly in a historic bandstand. Other summer activities include Art on the Square and Sweet Corn Serenade. Oskyfest celebrates the coming of autumn, and Oskaloosa's lighted Christmas parade is known as one of the best holiday events in the Midwest.

The area also has parks and playgrounds, lighted ballparks, and tennis courts as well as a movie theater, bowling alley, roller-skating rink, and YMCA. Hiking, boating, fishing, swimming, and camping are located nearby at Lake Keomah State Park and Red Rock Lake.

Majors and Degrees

The College of Arts, Sciences, and Professional Studies awards the Bachelor of Arts degree in accounting; applied computer science (communications applications, computer information systems, engineering applications); biology (bioprocess technology, environmental studies, general biology, preprofessional studies); business management; communications (English, fine arts, journalism/electronic media, public relations, technical); contemporary business; elementary education, with endorsements in K–6 elementary education, health, reading, and special education; history/government (American government, American history, general history/government, prelaw); industrial technology (engineering technology, industrial management, technical); information management; information technology; mathematics; mechanical engineering; physical education (sports administration, strength and conditioning, wellness and recreation); psychology (general psychology, human services); sociology (criminology, general sociology); and secondary education, with endorsements in American government, American history, athletics coaching, biology, biology with chemistry, biology with earth science, biology with general science, biology with physical science, biology with physics, driver and safety education, English as a second language, English/language arts, general business, general science, health, industrial technology, journalism, math, multicategorical, natural science combinations, physical education, physics, psychology, sociology, special education, and speech/theater.

The College for Working Adults offers programs in business (management, marketing, finance), information management (business applications, decision support systems), and public administration (health services administration, nonprofit management, human resources management/organizational effectiveness), and an Associate of Arts degree in leadership studies.

Academic Programs

William Penn University, accredited by the Higher Learning Commission of the North Central Association of Colleges and Schools, offers two full semesters and three summer sessions every academic year. The academic program is based on four foundational concepts: leadership, ethical practice, lifelong learning, and commitment to service. These concepts are emphasized throughout the University experience. Majors consist of at least 30 hours in the student's area of concentration and must be completed with a cumulative GPA of at least 2.0 (on a 4.0 scale). The Leadership Core, William Penn University's general education requirement, has been named by the John Templeton Foundation to the Honor Roll for Character Building Colleges. Penn was one of only thirty-five colleges in the nation cited for exemplary programming in leadership.

William Penn's teacher-education program offers a major in elementary education and twenty secondary education endorsements. Penn is one of only a few universities in Iowa that offers the ESL endorsement and has received a federal grant to expand the availability of the English as a second language K–12 endorsement. William Penn is one of only two institutions in the state to offer certification for industrial technology teachers and is the only private institution in the state to offer a four-year major in industrial technology.

Academic Facilities

Wilcox Library currently holds nearly 57,000 volumes plus audiovisual materials and electronic books. The library subscribes to 212 periodicals and more than 12,000 electronic journals. The Quaker Collection, an extensive holding of Quaker monographs, photographs, and other materials, is also part of Wilcox Library. In addition, the Academic Resource Center and the Jones Mid-East Collection are located in the library. The library has a wireless network with laptops available for student use. In the lower level is an electronic classroom that all instructors can use. It is equipped with a smart board and additional computers.

William Penn's computer facilities contain up-to-date equipment. Networked Macintosh and IBM-compatible microcomputers are available in the computer lab and connect students with e-mail and the Internet. Students also have access to the University's Hewlett-Packard 3000 superminicomputer through terminals located in the computer lab. Knowledgeable lab assistants are always on duty in the computer lab to answer questions and help students understand the computers and software. The dorms are part of the campus' local area network, and students with their own computers can access the Internet directly from their rooms for a small, one-time connection fee.

Most classes are held in Penn Hall, which was built in 1917. This building stands in the center of Penn's 40-acre campus. Ware Recital Hall, a 100-seat auditorium in McGrew Fine Arts Center, is the setting for many theatrical productions, concerts, classes, and lectures. A 255-seat auditorium in Penn Hall also hosts special events and guest speakers.

Costs

Full-time tuition for 2004–05 is $14,234. The room fee is $1852. Board is $2894.

Financial Aid

William Penn University seeks to make it financially possible for qualified students to experience the advantages of a college education. Generous gifts from alumni, trustees, and friends of the University, in addition to state and federal student aid programs, make this opportunity possible. Ninety-eight percent of William Penn University's students receive financial aid, such as academic scholarships, performing arts scholarships, athletic scholarships, international scholarships, work-study, federal and state grants, and government loans.

To apply for assistance, students must first apply for admission and be accepted to a degree-granting program. In addition, students are strongly encouraged to file the Free Application for Federal Student Aid (FAFSA) after January 1. Iowa residents must file prior to July 1 to qualify for state student financial aid. Students must name William Penn University (code 001900) in order for the University to receive the needs analysis report. To receive the results more quickly, students should file electronically at http://www.fafsa.ed.gov.

Students who apply for aid after April 15 are funded on a funds-available basis.

Faculty

William Penn University's faculty is made up of 45 full-time and 22 part-time members. The emphasis at William Penn is on teaching, but students are often able to become involved and work with faculty members on individual research projects. Faculty members are encouraged to get to know students both in the classroom and through cocurricular activities. The faculty-student ratio is 1:14.

Student Government

The Student Government Association (SGA) serves as the governing organization for all students and student organizations. The SGA, led by the student body president, is very active in planning campus activities and events, including Homecoming. The student body is represented by the student body president at all Board of Trustees meetings, and students are a part of many campus committees.

Admission Requirements

Students from accredited high schools and college transfers are considered for admission to William Penn University based on their grade point average, class rank, ACT or SAT I scores, and likelihood of academic success. William Penn University has a rolling admissions policy.

Application and Information

Applications are accepted on a rolling basis and are reviewed as soon as they are complete. Students should send a completed application, the $20 application fee, official copies of all high school and/or college transcripts or the GED score, and ACT or SAT I results to the Office of Admissions.

International students should submit TOEFL scores along with an international student application and a statement of financial support. An ESL program is available for students seeking to improve their English skills.

Campus tours and information sessions are available throughout the week.

Office of Admissions
William Penn University
201 Trueblood Avenue
Oskaloosa, Iowa 52577
Telephone: 641-673-1012
800-779-7366 (toll-free)
E-mail: admissions@wmpenn.edu
World Wide Web: http://www.wmpenn.edu

William Penn University students look forward to a successful future.

WILLIAM WOODS UNIVERSITY

FULTON, MISSOURI

The University

As an independent, selective, coeducational institution, William Woods University (WWU) serves a total enrollment of 1,813 students and offers degrees in more than forty undergraduate and graduate majors in both traditional and nontraditional settings. Chartered in 1870 as an all-female institution serving young women orphaned by the Civil War, the school moved to its Fulton, Missouri, location in 1890, changing its name to Daughter's College of the Christian Church. By the turn of the twentieth century, the school adopted the William Woods College name and began offering undergraduate programs. In 1962, William Woods officially became a four-year liberal arts college, and in 1993, William Woods became a university, awarding graduate degrees. In 1997, the University became a fully coeducational institution.

The diverse student body of William Woods University consists of 912 undergraduate and 901 graduate students from thirty-seven states and seventeen other countries. Eighty-eight percent of the students live in the twelve residence halls on campus.

More than 30,000 students from five nearby colleges and universities offer William Woods students abundant social opportunities in Fulton and the surrounding area. William Woods has more than forty clubs and six national fraternal organizations. Students have the opportunity to participate in a wide range of extracurricular activities. Intercollegiate sports include men's baseball, golf, soccer, and volleyball and women's basketball, golf, soccer, softball, and volleyball.

The Helen Stephens Sports Complex houses a gymnasium, classrooms, a weight room, and a whirlpool and sauna. The University's Weider Fitness Center also contains aerobic fitness equipment for student use.

The on-campus Equine Center includes four stables, two indoor arenas, an outdoor arena, a blacksmith's shop, and a 30-acre cross-country course. The McNutt Student Center, a multipurpose geodesic domed structure, houses the student activities center and the admission office, as well as a 1,251-seat auditorium.

A $1.5 million Center for Human Performance provides a home for the new Department of Human Performance, which includes athletic training, sports management, and physical education. The one-story, 12,000-square-foot facility provides ten times the amount of space previously dedicated to athletic training. It serves the two-fold purpose of providing state-of-the-art care to WWU athletes and, at the same time, enhancing the University's ability to provide clinical experiences for athletic-training students.

The University's Graduate and Adult Studies Division offers programs leading to the Master of Business Administration, Master of Education in administration, Master of Education in curriculum and instruction, and the Education Specialist degree.

Location

The beautiful 170-acre William Woods campus is located in Fulton, Missouri, a historic community of 12,000. William Woods students enjoy the charm and safety that a small town offers, along with the cultural and recreational facilities of nearby cities and educational institutions. Columbia, home of the University of Missouri and its 25,000 students, is 25 miles west. Fulton sits midway between Kansas City and St. Louis and is a scenic hour's drive north of mid-Missouri's premier recreational area, the Lake of the Ozarks.

Majors and Degrees

William Woods University offers programs leading to the Bachelor of Arts, Bachelor of Science, Bachelor of Social Work, and Bachelor of Fine Arts degrees. Majors and minors include accounting, advertising/marketing, art, art education, athletic training, biology, biology education, broadcasting, business administration, chemistry, communications, computer and information systems, criminal justice, early childhood education, economics/finance, elementary education, English, English education, equestrian science, equine administration, film studies, graphic design, history, history education, interdisciplinary studies, international business, interpreting/American Sign Language (ASL), journalism, management, math education, mathematics, middle school education, music, paralegal studies, philosophy, physical education, physical science, political and legal studies, psychology, public relations, secondary education, social work, sociology, Spanish, special education, speech/theater education, sports management, theater, and visual communications. WVU is one of only twenty-five schools in the country to offer a four-year degree in American Sign Language interpreting.

Academic Program

At William Woods, students are encouraged to develop a comprehensive, global vision of the world. The workplace is expanding globally, and so must a student's education. Academic programs are designed to prepare the graduate for an active role in a profession or graduate study as well as in society. William Woods purposely remains a small university because it wishes to emphasize the recognition of each student as an individual and to provide the advantages of small classes. The University encourages a close relationship between students, professors, and faculty advisers.

A minimum of 122 credit hours is required for the baccalaureate degree; these include both departmental and general education requirements. The University requires all students to complete a core of common studies. These courses include English, communications, mathematics, fine and performing arts, humanities, history, cultural diversity, natural science, and behavioral/social science. In addition, students gain practical experience through internships offered in many programs of study.

The University grants advanced placement and appropriate credit to qualified students on the basis of College Board Advanced Placement examinations, advanced-placement high school courses, CLEP scores, community college courses, International Baccalaureate, or other supporting evidence of superior scholarship and accomplishments. William Woods also offers an honors program, the Mentor-Mentee Program, and accelerated and independent study for advanced students.

Off-Campus Programs

William Woods participates in exchange agreements with four other regional institutions, providing many academic and cocurricular opportunities. Through cooperative agreements and direct affiliations with institutions abroad, opportunities for fully accredited study abroad are available to qualified students. Approved programs currently are available through the following organizations: American Institute for Foreign Study, Council International Education, and Beaver College. Direct affiliation programs are available at the following institutions: Regent's College in London, Espiritu Santo University in Ecuador, Altai State University in Russia, and Nagoya Women's University in Japan.

Academic Facilities

The William Woods University Library contains more than 122,000 printed volumes, more than 4,000 journal titles in printed and full-text electronic form, and thousands of nonprint items, including videos, CD-ROMs, and computer software. A separate law library is located within the library building. WWU is a charter member of MOBIUS, a statewide consortium of academic libraries that provides online patron-initiated borrowing to WWU students and faculty members from all participating libraries in Missouri. WWU has twelve computer labs for instructional and student use. The library, all classroom buildings, and all residence halls have direct connections to the Internet through the campus network. Distance education students also have access to electronic library resources from remote sites.

The Burton Business and Economics Building, a three-level structure of 35,000 square feet, houses the Division of Business and the Departments of Legal Studies and Interpreting/American Sign Language. A model courtroom provides space for mock trials. The campus also has a 40,000-square-foot Center for the Arts, which houses the Division of Visual, Performing and Communication Arts. Built with a glassed-in main foyer and sculpture garden, the facility contains a performance theater, a television studio, an art gallery for exhibitions, foundry and kilns, and computer labs, as well as numerous classrooms dedicated to studio art, jewelry, sculpture, printing, graphic design, photography, ceramics, music, weaving, and other activities.

Costs

Resident student fees for the 2003–04 academic year were as follows: tuition and fees, $14,000, and room and board, $5700. The application fee is $25.

Financial Aid

Approximately 90 percent of the University's students receive some form of financial assistance. William Woods participates in the Federal Pell Grant, Federal Supplemental Educational Opportunity Grant, Gallagher State Grant, Federal Perkins Loan, Federal Stafford Student Loan, and Federal Work-Study programs. Parents of students applying for need-based assistance are required to file the Free Application for Federal Student Aid (FAFSA). In addition to providing awards for achievement in art, athletics, equestrian science, and performing arts, William Woods also offers academic scholarships based on class rank and ACT or SAT I scores. Scholarships are offered to students graduating first in their class as well as to those students who have achieved National Merit Finalist status. William Woods has designed a program intended to make the University more affordable and, at the same time, to encourage and reward campus and community involvement that makes a complete, well-rounded liberal arts background. This $5000 LEAD (Leading, Educating, Achieving, and Developing) award is available to any student, regardless of financial need, who agrees to make a commitment to campus and community involvement. Information, instructions about applying, and necessary forms are available in the Office of Enrollment Services or on the University's Web site, listed below.

Faculty

William Woods has 57 full-time and 12 part-time faculty members; no classes are taught by graduate students. Students enjoy the relaxed and informal atmosphere of small classes conducted by a diverse teaching faculty; the student-faculty ratio is 16:1. Most of the professors are experienced professionals, and more than 84 percent hold Ph.D.'s or other terminal degrees. The faculty's enthusiasm and dedication to students are among the University's greatest assets.

Admission Requirements

The Enrollment Council at William Woods considers each application individually. The council reviews an applicant's high school courses, grades, activities, performance on the SAT I or ACT, rank in class, and personal references. Early admission and early acceptance policies exist at William Woods. Transfer students who have cumulative grade point averages of C (2.0) or above are eligible for acceptance. Enrollment representatives arrange visits for prospective students and their parents. The Office of Enrollment Services arranges campus tours and interviews during the regular school terms and summer months.

William Woods University welcomes qualified students of any race, color, gender, and national or ethnic origin and persons with disabilities, according to the definition in Section 504 of the Rehabilitation Act of 1973.

Application and Information

To apply for admission, students should submit a current application with a $25 application fee, authorize their high school to send an academic transcript to William Woods, and request that SAT I or ACT scores be sent to the University. Students are accepted on a rolling admission basis after all necessary credentials have been received. While there is no deadline for applying, the University encourages students to apply as early as possible. For an application form, financial assistance information, and brochures, students should contact:

Office of Enrollment Services
William Woods University
1 University Avenue
Fulton, Missouri 65251-1098

Telephone: 573-592-4221
800-995-3159 (toll-free)

E-mail: admissions@williamwoods.edu
World Wide Web: http://www.williamwoods.edu

William Woods is located on a self-contained, 170-acre campus.

WILMINGTON COLLEGE

NEW CASTLE, DELAWARE

The College

Wilmington College, founded in 1967, is a private career-oriented institution offering undergraduate and graduate degrees. The College is accredited by the Middle States Association of Colleges and Schools. The educational programs are designed to help students of varied academic backgrounds achieve their potential in a small-college environment where individual attention plays an important part in the academic and personal growth of each student. The current enrollment is 8,800 men and women. The student body consists of a combination of recent high school graduates and returning adult students who wish to upgrade their educational levels and enhance their learning capabilities.

At the graduate level, master's degrees are offered in administration of justice, business, community counseling, education, information system technologies, nursing, and organizational leadership. A doctoral program in education is also offered.

The College is a member of both the National Association of Intercollegiate Athletics (NAIA) and the National Collegiate Athletic Association (NCAA). Wilmington College offers intercollegiate teams for cross-country and soccer for men and women, baseball and basketball for men, and basketball, softball, and volleyball for women. Intramural sports for men and women are provided during the fall and spring semesters.

Location

Wilmington College's main campus is located near the historic town of New Castle, approximately 6 miles from the city of Wilmington. New Castle is filled with museums, buildings, and other sites of interest dating back to before the Revolutionary War. To serve the educational needs of Delaware's population, Wilmington College offers many of its programs at five other convenient locations—Dover Air Force Base, North Dover, Georgetown, the Wilmington Graduate Center, and a site at Rehoboth Beach.

Majors and Degrees

Wilmington College offers an Associate of Arts degree in general studies and Associate of Science degrees in early childhood education and media art, design, and technology. The College confers the Bachelor of Arts degree in behavioral science and the Bachelor of Science degree in accounting, business management, criminal justice, elementary education, finance, human resources management, interactive multimedia design and communication, Internet and networking design and technology, legal studies, marketing, nursing (RNs only), psychology, sports management, and television and video production design.

Academic Programs

The academic program of the College has been developed to provide a personal approach to career education. Each student is assigned an academic adviser to assist with curriculum and career development. Representatives from business, industry, health care, and education serve as adjunct faculty members. They work closely with faculty members to design practical experiences and special interest courses to meet student needs. A personalized education and a well-trained faculty give students the skills that will make them competitive in the job market. Wilmington College offers programs on a year-round basis that are designed to fit a student's schedule. Courses at the New Castle campus are offered both during the day and in the evening. In addition to the traditional fifteen-week semester, many courses are offered in a seven-week accelerated format and a weekend format. The fall semester begins in September and ends before Christmas. The spring semester begins in January and ends in April. The summer sessions are offered in the seven-week accelerated format during the months of May, June, July, and August.

Academic Facilities

The College's nine buildings house classrooms, offices, the bookstore, a radio station and TV studio, computer labs, the gymnasium, and the Wilmington College Cafe. The latest addition to the campus is an 80,000-square-foot building that houses admissions, academic advising, financial aid, the registrar, and the bursar. In addition to these student services, the building also holds classrooms, a video screening room, and state-of-the-art computer labs. The library houses 196,000 volumes.

The Wilmington College Library houses a collection of more than 142,000 bound volumes and subscribes to more than 500 periodicals. Also available in the library are microcomputers, electronic links to other libraries, and a growing collection of software programs and nonprint media for student use.

Costs

For the 2003–04 academic year, tuition was $693 per 3-credit course at the New Castle campus. The registration fee was $25 per term, and the graduation fee was $50. For certain courses, there may be additional laboratory fees. These fees are provided in the appropriate registration program.

Tuition at various Wilmington College sites varies. For current costs, students should contact the site of attendance.

Financial Aid

The purpose of the financial aid program at Wilmington College is to supplement the resources of the students and their family in order to give needy students the opportunity to obtain a college education. Applicants for financial aid are urged to apply early, since funds are limited. Financial aid is generally awarded in a combination of loan, grant, and employment. The major student financial aid programs in which the College participates are Federal Pell Grants, Federal Supplemental Educational Opportunity Grants, Federal Work-Study, and Federal Stafford Student Loans. Delaware students may be eligible for assistance from the Delaware Postsecondary Scholarship Fund Program. Academic, service, and athletics scholarships are also available.

Applicants for aid should request the necessary application forms from the Financial Aid Office. Awards are not made until a student has been officially accepted by the College. For further information, students should contact the financial aid officer at the College.

Faculty

There are 460 full- and part-time faculty members at Wilmington College who offer personalized attention to each student. Full-time professors, as well as adjunct faculty members from business, industry, health care, and education, serve as faculty advisers in diversified career fields. The student-faculty ratio is 22:1.

Admission Requirements

Wilmington College welcomes applications from men and women of all ages and of every race, color, and creed who, in its judgment, show promise of academic achievement regardless of past performance. The College seeks a diversified student body and encourages the submission of applications from students of widely differing backgrounds, aptitudes, and interests, including career-minded adults who wish to upgrade their skills or complete a degree program.

In addition to considering an applicant's academic record, the Admissions Committee relies heavily upon the recommendation of the student's guidance counselor or principal as to the applicant's desire to attend Wilmington College and ability to benefit from the programs and services offered. The College recognizes the effect of determination and motivation on students' performance in college and is eager to give them a chance to prove themselves.

Candidates must be graduates of an accredited high school or have successfully completed a General Educational Development (GED) program. SAT I scores are preferred and are taken into consideration for admission to the College, but they are not required. Applications are reviewed and accepted on a continuous basis. Freshmen are admitted to the fall, spring, and summer sessions.

Application and Information

Applications for admission, along with a $25 application fee and all other required materials, should be submitted no later than one month prior to the beginning of a semester. The College uses a rolling admission plan, and applicants are notified of the admission decision within three weeks of the receipt of all materials.

Requests for additional information and for application forms should be directed to:

Admissions Office
Wilmington College
320 DuPont Highway
New Castle, Delaware 19720-6491
Telephone: 302-328-9407
E-mail: inquire@wilmcoll.edu

The Pratt Student Center.

WILSON COLLEGE

CHAMBERSBURG, PENNSYLVANIA

The College

Wilson College, an independent college founded in 1869, is dedicated to the education of women, rigorous study in the liberal arts and sciences, and strong career preparation. Students from twenty-one different states and fourteen countries join a cooperative learning community that embraces educational opportunities both inside and outside of the classroom. Wilson is committed to the life of the mind and spirit, to environmental sustainability and preparing articulate, ethical leaders who will serve their communities and professions effectively in an increasingly complex, interdependent, and global world. The College is distinguished by its supportive, diverse, and close-knit community, which is guided by the Wilson Honor Principle.

The College is accredited by the Middle States Association of Colleges and Schools, the Pennsylvania Department of Education, and the American Veterinary Medical Association. Programs in the College for Women celebrate, reflect upon, and critique women's contributions to society and offer women unique opportunities to grow in intellect, self-confidence, leadership, and feelings of self-worth in their chosen roles. Offerings in the College for Continuing Education draw upon the strengths of the Women's College, while recognizing the needs of older adults, both women and men. The total College enrollment in fall 2003 was approximately 800, with an enrollment of 350 in the College for Women.

Within Wilson's intentionally small, close-knit community, built upon shared governance under an Honor Principle, students learn by direct participation and initiative to maintain a lifestyle based on mutual trust, empathetic understanding, and respect for others and the natural world. With a history of tradition, Wilson also has many clubs and athletic teams (field hockey, soccer, volleyball, basketball, gymnastics, hunt seat equitation, softball, and tennis) for students.

In 2003–04, students benefit from completed campus renovations, including the Lenfest Commons, a state-of-the-art student center that is the hub for community conversation, dining, recreation, fitness, and campus activities. Renovations have been completed for the Hankey Center, which houses the Wilson archives and is a center for research on the education of women and girls. Expanded athletic facilities in Kris's Meadow include the Rhonda Brake Shreiner Soccer Field and Softball Field.

Wilson's residential Women with Children Program (WWC) provides on-campus residential housing year-round to single mothers and their children so that the mother can pursue a bachelor's degree full-time. The program provides today's women with the tools to become academically, financially, and personally successful. The Women with Children program is nationally recognized as a model program for providing college access for single women with children.

Wilson is also known as a leader in the study of sustainable agricultural practices. The Fulton Center for Sustainable Living at Wilson College is dedicated to the sustainable use of natural resources and the protection of the environment, promoting these principles through education, research, and community outreach. It has been recognized internationally as a model of sustainable agricultural practices.

Location

Wilson College is located in a residential neighborhood of historic Chambersburg (population about 22,000) in Franklin County. It is located in the scenic Cumberland Valley approximately 1 mile north of downtown Chambersburg on Philadelphia Avenue (State Route 11) and is easily accessible from Interstate 81 and U.S. Route 30. Wilson College sits approximately 50 miles southwest of Harrisburg, Pennsylvania, and 95 miles northwest of Washington, D.C., and Baltimore, Maryland.

Majors and Degrees

Wilson offers programs leading to the Bachelor of Arts or Bachelor of Science degree. Majors are available in the following fields: accounting, behavioral sciences (psychology and sociology), biology, business and economics (economics, international business, management, management information systems, and marketing), chemistry, education (elementary and secondary), English, environmental studies (ecological perspectives, natural and sustainable systems, and social systems), equestrian studies (equestrian management and equine management), equine facilitated therapeutics, exercise and sport science, fine arts (art history and studio art), French, history and political science (history, international relations, and political science), international studies, mass communications, mathematics, philosophy and religion studies, psychobiology, Spanish, and veterinary medical technology.

Preprofessional programs include health studies, law, medicine, and veterinary medicine.

Minors are available in archaeology, art history, athletic coaching, biology, business, chemistry, computer science, dance, economics, English, entrepreneurship and small business management, environmental studies, film studies, French, German, historic preservation, history, international studies, Latin, management information systems, mass communications, mathematics, music, peace and conflict studies, philosophy, philosophy and religion, political science, psychology, social ethics, sociology, Spanish, studio art, and women's studies.

Academic Programs

The Bachelor of Arts and the Bachelor of Science degrees require the successful completion of a minimum of thirty-six courses, at least eighteen of which must be outside any single discipline. All students follow a liberal studies curriculum that includes a first-year seminar; foundational courses in writing, foreign language, computer studies, quantitative skills, and physical activity and wellness; and transdisciplinary studies courses in art and literature, environmental studies, multicultural studies, natural science, and women's studies. Students have the opportunity to pursue specialized interests through independent studies, advanced study or research, and internships in professional settings.

The Wilson College calendar includes two semesters and the January term. First-semester final examinations come before the winter vacation. The January term is often used for internships, independent studies, field experiences, special courses, and travel.

Off-Campus Programs

Opportunities for off-campus study, including study-abroad and other special programs, are available to qualified students. In addition, internships, independent studies, and other field experiences may be arranged off campus for the summer, for regular semesters, or for the January term.

Academic Facilities

Wilson's library has a Web-based online catalog for accessing its collection as well as several electronic databases for locating articles. In addition, students have access to the resources of libraries worldwide through the interlibrary loan service. Academic facilities include student research laboratories, veterinary medical technology laboratories, X-ray and surgical facilities, an electron microscope, a nuclear magnetic resonance spectrometer, computer facilities, a learning resource center, an equestrian center, and a unique Center for Environmental Education and Sustainable Living. Personal computers are available to students in residence halls, academic buildings, and the library. The fine arts department houses a gallery and individual studios for painting and graphics as well as an art annex with ceramics, sculpture, and printmaking facilities. The Hankey Center, which houses the C. Elizabeth Boyd '33 Archives and the Barron Blewett Hunnicutt Classics Gallery, allows students the opportunity to conduct research.

Costs

The cost for a full-time student in residence at Wilson College in 2003–04 was $23,912, including $16,466 for tuition, $6996 for room and board, and $450 for fees. All costs and fees are subject to change.

Financial Aid

Approximately 90 percent of the students at Wilson benefit from a strong financial aid program that provides assistance through a combination of grants, loans, and student employment. Awards are based on financial need, which is determined from information provided through the Free Application for Federal Student Aid (FAFSA) form. A brochure describing the financial aid program is available from the Financial Aid Office.

Merit scholarships are awarded to incoming freshmen and transfer students. The Curran Scholarships are awarded on a competitive basis to incoming students with a record of community service. Recipients must be enrolled full-time, i.e., at least four courses per semester. These scholarships are renewable. The College awards more than $3 million from institutional funds.

Faculty

The faculty at Wilson is organized into three divisions: Humanities, Sciences, and Social Sciences. This structure facilitates communication among the disciplines and encourages the development of interdisciplinary courses. There are 37 full-time and 53 part-time faculty members. Of the full-time faculty members, 89 percent have doctorates or other terminal degrees in their fields; 51 percent are women. The student-faculty ratio of 10:1 allows for small classes and close working relationships. Primarily concerned with their role as teachers, Wilson's faculty members are responsive to students' needs and interests, while pursuing their own interests in research, publishing, or artistic achievement.

Student Government

Every student at Wilson is a member of the Wilson College Government Association. Senators chosen from each residence hall represent their constituents in all areas of College government. Students also serve on faculty committees and on committees of the Board of Trustees.

Admission Requirements

Wilson admits students of any race, color, religion, national or ethnic origin, or geographical location. An applicant's secondary program should include 4 years of English, 4 years of social studies, 3 years of mathematics, 2 years of lab science, and 2 years of a foreign language. The Admissions Committee also carefully considers applicants whose credentials vary from this pattern. In addition, early admission is available to well-qualified students who wish to enter college after three years of secondary school. Home-schooled students are encouraged to apply. Neither the number of applications from a single school or region nor the need for financial aid is considered in the admission process.

The Admissions Committee reviews an application after receiving all required documents. These include the candidate's application, an essay, an official secondary school transcript, a counselor or teacher recommendation, and SAT I or ACT scores. Transfer students must also submit all official college transcripts. International students from non-English-speaking countries are required to submit results from the TOEFL.

Application and Information

Applications are accepted for both the fall and spring semesters. Wilson College uses a rolling admission plan, which enables the Admissions Committee to act upon a candidate's application as soon as possible after it is completed. Although there are no deadlines for application, candidates are encouraged to apply as early as possible. Students may also apply online.

For further information and application forms, students should contact:

Kathleen H. Berard
Vice President and Dean of Enrollment
Wilson College
1015 Philadelphia Avenue
Chambersburg, Pennsylvania 17201-1285
Telephone: 717-262-2002
800-421-8402 (toll-free)
E-mail: admissions@wilson.edu
World Wide Web: http://www.wilson.edu

Students enjoy the nice weather during a class held outdoors.

WINGATE UNIVERSITY

WINGATE, NORTH CAROLINA

The University

Wingate University was founded in 1896 and offers an excellent educational experience in a traditional environment. Students are respected, and there is concern for the individual. Wingate enrolls both resident and commuting students, and students come from more than thirty states and fifteen other countries. There are more than 1,400 men and women currently enrolled and 92 percent of the students live on campus. There are several traditional residence halls for freshmen students. Most upperclass students reside in fully furnished on-campus student apartments with private bedrooms, built-in washers and dryers, a living room, an eating area, and full kitchens, including microwave ovens.

Social life at Wingate University includes a full schedule of activities planned by the Student Government Association (SGA) and the Activities Program Board of the Dickson-Palmer Student Center. There are more than thirty-five clubs on campus, including the Christian Student Union. An active Greek system includes four national fraternities and two national sororities. For men, Wingate University participates in NCAA Division II intercollegiate baseball, basketball, cross-country, football, golf, lacrosse, soccer, and tennis. For women, NCAA Division II intercollegiate basketball, cross-country, golf, soccer, softball, swimming, tennis, and volleyball are available. An active year-round intramural program is also carried on at Wingate. The Cannon Athletic Complex houses a basketball arena, an Olympic-size indoor pool, racquetball courts, and physical fitness facilities, including a second full-size gym.

Austin Memorial Auditorium seats 1,100 and serves as a cultural center for the University and the area. Each year, the University Lyceum Series brings outstanding programs to the campus. The Dickson-Palmer Student Center houses the campus store, game rooms, a lounge, a fitness center, the Klondike Grill, the campus post office, a social hall, facilities for student organizations, and other multipurpose rooms. A clubhouse, a student health center, an outdoor pool, and a sand volleyball court were recently added. An $8.3-million Fine Arts Center and a $3.5-million football stadium and field house were dedicated and used for the first time during the 2000–01 academic year.

Wingate University is affiliated with the Baptist State Convention of North Carolina and is accredited by the Southern Association of Colleges and Schools, NCATE, the North Carolina Department of Public Instruction, the Association of Collegiate Business Schools and Programs (ACBSP), and the Commission on Accreditation of Allied Health Education Programs (CAAHEP).

The School of Education and the School of Business and Economics offer master's degrees, and the new School of Pharmacy awards the Pharm.D. degree.

Location

Wingate's beautiful 390-acre campus is nestled halfway between the North Carolina mountains and seashore. Wingate's location offers unlimited opportunities for students. Wingate University is in Wingate, North Carolina, 4 miles from Monroe (population 25,000) and just 25 miles east of Metropolitan Charlotte, one of the most vibrant cities in the U.S. Many venues, including Ovens Auditorium, Blumenthal Arts Center, Carolina Panthers Stadium (Ericsson Stadium), Verizon Wireless Amphitheater, Lowes Motor Speedway, Independence Arena, and the Charlotte Coliseum, sites of cultural and sports events, are accessible in 45 minutes or less. The Charlotte/Douglas International Airport provides easy access to the Wingate campus.

Majors and Degrees

Wingate University offers five undergraduate degrees: Bachelor of Arts, Bachelor of Science, Bachelor of Music Education, Bachelor of Fine Arts, and Bachelor of Liberal Studies. Majors are offered in accounting; American studies; art, with concentrations in computer graphics and 2-D and 3-D studio art; athletic training/sports medicine; biology; business administration; business mathematics; chemistry; chemistry business; communication studies, with concentrations in broadcast journalism, media arts, organizational communications, public relations, and speech; education, with concentrations in art (K–12), elementary (K–6), middle grades (6–9), music (K–12), physical education (K–12), reading (K–12), and secondary (9–12 in biology/chemistry, English, history, and mathematics); English; environmental biology; finance; general studies; history; human services; management; marketing; mathematics, with a concentration in computer science; music, with concentrations in business, communications, and performance; parks and recreation administration; philosophy; religious studies; sociology; Spanish; and sport management. Preprofessional programs are offered in dentistry, law, medicine, ministerial, pharmacy, and veterinary medicine.

Academic Program

All students complete core education courses in the humanities, the fine arts, foreign language, mathematics, the sciences, and the social sciences. Students then choose from a variety of majors—planned programs of study. In addition, they may select a concentration (minimum requirement of 18 hours) from one of thirty-two academic areas. Concentrations are optional in all programs except intermediate education, which has a built-in requirement. Almost all programs offer a component of independent study if a student desires it.

Wingate has an honors program for its most qualified students.

All students are given the opportunity to receive credit through International Baccalaureate, Advanced Placement, the College-Level Examination Program (CLEP), or departmental examinations.

The Wingate 101 course helps freshmen successfully adjust to the challenges of college life and explore career opportunities, academic concerns, and social issues. The course is taught by the student's faculty adviser with the assistance of student peer advisers.

Summer research grants provide stipends for teams of top students and faculty members to study a broad range of topics each summer.

Other important aspects of the University's overall program are academic advising, career planning, and placement services. The liberal arts emphasis at Wingate is ensured through the Lyceum Events Series. Students attend forty of these events (which include arts, religious, political, dramatic, musical, literary, and other entertaining and cultural events) during their four years at Wingate.

Wingate's calendar year includes a fall semester, a spring semester, and two 4-week summer sessions.

Off-Campus Programs

More than 25 years ago, Wingate pioneered an annual program of international study called W'International. This program offers all qualifying juniors an international study experience at virtually no cost above regular tuition and fees. Students who complete both the W'International seminar and the travel component with a Wingate University professor receive 2 hours of credit. In addition, a semester-long international program in

London allows students to live in London and complete a full semester's work there under the tutelage of Wingate professors. Wingate also offers full semester programs in Hong Kong and Copenhagen.

More than 60 percent of Wingate graduates have studied abroad at least once during their four years at Wingate.

Academic Facilities

The Ethel K. Smith Library is the heart of academic life on campus. The large air-conditioned building, enlarged and remodeled in 1992, is equipped with study tables and carrels and has more than 110,000 volumes, 500 periodicals, 300,000 titles on microfiche and CD-ROM, and a special collection of children's literature. Wingate was the first independent college in North Carolina to install the Integrated On-line Catalog and Circulation System, which greatly assists students' research projects. The library recently added twenty-five new Pentium PC terminals and several high-speed printers, which provide students with access to the Internet and the World Wide Web, as well as virtual library access to more than 2,000 full-text online journals and 6,000 indexes.

The Academic Resources Center, which opened in 1992, houses all campus tutorial programs and student support services, including LSAT and GRE review programs.

The $8.3-million George A. Batte, Jr. Fine Arts Center houses a 550-seat theater, a 175-seat recital hall, a secure art gallery, music practice rooms, music classrooms, and performance areas.

The Computing Center directs both the administrative and academic systems for the whole campus. In addition, microcomputer labs are available for student use in several campus locations. All PCs in the computer labs provide direct access to the library's online system and to the Internet. These facilities are open long hours to accommodate student needs.

Costs

The basic charge for tuition and general fees in 2004–05 is $16,020. Room and board fees are $6250. The total cost for 2004–05 is $22,250. There is no additional charge for out-of-state residents.

Financial Aid

Approximately 85 percent of the students at Wingate University receive financial aid. Students must apply each year by filing the Free Application for Federal Student Aid. Students are expected to file by April 15.

Wingate offers generous merit-based academic, athletic, and music scholarships to excellent students who qualify. There are also scholarships for transfer students. Additional aid for students comes from Federal Pell Grants, Federal Supplemental Educational Opportunity Grants, North Carolina Contract Grants, and North Carolina Student Incentive Grants. Federal Stafford Student Loans are available, if needed. Most aid packages are renewable each undergraduate year, assuming students' family circumstances remain about the same. A convenient monthly payment plan is also available. Jobs in the library, the student center, the cafeteria, and other areas are available; earnings are paid directly to the students.

Faculty

The University has 86 full-time faculty members. More than 90 percent of these hold earned doctorates or terminal degrees. Faculty emphasis is on teaching, and the majority of the faculty members serve as academic advisers. The average class size is 20 students, and all classes are taught by professors, not by graduate assistants. Student-faculty dialogue is encouraged, and the student-faculty ratio is kept low (less than 13:1) to stimulate interaction between the two groups. Summer research grants provide an opportunity for faculty members and students to collaborate on independent research in their fields of interest.

Student Government

Students are actively involved in institutional government. Student Government Association members are elected in campuswide elections, and the SGA has authority in matters relating to student discipline and the campus honor code. Campus rules reflect North Carolina laws and the Christian heritage of Wingate University. Student government also plays an active role in planning campus activities. Students serve as voting members of each University Assembly committee that deals directly with student life.

Admission Requirements

Freshman applicants should be qualified graduates of an accredited high school. Freshman applicants are considered on the basis of class rank, high school average, curriculum, and test scores (SAT I or ACT).

Transfer students are encouraged to apply. To qualify for admission, they must be academically eligible to return to their previous institution, have a minimum 2.0 GPA, and must provide official transcripts of all previous work.

Campus interviews are strongly encouraged but not required.

Application and Information

When students are applying for admission, the following must be sent in and must be complete: the application and $25 processing fee, transcripts of all work attempted, SAT I or ACT scores, and two letters of recommendation. Applications for freshman admission should be sent in as soon as possible during the senior year of high school. Wingate uses a rolling admission policy. In most cases, students are notified of the admission decision within two weeks after their application file has been completed. Wingate University is operated on a nondiscriminatory basis. Online applications are available on the Wingate Web site (see below).

Application materials should be sent to:

Wingate University Admissions Office
Campus Box 3059
Wingate University
Wingate, North Carolina 28174

Telephone: 704-233-8200
800-755-5550 (toll-free)
Fax: 704-233-8110
E-mail: admit@wingate.edu
World Wide Web: http://www.wingate.edu

The Stegall Administration Building at Wingate University.

WINTHROP UNIVERSITY

ROCK HILL, SOUTH CAROLINA

The University

Founded in 1886, Winthrop University has become a national-caliber university with regional prominence in the Southeast. Winthrop has achieved its present reputation for overall excellence by working consistently to be market-wise, values-centered, and vision-driven. Winthrop's achievements have been recognized by *U.S. News & World Report,* which ranks the school as a top ten southern regional public university and was listed among the best Southeastern public universities in the *Princeton Review.*

The University's distinctive mission is to offer challenging academic programs to a high-achieving, culturally diverse, socially responsible student body. More than 6,500 students, representing forty-two states and thirty-nine countries, pursue degrees in the school's four academic divisions—arts and sciences, business administration, education, and visual and performing arts, all of which are supported by Winthrop newest academic division, University College. The University offers eighty-two undergraduate and forty-nine graduate degrees and options.

The University features 100 percent national accreditation of all eligible academic programs. Such accreditations have enabled Winthrop to join an elite group of universities and colleges nationwide with accreditations by the National Associations of Schools of Art and Design, Dance, Music, and Theatre, establishing the University as a regional center for the arts.

Some of the most significant educational experiences at Winthrop occur outside the classroom as students actively participate in the life of the campus. More than 100 campus organizations offer outlets for special interests or talents and provide opportunities to hone leadership skills and build confidence and interpersonal skills. In addition, students enjoy recreational sports and NCAA Division I intercollegiate competition in men's and women's basketball, cross-country, golf, indoor and outdoor track, soccer, and tennis; women's softball and volleyball; and men's baseball.

Winthrop's students also benefit from the nationally recognized Dinkins Student Union (DSU), the University's activities board. DSU schedules a broad array of fun and interesting entertainment, including bands, comedians, lecturers, and novelty acts for student enjoyment.

Upon graduation, Winthrop students successfully continue their education in prestigious graduate and professional programs or enter a wide variety of positions in the arts, business, education, medicine, government, law, or other professions.

Location

Winthrop's beautiful, tree-lined campus is included on the National Register of Historic Places. The 100-acre central campus, complemented by a 325-acre athletics and recreational area, including a lake and coliseum, provides an ideal collegiate setting. Winthrop's location in Rock Hill, South Carolina, offers the friendly atmosphere of a college town with attractions such as professional sports and entertainment only 20 minutes away in Charlotte, North Carolina.

Majors and Degrees

At the undergraduate level, the University offers academic programs leading to the Bachelor of Arts, the Bachelor of Fine Arts, the Bachelor of Music, the Bachelor of Music Education, the Bachelor of Science, and the Bachelor of Social Work.

Majors that lead to the B.A. include art, art history, dance, English, environmental studies, general communication disorders, history, integrated marketing communication, mass communication (broadcast and journalism), mathematics, modern languages (French and Spanish), music, philosophy and religion, political science, psychology, public policy and administration, sociology: criminology, and theater (design/technical and performance).

The B.F.A. in art is offered with the following concentrations: ceramics, general studio, interior design, painting, photography (commercial and fine art), printmaking, sculpture (jewelry and metals), and visual communication design (graphic design and illustration). The Bachelor of Music in performance and the Bachelor of Music Education, with options in choral and instrumental music, are also offered.

Majors leading to the B.S. include biology (medical technology); business administration, with options in accounting, computer information systems, economics, entrepreneurship, finance, general business, health services management, international business, management, and marketing; chemistry; computer science; early childhood education; economics; elementary education; environmental sciences; family and consumer sciences; human nutrition (dietetics, food systems management, and nutrition science); integrated marketing communication; mathematics (statistics); middle-level education; physical education (fitness/wellness); science communication; special education (mild disabilities and severe disabilities); and sport management.

Teacher training programs leading to state certification are available in the fields of art, biology, dance, early childhood education, elementary education, English, history, mathematics, middle-level education, modern languages, music, physical education, political science, sociology, special education, and theater.

Academic Programs

The University is accredited by the Commission on Colleges of the Southern Association of Colleges and Schools (1866 Southern Lane, Decatur, Georgia 30033-4097; telephone: 404-697-4501) to award bachelor's, master's, and specialist degrees. Additional national accreditation of individual programs sets the University apart from its peers and assures Winthrop students of a top-notch curriculum taught by qualified faculty members using the best available resources.

A strong liberal arts core provides the foundation for Winthrop's undergraduate and graduate degree programs offered in the four academic divisions: the Colleges of Arts and Sciences, Business Administration, Education, and Visual and Performing Arts. A minimum of 124 credits is required for a baccalaureate degree, with a specified number of general education, major-specific, and elective hours for each degree.

Special student programs include the Honors Program; Academy 101 for freshmen; cooperative education and internships; New Start for adult learners; Leadership Winthrop; the Close Scholars Program; and Peer Mentoring, a first-year support program.

Off-Campus Programs

Winthrop students have experienced the excitement of studying abroad at a number of institutions in countries including Australia, Austria, China, Costa Rica, Egypt, England, France, Germany, Italy, Russia, Spain, and Sweden. In addition, Winthrop also participates in the National Student Exchange Program, which allows Winthrop students, paying Winthrop's tuition, to study for up to one year at one of more than 100 colleges and universities throughout the United States.

Academic Facilities

The faculty members and collections of the Dacus Library are an integral part of the University's instructional program. The Dacus Online Catalog system provides easy access to the library's collections. The library's holdings total more than 580,000 volumes and volume-equivalents, which are supplemented by resources available through the national interlibrary loan program.

Winthrop's academic computing department supports the instructional and research functions of the University. Students have access to diverse computing resources, including more than twenty-five computer laboratories that provide PC or Macintosh systems for open-access and instructional needs. All computer labs support Microsoft Windows 2000 professional standards. All campus buildings and residence halls are connected to the campus network and the Internet. Students are provided with consolidated computing services, including Web-based e-mail, central server storage space, and personal Web pages. The Academic Computing Center also provides computer access and Braille printing services to visually impaired students.

The Writing Center, Math Lab, and Language Lab facilities assist students who want to improve skills in specific areas. Multimedia classrooms and distance-learning facilities provide an added dimension to classroom instruction.

The University also maintains several versatile performing spaces. Byrnes Auditorium, which seats 3,500; the recently renovated 216-seat Frances May Barnes Recital Hall; and Tillman Auditorium, with a capacity of 700, are excellent facilities that are widely used for a variety of activities by the Winthrop community. In addition, Johnson Hall, which includes a 331-seat proscenium theater, a 100-seat studio theater, an actors' studio, and two dance studios, provides a comfortable home for the Department of Theatre and Dance. Johnson also houses the Department of Mass Communication and is equipped with broadcast facilities, including a student-operated radio station; editing booths; and equipment for its broadcasting and journalism students. Winthrop Galleries, in the Rutledge Building, include two professional exhibition spaces, and a student gallery in McLaurin provides space for art design students to show their work.

Costs

For 2003–04, the annual tuition cost for full-time South Carolina residents was $6652. Out-of-state tuition was $12,258. Room and board costs for all students for a double-occupancy room and a meal plan of unlimited meals was approximately $4600.

Financial Aid

At Winthrop, 65 percent of all students receive some form of financial assistance. The University offers a variety of scholarships to high-achieving freshmen with strong high school records and SAT or ACT scores. The scholarships range from $500 to full tuition and meals. The completed admissions application also serves as the application for academic scholarships. Additional scholarships are available to talented students in the visual and performing arts as well as in all of Winthrop's seventeen intercollegiate sports. Winthrop's financial aid packages, which are processed in the Office of Financial Aid, can include grants, loans, or student employment. Students should complete the Free Application for Federal Student Aid (FAFSA) and the Winthrop institutional aid form as soon as possible after January 1 of their senior year. Families often take advantage of the Winthrop Payment Plan, which divides each semester's costs into four convenient payments. For more information, students should contact the Office of Financial Aid at 803-323-2189 or by e-mail at wufrc@winthrop.edu.

Faculty

Effective, high-quality teaching is the number one priority of Winthrop's faculty members, who include renowned scholars, researchers, and creative artists. All classes are taught by faculty members, and class size typically ranges from 18 to 27 students, fostering close personal contact between student and teacher. Of the 264 full-time faculty members, 81 percent hold the highest degree in their field. With a student-faculty ratio of 15:1, Winthrop faculty members are able to take a personal interest in the individual needs and development of every student.

Student Government

The Council of Student Leaders is a representative body of Winthrop student leaders and other concerned students. It serves as a vehicle that provides students a significant role in institutional decision making and self-governance. Some of the council's purposes are to serve as the official student voice, to charter campus organizations, to distribute student activity funds to those organizations, and to promote campuswide events. The chair of the council serves as the student representative to the Winthrop University Board of Trustees.

Admission Requirements

Winthrop carefully reviews each applicant on an individual basis and the admissions process is designed to determine the right match between high-achieving students and the distinctive educational opportunities offered by Winthrop. Freshman applications are evaluated primarily by using high school performance, including class rank; level of course work; completion of high school prerequisites; standardized test scores (SAT or ACT); and guidance counselor recommendation. Other criteria, including letters of recommendation, essay or personal statement, and extracurricular activities, will be considered if presented.

Transfer applicants who have completed 30 semester hours/45 quarter hours or more of course work at an institution that is accredited by the commission on colleges of a regional accrediting agency must present a cumulative grade point ratio of at least 2.0 on a 4.0 scale. Applicants with fewer than 30 semester hours/45 quarter hours are additionally evaluated on their high school academic record and standardized test scores. Applicants who have been out of high school for five or more years are not required to submit standardized test scores.

Application and Information

The following admission credentials should be submitted by applicants: a completed application for admission, the $40 application fee, an official high school transcript or graduate equivalency diploma, and official results of the SAT I or ACT. Transfer applicants must submit transcripts from all colleges previously attended. Application deadlines are May 1 for fall enrollment and January 1 for spring enrollment. Applications are reviewed on a rolling basis. To be considered for academic scholarships, students should submit their completed admissions application by January 15.

For more information, students should contact:

Office of Admissions
Winthrop University
Rock Hill, South Carolina 29733
Telephone: 803-323-2191
800-763-0230 (toll-free)
E-mail: admissions@winthrop.edu
World Wide Web: http://www.winthrop.edu

The engraved sign at Winthrop's main entrance welcomes residents and visitors to the 108-year-old campus. In the background is Byrnes Auditorium, the site of Convocation and many other University events.

WITTENBERG UNIVERSITY

SPRINGFIELD, OHIO

The University

Wittenberg University is a four-year comprehensive liberal arts and sciences university. Founded in 1845, it is affiliated with the Evangelical Lutheran Church in America, a connection that helps the University preserve its commitment to producing graduates who have considered their own personal values and take an active interest in the health of their communities.

Wittenberg University strives to educate students by developing in harmony the intellectual, spiritual, aesthetic, social, and physical qualities that characterize broadly capable and effective teachers. Wittenberg's primary purpose is to provide a close, supportive, caring learning environment and a teaching faculty of superior-quality people committed to liberal arts education and designed to impart knowledge, inspire inquiry, and encourage independent thought.

Wittenberg is distinguished by its strong interdisciplinary programs such as East Asian studies and Russian area studies. Although Wittenberg's traditional strengths have been in the liberal arts, the sciences, management, and education have also developed into popular majors for students. One in four students choose a science major that is designed to emphasize collaborative problem solving among students and collaborative research among students and faculty members. Wittenberg is one of only a handful of colleges in the country to include community service as a graduation requirement. Also, Phi Beta Kappa is one of the many academic honoraries to grace the campus.

The University is accredited by the Higher Learning Commission of the North Central Association of Colleges and Schools and by the American Association of University Women.

Of Wittenberg's 2,200 students, 60 percent come from Ohio. Wittenberg hosts approximately 30–40 new international students each year from twenty to thirty countries. Deliberate efforts to maintain cultural, ethnic, social, and economic diversity avoid the homogeneity of many small private colleges. Wittenberg has a nonwhite population of at least 15 percent; it strives to have a student population that reflects the broader society.

Wittenberg's residential program is based on a philosophy of progressive responsibility. First- and second-year students reside in the residence halls. After the second year, students have the opportunity to live in Greek housing or one of the many University-owned rental units in the University district and other theme housing. The award-winning food service catered by Marriott serves food in the Central Dining Room, a cafeteria-style eatery, and the Commons, a deli-style eatery.

Location

Wittenberg's 100-acre parklike campus is as functional as it is attractive, with beautiful rolling hills, lush green spaces, and many trees. Its twenty-seven buildings include outstanding facilities for the sciences, arts, and music, as well as comfortable residence halls and excellent recreational and athletics facilities. The school is located in Springfield, Ohio, which is a small city with a population of 65,000 that provides easy access to big-city excitement in nearby Columbus and Dayton.

While Wittenberg plays a major role in the lives of Springfield residents, the community also provides much opportunity to the University's students. Wittenberg is a major leader in the community's cultural, academic, and athletic life, yet Wittenberg people see a great benefit to being in Springfield. The community offers an area rich in cultural opportunities and recreational activities, with lakes, public parkland, nature preserves, bike trails, and public golf courses.

Majors and Degrees

Wittenberg offers the degrees of Bachelor of Arts, Bachelor of Fine Arts, Bachelor of Music, Bachelor of Music Education, and Bachelor of Science. Many students increase the power of their degree by double majoring or adding a minor. The Bachelor of Arts degree may be earned in American studies, art, biochemistry/molecular biology, chemistry, communications, computer science, East Asian studies, economics, education (early childhood, elementary, and middle childhood licensing), English, geography, geology, history, languages (French, Spanish, and German), management (with concentrations in accounting, finance, human resources, international business, and marketing), mathematics, music, philosophy, physics, political science, psychology, religion, Russian area studies, sociology, and theater. The Bachelor of Science degree is offered in biology, chemistry, computer science, geology, mathematics, physics, and psychology. Minors may be completed in all the above majors and the following: Africana studies, creative writing, dance, environmental studies, global studies, urban studies, and women's studies.

Special areas of study include forestry and environmental studies, international education, languages (Chinese, Japanese, and Russian), and marine biology/freshwater ecology. Through one of the comprehensive preprofessional programs, Wittenberg students can prepare for law school, medical school (including dental, optometry, or veterinary school), physical therapy, theology, nursing, or another postgraduate program. Wittenberg also offers 3-2 programs in computer engineering, engineering, environmental studies, nursing, and occupational therapy. Advanced study during the two years is completed at schools such as Case Western Reserve, Columbia, Duke, Georgia Tech, and Washington (St. Louis).

Academic Programs

Wittenberg graduates are critical thinkers who are equipped for a lifetime of success in a changing world. A Wittenberg education exposes students to a broad range of ideas and inquiries, from scientific investigations to philosophical explorations. Developing excellent communication, writing, and critical-thinking skills, as well as engaging diverse subjects, improves students as scholars and people.

Wittenberg students must complete a course of study in two broad categories—comprehensive education in the liberal arts and sciences and a major program of study. Each of these categories makes up one third of the total credits required for graduation. To make up the remaining one third of the credits, students may choose either elective courses from across the curriculum or courses required for a minor within one or more particular areas. The comprehensive program is based upon general education learning goals. These goals reflect Wittenberg's emphasis on teaching and student learning.

All candidates for the Bachelor of Arts, Music, Science, and Fine

Arts degrees must complete 130 semester hours of credit. Generally, a major consists of 32 to 42 semester hours of credit, and a minor consists of 20 to 22 semester hours of credit.

Off-Campus Programs

Every year, around 100 students from Wittenberg study abroad in more than twenty countries. Some programs last for only a few weeks during semester break or take place over the summer for one to two months; other programs last for a semester or an entire academic year. In addition, some students choose to study off campus with cooperative programs in such places as Washington, D.C., and Duke University.

Academic Facilities

Wittenberg's twenty-seven buildings combine the best of tradition (Myers Hall and Recitation Hall are on the National Register of Historic Places) and the best of tomorrow. Hollenbeck Hall, a state-of-the-art academic building, opened in 2000, and the new Barbara C. Kuss Science Center is expected to open soon. The new science center is to be equipped with the newest technology in the laboratories and classrooms. The Wittenberg Department of Music is housed in Krieg Hall, a spacious structure specially designed to provide state-of-the-art instruction in music. The Music Building houses a sixteen-unit electronic keyboard laboratory that students use for advanced music composition.

All of the residence halls have computer labs open to the residents around the clock. In Hollenbeck Hall, the computer lab is open 24 hours a day. Departmental labs set their own hours, and the computer lab in the Thomas Library is available during open hours. A fiber-optic network connects classroom and administration buildings, the library, and residence halls. All students are given a network account and an e-mail account. Thomas Library has 367,000 volumes and access to millions more through a statewide electronic library catalog, OhioLINK.

Costs

Total annual charges for the 2004–05 academic year are $32,726. This amount includes tuition ($26,040), room ($3454), and board ($3232). Estimated costs for books, travel, miscellaneous expenses, and entertainment are $1800 for in-state students. Wittenberg estimates a total of $2800 for out-of-state students to account for additional travel expenses.

Financial Aid

Two features that keep Wittenberg affordable for many families are that more than 80 percent of Wittenberg students receive nearly $24 million each year in scholarships and financial assistance and that Wittenberg's four-year graduation guarantee states that with proper planning, students should be able to graduate in four years rather than the five- to six-year average of many universities. Students are not charged additional tuition or fees if they have met minimum criteria. Financial aid packages are made up of scholarships, grants, loans, and employment on campus. In order to be considered for financial aid, students must complete the Free Application for Federal Student Aid (FAFSA). Academic and talent-based scholarships are available from $500 per year to full tuition regardless of financial need.

Faculty

Wittenberg faculty members are outstanding classroom instructors, true mentors who consider students their top priority and have a genuine interest in teaching undergraduates. Many of the faculty members are renowned experts in their fields. Robert P. Welker, an education professor, was named Ohio Professor of the Year in 2001. He is the fourth professor from Wittenberg in fifteen years to win this prestigious award. Ninety-seven percent of the faculty members have the highest degree in their field; full-time faculty members number 156, and part-time faculty members number 67. The faculty-student ratio is 1:13, which allows for the average class size of 19 students.

Student Government

The student government for the undergraduate student body is the Student Senate. The Student Senate operates primarily as a legislative body. The senate is elected/selected each spring. Through its committees this body addresses each aspect of student life.

Admission Requirements

Admission to Wittenberg is selective and is based on the following information: high school record, including the strength of the high school and its curriculum and trends in the student's academic work; SAT or ACT scores; cocurricular activities and community participation; recommendations; and an essay. International students and transfer students are encouraged to apply. An on-campus interview is not required but is highly recommended. Students may apply using the regular application or online at the Web site address listed below.

Application and Information

The deadlines for applying are as follows for incoming freshmen: early decision is November 15, early action I is December 1, early action II is January 15, and regular action is March 15. Students must apply by February 15 to be considered for merit-based scholarships. Transfer student application deadlines are December 1 for the spring semester and July 1 for the fall semester. The international student application deadline is March 15. More information may be obtained by contacting:

Office of Admission
Wittenberg University
Ward Street at North Wittenberg Avenue
Post Office Box 720
Springfield, Ohio 45501-0720
Telephone: 937-327-6314
800-677-7558 (toll-free)
E-mail: admission@wittenberg.edu
World Wide Web: http://www.wittenberg.edu

On the campus of Wittenberg University.

WOODBURY UNIVERSITY

BURBANK, CALIFORNIA

The University

Woodbury University offers students practical, applied education; high academic standards; and small classes. The University is an accredited, independent, nonprofit, coeducational, nonsectarian institution.

Students attend Woodbury because of its specialization in the areas of architecture, business, computers, professional design, and arts and sciences. Also offered is a Master of Business Administration program. The carefully designed curricula at Woodbury give students hands-on experience in their majors in addition to an effective general education. Woodbury maintains small classes to ensure individual student attention.

The University presents a variety of opportunities for all students to join cultural, social, and professional organizations, both on and off campus. The Office of Student Services at Woodbury helps meet students' needs through career planning and job placement workshops; educational, cultural, social, and recreational programs; the sponsorship of various student groups; and special services for international students. The career services office provides Woodbury students and alumni with lifetime employment assistance.

Woodbury's 22-acre campus in Burbank provides students with such on-campus amenities as a swimming pool, gymnasium, residence halls, an athletic field, and food services, all situated on beautifully landscaped grounds.

Founded in 1884, Woodbury's primary mission is to provide the highest level of professional education in its undergraduate and graduate programs. The goal is to prepare graduates who are articulate, ethical, and innovative lifelong learners. The University is accredited by the Senior Commission of the Western Association of Schools and Colleges and is approved by the Postsecondary Commission, California Department of Education. The Interior Design Program is accredited by the Foundation for Interior Design Education Research. The Architecture Program is accredited by the National Architectural Accrediting Board. The School of Business is accredited by the Association of Collegiate Business Schools and Programs.

Location

The Los Angeles metropolitan area serves not only as a business, financial, and design center but also as one of the great shipping centers of the world. The University is closely linked to these resources and commercial communities, which provide students with a firsthand laboratory in which to study the professional positions they have set as their goals.

The campus location offers students beaches, mountains, and deserts within a 90-minute drive. Art, history, and science museums; professional sporting events; and world-class entertainment are local attractions students can enjoy.

Majors and Degrees

The Bachelor of Science degree is offered in accounting, business and management, communication, computer information systems, fashion marketing, history and politics, interdisciplinary studies, management, marketing, and psychology. The Bachelor of Fine Arts degree is offered in animation arts, fashion design, and graphic design. In addition, the Bachelor of Architecture and Bachelor of Interior Architecture degrees are offered.

Academic Program

The academic programs at Woodbury are designed to provide students with the higher education necessary for success and leadership in their chosen fields. The principal emphasis is on relevance of subject matter and personalized instruction, complemented by a strong focus on general education. The academic calendar is based on the semester system. The number of elective units varies depending on the major.

To encourage the achievement of academic excellence, Woodbury University recognizes students who demonstrate the initiative and sense of responsibility to excel. Such superior performance is recognized with special awards.

Academic Facilities

The University library houses a collection of books, magazines, technical reports, trade journals, and reading materials carefully selected to meet fully the curricular needs of students. Microfilm reader-printers, film printers, and copying machines are available, as are special library services, including reference materials on line and on CD-ROM.

Special design facilities provide for the needs of students majoring in animation arts, architecture, fashion design, graphic design, and interior design. Included are darkrooms, design studios, a critique and presentation area, and display areas.

Computer facilities include IBM PC compatibles with Internet access, Macintoshes, and a terminal lab for student access to two Digital VAX 4200 systems. The facility includes classrooms and laboratories with terminals and printers exclusively for student use.

Costs

Tuition for full-time study (two semesters) for 2003–04 was $20,070 for the Bachelor of Science program and $21,122 for the Bachelor of Architecture program. The cost of room and board (eight to ten meals per week) was $7183 for 2003–04. Estimated expenses for a year (two semesters) were $1224 for books and supplies, $612 for transportation, and $1872 for personal expenses.

Financial Aid

Assisting students who lack adequate financial resources to attend Woodbury is a primary concern of the University. Various sources of financial aid are available to help meet education costs. Eligible students generally are awarded a financial aid package consisting of a combination of available funds.

Financial aid for eligible U.S. citizens and permanent residents includes Federal Pell Grants, California Grants A and B for California residents, Federal Family Educational Loans, veterans' educational benefits, Federal Supplemental Educational Opportunity Grants, Federal Work-Study awards, Federal Perkins Loans, local scholarships, and Woodbury grants. The University offers financial aid and counseling, as well as part-time employment and full-time placement services. Classes are scheduled to permit students to work part-time, usually in the area of their major interest, so that they may not only meet financial needs but also gain excellent experience.

Faculty

Students benefit from faculty members who are both experts and practitioners in their fields. A student-faculty ratio of 18:1 allows students to work individually with advisers and instructors to structure their course selections, arrange internships, and plan for the future.

Student Government

The student government at Woodbury, known as the Associated Student Government (ASG), represents the entire student body. The ASG consists of 11 undergraduate students who serve as members of the governing board. These students are elected each spring for a year's term. The purpose of the organization is to promote educational advancement, to further intercultural relations, to enhance cooperation among students, and to serve the best interests of the students of Woodbury University.

Admission Requirements

The Admissions Committee evaluates each application on an individual basis. Academic course load and achievement have a significant impact on the admission decision, and interviews are strongly recommended. Each applicant must submit a completed application form and fee or fee waiver, and official transcripts from all schools attended. Each applicant may also submit an optional essay or personal statement and optional academic reference. Students applying to the animation arts major are also required to submit a portfolio. SAT I or ACT scores are required for all freshman applicants and transfer applicants with fewer than 30 semester or 45 quarter units.

Application and Information

Applications are accepted throughout the year for entrance in the fall, spring, and summer terms. Freshman applicants are encouraged to apply before the priority dates, March 1 (for fall admission) and October 1 (for winter admission). The priority application deadline for transfer students is April 15. Students should direct all materials and inquiries to the Office of Admission at the address below.

Office of Admission
Woodbury University
7500 Glenoaks Boulevard
Burbank, California 91510-7846
Telephone: 818-767-0888, ext. 221
800-784-WOOD (toll-free)
E-mail: info@woodbury.edu
World Wide Web: http://www.woodbury.edu

The Woodbury University Los Angeles Times Library.

WORCESTER STATE COLLEGE

WORCESTER, MASSACHUSETTS

The College

Founded in 1874, Worcester State College (WSC) has a long, impressive record of teacher education. Worcester State College has developed into a comprehensive liberal arts institution with more than 3,200 undergraduates and 850 graduate and professional students and a full-time faculty of 168. A wide range of four-year degree programs are offered, as are a number of graduate programs leading to master's degrees. An emphasis on allied health and biotechnology programs leads the College into the twenty-first century. Worcester State's signature program is education, and the College recently embarked on a program to strengthen its leadership in teacher training.

Worcester State College is located on 58 acres on the outskirts of New England's third-largest city and consists of eight major complexes: the Administration Building, the Sullivan Academic Center, the Learning Resource Center, the Ghosh Center for Science and Technology, the Gymnasium, the Student Center, Dowden Hall, and Chandler Village. The Student Center provides cultural, social, and personal growth and opportunities and offers many services and conveniences for students. The center serves as the "hearthstone" of the campus community.

Worcester State College broke ground on a new 348-bed residence hall in May 2003. Located in front of Chandler Village and Dowden Hall, the new residence hall will serve as a focal point for residential life on WSC's upper campus. The six-story structure will provide a spectacular view of the campus below. The three residential halls will be linked by walking paths. The residence hall is scheduled for occupancy beginning in fall 2004.

The College's athletic department provides numerous opportunities for all students to participate in intercollegiate and intramural athletics. Varsity sports for men are baseball, basketball, cross-country, football, golf, hockey, lacrosse, soccer, tennis, and track (indoor and outdoor). Varsity sports for women are basketball, cross-country, field hockey, soccer, softball, tennis, track (indoor and outdoor), and volleyball. Club sports include men's and women's crew. Other extracurricular offerings include numerous clubs and organizations, lectures, films, arts and crafts exhibits, performing artists, dances, and charter travel service. Students operate their own weekly newspaper, TV station (closed-circuit), and daily radio station (WSCW). The College also has its own Web site. Services of the professionally staffed Career Development and Counseling Center are available to students, as is the Academic Success Center. Students also have access to the center's library of information on careers and graduate schools.

Location

Through a shuttle service, students have easy access to Worcester, which is called the "Heart of New England" because of its location at the geographic center of the six-state region. Rich in history, the city has a population of 170,000 and is about 40 miles west of Boston; 45 miles north of Providence, Rhode Island; and 60 miles northeast of Hartford, Connecticut. More than 700,000 people live less than an hour's drive from the city. The Worcester Art Museum is one of the finest in the country. The Higgins Armory Museum has the greatest collection of armor east of the Mississippi. Other cultural benefits are provided by the Worcester Science Center and the American Antiquarian Society. The Worcester Centrum and Convention Center has a seating capacity of 15,500 and hosts a variety of national sports and entertainment events and exhibits. The Worcester Music Festival, an annual event since 1858, attracts nationally and internationally known performers. The city's parks total 1,290 acres, and there are seven city beaches. Boating and fishing are available in Worcester.

Majors and Degrees

Worcester State College confers the Bachelor of Arts, Bachelor of Science, and Bachelor of Science in Education degrees. Majors are offered in biology, biotechnology, business administration, chemistry, communication disorders, communications, community health, computer science, criminal justice, economics, education, English, geography, health education, history, mathematics, natural science, nursing (a four-year program and an upper-division program for RNs), occupational therapy, psychology, sociology, Spanish, and urban studies. Minors are available in art, biology, business administration, chemistry, communication disorders, communications, community health, computer science, economics, English, French, geography, health education, history, mathematics, Middle East studies, music, natural science, philosophy, physics, political science, psychology, sociology, Spanish, theater, and urban studies. Provisional certification programs are offered in early childhood and elementary education, with a minor available in secondary education.

Academic Programs

The academic year is divided into two semesters, the first beginning in early September and ending in late December and the second beginning in mid-January and ending in late May. The College offers a strong futuristic focus in health and biomedical sciences while continuing its traditional commitment to liberal arts and sciences, business, and teacher education. Volunteer internships, which can be undertaken for college credit, are available in business and social service agencies, in biomedical and biotechnology firms, and in government and the media. Internships are available locally as well as in Washington, D.C., and at Disney World.

Off-Campus Programs

Each semester, full-time students at Worcester State may take one course free of charge on a space-available basis at any of the other institutions in the Colleges of Worcester Consortium. Because Worcester State is one of nine state colleges participating in College Academic Program Sharing (CAPS), students may study for a semester or a year at another of the state colleges. Worcester State College has joint admissions agreements with all of the Massachusetts public community colleges.

Full-time students at Worcester State may spend one semester abroad at Worcester College in Worcester, England, or at the University of Puerto Rico in Cayey as part of a student exchange program. In addition, opportunities to study abroad in any one of more than twenty different countries are open to students from any public institution of higher education in Massachusetts under the auspices of the Massachusetts Council for International Education, which is headquartered at the University of Massachusetts Amherst.

Academic Facilities

The Science and Technology Building is a state-of-the-art building designed to house the science and allied health programs. The building contains thirty science, therapy, and computer labs; administrative and faculty offices; conference/seminar rooms; and student discussion areas. Also located in the building are a Speech/Language/Hearing Clinic, a 200-seat multimedia classroom, and an eighty-seat general-use computer lab. The Sullivan Academic Center houses classrooms, administrative and faculty offices, and the Learning Assistance Center, which offers tutoring in several subject areas. The Administration Building houses administrative and faculty offices, classrooms, and psychology laboratories. In addition to its fitness and athletic facilities, the Gymnasium Building includes general classrooms and art studios.

The Learning Resources Center (LRC) houses the library, a comfortable place for study and research, with more than 150,000 volumes and approximately 800 current periodicals. A CD-ROM network electronically provides ready access to several resources. The library is part of a joint effort of fifteen academic, public, and special-collection libraries that share advanced technologies in library and information sciences. In addition, the building houses the Media Center, which provides student access to television, radio, and film production facilities. The LRC also houses a complex of modern telecommunications and electronic learning facilities. Among these are a writing classroom, a math lab, and several labs for use in computer science classes. In addition, a bank of computers is available for general use by members of the campus community. The College supports both PCs and Macintoshes. All labs are networked and are tied to the campus fiber-optic network; this provides students with Internet connections and access to the World Wide Web. Additional computer labs are located in the various academic departments to afford the opportunity to integrate computer technology throughout the curriculum.

The Academic Success Center, located in the Sullivan Academic Center, is dedicated to fostering a healthy academic climate on campus. The Success Center operates the orientation program and is also responsible for academic advising, minority affairs, disability services, and international student services. In addition, the Learning Assistance Center provides individual tutoring services designed to increase student academic effectiveness. The Counseling and Career Service Centers provide services to all students seeking assistance in the areas of personal and career development.

Costs

Tuition for full-time study in 2002–03 was $970 for in-state residents and $7050 for out-of-state students. Yearly fees were $2303 and the cost of books and supplies averaged $650. Annual campus housing costs were $5186 (room and board) for a double room and nineteen meals per week. Apartments and single rooms are available at a higher cost. All costs are subject to change.

Financial Aid

Students at Worcester State College may apply for all forms of federal, state, and institutional grant and loan assistance by submitting prior to March 1 a Free Application for Federal Student Aid (FAFSA) and a Worcester State College Financial Aid Application. In addition to need-based financial aid and academic scholarships, the College also offers a tuition payment plan. Academic scholarships, offered to promising freshmen at the time of their acceptance, are also available to upperclass students who demonstrate scholarly excellence.

Faculty

There are 168 full-time faculty members, of whom almost 64 percent hold earned doctorates. With the student-faculty ratio of 19:1, there is ample opportunity for interaction between students and faculty members. Upon matriculation and declaration of a major, each student is assigned a faculty adviser, who assists him or her in developing an educational program. The major adviser also guides students throughout their years at the College.

Student Government

The Student Government Association (SGA) is the representative body of the undergraduate student population. Its goals include advocacy of student concerns and rights, involvement in academic and administrative policy decisions, and facilitation of communications between administration, faculty members, staff members, and students. Payment of the activity fee entitles any undergraduate student to participate in the Association through selection of representation, involvement in legislative and administrative meetings, seeking of elected office, appointment to institutional committees, and involvement in other activities of the Association. The SGA annually elects a student representative to sit as a voting member of the College's Board of Trustees.

Admission Requirements

The College admits applicants who have demonstrated strong academic ability. Acceptance of high school seniors and those who have graduated within the past two years is determined by the high school transcript, academic units, and a minimum grade point average (GPA) of 3.0. This GPA is recalculated using only college-preparatory course work. Applicants with GPAs below 3.0 may be considered for admission by using a sliding scale that includes the GPA and total SAT I scores. A total SAT I score of 920 is the minimum for applicants in this category. For those students whose primary language is not English, a minimum TOEFL score of 550 on the paper-based test or 213 on the computer-based test is required. Additional standards for admission are a minimum of sixteen college-preparatory courses taken in the following subject areas: English (four), mathematics (three), natural science (three), social science (two), foreign language (two), and elective courses (two) from these same disciplines, as well as computer science, visual/performing arts, and humanities.

Worcester State College also welcomes applications from transfer students. In order to be eligible, students must meet one of the following sets of criteria: 12 or more transferable college credits and a 2.5 college GPA; up to 24 transferable college credits, a 2.0 college GPA, and a high school transcript that meets the admission standards for freshman applicants; or 24 or more transferable college credits and a 2.0 college GPA. Transfer applicants should arrange to have all college transcripts as well as a final high school transcript sent directly to the Admissions Office.

Although admission interviews are not required, applicants are urged to visit the College during scheduled information sessions, campus tours, or to seek information from the offices concerned with academic advising, athletics, financial aid, housing, and student activities. For information on campus tours or open campus events, students should contact the Admission Office.

Application and Information

The application deadline for the January semester is November 15. The application priority deadline for September is June 1. Applications received after this date are reviewed on the basis of vacancies. High school candidates are strongly encouraged to apply after the first marking period of the senior year. Applicants are notified of admission decisions on a rolling basis. Letters of notification are forwarded starting in early November for the spring semester and mid-January for the fall semester.

Candidates to either the occupational therapy or nursing programs must submit their applications by January 15; notifications are forwarded in early March.

International students are strongly encouraged to apply for the September semester with a priority deadline of April 1. Translations from a professional evaluating agency in the United States must be provided for all international transcripts. Candidates must also submit results of the SAT I (or a TOEFL score if English is not the primary language) and an affidavit of financial support.

Application forms may be obtained by contacting:

Alan Kines, Dean of Enrollment Management
Admission Office
Worcester State College
486 Chandler Street
Worcester, Massachusetts 01602
Telephone: 508-929-8040
866-WSC-CALL (toll-free)
Fax: 508-929-8183
E-mail: admissions@worcester.edu
World Wide Web: http://www.worcester.edu

WRIGHT STATE UNIVERSITY

DAYTON, OHIO

The University

Wright State University (WSU) is an easily accessible campus that supports a diverse student body of more than 15,000 students. Wright State offers bachelor's degrees in more than 100 undergraduate majors as well as more than forty graduate and professional degree programs. The University continues to grow and mature as an institution, while striving to maintain an innovative spirit between its faculty members and students and programs and research. Wright State is currently ranked third in research funding among Ohio's thirteen state universities and colleges.

The growing reputation of Wright State has attracted students from throughout Ohio as well as forty-six other states and sixty-nine countries. The creation of additional on-campus housing for students has increased the opportunity for students from across Ohio and other states to attend Wright State. Currently, the University has modern suite-style residence halls and apartments for more than 3,500 students. The majority of new freshmen live on campus. A variety of coeducational living environments, including alcohol- and smoke-free environments, are available. A new honors residence hall was recently opened.

State-of-the-art computer facilities are located in each academic building and the University library. All residence hall rooms have Internet access, and 24-hour computer labs are located in each of the residence halls. Many classrooms have advanced audiovisual equipment, which has increased the use of technology for instructional purposes by faculty members.

Wright State is a comprehensive University in terms of both academic programs and extracurricular activities. There are more than 130 student clubs, organizations, and activities that provide opportunities for students to meet new people, explore different cultures, and gain leadership skills. Recreational facilities are located in the Student Union, the Nutter Center, and the residence halls. Adding excitement and energy to campus life, Wright State's varsity athletics teams compete at the NCAA Division I level through the Horizon League.

Wright State has a particularly active Disability Services program and encourages disabled students to participate in all facets of University life. WSU facilities have been designed to remove architectural barriers and permit more effective and independent use of the facilities. Applicants who require supportive services should arrange for an interview with the Office of Disability Services at least three months prior to enrollment.

Location

The 557-acre main campus, surrounded by a lush biological preserve, is located in a Miami Valley suburban community 12 miles northeast of Dayton, Ohio. The Miami Valley area has a tradition of innovation and is rich in industry and research, including nearby Wright Patterson Air Force Base. The University has convenient highway access and is less than a 2-hour drive from Cincinnati and Columbus. Wright State University Lake Campus is located in Celina, Ohio, approximately 70 miles northwest of Dayton. The Lake Campus is on the shore of beautiful Grand Lake St. Marys.

Majors and Degrees

Fully accredited by the North Central Association of Colleges and Schools, Wright State's main campus grants the Bachelor of Arts, Bachelor of Fine Arts, Bachelor of Music, Bachelor of Science, Bachelor of Science in Business, Bachelor of Science in Clinical Laboratory Science, Bachelor of Science in Computer Engineering, Bachelor of Science in Computer Science, B Bachelor of Science in Education, Bachelor of Science in Electrical Engineering, Bachelor of Science in Engineering Physics, Bachelor of Science in Materials Science and Engineering, Bachelor of Science in Mechanical Engineering, and Bachelor of Science in Nursing. Majors and programs of study include the Raj Soin College of Business—accountancy, business economics, finance, financial services, human resource management, international business, management, management information systems, marketing, and operations management; College of Education and Human Services—athletic training, early childhood education, health and physical education, integrated business education, marketing education, middle childhood education, organizational leadership, rehabilitation services, and vocational education; College of Engineering and Computer Science—biomedical engineering, computer engineering, computer science, electrical engineering, engineering physics, industrial and systems engineering, materials science and engineering, and mechanical engineering; College of Liberal Arts—acting, acting/musical theater, African and African-American studies, anthropology, art, art history, art history/studio art, classical humanities, communication studies, criminal justice, dance, economics, English, French, geography, German, Greek, history, integrated language arts/English education, international studies, Latin, liberal studies, mass communications, modern languages, motion picture history/theory/criticism, motion picture production, music, music education, music history and literature, music performance, organizational communication, philosophy, political science, religion, selected studies, social and industrial communication, social science education, social work, sociology, Spanish, theater design/technology/stage management, theater studies, urban affairs, visual arts education, and women's studies; and College of Science and Mathematics—biological sciences, biological sciences education, chemistry, chemistry education, clinical laboratory science, environmental sciences, geological sciences, geological sciences education, integrated science education, mathematics, mathematics education, physics, physics education, and psychology. The College of Nursing and Health offers the Bachelor of Science in Nursing.

Wright State grants the Associate of Arts, Associate of Science, Associate of Applied Business, Associate of Applied Science, Associate of Technical Study, Bachelor of Science in Education, and Bachelor of Science in Organizational Leadership through the Lake campus in Celina, Ohio.

The Wright State University Lake Campus also offers associate degrees with course work in the following fields of study: biological sciences, business and administration, chemistry, financial management technology, geography, history, management information systems, mechanical engineering technology (computer-aided drafting design and manufacturing options), office information systems (administrative assistant, legal administrative assistant, and medical administrative assistant options), psychology, social work, and sociology.

Academic Programs

University College serves as the academic home of many first-year students. It can help students determine and achieve their academic and career goals. Academic advisers in University College provide students with assistance in scheduling courses and meeting entry requirements for their major. All students, regardless of their intended major, must complete a core group of general education requirements.

Students who complete Advanced Placement (AP) course work while in high school may be granted University credit on the basis of their examination scores. Wright State University accepts credits from accredited institutions earned through dual-enrollment programs, such as Ohio's Post Secondary Enrollment Program.

The University honors program creates a learning environment that students can expect to find at a small liberal arts college rather than within a large university. Honors students benefit from small, discussion-centered courses with experienced faculty members; opportunities for leadership in the Student Honors Association and the Mid-East Honor Association; self-directed research with faculty members; and honors housing. Admission to the honors program is based on ACT and SAT scores, high school grade point average, and class rank. Upon admission to the University, eligible students will be sent an application for the honors program.

Other academic programs of note include Air Force and Army ROTC and adult education programs.

Off-Campus Programs

Wright State's membership in the Southwestern Ohio Council for Higher Education enables full-time students to take courses at many area colleges and universities at Wright State's tuition rates. Wright State students can gain hands-on experience through cooperative education and internships. Students who have attained sophomore standing can work with the Office of Career Services and faculty members in their major to find co-op and internship opportunities. Many majors include courses that require students to work with community agencies, businesses, and industries to solve real-world problems.

Wright State students who desire an international experience can spend a quarter or more overseas in one of more than twenty countries or travel with a group of Wright State students and faculty members to Brazil or Japan during the summer.

Academic Facilities

Major academic buildings on the main campus include the Creative Arts Center, the Paul Lawrence Dunbar Library, the Telecommunications Center, four main classroom buildings, the Brehm Laboratory, the Bio-Science Building, the Russ Engineering Center, the Mathematical and Microbiological Sciences Building, the Health Sciences Building, the Medical Sciences Building, the Rike Hall Raj Soin Business Building, the Student Union, and University Hall. Other facilities are available in downtown Dayton and Celina. Wright State students also have access to the libraries of all the institutions in the Southwestern Ohio Council for Higher Education. The combined library holdings total more than a million volumes.

Costs

For 2003–04, tuition and fees for Ohio residents were $1964 per quarter. Tuition and fees for out-of-state students were $3788 per quarter. Room and board were $1800 per quarter, and additional expenses, including books and supplies, cost approximately $900 per year.

Financial Aid

Three forms of financial aid are available: grants and scholarships, which do not require repayment; long-term and short-term loans, which must be repaid; and part-time student employment. Students applying for financial aid must complete the Free Application for Federal Student Aid (FAFSA). Sixty-five percent of Wright State's students receive financial aid. University scholarships, based solely on academic ability, are awarded each fall. A special scholarship application must be filed and additional credentials such as letters of recommendation may be required. Further details concerning financial aid and scholarship programs are available through the Office of Financial Aid.

Faculty

The WSU faculty has 670 full-time and 22 part-time members. Approximately 80 percent hold the highest degrees in their fields. More than 75 percent of classes have less than 50 students.

Student Government

The Student Government Association is the representative body for Wright State students. Leaders and representatives are elected by the entire student body and members participate in the University Senate, which is composed of faculty members, administration, and student representatives. The Student Government Association deals with academic regulations, curriculum changes, and other matters of University-wide policy.

Admission Requirements

Ohio students who have graduated from an accredited high school with a college-preparatory curriculum, a minimum 2.0 grade point average (on a 4.0 scale), and a minimum ACT composite score of 18 or a minimum SAT I combined score of 840 are eligible to enter Wright State. Applications from students not meeting these requirements or from students who hold a state-approved high school equivalency certificate are reviewed on an individual basis. Out-of-state students must have a minimum GPA of 2.5 and an ACT score of 20 or an SAT score of 960. Students applying as freshmen should submit a WSU application form, a nonrefundable $30 application fee, a copy of their high school transcript, a College-Preparatory Curriculum Completion Form, and ACT or SAT I scores.

The transfer policies among the University's academic divisions vary and depend on the number of transfer hours applicants have acquired and their cumulative GPA. The Office of Admissions can provide specific requirements for each college. Transfer applicants must submit official transcripts from each college and university attended and must have at least a 2.0 GPA for admission to the University. The appropriate college of the University determines how a student's credit is to be applied to the Wright State academic credit requirements.

Application and Information

Application deadlines vary depending on the quarter for which a student is applying. In general, students should submit the completed application and appropriate fee, transcripts, and test scores (where applicable) as soon as possible to ensure a good selection of courses. International students and others with questions about exceptional circumstances should contact the Office of Admissions.

Cathy Davis
Director of Admissions
E 148 Student Union
Wright State University
Dayton, Ohio 45435
Telephone: 937-775-5700
800-247-1770 (toll-free)
E-mail: admissions@wright.edu
World Wide Web: http://www.wright.edu

The Student Union includes a fitness center with aerobic and weight-training equipment, a small gymnasium, and a pool for open recreational activities.

XAVIER UNIVERSITY

CINCINNATI, OHIO

The University

Founded in 1831, Xavier University is the fourth oldest of the twenty-eight Jesuit colleges and universities in the United States. There are approximately 4,000 undergraduate students attending Xavier during the day, and the total University enrollment is 6,500. Coeducational in all divisions, the University has students from forty-three states and forty-three countries. Students may choose from more than sixty undergraduate majors in three colleges and can later pursue graduate degrees in twenty areas. Xavier is nationally recognized for providing a high-quality personalized education rooted in the Catholic Jesuit tradition. Major University divisions include the College of Arts and Sciences, the Williams College of Business, the College of Social Sciences, the Center for Adult and Part-Time Students, and the graduate programs.

Location

Xavier University's 125-acre campus is located in a residential neighborhood that is a short drive from downtown Cincinnati, a diverse, bustling community that *Places Rated Almanac* calls America's eleventh most livable city. The nation's twenty-third-largest region, Greater Cincinnati, is home to 2 million people, two major league sports teams, and eight Fortune 500 companies. Cincinnati is located on the banks of the Ohio River and at the convergence of three states—Ohio, Kentucky, and Indiana.

Majors and Degrees

Xavier's College of Arts and Sciences awards the Bachelor of Arts or Bachelor of Science degree in applied science (biology, chemistry, or physics/engineering), art, biology, chemical science, chemistry, classical humanities, classics, communication arts, computer science, English, history, mathematics, medical technology, modern languages (French, German, Spanish), music, music education, natural science (preprofessional programs in dentistry, medicine, and veterinary studies), philosophy, physics, and theology. Students studying the preprofessional programs in the natural sciences are assisted with entrance into a health career or medical school by the preprofessional health advising office. Xavier also offers an associate degree in radiologic technology.

The Williams College of Business awards the Bachelor of Science in Business Administration degree in accounting, economics, entrepreneurial studies, finance, general business, human resources, information systems, international business, management, and marketing. Cooperative education (co-op) opportunities are offered to qualified students.

Majors and areas of study offered through Xavier's College of Social Sciences include athletic training, criminal justice, economics, education (early childhood, middle childhood, Montessori, secondary, and special education), international affairs, nursing, occupational therapy, political science, psychology, social work, sociology, and sports management/sports marketing.

Xavier offers a preprofessional program in law. Students in the program are free to select any major of interest to them. The prelaw adviser assists students in their course selection and preparation for law school.

A two-year preprofessional program in pharmacy is also offered, preparing students for entrance into a school of pharmacy. Students who decide not to go on in pharmacy may continue at Xavier for a four-year degree in science.

Xavier offers pre-engineering programs in conjunction with the University of Cincinnati. In addition, an environmental management program is offered in conjunction with Duke University. After spending three years at Xavier in biology and two years at Duke in environmental management, students graduate with a Bachelor of Science in applied biology from Xavier and either a Master of Environmental Management or a Master of Forestry from Duke.

Students may select minor areas of study in art history, biology, business, chemistry, classical studies, communication arts, computer science, corrections, criminal justice, economics, education (Montessori and secondary), English, environmental studies, French, German, Greek, history, information technology, international affairs, international business, international studies, jazz, Latin, Latin American studies, mathematics, music, natural sciences, peace studies, performance studies, philosophy, physics, political science, psychology, Spanish, studio art, theology, and women's and minorities' studies. The Center for Adult and Part-Time Students serves those who wish to continue their education but are not in a position to attend regular daytime classes. In addition to the bachelor's degrees, the division offers two-year associate degree programs in a number of fields.

Academic Program

The academic year consists of two semesters, and summer courses are available. While the number of semester hours required for graduation varies with the program chosen, a minimum of 120 hours are required for a degree. A student must fulfill the required semester hours in a major as well as the basic requirements of the core curriculum. With an emphasis on liberal arts education, the curriculum serves to prepare the individual for a full and purposeful life as well as for a career. The student must complete a designated number of hours in the humanities, mathematics, philosophy, sciences, social sciences, and theology, and considerable freedom is permitted in the selection of courses in these areas.

Special programs include three challenging honors programs: the Honors Bachelor of Arts, University Scholars, and the newest program, Philosophy, Politics and the Public (PPP). The PPP includes a rich academic curriculum in a multidisciplinary study of the many meanings of "public." Students earn an honors degree and are well-prepared for graduate study or careers in many professions, including business, law, economics, and public policy. Other special programs include programs in peace and justice and the women's and minorities' studies minor.

Off-Campus Programs

Fifteen area colleges, including Xavier, have formed the Greater Cincinnati Consortium of Colleges and Universities through which all students at member colleges may take courses not available at their home institution. Xavier encourages full-time students to take advantage of this opportunity for curriculum enrichment through cross-registration. In addition, students who wish to spend a semester or year abroad as part of their undergraduate education have a number of possibilities open to them through the Xavier Study-Abroad Programs and Service Learning.

Academic Facilities

The McDonald Memorial Library supports all of the University's programs and offers a wireless computer environment with laptops available to check out. McDonald Memorial Library also offers extensive computerized research, including online and CD-ROM resources. XPLORE, the library's computerized catalog, allows students to search online for books, periodicals, articles, and videos. XPLORE can be reached from any terminal on the campus or from home. Students also have access to a variety of university and public libraries through a consortium and a computer program called OhioLINK. The Cintas Center is a multipurpose facility with a 10,250-seat arena, a conference center, banquet space, and a student dining center. The Gallagher Student Center has a wireless computer environment with laptops available for checkout. The center also houses a state-of-the-art 350-seat theater, where students can attend a variety of performances including the University's drama group, the Xavier Players. The Science Center provides a modern science facility that serves the needs of today's students. The center comprises a physics building and recently renovated buildings for the biology and chemistry departments.

Costs

Annual tuition for full-time undergraduates for 2003–04 was $18,850. Room and board costs averaged $3730 per semester, depending on accommodations. Costs are subject to change.

Financial Aid

Xavier is committed to helping students afford to attend Xavier University. Each year, nearly 95 percent of undergraduates receive financial assistance, and approximately half of all freshmen receive an academic scholarship. All applicants are automatically considered for academic scholarships, and decisions are typically sent with admission decisions, as are notifications to students who are selected to compete for Xavier Service Fellowships, St. Francis Xavier Scholarships, or Chancellor Scholarships. Ten 4-year, non-need, full tuition St. Francis Xavier Scholarships are awarded annually to students of superior academic ability. The Xavier Service Fellowships are awarded based on high academic ability and a demonstration of exemplary involvement in voluntary service. These awards pay full tuition, room, and board. In addition, Xavier offers departmental scholarships, music and art scholarships, performing arts grants, athletic scholarships, minority awards, and ROTC scholarships. The University also participates in the following federally sponsored aid programs: the Federal Perkins Loan, Federal Pell Grant, Federal Supplemental Educational Opportunity Grant, Federal Work-Study, and Federal Stafford Student Loan programs. Residents of Ohio may qualify for assistance under the Ohio Instructional Grant Program. In order to be considered for financial aid, one must complete the Free Application for Federal Student Aid (FAFSA).

Faculty

The faculty for all divisions numbers 591 members, of whom 278 are full-time. There are no teaching assistants and graduate students do not teach. Eighty-five percent of the full-time faculty members hold doctoral degrees. The student-faculty ratio is 13:1 and the average class size is 22 students. Academic, vocational, and personal counseling and counseling for veterans are readily available. The University has always enjoyed a reputation for good rapport and excellent personal relationships between faculty members and students.

Student Government

The Student Government is the principal agency of student participation in University governance and is devoted to improving the quality of student life. Students choose from more than 100 different academic clubs, social organizations, and intramural group teams. The Student Senate, the main governing organization of the student body, is composed of 16 elected members. Xavier students sit on numerous University committees.

Admission Requirements

Xavier is open to qualified men and women regardless of age, race, religion, handicap, or national origin. Undergraduate students may apply to commence their studies at Xavier for either the fall or spring semesters. While applications are accepted year-round, all students are encouraged to apply by the appropriate deadlines. Each student who applies to Xavier is given a thorough, individual evaluation. Factors considered in making admissions decisions include, but are not limited to, the following: the candidate's previous academic performance, including the rigor of the curriculum pursued and the grades achieved; results from the SAT and/or ACT exams; the candidate's rank in class (when available); the application essay; letters of recommendation; the candidate's extracurricular profile; life or work experience; and any other factors that help to determine the candidate's potential to be successful academically at Xavier and to contribute positively to the Xavier community as a whole.

Transfer applicants with fewer than 30 transferable semester hour credits must follow the instructions for freshman applicants. Transfer applicants with 30 or more hours do not need to submit the application essay, the counselor recommendation, or SAT/ACT results. In addition to the application, transfer candidates must submit official copies of academic and financial aid transcripts from all colleges previously attended, as well as a list of any courses in progress.

Application and Information

To be considered for admission, a student must submit the application form with the $35 application fee; the official high school transcript sent by the school with a counselor recommendation; and scores on the SAT I or ACT, which may be included on the high school record. Students may also apply online, where the application fee is waived. Students should check with the University for application deadlines.

An application and additional information may be obtained by contacting:

Office of Admission
Xavier University
3800 Victory Parkway
Cincinnati, Ohio 45207-5311
Telephone: 513-745-3301
877-XUADMIT (982-3648) (toll-free)
E-mail: xuadmit@xavier.edu
transfer@xavier.edu (transfer students)
xuglobal@xavier.edu (international students)
World Wide Web: http://www.xavier.edu

Xavier University's academic mall.

YALE UNIVERSITY

NEW HAVEN, CONNECTICUT

The University

Yale University was founded in 1701 as the Collegiate School in Branford, Connecticut, with a gift of books from 10 clergymen. In 1716 it moved to New Haven; it was renamed Yale College in 1718 to honor a generous benefactor, Elihu Yale. Today, the University enrolls more than 10,000 students in the eleven graduate and professional schools and in the undergraduate college. Diversity is a hallmark of the student population; its more than 5,000 undergraduates come from every state and from almost fifty countries and represent a wide economic, social, and ethnic mix.

Yale's residential college system is the most pervasive influence on undergraduate life and work. The twelve residential colleges are much more than bed, board, and books: they are self-sufficient communities within Yale College. Each college has its own dining hall, library, courtyard, seminar rooms, practice rooms for musicians, and computer cluster and numerous other facilities that range from darkrooms to printing presses to game rooms and saunas. Although students are assigned to a residential college before entrance, most freshmen live on the Old Campus and move into their residential college during the sophomore year. Freshmen participate fully in all aspects of residential college life. The colleges sponsor a wide variety of activities, such as intramural sports, dramatic societies, and newspapers. Most activities, such as the *Yale Daily News*, the Yale Symphony Orchestra, and thirty-five varsity sports, draw students from all of the residential colleges.

Undergraduates are encouraged to enroll in courses that are sufficiently challenging and to pursue an education that covers a wide range of subjects while studying some subjects in great depth. Students may cross-register with most of the graduate and professional schools to take highly advanced courses. In some areas, it is possible to take a combined-degree program. Yale's hope is that the undergraduates use the vast resources of a major research university in every way possible.

The University offers graduate and professional degrees in the Schools of Architecture, Art, Divinity, Drama, Forestry and Environmental Studies, Law, Management, Medicine, Music, and Nursing and in the Graduate School of Arts and Sciences.

Location

Yale University is located in the heart of New Haven, Connecticut, a city of 120,000 on Long Island Sound. Founded in 1658, New Haven was the first planned municipality in the United States. Today, its diversity is manifested in a wide variety of neighborhoods, restaurants, and recreation. Two nationally distinguished theaters, the Yale Repertory and the Long Wharf Theatres, make their homes there. More than 2,000 students each year are involved in the community through volunteer or work-study projects, tutoring in city schools, working in a halfway house or in the local hospitals, or doing an internship in business, journalism, or city government. The University and the city are vitally interdependent.

Majors and Degrees

Yale University confers the Bachelor of Arts (B.A.) and Bachelor of Science (B.S.) degrees. Majors, usually selected at the end of the sophomore or the beginning of the junior year, are available in the following areas: African and African-American studies; American studies; anthropology; applied mathematics; applied physics; archaeological studies; architecture; art; astronomy; astronomy and physics; biology; chemistry; Chinese; classical civilization; classical languages and literatures; cognitive science; computer science; computer science and mathematics; computer science and psychology; East Asian languages and literatures; East Asian studies (China or Japan); economics; economics and mathematics; electrical engineering and computer science; engineering (biomedical engineering, chemical engineering, electrical engineering, engineering sciences (chemical, electrical, mechanical), environmental engineering, mechanical engineering); English; environmental studies; ethics, politics, and economics; ethnicity, race, and migration; film studies; French; geology and geophysics; Germanic languages and literatures; German studies; history; history of art; history of science and medicine; humanities; international studies; Italian; Japanese; Judaic studies; Latin American studies; linguistics; literature; mathematics; mathematics and philosophy; mathematics and physics; molecular biophysics and biochemistry; music; Near Eastern languages and civilizations; philosophy; physics; physics and philosophy; political science; Portuguese; psychology; religious studies; Renaissance studies; Russian; Russian and East European studies; sociology; Spanish; theater studies; and women's and gender studies. In addition, students may create their own programs in a special divisional major. Yale offers a double major, but no minor.

Academic Programs

Yale's academic goal is to provide students with a liberal education by encouraging curiosity, inquiry, and the development of expressive and analytical intellectual skills. In the belief that a liberal education should be neither too focused nor too diffuse, Yale supports the principle of distribution as well as concentration. Courses at Yale are divided into four distributional groups: languages and literatures, the other humanities, social sciences, and natural sciences, engineering, and mathematics. Thirty-six term courses or the equivalent are required for graduation. There are usually eleven to fourteen courses in a student's major, with the exception of certain intensive majors that require more course work. A student must earn at least 12 course credits drawn from outside the distributional group that includes the major. At least 3 course credits must be drawn from each of the four groups. An intermediate proficiency in a foreign language is required for graduation.

All students, except transfers, enter Yale as freshmen, but a student may graduate as much as a year early through the accumulation of acceleration credits. Acceleration credits are given in most subjects for a score of 4 or 5 on the College Board Advanced Placement tests and/or for advanced course work done in the freshman year. Yale also offers special programs such as Directed Studies, a freshman program that surveys the Western cultural tradition.

Yale operates on a semester calendar. The first semester runs from September through December, and final examinations are held before Winter Break. The second semester begins in mid-January and runs through early May.

Off-Campus Programs

Yale sponsors a program in British culture at the Mellon Centre for Studies in British Art in London. The program is open to students in all disciplines and is available for either a single term or a full academic year. Students may also register directly at an international university or participate in a program sponsored by another American college if given prior approval from Yale. Many students use the Office of International Education and Fellowship Programs as a resource for pursuing opportunities abroad beyond the standard junior term abroad.

Academic Facilities

The Yale Library is the second-largest university library and the second-largest research library in the world, containing more than 10 million volumes. Although it is centered in Sterling Memorial Library, the open-stack system provides access to facilities throughout the campus, including the Kline Science Library and the Beinecke Rare Book and Manuscript Library, one of the country's most important and heavily used resources for original scholarship in the humanities.

Science facilities include the Chemical Instrumentation Center in the Sterling Chemistry Laboratory, part of Yale's fifteen-building complex for teaching and research in science. With the commissioning of an ESTU Van de Graaff accelerator, Yale continues its preeminence in nuclear physics. The astronomy department maintains research and teaching facilities in New Haven and nearby Bethany, Connecticut; in Cerro Tololo, Chile; and also at Kitt Peak National Observatory in Arizona.

Yale offers numerous galleries and special collections, among which are the Yale Art Gallery (the oldest college-affiliated gallery in the country), the Peabody Museum of Natural History, and the Yale Center for British Art, which houses the largest collection of British art outside the United Kingdom.

Costs

Tuition for the 2003–04 academic year was $28,400 and room and board was $8600. Books, supplies and personal expenses were estimated at $2520, bringing the estimated total annual cost to $39,520.

Financial Aid

Admission and financial aid decisions are made independently, and an application for aid in no way affects a student's chances for admission.

Financial need is the only consideration in determining who receives financial aid; there are no athletic or academic scholarships. More than 40 percent of Yale's undergraduates receive aid in the form of gift scholarships, loans, and employment. Furthermore, many students who are not eligible for financial aid participate in the campus employment program or in loan programs to help meet their expenses.

Applicants for financial aid should file the Free Application for Federal Student Aid (FAFSA) and the PROFILE with the College Scholarship Service (CSS) by February 1 and should follow the financial aid application procedures outlined in the Yale Application for Admission by January 16. Award notifications are mailed with the decision letters in early April.

Faculty

The Yale faculty is made up of eminent scholars in every field who usually teach on both the graduate and undergraduate levels. Yale takes pride in the faculty's commitment to undergraduate teaching and in its accessibility to the students. Freshmen frequently have as much access to senior faculty members as upperclass students do; senior faculty members and even department chairs regularly teach introductory-level courses. Eighty-five percent of the courses offered enroll fewer than 25 students. Faculty members hold regular office hours and act as academic advisers to individual students. Most are fellows of the residential colleges and frequently take meals in the college dining halls. A few faculty members live in separate residences within the residential colleges, and many maintain offices there.

Student Government

Each of the twelve residential colleges has its own college council, which has representatives from all four classes. The Yale College Council draws representatives from each residential college and acts as a forum for student opinion and counsel. In addition, students serve on various college and University committees.

Admission Requirements

In selecting a class of 1,300 from more than 19,000 applicants, the Admissions Committee looks for academic ability and achievement combined with such personal strengths as motivation, curiosity, energy, sense of humor, and leadership ability. No two individuals offer these in like proportions; thus, no simple profile of grades, scores, and activities can guarantee admission.

For evidence of academic strength, Yale looks to a student's high school record (quality and breadth of courses selected, as well as grades achieved), test scores on the SAT I and three SAT II Subject Tests or on the ACT, and recommendations submitted by a counselor and 2 academic teachers. In addition, applicants are asked to supply information about their interests and activities and must write two essays. The personal recommendations and essays are important parts of the application process and should not be underrated by applicants. Interviews are not required; most applicants are interviewed by alumni representatives, although a limited number of appointments are available in New Haven on a first-come, first-served basis. Applicants are urged to visit the campus, preferably during the school year, and are welcome to visit classes, take a tour, and attend an information session in the admissions office.

Application and Information

Application forms may be obtained from the admissions office at Yale. Students who apply only to Yale under early action must file by November 1, and they receive a nonbinding decision in mid-December. Students who apply under the regular decision program must file by December 31; decision letters are mailed in early April. Students are encouraged to submit their applications online at the Web site listed below. Yale does accept the Common Application. All Common Application forms must be mailed to the admissions office. Students applying to Yale using the Common Application also need to complete Yale's Common Application Supplement, which is available at the University's Web site.

For an application form or additional information, prospective students are encouraged to visit the Web site or to contact:

Office of Undergraduate Admissions
Yale University
P.O. Box 208234
New Haven, Connecticut 06520-8234
Telephone: 203-432-9316
E-mail: student.questions@yale.edu
World Wide Web: http://www.yale.edu/admit

YORK COLLEGE OF THE CITY UNIVERSITY OF NEW YORK

JAMAICA, NEW YORK

The College

Founded in 1966, York College offers a distinctive educational experience within the City University of New York (CUNY) system. This small, modernized institution embodies the essential qualities of a major university: a strong liberal arts foundation, a distinguished faculty, preprofessional programs, and career planning. At the same time, students are offered the intimacy, individualized attention, and sense of community unavailable at larger universities.

More than fifty student organizations, representing various academic and ethnic interests and including student publications, welcome student participation. Students participate in intercollegiate and intramural athletics and a variety of recreational activities.

In 1986, York College opened a new facility in Jamaica, New York, constituting the academic core of its new campus. The structure—which includes an interior mall that covers four levels and is topped by a glass skylight—houses up-to-date laboratory, computer, and library facilities. It provides an excellent academic and social environment for York College students. Work was completed on an athletic and physical education complex, as well as on a performing arts center with a 1,500-seat theater, in 1990.

York College also has a master's program in occupational therapy.

Location

Centrally located in Queens, New York, York College is accessible by car, bus, subway, and the Long Island Rail Road. Easy access to the rest of Queens and New York City enables York College students to engage in extensive community service as a part of their curriculum. The College is 4 miles from John F. Kennedy Airport.

Majors and Degrees

York College awards Bachelor of Arts and Bachelor of Science degrees in the following liberal arts and career-oriented majors: accounting, Afro-American studies, anthropology, art history, biology, biotechnology, business administration, chemistry, communications technology, community health, computer science, economics, education (bilingual, early childhood, and elementary), English, environmental health science, French, geology, gerontology, health education, health promotion management, history, information systems management, marketing, mathematics, medical technology, movement science (nonteaching physical education), music, nursing, occupational therapy, philosophy, physical education (teaching), physics, political science, psychology, social work, sociology, Spanish, speech, and studio art. York College also offers certificates in survey research and mortgage finance.

Many majors have an integral cooperative education component that enables students in the junior and senior years to alternate semesters between school and paid internships.

Academic Programs

The curriculum at York College is designed to give students a firm and broad base in the liberal arts as well as to permit specialization in a career or professional area. The required liberal arts core includes courses in the humanities, social sciences, and natural sciences, and selections may be made from a range of courses. At least 120 credits are required to earn a bachelor's degree. Students should refer to the College's current catalog for the credit requirements for each major.

Cooperative education is designed to give students practical work experience to supplement the theoretical work in the classroom. Three job placements are made, giving students a range of opportunities. Upon graduation, students are better prepared for the labor market, have significant job experience and references, and are well equipped to seek employment in their field.

York College has an ongoing commitment to its community, and community service is an integral part of many of the academic programs. Students in the areas of community health, education, gerontology, health promotion management, occupational therapy, physical education, political science, psychology, and social work have the opportunity to become involved in community service fieldwork and internships. They gain valuable experience while making a contribution to the community.

Academic Facilities

York College's modern facility on Guy R. Brewer Boulevard and Liberty Avenue provides extensive science and computer laboratories, a large library, and up-to-date education technology. Music majors studying electronic music and jazz have access to a computer music studio that has microcomputers, digital synthesizers, MIDI interfaces, sound sampling systems, and multitrack tape recorders. The Computer Graphics Lab of York College is the most modern graphics lab in the City University system. In this advanced facility, students can display three-dimensional scientific figures, create graphic business charts and presentations, develop desktop publishing skills, or utilize computer-aided design in other disciplines and fields of study. Students interested in media and the communication arts have access to a fully equipped television production studio, including audio production. There are also a theater complex and a physical education facility that includes an Olympic-size swimming pool, an athletic field, tennis and handball courts, a health promotion center, a health promotion lab, and biofeedback facilities.

Costs

For 2003–04, the cost of tuition for newly enrolled full-time students was $4241 per year for in-state residents and $8484 per year for newly enrolled out-of-state residents. The student activity fee was $120.85 per year. Room and board are not available at York College. Tuition is subject to change.

Financial Aid

Financial aid is available for qualified students on the basis of need through state and federal aid programs. For full consideration, applicants should file the City University of New

York Application for Federal State Student Aid (CUNY AFSSA). Applications for the fall semester should be submitted by the preceding June.

Faculty

More than 85 percent of the full-time faculty members hold a doctoral degree. The faculty is dedicated to scholarship, research, and high-quality teaching. Faculty members work closely with students to provide the academic and intellectual support necessary for the students' successful development.

Student Government

The student government, composed of elected student representatives, is responsible for the allocation of money for student activities. Members of the student government serve on College-wide committees that decide College policy.

Admission Requirements

Admission is based upon the applicant's academic average and academic units. Classwork and SAT I or ACT scores may be considered in the admission decision; SAT or ACT scores are required for recent high school graduates. Admission is centrally processed by the City University of New York and directly at the Admissions Office of York College.

Application and Information

Applicants to the freshman class are admitted on a monthly basis starting in February for the fall semester; transfer applicants are admitted starting in April. The application fee for freshmen and transfer students is $50. Application forms may be obtained by contacting the Admissions Office at the address below.

For further information, students should contact:

Admissions Office 1B07
York College of the
City University of New York
Jamaica, New York 11451
Telephone: 718-262-2165
Fax: 718-262-2601
E-mail: admissions@york.cuny.edu
World Wide Web: http://www.york.cuny.edu

On the campus of York College of the City University of New York.

YORK UNIVERSITY

TORONTO, ONTARIO, CANADA

The University

Students at York University find some of the best and brightest within its community. That is because York has a national and international reputation for innovation that expands its students' horizons with unique programs, inspired teaching, and groundbreaking results. Students chart their own paths, find mentors among the best professors, and gain a degree that is respected around the world. York offers undergraduate and graduate degrees in the humanities, social sciences, business, education, engineering, environmental studies, fine arts, Internet studies, law, nursing, pure and applied science, and social work. It is home to twenty leading research centres. There are slightly more than 40,000 students at York, making it the third-largest university in Canada. Because of its size, York can offer a wide range of opportunities and services and two very different campuses. The Keele campus, in Toronto's north end, is a modern learning environment with extensive facilities, including forty restaurants, a retail mall, an athletics complex, on-campus housing, and hundreds of events and cultural activities. The Glendon campus, among the parks and boutiques of midtown Toronto, is a small liberal arts community with an international flair. Classes are taught in English and French.

Location

York University is located in Toronto, Canada's largest city and main financial centre. Known for its multiculturalism, friendly people, beautiful spaces, and vibrant cities, Canada is often recognized as one of the best places in the world to live. As one of the world's most multicultural cities, Toronto has theater, music, and restaurants from all around the globe. From art galleries and museums to restaurants and major-league sports, Toronto has all the elements of a world-class city. Toronto is convenient—it is a 1-hour flight from New York City, Boston, Chicago, or Detroit and a 90-minute drive from the Canadian-U.S. border at Buffalo, New York.

Majors and Degrees

The Bachelor of Arts (daytime studies, Keele campus) is offered in African studies, anthropology, applied geography, applied mathematics, business and society, classical studies (includes Greek and Latin), classics, cognitive science, communication studies, computer science, creative writing, criminology, East Asian studies, economics, economics and business, English, European studies, French studies, geography, German studies, global political studies, health and society, history, humanities, individualized studies, information technology, international development studies, kinesiology and health science, labour studies, languages/literatures and linguistics (includes courses in Chinese, German, Hebrew, Italian, Japanese, Portuguese, Russian, and Spanish), Latin American and Caribbean studies, law and society, linguistics, mathematics, mathematics for commerce, philosophy, political science, professional writing, psychology, public policy and administration, religious studies, science and society, social and political thought, sociology, South Asian studies, statistics, urban studies, and women's studies. Joint programs with some Ontario community colleges are available in communication arts, early childhood education, gerontology, and rehabilitation services. The Schulich School of Business offers a Bachelor of Business Administration degree in accounting, economics, entrepreneurship and family business, finance, information technology, marketing, organizational behaviour and industrial relations, and management science. An International Bachelor of Business Administration degree is also offered. The Bachelor of Environmental Studies degree is offered in environmental management, environmental politics, environment and culture, and urban and regional environments; certificates are offered in environmental landscape design and geographical information systems. Joint college programs also offer ecosystem management, international project management, and urban sustainability. The Faculty of Fine Arts offers Bachelor of Design (B.D.), Bachelor of Fine Arts (B.F.A.), and Bachelor of Arts (B.A.) degrees in the following programs: cultural studies, dance, film and video, music, theater, and visual arts (includes art history, drawing, media arts, painting, photography, printmaking, and sculpture). The Bachelor of Arts at the Glendon campus (courses taught in English and/or French) is offered in business economics, Canadian studies, computer science, drama studies, economics, English, environmental and health sciences, études françaises, Hispanic studies, history, information technology, international studies, linguistics and language studies, mathematics, mathematics for commerce, multidisciplinary studies, philosophy, political science, psychology, sociology, translation, and women's studies. A joint program with Seneca College is available in early childhood education. Certificates are available in intercultural studies, refugee and migration studies, Spanish/English and English/Spanish translation, teaching English as an international language, and technical and professional writing. The Bachelor of Science is offered in atmospheric chemistry, biology, biotechnology, chemistry, computer engineering, computer science, earth and atmospheric science, environmental science, geography, geomatics engineering, kinesiology and health science, mathematics, physics and astronomy, psychology, space and communication sciences, and space engineering. A joint program with Seneca College is available in rehabilitation services. The Atkinson Faculty of Liberal and Professional Studies offers the following degrees: Bachelor of Administrative Studies (accounting*, business research*, general management*, human resources management*, information technology, and marketing), Bachelor of Arts (business economics, Canadian studies, classical studies, computer science, creative arts and cultural expression, economics, English, health studies, history, humanities, individualized studies, information technology, mathematics, mathematics for commerce, philosophy, political science, psychology, public administration and management, public service studies*, religious studies, science and technology studies, social and political thought, social science, sociology, and women's studies), Bachelor of Health Studies, Bachelor of Human Resources Management, Bachelor of Science (computer science, general science, mathematics, and psychology), Bachelor of Science in Nursing, and Bachelor of Social Work. The Bachelor of Education (concurrent) is offered in primary-junior (junior kindergarten–grade 6), junior-intermediate (grades 4–10), and intermediate-senior (grades 7–final year of high school) levels. The Bachelor of Education (consecutive) is offered in primary-junior (junior kindergarten–grade 6), junior-intermediate (grades 4–10, with options in biology, chemistry, computer science, English, environmental science, fine arts dance, fine arts drama, fine arts music, fine arts visual arts, French as a second language, geography, history, mathematics, physical education, religious studies, and science general), and intermediate-senior (grades 7–final year of high school, with options in computer science, economics, English, environmental science, fine arts dance, fine arts drama, fine arts music, fine arts visual arts, French as a second language, geography, history, individual and society, Italian, mathematics, physical education, physics, religious studies, science general, and Spanish). York's Osgoode Hall Law School offers a Bachelor of Laws. An asterisk (*) indicates that a program is available through distance education.

Academic Program

Students can begin their studies at York in September (all programs) or, in a limited number of programs, in May or January. Students can study on a full- or part-time basis during the day or evening. All undergraduate and professional degrees have specific requirements that students are required to complete prior to graduating. Detailed information on program requirements can be found in the University calendars on York's Web site, which is listed below.

Off-Campus Programs

York offers more than 100 exchange and study-abroad opportunities in thirty-five countries around the world. All undergraduate students can take part in an academic exchange for one year or semester if they are in an honors program, have completed two years of study, maintained at least an overall B average, and, in some cases, have proficiency in the host country's language.

Academic Facilities

York offers eight libraries with a total collection of more than 4.4 million items, including 2.2 million books as well as maps, films, videos, archives, sound recordings, and compact disks. There are visual arts studios, three theaters, two art galleries, state-of-the-art science laboratories, and an observatory with two telescopes. York students have access to a wide range of computer facilities, including forty-two computer labs and 2,500 workstations. Seven new buildings are currently under construction, in addition to the new computer science building, which has won international acclaim for environmental design. All students receive free e-mail and Internet access. To help students succeed in their studies, there are academic tutors, advisers to help with course selection, and an extensive learning disabilities program. Students whose first language is not English can get extra help at the English as a Second Language Tutoring Centre and take ESL courses that count toward their degrees. Those who need to improve their English to attend university can take intensive ESL courses at the York University English Language Institute before starting a regular degree program.

Costs

For the 2003–04 academic year, tuition fees for a full-time student were a minimum of Can$4824 for Canadian citizens and permanent residents or Can$11,647 for international students. Room and board, including a meal plan that costs Can$2400, cost approximately Can$3207 for a double room. Students living in residence must purchase a meal plan. Course materials, books, health insurance, and supplies generally average approximately Can$2000. Students should visit http://www.yorku.ca/osfs for details. All fees are subject to change.

Financial Aid

York offers entrance scholarships to undergraduate candidates with excellent academic grades. These scholarships range in value from Can$500 to Can$6000. The scholarships are for first-year study only and are not renewable. Applicants are considered for scholarships at the time of admission. International candidates can also compete for the prestigious Global Leader of Tomorrow Award, worth Can$10,500 and renewable for up to four years of undergraduate study as long as excellent grades are maintained. An application for this award is necessary. Once at York, international students are eligible for continuing student scholarships worth up to Can$3000 based on their performance in York courses. U.S. citizens may be eligible to receive U.S. federal funding to study at York (York's FAFSA code is G07679). All full-time international students may work part-time on campus.

Faculty

York's professors are mentors, but they are also eager to learn from their students. They are known internationally for excellence and innovation in teaching and research. Innovative teaching allows hands-on learning and dynamic classroom discussion. More than 30 professors have received Killam Research Fellowships—Canada's most prestigious research award. More than 55 York faculty members have received provincial and national awards for teaching excellence, and more than 70 percent of all first-year courses are taught by tenured professors. That means professors are accessible starting the first year.

Student Government

There are sixteen recognized student governments at York located within the residential colleges and Faculties. There is also a central student government, the York Federation of Students, which offers many services, including a health plan, a course evaluation guide, International Identity Cards, and Student Saver Cards. York University students also have representation on the Board of Governors, Senate, Faculty Councils, Council of Masters, and other advisory committees.

Admission Requirements

York is a selective university; therefore, only those candidates who show potential for academic success are considered. Meeting minimum requirements does not guarantee admission. Some programs may require specific preparation in certain subject areas. York's CEEB Code is 0894. Academically outstanding students with a minimum SAT score of 1300 may receive early admission.

Application and Information

Applications are available online at http://www.ouac.on.ca. All undergraduate programs begin in September. Some programs also start in May or January. The early deadline for September entry is February 1; the final deadline is March 1. International applicants are strongly encouraged to apply by February 1, especially for fine arts and the Schulich School of Business. Deadline dates for January and May are posted on the York Web site. For additional information about admissions, academic programs, or University visits and tours, students may visit http://www.myfuture.yorku.ca.

Office of International Admissions
York University
4700 Keele Street
Toronto, Ontario M3J 1P3
Canada
Telephone: 416-736-5825
Fax: 416-650-8195
World Wide Web: http://www.yorku.ca/admissions

Vari Hall, the focal point of the Keele campus.

YOUNGSTOWN STATE UNIVERSITY

YOUNGSTOWN, OHIO

The University

For almost a century, Youngstown State University (YSU) has prepared its graduates to become leaders in the region, the state, and the nation. Located on a beautiful 140-acre campus near downtown Youngstown, Ohio, YSU offers its students a comprehensive selection of major programs backed by a strong tradition of teaching and scholarship. YSU's diverse student body of 12,698 and a student-faculty ratio of 19:1 provide the personal contact associated with a smaller institution, and its connection to the Ohio state system of higher education enables it to draw on the vast resources of that system. The average undergraduate class size is 27 for lectures and 9 for labs.

Youngstown State seeks to offer its students a vital living and learning environment with a relatively small, cohesive campus and a wealth of curricular and cocurricular activities. Attractive residence halls house close to 1,000 students and include a special residential honors facility. The new University Courtyard Apartments, located adjacent to the campus, offer 400 students spacious, apartment-style living. Campus activities abound, with more than 130 student organizations, including social sororities and fraternities and opportunities for participation in theater, performing groups, student publications, intramural and intercollegiate athletics, and activity planning.

Youngstown State University competes in NCAA athletics. Since 1991, it has captured four Division I-AA national football championships. During the past decade, the women's basketball team won five Mid-Continent Conference titles and played three years in the NCAA tournament. The University fields ten women's and eight men's intercollegiate Division I teams. Fitness and recreational facilities are free to all YSU students in the Beeghly Physical Education Center and the Stambaugh Sports Complex, including track, tennis, swimming, racquetball, basketball, handball, Nautilus, aerobic conditioning, and free weights. A new wellness and recreation center is scheduled to open as part of the student center in 2005.

Of the 12,858 students at YSU, 11,598 are undergraduates. Multicultural students make up 13 percent of the student body and international students hail from fifty-five countries. Students benefit from a wide range of student services: complete tutorial assistance in all subject areas, with special centers for writing, study skills, reading, and mathematics; counseling and health services; career testing, planning, and placement; special programs for multicultural, women, and adult students (those older than 25); and an orientation program that includes mentoring by faculty and staff members and upperclass students.

The University seeks a balance between teaching, service, and scholarly activity that serves both its students and the larger community of scholars. The University is committed to keeping its doors open to all who seek higher education and equally committed to giving students every opportunity to enrich their minds, develop their creativity and problem-solving abilities, and become informed, conscientious citizens of the world.

The University's School of Graduate Studies and Research offers more than thirty master's degree programs, including one in physical therapy, and a doctoral degree in educational leadership.

Location

Youngstown is at the center of a metropolitan area of 600,000, located 60 miles from both Pittsburgh and Cleveland. The campus is within easy driving or walking distance of restaurants, shopping centers, museums, and parks. The University is a major contributor to the city's cultural and recreational vitality, each year presenting hundreds of concerts, exhibits, lectures, performances, and athletic contests. The city offers an outstanding symphony orchestra, three community theaters, a vital arts community, and unlimited recreational options provided by 2,500-acre Mill Creek Park that is located 1 mile from the campus. YSU students can take advantage of close ties to area businesses for internships and work co-op programs, which provide valuable on-the-job experience.

Majors and Degrees

The College of Arts and Sciences offers majors in Africana studies, American studies, anthropology, biology, chemistry, computer information systems, computer science, earth science, economics, English, environmental studies, French, geography, geology, German, history, information technology, Italian, journalism, mathematics, philosophy, physics/astronomy, political science, professional writing and editing, psychology, religious studies, social studies, sociology, and Spanish, as well as predentistry, preforestry, prelaw, premedicine, and pre–veterinary medicine.

The Beeghly College of Education offers majors in adolescent/young adult education (in specialized teaching fields), early and middle childhood education, multiage education (in specialized teaching fields), special education, and vocational education.

The Rayen College of Engineering and Technology offers majors in chemical engineering, civil engineering (structural and transportation option and environmental option), civil and construction engineering technology, drafting and design technology, electrical and computer engineering, electrical engineering technology, electric utility technology, industrial and systems engineering, mechanical engineering, mechanical engineering technology, and power-plant technology.

The College of Fine and Performing Arts offers majors in studio art, art history, music/history and literature, music education, music/performance, music theory, music composition, communications studies, telecommunication studies, and theater.

The Bitonte College of Health and Human Services offers majors in allied health, Army and Air Force ROTC, clinical laboratory science, clinical laboratory technology, community health, criminal justice, dental hygiene, dietetic technology, emergency medical technology, family and consumer sciences education, exercise science, family and consumer studies, food and nutrition, histotechnology, hospitality management, medical assisting technology, merchandising (fashion and interiors), nursing, nursing home administration, physical education, prekindergarten, respiratory care, school health education, social service technology, and social work.

The Williamson College of Business Administration offers majors in accounting, advertising and public relations, business economics, finance, general administration, human resource management, management, management information systems, and marketing management. Associate degrees are offered with concentrations in accounting, finance, labor studies, management, and marketing.

Interdisciplinary minors are offered in gerontology, linguistics, peace and conflict studies, professional ethics, statistics, and women's studies.

Students may also enroll for a combined B.S./M.D. program with the Northeastern Ohio Universities College of Medicine. Each student successfully completing this program is awarded the Bachelor of Science degree from Youngstown State University and the M.D. degree from the College of Medicine.

Academic Programs

Youngstown State University is one of a few comprehensive metropolitan institutions in Ohio that provide associate, baccalaureate, and graduate instruction and continuing education in one location. Currently, the University offers a broad curriculum in the School of Graduate Studies and Research and six colleges:

Arts and Sciences, Business Administration, Education, Engineering and Technology, Fine and Performing Arts, and Health and Human Services. The spirit of cooperation among departments and colleges permits students to pursue interdisciplinary majors and minors, to major in one department or college and minor in another, or to pursue double majors. Youngstown State University provides for a broad-based education through a core curriculum of 45 semester hours spread across five areas of concentration and emphasizing the development of writing, speaking, and critical-thinking skills. In addition to fulfilling this general education requirement, each student must complete the major and/or minor requirements and meet the semester hours required for the baccalaureate degree.

Application of associate degree credits to baccalaureate programs is possible within the University. Transfer and dual-admission agreements with two-year institutions and community colleges provide opportunities for transfer into baccalaureate programs at Youngstown State.

An individualized curriculum program is available to students whose needs are not met by existing conventional programs. Students may design curricula to suit their particular needs, allowing alternative paths for earning the undergraduate degrees currently offered.

Off-Campus Programs

YSU offers cooperative/internship education programs in which students participate in both classroom and experiential study via employment in a government, industry, or business setting. Opportunities for international studies for academic credit are available in several majors.

Academic Facilities

Maag Library houses more than a half-million books and more than 200,000 government documents and subscribes to more than 2,500 periodicals and scholarly journals. Online research services provide access to all state university libraries in Ohio and a wide range of other information sources. The library's resources are augmented by the Curriculum Resource Center in the College of Education. A Multimedia Center, housed in Maag Library, offers research materials in a variety of formats.

Comprehensive computing facilities are readily available to students throughout the campus. Scientific laboratories at YSU are fully outfitted with up-to-date instructional and research equipment. Studios and performance halls in the College of Fine and Performing Arts have been recently renovated for acoustic excellence, and the McDonough Museum of Art is an innovative exhibit space for student and faculty work.

Costs

Tuition and fees for an Ohio resident for the 2004 fall semester are $2941 for full-time (12–16 credits) attendance. For students residing in certain counties in New York, West Virginia, and western Pennsylvania, the out-of-state tuition surcharge is reduced, making the total semester cost $4177 for full-time attendance. The charge for University housing, including meals, is $6100 per year. The University estimates books and supplies at $860 per year, and on-campus parking is $68 per semester. Some laboratory and computer classes entail a lab/materials fee, ranging from $35 to $65. All fees and charges are subject to change.

Financial Aid

Financial aid is awarded in four basic forms: scholarships, grants, loans, and on-campus employment. Depending on the student's computed financial need, the award may include a package of any or all of these components in varying amounts. Financial aid applications should be submitted to the University by February 15 for fall-semester assistance and must be resubmitted each year. About 82 percent of Youngstown State's full-time students receive some form of financial aid through a comprehensive program that includes need-based and performance-based aid. Youngstown State prides itself on an exemplary scholarship program that rewards academic performance and promise. The University Scholars program provides full-cost scholarships for 160 high-achieving students, and numerous other scholarships are available under a wide range of criteria.

Faculty

Eighty percent of YSU's 360 full-time faculty members hold the highest degree in their field and most are engaged in active, cutting-edge research that they bring to their instruction. YSU classes are small—76 percent of undergraduate classes have fewer than 30 students—creating many opportunities for class discussion, projects, and interaction between faculty members and students.

Student Government

Student Government exercises the power to conduct student elections, to recommend student representatives to serve on joint faculty-student committees, and to supervise programs funded from its operating budget. Members are elected by the student body to executive positions and to the legislative branch in proportion to the enrollment in each college. Student Government nominates students for two nonvoting gubernatorial appointments to the University Board of Trustees.

Admission Requirements

Ohio residents and residents of Mercer and Lawrence Counties in Pennsylvania must have graduated from a public or chartered high school or passed the General Educational Development (GED) test. Home-schooled applicants should contact the Office of Undergraduate Admissions for information. Nonresidents must have graduated from a public or chartered high school and be ranked in the upper two thirds of their high school class, have a minimum ACT composite score of 17 or a minimum combined SAT score of 820, or have passed the GED test. Transfer applicants must have earned at least a 2.0 accumulated point average and be in good standing at the last institution attended.

Application and Information

Application deadlines vary depending on the semester and the program for which a student is applying. Under the program, students who are admitted by February 15 become eligible for advance advisement and registration for fall classes. Applications must be accompanied by a nonrefundable fee. For more information and an application, students should contact:

Undergraduate Admissions
Youngstown State University
One University Plaza
Youngstown, Ohio 44555

Telephone: 330-941-2000
330-941-1564 (TTY/TDD)
877-468-6978 (toll-free)
Fax: 330-941-3674
E-mail: enroll@ysu.edu
World Wide Web: http://www.ysu.edu

YSU's beautiful, safe campus provides a pleasant backdrop for the students' college experience.

Appendix

2003–04 Changes in Institutions

Following is an alphabetical listing of institutions that have recently closed, merged with other institutions, or changed their name or status. In the case of a name change, the former name appears first, followed by the new name.

Academy of Art College (San Francisco, CA); name changed to Academy of Art University.

American University of Rome (Rome, Italy); name changed to The American University of Rome.

Armstrong University (Oakland, CA); no longer eligible for inclusion.

Bethel College (St. Paul, MN); name changed to Bethel University.

California College of Arts and Crafts (San Francisco, CA); name changed to California College of the Arts.

Canadian Bible College (Calgary, AB, Canada); name changed to Alliance University College.

Chipola Junior College (Marianna, FL); name changed to Chipola College.

Columbia Junior College (Columbia, SC); name changed to South University.

Community Hospital of Roanoke Valley–College of Health Sciences (Roanoke, VA); name changed to Jefferson College of Health Sciences.

Concordia University (St. Paul, MN); name changed to Concordia University, St. Paul.

Coppin State College (Baltimore, MD); name changed to Coppin State University.

DeVry College of Technology (North Brunswick, NJ); name changed to DeVry University.

DeVry University-Keller Graduate School of Management (Oakbrook Terrace, IL); name changed to DeVry University.

École des Hautes Études Commerciales de Montréal (Montréal, QC, Canada); name changed to HEC Montréal.

Everglades College (Ft. Lauderdale, FL); name changed to Everglades University.

Fountainhead College of Electronics (Knoxville, TN); name changed to Fountainhead College of Technology.

Georgia Baptist College of Nursing of Mercer University (Atlanta, GA); closed.

Georgian Court College (Lakewood, NJ); name changed to Georgian Court University.

Harrington Institute of Interior Design (Chicago, IL); name changed to Harrington College of Design.

Herzing College, Minneapolis Drafting School Campus (Minneapolis, MN); name changed to Herzing College, Minneapolis Drafting School Division.

Hsi Lai University (Rosemead, CA); name changed to University of the West.

ISIM University (Denver, CO); name changed to Aspen University.

Johns Hopkins University (Baltimore, MD); name changed to The Johns Hopkins University.

Johnson & Wales University (Charleston, SC); closed.

Johnson & Wales University (Norfolk, VA); closed.

Kendall College of Art and Design of Ferris State University (Grand Rapids, MI); closed.

The King's College (Van Nuys, CA); name changed to The King's College and Seminary.

Long Island University, Southampton College, Friends World Program (Southampton, NY); name changed to Long Island University, Friends World Program.

Miami University–Hamilton Campus (Hamilton, OH); name changed to Miami University Hamilton.

Miami-Dade Community College (Miami, FL); name changed to Miami Dade College.

Minnesota State University, Moorhead (Moorhead, MN); name changed to Minnesota State University Moorhead.

Missouri Southern State College (Joplin, MO); name changed to Missouri Southern State University.

National American University–St. Paul Campus (St. Paul, MN); closed.

New England Institute of Art & Communications (Brookline, MA); name changed to The New England Institute of Art.

Patten College (Oakland, CA); name changed to Patten University.

Plattsburgh State University of New York (Plattsburgh, NY); name changed to State University of New York at Plattsburgh.

Plymouth State College (Plymouth, NH); name changed to Plymouth State University.

Point Park College (Pittsburgh, PA); name changed to Point Park University.

Rutgers, The State University of New Jersey, New Brunswick (New Brunswick, NJ); name changed to Rutgers, The State University of New Jersey, New Brunswick/Piscataway.

Saint Mary College (Leavenworth, KS); name changed to University of Saint Mary.

Saint Mary's College of Madonna University (Orchard Lake, MI); closed.

San Jose Christian College (San Jose, CA); name changed to William Jessup University.

School of the Museum of Fine Arts (Boston, MA); name changed to School of the Museum of Fine Arts, Boston.

Shepherd College (Shepherdstown, WV); name changed to Shepherd University.

Silicon Valley College-Emeryville Campus (Emeryville, CA); name changed to Silicon Valley College.

South University (Columbia, SC); closed.

Southwest State University (Marshall, MN); name changed to Southwest Minnesota State University.

Southwest Texas State University (San Marcos, TX); name changed to Texas State University-San Marcos.

State University of New York at Albany (Albany, NY); name changed to University at Albany, State University of New York.

State University of New York College at Buffalo (Buffalo, NY); name changed to Buffalo State College, State University of New York.

State University of New York Health Science Center at Brooklyn (Brooklyn, NY); name changed to State University of New York Downstate Medical Center.

Swedish Institute of Massage (New York, NY); name changed to Swedish Institute, College of Health Sciences.

Tyndale College & Seminary (Toronto, ON, Canada); name changed to Tyndale University College & Seminary.

University of Action Learning at Boulder (Boulder, CO); name changed to Revans University–The University of Action Learning.

University of Monaco (Monte Carlo, Monaco); name changed to The International University of Monaco.

University of Phoenix–Ohio Campus (Independence, OH); name changed to University of Phoenix–Cleveland Campus.

University System College for Lifelong Learning (Concord, NH); name changed to College for Lifelong Learning.

Vermont College (Montpelier, VT); closed.

Virginia College (Lynchburg, VA); name changed to Virginia University of Lynchburg.

Washburn University of Topeka (Topeka, KS); name changed to Washburn University.

Western Pentecostal Bible College (Abbotsford, BC, Canada); name changed to Summit Pacific College.

Indexes

Entrance Difficulty

This index groups colleges by their own assessment of their entrance difficulty level. The colleges were asked to select the level that most closely corresponds to their entrance difficulty, according to the guidelines below. Institutions for which high school class rank and/or standardized test scores do not apply as admission criteria were asked to select the level that best indicates their entrance difficulty as compared to other institutions.

Most Difficult

More than 75% of the freshmen were in the top 10% of their high school class and scored over 1310 on the SAT I (verbal and mathematical combined) or over 29 on the ACT (composite); about 30% or fewer of the applicants were accepted.

Amherst Coll (MA)
Barnard Coll (NY)
Bates Coll (ME)
Bowdoin Coll (ME)
Brandeis U (MA)
Brown U (RI)
Bryn Mawr Coll (PA)
California Inst of Technology (CA)
Colby Coll (ME)
Columbia Coll (NY)
Columbia U, School of General Studies (NY)
Columbia U, The Fu Foundation School of Eng and Applied Science (NY)
Cooper Union for the Advancement of Science and Art (NY)
Cornell U (NY)
Dartmouth Coll (NH)
Duke U (NC)
Emory U (GA)
Georgetown U (DC)
Gettysburg Coll (PA)
Grove City Coll (PA)
Harvard U (MA)
Harvey Mudd Coll (CA)
Haverford Coll (PA)
The Johns Hopkins U (MD)
The Juilliard School (NY)
Lafayette Coll (PA)
Lehigh U (PA)
Massachusetts Inst of Technology (MA)
Middlebury Coll (VT)
New York U (NY)
Northwestern U (IL)
Pomona Coll (CA)
Princeton U (NJ)
Queen's U at Kingston (ON, Canada)
Reed Coll (OR)
Rice U (TX)
Stanford U (CA)
Swarthmore Coll (PA)
Trinity Coll of Nursing and Health Sciences (IL)
Tufts U (MA)
United States Air Force Acad (CO)
United States Military Acad (NY)
U of Chicago (IL)
U of Notre Dame (IN)
U of Pennsylvania (PA)
U of Southern California (CA)
U of Virginia (VA)
Washington and Lee U (VA)
Washington U in St. Louis (MO)
Webb Inst (NY)
Wellesley Coll (MA)
Wesleyan U (CT)
Williams Coll (MA)
Yale U (CT)

Very Difficult

More than 50% of the freshmen were in the top 10% of their high school class and scored over 1230 on the SAT I or over 26 on the ACT; about 60% or fewer applicants were accepted.

Agnes Scott Coll (GA)
Allegheny Coll (PA)
American U (DC)
The American U in Cairo (Egypt)
Art Center Coll of Design (CA)
Austin Coll (TX)
Ave Maria Coll (MI)
Babson Coll (MA)
Bard Coll (NY)
Beloit Coll (WI)
Bennington Coll (VT)
Berea Coll (KY)
Bernard M. Baruch Coll of the City U of New York (NY)
Boston Coll (MA)
Boston U (MA)
Bucknell U (PA)
California Inst of the Arts (CA)
Carleton Coll (MN)
Carnegie Mellon U (PA)
Case Western Reserve U (OH)
Centre Coll (KY)
Christendom Coll (VA)
Claremont McKenna Coll (CA)
Clarkson U (NY)
Cleveland Inst of Music (OH)
Colgate U (NY)
The Coll of New Jersey (NJ)
Coll of the Atlantic (ME)
Coll of the Holy Cross (MA)
The Coll of William and Mary (VA)
The Colorado Coll (CO)
Colorado School of Mines (CO)
Connecticut Coll (CT)
Davidson Coll (NC)
Dickinson Coll (PA)
Emerson Coll (MA)
Florida State U (FL)
Fordham U (NY)
Franklin and Marshall Coll (PA)
Furman U (SC)
The George Washington U (DC)
Georgia Inst of Technology (GA)
Grinnell Coll (IA)
Gustavus Adolphus Coll (MN)
Hamilton Coll (NY)
Hendrix Coll (AR)
Hillsdale Coll (MI)
Hiram Coll (OH)
Hobart and William Smith Colls (NY)
Illinois Inst of Technology (IL)
Illinois Wesleyan U (IL)
James Madison U (VA)
Jewish Theological Sem of America (NY)
Kalamazoo Coll (MI)
Kenyon Coll (OH)
Kettering U (MI)
Knox Coll (IL)
Laguna Coll of Art & Design (CA)
Lake Forest Coll (IL)
Lawrence U (WI)
Lewis & Clark Coll (OR)
Loyola Marymount U (CA)
Lyon Coll (AR)
Macalester Coll (MN)
Manhattan School of Music (NY)
Mannes Coll of Music, New School U (NY)
Maryland Inst Coll of Art (MD)
Mary Washington Coll (VA)
Massachusetts Coll of Art (MA)
McGill U (QC, Canada)
Medical U of South Carolina (SC)
Mount Holyoke Coll (MA)
Muhlenberg Coll (PA)
New Coll of Florida (FL)
New England Conservatory of Music (MA)
North Carolina School of the Arts (NC)
North Carolina State U (NC)
Nova Scotia Coll of Art and Design (NS, Canada)
Oberlin Coll (OH)
Occidental Coll (CA)
Oglethorpe U (GA)
Ohio Wesleyan U (OH)
Parsons School of Design, New School U (NY)
Peabody Conservatory of Music of The Johns Hopkins U (MD)
The Pennsylvania State U at Erie, The Behrend Coll (PA)
The Pennsylvania State U U Park Campus (PA)
Pepperdine U, Malibu (CA)
Polytechnic U, Brooklyn Campus (NY)
Pratt Inst (NY)
Presbyterian Coll (SC)
Providence Coll (RI)
Queens Coll of the City U of New York (NY)
Rensselaer Polytechnic Inst (NY)
Rhode Island School of Design (RI)
Rhodes Coll (TN)
The Richard Stockton Coll of New Jersey (NJ)
Rollins Coll (FL)
Rose-Hulman Inst of Technology (IN)
St. John's Coll (NM)
Saint Joseph's U (PA)
St. Lawrence U (NY)
Saint Luke's Coll (MO)
St. Mary's Coll of Maryland (MD)
St. Olaf Coll (MN)
Sarah Lawrence Coll (NY)
Scripps Coll (CA)
Simon's Rock Coll of Bard (MA)
Skidmore Coll (NY)
Smith Coll (MA)
Southwestern U (TX)
Spelman Coll (GA)
State U of New York at Binghamton (NY)
State U of New York Coll at Geneseo (NY)
State U of New York Coll of Environmental Science and Forestry (NY)
Stevens Inst of Technology (NJ)
Stonehill Coll (MA)
Stony Brook U, State U of New York (NY)
Syracuse U (NY)
Taylor U (IN)
Thomas Aquinas Coll (CA)
Transylvania U (KY)
Trinity Coll (CT)
Trinity U (TX)
Tulane U (LA)
Union Coll (NY)
United States Coast Guard Acad (CT)
United States Merchant Marine Acad (NY)
United States Naval Acad (MD)
The U of British Columbia (BC, Canada)
U of California, Berkeley (CA)
U of California, Davis (CA)
U of California, Los Angeles (CA)
U of California, Riverside (CA)
U of California, San Diego (CA)
U of California, Santa Barbara (CA)
U of California, Santa Cruz (CA)
U of Florida (FL)
U of Illinois at Urbana–Champaign (IL)
U of Miami (FL)
U of Michigan (MI)
U of Missouri–Rolla (MO)
The U of North Carolina at Chapel Hill (NC)
U of North Florida (FL)
U of Puerto Rico, Cayey U Coll (PR)
U of Puget Sound (WA)
U of Richmond (VA)
U of Rochester (NY)
U of San Diego (CA)
The U of Texas at Austin (TX)
The U of Texas at Dallas (TX)
The U of Texas Medical Branch (TX)
U of the South (TN)
U of Toronto (ON, Canada)
U of Tulsa (OK)
The U of Western Ontario (ON, Canada)
U of Wisconsin–Madison (WI)
Ursinus Coll (PA)
Vanderbilt U (TN)
Vassar Coll (NY)
Villanova U (PA)
Wake Forest U (NC)
Washington & Jefferson Coll (PA)
Wheaton Coll (IL)
Whitman Coll (WA)
Whitworth Coll (WA)
Willamette U (OR)
Wofford Coll (SC)
Worcester Polytechnic Inst (MA)

Moderately Difficult

More than 75% of the freshmen were in the top half of their high school class and scored over 1010 on the SAT I or over 18 on the ACT; about 85% or fewer of the applicants were accepted.

Abilene Christian U (TX)
Acadia U (NS, Canada)
Adams State Coll (CO)
Adelphi U (NY)

Adrian Coll (MI)
Alaska Pacific U (AK)
Albany Coll of Pharmacy of Union U (NY)
Alberta Coll of Art & Design (AB, Canada)
Albertson Coll of Idaho (ID)
Albertus Magnus Coll (CT)
Albion Coll (MI)
Albright Coll (PA)
Alderson-Broaddus Coll (WV)
Alfred U (NY)
Alice Lloyd Coll (KY)
Allen Coll (IA)
Alliant Intl U (CA)
Alliant Intl U–México City (Mexico)
Alma Coll (MI)
Alvernia Coll (PA)
Alverno Coll (WI)
American Acad of Art (IL)
American Coll of Computer & Information Sciences (AL)
American Intl Coll (MA)
The American U of Rome (Italy)
Anderson Coll (SC)
Andrews U (MI)
Angelo State U (TX)
Anna Maria Coll (MA)
Antioch Coll (OH)
Antioch U Los Angeles (CA)
Appalachian State U (NC)
Aquinas Coll (MI)
Arcadia U (PA)
Argosy U/Orange County (CA)
Arizona State U (AZ)
Arizona State U East (AZ)
Arizona State U West (AZ)
Arkansas State U (AR)
Arkansas Tech U (AR)
Art Acad of Cincinnati (OH)
The Art Inst of Boston at Lesley U (MA)
The Art Inst of California–San Francisco (CA)
Asbury Coll (KY)
Ashland U (OH)
Assumption Coll (MA)
Atlanta Christian Coll (GA)
Atlanta Coll of Art (GA)
Atlantic Union Coll (MA)
Auburn U (AL)
Auburn U Montgomery (AL)
Augsburg Coll (MN)
Augustana Coll (IL)
Augustana Coll (SD)
Aurora U (IL)
Austin Peay State U (TN)
Averett U (VA)
Azusa Pacific U (CA)
Baker U (KS)
Baldwin-Wallace Coll (OH)
Ball State U (IN)
Barry U (FL)
Baylor U (TX)
Bay Path Coll (MA)
Belhaven Coll (MS)
Bellarmine U (KY)
Bellin Coll of Nursing (WI)
Belmont Abbey Coll (NC)
Belmont U (TN)
Bemidji State U (MN)
Benedictine Coll (KS)
Benedictine U (IL)
Bentley Coll (MA)
Berklee Coll of Music (MA)
Berry Coll (GA)
Bethany Bible Coll (NB, Canada)
Bethany Coll (KS)
Bethany Coll (WV)
Bethany Lutheran Coll (MN)
Bethel Coll (KS)
Bethel U (MN)
Biola U (CA)
Birmingham-Southern Coll (AL)
Bishop's U (QC, Canada)
Blackburn Coll (IL)
Blessing-Rieman Coll of Nursing (IL)
Bloomsburg U of Pennsylvania (PA)
Bluefield Coll (VA)
Bluffton Coll (OH)
Bowling Green State U (OH)
Bradley U (IL)
Brenau U (GA)
Brescia U (KY)
Briarcliffe Coll (NY)
Briar Cliff U (IA)
Bridgewater Coll (VA)
Bridgewater State Coll (MA)
Brigham Young U (UT)
Brigham Young U–Hawaii (HI)
Brock U (ON, Canada)
Brooklyn Coll of the City U of New York (NY)
Bryan Coll (TN)
Bryant Coll (RI)
Buena Vista U (IA)
Buffalo State Coll, State U of New York (NY)
Butler U (IN)
Caldwell Coll (NJ)
California Coll of the Arts (CA)
California Lutheran U (CA)
California Maritime Acad (CA)
California Polytechnic State U, San Luis Obispo (CA)
California State Polytechnic U, Pomona (CA)
California State U, Chico (CA)
California State U, Dominguez Hills (CA)
California State U, Fresno (CA)
California State U, Fullerton (CA)
California State U, Hayward (CA)
California State U, Long Beach (CA)
California State U, Los Angeles (CA)
California State U, Sacramento (CA)
California State U, San Bernardino (CA)
California State U, San Marcos (CA)
California State U, Stanislaus (CA)
California U of Pennsylvania (PA)
Calvin Coll (MI)
Campbellsville U (KY)
Campbell U (NC)
Canadian Mennonite U (MB, Canada)
Canisius Coll (NY)
Capella U (MN)
Capital U (OH)
Cardinal Stritch U (WI)
Carleton U (ON, Canada)
Carlow Coll (PA)
Carroll Coll (MT)
Carroll Coll (WI)
Carson-Newman Coll (TN)
Carthage Coll (WI)
Castleton State Coll (VT)
Catawba Coll (NC)
The Catholic U of America (DC)
Cedar Crest Coll (PA)
Cedarville U (OH)
Centenary Coll (NJ)
Centenary Coll of Louisiana (LA)
Central Christian Coll of Kansas (KS)
Central Coll (IA)
Central Connecticut State U (CT)
Central Methodist Coll (MO)
Central Michigan U (MI)
Central Missouri State U (MO)
Central Washington U (WA)
Chaminade U of Honolulu (HI)
Champlain Coll (VT)
Chapman U (CA)
Charleston Southern U (SC)
Chatham Coll (PA)
Chester Coll of New England (NH)
Chestnut Hill Coll (PA)
Chicago State U (IL)
Christian Brothers U (TN)
Christian Heritage Coll (CA)
Christopher Newport U (VA)
The Citadel, The Military Coll of South Carolina (SC)
City Coll of the City U of New York (NY)
Clark Atlanta U (GA)
Clarke Coll (IA)
Clark U (MA)
Cleary U (MI)
Clemson U (SC)
The Cleveland Inst of Art (OH)
Coastal Carolina U (SC)
Coe Coll (IA)
Cogswell Polytechnical Coll (CA)
Coker Coll (SC)
Colby-Sawyer Coll (NH)
Coleman Coll, La Mesa (CA)
Coll for Creative Studies (MI)
Coll Misericordia (PA)
Coll of Charleston (SC)
Coll of Mount St. Joseph (OH)
Coll of Mount Saint Vincent (NY)
The Coll of New Rochelle (NY)
Coll of Notre Dame of Maryland (MD)
Coll of Saint Benedict (MN)
Coll of St. Catherine (MN)
Coll of Saint Elizabeth (NJ)
The Coll of Saint Rose (NY)
The Coll of St. Scholastica (MN)
Coll of Santa Fe (NM)
The Coll of Southeastern Europe, The American U of Athens (Greece)
Coll of Staten Island of the City U of New York (NY)
Coll of the Ozarks (MO)
Coll of the Southwest (NM)
Coll of Visual Arts (MN)
The Coll of Wooster (OH)
Colorado Christian U (CO)
Colorado State U (CO)
Colorado State U-Pueblo (CO)
Columbia Coll (SC)
Columbia Coll of Nursing (WI)
Columbus Coll of Art & Design (OH)
Concordia Coll (MN)
Concordia Coll (NY)
Concordia U (CA)
Concordia U (IL)
Concordia U (MI)
Concordia U (NE)
Concordia U (OR)
Concordia U (QC, Canada)
Concordia U at Austin (TX)
Concordia U Coll of Alberta (AB, Canada)
Concordia U Wisconsin (WI)
Converse Coll (SC)
Cornell Coll (IA)
Cornerstone U (MI)
Cornish Coll of the Arts (WA)
Covenant Coll (GA)
Creighton U (NE)
Crichton Coll (TN)
The Culinary Inst of America (NY)
Culver-Stockton Coll (MO)
Cumberland Coll (KY)
Cumberland U (TN)
Curry Coll (MA)
Daemen Coll (NY)
Dakota Wesleyan U (SD)
Dalhousie U (NS, Canada)
Dallas Baptist U (TX)
Dana Coll (NE)
Daniel Webster Coll (NH)
Defiance Coll (OH)
Delaware State U (DE)
Delaware Valley Coll (PA)
Denison U (OH)
DePaul U (IL)
DePauw U (IN)
DeSales U (PA)
Dillard U (LA)
Doane Coll (NE)
Dominican Coll (NY)
Dominican U (IL)
Dominican U of California (CA)
Dordt Coll (IA)
Dowling Coll (NY)
Drake U (IA)
Drew U (NJ)
Drexel U (PA)
Drury U (MO)
Duquesne U (PA)
D'Youville Coll (NY)
Earlham Coll (IN)
East Carolina U (NC)
East Central U (OK)
Eastern Connecticut State U (CT)
Eastern Illinois U (IL)
Eastern Mennonite U (VA)
Eastern Michigan U (MI)
Eastern Nazarene Coll (MA)
Eastern Oregon U (OR)
Eastern U (PA)
Eastern Washington U (WA)
East Stroudsburg U of Pennsylvania (PA)
East Texas Baptist U (TX)
Eckerd Coll (FL)
Edgewood Coll (WI)
Edinboro U of Pennsylvania (PA)
Elizabeth City State U (NC)
Elizabethtown Coll (PA)
Elmhurst Coll (IL)
Elmira Coll (NY)
Elms Coll (MA)
Elon U (NC)
Embry-Riddle Aeronautical U (AZ)
Embry-Riddle Aeronautical U (FL)
Emory & Henry Coll (VA)
Endicott Coll (MA)
Erskine Coll (SC)
Escuela de Artes Plasticas de Puerto Rico (PR)
Eugene Lang Coll, New School U (NY)
Eureka Coll (IL)
Evangel U (MO)
The Evergreen State Coll (WA)
Fairfield U (CT)
Fairleigh Dickinson U, Coll at Florham (NJ)
Fairleigh Dickinson U, Metropolitan Campus (NJ)
Farmingdale State U of New York (NY)
Fashion Inst of Technology (NY)
Five Towns Coll (NY)
Flagler Coll (FL)
Florida Ag and Mech U (FL)
Florida Atlantic U (FL)
Florida Coll (FL)
Florida Gulf Coast U (FL)
Florida Inst of Technology (FL)
Florida Intl U (FL)
Florida Southern Coll (FL)
Fontbonne U (MO)
Fort Lewis Coll (CO)
Fort Valley State U (GA)
Framingham State Coll (MA)
Franciscan U of Steubenville (OH)
Francis Marion U (SC)
Franklin Coll (IN)
Franklin Coll Switzerland (Switzerland)
Franklin Pierce Coll (NH)
Freed-Hardeman U (TN)
Fresno Pacific U (CA)
Frostburg State U (MD)
Gallaudet U (DC)
Gannon U (PA)
Gardner-Webb U (NC)
Geneva Coll (PA)
George Fox U (OR)
George Mason U (VA)
Georgetown Coll (KY)
Georgia Coll & State U (GA)

Georgian Court U (NJ)
Georgia Southern U (GA)
Georgia Southwestern State U (GA)
Georgia State U (GA)
Goddard Coll (VT)
Golden Gate U (CA)
Goldey-Beacom Coll (DE)
Gonzaga U (WA)
Gordon Coll (MA)
Goshen Coll (IN)
Goucher Coll (MD)
Governors State U (IL)
Grace Coll (IN)
Graceland U (IA)
Grace U (NE)
Grand Canyon U (AZ)
Grand Valley State U (MI)
Gratz Coll (PA)
Greensboro Coll (NC)
Greenville Coll (IL)
Guilford Coll (NC)
Gwynedd-Mercy Coll (PA)
Hamline U (MN)
Hampden-Sydney Coll (VA)
Hampshire Coll (MA)
Hampton U (VA)
Hannibal-LaGrange Coll (MO)
Hanover Coll (IN)
Harding U (AR)
Hardin-Simmons U (TX)
Harris-Stowe State Coll (MO)
Hartwick Coll (NY)
Hastings Coll (NE)
Hawai'i Pacific U (HI)
HEC Montreal (QC, Canada)
Heidelberg Coll (OH)
Henderson State U (AR)
Herzing Coll, Minneapolis Drafting School Division (MN)
Hesser Coll (NH)
High Point U (NC)
Hofstra U (NY)
Hollins U (VA)
Holy Names Coll (CA)
Hood Coll (MD)
Hope Coll (MI)
Houghton Coll (NY)
Houston Baptist U (TX)
Howard U (DC)
Humboldt State U (CA)
Hunter Coll of the City U of New York (NY)
Huntingdon Coll (AL)
Huntington Coll (IN)
Huron U USA in London (United Kingdom)
Husson Coll (ME)
Huston-Tillotson Coll (TX)
Illinois Coll (IL)
Illinois State U (IL)
Immaculata U (PA)
Indiana Inst of Technology (IN)
Indiana State U (IN)
Indiana U Bloomington (IN)
Indiana U East (IN)
Indiana U of Pennsylvania (PA)
Indiana U–Purdue U Indianapolis (IN)
Indiana U South Bend (IN)
Inter American U of Puerto Rico, Aguadilla Campus (PR)
Inter American U of Puerto Rico, Barranquitas Campus (PR)
Inter American U of Puerto Rico, Fajardo Campus (PR)
Inter American U of Puerto Rico, Ponce Campus (PR)
Inter American U of Puerto Rico, San Germán Campus (PR)
Intl U in Geneva (Switzerland)
Iona Coll (NY)
Iowa State U of Science and Technology (IA)
Iowa Wesleyan Coll (IA)
Ithaca Coll (NY)
Jacksonville U (FL)
Jewish Hospital Coll of Nursing and Allied Health (MO)
John Brown U (AR)
John Cabot U (Italy)
John Carroll U (OH)
John Jay Coll of Criminal Justice of the City U of New York (NY)
Johnson State Coll (VT)
Judson Coll (AL)
Judson Coll (IL)
Juniata Coll (PA)
Kansas City Art Inst (MO)
Kansas Wesleyan U (KS)
Kean U (NJ)
Keene State Coll (NH)
Kennesaw State U (GA)
Kent State U (OH)
Kentucky Christian Coll (KY)
Kentucky Mountain Bible Coll (KY)
Kentucky Wesleyan Coll (KY)
Keuka Coll (NY)
King Coll (TN)
King's Coll (PA)
The King's U Coll (AB, Canada)
Kutztown U of Pennsylvania (PA)
Laboratory Inst of Merchandising (NY)
LaGrange Coll (GA)
Lakehead U (ON, Canada)
Lake Superior State U (MI)
Lambuth U (TN)
Lander U (SC)
La Salle U (PA)
Lasell Coll (MA)
Lawrence Technological U (MI)
Lebanon Valley Coll (PA)
Lehman Coll of the City U of New York (NY)
Le Moyne Coll (NY)
Lenoir-Rhyne Coll (NC)
Lesley U (MA)
Lewis U (IL)
Life Pacific Coll (CA)
Lincoln Memorial U (TN)
Lincoln U (PA)
Lindenwood U (MO)
Linfield Coll (OR)
Lipscomb U (TN)
Lock Haven U of Pennsylvania (PA)
Logan U-Coll of Chiropractic (MO)
Long Island U, C.W. Post Campus (NY)
Long Island U, Southampton Coll (NY)
Longwood U (VA)
Loras Coll (IA)
Louisiana Coll (LA)
Louisiana State U and Ag and Mech Coll (LA)
Louisiana Tech U (LA)
Lourdes Coll (OH)
Loyola Coll in Maryland (MD)
Loyola U Chicago (IL)
Loyola U New Orleans (LA)
Lubbock Christian U (TX)
Luther Coll (IA)
Lycoming Coll (PA)
Lyme Acad Coll of Fine Arts (CT)
Lynchburg Coll (VA)
Lyndon State Coll (VT)
MacMurray Coll (IL)
Madonna U (MI)
Magdalen Coll (NH)
Maharishi U of Management (IA)
Maine Coll of Art (ME)
Maine Maritime Acad (ME)
Malone Coll (OH)
Manchester Coll (IN)
Manhattan Coll (NY)
Manhattanville Coll (NY)
Mansfield U of Pennsylvania (PA)
Marian Coll (IN)
Marian Coll of Fond du Lac (WI)
Marietta Coll (OH)
Marist Coll (NY)
Marlboro Coll (VT)
Marquette U (WI)
Mars Hill Coll (NC)
Martin Luther Coll (MN)
Mary Baldwin Coll (VA)
Marygrove Coll (MI)
Marymount Coll of Fordham U (NY)
Marymount Manhattan Coll (NY)
Marymount U (VA)
Maryville Coll (TN)
Maryville U of Saint Louis (MO)
Marywood U (PA)
Massachusetts Coll of Liberal Arts (MA)
Massachusetts Coll of Pharmacy and Health Sciences (MA)
Massachusetts Maritime Acad (MA)
The Master's Coll and Sem (CA)
McDaniel Coll (MD)
McKendree Coll (IL)
McMurry U (TX)
McNeese State U (LA)
McPherson Coll (KS)
Medaille Coll (NY)
Medcenter One Coll of Nursing (ND)
Medical Coll of Georgia (GA)
Memorial U of Newfoundland (NL, Canada)
Memphis Coll of Art (TN)
Menlo Coll (CA)
Mercer U (GA)
Mercyhurst Coll (PA)
Meredith Coll (NC)
Merrimack Coll (MA)
Messenger Coll (MO)
Messiah Coll (PA)
Methodist Coll (NC)
Miami Intl U of Art & Design (FL)
Miami U (OH)
Michigan State U (MI)
Michigan Technological U (MI)
Middle Tennessee State U (TN)
Millersville U of Pennsylvania (PA)
Milligan Coll (TN)
Millikin U (IL)
Millsaps Coll (MS)
Mills Coll (CA)
Milwaukee Inst of Art and Design (WI)
Milwaukee School of Eng (WI)
Minneapolis Coll of Art and Design (MN)
Minnesota State U Mankato (MN)
Minnesota State U Moorhead (MN)
Mississippi Coll (MS)
Mississippi State U (MS)
Missouri Baptist U (MO)
Missouri Southern State U (MO)
Missouri Tech (MO)
Molloy Coll (NY)
Monmouth Coll (IL)
Monmouth U (NJ)
Montana State U–Billings (MT)
Montana State U–Bozeman (MT)
Montana Tech of The U of Montana (MT)
Montclair State U (NJ)
Montreat Coll (NC)
Montserrat Coll of Art (MA)
Moody Bible Inst (IL)
Moore Coll of Art & Design (PA)
Moravian Coll (PA)
Morehouse Coll (GA)
Morgan State U (MD)
Morningside Coll (IA)
Mount Allison U (NB, Canada)
Mount Ida Coll (MA)
Mount Marty Coll (SD)
Mount Mary Coll (WI)
Mount Mercy Coll (IA)
Mount Saint Mary Coll (NY)
Mount St. Mary's Coll (CA)
Mount Saint Mary's Coll and Sem (MD)
Mount Saint Vincent U (NS, Canada)
Mt. Sierra Coll (CA)
Mount Union Coll (OH)
Mount Vernon Nazarene U (OH)
Multnomah Bible Coll and Biblical Sem (OR)
Murray State U (KY)
Naropa U (CO)
Nazareth Coll of Rochester (NY)
Nebraska Methodist Coll (NE)
Nebraska Wesleyan U (NE)
Neumann Coll (PA)
Newberry Coll (SC)
New Jersey City U (NJ)
New Jersey Inst of Technology (NJ)
New Mexico Inst of Mining and Technology (NM)
New Mexico State U (NM)
New School Bachelor of Arts, New School U (NY)
New York Inst of Technology (NY)
New York School of Interior Design (NY)
Niagara U (NY)
Nichols Coll (MA)
Norfolk State U (VA)
North Carolina Wesleyan Coll (NC)
North Central Coll (IL)
North Dakota State U (ND)
Northeastern State U (OK)
Northeastern U (MA)
Northern Arizona U (AZ)
Northern Illinois U (IL)
North Georgia Coll & State U (GA)
Northland Coll (WI)
North Park U (IL)
Northwest Christian Coll (OR)
Northwest Coll of Art (WA)
Northwestern Coll (IA)
Northwestern Coll (MN)
Northwestern Oklahoma State U (OK)
Northwest Nazarene U (ID)
Northwood U (MI)
Northwood U, Florida Campus (FL)
Northwood U, Texas Campus (TX)
Notre Dame Coll (OH)
Notre Dame de Namur U (CA)
Nova Southeastern U (FL)
Nyack Coll (NY)
Oakland U (MI)
Ohio Dominican U (OH)
Ohio Northern U (OH)
The Ohio State U (OH)
Ohio U (OH)
Ohr Somayach/Joseph Tanenbaum Educational Center (NY)
Oklahoma Baptist U (OK)
Oklahoma City U (OK)
Oklahoma State U (OK)
O'More Coll of Design (TN)
Oral Roberts U (OK)
Oregon Inst of Technology (OR)
Oregon State U (OR)
Otis Coll of Art and Design (CA)
Ottawa U (KS)
Otterbein Coll (OH)
Ouachita Baptist U (AR)
Our Lady of the Lake U of San Antonio (TX)
Pace U (NY)
Pacific Lutheran U (WA)
Pacific Northwest Coll of Art (OR)
Pacific Union Coll (CA)
Pacific U (OR)
Palm Beach Atlantic U (FL)
Palmer Coll of Chiropractic (IA)
Park U (MO)
Peace Coll (NC)
The Pennsylvania State U Abington Coll (PA)
The Pennsylvania State U Altoona Coll (PA)
The Pennsylvania State U Beaver Campus of the Commonwealth Coll (PA)

The Pennsylvania State U Berks Campus of the Berks–Lehigh Valley Coll (PA)
The Pennsylvania State U Delaware County Campus of the Commonwealth Coll (PA)
The Pennsylvania State U DuBois Campus of the Commonwealth Coll (PA)
The Pennsylvania State U Fayette Campus of the Commonwealth Coll (PA)
The Pennsylvania State U Harrisburg Campus of the Capital Coll (PA)
The Pennsylvania State U Hazleton Campus of the Commonwealth Coll (PA)
The Pennsylvania State U, Lehigh Valley Campus of the Berks-Lehigh Valley Coll (PA)
The Pennsylvania State U McKeesport Campus of the Commonwealth Coll (PA)
The Pennsylvania State U Mont Alto Campus of the Commonwealth Coll (PA)
The Pennsylvania State U New Kensington Campus of the Commonwealth Coll (PA)
The Pennsylvania State U Schuylkill Campus of the Capital Coll (PA)
The Pennsylvania State U Shenango Campus of the Commonwealth Coll (PA)
The Pennsylvania State U Wilkes-Barre Campus of the Commonwealth Coll (PA)
The Pennsylvania State U Worthington Scranton Campus of the Commonwealth Coll (PA)
The Pennsylvania State U York Campus of the Commonwealth Coll (PA)
Pfeiffer U (NC)
Philadelphia Biblical U (PA)
Philadelphia U (PA)
Piedmont Coll (GA)
Pine Manor Coll (MA)
Pitzer Coll (CA)
Plymouth State U (NH)
Point Loma Nazarene U (CA)
Point Park U (PA)
Pontifical Catholic U of Puerto Rico (PR)
Prairie View A&M U (TX)
Principia Coll (IL)
Purdue U (IN)
Queens U of Charlotte (NC)
Quincy U (IL)
Quinnipiac U (CT)
Radford U (VA)
Ramapo Coll of New Jersey (NJ)
Randolph-Macon Coll (VA)
Randolph-Macon Woman's Coll (VA)
Redeemer U Coll (ON, Canada)
Reformed Bible Coll (MI)
Regis Coll (MA)
Regis U (CO)
Reinhardt Coll (GA)
Research Coll of Nursing (MO)
Rhode Island Coll (RI)
Richmond, The American Intl U in London (United Kingdom)
Rider U (NJ)
Ringling School of Art and Design (FL)
Ripon Coll (WI)
Rivier Coll (NH)
Roanoke Coll (VA)
Robert Morris U (PA)
Roberts Wesleyan Coll (NY)
Rochester Inst of Technology (NY)
Rockford Coll (IL)
Rockhurst U (MO)
Rocky Mountain Coll (MT)
Rocky Mountain Coll of Art & Design (CO)
Roger Williams U (RI)
Roosevelt U (IL)
Rosemont Coll (PA)
Rowan U (NJ)
Rush U (IL)
Russell Sage Coll (NY)
Rutgers, The State U of New Jersey, Camden (NJ)
Rutgers, The State U of New Jersey, Newark (NJ)
Rutgers, The State U of New Jersey, New Brunswick/Piscataway (NJ)
Ryerson U (ON, Canada)
Sacred Heart Major Sem (MI)
Sacred Heart U (CT)
Saginaw Valley State U (MI)
St. Ambrose U (IA)
St. Andrews Presbyterian Coll (NC)
Saint Anselm Coll (NH)
Saint Anthony Coll of Nursing (IL)
St. Bonaventure U (NY)
St. Charles Borromeo Sem, Overbrook (PA)
St. Cloud State U (MN)
St. Edward's U (TX)
St. Francis Coll (NY)
Saint Francis Medical Center Coll of Nursing (IL)
Saint Francis U (PA)
St. Francis Xavier U (NS, Canada)
St. John Fisher Coll (NY)
St. John's Coll (IL)
St. John's Coll (MD)
Saint John's U (MN)
St. John's U (NY)
Saint Joseph Coll (CT)
Saint Joseph's Coll (IN)
St. Joseph's Coll, New York (NY)
Saint Joseph's Coll of Maine (ME)
St. Joseph's Coll, Suffolk Campus (NY)
Saint Leo U (FL)
St. Louis Coll of Pharmacy (MO)
Saint Louis U (MO)
Saint Martin's Coll (WA)
Saint Mary-of-the-Woods Coll (IN)
Saint Mary's Coll (IN)
Saint Mary's Coll of California (CA)
Saint Mary's U of Minnesota (MN)
St. Mary's U of San Antonio (TX)
Saint Michael's Coll (VT)
St. Norbert Coll (WI)
St. Thomas Aquinas Coll (NY)
St. Thomas U (FL)
St. Thomas U (NB, Canada)
Saint Vincent Coll (PA)
Saint Xavier U (IL)
Salem Coll (NC)
Salisbury U (MD)
Salve Regina U (RI)
Samford U (AL)
Sam Houston State U (TX)
Samuel Merritt Coll (CA)
San Diego State U (CA)
San Francisco Art Inst (CA)
San Francisco State U (CA)
San Jose State U (CA)
Santa Clara U (CA)
Savannah Coll of Art and Design (GA)
School of the Art Inst of Chicago (IL)
School of the Museum of Fine Arts, Boston (MA)
Schreiner U (TX)
Seattle Pacific U (WA)
Seattle U (WA)
Seton Hall U (NJ)
Seton Hill U (PA)
Shenandoah U (VA)
Shepherd U (WV)
Shimer Coll (IL)
Shippensburg U of Pennsylvania (PA)
Shorter Coll (GA)
Siena Coll (NY)
Siena Heights U (MI)
Sierra Nevada Coll (NV)
Simmons Coll (MA)
Simon Fraser U (BC, Canada)
Simpson Coll (IA)
Simpson Coll and Graduate School (CA)
Slippery Rock U of Pennsylvania (PA)
Sonoma State U (CA)
South Dakota School of Mines and Technology (SD)
South Dakota State U (SD)
Southeastern Bible Coll (AL)
Southeastern Oklahoma State U (OK)
Southeast Missouri State U (MO)
Southern Adventist U (TN)
Southern Arkansas U–Magnolia (AR)
Southern California Inst of Architecture (CA)
Southern Connecticut State U (CT)
Southern Illinois U Carbondale (IL)
Southern Illinois U Edwardsville (IL)
Southern Methodist U (TX)
Southern Oregon U (OR)
Southern Polytechnic State U (GA)
Southern U and Ag and Mech Coll (LA)
Southern Utah U (UT)
Southwest Baptist U (MO)
Southwestern Coll (KS)
Southwestern Oklahoma State U (OK)
Southwest Missouri State U (MO)
Spring Arbor U (MI)
Springfield Coll (MA)
Spring Hill Coll (AL)
State U of New York at New Paltz (NY)
State U of New York at Oswego (NY)
State U of New York at Plattsburgh (NY)
State U of New York Coll at Brockport (NY)
State U of New York Coll at Cortland (NY)
State U of New York Coll at Fredonia (NY)
State U of New York Coll at Old Westbury (NY)
State U of New York Coll at Oneonta (NY)
State U of New York Coll at Potsdam (NY)
State U of New York Coll of Agriculture and Technology at Cobleskill (NY)
State U of New York Coll of Technology at Alfred (NY)
State U of New York Downstate Medical Center (NY)
State U of New York Upstate Medical U (NY)
Stephens Coll (MO)
Sterling Coll (KS)
Sterling Coll (VT)
Stetson U (FL)
Suffolk U (MA)
Susquehanna U (PA)
Sweet Briar Coll (VA)
Tabor Coll (KS)
Talmudic Coll of Florida (FL)
Tarleton State U (TX)
Taylor U, Fort Wayne Campus (IN)
Tennessee Technological U (TN)
Tennessee Wesleyan Coll (TN)
Texas A&M Intl U (TX)
Texas A&M U (TX)
Texas A&M U at Galveston (TX)
Texas A&M U–Commerce (TX)
Texas A&M U–Corpus Christi (TX)
Texas A&M U–Kingsville (TX)
Texas Chiropractic Coll (TX)
Texas Christian U (TX)
Texas Lutheran U (TX)
Texas State U-San Marcos (TX)
Texas Tech U (TX)
Texas Wesleyan U (TX)
Thiel Coll (PA)
Thomas Jefferson U (PA)
Thomas More Coll (KY)
Thomas More Coll of Liberal Arts (NH)
Toccoa Falls Coll (GA)
Towson U (MD)
Trent U (ON, Canada)
Trevecca Nazarene U (TN)
Trinity Baptist Coll (FL)
Trinity Christian Coll (IL)
Trinity Coll (DC)
Trinity Intl U (IL)
Trinity Western U (BC, Canada)
Tri-State U (IN)
Troy State U (AL)
Truman State U (MO)
Tusculum Coll (TN)
Tuskegee U (AL)
Tyndale U Coll & Sem (ON, Canada)
Union Coll (KY)
Union Coll (NE)
Union Inst & U (OH)
Union U (TN)
United States Intl U (Kenya)
Unity Coll (ME)
Université de Montréal (QC, Canada)
Université de Sherbrooke (QC, Canada)
U at Albany, State U of New York (NY)
U at Buffalo, The State U of New York (NY)
The U of Alabama (AL)
The U of Alabama at Birmingham (AL)
The U of Alabama in Huntsville (AL)
U of Alberta (AB, Canada)
The U of Arizona (AZ)
U of Arkansas (AR)
U of Bridgeport (CT)
U of Calgary (AB, Canada)
U of California, Irvine (CA)
U of Central Arkansas (AR)
U of Central Florida (FL)
U of Charleston (WV)
U of Cincinnati (OH)
U of Colorado at Boulder (CO)
U of Colorado at Colorado Springs (CO)
U of Colorado at Denver (CO)
U of Colorado Health Sciences Center (CO)
U of Connecticut (CT)
U of Dallas (TX)
U of Dayton (OH)
U of Delaware (DE)
U of Denver (CO)
U of Detroit Mercy (MI)
U of Dubuque (IA)
U of Evansville (IN)
The U of Findlay (OH)
U of Georgia (GA)
U of Guelph (ON, Canada)
U of Hartford (CT)
U of Hawaii at Hilo (HI)
U of Hawaii at Manoa (HI)
U of Houston (TX)
U of Idaho (ID)
U of Illinois at Chicago (IL)
U of Indianapolis (IN)
The U of Iowa (IA)
U of Judaism (CA)
U of Kansas (KS)
U of Kentucky (KY)
U of King's Coll (NS, Canada)
U of La Verne (CA)
The U of Lethbridge (AB, Canada)
U of Louisiana at Lafayette (LA)
U of Louisville (KY)
U of Maine (ME)
U of Maine at Farmington (ME)
U of Maine at Fort Kent (ME)
U of Maine at Machias (ME)
U of Manitoba (MB, Canada)
U of Mary (ND)
U of Mary Hardin-Baylor (TX)
U of Maryland, Baltimore County (MD)
U of Maryland, Coll Park (MD)
U of Maryland Eastern Shore (MD)
U of Massachusetts Amherst (MA)
U of Massachusetts Boston (MA)
U of Massachusetts Dartmouth (MA)
U of Massachusetts Lowell (MA)
The U of Memphis (TN)
U of Michigan–Dearborn (MI)
U of Michigan–Flint (MI)
U of Minnesota, Crookston (MN)
U of Minnesota, Duluth (MN)
U of Minnesota, Morris (MN)
U of Minnesota, Twin Cities Campus (MN)
U of Mississippi (MS)

U of Missouri–Columbia (MO)
U of Missouri–Kansas City (MO)
U of Missouri–St. Louis (MO)
U of Mobile (AL)
The U of Montana–Missoula (MT)
U of Montevallo (AL)
U of Nebraska–Lincoln (NE)
U of Nebraska Medical Center (NE)
U of Nevada, Las Vegas (NV)
U of Nevada, Reno (NV)
U of New Brunswick Fredericton (NB, Canada)
U of New Hampshire (NH)
U of New Hampshire at Manchester (NH)
U of New Haven (CT)
U of New Mexico (NM)
U of New Orleans (LA)
The U of North Carolina at Asheville (NC)
The U of North Carolina at Charlotte (NC)
The U of North Carolina at Greensboro (NC)
The U of North Carolina at Pembroke (NC)
The U of North Carolina at Wilmington (NC)
U of Northern Colorado (CO)
U of Northern Iowa (IA)
U of North Texas (TX)
U of Oklahoma (OK)
U of Oklahoma Health Sciences Center (OK)
U of Oregon (OR)
U of Ottawa (ON, Canada)
U of Pittsburgh (PA)
U of Pittsburgh at Greensburg (PA)
U of Pittsburgh at Johnstown (PA)
U of Portland (OR)
U of Prince Edward Island (PE, Canada)
U of Redlands (CA)
U of Rhode Island (RI)
U of St. Francis (IL)
U of Saint Francis (IN)
U of Saint Mary (KS)
U of St. Thomas (MN)
U of St. Thomas (TX)
U of San Francisco (CA)
U of Saskatchewan (SK, Canada)
U of Science and Arts of Oklahoma (OK)
The U of Scranton (PA)
U of Sioux Falls (SD)
U of South Alabama (AL)
U of South Carolina (SC)
U of South Carolina Spartanburg (SC)
The U of South Dakota (SD)
U of Southern Maine (ME)
U of South Florida (FL)
The U of Tampa (FL)
The U of Tennessee (TN)
The U of Tennessee at Chattanooga (TN)
The U of Tennessee at Martin (TN)
The U of Texas at Arlington (TX)
The U of Texas Health Science Center at Houston (TX)
The U of Texas Health Science Center at San Antonio (TX)
The U of Texas Southwestern Medical Center at Dallas (TX)
The U of the Arts (PA)
U of the Incarnate Word (TX)
U of the Ozarks (AR)
U of the Pacific (CA)
U of the Sacred Heart (PR)
U of the Sciences in Philadelphia (PA)
U of Utah (UT)
U of Vermont (VT)
U of Victoria (BC, Canada)
The U of Virginia's Coll at Wise (VA)
U of Washington (WA)
U of Waterloo (ON, Canada)
U of West Florida (FL)
U of Windsor (ON, Canada)
U of Wisconsin–Eau Claire (WI)
U of Wisconsin–Green Bay (WI)
U of Wisconsin–La Crosse (WI)
U of Wisconsin–Milwaukee (WI)
U of Wisconsin–Oshkosh (WI)
U of Wisconsin–Parkside (WI)
U of Wisconsin–Platteville (WI)
U of Wisconsin–River Falls (WI)
U of Wisconsin–Stevens Point (WI)
U of Wisconsin–Stout (WI)
U of Wisconsin–Superior (WI)
U of Wisconsin–Whitewater (WI)
U of Wyoming (WY)
Upper Iowa U (IA)
Urbana U (OH)
Utah State U (UT)
Utica Coll (NY)
Valdosta State U (GA)
Valparaiso U (IN)
Vanguard U of Southern California (CA)
Villa Julie Coll (MD)
Virginia Coll at Birmingham (AL)
Virginia Commonwealth U (VA)
Virginia Military Inst (VA)
Virginia Polytechnic Inst and State U (VA)
Virginia Union U (VA)
Virginia Wesleyan Coll (VA)
Viterbo U (WI)
Voorhees Coll (SC)
Wabash Coll (IN)
Wagner Coll (NY)
Waldorf Coll (IA)
Walla Walla Coll (WA)
Walsh U (OH)
Warner Pacific Coll (OR)
Warren Wilson Coll (NC)
Wartburg Coll (IA)
Washington Bible Coll (MD)
Washington Coll (MD)
Washington State U (WA)
Watkins Coll of Art and Design (TN)
Waynesburg Coll (PA)
Wayne State U (MI)
Webber Intl U (FL)
Webster U (MO)
Wells Coll (NY)
Wentworth Inst of Technology (MA)
Wesleyan Coll (GA)
Wesley Coll (DE)
West Chester U of Pennsylvania (PA)
Western Baptist Coll (OR)
Western Carolina U (NC)
Western Connecticut State U (CT)
Western Illinois U (IL)
Western Kentucky U (KY)
Western Michigan U (MI)
Western New England Coll (MA)
Western Oregon U (OR)
Western State Coll of Colorado (CO)
Western Washington U (WA)
Westfield State Coll (MA)
Westminster Choir Coll of Rider U (NJ)
Westminster Coll (MO)
Westminster Coll (PA)
Westminster Coll (UT)
Westmont Coll (CA)
West Texas A&M U (TX)
West Virginia U (WV)
West Virginia Wesleyan Coll (WV)
Wheaton Coll (MA)
Wheeling Jesuit U (WV)
Wheelock Coll (MA)
Widener U (PA)
Wilkes U (PA)
William Carey Coll (MS)
William Jewell Coll (MO)
William Paterson U of New Jersey (NJ)
William Penn U (IA)
William Woods U (MO)
Wilson Coll (PA)
Wingate U (NC)
Winona State U (MN)
Winthrop U (SC)
Wisconsin Lutheran Coll (WI)
Wittenberg U (OH)
Worcester State Coll (MA)
Xavier U (OH)
Xavier U of Louisiana (LA)
York Coll (NE)
York Coll of Pennsylvania (PA)
York Coll of the City U of New York (NY)
York U (ON, Canada)

Minimally Difficult

Most freshmen were not in the top half of their high school class and scored somewhat below 1010 on the SAT I or below 19 on the ACT; up to 95% of the applicants were accepted.

Alabama Ag and Mech U (AL)
Alabama State U (AL)
Alaska Bible Coll (AK)
Albany State U (GA)
Alcorn State U (MS)
Allen U (SC)
Amberton U (TX)
American Coll of Thessaloniki (Greece)
American Indian Coll of the Assemblies of God, Inc. (AZ)
Antioch U Santa Barbara (CA)
Appalachian Bible Coll (WV)
Arkansas Baptist Coll (AR)
Armstrong Atlantic State U (GA)
The Art Inst of Atlanta (GA)
The Art Inst of California–San Diego (CA)
The Art Inst of Colorado (CO)
The Art Inst of Phoenix (AZ)
The Art Inst of Portland (OR)
Atlantic Baptist U (NB, Canada)
Augusta State U (GA)
Austin Graduate School of Theology (TX)
Avila U (MO)
Bacone Coll (OK)
Baltimore Intl Coll (MD)
Barber-Scotia Coll (NC)
Barclay Coll (KS)
Barton Coll (NC)
Becker Coll (MA)
Berkeley Coll (NJ)
Berkeley Coll-New York City Campus (NY)
Berkeley Coll-Westchester Campus (NY)
Bethel Coll (IN)
Bethel Coll (TN)
Bethesda Christian U (CA)
Bethune-Cookman Coll (FL)
Black Hills State U (SD)
Bloomfield Coll (NJ)
Blue Mountain Coll (MS)
Boise State U (ID)
Bowie State U (MD)
Brevard Coll (NC)
Brewton-Parker Coll (GA)
Bryn Athyn Coll of the New Church (PA)
Cabrini Coll (PA)
California Baptist U (CA)
Calumet Coll of Saint Joseph (IN)
Calvary Bible Coll and Theological Sem (MO)
Cambridge Coll (MA)
Cameron U (OK)
Capitol Coll (MD)
Cazenovia Coll (NY)
Central Baptist Coll (AR)
Central Pentecostal Coll (SK, Canada)
Central State U (OH)
Cheyney U of Pennsylvania (PA)
Chowan Coll (NC)
Clarion U of Pennsylvania (PA)
Clayton Coll & State U (GA)
Clearwater Christian Coll (FL)
Coll of St. Joseph (VT)
Coll of Saint Mary (NE)
Colorado Tech U Sioux Falls Campus (SD)
Columbia Coll (MO)
Columbia Coll Hollywood (CA)
Columbia Intl U (SC)
Columbia Union Coll (MD)
Columbus State U (GA)
Concord Coll (WV)
Concordia U, St. Paul (MN)
Crown Coll (MN)
Dakota State U (SD)
Dallas Christian Coll (TX)
Davis & Elkins Coll (WV)
Delta State U (MS)
Eastern New Mexico U (NM)
Embry-Riddle Aeronautical U, Extended Campus (FL)
Emmanuel Coll (GA)
Eugene Bible Coll (OR)
Fairmont State Coll (WV)
Faith Baptist Bible Coll and Theological Sem (IA)
Faulkner U (AL)
Fayetteville State U (NC)
Ferris State U (MI)
Ferrum Coll (VA)
Fisher Coll (MA)
Florida Metropolitan U–Brandon Campus (FL)
Florida Metropolitan U–Fort Lauderdale Campus (FL)
Florida Metropolitan U–Lakeland Campus (FL)
Florida Metropolitan U–Tampa Campus (FL)
The Franciscan U (IA)
God's Bible School and Coll (OH)
Grace Bible Coll (MI)
Grand View Coll (IA)
Griggs U (MD)
Haskell Indian Nations U (KS)
Hellenic Coll (MA)
Heritage Bible Coll (NC)
Hilbert Coll (NY)
Howard Payne U (TX)
Idaho State U (ID)
The Illinois Inst of Art (IL)
The Illinois Inst of Art-Schaumburg (IL)
Indiana U Kokomo (IN)
Indiana U Northwest (IN)
Indiana U–Purdue U Fort Wayne (IN)
Indiana U Southeast (IN)
Intl Acad of Design & Technology (IL)
Intl Coll (FL)
Jacksonville State U (AL)
Jamestown Coll (ND)
Jarvis Christian Coll (TX)
Johnson & Wales U (CO)
Johnson & Wales U (FL)
Johnson & Wales U (RI)
Johnson Bible Coll (TN)
Johnson C. Smith U (NC)
John Wesley Coll (NC)
Kaplan Coll (IA)
Kendall Coll (IL)
Kentucky State U (KY)
Keystone Coll (PA)
Lake Erie Coll (OH)
Lakeland Coll (WI)
Lamar U (TX)
Lancaster Bible Coll (PA)
Lane Coll (TN)
La Roche Coll (PA)
Laurentian U (ON, Canada)
Lewis-Clark State Coll (ID)
Liberty U (VA)
Limestone Coll (SC)
Lindsey Wilson Coll (KY)
Livingstone Coll (NC)
Long Island U, Brooklyn Campus (NY)
Lynn U (FL)
Macon State Coll (GA)
Manhattan Christian Coll (KS)

Marshall U (WV)
Metropolitan Coll, Tulsa (OK)
Metropolitan State Coll of Denver (CO)
Metropolitan State U (MN)
MidAmerica Nazarene U (KS)
Mid-Continent Coll (KY)
Midway Coll (KY)
Midwestern State U (TX)
Minot State U (ND)
Mississippi Valley State U (MS)
Missouri Valley Coll (MO)
Mitchell Coll (CT)
Morehead State U (KY)
Morris Coll (SC)
Mount Aloysius Coll (PA)
Musicians Inst (CA)
National-Louis U (IL)
Newbury Coll (MA)
The New England Inst of Art (MA)
New England School of Communications (ME)
New Hampshire Inst of Art (NH)
Newman U (KS)
New Mexico Highlands U (NM)
Nipissing U (ON, Canada)
North Carolina Central U (NC)
Northcentral U (AZ)
Northeastern Illinois U (IL)
Northern Michigan U (MI)
Northern State U (SD)
North Greenville Coll (SC)
Nova Scotia Ag Coll (NS, Canada)
Oak Hills Christian Coll (MN)
Oakland City U (IN)
Ohio Valley Coll (WV)
Olivet Coll (MI)
Olivet Nazarene U (IL)
Oregon Coll of Art & Craft (OR)
Our Lady of Holy Cross Coll (LA)
Pacific States U (CA)
Paier Coll of Art, Inc. (CT)
Paine Coll (GA)
Paul Smith's Coll of Arts and Sciences (NY)
Peirce Coll (PA)
Polytechnic U of Puerto Rico (PR)
Pontifical Coll Josephinum (OH)
Portland State U (OR)
Practical Bible Coll (NY)
Prairie Bible Coll (AB, Canada)
Purdue U North Central (IN)
Robert Morris Coll (IL)
Rochester Coll (MI)
Sage Coll of Albany (NY)
Saint Augustine's Coll (NC)
St. Gregory's U (OK)
Saint Joseph Sem Coll (LA)
St. Louis Christian Coll (MO)
Salem State Coll (MA)
Schiller Intl U, American Coll of Switzerland (Switzerland)
Shaw U (NC)
Silver Lake Coll (WI)
South Carolina State U (SC)
Southeastern Coll of the Assemblies of God (FL)
Southern Christian U (AL)
Southern Vermont Coll (VT)
Southern Wesleyan U (SC)
South U (AL)
South U (GA)
Southwestern Coll (AZ)
State U of New York Empire State Coll (NY)
State U of New York Inst of Technology at Utica/Rome (NY)
State U of West Georgia (GA)
Steinbach Bible Coll (MB, Canada)
Stratford U (VA)
Sullivan U (KY)
Talladega Coll (AL)
Teikyo Post U (CT)
Tennessee State U (TN)
Texas Woman's U (TX)
Thomas Coll (ME)
Tiffin U (OH)
Tougaloo Coll (MS)
Touro U Intl (CA)
Trinity Coll of Florida (FL)
Troy State U Dothan (AL)
Universidad Adventista de las Antillas (PR)
Université Laval (QC, Canada)
The U of Akron (OH)
U of Alaska Fairbanks (AK)
U of Arkansas at Little Rock (AR)
U of Houston–Clear Lake (TX)
U of Houston–Victoria (TX)
U of Illinois at Springfield (IL)
U of Maine at Presque Isle (ME)
The U of Montana–Western (MT)
U of Nebraska at Omaha (NE)
U of North Alabama (AL)
U of North Dakota (ND)
U of Pittsburgh at Bradford (PA)
U of Regina (SK, Canada)
U of South Carolina Aiken (SC)
U of the Virgin Islands (VI)
The U of West Alabama (AL)
U of West Los Angeles (CA)
Ursuline Coll (OH)
Vermont Tech Coll (VT)
Virginia Intermont Coll (VA)
Virginia State U (VA)
Warner Southern Coll (FL)
Wayland Baptist U (TX)
West Liberty State Coll (WV)
West Virginia State Coll (WV)
Wilberforce U (OH)
Williams Baptist Coll (AR)
William Tyndale Coll (MI)
Winston-Salem State U (NC)
Wright State U (OH)

Noncompetitive

Virtually all applicants were accepted regardless of high school rank or test scores.

Acad of Art U (CA)
American Baptist Coll of American Baptist Theological Sem (TN)
American InterContinental U (CA)
American InterContinental U, Atlanta (GA)
American InterContinental U-London (United Kingdom)
American Public U System (WV)
American U of Puerto Rico (PR)
Antioch U Seattle (WA)
Arlington Baptist Coll (TX)
Athabasca U (AB, Canada)
Athens State U (AL)
Baker Coll of Auburn Hills (MI)
Baker Coll of Cadillac (MI)
Baker Coll of Clinton Township (MI)
Baker Coll of Flint (MI)
Baker Coll of Jackson (MI)
Baker Coll of Muskegon (MI)
Baker Coll of Owosso (MI)
Baker Coll of Port Huron (MI)
Baptist Bible Coll (MO)
The Baptist Coll of Florida (FL)
Bellevue U (NE)
Bluefield State Coll (WV)
Boston Architectural Center (MA)
Briercrest Bible Coll (SK, Canada)
Burlington Coll (VT)
California Christian Coll (CA)
Cascade Coll (OR)
Chadron State Coll (NE)
Chaparral Coll (AZ)
Charter Oak State Coll (CT)
City U (WA)
Clear Creek Baptist Bible Coll (KY)
Cleveland State U (OH)
CollAmerica–Fort Collins (CO)
Coll for Lifelong Learning (NH)
Coll of Biblical Studies–Houston (TX)
Coll of Emmanuel and St. Chad (SK, Canada)
Columbia Coll, Caguas (PR)
Columbia Coll Chicago (IL)
Columbia Southern U (AL)
Conception Sem Coll (MO)
Concordia Coll (AL)
Crossroads Bible Coll (IN)
Crossroads Coll (MN)
Dalton State Coll (GA)
Davenport U, Dearborn (MI)
Davenport U, Grand Rapids (MI)
Davenport U, Kalamazoo (MI)
Davenport U, Lansing (MI)
Davenport U, Warren (MI)
Design Inst of San Diego (CA)
Dickinson State U (ND)
Eastern Kentucky U (KY)
Emporia State U (KS)
Everglades U, Boca Raton (FL)
Excelsior Coll (NY)
Fort Hays State U (KS)
Franklin U (OH)
Glenville State Coll (WV)
Global U of the Assemblies of God (MO)
Grambling State U (LA)
Grantham U (LA)
Hamilton Tech Coll (IA)
Harrington Coll of Design (IL)
Henry Cogswell Coll (WA)
Heritage Christian U (AL)
Hillsdale Free Will Baptist Coll (OK)
Holy Trinity Orthodox Sem (NY)
Intl Acad of Design & Technology (FL)
John F. Kennedy U (CA)
Jones Coll, Jacksonville (FL)
Jones Intl U (CO)
Kansas State U (KS)
Laura and Alvin Siegal Coll of Judaic Studies (OH)
Lexington Coll (IL)
Life U (GA)
Lincoln U (MO)
Long Island U, Friends World Program (NY)
Louisiana State U in Shreveport (LA)
Magnolia Bible Coll (MS)
Martin U (IN)
Marylhurst U (OR)
Master's Coll and Sem (ON, Canada)
Mayville State U (ND)
Medgar Evers Coll of the City U of New York (NY)
Miami Dade Coll (FL)
Miami U Hamilton (OH)
Miles Coll (AL)
Morrison U (NV)
Mountain State U (WV)
National American U, Colorado Springs (CO)
National American U, Denver (CO)
National American U (NM)
National American U (SD)
National American U–Sioux Falls Branch (SD)
National U (CA)
New Coll of California (CA)
New World School of the Arts (FL)
Nicholls State U (LA)
North Central U (MN)
North Dakota State Coll of Science (ND)
Northwestern State U of Louisiana (LA)
The Ohio State U at Lima (OH)
The Ohio State U at Marion (OH)
The Ohio State U–Mansfield Campus (OH)
The Ohio State U–Newark Campus (OH)
Ohio U–Chillicothe (OH)
Ohio U–Southern Campus (OH)
Ohio U–Zanesville (OH)
Oklahoma Christian U (OK)
Oklahoma Panhandle State U (OK)
Our Lady of the Lake Coll (LA)
Pennsylvania Coll of Technology (PA)
Pikeville Coll (KY)
Pillsbury Baptist Bible Coll (MN)
Pittsburg State U (KS)
Presentation Coll (SD)
Providence Coll and Theological Sem (MB, Canada)
Remington Coll–Colorado Springs Campus (CO)
Rocky Mountain Coll (AB, Canada)
St. Augustine Coll (IL)
Schiller Intl U (FL)
Schiller Intl U (France)
Schiller Intl U (Germany)
Schiller Intl U (Spain)
Schiller Intl U (United Kingdom)
Shasta Bible Coll (CA)
Shawnee State U (OH)
Sheldon Jackson Coll (AK)
Southern Nazarene U (OK)
Strayer U (DC)
Texas A&M U–Texarkana (TX)
Texas Southern U (TX)
Thomas Edison State Coll (NJ)
Thomas U (GA)
Trinity Bible Coll (ND)
Troy State U Montgomery (AL)
Université du Québec en Outaouais (QC, Canada)
U of Alaska Southeast (AK)
U of Arkansas at Fort Smith (AR)
U of Arkansas at Monticello (AR)
U of Baltimore (MD)
U of Great Falls (MT)
The U of Maine at Augusta (ME)
U of Maryland U Coll (MD)
U of Northwestern Ohio (OH)
U of Phoenix–Atlanta Campus (GA)
U of Phoenix–Boston Campus (MA)
U of Phoenix–Chicago Campus (IL)
U of Phoenix–Cleveland Campus (OH)
U of Phoenix–Colorado Campus (CO)
U of Phoenix–Dallas Campus (TX)
U of Phoenix–Fort Lauderdale Campus (FL)
U of Phoenix–Hawaii Campus (HI)
U of Phoenix–Houston Campus (TX)
U of Phoenix–Idaho Campus (ID)
U of Phoenix–Jacksonville Campus (FL)
U of Phoenix–Kansas City Campus (MO)
U of Phoenix–Louisiana Campus (LA)
U of Phoenix–Maryland Campus (MD)
U of Phoenix–Metro Detroit Campus (MI)
U of Phoenix–Nevada Campus (NV)
U of Phoenix–New Mexico Campus (NM)
U of Phoenix–Northern California Campus (CA)
U of Phoenix–Oklahoma City Campus (OK)
U of Phoenix Online Campus (AZ)
U of Phoenix–Oregon Campus (OR)
U of Phoenix–Orlando Campus (FL)
U of Phoenix–Philadelphia Campus (PA)
U of Phoenix–Phoenix Campus (AZ)
U of Phoenix–Pittsburgh Campus (PA)
U of Phoenix–Puerto Rico Campus (PR)
U of Phoenix–Sacramento Campus (CA)
U of Phoenix–St. Louis Campus (MO)
U of Phoenix–San Diego Campus (CA)
U of Phoenix–Southern Arizona Campus (AZ)
U of Phoenix–Southern California Campus (CA)
U of Phoenix–Southern Colorado Campus (CO)
U of Phoenix–Tampa Campus (FL)
U of Phoenix–Tulsa Campus (OK)
U of Phoenix–Utah Campus (UT)
U of Phoenix–Vancouver Campus (BC, Canada)
U of Phoenix–Washington Campus (WA)
U of Phoenix–West Michigan Campus (MI)
U of Phoenix–Wisconsin Campus (WI)

Noncompetitive

U of Southern Indiana (IN)
The U of Texas at Brownsville (TX)
The U of Texas–Pan American (TX)
U of the District of Columbia (DC)
U of Toledo (OH)
Valley City State U (ND)
Walsh Coll of Accountancy and Business Administration (MI)
Washburn U (KS)
Wayne State Coll (NE)
Weber State U (UT)
Wichita State U (KS)
William Jessup U (CA)
Williamson Christian Coll (TN)
Wilmington Coll (DE)
World Coll (VA)
Youngstown State U (OH)

Cost Ranges

Less than $2000

Colleges with No Room and Board or with Room Only
Apex School of Theology (NC)
Charter Oak State Coll (CT)
Dalton State Coll (GA)
Macon State Coll (GA)
Miami Dade Coll (FL)
U of Arkansas at Fort Smith (AR)
U of Puerto Rico, Cayey U Coll (PR)

Colleges with Room and Board
The Colburn School of Performing Arts (CA)
Haskell Indian Nations U (KS)

$2000–$3999

Colleges with No Room and Board or with Room Only
American U of Puerto Rico (PR)
Augusta State U (GA)
Beacon Coll and Graduate School (GA)
Bluefield State Coll (WV)
Clayton Coll & State U (GA)
Cleveland Chiropractic Coll-Kansas City Campus (MO)
Columbia Coll, Caguas (PR)
Columbia Southern U (AL)
Escuela de Artes Plasticas de Puerto Rico (PR)
Global U of the Assemblies of God (MO)
Governors State U (IL)
Grantham U (LA)
Harris-Stowe State Coll (MO)
Inter American U of Puerto Rico, Aguadilla Campus (PR)
Inter American U of Puerto Rico, Bayamón Campus (PR)
Logan U-Coll of Chiropractic (MO)
Metropolitan State Coll of Denver (CO)
Metropolitan State U (MN)
Miami U Hamilton (OH)
New World School of the Arts (FL)
Ohio U–Southern Campus (OH)
Texas A&M U–Texarkana (TX)
Troy State U Dothan (AL)
Troy State U Montgomery (AL)
U Coll of the Fraser Valley (BC, Canada)
U of Colorado at Denver (CO)
U of Houston–Clear Lake (TX)
U of Houston–Victoria (TX)
U of Oklahoma Health Sciences Center (OK)
The U of Texas Health Science Center at San Antonio (TX)
The U of Texas Southwestern Medical Center at Dallas (TX)
U of the District of Columbia (DC)
World Coll (VA)

Colleges with Room and Board
Coll of the Ozarks (MO)
Inter American U of Puerto Rico, Fajardo Campus (PR)

$4000–$5999

Colleges with No Room and Board or with Room Only
American Baptist Coll of American Baptist Theological Sem (TN) **(room only)**
Argosy U/Atlanta (GA)
Athens State U (AL) **(room only)**
Austin Graduate School of Theology (TX)
Baker Coll of Allen Park (MI)
Baker Coll of Auburn Hills (MI)
Baker Coll of Cadillac (MI)
Baker Coll of Clinton Township (MI)
Baker Coll of Jackson (MI)
Baker Coll of Port Huron (MI)
Bellevue U (NE)
Bernard M. Baruch Coll of the City U of New York (NY)
Brooklyn Coll of the City U of New York (NY)
California State U, Los Angeles (CA) **(room only)**
City Coll of the City U of New York (NY)
Cleveland Chiropractic Coll-Los Angeles Campus (CA)
Coll for Lifelong Learning (NH)
Coll of Biblical Studies–Houston (TX)
Coll of Staten Island of the City U of New York (NY)
Hunter Coll of the City U of New York (NY)
Indiana U East (IN)
Indiana U Kokomo (IN)
Indiana U Northwest (IN)
Indiana U–Purdue U Fort Wayne (IN)
Indiana U South Bend (IN)
Indiana U Southeast (IN)
Inter American U of Puerto Rico, Barranquitas Campus (PR)
Inter American U of Puerto Rico, Ponce Campus (PR)
John Jay Coll of Criminal Justice of the City U of New York (NY)
Lehman Coll of the City U of New York (NY)
Life U (GA)
Louisiana State U Health Sciences Center (LA) **(room only)**
Louisiana State U in Shreveport (LA) **(room only)**
Medgar Evers Coll of the City U of New York (NY)
Nevada State Coll at Henderson (NV)
Northeastern Illinois U (IL)
The Ohio State U at Lima (OH)
The Ohio State U at Marion (OH)
The Ohio State U–Mansfield Campus (OH)
The Ohio State U–Newark Campus (OH)
Ohio U–Chillicothe (OH)
Ohio U–Zanesville (OH)
Our Lady of Holy Cross Coll (LA)
Palmer Coll of Chiropractic (IA)
Polytechnic U of Puerto Rico (PR)
Purdue U North Central (IN)
Queens Coll of the City U of New York (NY)
State U of New York Empire State Coll (NY)
U of Baltimore (MD)
U of Maryland U Coll (MD)
U of Michigan–Dearborn (MI)
U of Michigan–Flint (MI)
U of Mississippi Medical Center (MS) **(room only)**
U of Nebraska Medical Center (NE)
U of Phoenix–Puerto Rico Campus (PR)
The U of Texas Health Science Center at Houston (TX)
U of the Virgin Islands (VI) **(room only)**
York Coll of the City U of New York (NY)

Colleges with Room and Board
Alice Lloyd Coll (KY)
Berea Coll (KY)
Cameron U (OK)
Holy Trinity Orthodox Sem (NY)
Northeastern State U (OK)
Northwestern Oklahoma State U (OK)
Okanagan U Coll (BC, Canada)
Oklahoma Panhandle State U (OK)
Southwestern Oklahoma State U (OK)
U of Louisiana at Lafayette (LA)

$6000–$7999

Colleges with No Room and Board or with Room Only
Amberton U (TX)
Arizona State U West (AZ) **(room only)**
Armstrong Atlantic State U (GA) **(room only)**
Bethesda Christian U (CA)
British Columbia Inst of Technology (BC, Canada) **(room only)**
California State U, Dominguez Hills (CA) **(room only)**
California State U, Fullerton (CA) **(room only)**
California State U, Hayward (CA) **(room only)**
Franklin U (OH)
Griggs U (MD)
Hamilton Tech Coll (IA)
Jones Coll, Jacksonville (FL)
Jones Coll, Miami (FL)
Kennesaw State U (GA) **(room only)**
Magnolia Bible Coll (MS) **(room only)**
MedCentral Coll of Nursing (OH)
Medical Coll of Georgia (GA) **(room only)**
Metropolitan Coll, Tulsa (OK)
National American U–Sioux Falls Branch (SD)
National Coll of Midwifery (NM)
Our Lady of the Lake Coll (LA)
St. Augustine Coll (IL)
Shasta Bible Coll (CA) **(room only)**
Touro U Intl (CA)
Union Inst & U (OH)
The U of Alabama at Birmingham (AL) **(room only)**
U of Arkansas at Little Rock (AR) **(room only)**
U of Colorado Health Sciences Center (CO)
The U of Maine at Augusta (ME)
U of Massachusetts Boston (MA)
U of New Hampshire at Manchester (NH)
U of New Orleans (LA) **(room only)**
U of Northern British Columbia (BC, Canada) **(room only)**
U of Regina (SK Canada) **(room only)**
The U of Tennessee at Chattanooga (TN) **(room only)**
The U of Texas at Tyler (TX) **(room only)**
U of the Sacred Heart (PR) **(room only)**
Walsh Coll of Accountancy and Business Administration (MI)
Williamson Christian Coll (TN)
Wilmington Coll (DE)

Colleges with Room and Board
Alabama State U (AL)
Albany State U (GA)
Angelo State U (TX)
Appalachian State U (NC)
Arkansas Tech U (AR)
Boise State U (ID)
Brigham Young U–Hawaii (HI)
California State U, San Bernardino (CA)
Chadron State Coll (NE)
Clear Creek Baptist Bible Coll (KY)
Columbus State U (GA)
Dakota State U (SD)
Delta State U (MS)
Dickinson State U (ND)
East Central U (OK)
Eastern New Mexico U (NM)
Elizabeth City State U (NC)
Emporia State U (KS)
Fayetteville State U (NC)
Fort Hays State U (KS)
Fort Valley State U (GA)
Georgia Southwestern State U (GA)
Glenville State Coll (WV)
God's Bible School and Coll (OH)
Henderson State U (AR)
Heritage Bible Coll (NC)
Inter American U of Puerto Rico, San Germán Campus (PR)
Jacksonville State U (AL)
Kentucky Mountain Bible Coll (KY)
Lewis-Clark State Coll (ID)
Louisiana Tech U (LA)
Mayville State U (ND)
McNeese State U (LA)
Messenger Coll (MO)
Minot State U (ND)
Mississippi Valley State U (MS)
Moody Bible Inst (IL)
Morehead State U (KY)
Murray State U (KY)
New Mexico Highlands U (NM)
New Mexico Inst of Mining and Technology (NM)
New Mexico State U (NM)
Nicholls State U (LA)
North Carolina Central U (NC)
North Dakota State Coll of Science (ND)
Northern State U (SD)
North Georgia Coll & State U (GA)
Northwestern State U of Louisiana (LA)
Pittsburg State U (KS)
Pontifical Catholic U of Puerto Rico (PR)
Sam Houston State U (TX)
South Dakota School of Mines and Technology (SD)
Southeastern Louisiana U (LA)
Southeastern Oklahoma State U (OK)
Southern Arkansas U–Magnolia (AR)
Southern Polytechnic State U (GA)
Southern U and Ag and Mech Coll (LA)
State U of West Georgia (GA)
Texas A&M U–Kingsville (TX)
Texas Woman's U (TX)
United States Intl U (Kenya)
Universidad Adventista de las Antillas (PR)
U of Arkansas at Monticello (AR)
U of Hawaii at Hilo (HI)
U of North Alabama (AL)
The U of North Carolina at Greensboro (NC)
The U of North Carolina at Pembroke (NC)

U of Science and Arts of Oklahoma (OK)
U of South Alabama (AL)
The U of South Dakota (SD)
The U of Tennessee at Martin (TN)
The U of Texas–Pan American (TX)
The U of West Alabama (AL)
Utah State U (UT)
Valdosta State U (GA)
Valley City State U (ND)
Wayne State Coll (NE)
Webb Inst (NY)
Western Carolina U (NC)
West Liberty State Coll (WV)
West Texas A&M U (TX)
West Virginia State Coll (WV)
Winston-Salem State U (NC)

$8000–$9999

Colleges with No Room and Board or with Room Only
American Public U System (WV)
Argosy U/Dallas (TX)
Baker Coll of Flint (MI) **(room only)**
Baker Coll of Muskegon (MI) **(room only)**
Baker Coll of Owosso (MI) **(room only)**
Boston Architectural Center (MA)
California State U, San Marcos (CA) **(room only)**
Calumet Coll of Saint Joseph (IN)
Cambridge Coll (MA)
Carlos Albizu U, Miami Campus (FL)
City U (WA)
Colorado Tech U Sioux Falls Campus (SD)
Crossroads Bible Coll (IN) **(room only)**
Everglades U, Boca Raton (FL)
Florida Metropolitan U–Brandon Campus (FL)
Florida Metropolitan U–Fort Lauderdale Campus (FL)
Florida Metropolitan U–Lakeland Campus (FL)
Florida Metropolitan U–Tampa Campus (FL)
Goddard Coll (VT)
Golden Gate U (CA)
Heritage Christian U (AL) **(room only)**
Herzing Coll, Minneapolis Drafting School Division (MN)
Indiana U–Purdue U Indianapolis (IN) **(room only)**
Intl Coll (FL)
John Wesley Coll (NC) **(room only)**
Laura and Alvin Siegal Coll of Judaic Studies (OH)
Medcenter One Coll of Nursing (ND) **(room only)**
Medical U of South Carolina (SC)
National American U, Denver (CO)
National U (CA)
New Hampshire Inst of Art (NH)
Northwestern Polytechnic U (CA) **(room only)**
Pacific States U (CA)
The Pennsylvania State U Abington Coll (PA)
The Pennsylvania State U Delaware County Campus of the Commonwealth Coll (PA)
The Pennsylvania State U DuBois Campus of the Commonwealth Coll (PA)
The Pennsylvania State U Fayette Campus of the Commonwealth Coll (PA)
The Pennsylvania State U, Lehigh Valley Campus of the Berks-Lehigh Valley Coll (PA)
The Pennsylvania State U New Kensington Campus of the Commonwealth Coll (PA)
The Pennsylvania State U Shenango Campus of the Commonwealth Coll (PA)
The Pennsylvania State U Wilkes-Barre Campus of the Commonwealth Coll (PA)
The Pennsylvania State U Worthington Scranton Campus of the Commonwealth Coll (PA)
The Pennsylvania State U York Campus of the Commonwealth Coll (PA)
St. John's Coll (IL)
Saint Luke's Coll (MO)
Southern Christian U (AL)
Strayer U (DC)
Trinity Coll of Nursing and Health Sciences (IL)
U of Phoenix–Atlanta Campus (GA)
U of Phoenix–Chicago Campus (IL)
U of Phoenix–Colorado Campus (CO)
U of Phoenix–Dallas Campus (TX)
U of Phoenix–Fort Lauderdale Campus (FL)
U of Phoenix–Houston Campus (TX)
U of Phoenix–Idaho Campus (ID)
U of Phoenix–Jacksonville Campus (FL)
U of Phoenix–Kansas City Campus (MO)
U of Phoenix–Louisiana Campus (LA)
U of Phoenix–Nevada Campus (NV)
U of Phoenix–New Mexico Campus (NM)
U of Phoenix–Oklahoma City Campus (OK)
U of Phoenix–Oregon Campus (OR)
U of Phoenix–Orlando Campus (FL)
U of Phoenix–Phoenix Campus (AZ)
U of Phoenix–Southern Arizona Campus (AZ)
U of Phoenix–Southern Colorado Campus (CO)
U of Phoenix–Tampa Campus (FL)
U of Phoenix–Tulsa Campus (OK)
U of Phoenix–Utah Campus (UT)
U of Phoenix–Washington Campus (WA)
U of Phoenix–West Michigan Campus (MI)
U of Phoenix–Wisconsin Campus (WI)
U of West Los Angeles (CA)
Virginia Coll at Birmingham (AL)

Colleges with Room and Board
Adams State Coll (CO)
Alabama Ag and Mech U (AL)
Alaska Bible Coll (AK)
Alcorn State U (MS)
Allen U (SC)
American Indian Coll of the Assemblies of God, Inc. (AZ)
Arizona State U East (AZ)
Arkansas Baptist Coll (AR)
Arkansas State U (AR)
Arlington Baptist Coll (TX)
Auburn U Montgomery (AL)
Austin Peay State U (TN)
Baptist Bible Coll (MO)
The Baptist Coll of Florida (FL)
Bemidji State U (MN)
Black Hills State U (SD)
Brigham Young U (UT)
California Christian Coll (CA)
California Maritime Acad (CA)
California State Polytechnic U, Pomona (CA)
California State U, Fresno (CA)
California State U, Long Beach (CA)
California State U, Sacramento (CA)
California State U, Stanislaus (CA)
Central Washington U (WA)
Colorado State U (CO)
Colorado State U-Pueblo (CO)
Concord Coll (WV)
Concordia Coll (AL)
East Carolina U (NC)
Eastern Kentucky U (KY)
Eastern Washington U (WA)
The Evergreen State Coll (WA)
Fairmont State Coll (WV)
Florida Ag and Mech U (FL)
Florida Atlantic U (FL)
Florida State U (FL)
Fort Lewis Coll (CO)
Framingham State Coll (MA)
Francis Marion U (SC)
Georgia Coll & State U (GA)
Georgia Southern U (GA)
Humboldt State U (CA)
Idaho State U (ID)
Jarvis Christian Coll (TX)
Jones Intl U (CO)
Kansas State U (KS)
Kentucky State U (KY)
Lamar U (TX)
Lincoln U (MO)
Louisiana State U and Ag and Mech Coll (LA)
Marshall U (WV)
Mary Washington Coll (VA)
Middle Tennessee State U (TN)
Midwestern State U (TX)
Miles Coll (AL)
Minnesota State U Mankato (MN)
Minnesota State U Moorhead (MN)
Mississippi State U (MS)
Missouri Southern State U (MO)
Missouri Western State Coll (MO)
Montana State U–Billings (MT)
Montana State U–Bozeman (MT)
Montana Tech of The U of Montana (MT)
New Coll of Florida (FL)
Norfolk State U (VA)
North Carolina School of the Arts (NC)
North Dakota State U (ND)
Northern Arizona U (AZ)
Oklahoma State U (OK)
Prairie View A&M U (TX)
Providence Coll and Theological Sem (MB, Canada)
Radford U (VA)
St. Cloud State U (MN)
St. Thomas U (NB, Canada)
Shepherd U (WV)
South Dakota State U (SD)
Southern Illinois U Edwardsville (IL)
Southern Utah U (UT)
Southwest Missouri State U (MO)
Steinbach Bible Coll (MB, Canada)
Tarleton State U (TX)
Tennessee State U (TN)
Tennessee Technological U (TN)
Texas A&M Intl U (TX)
Texas A&M U at Galveston (TX)
Texas A&M U–Commerce (TX)
Texas Southern U (TX)
Texas State U-San Marcos (TX)
Trinity Baptist Coll (FL)
Troy State U (AL)
Truman State U (MO)
The U of Alabama (AL)
The U of Alabama in Huntsville (AL)
U of Alaska Fairbanks (AK)
U of Alaska Southeast (AK)
U of Arkansas (AR)
U of Central Arkansas (AR)
U of Florida (FL)
U of Georgia (GA)
U of Hawaii at Manoa (HI)
U of Houston (TX)
U of Idaho (ID)
U of Kansas (KS)
U of Kentucky (KY)
U of Louisville (KY)
U of Maine at Machias (ME)
U of Maine at Presque Isle (ME)
The U of Memphis (TN)
U of Mississippi (MS)
The U of Montana–Missoula (MT)
The U of Montana–Western (MT)
U of Montevallo (AL)
U of Nebraska at Omaha (NE)
U of Nebraska–Lincoln (NE)
U of New Mexico (NM)
The U of North Carolina at Asheville (NC)
The U of North Carolina at Charlotte (NC)
The U of North Carolina at Wilmington (NC)
U of North Dakota (ND)
U of Northern Colorado (CO)
U of Northern Iowa (IA)
U of North Florida (FL)
U of North Texas (TX)
U of Oklahoma (OK)
U of South Carolina Aiken (SC)
U of South Carolina Spartanburg (SC)
U of Southern Indiana (IN)
U of South Florida (FL)
The U of Texas at Arlington (TX)
The U of Texas at Brownsville (TX)
U of Toronto (ON, Canada)
U of Utah (UT)
U of West Florida (FL)
U of Wisconsin–Eau Claire (WI)
U of Wisconsin–Green Bay (WI)
U of Wisconsin–La Crosse (WI)
U of Wisconsin–Milwaukee (WI)
U of Wisconsin–Oshkosh (WI)
U of Wisconsin–Parkside (WI)
U of Wisconsin–Platteville (WI)
U of Wisconsin–River Falls (WI)
U of Wisconsin–Stevens Point (WI)
U of Wisconsin–Stout (WI)
U of Wisconsin–Superior (WI)
U of Wisconsin–Whitewater (WI)
U of Wyoming (WY)
Virginia Polytechnic Inst and State U (VA)
Weber State U (UT)
Western State Coll of Colorado (CO)
Westfield State Coll (MA)
West Virginia U (WV)
Wichita State U (KS)
Winona State U (MN)
Worcester State Coll (MA)

$10,000–$11,999

Colleges with No Room and Board or with Room Only
Cleary U (MI)
Columbia Coll Hollywood (CA)
Crossroads Coll (MN) **(room only)**
Design Inst of San Diego (CA)
Gratz Coll (PA)
Jewish Hospital Coll of Nursing and Allied Health (MO) **(room only)**
Kaplan Coll (IA)
Lester L. Cox Coll of Nursing and Health Sciences (MO) **(room only)**
Martin U (IN)
National American U, Colorado Springs (CO)
Nebraska Methodist Coll (NE) **(room only)**
Ohr Somayach/Joseph Tanenbaum Educational Center (NY)
O'More Coll of Design (TN)
Paier Coll of Art, Inc. (CT)
Peirce Coll (PA)
St. Francis Coll (NY)
Saint Francis Medical Center Coll of Nursing (IL) **(room only)**
St. Joseph's Coll, New York (NY)
St. Joseph's Coll, Suffolk Campus (NY)
South U (AL)
South U (GA)
Thomas U (GA) **(room only)**
U of Phoenix–Boston Campus (MA)
U of Phoenix–Cleveland Campus (OH)
U of Phoenix–Hawaii Campus (HI)
U of Phoenix–Maryland Campus (MD)
U of Phoenix–Metro Detroit Campus (MI)
U of Phoenix–Philadelphia Campus (PA)
U of Phoenix–Pittsburgh Campus (PA)
U of Phoenix–St. Louis Campus (MO)
U of Phoenix–San Diego Campus (CA)
U of Phoenix–Vancouver Campus (BC, Canada)
Watkins Coll of Art and Design (TN)

Colleges with Room and Board
Arizona State U (AZ)
Auburn U (AL)
Ball State U (IN)

Bloomsburg U of Pennsylvania (PA)
Blue Mountain Coll (MS)
Bowie State U (MD)
Bridgewater State Coll (MA)
Buffalo State Coll, State U of New York (NY)
California Polytechnic State U, San Luis Obispo (CA)
California State U, Chico (CA)
California U of Pennsylvania (PA)
Calvary Bible Coll and Theological Sem (MO)
Carleton U (ON, Canada)
Castleton State Coll (VT)
Central Baptist Coll (AR)
Central Michigan U (MI)
Central Missouri State U (MO)
Central State U (OH)
Cheyney U of Pennsylvania (PA)
Christopher Newport U (VA)
The Citadel, The Military Coll of South Carolina (SC)
Clarion U of Pennsylvania (PA)
Clemson U (SC)
Coastal Carolina U (SC)
Coll of Charleston (SC)
Concordia U Coll of Alberta (AB, Canada)
Dallas Christian Coll (TX)
Delaware State U (DE)
Eastern Illinois U (IL)
Eastern Michigan U (MI)
Eastern Oregon U (OR)
East Stroudsburg U of Pennsylvania (PA)
Edinboro U of Pennsylvania (PA)
Eugene Bible Coll (OR)
Fashion Inst of Technology (NY)
Florida Gulf Coast U (FL)
Florida Intl U (FL)
Frostburg State U (MD)
George Mason U (VA)
Georgia Inst of Technology (GA)
Georgia State U (GA)
Grand Valley State U (MI)
Hillsdale Free Will Baptist Coll (OK)
Illinois State U (IL)
Indiana State U (IN)
Indiana U of Pennsylvania (PA)
Iowa State U of Science and Technology (IA)
James Madison U (VA)
Johnson Bible Coll (TN)
Johnson State Coll (VT)
Kutztown U of Pennsylvania (PA)
Lake Superior State U (MI)
Lander U (SC)
Lane Coll (TN)
Life Pacific Coll (CA)
Lock Haven U of Pennsylvania (PA)
Longwood U (VA)
Lyndon State Coll (VT)
Mansfield U of Pennsylvania (PA)
Martin Luther Coll (MN)
Massachusetts Coll of Liberal Arts (MA)
Massachusetts Maritime Acad (MA)
Michigan State U (MI)
Millersville U of Pennsylvania (PA)
Morris Coll (SC)
Mountain State U (WV)
North Carolina State U (NC)
Northern Illinois U (IL)
Northern Michigan U (MI)
Oakland U (MI)
Old Dominion U (VA)
Oregon Inst of Technology (OR)
Oregon State U (OR)
Park U (MO)
Pillsbury Baptist Bible Coll (MN)
Rhode Island Coll (RI)
Saginaw Valley State U (MI)
Salem State Coll (MA)
San Diego State U (CA)
San Francisco State U (CA)
San Jose State U (CA)
Shawnee State U (OH)
Shippensburg U of Pennsylvania (PA)
Slippery Rock U of Pennsylvania (PA)
Sonoma State U (CA)
South Carolina State U (SC)
Southeastern Bible Coll (AL)
Southeast Missouri State U (MO)
Southern Illinois U Carbondale (IL)
Southern Oregon U (OR)
State U of New York at New Paltz (NY)
State U of New York at Plattsburgh (NY)
State U of New York Coll at Fredonia (NY)
State U of New York Coll at Oneonta (NY)
State U of New York Coll of Technology at Alfred (NY)
State U of New York Inst of Technology at Utica/Rome (NY)
Talladega Coll (AL)
Texas A&M U (TX)
Texas A&M U–Corpus Christi (TX)
Texas Tech U (TX)
Trent U (ON, Canada)
Trinity Coll of Florida (FL)
The U of Arizona (AZ)
U of Central Florida (FL)
U of Colorado at Boulder (CO)
U of Colorado at Colorado Springs (CO)
U of Illinois at Springfield (IL)
The U of Iowa (IA)
U of Maine at Farmington (ME)
U of Maine at Fort Kent (ME)
U of Maryland Eastern Shore (MD)
U of Massachusetts Lowell (MA)
U of Minnesota, Crookston (MN)
U of Nevada, Las Vegas (NV)
U of New Brunswick Fredericton (NB, Canada)
The U of North Carolina at Chapel Hill (NC)
U of Oregon (OR)
U of South Carolina (SC)
U of Southern Maine (ME)
The U of Tennessee (TN)
The U of Texas at Austin (TX)
The U of Texas at Dallas (TX)
U of the West (CA)
U of Virginia (VA)
The U of Virginia's Coll at Wise (VA)
U of Washington (WA)
U of Wisconsin–Madison (WI)
Virginia Commonwealth U (VA)
Virginia Military Inst (VA)
Virginia State U (VA)
Voorhees Coll (SC)
Washington State U (WA)
Wayland Baptist U (TX)
Wayne State U (MI)
West Chester U of Pennsylvania (PA)
Western Connecticut State U (CT)
Western Illinois U (IL)
Western Oregon U (OR)
Western Washington U (WA)
William Carey Coll (MS)
Winthrop U (SC)
Wright State U (OH)
Youngstown State U (OH)

$12,000–$13,999

Colleges with No Room and Board or with Room Only
Antioch U Santa Barbara (CA)
Argosy U/Chicago (IL)
Argosy U/Phoenix (AZ)
Argosy U/Sarasota (FL)
Bellin Coll of Nursing (WI)
Capella U (MN)
Davenport U, Dearborn (MI) **(room only)**
Davenport U, Gaylord (MI) **(room only)**
Davenport U, Grand Rapids (MI) **(room only)**
Davenport U, Holland (MI) **(room only)**
Davenport U, Kalamazoo (MI) **(room only)**
Davenport U, Lansing (MI) **(room only)**
Davenport U, Lapeer (MI) **(room only)**
Davenport U, Traverse City (MI) **(room only)**
Davenport U, Warren (MI) **(room only)**
Globe Inst of Technology (NY) **(room only)**
John F. Kennedy U (CA)
Lexington Coll (IL)
Marylhurst U (OR)
Morrison U (NV)
Musicians Inst (CA)
New Coll of California (CA)
Northwest Coll of Art (WA)
The Pennsylvania State U Schuylkill Campus of the Capital Coll (PA) **(room only)**
Silicon Valley Coll, Walnut Creek (CA)
U of Northwestern Ohio (OH) **(room only)**
U of Phoenix–Northern California Campus (CA)
U of Phoenix Online Campus (AZ)
U of Phoenix–Sacramento Campus (CA)
U of Phoenix–Southern California Campus (CA)

Colleges with Room and Board
American U in Bulgaria (Bulgaria)
Appalachian Bible Coll (WV)
Bowling Green State U (OH)
Bryn Athyn Coll of the New Church (PA)
Central Connecticut State U (CT)
Chicago State U (IL)
Cleveland State U (OH)
The Coll of Southeastern Europe, The American U of Athens (Greece)
Coll of the Southwest (NM)
The Coll of William and Mary (VA)
Colorado School of Mines (CO)
Eastern Connecticut State U (CT)
East Texas Baptist U (TX)
Emmanuel Coll (GA)
Farmingdale State U of New York (NY)
Ferris State U (MI)
Flagler Coll (FL)
Hannibal-LaGrange Coll (MO)
Huston-Tillotson Coll (TX)
Indiana U Bloomington (IN)
Jamestown Coll (ND)
Keene State Coll (NH)
Lincoln U (PA)
Louisiana Coll (LA)
Maine Maritime Acad (ME)
Manhattan Christian Coll (KS)
Michigan Technological U (MI)
Morgan State U (MD)
National American U (SD)
New Jersey City U (NJ)
Oak Hills Christian Coll (MN)
The Ohio State U (OH)
Paine Coll (GA)
Plymouth State U (NH)
Portland State U (OR)
Practical Bible Coll (NY)
Purdue U (IN)
The Richard Stockton Coll of New Jersey (NJ)
St. Louis Christian Coll (MO)
Salisbury U (MD)
Southern Connecticut State U (CT)
State U of New York at Binghamton (NY)
State U of New York at Oswego (NY)
State U of New York Coll at Brockport (NY)
State U of New York Coll at Cortland (NY)
State U of New York Coll at Geneseo (NY)
State U of New York Coll at Old Westbury (NY)
State U of New York Coll at Potsdam (NY)
State U of New York Coll of Agriculture and Technology at Cobleskill (NY)
State U of New York Upstate Medical U (NY)
Stony Brook U, State U of New York (NY)
Talmudic Coll of Florida (FL)
Tougaloo Coll (MS)
Towson U (MD)
U at Albany, State U of New York (NY)
U at Buffalo, The State U of New York (NY)
U of Delaware (DE)
U of Maine (ME)
U of Massachusetts Dartmouth (MA)
U of Minnesota, Duluth (MN)
U of Minnesota, Morris (MN)
U of Minnesota, Twin Cities Campus (MN)
U of Missouri–Columbia (MO)
U of Missouri–Kansas City (MO)
U of Missouri–Rolla (MO)
U of Missouri–St. Louis (MO)
U of Rhode Island (RI)
U of Toledo (OH)
Vermont Tech Coll (VT)
Western Michigan U (MI)
Williams Baptist Coll (AR)
William Tyndale Coll (MI)

$14,000–$15,999

Colleges with No Room and Board or with Room Only
The American U in Cairo (Egypt) **(room only)**
The American U in Dubai (United Arab Emirates) **(room only)**
Berkeley Coll-New York City Campus (NY)
Briarcliffe Coll (NY)
Crichton Coll (TN) **(room only)**
Goldey-Beacom Coll (DE) **(room only)**
Henry Cogswell Coll (WA)
Lourdes Coll (OH)
Lyme Acad Coll of Fine Arts (CT)
Missouri Tech (MO) **(room only)**
Molloy Coll (NY)
Oregon Coll of Art & Craft (OR)
Pacific Northwest Coll of Art (OR)
Remington Coll–Colorado Springs Campus (CO)
Robert Morris Coll (IL)
Saint Anthony Coll of Nursing (IL)
Saint Louis U, Madrid Campus (Spain)

Colleges with Room and Board
Allen Coll (IA)
Atlanta Christian Coll (GA)
Ave Maria Coll (MI)
Ave Maria U (FL)
Bacone Coll (OK)
Barber-Scotia Coll (NC)
Barclay Coll (KS)
Bethel Coll (TN)
Blackburn Coll (IL)
Bluefield Coll (VA)
Brescia U (KY)
Brewton-Parker Coll (GA)
Clearwater Christian Coll (FL)
CollAmerica–Fort Collins (CO)
The Coll of New Jersey (NJ)
Cooper Union for the Advancement of Science and Art (NY)
Dallas Baptist U (TX)
Faith Baptist Bible Coll and Theological Sem (IA)
Faulkner U (AL)
Florida Coll (FL)
Grace Bible Coll (MI)
Grace U (NE)
Grambling State U (LA)
Grove City Coll (PA)
Harding U (AR)
Howard Payne U (TX)
Judson Coll (AL)
Kean U (NJ)
Kent State U (OH)
Kentucky Christian Coll (KY)
Lubbock Christian U (TX)
Madonna U (MI)
Magdalen Coll (NH)
Massachusetts Coll of Art (MA)

Miami U (OH)
Mid-Continent Coll (KY)
Montclair State U (NJ)
Multnomah Bible Coll and Biblical Sem (OR)
New England School of Communications (ME)
North Central U (MN)
North Greenville Coll (SC)
Ohio U (OH)
Oklahoma Baptist U (OK)
Pennsylvania Coll of Technology (PA)
The Pennsylvania State U Altoona Coll (PA)
The Pennsylvania State U at Erie, The Behrend Coll (PA)
The Pennsylvania State U Beaver Campus of the Commonwealth Coll (PA)
The Pennsylvania State U Berks Campus of the Berks–Lehigh Valley Coll (PA)
The Pennsylvania State U Hazleton Campus of the Commonwealth Coll (PA)
The Pennsylvania State U McKeesport Campus of the Commonwealth Coll (PA)
The Pennsylvania State U Mont Alto Campus of the Commonwealth Coll (PA)
The Pennsylvania State U U Park Campus (PA)
Pikeville Coll (KY)
Presentation Coll (SD)
Ramapo Coll of New Jersey (NJ)
Reformed Bible Coll (MI)
Rowan U (NJ)
Rutgers, The State U of New Jersey, Camden (NJ)
Rutgers, The State U of New Jersey, Newark (NJ)
Rutgers, The State U of New Jersey, New Brunswick/Piscataway (NJ)
Sacred Heart Major Sem (MI)
Saint Augustine's Coll (NC)
St. Gregory's U (OK)
Saint Joseph Sem Coll (LA)
Shaw U (NC)
Southeastern Coll of the Assemblies of God (FL)
Southwestern Coll (AZ)
State U of New York Coll of Environmental Science and Forestry (NY)
Toccoa Falls Coll (GA)
Trinity Bible Coll (ND)
The U of Akron (OH)
U of California, Davis (CA)
U of California, Irvine (CA)
U of California, Riverside (CA)
U of California, San Diego (CA)
U of California, Santa Barbara (CA)
U of California, Santa Cruz (CA)
U of Cincinnati (OH)
U of Connecticut (CT)
U of Illinois at Chicago (IL)
U of Mary (ND)
U of Mary Hardin-Baylor (TX)
U of Maryland, Baltimore County (MD)
U of Maryland, Coll Park (MD)
U of Massachusetts Amherst (MA)
U of Michigan (MI)
U of Mobile (AL)
U of New Hampshire (NH)
U of Pittsburgh at Bradford (PA)
U of Pittsburgh at Greensburg (PA)
U of Pittsburgh at Johnstown (PA)
William Paterson U of New Jersey (NJ)
York Coll (NE)
York Coll of Pennsylvania (PA)

$16,000–$17,999

Colleges with No Room and Board or with Room Only

American Acad of Art (IL)
Antioch U Los Angeles (CA)
The Art Inst of California–San Francisco (CA)
The Art Inst of Phoenix (AZ)
Bastyr U (WA) **(room only)**
Cogswell Polytechnical Coll (CA) **(room only)**
Coleman Coll, La Mesa (CA)
Coll of Visual Arts (MN)
Harrington Coll of Design (IL) **(room only)**
The Illinois Inst of Art (IL)
The Illinois Inst of Art-Schaumburg (IL)
Intl Acad of Design & Technology (FL)
Jewish Theological Sem of America (NY) **(room only)**
Laguna Coll of Art & Design (CA)
Mt. Sierra Coll (CA)
Stratford U (VA)
Sullivan U (KY) **(room only)**

Colleges with Room and Board

Bethune-Cookman Coll (FL)
Bryan Coll (TN)
Campbellsville U (KY)
Cascade Coll (OR)
Central Christian Coll of Kansas (KS)
Columbia Coll (MO)
Culver-Stockton Coll (MO)
Cumberland Coll (KY)
Cumberland U (TN)
Dillard U (LA)
Evangel U (MO)
Freed-Hardeman U (TN)
Gallaudet U (DC)
Hardin-Simmons U (TX)
Hesser Coll (NH)
Houston Baptist U (TX)
Howard U (DC)
Husson Coll (ME)
Kentucky Wesleyan Coll (KY)
Lambuth U (TN)
Lancaster Bible Coll (PA)
Lincoln Memorial U (TN)
Lindenwood U (MO)
Marygrove Coll (MI)
Midway Coll (KY)
Mississippi Coll (MS)
New Jersey Inst of Technology (NJ)
Oakland City U (IN)
Ohio Valley Coll (WV)
Oklahoma Christian U (OK)
The Pennsylvania State U Harrisburg Campus of the Capital Coll (PA)
Pontifical Coll Josephinum (OH)
Reinhardt Coll (GA)
Rochester Coll (MI)
St. Charles Borromeo Sem, Overbrook (PA)
St. Mary's Coll of Maryland (MD)
Shorter Coll (GA)
Southern Adventist U (TN)
Southern Nazarene U (OK)
Southwest Baptist U (MO)
State U of New York Downstate Medical Center (NY)
Tennessee Wesleyan Coll (TN)
Texas Chiropractic Coll (TX)
Texas Wesleyan U (TX)
Tuskegee U (AL)
Union Coll (KY)
Union Coll (NE)
U of California, Berkeley (CA)
U of California, Los Angeles (CA)
U of Great Falls (MT)
U of Illinois at Urbana–Champaign (IL)
U of Pittsburgh (PA)
U of the Ozarks (AR)
U of Vermont (VT)
Virginia Union U (VA)
Waldorf Coll (IA)
Warner Southern Coll (FL)
Webber Intl U (FL)
Wesleyan Coll (GA)
Wilberforce U (OH)
William Jessup U (CA)
Xavier U of Louisiana (LA)

$18,000–$19,999

Colleges with No Room and Board or with Room Only

American InterContinental U, Atlanta (GA) **(room only)**
The American U of Rome (Italy) **(room only)**
Antioch U Seattle (WA)
Art Acad of Cincinnati (OH)
Burlington Coll (VT) **(room only)**
Cornish Coll of the Arts (WA)
Intl Acad of Design & Technology (IL)
New York School of Interior Design (NY)
Pacific Oaks Coll (CA)
Rocky Mountain Coll of Art & Design (CO) **(room only)**
Silver Lake Coll (WI) **(room only)**
Southern California Inst of Architecture (CA)
Villa Julie Coll (MD) **(room only)**

Colleges with Room and Board

Abilene Christian U (TX)
Albertson Coll of Idaho (ID)
Alverno Coll (WI)
Anderson Coll (SC)
Atlantic Union Coll (MA)
Baker U (KS)
Barton Coll (NC)
Belhaven Coll (MS)
Bethany Coll (KS)
Bethany Coll (WV)
Bethany Lutheran Coll (MN)
Bethel Coll (IN)
Bethel Coll (KS)
Blessing-Rieman Coll of Nursing (IL)
Brevard Coll (NC)
Campbell U (NC)
Cardinal Stritch U (WI)
Carson-Newman Coll (TN)
Cedarville U (OH)
Central Methodist Coll (MO)
Christendom Coll (VA)
Christian Heritage Coll (CA)
Clark Atlanta U (GA)
Coll of St. Joseph (VT)
Columbia Coll of Nursing (WI)
Columbia Intl U (SC)
Conception Sem Coll (MO)
Cornerstone U (MI)
Crown Coll (MN)
Dakota Wesleyan U (SD)
Drury U (MO)
Eureka Coll (IL)
The Franciscan U (IA)
Gardner-Webb U (NC)
Grace Coll (IN)
Graceland U (IA)
Grand View Coll (IA)
Hampton U (VA)
Hastings Coll (NE)
Hawai'i Pacific U (HI)
Hilbert Coll (NY)
Illinois Coll (IL)
John Brown U (AR)
Johnson C. Smith U (NC)
Liberty U (VA)
Limestone Coll (SC)
Lindsey Wilson Coll (KY)
Lipscomb U (TN)
Livingstone Coll (NC)
Lyon Coll (AR)
Marian Coll of Fond du Lac (WI)
McMurry U (TX)
Mercy Coll (NY)
MidAmerica Nazarene U (KS)
Milligan Coll (TN)
Missouri Baptist U (MO)
Missouri Valley Coll (MO)
Montreat Coll (NC)
Mount Marty Coll (SD)
Mount Vernon Nazarene U (OH)
Newman U (KS)
North Carolina Wesleyan Coll (NC)
Northwestern Coll (IA)
Northwood U, Texas Campus (TX)
Oklahoma City U (OK)
Oral Roberts U (OK)
Ottawa U (KS)
Ouachita Baptist U (AR)
Patrick Henry Coll (VA)
Philadelphia Biblical U (PA)
Piedmont Coll (GA)
Rocky Mountain Coll (MT)
Samford U (AL)
Sheldon Jackson Coll (AK)
Shimer Coll (IL)
Southern Vermont Coll (VT)
Southern Virginia U (VA)
Southern Wesleyan U (SC)
Sterling Coll (KS)
Tabor Coll (KS)
Thomas More Coll of Liberal Arts (NH)
Trevecca Nazarene U (TN)
U of Saint Mary (KS)
U of Sioux Falls (SD)
Urbana U (OH)
Virginia Intermont Coll (VA)
Washington Bible Coll (MD)
Waynesburg Coll (PA)
Westminster Coll (MO)
William Penn U (IA)

$20,000 and over

Colleges with No Room and Board or with Room Only

Art Center Coll of Design (CA)
The Art Inst of Atlanta (GA) **(room only)**
The Art Inst of California–San Diego (CA) **(room only)**
The Art Inst of Washington (VA) **(room only)**
Atlanta Coll of Art (GA) **(room only)**
Capitol Coll (MD) **(room only)**
Coll for Creative Studies (MI) **(room only)**
Columbia U, School of General Studies (NY) **(room only)**
Dowling Coll (NY) **(room only)**
Huron U USA in London (United Kingdom) **(room only)**
John Cabot U (Italy) **(room only)**
Johnson & Wales U (FL) **(room only)**
The King's Coll (NY) **(room only)**
Laboratory Inst of Merchandising (NY) **(room only)**
Loma Linda U (CA) **(room only)**
Long Island U, Brentwood Campus (NY)
Manhattan School of Music (NY) **(room only)**
Miami Intl U of Art & Design (FL) **(room only)**
Montserrat Coll of Art (MA) **(room only)**
Otis Coll of Art and Design (CA)
Rockford Coll (IL)
Rush U (IL) **(room only)**
School of the Art Inst of Chicago (IL) **(room only)**
The U of the Arts (PA) **(room only)**
Westwood Coll of Technology–Long Beach (CA)

Colleges with Room and Board

Acad of Art U (CA)
Adelphi U (NY)
Adrian Coll (MI)
Agnes Scott Coll (GA)
Alaska Pacific U (AK)
Albany Coll of Pharmacy of Union U (NY)
Albertus Magnus Coll (CT)
Albion Coll (MI)
Albright Coll (PA)

Alderson-Broaddus Coll (WV)
Alfred U (NY)
Allegheny Coll (PA)
Alliant Intl U (CA)
Alma Coll (MI)
Alvernia Coll (PA)
American Intl Coll (MA)
American U (DC)
Amherst Coll (MA)
Andrews U (MI)
Anna Maria Coll (MA)
Antioch Coll (OH)
Aquinas Coll (MI)
Arcadia U (PA)
The Art Inst of Boston at Lesley U (MA)
The Art Inst of Colorado (CO)
The Art Inst of Portland (OR)
Asbury Coll (KY)
Ashland U (OH)
Assumption Coll (MA)
Augsburg Coll (MN)
Augustana Coll (IL)
Augustana Coll (SD)
Aurora U (IL)
Austin Coll (TX)
Averett U (VA)
Avila U (MO)
Azusa Pacific U (CA)
Babson Coll (MA)
Baldwin-Wallace Coll (OH)
Baltimore Intl Coll (MD)
Bard Coll (NY)
Barnard Coll (NY)
Barry U (FL)
Bates Coll (ME)
Baylor U (TX)
Bay Path Coll (MA)
Beacon Coll (FL)
Becker Coll (MA)
Bellarmine U (KY)
Belmont Abbey Coll (NC)
Belmont U (TN)
Beloit Coll (WI)
Benedictine Coll (KS)
Benedictine U (IL)
Bennington Coll (VT)
Bentley Coll (MA)
Berkeley Coll (NJ)
Berkeley Coll-Westchester Campus (NY)
Berklee Coll of Music (MA)
Berry Coll (GA)
Bethel U (MN)
Biola U (CA)
Birmingham-Southern Coll (AL)
Bloomfield Coll (NJ)
Bluffton Coll (OH)
Boston Coll (MA)
Boston U (MA)
Bowdoin Coll (ME)
Bradley U (IL)
Brandeis U (MA)
Brenau U (GA)
Briar Cliff U (IA)
Bridgewater Coll (VA)
Brown U (RI)
Bryant Coll (RI)
Bryn Mawr Coll (PA)
Bucknell U (PA)
Buena Vista U (IA)
Butler U (IN)
Cabrini Coll (PA)
Caldwell Coll (NJ)
California Baptist U (CA)
California Coll of the Arts (CA)
California Inst of Technology (CA)
California Inst of the Arts (CA)
California Lutheran U (CA)
Calvin Coll (MI)
Canisius Coll (NY)
Capital U (OH)
Carleton Coll (MN)
Carlow Coll (PA)
Carnegie Mellon U (PA)
Carroll Coll (MT)
Carroll Coll (WI)
Carthage Coll (WI)
Case Western Reserve U (OH)
Catawba Coll (NC)
The Catholic U of America (DC)
Cazenovia Coll (NY)
Cedar Crest Coll (PA)
Centenary Coll (NJ)
Centenary Coll of Louisiana (LA)
Central Coll (IA)
Centre Coll (KY)
Chaminade U of Honolulu (HI)
Champlain Coll (VT)
Chapman U (CA)
Charleston Southern U (SC)
Chatham Coll (PA)
Chester Coll of New England (NH)
Chestnut Hill Coll (PA)
Chowan Coll (NC)
Christian Brothers U (TN)
Claremont McKenna Coll (CA)
Clarke Coll (IA)
Clarkson U (NY)
Clark U (MA)
The Cleveland Inst of Art (OH)
Cleveland Inst of Music (OH)
Coe Coll (IA)
Coker Coll (SC)
Colby Coll (ME)
Colby-Sawyer Coll (NH)
Colgate U (NY)
Coll Misericordia (PA)
Coll of Mount St. Joseph (OH)
Coll of Mount Saint Vincent (NY)
The Coll of New Rochelle (NY)
Coll of Notre Dame of Maryland (MD)
Coll of Saint Benedict (MN)
Coll of St. Catherine (MN)
Coll of Saint Elizabeth (NJ)
Coll of Saint Mary (NE)
The Coll of Saint Rose (NY)
The Coll of St. Scholastica (MN)
Coll of Santa Fe (NM)
Coll of the Atlantic (ME)
Coll of the Holy Cross (MA)
The Coll of Wooster (OH)
Colorado Christian U (CO)
The Colorado Coll (CO)
Columbia Coll (NY)
Columbia Coll (SC)
Columbia Coll Chicago (IL)
Columbia Union Coll (MD)
Columbia U, The Fu Foundation School of Eng and Applied Science (NY)
Columbus Coll of Art & Design (OH)
Concordia Coll (MN)
Concordia Coll (NY)
Concordia U (CA)
Concordia U (IL)
Concordia U (MI)
Concordia U (NE)
Concordia U (OR)
Concordia U at Austin (TX)
Concordia U, St. Paul (MN)
Concordia U Wisconsin (WI)
Connecticut Coll (CT)
Converse Coll (SC)
Cornell Coll (IA)
Cornell U (NY)
Covenant Coll (GA)
Creighton U (NE)
The Culinary Inst of America (NY)
Curry Coll (MA)
Daemen Coll (NY)
Dana Coll (NE)
Daniel Webster Coll (NH)
Dartmouth Coll (NH)
Davidson Coll (NC)
Davis & Elkins Coll (WV)
Defiance Coll (OH)
Delaware Valley Coll (PA)
Denison U (OH)
DePaul U (IL)
DePauw U (IN)
DeSales U (PA)
Dickinson Coll (PA)
Doane Coll (NE)
Dominican Coll (NY)
Dominican U (IL)
Dominican U of California (CA)
Dordt Coll (IA)
Drake U (IA)
Drew U (NJ)
Drexel U (PA)
Duke U (NC)
Duquesne U (PA)
D'Youville Coll (NY)
Earlham Coll (IN)
Eastern Mennonite U (VA)
Eastern Nazarene Coll (MA)
Eastern U (PA)
Eckerd Coll (FL)
Edgewood Coll (WI)
Elizabethtown Coll (PA)
Elmhurst Coll (IL)
Elmira Coll (NY)
Elms Coll (MA)
Elon U (NC)
Embry-Riddle Aeronautical U (AZ)
Embry-Riddle Aeronautical U (FL)
Embry-Riddle Aeronautical U, Extended Campus (FL)
Emerson Coll (MA)
Emory & Henry Coll (VA)
Emory U (GA)
Endicott Coll (MA)
Erskine Coll (SC)
Eugene Lang Coll, New School U (NY)
Fairfield U (CT)
Fairleigh Dickinson U, Coll at Florham (NJ)
Fairleigh Dickinson U, Metropolitan Campus (NJ)
Ferrum Coll (VA)
Fisher Coll (MA)
Five Towns Coll (NY)
Florida Inst of Technology (FL)
Florida Southern Coll (FL)
Fontbonne U (MO)
Fordham U (NY)
Franciscan U of Steubenville (OH)
Franklin and Marshall Coll (PA)
Franklin Coll (IN)
Franklin Coll Switzerland (Switzerland)
Franklin Pierce Coll (NH)
Fresno Pacific U (CA)
Furman U (SC)
Gannon U (PA)
Geneva Coll (PA)
George Fox U (OR)
Georgetown Coll (KY)
Georgetown U (DC)
The George Washington U (DC)
Georgian Court U (NJ)
Gettysburg Coll (PA)
Gonzaga U (WA)
Gordon Coll (MA)
Goshen Coll (IN)
Goucher Coll (MD)
Grand Canyon U (AZ)
Greensboro Coll (NC)
Greenville Coll (IL)
Grinnell Coll (IA)
Gustavus Adolphus Coll (MN)
Gwynedd-Mercy Coll (PA)
Hamilton Coll (NY)
Hamline U (MN)
Hampden-Sydney Coll (VA)
Hampshire Coll (MA)
Hanover Coll (IN)
Hartwick Coll (NY)
Harvard U (MA)
Harvey Mudd Coll (CA)
Haverford Coll (PA)
Heidelberg Coll (OH)
Hellenic Coll (MA)
Hendrix Coll (AR)
High Point U (NC)
Hillsdale Coll (MI)
Hiram Coll (OH)
Hobart and William Smith Colls (NY)
Hofstra U (NY)
Hollins U (VA)
Holy Names Coll (CA)
Hood Coll (MD)
Hope Coll (MI)
Houghton Coll (NY)
Huntingdon Coll (AL)
Huntington Coll (IN)
Illinois Inst of Technology (IL)
Illinois Wesleyan U (IL)
Immaculata U (PA)
Indiana Inst of Technology (IN)
Iona Coll (NY)
Iowa Wesleyan Coll (IA)
Ithaca Coll (NY)
Jacksonville U (FL)
John Carroll U (OH)
The Johns Hopkins U (MD)
Johnson & Wales U (CO)
Johnson & Wales U (RI)
Judson Coll (IL)
The Juilliard School (NY)
Juniata Coll (PA)
Kalamazoo Coll (MI)
Kansas City Art Inst (MO)
Kansas Wesleyan U (KS)
Kendall Coll (IL)
Kenyon Coll (OH)
Kettering U (MI)
Keuka Coll (NY)
Keystone Coll (PA)
King Coll (TN)
King's Coll (PA)
Knox Coll (IL)
Lafayette Coll (PA)
LaGrange Coll (GA)
Lake Erie Coll (OH)
Lake Forest Coll (IL)
Lakeland Coll (WI)
La Roche Coll (PA)
La Salle U (PA)
Lasell Coll (MA)
Lawrence Technological U (MI)
Lawrence U (WI)
Lebanon Valley Coll (PA)
Lehigh U (PA)
Le Moyne Coll (NY)
Lenoir-Rhyne Coll (NC)
Lesley U (MA)
LeTourneau U (TX)
Lewis & Clark Coll (OR)
Lewis U (IL)
Linfield Coll (OR)
Long Island U, Brooklyn Campus (NY)
Long Island U, C.W. Post Campus (NY)
Long Island U, Friends World Program (NY)
Long Island U, Southampton Coll (NY)
Loras Coll (IA)
Loyola Coll in Maryland (MD)
Loyola Marymount U (CA)
Loyola U Chicago (IL)
Loyola U New Orleans (LA)
Luther Coll (IA)
Lycoming Coll (PA)
Lynchburg Coll (VA)

Lynn U (FL)
Macalester Coll (MN)
MacMurray Coll (IL)
Maharishi U of Management (IA)
Maine Coll of Art (ME)
Malone Coll (OH)
Manchester Coll (IN)
Manhattan Coll (NY)
Manhattanville Coll (NY)
Mannes Coll of Music, New School U (NY)
Marian Coll (IN)
Marietta Coll (OH)
Marist Coll (NY)
Marlboro Coll (VT)
Marquette U (WI)
Mars Hill Coll (NC)
Mary Baldwin Coll (VA)
Maryland Inst Coll of Art (MD)
Marymount Coll of Fordham U (NY)
Marymount Manhattan Coll (NY)
Marymount U (VA)
Maryville Coll (TN)
Maryville U of Saint Louis (MO)
Marywood U (PA)
Massachusetts Coll of Pharmacy and Health Sciences (MA)
Massachusetts Inst of Technology (MA)
The Master's Coll and Sem (CA)
McDaniel Coll (MD)
McKendree Coll (IL)
McPherson Coll (KS)
Medaille Coll (NY)
Memphis Coll of Art (TN)
Menlo Coll (CA)
Mercer U (GA)
Mercyhurst Coll (PA)
Meredith Coll (NC)
Merrimack Coll (MA)
Messiah Coll (PA)
Methodist Coll (NC)
Middlebury Coll (VT)
Millikin U (IL)
Millsaps Coll (MS)
Mills Coll (CA)
Milwaukee Inst of Art and Design (WI)
Milwaukee School of Eng (WI)
Minneapolis Coll of Art and Design (MN)
Mitchell Coll (CT)
Monmouth Coll (IL)
Monmouth U (NJ)
Moore Coll of Art & Design (PA)
Moravian Coll (PA)
Morehouse Coll (GA)
Morningside Coll (IA)
Mount Aloysius Coll (PA)
Mount Holyoke Coll (MA)
Mount Ida Coll (MA)
Mount Mary Coll (WI)
Mount Mercy Coll (IA)
Mount Saint Mary Coll (NY)
Mount St. Mary's Coll (CA)
Mount Saint Mary's Coll and Sem (MD)
Mount Union Coll (OH)
Muhlenberg Coll (PA)
Naropa U (CO)
National-Louis U (IL)
Nazareth Coll of Rochester (NY)
Nebraska Wesleyan U (NE)
Neumann Coll (PA)
Newberry Coll (SC)
Newbury Coll (MA)
New England Conservatory of Music (MA)
The New England Inst of Art (MA)
New School Bachelor of Arts, New School U (NY)
New York Inst of Technology (NY)
New York U (NY)
Niagara U (NY)
Nichols Coll (MA)
North Central Coll (IL)
Northeastern U (MA)
Northface U (UT)
Northland Coll (WI)
North Park U (IL)
Northwest Christian Coll (OR)
Northwestern Coll (MN)
Northwestern U (IL)
Northwest Nazarene U (ID)
Northwood U (MI)
Northwood U, Florida Campus (FL)
Notre Dame Coll (OH)
Notre Dame de Namur U (CA)
Nova Southeastern U (FL)
Nyack Coll (NY)
Oberlin Coll (OH)
Occidental Coll (CA)
Oglethorpe U (GA)
Ohio Dominican U (OH)
Ohio Northern U (OH)
Ohio Wesleyan U (OH)
Olivet Coll (MI)
Olivet Nazarene U (IL)
Otterbein Coll (OH)
Our Lady of the Lake U of San Antonio (TX)
Pace U (NY)
Pacific Lutheran U (WA)
Pacific Union Coll (CA)
Pacific U (OR)
Palm Beach Atlantic U (FL)
Parsons School of Design, New School U (NY)
Paul Smith's Coll of Arts and Sciences (NY)
Peabody Conservatory of Music of The Johns Hopkins U (MD)
Peace Coll (NC)
Pepperdine U, Malibu (CA)
Pfeiffer U (NC)
Philadelphia U (PA)
Pine Manor Coll (MA)
Pitzer Coll (CA)
Point Loma Nazarene U (CA)
Point Park U (PA)
Polytechnic U, Brooklyn Campus (NY)
Pomona Coll (CA)
Pratt Inst (NY)
Presbyterian Coll (SC)
Princeton U (NJ)
Principia Coll (IL)
Providence Coll (RI)
Queens U of Charlotte (NC)
Quincy U (IL)
Quinnipiac U (CT)
Randolph-Macon Coll (VA)
Randolph-Macon Woman's Coll (VA)
Reed Coll (OR)
Regis Coll (MA)
Regis U (CO)
Rensselaer Polytechnic Inst (NY)
Research Coll of Nursing (MO)
Rhode Island School of Design (RI)
Rhodes Coll (TN)
Rice U (TX)
Richmond, The American Intl U in London (United Kingdom)
Rider U (NJ)
Ringling School of Art and Design (FL)
Ripon Coll (WI)
Rivier Coll (NH)
Roanoke Coll (VA)
Robert Morris U (PA)
Roberts Wesleyan Coll (NY)
Rochester Inst of Technology (NY)
Rockhurst U (MO)
Roger Williams U (RI)
Rollins Coll (FL)
Roosevelt U (IL)
Rose-Hulman Inst of Technology (IN)
Rosemont Coll (PA)
Russell Sage Coll (NY)
Sacred Heart U (CT)
Sage Coll of Albany (NY)
St. Ambrose U (IA)
St. Andrews Presbyterian Coll (NC)
Saint Anselm Coll (NH)
St. Bonaventure U (NY)
St. Edward's U (TX)
Saint Francis U (PA)
St. John Fisher Coll (NY)
St. John's Coll (MD)
St. John's Coll (NM)
Saint John's U (MN)
St. John's U (NY)
Saint Joseph Coll (CT)
Saint Joseph's Coll (IN)
Saint Joseph's Coll of Maine (ME)
Saint Joseph's U (PA)
St. Lawrence U (NY)
Saint Leo U (FL)
St. Louis Coll of Pharmacy (MO)
Saint Louis U (MO)
Saint Martin's Coll (WA)
Saint Mary-of-the-Woods Coll (IN)
Saint Mary's Coll (IN)
Saint Mary's Coll of California (CA)
Saint Mary's U of Minnesota (MN)
St. Mary's U of San Antonio (TX)
Saint Michael's Coll (VT)
St. Norbert Coll (WI)
St. Olaf Coll (MN)
St. Thomas Aquinas Coll (NY)
St. Thomas U (FL)
Saint Vincent Coll (PA)
Saint Xavier U (IL)
Salem Coll (NC)
Salve Regina U (RI)
Samuel Merritt Coll (CA)
San Francisco Art Inst (CA)
Santa Clara U (CA)
Sarah Lawrence Coll (NY)
Savannah Coll of Art and Design (GA)
Schiller Intl U (FL)
Schiller Intl U (United Kingdom)
School of the Museum of Fine Arts, Boston (MA)
Schreiner U (TX)
Scripps Coll (CA)
Seattle Pacific U (WA)
Seattle U (WA)
Seton Hall U (NJ)
Seton Hill U (PA)
Shenandoah U (VA)
Siena Coll (NY)
Siena Heights U (MI)
Sierra Nevada Coll (NV)
Simmons Coll (MA)
Simon's Rock Coll of Bard (MA)
Simpson Coll (IA)
Simpson Coll and Graduate School (CA)
Skidmore Coll (NY)
Smith Coll (MA)
Southern Methodist U (TX)
Southwestern Coll (KS)
Southwestern U (TX)
Spelman Coll (GA)
Spring Arbor U (MI)
Springfield Coll (MA)
Spring Hill Coll (AL)
Stanford U (CA)
Stephens Coll (MO)
Sterling Coll (VT)
Stetson U (FL)
Stevens Inst of Technology (NJ)
Stonehill Coll (MA)
Suffolk U (MA)
Susquehanna U (PA)
Swarthmore Coll (PA)
Sweet Briar Coll (VA)
Syracuse U (NY)
Taylor U (IN)
Taylor U, Fort Wayne Campus (IN)
Teikyo Post U (CT)
Texas Christian U (TX)
Texas Lutheran U (TX)
Thiel Coll (PA)
Thomas Aquinas Coll (CA)
Thomas Coll (ME)
Thomas Jefferson U (PA)
Thomas More Coll (KY)
Tiffin U (OH)
Transylvania U (KY)
Trinity Christian Coll (IL)
Trinity Coll (CT)
Trinity Coll (DC)
Trinity Intl U (IL)
Trinity U (TX)
Tri-State U (IN)
Tufts U (MA)
Tulane U (LA)
Tusculum Coll (TN)
Union Coll (NY)
Union U (TN)
Unity Coll (ME)
U of Advancing Technology (AZ)
U of Bridgeport (CT)
U of Charleston (WV)
U of Chicago (IL)
U of Dallas (TX)
U of Dayton (OH)
U of Denver (CO)
U of Detroit Mercy (MI)
U of Dubuque (IA)
U of Evansville (IN)
The U of Findlay (OH)
U of Hartford (CT)
U of Indianapolis (IN)
U of Judaism (CA)
U of La Verne (CA)
U of Miami (FL)
U of New Haven (CT)
U of Notre Dame (IN)
U of Pennsylvania (PA)
U of Portland (OR)
U of Puget Sound (WA)
U of Redlands (CA)
U of Richmond (VA)
U of Rochester (NY)
U of St. Francis (IL)
U of Saint Francis (IN)
U of St. Thomas (MN)
U of St. Thomas (TX)
U of San Diego (CA)
U of San Francisco (CA)
The U of Scranton (PA)
U of Southern California (CA)
The U of Tampa (FL)
U of the Incarnate Word (TX)
U of the Pacific (CA)
U of the Sciences in Philadelphia (PA)
U of the South (TN)
U of Tulsa (OK)
Upper Iowa U (IA)
Ursinus Coll (PA)
Ursuline Coll (OH)
Utica Coll (NY)
Valparaiso U (IN)
Vanderbilt U (TN)
Vanguard U of Southern California (CA)
Vassar Coll (NY)
Villanova U (PA)
Virginia Wesleyan Coll (VA)
Viterbo U (WI)
Wabash Coll (IN)
Wagner Coll (NY)
Wake Forest U (NC)
Walla Walla Coll (WA)
Walsh U (OH)
Warner Pacific Coll (OR)
Warren Wilson Coll (NC)
Wartburg Coll (IA)
Washington & Jefferson Coll (PA)

Washington and Lee U (VA)
Washington Coll (MD)
Washington U in St. Louis (MO)
Webster U (MO)
Wellesley Coll (MA)
Wells Coll (NY)
Wentworth Inst of Technology (MA)
Wesleyan U (CT)
Wesley Coll (DE)
Western Baptist Coll (OR)
Western New England Coll (MA)
Westminster Choir Coll of Rider U (NJ)
Westminster Coll (PA)
Westminster Coll (UT)
Westmont Coll (CA)
West Virginia Wesleyan Coll (WV)
Wheaton Coll (IL)
Wheaton Coll (MA)
Wheeling Jesuit U (WV)
Wheelock Coll (MA)
Whitman Coll (WA)
Whitworth Coll (WA)
Widener U (PA)
Wilkes U (PA)
Willamette U (OR)
William Jewell Coll (MO)
Williams Coll (MA)
William Woods U (MO)
Wilson Coll (PA)
Wingate U (NC)
Wisconsin Lutheran Coll (WI)
Wittenberg U (OH)
Wofford Coll (SC)
Worcester Polytechnic Inst (MA)
Xavier U (OH)
Yale U (CT)

Majors

ACCOUNTING
Abilene Christian U (TX)
Adelphi U (NY)
Adrian Coll (MI)
Alabama Ag and Mech U (AL)
Alabama State U (AL)
Albany State U (GA)
Albertson Coll of Idaho (ID)
Albertus Magnus Coll (CT)
Albright Coll (PA)
Alcorn State U (MS)
Alderson-Broaddus Coll (WV)
Alfred U (NY)
Alma Coll (MI)
Alvernia Coll (PA)
Amberton U (TX)
American Intl Coll (MA)
The American U in Cairo(Egypt)
American U of Puerto Rico (PR)
Anderson Coll (SC)
Andrews U (MI)
Angelo State U (TX)
Appalachian State U (NC)
Aquinas Coll (MI)
Arcadia U (PA)
Arizona State U (AZ)
Arizona State U West (AZ)
Arkansas State U (AR)
Arkansas Tech U (AR)
Asbury Coll (KY)
Ashland U (OH)
Assumption Coll (MA)
Athabasca U (AB, Canada)
Athens State U (AL)
Atlantic Union Coll (MA)
Auburn U (AL)
Auburn U Montgomery (AL)
Augsburg Coll (MN)
Augustana Coll (IL)
Augustana Coll (SD)
Augusta State U (GA)
Aurora U (IL)
Averett U (VA)
Avila U (MO)
Azusa Pacific U (CA)
Babson Coll (MA)
Bacone Coll (OK)
Baker Coll of Auburn Hills (MI)
Baker Coll of Cadillac (MI)
Baker Coll of Flint (MI)
Baker Coll of Jackson (MI)
Baker Coll of Muskegon (MI)
Baker Coll of Owosso (MI)
Baker Coll of Port Huron (MI)
Baker U (KS)
Ball State U (IN)
Barber-Scotia Coll (NC)
Barry U (FL)
Barton Coll (NC)
Baylor U (TX)
Becker Coll (MA)
Belhaven Coll (MS)
Bellarmine U (KY)
Bellevue U (NE)
Belmont Abbey Coll (NC)
Belmont U (TN)
Bemidji State U (MN)
Benedictine Coll (KS)
Benedictine U (IL)
Bentley Coll (MA)
Berkeley Coll-New York City Campus (NY)
Berkeley Coll-Westchester Campus (NY)
Baruch Coll of the City U of NY (NY)
Berry Coll (GA)
Bethany Coll (KS)
Bethany Coll (WV)
Bethel Coll (IN)
Bethel Coll (TN)
Bethune-Cookman Coll (FL)
Birmingham-Southern Coll (AL)
Bishop's U (QC, Canada)
Blackburn Coll (IL)
Black Hills State U (SD)
Bloomfield Coll (NJ)
Bloomsburg U of Pennsylvania (PA)
Bluefield Coll (VA)
Bluefield State Coll (WV)
Bluffton Coll (OH)
Boise State U (ID)
Boston Coll (MA)
Boston U (MA)
Bowie State U (MD)
Bowling Green State U (OH)
Bradley U (IL)
Brenau U (GA)
Brescia U (KY)
Brewton-Parker Coll (GA)
Briarcliffe Coll (NY)
Briar Cliff U (IA)
Bridgewater Coll (VA)
Bridgewater State Coll (MA)
Briercrest Bible Coll (SK, Canada)
Brigham Young U (UT)
Brigham Young U–Hawaii (HI)
British Columbia Inst of Technology (BC, Canada)
Brock U (ON, Canada)
Brooklyn Coll of the City U of NY (NY)
Bryant Coll (RI)
Bucknell U (PA)
Buena Vista U (IA)
Butler U (IN)
Cabrini Coll (PA)
Caldwell Coll (NJ)
California Lutheran U (CA)
California State Polytechnic U, Pomona (CA)
California State U, Chico (CA)
California State U, Dominguez Hills (CA)
California State U, Fresno (CA)
California State U, Fullerton (CA)
California State U, Hayward (CA)
California State U, Long Beach (CA)
California State U, Sacramento (CA)
California State U, San Bernardino (CA)
California State U, San Marcos (CA)
California U of Pennsylvania (PA)
Calumet Coll of Saint Joseph (IN)
Calvin Coll (MI)
Cameron U (OK)
Campbellsville U (KY)
Campbell U (NC)
Canisius Coll (NY)
Capital U (OH)
Cardinal Stritch U (WI)
Carleton U (ON, Canada)
Carlow Coll (PA)
Carroll Coll (MT)
Carroll Coll (WI)
Carson-Newman Coll (TN)
Carthage Coll (WI)
Case Western Reserve U (OH)
Castleton State Coll (VT)
The Catholic U of America (DC)
Cazenovia Coll (NY)
Cedar Crest Coll (PA)
Cedarville U (OH)
Centenary Coll (NJ)
Centenary Coll of Louisiana (LA)
Central Christian Coll of Kansas (KS)
Central Coll (IA)
Central Connecticut State U (CT)
Central Methodist Coll (MO)
Central Michigan U (MI)
Central Missouri State U (MO)
Central State U (OH)
Central Washington U (WA)
Chaminade U of Honolulu (HI)
Champlain Coll (VT)
Chaparral Coll (AZ)
Chapman U (CA)
Charleston Southern U (SC)
Chatham Coll (PA)
Chestnut Hill Coll (PA)
Chicago State U (IL)
Chowan Coll (NC)
Christian Brothers U (TN)
Christopher Newport U (VA)
City U (WA)
Claremont McKenna Coll (CA)
Clarion U of Pennsylvania (PA)
Clark Atlanta U (GA)
Clarke Coll (IA)
Clarkson U (NY)
Clayton Coll & State U (GA)
Clearwater Christian Coll (FL)
Cleary U (MI)
Clemson U (SC)
Cleveland State U (OH)
Coastal Carolina U (SC)
Coe Coll (IA)
Coker Coll (SC)
CollAmerica–Fort Collins (CO)
Coll Misericordia (PA)
Coll of Charleston (SC)
Coll of Mount St. Joseph (OH)
The Coll of New Jersey (NJ)
Coll of Saint Benedict (MN)
Coll of St. Catherine (MN)
Coll of Saint Elizabeth (NJ)
Coll of St. Joseph (VT)
The Coll of Saint Rose (NY)
The Coll of St. Scholastica (MN)
Coll of Santa Fe (NM)
The Coll of Southeastern Europe, The American U of Athens(Greece)
Coll of Staten Island of the City U of NY (NY)
Coll of the Holy Cross (MA)
Coll of the Ozarks (MO)
Coll of the Southwest (NM)
Colorado Christian U (CO)
Colorado State U (CO)
Colorado State U-Pueblo (CO)
Colorado Tech U Sioux Falls Campus (SD)
Columbia Coll (MO)
Columbia Coll (SC)
Columbia Union Coll (MD)
Columbus State U (GA)
Concord Coll (WV)
Concordia Coll (MN)
Concordia U (IL)
Concordia U (NE)
Concordia U (QC, Canada)
Concordia U, St. Paul (MN)
Concordia U Wisconsin (WI)
Converse Coll (SC)
Cornell U (NY)
Cornerstone U (MI)
Creighton U (NE)
Culver-Stockton Coll (MO)
Cumberland Coll (KY)
Cumberland U (TN)
Daemen Coll (NY)
Dakota State U (SD)
Dakota Wesleyan U (SD)
Dalhousie U (NS, Canada)
Dallas Baptist U (TX)
Dana Coll (NE)
Davenport U, Dearborn (MI)
Davenport U, Grand Rapids (MI)
Davenport U, Kalamazoo (MI)
Davenport U, Lansing (MI)
Davenport U, Lapeer (MI)
Davenport U, Warren (MI)
Davis & Elkins Coll (WV)
Defiance Coll (OH)
Delaware State U (DE)
Delaware Valley Coll (PA)
Delta State U (MS)
DePaul U (IL)
DeSales U (PA)
Dickinson State U (ND)
Dillard U (LA)
Doane Coll (NE)
Dominican Coll (NY)
Dominican U (IL)
Dordt Coll (IA)
Dowling Coll (NY)
Drake U (IA)
Drexel U (PA)
Drury U (MO)
Duquesne U (PA)
D'Youville Coll (NY)
East Carolina U (NC)
East Central U (OK)
Eastern Connecticut State U (CT)
Eastern Illinois U (IL)
Eastern Kentucky U (KY)
Eastern Mennonite U (VA)
Eastern Michigan U (MI)
Eastern New Mexico U (NM)
Eastern Oregon U (OR)
Eastern U (PA)
Eastern Washington U (WA)
East Texas Baptist U (TX)
Edgewood Coll (WI)
Elizabeth City State U (NC)
Elizabethtown Coll (PA)
Elmhurst Coll (IL)
Elmira Coll (NY)
Elms Coll (MA)
Elon U (NC)
Emory & Henry Coll (VA)
Emory U (GA)
Emporia State U (KS)
Eureka Coll (IL)
Evangel U (MO)
Excelsior Coll (NY)
Fairfield U (CT)
Fairleigh Dickinson U, Florham (NJ)
Fairleigh Dickinson U, Teaneck-Metro Campus (NJ)
Fairmont State Coll (WV)
Faulkner U (AL)
Fayetteville State U (NC)
Ferris State U (MI)
Ferrum Coll (VA)
Flagler Coll (FL)
Florida Ag and Mech U (FL)
Florida Atlantic U (FL)
Florida Gulf Coast U (FL)
Florida Inst of Technology (FL)
Florida Intl U (FL)
Florida Metropolitan U-Tampa Coll, Brandon (FL)
Florida Metropolitan U-Fort Lauderdale Coll (FL)
Florida Metropolitan U-Tampa Coll, Lakeland (FL)
Florida Metropolitan U-Tampa Coll (FL)
Florida Southern Coll (FL)
Florida State U (FL)
Fontbonne U (MO)
Fordham U (NY)
Fort Hays State U (KS)
Fort Lewis Coll (CO)
Fort Valley State U (GA)
Framingham State Coll (MA)
The Franciscan U (IA)
Franciscan U of Steubenville (OH)
Francis Marion U (SC)
Franklin Coll (IN)
Franklin Pierce Coll (NH)
Franklin U (OH)
Freed-Hardeman U (TN)
Fresno Pacific U (CA)
Frostburg State U (MD)
Furman U (SC)
Gallaudet U (DC)
Gannon U (PA)
Gardner-Webb U (NC)
Geneva Coll (PA)
George Mason U (VA)
Georgetown Coll (KY)
Georgetown U (DC)
The George Washington U (DC)
Georgia Coll & State U (GA)
Georgian Court U (NJ)
Georgia Southern U (GA)
Georgia Southwestern State U (GA)
Georgia State U (GA)
Gettysburg Coll (PA)
Glenville State Coll (WV)
Globe Inst of Technology (NY)
Golden Gate U (CA)
Goldey-Beacom Coll (DE)
Gonzaga U (WA)
Gordon Coll (MA)
Goshen Coll (IN)
Governors State U (IL)
Grace Bible Coll (MI)
Grace Coll (IN)
Graceland U (IA)
Grace U (NE)
Grambling State U (LA)
Grand Canyon U (AZ)
Grand Valley State U (MI)
Grand View Coll (IA)
Greensboro Coll (NC)
Greenville Coll (IL)
Grove City Coll (PA)
Guilford Coll (NC)
Gustavus Adolphus Coll (MN)
Gwynedd-Mercy Coll (PA)
Hampton U (VA)
Harding U (AR)
Hardin-Simmons U (TX)
Harris-Stowe State Coll (MO)
Hartwick Coll (NY)
Hastings Coll (NE)
Hawai'i Pacific U (HI)
HEC Montreal (QC, Canada)
Heidelberg Coll (OH)
Henderson State U (AR)
Hendrix Coll (AR)
Hesser Coll (NH)
High Point U (NC)
Hilbert Coll (NY)
Hillsdale Coll (MI)
Hofstra U (NY)
Hope Coll (MI)
Houghton Coll (NY)
Houston Baptist U (TX)
Howard Payne U (TX)
Howard U (DC)
Humboldt State U (CA)
Hunter Coll of the City U of NY (NY)
Huntingdon Coll (AL)
Huntington Coll (IN)
Husson Coll (ME)
Huston-Tillotson Coll (TX)
Idaho State U (ID)
Illinois Coll (IL)
Illinois State U (IL)
Illinois Wesleyan U (IL)
Immaculata U (PA)
Indiana Inst of Technology (IN)
Indiana State U (IN)
Indiana U Bloomington (IN)
Indiana U Northwest (IN)
Indiana U of Pennsylvania (PA)
Indiana U–Purdue U Fort Wayne (IN)
Inter American U of PR, Aguadilla Campus (PR)
Inter Amer U of PR, Barranquitas Campus (PR)
Inter American U of PR, Bayamón Campus (PR)
Inter American U of PR, Ponce Campus (PR)
Inter American U of PR, San Germán Campus (PR)
Intl Coll (FL)
Iona Coll (NY)
Iowa State U of Science and Technology (IA)
Iowa Wesleyan Coll (IA)
Ithaca Coll (NY)
Jacksonville State U (AL)
Jacksonville U (FL)
James Madison U (VA)
Jamestown Coll (ND)
Jarvis Christian Coll (TX)
John Brown U (AR)
John Carroll U (OH)
John F. Kennedy U (CA)
Johnson & Wales U (RI)
Johnson State Coll (VT)
Jones Coll, Jacksonville (FL)
Judson Coll (IL)
Juniata Coll (PA)
Kansas State U (KS)
Kansas Wesleyan U (KS)
Kean U (NJ)
Kennesaw State U (GA)
Kent State U (OH)
Kentucky Wesleyan Coll (KY)
Kettering U (MI)
Keuka Coll (NY)
Keystone Coll (PA)
King Coll (TN)
King's Coll (PA)
Kutztown U of Pennsylvania (PA)
Kwantlen U Coll (BC, Canada)
LaGrange Coll (GA)
Lake Erie Coll (OH)
Lakehead U (ON, Canada)
Lakeland Coll (WI)
Lake Superior State U (MI)
Lamar U (TX)
Lambuth U (TN)

La Roche Coll (PA)
La Salle U (PA)
Lasell Coll (MA)
Lebanon Valley Coll (PA)
Lehigh U (PA)
Lehman Coll of the City U of NY (NY)
Le Moyne Coll (NY)
Lenoir-Rhyne Coll (NC)
LeTourneau U (TX)
Lewis U (IL)
Liberty U (VA)
Limestone Coll (SC)
Lincoln Memorial U (TN)
Lincoln U (MO)
Lincoln U (PA)
Lindenwood U (MO)
Lindsey Wilson Coll (KY)
Linfield Coll (OR)
Lipscomb U (TN)
Livingstone Coll (NC)
Lock Haven U of Pennsylvania (PA)
Long Island U, Brentwood Campus (NY)
Long Island U, Brooklyn Campus (NY)
Long Island U, C.W. Post Campus (NY)
Long Island U, Southampton Coll (NY)
Longwood U (VA)
Loras Coll (IA)
Louisiana Coll (LA)
Louisiana State U and A&M Coll (LA)
Louisiana State U in Shreveport (LA)
Louisiana Tech U (LA)
Lourdes Coll (OH)
Loyola Coll in Maryland (MD)
Loyola Marymount U (CA)
Loyola U Chicago (IL)
Loyola U New Orleans (LA)
Lubbock Christian U (TX)
Luther Coll (IA)
Lycoming Coll (PA)
Lynchburg Coll (VA)
Lyndon State Coll (VT)
Lynn U (FL)
Lyon Coll (AR)
MacMurray Coll (IL)
Madonna U (MI)
Malone Coll (OH)
Manchester Coll (IN)
Manhattan Coll (NY)
Mansfield U of Pennsylvania (PA)
Marian Coll (IN)
Marian Coll of Fond du Lac (WI)
Marietta Coll (OH)
Marist Coll (NY)
Marquette U (WI)
Marshall U (WV)
Mars Hill Coll (NC)
Martin U (IN)
Marymount Coll of Fordham U (NY)
Marymount Manhattan Coll (NY)
Marymount U (VA)
Maryville U of Saint Louis (MO)
Marywood U (PA)
Massachusetts Coll of Liberal Arts (MA)
The Master's Coll and Sem (CA)
McGill U (QC, Canada)
McKendree Coll (IL)
McMurry U (TX)
McNeese State U (LA)
McPherson Coll (KS)
Medaille Coll (NY)
Medgar Evers Coll of the City U of NY (NY)
Memorial U of Newfoundland (NL, Canada)
Mercy Coll (NY)
Mercyhurst Coll (PA)
Meredith Coll (NC)
Merrimack Coll (MA)
Messiah Coll (PA)
Methodist Coll (NC)
Metropolitan State Coll of Denver (CO)
Metropolitan State U (MN)
Miami U (OH)
Miami U Hamilton (OH)
Michigan State U (MI)
Michigan Technological U (MI)
MidAmerica Nazarene U (KS)
Middle Tennessee State U (TN)
Midwestern State U (TX)
Milligan Coll (TN)
Millikin U (IL)
Millsaps Coll (MS)
Minnesota State U Mankato (MN)
Minnesota State U Moorhead (MN)
Minot State U (ND)
Mississippi Coll (MS)
Mississippi State U (MS)
Mississippi Valley State U (MS)
Missouri Baptist U (MO)
Missouri Southern State U (MO)
Missouri Valley Coll (MO)
Missouri Western State Coll (MO)
Molloy Coll (NY)
Monmouth Coll (IL)
Montana State U–Billings (MT)
Montana Tech of The U of Montana (MT)
Montclair State U (NJ)
Moravian Coll (PA)
Morehead State U (KY)
Morehouse Coll (GA)
Morgan State U (MD)
Morningside Coll (IA)
Morrison U (NV)
Mountain State U (WV)
Mount Allison U (NB, Canada)
Mount Aloysius Coll (PA)
Mount Marty Coll (SD)
Mount Mary Coll (WI)
Mount Mercy Coll (IA)
Mount Saint Mary Coll (NY)
Mount St. Mary's Coll (CA)
Mount Saint Mary's Coll and Sem (MD)
Mount Saint Vincent U (NS, Canada)
Mount Union Coll (OH)
Mount Vernon Nazarene U (OH)
Muhlenberg Coll (PA)
Murray State U (KY)
National American U, Colorado Springs (CO)
National American U, Denver (CO)
National American U (NM)
National American U (SD)
National American U–Sioux Falls Branch (SD)
National-Louis U (IL)
National U (CA)
Nazareth Coll of Rochester (NY)
Nebraska Wesleyan U (NE)
Neumann Coll (PA)
Newbury Coll (MA)
Newman U (KS)
New Mexico Highlands U (NM)
New Mexico State U (NM)
New York Inst of Technology (NY)
New York U (NY)
Niagara U (NY)
Nicholls State U (LA)
Nichols Coll (MA)
Norfolk State U (VA)
North Carolina Central U (NC)
North Carolina State U (NC)
North Carolina Wesleyan Coll (NC)
North Central Coll (IL)
North Dakota State U (ND)
Northeastern Illinois U (IL)
Northeastern State U (OK)
Northeastern U (MA)
Northern Arizona U (AZ)
Northern Illinois U (IL)
Northern Michigan U (MI)
Northern State U (SD)
North Georgia Coll & State U (GA)
North Park U (IL)
Northwestern Coll (IA)
Northwestern Coll (MN)
Northwestern Oklahoma State U (OK)
Northwestern State U of Louisiana (LA)
Northwest Nazarene U (ID)
Northwood U (MI)
Northwood U, Florida Campus (FL)
Northwood U, Texas Campus (TX)
Notre Dame Coll (OH)
Notre Dame de Namur U (CA)
Nova Southeastern U (FL)
Nyack Coll (NY)
Oakland City U (IN)
Oakland U (MI)
Oglethorpe U (GA)
Ohio Dominican U (OH)
Ohio Northern U (OH)
The Ohio State U (OH)
Ohio U (OH)
Ohio Valley Coll (WV)
Ohio Wesleyan U (OH)
Oklahoma Baptist U (OK)
Oklahoma Christian U (OK)
Oklahoma City U (OK)
Oklahoma Panhandle State U (OK)
Oklahoma State U (OK)
Old Dominion U (VA)
Olivet Coll (MI)
Olivet Nazarene U (IL)
Oral Roberts U (OK)
Oregon Inst of Technology (OR)
Oregon State U (OR)
Otterbein Coll (OH)
Ouachita Baptist U (AR)
Our Lady of Holy Cross Coll (LA)
Our Lady of the Lake U of San Antonio (TX)
Pace U (NY)
Pacific Lutheran U (WA)
Pacific Union Coll (CA)
Pacific U (OR)
Park U (MO)
Peirce Coll (PA)
Pennsylvania Coll of Technology (PA)
Penn State U Abington Coll (PA)
Penn State U Altoona Coll (PA)
Penn State U at Erie, The Behrend Coll (PA)
Penn State U Beaver Campus of the Commonwealth Coll (PA)
Penn State U Berks Cmps of Berks-Lehigh Valley Coll (PA)
Penn State U Delaware County Campus of the Commonwealth Coll (PA)
Penn State U DuBois Campus of the Commonwealth Coll (PA)
Penn State U Fayette Campus of the Commonwealth Coll (PA)
Penn State U Hazleton Campus of the Commonwealth Coll (PA)
Penn State U Lehigh Valley Cmps of Berks-Lehigh Valley Coll (PA)
Penn State U McKeesport Campus of the Commonwealth Coll (PA)
Penn State U Mont Alto Campus of the Commonwealth Coll (PA)
Penn State U New Kensington Campus of the Commonwealth Coll (PA)
Penn State U Schuylkill Campus of the Capital Coll (PA)
Penn State U Shenango Campus of the Commonwealth Coll (PA)
Penn State U Univ Park Campus (PA)
Penn State U Wilkes-Barre Campus of the Commonwealth Coll (PA)
Penn State U Worthington Scranton Cmps Commonwealth Coll (PA)
Penn State U York Campus of the Commonwealth Coll (PA)
Pepperdine U, Malibu (CA)
Pfeiffer U (NC)
Philadelphia U (PA)
Pittsburg State U (KS)
Plymouth State U (NH)
Point Loma Nazarene U (CA)
Point Park U (PA)
Polytechnic U of Puerto Rico (PR)
Pontifical Catholic U of Puerto Rico (PR)
Portland State U (OR)
Prairie View A&M U (TX)
Presbyterian Coll (SC)
Providence Coll (RI)
Purdue U (IN)
Queens Coll of the City U of NY (NY)
Queens U of Charlotte (NC)
Quincy U (IL)
Quinnipiac U (CT)
Radford U (VA)
Ramapo Coll of New Jersey (NJ)
Randolph-Macon Coll (VA)
Redeemer U Coll (ON, Canada)
Reformed Bible Coll (MI)
Regis U (CO)
Reinhardt Coll (GA)
Rhode Island Coll (RI)
Rider U (NJ)
Robert Morris U (PA)
Roberts Wesleyan Coll (NY)
Rochester Coll (MI)
Rochester Inst of Technology (NY)
Rockford Coll (IL)
Rockhurst U (MO)
Rocky Mountain Coll (MT)
Roger Williams U (RI)
Roosevelt U (IL)
Rosemont Coll (PA)
Rowan U (NJ)
Rutgers, The State U of New Jersey, Camden (NJ)
Rutgers, The State U of New Jersey, Newark (NJ)
Rutgers, The State U of New Jersey, New Brunswick/Piscataway (NJ)
Ryerson U (ON, Canada)
Sacred Heart U (CT)
Sage Coll of Albany (NY)
Saginaw Valley State U (MI)
St. Ambrose U (IA)
Saint Anselm Coll (NH)
Saint Augustine's Coll (NC)
St. Bonaventure U (NY)
St. Cloud State U (MN)
St. Edward's U (TX)
St. Francis Coll (NY)
Saint Francis U (PA)
St. Francis Xavier U (NS, Canada)
St. Gregory's U (OK)
St. John Fisher Coll (NY)
Saint John's U (MN)
St. John's U (NY)
Saint Joseph's Coll (IN)
St. Joseph's Coll, New York (NY)
Saint Joseph's Coll of Maine (ME)
St. Joseph's Coll, Suffolk Campus (NY)
Saint Joseph's U (PA)
Saint Leo U (FL)
Saint Louis U (MO)
Saint Martin's Coll (WA)
Saint Mary-of-the-Woods Coll (IN)
Saint Mary's Coll of California (CA)
Saint Mary's U of Minnesota (MN)
St. Mary's U of San Antonio (TX)
Saint Michael's Coll (VT)
St. Norbert Coll (WI)
St. Thomas Aquinas Coll (NY)
St. Thomas U (FL)
Saint Vincent Coll (PA)
Saint Xavier U (IL)
Salem Coll (NC)
Salem State Coll (MA)
Salisbury U (MD)
Salve Regina U (RI)
Samford U (AL)
Sam Houston State U (TX)
San Diego State U (CA)
San Francisco State U (CA)
San Jose State U (CA)
Santa Clara U (CA)
Schreiner U (TX)
Seattle Pacific U (WA)
Seattle U (WA)
Seton Hall U (NJ)
Seton Hill U (PA)
Shaw U (NC)
Shepherd U (WV)
Shippensburg U of Pennsylvania (PA)
Shorter Coll (GA)
Siena Coll (NY)
Siena Heights U (MI)
Silver Lake Coll (WI)
Simmons Coll (MA)
Simpson Coll (IA)
South Carolina State U (SC)
Southeastern Coll of the Assemblies of God (FL)
Southeastern Louisiana U (LA)
Southeastern Oklahoma State U (OK)
Southeast Missouri State U (MO)
Southern Adventist U (TN)
Southern Alberta Inst of Technology (AB, Canada)
Southern Arkansas U–Magnolia (AR)
Southern Connecticut State U (CT)
Southern Illinois U Carbondale (IL)
Southern Illinois U Edwardsville (IL)
Southern Methodist U (TX)
Southern Nazarene U (OK)
Southern Oregon U (OR)
Southern U and A&M Coll (LA)
Southern Utah U (UT)
Southern Wesleyan U (SC)
Southwest Baptist U (MO)
Southwestern Oklahoma State U (OK)
Southwestern U (TX)
Southwest Missouri State U (MO)
Spring Arbor U (MI)
Spring Hill Coll (AL)
State U of NY at Binghamton (NY)
State U of NY at New Paltz (NY)
State U of NY at Oswego (NY)
Plattsburgh State U of NY (NY)
State U of NY Coll at Brockport (NY)
State U of NY Coll at Fredonia (NY)
State U of NY Coll at Geneseo (NY)
State U of NY Coll at Old Westbury (NY)
State U of NY Coll at Oneonta (NY)
State U of NY Inst of Tech at Utica/Rome (NY)
State U of West Georgia (GA)
Stephens Coll (MO)
Stetson U (FL)
Stonehill Coll (MA)
Strayer U (DC)
Suffolk U (MA)
Sullivan U (KY)
Susquehanna U (PA)
Syracuse U (NY)
Tabor Coll (KS)
Talladega Coll (AL)
Tarleton State U (TX)
Taylor U (IN)
Teikyo Post U (CT)
Tennessee State U (TN)
Tennessee Technological U (TN)
Tennessee Wesleyan Coll (TN)
Texas A&M Intl U (TX)
Texas A&M U (TX)
Texas A&M U–Commerce (TX)
Texas A&M U–Corpus Christi (TX)
Texas A&M U–Kingsville (TX)
Texas A&M U–Texarkana (TX)
Texas Christian U (TX)
Texas Lutheran U (TX)
Texas Southern U (TX)
Texas State U-San Marcos (TX)
Texas Tech U (TX)
Texas Wesleyan U (TX)
Texas Woman's U (TX)
Thiel Coll (PA)
Thomas Coll (ME)
Thomas Edison State Coll (NJ)
Thomas More Coll (KY)
Thomas U (GA)
Tiffin U (OH)
Tougaloo Coll (MS)
Towson U (MD)
Transylvania U (KY)
Trevecca Nazarene U (TN)
Trinity Christian Coll (IL)
Trinity Intl U (IL)
Trinity U (TX)
Tri-State U (IN)
Troy State U (AL)
Troy State U Montgomery (AL)
Truman State U (MO)
Tulane U (LA)
Tusculum Coll (TN)
Tuskegee U (AL)
Union Coll (KY)
Union Coll (NE)
Union U (TN)
Université de Sherbrooke (QC, Canada)
U du Québec à Hull (QC, Canada)
State U of NY at Albany (NY)
U Coll of the Cariboo (BC, Canada)
The U of Akron (OH)
The U of Alabama (AL)
The U of Alabama at Birmingham (AL)
The U of Alabama in Huntsville (AL)
U of Alaska Fairbanks (AK)
U of Alaska Southeast (AK)
U of Alberta (AB, Canada)
The U of Arizona (AZ)
U of Arkansas (AR)
U of Arkansas at Fort Smith (AR)
U of Arkansas at Little Rock (AR)
U of Arkansas at Monticello (AR)
U of Baltimore (MD)
U of Bridgeport (CT)
The U of British Columbia (BC, Canada)
U of Calgary (AB, Canada)
U of Central Arkansas (AR)
U of Central Florida (FL)
U of Charleston (WV)
U of Cincinnati (OH)
U of Colorado at Boulder (CO)
U of Colorado at Colorado Springs (CO)
U of Connecticut (CT)
U of Dayton (OH)
U of Delaware (DE)
U of Denver (CO)
U of Detroit Mercy (MI)
U of Dubuque (IA)
U of Evansville (IN)
The U of Findlay (OH)
U of Florida (FL)
U of Georgia (GA)
U of Great Falls (MT)
U of Hartford (CT)
U of Hawaii at Manoa (HI)
U of Houston (TX)
U of Houston–Clear Lake (TX)
U of Houston–Victoria (TX)
U of Idaho (ID)
U of Illinois at Chicago (IL)
U of Illinois at Springfield (IL)
U of Illinois at Urbana–Champaign (IL)
U of Indianapolis (IN)
The U of Iowa (IA)
U of Kansas (KS)
U of Kentucky (KY)
U of La Verne (CA)
The U of Lethbridge (AB, Canada)
U of Louisiana at Lafayette (LA)
U of Louisville (KY)
The U of Maine at Augusta (ME)
U of Maine at Machias (ME)

U of Maine at Presque Isle (ME)
U of Manitoba (MB, Canada)
U of Mary (ND)
U of Mary Hardin-Baylor (TX)
U of Maryland, Coll Park (MD)
U of Maryland Eastern Shore (MD)
U of Maryland U Coll (MD)
U of Massachusetts Amherst (MA)
U of Massachusetts Dartmouth (MA)
The U of Memphis (TN)
U of Miami (FL)
U of Michigan (MI)
U of Michigan–Flint (MI)
U of Minnesota, Crookston (MN)
U of Minnesota, Duluth (MN)
U of Minnesota, Twin Cities Campus (MN)
U of Mississippi (MS)
U of Missouri–Columbia (MO)
U of Missouri–Kansas City (MO)
U of Missouri–St. Louis (MO)
U of Mobile (AL)
U of Montevallo (AL)
U of Nebraska at Omaha (NE)
U of Nebraska–Lincoln (NE)
U of Nevada, Las Vegas (NV)
U of Nevada, Reno (NV)
U of New Brunswick Fredericton (NB, Canada)
U of New Hampshire (NH)
U of New Haven (CT)
U of New Orleans (LA)
U of North Alabama (AL)
The U of North Carolina at Asheville (NC)
The U of North Carolina at Chapel Hill (NC)
The U of North Carolina at Charlotte (NC)
The U of North Carolina at Greensboro (NC)
The U of North Carolina at Pembroke (NC)
The U of North Carolina at Wilmington (NC)
U of North Dakota (ND)
U of Northern Iowa (IA)
U of North Florida (FL)
U of North Texas (TX)
U of Northwestern Ohio (OH)
U of Notre Dame (IN)
U of Oklahoma (OK)
U of Oregon (OR)
U of Ottawa (ON, Canada)
U of Pennsylvania (PA)
U of Phoenix–Atlanta Campus (GA)
U of Phoenix–Chicago Campus (IL)
U of Phoenix–Colorado Campus (CO)
U of Phoenix–Dallas Campus (TX)
U of Phoenix–Fort Lauderdale Campus (FL)
U of Phoenix–Hawaii Campus (HI)
U of Phoenix–Houston Campus (TX)
U of Phoenix–Idaho Campus (ID)
U of Phoenix–Jacksonville Campus (FL)
U of Phoenix–Kansas City Campus (MO)
U of Phoenix–Louisiana Campus (LA)
U of Phoenix–Maryland Campus (MD)
U of Phoenix–Metro Detroit Campus (MI)
U of Phoenix–Nevada Campus (NV)
U of Phoenix–New Mexico Campus (NM)
U of Phoenix–Northern California Campus (CA)
U of Phoenix–Oklahoma City Campus (OK)
U of Phoenix Online Campus (AZ)
U of Phoenix–Oregon Campus (OR)
U of Phoenix–Orlando Campus (FL)
U of Phoenix–Phoenix Campus (AZ)
U of Phoenix–Puerto Rico Campus (PR)
U of Phoenix–Sacramento Campus (CA)
U of Phoenix–San Diego Campus (CA)
U of Phoenix–Southern Arizona Campus (AZ)
U of Phoenix–Southern California Campus (CA)
U of Phoenix–Southern Colorado Campus (CO)
U of Phoenix–Tampa Campus (FL)
U of Phoenix–Tulsa Campus (OK)
U of Phoenix–Utah Campus (UT)
U of Phoenix–Washington Campus (WA)
U of Phoenix–West Michigan Campus (MI)
U of Phoenix–Wisconsin Campus (WI)
U of Pittsburgh (PA)
U of Pittsburgh at Greensburg (PA)
U of Pittsburgh at Johnstown (PA)
U of Portland (OR)
U of Puerto Rico, Cayey U Coll (PR)
U of Redlands (CA)
U of Regina (SK, Canada)
U of Rhode Island (RI)
U of Richmond (VA)
U of St. Francis (IL)
U of Saint Francis (IN)
U of Saint Mary (KS)
U of St. Thomas (MN)
U of St. Thomas (TX)
U of San Diego (CA)
U of San Francisco (CA)
U of Saskatchewan (SK, Canada)
The U of Scranton (PA)
U of Sioux Falls (SD)
U of South Alabama (AL)
U of South Carolina (SC)
The U of South Dakota (SD)
U of Southern California (CA)
U of Southern Indiana (IN)
U of Southern Maine (ME)
U of South Florida (FL)
The U of Tampa (FL)
The U of Tennessee (TN)
The U of Tennessee at Martin (TN)
The U of Texas at Arlington (TX)
The U of Texas at Austin (TX)
The U of Texas at Brownsville (TX)
The U of Texas at Dallas (TX)
The U of Texas at Tyler (TX)
The U of Texas–Pan American (TX)
U of the District of Columbia (DC)
U of the Incarnate Word (TX)
U of the Ozarks (AR)
U of the Sacred Heart (PR)
U of the Virgin Islands (VI)
U of Toledo (OH)
U of Tulsa (OK)
U of Utah (UT)
The U of Virginia's Coll at Wise (VA)
U of Washington (WA)
U of Waterloo (ON, Canada)
The U of West Alabama (AL)
U of West Florida (FL)
U of Windsor (ON, Canada)
U of Wisconsin–Eau Claire (WI)
U of Wisconsin–Green Bay (WI)
U of Wisconsin–La Crosse (WI)
U of Wisconsin–Madison (WI)
U of Wisconsin–Milwaukee (WI)
U of Wisconsin–Oshkosh (WI)
U of Wisconsin–Parkside (WI)
U of Wisconsin–Platteville (WI)
U of Wisconsin–River Falls (WI)
U of Wisconsin–Stevens Point (WI)
U of Wisconsin–Superior (WI)
U of Wisconsin–Whitewater (WI)
U of Wyoming (WY)
Upper Iowa U (IA)
Urbana U (OH)
Ursuline Coll (OH)
Utah State U (UT)
Utica Coll (NY)
Valdosta State U (GA)
Valparaiso U (IN)
Vanguard U of Southern California (CA)
Villa Julie Coll (MD)
Villanova U (PA)
Virginia Commonwealth U (VA)
Virginia Polytechnic Inst and State U (VA)
Virginia State U (VA)
Virginia Union U (VA)
Viterbo U (WI)
Voorhees Coll (SC)
Wagner Coll (NY)
Wake Forest U (NC)
Walla Walla Coll (WA)
Walsh Coll of Accountancy and Business Admin (MI)
Walsh U (OH)
Warner Southern Coll (FL)
Wartburg Coll (IA)
Washburn U (KS)
Washington & Jefferson Coll (PA)
Washington and Lee U (VA)
Washington State U (WA)
Washington U in St. Louis (MO)
Waynesburg Coll (PA)
Wayne State Coll (NE)
Wayne State U (MI)
Webber Intl U (FL)
Weber State U (UT)
Webster U (MO)
Wesley Coll (DE)
West Chester U of Pennsylvania (PA)
Western Baptist Coll (OR)
Western Carolina U (NC)
Western Connecticut State U (CT)
Western Illinois U (IL)
Western Kentucky U (KY)
Western Michigan U (MI)
Western New England Coll (MA)
Western State Coll of Colorado (CO)
Western Washington U (WA)
Westfield State Coll (MA)
West Liberty State Coll (WV)
Westminster Coll (MO)
Westminster Coll (PA)
Westminster Coll (UT)
West Texas A&M U (TX)
West Virginia State Coll (WV)
West Virginia U (WV)
West Virginia Wesleyan Coll (WV)
Wheeling Jesuit U (WV)
Whitworth Coll (WA)
Wichita State U (KS)
Widener U (PA)
Wilberforce U (OH)
Wilkes U (PA)
William Jewell Coll (MO)
William Paterson U of New Jersey (NJ)
William Penn U (IA)
William Woods U (MO)
Wilmington Coll (DE)
Wilson Coll (PA)
Wingate U (NC)
Winona State U (MN)
Winston-Salem State U (NC)
Wofford Coll (SC)
Wright State U (OH)
Xavier U (OH)
Xavier U of Louisiana (LA)
York Coll (NE)
York Coll of Pennsylvania (PA)
York Coll of the City U of New York (NY)
York U (ON, Canada)
Youngstown State U (OH)

ACCOUNTING AND BUSINESS/ MANAGEMENT

Alaska Pacific U (AK)
Babson Coll (MA)
Campbell U (NC)
Central Christian Coll of Kansas (KS)
Chestnut Hill Coll (PA)
Davis & Elkins Coll (WV)
Florida Ag and Mech U (FL)
Illinois State U (IL)
Keystone Coll (PA)
Miles Coll (AL)
Mount Aloysius Coll (PA)
National American U, Colorado Springs (CO)
North Greenville Coll (SC)
Paine Coll (GA)
Peirce Coll (PA)
U of Great Falls (MT)

ACCOUNTING AND COMPUTER SCIENCE

California State U, Chico (CA)
Fordham U (NY)
Husson Coll (ME)
San Jose State U (CA)
Western Washington U (WA)

ACCOUNTING AND FINANCE

Albertus Magnus Coll (CT)
American InterContinental U Online (IL)
Babson Coll (MA)
Campbell U (NC)
Drake U (IA)
Eastern Michigan U (MI)
Franklin and Marshall Coll (PA)
Kettering U (MI)
Palm Beach Atlantic U (FL)
Saint Francis U (PA)
U of North Dakota (ND)
U of Waterloo (ON, Canada)
U of Windsor (ON, Canada)
Wilberforce U (OH)

ACCOUNTING RELATED

Brigham Young U (UT)
California State U, Sacramento (CA)
Central Michigan U (MI)
Duquesne U (PA)
East Carolina U (NC)
Eastern Michigan U (MI)
Keystone Coll (PA)
Maryville U of Saint Louis (MO)
Park U (MO)
Peirce Coll (PA)
Rocky Mountain Coll (MT)
Saint Mary-of-the-Woods Coll (IN)
Saint Mary's Coll of California (CA)
State U of NY at Oswego (NY)
The U of Akron (OH)

ACCOUNTING TECHNOLOGY AND BOOKKEEPING

Bryant Coll (RI)
Canisius Coll (NY)
Lewis-Clark State Coll (ID)
Pace U (NY)
Peirce Coll (PA)
St. Edward's U (TX)
Washington State U (WA)

ACTING

Arcadia U (PA)
Bard Coll (NY)
Barry U (FL)
Baylor U (TX)
Boston U (MA)
Brigham Young U (UT)
California Inst of the Arts (CA)
California State U, Long Beach (CA)
Campbell U (NC)
Carroll Coll (MT)
Coe Coll (IA)
Coker Coll (SC)
Coll of Santa Fe (NM)
Coll of the Ozarks (MO)
Columbia Coll Chicago (IL)
Concordia U (QC, Canada)
Cornell U (NY)
Cornish Coll of the Arts (WA)
Dalhousie U (NS, Canada)
DePaul U (IL)
Drake U (IA)
Emerson Coll (MA)
Florida State U (FL)
Greensboro Coll (NC)
Hampshire Coll (MA)
Ithaca Coll (NY)
Johnson State Coll (VT)
The Juilliard School (NY)
Long Island U, C.W. Post Campus (NY)
Marymount Manhattan Coll (NY)
Memorial U of Newfoundland (NL, Canada)
Montclair State U (NJ)
New World School of the Arts (FL)
Ohio U (OH)
Old Dominion U (VA)
Palm Beach Atlantic U (FL)
Penn State U Abington Coll (PA)
Penn State U Altoona Coll (PA)
Penn State U at Erie, The Behrend Coll (PA)
Penn State U Beaver Campus of the Commonwealth Coll (PA)
Penn State U Berks Cmps of Berks-Lehigh Valley Coll (PA)
Penn State U Delaware County Campus of the Commonwealth Coll (PA)
Penn State U DuBois Campus of the Commonwealth Coll (PA)
Penn State U Fayette Campus of the Commonwealth Coll (PA)
Penn State U Hazleton Campus of the Commonwealth Coll (PA)
Penn State U Lehigh Valley Cmps of Berks-Lehigh Valley Coll (PA)
Penn State U McKeesport Campus of the Commonwealth Coll (PA)
Penn State U Mont Alto Campus of the Commonwealth Coll (PA)
Penn State U New Kensington Campus of the Commonwealth Coll (PA)
Penn State U Schuylkill Campus of the Capital Coll (PA)
Penn State U Shenango Campus of the Commonwealth Coll (PA)
Penn State U Univ Park Campus (PA)
Penn State U Wilkes-Barre Campus of the Commonwealth Coll (PA)
Penn State U Worthington Scranton Cmps Commonwealth Coll (PA)
Penn State U York Campus of the Commonwealth Coll (PA)
Ryerson U (ON, Canada)
St. Cloud State U (MN)
Sarah Lawrence Coll (NY)
Seton Hill U (PA)
Shenandoah U (VA)
Simon's Rock Coll of Bard (MA)
State U of NY Coll at Brockport (NY)
Syracuse U (NY)
Texas Tech U (TX)
Trinity U (TX)
The U of Akron (OH)
U of Connecticut (CT)
U of Northern Iowa (IA)
U of Regina (SK, Canada)
U of Southern California (CA)
The U of the Arts (PA)
U of Windsor (ON, Canada)
Western Michigan U (MI)
York U (ON, Canada)
Youngstown State U (OH)

ACTUARIAL SCIENCE

Ball State U (IN)
Bellarmine U (KY)
Baruch Coll of the City U of NY (NY)
Bradley U (IL)
Bryant Coll (RI)
Butler U (IN)
Carroll Coll (WI)
Central Michigan U (MI)
Concordia U (QC, Canada)
Drake U (IA)
Eastern Michigan U (MI)
Elmhurst Coll (IL)
Florida Ag and Mech U (FL)
Florida State U (FL)
Frostburg State U (MD)
Georgia State U (GA)
Hofstra U (NY)
Indiana U Northwest (IN)
Jamestown Coll (ND)
Lebanon Valley Coll (PA)
Lincoln U (PA)
Lycoming Coll (PA)
Maryville U of Saint Louis (MO)
The Master's Coll and Sem (CA)
Mercy Coll (NY)
New Jersey Inst of Technology (NJ)
New York U (NY)
North Central Coll (IL)
Northwestern Coll (IA)
The Ohio State U (OH)
Ohio U (OH)
Oregon State U (OR)
Penn State U Abington Coll (PA)
Penn State U Altoona Coll (PA)
Penn State U at Erie, The Behrend Coll (PA)
Penn State U Beaver Campus of the Commonwealth Coll (PA)
Penn State U Berks Cmps of Berks-Lehigh Valley Coll (PA)
Penn State U Delaware County Campus of the Commonwealth Coll (PA)
Penn State U DuBois Campus of the Commonwealth Coll (PA)
Penn State U Fayette Campus of the Commonwealth Coll (PA)
Penn State U Hazleton Campus of the Commonwealth Coll (PA)
Penn State U Lehigh Valley Cmps of Berks-Lehigh Valley Coll (PA)
Penn State U McKeesport Campus of the Commonwealth Coll (PA)
Penn State U Mont Alto Campus of the Commonwealth Coll (PA)
Penn State U New Kensington Campus of the Commonwealth Coll (PA)
Penn State U Schuylkill Campus of the Capital Coll (PA)
Penn State U Shenango Campus of the Commonwealth Coll (PA)
Penn State U Univ Park Campus (PA)
Penn State U Wilkes-Barre Campus of the Commonwealth Coll (PA)
Penn State U Worthington Scranton Cmps Commonwealth Coll (PA)
Penn State U York Campus of the Commonwealth Coll (PA)
Queens Coll of the City U of NY (NY)
Quinnipiac U (CT)
Rider U (NJ)
Robert Morris U (PA)
Roosevelt U (IL)
St. John's U (NY)
Seton Hill U (PA)
Simon Fraser U (BC, Canada)
Southern Adventist U (TN)
Tabor Coll (KS)
Thiel Coll (PA)
Université de Montréal (QC, Canada)
Université Laval (QC, Canada)
State U of NY at Albany (NY)

U of Calgary (AB, Canada)
U of Central Florida (FL)
U of Connecticut (CT)
U of Illinois at Urbana–Champaign (IL)
The U of Iowa (IA)
U of Manitoba (MB, Canada)
U of Michigan–Flint (MI)
U of Minnesota, Duluth (MN)
U of Minnesota, Twin Cities Campus (MN)
U of Nebraska–Lincoln (NE)
U of Northern Iowa (IA)
U of Pennsylvania (PA)
U of Regina (SK, Canada)
U of St. Thomas (MN)
U of Toronto (ON, Canada)
U of Waterloo (ON, Canada)
The U of Western Ontario (ON, Canada)
U of Wisconsin–Madison (WI)
U of Wisconsin–Stevens Point (WI)
Valparaiso U (IN)
Washburn U (KS)
Worcester Polytechnic Inst (MA)
York U (ON, Canada)

ADMINISTRATIVE ASSISTANT AND SECRETARIAL SCIENCE
Alabama State U (AL)
Albany State U (GA)
Alcorn State U (MS)
American U of Puerto Rico (PR)
Baker Coll of Flint (MI)
Baker Coll of Muskegon (MI)
Baker Coll of Owosso (MI)
Baker Coll of Port Huron (MI)
Baptist Bible Coll (MO)
Belmont U (TN)
Bluefield State Coll (WV)
Campbellsville U (KY)
Clearwater Christian Coll (FL)
East Central U (OK)
Eastern Kentucky U (KY)
Evangel U (MO)
Florida Ag and Mech U (FL)
Fort Hays State U (KS)
Fort Valley State U (GA)
Hofstra U (NY)
Inter American U of PR, Aguadilla Campus (PR)
Inter Amer U of PR, Barranquitas Campus (PR)
Inter American U of PR, Bayamón Campus (PR)
Inter American U of PR, Fajardo Campus (PR)
Inter American U of PR, Ponce Campus (PR)
Inter American U of PR, San Germán Campus (PR)
Jones Coll, Jacksonville (FL)
Lake Superior State U (MI)
Lamar U (TX)
Lewis-Clark State Coll (ID)
Lincoln U (MO)
Mayville State U (ND)
Mercyhurst Coll (PA)
Mount Vernon Nazarene U (OH)
Northern State U (SD)
Pillsbury Baptist Bible Coll (MN)
Pontifical Catholic U of Puerto Rico (PR)
Ryerson U (ON, Canada)
Salem State Coll (MA)
South Carolina State U (SC)
Southeast Missouri State U (MO)
Suffolk U (MA)
Tabor Coll (KS)
Tennessee State U (TN)
Texas A&M U–Commerce (TX)
Texas Woman's U (TX)
Trinity Bible Coll (ND)
Universidad Adventista de las Antillas (PR)
U of Idaho (ID)
U of Maine at Machias (ME)
The U of Montana–Missoula (MT)
U of Puerto Rico, Cayey U Coll (PR)
U of Sioux Falls (SD)
U of the Sacred Heart (PR)
U of Wisconsin–Superior (WI)
Utah State U (UT)
Valdosta State U (GA)
Weber State U (UT)
Winona State U (MN)
Youngstown State U (OH)

ADULT AND CONTINUING EDUCATION
American Intl Coll (MA)
Arkansas Baptist Coll (AR)
Atlantic Union Coll (MA)
Auburn U (AL)
Biola U (CA)
Brock U (ON, Canada)
Christian Heritage Coll (CA)
Dakota Wesleyan U (SD)
DePaul U (IL)
Franklin Pierce Coll (NH)
Immaculata U (PA)
Iowa Wesleyan Coll (IA)
Laurentian U (ON, Canada)
Lenoir-Rhyne Coll (NC)
Louisiana Coll (LA)
Lynn U (FL)
Mars Hill Coll (NC)
Martin U (IN)
Massachusetts Coll of Liberal Arts (MA)
Memorial U of Newfoundland (NL, Canada)
Morehouse Coll (GA)
Pittsburg State U (KS)
Pratt Inst (NY)
St. Joseph's Coll, Suffolk Campus (NY)
Tabor Coll (KS)
Tennessee State U (TN)
Université de Sherbrooke (QC, Canada)
U Coll of the Fraser Valley (BC, Canada)
U of Alberta (AB, Canada)
U of Arkansas (AR)
U of Nevada, Las Vegas (NV)
U of New Brunswick Fredericton (NB, Canada)
U of New Hampshire (NH)
U of Regina (SK, Canada)
U of San Francisco (CA)
U of the Incarnate Word (TX)
U of Toledo (OH)
Urbana U (OH)

ADULT AND CONTINUING EDUCATION ADMINISTRATION
Marshall U (WV)
Penn State U Abington Coll (PA)
Penn State U Altoona Coll (PA)
Penn State U at Erie, The Behrend Coll (PA)
Penn State U Beaver Campus of the Commonwealth Coll (PA)
Penn State U Berks Cmps of Berks-Lehigh Valley Coll (PA)
Penn State U Delaware County Campus of the Commonwealth Coll (PA)
Penn State U DuBois Campus of the Commonwealth Coll (PA)
Penn State U Fayette Campus of the Commonwealth Coll (PA)
Penn State U Hazleton Campus of the Commonwealth Coll (PA)
Penn State U Lehigh Valley Cmps of Berks-Lehigh Valley Coll (PA)
Penn State U McKeesport Campus of the Commonwealth Coll (PA)
Penn State U Mont Alto Campus of the Commonwealth Coll (PA)
Penn State U New Kensington Campus of the Commonwealth Coll (PA)
Penn State U Schuylkill Campus of the Capital Coll (PA)
Penn State U Shenango Campus of the Commonwealth Coll (PA)
Penn State U Univ Park Campus (PA)
Penn State U Wilkes-Barre Campus of the Commonwealth Coll (PA)
Penn State U Worthington Scranton Cmps Commonwealth Coll (PA)
Penn State U York Campus of the Commonwealth Coll (PA)
Saint Joseph's Coll of Maine (ME)
U Coll of the Fraser Valley (BC, Canada)

ADULT DEVELOPMENT AND AGING
Bowling Green State U (OH)
Chestnut Hill Coll (PA)
Eastern Michigan U (MI)
Liberty U (VA)
Madonna U (MI)
Mount Saint Vincent U (NS, Canada)
Saint Mary-of-the-Woods Coll (IN)
St. Thomas U (NB, Canada)
U of Guelph (ON, Canada)
U of Northern Colorado (CO)
Washington State U (WA)

ADULT HEALTH NURSING
Okanagan U Coll (BC, Canada)
Pennsylvania Coll of Technology (PA)
U at Buffalo, The State U of New York (NY)
Wright State U (OH)

ADVANCED/GRADUATE DENTISTRY AND ORAL SCIENCES RELATED
Dalhousie U (NS, Canada)

ADVERTISING
Acad of Art U (CA)
American Acad of Art (IL)
Appalachian State U (NC)
Art Center Coll of Design (CA)
The Art Inst of Atlanta (GA)
The Art Inst of California–San Diego (CA)
The Art Inst of California–San Francisco (CA)
The Art Inst of Colorado (CO)
The Art Inst of Phoenix (AZ)
The Art Inst of Portland (OR)
The Art Inst of Washington (VA)
Ball State U (IN)
Barry U (FL)
Belmont U (TN)
Baruch Coll of the City U of NY (NY)
Boise State U (ID)
Bradley U (IL)
Brigham Young U (UT)
California State U, Fullerton (CA)
California State U, Hayward (CA)
Campbell U (NC)
Central Michigan U (MI)
Chapman U (CA)
Clarke Coll (IA)
The Coll of Southeastern Europe, The American U of Athens(Greece)
Colorado State U-Pueblo (CO)
Columbia Coll Chicago (IL)
Concordia Coll (MN)
DePaul U (IL)
Drake U (IA)
Drury U (MO)
East Central U (OK)
Eastern Nazarene Coll (MA)
Emerson Coll (MA)
Ferris State U (MI)
Florida Southern Coll (FL)
Florida State U (FL)
Fontbonne U (MO)
Franklin Pierce Coll (NH)
Gannon U (PA)
Grand Valley State U (MI)
Hampton U (VA)
Harding U (AR)
Hastings Coll (NE)
Hawai'i Pacific U (HI)
The Illinois Inst of Art-Schaumburg (IL)
Iona Coll (NY)
Iowa State U of Science and Technology (IA)
Johnson & Wales U (RI)
Kent State U (OH)
Liberty U (VA)
Louisiana Coll (LA)
Marist Coll (NY)
Marquette U (WI)
Marywood U (PA)
Memphis Coll of Art (TN)
Mercyhurst Coll (PA)
Metropolitan State U (MN)
Michigan State U (MI)
Minneapolis Coll of Art and Design (MN)
Minnesota State U Moorhead (MN)
New England School of Communications (ME)
New York Inst of Technology (NY)
Northern Arizona U (AZ)
Northwood U (MI)
Northwood U, Florida Campus (FL)
Northwood U, Texas Campus (TX)
Notre Dame de Namur U (CA)
Ohio U (OH)
Oklahoma Baptist U (OK)
Oklahoma Christian U (OK)
Oklahoma City U (OK)
Oklahoma State U (OK)
Pace U (NY)
Pacific Union Coll (CA)
Penn State U Abington Coll (PA)
Penn State U Altoona Coll (PA)
Penn State U at Erie, The Behrend Coll (PA)
Penn State U Beaver Campus of the Commonwealth Coll (PA)
Penn State U Berks Cmps of Berks-Lehigh Valley Coll (PA)
Penn State U Delaware County Campus of the Commonwealth Coll (PA)
Penn State U DuBois Campus of the Commonwealth Coll (PA)
Penn State U Fayette Campus of the Commonwealth Coll (PA)
Penn State U Hazleton Campus of the Commonwealth Coll (PA)
Penn State U Lehigh Valley Cmps of Berks-Lehigh Valley Coll (PA)
Penn State U McKeesport Campus of the Commonwealth Coll (PA)
Penn State U Mont Alto Campus of the Commonwealth Coll (PA)
Penn State U New Kensington Campus of the Commonwealth Coll (PA)
Penn State U Schuylkill Campus of the Capital Coll (PA)
Penn State U Shenango Campus of the Commonwealth Coll (PA)
Penn State U Univ Park Campus (PA)
Penn State U Wilkes-Barre Campus of the Commonwealth Coll (PA)
Penn State U Worthington Scranton Cmps Commonwealth Coll (PA)
Penn State U York Campus of the Commonwealth Coll (PA)
Pepperdine U, Malibu (CA)
Pittsburg State U (KS)
Point Park U (PA)
Portland State U (OR)
Quinnipiac U (CT)
Rider U (NJ)
Rochester Inst of Technology (NY)
St. Ambrose U (IA)
St. Cloud State U (MN)
Saint Joseph's Coll of Maine (ME)
Sam Houston State U (TX)
San Jose State U (CA)
Simmons Coll (MA)
Simpson Coll (IA)
Southern Methodist U (TX)
Stephens Coll (MO)
Syracuse U (NY)
Texas A&M U–Commerce (TX)
Texas Christian U (TX)
Texas State U-San Marcos (TX)
Texas Tech U (TX)
Texas Wesleyan U (TX)
Thomas Edison State Coll (NJ)
Union U (TN)
The U of Alabama (AL)
U of Arkansas at Little Rock (AR)
U of Central Florida (FL)
U of Colorado at Boulder (CO)
U of Florida (FL)
U of Georgia (GA)
U of Illinois at Urbana–Champaign (IL)
U of Kansas (KS)
U of Kentucky (KY)
U of Miami (FL)
U of Mississippi (MS)
U of Missouri–Columbia (MO)
U of Nebraska–Lincoln (NE)
U of Nevada, Reno (NV)
U of North Texas (TX)
U of Oklahoma (OK)
U of Oregon (OR)
U of South Carolina (SC)
U of Southern Indiana (IN)
The U of Tennessee (TN)
The U of Texas at Arlington (TX)
The U of Texas at Austin (TX)
U of the Sacred Heart (PR)
U of Wisconsin–Madison (WI)
Washington State U (WA)
Washington U in St. Louis (MO)
Waynesburg Coll (PA)
Wayne State Coll (NE)
Webster U (MO)
Wesleyan Coll (GA)
Western Kentucky U (KY)
Western New England Coll (MA)
West Texas A&M U (TX)
West Virginia U (WV)
Widener U (PA)
William Woods U (MO)
Winona State U (MN)
Xavier U (OH)
Youngstown State U (OH)

AERONAUTICAL/AEROSPACE ENGINEERING TECHNOLOGY
Arizona State U East (AZ)
Central Missouri State U (MO)
Embry-Riddle Aeronautical U (FL)
New York Inst of Technology (NY)
Northeastern U (MA)
Ohio U (OH)
Saint Louis U (MO)
Utah State U (UT)

AERONAUTICS/AVIATION/AEROSPACE SCIENCE AND TECHNOLOGY
Augsburg Coll (MN)
Central Washington U (WA)
Daniel Webster Coll (NH)
Delta State U (MS)
Eastern Michigan U (MI)
Elizabeth City State U (NC)
Embry-Riddle Aeronautical U (AZ)
Embry-Riddle Aeronautical U (FL)
Embry-Riddle Aeronautical U, Extended Campus (FL)
Florida Inst of Technology (FL)
Inter American U of PR, Bayamón Campus (PR)
Kansas State U (KS)
Kent State U (OH)
Louisiana Tech U (LA)
Middle Tennessee State U (TN)
Ohio U (OH)
Purdue U (IN)
St. Francis Coll (NY)
San Jose State U (CA)
U of Nebraska at Omaha (NE)
U of North Dakota (ND)
U of Oklahoma (OK)
U of the District of Columbia (DC)
York U (ON, Canada)

AEROSPACE, AERONAUTICAL AND ASTRONAUTICAL ENGINEERING
Arizona State U (AZ)
Auburn U (AL)
Bethel Coll (IN)
Boston U (MA)
California Inst of Technology (CA)
California Polytechnic State U, San Luis Obispo (CA)
California State Polytechnic U, Pomona (CA)
California State U, Long Beach (CA)
Carleton U (ON, Canada)
Case Western Reserve U (OH)
Clarkson U (NY)
Cornell U (NY)
Dowling Coll (NY)
Eastern Nazarene Coll (MA)
Embry-Riddle Aeronautical U (AZ)
Embry-Riddle Aeronautical U (FL)
Florida Inst of Technology (FL)
Georgia Inst of Technology (GA)
Illinois Inst of Technology (IL)
Inter American U of PR, Bayamón Campus (PR)
Iowa State U of Science and Technology (IA)
Massachusetts Inst of Technology (MA)
Miami U (OH)
Mississippi State U (MS)
New Mexico State U (NM)
North Carolina State U (NC)
The Ohio State U (OH)
Oklahoma State U (OK)
Penn State U Abington Coll (PA)
Penn State U Altoona Coll (PA)
Penn State U at Erie, The Behrend Coll (PA)
Penn State U Beaver Campus of the Commonwealth Coll (PA)
Penn State U Berks Cmps of Berks-Lehigh Valley Coll (PA)
Penn State U Delaware County Campus of the Commonwealth Coll (PA)
Penn State U DuBois Campus of the Commonwealth Coll (PA)
Penn State U Fayette Campus of the Commonwealth Coll (PA)
Penn State U Hazleton Campus of the Commonwealth Coll (PA)
Penn State U Lehigh Valley Cmps of Berks-Lehigh Valley Coll (PA)
Penn State U McKeesport Campus of the Commonwealth Coll (PA)
Penn State U Mont Alto Campus of the Commonwealth Coll (PA)
Penn State U New Kensington Campus of the Commonwealth Coll (PA)
Penn State U Schuylkill Campus of the Capital Coll (PA)
Penn State U Shenango Campus of the Commonwealth Coll (PA)
Penn State U Univ Park Campus (PA)
Penn State U Wilkes-Barre Campus of the Commonwealth Coll (PA)
Penn State U Worthington Scranton Cmps Commonwealth Coll (PA)

Penn State U York Campus of the Commonwealth Coll (PA)
Purdue U (IN)
Rensselaer Polytechnic Inst (NY)
Rochester Inst of Technology (NY)
Ryerson U (ON, Canada)
Saint Louis U (MO)
San Diego State U (CA)
San Jose State U (CA)
Stanford U (CA)
Syracuse U (NY)
Texas A&M U (TX)
Tuskegee U (AL)
United States Air Force Acad (CO)
United States Military Acad (NY)
United States Naval Acad (MD)
U at Buffalo, The State U of New York (NY)
The U of Alabama (AL)
The U of Arizona (AZ)
U of Calif, Davis (CA)
U of Calif, Irvine (CA)
U of Calif, Los Angeles (CA)
U of Calif, San Diego (CA)
U of Central Florida (FL)
U of Cincinnati (OH)
U of Colorado at Boulder (CO)
U of Florida (FL)
U of Illinois at Urbana–Champaign (IL)
U of Kansas (KS)
U of Maryland, Coll Park (MD)
U of Miami (FL)
U of Michigan (MI)
U of Minnesota, Twin Cities Campus (MN)
U of Missouri–Rolla (MO)
U of Notre Dame (IN)
U of Oklahoma (OK)
U of Southern California (CA)
The U of Tennessee (TN)
The U of Texas at Arlington (TX)
The U of Texas at Austin (TX)
U of Toronto (ON, Canada)
U of Virginia (VA)
U of Washington (WA)
Utah State U (UT)
Virginia Polytechnic Inst and State U (VA)
Washington U in St. Louis (MO)
Weber State U (UT)
Western Michigan U (MI)
West Virginia U (WV)
Wichita State U (KS)
Worcester Polytechnic Inst (MA)
York U (ON, Canada)

AFRICAN-AMERICAN/BLACK STUDIES

Amherst Coll (MA)
Antioch Coll (OH)
Arizona State U (AZ)
Bates Coll (ME)
Bowdoin Coll (ME)
Brandeis U (MA)
Brown U (RI)
California State U, Dominguez Hills (CA)
California State U, Fresno (CA)
California State U, Fullerton (CA)
California State U, Hayward (CA)
California State U, Long Beach (CA)
California State U, Los Angeles (CA)
California State U, San Bernardino (CA)
City Coll of the City U of NY (NY)
Claremont McKenna Coll (CA)
Coe Coll (IA)
Colby Coll (ME)
Colgate U (NY)
Coll of Staten Island of the City U of NY (NY)
Coll of the Holy Cross (MA)
The Coll of William and Mary (VA)
The Coll of Wooster (OH)
Columbia Coll (NY)
Columbia U, School of General Studies (NY)
Cornell U (NY)
Dartmouth Coll (NH)
Denison U (OH)
DePaul U (IL)
DePauw U (IN)
Duke U (NC)
Earlham Coll (IN)
Eastern Illinois U (IL)
Eastern Michigan U (MI)
Emory U (GA)
Florida Ag and Mech U (FL)
Florida State U (FL)
Fordham U (NY)
Georgia State U (GA)
Gettysburg Coll (PA)
Grinnell Coll (IA)
Guilford Coll (NC)
Hampshire Coll (MA)
Harvard U (MA)
Hobart and William Smith Colls (NY)
Howard U (DC)
Hunter Coll of the City U of NY (NY)
Indiana State U (IN)
Indiana U Bloomington (IN)
Indiana U Northwest (IN)
Kent State U (OH)
Kenyon Coll (OH)
Knox Coll (IL)
Lehman Coll of the City U of NY (NY)
Lincoln U (PA)
Loyola Marymount U (CA)
Luther Coll (IA)
Marquette U (WI)
Martin U (IN)
Mercer U (GA)
Metropolitan State Coll of Denver (CO)
Miami U (OH)
Morehouse Coll (GA)
Morgan State U (MD)
Mount Holyoke Coll (MA)
New York U (NY)
Northeastern U (MA)
Northwestern U (IL)
Oberlin Coll (OH)
The Ohio State U (OH)
Ohio U (OH)
Ohio Wesleyan U (OH)
Penn State U Abington Coll (PA)
Penn State U Altoona Coll (PA)
Penn State U at Erie, The Behrend Coll (PA)
Penn State U Beaver Campus of the Commonwealth Coll (PA)
Penn State U Berks Cmps of Berks-Lehigh Valley Coll (PA)
Penn State U Delaware County Campus of the Commonwealth Coll (PA)
Penn State U DuBois Campus of the Commonwealth Coll (PA)
Penn State U Fayette Campus of the Commonwealth Coll (PA)
Penn State U Hazleton Campus of the Commonwealth Coll (PA)
Penn State U Lehigh Valley Cmps of Berks-Lehigh Valley Coll (PA)
Penn State U McKeesport Campus of the Commonwealth Coll (PA)
Penn State U Mont Alto Campus of the Commonwealth Coll (PA)
Penn State U New Kensington Campus of the Commonwealth Coll (PA)
Penn State U Schuylkill Campus of the Capital Coll (PA)
Penn State U Shenango Campus of the Commonwealth Coll (PA)
Penn State U Univ Park Campus (PA)
Penn State U Wilkes-Barre Campus of the Commonwealth Coll (PA)
Penn State U Worthington Scranton Cmps Commonwealth Coll (PA)
Penn State U York Campus of the Commonwealth Coll (PA)
Pitzer Coll (CA)
Pomona Coll (CA)
Purdue U (IN)
Rhode Island Coll (RI)
Roosevelt U (IL)
Rutgers, The State U of New Jersey, Camden (NJ)
Rutgers, The State U of New Jersey, Newark (NJ)
Saint Augustine's Coll (NC)
San Diego State U (CA)
San Francisco State U (CA)
San Jose State U (CA)
Sarah Lawrence Coll (NY)
Scripps Coll (CA)
Seton Hall U (NJ)
Simmons Coll (MA)
Simon's Rock Coll of Bard (MA)
Smith Coll (MA)
Sonoma State U (CA)
Southern Methodist U (TX)
State U of NY at Binghamton (NY)
State U of NY at New Paltz (NY)
State U of NY Coll at Brockport (NY)
State U of NY Coll at Cortland (NY)
State U of NY Coll at Geneseo (NY)
State U of NY Coll at Oneonta (NY)
Stony Brook U, State U of New York (NY)
Suffolk U (MA)
Syracuse U (NY)
Talladega Coll (AL)
Texas Southern U (TX)
Tougaloo Coll (MS)
Tufts U (MA)
State U of NY at Albany (NY)
U at Buffalo, The State U of New York (NY)
The U of Alabama at Birmingham (AL)
U of Calif, Berkeley (CA)
U of Calif, Davis (CA)
U of Calif, Irvine (CA)
U of Calif, Los Angeles (CA)
U of Calif, Riverside (CA)
U of Calif, Santa Barbara (CA)
U of Chicago (IL)
U of Cincinnati (OH)
U of Delaware (DE)
U of Georgia (GA)
U of Illinois at Chicago (IL)
The U of Iowa (IA)
U of Kansas (KS)
U of Louisville (KY)
U of Maryland, Baltimore County (MD)
U of Maryland, Coll Park (MD)
U of Massachusetts Amherst (MA)
U of Massachusetts Boston (MA)
The U of Memphis (TN)
U of Miami (FL)
U of Michigan (MI)
U of Michigan–Flint (MI)
U of Minnesota, Twin Cities Campus (MN)
The U of Montana–Missoula (MT)
U of Nebraska at Omaha (NE)
U of Nevada, Las Vegas (NV)
U of New Mexico (NM)
The U of North Carolina at Chapel Hill (NC)
The U of North Carolina at Charlotte (NC)
The U of North Carolina at Greensboro (NC)
U of Northern Colorado (CO)
U of Oklahoma (OK)
U of Pennsylvania (PA)
U of Pittsburgh (PA)
U of Rochester (NY)
U of South Carolina (SC)
U of Southern California (CA)
U of South Florida (FL)
U of Toledo (OH)
U of Virginia (VA)
U of Washington (WA)
U of Wisconsin–Madison (WI)
U of Wisconsin–Milwaukee (WI)
Vanderbilt U (TN)
Virginia Commonwealth U (VA)
Washington U in St. Louis (MO)
Wayne State U (MI)
Wellesley Coll (MA)
Wells Coll (NY)
Wesleyan U (CT)
Western Illinois U (IL)
William Paterson U of New Jersey (NJ)
Wright State U (OH)
Yale U (CT)
York Coll of the City U of New York (NY)
Youngstown State U (OH)

AFRICAN LANGUAGES

Harvard U (MA)
Lincoln U (PA)
Ohio U (OH)
U of Calif, Los Angeles (CA)
U of Wisconsin–Madison (WI)

AFRICAN STUDIES

American Public U System (WV)
American U (DC)
Antioch Coll (OH)
Bard Coll (NY)
Barnard Coll (NY)
Bowdoin Coll (ME)
Bowling Green State U (OH)
Brandeis U (MA)
Brooklyn Coll of the City U of NY (NY)
Carleton Coll (MN)
Carleton U (ON, Canada)
Chicago State U (IL)
Colgate U (NY)
Coll of the Holy Cross (MA)
Connecticut Coll (CT)
Dartmouth Coll (NH)
DePaul U (IL)
Emory U (GA)
Fordham U (NY)
Franklin and Marshall Coll (PA)
Hamilton Coll (NY)
Hampshire Coll (MA)
Harvard U (MA)
Haverford Coll (PA)
Hobart and William Smith Colls (NY)
Hofstra U (NY)
Indiana U Bloomington (IN)
Kenyon Coll (OH)
Marlboro Coll (VT)
McGill U (QC, Canada)
Miles Coll (AL)
Morgan State U (MD)
Northwestern U (IL)
The Ohio State U (OH)
Ohio U (OH)
Portland State U (OR)
Queens Coll of the City U of NY (NY)
Rutgers, The State U of New Jersey, New Brunswick/Piscataway (NJ)
St. Lawrence U (NY)
Sarah Lawrence Coll (NY)
Shaw U (NC)
Stanford U (CA)
State U of NY at Binghamton (NY)
State U of NY Coll at Brockport (NY)
Tennessee State U (TN)
Tulane U (LA)
U of Calif, Davis (CA)
U of Calif, Los Angeles (CA)
U of Chicago (IL)
The U of Iowa (IA)
U of Kansas (KS)
U of Michigan (MI)
U of Minnesota, Twin Cities Campus (MN)
U of Pennsylvania (PA)
U of Toronto (ON, Canada)
U of Wisconsin–Madison (WI)
Vanderbilt U (TN)
Vassar Coll (NY)
Washington U in St. Louis (MO)
Wellesley Coll (MA)
William Paterson U of New Jersey (NJ)
Yale U (CT)
York U (ON, Canada)
Youngstown State U (OH)

AGRIBUSINESS

Abilene Christian U (TX)
Andrews U (MI)
Arkansas State U (AR)
Arkansas Tech U (AR)
Brigham Young U (UT)
Central Missouri State U (MO)
Coll of the Ozarks (MO)
Colorado State U (CO)
Delaware Valley Coll (PA)
Illinois State U (IL)
Lindenwood U (MO)
McGill U (QC, Canada)
Middle Tennessee State U (TN)
Mississippi State U (MS)
North Carolina State U (NC)
North Dakota State U (ND)
Northwestern Coll (IA)
Penn State U Abington Coll (PA)
Penn State U Altoona Coll (PA)
Penn State U at Erie, The Behrend Coll (PA)
Penn State U Beaver Campus of the Commonwealth Coll (PA)
Penn State U Berks Cmps of Berks-Lehigh Valley Coll (PA)
Penn State U Delaware County Campus of the Commonwealth Coll (PA)
Penn State U DuBois Campus of the Commonwealth Coll (PA)
Penn State U Fayette Campus of the Commonwealth Coll (PA)
Penn State U Hazleton Campus of the Commonwealth Coll (PA)
Penn State U Lehigh Valley Cmps of Berks-Lehigh Valley Coll (PA)
Penn State U McKeesport Campus of the Commonwealth Coll (PA)
Penn State U Mont Alto Campus of the Commonwealth Coll (PA)
Penn State U New Kensington Campus of the Commonwealth Coll (PA)
Penn State U Schuylkill Campus of the Capital Coll (PA)
Penn State U Shenango Campus of the Commonwealth Coll (PA)
Penn State U Univ Park Campus (PA)
Penn State U Wilkes-Barre Campus of the Commonwealth Coll (PA)
Penn State U Worthington Scranton Cmps Commonwealth Coll (PA)
Penn State U York Campus of the Commonwealth Coll (PA)
Sam Houston State U (TX)
South Dakota State U (SD)
Southeast Missouri State U (MO)
Southwest Missouri State U (MO)
Texas A&M U (TX)
Texas State U-San Marcos (TX)
U of Arkansas (AR)
U of Delaware (DE)
U of Illinois at Urbana–Champaign (IL)
U of Louisiana at Lafayette (LA)
U of Saskatchewan (SK, Canada)
U of Wyoming (WY)
West Texas A&M U (TX)

AGRICULTURAL AND DOMESTIC ANIMALS SERVICES RELATED

Sterling Coll (VT)
Tarleton State U (TX)

AGRICULTURAL AND EXTENSION EDUCATION

Colorado State U (CO)
Cornell U (NY)
North Carolina State U (NC)
Penn State U Abington Coll (PA)
Penn State U Altoona Coll (PA)
Penn State U at Erie, The Behrend Coll (PA)
Penn State U Beaver Campus of the Commonwealth Coll (PA)
Penn State U Berks Cmps of Berks-Lehigh Valley Coll (PA)
Penn State U Delaware County Campus of the Commonwealth Coll (PA)
Penn State U DuBois Campus of the Commonwealth Coll (PA)
Penn State U Fayette Campus of the Commonwealth Coll (PA)
Penn State U Hazleton Campus of the Commonwealth Coll (PA)
Penn State U Lehigh Valley Cmps of Berks-Lehigh Valley Coll (PA)
Penn State U McKeesport Campus of the Commonwealth Coll (PA)
Penn State U Mont Alto Campus of the Commonwealth Coll (PA)
Penn State U New Kensington Campus of the Commonwealth Coll (PA)
Penn State U Schuylkill Campus of the Capital Coll (PA)
Penn State U Shenango Campus of the Commonwealth Coll (PA)
Penn State U Univ Park Campus (PA)
Penn State U Wilkes-Barre Campus of the Commonwealth Coll (PA)
Penn State U Worthington Scranton Cmps Commonwealth Coll (PA)
Penn State U York Campus of the Commonwealth Coll (PA)

AGRICULTURAL AND FOOD PRODUCTS PROCESSING

Kansas State U (KS)
The Ohio State U (OH)
Texas A&M U (TX)
The U of British Columbia (BC, Canada)
U of Florida (FL)

AGRICULTURAL AND HORTICULTURAL PLANT BREEDING

Colorado State U (CO)
Cornell U (NY)
Delaware State U (DE)
Sterling Coll (VT)

AGRICULTURAL ANIMAL BREEDING

Cornell U (NY)
Sterling Coll (VT)
Texas A&M U (TX)
U of Nevada, Reno (NV)

AGRICULTURAL/BIOLOGICAL ENGINEERING AND BIOENGINEERING

Auburn U (AL)
California Polytechnic State U, San Luis Obispo (CA)
California State Polytechnic U, Pomona (CA)
Clemson U (SC)

Cornell U (NY)
Dalhousie U (NS, Canada)
Fort Valley State U (GA)
Iowa State U of Science and Technology (IA)
Kansas State U (KS)
McGill U (QC, Canada)
Michigan State U (MI)
Mississippi State U (MS)
North Carolina State U (NC)
North Dakota State U (ND)
The Ohio State U (OH)
Penn State U Abington Coll (PA)
Penn State U Altoona Coll (PA)
Penn State U at Erie, The Behrend Coll (PA)
Penn State U Beaver Campus of the Commonwealth Coll (PA)
Penn State U Berks Cmps of Berks-Lehigh Valley Coll (PA)
Penn State U Delaware County Campus of the Commonwealth Coll (PA)
Penn State U DuBois Campus of the Commonwealth Coll (PA)
Penn State U Fayette Campus of the Commonwealth Coll (PA)
Penn State U Hazleton Campus of the Commonwealth Coll (PA)
Penn State U Lehigh Valley Cmps of Berks-Lehigh Valley Coll (PA)
Penn State U McKeesport Campus of the Commonwealth Coll (PA)
Penn State U Mont Alto Campus of the Commonwealth Coll (PA)
Penn State U New Kensington Campus of the Commonwealth Coll (PA)
Penn State U Schuylkill Campus of the Capital Coll (PA)
Penn State U Shenango Campus of the Commonwealth Coll (PA)
Penn State U Univ Park Campus (PA)
Penn State U Wilkes-Barre Campus of the Commonwealth Coll (PA)
Penn State U Worthington Scranton Cmps Commonwealth Coll (PA)
Penn State U York Campus of the Commonwealth Coll (PA)
Purdue U (IN)
Rutgers, The State U of New Jersey, New Brunswick/Piscataway (NJ)
South Dakota State U (SD)
Tennessee Technological U (TN)
Texas A&M U (TX)
The U of Arizona (AZ)
U of Arkansas (AR)
U of Calif, Davis (CA)
U of Calif, Los Angeles (CA)
U of Delaware (DE)
U of Florida (FL)
U of Georgia (GA)
U of Guelph (ON, Canada)
U of Hawaii at Manoa (HI)
U of Idaho (ID)
U of Illinois at Urbana–Champaign (IL)
U of Kentucky (KY)
U of Maine (ME)
U of Manitoba (MB, Canada)
U of Maryland, Coll Park (MD)
U of Minnesota, Twin Cities Campus (MN)
U of Missouri–Rolla (MO)
U of Nebraska–Lincoln (NE)
U of Saskatchewan (SK, Canada)
The U of Tennessee (TN)
U of Wisconsin–Madison (WI)
U of Wisconsin–River Falls (WI)
Utah State U (UT)
Washington State U (WA)

AGRICULTURAL BUSINESS AND MANAGEMENT

Alcorn State U (MS)
Andrews U (MI)
Arizona State U East (AZ)
Berea Coll (KY)
Brigham Young U (UT)
California Polytechnic State U, San Luis Obispo (CA)
California State Polytechnic U, Pomona (CA)
California State U, Chico (CA)
California State U, Fresno (CA)
Capital U (OH)
Central Missouri State U (MO)
Clemson U (SC)
Cornell U (NY)
Delaware State U (DE)
Dickinson State U (ND)
Dordt Coll (IA)
Eastern Kentucky U (KY)
Eastern New Mexico U (NM)
Eastern Oregon U (OR)
Florida Ag and Mech U (FL)
Florida Southern Coll (FL)
Fort Hays State U (KS)
Fort Lewis Coll (CO)
Freed-Hardeman U (TN)
Grace U (NE)
Hardin-Simmons U (TX)
Iowa State U of Science and Technology (IA)
Kansas State U (KS)
Lincoln U (MO)
Louisiana State U and A&M Coll (LA)
Louisiana Tech U (LA)
Lubbock Christian U (TX)
McGill U (QC, Canada)
McPherson Coll (KS)
Michigan State U (MI)
MidAmerica Nazarene U (KS)
Montana State U–Bozeman (MT)
Murray State U (KY)
Nicholls State U (LA)
North Dakota State U (ND)
Northwestern Oklahoma State U (OK)
Nova Scotia Ag Coll (NS, Canada)
The Ohio State U (OH)
Oklahoma Panhandle State U (OK)
Oklahoma State U (OK)
Oregon State U (OR)
Rocky Mountain Coll (MT)
Sam Houston State U (TX)
San Diego State U (CA)
Simon's Rock Coll of Bard (MA)
South Carolina State U (SC)
Southern Arkansas U–Magnolia (AR)
State U of NY Coll of A&T at Cobleskill (NY)
Sterling Coll (VT)
Tabor Coll (KS)
Tennessee Technological U (TN)
Texas A&M U (TX)
Texas A&M U–Kingsville (TX)
Texas Tech U (TX)
Truman State U (MO)
Tuskegee U (AL)
U of Alberta (AB, Canada)
U of Calif, Davis (CA)
U of Delaware (DE)
U of Georgia (GA)
U of Guelph (ON, Canada)
U of Hawaii at Hilo (HI)
U of Idaho (ID)
The U of Lethbridge (AB, Canada)
U of Maryland Eastern Shore (MD)
U of Minnesota, Crookston (MN)
U of Minnesota, Twin Cities Campus (MN)
U of Missouri–Columbia (MO)
U of Nebraska–Lincoln (NE)
U of New Hampshire (NH)
The U of Tennessee at Martin (TN)
U of Vermont (VT)
U of Wisconsin–Madison (WI)
U of Wisconsin–Platteville (WI)
U of Wisconsin–River Falls (WI)
Upper Iowa U (IA)
Utah State U (UT)
Washington State U (WA)
Wayne State Coll (NE)
West Texas A&M U (TX)

AGRICULTURAL BUSINESS AND MANAGEMENT RELATED

Sterling Coll (VT)
The U of Tennessee (TN)
Utah State U (UT)

AGRICULTURAL BUSINESS TECHNOLOGY

U of Alaska Fairbanks (AK)

AGRICULTURAL COMMUNICATION/JOURNALISM

Michigan State U (MI)
Oklahoma State U (OK)
Sterling Coll (VT)
U of Illinois at Urbana–Champaign (IL)
U of Missouri–Columbia (MO)
U of Nebraska–Lincoln (NE)
U of Wyoming (WY)
Washington State U (WA)

AGRICULTURAL ECONOMICS

Alabama Ag and Mech U (AL)
Alcorn State U (MS)
Auburn U (AL)
Brigham Young U (UT)
Central Missouri State U (MO)
Clemson U (SC)
Colorado State U (CO)
Cornell U (NY)
Eastern Oregon U (OR)
Fort Valley State U (GA)
Hampshire Coll (MA)
Kansas State U (KS)
McGill U (QC, Canada)
McPherson Coll (KS)
Michigan State U (MI)
Mississippi State U (MS)
New Mexico State U (NM)
North Carolina State U (NC)
North Dakota State U (ND)
Nova Scotia Ag Coll (NS, Canada)
The Ohio State U (OH)
Oklahoma State U (OK)
Oregon State U (OR)
Purdue U (IN)
South Dakota State U (SD)
Southern Illinois U Carbondale (IL)
Southern U and A&M Coll (LA)
Tarleton State U (TX)
Texas A&M U (TX)
Texas A&M U–Commerce (TX)
Texas Tech U (TX)
Truman State U (MO)
Université Laval (QC, Canada)
U of Alberta (AB, Canada)
The U of Arizona (AZ)
U of Arkansas (AR)
U of Calif, Davis (CA)
U of Connecticut (CT)
U of Delaware (DE)
U of Florida (FL)
U of Georgia (GA)
U of Guelph (ON, Canada)
U of Hawaii at Manoa (HI)
U of Idaho (ID)
U of Illinois at Urbana–Champaign (IL)
U of Kentucky (KY)
U of Maine (ME)
U of Manitoba (MB, Canada)
U of Maryland, Coll Park (MD)
U of Missouri–Columbia (MO)
U of Nebraska–Lincoln (NE)
U of Nevada, Reno (NV)
U of Saskatchewan (SK, Canada)
The U of Tennessee (TN)
U of Vermont (VT)
U of Wisconsin–Madison (WI)
Utah State U (UT)
Virginia Polytechnic Inst and State U (VA)
Washington State U (WA)
West Virginia U (WV)

AGRICULTURAL/FARM SUPPLIES RETAILING AND WHOLESALING

Texas A&M U (TX)

AGRICULTURAL MECHANIZATION

Andrews U (MI)
Central Missouri State U (MO)
Coll of the Ozarks (MO)
Iowa State U of Science and Technology (IA)
Kansas State U (KS)
Montana State U–Bozeman (MT)
North Dakota State U (ND)
Nova Scotia Ag Coll (NS, Canada)
Penn State U Abington Coll (PA)
Penn State U at Erie, The Behrend Coll (PA)
Penn State U Beaver Campus of the Commonwealth Coll (PA)
Penn State U Berks Cmps of Berks-Lehigh Valley Coll (PA)
Penn State U Delaware County Campus of the Commonwealth Coll (PA)
Penn State U DuBois Campus of the Commonwealth Coll (PA)
Penn State U Fayette Campus of the Commonwealth Coll (PA)
Penn State U Hazleton Campus of the Commonwealth Coll (PA)
Penn State U Lehigh Valley Cmps of Berks-Lehigh Valley Coll (PA)
Penn State U McKeesport Campus of the Commonwealth Coll (PA)
Penn State U Mont Alto Campus of the Commonwealth Coll (PA)
Penn State U New Kensington Campus of the Commonwealth Coll (PA)
Penn State U Schuylkill Campus of the Capital Coll (PA)
Penn State U Shenango Campus of the Commonwealth Coll (PA)
Penn State U Univ Park Campus (PA)
Penn State U Wilkes-Barre Campus of the Commonwealth Coll (PA)
Penn State U Worthington Scranton Cmps Commonwealth Coll (PA)
Penn State U York Campus of the Commonwealth Coll (PA)
Purdue U (IN)
Sam Houston State U (TX)
South Dakota State U (SD)
State U of NY Coll of A&T at Cobleskill (NY)
U of Idaho (ID)
U of Illinois at Urbana–Champaign (IL)
U of Missouri–Columbia (MO)
U of Nebraska–Lincoln (NE)
Washington State U (WA)

AGRICULTURAL MECHANIZATION RELATED

Coll of the Ozarks (MO)

AGRICULTURAL POWER MACHINERY OPERATION

U of Minnesota, Crookston (MN)

AGRICULTURAL PRODUCTION

Eastern Kentucky U (KY)
Texas A&M U (TX)
Texas Tech U (TX)
U of Arkansas (AR)
U of Hawaii at Manoa (HI)
Washington State U (WA)

AGRICULTURAL PRODUCTION RELATED

Sterling Coll (VT)
Tarleton State U (TX)

AGRICULTURAL PUBLIC SERVICES RELATED

Sterling Coll (VT)

AGRICULTURAL SCIENCES

Cameron U (OK)

AGRICULTURAL TEACHER EDUCATION

Andrews U (MI)
Arkansas State U (AR)
Auburn U (AL)
California State Polytechnic U, Pomona (CA)
California State U, Chico (CA)
California State U, Fresno (CA)
Central Missouri State U (MO)
Clemson U (SC)
Coll of the Ozarks (MO)
Colorado State U (CO)
Cornell U (NY)
Dordt Coll (IA)
Eastern New Mexico U (NM)
Iowa State U of Science and Technology (IA)
Louisiana Tech U (LA)
McNeese State U (LA)
Mississippi State U (MS)
Montana State U–Bozeman (MT)
Murray State U (KY)
New Mexico State U (NM)
North Carolina State U (NC)
North Dakota State U (ND)
The Ohio State U (OH)
Oklahoma Panhandle State U (OK)
Oklahoma State U (OK)
Prairie View A&M U (TX)
Purdue U (IN)
Sam Houston State U (TX)
South Dakota State U (SD)
Southern Arkansas U–Magnolia (AR)
Southwest Missouri State U (MO)
State U of NY at Oswego (NY)
Sterling Coll (VT)
Tarleton State U (TX)
Tennessee Technological U (TN)
Texas A&M U–Commerce (TX)
Texas A&M U–Kingsville (TX)
The U of Akron (OH)
The U of Arizona (AZ)
U of Arkansas (AR)
U of Calif, Davis (CA)
U of Connecticut (CT)
U of Delaware (DE)
U of Florida (FL)
U of Georgia (GA)
U of Hawaii at Manoa (HI)
U of Idaho (ID)
U of Maryland Eastern Shore (MD)
U of Minnesota, Crookston (MN)
U of Minnesota, Twin Cities Campus (MN)
U of Missouri–Columbia (MO)
U of Nebraska–Lincoln (NE)
U of Nevada, Reno (NV)
U of New Hampshire (NH)
The U of Tennessee (TN)
The U of Tennessee at Martin (TN)
U of Wisconsin–Madison (WI)
U of Wisconsin–River Falls (WI)
U of Wyoming (WY)
Utah State U (UT)
Virginia Polytechnic Inst and State U (VA)
Washington State U (WA)
West Virginia U (WV)

AGRICULTURE

Alcorn State U (MS)
Andrews U (MI)
Arkansas State U (AR)
Auburn U (AL)
Austin Peay State U (TN)
Berea Coll (KY)
California Polytechnic State U, San Luis Obispo (CA)
California State Polytechnic U, Pomona (CA)
California State U, Stanislaus (CA)
Colorado State U (CO)
Cornell U (NY)
Delaware State U (DE)
Dordt Coll (IA)
Eastern Kentucky U (KY)
Ferrum Coll (VA)
Florida Ag and Mech U (FL)
Fort Hays State U (KS)
Hampshire Coll (MA)
Illinois State U (IL)
Iowa State U of Science and Technology (IA)
Knox Coll (IL)
Lincoln U (MO)
Lubbock Christian U (TX)
McNeese State U (LA)
Mississippi State U (MS)
Morehead State U (KY)
Murray State U (KY)
New Mexico State U (NM)
North Dakota State U (ND)
Northwestern Oklahoma State U (OK)
Nova Scotia Ag Coll (NS, Canada)
Oklahoma State U (OK)
Oregon State U (OR)
Penn State U Abington Coll (PA)
Penn State U Altoona Coll (PA)
Penn State U at Erie, The Behrend Coll (PA)
Penn State U Beaver Campus of the Commonwealth Coll (PA)
Penn State U Berks Cmps of Berks-Lehigh Valley Coll (PA)
Penn State U Delaware County Campus of the Commonwealth Coll (PA)
Penn State U DuBois Campus of the Commonwealth Coll (PA)
Penn State U Fayette Campus of the Commonwealth Coll (PA)
Penn State U Hazleton Campus of the Commonwealth Coll (PA)
Penn State U Lehigh Valley Cmps of Berks-Lehigh Valley Coll (PA)
Penn State U McKeesport Campus of the Commonwealth Coll (PA)
Penn State U Mont Alto Campus of the Commonwealth Coll (PA)
Penn State U New Kensington Campus of the Commonwealth Coll (PA)
Penn State U Schuylkill Campus of the Capital Coll (PA)
Penn State U Shenango Campus of the Commonwealth Coll (PA)
Penn State U Univ Park Campus (PA)
Penn State U Wilkes-Barre Campus of the Commonwealth Coll (PA)
Penn State U Worthington Scranton Cmps Commonwealth Coll (PA)
Penn State U York Campus of the Commonwealth Coll (PA)
Prairie View A&M U (TX)
Purdue U (IN)
Rutgers, The State U of New Jersey, New Brunswick/Piscataway (NJ)
Sam Houston State U (TX)
South Dakota State U (SD)
Southeast Missouri State U (MO)
Southern Arkansas U–Magnolia (AR)
Southern Illinois U Carbondale (IL)
Southwest Missouri State U (MO)
Sterling Coll (VT)
Tennessee State U (TN)

Texas A&M U (TX)
Texas A&M U–Commerce (TX)
Texas A&M U–Kingsville (TX)
Texas State U-San Marcos (TX)
Texas Tech U (TX)
Truman State U (MO)
Tuskegee U (AL)
U of Alberta (AB, Canada)
The U of Arizona (AZ)
U of Arkansas at Monticello (AR)
The U of British Columbia (BC, Canada)
U of Connecticut (CT)
U of Delaware (DE)
U of Guelph (ON, Canada)
U of Hawaii at Hilo (HI)
U of Idaho (ID)
U of Illinois at Urbana–Champaign (IL)
The U of Lethbridge (AB, Canada)
U of Louisiana at Lafayette (LA)
U of Manitoba (MB, Canada)
U of Maryland, Coll Park (MD)
U of Maryland Eastern Shore (MD)
U of Minnesota, Crookston (MN)
U of Minnesota, Twin Cities Campus (MN)
U of Missouri–Columbia (MO)
U of Nebraska–Lincoln (NE)
U of New Hampshire (NH)
U of Saskatchewan (SK, Canada)
The U of Tennessee at Martin (TN)
U of Vermont (VT)
U of Wisconsin–Madison (WI)
U of Wisconsin–River Falls (WI)
Utah State U (UT)
Virginia State U (VA)
Washington State U (WA)
Western Illinois U (IL)
Western Kentucky U (KY)
West Texas A&M U (TX)

AGRICULTURE AND AGRICULTURE OPERATIONS RELATED
Bethel Coll (IN)
Michigan State U (MI)
Sterling Coll (VT)
Tarleton State U (TX)
U of Guelph (ON, Canada)
U of Kentucky (KY)
U of Maryland, Coll Park (MD)
U of Wyoming (WY)
Washington State U (WA)

AGRONOMY AND CROP SCIENCE
Alcorn State U (MS)
Andrews U (MI)
Auburn U (AL)
California Polytechnic State U, San Luis Obispo (CA)
California State Polytechnic U, Pomona (CA)
California State U, Chico (CA)
California State U, Fresno (CA)
Coll of the Ozarks (MO)
Colorado State U (CO)
Cornell U (NY)
Delaware State U (DE)
Delaware Valley Coll (PA)
Eastern Oregon U (OR)
Fort Hays State U (KS)
Fort Valley State U (GA)
Hardin-Simmons U (TX)
Iowa State U of Science and Technology (IA)
Kansas State U (KS)
Mississippi State U (MS)
New Mexico State U (NM)
North Carolina State U (NC)
The Ohio State U (OH)
Oklahoma Panhandle State U (OK)
Oregon State U (OR)
Purdue U (IN)
South Dakota State U (SD)
Southwest Missouri State U (MO)
State U of NY Coll of A&T at Cobleskill (NY)
Sterling Coll (VT)
Tennessee Technological U (TN)
Texas A&M U (TX)
Texas A&M U–Commerce (TX)
Texas A&M U–Kingsville (TX)
Texas Tech U (TX)
Truman State U (MO)
Tuskegee U (AL)
Université Laval (QC, Canada)
U of Alberta (AB, Canada)
U of Arkansas (AR)
U of Connecticut (CT)
U of Delaware (DE)
U of Florida (FL)
U of Georgia (GA)
U of Guelph (ON, Canada)
U of Illinois at Urbana–Champaign (IL)
U of Kentucky (KY)
U of Manitoba (MB, Canada)
U of Maryland, Coll Park (MD)
U of Minnesota, Crookston (MN)
U of Minnesota, Twin Cities Campus (MN)
U of Nebraska–Lincoln (NE)
U of New Hampshire (NH)
U of Saskatchewan (SK, Canada)
The U of Tennessee at Martin (TN)
U of Wisconsin–Madison (WI)
U of Wisconsin–Platteville (WI)
U of Wisconsin–River Falls (WI)
Utah State U (UT)
Virginia Polytechnic Inst and State U (VA)
Washington State U (WA)
West Texas A&M U (TX)

AGRONOMY/CROP SCIENCE
Coll of the Ozarks (MO)

AIRCRAFT POWERPLANT TECHNOLOGY
Thomas Edison State Coll (NJ)

AIR FORCE R.O.T.C./AIR SCIENCE
La Salle U (PA)
Rensselaer Polytechnic Inst (NY)
The U of Iowa (IA)
U of Washington (WA)
Weber State U (UT)

AIRFRAME MECHANICS AND AIRCRAFT MAINTENANCE TECHNOLOGY
LeTourneau U (TX)
Lewis U (IL)
Utah State U (UT)
Wilmington Coll (DE)

AIRLINE PILOT AND FLIGHT CREW
Andrews U (MI)
Auburn U (AL)
Averett U (VA)
Baylor U (TX)
Bowling Green State U (OH)
Bridgewater State Coll (MA)
Cornerstone U (MI)
Daniel Webster Coll (NH)
Delaware State U (DE)
Delta State U (MS)
Eastern Kentucky U (KY)
Embry-Riddle Aeronautical U (AZ)
Embry-Riddle Aeronautical U (FL)
Embry-Riddle Aeronautical U, Extended Campus (FL)
Everglades U, Boca Raton (FL)
State U of NY at Farmingdale (NY)
Grace U (NE)
Henderson State U (AR)
Indiana State U (IN)
Inter American U of PR, Bayamón Campus (PR)
Jacksonville U (FL)
Kansas State U (KS)
LeTourneau U (TX)
Lewis U (IL)
Lynn U (FL)
Oklahoma State U (OK)
Providence Coll and Theological Sem (MB, Canada)
Quincy U (IL)
Rocky Mountain Coll (MT)
St. Cloud State U (MN)
Saint Louis U (MO)
Southeastern Oklahoma State U (OK)
Thomas Edison State Coll (NJ)
Trinity Western U (BC, Canada)
U of Dubuque (IA)
Western Michigan U (MI)
Westminster Coll (UT)

AIR TRAFFIC CONTROL
Daniel Webster Coll (NH)
Embry-Riddle Aeronautical U (FL)
Hampton U (VA)
Inter American U of PR, Bayamón Campus (PR)
St. Cloud State U (MN)
Texas Southern U (TX)
Thomas Edison State Coll (NJ)
U of Maryland Eastern Shore (MD)
U of North Dakota (ND)

AIR TRANSPORTATION RELATED
Averett U (VA)
Florida Inst of Technology (FL)

ALLIED HEALTH AND MEDICAL ASSISTING SERVICES RELATED
Bloomfield Coll (NJ)
Wayne State U (MI)

ALLIED HEALTH DIAGNOSTIC, INTERVENTION, AND TREATMENT PROFESSIONS RELATED
Fairleigh Dickinson U, Florham (NJ)
Fairleigh Dickinson U, Teaneck-Metro Campus (NJ)
Georgian Court U (NJ)
Gwynedd-Mercy Coll (PA)
Ramapo Coll of New Jersey (NJ)
Rutgers, The State U of New Jersey, Newark (NJ)
U of Connecticut (CT)
U of Toledo (OH)

AMERICAN GOVERNMENT AND POLITICS
Bard Coll (NY)
Bridgewater State Coll (MA)
Chapman U (CA)
Claremont McKenna Coll (CA)
Cornell U (NY)
Drury U (MO)
Framingham State Coll (MA)
Gallaudet U (DC)
Huston-Tillotson Coll (TX)
Lipscomb U (TN)
The Master's Coll and Sem (CA)
North Carolina State U (NC)
Northern Arizona U (AZ)
Oklahoma Christian U (OK)
Patrick Henry Coll (VA)
Rivier Coll (NH)
The U of Akron (OH)
The U of Montana–Missoula (MT)

AMERICAN HISTORY
Ave Maria U (FL)
Bard Coll (NY)
Bridgewater Coll (VA)
Calvin Coll (MI)
Chapman U (CA)
Charleston Southern U (SC)
Cornell U (NY)
Framingham State Coll (MA)
Gettysburg Coll (PA)
Hampshire Coll (MA)
North Central Coll (IL)
Pitzer Coll (CA)
Saint Joseph's Coll of Maine (ME)
Sarah Lawrence Coll (NY)
U of Regina (SK, Canada)

AMERICAN INDIAN/NATIVE AMERICAN STUDIES
Arizona State U (AZ)
Bemidji State U (MN)
Black Hills State U (SD)
California State U, Hayward (CA)
Colgate U (NY)
Cornell U (NY)
Creighton U (NE)
Dartmouth Coll (NH)
The Evergreen State Coll (WA)
Hampshire Coll (MA)
Haskell Indian Nations U (KS)
Humboldt State U (CA)
Lake Superior State U (MI)
Laurentian U (ON, Canada)
Naropa U (CO)
Northeastern State U (OK)
Northern Arizona U (AZ)
Northland Coll (WI)
Portland State U (OR)
St. Thomas U (NB, Canada)
Sonoma State U (CA)
Stanford U (CA)
Trent U (ON, Canada)
U of Alaska Fairbanks (AK)
U of Alberta (AB, Canada)
U of Calgary (AB, Canada)
U of Calif, Berkeley (CA)
U of Calif, Davis (CA)
U of Calif, Los Angeles (CA)
U of Calif, Riverside (CA)
The U of Iowa (IA)
The U of Lethbridge (AB, Canada)
U of Minnesota, Duluth (MN)
U of Minnesota, Twin Cities Campus (MN)
The U of Montana–Missoula (MT)
The U of North Carolina at Pembroke (NC)
U of North Dakota (ND)
U of Oklahoma (OK)
U of Regina (SK, Canada)
U of Saskatchewan (SK, Canada)
U of Science and Arts of Oklahoma (OK)
The U of South Dakota (SD)
U of the Incarnate Word (TX)
U of Toronto (ON, Canada)
U of Washington (WA)
U of Wisconsin–Eau Claire (WI)
U of Wisconsin–Milwaukee (WI)

AMERICAN LITERATURE
Ave Maria U (FL)
Castleton State Coll (VT)
Cornell U (NY)
Hampshire Coll (MA)
Huron U USA in London(United Kingdom)
Middlebury Coll (VT)
Queens U of Charlotte (NC)
Saint Mary's U of Minnesota (MN)
Sarah Lawrence Coll (NY)
Simon's Rock Coll of Bard (MA)
State U of NY Coll at Brockport (NY)
U of Calif, Los Angeles (CA)
U of Great Falls (MT)
U of Southern California (CA)
Washington U in St. Louis (MO)

AMERICAN NATIVE/NATIVE AMERICAN EDUCATION
Simon's Rock Coll of Bard (MA)
The U of Lethbridge (AB, Canada)
U of Mary Hardin-Baylor (TX)
U of Regina (SK, Canada)

AMERICAN NATIVE/NATIVE AMERICAN LANGUAGES
Bemidji State U (MN)
The U of Lethbridge (AB, Canada)
U of Regina (SK, Canada)

AMERICAN SIGN LANGUAGE (ASL)
Bethel Coll (IN)
Coll of the Holy Cross (MA)
Madonna U (MI)
Maryville Coll (TN)
North Central U (MN)
Rochester Inst of Technology (NY)
U of Rochester (NY)

AMERICAN SIGN LANGUAGE RELATED
U of Arkansas (AR)
U of Chicago (IL)
The U of Iowa (IA)

AMERICAN STUDIES
Albion Coll (MI)
Albright Coll (PA)
American Public U System (WV)
American U (DC)
American U in Bulgaria(Bulgaria)
Amherst Coll (MA)
Arizona State U West (AZ)
Ashland U (OH)
Austin Coll (TX)
Bard Coll (NY)
Barnard Coll (NY)
Bates Coll (ME)
Baylor U (TX)
Boston U (MA)
Bowling Green State U (OH)
Brandeis U (MA)
Brigham Young U (UT)
Brooklyn Coll of the City U of NY (NY)
Brown U (RI)
Cabrini Coll (PA)
California State U, Chico (CA)
California State U, Fullerton (CA)
California State U, Long Beach (CA)
California State U, San Bernardino (CA)
Carleton Coll (MN)
Case Western Reserve U (OH)
Cedarville U (OH)
Claremont McKenna Coll (CA)
Coe Coll (IA)
Colby Coll (ME)
Coll of Saint Elizabeth (NJ)
Coll of St. Joseph (VT)
The Coll of Saint Rose (NY)
Coll of Staten Island of the City U of NY (NY)
The Coll of William and Mary (VA)
Colorado State U (CO)
Columbia Coll (NY)
Connecticut Coll (CT)
Cornell U (NY)
Creighton U (NE)
Cumberland U (TN)
DePaul U (IL)
Dickinson Coll (PA)
Dominican Coll (NY)
Dominican U (IL)
Eckerd Coll (FL)
Elmhurst Coll (IL)
Elmira Coll (NY)
Elms Coll (MA)
Erskine Coll (SC)
Fairfield U (CT)
Florida State U (FL)
Fordham U (NY)
Franklin and Marshall Coll (PA)
Franklin Coll (IN)
Franklin Pierce Coll (NH)
Georgetown Coll (KY)
Georgetown U (DC)
The George Washington U (DC)
Gettysburg Coll (PA)
Goucher Coll (MD)
Grinnell Coll (IA)
Hamilton Coll (NY)
Hampshire Coll (MA)
Harding U (AR)
Harvard U (MA)
High Point U (NC)
Hillsdale Coll (MI)
Hobart and William Smith Colls (NY)
Hofstra U (NY)
Howard Payne U (TX)
Huntingdon Coll (AL)
Idaho State U (ID)
Illinois Wesleyan U (IL)
The Johns Hopkins U (MD)
Keene State Coll (NH)
Kent State U (OH)
Kenyon Coll (OH)
King Coll (TN)
Knox Coll (IL)
Lafayette Coll (PA)
Lake Forest Coll (IL)
Lebanon Valley Coll (PA)
Lehigh U (PA)
Lehman Coll of the City U of NY (NY)
Lesley U (MA)
Lewis U (IL)
Lindsey Wilson Coll (KY)
Lipscomb U (TN)
Long Island U, C.W. Post Campus (NY)
Lycoming Coll (PA)
Manhattanville Coll (NY)
Marist Coll (NY)
Marlboro Coll (VT)
Marymount Coll of Fordham U (NY)
Mary Washington Coll (VA)
Meredith Coll (NC)
Miami U (OH)
Miami U Hamilton (OH)
Michigan State U (MI)
Middlebury Coll (VT)
Millikin U (IL)
Mills Coll (CA)
Minnesota State U Moorhead (MN)
Montreat Coll (NC)
Mount Allison U (NB, Canada)
Mount Holyoke Coll (MA)
Mount Ida Coll (MA)
Mount St. Mary's Coll (CA)
Mount Union Coll (OH)
Muhlenberg Coll (PA)
Nazareth Coll of Rochester (NY)
Northwestern U (IL)
Oakland U (MI)
Occidental Coll (CA)
Oglethorpe U (GA)
Oklahoma City U (OK)
Oklahoma State U (OK)
Oregon State U (OR)
Our Lady of the Lake U of San Antonio (TX)
Penn State U Abington Coll (PA)
Penn State U Altoona Coll (PA)
Penn State U at Erie, The Behrend Coll (PA)
Penn State U Beaver Campus of the Commonwealth Coll (PA)
Penn State U Berks Cmps of Berks-Lehigh Valley Coll (PA)
Penn State U Delaware County Campus of the Commonwealth Coll (PA)
Penn State U DuBois Campus of the Commonwealth Coll (PA)
Penn State U Fayette Campus of the Commonwealth Coll (PA)
Penn State U Harrisburg Campus of the Capital Coll (PA)
Penn State U Hazleton Campus of the Commonwealth Coll (PA)
Penn State U Lehigh Valley Cmps of Berks-Lehigh Valley Coll (PA)
Penn State U McKeesport Campus of the Commonwealth Coll (PA)
Penn State U Mont Alto Campus of the Commonwealth Coll (PA)

Penn State U New Kensington Campus of the Commonwealth Coll (PA)
Penn State U Schuylkill Campus of the Capital Coll (PA)
Penn State U Shenango Campus of the Commonwealth Coll (PA)
Penn State U Univ Park Campus (PA)
Penn State U Wilkes-Barre Campus of the Commonwealth Coll (PA)
Penn State U Worthington Scranton Cmps Commonwealth Coll (PA)
Penn State U York Campus of the Commonwealth Coll (PA)
Pine Manor Coll (MA)
Pitzer Coll (CA)
Pomona Coll (CA)
Providence Coll (RI)
Queens Coll of the City U of NY (NY)
Queens U of Charlotte (NC)
Ramapo Coll of New Jersey (NJ)
Randolph-Macon Woman's Coll (VA)
Reed Coll (OR)
Rider U (NJ)
Roger Williams U (RI)
Roosevelt U (IL)
Rutgers, The State U of New Jersey, Newark (NJ)
Rutgers, The State U of New Jersey, New Brunswick/Piscataway (NJ)
St. Cloud State U (MN)
Saint Francis U (PA)
St. John Fisher Coll (NY)
Saint Joseph Coll (CT)
Saint Louis U (MO)
Saint Mary's Coll of California (CA)
Saint Michael's Coll (VT)
St. Olaf Coll (MN)
Salem Coll (NC)
Salve Regina U (RI)
San Diego State U (CA)
San Francisco State U (CA)
San Jose State U (CA)
Sarah Lawrence Coll (NY)
Scripps Coll (CA)
Shenandoah U (VA)
Siena Coll (NY)
Simon's Rock Coll of Bard (MA)
Smith Coll (MA)
Sonoma State U (CA)
Southeast Missouri State U (MO)
Southern Nazarene U (OK)
Southwestern U (TX)
Stanford U (CA)
State U of NY at Oswego (NY)
State U of NY Coll at Fredonia (NY)
State U of NY Coll at Geneseo (NY)
State U of NY Coll at Old Westbury (NY)
Stetson U (FL)
Stonehill Coll (MA)
Stony Brook U, State U of New York (NY)
Syracuse U (NY)
Texas A&M U (TX)
Texas State U-San Marcos (TX)
Trinity Coll (CT)
Tufts U (MA)
Tulane U (LA)
Union Coll (NY)
United States Military Acad (NY)
U at Buffalo, The State U of New York (NY)
The U of Alabama (AL)
U of Arkansas (AR)
U of Calif, Berkeley (CA)
U of Calif, Davis (CA)
U of Calif, Los Angeles (CA)
U of Calif, Santa Cruz (CA)
U of Chicago (IL)
U of Dayton (OH)
U of Florida (FL)
U of Hawaii at Manoa (HI)
U of Idaho (ID)
The U of Iowa (IA)
U of Kansas (KS)
U of Maryland, Baltimore County (MD)
U of Maryland, Coll Park (MD)
U of Massachusetts Boston (MA)
U of Massachusetts Lowell (MA)
U of Miami (FL)
U of Michigan (MI)
U of Michigan–Dearborn (MI)
U of Minnesota, Twin Cities Campus (MN)
U of Mississippi (MS)
U of Missouri–Kansas City (MO)
U of New Hampshire (NH)
U of New Mexico (NM)
The U of North Carolina at Chapel Hill (NC)
The U of North Carolina at Pembroke (NC)
U of Northern Iowa (IA)
U of Notre Dame (IN)
U of Pennsylvania (PA)
U of Pittsburgh at Bradford (PA)
U of Pittsburgh at Greensburg (PA)
U of Pittsburgh at Johnstown (PA)
U of Richmond (VA)
U of Saskatchewan (SK, Canada)
U of Southern California (CA)
U of South Florida (FL)
The U of Texas at Austin (TX)
The U of Texas at Dallas (TX)
The U of Texas–Pan American (TX)
U of the South (TN)
U of Toledo (OH)
U of Toronto (ON, Canada)
U of Wisconsin–Madison (WI)
U of Wyoming (WY)
Ursinus Coll (PA)
Ursuline Coll (OH)
Utah State U (UT)
Valparaiso U (IN)
Vanderbilt U (TN)
Vassar Coll (NY)
Virginia Wesleyan Coll (VA)
Warner Pacific Coll (OR)
Washington Coll (MD)
Washington State U (WA)
Washington U in St. Louis (MO)
Wayne State U (MI)
Wellesley Coll (MA)
Wells Coll (NY)
Wesleyan Coll (GA)
Wesleyan U (CT)
Wesley Coll (DE)
West Chester U of Pennsylvania (PA)
Western Connecticut State U (CT)
Western Michigan U (MI)
Western State Coll of Colorado (CO)
Western Washington U (WA)
Wheaton Coll (MA)
Whitworth Coll (WA)
Williams Coll (MA)
Wingate U (NC)
Wittenberg U (OH)
Yale U (CT)
Youngstown State U (OH)

ANALYSIS AND FUNCTIONAL ANALYSIS
Cornell U (NY)

ANALYTICAL CHEMISTRY
Cornell U (NY)
Florida Inst of Technology (FL)

ANATOMY
Andrews U (MI)
Duke U (NC)
Hampshire Coll (MA)
Howard U (DC)
Minnesota State U Mankato (MN)
Tulane U (LA)
U of Indianapolis (IN)
U of Saskatchewan (SK, Canada)
U of Toronto (ON, Canada)
Wright State U (OH)

ANCIENT/CLASSICAL GREEK
Amherst Coll (MA)
Asbury Coll (KY)
Bard Coll (NY)
Barnard Coll (NY)
Baylor U (TX)
Boston U (MA)
Brandeis U (MA)
Brigham Young U (UT)
Brock U (ON, Canada)
Bryn Mawr Coll (PA)
California State U, Long Beach (CA)
Carleton Coll (MN)
Columbia Coll (NY)
Creighton U (NE)
Dartmouth Coll (NH)
DePauw U (IN)
Duke U (NC)
Duquesne U (PA)
Franklin and Marshall Coll (PA)
Gettysburg Coll (PA)
Hampden-Sydney Coll (VA)
Hobart and William Smith Colls (NY)
Hunter Coll of the City U of NY (NY)
Indiana U Bloomington (IN)
Kenyon Coll (OH)
Lawrence U (WI)
Lehigh U (PA)
Loyola U Chicago (IL)
Luther Coll (IA)
Miami U (OH)
Mount Allison U (NB, Canada)
Multnomah Bible Coll and Biblical Sem (OR)
Ohio U (OH)
Queens Coll of the City U of NY (NY)
Randolph-Macon Coll (VA)
Randolph-Macon Woman's Coll (VA)
Rice U (TX)
Rutgers, The State U of New Jersey, New Brunswick/Piscataway (NJ)
St. John's Coll (NM)
St. Olaf Coll (MN)
Santa Clara U (CA)
Smith Coll (MA)
Swarthmore Coll (PA)
U of Calif, Berkeley (CA)
U of Calif, Los Angeles (CA)
U of Calif, Santa Cruz (CA)
U of Chicago (IL)
U of Georgia (GA)
U of Hawaii at Manoa (HI)
The U of Iowa (IA)
U of Nebraska–Lincoln (NE)
U of Notre Dame (IN)
U of St. Thomas (MN)
The U of Scranton (PA)
The U of Texas at Austin (TX)
U of Vermont (VT)
U of Victoria (BC, Canada)
U of Washington (WA)
The U of Western Ontario (ON, Canada)
Vassar Coll (NY)
Wake Forest U (NC)
Washington U in St. Louis (MO)
Wellesley Coll (MA)
Yale U (CT)

ANCIENT NEAR EASTERN AND BIBLICAL LANGUAGES
Baylor U (TX)
Belmont U (TN)
Bethel Coll (IN)
Carson-Newman Coll (TN)
Columbia Intl U (SC)
Concordia U (IL)
Concordia U (MI)
Concordia U Wisconsin (WI)
Cornerstone U (MI)
Harvard U (MA)
Howard Payne U (TX)
Jewish Theological Sem of America (NY)
Laura and Alvin Siegal Coll of Judaic Studies (OH)
Lipscomb U (TN)
Lubbock Christian U (TX)
Luther Coll (IA)
The Master's Coll and Sem (CA)
Mid-Continent Coll (KY)
North Greenville Coll (SC)
Northwest Nazarene U (ID)
Oklahoma Baptist U (OK)
Prairie Bible Coll (AB, Canada)
Taylor U (IN)
Union U (TN)
U of Chicago (IL)
U of Toronto (ON, Canada)
Walla Walla Coll (WA)
York Coll (NE)
York U (ON, Canada)

ANCIENT STUDIES
Barnard Coll (NY)
Columbia Coll (NY)
Michigan State U (MI)
St. Olaf Coll (MN)
Southwest Missouri State U (MO)
The U of Iowa (IA)
U of Kansas (KS)
U of Maryland, Baltimore County (MD)
The U of Texas at Austin (TX)

ANIMAL BEHAVIOR AND ETHOLOGY
Carroll Coll (WI)
Franklin and Marshall Coll (PA)
Hampshire Coll (MA)

ANIMAL GENETICS
Ball State U (IN)
Cedar Crest Coll (PA)
Clemson U (SC)
Cornell U (NY)
Dartmouth Coll (NH)
Hampshire Coll (MA)
Harvard U (MA)
Jacksonville State U (AL)
McGill U (QC, Canada)
Missouri Southern State U (MO)
The Ohio State U (OH)
Ohio Wesleyan U (OH)
Rutgers, The State U of New Jersey, New Brunswick/Piscataway (NJ)
Sarah Lawrence Coll (NY)
U of Alberta (AB, Canada)
The U of British Columbia (BC, Canada)
U of Calif, Davis (CA)
U of Georgia (GA)
U of Manitoba (MB, Canada)
U of Minnesota, Twin Cities Campus (MN)
U of Toronto (ON, Canada)
The U of Western Ontario (ON, Canada)
U of Wisconsin–Madison (WI)
Washington State U (WA)
Worcester Polytechnic Inst (MA)

ANIMAL HEALTH
Sterling Coll (VT)

ANIMAL/LIVESTOCK HUSBANDRY AND PRODUCTION
Dordt Coll (IA)
Rutgers, The State U of New Jersey, New Brunswick/Piscataway (NJ)
Saint Mary-of-the-Woods Coll (IN)
Sterling Coll (VT)
Tarleton State U (TX)
Texas A&M U (TX)
Texas Tech U (TX)
The U of British Columbia (BC, Canada)
U of New Hampshire (NH)
The U of Tennessee at Martin (TN)

ANIMAL NUTRITION
Cornell U (NY)
Sterling Coll (VT)

ANIMAL PHYSIOLOGY
Boston U (MA)
California State U, Fresno (CA)
Cornell U (NY)
Hampshire Coll (MA)
McGill U (QC, Canada)
Minnesota State U Mankato (MN)
Northern Michigan U (MI)
Okanagan U Coll (BC, Canada)
Rutgers, The State U of New Jersey, New Brunswick/Piscataway (NJ)
San Francisco State U (CA)
Sonoma State U (CA)
The U of Akron (OH)
U of Alberta (AB, Canada)
The U of Arizona (AZ)
U of Calif, Davis (CA)
U of Calif, San Diego (CA)
U of Calif, Santa Barbara (CA)
U of Connecticut (CT)
U of Minnesota, Twin Cities Campus (MN)
U of New Brunswick Fredericton (NB, Canada)
U of Ottawa (ON, Canada)
U of Saskatchewan (SK, Canada)
U of Toronto (ON, Canada)
The U of Western Ontario (ON, Canada)
Utah State U (UT)

ANIMAL SCIENCES
Abilene Christian U (TX)
Alabama Ag and Mech U (AL)
Alcorn State U (MS)
Angelo State U (TX)
Arkansas State U (AR)
Auburn U (AL)
Berry Coll (GA)
California Polytechnic State U, San Luis Obispo (CA)
California State Polytechnic U, Pomona (CA)
California State U, Chico (CA)
California State U, Fresno (CA)
Clemson U (SC)
Coll of the Ozarks (MO)
Colorado State U (CO)
Cornell U (NY)
Delaware State U (DE)
Delaware Valley Coll (PA)
Dordt Coll (IA)
Florida Ag and Mech U (FL)
Fort Hays State U (KS)
Fort Valley State U (GA)
Hampshire Coll (MA)
Hardin-Simmons U (TX)
Iowa State U of Science and Technology (IA)
Kansas State U (KS)
Louisiana State U and A&M Coll (LA)
Louisiana Tech U (LA)
Lubbock Christian U (TX)
McGill U (QC, Canada)
Michigan State U (MI)
Middle Tennessee State U (TN)
Mississippi State U (MS)
Montana State U–Bozeman (MT)
Mount Ida Coll (MA)
New Mexico State U (NM)
North Carolina State U (NC)
North Dakota State U (ND)
Nova Scotia Ag Coll (NS, Canada)
The Ohio State U (OH)
Oklahoma Panhandle State U (OK)
Oklahoma State U (OK)
Oregon State U (OR)
Penn State U Abington Coll (PA)
Penn State U Altoona Coll (PA)
Penn State U at Erie, The Behrend Coll (PA)
Penn State U Beaver Campus of the Commonwealth Coll (PA)
Penn State U Berks Cmps of Berks-Lehigh Valley Coll (PA)
Penn State U Delaware County Campus of the Commonwealth Coll (PA)
Penn State U DuBois Campus of the Commonwealth Coll (PA)
Penn State U Fayette Campus of the Commonwealth Coll (PA)
Penn State U Hazleton Campus of the Commonwealth Coll (PA)
Penn State U Lehigh Valley Cmps of Berks-Lehigh Valley Coll (PA)
Penn State U McKeesport Campus of the Commonwealth Coll (PA)
Penn State U Mont Alto Campus of the Commonwealth Coll (PA)
Penn State U New Kensington Campus of the Commonwealth Coll (PA)
Penn State U Schuylkill Campus of the Capital Coll (PA)
Penn State U Shenango Campus of the Commonwealth Coll (PA)
Penn State U Univ Park Campus (PA)
Penn State U Wilkes-Barre Campus of the Commonwealth Coll (PA)
Penn State U Worthington Scranton Cmps Commonwealth Coll (PA)
Penn State U York Campus of the Commonwealth Coll (PA)
Purdue U (IN)
Rutgers, The State U of New Jersey, New Brunswick/Piscataway (NJ)
Sam Houston State U (TX)
South Dakota State U (SD)
Southern Illinois U Carbondale (IL)
Southern U and A&M Coll (LA)
Southwestern U (TX)
Southwest Missouri State U (MO)
Sterling Coll (VT)
Tennessee State U (TN)
Tennessee Technological U (TN)
Texas A&M U (TX)
Texas A&M U–Commerce (TX)
Texas A&M U–Kingsville (TX)
Texas State U-San Marcos (TX)
Texas Tech U (TX)
Truman State U (MO)
Tuskegee U (AL)
U Coll of the Cariboo (BC, Canada)
U of Alberta (AB, Canada)
The U of Arizona (AZ)
U of Arkansas (AR)
The U of British Columbia (BC, Canada)
U of Calif, Davis (CA)
U of Connecticut (CT)
U of Delaware (DE)
U of Denver (CO)
U of Florida (FL)
U of Georgia (GA)
U of Guelph (ON, Canada)
U of Hawaii at Hilo (HI)
U of Idaho (ID)
U of Illinois at Urbana–Champaign (IL)
U of Kentucky (KY)
U of Louisiana at Lafayette (LA)
U of Maine (ME)
U of Manitoba (MB, Canada)
U of Maryland, Coll Park (MD)
U of Massachusetts Amherst (MA)
U of Minnesota, Crookston (MN)

U of Minnesota, Twin Cities Campus (MN)
U of Missouri–Columbia (MO)
U of Nebraska–Lincoln (NE)
U of Nevada, Reno (NV)
U of New Hampshire (NH)
U of Rhode Island (RI)
U of Saskatchewan (SK, Canada)
The U of Tennessee (TN)
The U of Tennessee at Martin (TN)
U of Vermont (VT)
U of Wisconsin–Madison (WI)
U of Wisconsin–Platteville (WI)
U of Wisconsin–River Falls (WI)
Utah State U (UT)
Virginia Polytechnic Inst and State U (VA)
Washington State U (WA)
West Texas A&M U (TX)
West Virginia U (WV)

ANIMAL SCIENCES RELATED

Cornell U (NY)
Delaware Valley Coll (PA)
McGill U (QC, Canada)
Penn State U Abington Coll (PA)
Penn State U Altoona Coll (PA)
Penn State U at Erie, The Behrend Coll (PA)
Penn State U Beaver Campus of the Commonwealth Coll (PA)
Penn State U Berks Cmps of Berks-Lehigh Valley Coll (PA)
Penn State U Delaware County Campus of the Commonwealth Coll (PA)
Penn State U DuBois Campus of the Commonwealth Coll (PA)
Penn State U Fayette Campus of the Commonwealth Coll (PA)
Penn State U Hazleton Campus of the Commonwealth Coll (PA)
Penn State U Lehigh Valley Cmps of Berks-Lehigh Valley Coll (PA)
Penn State U McKeesport Campus of the Commonwealth Coll (PA)
Penn State U Mont Alto Campus of the Commonwealth Coll (PA)
Penn State U New Kensington Campus of the Commonwealth Coll (PA)
Penn State U Schuylkill Campus of the Capital Coll (PA)
Penn State U Shenango Campus of the Commonwealth Coll (PA)
Penn State U Univ Park Campus (PA)
Penn State U Wilkes-Barre Campus of the Commonwealth Coll (PA)
Penn State U Worthington Scranton Cmps Commonwealth Coll (PA)
Penn State U York Campus of the Commonwealth Coll (PA)
Southern U and A&M Coll (LA)
Sterling Coll (VT)
U of Wyoming (WY)

ANIMAL TRAINING

Sterling Coll (VT)

ANIMATION, INTERACTIVE TECHNOLOGY, VIDEO GRAPHICS AND SPECIAL EFFECTS

Acad of Art U (CA)
The Art Inst of Atlanta (GA)
The Art Inst of California–San Francisco (CA)
The Art Inst of Phoenix (AZ)
The Art Inst of Portland (OR)
Brigham Young U (UT)
Burlington Coll (VT)
Champlain Coll (VT)
Hampshire Coll (MA)
The Illinois Inst of Art-Schaumburg (IL)
Nevada State Coll at Henderson (NV)
The New England Inst of Art (MA)
New England School of Communications (ME)
Rochester Inst of Technology (NY)
Savannah Coll of Art and Design (GA)
School of the Art Inst of Chicago (IL)
Silicon Valley Coll, Walnut Creek (CA)
U of Dubuque (IA)

ANTHROPOLOGY

Adelphi U (NY)
Agnes Scott Coll (GA)
Albertson Coll of Idaho (ID)
Albion Coll (MI)
Alma Coll (MI)
American U (DC)
The American U in Cairo(Egypt)
Amherst Coll (MA)
Antioch Coll (OH)
Appalachian State U (NC)
Arizona State U (AZ)
Athabasca U (AB, Canada)
Auburn U (AL)
Augustana Coll (IL)
Ball State U (IN)
Bard Coll (NY)
Barnard Coll (NY)
Bates Coll (ME)
Baylor U (TX)
Beloit Coll (WI)
Bennington Coll (VT)
Berry Coll (GA)
Biola U (CA)
Bloomsburg U of Pennsylvania (PA)
Boise State U (ID)
Boston U (MA)
Bowdoin Coll (ME)
Brandeis U (MA)
Bridgewater State Coll (MA)
Brigham Young U (UT)
Brigham Young U–Hawaii (HI)
Brooklyn Coll of the City U of NY (NY)
Brown U (RI)
Bryn Mawr Coll (PA)
Bucknell U (PA)
State U of NY Coll at Buffalo (NY)
Butler U (IN)
California State Polytechnic U, Pomona (CA)
California State U, Chico (CA)
California State U, Dominguez Hills (CA)
California State U, Fresno (CA)
California State U, Fullerton (CA)
California State U, Hayward (CA)
California State U, Long Beach (CA)
California State U, Los Angeles (CA)
California State U, Sacramento (CA)
California State U, San Bernardino (CA)
California State U, Stanislaus (CA)
California U of Pennsylvania (PA)
Canisius Coll (NY)
Carleton Coll (MN)
Carleton U (ON, Canada)
Case Western Reserve U (OH)
The Catholic U of America (DC)
Central Connecticut State U (CT)
Central Michigan U (MI)
Central Washington U (WA)
Centre Coll (KY)
Chicago State U (IL)
City Coll of the City U of NY (NY)
Claremont McKenna Coll (CA)
Clarion U of Pennsylvania (PA)
Cleveland State U (OH)
Colby Coll (ME)
Colgate U (NY)
Coll of Charleston (SC)
Coll of the Holy Cross (MA)
The Coll of William and Mary (VA)
The Colorado Coll (CO)
Colorado State U (CO)
Columbia Coll (NY)
Columbia U, School of General Studies (NY)
Concordia U (QC, Canada)
Connecticut Coll (CT)
Cornell U (NY)
Dalhousie U (NS, Canada)
Dartmouth Coll (NH)
Davidson Coll (NC)
Denison U (OH)
DePaul U (IL)
DePauw U (IN)
Dickinson Coll (PA)
Dowling Coll (NY)
Drake U (IA)
Drew U (NJ)
Duke U (NC)
East Carolina U (NC)
Eastern Kentucky U (KY)
Eastern Michigan U (MI)
Eastern New Mexico U (NM)
Eastern Oregon U (OR)
Eastern Washington U (WA)
Eckerd Coll (FL)
Edinboro U of Pennsylvania (PA)
Elizabethtown Coll (PA)
Elmira Coll (NY)
Emory U (GA)
Eugene Lang Coll, New School U (NY)
Florida Atlantic U (FL)
Florida State U (FL)
Fordham U (NY)
Fort Lewis Coll (CO)
Framingham State Coll (MA)
Franciscan U of Steubenville (OH)
Franklin and Marshall Coll (PA)
Franklin Pierce Coll (NH)
George Mason U (VA)
The George Washington U (DC)
Georgia Southern U (GA)
Georgia State U (GA)
Gettysburg Coll (PA)
Grand Valley State U (MI)
Grinnell Coll (IA)
Gustavus Adolphus Coll (MN)
Hamilton Coll (NY)
Hamline U (MN)
Hampshire Coll (MA)
Hanover Coll (IN)
Hartwick Coll (NY)
Harvard U (MA)
Haverford Coll (PA)
Hawai'i Pacific U (HI)
Heidelberg Coll (OH)
Hendrix Coll (AR)
Hobart and William Smith Colls (NY)
Hofstra U (NY)
Howard U (DC)
Humboldt State U (CA)
Hunter Coll of the City U of NY (NY)
Idaho State U (ID)
Illinois State U (IL)
Indiana State U (IN)
Indiana U Bloomington (IN)
Indiana U of Pennsylvania (PA)
Indiana U–Purdue U Fort Wayne (IN)
Indiana U–Purdue U Indianapolis (IN)
Iowa State U of Science and Technology (IA)
Ithaca Coll (NY)
Jacksonville State U (AL)
James Madison U (VA)
The Johns Hopkins U (MD)
Johnson State Coll (VT)
Judson Coll (IL)
Juniata Coll (PA)
Kalamazoo Coll (MI)
Kansas State U (KS)
Kent State U (OH)
Kenyon Coll (OH)
Knox Coll (IL)
Kutztown U of Pennsylvania (PA)
Lafayette Coll (PA)
Lake Forest Coll (IL)
Lakehead U (ON, Canada)
Laurentian U (ON, Canada)
Lawrence U (WI)
Lehigh U (PA)
Lehman Coll of the City U of NY (NY)
Lewis & Clark Coll (OR)
Lincoln U (PA)
Linfield Coll (OR)
Lock Haven U of Pennsylvania (PA)
Longwood U (VA)
Louisiana State U and A&M Coll (LA)
Loyola U Chicago (IL)
Luther Coll (IA)
Lycoming Coll (PA)
Macalester Coll (MN)
Malaspina U-Coll (BC, Canada)
Mansfield U of Pennsylvania (PA)
Marlboro Coll (VT)
Marquette U (WI)
Massachusetts Coll of Liberal Arts (MA)
Massachusetts Inst of Technology (MA)
McGill U (QC, Canada)
Memorial U of Newfoundland (NL, Canada)
Mercyhurst Coll (PA)
Metropolitan State Coll of Denver (CO)
Miami U (OH)
Miami U Hamilton (OH)
Michigan State U (MI)
Middle Tennessee State U (TN)
Millersville U of Pennsylvania (PA)
Millsaps Coll (MS)
Mills Coll (CA)
Minnesota State U Mankato (MN)
Minnesota State U Moorhead (MN)
Mississippi State U (MS)
Monmouth U (NJ)
Montana State U–Bozeman (MT)
Montclair State U (NJ)
Mount Allison U (NB, Canada)
Mount Holyoke Coll (MA)
Mount Saint Vincent U (NS, Canada)
Muhlenberg Coll (PA)
National-Louis U (IL)
Nazareth Coll of Rochester (NY)
New Coll of Florida (FL)
New Mexico Highlands U (NM)
New Mexico State U (NM)
New York U (NY)
North Carolina State U (NC)
North Carolina Wesleyan Coll (NC)
Northeastern Illinois U (IL)
Northeastern U (MA)
Northern Arizona U (AZ)
Northern Illinois U (IL)
North Park U (IL)
Northwestern State U of Louisiana (LA)
Northwestern U (IL)
Oakland U (MI)
Oberlin Coll (OH)
Occidental Coll (CA)
The Ohio State U (OH)
Ohio U (OH)
Ohio Wesleyan U (OH)
Okanagan U Coll (BC, Canada)
Old Dominion U (VA)
Oregon State U (OR)
Pacific Lutheran U (WA)
Penn State U Abington Coll (PA)
Penn State U Altoona Coll (PA)
Penn State U at Erie, The Behrend Coll (PA)
Penn State U Beaver Campus of the Commonwealth Coll (PA)
Penn State U Berks Cmps of Berks-Lehigh Valley Coll (PA)
Penn State U Delaware County Campus of the Commonwealth Coll (PA)
Penn State U DuBois Campus of the Commonwealth Coll (PA)
Penn State U Fayette Campus of the Commonwealth Coll (PA)
Penn State U Hazleton Campus of the Commonwealth Coll (PA)
Penn State U Lehigh Valley Cmps of Berks-Lehigh Valley Coll (PA)
Penn State U McKeesport Campus of the Commonwealth Coll (PA)
Penn State U Mont Alto Campus of the Commonwealth Coll (PA)
Penn State U New Kensington Campus of the Commonwealth Coll (PA)
Penn State U Schuylkill Campus of the Capital Coll (PA)
Penn State U Shenango Campus of the Commonwealth Coll (PA)
Penn State U Univ Park Campus (PA)
Penn State U Wilkes-Barre Campus of the Commonwealth Coll (PA)
Penn State U Worthington Scranton Cmps Commonwealth Coll (PA)
Penn State U York Campus of the Commonwealth Coll (PA)
Pitzer Coll (CA)
Pomona Coll (CA)
Portland State U (OR)
Princeton U (NJ)
Principia Coll (IL)
Queens Coll of the City U of NY (NY)
Radford U (VA)
Reed Coll (OR)
Rhode Island Coll (RI)
Rhodes Coll (TN)
Rice U (TX)
Richmond, The American Intl U in London(United Kingdom)
Ripon Coll (WI)
Rockford Coll (IL)
Roger Williams U (RI)
Rollins Coll (FL)
Rutgers, The State U of New Jersey, Newark (NJ)
Rutgers, The State U of New Jersey, New Brunswick/Piscataway (NJ)
St. Cloud State U (MN)
Saint Francis U (PA)
St. Francis Xavier U (NS, Canada)
St. John Fisher Coll (NY)
St. John's U (NY)
St. Lawrence U (NY)
Saint Mary's Coll of California (CA)
St. Mary's Coll of Maryland (MD)
St. Thomas U (NB, Canada)
Saint Vincent Coll (PA)
Salve Regina U (RI)
San Diego State U (CA)
San Francisco State U (CA)
San Jose State U (CA)
Santa Clara U (CA)
Sarah Lawrence Coll (NY)
Scripps Coll (CA)
Seton Hall U (NJ)
Simon's Rock Coll of Bard (MA)
Skidmore Coll (NY)
Slippery Rock U of Pennsylvania (PA)
Smith Coll (MA)
Sonoma State U (CA)
Southeast Missouri State U (MO)
Southern Illinois U Carbondale (IL)
Southern Illinois U Edwardsville (IL)
Southern Methodist U (TX)
Southern Oregon U (OR)
Southwest Missouri State U (MO)
Spelman Coll (GA)
Stanford U (CA)
State U of NY at Binghamton (NY)
State U of NY at New Paltz (NY)
State U of NY at Oswego (NY)
Plattsburgh State U of NY (NY)
State U of NY Coll at Brockport (NY)
State U of NY Coll at Cortland (NY)
State U of NY Coll at Geneseo (NY)
State U of NY Coll at Oneonta (NY)
State U of NY Coll at Potsdam (NY)
State U of West Georgia (GA)
Stony Brook U, State U of New York (NY)
Sweet Briar Coll (VA)
Syracuse U (NY)
Texas A&M U (TX)
Texas A&M U–Commerce (TX)
Texas A&M U–Kingsville (TX)
Texas Christian U (TX)
Texas State U-San Marcos (TX)
Texas Tech U (TX)
Thomas Edison State Coll (NJ)
Transylvania U (KY)
Trent U (ON, Canada)
Trinity Coll (CT)
Trinity U (TX)
Tufts U (MA)
Tulane U (LA)
Union Coll (NY)
Université de Montréal (QC, Canada)
Université Laval (QC, Canada)
State U of NY at Albany (NY)
U at Buffalo, The State U of New York (NY)
U Coll of the Fraser Valley (BC, Canada)
The U of Alabama (AL)
The U of Alabama at Birmingham (AL)
U of Alaska Fairbanks (AK)
U of Alberta (AB, Canada)
The U of Arizona (AZ)
U of Arkansas (AR)
U of Arkansas at Little Rock (AR)
The U of British Columbia (BC, Canada)
U of Calgary (AB, Canada)
U of Calif, Berkeley (CA)
U of Calif, Davis (CA)
U of Calif, Irvine (CA)
U of Calif, Los Angeles (CA)
U of Calif, Riverside (CA)
U of Calif, San Diego (CA)
U of Calif, Santa Barbara (CA)
U of Calif, Santa Cruz (CA)
U of Central Florida (FL)
U of Chicago (IL)
U of Cincinnati (OH)
U of Colorado at Boulder (CO)
U of Colorado at Colorado Springs (CO)
U of Colorado at Denver (CO)
U of Connecticut (CT)
U of Delaware (DE)
U of Denver (CO)
U of Evansville (IN)
U of Florida (FL)
U of Georgia (GA)
U of Guelph (ON, Canada)
U of Hawaii at Hilo (HI)
U of Hawaii at Manoa (HI)
U of Houston (TX)
U of Houston–Clear Lake (TX)
U of Idaho (ID)
U of Illinois at Chicago (IL)
U of Illinois at Springfield (IL)
U of Illinois at Urbana–Champaign (IL)
U of Indianapolis (IN)
The U of Iowa (IA)
U of Kansas (KS)
U of Kentucky (KY)
U of King's Coll (NS, Canada)
U of La Verne (CA)

The U of Lethbridge (AB, Canada)
U of Louisiana at Lafayette (LA)
U of Louisville (KY)
U of Maine (ME)
U of Maine at Farmington (ME)
U of Manitoba (MB, Canada)
U of Maryland, Baltimore County (MD)
U of Maryland, Coll Park (MD)
U of Massachusetts Amherst (MA)
U of Massachusetts Boston (MA)
The U of Memphis (TN)
U of Miami (FL)
U of Michigan (MI)
U of Michigan–Dearborn (MI)
U of Michigan–Flint (MI)
U of Minnesota, Duluth (MN)
U of Minnesota, Morris (MN)
U of Minnesota, Twin Cities Campus (MN)
U of Mississippi (MS)
U of Missouri–Columbia (MO)
U of Missouri–St. Louis (MO)
The U of Montana–Missoula (MT)
U of Nebraska–Lincoln (NE)
U of Nevada, Las Vegas (NV)
U of Nevada, Reno (NV)
U of New Brunswick Fredericton (NB, Canada)
U of New Hampshire (NH)
U of New Mexico (NM)
U of New Orleans (LA)
The U of North Carolina at Chapel Hill (NC)
The U of North Carolina at Charlotte (NC)
The U of North Carolina at Greensboro (NC)
The U of North Carolina at Wilmington (NC)
U of North Dakota (ND)
U of Northern Iowa (IA)
U of North Florida (FL)
U of North Texas (TX)
U of Notre Dame (IN)
U of Oklahoma (OK)
U of Oregon (OR)
U of Pennsylvania (PA)
U of Pittsburgh (PA)
U of Pittsburgh at Greensburg (PA)
U of Prince Edward Island (PE, Canada)
U of Redlands (CA)
U of Regina (SK, Canada)
U of Rhode Island (RI)
U of Rochester (NY)
U of San Diego (CA)
U of Saskatchewan (SK, Canada)
U of South Alabama (AL)
U of South Carolina (SC)
The U of South Dakota (SD)
U of Southern California (CA)
U of Southern Maine (ME)
U of South Florida (FL)
The U of Tennessee (TN)
The U of Texas at Arlington (TX)
The U of Texas at Austin (TX)
The U of Texas–Pan American (TX)
U of the District of Columbia (DC)
U of the South (TN)
U of Toledo (OH)
U of Toronto (ON, Canada)
U of Tulsa (OK)
U of Utah (UT)
U of Vermont (VT)
U of Victoria (BC, Canada)
U of Virginia (VA)
U of Washington (WA)
U of Waterloo (ON, Canada)
The U of Western Ontario (ON, Canada)
U of West Florida (FL)
U of Windsor (ON, Canada)
U of Wisconsin–Madison (WI)
U of Wisconsin–Milwaukee (WI)
U of Wisconsin–Oshkosh (WI)
U of Wyoming (WY)
Ursinus Coll (PA)
Utah State U (UT)
Vanderbilt U (TN)
Vanguard U of Southern California (CA)
Vassar Coll (NY)
Wagner Coll (NY)
Wake Forest U (NC)
Washburn U (KS)
Washington and Lee U (VA)
Washington Coll (MD)
Washington State U (WA)
Washington U in St. Louis (MO)
Wayne State U (MI)
Webster U (MO)
Wellesley Coll (MA)
Wells Coll (NY)
Wesleyan U (CT)
West Chester U of Pennsylvania (PA)
Western Carolina U (NC)
Western Connecticut State U (CT)
Western Kentucky U (KY)
Western Michigan U (MI)
Western Oregon U (OR)
Western State Coll of Colorado (CO)
Western Washington U (WA)
Westminster Coll (MO)
Westmont Coll (CA)
West Virginia U (WV)
Wheaton Coll (IL)
Wheaton Coll (MA)
Whitman Coll (WA)
Wichita State U (KS)
Widener U (PA)
Willamette U (OR)
William Paterson U of New Jersey (NJ)
Williams Coll (MA)
Wright State U (OH)
Yale U (CT)
York Coll of the City U of New York (NY)
York U (ON, Canada)
Youngstown State U (OH)

ANTHROPOLOGY RELATED
U of Southern California (CA)

APPAREL AND ACCESSORIES MARKETING
The Art Inst of Phoenix (AZ)
Bluffton Coll (OH)
Philadelphia U (PA)
U of Rhode Island (RI)
Youngstown State U (OH)

APPAREL AND TEXTILE MANUFACTURING
North Carolina State U (NC)

APPAREL AND TEXTILE MARKETING MANAGEMENT
Florida State U (FL)
North Carolina State U (NC)
Wayne State U (MI)

APPAREL AND TEXTILES
Acad of Art U (CA)
Albright Coll (PA)
Appalachian State U (NC)
Auburn U (AL)
California State U, Long Beach (CA)
Central Missouri State U (MO)
Coll of the Ozarks (MO)
Colorado State U (CO)
Cornell U (NY)
East Carolina U (NC)
Fashion Inst of Technology (NY)
Florida State U (FL)
Freed-Hardeman U (TN)
Gallaudet U (DC)
Georgia Southern U (GA)
Indiana State U (IN)
Indiana U Bloomington (IN)
Iowa State U of Science and Technology (IA)
Kansas State U (KS)
Kentucky State U (KY)
Michigan State U (MI)
Middle Tennessee State U (TN)
Murray State U (KY)
New Mexico State U (NM)
North Dakota State U (ND)
Northern Illinois U (IL)
The Ohio State U (OH)
Ohio U (OH)
Oklahoma State U (OK)
Purdue U (IN)
Seattle Pacific U (WA)
Southern Illinois U Carbondale (IL)
Southwest Missouri State U (MO)
Syracuse U (NY)
Texas Tech U (TX)
The U of Akron (OH)
The U of Alabama (AL)
U of Arkansas (AR)
U of Calif, Davis (CA)
U of Georgia (GA)
U of Hawaii at Manoa (HI)
U of Idaho (ID)
U of Kentucky (KY)
U of Missouri–Columbia (MO)
U of Nebraska–Lincoln (NE)
The U of North Carolina at Greensboro (NC)
U of Northern Iowa (IA)
U of Rhode Island (RI)
The U of Texas at Austin (TX)
U of Wisconsin–Stout (WI)
Washington State U (WA)
Western Kentucky U (KY)
Western Michigan U (MI)
Youngstown State U (OH)

APPAREL AND TEXTILES RELATED
California State U, Sacramento (CA)
Framingham State Coll (MA)
U of Louisiana at Lafayette (LA)

APPLIED ART
Acad of Art U (CA)
Alfred U (NY)
American Acad of Art (IL)
Athabasca U (AB, Canada)
Azusa Pacific U (CA)
Bemidji State U (MN)
State U of NY Coll at Buffalo (NY)
California Coll of the Arts (CA)
California Polytechnic State U, San Luis Obispo (CA)
California State U, Dominguez Hills (CA)
Carthage Coll (WI)
Chicago State U (IL)
Cleveland State U (OH)
Col for Creative Studies (MI)
Colorado State U-Pueblo (CO)
Columbia Coll (SC)
Columbia U, School of General Studies (NY)
Converse Coll (SC)
Cornell U (NY)
Daemen Coll (NY)
DePaul U (IL)
Dowling Coll (NY)
Elizabeth City State U (NC)
Elms Coll (MA)
Franklin Pierce Coll (NH)
Howard Payne U (TX)
Howard U (DC)
Huntingdon Coll (AL)
Indiana U Bloomington (IN)
Inter American U of PR, San Germán Campus (PR)
Lamar U (TX)
Lindenwood U (MO)
Lubbock Christian U (TX)
Mansfield U of Pennsylvania (PA)
Marygrove Coll (MI)
Marywood U (PA)
McNeese State U (LA)
Memphis Coll of Art (TN)
Midwestern State U (TX)
Minnesota State U Mankato (MN)
Minnesota State U Moorhead (MN)
Mount Vernon Nazarene U (OH)
National American U (NM)
New World School of the Arts (FL)
Northern Michigan U (MI)
Oakland City U (IN)
Oklahoma Baptist U (OK)
Olivet Coll (MI)
Oregon State U (OR)
Otis Coll of Art and Design (CA)
Portland State U (OR)
Pratt Inst (NY)
Rochester Inst of Technology (NY)
St. Cloud State U (MN)
St. Thomas Aquinas Coll (NY)
Savannah Coll of Art and Design (GA)
School of the Museum of Fine Arts, Boston (MA)
Springfield Coll (MA)
State U of NY Coll at Fredonia (NY)
Syracuse U (NY)
Truman State U (MO)
The U of Akron (OH)
U of Dayton (OH)
U of Delaware (DE)
U of Michigan (MI)
The U of Montana–Western (MT)
U of Oregon (OR)
U of Ottawa (ON, Canada)
U of Sioux Falls (SD)
The U of Texas at Brownsville (TX)
U of the South (TN)
U of Toledo (OH)
U of Wisconsin–Madison (WI)
Washington U in St. Louis (MO)
William Paterson U of New Jersey (NJ)
Winona State U (MN)
York U (ON, Canada)

APPLIED ECONOMICS
Allegheny Coll (PA)
Brigham Young U (UT)
The Coll of St. Scholastica (MN)
Cornell U (NY)
Florida State U (FL)
HEC Montreal (QC, Canada)
Ithaca Coll (NY)
Michigan State U (MI)
Penn State U Abington Coll (PA)
Penn State U Altoona Coll (PA)
Penn State U at Erie, The Behrend Coll (PA)
Penn State U Beaver Campus of the Commonwealth Coll (PA)
Penn State U Berks Cmps of Berks-Lehigh Valley Coll (PA)
Penn State U Delaware County Campus of the Commonwealth Coll (PA)
Penn State U DuBois Campus of the Commonwealth Coll (PA)
Penn State U Fayette Campus of the Commonwealth Coll (PA)
Penn State U Hazleton Campus of the Commonwealth Coll (PA)
Penn State U Lehigh Valley Cmps of Berks-Lehigh Valley Coll (PA)
Penn State U McKeesport Campus of the Commonwealth Coll (PA)
Penn State U Mont Alto Campus of the Commonwealth Coll (PA)
Penn State U New Kensington Campus of the Commonwealth Coll (PA)
Penn State U Schuylkill Campus of the Capital Coll (PA)
Penn State U Shenango Campus of the Commonwealth Coll (PA)
Penn State U Univ Park Campus (PA)
Penn State U Wilkes-Barre Campus of the Commonwealth Coll (PA)
Penn State U Worthington Scranton Cmps Commonwealth Coll (PA)
Penn State U York Campus of the Commonwealth Coll (PA)
Plymouth State U (NH)
Southern Methodist U (TX)
U of Guelph (ON, Canada)
U of Massachusetts Amherst (MA)
U of Northern Iowa (IA)
U of Rhode Island (RI)
U of San Francisco (CA)
U of Waterloo (ON, Canada)

APPLIED HORTICULTURE
Coll of the Ozarks (MO)
Colorado State U (CO)
Ferrum Coll (VA)
Iowa State U of Science and Technology (IA)
Nova Scotia Ag Coll (NS, Canada)
South Dakota State U (SD)
Sterling Coll (VT)
Texas A&M U (TX)
Texas Tech U (TX)
U of Georgia (GA)
U of Hawaii at Manoa (HI)
U of Vermont (VT)

APPLIED HORTICULTURE/ HORTICULTURAL BUSINESS SERVICES RELATED
Delaware Valley Coll (PA)
U of Vermont (VT)

APPLIED MATHEMATICS
Alderson-Broaddus Coll (WV)
American U (DC)
Asbury Coll (KY)
Auburn U (AL)
Barnard Coll (NY)
Baylor U (TX)
Belmont U (TN)
Bloomfield Coll (NJ)
Bowie State U (MD)
Brescia U (KY)
Brock U (ON, Canada)
Brown U (RI)
California Inst of Technology (CA)
California State Polytechnic U, Pomona (CA)
California State U, Chico (CA)
California State U, Fullerton (CA)
California State U, Hayward (CA)
California State U, Long Beach (CA)
California State U, Los Angeles (CA)
Carleton U (ON, Canada)
Carnegie Mellon U (PA)
Case Western Reserve U (OH)
Charleston Southern U (SC)
Clarkson U (NY)
Coastal Carolina U (SC)
Coll of Mount St. Joseph (OH)
Colorado State U (CO)
Columbia U, School of General Studies (NY)
Columbia U, School of Eng & Applied Sci (NY)
Columbus State U (GA)
Concordia U (QC, Canada)
Cornell U (NY)
Creighton U (NE)
DePaul U (IL)
Eastern Kentucky U (KY)
Elms Coll (MA)
Emory & Henry Coll (VA)
State U of NY at Farmingdale (NY)
Ferris State U (MI)
Florida Inst of Technology (FL)
Florida Intl U (FL)
Florida State U (FL)
Fresno Pacific U (CA)
Geneva Coll (PA)
The George Washington U (DC)
Grand Valley State U (MI)
Grand View Coll (IA)
Hampden-Sydney Coll (VA)
Hampshire Coll (MA)
Harvard U (MA)
Hawai'i Pacific U (HI)
Hofstra U (NY)
Humboldt State U (CA)
Illinois Inst of Technology (IL)
Indiana U of Pennsylvania (PA)
Indiana U South Bend (IN)
Inter American U of PR, Bayamón Campus (PR)
Inter American U of PR, San Germán Campus (PR)
Iona Coll (NY)
Ithaca Coll (NY)
Jamestown Coll (ND)
The Johns Hopkins U (MD)
Johnson C. Smith U (NC)
Kent State U (OH)
Kentucky State U (KY)
Kettering U (MI)
Lamar U (TX)
La Roche Coll (PA)
La Salle U (PA)
Le Moyne Coll (NY)
Long Island U, C.W. Post Campus (NY)
Longwood U (VA)
Loyola Coll in Maryland (MD)
Marlboro Coll (VT)
Mary Baldwin Coll (VA)
Maryville U of Saint Louis (MO)
The Master's Coll and Sem (CA)
McGill U (QC, Canada)
Medgar Evers Coll of the City U of NY (NY)
Memorial U of Newfoundland (NL, Canada)
Metropolitan State U (MN)
Michigan State U (MI)
Michigan Technological U (MI)
Montana Tech of The U of Montana (MT)
Montclair State U (NJ)
Mount Allison U (NB, Canada)
Mount Saint Vincent U (NS, Canada)
New Jersey Inst of Technology (NJ)
New Mexico Inst of Mining and Technology (NM)
North Carolina State U (NC)
North Central Coll (IL)
Northern Illinois U (IL)
Northern Michigan U (MI)
Northland Coll (WI)
Northwestern U (IL)
Oakland City U (IN)
Oakland U (MI)
Ohio U (OH)
Oregon State U (OR)
Pacific Union Coll (CA)
Penn State U Harrisburg Campus of the Capital Coll (PA)
Queens Coll of the City U of NY (NY)
Queens U of Charlotte (NC)
Quinnipiac U (CT)
Rensselaer Polytechnic Inst (NY)
Rice U (TX)
Robert Morris U (PA)
Rochester Inst of Technology (NY)
Rutgers, The State U of New Jersey, Newark (NJ)
Saint Louis U (MO)
St. Thomas Aquinas Coll (NY)
Salem State Coll (MA)
San Diego State U (CA)
San Francisco State U (CA)
San Jose State U (CA)
Seattle U (WA)
Shawnee State U (OH)
Simon Fraser U (BC, Canada)
Simon's Rock Coll of Bard (MA)
Sonoma State U (CA)
State U of NY at New Paltz (NY)
State U of NY at Oswego (NY)
State U of NY Inst of Tech at Utica/Rome (NY)

Stony Brook U, State U of New York (NY)
Texas A&M U (TX)
Texas State U-San Marcos (TX)
Trent U (ON, Canada)
Trinity Western U (BC, Canada)
United States Military Acad (NY)
Université de Montréal (QC, Canada)
Université de Sherbrooke (QC, Canada)
State U of NY at Albany (NY)
The U of Akron (OH)
U of Alaska Fairbanks (AK)
U of Alberta (AB, Canada)
The U of British Columbia (BC, Canada)
U of Calgary (AB, Canada)
U of Calif, Berkeley (CA)
U of Calif, Los Angeles (CA)
U of Calif, San Diego (CA)
U of Calif, Santa Cruz (CA)
U of Chicago (IL)
U of Colorado at Boulder (CO)
U of Colorado at Colorado Springs (CO)
U of Connecticut (CT)
U of Guelph (ON, Canada)
U of Houston (TX)
U of Idaho (ID)
U of Manitoba (MB, Canada)
U of Maryland, Baltimore County (MD)
U of Massachusetts Lowell (MA)
U of Michigan (MI)
U of Missouri–Rolla (MO)
U of Missouri–St. Louis (MO)
The U of Montana–Missoula (MT)
U of Nevada, Las Vegas (NV)
U of New Brunswick Fredericton (NB, Canada)
The U of North Carolina at Chapel Hill (NC)
The U of North Carolina at Greensboro (NC)
U of Northern Iowa (IA)
U of Ottawa (ON, Canada)
U of Pittsburgh (PA)
U of Pittsburgh at Bradford (PA)
U of Pittsburgh at Greensburg (PA)
U of Rochester (NY)
U of Sioux Falls (SD)
U of South Carolina Aiken (SC)
The U of Tennessee at Chattanooga (TN)
The U of Texas at Dallas (TX)
U of Toronto (ON, Canada)
U of Tulsa (OK)
U of Virginia (VA)
U of Washington (WA)
U of Waterloo (ON, Canada)
The U of Western Ontario (ON, Canada)
U of Windsor (ON, Canada)
U of Wisconsin–Madison (WI)
U of Wisconsin–Milwaukee (WI)
U of Wisconsin–Stout (WI)
Valdosta State U (GA)
Washington State U (WA)
Washington U in St. Louis (MO)
Wayne State Coll (NE)
Weber State U (UT)
Western Michigan U (MI)
West Virginia State Coll (WV)
William Paterson U of New Jersey (NJ)
Winona State U (MN)
Worcester Polytechnic Inst (MA)
Wright State U (OH)
Yale U (CT)
York U (ON, Canada)

APPLIED MATHEMATICS RELATED
Arizona State U (AZ)
Averett U (VA)
Carroll Coll (WI)
Georgia Inst of Technology (GA)
Saint Mary's Coll (IN)
The U of Akron (OH)
U of Dayton (OH)
The U of Iowa (IA)
U of Waterloo (ON, Canada)
U of Wyoming (WY)

AQUACULTURE
Auburn U (AL)
Clemson U (SC)
Hampshire Coll (MA)
Texas A&M U (TX)

AQUATIC BIOLOGY/LIMNOLOGY
Eastern Michigan U (MI)
Florida Inst of Technology (FL)
Stetson U (FL)
Texas State U-San Marcos (TX)

U of Calif, Santa Barbara (CA)

ARABIC
Claremont McKenna Coll (CA)
Dartmouth Coll (NH)
Georgetown U (DC)
Harvard U (MA)
Middlebury Coll (VT)
The Ohio State U (OH)
State U of NY at Binghamton (NY)
United States Military Acad (NY)
U of Alberta (AB, Canada)
U of Calif, Los Angeles (CA)
U of Chicago (IL)
U of Michigan (MI)
U of Notre Dame (IN)
The U of Texas at Austin (TX)
U of Toronto (ON, Canada)
U of Utah (UT)
Washington U in St. Louis (MO)

ARCHEOLOGY
The American U in Cairo(Egypt)
Bard Coll (NY)
Baylor U (TX)
Boston U (MA)
Bowdoin Coll (ME)
Bridgewater State Coll (MA)
Brock U (ON, Canada)
Brown U (RI)
Bryn Mawr Coll (PA)
Claremont McKenna Coll (CA)
The Coll of Southeastern Europe, The American U of Athens(Greece)
The Coll of Wooster (OH)
Columbia Coll (NY)
Cornell U (NY)
Dartmouth Coll (NH)
Dickinson Coll (PA)
Fort Lewis Coll (CO)
Franklin Pierce Coll (NH)
The George Washington U (DC)
Grinnell Coll (IA)
Hamilton Coll (NY)
Hampshire Coll (MA)
Harvard U (MA)
Haverford Coll (PA)
Hunter Coll of the City U of NY (NY)
Lawrence U (WI)
Lycoming Coll (PA)
Memorial U of Newfoundland (NL, Canada)
Mercyhurst Coll (PA)
Minnesota State U Moorhead (MN)
New York U (NY)
Oberlin Coll (OH)
Oregon State U (OR)
Penn State U Abington Coll (PA)
Penn State U Altoona Coll (PA)
Penn State U at Erie, The Behrend Coll (PA)
Penn State U Beaver Campus of the Commonwealth Coll (PA)
Penn State U Berks Cmps of Berks-Lehigh Valley Coll (PA)
Penn State U Delaware County Campus of the Commonwealth Coll (PA)
Penn State U DuBois Campus of the Commonwealth Coll (PA)
Penn State U Fayette Campus of the Commonwealth Coll (PA)
Penn State U Hazleton Campus of the Commonwealth Coll (PA)
Penn State U Lehigh Valley Cmps of Berks-Lehigh Valley Coll (PA)
Penn State U McKeesport Campus of the Commonwealth Coll (PA)
Penn State U Mont Alto Campus of the Commonwealth Coll (PA)
Penn State U New Kensington Campus of the Commonwealth Coll (PA)
Penn State U Schuylkill Campus of the Capital Coll (PA)
Penn State U Shenango Campus of the Commonwealth Coll (PA)
Penn State U Univ Park Campus (PA)
Penn State U Wilkes-Barre Campus of the Commonwealth Coll (PA)
Penn State U Worthington Scranton Cmps Commonwealth Coll (PA)
Penn State U York Campus of the Commonwealth Coll (PA)
Saint Mary's Coll of California (CA)
Sarah Lawrence Coll (NY)
Simon Fraser U (BC, Canada)
Stanford U (CA)
State U of NY Coll at Potsdam (NY)
Tufts U (MA)

Université de Montréal (QC, Canada)
Université Laval (QC, Canada)
The U of British Columbia (BC, Canada)
U of Calgary (AB, Canada)
U of Calif, Los Angeles (CA)
U of Calif, San Diego (CA)
U of Evansville (IN)
U of Indianapolis (IN)
U of Michigan (MI)
U of Missouri–Columbia (MO)
The U of North Carolina at Greensboro (NC)
U of Saskatchewan (SK, Canada)
The U of Texas at Austin (TX)
U of Toronto (ON, Canada)
U of Wisconsin–La Crosse (WI)
Washington and Lee U (VA)
Washington U in St. Louis (MO)
Wellesley Coll (MA)
Western Washington U (WA)
Wheaton Coll (IL)
Yale U (CT)

ARCHITECTURAL ENGINEERING
Andrews U (MI)
Auburn U (AL)
California Polytechnic State U, San Luis Obispo (CA)
The Coll of Southeastern Europe, The American U of Athens(Greece)
Drexel U (PA)
Harvard U (MA)
Illinois Inst of Technology (IL)
Kansas State U (KS)
Milwaukee School of Eng (WI)
Oklahoma State U (OK)
Penn State U Abington Coll (PA)
Penn State U Altoona Coll (PA)
Penn State U at Erie, The Behrend Coll (PA)
Penn State U Beaver Campus of the Commonwealth Coll (PA)
Penn State U Berks Cmps of Berks-Lehigh Valley Coll (PA)
Penn State U Delaware County Campus of the Commonwealth Coll (PA)
Penn State U DuBois Campus of the Commonwealth Coll (PA)
Penn State U Fayette Campus of the Commonwealth Coll (PA)
Penn State U Hazleton Campus of the Commonwealth Coll (PA)
Penn State U Lehigh Valley Cmps of Berks-Lehigh Valley Coll (PA)
Penn State U McKeesport Campus of the Commonwealth Coll (PA)
Penn State U Mont Alto Campus of the Commonwealth Coll (PA)
Penn State U New Kensington Campus of the Commonwealth Coll (PA)
Penn State U Schuylkill Campus of the Capital Coll (PA)
Penn State U Shenango Campus of the Commonwealth Coll (PA)
Penn State U Univ Park Campus (PA)
Penn State U Wilkes-Barre Campus of the Commonwealth Coll (PA)
Penn State U Worthington Scranton Cmps Commonwealth Coll (PA)
Penn State U York Campus of the Commonwealth Coll (PA)
Tennessee State U (TN)
Tufts U (MA)
U of Cincinnati (OH)
U of Colorado at Boulder (CO)
U of Kansas (KS)
U of Miami (FL)
U of Missouri–Rolla (MO)
U of Nebraska at Omaha (NE)
U of Nebraska–Lincoln (NE)
The U of Texas at Austin (TX)
U of Wyoming (WY)

ARCHITECTURAL ENGINEERING TECHNOLOGY
Bluefield State Coll (WV)
Central Missouri State U (MO)
Eastern Kentucky U (KY)
State U of NY at Farmingdale (NY)
Florida Ag and Mech U (FL)
Grambling State U (LA)
Indiana State U (IN)
Indiana U–Purdue U Indianapolis (IN)
Purdue U (IN)
Southern Polytechnic State U (GA)
State U of NY Coll of Technology at Alfred (NY)

Texas Southern U (TX)
Texas Tech U (TX)
Thomas Edison State Coll (NJ)
U of Cincinnati (OH)
U of Hartford (CT)
Vermont Tech Coll (VT)
Washington U in St. Louis (MO)
Wentworth Inst of Technology (MA)

ARCHITECTURAL HISTORY AND CRITICISM
Barnard Coll (NY)
Brown U (RI)
Cornell U (NY)
Hampshire Coll (MA)
Miami U Hamilton (OH)
Sarah Lawrence Coll (NY)
Savannah Coll of Art and Design (GA)
U of Kansas (KS)
U of Virginia (VA)

ARCHITECTURAL TECHNOLOGY
Washington U in St. Louis (MO)

ARCHITECTURE
Andrews U (MI)
Arizona State U (AZ)
Auburn U (AL)
Ball State U (IN)
Barnard Coll (NY)
Baylor U (TX)
Bennington Coll (VT)
Boston Architectural Center (MA)
California Coll of the Arts (CA)
California Polytechnic State U, San Luis Obispo (CA)
California State Polytechnic U, Pomona (CA)
Carleton U (ON, Canada)
Carnegie Mellon U (PA)
The Catholic U of America (DC)
City Coll of the City U of NY (NY)
Clemson U (SC)
Coe Coll (IA)
Columbia Coll (NY)
Columbia U, School of General Studies (NY)
Connecticut Coll (CT)
Cooper Union for the Advancement of Science & Art (NY)
Cornell Coll (IA)
Cornell U (NY)
Dalhousie U (NS, Canada)
Drexel U (PA)
Drury U (MO)
Eastern Michigan U (MI)
Florida Ag and Mech U (FL)
Florida Atlantic U (FL)
Georgia Inst of Technology (GA)
Hampshire Coll (MA)
Hampton U (VA)
Hobart and William Smith Colls (NY)
Howard U (DC)
Illinois Inst of Technology (IL)
Iowa State U of Science and Technology (IA)
Judson Coll (IL)
Kansas State U (KS)
Kent State U (OH)
Lawrence Technological U (MI)
Lehigh U (PA)
Louisiana State U and A&M Coll (LA)
Louisiana Tech U (LA)
Massachusetts Coll of Art (MA)
Massachusetts Inst of Technology (MA)
McGill U (QC, Canada)
Miami U (OH)
Miami U Hamilton (OH)
Mississippi State U (MS)
New Jersey Inst of Technology (NJ)
New York Inst of Technology (NY)
North Carolina State U (NC)
North Dakota State U (ND)
Northeastern U (MA)
The Ohio State U (OH)
Oklahoma State U (OK)
Parsons School of Design, New School U (NY)
Penn State U Univ Park Campus (PA)
Philadelphia U (PA)
Polytechnic U of Puerto Rico (PR)
Portland State U (OR)
Prairie View A&M U (TX)
Pratt Inst (NY)
Princeton U (NJ)
Rensselaer Polytechnic Inst (NY)
Rhode Island School of Design (RI)
Rice U (TX)
Roger Williams U (RI)
Ryerson U (ON, Canada)

Savannah Coll of Art and Design (GA)
Smith Coll (MA)
Southern California Inst of Architecture (CA)
Southern Illinois U Carbondale (IL)
Southern Polytechnic State U (GA)
Southern U and A&M Coll (LA)
Syracuse U (NY)
Texas A&M U (TX)
Texas Tech U (TX)
Tulane U (LA)
Tuskegee U (AL)
Université de Montréal (QC, Canada)
Université Laval (QC, Canada)
U at Buffalo, The State U of New York (NY)
The U of Arizona (AZ)
U of Arkansas (AR)
U of Calif, Berkeley (CA)
U of Calif, Los Angeles (CA)
U of Cincinnati (OH)
U of Detroit Mercy (MI)
U of Florida (FL)
U of Hawaii at Manoa (HI)
U of Houston (TX)
U of Idaho (ID)
U of Illinois at Chicago (IL)
U of Kansas (KS)
U of Kentucky (KY)
U of Louisiana at Lafayette (LA)
U of Manitoba (MB, Canada)
U of Maryland, Coll Park (MD)
The U of Memphis (TN)
U of Miami (FL)
U of Michigan (MI)
U of Minnesota, Twin Cities Campus (MN)
U of Nebraska–Lincoln (NE)
U of Nevada, Las Vegas (NV)
U of New Mexico (NM)
The U of North Carolina at Charlotte (NC)
U of Notre Dame (IN)
U of Oklahoma (OK)
U of Oregon (OR)
U of Pennsylvania (PA)
U of San Francisco (CA)
U of Southern California (CA)
The U of Tennessee (TN)
The U of Texas at Arlington (TX)
The U of Texas at Austin (TX)
U of the District of Columbia (DC)
U of Toronto (ON, Canada)
U of Utah (UT)
U of Virginia (VA)
U of Washington (WA)
U of Waterloo (ON, Canada)
U of Wisconsin–Milwaukee (WI)
Virginia Polytechnic Inst and State U (VA)
Washington State U (WA)
Washington U in St. Louis (MO)
Wellesley Coll (MA)
Wentworth Inst of Technology (MA)
Western Michigan U (MI)
Yale U (CT)

ARCHITECTURE RELATED
Columbia Coll (NY)
Cornell U (NY)
Florida Intl U (FL)
Georgia Inst of Technology (GA)
New York Inst of Technology (NY)
Rensselaer Polytechnic Inst (NY)
School of the Art Inst of Chicago (IL)
U of Houston (TX)
U of Illinois at Urbana–Champaign (IL)
U of Louisiana at Lafayette (LA)
U of Oklahoma (OK)
U of Utah (UT)
Washington U in St. Louis (MO)

AREA, ETHNIC, CULTURAL, AND GENDER STUDIES RELATED
Bethel U (MN)
Brandeis U (MA)
Brigham Young U–Hawaii (HI)
Chatham Coll (PA)
Claremont McKenna Coll (CA)
Coe Coll (IA)
The Coll of Wooster (OH)
Columbia Coll Chicago (IL)
The Evergreen State Coll (WA)
Gettysburg Coll (PA)
Kent State U (OH)
Linfield Coll (OR)
New York U (NY)
Northwest Christian Coll (OR)
Pratt Inst (NY)
St. John's U (NY)
Saint Mary's Coll of California (CA)
Skidmore Coll (NY)

Sterling Coll (VT)
Syracuse U (NY)
U of Calif, Irvine (CA)
U of Chicago (IL)
The U of North Carolina at Chapel Hill (NC)
The U of North Carolina at Charlotte (NC)
The U of Tennessee (TN)
U of the Incarnate Word (TX)
Washington U in St. Louis (MO)

AREA STUDIES

Abilene Christian U (TX)
The American U in Cairo(Egypt)
Bard Coll (NY)
Bucknell U (PA)
Denison U (OH)
Eastern Michigan U (MI)
Excelsior Coll (NY)
Gettysburg Coll (PA)
Hawai'i Pacific U (HI)
Marymount Coll of Fordham U (NY)
Memorial U of Newfoundland (NL, Canada)
Millersville U of Pennsylvania (PA)
United States Air Force Acad (CO)
The U of Montana–Missoula (MT)
U of Oklahoma (OK)

AREA STUDIES RELATED

Barnard Coll (NY)
Boston U (MA)
Bridgewater State Coll (MA)
Claremont McKenna Coll (CA)
Colby Coll (ME)
Drexel U (PA)
Eastern Michigan U (MI)
Gettysburg Coll (PA)
Hampshire Coll (MA)
Hawai'i Pacific U (HI)
Hofstra U (NY)
Illinois Wesleyan U (IL)
Kent State U (OH)
Lewis U (IL)
McGill U (QC, Canada)
Millersville U of Pennsylvania (PA)
Northwestern U (IL)
Oakland U (MI)
Ramapo Coll of New Jersey (NJ)
St. Francis Coll (NY)
St. John's U (NY)
Swarthmore Coll (PA)
U of Alaska Fairbanks (AK)
U of Calif, Los Angeles (CA)
U of Illinois at Urbana–Champaign (IL)
U of Oklahoma (OK)
U of Virginia (VA)
Utah State U (UT)
Virginia Commonwealth U (VA)
Washington U in St. Louis (MO)
Wright State U (OH)

ARMY R.O.T.C./MILITARY SCIENCE

American Public U System (WV)
Campbell U (NC)
Drake U (IA)
Hampton U (VA)
Jacksonville State U (AL)
La Salle U (PA)
Longwood U (VA)
Minnesota State U Mankato (MN)
Rensselaer Polytechnic Inst (NY)
Rhode Island Coll (RI)
United States Military Acad (NY)
The U of Iowa (IA)
U of Puerto Rico, Cayey U Coll (PR)
U of Washington (WA)

ART

Abilene Christian U (TX)
Acad of Art U (CA)
Adams State Coll (CO)
Adrian Coll (MI)
Agnes Scott Coll (GA)
Alabama State U (AL)
Albany State U (GA)
Alberta Coll of Art & Design (AB, Canada)
Albertson Coll of Idaho (ID)
Albertus Magnus Coll (CT)
Albion Coll (MI)
Albright Coll (PA)
Alfred U (NY)
Allegheny Coll (PA)
Alma Coll (MI)
Alverno Coll (WI)
American Acad of Art (IL)
American U (DC)
The American U in Cairo(Egypt)
Amherst Coll (MA)
Anderson Coll (SC)
Andrews U (MI)
Angelo State U (TX)
Anna Maria Coll (MA)
Appalachian State U (NC)
Aquinas Coll (MI)
Arcadia U (PA)
Arizona State U (AZ)
Arkansas State U (AR)
Arkansas Tech U (AR)
Armstrong Atlantic State U (GA)
Art Acad of Cincinnati (OH)
Art Center Coll of Design (CA)
The Art Inst of Colorado (CO)
Ashland U (OH)
Athens State U (AL)
Atlantic Union Coll (MA)
Auburn U (AL)
Auburn U Montgomery (AL)
Augsburg Coll (MN)
Augustana Coll (IL)
Augustana Coll (SD)
Austin Coll (TX)
Austin Peay State U (TN)
Averett U (VA)
Azusa Pacific U (CA)
Ball State U (IN)
Bard Coll (NY)
Bates Coll (ME)
Baylor U (TX)
Belhaven Coll (MS)
Bellarmine U (KY)
Belmont U (TN)
Bemidji State U (MN)
Bennington Coll (VT)
Berea Coll (KY)
Berry Coll (GA)
Bethany Coll (KS)
Bethany Coll (WV)
Bethany Lutheran Coll (MN)
Bethel Coll (IN)
Bethel U (MN)
Biola U (CA)
Birmingham-Southern Coll (AL)
Bishop's U (QC, Canada)
Blackburn Coll (IL)
Black Hills State U (SD)
Bluefield Coll (VA)
Bluffton Coll (OH)
Boise State U (ID)
Bowdoin Coll (ME)
Bowie State U (MD)
Bradley U (IL)
Brandeis U (MA)
Brescia U (KY)
Brevard Coll (NC)
Briar Cliff U (IA)
Bridgewater State Coll (MA)
Brigham Young U (UT)
Brigham Young U–Hawaii (HI)
Brock U (ON, Canada)
Brooklyn Coll of the City U of NY (NY)
Brown U (RI)
Bryn Mawr Coll (PA)
Bucknell U (PA)
Buena Vista U (IA)
State U of NY Coll at Buffalo (NY)
Burlington Coll (VT)
Caldwell Coll (NJ)
California Baptist U (CA)
California Coll of the Arts (CA)
California Inst of the Arts (CA)
California Lutheran U (CA)
California Polytechnic State U, San Luis Obispo (CA)
California State Polytechnic U, Pomona (CA)
California State U, Chico (CA)
California State U, Dominguez Hills (CA)
California State U, Fresno (CA)
California State U, Fullerton (CA)
California State U, Long Beach (CA)
California State U, Los Angeles (CA)
California State U, Sacramento (CA)
California State U, San Bernardino (CA)
California State U, Stanislaus (CA)
California U of Pennsylvania (PA)
Calvin Coll (MI)
Cameron U (OK)
Campbellsville U (KY)
Campbell U (NC)
Capital U (OH)
Cardinal Stritch U (WI)
Carlow Coll (PA)
Carnegie Mellon U (PA)
Carroll Coll (WI)
Carson-Newman Coll (TN)
Castleton State Coll (VT)
The Catholic U of America (DC)
Cedar Crest Coll (PA)
Centenary Coll of Louisiana (LA)
Central Coll (IA)
Central Connecticut State U (CT)
Central Michigan U (MI)
Central State U (OH)
Central Washington U (WA)
Centre Coll (KY)
Chadron State Coll (NE)
Chapman U (CA)
Cheyney U of Pennsylvania (PA)
Chowan Coll (NC)
Christopher Newport U (VA)
City Coll of the City U of NY (NY)
Claremont McKenna Coll (CA)
Clarion U of Pennsylvania (PA)
Clark Atlanta U (GA)
Clarke Coll (IA)
Clark U (MA)
Clemson U (SC)
Cleveland State U (OH)
Coe Coll (IA)
Coker Coll (SC)
Colby Coll (ME)
Colby-Sawyer Coll (NH)
Colgate U (NY)
Col for Creative Studies (MI)
The Coll of New Jersey (NJ)
Coll of Notre Dame of Maryland (MD)
Coll of Saint Benedict (MN)
Coll of St. Catherine (MN)
Coll of Saint Elizabeth (NJ)
Coll of Saint Mary (NE)
Coll of the Atlantic (ME)
Coll of the Ozarks (MO)
Coll of Visual Arts (MN)
The Coll of William and Mary (VA)
Colorado Christian U (CO)
Colorado State U (CO)
Colorado State U-Pueblo (CO)
Columbia Coll (MO)
Columbia Coll Chicago (IL)
Columbus State U (GA)
Concordia Coll (MN)
Concordia U (CA)
Concordia U (IL)
Concordia U (MI)
Concordia U (NE)
Concordia U (QC, Canada)
Concordia U Wisconsin (WI)
Connecticut Coll (CT)
Converse Coll (SC)
Cornell Coll (IA)
Cornell U (NY)
Cornish Coll of the Arts (WA)
Covenant Coll (GA)
Creighton U (NE)
Culver-Stockton Coll (MO)
Curry Coll (MA)
Daemen Coll (NY)
Dakota Wesleyan U (SD)
Dallas Baptist U (TX)
Dana Coll (NE)
Davidson Coll (NC)
Defiance Coll (OH)
Delaware State U (DE)
Denison U (OH)
DePaul U (IL)
Dickinson State U (ND)
Dillard U (LA)
Doane Coll (NE)
Dominican U (IL)
Dominican U of California (CA)
Dordt Coll (IA)
Drake U (IA)
Drew U (NJ)
Drury U (MO)
Duke U (NC)
Earlham Coll (IN)
East Carolina U (NC)
East Central U (OK)
Eastern Connecticut State U (CT)
Eastern Illinois U (IL)
Eastern Kentucky U (KY)
Eastern Mennonite U (VA)
Eastern Michigan U (MI)
Eastern New Mexico U (NM)
Eastern Oregon U (OR)
Eckerd Coll (FL)
Edgewood Coll (WI)
Edinboro U of Pennsylvania (PA)
Elizabeth City State U (NC)
Elizabethtown Coll (PA)
Elmhurst Coll (IL)
Elmira Coll (NY)
Elms Coll (MA)
Elon U (NC)
Emory & Henry Coll (VA)
Emporia State U (KS)
Erskine Coll (SC)
Eureka Coll (IL)
Evangel U (MO)
The Evergreen State Coll (WA)
Fairfield U (CT)
Fayetteville State U (NC)
Ferrum Coll (VA)
Florida Ag and Mech U (FL)
Florida Atlantic U (FL)
Florida Southern Coll (FL)
Florida State U (FL)
Fontbonne U (MO)
Fordham U (NY)
Fort Hays State U (KS)
Fort Lewis Coll (CO)
Francis Marion U (SC)
Franklin Pierce Coll (NH)
Freed-Hardeman U (TN)
Furman U (SC)
Gallaudet U (DC)
Gardner-Webb U (NC)
George Fox U (OR)
George Mason U (VA)
Georgetown Coll (KY)
Georgetown U (DC)
The George Washington U (DC)
Georgia Coll & State U (GA)
Georgian Court U (NJ)
Georgia Southern U (GA)
Georgia Southwestern State U (GA)
Georgia State U (GA)
Gettysburg Coll (PA)
Gonzaga U (WA)
Gordon Coll (MA)
Goshen Coll (IN)
Goucher Coll (MD)
Governors State U (IL)
Grace Coll (IN)
Graceland U (IA)
Grambling State U (LA)
Grand Canyon U (AZ)
Grand Valley State U (MI)
Grand View Coll (IA)
Greensboro Coll (NC)
Greenville Coll (IL)
Grinnell Coll (IA)
Guilford Coll (NC)
Gustavus Adolphus Coll (MN)
Hamilton Coll (NY)
Hamline U (MN)
Hampshire Coll (MA)
Hampton U (VA)
Hannibal-LaGrange Coll (MO)
Hanover Coll (IN)
Hartwick Coll (NY)
Harvard U (MA)
Hastings Coll (NE)
Haverford Coll (PA)
Henderson State U (AR)
Hendrix Coll (AR)
Hillsdale Coll (MI)
Hiram Coll (OH)
Hobart and William Smith Colls (NY)
Hood Coll (MD)
Houghton Coll (NY)
Howard Payne U (TX)
Howard U (DC)
Humboldt State U (CA)
Hunter Coll of the City U of NY (NY)
Huntingdon Coll (AL)
Huntington Coll (IN)
Huron U USA in London(United Kingdom)
Idaho State U (ID)
Illinois Coll (IL)
Illinois State U (IL)
Illinois Wesleyan U (IL)
Indiana State U (IN)
Indiana U Bloomington (IN)
Indiana U Northwest (IN)
Indiana U of Pennsylvania (PA)
Indiana U South Bend (IN)
Indiana U Southeast (IN)
Inter American U of PR, San Germán Campus (PR)
Iowa State U of Science and Technology (IA)
Iowa Wesleyan Coll (IA)
Ithaca Coll (NY)
Jacksonville State U (AL)
Jacksonville U (FL)
James Madison U (VA)
Jamestown Coll (ND)
Johnson State Coll (VT)
Judson Coll (AL)
Judson Coll (IL)
Kalamazoo Coll (MI)
Kansas State U (KS)
Kansas Wesleyan U (KS)
Kean U (NJ)
Keene State Coll (NH)
Kennesaw State U (GA)
Kenyon Coll (OH)
Keystone Coll (PA)
Knox Coll (IL)
Kutztown U of Pennsylvania (PA)
Lafayette Coll (PA)
Laguna Coll of Art & Design (CA)
Lake Erie Coll (OH)
Lakehead U (ON, Canada)
Lakeland Coll (WI)
Lamar U (TX)
Lambuth U (TN)
Lander U (SC)
Lehman Coll of the City U of NY (NY)
Lesley U (MA)
Lewis & Clark Coll (OR)
Lewis U (IL)
Lincoln Memorial U (TN)
Lincoln U (MO)
Lindenwood U (MO)
Lindsey Wilson Coll (KY)
Linfield Coll (OR)
Lipscomb U (TN)
Lock Haven U of Pennsylvania (PA)
Long Island U, Brooklyn Campus (NY)
Longwood U (VA)
Louisiana Coll (LA)
Louisiana State U in Shreveport (LA)
Louisiana Tech U (LA)
Lourdes Coll (OH)
Loyola Coll in Maryland (MD)
Loyola U Chicago (IL)
Loyola U New Orleans (LA)
Luther Coll (IA)
Lycoming Coll (PA)
Lynchburg Coll (VA)
Lyon Coll (AR)
MacMurray Coll (IL)
Madonna U (MI)
Manchester Coll (IN)
Mansfield U of Pennsylvania (PA)
Marian Coll (IN)
Marietta Coll (OH)
Marist Coll (NY)
Marlboro Coll (VT)
Marshall U (WV)
Mars Hill Coll (NC)
Mary Baldwin Coll (VA)
Marygrove Coll (MI)
Maryland Inst Coll of Art (MD)
Marylhurst U (OR)
Marymount Coll of Fordham U (NY)
Marymount Manhattan Coll (NY)
Mary Washington Coll (VA)
Massachusetts Coll of Liberal Arts (MA)
McDaniel Coll (MD)
McKendree Coll (IL)
McMurry U (TX)
McNeese State U (LA)
McPherson Coll (KS)
Medaille Coll (NY)
Memorial U of Newfoundland (NL, Canada)
Memphis Coll of Art (TN)
Mercer U (GA)
Mercy Coll (NY)
Mercyhurst Coll (PA)
Methodist Coll (NC)
Metropolitan State Coll of Denver (CO)
Miami U (OH)
Miami U Hamilton (OH)
Michigan State U (MI)
Middle Tennessee State U (TN)
Midwestern State U (TX)
Millersville U of Pennsylvania (PA)
Millsaps Coll (MS)
Mills Coll (CA)
Milwaukee Inst of Art and Design (WI)
Minnesota State U Mankato (MN)
Minnesota State U Moorhead (MN)
Minot State U (ND)
Mississippi Coll (MS)
Mississippi Valley State U (MS)
Missouri Valley Coll (MO)
Missouri Western State Coll (MO)
Molloy Coll (NY)
Monmouth Coll (IL)
Monmouth U (NJ)
Montana State U–Billings (MT)
Montana State U–Bozeman (MT)
Montclair State U (NJ)
Moore Coll of Art & Design (PA)
Moravian Coll (PA)
Morehouse Coll (GA)
Morgan State U (MD)
Morningside Coll (IA)
Mount Mary Coll (WI)
Mount Mercy Coll (IA)
Mount St. Mary's Coll (CA)
Mount Saint Mary's Coll and Sem (MD)
Mount Union Coll (OH)
Mount Vernon Nazarene U (OH)
Muhlenberg Coll (PA)
Naropa U (CO)
National-Louis U (IL)
Nazareth Coll of Rochester (NY)
Nebraska Wesleyan U (NE)
Newberry Coll (SC)
New Jersey City U (NJ)

Newman U (KS)
New Mexico Highlands U (NM)
New York U (NY)
Nicholls State U (LA)
Norfolk State U (VA)
North Carolina Central U (NC)
North Central Coll (IL)
North Dakota State U (ND)
Northeastern Illinois U (IL)
Northeastern State U (OK)
Northeastern U (MA)
Northern Arizona U (AZ)
Northern Illinois U (IL)
Northern Michigan U (MI)
Northern State U (SD)
North Georgia Coll & State U (GA)
Northland Coll (WI)
North Park U (IL)
Northwest Coll of Art (WA)
Northwestern Coll (IA)
Northwestern State U of Louisiana (LA)
Northwestern U (IL)
Northwest Nazarene U (ID)
Notre Dame Coll (OH)
Notre Dame de Namur U (CA)
Nova Scotia Coll of Art and Design (NS, Canada)
Oakland City U (IN)
Oberlin Coll (OH)
Oglethorpe U (GA)
Ohio Northern U (OH)
The Ohio State U (OH)
Ohio U (OH)
Oklahoma Baptist U (OK)
Oklahoma Christian U (OK)
Oklahoma City U (OK)
Oklahoma State U (OK)
Old Dominion U (VA)
Olivet Coll (MI)
Olivet Nazarene U (IL)
Oregon State U (OR)
Otis Coll of Art and Design (CA)
Ottawa U (KS)
Otterbein Coll (OH)
Our Lady of the Lake U of San Antonio (TX)
Pace U (NY)
Pacific Lutheran U (WA)
Pacific Union Coll (CA)
Pacific U (OR)
Paier Coll of Art, Inc. (CT)
Parsons School of Design, New School U (NY)
Penn State U Abington Coll (PA)
Penn State U Altoona Coll (PA)
Penn State U at Erie, The Behrend Coll (PA)
Penn State U Beaver Campus of the Commonwealth Coll (PA)
Penn State U Berks Cmps of Berks-Lehigh Valley Coll (PA)
Penn State U Delaware County Campus of the Commonwealth Coll (PA)
Penn State U DuBois Campus of the Commonwealth Coll (PA)
Penn State U Fayette Campus of the Commonwealth Coll (PA)
Penn State U Hazleton Campus of the Commonwealth Coll (PA)
Penn State U Lehigh Valley Cmps of Berks-Lehigh Valley Coll (PA)
Penn State U McKeesport Campus of the Commonwealth Coll (PA)
Penn State U Mont Alto Campus of the Commonwealth Coll (PA)
Penn State U New Kensington Campus of the Commonwealth Coll (PA)
Penn State U Schuylkill Campus of the Capital Coll (PA)
Penn State U Shenango Campus of the Commonwealth Coll (PA)
Penn State U Univ Park Campus (PA)
Penn State U Wilkes-Barre Campus of the Commonwealth Coll (PA)
Penn State U Worthington Scranton Cmps Commonwealth Coll (PA)
Penn State U York Campus of the Commonwealth Coll (PA)
Pepperdine U, Malibu (CA)
Pikeville Coll (KY)
Pittsburg State U (KS)
Pitzer Coll (CA)
Plymouth State U (NH)
Point Loma Nazarene U (CA)
Pomona Coll (CA)
Pontifical Catholic U of Puerto Rico (PR)
Portland State U (OR)
Pratt Inst (NY)
Presbyterian Coll (SC)
Purdue U (IN)
Queens Coll of the City U of NY (NY)
Queens U of Charlotte (NC)
Radford U (VA)
Randolph-Macon Woman's Coll (VA)
Redeemer U Coll (ON, Canada)
Reed Coll (OR)
Regis Coll (MA)
Reinhardt Coll (GA)
Rhode Island Coll (RI)
Rhodes Coll (TN)
Rice U (TX)
Richmond, The American Intl U in London(United Kingdom)
Ripon Coll (WI)
Rivier Coll (NH)
Roanoke Coll (VA)
Roberts Wesleyan Coll (NY)
Rochester Inst of Technology (NY)
Rockford Coll (IL)
Rocky Mountain Coll (MT)
Roger Williams U (RI)
Roosevelt U (IL)
Rowan U (NJ)
Rutgers, The State U of New Jersey, Camden (NJ)
Rutgers, The State U of New Jersey, Newark (NJ)
Rutgers, The State U of New Jersey, New Brunswick/Piscataway (NJ)
Sacred Heart U (CT)
Saginaw Valley State U (MI)
St. Ambrose U (IA)
St. Andrews Presbyterian Coll (NC)
Saint Anselm Coll (NH)
Saint Augustine's Coll (NC)
St. Cloud State U (MN)
St. Edward's U (TX)
Saint John's U (MN)
St. Lawrence U (NY)
Saint Mary-of-the-Woods Coll (IN)
Saint Mary's Coll (IN)
Saint Mary's Coll of California (CA)
St. Mary's Coll of Maryland (MD)
Saint Michael's Coll (VT)
St. Norbert Coll (WI)
St. Olaf Coll (MN)
St. Thomas Aquinas Coll (NY)
Saint Xavier U (IL)
Salem State Coll (MA)
Salisbury U (MD)
Samford U (AL)
Sam Houston State U (TX)
San Diego State U (CA)
San Francisco State U (CA)
San Jose State U (CA)
Santa Clara U (CA)
Sarah Lawrence Coll (NY)
School of the Art Inst of Chicago (IL)
School of the Museum of Fine Arts, Boston (MA)
Scripps Coll (CA)
Seattle Pacific U (WA)
Seattle U (WA)
Shawnee State U (OH)
Shepherd U (WV)
Shippensburg U of Pennsylvania (PA)
Shorter Coll (GA)
Siena Heights U (MI)
Sierra Nevada Coll (NV)
Silver Lake Coll (WI)
Simmons Coll (MA)
Simon Fraser U (BC, Canada)
Simpson Coll (IA)
Slippery Rock U of Pennsylvania (PA)
Smith Coll (MA)
Sonoma State U (CA)
South Dakota State U (SD)
Southeastern Louisiana U (LA)
Southeastern Oklahoma State U (OK)
Southeast Missouri State U (MO)
Southern Adventist U (TN)
Southern Arkansas U–Magnolia (AR)
Southern Illinois U Carbondale (IL)
Southern Illinois U Edwardsville (IL)
Southern Oregon U (OR)
Southern U and A&M Coll (LA)
Southern Utah U (UT)
Southern Virginia U (VA)
Southwest Baptist U (MO)
Southwestern U (TX)
Southwest Missouri State U (MO)
Spelman Coll (GA)
Spring Arbor U (MI)
Stanford U (CA)
State U of NY at Binghamton (NY)
State U of NY at New Paltz (NY)
State U of NY at Oswego (NY)
State U of NY Coll at Brockport (NY)
State U of NY Coll at Fredonia (NY)
State U of NY Coll at Geneseo (NY)
State U of NY Coll at Old Westbury (NY)
State U of NY Coll at Oneonta (NY)
State U of NY Coll at Potsdam (NY)
State U of NY Empire State Coll (NY)
State U of West Georgia (GA)
Sterling Coll (KS)
Stetson U (FL)
Suffolk U (MA)
Susquehanna U (PA)
Syracuse U (NY)
Tarleton State U (TX)
Taylor U (IN)
Tennessee State U (TN)
Tennessee Technological U (TN)
Texas A&M U–Commerce (TX)
Texas A&M U–Corpus Christi (TX)
Texas A&M U–Kingsville (TX)
Texas Lutheran U (TX)
Texas Southern U (TX)
Texas State U-San Marcos (TX)
Texas Tech U (TX)
Texas Wesleyan U (TX)
Texas Woman's U (TX)
Thiel Coll (PA)
Thomas Edison State Coll (NJ)
Tougaloo Coll (MS)
Towson U (MD)
Transylvania U (KY)
Trinity Christian Coll (IL)
Trinity Coll (CT)
Trinity U (TX)
Troy State U (AL)
Truman State U (MO)
Tulane U (LA)
Tusculum Coll (TN)
Union U (TN)
Université de Montréal (QC, Canada)
U du Québec à Hull (QC, Canada)
State U of NY at Albany (NY)
U at Buffalo, The State U of New York (NY)
The U of Akron (OH)
The U of Alabama in Huntsville (AL)
U of Alaska Fairbanks (AK)
U of Alberta (AB, Canada)
U of Arkansas (AR)
U of Arkansas at Little Rock (AR)
U of Arkansas at Monticello (AR)
U of Calgary (AB, Canada)
U of Calif, Berkeley (CA)
U of Calif, Davis (CA)
U of Calif, Irvine (CA)
U of Calif, Los Angeles (CA)
U of Calif, San Diego (CA)
U of Calif, Santa Cruz (CA)
U of Central Arkansas (AR)
U of Central Florida (FL)
U of Charleston (WV)
U of Chicago (IL)
U of Cincinnati (OH)
U of Colorado at Colorado Springs (CO)
U of Dallas (TX)
U of Dayton (OH)
U of Delaware (DE)
U of Denver (CO)
U of Evansville (IN)
The U of Findlay (OH)
U of Georgia (GA)
U of Great Falls (MT)
U of Hawaii at Hilo (HI)
U of Hawaii at Manoa (HI)
U of Houston (TX)
U of Houston–Clear Lake (TX)
U of Idaho (ID)
U of Illinois at Springfield (IL)
U of Indianapolis (IN)
The U of Iowa (IA)
U of La Verne (CA)
The U of Lethbridge (AB, Canada)
U of Louisiana at Lafayette (LA)
U of Maine (ME)
U of Maine at Farmington (ME)
U of Maine at Machias (ME)
U of Maine at Presque Isle (ME)
U of Manitoba (MB, Canada)
U of Mary Hardin-Baylor (TX)
U of Maryland, Baltimore County (MD)
U of Massachusetts Boston (MA)
The U of Memphis (TN)
U of Miami (FL)
U of Minnesota, Duluth (MN)
U of Minnesota, Twin Cities Campus (MN)
U of Mississippi (MS)
U of Missouri–Columbia (MO)
U of Missouri–Kansas City (MO)
U of Mobile (AL)
The U of Montana–Missoula (MT)
U of Montevallo (AL)
U of Nebraska at Omaha (NE)
U of Nevada, Las Vegas (NV)
U of Nevada, Reno (NV)
U of New Hampshire (NH)
U of New Haven (CT)
U of New Mexico (NM)
The U of North Carolina at Asheville (NC)
The U of North Carolina at Charlotte (NC)
The U of North Carolina at Greensboro (NC)
U of North Dakota (ND)
U of Northern Iowa (IA)
U of North Florida (FL)
U of North Texas (TX)
U of Oklahoma (OK)
U of Oregon (OR)
U of Ottawa (ON, Canada)
U of Puget Sound (WA)
U of Regina (SK, Canada)
U of Rhode Island (RI)
U of Richmond (VA)
U of Saint Francis (IN)
U of Saint Mary (KS)
U of San Diego (CA)
U of San Francisco (CA)
U of Science and Arts of Oklahoma (OK)
U of South Alabama (AL)
The U of South Dakota (SD)
U of Southern California (CA)
U of Southern Indiana (IN)
U of Southern Maine (ME)
U of South Florida (FL)
The U of Tampa (FL)
The U of Tennessee at Chattanooga (TN)
The U of Texas at Arlington (TX)
The U of Texas at Austin (TX)
The U of Texas at Brownsville (TX)
The U of Texas at Tyler (TX)
The U of Texas–Pan American (TX)
U of the District of Columbia (DC)
U of the Incarnate Word (TX)
U of the Ozarks (AR)
U of the Pacific (CA)
U of the South (TN)
U of Toledo (OH)
U of Toronto (ON, Canada)
U of Utah (UT)
U of Virginia (VA)
The U of Virginia's Coll at Wise (VA)
U of Washington (WA)
The U of Western Ontario (ON, Canada)
U of West Florida (FL)
U of Windsor (ON, Canada)
U of Wisconsin–Eau Claire (WI)
U of Wisconsin–Green Bay (WI)
U of Wisconsin–La Crosse (WI)
U of Wisconsin–Madison (WI)
U of Wisconsin–Milwaukee (WI)
U of Wisconsin–Oshkosh (WI)
U of Wisconsin–Parkside (WI)
U of Wisconsin–Platteville (WI)
U of Wisconsin–River Falls (WI)
U of Wisconsin–Stevens Point (WI)
U of Wisconsin–Whitewater (WI)
U of Wyoming (WY)
Upper Iowa U (IA)
Ursinus Coll (PA)
Utah State U (UT)
Valdosta State U (GA)
Valley City State U (ND)
Valparaiso U (IN)
Vanderbilt U (TN)
Virginia Intermont Coll (VA)
Virginia Polytechnic Inst and State U (VA)
Virginia Wesleyan Coll (VA)
Viterbo U (WI)
Wabash Coll (IN)
Wagner Coll (NY)
Walla Walla Coll (WA)
Warren Wilson Coll (NC)
Wartburg Coll (IA)
Washburn U (KS)
Washington & Jefferson Coll (PA)
Washington Coll (MD)
Washington U in St. Louis (MO)
Wayland Baptist U (TX)
Waynesburg Coll (PA)
Wayne State Coll (NE)
Wayne State U (MI)
Weber State U (UT)
Webster U (MO)
Wells Coll (NY)
West Chester U of Pennsylvania (PA)
Western Carolina U (NC)
Western Connecticut State U (CT)
Western Illinois U (IL)
Western Michigan U (MI)
Western Oregon U (OR)
Western State Coll of Colorado (CO)
Western Washington U (WA)
Westfield State Coll (MA)
Westminster Coll (PA)
Westminster Coll (UT)
Westmont Coll (CA)
West Texas A&M U (TX)
West Virginia State Coll (WV)
West Virginia U (WV)
West Virginia Wesleyan Coll (WV)
Wheaton Coll (IL)
Wheaton Coll (MA)
Whitman Coll (WA)
Whitworth Coll (WA)
Wichita State U (KS)
Willamette U (OR)
William Carey Coll (MS)
William Jewell Coll (MO)
William Paterson U of New Jersey (NJ)
Williams Baptist Coll (AR)
William Woods U (MO)
Wilson Coll (PA)
Wingate U (NC)
Winona State U (MN)
Winston-Salem State U (NC)
Winthrop U (SC)
Wisconsin Lutheran Coll (WI)
Wittenberg U (OH)
Wright State U (OH)
Xavier U (OH)
Xavier U of Louisiana (LA)
Yale U (CT)
York Coll of the City U of New York (NY)
York U (ON, Canada)
Youngstown State U (OH)

ART HISTORY, CRITICISM AND CONSERVATION

Adelphi U (NY)
Albertus Magnus Coll (CT)
Allegheny Coll (PA)
American U (DC)
Andrews U (MI)
Aquinas Coll (MI)
Arcadia U (PA)
Arizona State U (AZ)
Art Acad of Cincinnati (OH)
Augsburg Coll (MN)
Augustana Coll (IL)
Baker U (KS)
Baldwin-Wallace Coll (OH)
Bard Coll (NY)
Barnard Coll (NY)
Baylor U (TX)
Beloit Coll (WI)
Berea Coll (KY)
Birmingham-Southern Coll (AL)
Blackburn Coll (IL)
Bloomsburg U of Pennsylvania (PA)
Boise State U (ID)
Boston Coll (MA)
Boston U (MA)
Bowdoin Coll (ME)
Bowling Green State U (OH)
Bradley U (IL)
Brigham Young U (UT)
Brooklyn Coll of the City U of NY (NY)
Brown U (RI)
Bryn Mawr Coll (PA)
Bucknell U (PA)
State U of NY Coll at Buffalo (NY)
California State U, Chico (CA)
California State U, Dominguez Hills (CA)
California State U, Fullerton (CA)
California State U, Hayward (CA)
California State U, Long Beach (CA)
California State U, San Bernardino (CA)
Calvin Coll (MI)
Canisius Coll (NY)
Carleton Coll (MN)
Carleton U (ON, Canada)
Carlow Coll (PA)
Case Western Reserve U (OH)
The Catholic U of America (DC)
Centre Coll (KY)
Chapman U (CA)
Chatham Coll (PA)
Chicago State U (IL)
City Coll of the City U of NY (NY)
Claremont McKenna Coll (CA)

Clarke Coll (IA)
Clark U (MA)
Colby Coll (ME)
Colgate U (NY)
Coll of Charleston (SC)
The Coll of New Jersey (NJ)
The Coll of New Rochelle (NY)
Coll of Saint Benedict (MN)
Coll of St. Catherine (MN)
Coll of Santa Fe (NM)
The Coll of Southeastern Europe, The American U of Athens(Greece)
Coll of the Holy Cross (MA)
The Coll of William and Mary (VA)
The Coll of Wooster (OH)
The Colorado Coll (CO)
Colorado State U (CO)
Columbia Coll (NY)
Columbia U, School of General Studies (NY)
Concordia Coll (MN)
Concordia U (QC, Canada)
Connecticut Coll (CT)
Converse Coll (SC)
Cornell Coll (IA)
Cornell U (NY)
Dartmouth Coll (NH)
Denison U (OH)
DePaul U (IL)
DePauw U (IN)
Dominican U (IL)
Dominican U of California (CA)
Drake U (IA)
Drury U (MO)
Duke U (NC)
Duquesne U (PA)
East Carolina U (NC)
Eastern Michigan U (MI)
Eastern U (PA)
Eastern Washington U (WA)
Edinboro U of Pennsylvania (PA)
Emory U (GA)
Fashion Inst of Technology (NY)
Florida Intl U (FL)
Florida State U (FL)
Fordham U (NY)
Framingham State Coll (MA)
Franklin and Marshall Coll (PA)
Franklin Coll Switzerland(Switzerland)
Furman U (SC)
Gallaudet U (DC)
George Mason U (VA)
The George Washington U (DC)
Georgian Court U (NJ)
Gettysburg Coll (PA)
Governors State U (IL)
Grand Valley State U (MI)
Gustavus Adolphus Coll (MN)
Hamilton Coll (NY)
Hamline U (MN)
Hampshire Coll (MA)
Hanover Coll (IN)
Hartwick Coll (NY)
Harvard U (MA)
Hastings Coll (NE)
Haverford Coll (PA)
Hiram Coll (OH)
Hobart and William Smith Colls (NY)
Hofstra U (NY)
Hollins U (VA)
Hope Coll (MI)
Humboldt State U (CA)
Hunter Coll of the City U of NY (NY)
Huron U USA in London(United Kingdom)
Indiana U Bloomington (IN)
Indiana U–Purdue U Indianapolis (IN)
Inter American U of PR, San Germán Campus (PR)
Ithaca Coll (NY)
Jacksonville U (FL)
James Madison U (VA)
John Cabot U(Italy)
John Carroll U (OH)
The Johns Hopkins U (MD)
Juniata Coll (PA)
Kalamazoo Coll (MI)
Kansas City Art Inst (MO)
Kean U (NJ)
Kent State U (OH)
Kenyon Coll (OH)
Knox Coll (IL)
Lafayette Coll (PA)
Lake Forest Coll (IL)
Lambuth U (TN)
La Salle U (PA)
Lawrence U (WI)
Lebanon Valley Coll (PA)
Lehman Coll of the City U of NY (NY)
Lindenwood U (MO)
Long Island U, C.W. Post Campus (NY)
Longwood U (VA)
Lourdes Coll (OH)
Loyola Marymount U (CA)
Loyola U Chicago (IL)
Lycoming Coll (PA)
Macalester Coll (MN)
MacMurray Coll (IL)
Manhattanville Coll (NY)
Marian Coll (IN)
Marlboro Coll (VT)
Mars Hill Coll (NC)
Marymount Coll of Fordham U (NY)
Marymount Manhattan Coll (NY)
Mary Washington Coll (VA)
Massachusetts Coll of Art (MA)
McDaniel Coll (MD)
McGill U (QC, Canada)
Memorial U of Newfoundland (NL, Canada)
Meredith Coll (NC)
Messiah Coll (PA)
Miami U (OH)
Michigan State U (MI)
Middlebury Coll (VT)
Mills Coll (CA)
Minnesota State U Mankato (MN)
Minnesota State U Moorhead (MN)
Mississippi Coll (MS)
Montclair State U (NJ)
Moore Coll of Art & Design (PA)
Moravian Coll (PA)
Morgan State U (MD)
Mount Allison U (NB, Canada)
Mount Holyoke Coll (MA)
Muhlenberg Coll (PA)
Nazareth Coll of Rochester (NY)
New Coll of Florida (FL)
New York U (NY)
Northern Arizona U (AZ)
Northern Illinois U (IL)
Northwestern U (IL)
Nova Scotia Coll of Art and Design (NS, Canada)
Oakland U (MI)
Oberlin Coll (OH)
Occidental Coll (CA)
The Ohio State U (OH)
Ohio U (OH)
Ohio Wesleyan U (OH)
Oklahoma City U (OK)
Old Dominion U (VA)
Oregon State U (OR)
Pace U (NY)
Pacific Lutheran U (WA)
Pacific Union Coll (CA)
Penn State U Abington Coll (PA)
Penn State U at Erie, The Behrend Coll (PA)
Penn State U Beaver Campus of the Commonwealth Coll (PA)
Penn State U Berks Cmps of Berks-Lehigh Valley Coll (PA)
Penn State U Delaware County Campus of the Commonwealth Coll (PA)
Penn State U DuBois Campus of the Commonwealth Coll (PA)
Penn State U Fayette Campus of the Commonwealth Coll (PA)
Penn State U Hazleton Campus of the Commonwealth Coll (PA)
Penn State U Lehigh Valley Cmps of Berks-Lehigh Valley Coll (PA)
Penn State U McKeesport Campus of the Commonwealth Coll (PA)
Penn State U Mont Alto Campus of the Commonwealth Coll (PA)
Penn State U New Kensington Campus of the Commonwealth Coll (PA)
Penn State U Schuylkill Campus of the Capital Coll (PA)
Penn State U Shenango Campus of the Commonwealth Coll (PA)
Penn State U Univ Park Campus (PA)
Penn State U Wilkes-Barre Campus of the Commonwealth Coll (PA)
Penn State U Worthington Scranton Cmps Commonwealth Coll (PA)
Penn State U York Campus of the Commonwealth Coll (PA)
Pine Manor Coll (MA)
Pitzer Coll (CA)
Pomona Coll (CA)
Portland State U (OR)
Pratt Inst (NY)
Princeton U (NJ)
Principia Coll (IL)
Providence Coll (RI)
Queens Coll of the City U of NY (NY)
Queen's U at Kingston (ON, Canada)
Randolph-Macon Coll (VA)
Randolph-Macon Woman's Coll (VA)
Rhode Island Coll (RI)
Rhodes Coll (TN)
Rice U (TX)
Rockford Coll (IL)
Roger Williams U (RI)
Rollins Coll (FL)
Roosevelt U (IL)
Rosemont Coll (PA)
Rutgers, The State U of New Jersey, New Brunswick/Piscataway (NJ)
St. Cloud State U (MN)
Saint John's U (MN)
Saint Joseph Coll (CT)
St. Lawrence U (NY)
Saint Louis U (MO)
Saint Mary's Coll of California (CA)
St. Olaf Coll (MN)
Saint Vincent Coll (PA)
Salem Coll (NC)
Salve Regina U (RI)
San Diego State U (CA)
San Jose State U (CA)
Santa Clara U (CA)
Sarah Lawrence Coll (NY)
Savannah Coll of Art and Design (GA)
School of the Art Inst of Chicago (IL)
Scripps Coll (CA)
Seattle U (WA)
Seton Hall U (NJ)
Seton Hill U (PA)
Simon's Rock Coll of Bard (MA)
Skidmore Coll (NY)
Smith Coll (MA)
Sonoma State U (CA)
Southern Connecticut State U (CT)
Southern Methodist U (TX)
Southwestern U (TX)
State U of NY at Binghamton (NY)
State U of NY at New Paltz (NY)
Plattsburgh State U of NY (NY)
State U of NY Coll at Cortland (NY)
State U of NY Coll at Fredonia (NY)
State U of NY Coll at Geneseo (NY)
State U of NY Coll at Oneonta (NY)
State U of NY Coll at Potsdam (NY)
Stony Brook U, State U of New York (NY)
Susquehanna U (PA)
Swarthmore Coll (PA)
Sweet Briar Coll (VA)
Syracuse U (NY)
Texas A&M U–Commerce (TX)
Texas Christian U (TX)
Texas Tech U (TX)
Trinity Coll (CT)
Trinity Coll (DC)
Trinity U (TX)
Troy State U (AL)
Truman State U (MO)
Tufts U (MA)
Tulane U (LA)
Université de Montréal (QC, Canada)
Université Laval (QC, Canada)
State U of NY at Albany (NY)
U at Buffalo, The State U of New York (NY)
The U of Akron (OH)
The U of Alabama (AL)
U of Alberta (AB, Canada)
The U of Arizona (AZ)
U of Arkansas at Little Rock (AR)
The U of British Columbia (BC, Canada)
U of Calgary (AB, Canada)
U of Calif, Berkeley (CA)
U of Calif, Davis (CA)
U of Calif, Irvine (CA)
U of Calif, Los Angeles (CA)
U of Calif, Riverside (CA)
U of Calif, San Diego (CA)
U of Calif, Santa Barbara (CA)
U of Calif, Santa Cruz (CA)
U of Chicago (IL)
U of Cincinnati (OH)
U of Connecticut (CT)
U of Dallas (TX)
U of Dayton (OH)
U of Delaware (DE)
U of Denver (CO)
U of Evansville (IN)
U of Florida (FL)
U of Georgia (GA)
U of Guelph (ON, Canada)
U of Hartford (CT)
U of Houston (TX)
U of Illinois at Chicago (IL)
U of Illinois at Urbana–Champaign (IL)
U of Indianapolis (IN)
The U of Iowa (IA)
U of Kansas (KS)
U of Kentucky (KY)
U of La Verne (CA)
U of Louisville (KY)
U of Maine (ME)
U of Manitoba (MB, Canada)
U of Maryland, Baltimore County (MD)
U of Maryland, Coll Park (MD)
U of Massachusetts Amherst (MA)
U of Massachusetts Dartmouth (MA)
The U of Memphis (TN)
U of Miami (FL)
U of Michigan (MI)
U of Michigan–Dearborn (MI)
U of Minnesota, Duluth (MN)
U of Minnesota, Morris (MN)
U of Minnesota, Twin Cities Campus (MN)
U of Mississippi (MS)
U of Missouri–Columbia (MO)
U of Missouri–Kansas City (MO)
U of Missouri–St. Louis (MO)
The U of Montana–Missoula (MT)
U of Nebraska at Omaha (NE)
U of Nebraska–Lincoln (NE)
U of Nevada, Las Vegas (NV)
U of Nevada, Reno (NV)
U of New Hampshire (NH)
U of New Mexico (NM)
U of New Orleans (LA)
The U of North Carolina at Chapel Hill (NC)
The U of North Carolina at Greensboro (NC)
The U of North Carolina at Wilmington (NC)
U of Northern Iowa (IA)
U of North Texas (TX)
U of Notre Dame (IN)
U of Oklahoma (OK)
U of Oregon (OR)
U of Pennsylvania (PA)
U of Pittsburgh (PA)
U of Redlands (CA)
U of Regina (SK, Canada)
U of Rhode Island (RI)
U of Richmond (VA)
U of Rochester (NY)
U of St. Thomas (MN)
U of San Francisco (CA)
U of Saskatchewan (SK, Canada)
U of South Carolina (SC)
U of Southern California (CA)
The U of Tennessee (TN)
The U of Texas at Arlington (TX)
The U of Texas at Austin (TX)
U of the Pacific (CA)
U of the South (TN)
U of Toledo (OH)
U of Toronto (ON, Canada)
U of Tulsa (OK)
U of Utah (UT)
U of Vermont (VT)
U of Victoria (BC, Canada)
U of Washington (WA)
U of Waterloo (ON, Canada)
The U of Western Ontario (ON, Canada)
U of West Florida (FL)
U of Windsor (ON, Canada)
U of Wisconsin–Madison (WI)
U of Wisconsin–Milwaukee (WI)
U of Wisconsin–Superior (WI)
U of Wisconsin–Whitewater (WI)
Ursuline Coll (OH)
Valparaiso U (IN)
Vassar Coll (NY)
Villanova U (PA)
Virginia Commonwealth U (VA)
Wake Forest U (NC)
Washburn U (KS)
Washington and Lee U (VA)
Washington State U (WA)
Washington U in St. Louis (MO)
Wayne State U (MI)
Webster U (MO)
Wellesley Coll (MA)
Wells Coll (NY)
Wesleyan Coll (GA)
Wesleyan U (CT)
Western Michigan U (MI)
Western Washington U (WA)
West Virginia Wesleyan Coll (WV)
Wheaton Coll (MA)
Whitman Coll (WA)
Whitworth Coll (WA)
Wichita State U (KS)
Willamette U (OR)
William Paterson U of New Jersey (NJ)
Williams Coll (MA)
Winthrop U (SC)
Wofford Coll (SC)
Wright State U (OH)
Yale U (CT)
York U (ON, Canada)
Youngstown State U (OH)

ARTIFICIAL INTELLIGENCE AND ROBOTICS

Eastern Michigan U (MI)
Hampshire Coll (MA)
Harvard U (MA)
Huron U USA in London(United Kingdom)
Montana Tech of The U of Montana (MT)
Pacific Union Coll (CA)
Queen's U at Kingston (ON, Canada)
Southern Alberta Inst of Technology (AB, Canada)
U of New Mexico (NM)
U of Windsor (ON, Canada)

ARTS MANAGEMENT

Adrian Coll (MI)
Appalachian State U (NC)
Aquinas Coll (MI)
Bellarmine U (KY)
Benedictine Coll (KS)
Benedictine U (IL)
Baruch Coll of the City U of NY (NY)
Bishop's U (QC, Canada)
Brenau U (GA)
Buena Vista U (IA)
Butler U (IN)
California State U, Hayward (CA)
Chatham Coll (PA)
Coll of Charleston (SC)
Coll of Santa Fe (NM)
Columbia Coll Chicago (IL)
Concordia Coll (NY)
Culver-Stockton Coll (MO)
Dakota State U (SD)
Delaware State U (DE)
DePaul U (IL)
Drury U (MO)
Eastern Michigan U (MI)
Fontbonne U (MO)
Georgia Coll & State U (GA)
Illinois Wesleyan U (IL)
Ithaca Coll (NY)
Kansas Wesleyan U (KS)
Long Island U, C.W. Post Campus (NY)
Luther Coll (IA)
Mary Baldwin Coll (VA)
Marywood U (PA)
Mercyhurst Coll (PA)
Millikin U (IL)
North Carolina State U (NC)
Northern Arizona U (AZ)
Ohio U (OH)
Oklahoma City U (OK)
Pfeiffer U (NC)
Point Park U (PA)
Quincy U (IL)
Randolph-Macon Coll (VA)
Salem Coll (NC)
Seton Hill U (PA)
Shenandoah U (VA)
Simmons Coll (MA)
Southeastern Louisiana U (LA)
Spring Hill Coll (AL)
State U of NY Coll at Fredonia (NY)
U of Evansville (IN)
The U of Iowa (IA)
U of Kentucky (KY)
U of Michigan–Dearborn (MI)
U of Ottawa (ON, Canada)
U of Portland (OR)
U of San Francisco (CA)
U of Toronto (ON, Canada)
U of Tulsa (OK)
U of Waterloo (ON, Canada)
U of Windsor (ON, Canada)
U of Wisconsin–Stevens Point (WI)
Upper Iowa U (IA)
Viterbo U (WI)
Wagner Coll (NY)
Wartburg Coll (IA)
Waynesburg Coll (PA)
Whitworth Coll (WA)
Wright State U (OH)

ART TEACHER EDUCATION

Abilene Christian U (TX)
Adelphi U (NY)
Adrian Coll (MI)
Alabama State U (AL)

Albright Coll (PA)
Alfred U (NY)
Alma Coll (MI)
Alverno Coll (WI)
Anderson Coll (SC)
Andrews U (MI)
Anna Maria Coll (MA)
Appalachian State U (NC)
Aquinas Coll (MI)
Arcadia U (PA)
Arkansas State U (AR)
Arkansas Tech U (AR)
Armstrong Atlantic State U (GA)
Asbury Coll (KY)
Ashland U (OH)
Atlantic Union Coll (MA)
Augsburg Coll (MN)
Augustana Coll (IL)
Augustana Coll (SD)
Averett U (VA)
Baker U (KS)
Baldwin-Wallace Coll (OH)
Ball State U (IN)
Barton Coll (NC)
Baylor U (TX)
Belmont U (TN)
Beloit Coll (WI)
Bemidji State U (MN)
Berea Coll (KY)
Bethany Coll (KS)
Bethel U (MN)
Birmingham-Southern Coll (AL)
Bishop's U (QC, Canada)
Bloomfield Coll (NJ)
Boise State U (ID)
Boston U (MA)
Bowling Green State U (OH)
Brenau U (GA)
Brescia U (KY)
Briar Cliff U (IA)
Brigham Young U (UT)
Brigham Young U–Hawaii (HI)
Brooklyn Coll of the City U of NY (NY)
Buena Vista U (IA)
State U of NY Coll at Buffalo (NY)
California Lutheran U (CA)
California State U, Chico (CA)
California State U, Fullerton (CA)
California State U, Long Beach (CA)
Calumet Coll of Saint Joseph (IN)
Calvin Coll (MI)
Cameron U (OK)
Campbellsville U (KY)
Capital U (OH)
Cardinal Stritch U (WI)
Carlow Coll (PA)
Carroll Coll (WI)
Carson-Newman Coll (TN)
Case Western Reserve U (OH)
The Catholic U of America (DC)
Centenary Coll of Louisiana (LA)
Central Connecticut State U (CT)
Central Michigan U (MI)
Central Missouri State U (MO)
Central State U (OH)
Central Washington U (WA)
Chadron State Coll (NE)
Chicago State U (IL)
City Coll of the City U of NY (NY)
Clark Atlanta U (GA)
Clarke Coll (IA)
Coe Coll (IA)
Coker Coll (SC)
Colby-Sawyer Coll (NH)
Coll of Mount St. Joseph (OH)
The Coll of New Jersey (NJ)
The Coll of New Rochelle (NY)
Coll of Saint Benedict (MN)
Coll of St. Catherine (MN)
The Coll of Saint Rose (NY)
Coll of the Ozarks (MO)
Colorado State U (CO)
Colorado State U-Pueblo (CO)
Columbus State U (GA)
Concord Coll (WV)
Concordia Coll (MN)
Concordia U (IL)
Concordia U (MI)
Concordia U (NE)
Concordia U (QC, Canada)
Concordia U Wisconsin (WI)
Converse Coll (SC)
Culver-Stockton Coll (MO)
Cumberland Coll (KY)
Daemen Coll (NY)
Dakota State U (SD)
Dakota Wesleyan U (SD)
Dana Coll (NE)
Davis & Elkins Coll (WV)
Defiance Coll (OH)
Delaware State U (DE)
Delta State U (MS)
Dickinson State U (ND)
Dillard U (LA)
Dowling Coll (NY)
East Carolina U (NC)
East Central U (OK)
Eastern Kentucky U (KY)
Eastern Mennonite U (VA)
Eastern Michigan U (MI)
Eastern Washington U (WA)
Edgewood Coll (WI)
Edinboro U of Pennsylvania (PA)
Elizabeth City State U (NC)
Elmhurst Coll (IL)
Elmira Coll (NY)
Elms Coll (MA)
Escuela de Artes Plasticas de Puerto Rico (PR)
Evangel U (MO)
Fairmont State Coll (WV)
Flagler Coll (FL)
Florida Ag and Mech U (FL)
Florida Intl U (FL)
Florida Southern Coll (FL)
Florida State U (FL)
Fontbonne U (MO)
Fort Hays State U (KS)
Fort Lewis Coll (CO)
Framingham State Coll (MA)
Francis Marion U (SC)
Franklin Pierce Coll (NH)
Freed-Hardeman U (TN)
Gallaudet U (DC)
Georgian Court U (NJ)
Georgia Southern U (GA)
Georgia State U (GA)
Goshen Coll (IN)
Grace Coll (IN)
Graceland U (IA)
Grambling State U (LA)
Grand Canyon U (AZ)
Grand Valley State U (MI)
Greensboro Coll (NC)
Greenville Coll (IL)
Gustavus Adolphus Coll (MN)
Hampton U (VA)
Hannibal-LaGrange Coll (MO)
Harding U (AR)
Hardin-Simmons U (TX)
Hastings Coll (NE)
Henderson State U (AR)
High Point U (NC)
Hofstra U (NY)
Hope Coll (MI)
Houghton Coll (NY)
Houston Baptist U (TX)
Howard Payne U (TX)
Humboldt State U (CA)
Huntingdon Coll (AL)
Huntington Coll (IN)
Indiana State U (IN)
Indiana U Bloomington (IN)
Indiana U of Pennsylvania (PA)
Indiana U–Purdue U Fort Wayne (IN)
Indiana U–Purdue U Indianapolis (IN)
Inter American U of PR, Fajardo Campus (PR)
Inter American U of PR, San Germán Campus (PR)
Iowa Wesleyan Coll (IA)
Ithaca Coll (NY)
Johnson State Coll (VT)
Kansas Wesleyan U (KS)
Kennesaw State U (GA)
Kent State U (OH)
Kentucky State U (KY)
Kentucky Wesleyan Coll (KY)
Keystone Coll (PA)
Kutztown U of Pennsylvania (PA)
Lamar U (TX)
Lambuth U (TN)
Lawrence U (WI)
Lehman Coll of the City U of NY (NY)
Lenoir-Rhyne Coll (NC)
Lewis U (IL)
Limestone Coll (SC)
Lincoln Memorial U (TN)
Lincoln U (MO)
Lincoln U (PA)
Lindenwood U (MO)
Lindsey Wilson Coll (KY)
Long Island U, Brooklyn Campus (NY)
Long Island U, C.W. Post Campus (NY)
Long Island U, Southampton Coll (NY)
Longwood U (VA)
Loras Coll (IA)
Louisiana Coll (LA)
Louisiana State U in Shreveport (LA)
Louisiana Tech U (LA)
Lubbock Christian U (TX)
Lycoming Coll (PA)
Madonna U (MI)
Malone Coll (OH)
Manchester Coll (IN)
Manhattanville Coll (NY)
Mansfield U of Pennsylvania (PA)
Marian Coll (IN)
Marian Coll of Fond du Lac (WI)
Mars Hill Coll (NC)
Maryland Inst Coll of Art (MD)
Marymount Coll of Fordham U (NY)
Maryville Coll (TN)
Maryville U of Saint Louis (MO)
Marywood U (PA)
Massachusetts Coll of Art (MA)
McKendree Coll (IL)
McMurry U (TX)
McNeese State U (LA)
McPherson Coll (KS)
Mercyhurst Coll (PA)
Meredith Coll (NC)
Messiah Coll (PA)
Methodist Coll (NC)
Miami U (OH)
Miami U Hamilton (OH)
Michigan State U (MI)
Middle Tennessee State U (TN)
Millersville U of Pennsylvania (PA)
Millikin U (IL)
Minnesota State U Mankato (MN)
Minnesota State U Moorhead (MN)
Minot State U (ND)
Mississippi Coll (MS)
Missouri Western State Coll (MO)
Montana State U–Billings (MT)
Montclair State U (NJ)
Montserrat Coll of Art (MA)
Moore Coll of Art & Design (PA)
Moravian Coll (PA)
Morningside Coll (IA)
Mount Mary Coll (WI)
Mount Mercy Coll (IA)
Mount St. Mary's Coll (CA)
Mount Saint Vincent U (NS, Canada)
Mount Vernon Nazarene U (OH)
Murray State U (KY)
Nazareth Coll of Rochester (NY)
New Jersey City U (NJ)
New Mexico Highlands U (NM)
New York Inst of Technology (NY)
Nicholls State U (LA)
North Carolina Central U (NC)
North Central Coll (IL)
Northeastern State U (OK)
Northern Arizona U (AZ)
Northern Illinois U (IL)
Northern Michigan U (MI)
Northern State U (SD)
North Georgia Coll & State U (GA)
Northland Coll (WI)
North Park U (IL)
Northwestern Coll (IA)
Northwestern Coll (MN)
Northwest Nazarene U (ID)
Notre Dame Coll (OH)
Oakland City U (IN)
Ohio Dominican U (OH)
Ohio Northern U (OH)
The Ohio State U (OH)
Ohio U (OH)
Ohio Wesleyan U (OH)
Oklahoma Baptist U (OK)
Oklahoma City U (OK)
Olivet Coll (MI)
Olivet Nazarene U (IL)
Oral Roberts U (OK)
Ottawa U (KS)
Otterbein Coll (OH)
Ouachita Baptist U (AR)
Pacific Lutheran U (WA)
Pacific U (OR)
Palm Beach Atlantic U (FL)
Parsons School of Design, New School U (NY)
Penn State U Abington Coll (PA)
Penn State U Altoona Coll (PA)
Penn State U at Erie, The Behrend Coll (PA)
Penn State U Beaver Campus of the Commonwealth Coll (PA)
Penn State U Berks Cmps of Berks-Lehigh Valley Coll (PA)
Penn State U Delaware County Campus of the Commonwealth Coll (PA)
Penn State U DuBois Campus of the Commonwealth Coll (PA)
Penn State U Fayette Campus of the Commonwealth Coll (PA)
Penn State U Hazleton Campus of the Commonwealth Coll (PA)
Penn State U Lehigh Valley Cmps of Berks-Lehigh Valley Coll (PA)
Penn State U McKeesport Campus of the Commonwealth Coll (PA)
Penn State U Mont Alto Campus of the Commonwealth Coll (PA)
Penn State U New Kensington Campus of the Commonwealth Coll (PA)
Penn State U Schuylkill Campus of the Capital Coll (PA)
Penn State U Shenango Campus of the Commonwealth Coll (PA)
Penn State U Univ Park Campus (PA)
Penn State U Wilkes-Barre Campus of the Commonwealth Coll (PA)
Penn State U Worthington Scranton Cmps Commonwealth Coll (PA)
Penn State U York Campus of the Commonwealth Coll (PA)
Pittsburg State U (KS)
Plymouth State U (NH)
Pontifical Catholic U of Puerto Rico (PR)
Pratt Inst (NY)
Queens Coll of the City U of NY (NY)
Queen's U at Kingston (ON, Canada)
Rhode Island Coll (RI)
Roberts Wesleyan Coll (NY)
Rockford Coll (IL)
Rocky Mountain Coll (MT)
Rocky Mountain Coll of Art & Design (CO)
St. Ambrose U (IA)
St. Bonaventure U (NY)
St. Cloud State U (MN)
St. Edward's U (TX)
Saint John's U (MN)
St. John's U (NY)
Saint Joseph's Coll (IN)
Saint Mary-of-the-Woods Coll (IN)
Saint Mary's Coll (IN)
St. Mary's U of San Antonio (TX)
Saint Michael's Coll (VT)
St. Thomas Aquinas Coll (NY)
Saint Vincent Coll (PA)
Saint Xavier U (IL)
Salem State Coll (MA)
Sam Houston State U (TX)
San Diego State U (CA)
School of the Art Inst of Chicago (IL)
School of the Museum of Fine Arts, Boston (MA)
Seattle Pacific U (WA)
Seton Hall U (NJ)
Seton Hill U (PA)
Shawnee State U (OH)
Shorter Coll (GA)
Siena Heights U (MI)
Silver Lake Coll (WI)
Simpson Coll (IA)
South Carolina State U (SC)
South Dakota State U (SD)
Southeastern Louisiana U (LA)
Southeastern Oklahoma State U (OK)
Southeast Missouri State U (MO)
Southern Arkansas U–Magnolia (AR)
Southern Connecticut State U (CT)
Southern Nazarene U (OK)
Southern Utah U (UT)
Southwest Baptist U (MO)
Southwestern Oklahoma State U (OK)
Southwestern U (TX)
Southwest Missouri State U (MO)
State U of NY at New Paltz (NY)
Syracuse U (NY)
Tabor Coll (KS)
Taylor U (IN)
Tennessee Technological U (TN)
Texas A&M U–Commerce (TX)
Texas Christian U (TX)
Texas Lutheran U (TX)
Texas Southern U (TX)
Texas Wesleyan U (TX)
Thomas More Coll (KY)
Towson U (MD)
Transylvania U (KY)
Trinity Christian Coll (IL)
Troy State U (AL)
Tusculum Coll (TN)
Union Coll (NE)
Union U (TN)
Université Laval (QC, Canada)
The U of Akron (OH)
U of Alberta (AB, Canada)
The U of Arizona (AZ)
The U of British Columbia (BC, Canada)
U of Calgary (AB, Canada)
U of Central Florida (FL)
U of Cincinnati (OH)
U of Dallas (TX)
U of Dayton (OH)
U of Denver (CO)
U of Evansville (IN)
The U of Findlay (OH)
U of Florida (FL)
U of Georgia (GA)
U of Great Falls (MT)
U of Hawaii at Manoa (HI)
U of Idaho (ID)
U of Illinois at Chicago (IL)
U of Illinois at Urbana–Champaign (IL)
U of Indianapolis (IN)
The U of Iowa (IA)
U of Kansas (KS)
U of Kentucky (KY)
The U of Lethbridge (AB, Canada)
U of Maine (ME)
U of Maine at Presque Isle (ME)
U of Mary Hardin-Baylor (TX)
U of Maryland, Coll Park (MD)
U of Maryland Eastern Shore (MD)
U of Massachusetts Dartmouth (MA)
U of Michigan (MI)
U of Michigan–Dearborn (MI)
U of Michigan–Flint (MI)
U of Minnesota, Duluth (MN)
U of Minnesota, Twin Cities Campus (MN)
U of Missouri–Columbia (MO)
The U of Montana–Missoula (MT)
The U of Montana–Western (MT)
U of Montevallo (AL)
U of Nebraska–Lincoln (NE)
U of Nevada, Reno (NV)
U of New Brunswick Fredericton (NB, Canada)
U of New Hampshire (NH)
U of New Mexico (NM)
The U of North Carolina at Charlotte (NC)
The U of North Carolina at Greensboro (NC)
The U of North Carolina at Pembroke (NC)
U of North Dakota (ND)
U of Northern Iowa (IA)
U of North Florida (FL)
U of Regina (SK, Canada)
U of Richmond (VA)
U of Saint Francis (IN)
U of Sioux Falls (SD)
U of South Carolina (SC)
The U of South Dakota (SD)
U of Southern Maine (ME)
U of South Florida (FL)
The U of Tennessee (TN)
The U of Tennessee at Chattanooga (TN)
The U of Tennessee at Martin (TN)
U of the District of Columbia (DC)
U of the Incarnate Word (TX)
U of the Ozarks (AR)
U of Toledo (OH)
U of Vermont (VT)
U of Victoria (BC, Canada)
The U of Western Ontario (ON, Canada)
U of West Florida (FL)
U of Windsor (ON, Canada)
U of Wisconsin–La Crosse (WI)
U of Wisconsin–Madison (WI)
U of Wisconsin–Milwaukee (WI)
U of Wisconsin–Oshkosh (WI)
U of Wisconsin–River Falls (WI)
U of Wisconsin–Stout (WI)
U of Wisconsin–Superior (WI)
U of Wisconsin–Whitewater (WI)
Upper Iowa U (IA)
Ursuline Coll (OH)
Valdosta State U (GA)
Valley City State U (ND)
Valparaiso U (IN)
Virginia Commonwealth U (VA)
Virginia Intermont Coll (VA)
Virginia Wesleyan Coll (VA)
Viterbo U (WI)
Waldorf Coll (IA)
Walla Walla Coll (WA)
Wartburg Coll (IA)
Washburn U (KS)
Washington & Jefferson Coll (PA)
Washington U in St. Louis (MO)
Wayne State U (MI)
Weber State U (UT)
Western Carolina U (NC)
Western Kentucky U (KY)
Western Michigan U (MI)
Western State Coll of Colorado (CO)
Western Washington U (WA)
Westfield State Coll (MA)
West Liberty State Coll (WV)
Westmont Coll (CA)
West Virginia State Coll (WV)
West Virginia Wesleyan Coll (WV)

Whitworth Coll (WA)
Wichita State U (KS)
William Carey Coll (MS)
William Paterson U of New Jersey (NJ)
Williams Baptist Coll (AR)
William Woods U (MO)
Wingate U (NC)
Winona State U (MN)
Winston-Salem State U (NC)
Wright State U (OH)
Xavier U of Louisiana (LA)
York Coll (NE)
York U (ON, Canada)
Youngstown State U (OH)

ART THERAPY
Albertus Magnus Coll (CT)
Alverno Coll (WI)
Anna Maria Coll (MA)
Bowling Green State U (OH)
Brescia U (KY)
Capital U (OH)
The Coll of New Rochelle (NY)
Coll of Santa Fe (NM)
Concordia U (QC, Canada)
Converse Coll (SC)
Edgewood Coll (WI)
Elms Coll (MA)
Endicott Coll (MA)
Goshen Coll (IN)
Harding U (AR)
Howard U (DC)
Lesley U (MA)
Long Island U, C.W. Post Campus (NY)
Marian Coll of Fond du Lac (WI)
Marygrove Coll (MI)
Marymount Coll of Fordham U (NY)
Marywood U (PA)
Mercyhurst Coll (PA)
Millikin U (IL)
Mount Mary Coll (WI)
Nazareth Coll of Rochester (NY)
Ohio U (OH)
Ohio Wesleyan U (OH)
Russell Sage Coll (NY)
St. Thomas Aquinas Coll (NY)
Seton Hill U (PA)
Springfield Coll (MA)
Spring Hill Coll (AL)
U of Indianapolis (IN)
U of Wisconsin–Superior (WI)
Webster U (MO)
Wright State U (OH)

ASIAN-AMERICAN STUDIES
California State U, Fullerton (CA)
California State U, Hayward (CA)
California State U, Long Beach (CA)
Claremont McKenna Coll (CA)
Colorado State U (CO)
Columbia Coll (NY)
Hampshire Coll (MA)
Loyola Marymount U (CA)
The Ohio State U (OH)
Pitzer Coll (CA)
Scripps Coll (CA)
State U of NY at Binghamton (NY)
U of Calif, Berkeley (CA)
U of Calif, Irvine (CA)
U of Calif, Los Angeles (CA)
U of Calif, Riverside (CA)
U of Calif, Santa Barbara (CA)
U of Denver (CO)
U of Southern California (CA)

ASIAN HISTORY
Bard Coll (NY)
Cornell U (NY)
Gettysburg Coll (PA)
Sarah Lawrence Coll (NY)
U of Regina (SK, Canada)
U of the West (CA)

ASIAN STUDIES
American Public U System (WV)
American U (DC)
Amherst Coll (MA)
Augustana Coll (IL)
Bard Coll (NY)
Barnard Coll (NY)
Baylor U (TX)
Beloit Coll (WI)
Birmingham-Southern Coll (AL)
Bowdoin Coll (ME)
Bowling Green State U (OH)
Brigham Young U (UT)
California State U, Chico (CA)
California State U, Long Beach (CA)
California State U, Sacramento (CA)
Carleton Coll (MN)
Carleton U (ON, Canada)
Case Western Reserve U (OH)
Central Washington U (WA)
City Coll of the City U of NY (NY)
Claremont McKenna Coll (CA)
Clark U (MA)
Coe Coll (IA)
Colgate U (NY)
Coll of the Holy Cross (MA)
The Colorado Coll (CO)
Colorado State U (CO)
Cornell U (NY)
Dartmouth Coll (NH)
Duke U (NC)
Emory U (GA)
Florida Intl U (FL)
Florida State U (FL)
Fort Lewis Coll (CO)
Furman U (SC)
The George Washington U (DC)
Gonzaga U (WA)
Hamilton Coll (NY)
Hamline U (MN)
Hampshire Coll (MA)
Harvard U (MA)
Hobart and William Smith Colls (NY)
Hofstra U (NY)
Illinois Wesleyan U (IL)
Indiana U Bloomington (IN)
John Carroll U (OH)
Kenyon Coll (OH)
Lake Forest Coll (IL)
Macalester Coll (MN)
Manhattanville Coll (NY)
Marlboro Coll (VT)
Mary Baldwin Coll (VA)
Mount Holyoke Coll (MA)
Mount Union Coll (OH)
Northwestern U (IL)
Occidental Coll (CA)
Ohio U (OH)
Pitzer Coll (CA)
Pomona Coll (CA)
Rice U (TX)
St. Andrews Presbyterian Coll (NC)
St. John's U (NY)
St. Lawrence U (NY)
St. Olaf Coll (MN)
Samford U (AL)
San Diego State U (CA)
Sarah Lawrence Coll (NY)
Scripps Coll (CA)
Seton Hall U (NJ)
Simon's Rock Coll of Bard (MA)
Skidmore Coll (NY)
Stanford U (CA)
State U of NY Coll at Brockport (NY)
Swarthmore Coll (PA)
Texas State U-San Marcos (TX)
Trinity U (TX)
Tufts U (MA)
Tulane U (LA)
State U of NY at Albany (NY)
U at Buffalo, The State U of New York (NY)
The U of British Columbia (BC, Canada)
U of Calif, Berkeley (CA)
U of Calif, Los Angeles (CA)
U of Calif, Riverside (CA)
U of Calif, Santa Barbara (CA)
U of Calif, Santa Cruz (CA)
U of Chicago (IL)
U of Cincinnati (OH)
U of Colorado at Boulder (CO)
U of Florida (FL)
U of Hawaii at Manoa (HI)
The U of Iowa (IA)
U of Michigan (MI)
The U of Montana–Missoula (MT)
U of New Mexico (NM)
The U of North Carolina at Chapel Hill (NC)
U of Northern Iowa (IA)
U of Oregon (OR)
U of Puget Sound (WA)
U of Redlands (CA)
U of San Francisco (CA)
The U of Texas at Austin (TX)
U of the South (TN)
U of Toledo (OH)
U of Toronto (ON, Canada)
U of Utah (UT)
U of Vermont (VT)
U of Victoria (BC, Canada)
U of Washington (WA)
U of Wisconsin–Madison (WI)
Utah State U (UT)
Vassar Coll (NY)
Warren Wilson Coll (NC)
Washington State U (WA)
Washington U in St. Louis (MO)
Wayne State U (MI)
Western Michigan U (MI)
Western Washington U (WA)
Wheaton Coll (MA)
Whitman Coll (WA)
Williams Coll (MA)
York U (ON, Canada)

ASIAN STUDIES (EAST)
Augsburg Coll (MN)
Bates Coll (ME)
Boston U (MA)
Brown U (RI)
Bryn Mawr Coll (PA)
Bucknell U (PA)
Carleton U (ON, Canada)
Colby Coll (ME)
Colgate U (NY)
The Coll of William and Mary (VA)
Columbia Coll (NY)
Columbia U, School of General Studies (NY)
Connecticut Coll (CT)
Cornell U (NY)
Denison U (OH)
DePaul U (IL)
DePauw U (IN)
Dickinson Coll (PA)
Emory & Henry Coll (VA)
The George Washington U (DC)
Gettysburg Coll (PA)
Grinnell Coll (IA)
Hamilton Coll (NY)
Hamline U (MN)
Hampshire Coll (MA)
Harvard U (MA)
Haverford Coll (PA)
Indiana U Bloomington (IN)
John Carroll U (OH)
The Johns Hopkins U (MD)
Lawrence U (WI)
Lewis & Clark Coll (OR)
Marlboro Coll (VT)
McGill U (QC, Canada)
Middlebury Coll (VT)
New York U (NY)
Oberlin Coll (OH)
The Ohio State U (OH)
Ohio Wesleyan U (OH)
Penn State U Abington Coll (PA)
Penn State U Altoona Coll (PA)
Penn State U at Erie, The Behrend Coll (PA)
Penn State U Beaver Campus of the Commonwealth Coll (PA)
Penn State U Berks Cmps of Berks-Lehigh Valley Coll (PA)
Penn State U Delaware County Campus of the Commonwealth Coll (PA)
Penn State U DuBois Campus of the Commonwealth Coll (PA)
Penn State U Fayette Campus of the Commonwealth Coll (PA)
Penn State U Hazleton Campus of the Commonwealth Coll (PA)
Penn State U Lehigh Valley Cmps of Berks-Lehigh Valley Coll (PA)
Penn State U McKeesport Campus of the Commonwealth Coll (PA)
Penn State U Mont Alto Campus of the Commonwealth Coll (PA)
Penn State U New Kensington Campus of the Commonwealth Coll (PA)
Penn State U Schuylkill Campus of the Capital Coll (PA)
Penn State U Shenango Campus of the Commonwealth Coll (PA)
Penn State U Univ Park Campus (PA)
Penn State U Wilkes-Barre Campus of the Commonwealth Coll (PA)
Penn State U Worthington Scranton Cmps Commonwealth Coll (PA)
Penn State U York Campus of the Commonwealth Coll (PA)
Pomona Coll (CA)
Portland State U (OR)
Princeton U (NJ)
Queens Coll of the City U of NY (NY)
Rutgers, The State U of New Jersey, New Brunswick/Piscataway (NJ)
St. John's U (NY)
Sarah Lawrence Coll (NY)
Scripps Coll (CA)
Seattle U (WA)
Simmons Coll (MA)
Smith Coll (MA)
Stanford U (CA)
United States Military Acad (NY)
Université de Montréal (QC, Canada)
State U of NY at Albany (NY)
U of Alberta (AB, Canada)
The U of Arizona (AZ)
U of Calgary (AB, Canada)
U of Calif, Davis (CA)
U of Calif, Irvine (CA)
U of Calif, Los Angeles (CA)
U of Calif, Santa Cruz (CA)
U of Chicago (IL)
U of Delaware (DE)
U of Illinois at Urbana–Champaign (IL)
U of Minnesota, Twin Cities Campus (MN)
U of Missouri–Columbia (MO)
The U of Montana–Missoula (MT)
U of Oregon (OR)
U of Pennsylvania (PA)
U of St. Thomas (MN)
U of Southern California (CA)
U of Toronto (ON, Canada)
U of Washington (WA)
Ursinus Coll (PA)
Valparaiso U (IN)
Vanderbilt U (TN)
Washington and Lee U (VA)
Washington U in St. Louis (MO)
Wayne State U (MI)
Wellesley Coll (MA)
Wesleyan U (CT)
Western Washington U (WA)
Wittenberg U (OH)
Yale U (CT)
York U (ON, Canada)

ASIAN STUDIES (SOUTH)
Brown U (RI)
Concordia U (QC, Canada)
Gettysburg Coll (PA)
Hampshire Coll (MA)
Harvard U (MA)
Sarah Lawrence Coll (NY)
Syracuse U (NY)
The U of British Columbia (BC, Canada)
U of Calif, Santa Cruz (CA)
U of Chicago (IL)
U of Manitoba (MB, Canada)
U of Michigan (MI)
U of Minnesota, Twin Cities Campus (MN)
U of Missouri–Columbia (MO)
U of Pennsylvania (PA)
U of Toronto (ON, Canada)
U of Washington (WA)

ASIAN STUDIES (SOUTHEAST)
Hampshire Coll (MA)
Harvard U (MA)
Ohio U (OH)
Tufts U (MA)
U of Calif, Berkeley (CA)
U of Calif, Los Angeles (CA)
U of Calif, Santa Cruz (CA)
U of Chicago (IL)
U of Michigan (MI)
U of Washington (WA)
U of Wisconsin–Madison (WI)

ASIAN STUDIES (URAL-ALTAIC AND CENTRAL)
Stevens Inst of Technology (NJ)

ASTRONOMY
Amherst Coll (MA)
Barnard Coll (NY)
Benedictine Coll (KS)
Boston U (MA)
Brigham Young U (UT)
Bryn Mawr Coll (PA)
California Inst of Technology (CA)
Case Western Reserve U (OH)
Central Michigan U (MI)
Colgate U (NY)
Columbia Coll (NY)
Columbia U, School of General Studies (NY)
Cornell U (NY)
Dartmouth Coll (NH)
Drake U (IA)
Eastern U (PA)
Franklin and Marshall Coll (PA)
Hampshire Coll (MA)
Harvard U (MA)
Haverford Coll (PA)
Indiana U Bloomington (IN)
Laurentian U (ON, Canada)
Lycoming Coll (PA)
Marlboro Coll (VT)
Minnesota State U Mankato (MN)
Mount Holyoke Coll (MA)
Mount Union Coll (OH)
Northern Arizona U (AZ)
Northwestern U (IL)
The Ohio State U (OH)
Ohio Wesleyan U (OH)
Penn State U Abington Coll (PA)
Penn State U Altoona Coll (PA)
Penn State U at Erie, The Behrend Coll (PA)
Penn State U Beaver Campus of the Commonwealth Coll (PA)
Penn State U Berks Cmps of Berks-Lehigh Valley Coll (PA)
Penn State U Delaware County Campus of the Commonwealth Coll (PA)
Penn State U DuBois Campus of the Commonwealth Coll (PA)
Penn State U Fayette Campus of the Commonwealth Coll (PA)
Penn State U Hazleton Campus of the Commonwealth Coll (PA)
Penn State U Lehigh Valley Cmps of Berks-Lehigh Valley Coll (PA)
Penn State U McKeesport Campus of the Commonwealth Coll (PA)
Penn State U Mont Alto Campus of the Commonwealth Coll (PA)
Penn State U New Kensington Campus of the Commonwealth Coll (PA)
Penn State U Schuylkill Campus of the Capital Coll (PA)
Penn State U Shenango Campus of the Commonwealth Coll (PA)
Penn State U Univ Park Campus (PA)
Penn State U Wilkes-Barre Campus of the Commonwealth Coll (PA)
Penn State U Worthington Scranton Cmps Commonwealth Coll (PA)
Penn State U York Campus of the Commonwealth Coll (PA)
Pomona Coll (CA)
Rice U (TX)
San Diego State U (CA)
San Francisco State U (CA)
Sarah Lawrence Coll (NY)
Smith Coll (MA)
State U of NY Coll at Brockport (NY)
Stony Brook U, State U of New York (NY)
Swarthmore Coll (PA)
Tufts U (MA)
The U of Arizona (AZ)
The U of British Columbia (BC, Canada)
U of Calif, Los Angeles (CA)
U of Colorado at Boulder (CO)
U of Delaware (DE)
U of Florida (FL)
U of Georgia (GA)
U of Illinois at Urbana–Champaign (IL)
The U of Iowa (IA)
U of Kansas (KS)
U of Manitoba (MB, Canada)
U of Maryland, Coll Park (MD)
U of Massachusetts Amherst (MA)
U of Michigan (MI)
U of Minnesota, Twin Cities Campus (MN)
The U of Montana–Missoula (MT)
U of Oklahoma (OK)
U of Saskatchewan (SK, Canada)
U of Southern California (CA)
The U of Texas at Austin (TX)
U of Toledo (OH)
U of Toronto (ON, Canada)
U of Victoria (BC, Canada)
U of Virginia (VA)
U of Washington (WA)
The U of Western Ontario (ON, Canada)
U of Wisconsin–Madison (WI)
Valdosta State U (GA)
Valparaiso U (IN)
Vanderbilt U (TN)
Vassar Coll (NY)
Villanova U (PA)
Wellesley Coll (MA)
Wesleyan U (CT)
Wheaton Coll (MA)
Whitman Coll (WA)
Williams Coll (MA)
Yale U (CT)
York U (ON, Canada)
Youngstown State U (OH)

ASTRONOMY AND ASTROPHYSICS RELATED
Texas Christian U (TX)
U of Wyoming (WY)

ASTROPHYSICS
Agnes Scott Coll (GA)
Augsburg Coll (MN)
Barnard Coll (NY)
Boston U (MA)
Colgate U (NY)

Columbia Coll (NY)
Connecticut Coll (CT)
Cornell U (NY)
Florida Inst of Technology (FL)
Franklin and Marshall Coll (PA)
Hampshire Coll (MA)
Harvard U (MA)
Indiana U Bloomington (IN)
Lehigh U (PA)
Marlboro Coll (VT)
Michigan State U (MI)
New Mexico Inst of Mining and Technology (NM)
Ohio U (OH)
Pacific Union Coll (CA)
Princeton U (NJ)
Queen's U at Kingston (ON, Canada)
Rice U (TX)
Rutgers, The State U of New Jersey, New Brunswick/Piscataway (NJ)
San Francisco State U (CA)
Swarthmore Coll (PA)
U of Calgary (AB, Canada)
U of Calif, Berkeley (CA)
U of Calif, Los Angeles (CA)
U of Calif, Santa Cruz (CA)
U of Delaware (DE)
U of Minnesota, Twin Cities Campus (MN)
U of New Mexico (NM)
U of Oklahoma (OK)
Villanova U (PA)
Wellesley Coll (MA)
Williams Coll (MA)
Yale U (CT)

ATHLETIC TRAINING

Alderson-Broaddus Coll (WV)
Alfred U (NY)
Angelo State U (TX)
Appalachian State U (NC)
Aquinas Coll (MI)
Arkansas State U (AR)
Ashland U (OH)
Augsburg Coll (MN)
Augustana Coll (SD)
Averett U (VA)
Azusa Pacific U (CA)
Baldwin-Wallace Coll (OH)
Ball State U (IN)
Barton Coll (NC)
Baylor U (TX)
Belhaven Coll (MS)
Benedictine Coll (KS)
Bethany Coll (KS)
Bethel Coll (KS)
Bethel U (MN)
Bluefield Coll (VA)
Boise State U (ID)
Boston U (MA)
Bowling Green State U (OH)
Bridgewater Coll (VA)
Bridgewater State Coll (MA)
Brigham Young U (UT)
Buena Vista U (IA)
California Lutheran U (CA)
California State U, Hayward (CA)
California State U, Long Beach (CA)
Calvin Coll (MI)
Campbellsville U (KY)
Campbell U (NC)
Canisius Coll (NY)
Capital U (OH)
Carroll Coll (WI)
Carson-Newman Coll (TN)
Carthage Coll (WI)
Castleton State Coll (VT)
Catawba Coll (NC)
Cedarville U (OH)
Central Connecticut State U (CT)
Central Methodist Coll (MO)
Central Michigan U (MI)
Chapman U (CA)
Charleston Southern U (SC)
Chowan Coll (NC)
Christian Heritage Coll (CA)
Clarke Coll (IA)
Coe Coll (IA)
Colby-Sawyer Coll (NH)
Coll of Mount St. Joseph (OH)
Colorado State U (CO)
Colorado State U-Pueblo (CO)
Columbus State U (GA)
Concordia U (QC, Canada)
Concordia U Wisconsin (WI)
Creighton U (NE)
Culver-Stockton Coll (MO)
Cumberland U (TN)
Dakota Wesleyan U (SD)
Defiance Coll (OH)
DePauw U (IN)
Dominican Coll (NY)
Duquesne U (PA)
East Carolina U (NC)
Eastern Michigan U (MI)
Eastern Washington U (WA)
East Stroudsburg U of Pennsylvania (PA)
East Texas Baptist U (TX)
Elon U (NC)
Emporia State U (KS)
Endicott Coll (MA)
Erskine Coll (SC)
Eureka Coll (IL)
Faulkner U (AL)
Ferrum Coll (VA)
Florida Southern Coll (FL)
Florida State U (FL)
The Franciscan U (IA)
Franklin Coll (IN)
Fresno Pacific U (CA)
Gardner-Webb U (NC)
George Fox U (OR)
Georgia Southern U (GA)
Graceland U (IA)
Grand Canyon U (AZ)
Grand Valley State U (MI)
Greensboro Coll (NC)
Guilford Coll (NC)
Gustavus Adolphus Coll (MN)
Hamline U (MN)
Harding U (AR)
Heidelberg Coll (OH)
Henderson State U (AR)
High Point U (NC)
Hofstra U (NY)
Hope Coll (MI)
Howard Payne U (TX)
Huntingdon Coll (AL)
Illinois State U (IL)
Indiana State U (IN)
Indiana U Bloomington (IN)
Ithaca Coll (NY)
John Brown U (AR)
Johnson State Coll (VT)
Kansas State U (KS)
Keene State Coll (NH)
Kent State U (OH)
King's Coll (PA)
Lakehead U (ON, Canada)
Lake Superior State U (MI)
Lambuth U (TN)
Lander U (SC)
Lenoir-Rhyne Coll (NC)
Liberty U (VA)
Limestone Coll (SC)
Lincoln Memorial U (TN)
Lindenwood U (MO)
Linfield Coll (OR)
Lipscomb U (TN)
Lock Haven U of Pennsylvania (PA)
Long Island U, Brooklyn Campus (NY)
Longwood U (VA)
Loras Coll (IA)
Louisiana Coll (LA)
Lynchburg Coll (VA)
Lyndon State Coll (VT)
Manchester Coll (IN)
Marietta Coll (OH)
Marist Coll (NY)
Marquette U (WI)
Mars Hill Coll (NC)
Marywood U (PA)
Massachusetts Coll of Liberal Arts (MA)
McKendree Coll (IL)
McMurry U (TX)
Memorial U of Newfoundland (NL, Canada)
Mercyhurst Coll (PA)
Merrimack Coll (MA)
Messiah Coll (PA)
Methodist Coll (NC)
Miami U (OH)
Miami U Hamilton (OH)
MidAmerica Nazarene U (KS)
Middle Tennessee State U (TN)
Millikin U (IL)
Minnesota State U Mankato (MN)
Missouri Valley Coll (MO)
Montclair State U (NJ)
Mount Marty Coll (SD)
Mount Union Coll (OH)
National American U (SD)
Nebraska Wesleyan U (NE)
Newberry Coll (SC)
New Mexico State U (NM)
North Carolina Central U (NC)
North Central Coll (IL)
North Dakota State U (ND)
Northeastern U (MA)
Northern Michigan U (MI)
North Park U (IL)
Northwest Nazarene U (ID)
Nova Southeastern U (FL)
Ohio Northern U (OH)
The Ohio State U (OH)
Ohio U (OH)
Oklahoma Baptist U (OK)
Oklahoma State U (OK)
Olivet Nazarene U (IL)
Oregon State U (OR)
Otterbein Coll (OH)
Ouachita Baptist U (AR)
Pacific U (OR)
Park U (MO)
Pepperdine U, Malibu (CA)
Pfeiffer U (NC)
Plymouth State U (NH)
Point Loma Nazarene U (CA)
Quinnipiac U (CT)
Radford U (VA)
Roanoke Coll (VA)
Rocky Mountain Coll (MT)
Russell Sage Coll (NY)
Sacred Heart U (CT)
Salisbury U (MD)
Samford U (AL)
Shawnee State U (OH)
Simpson Coll (IA)
Slippery Rock U of Pennsylvania (PA)
South Dakota State U (SD)
Southeastern Louisiana U (LA)
Southern Connecticut State U (CT)
Southern Nazarene U (OK)
Southwest Baptist U (MO)
Southwestern Coll (KS)
Southwest Missouri State U (MO)
Springfield Coll (MA)
State U of NY Coll at Brockport (NY)
State U of NY Coll at Cortland (NY)
Sterling Coll (KS)
Stony Brook U, State U of New York (NY)
Tabor Coll (KS)
Taylor U (IN)
Tennessee Wesleyan Coll (TN)
Texas Lutheran U (TX)
Texas State U-San Marcos (TX)
Texas Wesleyan U (TX)
Towson U (MD)
Trinity Intl U (IL)
Troy State U (AL)
Tusculum Coll (TN)
Union U (TN)
Université de Sherbrooke (QC, Canada)
The U of Akron (OH)
The U of Alabama (AL)
U of Alberta (AB, Canada)
U of Central Arkansas (AR)
U of Charleston (WV)
U of Delaware (DE)
U of Evansville (IN)
The U of Findlay (OH)
U of Idaho (ID)
U of Indianapolis (IN)
The U of Iowa (IA)
U of Kansas (KS)
U of Louisiana at Lafayette (LA)
U of Maine at Presque Isle (ME)
U of Mary (ND)
U of Mary Hardin-Baylor (TX)
U of Miami (FL)
U of Michigan (MI)
U of Mobile (AL)
U of Nebraska–Lincoln (NE)
U of Nevada, Las Vegas (NV)
U of New Hampshire (NH)
The U of North Carolina at Wilmington (NC)
U of Northern Iowa (IA)
U of Pittsburgh at Bradford (PA)
U of Southern Maine (ME)
U of South Florida (FL)
The U of Tennessee at Martin (TN)
The U of Texas at Arlington (TX)
The U of Texas at Austin (TX)
U of the Incarnate Word (TX)
U of Tulsa (OK)
U of Vermont (VT)
The U of West Alabama (AL)
U of Windsor (ON, Canada)
U of Wisconsin–Eau Claire (WI)
U of Wisconsin–La Crosse (WI)
U of Wisconsin–Stevens Point (WI)
Upper Iowa U (IA)
Urbana U (OH)
Valparaiso U (IN)
Vanguard U of Southern California (CA)
Walsh U (OH)
Washington State U (WA)
Waynesburg Coll (PA)
Weber State U (UT)
West Chester U of Pennsylvania (PA)
Western State Coll of Colorado (CO)
Western Washington U (WA)
West Virginia Wesleyan Coll (WV)
Whitworth Coll (WA)
William Woods U (MO)
Wingate U (NC)
Winona State U (MN)
Xavier U (OH)
Youngstown State U (OH)

ATHLETIC TRAINING/SPORTS MEDICINE

Neumann Coll (PA)
The U of North Carolina at Charlotte (NC)
The U of North Carolina at Pembroke (NC)
U of North Dakota (ND)

ATMOSPHERIC SCIENCES AND METEOROLOGY

Cornell U (NY)
Creighton U (NE)
Dalhousie U (NS, Canada)
Embry-Riddle Aeronautical U (FL)
Florida State U (FL)
Georgia Inst of Technology (GA)
Harvard U (MA)
Iowa State U of Science and Technology (IA)
Lyndon State Coll (VT)
McGill U (QC, Canada)
Metropolitan State Coll of Denver (CO)
Millersville U of Pennsylvania (PA)
New Mexico Inst of Mining and Technology (NM)
Northern Illinois U (IL)
Northland Coll (WI)
Ohio U (OH)
Penn State U Abington Coll (PA)
Penn State U Altoona Coll (PA)
Penn State U at Erie, The Behrend Coll (PA)
Penn State U Beaver Campus of the Commonwealth Coll (PA)
Penn State U Berks Cmps of Berks-Lehigh Valley Coll (PA)
Penn State U Delaware County Campus of the Commonwealth Coll (PA)
Penn State U DuBois Campus of the Commonwealth Coll (PA)
Penn State U Fayette Campus of the Commonwealth Coll (PA)
Penn State U Hazleton Campus of the Commonwealth Coll (PA)
Penn State U Lehigh Valley Cmps of Berks-Lehigh Valley Coll (PA)
Penn State U McKeesport Campus of the Commonwealth Coll (PA)
Penn State U Mont Alto Campus of the Commonwealth Coll (PA)
Penn State U New Kensington Campus of the Commonwealth Coll (PA)
Penn State U Schuylkill Campus of the Capital Coll (PA)
Penn State U Shenango Campus of the Commonwealth Coll (PA)
Penn State U Univ Park Campus (PA)
Penn State U Wilkes-Barre Campus of the Commonwealth Coll (PA)
Penn State U Worthington Scranton Cmps Commonwealth Coll (PA)
Penn State U York Campus of the Commonwealth Coll (PA)
Plymouth State U (NH)
Rutgers, The State U of New Jersey, New Brunswick/Piscataway (NJ)
St. Cloud State U (MN)
Saint Louis U (MO)
San Francisco State U (CA)
San Jose State U (CA)
State U of NY at Oswego (NY)
State U of NY Coll at Brockport (NY)
State U of NY Coll at Oneonta (NY)
Texas A&M U (TX)
United States Air Force Acad (CO)
State U of NY at Albany (NY)
U of Alberta (AB, Canada)
The U of Arizona (AZ)
The U of British Columbia (BC, Canada)
U of Calif, Davis (CA)
U of Calif, Los Angeles (CA)
U of Hawaii at Manoa (HI)
U of Kansas (KS)
U of Miami (FL)
U of Michigan (MI)
U of Missouri–Columbia (MO)
U of Nebraska–Lincoln (NE)
The U of North Carolina at Asheville (NC)
U of North Dakota (ND)
U of Oklahoma (OK)
U of South Alabama (AL)
U of Utah (UT)
U of Victoria (BC, Canada)
U of Washington (WA)
U of Waterloo (ON, Canada)
U of Wisconsin–Milwaukee (WI)
Valparaiso U (IN)
Western Connecticut State U (CT)
York U (ON, Canada)

ATOMIC/MOLECULAR PHYSICS

The Catholic U of America (DC)
Columbia Coll (NY)
Maryville Coll (TN)
Ohio U (OH)
Queen's U at Kingston (ON, Canada)
Saint Mary's U of Minnesota (MN)
San Diego State U (CA)
The U of Akron (OH)
U of Calif, San Diego (CA)
U of Guelph (ON, Canada)
U of Waterloo (ON, Canada)

AUDIO ENGINEERING

American U (DC)
Berklee Coll of Music (MA)
Cleveland Inst of Music (OH)
Cogswell Polytechnical Coll (CA)
Five Towns Coll (NY)
New England School of Communications (ME)
Peabody Conserv of Music of Johns Hopkins U (MD)
State U of NY Coll at Fredonia (NY)
U of Hartford (CT)

AUDIOLOGY AND HEARING SCIENCES

California State U, Long Beach (CA)
Cleveland State U (OH)
Indiana U Bloomington (IN)
Indiana U–Purdue U Fort Wayne (IN)
Northwestern U (IL)
Texas Tech U (TX)
The U of Akron (OH)
The U of Iowa (IA)
U of Northern Colorado (CO)
U of Oklahoma Health Sciences Center (OK)
The U of Tennessee (TN)

AUDIOLOGY AND SPEECH-LANGUAGE PATHOLOGY

Adelphi U (NY)
Andrews U (MI)
Appalachian State U (NC)
Arkansas State U (AR)
Auburn U (AL)
Augustana Coll (SD)
Ball State U (IN)
Bloomsburg U of Pennsylvania (PA)
Brescia U (KY)
Brooklyn Coll of the City U of NY (NY)
State U of NY Coll at Buffalo (NY)
Butler U (IN)
California State U, Fresno (CA)
California State U, Fullerton (CA)
California State U, Hayward (CA)
California State U, Long Beach (CA)
California State U, Sacramento (CA)
Calvin Coll (MI)
Centenary Coll of Louisiana (LA)
Central Michigan U (MI)
Clarion U of Pennsylvania (PA)
The Coll of Saint Rose (NY)
Delta State U (MS)
East Carolina U (NC)
Eastern Kentucky U (KY)
Eastern New Mexico U (NM)
Eastern Washington U (WA)
East Stroudsburg U of Pennsylvania (PA)
Elmhurst Coll (IL)
Elmira Coll (NY)
Elms Coll (MA)
Emerson Coll (MA)
Florida State U (FL)
Fontbonne U (MO)
Fort Hays State U (KS)
Geneva Coll (PA)
The George Washington U (DC)
Governors State U (IL)
Hampton U (VA)

Hardin-Simmons U (TX)
Hofstra U (NY)
Hunter Coll of the City U of NY (NY)
Idaho State U (ID)
Illinois State U (IL)
Indiana State U (IN)
Indiana U Bloomington (IN)
Iona Coll (NY)
Ithaca Coll (NY)
Kent State U (OH)
Lamar U (TX)
Lambuth U (TN)
La Salle U (PA)
Lehman Coll of the City U of NY (NY)
Loma Linda U (CA)
Long Island U, C.W. Post Campus (NY)
Louisiana State U and A&M Coll (LA)
Louisiana State U in Shreveport (LA)
Louisiana Tech U (LA)
Marquette U (WI)
Marymount Manhattan Coll (NY)
Marywood U (PA)
Mercy Coll (NY)
Miami U (OH)
Miami U Hamilton (OH)
Michigan State U (MI)
Minnesota State U Mankato (MN)
Minnesota State U Moorhead (MN)
Molloy Coll (NY)
Murray State U (KY)
Nazareth Coll of Rochester (NY)
Nicholls State U (LA)
Northeastern State U (OK)
Northeastern U (MA)
Northern Michigan U (MI)
Northern State U (SD)
Northwestern U (IL)
The Ohio State U (OH)
Ohio U (OH)
Old Dominion U (VA)
Otterbein Coll (OH)
Our Lady of the Lake U of San Antonio (TX)
Pacific Union Coll (CA)
Purdue U (IN)
The Richard Stockton Coll of New Jersey (NJ)
St. Cloud State U (MN)
St. John's U (NY)
San Francisco State U (CA)
Shaw U (NC)
South Carolina State U (SC)
Southern Illinois U Edwardsville (IL)
Southern U and A&M Coll (LA)
Southwest Missouri State U (MO)
State U of NY at New Paltz (NY)
Plattsburgh State U of NY (NY)
State U of NY Coll at Cortland (NY)
State U of NY Coll at Fredonia (NY)
State U of NY Coll at Geneseo (NY)
Syracuse U (NY)
Tennessee State U (TN)
Texas State U-San Marcos (TX)
Texas Woman's U (TX)
Thiel Coll (PA)
Université de Montréal (QC, Canada)
U at Buffalo, The State U of New York (NY)
The U of Akron (OH)
The U of Alabama (AL)
U of Arkansas (AR)
U of Arkansas at Little Rock (AR)
U of Central Arkansas (AR)
U of Central Florida (FL)
U of Cincinnati (OH)
U of Florida (FL)
U of Hawaii at Manoa (HI)
U of Houston (TX)
U of Illinois at Urbana–Champaign (IL)
The U of Iowa (IA)
U of Kentucky (KY)
U of Louisiana at Lafayette (LA)
U of Minnesota, Duluth (MN)
U of Minnesota, Twin Cities Campus (MN)
U of Mississippi (MS)
The U of Montana–Missoula (MT)
U of Montevallo (AL)
U of New Hampshire (NH)
U of New Mexico (NM)
The U of North Carolina at Greensboro (NC)
U of North Dakota (ND)
U of North Texas (TX)
U of Oklahoma Health Sciences Center (OK)
U of Oregon (OR)
U of Pittsburgh (PA)
U of Redlands (CA)
U of South Alabama (AL)
U of South Florida (FL)
The U of Texas at Dallas (TX)
The U of Texas–Pan American (TX)
U of the District of Columbia (DC)
U of the Pacific (CA)
U of Toledo (OH)
U of Tulsa (OK)
U of Utah (UT)
U of Vermont (VT)
U of Virginia (VA)
U of Washington (WA)
U of Wisconsin–Milwaukee (WI)
U of Wisconsin–Oshkosh (WI)
U of Wisconsin–Stevens Point (WI)
U of Wyoming (WY)
Utah State U (UT)
Washington State U (WA)
West Chester U of Pennsylvania (PA)
Western Michigan U (MI)
Western Washington U (WA)
West Virginia U (WV)
Wichita State U (KS)

AUDIOVISUAL COMMUNICATIONS TECHNOLOGIES RELATED
Greenville Coll (IL)
Hofstra U (NY)
Nevada State Coll at Henderson (NV)

AUDITING
Babson Coll (MA)

AUTOBODY/COLLISION AND REPAIR TECHNOLOGY
Lewis-Clark State Coll (ID)

AUTOMOBILE/AUTOMOTIVE MECHANICS TECHNOLOGY
Andrews U (MI)
Colorado State U-Pueblo (CO)
Ferris State U (MI)
Lewis-Clark State Coll (ID)
Pittsburg State U (KS)
Walla Walla Coll (WA)
Weber State U (UT)

AUTOMOTIVE ENGINEERING TECHNOLOGY
Central Michigan U (MI)
Central Missouri State U (MO)
State U of NY at Farmingdale (NY)
Indiana State U (IN)
Minnesota State U Mankato (MN)
Pennsylvania Coll of Technology (PA)
Pittsburg State U (KS)
Southern Illinois U Carbondale (IL)
Weber State U (UT)
Western Washington U (WA)

AVIATION/AIRWAY MANAGEMENT
Auburn U (AL)
Averett U (VA)
Baker Coll of Muskegon (MI)
Bowling Green State U (OH)
Bridgewater State Coll (MA)
Daniel Webster Coll (NH)
Delaware State U (DE)
Embry-Riddle Aeronautical U (FL)
Embry-Riddle Aeronautical U, Extended Campus (FL)
Everglades U, Boca Raton (FL)
Fairmont State Coll (WV)
State U of NY at Farmingdale (NY)
Florida Inst of Technology (FL)
Geneva Coll (PA)
Hampton U (VA)
Indiana State U (IN)
Inter American U of PR, Bayamón Campus (PR)
Inter American U of PR, Fajardo Campus (PR)
Jacksonville U (FL)
Lewis U (IL)
Louisiana Tech U (LA)
Lynn U (FL)
Marywood U (PA)
Metropolitan State Coll of Denver (CO)
Minnesota State U Mankato (MN)
Mountain State U (WV)
The Ohio State U (OH)
Ohio U (OH)
Oklahoma State U (OK)
Park U (MO)
Quincy U (IL)
Robert Morris U (PA)
Rocky Mountain Coll (MT)
St. Cloud State U (MN)
St. Francis Coll (NY)
Saint Louis U (MO)
Salem State Coll (MA)
Southeastern Oklahoma State U (OK)
Southern Illinois U Carbondale (IL)
Southern Nazarene U (OK)
Tarleton State U (TX)
Texas Southern U (TX)
U Coll of the Fraser Valley (BC, Canada)
U of Dubuque (IA)
U of Minnesota, Crookston (MN)
U of New Haven (CT)
U of North Dakota (ND)
Western Michigan U (MI)
Westminster Coll (UT)
Wilmington Coll (DE)
Winona State U (MN)

AVIONICS MAINTENANCE TECHNOLOGY
Andrews U (MI)
Averett U (VA)
Coll of the Ozarks (MO)
Elizabeth City State U (NC)
Fairmont State Coll (WV)
Grace U (NE)
Hampton U (VA)
Inter American U of PR, Fajardo Campus (PR)
LeTourneau U (TX)
Lewis U (IL)
Moody Bible Inst (IL)
The Ohio State U (OH)
Oklahoma State U (OK)
Pennsylvania Coll of Technology (PA)
Southern Illinois U Carbondale (IL)
Walla Walla Coll (WA)
Western Michigan U (MI)
Wilmington Coll (DE)

AYURVEDIC MEDICINE
Maharishi U of Management (IA)

BAKING AND PASTRY ARTS
The Art Inst of California–San Diego (CA)
The Culinary Inst of America (NY)
Johnson & Wales U (RI)

BALKANS STUDIES
American Coll of Thessaloniki(Greece)

BALLET
Brigham Young U (UT)
Texas Christian U (TX)
U of Utah (UT)

BANKING AND FINANCIAL SUPPORT SERVICES
Buena Vista U (IA)
Central Michigan U (MI)
Clearwater Christian Coll (FL)
Delaware State U (DE)
Husson Coll (ME)
National U (CA)
Northwood U (MI)
Northwood U, Florida Campus (FL)
Northwood U, Texas Campus (TX)
Saint Joseph's Coll of Maine (ME)
Texas Southern U (TX)
Thomas Edison State Coll (NJ)
U of Indianapolis (IN)
U of Nebraska at Omaha (NE)
U of North Florida (FL)
U of North Texas (TX)
The U of Texas at Arlington (TX)
West Liberty State Coll (WV)
Youngstown State U (OH)

BEHAVIORAL SCIENCES
Andrews U (MI)
Anna Maria Coll (MA)
Antioch Coll (OH)
Athens State U (AL)
Augsburg Coll (MN)
Belmont U (TN)
Bemidji State U (MN)
Brown U (RI)
California Baptist U (CA)
California State Polytechnic U, Pomona (CA)
California State U, Dominguez Hills (CA)
Cedar Crest Coll (PA)
Chaminade U of Honolulu (HI)
Coll for Lifelong Learning (NH)
Concordia U (CA)
Concordia U (NE)
Concordia U (QC, Canada)
Dakota Wesleyan U (SD)
Drew U (NJ)
Drury U (MO)
Erskine Coll (SC)
Evangel U (MO)
Freed-Hardeman U (TN)
Glenville State Coll (WV)
Grand Valley State U (MI)
Hampshire Coll (MA)
Harvard U (MA)
Hawai'i Pacific U (HI)
Howard Payne U (TX)
Indiana U Kokomo (IN)
Inter American U of PR, San Germán Campus (PR)
Iona Coll (NY)
John Jay Coll of Criminal Justice, the City U of NY (NY)
The Johns Hopkins U (MD)
King Coll (TN)
Laurentian U (ON, Canada)
Loyola U New Orleans (LA)
Marist Coll (NY)
Marlboro Coll (VT)
Mars Hill Coll (NC)
McPherson Coll (KS)
Mercy Coll (NY)
Methodist Coll (NC)
Metropolitan State Coll of Denver (CO)
Miles Coll (AL)
Minnesota State U Mankato (MN)
Morgan State U (MD)
Mountain State U (WV)
Mount Aloysius Coll (PA)
Mount Marty Coll (SD)
Mount Mary Coll (WI)
National-Louis U (IL)
National U (CA)
New Mexico Inst of Mining and Technology (NM)
Northeastern U (MA)
Northern Michigan U (MI)
Notre Dame de Namur U (CA)
Our Lady of Holy Cross Coll (LA)
Pacific Union Coll (CA)
Point Park U (PA)
Rhode Island Coll (RI)
Rochester Coll (MI)
St. Cloud State U (MN)
St. Joseph's Coll, Suffolk Campus (NY)
San Jose State U (CA)
Sterling Coll (KS)
Tennessee Wesleyan Coll (TN)
Texas Wesleyan U (TX)
Trevecca Nazarene U (TN)
Tufts U (MA)
United States Air Force Acad (CO)
United States Military Acad (NY)
The U of Akron (OH)
U of Chicago (IL)
U of Detroit Mercy (MI)
U of Houston–Clear Lake (TX)
U of Kansas (KS)
U of La Verne (CA)
U of Maine at Fort Kent (ME)
U of Maine at Machias (ME)
U of Maine at Presque Isle (ME)
U of Mary (ND)
U of Mary Hardin-Baylor (TX)
U of Michigan–Dearborn (MI)
U of Missouri–Columbia (MO)
U of Mobile (AL)
U of North Texas (TX)
U of Ottawa (ON, Canada)
U of Sioux Falls (SD)
U of Utah (UT)
Ursuline Coll (OH)
Walsh U (OH)
Westminster Coll (PA)
Widener U (PA)
William Paterson U of New Jersey (NJ)
Wilmington Coll (DE)
Wilson Coll (PA)
York Coll of Pennsylvania (PA)
York U (ON, Canada)

BENGALI
U of Chicago (IL)

BIBLICAL STUDIES
Abilene Christian U (TX)
Alaska Bible Coll (AK)
American Baptist Coll of American Baptist Theol Sem (TN)
Andrews U (MI)
Appalachian Bible Coll (WV)
Arlington Baptist Coll (TX)
Asbury Coll (KY)
Atlanta Christian Coll (GA)
Atlantic Baptist U (NB, Canada)
Austin Graduate School of Theology (TX)
Azusa Pacific U (CA)
The Baptist Coll of Florida (FL)
Barclay Coll (KS)
Beacon Coll and Graduate School (GA)
Belhaven Coll (MS)
Belmont U (TN)
Bethany Bible Coll (NB, Canada)
Bethany Coll (SK, Canada)
Bethel Coll (IN)
Bethel U (MN)
Bethesda Christian U (CA)
Biola U (CA)
Bluefield Coll (VA)
Blue Mountain Coll (MS)
Briercrest Bible Coll (SK, Canada)
Bryan Coll (TN)
California Baptist U (CA)
California Christian Coll (CA)
Calvary Bible Coll and Theological Sem (MO)
Calvin Coll (MI)
Campbellsville U (KY)
Canadian Mennonite U (MB, Canada)
Carson-Newman Coll (TN)
Cascade Coll (OR)
Cedarville U (OH)
Central Baptist Coll (AR)
Central Christian Coll of Kansas (KS)
Central Pentecostal Coll (SK, Canada)
Christian Heritage Coll (CA)
Clear Creek Baptist Bible Coll (KY)
Clearwater Christian Coll (FL)
Coll of Biblical Studies–Houston (TX)
Colorado Christian U (CO)
Columbia Intl U (SC)
Cornerstone U (MI)
Covenant Coll (GA)
Crichton Coll (TN)
Crossroads Bible Coll (IN)
Crossroads Coll (MN)
Crown Coll (MN)
Dallas Baptist U (TX)
Dallas Christian Coll (TX)
Eastern Mennonite U (VA)
Eastern U (PA)
East Texas Baptist U (TX)
Emmanuel Coll (GA)
Erskine Coll (SC)
Eugene Bible Coll (OR)
Evangel U (MO)
Faith Baptist Bible Coll and Theological Sem (IA)
Faulkner U (AL)
Florida Coll (FL)
Freed-Hardeman U (TN)
Fresno Pacific U (CA)
Geneva Coll (PA)
George Fox U (OR)
Global U of the Assemblies of God (MO)
Goshen Coll (IN)
Grace Bible Coll (MI)
Grace Coll (IN)
Grace U (NE)
Grand Canyon U (AZ)
Hannibal-LaGrange Coll (MO)
Hardin-Simmons U (TX)
Harvard U (MA)
Heritage Christian U (AL)
Houghton Coll (NY)
Houston Baptist U (TX)
Howard Payne U (TX)
Huntington Coll (IN)
Jewish Theological Sem of America (NY)
John Brown U (AR)
Johnson Bible Coll (TN)
John Wesley Coll (NC)
Judson Coll (IL)
King Coll (TN)
Lancaster Bible Coll (PA)
Laura and Alvin Siegal Coll of Judaic Studies (OH)
LeTourneau U (TX)
Liberty U (VA)
Life Pacific Coll (CA)
Lipscomb U (TN)
Lubbock Christian U (TX)
Magnolia Bible Coll (MS)
Malone Coll (OH)
Manhattan Christian Coll (KS)
Marlboro Coll (VT)
The Master's Coll and Sem (CA)
Master's Coll and Sem (ON, Canada)
Messenger Coll (MO)
Messiah Coll (PA)
Methodist Coll (NC)
Mid-Continent Coll (KY)
Milligan Coll (TN)
Montreat Coll (NC)
Moody Bible Inst (IL)
Mount Vernon Nazarene U (OH)

Multnomah Bible Coll and Biblical Sem (OR)
North Central U (MN)
North Greenville Coll (SC)
North Park U (IL)
Northwest Christian Coll (OR)
Northwestern Coll (MN)
Nyack Coll (NY)
Oak Hills Christian Coll (MN)
Oakland City U (IN)
Ohio Valley Coll (WV)
Oklahoma Baptist U (OK)
Oklahoma Christian U (OK)
Olivet Nazarene U (IL)
Oral Roberts U (OK)
Ouachita Baptist U (AR)
Palm Beach Atlantic U (FL)
Philadelphia Biblical U (PA)
Pillsbury Baptist Bible Coll (MN)
Practical Bible Coll (NY)
Prairie Bible Coll (AB, Canada)
Providence Coll and Theological Sem (MB, Canada)
Redeemer U Coll (ON, Canada)
Reformed Bible Coll (MI)
Reinhardt Coll (GA)
Rochester Coll (MI)
Rocky Mountain Coll (AB, Canada)
St. Louis Christian Coll (MO)
Shasta Bible Coll (CA)
Simpson Coll and Graduate School (CA)
Southeastern Bible Coll (AL)
Southeastern Coll of the Assemblies of God (FL)
Southern Christian U (AL)
Southwest Baptist U (MO)
Southwestern Coll (AZ)
Steinbach Bible Coll (MB, Canada)
Tabor Coll (KS)
Talmudic Coll of Florida (FL)
Taylor U (IN)
Taylor U, Fort Wayne Campus (IN)
Toccoa Falls Coll (GA)
Trinity Baptist Coll (FL)
Trinity Bible Coll (ND)
Trinity Coll of Florida (FL)
Trinity Intl U (IL)
Trinity Western U (BC, Canada)
Tyndale U Coll & Sem (ON, Canada)
Union U (TN)
Universidad Adventista de las Antillas (PR)
Université de Montréal (QC, Canada)
U of Evansville (IN)
U of Michigan (MI)
U of Mobile (AL)
Vanguard U of Southern California (CA)
Vennard Coll (IA)
Warner Pacific Coll (OR)
Warner Southern Coll (FL)
Washington Bible Coll (MD)
Western Baptist Coll (OR)
Wheaton Coll (IL)
William Jessup U (CA)
Williamson Christian Coll (TN)
William Tyndale Coll (MI)
York Coll (NE)

BILINGUAL AND MULTILINGUAL EDUCATION

Adrian Coll (MI)
Belmont U (TN)
Biola U (CA)
Boise State U (ID)
Boston U (MA)
Brooklyn Coll of the City U of NY (NY)
California State Polytechnic U, Pomona (CA)
California State U, Dominguez Hills (CA)
Calvin Coll (MI)
Chicago State U (IL)
Coll of the Southwest (NM)
Concordia U, St. Paul (MN)
Elms Coll (MA)
Florida State U (FL)
Fordham U (NY)
Fresno Pacific U (CA)
Georgian Court U (NJ)
Goshen Coll (IN)
Hofstra U (NY)
Houston Baptist U (TX)
Indiana U Bloomington (IN)
Lehigh U (PA)
Long Island U, Brooklyn Campus (NY)
Mercy Coll (NY)
Mount Mary Coll (WI)
Nevada State Coll at Henderson (NV)
New Mexico Highlands U (NM)
Northeastern Illinois U (IL)
Rider U (NJ)
State U of NY Coll at Old Westbury (NY)
Texas A&M Intl U (TX)
Texas A&M U–Kingsville (TX)
Texas Christian U (TX)
Texas Southern U (TX)
Texas Wesleyan U (TX)
The U of Akron (OH)
U of Alberta (AB, Canada)
U of Delaware (DE)
The U of Findlay (OH)
U of Houston (TX)
U of Maine at Fort Kent (ME)
U of Michigan–Dearborn (MI)
U of Ottawa (ON, Canada)
U of Regina (SK, Canada)
U of San Francisco (CA)
The U of Texas at Brownsville (TX)
U of the Sacred Heart (PR)
U of Washington (WA)
U of Wisconsin–Milwaukee (WI)
Weber State U (UT)
Western Illinois U (IL)
York U (ON, Canada)

BILINGUAL, MULTILINGUAL, AND MULTICULTURAL EDUCATION RELATED

Florida State U (FL)
St. John's U (NY)
State U of NY Coll at Brockport (NY)

BIOCHEMICAL TECHNOLOGY

U at Buffalo, The State U of New York (NY)
U of Windsor (ON, Canada)

BIOCHEMISTRY

Abilene Christian U (TX)
Adelphi U (NY)
Agnes Scott Coll (GA)
Albright Coll (PA)
Allegheny Coll (PA)
Alma Coll (MI)
Alvernia Coll (PA)
American Intl Coll (MA)
American U (DC)
Andrews U (MI)
Angelo State U (TX)
Arizona State U (AZ)
Asbury Coll (KY)
Atlantic Union Coll (MA)
Auburn U (AL)
Azusa Pacific U (CA)
Bard Coll (NY)
Barnard Coll (NY)
Bates Coll (ME)
Baylor U (TX)
Belmont U (TN)
Beloit Coll (WI)
Benedictine Coll (KS)
Benedictine U (IL)
Bennington Coll (VT)
Berry Coll (GA)
Biola U (CA)
Bishop's U (QC, Canada)
Bloomfield Coll (NJ)
Boston Coll (MA)
Boston U (MA)
Bowdoin Coll (ME)
Bradley U (IL)
Brandeis U (MA)
Bridgewater State Coll (MA)
Brigham Young U (UT)
Brigham Young U–Hawaii (HI)
Brock U (ON, Canada)
Brown U (RI)
California Inst of Technology (CA)
California Lutheran U (CA)
California Polytechnic State U, San Luis Obispo (CA)
California State U, Chico (CA)
California State U, Dominguez Hills (CA)
California State U, Fullerton (CA)
California State U, Hayward (CA)
California State U, Long Beach (CA)
California State U, Los Angeles (CA)
California State U, San Bernardino (CA)
California State U, San Marcos (CA)
Calvin Coll (MI)
Campbell U (NC)
Canisius Coll (NY)
Capital U (OH)
Carleton U (ON, Canada)
Carnegie Mellon U (PA)
Carroll Coll (WI)
Case Western Reserve U (OH)
The Catholic U of America (DC)
Cedar Crest Coll (PA)
Centenary Coll of Louisiana (LA)
Centre Coll (KY)
Charleston Southern U (SC)
Chatham Coll (PA)
Chestnut Hill Coll (PA)
City Coll of the City U of NY (NY)
Claremont McKenna Coll (CA)
Clarkson U (NY)
Clark U (MA)
Clemson U (SC)
Coe Coll (IA)
Colby Coll (ME)
Colgate U (NY)
Coll Misericordia (PA)
Coll of Charleston (SC)
Coll of Mount St. Joseph (OH)
Coll of Mount Saint Vincent (NY)
Coll of Saint Benedict (MN)
Coll of St. Catherine (MN)
Coll of Saint Elizabeth (NJ)
The Coll of Saint Rose (NY)
The Coll of St. Scholastica (MN)
The Coll of Southeastern Europe, The American U of Athens(Greece)
Coll of Staten Island of the City U of NY (NY)
The Coll of Wooster (OH)
The Colorado Coll (CO)
Colorado State U (CO)
Columbia Coll (NY)
Columbia Union Coll (MD)
Concordia U (QC, Canada)
Connecticut Coll (CT)
Converse Coll (SC)
Cornell Coll (IA)
Cornell U (NY)
Daemen Coll (NY)
Dalhousie U (NS, Canada)
Dartmouth Coll (NH)
Denison U (OH)
DePaul U (IL)
DePauw U (IN)
Dickinson Coll (PA)
Dominican U (IL)
Drew U (NJ)
Duquesne U (PA)
East Carolina U (NC)
Eastern Connecticut State U (CT)
Eastern Mennonite U (VA)
Eastern Michigan U (MI)
Eastern U (PA)
Eastern Washington U (WA)
East Stroudsburg U of Pennsylvania (PA)
Edinboro U of Pennsylvania (PA)
Elizabethtown Coll (PA)
Elmira Coll (NY)
Fairleigh Dickinson U, Teaneck-Metro Campus (NJ)
Florida Inst of Technology (FL)
Florida State U (FL)
Fort Lewis Coll (CO)
Franklin and Marshall Coll (PA)
Freed-Hardeman U (TN)
Furman U (SC)
Georgetown U (DC)
Georgian Court U (NJ)
Gettysburg Coll (PA)
Gonzaga U (WA)
Grand Valley State U (MI)
Grinnell Coll (IA)
Grove City Coll (PA)
Gustavus Adolphus Coll (MN)
Hamilton Coll (NY)
Hamline U (MN)
Hampden-Sydney Coll (VA)
Hampshire Coll (MA)
Harding U (AR)
Hartwick Coll (NY)
Harvard U (MA)
Haverford Coll (PA)
Hobart and William Smith Colls (NY)
Hofstra U (NY)
Hood Coll (MD)
Humboldt State U (CA)
Idaho State U (ID)
Illinois State U (IL)
Immaculata U (PA)
Indiana U Bloomington (IN)
Indiana U of Pennsylvania (PA)
Inter American U of PR, Bayamón Campus (PR)
Iona Coll (NY)
Iowa State U of Science and Technology (IA)
Ithaca Coll (NY)
Jamestown Coll (ND)
John Brown U (AR)
Juniata Coll (PA)
Kansas State U (KS)
Kennesaw State U (GA)
Kenyon Coll (OH)
Keuka Coll (NY)
King Coll (TN)
Knox Coll (IL)
Lafayette Coll (PA)
LaGrange Coll (GA)
Lakeland Coll (WI)
La Salle U (PA)
Laurentian U (ON, Canada)
Lawrence U (WI)
Lebanon Valley Coll (PA)
Lehigh U (PA)
Lehman Coll of the City U of NY (NY)
Le Moyne Coll (NY)
Lewis & Clark Coll (OR)
Lewis U (IL)
Lipscomb U (TN)
Loras Coll (IA)
Louisiana State U and A&M Coll (LA)
Loyola Marymount U (CA)
Loyola U Chicago (IL)
Madonna U (MI)
Manhattan Coll (NY)
Manhattanville Coll (NY)
Mansfield U of Pennsylvania (PA)
Marietta Coll (OH)
Marist Coll (NY)
Marlboro Coll (VT)
Marquette U (WI)
Mary Baldwin Coll (VA)
Maryville Coll (TN)
McDaniel Coll (MD)
McGill U (QC, Canada)
McMurry U (TX)
Memorial U of Newfoundland (NL, Canada)
Mercer U (GA)
Mercyhurst Coll (PA)
Merrimack Coll (MA)
Messiah Coll (PA)
Miami U (OH)
Miami U Hamilton (OH)
Michigan State U (MI)
Michigan Technological U (MI)
Middlebury Coll (VT)
Mills Coll (CA)
Minnesota State U Mankato (MN)
Mississippi Coll (MS)
Mississippi State U (MS)
Monmouth Coll (IL)
Montclair State U (NJ)
Moravian Coll (PA)
Mount Allison U (NB, Canada)
Mount Holyoke Coll (MA)
Mount St. Mary's Coll (CA)
Mount Saint Mary's Coll and Sem (MD)
Muhlenberg Coll (PA)
Nazareth Coll of Rochester (NY)
Nebraska Wesleyan U (NE)
New Mexico State U (NM)
New York U (NY)
Niagara U (NY)
North Carolina State U (NC)
North Central Coll (IL)
Northeastern U (MA)
Northern Michigan U (MI)
Northwestern U (IL)
Northwest Nazarene U (ID)
Notre Dame Coll (OH)
Notre Dame de Namur U (CA)
Oakland U (MI)
Oberlin Coll (OH)
Occidental Coll (CA)
Ohio Northern U (OH)
The Ohio State U (OH)
Oklahoma Christian U (OK)
Oklahoma City U (OK)
Oklahoma State U (OK)
Old Dominion U (VA)
Olivet Coll (MI)
Olivet Nazarene U (IL)
Oral Roberts U (OK)
Oregon State U (OR)
Otterbein Coll (OH)
Pace U (NY)
Pacific Lutheran U (WA)
Pacific Union Coll (CA)
Penn State U Abington Coll (PA)
Penn State U Altoona Coll (PA)
Penn State U at Erie, The Behrend Coll (PA)
Penn State U Beaver Campus of the Commonwealth Coll (PA)
Penn State U Berks Cmps of Berks-Lehigh Valley Coll (PA)
Penn State U Delaware County Campus of the Commonwealth Coll (PA)
Penn State U DuBois Campus of the Commonwealth Coll (PA)
Penn State U Fayette Campus of the Commonwealth Coll (PA)
Penn State U Hazleton Campus of the Commonwealth Coll (PA)
Penn State U Lehigh Valley Cmps of Berks-Lehigh Valley Coll (PA)
Penn State U McKeesport Campus of the Commonwealth Coll (PA)
Penn State U Mont Alto Campus of the Commonwealth Coll (PA)
Penn State U New Kensington Campus of the Commonwealth Coll (PA)
Penn State U Schuylkill Campus of the Capital Coll (PA)
Penn State U Shenango Campus of the Commonwealth Coll (PA)
Penn State U Univ Park Campus (PA)
Penn State U Wilkes-Barre Campus of the Commonwealth Coll (PA)
Penn State U Worthington Scranton Cmps Commonwealth Coll (PA)
Penn State U York Campus of the Commonwealth Coll (PA)
Philadelphia U (PA)
Pitzer Coll (CA)
Point Loma Nazarene U (CA)
Pomona Coll (CA)
Portland State U (OR)
Purdue U (IN)
Queens Coll of the City U of NY (NY)
Queen's U at Kingston (ON, Canada)
Queens U of Charlotte (NC)
Quinnipiac U (CT)
Reed Coll (OR)
Regis Coll (MA)
Regis U (CO)
Rensselaer Polytechnic Inst (NY)
Rhodes Coll (TN)
Rice U (TX)
The Richard Stockton Coll of New Jersey (NJ)
Rider U (NJ)
Ripon Coll (WI)
Roanoke Coll (VA)
Roberts Wesleyan Coll (NY)
Rochester Inst of Technology (NY)
Rockford Coll (IL)
Rollins Coll (FL)
Rosemont Coll (PA)
Rowan U (NJ)
Russell Sage Coll (NY)
Rutgers, The State U of New Jersey, New Brunswick/Piscataway (NJ)
Sacred Heart U (CT)
Saginaw Valley State U (MI)
Saint Anselm Coll (NH)
St. Bonaventure U (NY)
St. Edward's U (TX)
St. John Fisher Coll (NY)
Saint John's U (MN)
Saint Joseph Coll (CT)
Saint Joseph's Coll (IN)
Saint Joseph's U (PA)
St. Lawrence U (NY)
Saint Mary's Coll of California (CA)
St. Mary's Coll of Maryland (MD)
St. Mary's U of San Antonio (TX)
Saint Michael's Coll (VT)
Saint Vincent Coll (PA)
Samford U (AL)
San Francisco State U (CA)
San Jose State U (CA)
Schreiner U (TX)
Scripps Coll (CA)
Seattle Pacific U (WA)
Seattle U (WA)
Seton Hall U (NJ)
Seton Hill U (PA)
Simmons Coll (MA)
Simon Fraser U (BC, Canada)
Simpson Coll (IA)
Skidmore Coll (NY)
Smith Coll (MA)
South Dakota State U (SD)
Southern Adventist U (TN)
Southern Connecticut State U (CT)
Southern Methodist U (TX)
Southern Nazarene U (OK)
Southern Oregon U (OR)
Southwestern Coll (KS)
Spelman Coll (GA)
Spring Arbor U (MI)
Spring Hill Coll (AL)
State U of NY at Binghamton (NY)
State U of NY at New Paltz (NY)
Plattsburgh State U of NY (NY)
State U of NY Coll at Brockport (NY)
State U of NY Coll at Fredonia (NY)
State U of NY Coll at Geneseo (NY)

State U of NY Coll at Oneonta (NY)
State U of NY Coll of Environ Sci and Forestry (NY)
Stetson U (FL)
Stevens Inst of Technology (NJ)
Stonehill Coll (MA)
Stony Brook U, State U of New York (NY)
Suffolk U (MA)
Susquehanna U (PA)
Swarthmore Coll (PA)
Syracuse U (NY)
Tennessee Technological U (TN)
Texas A&M U (TX)
Texas Christian U (TX)
Texas State U-San Marcos (TX)
Texas Tech U (TX)
Texas Wesleyan U (TX)
Trent U (ON, Canada)
Trinity Coll (CT)
Trinity Coll (DC)
Trinity U (TX)
Tulane U (LA)
Union Coll (NE)
Union Coll (NY)
United States Air Force Acad (CO)
Université de Montréal (QC, Canada)
Université de Sherbrooke (QC, Canada)
Université Laval (QC, Canada)
State U of NY at Albany (NY)
U at Buffalo, The State U of New York (NY)
U Coll of the Cariboo (BC, Canada)
U of Alberta (AB, Canada)
The U of Arizona (AZ)
The U of British Columbia (BC, Canada)
U of Calgary (AB, Canada)
U of Calif, Davis (CA)
U of Calif, Los Angeles (CA)
U of Calif, Riverside (CA)
U of Calif, San Diego (CA)
U of Calif, Santa Barbara (CA)
U of Calif, Santa Cruz (CA)
U of Chicago (IL)
U of Cincinnati (OH)
U of Colorado at Boulder (CO)
U of Dallas (TX)
U of Dayton (OH)
U of Delaware (DE)
U of Denver (CO)
U of Detroit Mercy (MI)
U of Evansville (IN)
U of Georgia (GA)
U of Guelph (ON, Canada)
U of Houston (TX)
U of Illinois at Chicago (IL)
U of Illinois at Urbana–Champaign (IL)
The U of Iowa (IA)
U of King's Coll (NS, Canada)
The U of Lethbridge (AB, Canada)
U of Maine (ME)
U of Maryland, Coll Park (MD)
U of Massachusetts Boston (MA)
U of Miami (FL)
U of Michigan (MI)
U of Michigan–Dearborn (MI)
U of Minnesota, Duluth (MN)
U of Minnesota, Twin Cities Campus (MN)
U of Missouri–Columbia (MO)
The U of Montana–Missoula (MT)
U of Nebraska–Lincoln (NE)
U of Nevada, Las Vegas (NV)
U of Nevada, Reno (NV)
U of New Brunswick Fredericton (NB, Canada)
U of New Hampshire (NH)
U of New Mexico (NM)
The U of North Carolina at Greensboro (NC)
U of Northern Iowa (IA)
U of North Texas (TX)
U of Notre Dame (IN)
U of Oregon (OR)
U of Ottawa (ON, Canada)
U of Pennsylvania (PA)
U of Regina (SK, Canada)
U of St. Thomas (MN)
U of Saskatchewan (SK, Canada)
U of Southern California (CA)
The U of Tampa (FL)
The U of Tennessee (TN)
The U of Texas at Arlington (TX)
The U of Texas at Austin (TX)
The U of Texas at Dallas (TX)
U of the Pacific (CA)
U of the Sciences in Philadelphia (PA)
U of Toronto (ON, Canada)
U of Tulsa (OK)
U of Vermont (VT)
U of Victoria (BC, Canada)
U of Washington (WA)
U of Waterloo (ON, Canada)
The U of Western Ontario (ON, Canada)
U of Windsor (ON, Canada)
U of Wisconsin–Madison (WI)
U of Wisconsin–Milwaukee (WI)
U of Wisconsin–River Falls (WI)
Valparaiso U (IN)
Vassar Coll (NY)
Virginia Polytechnic Inst and State U (VA)
Viterbo U (WI)
Wartburg Coll (IA)
Washington & Jefferson Coll (PA)
Washington and Lee U (VA)
Washington State U (WA)
Washington U in St. Louis (MO)
Wellesley Coll (MA)
Wells Coll (NY)
Wesleyan U (CT)
West Chester U of Pennsylvania (PA)
Western Kentucky U (KY)
Western Michigan U (MI)
Western Washington U (WA)
Wheaton Coll (MA)
Whitman Coll (WA)
Widener U (PA)
Wilkes U (PA)
William Jewell Coll (MO)
Wisconsin Lutheran Coll (WI)
Wittenberg U (OH)
Worcester Polytechnic Inst (MA)
Wright State U (OH)
Xavier U of Louisiana (LA)

BIOCHEMISTRY/BIOPHYSICS AND MOLECULAR BIOLOGY

California State U, Long Beach (CA)
Cornell U (NY)
Hardin-Simmons U (TX)
Illinois Inst of Technology (IL)
Michigan State U (MI)
Monmouth Coll (IL)
Nebraska Wesleyan U (NE)
North Dakota State U (ND)
The U of British Columbia (BC, Canada)
U of Kansas (KS)
U of Maryland, Baltimore County (MD)
U of Massachusetts Amherst (MA)
The U of Memphis (TN)
U of Waterloo (ON, Canada)

BIOCHEMISTRY, BIOPHYSICS AND MOLECULAR BIOLOGY RELATED

Mount Union Coll (OH)
Oklahoma State U (OK)
Ramapo Coll of New Jersey (NJ)
Sweet Briar Coll (VA)
Towson U (MD)
U of Waterloo (ON, Canada)
Washington State U (WA)

BIOETHICS/MEDICAL ETHICS

Cleveland State U (OH)

BIOINFORMATICS

Baylor U (TX)
Brigham Young U (UT)
Canisius Coll (NY)
Chatham Coll (PA)
Eastern Michigan U (MI)
Ramapo Coll of New Jersey (NJ)
Rensselaer Polytechnic Inst (NY)
Rochester Inst of Technology (NY)
St. Edward's U (TX)
U at Buffalo, The State U of New York (NY)
U of Alberta (AB, Canada)
U of Maryland, Baltimore County (MD)
U of Pennsylvania (PA)
U of Saskatchewan (SK, Canada)
U of the Sciences in Philadelphia (PA)
U of Waterloo (ON, Canada)
U of Windsor (ON, Canada)

BIOLOGICAL AND BIOMEDICAL SCIENCES RELATED

Arizona State U (AZ)
Boston U (MA)
Brandeis U (MA)
Capital U (OH)
Charleston Southern U (SC)
Cornell U (NY)
Davis & Elkins Coll (WV)
Fairleigh Dickinson U, Florham (NJ)
Fairleigh Dickinson U, Teaneck-Metro Campus (NJ)
State U of NY at Farmingdale (NY)
Guilford Coll (NC)
Holy Names Coll (CA)
Inter American U of PR, Bayamón Campus (PR)
Kent State U (OH)
Lehigh U (PA)
Louisiana State U in Shreveport (LA)
Lynchburg Coll (VA)
Monmouth Coll (IL)
National U (CA)
Our Lady of the Lake Coll (LA)
Park U (MO)
Penn State U Abington Coll (PA)
Penn State U Altoona Coll (PA)
Penn State U at Erie, The Behrend Coll (PA)
Penn State U Beaver Campus of the Commonwealth Coll (PA)
Penn State U Berks Cmps of Berks-Lehigh Valley Coll (PA)
Penn State U Delaware County Campus of the Commonwealth Coll (PA)
Penn State U DuBois Campus of the Commonwealth Coll (PA)
Penn State U Fayette Campus of the Commonwealth Coll (PA)
Penn State U Hazleton Campus of the Commonwealth Coll (PA)
Penn State U Lehigh Valley Cmps of Berks-Lehigh Valley Coll (PA)
Penn State U McKeesport Campus of the Commonwealth Coll (PA)
Penn State U Mont Alto Campus of the Commonwealth Coll (PA)
Penn State U New Kensington Campus of the Commonwealth Coll (PA)
Penn State U Schuylkill Campus of the Capital Coll (PA)
Penn State U Shenango Campus of the Commonwealth Coll (PA)
Penn State U Univ Park Campus (PA)
Penn State U Wilkes-Barre Campus of the Commonwealth Coll (PA)
Penn State U Worthington Scranton Cmps Commonwealth Coll (PA)
Penn State U York Campus of the Commonwealth Coll (PA)
Ramapo Coll of New Jersey (NJ)
Rensselaer Polytechnic Inst (NY)
Rochester Inst of Technology (NY)
Rutgers, The State U of New Jersey, Newark (NJ)
Saint Mary's Coll of California (CA)
Saint Mary's U of Minnesota (MN)
Skidmore Coll (NY)
Swarthmore Coll (PA)
Texas Wesleyan U (TX)
U of Illinois at Urbana–Champaign (IL)
U of Kansas (KS)
U of North Alabama (AL)
U of North Dakota (ND)
U of Wisconsin–Parkside (WI)
Ursuline Coll (OH)
Washington State U (WA)
Washington U in St. Louis (MO)
Wayland Baptist U (TX)

BIOLOGICAL AND PHYSICAL SCIENCES

Adams State Coll (CO)
Alfred U (NY)
Alice Lloyd Coll (KY)
Alma Coll (MI)
Alvernia Coll (PA)
Angelo State U (TX)
Antioch Coll (OH)
Athabasca U (AB, Canada)
Atlantic Union Coll (MA)
Augsburg Coll (MN)
Averett U (VA)
Avila U (MO)
Bard Coll (NY)
Belmont U (TN)
Bemidji State U (MN)
Bennington Coll (VT)
Bishop's U (QC, Canada)
Bloomsburg U of Pennsylvania (PA)
Bluefield State Coll (WV)
Brescia U (KY)
Brigham Young U (UT)
Brock U (ON, Canada)
Buena Vista U (IA)
California State U, Fresno (CA)
California U of Pennsylvania (PA)
Calvin Coll (MI)
Cameron U (OK)
Canisius Coll (NY)
Carleton U (ON, Canada)
Castleton State Coll (VT)
Cedar Crest Coll (PA)
Cedarville U (OH)
Charleston Southern U (SC)
Cheyney U of Pennsylvania (PA)
Chowan Coll (NC)
Clarion U of Pennsylvania (PA)
Coe Coll (IA)
Coll of Saint Benedict (MN)
Coll of the Atlantic (ME)
Colorado Christian U (CO)
Concordia U (IL)
Concordia U (MI)
Concordia U (OR)
Concordia U, St. Paul (MN)
Delta State U (MS)
Dowling Coll (NY)
Drexel U (PA)
Eastern Michigan U (MI)
Eastern Nazarene Coll (MA)
Eastern Oregon U (OR)
Eastern Washington U (WA)
East Stroudsburg U of Pennsylvania (PA)
Edinboro U of Pennsylvania (PA)
Erskine Coll (SC)
Eureka Coll (IL)
The Evergreen State Coll (WA)
Fairleigh Dickinson U, Teaneck-Metro Campus (NJ)
Florida Inst of Technology (FL)
Fordham U (NY)
Fort Hays State U (KS)
Freed-Hardeman U (TN)
Gannon U (PA)
Gettysburg Coll (PA)
Grand Valley State U (MI)
Grinnell Coll (IA)
Hampshire Coll (MA)
Harvard U (MA)
Houghton Coll (NY)
Huntington Coll (IN)
Indiana U Kokomo (IN)
Indiana U of Pennsylvania (PA)
Iowa Wesleyan Coll (IA)
John Carroll U (OH)
The Johns Hopkins U (MD)
Johnson C. Smith U (NC)
Judson Coll (IL)
Juniata Coll (PA)
Keystone Coll (PA)
King Coll (TN)
King's Coll (PA)
Kutztown U of Pennsylvania (PA)
Lakehead U (ON, Canada)
Lehigh U (PA)
Le Moyne Coll (NY)
Lock Haven U of Pennsylvania (PA)
Long Island U, Brooklyn Campus (NY)
Louisiana State U in Shreveport (LA)
Lyndon State Coll (VT)
Madonna U (MI)
Mansfield U of Pennsylvania (PA)
Marian Coll of Fond du Lac (WI)
Mars Hill Coll (NC)
Marygrove Coll (MI)
Marylhurst U (OR)
Marymount Coll of Fordham U (NY)
Maryville U of Saint Louis (MO)
Massachusetts Coll of Liberal Arts (MA)
The Master's Coll and Sem (CA)
McMurry U (TX)
Memorial U of Newfoundland (NL, Canada)
Methodist Coll (NC)
Michigan State U (MI)
Middle Tennessee State U (TN)
Minnesota State U Mankato (MN)
Mississippi State U (MS)
Montana Tech of The U of Montana (MT)
Mount Allison U (NB, Canada)
Mount Saint Vincent U (NS, Canada)
Mount Vernon Nazarene U (OH)
National-Louis U (IL)
New Mexico Inst of Mining and Technology (NM)
Northern State U (SD)
Northland Coll (WI)
North Park U (IL)
Northwestern U (IL)
Oakland City U (IN)
Oklahoma Baptist U (OK)
Oklahoma City U (OK)
Oklahoma Panhandle State U (OK)
Olivet Nazarene U (IL)
Oregon State U (OR)
Palmer Coll of Chiropractic (IA)
Penn State U Abington Coll (PA)
Penn State U Altoona Coll (PA)
Penn State U at Erie, The Behrend Coll (PA)
Penn State U Beaver Campus of the Commonwealth Coll (PA)
Penn State U Berks Cmps of Berks-Lehigh Valley Coll (PA)
Penn State U Delaware County Campus of the Commonwealth Coll (PA)
Penn State U DuBois Campus of the Commonwealth Coll (PA)
Penn State U Fayette Campus of the Commonwealth Coll (PA)
Penn State U Hazleton Campus of the Commonwealth Coll (PA)
Penn State U Lehigh Valley Cmps of Berks-Lehigh Valley Coll (PA)
Penn State U McKeesport Campus of the Commonwealth Coll (PA)
Penn State U Mont Alto Campus of the Commonwealth Coll (PA)
Penn State U New Kensington Campus of the Commonwealth Coll (PA)
Penn State U Schuylkill Campus of the Capital Coll (PA)
Penn State U Shenango Campus of the Commonwealth Coll (PA)
Penn State U Univ Park Campus (PA)
Penn State U Wilkes-Barre Campus of the Commonwealth Coll (PA)
Penn State U Worthington Scranton Cmps Commonwealth Coll (PA)
Penn State U York Campus of the Commonwealth Coll (PA)
Pontifical Catholic U of Puerto Rico (PR)
Portland State U (OR)
Purdue U (IN)
Quinnipiac U (CT)
Redeemer U Coll (ON, Canada)
Rensselaer Polytechnic Inst (NY)
Rhode Island Coll (RI)
Roberts Wesleyan Coll (NY)
Rochester Coll (MI)
Rockford Coll (IL)
Saginaw Valley State U (MI)
Saint Anselm Coll (NH)
St. Francis Xavier U (NS, Canada)
Saint Mary-of-the-Woods Coll (IN)
St. Mary's Coll of Maryland (MD)
St. Norbert Coll (WI)
Saint Xavier U (IL)
Sam Houston State U (TX)
San Francisco State U (CA)
Santa Clara U (CA)
Sarah Lawrence Coll (NY)
Seattle U (WA)
Shawnee State U (OH)
Sierra Nevada Coll (NV)
Simon Fraser U (BC, Canada)
Simpson Coll (IA)
Southern Arkansas U–Magnolia (AR)
State U of NY Coll at Fredonia (NY)
State U of NY Coll of Environ Sci and Forestry (NY)
State U of NY Empire State Coll (NY)
Sterling Coll (VT)
Tabor Coll (KS)
Texas A&M U at Galveston (TX)
Texas Southern U (TX)
Texas Tech U (TX)
Trent U (ON, Canada)
Trevecca Nazarene U (TN)
Trinity Western U (BC, Canada)
Union Coll (NY)
Union U (TN)
United States Air Force Acad (CO)
United States Military Acad (NY)
The U of Akron (OH)
The U of Alabama (AL)
The U of Alabama at Birmingham (AL)
U of Alaska Fairbanks (AK)
U of Alberta (AB, Canada)
U of Central Arkansas (AR)
U of Denver (CO)
U of Dubuque (IA)
The U of Findlay (OH)
U of Georgia (GA)
U of Guelph (ON, Canada)
The U of Lethbridge (AB, Canada)
U of Massachusetts Amherst (MA)
U of Michigan–Dearborn (MI)
U of Mobile (AL)
U of New Brunswick Fredericton (NB, Canada)
U of New Hampshire (NH)

U of Northern Iowa (IA)
U of North Florida (FL)
U of Oregon (OR)
U of Ottawa (ON, Canada)
U of Pittsburgh (PA)
U of Regina (SK, Canada)
U of Rochester (NY)
U of Saint Francis (IN)
U of Southern Indiana (IN)
U of South Florida (FL)
U of Toledo (OH)
U of Toronto (ON, Canada)
U of Waterloo (ON, Canada)
The U of Western Ontario (ON, Canada)
U of West Florida (FL)
U of Windsor (ON, Canada)
U of Wisconsin–Platteville (WI)
U of Wisconsin–Superior (WI)
U of Wisconsin–Whitewater (WI)
Upper Iowa U (IA)
Ursinus Coll (PA)
Vanguard U of Southern California (CA)
Villa Julie Coll (MD)
Virginia Commonwealth U (VA)
Walsh U (OH)
Warner Pacific Coll (OR)
Washington State U (WA)
Washington U in St. Louis (MO)
Western Washington U (WA)
Winona State U (MN)
Worcester State Coll (MA)
Wright State U (OH)
Xavier U (OH)
York Coll (NE)
York U (ON, Canada)
Youngstown State U (OH)

BIOLOGICAL SPECIALIZATIONS RELATED

Arizona State U (AZ)
Frostburg State U (MD)
King Coll (TN)
Marywood U (PA)
Okanagan U Coll (BC, Canada)
San Jose State U (CA)
U of Louisiana at Lafayette (LA)
Utah State U (UT)

BIOLOGY/BIOLOGICAL SCIENCES

Abilene Christian U (TX)
Acadia U (NS, Canada)
Adams State Coll (CO)
Adelphi U (NY)
Adrian Coll (MI)
Agnes Scott Coll (GA)
Alabama Ag and Mech U (AL)
Alabama State U (AL)
Albany State U (GA)
Albertson Coll of Idaho (ID)
Albertus Magnus Coll (CT)
Albion Coll (MI)
Albright Coll (PA)
Alcorn State U (MS)
Alderson-Broaddus Coll (WV)
Alfred U (NY)
Alice Lloyd Coll (KY)
Allegheny Coll (PA)
Allen U (SC)
Alma Coll (MI)
Alvernia Coll (PA)
Alverno Coll (WI)
American Intl Coll (MA)
American U (DC)
The American U in Cairo(Egypt)
Amherst Coll (MA)
Anderson Coll (SC)
Andrews U (MI)
Angelo State U (TX)
Anna Maria Coll (MA)
Antioch Coll (OH)
Appalachian State U (NC)
Aquinas Coll (MI)
Arcadia U (PA)
Arizona State U (AZ)
Arizona State U East (AZ)
Arizona State U West (AZ)
Arkansas State U (AR)
Arkansas Tech U (AR)
Armstrong Atlantic State U (GA)
Asbury Coll (KY)
Ashland U (OH)
Assumption Coll (MA)
Athens State U (AL)
Atlantic Baptist U (NB, Canada)
Atlantic Union Coll (MA)
Auburn U (AL)
Auburn U Montgomery (AL)
Augsburg Coll (MN)
Augustana Coll (IL)
Augustana Coll (SD)
Augusta State U (GA)
Aurora U (IL)
Austin Coll (TX)
Austin Peay State U (TN)
Ave Maria U (FL)
Averett U (VA)
Avila U (MO)
Azusa Pacific U (CA)
Baker U (KS)
Baldwin-Wallace Coll (OH)
Ball State U (IN)
Barber-Scotia Coll (NC)
Bard Coll (NY)
Barnard Coll (NY)
Barry U (FL)
Barton Coll (NC)
Bates Coll (ME)
Baylor U (TX)
Bay Path Coll (MA)
Becker Coll (MA)
Belhaven Coll (MS)
Bellarmine U (KY)
Belmont Abbey Coll (NC)
Belmont U (TN)
Beloit Coll (WI)
Bemidji State U (MN)
Benedictine Coll (KS)
Benedictine U (IL)
Bennington Coll (VT)
Berea Coll (KY)
Berry Coll (GA)
Bethany Coll (KS)
Bethany Coll (WV)
Bethany Lutheran Coll (MN)
Bethel Coll (IN)
Bethel Coll (KS)
Bethel Coll (TN)
Bethel U (MN)
Bethune-Cookman Coll (FL)
Biola U (CA)
Birmingham-Southern Coll (AL)
Bishop's U (QC, Canada)
Blackburn Coll (IL)
Black Hills State U (SD)
Bloomfield Coll (NJ)
Bloomsburg U of Pennsylvania (PA)
Bluefield Coll (VA)
Blue Mountain Coll (MS)
Bluffton Coll (OH)
Boise State U (ID)
Boston Coll (MA)
Boston U (MA)
Bowdoin Coll (ME)
Bowie State U (MD)
Bowling Green State U (OH)
Bradley U (IL)
Brandeis U (MA)
Brenau U (GA)
Brescia U (KY)
Brewton-Parker Coll (GA)
Briar Cliff U (IA)
Bridgewater Coll (VA)
Bridgewater State Coll (MA)
Brigham Young U (UT)
Brigham Young U–Hawaii (HI)
Brock U (ON, Canada)
Brooklyn Coll of the City U of NY (NY)
Brown U (RI)
Bryan Coll (TN)
Bryn Athyn Coll of the New Church (PA)
Bryn Mawr Coll (PA)
Bucknell U (PA)
Buena Vista U (IA)
State U of NY Coll at Buffalo (NY)
Butler U (IN)
Cabrini Coll (PA)
Caldwell Coll (NJ)
California Baptist U (CA)
California Inst of Technology (CA)
California Lutheran U (CA)
California Polytechnic State U, San Luis Obispo (CA)
California State Polytechnic U, Pomona (CA)
California State U, Chico (CA)
California State U, Dominguez Hills (CA)
California State U, Fresno (CA)
California State U, Fullerton (CA)
California State U, Hayward (CA)
California State U, Long Beach (CA)
California State U, Los Angeles (CA)
California State U, Sacramento (CA)
California State U, San Bernardino (CA)
California State U, San Marcos (CA)
California State U, Stanislaus (CA)
California U of Pennsylvania (PA)
Calvin Coll (MI)
Cameron U (OK)
Campbellsville U (KY)
Campbell U (NC)
Capital U (OH)
Cardinal Stritch U (WI)
Carleton Coll (MN)
Carleton U (ON, Canada)
Carlow Coll (PA)
Carnegie Mellon U (PA)
Carroll Coll (MT)
Carroll Coll (WI)
Carson-Newman Coll (TN)
Carthage Coll (WI)
Case Western Reserve U (OH)
Castleton State Coll (VT)
Catawba Coll (NC)
The Catholic U of America (DC)
Cedar Crest Coll (PA)
Cedarville U (OH)
Centenary Coll (NJ)
Centenary Coll of Louisiana (LA)
Central Coll (IA)
Central Connecticut State U (CT)
Central Methodist Coll (MO)
Central Michigan U (MI)
Central Missouri State U (MO)
Central State U (OH)
Central Washington U (WA)
Centre Coll (KY)
Chadron State Coll (NE)
Chaminade U of Honolulu (HI)
Chapman U (CA)
Charleston Southern U (SC)
Chatham Coll (PA)
Chestnut Hill Coll (PA)
Cheyney U of Pennsylvania (PA)
Chicago State U (IL)
Chowan Coll (NC)
Christian Brothers U (TN)
Christian Heritage Coll (CA)
Christopher Newport U (VA)
Citadel, The Military Coll of South Carolina (SC)
City Coll of the City U of NY (NY)
Claremont McKenna Coll (CA)
Clarion U of Pennsylvania (PA)
Clark Atlanta U (GA)
Clarke Coll (IA)
Clarkson U (NY)
Clark U (MA)
Clayton Coll & State U (GA)
Clearwater Christian Coll (FL)
Clemson U (SC)
Cleveland Chiropractic Coll-Kansas City Campus (MO)
Cleveland Chiropractic Coll-Los Angeles Campus (CA)
Cleveland State U (OH)
Coastal Carolina U (SC)
Coe Coll (IA)
Coker Coll (SC)
Colby Coll (ME)
Colby-Sawyer Coll (NH)
Colgate U (NY)
Coll Misericordia (PA)
Coll of Charleston (SC)
Coll of Mount St. Joseph (OH)
Coll of Mount Saint Vincent (NY)
The Coll of New Jersey (NJ)
The Coll of New Rochelle (NY)
Coll of Notre Dame of Maryland (MD)
Coll of Saint Benedict (MN)
Coll of St. Catherine (MN)
Coll of Saint Elizabeth (NJ)
Coll of Saint Mary (NE)
The Coll of Saint Rose (NY)
The Coll of St. Scholastica (MN)
The Coll of Southeastern Europe, The American U of Athens(Greece)
Coll of Staten Island of the City U of NY (NY)
Coll of the Atlantic (ME)
Coll of the Holy Cross (MA)
Coll of the Ozarks (MO)
Coll of the Southwest (NM)
The Coll of William and Mary (VA)
The Coll of Wooster (OH)
Colorado Christian U (CO)
The Colorado Coll (CO)
Colorado State U (CO)
Colorado State U-Pueblo (CO)
Columbia Coll (MO)
Columbia Coll (NY)
Columbia Coll (SC)
Columbia Union Coll (MD)
Columbia U, School of General Studies (NY)
Columbus State U (GA)
Concord Coll (WV)
Concordia Coll (MN)
Concordia Coll (NY)
Concordia U (CA)
Concordia U (IL)
Concordia U (MI)
Concordia U (NE)
Concordia U (OR)
Concordia U (QC, Canada)
Concordia U at Austin (TX)
Concordia U Coll of Alberta (AB, Canada)
Concordia U, St. Paul (MN)
Concordia U Wisconsin (WI)
Connecticut Coll (CT)
Converse Coll (SC)
Cornell Coll (IA)
Cornell U (NY)
Cornerstone U (MI)
Covenant Coll (GA)
Creighton U (NE)
Crichton Coll (TN)
Crown Coll (MN)
Culver-Stockton Coll (MO)
Cumberland Coll (KY)
Cumberland U (TN)
Curry Coll (MA)
Daemen Coll (NY)
Dakota State U (SD)
Dakota Wesleyan U (SD)
Dalhousie U (NS, Canada)
Dallas Baptist U (TX)
Dana Coll (NE)
Dartmouth Coll (NH)
Davidson Coll (NC)
Davis & Elkins Coll (WV)
Defiance Coll (OH)
Delaware State U (DE)
Delaware Valley Coll (PA)
Delta State U (MS)
Denison U (OH)
DePaul U (IL)
DePauw U (IN)
DeSales U (PA)
Dickinson Coll (PA)
Dickinson State U (ND)
Dillard U (LA)
Doane Coll (NE)
Dominican Coll (NY)
Dominican U (IL)
Dominican U of California (CA)
Dordt Coll (IA)
Dowling Coll (NY)
Drake U (IA)
Drew U (NJ)
Drexel U (PA)
Drury U (MO)
Duke U (NC)
Duquesne U (PA)
D'Youville Coll (NY)
Earlham Coll (IN)
East Carolina U (NC)
East Central U (OK)
Eastern Connecticut State U (CT)
Eastern Illinois U (IL)
Eastern Kentucky U (KY)
Eastern Mennonite U (VA)
Eastern Michigan U (MI)
Eastern Nazarene Coll (MA)
Eastern New Mexico U (NM)
Eastern Oregon U (OR)
Eastern U (PA)
Eastern Washington U (WA)
East Stroudsburg U of Pennsylvania (PA)
East Texas Baptist U (TX)
Eckerd Coll (FL)
Edgewood Coll (WI)
Edinboro U of Pennsylvania (PA)
Elizabeth City State U (NC)
Elizabethtown Coll (PA)
Elmhurst Coll (IL)
Elmira Coll (NY)
Elms Coll (MA)
Elon U (NC)
Emmanuel Coll (GA)
Emory & Henry Coll (VA)
Emory U (GA)
Emporia State U (KS)
Erskine Coll (SC)
Eureka Coll (IL)
Evangel U (MO)
The Evergreen State Coll (WA)
Excelsior Coll (NY)
Fairfield U (CT)
Fairleigh Dickinson U, Florham (NJ)
Fairleigh Dickinson U, Teaneck-Metro Campus (NJ)
Fairmont State Coll (WV)
Faulkner U (AL)
Fayetteville State U (NC)
Ferris State U (MI)
Ferrum Coll (VA)
Florida Ag and Mech U (FL)
Florida Atlantic U (FL)
Florida Inst of Technology (FL)
Florida Intl U (FL)
Florida Southern Coll (FL)
Florida State U (FL)
Fontbonne U (MO)
Fordham U (NY)
Fort Hays State U (KS)
Fort Lewis Coll (CO)
Fort Valley State U (GA)
Framingham State Coll (MA)
The Franciscan U (IA)
Franciscan U of Steubenville (OH)
Francis Marion U (SC)
Franklin and Marshall Coll (PA)
Franklin Coll (IN)
Franklin Pierce Coll (NH)
Freed-Hardeman U (TN)
Fresno Pacific U (CA)
Frostburg State U (MD)
Furman U (SC)
Gallaudet U (DC)
Gannon U (PA)
Gardner-Webb U (NC)
Geneva Coll (PA)
George Fox U (OR)
George Mason U (VA)
Georgetown Coll (KY)
Georgetown U (DC)
The George Washington U (DC)
Georgia Coll & State U (GA)
Georgia Inst of Technology (GA)
Georgian Court U (NJ)
Georgia Southern U (GA)
Georgia Southwestern State U (GA)
Georgia State U (GA)
Gettysburg Coll (PA)
Glenville State Coll (WV)
Gonzaga U (WA)
Gordon Coll (MA)
Goshen Coll (IN)
Goucher Coll (MD)
Governors State U (IL)
Grace Coll (IN)
Graceland U (IA)
Grambling State U (LA)
Grand Canyon U (AZ)
Grand Valley State U (MI)
Grand View Coll (IA)
Greensboro Coll (NC)
Greenville Coll (IL)
Grinnell Coll (IA)
Grove City Coll (PA)
Guilford Coll (NC)
Gustavus Adolphus Coll (MN)
Gwynedd-Mercy Coll (PA)
Hamilton Coll (NY)
Hamline U (MN)
Hampden-Sydney Coll (VA)
Hampshire Coll (MA)
Hampton U (VA)
Hannibal-LaGrange Coll (MO)
Hanover Coll (IN)
Harding U (AR)
Hardin-Simmons U (TX)
Hartwick Coll (NY)
Harvard U (MA)
Harvey Mudd Coll (CA)
Hastings Coll (NE)
Haverford Coll (PA)
Hawai'i Pacific U (HI)
Heidelberg Coll (OH)
Henderson State U (AR)
Hendrix Coll (AR)
High Point U (NC)
Hillsdale Coll (MI)
Hiram Coll (OH)
Hobart and William Smith Colls (NY)
Hofstra U (NY)
Hollins U (VA)
Holy Names Coll (CA)
Hood Coll (MD)
Hope Coll (MI)
Houghton Coll (NY)
Houston Baptist U (TX)
Howard Payne U (TX)
Howard U (DC)
Humboldt State U (CA)
Hunter Coll of the City U of NY (NY)
Huntingdon Coll (AL)
Huntington Coll (IN)
Husson Coll (ME)
Huston-Tillotson Coll (TX)
Idaho State U (ID)
Illinois Coll (IL)
Illinois Inst of Technology (IL)
Illinois State U (IL)
Illinois Wesleyan U (IL)
Immaculata U (PA)
Indiana State U (IN)
Indiana U Bloomington (IN)
Indiana U East (IN)
Indiana U Kokomo (IN)
Indiana U Northwest (IN)
Indiana U of Pennsylvania (PA)
Indiana U–Purdue U Fort Wayne (IN)
Indiana U–Purdue U Indianapolis (IN)
Indiana U South Bend (IN)
Indiana U Southeast (IN)
Inter American U of PR, Aguadilla Campus (PR)

Inter Amer U of PR, Barranquitas Campus (PR)
Inter American U of PR, Bayamón Campus (PR)
Inter American U of PR, Fajardo Campus (PR)
Inter American U of PR, Ponce Campus (PR)
Inter American U of PR, San Germán Campus (PR)
Iona Coll (NY)
Iowa State U of Science and Technology (IA)
Iowa Wesleyan Coll (IA)
Ithaca Coll (NY)
Jacksonville State U (AL)
Jacksonville U (FL)
James Madison U (VA)
Jamestown Coll (ND)
Jarvis Christian Coll (TX)
John Brown U (AR)
John Carroll U (OH)
The Johns Hopkins U (MD)
Johnson C. Smith U (NC)
Johnson State Coll (VT)
Judson Coll (AL)
Judson Coll (IL)
Juniata Coll (PA)
Kalamazoo Coll (MI)
Kansas State U (KS)
Kansas Wesleyan U (KS)
Kean U (NJ)
Keene State Coll (NH)
Kennesaw State U (GA)
Kent State U (OH)
Kentucky State U (KY)
Kentucky Wesleyan Coll (KY)
Kenyon Coll (OH)
Keuka Coll (NY)
Keystone Coll (PA)
King Coll (TN)
King's Coll (PA)
The King's U Coll (AB, Canada)
Knox Coll (IL)
Kutztown U of Pennsylvania (PA)
Lafayette Coll (PA)
LaGrange Coll (GA)
Lake Erie Coll (OH)
Lake Forest Coll (IL)
Lakehead U (ON, Canada)
Lakeland Coll (WI)
Lake Superior State U (MI)
Lamar U (TX)
Lambuth U (TN)
Lander U (SC)
Lane Coll (TN)
La Roche Coll (PA)
La Salle U (PA)
Laurentian U (ON, Canada)
Lawrence U (WI)
Lebanon Valley Coll (PA)
Lehigh U (PA)
Lehman Coll of the City U of NY (NY)
Le Moyne Coll (NY)
Lenoir-Rhyne Coll (NC)
LeTourneau U (TX)
Lewis & Clark Coll (OR)
Lewis-Clark State Coll (ID)
Lewis U (IL)
Liberty U (VA)
Life U (GA)
Limestone Coll (SC)
Lincoln Memorial U (TN)
Lincoln U (MO)
Lincoln U (PA)
Lindenwood U (MO)
Lindsey Wilson Coll (KY)
Linfield Coll (OR)
Lipscomb U (TN)
Livingstone Coll (NC)
Lock Haven U of Pennsylvania (PA)
Logan U-Coll of Chiropractic (MO)
Long Island U, Brooklyn Campus (NY)
Long Island U, C.W. Post Campus (NY)
Long Island U, Southampton Coll (NY)
Longwood U (VA)
Loras Coll (IA)
Louisiana Coll (LA)
Louisiana State U and A&M Coll (LA)
Louisiana State U in Shreveport (LA)
Louisiana Tech U (LA)
Lourdes Coll (OH)
Loyola Coll in Maryland (MD)
Loyola Marymount U (CA)
Loyola U Chicago (IL)
Loyola U New Orleans (LA)
Lubbock Christian U (TX)
Luther Coll (IA)
Lycoming Coll (PA)
Lynchburg Coll (VA)
Lyon Coll (AR)
Macalester Coll (MN)
MacMurray Coll (IL)
Madonna U (MI)
Malaspina U-Coll (BC, Canada)
Malone Coll (OH)
Manchester Coll (IN)
Manhattan Coll (NY)
Manhattanville Coll (NY)
Mansfield U of Pennsylvania (PA)
Marian Coll (IN)
Marian Coll of Fond du Lac (WI)
Marietta Coll (OH)
Marist Coll (NY)
Marlboro Coll (VT)
Marquette U (WI)
Marshall U (WV)
Mars Hill Coll (NC)
Martin U (IN)
Mary Baldwin Coll (VA)
Marygrove Coll (MI)
Marymount Coll of Fordham U (NY)
Marymount Manhattan Coll (NY)
Marymount U (VA)
Maryville Coll (TN)
Maryville U of Saint Louis (MO)
Mary Washington Coll (VA)
Marywood U (PA)
Massachusetts Coll of Liberal Arts (MA)
Massachusetts Inst of Technology (MA)
The Master's Coll and Sem (CA)
Mayville State U (ND)
McDaniel Coll (MD)
McGill U (QC, Canada)
McKendree Coll (IL)
McMurry U (TX)
McNeese State U (LA)
McPherson Coll (KS)
Medaille Coll (NY)
Medgar Evers Coll of the City U of NY (NY)
Memorial U of Newfoundland (NL, Canada)
Mercer U (GA)
Mercy Coll (NY)
Mercyhurst Coll (PA)
Meredith Coll (NC)
Merrimack Coll (MA)
Messiah Coll (PA)
Methodist Coll (NC)
Metropolitan State Coll of Denver (CO)
Metropolitan State U (MN)
Miami U (OH)
Michigan State U (MI)
Michigan Technological U (MI)
MidAmerica Nazarene U (KS)
Middlebury Coll (VT)
Middle Tennessee State U (TN)
Midway Coll (KY)
Midwestern State U (TX)
Miles Coll (AL)
Millersville U of Pennsylvania (PA)
Milligan Coll (TN)
Millikin U (IL)
Millsaps Coll (MS)
Mills Coll (CA)
Minnesota State U Mankato (MN)
Minnesota State U Moorhead (MN)
Minot State U (ND)
Mississippi Coll (MS)
Mississippi State U (MS)
Mississippi Valley State U (MS)
Missouri Baptist U (MO)
Missouri Southern State U (MO)
Missouri Valley Coll (MO)
Missouri Western State Coll (MO)
Molloy Coll (NY)
Monmouth Coll (IL)
Monmouth U (NJ)
Montana State U–Billings (MT)
Montana State U–Bozeman (MT)
Montana Tech of The U of Montana (MT)
Montclair State U (NJ)
Montreat Coll (NC)
Moravian Coll (PA)
Morehead State U (KY)
Morehouse Coll (GA)
Morgan State U (MD)
Morningside Coll (IA)
Morris Coll (SC)
Mount Allison U (NB, Canada)
Mount Holyoke Coll (MA)
Mount Marty Coll (SD)
Mount Mary Coll (WI)
Mount Mercy Coll (IA)
Mount Saint Mary Coll (NY)
Mount St. Mary's Coll (CA)
Mount Saint Mary's Coll and Sem (MD)
Mount Saint Vincent U (NS, Canada)
Mount Union Coll (OH)
Mount Vernon Nazarene U (OH)
Muhlenberg Coll (PA)
Murray State U (KY)
National-Louis U (IL)
Nazareth Coll of Rochester (NY)
Nebraska Wesleyan U (NE)
Neumann Coll (PA)
Nevada State Coll at Henderson (NV)
Newberry Coll (SC)
New Coll of Florida (FL)
New Jersey City U (NJ)
New Jersey Inst of Technology (NJ)
Newman U (KS)
New Mexico Highlands U (NM)
New Mexico Inst of Mining and Technology (NM)
New Mexico State U (NM)
New York Inst of Technology (NY)
New York U (NY)
Niagara U (NY)
Nicholls State U (LA)
Nipissing U (ON, Canada)
Norfolk State U (VA)
North Carolina Central U (NC)
North Carolina State U (NC)
North Carolina Wesleyan Coll (NC)
North Central Coll (IL)
North Dakota State U (ND)
Northeastern Illinois U (IL)
Northeastern State U (OK)
Northeastern U (MA)
Northern Arizona U (AZ)
Northern Illinois U (IL)
Northern Michigan U (MI)
Northern State U (SD)
North Georgia Coll & State U (GA)
North Greenville Coll (SC)
Northland Coll (WI)
North Park U (IL)
Northwestern Coll (IA)
Northwestern Coll (MN)
Northwestern Oklahoma State U (OK)
Northwestern State U of Louisiana (LA)
Northwestern U (IL)
Northwest Nazarene U (ID)
Notre Dame Coll (OH)
Notre Dame de Namur U (CA)
Nova Southeastern U (FL)
Oakland City U (IN)
Oakland U (MI)
Oberlin Coll (OH)
Occidental Coll (CA)
Oglethorpe U (GA)
Ohio Dominican U (OH)
Ohio Northern U (OH)
The Ohio State U (OH)
The Ohio State U at Lima (OH)
Ohio U (OH)
Ohio Wesleyan U (OH)
Okanagan U Coll (BC, Canada)
Oklahoma Baptist U (OK)
Oklahoma Christian U (OK)
Oklahoma City U (OK)
Oklahoma Panhandle State U (OK)
Oklahoma State U (OK)
Old Dominion U (VA)
Olivet Coll (MI)
Olivet Nazarene U (IL)
Oral Roberts U (OK)
Oregon State U (OR)
Ottawa U (KS)
Otterbein Coll (OH)
Ouachita Baptist U (AR)
Our Lady of Holy Cross Coll (LA)
Our Lady of the Lake Coll (LA)
Our Lady of the Lake U of San Antonio (TX)
Pace U (NY)
Pacific Lutheran U (WA)
Pacific Union Coll (CA)
Pacific U (OR)
Paine Coll (GA)
Palm Beach Atlantic U (FL)
Park U (MO)
Peace Coll (NC)
Penn State U Abington Coll (PA)
Penn State U Altoona Coll (PA)
Penn State U at Erie, The Behrend Coll (PA)
Penn State U Beaver Campus of the Commonwealth Coll (PA)
Penn State U Berks Cmps of Berks-Lehigh Valley Coll (PA)
Penn State U Delaware County Campus of the Commonwealth Coll (PA)
Penn State U DuBois Campus of the Commonwealth Coll (PA)
Penn State U Fayette Campus of the Commonwealth Coll (PA)
Penn State U Hazleton Campus of the Commonwealth Coll (PA)
Penn State U Lehigh Valley Cmps of Berks-Lehigh Valley Coll (PA)
Penn State U McKeesport Campus of the Commonwealth Coll (PA)
Penn State U Mont Alto Campus of the Commonwealth Coll (PA)
Penn State U New Kensington Campus of the Commonwealth Coll (PA)
Penn State U Schuylkill Campus of the Capital Coll (PA)
Penn State U Shenango Campus of the Commonwealth Coll (PA)
Penn State U Univ Park Campus (PA)
Penn State U Wilkes-Barre Campus of the Commonwealth Coll (PA)
Penn State U Worthington Scranton Cmps Commonwealth Coll (PA)
Penn State U York Campus of the Commonwealth Coll (PA)
Pepperdine U, Malibu (CA)
Pfeiffer U (NC)
Philadelphia U (PA)
Piedmont Coll (GA)
Pikeville Coll (KY)
Pine Manor Coll (MA)
Pittsburg State U (KS)
Pitzer Coll (CA)
Plymouth State U (NH)
Point Loma Nazarene U (CA)
Point Park U (PA)
Pomona Coll (CA)
Pontifical Catholic U of Puerto Rico (PR)
Portland State U (OR)
Prairie View A&M U (TX)
Presbyterian Coll (SC)
Presentation Coll (SD)
Principia Coll (IL)
Providence Coll (RI)
Purdue U (IN)
Purdue U North Central (IN)
Queens Coll of the City U of NY (NY)
Queen's U at Kingston (ON, Canada)
Queens U of Charlotte (NC)
Quincy U (IL)
Quinnipiac U (CT)
Radford U (VA)
Ramapo Coll of New Jersey (NJ)
Randolph-Macon Coll (VA)
Randolph-Macon Woman's Coll (VA)
Redeemer U Coll (ON, Canada)
Reed Coll (OR)
Regis Coll (MA)
Regis U (CO)
Reinhardt Coll (GA)
Rensselaer Polytechnic Inst (NY)
Rhode Island Coll (RI)
Rhodes Coll (TN)
Rice U (TX)
The Richard Stockton Coll of New Jersey (NJ)
Rider U (NJ)
Ripon Coll (WI)
Rivier Coll (NH)
Roanoke Coll (VA)
Roberts Wesleyan Coll (NY)
Rochester Inst of Technology (NY)
Rockford Coll (IL)
Rockhurst U (MO)
Rocky Mountain Coll (MT)
Roger Williams U (RI)
Rollins Coll (FL)
Roosevelt U (IL)
Rose-Hulman Inst of Technology (IN)
Rosemont Coll (PA)
Rowan U (NJ)
Russell Sage Coll (NY)
Rutgers, The State U of New Jersey, Camden (NJ)
Rutgers, The State U of New Jersey, Newark (NJ)
Rutgers, The State U of New Jersey, New Brunswick/Piscataway (NJ)
Ryerson U (ON, Canada)
Sacred Heart U (CT)
Saginaw Valley State U (MI)
St. Ambrose U (IA)
St. Andrews Presbyterian Coll (NC)
Saint Anselm Coll (NH)
Saint Augustine's Coll (NC)
St. Bonaventure U (NY)
St. Cloud State U (MN)
St. Edward's U (TX)
St. Francis Coll (NY)
Saint Francis U (PA)
St. Francis Xavier U (NS, Canada)
St. Gregory's U (OK)
St. John Fisher Coll (NY)
Saint John's U (MN)
St. John's U (NY)
Saint Joseph Coll (CT)
Saint Joseph's Coll (IN)
St. Joseph's Coll, New York (NY)
Saint Joseph's Coll of Maine (ME)
St. Joseph's Coll, Suffolk Campus (NY)
Saint Joseph's U (PA)
St. Lawrence U (NY)
Saint Leo U (FL)
Saint Louis U (MO)
Saint Martin's Coll (WA)
Saint Mary-of-the-Woods Coll (IN)
Saint Mary's Coll (IN)
Saint Mary's Coll of California (CA)
St. Mary's Coll of Maryland (MD)
Saint Mary's U of Minnesota (MN)
St. Mary's U of San Antonio (TX)
Saint Michael's Coll (VT)
St. Norbert Coll (WI)
St. Olaf Coll (MN)
St. Thomas Aquinas Coll (NY)
St. Thomas U (FL)
Saint Vincent Coll (PA)
Saint Xavier U (IL)
Salem Coll (NC)
Salem State Coll (MA)
Salisbury U (MD)
Salve Regina U (RI)
Samford U (AL)
Sam Houston State U (TX)
San Diego State U (CA)
San Francisco State U (CA)
San Jose State U (CA)
Santa Clara U (CA)
Sarah Lawrence Coll (NY)
Schreiner U (TX)
Scripps Coll (CA)
Seattle Pacific U (WA)
Seattle U (WA)
Seton Hall U (NJ)
Seton Hill U (PA)
Shawnee State U (OH)
Shaw U (NC)
Shenandoah U (VA)
Shepherd U (WV)
Shippensburg U of Pennsylvania (PA)
Shorter Coll (GA)
Siena Coll (NY)
Siena Heights U (MI)
Silver Lake Coll (WI)
Simmons Coll (MA)
Simon Fraser U (BC, Canada)
Simon's Rock Coll of Bard (MA)
Simpson Coll (IA)
Skidmore Coll (NY)
Slippery Rock U of Pennsylvania (PA)
Smith Coll (MA)
Sonoma State U (CA)
South Carolina State U (SC)
South Dakota State U (SD)
Southeastern Coll of the Assemblies of God (FL)
Southeastern Louisiana U (LA)
Southeastern Oklahoma State U (OK)
Southeast Missouri State U (MO)
Southern Adventist U (TN)
Southern Arkansas U–Magnolia (AR)
Southern Connecticut State U (CT)
Southern Illinois U Carbondale (IL)
Southern Illinois U Edwardsville (IL)
Southern Methodist U (TX)
Southern Nazarene U (OK)
Southern Oregon U (OR)
Southern Polytechnic State U (GA)
Southern U and A&M Coll (LA)
Southern Utah U (UT)
Southern Virginia U (VA)
Southern Wesleyan U (SC)
Southwest Baptist U (MO)
Southwestern Coll (KS)
Southwestern Oklahoma State U (OK)
Southwestern U (TX)
Southwest Missouri State U (MO)
Spelman Coll (GA)
Spring Arbor U (MI)
Springfield Coll (MA)
Spring Hill Coll (AL)
Stanford U (CA)
State U of NY at Binghamton (NY)
State U of NY at New Paltz (NY)
State U of NY at Oswego (NY)
Plattsburgh State U of NY (NY)
State U of NY Coll at Brockport (NY)
State U of NY Coll at Cortland (NY)
State U of NY Coll at Fredonia (NY)

State U of NY Coll at Geneseo (NY)
State U of NY Coll at Old Westbury (NY)
State U of NY Coll at Oneonta (NY)
State U of NY Coll at Potsdam (NY)
State U of NY Coll of Environ Sci and Forestry (NY)
State U of West Georgia (GA)
Stephens Coll (MO)
Sterling Coll (KS)
Stetson U (FL)
Stonehill Coll (MA)
Stony Brook U, State U of New York (NY)
Suffolk U (MA)
Susquehanna U (PA)
Swarthmore Coll (PA)
Sweet Briar Coll (VA)
Syracuse U (NY)
Tabor Coll (KS)
Talladega Coll (AL)
Tarleton State U (TX)
Taylor U (IN)
Teikyo Post U (CT)
Tennessee State U (TN)
Tennessee Technological U (TN)
Tennessee Wesleyan Coll (TN)
Texas A&M Intl U (TX)
Texas A&M U (TX)
Texas A&M U–Commerce (TX)
Texas A&M U–Corpus Christi (TX)
Texas A&M U–Kingsville (TX)
Texas A&M U–Texarkana (TX)
Texas Chiropractic Coll (TX)
Texas Christian U (TX)
Texas Lutheran U (TX)
Texas Southern U (TX)
Texas State U-San Marcos (TX)
Texas Tech U (TX)
Texas Wesleyan U (TX)
Texas Woman's U (TX)
Thiel Coll (PA)
Thomas Edison State Coll (NJ)
Thomas More Coll (KY)
Thomas More Coll of Liberal Arts (NH)
Thomas U (GA)
Tougaloo Coll (MS)
Towson U (MD)
Transylvania U (KY)
Trent U (ON, Canada)
Trevecca Nazarene U (TN)
Trinity Christian Coll (IL)
Trinity Coll (CT)
Trinity Coll (DC)
Trinity Intl U (IL)
Trinity U (TX)
Trinity Western U (BC, Canada)
Tri-State U (IN)
Troy State U (AL)
Troy State U Dothan (AL)
Truman State U (MO)
Tufts U (MA)
Tulane U (LA)
Tusculum Coll (TN)
Tuskegee U (AL)
Union Coll (KY)
Union Coll (NE)
Union Coll (NY)
Union U (TN)
United States Air Force Acad (CO)
United States Military Acad (NY)
Universidad Adventista de las Antillas (PR)
Université de Montréal (QC, Canada)
Université de Sherbrooke (QC, Canada)
Université Laval (QC, Canada)
State U of NY at Albany (NY)
U at Buffalo, The State U of New York (NY)
U Coll of the Cariboo (BC, Canada)
U Coll of the Fraser Valley (BC, Canada)
The U of Akron (OH)
The U of Alabama (AL)
The U of Alabama at Birmingham (AL)
The U of Alabama in Huntsville (AL)
U of Alaska Fairbanks (AK)
U of Alaska Southeast (AK)
U of Alberta (AB, Canada)
The U of Arizona (AZ)
U of Arkansas (AR)
U of Arkansas at Little Rock (AR)
U of Arkansas at Monticello (AR)
U of Bridgeport (CT)
The U of British Columbia (BC, Canada)
U of Calgary (AB, Canada)
U of Calif, Berkeley (CA)
U of Calif, Davis (CA)
U of Calif, Irvine (CA)
U of Calif, Los Angeles (CA)
U of Calif, Riverside (CA)
U of Calif, San Diego (CA)
U of Calif, Santa Barbara (CA)
U of Calif, Santa Cruz (CA)
U of Central Arkansas (AR)
U of Central Florida (FL)
U of Charleston (WV)
U of Chicago (IL)
U of Cincinnati (OH)
U of Colorado at Colorado Springs (CO)
U of Colorado at Denver (CO)
U of Connecticut (CT)
U of Dallas (TX)
U of Dayton (OH)
U of Delaware (DE)
U of Denver (CO)
U of Detroit Mercy (MI)
U of Dubuque (IA)
U of Evansville (IN)
The U of Findlay (OH)
U of Georgia (GA)
U of Great Falls (MT)
U of Guelph (ON, Canada)
U of Hartford (CT)
U of Hawaii at Hilo (HI)
U of Hawaii at Manoa (HI)
U of Houston (TX)
U of Houston–Clear Lake (TX)
U of Houston–Victoria (TX)
U of Idaho (ID)
U of Illinois at Chicago (IL)
U of Illinois at Springfield (IL)
U of Illinois at Urbana–Champaign (IL)
U of Indianapolis (IN)
The U of Iowa (IA)
U of Kansas (KS)
U of Kentucky (KY)
U of King's Coll (NS, Canada)
U of La Verne (CA)
The U of Lethbridge (AB, Canada)
U of Louisiana at Lafayette (LA)
U of Louisville (KY)
U of Maine (ME)
U of Maine at Farmington (ME)
U of Maine at Fort Kent (ME)
U of Maine at Machias (ME)
U of Maine at Presque Isle (ME)
U of Manitoba (MB, Canada)
U of Mary (ND)
U of Mary Hardin-Baylor (TX)
U of Maryland, Baltimore County (MD)
U of Maryland, Coll Park (MD)
U of Maryland Eastern Shore (MD)
U of Massachusetts Amherst (MA)
U of Massachusetts Boston (MA)
U of Massachusetts Dartmouth (MA)
U of Massachusetts Lowell (MA)
The U of Memphis (TN)
U of Miami (FL)
U of Michigan (MI)
U of Michigan–Dearborn (MI)
U of Michigan–Flint (MI)
U of Minnesota, Duluth (MN)
U of Minnesota, Morris (MN)
U of Minnesota, Twin Cities Campus (MN)
U of Mississippi (MS)
U of Missouri–Columbia (MO)
U of Missouri–Kansas City (MO)
U of Missouri–Rolla (MO)
U of Missouri–St. Louis (MO)
U of Mobile (AL)
The U of Montana–Missoula (MT)
U of Montevallo (AL)
U of Nebraska at Omaha (NE)
U of Nebraska–Lincoln (NE)
U of Nevada, Las Vegas (NV)
U of Nevada, Reno (NV)
U of New Brunswick Fredericton (NB, Canada)
U of New Hampshire (NH)
U of New Mexico (NM)
U of New Orleans (LA)
U of North Alabama (AL)
The U of North Carolina at Asheville (NC)
The U of North Carolina at Chapel Hill (NC)
The U of North Carolina at Charlotte (NC)
The U of North Carolina at Greensboro (NC)
The U of North Carolina at Pembroke (NC)
The U of North Carolina at Wilmington (NC)
U of North Dakota (ND)
U of Northern Colorado (CO)
U of Northern Iowa (IA)
U of North Florida (FL)
U of North Texas (TX)
U of Notre Dame (IN)
U of Oregon (OR)
U of Ottawa (ON, Canada)
U of Pennsylvania (PA)
U of Pittsburgh (PA)
U of Pittsburgh at Bradford (PA)
U of Pittsburgh at Greensburg (PA)
U of Pittsburgh at Johnstown (PA)
U of Portland (OR)
U of Prince Edward Island (PE, Canada)
U of Puerto Rico, Cayey U Coll (PR)
U of Puget Sound (WA)
U of Redlands (CA)
U of Regina (SK, Canada)
U of Rhode Island (RI)
U of Richmond (VA)
U of Rochester (NY)
U of St. Francis (IL)
U of Saint Francis (IN)
U of Saint Mary (KS)
U of St. Thomas (MN)
U of St. Thomas (TX)
U of San Diego (CA)
U of San Francisco (CA)
U of Saskatchewan (SK, Canada)
U of Science and Arts of Oklahoma (OK)
The U of Scranton (PA)
U of Sioux Falls (SD)
U of South Alabama (AL)
U of South Carolina (SC)
U of South Carolina Aiken (SC)
U of South Carolina Spartanburg (SC)
The U of South Dakota (SD)
U of Southern California (CA)
U of Southern Indiana (IN)
U of Southern Maine (ME)
U of South Florida (FL)
The U of Tampa (FL)
The U of Tennessee (TN)
The U of Tennessee at Chattanooga (TN)
The U of Tennessee at Martin (TN)
The U of Texas at Arlington (TX)
The U of Texas at Austin (TX)
The U of Texas at Brownsville (TX)
The U of Texas at Dallas (TX)
The U of Texas at Tyler (TX)
The U of Texas–Pan American (TX)
U of the District of Columbia (DC)
U of the Incarnate Word (TX)
U of the Ozarks (AR)
U of the Pacific (CA)
U of the Sacred Heart (PR)
U of the Sciences in Philadelphia (PA)
U of the South (TN)
U of the Virgin Islands (VI)
U of Toledo (OH)
U of Toronto (ON, Canada)
U of Tulsa (OK)
U of Utah (UT)
U of Vermont (VT)
U of Victoria (BC, Canada)
U of Virginia (VA)
The U of Virginia's Coll at Wise (VA)
U of Washington (WA)
U of Waterloo (ON, Canada)
The U of West Alabama (AL)
The U of Western Ontario (ON, Canada)
U of West Florida (FL)
U of Windsor (ON, Canada)
U of Wisconsin–Green Bay (WI)
U of Wisconsin–La Crosse (WI)
U of Wisconsin–Madison (WI)
U of Wisconsin–Milwaukee (WI)
U of Wisconsin–Oshkosh (WI)
U of Wisconsin–Platteville (WI)
U of Wisconsin–River Falls (WI)
U of Wisconsin–Stevens Point (WI)
U of Wisconsin–Superior (WI)
U of Wisconsin–Whitewater (WI)
U of Wyoming (WY)
Upper Iowa U (IA)
Urbana U (OH)
Ursinus Coll (PA)
Ursuline Coll (OH)
Utah State U (UT)
Utica Coll (NY)
Valdosta State U (GA)
Valley City State U (ND)
Valparaiso U (IN)
Vanderbilt U (TN)
Vanguard U of Southern California (CA)
Vassar Coll (NY)
Villa Julie Coll (MD)
Villanova U (PA)
Virginia Commonwealth U (VA)
Virginia Intermont Coll (VA)
Virginia Military Inst (VA)
Virginia Polytechnic Inst and State U (VA)
Virginia State U (VA)
Virginia Union U (VA)
Virginia Wesleyan Coll (VA)
Viterbo U (WI)
Voorhees Coll (SC)
Wabash Coll (IN)
Wagner Coll (NY)
Wake Forest U (NC)
Walla Walla Coll (WA)
Walsh U (OH)
Warner Pacific Coll (OR)
Warner Southern Coll (FL)
Warren Wilson Coll (NC)
Wartburg Coll (IA)
Washburn U (KS)
Washington & Jefferson Coll (PA)
Washington and Lee U (VA)
Washington Coll (MD)
Washington State U (WA)
Washington U in St. Louis (MO)
Wayland Baptist U (TX)
Waynesburg Coll (PA)
Wayne State Coll (NE)
Wayne State U (MI)
Webster U (MO)
Wellesley Coll (MA)
Wells Coll (NY)
Wesleyan Coll (GA)
Wesleyan U (CT)
Wesley Coll (DE)
West Chester U of Pennsylvania (PA)
Western Carolina U (NC)
Western Connecticut State U (CT)
Western Illinois U (IL)
Western Kentucky U (KY)
Western New England Coll (MA)
Western Oregon U (OR)
Western State Coll of Colorado (CO)
Western Washington U (WA)
Westfield State Coll (MA)
West Liberty State Coll (WV)
Westminster Coll (MO)
Westminster Coll (PA)
Westminster Coll (UT)
Westmont Coll (CA)
West Texas A&M U (TX)
West Virginia State Coll (WV)
West Virginia U (WV)
West Virginia Wesleyan Coll (WV)
Wheaton Coll (IL)
Wheaton Coll (MA)
Wheeling Jesuit U (WV)
Whitman Coll (WA)
Whitworth Coll (WA)
Wichita State U (KS)
Widener U (PA)
Wilberforce U (OH)
Wilkes U (PA)
Willamette U (OR)
William Carey Coll (MS)
William Jewell Coll (MO)
William Paterson U of New Jersey (NJ)
William Penn U (IA)
Williams Baptist Coll (AR)
Williams Coll (MA)
William Woods U (MO)
Wilson Coll (PA)
Wingate U (NC)
Winona State U (MN)
Winston-Salem State U (NC)
Winthrop U (SC)
Wisconsin Lutheran Coll (WI)
Wittenberg U (OH)
Wofford Coll (SC)
Worcester Polytechnic Inst (MA)
Worcester State Coll (MA)
Wright State U (OH)
Xavier U (OH)
Xavier U of Louisiana (LA)
Yale U (CT)
York Coll (NE)
York Coll of Pennsylvania (PA)
York Coll of the City U of New York (NY)
York U (ON, Canada)
Youngstown State U (OH)

BIOLOGY/BIOTECHNOLOGY LABORATORY TECHNICIAN

California State Polytechnic U, Pomona (CA)
California State U, Sacramento (CA)
Carleton U (ON, Canada)
Cleveland State U (OH)
Elizabeth City State U (NC)
Harvard U (MA)
Marywood U (PA)
Michigan Technological U (MI)
Minnesota State U Mankato (MN)
Niagara U (NY)
Northeastern U (MA)
Penn State U Abington Coll (PA)
Penn State U Altoona Coll (PA)
Penn State U at Erie, The Behrend Coll (PA)
Penn State U Beaver Campus of the Commonwealth Coll (PA)
Penn State U Berks Cmps of Berks-Lehigh Valley Coll (PA)
Penn State U Delaware County Campus of the Commonwealth Coll (PA)
Penn State U DuBois Campus of the Commonwealth Coll (PA)
Penn State U Fayette Campus of the Commonwealth Coll (PA)
Penn State U Hazleton Campus of the Commonwealth Coll (PA)
Penn State U Lehigh Valley Cmps of Berks-Lehigh Valley Coll (PA)
Penn State U McKeesport Campus of the Commonwealth Coll (PA)
Penn State U Mont Alto Campus of the Commonwealth Coll (PA)
Penn State U New Kensington Campus of the Commonwealth Coll (PA)
Penn State U Schuylkill Campus of the Capital Coll (PA)
Penn State U Shenango Campus of the Commonwealth Coll (PA)
Penn State U Univ Park Campus (PA)
Penn State U Wilkes-Barre Campus of the Commonwealth Coll (PA)
Penn State U Worthington Scranton Cmps Commonwealth Coll (PA)
Penn State U York Campus of the Commonwealth Coll (PA)
Point Park U (PA)
St. Cloud State U (MN)
State U of NY Coll at Brockport (NY)
State U of NY Coll at Fredonia (NY)
State U of NY Coll at Oneonta (NY)
Suffolk U (MA)
Université de Sherbrooke (QC, Canada)
U of Alberta (AB, Canada)
U of Delaware (DE)
U of New Haven (CT)
U of Ottawa (ON, Canada)
U of Vermont (VT)
Villa Julie Coll (MD)
Westminster Coll (PA)
Worcester Polytechnic Inst (MA)
York Coll of the City U of New York (NY)

BIOLOGY TEACHER EDUCATION

Abilene Christian U (TX)
Alma Coll (MI)
Alvernia Coll (PA)
Anderson Coll (SC)
Appalachian State U (NC)
Arkansas State U (AR)
Arkansas Tech U (AR)
Averett U (VA)
Baylor U (TX)
Berea Coll (KY)
Bethany Coll (KS)
Bethel Coll (TN)
Bethel U (MN)
Bethune-Cookman Coll (FL)
Bishop's U (QC, Canada)
Bloomfield Coll (NJ)
Bluefield Coll (VA)
Blue Mountain Coll (MS)
Bowling Green State U (OH)
Brewton-Parker Coll (GA)
Bridgewater Coll (VA)
Brigham Young U–Hawaii (HI)
Brooklyn Coll of the City U of NY (NY)
Buena Vista U (IA)
Cabrini Coll (PA)
California State U, Chico (CA)
California State U, Long Beach (CA)
Campbellsville U (KY)
Campbell U (NC)
Capital U (OH)
Carroll Coll (MT)
Carroll Coll (WI)
The Catholic U of America (DC)
Cedarville U (OH)
Centenary Coll of Louisiana (LA)
Central Methodist Coll (MO)
Central Michigan U (MI)
Central Missouri State U (MO)

Central Washington U (WA)
Chadron State Coll (NE)
Charleston Southern U (SC)
Christian Brothers U (TN)
Citadel, The Military Coll of South Carolina (SC)
City Coll of the City U of NY (NY)
Clearwater Christian Coll (FL)
Coker Coll (SC)
The Coll of New Jersey (NJ)
Coll of St. Catherine (MN)
The Coll of Saint Rose (NY)
The Coll of St. Scholastica (MN)
Coll of the Ozarks (MO)
Colorado State U (CO)
Columbus State U (GA)
Concordia Coll (MN)
Concordia U (IL)
Concordia U (MI)
Concordia U (NE)
Concordia U, St. Paul (MN)
Cornerstone U (MI)
Crichton Coll (TN)
Cumberland U (TN)
Daemen Coll (NY)
Dakota Wesleyan U (SD)
Delaware State U (DE)
Delta State U (MS)
Dillard U (LA)
Dominican Coll (NY)
Dordt Coll (IA)
Dowling Coll (NY)
Duquesne U (PA)
East Central U (OK)
Eastern Mennonite U (VA)
Eastern Michigan U (MI)
East Texas Baptist U (TX)
Elizabeth City State U (NC)
Elmhurst Coll (IL)
Elmira Coll (NY)
Evangel U (MO)
Fayetteville State U (NC)
Florida Inst of Technology (FL)
Framingham State Coll (MA)
Franklin Coll (IN)
Freed-Hardeman U (TN)
George Fox U (OR)
Georgian Court U (NJ)
Georgia Southern U (GA)
Glenville State Coll (WV)
Greensboro Coll (NC)
Greenville Coll (IL)
Gustavus Adolphus Coll (MN)
Harding U (AR)
Hardin-Simmons U (TX)
Hastings Coll (NE)
Hofstra U (NY)
Hope Coll (MI)
Houston Baptist U (TX)
Howard Payne U (TX)
Hunter Coll of the City U of NY (NY)
Husson Coll (ME)
Illinois Wesleyan U (IL)
Indiana U Bloomington (IN)
Indiana U Northwest (IN)
Indiana U–Purdue U Fort Wayne (IN)
Indiana U South Bend (IN)
Indiana U Southeast (IN)
Inter American U of PR, Aguadilla Campus (PR)
Iona Coll (NY)
Ithaca Coll (NY)
Jamestown Coll (ND)
Johnson State Coll (VT)
Juniata Coll (PA)
Kennesaw State U (GA)
Kentucky Wesleyan Coll (KY)
Keuka Coll (NY)
King Coll (TN)
Lambuth U (TN)
La Roche Coll (PA)
Lebanon Valley Coll (PA)
Le Moyne Coll (NY)
Liberty U (VA)
Limestone Coll (SC)
Lincoln Memorial U (TN)
Lindenwood U (MO)
Lindsey Wilson Coll (KY)
Lipscomb U (TN)
Long Island U, C.W. Post Campus (NY)
Long Island U, Southampton Coll (NY)
Louisiana State U in Shreveport (LA)
Louisiana Tech U (LA)
Manhattanville Coll (NY)
Mansfield U of Pennsylvania (PA)
Marian Coll of Fond du Lac (WI)
Marymount Coll of Fordham U (NY)
Maryville Coll (TN)
Maryville U of Saint Louis (MO)
Marywood U (PA)
Mayville State U (ND)
McGill U (QC, Canada)
McKendree Coll (IL)
McNeese State U (LA)
Mercyhurst Coll (PA)
Messiah Coll (PA)
Miami Dade Coll (FL)
Miami U (OH)
Minot State U (ND)
Molloy Coll (NY)
Montana State U–Billings (MT)
Moravian Coll (PA)
Morris Coll (SC)
Mount Mary Coll (WI)
Murray State U (KY)
Nazareth Coll of Rochester (NY)
Nevada State Coll at Henderson (NV)
New York Inst of Technology (NY)
New York U (NY)
Niagara U (NY)
North Carolina Central U (NC)
North Carolina State U (NC)
North Dakota State U (ND)
Northern Arizona U (AZ)
Northern Michigan U (MI)
Northwestern Coll (IA)
Northwest Nazarene U (ID)
Oakland City U (IN)
Ohio Northern U (OH)
Ohio U (OH)
Ohio Wesleyan U (OH)
Oklahoma Baptist U (OK)
Pace U (NY)
Paine Coll (GA)
Pikeville Coll (KY)
Pittsburg State U (KS)
Point Park U (PA)
Pontifical Catholic U of Puerto Rico (PR)
Rivier Coll (NH)
Roberts Wesleyan Coll (NY)
Rocky Mountain Coll (MT)
Sacred Heart U (CT)
St. Ambrose U (IA)
Saint Augustine's Coll (NC)
St. Bonaventure U (NY)
St. Edward's U (TX)
St. Francis Coll (NY)
Saint Francis U (PA)
St. Gregory's U (OK)
St. John's U (NY)
Saint Joseph's Coll of Maine (ME)
Saint Xavier U (IL)
Salve Regina U (RI)
Samford U (AL)
San Diego State U (CA)
Seattle Pacific U (WA)
Seton Hill U (PA)
Southern Arkansas U–Magnolia (AR)
Southwest Missouri State U (MO)
State U of NY Coll at Brockport (NY)
State U of NY Coll at Cortland (NY)
State U of NY Coll at Old Westbury (NY)
State U of NY Coll at Oneonta (NY)
State U of NY Coll at Potsdam (NY)
State U of NY Coll of Environ Sci and Forestry (NY)
State U of West Georgia (GA)
Syracuse U (NY)
Talladega Coll (AL)
Taylor U (IN)
Tennessee Wesleyan Coll (TN)
Texas A&M Intl U (TX)
Texas Wesleyan U (TX)
Trevecca Nazarene U (TN)
Trinity Christian Coll (IL)
Union Coll (NE)
Universidad Adventista de las Antillas (PR)
State U of NY at Albany (NY)
The U of Akron (OH)
The U of Arizona (AZ)
U of Arkansas at Fort Smith (AR)
U of Charleston (WV)
U of Delaware (DE)
U of Dubuque (IA)
U of Great Falls (MT)
U of Illinois at Chicago (IL)
The U of Iowa (IA)
U of Louisiana at Lafayette (LA)
U of Maine at Farmington (ME)
U of Maine at Machias (ME)
U of Mary (ND)
U of Michigan–Flint (MI)
U of Missouri–Columbia (MO)
U of Missouri–St. Louis (MO)
The U of Montana–Western (MT)
U of Nebraska–Lincoln (NE)
The U of North Carolina at Greensboro (NC)
The U of North Carolina at Pembroke (NC)
The U of North Carolina at Wilmington (NC)
U of Pittsburgh at Johnstown (PA)
U of Puerto Rico, Cayey U Coll (PR)
U of Regina (SK, Canada)
U of Saint Francis (IN)
U of St. Thomas (MN)
The U of South Dakota (SD)
The U of Tennessee at Martin (TN)
U of the Ozarks (AR)
U of Utah (UT)
U of Washington (WA)
U of Waterloo (ON, Canada)
U of Windsor (ON, Canada)
U of Wisconsin–River Falls (WI)
U of Wisconsin–Superior (WI)
Utah State U (UT)
Utica Coll (NY)
Valley City State U (ND)
Valparaiso U (IN)
Virginia Intermont Coll (VA)
Viterbo U (WI)
Washington U in St. Louis (MO)
Waynesburg Coll (PA)
Weber State U (UT)
West Chester U of Pennsylvania (PA)
Western Baptist Coll (OR)
Westminster Coll (UT)
Wheeling Jesuit U (WV)
Widener U (PA)
William Carey Coll (MS)
Xavier U (OH)
Xavier U of Louisiana (LA)
York Coll (NE)
York U (ON, Canada)
Youngstown State U (OH)

BIOMATHEMATICS AND BIOINFORMATICS RELATED
Cornell U (NY)
Florida State U (FL)
U of Calif, Los Angeles (CA)
The U of Scranton (PA)

BIOMEDICAL/MEDICAL ENGINEERING
Arizona State U (AZ)
Boston U (MA)
Brown U (RI)
Bucknell U (PA)
California Lutheran U (CA)
California State U, Long Beach (CA)
Carnegie Mellon U (PA)
Case Western Reserve U (OH)
The Catholic U of America (DC)
Cedar Crest Coll (PA)
City Coll of the City U of NY (NY)
Clemson U (SC)
The Coll of New Jersey (NJ)
Columbia U, School of Eng & Applied Sci (NY)
Cornell U (NY)
Dalhousie U (NS, Canada)
Drexel U (PA)
Duke U (NC)
Eastern Nazarene Coll (MA)
Florida Intl U (FL)
Florida State U (FL)
Georgia Inst of Technology (GA)
Harvard U (MA)
Hofstra U (NY)
Illinois Inst of Technology (IL)
Indiana U–Purdue U Indianapolis (IN)
The Johns Hopkins U (MD)
Kettering U (MI)
Lehigh U (PA)
LeTourneau U (TX)
Louisiana State U and A&M Coll (LA)
Louisiana Tech U (LA)
Marquette U (WI)
Michigan State U (MI)
Milwaukee School of Eng (WI)
Mississippi State U (MS)
New Jersey Inst of Technology (NJ)
North Carolina State U (NC)
Northwestern U (IL)
Oklahoma State U (OK)
Oral Roberts U (OK)
Penn State U Abington Coll (PA)
Penn State U Altoona Coll (PA)
Penn State U at Erie, The Behrend Coll (PA)
Penn State U Beaver Campus of the Commonwealth Coll (PA)
Penn State U Berks Cmps of Berks-Lehigh Valley Coll (PA)
Penn State U Delaware County Campus of the Commonwealth Coll (PA)
Penn State U DuBois Campus of the Commonwealth Coll (PA)
Penn State U Fayette Campus of the Commonwealth Coll (PA)
Penn State U Hazleton Campus of the Commonwealth Coll (PA)
Penn State U Lehigh Valley Cmps of Berks-Lehigh Valley Coll (PA)
Penn State U McKeesport Campus of the Commonwealth Coll (PA)
Penn State U Mont Alto Campus of the Commonwealth Coll (PA)
Penn State U New Kensington Campus of the Commonwealth Coll (PA)
Penn State U Schuylkill Campus of the Capital Coll (PA)
Penn State U Shenango Campus of the Commonwealth Coll (PA)
Penn State U Univ Park Campus (PA)
Penn State U Wilkes-Barre Campus of the Commonwealth Coll (PA)
Penn State U Worthington Scranton Cmps Commonwealth Coll (PA)
Penn State U York Campus of the Commonwealth Coll (PA)
Rensselaer Polytechnic Inst (NY)
Rice U (TX)
Rochester Inst of Technology (NY)
Rose-Hulman Inst of Technology (IN)
Rutgers, The State U of New Jersey, New Brunswick/Piscataway (NJ)
Saint Louis U (MO)
State U of NY at Binghamton (NY)
Stevens Inst of Technology (NJ)
Stony Brook U, State U of New York (NY)
Syracuse U (NY)
Texas A&M U (TX)
Trinity Coll (CT)
Trinity Coll (DC)
Tulane U (LA)
The U of Akron (OH)
The U of Alabama at Birmingham (AL)
The U of British Columbia (BC, Canada)
U of Calif, Berkeley (CA)
U of Calif, Davis (CA)
U of Calif, Irvine (CA)
U of Calif, Los Angeles (CA)
U of Calif, San Diego (CA)
U of Connecticut (CT)
U of Guelph (ON, Canada)
U of Hartford (CT)
U of Houston (TX)
U of Idaho (ID)
U of Illinois at Chicago (IL)
U of Illinois at Urbana–Champaign (IL)
The U of Iowa (IA)
U of Miami (FL)
U of Nebraska–Lincoln (NE)
U of Oklahoma (OK)
U of Pennsylvania (PA)
U of Pittsburgh (PA)
U of Rhode Island (RI)
U of Rochester (NY)
U of Southern California (CA)
The U of Texas at Austin (TX)
U of the Pacific (CA)
U of Toledo (OH)
U of Toronto (ON, Canada)
U of Utah (UT)
U of Virginia (VA)
U of Wisconsin–Madison (WI)
Vanderbilt U (TN)
Virginia Commonwealth U (VA)
Walla Walla Coll (WA)
Washington U in St. Louis (MO)
Western New England Coll (MA)
Worcester Polytechnic Inst (MA)
Wright State U (OH)
Yale U (CT)

BIOMEDICAL SCIENCE
U of Calgary (AB, Canada)

BIOMEDICAL SCIENCES
Albany Coll of Pharmacy of Union U (NY)
Antioch Coll (OH)
Auburn U (AL)
Brigham Young U (UT)
Brock U (ON, Canada)
Brown U (RI)
Cedar Crest Coll (PA)
City Coll of the City U of NY (NY)
Emory U (GA)
Florida Inst of Technology (FL)
Framingham State Coll (MA)
Grand Valley State U (MI)
Harvard U (MA)
Immaculata U (PA)
Inter American U of PR, San Germán Campus (PR)
Keuka Coll (NY)
Marquette U (WI)
Our Lady of the Lake Coll (LA)
Rutgers, The State U of New Jersey, New Brunswick/Piscataway (NJ)
St. Cloud State U (MN)
St. Francis Coll (NY)
St. Gregory's U (OK)
State U of NY Coll at Fredonia (NY)
Stephens Coll (MO)
Suffolk U (MA)
Texas A&M U (TX)
Université de Montréal (QC, Canada)
U of Calif, Riverside (CA)
U of Guelph (ON, Canada)
U of Michigan (MI)
U of Mississippi (MS)
U of Ottawa (ON, Canada)
U of Pennsylvania (PA)
U of South Alabama (AL)
U of Utah (UT)
U of Wisconsin–Eau Claire (WI)
U of Wisconsin–Green Bay (WI)
Worcester Polytechnic Inst (MA)

BIOMEDICAL TECHNOLOGY
Alfred U (NY)
Alvernia Coll (PA)
Andrews U (MI)
California State U, Hayward (CA)
Cedar Crest Coll (PA)
Colorado State U-Pueblo (CO)
New York Inst of Technology (NY)
Oral Roberts U (OK)
Rutgers, The State U of New Jersey, Camden (NJ)
Suffolk U (MA)
Texas Southern U (TX)
Thomas Edison State Coll (NJ)
U of New Hampshire (NH)
Walla Walla Coll (WA)
Wright State U (OH)

BIOMETRY/BIOMETRICS
Cornell U (NY)
Harvard U (MA)
Rutgers, The State U of New Jersey, New Brunswick/Piscataway (NJ)
U of Michigan (MI)

BIOPHYSICS
Andrews U (MI)
Barnard Coll (NY)
Brandeis U (MA)
Brigham Young U (UT)
Brown U (RI)
Carnegie Mellon U (PA)
Centenary Coll of Louisiana (LA)
Claremont McKenna Coll (CA)
Clarkson U (NY)
Columbia Coll (NY)
Cornell U (NY)
Freed-Hardeman U (TN)
Hampden-Sydney Coll (VA)
Hampshire Coll (MA)
Harvard U (MA)
Haverford Coll (PA)
Illinois Inst of Technology (IL)
Iowa State U of Science and Technology (IA)
The Johns Hopkins U (MD)
King Coll (TN)
Laurentian U (ON, Canada)
Longwood U (VA)
Oklahoma City U (OK)
Oregon State U (OR)
Pacific Union Coll (CA)
Rensselaer Polytechnic Inst (NY)
St. Bonaventure U (NY)
St. Lawrence U (NY)
Saint Mary's U of Minnesota (MN)
Southwestern Oklahoma State U (OK)
State U of NY Coll at Geneseo (NY)
Suffolk U (MA)
U at Buffalo, The State U of New York (NY)
The U of British Columbia (BC, Canada)
U of Calif, Los Angeles (CA)
U of Calif, San Diego (CA)
U of Connecticut (CT)
U of Guelph (ON, Canada)
U of Illinois at Urbana–Champaign (IL)
U of Miami (FL)

U of Michigan (MI)
U of New Brunswick Fredericton (NB, Canada)
U of Pennsylvania (PA)
The U of Scranton (PA)
U of Southern California (CA)
U of Southern Indiana (IN)
U of Toronto (ON, Canada)
The U of Western Ontario (ON, Canada)
U of Windsor (ON, Canada)
Walla Walla Coll (WA)
Washington State U (WA)
Washington U in St. Louis (MO)
Whitman Coll (WA)

BIOPSYCHOLOGY
Barnard Coll (NY)
Bucknell U (PA)
Chapman U (CA)
The Coll of William and Mary (VA)
Columbia Coll (NY)
Cornell U (NY)
Hastings Coll (NE)
Morningside Coll (IA)
Mount Allison U (NB, Canada)
Nebraska Wesleyan U (NE)
Philadelphia U (PA)
Rider U (NJ)
Rochester Inst of Technology (NY)
Russell Sage Coll (NY)
U of Calif, Santa Barbara (CA)
U of Denver (CO)
U of Pittsburgh at Johnstown (PA)
U of Windsor (ON, Canada)
Washington U in St. Louis (MO)

BIOSTATISTICS
Brigham Young U (UT)
Tulane U (LA)
U of Calif, Los Angeles (CA)
The U of North Carolina at Chapel Hill (NC)
U of Washington (WA)

BIOTECHNOLOGY
Assumption Coll (MA)
Bay Path Coll (MA)
Brigham Young U (UT)
British Columbia Inst of Technology (BC, Canada)
Brock U (ON, Canada)
Cabrini Coll (PA)
Calvin Coll (MI)
Clarkson U (NY)
Delaware State U (DE)
Eastern Washington U (WA)
East Stroudsburg U of Pennsylvania (PA)
Elizabethtown Coll (PA)
Florida Gulf Coast U (FL)
Framingham State Coll (MA)
Gannon U (PA)
Kent State U (OH)
Louisiana State U and A&M Coll (LA)
Manhattan Coll (NY)
Missouri Southern State U (MO)
Montana State U–Bozeman (MT)
North Dakota State U (ND)
The Ohio State U (OH)
Plymouth State U (NH)
Point Park U (PA)
Rochester Inst of Technology (NY)
Roosevelt U (IL)
Rutgers, The State U of New Jersey, New Brunswick/Piscataway (NJ)
Southeastern Oklahoma State U (OK)
State U of NY Coll at Brockport (NY)
State U of NY Coll of Environ Sci and Forestry (NY)
Thomas Jefferson U (PA)
Université de Sherbrooke (QC, Canada)
U at Buffalo, The State U of New York (NY)
The U of British Columbia (BC, Canada)
U of Calif, Los Angeles (CA)
U of Calif, San Diego (CA)
U of Delaware (DE)
U of Georgia (GA)
U of Guelph (ON, Canada)
The U of Lethbridge (AB, Canada)
U of Nebraska at Omaha (NE)
U of Nevada, Reno (NV)
U of Northern Iowa (IA)
U of Saskatchewan (SK, Canada)
U of Southern Maine (ME)
U of Waterloo (ON, Canada)
U of Windsor (ON, Canada)
U of Wisconsin–River Falls (WI)
Ursuline Coll (OH)
Washington State U (WA)
West Texas A&M U (TX)
Worcester State Coll (MA)
York U (ON, Canada)

BIOTECHNOLOGY RESEARCH
Hunter Coll of the City U of NY (NY)
Kennesaw State U (GA)

BOTANY/PLANT BIOLOGY
Andrews U (MI)
Arizona State U (AZ)
Auburn U (AL)
Ball State U (IN)
Brigham Young U (UT)
California State Polytechnic U, Pomona (CA)
California State U, Long Beach (CA)
Carleton U (ON, Canada)
Coll of the Atlantic (ME)
Colorado State U (CO)
Connecticut Coll (CT)
Cornell U (NY)
Fort Valley State U (GA)
Goddard Coll (VT)
Hampshire Coll (MA)
Humboldt State U (CA)
Idaho State U (ID)
Iowa State U of Science and Technology (IA)
Juniata Coll (PA)
Kent State U (OH)
Marlboro Coll (VT)
Mars Hill Coll (NC)
McGill U (QC, Canada)
Miami U (OH)
Michigan State U (MI)
Minnesota State U Mankato (MN)
North Carolina State U (NC)
North Dakota State U (ND)
Northern Arizona U (AZ)
Northern Michigan U (MI)
The Ohio State U (OH)
Ohio U (OH)
Ohio Wesleyan U (OH)
Oklahoma State U (OK)
Oregon State U (OR)
Purdue U (IN)
Rutgers, The State U of New Jersey, Newark (NJ)
St. Cloud State U (MN)
Saint Xavier U (IL)
San Francisco State U (CA)
Sonoma State U (CA)
Southeastern Oklahoma State U (OK)
Southern Connecticut State U (CT)
Southern Illinois U Carbondale (IL)
Southern Utah U (UT)
State U of NY Coll of Environ Sci and Forestry (NY)
Texas A&M U (TX)
Texas State U-San Marcos (TX)
The U of Akron (OH)
U of Alberta (AB, Canada)
U of Arkansas (AR)
U of Calgary (AB, Canada)
U of Calif, Berkeley (CA)
U of Calif, Davis (CA)
U of Calif, Los Angeles (CA)
U of Calif, Riverside (CA)
U of Calif, Santa Cruz (CA)
U of Delaware (DE)
U of Florida (FL)
U of Georgia (GA)
U of Great Falls (MT)
U of Guelph (ON, Canada)
U of Hawaii at Manoa (HI)
U of Idaho (ID)
U of Illinois at Urbana–Champaign (IL)
U of Maine (ME)
U of Manitoba (MB, Canada)
U of Michigan (MI)
U of Minnesota, Twin Cities Campus (MN)
The U of Montana–Missoula (MT)
U of New Brunswick Fredericton (NB, Canada)
U of New Hampshire (NH)
U of Oklahoma (OK)
The U of Tennessee (TN)
The U of Texas at Austin (TX)
U of Toronto (ON, Canada)
U of Vermont (VT)
U of Victoria (BC, Canada)
U of Washington (WA)
U of Wisconsin–Madison (WI)
U of Wyoming (WY)
Utah State U (UT)
Washington State U (WA)
Weber State U (UT)

BOTANY/PLANT BIOLOGY RELATED
McGill U (QC, Canada)
Miami U Hamilton (OH)

BROADCAST JOURNALISM
Adrian Coll (MI)
Alderson-Broaddus Coll (WV)
American U (DC)
Auburn U (AL)
Baldwin-Wallace Coll (OH)
Barry U (FL)
Belmont U (TN)
Bemidji State U (MN)
Bowie State U (MD)
Bowling Green State U (OH)
Bradley U (IL)
Brigham Young U (UT)
Brooklyn Coll of the City U of NY (NY)
State U of NY Coll at Buffalo (NY)
California State U, Hayward (CA)
California State U, Long Beach (CA)
Calvary Bible Coll and Theological Sem (MO)
Campbell U (NC)
Carson-Newman Coll (TN)
Cedarville U (OH)
Chapman U (CA)
Chicago State U (IL)
The Coll of New Rochelle (NY)
Coll of the Ozarks (MO)
Colorado State U-Pueblo (CO)
Columbia Coll Chicago (IL)
Columbia Coll Hollywood (CA)
Columbia Union Coll (MD)
Concordia Coll (MN)
Delaware State U (DE)
Drake U (IA)
Drury U (MO)
East Carolina U (NC)
Eastern Kentucky U (KY)
Edinboro U of Pennsylvania (PA)
Elon U (NC)
Emerson Coll (MA)
Evangel U (MO)
Florida Intl U (FL)
Florida Southern Coll (FL)
Fontbonne U (MO)
Fordham U (NY)
Gettysburg Coll (PA)
Gonzaga U (WA)
Goshen Coll (IN)
Grace U (NE)
Grand Valley State U (MI)
Hampton U (VA)
Harding U (AR)
Hardin-Simmons U (TX)
Hastings Coll (NE)
Hofstra U (NY)
Howard U (DC)
Humboldt State U (CA)
Huntington Coll (IN)
Indiana U Bloomington (IN)
Ithaca Coll (NY)
John Brown U (AR)
Lamar U (TX)
La Salle U (PA)
Lewis U (IL)
Liberty U (VA)
Lindenwood U (MO)
Long Island U, C.W. Post Campus (NY)
Louisiana Coll (LA)
Mansfield U of Pennsylvania (PA)
Marist Coll (NY)
Marquette U (WI)
Marywood U (PA)
Massachusetts Coll of Liberal Arts (MA)
Mercyhurst Coll (PA)
Minnesota State U Moorhead (MN)
Montclair State U (NJ)
Morris Coll (SC)
Mount Vernon Nazarene U (OH)
New England School of Communications (ME)
North Central Coll (IL)
North Central U (MN)
Northern Michigan U (MI)
Ohio U (OH)
Ohio Wesleyan U (OH)
Oklahoma Baptist U (OK)
Oklahoma Christian U (OK)
Oklahoma City U (OK)
Oklahoma State U (OK)
Olivet Nazarene U (IL)
Pacific Lutheran U (WA)
Pacific U (OR)
Paine Coll (GA)
Palm Beach Atlantic U (FL)
Pittsburg State U (KS)
Point Loma Nazarene U (CA)
Point Park U (PA)
Quinnipiac U (CT)
Reformed Bible Coll (MI)
Ryerson U (ON, Canada)
St. Cloud State U (MN)
St. Gregory's U (OK)
Southern Adventist U (TN)
Southern Arkansas U–Magnolia (AR)
Southern Methodist U (TX)
Southern Nazarene U (OK)
State U of NY at New Paltz (NY)
Plattsburgh State U of NY (NY)
State U of NY Coll at Brockport (NY)
State U of NY Coll at Fredonia (NY)
Stephens Coll (MO)
Suffolk U (MA)
Susquehanna U (PA)
Syracuse U (NY)
Texas Christian U (TX)
Troy State U (AL)
Union U (TN)
The U of Akron (OH)
U of Cincinnati (OH)
U of Colorado at Boulder (CO)
U of Dayton (OH)
U of Detroit Mercy (MI)
The U of Findlay (OH)
U of Georgia (GA)
U of Illinois at Urbana–Champaign (IL)
U of Kansas (KS)
U of La Verne (CA)
U of Miami (FL)
U of Missouri–Columbia (MO)
U of Montevallo (AL)
U of Nebraska at Omaha (NE)
U of Nebraska–Lincoln (NE)
U of Nevada, Reno (NV)
U of Northern Iowa (IA)
U of North Texas (TX)
U of Oklahoma (OK)
U of Oregon (OR)
U of St. Thomas (MN)
U of South Carolina (SC)
U of Southern California (CA)
The U of Tennessee at Martin (TN)
U of Utah (UT)
U of Windsor (ON, Canada)
U of Wisconsin–Madison (WI)
U of Wisconsin–Milwaukee (WI)
U of Wisconsin–Oshkosh (WI)
U of Wisconsin–Platteville (WI)
U of Wisconsin–River Falls (WI)
U of Wisconsin–Superior (WI)
Waldorf Coll (IA)
Wartburg Coll (IA)
Washington State U (WA)
Webster U (MO)
Western Washington U (WA)
Westminster Coll (PA)
West Texas A&M U (TX)
William Woods U (MO)
Winona State U (MN)

BUDDHIST STUDIES
Heritage Bible Coll (NC)
U of the West (CA)

BUILDING/CONSTRUCTION FINISHING, MANAGEMENT, AND INSPECTION RELATED
Central Connecticut State U (CT)

BUILDING/HOME/ CONSTRUCTION INSPECTION
Tuskegee U (AL)

BUSINESS ADMINISTRATION AND MANAGEMENT
Abilene Christian U (TX)
Acadia U (NS, Canada)
Adams State Coll (CO)
Adelphi U (NY)
Adrian Coll (MI)
Alabama Ag and Mech U (AL)
Alabama State U (AL)
Alaska Pacific U (AK)
Albany State U (GA)
Albertson Coll of Idaho (ID)
Albion Coll (MI)
Albright Coll (PA)
Alcorn State U (MS)
Alderson-Broaddus Coll (WV)
Alfred U (NY)
Alice Lloyd Coll (KY)
Allen U (SC)
Alliant Intl U (CA)
Alliant Intl U–México City(Mexico)
Alma Coll (MI)
Alvernia Coll (PA)
Alverno Coll (WI)
Amberton U (TX)
American Coll of Computer & Information Sciences (AL)
American Coll of Thessaloniki(Greece)
American InterContinental U (CA)
American InterContinental U-London(United Kingdom)
American Intl Coll (MA)
American Public U System (WV)
American U (DC)
American U in Bulgaria(Bulgaria)
The American U in Cairo(Egypt)
The American U in Dubai(United Arab Emirates)
American U of Puerto Rico (PR)
The American U of Rome(Italy)
Anderson Coll (SC)
Andrews U (MI)
Angelo State U (TX)
Anna Maria Coll (MA)
Antioch Coll (OH)
Appalachian State U (NC)
Aquinas Coll (MI)
Arcadia U (PA)
Argosy U/Chicago (IL)
Argosy U/Sarasota (FL)
Argosy U/Tampa (FL)
Arizona State U (AZ)
Arkansas Baptist Coll (AR)
Arkansas State U (AR)
Arkansas Tech U (AR)
Ashland U (OH)
Assumption Coll (MA)
Athabasca U (AB, Canada)
Athens State U (AL)
Atlanta Christian Coll (GA)
Atlantic Baptist U (NB, Canada)
Atlantic Union Coll (MA)
Auburn U (AL)
Auburn U Montgomery (AL)
Augsburg Coll (MN)
Augustana Coll (IL)
Augustana Coll (SD)
Augusta State U (GA)
Austin Coll (TX)
Averett U (VA)
Azusa Pacific U (CA)
Babson Coll (MA)
Bacone Coll (OK)
Baker Coll of Auburn Hills (MI)
Baker Coll of Cadillac (MI)
Baker Coll of Clinton Township (MI)
Baker Coll of Flint (MI)
Baker Coll of Jackson (MI)
Baker Coll of Muskegon (MI)
Baker Coll of Owosso (MI)
Baker Coll of Port Huron (MI)
Baker U (KS)
Baldwin-Wallace Coll (OH)
Ball State U (IN)
Baltimore Intl Coll (MD)
Baptist Bible Coll (MO)
Barber-Scotia Coll (NC)
Barclay Coll (KS)
Barry U (FL)
Barton Coll (NC)
Baylor U (TX)
Beacon Coll and Graduate School (GA)
Becker Coll (MA)
Belhaven Coll (MS)
Bellarmine U (KY)
Bellevue U (NE)
Belmont Abbey Coll (NC)
Belmont U (TN)
Beloit Coll (WI)
Bemidji State U (MN)
Benedictine Coll (KS)
Bentley Coll (MA)
Berea Coll (KY)
Berkeley Coll (NJ)
Berkeley Coll-New York City Campus (NY)
Berkeley Coll-Westchester Campus (NY)
Baruch Coll of the City U of NY (NY)
Berry Coll (GA)
Bethany Coll (KS)
Bethany Lutheran Coll (MN)
Bethel Coll (IN)
Bethel Coll (TN)
Bethel U (MN)
Bethune-Cookman Coll (FL)
Biola U (CA)
Birmingham-Southern Coll (AL)
Bishop's U (QC, Canada)
Blackburn Coll (IL)
Black Hills State U (SD)
Bloomfield Coll (NJ)
Bloomsburg U of Pennsylvania (PA)
Bluefield Coll (VA)
Bluefield State Coll (WV)
Blue Mountain Coll (MS)
Bluffton Coll (OH)
Boise State U (ID)
Boston Coll (MA)

Boston U (MA)
Bowie State U (MD)
Bradley U (IL)
Brenau U (GA)
Brevard Coll (NC)
Brewton-Parker Coll (GA)
Briar Cliff U (IA)
Bridgewater Coll (VA)
Bridgewater State Coll (MA)
Briercrest Bible Coll (SK, Canada)
Brigham Young U (UT)
Brigham Young U–Hawaii (HI)
British Columbia Inst of Technology (BC, Canada)
Brock U (ON, Canada)
Bryan Coll (TN)
Bryant Coll (RI)
Bucknell U (PA)
State U of NY Coll at Buffalo (NY)
Butler U (IN)
Cabrini Coll (PA)
Caldwell Coll (NJ)
California Baptist U (CA)
California Lutheran U (CA)
California Maritime Acad (CA)
California Polytechnic State U, San Luis Obispo (CA)
California State Polytechnic U, Pomona (CA)
California State U, Chico (CA)
California State U, Dominguez Hills (CA)
California State U, Fresno (CA)
California State U, Fullerton (CA)
California State U, Hayward (CA)
California State U, Long Beach (CA)
California State U, Los Angeles (CA)
California State U, Sacramento (CA)
California State U, San Bernardino (CA)
California State U, San Marcos (CA)
California State U, Stanislaus (CA)
California U of Pennsylvania (PA)
Calumet Coll of Saint Joseph (IN)
Calvin Coll (MI)
Cameron U (OK)
Campbellsville U (KY)
Campbell U (NC)
Canisius Coll (NY)
Capital U (OH)
Cardinal Stritch U (WI)
Carleton U (ON, Canada)
Carlos Albizu Univ—Miami (FL)
Carnegie Mellon U (PA)
Carroll Coll (MT)
Carroll Coll (WI)
Carson-Newman Coll (TN)
Carthage Coll (WI)
Cascade Coll (OR)
Case Western Reserve U (OH)
Castleton State Coll (VT)
Catawba Coll (NC)
The Catholic U of America (DC)
Cazenovia Coll (NY)
Cedar Crest Coll (PA)
Cedarville U (OH)
Centenary Coll (NJ)
Centenary Coll of Louisiana (LA)
Central Christian Coll of Kansas (KS)
Central Coll (IA)
Central Connecticut State U (CT)
Central Methodist Coll (MO)
Central Michigan U (MI)
Central Missouri State U (MO)
Central State U (OH)
Central Washington U (WA)
Chadron State Coll (NE)
Chaminade U of Honolulu (HI)
Champlain Coll (VT)
Chaparral Coll (AZ)
Chapman U (CA)
Charleston Southern U (SC)
Chatham Coll (PA)
Chestnut Hill Coll (PA)
Cheyney U of Pennsylvania (PA)
Chicago State U (IL)
Chowan Coll (NC)
Christian Brothers U (TN)
Christian Heritage Coll (CA)
Christopher Newport U (VA)
Citadel, The Military Coll of South Carolina (SC)
City Coll of the City U of NY (NY)
City U (WA)
Clarion U of Pennsylvania (PA)
Clark Atlanta U (GA)
Clarke Coll (IA)
Clarkson U (NY)
Clark U (MA)
Clayton Coll & State U (GA)
Clearwater Christian Coll (FL)
Cleary U (MI)
Clemson U (SC)
Cleveland State U (OH)
Coastal Carolina U (SC)
Coe Coll (IA)
Coker Coll (SC)
Colby-Sawyer Coll (NH)
CollAmerica–Fort Collins (CO)
Coll for Lifelong Learning (NH)
Coll Misericordia (PA)
Coll of Charleston (SC)
Coll of Mount St. Joseph (OH)
Coll of Mount Saint Vincent (NY)
The Coll of New Jersey (NJ)
The Coll of New Rochelle (NY)
Coll of Notre Dame of Maryland (MD)
Coll of Saint Benedict (MN)
Coll of St. Catherine (MN)
Coll of Saint Elizabeth (NJ)
Coll of St. Joseph (VT)
Coll of Saint Mary (NE)
The Coll of Saint Rose (NY)
The Coll of St. Scholastica (MN)
Coll of Santa Fe (NM)
The Coll of Southeastern Europe, The American U of Athens(Greece)
Coll of the Ozarks (MO)
Coll of the Southwest (NM)
The Coll of William and Mary (VA)
Colorado Christian U (CO)
Colorado State U (CO)
Colorado State U-Pueblo (CO)
Colorado Tech U Sioux Falls Campus (SD)
Columbia Coll (MO)
Columbia Coll (SC)
Columbia Coll Chicago (IL)
Columbia Southern U (AL)
Columbia Union Coll (MD)
Columbus State U (GA)
Concord Coll (WV)
Concordia Coll (AL)
Concordia Coll (MN)
Concordia Coll (NY)
Concordia U (CA)
Concordia U (IL)
Concordia U (MI)
Concordia U (NE)
Concordia U (OR)
Concordia U (QC, Canada)
Concordia U at Austin (TX)
Concordia U Coll of Alberta (AB, Canada)
Concordia U, St. Paul (MN)
Concordia U Wisconsin (WI)
Converse Coll (SC)
Cornell U (NY)
Cornerstone U (MI)
Covenant Coll (GA)
Crichton Coll (TN)
Crown Coll (MN)
Culver-Stockton Coll (MO)
Curry Coll (MA)
Daemen Coll (NY)
Dakota State U (SD)
Dakota Wesleyan U (SD)
Dalhousie U (NS, Canada)
Dallas Baptist U (TX)
Dallas Christian Coll (TX)
Dana Coll (NE)
Daniel Webster Coll (NH)
Davenport U, Dearborn (MI)
Davenport U, Grand Rapids (MI)
Davenport U, Kalamazoo (MI)
Davenport U, Lansing (MI)
Davenport U, Lapeer (MI)
Davenport U, Warren (MI)
Davis & Elkins Coll (WV)
Defiance Coll (OH)
Delaware State U (DE)
Delaware Valley Coll (PA)
Delta State U (MS)
DePaul U (IL)
DeSales U (PA)
Dickinson State U (ND)
Dillard U (LA)
Doane Coll (NE)
Dominican Coll (NY)
Dominican U (IL)
Dominican U of California (CA)
Dordt Coll (IA)
Dowling Coll (NY)
Drake U (IA)
Drury U (MO)
D'Youville Coll (NY)
Earlham Coll (IN)
East Carolina U (NC)
East Central U (OK)
Eastern Connecticut State U (CT)
Eastern Illinois U (IL)
Eastern Kentucky U (KY)
Eastern Mennonite U (VA)
Eastern Michigan U (MI)
Eastern Nazarene Coll (MA)
Eastern New Mexico U (NM)
Eastern Washington U (WA)
East Stroudsburg U of Pennsylvania (PA)
East Texas Baptist U (TX)
Eckerd Coll (FL)
Edgewood Coll (WI)
Edinboro U of Pennsylvania (PA)
Elizabeth City State U (NC)
Elizabethtown Coll (PA)
Elmhurst Coll (IL)
Elmira Coll (NY)
Elms Coll (MA)
Elon U (NC)
Emmanuel Coll (GA)
Emory & Henry Coll (VA)
Emory U (GA)
Emporia State U (KS)
Endicott Coll (MA)
Erskine Coll (SC)
Eureka Coll (IL)
Evangel U (MO)
Everglades U, Boca Raton (FL)
The Evergreen State Coll (WA)
Excelsior Coll (NY)
Fairfield U (CT)
Fairleigh Dickinson U, Florham (NJ)
Fairleigh Dickinson U, Teaneck-Metro Campus (NJ)
Fairmont State Coll (WV)
Faulkner U (AL)
Fayetteville State U (NC)
Ferris State U (MI)
Ferrum Coll (VA)
Fisher Coll (MA)
Five Towns Coll (NY)
Flagler Coll (FL)
Florida Ag and Mech U (FL)
Florida Atlantic U (FL)
Florida Gulf Coast U (FL)
Florida Inst of Technology (FL)
Florida Intl U (FL)
Florida Metropolitan U-Tampa Coll, Brandon (FL)
Florida Metropolitan U-Fort Lauderdale Coll (FL)
Florida Metropolitan U-Tampa Coll, Lakeland (FL)
Florida Metropolitan U-Tampa Coll (FL)
Florida Southern Coll (FL)
Florida State U (FL)
Fontbonne U (MO)
Fordham U (NY)
Fort Hays State U (KS)
Fort Lewis Coll (CO)
Fort Valley State U (GA)
Framingham State Coll (MA)
The Franciscan U (IA)
Franciscan U of Steubenville (OH)
Francis Marion U (SC)
Franklin and Marshall Coll (PA)
Franklin Pierce Coll (NH)
Franklin U (OH)
Freed-Hardeman U (TN)
Fresno Pacific U (CA)
Frostburg State U (MD)
Furman U (SC)
Gallaudet U (DC)
Gannon U (PA)
Gardner-Webb U (NC)
Geneva Coll (PA)
George Fox U (OR)
George Mason U (VA)
Georgetown Coll (KY)
Georgetown U (DC)
The George Washington U (DC)
Georgia Coll & State U (GA)
Georgia Inst of Technology (GA)
Georgian Court U (NJ)
Georgia Southern U (GA)
Georgia Southwestern State U (GA)
Georgia State U (GA)
Gettysburg Coll (PA)
Glenville State Coll (WV)
Globe Inst of Technology (NY)
Golden Gate U (CA)
Goldey-Beacom Coll (DE)
Gonzaga U (WA)
Gordon Coll (MA)
Goshen Coll (IN)
Governors State U (IL)
Grace Bible Coll (MI)
Grace Coll (IN)
Graceland U (IA)
Grace U (NE)
Grambling State U (LA)
Grand Canyon U (AZ)
Grand Valley State U (MI)
Grand View Coll (IA)
Grantham U (LA)
Greensboro Coll (NC)
Greenville Coll (IL)
Griggs U (MD)
Grove City Coll (PA)
Guilford Coll (NC)
Gustavus Adolphus Coll (MN)
Gwynedd-Mercy Coll (PA)
Hamline U (MN)
Hampton U (VA)
Hannibal-LaGrange Coll (MO)
Hanover Coll (IN)
Harding U (AR)
Hardin-Simmons U (TX)
Harris-Stowe State Coll (MO)
Hartwick Coll (NY)
Haskell Indian Nations U (KS)
Hastings Coll (NE)
Hawai'i Pacific U (HI)
HEC Montreal (QC, Canada)
Heidelberg Coll (OH)
Hellenic Coll (MA)
Henry Cogswell Coll (WA)
Hesser Coll (NH)
High Point U (NC)
Hilbert Coll (NY)
Hillsdale Coll (MI)
Hiram Coll (OH)
Hofstra U (NY)
Holy Names Coll (CA)
Hood Coll (MD)
Hope Coll (MI)
Houghton Coll (NY)
Houston Baptist U (TX)
Howard Payne U (TX)
Howard U (DC)
Humboldt State U (CA)
Huntingdon Coll (AL)
Huntington Coll (IN)
Huron U USA in London(United Kingdom)
Husson Coll (ME)
Huston-Tillotson Coll (TX)
Idaho State U (ID)
Illinois Coll (IL)
Illinois State U (IL)
Illinois Wesleyan U (IL)
Immaculata U (PA)
Indiana Inst of Technology (IN)
Indiana State U (IN)
Indiana U Bloomington (IN)
Indiana U Northwest (IN)
Indiana U of Pennsylvania (PA)
Indiana U–Purdue U Fort Wayne (IN)
Inter American U of PR, Aguadilla Campus (PR)
Inter Amer U of PR, Barranquitas Campus (PR)
Inter American U of PR, Bayamón Campus (PR)
Inter American U of PR, Fajardo Campus (PR)
Inter American U of PR, Ponce Campus (PR)
Inter American U of PR, San Germán Campus (PR)
Intl Coll (FL)
Intl U in Geneva(Switzerland)
Iona Coll (NY)
Iowa State U of Science and Technology (IA)
Iowa Wesleyan Coll (IA)
Ithaca Coll (NY)
Jacksonville State U (AL)
Jacksonville U (FL)
James Madison U (VA)
Jamestown Coll (ND)
Jarvis Christian Coll (TX)
John Brown U (AR)
John Cabot U(Italy)
John Carroll U (OH)
John F. Kennedy U (CA)
Johnson & Wales U (RI)
Johnson C. Smith U (NC)
Johnson State Coll (VT)
John Wesley Coll (NC)
Jones Coll, Jacksonville (FL)
Jones Coll, Miami (FL)
Jones Intl U (CO)
Judson Coll (IL)
Juniata Coll (PA)
Kansas State U (KS)
Kansas Wesleyan U (KS)
Kaplan Coll (IA)
Kean U (NJ)
Keene State Coll (NH)
Kendall Coll (IL)
Kennesaw State U (GA)
Kent State U (OH)
Kentucky Christian Coll (KY)
Kentucky State U (KY)
Kentucky Wesleyan Coll (KY)
Kettering U (MI)
Keuka Coll (NY)
Keystone Coll (PA)
King Coll (TN)
The King's Coll (NY)
King's Coll (PA)
The King's U Coll (AB, Canada)
Kutztown U of Pennsylvania (PA)
LaGrange Coll (GA)
Lake Erie Coll (OH)
Lakehead U (ON, Canada)
Lakeland Coll (WI)
Lake Superior State U (MI)
Lamar U (TX)
Lambuth U (TN)
Lander U (SC)
Lane Coll (TN)
La Roche Coll (PA)
La Salle U (PA)
Lasell Coll (MA)
Laurentian U (ON, Canada)
Lawrence Technological U (MI)
Lebanon Valley Coll (PA)
Lehigh U (PA)
Lehman Coll of the City U of NY (NY)
Le Moyne Coll (NY)
Lenoir-Rhyne Coll (NC)
Lesley U (MA)
LeTourneau U (TX)
Lewis-Clark State Coll (ID)
Lewis U (IL)
Liberty U (VA)
Life U (GA)
Limestone Coll (SC)
Lincoln Memorial U (TN)
Lincoln U (MO)
Lincoln U (PA)
Lindenwood U (MO)
Lindsey Wilson Coll (KY)
Lipscomb U (TN)
Livingstone Coll (NC)
Lock Haven U of Pennsylvania (PA)
Long Island U, Brentwood Campus (NY)
Long Island U, Brooklyn Campus (NY)
Long Island U, C.W. Post Campus (NY)
Long Island U, Southampton Coll (NY)
Longwood U (VA)
Loras Coll (IA)
Louisiana Coll (LA)
Louisiana State U and A&M Coll (LA)
Louisiana State U in Shreveport (LA)
Louisiana Tech U (LA)
Lourdes Coll (OH)
Loyola Marymount U (CA)
Loyola U Chicago (IL)
Loyola U New Orleans (LA)
Lubbock Christian U (TX)
Luther Coll (IA)
Lycoming Coll (PA)
Lynchburg Coll (VA)
Lyndon State Coll (VT)
Lynn U (FL)
Lyon Coll (AR)
MacMurray Coll (IL)
Macon State Coll (GA)
Madonna U (MI)
Maharishi U of Management (IA)
Maine Maritime Acad (ME)
Malone Coll (OH)
Manchester Coll (IN)
Manhattan Christian Coll (KS)
Manhattanville Coll (NY)
Mansfield U of Pennsylvania (PA)
Marian Coll (IN)
Marian Coll of Fond du Lac (WI)
Marietta Coll (OH)
Marist Coll (NY)
Marquette U (WI)
Marshall U (WV)
Mars Hill Coll (NC)
Martin U (IN)
Mary Baldwin Coll (VA)
Marygrove Coll (MI)
Marylhurst U (OR)
Marymount Coll of Fordham U (NY)
Marymount Manhattan Coll (NY)
Marymount U (VA)
Maryville Coll (TN)
Maryville U of Saint Louis (MO)
Mary Washington Coll (VA)
Marywood U (PA)
Massachusetts Coll of Liberal Arts (MA)
Massachusetts Inst of Technology (MA)
The Master's Coll and Sem (CA)
Mayville State U (ND)
McDaniel Coll (MD)
McGill U (QC, Canada)
McKendree Coll (IL)
McMurry U (TX)
McNeese State U (LA)
McPherson Coll (KS)
Medaille Coll (NY)

Medgar Evers Coll of the City U of NY (NY)
Memorial U of Newfoundland (NL, Canada)
Menlo Coll (CA)
Mercy Coll (NY)
Mercyhurst Coll (PA)
Meredith Coll (NC)
Merrimack Coll (MA)
Messenger Coll (MO)
Messiah Coll (PA)
Methodist Coll (NC)
Metropolitan State U (MN)
Miami U (OH)
Michigan State U (MI)
Michigan Technological U (MI)
MidAmerica Nazarene U (KS)
Mid-Continent Coll (KY)
Middle Tennessee State U (TN)
Midway Coll (KY)
Midwestern State U (TX)
Miles Coll (AL)
Millersville U of Pennsylvania (PA)
Milligan Coll (TN)
Millikin U (IL)
Millsaps Coll (MS)
Milwaukee School of Eng (WI)
Minnesota State U Mankato (MN)
Minnesota State U Moorhead (MN)
Minot State U (ND)
Mississippi Coll (MS)
Mississippi State U (MS)
Mississippi Valley State U (MS)
Missouri Baptist U (MO)
Missouri Southern State U (MO)
Missouri Valley Coll (MO)
Missouri Western State Coll (MO)
Mitchell Coll (CT)
Molloy Coll (NY)
Monmouth Coll (IL)
Monmouth U (NJ)
Montana State U–Billings (MT)
Montana Tech of The U of Montana (MT)
Montclair State U (NJ)
Montreat Coll (NC)
Moravian Coll (PA)
Morehead State U (KY)
Morehouse Coll (GA)
Morgan State U (MD)
Morningside Coll (IA)
Morris Coll (SC)
Morrison U (NV)
Mount Allison U (NB, Canada)
Mount Aloysius Coll (PA)
Mount Ida Coll (MA)
Mount Marty Coll (SD)
Mount Mary Coll (WI)
Mount Mercy Coll (IA)
Mount Saint Mary Coll (NY)
Mount St. Mary's Coll (CA)
Mount Saint Vincent U (NS, Canada)
Mt. Sierra Coll (CA)
Mount Union Coll (OH)
Muhlenberg Coll (PA)
Murray State U (KY)
National American U, Colorado Springs (CO)
National American U, Denver (CO)
National American U (NM)
National American U (SD)
National American U–Sioux Falls Branch (SD)
National-Louis U (IL)
National U (CA)
Nazareth Coll of Rochester (NY)
Nebraska Wesleyan U (NE)
Neumann Coll (PA)
Nevada State Coll at Henderson (NV)
Newberry Coll (SC)
Newbury Coll (MA)
New Jersey City U (NJ)
New Jersey Inst of Technology (NJ)
Newman U (KS)
New Mexico Highlands U (NM)
New Mexico Inst of Mining and Technology (NM)
New Mexico State U (NM)
New York Inst of Technology (NY)
New York U (NY)
Niagara U (NY)
Nicholls State U (LA)
Nichols Coll (MA)
Nipissing U (ON, Canada)
North Carolina Central U (NC)
North Carolina State U (NC)
North Carolina Wesleyan Coll (NC)
North Central Coll (IL)
Northcentral U (AZ)
North Central U (MN)
North Dakota State U (ND)
Northeastern Illinois U (IL)
Northeastern State U (OK)
Northeastern U (MA)
Northern Arizona U (AZ)
Northern Illinois U (IL)
Northern Michigan U (MI)
Northern State U (SD)
North Georgia Coll & State U (GA)
North Greenville Coll (SC)
Northland Coll (WI)
North Park U (IL)
Northwestern Coll (IA)
Northwestern Coll (MN)
Northwestern Oklahoma State U (OK)
Northwestern Polytechnic U (CA)
Northwestern State U of Louisiana (LA)
Northwest Nazarene U (ID)
Northwood U (MI)
Northwood U, Florida Campus (FL)
Northwood U, Texas Campus (TX)
Notre Dame Coll (OH)
Notre Dame de Namur U (CA)
Nova Southeastern U (FL)
Nyack Coll (NY)
Oak Hills Christian Coll (MN)
Oakland City U (IN)
Oakland U (MI)
Oglethorpe U (GA)
Ohio Dominican U (OH)
Ohio Northern U (OH)
The Ohio State U (OH)
The Ohio State U at Lima (OH)
The Ohio State U at Marion (OH)
The Ohio State U–Mansfield Campus (OH)
The Ohio State U–Newark Campus (OH)
Ohio U (OH)
Ohio U–Chillicothe (OH)
Ohio U–Southern Campus (OH)
Ohio Valley Coll (WV)
Ohio Wesleyan U (OH)
Okanagan U Coll (BC, Canada)
Oklahoma Baptist U (OK)
Oklahoma Christian U (OK)
Oklahoma City U (OK)
Oklahoma Panhandle State U (OK)
Old Dominion U (VA)
Olivet Coll (MI)
Olivet Nazarene U (IL)
Oral Roberts U (OK)
Oregon Inst of Technology (OR)
Oregon State U (OR)
Ottawa U (KS)
Otterbein Coll (OH)
Ouachita Baptist U (AR)
Our Lady of Holy Cross Coll (LA)
Our Lady of the Lake U of San Antonio (TX)
Pace U (NY)
Pacific Lutheran U (WA)
Pacific States U (CA)
Pacific Union Coll (CA)
Pacific U (OR)
Paine Coll (GA)
Palm Beach Atlantic U (FL)
Park U (MO)
Peace Coll (NC)
Peirce Coll (PA)
Pennsylvania Coll of Technology (PA)
Penn State U at Erie, The Behrend Coll (PA)
Penn State U Beaver Campus of the Commonwealth Coll (PA)
Penn State U Delaware County Campus of the Commonwealth Coll (PA)
Penn State U DuBois Campus of the Commonwealth Coll (PA)
Penn State U Fayette Campus of the Commonwealth Coll (PA)
Penn State U Harrisburg Campus of the Capital Coll (PA)
Penn State U Hazleton Campus of the Commonwealth Coll (PA)
Penn State U McKeesport Campus of the Commonwealth Coll (PA)
Penn State U Mont Alto Campus of the Commonwealth Coll (PA)
Penn State U New Kensington Campus of the Commonwealth Coll (PA)
Penn State U Shenango Campus of the Commonwealth Coll (PA)
Penn State U Wilkes-Barre Campus of the Commonwealth Coll (PA)
Penn State U Worthington Scranton Cmps Commonwealth Coll (PA)
Pepperdine U, Malibu (CA)
Pfeiffer U (NC)
Philadelphia Biblical U (PA)
Philadelphia U (PA)
Piedmont Coll (GA)
Pikeville Coll (KY)
Pillsbury Baptist Bible Coll (MN)
Pine Manor Coll (MA)
Pittsburg State U (KS)
Plymouth State U (NH)
Point Loma Nazarene U (CA)
Point Park U (PA)
Polytechnic U of Puerto Rico (PR)
Pontifical Catholic U of Puerto Rico (PR)
Portland State U (OR)
Prairie View A&M U (TX)
Presbyterian Coll (SC)
Presentation Coll (SD)
Principia Coll (IL)
Providence Coll (RI)
Providence Coll and Theological Sem (MB, Canada)
Purdue U (IN)
Purdue U North Central (IN)
Queen's U at Kingston (ON, Canada)
Queens U of Charlotte (NC)
Quincy U (IL)
Quinnipiac U (CT)
Radford U (VA)
Ramapo Coll of New Jersey (NJ)
Redeemer U Coll (ON, Canada)
Reformed Bible Coll (MI)
Regis U (CO)
Reinhardt Coll (GA)
Rensselaer Polytechnic Inst (NY)
Rhode Island Coll (RI)
Rhodes Coll (TN)
Rice U (TX)
The Richard Stockton Coll of New Jersey (NJ)
Richmond, The American Intl U in London(United Kingdom)
Rider U (NJ)
Ripon Coll (WI)
Rivier Coll (NH)
Roanoke Coll (VA)
Robert Morris Coll (IL)
Robert Morris U (PA)
Roberts Wesleyan Coll (NY)
Rochester Coll (MI)
Rochester Inst of Technology (NY)
Rockford Coll (IL)
Rockhurst U (MO)
Rocky Mountain Coll (MT)
Roger Williams U (RI)
Roosevelt U (IL)
Rosemont Coll (PA)
Rowan U (NJ)
Russell Sage Coll (NY)
Rutgers, The State U of New Jersey, Camden (NJ)
Rutgers, The State U of New Jersey, Newark (NJ)
Rutgers, The State U of New Jersey, New Brunswick/Piscataway (NJ)
Ryerson U (ON, Canada)
Sacred Heart U (CT)
Sage Coll of Albany (NY)
Saginaw Valley State U (MI)
St. Ambrose U (IA)
St. Andrews Presbyterian Coll (NC)
Saint Augustine's Coll (NC)
St. Bonaventure U (NY)
St. Cloud State U (MN)
St. Edward's U (TX)
St. Francis Coll (NY)
Saint Francis U (PA)
St. Francis Xavier U (NS, Canada)
St. Gregory's U (OK)
St. John Fisher Coll (NY)
Saint John's U (MN)
St. John's U (NY)
Saint Joseph Coll (CT)
St. Joseph's Coll, New York (NY)
Saint Joseph's Coll of Maine (ME)
St. Joseph's Coll, Suffolk Campus (NY)
Saint Joseph's U (PA)
Saint Leo U (FL)
Saint Louis U (MO)
Saint Martin's Coll (WA)
Saint Mary-of-the-Woods Coll (IN)
Saint Mary's Coll (IN)
Saint Mary's Coll of California (CA)
Saint Mary's U of Minnesota (MN)
St. Mary's U of San Antonio (TX)
Saint Michael's Coll (VT)
St. Thomas Aquinas Coll (NY)
St. Thomas U (FL)
Saint Vincent Coll (PA)
Salem Coll (NC)
Salem State Coll (MA)
Salisbury U (MD)
Salve Regina U (RI)
Samford U (AL)
Sam Houston State U (TX)
San Diego State U (CA)
San Francisco State U (CA)
San Jose State U (CA)
Schiller Intl U(France)
Schiller Intl U(Spain)
Schiller Intl U, American Coll of Switzerland(Switzerland)
Seattle Pacific U (WA)
Seattle U (WA)
Seton Hall U (NJ)
Seton Hill U (PA)
Shawnee State U (OH)
Shaw U (NC)
Sheldon Jackson Coll (AK)
Shenandoah U (VA)
Shepherd U (WV)
Shippensburg U of Pennsylvania (PA)
Shorter Coll (GA)
Siena Heights U (MI)
Sierra Nevada Coll (NV)
Silver Lake Coll (WI)
Simmons Coll (MA)
Simon Fraser U (BC, Canada)
Simpson Coll (IA)
Simpson Coll and Graduate School (CA)
Slippery Rock U of Pennsylvania (PA)
Sonoma State U (CA)
South Carolina State U (SC)
Southeastern Louisiana U (LA)
Southeastern Oklahoma State U (OK)
Southeast Missouri State U (MO)
Southern Adventist U (TN)
Southern Alberta Inst of Technology (AB, Canada)
Southern Connecticut State U (CT)
Southern Illinois U Carbondale (IL)
Southern Illinois U Edwardsville (IL)
Southern Methodist U (TX)
Southern Nazarene U (OK)
Southern Oregon U (OR)
Southern U and A&M Coll (LA)
Southern Utah U (UT)
Southern Vermont Coll (VT)
Southern Virginia U (VA)
Southern Wesleyan U (SC)
South U (AL)
South U (GA)
Southwest Baptist U (MO)
Southwestern Coll (AZ)
Southwestern Coll (KS)
Southwestern Oklahoma State U (OK)
Southwestern U (TX)
Southwest Missouri State U (MO)
Spring Arbor U (MI)
Springfield Coll (MA)
Spring Hill Coll (AL)
State U of NY at New Paltz (NY)
State U of NY at Oswego (NY)
Plattsburgh State U of NY (NY)
State U of NY Coll at Brockport (NY)
State U of NY Coll at Fredonia (NY)
State U of NY Coll at Geneseo (NY)
State U of NY Coll at Old Westbury (NY)
State U of NY Coll at Potsdam (NY)
State U of NY Empire State Coll (NY)
State U of NY Inst of Tech at Utica/Rome (NY)
State U of West Georgia (GA)
Stephens Coll (MO)
Sterling Coll (KS)
Stetson U (FL)
Stevens Inst of Technology (NJ)
Stonehill Coll (MA)
Stony Brook U, State U of New York (NY)
Strayer U (DC)
Suffolk U (MA)
Sullivan U (KY)
Susquehanna U (PA)
Syracuse U (NY)
Tabor Coll (KS)
Talladega Coll (AL)
Tarleton State U (TX)
Taylor U (IN)
Taylor U, Fort Wayne Campus (IN)
Teikyo Post U (CT)
Tennessee State U (TN)
Tennessee Technological U (TN)
Tennessee Wesleyan Coll (TN)
Texas A&M Intl U (TX)
Texas A&M U (TX)
Texas A&M U at Galveston (TX)
Texas A&M U–Commerce (TX)
Texas A&M U–Corpus Christi (TX)
Texas A&M U–Kingsville (TX)
Texas A&M U–Texarkana (TX)
Texas Lutheran U (TX)
Texas Southern U (TX)
Texas State U-San Marcos (TX)
Texas Tech U (TX)
Texas Wesleyan U (TX)
Texas Woman's U (TX)
Thiel Coll (PA)
Thomas Coll (ME)
Thomas Edison State Coll (NJ)
Thomas U (GA)
Tiffin U (OH)
Toccoa Falls Coll (GA)
Tougaloo Coll (MS)
Towson U (MD)
Transylvania U (KY)
Trent U (ON, Canada)
Trevecca Nazarene U (TN)
Trinity Bible Coll (ND)
Trinity Christian Coll (IL)
Trinity Coll (DC)
Trinity Intl U (IL)
Trinity U (TX)
Trinity Western U (BC, Canada)
Tri-State U (IN)
Troy State U (AL)
Troy State U Dothan (AL)
Troy State U Montgomery (AL)
Truman State U (MO)
Tulane U (LA)
Tusculum Coll (TN)
Tuskegee U (AL)
Union Coll (KY)
Union Coll (NE)
Union U (TN)
United States Air Force Acad (CO)
United States Intl U(Kenya)
United States Military Acad (NY)
Universidad Adventista de las Antillas (PR)
Université de Sherbrooke (QC, Canada)
U du Québec à Hull (QC, Canada)
Université Laval (QC, Canada)
State U of NY at Albany (NY)
U at Buffalo, The State U of New York (NY)
U Coll of the Cariboo (BC, Canada)
U Coll of the Fraser Valley (BC, Canada)
The U of Akron (OH)
The U of Alabama (AL)
The U of Alabama at Birmingham (AL)
The U of Alabama in Huntsville (AL)
U of Alaska Fairbanks (AK)
U of Alaska Southeast (AK)
U of Alberta (AB, Canada)
U of Arkansas (AR)
U of Arkansas at Fort Smith (AR)
U of Arkansas at Little Rock (AR)
U of Arkansas at Monticello (AR)
U of Baltimore (MD)
U of Bridgeport (CT)
The U of British Columbia (BC, Canada)
U of Calgary (AB, Canada)
U of Calif, Berkeley (CA)
U of Calif, Los Angeles (CA)
U of Calif, Riverside (CA)
U of Central Arkansas (AR)
U of Central Florida (FL)
U of Charleston (WV)
U of Cincinnati (OH)
U of Colorado at Colorado Springs (CO)
U of Dayton (OH)
U of Delaware (DE)
U of Denver (CO)
U of Detroit Mercy (MI)
U of Dubuque (IA)
U of Evansville (IN)
The U of Findlay (OH)
U of Florida (FL)
U of Georgia (GA)
U of Great Falls (MT)
U of Hartford (CT)
U of Hawaii at Hilo (HI)
U of Hawaii at Manoa (HI)
U of Houston (TX)
U of Houston–Clear Lake (TX)
U of Houston–Victoria (TX)
U of Illinois at Chicago (IL)
U of Illinois at Springfield (IL)
U of Indianapolis (IN)
The U of Iowa (IA)
U of La Verne (CA)
The U of Lethbridge (AB, Canada)
U of Louisiana at Lafayette (LA)
U of Louisville (KY)
U of Maine (ME)
The U of Maine at Augusta (ME)
U of Maine at Fort Kent (ME)
U of Maine at Machias (ME)
U of Maine at Presque Isle (ME)
U of Manitoba (MB, Canada)
U of Mary (ND)
U of Mary Hardin-Baylor (TX)

U of Maryland, Coll Park (MD)
U of Maryland Eastern Shore (MD)
U of Maryland U Coll (MD)
U of Massachusetts Amherst (MA)
U of Massachusetts Boston (MA)
U of Massachusetts Dartmouth (MA)
U of Massachusetts Lowell (MA)
U of Miami (FL)
U of Michigan (MI)
U of Michigan–Dearborn (MI)
U of Michigan–Flint (MI)
U of Minnesota, Crookston (MN)
U of Minnesota, Duluth (MN)
U of Minnesota, Morris (MN)
U of Mississippi (MS)
U of Missouri–Columbia (MO)
U of Missouri–Kansas City (MO)
U of Missouri–Rolla (MO)
U of Missouri–St. Louis (MO)
U of Mobile (AL)
U of Montevallo (AL)
U of Nebraska at Omaha (NE)
U of Nebraska–Lincoln (NE)
U of Nevada, Las Vegas (NV)
U of New Brunswick Fredericton (NB, Canada)
U of New Hampshire (NH)
U of New Hampshire at Manchester (NH)
U of New Haven (CT)
U of New Mexico (NM)
U of New Orleans (LA)
U of North Alabama (AL)
The U of North Carolina at Asheville (NC)
The U of North Carolina at Chapel Hill (NC)
The U of North Carolina at Charlotte (NC)
The U of North Carolina at Greensboro (NC)
The U of North Carolina at Pembroke (NC)
The U of North Carolina at Wilmington (NC)
U of Northern Colorado (CO)
U of Northern Iowa (IA)
U of North Florida (FL)
U of Northwestern Ohio (OH)
U of Oklahoma (OK)
U of Oregon (OR)
U of Ottawa (ON, Canada)
U of Pennsylvania (PA)
U of Phoenix–Atlanta Campus (GA)
U of Phoenix–Boston Campus (MA)
U of Phoenix–Chicago Campus (IL)
U of Phoenix–Cleveland Campus (OH)
U of Phoenix–Colorado Campus (CO)
U of Phoenix–Dallas Campus (TX)
U of Phoenix–Fort Lauderdale Campus (FL)
U of Phoenix–Houston Campus (TX)
U of Phoenix–Jacksonville Campus (FL)
U of Phoenix–Kansas City Campus (MO)
U of Phoenix–Louisiana Campus (LA)
U of Phoenix–Maryland Campus (MD)
U of Phoenix–Metro Detroit Campus (MI)
U of Phoenix–Nevada Campus (NV)
U of Phoenix–New Mexico Campus (NM)
U of Phoenix–Northern California Campus (CA)
U of Phoenix–Oklahoma City Campus (OK)
U of Phoenix Online Campus (AZ)
U of Phoenix–Oregon Campus (OR)
U of Phoenix–Orlando Campus (FL)
U of Phoenix–Philadelphia Campus (PA)
U of Phoenix–Phoenix Campus (AZ)
U of Phoenix–Pittsburgh Campus (PA)
U of Phoenix–Puerto Rico Campus (PR)
U of Phoenix–Sacramento Campus (CA)
U of Phoenix–St. Louis Campus (MO)
U of Phoenix–San Diego Campus (CA)
U of Phoenix–Southern Arizona Campus (AZ)
U of Phoenix–Southern California Campus (CA)
U of Phoenix–Southern Colorado Campus (CO)
U of Phoenix–Tampa Campus (FL)
U of Phoenix–Tulsa Campus (OK)
U of Phoenix–Utah Campus (UT)
U of Phoenix–Washington Campus (WA)
U of Phoenix–West Michigan Campus (MI)
U of Phoenix–Wisconsin Campus (WI)
U of Pittsburgh at Bradford (PA)
U of Pittsburgh at Greensburg (PA)
U of Pittsburgh at Johnstown (PA)
U of Portland (OR)
U of Prince Edward Island (PE, Canada)
U of Puerto Rico, Cayey U Coll (PR)
U of Redlands (CA)
U of Regina (SK, Canada)
U of Rhode Island (RI)
U of Richmond (VA)
U of St. Francis (IL)
U of Saint Francis (IN)
U of Saint Mary (KS)
U of St. Thomas (MN)
U of St. Thomas (TX)
U of San Diego (CA)
U of San Francisco (CA)
The U of Scranton (PA)
U of Sioux Falls (SD)
U of South Alabama (AL)
U of South Carolina (SC)
U of South Carolina Aiken (SC)
U of South Carolina Spartanburg (SC)
The U of South Dakota (SD)
U of Southern California (CA)
U of Southern Indiana (IN)
U of Southern Maine (ME)
U of South Florida (FL)
The U of Tampa (FL)
The U of Tennessee (TN)
The U of Tennessee at Chattanooga (TN)
The U of Tennessee at Martin (TN)
The U of Texas at Arlington (TX)
The U of Texas at Austin (TX)
The U of Texas at Brownsville (TX)
The U of Texas at Tyler (TX)
The U of Texas–Pan American (TX)
U of the District of Columbia (DC)
U of the Incarnate Word (TX)
U of the Ozarks (AR)
U of the Pacific (CA)
U of the Sacred Heart (PR)
U of the Virgin Islands (VI)
U of the West (CA)
U of Toledo (OH)
U of Toronto (ON, Canada)
U of Tulsa (OK)
U of Utah (UT)
U of Vermont (VT)
The U of Virginia's Coll at Wise (VA)
U of Washington (WA)
U of Waterloo (ON, Canada)
The U of West Alabama (AL)
The U of Western Ontario (ON, Canada)
U of West Florida (FL)
U of Windsor (ON, Canada)
U of Wisconsin–Eau Claire (WI)
U of Wisconsin–Green Bay (WI)
U of Wisconsin–La Crosse (WI)
U of Wisconsin–Madison (WI)
U of Wisconsin–Milwaukee (WI)
U of Wisconsin–Oshkosh (WI)
U of Wisconsin–Parkside (WI)
U of Wisconsin–Platteville (WI)
U of Wisconsin–River Falls (WI)
U of Wisconsin–Stevens Point (WI)
U of Wisconsin–Stout (WI)
U of Wisconsin–Superior (WI)
U of Wisconsin–Whitewater (WI)
U of Wyoming (WY)
Upper Iowa U (IA)
Urbana U (OH)
Ursinus Coll (PA)
Ursuline Coll (OH)
Utah State U (UT)
Utica Coll (NY)
Valdosta State U (GA)
Valley City State U (ND)
Vanguard U of Southern California (CA)
Vennard Coll (IA)
Vermont Tech Coll (VT)
Villa Julie Coll (MD)
Villanova U (PA)
Virginia Coll at Birmingham (AL)
Virginia Commonwealth U (VA)
Virginia Intermont Coll (VA)
Virginia Polytechnic Inst and State U (VA)
Virginia State U (VA)
Virginia Union U (VA)
Virginia Wesleyan Coll (VA)
Viterbo U (WI)
Voorhees Coll (SC)
Wagner Coll (NY)
Waldorf Coll (IA)
Walla Walla Coll (WA)
Walsh Coll of Accountancy and Business Admin (MI)
Walsh U (OH)
Warner Pacific Coll (OR)
Warner Southern Coll (FL)
Warren Wilson Coll (NC)
Wartburg Coll (IA)
Washburn U (KS)
Washington & Jefferson Coll (PA)
Washington and Lee U (VA)
Washington Coll (MD)
Washington State U (WA)
Washington U in St. Louis (MO)
Wayland Baptist U (TX)
Waynesburg Coll (PA)
Wayne State Coll (NE)
Wayne State U (MI)
Webber Intl U (FL)
Weber State U (UT)
Webster U (MO)
Wells Coll (NY)
Wentworth Inst of Technology (MA)
Wesleyan Coll (GA)
Wesley Coll (DE)
West Chester U of Pennsylvania (PA)
Western Baptist Coll (OR)
Western Carolina U (NC)
Western Connecticut State U (CT)
Western Illinois U (IL)
Western Kentucky U (KY)
Western Michigan U (MI)
Western New England Coll (MA)
Western State Coll of Colorado (CO)
Western Washington U (WA)
Westfield State Coll (MA)
West Liberty State Coll (WV)
Westminster Coll (MO)
Westminster Coll (PA)
Westminster Coll (UT)
West Texas A&M U (TX)
West Virginia State Coll (WV)
West Virginia U (WV)
West Virginia Wesleyan Coll (WV)
Wheeling Jesuit U (WV)
Whitworth Coll (WA)
Wichita State U (KS)
Widener U (PA)
Wilberforce U (OH)
Wilkes U (PA)
William Carey Coll (MS)
William Jewell Coll (MO)
William Paterson U of New Jersey (NJ)
William Penn U (IA)
Williams Baptist Coll (AR)
Williamson Christian Coll (TN)
William Tyndale Coll (MI)
William Woods U (MO)
Wilmington Coll (DE)
Wilson Coll (PA)
Wingate U (NC)
Winona State U (MN)
Winston-Salem State U (NC)
Winthrop U (SC)
Wittenberg U (OH)
Worcester Polytechnic Inst (MA)
Worcester State Coll (MA)
Wright State U (OH)
Xavier U (OH)
Xavier U of Louisiana (LA)
York Coll (NE)
York Coll of Pennsylvania (PA)
York Coll of the City U of New York (NY)
York U (ON, Canada)
Youngstown State U (OH)

BUSINESS ADMINISTRATION, MANAGEMENT AND OPERATIONS RELATED

Alverno Coll (WI)
American InterContinental U Online (IL)
Argosy U/Sarasota (FL)
Averett U (VA)
Babson Coll (MA)
Becker Coll (MA)
California State U, Chico (CA)
Canisius Coll (NY)
Capital U (OH)
Carlos Albizu Univ—Miami (FL)
Central Michigan U (MI)
Charleston Southern U (SC)
Cleveland State U (OH)
Coleman Coll, La Mesa (CA)
Cornerstone U (MI)
Davenport U, Dearborn (MI)
Davenport U, Grand Rapids (MI)
Davenport U, Holland (MI)
Davenport U, Lapeer (MI)
Davenport U, Warren (MI)
DePaul U (IL)
Duquesne U (PA)
Embry-Riddle Aeronautical U (FL)
Embry-Riddle Aeronautical U, Extended Campus (FL)
Florida Inst of Technology (FL)
Gettysburg Coll (PA)
Intl Coll (FL)
Keystone Coll (PA)
Malone Coll (OH)
Marymount U (VA)
Mayville State U (ND)
Mercer U (GA)
Miami U Hamilton (OH)
Missouri Baptist U (MO)
Morris Coll (SC)
Mountain State U (WV)
Northwest Christian Coll (OR)
Oakland City U (IN)
Oakland U (MI)
Palm Beach Atlantic U (FL)
Peirce Coll (PA)
Pennsylvania Coll of Technology (PA)
Point Park U (PA)
Saint Mary-of-the-Woods Coll (IN)
San Jose State U (CA)
Teikyo Post U (CT)
Texas Tech U (TX)
Towson U (MD)
Trinity Christian Coll (IL)
U of Charleston (WV)
U of Hawaii at Manoa (HI)
U of Houston–Clear Lake (TX)
U of Louisville (KY)
U of Miami (FL)
U of Notre Dame (IN)
U of Pennsylvania (PA)
U of Phoenix–Idaho Campus (ID)
U of St. Thomas (MN)
The U of Scranton (PA)
U of Southern California (CA)
The U of Texas at Austin (TX)
U of Toledo (OH)
U of Waterloo (ON, Canada)
Ursuline Coll (OH)
Viterbo U (WI)
Washington U in St. Louis (MO)
Widener U (PA)
William Jessup U (CA)

BUSINESS AND PERSONAL/ FINANCIAL SERVICES MARKETING

American Public U System (WV)
Nipissing U (ON, Canada)

BUSINESS AUTOMATION/ TECHNOLOGY/DATA ENTRY

East Carolina U (NC)
East Central U (OK)
Inter American U of PR, Bayamón Campus (PR)

BUSINESS/COMMERCE

Alabama Ag and Mech U (AL)
American Coll of Computer & Information Sciences (AL)
Argosy U/Chicago Northwest (IL)
Argosy U/Seattle (WA)
Arizona State U East (AZ)
Asbury Coll (KY)
Auburn U Montgomery (AL)
Aurora U (IL)
Austin Peay State U (TN)
Averett U (VA)
Avila U (MO)
Baker Coll of Jackson (MI)
Baylor U (TX)
Bay Path Coll (MA)
Benedictine U (IL)
Bentley Coll (MA)
Berkeley Coll-New York City Campus (NY)
Berkeley Coll-Westchester Campus (NY)
Bethel Coll (KS)
Bloomsburg U of Pennsylvania (PA)
Blue Mountain Coll (MS)
Bowling Green State U (OH)
Brescia U (KY)
Bridgewater State Coll (MA)
Brock U (ON, Canada)
Campbell U (NC)
Capella U (MN)
Capital U (OH)
Carlow Coll (PA)
The Catholic U of America (DC)
Central Christian Coll of Kansas (KS)
Central Michigan U (MI)
Champlain Coll (VT)
Christian Brothers U (TN)
The Coll of Southeastern Europe, The American U of Athens(Greece)
Coll of Staten Island of the City U of NY (NY)
Columbia Coll, Caguas (PR)
Columbus State U (GA)
Concordia Coll (MN)
Concordia U (NE)
Concordia U at Austin (TX)
Cornell U (NY)
Cumberland Coll (KY)
Cumberland U (TN)
Dalhousie U (NS, Canada)
Davenport U, Dearborn (MI)
Davenport U, Gaylord (MI)
Davenport U, Grand Rapids (MI)
Davenport U, Holland (MI)
Davenport U, Kalamazoo (MI)
Davenport U, Lansing (MI)
Davenport U, Lapeer (MI)
Davenport U, Traverse City (MI)
Davenport U, Warren (MI)
Delta State U (MS)
DePaul U (IL)
Drake U (IA)
Drexel U (PA)
Duquesne U (PA)
Eastern Connecticut State U (CT)
Eastern Kentucky U (KY)
Eastern Michigan U (MI)
East Texas Baptist U (TX)
Florida Southern Coll (FL)
Florida State U (FL)
Franklin Coll (IN)
Georgia Coll & State U (GA)
Glenville State Coll (WV)
Grace Coll (IN)
Harris-Stowe State Coll (MO)
HEC Montreal (QC, Canada)
Henderson State U (AR)
Hillsdale Free Will Baptist Coll (OK)
Hofstra U (NY)
Hollins U (VA)
Houston Baptist U (TX)
Howard Payne U (TX)
Idaho State U (ID)
Illinois Inst of Technology (IL)
Indiana U Bloomington (IN)
Indiana U East (IN)
Indiana U Kokomo (IN)
Indiana U–Purdue U Indianapolis (IN)
Indiana U South Bend (IN)
Indiana U Southeast (IN)
Ithaca Coll (NY)
Jacksonville U (FL)
The Johns Hopkins U (MD)
Johnson State Coll (VT)
Judson Coll (AL)
Juniata Coll (PA)
Kaplan Coll (IA)
Keystone Coll (PA)
LaGrange Coll (GA)
Lehigh U (PA)
Liberty U (VA)
Limestone Coll (SC)
Linfield Coll (OR)
Loras Coll (IA)
Loyola Coll in Maryland (MD)
Macon State Coll (GA)
Malaspina U-Coll (BC, Canada)
Manchester Coll (IN)
Marygrove Coll (MI)
Maryville U of Saint Louis (MO)
Massachusetts Inst of Technology (MA)
McMurry U (TX)
Mercer U (GA)
Miami U (OH)
Miami U Hamilton (OH)
Midwestern State U (TX)
Milwaukee School of Eng (WI)
Montana State U–Billings (MT)
Montana State U–Bozeman (MT)
Montana Tech of The U of Montana (MT)
Mount Allison U (NB, Canada)
Mount Saint Mary's Coll and Sem (MD)
Mt. Sierra Coll (CA)
Mount Vernon Nazarene U (OH)
Murray State U (KY)
New Mexico State U (NM)
Niagara U (NY)
Nichols Coll (MA)
Norfolk State U (VA)
Northeastern Illinois U (IL)
Northeastern U (MA)
Northern Arizona U (AZ)

Northern Illinois U (IL)
Ohio Northern U (OH)
Ohio U (OH)
Oklahoma Christian U (OK)
Oklahoma City U (OK)
Oklahoma State U (OK)
Peirce Coll (PA)
Penn State U Abington Coll (PA)
Penn State U Altoona Coll (PA)
Penn State U Berks Cmps of Berks-Lehigh Valley Coll (PA)
Penn State U Lehigh Valley Cmps of Berks-Lehigh Valley Coll (PA)
Penn State U Schuylkill Campus of the Capital Coll (PA)
Plymouth State U (NH)
Regis Coll (MA)
Reinhardt Coll (GA)
Rockhurst U (MO)
Roosevelt U (IL)
Saginaw Valley State U (MI)
St. Ambrose U (IA)
Saint Anselm Coll (NH)
St. Bonaventure U (NY)
Saint Joseph's Coll (IN)
Saint Mary's Coll of California (CA)
St. Norbert Coll (WI)
Saint Xavier U (IL)
Sam Houston State U (TX)
Schreiner U (TX)
Shippensburg U of Pennsylvania (PA)
Skidmore Coll (NY)
Southern Arkansas U–Magnolia (AR)
Southern Wesleyan U (SC)
Southwest Missouri State U (MO)
Sweet Briar Coll (VA)
Tarleton State U (TX)
Texas A&M U–Texarkana (TX)
Texas Tech U (TX)
Thomas More Coll (KY)
Touro U Intl (CA)
Trinity Christian Coll (IL)
Trinity Coll of Florida (FL)
Troy State U (AL)
Troy State U Montgomery (AL)
Tyndale U Coll & Sem (ON, Canada)
Union Inst & U (OH)
U Coll of the Cariboo (BC, Canada)
The U of Akron (OH)
The U of Arizona (AZ)
U of Arkansas (AR)
U of Arkansas at Little Rock (AR)
The U of British Columbia (BC, Canada)
U of Central Arkansas (AR)
U of Central Florida (FL)
U of Colorado at Boulder (CO)
U of Colorado at Denver (CO)
U of Connecticut (CT)
U of Denver (CO)
U of Georgia (GA)
U of Hawaii at Manoa (HI)
U of Houston–Clear Lake (TX)
U of Illinois at Urbana–Champaign (IL)
U of Kansas (KS)
U of Kentucky (KY)
U of Louisiana at Lafayette (LA)
U of Mary Hardin-Baylor (TX)
U of Maryland, Coll Park (MD)
U of Mississippi (MS)
U of Missouri–Rolla (MO)
U of Missouri–St. Louis (MO)
The U of Montana–Missoula (MT)
The U of Montana–Western (MT)
U of Nebraska at Omaha (NE)
U of Nevada, Reno (NV)
U of North Dakota (ND)
U of North Texas (TX)
U of Notre Dame (IN)
U of Pittsburgh (PA)
U of Puget Sound (WA)
U of Redlands (CA)
U of San Francisco (CA)
U of Saskatchewan (SK, Canada)
U of Science and Arts of Oklahoma (OK)
U of South Alabama (AL)
U of Southern Indiana (IN)
U of South Florida (FL)
The U of Tennessee (TN)
The U of Texas at Austin (TX)
The U of Texas at Dallas (TX)
U of the Incarnate Word (TX)
U of Toledo (OH)
U of Utah (UT)
U of Victoria (BC, Canada)
U of Virginia (VA)
U of Washington (WA)
U of Windsor (ON, Canada)
U of Wisconsin–Whitewater (WI)
Utah State U (UT)
Valdosta State U (GA)
Virginia Polytechnic Inst and State U (VA)
Wake Forest U (NC)
Washington State U (WA)
Washington U in St. Louis (MO)
Webber Intl U (FL)
Webster U (MO)
Western Michigan U (MI)
Western Oregon U (OR)
Westminster Coll (UT)
Westmont Coll (CA)
West Texas A&M U (TX)
Wright State U (OH)
Xavier U (OH)
York U (ON, Canada)
Youngstown State U (OH)

BUSINESS/CORPORATE COMMUNICATIONS

Aquinas Coll (MI)
Augustana Coll (SD)
Babson Coll (MA)
Bentley Coll (MA)
Brenau U (GA)
Brock U (ON, Canada)
Calvin Coll (MI)
Chestnut Hill Coll (PA)
Elon U (NC)
Grove City Coll (PA)
Harding U (AR)
Hawai'i Pacific U (HI)
Holy Names Coll (CA)
Jones Intl U (CO)
Marietta Coll (OH)
Morningside Coll (IA)
Ohio Dominican U (OH)
Penn State U Abington Coll (PA)
Point Loma Nazarene U (CA)
Point Park U (PA)
Rochester Coll (MI)
Rockhurst U (MO)
Simpson Coll (IA)
Southern Christian U (AL)
Southwestern Coll (KS)
State U of NY Coll of A&T at Cobleskill (NY)
The U of Findlay (OH)
U of Houston (TX)
U of Mary (ND)
The U of Montana–Western (MT)
U of St. Thomas (MN)

BUSINESS FAMILY AND CONSUMER SCIENCES/HUMAN SCIENCES

Brigham Young U (UT)
Cornell U (NY)
The Ohio State U (OH)
U of Houston (TX)

BUSINESS, MANAGEMENT, AND MARKETING RELATED

Adelphi U (NY)
Argosy U/Sarasota (FL)
Arizona State U (AZ)
The Art Inst of California–San Francisco (CA)
Athens State U (AL)
Baylor U (TX)
Benedictine U (IL)
Bowling Green State U (OH)
Bridgewater State Coll (MA)
California State U, Sacramento (CA)
California State U, Stanislaus (CA)
Central Michigan U (MI)
Clemson U (SC)
Coll of Mount St. Joseph (OH)
The Coll of St. Scholastica (MN)
Dowling Coll (NY)
Drexel U (PA)
Duquesne U (PA)
George Mason U (VA)
Inter American U of PR, Bayamón Campus (PR)
Iowa State U of Science and Technology (IA)
Mercyhurst Coll (PA)
Messiah Coll (PA)
Nebraska Wesleyan U (NE)
New York U (NY)
Ohio U (OH)
Park U (MO)
Saint Mary's U of Minnesota (MN)
Saint Vincent Coll (PA)
Skidmore Coll (NY)
Southeastern Coll of the Assemblies of God (FL)
Sweet Briar Coll (VA)
Texas Wesleyan U (TX)
Troy State U Dothan (AL)
U of Denver (CO)
U of Maryland, Coll Park (MD)
U of Phoenix–Kansas City Campus (MO)
U of Phoenix–Nevada Campus (NV)
U of Southern California (CA)
U of Toledo (OH)
U of Utah (UT)
Utica Coll (NY)
Western Baptist Coll (OR)
York Coll of Pennsylvania (PA)

BUSINESS/MANAGERIAL ECONOMICS

Alabama Ag and Mech U (AL)
Albertus Magnus Coll (CT)
Allegheny Coll (PA)
American Intl Coll (MA)
American U (DC)
American U in Bulgaria(Bulgaria)
Andrews U (MI)
Arkansas State U (AR)
Auburn U (AL)
Auburn U Montgomery (AL)
Augsburg Coll (MN)
Aurora U (IL)
Ball State U (IN)
Baylor U (TX)
Bellarmine U (KY)
Belmont U (TN)
Beloit Coll (WI)
Benedictine U (IL)
Bentley Coll (MA)
Baruch Coll of the City U of NY (NY)
Bethany Coll (KS)
Bethany Coll (WV)
Bishop's U (QC, Canada)
Bloomsburg U of Pennsylvania (PA)
Boise State U (ID)
Bowling Green State U (OH)
Bradley U (IL)
Brock U (ON, Canada)
Buena Vista U (IA)
Butler U (IN)
California Inst of Technology (CA)
California State U, Fullerton (CA)
California State U, Hayward (CA)
California State U, Long Beach (CA)
California State U, San Bernardino (CA)
Campbellsville U (KY)
Capital U (OH)
Cardinal Stritch U (WI)
Carnegie Mellon U (PA)
Carroll Coll (MT)
Carson-Newman Coll (TN)
Catawba Coll (NC)
Cedar Crest Coll (PA)
Centenary Coll of Louisiana (LA)
Chapman U (CA)
Charleston Southern U (SC)
Christian Brothers U (TN)
Christopher Newport U (VA)
Clarion U of Pennsylvania (PA)
Cleveland State U (OH)
Coll of Mount Saint Vincent (NY)
The Coll of New Jersey (NJ)
The Coll of Southeastern Europe, The American U of Athens(Greece)
Coll of the Ozarks (MO)
The Coll of Wooster (OH)
Columbus State U (GA)
Concordia U (QC, Canada)
Dallas Baptist U (TX)
Delaware State U (DE)
DePaul U (IL)
Drexel U (PA)
Duquesne U (PA)
East Central U (OK)
Eastern Kentucky U (KY)
Eastern Michigan U (MI)
Eastern Oregon U (OR)
Eastern Washington U (WA)
Elmira Coll (NY)
Emory U (GA)
Fairleigh Dickinson U, Florham (NJ)
Fairleigh Dickinson U, Teaneck-Metro Campus (NJ)
Fayetteville State U (NC)
Ferris State U (MI)
Fordham U (NY)
Fort Hays State U (KS)
Framingham State Coll (MA)
Freed-Hardeman U (TN)
George Fox U (OR)
The George Washington U (DC)
Georgia Coll & State U (GA)
Georgia Inst of Technology (GA)
Georgia Southern U (GA)
Georgia State U (GA)
Gonzaga U (WA)
Grambling State U (LA)
Grand Canyon U (AZ)
Greensboro Coll (NC)
Grove City Coll (PA)
Gustavus Adolphus Coll (MN)
Hampden-Sydney Coll (VA)
Hampshire Coll (MA)
Hawai'i Pacific U (HI)
HEC Montreal (QC, Canada)
Hendrix Coll (AR)
Hofstra U (NY)
Hope Coll (MI)
Houston Baptist U (TX)
Huntingdon Coll (AL)
Huntington Coll (IN)
Illinois Coll (IL)
Immaculata U (PA)
Indiana U Bloomington (IN)
Indiana U–Purdue U Fort Wayne (IN)
Indiana U Southeast (IN)
Inter American U of PR, Bayamón Campus (PR)
Inter American U of PR, San Germán Campus (PR)
Ithaca Coll (NY)
James Madison U (VA)
Jamestown Coll (ND)
Kalamazoo Coll (MI)
Kennesaw State U (GA)
Kent State U (OH)
Kutztown U of Pennsylvania (PA)
Lafayette Coll (PA)
LaGrange Coll (GA)
Lake Forest Coll (IL)
Lake Superior State U (MI)
La Salle U (PA)
Lehigh U (PA)
Lewis U (IL)
Limestone Coll (SC)
Lincoln Memorial U (TN)
Lipscomb U (TN)
Lock Haven U of Pennsylvania (PA)
Longwood U (VA)
Louisiana State U and A&M Coll (LA)
Louisiana State U in Shreveport (LA)
Louisiana Tech U (LA)
Loyola U Chicago (IL)
Loyola U New Orleans (LA)
Marian Coll of Fond du Lac (WI)
Marquette U (WI)
Marshall U (WV)
Mars Hill Coll (NC)
Marymount Coll of Fordham U (NY)
McGill U (QC, Canada)
McMurry U (TX)
Mercy Coll (NY)
Meredith Coll (NC)
Merrimack Coll (MA)
Messiah Coll (PA)
Miami U (OH)
Miami U Hamilton (OH)
Michigan Technological U (MI)
Middle Tennessee State U (TN)
Mills Coll (CA)
Mississippi State U (MS)
Montana State U–Billings (MT)
Montclair State U (NJ)
Morehead State U (KY)
Morgan State U (MD)
Mount Allison U (NB, Canada)
New York U (NY)
Niagara U (NY)
Northern Arizona U (AZ)
Northern State U (SD)
North Georgia Coll & State U (GA)
North Greenville Coll (SC)
Northland Coll (WI)
Northwood U (MI)
Notre Dame de Namur U (CA)
Occidental Coll (CA)
Oglethorpe U (GA)
The Ohio State U (OH)
Ohio Wesleyan U (OH)
Oklahoma City U (OK)
Oklahoma State U (OK)
Old Dominion U (VA)
Olivet Nazarene U (IL)
Otterbein Coll (OH)
Park U (MO)
Penn State U Abington Coll (PA)
Penn State U Altoona Coll (PA)
Penn State U at Erie, The Behrend Coll (PA)
Penn State U Beaver Campus of the Commonwealth Coll (PA)
Penn State U Berks Cmps of Berks-Lehigh Valley Coll (PA)
Penn State U Delaware County Campus of the Commonwealth Coll (PA)
Penn State U DuBois Campus of the Commonwealth Coll (PA)
Penn State U Fayette Campus of the Commonwealth Coll (PA)
Penn State U Hazleton Campus of the Commonwealth Coll (PA)
Penn State U Lehigh Valley Cmps of Berks-Lehigh Valley Coll (PA)
Penn State U McKeesport Campus of the Commonwealth Coll (PA)
Penn State U Mont Alto Campus of the Commonwealth Coll (PA)
Penn State U New Kensington Campus of the Commonwealth Coll (PA)
Penn State U Schuylkill Campus of the Capital Coll (PA)
Penn State U Shenango Campus of the Commonwealth Coll (PA)
Penn State U Univ Park Campus (PA)
Penn State U Wilkes-Barre Campus of the Commonwealth Coll (PA)
Penn State U Worthington Scranton Cmps Commonwealth Coll (PA)
Penn State U York Campus of the Commonwealth Coll (PA)
Pfeiffer U (NC)
Pittsburg State U (KS)
Providence Coll (RI)
Quinnipiac U (CT)
Randolph-Macon Coll (VA)
Rider U (NJ)
Robert Morris U (PA)
Rockford Coll (IL)
Roosevelt U (IL)
Ryerson U (ON, Canada)
Sacred Heart U (CT)
Saginaw Valley State U (MI)
St. Bonaventure U (NY)
St. John's U (NY)
Salem State Coll (MA)
Sam Houston State U (TX)
Santa Clara U (CA)
Seattle U (WA)
Seton Hall U (NJ)
Seton Hill U (PA)
Shorter Coll (GA)
Sonoma State U (CA)
South Carolina State U (SC)
Southeast Missouri State U (MO)
Southern Connecticut State U (CT)
Southern Illinois U Carbondale (IL)
Southern Illinois U Edwardsville (IL)
Southern U and A&M Coll (LA)
State U of NY at New Paltz (NY)
Plattsburgh State U of NY (NY)
State U of NY Coll at Oneonta (NY)
State U of NY Coll at Potsdam (NY)
State U of West Georgia (GA)
Stetson U (FL)
Susquehanna U (PA)
Tennessee State U (TN)
Texas A&M Intl U (TX)
Texas A&M U–Kingsville (TX)
Texas State U-San Marcos (TX)
Texas Wesleyan U (TX)
Union U (TN)
The U of Alabama (AL)
The U of Alabama at Birmingham (AL)
The U of Arizona (AZ)
U of Arkansas (AR)
U of Calif, Los Angeles (CA)
U of Calif, Riverside (CA)
U of Calif, Santa Barbara (CA)
U of Calif, Santa Cruz (CA)
U of Central Florida (FL)
U of Dayton (OH)
U of Delaware (DE)
U of Denver (CO)
U of Evansville (IN)
U of Georgia (GA)
U of Guelph (ON, Canada)
U of Hartford (CT)
U of Hawaii at Manoa (HI)
U of Indianapolis (IN)
The U of Iowa (IA)
U of Judaism (CA)
U of Kentucky (KY)
U of La Verne (CA)
U of Louisiana at Lafayette (LA)
U of Louisville (KY)
U of Maine at Farmington (ME)
U of Manitoba (MB, Canada)
The U of Memphis (TN)
U of Miami (FL)
U of Mississippi (MS)
U of Missouri–Columbia (MO)
U of Nebraska at Omaha (NE)
U of Nebraska–Lincoln (NE)
U of Nevada, Reno (NV)
U of New Brunswick Fredericton (NB, Canada)
U of New Haven (CT)
U of New Orleans (LA)

U of North Alabama (AL)
The U of North Carolina at Charlotte (NC)
The U of North Carolina at Wilmington (NC)
U of North Dakota (ND)
U of North Florida (FL)
U of North Texas (TX)
U of Oklahoma (OK)
U of Ottawa (ON, Canada)
U of Pittsburgh at Johnstown (PA)
U of Richmond (VA)
U of San Diego (CA)
U of Saskatchewan (SK, Canada)
U of South Carolina (SC)
The U of South Dakota (SD)
U of South Florida (FL)
The U of Tennessee (TN)
The U of Tennessee at Martin (TN)
The U of Texas at Arlington (TX)
The U of Texas at Tyler (TX)
U of Toledo (OH)
U of West Florida (FL)
U of Windsor (ON, Canada)
U of Wisconsin–Platteville (WI)
U of Wisconsin–Superior (WI)
U of Wisconsin–Whitewater (WI)
U of Wyoming (WY)
Urbana U (OH)
Utica Coll (NY)
Valdosta State U (GA)
Villanova U (PA)
Virginia Commonwealth U (VA)
Virginia State U (VA)
Washington State U (WA)
Washington U in St. Louis (MO)
Wayne State Coll (NE)
Weber State U (UT)
West Chester U of Pennsylvania (PA)
Western Illinois U (IL)
Western Kentucky U (KY)
Western Michigan U (MI)
Western Washington U (WA)
West Liberty State Coll (WV)
Westminster Coll (UT)
Westmont Coll (CA)
West Texas A&M U (TX)
West Virginia U (WV)
West Virginia Wesleyan Coll (WV)
Wheaton Coll (IL)
Widener U (PA)
Wilberforce U (OH)
William Paterson U of New Jersey (NJ)
William Woods U (MO)
Wingate U (NC)
Winona State U (MN)
Wisconsin Lutheran Coll (WI)
Wittenberg U (OH)
Wofford Coll (SC)
Wright State U (OH)
Xavier U (OH)
York Coll of Pennsylvania (PA)
York U (ON, Canada)
Youngstown State U (OH)

BUSINESS OPERATIONS SUPPORT AND SECRETARIAL SERVICES RELATED
Roosevelt U (IL)

BUSINESS STATISTICS
Alabama Ag and Mech U (AL)
Baylor U (TX)
Brigham Young U (UT)
Central Missouri State U (MO)
Cleveland State U (OH)
HEC Montreal (QC, Canada)
Southern Oregon U (OR)
U of Houston (TX)
Western Michigan U (MI)
Wright State U (OH)
York U (ON, Canada)

BUSINESS SYSTEMS ANALYSIS/ DESIGN
U of North Dakota (ND)

BUSINESS TEACHER EDUCATION
Adrian Coll (MI)
Alabama State U (AL)
Albany State U (GA)
Alfred U (NY)
American Intl Coll (MA)
Appalachian State U (NC)
Arkansas State U (AR)
Arkansas Tech U (AR)
Armstrong Atlantic State U (GA)
Atlantic Union Coll (MA)
Auburn U (AL)
Baldwin-Wallace Coll (OH)
Ball State U (IN)
Baylor U (TX)
Belmont U (TN)
Bethany Coll (KS)
Bethel Coll (IN)
Bethune-Cookman Coll (FL)
Black Hills State U (SD)
Bluefield Coll (VA)
Blue Mountain Coll (MS)
Boise State U (ID)
Bowling Green State U (OH)
Brigham Young U–Hawaii (HI)
Buena Vista U (IA)
State U of NY Coll at Buffalo (NY)
California State U, Fresno (CA)
Calumet Coll of Saint Joseph (IN)
Campbellsville U (KY)
Carson-Newman Coll (TN)
Centenary Coll of Louisiana (LA)
Central Michigan U (MI)
Central Missouri State U (MO)
Central Washington U (WA)
Chadron State Coll (NE)
Chicago State U (IL)
Clark Atlanta U (GA)
Clearwater Christian Coll (FL)
Coll of Santa Fe (NM)
Coll of the Ozarks (MO)
Coll of the Southwest (NM)
Colorado State U (CO)
Concord Coll (WV)
Concordia Coll (MN)
Concordia Coll (NY)
Concordia U (NE)
Concordia U Wisconsin (WI)
Cumberland Coll (KY)
Dakota State U (SD)
Dakota Wesleyan U (SD)
Dana Coll (NE)
Davis & Elkins Coll (WV)
Defiance Coll (OH)
Delaware State U (DE)
Delta State U (MS)
Dickinson State U (ND)
Doane Coll (NE)
Dordt Coll (IA)
Dowling Coll (NY)
Drake U (IA)
D'Youville Coll (NY)
East Carolina U (NC)
East Central U (OK)
Eastern Kentucky U (KY)
Eastern Michigan U (MI)
Eastern New Mexico U (NM)
Eastern Washington U (WA)
Elizabeth City State U (NC)
Emmanuel Coll (GA)
Evangel U (MO)
Fairmont State Coll (WV)
Fayetteville State U (NC)
Ferris State U (MI)
Florida Ag and Mech U (FL)
Fort Hays State U (KS)
The Franciscan U (IA)
Frostburg State U (MD)
Geneva Coll (PA)
Georgia Southern U (GA)
Glenville State Coll (WV)
Goshen Coll (IN)
Grace U (NE)
Grambling State U (LA)
Grand Canyon U (AZ)
Gwynedd-Mercy Coll (PA)
Hampton U (VA)
Hannibal-LaGrange Coll (MO)
Hardin-Simmons U (TX)
Hastings Coll (NE)
Henderson State U (AR)
Hofstra U (NY)
Howard Payne U (TX)
Huntington Coll (IN)
Illinois State U (IL)
Indiana State U (IN)
Indiana U of Pennsylvania (PA)
Inter American U of PR, Fajardo Campus (PR)
James Madison U (VA)
Jarvis Christian Coll (TX)
John Brown U (AR)
Kent State U (OH)
Lakeland Coll (WI)
Lambuth U (TN)
La Salle U (PA)
Lehman Coll of the City U of NY (NY)
Le Moyne Coll (NY)
Lenoir-Rhyne Coll (NC)
Liberty U (VA)
Lincoln Memorial U (TN)
Lincoln U (MO)
Lindenwood U (MO)
Louisiana Coll (LA)
Louisiana Tech U (LA)
Mayville State U (ND)
McGill U (QC, Canada)
McKendree Coll (IL)
McNeese State U (LA)
McPherson Coll (KS)
Mercyhurst Coll (PA)
MidAmerica Nazarene U (KS)
Middle Tennessee State U (TN)
Minot State U (ND)
Mississippi Coll (MS)
Mississippi State U (MS)
Missouri Baptist U (MO)
Morehead State U (KY)
Morgan State U (MD)
Morningside Coll (IA)
Mount Mary Coll (WI)
Mount St. Mary's Coll (CA)
Mount Vernon Nazarene U (OH)
Murray State U (KY)
Nazareth Coll of Rochester (NY)
New York Inst of Technology (NY)
Niagara U (NY)
Nicholls State U (LA)
Norfolk State U (VA)
Northeastern State U (OK)
Northern Michigan U (MI)
Northern State U (SD)
Northwestern Coll (IA)
Northwestern Oklahoma State U (OK)
Oakland City U (IN)
Oklahoma Panhandle State U (OK)
Ouachita Baptist U (AR)
Our Lady of Holy Cross Coll (LA)
Pace U (NY)
Pacific Union Coll (CA)
Pillsbury Baptist Bible Coll (MN)
Pontifical Catholic U of Puerto Rico (PR)
Rider U (NJ)
Robert Morris U (PA)
St. Ambrose U (IA)
Saint Augustine's Coll (NC)
St. Francis Coll (NY)
Saint Mary's Coll (IN)
St. Mary's U of San Antonio (TX)
Saint Vincent Coll (PA)
Salem State Coll (MA)
Sam Houston State U (TX)
Siena Heights U (MI)
South Carolina State U (SC)
Southeastern Oklahoma State U (OK)
Southeast Missouri State U (MO)
Southern Arkansas U–Magnolia (AR)
Southern Nazarene U (OK)
Southern Utah U (UT)
Southwest Baptist U (MO)
Southwest Missouri State U (MO)
State U of West Georgia (GA)
Suffolk U (MA)
Tabor Coll (KS)
Tennessee State U (TN)
Texas A&M U–Commerce (TX)
Texas Southern U (TX)
Texas Wesleyan U (TX)
Thomas Coll (ME)
Thomas More Coll (KY)
Trinity Christian Coll (IL)
Troy State U (AL)
Union Coll (KY)
Union Coll (NE)
Union U (TN)
The U of Akron (OH)
U of Alberta (AB, Canada)
U of Arkansas at Monticello (AR)
The U of British Columbia (BC, Canada)
U of Central Arkansas (AR)
U of Central Florida (FL)
The U of Findlay (OH)
U of Georgia (GA)
U of Hawaii at Manoa (HI)
U of Idaho (ID)
U of Illinois at Urbana–Champaign (IL)
U of Indianapolis (IN)
The U of Lethbridge (AB, Canada)
U of Maine at Fort Kent (ME)
U of Maine at Machias (ME)
U of Mary Hardin-Baylor (TX)
U of Maryland Eastern Shore (MD)
U of Minnesota, Twin Cities Campus (MN)
U of Missouri–Columbia (MO)
U of Missouri–St. Louis (MO)
The U of Montana–Missoula (MT)
The U of Montana–Western (MT)
U of Nebraska–Lincoln (NE)
U of Nevada, Reno (NV)
U of New Brunswick Fredericton (NB, Canada)
U of New Mexico (NM)
The U of North Carolina at Greensboro (NC)
U of North Dakota (ND)
U of Northern Iowa (IA)
U of Regina (SK, Canada)
U of Saint Francis (IN)
U of Southern Indiana (IN)
U of South Florida (FL)
The U of Tennessee (TN)
The U of Tennessee at Martin (TN)
U of the District of Columbia (DC)
U of the Ozarks (AR)
U of Toledo (OH)
The U of Western Ontario (ON, Canada)
U of Wisconsin–Superior (WI)
U of Wisconsin–Whitewater (WI)
Upper Iowa U (IA)
Utah State U (UT)
Utica Coll (NY)
Valdosta State U (GA)
Valley City State U (ND)
Virginia Polytechnic Inst and State U (VA)
Virginia State U (VA)
Virginia Union U (VA)
Viterbo U (WI)
Walla Walla Coll (WA)
Warner Southern Coll (FL)
Wayne State Coll (NE)
Weber State U (UT)
Western Baptist Coll (OR)
Western Kentucky U (KY)
Western Michigan U (MI)
Westfield State Coll (MA)
West Virginia State Coll (WV)
William Penn U (IA)
Winona State U (MN)
Winthrop U (SC)
Wright State U (OH)
York Coll (NE)
Youngstown State U (OH)

CAD/CADD DRAFTING/DESIGN TECHNOLOGY
Eastern Michigan U (MI)

CANADIAN GOVERNMENT AND POLITICS
The U of British Columbia (BC, Canada)

CANADIAN HISTORY
U of Regina (SK, Canada)

CANADIAN STUDIES
Acadia U (NS, Canada)
Athabasca U (AB, Canada)
Bishop's U (QC, Canada)
Brock U (ON, Canada)
Carleton U (ON, Canada)
Concordia U Coll of Alberta (AB, Canada)
Dalhousie U (NS, Canada)
Duke U (NC)
Franklin Coll (IN)
Hampshire Coll (MA)
McGill U (QC, Canada)
Memorial U of Newfoundland (NL, Canada)
Mount Allison U (NB, Canada)
Queen's U at Kingston (ON, Canada)
St. Francis Xavier U (NS, Canada)
St. Lawrence U (NY)
Simon Fraser U (BC, Canada)
Plattsburgh State U of NY (NY)
Sterling Coll (VT)
Trent U (ON, Canada)
U Coll of the Cariboo (BC, Canada)
U of Alberta (AB, Canada)
The U of British Columbia (BC, Canada)
U of Calgary (AB, Canada)
The U of Lethbridge (AB, Canada)
U of Manitoba (MB, Canada)
U of New Brunswick Fredericton (NB, Canada)
U of Ottawa (ON, Canada)
U of Prince Edward Island (PE, Canada)
U of Regina (SK, Canada)
U of Toronto (ON, Canada)
U of Vermont (VT)
U of Washington (WA)
U of Waterloo (ON, Canada)
Western Washington U (WA)
York U (ON, Canada)

CARDIOPULMONARY TECHNOLOGY
Bellarmine U (KY)

CARDIOVASCULAR TECHNOLOGY
Gwynedd-Mercy Coll (PA)
Louisiana State U Health Sciences Center (LA)
Nebraska Methodist Coll (NE)
Pennsylvania Coll of Technology (PA)
State U of New York Upstate Medical U (NY)
Thomas Jefferson U (PA)

CARIBBEAN STUDIES
Brooklyn Coll of the City U of NY (NY)
Florida State U (FL)
Hofstra U (NY)
Northwestern U (IL)

CARTOGRAPHY
Ball State U (IN)
Brigham Young U (UT)
East Central U (OK)
Kennesaw State U (GA)
Mansfield U of Pennsylvania (PA)
Memorial U of Newfoundland (NL, Canada)
Salem State Coll (MA)
Samford U (AL)
Southwest Missouri State U (MO)
State U of NY Coll at Oneonta (NY)
Texas A&M U (TX)
Texas A&M U–Corpus Christi (TX)
Texas State U-San Marcos (TX)
The U of Akron (OH)
U of Alberta (AB, Canada)
U of Idaho (ID)
U of Wisconsin–Madison (WI)
U of Wisconsin–Platteville (WI)

CELL AND MOLECULAR BIOLOGY
Connecticut Coll (CT)
Eastern Michigan U (MI)
Florida State U (FL)
Grand Valley State U (MI)
Marymount U (VA)
Pittsburg State U (KS)
Southwest Missouri State U (MO)
State U of NY Coll at Brockport (NY)
Texas A&M U (TX)
Texas Tech U (TX)
U Coll of the Cariboo (BC, Canada)
U of Calif, Berkeley (CA)
U of Calif, Los Angeles (CA)
U of Colorado at Boulder (CO)
U of Illinois at Urbana–Champaign (IL)
Western Washington U (WA)

CELL BIOLOGY AND ANATOMICAL SCIENCES RELATED
Brandeis U (MA)
Bridgewater State Coll (MA)
Connecticut Coll (CT)
Huntingdon Coll (AL)
Northern Arizona U (AZ)
Rutgers, The State U of New Jersey, New Brunswick/Piscataway (NJ)
Tulane U (LA)
U of Arkansas (AR)
U of Connecticut (CT)
U of Kentucky (KY)
Yale U (CT)

CELL BIOLOGY AND HISTOLOGY
Ball State U (IN)
Beloit Coll (WI)
California State U, Fresno (CA)
California State U, Long Beach (CA)
California State U, San Marcos (CA)
Clarkson U (NY)
Colby Coll (ME)
The Coll of Saint Rose (NY)
Concordia U (QC, Canada)
Cornell U (NY)
Fort Lewis Coll (CO)
Hampshire Coll (MA)
Harvard U (MA)
Humboldt State U (CA)
Juniata Coll (PA)
Lindenwood U (MO)
Mansfield U of Pennsylvania (PA)
Marlboro Coll (VT)
Memorial U of Newfoundland (NL, Canada)
Northeastern State U (OK)
Northwestern U (IL)
Ohio U (OH)
Okanagan U Coll (BC, Canada)
Oklahoma State U (OK)
Oregon State U (OR)
Pomona Coll (CA)
Rutgers, The State U of New Jersey, New Brunswick/Piscataway (NJ)

San Francisco State U (CA)
Sonoma State U (CA)
State U of NY Coll at Brockport (NY)
Texas Tech U (TX)
Tulane U (LA)
U Coll of the Cariboo (BC, Canada)
U of Alberta (AB, Canada)
The U of Arizona (AZ)
The U of British Columbia (BC, Canada)
U of Calgary (AB, Canada)
U of Calif, Davis (CA)
U of Calif, San Diego (CA)
U of Calif, Santa Barbara (CA)
U of Calif, Santa Cruz (CA)
U of Georgia (GA)
U of Illinois at Urbana–Champaign (IL)
U of Michigan (MI)
U of Minnesota, Duluth (MN)
U of Minnesota, Twin Cities Campus (MN)
U of New Hampshire (NH)
U of Utah (UT)
U of Washington (WA)
The U of Western Ontario (ON, Canada)
U of Wisconsin–Madison (WI)
U of Wisconsin–Superior (WI)
Western Washington U (WA)
William Jewell Coll (MO)
Worcester Polytechnic Inst (MA)

CELTIC LANGUAGES
U of Calif, Berkeley (CA)

CERAMIC ARTS AND CERAMICS
Alberta Coll of Art & Design (AB, Canada)
Alfred U (NY)
Arcadia U (PA)
Arizona State U (AZ)
Ball State U (IN)
Bennington Coll (VT)
Bethany Coll (KS)
Bowling Green State U (OH)
Brigham Young U (UT)
California Coll of the Arts (CA)
California State U, Fullerton (CA)
California State U, Hayward (CA)
California State U, Long Beach (CA)
Carnegie Mellon U (PA)
Chicago State U (IL)
The Cleveland Inst of Art (OH)
Coe Coll (IA)
Col for Creative Studies (MI)
Coll of the Atlantic (ME)
Colorado State U (CO)
Concord Coll (WV)
Concordia U (QC, Canada)
Franklin Pierce Coll (NH)
Grand Valley State U (MI)
Hampton U (VA)
Hofstra U (NY)
Howard U (DC)
Indiana U Bloomington (IN)
Inter American U of PR, San Germán Campus (PR)
Kansas City Art Inst (MO)
Loyola U Chicago (IL)
Maine Coll of Art (ME)
Marlboro Coll (VT)
Maryland Inst Coll of Art (MD)
Massachusetts Coll of Art (MA)
McMurry U (TX)
McNeese State U (LA)
Memphis Coll of Art (TN)
Minnesota State U Mankato (MN)
Minnesota State U Moorhead (MN)
Nazareth Coll of Rochester (NY)
Northern Michigan U (MI)
Northwest Nazarene U (ID)
Nova Scotia Coll of Art and Design (NS, Canada)
Ohio Northern U (OH)
The Ohio State U (OH)
Ohio U (OH)
Pratt Inst (NY)
Rhode Island School of Design (RI)
Rochester Inst of Technology (NY)
Rutgers, The State U of New Jersey, New Brunswick/Piscataway (NJ)
St. Cloud State U (MN)
San Francisco Art Inst (CA)
School of the Art Inst of Chicago (IL)
School of the Museum of Fine Arts, Boston (MA)
Seton Hill U (PA)
Shawnee State U (OH)
Simon's Rock Coll of Bard (MA)
State U of NY at New Paltz (NY)
State U of NY Coll at Brockport (NY)
State U of NY Coll at Potsdam (NY)
Syracuse U (NY)
Trinity Christian Coll (IL)
The U of Akron (OH)
U of Dallas (TX)
U of Evansville (IN)
U of Hartford (CT)
The U of Iowa (IA)
U of Kansas (KS)
U of Massachusetts Dartmouth (MA)
U of Miami (FL)
U of Michigan (MI)
U of Michigan–Flint (MI)
U of Montevallo (AL)
U of North Texas (TX)
U of Oregon (OR)
U of Regina (SK, Canada)
U of the District of Columbia (DC)
U of Washington (WA)
U of Wisconsin–Milwaukee (WI)
Washington U in St. Louis (MO)
Western Washington U (WA)
West Virginia Wesleyan Coll (WV)

CERAMIC SCIENCES AND ENGINEERING
Alfred U (NY)
Clemson U (SC)
The Ohio State U (OH)
Rutgers, The State U of New Jersey, New Brunswick/Piscataway (NJ)
U of Missouri–Rolla (MO)
U of Washington (WA)

CHEMICAL ENGINEERING
Arizona State U (AZ)
Auburn U (AL)
Bethel Coll (IN)
Brigham Young U (UT)
Brown U (RI)
Bucknell U (PA)
California Inst of Technology (CA)
California State Polytechnic U, Pomona (CA)
California State U, Long Beach (CA)
Calvin Coll (MI)
Carlow Coll (PA)
Carnegie Mellon U (PA)
Case Western Reserve U (OH)
Christian Brothers U (TN)
City Coll of the City U of NY (NY)
Clarkson U (NY)
Clemson U (SC)
Cleveland State U (OH)
Colorado School of Mines (CO)
Colorado State U (CO)
Columbia U, School of Eng & Applied Sci (NY)
Cooper Union for the Advancement of Science & Art (NY)
Cornell U (NY)
Dalhousie U (NS, Canada)
Drexel U (PA)
Excelsior Coll (NY)
Florida Ag and Mech U (FL)
Florida Inst of Technology (FL)
Florida Intl U (FL)
Florida State U (FL)
Gallaudet U (DC)
Geneva Coll (PA)
Georgia Inst of Technology (GA)
Hampton U (VA)
Harvard U (MA)
Howard U (DC)
Illinois Inst of Technology (IL)
Iowa State U of Science and Technology (IA)
The Johns Hopkins U (MD)
Kansas State U (KS)
Lafayette Coll (PA)
Lakehead U (ON, Canada)
Lamar U (TX)
Lehigh U (PA)
Louisiana State U and A&M Coll (LA)
Louisiana Tech U (LA)
Manhattan Coll (NY)
Massachusetts Inst of Technology (MA)
McGill U (QC, Canada)
Memorial U of Newfoundland (NL, Canada)
Michigan State U (MI)
Michigan Technological U (MI)
Mississippi State U (MS)
Montana State U–Bozeman (MT)
Murray State U (KY)
New Jersey Inst of Technology (NJ)
New Mexico Inst of Mining and Technology (NM)
New Mexico State U (NM)
North Carolina State U (NC)
Northeastern U (MA)
Northwestern U (IL)
The Ohio State U (OH)
Ohio U (OH)
Oklahoma State U (OK)
Oregon State U (OR)
Penn State U Abington Coll (PA)
Penn State U Altoona Coll (PA)
Penn State U at Erie, The Behrend Coll (PA)
Penn State U Beaver Campus of the Commonwealth Coll (PA)
Penn State U Berks Cmps of Berks-Lehigh Valley Coll (PA)
Penn State U Delaware County Campus of the Commonwealth Coll (PA)
Penn State U DuBois Campus of the Commonwealth Coll (PA)
Penn State U Fayette Campus of the Commonwealth Coll (PA)
Penn State U Hazleton Campus of the Commonwealth Coll (PA)
Penn State U Lehigh Valley Cmps of Berks-Lehigh Valley Coll (PA)
Penn State U McKeesport Campus of the Commonwealth Coll (PA)
Penn State U Mont Alto Campus of the Commonwealth Coll (PA)
Penn State U New Kensington Campus of the Commonwealth Coll (PA)
Penn State U Schuylkill Campus of the Capital Coll (PA)
Penn State U Shenango Campus of the Commonwealth Coll (PA)
Penn State U Univ Park Campus (PA)
Penn State U Wilkes-Barre Campus of the Commonwealth Coll (PA)
Penn State U Worthington Scranton Cmps Commonwealth Coll (PA)
Penn State U York Campus of the Commonwealth Coll (PA)
Polytechnic U, Brooklyn Campus (NY)
Polytechnic U of Puerto Rico (PR)
Prairie View A&M U (TX)
Princeton U (NJ)
Purdue U (IN)
Queen's U at Kingston (ON, Canada)
Rensselaer Polytechnic Inst (NY)
Rice U (TX)
Rose-Hulman Inst of Technology (IN)
Rowan U (NJ)
Rutgers, The State U of New Jersey, New Brunswick/Piscataway (NJ)
Ryerson U (ON, Canada)
San Diego State U (CA)
San Jose State U (CA)
South Dakota School of Mines and Technology (SD)
Stanford U (CA)
State U of NY Coll of Environ Sci and Forestry (NY)
Stevens Inst of Technology (NJ)
Syracuse U (NY)
Tennessee Technological U (TN)
Texas A&M U (TX)
Texas A&M U–Kingsville (TX)
Texas Tech U (TX)
Thiel Coll (PA)
Tri-State U (IN)
Tufts U (MA)
Tulane U (LA)
Tuskegee U (AL)
United States Military Acad (NY)
Université de Montréal (QC, Canada)
Université de Sherbrooke (QC, Canada)
Université Laval (QC, Canada)
U at Buffalo, The State U of New York (NY)
The U of Akron (OH)
The U of Alabama (AL)
The U of Alabama in Huntsville (AL)
U of Alberta (AB, Canada)
The U of Arizona (AZ)
U of Arkansas (AR)
The U of British Columbia (BC, Canada)
U of Calgary (AB, Canada)
U of Calif, Berkeley (CA)
U of Calif, Davis (CA)
U of Calif, Irvine (CA)
U of Calif, Los Angeles (CA)
U of Calif, Riverside (CA)
U of Calif, San Diego (CA)
U of Calif, Santa Barbara (CA)
U of Cincinnati (OH)
U of Colorado at Boulder (CO)
U of Connecticut (CT)
U of Dayton (OH)
U of Delaware (DE)
U of Florida (FL)
U of Guelph (ON, Canada)
U of Houston (TX)
U of Idaho (ID)
U of Illinois at Chicago (IL)
U of Illinois at Urbana–Champaign (IL)
The U of Iowa (IA)
U of Kansas (KS)
U of Kentucky (KY)
U of Louisiana at Lafayette (LA)
U of Louisville (KY)
U of Maine (ME)
U of Maryland, Baltimore County (MD)
U of Maryland, Coll Park (MD)
U of Massachusetts Amherst (MA)
U of Massachusetts Lowell (MA)
U of Michigan (MI)
U of Minnesota, Duluth (MN)
U of Minnesota, Twin Cities Campus (MN)
U of Mississippi (MS)
U of Missouri–Columbia (MO)
U of Missouri–Rolla (MO)
U of Nebraska–Lincoln (NE)
U of Nevada, Reno (NV)
U of New Brunswick Fredericton (NB, Canada)
U of New Hampshire (NH)
U of New Haven (CT)
U of New Mexico (NM)
U of North Dakota (ND)
U of Notre Dame (IN)
U of Oklahoma (OK)
U of Ottawa (ON, Canada)
U of Pennsylvania (PA)
U of Pittsburgh (PA)
U of Rhode Island (RI)
U of Rochester (NY)
U of Saskatchewan (SK, Canada)
U of South Alabama (AL)
U of South Carolina (SC)
U of Southern California (CA)
U of South Florida (FL)
The U of Tennessee (TN)
The U of Texas at Austin (TX)
U of Toledo (OH)
U of Toronto (ON, Canada)
U of Tulsa (OK)
U of Utah (UT)
U of Virginia (VA)
U of Washington (WA)
U of Waterloo (ON, Canada)
The U of Western Ontario (ON, Canada)
U of Wisconsin–Madison (WI)
U of Wyoming (WY)
Vanderbilt U (TN)
Villanova U (PA)
Virginia Commonwealth U (VA)
Virginia Polytechnic Inst and State U (VA)
Waldorf Coll (IA)
Washington and Lee U (VA)
Washington State U (WA)
Washington U in St. Louis (MO)
Wayne State U (MI)
Western Michigan U (MI)
West Virginia U (WV)
Widener U (PA)
Winona State U (MN)
Worcester Polytechnic Inst (MA)
Xavier U (OH)
Yale U (CT)
Youngstown State U (OH)

CHEMICAL PHYSICS
Barnard Coll (NY)
Bowdoin Coll (ME)
California Inst of Technology (CA)
Michigan State U (MI)
Simon Fraser U (BC, Canada)
Swarthmore Coll (PA)
U of Waterloo (ON, Canada)

CHEMICAL TECHNOLOGY
Inter American U of PR, Bayamón Campus (PR)
Murray State U (KY)
U of Regina (SK, Canada)

CHEMISTRY
Abilene Christian U (TX)
Acadia U (NS, Canada)
Adams State Coll (CO)
Adelphi U (NY)
Adrian Coll (MI)
Agnes Scott Coll (GA)
Alabama Ag and Mech U (AL)
Alabama State U (AL)
Albany State U (GA)
Albertson Coll of Idaho (ID)
Albertus Magnus Coll (CT)
Albion Coll (MI)
Albright Coll (PA)
Alcorn State U (MS)
Alderson-Broaddus Coll (WV)
Alfred U (NY)
Allegheny Coll (PA)
Allen U (SC)
Alma Coll (MI)
Alvernia Coll (PA)
Alverno Coll (WI)
American Intl Coll (MA)
American U (DC)
The American U in Cairo(Egypt)
Amherst Coll (MA)
Andrews U (MI)
Angelo State U (TX)
Antioch Coll (OH)
Appalachian State U (NC)
Aquinas Coll (MI)
Arcadia U (PA)
Arizona State U (AZ)
Arkansas State U (AR)
Arkansas Tech U (AR)
Armstrong Atlantic State U (GA)
Asbury Coll (KY)
Ashland U (OH)
Assumption Coll (MA)
Athens State U (AL)
Atlantic Union Coll (MA)
Auburn U (AL)
Augsburg Coll (MN)
Augustana Coll (IL)
Augustana Coll (SD)
Augusta State U (GA)
Aurora U (IL)
Austin Coll (TX)
Austin Peay State U (TN)
Averett U (VA)
Avila U (MO)
Azusa Pacific U (CA)
Baker U (KS)
Baldwin-Wallace Coll (OH)
Ball State U (IN)
Bard Coll (NY)
Barnard Coll (NY)
Barry U (FL)
Barton Coll (NC)
Bates Coll (ME)
Baylor U (TX)
Belhaven Coll (MS)
Bellarmine U (KY)
Belmont U (TN)
Beloit Coll (WI)
Bemidji State U (MN)
Benedictine Coll (KS)
Benedictine U (IL)
Bennington Coll (VT)
Berea Coll (KY)
Berry Coll (GA)
Bethany Coll (KS)
Bethany Coll (WV)
Bethany Lutheran Coll (MN)
Bethel Coll (IN)
Bethel Coll (KS)
Bethel Coll (TN)
Bethel U (MN)
Bethune-Cookman Coll (FL)
Birmingham-Southern Coll (AL)
Bishop's U (QC, Canada)
Blackburn Coll (IL)
Black Hills State U (SD)
Bloomfield Coll (NJ)
Bloomsburg U of Pennsylvania (PA)
Bluefield Coll (VA)
Blue Mountain Coll (MS)
Bluffton Coll (OH)
Boise State U (ID)
Boston Coll (MA)
Boston U (MA)
Bowdoin Coll (ME)
Bowling Green State U (OH)
Bradley U (IL)
Brandeis U (MA)
Brescia U (KY)
Briar Cliff U (IA)
Bridgewater Coll (VA)
Bridgewater State Coll (MA)
Brigham Young U (UT)
Brigham Young U–Hawaii (HI)
Brock U (ON, Canada)
Brooklyn Coll of the City U of NY (NY)
Brown U (RI)
Bryn Mawr Coll (PA)
Bucknell U (PA)
Buena Vista U (IA)
State U of NY Coll at Buffalo (NY)
Butler U (IN)
Cabrini Coll (PA)
Caldwell Coll (NJ)

California Inst of Technology (CA)
California Lutheran U (CA)
California Polytechnic State U, San Luis Obispo (CA)
California State Polytechnic U, Pomona (CA)
California State U, Chico (CA)
California State U, Dominguez Hills (CA)
California State U, Fresno (CA)
California State U, Fullerton (CA)
California State U, Hayward (CA)
California State U, Long Beach (CA)
California State U, Los Angeles (CA)
California State U, Sacramento (CA)
California State U, San Bernardino (CA)
California State U, San Marcos (CA)
California State U, Stanislaus (CA)
California U of Pennsylvania (PA)
Calvin Coll (MI)
Cameron U (OK)
Campbellsville U (KY)
Campbell U (NC)
Canisius Coll (NY)
Capital U (OH)
Cardinal Stritch U (WI)
Carleton Coll (MN)
Carleton U (ON, Canada)
Carlow Coll (PA)
Carnegie Mellon U (PA)
Carroll Coll (MT)
Carroll Coll (WI)
Carson-Newman Coll (TN)
Carthage Coll (WI)
Case Western Reserve U (OH)
Catawba Coll (NC)
The Catholic U of America (DC)
Cedar Crest Coll (PA)
Cedarville U (OH)
Centenary Coll of Louisiana (LA)
Central Coll (IA)
Central Connecticut State U (CT)
Central Methodist Coll (MO)
Central Michigan U (MI)
Central Missouri State U (MO)
Central State U (OH)
Central Washington U (WA)
Centre Coll (KY)
Chadron State Coll (NE)
Chapman U (CA)
Charleston Southern U (SC)
Chatham Coll (PA)
Chestnut Hill Coll (PA)
Cheyney U of Pennsylvania (PA)
Chicago State U (IL)
Christian Brothers U (TN)
Citadel, The Military Coll of South Carolina (SC)
City Coll of the City U of NY (NY)
Claremont McKenna Coll (CA)
Clarion U of Pennsylvania (PA)
Clark Atlanta U (GA)
Clarke Coll (IA)
Clarkson U (NY)
Clark U (MA)
Clemson U (SC)
Cleveland State U (OH)
Coastal Carolina U (SC)
Coe Coll (IA)
Coker Coll (SC)
Colby Coll (ME)
Colgate U (NY)
Coll Misericordia (PA)
Coll of Charleston (SC)
Coll of Mount St. Joseph (OH)
Coll of Mount Saint Vincent (NY)
The Coll of New Jersey (NJ)
The Coll of New Rochelle (NY)
Coll of Notre Dame of Maryland (MD)
Coll of Saint Benedict (MN)
Coll of St. Catherine (MN)
Coll of Saint Elizabeth (NJ)
Coll of Saint Mary (NE)
The Coll of Saint Rose (NY)
The Coll of St. Scholastica (MN)
The Coll of Southeastern Europe, The American U of Athens(Greece)
Coll of Staten Island of the City U of NY (NY)
Coll of the Holy Cross (MA)
Coll of the Ozarks (MO)
The Coll of William and Mary (VA)
The Coll of Wooster (OH)
The Colorado Coll (CO)
Colorado School of Mines (CO)
Colorado State U (CO)
Colorado State U-Pueblo (CO)
Columbia Coll (MO)
Columbia Coll (NY)
Columbia Coll (SC)
Columbia Union Coll (MD)
Columbia U, School of General Studies (NY)
Columbus State U (GA)
Concord Coll (WV)
Concordia Coll (MN)
Concordia U (CA)
Concordia U (IL)
Concordia U (NE)
Concordia U (OR)
Concordia U (QC, Canada)
Concordia U Coll of Alberta (AB, Canada)
Connecticut Coll (CT)
Converse Coll (SC)
Cornell Coll (IA)
Cornell U (NY)
Covenant Coll (GA)
Creighton U (NE)
Crichton Coll (TN)
Culver-Stockton Coll (MO)
Cumberland Coll (KY)
Dakota State U (SD)
Dalhousie U (NS, Canada)
Dana Coll (NE)
Dartmouth Coll (NH)
Davidson Coll (NC)
Davis & Elkins Coll (WV)
Defiance Coll (OH)
Delaware State U (DE)
Delaware Valley Coll (PA)
Delta State U (MS)
Denison U (OH)
DePaul U (IL)
DePauw U (IN)
DeSales U (PA)
Dickinson Coll (PA)
Dickinson State U (ND)
Dillard U (LA)
Doane Coll (NE)
Dominican U (IL)
Dordt Coll (IA)
Drake U (IA)
Drew U (NJ)
Drexel U (PA)
Drury U (MO)
Duke U (NC)
Duquesne U (PA)
Earlham Coll (IN)
East Carolina U (NC)
East Central U (OK)
Eastern Illinois U (IL)
Eastern Kentucky U (KY)
Eastern Mennonite U (VA)
Eastern Michigan U (MI)
Eastern Nazarene Coll (MA)
Eastern New Mexico U (NM)
Eastern Oregon U (OR)
Eastern U (PA)
Eastern Washington U (WA)
East Stroudsburg U of Pennsylvania (PA)
East Texas Baptist U (TX)
Eckerd Coll (FL)
Edgewood Coll (WI)
Edinboro U of Pennsylvania (PA)
Elizabeth City State U (NC)
Elizabethtown Coll (PA)
Elmhurst Coll (IL)
Elmira Coll (NY)
Elms Coll (MA)
Elon U (NC)
Emory & Henry Coll (VA)
Emory U (GA)
Emporia State U (KS)
Erskine Coll (SC)
Eureka Coll (IL)
Evangel U (MO)
Excelsior Coll (NY)
Fairfield U (CT)
Fairleigh Dickinson U, Florham (NJ)
Fairleigh Dickinson U, Teaneck-Metro Campus (NJ)
Fairmont State Coll (WV)
Fayetteville State U (NC)
Ferrum Coll (VA)
Florida Ag and Mech U (FL)
Florida Atlantic U (FL)
Florida Inst of Technology (FL)
Florida Intl U (FL)
Florida Southern Coll (FL)
Florida State U (FL)
Fordham U (NY)
Fort Hays State U (KS)
Fort Lewis Coll (CO)
Fort Valley State U (GA)
Framingham State Coll (MA)
Franciscan U of Steubenville (OH)
Francis Marion U (SC)
Franklin and Marshall Coll (PA)
Franklin Coll (IN)
Freed-Hardeman U (TN)
Fresno Pacific U (CA)
Frostburg State U (MD)
Furman U (SC)
Gallaudet U (DC)
Gannon U (PA)
Gardner-Webb U (NC)
Geneva Coll (PA)
George Fox U (OR)
George Mason U (VA)
Georgetown Coll (KY)
Georgetown U (DC)
The George Washington U (DC)
Georgia Coll & State U (GA)
Georgia Inst of Technology (GA)
Georgian Court U (NJ)
Georgia Southern U (GA)
Georgia Southwestern State U (GA)
Georgia State U (GA)
Gettysburg Coll (PA)
Glenville State Coll (WV)
Gonzaga U (WA)
Gordon Coll (MA)
Goshen Coll (IN)
Goucher Coll (MD)
Governors State U (IL)
Graceland U (IA)
Grambling State U (LA)
Grand Canyon U (AZ)
Grand Valley State U (MI)
Greensboro Coll (NC)
Greenville Coll (IL)
Grinnell Coll (IA)
Grove City Coll (PA)
Guilford Coll (NC)
Gustavus Adolphus Coll (MN)
Hamilton Coll (NY)
Hamline U (MN)
Hampden-Sydney Coll (VA)
Hampshire Coll (MA)
Hampton U (VA)
Hanover Coll (IN)
Harding U (AR)
Hardin-Simmons U (TX)
Hartwick Coll (NY)
Harvard U (MA)
Harvey Mudd Coll (CA)
Hastings Coll (NE)
Haverford Coll (PA)
Heidelberg Coll (OH)
Henderson State U (AR)
Hendrix Coll (AR)
High Point U (NC)
Hillsdale Coll (MI)
Hiram Coll (OH)
Hobart and William Smith Colls (NY)
Hofstra U (NY)
Hollins U (VA)
Hood Coll (MD)
Hope Coll (MI)
Houghton Coll (NY)
Houston Baptist U (TX)
Howard Payne U (TX)
Howard U (DC)
Humboldt State U (CA)
Hunter Coll of the City U of NY (NY)
Huntingdon Coll (AL)
Huntington Coll (IN)
Huston-Tillotson Coll (TX)
Idaho State U (ID)
Illinois Coll (IL)
Illinois Inst of Technology (IL)
Illinois State U (IL)
Illinois Wesleyan U (IL)
Immaculata U (PA)
Indiana State U (IN)
Indiana U Bloomington (IN)
Indiana U Northwest (IN)
Indiana U of Pennsylvania (PA)
Indiana U–Purdue U Fort Wayne (IN)
Indiana U–Purdue U Indianapolis (IN)
Indiana U South Bend (IN)
Indiana U Southeast (IN)
Inter American U of PR, Bayamón Campus (PR)
Inter American U of PR, San Germán Campus (PR)
Iona Coll (NY)
Iowa State U of Science and Technology (IA)
Iowa Wesleyan Coll (IA)
Ithaca Coll (NY)
Jacksonville State U (AL)
Jacksonville U (FL)
James Madison U (VA)
Jamestown Coll (ND)
Jarvis Christian Coll (TX)
John Brown U (AR)
John Carroll U (OH)
The Johns Hopkins U (MD)
Johnson C. Smith U (NC)
Judson Coll (AL)
Judson Coll (IL)
Juniata Coll (PA)
Kalamazoo Coll (MI)
Kansas State U (KS)
Kansas Wesleyan U (KS)
Kean U (NJ)
Keene State Coll (NH)
Kennesaw State U (GA)
Kent State U (OH)
Kentucky State U (KY)
Kentucky Wesleyan Coll (KY)
Kenyon Coll (OH)
Kettering U (MI)
King Coll (TN)
King's Coll (PA)
The King's U Coll (AB, Canada)
Knox Coll (IL)
Kutztown U of Pennsylvania (PA)
Lafayette Coll (PA)
LaGrange Coll (GA)
Lake Erie Coll (OH)
Lake Forest Coll (IL)
Lakehead U (ON, Canada)
Lakeland Coll (WI)
Lamar U (TX)
Lambuth U (TN)
Lander U (SC)
Lane Coll (TN)
La Roche Coll (PA)
La Salle U (PA)
Laurentian U (ON, Canada)
Lawrence Technological U (MI)
Lawrence U (WI)
Lebanon Valley Coll (PA)
Lehigh U (PA)
Lehman Coll of the City U of NY (NY)
Le Moyne Coll (NY)
Lenoir-Rhyne Coll (NC)
LeTourneau U (TX)
Lewis & Clark Coll (OR)
Lewis-Clark State Coll (ID)
Lewis U (IL)
Limestone Coll (SC)
Lincoln Memorial U (TN)
Lincoln U (MO)
Lincoln U (PA)
Lindenwood U (MO)
Linfield Coll (OR)
Lipscomb U (TN)
Livingstone Coll (NC)
Lock Haven U of Pennsylvania (PA)
Long Island U, Brooklyn Campus (NY)
Long Island U, C.W. Post Campus (NY)
Long Island U, Southampton Coll (NY)
Longwood U (VA)
Loras Coll (IA)
Louisiana Coll (LA)
Louisiana State U and A&M Coll (LA)
Louisiana State U in Shreveport (LA)
Louisiana Tech U (LA)
Lourdes Coll (OH)
Loyola Coll in Maryland (MD)
Loyola Marymount U (CA)
Loyola U Chicago (IL)
Loyola U New Orleans (LA)
Lubbock Christian U (TX)
Luther Coll (IA)
Lycoming Coll (PA)
Lynchburg Coll (VA)
Lyon Coll (AR)
Macalester Coll (MN)
MacMurray Coll (IL)
Madonna U (MI)
Malone Coll (OH)
Manchester Coll (IN)
Manhattan Coll (NY)
Manhattanville Coll (NY)
Mansfield U of Pennsylvania (PA)
Marian Coll (IN)
Marian Coll of Fond du Lac (WI)
Marietta Coll (OH)
Marist Coll (NY)
Marlboro Coll (VT)
Marquette U (WI)
Marshall U (WV)
Mars Hill Coll (NC)
Martin U (IN)
Mary Baldwin Coll (VA)
Marygrove Coll (MI)
Marymount Coll of Fordham U (NY)
Maryville Coll (TN)
Maryville U of Saint Louis (MO)
Mary Washington Coll (VA)
Massachusetts Coll of Liberal Arts (MA)
Mass Coll of Pharmacy and Allied Health Sciences (MA)
Massachusetts Inst of Technology (MA)
Mayville State U (ND)
McDaniel Coll (MD)
McGill U (QC, Canada)
McKendree Coll (IL)
McMurry U (TX)
McNeese State U (LA)
McPherson Coll (KS)
Memorial U of Newfoundland (NL, Canada)
Mercer U (GA)
Mercyhurst Coll (PA)
Meredith Coll (NC)
Merrimack Coll (MA)
Messiah Coll (PA)
Methodist Coll (NC)
Metropolitan State Coll of Denver (CO)
Miami U (OH)
Miami U Hamilton (OH)
Michigan State U (MI)
Michigan Technological U (MI)
MidAmerica Nazarene U (KS)
Middlebury Coll (VT)
Middle Tennessee State U (TN)
Midway Coll (KY)
Midwestern State U (TX)
Miles Coll (AL)
Millersville U of Pennsylvania (PA)
Milligan Coll (TN)
Millikin U (IL)
Millsaps Coll (MS)
Mills Coll (CA)
Minnesota State U Mankato (MN)
Minnesota State U Moorhead (MN)
Minot State U (ND)
Mississippi Coll (MS)
Mississippi State U (MS)
Mississippi Valley State U (MS)
Missouri Baptist U (MO)
Missouri Southern State U (MO)
Missouri Western State Coll (MO)
Monmouth Coll (IL)
Monmouth U (NJ)
Montana State U–Billings (MT)
Montana State U–Bozeman (MT)
Montana Tech of The U of Montana (MT)
Montclair State U (NJ)
Moravian Coll (PA)
Morehead State U (KY)
Morehouse Coll (GA)
Morgan State U (MD)
Morningside Coll (IA)
Mount Allison U (NB, Canada)
Mount Holyoke Coll (MA)
Mount Marty Coll (SD)
Mount Mary Coll (WI)
Mount Saint Mary Coll (NY)
Mount St. Mary's Coll (CA)
Mount Saint Mary's Coll and Sem (MD)
Mount Saint Vincent U (NS, Canada)
Mount Union Coll (OH)
Mount Vernon Nazarene U (OH)
Muhlenberg Coll (PA)
Murray State U (KY)
Nazareth Coll of Rochester (NY)
Nebraska Wesleyan U (NE)
Newberry Coll (SC)
New Coll of Florida (FL)
New Jersey City U (NJ)
New Jersey Inst of Technology (NJ)
Newman U (KS)
New Mexico Highlands U (NM)
New Mexico Inst of Mining and Technology (NM)
New Mexico State U (NM)
New York Inst of Technology (NY)
New York U (NY)
Niagara U (NY)
Nicholls State U (LA)
Norfolk State U (VA)
North Carolina Central U (NC)
North Carolina State U (NC)
North Carolina Wesleyan Coll (NC)
North Central Coll (IL)
North Dakota State U (ND)
Northeastern Illinois U (IL)
Northeastern State U (OK)
Northeastern U (MA)
Northern Arizona U (AZ)
Northern Illinois U (IL)
Northern Michigan U (MI)
Northern State U (SD)
North Georgia Coll & State U (GA)
Northland Coll (WI)
North Park U (IL)
Northwestern Coll (IA)
Northwestern Oklahoma State U (OK)
Northwestern State U of Louisiana (LA)
Northwestern U (IL)
Northwest Nazarene U (ID)
Notre Dame Coll (OH)
Oakland City U (IN)
Oakland U (MI)

Oberlin Coll (OH)
Occidental Coll (CA)
Oglethorpe U (GA)
Ohio Dominican U (OH)
Ohio Northern U (OH)
The Ohio State U (OH)
Ohio U (OH)
Ohio Wesleyan U (OH)
Okanagan U Coll (BC, Canada)
Oklahoma Baptist U (OK)
Oklahoma Christian U (OK)
Oklahoma City U (OK)
Oklahoma Panhandle State U (OK)
Oklahoma State U (OK)
Old Dominion U (VA)
Olivet Coll (MI)
Olivet Nazarene U (IL)
Oral Roberts U (OK)
Oregon State U (OR)
Otterbein Coll (OH)
Ouachita Baptist U (AR)
Our Lady of the Lake U of San Antonio (TX)
Pace U (NY)
Pacific Lutheran U (WA)
Pacific Union Coll (CA)
Pacific U (OR)
Paine Coll (GA)
Park U (MO)
Penn State U Abington Coll (PA)
Penn State U Altoona Coll (PA)
Penn State U at Erie, The Behrend Coll (PA)
Penn State U Beaver Campus of the Commonwealth Coll (PA)
Penn State U Berks Cmps of Berks-Lehigh Valley Coll (PA)
Penn State U Delaware County Campus of the Commonwealth Coll (PA)
Penn State U DuBois Campus of the Commonwealth Coll (PA)
Penn State U Fayette Campus of the Commonwealth Coll (PA)
Penn State U Hazleton Campus of the Commonwealth Coll (PA)
Penn State U Lehigh Valley Cmps of Berks-Lehigh Valley Coll (PA)
Penn State U McKeesport Campus of the Commonwealth Coll (PA)
Penn State U Mont Alto Campus of the Commonwealth Coll (PA)
Penn State U New Kensington Campus of the Commonwealth Coll (PA)
Penn State U Schuylkill Campus of the Capital Coll (PA)
Penn State U Shenango Campus of the Commonwealth Coll (PA)
Penn State U Univ Park Campus (PA)
Penn State U Wilkes-Barre Campus of the Commonwealth Coll (PA)
Penn State U Worthington Scranton Cmps Commonwealth Coll (PA)
Penn State U York Campus of the Commonwealth Coll (PA)
Pepperdine U, Malibu (CA)
Pfeiffer U (NC)
Philadelphia U (PA)
Piedmont Coll (GA)
Pikeville Coll (KY)
Pittsburg State U (KS)
Pitzer Coll (CA)
Plymouth State U (NH)
Point Loma Nazarene U (CA)
Polytechnic U, Brooklyn Campus (NY)
Pomona Coll (CA)
Pontifical Catholic U of Puerto Rico (PR)
Portland State U (OR)
Prairie View A&M U (TX)
Presbyterian Coll (SC)
Princeton U (NJ)
Principia Coll (IL)
Providence Coll (RI)
Purdue U (IN)
Queens Coll of the City U of NY (NY)
Queen's U at Kingston (ON, Canada)
Quincy U (IL)
Quinnipiac U (CT)
Radford U (VA)
Ramapo Coll of New Jersey (NJ)
Randolph-Macon Coll (VA)
Randolph-Macon Woman's Coll (VA)
Reed Coll (OR)
Regis U (CO)
Rensselaer Polytechnic Inst (NY)
Rhode Island Coll (RI)
Rhodes Coll (TN)
Rice U (TX)
The Richard Stockton Coll of New Jersey (NJ)
Rider U (NJ)
Ripon Coll (WI)
Rivier Coll (NH)
Roanoke Coll (VA)
Roberts Wesleyan Coll (NY)
Rochester Inst of Technology (NY)
Rockford Coll (IL)
Rockhurst U (MO)
Rocky Mountain Coll (MT)
Roger Williams U (RI)
Rollins Coll (FL)
Roosevelt U (IL)
Rose-Hulman Inst of Technology (IN)
Rosemont Coll (PA)
Rowan U (NJ)
Russell Sage Coll (NY)
Rutgers, The State U of New Jersey, Camden (NJ)
Rutgers, The State U of New Jersey, Newark (NJ)
Rutgers, The State U of New Jersey, New Brunswick/Piscataway (NJ)
Ryerson U (ON, Canada)
Sacred Heart U (CT)
Saginaw Valley State U (MI)
St. Ambrose U (IA)
St. Andrews Presbyterian Coll (NC)
Saint Augustine's Coll (NC)
St. Bonaventure U (NY)
St. Cloud State U (MN)
St. Edward's U (TX)
St. Francis Coll (NY)
Saint Francis U (PA)
St. Francis Xavier U (NS, Canada)
St. Gregory's U (OK)
St. John Fisher Coll (NY)
Saint John's U (MN)
St. John's U (NY)
Saint Joseph Coll (CT)
Saint Joseph's Coll (IN)
St. Joseph's Coll, New York (NY)
Saint Joseph's Coll of Maine (ME)
Saint Joseph's U (PA)
St. Lawrence U (NY)
Saint Louis U (MO)
Saint Martin's Coll (WA)
Saint Mary's Coll (IN)
Saint Mary's Coll of California (CA)
St. Mary's Coll of Maryland (MD)
Saint Mary's U of Minnesota (MN)
St. Mary's U of San Antonio (TX)
Saint Michael's Coll (VT)
St. Norbert Coll (WI)
St. Olaf Coll (MN)
St. Thomas U (FL)
Saint Vincent Coll (PA)
Saint Xavier U (IL)
Salem Coll (NC)
Salem State Coll (MA)
Salisbury U (MD)
Salve Regina U (RI)
Samford U (AL)
Sam Houston State U (TX)
San Diego State U (CA)
San Francisco State U (CA)
San Jose State U (CA)
Santa Clara U (CA)
Sarah Lawrence Coll (NY)
Schreiner U (TX)
Scripps Coll (CA)
Seattle Pacific U (WA)
Seattle U (WA)
Seton Hall U (NJ)
Seton Hill U (PA)
Shawnee State U (OH)
Shaw U (NC)
Shenandoah U (VA)
Shepherd U (WV)
Shippensburg U of Pennsylvania (PA)
Shorter Coll (GA)
Siena Coll (NY)
Siena Heights U (MI)
Simmons Coll (MA)
Simon Fraser U (BC, Canada)
Simon's Rock Coll of Bard (MA)
Simpson Coll (IA)
Skidmore Coll (NY)
Slippery Rock U of Pennsylvania (PA)
Smith Coll (MA)
Sonoma State U (CA)
South Carolina State U (SC)
South Dakota School of Mines and Technology (SD)
South Dakota State U (SD)
Southeastern Louisiana U (LA)
Southeastern Oklahoma State U (OK)
Southeast Missouri State U (MO)
Southern Adventist U (TN)
Southern Arkansas U–Magnolia (AR)
Southern Connecticut State U (CT)
Southern Illinois U Carbondale (IL)
Southern Illinois U Edwardsville (IL)
Southern Methodist U (TX)
Southern Nazarene U (OK)
Southern Oregon U (OR)
Southern U and A&M Coll (LA)
Southern Utah U (UT)
Southern Wesleyan U (SC)
Southwest Baptist U (MO)
Southwestern Coll (KS)
Southwestern Oklahoma State U (OK)
Southwestern U (TX)
Southwest Missouri State U (MO)
Spelman Coll (GA)
Spring Arbor U (MI)
Springfield Coll (MA)
Spring Hill Coll (AL)
Stanford U (CA)
State U of NY at Binghamton (NY)
State U of NY at New Paltz (NY)
State U of NY at Oswego (NY)
Plattsburgh State U of NY (NY)
State U of NY Coll at Brockport (NY)
State U of NY Coll at Cortland (NY)
State U of NY Coll at Fredonia (NY)
State U of NY Coll at Geneseo (NY)
State U of NY Coll at Old Westbury (NY)
State U of NY Coll at Oneonta (NY)
State U of NY Coll at Potsdam (NY)
State U of NY Coll of Environ Sci and Forestry (NY)
State U of West Georgia (GA)
Stetson U (FL)
Stevens Inst of Technology (NJ)
Stonehill Coll (MA)
Stony Brook U, State U of New York (NY)
Suffolk U (MA)
Susquehanna U (PA)
Swarthmore Coll (PA)
Sweet Briar Coll (VA)
Syracuse U (NY)
Tabor Coll (KS)
Talladega Coll (AL)
Tarleton State U (TX)
Taylor U (IN)
Tennessee State U (TN)
Tennessee Technological U (TN)
Tennessee Wesleyan Coll (TN)
Texas A&M Intl U (TX)
Texas A&M U (TX)
Texas A&M U–Commerce (TX)
Texas A&M U–Corpus Christi (TX)
Texas A&M U–Kingsville (TX)
Texas Christian U (TX)
Texas Lutheran U (TX)
Texas Southern U (TX)
Texas State U-San Marcos (TX)
Texas Tech U (TX)
Texas Wesleyan U (TX)
Texas Woman's U (TX)
Thiel Coll (PA)
Thomas Edison State Coll (NJ)
Thomas More Coll (KY)
Tougaloo Coll (MS)
Towson U (MD)
Transylvania U (KY)
Trent U (ON, Canada)
Trevecca Nazarene U (TN)
Trinity Christian Coll (IL)
Trinity Coll (CT)
Trinity Coll (DC)
Trinity Intl U (IL)
Trinity U (TX)
Trinity Western U (BC, Canada)
Tri-State U (IN)
Troy State U (AL)
Truman State U (MO)
Tufts U (MA)
Tulane U (LA)
Tuskegee U (AL)
Union Coll (KY)
Union Coll (NE)
Union Coll (NY)
Union U (TN)
United States Air Force Acad (CO)
United States Military Acad (NY)
United States Naval Acad (MD)
Universidad Adventista de las Antillas (PR)
Université de Montréal (QC, Canada)
Université de Sherbrooke (QC, Canada)
Université Laval (QC, Canada)
State U of NY at Albany (NY)
U at Buffalo, The State U of New York (NY)
U Coll of the Cariboo (BC, Canada)
U Coll of the Fraser Valley (BC, Canada)
The U of Akron (OH)
The U of Alabama (AL)
The U of Alabama at Birmingham (AL)
The U of Alabama in Huntsville (AL)
U of Alaska Fairbanks (AK)
U of Alberta (AB, Canada)
The U of Arizona (AZ)
U of Arkansas (AR)
U of Arkansas at Little Rock (AR)
U of Arkansas at Monticello (AR)
The U of British Columbia (BC, Canada)
U of Calgary (AB, Canada)
U of Calif, Berkeley (CA)
U of Calif, Davis (CA)
U of Calif, Irvine (CA)
U of Calif, Los Angeles (CA)
U of Calif, Riverside (CA)
U of Calif, San Diego (CA)
U of Calif, Santa Barbara (CA)
U of Calif, Santa Cruz (CA)
U of Central Arkansas (AR)
U of Central Florida (FL)
U of Charleston (WV)
U of Chicago (IL)
U of Cincinnati (OH)
U of Colorado at Boulder (CO)
U of Colorado at Colorado Springs (CO)
U of Colorado at Denver (CO)
U of Connecticut (CT)
U of Dallas (TX)
U of Dayton (OH)
U of Delaware (DE)
U of Denver (CO)
U of Detroit Mercy (MI)
U of Evansville (IN)
U of Florida (FL)
U of Georgia (GA)
U of Great Falls (MT)
U of Guelph (ON, Canada)
U of Hartford (CT)
U of Hawaii at Hilo (HI)
U of Hawaii at Manoa (HI)
U of Houston (TX)
U of Houston–Clear Lake (TX)
U of Idaho (ID)
U of Illinois at Chicago (IL)
U of Illinois at Springfield (IL)
U of Illinois at Urbana–Champaign (IL)
U of Indianapolis (IN)
The U of Iowa (IA)
U of Kansas (KS)
U of Kentucky (KY)
U of King's Coll (NS, Canada)
U of La Verne (CA)
The U of Lethbridge (AB, Canada)
U of Louisiana at Lafayette (LA)
U of Louisville (KY)
U of Maine (ME)
U of Manitoba (MB, Canada)
U of Mary Hardin-Baylor (TX)
U of Maryland, Baltimore County (MD)
U of Maryland, Coll Park (MD)
U of Maryland Eastern Shore (MD)
U of Massachusetts Amherst (MA)
U of Massachusetts Boston (MA)
U of Massachusetts Dartmouth (MA)
U of Massachusetts Lowell (MA)
The U of Memphis (TN)
U of Miami (FL)
U of Michigan (MI)
U of Michigan–Dearborn (MI)
U of Michigan–Flint (MI)
U of Minnesota, Duluth (MN)
U of Minnesota, Morris (MN)
U of Minnesota, Twin Cities Campus (MN)
U of Mississippi (MS)
U of Missouri–Columbia (MO)
U of Missouri–Kansas City (MO)
U of Missouri–Rolla (MO)
U of Missouri–St. Louis (MO)
U of Mobile (AL)
The U of Montana–Missoula (MT)
U of Montevallo (AL)
U of Nebraska at Omaha (NE)
U of Nebraska–Lincoln (NE)
U of Nevada, Las Vegas (NV)
U of Nevada, Reno (NV)
U of New Brunswick Fredericton (NB, Canada)
U of New Hampshire (NH)
U of New Haven (CT)
U of New Mexico (NM)
U of New Orleans (LA)
U of North Alabama (AL)
The U of North Carolina at Asheville (NC)
The U of North Carolina at Chapel Hill (NC)
The U of North Carolina at Charlotte (NC)
The U of North Carolina at Greensboro (NC)
The U of North Carolina at Pembroke (NC)
The U of North Carolina at Wilmington (NC)
U of North Dakota (ND)
U of Northern Colorado (CO)
U of Northern Iowa (IA)
U of North Florida (FL)
U of North Texas (TX)
U of Notre Dame (IN)
U of Oklahoma (OK)
U of Oregon (OR)
U of Ottawa (ON, Canada)
U of Pennsylvania (PA)
U of Pittsburgh (PA)
U of Pittsburgh at Bradford (PA)
U of Pittsburgh at Johnstown (PA)
U of Portland (OR)
U of Prince Edward Island (PE, Canada)
U of Puerto Rico, Cayey U Coll (PR)
U of Puget Sound (WA)
U of Redlands (CA)
U of Regina (SK, Canada)
U of Rhode Island (RI)
U of Richmond (VA)
U of Rochester (NY)
U of Saint Francis (IN)
U of Saint Mary (KS)
U of St. Thomas (MN)
U of St. Thomas (TX)
U of San Diego (CA)
U of San Francisco (CA)
U of Saskatchewan (SK, Canada)
U of Science and Arts of Oklahoma (OK)
The U of Scranton (PA)
U of Sioux Falls (SD)
U of South Alabama (AL)
U of South Carolina (SC)
U of South Carolina Aiken (SC)
U of South Carolina Spartanburg (SC)
The U of South Dakota (SD)
U of Southern California (CA)
U of Southern Indiana (IN)
U of Southern Maine (ME)
U of South Florida (FL)
The U of Tampa (FL)
The U of Tennessee (TN)
The U of Tennessee at Chattanooga (TN)
The U of Tennessee at Martin (TN)
The U of Texas at Arlington (TX)
The U of Texas at Austin (TX)
The U of Texas at Brownsville (TX)
The U of Texas at Dallas (TX)
The U of Texas at Tyler (TX)
The U of Texas–Pan American (TX)
U of the District of Columbia (DC)
U of the Incarnate Word (TX)
U of the Ozarks (AR)
U of the Pacific (CA)
U of the Sacred Heart (PR)
U of the Sciences in Philadelphia (PA)
U of the South (TN)
U of the Virgin Islands (VI)
U of Toledo (OH)
U of Toronto (ON, Canada)
U of Tulsa (OK)
U of Utah (UT)
U of Vermont (VT)
U of Victoria (BC, Canada)
U of Virginia (VA)
The U of Virginia's Coll at Wise (VA)
U of Washington (WA)
U of Waterloo (ON, Canada)
The U of West Alabama (AL)
The U of Western Ontario (ON, Canada)
U of West Florida (FL)
U of Windsor (ON, Canada)
U of Wisconsin–Eau Claire (WI)
U of Wisconsin–Green Bay (WI)
U of Wisconsin–La Crosse (WI)
U of Wisconsin–Madison (WI)
U of Wisconsin–Milwaukee (WI)
U of Wisconsin–Oshkosh (WI)
U of Wisconsin–Parkside (WI)
U of Wisconsin–River Falls (WI)
U of Wisconsin–Stevens Point (WI)
U of Wisconsin–Superior (WI)
U of Wisconsin–Whitewater (WI)
U of Wyoming (WY)

Upper Iowa U (IA)
Urbana U (OH)
Ursinus Coll (PA)
Utah State U (UT)
Utica Coll (NY)
Valdosta State U (GA)
Valley City State U (ND)
Valparaiso U (IN)
Vanderbilt U (TN)
Vanguard U of Southern California (CA)
Vassar Coll (NY)
Villa Julie Coll (MD)
Villanova U (PA)
Virginia Commonwealth U (VA)
Virginia Military Inst (VA)
Virginia Polytechnic Inst and State U (VA)
Virginia State U (VA)
Virginia Union U (VA)
Virginia Wesleyan Coll (VA)
Viterbo U (WI)
Voorhees Coll (SC)
Wabash Coll (IN)
Wagner Coll (NY)
Wake Forest U (NC)
Walla Walla Coll (WA)
Walsh U (OH)
Warren Wilson Coll (NC)
Wartburg Coll (IA)
Washburn U (KS)
Washington & Jefferson Coll (PA)
Washington and Lee U (VA)
Washington Coll (MD)
Washington State U (WA)
Washington U in St. Louis (MO)
Wayland Baptist U (TX)
Waynesburg Coll (PA)
Wayne State Coll (NE)
Wayne State U (MI)
Weber State U (UT)
Wellesley Coll (MA)
Wells Coll (NY)
Wesleyan Coll (GA)
Wesleyan U (CT)
West Chester U of Pennsylvania (PA)
Western Carolina U (NC)
Western Connecticut State U (CT)
Western Illinois U (IL)
Western Kentucky U (KY)
Western Michigan U (MI)
Western New England Coll (MA)
Western Oregon U (OR)
Western State Coll of Colorado (CO)
Western Washington U (WA)
West Liberty State Coll (WV)
Westminster Coll (MO)
Westminster Coll (PA)
Westminster Coll (UT)
Westmont Coll (CA)
West Texas A&M U (TX)
West Virginia State Coll (WV)
West Virginia U (WV)
West Virginia Wesleyan Coll (WV)
Wheaton Coll (IL)
Wheaton Coll (MA)
Wheeling Jesuit U (WV)
Whitman Coll (WA)
Whitworth Coll (WA)
Wichita State U (KS)
Widener U (PA)
Wilberforce U (OH)
Wilkes U (PA)
Willamette U (OR)
William Carey Coll (MS)
William Jewell Coll (MO)
Williams Coll (MA)
Wilson Coll (PA)
Wingate U (NC)
Winona State U (MN)
Winston-Salem State U (NC)
Winthrop U (SC)
Wisconsin Lutheran Coll (WI)
Wittenberg U (OH)
Wofford Coll (SC)
Worcester Polytechnic Inst (MA)
Worcester State Coll (MA)
Wright State U (OH)
Xavier U (OH)
Xavier U of Louisiana (LA)
Yale U (CT)
York Coll of Pennsylvania (PA)
York Coll of the City U of New York (NY)
York U (ON, Canada)
Youngstown State U (OH)

CHEMISTRY RELATED
Bridgewater State Coll (MA)
California State U, Chico (CA)
California State U, Sacramento (CA)
Clemson U (SC)
Coll of Mount St. Joseph (OH)
Connecticut Coll (CT)
Cornell U (NY)
Dartmouth Coll (NH)
Duquesne U (PA)
Edinboro U of Pennsylvania (PA)
Florida Inst of Technology (FL)
Florida State U (FL)
Georgia Inst of Technology (GA)
Hofstra U (NY)
Lawrence Technological U (MI)
Lehigh U (PA)
McGill U (QC, Canada)
Northern Arizona U (AZ)
Ohio Northern U (OH)
Okanagan U Coll (BC, Canada)
Roger Williams U (RI)
Saint Anselm Coll (NH)
Saint Mary's Coll of California (CA)
San Diego State U (CA)
Stony Brook U, State U of New York (NY)
Texas Wesleyan U (TX)
Towson U (MD)
U of Calif, Berkeley (CA)
U of Massachusetts Dartmouth (MA)
U of Miami (FL)
U of Northern Iowa (IA)
U of Notre Dame (IN)
The U of Scranton (PA)
U of the Pacific (CA)
U of Wisconsin–Eau Claire (WI)
U of Wisconsin–Whitewater (WI)
Washington & Jefferson Coll (PA)
Washington U in St. Louis (MO)
Western Michigan U (MI)

CHEMISTRY TEACHER EDUCATION
Alma Coll (MI)
Alvernia Coll (PA)
Appalachian State U (NC)
Arkansas State U (AR)
Arkansas Tech U (AR)
Averett U (VA)
Baylor U (TX)
Bethany Coll (KS)
Bethel U (MN)
Bethune-Cookman Coll (FL)
Bishop's U (QC, Canada)
Bloomfield Coll (NJ)
Bluefield Coll (VA)
Blue Mountain Coll (MS)
Boston U (MA)
Bridgewater Coll (VA)
Brigham Young U (UT)
Brigham Young U–Hawaii (HI)
Brooklyn Coll of the City U of NY (NY)
Buena Vista U (IA)
Cabrini Coll (PA)
California State U, Chico (CA)
Campbellsville U (KY)
Capital U (OH)
Carroll Coll (WI)
The Catholic U of America (DC)
Centenary Coll of Louisiana (LA)
Central Methodist Coll (MO)
Central Michigan U (MI)
Central Missouri State U (MO)
Central Washington U (WA)
Chadron State Coll (NE)
Chapman U (CA)
Chatham Coll (PA)
Christian Brothers U (TN)
City Coll of the City U of NY (NY)
Coker Coll (SC)
The Coll of New Jersey (NJ)
Coll of St. Catherine (MN)
The Coll of Saint Rose (NY)
The Coll of St. Scholastica (MN)
Coll of the Ozarks (MO)
Colorado State U (CO)
Columbus State U (GA)
Concordia Coll (MN)
Concordia U (NE)
Concordia U, St. Paul (MN)
Crichton Coll (TN)
Delaware State U (DE)
Delta State U (MS)
Dordt Coll (IA)
Duquesne U (PA)
East Central U (OK)
Eastern Mennonite U (VA)
Eastern Michigan U (MI)
Eastern Washington U (WA)
East Texas Baptist U (TX)
Elizabeth City State U (NC)
Elmhurst Coll (IL)
Elmira Coll (NY)
Evangel U (MO)
Florida Inst of Technology (FL)
Framingham State Coll (MA)
Franklin Coll (IN)
George Fox U (OR)
Georgia Southern U (GA)
Glenville State Coll (WV)
Greenville Coll (IL)
Gustavus Adolphus Coll (MN)
Hardin-Simmons U (TX)
Hastings Coll (NE)
Hofstra U (NY)
Hope Coll (MI)
Huntingdon Coll (AL)
Illinois Wesleyan U (IL)
Indiana U Bloomington (IN)
Indiana U Northwest (IN)
Indiana U–Purdue U Fort Wayne (IN)
Indiana U South Bend (IN)
Ithaca Coll (NY)
Juniata Coll (PA)
Kennesaw State U (GA)
Kent State U (OH)
Kentucky Wesleyan Coll (KY)
King Coll (TN)
Lambuth U (TN)
La Roche Coll (PA)
Lebanon Valley Coll (PA)
Le Moyne Coll (NY)
Lincoln Memorial U (TN)
Lindenwood U (MO)
Long Island U, Brooklyn Campus (NY)
Long Island U, C.W. Post Campus (NY)
Louisiana State U in Shreveport (LA)
Louisiana Tech U (LA)
Manhattanville Coll (NY)
Mansfield U of Pennsylvania (PA)
Marian Coll of Fond du Lac (WI)
Marymount Coll of Fordham U (NY)
Maryville Coll (TN)
Maryville U of Saint Louis (MO)
Mayville State U (ND)
McGill U (QC, Canada)
McNeese State U (LA)
Mercyhurst Coll (PA)
Messiah Coll (PA)
Miami Dade Coll (FL)
Miami U Hamilton (OH)
Michigan State U (MI)
Minot State U (ND)
Montana State U–Billings (MT)
Moravian Coll (PA)
Mount Marty Coll (SD)
Murray State U (KY)
Nazareth Coll of Rochester (NY)
New York Inst of Technology (NY)
New York U (NY)
Niagara U (NY)
North Carolina Central U (NC)
North Carolina State U (NC)
North Dakota State U (ND)
Northern Michigan U (MI)
Northwest Nazarene U (ID)
Ohio Dominican U (OH)
Ohio Northern U (OH)
Ohio Wesleyan U (OH)
Oklahoma Baptist U (OK)
Pace U (NY)
Pikeville Coll (KY)
Pittsburg State U (KS)
Rivier Coll (NH)
Roberts Wesleyan Coll (NY)
Rocky Mountain Coll (MT)
Sacred Heart U (CT)
St. Ambrose U (IA)
St. Bonaventure U (NY)
St. Francis Coll (NY)
Saint Francis U (PA)
St. John's U (NY)
Saint Joseph's Coll of Maine (ME)
Saint Mary's U of Minnesota (MN)
San Diego State U (CA)
Seton Hill U (PA)
Southern Arkansas U–Magnolia (AR)
Southwest Baptist U (MO)
Southwest Missouri State U (MO)
State U of NY Coll at Brockport (NY)
State U of NY Coll at Cortland (NY)
State U of NY Coll at Old Westbury (NY)
State U of NY Coll at Oneonta (NY)
State U of NY Coll at Potsdam (NY)
State U of NY Coll of Environ Sci and Forestry (NY)
State U of West Georgia (GA)
Syracuse U (NY)
Talladega Coll (AL)
Tennessee Wesleyan Coll (TN)
Trevecca Nazarene U (TN)
Trinity Christian Coll (IL)
Union Coll (NE)
State U of NY at Albany (NY)
The U of Akron (OH)
The U of Arizona (AZ)
U of Calif, San Diego (CA)
U of Delaware (DE)
U of Great Falls (MT)
U of Illinois at Chicago (IL)
The U of Iowa (IA)
U of Louisiana at Lafayette (LA)
U of Michigan–Flint (MI)
U of Missouri–Columbia (MO)
U of Missouri–St. Louis (MO)
U of Nebraska–Lincoln (NE)
The U of North Carolina at Charlotte (NC)
The U of North Carolina at Wilmington (NC)
U of Pittsburgh at Johnstown (PA)
U of Puerto Rico, Cayey U Coll (PR)
U of Regina (SK, Canada)
U of Saint Francis (IN)
U of St. Thomas (MN)
The U of Tennessee at Martin (TN)
U of Waterloo (ON, Canada)
U of Windsor (ON, Canada)
U of Wisconsin–River Falls (WI)
U of Wisconsin–Superior (WI)
Utah State U (UT)
Utica Coll (NY)
Valdosta State U (GA)
Valley City State U (ND)
Valparaiso U (IN)
Viterbo U (WI)
Washington U in St. Louis (MO)
Waynesburg Coll (PA)
Weber State U (UT)
West Chester U of Pennsylvania (PA)
Western Michigan U (MI)
Western Washington U (WA)
Wheeling Jesuit U (WV)
Widener U (PA)
Xavier U (OH)
Xavier U of Louisiana (LA)
York U (ON, Canada)
Youngstown State U (OH)

CHILD CARE AND SUPPORT SERVICES MANAGEMENT
Brigham Young U (UT)
Central Michigan U (MI)
Chestnut Hill Coll (PA)
Concordia U, St. Paul (MN)
Eastern Washington U (WA)
Malaspina U-Coll (BC, Canada)
Pacific Union Coll (CA)
Saint Mary-of-the-Woods Coll (IN)
Seton Hill U (PA)
U Coll of the Fraser Valley (BC, Canada)

CHILD CARE/GUIDANCE
Coll of the Ozarks (MO)

CHILD CARE PROVISION
Brigham Young U (UT)

CHILD DEVELOPMENT
Albertus Magnus Coll (CT)
Appalachian State U (NC)
Ashland U (OH)
Auburn U (AL)
Berea Coll (KY)
Bowling Green State U (OH)
Briercrest Bible Coll (SK, Canada)
Brigham Young U (UT)
California State U, Dominguez Hills (CA)
California State U, Fresno (CA)
California State U, Hayward (CA)
California State U, Long Beach (CA)
Campbell U (NC)
Carleton U (ON, Canada)
Carson-Newman Coll (TN)
Coll of the Ozarks (MO)
Concordia Coll (MN)
East Carolina U (NC)
Eastern Kentucky U (KY)
Eastern Washington U (WA)
Florida State U (FL)
Freed-Hardeman U (TN)
Gallaudet U (DC)
Goshen Coll (IN)
Hampshire Coll (MA)
Hampton U (VA)
Houston Baptist U (TX)
Humboldt State U (CA)
Indiana U Bloomington (IN)
Kansas State U (KS)
Lasell Coll (MA)
Lesley U (MA)
Lewis-Clark State Coll (ID)
Louisiana Tech U (LA)
Madonna U (MI)
Meredith Coll (NC)
Miami U (OH)
Michigan State U (MI)
Minnesota State U Mankato (MN)
Missouri Baptist U (MO)
Mitchell Coll (CT)
Montclair State U (NJ)
Mount Ida Coll (MA)
Mount Saint Vincent U (NS, Canada)
Northern Michigan U (MI)
Ohio U (OH)
Oklahoma Baptist U (OK)
Oklahoma Christian U (OK)
Oklahoma State U (OK)
Olivet Nazarene U (IL)
Oregon State U (OR)
Pacific Oaks Coll (CA)
Pittsburg State U (KS)
Point Loma Nazarene U (CA)
Portland State U (OR)
Quinnipiac U (CT)
Reformed Bible Coll (MI)
Ryerson U (ON, Canada)
St. Cloud State U (MN)
Saint Joseph Coll (CT)
San Diego State U (CA)
Seton Hill U (PA)
South Dakota State U (SD)
Plattsburgh State U of NY (NY)
State U of NY Coll at Oneonta (NY)
Stephens Coll (MO)
Syracuse U (NY)
Tennessee Technological U (TN)
Texas A&M U–Kingsville (TX)
Texas Southern U (TX)
Texas Tech U (TX)
Texas Woman's U (TX)
Tufts U (MA)
The U of Akron (OH)
U of Alberta (AB, Canada)
U of Delaware (DE)
U of Guelph (ON, Canada)
U of Idaho (ID)
U of Illinois at Springfield (IL)
U of La Verne (CA)
U of Maine (ME)
U of Manitoba (MB, Canada)
U of Maryland Eastern Shore (MD)
U of Michigan–Dearborn (MI)
U of Nevada, Reno (NV)
U of New Hampshire (NH)
The U of North Carolina at Greensboro (NC)
U of Pittsburgh (PA)
U of Saint Mary (KS)
The U of Tennessee at Martin (TN)
The U of Texas at Arlington (TX)
U of Utah (UT)
U of Victoria (BC, Canada)
U of Wisconsin–Madison (WI)
Villa Julie Coll (MD)
Washington & Jefferson Coll (PA)
Weber State U (UT)
Western Michigan U (MI)
Wheelock Coll (MA)
Youngstown State U (OH)

CHILD GUIDANCE
Alcorn State U (MS)
Coll of the Ozarks (MO)
Oklahoma Baptist U (OK)
Pace U (NY)
Reformed Bible Coll (MI)
Rochester Coll (MI)
St. Joseph's Coll, New York (NY)
Siena Heights U (MI)
Thomas Edison State Coll (NJ)
Tougaloo Coll (MS)
U of North Texas (TX)

CHINESE
Augustana Coll (IL)
Bard Coll (NY)
Bates Coll (ME)
Bennington Coll (VT)
Brigham Young U (UT)
Brooklyn Coll of the City U of NY (NY)
California State U, Long Beach (CA)
California State U, Los Angeles (CA)
Claremont McKenna Coll (CA)
Colgate U (NY)
Connecticut Coll (CT)
Cornell U (NY)
Dartmouth Coll (NH)
Eckerd Coll (FL)
Emory U (GA)
Georgetown U (DC)
The George Washington U (DC)
Grinnell Coll (IA)
Harvard U (MA)
Hobart and William Smith Colls (NY)
Hunter Coll of the City U of NY (NY)

Indiana U Bloomington (IN)
Lawrence U (WI)
Lincoln U (PA)
Middlebury Coll (VT)
Oakland U (MI)
The Ohio State U (OH)
Pacific Lutheran U (WA)
Pacific U (OR)
Pomona Coll (CA)
Portland State U (OR)
Reed Coll (OR)
Rutgers, The State U of New Jersey, New Brunswick/Piscataway (NJ)
San Francisco State U (CA)
San Jose State U (CA)
Scripps Coll (CA)
Simon's Rock Coll of Bard (MA)
Stanford U (CA)
Swarthmore Coll (PA)
Trinity U (TX)
Tufts U (MA)
United States Military Acad (NY)
State U of NY at Albany (NY)
U of Alberta (AB, Canada)
The U of British Columbia (BC, Canada)
U of Calif, Berkeley (CA)
U of Calif, Davis (CA)
U of Calif, Irvine (CA)
U of Calif, Los Angeles (CA)
U of Calif, Riverside (CA)
U of Calif, San Diego (CA)
U of Calif, Santa Barbara (CA)
U of Calif, Santa Cruz (CA)
U of Chicago (IL)
U of Colorado at Boulder (CO)
U of Hawaii at Manoa (HI)
The U of Iowa (IA)
U of Maryland, Coll Park (MD)
U of Massachusetts Amherst (MA)
U of Michigan (MI)
U of Minnesota, Twin Cities Campus (MN)
The U of Montana–Missoula (MT)
U of Notre Dame (IN)
U of Oregon (OR)
U of Pittsburgh (PA)
U of Regina (SK, Canada)
U of Toronto (ON, Canada)
U of Utah (UT)
U of Victoria (BC, Canada)
U of Washington (WA)
U of Wisconsin–Madison (WI)
Washington U in St. Louis (MO)
Wellesley Coll (MA)
Williams Coll (MA)
Yale U (CT)

CHINESE STUDIES
Claremont McKenna Coll (CA)
Sarah Lawrence Coll (NY)
Simon's Rock Coll of Bard (MA)
U of the West (CA)

CHRISTIAN STUDIES
Bethany Coll (KS)
Bethel Coll (IN)
California Baptist U (CA)
Central Pentecostal Coll (SK, Canada)
Coll of Biblical Studies–Houston (TX)
Crown Coll (MN)
God's Bible School and Coll (OH)
Gordon Coll (MA)
Harding U (AR)
Heritage Bible Coll (NC)
Hillsdale Coll (MI)
Houston Baptist U (TX)
Lindenwood U (MO)
Mercer U (GA)
Mississippi Coll (MS)
Seton Hall U (NJ)
Ursuline Coll (OH)
Vennard Coll (IA)
Wayland Baptist U (TX)

CINEMATOGRAPHY AND FILM/ VIDEO PRODUCTION
Acad of Art U (CA)
American InterContinental U (CA)
American InterContinental U, Atlanta (GA)
American InterContinental U-London(United Kingdom)
American U (DC)
Antioch Coll (OH)
Art Center Coll of Design (CA)
The Art Inst of Atlanta (GA)
Atlanta Coll of Art (GA)
Bard Coll (NY)
Boston U (MA)
Brigham Young U (UT)
Brooklyn Coll of the City U of NY (NY)
Burlington Coll (VT)
California State U, Long Beach (CA)
Chapman U (CA)
City Coll of the City U of NY (NY)
Col for Creative Studies (MI)
Coll of Staten Island of the City U of NY (NY)
Coll of the Holy Cross (MA)
Colorado State U-Pueblo (CO)
Columbia Coll Chicago (IL)
Columbia Coll Hollywood (CA)
Concordia U (QC, Canada)
DeSales U (PA)
Drexel U (PA)
Emerson Coll (MA)
The Evergreen State Coll (WA)
Fairleigh Dickinson U, Florham (NJ)
Five Towns Coll (NY)
Florida State U (FL)
Grand Valley State U (MI)
Hampshire Coll (MA)
Hofstra U (NY)
Hunter Coll of the City U of NY (NY)
Ithaca Coll (NY)
Long Island U, C.W. Post Campus (NY)
Loyola Marymount U (CA)
Maharishi U of Management (IA)
Massachusetts Coll of Art (MA)
Middlebury Coll (VT)
Minneapolis Coll of Art and Design (MN)
Montana State U–Bozeman (MT)
New England School of Communications (ME)
New York U (NY)
North Carolina School of the Arts (NC)
Northern Michigan U (MI)
Ohio U (OH)
Oklahoma City U (OK)
Point Park U (PA)
Pratt Inst (NY)
Quinnipiac U (CT)
Rochester Inst of Technology (NY)
Sacred Heart U (CT)
Sarah Lawrence Coll (NY)
Savannah Coll of Art and Design (GA)
School of the Art Inst of Chicago (IL)
School of the Museum of Fine Arts, Boston (MA)
Southern Adventist U (TN)
Southern Illinois U Carbondale (IL)
Syracuse U (NY)
U of Advancing Technology (AZ)
U of Calif, Santa Cruz (CA)
U of Central Florida (FL)
U of Hartford (CT)
U of Illinois at Chicago (IL)
The U of Iowa (IA)
U of Miami (FL)
The U of North Carolina at Greensboro (NC)
The U of North Carolina at Wilmington (NC)
U of Oklahoma (OK)
U of Regina (SK, Canada)
U of Southern California (CA)
The U of the Arts (PA)
Vanguard U of Southern California (CA)
Villa Julie Coll (MD)
Waldorf Coll (IA)
Watkins Coll of Art and Design (TN)
Webster U (MO)
York U (ON, Canada)

CITY/URBAN, COMMUNITY AND REGIONAL PLANNING
Alabama Ag and Mech U (AL)
Appalachian State U (NC)
Arizona State U (AZ)
Ball State U (IN)
Bridgewater State Coll (MA)
State U of NY Coll at Buffalo (NY)
Burlington Coll (VT)
California Polytechnic State U, San Luis Obispo (CA)
California State Polytechnic U, Pomona (CA)
California State U, Chico (CA)
Carleton U (ON, Canada)
Cornell U (NY)
Dalhousie U (NS, Canada)
DePaul U (IL)
East Carolina U (NC)
Eastern Michigan U (MI)
Eastern Oregon U (OR)
Eastern Washington U (WA)
Florida Atlantic U (FL)
Framingham State Coll (MA)
Frostburg State U (MD)
Hampshire Coll (MA)
Harvard U (MA)
Indiana U Bloomington (IN)
Indiana U of Pennsylvania (PA)
Iowa State U of Science and Technology (IA)
Mansfield U of Pennsylvania (PA)
Massachusetts Inst of Technology (MA)
Miami U (OH)
Miami U Hamilton (OH)
Michigan State U (MI)
Minnesota State U Mankato (MN)
New Mexico State U (NM)
New York U (NY)
Northern Michigan U (MI)
The Ohio State U (OH)
Plymouth State U (NH)
Portland State U (OR)
Pratt Inst (NY)
Ryerson U (ON, Canada)
St. Cloud State U (MN)
Saint Louis U (MO)
Salem State Coll (MA)
Southwest Missouri State U (MO)
State U of NY at New Paltz (NY)
State U of NY Coll of Environ Sci and Forestry (NY)
Texas State U-San Marcos (TX)
The U of Arizona (AZ)
U of Calif, Los Angeles (CA)
U of Cincinnati (OH)
U of Illinois at Urbana–Champaign (IL)
U of Missouri–Kansas City (MO)
The U of Montana–Missoula (MT)
U of Nevada, Las Vegas (NV)
U of New Hampshire (NH)
U of North Texas (TX)
U of Oregon (OR)
U of San Francisco (CA)
U of Southern California (CA)
U of the District of Columbia (DC)
U of Virginia (VA)
U of Washington (WA)
U of Waterloo (ON, Canada)
The U of Western Ontario (ON, Canada)
U of Windsor (ON, Canada)
West Chester U of Pennsylvania (PA)
Western Washington U (WA)
Westfield State Coll (MA)
Winona State U (MN)
Wright State U (OH)

CIVIL ENGINEERING
Alabama Ag and Mech U (AL)
Arizona State U (AZ)
Auburn U (AL)
Bethel Coll (IN)
Boise State U (ID)
Bradley U (IL)
Brigham Young U (UT)
Brown U (RI)
Bucknell U (PA)
California Inst of Technology (CA)
California Polytechnic State U, San Luis Obispo (CA)
California State Polytechnic U, Pomona (CA)
California State U, Chico (CA)
California State U, Fresno (CA)
California State U, Fullerton (CA)
California State U, Long Beach (CA)
California State U, Los Angeles (CA)
Calvin Coll (MI)
Carleton U (ON, Canada)
Carnegie Mellon U (PA)
Carroll Coll (MT)
Case Western Reserve U (OH)
The Catholic U of America (DC)
Christian Brothers U (TN)
Citadel, The Military Coll of South Carolina (SC)
City Coll of the City U of NY (NY)
Clarkson U (NY)
Clemson U (SC)
Cleveland State U (OH)
The Coll of Southeastern Europe, The American U of Athens(Greece)
Colorado School of Mines (CO)
Colorado State U (CO)
Columbia U, School of Eng & Applied Sci (NY)
Concordia U (QC, Canada)
Cooper Union for the Advancement of Science & Art (NY)
Cornell U (NY)
Dalhousie U (NS, Canada)
Delaware State U (DE)
Drexel U (PA)
Duke U (NC)
Florida Ag and Mech U (FL)
Florida Atlantic U (FL)
Florida Inst of Technology (FL)
Florida Intl U (FL)
Florida State U (FL)
Gallaudet U (DC)
The George Washington U (DC)
Georgia Inst of Technology (GA)
Gonzaga U (WA)
Harvard U (MA)
Hofstra U (NY)
Howard U (DC)
Idaho State U (ID)
Illinois Inst of Technology (IL)
Iowa State U of Science and Technology (IA)
The Johns Hopkins U (MD)
Kansas State U (KS)
Lafayette Coll (PA)
Lakehead U (ON, Canada)
Lamar U (TX)
Lawrence Technological U (MI)
Lehigh U (PA)
Louisiana State U and A&M Coll (LA)
Louisiana Tech U (LA)
Loyola Marymount U (CA)
Manhattan Coll (NY)
Marquette U (WI)
Massachusetts Inst of Technology (MA)
Memorial U of Newfoundland (NL, Canada)
Merrimack Coll (MA)
Messiah Coll (PA)
Michigan State U (MI)
Michigan Technological U (MI)
Minnesota State U Mankato (MN)
Mississippi State U (MS)
Montana State U–Bozeman (MT)
Montana Tech of The U of Montana (MT)
Morgan State U (MD)
New Jersey Inst of Technology (NJ)
New Mexico Inst of Mining and Technology (NM)
New Mexico State U (NM)
North Carolina State U (NC)
North Dakota State U (ND)
Northeastern U (MA)
Northern Arizona U (AZ)
Northwestern U (IL)
Ohio Northern U (OH)
The Ohio State U (OH)
Ohio U (OH)
Oklahoma State U (OK)
Old Dominion U (VA)
Oregon Inst of Technology (OR)
Oregon State U (OR)
Penn State U Abington Coll (PA)
Penn State U Altoona Coll (PA)
Penn State U at Erie, The Behrend Coll (PA)
Penn State U Beaver Campus of the Commonwealth Coll (PA)
Penn State U Berks Cmps of Berks-Lehigh Valley Coll (PA)
Penn State U Delaware County Campus of the Commonwealth Coll (PA)
Penn State U DuBois Campus of the Commonwealth Coll (PA)
Penn State U Fayette Campus of the Commonwealth Coll (PA)
Penn State U Hazleton Campus of the Commonwealth Coll (PA)
Penn State U Lehigh Valley Cmps of Berks-Lehigh Valley Coll (PA)
Penn State U McKeesport Campus of the Commonwealth Coll (PA)
Penn State U Mont Alto Campus of the Commonwealth Coll (PA)
Penn State U New Kensington Campus of the Commonwealth Coll (PA)
Penn State U Schuylkill Campus of the Capital Coll (PA)
Penn State U Shenango Campus of the Commonwealth Coll (PA)
Penn State U Univ Park Campus (PA)
Penn State U Wilkes-Barre Campus of the Commonwealth Coll (PA)
Penn State U Worthington Scranton Cmps Commonwealth Coll (PA)
Penn State U York Campus of the Commonwealth Coll (PA)
Polytechnic U, Brooklyn Campus (NY)
Polytechnic U of Puerto Rico (PR)
Portland State U (OR)
Prairie View A&M U (TX)
Princeton U (NJ)
Purdue U (IN)
Queen's U at Kingston (ON, Canada)
Rensselaer Polytechnic Inst (NY)
Rice U (TX)
Rose-Hulman Inst of Technology (IN)
Rowan U (NJ)
Rutgers, The State U of New Jersey, New Brunswick/Piscataway (NJ)
Ryerson U (ON, Canada)
Saint Martin's Coll (WA)
San Diego State U (CA)
San Francisco State U (CA)
San Jose State U (CA)
Santa Clara U (CA)
Seattle U (WA)
South Dakota School of Mines and Technology (SD)
South Dakota State U (SD)
Southern Illinois U Carbondale (IL)
Southern Illinois U Edwardsville (IL)
Southern U and A&M Coll (LA)
Stanford U (CA)
Stevens Inst of Technology (NJ)
Syracuse U (NY)
Tennessee State U (TN)
Tennessee Technological U (TN)
Texas A&M U (TX)
Texas A&M U–Kingsville (TX)
Texas Tech U (TX)
Tri-State U (IN)
Tufts U (MA)
Tulane U (LA)
United States Air Force Acad (CO)
United States Coast Guard Acad (CT)
United States Military Acad (NY)
Université de Sherbrooke (QC, Canada)
Université Laval (QC, Canada)
U at Buffalo, The State U of New York (NY)
The U of Akron (OH)
The U of Alabama (AL)
The U of Alabama at Birmingham (AL)
The U of Alabama in Huntsville (AL)
U of Alaska Fairbanks (AK)
U of Alberta (AB, Canada)
The U of Arizona (AZ)
U of Arkansas (AR)
The U of British Columbia (BC, Canada)
U of Calgary (AB, Canada)
U of Calif, Berkeley (CA)
U of Calif, Davis (CA)
U of Calif, Irvine (CA)
U of Calif, Los Angeles (CA)
U of Central Florida (FL)
U of Cincinnati (OH)
U of Colorado at Boulder (CO)
U of Colorado at Denver (CO)
U of Connecticut (CT)
U of Dayton (OH)
U of Delaware (DE)
U of Detroit Mercy (MI)
U of Evansville (IN)
U of Florida (FL)
U of Hartford (CT)
U of Hawaii at Manoa (HI)
U of Houston (TX)
U of Idaho (ID)
U of Illinois at Chicago (IL)
U of Illinois at Urbana–Champaign (IL)
The U of Iowa (IA)
U of Kansas (KS)
U of Kentucky (KY)
U of Louisiana at Lafayette (LA)
U of Louisville (KY)
U of Maine (ME)
U of Manitoba (MB, Canada)
U of Maryland, Coll Park (MD)
U of Massachusetts Amherst (MA)
U of Massachusetts Dartmouth (MA)
U of Massachusetts Lowell (MA)
The U of Memphis (TN)
U of Miami (FL)
U of Michigan (MI)
U of Minnesota, Twin Cities Campus (MN)
U of Mississippi (MS)
U of Missouri–Columbia (MO)
U of Missouri–Kansas City (MO)
U of Missouri–Rolla (MO)
U of Missouri–St. Louis (MO)
U of Nebraska at Omaha (NE)
U of Nebraska–Lincoln (NE)
U of Nevada, Las Vegas (NV)
U of Nevada, Reno (NV)

U of New Brunswick Fredericton (NB, Canada)
U of New Hampshire (NH)
U of New Haven (CT)
U of New Mexico (NM)
U of New Orleans (LA)
The U of North Carolina at Charlotte (NC)
U of North Dakota (ND)
U of North Florida (FL)
U of Notre Dame (IN)
U of Oklahoma (OK)
U of Ottawa (ON, Canada)
U of Pennsylvania (PA)
U of Pittsburgh (PA)
U of Portland (OR)
U of Rhode Island (RI)
U of Saskatchewan (SK, Canada)
U of South Alabama (AL)
U of South Carolina (SC)
U of Southern California (CA)
U of South Florida (FL)
The U of Tennessee (TN)
The U of Texas at Arlington (TX)
The U of Texas at Austin (TX)
U of the District of Columbia (DC)
U of the Pacific (CA)
U of Toledo (OH)
U of Toronto (ON, Canada)
U of Utah (UT)
U of Vermont (VT)
U of Virginia (VA)
U of Washington (WA)
U of Waterloo (ON, Canada)
The U of Western Ontario (ON, Canada)
U of Windsor (ON, Canada)
U of Wisconsin–Madison (WI)
U of Wisconsin–Milwaukee (WI)
U of Wisconsin–Platteville (WI)
U of Wyoming (WY)
Ursinus Coll (PA)
Utah State U (UT)
Valparaiso U (IN)
Vanderbilt U (TN)
Villanova U (PA)
Virginia Military Inst (VA)
Virginia Polytechnic Inst and State U (VA)
Walla Walla Coll (WA)
Washington State U (WA)
Washington U in St. Louis (MO)
Wayne State U (MI)
Western Kentucky U (KY)
Western Michigan U (MI)
West Virginia U (WV)
Widener U (PA)
Worcester Polytechnic Inst (MA)
Youngstown State U (OH)

CIVIL ENGINEERING RELATED

Bradley U (IL)
California State U, Sacramento (CA)
Drexel U (PA)
Embry-Riddle Aeronautical U (FL)
George Mason U (VA)
Ohio Northern U (OH)
U of Southern California (CA)

CIVIL ENGINEERING TECHNOLOGY

Alabama Ag and Mech U (AL)
Bluefield State Coll (WV)
Central Connecticut State U (CT)
Colorado State U-Pueblo (CO)
Fairleigh Dickinson U, Teaneck-Metro Campus (NJ)
Fairmont State Coll (WV)
Florida Ag and Mech U (FL)
Fontbonne U (MO)
Georgia Southern U (GA)
Lakehead U (ON, Canada)
Metropolitan State Coll of Denver (CO)
Missouri Western State Coll (MO)
Murray State U (KY)
Old Dominion U (VA)
Pennsylvania Coll of Technology (PA)
Point Park U (PA)
Rochester Inst of Technology (NY)
South Carolina State U (SC)
Southern Polytechnic State U (GA)
State U of NY Inst of Tech at Utica/Rome (NY)
Texas Southern U (TX)
Thomas Edison State Coll (NJ)
U of Cincinnati (OH)
U of Houston (TX)
U of Massachusetts Lowell (MA)
The U of North Carolina at Charlotte (NC)
U of North Texas (TX)
U of Pittsburgh at Johnstown (PA)
U of Toledo (OH)
Washington U in St. Louis (MO)
Wentworth Inst of Technology (MA)
Youngstown State U (OH)

CLASSICAL, ANCIENT MEDITERRANEAN AND NEAR EASTERN STUDIES AND ARCHAEOLOGY

Bates Coll (ME)
Columbia Coll (NY)
Creighton U (NE)
Samford U (AL)
U of Calif, Berkeley (CA)
U of Calif, Irvine (CA)
U of Calif, Los Angeles (CA)
U of Guelph (ON, Canada)

CLASSICS

Hunter Coll of the City U of NY (NY)
The U of North Carolina at Greensboro (NC)
Ursinus Coll (PA)
Washington and Lee U (VA)

CLASSICS AND CLASSICAL LANGUAGES RELATED

Austin Coll (TX)
Brandeis U (MA)
California State U, Long Beach (CA)
The Catholic U of America (DC)
Concordia Coll (MN)
Lawrence U (WI)
New Coll of Florida (FL)
Rutgers, The State U of New Jersey, Newark (NJ)
St. Bonaventure U (NY)
Saint Louis U (MO)
Tulane U (LA)
Université Laval (QC, Canada)
U of Calif, Los Angeles (CA)
U of St. Thomas (MN)

CLASSICS AND LANGUAGES, LITERATURES AND LINGUISTICS

Acadia U (NS, Canada)
Agnes Scott Coll (GA)
Albertus Magnus Coll (CT)
Amherst Coll (MA)
Asbury Coll (KY)
Assumption Coll (MA)
Augustana Coll (IL)
Austin Coll (TX)
Ave Maria Coll (MI)
Ave Maria U (FL)
Ball State U (IN)
Bard Coll (NY)
Barnard Coll (NY)
Baylor U (TX)
Beloit Coll (WI)
Berea Coll (KY)
Bishop's U (QC, Canada)
Boston Coll (MA)
Boston U (MA)
Bowdoin Coll (ME)
Bowling Green State U (OH)
Brigham Young U (UT)
Brock U (ON, Canada)
Brooklyn Coll of the City U of NY (NY)
Brown U (RI)
Bryn Mawr Coll (PA)
Bucknell U (PA)
Calvin Coll (MI)
Carleton Coll (MN)
Carleton U (ON, Canada)
Carthage Coll (WI)
Case Western Reserve U (OH)
The Catholic U of America (DC)
Centre Coll (KY)
Christendom Coll (VA)
Claremont McKenna Coll (CA)
Clark U (MA)
Coe Coll (IA)
Colby Coll (ME)
Colgate U (NY)
Coll of Charleston (SC)
The Coll of New Rochelle (NY)
Coll of Notre Dame of Maryland (MD)
Coll of Saint Benedict (MN)
Coll of the Holy Cross (MA)
The Coll of William and Mary (VA)
The Coll of Wooster (OH)
The Colorado Coll (CO)
Columbia Coll (NY)
Columbia U, School of General Studies (NY)
Concordia U (QC, Canada)
Connecticut Coll (CT)
Cornell Coll (IA)
Cornell U (NY)
Dalhousie U (NS, Canada)
Dartmouth Coll (NH)
Davidson Coll (NC)
Denison U (OH)
DePauw U (IN)
Dickinson Coll (PA)
Drew U (NJ)
Duke U (NC)
Duquesne U (PA)
Earlham Coll (IN)
Elmira Coll (NY)
Emory U (GA)
The Evergreen State Coll (WA)
Florida State U (FL)
Fordham U (NY)
Franciscan U of Steubenville (OH)
Franklin and Marshall Coll (PA)
Georgetown U (DC)
The George Washington U (DC)
Georgia State U (GA)
Gettysburg Coll (PA)
Grand Valley State U (MI)
Grinnell Coll (IA)
Gustavus Adolphus Coll (MN)
Hamilton Coll (NY)
Hampden-Sydney Coll (VA)
Hampshire Coll (MA)
Hanover Coll (IN)
Harvard U (MA)
Haverford Coll (PA)
Hellenic Coll (MA)
Hillsdale Coll (MI)
Hiram Coll (OH)
Hobart and William Smith Colls (NY)
Hofstra U (NY)
Hollins U (VA)
Hope Coll (MI)
Howard U (DC)
Hunter Coll of the City U of NY (NY)
Illinois Wesleyan U (IL)
Indiana U Bloomington (IN)
John Carroll U (OH)
The Johns Hopkins U (MD)
Kalamazoo Coll (MI)
Kent State U (OH)
Kenyon Coll (OH)
Knox Coll (IL)
La Salle U (PA)
Laurentian U (ON, Canada)
Lawrence U (WI)
Lehigh U (PA)
Lehman Coll of the City U of NY (NY)
Lenoir-Rhyne Coll (NC)
Loyola Coll in Maryland (MD)
Loyola Marymount U (CA)
Loyola U Chicago (IL)
Loyola U New Orleans (LA)
Luther Coll (IA)
Macalester Coll (MN)
Manhattan Coll (NY)
Manhattanville Coll (NY)
Marlboro Coll (VT)
Marquette U (WI)
Mary Washington Coll (VA)
McGill U (QC, Canada)
Memorial U of Newfoundland (NL, Canada)
Mercer U (GA)
Miami U (OH)
Miami U Hamilton (OH)
Middlebury Coll (VT)
Millsaps Coll (MS)
Monmouth Coll (IL)
Montclair State U (NJ)
Moravian Coll (PA)
Mount Allison U (NB, Canada)
Mount Holyoke Coll (MA)
New York U (NY)
Nipissing U (ON, Canada)
North Dakota State U (ND)
Northwestern U (IL)
Oakland U (MI)
Oberlin Coll (OH)
The Ohio State U (OH)
Ohio U (OH)
Ohio Wesleyan U (OH)
Pacific Lutheran U (WA)
Penn State U Abington Coll (PA)
Penn State U Altoona Coll (PA)
Penn State U at Erie, The Behrend Coll (PA)
Penn State U Beaver Campus of the Commonwealth Coll (PA)
Penn State U Berks Cmps of Berks-Lehigh Valley Coll (PA)
Penn State U Delaware County Campus of the Commonwealth Coll (PA)
Penn State U DuBois Campus of the Commonwealth Coll (PA)
Penn State U Fayette Campus of the Commonwealth Coll (PA)
Penn State U Hazleton Campus of the Commonwealth Coll (PA)
Penn State U Lehigh Valley Cmps of Berks-Lehigh Valley Coll (PA)
Penn State U McKeesport Campus of the Commonwealth Coll (PA)
Penn State U Mont Alto Campus of the Commonwealth Coll (PA)
Penn State U New Kensington Campus of the Commonwealth Coll (PA)
Penn State U Schuylkill Campus of the Capital Coll (PA)
Penn State U Shenango Campus of the Commonwealth Coll (PA)
Penn State U Univ Park Campus (PA)
Penn State U Wilkes-Barre Campus of the Commonwealth Coll (PA)
Penn State U Worthington Scranton Cmps Commonwealth Coll (PA)
Penn State U York Campus of the Commonwealth Coll (PA)
Pitzer Coll (CA)
Pomona Coll (CA)
Princeton U (NJ)
Queen's U at Kingston (ON, Canada)
Randolph-Macon Coll (VA)
Randolph-Macon Woman's Coll (VA)
Reed Coll (OR)
Rhodes Coll (TN)
Rice U (TX)
Rockford Coll (IL)
Rollins Coll (FL)
Rutgers, The State U of New Jersey, Newark (NJ)
Rutgers, The State U of New Jersey, New Brunswick/Piscataway (NJ)
Saint Anselm Coll (NH)
St. Bonaventure U (NY)
St. Francis Xavier U (NS, Canada)
St. John's Coll (NM)
Saint John's U (MN)
Saint Michael's Coll (VT)
St. Olaf Coll (MN)
Samford U (AL)
San Diego State U (CA)
San Francisco State U (CA)
Santa Clara U (CA)
Sarah Lawrence Coll (NY)
Scripps Coll (CA)
Seattle Pacific U (WA)
Seton Hall U (NJ)
Siena Coll (NY)
Skidmore Coll (NY)
Smith Coll (MA)
Southern Illinois U Carbondale (IL)
Stanford U (CA)
State U of NY at Binghamton (NY)
Swarthmore Coll (PA)
Sweet Briar Coll (VA)
Syracuse U (NY)
Texas Tech U (TX)
Trent U (ON, Canada)
Trinity Coll (CT)
Trinity U (TX)
Truman State U (MO)
Tufts U (MA)
Tulane U (LA)
Union Coll (NY)
Université de Montréal (QC, Canada)
State U of NY at Albany (NY)
U at Buffalo, The State U of New York (NY)
The U of Akron (OH)
The U of Alabama (AL)
U of Alberta (AB, Canada)
The U of Arizona (AZ)
U of Arkansas (AR)
The U of British Columbia (BC, Canada)
U of Calgary (AB, Canada)
U of Calif, Berkeley (CA)
U of Calif, Irvine (CA)
U of Calif, Los Angeles (CA)
U of Calif, Riverside (CA)
U of Calif, San Diego (CA)
U of Calif, Santa Barbara (CA)
U of Calif, Santa Cruz (CA)
U of Chicago (IL)
U of Cincinnati (OH)
U of Colorado at Boulder (CO)
U of Connecticut (CT)
U of Dallas (TX)
U of Delaware (DE)
U of Evansville (IN)
U of Florida (FL)
U of Georgia (GA)
U of Guelph (ON, Canada)
U of Houston (TX)
U of Idaho (ID)
U of Illinois at Chicago (IL)
U of Illinois at Urbana–Champaign (IL)
The U of Iowa (IA)
U of Kansas (KS)
U of Kentucky (KY)
U of King's Coll (NS, Canada)
U of Maine (ME)
U of Manitoba (MB, Canada)
U of Maryland, Baltimore County (MD)
U of Maryland, Coll Park (MD)
U of Massachusetts Amherst (MA)
U of Massachusetts Boston (MA)
U of Michigan (MI)
U of Mississippi (MS)
U of Missouri–Columbia (MO)
The U of Montana–Missoula (MT)
U of Nebraska–Lincoln (NE)
U of New Brunswick Fredericton (NB, Canada)
U of New Hampshire (NH)
U of New Mexico (NM)
The U of North Carolina at Asheville (NC)
The U of North Carolina at Chapel Hill (NC)
The U of North Carolina at Greensboro (NC)
U of Notre Dame (IN)
U of Oklahoma (OK)
U of Oregon (OR)
U of Ottawa (ON, Canada)
U of Pennsylvania (PA)
U of Pittsburgh (PA)
U of Puget Sound (WA)
U of Regina (SK, Canada)
U of Rhode Island (RI)
U of Richmond (VA)
U of Rochester (NY)
U of St. Thomas (MN)
U of Saskatchewan (SK, Canada)
U of South Carolina (SC)
The U of South Dakota (SD)
U of Southern California (CA)
U of Southern Maine (ME)
U of South Florida (FL)
The U of Tennessee (TN)
The U of Texas at Arlington (TX)
The U of Texas at Austin (TX)
U of the Pacific (CA)
U of the South (TN)
U of Toledo (OH)
U of Toronto (ON, Canada)
U of Utah (UT)
U of Vermont (VT)
U of Victoria (BC, Canada)
U of Virginia (VA)
U of Washington (WA)
U of Waterloo (ON, Canada)
The U of Western Ontario (ON, Canada)
U of Windsor (ON, Canada)
U of Wisconsin–Madison (WI)
U of Wisconsin–Milwaukee (WI)
Ursinus Coll (PA)
Valparaiso U (IN)
Vanderbilt U (TN)
Vassar Coll (NY)
Villanova U (PA)
Wabash Coll (IN)
Wake Forest U (NC)
Washington State U (WA)
Washington U in St. Louis (MO)
Wayne State U (MI)
Wellesley Coll (MA)
Wesleyan U (CT)
Western Washington U (WA)
Westminster Coll (PA)
Wheaton Coll (MA)
Whitman Coll (WA)
Willamette U (OR)
Williams Coll (MA)
Wright State U (OH)
Xavier U (OH)
Yale U (CT)
York U (ON, Canada)

CLINICAL CHILD PSYCHOLOGY

St. John's U (NY)
U of Windsor (ON, Canada)

CLINICAL LABORATORY SCIENCE/MEDICAL TECHNOLOGY

Abilene Christian U (TX)
Alcorn State U (MS)
Alderson-Broaddus Coll (WV)
Alvernia Coll (PA)
American Intl Coll (MA)
Andrews U (MI)
Angelo State U (TX)
Appalachian State U (NC)
Aquinas Coll (MI)
Arizona State U (AZ)
Arkansas State U (AR)
Arkansas Tech U (AR)

Armstrong Atlantic State U (GA)
Atlantic Union Coll (MA)
Auburn U (AL)
Augustana Coll (SD)
Augusta State U (GA)
Aurora U (IL)
Austin Peay State U (TN)
Averett U (VA)
Ball State U (IN)
Barry U (FL)
Baylor U (TX)
Bellarmine U (KY)
Belmont Abbey Coll (NC)
Belmont U (TN)
Bemidji State U (MN)
Benedictine U (IL)
Bethune-Cookman Coll (FL)
Blackburn Coll (IL)
Bloomfield Coll (NJ)
Bloomsburg U of Pennsylvania (PA)
Blue Mountain Coll (MS)
Boise State U (ID)
Boston U (MA)
Bowling Green State U (OH)
Bradley U (IL)
Brescia U (KY)
Briar Cliff U (IA)
Bridgewater Coll (VA)
Brigham Young U (UT)
Cabrini Coll (PA)
Caldwell Coll (NJ)
California State U, Chico (CA)
California State U, Dominguez Hills (CA)
Cameron U (OK)
Campbellsville U (KY)
Carroll Coll (MT)
Carroll Coll (WI)
Carson-Newman Coll (TN)
Catawba Coll (NC)
The Catholic U of America (DC)
Cedar Crest Coll (PA)
Cedarville U (OH)
Central Michigan U (MI)
Central Missouri State U (MO)
Cheyney U of Pennsylvania (PA)
Clarion U of Pennsylvania (PA)
Clemson U (SC)
Coker Coll (SC)
Coll Misericordia (PA)
Coll of Mount St. Joseph (OH)
Coll of St. Catherine (MN)
Coll of Saint Elizabeth (NJ)
Coll of Saint Mary (NE)
The Coll of Saint Rose (NY)
Coll of Staten Island of the City U of NY (NY)
Coll of the Ozarks (MO)
Concord Coll (WV)
Concordia Coll (MN)
Culver-Stockton Coll (MO)
Cumberland Coll (KY)
Defiance Coll (OH)
Delta State U (MS)
DePaul U (IL)
DeSales U (PA)
Dominican U (IL)
Dordt Coll (IA)
East Carolina U (NC)
Eastern Illinois U (IL)
Eastern Kentucky U (KY)
Eastern Mennonite U (VA)
Eastern Michigan U (MI)
Eastern New Mexico U (NM)
East Stroudsburg U of Pennsylvania (PA)
East Texas Baptist U (TX)
Eckerd Coll (FL)
Edgewood Coll (WI)
Elmhurst Coll (IL)
Elmira Coll (NY)
Elms Coll (MA)
Elon U (NC)
Emory & Henry Coll (VA)
Erskine Coll (SC)
Eureka Coll (IL)
Evangel U (MO)
Fairleigh Dickinson U, Florham (NJ)
Fairleigh Dickinson U, Teaneck-Metro Campus (NJ)
Ferris State U (MI)
Ferrum Coll (VA)
Florida Atlantic U (FL)
Fort Hays State U (KS)
Gannon U (PA)
Gardner-Webb U (NC)
George Mason U (VA)
The George Washington U (DC)
Georgia Southern U (GA)
Georgia Southwestern State U (GA)
Graceland U (IA)
Grand Valley State U (MI)
Greensboro Coll (NC)
Gwynedd-Mercy Coll (PA)
Harding U (AR)
Hardin-Simmons U (TX)
Hartwick Coll (NY)
Henderson State U (AR)
High Point U (NC)
Houghton Coll (NY)
Howard U (DC)
Humboldt State U (CA)
Idaho State U (ID)
Illinois Coll (IL)
Illinois State U (IL)
Indiana State U (IN)
Indiana U East (IN)
Indiana U Kokomo (IN)
Indiana U of Pennsylvania (PA)
Indiana U–Purdue U Fort Wayne (IN)
Indiana U–Purdue U Indianapolis (IN)
Indiana U Southeast (IN)
Inter American U of PR, Fajardo Campus (PR)
Inter American U of PR, San Germán Campus (PR)
Iona Coll (NY)
Jamestown Coll (ND)
Jewish Hospital Coll of Nursing and Allied Health (MO)
John Brown U (AR)
Kansas State U (KS)
Kean U (NJ)
Kent State U (OH)
Kentucky State U (KY)
Kentucky Wesleyan Coll (KY)
Keuka Coll (NY)
King Coll (TN)
King's Coll (PA)
Kutztown U of Pennsylvania (PA)
Lake Superior State U (MI)
Lamar U (TX)
Lenoir-Rhyne Coll (NC)
Lewis U (IL)
Lincoln Memorial U (TN)
Lincoln U (MO)
Lindenwood U (MO)
Loma Linda U (CA)
Long Island U, Brooklyn Campus (NY)
Long Island U, C.W. Post Campus (NY)
Longwood U (VA)
Loras Coll (IA)
Louisiana Coll (LA)
Louisiana State U Health Sciences Center (LA)
Louisiana Tech U (LA)
Lubbock Christian U (TX)
Lycoming Coll (PA)
Madonna U (MI)
Malone Coll (OH)
Manchester Coll (IN)
Mansfield U of Pennsylvania (PA)
Marian Coll of Fond du Lac (WI)
Marist Coll (NY)
Marshall U (WV)
Mary Baldwin Coll (VA)
Marymount Coll of Fordham U (NY)
Maryville U of Saint Louis (MO)
Marywood U (PA)
Massachusetts Coll of Liberal Arts (MA)
McKendree Coll (IL)
McNeese State U (LA)
Medical Coll of Georgia (GA)
Mercy Coll (NY)
Mercyhurst Coll (PA)
Miami U (OH)
Miami U Hamilton (OH)
Michigan State U (MI)
Michigan Technological U (MI)
Midwestern State U (TX)
Minnesota State U Mankato (MN)
Minnesota State U Moorhead (MN)
Minot State U (ND)
Mississippi State U (MS)
Missouri Southern State U (MO)
Missouri Western State Coll (MO)
Monmouth U (NJ)
Moravian Coll (PA)
Morehead State U (KY)
Morgan State U (MD)
Morningside Coll (IA)
Mount Marty Coll (SD)
Mount Mercy Coll (IA)
Mount Saint Mary Coll (NY)
Mount Vernon Nazarene U (OH)
Murray State U (KY)
National-Louis U (IL)
New Mexico Inst of Mining and Technology (NM)
Norfolk State U (VA)
North Dakota State U (ND)
Northeastern State U (OK)
Northern Illinois U (IL)
Northern Michigan U (MI)
Northern State U (SD)
North Park U (IL)
Northwestern Coll (IA)
Northwestern State U of Louisiana (LA)
Oakland U (MI)
Ohio Northern U (OH)
The Ohio State U (OH)
Oklahoma Christian U (OK)
Oklahoma Panhandle State U (OK)
Oklahoma State U (OK)
Old Dominion U (VA)
Olivet Nazarene U (IL)
Oregon State U (OR)
Our Lady of Holy Cross Coll (LA)
Our Lady of the Lake Coll (LA)
Pace U (NY)
Pacific Union Coll (CA)
Pittsburg State U (KS)
Pontifical Catholic U of Puerto Rico (PR)
Prairie View A&M U (TX)
Purdue U (IN)
Quincy U (IL)
Radford U (VA)
Rhode Island Coll (RI)
Roanoke Coll (VA)
Roberts Wesleyan Coll (NY)
Rochester Inst of Technology (NY)
Roosevelt U (IL)
Rush U (IL)
Rutgers, The State U of New Jersey, Camden (NJ)
Rutgers, The State U of New Jersey, Newark (NJ)
Rutgers, The State U of New Jersey, New Brunswick/Piscataway (NJ)
Saginaw Valley State U (MI)
St. Cloud State U (MN)
St. Francis Coll (NY)
Saint Francis U (PA)
St. John's U (NY)
Saint Joseph's Coll (IN)
Saint Leo U (FL)
Saint Louis U (MO)
Saint Mary-of-the-Woods Coll (IN)
Saint Mary's Coll (IN)
Saint Mary's U of Minnesota (MN)
St. Thomas Aquinas Coll (NY)
Salem Coll (NC)
Salem State Coll (MA)
Salisbury U (MD)
Salve Regina U (RI)
Sam Houston State U (TX)
Seattle U (WA)
Seton Hill U (PA)
Simpson Coll (IA)
South Dakota State U (SD)
Southeastern Oklahoma State U (OK)
Southeast Missouri State U (MO)
Southern Adventist U (TN)
Southern Arkansas U–Magnolia (AR)
Southern Wesleyan U (SC)
Southwest Baptist U (MO)
Southwestern Oklahoma State U (OK)
Southwest Missouri State U (MO)
Springfield Coll (MA)
Plattsburgh State U of NY (NY)
State U of NY Coll at Brockport (NY)
State U of NY Coll at Fredonia (NY)
State U of New York Upstate Medical U (NY)
Stetson U (FL)
Stony Brook U, State U of New York (NY)
Suffolk U (MA)
Tabor Coll (KS)
Tarleton State U (TX)
Taylor U (IN)
Tennessee State U (TN)
Texas A&M U–Corpus Christi (TX)
Texas Southern U (TX)
Texas State U-San Marcos (TX)
Texas Woman's U (TX)
Thiel Coll (PA)
Thomas Jefferson U (PA)
Thomas More Coll (KY)
Trevecca Nazarene U (TN)
Tusculum Coll (TN)
Tuskegee U (AL)
Union Coll (NE)
Union U (TN)
U at Buffalo, The State U of New York (NY)
The U of Akron (OH)
The U of Alabama at Birmingham (AL)
The U of Arizona (AZ)
U of Bridgeport (CT)
U of Central Arkansas (AR)
U of Central Florida (FL)
U of Cincinnati (OH)
U of Connecticut (CT)
U of Delaware (DE)
U of Evansville (IN)
The U of Findlay (OH)
U of Hartford (CT)
U of Hawaii at Manoa (HI)
U of Houston (TX)
U of Idaho (ID)
U of Illinois at Chicago (IL)
U of Indianapolis (IN)
The U of Iowa (IA)
U of Kansas (KS)
U of Kentucky (KY)
U of Maine (ME)
U of Mary (ND)
U of Mary Hardin-Baylor (TX)
U of Maryland Eastern Shore (MD)
U of Massachusetts Amherst (MA)
U of Massachusetts Boston (MA)
U of Massachusetts Dartmouth (MA)
U of Massachusetts Lowell (MA)
U of Michigan (MI)
U of Michigan–Flint (MI)
U of Minnesota, Twin Cities Campus (MN)
U of Mississippi (MS)
U of Mississippi Medical Center (MS)
U of Missouri–St. Louis (MO)
The U of Montana–Missoula (MT)
U of Nebraska Medical Center (NE)
U of Nevada, Las Vegas (NV)
U of New Haven (CT)
U of New Orleans (LA)
The U of North Carolina at Chapel Hill (NC)
The U of North Carolina at Charlotte (NC)
The U of North Carolina at Greensboro (NC)
The U of North Carolina at Wilmington (NC)
U of North Dakota (ND)
U of Northern Colorado (CO)
U of North Texas (TX)
U of Pittsburgh (PA)
U of Rhode Island (RI)
U of St. Francis (IL)
U of Saint Francis (IN)
The U of Scranton (PA)
U of Sioux Falls (SD)
U of South Alabama (AL)
U of South Florida (FL)
The U of Tennessee (TN)
The U of Tennessee at Chattanooga (TN)
The U of Texas at Arlington (TX)
The U of Texas at Austin (TX)
The U of Texas at Tyler (TX)
U of Texas Health Science Center at San Antonio (TX)
U of Texas Medical Branch at Galveston (TX)
The U of Texas–Pan American (TX)
U of Texas Southwestern Medical Center at Dallas (TX)
U of the District of Columbia (DC)
U of the Incarnate Word (TX)
U of the Sacred Heart (PR)
U of the Sciences in Philadelphia (PA)
U of Toledo (OH)
U of Utah (UT)
U of Vermont (VT)
The U of Virginia's Coll at Wise (VA)
U of Washington (WA)
U of West Florida (FL)
U of Wisconsin–La Crosse (WI)
U of Wisconsin–Madison (WI)
U of Wisconsin–Milwaukee (WI)
U of Wisconsin–Oshkosh (WI)
U of Wisconsin–Stevens Point (WI)
Utah State U (UT)
Virginia Commonwealth U (VA)
Wake Forest U (NC)
Walla Walla Coll (WA)
Wartburg Coll (IA)
Washburn U (KS)
Wayne State Coll (NE)
Weber State U (UT)
Wesley Coll (DE)
Western Carolina U (NC)
Western Connecticut State U (CT)
Western Illinois U (IL)
Western Kentucky U (KY)
Westfield State Coll (MA)
West Liberty State Coll (WV)
West Texas A&M U (TX)
West Virginia U (WV)
Wichita State U (KS)
Wilkes U (PA)
William Jewell Coll (MO)
Winona State U (MN)
Winston-Salem State U (NC)
Winthrop U (SC)
Wright State U (OH)
Xavier U (OH)
York Coll of Pennsylvania (PA)
York Coll of the City U of New York (NY)
Youngstown State U (OH)

CLINICAL/MEDICAL LABORATORY ASSISTANT

Saint Joseph's Coll of Maine (ME)
U of Vermont (VT)

CLINICAL/MEDICAL LABORATORY SCIENCE AND ALLIED PROFESSIONS RELATED

Abilene Christian U (TX)
Bellarmine U (KY)
Hunter Coll of the City U of NY (NY)
Lebanon Valley Coll (PA)
Roosevelt U (IL)
Saint Louis U (MO)

CLINICAL/MEDICAL LABORATORY TECHNOLOGY

Alabama State U (AL)
Alfred U (NY)
Andrews U (MI)
Auburn U (AL)
Baldwin-Wallace Coll (OH)
Barry U (FL)
Bloomsburg U of Pennsylvania (PA)
California State U, Dominguez Hills (CA)
California State U, Hayward (CA)
California U of Pennsylvania (PA)
DePaul U (IL)
East Central U (OK)
Edinboro U of Pennsylvania (PA)
Ferris State U (MI)
Gardner-Webb U (NC)
Long Island U, C.W. Post Campus (NY)
Longwood U (VA)
Madonna U (MI)
Marquette U (WI)
Massachusetts Coll of Liberal Arts (MA)
Morgan State U (MD)
Mount Saint Mary Coll (NY)
Northeastern U (MA)
Northern Michigan U (MI)
Northern State U (SD)
Our Lady of the Lake Coll (LA)
Penn State U DuBois Campus of the Commonwealth Coll (PA)
St. Thomas Aquinas Coll (NY)
Slippery Rock U of Pennsylvania (PA)
Sonoma State U (CA)
U of Alberta (AB, Canada)
The U of British Columbia (BC, Canada)
U of Maryland Eastern Shore (MD)
U of Missouri–Kansas City (MO)
The U of Montana–Missoula (MT)
U of New Hampshire (NH)
U of Oklahoma (OK)
U of Science and Arts of Oklahoma (OK)
U of Utah (UT)
Weber State U (UT)
Winona State U (MN)

CLINICAL/MEDICAL SOCIAL WORK

Arkansas Tech U (AR)
Slippery Rock U of Pennsylvania (PA)
U of St. Thomas (MN)

CLINICAL NUTRITION

Framingham State Coll (MA)
Messiah Coll (PA)
West Chester U of Pennsylvania (PA)

CLINICAL PSYCHOLOGY

Averett U (VA)
Biola U (CA)
Blackburn Coll (IL)
Bridgewater State Coll (MA)
California State U, Fullerton (CA)
Colorado State U-Pueblo (CO)
Crichton Coll (TN)
Eastern Nazarene Coll (MA)
Fairfield U (CT)
Franklin Pierce Coll (NH)
George Fox U (OR)
Husson Coll (ME)

Lakehead U (ON, Canada)
Lamar U (TX)
Liberty U (VA)
Mansfield U of Pennsylvania (PA)
Moravian Coll (PA)
Sam Houston State U (TX)
Simon Fraser U (BC, Canada)
Tennessee State U (TN)
U of Alberta (AB, Canada)
The U of British Columbia (BC, Canada)
U of Houston–Clear Lake (TX)
U of Michigan–Flint (MI)
U of New Brunswick Fredericton (NB, Canada)
U of Windsor (ON, Canada)
Western State Coll of Colorado (CO)

CLOTHING/TEXTILES
Bluffton Coll (OH)
Bowling Green State U (OH)
Cheyney U of Pennsylvania (PA)
Delaware State U (DE)
Framingham State Coll (MA)
Indiana U Bloomington (IN)
Jacksonville State U (AL)
Marymount Coll of Fordham U (NY)
Mercyhurst Coll (PA)
Minnesota State U Mankato (MN)
New Mexico State U (NM)
The Ohio State U (OH)
Oklahoma State U (OK)
Olivet Nazarene U (IL)
Oregon State U (OR)
Philadelphia U (PA)
San Francisco State U (CA)
Syracuse U (NY)
Tennessee Technological U (TN)
Texas Southern U (TX)
The U of Akron (OH)
U of Alberta (AB, Canada)
U of Manitoba (MB, Canada)
U of Minnesota, Twin Cities Campus (MN)
The U of North Carolina at Greensboro (NC)
U of the District of Columbia (DC)
The U of Western Ontario (ON, Canada)
U of Wisconsin–Madison (WI)
Virginia Polytechnic Inst and State U (VA)

COGNITIVE PSYCHOLOGY AND PSYCHOLINGUISTICS
Averett U (VA)
Brown U (RI)
California State U, Stanislaus (CA)
Carleton U (ON, Canada)
Carnegie Mellon U (PA)
Dartmouth Coll (NH)
George Fox U (OR)
Hampshire Coll (MA)
Harvard U (MA)
Indiana U Bloomington (IN)
The Johns Hopkins U (MD)
Lawrence U (WI)
Massachusetts Inst of Technology (MA)
Northwestern U (IL)
Occidental Coll (CA)
Queen's U at Kingston (ON, Canada)
Simon's Rock Coll of Bard (MA)
State U of NY at Oswego (NY)
Tulane U (LA)
U of Calif, San Diego (CA)
U of Calif, Santa Cruz (CA)
U of Georgia (GA)
U of Kansas (KS)
The U of Texas at Dallas (TX)
Vanderbilt U (TN)
Vassar Coll (NY)
Washington U in St. Louis (MO)
Wellesley Coll (MA)
Yale U (CT)

COGNITIVE SCIENCE
Cornell U (NY)
Hampshire Coll (MA)
Harvard U (MA)
Lawrence U (WI)
Simon Fraser U (BC, Canada)
State U of NY at Oswego (NY)
The U of British Columbia (BC, Canada)
U of Calif, Berkeley (CA)
U of Calif, Los Angeles (CA)
U of Pennsylvania (PA)
U of Rochester (NY)

COLLEGE STUDENT COUNSELING AND PERSONNEL SERVICES
Eastern Michigan U (MI)
Kutztown U of Pennsylvania (PA)

COMMERCIAL AND ADVERTISING ART
Abilene Christian U (TX)
Acad of Art U (CA)
Alberta Coll of Art & Design (AB, Canada)
Albertus Magnus Coll (CT)
American Acad of Art (IL)
American InterContinental U (CA)
American U (DC)
Anderson Coll (SC)
Andrews U (MI)
Arcadia U (PA)
Arizona State U (AZ)
Arkansas State U (AR)
Art Center Coll of Design (CA)
The Art Inst of Atlanta (GA)
The Art Inst of California–San Diego (CA)
The Art Inst of California–San Francisco (CA)
The Art Inst of Colorado (CO)
The Art Inst of Washington (VA)
Ashland U (OH)
Atlanta Coll of Art (GA)
Auburn U (AL)
Baker Coll of Flint (MI)
Baker Coll of Owosso (MI)
Ball State U (IN)
Becker Coll (MA)
Bemidji State U (MN)
Biola U (CA)
Black Hills State U (SD)
Boise State U (ID)
Boston U (MA)
Brenau U (GA)
Brescia U (KY)
Briar Cliff U (IA)
Bridgewater State Coll (MA)
Buena Vista U (IA)
State U of NY Coll at Buffalo (NY)
California Inst of the Arts (CA)
California Inst of the Arts (CA)
California Polytechnic State U, San Luis Obispo (CA)
California State Polytechnic U, Pomona (CA)
California State U, Dominguez Hills (CA)
California State U, Fresno (CA)
California State U, Fullerton (CA)
California State U, Hayward (CA)
California State U, Long Beach (CA)
California State U, San Bernardino (CA)
Campbell U (NC)
Cardinal Stritch U (WI)
Carnegie Mellon U (PA)
Carroll Coll (WI)
Carson-Newman Coll (TN)
Carthage Coll (WI)
Centenary Coll (NJ)
Central Michigan U (MI)
Central Missouri State U (MO)
Champlain Coll (VT)
Chicago State U (IL)
Chowan Coll (NC)
Clark U (MA)
The Cleveland Inst of Art (OH)
Cogswell Polytechnical Coll (CA)
Col for Creative Studies (MI)
The Coll of New Jersey (NJ)
The Coll of Saint Rose (NY)
Coll of Visual Arts (MN)
Colorado State U (CO)
Columbia Coll Chicago (IL)
Concord Coll (WV)
Concordia U (IL)
Concordia U (NE)
Concordia U (QC, Canada)
Concordia U Wisconsin (WI)
Curry Coll (MA)
DePaul U (IL)
Dominican U (IL)
Dordt Coll (IA)
Dowling Coll (NY)
Drake U (IA)
Drexel U (PA)
Eastern Kentucky U (KY)
Edgewood Coll (WI)
Elms Coll (MA)
Escuela de Artes Plasticas de Puerto Rico (PR)
Fairmont State Coll (WV)
Fashion Inst of Technology (NY)
Florida Ag and Mech U (FL)
Florida Southern Coll (FL)
Florida State U (FL)
Fontbonne U (MO)
Fordham U (NY)
Fort Hays State U (KS)
Franklin Pierce Coll (NH)
Freed-Hardeman U (TN)
Gallaudet U (DC)
Grace Coll (IN)
Graceland U (IA)
Grand Canyon U (AZ)
Grand Valley State U (MI)
Hampton U (VA)
Huntington Coll (IN)
The Illinois Inst of Art (IL)
Indiana U Bloomington (IN)
Indiana U–Purdue U Fort Wayne (IN)
Intl Acad of Design & Technology (FL)
Intl Acad of Merchandising & Design, Ltd (IL)
Iowa State U of Science and Technology (IA)
John Brown U (AR)
Judson Coll (IL)
Kansas City Art Inst (MO)
Keene State Coll (NH)
Kent State U (OH)
Kutztown U of Pennsylvania (PA)
Laguna Coll of Art & Design (CA)
Lamar U (TX)
Lasell Coll (MA)
Lewis U (IL)
Lipscomb U (TN)
Longwood U (VA)
Louisiana Coll (LA)
Louisiana Tech U (LA)
Loyola U New Orleans (LA)
Lycoming Coll (PA)
Lyndon State Coll (VT)
Lynn U (FL)
Marietta Coll (OH)
Massachusetts Coll of Art (MA)
Memphis Coll of Art (TN)
Mercy Coll (NY)
Meredith Coll (NC)
Millikin U (IL)
Milwaukee Inst of Art and Design (WI)
Minneapolis Coll of Art and Design (MN)
Minnesota State U Mankato (MN)
Minnesota State U Moorhead (MN)
Missouri Southern State U (MO)
Moore Coll of Art & Design (PA)
Morningside Coll (IA)
Mount Ida Coll (MA)
Mount Mary Coll (WI)
Mt. Sierra Coll (CA)
Nazareth Coll of Rochester (NY)
The New England Inst of Art (MA)
New Mexico Highlands U (NM)
New York Inst of Technology (NY)
Northeastern State U (OK)
Northeastern U (MA)
Northern Michigan U (MI)
Northwest Coll of Art (WA)
Northwest Nazarene U (ID)
Notre Dame de Namur U (CA)
Nova Scotia Coll of Art and Design (NS, Canada)
Ohio Northern U (OH)
The Ohio State U (OH)
Ohio U (OH)
Oklahoma Christian U (OK)
Oklahoma City U (OK)
Oklahoma State U (OK)
Olivet Coll (MI)
Olivet Nazarene U (IL)
O'More Coll of Design (TN)
Oral Roberts U (OK)
Otis Coll of Art and Design (CA)
Paier Coll of Art, Inc. (CT)
Park U (MO)
Parsons School of Design, New School U (NY)
Pennsylvania Coll of Technology (PA)
Philadelphia U (PA)
Pittsburg State U (KS)
Plymouth State U (NH)
Portland State U (OR)
Pratt Inst (NY)
Rivier Coll (NH)
Rutgers, The State U of New Jersey, New Brunswick/Piscataway (NJ)
Ryerson U (ON, Canada)
Sacred Heart U (CT)
St. John's U (NY)
Saint Mary's U of Minnesota (MN)
St. Norbert Coll (WI)
St. Thomas Aquinas Coll (NY)
Salem State Coll (MA)
Samford U (AL)
Sam Houston State U (TX)
School of the Art Inst of Chicago (IL)
School of the Museum of Fine Arts, Boston (MA)
Seton Hall U (NJ)
Seton Hill U (PA)
Simmons Coll (MA)
Simpson Coll (IA)
Southern Connecticut State U (CT)
Southwest Baptist U (MO)
Southwestern Oklahoma State U (OK)
State U of NY at New Paltz (NY)
State U of NY at Oswego (NY)
State U of NY Coll at Fredonia (NY)
Suffolk U (MA)
Syracuse U (NY)
Taylor U (IN)
Texas A&M U–Commerce (TX)
Texas State U-San Marcos (TX)
Texas Tech U (TX)
Trinity Christian Coll (IL)
Truman State U (MO)
Union Coll (NE)
Université Laval (QC, Canada)
U of Advancing Technology (AZ)
The U of Akron (OH)
U of Cincinnati (OH)
U of Dayton (OH)
U of Delaware (DE)
U of Denver (CO)
U of Evansville (IN)
U of Hartford (CT)
U of Illinois at Chicago (IL)
U of Indianapolis (IN)
U of Mary Hardin-Baylor (TX)
U of Massachusetts Dartmouth (MA)
U of Miami (FL)
U of Michigan (MI)
U of Minnesota, Duluth (MN)
U of Minnesota, Twin Cities Campus (MN)
U of Montevallo (AL)
U of Oregon (OR)
U of Saint Francis (IN)
U of Sioux Falls (SD)
The U of Tennessee (TN)
The U of Tennessee at Martin (TN)
The U of Texas–Pan American (TX)
U of the Incarnate Word (TX)
U of the Pacific (CA)
U of Washington (WA)
U of Wisconsin–Platteville (WI)
U of Wisconsin–Stevens Point (WI)
Upper Iowa U (IA)
Villa Julie Coll (MD)
Walla Walla Coll (WA)
Wartburg Coll (IA)
Washington U in St. Louis (MO)
Waynesburg Coll (PA)
Wayne State Coll (NE)
Weber State U (UT)
Western Connecticut State U (CT)
Western Kentucky U (KY)
Western Michigan U (MI)
Western State Coll of Colorado (CO)
Western Washington U (WA)
Westfield State Coll (MA)
West Liberty State Coll (WV)
West Texas A&M U (TX)
West Virginia Wesleyan Coll (WV)
Wichita State U (KS)
William Paterson U of New Jersey (NJ)
William Woods U (MO)
Winona State U (MN)
York Coll of Pennsylvania (PA)
York U (ON, Canada)
Youngstown State U (OH)

COMMERCIAL PHOTOGRAPHY
Art Center Coll of Design (CA)
The Art Inst of Atlanta (GA)
Col for Creative Studies (MI)
Memphis Coll of Art (TN)
Minnesota State U Moorhead (MN)
Ohio U (OH)
Rochester Inst of Technology (NY)

COMMUNICATION AND JOURNALISM RELATED
Abilene Christian U (TX)
Alfred U (NY)
Arizona State U East (AZ)
The Art Inst of California–San Diego (CA)
Auburn U (AL)
Berry Coll (GA)
Bowling Green State U (OH)
Bradley U (IL)
Brigham Young U (UT)
Brigham Young U–Hawaii (HI)
California Baptist U (CA)
Campbell U (NC)
Centenary Coll of Louisiana (LA)
Champlain Coll (VT)
Chestnut Hill Coll (PA)
Clemson U (SC)
Coll of the Ozarks (MO)
Columbia Coll (SC)
Dalhousie U (NS, Canada)
Drexel U (PA)
Eastern Washington U (WA)
Framingham State Coll (MA)
The Franciscan U (IA)
Hannibal-LaGrange Coll (MO)
Hawai'i Pacific U (HI)
Illinois Inst of Technology (IL)
Indiana State U (IN)
Inter American U of PR, Ponce Campus (PR)
Ithaca Coll (NY)
Juniata Coll (PA)
Keystone Coll (PA)
Lehigh U (PA)
Lehman Coll of the City U of NY (NY)
Loyola U Chicago (IL)
Luther Coll (IA)
Malone Coll (OH)
Marquette U (WI)
Mary Baldwin Coll (VA)
Mercer U (GA)
Milwaukee School of Eng (WI)
Mississippi Coll (MS)
New England School of Communications (ME)
Norfolk State U (VA)
Northern Arizona U (AZ)
Notre Dame de Namur U (CA)
Ohio Northern U (OH)
The Ohio State U (OH)
Ohio U (OH)
Oklahoma State U (OK)
Old Dominion U (VA)
Pace U (NY)
Penn State U Abington Coll (PA)
Penn State U Altoona Coll (PA)
Penn State U at Erie, The Behrend Coll (PA)
Penn State U Beaver Campus of the Commonwealth Coll (PA)
Penn State U Berks Cmps of Berks-Lehigh Valley Coll (PA)
Penn State U Delaware County Campus of the Commonwealth Coll (PA)
Penn State U DuBois Campus of the Commonwealth Coll (PA)
Penn State U Fayette Campus of the Commonwealth Coll (PA)
Penn State U Hazleton Campus of the Commonwealth Coll (PA)
Penn State U Lehigh Valley Cmps of Berks-Lehigh Valley Coll (PA)
Penn State U McKeesport Campus of the Commonwealth Coll (PA)
Penn State U Mont Alto Campus of the Commonwealth Coll (PA)
Penn State U New Kensington Campus of the Commonwealth Coll (PA)
Penn State U Schuylkill Campus of the Capital Coll (PA)
Penn State U Shenango Campus of the Commonwealth Coll (PA)
Penn State U Univ Park Campus (PA)
Penn State U Wilkes-Barre Campus of the Commonwealth Coll (PA)
Penn State U Worthington Scranton Cmps Commonwealth Coll (PA)
Penn State U York Campus of the Commonwealth Coll (PA)
Pittsburg State U (KS)
Quinnipiac U (CT)
Saint Louis U (MO)
Saint Mary's Coll of California (CA)
San Diego State U (CA)
Southeastern Oklahoma State U (OK)
Spring Hill Coll (AL)
State U of NY Coll at Brockport (NY)
State U of NY Inst of Tech at Utica/Rome (NY)
Sterling Coll (KS)
Syracuse U (NY)
Taylor U, Fort Wayne Campus (IN)
Université de Sherbrooke (QC, Canada)
The U of Akron (OH)
U of Illinois at Urbana–Champaign (IL)
U of Miami (FL)
U of Oklahoma (OK)
The U of the Arts (PA)

U of Wisconsin–Green Bay (WI)
Valparaiso U (IN)
Virginia Intermont Coll (VA)
Washington U in St. Louis (MO)
Webster U (MO)
Western Kentucky U (KY)
West Virginia U (WV)
Wheeling Jesuit U (WV)
Wisconsin Lutheran Coll (WI)

COMMUNICATION AND MEDIA RELATED

Alma Coll (MI)
Athabasca U (AB, Canada)
Bellevue U (NE)
Calumet Coll of Saint Joseph (IN)
Campbell U (NC)
Canisius Coll (NY)
Centenary Coll of Louisiana (LA)
Central Missouri State U (MO)
Champlain Coll (VT)
Clayton Coll & State U (GA)
Crown Coll (MN)
Florida State U (FL)
Framingham State Coll (MA)
Franklin Coll Switzerland(Switzerland)
Greenville Coll (IL)
Harding U (AR)
Hood Coll (MD)
Houston Baptist U (TX)
Indiana U–Purdue U Fort Wayne (IN)
Lane Coll (TN)
Macon State Coll (GA)
Miles Coll (AL)
Milligan Coll (TN)
Missouri Western State Coll (MO)
Northwestern U (IL)
Penn State U at Erie, The Behrend Coll (PA)
Point Loma Nazarene U (CA)
Point Park U (PA)
Providence Coll and Theological Sem (MB, Canada)
Rochester Inst of Technology (NY)
Roger Williams U (RI)
St. Edward's U (TX)
St. Gregory's U (OK)
Southwestern Coll (KS)
State U of NY Coll at Brockport (NY)
Trinity Intl U (IL)
Université de Sherbrooke (QC, Canada)
U of Ottawa (ON, Canada)
The U of the Arts (PA)
Walsh U (OH)
Washington State U (WA)
Wilmington Coll (DE)

COMMUNICATION DISORDERS

Appalachian State U (NC)
Arizona State U (AZ)
Baldwin-Wallace Coll (OH)
Baylor U (TX)
Biola U (CA)
Boston U (MA)
Bowling Green State U (OH)
Bridgewater State Coll (MA)
Brock U (ON, Canada)
California State U, Chico (CA)
California State U, Fresno (CA)
California State U, Fullerton (CA)
California State U, Long Beach (CA)
California State U, Los Angeles (CA)
Case Western Reserve U (OH)
The Coll of Saint Rose (NY)
Eastern Illinois U (IL)
Eastern Washington U (WA)
Edinboro U of Pennsylvania (PA)
Emerson Coll (MA)
Harding U (AR)
Kansas State U (KS)
Longwood U (VA)
Marshall U (WV)
Minnesota State U Mankato (MN)
Minot State U (ND)
Northern Illinois U (IL)
Northwestern U (IL)
Oklahoma State U (OK)
Pace U (NY)
Penn State U Abington Coll (PA)
Penn State U at Erie, The Behrend Coll (PA)
Penn State U Berks Cmps of Berks-Lehigh Valley Coll (PA)
Penn State U Delaware County Campus of the Commonwealth Coll (PA)
Penn State U DuBois Campus of the Commonwealth Coll (PA)
Penn State U Fayette Campus of the Commonwealth Coll (PA)
Penn State U Hazleton Campus of the Commonwealth Coll (PA)
Penn State U Lehigh Valley Cmps of Berks-Lehigh Valley Coll (PA)
Penn State U McKeesport Campus of the Commonwealth Coll (PA)
Penn State U Mont Alto Campus of the Commonwealth Coll (PA)
Penn State U New Kensington Campus of the Commonwealth Coll (PA)
Penn State U Schuylkill Campus of the Capital Coll (PA)
Penn State U Shenango Campus of the Commonwealth Coll (PA)
Penn State U Univ Park Campus (PA)
Penn State U Wilkes-Barre Campus of the Commonwealth Coll (PA)
Penn State U Worthington Scranton Cmps Commonwealth Coll (PA)
Penn State U York Campus of the Commonwealth Coll (PA)
Queens Coll of the City U of NY (NY)
St. Cloud State U (MN)
San Diego State U (CA)
San Jose State U (CA)
Southeast Missouri State U (MO)
Southern Illinois U Carbondale (IL)
Plattsburgh State U of NY (NY)
State U of NY Coll at Fredonia (NY)
Truman State U (MO)
The U of Akron (OH)
The U of Arizona (AZ)
U of Colorado at Boulder (CO)
U of Georgia (GA)
U of Houston (TX)
U of Kansas (KS)
U of Maine (ME)
U of Massachusetts Amherst (MA)
U of Rhode Island (RI)
The U of South Dakota (SD)
The U of Texas at Austin (TX)
U of Vermont (VT)
U of Wisconsin–Eau Claire (WI)
U of Wisconsin–River Falls (WI)
Western Carolina U (NC)
Western Illinois U (IL)
West Texas A&M U (TX)
Winthrop U (SC)
Worcester State Coll (MA)

COMMUNICATION DISORDERS SCIENCES AND SERVICES RELATED

Long Island U, Brooklyn Campus (NY)
Ohio U (OH)
Ouachita Baptist U (AR)
Radford U (VA)
St. Cloud State U (MN)
Syracuse U (NY)
U of Missouri–Columbia (MO)
U of Oklahoma Health Sciences Center (OK)

COMMUNICATION/SPEECH COMMUNICATION AND RHETORIC

Adams State Coll (CO)
Adelphi U (NY)
Albright Coll (PA)
Allegheny Coll (PA)
Alvernia Coll (PA)
Alverno Coll (WI)
The American U of Rome(Italy)
Angelo State U (TX)
Antioch Coll (OH)
Aquinas Coll (MI)
Arizona State U (AZ)
Arizona State U West (AZ)
Auburn U Montgomery (AL)
Augustana Coll (SD)
Augusta State U (GA)
Aurora U (IL)
Austin Coll (TX)
Avila U (MO)
Azusa Pacific U (CA)
Baldwin-Wallace Coll (OH)
Barry U (FL)
Baylor U (TX)
Belhaven Coll (MS)
Bellarmine U (KY)
Benedictine U (IL)
Bethany Coll (KS)
Bethany Coll (WV)
Bethany Lutheran Coll (MN)
Bethel Coll (IN)
Bethel U (MN)
Blackburn Coll (IL)
Bloomfield Coll (NJ)
Bloomsburg U of Pennsylvania (PA)
Bluffton Coll (OH)
Boston U (MA)
Bowling Green State U (OH)
Bradley U (IL)
Brewton-Parker Coll (GA)
Brock U (ON, Canada)
Brooklyn Coll of the City U of NY (NY)
Bryant Coll (RI)
Buena Vista U (IA)
State U of NY Coll at Buffalo (NY)
Cabrini Coll (PA)
Caldwell Coll (NJ)
California Baptist U (CA)
California State U, Fullerton (CA)
California State U, Los Angeles (CA)
California State U, Sacramento (CA)
California State U, San Marcos (CA)
California State U, Stanislaus (CA)
California U of Pennsylvania (PA)
Calumet Coll of Saint Joseph (IN)
Calvin Coll (MI)
Cameron U (OK)
Campbell U (NC)
Capital U (OH)
Cardinal Stritch U (WI)
Carlow Coll (PA)
Carroll Coll (MT)
Carroll Coll (WI)
The Catholic U of America (DC)
Cedar Crest Coll (PA)
Cedarville U (OH)
Central Coll (IA)
Central Connecticut State U (CT)
Central Methodist Coll (MO)
Chapman U (CA)
Chatham Coll (PA)
Christian Heritage Coll (CA)
Christopher Newport U (VA)
Clarion U of Pennsylvania (PA)
Clarkson U (NY)
Clearwater Christian Coll (FL)
Cleveland State U (OH)
Coll Misericordia (PA)
Coll of Charleston (SC)
Coll of Mount St. Joseph (OH)
Coll of Saint Elizabeth (NJ)
Coll of St. Joseph (VT)
The Coll of Saint Rose (NY)
The Coll of St. Scholastica (MN)
Coll of Staten Island of the City U of NY (NY)
The Coll of Wooster (OH)
Colorado Christian U (CO)
Columbia Coll (SC)
Columbia Intl U (SC)
Concordia Coll (MN)
Concordia U (CA)
Concordia U (IL)
Concordia U (MI)
Concordia U (NE)
Concordia U (QC, Canada)
Cornell U (NY)
Creighton U (NE)
Cumberland Coll (KY)
Dallas Baptist U (TX)
Dana Coll (NE)
Davis & Elkins Coll (WV)
DePaul U (IL)
Doane Coll (NE)
Dominican U of California (CA)
Dowling Coll (NY)
Duquesne U (PA)
East Carolina U (NC)
Eastern Connecticut State U (CT)
Eastern Mennonite U (VA)
Eastern New Mexico U (NM)
Eastern U (PA)
Eastern Washington U (WA)
East Stroudsburg U of Pennsylvania (PA)
Eckerd Coll (FL)
Edinboro U of Pennsylvania (PA)
Elizabethtown Coll (PA)
Elmhurst Coll (IL)
Elon U (NC)
Embry-Riddle Aeronautical U (FL)
Emerson Coll (MA)
Emporia State U (KS)
Fairleigh Dickinson U, Florham (NJ)
Fairleigh Dickinson U, Teaneck-Metro Campus (NJ)
Flagler Coll (FL)
Florida Inst of Technology (FL)
Florida Intl U (FL)
Florida Southern Coll (FL)
Florida State U (FL)
Fontbonne U (MO)
Framingham State Coll (MA)
Franciscan U of Steubenville (OH)
Frostburg State U (MD)
Furman U (SC)
Gallaudet U (DC)
Gannon U (PA)
Geneva Coll (PA)
George Fox U (OR)
Georgia Southern U (GA)
Gordon Coll (MA)
Governors State U (IL)
Grace U (NE)
Greensboro Coll (NC)
Hannibal-LaGrange Coll (MO)
Harding U (AR)
Hardin-Simmons U (TX)
Hastings Coll (NE)
Hawai'i Pacific U (HI)
Hofstra U (NY)
Hollins U (VA)
Hope Coll (MI)
Houston Baptist U (TX)
Howard Payne U (TX)
Humboldt State U (CA)
Huntington Coll (IN)
Huron U USA in London(United Kingdom)
Idaho State U (ID)
Indiana State U (IN)
Indiana U Bloomington (IN)
Indiana U East (IN)
Indiana U Kokomo (IN)
Indiana U of Pennsylvania (PA)
Indiana U–Purdue U Indianapolis (IN)
Indiana U Southeast (IN)
Inter American U of PR, Bayamón Campus (PR)
Iona Coll (NY)
Jacksonville State U (AL)
Jacksonville U (FL)
James Madison U (VA)
Jamestown Coll (ND)
Juniata Coll (PA)
Kansas State U (KS)
Kean U (NJ)
Kennesaw State U (GA)
Kentucky Wesleyan Coll (KY)
Keuka Coll (NY)
Keystone Coll (PA)
King Coll (TN)
King's Coll (PA)
Lake Forest Coll (IL)
La Roche Coll (PA)
Lasell Coll (MA)
Le Moyne Coll (NY)
Lewis & Clark Coll (OR)
Lewis-Clark State Coll (ID)
Liberty U (VA)
Lincoln U (PA)
Linfield Coll (OR)
Long Island U, Brooklyn Campus (NY)
Long Island U, C.W. Post Campus (NY)
Long Island U, Southampton Coll (NY)
Longwood U (VA)
Loyola Coll in Maryland (MD)
Loyola U Chicago (IL)
Loyola U New Orleans (LA)
Lynchburg Coll (VA)
Macalester Coll (MN)
Marian Coll of Fond du Lac (WI)
Marietta Coll (OH)
Marist Coll (NY)
Marquette U (WI)
Martin U (IN)
Mary Baldwin Coll (VA)
Marymount U (VA)
McDaniel Coll (MD)
McMurry U (TX)
Meredith Coll (NC)
Merrimack Coll (MA)
Messiah Coll (PA)
Metropolitan State U (MN)
Miami U Hamilton (OH)
Michigan State U (MI)
Michigan Technological U (MI)
Millersville U of Pennsylvania (PA)
Millikin U (IL)
Mississippi Coll (MS)
Mississippi State U (MS)
Missouri Baptist U (MO)
Missouri Southern State U (MO)
Molloy Coll (NY)
Monmouth U (NJ)
Montana Tech of The U of Montana (MT)
Montclair State U (NJ)
Moody Bible Inst (IL)
Morehead State U (KY)
Mount Mary Coll (WI)
Mount Mercy Coll (IA)
Mount Saint Mary's Coll and Sem (MD)
Mount Union Coll (OH)
Mount Vernon Nazarene U (OH)
Multnomah Bible Coll and Biblical Sem (OR)
Nebraska Wesleyan U (NE)
Neumann Coll (PA)
New Jersey City U (NJ)
New York U (NY)
North Carolina State U (NC)
Northeastern U (MA)
Northern Arizona U (AZ)
Northern Illinois U (IL)
Northern Michigan U (MI)
Northwest Christian Coll (OR)
Northwestern Coll (MN)
Northwestern U (IL)
Northwest Nazarene U (ID)
Notre Dame Coll (OH)
Notre Dame de Namur U (CA)
Nyack Coll (NY)
Oakland U (MI)
Ohio Dominican U (OH)
Ohio Northern U (OH)
The Ohio State U (OH)
Ohio U (OH)
Oral Roberts U (OK)
Oregon Inst of Technology (OR)
Our Lady of the Lake U of San Antonio (TX)
Pace U (NY)
Palm Beach Atlantic U (FL)
Park U (MO)
Peace Coll (NC)
Penn State U Abington Coll (PA)
Penn State U Altoona Coll (PA)
Penn State U at Erie, The Behrend Coll (PA)
Penn State U Beaver Campus of the Commonwealth Coll (PA)
Penn State U Berks Cmps of Berks-Lehigh Valley Coll (PA)
Penn State U Delaware County Campus of the Commonwealth Coll (PA)
Penn State U DuBois Campus of the Commonwealth Coll (PA)
Penn State U Fayette Campus of the Commonwealth Coll (PA)
Penn State U Harrisburg Campus of the Capital Coll (PA)
Penn State U Hazleton Campus of the Commonwealth Coll (PA)
Penn State U Lehigh Valley Cmps of Berks-Lehigh Valley Coll (PA)
Penn State U McKeesport Campus of the Commonwealth Coll (PA)
Penn State U Mont Alto Campus of the Commonwealth Coll (PA)
Penn State U New Kensington Campus of the Commonwealth Coll (PA)
Penn State U Schuylkill Campus of the Capital Coll (PA)
Penn State U Shenango Campus of the Commonwealth Coll (PA)
Penn State U Univ Park Campus (PA)
Penn State U Wilkes-Barre Campus of the Commonwealth Coll (PA)
Penn State U Worthington Scranton Cmps Commonwealth Coll (PA)
Penn State U York Campus of the Commonwealth Coll (PA)
Pepperdine U, Malibu (CA)
Pfeiffer U (NC)
Pikeville Coll (KY)
Pine Manor Coll (MA)
Plymouth State U (NH)
Point Loma Nazarene U (CA)
Presentation Coll (SD)
Purdue U (IN)
Queens Coll of the City U of NY (NY)
Quincy U (IL)
Radford U (VA)
Ramapo Coll of New Jersey (NJ)
Randolph-Macon Woman's Coll (VA)
Reformed Bible Coll (MI)
Regis Coll (MA)
Regis U (CO)
Rensselaer Polytechnic Inst (NY)
The Richard Stockton Coll of New Jersey (NJ)
Ripon Coll (WI)
Rivier Coll (NH)
Robert Morris U (PA)
Roberts Wesleyan Coll (NY)
Rochester Coll (MI)
Rockhurst U (MO)
Rocky Mountain Coll (MT)
Roosevelt U (IL)
Rosemont Coll (PA)
Rowan U (NJ)

Rutgers, The State U of New Jersey, New Brunswick/Piscataway (NJ)
Saginaw Valley State U (MI)
Saint Augustine's Coll (NC)
St. Francis Coll (NY)
St. John's U (NY)
Saint Joseph's Coll (IN)
Saint Joseph's U (PA)
Saint Louis U (MO)
Saint Mary's Coll (IN)
Saint Mary's Coll of California (CA)
St. Mary's U of San Antonio (TX)
St. Norbert Coll (WI)
Saint Vincent Coll (PA)
Saint Xavier U (IL)
Salisbury U (MD)
Santa Clara U (CA)
Seattle Pacific U (WA)
Seton Hall U (NJ)
Seton Hill U (PA)
Shenandoah U (VA)
Shepherd U (WV)
Simon Fraser U (BC, Canada)
Simpson Coll and Graduate School (CA)
Slippery Rock U of Pennsylvania (PA)
Southeastern Coll of the Assemblies of God (FL)
Southeastern Louisiana U (LA)
Southeastern Oklahoma State U (OK)
Southeast Missouri State U (MO)
Southern Connecticut State U (CT)
Southern Oregon U (OR)
Southern Vermont Coll (VT)
Southwest Baptist U (MO)
Southwest Missouri State U (MO)
Spring Arbor U (MI)
Stanford U (CA)
Plattsburgh State U of NY (NY)
State U of NY Coll at Brockport (NY)
State U of NY Coll at Cortland (NY)
State U of NY Coll at Geneseo (NY)
State U of NY Coll at Old Westbury (NY)
Stetson U (FL)
Stonehill Coll (MA)
Susquehanna U (PA)
Sweet Briar Coll (VA)
Syracuse U (NY)
Tabor Coll (KS)
Taylor U (IN)
Texas A&M Intl U (TX)
Texas A&M U–Corpus Christi (TX)
Texas Christian U (TX)
Texas Lutheran U (TX)
Texas Southern U (TX)
Thiel Coll (PA)
Thomas Edison State Coll (NJ)
Thomas More Coll (KY)
Thomas U (GA)
Tiffin U (OH)
Towson U (MD)
Trevecca Nazarene U (TN)
Trinity Christian Coll (IL)
Trinity U (TX)
Trinity Western U (BC, Canada)
Tri-State U (IN)
Truman State U (MO)
Union Coll (KY)
Union Inst & U (OH)
U at Buffalo, The State U of New York (NY)
The U of Akron (OH)
The U of Alabama at Birmingham (AL)
U of Alaska Fairbanks (AK)
The U of Arizona (AZ)
U of Arkansas (AR)
U of Calgary (AB, Canada)
U of Calif, Los Angeles (CA)
U of Calif, Santa Barbara (CA)
U of Colorado at Boulder (CO)
U of Colorado at Colorado Springs (CO)
U of Colorado at Denver (CO)
U of Connecticut (CT)
U of Delaware (DE)
U of Denver (CO)
U of Hartford (CT)
U of Hawaii at Manoa (HI)
U of Houston (TX)
U of Houston–Clear Lake (TX)
U of Idaho (ID)
U of Indianapolis (IN)
The U of Iowa (IA)
U of Kentucky (KY)
U of La Verne (CA)
U of Louisiana at Lafayette (LA)
U of Louisville (KY)
U of Maine (ME)
U of Mary Hardin-Baylor (TX)
U of Maryland, Coll Park (MD)
U of Maryland U Coll (MD)
U of Massachusetts Amherst (MA)
The U of Memphis (TN)
U of Miami (FL)
U of Michigan–Flint (MI)
U of Missouri–Columbia (MO)
U of Missouri–St. Louis (MO)
U of Nebraska at Omaha (NE)
U of Nebraska–Lincoln (NE)
U of Nevada, Las Vegas (NV)
U of Nevada, Reno (NV)
U of New Orleans (LA)
The U of North Carolina at Chapel Hill (NC)
The U of North Carolina at Charlotte (NC)
U of North Dakota (ND)
U of Northern Colorado (CO)
U of Northern Iowa (IA)
U of North Florida (FL)
U of North Texas (TX)
U of Oklahoma (OK)
U of Pennsylvania (PA)
U of Pittsburgh (PA)
U of Puget Sound (WA)
U of Rhode Island (RI)
U of Saint Francis (IN)
U of St. Thomas (MN)
U of St. Thomas (TX)
U of San Francisco (CA)
U of Science and Arts of Oklahoma (OK)
The U of Scranton (PA)
U of South Alabama (AL)
U of South Carolina Aiken (SC)
U of South Carolina Spartanburg (SC)
U of Southern California (CA)
U of Southern Indiana (IN)
U of Southern Maine (ME)
U of South Florida (FL)
The U of Texas at Austin (TX)
The U of Texas–Pan American (TX)
The U of the Arts (PA)
U of the Incarnate Word (TX)
U of the Ozarks (AR)
U of the Pacific (CA)
U of the Sacred Heart (PR)
U of Toledo (OH)
U of Tulsa (OK)
U of Utah (UT)
The U of Virginia's Coll at Wise (VA)
U of Washington (WA)
U of Waterloo (ON, Canada)
U of West Florida (FL)
U of Windsor (ON, Canada)
U of Wisconsin–Eau Claire (WI)
U of Wisconsin–La Crosse (WI)
U of Wisconsin–Parkside (WI)
U of Wisconsin–Stevens Point (WI)
U of Wisconsin–Whitewater (WI)
U of Wyoming (WY)
Utica Coll (NY)
Valdosta State U (GA)
Valparaiso U (IN)
Vanguard U of Southern California (CA)
Virginia Polytechnic Inst and State U (VA)
Virginia Wesleyan Coll (VA)
Wake Forest U (NC)
Warner Southern Coll (FL)
Washburn U (KS)
Washington State U (WA)
Washington U in St. Louis (MO)
Waynesburg Coll (PA)
Wayne State U (MI)
Wesleyan Coll (GA)
West Chester U of Pennsylvania (PA)
Western Baptist Coll (OR)
Western Carolina U (NC)
Western Illinois U (IL)
Western Kentucky U (KY)
Western Michigan U (MI)
Western New England Coll (MA)
Western Washington U (WA)
Westminster Coll (UT)
Westmont Coll (CA)
West Virginia State Coll (WV)
West Virginia Wesleyan Coll (WV)
Wheaton Coll (IL)
Wichita State U (KS)
Wilkes U (PA)
William Carey Coll (MS)
William Penn U (IA)
William Woods U (MO)
Wisconsin Lutheran Coll (WI)
Wittenberg U (OH)
Wright State U (OH)
York U (ON, Canada)
Youngstown State U (OH)

COMMUNICATIONS TECHNOLOGIES AND SUPPORT SERVICES RELATED

Alverno Coll (WI)
Chestnut Hill Coll (PA)
Hofstra U (NY)
Lesley U (MA)
New England School of Communications (ME)
Saint Mary-of-the-Woods Coll (IN)
The U of Scranton (PA)
U of Windsor (ON, Canada)

COMMUNICATIONS TECHNOLOGY

Becker Coll (MA)
Cheyney U of Pennsylvania (PA)
The Coll of Saint Rose (NY)
Eastern Michigan U (MI)
East Stroudsburg U of Pennsylvania (PA)
Hastings Coll (NE)
Inter American U of PR, Bayamón Campus (PR)
Lawrence Technological U (MI)
Saint Mary-of-the-Woods Coll (IN)
Salve Regina U (RI)
U of Michigan–Dearborn (MI)

COMMUNITY COLLEGE EDUCATION

Eastern Michigan U (MI)

COMMUNITY HEALTH AND PREVENTIVE MEDICINE

Hofstra U (NY)
Tufts U (MA)
U of Calif, Los Angeles (CA)
U of Illinois at Urbana–Champaign (IL)
U of Massachusetts Lowell (MA)

COMMUNITY HEALTH LIAISON

Delaware State U (DE)
Eastern Kentucky U (KY)
Texas Woman's U (TX)

COMMUNITY HEALTH SERVICES COUNSELING

Bethel U (MN)
California State U, Sacramento (CA)
Central Washington U (WA)
Cleveland State U (OH)
Cumberland Coll (KY)
Eastern Kentucky U (KY)
Florida State U (FL)
Indiana State U (IN)
Indiana U–Purdue U Fort Wayne (IN)
James Madison U (VA)
Long Island U, Brooklyn Campus (NY)
Longwood U (VA)
Marymount Coll of Fordham U (NY)
Minnesota State U Moorhead (MN)
Morris Coll (SC)
Northeastern Illinois U (IL)
Ohio U (OH)
Prairie View A&M U (TX)
Sam Houston State U (TX)
Seton Hill U (PA)
Texas A&M U (TX)
Texas State U-San Marcos (TX)
Texas Tech U (TX)
U of Arkansas (AR)
U of Florida (FL)
U of Houston (TX)
U of Kansas (KS)
U of Michigan–Flint (MI)
U of Nebraska at Omaha (NE)
U of Nebraska–Lincoln (NE)
U of Northern Iowa (IA)
U of Pennsylvania (PA)
U of West Florida (FL)
Western Kentucky U (KY)
Western Washington U (WA)
Youngstown State U (OH)

COMMUNITY ORGANIZATION AND ADVOCACY

Alverno Coll (WI)
Bellarmine U (KY)
Bemidji State U (MN)
Cazenovia Coll (NY)
Central Michigan U (MI)
Cleveland State U (OH)
Concordia U, St. Paul (MN)
Cornell U (NY)
Eastern Michigan U (MI)
Emory & Henry Coll (VA)
Hampshire Coll (MA)
High Point U (NC)
Marywood U (PA)
Mercer U (GA)
New Mexico State U (NM)
Northern State U (SD)
North Park U (IL)
Northwestern U (IL)
Pace U (NY)
Providence Coll (RI)
Rockhurst U (MO)
Roosevelt U (IL)
Saint Leo U (FL)
Saint Martin's Coll (WA)
Samford U (AL)
Siena Heights U (MI)
Southern Arkansas U–Magnolia (AR)
Southern Connecticut State U (CT)
Springfield Coll (MA)
State U of NY Empire State Coll (NY)
Thomas Edison State Coll (NJ)
The U of Akron (OH)
U of Alaska Fairbanks (AK)
U of Baltimore (MD)
U of Delaware (DE)
U of Hartford (CT)
U of Massachusetts Boston (MA)
U of Oregon (OR)
U of Saint Mary (KS)
U of Toledo (OH)
Western Baptist Coll (OR)

COMMUNITY PSYCHOLOGY

Kwantlen U Coll (BC, Canada)
Montana State U–Billings (MT)
New York Inst of Technology (NY)
Northwestern U (IL)
Pikeville Coll (KY)
Seton Hill U (PA)
U of Saint Mary (KS)
Wright State U (OH)

COMPARATIVE LITERATURE

The American U in Cairo(Egypt)
Antioch Coll (OH)
Bard Coll (NY)
Barnard Coll (NY)
Beloit Coll (WI)
Bennington Coll (VT)
Brandeis U (MA)
Brigham Young U (UT)
Brooklyn Coll of the City U of NY (NY)
Brown U (RI)
Bryn Mawr Coll (PA)
California State U, Fullerton (CA)
California State U, Long Beach (CA)
Carleton U (ON, Canada)
Case Western Reserve U (OH)
Clark U (MA)
The Coll of Wooster (OH)
The Colorado Coll (CO)
Columbia Coll (NY)
Columbia U, School of General Studies (NY)
Cornell U (NY)
Dartmouth Coll (NH)
DePaul U (IL)
Eckerd Coll (FL)
Emory U (GA)
Fordham U (NY)
Georgetown U (DC)
Hamilton Coll (NY)
Hampshire Coll (MA)
Harvard U (MA)
Haverford Coll (PA)
Hillsdale Coll (MI)
Hobart and William Smith Colls (NY)
Hofstra U (NY)
Hunter Coll of the City U of NY (NY)
Hunter Coll of the City U of NY (NY)
Indiana U Bloomington (IN)
Marlboro Coll (VT)
Mills Coll (CA)
New Coll of Florida (FL)
New York U (NY)
Northwestern U (IL)
Oakland U (MI)
Oberlin Coll (OH)
Occidental Coll (CA)
The Ohio State U (OH)
Oregon State U (OR)
Penn State U Abington Coll (PA)
Penn State U Altoona Coll (PA)
Penn State U at Erie, The Behrend Coll (PA)
Penn State U Beaver Campus of the Commonwealth Coll (PA)
Penn State U Berks Cmps of Berks-Lehigh Valley Coll (PA)
Penn State U Delaware County Campus of the Commonwealth Coll (PA)
Penn State U DuBois Campus of the Commonwealth Coll (PA)
Penn State U Fayette Campus of the Commonwealth Coll (PA)
Penn State U Hazleton Campus of the Commonwealth Coll (PA)
Penn State U Lehigh Valley Cmps of Berks-Lehigh Valley Coll (PA)
Penn State U McKeesport Campus of the Commonwealth Coll (PA)
Penn State U Mont Alto Campus of the Commonwealth Coll (PA)
Penn State U New Kensington Campus of the Commonwealth Coll (PA)
Penn State U Schuylkill Campus of the Capital Coll (PA)
Penn State U Shenango Campus of the Commonwealth Coll (PA)
Penn State U Univ Park Campus (PA)
Penn State U Wilkes-Barre Campus of the Commonwealth Coll (PA)
Penn State U Worthington Scranton Cmps Commonwealth Coll (PA)
Penn State U York Campus of the Commonwealth Coll (PA)
Princeton U (NJ)
Queens Coll of the City U of NY (NY)
Ramapo Coll of New Jersey (NJ)
Roosevelt U (IL)
Rutgers, The State U of New Jersey, New Brunswick/Piscataway (NJ)
St. Cloud State U (MN)
Salem State Coll (MA)
San Diego State U (CA)
San Francisco State U (CA)
Sarah Lawrence Coll (NY)
Simmons Coll (MA)
Smith Coll (MA)
Stanford U (CA)
State U of NY at Binghamton (NY)
State U of NY at New Paltz (NY)
State U of NY Coll at Geneseo (NY)
Stony Brook U, State U of New York (NY)
Swarthmore Coll (PA)
Trinity Coll (CT)
U of Alberta (AB, Canada)
U of Arkansas (AR)
U of Calif, Berkeley (CA)
U of Calif, Davis (CA)
U of Calif, Irvine (CA)
U of Calif, Los Angeles (CA)
U of Calif, Riverside (CA)
U of Calif, Santa Barbara (CA)
U of Calif, Santa Cruz (CA)
U of Chicago (IL)
U of Cincinnati (OH)
U of Delaware (DE)
U of Georgia (GA)
U of Illinois at Urbana–Champaign (IL)
The U of Iowa (IA)
U of La Verne (CA)
U of Massachusetts Amherst (MA)
U of Michigan (MI)
U of Michigan–Dearborn (MI)
U of Minnesota, Twin Cities Campus (MN)
U of Nevada, Las Vegas (NV)
U of New Brunswick Fredericton (NB, Canada)
U of New Mexico (NM)
The U of North Carolina at Chapel Hill (NC)
U of Oregon (OR)
U of Pennsylvania (PA)
U of Rhode Island (RI)
U of Rochester (NY)
U of Southern California (CA)
U of the South (TN)
U of Virginia (VA)
U of Washington (WA)
The U of Western Ontario (ON, Canada)
U of Windsor (ON, Canada)
U of Wisconsin–Madison (WI)
U of Wisconsin–Milwaukee (WI)
Washington U in St. Louis (MO)
Wellesley Coll (MA)
West Chester U of Pennsylvania (PA)
Western Washington U (WA)
Willamette U (OR)
William Woods U (MO)

COMPUTATIONAL MATHEMATICS

Brooklyn Coll of the City U of NY (NY)

Indiana U–Purdue U Fort Wayne (IN)
Marquette U (WI)
Michigan State U (MI)
Northern Illinois U (IL)
Stevens Inst of Technology (NJ)
U of Calif, Los Angeles (CA)
U of Waterloo (ON, Canada)

COMPUTER AND INFORMATION SCIENCES

Adelphi U (NY)
Alabama Ag and Mech U (AL)
Albany State U (GA)
Alcorn State U (MS)
Alfred U (NY)
Alverno Coll (WI)
Amberton U (TX)
American Coll of Computer & Information Sciences (AL)
American U in Bulgaria(Bulgaria)
Andrews U (MI)
Angelo State U (TX)
Aquinas Coll (MI)
Arcadia U (PA)
Arkansas State U (AR)
Arkansas Tech U (AR)
Athabasca U (AB, Canada)
Auburn U (AL)
Augusta State U (GA)
Aurora U (IL)
Austin Peay State U (TN)
Avila U (MO)
Baker Coll of Muskegon (MI)
Barnard Coll (NY)
Barton Coll (NC)
Bellarmine U (KY)
Bellevue U (NE)
Bentley Coll (MA)
Bethel Coll (IN)
Bethel U (MN)
Biola U (CA)
Bishop's U (QC, Canada)
Bloomsburg U of Pennsylvania (PA)
Bluefield State Coll (WV)
Boise State U (ID)
Bowie State U (MD)
Bowling Green State U (OH)
Bradley U (IL)
Brewton-Parker Coll (GA)
Brooklyn Coll of the City U of NY (NY)
Bryant Coll (RI)
Bucknell U (PA)
Cabrini Coll (PA)
Caldwell Coll (NJ)
California Lutheran U (CA)
California State Polytechnic U, Pomona (CA)
California State U, Los Angeles (CA)
California State U, Sacramento (CA)
California State U, San Bernardino (CA)
California State U, Stanislaus (CA)
Cameron U (OK)
Campbell U (NC)
Carnegie Mellon U (PA)
Carroll Coll (WI)
Castleton State Coll (VT)
Cedar Crest Coll (PA)
Central Connecticut State U (CT)
Central Michigan U (MI)
Central Missouri State U (MO)
Central State U (OH)
Central Washington U (WA)
Chaminade U of Honolulu (HI)
Champlain Coll (VT)
Chapman U (CA)
Chatham Coll (PA)
Chestnut Hill Coll (PA)
Christopher Newport U (VA)
Claremont McKenna Coll (CA)
Clarion U of Pennsylvania (PA)
Clark Atlanta U (GA)
Clarkson U (NY)
Clemson U (SC)
Cleveland State U (OH)
Coastal Carolina U (SC)
Coleman Coll, La Mesa (CA)
CollAmerica–Fort Collins (CO)
Coll of Charleston (SC)
The Coll of New Jersey (NJ)
Coll of St. Catherine (MN)
The Coll of Saint Rose (NY)
The Coll of St. Scholastica (MN)
The Coll of Southeastern Europe, The American U of Athens(Greece)
Coll of Staten Island of the City U of NY (NY)
Coll of the Ozarks (MO)
The Coll of William and Mary (VA)
Colorado Christian U (CO)
Colorado State U (CO)
Colorado State U-Pueblo (CO)
Columbia Coll (MO)
Concordia U (MI)
Concordia U (NE)
Connecticut Coll (CT)
Cornell U (NY)
Cumberland Coll (KY)
Dallas Baptist U (TX)
Delaware State U (DE)
DePaul U (IL)
Doane Coll (NE)
Dominican Coll (NY)
Dowling Coll (NY)
Drury U (MO)
Eastern Connecticut State U (CT)
Eastern Kentucky U (KY)
Eastern Michigan U (MI)
Eastern New Mexico U (NM)
Eastern Washington U (WA)
East Stroudsburg U of Pennsylvania (PA)
East Texas Baptist U (TX)
Edinboro U of Pennsylvania (PA)
Emmanuel Coll (GA)
Emporia State U (KS)
The Evergreen State Coll (WA)
Fairleigh Dickinson U, Florham (NJ)
Fairleigh Dickinson U, Teaneck-Metro Campus (NJ)
Florida Ag and Mech U (FL)
Florida Atlantic U (FL)
Florida Gulf Coast U (FL)
Florida Intl U (FL)
Florida Metropolitan U-Tampa Coll, Brandon (FL)
Florida State U (FL)
Fordham U (NY)
The Franciscan U (IA)
Franciscan U of Steubenville (OH)
Francis Marion U (SC)
Franklin Coll (IN)
Franklin U (OH)
Freed-Hardeman U (TN)
Fresno Pacific U (CA)
Frostburg State U (MD)
Gallaudet U (DC)
Gannon U (PA)
George Fox U (OR)
George Mason U (VA)
Georgetown Coll (KY)
The George Washington U (DC)
Georgia Coll & State U (GA)
Georgia Inst of Technology (GA)
Georgia Southern U (GA)
Georgia Southwestern State U (GA)
Georgia State U (GA)
Globe Inst of Technology (NY)
Grace Bible Coll (MI)
Grace U (NE)
Grand Valley State U (MI)
Grove City Coll (PA)
Guilford Coll (NC)
Gwynedd-Mercy Coll (PA)
Hampshire Coll (MA)
Hannibal-LaGrange Coll (MO)
Harding U (AR)
Hartwick Coll (NY)
Harvard U (MA)
Haskell Indian Nations U (KS)
Hastings Coll (NE)
Hawai'i Pacific U (HI)
Henderson State U (AR)
High Point U (NC)
Hood Coll (MD)
Houston Baptist U (TX)
Huntingdon Coll (AL)
Huron U USA in London(United Kingdom)
Idaho State U (ID)
Immaculata U (PA)
Indiana State U (IN)
Indiana U Bloomington (IN)
Indiana U of Pennsylvania (PA)
Indiana U–Purdue U Indianapolis (IN)
Inter Amer U of PR, Barranquitas Campus (PR)
Iowa State U of Science and Technology (IA)
Ithaca Coll (NY)
Jacksonville State U (AL)
Jacksonville U (FL)
James Madison U (VA)
The Johns Hopkins U (MD)
Johnson & Wales U (RI)
Jones Coll, Miami (FL)
Juniata Coll (PA)
Kansas State U (KS)
Kaplan Coll (IA)
Kean U (NJ)
Kennesaw State U (GA)
Kentucky State U (KY)
Kentucky Wesleyan Coll (KY)
King's Coll (PA)
Knox Coll (IL)
LaGrange Coll (GA)
Lambuth U (TN)
Lancaster Bible Coll (PA)
Lander U (SC)
Lane Coll (TN)
La Roche Coll (PA)
La Salle U (PA)
Lehman Coll of the City U of NY (NY)
Lewis-Clark State Coll (ID)
Liberty U (VA)
Lincoln Memorial U (TN)
Lincoln U (PA)
Lock Haven U of Pennsylvania (PA)
Long Island U, Brooklyn Campus (NY)
Long Island U, C.W. Post Campus (NY)
Loyola Coll in Maryland (MD)
Loyola U New Orleans (LA)
Lubbock Christian U (TX)
Lyndon State Coll (VT)
Madonna U (MI)
Malaspina U-Coll (BC, Canada)
Mansfield U of Pennsylvania (PA)
Marshall U (WV)
Mary Baldwin Coll (VA)
Marygrove Coll (MI)
Marymount Coll of Fordham U (NY)
Marymount U (VA)
Marywood U (PA)
Massachusetts Coll of Liberal Arts (MA)
The Master's Coll and Sem (CA)
Mayville State U (ND)
McDaniel Coll (MD)
McGill U (QC, Canada)
McMurry U (TX)
Medaille Coll (NY)
Mercyhurst Coll (PA)
Meredith Coll (NC)
Metropolitan State Coll of Denver (CO)
Miami U (OH)
Michigan State U (MI)
Miles Coll (AL)
Millersville U of Pennsylvania (PA)
Milligan Coll (TN)
Millikin U (IL)
Minnesota State U Moorhead (MN)
Mississippi Coll (MS)
Mississippi State U (MS)
Missouri Baptist U (MO)
Missouri Southern State U (MO)
Missouri Western State Coll (MO)
Monmouth U (NJ)
Montana Tech of The U of Montana (MT)
Montclair State U (NJ)
Montreat Coll (NC)
Morehead State U (KY)
Morehouse Coll (GA)
Mount Mercy Coll (IA)
Mount Saint Mary Coll (NY)
Mount Saint Mary's Coll and Sem (MD)
Mount Saint Vincent U (NS, Canada)
Mt. Sierra Coll (CA)
Mount Vernon Nazarene U (OH)
Murray State U (KY)
National American U, Denver (CO)
Neumann Coll (PA)
New Jersey City U (NJ)
New Jersey Inst of Technology (NJ)
New Mexico State U (NM)
New York Inst of Technology (NY)
New York U (NY)
Norfolk State U (VA)
Northeastern Illinois U (IL)
Northern Arizona U (AZ)
Northern Michigan U (MI)
Northface U (UT)
North Georgia Coll & State U (GA)
Northwest Christian Coll (OR)
Northwestern U (IL)
Northwood U (MI)
Northwood U, Florida Campus (FL)
Northwood U, Texas Campus (TX)
Nova Southeastern U (FL)
Oakland U (MI)
The Ohio State U (OH)
Oklahoma Baptist U (OK)
Oklahoma State U (OK)
Old Dominion U (VA)
Olivet Coll (MI)
Oregon Inst of Technology (OR)
Pace U (NY)
Pacific Union Coll (CA)
Palm Beach Atlantic U (FL)
Park U (MO)
Penn State U Abington Coll (PA)
Penn State U Altoona Coll (PA)
Penn State U at Erie, The Behrend Coll (PA)
Penn State U Beaver Campus of the Commonwealth Coll (PA)
Penn State U Berks Cmps of Berks-Lehigh Valley Coll (PA)
Penn State U Delaware County Campus of the Commonwealth Coll (PA)
Penn State U DuBois Campus of the Commonwealth Coll (PA)
Penn State U Fayette Campus of the Commonwealth Coll (PA)
Penn State U Harrisburg Campus of the Capital Coll (PA)
Penn State U Hazleton Campus of the Commonwealth Coll (PA)
Penn State U Lehigh Valley Cmps of Berks-Lehigh Valley Coll (PA)
Penn State U McKeesport Campus of the Commonwealth Coll (PA)
Penn State U Mont Alto Campus of the Commonwealth Coll (PA)
Penn State U New Kensington Campus of the Commonwealth Coll (PA)
Penn State U Schuylkill Campus of the Capital Coll (PA)
Penn State U Shenango Campus of the Commonwealth Coll (PA)
Penn State U Univ Park Campus (PA)
Penn State U Wilkes-Barre Campus of the Commonwealth Coll (PA)
Penn State U Worthington Scranton Cmps Commonwealth Coll (PA)
Penn State U York Campus of the Commonwealth Coll (PA)
Philadelphia U (PA)
Pikeville Coll (KY)
Pittsburg State U (KS)
Portland State U (OR)
Principia Coll (IL)
Purdue U (IN)
Queen's U at Kingston (ON, Canada)
Quincy U (IL)
Ramapo Coll of New Jersey (NJ)
Reformed Bible Coll (MI)
Regis Coll (MA)
Rensselaer Polytechnic Inst (NY)
Rice U (TX)
The Richard Stockton Coll of New Jersey (NJ)
Rochester Inst of Technology (NY)
Rowan U (NJ)
Rutgers, The State U of New Jersey, Camden (NJ)
Rutgers, The State U of New Jersey, Newark (NJ)
Sacred Heart U (CT)
Sage Coll of Albany (NY)
Saginaw Valley State U (MI)
Saint Augustine's Coll (NC)
St. Edward's U (TX)
St. Francis Xavier U (NS, Canada)
St. John's U (NY)
Saint Joseph's Coll (IN)
Saint Joseph's Coll of Maine (ME)
Saint Joseph's U (PA)
Saint Louis U (MO)
Saint Mary-of-the-Woods Coll (IN)
St. Mary's Coll of Maryland (MD)
Saint Vincent Coll (PA)
Saint Xavier U (IL)
Salisbury U (MD)
Sam Houston State U (TX)
San Diego State U (CA)
Seton Hall U (NJ)
Shaw U (NC)
Shepherd U (WV)
Shippensburg U of Pennsylvania (PA)
Shorter Coll (GA)
Siena Coll (NY)
Sierra Nevada Coll (NV)
Silver Lake Coll (WI)
Simon's Rock Coll of Bard (MA)
Skidmore Coll (NY)
Slippery Rock U of Pennsylvania (PA)
South Dakota State U (SD)
Southeastern Oklahoma State U (OK)
Southeast Missouri State U (MO)
Southern Arkansas U–Magnolia (AR)
Southern Polytechnic State U (GA)
Southern Wesleyan U (SC)
Southwestern Oklahoma State U (OK)
Spring Hill Coll (AL)
State U of NY Coll at Old Westbury (NY)
State U of NY Coll at Potsdam (NY)
State U of NY Coll of Technology at Alfred (NY)
State U of NY Inst of Tech at Utica/Rome (NY)
State U of West Georgia (GA)
Sterling Coll (KS)
Suffolk U (MA)
Swarthmore Coll (PA)
Syracuse U (NY)
Tarleton State U (TX)
Taylor U, Fort Wayne Campus (IN)
Texas Christian U (TX)
Texas Southern U (TX)
Texas State U-San Marcos (TX)
Texas Tech U (TX)
Texas Wesleyan U (TX)
Texas Woman's U (TX)
Thomas Coll (ME)
Thomas Edison State Coll (NJ)
Thomas More Coll (KY)
Trinity U (TX)
Troy State U (AL)
Troy State U Dothan (AL)
Troy State U Montgomery (AL)
Tulane U (LA)
Union Coll (NY)
United States Naval Acad (MD)
Université de Sherbrooke (QC, Canada)
State U of NY at Albany (NY)
U Coll of the Cariboo (BC, Canada)
U Coll of the Fraser Valley (BC, Canada)
The U of Alabama (AL)
The U of Alabama at Birmingham (AL)
The U of Alabama in Huntsville (AL)
U of Alaska Fairbanks (AK)
The U of Arizona (AZ)
U of Arkansas (AR)
U of Arkansas at Fort Smith (AR)
U of Baltimore (MD)
U of Calif, Irvine (CA)
U of Central Arkansas (AR)
U of Central Florida (FL)
U of Charleston (WV)
U of Cincinnati (OH)
U of Colorado at Colorado Springs (CO)
U of Colorado at Denver (CO)
U of Delaware (DE)
U of Denver (CO)
U of Detroit Mercy (MI)
U of Dubuque (IA)
U of Florida (FL)
U of Georgia (GA)
U of Great Falls (MT)
U of Guelph (ON, Canada)
U of Hartford (CT)
U of Hawaii at Manoa (HI)
U of Houston (TX)
U of Houston–Clear Lake (TX)
U of Illinois at Chicago (IL)
The U of Iowa (IA)
U of Kansas (KS)
U of Kentucky (KY)
U of Louisiana at Lafayette (LA)
The U of Maine at Augusta (ME)
U of Mary Hardin-Baylor (TX)
U of Maryland, Coll Park (MD)
U of Maryland U Coll (MD)
U of Massachusetts Dartmouth (MA)
U of Miami (FL)
U of Michigan–Dearborn (MI)
U of Mississippi (MS)
U of Missouri–Columbia (MO)
U of Missouri–St. Louis (MO)
The U of Montana–Missoula (MT)
U of Nebraska–Lincoln (NE)
U of Nevada, Reno (NV)
U of New Haven (CT)
U of New Mexico (NM)
U of North Alabama (AL)
The U of North Carolina at Greensboro (NC)
U of North Dakota (ND)
U of North Florida (FL)
U of North Texas (TX)
U of Notre Dame (IN)
U of Oklahoma (OK)
U of Oregon (OR)
U of Ottawa (ON, Canada)
U of Phoenix–Atlanta Campus (GA)
U of Phoenix–Cleveland Campus (OH)
U of Phoenix–Fort Lauderdale Campus (FL)
U of Phoenix–Idaho Campus (ID)
U of Phoenix–Kansas City Campus (MO)
U of Phoenix–Louisiana Campus (LA)

U of Phoenix–Nevada Campus (NV)
U of Phoenix–Orlando Campus (FL)
U of Phoenix–Tampa Campus (FL)
U of Phoenix–Tulsa Campus (OK)
U of Phoenix–Utah Campus (UT)
U of Phoenix–Vancouver Campus (BC, Canada)
U of Phoenix–Washington Campus (WA)
U of Phoenix–Wisconsin Campus (WI)
U of Pittsburgh at Greensburg (PA)
U of Rhode Island (RI)
U of Saint Mary (KS)
U of St. Thomas (MN)
U of San Francisco (CA)
U of Science and Arts of Oklahoma (OK)
U of South Alabama (AL)
U of South Carolina (SC)
U of South Carolina Spartanburg (SC)
The U of South Dakota (SD)
U of Southern California (CA)
U of Southern Indiana (IN)
U of South Florida (FL)
The U of Texas at Arlington (TX)
The U of Texas at Austin (TX)
The U of Texas at Brownsville (TX)
The U of Texas at Dallas (TX)
The U of Texas at Tyler (TX)
U of Vermont (VT)
U of Virginia (VA)
The U of Virginia's Coll at Wise (VA)
U of Washington (WA)
The U of Western Ontario (ON, Canada)
U of West Florida (FL)
U of Windsor (ON, Canada)
U of Wisconsin–Eau Claire (WI)
U of Wisconsin–River Falls (WI)
U of Wisconsin–Stevens Point (WI)
U of Wisconsin–Superior (WI)
U of Wisconsin–Whitewater (WI)
Utah State U (UT)
Utica Coll (NY)
Valdosta State U (GA)
Valley City State U (ND)
Vassar Coll (NY)
Virginia Commonwealth U (VA)
Virginia Intermont Coll (VA)
Viterbo U (WI)
Wake Forest U (NC)
Walsh Coll of Accountancy and Business Admin (MI)
Warner Southern Coll (FL)
Washington U in St. Louis (MO)
Waynesburg Coll (PA)
Wayne State U (MI)
Webber Intl U (FL)
Weber State U (UT)
Wesleyan Coll (GA)
West Chester U of Pennsylvania (PA)
Western Illinois U (IL)
Western Kentucky U (KY)
Western Michigan U (MI)
West Texas A&M U (TX)
West Virginia Wesleyan Coll (WV)
Wichita State U (KS)
Widener U (PA)
Wilkes U (PA)
Williams Baptist Coll (AR)
William Woods U (MO)
Winona State U (MN)
Worcester Polytechnic Inst (MA)
Worcester State Coll (MA)
Wright State U (OH)
Xavier U of Louisiana (LA)
Yale U (CT)
York Coll of Pennsylvania (PA)
York U (ON, Canada)
Youngstown State U (OH)

COMPUTER AND INFORMATION SCIENCES AND SUPPORT SERVICES RELATED

Anna Maria Coll (MA)
Becker Coll (MA)
California State U, Chico (CA)
California State U, Los Angeles (CA)
City U (WA)
Coll of Mount St. Joseph (OH)
Coll of Staten Island of the City U of NY (NY)
Columbia Coll (SC)
Columbia Coll Chicago (IL)
Delaware Valley Coll (PA)
Dowling Coll (NY)
Fairleigh Dickinson U, Teaneck-Metro Campus (NJ)
Georgian Court U (NJ)
Greenville Coll (IL)
Huron U USA in London(United Kingdom)
Inter American U of PR, Bayamón Campus (PR)
Intl Acad of Merchandising & Design, Ltd (IL)
Lehigh U (PA)
Long Island U, C.W. Post Campus (NY)
Mayville State U (ND)
Mountain State U (WV)
Mt. Sierra Coll (CA)
New Jersey Inst of Technology (NJ)
Park U (MO)
Purdue U (IN)
Roberts Wesleyan Coll (NY)
Saint Louis U (MO)
Southern Polytechnic State U (GA)
Strayer U (DC)
Tiffin U (OH)
U of Calif, Irvine (CA)
U of Great Falls (MT)
U of Missouri–Rolla (MO)
U of Notre Dame (IN)
U of Pittsburgh (PA)
The U of Scranton (PA)
Utah State U (UT)
Valley City State U (ND)
Washington U in St. Louis (MO)
York Coll of Pennsylvania (PA)

COMPUTER AND INFORMATION SCIENCES RELATED

Bellevue U (NE)
Campbell U (NC)
Central Michigan U (MI)
DePaul U (IL)
Eastern Illinois U (IL)
Grace U (NE)
Huron U USA in London(United Kingdom)
Indiana State U (IN)
Maryville Coll (TN)
McGill U (QC, Canada)
Miami U Hamilton (OH)
National American U, Denver (CO)
Northface U (UT)
Pittsburg State U (KS)
Queen's U at Kingston (ON, Canada)
Texas Christian U (TX)
Université de Sherbrooke (QC, Canada)
U of Great Falls (MT)
The U of Lethbridge (AB, Canada)
U of Northern Iowa (IA)
U of Windsor (ON, Canada)
West Virginia U (WV)

COMPUTER AND INFORMATION SYSTEMS SECURITY

Briar Cliff U (IA)
Champlain Coll (VT)
Dakota State U (SD)
Davenport U, Dearborn (MI)
Davenport U, Grand Rapids (MI)
Davenport U, Lansing (MI)
Davenport U, Warren (MI)
East Stroudsburg U of Pennsylvania (PA)
Huron U USA in London(United Kingdom)
Mt. Sierra Coll (CA)
Rochester Inst of Technology (NY)
U of Great Falls (MT)

COMPUTER ENGINEERING

Arizona State U (AZ)
Auburn U (AL)
Bellarmine U (KY)
Bethel Coll (IN)
Bethune-Cookman Coll (FL)
Boston U (MA)
Brigham Young U (UT)
Brown U (RI)
Bucknell U (PA)
California Inst of Technology (CA)
California Polytechnic State U, San Luis Obispo (CA)
California State Polytechnic U, Pomona (CA)
California State U, Chico (CA)
California State U, Fresno (CA)
California State U, Long Beach (CA)
California State U, Sacramento (CA)
Capital U (OH)
Capitol Coll (MD)
Carleton U (ON, Canada)
Carnegie Mellon U (PA)
Case Western Reserve U (OH)
The Catholic U of America (DC)
Cedarville U (OH)
Christian Brothers U (TN)
Christopher Newport U (VA)
Clarkson U (NY)
Clemson U (SC)
Cleveland State U (OH)
The Coll of New Jersey (NJ)
Colorado State U (CO)
Columbia U, School of Eng & Applied Sci (NY)
Concordia U (QC, Canada)
Dalhousie U (NS, Canada)
Dominican U (IL)
Dordt Coll (IA)
Drexel U (PA)
Eastern Michigan U (MI)
Eastern Nazarene Coll (MA)
Elizabethtown Coll (PA)
Embry-Riddle Aeronautical U (AZ)
Embry-Riddle Aeronautical U (FL)
Florida Ag and Mech U (FL)
Florida Atlantic U (FL)
Florida Inst of Technology (FL)
Florida Intl U (FL)
Florida State U (FL)
Gallaudet U (DC)
George Mason U (VA)
The George Washington U (DC)
Georgia Inst of Technology (GA)
Gonzaga U (WA)
Grand Valley State U (MI)
Harding U (AR)
Harvard U (MA)
Hofstra U (NY)
Illinois Inst of Technology (IL)
Indiana Inst of Technology (IN)
Indiana U–Purdue U Fort Wayne (IN)
Indiana U–Purdue U Indianapolis (IN)
Iowa State U of Science and Technology (IA)
The Johns Hopkins U (MD)
Johnson & Wales U (RI)
Johnson C. Smith U (NC)
Kansas State U (KS)
Kettering U (MI)
Lakehead U (ON, Canada)
Lawrence Technological U (MI)
Lehigh U (PA)
LeTourneau U (TX)
Louisiana State U and A&M Coll (LA)
Loyola Marymount U (CA)
Manhattan Coll (NY)
Marquette U (WI)
McGill U (QC, Canada)
Merrimack Coll (MA)
Miami U Hamilton (OH)
Michigan State U (MI)
Michigan Technological U (MI)
Midwestern State U (TX)
Milwaukee School of Eng (WI)
Minnesota State U Mankato (MN)
Mississippi State U (MS)
Missouri Tech (MO)
Montana State U–Bozeman (MT)
Montana Tech of The U of Montana (MT)
New Jersey Inst of Technology (NJ)
North Carolina State U (NC)
North Dakota State U (ND)
Northeastern U (MA)
Northwestern Polytechnic U (CA)
Northwestern U (IL)
Ohio Northern U (OH)
The Ohio State U (OH)
Ohio U (OH)
Oklahoma Christian U (OK)
Oklahoma State U (OK)
Old Dominion U (VA)
Oral Roberts U (OK)
Oregon State U (OR)
Pacific Lutheran U (WA)
Penn State U Abington Coll (PA)
Penn State U Altoona Coll (PA)
Penn State U at Erie, The Behrend Coll (PA)
Penn State U Beaver Campus of the Commonwealth Coll (PA)
Penn State U Berks Cmps of Berks-Lehigh Valley Coll (PA)
Penn State U Delaware County Campus of the Commonwealth Coll (PA)
Penn State U DuBois Campus of the Commonwealth Coll (PA)
Penn State U Fayette Campus of the Commonwealth Coll (PA)
Penn State U Hazleton Campus of the Commonwealth Coll (PA)
Penn State U Lehigh Valley Cmps of Berks-Lehigh Valley Coll (PA)
Penn State U McKeesport Campus of the Commonwealth Coll (PA)
Penn State U Mont Alto Campus of the Commonwealth Coll (PA)
Penn State U New Kensington Campus of the Commonwealth Coll (PA)
Penn State U Schuylkill Campus of the Capital Coll (PA)
Penn State U Shenango Campus of the Commonwealth Coll (PA)
Penn State U Univ Park Campus (PA)
Penn State U Wilkes-Barre Campus of the Commonwealth Coll (PA)
Penn State U Worthington Scranton Cmps Commonwealth Coll (PA)
Penn State U York Campus of the Commonwealth Coll (PA)
Polytechnic U, Brooklyn Campus (NY)
Polytechnic U of Puerto Rico (PR)
Portland State U (OR)
Princeton U (NJ)
Purdue U (IN)
Queen's U at Kingston (ON, Canada)
Rensselaer Polytechnic Inst (NY)
Rice U (TX)
Richmond, The American Intl U in London(United Kingdom)
Robert Morris U (PA)
Rochester Inst of Technology (NY)
Rose-Hulman Inst of Technology (IN)
Rutgers, The State U of New Jersey, New Brunswick/Piscataway (NJ)
St. Cloud State U (MN)
Saint Mary's U of Minnesota (MN)
St. Mary's U of San Antonio (TX)
San Diego State U (CA)
San Jose State U (CA)
Santa Clara U (CA)
South Dakota School of Mines and Technology (SD)
Southern Illinois U Carbondale (IL)
Southern Illinois U Edwardsville (IL)
Southern Methodist U (TX)
State U of NY at Binghamton (NY)
State U of NY at New Paltz (NY)
Stevens Inst of Technology (NJ)
Stonehill Coll (MA)
Suffolk U (MA)
Syracuse U (NY)
Taylor U (IN)
Tennessee Technological U (TN)
Texas A&M U (TX)
Texas Tech U (TX)
Trinity Coll (CT)
Tri-State U (IN)
Tufts U (MA)
Tulane U (LA)
United States Military Acad (NY)
Université de Sherbrooke (QC, Canada)
U du Québec à Hull (QC, Canada)
Université Laval (QC, Canada)
U at Buffalo, The State U of New York (NY)
The U of Akron (OH)
The U of Alabama in Huntsville (AL)
U of Alberta (AB, Canada)
The U of Arizona (AZ)
U of Arkansas (AR)
U of Bridgeport (CT)
The U of British Columbia (BC, Canada)
U of Calgary (AB, Canada)
U of Calif, Davis (CA)
U of Calif, Irvine (CA)
U of Calif, Los Angeles (CA)
U of Calif, San Diego (CA)
U of Calif, Santa Barbara (CA)
U of Calif, Santa Cruz (CA)
U of Central Florida (FL)
U of Cincinnati (OH)
U of Colorado at Boulder (CO)
U of Colorado at Colorado Springs (CO)
U of Connecticut (CT)
U of Dayton (OH)
U of Delaware (DE)
U of Denver (CO)
U of Detroit Mercy (MI)
U of Evansville (IN)
U of Florida (FL)
U of Hartford (CT)
U of Houston (TX)
U of Houston–Clear Lake (TX)
U of Idaho (ID)
U of Illinois at Chicago (IL)
U of Illinois at Urbana–Champaign (IL)
U of Kansas (KS)
U of Louisiana at Lafayette (LA)
U of Louisville (KY)
U of Maine (ME)
U of Manitoba (MB, Canada)
U of Maryland, Baltimore County (MD)
U of Maryland, Coll Park (MD)
U of Massachusetts Amherst (MA)
U of Massachusetts Dartmouth (MA)
U of Massachusetts Lowell (MA)
The U of Memphis (TN)
U of Miami (FL)
U of Michigan (MI)
U of Minnesota, Duluth (MN)
U of Missouri–Columbia (MO)
U of Missouri–Rolla (MO)
U of Nebraska at Omaha (NE)
U of Nebraska–Lincoln (NE)
U of Nevada, Las Vegas (NV)
U of Nevada, Reno (NV)
U of New Brunswick Fredericton (NB, Canada)
U of New Hampshire (NH)
U of New Mexico (NM)
The U of North Carolina at Charlotte (NC)
U of North Texas (TX)
U of Notre Dame (IN)
U of Oklahoma (OK)
U of Ottawa (ON, Canada)
U of Pennsylvania (PA)
U of Pittsburgh (PA)
U of Portland (OR)
U of Rhode Island (RI)
The U of Scranton (PA)
U of South Alabama (AL)
U of South Carolina (SC)
U of Southern California (CA)
U of South Florida (FL)
The U of Tennessee (TN)
The U of Texas at Arlington (TX)
The U of Texas at Dallas (TX)
U of the Pacific (CA)
U of Toledo (OH)
U of Toronto (ON, Canada)
U of Utah (UT)
U of Victoria (BC, Canada)
U of Virginia (VA)
U of Washington (WA)
U of Waterloo (ON, Canada)
U of West Florida (FL)
U of Windsor (ON, Canada)
U of Wisconsin–Madison (WI)
U of Wyoming (WY)
Utah State U (UT)
Valparaiso U (IN)
Vanderbilt U (TN)
Villanova U (PA)
Virginia Commonwealth U (VA)
Virginia Polytechnic Inst and State U (VA)
Virginia State U (VA)
Washington State U (WA)
Washington U in St. Louis (MO)
Western Michigan U (MI)
West Virginia U (WV)
Wichita State U (KS)
Wilberforce U (OH)
Worcester Polytechnic Inst (MA)
Wright State U (OH)
Xavier U of Louisiana (LA)
York U (ON, Canada)

COMPUTER ENGINEERING RELATED

Auburn U (AL)
Ohio Northern U (OH)
Queen's U at Kingston (ON, Canada)
Ryerson U (ON, Canada)
U of Southern California (CA)

COMPUTER ENGINEERING TECHNOLOGIES RELATED

Old Dominion U (VA)

COMPUTER ENGINEERING TECHNOLOGY

Andrews U (MI)
Arizona State U East (AZ)
Brock U (ON, Canada)
California State U, Long Beach (CA)
Capitol Coll (MD)
Central Michigan U (MI)
Colorado State U-Pueblo (CO)
East Carolina U (NC)
Eastern Kentucky U (KY)
Eastern Washington U (WA)
Excelsior Coll (NY)
State U of NY at Farmingdale (NY)
Georgia Southwestern State U (GA)
Grantham U (LA)
Harvard U (MA)
Indiana State U (IN)

Indiana U–Purdue U Fort Wayne (IN)
Lake Superior State U (MI)
LeTourneau U (TX)
Marist Coll (NY)
Marshall U (WV)
Martin U (IN)
Minnesota State U Mankato (MN)
Murray State U (KY)
Norfolk State U (VA)
Northeastern U (MA)
Oregon Inst of Technology (OR)
Peirce Coll (PA)
Pittsburg State U (KS)
Purdue U North Central (IN)
Rochester Inst of Technology (NY)
Shawnee State U (OH)
Southern Polytechnic State U (GA)
State U of NY Coll of Technology at Alfred (NY)
State U of NY Inst of Tech at Utica/Rome (NY)
Texas Southern U (TX)
U of Arkansas at Little Rock (AR)
U of Dayton (OH)
U of Guelph (ON, Canada)
U of Houston (TX)
The U of Memphis (TN)
Utah State U (UT)
Vermont Tech Coll (VT)
Wentworth Inst of Technology (MA)

COMPUTER GRAPHICS
Acad of Art U (CA)
Alberta Coll of Art & Design (AB, Canada)
American Acad of Art (IL)
The Art Inst of California–San Francisco (CA)
The Art Inst of Colorado (CO)
Atlanta Coll of Art (GA)
Baker Coll of Flint (MI)
Bloomfield Coll (NJ)
Bowie State U (MD)
Brooklyn Coll of the City U of NY (NY)
California Inst of the Arts (CA)
California State U, Chico (CA)
California State U, Hayward (CA)
Capella U (MN)
Champlain Coll (VT)
Cogswell Polytechnical Coll (CA)
Col for Creative Studies (MI)
The Coll of Southeastern Europe, The American U of Athens(Greece)
Coll of the Atlantic (ME)
Dakota State U (SD)
DePaul U (IL)
Dominican U (IL)
Dominican U of California (CA)
Hampshire Coll (MA)
Harvard U (MA)
Huntingdon Coll (AL)
Huron U USA in London(United Kingdom)
The Illinois Inst of Art (IL)
John Brown U (AR)
Judson Coll (IL)
Memphis Coll of Art (TN)
The New England Inst of Art (MA)
New England School of Communications (ME)
Northern Michigan U (MI)
Oakland City U (IN)
Pittsburg State U (KS)
Pratt Inst (NY)
Rochester Inst of Technology (NY)
Savannah Coll of Art and Design (GA)
School of the Art Inst of Chicago (IL)
School of the Museum of Fine Arts, Boston (MA)
Simon's Rock Coll of Bard (MA)
South Dakota State U (SD)
Southern Adventist U (TN)
Springfield Coll (MA)
State U of NY Coll at Fredonia (NY)
State U of NY Coll at Oneonta (NY)
Syracuse U (NY)
Taylor U (IN)
U of Advancing Technology (AZ)
U of Dubuque (IA)
U of Great Falls (MT)
U of Mary Hardin-Baylor (TX)
U of Pennsylvania (PA)
The U of Tampa (FL)
Villa Julie Coll (MD)
Wingate U (NC)

COMPUTER HARDWARE ENGINEERING
Abilene Christian U (TX)
Auburn U (AL)
Queen's U at Kingston (ON, Canada)
Rochester Inst of Technology (NY)
State U of NY Coll of Technology at Alfred (NY)
Stony Brook U, State U of New York (NY)
Westwood Coll of Technology–Long Beach (CA)
York U (ON, Canada)

COMPUTER/INFORMATION TECHNOLOGY SERVICES ADMINISTRATION RELATED
Bellevue U (NE)
California Baptist U (CA)
Capella U (MN)
Champlain Coll (VT)
Chestnut Hill Coll (PA)
Clayton Coll & State U (GA)
Dalhousie U (NS, Canada)
Dordt Coll (IA)
Eastern Illinois U (IL)
Golden Gate U (CA)
Holy Names Coll (CA)
Huron U USA in London(United Kingdom)
Intl Coll (FL)
Kettering U (MI)
Keystone Coll (PA)
Lindenwood U (MO)
Mt. Sierra Coll (CA)
National American U, Denver (CO)
Point Park U (PA)
Queens U of Charlotte (NC)
Saint Augustine's Coll (NC)
Seattle Pacific U (WA)
Southern Alberta Inst of Technology (AB, Canada)
State U of NY Coll of Technology at Alfred (NY)
U of Great Falls (MT)
U of South Florida (FL)
Washington U in St. Louis (MO)

COMPUTER INSTALLATION AND REPAIR TECHNOLOGY
Inter American U of PR, Bayamón Campus (PR)

COMPUTER MANAGEMENT
American InterContinental U (CA)
American InterContinental U-London(United Kingdom)
Belmont U (TN)
Champlain Coll (VT)
Coll of Saint Mary (NE)
Columbia Southern U (AL)
Columbus State U (GA)
Daniel Webster Coll (NH)
Faulkner U (AL)
Fordham U (NY)
Grove City Coll (PA)
HEC Montreal (QC, Canada)
Lehman Coll of the City U of NY (NY)
Life U (GA)
Luther Coll (IA)
National American U (SD)
National-Louis U (IL)
Northwood U (MI)
Oakland City U (IN)
Oklahoma Baptist U (OK)
Oklahoma State U (OK)
Pacific Union Coll (CA)
Pontifical Catholic U of Puerto Rico (PR)
Rochester Coll (MI)
St. Mary's U of San Antonio (TX)
Simpson Coll (IA)
Thomas Coll (ME)
Université de Sherbrooke (QC, Canada)
U of Cincinnati (OH)
U of Great Falls (MT)
U of the Incarnate Word (TX)
Webster U (MO)
Western Washington U (WA)
York Coll of the City U of New York (NY)

COMPUTER PROGRAMMING
American InterContinental U Online (IL)
Andrews U (MI)
Arcadia U (PA)
Baker Coll of Flint (MI)
Baker Coll of Owosso (MI)
Belmont U (TN)
Bishop's U (QC, Canada)
Brigham Young U–Hawaii (HI)
Brock U (ON, Canada)
Carleton U (ON, Canada)
Charleston Southern U (SC)
City U (WA)
Clemson U (SC)
Coll for Lifelong Learning (NH)
Creighton U (NE)
Daniel Webster Coll (NH)
DePaul U (IL)
Dordt Coll (IA)
State U of NY at Farmingdale (NY)
Ferris State U (MI)
Florida Metropolitan U-Fort Lauderdale Coll (FL)
Florida Metropolitan U-Tampa Coll, Lakeland (FL)
Florida Metropolitan U-Tampa Coll (FL)
Florida State U (FL)
Framingham State Coll (MA)
Franklin Pierce Coll (NH)
Globe Inst of Technology (NY)
Grace U (NE)
Grand Valley State U (MI)
Hampshire Coll (MA)
Hardin-Simmons U (TX)
Harvard U (MA)
Huron U USA in London(United Kingdom)
Husson Coll (ME)
Inter American U of PR, Bayamón Campus (PR)
Inter American U of PR, San Germán Campus (PR)
Iowa Wesleyan Coll (IA)
Kent State U (OH)
Lamar U (TX)
La Salle U (PA)
Limestone Coll (SC)
McPherson Coll (KS)
Medaille Coll (NY)
Memorial U of Newfoundland (NL, Canada)
Michigan Technological U (MI)
Minnesota State U Mankato (MN)
Montana Tech of The U of Montana (MT)
Mt. Sierra Coll (CA)
National American U, Denver (CO)
National American U (SD)
National American U–Sioux Falls Branch (SD)
Nevada State Coll at Henderson (NV)
Newbury Coll (MA)
New Mexico Highlands U (NM)
New Mexico Inst of Mining and Technology (NM)
Northern Michigan U (MI)
Northface U (UT)
Ohio Dominican U (OH)
Oregon Inst of Technology (OR)
Pacific Union Coll (CA)
Pittsburg State U (KS)
Richmond, The American Intl U in London(United Kingdom)
Rockhurst U (MO)
Saint Francis U (PA)
Southeast Missouri State U (MO)
Southwestern Coll (KS)
Taylor U (IN)
Texas Southern U (TX)
Thomas Coll (ME)
Université de Sherbrooke (QC, Canada)
U Coll of the Cariboo (BC, Canada)
U of Advancing Technology (AZ)
U of Cincinnati (OH)
U of Detroit Mercy (MI)
U of Great Falls (MT)
U of Phoenix–Atlanta Campus (GA)
U of Phoenix Online Campus (AZ)
U of Phoenix–Washington Campus (WA)
The U of Tampa (FL)
U of Toledo (OH)
Villa Julie Coll (MD)
Western Washington U (WA)
Wheeling Jesuit U (WV)
Winona State U (MN)
York U (ON, Canada)
Youngstown State U (OH)

COMPUTER PROGRAMMING RELATED
State U of NY at Farmingdale (NY)
Huron U USA in London(United Kingdom)
Inter Amer U of PR, Barranquitas Campus (PR)
National American U, Denver (CO)
Northface U (UT)

COMPUTER PROGRAMMING (SPECIFIC APPLICATIONS)
The Art Inst of California–San Francisco (CA)
DePaul U (IL)
Georgia Southwestern State U (GA)
Huron U USA in London(United Kingdom)
Husson Coll (ME)
Kent State U (OH)
Keystone Coll (PA)
National American U, Denver (CO)
Northface U (UT)
Oklahoma Baptist U (OK)
Peirce Coll (PA)
Rochester Inst of Technology (NY)
St. Norbert Coll (WI)
U of Puget Sound (WA)
U of Windsor (ON, Canada)

COMPUTER PROGRAMMING (VENDOR/PRODUCT CERTIFICATION)
Davenport U, Dearborn (MI)
Davenport U, Gaylord (MI)
Davenport U, Grand Rapids (MI)
Davenport U, Kalamazoo (MI)
Davenport U, Warren (MI)
Huron U USA in London(United Kingdom)
National American U–Sioux Falls Branch (SD)
Northface U (UT)

COMPUTER SCIENCE
Abilene Christian U (TX)
Acadia U (NS, Canada)
Alabama State U (AL)
Albertson Coll of Idaho (ID)
Albion Coll (MI)
Albright Coll (PA)
Alderson-Broaddus Coll (WV)
Allegheny Coll (PA)
Alma Coll (MI)
Alverno Coll (WI)
American Coll of Computer & Information Sciences (AL)
American Coll of Thessaloniki(Greece)
American Public U System (WV)
American U (DC)
The American U in Cairo(Egypt)
Amherst Coll (MA)
Andrews U (MI)
Antioch Coll (OH)
Appalachian State U (NC)
Aquinas Coll (MI)
Arcadia U (PA)
Arizona State U (AZ)
Arkansas Baptist Coll (AR)
Armstrong Atlantic State U (GA)
Ashland U (OH)
Assumption Coll (MA)
Athens State U (AL)
Atlantic Union Coll (MA)
Augsburg Coll (MN)
Augustana Coll (IL)
Augustana Coll (SD)
Austin Coll (TX)
Azusa Pacific U (CA)
Baker Coll of Muskegon (MI)
Baker Coll of Owosso (MI)
Baker U (KS)
Baldwin-Wallace Coll (OH)
Ball State U (IN)
Barber-Scotia Coll (NC)
Bard Coll (NY)
Barry U (FL)
Baylor U (TX)
Belhaven Coll (MS)
Bellarmine U (KY)
Belmont U (TN)
Beloit Coll (WI)
Bemidji State U (MN)
Benedictine Coll (KS)
Benedictine U (IL)
Bennington Coll (VT)
Berry Coll (GA)
Bethany Coll (WV)
Bethel Coll (IN)
Bethel Coll (KS)
Bethune-Cookman Coll (FL)
Birmingham-Southern Coll (AL)
Bishop's U (QC, Canada)
Blackburn Coll (IL)
Bloomsburg U of Pennsylvania (PA)
Bluefield Coll (VA)
Bluffton Coll (OH)
Boise State U (ID)
Boston Coll (MA)
Boston U (MA)
Bowdoin Coll (ME)
Brandeis U (MA)
Briar Cliff U (IA)
Bridgewater Coll (VA)
Bridgewater State Coll (MA)
Brigham Young U (UT)
Brigham Young U–Hawaii (HI)
British Columbia Inst of Technology (BC, Canada)
Brock U (ON, Canada)
Brown U (RI)
Bryan Coll (TN)
Buena Vista U (IA)
Butler U (IN)
Caldwell Coll (NJ)
California Inst of Technology (CA)
California Lutheran U (CA)
California Polytechnic State U, San Luis Obispo (CA)
California State Polytechnic U, Pomona (CA)
California State U, Chico (CA)
California State U, Dominguez Hills (CA)
California State U, Fresno (CA)
California State U, Fullerton (CA)
California State U, Hayward (CA)
California State U, Long Beach (CA)
California State U, Los Angeles (CA)
California State U, San Bernardino (CA)
California State U, San Marcos (CA)
Calumet Coll of Saint Joseph (IN)
Calvin Coll (MI)
Canadian Mennonite U (MB, Canada)
Canisius Coll (NY)
Capital U (OH)
Cardinal Stritch U (WI)
Carleton Coll (MN)
Carleton U (ON, Canada)
Carlow Coll (PA)
Carnegie Mellon U (PA)
Carroll Coll (MT)
Carroll Coll (WI)
Carson-Newman Coll (TN)
Carthage Coll (WI)
Case Western Reserve U (OH)
Catawba Coll (NC)
The Catholic U of America (DC)
Cedarville U (OH)
Central Coll (IA)
Central Methodist Coll (MO)
Centre Coll (KY)
Chapman U (CA)
Charleston Southern U (SC)
Chestnut Hill Coll (PA)
Cheyney U of Pennsylvania (PA)
Chicago State U (IL)
Christian Brothers U (TN)
Christopher Newport U (VA)
Citadel, The Military Coll of South Carolina (SC)
City Coll of the City U of NY (NY)
Claremont McKenna Coll (CA)
Clark Atlanta U (GA)
Clarke Coll (IA)
Clarkson U (NY)
Clark U (MA)
Cleveland State U (OH)
Coe Coll (IA)
Coker Coll (SC)
Colby Coll (ME)
Colgate U (NY)
Coll Misericordia (PA)
Coll of Mount St. Joseph (OH)
Coll of Mount Saint Vincent (NY)
Coll of Notre Dame of Maryland (MD)
Coll of Saint Benedict (MN)
Coll of Saint Elizabeth (NJ)
Coll of Santa Fe (NM)
The Coll of Southeastern Europe, The American U of Athens(Greece)
Coll of the Ozarks (MO)
Coll of the Southwest (NM)
The Coll of Wooster (OH)
Colorado School of Mines (CO)
Colorado State U (CO)
Colorado Tech U Sioux Falls Campus (SD)
Columbia Coll (MO)
Columbia Coll (NY)
Columbia Union Coll (MD)
Columbia U, School of General Studies (NY)
Columbia U, School of Eng & Applied Sci (NY)
Columbus State U (GA)
Concord Coll (WV)
Concordia Coll (MN)
Concordia U (IL)
Concordia U (NE)
Concordia U (QC, Canada)

Concordia U at Austin (TX)
Concordia U Wisconsin (WI)
Converse Coll (SC)
Cornell Coll (IA)
Cornell U (NY)
Covenant Coll (GA)
Creighton U (NE)
Dakota State U (SD)
Dalhousie U (NS, Canada)
Dallas Baptist U (TX)
Dana Coll (NE)
Daniel Webster Coll (NH)
Dartmouth Coll (NH)
Davis & Elkins Coll (WV)
Defiance Coll (OH)
Delaware State U (DE)
Denison U (OH)
DePaul U (IL)
DePauw U (IN)
DeSales U (PA)
Dickinson Coll (PA)
Dickinson State U (ND)
Dillard U (LA)
Doane Coll (NE)
Dominican U (IL)
Dordt Coll (IA)
Drake U (IA)
Drew U (NJ)
Drexel U (PA)
Drury U (MO)
Duke U (NC)
Duquesne U (PA)
Earlham Coll (IN)
East Carolina U (NC)
East Central U (OK)
Eastern Kentucky U (KY)
Eastern Mennonite U (VA)
Eastern Nazarene Coll (MA)
Eastern Oregon U (OR)
Eckerd Coll (FL)
Elizabeth City State U (NC)
Elizabethtown Coll (PA)
Elmhurst Coll (IL)
Elms Coll (MA)
Elon U (NC)
Emory & Henry Coll (VA)
Emory U (GA)
Eureka Coll (IL)
Evangel U (MO)
Excelsior Coll (NY)
Fairfield U (CT)
Fairmont State Coll (WV)
Fayetteville State U (NC)
Ferrum Coll (VA)
Florida Inst of Technology (FL)
Florida Intl U (FL)
Florida Metropolitan U-Tampa Coll, Lakeland (FL)
Florida Metropolitan U-Tampa Coll (FL)
Florida Southern Coll (FL)
Florida State U (FL)
Fontbonne U (MO)
Fordham U (NY)
Fort Lewis Coll (CO)
Fort Valley State U (GA)
Framingham State Coll (MA)
Franciscan U of Steubenville (OH)
Franklin Coll (IN)
Franklin Pierce Coll (NH)
Freed-Hardeman U (TN)
Furman U (SC)
Gallaudet U (DC)
Gardner-Webb U (NC)
Geneva Coll (PA)
Georgetown Coll (KY)
Georgetown U (DC)
The George Washington U (DC)
Georgian Court U (NJ)
Georgia Southwestern State U (GA)
Gettysburg Coll (PA)
Glenville State Coll (WV)
Gonzaga U (WA)
Gordon Coll (MA)
Goshen Coll (IN)
Goucher Coll (MD)
Governors State U (IL)
Graceland U (IA)
Grace U (NE)
Grambling State U (LA)
Grand Valley State U (MI)
Grand View Coll (IA)
Grantham U (LA)
Greenville Coll (IL)
Grinnell Coll (IA)
Gustavus Adolphus Coll (MN)
Hamilton Coll (NY)
Hampden-Sydney Coll (VA)
Hampshire Coll (MA)
Hampton U (VA)
Hanover Coll (IN)
Harding U (AR)
Hartwick Coll (NY)
Harvard U (MA)
Harvey Mudd Coll (CA)
Hastings Coll (NE)
Haverford Coll (PA)
Hawai'i Pacific U (HI)
Heidelberg Coll (OH)
Hendrix Coll (AR)
Henry Cogswell Coll (WA)
High Point U (NC)
Hillsdale Coll (MI)
Hiram Coll (OH)
Hobart and William Smith Colls (NY)
Hofstra U (NY)
Hollins U (VA)
Hope Coll (MI)
Houghton Coll (NY)
Houston Baptist U (TX)
Howard Payne U (TX)
Humboldt State U (CA)
Hunter Coll of the City U of NY (NY)
Huntingdon Coll (AL)
Huntington Coll (IN)
Huron U USA in London(United Kingdom)
Huston-Tillotson Coll (TX)
Illinois Coll (IL)
Illinois Inst of Technology (IL)
Illinois State U (IL)
Illinois Wesleyan U (IL)
Immaculata U (PA)
Indiana Inst of Technology (IN)
Indiana U–Purdue U Fort Wayne (IN)
Indiana U South Bend (IN)
Indiana U Southeast (IN)
Inter American U of PR, Aguadilla Campus (PR)
Inter American U of PR, Bayamón Campus (PR)
Inter American U of PR, Fajardo Campus (PR)
Inter American U of PR, Ponce Campus (PR)
Inter American U of PR, San Germán Campus (PR)
Iona Coll (NY)
Iowa Wesleyan Coll (IA)
Ithaca Coll (NY)
Jamestown Coll (ND)
Jarvis Christian Coll (TX)
John Carroll U (OH)
Johnson & Wales U (RI)
Johnson C. Smith U (NC)
Judson Coll (IL)
Kalamazoo Coll (MI)
Kansas Wesleyan U (KS)
Keene State Coll (NH)
Kennesaw State U (GA)
Kent State U (OH)
Kentucky Wesleyan Coll (KY)
Kettering U (MI)
King's Coll (PA)
The King's U Coll (AB, Canada)
Lafayette Coll (PA)
LaGrange Coll (GA)
Lake Forest Coll (IL)
Lakehead U (ON, Canada)
Lakeland Coll (WI)
Lake Superior State U (MI)
Lamar U (TX)
La Salle U (PA)
Laurentian U (ON, Canada)
Lawrence Technological U (MI)
Lawrence U (WI)
Lebanon Valley Coll (PA)
Lehigh U (PA)
Lehman Coll of the City U of NY (NY)
Lenoir-Rhyne Coll (NC)
LeTourneau U (TX)
Lewis & Clark Coll (OR)
Lewis-Clark State Coll (ID)
Lewis U (IL)
Limestone Coll (SC)
Lindenwood U (MO)
Linfield Coll (OR)
Lipscomb U (TN)
Livingstone Coll (NC)
Lock Haven U of Pennsylvania (PA)
Long Island U, Brooklyn Campus (NY)
Long Island U, C.W. Post Campus (NY)
Longwood U (VA)
Loras Coll (IA)
Louisiana State U and A&M Coll (LA)
Louisiana State U in Shreveport (LA)
Louisiana Tech U (LA)
Loyola Marymount U (CA)
Loyola U Chicago (IL)
Lubbock Christian U (TX)
Luther Coll (IA)
Lycoming Coll (PA)
Lynchburg Coll (VA)
Lyon Coll (AR)
Macalester Coll (MN)
Madonna U (MI)
Maharishi U of Management (IA)
Malone Coll (OH)
Manchester Coll (IN)
Manhattan Coll (NY)
Manhattanville Coll (NY)
Mansfield U of Pennsylvania (PA)
Marietta Coll (OH)
Marist Coll (NY)
Marlboro Coll (VT)
Marquette U (WI)
Mars Hill Coll (NC)
Marymount U (VA)
Maryville Coll (TN)
Maryville U of Saint Louis (MO)
Mary Washington Coll (VA)
Massachusetts Coll of Liberal Arts (MA)
Massachusetts Inst of Technology (MA)
McGill U (QC, Canada)
McKendree Coll (IL)
McPherson Coll (KS)
Memorial U of Newfoundland (NL, Canada)
Mercer U (GA)
Mercy Coll (NY)
Mercyhurst Coll (PA)
Meredith Coll (NC)
Merrimack Coll (MA)
Messiah Coll (PA)
Methodist Coll (NC)
Metropolitan State Coll of Denver (CO)
Metropolitan State U (MN)
Miami U Hamilton (OH)
Michigan Technological U (MI)
MidAmerica Nazarene U (KS)
Middlebury Coll (VT)
Middle Tennessee State U (TN)
Midwestern State U (TX)
Millersville U of Pennsylvania (PA)
Milligan Coll (TN)
Millsaps Coll (MS)
Mills Coll (CA)
Minnesota State U Mankato (MN)
Minnesota State U Moorhead (MN)
Minot State U (ND)
Mississippi Coll (MS)
Mississippi Valley State U (MS)
Missouri Southern State U (MO)
Missouri Valley Coll (MO)
Molloy Coll (NY)
Monmouth Coll (IL)
Montana State U–Bozeman (MT)
Montana Tech of The U of Montana (MT)
Montclair State U (NJ)
Moravian Coll (PA)
Morgan State U (MD)
Morningside Coll (IA)
Mountain State U (WV)
Mount Allison U (NB, Canada)
Mount Holyoke Coll (MA)
Mount Marty Coll (SD)
Mount Mary Coll (WI)
Mount Mercy Coll (IA)
Mount Saint Mary Coll (NY)
Mt. Sierra Coll (CA)
Mount Union Coll (OH)
Muhlenberg Coll (PA)
National U (CA)
Nebraska Wesleyan U (NE)
Newberry Coll (SC)
Newbury Coll (MA)
New Mexico Highlands U (NM)
New Mexico Inst of Mining and Technology (NM)
New York U (NY)
Niagara U (NY)
Nicholls State U (LA)
Nipissing U (ON, Canada)
North Carolina Central U (NC)
North Carolina State U (NC)
North Central Coll (IL)
North Dakota State U (ND)
Northeastern Illinois U (IL)
Northeastern State U (OK)
Northeastern U (MA)
Northern Illinois U (IL)
Northern Michigan U (MI)
Northface U (UT)
North Georgia Coll & State U (GA)
Northwestern Coll (IA)
Northwestern Oklahoma State U (OK)
Northwestern Polytechnic U (CA)
Northwestern U (IL)
Northwest Nazarene U (ID)
Notre Dame de Namur U (CA)
Nova Southeastern U (FL)
Nyack Coll (NY)
Oberlin Coll (OH)
Oglethorpe U (GA)
Ohio Dominican U (OH)
Ohio Northern U (OH)
The Ohio State U (OH)
Ohio U (OH)
Ohio Wesleyan U (OH)
Oklahoma Baptist U (OK)
Oklahoma Christian U (OK)
Oklahoma City U (OK)
Oklahoma State U (OK)
Olivet Coll (MI)
Olivet Nazarene U (IL)
Oral Roberts U (OK)
Oregon State U (OR)
Otterbein Coll (OH)
Ouachita Baptist U (AR)
Pacific Lutheran U (WA)
Pacific States U (CA)
Pacific Union Coll (CA)
Pacific U (OR)
Park U (MO)
Penn State U at Erie, The Behrend Coll (PA)
Pepperdine U, Malibu (CA)
Philadelphia U (PA)
Piedmont Coll (GA)
Pittsburg State U (KS)
Plymouth State U (NH)
Point Loma Nazarene U (CA)
Polytechnic U, Brooklyn Campus (NY)
Pomona Coll (CA)
Pontifical Catholic U of Puerto Rico (PR)
Portland State U (OR)
Prairie View A&M U (TX)
Presbyterian Coll (SC)
Providence Coll (RI)
Queens Coll of the City U of NY (NY)
Queen's U at Kingston (ON, Canada)
Quincy U (IL)
Quinnipiac U (CT)
Radford U (VA)
Randolph-Macon Coll (VA)
Redeemer U Coll (ON, Canada)
Regis U (CO)
Rensselaer Polytechnic Inst (NY)
Rhode Island Coll (RI)
Rhodes Coll (TN)
The Richard Stockton Coll of New Jersey (NJ)
Richmond, The American Intl U in London(United Kingdom)
Rider U (NJ)
Ripon Coll (WI)
Rivier Coll (NH)
Roanoke Coll (VA)
Roberts Wesleyan Coll (NY)
Rochester Inst of Technology (NY)
Rockford Coll (IL)
Rockhurst U (MO)
Rocky Mountain Coll (MT)
Roger Williams U (RI)
Rollins Coll (FL)
Roosevelt U (IL)
Rose-Hulman Inst of Technology (IN)
Rowan U (NJ)
Rutgers, The State U of New Jersey, New Brunswick/Piscataway (NJ)
Ryerson U (ON, Canada)
Sacred Heart U (CT)
St. Ambrose U (IA)
Saint Anselm Coll (NH)
Saint Augustine's Coll (NC)
St. Bonaventure U (NY)
St. Cloud State U (MN)
St. Edward's U (TX)
Saint Francis U (PA)
St. John Fisher Coll (NY)
Saint John's U (MN)
St. Joseph's Coll, Suffolk Campus (NY)
Saint Joseph's U (PA)
St. Lawrence U (NY)
Saint Martin's Coll (WA)
Saint Mary's U of Minnesota (MN)
St. Mary's U of San Antonio (TX)
Saint Michael's Coll (VT)
St. Olaf Coll (MN)
St. Thomas U (FL)
Saint Xavier U (IL)
Salem State Coll (MA)
Samford U (AL)
San Francisco State U (CA)
San Jose State U (CA)
Santa Clara U (CA)
Sarah Lawrence Coll (NY)
Scripps Coll (CA)
Seattle Pacific U (WA)
Seattle U (WA)
Seton Hill U (PA)
Shaw U (NC)
Simmons Coll (MA)
Simon Fraser U (BC, Canada)
Simon's Rock Coll of Bard (MA)
Simpson Coll (IA)
Smith Coll (MA)
Sonoma State U (CA)
South Carolina State U (SC)
South Dakota School of Mines and Technology (SD)
Southeastern Louisiana U (LA)
Southern Adventist U (TN)
Southern Connecticut State U (CT)
Southern Illinois U Carbondale (IL)
Southern Illinois U Edwardsville (IL)
Southern Methodist U (TX)
Southern Nazarene U (OK)
Southern Oregon U (OR)
Southern U and A&M Coll (LA)
Southern Utah U (UT)
Southwest Baptist U (MO)
Southwestern Coll (KS)
Southwestern Oklahoma State U (OK)
Southwestern U (TX)
Southwest Missouri State U (MO)
Spelman Coll (GA)
Spring Arbor U (MI)
Springfield Coll (MA)
Stanford U (CA)
State U of NY at Binghamton (NY)
State U of NY at New Paltz (NY)
State U of NY at Oswego (NY)
Plattsburgh State U of NY (NY)
State U of NY Coll at Brockport (NY)
State U of NY Coll at Fredonia (NY)
State U of NY Coll at Geneseo (NY)
State U of NY Coll at Oneonta (NY)
State U of NY Inst of Tech at Utica/Rome (NY)
Stetson U (FL)
Stevens Inst of Technology (NJ)
Stonehill Coll (MA)
Stony Brook U, State U of New York (NY)
Suffolk U (MA)
Sullivan U (KY)
Susquehanna U (PA)
Sweet Briar Coll (VA)
Tabor Coll (KS)
Talladega Coll (AL)
Taylor U (IN)
Tennessee State U (TN)
Tennessee Technological U (TN)
Texas A&M U (TX)
Texas A&M U–Commerce (TX)
Texas A&M U–Corpus Christi (TX)
Texas A&M U–Kingsville (TX)
Texas Lutheran U (TX)
Texas Southern U (TX)
Thiel Coll (PA)
Thomas Coll (ME)
Thomas Edison State Coll (NJ)
Tougaloo Coll (MS)
Transylvania U (KY)
Trent U (ON, Canada)
Trinity Christian Coll (IL)
Trinity Coll (CT)
Trinity Intl U (IL)
Trinity Western U (BC, Canada)
Tri-State U (IN)
Truman State U (MO)
Tufts U (MA)
Tulane U (LA)
Tusculum Coll (TN)
Tuskegee U (AL)
Union Coll (NE)
Union U (TN)
United States Air Force Acad (CO)
United States Military Acad (NY)
United States Naval Acad (MD)
Universidad Adventista de las Antillas (PR)
Université de Montréal (QC, Canada)
Université de Sherbrooke (QC, Canada)
U du Québec à Hull (QC, Canada)
Université Laval (QC, Canada)
State U of NY at Albany (NY)
U at Buffalo, The State U of New York (NY)
U Coll of the Cariboo (BC, Canada)
The U of Akron (OH)
U of Alaska Fairbanks (AK)
U of Alberta (AB, Canada)
U of Arkansas at Little Rock (AR)
U of Bridgeport (CT)
The U of British Columbia (BC, Canada)
U of Calgary (AB, Canada)
U of Calif, Berkeley (CA)
U of Calif, Irvine (CA)

U of Calif, Los Angeles (CA)
U of Calif, Riverside (CA)
U of Calif, San Diego (CA)
U of Calif, Santa Barbara (CA)
U of Calif, Santa Cruz (CA)
U of Chicago (IL)
U of Cincinnati (OH)
U of Colorado at Boulder (CO)
U of Colorado at Colorado Springs (CO)
U of Connecticut (CT)
U of Dallas (TX)
U of Dayton (OH)
U of Delaware (DE)
U of Detroit Mercy (MI)
U of Dubuque (IA)
U of Evansville (IN)
The U of Findlay (OH)
U of Great Falls (MT)
U of Guelph (ON, Canada)
U of Hawaii at Hilo (HI)
U of Houston–Clear Lake (TX)
U of Houston–Victoria (TX)
U of Idaho (ID)
U of Illinois at Springfield (IL)
U of Illinois at Urbana–Champaign (IL)
U of Indianapolis (IN)
The U of Iowa (IA)
U of King's Coll (NS, Canada)
U of La Verne (CA)
The U of Lethbridge (AB, Canada)
U of Louisiana at Lafayette (LA)
U of Maine (ME)
U of Maine at Farmington (ME)
U of Maine at Fort Kent (ME)
U of Manitoba (MB, Canada)
U of Mary Hardin-Baylor (TX)
U of Maryland, Baltimore County (MD)
U of Maryland Eastern Shore (MD)
U of Maryland U Coll (MD)
U of Massachusetts Amherst (MA)
U of Massachusetts Boston (MA)
U of Massachusetts Lowell (MA)
The U of Memphis (TN)
U of Miami (FL)
U of Michigan (MI)
U of Michigan–Dearborn (MI)
U of Michigan–Flint (MI)
U of Minnesota, Duluth (MN)
U of Minnesota, Morris (MN)
U of Minnesota, Twin Cities Campus (MN)
U of Missouri–Columbia (MO)
U of Missouri–Kansas City (MO)
U of Missouri–Rolla (MO)
U of Missouri–St. Louis (MO)
U of Mobile (AL)
The U of Montana–Missoula (MT)
U of Nebraska at Omaha (NE)
U of Nevada, Las Vegas (NV)
U of Nevada, Reno (NV)
U of New Brunswick Fredericton (NB, Canada)
U of New Hampshire (NH)
U of New Mexico (NM)
U of New Orleans (LA)
The U of North Carolina at Asheville (NC)
The U of North Carolina at Chapel Hill (NC)
The U of North Carolina at Charlotte (NC)
The U of North Carolina at Greensboro (NC)
The U of North Carolina at Pembroke (NC)
The U of North Carolina at Wilmington (NC)
U of Northern Iowa (IA)
U of Oregon (OR)
U of Ottawa (ON, Canada)
U of Pittsburgh (PA)
U of Pittsburgh at Bradford (PA)
U of Pittsburgh at Johnstown (PA)
U of Portland (OR)
U of Prince Edward Island (PE, Canada)
U of Puget Sound (WA)
U of Redlands (CA)
U of Regina (SK, Canada)
U of Richmond (VA)
U of Rochester (NY)
U of St. Francis (IL)
U of San Diego (CA)
U of San Francisco (CA)
U of Saskatchewan (SK, Canada)
The U of Scranton (PA)
U of Sioux Falls (SD)
U of Southern California (CA)
U of Southern Maine (ME)
The U of Tennessee (TN)
The U of Tennessee at Chattanooga (TN)
The U of Tennessee at Martin (TN)
The U of Texas at Arlington (TX)
The U of Texas at Dallas (TX)
The U of Texas–Pan American (TX)
U of the District of Columbia (DC)
U of the Pacific (CA)
U of the Sacred Heart (PR)
U of the Sciences in Philadelphia (PA)
U of the South (TN)
U of Toledo (OH)
U of Toronto (ON, Canada)
U of Tulsa (OK)
U of Utah (UT)
U of Vermont (VT)
U of Victoria (BC, Canada)
U of Washington (WA)
U of Waterloo (ON, Canada)
The U of Western Ontario (ON, Canada)
U of Windsor (ON, Canada)
U of Wisconsin–Green Bay (WI)
U of Wisconsin–La Crosse (WI)
U of Wisconsin–Madison (WI)
U of Wisconsin–Milwaukee (WI)
U of Wisconsin–Oshkosh (WI)
U of Wisconsin–Parkside (WI)
U of Wisconsin–Platteville (WI)
U of Wisconsin–River Falls (WI)
U of Wisconsin–Superior (WI)
U of Wyoming (WY)
Ursinus Coll (PA)
Valparaiso U (IN)
Vanderbilt U (TN)
Villanova U (PA)
Virginia Military Inst (VA)
Virginia Polytechnic Inst and State U (VA)
Virginia State U (VA)
Virginia Wesleyan Coll (VA)
Voorhees Coll (SC)
Wagner Coll (NY)
Walla Walla Coll (WA)
Walsh U (OH)
Wartburg Coll (IA)
Washington and Lee U (VA)
Washington Coll (MD)
Washington State U (WA)
Washington U in St. Louis (MO)
Waynesburg Coll (PA)
Wayne State Coll (NE)
Weber State U (UT)
Webster U (MO)
Wellesley Coll (MA)
Wells Coll (NY)
Wentworth Inst of Technology (MA)
Wesleyan U (CT)
Western Baptist Coll (OR)
Western Carolina U (NC)
Western Connecticut State U (CT)
Western Michigan U (MI)
Western New England Coll (MA)
Western Oregon U (OR)
Western State Coll of Colorado (CO)
Western Washington U (WA)
Westfield State Coll (MA)
Westminster Coll (MO)
Westminster Coll (PA)
Westminster Coll (UT)
Westmont Coll (CA)
West Virginia U (WV)
West Virginia Wesleyan Coll (WV)
Wheaton Coll (IL)
Wheaton Coll (MA)
Wheeling Jesuit U (WV)
Whitworth Coll (WA)
Widener U (PA)
Wilberforce U (OH)
Willamette U (OR)
William Jewell Coll (MO)
William Paterson U of New Jersey (NJ)
William Penn U (IA)
Williams Coll (MA)
Winona State U (MN)
Winston-Salem State U (NC)
Winthrop U (SC)
Wittenberg U (OH)
Wofford Coll (SC)
Worcester Polytechnic Inst (MA)
Wright State U (OH)
Xavier U (OH)
Xavier U of Louisiana (LA)
York Coll of Pennsylvania (PA)
York U (ON, Canada)
Youngstown State U (OH)

COMPUTER SOFTWARE AND MEDIA APPLICATIONS RELATED

Baldwin-Wallace Coll (OH)
Carleton U (ON, Canada)
Champlain Coll (VT)
Dakota Wesleyan U (SD)
Eastern Washington U (WA)
Florida State U (FL)
Holy Names Coll (CA)
Huron U USA in London(United Kingdom)
Indiana U–Purdue U Fort Wayne (IN)
McMurry U (TX)
New England School of Communications (ME)
Northface U (UT)
Southern Alberta Inst of Technology (AB, Canada)
U of Great Falls (MT)
U of Windsor (ON, Canada)

COMPUTER SOFTWARE ENGINEERING

Allegheny Coll (PA)
Auburn U (AL)
Brock U (ON, Canada)
Carroll Coll (WI)
Champlain Coll (VT)
Clarkson U (NY)
Embry-Riddle Aeronautical U (AZ)
Embry-Riddle Aeronautical U (FL)
Fairfield U (CT)
Florida Inst of Technology (FL)
Florida State U (FL)
Grantham U (LA)
Michigan Technological U (MI)
Milwaukee School of Eng (WI)
Mississippi State U (MS)
National U (CA)
Notre Dame de Namur U (CA)
Penn State U at Erie, The Behrend Coll (PA)
Queen's U at Kingston (ON, Canada)
Rochester Inst of Technology (NY)
Rose-Hulman Inst of Technology (IN)
South Dakota State U (SD)
Université Laval (QC, Canada)
U of Houston–Clear Lake (TX)
U of Regina (SK, Canada)
The U of Texas at Arlington (TX)
U of Victoria (BC, Canada)
U of Waterloo (ON, Canada)
The U of Western Ontario (ON, Canada)
Washington State U (WA)
York U (ON, Canada)

COMPUTER SYSTEMS ANALYSIS

Arkansas Tech U (AR)
Baker Coll of Flint (MI)
Baldwin-Wallace Coll (OH)
British Columbia Inst of Technology (BC, Canada)
Coll for Lifelong Learning (NH)
Davenport U, Dearborn (MI)
Davenport U, Grand Rapids (MI)
Davenport U, Holland (MI)
Davenport U, Kalamazoo (MI)
Davenport U, Warren (MI)
Eastern Mennonite U (VA)
HEC Montreal (QC, Canada)
Huron U USA in London(United Kingdom)
Inter American U of PR, Bayamón Campus (PR)
Kent State U (OH)
Metropolitan State U (MN)
Miami U (OH)
Miami U Hamilton (OH)
Montana Tech of The U of Montana (MT)
Mount Saint Vincent U (NS, Canada)
Oklahoma Baptist U (OK)
Pennsylvania Coll of Technology (PA)
Rochester Inst of Technology (NY)
Rockhurst U (MO)
Saginaw Valley State U (MI)
St. Ambrose U (IA)
Seattle Pacific U (WA)
Shippensburg U of Pennsylvania (PA)
U Coll of the Cariboo (BC, Canada)
U Coll of the Fraser Valley (BC, Canada)
U of Advancing Technology (AZ)
U of Arkansas (AR)
U of Denver (CO)
U of Great Falls (MT)
U of Houston (TX)
U of Louisiana at Lafayette (LA)
U of Miami (FL)
Valdosta State U (GA)

COMPUTER SYSTEMS NETWORKING AND TELECOMMUNICATIONS

Aurora U (IL)
Baldwin-Wallace Coll (OH)
Boise State U (ID)
California State U, Hayward (CA)
Capella U (MN)
Champlain Coll (VT)
Chaparral Coll (AZ)
Coleman Coll, La Mesa (CA)
The Coll of Southeastern Europe, The American U of Athens(Greece)
Davenport U, Dearborn (MI)
Davenport U, Grand Rapids (MI)
Davenport U, Holland (MI)
Davenport U, Kalamazoo (MI)
Davenport U, Lansing (MI)
Davenport U, Warren (MI)
DePaul U (IL)
Huron U USA in London(United Kingdom)
Illinois State U (IL)
Kean U (NJ)
Keystone Coll (PA)
Mt. Sierra Coll (CA)
National American U, Denver (CO)
Northern Michigan U (MI)
Northwestern Oklahoma State U (OK)
Our Lady of the Lake U of San Antonio (TX)
Pennsylvania Coll of Technology (PA)
Rochester Inst of Technology (NY)
Roosevelt U (IL)
Ryerson U (ON, Canada)
Sage Coll of Albany (NY)
St. Ambrose U (IA)
Southern Alberta Inst of Technology (AB, Canada)
Strayer U (DC)
The U of Findlay (OH)
U of Great Falls (MT)
U of Houston–Clear Lake (TX)
U of Pennsylvania (PA)
U of Phoenix–Atlanta Campus (GA)
U of St. Francis (IL)
U of Windsor (ON, Canada)
U of Wisconsin–Stout (WI)
Weber State U (UT)

COMPUTER TEACHER EDUCATION

Alma Coll (MI)
Baylor U (TX)
Bishop's U (QC, Canada)
Bridgewater Coll (VA)
Buena Vista U (IA)
Capital U (OH)
Central Michigan U (MI)
Concordia U (IL)
Concordia U (NE)
Dordt Coll (IA)
Eastern Michigan U (MI)
Eastern Washington U (WA)
Emmanuel Coll (GA)
Florida Inst of Technology (FL)
Hardin-Simmons U (TX)
Liberty U (VA)
Long Island U, Brooklyn Campus (NY)
Northern Michigan U (MI)
Pillsbury Baptist Bible Coll (MN)
Pontifical Catholic U of Puerto Rico (PR)
San Diego State U (CA)
South Dakota State U (SD)
Union Coll (NE)
The U of Akron (OH)
U of Illinois at Urbana–Champaign (IL)
U of Nebraska–Lincoln (NE)
U of North Texas (TX)
U of Wisconsin–River Falls (WI)
Utica Coll (NY)
Viterbo U (WI)
Wright State U (OH)
Youngstown State U (OH)

COMPUTER/TECHNICAL SUPPORT

State U of NY Coll of Technology at Alfred (NY)

COMPUTER TECHNOLOGY/ COMPUTER SYSTEMS TECHNOLOGY

Peirce Coll (PA)
Prairie View A&M U (TX)
Southwestern Coll (KS)
U of Central Florida (FL)

CONDUCTING

Bethesda Christian U (CA)
Calvin Coll (MI)
Canadian Mennonite U (MB, Canada)
Loyola Marymount U (CA)
Mannes Coll of Music, New School U (NY)
Ohio U (OH)
Sam Houston State U (TX)
U of Miami (FL)
Westminster Choir Coll of Rider U (NJ)

CONSERVATION BIOLOGY

Arizona State U (AZ)
Brigham Young U (UT)
California State U, Sacramento (CA)
Philadelphia U (PA)
St. Gregory's U (OK)
Sterling Coll (VT)
Texas State U-San Marcos (TX)
U of Maine at Machias (ME)

CONSTRUCTION ENGINEERING

The American U in Cairo(Egypt)
Andrews U (MI)
Arizona State U (AZ)
Bradley U (IL)
California State U, Long Beach (CA)
Clarkson U (NY)
John Brown U (AR)
Michigan Technological U (MI)
National U (CA)
North Carolina State U (NC)
North Dakota State U (ND)
Oregon State U (OR)
Purdue U (IN)
State U of NY Coll of Environ Sci and Forestry (NY)
State U of NY Coll of Technology at Alfred (NY)
Texas A&M U–Commerce (TX)
U of Alberta (AB, Canada)
U of Cincinnati (OH)
U of Nevada, Las Vegas (NV)
U of New Brunswick Fredericton (NB, Canada)
U of Southern California (CA)
Western Michigan U (MI)

CONSTRUCTION ENGINEERING TECHNOLOGY

Bemidji State U (MN)
Bowling Green State U (OH)
California State Polytechnic U, Pomona (CA)
California State U, Chico (CA)
California State U, Fresno (CA)
California State U, Long Beach (CA)
California State U, Sacramento (CA)
Central Michigan U (MI)
Central Missouri State U (MO)
Colorado State U-Pueblo (CO)
Eastern Kentucky U (KY)
Eastern Michigan U (MI)
Eastern Washington U (WA)
Fairleigh Dickinson U, Teaneck-Metro Campus (NJ)
State U of NY at Farmingdale (NY)
Florida Ag and Mech U (FL)
Florida Intl U (FL)
Georgia Southern U (GA)
Hampton U (VA)
Indiana U–Purdue U Fort Wayne (IN)
Louisiana Tech U (LA)
Minnesota State U Moorhead (MN)
Montana State U–Bozeman (MT)
Norfolk State U (VA)
Northern Arizona U (AZ)
Northern Michigan U (MI)
Oklahoma State U (OK)
Pennsylvania Coll of Technology (PA)
Pittsburg State U (KS)
Sam Houston State U (TX)
South Dakota State U (SD)
Southeast Missouri State U (MO)
Southern Illinois U Carbondale (IL)
Southern Illinois U Edwardsville (IL)
Southern Polytechnic State U (GA)
Southern Utah U (UT)
Texas A&M U (TX)
Texas Southern U (TX)
Texas State U-San Marcos (TX)
Thomas Edison State Coll (NJ)
Tuskegee U (AL)
U of Arkansas at Little Rock (AR)
U of Cincinnati (OH)
U of Florida (FL)
U of Houston (TX)
U of Maine (ME)
U of Maryland Eastern Shore (MD)
U of Nebraska at Omaha (NE)
U of Nebraska–Lincoln (NE)
U of Nevada, Reno (NV)
U of New Mexico (NM)

U of North Florida (FL)
U of North Texas (TX)
U of Toledo (OH)
U of Wisconsin–Stout (WI)
Virginia Polytechnic Inst and State U (VA)
Washington State U (WA)
Wentworth Inst of Technology (MA)
Western Carolina U (NC)
Western Michigan U (MI)

CONSTRUCTION/HEAVY EQUIPMENT/EARTHMOVING EQUIPMENT OPERATION
Oklahoma State U (OK)

CONSTRUCTION MANAGEMENT
Boise State U (ID)
California State U, Long Beach (CA)
Eastern Michigan U (MI)
State U of NY at Farmingdale (NY)
Ferris State U (MI)
Hampton U (VA)
John Brown U (AR)
Lawrence Technological U (MI)
Louisiana State U and A&M Coll (LA)
Michigan State U (MI)
Milwaukee School of Eng (WI)
Minnesota State U Mankato (MN)
Mississippi State U (MS)
North Carolina State U (NC)
North Dakota State U (ND)
Oklahoma State U (OK)
Oklahoma State U (OK)
Oregon State U (OR)
Pittsburg State U (KS)
Polytechnic U, Brooklyn Campus (NY)
Pratt Inst (NY)
Roger Williams U (RI)
Sam Houston State U (TX)
U of Cincinnati (OH)
U of Denver (CO)
U of Maryland Eastern Shore (MD)
U of Minnesota, Twin Cities Campus (MN)
U of Northern Iowa (IA)
U of the District of Columbia (DC)
U of Washington (WA)
U of Wisconsin–Madison (WI)
U of Wisconsin–Platteville (WI)
Wentworth Inst of Technology (MA)
Western Michigan U (MI)

CONSUMER ECONOMICS
Cornell U (NY)
Indiana U of Pennsylvania (PA)
Louisiana Tech U (LA)
The U of Alabama (AL)
The U of Arizona (AZ)
U of Delaware (DE)
U of Georgia (GA)
U of Rhode Island (RI)
The U of Tennessee (TN)

CONSUMER/HOMEMAKING EDUCATION
Virginia Polytechnic Inst and State U (VA)

CONSUMER MERCHANDISING/ RETAILING MANAGEMENT
Belmont U (TN)
Chicago State U (IL)
East Central U (OK)
Eastern Kentucky U (KY)
Ferris State U (MI)
Fontbonne U (MO)
Governors State U (IL)
HEC Montreal (QC, Canada)
Indiana U Bloomington (IN)
John F. Kennedy U (CA)
Johnson & Wales U (RI)
Lasell Coll (MA)
Lindenwood U (MO)
Madonna U (MI)
Montclair State U (NJ)
Mount Ida Coll (MA)
Northern Michigan U (MI)
Ryerson U (ON, Canada)
Salem State Coll (MA)
San Francisco State U (CA)
Simmons Coll (MA)
Syracuse U (NY)
Thomas Coll (ME)
Thomas Edison State Coll (NJ)
The U of Memphis (TN)
U of Montevallo (AL)
Winona State U (MN)
Youngstown State U (OH)

CONSUMER SERVICES AND ADVOCACY
Carson-Newman Coll (TN)
Coll of the Ozarks (MO)
South Dakota State U (SD)
State U of NY Coll at Oneonta (NY)
Syracuse U (NY)
Tennessee State U (TN)
Université Laval (QC, Canada)
U of Wisconsin–Madison (WI)

COOKING AND RELATED CULINARY ARTS
The Art Inst of California–San Diego (CA)
Kendall Coll (IL)
Lexington Coll (IL)

CORRECTIONS
Bluefield State Coll (WV)
California State U, Hayward (CA)
Chicago State U (IL)
Coker Coll (SC)
Coll of the Ozarks (MO)
Colorado State U-Pueblo (CO)
East Central U (OK)
Eastern Kentucky U (KY)
Eastern Washington U (WA)
Hardin-Simmons U (TX)
Jacksonville State U (AL)
John Jay Coll of Criminal Justice, the City U of NY (NY)
Lake Superior State U (MI)
Lamar U (TX)
Lewis-Clark State Coll (ID)
Limestone Coll (SC)
Mercyhurst Coll (PA)
Minnesota State U Mankato (MN)
Northeastern U (MA)
Oklahoma City U (OK)
Saint Louis U (MO)
Sam Houston State U (TX)
Southeast Missouri State U (MO)
State U of NY Coll at Brockport (NY)
Texas State U-San Marcos (TX)
Tiffin U (OH)
Troy State U (AL)
Tulane U (LA)
The U of Akron (OH)
U of Great Falls (MT)
U of Indianapolis (IN)
U of New Haven (CT)
U of New Mexico (NM)
U of Pittsburgh (PA)
The U of Texas at Brownsville (TX)
The U of Texas–Pan American (TX)
Washburn U (KS)
Weber State U (UT)
Western Oregon U (OR)
Westfield State Coll (MA)
Winona State U (MN)
York Coll of Pennsylvania (PA)
Youngstown State U (OH)

CORRECTIONS ADMINISTRATION
U of Great Falls (MT)

CORRECTIONS AND CRIMINAL JUSTICE RELATED
American InterContinental U Online (IL)
Averett U (VA)
Bethune-Cookman Coll (FL)
Chadron State Coll (NE)
Coll for Lifelong Learning (NH)
Harding U (AR)
Hastings Coll (NE)
John Jay Coll of Criminal Justice, the City U of NY (NY)
Limestone Coll (SC)
Mercyhurst Coll (PA)
Mount Mary Coll (WI)
North Dakota State U (ND)
Sam Houston State U (TX)
State U of NY Coll at Brockport (NY)
The U of Alabama at Birmingham (AL)
U of Alaska Fairbanks (AK)
U of Great Falls (MT)
U of Michigan–Flint (MI)
U of Phoenix–Northern California Campus (CA)
U of Phoenix Online Campus (AZ)
U of Phoenix–Orlando Campus (FL)
U of Phoenix–Pittsburgh Campus (PA)
U of Phoenix–Sacramento Campus (CA)
U of Phoenix–St. Louis Campus (MO)
U of Phoenix–San Diego Campus (CA)
U of Phoenix–Southern Arizona Campus (AZ)
U of Phoenix–Southern California Campus (CA)
U of Phoenix–Southern Colorado Campus (CO)
U of Phoenix–Tampa Campus (FL)
U of Phoenix–Tulsa Campus (OK)
U of Phoenix–Utah Campus (UT)
U of Phoenix–Vancouver Campus (BC, Canada)
U of Phoenix–West Michigan Campus (MI)

COUNSELING PSYCHOLOGY
Atlanta Christian Coll (GA)
Central Baptist Coll (AR)
Chatham Coll (PA)
Christian Heritage Coll (CA)
Coker Coll (SC)
Coll of Santa Fe (NM)
Columbia Union Coll (MD)
Crichton Coll (TN)
Crossroads Coll (MN)
Grace Coll (IN)
Huntingdon Coll (AL)
Jamestown Coll (ND)
Kutztown U of Pennsylvania (PA)
Lesley U (MA)
Liberty U (VA)
Marywood U (PA)
Mid-Continent Coll (KY)
Morningside Coll (IA)
Newman U (KS)
Northwestern U (IL)
Oregon Inst of Technology (OR)
Paine Coll (GA)
Rochester Coll (MI)
Rocky Mountain Coll (AB, Canada)
St. Andrews Presbyterian Coll (NC)
Saint Xavier U (IL)
Samford U (AL)
Sam Houston State U (TX)
Southwestern Coll (AZ)
Texas Wesleyan U (TX)
Toccoa Falls Coll (GA)
Trinity Coll of Florida (FL)
U of Great Falls (MT)
The U of Lethbridge (AB, Canada)
U of North Alabama (AL)
U of Phoenix–Phoenix Campus (AZ)

COUNSELOR EDUCATION/ SCHOOL COUNSELING AND GUIDANCE
Amberton U (TX)
Belmont U (TN)
California State Polytechnic U, Pomona (CA)
Clemson U (SC)
Cornell U (NY)
DePaul U (IL)
East Central U (OK)
Eastern Michigan U (MI)
Franklin Pierce Coll (NH)
Harding U (AR)
Houston Baptist U (TX)
Howard U (DC)
Kutztown U of Pennsylvania (PA)
Lamar U (TX)
Lancaster Bible Coll (PA)
Marshall U (WV)
Martin U (IN)
Memorial U of Newfoundland (NL, Canada)
Northern Arizona U (AZ)
Oakland U (MI)
Pittsburg State U (KS)
Radford U (VA)
St. Cloud State U (MN)
St. John's U (NY)
Sam Houston State U (TX)
Tarleton State U (TX)
Texas A&M U–Commerce (TX)
Texas Christian U (TX)
Texas Southern U (TX)
Université de Sherbrooke (QC, Canada)
Université Laval (QC, Canada)
U of Arkansas (AR)
The U of British Columbia (BC, Canada)
U of Hawaii at Manoa (HI)
U of Houston–Clear Lake (TX)
U of New Brunswick Fredericton (NB, Canada)
U of Windsor (ON, Canada)
U of Wisconsin–Superior (WI)
Wayne State Coll (NE)
Western Washington U (WA)
Westfield State Coll (MA)
Wright State U (OH)

COURT REPORTING
Johnson & Wales U (RI)
Metropolitan Coll, Tulsa (OK)
U of Mississippi (MS)

CRAFTS, FOLK ART AND ARTISANRY
Bowling Green State U (OH)
Bridgewater State Coll (MA)
Brigham Young U (UT)
The Cleveland Inst of Art (OH)
Indiana U–Purdue U Fort Wayne (IN)
Kent State U (OH)
Kutztown U of Pennsylvania (PA)
North Georgia Coll & State U (GA)
Nova Scotia Coll of Art and Design (NS, Canada)
Oregon Coll of Art & Craft (OR)
Rochester Inst of Technology (NY)
School of the Art Inst of Chicago (IL)
The U of Akron (OH)
U of Illinois at Urbana–Champaign (IL)
The U of the Arts (PA)
Virginia Commonwealth U (VA)

CREATIVE WRITING
Agnes Scott Coll (GA)
Albertson Coll of Idaho (ID)
Alderson-Broaddus Coll (WV)
Allegheny Coll (PA)
Anderson Coll (SC)
Antioch Coll (OH)
Arkansas Tech U (AR)
Ashland U (OH)
Augustana Coll (IL)
Bard Coll (NY)
Beloit Coll (WI)
Bennington Coll (VT)
Baruch Coll of the City U of NY (NY)
Bloomfield Coll (NJ)
Bluffton Coll (OH)
Bowie State U (MD)
Bowling Green State U (OH)
Briar Cliff U (IA)
Bridgewater State Coll (MA)
Brooklyn Coll of the City U of NY (NY)
Brown U (RI)
California State U, Hayward (CA)
California State U, Long Beach (CA)
California State U, San Bernardino (CA)
Capital U (OH)
Cardinal Stritch U (WI)
Carlow Coll (PA)
Carnegie Mellon U (PA)
Carroll Coll (WI)
Carson-Newman Coll (TN)
Central Michigan U (MI)
Champlain Coll (VT)
Chapman U (CA)
Chatham Coll (PA)
Chester Coll of New England (NH)
Chicago State U (IL)
City Coll of the City U of NY (NY)
Coe Coll (IA)
Colby Coll (ME)
Coll of St. Catherine (MN)
Coll of Santa Fe (NM)
The Colorado Coll (CO)
Colorado State U (CO)
Columbia Coll (NY)
Columbia Coll Chicago (IL)
Columbus State U (GA)
Concordia Coll (MN)
Concordia U (QC, Canada)
Cornell U (NY)
Cornerstone U (MI)
Dartmouth Coll (NH)
Davis & Elkins Coll (WV)
Denison U (OH)
DePaul U (IL)
Dominican U of California (CA)
Drury U (MO)
Eastern Michigan U (MI)
Eastern U (PA)
Eastern Washington U (WA)
Eckerd Coll (FL)
Emerson Coll (MA)
Emory & Henry Coll (VA)
Emory U (GA)
Eugene Lang Coll, New School U (NY)
Florida State U (FL)
Fordham U (NY)
Framingham State Coll (MA)
Franklin and Marshall Coll (PA)
Franklin Pierce Coll (NH)
Geneva Coll (PA)
Georgia Coll & State U (GA)
Gettysburg Coll (PA)
Grand Valley State U (MI)
Hamilton Coll (NY)
Hampshire Coll (MA)
Harvard U (MA)
Hastings Coll (NE)
High Point U (NC)
Hofstra U (NY)
Hollins U (VA)
Houghton Coll (NY)
Huntingdon Coll (AL)
Huron U USA in London(United Kingdom)
Indiana U–Purdue U Fort Wayne (IN)
Ithaca Coll (NY)
The Johns Hopkins U (MD)
Johnson State Coll (VT)
Kenyon Coll (OH)
King Coll (TN)
Knox Coll (IL)
Lehman Coll of the City U of NY (NY)
Le Moyne Coll (NY)
Lewis-Clark State Coll (ID)
Linfield Coll (OR)
Loras Coll (IA)
Loyola Coll in Maryland (MD)
Loyola U New Orleans (LA)
Lycoming Coll (PA)
Lynchburg Coll (VA)
Malaspina U-Coll (BC, Canada)
Marlboro Coll (VT)
Marquette U (WI)
Marylhurst U (OR)
Marymount Coll of Fordham U (NY)
Massachusetts Coll of Liberal Arts (MA)
Massachusetts Inst of Technology (MA)
McMurry U (TX)
Medaille Coll (NY)
Mercyhurst Coll (PA)
Methodist Coll (NC)
Miami U (OH)
Miami U Hamilton (OH)
Millikin U (IL)
Mills Coll (CA)
Minnesota State U Mankato (MN)
Montclair State U (NJ)
Moravian Coll (PA)
Naropa U (CO)
Nazareth Coll of Rochester (NY)
New Coll of California (CA)
North Carolina State U (NC)
Northern Michigan U (MI)
Northland Coll (WI)
Northwestern Coll (MN)
Oberlin Coll (OH)
Ohio Northern U (OH)
The Ohio State U (OH)
Ohio U (OH)
Ohio Wesleyan U (OH)
Oklahoma Christian U (OK)
Oklahoma State U (OK)
Pacific U (OR)
Patrick Henry Coll (VA)
Pine Manor Coll (MA)
Pitzer Coll (CA)
Pratt Inst (NY)
Randolph-Macon Woman's Coll (VA)
Rockhurst U (MO)
Roger Williams U (RI)
St. Andrews Presbyterian Coll (NC)
St. Cloud State U (MN)
Saint Joseph's Coll (IN)
St. Lawrence U (NY)
Saint Leo U (FL)
Saint Mary's Coll (IN)
San Diego State U (CA)
San Francisco State U (CA)
Sarah Lawrence Coll (NY)
Seattle U (WA)
Seton Hill U (PA)
Simon's Rock Coll of Bard (MA)
Southern Connecticut State U (CT)
Southern Methodist U (TX)
Southern Vermont Coll (VT)
State U of NY at New Paltz (NY)
State U of NY at Oswego (NY)
State U of NY Coll at Brockport (NY)
Stephens Coll (MO)
Susquehanna U (PA)
Sweet Briar Coll (VA)
Taylor U (IN)
Trinity Coll (CT)
The U of Arizona (AZ)
U of Arkansas (AR)
The U of British Columbia (BC, Canada)
U of Calif, Riverside (CA)
U of Calif, San Diego (CA)
U of Calif, Santa Cruz (CA)
U of Charleston (WV)
U of Chicago (IL)

U of Denver (CO)
U of Evansville (IN)
The U of Findlay (OH)
U of Great Falls (MT)
U of Houston (TX)
U of Maine at Farmington (ME)
U of Maine at Machias (ME)
U of Miami (FL)
U of Michigan (MI)
The U of Montana–Missoula (MT)
U of Nebraska at Omaha (NE)
U of New Mexico (NM)
The U of North Carolina at Wilmington (NC)
U of Pittsburgh (PA)
U of Pittsburgh at Bradford (PA)
U of Pittsburgh at Greensburg (PA)
U of Pittsburgh at Johnstown (PA)
U of Puget Sound (WA)
U of Redlands (CA)
U of St. Thomas (MN)
U of Southern California (CA)
The U of Tampa (FL)
U of Victoria (BC, Canada)
U of Washington (WA)
U of Windsor (ON, Canada)
U of Wisconsin–Parkside (WI)
Waldorf Coll (IA)
Warren Wilson Coll (NC)
Washington U in St. Louis (MO)
Waynesburg Coll (PA)
Wayne State Coll (NE)
Wells Coll (NY)
Western Michigan U (MI)
Western Washington U (WA)
Westminster Coll (PA)
West Virginia Wesleyan Coll (WV)
Wofford Coll (SC)
York U (ON, Canada)

CRIMINALISTICS AND CRIMINAL SCIENCE

U of New Haven (CT)
West Virginia U (WV)

CRIMINAL JUSTICE/LAW ENFORCEMENT ADMINISTRATION

Adelphi U (NY)
Adrian Coll (MI)
Alabama State U (AL)
Albertus Magnus Coll (CT)
Alfred U (NY)
Alvernia Coll (PA)
American InterContinental U (CA)
American Intl Coll (MA)
Anna Maria Coll (MA)
Arizona State U West (AZ)
Ashland U (OH)
Athens State U (AL)
Aurora U (IL)
Averett U (VA)
Baldwin-Wallace Coll (OH)
Ball State U (IN)
Barber-Scotia Coll (NC)
Barton Coll (NC)
Bay Path Coll (MA)
Becker Coll (MA)
Bellevue U (NE)
Bemidji State U (MN)
Blackburn Coll (IL)
Bloomfield Coll (NJ)
Bluefield Coll (VA)
Boise State U (ID)
Bowie State U (MD)
Bradley U (IL)
Briar Cliff U (IA)
State U of NY Coll at Buffalo (NY)
California Baptist U (CA)
California Lutheran U (CA)
California State U, Dominguez Hills (CA)
California State U, Fullerton (CA)
California State U, Hayward (CA)
California State U, Long Beach (CA)
California State U, Sacramento (CA)
California State U, San Bernardino (CA)
California State U, Stanislaus (CA)
Calumet Coll of Saint Joseph (IN)
Campbellsville U (KY)
Campbell U (NC)
Canisius Coll (NY)
Carleton U (ON, Canada)
Carroll Coll (WI)
Carthage Coll (WI)
Castleton State Coll (VT)
Cedarville U (OH)
Central Missouri State U (MO)
Central Washington U (WA)
Champlain Coll (VT)
Charleston Southern U (SC)
Chestnut Hill Coll (PA)
Chicago State U (IL)
Citadel, The Military Coll of South Carolina (SC)
Clark Atlanta U (GA)
Coker Coll (SC)
Coll for Lifelong Learning (NH)
The Coll of New Jersey (NJ)
The Coll of Saint Rose (NY)
Coll of Santa Fe (NM)
Coll of the Ozarks (MO)
Columbia Coll (MO)
Columbus State U (GA)
Concordia U (MI)
Concordia U at Austin (TX)
Concordia U Wisconsin (WI)
Culver-Stockton Coll (MO)
Cumberland U (TN)
Curry Coll (MA)
Dakota Wesleyan U (SD)
Dallas Baptist U (TX)
Dana Coll (NE)
Defiance Coll (OH)
Delaware State U (DE)
Delaware Valley Coll (PA)
DeSales U (PA)
Dordt Coll (IA)
East Central U (OK)
Eastern Kentucky U (KY)
Eastern Washington U (WA)
Edgewood Coll (WI)
Elizabeth City State U (NC)
Elmira Coll (NY)
Evangel U (MO)
Faulkner U (AL)
Fayetteville State U (NC)
Ferris State U (MI)
Florida Ag and Mech U (FL)
Florida Metropolitan U-Tampa Coll (FL)
Fordham U (NY)
Fort Valley State U (GA)
Franklin Pierce Coll (NH)
Frostburg State U (MD)
Gardner-Webb U (NC)
The George Washington U (DC)
Georgia Coll & State U (GA)
Georgian Court U (NJ)
Gonzaga U (WA)
Governors State U (IL)
Grace Coll (IN)
Graceland U (IA)
Grambling State U (LA)
Grand Canyon U (AZ)
Grand Valley State U (MI)
Grand View Coll (IA)
Greenville Coll (IL)
Gustavus Adolphus Coll (MN)
Hamline U (MN)
Hampton U (VA)
Hannibal-LaGrange Coll (MO)
Harris-Stowe State Coll (MO)
Hawai'i Pacific U (HI)
Hesser Coll (NH)
Hilbert Coll (NY)
Indiana U Northwest (IN)
Indiana U South Bend (IN)
Inter Amer U of PR, Barranquitas Campus (PR)
Inter American U of PR, Fajardo Campus (PR)
Inter American U of PR, Ponce Campus (PR)
Iona Coll (NY)
Iowa Wesleyan Coll (IA)
Jacksonville State U (AL)
John Jay Coll of Criminal Justice, the City U of NY (NY)
Johnson & Wales U (RI)
Johnson C. Smith U (NC)
Judson Coll (AL)
Kansas Wesleyan U (KS)
Kean U (NJ)
Keuka Coll (NY)
Keystone Coll (PA)
Lake Superior State U (MI)
Lamar U (TX)
Lambuth U (TN)
Lewis U (IL)
Liberty U (VA)
Lincoln Memorial U (TN)
Lincoln U (MO)
Lindenwood U (MO)
Lindsey Wilson Coll (KY)
Lock Haven U of Pennsylvania (PA)
Long Island U, C.W. Post Campus (NY)
Longwood U (VA)
Louisiana Coll (LA)
Lourdes Coll (OH)
Lycoming Coll (PA)
MacMurray Coll (IL)
Mansfield U of Pennsylvania (PA)
Marian Coll of Fond du Lac (WI)
Marist Coll (NY)
Mars Hill Coll (NC)
Martin U (IN)
Marywood U (PA)
McKendree Coll (IL)
Mercy Coll (NY)
Mercyhurst Coll (PA)
Methodist Coll (NC)
Metropolitan State Coll of Denver (CO)
Metropolitan State U (MN)
Michigan State U (MI)
MidAmerica Nazarene U (KS)
Middle Tennessee State U (TN)
Midwestern State U (TX)
Miles Coll (AL)
Mississippi Coll (MS)
Mississippi Valley State U (MS)
Missouri Southern State U (MO)
Missouri Valley Coll (MO)
Mitchell Coll (CT)
Moravian Coll (PA)
Morris Coll (SC)
Mountain State U (WV)
Mount Ida Coll (MA)
Mount Mercy Coll (IA)
Mount Vernon Nazarene U (OH)
National U (CA)
Nevada State Coll at Henderson (NV)
Newbury Coll (MA)
Newman U (KS)
New York Inst of Technology (NY)
Niagara U (NY)
North Carolina Central U (NC)
North Carolina Wesleyan Coll (NC)
Northeastern State U (OK)
Northern Arizona U (AZ)
Northern Michigan U (MI)
North Georgia Coll & State U (GA)
Oakland City U (IN)
Ohio Dominican U (OH)
Ohio Northern U (OH)
Ohio U (OH)
Ohio U–Chillicothe (OH)
Ohio U–Southern Campus (OH)
Ohio U–Zanesville (OH)
Oklahoma City U (OK)
Olivet Nazarene U (IL)
Pace U (NY)
Park U (MO)
Penn State U Abington Coll (PA)
Penn State U Altoona Coll (PA)
Penn State U at Erie, The Behrend Coll (PA)
Penn State U Beaver Campus of the Commonwealth Coll (PA)
Penn State U Berks Cmps of Berks-Lehigh Valley Coll (PA)
Penn State U Delaware County Campus of the Commonwealth Coll (PA)
Penn State U DuBois Campus of the Commonwealth Coll (PA)
Penn State U Fayette Campus of the Commonwealth Coll (PA)
Penn State U Hazleton Campus of the Commonwealth Coll (PA)
Penn State U Lehigh Valley Cmps of Berks-Lehigh Valley Coll (PA)
Penn State U McKeesport Campus of the Commonwealth Coll (PA)
Penn State U Mont Alto Campus of the Commonwealth Coll (PA)
Penn State U New Kensington Campus of the Commonwealth Coll (PA)
Penn State U Schuylkill Campus of the Capital Coll (PA)
Penn State U Shenango Campus of the Commonwealth Coll (PA)
Penn State U Univ Park Campus (PA)
Penn State U Wilkes-Barre Campus of the Commonwealth Coll (PA)
Penn State U Worthington Scranton Cmps Commonwealth Coll (PA)
Penn State U York Campus of the Commonwealth Coll (PA)
Pfeiffer U (NC)
Piedmont Coll (GA)
Pittsburg State U (KS)
Point Park U (PA)
Pontifical Catholic U of Puerto Rico (PR)
Portland State U (OR)
Radford U (VA)
Regis U (CO)
Remington Coll–Colorado Springs Campus (CO)
Roberts Wesleyan Coll (NY)
Rochester Inst of Technology (NY)
Rockford Coll (IL)
Roger Williams U (RI)
Russell Sage Coll (NY)
Rutgers, The State U of New Jersey, New Brunswick/Piscataway (NJ)
Ryerson U (ON, Canada)
Sacred Heart U (CT)
Sage Coll of Albany (NY)
Saint Augustine's Coll (NC)
St. Cloud State U (MN)
Saint Francis U (PA)
St. John's U (NY)
Saint Joseph's U (PA)
Saint Louis U (MO)
Saint Martin's Coll (WA)
Saint Mary's U of Minnesota (MN)
St. Mary's U of San Antonio (TX)
St. Thomas Aquinas Coll (NY)
St. Thomas U (FL)
Salem State Coll (MA)
Salve Regina U (RI)
Samford U (AL)
Sam Houston State U (TX)
San Diego State U (CA)
San Francisco State U (CA)
Seattle U (WA)
Shenandoah U (VA)
Siena Heights U (MI)
Simpson Coll (IA)
Sonoma State U (CA)
South Carolina State U (SC)
Southern Illinois U Carbondale (IL)
Southern Vermont Coll (VT)
Southwest Baptist U (MO)
Southwestern Coll (KS)
Southwestern Oklahoma State U (OK)
State U of NY at Oswego (NY)
State U of NY Coll at Brockport (NY)
State U of NY Coll at Fredonia (NY)
Suffolk U (MA)
Taylor U, Fort Wayne Campus (IN)
Teikyo Post U (CT)
Tennessee State U (TN)
Texas A&M U–Commerce (TX)
Texas A&M U–Corpus Christi (TX)
Texas Southern U (TX)
Thomas Coll (ME)
Thomas Edison State Coll (NJ)
Thomas More Coll (KY)
Thomas U (GA)
Tiffin U (OH)
Tri-State U (IN)
Truman State U (MO)
Union Coll (KY)
Union Inst & U (OH)
State U of NY at Albany (NY)
The U of Akron (OH)
U of Alberta (AB, Canada)
The U of Arizona (AZ)
U of Arkansas at Little Rock (AR)
U of Baltimore (MD)
U of Cincinnati (OH)
U of Dayton (OH)
U of Delaware (DE)
U of Detroit Mercy (MI)
U of Dubuque (IA)
U of Evansville (IN)
The U of Findlay (OH)
U of Great Falls (MT)
U of Guelph (ON, Canada)
U of Illinois at Springfield (IL)
U of Indianapolis (IN)
U of Louisville (KY)
The U of Maine at Augusta (ME)
U of Maine at Presque Isle (ME)
U of Mary Hardin-Baylor (TX)
U of Maryland Eastern Shore (MD)
U of Maryland U Coll (MD)
U of Massachusetts Lowell (MA)
The U of Memphis (TN)
U of Missouri–Kansas City (MO)
U of Nevada, Las Vegas (NV)
U of New Hampshire (NH)
U of New Haven (CT)
U of North Alabama (AL)
U of Ottawa (ON, Canada)
U of Phoenix–Colorado Campus (CO)
U of Phoenix–New Mexico Campus (NM)
U of Phoenix–Phoenix Campus (AZ)
U of Phoenix–Washington Campus (WA)
U of Pittsburgh at Bradford (PA)
U of Pittsburgh at Greensburg (PA)
U of Regina (SK, Canada)
U of Richmond (VA)
U of South Alabama (AL)
U of South Carolina (SC)
U of South Carolina Spartanburg (SC)
The U of South Dakota (SD)
The U of Tennessee at Chattanooga (TN)
The U of Tennessee at Martin (TN)
The U of Texas at Brownsville (TX)
The U of Texas–Pan American (TX)
U of the District of Columbia (DC)
U of Washington (WA)
U of Wisconsin–Milwaukee (WI)
U of Wisconsin–Oshkosh (WI)
U of Wisconsin–Parkside (WI)
U of Wisconsin–Platteville (WI)
Urbana U (OH)
Utica Coll (NY)
Villanova U (PA)
Virginia Commonwealth U (VA)
Virginia Intermont Coll (VA)
Voorhees Coll (SC)
Washburn U (KS)
Washington State U (WA)
Waynesburg Coll (PA)
Wayne State Coll (NE)
Western Illinois U (IL)
Western New England Coll (MA)
Western Oregon U (OR)
Westfield State Coll (MA)
West Liberty State Coll (WV)
Westminster Coll (PA)
West Texas A&M U (TX)
West Virginia State Coll (WV)
West Virginia Wesleyan Coll (WV)
Wheeling Jesuit U (WV)
Widener U (PA)
Wilmington Coll (DE)
Winona State U (MN)
Youngstown State U (OH)

CRIMINAL JUSTICE/POLICE SCIENCE

American Intl Coll (MA)
Athabasca U (AB, Canada)
Becker Coll (MA)
Bemidji State U (MN)
California State U, Hayward (CA)
Carleton U (ON, Canada)
Chicago State U (IL)
Coll of the Ozarks (MO)
Defiance Coll (OH)
East Central U (OK)
Eastern Kentucky U (KY)
Fairmont State Coll (WV)
Ferris State U (MI)
Florida Metropolitan U-Fort Lauderdale Coll (FL)
Frostburg State U (MD)
George Mason U (VA)
Grambling State U (LA)
Grand Valley State U (MI)
Hardin-Simmons U (TX)
Hesser Coll (NH)
Hilbert Coll (NY)
Howard U (DC)
Husson Coll (ME)
Jacksonville State U (AL)
John Jay Coll of Criminal Justice, the City U of NY (NY)
Lake Superior State U (MI)
Lamar U (TX)
Louisiana Coll (LA)
MacMurray Coll (IL)
Memorial U of Newfoundland (NL, Canada)
Mercyhurst Coll (PA)
Metropolitan State U (MN)
Minnesota State U Mankato (MN)
Mountain State U (WV)
Northeastern State U (OK)
Northeastern U (MA)
Northern Michigan U (MI)
Northern State U (SD)
Northwestern Oklahoma State U (OK)
Ohio Northern U (OH)
Oklahoma City U (OK)
Rowan U (NJ)
St. Gregory's U (OK)
Saint Louis U (MO)
Saint Mary's U of Minnesota (MN)
Sam Houston State U (TX)
State U of NY Coll at Brockport (NY)
Texas A&M U–Commerce (TX)
Texas State U-San Marcos (TX)
Tiffin U (OH)
Truman State U (MO)
U of Cincinnati (OH)
U of Great Falls (MT)
U of Hartford (CT)
U of Mary (ND)
U of New Haven (CT)
U of Pittsburgh at Greensburg (PA)
U of Regina (SK, Canada)
The U of Tennessee at Chattanooga (TN)
The U of Texas at Brownsville (TX)
The U of Texas–Pan American (TX)
U of Toronto (ON, Canada)
U of Wisconsin–Milwaukee (WI)
Washburn U (KS)

Wayne State Coll (NE)
Weber State U (UT)
Western Connecticut State U (CT)
Western Oregon U (OR)
Western State Coll of Colorado (CO)
Winona State U (MN)
Wright State U (OH)
York Coll of Pennsylvania (PA)
Youngstown State U (OH)

CRIMINAL JUSTICE/SAFETY
Albany State U (GA)
Alcorn State U (MS)
American Public U System (WV)
American U (DC)
Angelo State U (TX)
Appalachian State U (NC)
Arizona State U (AZ)
Auburn U Montgomery (AL)
Augsburg Coll (MN)
Augusta State U (GA)
Aurora U (IL)
Bellarmine U (KY)
Bethany Coll (KS)
Bethel Coll (IN)
Bloomsburg U of Pennsylvania (PA)
Bluefield State Coll (WV)
Bluffton Coll (OH)
Bowling Green State U (OH)
Bridgewater State Coll (MA)
Buena Vista U (IA)
Butler U (IN)
Caldwell Coll (NJ)
California State U, Chico (CA)
California State U, Los Angeles (CA)
Capital U (OH)
Cazenovia Coll (NY)
Central Methodist Coll (MO)
Champlain Coll (VT)
Chaparral Coll (AZ)
Charleston Southern U (SC)
Chowan Coll (NC)
Coll of the Southwest (NM)
Colorado State U (CO)
Colorado Tech U Sioux Falls Campus (SD)
Columbia Southern U (AL)
Concordia U, St. Paul (MN)
Delta State U (MS)
DeSales U (PA)
East Carolina U (NC)
Eastern New Mexico U (NM)
Edinboro U of Pennsylvania (PA)
Elizabeth City State U (NC)
Elizabethtown Coll (PA)
Endicott Coll (MA)
Fairleigh Dickinson U, Teaneck-Metro Campus (NJ)
Ferrum Coll (VA)
Florida Atlantic U (FL)
Florida Gulf Coast U (FL)
Florida Intl U (FL)
Florida Metropolitan U-Tampa Coll, Brandon (FL)
Florida Metropolitan U-Tampa Coll, Lakeland (FL)
Florida Southern Coll (FL)
Florida State U (FL)
Fort Hays State U (KS)
The Franciscan U (IA)
Gannon U (PA)
Georgia Southern U (GA)
Georgia State U (GA)
Guilford Coll (NC)
Harding U (AR)
Hesser Coll (NH)
High Point U (NC)
Husson Coll (ME)
Illinois State U (IL)
Indiana U Bloomington (IN)
Indiana U Kokomo (IN)
Indiana U–Purdue U Fort Wayne (IN)
Indiana U–Purdue U Indianapolis (IN)
Inter American U of PR, Aguadilla Campus (PR)
Intl Coll (FL)
Jamestown Coll (ND)
Judson Coll (IL)
Juniata Coll (PA)
Kaplan Coll (IA)
Kennesaw State U (GA)
Kent State U (OH)
Kentucky State U (KY)
Kentucky Wesleyan Coll (KY)
King's Coll (PA)
Kutztown U of Pennsylvania (PA)
Lakeland Coll (WI)
Lane Coll (TN)
La Roche Coll (PA)
La Salle U (PA)
Lasell Coll (MA)
Limestone Coll (SC)
Lincoln U (PA)
Long Island U, Brentwood Campus (NY)
Long Island U, C.W. Post Campus (NY)
Loras Coll (IA)
Louisiana State U in Shreveport (LA)
Loyola U Chicago (IL)
Loyola U New Orleans (LA)
Lubbock Christian U (TX)
Madonna U (MI)
Marshall U (WV)
Marymount U (VA)
Marywood U (PA)
McNeese State U (LA)
Medaille Coll (NY)
Mercer U (GA)
Mercyhurst Coll (PA)
Metropolitan State U (MN)
Michigan State U (MI)
Minnesota State U Moorhead (MN)
Minot State U (ND)
Missouri Baptist U (MO)
Missouri Western State Coll (MO)
Molloy Coll (NY)
Monmouth U (NJ)
Mountain State U (WV)
Mount Aloysius Coll (PA)
Mount Marty Coll (SD)
Mount Saint Mary Coll (NY)
Mount Saint Mary's Coll and Sem (MD)
Murray State U (KY)
Neumann Coll (PA)
New Jersey City U (NJ)
New Mexico Highlands U (NM)
New Mexico State U (NM)
Northeastern Illinois U (IL)
Northeastern U (MA)
Northern Michigan U (MI)
North Georgia Coll & State U (GA)
Northwestern Coll (MN)
Northwestern State U of Louisiana (LA)
Ohio Northern U (OH)
The Ohio State U (OH)
Ohio U (OH)
Olivet Coll (MI)
Penn State U Abington Coll (PA)
Penn State U Altoona Coll (PA)
Penn State U Fayette Campus of the Commonwealth Coll (PA)
Penn State U Harrisburg Campus of the Capital Coll (PA)
Penn State U Schuylkill Campus of the Capital Coll (PA)
Pikeville Coll (KY)
Pittsburg State U (KS)
Plymouth State U (NH)
Point Park U (PA)
Prairie View A&M U (TX)
Quincy U (IL)
Quinnipiac U (CT)
Rhode Island Coll (RI)
Roanoke Coll (VA)
Rochester Inst of Technology (NY)
Roosevelt U (IL)
Rutgers, The State U of New Jersey, Camden (NJ)
Rutgers, The State U of New Jersey, Newark (NJ)
Saginaw Valley State U (MI)
St. Ambrose U (IA)
Saint Anselm Coll (NH)
St. Edward's U (TX)
St. Francis Coll (NY)
Saint Joseph's Coll (IN)
Saint Joseph's Coll of Maine (ME)
Saint Leo U (FL)
Saint Xavier U (IL)
Sam Houston State U (TX)
San Jose State U (CA)
Seton Hall U (NJ)
Shaw U (NC)
Shippensburg U of Pennsylvania (PA)
Southeastern Louisiana U (LA)
Southeastern Oklahoma State U (OK)
Southern Arkansas U–Magnolia (AR)
Southern Illinois U Edwardsville (IL)
Southern Nazarene U (OK)
Southern U and A&M Coll (LA)
Southwest Missouri State U (MO)
State U of NY Coll at Oneonta (NY)
State U of NY Coll at Potsdam (NY)
State U of West Georgia (GA)
Stonehill Coll (MA)
Tarleton State U (TX)
Taylor U, Fort Wayne Campus (IN)
Texas A&M Intl U (TX)
Texas A&M U–Texarkana (TX)
Texas Christian U (TX)
Texas State U-San Marcos (TX)
Texas Wesleyan U (TX)
Texas Woman's U (TX)
Thiel Coll (PA)
Tiffin U (OH)
Troy State U Dothan (AL)
Tulane U (LA)
U Coll of the Fraser Valley (BC, Canada)
The U of Akron (OH)
The U of Alabama (AL)
U of Arkansas (AR)
U of Arkansas at Monticello (AR)
U of Central Florida (FL)
U of Georgia (GA)
U of Great Falls (MT)
U of Idaho (ID)
U of Illinois at Chicago (IL)
U of Louisiana at Lafayette (LA)
U of Massachusetts Boston (MA)
U of Nebraska at Omaha (NE)
U of New Haven (CT)
The U of North Carolina at Charlotte (NC)
The U of North Carolina at Pembroke (NC)
The U of North Carolina at Wilmington (NC)
U of North Dakota (ND)
U of Northern Colorado (CO)
U of North Florida (FL)
U of North Texas (TX)
U of Portland (OR)
U of Regina (SK, Canada)
The U of Scranton (PA)
U of South Florida (FL)
The U of Texas at Arlington (TX)
The U of Texas at Tyler (TX)
U of the Sacred Heart (PR)
U of Toledo (OH)
The U of Virginia's Coll at Wise (VA)
U of West Florida (FL)
U of Windsor (ON, Canada)
U of Wisconsin–Eau Claire (WI)
U of Wisconsin–Superior (WI)
U of Wyoming (WY)
Valdosta State U (GA)
Virginia State U (VA)
Viterbo U (WI)
Wayland Baptist U (TX)
Wayne State U (MI)
Weber State U (UT)
West Chester U of Pennsylvania (PA)
Western Carolina U (NC)
Western Michigan U (MI)
Wichita State U (KS)
Wilkes U (PA)
Worcester State Coll (MA)
Xavier U (OH)
Youngstown State U (OH)

CRIMINOLOGY
Albright Coll (PA)
Arkansas State U (AR)
Auburn U (AL)
Ball State U (IN)
Barry U (FL)
Bethel Coll (KS)
Bridgewater State Coll (MA)
California State U, Fresno (CA)
Cameron U (OK)
Capital U (OH)
Carleton U (ON, Canada)
Castleton State Coll (VT)
Centenary Coll (NJ)
Central Connecticut State U (CT)
Central Michigan U (MI)
Chaminade U of Honolulu (HI)
Coker Coll (SC)
Coll of Mount St. Joseph (OH)
Coll of the Ozarks (MO)
Colorado State U-Pueblo (CO)
Dominican U (IL)
Drury U (MO)
Eastern Michigan U (MI)
Florida State U (FL)
Gallaudet U (DC)
Husson Coll (ME)
Indiana State U (IN)
Indiana U of Pennsylvania (PA)
Juniata Coll (PA)
Kwantlen U Coll (BC, Canada)
Le Moyne Coll (NY)
Lindenwood U (MO)
Marquette U (WI)
Marymount U (VA)
Maryville U of Saint Louis (MO)
Marywood U (PA)
Memorial U of Newfoundland (NL, Canada)
Mount Aloysius Coll (PA)
New Mexico Highlands U (NM)
Niagara U (NY)
North Carolina State U (NC)
The Ohio State U (OH)
Ohio U (OH)
Old Dominion U (VA)
Paine Coll (GA)
Pontifical Catholic U of Puerto Rico (PR)
The Richard Stockton Coll of New Jersey (NJ)
Rivier Coll (NH)
St. Cloud State U (MN)
Saint Francis U (PA)
St. John's U (NY)
Saint Joseph's U (PA)
St. Mary's U of San Antonio (TX)
St. Thomas U (NB, Canada)
Simon Fraser U (BC, Canada)
Southern Oregon U (OR)
Plattsburgh State U of NY (NY)
State U of NY Coll at Brockport (NY)
State U of NY Coll at Cortland (NY)
State U of NY Coll at Old Westbury (NY)
Stonehill Coll (MA)
Texas A&M U–Kingsville (TX)
Thomas U (GA)
Université de Montréal (QC, Canada)
U of Alberta (AB, Canada)
U of Calif, Irvine (CA)
U of Denver (CO)
U of Florida (FL)
U of La Verne (CA)
U of Maryland, Coll Park (MD)
The U of Memphis (TN)
U of Miami (FL)
U of Minnesota, Duluth (MN)
U of Missouri–St. Louis (MO)
U of Nevada, Reno (NV)
U of Northern Iowa (IA)
U of Oklahoma (OK)
U of Ottawa (ON, Canada)
U of St. Thomas (MN)
U of Southern Maine (ME)
The U of Tampa (FL)
The U of Texas at Dallas (TX)
U of Windsor (ON, Canada)
Upper Iowa U (IA)
Valparaiso U (IN)
Virginia Union U (VA)
Virginia Wesleyan Coll (VA)
Western Michigan U (MI)
William Penn U (IA)
Wright State U (OH)

CRITICAL CARE NURSING
British Columbia Inst of Technology (BC, Canada)
U at Buffalo, The State U of New York (NY)

CROP PRODUCTION
Colorado State U (CO)
Cornell U (NY)
Delaware Valley Coll (PA)
North Dakota State U (ND)
Sterling Coll (VT)
Washington State U (WA)

CULINARY ARTS
The Art Inst of Colorado (CO)
The Art Inst of Washington (VA)
Baltimore Intl Coll (MD)
The Culinary Inst of America (NY)
Drexel U (PA)
Johnson & Wales U (FL)
Johnson & Wales U (RI)
Kendall Coll (IL)
Lexington Coll (IL)
Mercyhurst Coll (PA)
Metropolitan State U (MN)
Nicholls State U (LA)
Northern Michigan U (MI)
Paul Smith's Coll of Arts and Sciences (NY)
Pennsylvania Coll of Technology (PA)
Sullivan U (KY)
U of Nevada, Las Vegas (NV)
Virginia Intermont Coll (VA)

CULINARY ARTS RELATED
The Culinary Inst of America (NY)
Lexington Coll (IL)
Newbury Coll (MA)

CULTURAL RESOURCE MANAGEMENT AND POLICY ANALYSIS
Eastern Michigan U (MI)
Sterling Coll (VT)
U of Waterloo (ON, Canada)

CULTURAL STUDIES
Azusa Pacific U (CA)
Bard Coll (NY)
Boise State U (ID)
Bridgewater Coll (VA)
Briercrest Bible Coll (SK, Canada)
Brigham Young U–Hawaii (HI)
California State Polytechnic U, Pomona (CA)
California State U, Fullerton (CA)
California State U, Hayward (CA)
California State U, Sacramento (CA)
Clark U (MA)
The Coll of William and Mary (VA)
Concordia U (QC, Canada)
Cornell Coll (IA)
The Evergreen State Coll (WA)
Fort Lewis Coll (CO)
Hampshire Coll (MA)
Harvard U (MA)
Houghton Coll (NY)
Jewish Theological Sem of America (NY)
Kent State U (OH)
Marlboro Coll (VT)
Mills Coll (CA)
Minnesota State U Mankato (MN)
New Coll of California (CA)
The Ohio State U (OH)
Ohio Wesleyan U (OH)
Oregon State U (OR)
Penn State U Univ Park Campus (PA)
Reformed Bible Coll (MI)
Rutgers, The State U of New Jersey, Newark (NJ)
Rutgers, The State U of New Jersey, New Brunswick/Piscataway (NJ)
St. Francis Xavier U (NS, Canada)
Saint Mary-of-the-Woods Coll (IN)
St. Olaf Coll (MN)
Simon's Rock Coll of Bard (MA)
Sonoma State U (CA)
The U of British Columbia (BC, Canada)
U of Calif, Irvine (CA)
U of Calif, Riverside (CA)
U of Calif, San Diego (CA)
U of Colorado at Boulder (CO)
U of Nevada, Las Vegas (NV)
U of Oregon (OR)
U of Southern California (CA)
The U of Tennessee (TN)
U of Toronto (ON, Canada)
U of Virginia (VA)
U of Washington (WA)
U of Wisconsin–Milwaukee (WI)
Washington U in St. Louis (MO)
Western Washington U (WA)
Yale U (CT)
York U (ON, Canada)

CURRICULUM AND INSTRUCTION
Albertus Magnus Coll (CT)
Eastern Michigan U (MI)
Lock Haven U of Pennsylvania (PA)
Ohio U (OH)
St. John's U (NY)
Sam Houston State U (TX)
Sterling Coll (VT)
Tarleton State U (TX)
Texas A&M U (TX)
Texas Southern U (TX)
U of Arkansas (AR)
U of Houston–Clear Lake (TX)
The U of Montana–Missoula (MT)
U of Saint Mary (KS)
The U of South Dakota (SD)
Utah State U (UT)
Wright State U (OH)
York U (ON, Canada)

CUSTOMER SERVICE MANAGEMENT
U of Wisconsin–Stout (WI)

CUSTOMER SERVICE SUPPORT/ CALL CENTER/TELESERVICE OPERATION
National American U–Sioux Falls Branch (SD)

CYTOTECHNOLOGY
Alderson-Broaddus Coll (WV)
Anderson Coll (SC)
Barry U (FL)
Bellarmine U (KY)
Bloomfield Coll (NJ)
California State U, Dominguez Hills (CA)
Coll of Saint Elizabeth (NJ)

The Coll of Saint Rose (NY)
Edgewood Coll (WI)
Elmhurst Coll (IL)
The Franciscan U (IA)
Illinois Coll (IL)
Indiana U–Purdue U Indianapolis (IN)
Indiana U Southeast (IN)
Jewish Hospital Coll of Nursing and Allied Health (MO)
Loma Linda U (CA)
Long Island U, Brooklyn Campus (NY)
Long Island U, C.W. Post Campus (NY)
Louisiana State U Health Sciences Center (LA)
Marian Coll of Fond du Lac (WI)
Marshall U (WV)
Minnesota State U Moorhead (MN)
Monmouth U (NJ)
Northern Michigan U (MI)
Oakland U (MI)
Old Dominion U (VA)
Roosevelt U (IL)
St. John's U (NY)
Saint Mary's Coll (IN)
Saint Mary's U of Minnesota (MN)
Salve Regina U (RI)
Slippery Rock U of Pennsylvania (PA)
State U of New York Upstate Medical U (NY)
Stony Brook U, State U of New York (NY)
Thiel Coll (PA)
Thomas Edison State Coll (NJ)
Thomas Jefferson U (PA)
The U of Akron (OH)
The U of Alabama at Birmingham (AL)
U of Connecticut (CT)
U of Kansas (KS)
U of Mississippi Medical Center (MS)
U of Missouri–St. Louis (MO)
U of North Dakota (ND)
U of North Texas (TX)
Winona State U (MN)

CZECH
The U of Texas at Austin (TX)

DAIRY HUSBANDRY AND PRODUCTION
Sterling Coll (VT)
U of Vermont (VT)

DAIRY SCIENCE
Auburn U (AL)
California Polytechnic State U, San Luis Obispo (CA)
Cornell U (NY)
Delaware Valley Coll (PA)
Iowa State U of Science and Technology (IA)
Oregon State U (OR)
South Dakota State U (SD)
State U of NY Coll of A&T at Cobleskill (NY)
Sterling Coll (VT)
Texas A&M U (TX)
U of Alberta (AB, Canada)
U of Florida (FL)
U of Georgia (GA)
U of New Hampshire (NH)
U of Wisconsin–Madison (WI)
U of Wisconsin–River Falls (WI)
Utah State U (UT)
Virginia Polytechnic Inst and State U (VA)

DANCE
Adelphi U (NY)
Alma Coll (MI)
Amherst Coll (MA)
Antioch Coll (OH)
Arizona State U (AZ)
Baldwin-Wallace Coll (OH)
Ball State U (IN)
Bard Coll (NY)
Barnard Coll (NY)
Belhaven Coll (MS)
Bennington Coll (VT)
Birmingham-Southern Coll (AL)
Bowling Green State U (OH)
Brenau U (GA)
Brigham Young U (UT)
Butler U (IN)
California Inst of the Arts (CA)
California State U, Fresno (CA)
California State U, Fullerton (CA)
California State U, Hayward (CA)
California State U, Long Beach (CA)
California State U, Los Angeles (CA)
California State U, Sacramento (CA)
Cedar Crest Coll (PA)
Centenary Coll of Louisiana (LA)
Chapman U (CA)
Claremont McKenna Coll (CA)
Cleveland State U (OH)
Coker Coll (SC)
The Colorado Coll (CO)
Colorado State U (CO)
Columbia Coll (NY)
Columbia Coll (SC)
Columbia Coll Chicago (IL)
Columbia U, School of General Studies (NY)
Concordia U (QC, Canada)
Connecticut Coll (CT)
Cornell U (NY)
Cornish Coll of the Arts (WA)
Denison U (OH)
DeSales U (PA)
Dickinson Coll (PA)
East Carolina U (NC)
Eastern Michigan U (MI)
Emory U (GA)
Florida Intl U (FL)
Florida State U (FL)
Fordham U (NY)
Frostburg State U (MD)
George Mason U (VA)
The George Washington U (DC)
Goucher Coll (MD)
Gustavus Adolphus Coll (MN)
Hamilton Coll (NY)
Hampshire Coll (MA)
Hobart and William Smith Colls (NY)
Hofstra U (NY)
Hollins U (VA)
Hope Coll (MI)
Hunter Coll of the City U of NY (NY)
Indiana U Bloomington (IN)
Ithaca Coll (NY)
Jacksonville U (FL)
Johnson State Coll (VT)
The Juilliard School (NY)
Kent State U (OH)
Kenyon Coll (OH)
Lake Erie Coll (OH)
Lamar U (TX)
La Roche Coll (PA)
Lehman Coll of the City U of NY (NY)
Lindenwood U (MO)
Long Island U, Brooklyn Campus (NY)
Long Island U, C.W. Post Campus (NY)
Loyola Marymount U (CA)
Luther Coll (IA)
Manhattanville Coll (NY)
Marlboro Coll (VT)
Marygrove Coll (MI)
Marymount Manhattan Coll (NY)
Mercyhurst Coll (PA)
Meredith Coll (NC)
Middlebury Coll (VT)
Mills Coll (CA)
Montclair State U (NJ)
Mount Holyoke Coll (MA)
Muhlenberg Coll (PA)
Naropa U (CO)
New Mexico State U (NM)
New World School of the Arts (FL)
New York U (NY)
North Carolina School of the Arts (NC)
Northwestern U (IL)
Oakland U (MI)
Oberlin Coll (OH)
The Ohio State U (OH)
Ohio U (OH)
Oklahoma City U (OK)
Old Dominion U (VA)
Palm Beach Atlantic U (FL)
Pitzer Coll (CA)
Point Park U (PA)
Pomona Coll (CA)
Queens Coll of the City U of NY (NY)
Radford U (VA)
Randolph-Macon Woman's Coll (VA)
Reed Coll (OR)
Rhode Island Coll (RI)
Roger Williams U (RI)
Rutgers, The State U of New Jersey, New Brunswick/Piscataway (NJ)
Ryerson U (ON, Canada)
St. Gregory's U (OK)
Saint Mary's Coll of California (CA)
St. Olaf Coll (MN)
Sam Houston State U (TX)
San Diego State U (CA)
San Francisco State U (CA)
San Jose State U (CA)
Sarah Lawrence Coll (NY)
Scripps Coll (CA)
Shenandoah U (VA)
Simon Fraser U (BC, Canada)
Simon's Rock Coll of Bard (MA)
Skidmore Coll (NY)
Slippery Rock U of Pennsylvania (PA)
Smith Coll (MA)
Southern Methodist U (TX)
Southern Utah U (UT)
Southwest Missouri State U (MO)
State U of NY Coll at Brockport (NY)
State U of NY Coll at Fredonia (NY)
State U of NY Coll at Potsdam (NY)
Stephens Coll (MO)
Swarthmore Coll (PA)
Sweet Briar Coll (VA)
Texas State U-San Marcos (TX)
Texas Tech U (TX)
Texas Woman's U (TX)
Thomas Edison State Coll (NJ)
Towson U (MD)
Trinity Coll (CT)
U at Buffalo, The State U of New York (NY)
The U of Akron (OH)
The U of Alabama (AL)
U of Alberta (AB, Canada)
The U of Arizona (AZ)
U of Calgary (AB, Canada)
U of Calif, Berkeley (CA)
U of Calif, Irvine (CA)
U of Calif, Los Angeles (CA)
U of Calif, Riverside (CA)
U of Calif, San Diego (CA)
U of Calif, Santa Barbara (CA)
U of Calif, Santa Cruz (CA)
U of Cincinnati (OH)
U of Colorado at Boulder (CO)
U of Florida (FL)
U of Hartford (CT)
U of Hawaii at Manoa (HI)
U of Idaho (ID)
U of Illinois at Urbana–Champaign (IL)
The U of Iowa (IA)
U of Kansas (KS)
U of Maryland, Baltimore County (MD)
U of Maryland, Coll Park (MD)
U of Massachusetts Amherst (MA)
U of Miami (FL)
U of Michigan (MI)
U of Minnesota, Twin Cities Campus (MN)
U of Missouri–Kansas City (MO)
The U of Montana–Missoula (MT)
U of Nebraska–Lincoln (NE)
U of Nevada, Las Vegas (NV)
U of New Mexico (NM)
The U of North Carolina at Charlotte (NC)
The U of North Carolina at Greensboro (NC)
U of North Texas (TX)
U of Oklahoma (OK)
U of Oregon (OR)
U of South Florida (FL)
The U of Texas at Austin (TX)
The U of the Arts (PA)
U of Utah (UT)
U of Washington (WA)
U of Wisconsin–Milwaukee (WI)
U of Wisconsin–Stevens Point (WI)
Utah State U (UT)
Virginia Commonwealth U (VA)
Virginia Intermont Coll (VA)
Washington U in St. Louis (MO)
Wayne State U (MI)
Weber State U (UT)
Webster U (MO)
Wells Coll (NY)
Wesleyan U (CT)
Western Michigan U (MI)
Western Oregon U (OR)
Westmont Coll (CA)
West Texas A&M U (TX)
Winthrop U (SC)
Wright State U (OH)
York U (ON, Canada)

DANCE RELATED
Brigham Young U (UT)
California State U, Long Beach (CA)
Chapman U (CA)
New World School of the Arts (FL)
Sarah Lawrence Coll (NY)

DANCE THERAPY
Columbia Coll Chicago (IL)

DATA ENTRY/MICROCOMPUTER APPLICATIONS
Huron U USA in London(United Kingdom)
National American U, Denver (CO)

DATA ENTRY/MICROCOMPUTER APPLICATIONS RELATED
Huron U USA in London(United Kingdom)

DATA MODELING/ WAREHOUSING AND DATABASE ADMINISTRATION
Huron U USA in London(United Kingdom)
Northface U (UT)
Rochester Inst of Technology (NY)
U of Phoenix–Atlanta Campus (GA)

DATA PROCESSING AND DATA PROCESSING TECHNOLOGY
Arkansas State U (AR)
Bemidji State U (MN)
Central Baptist Coll (AR)
Chicago State U (IL)
Florida Metropolitan U-Tampa Coll (FL)
Gardner-Webb U (NC)
Huron U USA in London(United Kingdom)
Indiana U Kokomo (IN)
Indiana U Northwest (IN)
Long Island U, Brooklyn Campus (NY)
Minnesota State U Mankato (MN)
Mount Vernon Nazarene U (OH)
Northern Michigan U (MI)
Pacific Union Coll (CA)
Texas State U-San Marcos (TX)
U of Advancing Technology (AZ)
U of Arkansas (AR)
U of Mary Hardin-Baylor (TX)
U of New Brunswick Fredericton (NB, Canada)
U of Southern Indiana (IN)
U of Washington (WA)

DEMOGRAPHY AND POPULATION
Cornell U (NY)
Plymouth State U (NH)

DENTAL ASSISTING
Louisiana State U Health Sciences Center (LA)

DENTAL HYGIENE
Armstrong Atlantic State U (GA)
Clayton Coll & State U (GA)
Dalhousie U (NS, Canada)
Eastern Washington U (WA)
State U of NY at Farmingdale (NY)
Howard U (DC)
Idaho State U (ID)
Indiana U–Purdue U Indianapolis (IN)
Loma Linda U (CA)
Louisiana State U Health Sciences Center (LA)
Marquette U (WI)
Mars Hill Coll (NC)
Mass Coll of Pharmacy and Allied Health Sciences (MA)
Medical Coll of Georgia (GA)
Midwestern State U (TX)
Minnesota State U Mankato (MN)
New York U (NY)
Northeastern U (MA)
Northern Arizona U (AZ)
The Ohio State U (OH)
Old Dominion U (VA)
Oregon Inst of Technology (OR)
Pennsylvania Coll of Technology (PA)
Southern Illinois U Carbondale (IL)
Tennessee State U (TN)
Texas A&M U System Health Science Center (TX)
Texas Woman's U (TX)
Thomas Edison State Coll (NJ)
U of Alberta (AB, Canada)
U of Bridgeport (CT)
The U of British Columbia (BC, Canada)
U of Colorado Health Sciences Center (CO)
U of Detroit Mercy (MI)
U of Hawaii at Manoa (HI)
U of Louisiana at Lafayette (LA)
U of Louisville (KY)
The U of Maine at Augusta (ME)
U of Manitoba (MB, Canada)
U of Michigan (MI)
U of Minnesota, Twin Cities Campus (MN)
U of Mississippi Medical Center (MS)
U of Missouri–Kansas City (MO)
U of Nebraska Medical Center (NE)
U of New Haven (CT)
U of New Mexico (NM)
The U of North Carolina at Chapel Hill (NC)
U of Oklahoma Health Sciences Center (OK)
U of Pittsburgh (PA)
U of Rhode Island (RI)
The U of South Dakota (SD)
U of Southern California (CA)
U of Southern Indiana (IN)
U of Texas-Houston Health Science Center (TX)
U of Texas Health Science Center at San Antonio (TX)
U of Washington (WA)
U of Wyoming (WY)
Virginia Commonwealth U (VA)
Weber State U (UT)
Western Kentucky U (KY)
West Liberty State Coll (WV)
West Virginia U (WV)
Wichita State U (KS)

DENTAL LABORATORY TECHNOLOGY
Boston U (MA)
Central Missouri State U (MO)
Louisiana State U Health Sciences Center (LA)

DESIGN AND APPLIED ARTS RELATED
Art Center Coll of Design (CA)
The Art Inst of California–San Diego (CA)
Bennington Coll (VT)
Col for Creative Studies (MI)
Daemen Coll (NY)
Drexel U (PA)
Fashion Inst of Technology (NY)
Hampshire Coll (MA)
Harding U (AR)
Laguna Coll of Art & Design (CA)
Lehigh U (PA)
Mt. Sierra Coll (CA)
The New England Inst of Art (MA)
New York Inst of Technology (NY)
North Carolina State U (NC)
Nova Scotia Coll of Art and Design (NS, Canada)
Ohio U (OH)
Point Park U (PA)
Pratt Inst (NY)
Ringling School of Art and Design (FL)
Robert Morris Coll (IL)
St. Cloud State U (MN)
Savannah Coll of Art and Design (GA)
School of the Art Inst of Chicago (IL)
The U of Akron (OH)
U of Calif, Los Angeles (CA)
U of Massachusetts Dartmouth (MA)
U of Saint Francis (IN)
U of Wisconsin–Stout (WI)

DESIGN AND VISUAL COMMUNICATIONS
Alberta Coll of Art & Design (AB, Canada)
Albright Coll (PA)
Alma Coll (MI)
American Acad of Art (IL)
American InterContinental U, Atlanta (GA)
American InterContinental U Online (IL)
The American U in Dubai(United Arab Emirates)
The Art Inst of Washington (VA)
Atlanta Coll of Art (GA)
Bethel Coll (IN)
Bethesda Christian U (CA)
Bowling Green State U (OH)
Brigham Young U (UT)
State U of NY Coll at Buffalo (NY)
California State U, Chico (CA)
Carlow Coll (PA)
Cazenovia Coll (NY)
Central Connecticut State U (CT)
Champlain Coll (VT)
Col for Creative Studies (MI)
Cornell U (NY)

Drury U (MO)
Duke U (NC)
Endicott Coll (MA)
State U of NY at Farmingdale (NY)
Henry Cogswell Coll (WA)
The Illinois Inst of Art-Schaumburg (IL)
Illinois Inst of Technology (IL)
Intl Acad of Design & Technology (FL)
Intl Acad of Merchandising & Design, Ltd (IL)
Iowa State U of Science and Technology (IA)
Jacksonville U (FL)
Kean U (NJ)
Laguna Coll of Art & Design (CA)
Lambuth U (TN)
Lubbock Christian U (TX)
Marywood U (PA)
Memphis Coll of Art (TN)
Mount Union Coll (OH)
Mount Vernon Nazarene U (OH)
North Carolina State U (NC)
Nova Scotia Coll of Art and Design (NS, Canada)
Ohio Northern U (OH)
The Ohio State U (OH)
Ohio U (OH)
Paier Coll of Art, Inc. (CT)
Peace Coll (NC)
Purdue U (IN)
Robert Morris U (PA)
Rochester Inst of Technology (NY)
Saginaw Valley State U (MI)
St. Ambrose U (IA)
Saint Mary-of-the-Woods Coll (IN)
San Diego State U (CA)
Savannah Coll of Art and Design (GA)
School of the Art Inst of Chicago (IL)
Silicon Valley Coll, Walnut Creek (CA)
Southern Illinois U Carbondale (IL)
Southwest Missouri State U (MO)
Syracuse U (NY)
Truman State U (MO)
U du Québec à Hull (QC, Canada)
U of Advancing Technology (AZ)
U of Calif, Davis (CA)
U of Kansas (KS)
U of Massachusetts Dartmouth (MA)
U of Michigan (MI)
U of Notre Dame (IN)
U of Oklahoma (OK)
The U of Texas at Austin (TX)
Virginia Commonwealth U (VA)
Viterbo U (WI)
Washington U in St. Louis (MO)
Weber State U (UT)
Western Washington U (WA)
Westwood Coll of Technology–Long Beach (CA)
William Woods U (MO)
Wilmington Coll (DE)
York U (ON, Canada)

DESKTOP PUBLISHING AND DIGITAL IMAGING DESIGN
California State U, Chico (CA)
Silicon Valley Coll, Walnut Creek (CA)
Texas State U-San Marcos (TX)

DEVELOPMENTAL AND CHILD PSYCHOLOGY
Belmont U (TN)
Bennington Coll (VT)
Berea Coll (KY)
Brooklyn Coll of the City U of NY (NY)
California Polytechnic State U, San Luis Obispo (CA)
California State U, Hayward (CA)
California State U, San Bernardino (CA)
Carson-Newman Coll (TN)
Castleton State Coll (VT)
Christopher Newport U (VA)
Clark Atlanta U (GA)
Colby-Sawyer Coll (NH)
Colorado State U-Pueblo (CO)
Concordia U (QC, Canada)
Cornell U (NY)
Eastern Connecticut State U (CT)
Eastern Washington U (WA)
Edgewood Coll (WI)
Fort Valley State U (GA)
Framingham State Coll (MA)
Fresno Pacific U (CA)
Hampshire Coll (MA)
Hampton U (VA)
Houston Baptist U (TX)
Humboldt State U (CA)
Liberty U (VA)
Longwood U (VA)
Marlboro Coll (VT)
Maryville Coll (TN)
Marywood U (PA)
Metropolitan State U (MN)
Mills Coll (CA)
Minnesota State U Mankato (MN)
Mount Ida Coll (MA)
Mount St. Mary's Coll (CA)
Mount Saint Vincent U (NS, Canada)
Northern Michigan U (MI)
Oklahoma Baptist U (OK)
Olivet Nazarene U (IL)
Quinnipiac U (CT)
Rockford Coll (IL)
St. Joseph's Coll, New York (NY)
St. Joseph's Coll, Suffolk Campus (NY)
Sarah Lawrence Coll (NY)
Simon's Rock Coll of Bard (MA)
Sonoma State U (CA)
Spelman Coll (GA)
Suffolk U (MA)
Tufts U (MA)
Université de Montréal (QC, Canada)
The U of Akron (OH)
U of Alberta (AB, Canada)
The U of British Columbia (BC, Canada)
U of Calif, Santa Cruz (CA)
U of Delaware (DE)
U of Detroit Mercy (MI)
U of Michigan–Dearborn (MI)
U of Minnesota, Twin Cities Campus (MN)
U of New Brunswick Fredericton (NB, Canada)
U of Ottawa (ON, Canada)
U of the District of Columbia (DC)
U of the Incarnate Word (TX)
U of Toledo (OH)
U of Utah (UT)
U of Windsor (ON, Canada)
U of Wisconsin–Green Bay (WI)
U of Wisconsin–Madison (WI)
Utica Coll (NY)
Villa Julie Coll (MD)
Western Washington U (WA)

DEVELOPMENT ECONOMICS AND INTERNATIONAL DEVELOPMENT
American U (DC)
Arkansas State U (AR)
Brown U (RI)
Canadian Mennonite U (MB, Canada)
Clark U (MA)
Dalhousie U (NS, Canada)
Eastern Mennonite U (VA)
Georgia Southern U (GA)
The Ohio State U (OH)
Point Loma Nazarene U (CA)
U of Calif, Los Angeles (CA)
U of Guelph (ON, Canada)
U of King's Coll (NS, Canada)
U of Windsor (ON, Canada)
York U (ON, Canada)

DIAGNOSTIC MEDICAL SONOGRAPHY AND ULTRASOUND TECHNOLOGY
Baptist Coll of Health Sciences (TN)
Dalhousie U (NS, Canada)
Medical Coll of Georgia (GA)
Mountain State U (WV)
Nebraska Methodist Coll (NE)
Rochester Inst of Technology (NY)
Seattle U (WA)
State U of NY Health Science Center at Brooklyn (NY)
U of Missouri–Columbia (MO)
U of Nebraska Medical Center (NE)
Weber State U (UT)

DIESEL MECHANICS TECHNOLOGY
Lewis-Clark State Coll (ID)

DIETETICS
Abilene Christian U (TX)
Acadia U (NS, Canada)
Andrews U (MI)
Ashland U (OH)
Ball State U (IN)
Bastyr U (WA)
Berea Coll (KY)
Bowling Green State U (OH)
Brigham Young U (UT)
State U of NY Coll at Buffalo (NY)
California State Polytechnic U, Pomona (CA)
California State U, Chico (CA)
California State U, Fresno (CA)
California State U, Long Beach (CA)
California State U, Los Angeles (CA)
California State U, San Bernardino (CA)
Carson-Newman Coll (TN)
Case Western Reserve U (OH)
Central Michigan U (MI)
Central Missouri State U (MO)
Coll of Saint Benedict (MN)
Coll of St. Catherine (MN)
Coll of Saint Elizabeth (NJ)
Coll of the Ozarks (MO)
Colorado State U (CO)
Concordia Coll (MN)
Delaware State U (DE)
Dominican U (IL)
D'Youville Coll (NY)
East Carolina U (NC)
Eastern Kentucky U (KY)
Eastern Michigan U (MI)
Florida Intl U (FL)
Florida State U (FL)
Fontbonne U (MO)
Framingham State Coll (MA)
Gannon U (PA)
Harding U (AR)
Idaho State U (ID)
Immaculata U (PA)
Indiana U Bloomington (IN)
Indiana U of Pennsylvania (PA)
Iowa State U of Science and Technology (IA)
Jacksonville State U (AL)
Kansas State U (KS)
Keene State Coll (NH)
Lamar U (TX)
Lehman Coll of the City U of NY (NY)
Lipscomb U (TN)
Loma Linda U (CA)
Louisiana Tech U (LA)
Mansfield U of Pennsylvania (PA)
Marshall U (WV)
Marymount Coll of Fordham U (NY)
Marywood U (PA)
McGill U (QC, Canada)
Memorial U of Newfoundland (NL, Canada)
Mercyhurst Coll (PA)
Meredith Coll (NC)
Miami U (OH)
Miami U Hamilton (OH)
Michigan State U (MI)
Minnesota State U Mankato (MN)
Montclair State U (NJ)
Morgan State U (MD)
Mount Mary Coll (WI)
Mount Saint Vincent U (NS, Canada)
Nicholls State U (LA)
North Dakota State U (ND)
Northern Michigan U (MI)
The Ohio State U (OH)
Ohio U (OH)
Oklahoma State U (OK)
Olivet Nazarene U (IL)
Oregon State U (OR)
Ouachita Baptist U (AR)
Rochester Inst of Technology (NY)
Saint John's U (MN)
Saint Joseph Coll (CT)
San Francisco State U (CA)
San Jose State U (CA)
Seton Hill U (PA)
Simmons Coll (MA)
South Dakota State U (SD)
Southwest Missouri State U (MO)
State U of NY Coll at Oneonta (NY)
Syracuse U (NY)
Tennessee Technological U (TN)
Texas A&M U–Kingsville (TX)
Texas Christian U (TX)
Texas Southern U (TX)
Texas Tech U (TX)
Tuskegee U (AL)
The U of Akron (OH)
The U of British Columbia (BC, Canada)
U of Connecticut (CT)
U of Dayton (OH)
U of Delaware (DE)
U of Georgia (GA)
U of Guelph (ON, Canada)
U of Illinois at Chicago (IL)
U of Louisiana at Lafayette (LA)
U of Maryland, Coll Park (MD)
U of Maryland Eastern Shore (MD)
U of Missouri–Columbia (MO)
U of Montevallo (AL)
U of New Hampshire (NH)
U of New Haven (CT)
The U of North Carolina at Greensboro (NC)
U of North Dakota (ND)
U of Northern Colorado (CO)
U of Oklahoma Health Sciences Center (OK)
U of Pittsburgh (PA)
U of Rhode Island (RI)
The U of Tennessee at Martin (TN)
The U of Texas–Pan American (TX)
U of Texas Southwestern Medical Center at Dallas (TX)
U of Vermont (VT)
The U of Western Ontario (ON, Canada)
U of Wisconsin–Madison (WI)
U of Wisconsin–Stevens Point (WI)
U of Wisconsin–Stout (WI)
Virginia Polytechnic Inst and State U (VA)
Viterbo U (WI)
Wayne State U (MI)
West Chester U of Pennsylvania (PA)
Western Carolina U (NC)
Western Michigan U (MI)
Youngstown State U (OH)

DIETETICS AND CLINICAL NUTRITION SERVICES RELATED
Madonna U (MI)
Texas Christian U (TX)

DIGITAL COMMUNICATION AND MEDIA/MULTIMEDIA
Abilene Christian U (TX)
Acad of Art U (CA)
The Art Inst of California–San Diego (CA)
The Art Inst of Washington (VA)
California Lutheran U (CA)
California State U, Sacramento (CA)
Calvin Coll (MI)
Canisius Coll (NY)
Champlain Coll (VT)
Clarkson U (NY)
Eastern Washington U (WA)
Florida Atlantic U (FL)
Grace Bible Coll (MI)
Hampshire Coll (MA)
Harding U (AR)
Huntington Coll (IN)
The Illinois Inst of Art-Schaumburg (IL)
Kent State U (OH)
Kutztown U of Pennsylvania (PA)
Lebanon Valley Coll (PA)
Lindenwood U (MO)
Marist Coll (NY)
Minot State U (ND)
The New England Inst of Art (MA)
New York U (NY)
Saint Joseph's Coll of Maine (ME)
Sam Houston State U (TX)
Savannah Coll of Art and Design (GA)
School of the Art Inst of Chicago (IL)
Stevens Inst of Technology (NJ)
Texas A&M U (TX)
Université de Sherbrooke (QC, Canada)
U of Baltimore (MD)
The U of Lethbridge (AB, Canada)
U of Northern Iowa (IA)
The U of Texas at Arlington (TX)
The U of the Arts (PA)
U of Waterloo (ON, Canada)
Wheeling Jesuit U (WV)

DIRECT ENTRY MIDWIFERY
Utah Coll of Midwifery (UT)

DIRECTING AND THEATRICAL PRODUCTION
Brigham Young U (UT)
California State U, Long Beach (CA)
Campbell U (NC)
Coe Coll (IA)
Cornish Coll of the Arts (WA)
Drake U (IA)
Elizabethtown Coll (PA)
Hampshire Coll (MA)
Marywood U (PA)
Ohio U (OH)
Sarah Lawrence Coll (NY)
U of Southern California (CA)
Western Michigan U (MI)

DIVINITY/MINISTRY
Atlantic Union Coll (MA)
Azusa Pacific U (CA)
Baptist Bible Coll (MO)
Barclay Coll (KS)
Belmont U (TN)
Bethany Bible Coll (NB, Canada)
Bethel Coll (IN)
Bethesda Christian U (CA)
Biola U (CA)
Bluefield Coll (VA)
Briercrest Bible Coll (SK, Canada)
Campbellsville U (KY)
Campbell U (NC)
Canadian Mennonite U (MB, Canada)
Cardinal Stritch U (WI)
Central Christian Coll of Kansas (KS)
Christian Heritage Coll (CA)
Clear Creek Baptist Bible Coll (KY)
Coll of Biblical Studies–Houston (TX)
Concordia U (CA)
Eugene Bible Coll (OR)
Faith Baptist Bible Coll and Theological Sem (IA)
Faulkner U (AL)
Fresno Pacific U (CA)
Global U of the Assemblies of God (MO)
Grace Coll (IN)
Grace U (NE)
Grand Canyon U (AZ)
Grove City Coll (PA)
Harding U (AR)
Hardin-Simmons U (TX)
Huntington Coll (IN)
John Brown U (AR)
John Wesley Coll (NC)
Liberty U (VA)
Lipscomb U (TN)
Manhattan Christian Coll (KS)
Marylhurst U (OR)
The Master's Coll and Sem (CA)
Master's Coll and Sem (ON, Canada)
Messenger Coll (MO)
North Central U (MN)
North Park U (IL)
Northwest Nazarene U (ID)
Oakland City U (IN)
Oklahoma Baptist U (OK)
Providence Coll and Theological Sem (MB, Canada)
Reformed Bible Coll (MI)
Roberts Wesleyan Coll (NY)
St. John's U (NY)
St. Louis Christian Coll (MO)
Shorter Coll (GA)
Southern Wesleyan U (SC)
Tabor Coll (KS)
Trinity Western U (BC, Canada)
Tyndale U Coll & Sem (ON, Canada)
Warner Pacific Coll (OR)
Wayland Baptist U (TX)
Western Baptist Coll (OR)
William Jessup U (CA)
Williams Baptist Coll (AR)

DRAFTING AND DESIGN TECHNOLOGY
Baker Coll of Flint (MI)
Baker Coll of Owosso (MI)
Central Missouri State U (MO)
East Central U (OK)
Grambling State U (LA)
Hillsdale Coll (MI)
Keene State Coll (NH)
Lewis-Clark State Coll (ID)
Lynn U (FL)
Norfolk State U (VA)
Northern Michigan U (MI)
Northern State U (SD)
Pacific Union Coll (CA)
Prairie View A&M U (TX)
Sam Houston State U (TX)
Texas Southern U (TX)
Thomas Edison State Coll (NJ)
Tri-State U (IN)
U of Houston (TX)

DRAFTING/DESIGN ENGINEERING TECHNOLOGIES RELATED
Eastern Washington U (WA)
National U (CA)

DRAMA AND DANCE TEACHER EDUCATION
Appalachian State U (NC)
Baylor U (TX)
Bishop's U (QC, Canada)
Boston U (MA)

Bowling Green State U (OH)
Brenau U (GA)
Bridgewater State Coll (MA)
Brigham Young U (UT)
Capital U (OH)
Carroll Coll (WI)
The Catholic U of America (DC)
Centenary Coll of Louisiana (LA)
Central Washington U (WA)
Chadron State Coll (NE)
Coll of St. Catherine (MN)
Columbia Coll (SC)
Columbus State U (GA)
Concordia U (NE)
Concordia U (QC, Canada)
Dana Coll (NE)
Davis & Elkins Coll (WV)
Dordt Coll (IA)
East Carolina U (NC)
Eastern Washington U (WA)
East Texas Baptist U (TX)
Emerson Coll (MA)
Greensboro Coll (NC)
Hardin-Simmons U (TX)
Hastings Coll (NE)
Hope Coll (MI)
Howard Payne U (TX)
Indiana U–Purdue U Fort Wayne (IN)
Jacksonville U (FL)
Johnson State Coll (VT)
Meredith Coll (NC)
Minnesota State U Moorhead (MN)
Northern Arizona U (AZ)
The Ohio State U (OH)
Ohio Wesleyan U (OH)
Oklahoma Baptist U (OK)
Point Park U (PA)
Ryerson U (ON, Canada)
St. Edward's U (TX)
Salve Regina U (RI)
San Diego State U (CA)
Texas Wesleyan U (TX)
The U of Akron (OH)
The U of Arizona (AZ)
U of Calgary (AB, Canada)
U of Georgia (GA)
The U of Iowa (IA)
The U of Lethbridge (AB, Canada)
The U of North Carolina at Charlotte (NC)
The U of North Carolina at Greensboro (NC)
U of St. Thomas (MN)
The U of South Dakota (SD)
U of South Florida (FL)
The U of the Arts (PA)
U of Utah (UT)
U of Windsor (ON, Canada)
Valparaiso U (IN)
Viterbo U (WI)
Waldorf Coll (IA)
Washington U in St. Louis (MO)
Weber State U (UT)
William Carey Coll (MS)
William Jewell Coll (MO)
York U (ON, Canada)
Youngstown State U (OH)

DRAMA THERAPY

Howard U (DC)
Virginia Union U (VA)

DRAMATIC/THEATRE ARTS

Abilene Christian U (TX)
Acadia U (NS, Canada)
Adams State Coll (CO)
Adelphi U (NY)
Adrian Coll (MI)
Agnes Scott Coll (GA)
Alabama State U (AL)
Albertson Coll of Idaho (ID)
Albertus Magnus Coll (CT)
Albion Coll (MI)
Albright Coll (PA)
Alderson-Broaddus Coll (WV)
Alfred U (NY)
Allegheny Coll (PA)
Alma Coll (MI)
American U (DC)
The American U in Cairo(Egypt)
Amherst Coll (MA)
Anderson Coll (SC)
Angelo State U (TX)
Antioch Coll (OH)
Appalachian State U (NC)
Arcadia U (PA)
Arizona State U (AZ)
Arkansas State U (AR)
Armstrong Atlantic State U (GA)
Ashland U (OH)
Auburn U (AL)
Augsburg Coll (MN)
Augustana Coll (IL)
Augustana Coll (SD)
Averett U (VA)
Avila U (MO)
Baker U (KS)
Ball State U (IN)
Bard Coll (NY)
Barnard Coll (NY)
Barry U (FL)
Barton Coll (NC)
Bates Coll (ME)
Baylor U (TX)
Belhaven Coll (MS)
Belmont U (TN)
Beloit Coll (WI)
Bemidji State U (MN)
Benedictine Coll (KS)
Bennington Coll (VT)
Berea Coll (KY)
Bethany Coll (WV)
Bethany Lutheran Coll (MN)
Bethel Coll (IN)
Bethel Coll (KS)
Bethel Coll (TN)
Bethel U (MN)
Birmingham-Southern Coll (AL)
Bishop's U (QC, Canada)
Bloomfield Coll (NJ)
Bloomsburg U of Pennsylvania (PA)
Bluefield Coll (VA)
Blue Mountain Coll (MS)
Boise State U (ID)
Boston Coll (MA)
Bowling Green State U (OH)
Bradley U (IL)
Brandeis U (MA)
Brenau U (GA)
Briar Cliff U (IA)
Bridgewater State Coll (MA)
Brigham Young U (UT)
Brock U (ON, Canada)
Brown U (RI)
Bucknell U (PA)
State U of NY Coll at Buffalo (NY)
Butler U (IN)
California Inst of the Arts (CA)
California Lutheran U (CA)
California State Polytechnic U, Pomona (CA)
California State U, Chico (CA)
California State U, Dominguez Hills (CA)
California State U, Fresno (CA)
California State U, Fullerton (CA)
California State U, Hayward (CA)
California State U, Long Beach (CA)
California State U, Los Angeles (CA)
California State U, Sacramento (CA)
California State U, San Bernardino (CA)
California State U, Stanislaus (CA)
California U of Pennsylvania (PA)
Calvin Coll (MI)
Campbell U (NC)
Capital U (OH)
Cardinal Stritch U (WI)
Carleton U (ON, Canada)
Carnegie Mellon U (PA)
Carroll Coll (MT)
Carroll Coll (WI)
Carson-Newman Coll (TN)
Carthage Coll (WI)
Case Western Reserve U (OH)
Castleton State Coll (VT)
Catawba Coll (NC)
The Catholic U of America (DC)
Cedar Crest Coll (PA)
Cedarville U (OH)
Centenary Coll of Louisiana (LA)
Central Coll (IA)
Central Connecticut State U (CT)
Central Methodist Coll (MO)
Central Michigan U (MI)
Central Missouri State U (MO)
Central Washington U (WA)
Centre Coll (KY)
Chadron State Coll (NE)
Chapman U (CA)
Chatham Coll (PA)
Cheyney U of Pennsylvania (PA)
Christopher Newport U (VA)
City Coll of the City U of NY (NY)
Claremont McKenna Coll (CA)
Clarion U of Pennsylvania (PA)
Clark Atlanta U (GA)
Clarke Coll (IA)
Clark U (MA)
Cleveland State U (OH)
Coastal Carolina U (SC)
Coe Coll (IA)
Coker Coll (SC)
Colby Coll (ME)
Colgate U (NY)
Coll of Charleston (SC)
Coll of Saint Benedict (MN)
Coll of St. Catherine (MN)
Coll of Santa Fe (NM)
Coll of Staten Island of the City U of NY (NY)
Coll of the Holy Cross (MA)
Coll of the Ozarks (MO)
Coll of the Southwest (NM)
The Coll of William and Mary (VA)
The Coll of Wooster (OH)
Colorado Christian U (CO)
The Colorado Coll (CO)
Colorado State U (CO)
Columbia Coll (NY)
Columbia Coll Chicago (IL)
Columbia U, School of General Studies (NY)
Columbus State U (GA)
Concordia Coll (MN)
Concordia U (CA)
Concordia U (IL)
Concordia U (NE)
Concordia U (OR)
Concordia U (QC, Canada)
Concordia U, St. Paul (MN)
Connecticut Coll (CT)
Converse Coll (SC)
Cornell Coll (IA)
Cornell U (NY)
Cornish Coll of the Arts (WA)
Creighton U (NE)
Culver-Stockton Coll (MO)
Cumberland Coll (KY)
Cumberland U (TN)
Dakota Wesleyan U (SD)
Dalhousie U (NS, Canada)
Dartmouth Coll (NH)
Davidson Coll (NC)
Davis & Elkins Coll (WV)
Denison U (OH)
DePaul U (IL)
DePauw U (IN)
DeSales U (PA)
Dickinson Coll (PA)
Dickinson State U (ND)
Dillard U (LA)
Doane Coll (NE)
Dominican U (IL)
Dordt Coll (IA)
Drake U (IA)
Drew U (NJ)
Drury U (MO)
Duke U (NC)
Duquesne U (PA)
Earlham Coll (IN)
East Carolina U (NC)
Eastern Illinois U (IL)
Eastern Kentucky U (KY)
Eastern Mennonite U (VA)
Eastern Michigan U (MI)
Eastern Nazarene Coll (MA)
Eastern New Mexico U (NM)
Eastern Oregon U (OR)
Eastern Washington U (WA)
East Stroudsburg U of Pennsylvania (PA)
East Texas Baptist U (TX)
Eckerd Coll (FL)
Edgewood Coll (WI)
Edinboro U of Pennsylvania (PA)
Elmhurst Coll (IL)
Elmira Coll (NY)
Elon U (NC)
Emerson Coll (MA)
Emory & Henry Coll (VA)
Emory U (GA)
Emporia State U (KS)
Eugene Lang Coll, New School U (NY)
Eureka Coll (IL)
The Evergreen State Coll (WA)
Fairleigh Dickinson U, Florham (NJ)
Fairleigh Dickinson U, Teaneck-Metro Campus (NJ)
Fairmont State Coll (WV)
Faulkner U (AL)
Ferrum Coll (VA)
Five Towns Coll (NY)
Flagler Coll (FL)
Florida Ag and Mech U (FL)
Florida Atlantic U (FL)
Florida Intl U (FL)
Florida Southern Coll (FL)
Florida State U (FL)
Fontbonne U (MO)
Fordham U (NY)
Fort Lewis Coll (CO)
Francis Marion U (SC)
Franklin and Marshall Coll (PA)
Franklin Coll (IN)
Franklin Pierce Coll (NH)
Freed-Hardeman U (TN)
Frostburg State U (MD)
Furman U (SC)
Gallaudet U (DC)
Gannon U (PA)
Gardner-Webb U (NC)
George Mason U (VA)
Georgetown Coll (KY)
The George Washington U (DC)
Georgia Coll & State U (GA)
Georgia Southern U (GA)
Georgia Southwestern State U (GA)
Georgia State U (GA)
Gettysburg Coll (PA)
Gonzaga U (WA)
Goshen Coll (IN)
Goucher Coll (MD)
Graceland U (IA)
Grambling State U (LA)
Grand Canyon U (AZ)
Grand Valley State U (MI)
Grand View Coll (IA)
Greensboro Coll (NC)
Greenville Coll (IL)
Grinnell Coll (IA)
Guilford Coll (NC)
Gustavus Adolphus Coll (MN)
Hamilton Coll (NY)
Hamline U (MN)
Hampshire Coll (MA)
Hampton U (VA)
Hannibal-LaGrange Coll (MO)
Hanover Coll (IN)
Harding U (AR)
Hardin-Simmons U (TX)
Hartwick Coll (NY)
Harvard U (MA)
Hastings Coll (NE)
Heidelberg Coll (OH)
Henderson State U (AR)
Hendrix Coll (AR)
High Point U (NC)
Hillsdale Coll (MI)
Hiram Coll (OH)
Hobart and William Smith Colls (NY)
Hofstra U (NY)
Hollins U (VA)
Hope Coll (MI)
Howard Payne U (TX)
Howard U (DC)
Humboldt State U (CA)
Hunter Coll of the City U of NY (NY)
Huntingdon Coll (AL)
Huntington Coll (IN)
Idaho State U (ID)
Illinois Coll (IL)
Illinois State U (IL)
Illinois Wesleyan U (IL)
Indiana State U (IN)
Indiana U Bloomington (IN)
Indiana U Northwest (IN)
Indiana U of Pennsylvania (PA)
Indiana U–Purdue U Fort Wayne (IN)
Indiana U South Bend (IN)
Iona Coll (NY)
Iowa State U of Science and Technology (IA)
Ithaca Coll (NY)
Jacksonville State U (AL)
Jacksonville U (FL)
James Madison U (VA)
Jamestown Coll (ND)
Johnson State Coll (VT)
Judson Coll (IL)
Kalamazoo Coll (MI)
Kansas State U (KS)
Kansas Wesleyan U (KS)
Kean U (NJ)
Keene State Coll (NH)
Kennesaw State U (GA)
Kent State U (OH)
Kenyon Coll (OH)
King's Coll (PA)
Knox Coll (IL)
Kutztown U of Pennsylvania (PA)
LaGrange Coll (GA)
Lake Erie Coll (OH)
Lamar U (TX)
Lambuth U (TN)
Laurentian U (ON, Canada)
Lawrence U (WI)
Lehman Coll of the City U of NY (NY)
Le Moyne Coll (NY)
Lenoir-Rhyne Coll (NC)
Lewis & Clark Coll (OR)
Lewis U (IL)
Limestone Coll (SC)
Lindenwood U (MO)
Linfield Coll (OR)
Lock Haven U of Pennsylvania (PA)
Long Island U, C.W. Post Campus (NY)
Longwood U (VA)
Louisiana Coll (LA)
Louisiana State U and A&M Coll (LA)
Loyola Marymount U (CA)
Loyola U Chicago (IL)
Loyola U New Orleans (LA)
Lycoming Coll (PA)
Lynchburg Coll (VA)
Lyon Coll (AR)
Macalester Coll (MN)
MacMurray Coll (IL)
Manchester Coll (IN)
Marietta Coll (OH)
Marist Coll (NY)
Marlboro Coll (VT)
Marquette U (WI)
Mars Hill Coll (NC)
Mary Baldwin Coll (VA)
Marymount Coll of Fordham U (NY)
Marymount Manhattan Coll (NY)
Maryville Coll (TN)
Mary Washington Coll (VA)
Marywood U (PA)
Massachusetts Coll of Liberal Arts (MA)
McDaniel Coll (MD)
McGill U (QC, Canada)
McMurry U (TX)
McNeese State U (LA)
McPherson Coll (KS)
Memorial U of Newfoundland (NL, Canada)
Mercer U (GA)
Meredith Coll (NC)
Messiah Coll (PA)
Methodist Coll (NC)
Metropolitan State U (MN)
Miami U (OH)
Michigan State U (MI)
Middlebury Coll (VT)
Middle Tennessee State U (TN)
Midwestern State U (TX)
Millikin U (IL)
Millsaps Coll (MS)
Minnesota State U Mankato (MN)
Minnesota State U Moorhead (MN)
Missouri Southern State U (MO)
Missouri Valley Coll (MO)
Monmouth Coll (IL)
Montana State U–Billings (MT)
Montclair State U (NJ)
Morehead State U (KY)
Morehouse Coll (GA)
Morgan State U (MD)
Morningside Coll (IA)
Mount Allison U (NB, Canada)
Mount Holyoke Coll (MA)
Mount Mercy Coll (IA)
Mount Union Coll (OH)
Mount Vernon Nazarene U (OH)
Muhlenberg Coll (PA)
Naropa U (CO)
National-Louis U (IL)
Nazareth Coll of Rochester (NY)
Nebraska Wesleyan U (NE)
Newberry Coll (SC)
New Mexico State U (NM)
New York U (NY)
Niagara U (NY)
North Carolina Central U (NC)
North Carolina School of the Arts (NC)
North Carolina Wesleyan Coll (NC)
North Central Coll (IL)
North Central U (MN)
North Dakota State U (ND)
Northeastern State U (OK)
Northeastern U (MA)
Northern Arizona U (AZ)
Northern Illinois U (IL)
Northern Michigan U (MI)
Northern State U (SD)
North Park U (IL)
Northwestern Coll (IA)
Northwestern Coll (MN)
Northwestern State U of Louisiana (LA)
Northwestern U (IL)
Notre Dame de Namur U (CA)
Oakland U (MI)
Oberlin Coll (OH)
Occidental Coll (CA)
Ohio Northern U (OH)
The Ohio State U (OH)
Ohio U (OH)
Ohio Wesleyan U (OH)
Oklahoma Baptist U (OK)
Oklahoma Christian U (OK)
Oklahoma City U (OK)
Oklahoma State U (OK)
Old Dominion U (VA)
Oral Roberts U (OK)
Oregon State U (OR)
Ottawa U (KS)
Otterbein Coll (OH)
Ouachita Baptist U (AR)

Our Lady of the Lake U of San Antonio (TX)
Pacific Lutheran U (WA)
Pacific U (OR)
Paine Coll (GA)
Palm Beach Atlantic U (FL)
Pepperdine U, Malibu (CA)
Piedmont Coll (GA)
Pitzer Coll (CA)
Plymouth State U (NH)
Point Loma Nazarene U (CA)
Point Park U (PA)
Pomona Coll (CA)
Portland State U (OR)
Prairie Bible Coll (AB, Canada)
Prairie View A&M U (TX)
Presbyterian Coll (SC)
Principia Coll (IL)
Providence Coll and Theological Sem (MB, Canada)
Purdue U (IN)
Queens Coll of the City U of NY (NY)
Queen's U at Kingston (ON, Canada)
Queens U of Charlotte (NC)
Radford U (VA)
Randolph-Macon Coll (VA)
Randolph-Macon Woman's Coll (VA)
Redeemer U Coll (ON, Canada)
Reed Coll (OR)
Regis Coll (MA)
Rhode Island Coll (RI)
Rhodes Coll (TN)
Ripon Coll (WI)
Roanoke Coll (VA)
Rockford Coll (IL)
Rockhurst U (MO)
Rocky Mountain Coll (MT)
Roger Williams U (RI)
Rollins Coll (FL)
Roosevelt U (IL)
Rowan U (NJ)
Russell Sage Coll (NY)
Rutgers, The State U of New Jersey, Camden (NJ)
Rutgers, The State U of New Jersey, Newark (NJ)
Rutgers, The State U of New Jersey, New Brunswick/Piscataway (NJ)
Ryerson U (ON, Canada)
Sacred Heart U (CT)
Saginaw Valley State U (MI)
St. Ambrose U (IA)
St. Cloud State U (MN)
St. Edward's U (TX)
Saint John's U (MN)
St. Lawrence U (NY)
Saint Louis U (MO)
Saint Martin's Coll (WA)
Saint Mary-of-the-Woods Coll (IN)
Saint Mary's Coll (IN)
Saint Mary's Coll of California (CA)
St. Mary's Coll of Maryland (MD)
Saint Mary's U of Minnesota (MN)
Saint Michael's Coll (VT)
St. Olaf Coll (MN)
Saint Vincent Coll (PA)
Salem State Coll (MA)
Salisbury U (MD)
Salve Regina U (RI)
Samford U (AL)
Sam Houston State U (TX)
San Diego State U (CA)
San Francisco State U (CA)
San Jose State U (CA)
Santa Clara U (CA)
Sarah Lawrence Coll (NY)
Savannah Coll of Art and Design (GA)
Schreiner U (TX)
Scripps Coll (CA)
Seattle Pacific U (WA)
Seattle U (WA)
Seton Hill U (PA)
Shawnee State U (OH)
Shaw U (NC)
Shenandoah U (VA)
Shorter Coll (GA)
Siena Heights U (MI)
Simon Fraser U (BC, Canada)
Simon's Rock Coll of Bard (MA)
Simpson Coll (IA)
Skidmore Coll (NY)
Slippery Rock U of Pennsylvania (PA)
Smith Coll (MA)
Sonoma State U (CA)
South Carolina State U (SC)
South Dakota State U (SD)
Southeastern Coll of the Assemblies of God (FL)
Southeastern Oklahoma State U (OK)
Southeast Missouri State U (MO)
Southern Arkansas U–Magnolia (AR)
Southern Connecticut State U (CT)
Southern Illinois U Carbondale (IL)
Southern Illinois U Edwardsville (IL)
Southern Methodist U (TX)
Southern Oregon U (OR)
Southern U and A&M Coll (LA)
Southern Utah U (UT)
Southern Virginia U (VA)
Southwest Baptist U (MO)
Southwestern U (TX)
Southwest Missouri State U (MO)
Spelman Coll (GA)
Spring Hill Coll (AL)
Stanford U (CA)
State U of NY at Binghamton (NY)
State U of NY at New Paltz (NY)
State U of NY at Oswego (NY)
Plattsburgh State U of NY (NY)
State U of NY Coll at Brockport (NY)
State U of NY Coll at Fredonia (NY)
State U of NY Coll at Geneseo (NY)
State U of NY Coll at Oneonta (NY)
State U of NY Coll at Potsdam (NY)
State U of West Georgia (GA)
Stephens Coll (MO)
Sterling Coll (KS)
Stetson U (FL)
Stony Brook U, State U of New York (NY)
Suffolk U (MA)
Susquehanna U (PA)
Swarthmore Coll (PA)
Sweet Briar Coll (VA)
Syracuse U (NY)
Tarleton State U (TX)
Taylor U (IN)
Texas A&M U (TX)
Texas A&M U–Commerce (TX)
Texas A&M U–Kingsville (TX)
Texas Christian U (TX)
Texas Lutheran U (TX)
Texas Southern U (TX)
Texas State U-San Marcos (TX)
Texas Tech U (TX)
Texas Wesleyan U (TX)
Texas Woman's U (TX)
Thomas Edison State Coll (NJ)
Thomas More Coll (KY)
Towson U (MD)
Transylvania U (KY)
Trevecca Nazarene U (TN)
Trinity Coll (CT)
Trinity U (TX)
Trinity Western U (BC, Canada)
Troy State U (AL)
Truman State U (MO)
Tufts U (MA)
Tulane U (LA)
Union U (TN)
Université Laval (QC, Canada)
State U of NY at Albany (NY)
U at Buffalo, The State U of New York (NY)
U Coll of the Cariboo (BC, Canada)
The U of Akron (OH)
The U of Alabama (AL)
U of Alaska Fairbanks (AK)
U of Alberta (AB, Canada)
The U of Arizona (AZ)
U of Arkansas (AR)
U of Arkansas at Little Rock (AR)
The U of British Columbia (BC, Canada)
U of Calgary (AB, Canada)
U of Calif, Berkeley (CA)
U of Calif, Davis (CA)
U of Calif, Irvine (CA)
U of Calif, Los Angeles (CA)
U of Calif, Riverside (CA)
U of Calif, San Diego (CA)
U of Calif, Santa Barbara (CA)
U of Calif, Santa Cruz (CA)
U of Central Florida (FL)
U of Cincinnati (OH)
U of Colorado at Boulder (CO)
U of Colorado at Denver (CO)
U of Connecticut (CT)
U of Dallas (TX)
U of Dayton (OH)
U of Denver (CO)
U of Detroit Mercy (MI)
U of Evansville (IN)
The U of Findlay (OH)
U of Florida (FL)
U of Georgia (GA)
U of Guelph (ON, Canada)
U of Hartford (CT)
U of Hawaii at Manoa (HI)
U of Houston (TX)
U of Idaho (ID)
U of Illinois at Chicago (IL)
U of Illinois at Urbana–Champaign (IL)
U of Indianapolis (IN)
The U of Iowa (IA)
U of Kansas (KS)
U of Kentucky (KY)
U of King's Coll (NS, Canada)
U of La Verne (CA)
The U of Lethbridge (AB, Canada)
U of Louisiana at Lafayette (LA)
U of Louisville (KY)
U of Maine (ME)
U of Maine at Farmington (ME)
U of Maine at Machias (ME)
U of Manitoba (MB, Canada)
U of Mary Hardin-Baylor (TX)
U of Maryland, Baltimore County (MD)
U of Maryland, Coll Park (MD)
U of Massachusetts Amherst (MA)
U of Massachusetts Boston (MA)
The U of Memphis (TN)
U of Miami (FL)
U of Michigan (MI)
U of Michigan–Flint (MI)
U of Minnesota, Duluth (MN)
U of Minnesota, Morris (MN)
U of Minnesota, Twin Cities Campus (MN)
U of Mississippi (MS)
U of Missouri–Columbia (MO)
U of Missouri–Kansas City (MO)
U of Mobile (AL)
The U of Montana–Missoula (MT)
The U of Montana–Western (MT)
U of Montevallo (AL)
U of Nebraska at Omaha (NE)
U of Nebraska–Lincoln (NE)
U of Nevada, Las Vegas (NV)
U of Nevada, Reno (NV)
U of New Brunswick Fredericton (NB, Canada)
U of New Hampshire (NH)
U of New Mexico (NM)
The U of North Carolina at Asheville (NC)
The U of North Carolina at Chapel Hill (NC)
The U of North Carolina at Charlotte (NC)
The U of North Carolina at Greensboro (NC)
The U of North Carolina at Pembroke (NC)
The U of North Carolina at Wilmington (NC)
U of North Dakota (ND)
U of Northern Colorado (CO)
U of Northern Iowa (IA)
U of North Texas (TX)
U of Notre Dame (IN)
U of Oklahoma (OK)
U of Oregon (OR)
U of Ottawa (ON, Canada)
U of Pennsylvania (PA)
U of Pittsburgh (PA)
U of Pittsburgh at Johnstown (PA)
U of Portland (OR)
U of Puget Sound (WA)
U of Regina (SK, Canada)
U of Richmond (VA)
U of Saint Mary (KS)
U of St. Thomas (MN)
U of St. Thomas (TX)
U of Saskatchewan (SK, Canada)
U of Science and Arts of Oklahoma (OK)
The U of Scranton (PA)
U of Sioux Falls (SD)
U of South Alabama (AL)
U of South Carolina (SC)
The U of South Dakota (SD)
U of Southern California (CA)
U of Southern Indiana (IN)
U of Southern Maine (ME)
U of South Florida (FL)
The U of Tampa (FL)
The U of Tennessee (TN)
The U of Tennessee at Chattanooga (TN)
The U of Texas at Arlington (TX)
The U of Texas at Austin (TX)
The U of Texas at Tyler (TX)
The U of Texas–Pan American (TX)
The U of the Arts (PA)
U of the District of Columbia (DC)
U of the Incarnate Word (TX)
U of the Ozarks (AR)
U of the Pacific (CA)
U of the Sacred Heart (PR)
U of the South (TN)
U of the Virgin Islands (VI)
U of Toledo (OH)
U of Toronto (ON, Canada)
U of Tulsa (OK)
U of Utah (UT)
U of Vermont (VT)
U of Victoria (BC, Canada)
U of Virginia (VA)
The U of Virginia's Coll at Wise (VA)
U of Washington (WA)
U of Waterloo (ON, Canada)
U of West Florida (FL)
U of Windsor (ON, Canada)
U of Wisconsin–Eau Claire (WI)
U of Wisconsin–Green Bay (WI)
U of Wisconsin–La Crosse (WI)
U of Wisconsin–Madison (WI)
U of Wisconsin–Milwaukee (WI)
U of Wisconsin–Oshkosh (WI)
U of Wisconsin–Parkside (WI)
U of Wisconsin–River Falls (WI)
U of Wisconsin–Stevens Point (WI)
U of Wisconsin–Superior (WI)
U of Wisconsin–Whitewater (WI)
U of Wyoming (WY)
Utah State U (UT)
Valparaiso U (IN)
Vanderbilt U (TN)
Vanguard U of Southern California (CA)
Vassar Coll (NY)
Virginia Commonwealth U (VA)
Virginia Intermont Coll (VA)
Virginia Polytechnic Inst and State U (VA)
Virginia Wesleyan Coll (VA)
Viterbo U (WI)
Wabash Coll (IN)
Wagner Coll (NY)
Wake Forest U (NC)
Waldorf Coll (IA)
Washburn U (KS)
Washington & Jefferson Coll (PA)
Washington and Lee U (VA)
Washington Coll (MD)
Washington State U (WA)
Washington U in St. Louis (MO)
Wayland Baptist U (TX)
Wayne State Coll (NE)
Wayne State U (MI)
Weber State U (UT)
Webster U (MO)
Wellesley Coll (MA)
Wells Coll (NY)
Wesleyan U (CT)
West Chester U of Pennsylvania (PA)
Western Carolina U (NC)
Western Connecticut State U (CT)
Western Illinois U (IL)
Western Kentucky U (KY)
Western Michigan U (MI)
Western Oregon U (OR)
Western State Coll of Colorado (CO)
Western Washington U (WA)
Westminster Coll (PA)
Westmont Coll (CA)
West Texas A&M U (TX)
West Virginia U (WV)
West Virginia Wesleyan Coll (WV)
Wheaton Coll (MA)
Whitman Coll (WA)
Whitworth Coll (WA)
Wichita State U (KS)
Wilkes U (PA)
Willamette U (OR)
William Carey Coll (MS)
William Jewell Coll (MO)
William Paterson U of New Jersey (NJ)
Williams Coll (MA)
William Woods U (MO)
Winona State U (MN)
Winthrop U (SC)
Wisconsin Lutheran Coll (WI)
Wittenberg U (OH)
Wofford Coll (SC)
Wright State U (OH)
Yale U (CT)
York Coll of the City U of New York (NY)
York U (ON, Canada)
Youngstown State U (OH)

DRAMATIC/THEATRE ARTS AND STAGECRAFT RELATED

Baldwin-Wallace Coll (OH)
Bowdoin Coll (ME)
Bowling Green State U (OH)
Brevard Coll (NC)
Brigham Young U (UT)
California Inst of the Arts (CA)
California State U, Chico (CA)
Charleston Southern U (SC)
Coastal Carolina U (SC)
Coker Coll (SC)
Coll of Santa Fe (NM)
Dalhousie U (NS, Canada)
DePaul U (IL)
Drake U (IA)
Fayetteville State U (NC)
Hampshire Coll (MA)
Nebraska Wesleyan U (NE)
Ohio U (OH)
Ramapo Coll of New Jersey (NJ)
Saint Augustine's Coll (NC)
St. Cloud State U (MN)
Seton Hill U (PA)
Shenandoah U (VA)
U at Buffalo, The State U of New York (NY)
U Coll of the Cariboo (BC, Canada)
The U of Akron (OH)
U of Connecticut (CT)
U of Nevada, Las Vegas (NV)
U of Northern Colorado (CO)
U of Regina (SK, Canada)
The U of the Arts (PA)

DRAWING

Acad of Art U (CA)
Alberta Coll of Art & Design (AB, Canada)
American Acad of Art (IL)
Anderson Coll (SC)
Antioch Coll (OH)
Aquinas Coll (MI)
Arcadia U (PA)
Arizona State U (AZ)
Art Acad of Cincinnati (OH)
Atlanta Coll of Art (GA)
Ball State U (IN)
Bard Coll (NY)
Bennington Coll (VT)
Bethany Coll (KS)
Biola U (CA)
Birmingham-Southern Coll (AL)
Boise State U (ID)
Boston U (MA)
Bowling Green State U (OH)
Brigham Young U (UT)
Brock U (ON, Canada)
State U of NY Coll at Buffalo (NY)
California Coll of the Arts (CA)
California State U, Fullerton (CA)
California State U, Hayward (CA)
California State U, Long Beach (CA)
Carson-Newman Coll (TN)
Chicago State U (IL)
The Cleveland Inst of Art (OH)
Col for Creative Studies (MI)
Coll of the Atlantic (ME)
Coll of Visual Arts (MN)
Colorado State U (CO)
Columbia Coll (MO)
Concordia U (QC, Canada)
DePaul U (IL)
Drake U (IA)
Governors State U (IL)
Grace Coll (IN)
Grand Valley State U (MI)
Hampshire Coll (MA)
Hampton U (VA)
Indiana U Bloomington (IN)
Indiana U–Purdue U Fort Wayne (IN)
Inter American U of PR, San Germán Campus (PR)
Judson Coll (IL)
Laguna Coll of Art & Design (CA)
Lewis U (IL)
Lindenwood U (MO)
Longwood U (VA)
Lyme Acad Coll of Fine Arts (CT)
Marlboro Coll (VT)
Maryland Inst Coll of Art (MD)
McNeese State U (LA)
Memorial U of Newfoundland (NL, Canada)
Memphis Coll of Art (TN)
Milwaukee Inst of Art and Design (WI)
Minneapolis Coll of Art and Design (MN)
Minnesota State U Mankato (MN)
Montserrat Coll of Art (MA)
Mount Allison U (NB, Canada)
Nazareth Coll of Rochester (NY)
New World School of the Arts (FL)
Northern Michigan U (MI)
North Georgia Coll & State U (GA)
Nova Scotia Coll of Art and Design (NS, Canada)
The Ohio State U (OH)
Ohio U (OH)
Otis Coll of Art and Design (CA)
Parsons School of Design, New School U (NY)
Portland State U (OR)
Pratt Inst (NY)
Rivier Coll (NH)

Rutgers, The State U of New Jersey, New Brunswick/Piscataway (NJ)
Sacred Heart U (CT)
St. Cloud State U (MN)
Salem State Coll (MA)
San Francisco Art Inst (CA)
Sarah Lawrence Coll (NY)
School of the Art Inst of Chicago (IL)
School of the Museum of Fine Arts, Boston (MA)
Seton Hill U (PA)
Shawnee State U (OH)
Simon's Rock Coll of Bard (MA)
Sonoma State U (CA)
State U of NY at Binghamton (NY)
State U of NY at New Paltz (NY)
State U of NY Coll at Brockport (NY)
State U of NY Coll at Fredonia (NY)
Texas A&M U–Commerce (TX)
Trinity Christian Coll (IL)
The U of Akron (OH)
U of Alberta (AB, Canada)
U of Calif, Santa Cruz (CA)
U of Evansville (IN)
U of Hartford (CT)
The U of Iowa (IA)
U of Michigan (MI)
U of Missouri–St. Louis (MO)
The U of Montana–Missoula (MT)
U of Montevallo (AL)
U of North Texas (TX)
U of Oregon (OR)
U of Regina (SK, Canada)
U of San Francisco (CA)
U of the South (TN)
U of Toledo (OH)
U of Windsor (ON, Canada)
Washington U in St. Louis (MO)
Western Washington U (WA)
West Virginia Wesleyan Coll (WV)
Wingate U (NC)
Winona State U (MN)
Wright State U (OH)
York U (ON, Canada)

DRIVER AND SAFETY TEACHER EDUCATION

Bridgewater Coll (VA)
U of Northern Iowa (IA)
William Penn U (IA)

DUTCH/FLEMISH

U of Calif, Berkeley (CA)

EARLY CHILDHOOD EDUCATION

Alma Coll (MI)
Arcadia U (PA)
Arlington Baptist Coll (TX)
Auburn U (AL)
Bacone Coll (OK)
Baldwin-Wallace Coll (OH)
Berry Coll (GA)
Bethel U (MN)
Bethesda Christian U (CA)
Bloomsburg U of Pennsylvania (PA)
Brewton-Parker Coll (GA)
Brigham Young U (UT)
Brooklyn Coll of the City U of NY (NY)
Cabrini Coll (PA)
California State U, Chico (CA)
California State U, Fullerton (CA)
California State U, Los Angeles (CA)
Canisius Coll (NY)
Capital U (OH)
Carroll Coll (WI)
Cascade Coll (OR)
Cazenovia Coll (NY)
Cedarville U (OH)
Cedarville U (OH)
Central Connecticut State U (CT)
Central Methodist Coll (MO)
Central Washington U (WA)
Chaminade U of Honolulu (HI)
Charleston Southern U (SC)
Chestnut Hill Coll (PA)
City Coll of the City U of NY (NY)
Clark Atlanta U (GA)
Cleveland State U (OH)
Coastal Carolina U (SC)
Coker Coll (SC)
Colby-Sawyer Coll (NH)
Coll for Lifelong Learning (NH)
Coll of Charleston (SC)
Coll of Saint Mary (NE)
Coll of Santa Fe (NM)
Columbia Coll Chicago (IL)
Columbus State U (GA)
Concordia Coll (AL)
Concordia U (NE)
Concordia U, St. Paul (MN)
Connecticut Coll (CT)
Cornerstone U (MI)
Crown Coll (MN)
Daemen Coll (NY)
Delaware State U (DE)
Duquesne U (PA)
East Central U (OK)
Eastern Connecticut State U (CT)
Eastern Michigan U (MI)
Eastern Washington U (WA)
East Stroudsburg U of Pennsylvania (PA)
Endicott Coll (MA)
Evangel U (MO)
Florida Gulf Coast U (FL)
Florida State U (FL)
Francis Marion U (SC)
Gardner-Webb U (NC)
Georgia Coll & State U (GA)
Georgia State U (GA)
Governors State U (IL)
Grace Bible Coll (MI)
Greensboro Coll (NC)
Greenville Coll (IL)
Hannibal-LaGrange Coll (MO)
Harding U (AR)
Harris-Stowe State Coll (MO)
Hastings Coll (NE)
Hillsdale Coll (MI)
Hofstra U (NY)
Houston Baptist U (TX)
Illinois Coll (IL)
Indiana State U (IN)
Inter American U of PR, Aguadilla Campus (PR)
Iona Coll (NY)
Iowa State U of Science and Technology (IA)
Johnson C. Smith U (NC)
Juniata Coll (PA)
Kean U (NJ)
Kendall Coll (IL)
Kennesaw State U (GA)
Keystone Coll (PA)
King's Coll (PA)
LaGrange Coll (GA)
Lancaster Bible Coll (PA)
Lander U (SC)
Loras Coll (IA)
Louisiana State U and A&M Coll (LA)
Louisiana Tech U (LA)
Lubbock Christian U (TX)
Malone Coll (OH)
McNeese State U (LA)
Mercyhurst Coll (PA)
Messiah Coll (PA)
Miami U Hamilton (OH)
Midwestern State U (TX)
Miles Coll (AL)
Millersville U of Pennsylvania (PA)
Milligan Coll (TN)
Montclair State U (NJ)
Morris Coll (SC)
Mount Union Coll (OH)
Mount Vernon Nazarene U (OH)
Murray State U (KY)
New Mexico State U (NM)
Nicholls State U (LA)
Northeastern Illinois U (IL)
Northern Michigan U (MI)
Northwestern Coll (MN)
Northwestern State U of Louisiana (LA)
Notre Dame Coll (OH)
Oakland U (MI)
Ohio Dominican U (OH)
Ohio Northern U (OH)
The Ohio State U–Mansfield Campus (OH)
Ohio U (OH)
Ohio U–Southern Campus (OH)
Ohio Wesleyan U (OH)
Oklahoma Christian U (OK)
Ouachita Baptist U (AR)
Park U (MO)
Plymouth State U (NH)
Point Park U (PA)
Purdue U (IN)
Ripon Coll (WI)
St. Ambrose U (IA)
Saint Augustine's Coll (NC)
St. Bonaventure U (NY)
St. John's U (NY)
St. Joseph's Coll, Suffolk Campus (NY)
Salve Regina U (RI)
San Jose State U (CA)
Sarah Lawrence Coll (NY)
Schreiner U (TX)
Shawnee State U (OH)
Southern Illinois U Edwardsville (IL)
Southern Nazarene U (OK)
Southwestern Coll (KS)
Southwest Missouri State U (MO)
Spring Hill Coll (AL)
State U of NY Coll at Brockport (NY)
State U of NY Coll at Old Westbury (NY)
State U of NY Coll at Oneonta (NY)
Stephens Coll (MO)
Texas Christian U (TX)
Thomas U (GA)
Toccoa Falls Coll (GA)
Towson U (MD)
U of Arkansas at Fort Smith (AR)
U of Central Florida (FL)
U of Hartford (CT)
U of Houston–Clear Lake (TX)
U of Mary (ND)
U of Michigan–Flint (MI)
U of Minnesota, Crookston (MN)
U of Missouri–Columbia (MO)
U of Missouri–St. Louis (MO)
U of New Orleans (LA)
The U of North Carolina at Chapel Hill (NC)
The U of North Carolina at Greensboro (NC)
The U of North Carolina at Pembroke (NC)
U of North Dakota (ND)
U of Oklahoma (OK)
U of Regina (SK, Canada)
U of Science and Arts of Oklahoma (OK)
The U of Scranton (PA)
U of South Alabama (AL)
U of South Carolina Aiken (SC)
U of Vermont (VT)
The U of West Alabama (AL)
U of West Florida (FL)
U of Wisconsin–Stout (WI)
U of Wisconsin–Whitewater (WI)
Ursuline Coll (OH)
Valdosta State U (GA)
Waldorf Coll (IA)
Wesleyan Coll (GA)
Western Carolina U (NC)
Widener U (PA)
Wilmington Coll (DE)
Xavier U of Louisiana (LA)

EARTH SCIENCES

The U of North Carolina at Charlotte (NC)

EAST ASIAN LANGUAGES

Columbia Coll (NY)
Cornell U (NY)
Eckerd Coll (FL)
Smith Coll (MA)
U of Calif, Los Angeles (CA)
U of Kansas (KS)
U of Oregon (OR)
U of Southern California (CA)
The U of Texas at Austin (TX)

EAST ASIAN LANGUAGES RELATED

Arizona State U (AZ)
Claremont McKenna Coll (CA)
Dartmouth Coll (NH)
Michigan State U (MI)
Northwestern U (IL)
U of Florida (FL)
U of Hawaii at Manoa (HI)
Washington U in St. Louis (MO)

ECOLOGY

Adelphi U (NY)
Appalachian State U (NC)
Averett U (VA)
Ball State U (IN)
Bard Coll (NY)
Barry U (FL)
Bemidji State U (MN)
Bennington Coll (VT)
Boston U (MA)
Bradley U (IL)
Brevard Coll (NC)
California State U, Chico (CA)
California State U, Fresno (CA)
California State U, Hayward (CA)
California State U, Long Beach (CA)
California State U, San Marcos (CA)
Carleton U (ON, Canada)
Carlow Coll (PA)
Clarkson U (NY)
Clark U (MA)
Coll of the Atlantic (ME)
Concordia Coll (NY)
Concordia U (QC, Canada)
Connecticut Coll (CT)
Cornell U (NY)
Dartmouth Coll (NH)
Defiance Coll (OH)
East Central U (OK)
Eastern Kentucky U (KY)
Florida Inst of Technology (FL)
Florida State U (FL)
Franklin Pierce Coll (NH)
Georgetown Coll (KY)
Hampshire Coll (MA)
Harvard U (MA)
Idaho State U (ID)
Iona Coll (NY)
Iowa State U of Science and Technology (IA)
Jacksonville State U (AL)
Juniata Coll (PA)
Keene State Coll (NH)
Kent State U (OH)
Lawrence U (WI)
Lehigh U (PA)
Lenoir-Rhyne Coll (NC)
Manchester Coll (IN)
Marlboro Coll (VT)
McGill U (QC, Canada)
Memorial U of Newfoundland (NL, Canada)
Michigan Technological U (MI)
Minnesota State U Mankato (MN)
Missouri Southern State U (MO)
Morehead State U (KY)
Naropa U (CO)
New Coll of California (CA)
North Carolina State U (NC)
Northern Arizona U (AZ)
Northern Michigan U (MI)
Northland Coll (WI)
Northwestern U (IL)
Oberlin Coll (OH)
Okanagan U Coll (BC, Canada)
Pace U (NY)
Pomona Coll (CA)
Princeton U (NJ)
Rice U (TX)
Rutgers, The State U of New Jersey, New Brunswick/Piscataway (NJ)
St. Cloud State U (MN)
St. John's U (NY)
San Diego State U (CA)
San Francisco State U (CA)
Sarah Lawrence Coll (NY)
Siena Coll (NY)
Sierra Nevada Coll (NV)
Simon's Rock Coll of Bard (MA)
Sonoma State U (CA)
Springfield Coll (MA)
State U of NY Coll of Environ Sci and Forestry (NY)
Sterling Coll (VT)
Susquehanna U (PA)
Texas A&M U (TX)
Tufts U (MA)
Tulane U (LA)
Unity Coll (ME)
Université de Montréal (QC, Canada)
Université de Sherbrooke (QC, Canada)
U Coll of the Cariboo (BC, Canada)
The U of Akron (OH)
The U of Arizona (AZ)
U of Calgary (AB, Canada)
U of Calif, Irvine (CA)
U of Calif, Los Angeles (CA)
U of Calif, San Diego (CA)
U of Calif, Santa Barbara (CA)
U of Calif, Santa Cruz (CA)
U of Colorado at Colorado Springs (CO)
U of Connecticut (CT)
U of Delaware (DE)
U of Georgia (GA)
U of Guelph (ON, Canada)
U of Illinois at Urbana–Champaign (IL)
U of Maine at Machias (ME)
U of Manitoba (MB, Canada)
U of Maryland, Coll Park (MD)
U of Maryland Eastern Shore (MD)
U of Michigan (MI)
U of Michigan–Flint (MI)
U of Minnesota, Twin Cities Campus (MN)
U of New Brunswick Fredericton (NB, Canada)
U of New Hampshire (NH)
U of Northern Iowa (IA)
U of Pittsburgh (PA)
U of Pittsburgh at Johnstown (PA)
The U of Tennessee (TN)
The U of Texas at Austin (TX)
U of Toronto (ON, Canada)
U of Victoria (BC, Canada)
U of Waterloo (ON, Canada)
The U of Western Ontario (ON, Canada)
U of Wisconsin–Milwaukee (WI)
Utah State U (UT)
Vanderbilt U (TN)
Washington Coll (MD)
Washington State U (WA)
West Chester U of Pennsylvania (PA)
Western Washington U (WA)
William Paterson U of New Jersey (NJ)
Winona State U (MN)
Yale U (CT)
York U (ON, Canada)

ECOLOGY, EVOLUTION, SYSTEMATICS AND POPULATION BIOLOGY RELATED

Brigham Young U (UT)
Marywood U (PA)
Sterling Coll (VT)
U of Colorado at Boulder (CO)

E-COMMERCE

Argosy U/Sarasota (FL)
Argosy U/Tampa (FL)
Averett U (VA)
Champlain Coll (VT)
Delaware State U (DE)
DeSales U (PA)
Dominican U of California (CA)
Eastern Michigan U (MI)
Maryville U of Saint Louis (MO)
Messiah Coll (PA)
Mt. Sierra Coll (CA)
Philadelphia U (PA)
Saint Mary's U of Minnesota (MN)
Stetson U (FL)
Texas Christian U (TX)
U of Pennsylvania (PA)
U of Phoenix–Hawaii Campus (HI)
U of Phoenix–Houston Campus (TX)
U of Phoenix–Idaho Campus (ID)
U of Phoenix–Jacksonville Campus (FL)
U of South Alabama (AL)
U of Southern Indiana (IN)
Wilkes U (PA)

ECONOMETRICS AND QUANTITATIVE ECONOMICS

The Colorado Coll (CO)
Hampden-Sydney Coll (VA)
Haverford Coll (PA)
Miami U Hamilton (OH)
San Diego State U (CA)
Southern Methodist U (TX)
State U of NY at Oswego (NY)
United States Naval Acad (MD)
Université Laval (QC, Canada)
U of Calif, San Diego (CA)
U of Guelph (ON, Canada)
U of Northern Iowa (IA)
U of Rhode Island (RI)
U of St. Thomas (MN)
Wake Forest U (NC)
Youngstown State U (OH)

ECONOMICS

Acadia U (NS, Canada)
Adelphi U (NY)
Adrian Coll (MI)
Agnes Scott Coll (GA)
Alabama Ag and Mech U (AL)
Alabama State U (AL)
Albertson Coll of Idaho (ID)
Albertus Magnus Coll (CT)
Albion Coll (MI)
Albright Coll (PA)
Alcorn State U (MS)
Alfred U (NY)
Allegheny Coll (PA)
Alma Coll (MI)
American Intl Coll (MA)
American U (DC)
The American U in Cairo(Egypt)
Amherst Coll (MA)
Andrews U (MI)
Antioch Coll (OH)
Appalachian State U (NC)
Aquinas Coll (MI)
Arizona State U (AZ)
Arkansas State U (AR)
Arkansas Tech U (AR)
Armstrong Atlantic State U (GA)
Ashland U (OH)
Assumption Coll (MA)
Auburn U (AL)
Augsburg Coll (MN)
Augustana Coll (IL)
Augustana Coll (SD)
Aurora U (IL)
Austin Coll (TX)
Ave Maria Coll (MI)
Babson Coll (MA)
Baker U (KS)

Baldwin-Wallace Coll (OH)
Ball State U (IN)
Bard Coll (NY)
Barnard Coll (NY)
Barry U (FL)
Barton Coll (NC)
Bates Coll (ME)
Baylor U (TX)
Bellarmine U (KY)
Belmont Abbey Coll (NC)
Belmont U (TN)
Beloit Coll (WI)
Bemidji State U (MN)
Benedictine Coll (KS)
Benedictine U (IL)
Bentley Coll (MA)
Berea Coll (KY)
Baruch Coll of the City U of NY (NY)
Berry Coll (GA)
Bethany Coll (WV)
Bethel U (MN)
Birmingham-Southern Coll (AL)
Bishop's U (QC, Canada)
Bloomfield Coll (NJ)
Bloomsburg U of Pennsylvania (PA)
Bluffton Coll (OH)
Boise State U (ID)
Boston Coll (MA)
Boston U (MA)
Bowdoin Coll (ME)
Bowie State U (MD)
Bowling Green State U (OH)
Bradley U (IL)
Brandeis U (MA)
Bridgewater Coll (VA)
Bridgewater State Coll (MA)
Brigham Young U (UT)
Brock U (ON, Canada)
Brooklyn Coll of the City U of NY (NY)
Brown U (RI)
Bryant Coll (RI)
Bryn Mawr Coll (PA)
Bucknell U (PA)
State U of NY Coll at Buffalo (NY)
Butler U (IN)
California Inst of Technology (CA)
California Lutheran U (CA)
California Polytechnic State U, San Luis Obispo (CA)
California State Polytechnic U, Pomona (CA)
California State U, Chico (CA)
California State U, Dominguez Hills (CA)
California State U, Fresno (CA)
California State U, Fullerton (CA)
California State U, Hayward (CA)
California State U, Long Beach (CA)
California State U, Los Angeles (CA)
California State U, Sacramento (CA)
California State U, San Bernardino (CA)
California State U, San Marcos (CA)
California State U, Stanislaus (CA)
California U of Pennsylvania (PA)
Calvin Coll (MI)
Campbellsville U (KY)
Campbell U (NC)
Canadian Mennonite U (MB, Canada)
Canisius Coll (NY)
Capital U (OH)
Carleton Coll (MN)
Carleton U (ON, Canada)
Carnegie Mellon U (PA)
Carson-Newman Coll (TN)
Carthage Coll (WI)
Case Western Reserve U (OH)
The Catholic U of America (DC)
Centenary Coll of Louisiana (LA)
Central Coll (IA)
Central Connecticut State U (CT)
Central Methodist Coll (MO)
Central Michigan U (MI)
Central Missouri State U (MO)
Central State U (OH)
Central Washington U (WA)
Centre Coll (KY)
Charleston Southern U (SC)
Chatham Coll (PA)
Cheyney U of Pennsylvania (PA)
Chicago State U (IL)
Christian Brothers U (TN)
Christopher Newport U (VA)
City Coll of the City U of NY (NY)
Claremont McKenna Coll (CA)
Clarion U of Pennsylvania (PA)
Clark Atlanta U (GA)
Clarke Coll (IA)
Clark U (MA)
Clemson U (SC)
Cleveland State U (OH)
Coe Coll (IA)
Colby Coll (ME)
Colgate U (NY)
Coll of Charleston (SC)
Coll of Mount Saint Vincent (NY)
The Coll of New Jersey (NJ)
The Coll of New Rochelle (NY)
Coll of Notre Dame of Maryland (MD)
Coll of Saint Benedict (MN)
Coll of St. Catherine (MN)
Coll of Saint Elizabeth (NJ)
Coll of Staten Island of the City U of NY (NY)
Coll of the Atlantic (ME)
Coll of the Holy Cross (MA)
The Coll of William and Mary (VA)
The Coll of Wooster (OH)
The Colorado Coll (CO)
Colorado School of Mines (CO)
Colorado State U (CO)
Columbia Coll (NY)
Columbia U, School of General Studies (NY)
Concordia Coll (MN)
Concordia U (QC, Canada)
Concordia U Wisconsin (WI)
Connecticut Coll (CT)
Converse Coll (SC)
Cornell Coll (IA)
Cornell U (NY)
Covenant Coll (GA)
Creighton U (NE)
Dalhousie U (NS, Canada)
Dartmouth Coll (NH)
Davidson Coll (NC)
Davis & Elkins Coll (WV)
Denison U (OH)
DePaul U (IL)
DePauw U (IN)
Dickinson Coll (PA)
Dillard U (LA)
Doane Coll (NE)
Dominican Coll (NY)
Dominican U (IL)
Dowling Coll (NY)
Drake U (IA)
Drew U (NJ)
Drury U (MO)
Duke U (NC)
Duquesne U (PA)
Earlham Coll (IN)
East Carolina U (NC)
Eastern Connecticut State U (CT)
Eastern Illinois U (IL)
Eastern Kentucky U (KY)
Eastern Mennonite U (VA)
Eastern Michigan U (MI)
Eastern Oregon U (OR)
Eastern Washington U (WA)
East Stroudsburg U of Pennsylvania (PA)
Eckerd Coll (FL)
Edgewood Coll (WI)
Edinboro U of Pennsylvania (PA)
Elizabethtown Coll (PA)
Elmhurst Coll (IL)
Elmira Coll (NY)
Elon U (NC)
Emory & Henry Coll (VA)
Emory U (GA)
Emporia State U (KS)
Eugene Lang Coll, New School U (NY)
Eureka Coll (IL)
Excelsior Coll (NY)
Fairfield U (CT)
Fairleigh Dickinson U, Florham (NJ)
Fairmont State Coll (WV)
Florida Ag and Mech U (FL)
Florida Atlantic U (FL)
Florida Intl U (FL)
Florida Southern Coll (FL)
Florida State U (FL)
Fordham U (NY)
Fort Hays State U (KS)
Fort Lewis Coll (CO)
Fort Valley State U (GA)
Framingham State Coll (MA)
Franciscan U of Steubenville (OH)
Francis Marion U (SC)
Franklin and Marshall Coll (PA)
Franklin Coll (IN)
Franklin Pierce Coll (NH)
Frostburg State U (MD)
Furman U (SC)
Gallaudet U (DC)
George Mason U (VA)
Georgetown Coll (KY)
Georgetown U (DC)
The George Washington U (DC)
Georgia Southern U (GA)
Georgia State U (GA)
Gettysburg Coll (PA)
Gonzaga U (WA)
Gordon Coll (MA)
Goshen Coll (IN)
Goucher Coll (MD)
Graceland U (IA)
Grand Canyon U (AZ)
Grand Valley State U (MI)
Grinnell Coll (IA)
Grove City Coll (PA)
Guilford Coll (NC)
Gustavus Adolphus Coll (MN)
Hamilton Coll (NY)
Hamline U (MN)
Hampden-Sydney Coll (VA)
Hampshire Coll (MA)
Hampton U (VA)
Hanover Coll (IN)
Harding U (AR)
Hardin-Simmons U (TX)
Hartwick Coll (NY)
Harvard U (MA)
Hastings Coll (NE)
Haverford Coll (PA)
Hawai'i Pacific U (HI)
Heidelberg Coll (OH)
Hendrix Coll (AR)
Hillsdale Coll (MI)
Hiram Coll (OH)
Hobart and William Smith Colls (NY)
Hofstra U (NY)
Hollins U (VA)
Hood Coll (MD)
Hope Coll (MI)
Houston Baptist U (TX)
Howard U (DC)
Humboldt State U (CA)
Hunter Coll of the City U of NY (NY)
Huntington Coll (IN)
Idaho State U (ID)
Illinois Coll (IL)
Illinois State U (IL)
Illinois Wesleyan U (IL)
Immaculata U (PA)
Indiana State U (IN)
Indiana U Bloomington (IN)
Indiana U Northwest (IN)
Indiana U of Pennsylvania (PA)
Indiana U–Purdue U Fort Wayne (IN)
Indiana U–Purdue U Indianapolis (IN)
Indiana U South Bend (IN)
Indiana U Southeast (IN)
Inter American U of PR, Fajardo Campus (PR)
Inter American U of PR, San Germán Campus (PR)
Iona Coll (NY)
Iowa State U of Science and Technology (IA)
Ithaca Coll (NY)
Jacksonville State U (AL)
Jacksonville U (FL)
James Madison U (VA)
Jarvis Christian Coll (TX)
John Carroll U (OH)
The Johns Hopkins U (MD)
Johnson C. Smith U (NC)
Juniata Coll (PA)
Kansas State U (KS)
Kean U (NJ)
Keene State Coll (NH)
Kennesaw State U (GA)
Kent State U (OH)
Kenyon Coll (OH)
King Coll (TN)
King's Coll (PA)
Knox Coll (IL)
Kutztown U of Pennsylvania (PA)
Lafayette Coll (PA)
LaGrange Coll (GA)
Lake Forest Coll (IL)
Lakehead U (ON, Canada)
Lake Superior State U (MI)
Lamar U (TX)
La Salle U (PA)
Laurentian U (ON, Canada)
Lawrence U (WI)
Lebanon Valley Coll (PA)
Lehman Coll of the City U of NY (NY)
Le Moyne Coll (NY)
Lenoir-Rhyne Coll (NC)
Lewis & Clark Coll (OR)
Lewis U (IL)
Liberty U (VA)
Lincoln Memorial U (TN)
Lincoln U (MO)
Lincoln U (PA)
Lindenwood U (MO)
Linfield Coll (OR)
Lock Haven U of Pennsylvania (PA)
Long Island U, Brooklyn Campus (NY)
Long Island U, C.W. Post Campus (NY)
Longwood U (VA)
Loras Coll (IA)
Louisiana Coll (LA)
Louisiana State U and A&M Coll (LA)
Loyola Coll in Maryland (MD)
Loyola Marymount U (CA)
Loyola U Chicago (IL)
Loyola U New Orleans (LA)
Luther Coll (IA)
Lycoming Coll (PA)
Lynchburg Coll (VA)
Lyon Coll (AR)
Macalester Coll (MN)
Manchester Coll (IN)
Manhattan Coll (NY)
Manhattanville Coll (NY)
Mansfield U of Pennsylvania (PA)
Marietta Coll (OH)
Marist Coll (NY)
Marlboro Coll (VT)
Marquette U (WI)
Marshall U (WV)
Mary Baldwin Coll (VA)
Marymount Coll of Fordham U (NY)
Marymount U (VA)
Maryville Coll (TN)
Mary Washington Coll (VA)
Massachusetts Coll of Liberal Arts (MA)
Massachusetts Inst of Technology (MA)
McDaniel Coll (MD)
McGill U (QC, Canada)
McKendree Coll (IL)
Memorial U of Newfoundland (NL, Canada)
Mercer U (GA)
Meredith Coll (NC)
Merrimack Coll (MA)
Messiah Coll (PA)
Methodist Coll (NC)
Metropolitan State Coll of Denver (CO)
Metropolitan State U (MN)
Miami U (OH)
Miami U Hamilton (OH)
Michigan State U (MI)
Middlebury Coll (VT)
Middle Tennessee State U (TN)
Midwestern State U (TX)
Millersville U of Pennsylvania (PA)
Millsaps Coll (MS)
Mills Coll (CA)
Minnesota State U Mankato (MN)
Minnesota State U Moorhead (MN)
Minot State U (ND)
Mississippi State U (MS)
Missouri Valley Coll (MO)
Missouri Western State Coll (MO)
Monmouth Coll (IL)
Monmouth U (NJ)
Montana State U–Bozeman (MT)
Montclair State U (NJ)
Moravian Coll (PA)
Morehouse Coll (GA)
Morgan State U (MD)
Mount Allison U (NB, Canada)
Mount Holyoke Coll (MA)
Mount Saint Mary's Coll and Sem (MD)
Mount Saint Vincent U (NS, Canada)
Mount Union Coll (OH)
Muhlenberg Coll (PA)
Murray State U (KY)
Nazareth Coll of Rochester (NY)
Nebraska Wesleyan U (NE)
New Coll of Florida (FL)
New Jersey City U (NJ)
New Mexico State U (NM)
New York Inst of Technology (NY)
New York U (NY)
Niagara U (NY)
Nichols Coll (MA)
Nipissing U (ON, Canada)
North Carolina State U (NC)
North Central Coll (IL)
North Dakota State U (ND)
Northeastern Illinois U (IL)
Northeastern U (MA)
Northern Arizona U (AZ)
Northern Illinois U (IL)
Northern Michigan U (MI)
Northern State U (SD)
Northland Coll (WI)
North Park U (IL)
Northwestern Coll (IA)
Northwestern U (IL)
Oakland U (MI)
Oberlin Coll (OH)
Occidental Coll (CA)
Oglethorpe U (GA)
Ohio Dominican U (OH)
The Ohio State U (OH)
Ohio U (OH)
Ohio Wesleyan U (OH)
Okanagan U Coll (BC, Canada)
Oklahoma State U (OK)
Old Dominion U (VA)
Olivet Coll (MI)
Olivet Nazarene U (IL)
Oregon State U (OR)
Otterbein Coll (OH)
Pace U (NY)
Pacific Lutheran U (WA)
Pacific U (OR)
Park U (MO)
Penn State U Abington Coll (PA)
Penn State U Altoona Coll (PA)
Penn State U at Erie, The Behrend Coll (PA)
Penn State U Beaver Campus of the Commonwealth Coll (PA)
Penn State U Berks Cmps of Berks-Lehigh Valley Coll (PA)
Penn State U Delaware County Campus of the Commonwealth Coll (PA)
Penn State U DuBois Campus of the Commonwealth Coll (PA)
Penn State U Fayette Campus of the Commonwealth Coll (PA)
Penn State U Hazleton Campus of the Commonwealth Coll (PA)
Penn State U Lehigh Valley Cmps of Berks-Lehigh Valley Coll (PA)
Penn State U McKeesport Campus of the Commonwealth Coll (PA)
Penn State U Mont Alto Campus of the Commonwealth Coll (PA)
Penn State U New Kensington Campus of the Commonwealth Coll (PA)
Penn State U Schuylkill Campus of the Capital Coll (PA)
Penn State U Shenango Campus of the Commonwealth Coll (PA)
Penn State U Univ Park Campus (PA)
Penn State U Wilkes-Barre Campus of the Commonwealth Coll (PA)
Penn State U Worthington Scranton Cmps Commonwealth Coll (PA)
Penn State U York Campus of the Commonwealth Coll (PA)
Pepperdine U, Malibu (CA)
Pfeiffer U (NC)
Pittsburg State U (KS)
Pitzer Coll (CA)
Pomona Coll (CA)
Pontifical Catholic U of Puerto Rico (PR)
Portland State U (OR)
Presbyterian Coll (SC)
Princeton U (NJ)
Principia Coll (IL)
Providence Coll (RI)
Purdue U (IN)
Queens Coll of the City U of NY (NY)
Queen's U at Kingston (ON, Canada)
Quinnipiac U (CT)
Radford U (VA)
Ramapo Coll of New Jersey (NJ)
Randolph-Macon Coll (VA)
Randolph-Macon Woman's Coll (VA)
Reed Coll (OR)
Regis U (CO)
Rensselaer Polytechnic Inst (NY)
Rhode Island Coll (RI)
Rhodes Coll (TN)
Rice U (TX)
The Richard Stockton Coll of New Jersey (NJ)
Richmond, The American Intl U in London(United Kingdom)
Rider U (NJ)
Ripon Coll (WI)
Roanoke Coll (VA)
Robert Morris U (PA)
Rochester Inst of Technology (NY)
Rockford Coll (IL)
Rockhurst U (MO)
Rocky Mountain Coll (MT)
Rollins Coll (FL)
Roosevelt U (IL)
Rose-Hulman Inst of Technology (IN)
Rosemont Coll (PA)
Rowan U (NJ)

Rutgers, The State U of New Jersey, Camden (NJ)
Rutgers, The State U of New Jersey, Newark (NJ)
Rutgers, The State U of New Jersey, New Brunswick/Piscataway (NJ)
Ryerson U (ON, Canada)
Sacred Heart U (CT)
Saginaw Valley State U (MI)
St. Ambrose U (IA)
Saint Anselm Coll (NH)
St. Cloud State U (MN)
St. Edward's U (TX)
St. Francis Coll (NY)
Saint Francis U (PA)
St. Francis Xavier U (NS, Canada)
St. John Fisher Coll (NY)
Saint John's U (MN)
St. John's U (NY)
Saint Joseph Coll (CT)
Saint Joseph's Coll (IN)
St. Joseph's Coll, Suffolk Campus (NY)
Saint Joseph's U (PA)
St. Lawrence U (NY)
Saint Louis U (MO)
Saint Martin's Coll (WA)
Saint Mary's Coll (IN)
Saint Mary's Coll of California (CA)
St. Mary's Coll of Maryland (MD)
St. Mary's U of San Antonio (TX)
Saint Michael's Coll (VT)
St. Norbert Coll (WI)
St. Olaf Coll (MN)
St. Thomas U (NB, Canada)
Saint Vincent Coll (PA)
Salem Coll (NC)
Salem State Coll (MA)
Salisbury U (MD)
Salve Regina U (RI)
San Diego State U (CA)
San Francisco State U (CA)
San Jose State U (CA)
Santa Clara U (CA)
Sarah Lawrence Coll (NY)
Schiller Intl U(Germany)
Schiller Intl U(United Kingdom)
Schiller Intl U, American Coll of Switzerland(Switzerland)
Scripps Coll (CA)
Seattle Pacific U (WA)
Seattle U (WA)
Seton Hall U (NJ)
Seton Hill U (PA)
Shepherd U (WV)
Shippensburg U of Pennsylvania (PA)
Shorter Coll (GA)
Siena Coll (NY)
Simmons Coll (MA)
Simon Fraser U (BC, Canada)
Simpson Coll (IA)
Skidmore Coll (NY)
Slippery Rock U of Pennsylvania (PA)
Smith Coll (MA)
Sonoma State U (CA)
South Carolina State U (SC)
South Dakota State U (SD)
Southeastern Oklahoma State U (OK)
Southeast Missouri State U (MO)
Southern Connecticut State U (CT)
Southern Illinois U Carbondale (IL)
Southern Illinois U Edwardsville (IL)
Southern Methodist U (TX)
Southern Oregon U (OR)
Southern Utah U (UT)
Southwestern U (TX)
Southwest Missouri State U (MO)
Spelman Coll (GA)
Stanford U (CA)
State U of NY at Binghamton (NY)
State U of NY at New Paltz (NY)
State U of NY at Oswego (NY)
Plattsburgh State U of NY (NY)
State U of NY Coll at Brockport (NY)
State U of NY Coll at Cortland (NY)
State U of NY Coll at Fredonia (NY)
State U of NY Coll at Geneseo (NY)
State U of NY Coll at Oneonta (NY)
State U of NY Coll at Potsdam (NY)
State U of NY Empire State Coll (NY)
State U of West Georgia (GA)
Stetson U (FL)
Stonehill Coll (MA)
Stony Brook U, State U of New York (NY)
Strayer U (DC)
Suffolk U (MA)
Susquehanna U (PA)
Swarthmore Coll (PA)
Sweet Briar Coll (VA)
Syracuse U (NY)
Talladega Coll (AL)
Tarleton State U (TX)
Taylor U (IN)
Tennessee Technological U (TN)
Texas A&M U (TX)
Texas A&M U–Commerce (TX)
Texas A&M U–Kingsville (TX)
Texas Christian U (TX)
Texas Lutheran U (TX)
Texas Southern U (TX)
Texas State U-San Marcos (TX)
Texas Tech U (TX)
Texas Wesleyan U (TX)
Thomas Edison State Coll (NJ)
Thomas More Coll (KY)
Tougaloo Coll (MS)
Towson U (MD)
Transylvania U (KY)
Trent U (ON, Canada)
Trinity Coll (CT)
Trinity Coll (DC)
Trinity U (TX)
Truman State U (MO)
Tufts U (MA)
Tulane U (LA)
Tuskegee U (AL)
Union Coll (NY)
Union U (TN)
United States Air Force Acad (CO)
United States Military Acad (NY)
United States Naval Acad (MD)
Université de Montréal (QC, Canada)
Université de Sherbrooke (QC, Canada)
Université Laval (QC, Canada)
State U of NY at Albany (NY)
U at Buffalo, The State U of New York (NY)
U Coll of the Cariboo (BC, Canada)
The U of Akron (OH)
U of Alaska Fairbanks (AK)
U of Alberta (AB, Canada)
The U of Arizona (AZ)
U of Arkansas (AR)
U of Arkansas at Little Rock (AR)
U of Baltimore (MD)
U of Bridgeport (CT)
The U of British Columbia (BC, Canada)
U of Calgary (AB, Canada)
U of Calif, Berkeley (CA)
U of Calif, Davis (CA)
U of Calif, Irvine (CA)
U of Calif, Los Angeles (CA)
U of Calif, Riverside (CA)
U of Calif, San Diego (CA)
U of Calif, Santa Barbara (CA)
U of Calif, Santa Cruz (CA)
U of Central Arkansas (AR)
U of Central Florida (FL)
U of Chicago (IL)
U of Cincinnati (OH)
U of Colorado at Boulder (CO)
U of Colorado at Colorado Springs (CO)
U of Colorado at Denver (CO)
U of Connecticut (CT)
U of Dallas (TX)
U of Dayton (OH)
U of Delaware (DE)
U of Denver (CO)
U of Detroit Mercy (MI)
U of Evansville (IN)
The U of Findlay (OH)
U of Florida (FL)
U of Georgia (GA)
U of Guelph (ON, Canada)
U of Hartford (CT)
U of Hawaii at Hilo (HI)
U of Hawaii at Manoa (HI)
U of Houston (TX)
U of Idaho (ID)
U of Illinois at Chicago (IL)
U of Illinois at Springfield (IL)
U of Illinois at Urbana–Champaign (IL)
The U of Iowa (IA)
U of Kansas (KS)
U of Kentucky (KY)
U of King's Coll (NS, Canada)
The U of Lethbridge (AB, Canada)
U of Louisville (KY)
U of Maine (ME)
U of Manitoba (MB, Canada)
U of Mary Hardin-Baylor (TX)
U of Maryland, Baltimore County (MD)
U of Maryland, Coll Park (MD)
U of Massachusetts Amherst (MA)
U of Massachusetts Boston (MA)
U of Massachusetts Dartmouth (MA)
U of Massachusetts Lowell (MA)
The U of Memphis (TN)
U of Michigan (MI)
U of Michigan–Dearborn (MI)
U of Michigan–Flint (MI)
U of Minnesota, Duluth (MN)
U of Minnesota, Morris (MN)
U of Minnesota, Twin Cities Campus (MN)
U of Mississippi (MS)
U of Missouri–Columbia (MO)
U of Missouri–Kansas City (MO)
U of Missouri–Rolla (MO)
U of Missouri–St. Louis (MO)
U of Mobile (AL)
The U of Montana–Missoula (MT)
U of Nebraska–Lincoln (NE)
U of Nevada, Las Vegas (NV)
U of New Brunswick Fredericton (NB, Canada)
U of New Hampshire (NH)
U of New Haven (CT)
U of New Mexico (NM)
U of New Orleans (LA)
The U of North Carolina at Asheville (NC)
The U of North Carolina at Chapel Hill (NC)
The U of North Carolina at Charlotte (NC)
The U of North Carolina at Greensboro (NC)
The U of North Carolina at Wilmington (NC)
U of North Dakota (ND)
U of Northern Colorado (CO)
U of Northern Iowa (IA)
U of North Florida (FL)
U of North Texas (TX)
U of Notre Dame (IN)
U of Oklahoma (OK)
U of Oregon (OR)
U of Ottawa (ON, Canada)
U of Pennsylvania (PA)
U of Pittsburgh (PA)
U of Pittsburgh at Bradford (PA)
U of Pittsburgh at Johnstown (PA)
U of Prince Edward Island (PE, Canada)
U of Puerto Rico, Cayey U Coll (PR)
U of Puget Sound (WA)
U of Redlands (CA)
U of Regina (SK, Canada)
U of Rhode Island (RI)
U of Richmond (VA)
U of Rochester (NY)
U of Saint Francis (IN)
U of St. Thomas (MN)
U of St. Thomas (TX)
U of San Diego (CA)
U of San Francisco (CA)
U of Saskatchewan (SK, Canada)
U of Science and Arts of Oklahoma (OK)
The U of Scranton (PA)
U of Sioux Falls (SD)
U of South Carolina (SC)
The U of South Dakota (SD)
U of Southern California (CA)
U of Southern Indiana (IN)
U of Southern Maine (ME)
U of South Florida (FL)
The U of Tampa (FL)
The U of Tennessee (TN)
The U of Tennessee at Chattanooga (TN)
The U of Tennessee at Martin (TN)
The U of Texas at Arlington (TX)
The U of Texas at Austin (TX)
The U of Texas at Dallas (TX)
The U of Texas–Pan American (TX)
U of the District of Columbia (DC)
U of the Pacific (CA)
U of the South (TN)
U of Toledo (OH)
U of Toronto (ON, Canada)
U of Tulsa (OK)
U of Utah (UT)
U of Vermont (VT)
U of Victoria (BC, Canada)
U of Virginia (VA)
The U of Virginia's Coll at Wise (VA)
U of Washington (WA)
U of Waterloo (ON, Canada)
The U of Western Ontario (ON, Canada)
U of Windsor (ON, Canada)
U of Wisconsin–Eau Claire (WI)
U of Wisconsin–Green Bay (WI)
U of Wisconsin–La Crosse (WI)
U of Wisconsin–Madison (WI)
U of Wisconsin–Milwaukee (WI)
U of Wisconsin–Oshkosh (WI)
U of Wisconsin–Parkside (WI)
U of Wisconsin–Platteville (WI)
U of Wisconsin–River Falls (WI)
U of Wisconsin–Stevens Point (WI)
U of Wisconsin–Superior (WI)
Ursinus Coll (PA)
Utah State U (UT)
Utica Coll (NY)
Valdosta State U (GA)
Valparaiso U (IN)
Vanderbilt U (TN)
Vassar Coll (NY)
Villanova U (PA)
Virginia Military Inst (VA)
Virginia Polytechnic Inst and State U (VA)
Wabash Coll (IN)
Wake Forest U (NC)
Walla Walla Coll (WA)
Warren Wilson Coll (NC)
Wartburg Coll (IA)
Washburn U (KS)
Washington & Jefferson Coll (PA)
Washington and Lee U (VA)
Washington Coll (MD)
Washington State U (WA)
Washington U in St. Louis (MO)
Wayne State U (MI)
Weber State U (UT)
Webster U (MO)
Wellesley Coll (MA)
Wells Coll (NY)
Wesleyan Coll (GA)
Wesleyan U (CT)
Western Connecticut State U (CT)
Western Illinois U (IL)
Western Kentucky U (KY)
Western Michigan U (MI)
Western New England Coll (MA)
Western Oregon U (OR)
Western State Coll of Colorado (CO)
Western Washington U (WA)
Westfield State Coll (MA)
Westminster Coll (MO)
Westminster Coll (PA)
Westmont Coll (CA)
West Texas A&M U (TX)
West Virginia State Coll (WV)
West Virginia U (WV)
West Virginia Wesleyan Coll (WV)
Wheaton Coll (IL)
Wheaton Coll (MA)
Whitman Coll (WA)
Whitworth Coll (WA)
Wichita State U (KS)
Widener U (PA)
Wilberforce U (OH)
Willamette U (OR)
William Jewell Coll (MO)
Williams Coll (MA)
Wingate U (NC)
Winona State U (MN)
Winston-Salem State U (NC)
Wittenberg U (OH)
Wofford Coll (SC)
Worcester Polytechnic Inst (MA)
Worcester State Coll (MA)
Wright State U (OH)
Xavier U (OH)
Yale U (CT)
York Coll of Pennsylvania (PA)
York Coll of the City U of New York (NY)
York U (ON, Canada)
Youngstown State U (OH)

ECONOMICS RELATED

Assumption Coll (MA)
Barnard Coll (NY)
Bloomsburg U of Pennsylvania (PA)
California State U, Chico (CA)
Claremont McKenna Coll (CA)
The Colorado Coll (CO)
Eastern Michigan U (MI)
Marymount U (VA)
Nevada State Coll at Henderson (NV)
Simon's Rock Coll of Bard (MA)
State U of West Georgia (GA)
Truman State U (MO)
U at Buffalo, The State U of New York (NY)
The U of Akron (OH)
U of Dallas (TX)
U of Hartford (CT)
U of Illinois at Urbana–Champaign (IL)
Valparaiso U (IN)
Wright State U (OH)

EDUCATION

Acadia U (NS, Canada)
Adelphi U (NY)
Adrian Coll (MI)
Alabama State U (AL)
Albertus Magnus Coll (CT)
Albion Coll (MI)
Alderson-Broaddus Coll (WV)
Allegheny Coll (PA)
Allen U (SC)
Alma Coll (MI)
Alvernia Coll (PA)
Alverno Coll (WI)
American Intl Coll (MA)
American U of Puerto Rico (PR)
Anderson Coll (SC)
Andrews U (MI)
Antioch Coll (OH)
Aquinas Coll (MI)
Arcadia U (PA)
Arlington Baptist Coll (TX)
Ashland U (OH)
Atlantic Baptist U (NB, Canada)
Atlantic Union Coll (MA)
Augsburg Coll (MN)
Augustana Coll (IL)
Bacone Coll (OK)
Baldwin-Wallace Coll (OH)
Ball State U (IN)
The Baptist Coll of Florida (FL)
Barry U (FL)
Baylor U (TX)
Becker Coll (MA)
Bellarmine U (KY)
Belmont Abbey Coll (NC)
Belmont U (TN)
Beloit Coll (WI)
Bemidji State U (MN)
Benedictine U (IL)
Berea Coll (KY)
Baruch Coll of the City U of NY (NY)
Bethany Coll (KS)
Bethany Coll (WV)
Bethel Coll (IN)
Bethel Coll (TN)
Biola U (CA)
Birmingham-Southern Coll (AL)
Bishop's U (QC, Canada)
Bluefield Coll (VA)
Boise State U (ID)
Boston U (MA)
Bowie State U (MD)
Bowling Green State U (OH)
Brenau U (GA)
Brescia U (KY)
Brevard Coll (NC)
Brewton-Parker Coll (GA)
Briar Cliff U (IA)
Bridgewater State Coll (MA)
Brigham Young U–Hawaii (HI)
Brock U (ON, Canada)
Brooklyn Coll of the City U of NY (NY)
Brown U (RI)
Bryan Coll (TN)
Bucknell U (PA)
Cabrini Coll (PA)
California U of Pennsylvania (PA)
Cameron U (OK)
Campbell U (NC)
Capital U (OH)
Cardinal Stritch U (WI)
Carroll Coll (MT)
Carroll Coll (WI)
Carson-Newman Coll (TN)
Carthage Coll (WI)
Catawba Coll (NC)
The Catholic U of America (DC)
Cedar Crest Coll (PA)
Centenary Coll (NJ)
Central Methodist Coll (MO)
Central Missouri State U (MO)
Charleston Southern U (SC)
Cheyney U of Pennsylvania (PA)
Chicago State U (IL)
Christian Brothers U (TN)
Christian Heritage Coll (CA)
Christopher Newport U (VA)
City Coll of the City U of NY (NY)
Clarion U of Pennsylvania (PA)
Clark Atlanta U (GA)
Clarke Coll (IA)
Clark U (MA)
Clearwater Christian Coll (FL)
Cleveland State U (OH)
Coe Coll (IA)
Coker Coll (SC)
Colgate U (NY)
Coll of Mount Saint Vincent (NY)
The Coll of New Jersey (NJ)
The Coll of New Rochelle (NY)
Coll of Notre Dame of Maryland (MD)
Coll of Saint Benedict (MN)
Coll of St. Catherine (MN)
Coll of St. Joseph (VT)
Coll of Saint Mary (NE)
Coll of the Atlantic (ME)

Coll of the Ozarks (MO)
Coll of the Southwest (NM)
Colorado State U-Pueblo (CO)
Columbia Coll (MO)
Concord Coll (WV)
Concordia Coll (MN)
Concordia Coll (NY)
Concordia U (IL)
Concordia U (NE)
Concordia U (OR)
Concordia U Coll of Alberta (AB, Canada)
Concordia U, St. Paul (MN)
Concordia U Wisconsin (WI)
Converse Coll (SC)
Cornell U (NY)
Cornerstone U (MI)
Cumberland U (TN)
Curry Coll (MA)
Dakota State U (SD)
Dakota Wesleyan U (SD)
Dallas Baptist U (TX)
Dallas Christian Coll (TX)
Dana Coll (NE)
Davis & Elkins Coll (WV)
Defiance Coll (OH)
Delta State U (MS)
DePaul U (IL)
Dickinson State U (ND)
Dillard U (LA)
Dominican Coll (NY)
Dordt Coll (IA)
Dowling Coll (NY)
Drury U (MO)
Duquesne U (PA)
D'Youville Coll (NY)
Earlham Coll (IN)
East Central U (OK)
Eastern Kentucky U (KY)
Eastern Nazarene Coll (MA)
Eastern Oregon U (OR)
East Texas Baptist U (TX)
Edgewood Coll (WI)
Elizabeth City State U (NC)
Elizabethtown Coll (PA)
Elmhurst Coll (IL)
Elmira Coll (NY)
Elms Coll (MA)
Elon U (NC)
Emory U (GA)
Eugene Lang Coll, New School U (NY)
Eureka Coll (IL)
Evangel U (MO)
Fairmont State Coll (WV)
Faulkner U (AL)
Fayetteville State U (NC)
Ferris State U (MI)
Ferrum Coll (VA)
Florida Ag and Mech U (FL)
Florida Southern Coll (FL)
Fontbonne U (MO)
Fordham U (NY)
Fort Lewis Coll (CO)
Framingham State Coll (MA)
The Franciscan U (IA)
Franklin Pierce Coll (NH)
Freed-Hardeman U (TN)
Fresno Pacific U (CA)
Furman U (SC)
Gallaudet U (DC)
Gardner-Webb U (NC)
Georgetown Coll (KY)
Georgia Southern U (GA)
Georgia Southwestern State U (GA)
Gettysburg Coll (PA)
Glenville State Coll (WV)
Goshen Coll (IN)
Goucher Coll (MD)
Graceland U (IA)
Grand Valley State U (MI)
Greensboro Coll (NC)
Grinnell Coll (IA)
Gustavus Adolphus Coll (MN)
Gwynedd-Mercy Coll (PA)
Hamline U (MN)
Hampshire Coll (MA)
Hampton U (VA)
Hannibal-LaGrange Coll (MO)
Hardin-Simmons U (TX)
Hastings Coll (NE)
Haverford Coll (PA)
Heidelberg Coll (OH)
High Point U (NC)
Hillsdale Coll (MI)
Hofstra U (NY)
Houston Baptist U (TX)
Howard Payne U (TX)
Howard U (DC)
Humboldt State U (CA)
Huntingdon Coll (AL)
Huntington Coll (IN)
Huston-Tillotson Coll (TX)
Illinois Coll (IL)
Illinois Wesleyan U (IL)
Immaculata U (PA)
Indiana U Bloomington (IN)
Indiana U East (IN)
Indiana U Northwest (IN)
Indiana U–Purdue U Fort Wayne (IN)
Indiana U–Purdue U Indianapolis (IN)
Indiana U South Bend (IN)
Indiana U Southeast (IN)
Inter Amer U of PR, Barranquitas Campus (PR)
Inter American U of PR, Fajardo Campus (PR)
Inter American U of PR, Ponce Campus (PR)
Inter American U of PR, San Germán Campus (PR)
Iona Coll (NY)
Iowa State U of Science and Technology (IA)
Iowa Wesleyan Coll (IA)
Jacksonville State U (AL)
John Brown U (AR)
John Carroll U (OH)
Johnson C. Smith U (NC)
Johnson State Coll (VT)
Judson Coll (AL)
Judson Coll (IL)
Juniata Coll (PA)
Kansas Wesleyan U (KS)
Keene State Coll (NH)
Kendall Coll (IL)
Kent State U (OH)
Keystone Coll (PA)
King Coll (TN)
The King's Coll (NY)
Knox Coll (IL)
Kutztown U of Pennsylvania (PA)
LaGrange Coll (GA)
Lake Forest Coll (IL)
Lakehead U (ON, Canada)
Lake Superior State U (MI)
Lamar U (TX)
Lambuth U (TN)
Lancaster Bible Coll (PA)
La Salle U (PA)
Lasell Coll (MA)
Laurentian U (ON, Canada)
Lehigh U (PA)
Lenoir-Rhyne Coll (NC)
Lesley U (MA)
Lewis U (IL)
Limestone Coll (SC)
Lincoln Memorial U (TN)
Lincoln U (PA)
Lindenwood U (MO)
Lindsey Wilson Coll (KY)
Lipscomb U (TN)
Livingstone Coll (NC)
Lock Haven U of Pennsylvania (PA)
Long Island U, Brooklyn Campus (NY)
Long Island U, C.W. Post Campus (NY)
Longwood U (VA)
Loras Coll (IA)
Loyola Coll in Maryland (MD)
Loyola U New Orleans (LA)
Lubbock Christian U (TX)
Lycoming Coll (PA)
Lynchburg Coll (VA)
Lynn U (FL)
Madonna U (MI)
Malaspina U-Coll (BC, Canada)
Manchester Coll (IN)
Manhattan Coll (NY)
Manhattanville Coll (NY)
Mansfield U of Pennsylvania (PA)
Marian Coll (IN)
Marian Coll of Fond du Lac (WI)
Marietta Coll (OH)
Marquette U (WI)
Mars Hill Coll (NC)
Martin U (IN)
Marygrove Coll (MI)
Marymount Coll of Fordham U (NY)
Maryville Coll (TN)
Massachusetts Coll of Liberal Arts (MA)
The Master's Coll and Sem (CA)
Mayville State U (ND)
McGill U (QC, Canada)
McNeese State U (LA)
McPherson Coll (KS)
Medaille Coll (NY)
Medgar Evers Coll of the City U of NY (NY)
Memorial U of Newfoundland (NL, Canada)
Mercy Coll (NY)
Mercyhurst Coll (PA)
Methodist Coll (NC)
Michigan State U (MI)
Middlebury Coll (VT)
Midway Coll (KY)
Miles Coll (AL)
Milligan Coll (TN)
Millsaps Coll (MS)
Minnesota State U Mankato (MN)
Mississippi Coll (MS)
Mississippi Valley State U (MS)
Missouri Southern State U (MO)
Missouri Valley Coll (MO)
Molloy Coll (NY)
Monmouth Coll (IL)
Monmouth U (NJ)
Montana State U–Billings (MT)
Moravian Coll (PA)
Morgan State U (MD)
Morningside Coll (IA)
Mount Holyoke Coll (MA)
Mount Marty Coll (SD)
Mount Mary Coll (WI)
Mount Mercy Coll (IA)
Mount Saint Mary Coll (NY)
Mount St. Mary's Coll (CA)
Mount Saint Vincent U (NS, Canada)
Mount Vernon Nazarene U (OH)
Nazareth Coll of Rochester (NY)
Nevada State Coll at Henderson (NV)
Newberry Coll (SC)
New Coll of California (CA)
Newman U (KS)
New Mexico Highlands U (NM)
New York Inst of Technology (NY)
New York U (NY)
Niagara U (NY)
Nicholls State U (LA)
Nipissing U (ON, Canada)
North Carolina State U (NC)
North Carolina Wesleyan Coll (NC)
North Central Coll (IL)
Northeastern State U (OK)
Northeastern U (MA)
Northern Arizona U (AZ)
Northern Illinois U (IL)
Northern Michigan U (MI)
Northern State U (SD)
North Georgia Coll & State U (GA)
Northland Coll (WI)
North Park U (IL)
Northwestern U (IL)
Notre Dame de Namur U (CA)
Oakland City U (IN)
Oakland U (MI)
Oglethorpe U (GA)
Ohio Northern U (OH)
Ohio U (OH)
Ohio U–Southern Campus (OH)
Ohio Valley Coll (WV)
Ohio Wesleyan U (OH)
Okanagan U Coll (BC, Canada)
Oklahoma Baptist U (OK)
Oklahoma City U (OK)
Oklahoma State U (OK)
Olivet Coll (MI)
Olivet Nazarene U (IL)
Oral Roberts U (OK)
Otterbein Coll (OH)
Ouachita Baptist U (AR)
Our Lady of Holy Cross Coll (LA)
Pacific Lutheran U (WA)
Pacific Union Coll (CA)
Pacific U (OR)
Palm Beach Atlantic U (FL)
Patrick Henry Coll (VA)
Pepperdine U, Malibu (CA)
Pfeiffer U (NC)
Pillsbury Baptist Bible Coll (MN)
Pittsburg State U (KS)
Point Park U (PA)
Pontifical Catholic U of Puerto Rico (PR)
Prairie Bible Coll (AB, Canada)
Presbyterian Coll (SC)
Providence Coll and Theological Sem (MB, Canada)
Purdue U (IN)
Queen's U at Kingston (ON, Canada)
Queens U of Charlotte (NC)
Quinnipiac U (CT)
Redeemer U Coll (ON, Canada)
Regis U (CO)
Rhode Island Coll (RI)
Rider U (NJ)
Ripon Coll (WI)
Rivier Coll (NH)
Roberts Wesleyan Coll (NY)
Rockford Coll (IL)
Rockhurst U (MO)
Rocky Mountain Coll (MT)
Rocky Mountain Coll (AB, Canada)
Rollins Coll (FL)
Roosevelt U (IL)
Sacred Heart U (CT)
St. Ambrose U (IA)
St. Cloud State U (MN)
Saint Francis U (PA)
St. Francis Xavier U (NS, Canada)
Saint John's U (MN)
Saint Joseph Coll (CT)
St. Joseph's Coll, New York (NY)
Saint Joseph's Coll of Maine (ME)
St. Joseph's Coll, Suffolk Campus (NY)
Saint Joseph's U (PA)
Saint Louis U (MO)
Saint Martin's Coll (WA)
Saint Mary-of-the-Woods Coll (IN)
Saint Mary's Coll (IN)
St. Mary's U of San Antonio (TX)
Saint Michael's Coll (VT)
St. Thomas Aquinas Coll (NY)
St. Thomas U (NB, Canada)
Salem Coll (NC)
Salem State Coll (MA)
Salisbury U (MD)
Sam Houston State U (TX)
Sarah Lawrence Coll (NY)
Schreiner U (TX)
Shasta Bible Coll (CA)
Shawnee State U (OH)
Simmons Coll (MA)
Simon Fraser U (BC, Canada)
Simpson Coll (IA)
Smith Coll (MA)
South Carolina State U (SC)
South Dakota State U (SD)
Southeastern Bible Coll (AL)
Southeastern Oklahoma State U (OK)
Southern Connecticut State U (CT)
Southern Nazarene U (OK)
Southern Utah U (UT)
Southern Wesleyan U (SC)
Southwestern Oklahoma State U (OK)
Springfield Coll (MA)
State U of NY at New Paltz (NY)
State U of NY at Oswego (NY)
Plattsburgh State U of NY (NY)
State U of NY Coll at Brockport (NY)
State U of NY Coll at Fredonia (NY)
State U of NY Coll at Geneseo (NY)
State U of NY Coll at Oneonta (NY)
State U of NY Empire State Coll (NY)
Stetson U (FL)
Suffolk U (MA)
Tabor Coll (KS)
Talladega Coll (AL)
Tarleton State U (TX)
Taylor U (IN)
Tennessee State U (TN)
Tennessee Technological U (TN)
Tennessee Wesleyan Coll (TN)
Texas A&M U–Commerce (TX)
Texas A&M U–Kingsville (TX)
Texas Lutheran U (TX)
Texas Southern U (TX)
Texas Wesleyan U (TX)
Tougaloo Coll (MS)
Trent U (ON, Canada)
Trinity Christian Coll (IL)
Trinity Coll (CT)
Trinity Coll (DC)
Trinity Intl U (IL)
Trinity Western U (BC, Canada)
Tri-State U (IN)
Troy State U (AL)
Tusculum Coll (TN)
Union Coll (KY)
Union Coll (NE)
Union Inst & U (OH)
Union U (TN)
Université de Montréal (QC, Canada)
Université de Sherbrooke (QC, Canada)
U du Québec à Hull (QC, Canada)
The U of Akron (OH)
U of Alaska Fairbanks (AK)
U of Alaska Southeast (AK)
U of Alberta (AB, Canada)
U of Arkansas at Little Rock (AR)
U of Arkansas at Monticello (AR)
The U of British Columbia (BC, Canada)
U of Calgary (AB, Canada)
U of Calif, Los Angeles (CA)
U of Charleston (WV)
U of Cincinnati (OH)
U of Dallas (TX)
U of Dayton (OH)
U of Delaware (DE)
U of Detroit Mercy (MI)
The U of Findlay (OH)
U of Hawaii at Manoa (HI)
U of Houston (TX)
U of Houston–Victoria (TX)
U of Indianapolis (IN)
U of La Verne (CA)
The U of Lethbridge (AB, Canada)
U of Louisiana at Lafayette (LA)
U of Maine (ME)
U of Maine at Fort Kent (ME)
U of Maine at Machias (ME)
U of Maine at Presque Isle (ME)
U of Manitoba (MB, Canada)
U of Mary Hardin-Baylor (TX)
U of Maryland, Coll Park (MD)
U of Maryland Eastern Shore (MD)
U of Massachusetts Amherst (MA)
U of Miami (FL)
U of Michigan (MI)
U of Michigan–Dearborn (MI)
U of Michigan–Flint (MI)
U of Minnesota, Duluth (MN)
U of Minnesota, Morris (MN)
U of Minnesota, Twin Cities Campus (MN)
U of Missouri–Columbia (MO)
U of Missouri–Kansas City (MO)
U of Missouri–St. Louis (MO)
The U of Montana–Missoula (MT)
The U of Montana–Western (MT)
U of Nevada, Las Vegas (NV)
U of New Brunswick Fredericton (NB, Canada)
U of New Mexico (NM)
U of Oregon (OR)
U of Ottawa (ON, Canada)
U of Pittsburgh at Greensburg (PA)
U of Pittsburgh at Johnstown (PA)
U of Portland (OR)
U of Prince Edward Island (PE, Canada)
U of Redlands (CA)
U of Regina (SK, Canada)
U of Richmond (VA)
U of Saint Francis (IN)
U of Saint Mary (KS)
U of St. Thomas (TX)
U of San Diego (CA)
U of San Francisco (CA)
U of Saskatchewan (SK, Canada)
U of Sioux Falls (SD)
The U of South Dakota (SD)
U of Southern California (CA)
U of South Florida (FL)
U of the Incarnate Word (TX)
U of the Pacific (CA)
U of the Sacred Heart (PR)
U of Toledo (OH)
U of Toronto (ON, Canada)
U of Tulsa (OK)
U of Utah (UT)
U of Vermont (VT)
U of Victoria (BC, Canada)
U of Washington (WA)
The U of Western Ontario (ON, Canada)
U of Windsor (ON, Canada)
U of Wisconsin–La Crosse (WI)
U of Wisconsin–Milwaukee (WI)
U of Wisconsin–Oshkosh (WI)
U of Wisconsin–Platteville (WI)
U of Wisconsin–River Falls (WI)
U of Wisconsin–Stevens Point (WI)
U of Wisconsin–Superior (WI)
U of Wisconsin–Whitewater (WI)
Upper Iowa U (IA)
Urbana U (OH)
Valley City State U (ND)
Vanderbilt U (TN)
Vanguard U of Southern California (CA)
Villanova U (PA)
Virginia Intermont Coll (VA)
Voorhees Coll (SC)
Wagner Coll (NY)
Waldorf Coll (IA)
Walsh U (OH)
Warner Pacific Coll (OR)
Warren Wilson Coll (NC)
Washburn U (KS)
Washington U in St. Louis (MO)
Wayne State Coll (NE)
Webster U (MO)
Wells Coll (NY)
Wesleyan Coll (GA)
Wesley Coll (DE)
Western Baptist Coll (OR)
Western Connecticut State U (CT)
Western State Coll of Colorado (CO)
Western Washington U (WA)
Westfield State Coll (MA)
West Liberty State Coll (WV)
Westminster Coll (PA)
Westmont Coll (CA)
West Virginia State Coll (WV)
West Virginia Wesleyan Coll (WV)
Wheeling Jesuit U (WV)
Wheelock Coll (MA)

Wilkes U (PA)
William Jessup U (CA)
William Jewell Coll (MO)
William Paterson U of New Jersey (NJ)
William Penn U (IA)
Williams Baptist Coll (AR)
William Woods U (MO)
Wingate U (NC)
Winona State U (MN)
Winston-Salem State U (NC)
Wittenberg U (OH)
Wright State U (OH)
Xavier U (OH)
Xavier U of Louisiana (LA)
York Coll (NE)
York U (ON, Canada)
Youngstown State U (OH)

EDUCATIONAL ADMINISTRATION AND SUPERVISION RELATED
Cazenovia Coll (NY)
Kendall Coll (IL)
Troy State U Dothan (AL)

EDUCATIONAL ASSESSMENT, EVALUATION, AND RESEARCH RELATED
Jones Intl U (CO)

EDUCATIONAL ASSESSMENT, TESTING, AND MEASUREMENT
U of Arkansas (AR)

EDUCATIONAL EVALUATION AND RESEARCH
U of Arkansas (AR)

EDUCATIONAL, INSTRUCTIONAL, AND CURRICULUM SUPERVISION
Sterling Coll (VT)
Wright State U (OH)

EDUCATIONAL/INSTRUCTIONAL MEDIA DESIGN
Ball State U (IN)
California State U, Chico (CA)
Capital U (OH)
Eastern Michigan U (MI)
Indiana State U (IN)
Ithaca Coll (NY)
Jacksonville State U (AL)
Jones Intl U (CO)
Kutztown U of Pennsylvania (PA)
Lindenwood U (MO)
St. Cloud State U (MN)
Seton Hill U (PA)
U of Arkansas (AR)
U of Houston–Clear Lake (TX)
U of Maine (ME)
U of Toledo (OH)
U of Wisconsin–Superior (WI)
Western Illinois U (IL)
Western Oregon U (OR)
Widener U (PA)

EDUCATIONAL LEADERSHIP AND ADMINISTRATION
Baldwin-Wallace Coll (OH)
Campbell U (NC)
Charleston Southern U (SC)
Cleveland State U (OH)
Cornell U (NY)
Eastern Michigan U (MI)
Eureka Coll (IL)
Harding U (AR)
Jamestown Coll (ND)
Jones Intl U (CO)
Kendall Coll (IL)
Lamar U (TX)
Liberty U (VA)
Lindenwood U (MO)
McNeese State U (LA)
Northern Arizona U (AZ)
North Georgia Coll & State U (GA)
Oakland U (MI)
Ohio U (OH)
Oral Roberts U (OK)
St. Cloud State U (MN)
St. John's U (NY)
Sterling Coll (VT)
Tarleton State U (TX)
Tennessee State U (TN)
Texas Christian U (TX)
Texas Southern U (TX)
U of Arkansas (AR)
The U of British Columbia (BC, Canada)
U of Calif, Los Angeles (CA)
U of Houston–Clear Lake (TX)
The U of Lethbridge (AB, Canada)
U of Oregon (OR)
U of San Francisco (CA)
U of Windsor (ON, Canada)
U of Wisconsin–Superior (WI)
Western Washington U (WA)
Wright State U (OH)

EDUCATIONAL PSYCHOLOGY
Alcorn State U (MS)
The Catholic U of America (DC)
Christian Brothers U (TN)
Cornell U (NY)
Eastern Michigan U (MI)
Jacksonville State U (AL)
Marymount U (VA)
Mississippi State U (MS)
Shenandoah U (VA)
U of Georgia (GA)
U of Pittsburgh (PA)
U of Regina (SK, Canada)

EDUCATIONAL STATISTICS AND RESEARCH METHODS
Bucknell U (PA)
Cornell U (NY)
U of Arkansas (AR)

EDUCATION (K-12)
Adrian Coll (MI)
Atlantic Baptist U (NB, Canada)
Augustana Coll (SD)
Belmont U (TN)
Bethel Coll (TN)
Biola U (CA)
Briar Cliff U (IA)
Campbell U (NC)
Centenary Coll of Louisiana (LA)
Charleston Southern U (SC)
Christian Heritage Coll (CA)
Clearwater Christian Coll (FL)
Coll of Saint Mary (NE)
The Coll of St. Scholastica (MN)
Columbia Coll (NY)
Columbus State U (GA)
Dickinson State U (ND)
Dominican U (IL)
Dordt Coll (IA)
D'Youville Coll (NY)
Graceland U (IA)
Grace U (NE)
Gwynedd-Mercy Coll (PA)
Hamline U (MN)
Hastings Coll (NE)
Hillsdale Coll (MI)
Illinois Coll (IL)
Ithaca Coll (NY)
Jamestown Coll (ND)
John Carroll U (OH)
Keystone Coll (PA)
Lake Erie Coll (OH)
Lambuth U (TN)
Lewis U (IL)
Lindenwood U (MO)
McKendree Coll (IL)
McPherson Coll (KS)
Methodist Coll (NC)
Metropolitan State Coll of Denver (CO)
Mount Saint Mary Coll (NY)
Northwestern Coll (IA)
Ohio Dominican U (OH)
Ohio Wesleyan U (OH)
Our Lady of Holy Cross Coll (LA)
Pacific Union Coll (CA)
Pikeville Coll (KY)
Redeemer U Coll (ON, Canada)
St. Ambrose U (IA)
Saint Augustine's Coll (NC)
Saint Mary-of-the-Woods Coll (IN)
St. Norbert Coll (WI)
Southwest Baptist U (MO)
Syracuse U (NY)
Tabor Coll (KS)
Tennessee Wesleyan Coll (TN)
Thomas Coll (ME)
Trevecca Nazarene U (TN)
Trinity Intl U (IL)
The U of Lethbridge (AB, Canada)
U of Maine at Fort Kent (ME)
U of Minnesota, Morris (MN)
The U of Montana–Western (MT)
U of St. Thomas (MN)
The U of Tampa (FL)
The U of Tennessee at Martin (TN)
U of Windsor (ON, Canada)
U of Wisconsin–Superior (WI)
Walla Walla Coll (WA)
Washington U in St. Louis (MO)
West Virginia Wesleyan Coll (WV)
York U (ON, Canada)

EDUCATION (MULTIPLE LEVELS)
Averett U (VA)
Campbell U (NC)
Chestnut Hill Coll (PA)
Coll of Saint Elizabeth (NJ)
Columbia Intl U (SC)
Concordia U Wisconsin (WI)
Connecticut Coll (CT)
Dakota Wesleyan U (SD)
George Fox U (OR)
Harding U (AR)
Howard Payne U (TX)
Iona Coll (NY)
Ithaca Coll (NY)
Juniata Coll (PA)
Lake Superior State U (MI)
Liberty U (VA)
Manhattan Coll (NY)
Martin Luther Coll (MN)
Miami U Hamilton (OH)
Northwest Christian Coll (OR)
Ohio Northern U (OH)
Ohio Valley Coll (WV)
Ohio Wesleyan U (OH)
Oral Roberts U (OK)
The Richard Stockton Coll of New Jersey (NJ)
Saint Louis U (MO)
Shawnee State U (OH)
Tarleton State U (TX)
Texas Lutheran U (TX)
The U of Akron (OH)
U of Great Falls (MT)
The U of Memphis (TN)
U of Nebraska–Lincoln (NE)
U of North Alabama (AL)
U of the Ozarks (AR)
U of Washington (WA)
Utah State U (UT)
Wake Forest U (NC)
Waldorf Coll (IA)
Western Washington U (WA)
Wright State U (OH)
York Coll (NE)
Youngstown State U (OH)

EDUCATION RELATED
Albany State U (GA)
Alliant Intl U (CA)
Arkansas State U (AR)
Arkansas Tech U (AR)
Bowling Green State U (OH)
Brigham Young U (UT)
Campbell U (NC)
Centenary Coll of Louisiana (LA)
Cleveland State U (OH)
Concordia U, St. Paul (MN)
Dominican U of California (CA)
Eastern Washington U (WA)
Kendall Coll (IL)
Lancaster Bible Coll (PA)
Long Island U, Brooklyn Campus (NY)
Madonna U (MI)
Marylhurst U (OR)
Marywood U (PA)
McNeese State U (LA)
Mercer U (GA)
Messenger Coll (MO)
Oakland U (MI)
Ohio Northern U (OH)
Pace U (NY)
Park U (MO)
Pittsburg State U (KS)
Roosevelt U (IL)
State U of NY Coll at Potsdam (NY)
Sterling Coll (VT)
Swarthmore Coll (PA)
Syracuse U (NY)
Texas Southern U (TX)
Towson U (MD)
U of Missouri–Columbia (MO)
U of Waterloo (ON, Canada)
Wayland Baptist U (TX)
Wright State U (OH)
York Coll of Pennsylvania (PA)

EDUCATION (SPECIFIC LEVELS AND METHODS) RELATED
Boston U (MA)
Bowling Green State U (OH)
Brigham Young U (UT)
Columbia Coll Chicago (IL)
Kendall Coll (IL)
Oakland U (MI)
Rowan U (NJ)
St. Cloud State U (MN)
The U of Akron (OH)
U of Toledo (OH)
Washington U in St. Louis (MO)
Wright State U (OH)
Xavier U (OH)

EDUCATION (SPECIFIC SUBJECT AREAS) RELATED
Appalachian State U (NC)
Averett U (VA)
Avila U (MO)
Baylor U (TX)
Bowling Green State U (OH)
Bradley U (IL)
Brigham Young U (UT)
Cameron U (OK)
Central Michigan U (MI)
Chadron State Coll (NE)
Columbia Coll Chicago (IL)
Drexel U (PA)
Duquesne U (PA)
Eastern Kentucky U (KY)
Eastern Michigan U (MI)
Eastern Washington U (WA)
Henderson State U (AR)
Hofstra U (NY)
Hope Coll (MI)
Juniata Coll (PA)
Louisiana State U and A&M Coll (LA)
Louisiana Tech U (LA)
Madonna U (MI)
Marquette U (WI)
Marywood U (PA)
Miami Dade Coll (FL)
Minot State U (ND)
Northern Arizona U (AZ)
Ohio U (OH)
Oklahoma State U (OK)
Plymouth State U (NH)
Point Park U (PA)
St. Edward's U (TX)
San Diego State U (CA)
Schreiner U (TX)
Southwest Baptist U (MO)
Southwest Missouri State U (MO)
Syracuse U (NY)
Thomas More Coll (KY)
The U of Akron (OH)
The U of Arizona (AZ)
U of Hawaii at Manoa (HI)
U of Kentucky (KY)
U of Louisiana at Lafayette (LA)
U of Michigan–Flint (MI)
U of Nebraska–Lincoln (NE)
U of Nevada, Reno (NV)
The U of North Carolina at Wilmington (NC)
U of Oklahoma (OK)
U of St. Thomas (MN)
U of Toledo (OH)
U of Wisconsin–Eau Claire (WI)
Utah State U (UT)
Wright State U (OH)

ELECTRICAL AND ELECTRONIC ENGINEERING TECHNOLOGIES RELATED
Embry-Riddle Aeronautical U (FL)
Grove City Coll (PA)
New York Inst of Technology (NY)
Old Dominion U (VA)
Pennsylvania Coll of Technology (PA)
Pittsburg State U (KS)
Southern Illinois U Carbondale (IL)
Southern Polytechnic State U (GA)
U of Hartford (CT)
Western Carolina U (NC)

ELECTRICAL, ELECTRONIC AND COMMUNICATIONS ENGINEERING TECHNOLOGY
Andrews U (MI)
Appalachian State U (NC)
Arizona State U East (AZ)
Baker Coll of Muskegon (MI)
Baker Coll of Owosso (MI)
Bluefield State Coll (WV)
Bowling Green State U (OH)
Bradley U (IL)
British Columbia Inst of Technology (BC, Canada)
State U of NY Coll at Buffalo (NY)
California State Polytechnic U, Pomona (CA)
California State U, Long Beach (CA)
California U of Pennsylvania (PA)
Cameron U (OK)
Capitol Coll (MD)
Central Michigan U (MI)
Central Missouri State U (MO)
Central Washington U (WA)
Cleveland State U (OH)
Cogswell Polytechnical Coll (CA)
Delaware State U (DE)
East Carolina U (NC)
East Central U (OK)
Eastern Michigan U (MI)
Eastern Washington U (WA)
Edinboro U of Pennsylvania (PA)
Excelsior Coll (NY)
Fairleigh Dickinson U, Teaneck-Metro Campus (NJ)
Fairmont State Coll (WV)
State U of NY at Farmingdale (NY)
Ferris State U (MI)
Florida Ag and Mech U (FL)
Fort Valley State U (GA)
Georgia Southern U (GA)
Grambling State U (LA)
Grantham U (LA)
Hamilton Tech Coll (IA)
Hampton U (VA)
Indiana State U (IN)
Indiana U–Purdue U Fort Wayne (IN)
Indiana U–Purdue U Indianapolis (IN)
Inter American U of PR, Aguadilla Campus (PR)
Inter American U of PR, Bayamón Campus (PR)
Inter American U of PR, San Germán Campus (PR)
Jacksonville State U (AL)
Johnson & Wales U (RI)
Kansas State U (KS)
Keene State Coll (NH)
Lakehead U (ON, Canada)
Lake Superior State U (MI)
LeTourneau U (TX)
Louisiana Tech U (LA)
McNeese State U (LA)
Metropolitan State Coll of Denver (CO)
Michigan Technological U (MI)
Milwaukee School of Eng (WI)
Minnesota State U Mankato (MN)
Missouri Western State Coll (MO)
New York Inst of Technology (NY)
Norfolk State U (VA)
Northeastern State U (OK)
Northern Michigan U (MI)
Northern State U (SD)
Northwestern State U of Louisiana (LA)
Oklahoma State U (OK)
Oregon Inst of Technology (OR)
Pacific Union Coll (CA)
Penn State U at Erie, The Behrend Coll (PA)
Pittsburg State U (KS)
Point Park U (PA)
Prairie View A&M U (TX)
Purdue U (IN)
Rochester Inst of Technology (NY)
Roosevelt U (IL)
St. Cloud State U (MN)
Sam Houston State U (TX)
South Carolina State U (SC)
South Dakota State U (SD)
Southeastern Oklahoma State U (OK)
Southern Polytechnic State U (GA)
Southern U and A&M Coll (LA)
Southern Utah U (UT)
State U of NY Coll of Technology at Alfred (NY)
State U of NY Inst of Tech at Utica/Rome (NY)
Texas A&M U (TX)
Texas Southern U (TX)
Texas Tech U (TX)
Thomas Edison State Coll (NJ)
The U of Akron (OH)
U of Arkansas at Little Rock (AR)
U of Calif, Santa Barbara (CA)
U of Central Florida (FL)
U of Cincinnati (OH)
U of Dayton (OH)
U of Hartford (CT)
U of Maine (ME)
U of Maryland Eastern Shore (MD)
U of Massachusetts Dartmouth (MA)
U of Massachusetts Lowell (MA)
The U of Memphis (TN)
U of Nebraska–Lincoln (NE)
U of New Hampshire at Manchester (NH)
The U of North Carolina at Charlotte (NC)
U of North Texas (TX)
U of Pittsburgh at Johnstown (PA)
U of Regina (SK, Canada)
The U of Texas at Brownsville (TX)
U of Toledo (OH)
Wayne State U (MI)
Weber State U (UT)
Wentworth Inst of Technology (MA)
Western Carolina U (NC)
Western Washington U (WA)
World Coll (VA)
Youngstown State U (OH)

ELECTRICAL, ELECTRONICS AND COMMUNICATIONS ENGINEERING
Alabama Ag and Mech U (AL)
Alfred U (NY)
The American U in Cairo(Egypt)

Arizona State U (AZ)
Auburn U (AL)
Baylor U (TX)
Bethel Coll (IN)
Bloomsburg U of Pennsylvania (PA)
Boise State U (ID)
Boston U (MA)
Bradley U (IL)
Brigham Young U (UT)
Brown U (RI)
Bucknell U (PA)
California Inst of Technology (CA)
California Polytechnic State U, San Luis Obispo (CA)
California State Polytechnic U, Pomona (CA)
California State U, Chico (CA)
California State U, Fresno (CA)
California State U, Fullerton (CA)
California State U, Long Beach (CA)
California State U, Los Angeles (CA)
California State U, Sacramento (CA)
Calvin Coll (MI)
Capitol Coll (MD)
Carleton U (ON, Canada)
Carnegie Mellon U (PA)
Case Western Reserve U (OH)
The Catholic U of America (DC)
Cedarville U (OH)
Central Connecticut State U (CT)
Christian Brothers U (TN)
Citadel, The Military Coll of South Carolina (SC)
City Coll of the City U of NY (NY)
Clarkson U (NY)
Clemson U (SC)
Cleveland State U (OH)
Cogswell Polytechnical Coll (CA)
The Coll of New Jersey (NJ)
The Coll of Southeastern Europe, The American U of Athens(Greece)
Colorado School of Mines (CO)
Colorado State U (CO)
Columbia U, School of Eng & Applied Sci (NY)
Concordia U (QC, Canada)
Cooper Union for the Advancement of Science & Art (NY)
Cornell U (NY)
Dominican U (IL)
Dordt Coll (IA)
Drexel U (PA)
Duke U (NC)
Eastern Nazarene Coll (MA)
Embry-Riddle Aeronautical U (AZ)
Fairfield U (CT)
Fairleigh Dickinson U, Teaneck-Metro Campus (NJ)
Florida Ag and Mech U (FL)
Florida Atlantic U (FL)
Florida Inst of Technology (FL)
Florida Intl U (FL)
Florida State U (FL)
Frostburg State U (MD)
Gallaudet U (DC)
Gannon U (PA)
George Mason U (VA)
The George Washington U (DC)
Georgia Inst of Technology (GA)
Gonzaga U (WA)
Grand Valley State U (MI)
Grove City Coll (PA)
Hampton U (VA)
Harvard U (MA)
Henry Cogswell Coll (WA)
Hofstra U (NY)
Howard U (DC)
Idaho State U (ID)
Illinois Inst of Technology (IL)
Indiana Inst of Technology (IN)
Indiana U–Purdue U Fort Wayne (IN)
Indiana U–Purdue U Indianapolis (IN)
Inter American U of PR, Bayamón Campus (PR)
Inter American U of PR, Fajardo Campus (PR)
Iowa State U of Science and Technology (IA)
Jacksonville U (FL)
John Brown U (AR)
The Johns Hopkins U (MD)
Johnson & Wales U (RI)
Kansas State U (KS)
Kettering U (MI)
Lafayette Coll (PA)
Lakehead U (ON, Canada)
Lake Superior State U (MI)
Lamar U (TX)
Lawrence Technological U (MI)
Lehigh U (PA)
LeTourneau U (TX)
Louisiana State U and A&M Coll (LA)
Louisiana Tech U (LA)
Loyola Coll in Maryland (MD)
Loyola Marymount U (CA)
Manhattan Coll (NY)
Marquette U (WI)
Massachusetts Inst of Technology (MA)
McGill U (QC, Canada)
Memorial U of Newfoundland (NL, Canada)
Merrimack Coll (MA)
Miami U (OH)
Michigan State U (MI)
Michigan Technological U (MI)
Milwaukee School of Eng (WI)
Minnesota State U Mankato (MN)
Mississippi State U (MS)
Missouri Tech (MO)
Montana State U–Bozeman (MT)
Morgan State U (MD)
New Jersey Inst of Technology (NJ)
New Mexico Inst of Mining and Technology (NM)
New Mexico State U (NM)
New York Inst of Technology (NY)
Norfolk State U (VA)
North Carolina State U (NC)
North Dakota State U (ND)
Northeastern U (MA)
Northern Arizona U (AZ)
Northern Illinois U (IL)
Northwestern Polytechnic U (CA)
Northwestern U (IL)
Oakland U (MI)
Ohio Northern U (OH)
The Ohio State U (OH)
Ohio U (OH)
Oklahoma Christian U (OK)
Oklahoma State U (OK)
Old Dominion U (VA)
Oral Roberts U (OK)
Oregon State U (OR)
Pacific Lutheran U (WA)
Pacific States U (CA)
Penn State U Abington Coll (PA)
Penn State U Altoona Coll (PA)
Penn State U at Erie, The Behrend Coll (PA)
Penn State U Beaver Campus of the Commonwealth Coll (PA)
Penn State U Berks Cmps of Berks-Lehigh Valley Coll (PA)
Penn State U Delaware County Campus of the Commonwealth Coll (PA)
Penn State U DuBois Campus of the Commonwealth Coll (PA)
Penn State U Fayette Campus of the Commonwealth Coll (PA)
Penn State U Harrisburg Campus of the Capital Coll (PA)
Penn State U Hazleton Campus of the Commonwealth Coll (PA)
Penn State U Lehigh Valley Cmps of Berks-Lehigh Valley Coll (PA)
Penn State U McKeesport Campus of the Commonwealth Coll (PA)
Penn State U Mont Alto Campus of the Commonwealth Coll (PA)
Penn State U New Kensington Campus of the Commonwealth Coll (PA)
Penn State U Schuylkill Campus of the Capital Coll (PA)
Penn State U Shenango Campus of the Commonwealth Coll (PA)
Penn State U Univ Park Campus (PA)
Penn State U Wilkes-Barre Campus of the Commonwealth Coll (PA)
Penn State U Worthington Scranton Cmps Commonwealth Coll (PA)
Penn State U York Campus of the Commonwealth Coll (PA)
Polytechnic U, Brooklyn Campus (NY)
Polytechnic U of Puerto Rico (PR)
Portland State U (OR)
Prairie View A&M U (TX)
Princeton U (NJ)
Purdue U (IN)
Queen's U at Kingston (ON, Canada)
Rensselaer Polytechnic Inst (NY)
Rice U (TX)
Rochester Inst of Technology (NY)
Rose-Hulman Inst of Technology (IN)
Rowan U (NJ)
Rutgers, The State U of New Jersey, New Brunswick/Piscataway (NJ)
Ryerson U (ON, Canada)
Saginaw Valley State U (MI)
St. Cloud State U (MN)
Saint Louis U (MO)
St. Mary's U of San Antonio (TX)
San Diego State U (CA)
San Francisco State U (CA)
San Jose State U (CA)
Santa Clara U (CA)
Seattle Pacific U (WA)
Seattle U (WA)
South Dakota School of Mines and Technology (SD)
South Dakota State U (SD)
Southern Illinois U Carbondale (IL)
Southern Illinois U Edwardsville (IL)
Southern Methodist U (TX)
Southern U and A&M Coll (LA)
Stanford U (CA)
State U of NY at Binghamton (NY)
State U of NY at New Paltz (NY)
Stevens Inst of Technology (NJ)
Stony Brook U, State U of New York (NY)
Suffolk U (MA)
Syracuse U (NY)
Tennessee State U (TN)
Tennessee Technological U (TN)
Texas A&M U (TX)
Texas A&M U–Kingsville (TX)
Texas Tech U (TX)
Trinity Coll (CT)
Tri-State U (IN)
Tufts U (MA)
Tulane U (LA)
Tuskegee U (AL)
Union Coll (NY)
United States Air Force Acad (CO)
United States Coast Guard Acad (CT)
United States Military Acad (NY)
United States Naval Acad (MD)
Université de Sherbrooke (QC, Canada)
Université Laval (QC, Canada)
U at Buffalo, The State U of New York (NY)
The U of Akron (OH)
The U of Alabama (AL)
The U of Alabama at Birmingham (AL)
The U of Alabama in Huntsville (AL)
U of Alaska Fairbanks (AK)
U of Alberta (AB, Canada)
The U of Arizona (AZ)
U of Arkansas (AR)
The U of British Columbia (BC, Canada)
U of Calgary (AB, Canada)
U of Calif, Berkeley (CA)
U of Calif, Davis (CA)
U of Calif, Irvine (CA)
U of Calif, Los Angeles (CA)
U of Calif, Riverside (CA)
U of Calif, San Diego (CA)
U of Calif, Santa Barbara (CA)
U of Calif, Santa Cruz (CA)
U of Central Florida (FL)
U of Cincinnati (OH)
U of Colorado at Boulder (CO)
U of Colorado at Colorado Springs (CO)
U of Colorado at Denver (CO)
U of Connecticut (CT)
U of Dayton (OH)
U of Delaware (DE)
U of Denver (CO)
U of Detroit Mercy (MI)
U of Evansville (IN)
U of Florida (FL)
U of Hartford (CT)
U of Hawaii at Manoa (HI)
U of Houston (TX)
U of Idaho (ID)
U of Illinois at Chicago (IL)
U of Illinois at Urbana–Champaign (IL)
U of Indianapolis (IN)
The U of Iowa (IA)
U of Kansas (KS)
U of Kentucky (KY)
U of Louisiana at Lafayette (LA)
U of Louisville (KY)
U of Maine (ME)
U of Manitoba (MB, Canada)
U of Maryland, Coll Park (MD)
U of Massachusetts Amherst (MA)
U of Massachusetts Dartmouth (MA)
U of Massachusetts Lowell (MA)
The U of Memphis (TN)
U of Miami (FL)
U of Michigan (MI)
U of Michigan–Dearborn (MI)
U of Minnesota, Duluth (MN)
U of Minnesota, Twin Cities Campus (MN)
U of Mississippi (MS)
U of Missouri–Columbia (MO)
U of Missouri–Kansas City (MO)
U of Missouri–Rolla (MO)
U of Missouri–St. Louis (MO)
U of Nebraska at Omaha (NE)
U of Nebraska–Lincoln (NE)
U of Nevada, Las Vegas (NV)
U of Nevada, Reno (NV)
U of New Brunswick Fredericton (NB, Canada)
U of New Hampshire (NH)
U of New Haven (CT)
U of New Mexico (NM)
U of New Orleans (LA)
The U of North Carolina at Charlotte (NC)
U of North Florida (FL)
U of Notre Dame (IN)
U of Oklahoma (OK)
U of Ottawa (ON, Canada)
U of Pennsylvania (PA)
U of Pittsburgh (PA)
U of Portland (OR)
U of Regina (SK, Canada)
U of Rhode Island (RI)
U of Rochester (NY)
U of St. Thomas (MN)
U of San Diego (CA)
U of Saskatchewan (SK, Canada)
The U of Scranton (PA)
U of South Alabama (AL)
U of South Carolina (SC)
U of Southern California (CA)
U of Southern Maine (ME)
U of South Florida (FL)
The U of Tennessee (TN)
The U of Texas at Arlington (TX)
The U of Texas at Austin (TX)
The U of Texas at Dallas (TX)
The U of Texas at Tyler (TX)
The U of Texas–Pan American (TX)
U of the District of Columbia (DC)
U of the Pacific (CA)
U of Toledo (OH)
U of Toronto (ON, Canada)
U of Tulsa (OK)
U of Utah (UT)
U of Vermont (VT)
U of Victoria (BC, Canada)
U of Virginia (VA)
U of Washington (WA)
U of Waterloo (ON, Canada)
The U of Western Ontario (ON, Canada)
U of West Florida (FL)
U of Windsor (ON, Canada)
U of Wisconsin–Madison (WI)
U of Wisconsin–Milwaukee (WI)
U of Wisconsin–Platteville (WI)
U of Wyoming (WY)
Ursinus Coll (PA)
Utah State U (UT)
Valparaiso U (IN)
Vanderbilt U (TN)
Villanova U (PA)
Virginia Commonwealth U (VA)
Virginia Military Inst (VA)
Virginia Polytechnic Inst and State U (VA)
Walla Walla Coll (WA)
Washington State U (WA)
Washington U in St. Louis (MO)
Wayne State U (MI)
Wentworth Inst of Technology (MA)
Western Carolina U (NC)
Western Kentucky U (KY)
Western Michigan U (MI)
Western New England Coll (MA)
West Virginia U (WV)
Wichita State U (KS)
Widener U (PA)
Wilberforce U (OH)
Wilkes U (PA)
Worcester Polytechnic Inst (MA)
Wright State U (OH)
Yale U (CT)
Youngstown State U (OH)

ELECTRICAL/ELECTRONICS EQUIPMENT INSTALLATION AND REPAIR

Lewis-Clark State Coll (ID)

ELECTROMECHANICAL TECHNOLOGY

State U of NY Coll at Buffalo (NY)
Excelsior Coll (NY)
Miami U Hamilton (OH)
Murray State U (KY)
Rochester Inst of Technology (NY)
State U of NY Coll of Technology at Alfred (NY)
U of Houston (TX)
U of Northern Iowa (IA)
U of the District of Columbia (DC)
U of Toledo (OH)
Vermont Tech Coll (VT)
Wayne State U (MI)

ELECTRONEURODIAGNOSTIC/ ELECTROENCEPHALOGRAPHIC TECHNOLOGY

The Johns Hopkins U (MD)
Louisiana State U Health Sciences Center (LA)

ELEMENTARY AND MIDDLE SCHOOL ADMINISTRATION/ PRINCIPALSHIP

Campbell U (NC)
Charleston Southern U (SC)
Eastern Michigan U (MI)
Inter Amer U of PR, Barranquitas Campus (PR)
Ohio U (OH)
Piedmont Coll (GA)
U of Central Arkansas (AR)

ELEMENTARY EDUCATION

Abilene Christian U (TX)
Acadia U (NS, Canada)
Adams State Coll (CO)
Adrian Coll (MI)
Alabama Ag and Mech U (AL)
Alabama State U (AL)
Alaska Pacific U (AK)
Albertus Magnus Coll (CT)
Albion Coll (MI)
Albright Coll (PA)
Alcorn State U (MS)
Alderson-Broaddus Coll (WV)
Alfred U (NY)
Alice Lloyd Coll (KY)
Allen U (SC)
Alma Coll (MI)
Alvernia Coll (PA)
Alverno Coll (WI)
American Indian Coll of the Assemblies of God, Inc (AZ)
American Intl Coll (MA)
American U (DC)
American U of Puerto Rico (PR)
Anderson Coll (SC)
Andrews U (MI)
Anna Maria Coll (MA)
Appalachian State U (NC)
Aquinas Coll (MI)
Arcadia U (PA)
Arizona State U (AZ)
Arizona State U East (AZ)
Arizona State U West (AZ)
Arkansas Baptist Coll (AR)
Arkansas Tech U (AR)
Arlington Baptist Coll (TX)
Asbury Coll (KY)
Ashland U (OH)
Assumption Coll (MA)
Athens State U (AL)
Atlantic Union Coll (MA)
Auburn U (AL)
Auburn U Montgomery (AL)
Augsburg Coll (MN)
Augustana Coll (IL)
Augustana Coll (SD)
Augusta State U (GA)
Aurora U (IL)
Avila U (MO)
Bacone Coll (OK)
Baker U (KS)
Baldwin-Wallace Coll (OH)
Ball State U (IN)
Baptist Bible Coll (MO)
The Baptist Coll of Florida (FL)
Barber-Scotia Coll (NC)
Barclay Coll (KS)
Barry U (FL)
Barton Coll (NC)
Baylor U (TX)
Bay Path Coll (MA)
Becker Coll (MA)
Belhaven Coll (MS)
Bellarmine U (KY)
Belmont Abbey Coll (NC)
Belmont U (TN)
Beloit Coll (WI)
Bemidji State U (MN)
Benedictine Coll (KS)
Benedictine U (IL)
Berea Coll (KY)
Bethany Bible Coll (NB, Canada)
Bethany Coll (KS)
Bethany Lutheran Coll (MN)
Bethel Coll (IN)
Bethel Coll (KS)

Bethel Coll (TN)
Bethel U (MN)
Bethune-Cookman Coll (FL)
Biola U (CA)
Birmingham-Southern Coll (AL)
Bishop's U (QC, Canada)
Blackburn Coll (IL)
Black Hills State U (SD)
Bloomsburg U of Pennsylvania (PA)
Bluefield Coll (VA)
Bluefield State Coll (WV)
Blue Mountain Coll (MS)
Bluffton Coll (OH)
Boise State U (ID)
Boston Coll (MA)
Boston U (MA)
Bowie State U (MD)
Bowling Green State U (OH)
Bradley U (IL)
Brescia U (KY)
Brevard Coll (NC)
Briar Cliff U (IA)
Bridgewater State Coll (MA)
Brigham Young U (UT)
Brigham Young U–Hawaii (HI)
Brock U (ON, Canada)
Brooklyn Coll of the City U of NY (NY)
Bryan Coll (TN)
Bryn Athyn Coll of the New Church (PA)
Bucknell U (PA)
Buena Vista U (IA)
State U of NY Coll at Buffalo (NY)
Butler U (IN)
Cabrini Coll (PA)
Caldwell Coll (NJ)
California State U, Fresno (CA)
California U of Pennsylvania (PA)
Calumet Coll of Saint Joseph (IN)
Calvary Bible Coll and Theological Sem (MO)
Calvin Coll (MI)
Campbellsville U (KY)
Campbell U (NC)
Capital U (OH)
Cardinal Stritch U (WI)
Carlos Albizu Univ—Miami (FL)
Carlow Coll (PA)
Carroll Coll (MT)
Carroll Coll (WI)
Carson-Newman Coll (TN)
Carthage Coll (WI)
Cascade Coll (OR)
Catawba Coll (NC)
The Catholic U of America (DC)
Cedar Crest Coll (PA)
Centenary Coll (NJ)
Centenary Coll of Louisiana (LA)
Central Coll (IA)
Central Connecticut State U (CT)
Central Methodist Coll (MO)
Central Michigan U (MI)
Central Missouri State U (MO)
Central Washington U (WA)
Centre Coll (KY)
Chadron State Coll (NE)
Chaminade U of Honolulu (HI)
Champlain Coll (VT)
Charleston Southern U (SC)
Chatham Coll (PA)
Chestnut Hill Coll (PA)
Cheyney U of Pennsylvania (PA)
Chicago State U (IL)
Chowan Coll (NC)
Christian Brothers U (TN)
Christian Heritage Coll (CA)
City Coll of the City U of NY (NY)
City U (WA)
Clarion U of Pennsylvania (PA)
Clark Atlanta U (GA)
Clarke Coll (IA)
Clark U (MA)
Clearwater Christian Coll (FL)
Clemson U (SC)
Cleveland State U (OH)
Coastal Carolina U (SC)
Coe Coll (IA)
Coker Coll (SC)
Coll Misericordia (PA)
Coll of Charleston (SC)
Coll of Mount Saint Vincent (NY)
The Coll of New Jersey (NJ)
The Coll of New Rochelle (NY)
Coll of Notre Dame of Maryland (MD)
Coll of Saint Benedict (MN)
Coll of St. Catherine (MN)
Coll of St. Joseph (VT)
Coll of Saint Mary (NE)
The Coll of Saint Rose (NY)
The Coll of St. Scholastica (MN)
Coll of Santa Fe (NM)
Coll of the Atlantic (ME)
Coll of the Ozarks (MO)
Coll of the Southwest (NM)
Colorado State U-Pueblo (CO)
Columbia Coll (SC)
Columbia Union Coll (MD)
Concord Coll (WV)
Concordia Coll (AL)
Concordia Coll (MN)
Concordia Coll (NY)
Concordia U (IL)
Concordia U (MI)
Concordia U (NE)
Concordia U (OR)
Concordia U (QC, Canada)
Concordia U at Austin (TX)
Concordia U Coll of Alberta (AB, Canada)
Concordia U, St. Paul (MN)
Concordia U Wisconsin (WI)
Connecticut Coll (CT)
Converse Coll (SC)
Cornell Coll (IA)
Cornerstone U (MI)
Covenant Coll (GA)
Creighton U (NE)
Crichton Coll (TN)
Crossroads Bible Coll (IN)
Crown Coll (MN)
Culver-Stockton Coll (MO)
Cumberland Coll (KY)
Cumberland U (TN)
Curry Coll (MA)
Daemen Coll (NY)
Dakota State U (SD)
Dakota Wesleyan U (SD)
Dallas Baptist U (TX)
Dana Coll (NE)
Davis & Elkins Coll (WV)
Defiance Coll (OH)
Delaware State U (DE)
Delta State U (MS)
DePaul U (IL)
DePauw U (IN)
DeSales U (PA)
Dickinson State U (ND)
Dillard U (LA)
Doane Coll (NE)
Dominican Coll (NY)
Dominican U (IL)
Dordt Coll (IA)
Dowling Coll (NY)
Drake U (IA)
Drury U (MO)
Duquesne U (PA)
D'Youville Coll (NY)
East Carolina U (NC)
East Central U (OK)
Eastern Connecticut State U (CT)
Eastern Illinois U (IL)
Eastern Kentucky U (KY)
Eastern Mennonite U (VA)
Eastern Michigan U (MI)
Eastern Nazarene Coll (MA)
Eastern New Mexico U (NM)
Eastern U (PA)
Eastern Washington U (WA)
East Stroudsburg U of Pennsylvania (PA)
East Texas Baptist U (TX)
Edgewood Coll (WI)
Edinboro U of Pennsylvania (PA)
Elizabeth City State U (NC)
Elizabethtown Coll (PA)
Elmhurst Coll (IL)
Elmira Coll (NY)
Elms Coll (MA)
Elon U (NC)
Emmanuel Coll (GA)
Emory U (GA)
Emporia State U (KS)
Endicott Coll (MA)
Erskine Coll (SC)
Eureka Coll (IL)
Evangel U (MO)
Fairmont State Coll (WV)
Faith Baptist Bible Coll and Theological Sem (IA)
Faulkner U (AL)
Fayetteville State U (NC)
Five Towns Coll (NY)
Flagler Coll (FL)
Florida Ag and Mech U (FL)
Florida Atlantic U (FL)
Florida Coll (FL)
Florida Gulf Coast U (FL)
Florida Intl U (FL)
Florida Southern Coll (FL)
Florida State U (FL)
Fontbonne U (MO)
Fordham U (NY)
Fort Hays State U (KS)
Fort Lewis Coll (CO)
Framingham State Coll (MA)
The Franciscan U (IA)
Franciscan U of Steubenville (OH)
Francis Marion U (SC)
Franklin Coll (IN)
Franklin Pierce Coll (NH)
Freed-Hardeman U (TN)
Fresno Pacific U (CA)
Frostburg State U (MD)
Furman U (SC)
Gallaudet U (DC)
Gannon U (PA)
Gardner-Webb U (NC)
Geneva Coll (PA)
George Fox U (OR)
Georgetown Coll (KY)
Georgian Court U (NJ)
Georgia Southwestern State U (GA)
Georgia State U (GA)
Gettysburg Coll (PA)
Glenville State Coll (WV)
God's Bible School and Coll (OH)
Gonzaga U (WA)
Gordon Coll (MA)
Goshen Coll (IN)
Goucher Coll (MD)
Governors State U (IL)
Grace Bible Coll (MI)
Grace Coll (IN)
Graceland U (IA)
Grace U (NE)
Grambling State U (LA)
Grand Canyon U (AZ)
Grand Valley State U (MI)
Grand View Coll (IA)
Greensboro Coll (NC)
Greenville Coll (IL)
Grinnell Coll (IA)
Grove City Coll (PA)
Guilford Coll (NC)
Gustavus Adolphus Coll (MN)
Gwynedd-Mercy Coll (PA)
Hamline U (MN)
Hampshire Coll (MA)
Hampton U (VA)
Hannibal-LaGrange Coll (MO)
Harding U (AR)
Hardin-Simmons U (TX)
Harris-Stowe State Coll (MO)
Haskell Indian Nations U (KS)
Hastings Coll (NE)
Heidelberg Coll (OH)
Hellenic Coll (MA)
Henderson State U (AR)
Hendrix Coll (AR)
High Point U (NC)
Hillsdale Coll (MI)
Hiram Coll (OH)
Hofstra U (NY)
Hope Coll (MI)
Houghton Coll (NY)
Houston Baptist U (TX)
Howard Payne U (TX)
Humboldt State U (CA)
Hunter Coll of the City U of NY (NY)
Huntington Coll (IN)
Husson Coll (ME)
Huston-Tillotson Coll (TX)
Idaho State U (ID)
Illinois Coll (IL)
Illinois State U (IL)
Illinois Wesleyan U (IL)
Immaculata U (PA)
Indiana State U (IN)
Indiana U Bloomington (IN)
Indiana U East (IN)
Indiana U Kokomo (IN)
Indiana U Northwest (IN)
Indiana U of Pennsylvania (PA)
Indiana U–Purdue U Fort Wayne (IN)
Indiana U–Purdue U Indianapolis (IN)
Indiana U South Bend (IN)
Indiana U Southeast (IN)
Inter American U of PR, Aguadilla Campus (PR)
Inter Amer U of PR, Barranquitas Campus (PR)
Inter American U of PR, Fajardo Campus (PR)
Inter American U of PR, Ponce Campus (PR)
Inter American U of PR, San Germán Campus (PR)
Iona Coll (NY)
Iowa State U of Science and Technology (IA)
Iowa Wesleyan Coll (IA)
Jacksonville State U (AL)
Jacksonville U (FL)
Jamestown Coll (ND)
Jarvis Christian Coll (TX)
John Brown U (AR)
John Carroll U (OH)
Johnson Bible Coll (TN)
Johnson C. Smith U (NC)
Johnson State Coll (VT)
John Wesley Coll (NC)
Judson Coll (AL)
Judson Coll (IL)
Juniata Coll (PA)
Kansas State U (KS)
Kansas Wesleyan U (KS)
Kean U (NJ)
Keene State Coll (NH)
Kendall Coll (IL)
Kennesaw State U (GA)
Kentucky Christian Coll (KY)
Kentucky State U (KY)
Kentucky Wesleyan Coll (KY)
Keuka Coll (NY)
Keystone Coll (PA)
King Coll (TN)
The King's Coll (NY)
King's Coll (PA)
The King's U Coll (AB, Canada)
Kutztown U of Pennsylvania (PA)
LaGrange Coll (GA)
Lake Erie Coll (OH)
Lake Forest Coll (IL)
Lakehead U (ON, Canada)
Lakeland Coll (WI)
Lake Superior State U (MI)
Lamar U (TX)
Lambuth U (TN)
Lancaster Bible Coll (PA)
Lander U (SC)
La Roche Coll (PA)
La Salle U (PA)
Lasell Coll (MA)
Lebanon Valley Coll (PA)
Le Moyne Coll (NY)
Lenoir-Rhyne Coll (NC)
Lesley U (MA)
LeTourneau U (TX)
Lewis-Clark State Coll (ID)
Lewis U (IL)
Liberty U (VA)
Limestone Coll (SC)
Lincoln Memorial U (TN)
Lincoln U (MO)
Lincoln U (PA)
Lindenwood U (MO)
Lindsey Wilson Coll (KY)
Linfield Coll (OR)
Lipscomb U (TN)
Livingstone Coll (NC)
Lock Haven U of Pennsylvania (PA)
Long Island U, Brooklyn Campus (NY)
Long Island U, C.W. Post Campus (NY)
Long Island U, Southampton Coll (NY)
Longwood U (VA)
Loras Coll (IA)
Louisiana Coll (LA)
Louisiana State U and A&M Coll (LA)
Louisiana State U in Shreveport (LA)
Louisiana Tech U (LA)
Loyola Coll in Maryland (MD)
Loyola U Chicago (IL)
Loyola U New Orleans (LA)
Lubbock Christian U (TX)
Luther Coll (IA)
Lycoming Coll (PA)
Lynchburg Coll (VA)
Lyndon State Coll (VT)
Lynn U (FL)
MacMurray Coll (IL)
Madonna U (MI)
Maharishi U of Management (IA)
Manchester Coll (IN)
Manhattan Coll (NY)
Manhattanville Coll (NY)
Mansfield U of Pennsylvania (PA)
Marian Coll (IN)
Marian Coll of Fond du Lac (WI)
Marietta Coll (OH)
Marist Coll (NY)
Marquette U (WI)
Marshall U (WV)
Mars Hill Coll (NC)
Martin Luther Coll (MN)
Martin U (IN)
Marymount Coll of Fordham U (NY)
Maryville U of Saint Louis (MO)
Mary Washington Coll (VA)
Marywood U (PA)
Massachusetts Coll of Liberal Arts (MA)
The Master's Coll and Sem (CA)
Mayville State U (ND)
McGill U (QC, Canada)
McKendree Coll (IL)
McMurry U (TX)
McNeese State U (LA)
McPherson Coll (KS)
Medaille Coll (NY)
Memorial U of Newfoundland (NL, Canada)
Mercer U (GA)
Mercy Coll (NY)
Mercyhurst Coll (PA)
Merrimack Coll (MA)
Messiah Coll (PA)
Methodist Coll (NC)
Miami U (OH)
Michigan State U (MI)
MidAmerica Nazarene U (KS)
Mid-Continent Coll (KY)
Midway Coll (KY)
Miles Coll (AL)
Millersville U of Pennsylvania (PA)
Millikin U (IL)
Minnesota State U Mankato (MN)
Minnesota State U Moorhead (MN)
Minot State U (ND)
Mississippi Coll (MS)
Mississippi State U (MS)
Mississippi Valley State U (MS)
Missouri Baptist U (MO)
Missouri Southern State U (MO)
Missouri Valley Coll (MO)
Missouri Western State Coll (MO)
Molloy Coll (NY)
Monmouth Coll (IL)
Montana State U–Billings (MT)
Montana State U–Bozeman (MT)
Montreat Coll (NC)
Moravian Coll (PA)
Morehead State U (KY)
Morehouse Coll (GA)
Morgan State U (MD)
Morningside Coll (IA)
Morris Coll (SC)
Mount Marty Coll (SD)
Mount Mary Coll (WI)
Mount Mercy Coll (IA)
Mount Saint Mary Coll (NY)
Mount St. Mary's Coll (CA)
Mount Saint Mary's Coll and Sem (MD)
Mount Saint Vincent U (NS, Canada)
Mount Vernon Nazarene U (OH)
Muhlenberg Coll (PA)
Murray State U (KY)
National-Louis U (IL)
Nazareth Coll of Rochester (NY)
Nebraska Wesleyan U (NE)
Neumann Coll (PA)
Newberry Coll (SC)
New Jersey City U (NJ)
Newman U (KS)
New Mexico Highlands U (NM)
New Mexico State U (NM)
New York Inst of Technology (NY)
New York U (NY)
Niagara U (NY)
Nicholls State U (LA)
North Carolina Central U (NC)
North Carolina Wesleyan Coll (NC)
North Central Coll (IL)
North Central U (MN)
North Dakota State U (ND)
Northeastern Illinois U (IL)
Northeastern State U (OK)
Northeastern U (MA)
Northern Arizona U (AZ)
Northern Illinois U (IL)
Northern Michigan U (MI)
Northern State U (SD)
North Georgia Coll & State U (GA)
North Greenville Coll (SC)
Northland Coll (WI)
North Park U (IL)
Northwestern Coll (IA)
Northwestern Coll (MN)
Northwestern Oklahoma State U (OK)
Northwestern State U of Louisiana (LA)
Northwest Nazarene U (ID)
Notre Dame Coll (OH)
Notre Dame de Namur U (CA)
Nova Southeastern U (FL)
Nyack Coll (NY)
Oakland City U (IN)
Oakland U (MI)
Oglethorpe U (GA)
Ohio Northern U (OH)
The Ohio State U at Lima (OH)
The Ohio State U at Marion (OH)
The Ohio State U–Mansfield Campus (OH)
The Ohio State U–Newark Campus (OH)
Ohio U (OH)
Ohio U–Chillicothe (OH)
Ohio U–Zanesville (OH)
Ohio Valley Coll (WV)
Ohio Wesleyan U (OH)
Oklahoma Baptist U (OK)
Oklahoma Christian U (OK)
Oklahoma City U (OK)
Oklahoma Panhandle State U (OK)

Oklahoma State U (OK)
Olivet Coll (MI)
Olivet Nazarene U (IL)
Oral Roberts U (OK)
Ottawa U (KS)
Otterbein Coll (OH)
Our Lady of Holy Cross Coll (LA)
Pace U (NY)
Pacific Lutheran U (WA)
Pacific Oaks Coll (CA)
Pacific Union Coll (CA)
Pacific U (OR)
Paine Coll (GA)
Palm Beach Atlantic U (FL)
Park U (MO)
Penn State U Abington Coll (PA)
Penn State U Altoona Coll (PA)
Penn State U at Erie, The Behrend Coll (PA)
Penn State U Beaver Campus of the Commonwealth Coll (PA)
Penn State U Berks Cmps of Berks-Lehigh Valley Coll (PA)
Penn State U Delaware County Campus of the Commonwealth Coll (PA)
Penn State U DuBois Campus of the Commonwealth Coll (PA)
Penn State U Fayette Campus of the Commonwealth Coll (PA)
Penn State U Harrisburg Campus of the Capital Coll (PA)
Penn State U Hazleton Campus of the Commonwealth Coll (PA)
Penn State U Lehigh Valley Cmps of Berks-Lehigh Valley Coll (PA)
Penn State U McKeesport Campus of the Commonwealth Coll (PA)
Penn State U Mont Alto Campus of the Commonwealth Coll (PA)
Penn State U New Kensington Campus of the Commonwealth Coll (PA)
Penn State U Schuylkill Campus of the Capital Coll (PA)
Penn State U Shenango Campus of the Commonwealth Coll (PA)
Penn State U Univ Park Campus (PA)
Penn State U Wilkes-Barre Campus of the Commonwealth Coll (PA)
Penn State U Worthington Scranton Cmps Commonwealth Coll (PA)
Penn State U York Campus of the Commonwealth Coll (PA)
Pepperdine U, Malibu (CA)
Pfeiffer U (NC)
Philadelphia Biblical U (PA)
Pikeville Coll (KY)
Pillsbury Baptist Bible Coll (MN)
Pine Manor Coll (MA)
Pittsburg State U (KS)
Plymouth State U (NH)
Point Park U (PA)
Pontifical Catholic U of Puerto Rico (PR)
Presbyterian Coll (SC)
Principia Coll (IL)
Purdue U (IN)
Purdue U North Central (IN)
Queens Coll of the City U of NY (NY)
Queen's U at Kingston (ON, Canada)
Queens U of Charlotte (NC)
Quincy U (IL)
Randolph-Macon Woman's Coll (VA)
Redeemer U Coll (ON, Canada)
Reformed Bible Coll (MI)
Regis U (CO)
Rhode Island Coll (RI)
Rider U (NJ)
Ripon Coll (WI)
Rivier Coll (NH)
Robert Morris U (PA)
Roberts Wesleyan Coll (NY)
Rockford Coll (IL)
Rockhurst U (MO)
Rocky Mountain Coll (MT)
Roger Williams U (RI)
Roosevelt U (IL)
Rowan U (NJ)
Russell Sage Coll (NY)
Sacred Heart U (CT)
Saginaw Valley State U (MI)
St. Ambrose U (IA)
St. Andrews Presbyterian Coll (NC)
Saint Augustine's Coll (NC)
St. Bonaventure U (NY)
St. Cloud State U (MN)
Saint Francis U (PA)
St. Francis Xavier U (NS, Canada)
St. John Fisher Coll (NY)
Saint John's U (MN)
St. John's U (NY)
Saint Joseph Coll (CT)
Saint Joseph's Coll (IN)
Saint Joseph's Coll of Maine (ME)
St. Joseph's Coll, Suffolk Campus (NY)
Saint Joseph's U (PA)
Saint Leo U (FL)
Saint Martin's Coll (WA)
Saint Mary-of-the-Woods Coll (IN)
Saint Mary's Coll (IN)
Saint Mary's U of Minnesota (MN)
Saint Michael's Coll (VT)
St. Norbert Coll (WI)
St. Thomas Aquinas Coll (NY)
St. Thomas U (FL)
Saint Xavier U (IL)
Salem State Coll (MA)
Salisbury U (MD)
Salve Regina U (RI)
Sarah Lawrence Coll (NY)
Schreiner U (TX)
Seton Hall U (NJ)
Seton Hill U (PA)
Shawnee State U (OH)
Shaw U (NC)
Sheldon Jackson Coll (AK)
Shepherd U (WV)
Shippensburg U of Pennsylvania (PA)
Shorter Coll (GA)
Siena Heights U (MI)
Silver Lake Coll (WI)
Simmons Coll (MA)
Simpson Coll (IA)
Simpson Coll and Graduate School (CA)
Skidmore Coll (NY)
Slippery Rock U of Pennsylvania (PA)
South Carolina State U (SC)
Southeastern Coll of the Assemblies of God (FL)
Southeastern Louisiana U (LA)
Southeastern Oklahoma State U (OK)
Southeast Missouri State U (MO)
Southern Adventist U (TN)
Southern Arkansas U–Magnolia (AR)
Southern Connecticut State U (CT)
Southern Illinois U Carbondale (IL)
Southern Illinois U Edwardsville (IL)
Southern Nazarene U (OK)
Southern U and A&M Coll (LA)
Southern Utah U (UT)
Southern Wesleyan U (SC)
Southwest Baptist U (MO)
Southwestern Coll (AZ)
Southwestern Coll (KS)
Southwestern Oklahoma State U (OK)
Southwest Missouri State U (MO)
Spring Arbor U (MI)
Springfield Coll (MA)
Spring Hill Coll (AL)
State U of NY at New Paltz (NY)
State U of NY at Oswego (NY)
Plattsburgh State U of NY (NY)
State U of NY Coll at Brockport (NY)
State U of NY Coll at Cortland (NY)
State U of NY Coll at Fredonia (NY)
State U of NY Coll at Geneseo (NY)
State U of NY Coll at Old Westbury (NY)
State U of NY Coll at Oneonta (NY)
State U of NY Coll at Potsdam (NY)
State U of West Georgia (GA)
Stephens Coll (MO)
Sterling Coll (KS)
Stetson U (FL)
Stonehill Coll (MA)
Suffolk U (MA)
Susquehanna U (PA)
Tabor Coll (KS)
Taylor U (IN)
Taylor U, Fort Wayne Campus (IN)
Tennessee State U (TN)
Tennessee Technological U (TN)
Tennessee Wesleyan Coll (TN)
Texas A&M U–Commerce (TX)
Texas A&M U–Kingsville (TX)
Texas Christian U (TX)
Texas Lutheran U (TX)
Texas Southern U (TX)
Texas Wesleyan U (TX)
Texas Woman's U (TX)
Thiel Coll (PA)
Thomas Coll (ME)
Thomas More Coll (KY)
Tougaloo Coll (MS)
Towson U (MD)
Transylvania U (KY)
Trent U (ON, Canada)
Trinity Baptist Coll (FL)
Trinity Bible Coll (ND)
Trinity Christian Coll (IL)
Trinity Coll (DC)
Trinity Coll of Florida (FL)
Trinity Intl U (IL)
Trinity Western U (BC, Canada)
Tri-State U (IN)
Troy State U (AL)
Troy State U Dothan (AL)
Tufts U (MA)
Tusculum Coll (TN)
Tuskegee U (AL)
Union Coll (KY)
Union Coll (NE)
Union U (TN)
Universidad Adventista de las Antillas (PR)
Université de Montréal (QC, Canada)
Université de Sherbrooke (QC, Canada)
U du Québec à Hull (QC, Canada)
Université Laval (QC, Canada)
U Coll of the Cariboo (BC, Canada)
The U of Akron (OH)
The U of Alabama (AL)
The U of Alabama at Birmingham (AL)
The U of Alabama in Huntsville (AL)
U of Alaska Fairbanks (AK)
U of Alaska Southeast (AK)
U of Alberta (AB, Canada)
The U of Arizona (AZ)
U of Arkansas (AR)
U of Arkansas at Little Rock (AR)
U of Arkansas at Monticello (AR)
The U of British Columbia (BC, Canada)
U of Calgary (AB, Canada)
U of Central Arkansas (AR)
U of Central Florida (FL)
U of Charleston (WV)
U of Cincinnati (OH)
U of Connecticut (CT)
U of Dallas (TX)
U of Dayton (OH)
U of Delaware (DE)
U of Detroit Mercy (MI)
U of Dubuque (IA)
U of Evansville (IN)
The U of Findlay (OH)
U of Florida (FL)
U of Great Falls (MT)
U of Hartford (CT)
U of Hawaii at Hilo (HI)
U of Hawaii at Manoa (HI)
U of Idaho (ID)
U of Illinois at Chicago (IL)
U of Illinois at Springfield (IL)
U of Illinois at Urbana–Champaign (IL)
U of Indianapolis (IN)
The U of Iowa (IA)
U of Kansas (KS)
U of Kentucky (KY)
U of La Verne (CA)
U of Louisiana at Lafayette (LA)
U of Louisville (KY)
U of Maine (ME)
U of Maine at Farmington (ME)
U of Maine at Fort Kent (ME)
U of Maine at Machias (ME)
U of Maine at Presque Isle (ME)
U of Manitoba (MB, Canada)
U of Mary (ND)
U of Mary Hardin-Baylor (TX)
U of Maryland, Coll Park (MD)
U of Maryland Eastern Shore (MD)
U of Miami (FL)
U of Michigan (MI)
U of Michigan–Dearborn (MI)
U of Michigan–Flint (MI)
U of Minnesota, Duluth (MN)
U of Minnesota, Morris (MN)
U of Minnesota, Twin Cities Campus (MN)
U of Mississippi (MS)
U of Missouri–Columbia (MO)
U of Missouri–Kansas City (MO)
U of Missouri–St. Louis (MO)
U of Mobile (AL)
The U of Montana–Missoula (MT)
The U of Montana–Western (MT)
U of Montevallo (AL)
U of Nebraska at Omaha (NE)
U of Nebraska–Lincoln (NE)
U of Nevada, Las Vegas (NV)
U of Nevada, Reno (NV)
U of New Brunswick Fredericton (NB, Canada)
U of New Hampshire (NH)
U of New Mexico (NM)
U of New Orleans (LA)
U of North Alabama (AL)
The U of North Carolina at Chapel Hill (NC)
The U of North Carolina at Charlotte (NC)
The U of North Carolina at Greensboro (NC)
The U of North Carolina at Pembroke (NC)
The U of North Carolina at Wilmington (NC)
U of North Dakota (ND)
U of Northern Iowa (IA)
U of North Florida (FL)
U of Oklahoma (OK)
U of Ottawa (ON, Canada)
U of Pennsylvania (PA)
U of Pittsburgh at Johnstown (PA)
U of Portland (OR)
U of Prince Edward Island (PE, Canada)
U of Puerto Rico, Cayey U Coll (PR)
U of Redlands (CA)
U of Regina (SK, Canada)
U of Rhode Island (RI)
U of Richmond (VA)
U of St. Francis (IL)
U of Saint Francis (IN)
U of Saint Mary (KS)
U of St. Thomas (MN)
U of St. Thomas (TX)
U of San Francisco (CA)
U of Saskatchewan (SK, Canada)
U of Science and Arts of Oklahoma (OK)
The U of Scranton (PA)
U of Sioux Falls (SD)
U of South Alabama (AL)
U of South Carolina Aiken (SC)
U of South Carolina Spartanburg (SC)
The U of South Dakota (SD)
U of Southern Indiana (IN)
U of South Florida (FL)
The U of Tampa (FL)
The U of Tennessee at Martin (TN)
The U of Texas–Pan American (TX)
U of the District of Columbia (DC)
U of the Incarnate Word (TX)
U of the Sacred Heart (PR)
U of the Virgin Islands (VI)
U of Toledo (OH)
U of Tulsa (OK)
U of Utah (UT)
U of Vermont (VT)
U of Victoria (BC, Canada)
U of Washington (WA)
The U of West Alabama (AL)
The U of Western Ontario (ON, Canada)
U of West Florida (FL)
U of Windsor (ON, Canada)
U of Wisconsin–Eau Claire (WI)
U of Wisconsin–Green Bay (WI)
U of Wisconsin–La Crosse (WI)
U of Wisconsin–Madison (WI)
U of Wisconsin–Milwaukee (WI)
U of Wisconsin–Oshkosh (WI)
U of Wisconsin–Platteville (WI)
U of Wisconsin–River Falls (WI)
U of Wisconsin–Stevens Point (WI)
U of Wisconsin–Superior (WI)
U of Wisconsin–Whitewater (WI)
U of Wyoming (WY)
Upper Iowa U (IA)
Urbana U (OH)
Utah State U (UT)
Utica Coll (NY)
Valdosta State U (GA)
Valley City State U (ND)
Valparaiso U (IN)
Vanderbilt U (TN)
Vennard Coll (IA)
Villa Julie Coll (MD)
Villanova U (PA)
Virginia Intermont Coll (VA)
Virginia Union U (VA)
Virginia Wesleyan Coll (VA)
Viterbo U (WI)
Voorhees Coll (SC)
Wagner Coll (NY)
Waldorf Coll (IA)
Walla Walla Coll (WA)
Walsh U (OH)
Warner Pacific Coll (OR)
Warner Southern Coll (FL)
Warren Wilson Coll (NC)
Wartburg Coll (IA)
Washburn U (KS)
Washington Bible Coll (MD)
Washington State U (WA)
Washington U in St. Louis (MO)
Wayland Baptist U (TX)
Waynesburg Coll (PA)
Wayne State Coll (NE)
Wayne State U (MI)
Weber State U (UT)
Webster U (MO)
Wells Coll (NY)
West Chester U of Pennsylvania (PA)
Western Baptist Coll (OR)
Western Carolina U (NC)
Western Connecticut State U (CT)
Western Illinois U (IL)
Western Kentucky U (KY)
Western Michigan U (MI)
Western State Coll of Colorado (CO)
Western Washington U (WA)
Westfield State Coll (MA)
West Liberty State Coll (WV)
Westminster Coll (MO)
Westminster Coll (PA)
Westminster Coll (UT)
Westmont Coll (CA)
West Virginia State Coll (WV)
West Virginia U (WV)
West Virginia Wesleyan Coll (WV)
Wheaton Coll (IL)
Wheeling Jesuit U (WV)
Wheelock Coll (MA)
Whitworth Coll (WA)
Wichita State U (KS)
Widener U (PA)
Wilkes U (PA)
William Carey Coll (MS)
William Jewell Coll (MO)
William Paterson U of New Jersey (NJ)
William Penn U (IA)
Williams Baptist Coll (AR)
William Woods U (MO)
Wilmington Coll (DE)
Wilson Coll (PA)
Wingate U (NC)
Winona State U (MN)
Winston-Salem State U (NC)
Winthrop U (SC)
Wisconsin Lutheran Coll (WI)
Wittenberg U (OH)
Worcester State Coll (MA)
Wright State U (OH)
Xavier U (OH)
Xavier U of Louisiana (LA)
York Coll (NE)
York Coll of Pennsylvania (PA)
York U (ON, Canada)
Youngstown State U (OH)

EMERGENCY MEDICAL TECHNOLOGY (EMT PARAMEDIC)

Central Washington U (WA)
Creighton U (NE)
Eastern Kentucky U (KY)
The George Washington U (DC)
Loma Linda U (CA)
Nebraska Methodist Coll (NE)
Springfield Coll (MA)
U of Maryland, Baltimore County (MD)
U of Minnesota, Twin Cities Campus (MN)
U of the District of Columbia (DC)
Western Carolina U (NC)

ENERGY MANAGEMENT AND SYSTEMS TECHNOLOGY

Ferris State U (MI)
Lamar U (TX)
Sterling Coll (VT)

ENGINEERING

Abilene Christian U (TX)
The American U in Dubai(United Arab Emirates)
Arkansas State U (AR)
Arkansas Tech U (AR)
Auburn U (AL)
Baker U (KS)
Baldwin-Wallace Coll (OH)
Barry U (FL)
Bates Coll (ME)
Baylor U (TX)
Beloit Coll (WI)
Bethel Coll (IN)
Boston U (MA)
Brown U (RI)
State U of NY Coll at Buffalo (NY)
California Inst of Technology (CA)
California State U, Fullerton (CA)
California State U, Long Beach (CA)
California State U, Los Angeles (CA)
Calvin Coll (MI)

Carleton U (ON, Canada)
Carnegie Mellon U (PA)
Carroll Coll (MT)
Carthage Coll (WI)
Case Western Reserve U (OH)
The Catholic U of America (DC)
Chatham Coll (PA)
Claremont McKenna Coll (CA)
Clark Atlanta U (GA)
Clarkson U (NY)
Clark U (MA)
Cleveland State U (OH)
Cogswell Polytechnical Coll (CA)
Coll of Staten Island of the City U of NY (NY)
Coll of the Ozarks (MO)
Colorado School of Mines (CO)
Cooper Union for the Advancement of Science & Art (NY)
Cornell U (NY)
Dalhousie U (NS, Canada)
Dartmouth Coll (NH)
Dickinson Coll (PA)
Dordt Coll (IA)
Drexel U (PA)
Elizabethtown Coll (PA)
Elon U (NC)
Embry-Riddle Aeronautical U (AZ)
Embry-Riddle Aeronautical U (FL)
Fontbonne U (MO)
Gallaudet U (DC)
Gannon U (PA)
Geneva Coll (PA)
George Fox U (OR)
The George Washington U (DC)
Gonzaga U (WA)
Grand Valley State U (MI)
Harvard U (MA)
Harvey Mudd Coll (CA)
Hood Coll (MD)
Hope Coll (MI)
Idaho State U (ID)
Indiana U–Purdue U Indianapolis (IN)
Inter American U of PR, Bayamón Campus (PR)
Iowa State U of Science and Technology (IA)
John Brown U (AR)
The Johns Hopkins U (MD)
Johnson C. Smith U (NC)
Juniata Coll (PA)
Kansas Wesleyan U (KS)
Lafayette Coll (PA)
Lakehead U (ON, Canada)
LeTourneau U (TX)
Lipscomb U (TN)
Lock Haven U of Pennsylvania (PA)
Loyola Coll in Maryland (MD)
Lubbock Christian U (TX)
Maine Maritime Acad (ME)
Manhattan Coll (NY)
Marquette U (WI)
Maryville Coll (TN)
Massachusetts Maritime Acad (MA)
McNeese State U (LA)
Memorial U of Newfoundland (NL, Canada)
Mercer U (GA)
Messiah Coll (PA)
Michigan State U (MI)
Michigan Technological U (MI)
Mills Coll (CA)
Montana Tech of The U of Montana (MT)
Morehouse Coll (GA)
Morgan State U (MD)
National American U (NM)
New Mexico Highlands U (NM)
New Mexico Inst of Mining and Technology (NM)
North Carolina State U (NC)
North Dakota State U (ND)
Northeastern U (MA)
Northern Arizona U (AZ)
Northwestern U (IL)
Nova Scotia Ag Coll (NS, Canada)
Oakland U (MI)
Ohio Northern U (OH)
Ohio U (OH)
Oklahoma Christian U (OK)
Oklahoma State U (OK)
Olivet Nazarene U (IL)
Oregon State U (OR)
Pacific Union Coll (CA)
Pfeiffer U (NC)
Pitzer Coll (CA)
Queen's U at Kingston (ON, Canada)
Rensselaer Polytechnic Inst (NY)
Rochester Inst of Technology (NY)
Russell Sage Coll (NY)
Rutgers, The State U of New Jersey, Camden (NJ)
Rutgers, The State U of New Jersey, Newark (NJ)
Saint Anselm Coll (NH)
St. Cloud State U (MN)
Saint Francis U (PA)
Saint Mary's Coll of California (CA)
St. Mary's U of San Antonio (TX)
Saint Vincent Coll (PA)
San Diego State U (CA)
San Jose State U (CA)
Santa Clara U (CA)
Schreiner U (TX)
Seton Hill U (PA)
Spelman Coll (GA)
Stanford U (CA)
Stony Brook U, State U of New York (NY)
Swarthmore Coll (PA)
Tennessee State U (TN)
Texas Christian U (TX)
Texas Tech U (TX)
Trinity Coll (CT)
Tufts U (MA)
United States Air Force Acad (CO)
United States Military Acad (NY)
United States Naval Acad (MD)
Université de Sherbrooke (QC, Canada)
The U of Akron (OH)
U of Alberta (AB, Canada)
The U of Arizona (AZ)
U of Arkansas (AR)
U of Calif, Davis (CA)
U of Calif, Los Angeles (CA)
U of Calif, San Diego (CA)
U of Cincinnati (OH)
U of Delaware (DE)
U of Denver (CO)
U of Detroit Mercy (MI)
U of Hartford (CT)
U of Hawaii at Manoa (HI)
U of Idaho (ID)
U of Illinois at Urbana–Champaign (IL)
The U of Iowa (IA)
U of Louisiana at Lafayette (LA)
U of Louisville (KY)
U of Maryland, Coll Park (MD)
U of Massachusetts Amherst (MA)
U of Michigan (MI)
U of Michigan–Dearborn (MI)
U of Mississippi (MS)
U of New Brunswick Fredericton (NB, Canada)
U of New Haven (CT)
U of New Mexico (NM)
U of Oklahoma (OK)
U of Ottawa (ON, Canada)
U of Pittsburgh (PA)
U of Portland (OR)
U of Regina (SK, Canada)
U of Saskatchewan (SK, Canada)
U of Southern California (CA)
U of Southern Indiana (IN)
U of South Florida (FL)
The U of Tennessee at Chattanooga (TN)
The U of Tennessee at Martin (TN)
The U of Texas–Pan American (TX)
U of Toledo (OH)
U of Toronto (ON, Canada)
U of Utah (UT)
U of Virginia (VA)
U of Washington (WA)
U of Windsor (ON, Canada)
U of Wisconsin–Madison (WI)
U of Wisconsin–Milwaukee (WI)
Vanderbilt U (TN)
Virginia Polytechnic Inst and State U (VA)
Wake Forest U (NC)
Walla Walla Coll (WA)
Wartburg Coll (IA)
Washington U in St. Louis (MO)
Wells Coll (NY)
Western Michigan U (MI)
Western New England Coll (MA)
Widener U (PA)
Wilkes U (PA)
Winona State U (MN)
Wright State U (OH)
York U (ON, Canada)
Youngstown State U (OH)

ENGINEERING/INDUSTRIAL MANAGEMENT

California State U, Long Beach (CA)
Claremont McKenna Coll (CA)
Columbia U, School of Eng & Applied Sci (NY)
Eastern Michigan U (MI)
State U of NY at Farmingdale (NY)
Fort Lewis Coll (CO)
Grand Valley State U (MI)
Grantham U (LA)
Illinois Inst of Technology (IL)
John Brown U (AR)
Kettering U (MI)
Lake Superior State U (MI)
Lawrence Technological U (MI)
Miami U (OH)
Miami U Hamilton (OH)
Middle Tennessee State U (TN)
Missouri Tech (MO)
Robert Morris U (PA)
Saint Louis U (MO)
South Dakota State U (SD)
Stevens Inst of Technology (NJ)
Tri-State U (IN)
United States Merchant Marine Acad (NY)
United States Military Acad (NY)
U of Evansville (IN)
U of Illinois at Chicago (IL)
U of Massachusetts Lowell (MA)
U of Missouri–Rolla (MO)
U of Ottawa (ON, Canada)
U of Portland (OR)
The U of Tennessee at Chattanooga (TN)
U of the Pacific (CA)
U of Vermont (VT)
U of Wisconsin–Stout (WI)
Washington State U (WA)
Western Michigan U (MI)
Widener U (PA)
Wilkes U (PA)
Worcester Polytechnic Inst (MA)
York Coll of Pennsylvania (PA)

ENGINEERING MECHANICS

Clemson U (SC)
Cleveland State U (OH)
Columbia U, School of Eng & Applied Sci (NY)
Dordt Coll (IA)
The Johns Hopkins U (MD)
Lehigh U (PA)
Michigan Technological U (MI)
New Mexico Inst of Mining and Technology (NM)
Oral Roberts U (OK)
United States Air Force Acad (CO)
U of Cincinnati (OH)
U of Illinois at Urbana–Champaign (IL)
U of Windsor (ON, Canada)
U of Wisconsin–Madison (WI)
Wentworth Inst of Technology (MA)
West Virginia Wesleyan Coll (WV)
Worcester Polytechnic Inst (MA)

ENGINEERING PHYSICS

Abilene Christian U (TX)
Arkansas Tech U (AR)
Augustana Coll (IL)
Augustana Coll (SD)
Aurora U (IL)
Bemidji State U (MN)
Bradley U (IL)
Brandeis U (MA)
Brown U (RI)
California Inst of Technology (CA)
Case Western Reserve U (OH)
Christian Brothers U (TN)
Colorado School of Mines (CO)
Colorado State U (CO)
Columbia U, School of Eng & Applied Sci (NY)
Connecticut Coll (CT)
Cornell U (NY)
Dartmouth Coll (NH)
Delaware State U (DE)
Eastern Nazarene Coll (MA)
Elizabethtown Coll (PA)
Embry-Riddle Aeronautical U (FL)
Harvard U (MA)
Hope Coll (MI)
Jacksonville U (FL)
John Carroll U (OH)
Juniata Coll (PA)
Lehigh U (PA)
Loras Coll (IA)
Loyola Marymount U (CA)
Merrimack Coll (MA)
Miami U (OH)
Miami U Hamilton (OH)
Michigan Technological U (MI)
Morgan State U (MD)
Morningside Coll (IA)
Murray State U (KY)
Northeastern State U (OK)
Northern Arizona U (AZ)
Northwest Nazarene U (ID)
The Ohio State U (OH)
Oregon State U (OR)
Pacific Lutheran U (WA)
Point Loma Nazarene U (CA)
Queen's U at Kingston (ON, Canada)
Randolph-Macon Woman's Coll (VA)
Rensselaer Polytechnic Inst (NY)
Rose-Hulman Inst of Technology (IN)
St. Ambrose U (IA)
St. Bonaventure U (NY)
Saint Mary's U of Minnesota (MN)
Samford U (AL)
Santa Clara U (CA)
South Dakota State U (SD)
Southeast Missouri State U (MO)
Southern Arkansas U–Magnolia (AR)
Southwestern Coll (KS)
Southwestern Oklahoma State U (OK)
Southwest Missouri State U (MO)
State U of NY at New Paltz (NY)
Stevens Inst of Technology (NJ)
Syracuse U (NY)
Tarleton State U (TX)
Taylor U (IN)
Texas Tech U (TX)
Thiel Coll (PA)
Tufts U (MA)
United States Military Acad (NY)
Université Laval (QC, Canada)
U at Buffalo, The State U of New York (NY)
The U of Akron (OH)
U of Alberta (AB, Canada)
The U of Arizona (AZ)
The U of British Columbia (BC, Canada)
U of Calif, Berkeley (CA)
U of Calif, San Diego (CA)
U of Colorado at Boulder (CO)
U of Connecticut (CT)
U of Illinois at Chicago (IL)
U of Illinois at Urbana–Champaign (IL)
U of Kansas (KS)
U of Maine (ME)
U of Massachusetts Boston (MA)
U of Michigan (MI)
U of Nebraska at Omaha (NE)
U of Nevada, Reno (NV)
U of Northern Iowa (IA)
U of Oklahoma (OK)
U of Pittsburgh (PA)
U of Saskatchewan (SK, Canada)
The U of Tennessee (TN)
The U of Texas at Brownsville (TX)
U of the Pacific (CA)
U of Toledo (OH)
U of Tulsa (OK)
U of Wisconsin–Madison (WI)
Washington and Lee U (VA)
Washington U in St. Louis (MO)
Westmont Coll (CA)
West Virginia Wesleyan Coll (WV)
Wilberforce U (OH)
Worcester Polytechnic Inst (MA)
Wright State U (OH)
Yale U (CT)
York U (ON, Canada)

ENGINEERING RELATED

Augustana Coll (IL)
Boston U (MA)
California State U, Chico (CA)
California State U, Long Beach (CA)
Canisius Coll (NY)
Carnegie Mellon U (PA)
Charleston Southern U (SC)
Claremont McKenna Coll (CA)
Cleveland State U (OH)
Dowling Coll (NY)
Eastern Illinois U (IL)
Eastern Michigan U (MI)
Fairfield U (CT)
Gettysburg Coll (PA)
Hawai'i Pacific U (HI)
Idaho State U (ID)
Iowa State U of Science and Technology (IA)
Kentucky Wesleyan Coll (KY)
Lehigh U (PA)
Loras Coll (IA)
Madonna U (MI)
Marquette U (WI)
McGill U (QC, Canada)
Monmouth U (NJ)
New York U (NY)
Northwestern U (IL)
Ohio Northern U (OH)
Ohio U (OH)
Ohio Wesleyan U (OH)
Pacific Union Coll (CA)
Park U (MO)
Principia Coll (IL)
Purdue U (IN)
Rochester Inst of Technology (NY)
Rose-Hulman Inst of Technology (IN)
Samford U (AL)
Spring Hill Coll (AL)
Syracuse U (NY)
Texas Wesleyan U (TX)
Tufts U (MA)
Université Laval (QC, Canada)
The U of Alabama in Huntsville (AL)
The U of Arizona (AZ)
U of Arkansas (AR)
U of Connecticut (CT)
U of Maryland, Coll Park (MD)
U of Nebraska–Lincoln (NE)
U of Pennsylvania (PA)
U of the Incarnate Word (TX)
U of Waterloo (ON, Canada)
Waynesburg Coll (PA)
Western Washington U (WA)
Wheaton Coll (IL)
Worcester Polytechnic Inst (MA)
Wright State U (OH)

ENGINEERING-RELATED TECHNOLOGIES

Rochester Inst of Technology (NY)
United States Merchant Marine Acad (NY)

ENGINEERING SCIENCE

Abilene Christian U (TX)
Belmont U (TN)
Benedictine U (IL)
Bethel U (MN)
California Polytechnic State U, San Luis Obispo (CA)
California State U, Fullerton (CA)
Case Western Reserve U (OH)
Claremont McKenna Coll (CA)
Cleveland State U (OH)
The Coll of New Jersey (NJ)
Coll of Notre Dame of Maryland (MD)
The Coll of Southeastern Europe, The American U of Athens(Greece)
Colorado School of Mines (CO)
Colorado State U (CO)
Franciscan U of Steubenville (OH)
Gallaudet U (DC)
Harvard U (MA)
Hofstra U (NY)
Houston Baptist U (TX)
Iowa State U of Science and Technology (IA)
Lamar U (TX)
Lipscomb U (TN)
Manchester Coll (IN)
Montana Tech of The U of Montana (MT)
New Jersey Inst of Technology (NJ)
Northwestern U (IL)
Ohio Wesleyan U (OH)
Pacific Lutheran U (WA)
Penn State U Abington Coll (PA)
Penn State U Altoona Coll (PA)
Penn State U at Erie, The Behrend Coll (PA)
Penn State U Beaver Campus of the Commonwealth Coll (PA)
Penn State U Berks Cmps of Berks-Lehigh Valley Coll (PA)
Penn State U Delaware County Campus of the Commonwealth Coll (PA)
Penn State U DuBois Campus of the Commonwealth Coll (PA)
Penn State U Fayette Campus of the Commonwealth Coll (PA)
Penn State U Hazleton Campus of the Commonwealth Coll (PA)
Penn State U Lehigh Valley Cmps of Berks-Lehigh Valley Coll (PA)
Penn State U McKeesport Campus of the Commonwealth Coll (PA)
Penn State U Mont Alto Campus of the Commonwealth Coll (PA)
Penn State U New Kensington Campus of the Commonwealth Coll (PA)
Penn State U Schuylkill Campus of the Capital Coll (PA)
Penn State U Shenango Campus of the Commonwealth Coll (PA)
Penn State U Univ Park Campus (PA)
Penn State U Wilkes-Barre Campus of the Commonwealth Coll (PA)
Penn State U Worthington Scranton Cmps Commonwealth Coll (PA)
Penn State U York Campus of the Commonwealth Coll (PA)

Queen's U at Kingston (ON, Canada)
Rensselaer Polytechnic Inst (NY)
Rutgers, The State U of New Jersey, New Brunswick/Piscataway (NJ)
St. Mary's U of San Antonio (TX)
St. Thomas Aquinas Coll (NY)
Seattle Pacific U (WA)
Simon Fraser U (BC, Canada)
Smith Coll (MA)
State U of NY Coll at Oneonta (NY)
Sweet Briar Coll (VA)
Trinity U (TX)
Tufts U (MA)
Tulane U (LA)
United States Air Force Acad (CO)
U of Calif, Berkeley (CA)
U of Calif, San Diego (CA)
U of Cincinnati (OH)
U of Florida (FL)
U of Manitoba (MB, Canada)
U of Maryland, Baltimore County (MD)
U of Miami (FL)
U of Michigan (MI)
U of Michigan–Flint (MI)
U of New Mexico (NM)
U of New Orleans (LA)
U of Ottawa (ON, Canada)
U of Portland (OR)
U of Rochester (NY)
The U of Tennessee (TN)
U of Toronto (ON, Canada)
The U of Western Ontario (ON, Canada)
Vanderbilt U (TN)
Virginia Polytechnic Inst and State U (VA)
Washington State U (WA)
Washington U in St. Louis (MO)
Wright State U (OH)
Yale U (CT)

ENGINEERING TECHNOLOGIES RELATED
California Maritime Acad (CA)
California State Polytechnic U, Pomona (CA)
Cameron U (OK)
East Carolina U (NC)
Embry-Riddle Aeronautical U (FL)
New Jersey Inst of Technology (NJ)
Ohio U (OH)
Old Dominion U (VA)
Pennsylvania Coll of Technology (PA)
St. Cloud State U (MN)
The U of British Columbia (BC, Canada)
U of Hartford (CT)
U of Southern Indiana (IN)
Virginia State U (VA)
Western Michigan U (MI)

ENGINEERING TECHNOLOGY
Andrews U (MI)
Arkansas State U (AR)
Austin Peay State U (TN)
Berry Coll (GA)
Brigham Young U (UT)
State U of NY Coll at Buffalo (NY)
California State Polytechnic U, Pomona (CA)
California State U, Long Beach (CA)
California State U, Long Beach (CA)
Central Connecticut State U (CT)
Charleston Southern U (SC)
Cleveland State U (OH)
Colorado State U-Pueblo (CO)
Dordt Coll (IA)
Eastern Michigan U (MI)
Eastern New Mexico U (NM)
Eastern Washington U (WA)
Fairmont State Coll (WV)
Gallaudet U (DC)
Lawrence Technological U (MI)
LeTourneau U (TX)
Maine Maritime Acad (ME)
Massachusetts Maritime Acad (MA)
McNeese State U (LA)
Miami U (OH)
Miami U (OH)
Miami U Hamilton (OH)
Middle Tennessee State U (TN)
Midwestern State U (TX)
Missouri Tech (MO)
Murray State U (KY)
New Jersey Inst of Technology (NJ)
New Mexico State U (NM)
New Mexico State U (NM)
Northern Illinois U (IL)
Oklahoma State U (OK)
Oklahoma State U (OK)
Pacific Union Coll (CA)
Pittsburg State U (KS)
Prairie View A&M U (TX)
Rochester Inst of Technology (NY)
Rochester Inst of Technology (NY)
St. Cloud State U (MN)
Southern Illinois U Carbondale (IL)
Southwestern Oklahoma State U (OK)
Texas A&M U (TX)
Texas A&M U–Corpus Christi (TX)
Texas Southern U (TX)
Texas State U-San Marcos (TX)
Texas Tech U (TX)
Texas Tech U (TX)
Tuskegee U (AL)
The U of Akron (OH)
U of Central Florida (FL)
U of Hartford (CT)
U of Maine (ME)
U of Maryland Eastern Shore (MD)
U of North Texas (TX)
U of Pittsburgh at Johnstown (PA)
The U of Texas at Tyler (TX)
U of the District of Columbia (DC)
The U of West Alabama (AL)
U of West Florida (FL)
U of Wisconsin–River Falls (WI)
U of Wisconsin–Stout (WI)
Valdosta State U (GA)
Virginia State U (VA)
Walla Walla Coll (WA)
Wentworth Inst of Technology (MA)
Western Washington U (WA)
Western Washington U (WA)
William Penn U (IA)
Youngstown State U (OH)
Youngstown State U (OH)

ENGLISH
Abilene Christian U (TX)
Acadia U (NS, Canada)
Adams State Coll (CO)
Adelphi U (NY)
Adrian Coll (MI)
Agnes Scott Coll (GA)
Alabama Ag and Mech U (AL)
Alabama State U (AL)
Albany State U (GA)
Albertson Coll of Idaho (ID)
Albertus Magnus Coll (CT)
Albion Coll (MI)
Albright Coll (PA)
Alcorn State U (MS)
Alfred U (NY)
Alice Lloyd Coll (KY)
Allegheny Coll (PA)
Allen U (SC)
Alma Coll (MI)
Alvernia Coll (PA)
Alverno Coll (WI)
American Coll of Thessaloniki(Greece)
American Intl Coll (MA)
American U in Bulgaria(Bulgaria)
The American U in Cairo(Egypt)
Amherst Coll (MA)
Anderson Coll (SC)
Andrews U (MI)
Angelo State U (TX)
Anna Maria Coll (MA)
Antioch Coll (OH)
Appalachian State U (NC)
Aquinas Coll (MI)
Arcadia U (PA)
Arizona State U (AZ)
Arizona State U West (AZ)
Arkansas State U (AR)
Arkansas Tech U (AR)
Armstrong Atlantic State U (GA)
Asbury Coll (KY)
Ashland U (OH)
Assumption Coll (MA)
Athabasca U (AB, Canada)
Athens State U (AL)
Atlantic Baptist U (NB, Canada)
Atlantic Union Coll (MA)
Auburn U (AL)
Auburn U Montgomery (AL)
Augsburg Coll (MN)
Augustana Coll (IL)
Augustana Coll (SD)
Augusta State U (GA)
Aurora U (IL)
Austin Coll (TX)
Austin Peay State U (TN)
Ave Maria U (FL)
Averett U (VA)
Avila U (MO)
Azusa Pacific U (CA)
Baker U (KS)
Baldwin-Wallace Coll (OH)
Ball State U (IN)
Barber-Scotia Coll (NC)
Bard Coll (NY)
Barnard Coll (NY)
Barry U (FL)
Barton Coll (NC)
Bates Coll (ME)
Baylor U (TX)
Belhaven Coll (MS)
Bellarmine U (KY)
Belmont Abbey Coll (NC)
Belmont U (TN)
Beloit Coll (WI)
Bemidji State U (MN)
Benedictine Coll (KS)
Benedictine U (IL)
Bennington Coll (VT)
Bentley Coll (MA)
Berea Coll (KY)
Baruch Coll of the City U of NY (NY)
Berry Coll (GA)
Bethany Coll (KS)
Bethany Coll (WV)
Bethany Lutheran Coll (MN)
Bethel Coll (IN)
Bethel Coll (KS)
Bethel Coll (TN)
Bethel U (MN)
Bethune-Cookman Coll (FL)
Biola U (CA)
Birmingham-Southern Coll (AL)
Bishop's U (QC, Canada)
Blackburn Coll (IL)
Black Hills State U (SD)
Bloomfield Coll (NJ)
Bloomsburg U of Pennsylvania (PA)
Bluefield Coll (VA)
Blue Mountain Coll (MS)
Bluffton Coll (OH)
Boise State U (ID)
Boston Coll (MA)
Boston U (MA)
Bowdoin Coll (ME)
Bowie State U (MD)
Bowling Green State U (OH)
Bradley U (IL)
Brandeis U (MA)
Brenau U (GA)
Brescia U (KY)
Brevard Coll (NC)
Brewton-Parker Coll (GA)
Briar Cliff U (IA)
Bridgewater Coll (VA)
Bridgewater State Coll (MA)
Brigham Young U (UT)
Brigham Young U–Hawaii (HI)
Brock U (ON, Canada)
Brooklyn Coll of the City U of NY (NY)
Brown U (RI)
Bryan Coll (TN)
Bryant Coll (RI)
Bryn Athyn Coll of the New Church (PA)
Bryn Mawr Coll (PA)
Bucknell U (PA)
Buena Vista U (IA)
State U of NY Coll at Buffalo (NY)
Butler U (IN)
Cabrini Coll (PA)
Caldwell Coll (NJ)
California Baptist U (CA)
California Lutheran U (CA)
California Polytechnic State U, San Luis Obispo (CA)
California State Polytechnic U, Pomona (CA)
California State U, Chico (CA)
California State U, Dominguez Hills (CA)
California State U, Fresno (CA)
California State U, Fullerton (CA)
California State U, Hayward (CA)
California State U, Long Beach (CA)
California State U, Los Angeles (CA)
California State U, Sacramento (CA)
California State U, San Bernardino (CA)
California State U, San Marcos (CA)
California State U, Stanislaus (CA)
California U of Pennsylvania (PA)
Calumet Coll of Saint Joseph (IN)
Calvin Coll (MI)
Cameron U (OK)
Campbellsville U (KY)
Campbell U (NC)
Canadian Mennonite U (MB, Canada)
Canisius Coll (NY)
Capital U (OH)
Cardinal Stritch U (WI)
Carleton Coll (MN)
Carleton U (ON, Canada)
Carlow Coll (PA)
Carnegie Mellon U (PA)
Carroll Coll (MT)
Carroll Coll (WI)
Carson-Newman Coll (TN)
Carthage Coll (WI)
Cascade Coll (OR)
Case Western Reserve U (CH)
Catawba Coll (NC)
The Catholic U of America (DC)
Cazenovia Coll (NY)
Cedar Crest Coll (PA)
Cedarville U (OH)
Centenary Coll (NJ)
Centenary Coll of Louisiana (LA)
Central Coll (IA)
Central Connecticut State U (CT)
Central Methodist Coll (MO)
Central Michigan U (MI)
Central Missouri State U (MO)
Central State U (OH)
Central Washington U (WA)
Centre Coll (KY)
Chadron State Coll (NE)
Chaminade U of Honolulu (HI)
Chapman U (CA)
Charleston Southern U (SC)
Chatham Coll (PA)
Chestnut Hill Coll (PA)
Cheyney U of Pennsylvania (PA)
Chicago State U (IL)
Chowan Coll (NC)
Christian Brothers U (TN)
Christian Heritage Coll (CA)
Christopher Newport U (VA)
Citadel, The Military Coll of South Carolina (SC)
City Coll of the City U of NY (NY)
Claremont McKenna Coll (CA)
Clarion U of Pennsylvania (PA)
Clark Atlanta U (GA)
Clarke Coll (IA)
Clark U (MA)
Clearwater Christian Coll (FL)
Clemson U (SC)
Cleveland State U (OH)
Coastal Carolina U (SC)
Coe Coll (IA)
Coker Coll (SC)
Colby Coll (ME)
Colby-Sawyer Coll (NH)
Colgate U (NY)
Coll Misericordia (PA)
Coll of Charleston (SC)
Coll of Mount St. Joseph (OH)
Coll of Mount Saint Vincent (NY)
The Coll of New Jersey (NJ)
The Coll of New Rochelle (NY)
Coll of Notre Dame of Maryland (MD)
Coll of Saint Benedict (MN)
Coll of St. Catherine (MN)
Coll of Saint Elizabeth (NJ)
Coll of St. Joseph (VT)
Coll of Saint Mary (NE)
The Coll of Saint Rose (NY)
The Coll of St. Scholastica (MN)
Coll of Santa Fe (NM)
The Coll of Southeastern Europe, The American U of Athens(Greece)
Coll of Staten Island of the City U of NY (NY)
Coll of the Atlantic (ME)
Coll of the Holy Cross (MA)
Coll of the Ozarks (MO)
Coll of the Southwest (NM)
The Coll of William and Mary (VA)
The Coll of Wooster (OH)
Colorado Christian U (CO)
The Colorado Coll (CO)
Colorado State U (CO)
Colorado State U-Pueblo (CO)
Columbia Coll (MO)
Columbia Coll (NY)
Columbia Coll (SC)
Columbia Union Coll (MD)
Columbia U, School of General Studies (NY)
Columbus State U (GA)
Concord Coll (WV)
Concordia Coll (MN)
Concordia Coll (NY)
Concordia U (CA)
Concordia U (IL)
Concordia U (MI)
Concordia U (NE)
Concordia U (OR)
Concordia U (QC, Canada)
Concordia U at Austin (TX)
Concordia U Coll of Alberta (AB, Canada)
Concordia U, St. Paul (MN)
Concordia U Wisconsin (WI)
Connecticut Coll (CT)
Converse Coll (SC)
Cornell Coll (IA)
Cornell U (NY)
Cornerstone U (MI)
Covenant Coll (GA)
Creighton U (NE)
Crichton Coll (TN)
Crown Coll (MN)
Culver-Stockton Coll (MO)
Cumberland Coll (KY)
Cumberland U (TN)
Curry Coll (MA)
Daemen Coll (NY)
Dakota State U (SD)
Dakota Wesleyan U (SD)
Dalhousie U (NS, Canada)
Dallas Baptist U (TX)
Dana Coll (NE)
Dartmouth Coll (NH)
Davidson Coll (NC)
Davis & Elkins Coll (WV)
Defiance Coll (OH)
Delaware State U (DE)
Delaware Valley Coll (PA)
Delta State U (MS)
Denison U (OH)
DePaul U (IL)
DePauw U (IN)
DeSales U (PA)
Dickinson Coll (PA)
Dickinson State U (ND)
Dillard U (LA)
Doane Coll (NE)
Dominican Coll (NY)
Dominican U (IL)
Dominican U of California (CA)
Dordt Coll (IA)
Dowling Coll (NY)
Drake U (IA)
Drew U (NJ)
Drury U (MO)
Duke U (NC)
Duquesne U (PA)
D'Youville Coll (NY)
Earlham Coll (IN)
East Carolina U (NC)
East Central U (OK)
Eastern Connecticut State U (CT)
Eastern Illinois U (IL)
Eastern Kentucky U (KY)
Eastern Mennonite U (VA)
Eastern Michigan U (MI)
Eastern Nazarene Coll (MA)
Eastern New Mexico U (NM)
Eastern Oregon U (OR)
Eastern U (PA)
Eastern Washington U (WA)
East Stroudsburg U of Pennsylvania (PA)
East Texas Baptist U (TX)
Eckerd Coll (FL)
Edgewood Coll (WI)
Edinboro U of Pennsylvania (PA)
Elizabeth City State U (NC)
Elizabethtown Coll (PA)
Elmhurst Coll (IL)
Elmira Coll (NY)
Elms Coll (MA)
Elon U (NC)
Emmanuel Coll (GA)
Emory & Henry Coll (VA)
Emory U (GA)
Emporia State U (KS)
Endicott Coll (MA)
Erskine Coll (SC)
Eugene Lang Coll, New School U (NY)
Eureka Coll (IL)
Evangel U (MO)
Fairfield U (CT)
Fairleigh Dickinson U, Florham (NJ)
Fairleigh Dickinson U, Teaneck-Metro Campus (NJ)
Fairmont State Coll (WV)
Faulkner U (AL)
Fayetteville State U (NC)
Ferrum Coll (VA)
Flagler Coll (FL)
Florida Ag and Mech U (FL)
Florida Atlantic U (FL)
Florida Intl U (FL)
Florida Southern Coll (FL)
Florida State U (FL)
Fontbonne U (MO)
Fordham U (NY)
Fort Hays State U (KS)
Fort Lewis Coll (CO)
Framingham State Coll (MA)
The Franciscan U (IA)
Franciscan U of Steubenville (OH)
Francis Marion U (SC)
Franklin and Marshall Coll (PA)
Franklin Coll (IN)
Franklin Pierce Coll (NH)
Freed-Hardeman U (TN)
Fresno Pacific U (CA)

Frostburg State U (MD)
Furman U (SC)
Gallaudet U (DC)
Gardner-Webb U (NC)
Geneva Coll (PA)
George Fox U (OR)
George Mason U (VA)
Georgetown Coll (KY)
Georgetown U (DC)
The George Washington U (DC)
Georgia Coll & State U (GA)
Georgian Court U (NJ)
Georgia Southern U (GA)
Georgia Southwestern State U (GA)
Georgia State U (GA)
Gettysburg Coll (PA)
Glenville State Coll (WV)
Gonzaga U (WA)
Gordon Coll (MA)
Goshen Coll (IN)
Goucher Coll (MD)
Governors State U (IL)
Grace Coll (IN)
Graceland U (IA)
Grambling State U (LA)
Grand Canyon U (AZ)
Grand Valley State U (MI)
Grand View Coll (IA)
Greensboro Coll (NC)
Greenville Coll (IL)
Grinnell Coll (IA)
Grove City Coll (PA)
Guilford Coll (NC)
Gustavus Adolphus Coll (MN)
Gwynedd-Mercy Coll (PA)
Hamilton Coll (NY)
Hamline U (MN)
Hampden-Sydney Coll (VA)
Hampshire Coll (MA)
Hampton U (VA)
Hannibal-LaGrange Coll (MO)
Hanover Coll (IN)
Harding U (AR)
Hardin-Simmons U (TX)
Hartwick Coll (NY)
Harvard U (MA)
Hastings Coll (NE)
Haverford Coll (PA)
Hawai'i Pacific U (HI)
Heidelberg Coll (OH)
Henderson State U (AR)
Hendrix Coll (AR)
High Point U (NC)
Hilbert Coll (NY)
Hillsdale Coll (MI)
Hiram Coll (OH)
Hobart and William Smith Colls (NY)
Hofstra U (NY)
Hollins U (VA)
Holy Names Coll (CA)
Hood Coll (MD)
Hope Coll (MI)
Houghton Coll (NY)
Houston Baptist U (TX)
Howard Payne U (TX)
Howard U (DC)
Humboldt State U (CA)
Hunter Coll of the City U of NY (NY)
Huntingdon Coll (AL)
Huntington Coll (IN)
Huron U USA in London(United Kingdom)
Huston-Tillotson Coll (TX)
Idaho State U (ID)
Illinois Coll (IL)
Illinois State U (IL)
Illinois Wesleyan U (IL)
Immaculata U (PA)
Indiana State U (IN)
Indiana U Bloomington (IN)
Indiana U East (IN)
Indiana U Kokomo (IN)
Indiana U Northwest (IN)
Indiana U of Pennsylvania (PA)
Indiana U–Purdue U Fort Wayne (IN)
Indiana U–Purdue U Indianapolis (IN)
Indiana U South Bend (IN)
Indiana U Southeast (IN)
Inter American U of PR, San Germán Campus (PR)
Iona Coll (NY)
Iowa State U of Science and Technology (IA)
Iowa Wesleyan Coll (IA)
Ithaca Coll (NY)
Jacksonville State U (AL)
Jacksonville U (FL)
James Madison U (VA)
Jamestown Coll (ND)
Jarvis Christian Coll (TX)
John Brown U (AR)
John Carroll U (OH)
The Johns Hopkins U (MD)
Johnson C. Smith U (NC)
Johnson State Coll (VT)
Judson Coll (AL)
Judson Coll (IL)
Juniata Coll (PA)
Kalamazoo Coll (MI)
Kansas State U (KS)
Kansas Wesleyan U (KS)
Kean U (NJ)
Keene State Coll (NH)
Kennesaw State U (GA)
Kent State U (OH)
Kentucky State U (KY)
Kentucky Wesleyan Coll (KY)
Kenyon Coll (OH)
Keuka Coll (NY)
King Coll (TN)
King's Coll (PA)
The King's U Coll (AB, Canada)
Knox Coll (IL)
Kutztown U of Pennsylvania (PA)
Lafayette Coll (PA)
LaGrange Coll (GA)
Lake Erie Coll (OH)
Lake Forest Coll (IL)
Lakehead U (ON, Canada)
Lakeland Coll (WI)
Lake Superior State U (MI)
Lamar U (TX)
Lambuth U (TN)
Lander U (SC)
Lane Coll (TN)
La Roche Coll (PA)
La Salle U (PA)
Laurentian U (ON, Canada)
Lawrence U (WI)
Lebanon Valley Coll (PA)
Lehman Coll of the City U of NY (NY)
Le Moyne Coll (NY)
Lenoir-Rhyne Coll (NC)
Lesley U (MA)
LeTourneau U (TX)
Lewis & Clark Coll (OR)
Lewis-Clark State Coll (ID)
Lewis U (IL)
Liberty U (VA)
Limestone Coll (SC)
Lincoln Memorial U (TN)
Lincoln U (MO)
Lincoln U (PA)
Lindenwood U (MO)
Lindsey Wilson Coll (KY)
Linfield Coll (OR)
Lipscomb U (TN)
Livingstone Coll (NC)
Lock Haven U of Pennsylvania (PA)
Long Island U, Brooklyn Campus (NY)
Long Island U, C.W. Post Campus (NY)
Long Island U, Southampton Coll (NY)
Longwood U (VA)
Loras Coll (IA)
Louisiana Coll (LA)
Louisiana State U and A&M Coll (LA)
Louisiana State U in Shreveport (LA)
Louisiana Tech U (LA)
Lourdes Coll (OH)
Loyola Coll in Maryland (MD)
Loyola Marymount U (CA)
Loyola U Chicago (IL)
Loyola U New Orleans (LA)
Luther Coll (IA)
Lycoming Coll (PA)
Lynchburg Coll (VA)
Lyndon State Coll (VT)
Lynn U (FL)
Lyon Coll (AR)
Macalester Coll (MN)
MacMurray Coll (IL)
Madonna U (MI)
Maharishi U of Management (IA)
Malone Coll (OH)
Manchester Coll (IN)
Manhattan Coll (NY)
Manhattanville Coll (NY)
Mansfield U of Pennsylvania (PA)
Marian Coll (IN)
Marian Coll of Fond du Lac (WI)
Marietta Coll (OH)
Marist Coll (NY)
Marlboro Coll (VT)
Marquette U (WI)
Marshall U (WV)
Mars Hill Coll (NC)
Martin U (IN)
Mary Baldwin Coll (VA)
Marygrove Coll (MI)
Marymount Coll of Fordham U (NY)
Marymount Manhattan Coll (NY)
Marymount U (VA)
Maryville Coll (TN)
Maryville U of Saint Louis (MO)
Mary Washington Coll (VA)
Marywood U (PA)
Massachusetts Coll of Liberal Arts (MA)
Massachusetts Inst of Technology (MA)
The Master's Coll and Sem (CA)
Mayville State U (ND)
McDaniel Coll (MD)
McGill U (QC, Canada)
McKendree Coll (IL)
McMurry U (TX)
McNeese State U (LA)
McPherson Coll (KS)
Medaille Coll (NY)
Memorial U of Newfoundland (NL, Canada)
Mercer U (GA)
Mercy Coll (NY)
Mercyhurst Coll (PA)
Meredith Coll (NC)
Merrimack Coll (MA)
Messiah Coll (PA)
Methodist Coll (NC)
Metropolitan State Coll of Denver (CO)
Metropolitan State U (MN)
Miami U (OH)
Miami U Hamilton (OH)
Michigan State U (MI)
Michigan Technological U (MI)
MidAmerica Nazarene U (KS)
Mid-Continent Coll (KY)
Middlebury Coll (VT)
Middle Tennessee State U (TN)
Midway Coll (KY)
Midwestern State U (TX)
Miles Coll (AL)
Millersville U of Pennsylvania (PA)
Milligan Coll (TN)
Millikin U (IL)
Millsaps Coll (MS)
Mills Coll (CA)
Minnesota State U Mankato (MN)
Minnesota State U Moorhead (MN)
Minot State U (ND)
Mississippi Coll (MS)
Mississippi State U (MS)
Mississippi Valley State U (MS)
Missouri Baptist U (MO)
Missouri Southern State U (MO)
Missouri Valley Coll (MO)
Missouri Western State Coll (MO)
Molloy Coll (NY)
Monmouth Coll (IL)
Monmouth U (NJ)
Montana State U–Billings (MT)
Montana State U–Bozeman (MT)
Montclair State U (NJ)
Montreat Coll (NC)
Moravian Coll (PA)
Morehead State U (KY)
Morehouse Coll (GA)
Morgan State U (MD)
Morningside Coll (IA)
Morris Coll (SC)
Mount Allison U (NB, Canada)
Mount Aloysius Coll (PA)
Mount Holyoke Coll (MA)
Mount Marty Coll (SD)
Mount Mary Coll (WI)
Mount Mercy Coll (IA)
Mount Saint Mary Coll (NY)
Mount St. Mary's Coll (CA)
Mount Saint Mary's Coll and Sem (MD)
Mount Saint Vincent U (NS, Canada)
Mount Union Coll (OH)
Mount Vernon Nazarene U (OH)
Muhlenberg Coll (PA)
Murray State U (KY)
Naropa U (CO)
National-Louis U (IL)
National U (CA)
Nazareth Coll of Rochester (NY)
Nebraska Wesleyan U (NE)
Neumann Coll (PA)
Nevada State Coll at Henderson (NV)
Newberry Coll (SC)
New Coll of Florida (FL)
New Jersey City U (NJ)
Newman U (KS)
New Mexico Highlands U (NM)
New Mexico State U (NM)
New York Inst of Technology (NY)
New York U (NY)
Niagara U (NY)
Nicholls State U (LA)
Nichols Coll (MA)
Nipissing U (ON, Canada)
Norfolk State U (VA)
North Carolina Central U (NC)
North Carolina State U (NC)
North Carolina Wesleyan Coll (NC)
North Central Coll (IL)
North Central U (MN)
North Dakota State U (ND)
Northeastern Illinois U (IL)
Northeastern State U (OK)
Northeastern U (MA)
Northern Arizona U (AZ)
Northern Illinois U (IL)
Northern Michigan U (MI)
Northern State U (SD)
North Georgia Coll & State U (GA)
North Greenville Coll (SC)
Northland Coll (WI)
North Park U (IL)
Northwestern Coll (IA)
Northwestern Coll (MN)
Northwestern Oklahoma State U (OK)
Northwestern State U of Louisiana (LA)
Northwestern U (IL)
Northwest Nazarene U (ID)
Notre Dame Coll (OH)
Notre Dame de Namur U (CA)
Nova Southeastern U (FL)
Nyack Coll (NY)
Oakland City U (IN)
Oakland U (MI)
Oberlin Coll (OH)
Oglethorpe U (GA)
Ohio Dominican U (OH)
Ohio Northern U (OH)
The Ohio State U (OH)
The Ohio State U at Lima (OH)
The Ohio State U at Marion (OH)
The Ohio State U–Mansfield Campus (OH)
The Ohio State U–Newark Campus (OH)
Ohio U (OH)
Ohio Wesleyan U (OH)
Okanagan U Coll (BC, Canada)
Oklahoma Baptist U (OK)
Oklahoma Christian U (OK)
Oklahoma City U (OK)
Oklahoma Panhandle State U (OK)
Oklahoma State U (OK)
Old Dominion U (VA)
Olivet Coll (MI)
Olivet Nazarene U (IL)
Oregon State U (OR)
Ottawa U (KS)
Otterbein Coll (OH)
Ouachita Baptist U (AR)
Our Lady of Holy Cross Coll (LA)
Our Lady of the Lake U of San Antonio (TX)
Pace U (NY)
Pacific Lutheran U (WA)
Pacific Union Coll (CA)
Pacific U (OR)
Paine Coll (GA)
Palm Beach Atlantic U (FL)
Park U (MO)
Peace Coll (NC)
Penn State U Abington Coll (PA)
Penn State U Altoona Coll (PA)
Penn State U at Erie, The Behrend Coll (PA)
Penn State U Beaver Campus of the Commonwealth Coll (PA)
Penn State U Berks Cmps of Berks-Lehigh Valley Coll (PA)
Penn State U Delaware County Campus of the Commonwealth Coll (PA)
Penn State U DuBois Campus of the Commonwealth Coll (PA)
Penn State U Fayette Campus of the Commonwealth Coll (PA)
Penn State U Harrisburg Campus of the Capital Coll (PA)
Penn State U Hazleton Campus of the Commonwealth Coll (PA)
Penn State U Lehigh Valley Cmps of Berks-Lehigh Valley Coll (PA)
Penn State U McKeesport Campus of the Commonwealth Coll (PA)
Penn State U Mont Alto Campus of the Commonwealth Coll (PA)
Penn State U New Kensington Campus of the Commonwealth Coll (PA)
Penn State U Schuylkill Campus of the Capital Coll (PA)
Penn State U Shenango Campus of the Commonwealth Coll (PA)
Penn State U Univ Park Campus (PA)
Penn State U Wilkes-Barre Campus of the Commonwealth Coll (PA)
Penn State U Worthington Scranton Cmps Commonwealth Coll (PA)
Penn State U York Campus of the Commonwealth Coll (PA)
Pepperdine U, Malibu (CA)
Pfeiffer U (NC)
Piedmont Coll (GA)
Pikeville Coll (KY)
Pine Manor Coll (MA)
Pittsburg State U (KS)
Pitzer Coll (CA)
Plymouth State U (NH)
Point Loma Nazarene U (CA)
Point Park U (PA)
Pomona Coll (CA)
Pontifical Catholic U of Puerto Rico (PR)
Pontifical Coll Josephinum (OH)
Portland State U (OR)
Prairie View A&M U (TX)
Presbyterian Coll (SC)
Princeton U (NJ)
Principia Coll (IL)
Providence Coll (RI)
Purdue U (IN)
Purdue U North Central (IN)
Queens Coll of the City U of NY (NY)
Queen's U at Kingston (ON, Canada)
Queens U of Charlotte (NC)
Quincy U (IL)
Quinnipiac U (CT)
Radford U (VA)
Ramapo Coll of New Jersey (NJ)
Randolph-Macon Coll (VA)
Randolph-Macon Woman's Coll (VA)
Redeemer U Coll (ON, Canada)
Reed Coll (OR)
Regis Coll (MA)
Regis U (CO)
Reinhardt Coll (GA)
Rhode Island Coll (RI)
Rhodes Coll (TN)
Rice U (TX)
The Richard Stockton Coll of New Jersey (NJ)
Richmond, The American Intl U in London(United Kingdom)
Rider U (NJ)
Ripon Coll (WI)
Rivier Coll (NH)
Roanoke Coll (VA)
Robert Morris U (PA)
Roberts Wesleyan Coll (NY)
Rochester Coll (MI)
Rockford Coll (IL)
Rockhurst U (MO)
Rocky Mountain Coll (MT)
Roger Williams U (RI)
Rollins Coll (FL)
Roosevelt U (IL)
Rosemont Coll (PA)
Rowan U (NJ)
Russell Sage Coll (NY)
Rutgers, The State U of New Jersey, Camden (NJ)
Rutgers, The State U of New Jersey, Newark (NJ)
Rutgers, The State U of New Jersey, New Brunswick/Piscataway (NJ)
Sacred Heart U (CT)
Saginaw Valley State U (MI)
St. Ambrose U (IA)
St. Andrews Presbyterian Coll (NC)
Saint Anselm Coll (NH)
Saint Augustine's Coll (NC)
St. Bonaventure U (NY)
St. Cloud State U (MN)
St. Edward's U (TX)
St. Francis Coll (NY)
Saint Francis U (PA)
St. Francis Xavier U (NS, Canada)
St. Gregory's U (OK)
St. John Fisher Coll (NY)
St. John's Coll (NM)
Saint John's U (MN)
St. John's U (NY)
Saint Joseph Coll (CT)
Saint Joseph's Coll (IN)
St. Joseph's Coll, New York (NY)
Saint Joseph's Coll of Maine (ME)
St. Joseph's Coll, Suffolk Campus (NY)
Saint Joseph's U (PA)
St. Lawrence U (NY)
Saint Leo U (FL)
Saint Louis U (MO)
Saint Martin's Coll (WA)
Saint Mary-of-the-Woods Coll (IN)
Saint Mary's Coll of California (CA)
St. Mary's Coll of Maryland (MD)
Saint Mary's U of Minnesota (MN)

St. Mary's U of San Antonio (TX)
Saint Michael's Coll (VT)
St. Norbert Coll (WI)
St. Olaf Coll (MN)
St. Thomas Aquinas Coll (NY)
St. Thomas U (FL)
St. Thomas U (NB, Canada)
Saint Vincent Coll (PA)
Saint Xavier U (IL)
Salem Coll (NC)
Salem State Coll (MA)
Salisbury U (MD)
Salve Regina U (RI)
Samford U (AL)
Sam Houston State U (TX)
San Diego State U (CA)
San Francisco State U (CA)
San Jose State U (CA)
Santa Clara U (CA)
Sarah Lawrence Coll (NY)
Schreiner U (TX)
Scripps Coll (CA)
Seattle Pacific U (WA)
Seattle U (WA)
Seton Hall U (NJ)
Seton Hill U (PA)
Shawnee State U (OH)
Shaw U (NC)
Shenandoah U (VA)
Shepherd U (WV)
Shippensburg U of Pennsylvania (PA)
Shorter Coll (GA)
Siena Coll (NY)
Siena Heights U (MI)
Silver Lake Coll (WI)
Simmons Coll (MA)
Simon Fraser U (BC, Canada)
Simpson Coll (IA)
Simpson Coll and Graduate School (CA)
Slippery Rock U of Pennsylvania (PA)
Smith Coll (MA)
Sonoma State U (CA)
South Carolina State U (SC)
South Dakota State U (SD)
Southeastern Coll of the Assemblies of God (FL)
Southeastern Louisiana U (LA)
Southeastern Oklahoma State U (OK)
Southeast Missouri State U (MO)
Southern Adventist U (TN)
Southern Arkansas U–Magnolia (AR)
Southern Connecticut State U (CT)
Southern Illinois U Carbondale (IL)
Southern Illinois U Edwardsville (IL)
Southern Methodist U (TX)
Southern Nazarene U (OK)
Southern Oregon U (OR)
Southern U and A&M Coll (LA)
Southern Utah U (UT)
Southern Vermont Coll (VT)
Southern Virginia U (VA)
Southern Wesleyan U (SC)
Southwest Baptist U (MO)
Southwestern Coll (KS)
Southwestern Oklahoma State U (OK)
Southwestern U (TX)
Southwest Missouri State U (MO)
Spelman Coll (GA)
Spring Arbor U (MI)
Springfield Coll (MA)
Spring Hill Coll (AL)
Stanford U (CA)
State U of NY at Binghamton (NY)
State U of NY at New Paltz (NY)
State U of NY at Oswego (NY)
Plattsburgh State U of NY (NY)
State U of NY Coll at Brockport (NY)
State U of NY Coll at Cortland (NY)
State U of NY Coll at Fredonia (NY)
State U of NY Coll at Geneseo (NY)
State U of NY Coll at Oneonta (NY)
State U of NY Coll at Potsdam (NY)
State U of West Georgia (GA)
Stephens Coll (MO)
Sterling Coll (KS)
Stetson U (FL)
Stevens Inst of Technology (NJ)
Stonehill Coll (MA)
Stony Brook U, State U of New York (NY)
Suffolk U (MA)
Susquehanna U (PA)
Swarthmore Coll (PA)
Sweet Briar Coll (VA)
Syracuse U (NY)
Tabor Coll (KS)
Talladega Coll (AL)
Tarleton State U (TX)
Taylor U (IN)
Taylor U, Fort Wayne Campus (IN)
Teikyo Post U (CT)
Tennessee State U (TN)
Tennessee Technological U (TN)
Tennessee Wesleyan Coll (TN)
Texas A&M Intl U (TX)
Texas A&M U (TX)
Texas A&M U–Commerce (TX)
Texas A&M U–Corpus Christi (TX)
Texas A&M U–Kingsville (TX)
Texas A&M U–Texarkana (TX)
Texas Christian U (TX)
Texas Lutheran U (TX)
Texas Southern U (TX)
Texas State U-San Marcos (TX)
Texas Tech U (TX)
Texas Wesleyan U (TX)
Texas Woman's U (TX)
Thiel Coll (PA)
Thomas Edison State Coll (NJ)
Thomas More Coll (KY)
Thomas U (GA)
Tiffin U (OH)
Toccoa Falls Coll (GA)
Tougaloo Coll (MS)
Towson U (MD)
Transylvania U (KY)
Trent U (ON, Canada)
Trevecca Nazarene U (TN)
Trinity Christian Coll (IL)
Trinity Coll (CT)
Trinity Coll (DC)
Trinity Intl U (IL)
Trinity U (TX)
Trinity Western U (BC, Canada)
Tri-State U (IN)
Troy State U (AL)
Troy State U Dothan (AL)
Troy State U Montgomery (AL)
Truman State U (MO)
Tufts U (MA)
Tulane U (LA)
Tusculum Coll (TN)
Tuskegee U (AL)
Tyndale U Coll & Sem (ON, Canada)
Union Coll (NE)
Union Coll (NY)
Union U (TN)
United States Air Force Acad (CO)
United States Naval Acad (MD)
Université de Montréal (QC, Canada)
Université de Sherbrooke (QC, Canada)
Université Laval (QC, Canada)
State U of NY at Albany (NY)
U at Buffalo, The State U of New York (NY)
U Coll of the Cariboo (BC, Canada)
U Coll of the Fraser Valley (BC, Canada)
The U of Akron (OH)
The U of Alabama (AL)
The U of Alabama at Birmingham (AL)
The U of Alabama in Huntsville (AL)
U of Alaska Fairbanks (AK)
U of Alberta (AB, Canada)
The U of Arizona (AZ)
U of Arkansas (AR)
U of Arkansas at Little Rock (AR)
U of Arkansas at Monticello (AR)
U of Baltimore (MD)
U of Bridgeport (CT)
The U of British Columbia (BC, Canada)
U of Calgary (AB, Canada)
U of Calif, Berkeley (CA)
U of Calif, Davis (CA)
U of Calif, Irvine (CA)
U of Calif, Los Angeles (CA)
U of Calif, Riverside (CA)
U of Calif, San Diego (CA)
U of Calif, Santa Barbara (CA)
U of Central Arkansas (AR)
U of Central Florida (FL)
U of Charleston (WV)
U of Chicago (IL)
U of Cincinnati (OH)
U of Colorado at Boulder (CO)
U of Colorado at Colorado Springs (CO)
U of Colorado at Denver (CO)
U of Connecticut (CT)
U of Dallas (TX)
U of Dayton (OH)
U of Delaware (DE)
U of Denver (CO)
U of Detroit Mercy (MI)
U of Dubuque (IA)
U of Evansville (IN)
The U of Findlay (OH)
U of Florida (FL)
U of Georgia (GA)
U of Great Falls (MT)
U of Guelph (ON, Canada)
U of Hartford (CT)
U of Hawaii at Hilo (HI)
U of Hawaii at Manoa (HI)
U of Houston (TX)
U of Houston–Clear Lake (TX)
U of Idaho (ID)
U of Illinois at Chicago (IL)
U of Illinois at Springfield (IL)
U of Illinois at Urbana–Champaign (IL)
U of Indianapolis (IN)
The U of Iowa (IA)
U of Kansas (KS)
U of Kentucky (KY)
U of King's Coll (NS, Canada)
U of La Verne (CA)
The U of Lethbridge (AB, Canada)
U of Louisiana at Lafayette (LA)
U of Louisville (KY)
U of Maine (ME)
U of Maine at Farmington (ME)
U of Maine at Fort Kent (ME)
U of Maine at Machias (ME)
U of Maine at Presque Isle (ME)
U of Manitoba (MB, Canada)
U of Mary (ND)
U of Mary Hardin-Baylor (TX)
U of Maryland, Baltimore County (MD)
U of Maryland, Coll Park (MD)
U of Maryland Eastern Shore (MD)
U of Maryland U Coll (MD)
U of Massachusetts Amherst (MA)
U of Massachusetts Boston (MA)
U of Massachusetts Dartmouth (MA)
U of Massachusetts Lowell (MA)
The U of Memphis (TN)
U of Miami (FL)
U of Michigan (MI)
U of Michigan–Dearborn (MI)
U of Michigan–Flint (MI)
U of Minnesota, Duluth (MN)
U of Minnesota, Morris (MN)
U of Minnesota, Twin Cities Campus (MN)
U of Mississippi (MS)
U of Missouri–Columbia (MO)
U of Missouri–Kansas City (MO)
U of Missouri–Rolla (MO)
U of Missouri–St. Louis (MO)
U of Mobile (AL)
The U of Montana–Missoula (MT)
The U of Montana–Western (MT)
U of Montevallo (AL)
U of Nebraska at Omaha (NE)
U of Nebraska–Lincoln (NE)
U of Nevada, Las Vegas (NV)
U of Nevada, Reno (NV)
U of New Brunswick Fredericton (NB, Canada)
U of New Hampshire (NH)
U of New Hampshire at Manchester (NH)
U of New Haven (CT)
U of New Mexico (NM)
U of New Orleans (LA)
U of North Alabama (AL)
The U of North Carolina at Asheville (NC)
The U of North Carolina at Chapel Hill (NC)
The U of North Carolina at Charlotte (NC)
The U of North Carolina at Greensboro (NC)
The U of North Carolina at Pembroke (NC)
The U of North Carolina at Wilmington (NC)
U of North Dakota (ND)
U of Northern Colorado (CO)
U of Northern Iowa (IA)
U of North Florida (FL)
U of North Texas (TX)
U of Notre Dame (IN)
U of Oklahoma (OK)
U of Oregon (OR)
U of Ottawa (ON, Canada)
U of Pennsylvania (PA)
U of Pittsburgh (PA)
U of Pittsburgh at Bradford (PA)
U of Pittsburgh at Greensburg (PA)
U of Pittsburgh at Johnstown (PA)
U of Portland (OR)
U of Prince Edward Island (PE, Canada)
U of Puerto Rico, Cayey U Coll (PR)
U of Puget Sound (WA)
U of Redlands (CA)
U of Regina (SK, Canada)
U of Rhode Island (RI)
U of Richmond (VA)
U of Rochester (NY)
U of St. Francis (IL)
U of Saint Francis (IN)
U of Saint Mary (KS)
U of St. Thomas (MN)
U of St. Thomas (TX)
U of San Diego (CA)
U of San Francisco (CA)
U of Saskatchewan (SK, Canada)
U of Science and Arts of Oklahoma (OK)
The U of Scranton (PA)
U of Sioux Falls (SD)
U of South Alabama (AL)
U of South Carolina (SC)
U of South Carolina Aiken (SC)
U of South Carolina Spartanburg (SC)
The U of South Dakota (SD)
U of Southern California (CA)
U of Southern Indiana (IN)
U of Southern Maine (ME)
U of South Florida (FL)
The U of Tampa (FL)
The U of Tennessee (TN)
The U of Tennessee at Chattanooga (TN)
The U of Tennessee at Martin (TN)
The U of Texas at Arlington (TX)
The U of Texas at Austin (TX)
The U of Texas at Brownsville (TX)
The U of Texas at Tyler (TX)
The U of Texas–Pan American (TX)
U of the District of Columbia (DC)
U of the Incarnate Word (TX)
U of the Ozarks (AR)
U of the Pacific (CA)
U of the South (TN)
U of the Virgin Islands (VI)
U of the West (CA)
U of Toledo (OH)
U of Toronto (ON, Canada)
U of Tulsa (OK)
U of Utah (UT)
U of Vermont (VT)
U of Victoria (BC, Canada)
U of Virginia (VA)
The U of Virginia's Coll at Wise (VA)
U of Washington (WA)
U of Waterloo (ON, Canada)
The U of West Alabama (AL)
The U of Western Ontario (ON, Canada)
U of West Florida (FL)
U of Windsor (ON, Canada)
U of Wisconsin–Eau Claire (WI)
U of Wisconsin–Green Bay (WI)
U of Wisconsin–La Crosse (WI)
U of Wisconsin–Madison (WI)
U of Wisconsin–Milwaukee (WI)
U of Wisconsin–Oshkosh (WI)
U of Wisconsin–Parkside (WI)
U of Wisconsin–Platteville (WI)
U of Wisconsin–River Falls (WI)
U of Wisconsin–Stevens Point (WI)
U of Wisconsin–Superior (WI)
U of Wisconsin–Whitewater (WI)
U of Wyoming (WY)
Upper Iowa U (IA)
Urbana U (OH)
Ursinus Coll (PA)
Ursuline Coll (OH)
Utah State U (UT)
Utica Coll (NY)
Valdosta State U (GA)
Valley City State U (ND)
Valparaiso U (IN)
Vanderbilt U (TN)
Vanguard U of Southern California (CA)
Vassar Coll (NY)
Villa Julie Coll (MD)
Villanova U (PA)
Virginia Commonwealth U (VA)
Virginia Intermont Coll (VA)
Virginia Military Inst (VA)
Virginia Polytechnic Inst and State U (VA)
Virginia State U (VA)
Virginia Union U (VA)
Virginia Wesleyan Coll (VA)
Viterbo U (WI)
Voorhees Coll (SC)
Wabash Coll (IN)
Wagner Coll (NY)
Wake Forest U (NC)
Waldorf Coll (IA)
Walla Walla Coll (WA)
Walsh U (OH)
Warner Pacific Coll (OR)
Warner Southern Coll (FL)
Warren Wilson Coll (NC)
Wartburg Coll (IA)
Washburn U (KS)
Washington & Jefferson Coll (PA)
Washington and Lee U (VA)
Washington Coll (MD)
Washington State U (WA)
Washington U in St. Louis (MO)
Wayland Baptist U (TX)
Waynesburg Coll (PA)
Wayne State Coll (NE)
Wayne State U (MI)
Weber State U (UT)
Webster U (MO)
Wellesley Coll (MA)
Wells Coll (NY)
Wesleyan Coll (GA)
Wesleyan U (CT)
Wesley Coll (DE)
West Chester U of Pennsylvania (PA)
Western Baptist Coll (OR)
Western Carolina U (NC)
Western Connecticut State U (CT)
Western Illinois U (IL)
Western Kentucky U (KY)
Western Michigan U (MI)
Western New England Coll (MA)
Western Oregon U (OR)
Western State Coll of Colorado (CO)
Western Washington U (WA)
Westfield State Coll (MA)
West Liberty State Coll (WV)
Westminster Coll (MO)
Westminster Coll (PA)
Westminster Coll (UT)
Westmont Coll (CA)
West Texas A&M U (TX)
West Virginia State Coll (WV)
West Virginia U (WV)
West Virginia Wesleyan Coll (WV)
Wheaton Coll (IL)
Wheaton Coll (MA)
Wheeling Jesuit U (WV)
Whitman Coll (WA)
Whitworth Coll (WA)
Wichita State U (KS)
Widener U (PA)
Wilkes U (PA)
Willamette U (OR)
William Carey Coll (MS)
William Jewell Coll (MO)
William Paterson U of New Jersey (NJ)
Williams Baptist Coll (AR)
Williams Coll (MA)
William Tyndale Coll (MI)
William Woods U (MO)
Wilson Coll (PA)
Wingate U (NC)
Winona State U (MN)
Winston-Salem State U (NC)
Winthrop U (SC)
Wisconsin Lutheran Coll (WI)
Wittenberg U (OH)
Wofford Coll (SC)
Worcester State Coll (MA)
Wright State U (OH)
Xavier U (OH)
Xavier U of Louisiana (LA)
Yale U (CT)
York Coll (NE)
York Coll of Pennsylvania (PA)
York Coll of the City U of New York (NY)
York U (ON, Canada)
Youngstown State U (OH)

ENGLISH AS A SECOND/ FOREIGN LANGUAGE (TEACHING)

Alaska Bible Coll (AK)
Aquinas Coll (MI)
Auburn U (AL)
Bethel U (MN)
Bridgewater Coll (VA)
Brigham Young U (UT)
Brigham Young U–Hawaii (HI)
Brock U (ON, Canada)
Calvin Coll (MI)
Carleton U (ON, Canada)
Carroll Coll (MT)
Concordia U (NE)
Concordia U (QC, Canada)
Concordia U, St. Paul (MN)
Concordia U Wisconsin (WI)
Cornell U (NY)
Doane Coll (NE)
Eastern Michigan U (MI)
Eastern Washington U (WA)
Elms Coll (MA)
Georgian Court U (NJ)
Goshen Coll (IN)
Hawai'i Pacific U (HI)
Howard Payne U (TX)

Inter American U of PR, Aguadilla Campus (PR)
Inter American U of PR, Fajardo Campus (PR)
Inter American U of PR, San Germán Campus (PR)
John Brown U (AR)
Liberty U (VA)
Maryville Coll (TN)
McGill U (QC, Canada)
Mercy Coll (NY)
Moody Bible Inst (IL)
Murray State U (KY)
Northern Arizona U (AZ)
Northwestern Coll (MN)
Nyack Coll (NY)
Ohio Dominican U (OH)
Ohio U (OH)
Oklahoma Christian U (OK)
Oral Roberts U (OK)
Providence Coll and Theological Sem (MB, Canada)
Queens Coll of the City U of NY (NY)
St. John's U (NY)
Simmons Coll (MA)
Tarleton State U (TX)
Texas Wesleyan U (TX)
Union U (TN)
Université Laval (QC, Canada)
U of Alberta (AB, Canada)
The U of British Columbia (BC, Canada)
U of Calif, Los Angeles (CA)
U of Delaware (DE)
The U of Findlay (OH)
U of Hawaii at Manoa (HI)
The U of Iowa (IA)
The U of Montana–Missoula (MT)
U of Nebraska–Lincoln (NE)
U of New Brunswick Fredericton (NB, Canada)
U of Northern Iowa (IA)
U of Ottawa (ON, Canada)
U of Puerto Rico, Cayey U Coll (PR)
U of Saskatchewan (SK, Canada)
U of Victoria (BC, Canada)
U of Washington (WA)
U of Wisconsin–Oshkosh (WI)
U of Wisconsin–River Falls (WI)
William Penn U (IA)
Wright State U (OH)
York U (ON, Canada)

ENGLISH COMPOSITION

Aurora U (IL)
Baylor U (TX)
Bethel U (MN)
Brigham Young U (UT)
DePauw U (IN)
Dillard U (LA)
Eastern Michigan U (MI)
Florida Southern Coll (FL)
Gallaudet U (DC)
Gettysburg Coll (PA)
Graceland U (IA)
Huron U USA in London(United Kingdom)
Jamestown Coll (ND)
Lakeland Coll (WI)
Metropolitan State U (MN)
Miami U Hamilton (OH)
Mount Union Coll (OH)
Oakland U (MI)
Oklahoma Baptist U (OK)
Rochester Coll (MI)
St. Edward's U (TX)
Simon's Rock Coll of Bard (MA)
U of Central Arkansas (AR)
U of Colorado at Denver (CO)
U of Great Falls (MT)
U of Illinois at Urbana–Champaign (IL)
U of Michigan–Flint (MI)
U of Nevada, Reno (NV)
U of North Texas (TX)
Wartburg Coll (IA)
Western Michigan U (MI)
William Woods U (MO)

ENGLISH/FRENCH AS A SECOND/FOREIGN LANGUAGE (TEACHING) RELATED

Western Michigan U (MI)

ENGLISH LANGUAGE AND LITERATURE RELATED

American Public U System (WV)
Columbia Coll (SC)
Drexel U (PA)
Duquesne U (PA)
Fort Lewis Coll (CO)
McGill U (QC, Canada)
Milligan Coll (TN)
Moravian Coll (PA)
Patrick Henry Coll (VA)
St. Gregory's U (OK)
Saint Leo U (FL)
Saint Mary-of-the-Woods Coll (IN)
Saint Mary's Coll of California (CA)
Saint Mary's U of Minnesota (MN)
Sarah Lawrence Coll (NY)
Skidmore Coll (NY)
Spring Hill Coll (AL)
U of Calif, Los Angeles (CA)
U of Calif, Santa Cruz (CA)
U of Chicago (IL)
U of Great Falls (MT)
The U of Iowa (IA)
The U of Maine at Augusta (ME)
U of Nevada, Reno (NV)
U of North Texas (TX)
U of Oklahoma (OK)
U of Pennsylvania (PA)
Viterbo U (WI)
Washington U in St. Louis (MO)
Webster U (MO)
Western Kentucky U (KY)

ENGLISH/LANGUAGE ARTS TEACHER EDUCATION

Abilene Christian U (TX)
Alma Coll (MI)
Alvernia Coll (PA)
Alverno Coll (WI)
Anderson Coll (SC)
Appalachian State U (NC)
Aquinas Coll (MI)
Arkansas State U (AR)
Arkansas Tech U (AR)
Arlington Baptist Coll (TX)
Averett U (VA)
Barry U (FL)
Baylor U (TX)
Berea Coll (KY)
Bethany Coll (KS)
Bethel Coll (IN)
Bethel Coll (TN)
Bethel U (MN)
Bethune-Cookman Coll (FL)
Bishop's U (QC, Canada)
Bloomfield Coll (NJ)
Bluefield Coll (VA)
Blue Mountain Coll (MS)
Boston U (MA)
Bowling Green State U (OH)
Brewton-Parker Coll (GA)
Bridgewater Coll (VA)
Brigham Young U (UT)
Brigham Young U–Hawaii (HI)
Brooklyn Coll of the City U of NY (NY)
Buena Vista U (IA)
State U of NY Coll at Buffalo (NY)
Cabrini Coll (PA)
California State U, Chico (CA)
California State U, Long Beach (CA)
Calumet Coll of Saint Joseph (IN)
Campbellsville U (KY)
Capital U (OH)
Carroll Coll (MT)
Carroll Coll (WI)
The Catholic U of America (DC)
Cedarville U (OH)
Centenary Coll of Louisiana (LA)
Central Michigan U (MI)
Central Missouri State U (MO)
Central State U (OH)
Central Washington U (WA)
Chadron State Coll (NE)
Chapman U (CA)
Charleston Southern U (SC)
Chatham Coll (PA)
Chowan Coll (NC)
Christian Brothers U (TN)
Citadel, The Military Coll of South Carolina (SC)
Clearwater Christian Coll (FL)
Coker Coll (SC)
Colby-Sawyer Coll (NH)
The Coll of New Jersey (NJ)
Coll of St. Catherine (MN)
The Coll of Saint Rose (NY)
The Coll of St. Scholastica (MN)
Coll of Santa Fe (NM)
Coll of the Ozarks (MO)
Colorado State U (CO)
Columbia Union Coll (MD)
Columbus State U (GA)
Concordia Coll (MN)
Concordia U (IL)
Concordia U (MI)
Concordia U (NE)
Concordia U (OR)
Cornell U (NY)
Cornerstone U (MI)
Crichton Coll (TN)
Crown Coll (MN)
Culver-Stockton Coll (MO)
Daemen Coll (NY)
Dakota Wesleyan U (SD)
Dana Coll (NE)
Delaware State U (DE)
Delta State U (MS)
Dominican Coll (NY)
Dowling Coll (NY)
Duquesne U (PA)
East Carolina U (NC)
East Central U (OK)
Eastern Mennonite U (VA)
Eastern Michigan U (MI)
Eastern U (PA)
Eastern Washington U (WA)
East Texas Baptist U (TX)
Elizabeth City State U (NC)
Elmhurst Coll (IL)
Elmira Coll (NY)
Elms Coll (MA)
Emmanuel Coll (GA)
Faith Baptist Bible Coll and Theological Sem (IA)
Fayetteville State U (NC)
Florida Atlantic U (FL)
Florida Intl U (FL)
Florida State U (FL)
Framingham State Coll (MA)
Franklin Coll (IN)
Freed-Hardeman U (TN)
Gallaudet U (DC)
Gardner-Webb U (NC)
George Fox U (OR)
Georgian Court U (NJ)
Georgia Southern U (GA)
Glenville State Coll (WV)
Grace Coll (IN)
Grambling State U (LA)
Greensboro Coll (NC)
Greenville Coll (IL)
Hannibal-LaGrange Coll (MO)
Harding U (AR)
Hardin-Simmons U (TX)
Hastings Coll (NE)
Hofstra U (NY)
Hope Coll (MI)
Houston Baptist U (TX)
Howard Payne U (TX)
Huntingdon Coll (AL)
Illinois Wesleyan U (IL)
Indiana U Bloomington (IN)
Indiana U Northwest (IN)
Indiana U of Pennsylvania (PA)
Indiana U–Purdue U Fort Wayne (IN)
Indiana U–Purdue U Indianapolis (IN)
Indiana U South Bend (IN)
Indiana U Southeast (IN)
Iona Coll (NY)
Ithaca Coll (NY)
Jamestown Coll (ND)
Johnson State Coll (VT)
Judson Coll (AL)
Juniata Coll (PA)
Kennesaw State U (GA)
Kent State U (OH)
Kentucky Wesleyan Coll (KY)
Keuka Coll (NY)
King Coll (TN)
Lambuth U (TN)
La Roche Coll (PA)
Lebanon Valley Coll (PA)
Le Moyne Coll (NY)
Lewis-Clark State Coll (ID)
Liberty U (VA)
Limestone Coll (SC)
Lincoln U (PA)
Long Island U, Brooklyn Campus (NY)
Long Island U, C.W. Post Campus (NY)
Long Island U, Southampton Coll (NY)
Louisiana State U in Shreveport (LA)
Louisiana Tech U (LA)
Malone Coll (OH)
Manhattanville Coll (NY)
Mansfield U of Pennsylvania (PA)
Marian Coll of Fond du Lac (WI)
Marquette U (WI)
Maryville Coll (TN)
Maryville U of Saint Louis (MO)
Marywood U (PA)
Mayville State U (ND)
McGill U (QC, Canada)
McKendree Coll (IL)
McNeese State U (LA)
Mercyhurst Coll (PA)
Messiah Coll (PA)
Miami U (OH)
Miami U Hamilton (OH)
MidAmerica Nazarene U (KS)
Miles Coll (AL)
Millersville U of Pennsylvania (PA)
Minnesota State U Moorhead (MN)
Minot State U (ND)
Mississippi Valley State U (MS)
Missouri Western State Coll (MO)
Molloy Coll (NY)
Montana State U–Billings (MT)
Morris Coll (SC)
Mount Marty Coll (SD)
Mount Mary Coll (WI)
Mount Vernon Nazarene U (OH)
Murray State U (KY)
Nazareth Coll of Rochester (NY)
Nebraska Wesleyan U (NE)
Nevada State Coll at Henderson (NV)
New York Inst of Technology (NY)
New York U (NY)
North Carolina Central U (NC)
North Carolina State U (NC)
North Dakota State U (ND)
Northern Arizona U (AZ)
Northern Michigan U (MI)
North Georgia Coll & State U (GA)
Northwestern Coll (MN)
Northwest Nazarene U (ID)
Oakland City U (IN)
Ohio Northern U (OH)
Ohio Valley Coll (WV)
Oklahoma Baptist U (OK)
Oklahoma Christian U (OK)
Oral Roberts U (OK)
Pace U (NY)
Paine Coll (GA)
Penn State U Harrisburg Campus of the Capital Coll (PA)
Philadelphia Biblical U (PA)
Pikeville Coll (KY)
Pillsbury Baptist Bible Coll (MN)
Pittsburg State U (KS)
Point Park U (PA)
Pontifical Catholic U of Puerto Rico (PR)
Queens Coll of the City U of NY (NY)
Queens U of Charlotte (NC)
Rivier Coll (NH)
Roberts Wesleyan Coll (NY)
Rocky Mountain Coll (MT)
Sacred Heart U (CT)
St. Ambrose U (IA)
Saint Augustine's Coll (NC)
St. Bonaventure U (NY)
St. Francis Coll (NY)
Saint Francis U (PA)
St. Gregory's U (OK)
St. John's U (NY)
Saint Joseph's Coll of Maine (ME)
Saint Mary's U of Minnesota (MN)
Saint Xavier U (IL)
Salve Regina U (RI)
Samford U (AL)
Sam Houston State U (TX)
San Diego State U (CA)
Schreiner U (TX)
Seattle Pacific U (WA)
Seton Hill U (PA)
Shawnee State U (OH)
Shaw U (NC)
Simpson Coll and Graduate School (CA)
Southeastern Coll of the Assemblies of God (FL)
Southeastern Louisiana U (LA)
Southeastern Oklahoma State U (OK)
Southeast Missouri State U (MO)
Southern Adventist U (TN)
Southern Arkansas U–Magnolia (AR)
Southern Nazarene U (OK)
Southwest Baptist U (MO)
Southwestern Oklahoma State U (OK)
Southwest Missouri State U (MO)
State U of NY Coll at Brockport (NY)
State U of NY Coll at Oneonta (NY)
State U of NY Coll at Potsdam (NY)
Syracuse U (NY)
Talladega Coll (AL)
Tennessee Wesleyan Coll (TN)
Texas A&M Intl U (TX)
Texas Christian U (TX)
Texas Wesleyan U (TX)
Toccoa Falls Coll (GA)
Trevecca Nazarene U (TN)
Trinity Christian Coll (IL)
Tri-State U (IN)
Union Coll (NE)
State U of NY at Albany (NY)
The U of Akron (OH)
The U of Arizona (AZ)
U of Central Arkansas (AR)
U of Central Florida (FL)
U of Delaware (DE)
U of Dubuque (IA)
U of Georgia (GA)
U of Great Falls (MT)
U of Hawaii at Manoa (HI)
U of Illinois at Chicago (IL)
U of Illinois at Urbana–Champaign (IL)
U of Indianapolis (IN)
U of Maine at Farmington (ME)
U of Maine at Fort Kent (ME)
U of Maine at Machias (ME)
U of Mary (ND)
U of Maryland, Coll Park (MD)
U of Minnesota, Twin Cities Campus (MN)
U of Mississippi (MS)
U of Missouri–St. Louis (MO)
The U of Montana–Western (MT)
U of Nebraska–Lincoln (NE)
U of Nevada, Reno (NV)
U of New Orleans (LA)
The U of North Carolina at Chapel Hill (NC)
The U of North Carolina at Charlotte (NC)
The U of North Carolina at Greensboro (NC)
The U of North Carolina at Pembroke (NC)
The U of North Carolina at Wilmington (NC)
U of Oklahoma (OK)
U of Pittsburgh at Johnstown (PA)
U of Puerto Rico, Cayey U Coll (PR)
U of Regina (SK, Canada)
U of St. Francis (IL)
U of Saint Francis (IN)
U of St. Thomas (MN)
The U of South Dakota (SD)
U of South Florida (FL)
The U of Tennessee at Martin (TN)
U of the Ozarks (AR)
U of Toledo (OH)
U of Vermont (VT)
The U of Western Ontario (ON, Canada)
U of West Florida (FL)
U of Windsor (ON, Canada)
U of Wisconsin–River Falls (WI)
U of Wisconsin–Superior (WI)
Ursuline Coll (OH)
Utica Coll (NY)
Valdosta State U (GA)
Valley City State U (ND)
Valparaiso U (IN)
Virginia Intermont Coll (VA)
Viterbo U (WI)
Waldorf Coll (IA)
Warner Southern Coll (FL)
Washington U in St. Louis (MO)
Waynesburg Coll (PA)
Wayne State U (MI)
Weber State U (UT)
West Chester U of Pennsylvania (PA)
Western Baptist Coll (OR)
Western Carolina U (NC)
Western Michigan U (MI)
Westmont Coll (CA)
West Virginia Wesleyan Coll (WV)
Wheeling Jesuit U (WV)
Widener U (PA)
William Carey Coll (MS)
William Penn U (IA)
William Woods U (MO)
Winston-Salem State U (NC)
Wright State U (OH)
York Coll (NE)
York Coll of Pennsylvania (PA)
York U (ON, Canada)
Youngstown State U (OH)

ENGLISH LITERATURE (BRITISH AND COMMONWEALTH)

The Coll of Southeastern Europe, The American U of Athens(Greece)
Cornell U (NY)
Eastern Michigan U (MI)
Gannon U (PA)
Hampshire Coll (MA)
Hofstra U (NY)
Hunter Coll of the City U of NY (NY)
Huron U USA in London(United Kingdom)
Indiana U–Purdue U Fort Wayne (IN)
Marylhurst U (OR)
Oral Roberts U (OK)
Saint Mary's Coll (IN)
Sarah Lawrence Coll (NY)
Syracuse U (NY)
U of Miami (FL)
U of New Hampshire (NH)

U of Pittsburgh (PA)
U of Southern California (CA)
Washington U in St. Louis (MO)

ENTOMOLOGY
Clemson U (SC)
Colorado State U (CO)
Cornell U (NY)
Florida Ag and Mech U (FL)
Harvard U (MA)
Iowa State U of Science and Technology (IA)
Memorial U of Newfoundland (NL, Canada)
Michigan State U (MI)
The Ohio State U (OH)
Oklahoma State U (OK)
Oregon State U (OR)
Purdue U (IN)
State U of NY Coll of Environ Sci and Forestry (NY)
Texas A&M U (TX)
U of Alberta (AB, Canada)
U of Arkansas (AR)
U of Calif, Davis (CA)
U of Calif, Riverside (CA)
U of Delaware (DE)
U of Florida (FL)
U of Georgia (GA)
U of Hawaii at Manoa (HI)
U of Idaho (ID)
U of Illinois at Urbana–Champaign (IL)
U of Manitoba (MB, Canada)
U of New Brunswick Fredericton (NB, Canada)
U of Wisconsin–Madison (WI)
Utah State U (UT)
Washington State U (WA)

ENTREPRENEURIAL AND SMALL BUSINESS RELATED
Babson Coll (MA)
Florida State U (FL)
Kendall Coll (IL)
U of Alberta (AB, Canada)
U of Miami (FL)
Warren Wilson Coll (NC)

ENTREPRENEURSHIP
American U (DC)
Babson Coll (MA)
Bacone Coll (OK)
Baylor U (TX)
Bridgewater State Coll (MA)
Brigham Young U (UT)
Buena Vista U (IA)
California State U, Fullerton (CA)
Canisius Coll (NY)
Concordia U (QC, Canada)
Dalhousie U (NS, Canada)
Davenport U, Dearborn (MI)
Davenport U, Gaylord (MI)
Davenport U, Grand Rapids (MI)
Davenport U, Traverse City (MI)
Davenport U, Warren (MI)
Duquesne U (PA)
East Central U (OK)
Fordham U (NY)
Grove City Coll (PA)
Hawai'i Pacific U (HI)
HEC Montreal (QC, Canada)
Hofstra U (NY)
Houston Baptist U (TX)
Inter American U of PR, Bayamón Campus (PR)
Iowa State U of Science and Technology (IA)
Kendall Coll (IL)
Kwantlen U Coll (BC, Canada)
Lyndon State Coll (VT)
McGill U (QC, Canada)
Messiah Coll (PA)
Morris Coll (SC)
Northeastern U (MA)
Northern Michigan U (MI)
Northwood U (MI)
Northwood U, Texas Campus (TX)
Pace U (NY)
Palm Beach Atlantic U (FL)
Reinhardt Coll (GA)
Rensselaer Polytechnic Inst (NY)
St. Edward's U (TX)
Seton Hill U (PA)
Southern Polytechnic State U (GA)
Syracuse U (NY)
Union Coll (NE)
The U of Arizona (AZ)
U of Illinois at Chicago (IL)
The U of Iowa (IA)
U of Miami (FL)
U of Nevada, Reno (NV)
U of North Dakota (ND)
U of Oklahoma (OK)
U of Phoenix–Atlanta Campus (GA)
U of Phoenix–Fort Lauderdale Campus (FL)
U of Phoenix–Jacksonville Campus (FL)
U of Phoenix–Kansas City Campus (MO)
U of Phoenix–Louisiana Campus (LA)
U of Phoenix–Metro Detroit Campus (MI)
U of Phoenix–Phoenix Campus (AZ)
U of St. Thomas (MN)
The U of Scranton (PA)
U of Southern Indiana (IN)
U of Toledo (OH)
Washington State U (WA)
Washington U in St. Louis (MO)

ENVIRONMENTAL BIOLOGY
Antioch Coll (OH)
Arcadia U (PA)
Bard Coll (NY)
Barnard Coll (NY)
Beloit Coll (WI)
Bennington Coll (VT)
Bethel Coll (IN)
Bloomfield Coll (NJ)
Bridgewater State Coll (MA)
California Polytechnic State U, San Luis Obispo (CA)
Carlow Coll (PA)
Cedar Crest Coll (PA)
Cedarville U (OH)
Central Methodist Coll (MO)
Chowan Coll (NC)
Colgate U (NY)
Coll of the Atlantic (ME)
Colorado State U-Pueblo (CO)
Columbia Coll (NY)
Concordia U (QC, Canada)
Concordia U Coll of Alberta (AB, Canada)
Cornerstone U (MI)
Eastern Washington U (WA)
East Stroudsburg U of Pennsylvania (PA)
Florida State U (FL)
Fort Lewis Coll (CO)
Framingham State Coll (MA)
Franklin Pierce Coll (NH)
Grand Canyon U (AZ)
Greenville Coll (IL)
Grinnell Coll (IA)
Hampshire Coll (MA)
Harvard U (MA)
Heidelberg Coll (OH)
Humboldt State U (CA)
Inter American U of PR, Bayamón Campus (PR)
Iowa Wesleyan Coll (IA)
Jacksonville State U (AL)
Lakehead U (ON, Canada)
Mansfield U of Pennsylvania (PA)
Marist Coll (NY)
Marlboro Coll (VT)
Marygrove Coll (MI)
The Master's Coll and Sem (CA)
McGill U (QC, Canada)
Memorial U of Newfoundland (NL, Canada)
Michigan State U (MI)
Midway Coll (KY)
Minnesota State U Mankato (MN)
Mount Union Coll (OH)
New Mexico Inst of Mining and Technology (NM)
Nicholls State U (LA)
Nipissing U (ON, Canada)
Northland Coll (WI)
Ohio U (OH)
Oregon State U (OR)
Otterbein Coll (OH)
Philadelphia U (PA)
Pittsburg State U (KS)
Plymouth State U (NH)
Queens U of Charlotte (NC)
Sacred Heart U (CT)
St. Cloud State U (MN)
Simpson Coll (IA)
State U of NY Coll at Brockport (NY)
State U of NY Coll at Cortland (NY)
State U of NY Coll of Environ Sci and Forestry (NY)
Sterling Coll (VT)
Suffolk U (MA)
Tabor Coll (KS)
Taylor U (IN)
Trinity Western U (BC, Canada)
Tulane U (LA)
Unity Coll (ME)
U Coll of the Cariboo (BC, Canada)
U of Alberta (AB, Canada)
The U of British Columbia (BC, Canada)
U of Calif, Davis (CA)
U of Charleston (WV)
U of Dayton (OH)
U of Dubuque (IA)
U of Guelph (ON, Canada)
U of La Verne (CA)
U of Pittsburgh at Greensburg (PA)
U of Pittsburgh at Johnstown (PA)
U of Regina (SK, Canada)
The U of Tampa (FL)
U of Windsor (ON, Canada)
Ursuline Coll (OH)
Western Washington U (WA)
Westfield State Coll (MA)
William Penn U (IA)
Wingate U (NC)
Winona State U (MN)
York U (ON, Canada)

ENVIRONMENTAL CONTROL TECHNOLOGIES RELATED
Davis & Elkins Coll (WV)
Florida Intl U (FL)
Inter American U of PR, Bayamón Campus (PR)
New York Inst of Technology (NY)

ENVIRONMENTAL DESIGN/ ARCHITECTURE
Art Center Coll of Design (CA)
Auburn U (AL)
Ball State U (IN)
Bowling Green State U (OH)
Col for Creative Studies (MI)
The Coll of Southeastern Europe, The American U of Athens(Greece)
Coll of the Atlantic (ME)
Cornell U (NY)
Dalhousie U (NS, Canada)
Florida Intl U (FL)
Hampshire Coll (MA)
Harvard U (MA)
Kent State U (OH)
Lawrence Technological U (MI)
Miami U (OH)
Montana State U–Bozeman (MT)
North Carolina State U (NC)
North Dakota State U (ND)
Otis Coll of Art and Design (CA)
Parsons School of Design, New School U (NY)
Rutgers, The State U of New Jersey, New Brunswick/Piscataway (NJ)
State U of NY Coll of Environ Sci and Forestry (NY)
Sterling Coll (VT)
Texas A&M U (TX)
U at Buffalo, The State U of New York (NY)
U of Calif, Irvine (CA)
U of Colorado at Boulder (CO)
U of Hawaii at Manoa (HI)
U of Houston (TX)
U of Manitoba (MB, Canada)
U of Massachusetts Amherst (MA)
U of New Mexico (NM)
U of Oklahoma (OK)
U of Pennsylvania (PA)
York U (ON, Canada)

ENVIRONMENTAL EDUCATION
Coll of the Atlantic (ME)
Johnson State Coll (VT)
Northland Coll (WI)
The Ohio State U (OH)
Sonoma State U (CA)
State U of NY Coll of Environ Sci and Forestry (NY)
Unity Coll (ME)
U of Maine at Machias (ME)
The U of Montana–Missoula (MT)
Western Washington U (WA)
York U (ON, Canada)

ENVIRONMENTAL ENGINEERING TECHNOLOGY
British Columbia Inst of Technology (BC, Canada)
California State U, Long Beach (CA)
East Carolina U (NC)
Eastern Kentucky U (KY)
Lake Superior State U (MI)
Middle Tennessee State U (TN)
Murray State U (KY)
New York Inst of Technology (NY)
Pennsylvania Coll of Technology (PA)
Shawnee State U (OH)
Sterling Coll (VT)
Texas Southern U (TX)
Unity Coll (ME)
The U of British Columbia (BC, Canada)
U of Delaware (DE)
U of Guelph (ON, Canada)
U of Wisconsin–Whitewater (WI)
Western Kentucky U (KY)
Wright State U (OH)

ENVIRONMENTAL/ ENVIRONMENTAL HEALTH ENGINEERING
Bradley U (IL)
California Inst of Technology (CA)
California Polytechnic State U, San Luis Obispo (CA)
Carleton U (ON, Canada)
Carnegie Mellon U (PA)
Christian Brothers U (TN)
Clarkson U (NY)
Clemson U (SC)
Colorado School of Mines (CO)
Colorado State U (CO)
Columbia U, School of Eng & Applied Sci (NY)
Concordia U (QC, Canada)
Cornell U (NY)
Drexel U (PA)
Florida State U (FL)
Gannon U (PA)
The George Washington U (DC)
Harvard U (MA)
Hofstra U (NY)
Humboldt State U (CA)
Illinois Inst of Technology (IL)
The Johns Hopkins U (MD)
Lafayette Coll (PA)
Louisiana State U and A&M Coll (LA)
Manhattan Coll (NY)
Marquette U (WI)
Massachusetts Inst of Technology (MA)
Massachusetts Maritime Acad (MA)
Michigan Technological U (MI)
Montana Tech of The U of Montana (MT)
New Jersey Inst of Technology (NJ)
New Mexico Inst of Mining and Technology (NM)
North Carolina State U (NC)
Northern Arizona U (AZ)
Northwestern U (IL)
Old Dominion U (VA)
Oregon State U (OR)
Penn State U Abington Coll (PA)
Penn State U Altoona Coll (PA)
Penn State U at Erie, The Behrend Coll (PA)
Penn State U Beaver Campus of the Commonwealth Coll (PA)
Penn State U Berks Cmps of Berks-Lehigh Valley Coll (PA)
Penn State U Delaware County Campus of the Commonwealth Coll (PA)
Penn State U DuBois Campus of the Commonwealth Coll (PA)
Penn State U Fayette Campus of the Commonwealth Coll (PA)
Penn State U Harrisburg Campus of the Capital Coll (PA)
Penn State U Hazleton Campus of the Commonwealth Coll (PA)
Penn State U Lehigh Valley Cmps of Berks-Lehigh Valley Coll (PA)
Penn State U McKeesport Campus of the Commonwealth Coll (PA)
Penn State U Mont Alto Campus of the Commonwealth Coll (PA)
Penn State U New Kensington Campus of the Commonwealth Coll (PA)
Penn State U Schuylkill Campus of the Capital Coll (PA)
Penn State U Shenango Campus of the Commonwealth Coll (PA)
Penn State U Univ Park Campus (PA)
Penn State U Wilkes-Barre Campus of the Commonwealth Coll (PA)
Penn State U Worthington Scranton Cmps Commonwealth Coll (PA)
Penn State U York Campus of the Commonwealth Coll (PA)
Polytechnic U of Puerto Rico (PR)
Rensselaer Polytechnic Inst (NY)
Rice U (TX)
Roger Williams U (RI)
Seattle U (WA)
South Dakota School of Mines and Technology (SD)
South Dakota State U (SD)
Southern Methodist U (TX)
Stanford U (CA)
State U of NY Coll of Environ Sci and Forestry (NY)
Stevens Inst of Technology (NJ)
Syracuse U (NY)
Texas A&M U–Kingsville (TX)
Texas Tech U (TX)
Tufts U (MA)
Tulane U (LA)
United States Air Force Acad (CO)
United States Military Acad (NY)
Université Laval (QC, Canada)
U at Buffalo, The State U of New York (NY)
U of Alberta (AB, Canada)
U of Arkansas (AR)
U of Calif, Berkeley (CA)
U of Calif, Irvine (CA)
U of Calif, Riverside (CA)
U of Central Florida (FL)
U of Colorado at Boulder (CO)
U of Connecticut (CT)
U of Delaware (DE)
U of Florida (FL)
U of Guelph (ON, Canada)
U of Hartford (CT)
U of Miami (FL)
U of Michigan (MI)
U of Missouri–Rolla (MO)
U of Nevada, Reno (NV)
U of New Hampshire (NH)
U of North Dakota (ND)
U of Notre Dame (IN)
U of Oklahoma (OK)
U of Pennsylvania (PA)
U of Regina (SK, Canada)
U of Southern California (CA)
U of Utah (UT)
U of Vermont (VT)
U of Waterloo (ON, Canada)
The U of Western Ontario (ON, Canada)
U of Windsor (ON, Canada)
U of Wisconsin–Madison (WI)
Utah State U (UT)
Washington State U (WA)
Wentworth Inst of Technology (MA)
Wilkes U (PA)
Worcester Polytechnic Inst (MA)
Yale U (CT)
Youngstown State U (OH)

ENVIRONMENTAL HEALTH
Boise State U (ID)
Bowling Green State U (OH)
British Columbia Inst of Technology (BC, Canada)
Clarkson U (NY)
Colorado State U (CO)
Colorado State U-Pueblo (CO)
Concordia U Coll of Alberta (AB, Canada)
East Carolina U (NC)
East Central U (OK)
Eastern Kentucky U (KY)
Ferris State U (MI)
Hampshire Coll (MA)
Illinois State U (IL)
Indiana State U (IN)
Indiana U of Pennsylvania (PA)
Iowa Wesleyan Coll (IA)
Missouri Southern State U (MO)
New Mexico State U (NM)
Oakland U (MI)
Ohio U (OH)
Old Dominion U (VA)
Oregon State U (OR)
Ryerson U (ON, Canada)
Salisbury U (MD)
Springfield Coll (MA)
Texas Southern U (TX)
U of Arkansas at Little Rock (AR)
U of Calif, Los Angeles (CA)
U of Georgia (GA)
U of Michigan–Flint (MI)
The U of North Carolina at Chapel Hill (NC)
U of Southern Maine (ME)
U of Utah (UT)
U of Washington (WA)
U of Wisconsin–Eau Claire (WI)
West Chester U of Pennsylvania (PA)
Western Carolina U (NC)
Wright State U (OH)
York Coll of the City U of New York (NY)

ENVIRONMENTAL PSYCHOLOGY
Embry-Riddle Aeronautical U (FL)

ENVIRONMENTAL SCIENCE
Abilene Christian U (TX)
Alaska Pacific U (AK)
Albright Coll (PA)
Allegheny Coll (PA)

Aquinas Coll (MI)
Assumption Coll (MA)
Auburn U (AL)
Averett U (VA)
Barnard Coll (NY)
Berry Coll (GA)
Bethel U (MN)
Blackburn Coll (IL)
Bridgewater Coll (VA)
Brigham Young U (UT)
Brown U (RI)
California State U, Long Beach (CA)
Canisius Coll (NY)
Capital U (OH)
Carroll Coll (WI)
Central Methodist Coll (MO)
Chapman U (CA)
Colby Coll (ME)
Coll of Santa Fe (NM)
The Colorado Coll (CO)
Concordia U Coll of Alberta (AB, Canada)
Concordia U, St. Paul (MN)
Dalhousie U (NS, Canada)
Delaware State U (DE)
DeSales U (PA)
Dickinson Coll (PA)
Drake U (IA)
Duquesne U (PA)
East Central U (OK)
Eastern Connecticut State U (CT)
Eastern Mennonite U (VA)
Eastern Washington U (WA)
Florida Ag and Mech U (FL)
Florida Inst of Technology (FL)
Framingham State Coll (MA)
Franklin and Marshall Coll (PA)
Georgia Coll & State U (GA)
Gettysburg Coll (PA)
Hampshire Coll (MA)
Hardin-Simmons U (TX)
Haskell Indian Nations U (KS)
Hawai'i Pacific U (HI)
Heidelberg Coll (OH)
Hofstra U (NY)
Hunter Coll of the City U of NY (NY)
Inter American U of PR, Ponce Campus (PR)
John Brown U (AR)
Juniata Coll (PA)
Keuka Coll (NY)
King's Coll (PA)
Kutztown U of Pennsylvania (PA)
Lambuth U (TN)
Lander U (SC)
Lindenwood U (MO)
Long Island U, C.W. Post Campus (NY)
Long Island U, Southampton Coll (NY)
Louisiana State U and A&M Coll (LA)
Lubbock Christian U (TX)
Marietta Coll (OH)
Marshall U (WV)
Marymount U (VA)
Maryville U of Saint Louis (MO)
Marywood U (PA)
McMurry U (TX)
McNeese State U (LA)
Mercer U (GA)
Meredith Coll (NC)
Messiah Coll (PA)
Miami U Hamilton (OH)
Michigan State U (MI)
Midwestern State U (TX)
Miles Coll (AL)
Mills Coll (CA)
Monmouth Coll (IL)
Muhlenberg Coll (PA)
Nazareth Coll of Rochester (NY)
Nevada State Coll at Henderson (NV)
North Carolina State U (NC)
Northern Michigan U (MI)
Northwestern Coll (IA)
Northwestern U (IL)
Notre Dame Coll (OH)
Nova Southeastern U (FL)
Otterbein Coll (OH)
Paine Coll (GA)
Pfeiffer U (NC)
Piedmont Coll (GA)
Pitzer Coll (CA)
Point Park U (PA)
Queens Coll of the City U of NY (NY)
Queen's U at Kingston (ON, Canada)
Ramapo Coll of New Jersey (NJ)
Roanoke Coll (VA)
Rochester Inst of Technology (NY)
Rocky Mountain Coll (MT)
Roger Williams U (RI)
Roosevelt U (IL)
Sacred Heart U (CT)
Saint Francis U (PA)
Saint Joseph's Coll (IN)
Saint Joseph's Coll of Maine (ME)
Saint Joseph's U (PA)
Saint Louis U (MO)
Saint Vincent Coll (PA)
Samford U (AL)
Santa Clara U (CA)
Scripps Coll (CA)
Sheldon Jackson Coll (AK)
Simon Fraser U (BC, Canada)
Skidmore Coll (NY)
Slippery Rock U of Pennsylvania (PA)
Southeastern Oklahoma State U (OK)
Spring Hill Coll (AL)
State U of NY Coll at Cortland (NY)
Sweet Briar Coll (VA)
Teikyo Post U (CT)
Texas A&M U (TX)
Texas Christian U (TX)
Texas Southern U (TX)
Texas State U-San Marcos (TX)
Trinity Coll (CT)
Trinity Western U (BC, Canada)
Troy State U (AL)
State U of NY at Albany (NY)
U of Alberta (AB, Canada)
U of Arkansas (AR)
U of Calif, Berkeley (CA)
U of Calif, Los Angeles (CA)
U of Charleston (WV)
U of Dubuque (IA)
U of Florida (FL)
U of Houston–Clear Lake (TX)
U of Illinois at Urbana–Champaign (IL)
The U of Iowa (IA)
The U of Lethbridge (AB, Canada)
U of Maryland, Baltimore County (MD)
U of Massachusetts Amherst (MA)
U of Massachusetts Lowell (MA)
The U of North Carolina at Chapel Hill (NC)
The U of North Carolina at Wilmington (NC)
U of Northern Iowa (IA)
U of Oklahoma (OK)
U of Oregon (OR)
U of Ottawa (ON, Canada)
U of Rochester (NY)
U of St. Francis (IL)
U of San Francisco (CA)
U of the Sciences in Philadelphia (PA)
U of Vermont (VT)
U of Virginia (VA)
U of Waterloo (ON, Canada)
U of Windsor (ON, Canada)
U of Wisconsin–Green Bay (WI)
Upper Iowa U (IA)
Valparaiso U (IN)
Vassar Coll (NY)
Washington State U (WA)
Western Carolina U (NC)
Western Michigan U (MI)
Western Washington U (WA)
Westminster Coll (MO)
West Texas A&M U (TX)
West Virginia Wesleyan Coll (WV)
Willamette U (OR)
Wright State U (OH)
York U (ON, Canada)

ENVIRONMENTAL STUDIES

Acadia U (NS, Canada)
Adrian Coll (MI)
Albion Coll (MI)
Alderson-Broaddus Coll (WV)
Alfred U (NY)
Allegheny Coll (PA)
Alverno Coll (WI)
American Public U System (WV)
American U (DC)
Antioch Coll (OH)
Aquinas Coll (MI)
Ashland U (OH)
Auburn U (AL)
Augustana Coll (IL)
Aurora U (IL)
Ball State U (IN)
Bard Coll (NY)
Barnard Coll (NY)
Barton Coll (NC)
Bates Coll (ME)
Baylor U (TX)
Beloit Coll (WI)
Bemidji State U (MN)
Benedictine U (IL)
Bennington Coll (VT)
Bethany Coll (WV)
Black Hills State U (SD)
Boise State U (ID)
Boston Coll (MA)
Boston U (MA)
Bowdoin Coll (ME)
Brenau U (GA)
Brevard Coll (NC)
Briar Cliff U (IA)
Brock U (ON, Canada)
Brooklyn Coll of the City U of NY (NY)
Brown U (RI)
Bucknell U (PA)
California State U, Hayward (CA)
California State U, Sacramento (CA)
California State U, San Bernardino (CA)
California U of Pennsylvania (PA)
Calvin Coll (MI)
Carleton U (ON, Canada)
Carroll Coll (MT)
Carthage Coll (WI)
Case Western Reserve U (OH)
Castleton State Coll (VT)
Catawba Coll (NC)
Cazenovia Coll (NY)
Cedar Crest Coll (PA)
Centenary Coll of Louisiana (LA)
Central Coll (IA)
Central Michigan U (MI)
Chaminade U of Honolulu (HI)
Charleston Southern U (SC)
Chatham Coll (PA)
Chestnut Hill Coll (PA)
Christopher Newport U (VA)
Claremont McKenna Coll (CA)
Clarion U of Pennsylvania (PA)
Clarkson U (NY)
Clark U (MA)
Cleveland State U (OH)
Coe Coll (IA)
Colby Coll (ME)
Colby-Sawyer Coll (NH)
Colgate U (NY)
The Coll of New Rochelle (NY)
Coll of Saint Benedict (MN)
The Coll of Saint Rose (NY)
Coll of the Atlantic (ME)
Coll of the Holy Cross (MA)
Coll of the Southwest (NM)
The Coll of William and Mary (VA)
Columbia Coll (MO)
Columbia Coll (NY)
Columbia Southern U (AL)
Concordia Coll (MN)
Concordia U (IL)
Concordia U (OR)
Concordia U (QC, Canada)
Concordia U at Austin (TX)
Concordia U Coll of Alberta (AB, Canada)
Connecticut Coll (CT)
Cornell Coll (IA)
Cornell U (NY)
Creighton U (NE)
Curry Coll (MA)
Dalhousie U (NS, Canada)
Dana Coll (NE)
Dartmouth Coll (NH)
Defiance Coll (OH)
Denison U (OH)
DePaul U (IL)
DePauw U (IN)
DeSales U (PA)
Dickinson Coll (PA)
Dickinson State U (ND)
Doane Coll (NE)
Dominican U (IL)
Dominican U of California (CA)
Dordt Coll (IA)
Drake U (IA)
Drexel U (PA)
Drury U (MO)
Duke U (NC)
Earlham Coll (IN)
East Central U (OK)
Eastern Kentucky U (KY)
Eastern U (PA)
Eckerd Coll (FL)
Edinboro U of Pennsylvania (PA)
Elizabethtown Coll (PA)
Elmhurst Coll (IL)
Elmira Coll (NY)
Elon U (NC)
Emory & Henry Coll (VA)
Endicott Coll (MA)
The Evergreen State Coll (WA)
Fairleigh Dickinson U, Teaneck-Metro Campus (NJ)
Ferrum Coll (VA)
Florida Intl U (FL)
Florida Southern Coll (FL)
Florida State U (FL)
Framingham State Coll (MA)
Franklin and Marshall Coll (PA)
Franklin Pierce Coll (NH)
Frostburg State U (MD)
Furman U (SC)
Georgetown Coll (KY)
The George Washington U (DC)
Gettysburg Coll (PA)
Goshen Coll (IN)
Grinnell Coll (IA)
Guilford Coll (NC)
Gustavus Adolphus Coll (MN)
Hamline U (MN)
Hampshire Coll (MA)
Hampton U (VA)
Harvard U (MA)
Hawai'i Pacific U (HI)
Heidelberg Coll (OH)
Hiram Coll (OH)
Hobart and William Smith Colls (NY)
Hood Coll (MD)
Hope Coll (MI)
Humboldt State U (CA)
Illinois Coll (IL)
Illinois Wesleyan U (IL)
Indiana U Bloomington (IN)
Indiana U of Pennsylvania (PA)
Inter American U of PR, San Germán Campus (PR)
Iowa State U of Science and Technology (IA)
Ithaca Coll (NY)
Jacksonville U (FL)
John Brown U (AR)
John Carroll U (OH)
The Johns Hopkins U (MD)
Johnson State Coll (VT)
Juniata Coll (PA)
Keene State Coll (NH)
Kentucky Wesleyan Coll (KY)
Kenyon Coll (OH)
Keystone Coll (PA)
King's Coll (PA)
The King's U Coll (AB, Canada)
Knox Coll (IL)
Kutztown U of Pennsylvania (PA)
Lake Erie Coll (OH)
Lake Forest Coll (IL)
Lakehead U (ON, Canada)
Lake Superior State U (MI)
Lamar U (TX)
Lambuth U (TN)
La Salle U (PA)
Lawrence U (WI)
Lehigh U (PA)
Lenoir-Rhyne Coll (NC)
Lesley U (MA)
Lewis & Clark Coll (OR)
Lewis U (IL)
Lincoln Memorial U (TN)
Linfield Coll (OR)
Lipscomb U (TN)
Long Island U, C.W. Post Campus (NY)
Long Island U, Southampton Coll (NY)
Longwood U (VA)
Louisiana State U in Shreveport (LA)
Louisiana Tech U (LA)
Loyola U Chicago (IL)
Lynchburg Coll (VA)
Lynn U (FL)
Lyon Coll (AR)
Macalester Coll (MN)
Maharishi U of Management (IA)
Manchester Coll (IN)
Mansfield U of Pennsylvania (PA)
Marietta Coll (OH)
Marist Coll (NY)
Marlboro Coll (VT)
Marygrove Coll (MI)
Marylhurst U (OR)
Maryville Coll (TN)
Maryville U of Saint Louis (MO)
Mary Washington Coll (VA)
Massachusetts Coll of Liberal Arts (MA)
Massachusetts Maritime Acad (MA)
McGill U (QC, Canada)
McPherson Coll (KS)
Medgar Evers Coll of the City U of NY (NY)
Memorial U of Newfoundland (NL, Canada)
Mercer U (GA)
Meredith Coll (NC)
Merrimack Coll (MA)
Metropolitan State Coll of Denver (CO)
Miami U Hamilton (OH)
Michigan State U (MI)
Middlebury Coll (VT)
Mills Coll (CA)
Minnesota State U Mankato (MN)
Molloy Coll (NY)
Montana State U–Billings (MT)
Montana State U–Bozeman (MT)
Montclair State U (NJ)
Montreat Coll (NC)
Mount Allison U (NB, Canada)
Mount Holyoke Coll (MA)
Naropa U (CO)
Nazareth Coll of Rochester (NY)
Neumann Coll (PA)
New Coll of Florida (FL)
New Mexico Highlands U (NM)
New Mexico Inst of Mining and Technology (NM)
New Mexico State U (NM)
Nipissing U (ON, Canada)
North Carolina Central U (NC)
North Carolina State U (NC)
North Carolina Wesleyan Coll (NC)
Northeastern Illinois U (IL)
Northeastern U (MA)
Northern Arizona U (AZ)
Northern Michigan U (MI)
Northern State U (SD)
Northland Coll (WI)
Northwestern U (IL)
Nova Scotia Ag Coll (NS, Canada)
Nova Southeastern U (FL)
Oberlin Coll (OH)
Occidental Coll (CA)
Ohio Northern U (OH)
The Ohio State U (OH)
Ohio Wesleyan U (OH)
Oklahoma State U (OK)
Olivet Coll (MI)
Olivet Nazarene U (IL)
Oregon Inst of Technology (OR)
Oregon State U (OR)
Pacific Lutheran U (WA)
Pacific U (OR)
Paul Smith's Coll of Arts and Sciences (NY)
Penn State U Altoona Coll (PA)
Pfeiffer U (NC)
Piedmont Coll (GA)
Pittsburg State U (KS)
Pitzer Coll (CA)
Pomona Coll (CA)
Pontifical Catholic U of Puerto Rico (PR)
Portland State U (OR)
Principia Coll (IL)
Queens Coll of the City U of NY (NY)
Queen's U at Kingston (ON, Canada)
Ramapo Coll of New Jersey (NJ)
Randolph-Macon Coll (VA)
Randolph-Macon Woman's Coll (VA)
Regis U (CO)
The Richard Stockton Coll of New Jersey (NJ)
Rider U (NJ)
Ripon Coll (WI)
Rocky Mountain Coll (MT)
Rollins Coll (FL)
Roosevelt U (IL)
Rowan U (NJ)
Rutgers, The State U of New Jersey, Newark (NJ)
Rutgers, The State U of New Jersey, New Brunswick/Piscataway (NJ)
Saint Anselm Coll (NH)
St. Bonaventure U (NY)
Saint Francis U (PA)
St. Francis Xavier U (NS, Canada)
Saint John's U (MN)
St. John's U (NY)
Saint Joseph Coll (CT)
Saint Joseph's Coll of Maine (ME)
St. Lawrence U (NY)
Saint Leo U (FL)
St. Olaf Coll (MN)
Saint Vincent Coll (PA)
Samford U (AL)
Sam Houston State U (TX)
San Diego State U (CA)
San Jose State U (CA)
Santa Clara U (CA)
Sarah Lawrence Coll (NY)
Scripps Coll (CA)
Seattle U (WA)
Shaw U (NC)
Shenandoah U (VA)
Shepherd U (WV)
Shippensburg U of Pennsylvania (PA)
Shorter Coll (GA)
Sierra Nevada Coll (NV)
Simmons Coll (MA)
Simon's Rock Coll of Bard (MA)
Skidmore Coll (NY)
Slippery Rock U of Pennsylvania (PA)
Sonoma State U (CA)
Southern Methodist U (TX)
Southern Nazarene U (OK)

Southern Oregon U (OR)
Southern Vermont Coll (VT)
Spelman Coll (GA)
Springfield Coll (MA)
Stanford U (CA)
State U of NY at Binghamton (NY)
State U of NY at New Paltz (NY)
Plattsburgh State U of NY (NY)
State U of NY Coll at Brockport (NY)
State U of NY Coll at Cortland (NY)
State U of NY Coll at Fredonia (NY)
State U of NY Coll at Oneonta (NY)
State U of NY Coll at Potsdam (NY)
State U of NY Coll of A&T at Cobleskill (NY)
State U of NY Coll of Environ Sci and Forestry (NY)
State U of West Georgia (GA)
Stephens Coll (MO)
Sterling Coll (VT)
Stetson U (FL)
Stony Brook U, State U of New York (NY)
Suffolk U (MA)
Sweet Briar Coll (VA)
Taylor U (IN)
Teikyo Post U (CT)
Texas A&M U (TX)
Texas A&M U–Corpus Christi (TX)
Thiel Coll (PA)
Thomas Edison State Coll (NJ)
Trent U (ON, Canada)
Trinity Coll (DC)
Trinity Western U (BC, Canada)
Tri-State U (IN)
Tufts U (MA)
Tulane U (LA)
Tusculum Coll (TN)
Tuskegee U (AL)
United States Military Acad (NY)
Unity Coll (ME)
Université Laval (QC, Canada)
U of Alaska Southeast (AK)
U of Alberta (AB, Canada)
The U of Arizona (AZ)
The U of British Columbia (BC, Canada)
U of Calgary (AB, Canada)
U of Calif, Berkeley (CA)
U of Calif, Riverside (CA)
U of Calif, San Diego (CA)
U of Calif, Santa Barbara (CA)
U of Calif, Santa Cruz (CA)
U of Central Arkansas (AR)
U of Chicago (IL)
U of Colorado at Boulder (CO)
U of Connecticut (CT)
U of Dayton (OH)
U of Delaware (DE)
U of Denver (CO)
U of Dubuque (IA)
U of Evansville (IN)
The U of Findlay (OH)
U of Guelph (ON, Canada)
U of Houston (TX)
U of Idaho (ID)
U of Indianapolis (IN)
The U of Iowa (IA)
U of Kansas (KS)
U of Maine at Farmington (ME)
U of Maine at Fort Kent (ME)
U of Maine at Machias (ME)
U of Maine at Presque Isle (ME)
U of Manitoba (MB, Canada)
U of Maryland, Baltimore County (MD)
U of Maryland Eastern Shore (MD)
U of Maryland U Coll (MD)
U of Miami (FL)
U of Michigan (MI)
U of Michigan–Dearborn (MI)
U of Minnesota, Crookston (MN)
U of Minnesota, Duluth (MN)
U of Minnesota, Twin Cities Campus (MN)
U of Missouri–Columbia (MO)
U of Mobile (AL)
The U of Montana–Missoula (MT)
The U of Montana–Western (MT)
U of Nebraska at Omaha (NE)
U of Nebraska–Lincoln (NE)
U of Nevada, Las Vegas (NV)
U of New Hampshire (NH)
U of New Haven (CT)
U of New Orleans (LA)
The U of North Carolina at Asheville (NC)
The U of North Carolina at Chapel Hill (NC)
The U of North Carolina at Wilmington (NC)
U of Oregon (OR)
U of Ottawa (ON, Canada)
U of Pennsylvania (PA)
U of Pittsburgh at Bradford (PA)
U of Pittsburgh at Johnstown (PA)
U of Portland (OR)
U of Redlands (CA)
U of Regina (SK, Canada)
U of Rhode Island (RI)
U of Richmond (VA)
U of Rochester (NY)
U of Saint Francis (IN)
U of St. Thomas (TX)
U of San Francisco (CA)
U of Saskatchewan (SK, Canada)
U of Southern California (CA)
U of Southern Maine (ME)
U of South Florida (FL)
The U of Tampa (FL)
The U of Tennessee at Chattanooga (TN)
The U of Tennessee at Martin (TN)
U of the District of Columbia (DC)
U of the Incarnate Word (TX)
U of the Ozarks (AR)
U of the Pacific (CA)
U of the South (TN)
U of Toledo (OH)
U of Toronto (ON, Canada)
U of Tulsa (OK)
U of Utah (UT)
U of Vermont (VT)
U of Victoria (BC, Canada)
The U of Virginia's Coll at Wise (VA)
U of Washington (WA)
U of Waterloo (ON, Canada)
The U of Western Ontario (ON, Canada)
U of West Florida (FL)
U of Windsor (ON, Canada)
U of Wisconsin–Green Bay (WI)
U of Wisconsin–River Falls (WI)
U of Wyoming (WY)
Ursinus Coll (PA)
Vassar Coll (NY)
Villa Julie Coll (MD)
Virginia Intermont Coll (VA)
Virginia Polytechnic Inst and State U (VA)
Virginia Wesleyan Coll (VA)
Walla Walla Coll (WA)
Warren Wilson Coll (NC)
Washington Coll (MD)
Washington U in St. Louis (MO)
Waynesburg Coll (PA)
Webster U (MO)
Wellesley Coll (MA)
Wells Coll (NY)
Wesleyan U (CT)
Wesley Coll (DE)
West Chester U of Pennsylvania (PA)
Western Connecticut State U (CT)
Western Michigan U (MI)
Western State Coll of Colorado (CO)
Western Washington U (WA)
Westminster Coll (MO)
Westminster Coll (PA)
West Virginia U (WV)
Wheaton Coll (IL)
Wheaton Coll (MA)
Wheeling Jesuit U (WV)
Whitman Coll (WA)
Widener U (PA)
William Paterson U of New Jersey (NJ)
Wilson Coll (PA)
Wittenberg U (OH)
Worcester Polytechnic Inst (MA)
Xavier U of Louisiana (LA)
Yale U (CT)
York U (ON, Canada)
Youngstown State U (OH)

ENVIRONMENTAL TOXICOLOGY
Cornell U (NY)
U of Guelph (ON, Canada)

EPIDEMIOLOGY
Cornell U (NY)
U of Calif, Los Angeles (CA)

EQUESTRIAN STUDIES
Averett U (VA)
Cazenovia Coll (NY)
Centenary Coll (NJ)
Colorado State U (CO)
Johnson & Wales U (RI)
Lake Erie Coll (OH)
Midway Coll (KY)
Mount Ida Coll (MA)
National American U (SD)
North Dakota State U (ND)
Oregon State U (OR)
Otterbein Coll (OH)
Rocky Mountain Coll (MT)
Rutgers, The State U of New Jersey, New Brunswick/Piscataway (NJ)
St. Andrews Presbyterian Coll (NC)
Saint Mary-of-the-Woods Coll (IN)
Stephens Coll (MO)
Sterling Coll (VT)
Teikyo Post U (CT)
Truman State U (MO)
The U of Findlay (OH)
U of Minnesota, Crookston (MN)
U of New Hampshire (NH)
U of Vermont (VT)
U of Wisconsin–River Falls (WI)
Virginia Intermont Coll (VA)
West Texas A&M U (TX)
William Woods U (MO)
Wilson Coll (PA)

ETHICS
St. John's Coll (NM)
U of Michigan–Flint (MI)

ETHNIC, CULTURAL MINORITY, AND GENDER STUDIES RELATED
Boston U (MA)
Bowling Green State U (OH)
Bridgewater Coll (VA)
California State Polytechnic U, Pomona (CA)
California State U, Chico (CA)
California State U, Sacramento (CA)
Claremont McKenna Coll (CA)
The Colorado Coll (CO)
Connecticut Coll (CT)
Cornell Coll (IA)
Hampshire Coll (MA)
Kenyon Coll (OH)
Lawrence U (WI)
Marylhurst U (OR)
Metropolitan State U (MN)
Miami U Hamilton (OH)
St. Francis Coll (NY)
St. Olaf Coll (MN)
Simon's Rock Coll of Bard (MA)
Sterling Coll (VT)
U of Calif, Berkeley (CA)
U of Hawaii at Manoa (HI)
U of Oregon (OR)
U of Pittsburgh (PA)
U of Regina (SK, Canada)
The U of Texas at Austin (TX)
The U of Texas at Dallas (TX)
The U of Western Ontario (ON, Canada)
Washington State U (WA)
Washington U in St. Louis (MO)
Wellesley Coll (MA)
Yale U (CT)

EUROPEAN HISTORY
Ave Maria U (FL)
Bard Coll (NY)
Calvin Coll (MI)
Chapman U (CA)
Charleston Southern U (SC)
Cornell U (NY)
Framingham State Coll (MA)
Gettysburg Coll (PA)
Hampshire Coll (MA)
Pitzer Coll (CA)
Sarah Lawrence Coll (NY)
U of Calif, Santa Cruz (CA)
U of Regina (SK, Canada)

EUROPEAN STUDIES
American U (DC)
American U in Bulgaria(Bulgaria)
Amherst Coll (MA)
Antioch Coll (OH)
Bard Coll (NY)
Barnard Coll (NY)
Beloit Coll (WI)
Bennington Coll (VT)
Brandeis U (MA)
Brock U (ON, Canada)
Canisius Coll (NY)
Carleton U (ON, Canada)
Carnegie Mellon U (PA)
Central Michigan U (MI)
Claremont McKenna Coll (CA)
The Coll of William and Mary (VA)
Elmira Coll (NY)
Emory & Henry Coll (VA)
Fort Lewis Coll (CO)
Franklin Coll Switzerland(Switzerland)
Georgetown Coll (KY)
The George Washington U (DC)
Hamline U (MN)
Hampshire Coll (MA)
Harvard U (MA)
Hillsdale Coll (MI)
Hobart and William Smith Colls (NY)
Howard Payne U (TX)
Huntingdon Coll (AL)
Loyola Marymount U (CA)
Marlboro Coll (VT)
Middlebury Coll (VT)
Millsaps Coll (MS)
Mount Holyoke Coll (MA)
New York U (NY)
Ohio U (OH)
Pitzer Coll (CA)
Richmond, The American Intl U in London(United Kingdom)
Rollins Coll (FL)
Saint Mary's Coll of California (CA)
Salem State Coll (MA)
San Diego State U (CA)
Sarah Lawrence Coll (NY)
Scripps Coll (CA)
Seattle Pacific U (WA)
Simon's Rock Coll of Bard (MA)
Southern Methodist U (TX)
State U of NY Coll at Brockport (NY)
Texas State U-San Marcos (TX)
Trinity U (TX)
United States Military Acad (NY)
The U of British Columbia (BC, Canada)
U of Calif, Irvine (CA)
U of Calif, Los Angeles (CA)
U of Guelph (ON, Canada)
U of Kansas (KS)
U of Michigan (MI)
U of Minnesota, Morris (MN)
U of Minnesota, Twin Cities Campus (MN)
U of Missouri–Columbia (MO)
U of New Hampshire (NH)
U of New Mexico (NM)
The U of North Carolina at Greensboro (NC)
U of Northern Iowa (IA)
U of Richmond (VA)
U of South Carolina (SC)
U of the South (TN)
U of Toledo (OH)
U of Toronto (ON, Canada)
U of Vermont (VT)
U of Washington (WA)
Vanderbilt U (TN)
Washington U in St. Louis (MO)
York U (ON, Canada)

EUROPEAN STUDIES (CENTRAL AND EASTERN)
American U in Bulgaria(Bulgaria)
Bard Coll (NY)
Bowdoin Coll (ME)
Brigham Young U (UT)
Carleton U (ON, Canada)
Connecticut Coll (CT)
Emory U (GA)
Florida State U (FL)
Fordham U (NY)
Grinnell Coll (IA)
Hamline U (MN)
Hampshire Coll (MA)
Harvard U (MA)
Indiana U Bloomington (IN)
Kent State U (OH)
Marlboro Coll (VT)
McGill U (QC, Canada)
Middlebury Coll (VT)
Portland State U (OR)
Rutgers, The State U of New Jersey, New Brunswick/Piscataway (NJ)
Salem State Coll (MA)
Sarah Lawrence Coll (NY)
United States Military Acad (NY)
State U of NY at Albany (NY)
U of Alberta (AB, Canada)
The U of British Columbia (BC, Canada)
U of Chicago (IL)
U of Connecticut (CT)
U of Missouri–Columbia (MO)
U of Oregon (OR)
U of Richmond (VA)
U of Toronto (ON, Canada)
U of Vermont (VT)
U of Victoria (BC, Canada)
Wesleyan U (CT)

EUROPEAN STUDIES (WESTERN)
Central Coll (IA)
Claremont McKenna Coll (CA)
Grinnell Coll (IA)
Hampshire Coll (MA)
Illinois Wesleyan U (IL)
The Ohio State U (OH)
Seattle U (WA)
U of Houston (TX)
U of Nebraska–Lincoln (NE)

EVOLUTIONARY BIOLOGY
Case Western Reserve U (OH)
Coll of the Atlantic (ME)
Cornell U (NY)
Dartmouth Coll (NH)
Florida State U (FL)
Hampshire Coll (MA)
Harvard U (MA)
Oregon State U (OR)
Rice U (TX)
Rutgers, The State U of New Jersey, New Brunswick/Piscataway (NJ)
San Diego State U (CA)
Tulane U (LA)
The U of Arizona (AZ)
U of New Hampshire (NH)
Yale U (CT)

EXECUTIVE ASSISTANT/ EXECUTIVE SECRETARY
Cumberland Coll (KY)
Inter American U of PR, Bayamón Campus (PR)
Youngstown State U (OH)

EXERCISE PHYSIOLOGY
Baldwin-Wallace Coll (OH)
Chapman U (CA)
Concordia U Wisconsin (WI)
Miami U Hamilton (OH)
Pfeiffer U (NC)
State U of NY Coll at Brockport (NY)
West Virginia U (WV)

EXPERIMENTAL PSYCHOLOGY
Blackburn Coll (IL)
Cedar Crest Coll (PA)
Colorado State U-Pueblo (CO)
Huntingdon Coll (AL)
Longwood U (VA)
Marlboro Coll (VT)
Millikin U (IL)
Moravian Coll (PA)
New Mexico Inst of Mining and Technology (NM)
Northern Michigan U (MI)
Paine Coll (GA)
St. John's U (NY)
Southwestern U (TX)
Tufts U (MA)
U of Alberta (AB, Canada)
The U of British Columbia (BC, Canada)
U of South Carolina (SC)
U of Toledo (OH)
U of Wisconsin–Madison (WI)

FACILITIES PLANNING AND MANAGEMENT
Eastern Michigan U (MI)
North Dakota State U (ND)

FAMILY AND COMMUNITY SERVICES
Andrews U (MI)
Eastern Kentucky U (KY)
God's Bible School and Coll (OH)
Goshen Coll (IN)
Iowa State U of Science and Technology (IA)
Keystone Coll (PA)
Liberty U (VA)
Lubbock Christian U (TX)
Messiah Coll (PA)
Michigan State U (MI)
Oklahoma Christian U (OK)
Oklahoma State U (OK)
Olivet Nazarene U (IL)
Oregon State U (OR)
Our Lady of the Lake U of San Antonio (TX)
Prairie View A&M U (TX)
Southern Utah U (UT)
Syracuse U (NY)
Union U (TN)
U of Calif, Santa Cruz (CA)
U of Delaware (DE)
U of Florida (FL)
U of Maryland, Coll Park (MD)
U of Miami (FL)
U of Minnesota, Twin Cities Campus (MN)
The U of North Carolina at Greensboro (NC)
U of Northern Iowa (IA)
U of Utah (UT)
Youngstown State U (OH)

FAMILY AND CONSUMER ECONOMICS RELATED
Alabama Ag and Mech U (AL)
Andrews U (MI)
Ashland U (OH)
Baldwin-Wallace Coll (OH)
Ball State U (IN)
Berea Coll (KY)
Brigham Young U (UT)
California State U, Fresno (CA)
California State U, Sacramento (CA)
Carson-Newman Coll (TN)
Chadron State Coll (NE)
Fairmont State Coll (WV)
Florida State U (FL)
Framingham State Coll (MA)
Hampshire Coll (MA)
Howard U (DC)
Indiana U Bloomington (IN)
Iowa State U of Science and Technology (IA)
Lipscomb U (TN)
Louisiana Coll (LA)
Miami U (OH)
Minnesota State U Mankato (MN)
Montclair State U (NJ)
Mount Saint Vincent U (NS, Canada)
Murray State U (KY)
North Carolina Central U (NC)
Northern Michigan U (MI)
Oklahoma State U (OK)
Oregon State U (OR)
Ryerson U (ON, Canada)
Saint Joseph Coll (CT)
Seattle Pacific U (WA)
Tennessee State U (TN)
The U of Akron (OH)
U of Alberta (AB, Canada)
U of Delaware (DE)
U of Hawaii at Manoa (HI)
U of Maryland Eastern Shore (MD)
U of Missouri–Columbia (MO)
U of Montevallo (AL)
U of Nebraska–Lincoln (NE)
U of New Hampshire (NH)
U of Northern Iowa (IA)
U of Prince Edward Island (PE, Canada)
U of Utah (UT)
U of Vermont (VT)
U of Windsor (ON, Canada)
U of Wisconsin–Madison (WI)
U of Wisconsin–Stevens Point (WI)
Utah State U (UT)
Virginia State U (VA)
Wayne State Coll (NE)

FAMILY AND CONSUMER SCIENCES/HOME ECONOMICS TEACHER EDUCATION
Appalachian State U (NC)
Ashland U (OH)
Ball State U (IN)
Berea Coll (KY)
Bluffton Coll (OH)
Bowling Green State U (OH)
Bridgewater Coll (VA)
Campbell U (NC)
Carson-Newman Coll (TN)
Central Missouri State U (MO)
Chadron State Coll (NE)
Cheyney U of Pennsylvania (PA)
Coll of St. Catherine (MN)
Coll of the Ozarks (MO)
Colorado State U (CO)
Concordia U (NE)
Cornell U (NY)
Delta State U (MS)
East Carolina U (NC)
East Central U (OK)
Eastern Kentucky U (KY)
Fairmont State Coll (WV)
Ferris State U (MI)
Florida Intl U (FL)
Florida State U (FL)
Fontbonne U (MO)
Fort Valley State U (GA)
Framingham State Coll (MA)
George Fox U (OR)
Georgia Southern U (GA)
Grambling State U (LA)
Hampton U (VA)
Harding U (AR)
Henderson State U (AR)
Immaculata U (PA)
Indiana U of Pennsylvania (PA)
Iowa State U of Science and Technology (IA)
Jacksonville State U (AL)
Keene State Coll (NH)
Kent State U (OH)
Lamar U (TX)
Liberty U (VA)
Louisiana Tech U (LA)
Madonna U (MI)
Marymount Coll of Fordham U (NY)
Marywood U (PA)
McNeese State U (LA)
Mercyhurst Coll (PA)
Miami U (OH)
Michigan State U (MI)
Minnesota State U Mankato (MN)
Montclair State U (NJ)
Mount Vernon Nazarene U (OH)
Murray State U (KY)
New Mexico State U (NM)
North Carolina Central U (NC)
North Dakota State U (ND)
Northeastern State U (OK)
Northern Illinois U (IL)
Olivet Nazarene U (IL)
Pittsburg State U (KS)
Pontifical Catholic U of Puerto Rico (PR)
Queens Coll of the City U of NY (NY)
Saint Joseph Coll (CT)
Sam Houston State U (TX)
Seattle Pacific U (WA)
Seton Hill U (PA)
South Carolina State U (SC)
South Dakota State U (SD)
Southeast Missouri State U (MO)
Southern Utah U (UT)
Southwest Missouri State U (MO)
State U of NY Coll at Oneonta (NY)
Syracuse U (NY)
Tennessee Technological U (TN)
Texas A&M U–Kingsville (TX)
The U of Akron (OH)
U of Alberta (AB, Canada)
The U of Arizona (AZ)
U of Arkansas (AR)
The U of British Columbia (BC, Canada)
U of Central Arkansas (AR)
U of Georgia (GA)
U of Hawaii at Manoa (HI)
U of Idaho (ID)
U of Illinois at Springfield (IL)
U of Maryland Eastern Shore (MD)
U of Minnesota, Twin Cities Campus (MN)
U of Montevallo (AL)
U of Nevada, Reno (NV)
U of New Brunswick Fredericton (NB, Canada)
U of New Mexico (NM)
U of Saskatchewan (SK, Canada)
The U of Tennessee (TN)
The U of Tennessee at Martin (TN)
U of the District of Columbia (DC)
U of Utah (UT)
U of Wisconsin–Madison (WI)
U of Wisconsin–Stevens Point (WI)
U of Wisconsin–Stout (WI)
Utah State U (UT)
Wayne State Coll (NE)
Western Kentucky U (KY)
Western Michigan U (MI)
Winthrop U (SC)
Youngstown State U (OH)

FAMILY AND CONSUMER SCIENCES/HUMAN SCIENCES
Abilene Christian U (TX)
Alcorn State U (MS)
Ashland U (OH)
Auburn U (AL)
Ball State U (IN)
Baylor U (TX)
Bluffton Coll (OH)
Bridgewater Coll (VA)
Brigham Young U (UT)
California State Polytechnic U, Pomona (CA)
California State U, Long Beach (CA)
Cameron U (OK)
Campbell U (NC)
Carson-Newman Coll (TN)
Central Missouri State U (MO)
Central Washington U (WA)
Coll of St. Catherine (MN)
Coll of the Ozarks (MO)
Colorado State U (CO)
Cornell U (NY)
Delaware State U (DE)
Delta State U (MS)
East Central U (OK)
Eastern Illinois U (IL)
Eastern Kentucky U (KY)
Eastern Michigan U (MI)
Eastern New Mexico U (NM)
Fairmont State Coll (WV)
Florida State U (FL)
Fontbonne U (MO)
Framingham State Coll (MA)
Freed-Hardeman U (TN)
George Fox U (OR)
Harding U (AR)
Henderson State U (AR)
Idaho State U (ID)
Illinois State U (IL)
Immaculata U (PA)
Indiana State U (IN)
Iowa State U of Science and Technology (IA)
Jacksonville State U (AL)
Keene State Coll (NH)
Kent State U (OH)
Lamar U (TX)
Lambuth U (TN)
Liberty U (VA)
Lipscomb U (TN)
Louisiana State U and A&M Coll (LA)
Madonna U (MI)
Marshall U (WV)
Marymount Coll of Fordham U (NY)
Marywood U (PA)
The Master's Coll and Sem (CA)
McNeese State U (LA)
Mercyhurst Coll (PA)
Meredith Coll (NC)
Miami U (OH)
Michigan State U (MI)
Minnesota State U Mankato (MN)
Mississippi State U (MS)
Montana State U–Bozeman (MT)
Montclair State U (NJ)
Morgan State U (MD)
Mount Vernon Nazarene U (OH)
Nicholls State U (LA)
North Carolina Central U (NC)
Northeastern State U (OK)
Northwestern State U of Louisiana (LA)
Ohio U (OH)
Oklahoma State U (OK)
Olivet Nazarene U (IL)
Oregon State U (OR)
Pittsburg State U (KS)
Point Loma Nazarene U (CA)
Pontifical Catholic U of Puerto Rico (PR)
Purdue U (IN)
Queens Coll of the City U of NY (NY)
Saint Joseph Coll (CT)
Sam Houston State U (TX)
San Francisco State U (CA)
Seton Hill U (PA)
Shepherd U (WV)
South Carolina State U (SC)
Southeastern Louisiana U (LA)
Southeast Missouri State U (MO)
Southern Utah U (UT)
State U of NY Coll at Oneonta (NY)
Tarleton State U (TX)
Tennessee Technological U (TN)
Texas A&M U–Kingsville (TX)
Texas Southern U (TX)
Texas State U-San Marcos (TX)
Texas Tech U (TX)
Texas Woman's U (TX)
The U of Akron (OH)
The U of Alabama (AL)
U of Alberta (AB, Canada)
U of Arkansas (AR)
The U of British Columbia (BC, Canada)
U of Central Arkansas (AR)
U of Hawaii at Manoa (HI)
U of Houston (TX)
U of Kentucky (KY)
U of Manitoba (MB, Canada)
U of Maryland Eastern Shore (MD)
U of Mississippi (MS)
U of Montevallo (AL)
U of Nebraska at Omaha (NE)
U of New Hampshire (NH)
U of New Mexico (NM)
U of North Alabama (AL)
The U of North Carolina at Greensboro (NC)
The U of Tennessee at Martin (TN)
The U of Texas at Austin (TX)
U of the District of Columbia (DC)
U of Utah (UT)
U of Vermont (VT)
The U of Western Ontario (ON, Canada)
U of Wisconsin–Madison (WI)
U of Wyoming (WY)
Wayne State Coll (NE)
Western Illinois U (IL)
West Virginia U (WV)
Youngstown State U (OH)

FAMILY AND CONSUMER SCIENCES/HUMAN SCIENCES BUSINESS SERVICES RELATED
Brigham Young U (UT)

FAMILY AND CONSUMER SCIENCES/HUMAN SCIENCES COMMUNICATION
Framingham State Coll (MA)
U of Nebraska at Omaha (NE)

FAMILY AND CONSUMER SCIENCES/HUMAN SCIENCES RELATED
California State U, Long Beach (CA)
Framingham State Coll (MA)
Morehead State U (KY)
Norfolk State U (VA)
Southern Virginia U (VA)
The U of Alabama (AL)

FAMILY/COMMUNITY STUDIES
Coll of the Ozarks (MO)

FAMILY LIVING/PARENTHOOD
U of North Texas (TX)

FAMILY PRACTICE NURSING/NURSE PRACTITIONER
North Georgia Coll & State U (GA)
U at Buffalo, The State U of New York (NY)
The U of Virginia's Coll at Wise (VA)
U of Windsor (ON, Canada)

FAMILY PSYCHOLOGY
Western Baptist Coll (OR)

FAMILY RESOURCE MANAGEMENT
Arizona State U (AZ)
Bradley U (IL)
Brigham Young U (UT)
Cornell U (NY)
George Fox U (OR)
Iowa State U of Science and Technology (IA)
Middle Tennessee State U (TN)
The Ohio State U (OH)
Ohio U (OH)
U of Nebraska at Omaha (NE)
U of Utah (UT)

FAMILY SYSTEMS
Brigham Young U (UT)
Central Michigan U (MI)
Gallaudet U (DC)
Point Loma Nazarene U (CA)
Southern Adventist U (TN)
Spring Arbor U (MI)
Syracuse U (NY)
Texas Tech U (TX)
Towson U (MD)
The U of Akron (OH)
The U of Tennessee (TN)
Weber State U (UT)
Western Michigan U (MI)

FARM AND RANCH MANAGEMENT
California Polytechnic State U, San Luis Obispo (CA)
California State Polytechnic U, Pomona (CA)
Colorado State U (CO)
Cornell U (NY)
Eastern Kentucky U (KY)
Idaho State U (ID)
Iowa State U of Science and Technology (IA)
Johnson & Wales U (RI)
Sterling Coll (VT)
Tarleton State U (TX)
Texas A&M U (TX)
U of Alberta (AB, Canada)
The U of Findlay (OH)
U of Minnesota, Crookston (MN)
U of Wisconsin–Madison (WI)

FASHION/APPAREL DESIGN
Acad of Art U (CA)
American InterContinental U (CA)
American InterContinental U, Atlanta (GA)
American InterContinental U-London(United Kingdom)
The Art Inst of California–San Francisco (CA)
The Art Inst of Portland (OR)
Baylor U (TX)
State U of NY Coll at Buffalo (NY)
California Coll of the Arts (CA)
Cazenovia Coll (NY)
Centenary Coll (NJ)
Clark Atlanta U (GA)
Coll of St. Catherine (MN)
The Coll of Southeastern Europe, The American U of Athens(Greece)
Columbia Coll Chicago (IL)
Columbus Coll of Art & Design (OH)
Cornell U (NY)
Dominican U (IL)
Drexel U (PA)
Fashion Inst of Technology (NY)
Florida State U (FL)
Framingham State Coll (MA)
Hampton U (VA)
Howard U (DC)
The Illinois Inst of Art (IL)
Indiana U Bloomington (IN)
Intl Acad of Design & Technology (FL)
Intl Acad of Merchandising & Design, Ltd (IL)
Iowa State U of Science and Technology (IA)
Kent State U (OH)
Kwantlen U Coll (BC, Canada)
Lamar U (TX)
Lasell Coll (MA)
Lindenwood U (MO)
Lynn U (FL)
Marist Coll (NY)
Marymount Coll of Fordham U (NY)
Marymount U (VA)
Massachusetts Coll of Art (MA)
Meredith Coll (NC)
Michigan State U (MI)
Minnesota State U Mankato (MN)
Moore Coll of Art & Design (PA)
Mount Ida Coll (MA)
Mount Mary Coll (WI)
Oklahoma State U (OK)
O'More Coll of Design (TN)
Oregon State U (OR)
Otis Coll of Art and Design (CA)
Parsons School of Design, New School U (NY)
Philadelphia U (PA)
Pontifical Catholic U of Puerto Rico (PR)
Pratt Inst (NY)
Rhode Island School of Design (RI)
Ryerson U (ON, Canada)
Savannah Coll of Art and Design (GA)
School of the Art Inst of Chicago (IL)
Stephens Coll (MO)
Syracuse U (NY)
Texas Southern U (TX)
Texas Tech U (TX)
Texas Woman's U (TX)
U of Cincinnati (OH)
U of Delaware (DE)
U of Louisiana at Lafayette (LA)
U of Maryland Eastern Shore (MD)
U of North Texas (TX)
U of the Incarnate Word (TX)
Ursuline Coll (OH)
Virginia Commonwealth U (VA)
Washington U in St. Louis (MO)

FASHION MERCHANDISING
Acad of Art U (CA)
American InterContinental U (CA)
American InterContinental U, Atlanta (GA)
American InterContinental U-London(United Kingdom)
Ashland U (OH)
Ball State U (IN)
Baylor U (TX)
Bowling Green State U (OH)
Brenau U (GA)
Bridgewater Coll (VA)
State U of NY Coll at Buffalo (NY)
California State U, Long Beach (CA)
Carson-Newman Coll (TN)
Central Michigan U (MI)
Central Washington U (WA)
Coll of St. Catherine (MN)
Delaware State U (DE)
Delta State U (MS)
Dominican U (IL)
East Central U (OK)
Eastern Kentucky U (KY)
Eastern Michigan U (MI)
Fashion Inst of Technology (NY)
Florida State U (FL)
Fontbonne U (MO)
Framingham State Coll (MA)
Freed-Hardeman U (TN)
George Fox U (OR)
Hampton U (VA)

Harding U (AR)
The Illinois Inst of Art (IL)
Immaculata U (PA)
Indiana U Bloomington (IN)
Indiana U of Pennsylvania (PA)
Intl Acad of Merchandising & Design, Ltd (IL)
Kent State U (OH)
Laboratory Inst of Merchandising (NY)
Lamar U (TX)
Lambuth U (TN)
Lasell Coll (MA)
Liberty U (VA)
Lincoln U (MO)
Lindenwood U (MO)
Lipscomb U (TN)
Louisiana State U and A&M Coll (LA)
Lynn U (FL)
Marist Coll (NY)
Mars Hill Coll (NC)
Marymount Coll of Fordham U (NY)
Marymount U (VA)
Mercyhurst Coll (PA)
Meredith Coll (NC)
Montclair State U (NJ)
Mount Ida Coll (MA)
Mount Mary Coll (WI)
Northeastern State U (OK)
Northwood U (MI)
Northwood U, Texas Campus (TX)
Oklahoma State U (OK)
Olivet Nazarene U (IL)
O'More Coll of Design (TN)
Oregon State U (OR)
Our Lady of the Lake U of San Antonio (TX)
Parsons School of Design, New School U (NY)
Philadelphia U (PA)
Pittsburg State U (KS)
Ryerson U (ON, Canada)
Sam Houston State U (TX)
South Carolina State U (SC)
South Dakota State U (SD)
State U of NY Coll at Oneonta (NY)
Stephens Coll (MO)
Tennessee Technological U (TN)
Texas A&M U–Kingsville (TX)
Texas Christian U (TX)
Texas Southern U (TX)
Texas State U-San Marcos (TX)
Texas Tech U (TX)
Texas Woman's U (TX)
The U of Akron (OH)
U of Bridgeport (CT)
U of Delaware (DE)
U of Georgia (GA)
U of Illinois at Urbana–Champaign (IL)
U of Louisiana at Lafayette (LA)
U of Maryland Eastern Shore (MD)
The U of Montana–Missoula (MT)
U of Montevallo (AL)
U of North Texas (TX)
The U of Tennessee at Martin (TN)
U of the Incarnate Word (TX)
U of Wisconsin–Madison (WI)
Ursuline Coll (OH)
Utah State U (UT)
Wayne State Coll (NE)
Youngstown State U (OH)

FIBER, TEXTILE AND WEAVING ARTS

Acad of Art U (CA)
Alberta Coll of Art & Design (AB, Canada)
Bowling Green State U (OH)
California Coll of the Arts (CA)
California State U, Long Beach (CA)
The Cleveland Inst of Art (OH)
Col for Creative Studies (MI)
Colorado State U (CO)
Concordia U (QC, Canada)
Cornell U (NY)
Kansas City Art Inst (MO)
Maryland Inst Coll of Art (MD)
Massachusetts Coll of Art (MA)
Memphis Coll of Art (TN)
Mercyhurst Coll (PA)
Moore Coll of Art & Design (PA)
Northern Michigan U (MI)
Nova Scotia Coll of Art and Design (NS, Canada)
Oregon State U (OR)
Philadelphia U (PA)
Rhode Island School of Design (RI)
Savannah Coll of Art and Design (GA)
School of the Art Inst of Chicago (IL)
Syracuse U (NY)
U of Kansas (KS)
U of Massachusetts Dartmouth (MA)
U of Michigan (MI)
U of North Texas (TX)
U of Oregon (OR)
U of Washington (WA)
U of Wisconsin–Milwaukee (WI)
Western Washington U (WA)

FILIPINO/TAGALOG

U of Hawaii at Manoa (HI)

FILM/CINEMA STUDIES

Acad of Art U (CA)
Art Center Coll of Design (CA)
Bard Coll (NY)
Barnard Coll (NY)
Bennington Coll (VT)
Bowling Green State U (OH)
Brigham Young U (UT)
Brock U (ON, Canada)
Brooklyn Coll of the City U of NY (NY)
Brown U (RI)
Burlington Coll (VT)
California Coll of the Arts (CA)
California Inst of the Arts (CA)
California State U, Long Beach (CA)
Calvin Coll (MI)
Carleton U (ON, Canada)
Carson-Newman Coll (TN)
Centenary Coll of Louisiana (LA)
Chapman U (CA)
Claremont McKenna Coll (CA)
Clark U (MA)
Coll of Santa Fe (NM)
The Colorado Coll (CO)
Columbia Coll (NY)
Columbia Coll Chicago (IL)
Columbia Coll Hollywood (CA)
Columbia U, School of General Studies (NY)
Concordia U (QC, Canada)
Connecticut Coll (CT)
Cornell U (NY)
Curry Coll (MA)
Dartmouth Coll (NH)
Denison U (OH)
Emerson Coll (MA)
Emory U (GA)
Florida State U (FL)
Fordham U (NY)
Georgia State U (GA)
Grand Valley State U (MI)
Hampshire Coll (MA)
Harvard U (MA)
Hofstra U (NY)
Howard U (DC)
Hunter Coll of the City U of NY (NY)
Ithaca Coll (NY)
The Johns Hopkins U (MD)
Keene State Coll (NH)
La Salle U (PA)
Laurentian U (ON, Canada)
Marlboro Coll (VT)
Mount Holyoke Coll (MA)
New York U (NY)
North Carolina School of the Arts (NC)
North Carolina State U (NC)
Northern Michigan U (MI)
Northwestern U (IL)
Nova Scotia Coll of Art and Design (NS, Canada)
Oakland U (MI)
Ohio U (OH)
Olivet Nazarene U (IL)
Penn State U Abington Coll (PA)
Penn State U Altoona Coll (PA)
Penn State U at Erie, The Behrend Coll (PA)
Penn State U Beaver Campus of the Commonwealth Coll (PA)
Penn State U Berks Cmps of Berks-Lehigh Valley Coll (PA)
Penn State U Delaware County Campus of the Commonwealth Coll (PA)
Penn State U DuBois Campus of the Commonwealth Coll (PA)
Penn State U Fayette Campus of the Commonwealth Coll (PA)
Penn State U Hazleton Campus of the Commonwealth Coll (PA)
Penn State U Lehigh Valley Cmps of Berks-Lehigh Valley Coll (PA)
Penn State U McKeesport Campus of the Commonwealth Coll (PA)
Penn State U Mont Alto Campus of the Commonwealth Coll (PA)
Penn State U New Kensington Campus of the Commonwealth Coll (PA)
Penn State U Schuylkill Campus of the Capital Coll (PA)
Penn State U Shenango Campus of the Commonwealth Coll (PA)
Penn State U Univ Park Campus (PA)
Penn State U Wilkes-Barre Campus of the Commonwealth Coll (PA)
Penn State U Worthington Scranton Cmps Commonwealth Coll (PA)
Penn State U York Campus of the Commonwealth Coll (PA)
Pitzer Coll (CA)
Pomona Coll (CA)
Queens Coll of the City U of NY (NY)
Queen's U at Kingston (ON, Canada)
Quinnipiac U (CT)
Rhode Island Coll (RI)
Rhode Island School of Design (RI)
Rutgers, The State U of New Jersey, New Brunswick/Piscataway (NJ)
Ryerson U (ON, Canada)
Sacred Heart U (CT)
Saint Augustine's Coll (NC)
St. Cloud State U (MN)
San Francisco Art Inst (CA)
San Francisco State U (CA)
Sarah Lawrence Coll (NY)
School of the Art Inst of Chicago (IL)
School of the Museum of Fine Arts, Boston (MA)
Simon Fraser U (BC, Canada)
Southern Methodist U (TX)
State U of NY at Binghamton (NY)
State U of NY Coll at Fredonia (NY)
Université de Montréal (QC, Canada)
U at Buffalo, The State U of New York (NY)
U of Alberta (AB, Canada)
The U of British Columbia (BC, Canada)
U of Calif, Berkeley (CA)
U of Calif, Irvine (CA)
U of Calif, Los Angeles (CA)
U of Calif, San Diego (CA)
U of Calif, Santa Barbara (CA)
U of Calif, Santa Cruz (CA)
U of Chicago (IL)
U of Colorado at Boulder (CO)
U of Delaware (DE)
U of Georgia (GA)
U of Hartford (CT)
The U of Iowa (IA)
U of Manitoba (MB, Canada)
U of Maryland, Baltimore County (MD)
U of Miami (FL)
U of Michigan (MI)
U of Minnesota, Twin Cities Campus (MN)
U of Nebraska–Lincoln (NE)
U of Nevada, Las Vegas (NV)
U of New Mexico (NM)
U of Pittsburgh (PA)
U of Regina (SK, Canada)
U of Rochester (NY)
U of Southern California (CA)
U of Toledo (OH)
U of Toronto (ON, Canada)
U of Tulsa (OK)
U of Utah (UT)
U of Waterloo (ON, Canada)
The U of Western Ontario (ON, Canada)
U of Windsor (ON, Canada)
U of Wisconsin–Milwaukee (WI)
Vassar Coll (NY)
Washington U in St. Louis (MO)
Watkins Coll of Art and Design (TN)
Wayne State U (MI)
Webster U (MO)
Wellesley Coll (MA)
Wesleyan U (CT)
Whitman Coll (WA)
Wright State U (OH)
Yale U (CT)
York U (ON, Canada)

FILM/VIDEO AND PHOTOGRAPHIC ARTS RELATED

Art Center Coll of Design (CA)
Bloomfield Coll (NJ)
Brigham Young U (UT)
California Inst of the Arts (CA)
Col for Creative Studies (MI)
Hampshire Coll (MA)
Maryland Inst Coll of Art (MD)
New England School of Communications (ME)
Pratt Inst (NY)
Rocky Mountain Coll of Art & Design (CO)
School of the Art Inst of Chicago (IL)
School of the Museum of Fine Arts, Boston (MA)
Scripps Coll (CA)
The U of Iowa (IA)
The U of the Arts (PA)
Watkins Coll of Art and Design (TN)

FINANCE

Abilene Christian U (TX)
Adelphi U (NY)
Alabama Ag and Mech U (AL)
Alabama State U (AL)
Albertus Magnus Coll (CT)
Albright Coll (PA)
Alderson-Broaddus Coll (WV)
American Coll of Thessaloniki(Greece)
American Intl Coll (MA)
American U (DC)
Anderson Coll (SC)
Angelo State U (TX)
Appalachian State U (NC)
Arcadia U (PA)
Arizona State U (AZ)
Arkansas State U (AR)
Ashland U (OH)
Auburn U (AL)
Auburn U Montgomery (AL)
Augsburg Coll (MN)
Augustana Coll (IL)
Augusta State U (GA)
Aurora U (IL)
Averett U (VA)
Avila U (MO)
Babson Coll (MA)
Bacone Coll (OK)
Ball State U (IN)
Barber-Scotia Coll (NC)
Barry U (FL)
Baylor U (TX)
Belmont U (TN)
Benedictine U (IL)
Bentley Coll (MA)
Baruch Coll of the City U of NY (NY)
Berry Coll (GA)
Bishop's U (QC, Canada)
Bloomfield Coll (NJ)
Boise State U (ID)
Boston Coll (MA)
Boston U (MA)
Bowling Green State U (OH)
Bradley U (IL)
Brescia U (KY)
Bridgewater Coll (VA)
Bridgewater State Coll (MA)
Brock U (ON, Canada)
Bryant Coll (RI)
Butler U (IN)
Cabrini Coll (PA)
California State Polytechnic U, Pomona (CA)
California State U, Chico (CA)
California State U, Dominguez Hills (CA)
California State U, Fresno (CA)
California State U, Fullerton (CA)
California State U, Hayward (CA)
California State U, Long Beach (CA)
California State U, Sacramento (CA)
California State U, San Bernardino (CA)
Campbell U (NC)
Canisius Coll (NY)
Capital U (OH)
Carleton U (ON, Canada)
Carroll Coll (MT)
Carroll Coll (WI)
Castleton State Coll (VT)
The Catholic U of America (DC)
Cedarville U (OH)
Centenary Coll of Louisiana (LA)
Central Connecticut State U (CT)
Central Michigan U (MI)
Central Missouri State U (MO)
Central State U (OH)
Charleston Southern U (SC)
Chestnut Hill Coll (PA)
Chicago State U (IL)
Christian Brothers U (TN)
Christopher Newport U (VA)
Clarion U of Pennsylvania (PA)
Clarkson U (NY)
Cleary U (MI)
Clemson U (SC)
Cleveland State U (OH)
Coastal Carolina U (SC)
Coker Coll (SC)
Coll for Lifelong Learning (NH)
The Coll of New Jersey (NJ)
Coll of St. Joseph (VT)
The Coll of Southeastern Europe, The American U of Athens(Greece)
Colorado State U (CO)
Colorado State U-Pueblo (CO)
Colorado Tech U Sioux Falls Campus (SD)
Columbia Coll (MO)
Columbus State U (GA)
Concordia U (QC, Canada)
Concordia U, St. Paul (MN)
Cornell U (NY)
Creighton U (NE)
Culver-Stockton Coll (MO)
Dakota State U (SD)
Dakota Wesleyan U (SD)
Dalhousie U (NS, Canada)
Dallas Baptist U (TX)
Davenport U, Dearborn (MI)
Davenport U, Grand Rapids (MI)
Davenport U, Warren (MI)
Defiance Coll (OH)
Delaware State U (DE)
Delta State U (MS)
DePaul U (IL)
DeSales U (PA)
Dickinson State U (ND)
Dominican Coll (NY)
Dowling Coll (NY)
Drake U (IA)
Drexel U (PA)
Duquesne U (PA)
East Carolina U (NC)
East Central U (OK)
Eastern Illinois U (IL)
Eastern Kentucky U (KY)
Eastern Michigan U (MI)
Eastern New Mexico U (NM)
Eastern U (PA)
Eastern Washington U (WA)
Elmhurst Coll (IL)
Emory U (GA)
Eureka Coll (IL)
Excelsior Coll (NY)
Fairfield U (CT)
Fairmont State Coll (WV)
Fayetteville State U (NC)
Ferris State U (MI)
Ferrum Coll (VA)
Florida Ag and Mech U (FL)
Florida Atlantic U (FL)
Florida Gulf Coast U (FL)
Florida Intl U (FL)
Florida Southern Coll (FL)
Florida State U (FL)
Fontbonne U (MO)
Fordham U (NY)
Fort Hays State U (KS)
Fort Lewis Coll (CO)
Framingham State Coll (MA)
Francis Marion U (SC)
Franklin Pierce Coll (NH)
Franklin U (OH)
Freed-Hardeman U (TN)
Fresno Pacific U (CA)
Gannon U (PA)
George Mason U (VA)
Georgetown Coll (KY)
Georgetown U (DC)
The George Washington U (DC)
Georgia Southern U (GA)
Georgia State U (GA)
Globe Inst of Technology (NY)
Golden Gate U (CA)
Goldey-Beacom Coll (DE)
Gonzaga U (WA)
Governors State U (IL)
Grand Canyon U (AZ)
Grand Valley State U (MI)
Grove City Coll (PA)
Hampton U (VA)
Hardin-Simmons U (TX)
Hawai'i Pacific U (HI)
HEC Montreal (QC, Canada)
Hilbert Coll (NY)
Hillsdale Coll (MI)
Hofstra U (NY)
Houston Baptist U (TX)
Howard Payne U (TX)
Howard U (DC)
Husson Coll (ME)
Idaho State U (ID)
Illinois Coll (IL)
Illinois State U (IL)
Indiana State U (IN)
Indiana U Bloomington (IN)
Indiana U of Pennsylvania (PA)
Indiana U–Purdue U Fort Wayne (IN)

Inter American U of PR, Bayamón Campus (PR)
Inter American U of PR, Ponce Campus (PR)
Inter American U of PR, San Germán Campus (PR)
Iona Coll (NY)
Iowa State U of Science and Technology (IA)
Ithaca Coll (NY)
Jacksonville State U (AL)
Jacksonville U (FL)
James Madison U (VA)
John Carroll U (OH)
Juniata Coll (PA)
Kansas State U (KS)
Kean U (NJ)
Kennesaw State U (GA)
Kent State U (OH)
Kettering U (MI)
The King's Coll (NY)
King's Coll (PA)
Kutztown U of Pennsylvania (PA)
Lake Forest Coll (IL)
Lakehead U (ON, Canada)
Lake Superior State U (MI)
Lamar U (TX)
La Roche Coll (PA)
La Salle U (PA)
Lasell Coll (MA)
Lehigh U (PA)
LeTourneau U (TX)
Lewis U (IL)
Liberty U (VA)
Lincoln Memorial U (TN)
Lincoln U (PA)
Lindenwood U (MO)
Linfield Coll (OR)
Lipscomb U (TN)
Long Island U, Brentwood Campus (NY)
Long Island U, Brooklyn Campus (NY)
Long Island U, C.W. Post Campus (NY)
Longwood U (VA)
Loras Coll (IA)
Louisiana Coll (LA)
Louisiana State U and A&M Coll (LA)
Louisiana State U in Shreveport (LA)
Louisiana Tech U (LA)
Loyola Coll in Maryland (MD)
Loyola U Chicago (IL)
Loyola U New Orleans (LA)
Lubbock Christian U (TX)
Lycoming Coll (PA)
MacMurray Coll (IL)
Manchester Coll (IN)
Manhattan Coll (NY)
Manhattanville Coll (NY)
Marian Coll (IN)
Marian Coll of Fond du Lac (WI)
Marquette U (WI)
Marshall U (WV)
Mars Hill Coll (NC)
Marymount Coll of Fordham U (NY)
Marymount U (VA)
Massachusetts Coll of Liberal Arts (MA)
The Master's Coll and Sem (CA)
McGill U (QC, Canada)
McKendree Coll (IL)
McMurry U (TX)
McNeese State U (LA)
McPherson Coll (KS)
Memorial U of Newfoundland (NL, Canada)
Mercy Coll (NY)
Mercyhurst Coll (PA)
Meredith Coll (NC)
Merrimack Coll (MA)
Methodist Coll (NC)
Metropolitan State Coll of Denver (CO)
Metropolitan State U (MN)
Miami U (OH)
Miami U Hamilton (OH)
Michigan State U (MI)
Michigan Technological U (MI)
Middle Tennessee State U (TN)
Midwestern State U (TX)
Millikin U (IL)
Minnesota State U Mankato (MN)
Minnesota State U Moorhead (MN)
Minot State U (ND)
Mississippi State U (MS)
Missouri Southern State U (MO)
Missouri Western State Coll (MO)
Monmouth U (NJ)
Montana State U–Billings (MT)
Montana Tech of The U of Montana (MT)
Montclair State U (NJ)
Morehead State U (KY)
Morehouse Coll (GA)
Morgan State U (MD)
Murray State U (KY)
National U (CA)
Newbury Coll (MA)
New Mexico State U (NM)
New York Inst of Technology (NY)
New York U (NY)
Nicholls State U (LA)
Nichols Coll (MA)
North Carolina State U (NC)
North Central Coll (IL)
Northeastern Illinois U (IL)
Northeastern State U (OK)
Northeastern U (MA)
Northern Arizona U (AZ)
Northern Illinois U (IL)
Northern Michigan U (MI)
Northern State U (SD)
North Georgia Coll & State U (GA)
North Park U (IL)
Northwestern Coll (MN)
Northwest Nazarene U (ID)
Notre Dame de Namur U (CA)
Nova Southeastern U (FL)
Oakland U (MI)
Ohio Dominican U (OH)
The Ohio State U (OH)
Ohio U (OH)
Oklahoma Baptist U (OK)
Oklahoma City U (OK)
Oklahoma State U (OK)
Old Dominion U (VA)
Olivet Coll (MI)
Olivet Nazarene U (IL)
Oral Roberts U (OK)
Oregon State U (OR)
Otterbein Coll (OH)
Pacific Lutheran U (WA)
Pacific Union Coll (CA)
Pacific U (OR)
Penn State U Abington Coll (PA)
Penn State U Altoona Coll (PA)
Penn State U at Erie, The Behrend Coll (PA)
Penn State U Beaver Campus of the Commonwealth Coll (PA)
Penn State U Berks Cmps of Berks-Lehigh Valley Coll (PA)
Penn State U Delaware County Campus of the Commonwealth Coll (PA)
Penn State U DuBois Campus of the Commonwealth Coll (PA)
Penn State U Fayette Campus of the Commonwealth Coll (PA)
Penn State U Harrisburg Campus of the Capital Coll (PA)
Penn State U Hazleton Campus of the Commonwealth Coll (PA)
Penn State U Lehigh Valley Cmps of Berks-Lehigh Valley Coll (PA)
Penn State U McKeesport Campus of the Commonwealth Coll (PA)
Penn State U Mont Alto Campus of the Commonwealth Coll (PA)
Penn State U New Kensington Campus of the Commonwealth Coll (PA)
Penn State U Schuylkill Campus of the Capital Coll (PA)
Penn State U Shenango Campus of the Commonwealth Coll (PA)
Penn State U Univ Park Campus (PA)
Penn State U Wilkes-Barre Campus of the Commonwealth Coll (PA)
Penn State U Worthington Scranton Cmps Commonwealth Coll (PA)
Penn State U York Campus of the Commonwealth Coll (PA)
Pfeiffer U (NC)
Philadelphia U (PA)
Pittsburg State U (KS)
Polytechnic U of Puerto Rico (PR)
Pontifical Catholic U of Puerto Rico (PR)
Portland State U (OR)
Prairie View A&M U (TX)
Providence Coll (RI)
Queens Coll of the City U of NY (NY)
Quincy U (IL)
Quinnipiac U (CT)
Radford U (VA)
Rensselaer Polytechnic Inst (NY)
Rhode Island Coll (RI)
Rider U (NJ)
Robert Morris U (PA)
Rochester Inst of Technology (NY)
Rockford Coll (IL)
Rockhurst U (MO)
Roger Williams U (RI)
Roosevelt U (IL)
Rutgers, The State U of New Jersey, Camden (NJ)
Rutgers, The State U of New Jersey, Newark (NJ)
Rutgers, The State U of New Jersey, New Brunswick/Piscataway (NJ)
Ryerson U (ON, Canada)
Sacred Heart U (CT)
Saginaw Valley State U (MI)
St. Ambrose U (IA)
Saint Anselm Coll (NH)
St. Bonaventure U (NY)
St. Cloud State U (MN)
St. Edward's U (TX)
Saint Francis U (PA)
St. John Fisher Coll (NY)
St. John's U (NY)
Saint Joseph's Coll of Maine (ME)
Saint Joseph's U (PA)
Saint Louis U (MO)
Saint Martin's Coll (WA)
Saint Mary's Coll (IN)
St. Mary's U of San Antonio (TX)
St. Thomas Aquinas Coll (NY)
St. Thomas U (FL)
Saint Vincent Coll (PA)
Salem State Coll (MA)
Salisbury U (MD)
Sam Houston State U (TX)
San Diego State U (CA)
San Francisco State U (CA)
San Jose State U (CA)
Santa Clara U (CA)
Seattle U (WA)
Seton Hall U (NJ)
Seton Hill U (PA)
Shippensburg U of Pennsylvania (PA)
Siena Coll (NY)
Simmons Coll (MA)
Southeastern Louisiana U (LA)
Southeastern Oklahoma State U (OK)
Southeast Missouri State U (MO)
Southern Connecticut State U (CT)
Southern Illinois U Carbondale (IL)
Southern Methodist U (TX)
Southern Nazarene U (OK)
Southern U and A&M Coll (LA)
Southwestern Oklahoma State U (OK)
Southwest Missouri State U (MO)
Spring Hill Coll (AL)
State U of NY at New Paltz (NY)
State U of NY at Oswego (NY)
State U of NY Coll at Brockport (NY)
State U of NY Coll at Fredonia (NY)
State U of NY Coll at Old Westbury (NY)
State U of NY Inst of Tech at Utica/Rome (NY)
State U of West Georgia (GA)
Stetson U (FL)
Stonehill Coll (MA)
Suffolk U (MA)
Susquehanna U (PA)
Syracuse U (NY)
Talladega Coll (AL)
Tarleton State U (TX)
Taylor U (IN)
Teikyo Post U (CT)
Tennessee Technological U (TN)
Tennessee Wesleyan Coll (TN)
Texas A&M Intl U (TX)
Texas A&M U (TX)
Texas A&M U–Commerce (TX)
Texas A&M U–Corpus Christi (TX)
Texas A&M U–Kingsville (TX)
Texas A&M U–Texarkana (TX)
Texas Christian U (TX)
Texas Lutheran U (TX)
Texas Southern U (TX)
Texas State U-San Marcos (TX)
Texas Tech U (TX)
Thomas Coll (ME)
Thomas Edison State Coll (NJ)
Tiffin U (OH)
Trinity Bible Coll (ND)
Trinity U (TX)
Troy State U (AL)
Troy State U Montgomery (AL)
Truman State U (MO)
Tulane U (LA)
Tuskegee U (AL)
Union U (TN)
Université de Sherbrooke (QC, Canada)
U Coll of the Cariboo (BC, Canada)
The U of Akron (OH)
The U of Alabama (AL)
The U of Alabama at Birmingham (AL)
The U of Alabama in Huntsville (AL)
U of Alberta (AB, Canada)
The U of Arizona (AZ)
U of Arkansas (AR)
U of Arkansas at Little Rock (AR)
U of Baltimore (MD)
U of Bridgeport (CT)
The U of British Columbia (BC, Canada)
U of Calgary (AB, Canada)
U of Central Arkansas (AR)
U of Central Florida (FL)
U of Charleston (WV)
U of Cincinnati (OH)
U of Colorado at Boulder (CO)
U of Colorado at Colorado Springs (CO)
U of Connecticut (CT)
U of Dayton (OH)
U of Delaware (DE)
U of Denver (CO)
U of Detroit Mercy (MI)
U of Evansville (IN)
U of Florida (FL)
U of Georgia (GA)
U of Hartford (CT)
U of Hawaii at Manoa (HI)
U of Houston (TX)
U of Houston–Clear Lake (TX)
U of Idaho (ID)
U of Illinois at Chicago (IL)
U of Illinois at Urbana–Champaign (IL)
The U of Iowa (IA)
U of Kentucky (KY)
The U of Lethbridge (AB, Canada)
U of Louisiana at Lafayette (LA)
U of Louisville (KY)
U of Manitoba (MB, Canada)
U of Mary Hardin-Baylor (TX)
U of Maryland, Coll Park (MD)
U of Massachusetts Amherst (MA)
U of Massachusetts Dartmouth (MA)
The U of Memphis (TN)
U of Miami (FL)
U of Michigan–Dearborn (MI)
U of Michigan–Flint (MI)
U of Minnesota, Duluth (MN)
U of Minnesota, Twin Cities Campus (MN)
U of Mississippi (MS)
U of Missouri–Columbia (MO)
U of Missouri–St. Louis (MO)
U of Nebraska at Omaha (NE)
U of Nebraska–Lincoln (NE)
U of Nevada, Las Vegas (NV)
U of Nevada, Reno (NV)
U of New Brunswick Fredericton (NB, Canada)
U of New Hampshire (NH)
U of New Haven (CT)
U of New Orleans (LA)
U of North Alabama (AL)
The U of North Carolina at Charlotte (NC)
The U of North Carolina at Greensboro (NC)
The U of North Carolina at Wilmington (NC)
U of North Dakota (ND)
U of Northern Iowa (IA)
U of North Florida (FL)
U of North Texas (TX)
U of Notre Dame (IN)
U of Oklahoma (OK)
U of Oregon (OR)
U of Ottawa (ON, Canada)
U of Pennsylvania (PA)
U of Phoenix–Hawaii Campus (HI)
U of Phoenix Online Campus (AZ)
U of Phoenix–Phoenix Campus (AZ)
U of Phoenix–Southern Arizona Campus (AZ)
U of Phoenix–Utah Campus (UT)
U of Pittsburgh (PA)
U of Pittsburgh at Johnstown (PA)
U of Portland (OR)
U of Regina (SK, Canada)
U of Rhode Island (RI)
U of Richmond (VA)
U of St. Francis (IL)
U of Saint Francis (IN)
U of St. Thomas (MN)
U of St. Thomas (TX)
U of San Francisco (CA)
U of Saskatchewan (SK, Canada)
The U of Scranton (PA)
U of South Alabama (AL)
U of South Carolina (SC)
The U of South Dakota (SD)
U of Southern Indiana (IN)
U of South Florida (FL)
The U of Tampa (FL)
The U of Tennessee (TN)
The U of Tennessee at Martin (TN)
The U of Texas at Austin (TX)
The U of Texas at Brownsville (TX)
The U of Texas at Tyler (TX)
The U of Texas–Pan American (TX)
U of the District of Columbia (DC)
U of the Incarnate Word (TX)
U of Toledo (OH)
U of Toronto (ON, Canada)
U of Tulsa (OK)
U of Utah (UT)
U of West Florida (FL)
U of Windsor (ON, Canada)
U of Wisconsin–Eau Claire (WI)
U of Wisconsin–La Crosse (WI)
U of Wisconsin–Madison (WI)
U of Wisconsin–Milwaukee (WI)
U of Wisconsin–Oshkosh (WI)
U of Wisconsin–Parkside (WI)
U of Wisconsin–River Falls (WI)
U of Wisconsin–Whitewater (WI)
U of Wyoming (WY)
Utah State U (UT)
Valdosta State U (GA)
Valparaiso U (IN)
Vanguard U of Southern California (CA)
Villanova U (PA)
Virginia Polytechnic Inst and State U (VA)
Wagner Coll (NY)
Wake Forest U (NC)
Waldorf Coll (IA)
Walsh Coll of Accountancy and Business Admin (MI)
Walsh U (OH)
Warner Southern Coll (FL)
Wartburg Coll (IA)
Washburn U (KS)
Washington State U (WA)
Washington U in St. Louis (MO)
Waynesburg Coll (PA)
Wayne State Coll (NE)
Wayne State U (MI)
Webber Intl U (FL)
Weber State U (UT)
West Chester U of Pennsylvania (PA)
Western Baptist Coll (OR)
Western Carolina U (NC)
Western Connecticut State U (CT)
Western Illinois U (IL)
Western Kentucky U (KY)
Western Michigan U (MI)
Western New England Coll (MA)
Western Washington U (WA)
Westfield State Coll (MA)
Westminster Coll (UT)
West Texas A&M U (TX)
West Virginia U (WV)
West Virginia Wesleyan Coll (WV)
Wichita State U (KS)
Wilberforce U (OH)
Wilmington Coll (DE)
Wingate U (NC)
Winona State U (MN)
Wofford Coll (SC)
Wright State U (OH)
Xavier U (OH)
York Coll of Pennsylvania (PA)
York U (ON, Canada)
Youngstown State U (OH)

FINANCE AND FINANCIAL MANAGEMENT SERVICES RELATED

Babson Coll (MA)
Bryant Coll (RI)
Florida Ag and Mech U (FL)
Grace Bible Coll (MI)
Park U (MO)
Saint Mary's Coll of California (CA)
San Diego State U (CA)
San Jose State U (CA)
The U of Akron (OH)
Virginia Commonwealth U (VA)

FINANCIAL PLANNING AND SERVICES

Baylor U (TX)
Bethany Coll (KS)
Brigham Young U (UT)
Central Michigan U (MI)
Jamestown Coll (ND)
Marywood U (PA)
Medaille Coll (NY)
The Ohio State U at Lima (OH)
Roger Williams U (RI)
Trinity Christian Coll (IL)
U of Charleston (WV)
The U of Maine at Augusta (ME)
U of North Texas (TX)
Widener U (PA)

FINE ARTS RELATED

Abilene Christian U (TX)
Adelphi U (NY)
Allegheny Coll (PA)
Art Center Coll of Design (CA)
Bowling Green State U (OH)
Bridgewater State Coll (MA)
California State U, Long Beach (CA)
The Catholic U of America (DC)
Col for Creative Studies (MI)
Coll of Staten Island of the City U of NY (NY)
Dowling Coll (NY)
Indiana State U (IN)
Kentucky Wesleyan Coll (KY)
Lehigh U (PA)
Long Island U, Brooklyn Campus (NY)
Long Island U, C.W. Post Campus (NY)
Loyola U Chicago (IL)
Madonna U (MI)
Memphis Coll of Art (TN)
Monmouth U (NJ)
Montserrat Coll of Art (MA)
Mount Vernon Nazarene U (OH)
Okanagan U Coll (BC, Canada)
Oregon Coll of Art & Craft (OR)
Our Lady of the Lake U of San Antonio (TX)
Pratt Inst (NY)
Rhode Island School of Design (RI)
Rutgers, The State U of New Jersey, Newark (NJ)
St. John's U (NY)
Salisbury U (MD)
San Diego State U (CA)
School of the Art Inst of Chicago (IL)
School of the Museum of Fine Arts, Boston (MA)
Skidmore Coll (NY)
Syracuse U (NY)
The U of Akron (OH)
U of Calif, Los Angeles (CA)
U of Hartford (CT)
U of Massachusetts Dartmouth (MA)
U of North Alabama (AL)
U of Regina (SK, Canada)
U of Saint Francis (IN)
U of Science and Arts of Oklahoma (OK)
Ursinus Coll (PA)
Widener U (PA)
York Coll of Pennsylvania (PA)

FINE/STUDIO ARTS

Abilene Christian U (TX)
Acad of Art U (CA)
Alberta Coll of Art & Design (AB, Canada)
Albertus Magnus Coll (CT)
Alfred U (NY)
Allegheny Coll (PA)
Alma Coll (MI)
American Acad of Art (IL)
American U (DC)
Amherst Coll (MA)
Anderson Coll (SC)
Angelo State U (TX)
Anna Maria Coll (MA)
Appalachian State U (NC)
Aquinas Coll (MI)
Arcadia U (PA)
Arizona State U (AZ)
Art Acad of Cincinnati (OH)
Art Center Coll of Design (CA)
The Art Inst of Boston at Lesley U (MA)
Asbury Coll (KY)
Ashland U (OH)
Atlanta Coll of Art (GA)
Auburn U (AL)
Augsburg Coll (MN)
Augustana Coll (IL)
Baker U (KS)
Baldwin-Wallace Coll (OH)
Ball State U (IN)
Bard Coll (NY)
Barton Coll (NC)
Baylor U (TX)
Belmont U (TN)
Beloit Coll (WI)
Bemidji State U (MN)
Benedictine U (IL)
Bennington Coll (VT)
Berea Coll (KY)
Bethany Coll (WV)
Bethel Coll (KS)
Biola U (CA)
Birmingham-Southern Coll (AL)
Bishop's U (QC, Canada)
Bloomfield Coll (NJ)
Bloomsburg U of Pennsylvania (PA)
Boston Coll (MA)
Bowdoin Coll (ME)
Bowling Green State U (OH)
Bradley U (IL)
Brandeis U (MA)
Brenau U (GA)
Bridgewater Coll (VA)
Bridgewater State Coll (MA)
Brigham Young U (UT)
Brock U (ON, Canada)
Brooklyn Coll of the City U of NY (NY)
Brown U (RI)
Bucknell U (PA)
State U of NY Coll at Buffalo (NY)
Cabrini Coll (PA)
California Coll of the Arts (CA)
California Inst of the Arts (CA)
California State U, Chico (CA)
California State U, Dominguez Hills (CA)
California State U, Fullerton (CA)
California State U, Hayward (CA)
California State U, Long Beach (CA)
California State U, Stanislaus (CA)
Calvin Coll (MI)
Campbell U (NC)
Capital U (OH)
Cardinal Stritch U (WI)
Carleton Coll (MN)
Carnegie Mellon U (PA)
Carroll Coll (WI)
Carthage Coll (WI)
The Catholic U of America (DC)
Cazenovia Coll (NY)
Cedar Crest Coll (PA)
Centenary Coll of Louisiana (LA)
Central Missouri State U (MO)
Chapman U (CA)
Chatham Coll (PA)
Chester Coll of New England (NH)
Chicago State U (IL)
Chowan Coll (NC)
Claremont McKenna Coll (CA)
Clarke Coll (IA)
Clark U (MA)
Coastal Carolina U (SC)
Coe Coll (IA)
Coker Coll (SC)
Colby Coll (ME)
Colby-Sawyer Coll (NH)
Col for Creative Studies (MI)
Coll of Charleston (SC)
Coll of Mount St. Joseph (OH)
The Coll of New Jersey (NJ)
The Coll of New Rochelle (NY)
Coll of Saint Benedict (MN)
Coll of St. Catherine (MN)
The Coll of Saint Rose (NY)
Coll of Santa Fe (NM)
Coll of the Holy Cross (MA)
Coll of the Ozarks (MO)
The Coll of Wooster (OH)
Colorado Christian U (CO)
The Colorado Coll (CO)
Colorado State U (CO)
Columbia Coll (SC)
Columbia Coll Chicago (IL)
Columbus Coll of Art & Design (OH)
Concordia Coll (MN)
Concordia U (NE)
Concordia U (QC, Canada)
Concordia U, St. Paul (MN)
Converse Coll (SC)
Cooper Union for the Advancement of Science & Art (NY)
Cornell U (NY)
Cornish Coll of the Arts (WA)
Cumberland Coll (KY)
Cumberland U (TN)
Daemen Coll (NY)
Dartmouth Coll (NH)
Denison U (OH)
DePaul U (IL)
DePauw U (IN)
Dickinson Coll (PA)
Dominican U (IL)
Dowling Coll (NY)
Drake U (IA)
Drury U (MO)
Duquesne U (PA)
East Carolina U (NC)
Eastern Kentucky U (KY)
Eastern Michigan U (MI)
Eastern Washington U (WA)
Edinboro U of Pennsylvania (PA)
Elizabeth City State U (NC)
Elmira Coll (NY)
Endicott Coll (MA)
The Evergreen State Coll (WA)
Ferris State U (MI)
Ferrum Coll (VA)
Flagler Coll (FL)
Florida Intl U (FL)
Florida Southern Coll (FL)
Florida State U (FL)
Fontbonne U (MO)
Fordham U (NY)
Fort Lewis Coll (CO)
Framingham State Coll (MA)
Franklin and Marshall Coll (PA)
Franklin Pierce Coll (NH)
Furman U (SC)
Gallaudet U (DC)
Gardner-Webb U (NC)
George Mason U (VA)
Georgetown Coll (KY)
The George Washington U (DC)
Georgian Court U (NJ)
Georgia State U (GA)
Gettysburg Coll (PA)
Governors State U (IL)
Graceland U (IA)
Grand Canyon U (AZ)
Grand Valley State U (MI)
Grand View Coll (IA)
Hamilton Coll (NY)
Hamline U (MN)
Hampden-Sydney Coll (VA)
Hampshire Coll (MA)
Harding U (AR)
Hardin-Simmons U (TX)
Harvard U (MA)
High Point U (NC)
Hiram Coll (OH)
Hobart and William Smith Colls (NY)
Hofstra U (NY)
Hollins U (VA)
Hope Coll (MI)
Houston Baptist U (TX)
Howard Payne U (TX)
Humboldt State U (CA)
Hunter Coll of the City U of NY (NY)
Illinois State U (IL)
Indiana U Bloomington (IN)
Indiana U–Purdue U Fort Wayne (IN)
Indiana U–Purdue U Indianapolis (IN)
Indiana U South Bend (IN)
Indiana U Southeast (IN)
Iowa Wesleyan Coll (IA)
Ithaca Coll (NY)
Jacksonville U (FL)
Jamestown Coll (ND)
Johnson State Coll (VT)
Judson Coll (IL)
Juniata Coll (PA)
Kean U (NJ)
Kennesaw State U (GA)
Kent State U (OH)
Kentucky State U (KY)
Kenyon Coll (OH)
Keystone Coll (PA)
King Coll (TN)
Kutztown U of Pennsylvania (PA)
Lafayette Coll (PA)
Laguna Coll of Art & Design (CA)
Lake Erie Coll (OH)
Lake Forest Coll (IL)
Lamar U (TX)
Lambuth U (TN)
Lawrence U (WI)
Lebanon Valley Coll (PA)
Lewis U (IL)
Limestone Coll (SC)
Lindenwood U (MO)
Lipscomb U (TN)
Long Island U, C.W. Post Campus (NY)
Long Island U, Southampton Coll (NY)
Longwood U (VA)
Loras Coll (IA)
Louisiana Coll (LA)
Louisiana State U and A&M Coll (LA)
Loyola Marymount U (CA)
Lycoming Coll (PA)
Macalester Coll (MN)
MacMurray Coll (IL)
Maharishi U of Management (IA)
Malone Coll (OH)
Manchester Coll (IN)
Manhattanville Coll (NY)
Marian Coll (IN)
Marian Coll of Fond du Lac (WI)
Marietta Coll (OH)
Marist Coll (NY)
Marlboro Coll (VT)
Martin U (IN)
Marygrove Coll (MI)
Maryland Inst Coll of Art (MD)
Marymount Coll of Fordham U (NY)
Marymount Manhattan Coll (NY)
Marymount U (VA)
Maryville Coll (TN)
Maryville U of Saint Louis (MO)
Mary Washington Coll (VA)
Marywood U (PA)
Massachusetts Coll of Art (MA)
Memphis Coll of Art (TN)
Mercyhurst Coll (PA)
Meredith Coll (NC)
Merrimack Coll (MA)
Messiah Coll (PA)
Miami U (OH)
Middlebury Coll (VT)
Milligan Coll (TN)
Millikin U (IL)
Mills Coll (CA)
Minneapolis Coll of Art and Design (MN)
Minnesota State U Mankato (MN)
Minnesota State U Moorhead (MN)
Montana State U–Bozeman (MT)
Montclair State U (NJ)
Montserrat Coll of Art (MA)
Moore Coll of Art & Design (PA)
Moravian Coll (PA)
Morehead State U (KY)
Morningside Coll (IA)
Mount Allison U (NB, Canada)
Mount Holyoke Coll (MA)
Mount Saint Vincent U (NS, Canada)
Muhlenberg Coll (PA)
Murray State U (KY)
Naropa U (CO)
Nazareth Coll of Rochester (NY)
New Coll of Florida (FL)
New Hampshire Inst of Art (NH)
New Mexico State U (NM)
New York Inst of Technology (NY)
New York U (NY)
North Carolina Central U (NC)
Northeastern State U (OK)
Northern Illinois U (IL)
Northern Michigan U (MI)
Northland Coll (WI)
North Park U (IL)
Northwestern Coll (MN)
Notre Dame Coll (OH)
Notre Dame de Namur U (CA)
Nova Scotia Coll of Art and Design (NS, Canada)
Oakland U (MI)
Oberlin Coll (OH)
Occidental Coll (CA)
Ohio Dominican U (OH)
Ohio Northern U (OH)
The Ohio State U (OH)
Ohio U (OH)
Ohio Wesleyan U (OH)
Oklahoma Baptist U (OK)
Oklahoma City U (OK)
Oklahoma State U (OK)
Old Dominion U (VA)
Olivet Coll (MI)
Oral Roberts U (OK)
Oregon State U (OR)
Otis Coll of Art and Design (CA)
Ouachita Baptist U (AR)
Pacific Lutheran U (WA)
Pacific Union Coll (CA)
Paier Coll of Art, Inc. (CT)
Palm Beach Atlantic U (FL)
Park U (MO)
Piedmont Coll (GA)
Pine Manor Coll (MA)
Pittsburg State U (KS)
Pitzer Coll (CA)
Plymouth State U (NH)
Pomona Coll (CA)
Pratt Inst (NY)
Principia Coll (IL)
Providence Coll (RI)
Queens Coll of the City U of NY (NY)
Queen's U at Kingston (ON, Canada)
Queens U of Charlotte (NC)
Randolph-Macon Coll (VA)
Randolph-Macon Woman's Coll (VA)
Reed Coll (OR)
Rhode Island Coll (RI)
Rhodes Coll (TN)
Rice U (TX)
Richmond, The American Intl U in London(United Kingdom)
Ringling School of Art and Design (FL)
Rivier Coll (NH)
Roberts Wesleyan Coll (NY)
Rochester Inst of Technology (NY)
Rockford Coll (IL)
Rollins Coll (FL)
Rosemont Coll (PA)
Rowan U (NJ)
Saginaw Valley State U (MI)
St. Ambrose U (IA)
St. Andrews Presbyterian Coll (NC)
St. Cloud State U (MN)
St. Gregory's U (OK)
Saint John's U (MN)
St. John's U (NY)
Saint Joseph's Coll (IN)
Saint Louis U (MO)
Saint Mary-of-the-Woods Coll (IN)
Saint Mary's U of Minnesota (MN)
St. Thomas Aquinas Coll (NY)
Saint Vincent Coll (PA)
Salem Coll (NC)
Salve Regina U (RI)
Sam Houston State U (TX)
San Jose State U (CA)
Sarah Lawrence Coll (NY)
School of the Art Inst of Chicago (IL)
School of the Museum of Fine Arts, Boston (MA)
Scripps Coll (CA)
Seattle U (WA)
Seton Hill U (PA)
Shawnee State U (OH)
Shorter Coll (GA)
Siena Coll (NY)
Sierra Nevada Coll (NV)
Simon's Rock Coll of Bard (MA)
Smith Coll (MA)
Sonoma State U (CA)
Southern Connecticut State U (CT)
Southern Illinois U Carbondale (IL)
Southern Illinois U Edwardsville (IL)
Southern Methodist U (TX)
Southwestern U (TX)
Southwest Missouri State U (MO)
Spring Hill Coll (AL)
State U of NY at Binghamton (NY)
State U of NY at New Paltz (NY)
Plattsburgh State U of NY (NY)
State U of NY Coll at Brockport (NY)
State U of NY Coll at Cortland (NY)
State U of NY Coll at Fredonia (NY)
State U of NY Coll at Geneseo (NY)
State U of NY Coll at Oneonta (NY)
Stonehill Coll (MA)
Stony Brook U, State U of New York (NY)
Swarthmore Coll (PA)
Sweet Briar Coll (VA)
Syracuse U (NY)
Texas A&M U–Corpus Christi (TX)
Texas Christian U (TX)
Texas Southern U (TX)
Texas State U-San Marcos (TX)
Texas Tech U (TX)
Transylvania U (KY)
Trinity Coll (CT)
Troy State U (AL)
Truman State U (MO)
Tulane U (LA)
Union Coll (NE)
Union Coll (NY)
U du Québec à Hull (QC, Canada)
Université Laval (QC, Canada)
U at Buffalo, The State U of New York (NY)
U Coll of the Cariboo (BC, Canada)
The U of Akron (OH)
The U of Alabama (AL)
The U of Alabama at Birmingham (AL)
U of Alberta (AB, Canada)
The U of Arizona (AZ)
The U of British Columbia (BC, Canada)
U of Calif, Irvine (CA)
U of Calif, Riverside (CA)
U of Calif, San Diego (CA)
U of Calif, Santa Barbara (CA)
U of Central Florida (FL)
U of Chicago (IL)
U of Colorado at Boulder (CO)
U of Colorado at Colorado Springs (CO)
U of Colorado at Denver (CO)
U of Connecticut (CT)
U of Dallas (TX)
U of Dayton (OH)
U of Denver (CO)
U of Florida (FL)
U of Georgia (GA)
U of Great Falls (MT)
U of Guelph (ON, Canada)
U of Houston (TX)
U of Idaho (ID)
U of Illinois at Chicago (IL)
U of Indianapolis (IN)
The U of Iowa (IA)
U of Kansas (KS)
U of Kentucky (KY)
U of Louisville (KY)

U of Maine (ME)
The U of Maine at Augusta (ME)
U of Maine at Presque Isle (ME)
U of Mary Hardin-Baylor (TX)
U of Massachusetts Amherst (MA)
U of Massachusetts Lowell (MA)
U of Miami (FL)
U of Michigan–Flint (MI)
U of Minnesota, Duluth (MN)
U of Minnesota, Morris (MN)
U of Missouri–Kansas City (MO)
U of Missouri–St. Louis (MO)
U of Montevallo (AL)
U of Nebraska at Omaha (NE)
U of Nebraska–Lincoln (NE)
U of New Hampshire (NH)
U of New Orleans (LA)
U of North Alabama (AL)
The U of North Carolina at Asheville (NC)
The U of North Carolina at Chapel Hill (NC)
The U of North Carolina at Charlotte (NC)
The U of North Carolina at Greensboro (NC)
The U of North Carolina at Pembroke (NC)
The U of North Carolina at Wilmington (NC)
U of Northern Colorado (CO)
U of Northern Iowa (IA)
U of North Florida (FL)
U of Notre Dame (IN)
U of Oklahoma (OK)
U of Oregon (OR)
U of Ottawa (ON, Canada)
U of Pennsylvania (PA)
U of Pittsburgh (PA)
U of Redlands (CA)
U of Richmond (VA)
U of Rochester (NY)
U of St. Thomas (TX)
U of San Francisco (CA)
U of Saskatchewan (SK, Canada)
U of South Carolina (SC)
U of South Carolina Aiken (SC)
U of Southern California (CA)
The U of Tennessee (TN)
The U of Tennessee at Chattanooga (TN)
The U of Texas at Arlington (TX)
The U of Texas at Austin (TX)
The U of Texas–Pan American (TX)
U of the District of Columbia (DC)
U of the Pacific (CA)
U of the South (TN)
U of Toledo (OH)
U of Toronto (ON, Canada)
U of Tulsa (OK)
U of Vermont (VT)
U of Victoria (BC, Canada)
U of Waterloo (ON, Canada)
The U of Western Ontario (ON, Canada)
U of West Florida (FL)
U of Windsor (ON, Canada)
U of Wisconsin–Milwaukee (WI)
U of Wisconsin–Oshkosh (WI)
U of Wisconsin–Stevens Point (WI)
U of Wisconsin–Superior (WI)
Ursuline Coll (OH)
Valparaiso U (IN)
Vassar Coll (NY)
Viterbo U (WI)
Wake Forest U (NC)
Washburn U (KS)
Washington and Lee U (VA)
Washington State U (WA)
Washington U in St. Louis (MO)
Watkins Coll of Art and Design (TN)
Webster U (MO)
Wellesley Coll (MA)
Wells Coll (NY)
Wesleyan Coll (GA)
Wesleyan U (CT)
West Chester U of Pennsylvania (PA)
Western Carolina U (NC)
Western Illinois U (IL)
Western Kentucky U (KY)
Western State Coll of Colorado (CO)
Western Washington U (WA)
West Texas A&M U (TX)
West Virginia Wesleyan Coll (WV)
Wheaton Coll (MA)
Whitworth Coll (WA)
Wilberforce U (OH)
Willamette U (OR)
William Carey Coll (MS)
William Paterson U of New Jersey (NJ)
Williams Baptist Coll (AR)
Williams Coll (MA)
William Woods U (MO)
Wingate U (NC)
Winona State U (MN)
Xavier U (OH)
York U (ON, Canada)
Youngstown State U (OH)

FIRE PROTECTION AND SAFETY TECHNOLOGY
Columbia Southern U (AL)
Eastern Kentucky U (KY)
Oklahoma State U (OK)
Thomas Edison State Coll (NJ)
U of Cincinnati (OH)
U of New Haven (CT)

FIRE PROTECTION RELATED
The U of Akron (OH)

FIRE SCIENCE
Anna Maria Coll (MA)
Cogswell Polytechnical Coll (CA)
Eastern Oregon U (OR)
Hampton U (VA)
John Jay Coll of Criminal Justice, the City U of NY (NY)
Lake Superior State U (MI)
Lewis-Clark State Coll (ID)
Madonna U (MI)
Mercy Coll (NY)
U of Florida (FL)
U of Maryland U Coll (MD)
U of New Brunswick Fredericton (NB, Canada)
U of New Haven (CT)
U of the District of Columbia (DC)

FIRE SERVICES ADMINISTRATION
California State U, Los Angeles (CA)
Columbia Southern U (AL)
John Jay Coll of Criminal Justice, the City U of NY (NY)
Southern Illinois U Carbondale (IL)
U of New Haven (CT)
Western Oregon U (OR)

FISH/GAME MANAGEMENT
Delaware State U (DE)
Humboldt State U (CA)
Iowa State U of Science and Technology (IA)
Lake Superior State U (MI)
Lincoln Memorial U (TN)
Northland Coll (WI)
Oregon State U (OR)
Pittsburg State U (KS)
South Dakota State U (SD)
Southeastern Oklahoma State U (OK)
State U of NY Coll of Environ Sci and Forestry (NY)
Texas A&M U at Galveston (TX)
Texas A&M U–Kingsville (TX)
The U of British Columbia (BC, Canada)
U of Idaho (ID)
U of Minnesota, Duluth (MN)
U of Minnesota, Twin Cities Campus (MN)
U of Missouri–Columbia (MO)
U of New Brunswick Fredericton (NB, Canada)
U of Vermont (VT)
West Virginia U (WV)

FISHING AND FISHERIES SCIENCES AND MANAGEMENT
Colorado State U (CO)
Humboldt State U (CA)
Malaspina U-Coll (BC, Canada)
Mansfield U of Pennsylvania (PA)
Murray State U (KY)
North Carolina State U (NC)
The Ohio State U (OH)
State U of NY Coll of A&T at Cobleskill (NY)
State U of NY Coll of Environ Sci and Forestry (NY)
Sterling Coll (VT)
Texas A&M U (TX)
Texas Tech U (TX)
Unity Coll (ME)
U of Alaska Fairbanks (AK)
U of Georgia (GA)
U of Missouri–Columbia (MO)
U of Rhode Island (RI)
U of Washington (WA)

FLUID/THERMAL SCIENCES
Harvard U (MA)
Worcester Polytechnic Inst (MA)

FOLKLORE
Harvard U (MA)
Indiana U Bloomington (IN)
Laurentian U (ON, Canada)
Marlboro Coll (VT)
Memorial U of Newfoundland (NL, Canada)
The Ohio State U (OH)
U of Alberta (AB, Canada)
U of Oregon (OR)

FOOD/NUTRITION
Radford U (VA)

FOOD PREPARATION
Lexington Coll (IL)
Virginia Intermont Coll (VA)

FOODS AND NUTRITION RELATED
California State U, Long Beach (CA)
Framingham State Coll (MA)
Kent State U (OH)
Marywood U (PA)
The U of British Columbia (BC, Canada)
U of Wisconsin–Stout (WI)
Utah State U (UT)

FOOD SCIENCE
Acadia U (NS, Canada)
Alabama Ag and Mech U (AL)
Auburn U (AL)
Brigham Young U (UT)
California Polytechnic State U, San Luis Obispo (CA)
Clemson U (SC)
Cornell U (NY)
Dalhousie U (NS, Canada)
Delaware Valley Coll (PA)
Dominican U (IL)
Framingham State Coll (MA)
Kansas State U (KS)
Lamar U (TX)
Louisiana State U and A&M Coll (LA)
Marymount Coll of Fordham U (NY)
McGill U (QC, Canada)
Memorial U of Newfoundland (NL, Canada)
Michigan State U (MI)
Mississippi State U (MS)
North Carolina State U (NC)
North Dakota State U (ND)
The Ohio State U (OH)
Olivet Nazarene U (IL)
Oregon State U (OR)
Penn State U Abington Coll (PA)
Penn State U Altoona Coll (PA)
Penn State U at Erie, The Behrend Coll (PA)
Penn State U Beaver Campus of the Commonwealth Coll (PA)
Penn State U Berks Cmps of Berks-Lehigh Valley Coll (PA)
Penn State U Delaware County Campus of the Commonwealth Coll (PA)
Penn State U DuBois Campus of the Commonwealth Coll (PA)
Penn State U Fayette Campus of the Commonwealth Coll (PA)
Penn State U Hazleton Campus of the Commonwealth Coll (PA)
Penn State U Lehigh Valley Cmps of Berks-Lehigh Valley Coll (PA)
Penn State U McKeesport Campus of the Commonwealth Coll (PA)
Penn State U Mont Alto Campus of the Commonwealth Coll (PA)
Penn State U New Kensington Campus of the Commonwealth Coll (PA)
Penn State U Schuylkill Campus of the Capital Coll (PA)
Penn State U Shenango Campus of the Commonwealth Coll (PA)
Penn State U Univ Park Campus (PA)
Penn State U Wilkes-Barre Campus of the Commonwealth Coll (PA)
Penn State U Worthington Scranton Cmps Commonwealth Coll (PA)
Penn State U York Campus of the Commonwealth Coll (PA)
Purdue U (IN)
Rutgers, The State U of New Jersey, New Brunswick/Piscataway (NJ)
San Jose State U (CA)
South Dakota State U (SD)
Texas A&M U (TX)
Texas A&M U–Kingsville (TX)
Texas Tech U (TX)
Tuskegee U (AL)
Université Laval (QC, Canada)
The U of Akron (OH)
U of Alberta (AB, Canada)
U of Arkansas (AR)
The U of British Columbia (BC, Canada)
U of Calif, Davis (CA)
U of Delaware (DE)
U of Florida (FL)
U of Georgia (GA)
U of Guelph (ON, Canada)
U of Idaho (ID)
U of Illinois at Urbana–Champaign (IL)
U of Kentucky (KY)
U of Maine (ME)
U of Manitoba (MB, Canada)
U of Maryland, Coll Park (MD)
U of Massachusetts Amherst (MA)
U of Missouri–Columbia (MO)
U of Nebraska–Lincoln (NE)
U of Saskatchewan (SK, Canada)
The U of Tennessee (TN)
U of the District of Columbia (DC)
U of Utah (UT)
U of Wisconsin–Madison (WI)
U of Wisconsin–River Falls (WI)
Virginia Polytechnic Inst and State U (VA)
Washington State U (WA)

FOOD SCIENCE AND TECHNOLOGY RELATED
Framingham State Coll (MA)
The U of British Columbia (BC, Canada)

FOOD SERVICE AND DINING ROOM MANAGEMENT
Lexington Coll (IL)

FOOD SERVICES TECHNOLOGY
Iowa State U of Science and Technology (IA)
Johnson & Wales U (RI)
Madonna U (MI)
Mansfield U of Pennsylvania (PA)
Tennessee State U (TN)

FOODSERVICE SYSTEMS ADMINISTRATION
Central Michigan U (MI)
Cornell U (NY)
Dominican U (IL)
Johnson & Wales U (RI)
Rochester Inst of Technology (NY)
State U of NY Coll at Oneonta (NY)
The U of North Carolina at Greensboro (NC)
U of Wisconsin–Stout (WI)
Western Michigan U (MI)

FOODS, NUTRITION, AND WELLNESS
Acadia U (NS, Canada)
Alcorn State U (MS)
Andrews U (MI)
Appalachian State U (NC)
Arizona State U East (AZ)
Ashland U (OH)
Auburn U (AL)
Bastyr U (WA)
Bluffton Coll (OH)
Bowling Green State U (OH)
Bridgewater Coll (VA)
Brooklyn Coll of the City U of NY (NY)
California Polytechnic State U, San Luis Obispo (CA)
California State Polytechnic U, Pomona (CA)
California State U, Fresno (CA)
California State U, Los Angeles (CA)
California State U, San Bernardino (CA)
Carson-Newman Coll (TN)
Cedar Crest Coll (PA)
Central Washington U (WA)
Coll of Saint Benedict (MN)
Coll of St. Catherine (MN)
Coll of the Ozarks (MO)
Colorado State U (CO)
Concordia Coll (MN)
Cornell U (NY)
Delaware State U (DE)
Dominican U (IL)
Eastern Michigan U (MI)
Florida State U (FL)
Fort Valley State U (GA)
Framingham State Coll (MA)
Gallaudet U (DC)
Georgia Southern U (GA)
Georgia State U (GA)
Goddard Coll (VT)
Hampshire Coll (MA)
Howard U (DC)
Hunter Coll of the City U of NY (NY)
Idaho State U (ID)
Immaculata U (PA)
Indiana State U (IN)
Indiana U Bloomington (IN)
Indiana U of Pennsylvania (PA)
Iowa State U of Science and Technology (IA)
Ithaca Coll (NY)
Jacksonville State U (AL)
James Madison U (VA)
Kansas State U (KS)
Keene State Coll (NH)
Kent State U (OH)
Lambuth U (TN)
Lehman Coll of the City U of NY (NY)
Loyola U Chicago (IL)
Madonna U (MI)
Marymount Coll of Fordham U (NY)
The Master's Coll and Sem (CA)
McGill U (QC, Canada)
McNeese State U (LA)
Memorial U of Newfoundland (NL, Canada)
Middle Tennessee State U (TN)
Minnesota State U Mankato (MN)
Montclair State U (NJ)
Morgan State U (MD)
Mount Marty Coll (SD)
Mount Saint Vincent U (NS, Canada)
Murray State U (KY)
New Mexico State U (NM)
New York U (NY)
Northeastern State U (OK)
Northern Illinois U (IL)
The Ohio State U (OH)
Ohio U (OH)
Oklahoma State U (OK)
Oregon State U (OR)
Pepperdine U, Malibu (CA)
Point Loma Nazarene U (CA)
Prairie View A&M U (TX)
Purdue U (IN)
Ryerson U (ON, Canada)
St. Francis Xavier U (NS, Canada)
Saint John's U (MN)
Saint Joseph Coll (CT)
Saint Louis U (MO)
Sam Houston State U (TX)
San Diego State U (CA)
Seattle Pacific U (WA)
Simmons Coll (MA)
South Carolina State U (SC)
South Dakota State U (SD)
Southern Illinois U Carbondale (IL)
Plattsburgh State U of NY (NY)
Syracuse U (NY)
Tennessee Technological U (TN)
Texas A&M U (TX)
Texas A&M U–Kingsville (TX)
Texas Southern U (TX)
Texas State U-San Marcos (TX)
Texas Tech U (TX)
Texas Woman's U (TX)
Tuskegee U (AL)
Université de Montréal (QC, Canada)
Université Laval (QC, Canada)
The U of Akron (OH)
The U of Alabama (AL)
U of Alberta (AB, Canada)
U of Arkansas (AR)
The U of British Columbia (BC, Canada)
U of Calif, Davis (CA)
U of Cincinnati (OH)
U of Dayton (OH)
U of Delaware (DE)
U of Georgia (GA)
U of Houston (TX)
U of Idaho (ID)
U of Kentucky (KY)
U of Maine (ME)
U of Manitoba (MB, Canada)
U of Maryland, Coll Park (MD)
U of Michigan (MI)
U of Minnesota, Twin Cities Campus (MN)
U of Missouri–Columbia (MO)
U of Nebraska–Lincoln (NE)
U of Nevada, Reno (NV)
U of New Hampshire (NH)
U of New Mexico (NM)
The U of North Carolina at Chapel Hill (NC)
The U of North Carolina at Greensboro (NC)

U of Northern Iowa (IA)
U of Prince Edward Island (PE, Canada)
U of Rhode Island (RI)
The U of Tennessee (TN)
The U of Texas at Austin (TX)
U of the Incarnate Word (TX)
U of Toronto (ON, Canada)
U of Vermont (VT)
The U of Western Ontario (ON, Canada)
U of Wisconsin–Madison (WI)
Virginia Polytechnic Inst and State U (VA)
Washington State U (WA)
Wayne State U (MI)
Western Kentucky U (KY)
Winthrop U (SC)
Youngstown State U (OH)

FOOD TECHNOLOGY AND PROCESSING
Brigham Young U (UT)
Cornell U (NY)

FOREIGN LANGUAGES AND LITERATURES
Arkansas Tech U (AR)
Assumption Coll (MA)
Auburn U (AL)
Auburn U Montgomery (AL)
Augustana Coll (SD)
Austin Peay State U (TN)
Boston U (MA)
Cameron U (OK)
Campbell U (NC)
Centenary Coll of Louisiana (LA)
Central Methodist Coll (MO)
Central Washington U (WA)
Clemson U (SC)
The Coll of Southeastern Europe, The American U of Athens(Greece)
Colorado State U (CO)
Concordia U Coll of Alberta (AB, Canada)
Covenant Coll (GA)
Delta State U (MS)
Dominican U of California (CA)
Dowling Coll (NY)
Duquesne U (PA)
Eastern Illinois U (IL)
Eckerd Coll (FL)
Elmira Coll (NY)
Elon U (NC)
Emporia State U (KS)
Excelsior Coll (NY)
Framingham State Coll (MA)
Francis Marion U (SC)
Frostburg State U (MD)
Gannon U (PA)
George Mason U (VA)
Gordon Coll (MA)
Graceland U (IA)
Greenville Coll (IL)
Hastings Coll (NE)
Indiana State U (IN)
James Madison U (VA)
Juniata Coll (PA)
Kansas State U (KS)
Kenyon Coll (OH)
Knox Coll (IL)
Lambuth U (TN)
Lewis & Clark Coll (OR)
Long Island U, Brooklyn Campus (NY)
Long Island U, C.W. Post Campus (NY)
Marian Coll of Fond du Lac (WI)
Marshall U (WV)
Massachusetts Inst of Technology (MA)
McGill U (QC, Canada)
Mercyhurst Coll (PA)
Metropolitan State Coll of Denver (CO)
Middle Tennessee State U (TN)
Millikin U (IL)
Minnesota State U Moorhead (MN)
Mississippi Coll (MS)
Mississippi State U (MS)
Monmouth U (NJ)
Montana State U–Bozeman (MT)
New Coll of Florida (FL)
New Mexico State U (NM)
Oakland U (MI)
Old Dominion U (VA)
Pace U (NY)
Penn State U Berks Cmps of Berks-Lehigh Valley Coll (PA)
Penn State U Lehigh Valley Cmps of Berks-Lehigh Valley Coll (PA)
Principia Coll (IL)
Purdue U (IN)
Queens U of Charlotte (NC)
Radford U (VA)
The Richard Stockton Coll of New Jersey (NJ)
Roger Williams U (RI)
Roosevelt U (IL)
Rutgers, The State U of New Jersey, New Brunswick/Piscataway (NJ)
St. John's Coll (NM)
St. Lawrence U (NY)
Saint Louis U (MO)
St. Mary's Coll of Maryland (MD)
Saint Mary's U of Minnesota (MN)
Samford U (AL)
Sarah Lawrence Coll (NY)
Scripps Coll (CA)
Seton Hall U (NJ)
Simon's Rock Coll of Bard (MA)
Southern Adventist U (TN)
Southern Illinois U Edwardsville (IL)
Southern Methodist U (TX)
Stonehill Coll (MA)
Sweet Briar Coll (VA)
Syracuse U (NY)
Texas Southern U (TX)
Thomas Edison State Coll (NJ)
Tulane U (LA)
Union Coll (NY)
Union U (TN)
The U of Alabama in Huntsville (AL)
U of Alaska Fairbanks (AK)
U of Calif, San Diego (CA)
U of Calif, Santa Cruz (CA)
U of Central Florida (FL)
U of Delaware (DE)
U of Georgia (GA)
U of Hartford (CT)
U of Idaho (ID)
U of Maryland, Coll Park (MD)
U of Massachusetts Lowell (MA)
The U of Memphis (TN)
The U of Montana–Missoula (MT)
U of New Mexico (NM)
U of North Alabama (AL)
U of North Dakota (ND)
U of Northern Colorado (CO)
U of Northern Iowa (IA)
The U of Scranton (PA)
U of South Alabama (AL)
The U of Texas at Arlington (TX)
The U of Texas at Austin (TX)
The U of Texas at Tyler (TX)
U of Utah (UT)
The U of Virginia's Coll at Wise (VA)
Virginia Commonwealth U (VA)
Virginia Wesleyan Coll (VA)
Washington and Lee U (VA)
Washington Coll (MD)
Washington State U (WA)
Wayne State U (MI)
West Virginia U (WV)
Widener U (PA)
Wright State U (OH)
Youngstown State U (OH)

FOREIGN LANGUAGES RELATED
Clemson U (SC)
Colby Coll (ME)
The Coll of New Rochelle (NY)
Edinboro U of Pennsylvania (PA)
Hofstra U (NY)
Houston Baptist U (TX)
Marquette U (WI)
Mississippi Coll (MS)
Oakland U (MI)
Saint Mary's Coll of California (CA)
Southern Illinois U Carbondale (IL)
U of Calif, Berkeley (CA)
U of Calif, Los Angeles (CA)
U of Hawaii at Manoa (HI)
U of Michigan–Flint (MI)
U of Northern Iowa (IA)
U of St. Thomas (MN)
U of the Sacred Heart (PR)
Yale U (CT)

FOREIGN LANGUAGE TEACHER EDUCATION
Arkansas Tech U (AR)
Baylor U (TX)
Berea Coll (KY)
Boston U (MA)
Bowling Green State U (OH)
Brigham Young U (UT)
State U of NY Coll at Buffalo (NY)
Carroll Coll (WI)
The Catholic U of America (DC)
Central Methodist Coll (MO)
Cornell U (NY)
Dana Coll (NE)
Delta State U (MS)
Duquesne U (PA)
Elmira Coll (NY)
Florida Intl U (FL)
Florida State U (FL)
Gannon U (PA)
Gardner-Webb U (NC)
Greensboro Coll (NC)
Hastings Coll (NE)
Hofstra U (NY)
Juniata Coll (PA)
Kent State U (OH)
Le Moyne Coll (NY)
Lincoln U (PA)
Long Island U, C.W. Post Campus (NY)
Marquette U (WI)
McNeese State U (LA)
Mercyhurst Coll (PA)
Millersville U of Pennsylvania (PA)
Moravian Coll (PA)
Murray State U (KY)
Nazareth Coll of Rochester (NY)
New York U (NY)
North Carolina State U (NC)
Ohio Dominican U (OH)
Ohio Northern U (OH)
Ohio Wesleyan U (OH)
Queens Coll of the City U of NY (NY)
Rivier Coll (NH)
St. Bonaventure U (NY)
Saint Francis U (PA)
St. John's U (NY)
Sam Houston State U (TX)
San Diego State U (CA)
Seton Hill U (PA)
Southeast Missouri State U (MO)
Southern Nazarene U (OK)
State U of NY Coll at Brockport (NY)
State U of NY Coll at Old Westbury (NY)
State U of NY Coll at Potsdam (NY)
Texas Wesleyan U (TX)
State U of NY at Albany (NY)
The U of Akron (OH)
The U of Arizona (AZ)
U of Central Florida (FL)
U of Delaware (DE)
U of Georgia (GA)
U of Hawaii at Manoa (HI)
U of Illinois at Chicago (IL)
U of Illinois at Urbana–Champaign (IL)
The U of Lethbridge (AB, Canada)
U of Maryland, Coll Park (MD)
U of Minnesota, Twin Cities Campus (MN)
U of Nebraska–Lincoln (NE)
U of Nevada, Reno (NV)
U of New Orleans (LA)
U of Northern Iowa (IA)
U of Oklahoma (OK)
U of St. Thomas (MN)
The U of South Dakota (SD)
U of South Florida (FL)
U of Vermont (VT)
U of West Florida (FL)
U of Windsor (ON, Canada)
Valdosta State U (GA)
Valparaiso U (IN)
Virginia Wesleyan Coll (VA)
West Chester U of Pennsylvania (PA)
Western Michigan U (MI)
Wheeling Jesuit U (WV)
Wright State U (OH)
Youngstown State U (OH)

FORENSIC PSYCHOLOGY
Florida Inst of Technology (FL)
Gwynedd-Mercy Coll (PA)
John Jay Coll of Criminal Justice, the City U of NY (NY)
St. Ambrose U (IA)
Sam Houston State U (TX)
Tiffin U (OH)

FORENSIC SCIENCE AND TECHNOLOGY
Alvernia Coll (PA)
Baylor U (TX)
State U of NY Coll at Buffalo (NY)
Carroll Coll (WI)
Cedar Crest Coll (PA)
Chaminade U of Honolulu (HI)
Champlain Coll (VT)
Coll of the Ozarks (MO)
Columbia Coll (MO)
Eastern Kentucky U (KY)
Indiana U Bloomington (IN)
Inter American U of PR, Bayamón Campus (PR)
Jacksonville State U (AL)
John Jay Coll of Criminal Justice, the City U of NY (NY)
Keystone Coll (PA)
Long Island U, C.W. Post Campus (NY)
Loyola U New Orleans (LA)
Mercyhurst Coll (PA)
Mountain State U (WV)
Northwest Nazarene U (ID)
Our Lady of the Lake Coll (LA)
Saint Augustine's Coll (NC)
St. Edward's U (TX)
Saint Francis U (PA)
Sam Houston State U (TX)
Seattle U (WA)
Towson U (MD)
Tri-State U (IN)
U of Baltimore (MD)
U of Central Florida (FL)
U of Great Falls (MT)
U of Mississippi (MS)
U of New Haven (CT)
U of North Dakota (ND)
U of Windsor (ON, Canada)
Virginia Commonwealth U (VA)
Waynesburg Coll (PA)
West Virginia U (WV)

FOREST ENGINEERING
Oregon State U (OR)
State U of NY Coll of Environ Sci and Forestry (NY)
U of Maine (ME)
U of New Brunswick Fredericton (NB, Canada)
U of Washington (WA)

FOREST/FOREST RESOURCES MANAGEMENT
Clemson U (SC)
Louisiana State U and A&M Coll (LA)
North Carolina State U (NC)
State U of NY Coll of Environ Sci and Forestry (NY)
Sterling Coll (VT)
Texas A&M U (TX)
Université Laval (QC, Canada)
U of Alberta (AB, Canada)
The U of British Columbia (BC, Canada)
U of Minnesota, Twin Cities Campus (MN)
The U of Montana–Missoula (MT)
U of Washington (WA)
West Virginia U (WV)

FOREST HARVESTING PRODUCTION TECHNOLOGY
Saint Joseph's Coll of Maine (ME)

FOREST RESOURCES PRODUCTION AND MANAGEMENT
Sterling Coll (VT)

FORESTRY
Albright Coll (PA)
Baylor U (TX)
California Polytechnic State U, San Luis Obispo (CA)
Coll of Saint Benedict (MN)
Delaware State U (DE)
Humboldt State U (CA)
Iowa State U of Science and Technology (IA)
Lakehead U (ON, Canada)
Louisiana Tech U (LA)
Michigan State U (MI)
Michigan Technological U (MI)
Mississippi State U (MS)
Northland Coll (WI)
The Ohio State U (OH)
Oklahoma State U (OK)
Oregon State U (OR)
Purdue U (IN)
Saint John's U (MN)
Southern Illinois U Carbondale (IL)
State U of NY Coll of Environ Sci and Forestry (NY)
Sterling Coll (VT)
Texas A&M U (TX)
Thomas Edison State Coll (NJ)
Unity Coll (ME)
U of Alberta (AB, Canada)
U of Arkansas at Monticello (AR)
The U of British Columbia (BC, Canada)
U of Calif, Berkeley (CA)
U of Florida (FL)
U of Georgia (GA)
U of Idaho (ID)
U of Illinois at Urbana–Champaign (IL)
U of Maine (ME)
U of Massachusetts Amherst (MA)
U of Minnesota, Twin Cities Campus (MN)
U of Missouri–Columbia (MO)
The U of Montana–Missoula (MT)
U of Nevada, Reno (NV)
U of New Brunswick Fredericton (NB, Canada)
U of New Hampshire (NH)
The U of Tennessee (TN)
U of the District of Columbia (DC)
U of the South (TN)
U of Toronto (ON, Canada)
U of Vermont (VT)
U of Washington (WA)
U of Wisconsin–Madison (WI)
U of Wisconsin–Milwaukee (WI)
U of Wisconsin–Stevens Point (WI)
Utah State U (UT)
Virginia Polytechnic Inst and State U (VA)
Washington State U (WA)
West Virginia U (WV)

FORESTRY RELATED
Davis & Elkins Coll (WV)
Sterling Coll (VT)
Université Laval (QC, Canada)
Utah State U (UT)

FORESTRY TECHNOLOGY
Penn State U Abington Coll (PA)
Penn State U Altoona Coll (PA)
Penn State U at Erie, The Behrend Coll (PA)
Penn State U Beaver Campus of the Commonwealth Coll (PA)
Penn State U Berks Cmps of Berks-Lehigh Valley Coll (PA)
Penn State U Delaware County Campus of the Commonwealth Coll (PA)
Penn State U DuBois Campus of the Commonwealth Coll (PA)
Penn State U Fayette Campus of the Commonwealth Coll (PA)
Penn State U Hazleton Campus of the Commonwealth Coll (PA)
Penn State U Lehigh Valley Cmps of Berks-Lehigh Valley Coll (PA)
Penn State U McKeesport Campus of the Commonwealth Coll (PA)
Penn State U Mont Alto Campus of the Commonwealth Coll (PA)
Penn State U New Kensington Campus of the Commonwealth Coll (PA)
Penn State U Schuylkill Campus of the Capital Coll (PA)
Penn State U Shenango Campus of the Commonwealth Coll (PA)
Penn State U Univ Park Campus (PA)
Penn State U Wilkes-Barre Campus of the Commonwealth Coll (PA)
Penn State U Worthington Scranton Cmps Commonwealth Coll (PA)
Penn State U York Campus of the Commonwealth Coll (PA)

FOREST SCIENCES AND BIOLOGY
Auburn U (AL)
Canisius Coll (NY)
Colorado State U (CO)
Hampshire Coll (MA)
Memorial U of Newfoundland (NL, Canada)
Northern Arizona U (AZ)
Penn State U Abington Coll (PA)
Penn State U Altoona Coll (PA)
Penn State U at Erie, The Behrend Coll (PA)
Penn State U Beaver Campus of the Commonwealth Coll (PA)
Penn State U Berks Cmps of Berks-Lehigh Valley Coll (PA)
Penn State U Delaware County Campus of the Commonwealth Coll (PA)
Penn State U DuBois Campus of the Commonwealth Coll (PA)
Penn State U Fayette Campus of the Commonwealth Coll (PA)
Penn State U Hazleton Campus of the Commonwealth Coll (PA)
Penn State U Lehigh Valley Cmps of Berks-Lehigh Valley Coll (PA)
Penn State U McKeesport Campus of the Commonwealth Coll (PA)
Penn State U Mont Alto Campus of the Commonwealth Coll (PA)
Penn State U New Kensington Campus of the Commonwealth Coll (PA)
Penn State U Schuylkill Campus of the Capital Coll (PA)

Penn State U Shenango Campus of the Commonwealth Coll (PA)
Penn State U Univ Park Campus (PA)
Penn State U Wilkes-Barre Campus of the Commonwealth Coll (PA)
Penn State U Worthington Scranton Cmps Commonwealth Coll (PA)
Penn State U York Campus of the Commonwealth Coll (PA)
Sterling Coll (VT)
U of Georgia (GA)
U of Kentucky (KY)
U of Washington (WA)

FRENCH

Acadia U (NS, Canada)
Adelphi U (NY)
Adrian Coll (MI)
Agnes Scott Coll (GA)
Alabama State U (AL)
Albany State U (GA)
Albertus Magnus Coll (CT)
Albion Coll (MI)
Albright Coll (PA)
Alfred U (NY)
Allegheny Coll (PA)
Alma Coll (MI)
American U (DC)
Amherst Coll (MA)
Andrews U (MI)
Angelo State U (TX)
Antioch Coll (OH)
Appalachian State U (NC)
Aquinas Coll (MI)
Arizona State U (AZ)
Arkansas State U (AR)
Asbury Coll (KY)
Ashland U (OH)
Assumption Coll (MA)
Athabasca U (AB, Canada)
Atlantic Union Coll (MA)
Auburn U (AL)
Augsburg Coll (MN)
Augustana Coll (IL)
Augustana Coll (SD)
Augusta State U (GA)
Austin Coll (TX)
Baker U (KS)
Baldwin-Wallace Coll (OH)
Ball State U (IN)
Bard Coll (NY)
Barnard Coll (NY)
Barry U (FL)
Bates Coll (ME)
Baylor U (TX)
Bellarmine U (KY)
Beloit Coll (WI)
Benedictine Coll (KS)
Bennington Coll (VT)
Berea Coll (KY)
Berry Coll (GA)
Bethany Coll (WV)
Bethel U (MN)
Birmingham-Southern Coll (AL)
Bishop's U (QC, Canada)
Bloomsburg U of Pennsylvania (PA)
Boise State U (ID)
Boston Coll (MA)
Boston U (MA)
Bowdoin Coll (ME)
Bowling Green State U (OH)
Bradley U (IL)
Brandeis U (MA)
Bridgewater Coll (VA)
Brigham Young U (UT)
Brock U (ON, Canada)
Brooklyn Coll of the City U of NY (NY)
Brown U (RI)
Bryn Mawr Coll (PA)
Bucknell U (PA)
State U of NY Coll at Buffalo (NY)
Butler U (IN)
Cabrini Coll (PA)
Caldwell Coll (NJ)
California Lutheran U (CA)
California State U, Chico (CA)
California State U, Dominguez Hills (CA)
California State U, Fresno (CA)
California State U, Fullerton (CA)
California State U, Hayward (CA)
California State U, Long Beach (CA)
California State U, Los Angeles (CA)
California State U, Sacramento (CA)
California State U, San Bernardino (CA)
California State U, Stanislaus (CA)
California U of Pennsylvania (PA)
Calvin Coll (MI)
Campbell U (NC)
Canisius Coll (NY)
Capital U (OH)
Cardinal Stritch U (WI)
Carleton Coll (MN)
Carleton U (ON, Canada)
Carnegie Mellon U (PA)
Carroll Coll (MT)
Carson-Newman Coll (TN)
Carthage Coll (WI)
Case Western Reserve U (OH)
Catawba Coll (NC)
The Catholic U of America (DC)
Centenary Coll of Louisiana (LA)
Central Coll (IA)
Central Connecticut State U (CT)
Central Methodist Coll (MO)
Central Michigan U (MI)
Central Missouri State U (MO)
Centre Coll (KY)
Chapman U (CA)
Chatham Coll (PA)
Chestnut Hill Coll (PA)
Cheyney U of Pennsylvania (PA)
Christendom Coll (VA)
Christopher Newport U (VA)
Citadel, The Military Coll of South Carolina (SC)
City Coll of the City U of NY (NY)
Claremont McKenna Coll (CA)
Clarion U of Pennsylvania (PA)
Clark Atlanta U (GA)
Clarke Coll (IA)
Clark U (MA)
Cleveland State U (OH)
Coe Coll (IA)
Coker Coll (SC)
Colby Coll (ME)
Colgate U (NY)
Coll of Charleston (SC)
Coll of Mount Saint Vincent (NY)
The Coll of New Rochelle (NY)
Coll of Saint Benedict (MN)
Coll of St. Catherine (MN)
Coll of the Holy Cross (MA)
Coll of the Ozarks (MO)
The Coll of William and Mary (VA)
The Coll of Wooster (OH)
The Colorado Coll (CO)
Colorado State U (CO)
Columbia Coll (NY)
Columbia Coll (SC)
Columbia U, School of General Studies (NY)
Concordia Coll (MN)
Concordia U (QC, Canada)
Concordia U Coll of Alberta (AB, Canada)
Connecticut Coll (CT)
Converse Coll (SC)
Cornell Coll (IA)
Cornell U (NY)
Creighton U (NE)
Daemen Coll (NY)
Dalhousie U (NS, Canada)
Dartmouth Coll (NH)
Davidson Coll (NC)
Davis & Elkins Coll (WV)
Delaware State U (DE)
Denison U (OH)
DePaul U (IL)
DePauw U (IN)
Dickinson Coll (PA)
Dillard U (LA)
Doane Coll (NE)
Dominican U (IL)
Drew U (NJ)
Drury U (MO)
Duke U (NC)
Earlham Coll (IN)
East Carolina U (NC)
Eastern Kentucky U (KY)
Eastern Mennonite U (VA)
Eastern Michigan U (MI)
Eastern U (PA)
Eastern Washington U (WA)
East Stroudsburg U of Pennsylvania (PA)
Eckerd Coll (FL)
Edgewood Coll (WI)
Elizabethtown Coll (PA)
Elmhurst Coll (IL)
Elmira Coll (NY)
Elms Coll (MA)
Elon U (NC)
Emory & Henry Coll (VA)
Emory U (GA)
Erskine Coll (SC)
Fairfield U (CT)
Fairleigh Dickinson U, Florham (NJ)
Fairleigh Dickinson U, Teaneck-Metro Campus (NJ)
Fairmont State Coll (WV)
Florida Ag and Mech U (FL)
Florida Atlantic U (FL)
Florida Intl U (FL)
Florida State U (FL)
Fordham U (NY)
Fort Hays State U (KS)
Fort Valley State U (GA)
Franciscan U of Steubenville (OH)
Francis Marion U (SC)
Franklin and Marshall Coll (PA)
Franklin Coll (IN)
Furman U (SC)
Gallaudet U (DC)
Gardner-Webb U (NC)
Georgetown Coll (KY)
Georgetown U (DC)
The George Washington U (DC)
Georgia Coll & State U (GA)
Georgian Court U (NJ)
Georgia Southern U (GA)
Georgia State U (GA)
Gettysburg Coll (PA)
Gonzaga U (WA)
Gordon Coll (MA)
Goucher Coll (MD)
Grace Coll (IN)
Grambling State U (LA)
Grand Valley State U (MI)
Greensboro Coll (NC)
Greenville Coll (IL)
Grinnell Coll (IA)
Grove City Coll (PA)
Guilford Coll (NC)
Gustavus Adolphus Coll (MN)
Hamilton Coll (NY)
Hamline U (MN)
Hampden-Sydney Coll (VA)
Hanover Coll (IN)
Harding U (AR)
Hartwick Coll (NY)
Harvard U (MA)
Haverford Coll (PA)
Hendrix Coll (AR)
High Point U (NC)
Hillsdale Coll (MI)
Hiram Coll (OH)
Hobart and William Smith Colls (NY)
Hofstra U (NY)
Hollins U (VA)
Hood Coll (MD)
Hope Coll (MI)
Houghton Coll (NY)
Houston Baptist U (TX)
Howard U (DC)
Humboldt State U (CA)
Hunter Coll of the City U of NY (NY)
Idaho State U (ID)
Illinois Coll (IL)
Illinois State U (IL)
Illinois Wesleyan U (IL)
Immaculata U (PA)
Indiana State U (IN)
Indiana U Bloomington (IN)
Indiana U Northwest (IN)
Indiana U of Pennsylvania (PA)
Indiana U–Purdue U Fort Wayne (IN)
Indiana U–Purdue U Indianapolis (IN)
Indiana U South Bend (IN)
Indiana U Southeast (IN)
Iona Coll (NY)
Iowa State U of Science and Technology (IA)
Ithaca Coll (NY)
Jacksonville State U (AL)
Jacksonville U (FL)
John Carroll U (OH)
The Johns Hopkins U (MD)
Johnson C. Smith U (NC)
Juniata Coll (PA)
Kalamazoo Coll (MI)
Keene State Coll (NH)
Kennesaw State U (GA)
Kent State U (OH)
Kenyon Coll (OH)
King Coll (TN)
King's Coll (PA)
Knox Coll (IL)
Kutztown U of Pennsylvania (PA)
Lafayette Coll (PA)
Lake Erie Coll (OH)
Lake Forest Coll (IL)
Lakehead U (ON, Canada)
Lamar U (TX)
Lambuth U (TN)
Lane Coll (TN)
La Salle U (PA)
Laurentian U (ON, Canada)
Lawrence U (WI)
Lebanon Valley Coll (PA)
Lehigh U (PA)
Lehman Coll of the City U of NY (NY)
Le Moyne Coll (NY)
Lenoir-Rhyne Coll (NC)
Lewis & Clark Coll (OR)
Lincoln U (MO)
Lincoln U (PA)
Lindenwood U (MO)
Linfield Coll (OR)
Lipscomb U (TN)
Lock Haven U of Pennsylvania (PA)
Long Island U, C.W. Post Campus (NY)
Longwood U (VA)
Loras Coll (IA)
Louisiana Coll (LA)
Louisiana State U and A&M Coll (LA)
Louisiana State U in Shreveport (LA)
Louisiana Tech U (LA)
Loyola Coll in Maryland (MD)
Loyola Marymount U (CA)
Loyola U Chicago (IL)
Loyola U New Orleans (LA)
Luther Coll (IA)
Lycoming Coll (PA)
Lynchburg Coll (VA)
Macalester Coll (MN)
Madonna U (MI)
Manchester Coll (IN)
Manhattan Coll (NY)
Manhattanville Coll (NY)
Mansfield U of Pennsylvania (PA)
Marian Coll (IN)
Marist Coll (NY)
Marlboro Coll (VT)
Marquette U (WI)
Mary Baldwin Coll (VA)
Marymount Coll of Fordham U (NY)
Mary Washington Coll (VA)
Marywood U (PA)
McDaniel Coll (MD)
McGill U (QC, Canada)
McMurry U (TX)
McNeese State U (LA)
Memorial U of Newfoundland (NL, Canada)
Mercer U (GA)
Mercy Coll (NY)
Mercyhurst Coll (PA)
Meredith Coll (NC)
Merrimack Coll (MA)
Messiah Coll (PA)
Methodist Coll (NC)
Miami U (OH)
Miami U Hamilton (OH)
Michigan State U (MI)
Middlebury Coll (VT)
Millersville U of Pennsylvania (PA)
Millikin U (IL)
Millsaps Coll (MS)
Mills Coll (CA)
Minnesota State U Mankato (MN)
Minot State U (ND)
Mississippi Coll (MS)
Missouri Southern State U (MO)
Missouri Western State Coll (MO)
Molloy Coll (NY)
Monmouth Coll (IL)
Montclair State U (NJ)
Moravian Coll (PA)
Morehead State U (KY)
Morehouse Coll (GA)
Mount Allison U (NB, Canada)
Mount Holyoke Coll (MA)
Mount Mary Coll (WI)
Mount St. Mary's Coll (CA)
Mount Saint Mary's Coll and Sem (MD)
Mount Saint Vincent U (NS, Canada)
Mount Union Coll (OH)
Muhlenberg Coll (PA)
Murray State U (KY)
Nazareth Coll of Rochester (NY)
Nebraska Wesleyan U (NE)
Newberry Coll (SC)
New Coll of Florida (FL)
New York U (NY)
Niagara U (NY)
Nicholls State U (LA)
North Carolina Central U (NC)
North Carolina State U (NC)
North Central Coll (IL)
North Dakota State U (ND)
Northeastern Illinois U (IL)
Northeastern U (MA)
Northern Arizona U (AZ)
Northern Illinois U (IL)
Northern Michigan U (MI)
Northern State U (SD)
North Georgia Coll & State U (GA)
North Park U (IL)
Northwestern U (IL)
Notre Dame de Namur U (CA)
Oakland U (MI)
Oberlin Coll (OH)
Occidental Coll (CA)
Ohio Northern U (OH)
The Ohio State U (OH)
Ohio U (OH)
Ohio Wesleyan U (OH)
Oklahoma Baptist U (OK)
Oklahoma City U (OK)
Oklahoma State U (OK)
Old Dominion U (VA)
Oral Roberts U (OK)
Oregon State U (OR)
Otterbein Coll (OH)
Ouachita Baptist U (AR)
Pace U (NY)
Pacific Lutheran U (WA)
Pacific Union Coll (CA)
Pacific U (OR)
Penn State U Abington Coll (PA)
Penn State U Altoona Coll (PA)
Penn State U at Erie, The Behrend Coll (PA)
Penn State U Beaver Campus of the Commonwealth Coll (PA)
Penn State U Berks Cmps of Berks-Lehigh Valley Coll (PA)
Penn State U Delaware County Campus of the Commonwealth Coll (PA)
Penn State U DuBois Campus of the Commonwealth Coll (PA)
Penn State U Fayette Campus of the Commonwealth Coll (PA)
Penn State U Hazleton Campus of the Commonwealth Coll (PA)
Penn State U Lehigh Valley Cmps of Berks-Lehigh Valley Coll (PA)
Penn State U McKeesport Campus of the Commonwealth Coll (PA)
Penn State U Mont Alto Campus of the Commonwealth Coll (PA)
Penn State U New Kensington Campus of the Commonwealth Coll (PA)
Penn State U Schuylkill Campus of the Capital Coll (PA)
Penn State U Shenango Campus of the Commonwealth Coll (PA)
Penn State U Univ Park Campus (PA)
Penn State U Wilkes-Barre Campus of the Commonwealth Coll (PA)
Penn State U Worthington Scranton Cmps Commonwealth Coll (PA)
Penn State U York Campus of the Commonwealth Coll (PA)
Pepperdine U, Malibu (CA)
Pittsburg State U (KS)
Pitzer Coll (CA)
Plymouth State U (NH)
Pomona Coll (CA)
Pontifical Catholic U of Puerto Rico (PR)
Portland State U (OR)
Presbyterian Coll (SC)
Princeton U (NJ)
Principia Coll (IL)
Providence Coll (RI)
Queens Coll of the City U of NY (NY)
Queen's U at Kingston (ON, Canada)
Randolph-Macon Coll (VA)
Randolph-Macon Woman's Coll (VA)
Redeemer U Coll (ON, Canada)
Reed Coll (OR)
Regis U (CO)
Rhode Island Coll (RI)
Rhodes Coll (TN)
Rice U (TX)
Rider U (NJ)
Ripon Coll (WI)
Rivier Coll (NH)
Roanoke Coll (VA)
Rockford Coll (IL)
Rockhurst U (MO)
Rollins Coll (FL)
Roosevelt U (IL)
Rosemont Coll (PA)
Rutgers, The State U of New Jersey, Camden (NJ)
Rutgers, The State U of New Jersey, Newark (NJ)
Rutgers, The State U of New Jersey, New Brunswick/Piscataway (NJ)
Saginaw Valley State U (MI)
St. Ambrose U (IA)
Saint Anselm Coll (NH)
St. Bonaventure U (NY)
St. Cloud State U (MN)
St. Francis Coll (NY)
Saint Francis U (PA)
St. Francis Xavier U (NS, Canada)

St. John Fisher Coll (NY)
St. John's Coll (NM)
Saint John's U (MN)
St. John's U (NY)
Saint Joseph's U (PA)
St. Lawrence U (NY)
Saint Louis U (MO)
Saint Mary-of-the-Woods Coll (IN)
Saint Mary's Coll (IN)
Saint Mary's Coll of California (CA)
Saint Mary's U of Minnesota (MN)
St. Mary's U of San Antonio (TX)
Saint Michael's Coll (VT)
St. Norbert Coll (WI)
St. Olaf Coll (MN)
St. Thomas U (NB, Canada)
Saint Vincent Coll (PA)
Salem Coll (NC)
Salisbury U (MD)
Salve Regina U (RI)
Samford U (AL)
Sam Houston State U (TX)
San Diego State U (CA)
San Francisco State U (CA)
San Jose State U (CA)
Santa Clara U (CA)
Sarah Lawrence Coll (NY)
Scripps Coll (CA)
Seattle Pacific U (WA)
Seattle U (WA)
Seton Hall U (NJ)
Shippensburg U of Pennsylvania (PA)
Shorter Coll (GA)
Siena Coll (NY)
Simmons Coll (MA)
Simon Fraser U (BC, Canada)
Simon's Rock Coll of Bard (MA)
Simpson Coll (IA)
Skidmore Coll (NY)
Slippery Rock U of Pennsylvania (PA)
Smith Coll (MA)
Sonoma State U (CA)
South Carolina State U (SC)
South Dakota State U (SD)
Southeastern Louisiana U (LA)
Southeast Missouri State U (MO)
Southern Connecticut State U (CT)
Southern Illinois U Carbondale (IL)
Southern Methodist U (TX)
Southern Oregon U (OR)
Southern U and A&M Coll (LA)
Southern Utah U (UT)
Southwestern U (TX)
Southwest Missouri State U (MO)
Spelman Coll (GA)
Stanford U (CA)
State U of NY at Binghamton (NY)
State U of NY at New Paltz (NY)
State U of NY at Oswego (NY)
Plattsburgh State U of NY (NY)
State U of NY Coll at Brockport (NY)
State U of NY Coll at Cortland (NY)
State U of NY Coll at Fredonia (NY)
State U of NY Coll at Geneseo (NY)
State U of NY Coll at Oneonta (NY)
State U of NY Coll at Potsdam (NY)
State U of West Georgia (GA)
Stetson U (FL)
Stony Brook U, State U of New York (NY)
Suffolk U (MA)
Susquehanna U (PA)
Swarthmore Coll (PA)
Sweet Briar Coll (VA)
Syracuse U (NY)
Talladega Coll (AL)
Taylor U (IN)
Tennessee State U (TN)
Tennessee Technological U (TN)
Texas A&M U (TX)
Texas A&M U–Commerce (TX)
Texas Christian U (TX)
Texas Southern U (TX)
Texas State U-San Marcos (TX)
Texas Tech U (TX)
Towson U (MD)
Transylvania U (KY)
Trent U (ON, Canada)
Trinity Coll (CT)
Trinity Coll (DC)
Trinity U (TX)
Truman State U (MO)
Tufts U (MA)
Tulane U (LA)
Union Coll (NE)
Union U (TN)
United States Military Acad (NY)
Université de Montréal (QC, Canada)
Université de Sherbrooke (QC, Canada)
Université Laval (QC, Canada)
State U of NY at Albany (NY)
U at Buffalo, The State U of New York (NY)
The U of Akron (OH)
The U of Alabama (AL)
The U of Alabama at Birmingham (AL)
U of Alberta (AB, Canada)
The U of Arizona (AZ)
U of Arkansas (AR)
U of Arkansas at Little Rock (AR)
The U of British Columbia (BC, Canada)
U of Calgary (AB, Canada)
U of Calif, Berkeley (CA)
U of Calif, Davis (CA)
U of Calif, Irvine (CA)
U of Calif, Los Angeles (CA)
U of Calif, Riverside (CA)
U of Calif, San Diego (CA)
U of Calif, Santa Barbara (CA)
U of Calif, Santa Cruz (CA)
U of Central Arkansas (AR)
U of Central Florida (FL)
U of Chicago (IL)
U of Cincinnati (OH)
U of Colorado at Boulder (CO)
U of Colorado at Denver (CO)
U of Connecticut (CT)
U of Dallas (TX)
U of Dayton (OH)
U of Delaware (DE)
U of Denver (CO)
U of Evansville (IN)
U of Florida (FL)
U of Georgia (GA)
U of Guelph (ON, Canada)
U of Hawaii at Manoa (HI)
U of Houston (TX)
U of Idaho (ID)
U of Illinois at Chicago (IL)
U of Illinois at Urbana–Champaign (IL)
U of Indianapolis (IN)
The U of Iowa (IA)
U of Kansas (KS)
U of Kentucky (KY)
U of King's Coll (NS, Canada)
U of La Verne (CA)
The U of Lethbridge (AB, Canada)
U of Louisiana at Lafayette (LA)
U of Louisville (KY)
U of Maine (ME)
U of Maine at Fort Kent (ME)
U of Manitoba (MB, Canada)
U of Maryland, Baltimore County (MD)
U of Maryland, Coll Park (MD)
U of Massachusetts Amherst (MA)
U of Massachusetts Boston (MA)
U of Massachusetts Dartmouth (MA)
U of Miami (FL)
U of Michigan (MI)
U of Michigan–Dearborn (MI)
U of Michigan–Flint (MI)
U of Minnesota, Morris (MN)
U of Minnesota, Twin Cities Campus (MN)
U of Mississippi (MS)
U of Missouri–Columbia (MO)
U of Missouri–Kansas City (MO)
U of Missouri–St. Louis (MO)
The U of Montana–Missoula (MT)
U of Montevallo (AL)
U of Nebraska at Omaha (NE)
U of Nebraska–Lincoln (NE)
U of Nevada, Las Vegas (NV)
U of Nevada, Reno (NV)
U of New Brunswick Fredericton (NB, Canada)
U of New Hampshire (NH)
U of New Mexico (NM)
U of New Orleans (LA)
The U of North Carolina at Asheville (NC)
The U of North Carolina at Charlotte (NC)
The U of North Carolina at Greensboro (NC)
The U of North Carolina at Wilmington (NC)
U of North Dakota (ND)
U of Northern Colorado (CO)
U of Northern Iowa (IA)
U of North Texas (TX)
U of Notre Dame (IN)
U of Oklahoma (OK)
U of Oregon (OR)
U of Ottawa (ON, Canada)
U of Pennsylvania (PA)
U of Pittsburgh (PA)
U of Prince Edward Island (PE, Canada)
U of Puget Sound (WA)
U of Redlands (CA)
U of Regina (SK, Canada)
U of Rhode Island (RI)
U of Richmond (VA)
U of Rochester (NY)
U of St. Thomas (MN)
U of St. Thomas (TX)
U of San Diego (CA)
U of San Francisco (CA)
U of Saskatchewan (SK, Canada)
The U of Scranton (PA)
U of South Carolina (SC)
U of South Carolina Spartanburg (SC)
The U of South Dakota (SD)
U of Southern California (CA)
U of Southern Indiana (IN)
U of Southern Maine (ME)
U of South Florida (FL)
The U of Tennessee (TN)
The U of Tennessee at Chattanooga (TN)
The U of Tennessee at Martin (TN)
The U of Texas at Arlington (TX)
The U of Texas at Austin (TX)
U of the District of Columbia (DC)
U of the Pacific (CA)
U of the South (TN)
U of Toledo (OH)
U of Toronto (ON, Canada)
U of Tulsa (OK)
U of Utah (UT)
U of Vermont (VT)
U of Victoria (BC, Canada)
U of Virginia (VA)
The U of Virginia's Coll at Wise (VA)
U of Washington (WA)
U of Waterloo (ON, Canada)
The U of Western Ontario (ON, Canada)
U of Windsor (ON, Canada)
U of Wisconsin–Eau Claire (WI)
U of Wisconsin–Green Bay (WI)
U of Wisconsin–La Crosse (WI)
U of Wisconsin–Madison (WI)
U of Wisconsin–Milwaukee (WI)
U of Wisconsin–Oshkosh (WI)
U of Wisconsin–Parkside (WI)
U of Wisconsin–Platteville (WI)
U of Wisconsin–River Falls (WI)
U of Wisconsin–Stevens Point (WI)
U of Wisconsin–Whitewater (WI)
U of Wyoming (WY)
Ursinus Coll (PA)
Utah State U (UT)
Valdosta State U (GA)
Valparaiso U (IN)
Vanderbilt U (TN)
Vassar Coll (NY)
Villanova U (PA)
Virginia Polytechnic Inst and State U (VA)
Virginia Wesleyan Coll (VA)
Wabash Coll (IN)
Wake Forest U (NC)
Walla Walla Coll (WA)
Walsh U (OH)
Wartburg Coll (IA)
Washburn U (KS)
Washington & Jefferson Coll (PA)
Washington and Lee U (VA)
Washington Coll (MD)
Washington State U (WA)
Washington U in St. Louis (MO)
Wayne State Coll (NE)
Wayne State U (MI)
Weber State U (UT)
Webster U (MO)
Wellesley Coll (MA)
Wells Coll (NY)
Wesleyan Coll (GA)
Wesleyan U (CT)
West Chester U of Pennsylvania (PA)
Western Illinois U (IL)
Western Kentucky U (KY)
Western Michigan U (MI)
Western State Coll of Colorado (CO)
Western Washington U (WA)
Westminster Coll (MO)
Westminster Coll (PA)
Westmont Coll (CA)
Wheaton Coll (IL)
Wheaton Coll (MA)
Wheeling Jesuit U (WV)
Whitman Coll (WA)
Whitworth Coll (WA)
Wichita State U (KS)
Widener U (PA)
Wilkes U (PA)
Willamette U (OR)
William Jewell Coll (MO)
Williams Coll (MA)
Wilson Coll (PA)
Winona State U (MN)
Wittenberg U (OH)
Wofford Coll (SC)
Wright State U (OH)
Xavier U (OH)
Xavier U of Louisiana (LA)
Yale U (CT)
York Coll of the City U of New York (NY)
York U (ON, Canada)
Youngstown State U (OH)

FRENCH AS A SECOND/ FOREIGN LANGUAGE (TEACHING)

Bishop's U (QC, Canada)
Campbell U (NC)
Université Laval (QC, Canada)
U of Windsor (ON, Canada)
Western Michigan U (MI)

FRENCH LANGUAGE TEACHER EDUCATION

Alma Coll (MI)
Appalachian State U (NC)
Arkansas State U (AR)
Auburn U (AL)
Baylor U (TX)
Berea Coll (KY)
Bethel U (MN)
Bishop's U (QC, Canada)
Bridgewater Coll (VA)
Brigham Young U (UT)
Brooklyn Coll of the City U of NY (NY)
California Lutheran U (CA)
California State U, Chico (CA)
Carroll Coll (WI)
The Catholic U of America (DC)
Centenary Coll of Louisiana (LA)
Central Michigan U (MI)
Central Missouri State U (MO)
Central Washington U (WA)
Coll of St. Catherine (MN)
Coll of the Ozarks (MO)
Colorado State U (CO)
Columbus State U (GA)
Concordia Coll (MN)
Daemen Coll (NY)
Delaware State U (DE)
Duquesne U (PA)
East Carolina U (NC)
Eastern Mennonite U (VA)
Eastern Michigan U (MI)
Eastern Washington U (WA)
Elmhurst Coll (IL)
Elmira Coll (NY)
Franklin Coll (IN)
Gardner-Webb U (NC)
Georgian Court U (NJ)
Georgia Southern U (GA)
Grace Coll (IN)
Grambling State U (LA)
Hardin-Simmons U (TX)
Hofstra U (NY)
Hope Coll (MI)
Illinois Wesleyan U (IL)
Indiana U Bloomington (IN)
Indiana U Northwest (IN)
Indiana U–Purdue U Fort Wayne (IN)
Indiana U–Purdue U Indianapolis (IN)
Indiana U South Bend (IN)
Iona Coll (NY)
Ithaca Coll (NY)
Juniata Coll (PA)
Kennesaw State U (GA)
Kent State U (OH)
King Coll (TN)
Lebanon Valley Coll (PA)
Le Moyne Coll (NY)
Lindenwood U (MO)
Lipscomb U (TN)
Long Island U, C.W. Post Campus (NY)
Louisiana State U in Shreveport (LA)
Louisiana Tech U (LA)
Manhattanville Coll (NY)
Mansfield U of Pennsylvania (PA)
Marymount Coll of Fordham U (NY)
Marywood U (PA)
McGill U (QC, Canada)
Messiah Coll (PA)
Miami U Hamilton (OH)
Minot State U (ND)
Missouri Western State Coll (MO)
Molloy Coll (NY)
Moravian Coll (PA)
Murray State U (KY)
New York U (NY)
Niagara U (NY)
North Carolina Central U (NC)
North Carolina State U (NC)
North Dakota State U (ND)
Northern Michigan U (MI)
Ohio Northern U (OH)
Ohio U (OH)
Ohio Wesleyan U (OH)
Oklahoma Baptist U (OK)
Oral Roberts U (OK)
Pace U (NY)
St. Ambrose U (IA)
St. Bonaventure U (NY)
St. Francis Coll (NY)
Saint Francis U (PA)
St. John's U (NY)
Saint Mary's U of Minnesota (MN)
Salve Regina U (RI)
San Diego State U (CA)
Southeastern Louisiana U (LA)
Southwest Missouri State U (MO)
State U of NY Coll at Brockport (NY)
State U of NY Coll at Cortland (NY)
State U of NY Coll at Oneonta (NY)
State U of NY Coll at Potsdam (NY)
Talladega Coll (AL)
Université Laval (QC, Canada)
State U of NY at Albany (NY)
The U of Akron (OH)
The U of Arizona (AZ)
U of Illinois at Chicago (IL)
U of Illinois at Urbana–Champaign (IL)
U of Indianapolis (IN)
The U of Iowa (IA)
U of Louisiana at Lafayette (LA)
U of Maine at Fort Kent (ME)
U of Michigan–Flint (MI)
U of Minnesota, Duluth (MN)
U of Missouri–St. Louis (MO)
U of Nebraska–Lincoln (NE)
The U of North Carolina at Chapel Hill (NC)
The U of North Carolina at Charlotte (NC)
The U of North Carolina at Greensboro (NC)
The U of North Carolina at Wilmington (NC)
U of Regina (SK, Canada)
The U of South Dakota (SD)
The U of Tennessee at Martin (TN)
U of Toledo (OH)
U of Utah (UT)
U of Waterloo (ON, Canada)
U of Windsor (ON, Canada)
U of Wisconsin–River Falls (WI)
Valparaiso U (IN)
Washington U in St. Louis (MO)
Weber State U (UT)
West Chester U of Pennsylvania (PA)
Western Carolina U (NC)
Western Michigan U (MI)
Wheeling Jesuit U (WV)
Widener U (PA)
William Woods U (MO)
Xavier U of Louisiana (LA)
Youngstown State U (OH)

FRENCH STUDIES

Barnard Coll (NY)
Brock U (ON, Canada)
Brown U (RI)
Carleton Coll (MN)
Case Western Reserve U (OH)
Claremont McKenna Coll (CA)
Coe Coll (IA)
The Colorado Coll (CO)
Columbia Coll (NY)
Concordia U Coll of Alberta (AB, Canada)
Fordham U (NY)
Mills Coll (CA)
New Coll of Florida (FL)
Saint Joseph's U (PA)
Simon's Rock Coll of Bard (MA)
Smith Coll (MA)
U of Victoria (BC, Canada)
U of Waterloo (ON, Canada)
U of Windsor (ON, Canada)
York U (ON, Canada)

FUNERAL SERVICE AND MORTUARY SCIENCE

Eastern Michigan U (MI)
Gannon U (PA)
Lindenwood U (MO)
Mount Ida Coll (MA)
Point Park U (PA)
St. John's U (NY)
Southern Illinois U Carbondale (IL)
Thiel Coll (PA)

U of Minnesota, Twin Cities Campus (MN)
U of the District of Columbia (DC)
Wayne State U (MI)

FURNITURE DESIGN AND MANUFACTURING
Ferris State U (MI)
Rhode Island School of Design (RI)
Rochester Inst of Technology (NY)

GAY/LESBIAN STUDIES
Cornell U (NY)
Hobart and William Smith Colls (NY)
Sarah Lawrence Coll (NY)

GENERAL RETAILING/ WHOLESALING
U of South Carolina (SC)

GENERAL STUDIES
Albertus Magnus Coll (CT)
Alfred U (NY)
Alverno Coll (WI)
Angelo State U (TX)
Antioch U Santa Barbara (CA)
Arkansas State U (AR)
Arkansas Tech U (AR)
Athabasca U (AB, Canada)
Avila U (MO)
Bluefield State Coll (WV)
Brenau U (GA)
Brewton-Parker Coll (GA)
State U of NY Coll at Buffalo (NY)
California Inst of Technology (CA)
Calumet Coll of Saint Joseph (IN)
Campbell U (NC)
Canisius Coll (NY)
Carroll Coll (MT)
The Catholic U of America (DC)
Central Christian Coll of Kansas (KS)
Central Coll (IA)
City U (WA)
Clearwater Christian Coll (FL)
Cleveland State U (OH)
Coll of Saint Mary (NE)
Columbia Intl U (SC)
Columbia Union Coll (MD)
Concordia U, St. Paul (MN)
Concordia U Wisconsin (WI)
Crown Coll (MN)
Cumberland Coll (KY)
Dallas Baptist U (TX)
DePaul U (IL)
Dordt Coll (IA)
Drexel U (PA)
East Central U (OK)
Eastern Kentucky U (KY)
Emporia State U (KS)
Fairleigh Dickinson U, Teaneck-Metro Campus (NJ)
Ferrum Coll (VA)
Florida Gulf Coast U (FL)
The Franciscan U (IA)
Georgia Southern U (GA)
God's Bible School and Coll (OH)
Hampton U (VA)
Harding U (AR)
Howard Payne U (TX)
Huron U USA in London(United Kingdom)
Idaho State U (ID)
Indiana State U (IN)
Indiana U Bloomington (IN)
Indiana U East (IN)
Indiana U Kokomo (IN)
Indiana U Northwest (IN)
Indiana U of Pennsylvania (PA)
Indiana U–Purdue U Fort Wayne (IN)
Indiana U–Purdue U Indianapolis (IN)
Indiana U South Bend (IN)
Indiana U Southeast (IN)
Johnson C. Smith U (NC)
Kent State U (OH)
Kutztown U of Pennsylvania (PA)
La Roche Coll (PA)
Liberty U (VA)
Long Island U, C.W. Post Campus (NY)
Louisiana State U and A&M Coll (LA)
Louisiana State U in Shreveport (LA)
Louisiana Tech U (LA)
Loyola U New Orleans (LA)
Madonna U (MI)
Marshall U (WV)
Marygrove Coll (MI)
Mayville State U (ND)
McNeese State U (LA)
Metropolitan State U (MN)
Michigan Technological U (MI)
Mid-Continent Coll (KY)
Minot State U (ND)
Morehead State U (KY)
Mount Marty Coll (SD)
Murray State U (KY)
New Coll of Florida (FL)
New Mexico State U (NM)
Nicholls State U (LA)
Northcentral U (AZ)
Northern Arizona U (AZ)
Northwestern State U of Louisiana (LA)
Northwestern U (IL)
Oakland City U (IN)
Ohio Dominican U (OH)
Ohio Northern U (OH)
Ohio U (OH)
Ohio Wesleyan U (OH)
Our Lady of Holy Cross Coll (LA)
Palm Beach Atlantic U (FL)
Pittsburg State U (KS)
Point Park U (PA)
Rochester Inst of Technology (NY)
Saginaw Valley State U (MI)
St. John's Coll (NM)
St. Joseph's Coll, New York (NY)
Saint Joseph's Coll of Maine (ME)
Samford U (AL)
Seattle Pacific U (WA)
Seton Hill U (PA)
Shawnee State U (OH)
Shepherd U (WV)
Shimer Coll (IL)
Shorter Coll (GA)
Siena Heights U (MI)
Simon Fraser U (BC, Canada)
Southeastern Louisiana U (LA)
Southeastern Oklahoma State U (OK)
Southeast Missouri State U (MO)
Southern Nazarene U (OK)
Southwestern Coll (KS)
Springfield Coll (MA)
Spring Hill Coll (AL)
State U of NY Inst of Tech at Utica/Rome (NY)
Texas A&M U–Texarkana (TX)
Texas Christian U (TX)
Texas Southern U (TX)
Texas Tech U (TX)
Trinity Western U (BC, Canada)
U of Calgary (AB, Canada)
U of Charleston (WV)
U of Connecticut (CT)
U of Dayton (OH)
U of Hartford (CT)
U of Idaho (ID)
U of Louisiana at Lafayette (LA)
The U of Maine at Augusta (ME)
U of Maine at Farmington (ME)
U of Maine at Machias (ME)
U of Mary (ND)
U of Mary Hardin-Baylor (TX)
U of Massachusetts Amherst (MA)
The U of Memphis (TN)
U of Miami (FL)
U of Michigan (MI)
U of Missouri–Columbia (MO)
U of Missouri–St. Louis (MO)
U of Mobile (AL)
U of Nebraska at Omaha (NE)
U of Nevada, Reno (NV)
U of New Mexico (NM)
U of New Orleans (LA)
U of North Alabama (AL)
U of North Texas (TX)
U of Phoenix Online Campus (AZ)
U of St. Thomas (TX)
U of Southern California (CA)
U of South Florida (FL)
The U of Texas–Pan American (TX)
U of the Ozarks (AR)
U of Toledo (OH)
U of Washington (WA)
U of Windsor (ON, Canada)
U of Wisconsin–Green Bay (WI)
U of Wisconsin–Stevens Point (WI)
Valdosta State U (GA)
Virginia Commonwealth U (VA)
Western Kentucky U (KY)
Western Michigan U (MI)
Western Washington U (WA)
West Texas A&M U (TX)
West Virginia U (WV)
William Carey Coll (MS)
Wilmington Coll (DE)
Winston-Salem State U (NC)
York Coll (NE)

GENETICS
Cornell U (NY)
Hampshire Coll (MA)
Iowa State U of Science and Technology (IA)
Ohio Wesleyan U (OH)
Rochester Inst of Technology (NY)

GENETICS RELATED
Washington State U (WA)

GEOCHEMISTRY
Bowdoin Coll (ME)
Bridgewater State Coll (MA)
Brown U (RI)
California Inst of Technology (CA)
Columbia Coll (NY)
Cornell U (NY)
Hampshire Coll (MA)
Harvard U (MA)
New Mexico Inst of Mining and Technology (NM)
Northern Arizona U (AZ)
Pomona Coll (CA)
San Diego State U (CA)
State U of NY at Oswego (NY)
State U of NY Coll at Cortland (NY)
State U of NY Coll at Fredonia (NY)
State U of NY Coll at Geneseo (NY)
U of Calif, Los Angeles (CA)
U of New Brunswick Fredericton (NB, Canada)
U of Waterloo (ON, Canada)
Western Michigan U (MI)

GEOGRAPHY
Appalachian State U (NC)
Aquinas Coll (MI)
Arizona State U (AZ)
Arkansas State U (AR)
Auburn U (AL)
Augustana Coll (IL)
Austin Peay State U (TN)
Ball State U (IN)
Barnard Coll (NY)
Bemidji State U (MN)
Bishop's U (QC, Canada)
Bloomsburg U of Pennsylvania (PA)
Boston U (MA)
Bowling Green State U (OH)
Bridgewater State Coll (MA)
Brigham Young U (UT)
Brock U (ON, Canada)
Bucknell U (PA)
State U of NY Coll at Buffalo (NY)
California State Polytechnic U, Pomona (CA)
California State U, Chico (CA)
California State U, Dominguez Hills (CA)
California State U, Fresno (CA)
California State U, Fullerton (CA)
California State U, Hayward (CA)
California State U, Long Beach (CA)
California State U, Los Angeles (CA)
California State U, Sacramento (CA)
California State U, San Bernardino (CA)
California State U, Stanislaus (CA)
California U of Pennsylvania (PA)
Calvin Coll (MI)
Canadian Mennonite U (MB, Canada)
Carleton U (ON, Canada)
Carroll Coll (WI)
Carthage Coll (WI)
Central Connecticut State U (CT)
Central Michigan U (MI)
Central Missouri State U (MO)
Central Washington U (WA)
Cheyney U of Pennsylvania (PA)
Chicago State U (IL)
City Coll of the City U of NY (NY)
Clarion U of Pennsylvania (PA)
Clark U (MA)
Colgate U (NY)
Concord Coll (WV)
Concordia U (IL)
Concordia U (NE)
Concordia U (QC, Canada)
Dartmouth Coll (NH)
DePaul U (IL)
Dickinson State U (ND)
East Carolina U (NC)
Eastern Illinois U (IL)
Eastern Kentucky U (KY)
Eastern Michigan U (MI)
Eastern Washington U (WA)
East Stroudsburg U of Pennsylvania (PA)
Edinboro U of Pennsylvania (PA)
Elmhurst Coll (IL)
Emory & Henry Coll (VA)
Excelsior Coll (NY)
Fayetteville State U (NC)
Florida Ag and Mech U (FL)
Florida Atlantic U (FL)
Florida Intl U (FL)
Florida State U (FL)
Framingham State Coll (MA)
Francis Marion U (SC)
Frostburg State U (MD)
George Mason U (VA)
The George Washington U (DC)
Georgia Southern U (GA)
Georgia State U (GA)
Gustavus Adolphus Coll (MN)
Hampshire Coll (MA)
Hofstra U (NY)
Humboldt State U (CA)
Hunter Coll of the City U of NY (NY)
Illinois State U (IL)
Indiana State U (IN)
Indiana U Bloomington (IN)
Indiana U of Pennsylvania (PA)
Indiana U–Purdue U Indianapolis (IN)
Indiana U Southeast (IN)
Jacksonville State U (AL)
Jacksonville U (FL)
James Madison U (VA)
The Johns Hopkins U (MD)
Kansas State U (KS)
Keene State Coll (NH)
Kent State U (OH)
Kutztown U of Pennsylvania (PA)
Lakehead U (ON, Canada)
Laurentian U (ON, Canada)
Lehman Coll of the City U of NY (NY)
Lock Haven U of Pennsylvania (PA)
Long Island U, C.W. Post Campus (NY)
Longwood U (VA)
Louisiana State U and A&M Coll (LA)
Louisiana State U in Shreveport (LA)
Louisiana Tech U (LA)
Macalester Coll (MN)
Mansfield U of Pennsylvania (PA)
Marshall U (WV)
Mary Washington Coll (VA)
McGill U (QC, Canada)
Memorial U of Newfoundland (NL, Canada)
Miami U (OH)
Miami U Hamilton (OH)
Michigan State U (MI)
Middlebury Coll (VT)
Millersville U of Pennsylvania (PA)
Minnesota State U Mankato (MN)
Montclair State U (NJ)
Morehead State U (KY)
Mount Allison U (NB, Canada)
Mount Holyoke Coll (MA)
Murray State U (KY)
New Mexico State U (NM)
Nipissing U (ON, Canada)
North Carolina Central U (NC)
Northeastern Illinois U (IL)
Northeastern State U (OK)
Northern Arizona U (AZ)
Northern Illinois U (IL)
Northern Michigan U (MI)
Northwestern U (IL)
The Ohio State U (OH)
Ohio U (OH)
Ohio Wesleyan U (OH)
Oklahoma State U (OK)
Old Dominion U (VA)
Oregon State U (OR)
Penn State U Abington Coll (PA)
Penn State U Altoona Coll (PA)
Penn State U at Erie, The Behrend Coll (PA)
Penn State U Beaver Campus of the Commonwealth Coll (PA)
Penn State U Berks Cmps of Berks-Lehigh Valley Coll (PA)
Penn State U Delaware County Campus of the Commonwealth Coll (PA)
Penn State U DuBois Campus of the Commonwealth Coll (PA)
Penn State U Fayette Campus of the Commonwealth Coll (PA)
Penn State U Hazleton Campus of the Commonwealth Coll (PA)
Penn State U Lehigh Valley Cmps of Berks-Lehigh Valley Coll (PA)
Penn State U McKeesport Campus of the Commonwealth Coll (PA)
Penn State U Mont Alto Campus of the Commonwealth Coll (PA)
Penn State U New Kensington Campus of the Commonwealth Coll (PA)
Penn State U Schuylkill Campus of the Capital Coll (PA)
Penn State U Shenango Campus of the Commonwealth Coll (PA)
Penn State U Univ Park Campus (PA)
Penn State U Wilkes-Barre Campus of the Commonwealth Coll (PA)
Penn State U Worthington Scranton Cmps Commonwealth Coll (PA)
Penn State U York Campus of the Commonwealth Coll (PA)
Pittsburg State U (KS)
Plymouth State U (NH)
Portland State U (OR)
Queen's U at Kingston (ON, Canada)
Radford U (VA)
Rhode Island Coll (RI)
Roosevelt U (IL)
Rowan U (NJ)
Rutgers, The State U of New Jersey, New Brunswick/Piscataway (NJ)
Ryerson U (ON, Canada)
St. Cloud State U (MN)
Salem State Coll (MA)
Salisbury U (MD)
Samford U (AL)
Sam Houston State U (TX)
San Diego State U (CA)
San Francisco State U (CA)
San Jose State U (CA)
Shippensburg U of Pennsylvania (PA)
Simon Fraser U (BC, Canada)
Simon's Rock Coll of Bard (MA)
Slippery Rock U of Pennsylvania (PA)
Sonoma State U (CA)
South Dakota State U (SD)
Southeast Missouri State U (MO)
Southern Connecticut State U (CT)
Southern Illinois U Carbondale (IL)
Southern Illinois U Edwardsville (IL)
Southern Oregon U (OR)
Southwest Missouri State U (MO)
State U of NY at Binghamton (NY)
State U of NY at New Paltz (NY)
Plattsburgh State U of NY (NY)
State U of NY Coll at Cortland (NY)
State U of NY Coll at Geneseo (NY)
State U of NY Coll at Oneonta (NY)
State U of NY Coll at Potsdam (NY)
State U of West Georgia (GA)
Stetson U (FL)
Syracuse U (NY)
Texas A&M U (TX)
Texas A&M U–Commerce (TX)
Texas A&M U–Kingsville (TX)
Texas State U-San Marcos (TX)
Texas Tech U (TX)
Towson U (MD)
Trent U (ON, Canada)
Trinity Western U (BC, Canada)
United States Air Force Acad (CO)
United States Military Acad (NY)
Université de Montréal (QC, Canada)
Université de Sherbrooke (QC, Canada)
Université Laval (QC, Canada)
State U of NY at Albany (NY)
U at Buffalo, The State U of New York (NY)
U Coll of the Cariboo (BC, Canada)
U Coll of the Fraser Valley (BC, Canada)
The U of Akron (OH)
The U of Alabama (AL)
U of Alaska Fairbanks (AK)
U of Alberta (AB, Canada)
The U of Arizona (AZ)
U of Arkansas (AR)
The U of British Columbia (BC, Canada)
U of Calgary (AB, Canada)
U of Calif, Berkeley (CA)
U of Calif, Los Angeles (CA)
U of Calif, Santa Barbara (CA)
U of Central Arkansas (AR)
U of Chicago (IL)
U of Cincinnati (OH)
U of Colorado at Boulder (CO)
U of Colorado at Colorado Springs (CO)
U of Colorado at Denver (CO)
U of Connecticut (CT)
U of Delaware (DE)
U of Denver (CO)
U of Florida (FL)
U of Georgia (GA)
U of Guelph (ON, Canada)

U of Hawaii at Hilo (HI)
U of Hawaii at Manoa (HI)
U of Houston–Clear Lake (TX)
U of Idaho (ID)
U of Illinois at Urbana–Champaign (IL)
The U of Iowa (IA)
U of Kansas (KS)
U of Kentucky (KY)
The U of Lethbridge (AB, Canada)
U of Louisville (KY)
U of Maine at Farmington (ME)
U of Manitoba (MB, Canada)
U of Maryland, Baltimore County (MD)
U of Maryland, Coll Park (MD)
U of Massachusetts Amherst (MA)
U of Massachusetts Boston (MA)
The U of Memphis (TN)
U of Miami (FL)
U of Michigan (MI)
U of Michigan–Flint (MI)
U of Minnesota, Duluth (MN)
U of Minnesota, Twin Cities Campus (MN)
U of Missouri–Columbia (MO)
U of Missouri–Kansas City (MO)
The U of Montana–Missoula (MT)
U of Nebraska at Omaha (NE)
U of Nebraska–Lincoln (NE)
U of Nevada, Reno (NV)
U of New Hampshire (NH)
U of New Mexico (NM)
U of New Orleans (LA)
U of North Alabama (AL)
The U of North Carolina at Chapel Hill (NC)
The U of North Carolina at Charlotte (NC)
The U of North Carolina at Greensboro (NC)
The U of North Carolina at Wilmington (NC)
U of North Dakota (ND)
U of Northern Colorado (CO)
U of Northern Iowa (IA)
U of North Texas (TX)
U of Oklahoma (OK)
U of Oregon (OR)
U of Ottawa (ON, Canada)
U of Pittsburgh at Johnstown (PA)
U of Regina (SK, Canada)
U of St. Thomas (MN)
U of Saskatchewan (SK, Canada)
U of South Alabama (AL)
U of South Carolina (SC)
U of Southern California (CA)
U of Southern Maine (ME)
U of South Florida (FL)
The U of Tennessee (TN)
The U of Tennessee at Martin (TN)
The U of Texas at Austin (TX)
The U of Texas at Dallas (TX)
U of the District of Columbia (DC)
U of Toledo (OH)
U of Toronto (ON, Canada)
U of Utah (UT)
U of Vermont (VT)
U of Victoria (BC, Canada)
U of Washington (WA)
U of Waterloo (ON, Canada)
The U of Western Ontario (ON, Canada)
U of Wisconsin–Eau Claire (WI)
U of Wisconsin–La Crosse (WI)
U of Wisconsin–Madison (WI)
U of Wisconsin–Milwaukee (WI)
U of Wisconsin–Oshkosh (WI)
U of Wisconsin–Parkside (WI)
U of Wisconsin–Platteville (WI)
U of Wisconsin–River Falls (WI)
U of Wisconsin–Stevens Point (WI)
U of Wisconsin–Whitewater (WI)
U of Wyoming (WY)
Utah State U (UT)
Valparaiso U (IN)
Vassar Coll (NY)
Villanova U (PA)
Virginia Polytechnic Inst and State U (VA)
Wayne State Coll (NE)
Wayne State U (MI)
Weber State U (UT)
West Chester U of Pennsylvania (PA)
Western Carolina U (NC)
Western Illinois U (IL)
Western Kentucky U (KY)
Western Michigan U (MI)
Western Oregon U (OR)
Western Washington U (WA)
Westfield State Coll (MA)
West Texas A&M U (TX)
West Virginia U (WV)
William Paterson U of New Jersey (NJ)
Wittenberg U (OH)
Worcester State Coll (MA)
Wright State U (OH)
York U (ON, Canada)
Youngstown State U (OH)

GEOGRAPHY RELATED
Brigham Young U (UT)
Cornell U (NY)
U of Calif, Los Angeles (CA)

GEOGRAPHY TEACHER EDUCATION
Bishop's U (QC, Canada)
Carroll Coll (WI)
Concordia U (NE)
Cumberland U (TN)
Northern Michigan U (MI)
Shawnee State U (OH)
Université Laval (QC, Canada)
The U of Iowa (IA)
U of Windsor (ON, Canada)
Valparaiso U (IN)
Western Michigan U (MI)

GEOLOGICAL AND EARTH SCIENCES/GEOSCIENCES RELATED
Baylor U (TX)
Brigham Young U (UT)
Bucknell U (PA)
California State U, Chico (CA)
Cornell U (NY)
Georgia Inst of Technology (GA)
Lehigh U (PA)
Ohio U (OH)
Penn State U Abington Coll (PA)
Penn State U Altoona Coll (PA)
Penn State U at Erie, The Behrend Coll (PA)
Penn State U Beaver Campus of the Commonwealth Coll (PA)
Penn State U Berks Cmps of Berks-Lehigh Valley Coll (PA)
Penn State U Delaware County Campus of the Commonwealth Coll (PA)
Penn State U DuBois Campus of the Commonwealth Coll (PA)
Penn State U Fayette Campus of the Commonwealth Coll (PA)
Penn State U Hazleton Campus of the Commonwealth Coll (PA)
Penn State U Lehigh Valley Cmps of Berks-Lehigh Valley Coll (PA)
Penn State U McKeesport Campus of the Commonwealth Coll (PA)
Penn State U Mont Alto Campus of the Commonwealth Coll (PA)
Penn State U New Kensington Campus of the Commonwealth Coll (PA)
Penn State U Schuylkill Campus of the Capital Coll (PA)
Penn State U Shenango Campus of the Commonwealth Coll (PA)
Penn State U Univ Park Campus (PA)
Penn State U Wilkes-Barre Campus of the Commonwealth Coll (PA)
Penn State U Worthington Scranton Cmps Commonwealth Coll (PA)
Penn State U York Campus of the Commonwealth Coll (PA)
Princeton U (NJ)
San Diego State U (CA)
San Jose State U (CA)
Southeast Missouri State U (MO)
State U of NY Coll at Brockport (NY)
State U of West Georgia (GA)
Texas A&M U (TX)
Towson U (MD)
The U of Akron (OH)
U of Arkansas (AR)
U of Calif, Los Angeles (CA)
U of Hawaii at Manoa (HI)
U of Miami (FL)
U of Nevada, Las Vegas (NV)
U of Northern Iowa (IA)
U of Oklahoma (OK)
U of Pittsburgh (PA)
The U of Texas at Austin (TX)
U of Utah (UT)
U of Wyoming (WY)
Washington and Lee U (VA)
Western Michigan U (MI)
Yale U (CT)

GEOLOGICAL ENGINEERING
U of North Dakota (ND)

GEOLOGICAL/GEOPHYSICAL ENGINEERING
Auburn U (AL)
Colorado School of Mines (CO)
Cornell U (NY)
Harvard U (MA)
Laurentian U (ON, Canada)
Memorial U of Newfoundland (NL, Canada)
Michigan Technological U (MI)
Montana Tech of The U of Montana (MT)
New Jersey Inst of Technology (NJ)
Oregon State U (OR)
Queen's U at Kingston (ON, Canada)
Rutgers, The State U of New Jersey, Newark (NJ)
South Dakota School of Mines and Technology (SD)
Tufts U (MA)
Université Laval (QC, Canada)
The U of Akron (OH)
U of Alaska Fairbanks (AK)
The U of Arizona (AZ)
The U of British Columbia (BC, Canada)
U of Calgary (AB, Canada)
U of Calif, Berkeley (CA)
U of Calif, Los Angeles (CA)
U of Idaho (ID)
U of Manitoba (MB, Canada)
U of Minnesota, Twin Cities Campus (MN)
U of Mississippi (MS)
U of Missouri–Rolla (MO)
U of Nevada, Reno (NV)
U of New Brunswick Fredericton (NB, Canada)
U of Rochester (NY)
U of Saskatchewan (SK, Canada)
U of Utah (UT)
U of Waterloo (ON, Canada)

GEOLOGY/EARTH SCIENCE
Acadia U (NS, Canada)
Adams State Coll (CO)
Adrian Coll (MI)
Albion Coll (MI)
Alfred U (NY)
Allegheny Coll (PA)
Amherst Coll (MA)
Antioch Coll (OH)
Appalachian State U (NC)
Arizona State U (AZ)
Arkansas Tech U (AR)
Ashland U (OH)
Auburn U (AL)
Augustana Coll (IL)
Austin Peay State U (TN)
Baldwin-Wallace Coll (OH)
Ball State U (IN)
Barnard Coll (NY)
Bates Coll (ME)
Baylor U (TX)
Beloit Coll (WI)
Bemidji State U (MN)
Bloomsburg U of Pennsylvania (PA)
Boise State U (ID)
Boston Coll (MA)
Boston U (MA)
Bowdoin Coll (ME)
Bowling Green State U (OH)
Bradley U (IL)
Bridgewater State Coll (MA)
Brigham Young U (UT)
Brock U (ON, Canada)
Brooklyn Coll of the City U of NY (NY)
Brown U (RI)
Bryn Mawr Coll (PA)
Bucknell U (PA)
State U of NY Coll at Buffalo (NY)
California Inst of Technology (CA)
California Lutheran U (CA)
California State Polytechnic U, Pomona (CA)
California State U, Chico (CA)
California State U, Dominguez Hills (CA)
California State U, Fresno (CA)
California State U, Fullerton (CA)
California State U, Hayward (CA)
California State U, Long Beach (CA)
California State U, Los Angeles (CA)
California State U, Sacramento (CA)
California State U, San Bernardino (CA)
California State U, Stanislaus (CA)
California U of Pennsylvania (PA)
Calvin Coll (MI)
Carleton Coll (MN)
Carleton U (ON, Canada)
Case Western Reserve U (OH)
Castleton State Coll (VT)
Centenary Coll of Louisiana (LA)
Central Connecticut State U (CT)
Central Michigan U (MI)
Central Missouri State U (MO)
Central Washington U (WA)
City Coll of the City U of NY (NY)
Clarion U of Pennsylvania (PA)
Clark U (MA)
Clemson U (SC)
Cleveland State U (OH)
Colby Coll (ME)
Colgate U (NY)
Coll of Charleston (SC)
The Coll of William and Mary (VA)
The Coll of Wooster (OH)
The Colorado Coll (CO)
Colorado State U (CO)
Columbia Coll (NY)
Columbia U, School of General Studies (NY)
Columbus State U (GA)
Cornell Coll (IA)
Cornell U (NY)
Dalhousie U (NS, Canada)
Dartmouth Coll (NH)
Denison U (OH)
DePauw U (IN)
Dickinson Coll (PA)
Dickinson State U (ND)
Duke U (NC)
Earlham Coll (IN)
East Carolina U (NC)
Eastern Illinois U (IL)
Eastern Kentucky U (KY)
Eastern Michigan U (MI)
Eastern New Mexico U (NM)
Eastern Washington U (WA)
East Stroudsburg U of Pennsylvania (PA)
Edinboro U of Pennsylvania (PA)
Elizabeth City State U (NC)
Emporia State U (KS)
Excelsior Coll (NY)
Florida Atlantic U (FL)
Florida Intl U (FL)
Florida State U (FL)
Fort Hays State U (KS)
Fort Lewis Coll (CO)
Framingham State Coll (MA)
Franklin and Marshall Coll (PA)
Furman U (SC)
George Mason U (VA)
The George Washington U (DC)
Georgia Southern U (GA)
Georgia Southwestern State U (GA)
Georgia State U (GA)
Grand Valley State U (MI)
Guilford Coll (NC)
Gustavus Adolphus Coll (MN)
Hamilton Coll (NY)
Hampshire Coll (MA)
Hanover Coll (IN)
Hardin-Simmons U (TX)
Hartwick Coll (NY)
Harvard U (MA)
Haverford Coll (PA)
Hobart and William Smith Colls (NY)
Hofstra U (NY)
Hope Coll (MI)
Humboldt State U (CA)
Idaho State U (ID)
Illinois State U (IL)
Indiana State U (IN)
Indiana U Bloomington (IN)
Indiana U Northwest (IN)
Indiana U of Pennsylvania (PA)
Indiana U–Purdue U Fort Wayne (IN)
Indiana U–Purdue U Indianapolis (IN)
Iowa State U of Science and Technology (IA)
Jacksonville State U (AL)
James Madison U (VA)
The Johns Hopkins U (MD)
Juniata Coll (PA)
Kansas State U (KS)
Kean U (NJ)
Keene State Coll (NH)
Kent State U (OH)
Kutztown U of Pennsylvania (PA)
Lafayette Coll (PA)
Lakehead U (ON, Canada)
Lake Superior State U (MI)
Lamar U (TX)
La Salle U (PA)
Laurentian U (ON, Canada)
Lawrence U (WI)
Lehman Coll of the City U of NY (NY)
Lock Haven U of Pennsylvania (PA)
Long Island U, C.W. Post Campus (NY)
Longwood U (VA)
Louisiana State U and A&M Coll (LA)
Louisiana Tech U (LA)
Macalester Coll (MN)
Mansfield U of Pennsylvania (PA)
Marietta Coll (OH)
Marshall U (WV)
Mary Washington Coll (VA)
McGill U (QC, Canada)
McNeese State U (LA)
Memorial U of Newfoundland (NL, Canada)
Mercyhurst Coll (PA)
Miami U (OH)
Miami U Hamilton (OH)
Michigan State U (MI)
Michigan Technological U (MI)
Middlebury Coll (VT)
Middle Tennessee State U (TN)
Midwestern State U (TX)
Millersville U of Pennsylvania (PA)
Millsaps Coll (MS)
Minnesota State U Mankato (MN)
Minot State U (ND)
Mississippi State U (MS)
Montana State U–Bozeman (MT)
Montclair State U (NJ)
Moravian Coll (PA)
Morehead State U (KY)
Mount Allison U (NB, Canada)
Mount Holyoke Coll (MA)
Mount Union Coll (OH)
Murray State U (KY)
National U (CA)
New Jersey City U (NJ)
New Mexico Inst of Mining and Technology (NM)
New Mexico State U (NM)
North Carolina State U (NC)
North Dakota State U (ND)
Northeastern Illinois U (IL)
Northeastern U (MA)
Northern Arizona U (AZ)
Northern Illinois U (IL)
Northern Michigan U (MI)
Northland Coll (WI)
Northwestern U (IL)
Oberlin Coll (OH)
Occidental Coll (CA)
The Ohio State U (OH)
Ohio U (OH)
Ohio Wesleyan U (OH)
Oklahoma State U (OK)
Old Dominion U (VA)
Olivet Nazarene U (IL)
Oregon State U (OR)
Pace U (NY)
Pacific Lutheran U (WA)
Penn State U Abington Coll (PA)
Penn State U Altoona Coll (PA)
Penn State U at Erie, The Behrend Coll (PA)
Penn State U Beaver Campus of the Commonwealth Coll (PA)
Penn State U Berks Cmps of Berks-Lehigh Valley Coll (PA)
Penn State U Delaware County Campus of the Commonwealth Coll (PA)
Penn State U DuBois Campus of the Commonwealth Coll (PA)
Penn State U Fayette Campus of the Commonwealth Coll (PA)
Penn State U Hazleton Campus of the Commonwealth Coll (PA)
Penn State U Lehigh Valley Cmps of Berks-Lehigh Valley Coll (PA)
Penn State U McKeesport Campus of the Commonwealth Coll (PA)
Penn State U Mont Alto Campus of the Commonwealth Coll (PA)
Penn State U New Kensington Campus of the Commonwealth Coll (PA)
Penn State U Schuylkill Campus of the Capital Coll (PA)
Penn State U Shenango Campus of the Commonwealth Coll (PA)
Penn State U Univ Park Campus (PA)
Penn State U Wilkes-Barre Campus of the Commonwealth Coll (PA)
Penn State U Worthington Scranton Cmps Commonwealth Coll (PA)
Penn State U York Campus of the Commonwealth Coll (PA)
Pomona Coll (CA)
Portland State U (OR)
Purdue U (IN)

Queens Coll of the City U of NY (NY)
Queen's U at Kingston (ON, Canada)
Radford U (VA)
Rensselaer Polytechnic Inst (NY)
Rice U (TX)
The Richard Stockton Coll of New Jersey (NJ)
Rider U (NJ)
Rocky Mountain Coll (MT)
Rutgers, The State U of New Jersey, Newark (NJ)
Rutgers, The State U of New Jersey, New Brunswick/Piscataway (NJ)
St. Cloud State U (MN)
St. Francis Xavier U (NS, Canada)
St. Lawrence U (NY)
Saint Louis U (MO)
St. Mary's U of San Antonio (TX)
St. Norbert Coll (WI)
Salem State Coll (MA)
Sam Houston State U (TX)
San Diego State U (CA)
San Francisco State U (CA)
San Jose State U (CA)
Sarah Lawrence Coll (NY)
Scripps Coll (CA)
Shippensburg U of Pennsylvania (PA)
Simon Fraser U (BC, Canada)
Simon's Rock Coll of Bard (MA)
Skidmore Coll (NY)
Slippery Rock U of Pennsylvania (PA)
Smith Coll (MA)
Sonoma State U (CA)
South Dakota School of Mines and Technology (SD)
Southern Connecticut State U (CT)
Southern Illinois U Carbondale (IL)
Southern Methodist U (TX)
Southern Oregon U (OR)
Southern Utah U (UT)
Southwest Missouri State U (MO)
Stanford U (CA)
State U of NY at Binghamton (NY)
State U of NY at New Paltz (NY)
State U of NY at Oswego (NY)
Plattsburgh State U of NY (NY)
State U of NY Coll at Brockport (NY)
State U of NY Coll at Cortland (NY)
State U of NY Coll at Fredonia (NY)
State U of NY Coll at Geneseo (NY)
State U of NY Coll at Oneonta (NY)
State U of NY Coll at Potsdam (NY)
State U of West Georgia (GA)
Stony Brook U, State U of New York (NY)
Susquehanna U (PA)
Syracuse U (NY)
Tarleton State U (TX)
Tennessee Technological U (TN)
Texas A&M U (TX)
Texas A&M U–Commerce (TX)
Texas A&M U–Corpus Christi (TX)
Texas A&M U–Kingsville (TX)
Texas Christian U (TX)
Texas Tech U (TX)
Towson U (MD)
Trinity U (TX)
Tufts U (MA)
Tulane U (LA)
Union Coll (NY)
Université de Montréal (QC, Canada)
Université Laval (QC, Canada)
State U of NY at Albany (NY)
U at Buffalo, The State U of New York (NY)
The U of Akron (OH)
The U of Alabama (AL)
U of Alaska Fairbanks (AK)
U of Alberta (AB, Canada)
The U of Arizona (AZ)
U of Arkansas (AR)
U of Arkansas at Little Rock (AR)
The U of British Columbia (BC, Canada)
U of Calgary (AB, Canada)
U of Calif, Berkeley (CA)
U of Calif, Davis (CA)
U of Calif, Irvine (CA)
U of Calif, Los Angeles (CA)
U of Calif, Riverside (CA)
U of Calif, San Diego (CA)
U of Calif, Santa Barbara (CA)
U of Calif, Santa Cruz (CA)
U of Cincinnati (OH)
U of Colorado at Boulder (CO)
U of Connecticut (CT)
U of Dayton (OH)
U of Delaware (DE)
U of Florida (FL)
U of Georgia (GA)
U of Guelph (ON, Canada)
U of Hawaii at Hilo (HI)
U of Hawaii at Manoa (HI)
U of Houston (TX)
U of Idaho (ID)
U of Illinois at Chicago (IL)
U of Illinois at Urbana–Champaign (IL)
U of Indianapolis (IN)
The U of Iowa (IA)
U of Kansas (KS)
U of Kentucky (KY)
U of King's Coll (NS, Canada)
U of Louisiana at Lafayette (LA)
U of Maine (ME)
U of Maine at Farmington (ME)
U of Maine at Presque Isle (ME)
U of Manitoba (MB, Canada)
U of Maryland, Coll Park (MD)
U of Massachusetts Amherst (MA)
The U of Memphis (TN)
U of Miami (FL)
U of Michigan (MI)
U of Minnesota, Duluth (MN)
U of Minnesota, Morris (MN)
U of Minnesota, Twin Cities Campus (MN)
U of Mississippi (MS)
U of Missouri–Columbia (MO)
U of Missouri–Kansas City (MO)
U of Missouri–Rolla (MO)
The U of Montana–Missoula (MT)
U of Nebraska at Omaha (NE)
U of Nebraska–Lincoln (NE)
U of Nevada, Las Vegas (NV)
U of Nevada, Reno (NV)
U of New Brunswick Fredericton (NB, Canada)
U of New Hampshire (NH)
U of New Mexico (NM)
U of New Orleans (LA)
U of North Alabama (AL)
The U of North Carolina at Chapel Hill (NC)
The U of North Carolina at Charlotte (NC)
The U of North Carolina at Wilmington (NC)
U of North Dakota (ND)
U of Northern Colorado (CO)
U of Northern Iowa (IA)
U of North Texas (TX)
U of Notre Dame (IN)
U of Oklahoma (OK)
U of Oregon (OR)
U of Ottawa (ON, Canada)
U of Pennsylvania (PA)
U of Pittsburgh (PA)
U of Pittsburgh at Bradford (PA)
U of Pittsburgh at Johnstown (PA)
U of Puget Sound (WA)
U of Regina (SK, Canada)
U of Rhode Island (RI)
U of Rochester (NY)
U of St. Thomas (MN)
U of Saskatchewan (SK, Canada)
U of South Alabama (AL)
U of South Carolina (SC)
The U of South Dakota (SD)
U of Southern California (CA)
U of Southern Indiana (IN)
U of Southern Maine (ME)
U of South Florida (FL)
The U of Tennessee (TN)
The U of Tennessee at Chattanooga (TN)
The U of Tennessee at Martin (TN)
The U of Texas at Arlington (TX)
The U of Texas at Austin (TX)
The U of Texas at Dallas (TX)
U of the Pacific (CA)
U of the South (TN)
U of Toledo (OH)
U of Toronto (ON, Canada)
U of Tulsa (OK)
U of Utah (UT)
U of Vermont (VT)
U of Victoria (BC, Canada)
U of Washington (WA)
U of Waterloo (ON, Canada)
The U of Western Ontario (ON, Canada)
U of Windsor (ON, Canada)
U of Wisconsin–Eau Claire (WI)
U of Wisconsin–Green Bay (WI)
U of Wisconsin–Madison (WI)
U of Wisconsin–Milwaukee (WI)
U of Wisconsin–Oshkosh (WI)
U of Wisconsin–Parkside (WI)
U of Wisconsin–Platteville (WI)
U of Wisconsin–River Falls (WI)
U of Wyoming (WY)
Utah State U (UT)
Valparaiso U (IN)
Vanderbilt U (TN)
Vassar Coll (NY)
Virginia Polytechnic Inst and State U (VA)
Virginia Wesleyan Coll (VA)
Washington and Lee U (VA)
Washington State U (WA)
Washington U in St. Louis (MO)
Wayne State U (MI)
Weber State U (UT)
Wellesley Coll (MA)
Wesleyan U (CT)
West Chester U of Pennsylvania (PA)
Western Carolina U (NC)
Western Connecticut State U (CT)
Western Illinois U (IL)
Western Kentucky U (KY)
Western Michigan U (MI)
Western State Coll of Colorado (CO)
Western Washington U (WA)
West Texas A&M U (TX)
West Virginia U (WV)
Wheaton Coll (IL)
Whitman Coll (WA)
Wichita State U (KS)
Wilkes U (PA)
Williams Coll (MA)
Winona State U (MN)
Wittenberg U (OH)
Wright State U (OH)
York Coll of the City U of New York (NY)
York U (ON, Canada)
Youngstown State U (OH)

GEOPHYSICS AND SEISMOLOGY

Baylor U (TX)
Boise State U (ID)
Boston Coll (MA)
Bowdoin Coll (ME)
Brown U (RI)
California Inst of Technology (CA)
Cornell U (NY)
Eastern Michigan U (MI)
Hampshire Coll (MA)
Harvard U (MA)
Hope Coll (MI)
McGill U (QC, Canada)
Memorial U of Newfoundland (NL, Canada)
Michigan State U (MI)
Michigan Technological U (MI)
New Mexico Inst of Mining and Technology (NM)
Occidental Coll (CA)
Oregon State U (OR)
Rice U (TX)
St. Lawrence U (NY)
Saint Louis U (MO)
Southern Methodist U (TX)
Stanford U (CA)
State U of NY Coll at Fredonia (NY)
State U of NY Coll at Geneseo (NY)
Texas A&M U (TX)
Texas Tech U (TX)
Université de Sherbrooke (QC, Canada)
The U of Akron (OH)
U of Alberta (AB, Canada)
The U of British Columbia (BC, Canada)
U of Calgary (AB, Canada)
U of Calif, Los Angeles (CA)
U of Calif, Riverside (CA)
U of Calif, Santa Barbara (CA)
U of Calif, Santa Cruz (CA)
U of Chicago (IL)
U of Delaware (DE)
U of Houston (TX)
U of Minnesota, Twin Cities Campus (MN)
U of Missouri–Rolla (MO)
U of Nevada, Reno (NV)
U of New Brunswick Fredericton (NB, Canada)
U of New Orleans (LA)
U of Oklahoma (OK)
U of Saskatchewan (SK, Canada)
U of South Carolina (SC)
The U of Texas at Austin (TX)
U of Toronto (ON, Canada)
U of Tulsa (OK)
U of Utah (UT)
U of Victoria (BC, Canada)
U of Washington (WA)
U of Waterloo (ON, Canada)
The U of Western Ontario (ON, Canada)
U of Wisconsin–Madison (WI)
Western Michigan U (MI)
Western Washington U (WA)
Wright State U (OH)

GEOTECHNICAL ENGINEERING

Cornell U (NY)
Montana Tech of The U of Montana (MT)
York U (ON, Canada)

GERMAN

Adrian Coll (MI)
Agnes Scott Coll (GA)
Albion Coll (MI)
Alfred U (NY)
Allegheny Coll (PA)
Alma Coll (MI)
American U (DC)
Amherst Coll (MA)
Angelo State U (TX)
Antioch Coll (OH)
Aquinas Coll (MI)
Arizona State U (AZ)
Auburn U (AL)
Augsburg Coll (MN)
Augustana Coll (IL)
Augustana Coll (SD)
Austin Coll (TX)
Baker U (KS)
Baldwin-Wallace Coll (OH)
Ball State U (IN)
Bard Coll (NY)
Barnard Coll (NY)
Bates Coll (ME)
Baylor U (TX)
Bellarmine U (KY)
Beloit Coll (WI)
Bemidji State U (MN)
Bennington Coll (VT)
Berea Coll (KY)
Berry Coll (GA)
Bethany Coll (WV)
Birmingham-Southern Coll (AL)
Bishop's U (QC, Canada)
Bloomsburg U of Pennsylvania (PA)
Boise State U (ID)
Boston Coll (MA)
Boston U (MA)
Bowdoin Coll (ME)
Bowling Green State U (OH)
Bradley U (IL)
Brandeis U (MA)
Brigham Young U (UT)
Brock U (ON, Canada)
Brooklyn Coll of the City U of NY (NY)
Brown U (RI)
Bryn Mawr Coll (PA)
Bucknell U (PA)
Butler U (IN)
California Lutheran U (CA)
California State U, Chico (CA)
California State U, Fullerton (CA)
California State U, Long Beach (CA)
California U of Pennsylvania (PA)
Calvin Coll (MI)
Carleton Coll (MN)
Carleton U (ON, Canada)
Carnegie Mellon U (PA)
Carthage Coll (WI)
Case Western Reserve U (OH)
The Catholic U of America (DC)
Centenary Coll of Louisiana (LA)
Central Coll (IA)
Central Connecticut State U (CT)
Central Michigan U (MI)
Central Missouri State U (MO)
Centre Coll (KY)
Christopher Newport U (VA)
Citadel, The Military Coll of South Carolina (SC)
Claremont McKenna Coll (CA)
Coe Coll (IA)
Colby Coll (ME)
Colgate U (NY)
Coll of Charleston (SC)
Coll of Saint Benedict (MN)
Coll of the Holy Cross (MA)
Coll of the Ozarks (MO)
The Coll of William and Mary (VA)
The Coll of Wooster (OH)
The Colorado Coll (CO)
Colorado State U (CO)
Columbia Coll (NY)
Columbia U, School of General Studies (NY)
Concordia Coll (MN)
Concordia U (QC, Canada)
Concordia U Wisconsin (WI)
Connecticut Coll (CT)
Cornell Coll (IA)
Cornell U (NY)
Creighton U (NE)
Dalhousie U (NS, Canada)
Dana Coll (NE)
Dartmouth Coll (NH)
Davidson Coll (NC)
Denison U (OH)
DePaul U (IL)
DePauw U (IN)
Dickinson Coll (PA)
Dillard U (LA)
Doane Coll (NE)
Dordt Coll (IA)
Drew U (NJ)
Drury U (MO)
Duke U (NC)
Earlham Coll (IN)
East Carolina U (NC)
Eastern Mennonite U (VA)
Eastern Michigan U (MI)
Eckerd Coll (FL)
Edinboro U of Pennsylvania (PA)
Elizabethtown Coll (PA)
Elmhurst Coll (IL)
Emory U (GA)
Fairfield U (CT)
Florida Atlantic U (FL)
Florida Intl U (FL)
Florida State U (FL)
Fordham U (NY)
Fort Hays State U (KS)
Franciscan U of Steubenville (OH)
Franklin and Marshall Coll (PA)
Furman U (SC)
Georgetown Coll (KY)
Georgetown U (DC)
The George Washington U (DC)
Georgia Southern U (GA)
Georgia State U (GA)
Gettysburg Coll (PA)
Gonzaga U (WA)
Gordon Coll (MA)
Goshen Coll (IN)
Grace Coll (IN)
Graceland U (IA)
Grand Valley State U (MI)
Grinnell Coll (IA)
Guilford Coll (NC)
Gustavus Adolphus Coll (MN)
Hamilton Coll (NY)
Hamline U (MN)
Hampden-Sydney Coll (VA)
Hanover Coll (IN)
Hartwick Coll (NY)
Harvard U (MA)
Hastings Coll (NE)
Haverford Coll (PA)
Heidelberg Coll (OH)
Hendrix Coll (AR)
Hillsdale Coll (MI)
Hiram Coll (OH)
Hofstra U (NY)
Hollins U (VA)
Hood Coll (MD)
Hope Coll (MI)
Howard U (DC)
Humboldt State U (CA)
Hunter Coll of the City U of NY (NY)
Idaho State U (ID)
Illinois Coll (IL)
Illinois State U (IL)
Illinois Wesleyan U (IL)
Immaculata U (PA)
Indiana State U (IN)
Indiana U Bloomington (IN)
Indiana U of Pennsylvania (PA)
Indiana U–Purdue U Fort Wayne (IN)
Indiana U–Purdue U Indianapolis (IN)
Indiana U South Bend (IN)
Indiana U Southeast (IN)
Iowa State U of Science and Technology (IA)
Ithaca Coll (NY)
Jacksonville State U (AL)
John Carroll U (OH)
The Johns Hopkins U (MD)
Juniata Coll (PA)
Kalamazoo Coll (MI)
Kent State U (OH)
Kenyon Coll (OH)
Knox Coll (IL)
Kutztown U of Pennsylvania (PA)
Lafayette Coll (PA)
Lake Erie Coll (OH)
Lakeland Coll (WI)
Lambuth U (TN)
La Salle U (PA)
Lawrence U (WI)
Lebanon Valley Coll (PA)
Lehigh U (PA)
Lenoir-Rhyne Coll (NC)
Lewis & Clark Coll (OR)
Linfield Coll (OR)
Lipscomb U (TN)

Lock Haven U of Pennsylvania (PA)
Long Island U, C.W. Post Campus (NY)
Longwood U (VA)
Louisiana State U and A&M Coll (LA)
Loyola Coll in Maryland (MD)
Loyola U Chicago (IL)
Loyola U New Orleans (LA)
Luther Coll (IA)
Lycoming Coll (PA)
Manchester Coll (IN)
Mansfield U of Pennsylvania (PA)
Marlboro Coll (VT)
Marquette U (WI)
Mary Baldwin Coll (VA)
Mary Washington Coll (VA)
McDaniel Coll (MD)
McGill U (QC, Canada)
McMurry U (TX)
Memorial U of Newfoundland (NL, Canada)
Mercer U (GA)
Mercyhurst Coll (PA)
Messiah Coll (PA)
Miami U (OH)
Miami U Hamilton (OH)
Michigan State U (MI)
Middlebury Coll (VT)
Millersville U of Pennsylvania (PA)
Millikin U (IL)
Millsaps Coll (MS)
Minnesota State U Mankato (MN)
Minot State U (ND)
Missouri Southern State U (MO)
Moravian Coll (PA)
Morehouse Coll (GA)
Mount Allison U (NB, Canada)
Mount Holyoke Coll (MA)
Mount Saint Mary's Coll and Sem (MD)
Mount Saint Vincent U (NS, Canada)
Mount Union Coll (OH)
Muhlenberg Coll (PA)
Murray State U (KY)
Nazareth Coll of Rochester (NY)
Nebraska Wesleyan U (NE)
Newberry Coll (SC)
New Coll of Florida (FL)
New York U (NY)
North Central Coll (IL)
Northeastern U (MA)
Northern Arizona U (AZ)
Northern Illinois U (IL)
Northern State U (SD)
Northwestern U (IL)
Oakland U (MI)
Oberlin Coll (OH)
The Ohio State U (OH)
Ohio U (OH)
Ohio Wesleyan U (OH)
Oklahoma Baptist U (OK)
Oklahoma City U (OK)
Oklahoma State U (OK)
Old Dominion U (VA)
Oral Roberts U (OK)
Oregon State U (OR)
Pacific Lutheran U (WA)
Pacific U (OR)
Penn State U Abington Coll (PA)
Penn State U Altoona Coll (PA)
Penn State U at Erie, The Behrend Coll (PA)
Penn State U Beaver Campus of the Commonwealth Coll (PA)
Penn State U Berks Cmps of Berks-Lehigh Valley Coll (PA)
Penn State U Delaware County Campus of the Commonwealth Coll (PA)
Penn State U DuBois Campus of the Commonwealth Coll (PA)
Penn State U Fayette Campus of the Commonwealth Coll (PA)
Penn State U Hazleton Campus of the Commonwealth Coll (PA)
Penn State U Lehigh Valley Cmps of Berks-Lehigh Valley Coll (PA)
Penn State U McKeesport Campus of the Commonwealth Coll (PA)
Penn State U Mont Alto Campus of the Commonwealth Coll (PA)
Penn State U New Kensington Campus of the Commonwealth Coll (PA)
Penn State U Schuylkill Campus of the Capital Coll (PA)
Penn State U Shenango Campus of the Commonwealth Coll (PA)
Penn State U Univ Park Campus (PA)
Penn State U Wilkes-Barre Campus of the Commonwealth Coll (PA)
Penn State U Worthington Scranton Cmps Commonwealth Coll (PA)
Penn State U York Campus of the Commonwealth Coll (PA)
Pepperdine U, Malibu (CA)
Pitzer Coll (CA)
Pomona Coll (CA)
Portland State U (OR)
Presbyterian Coll (SC)
Princeton U (NJ)
Principia Coll (IL)
Queens Coll of the City U of NY (NY)
Queen's U at Kingston (ON, Canada)
Randolph-Macon Coll (VA)
Randolph-Macon Woman's Coll (VA)
Reed Coll (OR)
Rhodes Coll (TN)
Rice U (TX)
Rider U (NJ)
Ripon Coll (WI)
Rockford Coll (IL)
Rosemont Coll (PA)
Rutgers, The State U of New Jersey, Camden (NJ)
Rutgers, The State U of New Jersey, Newark (NJ)
Rutgers, The State U of New Jersey, New Brunswick/Piscataway (NJ)
St. Ambrose U (IA)
St. Cloud State U (MN)
St. John Fisher Coll (NY)
Saint John's U (MN)
Saint Joseph's U (PA)
St. Lawrence U (NY)
Saint Louis U (MO)
Saint Mary's Coll of California (CA)
St. Norbert Coll (WI)
St. Olaf Coll (MN)
Salem Coll (NC)
Samford U (AL)
Sam Houston State U (TX)
San Diego State U (CA)
San Francisco State U (CA)
San Jose State U (CA)
Sarah Lawrence Coll (NY)
Scripps Coll (CA)
Seattle Pacific U (WA)
Seattle U (WA)
Simon's Rock Coll of Bard (MA)
Simpson Coll (IA)
Skidmore Coll (NY)
Smith Coll (MA)
South Dakota State U (SD)
Southeast Missouri State U (MO)
Southern Connecticut State U (CT)
Southern Illinois U Carbondale (IL)
Southern Methodist U (TX)
Southern Oregon U (OR)
Southern Utah U (UT)
Southwestern U (TX)
Southwest Missouri State U (MO)
Stanford U (CA)
State U of NY at Binghamton (NY)
State U of NY at New Paltz (NY)
State U of NY at Oswego (NY)
State U of NY Coll at Cortland (NY)
State U of West Georgia (GA)
Stetson U (FL)
Stony Brook U, State U of New York (NY)
Susquehanna U (PA)
Swarthmore Coll (PA)
Sweet Briar Coll (VA)
Syracuse U (NY)
Tennessee Technological U (TN)
Texas A&M U (TX)
Texas Southern U (TX)
Texas State U-San Marcos (TX)
Texas Tech U (TX)
Towson U (MD)
Trent U (ON, Canada)
Trinity Coll (CT)
Trinity U (TX)
Truman State U (MO)
Tufts U (MA)
Tulane U (LA)
Union Coll (NE)
United States Military Acad (NY)
Université de Montréal (QC, Canada)
U at Buffalo, The State U of New York (NY)
The U of Akron (OH)
The U of Alabama (AL)
U of Alberta (AB, Canada)
The U of Arizona (AZ)
U of Arkansas (AR)
The U of British Columbia (BC, Canada)
U of Calgary (AB, Canada)
U of Calif, Berkeley (CA)
U of Calif, Davis (CA)
U of Calif, Irvine (CA)
U of Calif, Los Angeles (CA)
U of Calif, Riverside (CA)
U of Calif, San Diego (CA)
U of Calif, Santa Barbara (CA)
U of Calif, Santa Cruz (CA)
U of Chicago (IL)
U of Cincinnati (OH)
U of Connecticut (CT)
U of Dallas (TX)
U of Dayton (OH)
U of Delaware (DE)
U of Denver (CO)
U of Evansville (IN)
U of Florida (FL)
U of Georgia (GA)
U of Hawaii at Manoa (HI)
U of Houston (TX)
U of Idaho (ID)
U of Illinois at Chicago (IL)
U of Illinois at Urbana–Champaign (IL)
U of Indianapolis (IN)
The U of Iowa (IA)
U of Kentucky (KY)
U of King's Coll (NS, Canada)
U of La Verne (CA)
The U of Lethbridge (AB, Canada)
U of Maine (ME)
U of Manitoba (MB, Canada)
U of Maryland, Baltimore County (MD)
U of Maryland, Coll Park (MD)
U of Massachusetts Amherst (MA)
U of Massachusetts Boston (MA)
U of Miami (FL)
U of Michigan (MI)
U of Michigan–Dearborn (MI)
U of Minnesota, Morris (MN)
U of Minnesota, Twin Cities Campus (MN)
U of Mississippi (MS)
U of Missouri–Columbia (MO)
U of Missouri–Kansas City (MO)
U of Missouri–St. Louis (MO)
The U of Montana–Missoula (MT)
U of Nebraska at Omaha (NE)
U of Nebraska–Lincoln (NE)
U of Nevada, Las Vegas (NV)
U of Nevada, Reno (NV)
U of New Brunswick Fredericton (NB, Canada)
U of New Hampshire (NH)
U of New Mexico (NM)
The U of North Carolina at Asheville (NC)
The U of North Carolina at Chapel Hill (NC)
The U of North Carolina at Charlotte (NC)
The U of North Carolina at Greensboro (NC)
U of North Dakota (ND)
U of Northern Colorado (CO)
U of Northern Iowa (IA)
U of North Texas (TX)
U of Notre Dame (IN)
U of Oklahoma (OK)
U of Oregon (OR)
U of Ottawa (ON, Canada)
U of Pennsylvania (PA)
U of Pittsburgh (PA)
U of Prince Edward Island (PE, Canada)
U of Puget Sound (WA)
U of Redlands (CA)
U of Regina (SK, Canada)
U of Rhode Island (RI)
U of Richmond (VA)
U of Rochester (NY)
U of St. Thomas (MN)
U of Saskatchewan (SK, Canada)
The U of Scranton (PA)
U of South Carolina (SC)
The U of South Dakota (SD)
U of Southern California (CA)
U of Southern Indiana (IN)
U of South Florida (FL)
The U of Tennessee (TN)
The U of Texas at Arlington (TX)
The U of Texas at Austin (TX)
U of the Pacific (CA)
U of the South (TN)
U of Toledo (OH)
U of Toronto (ON, Canada)
U of Tulsa (OK)
U of Utah (UT)
U of Vermont (VT)
U of Victoria (BC, Canada)
U of Virginia (VA)
U of Washington (WA)
U of Waterloo (ON, Canada)
The U of Western Ontario (ON, Canada)
U of Windsor (ON, Canada)
U of Wisconsin–La Crosse (WI)
U of Wisconsin–Madison (WI)
U of Wisconsin–Milwaukee (WI)
U of Wisconsin–Oshkosh (WI)
U of Wisconsin–Parkside (WI)
U of Wisconsin–Platteville (WI)
U of Wisconsin–River Falls (WI)
U of Wisconsin–Stevens Point (WI)
U of Wisconsin–Whitewater (WI)
U of Wyoming (WY)
Ursinus Coll (PA)
Utah State U (UT)
Valparaiso U (IN)
Vanderbilt U (TN)
Vassar Coll (NY)
Villanova U (PA)
Virginia Polytechnic Inst and State U (VA)
Virginia Wesleyan Coll (VA)
Wabash Coll (IN)
Wake Forest U (NC)
Walla Walla Coll (WA)
Wartburg Coll (IA)
Washburn U (KS)
Washington & Jefferson Coll (PA)
Washington and Lee U (VA)
Washington Coll (MD)
Washington State U (WA)
Washington U in St. Louis (MO)
Wayne State Coll (NE)
Wayne State U (MI)
Weber State U (UT)
Webster U (MO)
Wellesley Coll (MA)
Wesleyan U (CT)
West Chester U of Pennsylvania (PA)
Western Carolina U (NC)
Western Kentucky U (KY)
Western Michigan U (MI)
Western Washington U (WA)
Westminster Coll (PA)
Wheaton Coll (IL)
Wheaton Coll (MA)
Whitman Coll (WA)
Willamette U (OR)
Williams Coll (MA)
Winona State U (MN)
Wittenberg U (OH)
Wofford Coll (SC)
Wright State U (OH)
Xavier U (OH)
Yale U (CT)
York U (ON, Canada)

GERMANIC LANGUAGES

Bethel Coll (KS)
Canisius Coll (NY)
Claremont McKenna Coll (CA)
Cleveland State U (OH)
Eastern Michigan U (MI)
New Coll of Florida (FL)
U of Colorado at Boulder (CO)
U of Kansas (KS)
U of Wisconsin–Eau Claire (WI)
U of Wisconsin–Green Bay (WI)
Washington U in St. Louis (MO)

GERMANIC LANGUAGES RELATED

Calvin Coll (MI)
Ohio Northern U (OH)
U of Calif, Los Angeles (CA)

GERMAN LANGUAGE TEACHER EDUCATION

Alma Coll (MI)
Auburn U (AL)
Baylor U (TX)
Berea Coll (KY)
Brigham Young U (UT)
California Lutheran U (CA)
California State U, Chico (CA)
Carroll Coll (WI)
The Catholic U of America (DC)
Centenary Coll of Louisiana (LA)
Central Michigan U (MI)
Central Missouri State U (MO)
Central Washington U (WA)
Colorado State U (CO)
Concordia Coll (MN)
Concordia U Wisconsin (WI)
East Carolina U (NC)
Eastern Mennonite U (VA)
Eastern Michigan U (MI)
Eastern Washington U (WA)
Elmhurst Coll (IL)
Georgia Southern U (GA)
Grace Coll (IN)
Hardin-Simmons U (TX)
Hofstra U (NY)
Hope Coll (MI)
Hunter Coll of the City U of NY (NY)
Indiana U Bloomington (IN)
Indiana U–Purdue U Fort Wayne (IN)
Indiana U–Purdue U Indianapolis (IN)
Indiana U South Bend (IN)
Ithaca Coll (NY)
Juniata Coll (PA)
Lebanon Valley Coll (PA)
Mansfield U of Pennsylvania (PA)
Messiah Coll (PA)
Miami U Hamilton (OH)
Minot State U (ND)
Moravian Coll (PA)
Murray State U (KY)
Ohio Northern U (OH)
Ohio U (OH)
Ohio Wesleyan U (OH)
Oklahoma Baptist U (OK)
Oral Roberts U (OK)
St. Ambrose U (IA)
St. Bonaventure U (NY)
San Diego State U (CA)
Southwest Missouri State U (MO)
The U of Akron (OH)
The U of Arizona (AZ)
U of Illinois at Chicago (IL)
U of Illinois at Urbana–Champaign (IL)
The U of Iowa (IA)
U of Louisiana at Lafayette (LA)
U of Minnesota, Duluth (MN)
U of Missouri–St. Louis (MO)
U of Nebraska–Lincoln (NE)
The U of North Carolina at Chapel Hill (NC)
The U of North Carolina at Charlotte (NC)
The U of North Carolina at Greensboro (NC)
The U of South Dakota (SD)
The U of Tennessee at Martin (TN)
U of Toledo (OH)
U of Utah (UT)
U of Windsor (ON, Canada)
U of Wisconsin–River Falls (WI)
Valparaiso U (IN)
Washington U in St. Louis (MO)
Weber State U (UT)
Western Carolina U (NC)
Western Michigan U (MI)
Youngstown State U (OH)

GERMAN STUDIES

Barnard Coll (NY)
Brock U (ON, Canada)
Brown U (RI)
Case Western Reserve U (OH)
Claremont McKenna Coll (CA)
Coe Coll (IA)
Coll of the Holy Cross (MA)
The Coll of Wooster (OH)
Columbia Coll (NY)
Connecticut Coll (CT)
Cornell U (NY)
Fordham U (NY)
Franklin and Marshall Coll (PA)
Manhattanville Coll (NY)
Simon's Rock Coll of Bard (MA)
Smith Coll (MA)
Swarthmore Coll (PA)
U of Calif, Irvine (CA)
U of Houston (TX)
U of Victoria (BC, Canada)
U of Windsor (ON, Canada)
York U (ON, Canada)

GERONTOLOGY

Alfred U (NY)
Alma Coll (MI)
Appalachian State U (NC)
Bethune-Cookman Coll (FL)
Bishop's U (QC, Canada)
Bowling Green State U (OH)
California State U, Chico (CA)
California State U, Dominguez Hills (CA)
California State U, Hayward (CA)
California State U, Los Angeles (CA)
California State U, Sacramento (CA)
California U of Pennsylvania (PA)
Case Western Reserve U (OH)
Cedar Crest Coll (PA)
Central Washington U (WA)
Cleveland State U (OH)
Coll of Mount St. Joseph (OH)
Coll of the Holy Cross (MA)
Coll of the Ozarks (MO)
Dominican U (IL)
Eastern Michigan U (MI)
Florida State U (FL)
Gwynedd-Mercy Coll (PA)
Ithaca Coll (NY)
John Carroll U (OH)
King's Coll (PA)

Lakehead U (ON, Canada)
Lindenwood U (MO)
Lynn U (FL)
Madonna U (MI)
Mars Hill Coll (NC)
Mercy Coll (NY)
Mercyhurst Coll (PA)
Miami U Hamilton (OH)
Mount St. Mary's Coll (CA)
Mount Saint Vincent U (NS, Canada)
National-Louis U (IL)
Nazareth Coll of Rochester (NY)
Pontifical Catholic U of Puerto Rico (PR)
Quinnipiac U (CT)
Roosevelt U (IL)
St. Cloud State U (MN)
Saint Mary-of-the-Woods Coll (IN)
St. Thomas U (NB, Canada)
San Diego State U (CA)
Shaw U (NC)
Southeastern Oklahoma State U (OK)
Southwest Missouri State U (MO)
Springfield Coll (MA)
State U of NY Coll at Fredonia (NY)
State U of NY Coll at Oneonta (NY)
Thomas Edison State Coll (NJ)
Towson U (MD)
The U of Akron (OH)
U of Arkansas (AR)
U of Evansville (IN)
U of Guelph (ON, Canada)
U of Massachusetts Boston (MA)
U of Nebraska at Omaha (NE)
U of Nevada, Las Vegas (NV)
The U of North Carolina at Greensboro (NC)
U of Northern Iowa (IA)
U of North Texas (TX)
The U of Scranton (PA)
U of Southern California (CA)
U of South Florida (FL)
Wagner Coll (NY)
Weber State U (UT)
Wichita State U (KS)
Winston-Salem State U (NC)
York Coll of the City U of New York (NY)
York U (ON, Canada)

GRAPHIC AND PRINTING EQUIPMENT OPERATION/ PRODUCTION
Appalachian State U (NC)
California Polytechnic State U, San Luis Obispo (CA)
Chowan Coll (NC)
Fairmont State Coll (WV)
Ferris State U (MI)
Florida Ag and Mech U (FL)
Georgia Southern U (GA)
Indiana State U (IN)
Lewis-Clark State Coll (ID)
Murray State U (KY)
Pennsylvania Coll of Technology (PA)
Pittsburg State U (KS)
Texas A&M U–Commerce (TX)
U of the District of Columbia (DC)
Western Illinois U (IL)

GRAPHIC COMMUNICATIONS
Acad of Art U (CA)
California State U, Los Angeles (CA)
Carroll Coll (WI)
Grand View Coll (IA)
Kean U (NJ)
Memphis Coll of Art (TN)
New England School of Communications (ME)
New York U (NY)
Notre Dame Coll (OH)
Point Loma Nazarene U (CA)
Rochester Inst of Technology (NY)
School of the Art Inst of Chicago (IL)
Silicon Valley Coll, Walnut Creek (CA)
U of Houston (TX)
U of Northern Iowa (IA)
Watkins Coll of Art and Design (TN)

GRAPHIC COMMUNICATIONS RELATED
U of the District of Columbia (DC)

GRAPHIC DESIGN
Acad of Art U (CA)
Alberta Coll of Art & Design (AB, Canada)
Albertus Magnus Coll (CT)
Alma Coll (MI)
Appalachian State U (NC)
Art Acad of Cincinnati (OH)
Art Center Coll of Design (CA)
The Art Inst of Boston at Lesley U (MA)
The Art Inst of California–San Diego (CA)
The Art Inst of California–San Francisco (CA)
The Art Inst of Phoenix (AZ)
The Art Inst of Portland (OR)
Becker Coll (MA)
Brigham Young U (UT)
Cabrini Coll (PA)
California Inst of the Arts (CA)
California State U, Chico (CA)
California State U, Fullerton (CA)
California State U, Long Beach (CA)
California State U, Sacramento (CA)
Campbell U (NC)
Cedarville U (OH)
Champlain Coll (VT)
Chapman U (CA)
Chester Coll of New England (NH)
City Coll of the City U of NY (NY)
The Cleveland Inst of Art (OH)
Coker Coll (SC)
Colby-Sawyer Coll (NH)
Col for Creative Studies (MI)
Coll of Mount St. Joseph (OH)
The Coll of Southeastern Europe, The American U of Athens(Greece)
Columbia Coll (MO)
Columbus Coll of Art & Design (OH)
Concordia U Wisconsin (WI)
Cornish Coll of the Arts (WA)
Creighton U (NE)
Daemen Coll (NY)
Dordt Coll (IA)
Drake U (IA)
East Stroudsburg U of Pennsylvania (PA)
Flagler Coll (FL)
Florida State U (FL)
Framingham State Coll (MA)
Grand View Coll (IA)
Harding U (AR)
Indiana U–Purdue U Fort Wayne (IN)
Iowa State U of Science and Technology (IA)
Kwantlen U Coll (BC, Canada)
Laguna Coll of Art & Design (CA)
La Roche Coll (PA)
Lasell Coll (MA)
Liberty U (VA)
Limestone Coll (SC)
Maine Coll of Art (ME)
Marietta Coll (OH)
Maryland Inst Coll of Art (MD)
Marymount U (VA)
Maryville U of Saint Louis (MO)
Marywood U (PA)
McMurry U (TX)
Memphis Coll of Art (TN)
Miami U Hamilton (OH)
MidAmerica Nazarene U (KS)
Mississippi Coll (MS)
Missouri Western State Coll (MO)
Montserrat Coll of Art (MA)
Moravian Coll (PA)
Mt. Sierra Coll (CA)
The New England Inst of Art (MA)
New World School of the Arts (FL)
North Carolina State U (NC)
Northwestern Coll (MN)
Northwest Nazarene U (ID)
Nova Scotia Coll of Art and Design (NS, Canada)
Ohio Dominican U (OH)
Ohio Northern U (OH)
Oklahoma State U (OK)
Old Dominion U (VA)
Ouachita Baptist U (AR)
Pacific Northwest Coll of Art (OR)
Palm Beach Atlantic U (FL)
Penn State U Abington Coll (PA)
Penn State U Altoona Coll (PA)
Penn State U at Erie, The Behrend Coll (PA)
Penn State U Beaver Campus of the Commonwealth Coll (PA)
Penn State U Berks Cmps of Berks-Lehigh Valley Coll (PA)
Penn State U Delaware County Campus of the Commonwealth Coll (PA)
Penn State U DuBois Campus of the Commonwealth Coll (PA)
Penn State U Fayette Campus of the Commonwealth Coll (PA)
Penn State U Hazleton Campus of the Commonwealth Coll (PA)
Penn State U Lehigh Valley Cmps of Berks-Lehigh Valley Coll (PA)
Penn State U McKeesport Campus of the Commonwealth Coll (PA)
Penn State U Mont Alto Campus of the Commonwealth Coll (PA)
Penn State U New Kensington Campus of the Commonwealth Coll (PA)
Penn State U Schuylkill Campus of the Capital Coll (PA)
Penn State U Shenango Campus of the Commonwealth Coll (PA)
Penn State U Univ Park Campus (PA)
Penn State U Wilkes-Barre Campus of the Commonwealth Coll (PA)
Penn State U Worthington Scranton Cmps Commonwealth Coll (PA)
Penn State U York Campus of the Commonwealth Coll (PA)
Philadelphia U (PA)
Pratt Inst (NY)
Quincy U (IL)
Rhode Island School of Design (RI)
Ringling School of Art and Design (FL)
Rochester Inst of Technology (NY)
Rocky Mountain Coll of Art & Design (CO)
St. Ambrose U (IA)
St. Edward's U (TX)
St. John's U (NY)
San Jose State U (CA)
Savannah Coll of Art and Design (GA)
School of the Art Inst of Chicago (IL)
School of the Museum of Fine Arts, Boston (MA)
Schreiner U (TX)
Shawnee State U (OH)
Spring Hill Coll (AL)
Susquehanna U (PA)
Texas Tech U (TX)
Union Coll (NE)
U of Bridgeport (CT)
U of Florida (FL)
U of Illinois at Chicago (IL)
U of Illinois at Urbana–Champaign (IL)
U of Kansas (KS)
U of Michigan–Flint (MI)
U of San Francisco (CA)
The U of the Arts (PA)
Ursuline Coll (OH)
Viterbo U (WI)
Washington U in St. Louis (MO)
Watkins Coll of Art and Design (TN)
Waynesburg Coll (PA)
Western Washington U (WA)

GRAPHIC/PRINTING EQUIPMENT
Coll of the Ozarks (MO)
Eastern Kentucky U (KY)

GREENHOUSE MANAGEMENT
Sterling Coll (VT)

HAZARDOUS MATERIALS MANAGEMENT AND WASTE TECHNOLOGY
Rochester Inst of Technology (NY)

HEALTH AND MEDICAL ADMINISTRATIVE SERVICES RELATED
Kent State U (OH)
Pennsylvania Coll of Technology (PA)
Robert Morris U (PA)
Saint Joseph's Coll of Maine (ME)
U of Baltimore (MD)
U of Miami (FL)
U of Michigan–Flint (MI)
Ursuline Coll (OH)

HEALTH AND PHYSICAL EDUCATION
Abilene Christian U (TX)
Angelo State U (TX)
Arkansas State U (AR)
Asbury Coll (KY)
Austin Peay State U (TN)
Averett U (VA)
Baldwin-Wallace Coll (OH)
Baylor U (TX)
Belmont U (TN)
Bethel Coll (IN)
Bethel Coll (KS)
Bethel Coll (TN)
Bethel U (MN)
Black Hills State U (SD)
Bluffton Coll (OH)
Bridgewater Coll (VA)
Bridgewater State Coll (MA)
Brigham Young U (UT)
Brigham Young U–Hawaii (HI)
California State U, Chico (CA)
California State U, Fullerton (CA)
California State U, Sacramento (CA)
Campbell U (NC)
Capital U (OH)
Carroll Coll (WI)
Castleton State Coll (VT)
Cedarville U (OH)
Chapman U (CA)
Coker Coll (SC)
Coll of St. Catherine (MN)
Coll of the Ozarks (MO)
Colorado Christian U (CO)
Columbia Union Coll (MD)
Concordia Coll (MN)
Concordia U (NE)
Concordia U Wisconsin (WI)
Cumberland Coll (KY)
Dalhousie U (NS, Canada)
Dana Coll (NE)
Doane Coll (NE)
Dordt Coll (IA)
Eastern Michigan U (MI)
Eastern U (PA)
Eastern Washington U (WA)
East Texas Baptist U (TX)
Edinboro U of Pennsylvania (PA)
Elmhurst Coll (IL)
Emory & Henry Coll (VA)
Evangel U (MO)
Florida Ag and Mech U (FL)
Freed-Hardeman U (TN)
Gardner-Webb U (NC)
Georgia Southern U (GA)
Guilford Coll (NC)
Hamline U (MN)
Hardin-Simmons U (TX)
Hastings Coll (NE)
Houghton Coll (NY)
Houston Baptist U (TX)
Howard Payne U (TX)
Indiana U of Pennsylvania (PA)
Iowa State U of Science and Technology (IA)
Ithaca Coll (NY)
Jacksonville State U (AL)
James Madison U (VA)
Jarvis Christian Coll (TX)
Johnson C. Smith U (NC)
Johnson State Coll (VT)
Kentucky State U (KY)
Liberty U (VA)
Lincoln Memorial U (TN)
Lincoln U (PA)
Lindenwood U (MO)
Linfield Coll (OR)
Loras Coll (IA)
Louisiana Tech U (LA)
Lubbock Christian U (TX)
Luther Coll (IA)
Lyndon State Coll (VT)
Malone Coll (OH)
Maryville Coll (TN)
The Master's Coll and Sem (CA)
Mayville State U (ND)
Miami U (OH)
Middle Tennessee State U (TN)
Milligan Coll (TN)
Minnesota State U Moorhead (MN)
Mississippi Coll (MS)
Montana State U–Billings (MT)
Montana State U–Bozeman (MT)
Nebraska Wesleyan U (NE)
North Carolina Central U (NC)
Northwest Nazarene U (ID)
Ohio Northern U (OH)
Ohio U (OH)
Oklahoma Baptist U (OK)
Oklahoma State U (OK)
Olivet Coll (MI)
Ouachita Baptist U (AR)
Pittsburg State U (KS)
Plymouth State U (NH)
Point Loma Nazarene U (CA)
Queens Coll of the City U of NY (NY)
Queen's U at Kingston (ON, Canada)
Radford U (VA)
Redeemer U Coll (ON, Canada)
Roanoke Coll (VA)
St. Ambrose U (IA)
Saint Mary's Coll of California (CA)
St. Mary's U of San Antonio (TX)
Salisbury U (MD)
Samford U (AL)
San Jose State U (CA)
Slippery Rock U of Pennsylvania (PA)
South Dakota State U (SD)
Southeast Missouri State U (MO)
Southern Illinois U Edwardsville (IL)
Southern Virginia U (VA)
Southern Wesleyan U (SC)
Southwestern Coll (KS)
Spring Arbor U (MI)
State U of NY Coll at Brockport (NY)
Sterling Coll (KS)
Tennessee Wesleyan Coll (TN)
Texas A&M Intl U (TX)
Texas A&M U (TX)
Texas Christian U (TX)
Texas Southern U (TX)
Texas State U-San Marcos (TX)
Texas Tech U (TX)
Texas Wesleyan U (TX)
Trinity Western U (BC, Canada)
U of Arkansas (AR)
U of Delaware (DE)
U of Great Falls (MT)
U of Hawaii at Manoa (HI)
U of Houston (TX)
U of Houston–Clear Lake (TX)
U of Kansas (KS)
U of Louisville (KY)
U of Mary (ND)
U of Missouri–Kansas City (MO)
U of Montevallo (AL)
U of Nebraska at Omaha (NE)
The U of North Carolina at Chapel Hill (NC)
The U of North Carolina at Charlotte (NC)
The U of North Carolina at Pembroke (NC)
The U of North Carolina at Wilmington (NC)
U of Northern Iowa (IA)
U of North Texas (TX)
U of Oklahoma (OK)
U of St. Thomas (MN)
U of San Francisco (CA)
U of Science and Arts of Oklahoma (OK)
The U of Tennessee at Martin (TN)
The U of Texas at Arlington (TX)
The U of Texas at Austin (TX)
The U of Texas at Brownsville (TX)
The U of Texas at Tyler (TX)
The U of Texas–Pan American (TX)
U of Utah (UT)
U of West Florida (FL)
U of Windsor (ON, Canada)
U of Wisconsin–Stevens Point (WI)
Ursinus Coll (PA)
Valdosta State U (GA)
Valparaiso U (IN)
Vanguard U of Southern California (CA)
Virginia Intermont Coll (VA)
Walla Walla Coll (WA)
Washington State U (WA)
Weber State U (UT)
West Chester U of Pennsylvania (PA)
West Texas A&M U (TX)
West Virginia U (WV)
West Virginia Wesleyan Coll (WV)
William Carey Coll (MS)
William Penn U (IA)
Wright State U (OH)
York U (ON, Canada)
Youngstown State U (OH)

HEALTH AND PHYSICAL EDUCATION RELATED
Arizona State U East (AZ)
Averett U (VA)
Avila U (MO)
Bloomsburg U of Pennsylvania (PA)
Bowling Green State U (OH)
Brewton-Parker Coll (GA)
Briar Cliff U (IA)
Bridgewater State Coll (MA)
Brigham Young U (UT)
California Baptist U (CA)
California State U, Long Beach (CA)
California State U, Sacramento (CA)
Campbell U (NC)
Capital U (OH)
Coe Coll (IA)
Coker Coll (SC)
Concordia U Wisconsin (WI)
Cornell Coll (IA)
East Carolina U (NC)

East Stroudsburg U of Pennsylvania (PA)
Greensboro Coll (NC)
Gustavus Adolphus Coll (MN)
Ithaca Coll (NY)
Lambuth U (TN)
Limestone Coll (SC)
Lincoln U (PA)
Mayville State U (ND)
Midwestern State U (TX)
Naropa U (CO)
Ohio Northern U (OH)
Reinhardt Coll (GA)
Rocky Mountain Coll (MT)
Saint Augustine's Coll (NC)
St. John Fisher Coll (NY)
Saint Mary's Coll of California (CA)
Sam Houston State U (TX)
State U of NY Coll at Brockport (NY)
Texas Christian U (TX)
Texas Lutheran U (TX)
Towson U (MD)
The U of Akron (OH)
U of Minnesota, Twin Cities Campus (MN)
U of Victoria (BC, Canada)
Washington State U (WA)

HEALTH COMMUNICATION
Juniata Coll (PA)

HEALTH/HEALTH CARE ADMINISTRATION
Albertus Magnus Coll (CT)
Alfred U (NY)
Alvernia Coll (PA)
American InterContinental U Online (IL)
Appalachian State U (NC)
Arcadia U (PA)
Auburn U (AL)
Augustana Coll (SD)
Baker Coll of Auburn Hills (MI)
Baker Coll of Flint (MI)
Baker Coll of Muskegon (MI)
Baker Coll of Owosso (MI)
Baker Coll of Port Huron (MI)
Baptist Coll of Health Sciences (TN)
Bellevue U (NE)
Belmont U (TN)
Benedictine U (IL)
Black Hills State U (SD)
Bowling Green State U (OH)
British Columbia Inst of Technology (BC, Canada)
Brock U (ON, Canada)
California State U, Dominguez Hills (CA)
California State U, Long Beach (CA)
California State U, Sacramento (CA)
California State U, San Bernardino (CA)
Calumet Coll of Saint Joseph (IN)
Cedar Crest Coll (PA)
Chestnut Hill Coll (PA)
Clayton Coll & State U (GA)
Coll for Lifelong Learning (NH)
Columbia Southern U (AL)
Columbia Union Coll (MD)
Concordia Coll (MN)
Concordia U (OR)
Concordia U Wisconsin (WI)
Creighton U (NE)
Dallas Baptist U (TX)
Davenport U, Dearborn (MI)
Davenport U, Lansing (MI)
Dillard U (LA)
Dominican Coll (NY)
Drexel U (PA)
Duquesne U (PA)
D'Youville Coll (NY)
Eastern Kentucky U (KY)
Eastern Michigan U (MI)
Eastern Washington U (WA)
Ferris State U (MI)
Florida Ag and Mech U (FL)
Florida Atlantic U (FL)
Florida Intl U (FL)
The Franciscan U (IA)
Franklin U (OH)
Governors State U (IL)
Harding U (AR)
Harris-Stowe State Coll (MO)
Hastings Coll (NE)
Heidelberg Coll (OH)
Howard Payne U (TX)
Idaho State U (ID)
Indiana U Northwest (IN)
Indiana U–Purdue U Indianapolis (IN)
Indiana U South Bend (IN)
Intl Coll (FL)
Iona Coll (NY)
Ithaca Coll (NY)
John Brown U (AR)
Johnson & Wales U (RI)
Lebanon Valley Coll (PA)
Lehman Coll of the City U of NY (NY)
Lewis U (IL)
Lindenwood U (MO)
Lynn U (FL)
Macon State Coll (GA)
Madonna U (MI)
Mary Baldwin Coll (VA)
Maryville U of Saint Louis (MO)
Marywood U (PA)
Mercy Coll (NY)
Methodist Coll (NC)
Metropolitan State Coll of Denver (CO)
Midway Coll (KY)
Minnesota State U Moorhead (MN)
Montana State U–Billings (MT)
Montana State U–Bozeman (MT)
Mountain State U (WV)
Mount St. Mary's Coll (CA)
National American U, Colorado Springs (CO)
National American U, Denver (CO)
National-Louis U (IL)
Newbury Coll (MA)
New Mexico Highlands U (NM)
New York U (NY)
Norfolk State U (VA)
Northeastern State U (OK)
Northeastern U (MA)
Ohio U (OH)
Ohio U–Southern Campus (OH)
Oregon State U (OR)
Our Lady of the Lake Coll (LA)
Penn State U Abington Coll (PA)
Penn State U at Erie, The Behrend Coll (PA)
Penn State U Beaver Campus of the Commonwealth Coll (PA)
Penn State U Berks Cmps of Berks-Lehigh Valley Coll (PA)
Penn State U Delaware County Campus of the Commonwealth Coll (PA)
Penn State U DuBois Campus of the Commonwealth Coll (PA)
Penn State U Fayette Campus of the Commonwealth Coll (PA)
Penn State U Harrisburg Campus of the Capital Coll (PA)
Penn State U Hazleton Campus of the Commonwealth Coll (PA)
Penn State U Lehigh Valley Cmps of Berks-Lehigh Valley Coll (PA)
Penn State U McKeesport Campus of the Commonwealth Coll (PA)
Penn State U Mont Alto Campus of the Commonwealth Coll (PA)
Penn State U New Kensington Campus of the Commonwealth Coll (PA)
Penn State U Schuylkill Campus of the Capital Coll (PA)
Penn State U Shenango Campus of the Commonwealth Coll (PA)
Penn State U Univ Park Campus (PA)
Penn State U Wilkes-Barre Campus of the Commonwealth Coll (PA)
Penn State U Worthington Scranton Cmps Commonwealth Coll (PA)
Penn State U York Campus of the Commonwealth Coll (PA)
Point Park U (PA)
Presentation Coll (SD)
Providence Coll (RI)
Robert Morris U (PA)
Roger Williams U (RI)
Roosevelt U (IL)
Ryerson U (ON, Canada)
St. Francis Coll (NY)
St. John's U (NY)
St. Joseph's Coll, New York (NY)
Saint Joseph's Coll of Maine (ME)
St. Joseph's Coll, Suffolk Campus (NY)
Saint Joseph's U (PA)
Saint Leo U (FL)
Saint Louis U (MO)
San Jose State U (CA)
Southern Adventist U (TN)
Southwestern Oklahoma State U (OK)
Spring Arbor U (MI)
Springfield Coll (MA)
State U of NY Coll at Brockport (NY)
State U of NY Coll at Fredonia (NY)
State U of NY Inst of Tech at Utica/Rome (NY)
Stonehill Coll (MA)
Tennessee State U (TN)
Texas Southern U (TX)
Texas State U-San Marcos (TX)
Thomas Edison State Coll (NJ)
Touro U Intl (CA)
Towson U (MD)
The U of Arizona (AZ)
U of Central Florida (FL)
U of Cincinnati (OH)
U of Connecticut (CT)
U of Detroit Mercy (MI)
U of Evansville (IN)
U of Great Falls (MT)
U of Houston–Clear Lake (TX)
U of Illinois at Springfield (IL)
U of Kentucky (KY)
U of La Verne (CA)
U of Maryland, Baltimore County (MD)
U of Michigan–Dearborn (MI)
U of Michigan–Flint (MI)
U of Minnesota, Crookston (MN)
U of Nevada, Las Vegas (NV)
U of New Hampshire (NH)
The U of North Carolina at Chapel Hill (NC)
U of Northwestern Ohio (OH)
U of Pennsylvania (PA)
U of Phoenix–Cleveland Campus (OH)
U of Phoenix–Hawaii Campus (HI)
U of Phoenix–Idaho Campus (ID)
U of Phoenix–Jacksonville Campus (FL)
U of Phoenix–Kansas City Campus (MO)
U of Phoenix–Nevada Campus (NV)
U of Phoenix–New Mexico Campus (NM)
U of Phoenix–Northern California Campus (CA)
U of Phoenix–Oklahoma City Campus (OK)
U of Phoenix Online Campus (AZ)
U of Phoenix–Phoenix Campus (AZ)
U of Phoenix–Sacramento Campus (CA)
U of Phoenix–San Diego Campus (CA)
U of Phoenix–Southern Arizona Campus (AZ)
U of Phoenix–Tampa Campus (FL)
U of Phoenix–Tulsa Campus (OK)
U of Phoenix–Vancouver Campus (BC, Canada)
U of Phoenix–Washington Campus (WA)
U of Phoenix–West Michigan Campus (MI)
U of Rhode Island (RI)
U of Saskatchewan (SK, Canada)
The U of Scranton (PA)
U of Texas Southwestern Medical Center at Dallas (TX)
U of Victoria (BC, Canada)
U of Wisconsin–Eau Claire (WI)
U of Wisconsin–Milwaukee (WI)
Upper Iowa U (IA)
Ursuline Coll (OH)
Waynesburg Coll (PA)
Weber State U (UT)
Webster U (MO)
West Chester U of Pennsylvania (PA)
Western Illinois U (IL)
Western Kentucky U (KY)
Western Michigan U (MI)
Wheeling Jesuit U (WV)
Wichita State U (KS)
Wilberforce U (OH)
Winona State U (MN)
Wright State U (OH)
York Coll of Pennsylvania (PA)

HEALTH INFORMATION/ MEDICAL RECORDS ADMINISTRATION
Alabama State U (AL)
Arkansas Tech U (AR)
Baker Coll of Auburn Hills (MI)
Baker Coll of Flint (MI)
Carroll Coll (MT)
Chicago State U (IL)
Clark Atlanta U (GA)
Coll of Saint Mary (NE)
The Coll of St. Scholastica (MN)
Dakota State U (SD)
Dalhousie U (NS, Canada)
East Carolina U (NC)
East Central U (OK)
Eastern Kentucky U (KY)
Ferris State U (MI)
Florida Ag and Mech U (FL)
Florida Intl U (FL)
Gwynedd-Mercy Coll (PA)
Illinois State U (IL)
Indiana U Northwest (IN)
Indiana U–Purdue U Indianapolis (IN)
Kean U (NJ)
Loma Linda U (CA)
Long Island U, C.W. Post Campus (NY)
Louisiana Tech U (LA)
Macon State Coll (GA)
Medical Coll of Georgia (GA)
Norfolk State U (VA)
The Ohio State U (OH)
Pace U (NY)
Regis U (CO)
Saint Louis U (MO)
Southwestern Oklahoma State U (OK)
Springfield Coll (MA)
State U of NY Health Science Center at Brooklyn (NY)
State U of NY Inst of Tech at Utica/Rome (NY)
Tennessee State U (TN)
Texas Southern U (TX)
Texas State U-San Marcos (TX)
The U of Alabama at Birmingham (AL)
U of Central Florida (FL)
U of Illinois at Chicago (IL)
U of Kansas (KS)
U of Louisiana at Lafayette (LA)
U of Mississippi Medical Center (MS)
U of Pittsburgh (PA)
U of Toledo (OH)
U of Wisconsin–Milwaukee (WI)
Western Carolina U (NC)

HEALTH INFORMATION/ MEDICAL RECORDS TECHNOLOGY
Gwynedd-Mercy Coll (PA)
Mercyhurst Coll (PA)

HEALTH/MEDICAL PHYSICS
Bloomsburg U of Pennsylvania (PA)
U of Nevada, Las Vegas (NV)

HEALTH/MEDICAL PREPARATORY PROGRAMS RELATED
Allegheny Coll (PA)
Asbury Coll (KY)
Aurora U (IL)
Avila U (MO)
Baylor U (TX)
Chadron State Coll (NE)
Charleston Southern U (SC)
Coll of the Ozarks (MO)
Concordia U (NE)
Cumberland U (TN)
DeSales U (PA)
Duquesne U (PA)
Eastern Michigan U (MI)
Emmanuel Coll (GA)
Fordham U (NY)
Guilford Coll (NC)
Intl Coll (FL)
Ithaca Coll (NY)
Juniata Coll (PA)
Lehigh U (PA)
Madonna U (MI)
Maryville U of Saint Louis (MO)
Mercer U (GA)
Mercyhurst Coll (PA)
Meredith Coll (NC)
Rhode Island Coll (RI)
Roosevelt U (IL)
St. Cloud State U (MN)
Salisbury U (MD)
The U of Akron (OH)
U of Louisville (KY)
U of Miami (FL)
U of Missouri–Columbia (MO)
U of Nevada, Reno (NV)
U of South Alabama (AL)
U of Waterloo (ON, Canada)
Utica Coll (NY)
Wheaton Coll (IL)
Wright State U (OH)

HEALTH/MEDICAL PSYCHOLOGY
Iona Coll (NY)
Mass Coll of Pharmacy and Allied Health Sciences (MA)
U of the Sciences in Philadelphia (PA)

HEALTH OCCUPATIONS TEACHER EDUCATION
Baylor U (TX)
New York Inst of Technology (NY)
North Carolina State U (NC)
U of Maine at Farmington (ME)

HEALTH PROFESSIONS RELATED
Albany Coll of Pharmacy of Union U (NY)
Albany State U (GA)
Alcorn State U (MS)
Arizona State U East (AZ)
Armstrong Atlantic State U (GA)
Baldwin-Wallace Coll (OH)
Bowling Green State U (OH)
Bradley U (IL)
California State U, Fullerton (CA)
California State U, Los Angeles (CA)
California State U, Sacramento (CA)
Chatham Coll (PA)
Clemson U (SC)
Cleveland State U (OH)
Dowling Coll (NY)
D'Youville Coll (NY)
East Carolina U (NC)
George Mason U (VA)
Hofstra U (NY)
King Coll (TN)
King's Coll (PA)
Lebanon Valley Coll (PA)
Long Island U, Brooklyn Campus (NY)
Long Island U, C.W. Post Campus (NY)
Marywood U (PA)
Mass Coll of Pharmacy and Allied Health Sciences (MA)
Mountain State U (WV)
Oakland U (MI)
The Ohio State U (OH)
Ohio U (OH)
Pennsylvania Coll of Technology (PA)
Purdue U (IN)
Randolph-Macon Woman's Coll (VA)
St. Francis Coll (NY)
Saint Joseph's U (PA)
Saint Mary's Coll of California (CA)
San Diego State U (CA)
Stony Brook U, State U of New York (NY)
Towson U (MD)
The U of Alabama (AL)
U of Arkansas (AR)
U of Louisiana at Lafayette (LA)
U of Miami (FL)
U of Nevada, Reno (NV)
U of Northern Iowa (IA)
U of Pennsylvania (PA)
U of Pittsburgh (PA)
U of Saint Francis (IN)
U of Southern Indiana (IN)
U of Utah (UT)
Washington U in St. Louis (MO)
William Carey Coll (MS)
Worcester State Coll (MA)

HEALTH SCIENCE
Alma Coll (MI)
American U (DC)
Armstrong Atlantic State U (GA)
Athens State U (AL)
Azusa Pacific U (CA)
Ball State U (IN)
Bastyr U (WA)
Benedictine U (IL)
Boise State U (ID)
Boston U (MA)
Bradley U (IL)
Brock U (ON, Canada)
California State U, Dominguez Hills (CA)
California State U, Fresno (CA)
California State U, Hayward (CA)
California State U, Long Beach (CA)
California State U, Los Angeles (CA)
California State U, San Bernardino (CA)
Carlow Coll (PA)
Castleton State Coll (VT)
Cedar Crest Coll (PA)
Centenary Coll of Louisiana (LA)
Chapman U (CA)
Coll Misericordia (PA)
Coll of Mount Saint Vincent (NY)
The Coll of St. Scholastica (MN)
Coll of the Ozarks (MO)
Columbus State U (GA)

Dalhousie U (NS, Canada)
Eastern Nazarene Coll (MA)
Erskine Coll (SC)
Fairmont State Coll (WV)
Florida Atlantic U (FL)
Florida Intl U (FL)
Gannon U (PA)
Gettysburg Coll (PA)
Graceland U (IA)
Grand Valley State U (MI)
Gwynedd-Mercy Coll (PA)
Hampshire Coll (MA)
Hiram Coll (OH)
Inter American U of PR, San Germán Campus (PR)
Johnson State Coll (VT)
Kalamazoo Coll (MI)
Kansas State U (KS)
Lamar U (TX)
Lock Haven U of Pennsylvania (PA)
Long Island U, Brooklyn Campus (NY)
Longwood U (VA)
Manchester Coll (IN)
Maryville U of Saint Louis (MO)
Merrimack Coll (MA)
Milligan Coll (TN)
Minnesota State U Mankato (MN)
Montana Tech of The U of Montana (MT)
Montclair State U (NJ)
New Jersey City U (NJ)
Newman U (KS)
Northeastern U (MA)
Northern Illinois U (IL)
Oakland U (MI)
Ohio U (OH)
Oklahoma State U (OK)
Oregon State U (OR)
Our Lady of Holy Cross Coll (LA)
Pacific U (OR)
Queen's U at Kingston (ON, Canada)
Roosevelt U (IL)
San Francisco State U (CA)
Sonoma State U (CA)
State U of NY Coll at Brockport (NY)
State U of NY Coll at Cortland (NY)
Syracuse U (NY)
Tennessee Wesleyan Coll (TN)
Texas A&M U–Corpus Christi (TX)
Texas Christian U (TX)
Texas Southern U (TX)
Truman State U (MO)
Union Inst & U (OH)
U of Arkansas at Little Rock (AR)
U of Central Florida (FL)
U of Colorado at Colorado Springs (CO)
U of Hartford (CT)
U of Maryland, Baltimore County (MD)
U of Nevada, Las Vegas (NV)
U of Saint Francis (IN)
U of St. Thomas (MN)
U of Southern California (CA)
U of Southern Maine (ME)
U of Waterloo (ON, Canada)
The U of Western Ontario (ON, Canada)
U of Wisconsin–Milwaukee (WI)
Waldorf Coll (IA)
Walla Walla Coll (WA)
Warner Pacific Coll (OR)
Wayne State U (MI)
Western Baptist Coll (OR)
West Liberty State Coll (WV)
William Paterson U of New Jersey (NJ)
Winona State U (MN)
York U (ON, Canada)
Youngstown State U (OH)

HEALTH SERVICES ADMINISTRATION
East Stroudsburg U of Pennsylvania (PA)
Freed-Hardeman U (TN)
Indiana U–Purdue U Fort Wayne (IN)
Marywood U (PA)
Medical U of South Carolina (SC)
Northwest Christian Coll (OR)
Ohio U–Southern Campus (OH)
U of Calif, Los Angeles (CA)
Ursuline Coll (OH)
Washburn U (KS)

HEALTH SERVICES/ALLIED HEALTH/HEALTH SCIENCES
Baptist Coll of Health Sciences (TN)
Bellarmine U (KY)
Brevard Coll (NC)
California State U, Chico (CA)
California State U, Sacramento (CA)
The Coll of St. Scholastica (MN)
Columbus State U (GA)
Daemen Coll (NY)
Dalhousie U (NS, Canada)
D'Youville Coll (NY)
Florida Atlantic U (FL)
Florida Gulf Coast U (FL)
Florida Intl U (FL)
Gwynedd-Mercy Coll (PA)
Idaho State U (ID)
Jones Coll, Miami (FL)
Kent State U (OH)
Lebanon Valley Coll (PA)
Liberty U (VA)
Marywood U (PA)
Mount Aloysius Coll (PA)
Nicholls State U (LA)
Nova Southeastern U (FL)
The Ohio State U at Lima (OH)
Old Dominion U (VA)
St. Cloud State U (MN)
Saint Joseph's Coll of Maine (ME)
San Jose State U (CA)
Stetson U (FL)
Texas State U-San Marcos (TX)
Texas Tech U (TX)
U Coll of the Cariboo (BC, Canada)
U of Central Florida (FL)
U of Florida (FL)
U of Minnesota, Crookston (MN)
U of North Florida (FL)
The U of Texas at Austin (TX)
The U of Texas at Brownsville (TX)
U of the Sciences in Philadelphia (PA)
U of Utah (UT)
U of Wyoming (WY)
Ursuline Coll (OH)
Western Baptist Coll (OR)
Widener U (PA)
York U (ON, Canada)

HEALTH TEACHER EDUCATION
Alma Coll (MI)
Appalachian State U (NC)
Aquinas Coll (MI)
Arkansas State U (AR)
Armstrong Atlantic State U (GA)
Ashland U (OH)
Auburn U (AL)
Augsburg Coll (MN)
Austin Peay State U (TN)
Averett U (VA)
Baldwin-Wallace Coll (OH)
Ball State U (IN)
Baylor U (TX)
Belmont U (TN)
Bemidji State U (MN)
Bethel U (MN)
Bluefield Coll (VA)
Bowling Green State U (OH)
Briar Cliff U (IA)
Bridgewater State Coll (MA)
Brooklyn Coll of the City U of NY (NY)
California State U, Chico (CA)
California State U, San Bernardino (CA)
Campbellsville U (KY)
Capital U (OH)
Carroll Coll (WI)
Cedarville U (OH)
Centenary Coll of Louisiana (LA)
Central Michigan U (MI)
Central State U (OH)
Central Washington U (WA)
Chicago State U (IL)
Clark Atlanta U (GA)
Coll of Mount Saint Vincent (NY)
Columbus State U (GA)
Concord Coll (WV)
Concordia Coll (MN)
Concordia U (NE)
Concordia U, St. Paul (MN)
Cumberland Coll (KY)
Curry Coll (MA)
Dalhousie U (NS, Canada)
Defiance Coll (OH)
Dillard U (LA)
East Carolina U (NC)
East Central U (OK)
Eastern Illinois U (IL)
Eastern Kentucky U (KY)
Eastern Mennonite U (VA)
Eastern Michigan U (MI)
Eastern Washington U (WA)
East Stroudsburg U of Pennsylvania (PA)
Elon U (NC)
Fayetteville State U (NC)
Florida Ag and Mech U (FL)
Florida Intl U (FL)
Florida State U (FL)
Fort Valley State U (GA)
Freed-Hardeman U (TN)
Gardner-Webb U (NC)
George Fox U (OR)
George Mason U (VA)
Georgia Coll & State U (GA)
Graceland U (IA)
Gustavus Adolphus Coll (MN)
Hamline U (MN)
Hampton U (VA)
Harding U (AR)
Heidelberg Coll (OH)
Hofstra U (NY)
Hunter Coll of the City U of NY (NY)
Idaho State U (ID)
Illinois State U (IL)
Indiana State U (IN)
Indiana U–Purdue U Indianapolis (IN)
Iowa State U of Science and Technology (IA)
Ithaca Coll (NY)
Jacksonville State U (AL)
John Brown U (AR)
Johnson C. Smith U (NC)
Kansas Wesleyan U (KS)
Keene State Coll (NH)
Kent State U (OH)
Lamar U (TX)
Lehman Coll of the City U of NY (NY)
Liberty U (VA)
Lincoln Memorial U (TN)
Lipscomb U (TN)
Long Island U, C.W. Post Campus (NY)
Longwood U (VA)
Louisiana Coll (LA)
Luther Coll (IA)
Lynchburg Coll (VA)
Malone Coll (OH)
Manchester Coll (IN)
Maryville Coll (TN)
Mayville State U (ND)
Miami U (OH)
Miami U Hamilton (OH)
Middle Tennessee State U (TN)
Minnesota State U Mankato (MN)
Minnesota State U Moorhead (MN)
Missouri Baptist U (MO)
Missouri Valley Coll (MO)
Montana State U–Billings (MT)
Montclair State U (NJ)
Morehead State U (KY)
Morgan State U (MD)
Mount Vernon Nazarene U (OH)
Murray State U (KY)
New Mexico Highlands U (NM)
Nicholls State U (LA)
North Carolina Central U (NC)
North Dakota State U (ND)
Northeastern State U (OK)
Northern Arizona U (AZ)
Northern Illinois U (IL)
Northern Michigan U (MI)
Northern State U (SD)
Northwestern Oklahoma State U (OK)
Ohio Northern U (OH)
Ohio Wesleyan U (OH)
Otterbein Coll (OH)
Pittsburg State U (KS)
Pontifical Catholic U of Puerto Rico (PR)
Portland State U (OR)
Queen's U at Kingston (ON, Canada)
Rhode Island Coll (RI)
Rocky Mountain Coll (MT)
St. Ambrose U (IA)
St. Cloud State U (MN)
Salem State Coll (MA)
Salisbury U (MD)
Sam Houston State U (TX)
San Francisco State U (CA)
South Carolina State U (SC)
Southeastern Oklahoma State U (OK)
Southern Illinois U Carbondale (IL)
Southern Illinois U Edwardsville (IL)
Southern Oregon U (OR)
Springfield Coll (MA)
State U of NY at Oswego (NY)
State U of NY Coll at Brockport (NY)
State U of NY Coll at Cortland (NY)
Tabor Coll (KS)
Tennessee State U (TN)
Tennessee Technological U (TN)
Texas A&M U–Commerce (TX)
Texas A&M U–Kingsville (TX)
Texas Southern U (TX)
Touro U Intl (CA)
Troy State U (AL)
Union Coll (KY)
The U of Akron (OH)
The U of Alabama at Birmingham (AL)
The U of Arizona (AZ)
U of Arkansas at Little Rock (AR)
U of Charleston (WV)
U of Cincinnati (OH)
U of Dayton (OH)
U of Delaware (DE)
U of Florida (FL)
U of Georgia (GA)
U of Great Falls (MT)
U of Hawaii at Manoa (HI)
U of Kentucky (KY)
The U of Lethbridge (AB, Canada)
U of Maine (ME)
U of Maine at Farmington (ME)
U of Maine at Presque Isle (ME)
U of Maryland, Coll Park (MD)
U of Minnesota, Duluth (MN)
The U of Montana–Missoula (MT)
The U of Montana–Western (MT)
U of Nebraska–Lincoln (NE)
U of Nevada, Las Vegas (NV)
U of Nevada, Reno (NV)
U of New Brunswick Fredericton (NB, Canada)
U of New Mexico (NM)
The U of North Carolina at Chapel Hill (NC)
The U of North Carolina at Greensboro (NC)
U of Northern Iowa (IA)
U of Regina (SK, Canada)
U of Richmond (VA)
U of Saint Francis (IN)
U of St. Thomas (MN)
U of Sioux Falls (SD)
The U of South Dakota (SD)
The U of Tennessee (TN)
U of the District of Columbia (DC)
U of Toledo (OH)
U of Toronto (ON, Canada)
U of Utah (UT)
U of Windsor (ON, Canada)
U of Wisconsin–La Crosse (WI)
U of Wyoming (WY)
Urbana U (OH)
Utah State U (UT)
Valley City State U (ND)
Virginia Commonwealth U (VA)
Virginia Polytechnic Inst and State U (VA)
Waldorf Coll (IA)
Washburn U (KS)
West Chester U of Pennsylvania (PA)
Western Connecticut State U (CT)
Western Illinois U (IL)
Western Michigan U (MI)
Western Washington U (WA)
West Liberty State Coll (WV)
West Virginia State Coll (WV)
West Virginia Wesleyan Coll (WV)
William Paterson U of New Jersey (NJ)
William Penn U (IA)
Winona State U (MN)
Wright State U (OH)
Xavier U of Louisiana (LA)
York Coll of the City U of New York (NY)
Youngstown State U (OH)

HEATING, AIR CONDITIONING AND REFRIGERATION TECHNOLOGY
Pennsylvania Coll of Technology (PA)

HEATING, AIR CONDITIONING, VENTILATION AND REFRIGERATION MAINTENANCE TECHNOLOGY
Ferris State U (MI)
Lewis-Clark State Coll (ID)

HEAVY EQUIPMENT MAINTENANCE TECHNOLOGY
Ferris State U (MI)
Pittsburg State U (KS)

HEBREW
Bard Coll (NY)
Brigham Young U (UT)
Brooklyn Coll of the City U of NY (NY)
Concordia U Wisconsin (WI)
Dartmouth Coll (NH)
Harvard U (MA)
Hofstra U (NY)
Hunter Coll of the City U of NY (NY)
Jewish Theological Sem of America (NY)
Laura and Alvin Siegal Coll of Judaic Studies (OH)
Lehman Coll of the City U of NY (NY)
Multnomah Bible Coll and Biblical Sem (OR)
New York U (NY)
The Ohio State U (OH)
Queens Coll of the City U of NY (NY)
State U of NY at Binghamton (NY)
U of Alberta (AB, Canada)
U of Calif, Los Angeles (CA)
U of Michigan (MI)
U of Minnesota, Twin Cities Campus (MN)
U of Oregon (OR)
U of Saskatchewan (SK, Canada)
The U of Texas at Austin (TX)
U of Toronto (ON, Canada)
U of Wisconsin–Madison (WI)
U of Wisconsin–Milwaukee (WI)
Washington U in St. Louis (MO)
York U (ON, Canada)

HERBALISM
Bastyr U (WA)

HIGHER EDUCATION/HIGHER EDUCATION ADMINISTRATION
Eastern Michigan U (MI)
U of Arkansas (AR)
Wright State U (OH)

HINDI
U of Chicago (IL)

HISPANIC-AMERICAN, PUERTO RICAN, AND MEXICAN-AMERICAN/CHICANO STUDIES
Arizona State U (AZ)
Boston Coll (MA)
Brooklyn Coll of the City U of NY (NY)
Brown U (RI)
California State U, Dominguez Hills (CA)
California State U, Fresno (CA)
California State U, Fullerton (CA)
California State U, Hayward (CA)
California State U, Long Beach (CA)
California State U, Los Angeles (CA)
California State U, San Bernardino (CA)
Claremont McKenna Coll (CA)
The Colorado Coll (CO)
Columbia Coll (NY)
Columbia U, School of General Studies (NY)
Connecticut Coll (CT)
Cornell U (NY)
Dartmouth Coll (NH)
Fordham U (NY)
Gettysburg Coll (PA)
Goshen Coll (IN)
Hampshire Coll (MA)
Harvard U (MA)
Hofstra U (NY)
Hunter Coll of the City U of NY (NY)
Lewis & Clark Coll (OR)
Loyola Marymount U (CA)
Metropolitan State Coll of Denver (CO)
Mills Coll (CA)
Mount Saint Mary Coll (NY)
Our Lady of the Lake U of San Antonio (TX)
Pitzer Coll (CA)
Pomona Coll (CA)
Pontifical Catholic U of Puerto Rico (PR)
Queen's U at Kingston (ON, Canada)
Rutgers, The State U of New Jersey, Newark (NJ)
Rutgers, The State U of New Jersey, New Brunswick/Piscataway (NJ)
St. Olaf Coll (MN)
San Diego State U (CA)
San Francisco State U (CA)
Scripps Coll (CA)
Sonoma State U (CA)
Southern Methodist U (TX)
Stanford U (CA)
State U of NY Coll at Oneonta (NY)
Trent U (ON, Canada)
Tulane U (LA)
Université de Montréal (QC, Canada)
State U of NY at Albany (NY)

The U of Arizona (AZ)
U of Calif, Berkeley (CA)
U of Calif, Davis (CA)
U of Calif, Irvine (CA)
U of Calif, Los Angeles (CA)
U of Calif, Riverside (CA)
U of Calif, Santa Barbara (CA)
U of Calif, Santa Cruz (CA)
U of Michigan (MI)
U of Michigan–Dearborn (MI)
U of Minnesota, Twin Cities Campus (MN)
U of Northern Colorado (CO)
U of San Diego (CA)
U of Southern California (CA)
U of Southern Maine (ME)
The U of Texas–Pan American (TX)
U of Washington (WA)
U of Windsor (ON, Canada)
U of Wisconsin–Madison (WI)
Wayne State U (MI)
Wheaton Coll (MA)
York U (ON, Canada)

HISTOLOGIC TECHNOLOGY/ HISTOTECHNOLOGIST
Northern Michigan U (MI)

HISTORIC PRESERVATION AND CONSERVATION
Coll of Charleston (SC)
Cornell U (NY)
Eastern Michigan U (MI)
Goucher Coll (MD)
Mary Washington Coll (VA)
Roger Williams U (RI)
Saint Mary's Coll of California (CA)
Salve Regina U (RI)
Savannah Coll of Art and Design (GA)
U of Delaware (DE)
Ursuline Coll (OH)

HISTORY
Abilene Christian U (TX)
Acadia U (NS, Canada)
Adams State Coll (CO)
Adelphi U (NY)
Adrian Coll (MI)
Agnes Scott Coll (GA)
Alabama State U (AL)
Albany State U (GA)
Albertson Coll of Idaho (ID)
Albertus Magnus Coll (CT)
Albion Coll (MI)
Albright Coll (PA)
Alcorn State U (MS)
Alderson-Broaddus Coll (WV)
Alfred U (NY)
Alice Lloyd Coll (KY)
Allegheny Coll (PA)
Alma Coll (MI)
Alvernia Coll (PA)
Alverno Coll (WI)
American Coll of Thessaloniki(Greece)
American Intl Coll (MA)
American Public U System (WV)
American U (DC)
American U in Bulgaria(Bulgaria)
The American U in Cairo(Egypt)
Amherst Coll (MA)
Anderson Coll (SC)
Andrews U (MI)
Angelo State U (TX)
Anna Maria Coll (MA)
Antioch Coll (OH)
Appalachian State U (NC)
Aquinas Coll (MI)
Arcadia U (PA)
Arizona State U (AZ)
Arizona State U West (AZ)
Arkansas State U (AR)
Armstrong Atlantic State U (GA)
Asbury Coll (KY)
Ashland U (OH)
Assumption Coll (MA)
Athabasca U (AB, Canada)
Athens State U (AL)
Atlantic Baptist U (NB, Canada)
Atlantic Union Coll (MA)
Auburn U (AL)
Auburn U Montgomery (AL)
Augsburg Coll (MN)
Augustana Coll (IL)
Augustana Coll (SD)
Augusta State U (GA)
Aurora U (IL)
Austin Coll (TX)
Austin Peay State U (TN)
Ave Maria Coll (MI)
Averett U (VA)
Avila U (MO)
Azusa Pacific U (CA)
Baker U (KS)
Baldwin-Wallace Coll (OH)
Ball State U (IN)
Bard Coll (NY)
Barnard Coll (NY)
Barry U (FL)
Barton Coll (NC)
Bates Coll (ME)
Baylor U (TX)
Belhaven Coll (MS)
Bellarmine U (KY)
Belmont Abbey Coll (NC)
Belmont U (TN)
Beloit Coll (WI)
Bemidji State U (MN)
Benedictine Coll (KS)
Benedictine U (IL)
Bennington Coll (VT)
Bentley Coll (MA)
Berea Coll (KY)
Baruch Coll of the City U of NY (NY)
Berry Coll (GA)
Bethany Coll (KS)
Bethany Coll (WV)
Bethany Lutheran Coll (MN)
Bethel Coll (IN)
Bethel Coll (KS)
Bethel Coll (TN)
Bethel U (MN)
Bethune-Cookman Coll (FL)
Biola U (CA)
Birmingham-Southern Coll (AL)
Bishop's U (QC, Canada)
Blackburn Coll (IL)
Black Hills State U (SD)
Bloomfield Coll (NJ)
Bloomsburg U of Pennsylvania (PA)
Bluefield Coll (VA)
Blue Mountain Coll (MS)
Bluffton Coll (OH)
Boise State U (ID)
Boston Coll (MA)
Boston U (MA)
Bowdoin Coll (ME)
Bowie State U (MD)
Bowling Green State U (OH)
Bradley U (IL)
Brandeis U (MA)
Brenau U (GA)
Brescia U (KY)
Brevard Coll (NC)
Brewton-Parker Coll (GA)
Briar Cliff U (IA)
Bridgewater Coll (VA)
Bridgewater State Coll (MA)
Brigham Young U (UT)
Brigham Young U–Hawaii (HI)
Brock U (ON, Canada)
Brooklyn Coll of the City U of NY (NY)
Brown U (RI)
Bryan Coll (TN)
Bryant Coll (RI)
Bryn Athyn Coll of the New Church (PA)
Bryn Mawr Coll (PA)
Bucknell U (PA)
Buena Vista U (IA)
State U of NY Coll at Buffalo (NY)
Butler U (IN)
Cabrini Coll (PA)
Caldwell Coll (NJ)
California Baptist U (CA)
California Inst of Technology (CA)
California Lutheran U (CA)
California Polytechnic State U, San Luis Obispo (CA)
California State Polytechnic U, Pomona (CA)
California State U, Chico (CA)
California State U, Dominguez Hills (CA)
California State U, Fresno (CA)
California State U, Fullerton (CA)
California State U, Hayward (CA)
California State U, Long Beach (CA)
California State U, Los Angeles (CA)
California State U, Sacramento (CA)
California State U, San Bernardino (CA)
California State U, San Marcos (CA)
California State U, Stanislaus (CA)
California U of Pennsylvania (PA)
Calvin Coll (MI)
Cameron U (OK)
Campbellsville U (KY)
Campbell U (NC)
Canadian Mennonite U (MB, Canada)
Canisius Coll (NY)
Capital U (OH)
Cardinal Stritch U (WI)
Carleton Coll (MN)
Carleton U (ON, Canada)
Carlow Coll (PA)
Carnegie Mellon U (PA)
Carroll Coll (MT)
Carroll Coll (WI)
Carson-Newman Coll (TN)
Carthage Coll (WI)
Case Western Reserve U (OH)
Castleton State Coll (VT)
Catawba Coll (NC)
The Catholic U of America (DC)
Cedar Crest Coll (PA)
Cedarville U (OH)
Centenary Coll (NJ)
Centenary Coll of Louisiana (LA)
Central Coll (IA)
Central Connecticut State U (CT)
Central Methodist Coll (MO)
Central Michigan U (MI)
Central Missouri State U (MO)
Central State U (OH)
Central Washington U (WA)
Centre Coll (KY)
Chadron State Coll (NE)
Chaminade U of Honolulu (HI)
Chapman U (CA)
Charleston Southern U (SC)
Chatham Coll (PA)
Chestnut Hill Coll (PA)
Chicago State U (IL)
Chowan Coll (NC)
Christendom Coll (VA)
Christian Brothers U (TN)
Christian Heritage Coll (CA)
Christopher Newport U (VA)
Citadel, The Military Coll of South Carolina (SC)
City Coll of the City U of NY (NY)
Claremont McKenna Coll (CA)
Clarion U of Pennsylvania (PA)
Clark Atlanta U (GA)
Clarke Coll (IA)
Clarkson U (NY)
Clark U (MA)
Clayton Coll & State U (GA)
Clearwater Christian Coll (FL)
Clemson U (SC)
Coastal Carolina U (SC)
Coe Coll (IA)
Coker Coll (SC)
Colby Coll (ME)
Colgate U (NY)
Coll Misericordia (PA)
Coll of Charleston (SC)
Coll of Mount St. Joseph (OH)
Coll of Mount Saint Vincent (NY)
The Coll of New Jersey (NJ)
The Coll of New Rochelle (NY)
Coll of Notre Dame of Maryland (MD)
Coll of Saint Benedict (MN)
Coll of St. Catherine (MN)
Coll of Saint Elizabeth (NJ)
Coll of St. Joseph (VT)
The Coll of Saint Rose (NY)
The Coll of St. Scholastica (MN)
The Coll of Southeastern Europe, The American U of Athens(Greece)
Coll of Staten Island of the City U of NY (NY)
Coll of the Holy Cross (MA)
Coll of the Ozarks (MO)
Coll of the Southwest (NM)
The Coll of William and Mary (VA)
The Coll of Wooster (OH)
Colorado Christian U (CO)
The Colorado Coll (CO)
Colorado State U (CO)
Colorado State U-Pueblo (CO)
Columbia Coll (MO)
Columbia Coll (NY)
Columbia Coll (SC)
Columbia Union Coll (MD)
Columbia U, School of General Studies (NY)
Columbus State U (GA)
Concord Coll (WV)
Concordia Coll (MN)
Concordia Coll (NY)
Concordia U (CA)
Concordia U (IL)
Concordia U (NE)
Concordia U (QC, Canada)
Concordia U at Austin (TX)
Concordia U Coll of Alberta (AB, Canada)
Concordia U, St. Paul (MN)
Concordia U Wisconsin (WI)
Connecticut Coll (CT)
Converse Coll (SC)
Cornell Coll (IA)
Cornell U (NY)
Cornerstone U (MI)
Covenant Coll (GA)
Creighton U (NE)
Crichton Coll (TN)
Crown Coll (MN)
Culver-Stockton Coll (MO)
Cumberland Coll (KY)
Cumberland U (TN)
Curry Coll (MA)
Daemen Coll (NY)
Dakota Wesleyan U (SD)
Dalhousie U (NS, Canada)
Dallas Baptist U (TX)
Dana Coll (NE)
Dartmouth Coll (NH)
Davidson Coll (NC)
Davis & Elkins Coll (WV)
Defiance Coll (OH)
Delaware State U (DE)
Delta State U (MS)
Denison U (OH)
DePaul U (IL)
DePauw U (IN)
DeSales U (PA)
Dickinson Coll (PA)
Dickinson State U (ND)
Dillard U (LA)
Doane Coll (NE)
Dominican Coll (NY)
Dominican U (IL)
Dominican U of California (CA)
Dordt Coll (IA)
Dowling Coll (NY)
Drake U (IA)
Drew U (NJ)
Drexel U (PA)
Drury U (MO)
Duke U (NC)
Duquesne U (PA)
D'Youville Coll (NY)
Earlham Coll (IN)
East Carolina U (NC)
East Central U (OK)
Eastern Connecticut State U (CT)
Eastern Illinois U (IL)
Eastern Kentucky U (KY)
Eastern Mennonite U (VA)
Eastern Michigan U (MI)
Eastern Nazarene Coll (MA)
Eastern New Mexico U (NM)
Eastern Oregon U (OR)
Eastern U (PA)
Eastern Washington U (WA)
East Stroudsburg U of Pennsylvania (PA)
East Texas Baptist U (TX)
Eckerd Coll (FL)
Edgewood Coll (WI)
Edinboro U of Pennsylvania (PA)
Elizabeth City State U (NC)
Elizabethtown Coll (PA)
Elmhurst Coll (IL)
Elmira Coll (NY)
Elms Coll (MA)
Elon U (NC)
Emory & Henry Coll (VA)
Emory U (GA)
Emporia State U (KS)
Erskine Coll (SC)
Eugene Lang Coll, New School U (NY)
Eureka Coll (IL)
Evangel U (MO)
Excelsior Coll (NY)
Fairfield U (CT)
Fairleigh Dickinson U, Florham (NJ)
Fairleigh Dickinson U, Teaneck-Metro Campus (NJ)
Fairmont State Coll (WV)
Faulkner U (AL)
Fayetteville State U (NC)
Ferrum Coll (VA)
Flagler Coll (FL)
Florida Ag and Mech U (FL)
Florida Atlantic U (FL)
Florida Intl U (FL)
Florida Southern Coll (FL)
Florida State U (FL)
Fontbonne U (MO)
Fordham U (NY)
Fort Hays State U (KS)
Fort Lewis Coll (CO)
Framingham State Coll (MA)
Franciscan U of Steubenville (OH)
Francis Marion U (SC)
Franklin and Marshall Coll (PA)
Franklin Coll (IN)
Franklin Coll Switzerland(Switzerland)
Franklin Pierce Coll (NH)
Freed-Hardeman U (TN)
Fresno Pacific U (CA)
Frostburg State U (MD)
Furman U (SC)
Gallaudet U (DC)
Gannon U (PA)
Gardner-Webb U (NC)
Geneva Coll (PA)
George Fox U (OR)
George Mason U (VA)
Georgetown Coll (KY)
Georgetown U (DC)
The George Washington U (DC)
Georgia Coll & State U (GA)
Georgian Court U (NJ)
Georgia Southern U (GA)
Georgia Southwestern State U (GA)
Georgia State U (GA)
Gettysburg Coll (PA)
Glenville State Coll (WV)
Gonzaga U (WA)
Gordon Coll (MA)
Goshen Coll (IN)
Goucher Coll (MD)
Graceland U (IA)
Grambling State U (LA)
Grand Canyon U (AZ)
Grand Valley State U (MI)
Grand View Coll (IA)
Greensboro Coll (NC)
Grinnell Coll (IA)
Grove City Coll (PA)
Guilford Coll (NC)
Gustavus Adolphus Coll (MN)
Gwynedd-Mercy Coll (PA)
Hamilton Coll (NY)
Hamline U (MN)
Hampden-Sydney Coll (VA)
Hampshire Coll (MA)
Hampton U (VA)
Hannibal-LaGrange Coll (MO)
Hanover Coll (IN)
Harding U (AR)
Hardin-Simmons U (TX)
Hartwick Coll (NY)
Harvard U (MA)
Hastings Coll (NE)
Haverford Coll (PA)
Hawai'i Pacific U (HI)
Heidelberg Coll (OH)
Henderson State U (AR)
Hendrix Coll (AR)
High Point U (NC)
Hillsdale Coll (MI)
Hiram Coll (OH)
Hobart and William Smith Colls (NY)
Hofstra U (NY)
Hollins U (VA)
Holy Names Coll (CA)
Hood Coll (MD)
Hope Coll (MI)
Houghton Coll (NY)
Houston Baptist U (TX)
Howard Payne U (TX)
Howard U (DC)
Humboldt State U (CA)
Hunter Coll of the City U of NY (NY)
Huntingdon Coll (AL)
Huntington Coll (IN)
Idaho State U (ID)
Illinois Coll (IL)
Illinois State U (IL)
Illinois Wesleyan U (IL)
Immaculata U (PA)
Indiana State U (IN)
Indiana U Bloomington (IN)
Indiana U Northwest (IN)
Indiana U of Pennsylvania (PA)
Indiana U–Purdue U Fort Wayne (IN)
Indiana U–Purdue U Indianapolis (IN)
Indiana U South Bend (IN)
Indiana U Southeast (IN)
Inter American U of PR, Fajardo Campus (PR)
Iona Coll (NY)
Iowa State U of Science and Technology (IA)
Iowa Wesleyan Coll (IA)
Ithaca Coll (NY)
Jacksonville State U (AL)
Jacksonville U (FL)
James Madison U (VA)
Jamestown Coll (ND)
Jarvis Christian Coll (TX)
Jewish Theological Sem of America (NY)
John Brown U (AR)
John Carroll U (OH)
The Johns Hopkins U (MD)
Johnson C. Smith U (NC)
Johnson State Coll (VT)
Judson Coll (AL)
Judson Coll (IL)
Juniata Coll (PA)
Kalamazoo Coll (MI)
Kansas State U (KS)
Kansas Wesleyan U (KS)
Kean U (NJ)

Keene State Coll (NH)
Kennesaw State U (GA)
Kent State U (OH)
Kentucky Christian Coll (KY)
Kentucky State U (KY)
Kentucky Wesleyan Coll (KY)
Kenyon Coll (OH)
Keuka Coll (NY)
King Coll (TN)
King's Coll (PA)
The King's U Coll (AB, Canada)
Knox Coll (IL)
Kutztown U of Pennsylvania (PA)
Lafayette Coll (PA)
LaGrange Coll (GA)
Lake Forest Coll (IL)
Lakehead U (ON, Canada)
Lakeland Coll (WI)
Lake Superior State U (MI)
Lamar U (TX)
Lambuth U (TN)
Lander U (SC)
Lane Coll (TN)
La Roche Coll (PA)
La Salle U (PA)
Lasell Coll (MA)
Laura and Alvin Siegal Coll of Judaic Studies (OH)
Laurentian U (ON, Canada)
Lawrence U (WI)
Lebanon Valley Coll (PA)
Lehigh U (PA)
Lehman Coll of the City U of NY (NY)
Le Moyne Coll (NY)
Lenoir-Rhyne Coll (NC)
LeTourneau U (TX)
Lewis & Clark Coll (OR)
Lewis U (IL)
Liberty U (VA)
Limestone Coll (SC)
Lincoln Memorial U (TN)
Lincoln U (MO)
Lincoln U (PA)
Lindenwood U (MO)
Lindsey Wilson Coll (KY)
Linfield Coll (OR)
Lipscomb U (TN)
Livingstone Coll (NC)
Lock Haven U of Pennsylvania (PA)
Long Island U, Brooklyn Campus (NY)
Long Island U, C.W. Post Campus (NY)
Longwood U (VA)
Loras Coll (IA)
Louisiana Coll (LA)
Louisiana State U and A&M Coll (LA)
Louisiana State U in Shreveport (LA)
Louisiana Tech U (LA)
Lourdes Coll (OH)
Loyola Coll in Maryland (MD)
Loyola Marymount U (CA)
Loyola U Chicago (IL)
Loyola U New Orleans (LA)
Luther Coll (IA)
Lycoming Coll (PA)
Lynchburg Coll (VA)
Lynn U (FL)
Lyon Coll (AR)
Macalester Coll (MN)
MacMurray Coll (IL)
Madonna U (MI)
Malaspina U-Coll (BC, Canada)
Malone Coll (OH)
Manchester Coll (IN)
Manhattan Coll (NY)
Manhattanville Coll (NY)
Mansfield U of Pennsylvania (PA)
Marian Coll (IN)
Marian Coll of Fond du Lac (WI)
Marietta Coll (OH)
Marist Coll (NY)
Marlboro Coll (VT)
Marquette U (WI)
Marshall U (WV)
Mars Hill Coll (NC)
Martin U (IN)
Mary Baldwin Coll (VA)
Marygrove Coll (MI)
Marymount Coll of Fordham U (NY)
Marymount Manhattan Coll (NY)
Marymount U (VA)
Maryville Coll (TN)
Maryville U of Saint Louis (MO)
Mary Washington Coll (VA)
Marywood U (PA)
Massachusetts Coll of Liberal Arts (MA)
Massachusetts Inst of Technology (MA)
The Master's Coll and Sem (CA)
McDaniel Coll (MD)
McGill U (QC, Canada)
McKendree Coll (IL)
McMurry U (TX)
McNeese State U (LA)
McPherson Coll (KS)
Memorial U of Newfoundland (NL, Canada)
Mercer U (GA)
Mercy Coll (NY)
Mercyhurst Coll (PA)
Meredith Coll (NC)
Merrimack Coll (MA)
Messiah Coll (PA)
Methodist Coll (NC)
Metropolitan State Coll of Denver (CO)
Metropolitan State U (MN)
Miami U (OH)
Miami U Hamilton (OH)
Michigan State U (MI)
MidAmerica Nazarene U (KS)
Middlebury Coll (VT)
Middle Tennessee State U (TN)
Midwestern State U (TX)
Miles Coll (AL)
Millersville U of Pennsylvania (PA)
Milligan Coll (TN)
Millikin U (IL)
Millsaps Coll (MS)
Mills Coll (CA)
Minnesota State U Mankato (MN)
Minnesota State U Moorhead (MN)
Minot State U (ND)
Mississippi Coll (MS)
Mississippi State U (MS)
Mississippi Valley State U (MS)
Missouri Baptist U (MO)
Missouri Southern State U (MO)
Missouri Valley Coll (MO)
Missouri Western State Coll (MO)
Molloy Coll (NY)
Monmouth Coll (IL)
Monmouth U (NJ)
Montana State U–Billings (MT)
Montana State U–Bozeman (MT)
Montclair State U (NJ)
Montreat Coll (NC)
Moravian Coll (PA)
Morehead State U (KY)
Morehouse Coll (GA)
Morgan State U (MD)
Morningside Coll (IA)
Morris Coll (SC)
Mount Allison U (NB, Canada)
Mount Aloysius Coll (PA)
Mount Holyoke Coll (MA)
Mount Marty Coll (SD)
Mount Mary Coll (WI)
Mount Mercy Coll (IA)
Mount Saint Mary Coll (NY)
Mount St. Mary's Coll (CA)
Mount Saint Mary's Coll and Sem (MD)
Mount Saint Vincent U (NS, Canada)
Mount Union Coll (OH)
Mount Vernon Nazarene U (OH)
Muhlenberg Coll (PA)
Multnomah Bible Coll and Biblical Sem (OR)
Murray State U (KY)
Nazareth Coll of Rochester (NY)
Nebraska Wesleyan U (NE)
Nevada State Coll at Henderson (NV)
Newberry Coll (SC)
New Coll of Florida (FL)
New Jersey City U (NJ)
New Jersey Inst of Technology (NJ)
Newman U (KS)
New Mexico Highlands U (NM)
New Mexico State U (NM)
New York U (NY)
Niagara U (NY)
Nicholls State U (LA)
Nichols Coll (MA)
Nipissing U (ON, Canada)
Norfolk State U (VA)
North Carolina Central U (NC)
North Carolina State U (NC)
North Carolina Wesleyan Coll (NC)
North Central Coll (IL)
North Dakota State U (ND)
Northeastern Illinois U (IL)
Northeastern State U (OK)
Northeastern U (MA)
Northern Arizona U (AZ)
Northern Illinois U (IL)
Northern Michigan U (MI)
Northern State U (SD)
North Georgia Coll & State U (GA)
Northland Coll (WI)
North Park U (IL)
Northwestern Coll (IA)
Northwestern Coll (MN)
Northwestern Oklahoma State U (OK)
Northwestern State U of Louisiana (LA)
Northwestern U (IL)
Northwest Nazarene U (ID)
Notre Dame Coll (OH)
Notre Dame de Namur U (CA)
Nova Southeastern U (FL)
Nyack Coll (NY)
Oakland U (MI)
Oberlin Coll (OH)
Occidental Coll (CA)
Oglethorpe U (GA)
Ohio Dominican U (OH)
Ohio Northern U (OH)
The Ohio State U (OH)
The Ohio State U at Lima (OH)
The Ohio State U at Marion (OH)
The Ohio State U–Mansfield Campus (OH)
The Ohio State U–Newark Campus (OH)
Ohio U (OH)
Ohio Wesleyan U (OH)
Okanagan U Coll (BC, Canada)
Oklahoma Baptist U (OK)
Oklahoma Christian U (OK)
Oklahoma City U (OK)
Oklahoma Panhandle State U (OK)
Oklahoma State U (OK)
Old Dominion U (VA)
Olivet Coll (MI)
Olivet Nazarene U (IL)
Oral Roberts U (OK)
Oregon State U (OR)
Ottawa U (KS)
Otterbein Coll (OH)
Ouachita Baptist U (AR)
Our Lady of Holy Cross Coll (LA)
Our Lady of the Lake U of San Antonio (TX)
Pace U (NY)
Pacific Lutheran U (WA)
Pacific Union Coll (CA)
Pacific U (OR)
Paine Coll (GA)
Palm Beach Atlantic U (FL)
Park U (MO)
Patrick Henry Coll (VA)
Penn State U Abington Coll (PA)
Penn State U Altoona Coll (PA)
Penn State U at Erie, The Behrend Coll (PA)
Penn State U Beaver Campus of the Commonwealth Coll (PA)
Penn State U Berks Cmps of Berks-Lehigh Valley Coll (PA)
Penn State U Delaware County Campus of the Commonwealth Coll (PA)
Penn State U DuBois Campus of the Commonwealth Coll (PA)
Penn State U Fayette Campus of the Commonwealth Coll (PA)
Penn State U Hazleton Campus of the Commonwealth Coll (PA)
Penn State U Lehigh Valley Cmps of Berks-Lehigh Valley Coll (PA)
Penn State U McKeesport Campus of the Commonwealth Coll (PA)
Penn State U Mont Alto Campus of the Commonwealth Coll (PA)
Penn State U New Kensington Campus of the Commonwealth Coll (PA)
Penn State U Schuylkill Campus of the Capital Coll (PA)
Penn State U Shenango Campus of the Commonwealth Coll (PA)
Penn State U Univ Park Campus (PA)
Penn State U Wilkes-Barre Campus of the Commonwealth Coll (PA)
Penn State U Worthington Scranton Cmps Commonwealth Coll (PA)
Penn State U York Campus of the Commonwealth Coll (PA)
Pepperdine U, Malibu (CA)
Pfeiffer U (NC)
Piedmont Coll (GA)
Pikeville Coll (KY)
Pine Manor Coll (MA)
Pittsburg State U (KS)
Pitzer Coll (CA)
Plymouth State U (NH)
Point Loma Nazarene U (CA)
Point Park U (PA)
Pomona Coll (CA)
Pontifical Catholic U of Puerto Rico (PR)
Portland State U (OR)
Prairie View A&M U (TX)
Presbyterian Coll (SC)
Princeton U (NJ)
Principia Coll (IL)
Providence Coll (RI)
Providence Coll and Theological Sem (MB, Canada)
Purdue U (IN)
Queens Coll of the City U of NY (NY)
Queen's U at Kingston (ON, Canada)
Queens U of Charlotte (NC)
Quincy U (IL)
Quinnipiac U (CT)
Radford U (VA)
Ramapo Coll of New Jersey (NJ)
Randolph-Macon Coll (VA)
Randolph-Macon Woman's Coll (VA)
Redeemer U Coll (ON, Canada)
Reed Coll (OR)
Regis Coll (MA)
Regis U (CO)
Reinhardt Coll (GA)
Rhode Island Coll (RI)
Rhodes Coll (TN)
Rice U (TX)
The Richard Stockton Coll of New Jersey (NJ)
Richmond, The American Intl U in London(United Kingdom)
Rider U (NJ)
Ripon Coll (WI)
Rivier Coll (NH)
Roanoke Coll (VA)
Roberts Wesleyan Coll (NY)
Rochester Coll (MI)
Rockford Coll (IL)
Rockhurst U (MO)
Rocky Mountain Coll (MT)
Roger Williams U (RI)
Rollins Coll (FL)
Roosevelt U (IL)
Rosemont Coll (PA)
Rowan U (NJ)
Russell Sage Coll (NY)
Rutgers, The State U of New Jersey, Camden (NJ)
Rutgers, The State U of New Jersey, Newark (NJ)
Rutgers, The State U of New Jersey, New Brunswick/Piscataway (NJ)
Sacred Heart U (CT)
Saginaw Valley State U (MI)
St. Ambrose U (IA)
St. Andrews Presbyterian Coll (NC)
Saint Anselm Coll (NH)
Saint Augustine's Coll (NC)
St. Bonaventure U (NY)
St. Cloud State U (MN)
St. Edward's U (TX)
St. Francis Coll (NY)
Saint Francis U (PA)
St. Francis Xavier U (NS, Canada)
St. Gregory's U (OK)
St. John Fisher Coll (NY)
St. John's Coll (NM)
Saint John's U (MN)
St. John's U (NY)
Saint Joseph Coll (CT)
Saint Joseph's Coll (IN)
St. Joseph's Coll, New York (NY)
Saint Joseph's Coll of Maine (ME)
St. Joseph's Coll, Suffolk Campus (NY)
Saint Joseph's U (PA)
St. Lawrence U (NY)
Saint Leo U (FL)
Saint Louis U (MO)
Saint Martin's Coll (WA)
Saint Mary-of-the-Woods Coll (IN)
Saint Mary's Coll (IN)
Saint Mary's Coll of California (CA)
St. Mary's Coll of Maryland (MD)
Saint Mary's U of Minnesota (MN)
St. Mary's U of San Antonio (TX)
Saint Michael's Coll (VT)
St. Norbert Coll (WI)
St. Olaf Coll (MN)
St. Thomas Aquinas Coll (NY)
St. Thomas U (FL)
St. Thomas U (NB, Canada)
Saint Vincent Coll (PA)
Saint Xavier U (IL)
Salem Coll (NC)
Salem State Coll (MA)
Salisbury U (MD)
Salve Regina U (RI)
Samford U (AL)
Sam Houston State U (TX)
San Diego State U (CA)
San Francisco State U (CA)
San Jose State U (CA)
Santa Clara U (CA)
Sarah Lawrence Coll (NY)
Schreiner U (TX)
Scripps Coll (CA)
Seattle Pacific U (WA)
Seattle U (WA)
Seton Hall U (NJ)
Seton Hill U (PA)
Shawnee State U (OH)
Shenandoah U (VA)
Shepherd U (WV)
Shippensburg U of Pennsylvania (PA)
Shorter Coll (GA)
Siena Coll (NY)
Siena Heights U (MI)
Silver Lake Coll (WI)
Simmons Coll (MA)
Simon Fraser U (BC, Canada)
Simpson Coll (IA)
Simpson Coll and Graduate School (CA)
Skidmore Coll (NY)
Slippery Rock U of Pennsylvania (PA)
Smith Coll (MA)
Sonoma State U (CA)
South Carolina State U (SC)
South Dakota State U (SD)
Southeastern Louisiana U (LA)
Southeastern Oklahoma State U (OK)
Southeast Missouri State U (MO)
Southern Adventist U (TN)
Southern Arkansas U–Magnolia (AR)
Southern Connecticut State U (CT)
Southern Illinois U Carbondale (IL)
Southern Illinois U Edwardsville (IL)
Southern Methodist U (TX)
Southern Nazarene U (OK)
Southern Oregon U (OR)
Southern U and A&M Coll (LA)
Southern Utah U (UT)
Southern Virginia U (VA)
Southern Wesleyan U (SC)
Southwest Baptist U (MO)
Southwestern Coll (KS)
Southwestern Oklahoma State U (OK)
Southwestern U (TX)
Southwest Missouri State U (MO)
Spelman Coll (GA)
Spring Arbor U (MI)
Springfield Coll (MA)
Spring Hill Coll (AL)
Stanford U (CA)
State U of NY at Binghamton (NY)
State U of NY at New Paltz (NY)
State U of NY at Oswego (NY)
Plattsburgh State U of NY (NY)
State U of NY Coll at Brockport (NY)
State U of NY Coll at Cortland (NY)
State U of NY Coll at Fredonia (NY)
State U of NY Coll at Geneseo (NY)
State U of NY Coll at Oneonta (NY)
State U of NY Coll at Potsdam (NY)
State U of NY Empire State Coll (NY)
State U of West Georgia (GA)
Sterling Coll (KS)
Stetson U (FL)
Stevens Inst of Technology (NJ)
Stonehill Coll (MA)
Stony Brook U, State U of New York (NY)
Suffolk U (MA)
Susquehanna U (PA)
Swarthmore Coll (PA)
Sweet Briar Coll (VA)
Syracuse U (NY)
Tabor Coll (KS)
Talladega Coll (AL)
Tarleton State U (TX)
Taylor U (IN)
Teikyo Post U (CT)
Tennessee State U (TN)
Tennessee Technological U (TN)
Tennessee Wesleyan Coll (TN)
Texas A&M Intl U (TX)
Texas A&M U (TX)
Texas A&M U–Commerce (TX)
Texas A&M U–Corpus Christi (TX)
Texas A&M U–Kingsville (TX)
Texas A&M U–Texarkana (TX)
Texas Christian U (TX)
Texas Lutheran U (TX)
Texas Southern U (TX)
Texas State U-San Marcos (TX)
Texas Tech U (TX)
Texas Wesleyan U (TX)
Texas Woman's U (TX)
Thiel Coll (PA)
Thomas Edison State Coll (NJ)

Thomas More Coll (KY)
Tougaloo Coll (MS)
Towson U (MD)
Transylvania U (KY)
Trent U (ON, Canada)
Trevecca Nazarene U (TN)
Trinity Christian Coll (IL)
Trinity Coll (CT)
Trinity Coll (DC)
Trinity Intl U (IL)
Trinity U (TX)
Trinity Western U (BC, Canada)
Troy State U (AL)
Troy State U Dothan (AL)
Troy State U Montgomery (AL)
Truman State U (MO)
Tufts U (MA)
Tulane U (LA)
Tusculum Coll (TN)
Tuskegee U (AL)
Tyndale U Coll & Sem (ON, Canada)
Union Coll (KY)
Union Coll (NE)
Union Coll (NY)
Union Inst & U (OH)
Union U (TN)
United States Air Force Acad (CO)
United States Military Acad (NY)
United States Naval Acad (MD)
Universidad Adventista de las Antillas (PR)
Université de Montréal (QC, Canada)
Université de Sherbrooke (QC, Canada)
Université Laval (QC, Canada)
State U of NY at Albany (NY)
U at Buffalo, The State U of New York (NY)
U Coll of the Cariboo (BC, Canada)
U Coll of the Fraser Valley (BC, Canada)
The U of Akron (OH)
The U of Alabama (AL)
The U of Alabama at Birmingham (AL)
The U of Alabama in Huntsville (AL)
U of Alaska Fairbanks (AK)
U of Alberta (AB, Canada)
The U of Arizona (AZ)
U of Arkansas (AR)
U of Arkansas at Little Rock (AR)
U of Arkansas at Monticello (AR)
U of Baltimore (MD)
The U of British Columbia (BC, Canada)
U of Calgary (AB, Canada)
U of Calif, Berkeley (CA)
U of Calif, Davis (CA)
U of Calif, Irvine (CA)
U of Calif, Los Angeles (CA)
U of Calif, Riverside (CA)
U of Calif, San Diego (CA)
U of Calif, Santa Barbara (CA)
U of Calif, Santa Cruz (CA)
U of Central Arkansas (AR)
U of Central Florida (FL)
U of Charleston (WV)
U of Chicago (IL)
U of Cincinnati (OH)
U of Colorado at Boulder (CO)
U of Colorado at Colorado Springs (CO)
U of Colorado at Denver (CO)
U of Connecticut (CT)
U of Dallas (TX)
U of Dayton (OH)
U of Delaware (DE)
U of Denver (CO)
U of Detroit Mercy (MI)
U of Evansville (IN)
The U of Findlay (OH)
U of Florida (FL)
U of Georgia (GA)
U of Great Falls (MT)
U of Guelph (ON, Canada)
U of Hartford (CT)
U of Hawaii at Hilo (HI)
U of Houston (TX)
U of Houston–Clear Lake (TX)
U of Houston–Victoria (TX)
U of Idaho (ID)
U of Illinois at Chicago (IL)
U of Illinois at Springfield (IL)
U of Illinois at Urbana–Champaign (IL)
U of Indianapolis (IN)
The U of Iowa (IA)
U of Kansas (KS)
U of Kentucky (KY)
U of King's Coll (NS, Canada)
U of La Verne (CA)
The U of Lethbridge (AB, Canada)
U of Louisiana at Lafayette (LA)
U of Louisville (KY)
U of Maine (ME)
U of Maine at Farmington (ME)
U of Maine at Machias (ME)
U of Manitoba (MB, Canada)
U of Mary (ND)
U of Mary Hardin-Baylor (TX)
U of Maryland, Baltimore County (MD)
U of Maryland, Coll Park (MD)
U of Maryland Eastern Shore (MD)
U of Maryland U Coll (MD)
U of Massachusetts Amherst (MA)
U of Massachusetts Boston (MA)
U of Massachusetts Dartmouth (MA)
U of Massachusetts Lowell (MA)
The U of Memphis (TN)
U of Miami (FL)
U of Michigan (MI)
U of Michigan–Dearborn (MI)
U of Michigan–Flint (MI)
U of Minnesota, Duluth (MN)
U of Minnesota, Morris (MN)
U of Minnesota, Twin Cities Campus (MN)
U of Mississippi (MS)
U of Missouri–Columbia (MO)
U of Missouri–Kansas City (MO)
U of Missouri–Rolla (MO)
U of Missouri–St. Louis (MO)
U of Mobile (AL)
The U of Montana–Missoula (MT)
U of Montevallo (AL)
U of Nebraska at Omaha (NE)
U of Nebraska–Lincoln (NE)
U of Nevada, Las Vegas (NV)
U of Nevada, Reno (NV)
U of New Brunswick Fredericton (NB, Canada)
U of New Hampshire (NH)
U of New Hampshire at Manchester (NH)
U of New Haven (CT)
U of New Mexico (NM)
U of New Orleans (LA)
U of North Alabama (AL)
The U of North Carolina at Asheville (NC)
The U of North Carolina at Chapel Hill (NC)
The U of North Carolina at Charlotte (NC)
The U of North Carolina at Greensboro (NC)
The U of North Carolina at Pembroke (NC)
The U of North Carolina at Wilmington (NC)
U of North Dakota (ND)
U of Northern Colorado (CO)
U of Northern Iowa (IA)
U of North Florida (FL)
U of North Texas (TX)
U of Notre Dame (IN)
U of Oklahoma (OK)
U of Oregon (OR)
U of Ottawa (ON, Canada)
U of Pennsylvania (PA)
U of Pittsburgh (PA)
U of Pittsburgh at Bradford (PA)
U of Pittsburgh at Johnstown (PA)
U of Portland (OR)
U of Prince Edward Island (PE, Canada)
U of Puerto Rico, Cayey U Coll (PR)
U of Puget Sound (WA)
U of Redlands (CA)
U of Regina (SK, Canada)
U of Rhode Island (RI)
U of Richmond (VA)
U of Rochester (NY)
U of St. Francis (IL)
U of Saint Francis (IN)
U of Saint Mary (KS)
U of St. Thomas (MN)
U of St. Thomas (TX)
U of San Diego (CA)
U of San Francisco (CA)
U of Saskatchewan (SK, Canada)
U of Science and Arts of Oklahoma (OK)
The U of Scranton (PA)
U of Sioux Falls (SD)
U of South Alabama (AL)
U of South Carolina (SC)
U of South Carolina Aiken (SC)
U of South Carolina Spartanburg (SC)
The U of South Dakota (SD)
U of Southern California (CA)
U of Southern Indiana (IN)
U of Southern Maine (ME)
U of South Florida (FL)
The U of Tampa (FL)
The U of Tennessee (TN)
The U of Tennessee at Chattanooga (TN)
The U of Tennessee at Martin (TN)
The U of Texas at Arlington (TX)
The U of Texas at Austin (TX)
The U of Texas at Brownsville (TX)
The U of Texas at Dallas (TX)
The U of Texas at Tyler (TX)
The U of Texas–Pan American (TX)
U of the District of Columbia (DC)
U of the Incarnate Word (TX)
U of the Ozarks (AR)
U of the Pacific (CA)
U of the South (TN)
U of the West (CA)
U of Toledo (OH)
U of Toronto (ON, Canada)
U of Tulsa (OK)
U of Utah (UT)
U of Vermont (VT)
U of Victoria (BC, Canada)
U of Virginia (VA)
The U of Virginia's Coll at Wise (VA)
U of Washington (WA)
U of Waterloo (ON, Canada)
The U of West Alabama (AL)
The U of Western Ontario (ON, Canada)
U of West Florida (FL)
U of Windsor (ON, Canada)
U of Wisconsin–Eau Claire (WI)
U of Wisconsin–Green Bay (WI)
U of Wisconsin–La Crosse (WI)
U of Wisconsin–Madison (WI)
U of Wisconsin–Milwaukee (WI)
U of Wisconsin–Oshkosh (WI)
U of Wisconsin–Parkside (WI)
U of Wisconsin–Platteville (WI)
U of Wisconsin–River Falls (WI)
U of Wisconsin–Stevens Point (WI)
U of Wisconsin–Superior (WI)
U of Wisconsin–Whitewater (WI)
U of Wyoming (WY)
Urbana U (OH)
Ursinus Coll (PA)
Ursuline Coll (OH)
Utah State U (UT)
Utica Coll (NY)
Valdosta State U (GA)
Valley City State U (ND)
Valparaiso U (IN)
Vanderbilt U (TN)
Vanguard U of Southern California (CA)
Villanova U (PA)
Virginia Commonwealth U (VA)
Virginia Intermont Coll (VA)
Virginia Military Inst (VA)
Virginia Polytechnic Inst and State U (VA)
Virginia State U (VA)
Virginia Union U (VA)
Virginia Wesleyan Coll (VA)
Wabash Coll (IN)
Wagner Coll (NY)
Wake Forest U (NC)
Waldorf Coll (IA)
Walla Walla Coll (WA)
Walsh U (OH)
Warner Pacific Coll (OR)
Warner Southern Coll (FL)
Warren Wilson Coll (NC)
Wartburg Coll (IA)
Washburn U (KS)
Washington & Jefferson Coll (PA)
Washington and Lee U (VA)
Washington Coll (MD)
Washington State U (WA)
Washington U in St. Louis (MO)
Wayland Baptist U (TX)
Waynesburg Coll (PA)
Wayne State Coll (NE)
Wayne State U (MI)
Weber State U (UT)
Webster U (MO)
Wellesley Coll (MA)
Wells Coll (NY)
Wesleyan Coll (GA)
Wesleyan U (CT)
Wesley Coll (DE)
West Chester U of Pennsylvania (PA)
Western Carolina U (NC)
Western Connecticut State U (CT)
Western Illinois U (IL)
Western Kentucky U (KY)
Western Michigan U (MI)
Western New England Coll (MA)
Western Oregon U (OR)
Western State Coll of Colorado (CO)
Western Washington U (WA)
Westfield State Coll (MA)
West Liberty State Coll (WV)
Westminster Coll (MO)
Westminster Coll (PA)
Westminster Coll (UT)
Westmont Coll (CA)
West Texas A&M U (TX)
West Virginia State Coll (WV)
West Virginia U (WV)
West Virginia Wesleyan Coll (WV)
Wheaton Coll (IL)
Wheaton Coll (MA)
Wheeling Jesuit U (WV)
Whitman Coll (WA)
Whitworth Coll (WA)
Wichita State U (KS)
Widener U (PA)
Wilkes U (PA)
Willamette U (OR)
William Carey Coll (MS)
William Jewell Coll (MO)
William Paterson U of New Jersey (NJ)
William Penn U (IA)
Williams Baptist Coll (AR)
Williams Coll (MA)
William Tyndale Coll (MI)
William Woods U (MO)
Wingate U (NC)
Winona State U (MN)
Winston-Salem State U (NC)
Winthrop U (SC)
Wisconsin Lutheran Coll (WI)
Wittenberg U (OH)
Wofford Coll (SC)
Worcester Polytechnic Inst (MA)
Worcester State Coll (MA)
Wright State U (OH)
Xavier U (OH)
Xavier U of Louisiana (LA)
Yale U (CT)
York Coll (NE)
York Coll of Pennsylvania (PA)
York Coll of the City U of New York (NY)
York U (ON, Canada)
Youngstown State U (OH)

HISTORY AND PHILOSOPHY OF SCIENCE AND TECHNOLOGY

Bard Coll (NY)
Case Western Reserve U (OH)
Cornell U (NY)
Dalhousie U (NS, Canada)
Georgia Inst of Technology (GA)
Hampshire Coll (MA)
Harvard U (MA)
The Johns Hopkins U (MD)
Oregon State U (OR)
Sarah Lawrence Coll (NY)
Stevens Inst of Technology (NJ)
U of Pennsylvania (PA)
U of Pittsburgh (PA)
U of Toronto (ON, Canada)
U of Washington (WA)
U of Wisconsin–Madison (WI)
Worcester Polytechnic Inst (MA)

HISTORY OF PHILOSOPHY

Bard Coll (NY)
Bennington Coll (VT)
Hampshire Coll (MA)
Harvard U (MA)
Marlboro Coll (VT)
Marquette U (WI)
St. John's Coll (NM)
Spring Arbor U (MI)
U of Regina (SK, Canada)
U of Toronto (ON, Canada)

HISTORY RELATED

Bard Coll (NY)
Bridgewater Coll (VA)
Coll of the Holy Cross (MA)
Coll of the Ozarks (MO)
The Colorado Coll (CO)
Cornell U (NY)
D'Youville Coll (NY)
Eastern Michigan U (MI)
The Franciscan U (IA)
Hamilton Coll (NY)
Hampshire Coll (MA)
Hawai'i Pacific U (HI)
Marquette U (WI)
Marylhurst U (OR)
Mercyhurst Coll (PA)
The Ohio State U (OH)
Ohio U (OH)
Saint Mary's U of Minnesota (MN)
Sarah Lawrence Coll (NY)
U of Regina (SK, Canada)

HISTORY TEACHER EDUCATION

Abilene Christian U (TX)
Alma Coll (MI)
Anderson Coll (SC)
Appalachian State U (NC)
Auburn U (AL)
Baylor U (TX)
Bethel Coll (TN)
Bishop's U (QC, Canada)
Bloomfield Coll (NJ)
Bluefield Coll (VA)
Brewton-Parker Coll (GA)
Bridgewater Coll (VA)
Brigham Young U (UT)
Buena Vista U (IA)
Campbellsville U (KY)
Campbell U (NC)
Carroll Coll (MT)
Carroll Coll (WI)
The Catholic U of America (DC)
Central Michigan U (MI)
Central Washington U (WA)
Chadron State Coll (NE)
Charleston Southern U (SC)
Christian Brothers U (TN)
Citadel, The Military Coll of South Carolina (SC)
Clark Atlanta U (GA)
Clearwater Christian Coll (FL)
Coker Coll (SC)
The Coll of New Jersey (NJ)
The Coll of St. Scholastica (MN)
Coll of the Ozarks (MO)
Columbus State U (GA)
Concordia U (IL)
Concordia U (NE)
Concordia U Wisconsin (WI)
Cornerstone U (MI)
Crown Coll (MN)
Culver-Stockton Coll (MO)
Cumberland U (TN)
Dakota Wesleyan U (SD)
Dana Coll (NE)
Dominican Coll (NY)
Dordt Coll (IA)
East Central U (OK)
Eastern Michigan U (MI)
East Texas Baptist U (TX)
Elizabeth City State U (NC)
Elmhurst Coll (IL)
Elmira Coll (NY)
Evangel U (MO)
Framingham State Coll (MA)
Georgia Southern U (GA)
Gwynedd-Mercy Coll (PA)
Hannibal-LaGrange Coll (MO)
Hardin-Simmons U (TX)
Hastings Coll (NE)
Hope Coll (MI)
Howard Payne U (TX)
Huntingdon Coll (AL)
Illinois Wesleyan U (IL)
Ithaca Coll (NY)
Jamestown Coll (ND)
Johnson State Coll (VT)
King Coll (TN)
Lambuth U (TN)
Liberty U (VA)
Lincoln Memorial U (TN)
Lindenwood U (MO)
Marian Coll of Fond du Lac (WI)
Maryville Coll (TN)
Maryville U of Saint Louis (MO)
Marywood U (PA)
McGill U (QC, Canada)
McKendree Coll (IL)
Minot State U (ND)
Montana State U–Billings (MT)
Moravian Coll (PA)
Mount Marty Coll (SD)
Murray State U (KY)
Nazareth Coll of Rochester (NY)
Nevada State Coll at Henderson (NV)
North Carolina Central U (NC)
North Carolina State U (NC)
North Dakota State U (ND)
Northern Arizona U (AZ)
Northern Michigan U (MI)
Northwest Nazarene U (ID)
Ohio Northern U (OH)
Ohio Wesleyan U (OH)
Oklahoma Baptist U (OK)
Paine Coll (GA)
Pittsburg State U (KS)
Pontifical Catholic U of Puerto Rico (PR)
Rocky Mountain Coll (MT)
Sacred Heart U (CT)
St. Ambrose U (IA)
St. Edward's U (TX)
Saint Francis U (PA)
Saint Joseph's Coll of Maine (ME)
Saint Xavier U (IL)
Salve Regina U (RI)
Samford U (AL)
Schreiner U (TX)
Shawnee State U (OH)
Southwest Baptist U (MO)
Southwestern Oklahoma State U (OK)
Southwest Missouri State U (MO)

State U of NY Coll at Brockport (NY)
Talladega Coll (AL)
Taylor U (IN)
Tennessee Wesleyan Coll (TN)
Texas A&M Intl U (TX)
Texas Lutheran U (TX)
Texas Wesleyan U (TX)
Toccoa Falls Coll (GA)
Trevecca Nazarene U (TN)
Trinity Christian Coll (IL)
Union Coll (NE)
Universidad Adventista de las Antillas (PR)
Université Laval (QC, Canada)
The U of Akron (OH)
The U of Arizona (AZ)
U of Delaware (DE)
U of Great Falls (MT)
U of Illinois at Chicago (IL)
The U of Iowa (IA)
U of Maine at Machias (ME)
U of Michigan–Flint (MI)
The U of Montana–Western (MT)
U of Nebraska–Lincoln (NE)
The U of North Carolina at Charlotte (NC)
The U of North Carolina at Wilmington (NC)
U of Pittsburgh at Johnstown (PA)
U of Puerto Rico, Cayey U Coll (PR)
The U of South Dakota (SD)
The U of Tennessee at Martin (TN)
U of Utah (UT)
U of Windsor (ON, Canada)
U of Wisconsin–River Falls (WI)
U of Wisconsin–Superior (WI)
Utica Coll (NY)
Valley City State U (ND)
Valparaiso U (IN)
Wartburg Coll (IA)
Washington U in St. Louis (MO)
Weber State U (UT)
West Chester U of Pennsylvania (PA)
Western Michigan U (MI)
Wheeling Jesuit U (WV)
Widener U (PA)
Xavier U of Louisiana (LA)
York Coll (NE)
York U (ON, Canada)
Youngstown State U (OH)

HOME FURNISHINGS AND EQUIPMENT INSTALLATION
Brigham Young U (UT)

HORSE HUSBANDRY/EQUINE SCIENCE AND MANAGEMENT
Bethany Coll (WV)
Mount Ida Coll (MA)
Stephens Coll (MO)
Sterling Coll (VT)

HORTICULTURAL SCIENCE
Auburn U (AL)
California Polytechnic State U, San Luis Obispo (CA)
California State Polytechnic U, Pomona (CA)
Christopher Newport U (VA)
Clemson U (SC)
Coll of the Ozarks (MO)
Colorado State U (CO)
Cornell U (NY)
Delaware Valley Coll (PA)
Eastern Kentucky U (KY)
Florida Ag and Mech U (FL)
Florida Southern Coll (FL)
Iowa State U of Science and Technology (IA)
Kansas State U (KS)
Michigan State U (MI)
Mississippi State U (MS)
Montana State U–Bozeman (MT)
Murray State U (KY)
Naropa U (CO)
New Mexico State U (NM)
North Carolina State U (NC)
North Dakota State U (ND)
The Ohio State U (OH)
Oklahoma State U (OK)
Oregon State U (OR)
Penn State U Abington Coll (PA)
Penn State U Altoona Coll (PA)
Penn State U at Erie, The Behrend Coll (PA)
Penn State U Beaver Campus of the Commonwealth Coll (PA)
Penn State U Berks Cmps of Berks-Lehigh Valley Coll (PA)
Penn State U Delaware County Campus of the Commonwealth Coll (PA)
Penn State U DuBois Campus of the Commonwealth Coll (PA)
Penn State U Fayette Campus of the Commonwealth Coll (PA)
Penn State U Hazleton Campus of the Commonwealth Coll (PA)
Penn State U Lehigh Valley Cmps of Berks-Lehigh Valley Coll (PA)
Penn State U McKeesport Campus of the Commonwealth Coll (PA)
Penn State U Mont Alto Campus of the Commonwealth Coll (PA)
Penn State U New Kensington Campus of the Commonwealth Coll (PA)
Penn State U Schuylkill Campus of the Capital Coll (PA)
Penn State U Shenango Campus of the Commonwealth Coll (PA)
Penn State U Univ Park Campus (PA)
Penn State U Wilkes-Barre Campus of the Commonwealth Coll (PA)
Penn State U Worthington Scranton Cmps Commonwealth Coll (PA)
Penn State U York Campus of the Commonwealth Coll (PA)
Purdue U (IN)
Sam Houston State U (TX)
Southeastern Louisiana U (LA)
Southwest Missouri State U (MO)
State U of NY Coll of A&T at Cobleskill (NY)
Sterling Coll (VT)
Tennessee Technological U (TN)
Texas A&M U (TX)
Texas A&M U–Kingsville (TX)
Texas Tech U (TX)
Thomas Edison State Coll (NJ)
Truman State U (MO)
U of Arkansas (AR)
The U of British Columbia (BC, Canada)
U of Calif, Davis (CA)
U of Connecticut (CT)
U of Delaware (DE)
U of Florida (FL)
U of Guelph (ON, Canada)
U of Hawaii at Hilo (HI)
U of Idaho (ID)
U of Illinois at Urbana–Champaign (IL)
U of Louisiana at Lafayette (LA)
U of Maryland, Coll Park (MD)
U of Minnesota, Crookston (MN)
U of Nebraska–Lincoln (NE)
U of New Hampshire (NH)
U of Saskatchewan (SK, Canada)
U of Wisconsin–Madison (WI)
U of Wisconsin–River Falls (WI)
Utah State U (UT)
Virginia Polytechnic Inst and State U (VA)
Washington State U (WA)

HOSPITAL AND HEALTH CARE FACILITIES ADMINISTRATION
Avila U (MO)
Black Hills State U (SD)
Carson-Newman Coll (TN)
Central Michigan U (MI)
Coll of Mount Saint Vincent (NY)
Eastern U (PA)
Gwynedd-Mercy Coll (PA)
Ithaca Coll (NY)
Long Island U, C.W. Post Campus (NY)
Marywood U (PA)
Ohio U (OH)
St. John's U (NY)
Saint Joseph's U (PA)
Saint Leo U (FL)
Texas State U-San Marcos (TX)
The U of Alabama (AL)
The U of South Dakota (SD)
U of Texas Southwestern Medical Center at Dallas (TX)
U of Toledo (OH)
Ursuline Coll (OH)
York U (ON, Canada)

HOSPITALITY ADMINISTRATION
American Coll of Thessaloniki(Greece)
Appalachian State U (NC)
Arkansas Tech U (AR)
Becker Coll (MA)
Belmont U (TN)
Boston U (MA)
Bowling Green State U (OH)
State U of NY Coll at Buffalo (NY)
Central Michigan U (MI)
Champlain Coll (VT)
The Coll of Southeastern Europe, The American U of Athens(Greece)
Concord Coll (WV)
Cornell U (NY)
Davis & Elkins Coll (WV)
Delaware State U (DE)
Delta State U (MS)
Eastern Michigan U (MI)
East Stroudsburg U of Pennsylvania (PA)
Endicott Coll (MA)
Ferris State U (MI)
Florida Atlantic U (FL)
Florida Intl U (FL)
Florida State U (FL)
Husson Coll (ME)
Indiana U–Purdue U Fort Wayne (IN)
James Madison U (VA)
Johnson & Wales U (FL)
Johnson & Wales U (RI)
Johnson State Coll (VT)
Kendall Coll (IL)
Lewis-Clark State Coll (ID)
Lexington Coll (IL)
Madonna U (MI)
Mercyhurst Coll (PA)
Metropolitan State Coll of Denver (CO)
Metropolitan State U (MN)
Michigan State U (MI)
Morgan State U (MD)
Mount Saint Vincent U (NS, Canada)
National American U (NM)
National U (CA)
New York U (NY)
North Carolina Central U (NC)
North Dakota State U (ND)
Northwestern State U of Louisiana (LA)
The Ohio State U (OH)
The Ohio State U at Lima (OH)
Robert Morris U (PA)
Rochester Inst of Technology (NY)
Roosevelt U (IL)
Rutgers, The State U of New Jersey, Camden (NJ)
Ryerson U (ON, Canada)
St. John's U (NY)
Saint Leo U (FL)
San Francisco State U (CA)
San Jose State U (CA)
Seton Hill U (PA)
Siena Heights U (MI)
Southwest Missouri State U (MO)
Syracuse U (NY)
Touro U Intl (CA)
Tuskegee U (AL)
U Coll of the Cariboo (BC, Canada)
U of Central Florida (FL)
U of Denver (CO)
U of Kentucky (KY)
U of Massachusetts Amherst (MA)
The U of Memphis (TN)
U of Nevada, Las Vegas (NV)
U of Nevada, Reno (NV)
U of New Hampshire (NH)
U of New Haven (CT)
U of New Orleans (LA)
U of North Texas (TX)
U of Prince Edward Island (PE, Canada)
U of South Carolina (SC)
U of South Florida (FL)
U of West Florida (FL)
U of Wisconsin–Stout (WI)
Virginia State U (VA)
Washington State U (WA)
Western Carolina U (NC)
Youngstown State U (OH)

HOSPITALITY ADMINISTRATION RELATED
Auburn U (AL)
Champlain Coll (VT)
Cornell U (NY)
Drexel U (PA)
Florida State U (FL)
Indiana U–Purdue U Indianapolis (IN)
Kendall Coll (IL)
Kent State U (OH)
Lexington Coll (IL)
Mountain State U (WV)
Niagara U (NY)
Penn State U Abington Coll (PA)
Penn State U Altoona Coll (PA)
Penn State U at Erie, The Behrend Coll (PA)
Penn State U Beaver Campus of the Commonwealth Coll (PA)
Penn State U Berks Cmps of Berks-Lehigh Valley Coll (PA)
Penn State U Delaware County Campus of the Commonwealth Coll (PA)
Penn State U DuBois Campus of the Commonwealth Coll (PA)
Penn State U Fayette Campus of the Commonwealth Coll (PA)
Penn State U Hazleton Campus of the Commonwealth Coll (PA)
Penn State U Lehigh Valley Cmps of Berks-Lehigh Valley Coll (PA)
Penn State U McKeesport Campus of the Commonwealth Coll (PA)
Penn State U Mont Alto Campus of the Commonwealth Coll (PA)
Penn State U New Kensington Campus of the Commonwealth Coll (PA)
Penn State U Schuylkill Campus of the Capital Coll (PA)
Penn State U Shenango Campus of the Commonwealth Coll (PA)
Penn State U Univ Park Campus (PA)
Penn State U Wilkes-Barre Campus of the Commonwealth Coll (PA)
Penn State U Worthington Scranton Cmps Commonwealth Coll (PA)
Penn State U York Campus of the Commonwealth Coll (PA)
Saint Leo U (FL)
San Diego State U (CA)
U Coll of the Cariboo (BC, Canada)
U of Hawaii at Manoa (HI)
U of Louisiana at Lafayette (LA)
U of the District of Columbia (DC)
Widener U (PA)

HOSPITALITY AND RECREATION MARKETING
Champlain Coll (VT)
Immaculata U (PA)
Johnson & Wales U (RI)
Kendall Coll (IL)
Methodist Coll (NC)
Tuskegee U (AL)
Tyndale U Coll & Sem (ON, Canada)
U of Delaware (DE)

HOSPITALITY/RECREATION MARKETING
Rochester Inst of Technology (NY)

HOTEL AND RESTAURANT MANAGEMENT
Coll of the Ozarks (MO)

HOTEL/MOTEL ADMINISTRATION
Alliant Intl U (CA)
Ashland U (OH)
Auburn U (AL)
Baltimore Intl Coll (MD)
Barber-Scotia Coll (NC)
Becker Coll (MA)
Belmont U (TN)
Bethune-Cookman Coll (FL)
Boston U (MA)
Brigham Young U–Hawaii (HI)
State U of NY Coll at Buffalo (NY)
California State Polytechnic U, Pomona (CA)
California State U, Long Beach (CA)
Central Missouri State U (MO)
Central State U (OH)
Champlain Coll (VT)
Cheyney U of Pennsylvania (PA)
Chicago State U (IL)
The Coll of Southeastern Europe, The American U of Athens(Greece)
Coll of the Ozarks (MO)
Colorado State U (CO)
Concord Coll (WV)
Cornell U (NY)
East Carolina U (NC)
Fairleigh Dickinson U, Florham (NJ)
Fairleigh Dickinson U, Teaneck-Metro Campus (NJ)
Florida Metropolitan U-Fort Lauderdale Coll (FL)
Florida Southern Coll (FL)
Georgia Southern U (GA)
Grambling State U (LA)
Grand Valley State U (MI)
Hampton U (VA)
Howard U (DC)
Indiana U of Pennsylvania (PA)
Inter American U of PR, Aguadilla Campus (PR)
Inter American U of PR, Fajardo Campus (PR)
Inter American U of PR, Ponce Campus (PR)
Iowa State U of Science and Technology (IA)
Johnson & Wales U (RI)
Kansas State U (KS)
Kendall Coll (IL)
Keuka Coll (NY)
Lasell Coll (MA)
Lexington Coll (IL)
Lynn U (FL)
Marywood U (PA)
Mercyhurst Coll (PA)
Michigan State U (MI)
Morgan State U (MD)
Mount Ida Coll (MA)
Mount Saint Vincent U (NS, Canada)
National American U (NM)
Newbury Coll (MA)
New York Inst of Technology (NY)
New York U (NY)
Niagara U (NY)
North Carolina Wesleyan Coll (NC)
Northern Arizona U (AZ)
Northwood U (MI)
Northwood U, Florida Campus (FL)
Northwood U, Texas Campus (TX)
Oklahoma State U (OK)
Pace U (NY)
Paul Smith's Coll of Arts and Sciences (NY)
Purdue U (IN)
Rochester Inst of Technology (NY)
Ryerson U (ON, Canada)
St. John's U (NY)
St. Thomas U (FL)
San Diego State U (CA)
Schiller Intl U (FL)
Schiller Intl U(Spain)
Schiller Intl U(United Kingdom)
Schiller Intl U, American Coll of Switzerland(Switzerland)
Sierra Nevada Coll (NV)
South Dakota State U (SD)
Southern Oregon U (OR)
Plattsburgh State U of NY (NY)
Sullivan U (KY)
Texas A&M U–Kingsville (TX)
Texas Tech U (TX)
Thomas Coll (ME)
Thomas Edison State Coll (NJ)
United States Intl U(Kenya)
The U of Alabama (AL)
U of Calgary (AB, Canada)
U of Delaware (DE)
U of Denver (CO)
The U of Findlay (OH)
U of Guelph (ON, Canada)
U of Houston (TX)
U of Maine at Machias (ME)
U of Maryland Eastern Shore (MD)
U of Minnesota, Crookston (MN)
U of Missouri–Columbia (MO)
U of New Hampshire (NH)
U of New Haven (CT)
U of San Francisco (CA)
The U of Tennessee (TN)
U of Victoria (BC, Canada)
Webber Intl U (FL)
Western Kentucky U (KY)
Widener U (PA)
Youngstown State U (OH)

HOUSING AND HUMAN ENVIRONMENTS
Auburn U (AL)
Cornell U (NY)
Eastern Kentucky U (KY)
Florida State U (FL)
Iowa State U of Science and Technology (IA)
Ohio U (OH)
Southwest Missouri State U (MO)
Syracuse U (NY)
The U of Akron (OH)
U of Arkansas (AR)
U of Georgia (GA)
U of Missouri–Columbia (MO)
U of Nebraska–Lincoln (NE)
U of Northern Iowa (IA)
U of the Incarnate Word (TX)
Utah State U (UT)
Western Kentucky U (KY)

HOUSING AND HUMAN ENVIRONMENTS RELATED
U of Nevada, Reno (NV)

HUMAN DEVELOPMENT AND FAMILY STUDIES
Abilene Christian U (TX)
Amberton U (TX)

Antioch Coll (OH)
Ashland U (OH)
Auburn U (AL)
Baylor U (TX)
Boston Coll (MA)
Brigham Young U (UT)
California State U, Hayward (CA)
California State U, Long Beach (CA)
California State U, San Bernardino (CA)
Christian Heritage Coll (CA)
Colorado State U (CO)
Concordia U (MI)
Cornell U (NY)
East Carolina U (NC)
Eastern Kentucky U (KY)
Eckerd Coll (FL)
Florida State U (FL)
Geneva Coll (PA)
Georgia Southern U (GA)
Hampshire Coll (MA)
Harvard U (MA)
Hawai'i Pacific U (HI)
Hellenic Coll (MA)
Indiana State U (IN)
Indiana U Bloomington (IN)
Indiana U of Pennsylvania (PA)
Kansas State U (KS)
Kent State U (OH)
Kentucky State U (KY)
Lesley U (MA)
Mercyhurst Coll (PA)
Miami U (OH)
Mitchell Coll (CT)
Murray State U (KY)
National-Louis U (IL)
New Mexico State U (NM)
North Dakota State U (ND)
Northern Illinois U (IL)
Northern Michigan U (MI)
The Ohio State U (OH)
Ohio U (OH)
Oklahoma State U (OK)
Oregon State U (OR)
Pacific Oaks Coll (CA)
Penn State U Abington Coll (PA)
Penn State U Altoona Coll (PA)
Penn State U at Erie, The Behrend Coll (PA)
Penn State U Beaver Campus of the Commonwealth Coll (PA)
Penn State U Berks Cmps of Berks-Lehigh Valley Coll (PA)
Penn State U Delaware County Campus of the Commonwealth Coll (PA)
Penn State U DuBois Campus of the Commonwealth Coll (PA)
Penn State U Fayette Campus of the Commonwealth Coll (PA)
Penn State U Hazleton Campus of the Commonwealth Coll (PA)
Penn State U Lehigh Valley Cmps of Berks-Lehigh Valley Coll (PA)
Penn State U McKeesport Campus of the Commonwealth Coll (PA)
Penn State U Mont Alto Campus of the Commonwealth Coll (PA)
Penn State U New Kensington Campus of the Commonwealth Coll (PA)
Penn State U Schuylkill Campus of the Capital Coll (PA)
Penn State U Shenango Campus of the Commonwealth Coll (PA)
Penn State U Univ Park Campus (PA)
Penn State U Wilkes-Barre Campus of the Commonwealth Coll (PA)
Penn State U Worthington Scranton Cmps Commonwealth Coll (PA)
Penn State U York Campus of the Commonwealth Coll (PA)
Purdue U (IN)
St. Olaf Coll (MN)
Samford U (AL)
Sarah Lawrence Coll (NY)
South Dakota State U (SD)
Southern Nazarene U (OK)
Southern U and A&M Coll (LA)
Southwest Missouri State U (MO)
State U of NY at Oswego (NY)
State U of NY Empire State Coll (NY)
Syracuse U (NY)
Texas State U-San Marcos (TX)
Texas Tech U (TX)
Texas Woman's U (TX)
Trinity Coll (DC)
The U of Alabama (AL)
The U of Arizona (AZ)
U of Arkansas (AR)
U of Calif, Davis (CA)
U of Calif, Riverside (CA)
U of Chicago (IL)
U of Connecticut (CT)
U of Delaware (DE)
U of Georgia (GA)
U of Guelph (ON, Canada)
U of Hawaii at Manoa (HI)
U of Houston (TX)
U of Illinois at Urbana–Champaign (IL)
U of Maine (ME)
The U of Memphis (TN)
U of Missouri–Columbia (MO)
U of Nevada, Reno (NV)
The U of North Carolina at Charlotte (NC)
The U of North Carolina at Greensboro (NC)
U of North Texas (TX)
U of Rhode Island (RI)
The U of Tennessee (TN)
The U of Texas at Austin (TX)
U of Utah (UT)
U of Vermont (VT)
U of Waterloo (ON, Canada)
U of Wisconsin–Stout (WI)
Utah State U (UT)
Vanderbilt U (TN)
Warner Pacific Coll (OR)
Washington State U (WA)
Wheelock Coll (MA)
Youngstown State U (OH)

HUMAN DEVELOPMENT AND FAMILY STUDIES RELATED

Columbia Coll (SC)
Harding U (AR)
Kent State U (OH)
Saint Joseph's Coll of Maine (ME)
U of Louisiana at Lafayette (LA)

HUMAN ECOLOGY

California State U, Hayward (CA)
Coll of the Atlantic (ME)
Connecticut Coll (CT)
Cornell U (NY)
Emory U (GA)
Kansas State U (KS)
Marymount Coll of Fordham U (NY)
Mercyhurst Coll (PA)
Morgan State U (MD)
Mount Saint Vincent U (NS, Canada)
Regis U (CO)
Rutgers, The State U of New Jersey, New Brunswick/Piscataway (NJ)
State U of NY Coll at Oneonta (NY)
Sterling Coll (VT)
U of Alberta (AB, Canada)
U of Calif, Irvine (CA)
U of Calif, San Diego (CA)
U of Manitoba (MB, Canada)
U of Maryland Eastern Shore (MD)
The U of Tennessee at Chattanooga (TN)

HUMANITIES

Adelphi U (NY)
Albertus Magnus Coll (CT)
Allen U (SC)
Alma Coll (MI)
Angelo State U (TX)
Antioch Coll (OH)
Arizona State U (AZ)
Arkansas Tech U (AR)
Athens State U (AL)
Atlanta Christian Coll (GA)
Augsburg Coll (MN)
Aurora U (IL)
Bard Coll (NY)
Baylor U (TX)
Becker Coll (MA)
Belhaven Coll (MS)
Bemidji State U (MN)
Bennington Coll (VT)
Biola U (CA)
Bishop's U (QC, Canada)
Bloomsburg U of Pennsylvania (PA)
Bluefield State Coll (WV)
Brigham Young U (UT)
Brigham Young U–Hawaii (HI)
Brock U (ON, Canada)
Bucknell U (PA)
Burlington Coll (VT)
California State Polytechnic U, Pomona (CA)
California State U, Chico (CA)
California State U, Dominguez Hills (CA)
California State U, Sacramento (CA)
California State U, San Bernardino (CA)
Carleton U (ON, Canada)
Carnegie Mellon U (PA)
Catawba Coll (NC)
Chaminade U of Honolulu (HI)
Charleston Southern U (SC)
Clarion U of Pennsylvania (PA)
Clarkson U (NY)
Clearwater Christian Coll (FL)
Colgate U (NY)
Coll of Saint Benedict (MN)
Coll of Saint Mary (NE)
The Coll of St. Scholastica (MN)
Coll of Santa Fe (NM)
Colorado State U (CO)
Columbia Intl U (SC)
Concordia Coll (MN)
Concordia U (CA)
Concordia U (OR)
Concordia U Wisconsin (WI)
Cornell U (NY)
Dominican Coll (NY)
Dominican U of California (CA)
Dowling Coll (NY)
Drexel U (PA)
Eastern Washington U (WA)
East Stroudsburg U of Pennsylvania (PA)
Eckerd Coll (FL)
Edinboro U of Pennsylvania (PA)
Elmira Coll (NY)
Eugene Lang Coll, New School U (NY)
The Evergreen State Coll (WA)
Fairleigh Dickinson U, Florham (NJ)
Fairleigh Dickinson U, Teaneck-Metro Campus (NJ)
Faulkner U (AL)
Florida Inst of Technology (FL)
Florida Intl U (FL)
Florida Southern Coll (FL)
Florida State U (FL)
Fort Lewis Coll (CO)
Framingham State Coll (MA)
The Franciscan U (IA)
Franciscan U of Steubenville (OH)
Freed-Hardeman U (TN)
Fresno Pacific U (CA)
Gannon U (PA)
The George Washington U (DC)
Georgian Court U (NJ)
Grace U (NE)
Grand Valley State U (MI)
Hampden-Sydney Coll (VA)
Hampshire Coll (MA)
Harding U (AR)
Harvard U (MA)
Hawai'i Pacific U (HI)
Hofstra U (NY)
Holy Names Coll (CA)
Hope Coll (MI)
Houghton Coll (NY)
Hunter Coll of the City U of NY (NY)
Huron U USA in London(United Kingdom)
Indiana State U (IN)
Indiana U Kokomo (IN)
Iona Coll (NY)
Jacksonville U (FL)
John Cabot U(Italy)
John Carroll U (OH)
John F. Kennedy U (CA)
Johnson State Coll (VT)
Juniata Coll (PA)
Kansas State U (KS)
Kenyon Coll (OH)
Lawrence Technological U (MI)
Lehigh U (PA)
Lesley U (MA)
Lincoln Memorial U (TN)
Lindsey Wilson Coll (KY)
Lock Haven U of Pennsylvania (PA)
Long Island U, Brooklyn Campus (NY)
Loyola Marymount U (CA)
Loyola U Chicago (IL)
Loyola U New Orleans (LA)
Lubbock Christian U (TX)
Lynn U (FL)
Macalester Coll (MN)
Marist Coll (NY)
Marlboro Coll (VT)
Marshall U (WV)
Martin U (IN)
McGill U (QC, Canada)
Memorial U of Newfoundland (NL, Canada)
Mercyhurst Coll (PA)
Messiah Coll (PA)
Michigan State U (MI)
Midwestern State U (TX)
Milligan Coll (TN)
Minnesota State U Mankato (MN)
Monmouth Coll (IL)
Montclair State U (NJ)
Mount Allison U (NB, Canada)
Mount Aloysius Coll (PA)
Mount Saint Vincent U (NS, Canada)
New Coll of California (CA)
New Coll of Florida (FL)
New York U (NY)
North Central Coll (IL)
North Dakota State U (ND)
Northern Arizona U (AZ)
North Greenville Coll (SC)
Northwestern Coll (IA)
Northwestern U (IL)
Notre Dame de Namur U (CA)
Nova Southeastern U (FL)
Oakland City U (IN)
The Ohio State U (OH)
Ohio Wesleyan U (OH)
Oklahoma Baptist U (OK)
Oklahoma City U (OK)
Oklahoma Panhandle State U (OK)
Our Lady of the Lake Coll (LA)
Pacific U (OR)
Penn State U Harrisburg Campus of the Capital Coll (PA)
Pepperdine U, Malibu (CA)
Plymouth State U (NH)
Pomona Coll (CA)
Pontifical Coll Josephinum (OH)
Portland State U (OR)
Principia Coll (IL)
Providence Coll (RI)
Providence Coll and Theological Sem (MB, Canada)
Purdue U (IN)
Quincy U (IL)
Ramapo Coll of New Jersey (NJ)
Redeemer U Coll (ON, Canada)
Regis U (CO)
Roberts Wesleyan Coll (NY)
Rockford Coll (IL)
Rosemont Coll (PA)
St. Gregory's U (OK)
St. John's Coll (NM)
Saint John's U (MN)
Saint Louis U (MO)
Saint Martin's Coll (WA)
Saint Mary-of-the-Woods Coll (IN)
Saint Mary's Coll (IN)
St. Norbert Coll (WI)
St. Thomas Aquinas Coll (NY)
San Diego State U (CA)
San Francisco State U (CA)
San Jose State U (CA)
Sarah Lawrence Coll (NY)
Schreiner U (TX)
Seattle U (WA)
Seton Hall U (NJ)
Shimer Coll (IL)
Siena Heights U (MI)
Sierra Nevada Coll (NV)
Simon Fraser U (BC, Canada)
Southeast Missouri State U (MO)
Southern Methodist U (TX)
Spring Hill Coll (AL)
State U of NY Coll at Old Westbury (NY)
State U of NY Empire State Coll (NY)
Stetson U (FL)
Stevens Inst of Technology (NJ)
Stony Brook U, State U of New York (NY)
Suffolk U (MA)
Syracuse U (NY)
Tabor Coll (KS)
Tennessee State U (TN)
Texas Wesleyan U (TX)
Thomas Edison State Coll (NJ)
Thomas U (GA)
Trent U (ON, Canada)
Trinity Intl U (IL)
Trinity U (TX)
Trinity Western U (BC, Canada)
Union Coll (NY)
Union Inst & U (OH)
United States Air Force Acad (CO)
United States Military Acad (NY)
The U of Akron (OH)
U of Alberta (AB, Canada)
The U of Arizona (AZ)
U of Bridgeport (CT)
U of Calgary (AB, Canada)
U of Calif, Irvine (CA)
U of Calif, Riverside (CA)
U of Central Florida (FL)
U of Chicago (IL)
U of Cincinnati (OH)
U of Colorado at Boulder (CO)
U of Detroit Mercy (MI)
U of Houston–Clear Lake (TX)
U of Houston–Victoria (TX)
U of Illinois at Urbana–Champaign (IL)
U of Kansas (KS)
The U of Lethbridge (AB, Canada)
U of Maryland U Coll (MD)
U of Massachusetts Amherst (MA)
U of Michigan (MI)
U of Michigan–Dearborn (MI)
U of Mobile (AL)
U of New Hampshire (NH)
U of New Hampshire at Manchester (NH)
U of New Mexico (NM)
U of Northern Iowa (IA)
U of Oregon (OR)
U of Ottawa (ON, Canada)
U of Pittsburgh (PA)
U of Pittsburgh at Greensburg (PA)
U of Pittsburgh at Johnstown (PA)
U of Puerto Rico, Cayey U Coll (PR)
U of Regina (SK, Canada)
U of San Diego (CA)
U of South Florida (FL)
The U of Tennessee at Chattanooga (TN)
The U of Texas at Austin (TX)
The U of Texas at Dallas (TX)
U of the Sacred Heart (PR)
U of the Virgin Islands (VI)
U of Toledo (OH)
U of Toronto (ON, Canada)
U of Utah (UT)
U of Washington (WA)
U of West Florida (FL)
U of Windsor (ON, Canada)
U of Wisconsin–Green Bay (WI)
U of Wisconsin–Parkside (WI)
U of Wyoming (WY)
Ursuline Coll (OH)
Valparaiso U (IN)
Villa Julie Coll (MD)
Virginia Wesleyan Coll (VA)
Waldorf Coll (IA)
Walla Walla Coll (WA)
Warren Wilson Coll (NC)
Washington Coll (MD)
Washington State U (WA)
Washington U in St. Louis (MO)
Wesleyan Coll (GA)
Wesleyan U (CT)
Western Baptist Coll (OR)
Western Oregon U (OR)
Western Washington U (WA)
Widener U (PA)
Willamette U (OR)
William Paterson U of New Jersey (NJ)
Wofford Coll (SC)
Worcester Polytechnic Inst (MA)
Wright State U (OH)
Yale U (CT)
York U (ON, Canada)

HUMAN/MEDICAL GENETICS

Sarah Lawrence Coll (NY)
U of Calif, Los Angeles (CA)

HUMAN NUTRITION

Baylor U (TX)
Case Western Reserve U (OH)
Cornell U (NY)
Framingham State Coll (MA)
Kent State U (OH)
Penn State U Abington Coll (PA)
Penn State U Altoona Coll (PA)
Penn State U at Erie, The Behrend Coll (PA)
Penn State U Beaver Campus of the Commonwealth Coll (PA)
Penn State U Berks Cmps of Berks-Lehigh Valley Coll (PA)
Penn State U Delaware County Campus of the Commonwealth Coll (PA)
Penn State U DuBois Campus of the Commonwealth Coll (PA)
Penn State U Fayette Campus of the Commonwealth Coll (PA)
Penn State U Hazleton Campus of the Commonwealth Coll (PA)
Penn State U Lehigh Valley Cmps of Berks-Lehigh Valley Coll (PA)
Penn State U McKeesport Campus of the Commonwealth Coll (PA)
Penn State U Mont Alto Campus of the Commonwealth Coll (PA)
Penn State U New Kensington Campus of the Commonwealth Coll (PA)
Penn State U Schuylkill Campus of the Capital Coll (PA)
Penn State U Shenango Campus of the Commonwealth Coll (PA)
Penn State U Univ Park Campus (PA)

Penn State U Wilkes-Barre Campus of the Commonwealth Coll (PA)
Penn State U Worthington Scranton Cmps Commonwealth Coll (PA)
Penn State U York Campus of the Commonwealth Coll (PA)
Rochester Inst of Technology (NY)
Samford U (AL)
Tarleton State U (TX)
The U of British Columbia (BC, Canada)
U of Guelph (ON, Canada)
U of Houston (TX)
U of Massachusetts Amherst (MA)
U of Missouri–Columbia (MO)
Washington State U (WA)

HUMAN RESOURCES DEVELOPMENT
Brigham Young U (UT)
Concordia U at Austin (TX)
Georgia State U (GA)
Limestone Coll (SC)
Oakland U (MI)
Trinity Intl U (IL)
U of Houston–Clear Lake (TX)

HUMAN RESOURCES MANAGEMENT
Amberton U (TX)
American InterContinental U Online (IL)
American Intl Coll (MA)
American U (DC)
Anderson Coll (SC)
Arcadia U (PA)
Athabasca U (AB, Canada)
Athens State U (AL)
Auburn U (AL)
Auburn U Montgomery (AL)
Baker Coll of Owosso (MI)
Ball State U (IN)
Barton Coll (NC)
Baylor U (TX)
Bellarmine U (KY)
Baruch Coll of the City U of NY (NY)
Birmingham-Southern Coll (AL)
Bishop's U (QC, Canada)
Black Hills State U (SD)
Bloomfield Coll (NJ)
Bluefield Coll (VA)
Boise State U (ID)
Boston Coll (MA)
Bowling Green State U (OH)
Brescia U (KY)
Briar Cliff U (IA)
Brigham Young U (UT)
Brock U (ON, Canada)
Cabrini Coll (PA)
California Polytechnic State U, San Luis Obispo (CA)
California State Polytechnic U, Pomona (CA)
California State U, Chico (CA)
California State U, Dominguez Hills (CA)
California State U, Fresno (CA)
California State U, Hayward (CA)
California State U, Long Beach (CA)
California State U, Sacramento (CA)
Capital U (OH)
Carleton U (ON, Canada)
The Catholic U of America (DC)
Central Michigan U (MI)
Central Missouri State U (MO)
Chestnut Hill Coll (PA)
Clarkson U (NY)
Cleary U (MI)
Coll for Lifelong Learning (NH)
Coll of Saint Elizabeth (NJ)
The Coll of Southeastern Europe, The American U of Athens(Greece)
Colorado Tech U Sioux Falls Campus (SD)
Concordia U (QC, Canada)
Crichton Coll (TN)
Davenport U, Lansing (MI)
Delaware State U (DE)
DePaul U (IL)
DeSales U (PA)
Dominican Coll (NY)
Dominican U of California (CA)
Drexel U (PA)
East Central U (OK)
Eastern Michigan U (MI)
Eastern New Mexico U (NM)
Eastern Washington U (WA)
Eckerd Coll (FL)
Excelsior Coll (NY)
Faulkner U (AL)
Florida Atlantic U (FL)
Florida Intl U (FL)
Florida Southern Coll (FL)
Florida State U (FL)
Fordham U (NY)
Framingham State Coll (MA)
Franklin U (OH)
Freed-Hardeman U (TN)
George Fox U (OR)
The George Washington U (DC)
Georgia Southwestern State U (GA)
Golden Gate U (CA)
Governors State U (IL)
Grace U (NE)
Grand Canyon U (AZ)
Grand Valley State U (MI)
Harding U (AR)
Hastings Coll (NE)
Hawai'i Pacific U (HI)
HEC Montreal (QC, Canada)
Holy Names Coll (CA)
Idaho State U (ID)
Indiana Inst of Technology (IN)
Indiana State U (IN)
Indiana U of Pennsylvania (PA)
Inter American U of PR, Bayamón Campus (PR)
Inter American U of PR, Ponce Campus (PR)
Inter American U of PR, San Germán Campus (PR)
Judson Coll (IL)
Juniata Coll (PA)
Keystone Coll (PA)
King's Coll (PA)
Kutztown U of Pennsylvania (PA)
Lakehead U (ON, Canada)
La Salle U (PA)
Lewis U (IL)
Lindenwood U (MO)
Loras Coll (IA)
Louisiana Tech U (LA)
Loyola U Chicago (IL)
Madonna U (MI)
Mansfield U of Pennsylvania (PA)
Marietta Coll (OH)
Marquette U (WI)
Martin U (IN)
Marymount U (VA)
McGill U (QC, Canada)
Medaille Coll (NY)
Mercyhurst Coll (PA)
Meredith Coll (NC)
Messiah Coll (PA)
Metropolitan State U (MN)
Miami U (OH)
Michigan State U (MI)
MidAmerica Nazarene U (KS)
Millikin U (IL)
Muhlenberg Coll (PA)
National U (CA)
Nazareth Coll of Rochester (NY)
Newbury Coll (MA)
New York Inst of Technology (NY)
Niagara U (NY)
Nichols Coll (MA)
North Carolina State U (NC)
Northeastern Illinois U (IL)
Northeastern State U (OK)
Northeastern U (MA)
Notre Dame Coll (OH)
Oakland City U (IN)
The Ohio State U (OH)
Ohio U (OH)
Ohio Valley Coll (WV)
Oklahoma Baptist U (OK)
Oklahoma State U (OK)
Olivet Nazarene U (IL)
Our Lady of the Lake U of San Antonio (TX)
Pace U (NY)
Palm Beach Atlantic U (FL)
Peace Coll (NC)
Point Park U (PA)
Pontifical Catholic U of Puerto Rico (PR)
Portland State U (OR)
Quinnipiac U (CT)
Redeemer U Coll (ON, Canada)
Rider U (NJ)
Robert Morris U (PA)
Roberts Wesleyan Coll (NY)
Rockhurst U (MO)
Roosevelt U (IL)
Ryerson U (ON, Canada)
St. Cloud State U (MN)
Saint Francis U (PA)
St. John Fisher Coll (NY)
St. Joseph's Coll, New York (NY)
St. Joseph's Coll, Suffolk Campus (NY)
Saint Leo U (FL)
Saint Louis U (MO)
Saint Mary-of-the-Woods Coll (IN)
Saint Mary's U of Minnesota (MN)
St. Mary's U of San Antonio (TX)
Samford U (AL)
Sam Houston State U (TX)
San Jose State U (CA)
Seton Hill U (PA)
Silver Lake Coll (WI)
Simpson Coll and Graduate School (CA)
Southern Christian U (AL)
Southern Wesleyan U (SC)
Southwestern Coll (KS)
Spring Arbor U (MI)
Springfield Coll (MA)
State U of NY at Oswego (NY)
Susquehanna U (PA)
Tarleton State U (TX)
Taylor U (IN)
Tennessee Wesleyan Coll (TN)
Texas A&M U–Commerce (TX)
Texas A&M U–Texarkana (TX)
Thomas Coll (ME)
Thomas Edison State Coll (NJ)
Trinity Christian Coll (IL)
Trinity Intl U (IL)
Troy State U Dothan (AL)
Troy State U Montgomery (AL)
Université de Montréal (QC, Canada)
U Coll of the Cariboo (BC, Canada)
The U of Akron (OH)
U of Alaska Fairbanks (AK)
U of Alberta (AB, Canada)
The U of Arizona (AZ)
U of Baltimore (MD)
U of Detroit Mercy (MI)
The U of Findlay (OH)
U of Guelph (ON, Canada)
U of Hawaii at Manoa (HI)
U of Idaho (ID)
U of Indianapolis (IN)
The U of Iowa (IA)
The U of Lethbridge (AB, Canada)
U of Maryland, Coll Park (MD)
U of Maryland U Coll (MD)
U of Miami (FL)
U of Michigan–Flint (MI)
U of Minnesota, Duluth (MN)
U of Nebraska at Omaha (NE)
U of Nevada, Las Vegas (NV)
U of Nevada, Reno (NV)
U of New Brunswick Fredericton (NB, Canada)
U of New Haven (CT)
The U of North Carolina at Chapel Hill (NC)
U of Ottawa (ON, Canada)
U of Pennsylvania (PA)
U of Saint Francis (IN)
U of St. Thomas (MN)
U of Saskatchewan (SK, Canada)
The U of Scranton (PA)
U of Toledo (OH)
U of Waterloo (ON, Canada)
U of Windsor (ON, Canada)
U of Wisconsin–Milwaukee (WI)
U of Wisconsin–Whitewater (WI)
Urbana U (OH)
Ursuline Coll (OH)
Utah State U (UT)
Valley City State U (ND)
Vanderbilt U (TN)
Virginia Polytechnic Inst and State U (VA)
Washington State U (WA)
Washington U in St. Louis (MO)
Weber State U (UT)
Webster U (MO)
Western Illinois U (IL)
Western Michigan U (MI)
Western State Coll of Colorado (CO)
Western Washington U (WA)
Westminster Coll (UT)
Wichita State U (KS)
Wilmington Coll (DE)
Winona State U (MN)
Wright State U (OH)
Xavier U (OH)
York Coll (NE)
York U (ON, Canada)

HUMAN RESOURCES MANAGEMENT AND SERVICES RELATED
Albertus Magnus Coll (CT)
Becker Coll (MA)
Bloomfield Coll (NJ)
Capella U (MN)
Columbia Southern U (AL)
Drake U (IA)
Miami U Hamilton (OH)
Mountain State U (WV)
Niagara U (NY)
Park U (MO)
U du Québec à Hull (QC, Canada)
U Coll of the Cariboo (BC, Canada)
The U of British Columbia (BC, Canada)
U of Oklahoma (OK)
U of the District of Columbia (DC)
Widener U (PA)

HUMAN SERVICES
Adrian Coll (MI)
Alaska Pacific U (AK)
Albertus Magnus Coll (CT)
Albertus Magnus Coll (CT)
Albion Coll (MI)
American Intl Coll (MA)
Anderson Coll (SC)
Arcadia U (PA)
Assumption Coll (MA)
Baldwin-Wallace Coll (OH)
Beacon Coll (FL)
Bethel Coll (IN)
Bethel Coll (TN)
Black Hills State U (SD)
Burlington Coll (VT)
Burlington Coll (VT)
California State U, Dominguez Hills (CA)
California State U, San Bernardino (CA)
Calumet Coll of Saint Joseph (IN)
Carson-Newman Coll (TN)
Cazenovia Coll (NY)
Champlain Coll (VT)
Chestnut Hill Coll (PA)
Clayton Coll & State U (GA)
Coll of Notre Dame of Maryland (MD)
Coll of St. Joseph (VT)
Coll of Saint Mary (NE)
Coll of Saint Mary (NE)
Concordia U, St. Paul (MN)
Dakota Wesleyan U (SD)
Dakota Wesleyan U (SD)
Doane Coll (NE)
Elmira Coll (NY)
Elon U (NC)
Endicott Coll (MA)
Fairmont State Coll (WV)
Florida Gulf Coast U (FL)
Florida Gulf Coast U (FL)
Fontbonne U (MO)
Framingham State Coll (MA)
Framingham State Coll (MA)
The Franciscan U (IA)
Geneva Coll (PA)
The George Washington U (DC)
Grace Bible Coll (MI)
Graceland U (IA)
Grand View Coll (IA)
Grand View Coll (IA)
Hannibal-LaGrange Coll (MO)
Hannibal-LaGrange Coll (MO)
Hastings Coll (NE)
Hawai'i Pacific U (HI)
High Point U (NC)
Hilbert Coll (NY)
Holy Names Coll (CA)
Indiana Inst of Technology (IN)
Indiana U–Purdue U Fort Wayne (IN)
Judson Coll (IL)
Kendall Coll (IL)
Kentucky Wesleyan Coll (KY)
LaGrange Coll (GA)
Lake Superior State U (MI)
La Roche Coll (PA)
Lasell Coll (MA)
Lenoir-Rhyne Coll (NC)
Lesley U (MA)
Lincoln U (PA)
Lincoln U (PA)
Lindenwood U (MO)
Lindenwood U (MO)
Lindsey Wilson Coll (KY)
Lindsey Wilson Coll (KY)
Livingstone Coll (NC)
Mansfield U of Pennsylvania (PA)
Marywood U (PA)
Medaille Coll (NY)
Medaille Coll (NY)
Mercer U (GA)
Merrimack Coll (MA)
Metropolitan State Coll of Denver (CO)
Metropolitan State U (MN)
Metropolitan State U (MN)
Millikin U (IL)
Missouri Baptist U (MO)
Missouri Valley Coll (MO)
Montreat Coll (NC)
Mount Ida Coll (MA)
Mount Saint Mary Coll (NY)
National-Louis U (IL)
Northeastern U (MA)
Northwest Christian Coll (OR)
Notre Dame de Namur U (CA)
Ottawa U (KS)
Pacific Oaks Coll (CA)
Park U (MO)
Pfeiffer U (NC)
Quinnipiac U (CT)
Roosevelt U (IL)
St. John's U (NY)
St. Joseph's Coll, New York (NY)
Saint Joseph's U (PA)
Saint Leo U (FL)
Saint Mary-of-the-Woods Coll (IN)
Saint Mary's U of Minnesota (MN)
Seton Hill U (PA)
Sheldon Jackson Coll (AK)
Siena Heights U (MI)
Simmons Coll (MA)
Southern Vermont Coll (VT)
Southwest Baptist U (MO)
Springfield Coll (MA)
State U of NY Coll at Cortland (NY)
State U of NY Empire State Coll (NY)
Suffolk U (MA)
Teikyo Post U (CT)
Teikyo Post U (CT)
Tennessee Wesleyan Coll (TN)
Texas A&M U–Kingsville (TX)
Tiffin U (OH)
Trinity Western U (BC, Canada)
Tyndale U Coll & Sem (ON, Canada)
U of Baltimore (MD)
U of Baltimore (MD)
U of Bridgeport (CT)
U of Detroit Mercy (MI)
U of Great Falls (MT)
U of Great Falls (MT)
U of Maine at Machias (ME)
U of Massachusetts Boston (MA)
U of Minnesota, Morris (MN)
U of Nevada, Las Vegas (NV)
U of Northern Colorado (CO)
U of Oregon (OR)
U of Phoenix–Sacramento Campus (CA)
U of Rhode Island (RI)
The U of Scranton (PA)
The U of Tennessee at Chattanooga (TN)
The U of Texas–Pan American (TX)
U of Wisconsin–Oshkosh (WI)
Upper Iowa U (IA)
Villanova U (PA)
Virginia Polytechnic Inst and State U (VA)
Virginia Wesleyan Coll (VA)
Walsh U (OH)
Western Washington U (WA)
William Penn U (IA)
Wingate U (NC)

HYDROLOGY AND WATER RESOURCES SCIENCE
California State U, Chico (CA)
Cornell U (NY)
East Central U (OK)
Florida Inst of Technology (FL)
Grand Valley State U (MI)
Heidelberg Coll (OH)
Humboldt State U (CA)
Lakehead U (ON, Canada)
North Carolina State U (NC)
Northern Michigan U (MI)
Northland Coll (WI)
Rensselaer Polytechnic Inst (NY)
St. Francis Xavier U (NS, Canada)
State U of NY Coll at Brockport (NY)
State U of NY Coll at Oneonta (NY)
State U of NY Coll of Environ Sci and Forestry (NY)
Tarleton State U (TX)
U of New Hampshire (NH)
The U of Texas at Austin (TX)
U of Wisconsin–Madison (WI)
U of Wisconsin–Stevens Point (WI)
Wright State U (OH)

ILLUSTRATION
Acad of Art U (CA)
Alberta Coll of Art & Design (AB, Canada)
Art Acad of Cincinnati (OH)
Art Center Coll of Design (CA)
The Art Inst of Boston at Lesley U (MA)
Atlanta Coll of Art (GA)
Becker Coll (MA)
Brigham Young U (UT)
California State U, Fullerton (CA)
California State U, Long Beach (CA)
The Cleveland Inst of Art (OH)
Col for Creative Studies (MI)
Columbia Coll (MO)
Columbus Coll of Art & Design (OH)

Cornish Coll of the Arts (WA)
Laguna Coll of Art & Design (CA)
Lawrence Technological U (MI)
Maryland Inst Coll of Art (MD)
Memphis Coll of Art (TN)
Montserrat Coll of Art (MA)
Mt. Sierra Coll (CA)
Pacific Northwest Coll of Art (OR)
Pratt Inst (NY)
Rhode Island School of Design (RI)
Ringling School of Art and Design (FL)
Rochester Inst of Technology (NY)
Rocky Mountain Coll of Art & Design (CO)
St. John's U (NY)
Savannah Coll of Art and Design (GA)
School of the Art Inst of Chicago (IL)
School of the Museum of Fine Arts, Boston (MA)
Syracuse U (NY)
U of Bridgeport (CT)
U of Kansas (KS)
U of San Francisco (CA)
The U of the Arts (PA)
Washington U in St. Louis (MO)

IMMUNOLOGY
Cornell U (NY)
U of Alberta (AB, Canada)

INDUSTRIAL AND ORGANIZATIONAL PSYCHOLOGY
Abilene Christian U (TX)
Albright Coll (PA)
Averett U (VA)
Bridgewater State Coll (MA)
Brooklyn Coll of the City U of NY (NY)
California State U, Hayward (CA)
California State U, Sacramento (CA)
Clarkson U (NY)
Coll of Santa Fe (NM)
Eastern Connecticut State U (CT)
East Texas Baptist U (TX)
Georgia Inst of Technology (GA)
Ithaca Coll (NY)
Lincoln U (PA)
Madonna U (MI)
Marymount U (VA)
Maryville U of Saint Louis (MO)
Marywood U (PA)
Middle Tennessee State U (TN)
Moravian Coll (PA)
Nebraska Wesleyan U (NE)
Northern Michigan U (MI)
Point Loma Nazarene U (CA)
Saint Mary's Coll of California (CA)
Saint Xavier U (IL)
Texas Wesleyan U (TX)
U of Illinois at Urbana–Champaign (IL)
Washington U in St. Louis (MO)
Western Baptist Coll (OR)
Wright State U (OH)

INDUSTRIAL ARTS
Andrews U (MI)
Ball State U (IN)
Bemidji State U (MN)
Berea Coll (KY)
State U of NY Coll at Buffalo (NY)
California State U, Fresno (CA)
Chicago State U (IL)
Coll of the Ozarks (MO)
Colorado State U-Pueblo (CO)
Eastern Kentucky U (KY)
Elizabeth City State U (NC)
Fairmont State Coll (WV)
Florida Ag and Mech U (FL)
Fort Hays State U (KS)
Humboldt State U (CA)
Keene State Coll (NH)
Lincoln U (MO)
McPherson Coll (KS)
Minnesota State U Mankato (MN)
New Mexico Highlands U (NM)
Northeastern State U (OK)
Northern State U (SD)
Ohio Northern U (OH)
Oklahoma Panhandle State U (OK)
Oklahoma State U (OK)
Pacific Union Coll (CA)
Pittsburg State U (KS)
Rhode Island Coll (RI)
St. Cloud State U (MN)
San Diego State U (CA)
San Francisco State U (CA)
South Carolina State U (SC)
Southern Utah U (UT)
Southwestern Oklahoma State U (OK)
State U of NY at Oswego (NY)
Tarleton State U (TX)
Tennessee State U (TN)
Texas A&M U–Commerce (TX)
U of Alberta (AB, Canada)
The U of British Columbia (BC, Canada)
U of Maryland Eastern Shore (MD)
The U of Montana–Western (MT)
U of Southern Maine (ME)
U of the District of Columbia (DC)
U of Wisconsin–Platteville (WI)
Walla Walla Coll (WA)
Western State Coll of Colorado (CO)
William Penn U (IA)

INDUSTRIAL DESIGN
Acad of Art U (CA)
Appalachian State U (NC)
Arizona State U (AZ)
Art Center Coll of Design (CA)
The Art Inst of Colorado (CO)
Auburn U (AL)
Brigham Young U (UT)
California Coll of the Arts (CA)
California State U, Long Beach (CA)
Carleton U (ON, Canada)
Carnegie Mellon U (PA)
Clemson U (SC)
The Cleveland Inst of Art (OH)
Col for Creative Studies (MI)
Columbia Coll Chicago (IL)
Columbus Coll of Art & Design (OH)
Escuela de Artes Plasticas de Puerto Rico (PR)
Fashion Inst of Technology (NY)
Georgia Inst of Technology (GA)
Kansas City Art Inst (MO)
Kean U (NJ)
Massachusetts Coll of Art (MA)
Metropolitan State Coll of Denver (CO)
Milwaukee Inst of Art and Design (WI)
North Carolina State U (NC)
Northern Michigan U (MI)
The Ohio State U (OH)
Parsons School of Design, New School U (NY)
Philadelphia U (PA)
Pittsburg State U (KS)
Pratt Inst (NY)
Rhode Island School of Design (RI)
Rochester Inst of Technology (NY)
San Francisco State U (CA)
San Jose State U (CA)
Savannah Coll of Art and Design (GA)
Syracuse U (NY)
Université de Montréal (QC, Canada)
U of Alberta (AB, Canada)
U of Bridgeport (CT)
U of Cincinnati (OH)
U of Illinois at Chicago (IL)
U of Illinois at Urbana–Champaign (IL)
U of Kansas (KS)
U of Louisiana at Lafayette (LA)
U of Michigan (MI)
The U of the Arts (PA)
U of Washington (WA)
U of Wisconsin–Platteville (WI)
Virginia Polytechnic Inst and State U (VA)
Wentworth Inst of Technology (MA)
Western Michigan U (MI)
Western Washington U (WA)

INDUSTRIAL ELECTRONICS TECHNOLOGY
Lewis-Clark State Coll (ID)

INDUSTRIAL ENGINEERING
Arizona State U (AZ)
Auburn U (AL)
Bethel Coll (IN)
Boston U (MA)
Bradley U (IL)
California Polytechnic State U, San Luis Obispo (CA)
California State Polytechnic U, Pomona (CA)
California State U, Fresno (CA)
California State U, Hayward (CA)
California State U, Long Beach (CA)
Central Michigan U (MI)
Central State U (OH)
Clemson U (SC)
Cleveland State U (OH)
The Coll of Southeastern Europe, The American U of Athens(Greece)
Colorado State U-Pueblo (CO)
Columbia U, School of Eng & Applied Sci (NY)
Concordia U (QC, Canada)
Cornell U (NY)
Dalhousie U (NS, Canada)
Drexel U (PA)
Eastern Nazarene Coll (MA)
Elizabethtown Coll (PA)
Ferris State U (MI)
Florida Ag and Mech U (FL)
Florida State U (FL)
Georgia Inst of Technology (GA)
Grand Valley State U (MI)
Hofstra U (NY)
Inter American U of PR, Bayamón Campus (PR)
Iowa State U of Science and Technology (IA)
The Johns Hopkins U (MD)
Kansas State U (KS)
Kent State U (OH)
Kettering U (MI)
Lamar U (TX)
Lehigh U (PA)
Louisiana State U and A&M Coll (LA)
Louisiana Tech U (LA)
Marquette U (WI)
Memorial U of Newfoundland (NL, Canada)
Miami U (OH)
Michigan Technological U (MI)
Milwaukee School of Eng (WI)
Mississippi State U (MS)
Montana State U–Bozeman (MT)
Morgan State U (MD)
New Jersey Inst of Technology (NJ)
New Mexico State U (NM)
New York Inst of Technology (NY)
North Carolina State U (NC)
North Dakota State U (ND)
Northeastern U (MA)
Northern Illinois U (IL)
Northwestern U (IL)
The Ohio State U (OH)
Ohio U (OH)
Oklahoma State U (OK)
Oregon State U (OR)
Penn State U Abington Coll (PA)
Penn State U Altoona Coll (PA)
Penn State U at Erie, The Behrend Coll (PA)
Penn State U Beaver Campus of the Commonwealth Coll (PA)
Penn State U Berks Cmps of Berks-Lehigh Valley Coll (PA)
Penn State U Delaware County Campus of the Commonwealth Coll (PA)
Penn State U DuBois Campus of the Commonwealth Coll (PA)
Penn State U Fayette Campus of the Commonwealth Coll (PA)
Penn State U Hazleton Campus of the Commonwealth Coll (PA)
Penn State U Lehigh Valley Cmps of Berks-Lehigh Valley Coll (PA)
Penn State U McKeesport Campus of the Commonwealth Coll (PA)
Penn State U Mont Alto Campus of the Commonwealth Coll (PA)
Penn State U New Kensington Campus of the Commonwealth Coll (PA)
Penn State U Schuylkill Campus of the Capital Coll (PA)
Penn State U Shenango Campus of the Commonwealth Coll (PA)
Penn State U Univ Park Campus (PA)
Penn State U Wilkes-Barre Campus of the Commonwealth Coll (PA)
Penn State U Worthington Scranton Cmps Commonwealth Coll (PA)
Penn State U York Campus of the Commonwealth Coll (PA)
Polytechnic U of Puerto Rico (PR)
Purdue U (IN)
Rensselaer Polytechnic Inst (NY)
Robert Morris U (PA)
Rochester Inst of Technology (NY)
Roosevelt U (IL)
Rutgers, The State U of New Jersey, New Brunswick/Piscataway (NJ)
Ryerson U (ON, Canada)
St. Ambrose U (IA)
St. Cloud State U (MN)
St. Mary's U of San Antonio (TX)
San Jose State U (CA)
Seattle U (WA)
South Dakota School of Mines and Technology (SD)
Southern Illinois U Edwardsville (IL)
Stanford U (CA)
State U of NY at Binghamton (NY)
Tennessee State U (TN)
Tennessee Technological U (TN)
Texas A&M U (TX)
Texas A&M U–Commerce (TX)
Texas A&M U–Kingsville (TX)
Texas Tech U (TX)
Tufts U (MA)
U at Buffalo, The State U of New York (NY)
The U of Alabama (AL)
The U of Alabama in Huntsville (AL)
U of Alaska Fairbanks (AK)
The U of Arizona (AZ)
U of Arkansas (AR)
U of Calgary (AB, Canada)
U of Central Florida (FL)
U of Cincinnati (OH)
U of Connecticut (CT)
U of Florida (FL)
U of Houston (TX)
U of Idaho (ID)
U of Illinois at Chicago (IL)
U of Illinois at Urbana–Champaign (IL)
The U of Iowa (IA)
U of Louisville (KY)
U of Manitoba (MB, Canada)
U of Massachusetts Amherst (MA)
U of Miami (FL)
U of Michigan (MI)
U of Michigan–Dearborn (MI)
U of Minnesota, Duluth (MN)
U of Minnesota, Twin Cities Campus (MN)
U of Missouri–Columbia (MO)
U of Missouri–Rolla (MO)
U of Nebraska–Lincoln (NE)
U of New Haven (CT)
U of New Mexico (NM)
U of Oklahoma (OK)
U of Pittsburgh (PA)
U of Regina (SK, Canada)
U of Rhode Island (RI)
U of San Diego (CA)
U of South Florida (FL)
The U of Tennessee (TN)
The U of Texas at Arlington (TX)
U of Toledo (OH)
U of Toronto (ON, Canada)
U of Washington (WA)
U of Windsor (ON, Canada)
U of Wisconsin–Madison (WI)
U of Wisconsin–Milwaukee (WI)
U of Wisconsin–Platteville (WI)
Virginia Polytechnic Inst and State U (VA)
Washington State U (WA)
Wayne State U (MI)
Western Michigan U (MI)
Western New England Coll (MA)
West Virginia U (WV)
Wichita State U (KS)
Worcester Polytechnic Inst (MA)
Youngstown State U (OH)

INDUSTRIAL PRODUCTION TECHNOLOGIES RELATED
Appalachian State U (NC)
Central Connecticut State U (CT)
Central Michigan U (MI)
Chadron State Coll (NE)
East Carolina U (NC)
Fashion Inst of Technology (NY)
Georgia Southern U (GA)
Indiana State U (IN)
Kean U (NJ)
Millersville U of Pennsylvania (PA)
Pennsylvania Coll of Technology (PA)
Southern Polytechnic State U (GA)
Southwestern Coll (KS)
Tarleton State U (TX)
The U of Akron (OH)
U of Nebraska–Lincoln (NE)
U of Wisconsin–Stout (WI)
Utah State U (UT)
Wayne State U (MI)
Western Kentucky U (KY)

INDUSTRIAL RADIOLOGIC TECHNOLOGY
Alderson-Broaddus Coll (WV)
Baker Coll of Owosso (MI)
Boise State U (ID)
Briar Cliff U (IA)
Concordia U Wisconsin (WI)
Howard U (DC)
Jamestown Coll (ND)
Madonna U (MI)
Mars Hill Coll (NC)
National-Louis U (IL)
Oregon Inst of Technology (OR)
Thomas Jefferson U (PA)
U of Maryland Eastern Shore (MD)
U of Sioux Falls (SD)

INDUSTRIAL SAFETY TECHNOLOGY
Rochester Inst of Technology (NY)
South Dakota State U (SD)

INDUSTRIAL TECHNOLOGY
Alcorn State U (MS)
Appalachian State U (NC)
Arizona State U East (AZ)
Baker Coll of Flint (MI)
Ball State U (IN)
Bemidji State U (MN)
Berea Coll (KY)
Black Hills State U (SD)
Boise State U (ID)
Bowling Green State U (OH)
Bradley U (IL)
State U of NY Coll at Buffalo (NY)
California Polytechnic State U, San Luis Obispo (CA)
California State U, Fresno (CA)
California State U, Long Beach (CA)
California State U, Los Angeles (CA)
California U of Pennsylvania (PA)
Central Missouri State U (MO)
Central State U (OH)
Central Washington U (WA)
Cheyney U of Pennsylvania (PA)
Cleveland State U (OH)
East Carolina U (NC)
Eastern Illinois U (IL)
Eastern Kentucky U (KY)
Eastern Michigan U (MI)
Elizabeth City State U (NC)
Excelsior Coll (NY)
Fairmont State Coll (WV)
Ferris State U (MI)
Georgia Southern U (GA)
Grambling State U (LA)
Illinois Inst of Technology (IL)
Illinois State U (IL)
Indiana State U (IN)
Indiana U–Purdue U Fort Wayne (IN)
Jacksonville State U (AL)
Kean U (NJ)
Keene State Coll (NH)
Kent State U (OH)
Lake Superior State U (MI)
Lamar U (TX)
Lawrence Technological U (MI)
Metropolitan State Coll of Denver (CO)
Middle Tennessee State U (TN)
Millersville U of Pennsylvania (PA)
Minnesota State U Mankato (MN)
Minnesota State U Moorhead (MN)
Mississippi State U (MS)
Mississippi Valley State U (MS)
Morehead State U (KY)
Murray State U (KY)
Northeastern State U (OK)
Northern Illinois U (IL)
Northern Michigan U (MI)
Northwestern State U of Louisiana (LA)
Ohio Northern U (OH)
Ohio U (OH)
Oklahoma Panhandle State U (OK)
Oklahoma State U (OK)
Pacific Union Coll (CA)
Pennsylvania Coll of Technology (PA)
Pittsburg State U (KS)
Prairie View A&M U (TX)
Rhode Island Coll (RI)
Saginaw Valley State U (MI)
Saint Mary's U of Minnesota (MN)
Sam Houston State U (TX)
South Carolina State U (SC)
South Dakota State U (SD)
Southeastern Louisiana U (LA)
Southeastern Oklahoma State U (OK)
Southeast Missouri State U (MO)
Southern Arkansas U–Magnolia (AR)
Southern Illinois U Carbondale (IL)
Southern Polytechnic State U (GA)
Southwestern Oklahoma State U (OK)
State U of NY Inst of Tech at Utica/Rome (NY)
Tennessee State U (TN)
Tennessee Technological U (TN)
Texas A&M U–Kingsville (TX)
Texas Southern U (TX)

Texas State U-San Marcos (TX)
Thomas Edison State Coll (NJ)
The U of Akron (OH)
U of Arkansas at Fort Smith (AR)
U of Dayton (OH)
U of Houston (TX)
U of Idaho (ID)
U of Louisiana at Lafayette (LA)
U of Massachusetts Lowell (MA)
U of Nebraska at Omaha (NE)
U of Nebraska–Lincoln (NE)
U of New Haven (CT)
The U of North Carolina at Charlotte (NC)
U of North Dakota (ND)
U of Northern Iowa (IA)
The U of Texas at Brownsville (TX)
The U of Texas at Tyler (TX)
U of Toledo (OH)
The U of West Alabama (AL)
U of Wisconsin–Platteville (WI)
Wayne State U (MI)
Weber State U (UT)
Western Illinois U (IL)
Western Kentucky U (KY)
Western Washington U (WA)
West Texas A&M U (TX)
William Penn U (IA)

INFORMATION RESOURCES MANAGEMENT
Clarkson U (NY)
Juniata Coll (PA)
Mount Saint Mary's Coll and Sem (MD)
U of Wisconsin–Eau Claire (WI)

INFORMATION SCIENCE/ STUDIES
Alabama State U (AL)
Albertus Magnus Coll (CT)
Albright Coll (PA)
Alvernia Coll (PA)
American Coll of Computer & Information Sciences (AL)
American Intl Coll (MA)
American U (DC)
The American U in Dubai(United Arab Emirates)
Andrews U (MI)
Armstrong Atlantic State U (GA)
Ashland U (OH)
Athabasca U (AB, Canada)
Athens State U (AL)
Atlantic Union Coll (MA)
Averett U (VA)
Baker Coll of Cadillac (MI)
Baker Coll of Flint (MI)
Baker Coll of Jackson (MI)
Baker Coll of Muskegon (MI)
Baker Coll of Owosso (MI)
Baker Coll of Port Huron (MI)
Baker U (KS)
Baldwin-Wallace Coll (OH)
Ball State U (IN)
Barry U (FL)
Belhaven Coll (MS)
Bellevue U (NE)
Belmont Abbey Coll (NC)
Belmont U (TN)
Bemidji State U (MN)
Benedictine U (IL)
Baruch Coll of the City U of NY (NY)
Bethune-Cookman Coll (FL)
Bloomfield Coll (NJ)
Bluffton Coll (OH)
Boise State U (ID)
Boston U (MA)
Bradley U (IL)
Brewton-Parker Coll (GA)
Brigham Young U–Hawaii (HI)
Brock U (ON, Canada)
Brooklyn Coll of the City U of NY (NY)
State U of NY Coll at Buffalo (NY)
Butler U (IN)
California Baptist U (CA)
California Lutheran U (CA)
California State Polytechnic U, Pomona (CA)
California State U, Dominguez Hills (CA)
California State U, Fullerton (CA)
California State U, Hayward (CA)
California State U, Stanislaus (CA)
Calumet Coll of Saint Joseph (IN)
Campbellsville U (KY)
Carleton U (ON, Canada)
Carlow Coll (PA)
Carnegie Mellon U (PA)
Carroll Coll (WI)
Carson-Newman Coll (TN)
Catawba Coll (NC)
Cedar Crest Coll (PA)
Cedarville U (OH)
Centenary Coll (NJ)
Central Coll (IA)
Chadron State Coll (NE)
Champlain Coll (VT)
Chicago State U (IL)
Chowan Coll (NC)
Christopher Newport U (VA)
Clarion U of Pennsylvania (PA)
Clark Atlanta U (GA)
Clarke Coll (IA)
Clayton Coll & State U (GA)
Clemson U (SC)
Cleveland State U (OH)
Coll Misericordia (PA)
Coll of Charleston (SC)
Coll of Notre Dame of Maryland (MD)
Coll of St. Joseph (VT)
The Coll of Saint Rose (NY)
Coll of Staten Island of the City U of NY (NY)
Colorado State U (CO)
Colorado Tech U Sioux Falls Campus (SD)
Columbia Union Coll (MD)
Columbus State U (GA)
Concord Coll (WV)
Concordia U (IL)
Cornell U (NY)
Cornerstone U (MI)
Culver-Stockton Coll (MO)
Dakota State U (SD)
Daniel Webster Coll (NH)
Davis & Elkins Coll (WV)
Delaware State U (DE)
DePaul U (IL)
Dillard U (LA)
Dominican U (IL)
Drake U (IA)
Drexel U (PA)
Eastern Kentucky U (KY)
Eastern Michigan U (MI)
Edgewood Coll (WI)
Elmira Coll (NY)
Emporia State U (KS)
Excelsior Coll (NY)
Fairfield U (CT)
Faulkner U (AL)
Ferris State U (MI)
Ferrum Coll (VA)
Florida Ag and Mech U (FL)
Florida Inst of Technology (FL)
Florida State U (FL)
Fordham U (NY)
Fort Hays State U (KS)
Fort Lewis Coll (CO)
Freed-Hardeman U (TN)
Frostburg State U (MD)
Gallaudet U (DC)
Georgetown Coll (KY)
Glenville State Coll (WV)
Golden Gate U (CA)
Goldey-Beacom Coll (DE)
Gonzaga U (WA)
Goshen Coll (IN)
Grambling State U (LA)
Grand Valley State U (MI)
Grand View Coll (IA)
Grantham U (LA)
Guilford Coll (NC)
Hampton U (VA)
Harris-Stowe State Coll (MO)
Harvard U (MA)
Hawai'i Pacific U (HI)
HEC Montreal (QC, Canada)
Heidelberg Coll (OH)
High Point U (NC)
Hofstra U (NY)
Hollins U (VA)
Houston Baptist U (TX)
Howard Payne U (TX)
Howard U (DC)
Humboldt State U (CA)
Huron U USA in London(United Kingdom)
Husson Coll (ME)
Idaho State U (ID)
Illinois Coll (IL)
Illinois Inst of Technology (IL)
Indiana Inst of Technology (IN)
Inter American U of PR, Ponce Campus (PR)
Inter American U of PR, San Germán Campus (PR)
Iowa Wesleyan Coll (IA)
James Madison U (VA)
John Jay Coll of Criminal Justice, the City U of NY (NY)
Johnson & Wales U (RI)
Johnson C. Smith U (NC)
Johnson State Coll (VT)
Jones Coll, Jacksonville (FL)
Judson Coll (IL)
Kansas State U (KS)
Kansas Wesleyan U (KS)
Kennesaw State U (GA)
Kettering U (MI)
King Coll (TN)
Lakehead U (ON, Canada)
Lamar U (TX)
La Salle U (PA)
Lasell Coll (MA)
Lehigh U (PA)
Le Moyne Coll (NY)
LeTourneau U (TX)
Limestone Coll (SC)
Lincoln U (MO)
Lipscomb U (TN)
Livingstone Coll (NC)
Long Island U, C.W. Post Campus (NY)
Louisiana State U in Shreveport (LA)
Loyola U Chicago (IL)
Loyola U New Orleans (LA)
MacMurray Coll (IL)
Macon State Coll (GA)
Madonna U (MI)
Mansfield U of Pennsylvania (PA)
Marietta Coll (OH)
Marist Coll (NY)
Marquette U (WI)
Marymount Coll of Fordham U (NY)
McGill U (QC, Canada)
McKendree Coll (IL)
McMurry U (TX)
Medgar Evers Coll of the City U of NY (NY)
Memorial U of Newfoundland (NL, Canada)
Mercer U (GA)
Mercy Coll (NY)
Mercyhurst Coll (PA)
Messiah Coll (PA)
Metropolitan State U (MN)
Michigan Technological U (MI)
Midwestern State U (TX)
Minnesota State U Mankato (MN)
Missouri Southern State U (MO)
Missouri Western State Coll (MO)
Montana Tech of The U of Montana (MT)
Morgan State U (MD)
Mountain State U (WV)
Mount Aloysius Coll (PA)
Mount Saint Vincent U (NS, Canada)
Mt. Sierra Coll (CA)
Mount Union Coll (OH)
Murray State U (KY)
National American U, Colorado Springs (CO)
National American U, Denver (CO)
National American U (NM)
National American U (SD)
National American U–Sioux Falls Branch (SD)
National-Louis U (IL)
National U (CA)
Nazareth Coll of Rochester (NY)
Nebraska Wesleyan U (NE)
New Jersey Inst of Technology (NJ)
Newman U (KS)
New Mexico Highlands U (NM)
New Mexico State U (NM)
New York Inst of Technology (NY)
New York U (NY)
Niagara U (NY)
North Carolina Central U (NC)
North Carolina Wesleyan Coll (NC)
Northeastern U (MA)
Northern Michigan U (MI)
North Georgia Coll & State U (GA)
Northland Coll (WI)
Northwestern Oklahoma State U (OK)
Northwestern State U of Louisiana (LA)
Northwestern U (IL)
Notre Dame Coll (OH)
Oakland City U (IN)
Ohio Dominican U (OH)
The Ohio State U (OH)
Oklahoma Baptist U (OK)
Oklahoma Christian U (OK)
Oklahoma Panhandle State U (OK)
Oklahoma State U (OK)
Olivet Nazarene U (IL)
Oregon State U (OR)
Ottawa U (KS)
Pace U (NY)
Pacific Union Coll (CA)
Penn State U Abington Coll (PA)
Penn State U Altoona Coll (PA)
Penn State U at Erie, The Behrend Coll (PA)
Penn State U Beaver Campus of the Commonwealth Coll (PA)
Penn State U Berks Cmps of Berks-Lehigh Valley Coll (PA)
Penn State U Delaware County Campus of the Commonwealth Coll (PA)
Penn State U DuBois Campus of the Commonwealth Coll (PA)
Penn State U Fayette Campus of the Commonwealth Coll (PA)
Penn State U Harrisburg Campus of the Capital Coll (PA)
Penn State U Lehigh Valley Cmps of Berks-Lehigh Valley Coll (PA)
Penn State U McKeesport Campus of the Commonwealth Coll (PA)
Penn State U Mont Alto Campus of the Commonwealth Coll (PA)
Penn State U New Kensington Campus of the Commonwealth Coll (PA)
Penn State U Schuylkill Campus of the Capital Coll (PA)
Penn State U Shenango Campus of the Commonwealth Coll (PA)
Penn State U Univ Park Campus (PA)
Penn State U Wilkes-Barre Campus of the Commonwealth Coll (PA)
Penn State U Worthington Scranton Cmps Commonwealth Coll (PA)
Penn State U York Campus of the Commonwealth Coll (PA)
Philadelphia U (PA)
Pittsburg State U (KS)
Queens U of Charlotte (NC)
Quincy U (IL)
Quinnipiac U (CT)
Radford U (VA)
Ramapo Coll of New Jersey (NJ)
Reinhardt Coll (GA)
Rhode Island Coll (RI)
The Richard Stockton Coll of New Jersey (NJ)
Richmond, The American Intl U in London(United Kingdom)
Rider U (NJ)
Rivier Coll (NH)
Roanoke Coll (VA)
Robert Morris U (PA)
Rockhurst U (MO)
Rutgers, The State U of New Jersey, Newark (NJ)
Rutgers, The State U of New Jersey, New Brunswick/Piscataway (NJ)
Ryerson U (ON, Canada)
St. Ambrose U (IA)
St. Cloud State U (MN)
St. Francis Xavier U (NS, Canada)
St. John's U (NY)
Saint Joseph's U (PA)
Saint Martin's Coll (WA)
Saint Mary-of-the-Woods Coll (IN)
Saint Mary's U of Minnesota (MN)
St. Mary's U of San Antonio (TX)
Saint Michael's Coll (VT)
St. Thomas Aquinas Coll (NY)
St. Thomas U (FL)
Salve Regina U (RI)
San Diego State U (CA)
San Francisco State U (CA)
Siena Heights U (MI)
Silver Lake Coll (WI)
Simpson Coll (IA)
South Dakota State U (SD)
Southeastern Oklahoma State U (OK)
Southern Illinois U Carbondale (IL)
Southern Nazarene U (OK)
Southern Polytechnic State U (GA)
South U (AL)
Southwest Baptist U (MO)
Springfield Coll (MA)
State U of NY at Binghamton (NY)
State U of NY at Oswego (NY)
State U of NY Coll at Fredonia (NY)
State U of NY Coll at Old Westbury (NY)
State U of NY Inst of Tech at Utica/Rome (NY)
Stony Brook U, State U of New York (NY)
Strayer U (DC)
Suffolk U (MA)
Susquehanna U (PA)
Syracuse U (NY)
Taylor U (IN)
Tennessee Technological U (TN)
Texas A&M Intl U (TX)
Texas A&M U–Commerce (TX)
Texas A&M U–Corpus Christi (TX)
Texas A&M U–Kingsville (TX)
Texas Lutheran U (TX)
Thiel Coll (PA)
Tiffin U (OH)
Towson U (MD)
Trevecca Nazarene U (TN)
Trinity Christian Coll (IL)
Tulane U (LA)
Tusculum Coll (TN)
Union Coll (NE)
Union U (TN)
United States Military Acad (NY)
Université de Sherbrooke (QC, Canada)
State U of NY at Albany (NY)
U of Alberta (AB, Canada)
U of Arkansas at Little Rock (AR)
U of Baltimore (MD)
U of Bridgeport (CT)
U of Calif, Los Angeles (CA)
U of Calif, Santa Cruz (CA)
U of Charleston (WV)
U of Cincinnati (OH)
U of Dayton (OH)
U of Detroit Mercy (MI)
U of Great Falls (MT)
U of Guelph (ON, Canada)
U of Hartford (CT)
U of Houston (TX)
U of Houston–Clear Lake (TX)
U of Indianapolis (IN)
U of Mary (ND)
U of Mary Hardin-Baylor (TX)
U of Maryland, Baltimore County (MD)
U of Maryland, Coll Park (MD)
U of Maryland U Coll (MD)
U of Miami (FL)
U of Michigan–Dearborn (MI)
U of Michigan–Flint (MI)
U of Minnesota, Crookston (MN)
U of Missouri–Rolla (MO)
U of Mobile (AL)
The U of Montana–Missoula (MT)
U of New Brunswick Fredericton (NB, Canada)
U of New Mexico (NM)
The U of North Carolina at Chapel Hill (NC)
U of North Texas (TX)
U of Ottawa (ON, Canada)
U of Phoenix–Jacksonville Campus (FL)
U of Pittsburgh (PA)
U of Saint Mary (KS)
U of San Francisco (CA)
U of Saskatchewan (SK, Canada)
The U of Scranton (PA)
U of Sioux Falls (SD)
U of South Florida (FL)
The U of Tampa (FL)
The U of Texas at Brownsville (TX)
U of the District of Columbia (DC)
U of the Pacific (CA)
U of the Sacred Heart (PR)
U of Toledo (OH)
U of Tulsa (OK)
U of Vermont (VT)
U of Washington (WA)
The U of Western Ontario (ON, Canada)
U of Windsor (ON, Canada)
U of Wisconsin–Green Bay (WI)
U of Wisconsin–River Falls (WI)
U of Wisconsin–Superior (WI)
Utah State U (UT)
Valdosta State U (GA)
Villa Julie Coll (MD)
Villanova U (PA)
Virginia Commonwealth U (VA)
Virginia Polytechnic Inst and State U (VA)
Waldorf Coll (IA)
Wartburg Coll (IA)
Washburn U (KS)
Washington U in St. Louis (MO)
Wayne State Coll (NE)
Wayne State U (MI)
Weber State U (UT)
Webster U (MO)
Western New England Coll (MA)
Westfield State Coll (MA)
West Liberty State Coll (WV)
Westminster Coll (PA)
West Virginia Wesleyan Coll (WV)
Widener U (PA)
Wilberforce U (OH)
Wilkes U (PA)
William Jewell Coll (MO)
Wingate U (NC)
Winona State U (MN)
Worcester Polytechnic Inst (MA)
Wright State U (OH)
York Coll of the City U of New York (NY)
Youngstown State U (OH)

INFORMATION TECHNOLOGY
American Coll of Computer & Information Sciences (AL)

American InterContinental U-London(United Kingdom)
American InterContinental U Online (IL)
American Public U System (WV)
Armstrong Atlantic State U (GA)
Bellevue U (NE)
Bluffton Coll (OH)
Brigham Young U (UT)
Bryant Coll (RI)
California State U, Chico (CA)
California State U, Los Angeles (CA)
Canisius Coll (NY)
Capella U (MN)
Coll of the Ozarks (MO)
Concordia U (CA)
Curry Coll (MA)
D'Youville Coll (NY)
Endicott Coll (MA)
Everglades U, Boca Raton (FL)
Florida Intl U (FL)
Framingham State Coll (MA)
Harding U (AR)
Huron U USA in London(United Kingdom)
Illinois Inst of Technology (IL)
Illinois State U (IL)
Intl Coll (FL)
Jones Intl U (CO)
Juniata Coll (PA)
Kaplan Coll (IA)
Keystone Coll (PA)
Kutztown U of Pennsylvania (PA)
Kwantlen U Coll (BC, Canada)
Lawrence Technological U (MI)
Long Island U, C.W. Post Campus (NY)
Marian Coll of Fond du Lac (WI)
Marist Coll (NY)
National American U, Denver (CO)
National American U–Sioux Falls Branch (SD)
Nazareth Coll of Rochester (NY)
New Mexico Inst of Mining and Technology (NM)
North Carolina State U (NC)
Northface U (UT)
Plymouth State U (NH)
Point Park U (PA)
Rensselaer Polytechnic Inst (NY)
Robert Morris Coll (IL)
Rochester Inst of Technology (NY)
Rocky Mountain Coll (MT)
Ryerson U (ON, Canada)
Sacred Heart U (CT)
St. Francis Coll (NY)
San Jose State U (CA)
Simmons Coll (MA)
Slippery Rock U of Pennsylvania (PA)
Southern Alberta Inst of Technology (AB, Canada)
South U (GA)
United States Intl U(Kenya)
Université de Sherbrooke (QC, Canada)
U of Central Florida (FL)
U of Great Falls (MT)
U of Houston (TX)
U of Massachusetts Lowell (MA)
U of Michigan–Flint (MI)
U of Missouri–Kansas City (MO)
U of Phoenix–Colorado Campus (CO)
U of Phoenix–Hawaii Campus (HI)
U of Phoenix–Maryland Campus (MD)
U of Phoenix–Metro Detroit Campus (MI)
U of Phoenix–New Mexico Campus (NM)
U of Phoenix–Northern California Campus (CA)
U of Phoenix–Oklahoma City Campus (OK)
U of Phoenix–Oregon Campus (OR)
U of Phoenix–Philadelphia Campus (PA)
U of Phoenix–Phoenix Campus (AZ)
U of Phoenix–Pittsburgh Campus (PA)
U of Phoenix–Sacramento Campus (CA)
U of Phoenix–San Diego Campus (CA)
U of Phoenix–Southern Arizona Campus (AZ)
U of Phoenix–Southern California Campus (CA)
U of Phoenix–Southern Colorado Campus (CO)
U of Phoenix–West Michigan Campus (MI)
U of St. Francis (IL)
U of Windsor (ON, Canada)
U of Wisconsin–Whitewater (WI)
Virginia Coll at Birmingham (AL)
Washington & Jefferson Coll (PA)
Wilmington Coll (DE)
York U (ON, Canada)

INORGANIC CHEMISTRY

California Inst of Technology (CA)
Cornell U (NY)

INSTITUTIONAL FOOD WORKERS

Grambling State U (LA)
Kendall Coll (IL)
Lexington Coll (IL)
Nicholls State U (LA)
Texas Woman's U (TX)

INSTRUMENTATION TECHNOLOGY

Colorado State U-Pueblo (CO)

INSURANCE

Appalachian State U (NC)
Ball State U (IN)
Baylor U (TX)
Bradley U (IL)
California State Polytechnic U, Pomona (CA)
California State U, Sacramento (CA)
Delta State U (MS)
Eastern Kentucky U (KY)
Excelsior Coll (NY)
Ferris State U (MI)
Florida Intl U (FL)
Florida State U (FL)
Georgia State U (GA)
Howard U (DC)
Illinois State U (IL)
Illinois Wesleyan U (IL)
Indiana State U (IN)
Martin U (IN)
Minnesota State U Mankato (MN)
Mississippi State U (MS)
The Ohio State U (OH)
Olivet Coll (MI)
Roosevelt U (IL)
St. Cloud State U (MN)
St. John's U (NY)
Seattle U (WA)
Southwest Missouri State U (MO)
Texas Southern U (TX)
Thomas Edison State Coll (NJ)
The U of Akron (OH)
U of Calgary (AB, Canada)
U of Central Arkansas (AR)
U of Cincinnati (OH)
U of Connecticut (CT)
U of Florida (FL)
U of Georgia (GA)
U of Hartford (CT)
U of Louisiana at Lafayette (LA)
The U of Memphis (TN)
U of Minnesota, Twin Cities Campus (MN)
U of Mississippi (MS)
U of North Texas (TX)
U of Pennsylvania (PA)
U of South Carolina (SC)
U of Wisconsin–Madison (WI)
Washington State U (WA)

INTERCULTURAL/ MULTICULTURAL AND DIVERSITY STUDIES

Coll of St. Catherine (MN)
Columbia Intl U (SC)
Evangel U (MO)
Marquette U (WI)
Sterling Coll (VT)
U of Houston–Clear Lake (TX)

INTERDISCIPLINARY STUDIES

Abilene Christian U (TX)
Agnes Scott Coll (GA)
Albertus Magnus Coll (CT)
Albright Coll (PA)
Alfred U (NY)
Alice Lloyd Coll (KY)
Amberton U (TX)
American U (DC)
The American U of Rome(Italy)
Amherst Coll (MA)
Angelo State U (TX)
Anna Maria Coll (MA)
Antioch Coll (OH)
Arizona State U (AZ)
Arizona State U East (AZ)
Arizona State U West (AZ)
Atlantic Baptist U (NB, Canada)
Augsburg Coll (MN)
Austin Peay State U (TN)
Bard Coll (NY)
Beloit Coll (WI)
Bennington Coll (VT)
Bentley Coll (MA)
Baruch Coll of the City U of NY (NY)
Bethany Coll (WV)
Bethel Coll (TN)
Birmingham-Southern Coll (AL)
Blackburn Coll (IL)
Bluefield Coll (VA)
Boise State U (ID)
Boston Coll (MA)
Boston U (MA)
Bowdoin Coll (ME)
Brevard Coll (NC)
Briar Cliff U (IA)
Brigham Young U–Hawaii (HI)
Brock U (ON, Canada)
Bucknell U (PA)
Burlington Coll (VT)
California Lutheran U (CA)
California State U, Dominguez Hills (CA)
California State U, Hayward (CA)
California State U, Long Beach (CA)
California State U, Los Angeles (CA)
California State U, San Bernardino (CA)
Calvin Coll (MI)
Capital U (OH)
Carleton Coll (MN)
Carleton U (ON, Canada)
Carnegie Mellon U (PA)
Carson-Newman Coll (TN)
Catawba Coll (NC)
The Catholic U of America (DC)
Centenary Coll of Louisiana (LA)
Central Coll (IA)
Central Connecticut State U (CT)
Central Methodist Coll (MO)
Chadron State Coll (NE)
Christian Heritage Coll (CA)
Christopher Newport U (VA)
Clark Atlanta U (GA)
Clarkson U (NY)
Clark U (MA)
Cleveland State U (OH)
Coe Coll (IA)
Coll Misericordia (PA)
Coll of Mount Saint Vincent (NY)
Coll of Notre Dame of Maryland (MD)
The Coll of Saint Rose (NY)
Coll of the Atlantic (ME)
Coll of the Ozarks (MO)
The Coll of William and Mary (VA)
The Coll of Wooster (OH)
Columbia Coll Chicago (IL)
Concordia U (OR)
Concordia U (QC, Canada)
Connecticut Coll (CT)
Cornell Coll (IA)
Cornell U (NY)
Cornerstone U (MI)
Covenant Coll (GA)
Dallas Baptist U (TX)
Dana Coll (NE)
DePaul U (IL)
DePauw U (IN)
Dowling Coll (NY)
D'Youville Coll (NY)
Earlham Coll (IN)
Eastern Michigan U (MI)
Eastern Washington U (WA)
Eckerd Coll (FL)
Elmhurst Coll (IL)
Elmira Coll (NY)
Elms Coll (MA)
Emerson Coll (MA)
Emory & Henry Coll (VA)
Eugene Lang Coll, New School U (NY)
Florida Inst of Technology (FL)
Fordham U (NY)
Franklin U (OH)
Freed-Hardeman U (TN)
George Fox U (OR)
George Mason U (VA)
Georgetown U (DC)
The George Washington U (DC)
Gettysburg Coll (PA)
Goddard Coll (VT)
Goucher Coll (MD)
Grand Valley State U (MI)
Greensboro Coll (NC)
Grinnell Coll (IA)
Guilford Coll (NC)
Gustavus Adolphus Coll (MN)
Hampshire Coll (MA)
Hardin-Simmons U (TX)
Harris-Stowe State Coll (MO)
Harvard U (MA)
Hastings Coll (NE)
Hawai'i Pacific U (HI)
Hendrix Coll (AR)
Hillsdale Coll (MI)
Hillsdale Free Will Baptist Coll (OK)
Hobart and William Smith Colls (NY)
Hofstra U (NY)
Hollins U (VA)
Hope Coll (MI)
Houston Baptist U (TX)
Huntingdon Coll (AL)
Illinois Coll (IL)
Illinois Wesleyan U (IL)
Iona Coll (NY)
Iowa State U of Science and Technology (IA)
Ithaca Coll (NY)
Jacksonville U (FL)
John Brown U (AR)
John Carroll U (OH)
The Johns Hopkins U (MD)
Johnson & Wales U (RI)
Jones Coll, Jacksonville (FL)
Jones Coll, Miami (FL)
Judson Coll (AL)
Juniata Coll (PA)
Kalamazoo Coll (MI)
Keene State Coll (NH)
Kentucky Christian Coll (KY)
Kentucky Wesleyan Coll (KY)
Kenyon Coll (OH)
Keuka Coll (NY)
Lake Superior State U (MI)
Lamar U (TX)
Lander U (SC)
Lane Coll (TN)
Lasell Coll (MA)
Lehman Coll of the City U of NY (NY)
LeTourneau U (TX)
Lewis-Clark State Coll (ID)
Liberty U (VA)
Long Island U, Brooklyn Campus (NY)
Long Island U, C.W. Post Campus (NY)
Long Island U, Southampton Coll, Friends World Program (NY)
Louisiana Coll (LA)
Loyola Coll in Maryland (MD)
Luther Coll (IA)
Lycoming Coll (PA)
Macalester Coll (MN)
Manchester Coll (IN)
Marlboro Coll (VT)
Marquette U (WI)
Mars Hill Coll (NC)
Martin Luther Coll (MN)
Marylhurst U (OR)
Marymount Coll of Fordham U (NY)
Maryville U of Saint Louis (MO)
Mary Washington Coll (VA)
Marywood U (PA)
Massachusetts Coll of Liberal Arts (MA)
McPherson Coll (KS)
Mercy Coll (NY)
Merrimack Coll (MA)
Miami U (OH)
Middle Tennessee State U (TN)
Midwestern State U (TX)
Millikin U (IL)
Mills Coll (CA)
Minneapolis Coll of Art and Design (MN)
Minnesota State U Moorhead (MN)
Molloy Coll (NY)
Monmouth U (NJ)
Morehouse Coll (GA)
Morningside Coll (IA)
Mountain State U (WV)
Mount Allison U (NB, Canada)
Mount Holyoke Coll (MA)
Mount Saint Mary Coll (NY)
Mount Saint Vincent U (NS, Canada)
Mount Union Coll (OH)
Naropa U (CO)
National U (CA)
Nazareth Coll of Rochester (NY)
Nebraska Wesleyan U (NE)
New Coll of California (CA)
New Mexico Inst of Mining and Technology (NM)
New Mexico State U (NM)
New York U (NY)
North Central U (MN)
North Greenville Coll (SC)
Northland Coll (WI)
Northwestern U (IL)
Nova Southeastern U (FL)
Nyack Coll (NY)
Oakland City U (IN)
Oakland U (MI)
Oberlin Coll (OH)
Oglethorpe U (GA)
Ohio Dominican U (OH)
Ohio U (OH)
Oklahoma Baptist U (OK)
Olivet Nazarene U (IL)
Oregon State U (OR)
Pace U (NY)
Pacific Union Coll (CA)
Pepperdine U, Malibu (CA)
Piedmont Coll (GA)
Pitzer Coll (CA)
Pomona Coll (CA)
Prairie View A&M U (TX)
Purdue U (IN)
Queens Coll of the City U of NY (NY)
Queen's U at Kingston (ON, Canada)
Radford U (VA)
Ramapo Coll of New Jersey (NJ)
Rensselaer Polytechnic Inst (NY)
Rhodes Coll (TN)
The Richard Stockton Coll of New Jersey (NJ)
Ripon Coll (WI)
Rochester Coll (MI)
Rochester Inst of Technology (NY)
Rocky Mountain Coll (MT)
Rollins Coll (FL)
Russell Sage Coll (NY)
Rutgers, The State U of New Jersey, New Brunswick/Piscataway (NJ)
St. Andrews Presbyterian Coll (NC)
St. Bonaventure U (NY)
St. Cloud State U (MN)
St. John's Coll (MD)
Saint Joseph's U (PA)
Saint Mary's Coll (IN)
Saint Mary's Coll of California (CA)
St. Norbert Coll (WI)
Salem Coll (NC)
San Francisco Art Inst (CA)
Santa Clara U (CA)
Sarah Lawrence Coll (NY)
Schiller Intl U (FL)
Schiller Intl U(France)
Schiller Intl U(Germany)
Schiller Intl U(Spain)
Schiller Intl U(United Kingdom)
Schiller Intl U, American Coll of Switzerland(Switzerland)
Silver Lake Coll (WI)
Simon's Rock Coll of Bard (MA)
Smith Coll (MA)
Sonoma State U (CA)
South Dakota School of Mines and Technology (SD)
Southeastern Coll of the Assemblies of God (FL)
Southeast Missouri State U (MO)
Southern Nazarene U (OK)
Southern Oregon U (OR)
Stanford U (CA)
State U of NY at Binghamton (NY)
Plattsburgh State U of NY (NY)
State U of NY Coll at Brockport (NY)
State U of NY Coll at Fredonia (NY)
State U of NY Coll at Oneonta (NY)
State U of NY Empire State Coll (NY)
Stephens Coll (MO)
Sterling Coll (KS)
Suffolk U (MA)
Syracuse U (NY)
Tabor Coll (KS)
Tarleton State U (TX)
Taylor U, Fort Wayne Campus (IN)
Tennessee Wesleyan Coll (TN)
Texas A&M U (TX)
Texas A&M U–Commerce (TX)
Texas A&M U–Corpus Christi (TX)
Texas A&M U–Texarkana (TX)
Texas Southern U (TX)
Texas Tech U (TX)
Texas Woman's U (TX)
Thomas Aquinas Coll (CA)
Tougaloo Coll (MS)
Towson U (MD)
Trent U (ON, Canada)
Trinity Coll (CT)
Trinity Coll (DC)
United States Air Force Acad (CO)
United States Military Acad (NY)
Unity Coll (ME)
Université de Montréal (QC, Canada)
Université de Sherbrooke (QC, Canada)
Université Laval (QC, Canada)
State U of NY at Albany (NY)
U Coll of the Fraser Valley (BC, Canada)
The U of Akron (OH)

The U of Alabama (AL)
U of Baltimore (MD)
U of Bridgeport (CT)
The U of British Columbia (BC, Canada)
U of Calif, San Diego (CA)
U of Calif, Santa Barbara (CA)
U of Chicago (IL)
U of Hartford (CT)
U of Hawaii at Hilo (HI)
U of Houston (TX)
U of Illinois at Springfield (IL)
The U of Iowa (IA)
U of Judaism (CA)
U of Kentucky (KY)
U of Maine at Farmington (ME)
U of Mary (ND)
U of Maryland, Baltimore County (MD)
U of Massachusetts Boston (MA)
U of Massachusetts Dartmouth (MA)
The U of Memphis (TN)
U of Michigan (MI)
U of Michigan–Dearborn (MI)
U of Minnesota, Crookston (MN)
U of Minnesota, Duluth (MN)
U of Missouri–Columbia (MO)
U of Missouri–Kansas City (MO)
The U of Montana–Missoula (MT)
U of Nevada, Las Vegas (NV)
U of New Hampshire (NH)
The U of North Carolina at Greensboro (NC)
U of Northern Colorado (CO)
U of North Texas (TX)
U of Ottawa (ON, Canada)
U of Pittsburgh (PA)
U of Portland (OR)
U of Puget Sound (WA)
U of Redlands (CA)
U of Rhode Island (RI)
U of Richmond (VA)
U of Saint Mary (KS)
U of St. Thomas (MN)
U of San Francisco (CA)
U of Sioux Falls (SD)
U of South Carolina Spartanburg (SC)
U of Southern California (CA)
The U of Tennessee at Martin (TN)
The U of Texas at Arlington (TX)
The U of Texas at Dallas (TX)
The U of Texas at Tyler (TX)
The U of Texas–Pan American (TX)
U of the Incarnate Word (TX)
U of the Pacific (CA)
U of the Sacred Heart (PR)
U of Vermont (VT)
The U of Virginia's Coll at Wise (VA)
U of Washington (WA)
U of Waterloo (ON, Canada)
U of Wisconsin–Green Bay (WI)
U of Wisconsin–Milwaukee (WI)
U of Wisconsin–Parkside (WI)
Vanderbilt U (TN)
Vanguard U of Southern California (CA)
Vassar Coll (NY)
Villa Julie Coll (MD)
Virginia Intermont Coll (VA)
Virginia Polytechnic Inst and State U (VA)
Virginia State U (VA)
Virginia Wesleyan Coll (VA)
Warren Wilson Coll (NC)
Washington and Lee U (VA)
Washington U in St. Louis (MO)
Wayne State Coll (NE)
Wayne State U (MI)
Webster U (MO)
Wesleyan Coll (GA)
Wesleyan U (CT)
Western Baptist Coll (OR)
Western Oregon U (OR)
Western Washington U (WA)
West Liberty State Coll (WV)
Westminster Coll (PA)
West Texas A&M U (TX)
West Virginia U (WV)
Wheaton Coll (MA)
William Jewell Coll (MO)
William Woods U (MO)
Wingate U (NC)
Wisconsin Lutheran Coll (WI)
Worcester Polytechnic Inst (MA)
York U (ON, Canada)

INTERIOR ARCHITECTURE

Arizona State U (AZ)
The Art Inst of California–San Diego (CA)
Auburn U (AL)
California Coll of the Arts (CA)
Central Michigan U (MI)
Central Missouri State U (MO)
Fashion Inst of Technology (NY)
Indiana State U (IN)
Indiana U of Pennsylvania (PA)
Kansas State U (KS)
Lawrence Technological U (MI)
Louisiana State U and A&M Coll (LA)
Louisiana Tech U (LA)
Philadelphia U (PA)
Rhode Island School of Design (RI)
School of the Art Inst of Chicago (IL)
Syracuse U (NY)
Texas State U-San Marcos (TX)
Texas Tech U (TX)
U of Bridgeport (CT)
U of Hawaii at Manoa (HI)
U of Houston (TX)
U of Idaho (ID)
U of Louisiana at Lafayette (LA)
U of Missouri–Columbia (MO)
U of Nebraska–Lincoln (NE)
U of Nevada, Las Vegas (NV)
U of New Haven (CT)
U of Oregon (OR)
The U of Texas at Arlington (TX)
U of Washington (WA)
Washington State U (WA)
Watkins Coll of Art and Design (TN)

INTERIOR DESIGN

Abilene Christian U (TX)
Acad of Art U (CA)
Adrian Coll (MI)
American InterContinental U (CA)
American InterContinental U, Atlanta (GA)
American InterContinental U-London(United Kingdom)
The American U in Dubai(United Arab Emirates)
Anderson Coll (SC)
Arcadia U (PA)
Art Center Coll of Design (CA)
The Art Inst of Atlanta (GA)
The Art Inst of California–San Diego (CA)
The Art Inst of California–San Francisco (CA)
The Art Inst of Colorado (CO)
The Art Inst of Phoenix (AZ)
The Art Inst of Portland (OR)
The Art Inst of Washington (VA)
Atlantic Union Coll (MA)
Baker Coll of Flint (MI)
Baylor U (TX)
Becker Coll (MA)
Bethel Coll (IN)
Boston Architectural Center (MA)
Brenau U (GA)
Bridgewater Coll (VA)
Brigham Young U (UT)
California State U, Chico (CA)
California State U, Fresno (CA)
California State U, Long Beach (CA)
California State U, Sacramento (CA)
Carson-Newman Coll (TN)
Cazenovia Coll (NY)
Central Missouri State U (MO)
Chaminade U of Honolulu (HI)
The Cleveland Inst of Art (OH)
Col for Creative Studies (MI)
Coll of Mount St. Joseph (OH)
Colorado State U (CO)
Columbia Coll Chicago (IL)
Columbus Coll of Art & Design (OH)
Concordia U Wisconsin (WI)
Converse Coll (SC)
Cornish Coll of the Arts (WA)
Design Inst of San Diego (CA)
Drexel U (PA)
East Carolina U (NC)
Eastern Kentucky U (KY)
Eastern Michigan U (MI)
Ferris State U (MI)
Florida Intl U (FL)
Florida State U (FL)
Georgia Southern U (GA)
Hampton U (VA)
Harding U (AR)
Harrington Coll of Design (IL)
High Point U (NC)
Howard U (DC)
The Illinois Inst of Art (IL)
The Illinois Inst of Art-Schaumburg (IL)
Indiana U Bloomington (IN)
Indiana U–Purdue U Indianapolis (IN)
Intl Acad of Design & Technology (FL)
Intl Acad of Merchandising & Design, Ltd (IL)
Iowa State U of Science and Technology (IA)
Kansas State U (KS)
Kean U (NJ)
Kent State U (OH)
Kwantlen U Coll (BC, Canada)
Lamar U (TX)
Lambuth U (TN)
La Roche Coll (PA)
Longwood U (VA)
Maryland Inst Coll of Art (MD)
Marylhurst U (OR)
Marymount Coll of Fordham U (NY)
Marymount U (VA)
Maryville U of Saint Louis (MO)
Mercyhurst Coll (PA)
Meredith Coll (NC)
Miami U (OH)
Miami U Hamilton (OH)
Michigan State U (MI)
Middle Tennessee State U (TN)
Milwaukee Inst of Art and Design (WI)
Minnesota State U Mankato (MN)
Mississippi Coll (MS)
Moore Coll of Art & Design (PA)
Mount Ida Coll (MA)
Mount Mary Coll (WI)
Newbury Coll (MA)
The New England Inst of Art (MA)
New York Inst of Technology (NY)
New York School of Interior Design (NY)
North Dakota State U (ND)
Northern Arizona U (AZ)
The Ohio State U (OH)
Oklahoma Christian U (OK)
Oklahoma State U (OK)
O'More Coll of Design (TN)
Oregon State U (OR)
Otis Coll of Art and Design (CA)
Paier Coll of Art, Inc. (CT)
Park U (MO)
Parsons School of Design, New School U (NY)
Philadelphia U (PA)
Pittsburg State U (KS)
Pratt Inst (NY)
Radford U (VA)
Rhode Island School of Design (RI)
Ringling School of Art and Design (FL)
Rochester Inst of Technology (NY)
Rocky Mountain Coll of Art & Design (CO)
Ryerson U (ON, Canada)
Salem Coll (NC)
Samford U (AL)
Sam Houston State U (TX)
San Diego State U (CA)
San Francisco State U (CA)
San Jose State U (CA)
Savannah Coll of Art and Design (GA)
School of the Art Inst of Chicago (IL)
South Dakota State U (SD)
Southern Illinois U Carbondale (IL)
Suffolk U (MA)
Syracuse U (NY)
Texas A&M U–Kingsville (TX)
Texas Christian U (TX)
The U of Akron (OH)
The U of Alabama (AL)
U of Bridgeport (CT)
U of Charleston (WV)
U of Cincinnati (OH)
U of Florida (FL)
U of Houston (TX)
U of Idaho (ID)
U of Kansas (KS)
U of Kentucky (KY)
U of Manitoba (MB, Canada)
U of Massachusetts Amherst (MA)
U of Michigan (MI)
U of Minnesota, Twin Cities Campus (MN)
U of Montevallo (AL)
The U of North Carolina at Greensboro (NC)
U of Northern Iowa (IA)
U of Oklahoma (OK)
U of Oregon (OR)
The U of Tennessee (TN)
The U of Tennessee at Martin (TN)
The U of Texas at Austin (TX)
U of the Incarnate Word (TX)
U of Wisconsin–Madison (WI)
U of Wisconsin–Stevens Point (WI)
Ursuline Coll (OH)
Utah State U (UT)
Valdosta State U (GA)
Virginia Coll at Birmingham (AL)
Virginia Commonwealth U (VA)
Watkins Coll of Art and Design (TN)
Wayne State Coll (NE)
Wentworth Inst of Technology (MA)
Western Carolina U (NC)
Western Michigan U (MI)
William Woods U (MO)

INTERMEDIA/MULTIMEDIA

Alberta Coll of Art & Design (AB, Canada)
American U (DC)
Art Acad of Cincinnati (OH)
Art Center Coll of Design (CA)
The Art Inst of California–San Diego (CA)
The Art Inst of Portland (OR)
The Art Inst of Washington (VA)
Augusta State U (GA)
Calumet Coll of Saint Joseph (IN)
Champlain Coll (VT)
City Coll of the City U of NY (NY)
The Cleveland Inst of Art (OH)
Col for Creative Studies (MI)
The Coll of New Jersey (NJ)
Coll of Santa Fe (NM)
Columbia Coll Chicago (IL)
Eastern U (PA)
Emerson Coll (MA)
The Evergreen State Coll (WA)
Hampshire Coll (MA)
Indiana U of Pennsylvania (PA)
Laguna Coll of Art & Design (CA)
Long Island U, C.W. Post Campus (NY)
Maine Coll of Art (ME)
Maryland Inst Coll of Art (MD)
Massachusetts Coll of Art (MA)
Memphis Coll of Art (TN)
Mills Coll (CA)
Minneapolis Coll of Art and Design (MN)
Mt. Sierra Coll (CA)
National U (CA)
The New England Inst of Art (MA)
New England School of Communications (ME)
New World School of the Arts (FL)
Pacific Northwest Coll of Art (OR)
Radford U (VA)
Ramapo Coll of New Jersey (NJ)
School of the Art Inst of Chicago (IL)
School of the Museum of Fine Arts, Boston (MA)
State U of NY Coll at Fredonia (NY)
Stevens Inst of Technology (NJ)
U of Calif, San Diego (CA)
U of Central Florida (FL)
U of Florida (FL)
U of Massachusetts Dartmouth (MA)
U of Michigan (MI)
U of Oregon (OR)
U of Regina (SK, Canada)
U of Windsor (ON, Canada)
Western Washington U (WA)

INTERNATIONAL AGRICULTURE

Cornell U (NY)
Eastern Mennonite U (VA)
Iowa State U of Science and Technology (IA)
McGill U (QC, Canada)
MidAmerica Nazarene U (KS)
Sterling Coll (VT)
Tarleton State U (TX)
U of Calif, Davis (CA)
U of Missouri–Columbia (MO)
Utah State U (UT)

INTERNATIONAL AND COMPARATIVE EDUCATION

Sterling Coll (VT)

INTERNATIONAL BUSINESS/ TRADE/COMMERCE

Adrian Coll (MI)
Albertson Coll of Idaho (ID)
Albertus Magnus Coll (CT)
Albright Coll (PA)
Alliant Intl U (CA)
Alliant Intl U–México City(Mexico)
Alma Coll (MI)
Alverno Coll (WI)
American Coll of Thessaloniki(Greece)
American InterContinental U, Atlanta (GA)
American Intl Coll (MA)
American U (DC)
The American U of Rome(Italy)
Appalachian State U (NC)
Aquinas Coll (MI)
Arcadia U (PA)
Arizona State U West (AZ)
Arkansas State U (AR)
Assumption Coll (MA)
Auburn U (AL)
Augsburg Coll (MN)
Avila U (MO)
Babson Coll (MA)
Baker U (KS)
Barry U (FL)
Baylor U (TX)
Bay Path Coll (MA)
Bellarmine U (KY)
Belmont Abbey Coll (NC)
Belmont U (TN)
Benedictine U (IL)
Berkeley Coll (NJ)
Berkeley Coll-New York City Campus (NY)
Berkeley Coll-Westchester Campus (NY)
Baruch Coll of the City U of NY (NY)
Bethany Coll (KS)
Bethel Coll (IN)
Bethune-Cookman Coll (FL)
Birmingham-Southern Coll (AL)
Bishop's U (QC, Canada)
Boise State U (ID)
Boston U (MA)
Bowling Green State U (OH)
Bradley U (IL)
Bridgewater Coll (VA)
Bridgewater State Coll (MA)
Brigham Young U–Hawaii (HI)
Brock U (ON, Canada)
Buena Vista U (IA)
Butler U (IN)
Caldwell Coll (NJ)
California State Polytechnic U, Pomona (CA)
California State U, Dominguez Hills (CA)
California State U, Fresno (CA)
California State U, Long Beach (CA)
California State U, Sacramento (CA)
Campbell U (NC)
Canisius Coll (NY)
Cardinal Stritch U (WI)
Carleton U (ON, Canada)
Cedarville U (OH)
Central Coll (IA)
Central Connecticut State U (CT)
Central Michigan U (MI)
Champlain Coll (VT)
Chapman U (CA)
Chatham Coll (PA)
Chestnut Hill Coll (PA)
Christopher Newport U (VA)
City U (WA)
Claremont McKenna Coll (CA)
Clarion U of Pennsylvania (PA)
Clarke Coll (IA)
Clarkson U (NY)
Coker Coll (SC)
Coll of Charleston (SC)
The Coll of New Jersey (NJ)
Coll of Notre Dame of Maryland (MD)
Coll of St. Catherine (MN)
The Coll of St. Scholastica (MN)
Coll of Santa Fe (NM)
The Coll of Southeastern Europe, The American U of Athens(Greece)
Coll of the Ozarks (MO)
Columbia Coll (MO)
Columbia Southern U (AL)
Concordia Coll (MN)
Concordia U (QC, Canada)
Converse Coll (SC)
Cornell Coll (IA)
Creighton U (NE)
Dalhousie U (NS, Canada)
Davenport U, Dearborn (MI)
Davenport U, Grand Rapids (MI)
Davenport U, Warren (MI)
Davis & Elkins Coll (WV)
DePaul U (IL)
Dickinson Coll (PA)
Dickinson State U (ND)
Dillard U (LA)
Dominican Coll (NY)
Dominican U (IL)
Dominican U of California (CA)
Dowling Coll (NY)
Drake U (IA)
Drexel U (PA)
Drury U (MO)
Duquesne U (PA)
D'Youville Coll (NY)
Eastern Mennonite U (VA)
Eastern Michigan U (MI)
Eckerd Coll (FL)

Elizabethtown Coll (PA)
Elmhurst Coll (IL)
Elmira Coll (NY)
Excelsior Coll (NY)
Ferris State U (MI)
Florida Atlantic U (FL)
Florida Intl U (FL)
Florida Metropolitan U-Fort Lauderdale Coll (FL)
Florida Southern Coll (FL)
Florida State U (FL)
Fordham U (NY)
Fort Lewis Coll (CO)
Framingham State Coll (MA)
Franklin Coll Switzerland(Switzerland)
Fresno Pacific U (CA)
Gannon U (PA)
Georgetown Coll (KY)
Georgetown U (DC)
The George Washington U (DC)
Georgia Coll & State U (GA)
Georgia Southern U (GA)
Gettysburg Coll (PA)
Golden Gate U (CA)
Goldey-Beacom Coll (DE)
Gonzaga U (WA)
Grace Coll (IN)
Graceland U (IA)
Grand Canyon U (AZ)
Grand Valley State U (MI)
Grove City Coll (PA)
Gustavus Adolphus Coll (MN)
Hamline U (MN)
Hampshire Coll (MA)
Harding U (AR)
Hardin-Simmons U (TX)
Hawai'i Pacific U (HI)
HEC Montreal (QC, Canada)
High Point U (NC)
Hiram Coll (OH)
Hofstra U (NY)
Howard U (DC)
Huntingdon Coll (AL)
Husson Coll (ME)
Illinois State U (IL)
Illinois Wesleyan U (IL)
Immaculata U (PA)
Indiana U of Pennsylvania (PA)
Inter American U of PR, Ponce Campus (PR)
Iona Coll (NY)
Iowa State U of Science and Technology (IA)
Ithaca Coll (NY)
Jacksonville U (FL)
James Madison U (VA)
Jamestown Coll (ND)
John Brown U (AR)
Johnson & Wales U (FL)
Johnson & Wales U (RI)
Judson Coll (IL)
Juniata Coll (PA)
King Coll (TN)
King's Coll (PA)
Kutztown U of Pennsylvania (PA)
Lake Erie Coll (OH)
Lakeland Coll (WI)
La Roche Coll (PA)
Lasell Coll (MA)
Lenoir-Rhyne Coll (NC)
LeTourneau U (TX)
Liberty U (VA)
Linfield Coll (OR)
Long Island U, C.W. Post Campus (NY)
Loras Coll (IA)
Louisiana State U and A&M Coll (LA)
Loyola Coll in Maryland (MD)
Loyola U New Orleans (LA)
Lycoming Coll (PA)
Lynn U (FL)
Madonna U (MI)
Maine Maritime Acad (ME)
Mansfield U of Pennsylvania (PA)
Marietta Coll (OH)
Marquette U (WI)
Mars Hill Coll (NC)
Marygrove Coll (MI)
Marymount Coll of Fordham U (NY)
Marymount U (VA)
Maryville Coll (TN)
Marywood U (PA)
Massachusetts Maritime Acad (MA)
McGill U (QC, Canada)
McPherson Coll (KS)
Meredith Coll (NC)
Merrimack Coll (MA)
Messiah Coll (PA)
Metropolitan State U (MN)
Midwestern State U (TX)
Millikin U (IL)
Milwaukee School of Eng (WI)
Minnesota State U Mankato (MN)
Minnesota State U Moorhead (MN)
Minot State U (ND)
Missouri Southern State U (MO)
Montclair State U (NJ)
Moravian Coll (PA)
Mount Allison U (NB, Canada)
Mount Saint Mary Coll (NY)
Mount St. Mary's Coll (CA)
Mount Union Coll (OH)
Murray State U (KY)
National-Louis U (IL)
Nebraska Wesleyan U (NE)
Neumann Coll (PA)
Newbury Coll (MA)
New Mexico State U (NM)
New York Inst of Technology (NY)
New York U (NY)
Niagara U (NY)
North Central Coll (IL)
Northeastern U (MA)
Northern State U (SD)
North Park U (IL)
Northwestern Coll (MN)
Northwest Nazarene U (ID)
Northwood U (MI)
Northwood U, Florida Campus (FL)
Northwood U, Texas Campus (TX)
Notre Dame de Namur U (CA)
Ohio Dominican U (OH)
Ohio Northern U (OH)
The Ohio State U (OH)
Ohio U (OH)
Ohio Wesleyan U (OH)
Oklahoma Baptist U (OK)
Oklahoma City U (OK)
Oklahoma State U (OK)
Old Dominion U (VA)
Oregon State U (OR)
Otterbein Coll (OH)
Pace U (NY)
Pacific Lutheran U (WA)
Pacific Union Coll (CA)
Paine Coll (GA)
Palm Beach Atlantic U (FL)
Penn State U Abington Coll (PA)
Penn State U Altoona Coll (PA)
Penn State U at Erie, The Behrend Coll (PA)
Penn State U Beaver Campus of the Commonwealth Coll (PA)
Penn State U Berks Cmps of Berks-Lehigh Valley Coll (PA)
Penn State U Delaware County Campus of the Commonwealth Coll (PA)
Penn State U DuBois Campus of the Commonwealth Coll (PA)
Penn State U Fayette Campus of the Commonwealth Coll (PA)
Penn State U Harrisburg Campus of the Capital Coll (PA)
Penn State U Hazleton Campus of the Commonwealth Coll (PA)
Penn State U Lehigh Valley Cmps of Berks-Lehigh Valley Coll (PA)
Penn State U McKeesport Campus of the Commonwealth Coll (PA)
Penn State U Mont Alto Campus of the Commonwealth Coll (PA)
Penn State U New Kensington Campus of the Commonwealth Coll (PA)
Penn State U Schuylkill Campus of the Capital Coll (PA)
Penn State U Shenango Campus of the Commonwealth Coll (PA)
Penn State U Univ Park Campus (PA)
Penn State U Wilkes-Barre Campus of the Commonwealth Coll (PA)
Penn State U Worthington Scranton Cmps Commonwealth Coll (PA)
Penn State U York Campus of the Commonwealth Coll (PA)
Pepperdine U, Malibu (CA)
Pfeiffer U (NC)
Philadelphia U (PA)
Pontifical Catholic U of Puerto Rico (PR)
Queens Coll of the City U of NY (NY)
Quinnipiac U (CT)
Ramapo Coll of New Jersey (NJ)
Rhodes Coll (TN)
Richmond, The American Intl U in London(United Kingdom)
Rider U (NJ)
Rochester Inst of Technology (NY)
Roger Williams U (RI)
Rollins Coll (FL)
Roosevelt U (IL)
Ryerson U (ON, Canada)
Sacred Heart U (CT)
St. Ambrose U (IA)
St. Andrews Presbyterian Coll (NC)
Saint Augustine's Coll (NC)
St. Bonaventure U (NY)
St. Cloud State U (MN)
St. Edward's U (TX)
Saint Francis U (PA)
St. John Fisher Coll (NY)
St. John's U (NY)
Saint Joseph's Coll of Maine (ME)
Saint Leo U (FL)
Saint Louis U (MO)
Saint Mary's Coll (IN)
Saint Mary's Coll of California (CA)
Saint Mary's U of Minnesota (MN)
St. Mary's U of San Antonio (TX)
St. Norbert Coll (WI)
St. Thomas U (FL)
Saint Vincent Coll (PA)
Saint Xavier U (IL)
Salem Coll (NC)
Samford U (AL)
Sam Houston State U (TX)
San Diego State U (CA)
San Francisco State U (CA)
San Jose State U (CA)
Schiller Intl U (FL)
Schiller Intl U(France)
Schiller Intl U(Germany)
Schiller Intl U(Spain)
Schiller Intl U(United Kingdom)
Schiller Intl U, American Coll of Switzerland(Switzerland)
Seattle U (WA)
Seton Hill U (PA)
Shaw U (NC)
Simpson Coll (IA)
Southern Adventist U (TN)
Spring Hill Coll (AL)
State U of NY at New Paltz (NY)
Plattsburgh State U of NY (NY)
State U of NY Coll at Brockport (NY)
Stetson U (FL)
Strayer U (DC)
Tarleton State U (TX)
Taylor U (IN)
Taylor U, Fort Wayne Campus (IN)
Teikyo Post U (CT)
Tennessee Technological U (TN)
Texas A&M U–Kingsville (TX)
Texas A&M U–Texarkana (TX)
Texas Christian U (TX)
Texas Tech U (TX)
Texas Wesleyan U (TX)
Thiel Coll (PA)
Thomas Coll (ME)
Thomas Edison State Coll (NJ)
Trinity Intl U (IL)
Trinity U (TX)
United States Intl U(Kenya)
U du Québec à Hull (QC, Canada)
The U of Akron (OH)
U of Alberta (AB, Canada)
U of Arkansas (AR)
U of Arkansas at Little Rock (AR)
U of Baltimore (MD)
U of Bridgeport (CT)
The U of British Columbia (BC, Canada)
U of Dayton (OH)
U of Denver (CO)
U of Detroit Mercy (MI)
U of Evansville (IN)
The U of Findlay (OH)
U of Georgia (GA)
U of Hawaii at Manoa (HI)
U of Indianapolis (IN)
U of La Verne (CA)
The U of Lethbridge (AB, Canada)
The U of Memphis (TN)
U of Miami (FL)
U of Minnesota, Twin Cities Campus (MN)
U of Mississippi (MS)
U of Missouri–Columbia (MO)
U of Missouri–St. Louis (MO)
The U of Montana–Missoula (MT)
U of Nebraska–Lincoln (NE)
U of Nevada, Las Vegas (NV)
U of Nevada, Reno (NV)
U of New Brunswick Fredericton (NB, Canada)
U of New Haven (CT)
The U of North Carolina at Charlotte (NC)
U of North Florida (FL)
U of Oklahoma (OK)
U of Oregon (OR)
U of Ottawa (ON, Canada)
U of Pennsylvania (PA)
U of Portland (OR)
U of Puget Sound (WA)
U of Rhode Island (RI)
U of Richmond (VA)
U of St. Thomas (MN)
U of San Francisco (CA)
The U of Scranton (PA)
U of Southern California (CA)
U of South Florida (FL)
The U of Tampa (FL)
The U of Tennessee at Martin (TN)
The U of Texas at Arlington (TX)
The U of Texas at Dallas (TX)
The U of Texas–Pan American (TX)
U of the Incarnate Word (TX)
U of Toledo (OH)
U of Tulsa (OK)
U of Victoria (BC, Canada)
U of Washington (WA)
U of Waterloo (ON, Canada)
U of Wisconsin–La Crosse (WI)
Utica Coll (NY)
Valparaiso U (IN)
Vanguard U of Southern California (CA)
Villanova U (PA)
Virginia Intermont Coll (VA)
Warren Wilson Coll (NC)
Wartburg Coll (IA)
Washington & Jefferson Coll (PA)
Washington State U (WA)
Washington U in St. Louis (MO)
Waynesburg Coll (PA)
Wayne State Coll (NE)
Webber Intl U (FL)
Webster U (MO)
Wesleyan Coll (GA)
Western Carolina U (NC)
Western State Coll of Colorado (CO)
Western Washington U (WA)
Westminster Coll (MO)
Westminster Coll (PA)
Westminster Coll (UT)
Wheeling Jesuit U (WV)
Whitworth Coll (WA)
Wichita State U (KS)
Widener U (PA)
William Jewell Coll (MO)
William Paterson U of New Jersey (NJ)
William Woods U (MO)
Wofford Coll (SC)
Wright State U (OH)
York Coll of Pennsylvania (PA)
York U (ON, Canada)

INTERNATIONAL ECONOMICS

Albertson Coll of Idaho (ID)
Albertus Magnus Coll (CT)
American U (DC)
Assumption Coll (MA)
Austin Coll (TX)
Bard Coll (NY)
Bentley Coll (MA)
Brock U (ON, Canada)
California State U, Chico (CA)
Carson-Newman Coll (TN)
Carthage Coll (WI)
The Catholic U of America (DC)
Claremont McKenna Coll (CA)
Coll of St. Catherine (MN)
The Colorado Coll (CO)
Eastern Michigan U (MI)
Fordham U (NY)
Franklin Coll Switzerland(Switzerland)
Georgetown U (DC)
Georgia Inst of Technology (GA)
Gettysburg Coll (PA)
Hamline U (MN)
Hampshire Coll (MA)
Harvard U (MA)
HEC Montreal (QC, Canada)
Hiram Coll (OH)
Howard U (DC)
John Carroll U (OH)
Lawrence U (WI)
Longwood U (VA)
Loyola Marymount U (CA)
Marlboro Coll (VT)
Muhlenberg Coll (PA)
Ohio U (OH)
Rhodes Coll (TN)
Rockford Coll (IL)
Ryerson U (ON, Canada)
San Diego State U (CA)
Schiller Intl U, American Coll of Switzerland(Switzerland)
Seattle U (WA)
State U of NY at New Paltz (NY)
State U of NY at Oswego (NY)
State U of West Georgia (GA)
Suffolk U (MA)
Taylor U (IN)
Texas Christian U (TX)
U of Calif, Los Angeles (CA)
U of Calif, Santa Cruz (CA)
U of Missouri–Columbia (MO)
U of Puget Sound (WA)
U of Richmond (VA)
U of St. Thomas (MN)
Valparaiso U (IN)
Washington U in St. Louis (MO)
Westminster Coll (PA)
Youngstown State U (OH)

INTERNATIONAL FINANCE

American U (DC)
Babson Coll (MA)
Boston U (MA)
Brigham Young U (UT)
The Catholic U of America (DC)
Franklin Coll Switzerland(Switzerland)
HEC Montreal (QC, Canada)
Ryerson U (ON, Canada)
Texas Christian U (TX)
The U of Akron (OH)
Washington U in St. Louis (MO)
York U (ON, Canada)

INTERNATIONAL/GLOBAL STUDIES

Abilene Christian U (TX)
Adelphi U (NY)
Allegheny Coll (PA)
Alverno Coll (WI)
Assumption Coll (MA)
Baldwin-Wallace Coll (OH)
Case Western Reserve U (OH)
Chatham Coll (PA)
City Coll of the City U of NY (NY)
The Coll of New Rochelle (NY)
The Coll of St. Scholastica (MN)
Colorado Christian U (CO)
Concordia Coll (MN)
Dominican U of California (CA)
Endicott Coll (MA)
The Evergreen State Coll (WA)
Grinnell Coll (IA)
Hampshire Coll (MA)
Hanover Coll (IN)
Harding U (AR)
Hope Coll (MI)
Illinois Wesleyan U (IL)
Iona Coll (NY)
Juniata Coll (PA)
Kenyon Coll (OH)
Louisiana State U and A&M Coll (LA)
Marquette U (WI)
Miami U Hamilton (OH)
Michigan State U (MI)
Midwestern State U (TX)
Nebraska Wesleyan U (NE)
New Coll of Florida (FL)
North Dakota State U (ND)
Randolph-Macon Coll (VA)
State U of NY Coll at Cortland (NY)
Sterling Coll (VT)
Texas A&M U (TX)
Texas State U-San Marcos (TX)
U of Calif, Irvine (CA)
U of Chicago (IL)
U of Colorado at Boulder (CO)
The U of Iowa (IA)
U of Nebraska at Omaha (NE)
U of New Hampshire (NH)
U of New Orleans (LA)
U of North Texas (TX)
U of Pennsylvania (PA)
U of Utah (UT)
U of Waterloo (ON, Canada)
U of Wisconsin–Whitewater (WI)
Warren Wilson Coll (NC)
Willamette U (OR)

INTERNATIONAL MARKETING

American InterContinental U-London(United Kingdom)
American U (DC)
Brigham Young U (UT)
Davis & Elkins Coll (WV)
Oklahoma Baptist U (OK)
Pace U (NY)
Texas Christian U (TX)
The U of Akron (OH)
York U (ON, Canada)

INTERNATIONAL RELATIONS AND AFFAIRS

Adrian Coll (MI)
Agnes Scott Coll (GA)
Albion Coll (MI)
Allegheny Coll (PA)
Alliant Intl U (CA)
Alliant Intl U–México City(Mexico)
Alverno Coll (WI)
American Coll of Thessaloniki(Greece)
American Intl Coll (MA)
American U (DC)
American U in Bulgaria(Bulgaria)
The American U of Rome(Italy)
Antioch Coll (OH)
Aquinas Coll (MI)
Ashland U (OH)

Augsburg Coll (MN)
Augustana Coll (SD)
Austin Coll (TX)
Azusa Pacific U (CA)
Bard Coll (NY)
Barry U (FL)
Baylor U (TX)
Bellarmine U (KY)
Beloit Coll (WI)
Benedictine U (IL)
Bennington Coll (VT)
Berry Coll (GA)
Bethany Coll (WV)
Bethel U (MN)
Bethune-Cookman Coll (FL)
Boston U (MA)
Bowling Green State U (OH)
Bradley U (IL)
Brenau U (GA)
Bridgewater Coll (VA)
Bridgewater State Coll (MA)
Brigham Young U (UT)
Brown U (RI)
Bryant Coll (RI)
Bucknell U (PA)
Butler U (IN)
California Lutheran U (CA)
California State U, Chico (CA)
California State U, Hayward (CA)
California State U, Long Beach (CA)
Calvin Coll (MI)
Campbell U (NC)
Canadian Mennonite U (MB, Canada)
Canisius Coll (NY)
Capital U (OH)
Carleton Coll (MN)
Carleton U (ON, Canada)
Carroll Coll (MT)
Carroll Coll (WI)
Case Western Reserve U (OH)
Catawba Coll (NC)
The Catholic U of America (DC)
Cedar Crest Coll (PA)
Cedarville U (OH)
Centenary Coll (NJ)
Central Michigan U (MI)
Centre Coll (KY)
Chaminade U of Honolulu (HI)
Chatham Coll (PA)
Christopher Newport U (VA)
City Coll of the City U of NY (NY)
Claremont McKenna Coll (CA)
Clark U (MA)
Cleveland State U (OH)
Colby Coll (ME)
Colgate U (NY)
The Coll of New Jersey (NJ)
Coll of Notre Dame of Maryland (MD)
Coll of St. Catherine (MN)
Coll of Saint Elizabeth (NJ)
Coll of Staten Island of the City U of NY (NY)
The Coll of William and Mary (VA)
The Coll of Wooster (OH)
Concordia Coll (NY)
Connecticut Coll (CT)
Cornell Coll (IA)
Cornell U (NY)
Creighton U (NE)
Dalhousie U (NS, Canada)
Denison U (OH)
DePaul U (IL)
Dickinson Coll (PA)
Doane Coll (NE)
Drake U (IA)
Duke U (NC)
Duquesne U (PA)
Earlham Coll (IN)
Eastern Washington U (WA)
Eckerd Coll (FL)
Edgewood Coll (WI)
Elmira Coll (NY)
Elms Coll (MA)
Elon U (NC)
Embry-Riddle Aeronautical U (AZ)
Emory & Henry Coll (VA)
Emory U (GA)
Eugene Lang Coll, New School U (NY)
Fairfield U (CT)
Fairleigh Dickinson U, Teaneck-Metro Campus (NJ)
Ferrum Coll (VA)
Florida Intl U (FL)
Florida State U (FL)
Fordham U (NY)
Francis Marion U (SC)
Franklin Coll Switzerland(Switzerland)
Frostburg State U (MD)
Gallaudet U (DC)
George Fox U (OR)
George Mason U (VA)
Georgetown U (DC)
The George Washington U (DC)
Georgia Inst of Technology (GA)
Georgia Southern U (GA)
Gettysburg Coll (PA)
Gonzaga U (WA)
Gordon Coll (MA)
Goucher Coll (MD)
Graceland U (IA)
Grand Canyon U (AZ)
Grand Valley State U (MI)
Guilford Coll (NC)
Hamilton Coll (NY)
Hamline U (MN)
Hampden-Sydney Coll (VA)
Hampshire Coll (MA)
Harding U (AR)
Harvard U (MA)
Hastings Coll (NE)
Hawai'i Pacific U (HI)
Heidelberg Coll (OH)
Hendrix Coll (AR)
High Point U (NC)
Hillsdale Coll (MI)
Hobart and William Smith Colls (NY)
Hollins U (VA)
Holy Names Coll (CA)
Houghton Coll (NY)
Huntingdon Coll (AL)
Huron U USA in London(United Kingdom)
Illinois Coll (IL)
Immaculata U (PA)
Indiana U of Pennsylvania (PA)
Intl U in Geneva(Switzerland)
Iowa State U of Science and Technology (IA)
Jacksonville U (FL)
James Madison U (VA)
John Brown U (AR)
John Cabot U(Italy)
John Carroll U (OH)
The Johns Hopkins U (MD)
Juniata Coll (PA)
Kennesaw State U (GA)
Kent State U (OH)
Kenyon Coll (OH)
Knox Coll (IL)
Lafayette Coll (PA)
Lake Forest Coll (IL)
Lambuth U (TN)
La Roche Coll (PA)
Lawrence U (WI)
Lehigh U (PA)
Le Moyne Coll (NY)
Lenoir-Rhyne Coll (NC)
Lewis & Clark Coll (OR)
Lincoln U (PA)
Lindenwood U (MO)
Lock Haven U of Pennsylvania (PA)
Long Island U, C.W. Post Campus (NY)
Longwood U (VA)
Loras Coll (IA)
Loyola U Chicago (IL)
Luther Coll (IA)
Lycoming Coll (PA)
Lynchburg Coll (VA)
Macalester Coll (MN)
Manhattan Coll (NY)
Manhattanville Coll (NY)
Mansfield U of Pennsylvania (PA)
Marian Coll of Fond du Lac (WI)
Marlboro Coll (VT)
Marquette U (WI)
Marshall U (WV)
Mars Hill Coll (NC)
Mary Baldwin Coll (VA)
Marymount Coll of Fordham U (NY)
Marymount Manhattan Coll (NY)
Maryville Coll (TN)
Mary Washington Coll (VA)
McKendree Coll (IL)
Mercer U (GA)
Meredith Coll (NC)
Methodist Coll (NC)
Miami U (OH)
Michigan State U (MI)
Middlebury Coll (VT)
Middle Tennessee State U (TN)
Millikin U (IL)
Mills Coll (CA)
Minnesota State U Mankato (MN)
Missouri Southern State U (MO)
Morehouse Coll (GA)
Mount Allison U (NB, Canada)
Mount Holyoke Coll (MA)
Mount Mary Coll (WI)
Mount Mercy Coll (IA)
Mount Saint Mary Coll (NY)
Mount Saint Mary's Coll and Sem (MD)
Muhlenberg Coll (PA)
Murray State U (KY)
Nazareth Coll of Rochester (NY)
New York U (NY)
Niagara U (NY)
Northeastern U (MA)
Northern Arizona U (AZ)
Northern Michigan U (MI)
North Park U (IL)
Northwestern U (IL)
Northwest Nazarene U (ID)
Occidental Coll (CA)
Oglethorpe U (GA)
Ohio Northern U (OH)
The Ohio State U (OH)
Ohio U (OH)
Ohio Wesleyan U (OH)
Okanagan U Coll (BC, Canada)
Old Dominion U (VA)
Oral Roberts U (OK)
Oregon State U (OR)
Otterbein Coll (OH)
Pace U (NY)
Pacific Lutheran U (WA)
Pacific U (OR)
Patrick Henry Coll (VA)
Penn State U Abington Coll (PA)
Penn State U Altoona Coll (PA)
Penn State U at Erie, The Behrend Coll (PA)
Penn State U Beaver Campus of the Commonwealth Coll (PA)
Penn State U Berks Cmps of Berks-Lehigh Valley Coll (PA)
Penn State U Delaware County Campus of the Commonwealth Coll (PA)
Penn State U DuBois Campus of the Commonwealth Coll (PA)
Penn State U Fayette Campus of the Commonwealth Coll (PA)
Penn State U Hazleton Campus of the Commonwealth Coll (PA)
Penn State U Lehigh Valley Cmps of Berks-Lehigh Valley Coll (PA)
Penn State U McKeesport Campus of the Commonwealth Coll (PA)
Penn State U Mont Alto Campus of the Commonwealth Coll (PA)
Penn State U New Kensington Campus of the Commonwealth Coll (PA)
Penn State U Schuylkill Campus of the Capital Coll (PA)
Penn State U Shenango Campus of the Commonwealth Coll (PA)
Penn State U Univ Park Campus (PA)
Penn State U Wilkes-Barre Campus of the Commonwealth Coll (PA)
Penn State U Worthington Scranton Cmps Commonwealth Coll (PA)
Penn State U York Campus of the Commonwealth Coll (PA)
Pepperdine U, Malibu (CA)
Pitzer Coll (CA)
Pomona Coll (CA)
Portland State U (OR)
Prairie Bible Coll (AB, Canada)
Queens U of Charlotte (NC)
Quinnipiac U (CT)
Randolph-Macon Coll (VA)
Randolph-Macon Woman's Coll (VA)
Reed Coll (OR)
Rhodes Coll (TN)
Richmond, The American Intl U in London(United Kingdom)
Roanoke Coll (VA)
Rochester Inst of Technology (NY)
Rockford Coll (IL)
Rockhurst U (MO)
Rollins Coll (FL)
Roosevelt U (IL)
Russell Sage Coll (NY)
Sacred Heart U (CT)
Saginaw Valley State U (MI)
Saint Augustine's Coll (NC)
St. Cloud State U (MN)
St. Edward's U (TX)
Saint Francis U (PA)
St. John Fisher Coll (NY)
St. John's U (NY)
Saint Joseph's Coll (IN)
Saint Joseph's U (PA)
Saint Leo U (FL)
Saint Louis U (MO)
Saint Mary's Coll of California (CA)
St. Norbert Coll (WI)
Saint Xavier U (IL)
Salem Coll (NC)
Samford U (AL)
San Diego State U (CA)
San Francisco State U (CA)
Sarah Lawrence Coll (NY)
Schiller Intl U (FL)
Schiller Intl U(France)
Schiller Intl U(Germany)
Schiller Intl U(Spain)
Schiller Intl U(United Kingdom)
Schiller Intl U, American Coll of Switzerland(Switzerland)
Scripps Coll (CA)
Seattle U (WA)
Seton Hall U (NJ)
Seton Hill U (PA)
Shawnee State U (OH)
Shaw U (NC)
Simmons Coll (MA)
Simpson Coll (IA)
Sonoma State U (CA)
Southern Methodist U (TX)
Southern Nazarene U (OK)
Southern Oregon U (OR)
Southern Polytechnic State U (GA)
Southwestern U (TX)
Spring Hill Coll (AL)
Stanford U (CA)
State U of NY at New Paltz (NY)
State U of NY at Oswego (NY)
State U of NY Coll at Brockport (NY)
State U of NY Coll at Cortland (NY)
State U of NY Coll at Geneseo (NY)
State U of NY Coll at Oneonta (NY)
State U of West Georgia (GA)
Stephens Coll (MO)
Stetson U (FL)
Stonehill Coll (MA)
Susquehanna U (PA)
Sweet Briar Coll (VA)
Syracuse U (NY)
Tabor Coll (KS)
Taylor U (IN)
Texas Christian U (TX)
Texas Lutheran U (TX)
Texas State U-San Marcos (TX)
Texas Wesleyan U (TX)
Thomas More Coll (KY)
Tiffin U (OH)
Towson U (MD)
Trent U (ON, Canada)
Trinity Coll (CT)
Trinity Coll (DC)
Trinity Western U (BC, Canada)
Tufts U (MA)
Tulane U (LA)
Union Coll (NE)
United States Intl U(Kenya)
The U of Alabama (AL)
U of Alberta (AB, Canada)
U of Arkansas (AR)
U of Arkansas at Little Rock (AR)
U of Bridgeport (CT)
The U of British Columbia (BC, Canada)
U of Calgary (AB, Canada)
U of Calif, Davis (CA)
U of Cincinnati (OH)
U of Dayton (OH)
U of Delaware (DE)
U of Denver (CO)
U of Evansville (IN)
U of Idaho (ID)
U of Indianapolis (IN)
U of Kansas (KS)
U of La Verne (CA)
U of Maine (ME)
U of Maine at Farmington (ME)
U of Maine at Presque Isle (ME)
The U of Memphis (TN)
U of Miami (FL)
U of Michigan (MI)
U of Michigan–Dearborn (MI)
U of Minnesota, Duluth (MN)
U of Minnesota, Twin Cities Campus (MN)
U of Mississippi (MS)
U of Nebraska–Lincoln (NE)
U of Nevada, Reno (NV)
U of New Brunswick Fredericton (NB, Canada)
U of New Hampshire (NH)
U of North Florida (FL)
U of Oregon (OR)
U of Ottawa (ON, Canada)
U of Pennsylvania (PA)
U of Puget Sound (WA)
U of Redlands (CA)
U of Richmond (VA)
U of St. Thomas (MN)
U of St. Thomas (TX)
U of San Diego (CA)
U of Saskatchewan (SK, Canada)
The U of Scranton (PA)
U of South Carolina (SC)
U of Southern California (CA)
U of Southern Indiana (IN)
U of Southern Maine (ME)
U of South Florida (FL)
The U of Tampa (FL)
The U of Tennessee at Martin (TN)
U of the Pacific (CA)
U of the South (TN)
U of Toledo (OH)
U of Toronto (ON, Canada)
U of Virginia (VA)
U of Washington (WA)
U of Waterloo (ON, Canada)
U of West Florida (FL)
U of Windsor (ON, Canada)
U of Wisconsin–Madison (WI)
U of Wisconsin–Milwaukee (WI)
U of Wisconsin–Oshkosh (WI)
U of Wisconsin–Parkside (WI)
U of Wisconsin–Platteville (WI)
U of Wisconsin–Stevens Point (WI)
U of Wisconsin–Whitewater (WI)
U of Wyoming (WY)
Ursinus Coll (PA)
Utica Coll (NY)
Valparaiso U (IN)
Vassar Coll (NY)
Virginia Military Inst (VA)
Virginia Polytechnic Inst and State U (VA)
Virginia Wesleyan Coll (VA)
Wartburg Coll (IA)
Washington Coll (MD)
Washington U in St. Louis (MO)
Wayne State U (MI)
Webster U (MO)
Wellesley Coll (MA)
Wells Coll (NY)
Wesleyan Coll (GA)
West Chester U of Pennsylvania (PA)
Western New England Coll (MA)
Western Oregon U (OR)
Westminster Coll (MO)
Westminster Coll (PA)
West Virginia U (WV)
West Virginia Wesleyan Coll (WV)
Wheaton Coll (IL)
Wheaton Coll (MA)
Wheeling Jesuit U (WV)
Whitworth Coll (WA)
Widener U (PA)
Wilkes U (PA)
William Jewell Coll (MO)
William Woods U (MO)
Wilson Coll (PA)
Winona State U (MN)
Wofford Coll (SC)
Wright State U (OH)
Xavier U (OH)
York Coll of Pennsylvania (PA)
York U (ON, Canada)

INVESTMENTS AND SECURITIES

Babson Coll (MA)
Duquesne U (PA)

IRANIAN/PERSIAN LANGUAGES

The U of Texas at Austin (TX)

ISLAMIC STUDIES

American U (DC)
Brandeis U (MA)
Hampshire Coll (MA)
Harvard U (MA)
The Ohio State U (OH)
U of Calif, Los Angeles (CA)
U of Calif, Santa Barbara (CA)
U of Michigan (MI)
The U of Texas at Austin (TX)
U of Toronto (ON, Canada)
Washington U in St. Louis (MO)
Wellesley Coll (MA)

ITALIAN

Albertus Magnus Coll (CT)
The American U of Rome(Italy)
Arizona State U (AZ)
Bard Coll (NY)
Barnard Coll (NY)
Bishop's U (QC, Canada)
Boston Coll (MA)
Boston U (MA)
Brigham Young U (UT)
Brock U (ON, Canada)
Brooklyn Coll of the City U of NY (NY)
Brown U (RI)
Bryn Mawr Coll (PA)
California State U, Long Beach (CA)
Carleton U (ON, Canada)
Central Connecticut State U (CT)
Claremont McKenna Coll (CA)
Coll of the Holy Cross (MA)
The Colorado Coll (CO)
Columbia Coll (NY)
Columbia U, School of General Studies (NY)
Concordia U (QC, Canada)

Connecticut Coll (CT)
Cornell U (NY)
Dartmouth Coll (NH)
DePaul U (IL)
Dickinson Coll (PA)
Dominican U (IL)
Duke U (NC)
Emory U (GA)
Florida Intl U (FL)
Florida State U (FL)
Fordham U (NY)
Georgetown U (DC)
Gettysburg Coll (PA)
Gonzaga U (WA)
Harvard U (MA)
Haverford Coll (PA)
Hofstra U (NY)
Hunter Coll of the City U of NY (NY)
Indiana U Bloomington (IN)
Iona Coll (NY)
The Johns Hopkins U (MD)
Lake Erie Coll (OH)
La Salle U (PA)
Laurentian U (ON, Canada)
Lehman Coll of the City U of NY (NY)
Long Island U, C.W. Post Campus (NY)
Loyola U Chicago (IL)
Marlboro Coll (VT)
McGill U (QC, Canada)
Mercy Coll (NY)
Middlebury Coll (VT)
Montclair State U (NJ)
Mount Holyoke Coll (MA)
Nazareth Coll of Rochester (NY)
New York U (NY)
Northeastern U (MA)
Northwestern U (IL)
Oakland U (MI)
The Ohio State U (OH)
Penn State U Abington Coll (PA)
Penn State U Altoona Coll (PA)
Penn State U at Erie, The Behrend Coll (PA)
Penn State U Beaver Campus of the Commonwealth Coll (PA)
Penn State U Berks Cmps of Berks-Lehigh Valley Coll (PA)
Penn State U Delaware County Campus of the Commonwealth Coll (PA)
Penn State U DuBois Campus of the Commonwealth Coll (PA)
Penn State U Fayette Campus of the Commonwealth Coll (PA)
Penn State U Hazleton Campus of the Commonwealth Coll (PA)
Penn State U Lehigh Valley Cmps of Berks-Lehigh Valley Coll (PA)
Penn State U McKeesport Campus of the Commonwealth Coll (PA)
Penn State U Mont Alto Campus of the Commonwealth Coll (PA)
Penn State U New Kensington Campus of the Commonwealth Coll (PA)
Penn State U Schuylkill Campus of the Capital Coll (PA)
Penn State U Shenango Campus of the Commonwealth Coll (PA)
Penn State U Univ Park Campus (PA)
Penn State U Wilkes-Barre Campus of the Commonwealth Coll (PA)
Penn State U Worthington Scranton Cmps Commonwealth Coll (PA)
Penn State U York Campus of the Commonwealth Coll (PA)
Providence Coll (RI)
Queens Coll of the City U of NY (NY)
Queen's U at Kingston (ON, Canada)
Rosemont Coll (PA)
Rutgers, The State U of New Jersey, Newark (NJ)
Rutgers, The State U of New Jersey, New Brunswick/Piscataway (NJ)
St. John Fisher Coll (NY)
St. John's U (NY)
Saint Mary's Coll of California (CA)
San Francisco State U (CA)
Santa Clara U (CA)
Sarah Lawrence Coll (NY)
Scripps Coll (CA)
Seton Hall U (NJ)
Smith Coll (MA)
Southern Connecticut State U (CT)
Stanford U (CA)
State U of NY at Binghamton (NY)
Stony Brook U, State U of New York (NY)
Sweet Briar Coll (VA)
Syracuse U (NY)
Trinity Coll (CT)
Tulane U (LA)
State U of NY at Albany (NY)
U at Buffalo, The State U of New York (NY)
U of Alberta (AB, Canada)
The U of Arizona (AZ)
The U of British Columbia (BC, Canada)
U of Calif, Berkeley (CA)
U of Calif, Davis (CA)
U of Calif, Los Angeles (CA)
U of Calif, San Diego (CA)
U of Calif, Santa Barbara (CA)
U of Calif, Santa Cruz (CA)
U of Chicago (IL)
U of Colorado at Boulder (CO)
U of Connecticut (CT)
U of Delaware (DE)
U of Denver (CO)
U of Georgia (GA)
U of Houston (TX)
U of Illinois at Chicago (IL)
U of Illinois at Urbana–Champaign (IL)
The U of Iowa (IA)
U of Maryland, Coll Park (MD)
U of Massachusetts Amherst (MA)
U of Massachusetts Boston (MA)
U of Miami (FL)
U of Michigan (MI)
U of Minnesota, Twin Cities Campus (MN)
U of Notre Dame (IN)
U of Oregon (OR)
U of Ottawa (ON, Canada)
U of Pennsylvania (PA)
U of Pittsburgh (PA)
U of Rhode Island (RI)
The U of Scranton (PA)
U of South Carolina (SC)
U of Southern California (CA)
U of South Florida (FL)
The U of Tennessee (TN)
The U of Texas at Austin (TX)
U of Toronto (ON, Canada)
U of Victoria (BC, Canada)
U of Virginia (VA)
U of Washington (WA)
U of Windsor (ON, Canada)
U of Wisconsin–Madison (WI)
U of Wisconsin–Milwaukee (WI)
Vassar Coll (NY)
Villanova U (PA)
Washington U in St. Louis (MO)
Wayne State U (MI)
Wellesley Coll (MA)
Wesleyan U (CT)
Yale U (CT)
York Coll of the City U of New York (NY)
York U (ON, Canada)
Youngstown State U (OH)

ITALIAN STUDIES

Bennington Coll (VT)
Brock U (ON, Canada)
Brown U (RI)
Columbia Coll (NY)
Connecticut Coll (CT)
Fordham U (NY)
John Cabot U(Italy)
U of Calif, Santa Cruz (CA)
U of Vermont (VT)
U of Victoria (BC, Canada)
U of Windsor (ON, Canada)
Wellesley Coll (MA)
York U (ON, Canada)

JAPANESE

Antioch Coll (OH)
Aquinas Coll (MI)
Augustana Coll (IL)
Ball State U (IN)
Bates Coll (ME)
Bennington Coll (VT)
Brigham Young U (UT)
California State U, Fullerton (CA)
California State U, Long Beach (CA)
California State U, Los Angeles (CA)
Carnegie Mellon U (PA)
Claremont McKenna Coll (CA)
Colgate U (NY)
Connecticut Coll (CT)
Dartmouth Coll (NH)
DePaul U (IL)
Dillard U (LA)
Eastern Michigan U (MI)
Emory U (GA)
Georgetown U (DC)
Gettysburg Coll (PA)
Gustavus Adolphus Coll (MN)
Harvard U (MA)
Hobart and William Smith Colls (NY)
Indiana U Bloomington (IN)
Lawrence U (WI)
Lehigh U (PA)
Lincoln U (PA)
Linfield Coll (OR)
Middlebury Coll (VT)
Mount Union Coll (OH)
North Central Coll (IL)
Oakland U (MI)
The Ohio State U (OH)
Pacific U (OR)
Penn State U Abington Coll (PA)
Penn State U Altoona Coll (PA)
Penn State U at Erie, The Behrend Coll (PA)
Penn State U Beaver Campus of the Commonwealth Coll (PA)
Penn State U Berks Cmps of Berks-Lehigh Valley Coll (PA)
Penn State U Delaware County Campus of the Commonwealth Coll (PA)
Penn State U DuBois Campus of the Commonwealth Coll (PA)
Penn State U Fayette Campus of the Commonwealth Coll (PA)
Penn State U Hazleton Campus of the Commonwealth Coll (PA)
Penn State U Lehigh Valley Cmps of Berks-Lehigh Valley Coll (PA)
Penn State U McKeesport Campus of the Commonwealth Coll (PA)
Penn State U Mont Alto Campus of the Commonwealth Coll (PA)
Penn State U New Kensington Campus of the Commonwealth Coll (PA)
Penn State U Schuylkill Campus of the Capital Coll (PA)
Penn State U Shenango Campus of the Commonwealth Coll (PA)
Penn State U Univ Park Campus (PA)
Penn State U Wilkes-Barre Campus of the Commonwealth Coll (PA)
Penn State U Worthington Scranton Cmps Commonwealth Coll (PA)
Penn State U York Campus of the Commonwealth Coll (PA)
Pomona Coll (CA)
Portland State U (OR)
San Diego State U (CA)
San Francisco State U (CA)
San Jose State U (CA)
Sarah Lawrence Coll (NY)
Scripps Coll (CA)
Stanford U (CA)
U of Alaska Fairbanks (AK)
U of Alberta (AB, Canada)
The U of British Columbia (BC, Canada)
U of Calif, Berkeley (CA)
U of Calif, Davis (CA)
U of Calif, Irvine (CA)
U of Calif, Los Angeles (CA)
U of Calif, San Diego (CA)
U of Calif, Santa Barbara (CA)
U of Calif, Santa Cruz (CA)
U of Chicago (IL)
U of Colorado at Boulder (CO)
The U of Findlay (OH)
U of Georgia (GA)
U of Hawaii at Hilo (HI)
U of Hawaii at Manoa (HI)
The U of Iowa (IA)
U of Maryland, Coll Park (MD)
U of Massachusetts Amherst (MA)
U of Michigan (MI)
U of Minnesota, Twin Cities Campus (MN)
The U of Montana–Missoula (MT)
U of Notre Dame (IN)
U of Oregon (OR)
U of Pittsburgh (PA)
U of Regina (SK, Canada)
U of Rochester (NY)
U of St. Thomas (MN)
U of the Pacific (CA)
U of Toronto (ON, Canada)
U of Utah (UT)
U of Victoria (BC, Canada)
U of Washington (WA)
U of Windsor (ON, Canada)
U of Wisconsin–Madison (WI)
Washington State U (WA)
Washington U in St. Louis (MO)
Wellesley Coll (MA)
Williams Coll (MA)
Yale U (CT)
York U (ON, Canada)

JAPANESE STUDIES

Case Western Reserve U (OH)
Claremont McKenna Coll (CA)
Earlham Coll (IN)
Gettysburg Coll (PA)
Gustavus Adolphus Coll (MN)
State U of NY at Albany (NY)
U of San Francisco (CA)
Willamette U (OR)

JAZZ/JAZZ STUDIES

Augustana Coll (IL)
Bard Coll (NY)
Barnard Coll (NY)
Bennington Coll (VT)
Berklee Coll of Music (MA)
Brigham Young U (UT)
California Inst of the Arts (CA)
Capital U (OH)
Central State U (OH)
Chicago State U (IL)
City Coll of the City U of NY (NY)
Concordia U (QC, Canada)
Cornish Coll of the Arts (WA)
DePaul U (IL)
Drake U (IA)
Five Towns Coll (NY)
Florida Ag and Mech U (FL)
Florida State U (FL)
Hampshire Coll (MA)
Hampton U (VA)
Hofstra U (NY)
Hope Coll (MI)
Indiana U Bloomington (IN)
Ithaca Coll (NY)
Johnson State Coll (VT)
The Juilliard School (NY)
Lamar U (TX)
Limestone Coll (SC)
Long Island U, Brooklyn Campus (NY)
Loyola U New Orleans (LA)
Manhattan School of Music (NY)
McGill U (QC, Canada)
Michigan State U (MI)
New England Conservatory of Music (MA)
North Carolina Central U (NC)
North Central Coll (IL)
Northwestern U (IL)
Oberlin Coll (OH)
The Ohio State U (OH)
Peabody Conserv of Music of Johns Hopkins U (MD)
Roosevelt U (IL)
Rowan U (NJ)
Rutgers, The State U of New Jersey, New Brunswick/Piscataway (NJ)
St. Cloud State U (MN)
St. Francis Xavier U (NS, Canada)
Sarah Lawrence Coll (NY)
Simon's Rock Coll of Bard (MA)
State U of NY at New Paltz (NY)
Texas Southern U (TX)
Texas State U-San Marcos (TX)
Université de Montréal (QC, Canada)
U of Cincinnati (OH)
U of Hartford (CT)
The U of Iowa (IA)
U of Louisiana at Lafayette (LA)
U of Michigan (MI)
U of Minnesota, Duluth (MN)
U of Nevada, Las Vegas (NV)
U of North Florida (FL)
U of North Texas (TX)
U of Oregon (OR)
U of Rochester (NY)
U of Southern California (CA)
Virginia Union U (VA)
Webster U (MO)
Western Washington U (WA)
Westfield State Coll (MA)
William Paterson U of New Jersey (NJ)
York U (ON, Canada)

JEWISH/JUDAIC STUDIES

American U (DC)
Bard Coll (NY)
Brandeis U (MA)
Brooklyn Coll of the City U of NY (NY)
Brown U (RI)
California State U, Chico (CA)
City Coll of the City U of NY (NY)
Clark U (MA)
DePaul U (IL)
Dickinson Coll (PA)
Emory U (GA)
Florida Atlantic U (FL)
The George Washington U (DC)
Gratz Coll (PA)
Hamline U (MN)
Hampshire Coll (MA)
Harvard U (MA)
Hofstra U (NY)
Hunter Coll of the City U of NY (NY)
Indiana U Bloomington (IN)
Jewish Theological Sem of America (NY)
Laura and Alvin Siegal Coll of Judaic Studies (OH)
Lehman Coll of the City U of NY (NY)
McGill U (QC, Canada)
Mount Holyoke Coll (MA)
New York U (NY)
Oberlin Coll (OH)
The Ohio State U (OH)
Penn State U Abington Coll (PA)
Penn State U Altoona Coll (PA)
Penn State U at Erie, The Behrend Coll (PA)
Penn State U Beaver Campus of the Commonwealth Coll (PA)
Penn State U Berks Cmps of Berks-Lehigh Valley Coll (PA)
Penn State U Delaware County Campus of the Commonwealth Coll (PA)
Penn State U DuBois Campus of the Commonwealth Coll (PA)
Penn State U Fayette Campus of the Commonwealth Coll (PA)
Penn State U Hazleton Campus of the Commonwealth Coll (PA)
Penn State U Lehigh Valley Cmps of Berks-Lehigh Valley Coll (PA)
Penn State U McKeesport Campus of the Commonwealth Coll (PA)
Penn State U Mont Alto Campus of the Commonwealth Coll (PA)
Penn State U New Kensington Campus of the Commonwealth Coll (PA)
Penn State U Schuylkill Campus of the Capital Coll (PA)
Penn State U Shenango Campus of the Commonwealth Coll (PA)
Penn State U Univ Park Campus (PA)
Penn State U Wilkes-Barre Campus of the Commonwealth Coll (PA)
Penn State U Worthington Scranton Cmps Commonwealth Coll (PA)
Penn State U York Campus of the Commonwealth Coll (PA)
Queens Coll of the City U of NY (NY)
Queen's U at Kingston (ON, Canada)
Rutgers, The State U of New Jersey, New Brunswick/Piscataway (NJ)
Scripps Coll (CA)
State U of NY at Binghamton (NY)
State U of NY at New Paltz (NY)
Talmudic Coll of Florida (FL)
Trinity Coll (CT)
Tufts U (MA)
Tulane U (LA)
State U of NY at Albany (NY)
The U of Arizona (AZ)
U of Calif, Los Angeles (CA)
U of Calif, San Diego (CA)
U of Chicago (IL)
U of Cincinnati (OH)
U of Florida (FL)
U of Hartford (CT)
U of Judaism (CA)
U of Manitoba (MB, Canada)
U of Maryland, Coll Park (MD)
U of Massachusetts Amherst (MA)
U of Miami (FL)
U of Michigan (MI)
U of Minnesota, Twin Cities Campus (MN)
U of Missouri–Kansas City (MO)
U of Oregon (OR)
U of Pennsylvania (PA)
U of Southern California (CA)
The U of Texas at Austin (TX)
U of Toronto (ON, Canada)
U of Washington (WA)
Vassar Coll (NY)
Washington U in St. Louis (MO)
Wellesley Coll (MA)
Yale U (CT)
York U (ON, Canada)

JOURNALISM

Abilene Christian U (TX)
Alabama State U (AL)
Allegheny Coll (PA)
Alliant Intl U (CA)

American U (DC)
American U in Bulgaria(Bulgaria)
The American U in Cairo(Egypt)
Anderson Coll (SC)
Andrews U (MI)
Angelo State U (TX)
Appalachian State U (NC)
Arizona State U (AZ)
Arkansas State U (AR)
Arkansas Tech U (AR)
Asbury Coll (KY)
Ashland U (OH)
Auburn U (AL)
Augustana Coll (SD)
Averett U (VA)
Ball State U (IN)
Barry U (FL)
Baylor U (TX)
Belmont U (TN)
Bemidji State U (MN)
Baruch Coll of the City U of NY (NY)
Boston U (MA)
Bowling Green State U (OH)
Bradley U (IL)
Brigham Young U (UT)
Brooklyn Coll of the City U of NY (NY)
State U of NY Coll at Buffalo (NY)
Butler U (IN)
California Lutheran U (CA)
California Polytechnic State U, San Luis Obispo (CA)
California State Polytechnic U, Pomona (CA)
California State U, Chico (CA)
California State U, Fresno (CA)
California State U, Fullerton (CA)
California State U, Hayward (CA)
California State U, Long Beach (CA)
California State U, Sacramento (CA)
Campbellsville U (KY)
Campbell U (NC)
Carleton U (ON, Canada)
Carroll Coll (WI)
Carson-Newman Coll (TN)
Castleton State Coll (VT)
Central Michigan U (MI)
Central Missouri State U (MO)
Central Washington U (WA)
Chester Coll of New England (NH)
Coll of St. Catherine (MN)
Coll of St. Joseph (VT)
The Coll of Southeastern Europe, The American U of Athens(Greece)
Coll of the Ozarks (MO)
Colorado State U (CO)
Colorado State U-Pueblo (CO)
Columbia Coll (SC)
Columbia Coll Chicago (IL)
Columbia Union Coll (MD)
Concordia Coll (MN)
Concordia U (QC, Canada)
Creighton U (NE)
Curry Coll (MA)
Delaware State U (DE)
Delta State U (MS)
Dordt Coll (IA)
Drake U (IA)
Drury U (MO)
Duquesne U (PA)
Eastern Illinois U (IL)
Eastern Kentucky U (KY)
Eastern Michigan U (MI)
Eastern Nazarene Coll (MA)
Eastern Washington U (WA)
Edinboro U of Pennsylvania (PA)
Elon U (NC)
Emerson Coll (MA)
Evangel U (MO)
Florida Ag and Mech U (FL)
Florida Southern Coll (FL)
Fordham U (NY)
Fort Hays State U (KS)
Framingham State Coll (MA)
The Franciscan U (IA)
Franklin Coll (IN)
Franklin Pierce Coll (NH)
Gardner-Webb U (NC)
The George Washington U (DC)
Georgia Coll & State U (GA)
Georgia Southern U (GA)
Georgia State U (GA)
Gettysburg Coll (PA)
Gonzaga U (WA)
Goshen Coll (IN)
Grace Coll (IN)
Grand Valley State U (MI)
Grand View Coll (IA)
Hampshire Coll (MA)
Hampton U (VA)
Hastings Coll (NE)
Hawai'i Pacific U (HI)
Henderson State U (AR)
Hofstra U (NY)
Howard U (DC)
Humboldt State U (CA)
Huntington Coll (IN)
Indiana State U (IN)
Indiana U Bloomington (IN)
Indiana U of Pennsylvania (PA)
Indiana U–Purdue U Indianapolis (IN)
Inter American U of PR, Ponce Campus (PR)
Iona Coll (NY)
Iowa State U of Science and Technology (IA)
Ithaca Coll (NY)
John Brown U (AR)
Johnson State Coll (VT)
Judson Coll (IL)
Kansas State U (KS)
Keene State Coll (NH)
Kent State U (OH)
Kentucky Wesleyan Coll (KY)
Kwantlen U Coll (BC, Canada)
Lamar U (TX)
La Salle U (PA)
Lehigh U (PA)
Lewis U (IL)
Liberty U (VA)
Lincoln U (MO)
Lincoln U (PA)
Lindenwood U (MO)
Lindsey Wilson Coll (KY)
Lock Haven U of Pennsylvania (PA)
Long Island U, Brooklyn Campus (NY)
Long Island U, C.W. Post Campus (NY)
Longwood U (VA)
Loras Coll (IA)
Louisiana Coll (LA)
Louisiana Tech U (LA)
Loyola U Chicago (IL)
Lynchburg Coll (VA)
Lyndon State Coll (VT)
Madonna U (MI)
Mansfield U of Pennsylvania (PA)
Marietta Coll (OH)
Marist Coll (NY)
Marquette U (WI)
Marshall U (WV)
Mars Hill Coll (NC)
Marymount Coll of Fordham U (NY)
Massachusetts Coll of Liberal Arts (MA)
Mercer U (GA)
Mercy Coll (NY)
Mercyhurst Coll (PA)
Messiah Coll (PA)
Metropolitan State Coll of Denver (CO)
Miami U (OH)
Miami U Hamilton (OH)
Michigan State U (MI)
Minnesota State U Mankato (MN)
Minnesota State U Moorhead (MN)
Morris Coll (SC)
Mount Vernon Nazarene U (OH)
Multnomah Bible Coll and Biblical Sem (OR)
Murray State U (KY)
New Mexico Highlands U (NM)
New Mexico State U (NM)
New York U (NY)
Norfolk State U (VA)
North Central U (MN)
Northeastern State U (OK)
Northeastern U (MA)
Northern Arizona U (AZ)
Northern Illinois U (IL)
North Greenville Coll (SC)
Northwestern Coll (MN)
Northwestern State U of Louisiana (LA)
Northwestern U (IL)
Oakland U (MI)
Ohio Northern U (OH)
The Ohio State U (OH)
Ohio U (OH)
Ohio Wesleyan U (OH)
Oklahoma Baptist U (OK)
Oklahoma Christian U (OK)
Oklahoma City U (OK)
Oklahoma State U (OK)
Olivet Coll (MI)
Olivet Nazarene U (IL)
Oral Roberts U (OK)
Otterbein Coll (OH)
Pacific Lutheran U (WA)
Pacific Union Coll (CA)
Pacific U (OR)
Paine Coll (GA)
Palm Beach Atlantic U (FL)
Patrick Henry Coll (VA)
Penn State U Abington Coll (PA)
Penn State U Altoona Coll (PA)
Penn State U at Erie, The Behrend Coll (PA)
Penn State U Beaver Campus of the Commonwealth Coll (PA)
Penn State U Berks Cmps of Berks-Lehigh Valley Coll (PA)
Penn State U Delaware County Campus of the Commonwealth Coll (PA)
Penn State U DuBois Campus of the Commonwealth Coll (PA)
Penn State U Fayette Campus of the Commonwealth Coll (PA)
Penn State U Hazleton Campus of the Commonwealth Coll (PA)
Penn State U Lehigh Valley Cmps of Berks-Lehigh Valley Coll (PA)
Penn State U McKeesport Campus of the Commonwealth Coll (PA)
Penn State U Mont Alto Campus of the Commonwealth Coll (PA)
Penn State U New Kensington Campus of the Commonwealth Coll (PA)
Penn State U Schuylkill Campus of the Capital Coll (PA)
Penn State U Shenango Campus of the Commonwealth Coll (PA)
Penn State U Univ Park Campus (PA)
Penn State U Wilkes-Barre Campus of the Commonwealth Coll (PA)
Penn State U Worthington Scranton Cmps Commonwealth Coll (PA)
Penn State U York Campus of the Commonwealth Coll (PA)
Pepperdine U, Malibu (CA)
Pfeiffer U (NC)
Pittsburg State U (KS)
Point Loma Nazarene U (CA)
Point Park U (PA)
Polytechnic U, Brooklyn Campus (NY)
Queens U of Charlotte (NC)
Quincy U (IL)
Quinnipiac U (CT)
Rider U (NJ)
Roosevelt U (IL)
Rutgers, The State U of New Jersey, Newark (NJ)
Rutgers, The State U of New Jersey, New Brunswick/Piscataway (NJ)
Ryerson U (ON, Canada)
Sacred Heart U (CT)
St. Ambrose U (IA)
St. Bonaventure U (NY)
St. Cloud State U (MN)
Saint Francis U (PA)
St. Gregory's U (OK)
St. John's U (NY)
Saint Joseph's Coll of Maine (ME)
Saint Mary-of-the-Woods Coll (IN)
Saint Michael's Coll (VT)
St. Thomas Aquinas Coll (NY)
St. Thomas U (NB, Canada)
Salem State Coll (MA)
Samford U (AL)
Sam Houston State U (TX)
San Diego State U (CA)
San Francisco State U (CA)
San Jose State U (CA)
Seattle U (WA)
Seton Hill U (PA)
Shippensburg U of Pennsylvania (PA)
South Dakota State U (SD)
Southern Adventist U (TN)
Southern Arkansas U–Magnolia (AR)
Southern Connecticut State U (CT)
Southern Illinois U Carbondale (IL)
Southern Methodist U (TX)
Southern Nazarene U (OK)
Southwest Missouri State U (MO)
Spring Arbor U (MI)
Spring Hill Coll (AL)
State U of NY at New Paltz (NY)
State U of NY at Oswego (NY)
State U of NY Coll at Brockport (NY)
State U of West Georgia (GA)
Suffolk U (MA)
Susquehanna U (PA)
Syracuse U (NY)
Tabor Coll (KS)
Tennessee Technological U (TN)
Texas A&M U (TX)
Texas A&M U–Commerce (TX)
Texas A&M U–Kingsville (TX)
Texas Christian U (TX)
Texas Southern U (TX)
Texas State U-San Marcos (TX)
Texas Tech U (TX)
Texas Wesleyan U (TX)
Texas Woman's U (TX)
Thomas Edison State Coll (NJ)
Troy State U (AL)
Truman State U (MO)
Union Coll (NE)
Union U (TN)
United States Intl U(Kenya)
U Coll of the Cariboo (BC, Canada)
The U of Alabama (AL)
U of Alaska Fairbanks (AK)
The U of Arizona (AZ)
U of Arkansas (AR)
U of Arkansas at Little Rock (AR)
U of Baltimore (MD)
U of Bridgeport (CT)
U of Calif, Irvine (CA)
U of Central Arkansas (AR)
U of Central Florida (FL)
U of Colorado at Boulder (CO)
U of Connecticut (CT)
U of Dayton (OH)
U of Delaware (DE)
U of Denver (CO)
U of Detroit Mercy (MI)
The U of Findlay (OH)
U of Florida (FL)
U of Georgia (GA)
U of Hawaii at Manoa (HI)
U of Houston (TX)
U of Idaho (ID)
U of Illinois at Urbana–Champaign (IL)
The U of Iowa (IA)
U of Kansas (KS)
U of Kentucky (KY)
U of King's Coll (NS, Canada)
U of La Verne (CA)
U of Maine (ME)
U of Maryland, Coll Park (MD)
U of Massachusetts Amherst (MA)
The U of Memphis (TN)
U of Miami (FL)
U of Michigan (MI)
U of Minnesota, Twin Cities Campus (MN)
U of Mississippi (MS)
U of Missouri–Columbia (MO)
The U of Montana–Missoula (MT)
U of Nebraska at Omaha (NE)
U of Nevada, Reno (NV)
U of New Hampshire (NH)
U of New Mexico (NM)
U of Northern Colorado (CO)
U of North Texas (TX)
U of Oklahoma (OK)
U of Oregon (OR)
U of Ottawa (ON, Canada)
U of Pittsburgh at Greensburg (PA)
U of Pittsburgh at Johnstown (PA)
U of Portland (OR)
U of Regina (SK, Canada)
U of Rhode Island (RI)
U of Richmond (VA)
U of St. Francis (IL)
U of St. Thomas (MN)
U of South Carolina (SC)
U of Southern California (CA)
U of Southern Indiana (IN)
The U of Tennessee (TN)
The U of Tennessee at Martin (TN)
The U of Texas at Arlington (TX)
The U of Texas at Austin (TX)
The U of Texas at Tyler (TX)
The U of Texas–Pan American (TX)
U of the Sacred Heart (PR)
U of Toledo (OH)
U of Utah (UT)
U of Windsor (ON, Canada)
U of Wisconsin–Eau Claire (WI)
U of Wisconsin–Madison (WI)
U of Wisconsin–Milwaukee (WI)
U of Wisconsin–Oshkosh (WI)
U of Wisconsin–River Falls (WI)
U of Wisconsin–Superior (WI)
U of Wisconsin–Whitewater (WI)
U of Wyoming (WY)
Utah State U (UT)
Utica Coll (NY)
Valparaiso U (IN)
Virginia Union U (VA)
Waldorf Coll (IA)
Walla Walla Coll (WA)
Wartburg Coll (IA)
Washburn U (KS)
Washington and Lee U (VA)
Waynesburg Coll (PA)
Wayne State Coll (NE)
Wayne State U (MI)
Weber State U (UT)
Webster U (MO)
Western Baptist Coll (OR)
Western Illinois U (IL)
Western Kentucky U (KY)
Western Michigan U (MI)
Western State Coll of Colorado (CO)
Western Washington U (WA)
West Texas A&M U (TX)
West Virginia U (WV)
Wheeling Jesuit U (WV)
Whitworth Coll (WA)
William Carey Coll (MS)
William Penn U (IA)
Wingate U (NC)
Winona State U (MN)
Youngstown State U (OH)

JOURNALISM RELATED
Averett U (VA)
Boston U (MA)
California State U, Long Beach (CA)
Campbell U (NC)
Central State U (OH)
Champlain Coll (VT)
City U (WA)
Columbia Coll (SC)
Eastern Washington U (WA)
Grace Coll (IN)
Kent State U (OH)
Liberty U (VA)
Ohio U (OH)
Roosevelt U (IL)
San Diego State U (CA)
Texas Southern U (TX)
U of Nebraska–Lincoln (NE)
The U of North Carolina at Asheville (NC)
U of St. Thomas (MN)
The U of Western Ontario (ON, Canada)

JUVENILE CORRECTIONS
East Central U (OK)
Harris-Stowe State Coll (MO)
U of New Haven (CT)

KINDERGARTEN/PRESCHOOL EDUCATION
Alabama Ag and Mech U (AL)
Alabama State U (AL)
Albany State U (GA)
Albright Coll (PA)
Alma Coll (MI)
Alvernia Coll (PA)
American Intl Coll (MA)
Anderson Coll (SC)
Anna Maria Coll (MA)
Appalachian State U (NC)
Arcadia U (PA)
Arizona State U (AZ)
Armstrong Atlantic State U (GA)
Ashland U (OH)
Athens State U (AL)
Atlanta Christian Coll (GA)
Atlantic Union Coll (MA)
Auburn U (AL)
Augsburg Coll (MN)
Augusta State U (GA)
Ball State U (IN)
Barry U (FL)
Baylor U (TX)
Bay Path Coll (MA)
Becker Coll (MA)
Belmont U (TN)
Bennington Coll (VT)
Berea Coll (KY)
Birmingham-Southern Coll (AL)
Black Hills State U (SD)
Bluefield Coll (VA)
Bluffton Coll (OH)
Boise State U (ID)
Boston Coll (MA)
Boston U (MA)
Bowie State U (MD)
Bowling Green State U (OH)
Bradley U (IL)
Brenau U (GA)
Bridgewater State Coll (MA)
Bryan Coll (TN)
Bucknell U (PA)
State U of NY Coll at Buffalo (NY)
Cabrini Coll (PA)
California Polytechnic State U, San Luis Obispo (CA)
California U of Pennsylvania (PA)
Cardinal Stritch U (WI)
Carlow Coll (PA)
Carroll Coll (WI)
Carson-Newman Coll (TN)
The Catholic U of America (DC)
Central Methodist Coll (MO)
Central State U (OH)
Central Washington U (WA)
Champlain Coll (VT)
Charleston Southern U (SC)
Cheyney U of Pennsylvania (PA)
Chicago State U (IL)
Clarion U of Pennsylvania (PA)
Clark Atlanta U (GA)

Clarke Coll (IA)
Clemson U (SC)
Coll Misericordia (PA)
Coll of Mount St. Joseph (OH)
The Coll of New Jersey (NJ)
Coll of Notre Dame of Maryland (MD)
Coll of St. Catherine (MN)
Coll of St. Joseph (VT)
Columbia Coll (SC)
Columbia Coll Chicago (IL)
Concord Coll (WV)
Concordia Coll (MN)
Concordia U (IL)
Concordia U (NE)
Concordia U (OR)
Concordia U (QC, Canada)
Concordia U, St. Paul (MN)
Concordia U Wisconsin (WI)
Connecticut Coll (CT)
Converse Coll (SC)
Crown Coll (MN)
Curry Coll (MA)
Dallas Baptist U (TX)
Delaware State U (DE)
Delta State U (MS)
DePaul U (IL)
Dillard U (LA)
East Carolina U (NC)
East Central U (OK)
Eastern Connecticut State U (CT)
Eastern Illinois U (IL)
Eastern Kentucky U (KY)
Eastern Mennonite U (VA)
Eastern Nazarene Coll (MA)
Eastern New Mexico U (NM)
Edgewood Coll (WI)
Edinboro U of Pennsylvania (PA)
Elizabeth City State U (NC)
Elizabethtown Coll (PA)
Elmhurst Coll (IL)
Elms Coll (MA)
Erskine Coll (SC)
Evangel U (MO)
Faulkner U (AL)
Fayetteville State U (NC)
Florida Ag and Mech U (FL)
Florida Southern Coll (FL)
Florida State U (FL)
Fontbonne U (MO)
Fort Hays State U (KS)
Fort Lewis Coll (CO)
Fort Valley State U (GA)
Framingham State Coll (MA)
The Franciscan U (IA)
Franklin Pierce Coll (NH)
Frostburg State U (MD)
Furman U (SC)
Gallaudet U (DC)
Gardner-Webb U (NC)
Georgetown Coll (KY)
Georgia Southern U (GA)
Glenville State Coll (WV)
Goshen Coll (IN)
Governors State U (IL)
Grambling State U (LA)
Greensboro Coll (NC)
Grove City Coll (PA)
Hampshire Coll (MA)
Hampton U (VA)
Hannibal-LaGrange Coll (MO)
Harding U (AR)
Harris-Stowe State Coll (MO)
Henderson State U (AR)
High Point U (NC)
Hillsdale Coll (MI)
Hofstra U (NY)
Hood Coll (MD)
Houston Baptist U (TX)
Howard Payne U (TX)
Howard U (DC)
Humboldt State U (CA)
Hunter Coll of the City U of NY (NY)
Illinois State U (IL)
Immaculata U (PA)
Indiana U Bloomington (IN)
Indiana U of Pennsylvania (PA)
Inter American U of PR, Aguadilla Campus (PR)
Inter American U of PR, Ponce Campus (PR)
Inter American U of PR, San Germán Campus (PR)
Iowa Wesleyan Coll (IA)
Jacksonville State U (AL)
Jarvis Christian Coll (TX)
John Brown U (AR)
John Carroll U (OH)
Johnson Bible Coll (TN)
Judson Coll (IL)
Juniata Coll (PA)
Keene State Coll (NH)
Kendall Coll (IL)
Kent State U (OH)
Keystone Coll (PA)

King Coll (TN)
Kutztown U of Pennsylvania (PA)
Lakeland Coll (WI)
Lamar U (TX)
La Roche Coll (PA)
Lasell Coll (MA)
Lenoir-Rhyne Coll (NC)
Lesley U (MA)
Lincoln Memorial U (TN)
Lincoln U (PA)
Lindenwood U (MO)
Livingstone Coll (NC)
Lock Haven U of Pennsylvania (PA)
Long Island U, C.W. Post Campus (NY)
Longwood U (VA)
Loras Coll (IA)
Louisiana Coll (LA)
Louisiana Tech U (LA)
Lourdes Coll (OH)
Loyola U Chicago (IL)
Lynchburg Coll (VA)
Lynn U (FL)
Mansfield U of Pennsylvania (PA)
Marian Coll (IN)
Marian Coll of Fond du Lac (WI)
Mars Hill Coll (NC)
Martin Luther Coll (MN)
Martin U (IN)
Marygrove Coll (MI)
Maryville U of Saint Louis (MO)
Massachusetts Coll of Liberal Arts (MA)
McNeese State U (LA)
McPherson Coll (KS)
Medaille Coll (NY)
Mercy Coll (NY)
Methodist Coll (NC)
Metropolitan State U (MN)
Miami U (OH)
Middle Tennessee State U (TN)
Minnesota State U Mankato (MN)
Minnesota State U Moorhead (MN)
Mississippi Valley State U (MS)
Missouri Baptist U (MO)
Missouri Southern State U (MO)
Mitchell Coll (CT)
Montclair State U (NJ)
Morehead State U (KY)
Mount Aloysius Coll (PA)
Mount Ida Coll (MA)
Mount Mary Coll (WI)
Mount Saint Vincent U (NS, Canada)
Mount Union Coll (OH)
Mount Vernon Nazarene U (OH)
Naropa U (CO)
National-Louis U (IL)
Neumann Coll (PA)
Newberry Coll (SC)
New Jersey City U (NJ)
New Mexico Highlands U (NM)
New Mexico State U (NM)
New York U (NY)
Nicholls State U (LA)
Norfolk State U (VA)
North Carolina Central U (NC)
Northeastern Illinois U (IL)
Northeastern State U (OK)
Northeastern U (MA)
Northern Illinois U (IL)
North Georgia Coll & State U (GA)
North Greenville Coll (SC)
North Park U (IL)
Northwestern Coll (MN)
Northwestern Oklahoma State U (OK)
Notre Dame Coll (OH)
Oglethorpe U (GA)
Ohio Northern U (OH)
The Ohio State U–Mansfield Campus (OH)
Ohio U (OH)
Ohio Wesleyan U (OH)
Oklahoma Baptist U (OK)
Oklahoma Christian U (OK)
Oklahoma City U (OK)
Olivet Nazarene U (IL)
Oral Roberts U (OK)
Oregon State U (OR)
Our Lady of the Lake U of San Antonio (TX)
Pacific Lutheran U (WA)
Pacific Oaks Coll (CA)
Pacific Union Coll (CA)
Pacific U (OR)
Philadelphia Biblical U (PA)
Piedmont Coll (GA)
Pine Manor Coll (MA)
Pittsburg State U (KS)
Pontifical Catholic U of Puerto Rico (PR)
Presbyterian Coll (SC)
Purdue U (IN)

Queens Coll of the City U of NY (NY)
Reinhardt Coll (GA)
Rhode Island Coll (RI)
Rider U (NJ)
Rivier Coll (NH)
Roosevelt U (IL)
Rowan U (NJ)
Ryerson U (ON, Canada)
Sacred Heart U (CT)
St. Bonaventure U (NY)
St. Cloud State U (MN)
Saint Joseph Coll (CT)
St. Joseph's Coll, Suffolk Campus (NY)
Saint Mary-of-the-Woods Coll (IN)
St. Thomas Aquinas Coll (NY)
Saint Xavier U (IL)
Salem State Coll (MA)
Sarah Lawrence Coll (NY)
Seton Hall U (NJ)
Seton Hill U (PA)
Shawnee State U (OH)
Siena Heights U (MI)
Silver Lake Coll (WI)
Simmons Coll (MA)
Simpson Coll (IA)
South Carolina State U (SC)
South Dakota State U (SD)
Southeastern Oklahoma State U (OK)
Southeast Missouri State U (MO)
Southern Adventist U (TN)
Southern Arkansas U–Magnolia (AR)
Southern Connecticut State U (CT)
Southern U and A&M Coll (LA)
Southern Wesleyan U (SC)
Spring Arbor U (MI)
Springfield Coll (MA)
State U of NY at New Paltz (NY)
State U of NY Coll at Cortland (NY)
State U of NY Coll at Fredonia (NY)
State U of NY Coll at Geneseo (NY)
Stephens Coll (MO)
Stonehill Coll (MA)
Susquehanna U (PA)
Syracuse U (NY)
Tabor Coll (KS)
Taylor U (IN)
Tennessee State U (TN)
Tennessee Technological U (TN)
Texas A&M Intl U (TX)
Texas A&M U–Commerce (TX)
Texas A&M U–Kingsville (TX)
Texas Southern U (TX)
Thomas U (GA)
Tougaloo Coll (MS)
Trinity Coll (DC)
Troy State U (AL)
Troy State U Dothan (AL)
Tufts U (MA)
Tusculum Coll (TN)
Union U (TN)
Université de Montréal (QC, Canada)
Université de Sherbrooke (QC, Canada)
U du Québec à Hull (QC, Canada)
Université Laval (QC, Canada)
The U of Akron (OH)
The U of Alabama (AL)
The U of Alabama at Birmingham (AL)
U of Alaska Southeast (AK)
U of Alberta (AB, Canada)
The U of Arizona (AZ)
U of Arkansas at Little Rock (AR)
The U of British Columbia (BC, Canada)
U of Cincinnati (OH)
U of Dayton (OH)
U of Delaware (DE)
U of Detroit Mercy (MI)
U of Georgia (GA)
U of Great Falls (MT)
U of Illinois at Urbana–Champaign (IL)
U of Kentucky (KY)
U of La Verne (CA)
U of Maine (ME)
U of Maine at Farmington (ME)
U of Manitoba (MB, Canada)
U of Mary Hardin-Baylor (TX)
U of Maryland, Coll Park (MD)
U of Maryland Eastern Shore (MD)
U of Michigan–Dearborn (MI)
U of Michigan–Flint (MI)
U of Minnesota, Duluth (MN)
U of Minnesota, Twin Cities Campus (MN)
U of Missouri–Columbia (MO)
U of Missouri–Kansas City (MO)
U of Mobile (AL)

U of Montevallo (AL)
U of Nevada, Las Vegas (NV)
U of New Brunswick Fredericton (NB, Canada)
U of New Hampshire (NH)
U of New Mexico (NM)
U of North Alabama (AL)
The U of North Carolina at Charlotte (NC)
The U of North Carolina at Wilmington (NC)
U of Northern Iowa (IA)
U of Ottawa (ON, Canada)
U of Regina (SK, Canada)
The U of Scranton (PA)
U of South Carolina Aiken (SC)
U of South Carolina Spartanburg (SC)
U of South Florida (FL)
The U of Tennessee at Martin (TN)
The U of Texas at Brownsville (TX)
U of the District of Columbia (DC)
U of the Incarnate Word (TX)
U of Toledo (OH)
U of Utah (UT)
U of Vermont (VT)
U of Victoria (BC, Canada)
The U of Western Ontario (ON, Canada)
U of Windsor (ON, Canada)
U of Wisconsin–La Crosse (WI)
U of Wisconsin–Madison (WI)
U of Wisconsin–Milwaukee (WI)
U of Wisconsin–Oshkosh (WI)
U of Wisconsin–Platteville (WI)
U of Wisconsin–Stevens Point (WI)
Utah State U (UT)
Vanderbilt U (TN)
Villa Julie Coll (MD)
Virginia Polytechnic Inst and State U (VA)
Virginia Union U (VA)
Voorhees Coll (SC)
Wagner Coll (NY)
Waldorf Coll (IA)
Walsh U (OH)
Warner Pacific Coll (OR)
Wartburg Coll (IA)
Washburn U (KS)
Washington Bible Coll (MD)
Wayne State Coll (NE)
Weber State U (UT)
Webster U (MO)
Western Kentucky U (KY)
Western Washington U (WA)
Westfield State Coll (MA)
West Liberty State Coll (WV)
Westminster Coll (UT)
West Virginia State Coll (WV)
West Virginia Wesleyan Coll (WV)
Wheelock Coll (MA)
Widener U (PA)
Williams Baptist Coll (AR)
Wingate U (NC)
Winona State U (MN)
Winston-Salem State U (NC)
Winthrop U (SC)
Worcester State Coll (MA)
Wright State U (OH)
York U (ON, Canada)
Youngstown State U (OH)

KINESIOLOGY AND EXERCISE SCIENCE

Acadia U (NS, Canada)
Adams State Coll (CO)
Adrian Coll (MI)
Albertson Coll of Idaho (ID)
Alma Coll (MI)
Appalachian State U (NC)
Arizona State U (AZ)
Arkansas State U (AR)
Augustana Coll (SD)
Ball State U (IN)
Barry U (FL)
Bastyr U (WA)
Becker Coll (MA)
Bethel Coll (IN)
Bethel U (MN)
Biola U (CA)
Bluefield Coll (VA)
Boise State U (ID)
Boston U (MA)
Brevard Coll (NC)
Bridgewater Coll (VA)
Bridgewater State Coll (MA)
Brigham Young U (UT)
Brigham Young U–Hawaii (HI)
Brock U (ON, Canada)
State U of NY Coll at Buffalo (NY)
Cabrini Coll (PA)
California Baptist U (CA)
California Lutheran U (CA)
California State U, Chico (CA)
California State U, Hayward (CA)

California State U, Long Beach (CA)
California State U, Sacramento (CA)
Calvin Coll (MI)
Campbell U (NC)
Capital U (OH)
Carroll Coll (WI)
Carson-Newman Coll (TN)
Castleton State Coll (VT)
Cedarville U (OH)
Centenary Coll of Louisiana (LA)
Central Coll (IA)
Central Washington U (WA)
Chatham Coll (PA)
Chowan Coll (NC)
Christian Heritage Coll (CA)
Cleveland State U (OH)
Coker Coll (SC)
Colby-Sawyer Coll (NH)
Coll of Mount Saint Vincent (NY)
The Coll of St. Scholastica (MN)
Colorado State U (CO)
Colorado State U-Pueblo (CO)
Columbus State U (GA)
Concordia Coll (MN)
Concordia U (CA)
Concordia U (IL)
Concordia U (NE)
Concordia U (QC, Canada)
Concordia U at Austin (TX)
Concordia U, St. Paul (MN)
Cornerstone U (MI)
Creighton U (NE)
Dakota State U (SD)
Dalhousie U (NS, Canada)
Davis & Elkins Coll (WV)
Defiance Coll (OH)
DePauw U (IN)
DeSales U (PA)
Dordt Coll (IA)
Drury U (MO)
East Carolina U (NC)
Eastern Washington U (WA)
East Stroudsburg U of Pennsylvania (PA)
Elmhurst Coll (IL)
Emmanuel Coll (GA)
Eureka Coll (IL)
Florida Atlantic U (FL)
Florida Gulf Coast U (FL)
Florida Intl U (FL)
Florida State U (FL)
Frostburg State U (MD)
Furman U (SC)
Gannon U (PA)
The George Washington U (DC)
Georgia Southern U (GA)
Gonzaga U (WA)
Gordon Coll (MA)
Grand Canyon U (AZ)
Greensboro Coll (NC)
Greenville Coll (IL)
Hamline U (MN)
Hampshire Coll (MA)
Harding U (AR)
Hardin-Simmons U (TX)
Hastings Coll (NE)
High Point U (NC)
Hofstra U (NY)
Hope Coll (MI)
Houston Baptist U (TX)
Howard Payne U (TX)
Humboldt State U (CA)
Huntingdon Coll (AL)
Huntington Coll (IN)
Iowa Wesleyan Coll (IA)
Ithaca Coll (NY)
Jacksonville State U (AL)
Jacksonville U (FL)
John Brown U (AR)
Johnson State Coll (VT)
Kansas State U (KS)
Kennesaw State U (GA)
Kent State U (OH)
Lake Superior State U (MI)
Lander U (SC)
Lasell Coll (MA)
Laurentian U (ON, Canada)
Lenoir-Rhyne Coll (NC)
Lewis-Clark State Coll (ID)
Liberty U (VA)
Lincoln Memorial U (TN)
Linfield Coll (OR)
Lipscomb U (TN)
Long Island U, Brooklyn Campus (NY)
Longwood U (VA)
Loras Coll (IA)
Louisiana Coll (LA)
Lubbock Christian U (TX)
Lynchburg Coll (VA)
Malone Coll (OH)
Marquette U (WI)
McDaniel Coll (MD)
McGill U (QC, Canada)

McNeese State U (LA)
Memorial U of Newfoundland (NL, Canada)
Meredith Coll (NC)
Messiah Coll (PA)
Metropolitan State Coll of Denver (CO)
Miami U (OH)
Michigan State U (MI)
MidAmerica Nazarene U (KS)
Midwestern State U (TX)
Mississippi Coll (MS)
Missouri Southern State U (MO)
Missouri Western State Coll (MO)
Morehead State U (KY)
Mount Union Coll (OH)
Mount Vernon Nazarene U (OH)
Murray State U (KY)
Nebraska Wesleyan U (NE)
Norfolk State U (VA)
Northern Arizona U (AZ)
Northern Michigan U (MI)
North Park U (IL)
Northwestern Coll (IA)
Northwestern Coll (MN)
Northwest Nazarene U (ID)
Oakland U (MI)
Occidental Coll (CA)
Ohio Northern U (OH)
The Ohio State U (OH)
Ohio U (OH)
Oklahoma Baptist U (OK)
Oklahoma City U (OK)
Old Dominion U (VA)
Olivet Nazarene U (IL)
Oral Roberts U (OK)
Oregon State U (OR)
Pacific Union Coll (CA)
Pacific U (OR)
Penn State U Abington Coll (PA)
Penn State U Altoona Coll (PA)
Penn State U at Erie, The Behrend Coll (PA)
Penn State U Beaver Campus of the Commonwealth Coll (PA)
Penn State U Berks Cmps of Berks-Lehigh Valley Coll (PA)
Penn State U Delaware County Campus of the Commonwealth Coll (PA)
Penn State U DuBois Campus of the Commonwealth Coll (PA)
Penn State U Fayette Campus of the Commonwealth Coll (PA)
Penn State U Hazleton Campus of the Commonwealth Coll (PA)
Penn State U Lehigh Valley Cmps of Berks-Lehigh Valley Coll (PA)
Penn State U McKeesport Campus of the Commonwealth Coll (PA)
Penn State U Mont Alto Campus of the Commonwealth Coll (PA)
Penn State U New Kensington Campus of the Commonwealth Coll (PA)
Penn State U Schuylkill Campus of the Capital Coll (PA)
Penn State U Shenango Campus of the Commonwealth Coll (PA)
Penn State U Univ Park Campus (PA)
Penn State U Wilkes-Barre Campus of the Commonwealth Coll (PA)
Penn State U Worthington Scranton Cmps Commonwealth Coll (PA)
Penn State U York Campus of the Commonwealth Coll (PA)
Point Loma Nazarene U (CA)
Queens Coll of the City U of NY (NY)
Radford U (VA)
Redeemer U Coll (ON, Canada)
Rice U (TX)
Rocky Mountain Coll (MT)
Rutgers, The State U of New Jersey, New Brunswick/Piscataway (NJ)
Sacred Heart U (CT)
St. Cloud State U (MN)
St. Edward's U (TX)
St. Francis Xavier U (NS, Canada)
Saint Joseph's Coll of Maine (ME)
Saint Louis U (MO)
Saint Mary's Coll of California (CA)
St. Mary's U of San Antonio (TX)
St. Olaf Coll (MN)
Salem State Coll (MA)
Samford U (AL)
Sam Houston State U (TX)
Schreiner U (TX)
Seattle Pacific U (WA)
Simon Fraser U (BC, Canada)
Skidmore Coll (NY)
Southern Adventist U (TN)
Southern Arkansas U–Magnolia (AR)
Southern Nazarene U (OK)
Springfield Coll (MA)
State U of NY Coll at Brockport (NY)
State U of NY Coll at Cortland (NY)
Stetson U (FL)
Syracuse U (NY)
Tarleton State U (TX)
Tennessee Wesleyan Coll (TN)
Texas Lutheran U (TX)
Texas Tech U (TX)
Texas Woman's U (TX)
Towson U (MD)
Transylvania U (KY)
Trevecca Nazarene U (TN)
Truman State U (MO)
Tulane U (LA)
Union Coll (NE)
Union U (TN)
Université de Sherbrooke (QC, Canada)
Université Laval (QC, Canada)
U at Buffalo, The State U of New York (NY)
U of Alaska Fairbanks (AK)
U of Alberta (AB, Canada)
U of Arkansas (AR)
The U of British Columbia (BC, Canada)
U of Calgary (AB, Canada)
U of Calif, Los Angeles (CA)
U of Central Arkansas (AR)
U of Colorado at Boulder (CO)
U of Dayton (OH)
U of Delaware (DE)
U of Evansville (IN)
U of Florida (FL)
U of Guelph (ON, Canada)
U of Hawaii at Manoa (HI)
U of Houston (TX)
U of Illinois at Chicago (IL)
U of Illinois at Urbana–Champaign (IL)
The U of Iowa (IA)
The U of Lethbridge (AB, Canada)
U of Mary (ND)
U of Massachusetts Amherst (MA)
U of Massachusetts Lowell (MA)
The U of Memphis (TN)
U of Miami (FL)
U of Michigan (MI)
U of Minnesota, Duluth (MN)
U of Mississippi (MS)
U of Nebraska–Lincoln (NE)
U of Nevada, Las Vegas (NV)
U of New Brunswick Fredericton (NB, Canada)
U of New Hampshire (NH)
The U of North Carolina at Greensboro (NC)
U of Northern Colorado (CO)
U of North Texas (TX)
U of Oregon (OR)
U of Puget Sound (WA)
U of Regina (SK, Canada)
U of Saskatchewan (SK, Canada)
The U of Scranton (PA)
U of Sioux Falls (SD)
U of South Carolina (SC)
U of South Carolina Aiken (SC)
U of Southern California (CA)
U of Southern Indiana (IN)
The U of Tampa (FL)
The U of Tennessee (TN)
The U of Tennessee at Chattanooga (TN)
The U of Texas at Brownsville (TX)
U of the Pacific (CA)
U of the Sacred Heart (PR)
U of Toledo (OH)
U of Tulsa (OK)
U of Utah (UT)
U of Victoria (BC, Canada)
U of Waterloo (ON, Canada)
The U of Western Ontario (ON, Canada)
U of Windsor (ON, Canada)
U of Wisconsin–Eau Claire (WI)
U of Wisconsin–La Crosse (WI)
U of Wyoming (WY)
Upper Iowa U (IA)
Valdosta State U (GA)
Valparaiso U (IN)
Vanguard U of Southern California (CA)
Voorhees Coll (SC)
Wake Forest U (NC)
Walla Walla Coll (WA)
Warner Pacific Coll (OR)
Warner Southern Coll (FL)
Washington State U (WA)
Waynesburg Coll (PA)
Wayne State Coll (NE)
Weber State U (UT)
West Chester U of Pennsylvania (PA)
Western Michigan U (MI)
Western State Coll of Colorado (CO)
Western Washington U (WA)
West Liberty State Coll (WV)
Westmont Coll (CA)
West Virginia U (WV)
Wheaton Coll (IL)
Willamette U (OR)
William Paterson U of New Jersey (NJ)
Wilson Coll (PA)
Winona State U (MN)
Winston-Salem State U (NC)
Youngstown State U (OH)

KINESIOTHERAPY
California State U, Long Beach (CA)
Université de Sherbrooke (QC, Canada)
U of Regina (SK, Canada)

KOREAN
Brigham Young U (UT)
U of Calif, Los Angeles (CA)

KOREAN STUDIES
Claremont McKenna Coll (CA)

LABOR AND INDUSTRIAL RELATIONS
Athabasca U (AB, Canada)
Bowling Green State U (OH)
Brock U (ON, Canada)
California State U, Dominguez Hills (CA)
Carleton U (ON, Canada)
Clarion U of Pennsylvania (PA)
Cleveland State U (OH)
Cornell U (NY)
Ferris State U (MI)
Governors State U (IL)
Grand Valley State U (MI)
Hampshire Coll (MA)
Indiana U Bloomington (IN)
Indiana U Kokomo (IN)
Indiana U Northwest (IN)
Indiana U–Purdue U Indianapolis (IN)
Indiana U South Bend (IN)
Indiana U Southeast (IN)
Ithaca Coll (NY)
Lakehead U (ON, Canada)
Le Moyne Coll (NY)
McGill U (QC, Canada)
Memorial U of Newfoundland (NL, Canada)
Penn State U Abington Coll (PA)
Penn State U Altoona Coll (PA)
Penn State U at Erie, The Behrend Coll (PA)
Penn State U Beaver Campus of the Commonwealth Coll (PA)
Penn State U Berks Cmps of Berks-Lehigh Valley Coll (PA)
Penn State U Delaware County Campus of the Commonwealth Coll (PA)
Penn State U DuBois Campus of the Commonwealth Coll (PA)
Penn State U Fayette Campus of the Commonwealth Coll (PA)
Penn State U Hazleton Campus of the Commonwealth Coll (PA)
Penn State U Lehigh Valley Cmps of Berks-Lehigh Valley Coll (PA)
Penn State U McKeesport Campus of the Commonwealth Coll (PA)
Penn State U Mont Alto Campus of the Commonwealth Coll (PA)
Penn State U New Kensington Campus of the Commonwealth Coll (PA)
Penn State U Schuylkill Campus of the Capital Coll (PA)
Penn State U Shenango Campus of the Commonwealth Coll (PA)
Penn State U Univ Park Campus (PA)
Penn State U Wilkes-Barre Campus of the Commonwealth Coll (PA)
Penn State U Worthington Scranton Cmps Commonwealth Coll (PA)
Penn State U York Campus of the Commonwealth Coll (PA)
Queens Coll of the City U of NY (NY)
Rhode Island Coll (RI)
Rockhurst U (MO)
Roosevelt U (IL)
Rutgers, The State U of New Jersey, New Brunswick/Piscataway (NJ)
Saint Francis U (PA)
San Francisco State U (CA)
Seton Hall U (NJ)
State U of NY Coll at Fredonia (NY)
State U of NY Coll at Old Westbury (NY)
State U of NY Coll at Potsdam (NY)
State U of NY Empire State Coll (NY)
Tennessee Technological U (TN)
Texas A&M U–Commerce (TX)
Thomas Edison State Coll (NJ)
Université de Montréal (QC, Canada)
U du Québec à Hull (QC, Canada)
Université Laval (QC, Canada)
U of Alberta (AB, Canada)
The U of British Columbia (BC, Canada)
U of Detroit Mercy (MI)
The U of Iowa (IA)
U of Manitoba (MB, Canada)
U of Massachusetts Boston (MA)
U of Toronto (ON, Canada)
U of Windsor (ON, Canada)
U of Wisconsin–Madison (WI)
U of Wisconsin–Milwaukee (WI)
Wayne State U (MI)
Westminster Coll (PA)
Winona State U (MN)
York U (ON, Canada)

LABOR STUDIES
Eastern Michigan U (MI)
Hofstra U (NY)
Indiana U–Purdue U Fort Wayne (IN)
U of Windsor (ON, Canada)

LANDSCAPE ARCHITECTURE
Arizona State U (AZ)
Auburn U (AL)
Ball State U (IN)
California Polytechnic State U, San Luis Obispo (CA)
California State Polytechnic U, Pomona (CA)
Chatham Coll (PA)
City Coll of the City U of NY (NY)
Clemson U (SC)
Coll of the Atlantic (ME)
Colorado State U (CO)
Cornell U (NY)
Eastern Kentucky U (KY)
Florida Ag and Mech U (FL)
Iowa State U of Science and Technology (IA)
Kansas State U (KS)
Louisiana State U and A&M Coll (LA)
Michigan State U (MI)
Mississippi State U (MS)
North Carolina State U (NC)
North Dakota State U (ND)
The Ohio State U (OH)
Oklahoma State U (OK)
Penn State U Abington Coll (PA)
Penn State U Altoona Coll (PA)
Penn State U at Erie, The Behrend Coll (PA)
Penn State U Beaver Campus of the Commonwealth Coll (PA)
Penn State U Berks Cmps of Berks-Lehigh Valley Coll (PA)
Penn State U Delaware County Campus of the Commonwealth Coll (PA)
Penn State U DuBois Campus of the Commonwealth Coll (PA)
Penn State U Fayette Campus of the Commonwealth Coll (PA)
Penn State U Hazleton Campus of the Commonwealth Coll (PA)
Penn State U Lehigh Valley Cmps of Berks-Lehigh Valley Coll (PA)
Penn State U McKeesport Campus of the Commonwealth Coll (PA)
Penn State U Mont Alto Campus of the Commonwealth Coll (PA)
Penn State U New Kensington Campus of the Commonwealth Coll (PA)
Penn State U Schuylkill Campus of the Capital Coll (PA)
Penn State U Shenango Campus of the Commonwealth Coll (PA)
Penn State U Univ Park Campus (PA)
Penn State U Wilkes-Barre Campus of the Commonwealth Coll (PA)
Penn State U Worthington Scranton Cmps Commonwealth Coll (PA)
Penn State U York Campus of the Commonwealth Coll (PA)
Philadelphia U (PA)
Purdue U (IN)
Ryerson U (ON, Canada)
State U of NY Coll of Environ Sci and Forestry (NY)
Texas A&M U (TX)
Texas Tech U (TX)
Université de Montréal (QC, Canada)
The U of Arizona (AZ)
U of Arkansas (AR)
The U of British Columbia (BC, Canada)
U of Calif, Berkeley (CA)
U of Calif, Davis (CA)
U of Connecticut (CT)
U of Florida (FL)
U of Georgia (GA)
U of Guelph (ON, Canada)
U of Hawaii at Manoa (HI)
U of Idaho (ID)
U of Illinois at Urbana–Champaign (IL)
U of Kentucky (KY)
U of Maryland, Coll Park (MD)
U of Massachusetts Amherst (MA)
U of Michigan (MI)
U of Minnesota, Twin Cities Campus (MN)
U of Nevada, Las Vegas (NV)
U of North Texas (TX)
U of Oregon (OR)
U of Rhode Island (RI)
U of Southern California (CA)
U of Washington (WA)
U of Wisconsin–Madison (WI)
Utah State U (UT)
Virginia Polytechnic Inst and State U (VA)
Washington State U (WA)
West Virginia U (WV)

LANDSCAPING AND GROUNDSKEEPING
Andrews U (MI)
Colorado State U (CO)
Mississippi State U (MS)
Oklahoma State U (OK)
Oregon State U (OR)
Penn State U Abington Coll (PA)
Penn State U Altoona Coll (PA)
Penn State U at Erie, The Behrend Coll (PA)
Penn State U Beaver Campus of the Commonwealth Coll (PA)
Penn State U Berks Cmps of Berks-Lehigh Valley Coll (PA)
Penn State U Delaware County Campus of the Commonwealth Coll (PA)
Penn State U DuBois Campus of the Commonwealth Coll (PA)
Penn State U Fayette Campus of the Commonwealth Coll (PA)
Penn State U Hazleton Campus of the Commonwealth Coll (PA)
Penn State U Lehigh Valley Cmps of Berks-Lehigh Valley Coll (PA)
Penn State U McKeesport Campus of the Commonwealth Coll (PA)
Penn State U Mont Alto Campus of the Commonwealth Coll (PA)
Penn State U New Kensington Campus of the Commonwealth Coll (PA)
Penn State U Schuylkill Campus of the Capital Coll (PA)
Penn State U Shenango Campus of the Commonwealth Coll (PA)
Penn State U Univ Park Campus (PA)
Penn State U Wilkes-Barre Campus of the Commonwealth Coll (PA)
Penn State U Worthington Scranton Cmps Commonwealth Coll (PA)
Penn State U York Campus of the Commonwealth Coll (PA)
South Dakota State U (SD)
Tennessee Technological U (TN)
U of Georgia (GA)
U of Maine (ME)
U of Nebraska–Lincoln (NE)
The U of Tennessee at Martin (TN)

LAND USE PLANNING AND MANAGEMENT
Burlington Coll (VT)
Grand Valley State U (MI)

Metropolitan State Coll of Denver (CO)
Northern Michigan U (MI)
Northland Coll (WI)
State U of NY Coll of Environ Sci and Forestry (NY)
Sterling Coll (VT)
U of Alberta (AB, Canada)
U of Michigan–Flint (MI)
U of Saskatchewan (SK, Canada)
U of Wisconsin–Platteville (WI)
U of Wisconsin–River Falls (WI)
Washington State U (WA)

LANGUAGE INTERPRETATION AND TRANSLATION
Brigham Young U (UT)
Concordia U (QC, Canada)
Laurentian U (ON, Canada)
Mississippi Coll (MS)
U du Québec à Hull (QC, Canada)
Université Laval (QC, Canada)
York U (ON, Canada)

LASER AND OPTICAL TECHNOLOGY
Excelsior Coll (NY)
Oregon Inst of Technology (OR)

LATIN
Acadia U (NS, Canada)
Amherst Coll (MA)
Asbury Coll (KY)
Augustana Coll (IL)
Austin Coll (TX)
Ave Maria U (FL)
Ball State U (IN)
Bard Coll (NY)
Barnard Coll (NY)
Baylor U (TX)
Boston U (MA)
Brandeis U (MA)
Brigham Young U (UT)
Brooklyn Coll of the City U of NY (NY)
Bryn Mawr Coll (PA)
Butler U (IN)
Calvin Coll (MI)
Carleton Coll (MN)
Carleton U (ON, Canada)
Carroll Coll (MT)
The Catholic U of America (DC)
Centenary Coll of Louisiana (LA)
Claremont McKenna Coll (CA)
Colgate U (NY)
The Coll of New Rochelle (NY)
The Coll of William and Mary (VA)
The Coll of Wooster (OH)
Concordia Coll (MN)
Cornell Coll (IA)
Creighton U (NE)
Dartmouth Coll (NH)
DePauw U (IN)
Duke U (NC)
Duquesne U (PA)
Emory U (GA)
Florida State U (FL)
Fordham U (NY)
Franklin and Marshall Coll (PA)
Furman U (SC)
Gettysburg Coll (PA)
Hamilton Coll (NY)
Hampden-Sydney Coll (VA)
Harvard U (MA)
Haverford Coll (PA)
Hobart and William Smith Colls (NY)
Hunter Coll of the City U of NY (NY)
Indiana U Bloomington (IN)
John Carroll U (OH)
Kent State U (OH)
Kenyon Coll (OH)
Lawrence U (WI)
Lehigh U (PA)
Lehman Coll of the City U of NY (NY)
Lenoir-Rhyne Coll (NC)
Louisiana State U and A&M Coll (LA)
Loyola Marymount U (CA)
Loyola U Chicago (IL)
Luther Coll (IA)
Macalester Coll (MN)
Marlboro Coll (VT)
Mary Washington Coll (VA)
Memorial U of Newfoundland (NL, Canada)
Mercer U (GA)
Miami U (OH)
Miami U Hamilton (OH)
Monmouth Coll (IL)
Montclair State U (NJ)
Mount Allison U (NB, Canada)
Mount Holyoke Coll (MA)
New York U (NY)
Oberlin Coll (OH)
Ohio U (OH)
Queens Coll of the City U of NY (NY)
Queen's U at Kingston (ON, Canada)
Randolph-Macon Coll (VA)
Randolph-Macon Woman's Coll (VA)
Rhodes Coll (TN)
Rice U (TX)
Rockford Coll (IL)
Rutgers, The State U of New Jersey, New Brunswick/Piscataway (NJ)
Saint Mary's Coll of California (CA)
St. Olaf Coll (MN)
Samford U (AL)
Santa Clara U (CA)
Sarah Lawrence Coll (NY)
Scripps Coll (CA)
Seattle Pacific U (WA)
Simon's Rock Coll of Bard (MA)
Smith Coll (MA)
Southwest Missouri State U (MO)
Swarthmore Coll (PA)
Trent U (ON, Canada)
Tufts U (MA)
Tulane U (LA)
State U of NY at Albany (NY)
U of Alberta (AB, Canada)
The U of British Columbia (BC, Canada)
U of Calif, Berkeley (CA)
U of Calif, Los Angeles (CA)
U of Calif, Santa Cruz (CA)
U of Chicago (IL)
U of Delaware (DE)
U of Georgia (GA)
U of Hawaii at Manoa (HI)
U of Houston (TX)
U of Idaho (ID)
The U of Iowa (IA)
U of Maine (ME)
U of Manitoba (MB, Canada)
U of Maryland, Coll Park (MD)
U of Michigan (MI)
U of Minnesota, Twin Cities Campus (MN)
U of Missouri–Columbia (MO)
The U of Montana–Missoula (MT)
U of Nebraska–Lincoln (NE)
U of New Brunswick Fredericton (NB, Canada)
U of New Hampshire (NH)
The U of North Carolina at Greensboro (NC)
U of Notre Dame (IN)
U of Oregon (OR)
U of Ottawa (ON, Canada)
U of Richmond (VA)
U of St. Thomas (MN)
U of Saskatchewan (SK, Canada)
The U of Scranton (PA)
The U of Tennessee at Chattanooga (TN)
The U of Texas at Austin (TX)
U of the South (TN)
U of Toronto (ON, Canada)
U of Vermont (VT)
U of Victoria (BC, Canada)
U of Washington (WA)
The U of Western Ontario (ON, Canada)
U of Windsor (ON, Canada)
U of Wisconsin–Madison (WI)
U of Wisconsin–Milwaukee (WI)
Vassar Coll (NY)
Wabash Coll (IN)
Wake Forest U (NC)
Washington U in St. Louis (MO)
Wellesley Coll (MA)
West Chester U of Pennsylvania (PA)
Western Michigan U (MI)
Westminster Coll (PA)
Wichita State U (KS)
Yale U (CT)
York U (ON, Canada)

LATIN AMERICAN STUDIES
Adelphi U (NY)
Albright Coll (PA)
Alliant Intl U (CA)
Alliant Intl U–México City(Mexico)
American Public U System (WV)
American U (DC)
Assumption Coll (MA)
Austin Coll (TX)
Ball State U (IN)
Bard Coll (NY)
Barnard Coll (NY)
Baylor U (TX)
Beloit Coll (WI)
Boston U (MA)
Bowdoin Coll (ME)
Brandeis U (MA)
Brigham Young U (UT)
Brown U (RI)
Bucknell U (PA)
Burlington Coll (VT)
California State U, Chico (CA)
California State U, Fullerton (CA)
California State U, Hayward (CA)
California State U, Los Angeles (CA)
Carleton Coll (MN)
Carleton U (ON, Canada)
Central Coll (IA)
City Coll of the City U of NY (NY)
Claremont McKenna Coll (CA)
Colby Coll (ME)
Colgate U (NY)
Coll of the Holy Cross (MA)
The Coll of William and Mary (VA)
Colorado State U (CO)
Columbia Coll (NY)
Connecticut Coll (CT)
Cornell Coll (IA)
Cornell U (NY)
Dartmouth Coll (NH)
Denison U (OH)
DePaul U (IL)
Earlham Coll (IN)
Emory U (GA)
Flagler Coll (FL)
Florida State U (FL)
Fordham U (NY)
Fort Lewis Coll (CO)
The George Washington U (DC)
Gettysburg Coll (PA)
Grinnell Coll (IA)
Gustavus Adolphus Coll (MN)
Hamline U (MN)
Hampshire Coll (MA)
Hanover Coll (IN)
Harvard U (MA)
Haverford Coll (PA)
Hobart and William Smith Colls (NY)
Hofstra U (NY)
Hood Coll (MD)
Hunter Coll of the City U of NY (NY)
Illinois Wesleyan U (IL)
Indiana U Bloomington (IN)
The Johns Hopkins U (MD)
Kent State U (OH)
Lake Forest Coll (IL)
Lehman Coll of the City U of NY (NY)
Lock Haven U of Pennsylvania (PA)
Macalester Coll (MN)
Marlboro Coll (VT)
McGill U (QC, Canada)
Middlebury Coll (VT)
Mount Holyoke Coll (MA)
New York U (NY)
Oberlin Coll (OH)
The Ohio State U (OH)
Ohio U (OH)
Penn State U Abington Coll (PA)
Penn State U Altoona Coll (PA)
Penn State U at Erie, The Behrend Coll (PA)
Penn State U Beaver Campus of the Commonwealth Coll (PA)
Penn State U Berks Cmps of Berks-Lehigh Valley Coll (PA)
Penn State U Delaware County Campus of the Commonwealth Coll (PA)
Penn State U DuBois Campus of the Commonwealth Coll (PA)
Penn State U Fayette Campus of the Commonwealth Coll (PA)
Penn State U Hazleton Campus of the Commonwealth Coll (PA)
Penn State U Lehigh Valley Cmps of Berks-Lehigh Valley Coll (PA)
Penn State U McKeesport Campus of the Commonwealth Coll (PA)
Penn State U Mont Alto Campus of the Commonwealth Coll (PA)
Penn State U New Kensington Campus of the Commonwealth Coll (PA)
Penn State U Schuylkill Campus of the Capital Coll (PA)
Penn State U Shenango Campus of the Commonwealth Coll (PA)
Penn State U Univ Park Campus (PA)
Penn State U Wilkes-Barre Campus of the Commonwealth Coll (PA)
Penn State U Worthington Scranton Cmps Commonwealth Coll (PA)
Penn State U York Campus of the Commonwealth Coll (PA)
Pitzer Coll (CA)
Pontifical Coll Josephinum (OH)
Portland State U (OR)
Queens Coll of the City U of NY (NY)
Queen's U at Kingston (ON, Canada)
Rice U (TX)
Ripon Coll (WI)
Rollins Coll (FL)
Rutgers, The State U of New Jersey, New Brunswick/Piscataway (NJ)
St. Cloud State U (MN)
St. Edward's U (TX)
Saint Mary's Coll of California (CA)
St. Olaf Coll (MN)
Samford U (AL)
San Diego State U (CA)
Sarah Lawrence Coll (NY)
Scripps Coll (CA)
Seattle Pacific U (WA)
Simon's Rock Coll of Bard (MA)
Smith Coll (MA)
Southern Methodist U (TX)
State U of NY at Binghamton (NY)
State U of NY at New Paltz (NY)
Plattsburgh State U of NY (NY)
State U of NY Coll at Brockport (NY)
Stetson U (FL)
Syracuse U (NY)
Texas Christian U (TX)
Texas Tech U (TX)
Trinity U (TX)
Tulane U (LA)
United States Military Acad (NY)
State U of NY at Albany (NY)
The U of Alabama (AL)
U of Alberta (AB, Canada)
The U of Arizona (AZ)
The U of British Columbia (BC, Canada)
U of Calgary (AB, Canada)
U of Calif, Berkeley (CA)
U of Calif, Los Angeles (CA)
U of Calif, Riverside (CA)
U of Calif, San Diego (CA)
U of Calif, Santa Barbara (CA)
U of Calif, Santa Cruz (CA)
U of Chicago (IL)
U of Cincinnati (OH)
U of Connecticut (CT)
U of Delaware (DE)
U of Denver (CO)
U of Idaho (ID)
U of Illinois at Chicago (IL)
U of Illinois at Urbana–Champaign (IL)
The U of Iowa (IA)
U of Kansas (KS)
U of Kentucky (KY)
U of Miami (FL)
U of Michigan (MI)
U of Minnesota, Morris (MN)
U of Minnesota, Twin Cities Campus (MN)
U of Missouri–Columbia (MO)
U of Nebraska at Omaha (NE)
U of Nebraska–Lincoln (NE)
U of New Mexico (NM)
The U of North Carolina at Chapel Hill (NC)
The U of North Carolina at Greensboro (NC)
U of Northern Iowa (IA)
U of Pennsylvania (PA)
U of Rhode Island (RI)
U of Richmond (VA)
U of San Francisco (CA)
U of South Carolina (SC)
The U of Texas at Austin (TX)
U of Toledo (OH)
U of Toronto (ON, Canada)
U of Vermont (VT)
U of Washington (WA)
U of Wisconsin–Eau Claire (WI)
U of Wisconsin–Madison (WI)
U of Wisconsin–Milwaukee (WI)
Vanderbilt U (TN)
Vassar Coll (NY)
Warren Wilson Coll (NC)
Washington Coll (MD)
Washington U in St. Louis (MO)
Wellesley Coll (MA)
Wesleyan U (CT)
Western Washington U (WA)
Willamette U (OR)
Yale U (CT)
York U (ON, Canada)

LATIN TEACHER EDUCATION
Baylor U (TX)
Bowling Green State U (OH)
Brigham Young U (UT)
Centenary Coll of Louisiana (LA)
Hope Coll (MI)
Kent State U (OH)
Miami U Hamilton (OH)
Ohio Wesleyan U (OH)
U of Illinois at Urbana–Champaign (IL)
The U of Iowa (IA)
Western Michigan U (MI)

LAW AND LEGAL STUDIES RELATED
U of Nebraska–Lincoln (NE)

LEGAL ADMINISTRATIVE ASSISTANT/SECRETARY
Ball State U (IN)
Lewis-Clark State Coll (ID)
Peirce Coll (PA)
Tabor Coll (KS)
Texas A&M U–Commerce (TX)
U of Detroit Mercy (MI)
U of West Los Angeles (CA)

LEGAL ASSISTANT/PARALEGAL
Anna Maria Coll (MA)
Avila U (MO)
Ball State U (IN)
Boston U (MA)
California State U, Chico (CA)
Calumet Coll of Saint Joseph (IN)
Cedar Crest Coll (PA)
Champlain Coll (VT)
Coll of Mount St. Joseph (OH)
Coll of Saint Mary (NE)
Concordia U Wisconsin (WI)
Davenport U, Grand Rapids (MI)
Davenport U, Kalamazoo (MI)
Eastern Kentucky U (KY)
Eastern Michigan U (MI)
Elms Coll (MA)
Faulkner U (AL)
Florida Gulf Coast U (FL)
Florida Metropolitan U-Tampa Coll, Brandon (FL)
Gannon U (PA)
Grand Valley State U (MI)
Hamline U (MN)
Hampton U (VA)
Hilbert Coll (NY)
Howard Payne U (TX)
Husson Coll (ME)
Johnson & Wales U (RI)
Jones Coll, Jacksonville (FL)
Jones Coll, Miami (FL)
Kaplan Coll (IA)
Kent State U (OH)
Lake Erie Coll (OH)
Lake Superior State U (MI)
Lewis-Clark State Coll (ID)
Lock Haven U of Pennsylvania (PA)
Madonna U (MI)
Marist Coll (NY)
Marymount U (VA)
Maryville U of Saint Louis (MO)
Marywood U (PA)
Mercy Coll (NY)
Minnesota State U Moorhead (MN)
Mississippi Coll (MS)
Morehead State U (KY)
National American U (SD)
National American U–Sioux Falls Branch (SD)
Nova Southeastern U (FL)
Peirce Coll (PA)
Quinnipiac U (CT)
Roger Williams U (RI)
Roosevelt U (IL)
St. John's U (NY)
Saint Mary-of-the-Woods Coll (IN)
Southern Illinois U Carbondale (IL)
South U (AL)
Suffolk U (MA)
Sullivan U (KY)
Teikyo Post U (CT)
Texas Woman's U (TX)
Thomas Edison State Coll (NJ)
U of Central Florida (FL)
U of Great Falls (MT)
U of Houston–Clear Lake (TX)
U of La Verne (CA)
U of Louisville (KY)
U of Maryland U Coll (MD)
The U of Memphis (TN)
The U of Tennessee at Chattanooga (TN)
U of West Los Angeles (CA)
U of Wisconsin–Superior (WI)
Ursuline Coll (OH)
Valdosta State U (GA)
Villa Julie Coll (MD)
Virginia Intermont Coll (VA)
Wesley Coll (DE)
William Woods U (MO)
Winona State U (MN)

LEGAL PROFESSIONS AND STUDIES RELATED

Bethany Coll (KS)
Brenau U (GA)
Hofstra U (NY)
Intl Coll (FL)
Peirce Coll (PA)
Pennsylvania Coll of Technology (PA)
Ramapo Coll of New Jersey (NJ)
Roger Williams U (RI)
Saint Joseph's U (PA)
Texas Wesleyan U (TX)
Tulane U (LA)
U of Nebraska–Lincoln (NE)
U of Pennsylvania (PA)
U of Tulsa (OK)
Washington State U (WA)

LEGAL STUDIES

American U (DC)
Amherst Coll (MA)
Bay Path Coll (MA)
Bay Path Coll (MA)
Becker Coll (MA)
Becker Coll (MA)
Burlington Coll (VT)
California State U, Chico (CA)
Chapman U (CA)
Chapman U (CA)
Christopher Newport U (VA)
Claremont McKenna Coll (CA)
The Coll of Southeastern Europe, The American U of Athens(Greece)
Coll of the Atlantic (ME)
Concordia U (IL)
East Central U (OK)
East Central U (OK)
Elms Coll (MA)
Franciscan U of Steubenville (OH)
Franciscan U of Steubenville (OH)
Gannon U (PA)
Grand Valley State U (MI)
Hamline U (MN)
Hampshire Coll (MA)
Hampshire Coll (MA)
Harding U (AR)
Hilbert Coll (NY)
Hood Coll (MD)
Indiana U–Purdue U Fort Wayne (IN)
John Jay Coll of Criminal Justice, the City U of NY (NY)
John Jay Coll of Criminal Justice, the City U of NY (NY)
Kenyon Coll (OH)
Lake Superior State U (MI)
Lasell Coll (MA)
Laurentian U (ON, Canada)
Manhattanville Coll (NY)
Marymount Coll of Fordham U (NY)
Methodist Coll (NC)
Mountain State U (WV)
Mountain State U (WV)
National U (CA)
Newbury Coll (MA)
North Carolina Wesleyan Coll (NC)
Northwestern U (IL)
Oberlin Coll (OH)
Park U (MO)
Park U (MO)
Pennsylvania Coll of Technology (PA)
Point Park U (PA)
Point Park U (PA)
Quinnipiac U (CT)
Ramapo Coll of New Jersey (NJ)
Rivier Coll (NH)
Roosevelt U (IL)
Sage Coll of Albany (NY)
St. John's U (NY)
Schreiner U (TX)
Scripps Coll (CA)
South U (AL)
South U (GA)
State U of NY Coll at Fredonia (NY)
Suffolk U (MA)
United States Air Force Acad (CO)
Université de Montréal (QC, Canada)
Université de Sherbrooke (QC, Canada)
Université Laval (QC, Canada)
U of Alberta (AB, Canada)
U of Baltimore (MD)
U of Calgary (AB, Canada)
U of Calif, Berkeley (CA)
U of Calif, Santa Cruz (CA)
U of Detroit Mercy (MI)
U of Evansville (IN)
U of Hartford (CT)
U of Hartford (CT)
U of Illinois at Springfield (IL)
U of Massachusetts Amherst (MA)
U of Massachusetts Boston (MA)
The U of Montana–Missoula (MT)
U of New Brunswick Fredericton (NB, Canada)
U of New Haven (CT)
U of Pittsburgh (PA)
U of West Los Angeles (CA)
U of Windsor (ON, Canada)
U of Windsor (ON, Canada)
U of Wisconsin–Superior (WI)
Villa Julie Coll (MD)
Virginia Intermont Coll (VA)
Webster U (MO)
Wilmington Coll (DE)
Winona State U (MN)
York U (ON, Canada)

LIBERAL ARTS AND SCIENCES AND HUMANITIES RELATED

Baldwin-Wallace Coll (OH)
Barton Coll (NC)
Beacon Coll (FL)
Brigham Young U (UT)
Central Christian Coll of Kansas (KS)
Chester Coll of New England (NH)
The Colorado Coll (CO)
Duquesne U (PA)
Florida Atlantic U (FL)
Geneva Coll (PA)
Goddard Coll (VT)
Howard Payne U (TX)
Huron U USA in London(United Kingdom)
The Johns Hopkins U (MD)
Keystone Coll (PA)
Lambuth U (TN)
Malone Coll (OH)
Northern Arizona U (AZ)
Northwest Christian Coll (OR)
Ohio U (OH)
Saint Anselm Coll (NH)
St. John's Coll (NM)
Saint Mary's Coll of California (CA)
Sarah Lawrence Coll (NY)
Shimer Coll (IL)
Southwestern Coll (KS)
Troy State U Montgomery (AL)
Tulane U (LA)
The U of Akron (OH)
U of Calif, Los Angeles (CA)
U of Louisville (KY)
U of Massachusetts Amherst (MA)
U of Nebraska–Lincoln (NE)
U of North Dakota (ND)
U of South Alabama (AL)
U of Utah (UT)
U of Wisconsin–Whitewater (WI)
Vassar Coll (NY)
Virginia Intermont Coll (VA)
Washington State U (WA)
Wright State U (OH)

LIBERAL ARTS AND SCIENCES/ LIBERAL STUDIES

Abilene Christian U (TX)
Adams State Coll (CO)
Alabama State U (AL)
Alaska Pacific U (AK)
Albertus Magnus Coll (CT)
Alcorn State U (MS)
Alderson-Broaddus Coll (WV)
Alliant Intl U–México City(Mexico)
Alma Coll (MI)
Alvernia Coll (PA)
Alverno Coll (WI)
American Intl Coll (MA)
Anderson Coll (SC)
Andrews U (MI)
Angelo State U (TX)
Antioch U Los Angeles (CA)
Antioch U Seattle (WA)
Appalachian State U (NC)
Aquinas Coll (MI)
Arcadia U (PA)
Arkansas Baptist Coll (AR)
Armstrong Atlantic State U (GA)
Ashland U (OH)
Athabasca U (AB, Canada)
Auburn U Montgomery (AL)
Augsburg Coll (MN)
Augustana Coll (IL)
Augustana Coll (SD)
Averett U (VA)
Azusa Pacific U (CA)
Ball State U (IN)
Barry U (FL)
Bay Path Coll (MA)
Beacon Coll (FL)
Becker Coll (MA)
Bellarmine U (KY)
Bemidji State U (MN)
Benedictine Coll (KS)
Bennington Coll (VT)
Bentley Coll (MA)
Bethany Lutheran Coll (MN)
Bethel Coll (IN)
Bethel Coll (TN)
Bethune-Cookman Coll (FL)
Bishop's U (QC, Canada)
Blackburn Coll (IL)
Bluefield Coll (VA)
Boise State U (ID)
Bowling Green State U (OH)
Bradley U (IL)
Brescia U (KY)
Bridgewater Coll (VA)
Brigham Young U (UT)
Brock U (ON, Canada)
Bryan Coll (TN)
State U of NY Coll at Buffalo (NY)
Burlington Coll (VT)
Cabrini Coll (PA)
California Baptist U (CA)
California Lutheran U (CA)
California Polytechnic State U, San Luis Obispo (CA)
California State Polytechnic U, Pomona (CA)
California State U, Chico (CA)
California State U, Dominguez Hills (CA)
California State U, Fresno (CA)
California State U, Fullerton (CA)
California State U, Hayward (CA)
California State U, Long Beach (CA)
California State U, Los Angeles (CA)
California State U, Sacramento (CA)
California State U, San Bernardino (CA)
California State U, San Marcos (CA)
California State U, Stanislaus (CA)
California U of Pennsylvania (PA)
Calumet Coll of Saint Joseph (IN)
Capital U (OH)
Cardinal Stritch U (WI)
Carlow Coll (PA)
Carnegie Mellon U (PA)
Carson-Newman Coll (TN)
Cascade Coll (OR)
Cazenovia Coll (NY)
Cedar Crest Coll (PA)
Centenary Coll of Louisiana (LA)
Central Christian Coll of Kansas (KS)
Chapman U (CA)
Charter Oak State Coll (CT)
Chowan Coll (NC)
Christian Heritage Coll (CA)
Clarion U of Pennsylvania (PA)
Clarkson U (NY)
Cleveland State U (OH)
Coastal Carolina U (SC)
Coe Coll (IA)
Coll for Lifelong Learning (NH)
Coll Misericordia (PA)
Coll of Mount St. Joseph (OH)
Coll of Mount Saint Vincent (NY)
The Coll of New Rochelle (NY)
Coll of Notre Dame of Maryland (MD)
Coll of Saint Benedict (MN)
Coll of St. Joseph (VT)
The Coll of Saint Rose (NY)
The Coll of St. Scholastica (MN)
Coll of Staten Island of the City U of NY (NY)
Coll of the Atlantic (ME)
Colorado Christian U (CO)
Colorado State U (CO)
Columbia Coll (MO)
Columbia Coll (SC)
Columbia Coll Chicago (IL)
Columbia Union Coll (MD)
Conception Sem Coll (MO)
Concordia Coll (NY)
Concordia U (CA)
Concordia U (OR)
Concordia U at Austin (TX)
Concordia U Wisconsin (WI)
Cornell Coll (IA)
Cornell U (NY)
Crichton Coll (TN)
Crossroads Coll (MN)
Crown Coll (MN)
Cumberland U (TN)
Dallas Baptist U (TX)
Defiance Coll (OH)
DeSales U (PA)
Dickinson State U (ND)
Dominican U of California (CA)
Dowling Coll (NY)
D'Youville Coll (NY)
East Carolina U (NC)
Eastern Illinois U (IL)
Eastern Mennonite U (VA)
Eastern Nazarene Coll (MA)
Eastern New Mexico U (NM)
Eastern Oregon U (OR)
Eastern Washington U (WA)
East Stroudsburg U of Pennsylvania (PA)
Edgewood Coll (WI)
Edinboro U of Pennsylvania (PA)
Elmira Coll (NY)
Elms Coll (MA)
Emory U (GA)
Endicott Coll (MA)
Eugene Lang Coll, New School U (NY)
Eureka Coll (IL)
The Evergreen State Coll (WA)
Excelsior Coll (NY)
Faulkner U (AL)
Ferrum Coll (VA)
Flagler Coll (FL)
Florida Atlantic U (FL)
Florida Coll (FL)
Florida Gulf Coast U (FL)
Florida Intl U (FL)
Fontbonne U (MO)
Fordham U (NY)
Fort Hays State U (KS)
Fort Lewis Coll (CO)
Framingham State Coll (MA)
The Franciscan U (IA)
Francis Marion U (SC)
Franklin Pierce Coll (NH)
Freed-Hardeman U (TN)
Fresno Pacific U (CA)
Frostburg State U (MD)
Gannon U (PA)
Gardner-Webb U (NC)
George Mason U (VA)
Georgetown U (DC)
The George Washington U (DC)
Georgian Court U (NJ)
Gettysburg Coll (PA)
Gonzaga U (WA)
Goshen Coll (IN)
Governors State U (IL)
Graceland U (IA)
Grace U (NE)
Grand Canyon U (AZ)
Grand Valley State U (MI)
Grand View Coll (IA)
Greenville Coll (IL)
Hampshire Coll (MA)
Hannibal-LaGrange Coll (MO)
Harvard U (MA)
Hastings Coll (NE)
Hawai'i Pacific U (HI)
Hobart and William Smith Colls (NY)
Hofstra U (NY)
Hollins U (VA)
Holy Names Coll (CA)
Houghton Coll (NY)
Houston Baptist U (TX)
Howard Payne U (TX)
Humboldt State U (CA)
Huntingdon Coll (AL)
Huron U USA in London(United Kingdom)
Husson Coll (ME)
Illinois Coll (IL)
Illinois State U (IL)
Indiana State U (IN)
Iowa State U of Science and Technology (IA)
Iowa Wesleyan Coll (IA)
Ithaca Coll (NY)
Jacksonville U (FL)
James Madison U (VA)
John F. Kennedy U (CA)
The Johns Hopkins U (MD)
Johnson C. Smith U (NC)
Johnson State Coll (VT)
Juniata Coll (PA)
Kansas Wesleyan U (KS)
Keene State Coll (NH)
Kent State U (OH)
Kentucky State U (KY)
Keuka Coll (NY)
Kutztown U of Pennsylvania (PA)
Lakehead U (ON, Canada)
Lamar U (TX)
Lander U (SC)
La Roche Coll (PA)
La Salle U (PA)
Lasell Coll (MA)
Laurentian U (ON, Canada)
Lebanon Valley Coll (PA)
Lesley U (MA)
Lewis U (IL)
Limestone Coll (SC)
Lincoln Memorial U (TN)
Lindenwood U (MO)
Lipscomb U (TN)
Lock Haven U of Pennsylvania (PA)
Long Island U, Brooklyn Campus (NY)
Long Island U, C.W. Post Campus (NY)
Long Island U, Southampton Coll, Friends World Program (NY)
Long Island U, Southampton Coll (NY)
Longwood U (VA)
Loras Coll (IA)
Louisiana Coll (LA)
Louisiana State U and A&M Coll (LA)
Lourdes Coll (OH)
Loyola Marymount U (CA)
Lyndon State Coll (VT)
Lynn U (FL)
MacMurray Coll (IL)
Magdalen Coll (NH)
Malaspina U-Coll (BC, Canada)
Manhattan Coll (NY)
Mansfield U of Pennsylvania (PA)
Marian Coll of Fond du Lac (WI)
Marietta Coll (OH)
Mars Hill Coll (NC)
Marymount Coll of Fordham U (NY)
Marymount Manhattan Coll (NY)
Marymount U (VA)
Maryville U of Saint Louis (MO)
Mary Washington Coll (VA)
Massachusetts Inst of Technology (MA)
The Master's Coll and Sem (CA)
McNeese State U (LA)
Medaille Coll (NY)
Menlo Coll (CA)
Mercer U (GA)
Mercyhurst Coll (PA)
Methodist Coll (NC)
Metropolitan State U (MN)
Middlebury Coll (VT)
Middle Tennessee State U (TN)
Midway Coll (KY)
Mills Coll (CA)
Minnesota State U Mankato (MN)
Mississippi Coll (MS)
Mississippi State U (MS)
Missouri Valley Coll (MO)
Mitchell Coll (CT)
Monmouth Coll (IL)
Montana State U–Billings (MT)
Montana Tech of The U of Montana (MT)
Morris Coll (SC)
Mount Allison U (NB, Canada)
Mount Aloysius Coll (PA)
Mount Ida Coll (MA)
Mount Marty Coll (SD)
Mount Mercy Coll (IA)
Mount Saint Mary Coll (NY)
Mount Saint Vincent U (NS, Canada)
Murray State U (KY)
National-Louis U (IL)
National U (CA)
Neumann Coll (PA)
Nevada State Coll at Henderson (NV)
New Coll of Florida (FL)
Newman U (KS)
New Mexico Inst of Mining and Technology (NM)
New Sch Bach of Arts, New Sch for Social Research (NY)
New York U (NY)
Niagara U (NY)
Nipissing U (ON, Canada)
North Carolina State U (NC)
North Central Coll (IL)
Northeastern Illinois U (IL)
Northeastern U (MA)
Northern Arizona U (AZ)
Northern Illinois U (IL)
Northern Michigan U (MI)
Northwestern State U of Louisiana (LA)
Northwestern U (IL)
Northwest Nazarene U (ID)
Notre Dame de Namur U (CA)
Nova Southeastern U (FL)
Nyack Coll (NY)
Oakland U (MI)
Ohio Dominican U (OH)
Ohio U (OH)
Ohio U–Chillicothe (OH)
Ohio U–Zanesville (OH)
Ohio Valley Coll (WV)
Okanagan U Coll (BC, Canada)
Oklahoma Christian U (OK)
Oklahoma City U (OK)
Oklahoma State U (OK)
Olivet Coll (MI)
Olivet Nazarene U (IL)
Oral Roberts U (OK)
Oregon State U (OR)
Our Lady of the Lake U of San Antonio (TX)
Pace U (NY)

Pacific Union Coll (CA)
Pacific U (OR)
Park U (MO)
Peace Coll (NC)
Penn State U Abington Coll (PA)
Penn State U Altoona Coll (PA)
Penn State U at Erie, The Behrend Coll (PA)
Penn State U Beaver Campus of the Commonwealth Coll (PA)
Penn State U Berks Cmps of Berks-Lehigh Valley Coll (PA)
Penn State U Delaware County Campus of the Commonwealth Coll (PA)
Penn State U DuBois Campus of the Commonwealth Coll (PA)
Penn State U Fayette Campus of the Commonwealth Coll (PA)
Penn State U Lehigh Valley Cmps of Berks-Lehigh Valley Coll (PA)
Penn State U McKeesport Campus of the Commonwealth Coll (PA)
Penn State U Mont Alto Campus of the Commonwealth Coll (PA)
Penn State U New Kensington Campus of the Commonwealth Coll (PA)
Penn State U Schuylkill Campus of the Capital Coll (PA)
Penn State U Shenango Campus of the Commonwealth Coll (PA)
Penn State U Univ Park Campus (PA)
Penn State U Wilkes-Barre Campus of the Commonwealth Coll (PA)
Penn State U Worthington Scranton Cmps Commonwealth Coll (PA)
Penn State U York Campus of the Commonwealth Coll (PA)
Pepperdine U, Malibu (CA)
Point Loma Nazarene U (CA)
Polytechnic U, Brooklyn Campus (NY)
Pomona Coll (CA)
Pontifical Catholic U of Puerto Rico (PR)
Portland State U (OR)
Providence Coll (RI)
Providence Coll and Theological Sem (MB, Canada)
Purdue U North Central (IN)
Quinnipiac U (CT)
Randolph-Macon Woman's Coll (VA)
Redeemer U Coll (ON, Canada)
Regis U (CO)
Reinhardt Coll (GA)
Rhode Island Coll (RI)
The Richard Stockton Coll of New Jersey (NJ)
Richmond, The American Intl U in London(United Kingdom)
Rivier Coll (NH)
Roger Williams U (RI)
Roosevelt U (IL)
Rowan U (NJ)
Rutgers, The State U of New Jersey, Camden (NJ)
Rutgers, The State U of New Jersey, New Brunswick/Piscataway (NJ)
Sacred Heart Major Sem (MI)
Sage Coll of Albany (NY)
St. Andrews Presbyterian Coll (NC)
St. Cloud State U (MN)
St. Edward's U (TX)
St. Francis Coll (NY)
St. Francis Xavier U (NS, Canada)
St. Gregory's U (OK)
St. John's Coll (MD)
St. John's Coll (NM)
St. John's U (NY)
Saint Joseph Coll (CT)
Saint Joseph's Coll of Maine (ME)
St. Joseph's Coll, Suffolk Campus (NY)
Saint Joseph Sem Coll (LA)
Saint Mary-of-the-Woods Coll (IN)
Saint Mary's Coll of California (CA)
St. Olaf Coll (MN)
St. Thomas U (FL)
Saint Vincent Coll (PA)
Saint Xavier U (IL)
Salem State Coll (MA)
Salisbury U (MD)
Salve Regina U (RI)
San Diego State U (CA)
San Francisco State U (CA)
San Jose State U (CA)
Santa Clara U (CA)
Sarah Lawrence Coll (NY)
Schreiner U (TX)
Seattle Pacific U (WA)
Seattle U (WA)
Seton Hall U (NJ)
Shaw U (NC)
Sheldon Jackson Coll (AK)
Shenandoah U (VA)
Shimer Coll (IL)
Shorter Coll (GA)
Simon Fraser U (BC, Canada)
Simpson Coll and Graduate School (CA)
Skidmore Coll (NY)
Sonoma State U (CA)
Southeastern Louisiana U (LA)
Southern Christian U (AL)
Southern Connecticut State U (CT)
Southern Illinois U Carbondale (IL)
Southern Illinois U Edwardsville (IL)
Southern Oregon U (OR)
Southern Vermont Coll (VT)
Southern Virginia U (VA)
Southwestern Coll (KS)
State U of NY Coll at Fredonia (NY)
State U of NY Coll at Oneonta (NY)
Stephens Coll (MO)
Sterling Coll (VT)
Suffolk U (MA)
Sweet Briar Coll (VA)
Syracuse U (NY)
Tarleton State U (TX)
Teikyo Post U (CT)
Tennessee State U (TN)
Texas A&M U–Commerce (TX)
Texas Christian U (TX)
Texas Southern U (TX)
Texas Tech U (TX)
Thomas Aquinas Coll (CA)
Thomas Edison State Coll (NJ)
Thomas More Coll (KY)
Thomas U (GA)
Trent U (ON, Canada)
Trinity Coll (DC)
Trinity Intl U (IL)
Trinity Western U (BC, Canada)
Tulane U (LA)
Tyndale U Coll & Sem (ON, Canada)
Union Coll (NY)
Union Inst & U (OH)
Université de Sherbrooke (QC, Canada)
The U of Akron (OH)
U of Alaska Southeast (AK)
U of Alberta (AB, Canada)
The U of Arizona (AZ)
U of Arkansas at Fort Smith (AR)
U of Arkansas at Little Rock (AR)
U of Baltimore (MD)
U of Bridgeport (CT)
The U of British Columbia (BC, Canada)
U of Calgary (AB, Canada)
U of Calif, Los Angeles (CA)
U of Calif, Riverside (CA)
U of Central Florida (FL)
U of Chicago (IL)
U of Cincinnati (OH)
U of Delaware (DE)
U of Evansville (IN)
U of Georgia (GA)
U of Hawaii at Manoa (HI)
U of Idaho (ID)
U of Illinois at Springfield (IL)
U of Illinois at Urbana–Champaign (IL)
U of Indianapolis (IN)
The U of Iowa (IA)
U of Judaism (CA)
U of Kansas (KS)
U of La Verne (CA)
U of Louisville (KY)
U of Maine at Farmington (ME)
U of Maine at Fort Kent (ME)
U of Maine at Presque Isle (ME)
U of Maryland Eastern Shore (MD)
U of Massachusetts Dartmouth (MA)
U of Massachusetts Lowell (MA)
The U of Memphis (TN)
U of Miami (FL)
U of Michigan (MI)
U of Michigan–Dearborn (MI)
U of Michigan–Flint (MI)
U of Minnesota, Morris (MN)
U of Mississippi (MS)
U of Missouri–Kansas City (MO)
The U of Montana–Missoula (MT)
The U of Montana–Western (MT)
U of Nebraska–Lincoln (NE)
U of New Brunswick Fredericton (NB, Canada)
U of New Haven (CT)
U of New Mexico (NM)
The U of North Carolina at Asheville (NC)
The U of North Carolina at Chapel Hill (NC)
The U of North Carolina at Greensboro (NC)
U of Northern Iowa (IA)
U of North Florida (FL)
U of Notre Dame (IN)
U of Oklahoma (OK)
U of Oregon (OR)
U of Ottawa (ON, Canada)
U of Pennsylvania (PA)
U of Pittsburgh (PA)
U of Pittsburgh at Bradford (PA)
U of Redlands (CA)
U of Regina (SK, Canada)
U of Rhode Island (RI)
U of St. Francis (IL)
U of Saint Francis (IN)
U of Saint Mary (KS)
U of St. Thomas (TX)
U of San Diego (CA)
U of San Francisco (CA)
U of Sioux Falls (SD)
U of South Carolina (SC)
U of South Carolina Aiken (SC)
The U of South Dakota (SD)
U of Southern Indiana (IN)
U of South Florida (FL)
The U of Tampa (FL)
The U of Texas at Austin (TX)
The U of Texas at Brownsville (TX)
The U of Texas at Tyler (TX)
U of the Incarnate Word (TX)
U of Toledo (OH)
U of Tulsa (OK)
U of Utah (UT)
U of Victoria (BC, Canada)
U of Virginia (VA)
The U of Virginia's Coll at Wise (VA)
U of Washington (WA)
U of Waterloo (ON, Canada)
U of Wisconsin–Oshkosh (WI)
U of Wisconsin–Platteville (WI)
U of Wisconsin–River Falls (WI)
U of Wisconsin–Whitewater (WI)
Urbana U (OH)
Utah State U (UT)
Utica Coll (NY)
Villa Julie Coll (MD)
Villanova U (PA)
Virginia Intermont Coll (VA)
Virginia State U (VA)
Virginia Wesleyan Coll (VA)
Viterbo U (WI)
Walsh U (OH)
Warner Pacific Coll (OR)
Washburn U (KS)
Washington Coll (MD)
Washington State U (WA)
Washington U in St. Louis (MO)
Weber State U (UT)
Webster U (MO)
Wesleyan U (CT)
Wesley Coll (DE)
West Chester U of Pennsylvania (PA)
Western Baptist Coll (OR)
Western Carolina U (NC)
Western Connecticut State U (CT)
Western Illinois U (IL)
Western New England Coll (MA)
Western Washington U (WA)
Westfield State Coll (MA)
Westminster Choir Coll of Rider U (NJ)
Westmont Coll (CA)
West Virginia U (WV)
Wheeling Jesuit U (WV)
Wichita State U (KS)
Wilberforce U (OH)
Wilkes U (PA)
William Jessup U (CA)
Williams Baptist Coll (AR)
Wingate U (NC)
Winona State U (MN)
Wittenberg U (OH)
Wright State U (OH)
Xavier U (OH)
York Coll (NE)
York Coll of the City U of New York (NY)
York U (ON, Canada)

LIBRARY SCIENCE
Appalachian State U (NC)
Chadron State Coll (NE)
Clarion U of Pennsylvania (PA)
Concord Coll (WV)
Kutztown U of Pennsylvania (PA)
Longwood U (VA)
Murray State U (KY)
Northeastern State U (OK)
St. Cloud State U (MN)
St. John's U (NY)
Southern Connecticut State U (CT)
Texas Woman's U (TX)
U of Houston–Clear Lake (TX)
The U of Maine at Augusta (ME)
U of Nebraska at Omaha (NE)
U of North Texas (TX)
U of Oklahoma (OK)
U of the District of Columbia (DC)

LIBRARY SCIENCE RELATED
Bethel U (MN)
U of Calif, Los Angeles (CA)
U of Great Falls (MT)

LINGUISTIC AND COMPARATIVE LANGUAGE STUDIES RELATED
Brigham Young U (UT)
U of Calif, Los Angeles (CA)

LINGUISTICS
Barnard Coll (NY)
Baylor U (TX)
Boston U (MA)
Brandeis U (MA)
Brigham Young U (UT)
Brock U (ON, Canada)
Brooklyn Coll of the City U of NY (NY)
Brown U (RI)
California State U, Chico (CA)
California State U, Dominguez Hills (CA)
California State U, Fresno (CA)
California State U, Fullerton (CA)
Carleton U (ON, Canada)
Central Coll (IA)
City Coll of the City U of NY (NY)
Cleveland State U (OH)
The Coll of William and Mary (VA)
Columbia Coll (NY)
Concordia U (QC, Canada)
Cornell U (NY)
Crown Coll (MN)
Dalhousie U (NS, Canada)
Dartmouth Coll (NH)
Duke U (NC)
Eastern Michigan U (MI)
Florida Atlantic U (FL)
Georgetown U (DC)
Grinnell Coll (IA)
Hampshire Coll (MA)
Harvard U (MA)
Indiana U Bloomington (IN)
Inter American U of PR, San Germán Campus (PR)
Iowa State U of Science and Technology (IA)
Judson Coll (IL)
Lawrence U (WI)
Lehman Coll of the City U of NY (NY)
Macalester Coll (MN)
Marlboro Coll (VT)
Massachusetts Inst of Technology (MA)
McGill U (QC, Canada)
Memorial U of Newfoundland (NL, Canada)
Miami U (OH)
Miami U Hamilton (OH)
Montclair State U (NJ)
Moody Bible Inst (IL)
Mount Saint Vincent U (NS, Canada)
New York U (NY)
Northeastern Illinois U (IL)
Northeastern U (MA)
Northwestern U (IL)
Oakland U (MI)
The Ohio State U (OH)
Ohio U (OH)
Pitzer Coll (CA)
Pomona Coll (CA)
Portland State U (OR)
Queens Coll of the City U of NY (NY)
Queen's U at Kingston (ON, Canada)
Reed Coll (OR)
Rice U (TX)
Rutgers, The State U of New Jersey, New Brunswick/Piscataway (NJ)
St. Cloud State U (MN)
San Diego State U (CA)
San Jose State U (CA)
Scripps Coll (CA)
Simon Fraser U (BC, Canada)
Southern Illinois U Carbondale (IL)
Stanford U (CA)
State U of NY at Binghamton (NY)
State U of NY at Oswego (NY)
Stony Brook U, State U of New York (NY)
Swarthmore Coll (PA)
Syracuse U (NY)
Trinity Western U (BC, Canada)
Tulane U (LA)
Université de Montréal (QC, Canada)
Université Laval (QC, Canada)
State U of NY at Albany (NY)
U at Buffalo, The State U of New York (NY)
U of Alaska Fairbanks (AK)
U of Alberta (AB, Canada)
The U of Arizona (AZ)
The U of British Columbia (BC, Canada)
U of Calgary (AB, Canada)
U of Calif, Berkeley (CA)
U of Calif, Davis (CA)
U of Calif, Irvine (CA)
U of Calif, Los Angeles (CA)
U of Calif, Riverside (CA)
U of Calif, San Diego (CA)
U of Calif, Santa Barbara (CA)
U of Calif, Santa Cruz (CA)
U of Chicago (IL)
U of Cincinnati (OH)
U of Colorado at Boulder (CO)
U of Connecticut (CT)
U of Delaware (DE)
U of Florida (FL)
U of Georgia (GA)
U of Hawaii at Hilo (HI)
U of Illinois at Urbana–Champaign (IL)
The U of Iowa (IA)
U of Kansas (KS)
U of Kentucky (KY)
U of King's Coll (NS, Canada)
U of Maryland, Baltimore County (MD)
U of Maryland, Coll Park (MD)
U of Massachusetts Amherst (MA)
U of Michigan (MI)
U of Minnesota, Twin Cities Campus (MN)
U of Mississippi (MS)
U of Missouri–Columbia (MO)
The U of Montana–Missoula (MT)
U of New Brunswick Fredericton (NB, Canada)
U of New Hampshire (NH)
U of New Mexico (NM)
The U of North Carolina at Chapel Hill (NC)
The U of North Carolina at Greensboro (NC)
U of Oklahoma (OK)
U of Oregon (OR)
U of Ottawa (ON, Canada)
U of Pennsylvania (PA)
U of Pittsburgh (PA)
U of Regina (SK, Canada)
U of Rochester (NY)
U of Saskatchewan (SK, Canada)
U of Southern California (CA)
U of Southern Maine (ME)
The U of Texas at Austin (TX)
U of Toledo (OH)
U of Toronto (ON, Canada)
U of Utah (UT)
U of Victoria (BC, Canada)
U of Washington (WA)
The U of Western Ontario (ON, Canada)
U of Windsor (ON, Canada)
U of Wisconsin–Madison (WI)
U of Wisconsin–Milwaukee (WI)
Washington State U (WA)
Wayne State U (MI)
Wellesley Coll (MA)
Western Washington U (WA)
Wright State U (OH)
Yale U (CT)
York U (ON, Canada)

LINGUISTICS OF ASL AND OTHER SIGN LANGUAGES
Kent State U (OH)

LITERATURE
Agnes Scott Coll (GA)
Alderson-Broaddus Coll (WV)
Alfred U (NY)
American U (DC)
Antioch Coll (OH)
Arcadia U (PA)
Augustana Coll (IL)
Ave Maria Coll (MI)
Bard Coll (NY)
Barry U (FL)
Beloit Coll (WI)
Bennington Coll (VT)
Baruch Coll of the City U of NY (NY)
Bishop's U (QC, Canada)
Blackburn Coll (IL)
Boise State U (ID)
Brock U (ON, Canada)
Brown U (RI)

Bryan Coll (TN)
Burlington Coll (VT)
California Inst of Technology (CA)
California State U, Dominguez Hills (CA)
California State U, Long Beach (CA)
Capital U (OH)
Carnegie Mellon U (PA)
Carson-Newman Coll (TN)
Castleton State Coll (VT)
Cazenovia Coll (NY)
Chapman U (CA)
Chicago State U (IL)
Christendom Coll (VA)
Christopher Newport U (VA)
City Coll of the City U of NY (NY)
Claremont McKenna Coll (CA)
Clark U (MA)
Coe Coll (IA)
Coll of St. Catherine (MN)
Coll of the Atlantic (ME)
Coll of the Holy Cross (MA)
Columbia U, School of General Studies (NY)
Columbus State U (GA)
Concordia U (QC, Canada)
Dalhousie U (NS, Canada)
Davis & Elkins Coll (WV)
Defiance Coll (OH)
DePaul U (IL)
Duke U (NC)
East Central U (OK)
Eastern Washington U (WA)
Eckerd Coll (FL)
Elmira Coll (NY)
Emory U (GA)
Eugene Lang Coll, New School U (NY)
Eureka Coll (IL)
Excelsior Coll (NY)
Florida State U (FL)
Fordham U (NY)
Fort Lewis Coll (CO)
Framingham State Coll (MA)
Franklin Coll Switzerland(Switzerland)
Franklin Pierce Coll (NH)
Fresno Pacific U (CA)
Gettysburg Coll (PA)
Gonzaga U (WA)
Graceland U (IA)
Grand Canyon U (AZ)
Grand Valley State U (MI)
Grove City Coll (PA)
Hamilton Coll (NY)
Hampshire Coll (MA)
Harvard U (MA)
Hastings Coll (NE)
Hawai'i Pacific U (HI)
High Point U (NC)
Houghton Coll (NY)
Hunter Coll of the City U of NY (NY)
Immaculata U (PA)
Indiana U Bloomington (IN)
Inter American U of PR, San Germán Campus (PR)
Jewish Theological Sem of America (NY)
John Cabot U(Italy)
John Carroll U (OH)
The Johns Hopkins U (MD)
Johnson State Coll (VT)
Judson Coll (IL)
Kansas Wesleyan U (KS)
Kenyon Coll (OH)
Lake Superior State U (MI)
Lycoming Coll (PA)
Marist Coll (NY)
Marlboro Coll (VT)
Marymount Coll of Fordham U (NY)
Massachusetts Coll of Liberal Arts (MA)
Memorial U of Newfoundland (NL, Canada)
Middlebury Coll (VT)
Minnesota State U Mankato (MN)
Morningside Coll (IA)
Mount Allison U (NB, Canada)
Mount Saint Vincent U (NS, Canada)
Mount Vernon Nazarene U (OH)
Naropa U (CO)
Nazareth Coll of Rochester (NY)
New Coll of California (CA)
New Coll of Florida (FL)
North Central Coll (IL)
North Park U (IL)
Ohio Wesleyan U (OH)
Olivet Nazarene U (IL)
Oregon State U (OR)
Otterbein Coll (OH)
Pace U (NY)
Pacific Lutheran U (WA)
Pacific U (OR)
Pitzer Coll (CA)
Quinnipiac U (CT)
Ramapo Coll of New Jersey (NJ)
Reed Coll (OR)
Rochester Coll (MI)
Rockford Coll (IL)
Roosevelt U (IL)
Sacred Heart U (CT)
Saint Francis U (PA)
St. John's Coll (NM)
Saint Leo U (FL)
Saint Mary's Coll of California (CA)
Salem State Coll (MA)
San Francisco State U (CA)
Sarah Lawrence Coll (NY)
Schreiner U (TX)
Shimer Coll (IL)
Simon's Rock Coll of Bard (MA)
Skidmore Coll (NY)
Sonoma State U (CA)
Southern Connecticut State U (CT)
Southern Nazarene U (OK)
Southern Vermont Coll (VT)
Southwestern U (TX)
State U of NY at Binghamton (NY)
State U of NY Coll at Brockport (NY)
State U of NY Coll at Old Westbury (NY)
Syracuse U (NY)
Taylor U (IN)
Thomas More Coll of Liberal Arts (NH)
Trent U (ON, Canada)
United States Military Acad (NY)
Université de Montréal (QC, Canada)
Université Laval (QC, Canada)
The U of Akron (OH)
U of Alberta (AB, Canada)
U of Baltimore (MD)
U of Calif, Irvine (CA)
U of Calif, San Diego (CA)
U of Calif, Santa Cruz (CA)
U of Cincinnati (OH)
U of Evansville (IN)
The U of Iowa (IA)
U of Judaism (CA)
U of Michigan (MI)
U of Missouri–St. Louis (MO)
The U of Montana–Western (MT)
U of New Brunswick Fredericton (NB, Canada)
U of New Hampshire (NH)
U of Ottawa (ON, Canada)
U of Pittsburgh at Greensburg (PA)
U of Pittsburgh at Johnstown (PA)
U of Redlands (CA)
The U of Texas at Dallas (TX)
U of the Sacred Heart (PR)
U of the South (TN)
U of Toledo (OH)
U of Toronto (ON, Canada)
U of Victoria (BC, Canada)
U of Windsor (ON, Canada)
U of Wisconsin–Milwaukee (WI)
Washington U in St. Louis (MO)
Wayne State Coll (NE)
Webster U (MO)
Western Washington U (WA)
Westfield State Coll (MA)
West Virginia Wesleyan Coll (WV)
Wheaton Coll (MA)
Wilberforce U (OH)
William Paterson U of New Jersey (NJ)
Williams Coll (MA)
Yale U (CT)
York U (ON, Canada)

LIVESTOCK MANAGEMENT

Sterling Coll (VT)

LOGISTICS AND MATERIALS MANAGEMENT

Auburn U (AL)
Bowling Green State U (OH)
Brigham Young U (UT)
Central Michigan U (MI)
Clarkson U (NY)
Duquesne U (PA)
Eastern Michigan U (MI)
Elmhurst Coll (IL)
Florida Intl U (FL)
Georgia Coll & State U (GA)
Georgia Southern U (GA)
Iowa State U of Science and Technology (IA)
Maine Maritime Acad (ME)
Michigan State U (MI)
Niagara U (NY)
Northeastern U (MA)
The Ohio State U (OH)
Park U (MO)
Penn State U Abington Coll (PA)
Penn State U Altoona Coll (PA)
Penn State U at Erie, The Behrend Coll (PA)
Penn State U Beaver Campus of the Commonwealth Coll (PA)
Penn State U Berks Cmps of Berks-Lehigh Valley Coll (PA)
Penn State U Delaware County Campus of the Commonwealth Coll (PA)
Penn State U DuBois Campus of the Commonwealth Coll (PA)
Penn State U Fayette Campus of the Commonwealth Coll (PA)
Penn State U Hazleton Campus of the Commonwealth Coll (PA)
Penn State U Lehigh Valley Cmps of Berks-Lehigh Valley Coll (PA)
Penn State U McKeesport Campus of the Commonwealth Coll (PA)
Penn State U Mont Alto Campus of the Commonwealth Coll (PA)
Penn State U New Kensington Campus of the Commonwealth Coll (PA)
Penn State U Schuylkill Campus of the Capital Coll (PA)
Penn State U Shenango Campus of the Commonwealth Coll (PA)
Penn State U Univ Park Campus (PA)
Penn State U Wilkes-Barre Campus of the Commonwealth Coll (PA)
Penn State U Worthington Scranton Cmps Commonwealth Coll (PA)
Penn State U York Campus of the Commonwealth Coll (PA)
Portland State U (OR)
Robert Morris U (PA)
St. John's U (NY)
Syracuse U (NY)
Thomas Edison State Coll (NJ)
U of Arkansas (AR)
The U of Findlay (OH)
U of Nevada, Reno (NV)
U of North Texas (TX)
The U of Tennessee (TN)
U of Toledo (OH)
Wayne State U (MI)
Weber State U (UT)
Wright State U (OH)

MANAGEMENT INFORMATION SYSTEMS

Albertus Magnus Coll (CT)
Alderson-Broaddus Coll (WV)
Alliant Intl U (CA)
Alliant Intl U–México City(Mexico)
Amberton U (TX)
American Coll of Thessaloniki(Greece)
American InterContinental U (CA)
American InterContinental U-London(United Kingdom)
American Intl Coll (MA)
American U (DC)
Angelo State U (TX)
Appalachian State U (NC)
Arcadia U (PA)
Arizona State U (AZ)
Auburn U (AL)
Auburn U Montgomery (AL)
Augsburg Coll (MN)
Augustana Coll (SD)
Aurora U (IL)
Azusa Pacific U (CA)
Babson Coll (MA)
Baker Coll of Flint (MI)
Ball State U (IN)
Barry U (FL)
Baylor U (TX)
Bellevue U (NE)
Baruch Coll of the City U of NY (NY)
Bethel Coll (KS)
Bishop's U (QC, Canada)
Boston Coll (MA)
Boston U (MA)
Bowling Green State U (OH)
Bradley U (IL)
Briar Cliff U (IA)
Bridgewater Coll (VA)
Bridgewater State Coll (MA)
Brigham Young U (UT)
Buena Vista U (IA)
Cabrini Coll (PA)
California Polytechnic State U, San Luis Obispo (CA)
California State U, Chico (CA)
California State U, Dominguez Hills (CA)
California State U, Fresno (CA)
California State U, Hayward (CA)
California State U, Long Beach (CA)
California State U, Sacramento (CA)
California State U, San Bernardino (CA)
Calvin Coll (MI)
Capitol Coll (MD)
Carleton U (ON, Canada)
Carson-Newman Coll (TN)
Central Connecticut State U (CT)
Central Michigan U (MI)
Central Missouri State U (MO)
Central State U (OH)
Charleston Southern U (SC)
Chatham Coll (PA)
Chicago State U (IL)
Christian Brothers U (TN)
Clarke Coll (IA)
Clarkson U (NY)
Clayton Coll & State U (GA)
Cleary U (MI)
Coker Coll (SC)
Coll Misericordia (PA)
Coll of St. Catherine (MN)
Coll of Saint Mary (NE)
Coll of Santa Fe (NM)
Colorado Christian U (CO)
Colorado Tech U Sioux Falls Campus (SD)
Concordia U (NE)
Concordia U (QC, Canada)
Concordia U, St. Paul (MN)
Cornerstone U (MI)
Creighton U (NE)
Dallas Baptist U (TX)
Dalton State Coll (GA)
Daniel Webster Coll (NH)
Davenport U, Dearborn (MI)
Davis & Elkins Coll (WV)
Delaware Valley Coll (PA)
Delta State U (MS)
DePaul U (IL)
DeSales U (PA)
Dominican Coll (NY)
Dordt Coll (IA)
Drexel U (PA)
Duquesne U (PA)
East Carolina U (NC)
East Central U (OK)
Eastern Connecticut State U (CT)
Eastern Illinois U (IL)
Eastern Kentucky U (KY)
Eastern Michigan U (MI)
Eastern New Mexico U (NM)
Eastern U (PA)
Eastern Washington U (WA)
Elmhurst Coll (IL)
Eureka Coll (IL)
Excelsior Coll (NY)
Fairfield U (CT)
Ferris State U (MI)
Florida Ag and Mech U (FL)
Florida Atlantic U (FL)
Florida Gulf Coast U (FL)
Florida Inst of Technology (FL)
Florida Intl U (FL)
Florida Metropolitan U-Fort Lauderdale Coll (FL)
Florida Southern Coll (FL)
Florida State U (FL)
Fontbonne U (MO)
Fordham U (NY)
Francis Marion U (SC)
Franklin U (OH)
Gannon U (PA)
Gardner-Webb U (NC)
George Fox U (OR)
Georgetown Coll (KY)
Georgia Southern U (GA)
Georgia Southwestern State U (GA)
Goldey-Beacom Coll (DE)
Governors State U (IL)
Grace Coll (IN)
Graceland U (IA)
Grand Valley State U (MI)
Grand View Coll (IA)
Greenville Coll (IL)
Hawai'i Pacific U (HI)
HEC Montreal (QC, Canada)
Henderson State U (AR)
Herzing Coll, Minneapolis Drafting School Division (MN)
Hofstra U (NY)
Husson Coll (ME)
Illinois Coll (IL)
Indiana State U (IN)
Indiana U Bloomington (IN)
Indiana U of Pennsylvania (PA)
Inter American U of PR, Aguadilla Campus (PR)
Inter American U of PR, Bayamón Campus (PR)
Iona Coll (NY)
Iowa State U of Science and Technology (IA)
Jacksonville U (FL)
Jamestown Coll (ND)
Johnson State Coll (VT)
Judson Coll (IL)
Kaplan Coll (IA)
Kettering U (MI)
Lakehead U (ON, Canada)
La Salle U (PA)
Lehigh U (PA)
Le Moyne Coll (NY)
LeTourneau U (TX)
Lewis U (IL)
Liberty U (VA)
Lindenwood U (MO)
Long Island U, C.W. Post Campus (NY)
Longwood U (VA)
Loras Coll (IA)
Louisiana Tech U (LA)
Loyola U Chicago (IL)
Luther Coll (IA)
MacMurray Coll (IL)
Madonna U (MI)
Marquette U (WI)
Maryville U of Saint Louis (MO)
The Master's Coll and Sem (CA)
McMurry U (TX)
Metropolitan State U (MN)
Miami U (OH)
Michigan Technological U (MI)
Middle Tennessee State U (TN)
Millikin U (IL)
Milwaukee School of Eng (WI)
Minnesota State U Moorhead (MN)
Minot State U (ND)
Mississippi State U (MS)
Montclair State U (NJ)
Morehead State U (KY)
Morgan State U (MD)
Morningside Coll (IA)
Mount Saint Vincent U (NS, Canada)
Murray State U (KY)
National American U, Denver (CO)
National American U (NM)
National American U (SD)
National American U–Sioux Falls Branch (SD)
Nazareth Coll of Rochester (NY)
Newman U (KS)
New Mexico Highlands U (NM)
New York Inst of Technology (NY)
New York U (NY)
Nicholls State U (LA)
Nichols Coll (MA)
North Central Coll (IL)
Northeastern U (MA)
Northern Arizona U (AZ)
Northern Illinois U (IL)
Northern Michigan U (MI)
Northern State U (SD)
Northwest Christian Coll (OR)
Northwestern Coll (MN)
Northwood U (MI)
Northwood U, Florida Campus (FL)
Northwood U, Texas Campus (TX)
Oakland U (MI)
The Ohio State U (OH)
Ohio U (OH)
Oklahoma Baptist U (OK)
Oklahoma City U (OK)
Oklahoma State U (OK)
Old Dominion U (VA)
Oral Roberts U (OK)
Oregon Inst of Technology (OR)
Oregon State U (OR)
Pacific Lutheran U (WA)
Pacific Union Coll (CA)
Paine Coll (GA)
Park U (MO)
Peirce Coll (PA)
Pennsylvania Coll of Technology (PA)
Penn State U Abington Coll (PA)
Penn State U Altoona Coll (PA)
Penn State U at Erie, The Behrend Coll (PA)
Penn State U Beaver Campus of the Commonwealth Coll (PA)
Penn State U Berks Cmps of Berks-Lehigh Valley Coll (PA)
Penn State U Delaware County Campus of the Commonwealth Coll (PA)
Penn State U DuBois Campus of the Commonwealth Coll (PA)
Penn State U Fayette Campus of the Commonwealth Coll (PA)
Penn State U Harrisburg Campus of the Capital Coll (PA)
Penn State U Hazleton Campus of the Commonwealth Coll (PA)
Penn State U Lehigh Valley Cmps of Berks-Lehigh Valley Coll (PA)
Penn State U McKeesport Campus of the Commonwealth Coll (PA)

Penn State U Mont Alto Campus of the Commonwealth Coll (PA)
Penn State U New Kensington Campus of the Commonwealth Coll (PA)
Penn State U Schuylkill Campus of the Capital Coll (PA)
Penn State U Shenango Campus of the Commonwealth Coll (PA)
Penn State U Univ Park Campus (PA)
Penn State U Wilkes-Barre Campus of the Commonwealth Coll (PA)
Penn State U Worthington Scranton Cmps Commonwealth Coll (PA)
Penn State U York Campus of the Commonwealth Coll (PA)
Pfeiffer U (NC)
Philadelphia U (PA)
Point Loma Nazarene U (CA)
Polytechnic U, Brooklyn Campus (NY)
Rensselaer Polytechnic Inst (NY)
Rhode Island Coll (RI)
Robert Morris U (PA)
Roberts Wesleyan Coll (NY)
Rochester Inst of Technology (NY)
Rockford Coll (IL)
Rocky Mountain Coll (MT)
Roger Williams U (RI)
Saint Francis U (PA)
St. Francis Xavier U (NS, Canada)
St. Gregory's U (OK)
St. John Fisher Coll (NY)
St. John's U (NY)
Saint Joseph's Coll (IN)
Saint Joseph's U (PA)
Saint Leo U (FL)
Saint Louis U (MO)
Saint Martin's Coll (WA)
Saint Mary's Coll (IN)
St. Norbert Coll (WI)
Salem State Coll (MA)
Salisbury U (MD)
Santa Clara U (CA)
Schreiner U (TX)
Seattle U (WA)
Seton Hall U (NJ)
Seton Hill U (PA)
Shawnee State U (OH)
Simmons Coll (MA)
Simon Fraser U (BC, Canada)
Simpson Coll and Graduate School (CA)
Southern Adventist U (TN)
Southern Illinois U Edwardsville (IL)
Southern Methodist U (TX)
Southern Nazarene U (OK)
Southwestern Coll (KS)
Southwest Missouri State U (MO)
Spring Arbor U (MI)
Springfield Coll (MA)
State U of West Georgia (GA)
Suffolk U (MA)
Tarleton State U (TX)
Teikyo Post U (CT)
Texas A&M U–Commerce (TX)
Texas A&M U–Texarkana (TX)
Texas State U-San Marcos (TX)
Texas Tech U (TX)
Texas Wesleyan U (TX)
Thiel Coll (PA)
Thomas Coll (ME)
Tiffin U (OH)
Touro U Intl (CA)
Trinity Christian Coll (IL)
Tri-State U (IN)
Troy State U (AL)
Université de Sherbrooke (QC, Canada)
U du Québec à Hull (QC, Canada)
The U of Alabama (AL)
The U of Alabama at Birmingham (AL)
The U of Alabama in Huntsville (AL)
U of Alberta (AB, Canada)
The U of Arizona (AZ)
U of Arkansas at Monticello (AR)
U of Baltimore (MD)
The U of British Columbia (BC, Canada)
U of Calgary (AB, Canada)
U of Central Arkansas (AR)
U of Central Florida (FL)
U of Cincinnati (OH)
U of Colorado at Boulder (CO)
U of Connecticut (CT)
U of Dayton (OH)
U of Denver (CO)
U of Georgia (GA)
U of Hartford (CT)
U of Hawaii at Manoa (HI)
U of Houston (TX)
U of Houston–Clear Lake (TX)
U of Idaho (ID)
U of Illinois at Chicago (IL)
The U of Iowa (IA)
The U of Lethbridge (AB, Canada)
U of Louisville (KY)
U of Mary Hardin-Baylor (TX)
U of Massachusetts Dartmouth (MA)
The U of Memphis (TN)
U of Minnesota, Twin Cities Campus (MN)
U of Mississippi (MS)
U of Missouri–Columbia (MO)
U of Missouri–St. Louis (MO)
U of Montevallo (AL)
U of Nebraska at Omaha (NE)
U of Nevada, Las Vegas (NV)
U of New Orleans (LA)
U of North Alabama (AL)
The U of North Carolina at Charlotte (NC)
The U of North Carolina at Greensboro (NC)
The U of North Carolina at Wilmington (NC)
U of Northern Iowa (IA)
U of North Texas (TX)
U of Notre Dame (IN)
U of Oklahoma (OK)
U of Ottawa (ON, Canada)
U of Pennsylvania (PA)
U of Phoenix–Atlanta Campus (GA)
U of Phoenix–Boston Campus (MA)
U of Phoenix–Chicago Campus (IL)
U of Phoenix–Cleveland Campus (OH)
U of Phoenix–Colorado Campus (CO)
U of Phoenix–Dallas Campus (TX)
U of Phoenix–Fort Lauderdale Campus (FL)
U of Phoenix–Hawaii Campus (HI)
U of Phoenix–Houston Campus (TX)
U of Phoenix–Jacksonville Campus (FL)
U of Phoenix–Maryland Campus (MD)
U of Phoenix–Metro Detroit Campus (MI)
U of Phoenix–New Mexico Campus (NM)
U of Phoenix–Northern California Campus (CA)
U of Phoenix–Oklahoma City Campus (OK)
U of Phoenix–Oregon Campus (OR)
U of Phoenix–Orlando Campus (FL)
U of Phoenix–Phoenix Campus (AZ)
U of Phoenix–Pittsburgh Campus (PA)
U of Phoenix–Puerto Rico Campus (PR)
U of Phoenix–Sacramento Campus (CA)
U of Phoenix–St. Louis Campus (MO)
U of Phoenix–San Diego Campus (CA)
U of Phoenix–Southern Arizona Campus (AZ)
U of Phoenix–Southern California Campus (CA)
U of Phoenix–Southern Colorado Campus (CO)
U of Phoenix–Tampa Campus (FL)
U of Phoenix–Tulsa Campus (OK)
U of Phoenix–Utah Campus (UT)
U of Phoenix–Vancouver Campus (BC, Canada)
U of Phoenix–Washington Campus (WA)
U of Phoenix–West Michigan Campus (MI)
U of Redlands (CA)
U of Rhode Island (RI)
U of Richmond (VA)
U of St. Thomas (TX)
U of San Francisco (CA)
U of Sioux Falls (SD)
U of South Florida (FL)
The U of Tennessee at Martin (TN)
The U of Texas at Arlington (TX)
The U of Texas at Austin (TX)
The U of Texas at Dallas (TX)
The U of Texas–Pan American (TX)
U of the Incarnate Word (TX)
U of Toledo (OH)
U of Tulsa (OK)
U of Utah (UT)
U of Washington (WA)
The U of West Alabama (AL)
U of West Florida (FL)
U of Windsor (ON, Canada)
U of Wisconsin–Green Bay (WI)
U of Wisconsin–La Crosse (WI)
U of Wisconsin–Milwaukee (WI)
U of Wisconsin–Oshkosh (WI)
U of Wisconsin–River Falls (WI)
U of Wisconsin–Whitewater (WI)
U of Wyoming (WY)
Upper Iowa U (IA)
Ursuline Coll (OH)
Villa Julie Coll (MD)
Villanova U (PA)
Virginia Polytechnic Inst and State U (VA)
Virginia State U (VA)
Virginia Union U (VA)
Viterbo U (WI)
Wake Forest U (NC)
Walla Walla Coll (WA)
Washington State U (WA)
Wayne State U (MI)
Weber State U (UT)
Webster U (MO)
Western Baptist Coll (OR)
Western Carolina U (NC)
Western Connecticut State U (CT)
Western Illinois U (IL)
Western Kentucky U (KY)
Western State Coll of Colorado (CO)
Western Washington U (WA)
Westfield State Coll (MA)
Westminster Coll (MO)
West Texas A&M U (TX)
Wichita State U (KS)
William Woods U (MO)
Wingate U (NC)
Winona State U (MN)
Winston-Salem State U (NC)
Worcester Polytechnic Inst (MA)
Wright State U (OH)
Xavier U (OH)
York U (ON, Canada)
Youngstown State U (OH)

MANAGEMENT INFORMATION SYSTEMS AND SERVICES RELATED

Anderson Coll (SC)
Argosy U/Sarasota (FL)
Bowling Green State U (OH)
Buena Vista U (IA)
California State U, Chico (CA)
Carroll Coll (WI)
Coll of Mount St. Joseph (OH)
Columbia Southern U (AL)
Crichton Coll (TN)
Florida Ag and Mech U (FL)
Fordham U (NY)
Greenville Coll (IL)
Lewis U (IL)
Midwestern State U (TX)
Oakland U (MI)
Purdue U (IN)
Rensselaer Polytechnic Inst (NY)
St. Bonaventure U (NY)
Southeastern Oklahoma State U (OK)
Southern Connecticut State U (CT)
Washington State U (WA)
Westminster Coll (UT)
Widener U (PA)

MANAGEMENT SCIENCE

American Coll of Thessaloniki(Greece)
American Public U System (WV)
Averett U (VA)
Caldwell Coll (NJ)
Capella U (MN)
Central Methodist Coll (MO)
Clarion U of Pennsylvania (PA)
The Coll of St. Scholastica (MN)
The Coll of Southeastern Europe, The American U of Athens(Greece)
Colorado Christian U (CO)
Columbia Coll (MO)
Cornell U (NY)
Dalhousie U (NS, Canada)
Duquesne U (PA)
Eastern Illinois U (IL)
Eastern U (PA)
Everglades U, Boca Raton (FL)
Franklin U (OH)
Georgia Inst of Technology (GA)
Goucher Coll (MD)
Grace Bible Coll (MI)
Hardin-Simmons U (TX)
HEC Montreal (QC, Canada)
Inter American U of PR, Bayamón Campus (PR)
Louisiana State U and A&M Coll (LA)
Louisiana Tech U (LA)
Lourdes Coll (OH)
Madonna U (MI)
Manhattan Coll (NY)
Marymount U (VA)
McGill U (QC, Canada)
Metropolitan State Coll of Denver (CO)
Miami U (OH)
Minnesota State U Mankato (MN)
Northeastern U (MA)
Nova Southeastern U (FL)
Oakland City U (IN)
Oakland U (MI)
Ohio Northern U (OH)
Oklahoma State U (OK)
Oral Roberts U (OK)
Rider U (NJ)
Rockhurst U (MO)
Rocky Mountain Coll (MT)
Roosevelt U (IL)
Rutgers, The State U of New Jersey, New Brunswick/Piscataway (NJ)
St. Ambrose U (IA)
St. Bonaventure U (NY)
St. Gregory's U (OK)
Saint Joseph's U (PA)
Saint Louis U (MO)
Salisbury U (MD)
Shippensburg U of Pennsylvania (PA)
Simon Fraser U (BC, Canada)
Southeastern Oklahoma State U (OK)
Southern Adventist U (TN)
Southern Illinois U Carbondale (IL)
Southern Methodist U (TX)
Southern Nazarene U (OK)
Southwestern Coll (KS)
State U of NY at Binghamton (NY)
State U of NY at Oswego (NY)
Stetson U (FL)
Texas A&M U (TX)
Texas Christian U (TX)
Trinity Intl U (IL)
Trinity U (TX)
Tuskegee U (AL)
United States Coast Guard Acad (CT)
The U of Alabama (AL)
U of Arkansas (AR)
U of Calif, San Diego (CA)
U of Connecticut (CT)
U of Florida (FL)
U of Great Falls (MT)
The U of Iowa (IA)
U of Kentucky (KY)
U of Mary (ND)
U of Maryland, Coll Park (MD)
U of Maryland U Coll (MD)
The U of Memphis (TN)
U of Minnesota, Morris (MN)
U of Missouri–St. Louis (MO)
U of Nebraska–Lincoln (NE)
U of Phoenix–Atlanta Campus (GA)
U of Phoenix–Chicago Campus (IL)
U of Phoenix–Colorado Campus (CO)
U of Phoenix–Dallas Campus (TX)
U of Phoenix–Fort Lauderdale Campus (FL)
U of Phoenix–Hawaii Campus (HI)
U of Phoenix–Houston Campus (TX)
U of Phoenix–Jacksonville Campus (FL)
U of Phoenix–Kansas City Campus (MO)
U of Phoenix–Maryland Campus (MD)
U of Phoenix–Metro Detroit Campus (MI)
U of Phoenix–New Mexico Campus (NM)
U of Phoenix–Northern California Campus (CA)
U of Phoenix–Oklahoma City Campus (OK)
U of Phoenix Online Campus (AZ)
U of Phoenix–Oregon Campus (OR)
U of Phoenix–Orlando Campus (FL)
U of Phoenix–Philadelphia Campus (PA)
U of Phoenix–Phoenix Campus (AZ)
U of Phoenix–Pittsburgh Campus (PA)
U of Phoenix–Sacramento Campus (CA)
U of Phoenix–St. Louis Campus (MO)
U of Phoenix–Southern Arizona Campus (AZ)
U of Phoenix–Southern Colorado Campus (CO)
U of Phoenix–Tampa Campus (FL)
U of Phoenix–Tulsa Campus (OK)
U of Phoenix–Utah Campus (UT)
U of Phoenix–Washington Campus (WA)
U of Phoenix–West Michigan Campus (MI)
U of Phoenix–Wisconsin Campus (WI)
The U of Scranton (PA)
U of South Carolina (SC)
U of South Florida (FL)
U of the Incarnate Word (TX)
U of Washington (WA)
U of Windsor (ON, Canada)
U of Wyoming (WY)
Valparaiso U (IN)
Wake Forest U (NC)
Washington State U (WA)
Wheeling Jesuit U (WV)
Wright State U (OH)
York U (ON, Canada)

MANAGEMENT SCIENCES AND QUANTITATIVE METHODS RELATED

The Coll of Southeastern Europe, The American U of Athens(Greece)
Georgia Coll & State U (GA)
Indiana State U (IN)
Ohio Northern U (OH)
Penn State U Abington Coll (PA)
Penn State U Altoona Coll (PA)
Penn State U at Erie, The Behrend Coll (PA)
Penn State U Beaver Campus of the Commonwealth Coll (PA)
Penn State U Berks Cmps of Berks-Lehigh Valley Coll (PA)
Penn State U Delaware County Campus of the Commonwealth Coll (PA)
Penn State U DuBois Campus of the Commonwealth Coll (PA)
Penn State U Fayette Campus of the Commonwealth Coll (PA)
Penn State U Hazleton Campus of the Commonwealth Coll (PA)
Penn State U Lehigh Valley Cmps of Berks-Lehigh Valley Coll (PA)
Penn State U McKeesport Campus of the Commonwealth Coll (PA)
Penn State U Mont Alto Campus of the Commonwealth Coll (PA)
Penn State U New Kensington Campus of the Commonwealth Coll (PA)
Penn State U Schuylkill Campus of the Capital Coll (PA)
Penn State U Shenango Campus of the Commonwealth Coll (PA)
Penn State U Univ Park Campus (PA)
Penn State U Wilkes-Barre Campus of the Commonwealth Coll (PA)
Penn State U Worthington Scranton Cmps Commonwealth Coll (PA)
Penn State U York Campus of the Commonwealth Coll (PA)
Rutgers, The State U of New Jersey, New Brunswick/Piscataway (NJ)
The U of Iowa (IA)
U of Pennsylvania (PA)
U of Toledo (OH)
Valparaiso U (IN)

MANUFACTURING ENGINEERING

Brigham Young U (UT)
California State U, Los Angeles (CA)
Clarkson U (NY)
Eastern Michigan U (MI)
Hofstra U (NY)
New Jersey Inst of Technology (NJ)
North Dakota State U (ND)
Northwestern U (IL)
Rensselaer Polytechnic Inst (NY)
Southern Illinois U Edwardsville (IL)
Texas State U-San Marcos (TX)
U of Calif, Berkeley (CA)
U of Calif, Los Angeles (CA)
U of Detroit Mercy (MI)
U of Hartford (CT)
U of Missouri–Rolla (MO)
The U of Texas–Pan American (TX)
U of Wisconsin–Stout (WI)
Virginia State U (VA)

MANUFACTURING TECHNOLOGY
Arizona State U East (AZ)
California State U, Long Beach (CA)
Central Connecticut State U (CT)
East Carolina U (NC)
Eastern Michigan U (MI)
Eastern Washington U (WA)
State U of NY at Farmingdale (NY)
Illinois Inst of Technology (IL)
Lewis-Clark State Coll (ID)
Midwestern State U (TX)
Morehead State U (KY)
Murray State U (KY)
Northern Michigan U (MI)
Pennsylvania Coll of Technology (PA)
Rochester Inst of Technology (NY)
Roger Williams U (RI)
Southwestern Coll (KS)
Tarleton State U (TX)
Texas A&M U (TX)
Texas State U-San Marcos (TX)
The U of Memphis (TN)
U of Nebraska at Omaha (NE)
U of Northern Iowa (IA)
The U of Texas at Brownsville (TX)
Western Carolina U (NC)
Western Illinois U (IL)
Western Washington U (WA)

MARINE BIOLOGY AND BIOLOGICAL OCEANOGRAPHY
Alabama State U (AL)
Alaska Pacific U (AK)
American U (DC)
Auburn U (AL)
Ball State U (IN)
Barry U (FL)
Bemidji State U (MN)
Boston U (MA)
Brown U (RI)
California State U, Long Beach (CA)
Coastal Carolina U (SC)
Coll of Charleston (SC)
Coll of the Atlantic (ME)
Dalhousie U (NS, Canada)
Dowling Coll (NY)
East Stroudsburg U of Pennsylvania (PA)
Eckerd Coll (FL)
Fairleigh Dickinson U, Florham (NJ)
Fairleigh Dickinson U, Teaneck-Metro Campus (NJ)
Florida Inst of Technology (FL)
Florida Intl U (FL)
Florida State U (FL)
Gettysburg Coll (PA)
Hampshire Coll (MA)
Hampton U (VA)
Harvard U (MA)
Hawai'i Pacific U (HI)
Humboldt State U (CA)
Jacksonville State U (AL)
Juniata Coll (PA)
Long Island U, Southampton Coll (NY)
Maine Maritime Acad (ME)
McGill U (QC, Canada)
Memorial U of Newfoundland (NL, Canada)
Mississippi State U (MS)
Missouri Southern State U (MO)
New Coll of Florida (FL)
Nicholls State U (LA)
Northeastern U (MA)
Northern Arizona U (AZ)
Nova Southeastern U (FL)
Old Dominion U (VA)
The Richard Stockton Coll of New Jersey (NJ)
Roger Williams U (RI)
Rutgers, The State U of New Jersey, New Brunswick/Piscataway (NJ)
Saint Francis U (PA)
Saint Joseph's Coll of Maine (ME)
Salem State Coll (MA)
Samford U (AL)
San Diego State U (CA)
San Francisco State U (CA)
San Jose State U (CA)
Sarah Lawrence Coll (NY)
Sonoma State U (CA)
Southern Connecticut State U (CT)
Southwestern Coll (KS)
Spring Hill Coll (AL)
Suffolk U (MA)
Texas A&M U at Galveston (TX)
Texas State U-San Marcos (TX)
Troy State U (AL)
Unity Coll (ME)
The U of Alabama (AL)
U of Alaska Southeast (AK)
The U of British Columbia (BC, Canada)
U of Calif, Los Angeles (CA)
U of Calif, Santa Barbara (CA)
U of Calif, Santa Cruz (CA)
U of Connecticut (CT)
U of Guelph (ON, Canada)
U of King's Coll (NS, Canada)
U of Maine (ME)
U of Maine at Machias (ME)
U of Maryland Eastern Shore (MD)
U of Miami (FL)
U of New Hampshire (NH)
U of New Haven (CT)
U of North Alabama (AL)
The U of North Carolina at Wilmington (NC)
U of Rhode Island (RI)
U of South Carolina (SC)
U of Southern California (CA)
U of the Virgin Islands (VI)
U of Victoria (BC, Canada)
The U of West Alabama (AL)
U of West Florida (FL)
U of Wisconsin–Superior (WI)
Waynesburg Coll (PA)
Western Washington U (WA)

MARINE SCIENCE/MERCHANT MARINE OFFICER
Hampton U (VA)
Jacksonville U (FL)
Maine Maritime Acad (ME)
Massachusetts Maritime Acad (MA)
Memorial U of Newfoundland (NL, Canada)
Oregon State U (OR)
Rider U (NJ)
Salem State Coll (MA)
Suffolk U (MA)
Texas A&M U at Galveston (TX)
United States Coast Guard Acad (CT)
United States Merchant Marine Acad (NY)
U of New Hampshire (NH)
U of San Diego (CA)
The U of Tampa (FL)

MARINE TECHNOLOGY
California Maritime Acad (CA)
Lamar U (TX)
Thomas Edison State Coll (NJ)

MARINE TRANSPORTATION RELATED
United States Merchant Marine Acad (NY)

MARITIME SCIENCE
Coll of the Atlantic (ME)
Maine Maritime Acad (ME)
Massachusetts Maritime Acad (MA)
Texas A&M U at Galveston (TX)
United States Merchant Marine Acad (NY)

MARKETING/MARKETING MANAGEMENT
Abilene Christian U (TX)
Alabama Ag and Mech U (AL)
Alabama State U (AL)
Albany State U (GA)
Albertus Magnus Coll (CT)
Albright Coll (PA)
Alderson-Broaddus Coll (WV)
Alma Coll (MI)
Alvernia Coll (PA)
Alverno Coll (WI)
Amberton U (TX)
American Coll of Thessaloniki(Greece)
American InterContinental U (CA)
American InterContinental U, Atlanta (GA)
American InterContinental U-London(United Kingdom)
American InterContinental U Online (IL)
American Intl Coll (MA)
American U (DC)
Anderson Coll (SC)
Andrews U (MI)
Angelo State U (TX)
Appalachian State U (NC)
Arcadia U (PA)
Arizona State U (AZ)
Arkansas State U (AR)
Ashland U (OH)
Assumption Coll (MA)
Athabasca U (AB, Canada)
Auburn U (AL)
Auburn U Montgomery (AL)
Augsburg Coll (MN)
Augustana Coll (IL)
Augusta State U (GA)
Aurora U (IL)
Averett U (VA)
Avila U (MO)
Azusa Pacific U (CA)
Babson Coll (MA)
Baker Coll of Auburn Hills (MI)
Baker Coll of Flint (MI)
Baker Coll of Jackson (MI)
Baker Coll of Muskegon (MI)
Baker Coll of Owosso (MI)
Baker Coll of Port Huron (MI)
Ball State U (IN)
Barber-Scotia Coll (NC)
Barry U (FL)
Barton Coll (NC)
Baylor U (TX)
Becker Coll (MA)
Bellevue U (NE)
Belmont U (TN)
Benedictine U (IL)
Bentley Coll (MA)
Berkeley Coll-New York City Campus (NY)
Berkeley Coll-Westchester Campus (NY)
Baruch Coll of the City U of NY (NY)
Berry Coll (GA)
Bishop's U (QC, Canada)
Blackburn Coll (IL)
Black Hills State U (SD)
Bloomfield Coll (NJ)
Bluefield State Coll (WV)
Boise State U (ID)
Boston Coll (MA)
Boston U (MA)
Bowie State U (MD)
Bradley U (IL)
Brenau U (GA)
Brescia U (KY)
Bridgewater Coll (VA)
Bridgewater State Coll (MA)
Brigham Young U (UT)
Brock U (ON, Canada)
Bryant Coll (RI)
Buena Vista U (IA)
Butler U (IN)
Cabrini Coll (PA)
Caldwell Coll (NJ)
California Lutheran U (CA)
California State Polytechnic U, Pomona (CA)
California State U, Chico (CA)
California State U, Dominguez Hills (CA)
California State U, Fresno (CA)
California State U, Fullerton (CA)
California State U, Hayward (CA)
California State U, Long Beach (CA)
California State U, Sacramento (CA)
California State U, San Bernardino (CA)
Campbellsville U (KY)
Campbell U (NC)
Capital U (OH)
Carleton U (ON, Canada)
Carroll Coll (WI)
Carson-Newman Coll (TN)
Castleton State Coll (VT)
Catawba Coll (NC)
Cedarville U (OH)
Centenary Coll (NJ)
Central Connecticut State U (CT)
Central Michigan U (MI)
Central Missouri State U (MO)
Central State U (OH)
Chaminade U of Honolulu (HI)
Champlain Coll (VT)
Charleston Southern U (SC)
Chatham Coll (PA)
Chestnut Hill Coll (PA)
Chicago State U (IL)
Chowan Coll (NC)
Christian Brothers U (TN)
Christopher Newport U (VA)
Clarion U of Pennsylvania (PA)
Clarke Coll (IA)
Clarkson U (NY)
Cleary U (MI)
Clemson U (SC)
Cleveland State U (OH)
Coastal Carolina U (SC)
Coker Coll (SC)
Coll Misericordia (PA)
Coll of St. Catherine (MN)
Coll of Saint Elizabeth (NJ)
The Coll of Southeastern Europe, The American U of Athens(Greece)
Coll of the Ozarks (MO)
Coll of the Southwest (NM)
Colorado State U (CO)
Colorado State U-Pueblo (CO)
Colorado Tech U Sioux Falls Campus (SD)
Columbia Coll (MO)
Columbia Coll Chicago (IL)
Columbia Southern U (AL)
Columbus State U (GA)
Concordia U (QC, Canada)
Concordia U Wisconsin (WI)
Converse Coll (SC)
Cornell U (NY)
Cornerstone U (MI)
Creighton U (NE)
Dakota State U (SD)
Dakota Wesleyan U (SD)
Dalhousie U (NS, Canada)
Dallas Baptist U (TX)
Dalton State Coll (GA)
Davenport U, Dearborn (MI)
Davenport U, Grand Rapids (MI)
Davenport U, Kalamazoo (MI)
Davenport U, Lansing (MI)
Davenport U, Warren (MI)
Davis & Elkins Coll (WV)
Defiance Coll (OH)
Delaware State U (DE)
Delaware Valley Coll (PA)
Delta State U (MS)
DePaul U (IL)
DeSales U (PA)
Dickinson State U (ND)
Dominican Coll (NY)
Drake U (IA)
Drexel U (PA)
Duquesne U (PA)
D'Youville Coll (NY)
East Carolina U (NC)
East Central U (OK)
Eastern Illinois U (IL)
Eastern Kentucky U (KY)
Eastern Michigan U (MI)
Eastern New Mexico U (NM)
Eastern U (PA)
Eastern Washington U (WA)
East Texas Baptist U (TX)
Elmhurst Coll (IL)
Elmira Coll (NY)
Elms Coll (MA)
Emerson Coll (MA)
Emory U (GA)
Emporia State U (KS)
Evangel U (MO)
Excelsior Coll (NY)
Fairfield U (CT)
Fairleigh Dickinson U, Florham (NJ)
Faulkner U (AL)
Fayetteville State U (NC)
Ferris State U (MI)
Florida Atlantic U (FL)
Florida Gulf Coast U (FL)
Florida Intl U (FL)
Florida Metropolitan U-Tampa Coll, Brandon (FL)
Florida Metropolitan U-Fort Lauderdale Coll (FL)
Florida Metropolitan U-Tampa Coll (FL)
Florida Southern Coll (FL)
Florida State U (FL)
Fontbonne U (MO)
Fordham U (NY)
Fort Hays State U (KS)
Fort Lewis Coll (CO)
Fort Valley State U (GA)
Framingham State Coll (MA)
Francis Marion U (SC)
Franklin Pierce Coll (NH)
Franklin U (OH)
Freed-Hardeman U (TN)
Fresno Pacific U (CA)
Gannon U (PA)
George Mason U (VA)
Georgetown Coll (KY)
Georgetown U (DC)
The George Washington U (DC)
Georgia Coll & State U (GA)
Georgia Southern U (GA)
Georgia Southwestern State U (GA)
Georgia State U (GA)
Glenville State Coll (WV)
Golden Gate U (CA)
Goldey-Beacom Coll (DE)
Gonzaga U (WA)
Governors State U (IL)
Grace Bible Coll (MI)
Grambling State U (LA)
Grand Canyon U (AZ)
Grand Valley State U (MI)
Greenville Coll (IL)
Grove City Coll (PA)
Hampton U (VA)
Hannibal-LaGrange Coll (MO)
Harding U (AR)
Hardin-Simmons U (TX)
Harris-Stowe State Coll (MO)
Hastings Coll (NE)
Hawai'i Pacific U (HI)
HEC Montreal (QC, Canada)
Hesser Coll (NH)
High Point U (NC)
Hillsdale Coll (MI)
Hofstra U (NY)
Holy Names Coll (CA)
Houston Baptist U (TX)
Howard Payne U (TX)
Howard U (DC)
Humboldt State U (CA)
Huntingdon Coll (AL)
Husson Coll (ME)
Idaho State U (ID)
Illinois State U (IL)
Immaculata U (PA)
Indiana Inst of Technology (IN)
Indiana State U (IN)
Indiana U Bloomington (IN)
Indiana U of Pennsylvania (PA)
Indiana U–Purdue U Fort Wayne (IN)
Indiana U South Bend (IN)
Inter American U of PR, Aguadilla Campus (PR)
Inter American U of PR, Bayamón Campus (PR)
Inter American U of PR, Ponce Campus (PR)
Inter American U of PR, San Germán Campus (PR)
Iona Coll (NY)
Iowa State U of Science and Technology (IA)
Ithaca Coll (NY)
Jacksonville State U (AL)
Jacksonville U (FL)
James Madison U (VA)
Jamestown Coll (ND)
Jarvis Christian Coll (TX)
John Carroll U (OH)
Johnson & Wales U (RI)
Johnson State Coll (VT)
Juniata Coll (PA)
Kansas State U (KS)
Kean U (NJ)
Kendall Coll (IL)
Kennesaw State U (GA)
Kent State U (OH)
Kettering U (MI)
Keuka Coll (NY)
The King's Coll (NY)
King's Coll (PA)
Kutztown U of Pennsylvania (PA)
Laboratory Inst of Merchandising (NY)
Lakehead U (ON, Canada)
Lakeland Coll (WI)
Lamar U (TX)
Lambuth U (TN)
La Salle U (PA)
Lasell Coll (MA)
Lehigh U (PA)
LeTourneau U (TX)
Lewis U (IL)
Liberty U (VA)
Limestone Coll (SC)
Lincoln Memorial U (TN)
Lincoln U (MO)
Lindenwood U (MO)
Lipscomb U (TN)
Long Island U, Brentwood Campus (NY)
Long Island U, C.W. Post Campus (NY)
Longwood U (VA)
Loras Coll (IA)
Louisiana Coll (LA)
Louisiana State U and A&M Coll (LA)
Louisiana State U in Shreveport (LA)
Louisiana Tech U (LA)
Loyola U Chicago (IL)
Loyola U New Orleans (LA)
Lubbock Christian U (TX)
Lycoming Coll (PA)
Lynchburg Coll (VA)
Lynn U (FL)
MacMurray Coll (IL)
Madonna U (MI)
Manchester Coll (IN)
Manhattan Coll (NY)
Mansfield U of Pennsylvania (PA)
Marian Coll of Fond du Lac (WI)
Marietta Coll (OH)
Marquette U (WI)
Marshall U (WV)
Mars Hill Coll (NC)
Martin U (IN)
Marygrove Coll (MI)
Marymount Coll of Fordham U (NY)
Marymount U (VA)
Maryville U of Saint Louis (MO)

Marywood U (PA)
Massachusetts Coll of Liberal Arts (MA)
McKendree Coll (IL)
McMurry U (TX)
McNeese State U (LA)
Medaille Coll (NY)
Memorial U of Newfoundland (NL, Canada)
Mercy Coll (NY)
Mercyhurst Coll (PA)
Meredith Coll (NC)
Merrimack Coll (MA)
Messiah Coll (PA)
Metropolitan State U (MN)
Miami U (OH)
Michigan State U (MI)
Michigan Technological U (MI)
Middle Tennessee State U (TN)
Midwestern State U (TX)
Millikin U (IL)
Minnesota State U Mankato (MN)
Minnesota State U Moorhead (MN)
Minot State U (ND)
Mississippi Coll (MS)
Mississippi State U (MS)
Missouri Baptist U (MO)
Missouri Southern State U (MO)
Missouri Valley Coll (MO)
Missouri Western State Coll (MO)
Monmouth U (NJ)
Montana State U–Billings (MT)
Montclair State U (NJ)
Morehead State U (KY)
Morehouse Coll (GA)
Morgan State U (MD)
Morningside Coll (IA)
Mount Ida Coll (MA)
Mount Mary Coll (WI)
Mount Mercy Coll (IA)
Mount St. Mary's Coll (CA)
Mount Saint Vincent U (NS, Canada)
Mount Vernon Nazarene U (OH)
Murray State U (KY)
National U (CA)
Nazareth Coll of Rochester (NY)
Neumann Coll (PA)
Newbury Coll (MA)
New England School of Communications (ME)
Newman U (KS)
New Mexico Highlands U (NM)
New Mexico State U (NM)
New York Inst of Technology (NY)
New York U (NY)
Niagara U (NY)
Nicholls State U (LA)
Nichols Coll (MA)
North Carolina State U (NC)
North Central Coll (IL)
Northeastern Illinois U (IL)
Northeastern State U (OK)
Northeastern U (MA)
Northern Arizona U (AZ)
Northern Illinois U (IL)
Northern Michigan U (MI)
Northern State U (SD)
North Georgia Coll & State U (GA)
North Park U (IL)
Northwestern Coll (MN)
Northwest Nazarene U (ID)
Northwood U (MI)
Northwood U, Florida Campus (FL)
Northwood U, Texas Campus (TX)
Notre Dame Coll (OH)
Notre Dame de Namur U (CA)
Oakland U (MI)
The Ohio State U (OH)
Ohio U (OH)
Ohio Valley Coll (WV)
Oklahoma Baptist U (OK)
Oklahoma Christian U (OK)
Oklahoma City U (OK)
Oklahoma State U (OK)
Old Dominion U (VA)
Olivet Coll (MI)
Olivet Nazarene U (IL)
Oral Roberts U (OK)
Oregon State U (OR)
Otterbein Coll (OH)
Our Lady of the Lake U of San Antonio (TX)
Pace U (NY)
Pacific Lutheran U (WA)
Pacific Union Coll (CA)
Pacific U (OR)
Palm Beach Atlantic U (FL)
Park U (MO)
Peirce Coll (PA)
Penn State U Abington Coll (PA)
Penn State U Altoona Coll (PA)
Penn State U at Erie, The Behrend Coll (PA)
Penn State U Beaver Campus of the Commonwealth Coll (PA)
Penn State U Berks Cmps of Berks-Lehigh Valley Coll (PA)
Penn State U Delaware County Campus of the Commonwealth Coll (PA)
Penn State U DuBois Campus of the Commonwealth Coll (PA)
Penn State U Fayette Campus of the Commonwealth Coll (PA)
Penn State U Harrisburg Campus of the Capital Coll (PA)
Penn State U Hazleton Campus of the Commonwealth Coll (PA)
Penn State U Lehigh Valley Cmps of Berks-Lehigh Valley Coll (PA)
Penn State U McKeesport Campus of the Commonwealth Coll (PA)
Penn State U Mont Alto Campus of the Commonwealth Coll (PA)
Penn State U New Kensington Campus of the Commonwealth Coll (PA)
Penn State U Schuylkill Campus of the Capital Coll (PA)
Penn State U Shenango Campus of the Commonwealth Coll (PA)
Penn State U Univ Park Campus (PA)
Penn State U Wilkes-Barre Campus of the Commonwealth Coll (PA)
Penn State U Worthington Scranton Cmps Commonwealth Coll (PA)
Penn State U York Campus of the Commonwealth Coll (PA)
Pfeiffer U (NC)
Philadelphia U (PA)
Pittsburg State U (KS)
Plymouth State U (NH)
Polytechnic U of Puerto Rico (PR)
Pontifical Catholic U of Puerto Rico (PR)
Portland State U (OR)
Prairie View A&M U (TX)
Providence Coll (RI)
Quincy U (IL)
Quinnipiac U (CT)
Radford U (VA)
Rensselaer Polytechnic Inst (NY)
Rhode Island Coll (RI)
Rider U (NJ)
Robert Morris U (PA)
Roberts Wesleyan Coll (NY)
Rochester Coll (MI)
Rochester Inst of Technology (NY)
Rockford Coll (IL)
Rockhurst U (MO)
Roger Williams U (RI)
Roosevelt U (IL)
Rutgers, The State U of New Jersey, Camden (NJ)
Rutgers, The State U of New Jersey, Newark (NJ)
Rutgers, The State U of New Jersey, New Brunswick/Piscataway (NJ)
Ryerson U (ON, Canada)
Sacred Heart U (CT)
St. Ambrose U (IA)
St. Bonaventure U (NY)
St. Cloud State U (MN)
St. Edward's U (TX)
Saint Francis U (PA)
St. Gregory's U (OK)
St. John Fisher Coll (NY)
St. John's U (NY)
Saint Joseph's Coll of Maine (ME)
Saint Joseph's U (PA)
Saint Leo U (FL)
Saint Louis U (MO)
Saint Martin's Coll (WA)
Saint Mary-of-the-Woods Coll (IN)
Saint Mary's Coll (IN)
Saint Mary's U of Minnesota (MN)
St. Mary's U of San Antonio (TX)
St. Thomas Aquinas Coll (NY)
St. Thomas U (FL)
Saint Vincent Coll (PA)
Salem State Coll (MA)
Salisbury U (MD)
Sam Houston State U (TX)
San Diego State U (CA)
San Francisco State U (CA)
San Jose State U (CA)
Santa Clara U (CA)
Schiller Intl U (FL)
Schiller Intl U(Spain)
Seattle U (WA)
Seton Hall U (NJ)
Seton Hill U (PA)
Shippensburg U of Pennsylvania (PA)
Siena Coll (NY)
Siena Heights U (MI)
Simmons Coll (MA)
South Carolina State U (SC)
Southeastern Coll of the Assemblies of God (FL)
Southeastern Louisiana U (LA)
Southeastern Oklahoma State U (OK)
Southeast Missouri State U (MO)
Southern Adventist U (TN)
Southern Illinois U Carbondale (IL)
Southern Methodist U (TX)
Southern Nazarene U (OK)
Southern Oregon U (OR)
Southern U and A&M Coll (LA)
Southwestern Oklahoma State U (OK)
Southwest Missouri State U (MO)
Spring Hill Coll (AL)
State U of NY at New Paltz (NY)
State U of NY at Oswego (NY)
Plattsburgh State U of NY (NY)
State U of NY Coll at Brockport (NY)
State U of NY Coll at Fredonia (NY)
State U of NY Coll at Old Westbury (NY)
State U of West Georgia (GA)
Stephens Coll (MO)
Stetson U (FL)
Stonehill Coll (MA)
Suffolk U (MA)
Sullivan U (KY)
Susquehanna U (PA)
Syracuse U (NY)
Tabor Coll (KS)
Taylor U (IN)
Teikyo Post U (CT)
Tennessee Technological U (TN)
Texas A&M Intl U (TX)
Texas A&M U (TX)
Texas A&M U–Commerce (TX)
Texas A&M U–Corpus Christi (TX)
Texas A&M U–Kingsville (TX)
Texas A&M U–Texarkana (TX)
Texas Christian U (TX)
Texas Southern U (TX)
Texas State U-San Marcos (TX)
Texas Tech U (TX)
Texas Wesleyan U (TX)
Texas Woman's U (TX)
Thomas Coll (ME)
Thomas Edison State Coll (NJ)
Tiffin U (OH)
Trevecca Nazarene U (TN)
Trinity Christian Coll (IL)
Trinity Intl U (IL)
Trinity U (TX)
Tri-State U (IN)
Tulane U (LA)
Tuskegee U (AL)
Union U (TN)
Université de Sherbrooke (QC, Canada)
U Coll of the Cariboo (BC, Canada)
The U of Akron (OH)
The U of Alabama (AL)
The U of Alabama at Birmingham (AL)
The U of Alabama in Huntsville (AL)
U of Alberta (AB, Canada)
The U of Arizona (AZ)
U of Arkansas (AR)
U of Arkansas at Little Rock (AR)
U of Baltimore (MD)
U of Bridgeport (CT)
The U of British Columbia (BC, Canada)
U of Calgary (AB, Canada)
U of Central Arkansas (AR)
U of Central Florida (FL)
U of Charleston (WV)
U of Cincinnati (OH)
U of Colorado at Boulder (CO)
U of Colorado at Colorado Springs (CO)
U of Connecticut (CT)
U of Dayton (OH)
U of Delaware (DE)
U of Denver (CO)
U of Detroit Mercy (MI)
U of Evansville (IN)
The U of Findlay (OH)
U of Florida (FL)
U of Georgia (GA)
U of Great Falls (MT)
U of Guelph (ON, Canada)
U of Hawaii at Manoa (HI)
U of Houston (TX)
U of Houston–Clear Lake (TX)
U of Houston–Victoria (TX)
U of Idaho (ID)
U of Illinois at Chicago (IL)
U of Indianapolis (IN)
The U of Iowa (IA)
U of Kentucky (KY)
U of La Verne (CA)
The U of Lethbridge (AB, Canada)
U of Louisiana at Lafayette (LA)
U of Louisville (KY)
U of Maine at Machias (ME)
U of Mary Hardin-Baylor (TX)
U of Maryland, Coll Park (MD)
U of Maryland U Coll (MD)
U of Massachusetts Amherst (MA)
U of Massachusetts Dartmouth (MA)
The U of Memphis (TN)
U of Miami (FL)
U of Michigan–Dearborn (MI)
U of Michigan–Flint (MI)
U of Minnesota, Duluth (MN)
U of Minnesota, Twin Cities Campus (MN)
U of Mississippi (MS)
U of Missouri–Columbia (MO)
U of Missouri–St. Louis (MO)
The U of Montana–Missoula (MT)
U of Montevallo (AL)
U of Nebraska at Omaha (NE)
U of Nebraska–Lincoln (NE)
U of Nevada, Las Vegas (NV)
U of Nevada, Reno (NV)
U of New Brunswick Fredericton (NB, Canada)
U of New Haven (CT)
U of New Orleans (LA)
U of North Alabama (AL)
The U of North Carolina at Charlotte (NC)
The U of North Carolina at Greensboro (NC)
The U of North Carolina at Wilmington (NC)
U of North Dakota (ND)
U of Northern Iowa (IA)
U of North Florida (FL)
U of North Texas (TX)
U of Northwestern Ohio (OH)
U of Notre Dame (IN)
U of Oklahoma (OK)
U of Oregon (OR)
U of Ottawa (ON, Canada)
U of Pennsylvania (PA)
U of Phoenix–Atlanta Campus (GA)
U of Phoenix–Boston Campus (MA)
U of Phoenix–Chicago Campus (IL)
U of Phoenix–Cleveland Campus (OH)
U of Phoenix–Dallas Campus (TX)
U of Phoenix–Fort Lauderdale Campus (FL)
U of Phoenix–Hawaii Campus (HI)
U of Phoenix–Houston Campus (TX)
U of Phoenix–Idaho Campus (ID)
U of Phoenix–Jacksonville Campus (FL)
U of Phoenix–Metro Detroit Campus (MI)
U of Phoenix–Nevada Campus (NV)
U of Phoenix–New Mexico Campus (NM)
U of Phoenix–Northern California Campus (CA)
U of Phoenix–Oregon Campus (OR)
U of Phoenix–Orlando Campus (FL)
U of Phoenix–Philadelphia Campus (PA)
U of Phoenix–Phoenix Campus (AZ)
U of Phoenix–Pittsburgh Campus (PA)
U of Phoenix–Puerto Rico Campus (PR)
U of Phoenix–Sacramento Campus (CA)
U of Phoenix–St. Louis Campus (MO)
U of Phoenix–San Diego Campus (CA)
U of Phoenix–Southern Arizona Campus (AZ)
U of Phoenix–Southern California Campus (CA)
U of Phoenix–Southern Colorado Campus (CO)
U of Phoenix–Tampa Campus (FL)
U of Phoenix–Tulsa Campus (OK)
U of Phoenix–Utah Campus (UT)
U of Phoenix–Washington Campus (WA)
U of Phoenix–Wisconsin Campus (WI)
U of Pittsburgh (PA)
U of Portland (OR)
U of Regina (SK, Canada)
U of Rhode Island (RI)
U of Richmond (VA)
U of St. Francis (IL)
U of Saint Francis (IN)
U of St. Thomas (MN)
U of San Francisco (CA)
U of Saskatchewan (SK, Canada)
The U of Scranton (PA)
U of Sioux Falls (SD)
U of South Alabama (AL)
U of South Carolina (SC)
The U of South Dakota (SD)
U of Southern Indiana (IN)
U of South Florida (FL)
The U of Tampa (FL)
The U of Tennessee (TN)
The U of Tennessee at Martin (TN)
The U of Texas at Arlington (TX)
The U of Texas at Austin (TX)
The U of Texas at Brownsville (TX)
The U of Texas at Dallas (TX)
The U of Texas at Tyler (TX)
The U of Texas–Pan American (TX)
U of the District of Columbia (DC)
U of the Incarnate Word (TX)
U of the Ozarks (AR)
U of the Sacred Heart (PR)
U of the Sciences in Philadelphia (PA)
U of Toledo (OH)
U of Tulsa (OK)
U of Utah (UT)
U of West Florida (FL)
U of Windsor (ON, Canada)
U of Wisconsin–Eau Claire (WI)
U of Wisconsin–La Crosse (WI)
U of Wisconsin–Milwaukee (WI)
U of Wisconsin–Oshkosh (WI)
U of Wisconsin–River Falls (WI)
U of Wisconsin–Superior (WI)
U of Wisconsin–Whitewater (WI)
U of Wyoming (WY)
Upper Iowa U (IA)
Urbana U (OH)
Ursuline Coll (OH)
Utah State U (UT)
Valdosta State U (GA)
Valparaiso U (IN)
Vanguard U of Southern California (CA)
Villanova U (PA)
Virginia Commonwealth U (VA)
Virginia Intermont Coll (VA)
Virginia Polytechnic Inst and State U (VA)
Virginia State U (VA)
Virginia Union U (VA)
Viterbo U (WI)
Waldorf Coll (IA)
Walla Walla Coll (WA)
Walsh Coll of Accountancy and Business Admin (MI)
Walsh U (OH)
Warner Southern Coll (FL)
Wartburg Coll (IA)
Washburn U (KS)
Washington State U (WA)
Washington U in St. Louis (MO)
Waynesburg Coll (PA)
Wayne State U (MI)
Webber Intl U (FL)
Weber State U (UT)
Webster U (MO)
Wesley Coll (DE)
Western Carolina U (NC)
Western Connecticut State U (CT)
Western Illinois U (IL)
Western Kentucky U (KY)
Western Michigan U (MI)
Western New England Coll (MA)
Western State Coll of Colorado (CO)
Western Washington U (WA)
Westfield State Coll (MA)
West Liberty State Coll (WV)
Westminster Coll (UT)
West Texas A&M U (TX)
West Virginia U (WV)
West Virginia Wesleyan Coll (WV)
Wheeling Jesuit U (WV)
Wichita State U (KS)
Widener U (PA)
Wilberforce U (OH)
Wilmington Coll (DE)
Wingate U (NC)
Winona State U (MN)
Wittenberg U (OH)
Wright State U (OH)
Xavier U (OH)
Xavier U of Louisiana (LA)
York Coll of Pennsylvania (PA)
York Coll of the City U of New York (NY)
York U (ON, Canada)
Youngstown State U (OH)

MARKETING RELATED
Babson Coll (MA)
Bowling Green State U (OH)
Canisius Coll (NY)
Capella U (MN)
Central Michigan U (MI)
Clark Atlanta U (GA)
Clayton Coll & State U (GA)
DeSales U (PA)
Duquesne U (PA)
Inter American U of PR, San Germán Campus (PR)
La Roche Coll (PA)
Macon State Coll (GA)
Miami U Hamilton (OH)
Mount Saint Mary Coll (NY)
Pace U (NY)
Saint Joseph's U (PA)
Troy State U (AL)
The U of Akron (OH)
U of Illinois at Urbana–Champaign (IL)
The U of Iowa (IA)
U of St. Thomas (TX)
U of Utah (UT)
Washington U in St. Louis (MO)
Western Carolina U (NC)
Western Michigan U (MI)

MARKETING RESEARCH
Ashland U (OH)
Baker Coll of Jackson (MI)
Boston U (MA)
Carthage Coll (WI)
Concordia U (QC, Canada)
Fairleigh Dickinson U, Teaneck-Metro Campus (NJ)
Inter American U of PR, Bayamón Campus (PR)
Ithaca Coll (NY)
McGill U (QC, Canada)
Methodist Coll (NC)
Metropolitan State Coll of Denver (CO)
Mount Saint Vincent U (NS, Canada)
Newbury Coll (MA)
Rochester Inst of Technology (NY)
Saginaw Valley State U (MI)
Talladega Coll (AL)
Troy State U Montgomery (AL)
U of Toledo (OH)
U of Windsor (ON, Canada)
York U (ON, Canada)

MARRIAGE AND FAMILY THERAPY/COUNSELING
Grace U (NE)
Harding U (AR)
Limestone Coll (SC)
Oklahoma Baptist U (OK)
Seton Hill U (PA)
Southern Christian U (AL)
U of Houston–Clear Lake (TX)
U of Nevada, Las Vegas (NV)
The U of North Carolina at Greensboro (NC)

MASS COMMUNICATION/MEDIA
Adrian Coll (MI)
Alabama State U (AL)
Albertus Magnus Coll (CT)
Albion Coll (MI)
Alcorn State U (MS)
Alderson-Broaddus Coll (WV)
Allegheny Coll (PA)
American Intl Coll (MA)
The American U in Cairo(Egypt)
Anderson Coll (SC)
Andrews U (MI)
Antioch Coll (OH)
Arcadia U (PA)
Ashland U (OH)
Atlantic Baptist U (NB, Canada)
Auburn U (AL)
Augsburg Coll (MN)
Augustana Coll (IL)
Austin Peay State U (TN)
Baker U (KS)
Baldwin-Wallace Coll (OH)
Barber-Scotia Coll (NC)
Barry U (FL)
Barton Coll (NC)
Becker Coll (MA)
Belmont U (TN)
Beloit Coll (WI)
Bemidji State U (MN)
Benedictine Coll (KS)
Berea Coll (KY)
Bethel Coll (KS)
Bethel U (MN)
Bethune-Cookman Coll (FL)
Black Hills State U (SD)
Bloomsburg U of Pennsylvania (PA)
Bluefield Coll (VA)
Boise State U (ID)
Boston Coll (MA)
Boston U (MA)
Bowie State U (MD)
Brenau U (GA)
Briar Cliff U (IA)
Bridgewater Coll (VA)
Brigham Young U (UT)
Brock U (ON, Canada)
Bryan Coll (TN)
Buena Vista U (IA)
State U of NY Coll at Buffalo (NY)
California Lutheran U (CA)
California State Polytechnic U, Pomona (CA)
California State U, Dominguez Hills (CA)
California State U, Fresno (CA)
California State U, Hayward (CA)
California State U, Long Beach (CA)
California State U, Sacramento (CA)
California State U, San Bernardino (CA)
Calvary Bible Coll and Theological Sem (MO)
Calvin Coll (MI)
Campbellsville U (KY)
Campbell U (NC)
Carleton U (ON, Canada)
Carnegie Mellon U (PA)
Carson-Newman Coll (TN)
Catawba Coll (NC)
Centenary Coll (NJ)
Central Washington U (WA)
Chaminade U of Honolulu (HI)
Champlain Coll (VT)
Cheyney U of Pennsylvania (PA)
City Coll of the City U of NY (NY)
City U (WA)
Clark Atlanta U (GA)
Clarke Coll (IA)
Clark U (MA)
Coker Coll (SC)
Colby-Sawyer Coll (NH)
Coll of Mount Saint Vincent (NY)
The Coll of New Rochelle (NY)
Coll of Notre Dame of Maryland (MD)
Coll of St. Catherine (MN)
Coll of the Ozarks (MO)
The Coll of Wooster (OH)
Colorado State U-Pueblo (CO)
Columbia Union Coll (MD)
Columbus State U (GA)
Concord Coll (WV)
Concordia Coll (MN)
Concordia U (NE)
Concordia U (QC, Canada)
Concordia U at Austin (TX)
Concordia U, St. Paul (MN)
Concordia U Wisconsin (WI)
Cornerstone U (MI)
Culver-Stockton Coll (MO)
Curry Coll (MA)
Defiance Coll (OH)
Denison U (OH)
DePaul U (IL)
DePauw U (IN)
DeSales U (PA)
Dillard U (LA)
Doane Coll (NE)
Dominican U (IL)
Dordt Coll (IA)
Drake U (IA)
Drury U (MO)
East Central U (OK)
Eastern Kentucky U (KY)
Eastern Nazarene Coll (MA)
Edgewood Coll (WI)
Emerson Coll (MA)
Emmanuel Coll (GA)
Emory & Henry Coll (VA)
Endicott Coll (MA)
Eureka Coll (IL)
Evangel U (MO)
Excelsior Coll (NY)
Fairfield U (CT)
Ferris State U (MI)
Florida Ag and Mech U (FL)
Florida State U (FL)
Fordham U (NY)
Fort Hays State U (KS)
Fort Valley State U (GA)
Francis Marion U (SC)
Franklin Pierce Coll (NH)
Fresno Pacific U (CA)
Frostburg State U (MD)
Gallaudet U (DC)
Gardner-Webb U (NC)
Georgetown Coll (KY)
The George Washington U (DC)
Gonzaga U (WA)
Goshen Coll (IN)
Goucher Coll (MD)
Governors State U (IL)
Grace Coll (IN)
Grace U (NE)
Grambling State U (LA)
Grand Canyon U (AZ)
Grand Valley State U (MI)
Grand View Coll (IA)
Greenville Coll (IL)
Grove City Coll (PA)
Gustavus Adolphus Coll (MN)
Hamilton Coll (NY)
Hamline U (MN)
Hampshire Coll (MA)
Hampton U (VA)
Hanover Coll (IN)
Hastings Coll (NE)
Hawai'i Pacific U (HI)
Heidelberg Coll (OH)
High Point U (NC)
Hiram Coll (OH)
Hobart and William Smith Colls (NY)
Hofstra U (NY)
Houston Baptist U (TX)
Howard U (DC)
Hunter Coll of the City U of NY (NY)
Huntington Coll (IN)
Idaho State U (ID)
Illinois Coll (IL)
Illinois State U (IL)
Indiana U Bloomington (IN)
Indiana U Northwest (IN)
Indiana U South Bend (IN)
Inter American U of PR, Bayamón Campus (PR)
Intl U in Geneva(Switzerland)
Iona Coll (NY)
Iowa State U of Science and Technology (IA)
Iowa Wesleyan Coll (IA)
Ithaca Coll (NY)
John Brown U (AR)
John Carroll U (OH)
Johnson & Wales U (RI)
Johnson C. Smith U (NC)
Judson Coll (IL)
Kansas Wesleyan U (KS)
Keene State Coll (NH)
Kent State U (OH)
Kentucky Mountain Bible Coll (KY)
Lamar U (TX)
Lambuth U (TN)
La Salle U (PA)
Lehman Coll of the City U of NY (NY)
Lenoir-Rhyne Coll (NC)
Lewis U (IL)
Lincoln Memorial U (TN)
Lindenwood U (MO)
Lindsey Wilson Coll (KY)
Lipscomb U (TN)
Long Island U, Southampton Coll (NY)
Loras Coll (IA)
Louisiana Coll (LA)
Louisiana State U and A&M Coll (LA)
Louisiana State U in Shreveport (LA)
Loyola Marymount U (CA)
Lubbock Christian U (TX)
Lycoming Coll (PA)
Lynchburg Coll (VA)
Lynn U (FL)
Madonna U (MI)
Manchester Coll (IN)
Mansfield U of Pennsylvania (PA)
Marian Coll (IN)
Marist Coll (NY)
Marquette U (WI)
Mars Hill Coll (NC)
Marylhurst U (OR)
Marymount Coll of Fordham U (NY)
Marymount Manhattan Coll (NY)
Maryville U of Saint Louis (MO)
Massachusetts Coll of Liberal Arts (MA)
Massachusetts Inst of Technology (MA)
The Master's Coll and Sem (CA)
McKendree Coll (IL)
McNeese State U (LA)
Medaille Coll (NY)
Menlo Coll (CA)
Mercer U (GA)
Mercyhurst Coll (PA)
Meredith Coll (NC)
Methodist Coll (NC)
Miami U (OH)
Miami U Hamilton (OH)
Michigan State U (MI)
MidAmerica Nazarene U (KS)
Middle Tennessee State U (TN)
Midwestern State U (TX)
Miles Coll (AL)
Minnesota State U Mankato (MN)
Minnesota State U Moorhead (MN)
Mississippi Coll (MS)
Mississippi Valley State U (MS)
Missouri Southern State U (MO)
Missouri Valley Coll (MO)
Montana State U–Billings (MT)
Morgan State U (MD)
Morningside Coll (IA)
Mount Saint Mary Coll (NY)
Mount Union Coll (OH)
Mount Vernon Nazarene U (OH)
Murray State U (KY)
Newberry Coll (SC)
Newbury Coll (MA)
Newman U (KS)
New Mexico Highlands U (NM)
New York U (NY)
Niagara U (NY)
Nicholls State U (LA)
North Carolina State U (NC)
North Central Coll (IL)
North Central U (MN)
North Dakota State U (ND)
Northeastern U (MA)
Northern Michigan U (MI)
North Greenville Coll (SC)
North Park U (IL)
Northwestern Coll (IA)
Northwestern Oklahoma State U (OK)
Northwest Nazarene U (ID)
Oglethorpe U (GA)
Ohio Northern U (OH)
Oklahoma Baptist U (OK)
Oklahoma Christian U (OK)
Oklahoma City U (OK)
Olivet Coll (MI)
Olivet Nazarene U (IL)
Oregon State U (OR)
Ottawa U (KS)
Ouachita Baptist U (AR)
Pacific Lutheran U (WA)
Pacific Union Coll (CA)
Pacific U (OR)
Piedmont Coll (GA)
Pine Manor Coll (MA)
Pittsburg State U (KS)
Point Park U (PA)
Pontifical Catholic U of Puerto Rico (PR)
Principia Coll (IL)
Queens Coll of the City U of NY (NY)
Queens U of Charlotte (NC)
Quinnipiac U (CT)
Reinhardt Coll (GA)
Rhode Island Coll (RI)
Richmond, The American Intl U in London(United Kingdom)
Robert Morris U (PA)
Russell Sage Coll (NY)
Rutgers, The State U of New Jersey, New Brunswick/Piscataway (NJ)
Sacred Heart U (CT)
St. Ambrose U (IA)
St. Andrews Presbyterian Coll (NC)
St. Bonaventure U (NY)
St. Cloud State U (MN)
Saint Francis U (PA)
St. John Fisher Coll (NY)
Saint Joseph's Coll (IN)
Saint Mary-of-the-Woods Coll (IN)
St. Mary's U of San Antonio (TX)
St. Thomas Aquinas Coll (NY)
St. Thomas U (FL)
Salem Coll (NC)
Salem State Coll (MA)
San Diego State U (CA)
Seattle U (WA)
Shaw U (NC)
Simmons Coll (MA)
Simpson Coll (IA)
Sonoma State U (CA)
South Dakota State U (SD)
Southern Adventist U (TN)
Southern Arkansas U–Magnolia (AR)
Southern Illinois U Edwardsville (IL)
Southern Nazarene U (OK)
Southern U and A&M Coll (LA)
Southern Utah U (UT)
Southern Vermont Coll (VT)
Southwestern Oklahoma State U (OK)
Southwestern U (TX)
Southwest Missouri State U (MO)
State U of NY at New Paltz (NY)
State U of NY at Oswego (NY)
Plattsburgh State U of NY (NY)
State U of NY Coll at Brockport (NY)
State U of NY Coll at Fredonia (NY)
State U of NY Coll at Oneonta (NY)
Stephens Coll (MO)
Suffolk U (MA)
Susquehanna U (PA)
Tabor Coll (KS)
Taylor U (IN)
Tennessee State U (TN)
Texas A&M U–Kingsville (TX)
Texas A&M U–Texarkana (TX)
Texas Christian U (TX)
Texas Southern U (TX)
Texas State U-San Marcos (TX)
Texas Wesleyan U (TX)
Toccoa Falls Coll (GA)
Towson U (MD)
Trevecca Nazarene U (TN)
Trinity Coll (DC)
Truman State U (MO)
Tulane U (LA)
Union U (TN)
Université de Montréal (QC, Canada)
Université de Sherbrooke (QC, Canada)
Université Laval (QC, Canada)
State U of NY at Albany (NY)
U at Buffalo, The State U of New York (NY)
The U of Akron (OH)
U of Baltimore (MD)
U of Bridgeport (CT)
U of Calif, Berkeley (CA)
U of Calif, San Diego (CA)
U of Central Florida (FL)
U of Charleston (WV)
U of Cincinnati (OH)
U of Dayton (OH)
U of Delaware (DE)
U of Detroit Mercy (MI)
U of Dubuque (IA)
U of Evansville (IN)
U of Georgia (GA)
U of Houston (TX)
U of Illinois at Springfield (IL)
U of Illinois at Urbana–Champaign (IL)
The U of Iowa (IA)
U of Louisiana at Lafayette (LA)
U of Maine (ME)
U of Mary (ND)
U of Mary Hardin-Baylor (TX)
U of Maryland Eastern Shore (MD)
U of Miami (FL)
U of Michigan (MI)
U of Michigan–Flint (MI)
U of Minnesota, Twin Cities Campus (MN)
U of Missouri–Columbia (MO)
U of Missouri–Kansas City (MO)
U of Missouri–St. Louis (MO)
U of Mobile (AL)
U of Montevallo (AL)
U of New Hampshire (NH)
U of New Hampshire at Manchester (NH)
U of New Mexico (NM)
The U of North Carolina at Chapel Hill (NC)
The U of North Carolina at Greensboro (NC)
U of Oregon (OR)
U of Ottawa (ON, Canada)
U of Pittsburgh at Bradford (PA)
U of Pittsburgh at Greensburg (PA)
U of Pittsburgh at Johnstown (PA)
U of Portland (OR)
U of St. Francis (IL)
U of Saint Francis (IN)
U of Saint Mary (KS)
U of San Diego (CA)
U of San Francisco (CA)
U of Sioux Falls (SD)
The U of South Dakota (SD)
U of Southern California (CA)
U of Southern Maine (ME)
The U of Tampa (FL)
The U of Tennessee at Chattanooga (TN)
The U of Texas–Pan American (TX)
U of the District of Columbia (DC)
U of the Incarnate Word (TX)
U of the Sacred Heart (PR)
U of Toledo (OH)
U of Toronto (ON, Canada)
U of Utah (UT)
The U of Western Ontario (ON, Canada)
U of Windsor (ON, Canada)
U of Wisconsin–Eau Claire (WI)
U of Wisconsin–Madison (WI)
U of Wisconsin–Milwaukee (WI)
U of Wisconsin–Oshkosh (WI)
U of Wisconsin–Platteville (WI)
U of Wisconsin–Superior (WI)
Upper Iowa U (IA)

Urbana U (OH)
Ursinus Coll (PA)
Valley City State U (ND)
Valparaiso U (IN)
Vanderbilt U (TN)
Villa Julie Coll (MD)
Villanova U (PA)
Virginia Commonwealth U (VA)
Virginia State U (VA)
Waldorf Coll (IA)
Walla Walla Coll (WA)
Wartburg Coll (IA)
Washburn U (KS)
Wayland Baptist U (TX)
Wayne State Coll (NE)
Wesley Coll (DE)
Western Connecticut State U (CT)
Western State Coll of Colorado (CO)
Western Washington U (WA)
Westfield State Coll (MA)
West Liberty State Coll (WV)
Westminster Coll (PA)
West Texas A&M U (TX)
West Virginia U (WV)
Whitworth Coll (WA)
Widener U (PA)
Wilberforce U (OH)
William Paterson U of New Jersey (NJ)
William Penn U (IA)
Wilson Coll (PA)
Wingate U (NC)
Winona State U (MN)
Winston-Salem State U (NC)
Winthrop U (SC)
Worcester State Coll (MA)
Wright State U (OH)
Xavier U of Louisiana (LA)
York Coll of Pennsylvania (PA)
York U (ON, Canada)

MASS COMMUNICATIONS

The U of North Carolina at Greensboro (NC)
The U of North Carolina at Pembroke (NC)

MATERIALS ENGINEERING

Arizona State U (AZ)
Auburn U (AL)
Brown U (RI)
California Polytechnic State U, San Luis Obispo (CA)
California State Polytechnic U, Pomona (CA)
California State U, Long Beach (CA)
Carnegie Mellon U (PA)
Case Western Reserve U (OH)
Clarkson U (NY)
Clemson U (SC)
Cornell U (NY)
Drexel U (PA)
Florida State U (FL)
Georgia Inst of Technology (GA)
Harvard U (MA)
Illinois Inst of Technology (IL)
Iowa State U of Science and Technology (IA)
The Johns Hopkins U (MD)
Lehigh U (PA)
Massachusetts Inst of Technology (MA)
Michigan Technological U (MI)
Montana Tech of The U of Montana (MT)
New Mexico Inst of Mining and Technology (NM)
North Carolina State U (NC)
Northwestern U (IL)
The Ohio State U (OH)
Purdue U (IN)
Rensselaer Polytechnic Inst (NY)
Rice U (TX)
San Jose State U (CA)
Stanford U (CA)
The U of Alabama at Birmingham (AL)
The U of British Columbia (BC, Canada)
U of Calif, Davis (CA)
U of Calif, Irvine (CA)
U of Calif, Los Angeles (CA)
U of Connecticut (CT)
U of Florida (FL)
U of Kentucky (KY)
U of Maryland, Coll Park (MD)
U of Michigan (MI)
U of Minnesota, Twin Cities Campus (MN)
U of Missouri–Rolla (MO)
U of Pennsylvania (PA)
U of Pittsburgh (PA)
The U of Tennessee (TN)
U of Toronto (ON, Canada)
U of Utah (UT)
U of Washington (WA)
The U of Western Ontario (ON, Canada)
U of Windsor (ON, Canada)
U of Wisconsin–Milwaukee (WI)
Virginia Polytechnic Inst and State U (VA)
Washington State U (WA)
Winona State U (MN)
Worcester Polytechnic Inst (MA)
Wright State U (OH)

MATERIALS SCIENCE

Alfred U (NY)
Carnegie Mellon U (PA)
Case Western Reserve U (OH)
Clarkson U (NY)
Columbia U, School of Eng & Applied Sci (NY)
Cornell U (NY)
Duke U (NC)
Harvard U (MA)
The Johns Hopkins U (MD)
Michigan State U (MI)
Montana Tech of The U of Montana (MT)
North Carolina State U (NC)
Northwestern U (IL)
The Ohio State U (OH)
Oregon State U (OR)
Penn State U Abington Coll (PA)
Penn State U Altoona Coll (PA)
Penn State U at Erie, The Behrend Coll (PA)
Penn State U Beaver Campus of the Commonwealth Coll (PA)
Penn State U Berks Cmps of Berks-Lehigh Valley Coll (PA)
Penn State U Delaware County Campus of the Commonwealth Coll (PA)
Penn State U DuBois Campus of the Commonwealth Coll (PA)
Penn State U Fayette Campus of the Commonwealth Coll (PA)
Penn State U Hazleton Campus of the Commonwealth Coll (PA)
Penn State U Lehigh Valley Cmps of Berks-Lehigh Valley Coll (PA)
Penn State U McKeesport Campus of the Commonwealth Coll (PA)
Penn State U Mont Alto Campus of the Commonwealth Coll (PA)
Penn State U New Kensington Campus of the Commonwealth Coll (PA)
Penn State U Schuylkill Campus of the Capital Coll (PA)
Penn State U Shenango Campus of the Commonwealth Coll (PA)
Penn State U Univ Park Campus (PA)
Penn State U Wilkes-Barre Campus of the Commonwealth Coll (PA)
Penn State U Worthington Scranton Cmps Commonwealth Coll (PA)
Penn State U York Campus of the Commonwealth Coll (PA)
Rice U (TX)
Stanford U (CA)
United States Air Force Acad (CO)
The U of Arizona (AZ)
U of Calif, Berkeley (CA)
U of Calif, Los Angeles (CA)
U of Illinois at Urbana–Champaign (IL)
U of Michigan (MI)
U of Minnesota, Twin Cities Campus (MN)
U of Pennsylvania (PA)
U of Southern California (CA)
U of Toronto (ON, Canada)
U of Utah (UT)
Washington State U (WA)
Worcester Polytechnic Inst (MA)

MATERNAL/CHILD HEALTH AND NEONATAL NURSING

U at Buffalo, The State U of New York (NY)
U of Washington (WA)

MATHEMATICAL STATISTICS AND PROBABILITY

Northern Illinois U (IL)

MATHEMATICS

Abilene Christian U (TX)
Acadia U (NS, Canada)
Adams State Coll (CO)
Adelphi U (NY)
Adrian Coll (MI)
Agnes Scott Coll (GA)
Alabama Ag and Mech U (AL)
Alabama State U (AL)
Albany State U (GA)
Albertson Coll of Idaho (ID)
Albertus Magnus Coll (CT)
Albion Coll (MI)
Albright Coll (PA)
Alcorn State U (MS)
Alderson-Broaddus Coll (WV)
Alfred U (NY)
Allegheny Coll (PA)
Allen U (SC)
Alma Coll (MI)
Alvernia Coll (PA)
Alverno Coll (WI)
American Intl Coll (MA)
American U (DC)
American U in Bulgaria(Bulgaria)
The American U in Cairo(Egypt)
Amherst Coll (MA)
Anderson Coll (SC)
Andrews U (MI)
Angelo State U (TX)
Antioch Coll (OH)
Appalachian State U (NC)
Aquinas Coll (MI)
Arcadia U (PA)
Arizona State U (AZ)
Arkansas State U (AR)
Arkansas Tech U (AR)
Armstrong Atlantic State U (GA)
Asbury Coll (KY)
Ashland U (OH)
Assumption Coll (MA)
Athens State U (AL)
Atlantic Union Coll (MA)
Auburn U (AL)
Auburn U Montgomery (AL)
Augsburg Coll (MN)
Augustana Coll (IL)
Augustana Coll (SD)
Augusta State U (GA)
Aurora U (IL)
Austin Coll (TX)
Austin Peay State U (TN)
Ave Maria Coll (MI)
Ave Maria U (FL)
Averett U (VA)
Avila U (MO)
Azusa Pacific U (CA)
Baker U (KS)
Baldwin-Wallace Coll (OH)
Ball State U (IN)
Barber-Scotia Coll (NC)
Bard Coll (NY)
Barnard Coll (NY)
Barry U (FL)
Barton Coll (NC)
Bates Coll (ME)
Baylor U (TX)
Belhaven Coll (MS)
Bellarmine U (KY)
Belmont U (TN)
Beloit Coll (WI)
Bemidji State U (MN)
Benedictine Coll (KS)
Benedictine U (IL)
Bennington Coll (VT)
Bentley Coll (MA)
Berea Coll (KY)
Baruch Coll of the City U of NY (NY)
Berry Coll (GA)
Bethany Coll (KS)
Bethany Coll (WV)
Bethel Coll (IN)
Bethel Coll (KS)
Bethel Coll (TN)
Bethel U (MN)
Bethune-Cookman Coll (FL)
Biola U (CA)
Birmingham-Southern Coll (AL)
Bishop's U (QC, Canada)
Blackburn Coll (IL)
Black Hills State U (SD)
Bloomsburg U of Pennsylvania (PA)
Bluefield Coll (VA)
Blue Mountain Coll (MS)
Bluffton Coll (OH)
Boise State U (ID)
Boston Coll (MA)
Boston U (MA)
Bowdoin Coll (ME)
Bowie State U (MD)
Bowling Green State U (OH)
Bradley U (IL)
Brandeis U (MA)
Brevard Coll (NC)
Brewton-Parker Coll (GA)
Briar Cliff U (IA)
Bridgewater Coll (VA)
Bridgewater State Coll (MA)
Brigham Young U (UT)
Brigham Young U–Hawaii (HI)
Brock U (ON, Canada)
Brooklyn Coll of the City U of NY (NY)
Brown U (RI)
Bryan Coll (TN)
Bryn Mawr Coll (PA)
Bucknell U (PA)
Buena Vista U (IA)
State U of NY Coll at Buffalo (NY)
Butler U (IN)
Cabrini Coll (PA)
Caldwell Coll (NJ)
California Baptist U (CA)
California Inst of Technology (CA)
California Lutheran U (CA)
California Polytechnic State U, San Luis Obispo (CA)
California State Polytechnic U, Pomona (CA)
California State U, Chico (CA)
California State U, Dominguez Hills (CA)
California State U, Fresno (CA)
California State U, Fullerton (CA)
California State U, Hayward (CA)
California State U, Long Beach (CA)
California State U, Los Angeles (CA)
California State U, Sacramento (CA)
California State U, San Bernardino (CA)
California State U, San Marcos (CA)
California State U, Stanislaus (CA)
California U of Pennsylvania (PA)
Calvin Coll (MI)
Cameron U (OK)
Campbellsville U (KY)
Campbell U (NC)
Canadian Mennonite U (MB, Canada)
Capital U (OH)
Cardinal Stritch U (WI)
Carleton Coll (MN)
Carleton U (ON, Canada)
Carlow Coll (PA)
Carnegie Mellon U (PA)
Carroll Coll (MT)
Carroll Coll (WI)
Carson-Newman Coll (TN)
Carthage Coll (WI)
Case Western Reserve U (OH)
Castleton State Coll (VT)
Catawba Coll (NC)
The Catholic U of America (DC)
Cedar Crest Coll (PA)
Cedarville U (OH)
Centenary Coll (NJ)
Centenary Coll of Louisiana (LA)
Central Coll (IA)
Central Connecticut State U (CT)
Central Methodist Coll (MO)
Central Michigan U (MI)
Central Missouri State U (MO)
Central State U (OH)
Central Washington U (WA)
Centre Coll (KY)
Chadron State Coll (NE)
Chapman U (CA)
Charleston Southern U (SC)
Chatham Coll (PA)
Cheyney U of Pennsylvania (PA)
Chicago State U (IL)
Chowan Coll (NC)
Christian Brothers U (TN)
Christian Heritage Coll (CA)
Christopher Newport U (VA)
Citadel, The Military Coll of South Carolina (SC)
City Coll of the City U of NY (NY)
Claremont McKenna Coll (CA)
Clarion U of Pennsylvania (PA)
Clark Atlanta U (GA)
Clarke Coll (IA)
Clarkson U (NY)
Clark U (MA)
Clearwater Christian Coll (FL)
Clemson U (SC)
Cleveland State U (OH)
Coe Coll (IA)
Coker Coll (SC)
Colby Coll (ME)
Colgate U (NY)
Coll Misericordia (PA)
Coll of Charleston (SC)
Coll of Mount St. Joseph (OH)
Coll of Mount Saint Vincent (NY)
The Coll of New Jersey (NJ)
The Coll of New Rochelle (NY)
Coll of Notre Dame of Maryland (MD)
Coll of Saint Benedict (MN)
Coll of St. Catherine (MN)
Coll of Saint Elizabeth (NJ)
Coll of Saint Mary (NE)
The Coll of Saint Rose (NY)
The Coll of St. Scholastica (MN)
The Coll of Southeastern Europe, The American U of Athens(Greece)
Coll of Staten Island of the City U of NY (NY)
Coll of the Holy Cross (MA)
Coll of the Ozarks (MO)
Coll of the Southwest (NM)
The Coll of William and Mary (VA)
The Coll of Wooster (OH)
Colorado Christian U (CO)
The Colorado Coll (CO)
Colorado School of Mines (CO)
Colorado State U (CO)
Colorado State U-Pueblo (CO)
Columbia Coll (MO)
Columbia Coll (NY)
Columbia Coll (SC)
Columbia Union Coll (MD)
Columbia U, School of General Studies (NY)
Columbus State U (GA)
Concord Coll (WV)
Concordia Coll (MN)
Concordia Coll (NY)
Concordia U (CA)
Concordia U (IL)
Concordia U (MI)
Concordia U (NE)
Concordia U (QC, Canada)
Concordia U at Austin (TX)
Concordia U Coll of Alberta (AB, Canada)
Concordia U, St. Paul (MN)
Concordia U Wisconsin (WI)
Connecticut Coll (CT)
Converse Coll (SC)
Cornell Coll (IA)
Cornell U (NY)
Cornerstone U (MI)
Covenant Coll (GA)
Creighton U (NE)
Culver-Stockton Coll (MO)
Cumberland Coll (KY)
Cumberland U (TN)
Daemen Coll (NY)
Dakota State U (SD)
Dakota Wesleyan U (SD)
Dalhousie U (NS, Canada)
Dallas Baptist U (TX)
Dana Coll (NE)
Dartmouth Coll (NH)
Davidson Coll (NC)
Davis & Elkins Coll (WV)
Defiance Coll (OH)
Delaware State U (DE)
Delaware Valley Coll (PA)
Delta State U (MS)
Denison U (OH)
DePaul U (IL)
DePauw U (IN)
DeSales U (PA)
Dickinson Coll (PA)
Dickinson State U (ND)
Dillard U (LA)
Doane Coll (NE)
Dominican Coll (NY)
Dominican U (IL)
Dordt Coll (IA)
Dowling Coll (NY)
Drake U (IA)
Drew U (NJ)
Drexel U (PA)
Drury U (MO)
Duke U (NC)
Duquesne U (PA)
Earlham Coll (IN)
East Carolina U (NC)
East Central U (OK)
Eastern Connecticut State U (CT)
Eastern Illinois U (IL)
Eastern Kentucky U (KY)
Eastern Mennonite U (VA)
Eastern Michigan U (MI)
Eastern Nazarene Coll (MA)
Eastern Oregon U (OR)
Eastern U (PA)
Eastern Washington U (WA)
East Stroudsburg U of Pennsylvania (PA)
East Texas Baptist U (TX)
Eckerd Coll (FL)
Edgewood Coll (WI)
Edinboro U of Pennsylvania (PA)
Elizabeth City State U (NC)
Elizabethtown Coll (PA)
Elmhurst Coll (IL)
Elmira Coll (NY)
Elms Coll (MA)
Elon U (NC)
Emmanuel Coll (GA)
Emory & Henry Coll (VA)
Emory U (GA)

Emporia State U (KS)
Erskine Coll (SC)
Eureka Coll (IL)
Evangel U (MO)
Excelsior Coll (NY)
Fairfield U (CT)
Fairleigh Dickinson U, Florham (NJ)
Fairleigh Dickinson U, Teaneck-Metro Campus (NJ)
Fairmont State Coll (WV)
Fayetteville State U (NC)
Ferris State U (MI)
Ferrum Coll (VA)
Florida Ag and Mech U (FL)
Florida Atlantic U (FL)
Florida Intl U (FL)
Florida Southern Coll (FL)
Florida State U (FL)
Fontbonne U (MO)
Fordham U (NY)
Fort Hays State U (KS)
Fort Lewis Coll (CO)
Fort Valley State U (GA)
Framingham State Coll (MA)
Franciscan U of Steubenville (OH)
Francis Marion U (SC)
Franklin and Marshall Coll (PA)
Franklin Coll (IN)
Franklin Pierce Coll (NH)
Freed-Hardeman U (TN)
Fresno Pacific U (CA)
Frostburg State U (MD)
Furman U (SC)
Gallaudet U (DC)
Gannon U (PA)
Gardner-Webb U (NC)
George Fox U (OR)
George Mason U (VA)
Georgetown Coll (KY)
Georgetown U (DC)
The George Washington U (DC)
Georgia Coll & State U (GA)
Georgia Inst of Technology (GA)
Georgian Court U (NJ)
Georgia Southern U (GA)
Georgia Southwestern State U (GA)
Georgia State U (GA)
Gettysburg Coll (PA)
Gonzaga U (WA)
Gordon Coll (MA)
Goshen Coll (IN)
Goucher Coll (MD)
Grace Coll (IN)
Graceland U (IA)
Grambling State U (LA)
Grand Canyon U (AZ)
Grand Valley State U (MI)
Greensboro Coll (NC)
Greenville Coll (IL)
Grinnell Coll (IA)
Grove City Coll (PA)
Guilford Coll (NC)
Gustavus Adolphus Coll (MN)
Gwynedd-Mercy Coll (PA)
Hamilton Coll (NY)
Hamline U (MN)
Hampden-Sydney Coll (VA)
Hampshire Coll (MA)
Hampton U (VA)
Hannibal-LaGrange Coll (MO)
Hanover Coll (IN)
Harding U (AR)
Hardin-Simmons U (TX)
Hartwick Coll (NY)
Harvard U (MA)
Harvey Mudd Coll (CA)
Hastings Coll (NE)
Haverford Coll (PA)
Heidelberg Coll (OH)
Henderson State U (AR)
Hendrix Coll (AR)
High Point U (NC)
Hillsdale Coll (MI)
Hiram Coll (OH)
Hobart and William Smith Colls (NY)
Hofstra U (NY)
Hollins U (VA)
Hood Coll (MD)
Hope Coll (MI)
Houghton Coll (NY)
Houston Baptist U (TX)
Howard Payne U (TX)
Howard U (DC)
Humboldt State U (CA)
Hunter Coll of the City U of NY (NY)
Huntingdon Coll (AL)
Huntington Coll (IN)
Huron U USA in London(United Kingdom)
Huston-Tillotson Coll (TX)
Idaho State U (ID)
Illinois Coll (IL)
Illinois State U (IL)
Illinois Wesleyan U (IL)
Immaculata U (PA)
Indiana State U (IN)
Indiana U Bloomington (IN)
Indiana U Kokomo (IN)
Indiana U Northwest (IN)
Indiana U of Pennsylvania (PA)
Indiana U–Purdue U Fort Wayne (IN)
Indiana U–Purdue U Indianapolis (IN)
Indiana U South Bend (IN)
Indiana U Southeast (IN)
Inter American U of PR, Bayamón Campus (PR)
Inter American U of PR, San Germán Campus (PR)
Iona Coll (NY)
Iowa State U of Science and Technology (IA)
Iowa Wesleyan Coll (IA)
Ithaca Coll (NY)
Jacksonville State U (AL)
Jacksonville U (FL)
James Madison U (VA)
Jamestown Coll (ND)
Jarvis Christian Coll (TX)
John Brown U (AR)
John Carroll U (OH)
The Johns Hopkins U (MD)
Johnson C. Smith U (NC)
Johnson State Coll (VT)
Judson Coll (AL)
Judson Coll (IL)
Juniata Coll (PA)
Kalamazoo Coll (MI)
Kansas State U (KS)
Kansas Wesleyan U (KS)
Kean U (NJ)
Keene State Coll (NH)
Kennesaw State U (GA)
Kent State U (OH)
Kentucky State U (KY)
Kentucky Wesleyan Coll (KY)
Kenyon Coll (OH)
Keuka Coll (NY)
King Coll (TN)
King's Coll (PA)
Knox Coll (IL)
Kutztown U of Pennsylvania (PA)
Lafayette Coll (PA)
LaGrange Coll (GA)
Lake Erie Coll (OH)
Lake Forest Coll (IL)
Lakehead U (ON, Canada)
Lakeland Coll (WI)
Lake Superior State U (MI)
Lamar U (TX)
Lambuth U (TN)
Lander U (SC)
Lane Coll (TN)
La Salle U (PA)
Laurentian U (ON, Canada)
Lawrence Technological U (MI)
Lawrence U (WI)
Lebanon Valley Coll (PA)
Lehigh U (PA)
Lehman Coll of the City U of NY (NY)
Le Moyne Coll (NY)
Lenoir-Rhyne Coll (NC)
LeTourneau U (TX)
Lewis & Clark Coll (OR)
Lewis-Clark State Coll (ID)
Lewis U (IL)
Liberty U (VA)
Limestone Coll (SC)
Lincoln Memorial U (TN)
Lincoln U (MO)
Lincoln U (PA)
Lindenwood U (MO)
Lindsey Wilson Coll (KY)
Linfield Coll (OR)
Lipscomb U (TN)
Livingstone Coll (NC)
Lock Haven U of Pennsylvania (PA)
Long Island U, Brooklyn Campus (NY)
Long Island U, C.W. Post Campus (NY)
Longwood U (VA)
Loras Coll (IA)
Louisiana Coll (LA)
Louisiana State U and A&M Coll (LA)
Louisiana State U in Shreveport (LA)
Louisiana Tech U (LA)
Loyola Coll in Maryland (MD)
Loyola Marymount U (CA)
Loyola U Chicago (IL)
Loyola U New Orleans (LA)
Lubbock Christian U (TX)
Luther Coll (IA)
Lycoming Coll (PA)
Lynchburg Coll (VA)
Lyndon State Coll (VT)
Lyon Coll (AR)
Macalester Coll (MN)
MacMurray Coll (IL)
Madonna U (MI)
Maharishi U of Management (IA)
Malone Coll (OH)
Manchester Coll (IN)
Manhattan Coll (NY)
Manhattanville Coll (NY)
Mansfield U of Pennsylvania (PA)
Marian Coll (IN)
Marian Coll of Fond du Lac (WI)
Marietta Coll (OH)
Marist Coll (NY)
Marlboro Coll (VT)
Marquette U (WI)
Marshall U (WV)
Mars Hill Coll (NC)
Martin U (IN)
Mary Baldwin Coll (VA)
Marygrove Coll (MI)
Marymount Coll of Fordham U (NY)
Marymount U (VA)
Maryville Coll (TN)
Maryville U of Saint Louis (MO)
Mary Washington Coll (VA)
Marywood U (PA)
Massachusetts Coll of Liberal Arts (MA)
Massachusetts Inst of Technology (MA)
The Master's Coll and Sem (CA)
Mayville State U (ND)
McDaniel Coll (MD)
McGill U (QC, Canada)
McKendree Coll (IL)
McMurry U (TX)
McNeese State U (LA)
McPherson Coll (KS)
Memorial U of Newfoundland (NL, Canada)
Mercer U (GA)
Mercy Coll (NY)
Mercyhurst Coll (PA)
Meredith Coll (NC)
Merrimack Coll (MA)
Messiah Coll (PA)
Methodist Coll (NC)
Metropolitan State Coll of Denver (CO)
Miami U (OH)
Miami U Hamilton (OH)
Michigan State U (MI)
Michigan Technological U (MI)
MidAmerica Nazarene U (KS)
Middlebury Coll (VT)
Middle Tennessee State U (TN)
Midway Coll (KY)
Midwestern State U (TX)
Miles Coll (AL)
Millersville U of Pennsylvania (PA)
Milligan Coll (TN)
Millikin U (IL)
Millsaps Coll (MS)
Mills Coll (CA)
Minnesota State U Mankato (MN)
Minnesota State U Moorhead (MN)
Minot State U (ND)
Mississippi Coll (MS)
Mississippi State U (MS)
Mississippi Valley State U (MS)
Missouri Baptist U (MO)
Missouri Southern State U (MO)
Missouri Valley Coll (MO)
Missouri Western State Coll (MO)
Molloy Coll (NY)
Monmouth Coll (IL)
Monmouth U (NJ)
Montana State U–Billings (MT)
Montana State U–Bozeman (MT)
Montana Tech of The U of Montana (MT)
Montclair State U (NJ)
Moravian Coll (PA)
Morehead State U (KY)
Morehouse Coll (GA)
Morgan State U (MD)
Morningside Coll (IA)
Morris Coll (SC)
Mount Allison U (NB, Canada)
Mount Holyoke Coll (MA)
Mount Marty Coll (SD)
Mount Mary Coll (WI)
Mount Mercy Coll (IA)
Mount Saint Mary Coll (NY)
Mount St. Mary's Coll (CA)
Mount Saint Mary's Coll and Sem (MD)
Mount Saint Vincent U (NS, Canada)
Mount Union Coll (OH)
Mount Vernon Nazarene U (OH)
Muhlenberg Coll (PA)
Murray State U (KY)
National-Louis U (IL)
National U (CA)
Nazareth Coll of Rochester (NY)
Nebraska Wesleyan U (NE)
Newberry Coll (SC)
New Coll of Florida (FL)
New Jersey City U (NJ)
Newman U (KS)
New Mexico Highlands U (NM)
New Mexico Inst of Mining and Technology (NM)
New Mexico State U (NM)
New York U (NY)
Niagara U (NY)
Nicholls State U (LA)
Nichols Coll (MA)
Nipissing U (ON, Canada)
Norfolk State U (VA)
North Carolina Central U (NC)
North Carolina State U (NC)
North Carolina Wesleyan Coll (NC)
North Central Coll (IL)
North Dakota State U (ND)
Northeastern Illinois U (IL)
Northeastern State U (OK)
Northeastern U (MA)
Northern Arizona U (AZ)
Northern Illinois U (IL)
Northern Michigan U (MI)
Northern State U (SD)
North Georgia Coll & State U (GA)
Northland Coll (WI)
North Park U (IL)
Northwestern Coll (IA)
Northwestern Coll (MN)
Northwestern Oklahoma State U (OK)
Northwestern State U of Louisiana (LA)
Northwestern U (IL)
Northwest Nazarene U (ID)
Notre Dame Coll (OH)
Nyack Coll (NY)
Oakland City U (IN)
Oakland U (MI)
Oberlin Coll (OH)
Occidental Coll (CA)
Oglethorpe U (GA)
Ohio Dominican U (OH)
Ohio Northern U (OH)
The Ohio State U (OH)
The Ohio State U at Lima (OH)
Ohio U (OH)
Ohio Wesleyan U (OH)
Okanagan U Coll (BC, Canada)
Oklahoma Baptist U (OK)
Oklahoma Christian U (OK)
Oklahoma City U (OK)
Oklahoma Panhandle State U (OK)
Oklahoma State U (OK)
Old Dominion U (VA)
Olivet Coll (MI)
Olivet Nazarene U (IL)
Oral Roberts U (OK)
Oregon State U (OR)
Ottawa U (KS)
Otterbein Coll (OH)
Ouachita Baptist U (AR)
Our Lady of Holy Cross Coll (LA)
Our Lady of the Lake U of San Antonio (TX)
Pace U (NY)
Pacific Lutheran U (WA)
Pacific Union Coll (CA)
Pacific U (OR)
Paine Coll (GA)
Palm Beach Atlantic U (FL)
Park U (MO)
Penn State U Abington Coll (PA)
Penn State U Altoona Coll (PA)
Penn State U at Erie, The Behrend Coll (PA)
Penn State U Beaver Campus of the Commonwealth Coll (PA)
Penn State U Berks Cmps of Berks-Lehigh Valley Coll (PA)
Penn State U Delaware County Campus of the Commonwealth Coll (PA)
Penn State U DuBois Campus of the Commonwealth Coll (PA)
Penn State U Fayette Campus of the Commonwealth Coll (PA)
Penn State U Hazleton Campus of the Commonwealth Coll (PA)
Penn State U Lehigh Valley Cmps of Berks-Lehigh Valley Coll (PA)
Penn State U McKeesport Campus of the Commonwealth Coll (PA)
Penn State U Mont Alto Campus of the Commonwealth Coll (PA)
Penn State U New Kensington Campus of the Commonwealth Coll (PA)
Penn State U Schuylkill Campus of the Capital Coll (PA)
Penn State U Shenango Campus of the Commonwealth Coll (PA)
Penn State U Univ Park Campus (PA)
Penn State U Wilkes-Barre Campus of the Commonwealth Coll (PA)
Penn State U Worthington Scranton Cmps Commonwealth Coll (PA)
Penn State U York Campus of the Commonwealth Coll (PA)
Pepperdine U, Malibu (CA)
Pfeiffer U (NC)
Piedmont Coll (GA)
Pikeville Coll (KY)
Pittsburg State U (KS)
Pitzer Coll (CA)
Plymouth State U (NH)
Point Loma Nazarene U (CA)
Polytechnic U, Brooklyn Campus (NY)
Pomona Coll (CA)
Pontifical Catholic U of Puerto Rico (PR)
Portland State U (OR)
Prairie View A&M U (TX)
Presbyterian Coll (SC)
Princeton U (NJ)
Principia Coll (IL)
Providence Coll (RI)
Purdue U (IN)
Queens Coll of the City U of NY (NY)
Queen's U at Kingston (ON, Canada)
Queens U of Charlotte (NC)
Quinnipiac U (CT)
Radford U (VA)
Ramapo Coll of New Jersey (NJ)
Randolph-Macon Coll (VA)
Randolph-Macon Woman's Coll (VA)
Redeemer U Coll (ON, Canada)
Reed Coll (OR)
Regis Coll (MA)
Regis U (CO)
Rensselaer Polytechnic Inst (NY)
Rhode Island Coll (RI)
Rhodes Coll (TN)
Rice U (TX)
The Richard Stockton Coll of New Jersey (NJ)
Richmond, The American Intl U in London(United Kingdom)
Rider U (NJ)
Ripon Coll (WI)
Rivier Coll (NH)
Roanoke Coll (VA)
Roberts Wesleyan Coll (NY)
Rochester Coll (MI)
Rochester Inst of Technology (NY)
Rockford Coll (IL)
Rockhurst U (MO)
Rocky Mountain Coll (MT)
Roger Williams U (RI)
Rollins Coll (FL)
Roosevelt U (IL)
Rose-Hulman Inst of Technology (IN)
Rosemont Coll (PA)
Rowan U (NJ)
Russell Sage Coll (NY)
Rutgers, The State U of New Jersey, Camden (NJ)
Rutgers, The State U of New Jersey, Newark (NJ)
Rutgers, The State U of New Jersey, New Brunswick/Piscataway (NJ)
Sacred Heart U (CT)
Saginaw Valley State U (MI)
St. Ambrose U (IA)
St. Andrews Presbyterian Coll (NC)
Saint Anselm Coll (NH)
Saint Augustine's Coll (NC)
St. Bonaventure U (NY)
St. Cloud State U (MN)
St. Edward's U (TX)
St. Francis Coll (NY)
Saint Francis U (PA)
St. Francis Xavier U (NS, Canada)
St. Gregory's U (OK)
St. John Fisher Coll (NY)
St. John's Coll (NM)
Saint John's U (MN)
St. John's U (NY)
Saint Joseph Coll (CT)
Saint Joseph's Coll (IN)
St. Joseph's Coll, New York (NY)
Saint Joseph's Coll of Maine (ME)
St. Joseph's Coll, Suffolk Campus (NY)
Saint Joseph's U (PA)

St. Lawrence U (NY)
Saint Louis U (MO)
Saint Martin's Coll (WA)
Saint Mary-of-the-Woods Coll (IN)
Saint Mary's Coll (IN)
Saint Mary's Coll of California (CA)
St. Mary's Coll of Maryland (MD)
Saint Mary's U of Minnesota (MN)
St. Mary's U of San Antonio (TX)
Saint Michael's Coll (VT)
St. Norbert Coll (WI)
St. Olaf Coll (MN)
St. Thomas Aquinas Coll (NY)
St. Thomas U (NB, Canada)
Saint Vincent Coll (PA)
Saint Xavier U (IL)
Salem Coll (NC)
Salem State Coll (MA)
Salisbury U (MD)
Salve Regina U (RI)
Samford U (AL)
Sam Houston State U (TX)
San Diego State U (CA)
San Francisco State U (CA)
San Jose State U (CA)
Santa Clara U (CA)
Sarah Lawrence Coll (NY)
Schreiner U (TX)
Scripps Coll (CA)
Seattle Pacific U (WA)
Seattle U (WA)
Seton Hall U (NJ)
Seton Hill U (PA)
Shawnee State U (OH)
Shaw U (NC)
Shenandoah U (VA)
Shepherd U (WV)
Shippensburg U of Pennsylvania (PA)
Shorter Coll (GA)
Siena Coll (NY)
Siena Heights U (MI)
Silver Lake Coll (WI)
Simmons Coll (MA)
Simon Fraser U (BC, Canada)
Simon's Rock Coll of Bard (MA)
Simpson Coll (IA)
Simpson Coll and Graduate School (CA)
Skidmore Coll (NY)
Slippery Rock U of Pennsylvania (PA)
Smith Coll (MA)
Sonoma State U (CA)
South Carolina State U (SC)
South Dakota School of Mines and Technology (SD)
South Dakota State U (SD)
Southeastern Louisiana U (LA)
Southeastern Oklahoma State U (OK)
Southeast Missouri State U (MO)
Southern Adventist U (TN)
Southern Arkansas U–Magnolia (AR)
Southern Connecticut State U (CT)
Southern Illinois U Carbondale (IL)
Southern Illinois U Edwardsville (IL)
Southern Methodist U (TX)
Southern Nazarene U (OK)
Southern Oregon U (OR)
Southern Polytechnic State U (GA)
Southern U and A&M Coll (LA)
Southern Utah U (UT)
Southern Wesleyan U (SC)
Southwest Baptist U (MO)
Southwestern Coll (KS)
Southwestern Oklahoma State U (OK)
Southwestern U (TX)
Southwest Missouri State U (MO)
Spelman Coll (GA)
Spring Arbor U (MI)
Springfield Coll (MA)
Spring Hill Coll (AL)
Stanford U (CA)
State U of NY at Binghamton (NY)
State U of NY at New Paltz (NY)
State U of NY at Oswego (NY)
Plattsburgh State U of NY (NY)
State U of NY Coll at Brockport (NY)
State U of NY Coll at Cortland (NY)
State U of NY Coll at Fredonia (NY)
State U of NY Coll at Geneseo (NY)
State U of NY Coll at Old Westbury (NY)
State U of NY Coll at Oneonta (NY)
State U of NY Coll at Potsdam (NY)
State U of NY Empire State Coll (NY)
State U of West Georgia (GA)
Sterling Coll (KS)
Stetson U (FL)
Stevens Inst of Technology (NJ)
Stonehill Coll (MA)
Stony Brook U, State U of New York (NY)
Suffolk U (MA)
Susquehanna U (PA)
Swarthmore Coll (PA)
Sweet Briar Coll (VA)
Syracuse U (NY)
Tabor Coll (KS)
Talladega Coll (AL)
Tarleton State U (TX)
Taylor U (IN)
Tennessee State U (TN)
Tennessee Technological U (TN)
Tennessee Wesleyan Coll (TN)
Texas A&M Intl U (TX)
Texas A&M U (TX)
Texas A&M U–Commerce (TX)
Texas A&M U–Corpus Christi (TX)
Texas A&M U–Kingsville (TX)
Texas A&M U–Texarkana (TX)
Texas Christian U (TX)
Texas Lutheran U (TX)
Texas Southern U (TX)
Texas State U-San Marcos (TX)
Texas Tech U (TX)
Texas Wesleyan U (TX)
Texas Woman's U (TX)
Thiel Coll (PA)
Thomas Edison State Coll (NJ)
Thomas More Coll (KY)
Tougaloo Coll (MS)
Towson U (MD)
Transylvania U (KY)
Trent U (ON, Canada)
Trevecca Nazarene U (TN)
Trinity Christian Coll (IL)
Trinity Coll (CT)
Trinity Coll (DC)
Trinity Intl U (IL)
Trinity U (TX)
Trinity Western U (BC, Canada)
Tri-State U (IN)
Troy State U (AL)
Troy State U Dothan (AL)
Troy State U Montgomery (AL)
Truman State U (MO)
Tufts U (MA)
Tulane U (LA)
Tusculum Coll (TN)
Tuskegee U (AL)
Union Coll (KY)
Union Coll (NE)
Union Coll (NY)
Union U (TN)
United States Air Force Acad (CO)
United States Military Acad (NY)
United States Naval Acad (MD)
Université de Montréal (QC, Canada)
Université de Sherbrooke (QC, Canada)
Université Laval (QC, Canada)
State U of NY at Albany (NY)
U at Buffalo, The State U of New York (NY)
U Coll of the Cariboo (BC, Canada)
U Coll of the Fraser Valley (BC, Canada)
The U of Akron (OH)
The U of Alabama (AL)
The U of Alabama at Birmingham (AL)
The U of Alabama in Huntsville (AL)
U of Alaska Fairbanks (AK)
U of Alberta (AB, Canada)
The U of Arizona (AZ)
U of Arkansas (AR)
U of Arkansas at Little Rock (AR)
U of Arkansas at Monticello (AR)
U of Bridgeport (CT)
The U of British Columbia (BC, Canada)
U of Calgary (AB, Canada)
U of Calif, Berkeley (CA)
U of Calif, Davis (CA)
U of Calif, Irvine (CA)
U of Calif, Los Angeles (CA)
U of Calif, Riverside (CA)
U of Calif, San Diego (CA)
U of Calif, Santa Barbara (CA)
U of Calif, Santa Cruz (CA)
U of Central Arkansas (AR)
U of Central Florida (FL)
U of Chicago (IL)
U of Cincinnati (OH)
U of Colorado at Boulder (CO)
U of Colorado at Colorado Springs (CO)
U of Colorado at Denver (CO)
U of Connecticut (CT)
U of Dallas (TX)
U of Dayton (OH)
U of Delaware (DE)
U of Denver (CO)
U of Detroit Mercy (MI)
U of Evansville (IN)
The U of Findlay (OH)
U of Florida (FL)
U of Georgia (GA)
U of Great Falls (MT)
U of Guelph (ON, Canada)
U of Hartford (CT)
U of Hawaii at Hilo (HI)
U of Hawaii at Manoa (HI)
U of Houston (TX)
U of Houston–Clear Lake (TX)
U of Houston–Victoria (TX)
U of Idaho (ID)
U of Illinois at Chicago (IL)
U of Illinois at Springfield (IL)
U of Illinois at Urbana–Champaign (IL)
U of Indianapolis (IN)
The U of Iowa (IA)
U of Kansas (KS)
U of Kentucky (KY)
U of King's Coll (NS, Canada)
U of La Verne (CA)
The U of Lethbridge (AB, Canada)
U of Louisiana at Lafayette (LA)
U of Louisville (KY)
U of Maine (ME)
U of Maine at Farmington (ME)
U of Manitoba (MB, Canada)
U of Mary (ND)
U of Mary Hardin-Baylor (TX)
U of Maryland, Baltimore County (MD)
U of Maryland, Coll Park (MD)
U of Maryland Eastern Shore (MD)
U of Massachusetts Amherst (MA)
U of Massachusetts Boston (MA)
U of Massachusetts Dartmouth (MA)
U of Massachusetts Lowell (MA)
The U of Memphis (TN)
U of Miami (FL)
U of Michigan (MI)
U of Michigan–Dearborn (MI)
U of Michigan–Flint (MI)
U of Minnesota, Duluth (MN)
U of Minnesota, Morris (MN)
U of Minnesota, Twin Cities Campus (MN)
U of Mississippi (MS)
U of Missouri–Columbia (MO)
U of Missouri–Kansas City (MO)
U of Missouri–St. Louis (MO)
U of Mobile (AL)
The U of Montana–Missoula (MT)
U of Montevallo (AL)
U of Nebraska at Omaha (NE)
U of Nebraska–Lincoln (NE)
U of Nevada, Las Vegas (NV)
U of Nevada, Reno (NV)
U of New Brunswick Fredericton (NB, Canada)
U of New Hampshire (NH)
U of New Haven (CT)
U of New Mexico (NM)
U of New Orleans (LA)
U of North Alabama (AL)
The U of North Carolina at Asheville (NC)
The U of North Carolina at Chapel Hill (NC)
The U of North Carolina at Charlotte (NC)
The U of North Carolina at Greensboro (NC)
The U of North Carolina at Pembroke (NC)
The U of North Carolina at Wilmington (NC)
U of North Dakota (ND)
U of Northern Colorado (CO)
U of Northern Iowa (IA)
U of North Florida (FL)
U of North Texas (TX)
U of Notre Dame (IN)
U of Oklahoma (OK)
U of Oregon (OR)
U of Ottawa (ON, Canada)
U of Pennsylvania (PA)
U of Pittsburgh (PA)
U of Pittsburgh at Johnstown (PA)
U of Portland (OR)
U of Prince Edward Island (PE, Canada)
U of Puerto Rico, Cayey U Coll (PR)
U of Puget Sound (WA)
U of Redlands (CA)
U of Regina (SK, Canada)
U of Rhode Island (RI)
U of Richmond (VA)
U of Rochester (NY)
U of St. Francis (IL)
U of Saint Mary (KS)
U of St. Thomas (MN)
U of St. Thomas (TX)
U of San Diego (CA)
U of San Francisco (CA)
U of Saskatchewan (SK, Canada)
U of Science and Arts of Oklahoma (OK)
The U of Scranton (PA)
U of Sioux Falls (SD)
U of South Carolina (SC)
U of South Carolina Spartanburg (SC)
The U of South Dakota (SD)
U of Southern California (CA)
U of Southern Indiana (IN)
U of Southern Maine (ME)
U of South Florida (FL)
The U of Tampa (FL)
The U of Tennessee (TN)
The U of Tennessee at Chattanooga (TN)
The U of Tennessee at Martin (TN)
The U of Texas at Arlington (TX)
The U of Texas at Austin (TX)
The U of Texas at Brownsville (TX)
The U of Texas at Dallas (TX)
The U of Texas at Tyler (TX)
The U of Texas–Pan American (TX)
U of the District of Columbia (DC)
U of the Incarnate Word (TX)
U of the Ozarks (AR)
U of the Pacific (CA)
U of the South (TN)
U of the Virgin Islands (VI)
U of Toledo (OH)
U of Toronto (ON, Canada)
U of Tulsa (OK)
U of Utah (UT)
U of Vermont (VT)
U of Victoria (BC, Canada)
U of Virginia (VA)
The U of Virginia's Coll at Wise (VA)
U of Washington (WA)
U of Waterloo (ON, Canada)
The U of West Alabama (AL)
The U of Western Ontario (ON, Canada)
U of West Florida (FL)
U of Windsor (ON, Canada)
U of Wisconsin–Eau Claire (WI)
U of Wisconsin–Green Bay (WI)
U of Wisconsin–La Crosse (WI)
U of Wisconsin–Madison (WI)
U of Wisconsin–Milwaukee (WI)
U of Wisconsin–Oshkosh (WI)
U of Wisconsin–Parkside (WI)
U of Wisconsin–Platteville (WI)
U of Wisconsin–River Falls (WI)
U of Wisconsin–Stevens Point (WI)
U of Wisconsin–Superior (WI)
U of Wisconsin–Whitewater (WI)
U of Wyoming (WY)
Upper Iowa U (IA)
Ursinus Coll (PA)
Ursuline Coll (OH)
Utah State U (UT)
Utica Coll (NY)
Valdosta State U (GA)
Valley City State U (ND)
Valparaiso U (IN)
Vanderbilt U (TN)
Vanguard U of Southern California (CA)
Vassar Coll (NY)
Villanova U (PA)
Virginia Commonwealth U (VA)
Virginia Military Inst (VA)
Virginia Polytechnic Inst and State U (VA)
Virginia State U (VA)
Virginia Union U (VA)
Virginia Wesleyan Coll (VA)
Viterbo U (WI)
Voorhees Coll (SC)
Wabash Coll (IN)
Wagner Coll (NY)
Wake Forest U (NC)
Walla Walla Coll (WA)
Walsh U (OH)
Warren Wilson Coll (NC)
Wartburg Coll (IA)
Washburn U (KS)
Washington & Jefferson Coll (PA)
Washington and Lee U (VA)
Washington Coll (MD)
Washington State U (WA)
Washington U in St. Louis (MO)
Wayland Baptist U (TX)
Waynesburg Coll (PA)
Wayne State Coll (NE)
Wayne State U (MI)
Weber State U (UT)
Webster U (MO)
Wellesley Coll (MA)
Wells Coll (NY)
Wesleyan Coll (GA)
Wesleyan U (CT)
West Chester U of Pennsylvania (PA)
Western Baptist Coll (OR)
Western Carolina U (NC)
Western Connecticut State U (CT)
Western Illinois U (IL)
Western Kentucky U (KY)
Western Michigan U (MI)
Western New England Coll (MA)
Western Oregon U (OR)
Western State Coll of Colorado (CO)
Western Washington U (WA)
Westfield State Coll (MA)
West Liberty State Coll (WV)
Westminster Coll (MO)
Westminster Coll (PA)
Westminster Coll (UT)
Westmont Coll (CA)
West Texas A&M U (TX)
West Virginia State Coll (WV)
West Virginia U (WV)
West Virginia Wesleyan Coll (WV)
Wheaton Coll (IL)
Wheaton Coll (MA)
Wheeling Jesuit U (WV)
Whitman Coll (WA)
Whitworth Coll (WA)
Wichita State U (KS)
Widener U (PA)
Wilberforce U (OH)
Wilkes U (PA)
Willamette U (OR)
William Carey Coll (MS)
William Jewell Coll (MO)
William Paterson U of New Jersey (NJ)
Williams Coll (MA)
William Tyndale Coll (MI)
William Woods U (MO)
Wilson Coll (PA)
Wingate U (NC)
Winona State U (MN)
Winston-Salem State U (NC)
Winthrop U (SC)
Wisconsin Lutheran Coll (WI)
Wittenberg U (OH)
Wofford Coll (SC)
Worcester Polytechnic Inst (MA)
Worcester State Coll (MA)
Wright State U (OH)
Xavier U (OH)
Xavier U of Louisiana (LA)
Yale U (CT)
York Coll of Pennsylvania (PA)
York Coll of the City U of New York (NY)
York U (ON, Canada)
Youngstown State U (OH)

MATHEMATICS AND COMPUTER SCIENCE

Alfred U (NY)
Augustana Coll (IL)
Averett U (VA)
Bethel Coll (IN)
Boston U (MA)
Bowdoin Coll (ME)
Brescia U (KY)
Brown U (RI)
Cardinal Stritch U (WI)
Carlow Coll (PA)
Central Coll (IA)
Chestnut Hill Coll (PA)
Coll of Saint Benedict (MN)
The Colorado Coll (CO)
Drew U (NJ)
Eastern Illinois U (IL)
Hampden-Sydney Coll (VA)
Harvard U (MA)
Hofstra U (NY)
Ithaca Coll (NY)
King Coll (TN)
Lake Superior State U (MI)
Lawrence Technological U (MI)
Lawrence U (WI)
Long Island U, C.W. Post Campus (NY)
Loyola U Chicago (IL)
Maryville Coll (TN)
Massachusetts Inst of Technology (MA)
McGill U (QC, Canada)
McMurry U (TX)
Mount Allison U (NB, Canada)
Mount Saint Vincent U (NS, Canada)
Paine Coll (GA)
Pfeiffer U (NC)
Piedmont Coll (GA)
Rochester Inst of Technology (NY)
Sacred Heart U (CT)

Saginaw Valley State U (MI)
Saint Francis U (PA)
St. Gregory's U (OK)
Saint John's U (MN)
Saint Joseph's Coll (IN)
St. Joseph's Coll, New York (NY)
Saint Mary's Coll (IN)
Saint Mary's Coll of California (CA)
Saint Mary's U of Minnesota (MN)
St. Norbert Coll (WI)
San Diego State U (CA)
Southern Oregon U (OR)
Stanford U (CA)
Swarthmore Coll (PA)
Trinity Western U (BC, Canada)
Université Laval (QC, Canada)
State U of NY at Albany (NY)
The U of Akron (OH)
U of Illinois at Chicago (IL)
U of Illinois at Urbana–Champaign (IL)
U of Oregon (OR)
U of Regina (SK, Canada)
U of Waterloo (ON, Canada)
U of Windsor (ON, Canada)
Washington State U (WA)
Washington U in St. Louis (MO)
Yale U (CT)
York U (ON, Canada)

MATHEMATICS AND STATISTICS RELATED

Barnard Coll (NY)
Bradley U (IL)
Canisius Coll (NY)
Coll of Mount St. Joseph (OH)
Coll of Saint Benedict (MN)
Hofstra U (NY)
Miami U Hamilton (OH)
New York U (NY)
The Ohio State U (OH)
Ohio U (OH)
Saint Mary's Coll of California (CA)
Seattle Pacific U (WA)
Tulane U (LA)
The U of Akron (OH)
U of Hartford (CT)
U of Miami (FL)
U of Pittsburgh (PA)
U of Regina (SK, Canada)
U of Rochester (NY)
The U of Scranton (PA)
U of South Alabama (AL)

MATHEMATICS RELATED

Bowdoin Coll (ME)
Eastern Washington U (WA)
Hillsdale Coll (MI)
Ohio Northern U (OH)
Seton Hill U (PA)
U at Buffalo, The State U of New York (NY)
U of Calif, Los Angeles (CA)
U of Waterloo (ON, Canada)

MATHEMATICS TEACHER EDUCATION

Abilene Christian U (TX)
Albertus Magnus Coll (CT)
Alma Coll (MI)
Alvernia Coll (PA)
Alverno Coll (WI)
Anderson Coll (SC)
Appalachian State U (NC)
Arkansas State U (AR)
Arkansas Tech U (AR)
Averett U (VA)
Baylor U (TX)
Berea Coll (KY)
Bethany Coll (KS)
Bethel Coll (IN)
Bethel U (MN)
Bethune-Cookman Coll (FL)
Bishop's U (QC, Canada)
Black Hills State U (SD)
Bloomfield Coll (NJ)
Bluefield Coll (VA)
Blue Mountain Coll (MS)
Boston U (MA)
Bowie State U (MD)
Bowling Green State U (OH)
Brewton-Parker Coll (GA)
Bridgewater Coll (VA)
Brigham Young U (UT)
Brigham Young U–Hawaii (HI)
Brock U (ON, Canada)
Brooklyn Coll of the City U of NY (NY)
Buena Vista U (IA)
State U of NY Coll at Buffalo (NY)
Cabrini Coll (PA)
California Lutheran U (CA)
California State U, Chico (CA)
California State U, Long Beach (CA)
Campbellsville U (KY)
Campbell U (NC)
Capital U (OH)
Carroll Coll (MT)
Carroll Coll (WI)
Castleton State Coll (VT)
The Catholic U of America (DC)
Cedarville U (OH)
Centenary Coll of Louisiana (LA)
Central Michigan U (MI)
Central Missouri State U (MO)
Central State U (OH)
Central Washington U (WA)
Chadron State Coll (NE)
Charleston Southern U (SC)
Chatham Coll (PA)
Chowan Coll (NC)
Christian Brothers U (TN)
Citadel, The Military Coll of South Carolina (SC)
City Coll of the City U of NY (NY)
Clearwater Christian Coll (FL)
Clemson U (SC)
Coker Coll (SC)
The Coll of New Jersey (NJ)
Coll of St. Catherine (MN)
The Coll of Saint Rose (NY)
The Coll of St. Scholastica (MN)
Coll of the Ozarks (MO)
Colorado State U (CO)
Colorado State U-Pueblo (CO)
Columbia Union Coll (MD)
Columbus State U (GA)
Concordia Coll (MN)
Concordia U (IL)
Concordia U (MI)
Concordia U (NE)
Concordia U (OR)
Concordia U, St. Paul (MN)
Cornell U (NY)
Cornerstone U (MI)
Culver-Stockton Coll (MO)
Cumberland U (TN)
Daemen Coll (NY)
Dakota Wesleyan U (SD)
Dana Coll (NE)
Davis & Elkins Coll (WV)
Delaware State U (DE)
Delta State U (MS)
Dominican Coll (NY)
Dowling Coll (NY)
Duquesne U (PA)
East Carolina U (NC)
East Central U (OK)
Eastern Mennonite U (VA)
Eastern Michigan U (MI)
Eastern Washington U (WA)
East Texas Baptist U (TX)
Elizabeth City State U (NC)
Elmhurst Coll (IL)
Elmira Coll (NY)
Elms Coll (MA)
Emmanuel Coll (GA)
Fayetteville State U (NC)
Florida Atlantic U (FL)
Florida Inst of Technology (FL)
Florida Intl U (FL)
Florida State U (FL)
Framingham State Coll (MA)
Franklin Coll (IN)
Freed-Hardeman U (TN)
Gardner-Webb U (NC)
Geneva Coll (PA)
George Fox U (OR)
Georgian Court U (NJ)
Georgia Southern U (GA)
Glenville State Coll (WV)
Grace Coll (IN)
Greensboro Coll (NC)
Greenville Coll (IL)
Gustavus Adolphus Coll (MN)
Gwynedd-Mercy Coll (PA)
Hannibal-LaGrange Coll (MO)
Harding U (AR)
Hardin-Simmons U (TX)
Hastings Coll (NE)
Hofstra U (NY)
Hope Coll (MI)
Houston Baptist U (TX)
Howard Payne U (TX)
Hunter Coll of the City U of NY (NY)
Huntingdon Coll (AL)
Illinois Wesleyan U (IL)
Indiana U Bloomington (IN)
Indiana U Northwest (IN)
Indiana U of Pennsylvania (PA)
Indiana U–Purdue U Fort Wayne (IN)
Indiana U South Bend (IN)
Indiana U Southeast (IN)
Iona Coll (NY)
Ithaca Coll (NY)
Jamestown Coll (ND)
Johnson C. Smith U (NC)
Johnson State Coll (VT)
Judson Coll (AL)
Juniata Coll (PA)
Kennesaw State U (GA)
Kentucky Wesleyan Coll (KY)
Keuka Coll (NY)
King Coll (TN)
Lambuth U (TN)
La Roche Coll (PA)
Lebanon Valley Coll (PA)
Le Moyne Coll (NY)
Lewis-Clark State Coll (ID)
Liberty U (VA)
Limestone Coll (SC)
Lincoln Memorial U (TN)
Lincoln U (PA)
Lindenwood U (MO)
Lindsey Wilson Coll (KY)
Long Island U, Brooklyn Campus (NY)
Long Island U, C.W. Post Campus (NY)
Louisiana State U in Shreveport (LA)
Louisiana Tech U (LA)
Lyndon State Coll (VT)
Madonna U (MI)
Manhattanville Coll (NY)
Mansfield U of Pennsylvania (PA)
Marian Coll of Fond du Lac (WI)
Marquette U (WI)
Marymount Coll of Fordham U (NY)
Maryville Coll (TN)
Maryville U of Saint Louis (MO)
Marywood U (PA)
Mayville State U (ND)
McGill U (QC, Canada)
McKendree Coll (IL)
McNeese State U (LA)
Mercyhurst Coll (PA)
Messiah Coll (PA)
Miami Dade Coll (FL)
Miami U Hamilton (OH)
MidAmerica Nazarene U (KS)
Miles Coll (AL)
Millersville U of Pennsylvania (PA)
Minnesota State U Moorhead (MN)
Minot State U (ND)
Mississippi Valley State U (MS)
Molloy Coll (NY)
Montana State U–Billings (MT)
Moravian Coll (PA)
Morris Coll (SC)
Mount Marty Coll (SD)
Mount Mary Coll (WI)
Mount Vernon Nazarene U (OH)
Murray State U (KY)
Nazareth Coll of Rochester (NY)
Nevada State Coll at Henderson (NV)
New York Inst of Technology (NY)
New York U (NY)
Niagara U (NY)
North Carolina Central U (NC)
North Carolina State U (NC)
North Dakota State U (ND)
Northern Arizona U (AZ)
Northern Michigan U (MI)
North Georgia Coll & State U (GA)
Northwestern Coll (MN)
Northwestern U (IL)
Northwest Nazarene U (ID)
Oakland City U (IN)
Oakland U (MI)
Ohio Dominican U (OH)
Ohio Northern U (OH)
Ohio U (OH)
Ohio Valley Coll (WV)
Ohio Wesleyan U (OH)
Oklahoma Baptist U (OK)
Oklahoma Christian U (OK)
Oral Roberts U (OK)
Pace U (NY)
Paine Coll (GA)
Philadelphia Biblical U (PA)
Pikeville Coll (KY)
Pillsbury Baptist Bible Coll (MN)
Pittsburg State U (KS)
Point Park U (PA)
Pontifical Catholic U of Puerto Rico (PR)
Queens Coll of the City U of NY (NY)
Queens U of Charlotte (NC)
Rivier Coll (NH)
Roberts Wesleyan Coll (NY)
Rocky Mountain Coll (MT)
Sacred Heart U (CT)
St. Ambrose U (IA)
Saint Augustine's Coll (NC)
St. Bonaventure U (NY)
St. Francis Coll (NY)
Saint Francis U (PA)
St. Gregory's U (OK)
St. John Fisher Coll (NY)
St. John's U (NY)
Saint Joseph's Coll of Maine (ME)
Saint Mary's U of Minnesota (MN)
Saint Xavier U (IL)
Salve Regina U (RI)
Sam Houston State U (TX)
San Diego State U (CA)
Schreiner U (TX)
Seattle Pacific U (WA)
Seton Hill U (PA)
Shawnee State U (OH)
Shaw U (NC)
Shorter Coll (GA)
Southeastern Coll of the Assemblies of God (FL)
Southeastern Louisiana U (LA)
Southeastern Oklahoma State U (OK)
Southeast Missouri State U (MO)
Southern Arkansas U–Magnolia (AR)
Southern Nazarene U (OK)
Southern Wesleyan U (SC)
Southwest Baptist U (MO)
Southwest Missouri State U (MO)
State U of NY Coll at Brockport (NY)
State U of NY Coll at Cortland (NY)
State U of NY Coll at Old Westbury (NY)
State U of NY Coll at Oneonta (NY)
State U of NY Coll at Potsdam (NY)
Syracuse U (NY)
Talladega Coll (AL)
Tennessee Wesleyan Coll (TN)
Texas A&M Intl U (TX)
Texas Christian U (TX)
Texas Lutheran U (TX)
Texas Wesleyan U (TX)
Thomas Coll (ME)
Trevecca Nazarene U (TN)
Trinity Christian Coll (IL)
Tri-State U (IN)
Union Coll (NE)
Universidad Adventista de las Antillas (PR)
Université Laval (QC, Canada)
State U of NY at Albany (NY)
The U of Akron (OH)
The U of Arizona (AZ)
U of Arkansas (AR)
U of Arkansas at Fort Smith (AR)
U of Calif, San Diego (CA)
U of Calif, Santa Cruz (CA)
U of Central Arkansas (AR)
U of Central Florida (FL)
U of Delaware (DE)
U of Georgia (GA)
U of Great Falls (MT)
U of Hawaii at Manoa (HI)
U of Illinois at Chicago (IL)
U of Indianapolis (IN)
The U of Iowa (IA)
The U of Lethbridge (AB, Canada)
U of Maine at Farmington (ME)
U of Maine at Fort Kent (ME)
U of Maine at Machias (ME)
U of Mary (ND)
U of Maryland, Coll Park (MD)
U of Minnesota, Duluth (MN)
U of Minnesota, Twin Cities Campus (MN)
U of Mississippi (MS)
U of Missouri–Columbia (MO)
U of Missouri–St. Louis (MO)
The U of Montana–Missoula (MT)
The U of Montana–Western (MT)
U of Nebraska–Lincoln (NE)
U of Nevada, Reno (NV)
U of New Hampshire (NH)
U of New Orleans (LA)
The U of North Carolina at Chapel Hill (NC)
The U of North Carolina at Charlotte (NC)
The U of North Carolina at Greensboro (NC)
The U of North Carolina at Pembroke (NC)
The U of North Carolina at Wilmington (NC)
U of North Dakota (ND)
U of Northern Iowa (IA)
U of North Florida (FL)
U of Oklahoma (OK)
U of Pittsburgh at Johnstown (PA)
U of Puerto Rico, Cayey U Coll (PR)
U of Regina (SK, Canada)
U of St. Francis (IL)
U of St. Thomas (MN)
The U of South Dakota (SD)
U of South Florida (FL)
The U of Tennessee at Martin (TN)
U of the Ozarks (AR)
U of Toledo (OH)
U of Utah (UT)
U of Vermont (VT)
U of Waterloo (ON, Canada)
The U of Western Ontario (ON, Canada)
U of West Florida (FL)
U of Windsor (ON, Canada)
U of Wisconsin–River Falls (WI)
U of Wisconsin–Superior (WI)
Ursuline Coll (OH)
Utah State U (UT)
Utica Coll (NY)
Valdosta State U (GA)
Valley City State U (ND)
Valparaiso U (IN)
Viterbo U (WI)
Wartburg Coll (IA)
Washington U in St. Louis (MO)
Waynesburg Coll (PA)
Wayne State U (MI)
West Chester U of Pennsylvania (PA)
Western Baptist Coll (OR)
Western Carolina U (NC)
Western Michigan U (MI)
Westmont Coll (CA)
West Virginia Wesleyan Coll (WV)
Wheeling Jesuit U (WV)
Widener U (PA)
William Carey Coll (MS)
William Penn U (IA)
William Woods U (MO)
Winston-Salem State U (NC)
Wright State U (OH)
York Coll (NE)
York Coll of Pennsylvania (PA)
York U (ON, Canada)
Youngstown State U (OH)

MECHANICAL DESIGN TECHNOLOGY

Bowling Green State U (OH)
Lincoln U (MO)
Pittsburg State U (KS)

MECHANICAL DRAFTING AND CAD/CADD

Eastern Michigan U (MI)
Murray State U (KY)
Pennsylvania Coll of Technology (PA)
Purdue U (IN)

MECHANICAL ENGINEERING

Alabama Ag and Mech U (AL)
Alfred U (NY)
The American U in Cairo(Egypt)
Andrews U (MI)
Arizona State U (AZ)
Arkansas Tech U (AR)
Auburn U (AL)
Baker Coll of Flint (MI)
Baylor U (TX)
Bethel Coll (IN)
Boston U (MA)
Bradley U (IL)
Brigham Young U (UT)
Brown U (RI)
Bucknell U (PA)
California Inst of Technology (CA)
California Maritime Acad (CA)
California Polytechnic State U, San Luis Obispo (CA)
California State Polytechnic U, Pomona (CA)
California State U, Chico (CA)
California State U, Fresno (CA)
California State U, Fullerton (CA)
California State U, Long Beach (CA)
California State U, Los Angeles (CA)
California State U, Sacramento (CA)
Calvin Coll (MI)
Carleton U (ON, Canada)
Carnegie Mellon U (PA)
Case Western Reserve U (OH)
The Catholic U of America (DC)
Cedarville U (OH)
Christian Brothers U (TN)
City Coll of the City U of NY (NY)
Clarkson U (NY)
Clemson U (SC)
Cleveland State U (OH)
The Coll of New Jersey (NJ)
The Coll of Southeastern Europe, The American U of Athens(Greece)
Colorado School of Mines (CO)
Colorado State U (CO)
Columbia U, School of Eng & Applied Sci (NY)
Concordia U (QC, Canada)
Cooper Union for the Advancement of Science & Art (NY)
Cornell U (NY)

Dalhousie U (NS, Canada)
Delaware State U (DE)
Dordt Coll (IA)
Drexel U (PA)
Duke U (NC)
Eastern Nazarene Coll (MA)
Florida Ag and Mech U (FL)
Florida Atlantic U (FL)
Florida Inst of Technology (FL)
Florida Intl U (FL)
Florida State U (FL)
Frostburg State U (MD)
Gallaudet U (DC)
Gannon U (PA)
The George Washington U (DC)
Georgia Inst of Technology (GA)
Gonzaga U (WA)
Grand Valley State U (MI)
Grove City Coll (PA)
Harvard U (MA)
Henry Cogswell Coll (WA)
Hofstra U (NY)
Howard U (DC)
Idaho State U (ID)
Illinois Inst of Technology (IL)
Indiana Inst of Technology (IN)
Indiana U–Purdue U Fort Wayne (IN)
Indiana U–Purdue U Indianapolis (IN)
Inter American U of PR, Bayamón Campus (PR)
Iowa State U of Science and Technology (IA)
Jacksonville U (FL)
John Brown U (AR)
The Johns Hopkins U (MD)
Johnson & Wales U (RI)
Kansas State U (KS)
Kettering U (MI)
Lafayette Coll (PA)
Lakehead U (ON, Canada)
Lake Superior State U (MI)
Lamar U (TX)
Lawrence Technological U (MI)
Lehigh U (PA)
LeTourneau U (TX)
Louisiana State U and A&M Coll (LA)
Louisiana Tech U (LA)
Loyola Marymount U (CA)
Manhattan Coll (NY)
Marquette U (WI)
Massachusetts Inst of Technology (MA)
McGill U (QC, Canada)
Memorial U of Newfoundland (NL, Canada)
Miami U (OH)
Michigan State U (MI)
Michigan Technological U (MI)
Milwaukee School of Eng (WI)
Minnesota State U Mankato (MN)
Mississippi State U (MS)
Montana State U–Bozeman (MT)
Montana Tech of The U of Montana (MT)
Murray State U (KY)
New Jersey Inst of Technology (NJ)
New Mexico Inst of Mining and Technology (NM)
New Mexico State U (NM)
New York Inst of Technology (NY)
North Carolina State U (NC)
North Dakota State U (ND)
Northeastern U (MA)
Northern Arizona U (AZ)
Northern Illinois U (IL)
Northern Michigan U (MI)
Northwestern U (IL)
Oakland U (MI)
Ohio Northern U (OH)
The Ohio State U (OH)
Ohio U (OH)
Oklahoma Christian U (OK)
Oklahoma State U (OK)
Old Dominion U (VA)
Oral Roberts U (OK)
Oregon State U (OR)
Penn State U Abington Coll (PA)
Penn State U Altoona Coll (PA)
Penn State U at Erie, The Behrend Coll (PA)
Penn State U Beaver Campus of the Commonwealth Coll (PA)
Penn State U Berks Cmps of Berks-Lehigh Valley Coll (PA)
Penn State U Delaware County Campus of the Commonwealth Coll (PA)
Penn State U DuBois Campus of the Commonwealth Coll (PA)
Penn State U Fayette Campus of the Commonwealth Coll (PA)
Penn State U Harrisburg Campus of the Capital Coll (PA)
Penn State U Hazleton Campus of the Commonwealth Coll (PA)
Penn State U Lehigh Valley Cmps of Berks-Lehigh Valley Coll (PA)
Penn State U McKeesport Campus of the Commonwealth Coll (PA)
Penn State U Mont Alto Campus of the Commonwealth Coll (PA)
Penn State U New Kensington Campus of the Commonwealth Coll (PA)
Penn State U Schuylkill Campus of the Capital Coll (PA)
Penn State U Shenango Campus of the Commonwealth Coll (PA)
Penn State U Univ Park Campus (PA)
Penn State U Wilkes-Barre Campus of the Commonwealth Coll (PA)
Penn State U Worthington Scranton Cmps Commonwealth Coll (PA)
Penn State U York Campus of the Commonwealth Coll (PA)
Polytechnic U, Brooklyn Campus (NY)
Polytechnic U of Puerto Rico (PR)
Portland State U (OR)
Prairie View A&M U (TX)
Princeton U (NJ)
Purdue U (IN)
Queen's U at Kingston (ON, Canada)
Rensselaer Polytechnic Inst (NY)
Rice U (TX)
Rochester Inst of Technology (NY)
Rose-Hulman Inst of Technology (IN)
Rowan U (NJ)
Rutgers, The State U of New Jersey, New Brunswick/Piscataway (NJ)
Ryerson U (ON, Canada)
Saginaw Valley State U (MI)
St. Cloud State U (MN)
Saint Louis U (MO)
Saint Martin's Coll (WA)
San Diego State U (CA)
San Francisco State U (CA)
San Jose State U (CA)
Santa Clara U (CA)
Seattle U (WA)
South Dakota School of Mines and Technology (SD)
South Dakota State U (SD)
Southern Illinois U Carbondale (IL)
Southern Illinois U Edwardsville (IL)
Southern Methodist U (TX)
Southern U and A&M Coll (LA)
Stanford U (CA)
State U of NY at Binghamton (NY)
Stevens Inst of Technology (NJ)
Stony Brook U, State U of New York (NY)
Syracuse U (NY)
Tennessee State U (TN)
Tennessee Technological U (TN)
Texas A&M U (TX)
Texas A&M U–Kingsville (TX)
Texas Tech U (TX)
Trinity Coll (CT)
Tri-State U (IN)
Tufts U (MA)
Tulane U (LA)
Tuskegee U (AL)
Union Coll (NY)
United States Air Force Acad (CO)
United States Coast Guard Acad (CT)
United States Military Acad (NY)
United States Naval Acad (MD)
Université de Sherbrooke (QC, Canada)
Université Laval (QC, Canada)
U at Buffalo, The State U of New York (NY)
The U of Akron (OH)
The U of Alabama (AL)
The U of Alabama at Birmingham (AL)
The U of Alabama in Huntsville (AL)
U of Alaska Fairbanks (AK)
U of Alberta (AB, Canada)
The U of Arizona (AZ)
U of Arkansas (AR)
The U of British Columbia (BC, Canada)
U of Calgary (AB, Canada)
U of Calif, Berkeley (CA)
U of Calif, Davis (CA)
U of Calif, Irvine (CA)
U of Calif, Los Angeles (CA)
U of Calif, Riverside (CA)
U of Calif, San Diego (CA)
U of Calif, Santa Barbara (CA)
U of Central Florida (FL)
U of Cincinnati (OH)
U of Colorado at Boulder (CO)
U of Colorado at Colorado Springs (CO)
U of Colorado at Denver (CO)
U of Connecticut (CT)
U of Dayton (OH)
U of Delaware (DE)
U of Denver (CO)
U of Detroit Mercy (MI)
U of Evansville (IN)
U of Florida (FL)
U of Hartford (CT)
U of Hawaii at Manoa (HI)
U of Houston (TX)
U of Idaho (ID)
U of Illinois at Chicago (IL)
U of Illinois at Urbana–Champaign (IL)
The U of Iowa (IA)
U of Kansas (KS)
U of Kentucky (KY)
U of Louisiana at Lafayette (LA)
U of Louisville (KY)
U of Maine (ME)
U of Manitoba (MB, Canada)
U of Maryland, Baltimore County (MD)
U of Maryland, Coll Park (MD)
U of Massachusetts Amherst (MA)
U of Massachusetts Dartmouth (MA)
U of Massachusetts Lowell (MA)
The U of Memphis (TN)
U of Miami (FL)
U of Michigan (MI)
U of Michigan–Dearborn (MI)
U of Minnesota, Twin Cities Campus (MN)
U of Mississippi (MS)
U of Missouri–Columbia (MO)
U of Missouri–Kansas City (MO)
U of Missouri–Rolla (MO)
U of Missouri–St. Louis (MO)
U of Nebraska–Lincoln (NE)
U of Nevada, Las Vegas (NV)
U of Nevada, Reno (NV)
U of New Brunswick Fredericton (NB, Canada)
U of New Hampshire (NH)
U of New Haven (CT)
U of New Mexico (NM)
U of New Orleans (LA)
The U of North Carolina at Charlotte (NC)
U of North Dakota (ND)
U of North Florida (FL)
U of Notre Dame (IN)
U of Oklahoma (OK)
U of Ottawa (ON, Canada)
U of Pennsylvania (PA)
U of Pittsburgh (PA)
U of Portland (OR)
U of Rhode Island (RI)
U of Rochester (NY)
U of St. Thomas (MN)
U of San Diego (CA)
U of Saskatchewan (SK, Canada)
U of South Alabama (AL)
U of South Carolina (SC)
U of Southern California (CA)
U of South Florida (FL)
The U of Tennessee (TN)
The U of Texas at Arlington (TX)
The U of Texas at Austin (TX)
The U of Texas at Tyler (TX)
The U of Texas–Pan American (TX)
U of the District of Columbia (DC)
U of the Pacific (CA)
U of Toledo (OH)
U of Toronto (ON, Canada)
U of Tulsa (OK)
U of Utah (UT)
U of Vermont (VT)
U of Victoria (BC, Canada)
U of Virginia (VA)
U of Washington (WA)
U of Waterloo (ON, Canada)
The U of Western Ontario (ON, Canada)
U of Windsor (ON, Canada)
U of Wisconsin–Madison (WI)
U of Wisconsin–Milwaukee (WI)
U of Wisconsin–Platteville (WI)
U of Wyoming (WY)
Ursinus Coll (PA)
Utah State U (UT)
Valparaiso U (IN)
Vanderbilt U (TN)
Villanova U (PA)
Virginia Commonwealth U (VA)
Virginia Military Inst (VA)
Virginia Polytechnic Inst and State U (VA)
Walla Walla Coll (WA)
Washington State U (WA)
Washington U in St. Louis (MO)
Wayne State U (MI)
Western Kentucky U (KY)
Western Michigan U (MI)
Western New England Coll (MA)
West Texas A&M U (TX)
West Virginia U (WV)
Wichita State U (KS)
Widener U (PA)
Wilkes U (PA)
William Penn U (IA)
Winona State U (MN)
Worcester Polytechnic Inst (MA)
Wright State U (OH)
Yale U (CT)
York Coll of Pennsylvania (PA)
Youngstown State U (OH)

MECHANICAL ENGINEERING/ MECHANICAL TECHNOLOGY

Alabama Ag and Mech U (AL)
Andrews U (MI)
Arizona State U East (AZ)
Bluefield State Coll (WV)
Boise State U (ID)
Bowling Green State U (OH)
British Columbia Inst of Technology (BC, Canada)
State U of NY Coll at Buffalo (NY)
California Polytechnic State U, San Luis Obispo (CA)
California State Polytechnic U, Pomona (CA)
California State U, Long Beach (CA)
California State U, Sacramento (CA)
Central Connecticut State U (CT)
Central Michigan U (MI)
Central Washington U (WA)
Colorado State U-Pueblo (CO)
Delaware State U (DE)
Eastern Michigan U (MI)
Eastern Washington U (WA)
Excelsior Coll (NY)
Fairleigh Dickinson U, Teaneck-Metro Campus (NJ)
Fairmont State Coll (WV)
State U of NY at Farmingdale (NY)
Georgia Southern U (GA)
Indiana U–Purdue U Fort Wayne (IN)
Indiana U–Purdue U Indianapolis (IN)
Johnson & Wales U (RI)
Kansas State U (KS)
Lakehead U (ON, Canada)
Lake Superior State U (MI)
LeTourneau U (TX)
Metropolitan State Coll of Denver (CO)
Miami U Hamilton (OH)
Michigan Technological U (MI)
Milwaukee School of Eng (WI)
Montana State U–Bozeman (MT)
New York Inst of Technology (NY)
Nicholls State U (LA)
Northeastern U (MA)
Ohio U (OH)
Oklahoma State U (OK)
Oregon Inst of Technology (OR)
Pennsylvania Coll of Technology (PA)
Penn State U at Erie, The Behrend Coll (PA)
Pittsburg State U (KS)
Point Park U (PA)
Purdue U North Central (IN)
Rochester Inst of Technology (NY)
South Carolina State U (SC)
Southern Polytechnic State U (GA)
State U of NY Coll of Technology at Alfred (NY)
State U of NY Inst of Tech at Utica/Rome (NY)
Texas A&M U (TX)
Texas Tech U (TX)
Thomas Edison State Coll (NJ)
The U of Akron (OH)
U of Arkansas at Little Rock (AR)
The U of British Columbia (BC, Canada)
U of Cincinnati (OH)
U of Dayton (OH)
U of Maine (ME)
U of Massachusetts Dartmouth (MA)
U of Massachusetts Lowell (MA)
U of New Hampshire at Manchester (NH)
The U of North Carolina at Charlotte (NC)
U of North Texas (TX)
U of Pittsburgh at Johnstown (PA)
The U of Texas at Brownsville (TX)
U of Toledo (OH)
Wayne State U (MI)
Weber State U (UT)
Wentworth Inst of Technology (MA)
Western Michigan U (MI)
Youngstown State U (OH)

MECHANICAL ENGINEERING TECHNOLOGIES RELATED

Cleveland State U (OH)
Grove City Coll (PA)
Indiana State U (IN)
New York Inst of Technology (NY)
Old Dominion U (VA)
Purdue U (IN)
U of Central Florida (FL)
U of Hartford (CT)

MECHANICS AND REPAIR

Lewis-Clark State Coll (ID)

MEDICAL ADMINISTRATIVE ASSISTANT AND MEDICAL SECRETARY

Baker Coll of Auburn Hills (MI)
Mercyhurst Coll (PA)
Tabor Coll (KS)

MEDICAL BASIC SCIENCES RELATED

Ramapo Coll of New Jersey (NJ)

MEDICAL/CLINICAL ASSISTANT

California State U, Dominguez Hills (CA)
Jones Coll, Jacksonville (FL)

MEDICAL/HEALTH MANAGEMENT AND CLINICAL ASSISTANT

Davenport U, Dearborn (MI)
Lewis-Clark State Coll (ID)

MEDICAL ILLUSTRATION

Alma Coll (MI)
Arcadia U (PA)
Clark Atlanta U (GA)
The Cleveland Inst of Art (OH)
Iowa State U of Science and Technology (IA)
Olivet Coll (MI)
Rochester Inst of Technology (NY)

MEDICAL ILLUSTRATION AND INFORMATICS RELATED

Florida Ag and Mech U (FL)

MEDICAL INFORMATICS

U of Waterloo (ON, Canada)

MEDICAL LABORATORY TECHNOLOGY

Abilene Christian U (TX)
Auburn U (AL)
The George Washington U (DC)
Oakland U (MI)
Quinnipiac U (CT)
Rockhurst U (MO)
Roosevelt U (IL)
Southeastern Oklahoma State U (OK)
Springfield Coll (MA)
U of Cincinnati (OH)
U of Illinois at Springfield (IL)
U of Nevada, Las Vegas (NV)
U of Oklahoma (OK)
U of Windsor (ON, Canada)

MEDICAL MICROBIOLOGY AND BACTERIOLOGY

Arizona State U (AZ)
Auburn U (AL)
Ball State U (IN)
Bowling Green State U (OH)
California Polytechnic State U, San Luis Obispo (CA)
California State Polytechnic U, Pomona (CA)
California State U, Dominguez Hills (CA)
California State U, Fresno (CA)
Central Michigan U (MI)
Colorado State U (CO)
Cornell U (NY)
Dalhousie U (NS, Canada)
Eastern Kentucky U (KY)
Hampshire Coll (MA)
Harvard U (MA)
Humboldt State U (CA)
Idaho State U (ID)
Indiana U Bloomington (IN)
Inter American U of PR, Bayamón Campus (PR)

Inter American U of PR, San Germán Campus (PR)
Juniata Coll (PA)
McGill U (QC, Canada)
Memorial U of Newfoundland (NL, Canada)
Miami U (OH)
Michigan Technological U (MI)
Minnesota State U Mankato (MN)
Mississippi State U (MS)
Missouri Southern State U (MO)
Montana State U–Bozeman (MT)
New Mexico State U (NM)
Northeastern State U (OK)
Northern Arizona U (AZ)
Northern Michigan U (MI)
The Ohio State U (OH)
Ohio U (OH)
Ohio Wesleyan U (OH)
Oklahoma State U (OK)
Oregon State U (OR)
Penn State U Abington Coll (PA)
Penn State U Altoona Coll (PA)
Penn State U at Erie, The Behrend Coll (PA)
Penn State U Beaver Campus of the Commonwealth Coll (PA)
Penn State U Berks Cmps of Berks-Lehigh Valley Coll (PA)
Penn State U Delaware County Campus of the Commonwealth Coll (PA)
Penn State U DuBois Campus of the Commonwealth Coll (PA)
Penn State U Fayette Campus of the Commonwealth Coll (PA)
Penn State U Hazleton Campus of the Commonwealth Coll (PA)
Penn State U Lehigh Valley Cmps of Berks-Lehigh Valley Coll (PA)
Penn State U McKeesport Campus of the Commonwealth Coll (PA)
Penn State U Mont Alto Campus of the Commonwealth Coll (PA)
Penn State U New Kensington Campus of the Commonwealth Coll (PA)
Penn State U Schuylkill Campus of the Capital Coll (PA)
Penn State U Shenango Campus of the Commonwealth Coll (PA)
Penn State U Univ Park Campus (PA)
Penn State U Wilkes-Barre Campus of the Commonwealth Coll (PA)
Penn State U Worthington Scranton Cmps Commonwealth Coll (PA)
Penn State U York Campus of the Commonwealth Coll (PA)
Pomona Coll (CA)
Quinnipiac U (CT)
Rutgers, The State U of New Jersey, New Brunswick/Piscataway (NJ)
St. Cloud State U (MN)
San Diego State U (CA)
San Francisco State U (CA)
Sonoma State U (CA)
South Dakota State U (SD)
Southern Connecticut State U (CT)
Texas Tech U (TX)
Université de Montréal (QC, Canada)
Université de Sherbrooke (QC, Canada)
Université Laval (QC, Canada)
The U of Akron (OH)
The U of Alabama (AL)
U of Alberta (AB, Canada)
The U of Arizona (AZ)
The U of British Columbia (BC, Canada)
U of Calif, Davis (CA)
U of Calif, Los Angeles (CA)
U of Calif, San Diego (CA)
U of Calif, Santa Barbara (CA)
U of Central Florida (FL)
U of Cincinnati (OH)
U of Florida (FL)
U of Georgia (GA)
U of Guelph (ON, Canada)
U of Idaho (ID)
U of King's Coll (NS, Canada)
U of Louisiana at Lafayette (LA)
U of Maine (ME)
U of Manitoba (MB, Canada)
U of Maryland, Coll Park (MD)
U of Miami (FL)
U of Michigan (MI)
U of Michigan–Dearborn (MI)
U of Minnesota, Twin Cities Campus (MN)
The U of Montana–Missoula (MT)
U of New Brunswick Fredericton (NB, Canada)
U of New Hampshire (NH)
U of Ottawa (ON, Canada)
U of Pittsburgh (PA)
U of Rhode Island (RI)
U of Saskatchewan (SK, Canada)
U of South Florida (FL)
The U of Tennessee (TN)
U of Toronto (ON, Canada)
U of Vermont (VT)
U of Victoria (BC, Canada)
U of Washington (WA)
The U of Western Ontario (ON, Canada)
U of Windsor (ON, Canada)
U of Wisconsin–La Crosse (WI)
U of Wisconsin–Madison (WI)
U of Wisconsin–Oshkosh (WI)
Utah State U (UT)
Wagner Coll (NY)
Weber State U (UT)
Worcester Polytechnic Inst (MA)
Xavier U of Louisiana (LA)

MEDICAL OFFICE ASSISTANT
Concordia U Wisconsin (WI)
Lewis-Clark State Coll (ID)
Mount Aloysius Coll (PA)

MEDICAL OFFICE MANAGEMENT
Eastern Kentucky U (KY)

MEDICAL PHARMACOLOGY AND PHARMACEUTICAL SCIENCES
Campbell U (NC)
The U of Montana–Missoula (MT)
U of the Sciences in Philadelphia (PA)

MEDICAL RADIOLOGIC TECHNOLOGY
Arkansas State U (AR)
Averett U (VA)
Avila U (MO)
Baptist Coll of Health Sciences (TN)
Bloomsburg U of Pennsylvania (PA)
British Columbia Inst of Technology (BC, Canada)
California State U, Long Beach (CA)
Coll Misericordia (PA)
Columbus State U (GA)
Fairleigh Dickinson U, Florham (NJ)
Fairleigh Dickinson U, Teaneck-Metro Campus (NJ)
Gannon U (PA)
Idaho State U (ID)
Indiana U Northwest (IN)
Indiana U–Purdue U Indianapolis (IN)
La Roche Coll (PA)
Loma Linda U (CA)
Long Island U, C.W. Post Campus (NY)
Marian Coll of Fond du Lac (WI)
Mass Coll of Pharmacy and Allied Health Sciences (MA)
McNeese State U (LA)
Minot State U (ND)
Morehead State U (KY)
Mount Marty Coll (SD)
Northwestern State U of Louisiana (LA)
The Ohio State U (OH)
Presentation Coll (SD)
Roosevelt U (IL)
St. Francis Coll (NY)
Saint Joseph's Coll of Maine (ME)
Southern Illinois U Carbondale (IL)
Southwest Missouri State U (MO)
State U of New York Upstate Medical U (NY)
Texas State U-San Marcos (TX)
Thomas Edison State Coll (NJ)
The U of Alabama at Birmingham (AL)
U of Central Arkansas (AR)
U of Central Florida (FL)
U of Hartford (CT)
U of Michigan–Flint (MI)
U of Missouri–Columbia (MO)
U of Nebraska Medical Center (NE)
U of Nevada, Las Vegas (NV)
The U of North Carolina at Chapel Hill (NC)
U of Prince Edward Island (PE, Canada)
U of St. Francis (IL)
U of Vermont (VT)
Wayne State U (MI)
Weber State U (UT)

MEDICAL STAFF SERVICES TECHNOLOGY
East Central U (OK)

MEDICAL TRANSCRIPTION
Mercyhurst Coll (PA)

MEDICINAL AND PHARMACEUTICAL CHEMISTRY
Butler U (IN)
Ohio Northern U (OH)
U at Buffalo, The State U of New York (NY)
U of Calif, San Diego (CA)
U of the Sciences in Philadelphia (PA)
Worcester Polytechnic Inst (MA)

MEDIEVAL AND RENAISSANCE STUDIES
Bard Coll (NY)
Barnard Coll (NY)
Brown U (RI)
Carleton U (ON, Canada)
The Catholic U of America (DC)
The Coll of William and Mary (VA)
Columbia Coll (NY)
Connecticut Coll (CT)
Cornell Coll (IA)
Cornell U (NY)
Dickinson Coll (PA)
Duke U (NC)
Eastern Michigan U (MI)
Emory U (GA)
Fordham U (NY)
Hamilton Coll (NY)
Hampshire Coll (MA)
Hanover Coll (IN)
Harvard U (MA)
Hobart and William Smith Colls (NY)
Marlboro Coll (VT)
Memorial U of Newfoundland (NL, Canada)
Mount Allison U (NB, Canada)
Mount Holyoke Coll (MA)
New Coll of Florida (FL)
New York U (NY)
Ohio Wesleyan U (OH)
Penn State U Abington Coll (PA)
Penn State U Altoona Coll (PA)
Penn State U at Erie, The Behrend Coll (PA)
Penn State U Beaver Campus of the Commonwealth Coll (PA)
Penn State U Berks Cmps of Berks-Lehigh Valley Coll (PA)
Penn State U Delaware County Campus of the Commonwealth Coll (PA)
Penn State U DuBois Campus of the Commonwealth Coll (PA)
Penn State U Fayette Campus of the Commonwealth Coll (PA)
Penn State U Hazleton Campus of the Commonwealth Coll (PA)
Penn State U Lehigh Valley Cmps of Berks-Lehigh Valley Coll (PA)
Penn State U McKeesport Campus of the Commonwealth Coll (PA)
Penn State U Mont Alto Campus of the Commonwealth Coll (PA)
Penn State U New Kensington Campus of the Commonwealth Coll (PA)
Penn State U Schuylkill Campus of the Capital Coll (PA)
Penn State U Shenango Campus of the Commonwealth Coll (PA)
Penn State U Univ Park Campus (PA)
Penn State U Wilkes-Barre Campus of the Commonwealth Coll (PA)
Penn State U Worthington Scranton Cmps Commonwealth Coll (PA)
Penn State U York Campus of the Commonwealth Coll (PA)
Plymouth State U (NH)
Queen's U at Kingston (ON, Canada)
Rutgers, The State U of New Jersey, New Brunswick/Piscataway (NJ)
Smith Coll (MA)
Southern Methodist U (TX)
State U of NY at Binghamton (NY)
Swarthmore Coll (PA)
Syracuse U (NY)
Tulane U (LA)
State U of NY at Albany (NY)
U of Calgary (AB, Canada)
U of Calif, Santa Barbara (CA)
U of Chicago (IL)
The U of Iowa (IA)
U of Manitoba (MB, Canada)
U of Michigan (MI)
U of Michigan–Dearborn (MI)
U of Nebraska–Lincoln (NE)
U of Notre Dame (IN)
U of Ottawa (ON, Canada)
U of the South (TN)
U of Toledo (OH)
U of Toronto (ON, Canada)
U of Victoria (BC, Canada)
U of Waterloo (ON, Canada)
Vassar Coll (NY)
Washington and Lee U (VA)
Washington U in St. Louis (MO)
Wellesley Coll (MA)
Wesleyan U (CT)

MENTAL AND SOCIAL HEALTH SERVICES AND ALLIED PROFESSIONS RELATED
Marymount U (VA)
Old Dominion U (VA)
Pennsylvania Coll of Technology (PA)
The U of Maine at Augusta (ME)
U of Toledo (OH)
Wright State U (OH)

MENTAL HEALTH COUNSELING
Florida Gulf Coast U (FL)
Marywood U (PA)

MENTAL HEALTH/ REHABILITATION
Elmira Coll (NY)
Evangel U (MO)
Governors State U (IL)
Kansas Wesleyan U (KS)
Morgan State U (MD)
Newman U (KS)
Pittsburg State U (KS)
St. Cloud State U (MN)
Springfield Coll (MA)
Thomas Edison State Coll (NJ)
Tufts U (MA)
U of Maine at Farmington (ME)
U of Puerto Rico, Cayey U Coll (PR)
Wright State U (OH)

MERCHANDISING
Michigan State U (MI)
Youngstown State U (OH)

MERCHANDISING, SALES, AND MARKETING OPERATIONS RELATED (GENERAL)
Brigham Young U (UT)
Eastern Michigan U (MI)
The U of Akron (OH)
Washington U in St. Louis (MO)

MERCHANDISING, SALES, AND MARKETING OPERATIONS RELATED (SPECIALIZED)
The U of Akron (OH)

METAL AND JEWELRY ARTS
Acad of Art U (CA)
Alberta Coll of Art & Design (AB, Canada)
Arcadia U (PA)
Arizona State U (AZ)
Bowling Green State U (OH)
California Coll of the Arts (CA)
California State U, Long Beach (CA)
The Cleveland Inst of Art (OH)
Col for Creative Studies (MI)
Colorado State U (CO)
Grand Valley State U (MI)
Hofstra U (NY)
Indiana U Bloomington (IN)
Loyola U Chicago (IL)
Maine Coll of Art (ME)
Massachusetts Coll of Art (MA)
Memphis Coll of Art (TN)
Northern Michigan U (MI)
Nova Scotia Coll of Art and Design (NS, Canada)
Pratt Inst (NY)
Rhode Island School of Design (RI)
Rochester Inst of Technology (NY)
Savannah Coll of Art and Design (GA)
School of the Art Inst of Chicago (IL)
School of the Museum of Fine Arts, Boston (MA)
Seton Hill U (PA)
Simon's Rock Coll of Bard (MA)
State U of NY at New Paltz (NY)
State U of NY Coll at Brockport (NY)
Syracuse U (NY)
The U of Akron (OH)
The U of Iowa (IA)
U of Kansas (KS)
U of Massachusetts Dartmouth (MA)
U of Michigan (MI)
U of North Texas (TX)
U of Oregon (OR)
U of Washington (WA)
U of Wisconsin–Milwaukee (WI)

METALLURGICAL ENGINEERING
Cleveland State U (OH)
Colorado School of Mines (CO)
Dalhousie U (NS, Canada)
Georgia Inst of Technology (GA)
Harvard U (MA)
Illinois Inst of Technology (IL)
Laurentian U (ON, Canada)
McGill U (QC, Canada)
Michigan Technological U (MI)
Montana Tech of The U of Montana (MT)
New Mexico Inst of Mining and Technology (NM)
The Ohio State U (OH)
Oregon State U (OR)
South Dakota School of Mines and Technology (SD)
Université Laval (QC, Canada)
The U of Alabama (AL)
U of Alberta (AB, Canada)
The U of British Columbia (BC, Canada)
U of Cincinnati (OH)
U of Idaho (ID)
U of Michigan (MI)
U of Missouri–Rolla (MO)
U of Nevada, Reno (NV)
U of Pittsburgh (PA)
U of Toronto (ON, Canada)
U of Utah (UT)
U of Washington (WA)
U of Wisconsin–Madison (WI)
Ursinus Coll (PA)

METALLURGICAL TECHNOLOGY
U of Cincinnati (OH)

METEOROLOGY
Cornell U (NY)
Florida Inst of Technology (FL)
Florida State U (FL)
North Carolina State U (NC)
State U of NY Coll at Brockport (NY)
U of Utah (UT)
Western Illinois U (IL)

MICROBIOLOGICAL SCIENCES AND IMMUNOLOGY RELATED
Dalhousie U (NS, Canada)
State U of West Georgia (GA)
U of Calif, Los Angeles (CA)
Wright State U (OH)

MICROBIOLOGY
Auburn U (AL)
Brigham Young U (UT)
California State U, Chico (CA)
California State U, Long Beach (CA)
California State U, Los Angeles (CA)
Clemson U (SC)
Cornell U (NY)
Duquesne U (PA)
Idaho State U (ID)
Inter American U of PR, Aguadilla Campus (PR)
Inter Amer U of PR, Barranquitas Campus (PR)
Iowa State U of Science and Technology (IA)
Juniata Coll (PA)
Louisiana State U and A&M Coll (LA)
Miami U Hamilton (OH)
Michigan State U (MI)
New Mexico State U (NM)
North Carolina State U (NC)
North Dakota State U (ND)
Northern Michigan U (MI)
Southern Illinois U Carbondale (IL)
Texas A&M U (TX)
Texas State U-San Marcos (TX)
U of Calif, Berkeley (CA)
U of Calif, Irvine (CA)
U of Guelph (ON, Canada)
U of Illinois at Urbana–Champaign (IL)
The U of Iowa (IA)

U of Kansas (KS)
U of Massachusetts Amherst (MA)
The U of Memphis (TN)
U of Missouri–Columbia (MO)
U of Northern Iowa (IA)
U of Oklahoma (OK)
U of Saskatchewan (SK, Canada)
The U of Texas at Arlington (TX)
The U of Texas at Austin (TX)
U of the Sciences in Philadelphia (PA)
U of Wyoming (WY)
Washington State U (WA)

MIDDLE/ NEAR EASTERN AND SEMITIC LANGUAGES RELATED
Sarah Lawrence Coll (NY)
U of Calif, Los Angeles (CA)

MIDDLE SCHOOL EDUCATION
Abilene Christian U (TX)
Albany State U (GA)
Albertus Magnus Coll (CT)
Alverno Coll (WI)
American Intl Coll (MA)
Antioch Coll (OH)
Appalachian State U (NC)
Arkansas State U (AR)
Arkansas Tech U (AR)
Arlington Baptist Coll (TX)
Armstrong Atlantic State U (GA)
Asbury Coll (KY)
Ashland U (OH)
Augusta State U (GA)
Avila U (MO)
Baldwin-Wallace Coll (OH)
Barton Coll (NC)
Bellarmine U (KY)
Berea Coll (KY)
Berry Coll (GA)
Bethel Coll (IN)
Black Hills State U (SD)
Bluefield Coll (VA)
Bluffton Coll (OH)
Bowling Green State U (OH)
Brenau U (GA)
Brescia U (KY)
Brevard Coll (NC)
Brewton-Parker Coll (GA)
Bridgewater State Coll (MA)
Bryan Coll (TN)
Campbell U (NC)
Capital U (OH)
Carroll Coll (WI)
Carthage Coll (WI)
Catawba Coll (NC)
Cedar Crest Coll (PA)
Central Methodist Coll (MO)
Central Missouri State U (MO)
Central State U (OH)
Chadron State Coll (NE)
Champlain Coll (VT)
Christopher Newport U (VA)
Clark Atlanta U (GA)
Clarke Coll (IA)
Clark U (MA)
Clayton Coll & State U (GA)
Clemson U (SC)
Cleveland State U (OH)
Coastal Carolina U (SC)
Coll of Charleston (SC)
Coll of Mount St. Joseph (OH)
Coll of Mount Saint Vincent (NY)
Coll of the Atlantic (ME)
Coll of the Ozarks (MO)
Coll of the Southwest (NM)
Colorado State U-Pueblo (CO)
Columbus State U (GA)
Concordia Coll (NY)
Concordia U (NE)
Concordia U at Austin (TX)
Concordia U, St. Paul (MN)
Concordia U Wisconsin (WI)
Connecticut Coll (CT)
Covenant Coll (GA)
Cumberland Coll (KY)
Dakota Wesleyan U (SD)
Delaware State U (DE)
East Carolina U (NC)
Eastern Illinois U (IL)
Eastern Kentucky U (KY)
Eastern Mennonite U (VA)
Eastern Michigan U (MI)
Eastern Nazarene Coll (MA)
Elizabeth City State U (NC)
Elmira Coll (NY)
Elon U (NC)
Emmanuel Coll (GA)
Evangel U (MO)
Fayetteville State U (NC)
Florida State U (FL)
Fontbonne U (MO)
Framingham State Coll (MA)
The Franciscan U (IA)
Georgetown Coll (KY)
Georgia Coll & State U (GA)
Georgia Southern U (GA)
Georgia Southwestern State U (GA)
Georgia State U (GA)
Gettysburg Coll (PA)
Gordon Coll (MA)
Governors State U (IL)
Grace U (NE)
Greensboro Coll (NC)
Hampton U (VA)
Harding U (AR)
Hardin-Simmons U (TX)
Harris-Stowe State Coll (MO)
Henderson State U (AR)
High Point U (NC)
Houston Baptist U (TX)
Illinois State U (IL)
Ithaca Coll (NY)
Jacksonville State U (AL)
John Brown U (AR)
Johnson Bible Coll (TN)
Johnson State Coll (VT)
Judson Coll (AL)
Kennesaw State U (GA)
Kent State U (OH)
Kentucky Christian Coll (KY)
Kentucky Wesleyan Coll (KY)
King Coll (TN)
LaGrange Coll (GA)
Lakeland Coll (WI)
Lake Superior State U (MI)
Lambuth U (TN)
Lesley U (MA)
Lindenwood U (MO)
Lindsey Wilson Coll (KY)
Lipscomb U (TN)
Louisiana Tech U (LA)
Lourdes Coll (OH)
Lubbock Christian U (TX)
Lynn U (FL)
Malone Coll (OH)
Manhattan Coll (NY)
Marian Coll of Fond du Lac (WI)
Marquette U (WI)
Marymount Coll of Fordham U (NY)
Maryville U of Saint Louis (MO)
Massachusetts Coll of Liberal Arts (MA)
The Master's Coll and Sem (CA)
McKendree Coll (IL)
McMurry U (TX)
Medaille Coll (NY)
Memorial U of Newfoundland (NL, Canada)
Mercer U (GA)
Merrimack Coll (MA)
Miami U (OH)
MidAmerica Nazarene U (KS)
Midway Coll (KY)
Minnesota State U Moorhead (MN)
Missouri Baptist U (MO)
Missouri Southern State U (MO)
Morehead State U (KY)
Morehouse Coll (GA)
Mount Mercy Coll (IA)
Mount Union Coll (OH)
Mount Vernon Nazarene U (OH)
Murray State U (KY)
Nebraska Wesleyan U (NE)
New York U (NY)
Nicholls State U (LA)
North Carolina Central U (NC)
North Carolina State U (NC)
North Carolina Wesleyan Coll (NC)
North Georgia Coll & State U (GA)
Northland Coll (WI)
Northwestern State U of Louisiana (LA)
Notre Dame Coll (OH)
Oakland City U (IN)
Oglethorpe U (GA)
Ohio Dominican U (OH)
Ohio Northern U (OH)
Ohio U (OH)
Ohio Wesleyan U (OH)
Otterbein Coll (OH)
Ouachita Baptist U (AR)
Paine Coll (GA)
Piedmont Coll (GA)
Pikeville Coll (KY)
Reinhardt Coll (GA)
Rhode Island Coll (RI)
Sacred Heart U (CT)
St. Bonaventure U (NY)
St. Cloud State U (MN)
St. John's U (NY)
Shawnee State U (OH)
Shorter Coll (GA)
Southeast Missouri State U (MO)
Southern Nazarene U (OK)
Southwest Baptist U (MO)
Southwest Missouri State U (MO)
Springfield Coll (MA)
State U of NY Coll at Brockport (NY)
State U of NY Coll at Cortland (NY)
State U of NY Coll at Old Westbury (NY)
State U of NY Coll at Oneonta (NY)
State U of West Georgia (GA)
Taylor U (IN)
Texas Lutheran U (TX)
Thomas More Coll (KY)
Thomas U (GA)
Toccoa Falls Coll (GA)
Transylvania U (KY)
Trinity Christian Coll (IL)
Tusculum Coll (TN)
Union Coll (KY)
The U of Akron (OH)
U of Arkansas (AR)
U of Arkansas at Fort Smith (AR)
U of Central Arkansas (AR)
U of Delaware (DE)
U of Florida (FL)
U of Georgia (GA)
U of Great Falls (MT)
U of Kansas (KS)
U of Kentucky (KY)
U of Mary Hardin-Baylor (TX)
U of Michigan–Dearborn (MI)
U of Minnesota, Duluth (MN)
U of Missouri–Columbia (MO)
U of Nebraska–Lincoln (NE)
U of New Orleans (LA)
The U of North Carolina at Chapel Hill (NC)
The U of North Carolina at Charlotte (NC)
The U of North Carolina at Greensboro (NC)
The U of North Carolina at Pembroke (NC)
The U of North Carolina at Wilmington (NC)
U of North Dakota (ND)
U of Northern Iowa (IA)
U of North Florida (FL)
U of Regina (SK, Canada)
U of Richmond (VA)
U of St. Thomas (MN)
U of Sioux Falls (SD)
The U of South Dakota (SD)
The U of Tennessee at Chattanooga (TN)
U of the Ozarks (AR)
U of Vermont (VT)
The U of Western Ontario (ON, Canada)
U of West Florida (FL)
U of Wisconsin–Platteville (WI)
Urbana U (OH)
Ursuline Coll (OH)
Valdosta State U (GA)
Valparaiso U (IN)
Villa Julie Coll (MD)
Virginia Wesleyan Coll (VA)
Wagner Coll (NY)
Waldorf Coll (IA)
Warner Pacific Coll (OR)
Washington U in St. Louis (MO)
Webster U (MO)
Wesleyan Coll (GA)
Western Carolina U (NC)
Western Kentucky U (KY)
Westminster Coll (MO)
West Virginia Wesleyan Coll (WV)
Wheeling Jesuit U (WV)
William Woods U (MO)
Wilmington Coll (DE)
Wingate U (NC)
Winona State U (MN)
Winston-Salem State U (NC)
Wright State U (OH)
Xavier U (OH)
Xavier U of Louisiana (LA)
York Coll (NE)
York U (ON, Canada)
Youngstown State U (OH)

MILITARY STUDIES
Hawai'i Pacific U (HI)
Texas Christian U (TX)
United States Air Force Acad (CO)

MILITARY TECHNOLOGIES
U of Idaho (ID)
Wright State U (OH)

MINING AND MINERAL ENGINEERING
Colorado School of Mines (CO)
Dalhousie U (NS, Canada)
Laurentian U (ON, Canada)
McGill U (QC, Canada)
Montana Tech of The U of Montana (MT)
New Mexico Inst of Mining and Technology (NM)
Oregon State U (OR)
Penn State U Abington Coll (PA)
Penn State U Altoona Coll (PA)
Penn State U at Erie, The Behrend Coll (PA)
Penn State U Beaver Campus of the Commonwealth Coll (PA)
Penn State U Berks Cmps of Berks-Lehigh Valley Coll (PA)
Penn State U Delaware County Campus of the Commonwealth Coll (PA)
Penn State U DuBois Campus of the Commonwealth Coll (PA)
Penn State U Fayette Campus of the Commonwealth Coll (PA)
Penn State U Hazleton Campus of the Commonwealth Coll (PA)
Penn State U Lehigh Valley Cmps of Berks-Lehigh Valley Coll (PA)
Penn State U McKeesport Campus of the Commonwealth Coll (PA)
Penn State U Mont Alto Campus of the Commonwealth Coll (PA)
Penn State U New Kensington Campus of the Commonwealth Coll (PA)
Penn State U Schuylkill Campus of the Capital Coll (PA)
Penn State U Shenango Campus of the Commonwealth Coll (PA)
Penn State U Univ Park Campus (PA)
Penn State U Wilkes-Barre Campus of the Commonwealth Coll (PA)
Penn State U Worthington Scranton Cmps Commonwealth Coll (PA)
Penn State U York Campus of the Commonwealth Coll (PA)
Queen's U at Kingston (ON, Canada)
South Dakota School of Mines and Technology (SD)
Southern Illinois U Carbondale (IL)
Université Laval (QC, Canada)
U of Alberta (AB, Canada)
The U of Arizona (AZ)
The U of British Columbia (BC, Canada)
U of Idaho (ID)
U of Kentucky (KY)
U of Missouri–Rolla (MO)
U of Nevada, Reno (NV)
U of Utah (UT)
U of Wisconsin–Madison (WI)
Virginia Polytechnic Inst and State U (VA)
West Virginia U (WV)

MINING AND PETROLEUM TECHNOLOGIES RELATED
U of Alaska Fairbanks (AK)

MINING TECHNOLOGY
Bluefield State Coll (WV)

MISSIONARY STUDIES AND MISSIOLOGY
Abilene Christian U (TX)
Asbury Coll (KY)
Bethany Coll (SK, Canada)
Bethel Coll (IN)
Bethesda Christian U (CA)
Biola U (CA)
Briercrest Bible Coll (SK, Canada)
Calvary Bible Coll and Theological Sem (MO)
Canadian Mennonite U (MB, Canada)
Cascade Coll (OR)
Cedarville U (OH)
Central Christian Coll of Kansas (KS)
Central Pentecostal Coll (SK, Canada)
Concordia U, St. Paul (MN)
Concordia U Wisconsin (WI)
Crossroads Bible Coll (IN)
Crossroads Coll (MN)
Crown Coll (MN)
Dordt Coll (IA)
Eastern U (PA)
East Texas Baptist U (TX)
Eugene Bible Coll (OR)
Faith Baptist Bible Coll and Theological Sem (IA)
Freed-Hardeman U (TN)
Gardner-Webb U (NC)
George Fox U (OR)
Global U of the Assemblies of God (MO)
God's Bible School and Coll (OH)
Grace U (NE)
Harding U (AR)
Hillsdale Free Will Baptist Coll (OK)
John Brown U (AR)
Kentucky Mountain Bible Coll (KY)
Lancaster Bible Coll (PA)
LeTourneau U (TX)
Liberty U (VA)
Lubbock Christian U (TX)
Manhattan Christian Coll (KS)
Master's Coll and Sem (ON, Canada)
Messenger Coll (MO)
MidAmerica Nazarene U (KS)
Mid-Continent Coll (KY)
Moody Bible Inst (IL)
Multnomah Bible Coll and Biblical Sem (OR)
North Central U (MN)
Northwestern Coll (MN)
Northwest Nazarene U (ID)
Nyack Coll (NY)
Oak Hills Christian Coll (MN)
Oklahoma Baptist U (OK)
Oklahoma Christian U (OK)
Oral Roberts U (OK)
Ouachita Baptist U (AR)
Pillsbury Baptist Bible Coll (MN)
Prairie Bible Coll (AB, Canada)
Providence Coll and Theological Sem (MB, Canada)
Reformed Bible Coll (MI)
Rocky Mountain Coll (AB, Canada)
Simpson Coll and Graduate School (CA)
Southeastern Coll of the Assemblies of God (FL)
Southern Nazarene U (OK)
Toccoa Falls Coll (GA)
Trinity Baptist Coll (FL)
Trinity Coll of Florida (FL)
Trinity Western U (BC, Canada)
Vanguard U of Southern California (CA)
Vennard Coll (IA)
Western Baptist Coll (OR)

MODERN GREEK
Ball State U (IN)
Bard Coll (NY)
Barnard Coll (NY)
Belmont U (TN)
Boston U (MA)
Brooklyn Coll of the City U of NY (NY)
Butler U (IN)
Calvin Coll (MI)
Carleton U (ON, Canada)
The Catholic U of America (DC)
Claremont McKenna Coll (CA)
Colgate U (NY)
The Coll of William and Mary (VA)
Columbia Coll (NY)
Concordia U Wisconsin (WI)
Cornell Coll (IA)
Emory U (GA)
Florida State U (FL)
Fordham U (NY)
Furman U (SC)
Hamilton Coll (NY)
Harvard U (MA)
Haverford Coll (PA)
John Carroll U (OH)
Kenyon Coll (OH)
Lehman Coll of the City U of NY (NY)
Loyola Marymount U (CA)
Macalester Coll (MN)
Marlboro Coll (VT)
Memorial U of Newfoundland (NL, Canada)
Monmouth Coll (IL)
Mount Holyoke Coll (MA)
New York U (NY)
Oberlin Coll (OH)
The Ohio State U (OH)
Queen's U at Kingston (ON, Canada)
Rhodes Coll (TN)
Rockford Coll (IL)
Saint Louis U (MO)
Saint Mary's Coll of California (CA)
Trent U (ON, Canada)
Tufts U (MA)
Tulane U (LA)
U of Alberta (AB, Canada)
U of Calif, Los Angeles (CA)
The U of Iowa (IA)
U of Manitoba (MB, Canada)
U of Michigan (MI)
U of Minnesota, Twin Cities Campus (MN)
U of Missouri–Columbia (MO)
U of New Brunswick Fredericton (NB, Canada)
U of New Hampshire (NH)
U of Oregon (OR)
U of Richmond (VA)
U of Saskatchewan (SK, Canada)

The U of Tennessee at Chattanooga (TN)
U of the South (TN)
U of Toronto (ON, Canada)
U of Utah (UT)
U of Windsor (ON, Canada)
U of Wisconsin–Madison (WI)
U of Wisconsin–Milwaukee (WI)
Wabash Coll (IN)
Wright State U (OH)
York U (ON, Canada)

MODERN LANGUAGES
Albion Coll (MI)
Alfred U (NY)
Alma Coll (MI)
Atlantic Union Coll (MA)
Ball State U (IN)
Bard Coll (NY)
Beloit Coll (WI)
Bemidji State U (MN)
Bennington Coll (VT)
Bishop's U (QC, Canada)
Buena Vista U (IA)
Carleton U (ON, Canada)
Carnegie Mellon U (PA)
Carthage Coll (WI)
Chicago State U (IL)
Claremont McKenna Coll (CA)
Clark U (MA)
Coll of Mount Saint Vincent (NY)
Coll of Notre Dame of Maryland (MD)
The Coll of William and Mary (VA)
Concordia U (QC, Canada)
Converse Coll (SC)
Cornell Coll (IA)
DePaul U (IL)
Dillard U (LA)
Eckerd Coll (FL)
Elizabethtown Coll (PA)
Elmira Coll (NY)
Fairfield U (CT)
Fordham U (NY)
Fort Lewis Coll (CO)
Franklin Coll Switzerland(Switzerland)
Gannon U (PA)
Georgia Inst of Technology (GA)
Gettysburg Coll (PA)
Greenville Coll (IL)
Grove City Coll (PA)
Hamilton Coll (NY)
Hampton U (VA)
Harvard U (MA)
Hastings Coll (NE)
Hobart and William Smith Colls (NY)
Howard Payne U (TX)
Immaculata U (PA)
Judson Coll (AL)
Kenyon Coll (OH)
King Coll (TN)
Lake Erie Coll (OH)
Lambuth U (TN)
La Salle U (PA)
Laurentian U (ON, Canada)
Lenoir-Rhyne Coll (NC)
Lewis & Clark Coll (OR)
Long Island U, Brooklyn Campus (NY)
Longwood U (VA)
Louisiana Coll (LA)
Marlboro Coll (VT)
Marymount Coll of Fordham U (NY)
Mary Washington Coll (VA)
Merrimack Coll (MA)
Middlebury Coll (VT)
Minnesota State U Mankato (MN)
Monmouth Coll (IL)
Mount Allison U (NB, Canada)
Mount Saint Vincent U (NS, Canada)
Nazareth Coll of Rochester (NY)
Northeastern U (MA)
North Park U (IL)
Oakland U (MI)
Olivet Nazarene U (IL)
Pace U (NY)
Pacific Lutheran U (WA)
Pacific U (OR)
Pomona Coll (CA)
Presbyterian Coll (SC)
Rivier Coll (NH)
St. Bonaventure U (NY)
Saint Francis U (PA)
St. Francis Xavier U (NS, Canada)
St. Lawrence U (NY)
Saint Mary's Coll of California (CA)
St. Mary's Coll of Maryland (MD)
Saint Michael's Coll (VT)
St. Thomas Aquinas Coll (NY)
Sarah Lawrence Coll (NY)
Scripps Coll (CA)
Slippery Rock U of Pennsylvania (PA)
Southwestern U (TX)
Stephens Coll (MO)
Suffolk U (MA)
Syracuse U (NY)
Trent U (ON, Canada)
Trinity Coll (CT)
United States Military Acad (NY)
Université de Montréal (QC, Canada)
Université Laval (QC, Canada)
U of Alberta (AB, Canada)
U of Chicago (IL)
The U of Lethbridge (AB, Canada)
U of Louisiana at Lafayette (LA)
U of Maine (ME)
U of Maryland, Baltimore County (MD)
U of New Brunswick Fredericton (NB, Canada)
U of New Hampshire (NH)
U of Ottawa (ON, Canada)
U of Southern Maine (ME)
U of South Florida (FL)
U of Toronto (ON, Canada)
U of Victoria (BC, Canada)
U of Windsor (ON, Canada)
Virginia Military Inst (VA)
Walla Walla Coll (WA)
Walsh U (OH)
Washington U in St. Louis (MO)
Wayne State Coll (NE)
Westminster Coll (PA)
Westmont Coll (CA)
Widener U (PA)
Winthrop U (SC)
Wright State U (OH)
York U (ON, Canada)

MOLECULAR BIOCHEMISTRY
Baker U (KS)
Polytechnic U, Brooklyn Campus (NY)
Simon Fraser U (BC, Canada)
U of Calif, Irvine (CA)
U of Calif, Los Angeles (CA)

MOLECULAR BIOLOGY
Alverno Coll (WI)
Arizona State U (AZ)
Assumption Coll (MA)
Auburn U (AL)
Ball State U (IN)
Bard Coll (NY)
Beloit Coll (WI)
Benedictine U (IL)
Bethel U (MN)
Blackburn Coll (IL)
Boston U (MA)
Bradley U (IL)
Bridgewater State Coll (MA)
Brigham Young U (UT)
Brown U (RI)
California Lutheran U (CA)
California State U, Fresno (CA)
California State U, Sacramento (CA)
California State U, San Marcos (CA)
Cedar Crest Coll (PA)
Centre Coll (KY)
Chapman U (CA)
Chestnut Hill Coll (PA)
Clarion U of Pennsylvania (PA)
Clarkson U (NY)
Clark U (MA)
Coe Coll (IA)
Colby Coll (ME)
Colgate U (NY)
The Coll of Southeastern Europe, The American U of Athens(Greece)
The Coll of Wooster (OH)
Concordia U (QC, Canada)
Cornell U (NY)
Dartmouth Coll (NH)
Elms Coll (MA)
Florida Ag and Mech U (FL)
Florida Inst of Technology (FL)
Fort Lewis Coll (CO)
Gettysburg Coll (PA)
Grove City Coll (PA)
Hamilton Coll (NY)
Hampshire Coll (MA)
Hampton U (VA)
Harvard U (MA)
Houston Baptist U (TX)
Humboldt State U (CA)
Juniata Coll (PA)
Kenyon Coll (OH)
Lehigh U (PA)
Long Island U, C.W. Post Campus (NY)
Marlboro Coll (VT)
Marquette U (WI)
McGill U (QC, Canada)
Meredith Coll (NC)
Middlebury Coll (VT)
Montclair State U (NJ)
Northwestern U (IL)
Ohio Northern U (OH)
Otterbein Coll (OH)
Pomona Coll (CA)
Princeton U (NJ)
Rutgers, The State U of New Jersey, New Brunswick/Piscataway (NJ)
San Francisco State U (CA)
San Jose State U (CA)
Sarah Lawrence Coll (NY)
Scripps Coll (CA)
Simon Fraser U (BC, Canada)
Southwest Missouri State U (MO)
State U of NY Coll at Brockport (NY)
Stetson U (FL)
Texas Lutheran U (TX)
Texas Tech U (TX)
Tulane U (LA)
State U of NY at Albany (NY)
U Coll of the Cariboo (BC, Canada)
U of Alberta (AB, Canada)
U of Calgary (AB, Canada)
U of Calif, Los Angeles (CA)
U of Calif, San Diego (CA)
U of Calif, Santa Barbara (CA)
U of Calif, Santa Cruz (CA)
U of Denver (CO)
U of Guelph (ON, Canada)
U of Idaho (ID)
U of Kansas (KS)
U of Maine (ME)
The U of Memphis (TN)
U of Michigan (MI)
U of Minnesota, Duluth (MN)
U of New Brunswick Fredericton (NB, Canada)
U of New Hampshire (NH)
U of Pittsburgh (PA)
U of Richmond (VA)
The U of Texas at Austin (TX)
The U of Texas at Dallas (TX)
U of Toronto (ON, Canada)
U of Washington (WA)
U of Wisconsin–Eau Claire (WI)
U of Wisconsin–Madison (WI)
U of Wisconsin–Parkside (WI)
U of Wisconsin–Superior (WI)
U of Wyoming (WY)
Vanderbilt U (TN)
Wells Coll (NY)
Wesleyan U (CT)
West Chester U of Pennsylvania (PA)
Western State Coll of Colorado (CO)
Western Washington U (WA)
Westminster Coll (PA)
Whitman Coll (WA)
William Jewell Coll (MO)
Winston-Salem State U (NC)
Worcester Polytechnic Inst (MA)
Yale U (CT)
York U (ON, Canada)

MOLECULAR BIOPHYSICS
The U of Arizona (AZ)

MOLECULAR GENETICS
Texas A&M U (TX)
U of Guelph (ON, Canada)
U of Vermont (VT)

MOLECULAR PHARMACOLOGY
U of Calif, Los Angeles (CA)

MOLECULAR PHYSIOLOGY
U of Calif, Los Angeles (CA)

MOLECULAR TOXICOLOGY
U of Calif, Los Angeles (CA)

MONTESSORI TEACHER EDUCATION
Oklahoma City U (OK)

MOVEMENT THERAPY AND MOVEMENT EDUCATION
Brock U (ON, Canada)
Texas Christian U (TX)

MULTICULTURAL EDUCATION
Florida State U (FL)

MULTI-/INTERDISCIPLINARY STUDIES RELATED
Abilene Christian U (TX)
Adelphi U (NY)
Albright Coll (PA)
Allegheny Coll (PA)
Angelo State U (TX)
Arizona State U (AZ)
Arizona State U East (AZ)
Arizona State U West (AZ)
Austin Coll (TX)
Baldwin-Wallace Coll (OH)
Barnard Coll (NY)
Bates Coll (ME)
Baylor U (TX)
Berry Coll (GA)
Bethel U (MN)
Bloomfield Coll (NJ)
Bloomsburg U of Pennsylvania (PA)
Bluffton Coll (OH)
Bowling Green State U (OH)
Brandeis U (MA)
Brevard Coll (NC)
Brigham Young U–Hawaii (HI)
Bucknell U (PA)
Buena Vista U (IA)
State U of NY Coll at Buffalo (NY)
Caldwell Coll (NJ)
California Lutheran U (CA)
California State U, Chico (CA)
California State U, Long Beach (CA)
California State U, Los Angeles (CA)
California State U, Stanislaus (CA)
Capital U (OH)
Central Connecticut State U (CT)
Chestnut Hill Coll (PA)
Christian Heritage Coll (CA)
Clayton Coll & State U (GA)
Cleveland State U (OH)
Colby Coll (ME)
The Coll of New Rochelle (NY)
Coll of Saint Elizabeth (NJ)
Coll of Santa Fe (NM)
Coll of the Ozarks (MO)
The Coll of William and Mary (VA)
The Coll of Wooster (OH)
The Colorado Coll (CO)
Columbia Coll (MO)
Columbia Coll (SC)
Columbia Coll Chicago (IL)
Cornell Coll (IA)
Cornell U (NY)
Cornerstone U (MI)
Dalhousie U (NS, Canada)
Dallas Baptist U (TX)
Dartmouth Coll (NH)
Davidson Coll (NC)
DePauw U (IN)
Dickinson Coll (PA)
Eastern Illinois U (IL)
Eastern Mennonite U (VA)
Eastern Michigan U (MI)
Eastern New Mexico U (NM)
Emporia State U (KS)
Endicott Coll (MA)
The Evergreen State Coll (WA)
Fairleigh Dickinson U, Teaneck-Metro Campus (NJ)
Florida Inst of Technology (FL)
The Franciscan U (IA)
Franklin and Marshall Coll (PA)
Frostburg State U (MD)
Georgetown Coll (KY)
Georgia Inst of Technology (GA)
Georgia State U (GA)
Glenville State Coll (WV)
Grace Bible Coll (MI)
Greenville Coll (IL)
Hampshire Coll (MA)
Hastings Coll (NE)
Hawai'i Pacific U (HI)
Hofstra U (NY)
Hood Coll (MD)
Hope Coll (MI)
Huntingdon Coll (AL)
Idaho State U (ID)
Illinois Inst of Technology (IL)
Intl Coll (FL)
Iowa State U of Science and Technology (IA)
Ithaca Coll (NY)
Judson Coll (AL)
Kent State U (OH)
Kentucky Wesleyan Coll (KY)
Kenyon Coll (OH)
Knox Coll (IL)
Lambuth U (TN)
Lane Coll (TN)
Lebanon Valley Coll (PA)
Lehigh U (PA)
Lewis-Clark State Coll (ID)
Liberty U (VA)
Long Island U, Brooklyn Campus (NY)
Long Island U, C.W. Post Campus (NY)
Long Island U, Southampton Coll, Friends World Program (NY)
Marquette U (WI)
Marshall U (WV)
Mary Baldwin Coll (VA)
Maryville Coll (TN)
Marywood U (PA)
Massachusetts Coll of Liberal Arts (MA)
McDaniel Coll (MD)
Mercer U (GA)
Mercyhurst Coll (PA)
Meredith Coll (NC)
Miami U (OH)
Miami U Hamilton (OH)
Mid-Continent Coll (KY)
Middle Tennessee State U (TN)
Midwestern State U (TX)
Mississippi State U (MS)
Missouri Baptist U (MO)
Missouri Western State Coll (MO)
Monmouth U (NJ)
Montana State U–Billings (MT)
Mountain State U (WV)
Mount Saint Mary's Coll and Sem (MD)
Naropa U (CO)
Nevada State Coll at Henderson (NV)
New York Inst of Technology (NY)
Norfolk State U (VA)
North Dakota State U (ND)
North Greenville Coll (SC)
Northwestern U (IL)
Notre Dame Coll (OH)
Nova Southeastern U (FL)
Ohio U–Southern Campus (OH)
Ohio Wesleyan U (OH)
Old Dominion U (VA)
Otterbein Coll (OH)
Pace U (NY)
Park U (MO)
Penn State U at Erie, The Behrend Coll (PA)
Plymouth State U (NH)
Princeton U (NJ)
Purdue U (IN)
Queens Coll of the City U of NY (NY)
Ramapo Coll of New Jersey (NJ)
Regis Coll (MA)
Rice U (TX)
Robert Morris U (PA)
Rocky Mountain Coll (MT)
Roger Williams U (RI)
Rutgers, The State U of New Jersey, Camden (NJ)
Rutgers, The State U of New Jersey, Newark (NJ)
Saginaw Valley State U (MI)
St. Ambrose U (IA)
St. Cloud State U (MN)
St. Edward's U (TX)
St. John Fisher Coll (NY)
Saint Mary's Coll of California (CA)
St. Mary's Coll of Maryland (MD)
St. Olaf Coll (MN)
Sam Houston State U (TX)
San Diego State U (CA)
San Jose State U (CA)
Scripps Coll (CA)
Sheldon Jackson Coll (AK)
Shippensburg U of Pennsylvania (PA)
Sonoma State U (CA)
Southeast Missouri State U (MO)
Southern Illinois U Carbondale (IL)
Spring Hill Coll (AL)
State U of NY Coll at Potsdam (NY)
Sterling Coll (VT)
Stonehill Coll (MA)
Stony Brook U, State U of New York (NY)
Tarleton State U (TX)
Texas A&M U (TX)
Texas A&M U at Galveston (TX)
Texas A&M U–Texarkana (TX)
Texas Southern U (TX)
Texas State U-San Marcos (TX)
Texas Tech U (TX)
Texas Wesleyan U (TX)
Thomas Aquinas Coll (CA)
Tulane U (LA)
Université Laval (QC, Canada)
U at Buffalo, The State U of New York (NY)
U of Alaska Fairbanks (AK)
The U of Arizona (AZ)
U of Arkansas (AR)
U of Arkansas at Fort Smith (AR)
U of Calif, Berkeley (CA)
U of Calif, Irvine (CA)
U of Calif, Los Angeles (CA)
U of Calif, Santa Barbara (CA)
U of Colorado at Boulder (CO)
U of Colorado at Denver (CO)
U of Connecticut (CT)
U of Denver (CO)
U of Florida (FL)
U of Hartford (CT)

U of Hawaii at Manoa (HI)
U of Houston–Clear Lake (TX)
U of Idaho (ID)
U of Kentucky (KY)
U of King's Coll (NS, Canada)
U of Maryland U Coll (MD)
U of Massachusetts Amherst (MA)
The U of Memphis (TN)
U of Nebraska at Omaha (NE)
U of North Dakota (ND)
U of Northern Colorado (CO)
U of North Texas (TX)
U of Oklahoma (OK)
U of Saint Mary (KS)
U of St. Thomas (MN)
U of South Alabama (AL)
The U of Tennessee (TN)
The U of Texas at Arlington (TX)
The U of Texas at Austin (TX)
The U of Texas at Brownsville (TX)
The U of Texas at Tyler (TX)
The U of Texas–Pan American (TX)
U of Toledo (OH)
U of Virginia (VA)
U of Waterloo (ON, Canada)
U of Wyoming (WY)
Ursinus Coll (PA)
Ursuline Coll (OH)
Utah State U (UT)
Valparaiso U (IN)
Vassar Coll (NY)
Vennard Coll (IA)
Virginia State U (VA)
Viterbo U (WI)
Washington and Lee U (VA)
Washington Coll (MD)
Washington U in St. Louis (MO)
Western Kentucky U (KY)
West Texas A&M U (TX)
Wheaton Coll (IL)
Wilkes U (PA)
Wisconsin Lutheran Coll (WI)
Wright State U (OH)
Yale U (CT)

MUSEUM STUDIES

Baylor U (TX)
Beloit Coll (WI)
Centenary Coll of Louisiana (LA)
Coll of the Atlantic (ME)
Connecticut Coll (CT)
Juniata Coll (PA)
Oklahoma Baptist U (OK)
Randolph-Macon Woman's Coll (VA)
Regis Coll (MA)
Texas A&M U (TX)
Tusculum Coll (TN)
The U of Iowa (IA)
The U of North Carolina at Greensboro (NC)

MUSIC

Abilene Christian U (TX)
Acadia U (NS, Canada)
Adams State Coll (CO)
Adelphi U (NY)
Adrian Coll (MI)
Agnes Scott Coll (GA)
Alabama State U (AL)
Albany State U (GA)
Albertson Coll of Idaho (ID)
Albion Coll (MI)
Albright Coll (PA)
Alderson-Broaddus Coll (WV)
Allegheny Coll (PA)
Allen U (SC)
Alma Coll (MI)
Alverno Coll (WI)
American U (DC)
Amherst Coll (MA)
Anderson Coll (SC)
Andrews U (MI)
Angelo State U (TX)
Anna Maria Coll (MA)
Antioch Coll (OH)
Aquinas Coll (MI)
Arizona State U (AZ)
Arkansas State U (AR)
Arkansas Tech U (AR)
Arlington Baptist Coll (TX)
Armstrong Atlantic State U (GA)
Asbury Coll (KY)
Ashland U (OH)
Atlanta Christian Coll (GA)
Atlantic Union Coll (MA)
Augsburg Coll (MN)
Augustana Coll (IL)
Augustana Coll (SD)
Augusta State U (GA)
Austin Coll (TX)
Austin Peay State U (TN)
Averett U (VA)
Azusa Pacific U (CA)
Baker U (KS)
Baldwin-Wallace Coll (OH)
Ball State U (IN)
Baptist Bible Coll (MO)
Bard Coll (NY)
Barnard Coll (NY)
Bates Coll (ME)
Baylor U (TX)
Belhaven Coll (MS)
Bellarmine U (KY)
Belmont U (TN)
Beloit Coll (WI)
Bemidji State U (MN)
Benedictine Coll (KS)
Benedictine U (IL)
Bennington Coll (VT)
Berea Coll (KY)
Berklee Coll of Music (MA)
Baruch Coll of the City U of NY (NY)
Berry Coll (GA)
Bethany Bible Coll (NB, Canada)
Bethany Coll (KS)
Bethany Coll (WV)
Bethany Lutheran Coll (MN)
Bethel Coll (IN)
Bethel U (MN)
Biola U (CA)
Birmingham-Southern Coll (AL)
Bishop's U (QC, Canada)
Blackburn Coll (IL)
Black Hills State U (SD)
Bloomsburg U of Pennsylvania (PA)
Bluefield Coll (VA)
Blue Mountain Coll (MS)
Bluffton Coll (OH)
Boise State U (ID)
Boston Coll (MA)
Bowdoin Coll (ME)
Bowling Green State U (OH)
Bradley U (IL)
Brandeis U (MA)
Brenau U (GA)
Brevard Coll (NC)
Brewton-Parker Coll (GA)
Briar Cliff U (IA)
Bridgewater State Coll (MA)
Briercrest Bible Coll (SK, Canada)
Brigham Young U (UT)
Brigham Young U–Hawaii (HI)
Brock U (ON, Canada)
Brooklyn Coll of the City U of NY (NY)
Brown U (RI)
Bryan Coll (TN)
Bryn Mawr Coll (PA)
Bucknell U (PA)
State U of NY Coll at Buffalo (NY)
Butler U (IN)
Caldwell Coll (NJ)
California Baptist U (CA)
California Inst of the Arts (CA)
California Lutheran U (CA)
California Polytechnic State U, San Luis Obispo (CA)
California State Polytechnic U, Pomona (CA)
California State U, Chico (CA)
California State U, Dominguez Hills (CA)
California State U, Fresno (CA)
California State U, Fullerton (CA)
California State U, Hayward (CA)
California State U, Long Beach (CA)
California State U, Los Angeles (CA)
California State U, Sacramento (CA)
California State U, San Bernardino (CA)
California State U, Stanislaus (CA)
Calvary Bible Coll and Theological Sem (MO)
Calvin Coll (MI)
Cameron U (OK)
Campbellsville U (KY)
Campbell U (NC)
Canadian Mennonite U (MB, Canada)
Capital U (OH)
Cardinal Stritch U (WI)
Carleton Coll (MN)
Carleton U (ON, Canada)
Carnegie Mellon U (PA)
Carroll Coll (WI)
Carson-Newman Coll (TN)
Carthage Coll (WI)
Case Western Reserve U (OH)
Castleton State Coll (VT)
Catawba Coll (NC)
The Catholic U of America (DC)
Cedar Crest Coll (PA)
Cedarville U (OH)
Centenary Coll of Louisiana (LA)
Central Coll (IA)
Central Connecticut State U (CT)
Central Methodist Coll (MO)
Central Michigan U (MI)
Central Missouri State U (MO)
Central State U (OH)
Central Washington U (WA)
Centre Coll (KY)
Chadron State Coll (NE)
Chapman U (CA)
Charleston Southern U (SC)
Chatham Coll (PA)
Cheyney U of Pennsylvania (PA)
Chicago State U (IL)
Chowan Coll (NC)
Christian Heritage Coll (CA)
Christopher Newport U (VA)
City Coll of the City U of NY (NY)
Claremont McKenna Coll (CA)
Clark Atlanta U (GA)
Clarke Coll (IA)
Clark U (MA)
Clayton Coll & State U (GA)
Clearwater Christian Coll (FL)
Cleveland Inst of Music (OH)
Cleveland State U (OH)
Coastal Carolina U (SC)
Coe Coll (IA)
Coker Coll (SC)
Colby Coll (ME)
Colgate U (NY)
Coll of Charleston (SC)
Coll of Mount St. Joseph (OH)
The Coll of New Jersey (NJ)
Coll of Notre Dame of Maryland (MD)
Coll of Saint Benedict (MN)
Coll of St. Catherine (MN)
Coll of Saint Elizabeth (NJ)
The Coll of Saint Rose (NY)
Coll of Staten Island of the City U of NY (NY)
Coll of the Atlantic (ME)
Coll of the Holy Cross (MA)
Coll of the Ozarks (MO)
The Coll of William and Mary (VA)
The Coll of Wooster (OH)
Colorado Christian U (CO)
The Colorado Coll (CO)
Colorado State U (CO)
Colorado State U-Pueblo (CO)
Columbia Coll (NY)
Columbia Coll (SC)
Columbia Coll Chicago (IL)
Columbia Intl U (SC)
Columbia Union Coll (MD)
Columbia U, School of General Studies (NY)
Columbus State U (GA)
Concordia Coll (MN)
Concordia Coll (NY)
Concordia U (CA)
Concordia U (IL)
Concordia U (MI)
Concordia U (NE)
Concordia U (QC, Canada)
Concordia U Coll of Alberta (AB, Canada)
Concordia U, St. Paul (MN)
Concordia U Wisconsin (WI)
Connecticut Coll (CT)
Converse Coll (SC)
Cornell Coll (IA)
Cornell U (NY)
Cornerstone U (MI)
Cornish Coll of the Arts (WA)
Covenant Coll (GA)
Creighton U (NE)
Crown Coll (MN)
Culver-Stockton Coll (MO)
Cumberland Coll (KY)
Cumberland U (TN)
Dakota Wesleyan U (SD)
Dalhousie U (NS, Canada)
Dallas Baptist U (TX)
Dana Coll (NE)
Dartmouth Coll (NH)
Davidson Coll (NC)
Davis & Elkins Coll (WV)
Delaware State U (DE)
Delta State U (MS)
Denison U (OH)
DePaul U (IL)
DePauw U (IN)
Dickinson Coll (PA)
Dickinson State U (ND)
Dillard U (LA)
Doane Coll (NE)
Dominican U of California (CA)
Dordt Coll (IA)
Dowling Coll (NY)
Drake U (IA)
Drew U (NJ)
Drexel U (PA)
Drury U (MO)
Duke U (NC)
Earlham Coll (IN)
East Central U (OK)
Eastern Illinois U (IL)
Eastern Kentucky U (KY)
Eastern Mennonite U (VA)
Eastern Michigan U (MI)
Eastern Nazarene Coll (MA)
Eastern New Mexico U (NM)
Eastern Oregon U (OR)
Eastern U (PA)
Eastern Washington U (WA)
East Texas Baptist U (TX)
Eckerd Coll (FL)
Edgewood Coll (WI)
Edinboro U of Pennsylvania (PA)
Elizabeth City State U (NC)
Elizabethtown Coll (PA)
Elmhurst Coll (IL)
Elmira Coll (NY)
Elon U (NC)
Emmanuel Coll (GA)
Emory & Henry Coll (VA)
Emory U (GA)
Emporia State U (KS)
Erskine Coll (SC)
Eureka Coll (IL)
Evangel U (MO)
Excelsior Coll (NY)
Five Towns Coll (NY)
Florida Ag and Mech U (FL)
Florida Atlantic U (FL)
Florida Intl U (FL)
Florida Southern Coll (FL)
Florida State U (FL)
Fordham U (NY)
Fort Hays State U (KS)
Fort Lewis Coll (CO)
The Franciscan U (IA)
Franklin and Marshall Coll (PA)
Franklin Pierce Coll (NH)
Freed-Hardeman U (TN)
Fresno Pacific U (CA)
Frostburg State U (MD)
Furman U (SC)
Gardner-Webb U (NC)
Geneva Coll (PA)
George Fox U (OR)
Georgetown Coll (KY)
The George Washington U (DC)
Georgia Coll & State U (GA)
Georgian Court U (NJ)
Georgia Southern U (GA)
Georgia Southwestern State U (GA)
Gettysburg Coll (PA)
Gonzaga U (WA)
Gordon Coll (MA)
Goshen Coll (IN)
Goucher Coll (MD)
Grace Bible Coll (MI)
Graceland U (IA)
Grace U (NE)
Grand Canyon U (AZ)
Grand Valley State U (MI)
Grand View Coll (IA)
Greensboro Coll (NC)
Greenville Coll (IL)
Grinnell Coll (IA)
Grove City Coll (PA)
Guilford Coll (NC)
Gustavus Adolphus Coll (MN)
Hamilton Coll (NY)
Hamline U (MN)
Hampshire Coll (MA)
Hampton U (VA)
Hannibal-LaGrange Coll (MO)
Hanover Coll (IN)
Harding U (AR)
Hartwick Coll (NY)
Harvard U (MA)
Hastings Coll (NE)
Haverford Coll (PA)
Heidelberg Coll (OH)
Henderson State U (AR)
Hendrix Coll (AR)
Hillsdale Coll (MI)
Hiram Coll (OH)
Hobart and William Smith Colls (NY)
Hofstra U (NY)
Hollins U (VA)
Holy Names Coll (CA)
Hood Coll (MD)
Hope Coll (MI)
Houghton Coll (NY)
Houston Baptist U (TX)
Howard Payne U (TX)
Howard U (DC)
Humboldt State U (CA)
Hunter Coll of the City U of NY (NY)
Huntingdon Coll (AL)
Huntington Coll (IN)
Huston-Tillotson Coll (TX)
Idaho State U (ID)
Illinois Coll (IL)
Illinois State U (IL)
Illinois Wesleyan U (IL)
Immaculata U (PA)
Indiana State U (IN)
Indiana U Bloomington (IN)
Indiana U of Pennsylvania (PA)
Indiana U–Purdue U Fort Wayne (IN)
Indiana U Southeast (IN)
Inter American U of PR, Fajardo Campus (PR)
Inter American U of PR, San Germán Campus (PR)
Iowa State U of Science and Technology (IA)
Iowa Wesleyan Coll (IA)
Ithaca Coll (NY)
Jacksonville State U (AL)
Jacksonville U (FL)
Jamestown Coll (ND)
Jarvis Christian Coll (TX)
Jewish Theological Sem of America (NY)
John Brown U (AR)
The Johns Hopkins U (MD)
Johnson C. Smith U (NC)
Johnson State Coll (VT)
Judson Coll (AL)
Judson Coll (IL)
The Juilliard School (NY)
Kalamazoo Coll (MI)
Kansas State U (KS)
Kean U (NJ)
Keene State Coll (NH)
Kennesaw State U (GA)
Kent State U (OH)
Kentucky Christian Coll (KY)
Kenyon Coll (OH)
King Coll (TN)
The King's U Coll (AB, Canada)
Knox Coll (IL)
Kutztown U of Pennsylvania (PA)
Lafayette Coll (PA)
LaGrange Coll (GA)
Lake Erie Coll (OH)
Lake Forest Coll (IL)
Lakehead U (ON, Canada)
Lakeland Coll (WI)
Lamar U (TX)
Lambuth U (TN)
Lander U (SC)
Lane Coll (TN)
Laurentian U (ON, Canada)
Lawrence U (WI)
Lehigh U (PA)
Lehman Coll of the City U of NY (NY)
Lenoir-Rhyne Coll (NC)
Lewis & Clark Coll (OR)
Lewis U (IL)
Liberty U (VA)
Limestone Coll (SC)
Lincoln U (PA)
Lindenwood U (MO)
Linfield Coll (OR)
Lipscomb U (TN)
Livingstone Coll (NC)
Lock Haven U of Pennsylvania (PA)
Long Island U, C.W. Post Campus (NY)
Longwood U (VA)
Loras Coll (IA)
Louisiana Coll (LA)
Louisiana State U and A&M Coll (LA)
Louisiana Tech U (LA)
Loyola Marymount U (CA)
Loyola U Chicago (IL)
Loyola U New Orleans (LA)
Lubbock Christian U (TX)
Luther Coll (IA)
Lycoming Coll (PA)
Lynchburg Coll (VA)
Lynn U (FL)
Lyon Coll (AR)
Macalester Coll (MN)
MacMurray Coll (IL)
Madonna U (MI)
Malone Coll (OH)
Manchester Coll (IN)
Manhattan School of Music (NY)
Manhattanville Coll (NY)
Mannes Coll of Music, New School U (NY)
Mansfield U of Pennsylvania (PA)
Marian Coll (IN)
Marian Coll of Fond du Lac (WI)
Marietta Coll (OH)
Marlboro Coll (VT)
Mars Hill Coll (NC)
Martin U (IN)
Mary Baldwin Coll (VA)
Marygrove Coll (MI)
Marylhurst U (OR)
Mary Washington Coll (VA)
Marywood U (PA)

Massachusetts Coll of Liberal Arts (MA)
Massachusetts Inst of Technology (MA)
The Master's Coll and Sem (CA)
McDaniel Coll (MD)
McGill U (QC, Canada)
McKendree Coll (IL)
McNeese State U (LA)
McPherson Coll (KS)
Memorial U of Newfoundland (NL, Canada)
Mercer U (GA)
Mercy Coll (NY)
Mercyhurst Coll (PA)
Meredith Coll (NC)
Messenger Coll (MO)
Messiah Coll (PA)
Methodist Coll (NC)
Miami U (OH)
Miami U Hamilton (OH)
Michigan State U (MI)
MidAmerica Nazarene U (KS)
Middlebury Coll (VT)
Middle Tennessee State U (TN)
Midwestern State U (TX)
Millersville U of Pennsylvania (PA)
Milligan Coll (TN)
Millikin U (IL)
Millsaps Coll (MS)
Mills Coll (CA)
Minnesota State U Mankato (MN)
Minnesota State U Moorhead (MN)
Minot State U (ND)
Mississippi Coll (MS)
Mississippi Valley State U (MS)
Missouri Southern State U (MO)
Missouri Valley Coll (MO)
Missouri Western State Coll (MO)
Molloy Coll (NY)
Monmouth Coll (IL)
Monmouth U (NJ)
Montana State U–Billings (MT)
Montana State U–Bozeman (MT)
Montclair State U (NJ)
Moravian Coll (PA)
Morehead State U (KY)
Morehouse Coll (GA)
Morgan State U (MD)
Morningside Coll (IA)
Mount Allison U (NB, Canada)
Mount Holyoke Coll (MA)
Mount Marty Coll (SD)
Mount Mary Coll (WI)
Mount Mercy Coll (IA)
Mount St. Mary's Coll (CA)
Mount Union Coll (OH)
Mount Vernon Nazarene U (OH)
Muhlenberg Coll (PA)
Murray State U (KY)
Musicians Inst (CA)
Naropa U (CO)
Nazareth Coll of Rochester (NY)
Nebraska Wesleyan U (NE)
Newberry Coll (SC)
New Coll of Florida (FL)
New Jersey City U (NJ)
New Mexico Highlands U (NM)
New York U (NY)
Nicholls State U (LA)
Norfolk State U (VA)
North Carolina Central U (NC)
North Central Coll (IL)
North Central U (MN)
North Dakota State U (ND)
Northeastern Illinois U (IL)
Northeastern State U (OK)
Northeastern U (MA)
Northern Arizona U (AZ)
Northern Illinois U (IL)
Northern Michigan U (MI)
Northern State U (SD)
North Georgia Coll & State U (GA)
North Greenville Coll (SC)
Northland Coll (WI)
North Park U (IL)
Northwestern Coll (IA)
Northwestern Coll (MN)
Northwestern Oklahoma State U (OK)
Northwestern U (IL)
Northwest Nazarene U (ID)
Notre Dame de Namur U (CA)
Nyack Coll (NY)
Oak Hills Christian Coll (MN)
Oakland City U (IN)
Oakland U (MI)
Oberlin Coll (OH)
Occidental Coll (CA)
Ohio Northern U (OH)
The Ohio State U (OH)
Ohio U (OH)
Ohio Wesleyan U (OH)
Oklahoma Baptist U (OK)
Oklahoma Christian U (OK)
Oklahoma City U (OK)
Oklahoma State U (OK)
Old Dominion U (VA)
Olivet Nazarene U (IL)
Oral Roberts U (OK)
Oregon State U (OR)
Ottawa U (KS)
Otterbein Coll (OH)
Ouachita Baptist U (AR)
Pacific Lutheran U (WA)
Pacific Union Coll (CA)
Pacific U (OR)
Palm Beach Atlantic U (FL)
Peabody Conserv of Music of Johns Hopkins U (MD)
Penn State U Univ Park Campus (PA)
Pepperdine U, Malibu (CA)
Pfeiffer U (NC)
Philadelphia Biblical U (PA)
Piedmont Coll (GA)
Pillsbury Baptist Bible Coll (MN)
Pittsburg State U (KS)
Plymouth State U (NH)
Point Loma Nazarene U (CA)
Pomona Coll (CA)
Pontifical Catholic U of Puerto Rico (PR)
Portland State U (OR)
Prairie Bible Coll (AB, Canada)
Prairie View A&M U (TX)
Presbyterian Coll (SC)
Princeton U (NJ)
Principia Coll (IL)
Providence Coll (RI)
Providence Coll and Theological Sem (MB, Canada)
Queens Coll of the City U of NY (NY)
Queen's U at Kingston (ON, Canada)
Queens U of Charlotte (NC)
Quincy U (IL)
Radford U (VA)
Ramapo Coll of New Jersey (NJ)
Randolph-Macon Coll (VA)
Redeemer U Coll (ON, Canada)
Reed Coll (OR)
Reinhardt Coll (GA)
Rhode Island Coll (RI)
Rhodes Coll (TN)
Rice U (TX)
Rider U (NJ)
Ripon Coll (WI)
Roanoke Coll (VA)
Roberts Wesleyan Coll (NY)
Rochester Coll (MI)
Rocky Mountain Coll (AB, Canada)
Rollins Coll (FL)
Roosevelt U (IL)
Rutgers, The State U of New Jersey, Camden (NJ)
Rutgers, The State U of New Jersey, Newark (NJ)
Rutgers, The State U of New Jersey, New Brunswick/Piscataway (NJ)
Saginaw Valley State U (MI)
St. Ambrose U (IA)
St. Cloud State U (MN)
St. Francis Xavier U (NS, Canada)
Saint John's U (MN)
St. Lawrence U (NY)
Saint Louis U (MO)
Saint Mary-of-the-Woods Coll (IN)
Saint Mary's Coll (IN)
Saint Mary's Coll of California (CA)
St. Mary's Coll of Maryland (MD)
Saint Mary's U of Minnesota (MN)
St. Mary's U of San Antonio (TX)
Saint Michael's Coll (VT)
St. Norbert Coll (WI)
St. Olaf Coll (MN)
Saint Vincent Coll (PA)
Saint Xavier U (IL)
Salem Coll (NC)
Salisbury U (MD)
Salve Regina U (RI)
Sam Houston State U (TX)
San Diego State U (CA)
San Francisco State U (CA)
San Jose State U (CA)
Santa Clara U (CA)
Sarah Lawrence Coll (NY)
Schreiner U (TX)
Scripps Coll (CA)
Seattle Pacific U (WA)
Seton Hall U (NJ)
Seton Hill U (PA)
Shaw U (NC)
Shenandoah U (VA)
Shepherd U (WV)
Shorter Coll (GA)
Siena Heights U (MI)
Sierra Nevada Coll (NV)
Silver Lake Coll (WI)
Simmons Coll (MA)
Simon Fraser U (BC, Canada)
Simon's Rock Coll of Bard (MA)
Simpson Coll (IA)
Simpson Coll and Graduate School (CA)
Slippery Rock U of Pennsylvania (PA)
Smith Coll (MA)
Sonoma State U (CA)
South Dakota State U (SD)
Southeastern Bible Coll (AL)
Southeastern Oklahoma State U (OK)
Southeast Missouri State U (MO)
Southern Adventist U (TN)
Southern Connecticut State U (CT)
Southern Illinois U Carbondale (IL)
Southern Illinois U Edwardsville (IL)
Southern Methodist U (TX)
Southern Oregon U (OR)
Southern Utah U (UT)
Southern Virginia U (VA)
Southern Wesleyan U (SC)
Southwest Baptist U (MO)
Southwestern Coll (KS)
Southwestern Oklahoma State U (OK)
Southwestern U (TX)
Southwest Missouri State U (MO)
Spelman Coll (GA)
Spring Arbor U (MI)
Stanford U (CA)
State U of NY at Binghamton (NY)
State U of NY at New Paltz (NY)
State U of NY at Oswego (NY)
Plattsburgh State U of NY (NY)
State U of NY Coll at Fredonia (NY)
State U of NY Coll at Geneseo (NY)
State U of NY Coll at Oneonta (NY)
State U of NY Coll at Potsdam (NY)
Steinbach Bible Coll (MB, Canada)
Sterling Coll (KS)
Stetson U (FL)
Stony Brook U, State U of New York (NY)
Susquehanna U (PA)
Swarthmore Coll (PA)
Sweet Briar Coll (VA)
Syracuse U (NY)
Tabor Coll (KS)
Talladega Coll (AL)
Tarleton State U (TX)
Taylor U (IN)
Taylor U, Fort Wayne Campus (IN)
Tennessee State U (TN)
Tennessee Technological U (TN)
Tennessee Wesleyan Coll (TN)
Texas A&M U (TX)
Texas A&M U–Commerce (TX)
Texas A&M U–Corpus Christi (TX)
Texas A&M U–Kingsville (TX)
Texas Christian U (TX)
Texas Lutheran U (TX)
Texas Southern U (TX)
Texas State U-San Marcos (TX)
Texas Tech U (TX)
Texas Wesleyan U (TX)
Texas Woman's U (TX)
Thomas Edison State Coll (NJ)
Toccoa Falls Coll (GA)
Tougaloo Coll (MS)
Towson U (MD)
Trevecca Nazarene U (TN)
Trinity Christian Coll (IL)
Trinity Coll (CT)
Trinity Intl U (IL)
Trinity U (TX)
Trinity Western U (BC, Canada)
Truman State U (MO)
Tufts U (MA)
Tulane U (LA)
Union Coll (NE)
Union U (TN)
Universidad Adventista de las Antillas (PR)
Université de Montréal (QC, Canada)
Université de Sherbrooke (QC, Canada)
Université Laval (QC, Canada)
State U of NY at Albany (NY)
U at Buffalo, The State U of New York (NY)
The U of Akron (OH)
The U of Alabama (AL)
The U of Alabama at Birmingham (AL)
The U of Alabama in Huntsville (AL)
U of Alaska Fairbanks (AK)
U of Alberta (AB, Canada)
The U of Arizona (AZ)
U of Arkansas at Little Rock (AR)
U of Arkansas at Monticello (AR)
U of Bridgeport (CT)
The U of British Columbia (BC, Canada)
U of Calgary (AB, Canada)
U of Calif, Berkeley (CA)
U of Calif, Davis (CA)
U of Calif, Irvine (CA)
U of Calif, Los Angeles (CA)
U of Calif, Riverside (CA)
U of Calif, San Diego (CA)
U of Calif, Santa Barbara (CA)
U of Calif, Santa Cruz (CA)
U of Central Arkansas (AR)
U of Charleston (WV)
U of Chicago (IL)
U of Cincinnati (OH)
U of Colorado at Boulder (CO)
U of Colorado at Denver (CO)
U of Connecticut (CT)
U of Dayton (OH)
U of Delaware (DE)
U of Denver (CO)
U of Evansville (IN)
U of Florida (FL)
U of Georgia (GA)
U of Guelph (ON, Canada)
U of Hartford (CT)
U of Hawaii at Hilo (HI)
U of Houston (TX)
U of Illinois at Chicago (IL)
U of Illinois at Urbana–Champaign (IL)
U of Indianapolis (IN)
The U of Iowa (IA)
U of Kansas (KS)
U of King's Coll (NS, Canada)
U of La Verne (CA)
The U of Lethbridge (AB, Canada)
U of Louisiana at Lafayette (LA)
U of Louisville (KY)
U of Maine (ME)
The U of Maine at Augusta (ME)
U of Maine at Farmington (ME)
U of Maine at Machias (ME)
U of Manitoba (MB, Canada)
U of Maryland, Baltimore County (MD)
U of Maryland, Coll Park (MD)
U of Massachusetts Amherst (MA)
U of Massachusetts Boston (MA)
U of Massachusetts Dartmouth (MA)
U of Massachusetts Lowell (MA)
The U of Memphis (TN)
U of Miami (FL)
U of Michigan (MI)
U of Michigan–Dearborn (MI)
U of Michigan–Flint (MI)
U of Minnesota, Duluth (MN)
U of Minnesota, Morris (MN)
U of Minnesota, Twin Cities Campus (MN)
U of Mississippi (MS)
U of Missouri–Columbia (MO)
U of Missouri–Kansas City (MO)
U of Missouri–St. Louis (MO)
U of Mobile (AL)
The U of Montana–Missoula (MT)
U of Montevallo (AL)
U of Nebraska at Omaha (NE)
U of Nebraska–Lincoln (NE)
U of Nevada, Las Vegas (NV)
U of Nevada, Reno (NV)
U of New Hampshire (NH)
U of New Haven (CT)
U of New Orleans (LA)
U of North Alabama (AL)
The U of North Carolina at Asheville (NC)
The U of North Carolina at Chapel Hill (NC)
The U of North Carolina at Charlotte (NC)
The U of North Carolina at Greensboro (NC)
The U of North Carolina at Pembroke (NC)
The U of North Carolina at Wilmington (NC)
U of North Dakota (ND)
U of Northern Colorado (CO)
U of Northern Iowa (IA)
U of North Florida (FL)
U of North Texas (TX)
U of Notre Dame (IN)
U of Oklahoma (OK)
U of Oregon (OR)
U of Ottawa (ON, Canada)
U of Pennsylvania (PA)
U of Pittsburgh (PA)
U of Portland (OR)
U of Prince Edward Island (PE, Canada)
U of Puget Sound (WA)
U of Redlands (CA)
U of Regina (SK, Canada)
U of Rhode Island (RI)
U of Richmond (VA)
U of Rochester (NY)
U of St. Thomas (MN)
U of St. Thomas (TX)
U of San Diego (CA)
U of Saskatchewan (SK, Canada)
U of Science and Arts of Oklahoma (OK)
U of Sioux Falls (SD)
U of South Alabama (AL)
U of South Carolina (SC)
The U of South Dakota (SD)
U of Southern California (CA)
U of Southern Maine (ME)
The U of Tampa (FL)
The U of Tennessee (TN)
The U of Tennessee at Chattanooga (TN)
The U of Tennessee at Martin (TN)
The U of Texas at Arlington (TX)
The U of Texas at Austin (TX)
The U of Texas at Brownsville (TX)
The U of Texas at Tyler (TX)
The U of Texas–Pan American (TX)
U of the District of Columbia (DC)
U of the Incarnate Word (TX)
U of the Ozarks (AR)
U of the Pacific (CA)
U of the South (TN)
U of Toledo (OH)
U of Toronto (ON, Canada)
U of Tulsa (OK)
U of Utah (UT)
U of Vermont (VT)
U of Victoria (BC, Canada)
U of Virginia (VA)
U of Washington (WA)
U of Waterloo (ON, Canada)
The U of Western Ontario (ON, Canada)
U of Windsor (ON, Canada)
U of Wisconsin–Eau Claire (WI)
U of Wisconsin–Green Bay (WI)
U of Wisconsin–La Crosse (WI)
U of Wisconsin–Madison (WI)
U of Wisconsin–Milwaukee (WI)
U of Wisconsin–Oshkosh (WI)
U of Wisconsin–Parkside (WI)
U of Wisconsin–Platteville (WI)
U of Wisconsin–River Falls (WI)
U of Wisconsin–Stevens Point (WI)
U of Wisconsin–Superior (WI)
U of Wisconsin–Whitewater (WI)
U of Wyoming (WY)
Utah State U (UT)
Valdosta State U (GA)
Valley City State U (ND)
Valparaiso U (IN)
Vanderbilt U (TN)
Vanguard U of Southern California (CA)
Vassar Coll (NY)
Virginia Polytechnic Inst and State U (VA)
Virginia Union U (VA)
Virginia Wesleyan Coll (VA)
Viterbo U (WI)
Wabash Coll (IN)
Wagner Coll (NY)
Wake Forest U (NC)
Walla Walla Coll (WA)
Warner Pacific Coll (OR)
Wartburg Coll (IA)
Washburn U (KS)
Washington & Jefferson Coll (PA)
Washington and Lee U (VA)
Washington Bible Coll (MD)
Washington Coll (MD)
Washington State U (WA)
Washington U in St. Louis (MO)
Wayland Baptist U (TX)
Wayne State Coll (NE)
Wayne State U (MI)
Weber State U (UT)
Webster U (MO)
Wellesley Coll (MA)
Wells Coll (NY)
Wesleyan Coll (GA)
Wesleyan U (CT)
West Chester U of Pennsylvania (PA)
Western Baptist Coll (OR)
Western Carolina U (NC)
Western Connecticut State U (CT)
Western Illinois U (IL)
Western Kentucky U (KY)
Western Michigan U (MI)
Western Oregon U (OR)
Western State Coll of Colorado (CO)
Western Washington U (WA)
Westfield State Coll (MA)

Westminster Choir Coll of Rider U (NJ)
Westminster Coll (PA)
Westmont Coll (CA)
West Texas A&M U (TX)
West Virginia U (WV)
West Virginia Wesleyan Coll (WV)
Wheaton Coll (IL)
Wheaton Coll (MA)
Whitman Coll (WA)
Whitworth Coll (WA)
Wichita State U (KS)
Willamette U (OR)
William Carey Coll (MS)
William Jessup U (CA)
William Jewell Coll (MO)
William Paterson U of New Jersey (NJ)
Williams Baptist Coll (AR)
Williams Coll (MA)
William Tyndale Coll (MI)
Wingate U (NC)
Winona State U (MN)
Winston-Salem State U (NC)
Winthrop U (SC)
Wisconsin Lutheran Coll (WI)
Wittenberg U (OH)
Worcester Polytechnic Inst (MA)
Wright State U (OH)
Xavier U (OH)
Xavier U of Louisiana (LA)
Yale U (CT)
York Coll (NE)
York Coll of Pennsylvania (PA)
York Coll of the City U of New York (NY)
York U (ON, Canada)
Youngstown State U (OH)

MUSICAL INSTRUMENT FABRICATION AND REPAIR

Ball State U (IN)
Barton Coll (NC)
Bellarmine U (KY)
Bloomfield Coll (NJ)
U of Washington (WA)

MUSICAL INSTRUMENT TECHNOLOGY

Delaware State U (DE)

MUSIC HISTORY, LITERATURE, AND THEORY

Baldwin-Wallace Coll (OH)
Bard Coll (NY)
Baylor U (TX)
Belmont U (TN)
Bennington Coll (VT)
Birmingham-Southern Coll (AL)
Boston U (MA)
Bridgewater Coll (VA)
Brigham Young U (UT)
Bucknell U (PA)
Butler U (IN)
California State U, Fresno (CA)
California State U, Fullerton (CA)
California State U, Long Beach (CA)
Calvin Coll (MI)
Canadian Mennonite U (MB, Canada)
The Catholic U of America (DC)
Central Michigan U (MI)
Christopher Newport U (VA)
The Coll of St. Scholastica (MN)
The Coll of Wooster (OH)
Converse Coll (SC)
Cornell U (NY)
Dalhousie U (NS, Canada)
Eastern Michigan U (MI)
Eugene Lang Coll, New School U (NY)
Fairfield U (CT)
Florida State U (FL)
Fordham U (NY)
Hampshire Coll (MA)
Hardin-Simmons U (TX)
Harvard U (MA)
Hastings Coll (NE)
Hofstra U (NY)
Indiana U Bloomington (IN)
Keene State Coll (NH)
Lafayette Coll (PA)
Loyola Marymount U (CA)
Marlboro Coll (VT)
McGill U (QC, Canada)
Memorial U of Newfoundland (NL, Canada)
Mount Allison U (NB, Canada)
Nazareth Coll of Rochester (NY)
New Coll of Florida (FL)
New England Conservatory of Music (MA)
Northeastern U (MA)
North Greenville Coll (SC)
Northwestern U (IL)
Oberlin Coll (OH)
The Ohio State U (OH)
Ohio U (OH)
Otterbein Coll (OH)
Ouachita Baptist U (AR)
Randolph-Macon Woman's Coll (VA)
Rice U (TX)
Rockford Coll (IL)
Roosevelt U (IL)
St. Cloud State U (MN)
Saint Joseph's Coll (IN)
Sarah Lawrence Coll (NY)
Seton Hall U (NJ)
Simmons Coll (MA)
Skidmore Coll (NY)
Southwestern U (TX)
State U of NY at New Paltz (NY)
State U of NY Coll at Fredonia (NY)
Trinity Intl U (IL)
The U of Akron (OH)
U of Alberta (AB, Canada)
The U of British Columbia (BC, Canada)
U of Calif, Los Angeles (CA)
U of Calif, San Diego (CA)
U of Chicago (IL)
U of Cincinnati (OH)
U of Hartford (CT)
U of Idaho (ID)
U of Illinois at Urbana–Champaign (IL)
U of Kansas (KS)
U of Kentucky (KY)
U of Michigan (MI)
U of Michigan–Dearborn (MI)
U of New Hampshire (NH)
The U of North Carolina at Greensboro (NC)
U of North Texas (TX)
U of Ottawa (ON, Canada)
U of Redlands (CA)
U of Regina (SK, Canada)
U of Richmond (VA)
The U of Texas at Austin (TX)
U of the Pacific (CA)
U of the South (TN)
U of Toronto (ON, Canada)
U of Vermont (VT)
U of Victoria (BC, Canada)
U of Washington (WA)
The U of Western Ontario (ON, Canada)
U of Windsor (ON, Canada)
U of Wisconsin–Milwaukee (WI)
Washington U in St. Louis (MO)
West Chester U of Pennsylvania (PA)
Western Connecticut State U (CT)
Western Michigan U (MI)
Western Washington U (WA)
Westfield State Coll (MA)
Wheaton Coll (IL)
Wright State U (OH)
York U (ON, Canada)
Youngstown State U (OH)

MUSIC MANAGEMENT AND MERCHANDISING

Appalachian State U (NC)
Bellarmine U (KY)
Belmont U (TN)
Berklee Coll of Music (MA)
Berry Coll (GA)
Bethesda Christian U (CA)
Boise State U (ID)
Bryan Coll (TN)
Butler U (IN)
California State U, Sacramento (CA)
Capital U (OH)
Central Washington U (WA)
Clarion U of Pennsylvania (PA)
Coker Coll (SC)
The Coll of St. Scholastica (MN)
Coll of the Ozarks (MO)
Columbia Coll Chicago (IL)
DePaul U (IL)
DePauw U (IN)
Drake U (IA)
Elizabeth City State U (NC)
Elmhurst Coll (IL)
Ferris State U (MI)
Five Towns Coll (NY)
Florida Southern Coll (FL)
Geneva Coll (PA)
Georgia State U (GA)
Grand Canyon U (AZ)
Grove City Coll (PA)
Hardin-Simmons U (TX)
Heidelberg Coll (OH)
Hofstra U (NY)
Jacksonville U (FL)
Johnson State Coll (VT)
Lebanon Valley Coll (PA)
Lewis U (IL)
Loyola U New Orleans (LA)
Madonna U (MI)
Mansfield U of Pennsylvania (PA)
Marian Coll of Fond du Lac (WI)
The Master's Coll and Sem (CA)
Methodist Coll (NC)
Middle Tennessee State U (TN)
Millikin U (IL)
Minnesota State U Mankato (MN)
Minnesota State U Moorhead (MN)
Montreat Coll (NC)
New York U (NY)
Northeastern U (MA)
North Park U (IL)
Northwest Christian Coll (OR)
Ohio Northern U (OH)
Ohio U (OH)
Oklahoma City U (OK)
Oklahoma State U (OK)
Otterbein Coll (OH)
Saint Joseph's Coll (IN)
Saint Mary's U of Minnesota (MN)
South Carolina State U (SC)
South Dakota State U (SD)
Southern Nazarene U (OK)
Southern Oregon U (OR)
Southwestern Oklahoma State U (OK)
State U of NY Coll at Fredonia (NY)
State U of NY Coll at Oneonta (NY)
State U of NY Coll at Potsdam (NY)
Syracuse U (NY)
Tabor Coll (KS)
Taylor U (IN)
Trevecca Nazarene U (TN)
Union U (TN)
U of Charleston (WV)
U of Evansville (IN)
U of Hartford (CT)
U of Idaho (ID)
The U of Iowa (IA)
The U of Memphis (TN)
U of Miami (FL)
U of New Haven (CT)
U of Puget Sound (WA)
U of Sioux Falls (SD)
U of Southern California (CA)
U of the Incarnate Word (TX)
U of the Pacific (CA)
Valparaiso U (IN)
Waldorf Coll (IA)
Warner Pacific Coll (OR)
Westfield State Coll (MA)
Wheaton Coll (IL)
William Paterson U of New Jersey (NJ)
Wingate U (NC)
Winona State U (MN)

MUSICOLOGY AND ETHNOMUSICOLOGY

Bowling Green State U (OH)
Brown U (RI)
Canadian Mennonite U (MB, Canada)
Cornell U (NY)
Hampshire Coll (MA)
Loyola Marymount U (CA)
Northwestern U (IL)
Prairie Bible Coll (AB, Canada)
The U of Akron (OH)
U of Calif, Los Angeles (CA)
U of Denver (CO)
U of Miami (FL)
U of Oregon (OR)
U of Regina (SK, Canada)
U of Washington (WA)
York U (ON, Canada)

MUSIC PEDAGOGY

Baylor U (TX)
Brigham Young U (UT)
California State U, Sacramento (CA)
Campbell U (NC)
Cedarville U (OH)
The Coll of St. Scholastica (MN)
Columbus State U (GA)
Connecticut Coll (CT)
Eastern Michigan U (MI)
Florida State U (FL)
Hastings Coll (NE)
Holy Names Coll (CA)
Lawrence U (WI)
Meredith Coll (NC)
Michigan State U (MI)
Montclair State U (NJ)
New England Conservatory of Music (MA)
Oklahoma State U (OK)
Roosevelt U (IL)
St. Cloud State U (MN)
Trinity Intl U (IL)
U of Louisiana at Lafayette (LA)
Viterbo U (WI)
Westminster Choir Coll of Rider U (NJ)
Willamette U (OR)

MUSIC PERFORMANCE

Adams State Coll (CO)
Alcorn State U (MS)
Allegheny Coll (PA)
Alma Coll (MI)
Appalachian State U (NC)
Aquinas Coll (MI)
Arizona State U (AZ)
Arkansas State U (AR)
Augustana Coll (IL)
Augusta State U (GA)
Averett U (VA)
Avila U (MO)
Baldwin-Wallace Coll (OH)
Bard Coll (NY)
Baylor U (TX)
Berklee Coll of Music (MA)
Bethany Coll (SK, Canada)
Bethel Coll (IN)
Bethel U (MN)
Bethune-Cookman Coll (FL)
Black Hills State U (SD)
Boston U (MA)
Bowling Green State U (OH)
Bradley U (IL)
Brewton-Parker Coll (GA)
Brigham Young U (UT)
Brigham Young U–Hawaii (HI)
Brooklyn Coll of the City U of NY (NY)
Bucknell U (PA)
Buena Vista U (IA)
California Baptist U (CA)
California Inst of the Arts (CA)
California State U, Chico (CA)
California State U, Fullerton (CA)
California State U, Long Beach (CA)
California State U, Los Angeles (CA)
California State U, Stanislaus (CA)
Calvin Coll (MI)
Campbell U (NC)
Canadian Mennonite U (MB, Canada)
Capital U (OH)
Carnegie Mellon U (PA)
The Catholic U of America (DC)
Cedarville U (OH)
Centenary Coll of Louisiana (LA)
Central Methodist Coll (MO)
Chapman U (CA)
Charleston Southern U (SC)
City Coll of the City U of NY (NY)
Clarion U of Pennsylvania (PA)
Clayton Coll & State U (GA)
Coe Coll (IA)
The Colburn School of Performing Arts (CA)
The Coll of St. Scholastica (MN)
The Coll of Wooster (OH)
Colorado Christian U (CO)
Colorado State U (CO)
Columbia Coll (SC)
Columbia Coll Chicago (IL)
Columbia Union Coll (MD)
Concordia Coll (MN)
Concordia U (QC, Canada)
Cornerstone U (MI)
Dalhousie U (NS, Canada)
DePaul U (IL)
DePauw U (IN)
Dillard U (LA)
Dominican U of California (CA)
Dordt Coll (IA)
Drake U (IA)
Drury U (MO)
Duquesne U (PA)
East Carolina U (NC)
Eastern Michigan U (MI)
Eastern Nazarene Coll (MA)
Eastern Washington U (WA)
Elon U (NC)
Florida Ag and Mech U (FL)
Florida State U (FL)
Gardner-Webb U (NC)
Geneva Coll (PA)
George Mason U (VA)
Georgia Southern U (GA)
Georgia State U (GA)
Gordon Coll (MA)
Grace Bible Coll (MI)
Grambling State U (LA)
Greensboro Coll (NC)
Grove City Coll (PA)
Hardin-Simmons U (TX)
Hastings Coll (NE)
Henderson State U (AR)
Hofstra U (NY)
Holy Names Coll (CA)
Hope Coll (MI)
Houston Baptist U (TX)
Howard Payne U (TX)
Idaho State U (ID)
Illinois State U (IL)
Indiana U of Pennsylvania (PA)
Indiana U South Bend (IN)
Ithaca Coll (NY)
Jacksonville U (FL)
James Madison U (VA)
Jamestown Coll (ND)
The Johns Hopkins U (MD)
Johnson State Coll (VT)
Kent State U (OH)
Kentucky State U (KY)
Lambuth U (TN)
Lawrence U (WI)
Lebanon Valley Coll (PA)
Long Island U, Brooklyn Campus (NY)
Long Island U, C.W. Post Campus (NY)
Louisiana State U and A&M Coll (LA)
Louisiana Tech U (LA)
Loyola U New Orleans (LA)
Lynchburg Coll (VA)
Mansfield U of Pennsylvania (PA)
Marygrove Coll (MI)
Maryville Coll (TN)
Marywood U (PA)
McGill U (QC, Canada)
McMurry U (TX)
McNeese State U (LA)
Mercer U (GA)
Mercyhurst Coll (PA)
Meredith Coll (NC)
Metropolitan State Coll of Denver (CO)
Miami U (OH)
Michigan State U (MI)
Millikin U (IL)
Mississippi Coll (MS)
Missouri Baptist U (MO)
Montclair State U (NJ)
Montreat Coll (NC)
Moravian Coll (PA)
Mount Allison U (NB, Canada)
Mount Union Coll (OH)
Nebraska Wesleyan U (NE)
New Mexico State U (NM)
New World School of the Arts (FL)
New York U (NY)
North Carolina School of the Arts (NC)
North Central U (MN)
Northern Arizona U (AZ)
Northwestern Coll (MN)
Northwestern State U of Louisiana (LA)
Northwestern U (IL)
Northwest Nazarene U (ID)
Notre Dame de Namur U (CA)
Oakland City U (IN)
Oakland U (MI)
Ohio Northern U (OH)
The Ohio State U (OH)
Ohio U (OH)
Ohio Wesleyan U (OH)
Old Dominion U (VA)
Oral Roberts U (OK)
Otterbein Coll (OH)
Ouachita Baptist U (AR)
Palm Beach Atlantic U (FL)
Peace Coll (NC)
Penn State U Univ Park Campus (PA)
Piedmont Coll (GA)
Pittsburg State U (KS)
Point Loma Nazarene U (CA)
Queens Coll of the City U of NY (NY)
Randolph-Macon Woman's Coll (VA)
Rice U (TX)
Rocky Mountain Coll (MT)
Roosevelt U (IL)
Rowan U (NJ)
Saint Augustine's Coll (NC)
St. Cloud State U (MN)
Saint Mary-of-the-Woods Coll (IN)
Saint Mary's U of Minnesota (MN)
St. Olaf Coll (MN)
Saint Vincent Coll (PA)
Saint Xavier U (IL)
Salem Coll (NC)
Salisbury U (MD)
Samford U (AL)
Sam Houston State U (TX)
San Jose State U (CA)
Sarah Lawrence Coll (NY)
Seton Hall U (NJ)
Seton Hill U (PA)
Shenandoah U (VA)

Simpson Coll (IA)
Slippery Rock U of Pennsylvania (PA)
Southeastern Coll of the Assemblies of God (FL)
Southeastern Louisiana U (LA)
Southeastern Oklahoma State U (OK)
Southern Adventist U (TN)
Southern Methodist U (TX)
Southern Nazarene U (OK)
Southern U and A&M Coll (LA)
Southwest Missouri State U (MO)
State U of NY at Binghamton (NY)
State U of NY Coll at Potsdam (NY)
State U of West Georgia (GA)
Stetson U (FL)
Stevens Inst of Technology (NJ)
Syracuse U (NY)
Taylor U (IN)
Texas Christian U (TX)
Texas State U-San Marcos (TX)
Texas Tech U (TX)
Toccoa Falls Coll (GA)
Transylvania U (KY)
Trinity Christian Coll (IL)
Trinity U (TX)
Truman State U (MO)
Union Coll (NE)
Union U (TN)
U at Buffalo, The State U of New York (NY)
The U of Akron (OH)
The U of Arizona (AZ)
U of Arkansas (AR)
U of Calif, Irvine (CA)
U of Central Arkansas (AR)
U of Central Florida (FL)
U of Colorado at Boulder (CO)
U of Denver (CO)
U of Georgia (GA)
U of Hartford (CT)
U of Hawaii at Manoa (HI)
U of Houston (TX)
U of Idaho (ID)
U of Illinois at Urbana–Champaign (IL)
U of Indianapolis (IN)
U of Kentucky (KY)
U of Louisiana at Lafayette (LA)
U of Mary (ND)
U of Mary Hardin-Baylor (TX)
U of Maryland, Coll Park (MD)
U of Massachusetts Amherst (MA)
U of Massachusetts Lowell (MA)
U of Miami (FL)
U of Missouri–St. Louis (MO)
The U of Montana–Missoula (MT)
U of Nebraska at Omaha (NE)
U of Nevada, Reno (NV)
U of New Mexico (NM)
The U of North Carolina at Chapel Hill (NC)
The U of North Carolina at Charlotte (NC)
The U of North Carolina at Greensboro (NC)
The U of North Carolina at Wilmington (NC)
U of North Dakota (ND)
U of Northern Iowa (IA)
U of North Florida (FL)
U of North Texas (TX)
U of Oklahoma (OK)
U of Oregon (OR)
U of Puget Sound (WA)
U of Redlands (CA)
U of Regina (SK, Canada)
U of Rhode Island (RI)
U of Southern California (CA)
U of Southern Maine (ME)
U of South Florida (FL)
The U of Texas at Austin (TX)
The U of the Arts (PA)
U of Vermont (VT)
U of Washington (WA)
U of West Florida (FL)
U of Windsor (ON, Canada)
U of Wyoming (WY)
Valdosta State U (GA)
Valparaiso U (IN)
Virginia Commonwealth U (VA)
Virginia State U (VA)
Viterbo U (WI)
Waldorf Coll (IA)
Wartburg Coll (IA)
Washington State U (WA)
Weber State U (UT)
Webster U (MO)
West Chester U of Pennsylvania (PA)
Western Baptist Coll (OR)
Western Carolina U (NC)
Western Michigan U (MI)
West Texas A&M U (TX)
Wheaton Coll (IL)
Wilkes U (PA)
Willamette U (OR)
William Carey Coll (MS)
William Jewell Coll (MO)
William Tyndale Coll (MI)
Wright State U (OH)
Xavier U of Louisiana (LA)
York U (ON, Canada)
Youngstown State U (OH)

MUSIC RELATED

Alverno Coll (WI)
Arizona State U (AZ)
Bethel Coll (KS)
Bowling Green State U (OH)
Brenau U (GA)
Brigham Young U (UT)
Brown U (RI)
California Inst of the Arts (CA)
California State U, Chico (CA)
California State U, Sacramento (CA)
Calvary Bible Coll and Theological Sem (MO)
Capital U (OH)
Central Baptist Coll (AR)
Central Michigan U (MI)
Claremont McKenna Coll (CA)
Coll of Santa Fe (NM)
Coll of the Ozarks (MO)
Colorado Christian U (CO)
Connecticut Coll (CT)
Dickinson Coll (PA)
Duquesne U (PA)
Greenville Coll (IL)
Hampton U (VA)
Indiana State U (IN)
Johnson C. Smith U (NC)
Lebanon Valley Coll (PA)
Long Island U, Brooklyn Campus (NY)
Malone Coll (OH)
Marylhurst U (OR)
McGill U (QC, Canada)
Mercer U (GA)
Milligan Coll (TN)
Northwest Christian Coll (OR)
Northwestern U (IL)
Ohio Northern U (OH)
Oklahoma State U (OK)
Roosevelt U (IL)
Saint Mary's U of Minnesota (MN)
St. Olaf Coll (MN)
San Diego State U (CA)
School of the Art Inst of Chicago (IL)
Shenandoah U (VA)
State U of NY Coll at Potsdam (NY)
The U of Arizona (AZ)
U of Hartford (CT)
U of Louisiana at Lafayette (LA)
U of Miami (FL)
The U of North Carolina at Asheville (NC)
U of Southern California (CA)
U of Tulsa (OK)
U of Wisconsin–Green Bay (WI)
Western Illinois U (IL)
Western Kentucky U (KY)
Westminster Choir Coll of Rider U (NJ)
Wheaton Coll (IL)

MUSIC TEACHER EDUCATION

Abilene Christian U (TX)
Acadia U (NS, Canada)
Adrian Coll (MI)
Alabama Ag and Mech U (AL)
Alabama State U (AL)
Alcorn State U (MS)
Alderson-Broaddus Coll (WV)
Alma Coll (MI)
Alverno Coll (WI)
Anderson Coll (SC)
Andrews U (MI)
Anna Maria Coll (MA)
Appalachian State U (NC)
Aquinas Coll (MI)
Arkansas State U (AR)
Arkansas Tech U (AR)
Arlington Baptist Coll (TX)
Armstrong Atlantic State U (GA)
Asbury Coll (KY)
Ashland U (OH)
Atlantic Union Coll (MA)
Auburn U (AL)
Augsburg Coll (MN)
Augustana Coll (IL)
Augustana Coll (SD)
Augusta State U (GA)
Baker U (KS)
Baldwin-Wallace Coll (OH)
Ball State U (IN)
Baptist Bible Coll (MO)
The Baptist Coll of Florida (FL)
Baylor U (TX)
Belmont U (TN)
Beloit Coll (WI)
Bemidji State U (MN)
Benedictine Coll (KS)
Benedictine U (IL)
Berea Coll (KY)
Berklee Coll of Music (MA)
Berry Coll (GA)
Bethany Coll (KS)
Bethel Coll (IN)
Bethel U (MN)
Bethune-Cookman Coll (FL)
Birmingham-Southern Coll (AL)
Bishop's U (QC, Canada)
Bluefield Coll (VA)
Blue Mountain Coll (MS)
Bluffton Coll (OH)
Boise State U (ID)
Boston U (MA)
Bowling Green State U (OH)
Bradley U (IL)
Brenau U (GA)
Brewton-Parker Coll (GA)
Bridgewater Coll (VA)
Brigham Young U (UT)
Brigham Young U–Hawaii (HI)
Brock U (ON, Canada)
Brooklyn Coll of the City U of NY (NY)
Bryan Coll (TN)
Bucknell U (PA)
Buena Vista U (IA)
Butler U (IN)
California Lutheran U (CA)
California State U, Chico (CA)
California State U, Dominguez Hills (CA)
California State U, Fresno (CA)
California State U, Fullerton (CA)
Calvary Bible Coll and Theological Sem (MO)
Calvin Coll (MI)
Campbellsville U (KY)
Campbell U (NC)
Capital U (OH)
Carroll Coll (WI)
Carson-Newman Coll (TN)
Carthage Coll (WI)
Case Western Reserve U (OH)
Castleton State Coll (VT)
Catawba Coll (NC)
The Catholic U of America (DC)
Cedarville U (OH)
Centenary Coll of Louisiana (LA)
Central Coll (IA)
Central Connecticut State U (CT)
Central Methodist Coll (MO)
Central Michigan U (MI)
Central Missouri State U (MO)
Central State U (OH)
Central Washington U (WA)
Chadron State Coll (NE)
Chapman U (CA)
Charleston Southern U (SC)
Chicago State U (IL)
Chowan Coll (NC)
Christian Heritage Coll (CA)
City Coll of the City U of NY (NY)
Clarion U of Pennsylvania (PA)
Clark Atlanta U (GA)
Clarke Coll (IA)
Clearwater Christian Coll (FL)
Cleveland Inst of Music (OH)
Coe Coll (IA)
Coker Coll (SC)
The Coll of New Jersey (NJ)
Coll of Saint Benedict (MN)
Coll of St. Catherine (MN)
The Coll of Saint Rose (NY)
The Coll of St. Scholastica (MN)
Coll of the Ozarks (MO)
The Coll of Wooster (OH)
Colorado Christian U (CO)
Colorado State U (CO)
Colorado State U-Pueblo (CO)
Columbia Coll (SC)
Columbia Union Coll (MD)
Columbus State U (GA)
Concord Coll (WV)
Concordia Coll (MN)
Concordia Coll (NY)
Concordia U (IL)
Concordia U (MI)
Concordia U (NE)
Concordia U, St. Paul (MN)
Concordia U Wisconsin (WI)
Connecticut Coll (CT)
Converse Coll (SC)
Cornell Coll (IA)
Cornerstone U (MI)
Crown Coll (MN)
Culver-Stockton Coll (MO)
Cumberland Coll (KY)
Cumberland U (TN)
Dakota State U (SD)
Dakota Wesleyan U (SD)
Dallas Baptist U (TX)
Dana Coll (NE)
Davis & Elkins Coll (WV)
Delaware State U (DE)
Delta State U (MS)
DePaul U (IL)
DePauw U (IN)
Dickinson State U (ND)
Dillard U (LA)
Dordt Coll (IA)
Dowling Coll (NY)
Drake U (IA)
Duquesne U (PA)
East Carolina U (NC)
East Central U (OK)
Eastern Kentucky U (KY)
Eastern Mennonite U (VA)
Eastern Michigan U (MI)
Eastern Nazarene Coll (MA)
Eastern New Mexico U (NM)
Eastern Washington U (WA)
East Texas Baptist U (TX)
Elizabeth City State U (NC)
Elizabethtown Coll (PA)
Elmhurst Coll (IL)
Elon U (NC)
Emmanuel Coll (GA)
Emporia State U (KS)
Erskine Coll (SC)
Eureka Coll (IL)
Evangel U (MO)
Fairmont State Coll (WV)
Faith Baptist Bible Coll and Theological Sem (IA)
Fayetteville State U (NC)
Five Towns Coll (NY)
Florida Ag and Mech U (FL)
Florida Atlantic U (FL)
Florida Intl U (FL)
Florida Southern Coll (FL)
Florida State U (FL)
Fort Hays State U (KS)
Fort Lewis Coll (CO)
The Franciscan U (IA)
Freed-Hardeman U (TN)
Fresno Pacific U (CA)
Furman U (SC)
Gardner-Webb U (NC)
Geneva Coll (PA)
George Fox U (OR)
Georgetown Coll (KY)
Georgia Coll & State U (GA)
Georgian Court U (NJ)
Georgia Southern U (GA)
Gettysburg Coll (PA)
Glenville State Coll (WV)
God's Bible School and Coll (OH)
Gonzaga U (WA)
Gordon Coll (MA)
Goshen Coll (IN)
Grace Bible Coll (MI)
Grace Coll (IN)
Graceland U (IA)
Grace U (NE)
Grambling State U (LA)
Grand Canyon U (AZ)
Grand Valley State U (MI)
Greensboro Coll (NC)
Greenville Coll (IL)
Grove City Coll (PA)
Gustavus Adolphus Coll (MN)
Hamline U (MN)
Hampton U (VA)
Hannibal-LaGrange Coll (MO)
Harding U (AR)
Hardin-Simmons U (TX)
Hartwick Coll (NY)
Hastings Coll (NE)
Heidelberg Coll (OH)
Henderson State U (AR)
Hofstra U (NY)
Hope Coll (MI)
Houghton Coll (NY)
Houston Baptist U (TX)
Howard Payne U (TX)
Humboldt State U (CA)
Huntingdon Coll (AL)
Huntington Coll (IN)
Idaho State U (ID)
Illinois State U (IL)
Illinois Wesleyan U (IL)
Immaculata U (PA)
Indiana U Bloomington (IN)
Indiana U of Pennsylvania (PA)
Indiana U–Purdue U Fort Wayne (IN)
Indiana U South Bend (IN)
Inter American U of PR, San Germán Campus (PR)
Iowa State U of Science and Technology (IA)
Iowa Wesleyan Coll (IA)
Ithaca Coll (NY)
Jacksonville State U (AL)
Jacksonville U (FL)
Jamestown Coll (ND)
Jarvis Christian Coll (TX)
John Brown U (AR)
The Johns Hopkins U (MD)
Johnson State Coll (VT)
Judson Coll (AL)
Judson Coll (IL)
Kansas State U (KS)
Kean U (NJ)
Keene State Coll (NH)
Kennesaw State U (GA)
Kent State U (OH)
Kentucky Christian Coll (KY)
Kentucky State U (KY)
Lakeland Coll (WI)
Lamar U (TX)
Lambuth U (TN)
Lancaster Bible Coll (PA)
Lawrence U (WI)
Lebanon Valley Coll (PA)
Lenoir-Rhyne Coll (NC)
Liberty U (VA)
Limestone Coll (SC)
Lincoln U (MO)
Lincoln U (PA)
Lindenwood U (MO)
Lipscomb U (TN)
Livingstone Coll (NC)
Long Island U, Brooklyn Campus (NY)
Long Island U, C.W. Post Campus (NY)
Longwood U (VA)
Louisiana Coll (LA)
Louisiana State U and A&M Coll (LA)
Louisiana Tech U (LA)
Loyola U New Orleans (LA)
Lubbock Christian U (TX)
Lycoming Coll (PA)
MacMurray Coll (IL)
Madonna U (MI)
Malone Coll (OH)
Manchester Coll (IN)
Manhattanville Coll (NY)
Mansfield U of Pennsylvania (PA)
Marian Coll (IN)
Marian Coll of Fond du Lac (WI)
Mars Hill Coll (NC)
Maryville Coll (TN)
Mary Washington Coll (VA)
Marywood U (PA)
The Master's Coll and Sem (CA)
McGill U (QC, Canada)
McKendree Coll (IL)
McMurry U (TX)
McNeese State U (LA)
McPherson Coll (KS)
Memorial U of Newfoundland (NL, Canada)
Mercer U (GA)
Mercy Coll (NY)
Mercyhurst Coll (PA)
Meredith Coll (NC)
Messiah Coll (PA)
Methodist Coll (NC)
Metropolitan State Coll of Denver (CO)
Miami U (OH)
Miami U Hamilton (OH)
Michigan State U (MI)
MidAmerica Nazarene U (KS)
Millersville U of Pennsylvania (PA)
Milligan Coll (TN)
Millikin U (IL)
Minnesota State U Mankato (MN)
Minnesota State U Moorhead (MN)
Minot State U (ND)
Mississippi Coll (MS)
Mississippi State U (MS)
Mississippi Valley State U (MS)
Missouri Baptist U (MO)
Missouri Western State Coll (MO)
Montana State U–Billings (MT)
Montana State U–Bozeman (MT)
Montclair State U (NJ)
Moravian Coll (PA)
Morningside Coll (IA)
Mount Marty Coll (SD)
Mount Mary Coll (WI)
Mount Mercy Coll (IA)
Mount St. Mary's Coll (CA)
Mount Union Coll (OH)
Mount Vernon Nazarene U (OH)
Murray State U (KY)
Nazareth Coll of Rochester (NY)
Nebraska Wesleyan U (NE)
Newberry Coll (SC)
New Jersey City U (NJ)
New Mexico Highlands U (NM)
New Mexico State U (NM)
New York U (NY)
Nicholls State U (LA)
North Carolina Central U (NC)
North Dakota State U (ND)

Northeastern State U (OK)
Northern Arizona U (AZ)
Northern Illinois U (IL)
Northern Michigan U (MI)
Northern State U (SD)
North Georgia Coll & State U (GA)
North Greenville Coll (SC)
Northland Coll (WI)
North Park U (IL)
Northwestern Coll (IA)
Northwestern Coll (MN)
Northwestern Oklahoma State U (OK)
Northwestern State U of Louisiana (LA)
Northwestern U (IL)
Northwest Nazarene U (ID)
Nyack Coll (NY)
Oakland City U (IN)
Oakland U (MI)
Oberlin Coll (OH)
Ohio Northern U (OH)
The Ohio State U (OH)
Ohio U (OH)
Ohio Wesleyan U (OH)
Oklahoma Baptist U (OK)
Oklahoma Christian U (OK)
Oklahoma City U (OK)
Oklahoma State U (OK)
Olivet Nazarene U (IL)
Oral Roberts U (OK)
Ottawa U (KS)
Otterbein Coll (OH)
Ouachita Baptist U (AR)
Pacific Lutheran U (WA)
Pacific Union Coll (CA)
Pacific U (OR)
Palm Beach Atlantic U (FL)
Peabody Conserv of Music of Johns Hopkins U (MD)
Penn State U Univ Park Campus (PA)
Pepperdine U, Malibu (CA)
Pfeiffer U (NC)
Pillsbury Baptist Bible Coll (MN)
Pittsburg State U (KS)
Plymouth State U (NH)
Point Loma Nazarene U (CA)
Pontifical Catholic U of Puerto Rico (PR)
Presbyterian Coll (SC)
Queens Coll of the City U of NY (NY)
Queen's U at Kingston (ON, Canada)
Quincy U (IL)
Reformed Bible Coll (MI)
Rhode Island Coll (RI)
Rider U (NJ)
Ripon Coll (WI)
Roberts Wesleyan Coll (NY)
Rochester Coll (MI)
Rocky Mountain Coll (MT)
Roosevelt U (IL)
Rutgers, The State U of New Jersey, New Brunswick/Piscataway (NJ)
St. Ambrose U (IA)
Saint Augustine's Coll (NC)
St. Cloud State U (MN)
Saint John's U (MN)
Saint Mary-of-the-Woods Coll (IN)
Saint Mary's Coll (IN)
Saint Mary's U of Minnesota (MN)
St. Norbert Coll (WI)
St. Olaf Coll (MN)
Saint Vincent Coll (PA)
Saint Xavier U (IL)
Salve Regina U (RI)
Samford U (AL)
Sam Houston State U (TX)
Seattle Pacific U (WA)
Seton Hill U (PA)
Shenandoah U (VA)
Shorter Coll (GA)
Siena Heights U (MI)
Silver Lake Coll (WI)
Simpson Coll (IA)
Simpson Coll and Graduate School (CA)
Sonoma State U (CA)
South Carolina State U (SC)
South Dakota State U (SD)
Southeastern Coll of the Assemblies of God (FL)
Southeastern Louisiana U (LA)
Southeastern Oklahoma State U (OK)
Southeast Missouri State U (MO)
Southern Adventist U (TN)
Southern Arkansas U–Magnolia (AR)
Southern Methodist U (TX)
Southern Nazarene U (OK)
Southern U and A&M Coll (LA)
Southern Utah U (UT)
Southern Wesleyan U (SC)
Southwest Baptist U (MO)
Southwestern Coll (AZ)
Southwestern Coll (KS)
Southwestern Oklahoma State U (OK)
Southwestern U (TX)
Southwest Missouri State U (MO)
Spring Arbor U (MI)
State U of NY Coll at Fredonia (NY)
State U of NY Coll at Potsdam (NY)
State U of West Georgia (GA)
Sterling Coll (KS)
Stetson U (FL)
Susquehanna U (PA)
Syracuse U (NY)
Tabor Coll (KS)
Talladega Coll (AL)
Tarleton State U (TX)
Taylor U (IN)
Tennessee Technological U (TN)
Tennessee Wesleyan Coll (TN)
Texas A&M U–Commerce (TX)
Texas A&M U–Kingsville (TX)
Texas Christian U (TX)
Texas Lutheran U (TX)
Texas Southern U (TX)
Texas Wesleyan U (TX)
Toccoa Falls Coll (GA)
Towson U (MD)
Transylvania U (KY)
Trevecca Nazarene U (TN)
Trinity Christian Coll (IL)
Trinity Intl U (IL)
Troy State U (AL)
Union Coll (NE)
Union U (TN)
Universidad Adventista de las Antillas (PR)
Université Laval (QC, Canada)
The U of Akron (OH)
The U of Alabama (AL)
U of Alberta (AB, Canada)
The U of Arizona (AZ)
U of Arkansas (AR)
U of Arkansas at Fort Smith (AR)
U of Arkansas at Monticello (AR)
The U of British Columbia (BC, Canada)
U of Central Florida (FL)
U of Charleston (WV)
U of Cincinnati (OH)
U of Colorado at Boulder (CO)
U of Connecticut (CT)
U of Dayton (OH)
U of Delaware (DE)
U of Evansville (IN)
U of Florida (FL)
U of Georgia (GA)
U of Hartford (CT)
U of Hawaii at Manoa (HI)
U of Idaho (ID)
U of Illinois at Urbana–Champaign (IL)
U of Indianapolis (IN)
The U of Iowa (IA)
U of Kansas (KS)
U of Kentucky (KY)
U of La Verne (CA)
The U of Lethbridge (AB, Canada)
U of Louisiana at Lafayette (LA)
U of Louisville (KY)
U of Maine (ME)
U of Mary (ND)
U of Mary Hardin-Baylor (TX)
U of Maryland, Coll Park (MD)
U of Maryland Eastern Shore (MD)
U of Miami (FL)
U of Michigan (MI)
U of Michigan–Flint (MI)
U of Minnesota, Duluth (MN)
U of Minnesota, Twin Cities Campus (MN)
U of Missouri–Columbia (MO)
U of Missouri–Kansas City (MO)
U of Missouri–St. Louis (MO)
The U of Montana–Missoula (MT)
The U of Montana–Western (MT)
U of Montevallo (AL)
U of Nebraska at Omaha (NE)
U of Nebraska–Lincoln (NE)
U of Nevada, Reno (NV)
U of New Brunswick Fredericton (NB, Canada)
U of New Hampshire (NH)
U of New Mexico (NM)
U of New Orleans (LA)
The U of North Carolina at Chapel Hill (NC)
The U of North Carolina at Charlotte (NC)
The U of North Carolina at Greensboro (NC)
The U of North Carolina at Pembroke (NC)
The U of North Carolina at Wilmington (NC)
U of North Dakota (ND)
U of Northern Colorado (CO)
U of Northern Iowa (IA)
U of North Florida (FL)
U of North Texas (TX)
U of Oregon (OR)
U of Ottawa (ON, Canada)
U of Portland (OR)
U of Prince Edward Island (PE, Canada)
U of Puget Sound (WA)
U of Redlands (CA)
U of Regina (SK, Canada)
U of Rhode Island (RI)
U of Rochester (NY)
U of St. Thomas (MN)
U of St. Thomas (TX)
U of Saskatchewan (SK, Canada)
U of Sioux Falls (SD)
U of South Carolina (SC)
The U of South Dakota (SD)
U of Southern California (CA)
U of Southern Maine (ME)
U of South Florida (FL)
The U of Tennessee (TN)
The U of Tennessee at Martin (TN)
U of the District of Columbia (DC)
U of the Incarnate Word (TX)
U of the Pacific (CA)
U of the Virgin Islands (VI)
U of Toledo (OH)
U of Toronto (ON, Canada)
U of Tulsa (OK)
U of Utah (UT)
U of Vermont (VT)
U of Victoria (BC, Canada)
U of Washington (WA)
The U of Western Ontario (ON, Canada)
U of West Florida (FL)
U of Windsor (ON, Canada)
U of Wisconsin–La Crosse (WI)
U of Wisconsin–Madison (WI)
U of Wisconsin–Milwaukee (WI)
U of Wisconsin–Oshkosh (WI)
U of Wisconsin–River Falls (WI)
U of Wisconsin–Stevens Point (WI)
U of Wisconsin–Superior (WI)
U of Wisconsin–Whitewater (WI)
U of Wyoming (WY)
Utah State U (UT)
Valdosta State U (GA)
Valley City State U (ND)
Valparaiso U (IN)
Viterbo U (WI)
Waldorf Coll (IA)
Walla Walla Coll (WA)
Warner Pacific Coll (OR)
Warner Southern Coll (FL)
Wartburg Coll (IA)
Washburn U (KS)
Washington Bible Coll (MD)
Washington State U (WA)
Wayland Baptist U (TX)
Wayne State Coll (NE)
Weber State U (UT)
Webster U (MO)
West Chester U of Pennsylvania (PA)
Western Baptist Coll (OR)
Western Carolina U (NC)
Western Connecticut State U (CT)
Western Kentucky U (KY)
Western Michigan U (MI)
Western State Coll of Colorado (CO)
Western Washington U (WA)
Westfield State Coll (MA)
West Liberty State Coll (WV)
Westminster Choir Coll of Rider U (NJ)
Westminster Coll (PA)
West Virginia State Coll (WV)
West Virginia Wesleyan Coll (WV)
Wheaton Coll (IL)
Whitworth Coll (WA)
Wichita State U (KS)
Wilkes U (PA)
William Carey Coll (MS)
William Jewell Coll (MO)
William Paterson U of New Jersey (NJ)
Williams Baptist Coll (AR)
Wingate U (NC)
Winona State U (MN)
Winston-Salem State U (NC)
Winthrop U (SC)
Wright State U (OH)
Xavier U (OH)
Xavier U of Louisiana (LA)
York Coll (NE)
York Coll of Pennsylvania (PA)
York U (ON, Canada)
Youngstown State U (OH)

MUSIC THEORY AND COMPOSITION

Arizona State U (AZ)
Baldwin-Wallace Coll (OH)
Bard Coll (NY)
Baylor U (TX)
Berklee Coll of Music (MA)
Bethesda Christian U (CA)
Boston U (MA)
Bowling Green State U (OH)
Bradley U (IL)
Brigham Young U (UT)
Brooklyn Coll of the City U of NY (NY)
Bucknell U (PA)
California Baptist U (CA)
California Inst of the Arts (CA)
California State U, Chico (CA)
California State U, Long Beach (CA)
California State U, Sacramento (CA)
Calvin Coll (MI)
Campbell U (NC)
Canadian Mennonite U (MB, Canada)
Capital U (OH)
Carnegie Mellon U (PA)
Carson-Newman Coll (TN)
The Catholic U of America (DC)
Cedarville U (OH)
Centenary Coll of Louisiana (LA)
Central Michigan U (MI)
Central Missouri State U (MO)
Central Washington U (WA)
Chapman U (CA)
Christopher Newport U (VA)
City Coll of the City U of NY (NY)
Clayton Coll & State U (GA)
Coe Coll (IA)
The Coll of Wooster (OH)
Concordia Coll (MN)
Cornell U (NY)
Cornerstone U (MI)
Dalhousie U (NS, Canada)
Dallas Baptist U (TX)
DePaul U (IL)
DePauw U (IN)
Drury U (MO)
East Carolina U (NC)
Eastern Washington U (WA)
Florida State U (FL)
Georgia Southern U (GA)
Grace U (NE)
Hampshire Coll (MA)
Hardin-Simmons U (TX)
Hofstra U (NY)
Hope Coll (MI)
Houghton Coll (NY)
Houston Baptist U (TX)
Ithaca Coll (NY)
Jacksonville U (FL)
The Johns Hopkins U (MD)
Lawrence U (WI)
Long Island U, Brooklyn Campus (NY)
Loyola Marymount U (CA)
Loyola U New Orleans (LA)
Lynchburg Coll (VA)
Mannes Coll of Music, New School U (NY)
McGill U (QC, Canada)
Memorial U of Newfoundland (NL, Canada)
Meredith Coll (NC)
Michigan State U (MI)
Minnesota State U Moorhead (MN)
Mississippi Coll (MS)
Montclair State U (NJ)
Moravian Coll (PA)
New England Conservatory of Music (MA)
New World School of the Arts (FL)
New York U (NY)
North Central U (MN)
Northwestern Coll (MN)
Northwestern U (IL)
Northwest Nazarene U (ID)
Nyack Coll (NY)
Oakland U (MI)
Oberlin Coll (OH)
The Ohio State U (OH)
Ohio U (OH)
Oklahoma Baptist U (OK)
Oklahoma City U (OK)
Oral Roberts U (OK)
Ouachita Baptist U (AR)
Palm Beach Atlantic U (FL)
Point Loma Nazarene U (CA)
Randolph-Macon Woman's Coll (VA)
Rice U (TX)
Rider U (NJ)
Roosevelt U (IL)
Rowan U (NJ)
St. Cloud State U (MN)
St. Olaf Coll (MN)
Samford U (AL)
Sarah Lawrence Coll (NY)
Seton Hill U (PA)
Shenandoah U (VA)
Simon's Rock Coll of Bard (MA)
Southern Adventist U (TN)
Southern Methodist U (TX)
Southwest Missouri State U (MO)
State U of NY Coll at Potsdam (NY)
State U of West Georgia (GA)
Stetson U (FL)
Stevens Inst of Technology (NJ)
Syracuse U (NY)
Texas Christian U (TX)
Texas Tech U (TX)
Trinity Intl U (IL)
Trinity U (TX)
The U of Akron (OH)
The U of British Columbia (BC, Canada)
U of Delaware (DE)
U of Georgia (GA)
U of Hartford (CT)
U of Houston (TX)
U of Idaho (ID)
U of Illinois at Urbana–Champaign (IL)
The U of Iowa (IA)
U of Kansas (KS)
U of Louisiana at Lafayette (LA)
U of Miami (FL)
U of Michigan (MI)
U of Nebraska at Omaha (NE)
U of Nevada, Las Vegas (NV)
The U of North Carolina at Greensboro (NC)
U of Northern Iowa (IA)
U of North Texas (TX)
U of Oklahoma (OK)
U of Redlands (CA)
U of Regina (SK, Canada)
U of Rhode Island (RI)
U of Rochester (NY)
U of Southern California (CA)
The U of Texas at Austin (TX)
The U of the Arts (PA)
U of the Pacific (CA)
U of Victoria (BC, Canada)
U of Washington (WA)
U of Windsor (ON, Canada)
U of Wyoming (WY)
Valparaiso U (IN)
Wartburg Coll (IA)
Washington State U (WA)
Washington U in St. Louis (MO)
Webster U (MO)
West Chester U of Pennsylvania (PA)
Western Michigan U (MI)
Westminster Choir Coll of Rider U (NJ)
West Texas A&M U (TX)
Wheaton Coll (IL)
Wilberforce U (OH)
Willamette U (OR)
William Jewell Coll (MO)
Wright State U (OH)
York U (ON, Canada)
Youngstown State U (OH)

MUSIC THERAPY

Alverno Coll (WI)
Anna Maria Coll (MA)
Appalachian State U (NC)
Arizona State U (AZ)
Augsburg Coll (MN)
Baldwin-Wallace Coll (OH)
Berklee Coll of Music (MA)
Canadian Mennonite U (MB, Canada)
Chapman U (CA)
Charleston Southern U (SC)
The Coll of Wooster (OH)
Colorado State U (CO)
Dillard U (LA)
Duquesne U (PA)
East Carolina U (NC)
Eastern Michigan U (MI)
Elizabethtown Coll (PA)
Florida State U (FL)
Georgia Coll & State U (GA)
Immaculata U (PA)
Indiana U–Purdue U Fort Wayne (IN)
Livingstone Coll (NC)
Mansfield U of Pennsylvania (PA)
Maryville U of Saint Louis (MO)
Marywood U (PA)
Michigan State U (MI)
Molloy Coll (NY)
Montclair State U (NJ)

Nazareth Coll of Rochester (NY)
Queens U of Charlotte (NC)
Saint Mary-of-the-Woods Coll (IN)
Sam Houston State U (TX)
Shenandoah U (VA)
Slippery Rock U of Pennsylvania (PA)
Southern Methodist U (TX)
Southwestern Oklahoma State U (OK)
State U of NY at New Paltz (NY)
State U of NY Coll at Fredonia (NY)
Texas Woman's U (TX)
U of Dayton (OH)
U of Evansville (IN)
U of Georgia (GA)
The U of Iowa (IA)
U of Kansas (KS)
U of Louisville (KY)
U of Miami (FL)
U of Minnesota, Twin Cities Campus (MN)
U of Missouri–Kansas City (MO)
U of the Incarnate Word (TX)
U of the Pacific (CA)
U of Windsor (ON, Canada)
U of Wisconsin–Eau Claire (WI)
U of Wisconsin–Milwaukee (WI)
U of Wisconsin–Oshkosh (WI)
Utah State U (UT)
Wartburg Coll (IA)
Western Michigan U (MI)
West Texas A&M U (TX)
William Carey Coll (MS)

MYCOLOGY
Cornell U (NY)

NATURAL RESOURCE ECONOMICS
Cornell U (NY)
Michigan State U (MI)

NATURAL RESOURCES AND CONSERVATION RELATED
Penn State U Abington Coll (PA)
Penn State U Altoona Coll (PA)
Penn State U at Erie, The Behrend Coll (PA)
Penn State U Beaver Campus of the Commonwealth Coll (PA)
Penn State U Berks Cmps of Berks-Lehigh Valley Coll (PA)
Penn State U Delaware County Campus of the Commonwealth Coll (PA)
Penn State U DuBois Campus of the Commonwealth Coll (PA)
Penn State U Fayette Campus of the Commonwealth Coll (PA)
Penn State U Hazleton Campus of the Commonwealth Coll (PA)
Penn State U Lehigh Valley Cmps of Berks-Lehigh Valley Coll (PA)
Penn State U McKeesport Campus of the Commonwealth Coll (PA)
Penn State U Mont Alto Campus of the Commonwealth Coll (PA)
Penn State U New Kensington Campus of the Commonwealth Coll (PA)
Penn State U Schuylkill Campus of the Capital Coll (PA)
Penn State U Shenango Campus of the Commonwealth Coll (PA)
Penn State U Univ Park Campus (PA)
Penn State U Wilkes-Barre Campus of the Commonwealth Coll (PA)
Penn State U Worthington Scranton Cmps Commonwealth Coll (PA)
Penn State U York Campus of the Commonwealth Coll (PA)
St. Gregory's U (OK)
Sterling Coll (VT)
U of Alaska Fairbanks (AK)
The U of British Columbia (BC, Canada)
U of Louisiana at Lafayette (LA)
U of Miami (FL)
U of Michigan–Flint (MI)
Utah State U (UT)

NATURAL RESOURCES/ CONSERVATION
California State U, Sacramento (CA)
Carroll Coll (WI)
Central Michigan U (MI)
Coll of Santa Fe (NM)
Cornell U (NY)
Frostburg State U (MD)
Harvard U (MA)
Humboldt State U (CA)
Kent State U (OH)
Louisiana Tech U (LA)
Marlboro Coll (VT)
McGill U (QC, Canada)
Montana State U–Bozeman (MT)
Mount Vernon Nazarene U (OH)
New Jersey Inst of Technology (NJ)
North Carolina State U (NC)
Northern Michigan U (MI)
Northland Coll (WI)
Penn State U Abington Coll (PA)
Penn State U Altoona Coll (PA)
Penn State U at Erie, The Behrend Coll (PA)
Penn State U Beaver Campus of the Commonwealth Coll (PA)
Penn State U Berks Cmps of Berks-Lehigh Valley Coll (PA)
Penn State U Delaware County Campus of the Commonwealth Coll (PA)
Penn State U DuBois Campus of the Commonwealth Coll (PA)
Penn State U Fayette Campus of the Commonwealth Coll (PA)
Penn State U Hazleton Campus of the Commonwealth Coll (PA)
Penn State U Lehigh Valley Cmps of Berks-Lehigh Valley Coll (PA)
Penn State U McKeesport Campus of the Commonwealth Coll (PA)
Penn State U Mont Alto Campus of the Commonwealth Coll (PA)
Penn State U New Kensington Campus of the Commonwealth Coll (PA)
Penn State U Schuylkill Campus of the Capital Coll (PA)
Penn State U Shenango Campus of the Commonwealth Coll (PA)
Penn State U Univ Park Campus (PA)
Penn State U Wilkes-Barre Campus of the Commonwealth Coll (PA)
Penn State U Worthington Scranton Cmps Commonwealth Coll (PA)
Penn State U York Campus of the Commonwealth Coll (PA)
Purdue U (IN)
Rutgers, The State U of New Jersey, New Brunswick/Piscataway (NJ)
Slippery Rock U of Pennsylvania (PA)
Southeastern Oklahoma State U (OK)
Springfield Coll (MA)
State U of NY Coll of Environ Sci and Forestry (NY)
Sterling Coll (VT)
Texas A&M U (TX)
Texas A&M U at Galveston (TX)
Texas Tech U (TX)
Unity Coll (ME)
U Coll of the Cariboo (BC, Canada)
U of Alberta (AB, Canada)
The U of British Columbia (BC, Canada)
U of Calif, Berkeley (CA)
U of Calif, Davis (CA)
U of Connecticut (CT)
U of Kentucky (KY)
U of Louisiana at Lafayette (LA)
U of Maryland, Coll Park (MD)
U of Michigan–Flint (MI)
U of Missouri–Columbia (MO)
The U of Montana–Missoula (MT)
U of Nebraska–Lincoln (NE)
U of Nevada, Reno (NV)
U of New Hampshire (NH)
U of Rhode Island (RI)
U of Vermont (VT)
U of Wisconsin–Milwaukee (WI)
U of Wisconsin–River Falls (WI)
U of Wisconsin–Stevens Point (WI)
U of Wyoming (WY)
Upper Iowa U (IA)
Valdosta State U (GA)
Washington State U (WA)
Washington U in St. Louis (MO)
Winona State U (MN)

NATURAL RESOURCES/ CONSERVATION RELATED
Sterling Coll (VT)

NATURAL RESOURCES MANAGEMENT
Burlington Coll (VT)
Central Washington U (WA)
Keystone Coll (PA)
McGill U (QC, Canada)
Moravian Coll (PA)
The Ohio State U (OH)
Rutgers, The State U of New Jersey, New Brunswick/Piscataway (NJ)
Sterling Coll (VT)
Unity Coll (ME)
The U of British Columbia (BC, Canada)

NATURAL RESOURCES MANAGEMENT AND POLICY
Alaska Pacific U (AK)
Albright Coll (PA)
Ball State U (IN)
Bowling Green State U (OH)
California State U, Chico (CA)
Charleston Southern U (SC)
Clark U (MA)
Coll of Santa Fe (NM)
Colorado State U (CO)
Eastern Oregon U (OR)
Fort Hays State U (KS)
Grand Valley State U (MI)
Humboldt State U (CA)
Huntington Coll (IN)
Iowa State U of Science and Technology (IA)
Johnson State Coll (VT)
McGill U (QC, Canada)
New Mexico Highlands U (NM)
North Carolina State U (NC)
North Dakota State U (ND)
Northland Coll (WI)
The Ohio State U (OH)
Oregon State U (OR)
Paul Smith's Coll of Arts and Sciences (NY)
Roanoke Coll (VA)
Rochester Inst of Technology (NY)
State U of NY Coll of Environ Sci and Forestry (NY)
Sterling Coll (VT)
Tuskegee U (AL)
Unity Coll (ME)
U of Alberta (AB, Canada)
The U of British Columbia (BC, Canada)
U of Calif, Berkeley (CA)
U of Calif, San Diego (CA)
U of Delaware (DE)
U of Guelph (ON, Canada)
U of Idaho (ID)
U of La Verne (CA)
U of Maine (ME)
U of Massachusetts Amherst (MA)
U of Miami (FL)
U of Michigan (MI)
U of Minnesota, Crookston (MN)
U of Minnesota, Twin Cities Campus (MN)
The U of Montana–Missoula (MT)
U of Nebraska–Lincoln (NE)
U of Nevada, Reno (NV)
U of New Hampshire (NH)
U of Rhode Island (RI)
U of the South (TN)
U of Vermont (VT)
U of Washington (WA)
The U of Western Ontario (ON, Canada)
U of Windsor (ON, Canada)
U of Wisconsin–Madison (WI)
U of Wisconsin–Stevens Point (WI)
Western Carolina U (NC)
Western Washington U (WA)
West Virginia U (WV)

NATURAL SCIENCES
Alderson-Broaddus Coll (WV)
Antioch Coll (OH)
Arcadia U (PA)
Atlantic Union Coll (MA)
Augsburg Coll (MN)
Avila U (MO)
Azusa Pacific U (CA)
Bard Coll (NY)
Bemidji State U (MN)
Benedictine Coll (KS)
Bennington Coll (VT)
Baruch Coll of the City U of NY (NY)
Bethel Coll (KS)
Bishop's U (QC, Canada)
Blue Mountain Coll (MS)
California State U, Fresno (CA)
California State U, Los Angeles (CA)
California State U, San Bernardino (CA)
Calvin Coll (MI)
Carthage Coll (WI)
Case Western Reserve U (OH)
Castleton State Coll (VT)
Cedar Crest Coll (PA)
Charleston Southern U (SC)
Christian Brothers U (TN)
Colgate U (NY)
Coll of Mount St. Joseph (OH)
Coll of Saint Benedict (MN)
Coll of Saint Mary (NE)
The Coll of St. Scholastica (MN)
Coll of the Atlantic (ME)
Concordia U (IL)
Concordia U (NE)
Concordia U (OR)
Concordia U, St. Paul (MN)
Covenant Coll (GA)
Daemen Coll (NY)
Davis & Elkins Coll (WV)
Defiance Coll (OH)
Doane Coll (NE)
Dordt Coll (IA)
Dowling Coll (NY)
Eastern Kentucky U (KY)
Eastern Washington U (WA)
Edgewood Coll (WI)
Elms Coll (MA)
Erskine Coll (SC)
Eureka Coll (IL)
The Evergreen State Coll (WA)
Florida Southern Coll (FL)
Fordham U (NY)
Fresno Pacific U (CA)
Goshen Coll (IN)
Grand Valley State U (MI)
Hampshire Coll (MA)
Hofstra U (NY)
Humboldt State U (CA)
Inter American U of PR, San Germán Campus (PR)
Iowa Wesleyan Coll (IA)
The Johns Hopkins U (MD)
Juniata Coll (PA)
Kenyon Coll (OH)
Lakehead U (ON, Canada)
Lesley U (MA)
LeTourneau U (TX)
Lewis-Clark State Coll (ID)
Lock Haven U of Pennsylvania (PA)
Longwood U (VA)
Loyola Marymount U (CA)
Loyola U Chicago (IL)
Lynn U (FL)
Madonna U (MI)
Marlboro Coll (VT)
The Master's Coll and Sem (CA)
Minnesota State U Mankato (MN)
Monmouth Coll (IL)
Mount Allison U (NB, Canada)
Muhlenberg Coll (PA)
New Coll of Florida (FL)
North Central Coll (IL)
Northland Coll (WI)
North Park U (IL)
Oklahoma Baptist U (OK)
Oklahoma Panhandle State U (OK)
Olivet Nazarene U (IL)
Our Lady of the Lake U of San Antonio (TX)
Park U (MO)
Pepperdine U, Malibu (CA)
Redeemer U Coll (ON, Canada)
St. Cloud State U (MN)
St. Gregory's U (OK)
Saint John's U (MN)
Saint Joseph Coll (CT)
St. Thomas Aquinas Coll (NY)
San Jose State U (CA)
Sarah Lawrence Coll (NY)
Shawnee State U (OH)
Shimer Coll (IL)
Shorter Coll (GA)
Siena Heights U (MI)
Simon's Rock Coll of Bard (MA)
Spelman Coll (GA)
State U of NY Coll at Geneseo (NY)
Stephens Coll (MO)
Sterling Coll (VT)
Tabor Coll (KS)
Taylor U (IN)
Thomas Edison State Coll (NJ)
Trent U (ON, Canada)
Trinity Western U (BC, Canada)
The U of Akron (OH)
U of Cincinnati (OH)
The U of Findlay (OH)
U of Hawaii at Hilo (HI)
U of La Verne (CA)
U of Mary (ND)
U of Michigan–Dearborn (MI)
U of Nebraska at Omaha (NE)
U of New Hampshire (NH)
U of Ottawa (ON, Canada)
U of Pennsylvania (PA)
U of Pittsburgh at Greensburg (PA)
U of Pittsburgh at Johnstown (PA)
U of Puerto Rico, Cayey U Coll (PR)
U of Puget Sound (WA)
U of Science and Arts of Oklahoma (OK)
U of Toledo (OH)
U of Wisconsin–River Falls (WI)
U of Wisconsin–Stevens Point (WI)
Villanova U (PA)
Virginia Wesleyan Coll (VA)
Washington U in St. Louis (MO)
Wayne State Coll (NE)
Western Oregon U (OR)
Winona State U (MN)
York Coll (NE)
York U (ON, Canada)

NAVAL ARCHITECTURE AND MARINE ENGINEERING
Maine Maritime Acad (ME)
Massachusetts Maritime Acad (MA)
Memorial U of Newfoundland (NL, Canada)
Texas A&M U at Galveston (TX)
United States Coast Guard Acad (CT)
United States Merchant Marine Acad (NY)
United States Naval Acad (MD)
U of Michigan (MI)
U of New Orleans (LA)
Webb Inst (NY)

NAVY/MARINE CORPS R.O.T.C./ NAVAL SCIENCE
Hampton U (VA)
Rensselaer Polytechnic Inst (NY)
U of Washington (WA)

NEAR AND MIDDLE EASTERN STUDIES
American U (DC)
The American U in Cairo(Egypt)
Barnard Coll (NY)
Brandeis U (MA)
Brown U (RI)
Carleton U (ON, Canada)
Claremont McKenna Coll (CA)
Coll of the Holy Cross (MA)
Columbia Coll (NY)
Columbia Intl U (SC)
Columbia U, School of General Studies (NY)
Cornell U (NY)
Dartmouth Coll (NH)
Emory & Henry Coll (VA)
Fordham U (NY)
The George Washington U (DC)
Hampshire Coll (MA)
Harvard U (MA)
Indiana U Bloomington (IN)
The Johns Hopkins U (MD)
McGill U (QC, Canada)
New York U (NY)
Oberlin Coll (OH)
The Ohio State U (OH)
Portland State U (OR)
Princeton U (NJ)
Queens Coll of the City U of NY (NY)
Rutgers, The State U of New Jersey, New Brunswick/Piscataway (NJ)
Sarah Lawrence Coll (NY)
Smith Coll (MA)
Stevens Inst of Technology (NJ)
Texas State U-San Marcos (TX)
United States Military Acad (NY)
The U of Arizona (AZ)
U of Arkansas (AR)
U of Calif, Berkeley (CA)
U of Calif, Los Angeles (CA)
U of Calif, Santa Barbara (CA)
U of Chicago (IL)
U of Connecticut (CT)
U of Massachusetts Amherst (MA)
U of Michigan (MI)
U of Minnesota, Twin Cities Campus (MN)
The U of Texas at Austin (TX)
U of Toledo (OH)
U of Toronto (ON, Canada)
U of Utah (UT)
U of Washington (WA)
Washington U in St. Louis (MO)
William Tyndale Coll (MI)

NEUROBIOLOGY AND NEUROPHYSIOLOGY
Andrews U (MI)
Connecticut Coll (CT)
Florida State U (FL)
New Coll of Florida (FL)
U of Calif, Los Angeles (CA)
U of Miami (FL)

NEUROSCIENCE
Allegheny Coll (PA)
Amherst Coll (MA)
Baldwin-Wallace Coll (OH)
Bates Coll (ME)
Baylor U (TX)
Bishop's U (QC, Canada)
Boston U (MA)
Bowdoin Coll (ME)
Bowling Green State U (OH)
Brandeis U (MA)
Brigham Young U (UT)
Brock U (ON, Canada)
Brown U (RI)
Carthage Coll (WI)
Cedar Crest Coll (PA)
Centenary Coll of Louisiana (LA)
Central Michigan U (MI)
Clark U (MA)
Colby Coll (ME)
Colgate U (NY)
The Colorado Coll (CO)
Concordia U (QC, Canada)
Connecticut Coll (CT)
Cornell U (NY)
Dalhousie U (NS, Canada)
Drew U (NJ)
Emory U (GA)
Franklin and Marshall Coll (PA)
Hamilton Coll (NY)
Hampshire Coll (MA)
Harvard U (MA)
Haverford Coll (PA)
John Carroll U (OH)
The Johns Hopkins U (MD)
Kenyon Coll (OH)
King's Coll (PA)
Lawrence U (WI)
Macalester Coll (MN)
Memorial U of Newfoundland (NL, Canada)
Middlebury Coll (VT)
New York U (NY)
Northwestern U (IL)
Oberlin Coll (OH)
Ohio Wesleyan U (OH)
Pitzer Coll (CA)
Pomona Coll (CA)
Regis U (CO)
Rice U (TX)
St. Lawrence U (NY)
Scripps Coll (CA)
Skidmore Coll (NY)
Smith Coll (MA)
Texas Christian U (TX)
Trinity Coll (CT)
Tulane U (LA)
Union Coll (NY)
U of Calif, Irvine (CA)
U of Calif, Los Angeles (CA)
U of Calif, Riverside (CA)
U of Delaware (DE)
U of King's Coll (NS, Canada)
The U of Lethbridge (AB, Canada)
U of Miami (FL)
U of Minnesota, Twin Cities Campus (MN)
U of Pennsylvania (PA)
U of Pittsburgh (PA)
The U of Scranton (PA)
The U of Texas at Dallas (TX)
U of Toronto (ON, Canada)
U of Windsor (ON, Canada)
Ursinus Coll (PA)
Washington and Lee U (VA)
Washington State U (WA)
Washington U in St. Louis (MO)
Wellesley Coll (MA)
Wesleyan U (CT)
Westmont Coll (CA)
Wofford Coll (SC)

NON-PROFIT MANAGEMENT
Austin Peay State U (TN)
Clarkson U (NY)
Concordia U Coll of Alberta (AB, Canada)
Crichton Coll (TN)
Dalhousie U (NS, Canada)
Davenport U, Dearborn (MI)
Eastern Michigan U (MI)
Fresno Pacific U (CA)
Gettysburg Coll (PA)
Lakeland Coll (WI)
Manchester Coll (IN)
Saint Mary-of-the-Woods Coll (IN)
Southern Adventist U (TN)
Trinity Intl U (IL)
U of Baltimore (MD)
U of Guelph (ON, Canada)
Warren Wilson Coll (NC)

NORWEGIAN
Brigham Young U (UT)

NUCLEAR AND INDUSTRIAL RADIOLOGIC TECHNOLOGIES RELATED
U of Vermont (VT)

NUCLEAR ENGINEERING
Cornell U (NY)
Georgia Inst of Technology (GA)
Kansas State U (KS)
Massachusetts Inst of Technology (MA)
North Carolina State U (NC)
Oregon State U (OR)
Penn State U Abington Coll (PA)
Penn State U Altoona Coll (PA)
Penn State U at Erie, The Behrend Coll (PA)
Penn State U Beaver Campus of the Commonwealth Coll (PA)
Penn State U Berks Cmps of Berks-Lehigh Valley Coll (PA)
Penn State U Delaware County Campus of the Commonwealth Coll (PA)
Penn State U DuBois Campus of the Commonwealth Coll (PA)
Penn State U Fayette Campus of the Commonwealth Coll (PA)
Penn State U Hazleton Campus of the Commonwealth Coll (PA)
Penn State U Lehigh Valley Cmps of Berks-Lehigh Valley Coll (PA)
Penn State U McKeesport Campus of the Commonwealth Coll (PA)
Penn State U Mont Alto Campus of the Commonwealth Coll (PA)
Penn State U New Kensington Campus of the Commonwealth Coll (PA)
Penn State U Schuylkill Campus of the Capital Coll (PA)
Penn State U Shenango Campus of the Commonwealth Coll (PA)
Penn State U Univ Park Campus (PA)
Penn State U Wilkes-Barre Campus of the Commonwealth Coll (PA)
Penn State U Worthington Scranton Cmps Commonwealth Coll (PA)
Penn State U York Campus of the Commonwealth Coll (PA)
Purdue U (IN)
Rensselaer Polytechnic Inst (NY)
South Carolina State U (SC)
Texas A&M U (TX)
United States Military Acad (NY)
The U of Arizona (AZ)
U of Calif, Berkeley (CA)
U of Cincinnati (OH)
U of Florida (FL)
U of Illinois at Urbana–Champaign (IL)
U of Maryland, Coll Park (MD)
U of Michigan (MI)
U of Missouri–Rolla (MO)
U of New Mexico (NM)
The U of Tennessee (TN)
U of Toronto (ON, Canada)
U of Wisconsin–Madison (WI)
Worcester Polytechnic Inst (MA)

NUCLEAR ENGINEERING TECHNOLOGY
Excelsior Coll (NY)
Old Dominion U (VA)
United States Merchant Marine Acad (NY)

NUCLEAR MEDICAL TECHNOLOGY
Baptist Coll of Health Sciences (TN)
Barry U (FL)
Benedictine U (IL)
California State U, Dominguez Hills (CA)
Cedar Crest Coll (PA)
Dalhousie U (NS, Canada)
Ferris State U (MI)
Indiana U of Pennsylvania (PA)
Indiana U–Purdue U Indianapolis (IN)
Long Island U, Brooklyn Campus (NY)
Long Island U, C.W. Post Campus (NY)
Loras Coll (IA)
Manhattan Coll (NY)
Mass Coll of Pharmacy and Allied Health Sciences (MA)
Medical Coll of Georgia (GA)
Oakland U (MI)
Old Dominion U (VA)
Rochester Inst of Technology (NY)
Roosevelt U (IL)
St. Cloud State U (MN)
Saint Louis U (MO)
Saint Mary's U of Minnesota (MN)
Salem State Coll (MA)
Thomas Edison State Coll (NJ)
U at Buffalo, The State U of New York (NY)
The U of Alabama at Birmingham (AL)
U of Central Arkansas (AR)
U of Cincinnati (OH)
The U of Findlay (OH)
The U of Iowa (IA)
U of Missouri–Columbia (MO)
U of Nebraska Medical Center (NE)
U of Nevada, Las Vegas (NV)
U of Oklahoma Health Sciences Center (OK)
U of St. Francis (IL)
U of the Incarnate Word (TX)
U of Wisconsin–La Crosse (WI)
Weber State U (UT)
Wheeling Jesuit U (WV)
York Coll of Pennsylvania (PA)

NUCLEAR/NUCLEAR POWER TECHNOLOGY
Thomas Edison State Coll (NJ)
U of North Texas (TX)

NUCLEAR PHYSICS
Harvard U (MA)

NURSE ANESTHETIST
U at Buffalo, The State U of New York (NY)
Webster U (MO)

NURSING ADMINISTRATION
Central Methodist Coll (MO)
Framingham State Coll (MA)
Nebraska Wesleyan U (NE)
Ryerson U (ON, Canada)
U of San Francisco (CA)
U of Saskatchewan (SK, Canada)
The U of Western Ontario (ON, Canada)
U of Windsor (ON, Canada)
Wheeling Jesuit U (WV)

NURSING MIDWIFERY
Ryerson U (ON, Canada)

NURSING (REGISTERED NURSE TRAINING)
Abilene Christian U (TX)
Adelphi U (NY)
Albany State U (GA)
Alcorn State U (MS)
Alderson-Broaddus Coll (WV)
Allen Coll (IA)
Alvernia Coll (PA)
Alverno Coll (WI)
American Intl Coll (MA)
Andrews U (MI)
Angelo State U (TX)
Anna Maria Coll (MA)
Arizona State U (AZ)
Arkansas State U (AR)
Arkansas Tech U (AR)
Armstrong Atlantic State U (GA)
Athabasca U (AB, Canada)
Atlantic Union Coll (MA)
Auburn U (AL)
Auburn U Montgomery (AL)
Augsburg Coll (MN)
Augustana Coll (SD)
Aurora U (IL)
Austin Peay State U (TN)
Azusa Pacific U (CA)
Bacone Coll (OK)
Baker U (KS)
Ball State U (IN)
Baptist Coll of Health Sciences (TN)
Barry U (FL)
Barton Coll (NC)
Baylor U (TX)
Bellarmine U (KY)
Bellin Coll of Nursing (WI)
Belmont U (TN)
Bemidji State U (MN)
Berea Coll (KY)
Berry Coll (GA)
Bethel Coll (IN)
Bethel Coll (KS)
Bethel U (MN)
Bethune-Cookman Coll (FL)
Biola U (CA)
Blessing-Rieman Coll of Nursing (IL)
Bloomfield Coll (NJ)
Bloomsburg U of Pennsylvania (PA)
Boise State U (ID)
Boston Coll (MA)
Bowie State U (MD)
Bowling Green State U (OH)
Bradley U (IL)
Brenau U (GA)
Briar Cliff U (IA)
Brigham Young U (UT)
British Columbia Inst of Technology (BC, Canada)
California State U, Chico (CA)
California State U, Dominguez Hills (CA)
California State U, Fresno (CA)
California State U, Fullerton (CA)
California State U, Hayward (CA)
California State U, Long Beach (CA)
California State U, Los Angeles (CA)
California State U, Sacramento (CA)
California State U, San Bernardino (CA)
California State U, Stanislaus (CA)
California U of Pennsylvania (PA)
Calvin Coll (MI)
Capital U (OH)
Cardinal Stritch U (WI)
Carlow Coll (PA)
Carroll Coll (MT)
Carroll Coll (WI)
Carson-Newman Coll (TN)
Case Western Reserve U (OH)
The Catholic U of America (DC)
Cedarville U (OH)
Central Connecticut State U (CT)
Central Methodist Coll (MO)
Central Missouri State U (MO)
Charleston Southern U (SC)
Chicago State U (IL)
Clarion U of Pennsylvania (PA)
Clayton Coll & State U (GA)
Clemson U (SC)
Cleveland State U (OH)
Coe Coll (IA)
Colby-Sawyer Coll (NH)
Coll Misericordia (PA)
Coll of Mount St. Joseph (OH)
Coll of Mount Saint Vincent (NY)
The Coll of New Jersey (NJ)
The Coll of New Rochelle (NY)
Coll of Notre Dame of Maryland (MD)
Coll of Saint Benedict (MN)
Coll of St. Catherine (MN)
Coll of Saint Mary (NE)
The Coll of St. Scholastica (MN)
Colorado State U-Pueblo (CO)
Columbia Coll of Nursing (WI)
Columbia Intl U (SC)
Columbia Union Coll (MD)
Columbus State U (GA)
Concordia Coll (MN)
Concordia U (IL)
Concordia U Wisconsin (WI)
Covenant Coll (GA)
Creighton U (NE)
Culver-Stockton Coll (MO)
Cumberland U (TN)
Curry Coll (MA)
Daemen Coll (NY)
Dalhousie U (NS, Canada)
Davenport U, Dearborn (MI)
Davenport U, Warren (MI)
Delaware State U (DE)
Delta State U (MS)
DePaul U (IL)
DeSales U (PA)
Dickinson State U (ND)
Dillard U (LA)
Dominican Coll (NY)
Dominican U of California (CA)
Dordt Coll (IA)
Duquesne U (PA)
D'Youville Coll (NY)
East Carolina U (NC)
East Central U (OK)
Eastern Kentucky U (KY)
Eastern Mennonite U (VA)
Eastern Michigan U (MI)
Eastern New Mexico U (NM)
Eastern U (PA)
Eastern Washington U (WA)
East Stroudsburg U of Pennsylvania (PA)
East Texas Baptist U (TX)
Edgewood Coll (WI)
Edinboro U of Pennsylvania (PA)
Elmhurst Coll (IL)
Elmira Coll (NY)
Elms Coll (MA)
Emory U (GA)
Emporia State U (KS)
Endicott Coll (MA)
Eureka Coll (IL)
Excelsior Coll (NY)
Fairfield U (CT)
Fairmont State Coll (WV)
Fayetteville State U (NC)
Ferris State U (MI)
Florida Ag and Mech U (FL)
Florida Atlantic U (FL)
Florida Gulf Coast U (FL)
Florida Intl U (FL)
Florida Southern Coll (FL)
Florida State U (FL)
Fort Hays State U (KS)
Franciscan U of Steubenville (OH)
Gannon U (PA)
Gardner-Webb U (NC)
George Mason U (VA)
Georgetown U (DC)
Georgia Coll & State U (GA)
Georgia Southern U (GA)
Georgia Southwestern State U (GA)
Georgia State U (GA)
Glenville State Coll (WV)
Gonzaga U (WA)
Goshen Coll (IN)
Governors State U (IL)
Graceland U (IA)
Grace U (NE)
Grambling State U (LA)
Grand Canyon U (AZ)
Grand Valley State U (MI)
Grand View Coll (IA)
Gustavus Adolphus Coll (MN)
Gwynedd-Mercy Coll (PA)
Hampton U (VA)
Hannibal-LaGrange Coll (MO)
Harding U (AR)
Hardin-Simmons U (TX)
Hartwick Coll (NY)
Hawai'i Pacific U (HI)
Henderson State U (AR)
Holy Names Coll (CA)
Hope Coll (MI)
Houston Baptist U (TX)
Howard U (DC)
Humboldt State U (CA)
Hunter Coll of the City U of NY (NY)
Husson Coll (ME)
Idaho State U (ID)
Illinois State U (IL)
Illinois Wesleyan U (IL)
Indiana State U (IN)
Indiana U East (IN)
Indiana U Kokomo (IN)
Indiana U Northwest (IN)
Indiana U of Pennsylvania (PA)
Indiana U–Purdue U Fort Wayne (IN)
Indiana U–Purdue U Indianapolis (IN)
Indiana U South Bend (IN)
Indiana U Southeast (IN)
Inter American U of PR, Fajardo Campus (PR)
Inter American U of PR, San Germán Campus (PR)
Iowa Wesleyan Coll (IA)
Jacksonville State U (AL)
Jacksonville U (FL)
James Madison U (VA)
Jamestown Coll (ND)
Jewish Hospital Coll of Nursing and Allied Health (MO)
The Johns Hopkins U (MD)
Judson Coll (IL)
Kansas Wesleyan U (KS)
Kean U (NJ)
Kennesaw State U (GA)
Kent State U (OH)
Kentucky Christian Coll (KY)
Kentucky State U (KY)
Keuka Coll (NY)
King Coll (TN)
Kutztown U of Pennsylvania (PA)
Kwantlen U Coll (BC, Canada)
LaGrange Coll (GA)
Lakehead U (ON, Canada)
Lake Superior State U (MI)
Lamar U (TX)
Lander U (SC)
La Salle U (PA)
Laurentian U (ON, Canada)
Lehman Coll of the City U of NY (NY)
Lenoir-Rhyne Coll (NC)
Lester L. Cox Coll of Nursing and Health Sciences (MO)
Lewis-Clark State Coll (ID)
Lewis U (IL)
Liberty U (VA)
Lincoln Memorial U (TN)
Lincoln U (MO)
Lipscomb U (TN)

Loma Linda U (CA)
Long Island U, Brooklyn Campus (NY)
Long Island U, C.W. Post Campus (NY)
Louisiana Coll (LA)
Louisiana State U Health Sciences Center (LA)
Lourdes Coll (OH)
Loyola U Chicago (IL)
Loyola U New Orleans (LA)
Luther Coll (IA)
Lynchburg Coll (VA)
Lynn U (FL)
MacMurray Coll (IL)
Macon State Coll (GA)
Madonna U (MI)
Malone Coll (OH)
Mansfield U of Pennsylvania (PA)
Marian Coll (IN)
Marian Coll of Fond du Lac (WI)
Marquette U (WI)
Marshall U (WV)
Mars Hill Coll (NC)
Marymount U (VA)
Maryville Coll (TN)
Maryville U of Saint Louis (MO)
Marywood U (PA)
McGill U (QC, Canada)
McKendree Coll (IL)
McMurry U (TX)
McNeese State U (LA)
Medcenter One Coll of Nursing (ND)
MedCentral Coll of Nursing (OH)
Medgar Evers Coll of the City U of NY (NY)
Medical Coll of Georgia (GA)
Medical U of South Carolina (SC)
Memorial U of Newfoundland (NL, Canada)
Mercer U (GA)
Mercy Coll (NY)
Mercyhurst Coll (PA)
Messiah Coll (PA)
Metropolitan State Coll of Denver (CO)
Metropolitan State U (MN)
Miami U (OH)
Michigan State U (MI)
MidAmerica Nazarene U (KS)
Middle Tennessee State U (TN)
Midway Coll (KY)
Midwestern State U (TX)
Millersville U of Pennsylvania (PA)
Milligan Coll (TN)
Millikin U (IL)
Milwaukee School of Eng (WI)
Minnesota State U Mankato (MN)
Minnesota State U Moorhead (MN)
Minot State U (ND)
Mississippi Coll (MS)
Missouri Southern State U (MO)
Missouri Western State Coll (MO)
Molloy Coll (NY)
Montana State U–Bozeman (MT)
Moravian Coll (PA)
Morehead State U (KY)
Morningside Coll (IA)
Mountain State U (WV)
Mount Marty Coll (SD)
Mount Mary Coll (WI)
Mount Mercy Coll (IA)
Mount Saint Mary Coll (NY)
Mount St. Mary's Coll (CA)
Murray State U (KY)
Nazareth Coll of Rochester (NY)
Nebraska Methodist Coll (NE)
Nebraska Wesleyan U (NE)
Neumann Coll (PA)
Nevada State Coll at Henderson (NV)
New Jersey Inst of Technology (NJ)
Newman U (KS)
New Mexico State U (NM)
New York Inst of Technology (NY)
New York U (NY)
Nicholls State U (LA)
Nipissing U (ON, Canada)
Norfolk State U (VA)
North Carolina Central U (NC)
North Dakota State U (ND)
Northeastern State U (OK)
Northern Arizona U (AZ)
Northern Illinois U (IL)
Northern Michigan U (MI)
North Georgia Coll & State U (GA)
North Park U (IL)
Northwestern Oklahoma State U (OK)
Northwestern State U of Louisiana (LA)
Northwest Nazarene U (ID)
Nova Southeastern U (FL)
Oakland U (MI)
The Ohio State U (OH)
Ohio U (OH)
Ohio U–Chillicothe (OH)
Ohio U–Southern Campus (OH)
Ohio U–Zanesville (OH)
Oklahoma Baptist U (OK)
Oklahoma City U (OK)
Oklahoma Panhandle State U (OK)
Old Dominion U (VA)
Olivet Nazarene U (IL)
Oral Roberts U (OK)
Otterbein Coll (OH)
Our Lady of Holy Cross Coll (LA)
Our Lady of the Lake Coll (LA)
Pace U (NY)
Pacific Lutheran U (WA)
Pacific Union Coll (CA)
Palm Beach Atlantic U (FL)
Penn State U Abington Coll (PA)
Penn State U Altoona Coll (PA)
Penn State U at Erie, The Behrend Coll (PA)
Penn State U Beaver Campus of the Commonwealth Coll (PA)
Penn State U Berks Cmps of Berks-Lehigh Valley Coll (PA)
Penn State U Delaware County Campus of the Commonwealth Coll (PA)
Penn State U DuBois Campus of the Commonwealth Coll (PA)
Penn State U Fayette Campus of the Commonwealth Coll (PA)
Penn State U Harrisburg Campus of the Capital Coll (PA)
Penn State U Hazleton Campus of the Commonwealth Coll (PA)
Penn State U Lehigh Valley Cmps of Berks-Lehigh Valley Coll (PA)
Penn State U McKeesport Campus of the Commonwealth Coll (PA)
Penn State U Mont Alto Campus of the Commonwealth Coll (PA)
Penn State U New Kensington Campus of the Commonwealth Coll (PA)
Penn State U Schuylkill Campus of the Capital Coll (PA)
Penn State U Shenango Campus of the Commonwealth Coll (PA)
Penn State U Univ Park Campus (PA)
Penn State U Wilkes-Barre Campus of the Commonwealth Coll (PA)
Penn State U Worthington Scranton Cmps Commonwealth Coll (PA)
Penn State U York Campus of the Commonwealth Coll (PA)
Piedmont Coll (GA)
Pittsburg State U (KS)
Point Loma Nazarene U (CA)
Pontifical Catholic U of Puerto Rico (PR)
Prairie View A&M U (TX)
Presentation Coll (SD)
Purdue U (IN)
Purdue U North Central (IN)
Queen's U at Kingston (ON, Canada)
Quincy U (IL)
Quinnipiac U (CT)
Radford U (VA)
Ramapo Coll of New Jersey (NJ)
Regis Coll (MA)
Regis U (CO)
Research Coll of Nursing (MO)
Rhode Island Coll (RI)
The Richard Stockton Coll of New Jersey (NJ)
Rivier Coll (NH)
Robert Morris U (PA)
Roberts Wesleyan Coll (NY)
Rockford Coll (IL)
Rockhurst U (MO)
Rush U (IL)
Russell Sage Coll (NY)
Rutgers, The State U of New Jersey, Camden (NJ)
Rutgers, The State U of New Jersey, Newark (NJ)
Rutgers, The State U of New Jersey, New Brunswick/Piscataway (NJ)
Ryerson U (ON, Canada)
Sacred Heart U (CT)
Saginaw Valley State U (MI)
St. Ambrose U (IA)
Saint Anthony Coll of Nursing (IL)
St. Cloud State U (MN)
Saint Francis Medical Center Coll of Nursing (IL)
Saint Francis U (PA)
St. Francis Xavier U (NS, Canada)
St. John Fisher Coll (NY)
St. John's Coll (IL)
Saint John's U (MN)
St. John's U (NY)
Saint Joseph Coll (CT)
Saint Joseph's Coll (IN)
St. Joseph's Coll, New York (NY)
Saint Joseph's Coll of Maine (ME)
St. Joseph's Coll, Suffolk Campus (NY)
Saint Louis U (MO)
Saint Luke's Coll (MO)
Saint Mary's Coll (IN)
Saint Mary's Coll of California (CA)
St. Olaf Coll (MN)
Saint Xavier U (IL)
Salem State Coll (MA)
Salisbury U (MD)
Salve Regina U (RI)
Samford U (AL)
Samuel Merritt Coll (CA)
San Diego State U (CA)
San Francisco State U (CA)
San Jose State U (CA)
Seattle Pacific U (WA)
Seattle U (WA)
Seton Hall U (NJ)
Seton Hill U (PA)
Shawnee State U (OH)
Shenandoah U (VA)
Shepherd U (WV)
Simmons Coll (MA)
Slippery Rock U of Pennsylvania (PA)
Sonoma State U (CA)
South Carolina State U (SC)
South Dakota State U (SD)
Southeastern Louisiana U (LA)
Southeast Missouri State U (MO)
Southern Connecticut State U (CT)
Southern Illinois U Edwardsville (IL)
Southern Nazarene U (OK)
Southern Oregon U (OR)
Southern U and A&M Coll (LA)
Southern Vermont Coll (VT)
Southwest Baptist U (MO)
Southwestern Coll (KS)
Southwestern Oklahoma State U (OK)
Southwest Missouri State U (MO)
Spring Hill Coll (AL)
State U of NY at Binghamton (NY)
State U of NY at New Paltz (NY)
Plattsburgh State U of NY (NY)
State U of NY Coll at Brockport (NY)
State U of NY Health Science Center at Brooklyn (NY)
State U of NY Inst of Tech at Utica/Rome (NY)
State U of West Georgia (GA)
Stony Brook U, State U of New York (NY)
Tarleton State U (TX)
Tennessee State U (TN)
Tennessee Technological U (TN)
Tennessee Wesleyan Coll (TN)
Texas A&M Intl U (TX)
Texas A&M U–Corpus Christi (TX)
Texas A&M U–Texarkana (TX)
Texas Christian U (TX)
Texas Southern U (TX)
Texas Woman's U (TX)
Thomas Jefferson U (PA)
Thomas More Coll (KY)
Thomas U (GA)
Towson U (MD)
Trent U (ON, Canada)
Trinity Christian Coll (IL)
Trinity Coll of Nursing and Health Sciences (IL)
Trinity Western U (BC, Canada)
Troy State U (AL)
Truman State U (MO)
Tuskegee U (AL)
Union Coll (NE)
Union U (TN)
Universidad Adventista de las Antillas (PR)
Université de Montréal (QC, Canada)
Université de Sherbrooke (QC, Canada)
U du Québec à Hull (QC, Canada)
Université Laval (QC, Canada)
U at Buffalo, The State U of New York (NY)
U Coll of the Cariboo (BC, Canada)
U Coll of the Fraser Valley (BC, Canada)
The U of Akron (OH)
The U of Alabama (AL)
The U of Alabama at Birmingham (AL)
The U of Alabama in Huntsville (AL)
U of Alberta (AB, Canada)
The U of Arizona (AZ)
U of Arkansas (AR)
U of Arkansas at Fort Smith (AR)
U of Arkansas at Monticello (AR)
The U of British Columbia (BC, Canada)
U of Calgary (AB, Canada)
U of Calif, Los Angeles (CA)
U of Central Arkansas (AR)
U of Central Florida (FL)
U of Charleston (WV)
U of Cincinnati (OH)
U of Colorado at Colorado Springs (CO)
U of Colorado Health Sciences Center (CO)
U of Connecticut (CT)
U of Delaware (DE)
U of Detroit Mercy (MI)
U of Dubuque (IA)
U of Evansville (IN)
U of Florida (FL)
U of Hartford (CT)
U of Hawaii at Hilo (HI)
U of Hawaii at Manoa (HI)
U of Illinois at Chicago (IL)
U of Illinois at Springfield (IL)
U of Indianapolis (IN)
The U of Iowa (IA)
U of Kansas (KS)
U of Kentucky (KY)
The U of Lethbridge (AB, Canada)
U of Louisiana at Lafayette (LA)
U of Louisville (KY)
U of Maine (ME)
U of Maine at Fort Kent (ME)
U of Manitoba (MB, Canada)
U of Mary (ND)
U of Mary Hardin-Baylor (TX)
U of Massachusetts Amherst (MA)
U of Massachusetts Boston (MA)
U of Massachusetts Dartmouth (MA)
U of Massachusetts Lowell (MA)
The U of Memphis (TN)
U of Miami (FL)
U of Michigan (MI)
U of Michigan–Flint (MI)
U of Minnesota, Twin Cities Campus (MN)
U of Mississippi Medical Center (MS)
U of Missouri–Columbia (MO)
U of Missouri–Kansas City (MO)
U of Missouri–St. Louis (MO)
U of Mobile (AL)
U of Nebraska Medical Center (NE)
U of Nevada, Las Vegas (NV)
U of Nevada, Reno (NV)
U of New Brunswick Fredericton (NB, Canada)
U of New Hampshire (NH)
U of New Mexico (NM)
U of North Alabama (AL)
The U of North Carolina at Chapel Hill (NC)
The U of North Carolina at Charlotte (NC)
The U of North Carolina at Greensboro (NC)
The U of North Carolina at Pembroke (NC)
The U of North Carolina at Wilmington (NC)
U of North Dakota (ND)
U of Northern Colorado (CO)
U of North Florida (FL)
U of Oklahoma Health Sciences Center (OK)
U of Ottawa (ON, Canada)
U of Pennsylvania (PA)
U of Phoenix–Hawaii Campus (HI)
U of Phoenix–New Mexico Campus (NM)
U of Phoenix–Oklahoma City Campus (OK)
U of Phoenix–St. Louis Campus (MO)
U of Phoenix–Southern Arizona Campus (AZ)
U of Phoenix–Tampa Campus (FL)
U of Phoenix–Tulsa Campus (OK)
U of Phoenix–Utah Campus (UT)
U of Phoenix–West Michigan Campus (MI)
U of Pittsburgh (PA)
U of Pittsburgh at Bradford (PA)
U of Portland (OR)
U of Prince Edward Island (PE, Canada)
U of Rhode Island (RI)
U of Rochester (NY)
U of St. Francis (IL)
U of Saint Francis (IN)
U of San Francisco (CA)
U of Saskatchewan (SK, Canada)
The U of Scranton (PA)
U of South Alabama (AL)
U of South Carolina (SC)
U of South Carolina Aiken (SC)
U of South Carolina Spartanburg (SC)
U of Southern Indiana (IN)
U of Southern Maine (ME)
U of South Florida (FL)
The U of Tampa (FL)
The U of Tennessee (TN)
The U of Tennessee at Chattanooga (TN)
The U of Tennessee at Martin (TN)
The U of Texas at Arlington (TX)
The U of Texas at Austin (TX)
The U of Texas at Brownsville (TX)
The U of Texas at Tyler (TX)
U of Texas-Houston Health Science Center (TX)
U of Texas Health Science Center at San Antonio (TX)
U of Texas Medical Branch at Galveston (TX)
The U of Texas–Pan American (TX)
U of the District of Columbia (DC)
U of the Incarnate Word (TX)
U of the Sacred Heart (PR)
U of the Virgin Islands (VI)
U of Toledo (OH)
U of Toronto (ON, Canada)
U of Tulsa (OK)
U of Utah (UT)
U of Vermont (VT)
U of Victoria (BC, Canada)
U of Virginia (VA)
U of Washington (WA)
The U of Western Ontario (ON, Canada)
U of West Florida (FL)
U of Windsor (ON, Canada)
U of Wisconsin–Eau Claire (WI)
U of Wisconsin–Madison (WI)
U of Wisconsin–Milwaukee (WI)
U of Wisconsin–Oshkosh (WI)
U of Wisconsin–Parkside (WI)
U of Wyoming (WY)
Ursuline Coll (OH)
Utica Coll (NY)
Valdosta State U (GA)
Valparaiso U (IN)
Villa Julie Coll (MD)
Villanova U (PA)
Virginia Commonwealth U (VA)
Viterbo U (WI)
Wagner Coll (NY)
Walla Walla Coll (WA)
Walsh U (OH)
Washburn U (KS)
Washington State U (WA)
Waynesburg Coll (PA)
Wayne State U (MI)
Weber State U (UT)
Webster U (MO)
Wesley Coll (DE)
West Chester U of Pennsylvania (PA)
Western Carolina U (NC)
Western Connecticut State U (CT)
Western Kentucky U (KY)
Western Michigan U (MI)
West Liberty State Coll (WV)
Westminster Coll (UT)
West Texas A&M U (TX)
West Virginia U (WV)
West Virginia Wesleyan Coll (WV)
Wheeling Jesuit U (WV)
Whitworth Coll (WA)
Widener U (PA)
Wilkes U (PA)
William Carey Coll (MS)
William Jewell Coll (MO)
William Paterson U of New Jersey (NJ)
Wilmington Coll (DE)
Winona State U (MN)
Winston-Salem State U (NC)
Worcester State Coll (MA)
Wright State U (OH)
York Coll of Pennsylvania (PA)
York Coll of the City U of New York (NY)
York U (ON, Canada)
Youngstown State U (OH)

NURSING RELATED

Adelphi U (NY)
Alverno Coll (WI)
Avila U (MO)
British Columbia Inst of Technology (BC, Canada)
California State U, Fullerton (CA)
Capital U (OH)
Coll of Staten Island of the City U of NY (NY)
Eastern Kentucky U (KY)
East Texas Baptist U (TX)

Inter American U of PR, Aguadilla Campus (PR)
Long Island U, Brooklyn Campus (NY)
Long Island U, C.W. Post Campus (NY)
Lubbock Christian U (TX)
Madonna U (MI)
Malaspina U-Coll (BC, Canada)
Minot State U (ND)
Monmouth U (NJ)
New York Inst of Technology (NY)
Northeastern U (MA)
Roberts Wesleyan Coll (NY)
Rowan U (NJ)
St. Francis Coll (NY)
Thomas More Coll (KY)
U at Buffalo, The State U of New York (NY)
The U of Akron (OH)
U of Calif, Los Angeles (CA)
U of Kentucky (KY)
U of Massachusetts Dartmouth (MA)
U of Pennsylvania (PA)
U of Saint Francis (IN)
U of Toledo (OH)
Western Kentucky U (KY)
Wright State U (OH)

NURSING SCIENCE
Benedictine U (IL)
Brock U (ON, Canada)
Cedar Crest Coll (PA)
Clarke Coll (IA)
Coll of Saint Elizabeth (NJ)
Columbia Coll, Caguas (PR)
Elmira Coll (NY)
Fairleigh Dickinson U, Teaneck-Metro Campus (NJ)
Holy Names Coll (CA)
Immaculata U (PA)
Kean U (NJ)
Kutztown U of Pennsylvania (PA)
La Roche Coll (PA)
Long Island U, C.W. Post Campus (NY)
Millersville U of Pennsylvania (PA)
Missouri Baptist U (MO)
Monmouth U (NJ)
Mount Aloysius Coll (PA)
National U (CA)
New Jersey City U (NJ)
New Jersey Inst of Technology (NJ)
The Ohio State U (OH)
Queens U of Charlotte (NC)
The Richard Stockton Coll of New Jersey (NJ)
St. Francis Xavier U (NS, Canada)
Southern Adventist U (TN)
State U of New York Upstate Medical U (NY)
Thomas Edison State Coll (NJ)
Trinity Coll of Nursing and Health Sciences (IL)
U Coll of the Cariboo (BC, Canada)
The U of Akron (OH)
U of Delaware (DE)
U of Kansas (KS)
U of New Hampshire at Manchester (NH)
U of Phoenix–Atlanta Campus (GA)
U of Phoenix–Colorado Campus (CO)
U of Phoenix–Fort Lauderdale Campus (FL)
U of Phoenix–Hawaii Campus (HI)
U of Phoenix–Jacksonville Campus (FL)
U of Phoenix–Louisiana Campus (LA)
U of Phoenix–Metro Detroit Campus (MI)
U of Phoenix–New Mexico Campus (NM)
U of Phoenix–Northern California Campus (CA)
U of Phoenix–Orlando Campus (FL)
U of Phoenix–Phoenix Campus (AZ)
U of Phoenix–Sacramento Campus (CA)
U of Phoenix–San Diego Campus (CA)
U of Phoenix–Southern Arizona Campus (AZ)
U of Phoenix–Southern California Campus (CA)
U of Phoenix–Southern Colorado Campus (CO)
U of Victoria (BC, Canada)
U of Wisconsin–Green Bay (WI)
Wichita State U (KS)
Xavier U (OH)
York U (ON, Canada)

NUTRITIONAL SCIENCES
Texas Woman's U (TX)

NUTRITION SCIENCE
Texas Woman's U (TX)

NUTRITION SCIENCES
Auburn U (AL)
Benedictine U (IL)
Boston U (MA)
Brigham Young U (UT)
Case Western Reserve U (OH)
Chapman U (CA)
Cornell U (NY)
Drexel U (PA)
Edinboro U of Pennsylvania (PA)
Elmhurst Coll (IL)
Florida State U (FL)
Goddard Coll (VT)
La Salle U (PA)
Louisiana State U and A&M Coll (LA)
McGill U (QC, Canada)
Michigan State U (MI)
Mount Saint Vincent U (NS, Canada)
New York Inst of Technology (NY)
Russell Sage Coll (NY)
Rutgers, The State U of New Jersey, New Brunswick/Piscataway (NJ)
Tulane U (LA)
Université Laval (QC, Canada)
U at Buffalo, The State U of New York (NY)
The U of Arizona (AZ)
U of Calif, Berkeley (CA)
U of Connecticut (CT)
U of Delaware (DE)
U of Guelph (ON, Canada)
U of Missouri–Columbia (MO)
U of Nevada, Las Vegas (NV)
U of Saskatchewan (SK, Canada)
U of the District of Columbia (DC)
U of Vermont (VT)
U of Wisconsin–Green Bay (WI)
Washington State U (WA)

OCCUPATIONAL AND ENVIRONMENTAL HEALTH NURSING
British Columbia Inst of Technology (BC, Canada)

OCCUPATIONAL HEALTH AND INDUSTRIAL HYGIENE
California State U, Fresno (CA)
Clarkson U (NY)
Illinois State U (IL)
Montana Tech of The U of Montana (MT)
Oakland U (MI)
Ryerson U (ON, Canada)
Saint Augustine's Coll (NC)

OCCUPATIONAL SAFETY AND HEALTH TECHNOLOGY
Ball State U (IN)
California State U, Fresno (CA)
Central Missouri State U (MO)
Central Washington U (WA)
Columbia Southern U (AL)
Embry-Riddle Aeronautical U (FL)
Fairmont State Coll (WV)
Ferris State U (MI)
Grand Valley State U (MI)
Indiana State U (IN)
Indiana U of Pennsylvania (PA)
Jacksonville State U (AL)
Keene State Coll (NH)
Marshall U (WV)
Mercy Coll (NY)
Millersville U of Pennsylvania (PA)
Montana Tech of The U of Montana (MT)
Murray State U (KY)
National U (CA)
Oregon State U (OR)
Rochester Inst of Technology (NY)
Slippery Rock U of Pennsylvania (PA)
Southeastern Oklahoma State U (OK)
Southwest Baptist U (MO)
Texas Southern U (TX)
U of New Haven (CT)
U of North Dakota (ND)
The U of Texas at Tyler (TX)
U of Wisconsin–Whitewater (WI)
Utah State U (UT)

OCCUPATIONAL THERAPIST ASSISTANT
Grand Valley State U (MI)
Penn State U Berks Cmps of Berks-Lehigh Valley Coll (PA)

OCCUPATIONAL THERAPY
Alabama State U (AL)
Alvernia Coll (PA)
American Intl Coll (MA)
Augustana Coll (IL)
Baker Coll of Flint (MI)
Bay Path Coll (MA)
Boston U (MA)
Brenau U (GA)
Calvin Coll (MI)
Carthage Coll (WI)
Centenary Coll of Louisiana (LA)
Chicago State U (IL)
Cleveland State U (OH)
Coll of Saint Benedict (MN)
Coll of St. Catherine (MN)
Coll of Saint Mary (NE)
Concordia Coll (MN)
Concordia U Wisconsin (WI)
Dalhousie U (NS, Canada)
Dominican Coll (NY)
Dominican U of California (CA)
Duquesne U (PA)
D'Youville Coll (NY)
East Carolina U (NC)
Eastern Kentucky U (KY)
Eastern Michigan U (MI)
Eastern Washington U (WA)
Elizabethtown Coll (PA)
Elmhurst Coll (IL)
Florida Ag and Mech U (FL)
Florida Gulf Coast U (FL)
Florida Intl U (FL)
Gannon U (PA)
Hamline U (MN)
Howard U (DC)
Husson Coll (ME)
Illinois Coll (IL)
Indiana U–Purdue U Indianapolis (IN)
Ithaca Coll (NY)
Kean U (NJ)
Keuka Coll (NY)
Lenoir-Rhyne Coll (NC)
Loma Linda U (CA)
Long Island U, Brooklyn Campus (NY)
McGill U (QC, Canada)
McKendree Coll (IL)
Medical Coll of Georgia (GA)
Mount Aloysius Coll (PA)
Mount Mary Coll (WI)
New York Inst of Technology (NY)
The Ohio State U (OH)
Penn State U Mont Alto Campus of the Commonwealth Coll (PA)
Quinnipiac U (CT)
Russell Sage Coll (NY)
Sacred Heart U (CT)
Saginaw Valley State U (MI)
Saint Francis U (PA)
Saint John's U (MN)
Saint Louis U (MO)
Saint Vincent Coll (PA)
San Jose State U (CA)
Shawnee State U (OH)
State U of NY Health Science Center at Brooklyn (NY)
Stephens Coll (MO)
Texas Woman's U (TX)
Thomas Jefferson U (PA)
Towson U (MD)
Tuskegee U (AL)
Université de Montréal (QC, Canada)
Université Laval (QC, Canada)
U at Buffalo, The State U of New York (NY)
U of Alberta (AB, Canada)
The U of British Columbia (BC, Canada)
U of Central Arkansas (AR)
The U of Findlay (OH)
U of Hartford (CT)
U of Kansas (KS)
U of Manitoba (MB, Canada)
U of Minnesota, Twin Cities Campus (MN)
U of Missouri–Columbia (MO)
U of New Hampshire (NH)
U of Ottawa (ON, Canada)
U of Pittsburgh (PA)
U of Southern California (CA)
U of Southern Indiana (IN)
U of Texas Health Science Center at San Antonio (TX)
U of Texas Medical Branch at Galveston (TX)
The U of Texas–Pan American (TX)
U of Utah (UT)
U of Washington (WA)
The U of Western Ontario (ON, Canada)
U of Wisconsin–La Crosse (WI)
U of Wisconsin–Madison (WI)
U of Wisconsin–Milwaukee (WI)
Utica Coll (NY)
Wartburg Coll (IA)
Wayne State U (MI)
Western Michigan U (MI)
West Virginia U (WV)
Winston-Salem State U (NC)
Worcester State Coll (MA)
Xavier U (OH)
York Coll of the City U of New York (NY)

OCEAN ENGINEERING
California State U, Long Beach (CA)
Florida Atlantic U (FL)
Florida Inst of Technology (FL)
Massachusetts Inst of Technology (MA)
Memorial U of Newfoundland (NL, Canada)
Texas A&M U (TX)
Texas A&M U at Galveston (TX)
United States Naval Acad (MD)
U of New Hampshire (NH)
U of Rhode Island (RI)
Virginia Polytechnic Inst and State U (VA)

OCEANOGRAPHY (CHEMICAL AND PHYSICAL)
Central Michigan U (MI)
Dalhousie U (NS, Canada)
Elizabeth City State U (NC)
Florida Inst of Technology (FL)
Hampshire Coll (MA)
Hawai'i Pacific U (HI)
Humboldt State U (CA)
Kutztown U of Pennsylvania (PA)
Lamar U (TX)
Maine Maritime Acad (ME)
Memorial U of Newfoundland (NL, Canada)
Millersville U of Pennsylvania (PA)
North Carolina State U (NC)
Old Dominion U (VA)
Rider U (NJ)
Texas A&M U at Galveston (TX)
United States Naval Acad (MD)
The U of British Columbia (BC, Canada)
U of Miami (FL)
U of Michigan (MI)
U of New Hampshire (NH)
U of San Diego (CA)
U of Victoria (BC, Canada)
U of Washington (WA)

OFFICE MANAGEMENT
Babson Coll (MA)
Baker Coll of Flint (MI)
Berkeley Coll-New York City Campus (NY)
Berkeley Coll-Westchester Campus (NY)
Central Michigan U (MI)
Central Missouri State U (MO)
Central Washington U (WA)
Davenport U, Dearborn (MI)
Davenport U, Warren (MI)
Delta State U (MS)
Eastern Kentucky U (KY)
Georgia Coll & State U (GA)
Indiana State U (IN)
Indiana U of Pennsylvania (PA)
Mayville State U (ND)
Metropolitan State U (MN)
Miami U Hamilton (OH)
Middle Tennessee State U (TN)
Mississippi Valley State U (MS)
Murray State U (KY)
Norfolk State U (VA)
Peirce Coll (PA)
Radford U (VA)
Southeastern Oklahoma State U (OK)
Southeast Missouri State U (MO)
State U of West Georgia (GA)
Tarleton State U (TX)
Texas Southern U (TX)
Tiffin U (OH)
U of Nebraska–Lincoln (NE)
U of Puerto Rico, Cayey U Coll (PR)
U of South Carolina (SC)
U of Southern Indiana (IN)
U of the Sacred Heart (PR)
Valley City State U (ND)
Weber State U (UT)
Wright State U (OH)
Youngstown State U (OH)

OFFICE OCCUPATIONS AND CLERICAL SERVICES
The U of Texas at Brownsville (TX)

OPERATIONS MANAGEMENT
Auburn U (AL)
Aurora U (IL)
Babson Coll (MA)
Baker Coll of Flint (MI)
Baylor U (TX)
Boise State U (ID)
Boston U (MA)
Bowling Green State U (OH)
California State U, Chico (CA)
California State U, Long Beach (CA)
California State U, Sacramento (CA)
Central Michigan U (MI)
Central Washington U (WA)
Clarkson U (NY)
Clemson U (SC)
Coker Coll (SC)
Dalton State Coll (GA)
Davenport U, Dearborn (MI)
Davenport U, Grand Rapids (MI)
Edinboro U of Pennsylvania (PA)
Excelsior Coll (NY)
State U of NY at Farmingdale (NY)
Florida Southern Coll (FL)
Franklin U (OH)
Georgia Inst of Technology (GA)
Golden Gate U (CA)
Indiana U–Purdue U Fort Wayne (IN)
Indiana U–Purdue U Indianapolis (IN)
Iowa State U of Science and Technology (IA)
Kennesaw State U (GA)
Kent State U (OH)
Kettering U (MI)
Louisiana Tech U (LA)
Loyola U Chicago (IL)
Metropolitan State U (MN)
Miami U (OH)
Michigan State U (MI)
Michigan Technological U (MI)
Missouri Baptist U (MO)
National U (CA)
Northern Illinois U (IL)
Oakland U (MI)
The Ohio State U (OH)
Purdue U (IN)
Remington Coll–Colorado Springs Campus (CO)
Robert Morris U (PA)
Saginaw Valley State U (MI)
Saint Leo U (FL)
Sam Houston State U (TX)
Seattle U (WA)
Tennessee Technological U (TN)
Texas Southern U (TX)
Thomas Edison State Coll (NJ)
Tri-State U (IN)
The U of Arizona (AZ)
U of Delaware (DE)
U of Houston (TX)
U of Idaho (ID)
U of Indianapolis (IN)
U of Michigan–Flint (MI)
The U of North Carolina at Asheville (NC)
The U of North Carolina at Charlotte (NC)
U of North Texas (TX)
U of Pennsylvania (PA)
U of St. Thomas (MN)
U of Saskatchewan (SK, Canada)
The U of Scranton (PA)
U of Toledo (OH)
U of Wisconsin–Stout (WI)
U of Wisconsin–Whitewater (WI)
Utah State U (UT)
Washington State U (WA)
Washington U in St. Louis (MO)
Western Washington U (WA)
Widener U (PA)
Wright State U (OH)
Youngstown State U (OH)

OPERATIONS RESEARCH
Babson Coll (MA)
Baruch Coll of the City U of NY (NY)
Boston Coll (MA)
California State U, Fullerton (CA)
Carleton U (ON, Canada)
Columbia U, School of Eng & Applied Sci (NY)
Cornell U (NY)
DePaul U (IL)
Long Island U, Brooklyn Campus (NY)
Mercy Coll (NY)
Miami U (OH)

New York U (NY)
Princeton U (NJ)
United States Air Force Acad (CO)
United States Coast Guard Acad (CT)
United States Military Acad (NY)
Université de Montréal (QC, Canada)
Université de Sherbrooke (QC, Canada)
U of Calif, Berkeley (CA)
U of Cincinnati (OH)
U of Denver (CO)
U of New Brunswick Fredericton (NB, Canada)
U of Waterloo (ON, Canada)
York U (ON, Canada)

OPHTHALMIC AND OPTOMETRIC SUPPORT SERVICES AND ALLIED PROFESSIONS RELATED
Concordia Coll (MN)
Tennessee Wesleyan Coll (TN)

OPHTHALMIC LABORATORY TECHNOLOGY
Abilene Christian U (TX)

OPHTHALMIC/OPTOMETRIC SERVICES
Gannon U (PA)
Indiana U Bloomington (IN)
Northeastern State U (OK)
State U of NY at New Paltz (NY)
State U of NY Coll at Oneonta (NY)
Université de Montréal (QC, Canada)
U of Waterloo (ON, Canada)

OPHTHALMIC TECHNOLOGY
Louisiana State U Health Sciences Center (LA)
Old Dominion U (VA)

OPTICAL SCIENCES
Saginaw Valley State U (MI)
The U of Arizona (AZ)
U of Rochester (NY)

OPTICIANRY
Ferris State U (MI)

ORGANIC CHEMISTRY
California Inst of Technology (CA)
Cornell U (NY)
Sarah Lawrence Coll (NY)

ORGANIZATIONAL BEHAVIOR
Athabasca U (AB, Canada)
Benedictine U (IL)
Bluffton Coll (OH)
Boston U (MA)
Bridgewater Coll (VA)
Brown U (RI)
Calvary Bible Coll and Theological Sem (MO)
Carroll Coll (WI)
Central Baptist Coll (AR)
Chapman U (CA)
The Coll of St. Scholastica (MN)
Concordia U, St. Paul (MN)
Cumberland Coll (KY)
Denison U (OH)
Greenville Coll (IL)
LaGrange Coll (GA)
Manhattan Coll (NY)
McGill U (QC, Canada)
Memorial U of Newfoundland (NL, Canada)
Miami U (OH)
Mid-Continent Coll (KY)
National U (CA)
Northwestern U (IL)
Oakland City U (IN)
Oakland U (MI)
Penn State U Abington Coll (PA)
Penn State U Altoona Coll (PA)
Penn State U at Erie, The Behrend Coll (PA)
Penn State U Beaver Campus of the Commonwealth Coll (PA)
Penn State U Berks Cmps of Berks-Lehigh Valley Coll (PA)
Penn State U Delaware County Campus of the Commonwealth Coll (PA)
Penn State U DuBois Campus of the Commonwealth Coll (PA)
Penn State U Fayette Campus of the Commonwealth Coll (PA)
Penn State U Harrisburg Campus of the Capital Coll (PA)
Penn State U Hazleton Campus of the Commonwealth Coll (PA)
Penn State U Lehigh Valley Cmps of Berks-Lehigh Valley Coll (PA)
Penn State U McKeesport Campus of the Commonwealth Coll (PA)
Penn State U Mont Alto Campus of the Commonwealth Coll (PA)
Penn State U New Kensington Campus of the Commonwealth Coll (PA)
Penn State U Schuylkill Campus of the Capital Coll (PA)
Penn State U Shenango Campus of the Commonwealth Coll (PA)
Penn State U Univ Park Campus (PA)
Penn State U Wilkes-Barre Campus of the Commonwealth Coll (PA)
Penn State U Worthington Scranton Cmps Commonwealth Coll (PA)
Penn State U York Campus of the Commonwealth Coll (PA)
Robert Morris U (PA)
St. Ambrose U (IA)
Saint Augustine's Coll (NC)
Saint Louis U (MO)
Scripps Coll (CA)
Simpson Coll and Graduate School (CA)
Southern Methodist U (TX)
Southern Polytechnic State U (GA)
Thomas Edison State Coll (NJ)
U of Houston (TX)
U of La Verne (CA)
U of Michigan–Flint (MI)
U of North Texas (TX)
U of San Francisco (CA)
The U of Texas at Dallas (TX)
U of the Incarnate Word (TX)
U of Toledo (OH)
Wayne State U (MI)
York U (ON, Canada)

ORGANIZATIONAL COMMUNICATION
Aquinas Coll (MI)
Assumption Coll (MA)
Brigham Young U (UT)
Buena Vista U (IA)
California State U, Chico (CA)
California State U, Sacramento (CA)
Capital U (OH)
Carroll Coll (WI)
The Coll of St. Scholastica (MN)
Dana Coll (NE)
Eastern Washington U (WA)
Emmanuel Coll (GA)
Indiana U–Purdue U Fort Wayne (IN)
Jones Intl U (CO)
Lynchburg Coll (VA)
McKendree Coll (IL)
Montclair State U (NJ)
Ohio Northern U (OH)
Ohio U–Southern Campus (OH)
Palm Beach Atlantic U (FL)
Pfeiffer U (NC)
Shorter Coll (GA)
State U of NY Coll at Brockport (NY)
Toccoa Falls Coll (GA)
U of Houston (TX)
U of Michigan–Flint (MI)
U of Northern Iowa (IA)
U of Windsor (ON, Canada)
Valparaiso U (IN)
Wright State U (OH)

ORNAMENTAL HORTICULTURE
Auburn U (AL)
California Polytechnic State U, San Luis Obispo (CA)
California State Polytechnic U, Pomona (CA)
California State U, Fresno (CA)
Cornell U (NY)
Delaware Valley Coll (PA)
Florida Ag and Mech U (FL)
Florida Southern Coll (FL)
Fort Valley State U (GA)
Iowa State U of Science and Technology (IA)
Tarleton State U (TX)
Texas A&M U (TX)
U of Arkansas (AR)
U of Delaware (DE)
U of Illinois at Urbana–Champaign (IL)
The U of Tennessee (TN)
U of the District of Columbia (DC)
Utah State U (UT)

ORTHOTICS/PROSTHETICS
Eastern Michigan U (MI)
Florida Intl U (FL)
U of Texas Southwestern Medical Center at Dallas (TX)
U of Washington (WA)

PACIFIC AREA/PACIFIC RIM STUDIES
Brigham Young U–Hawaii (HI)
Claremont McKenna Coll (CA)
U of Victoria (BC, Canada)

PAINTING
Acad of Art U (CA)
Alberta Coll of Art & Design (AB, Canada)
American Acad of Art (IL)
Art Acad of Cincinnati (OH)
Art Center Coll of Design (CA)
Atlanta Coll of Art (GA)
Bard Coll (NY)
Bellarmine U (KY)
Bethany Coll (KS)
Birmingham-Southern Coll (AL)
Boston U (MA)
Bowling Green State U (OH)
Brigham Young U (UT)
State U of NY Coll at Buffalo (NY)
California Coll of the Arts (CA)
California State U, Fullerton (CA)
California State U, Hayward (CA)
California State U, Long Beach (CA)
The Catholic U of America (DC)
The Cleveland Inst of Art (OH)
Coe Coll (IA)
Col for Creative Studies (MI)
Coll of Santa Fe (NM)
Coll of Visual Arts (MN)
Colorado State U (CO)
Columbia Coll (MO)
Concordia U (QC, Canada)
Cornell U (NY)
Davis & Elkins Coll (WV)
Drake U (IA)
Escuela de Artes Plasticas de Puerto Rico (PR)
Framingham State Coll (MA)
Grace Coll (IN)
Hampshire Coll (MA)
Harding U (AR)
Henderson State U (AR)
Hofstra U (NY)
Indiana U–Purdue U Fort Wayne (IN)
Kansas City Art Inst (MO)
Laguna Coll of Art & Design (CA)
Lewis U (IL)
Lyme Acad Coll of Fine Arts (CT)
Maine Coll of Art (ME)
Maryland Inst Coll of Art (MD)
Massachusetts Coll of Art (MA)
McMurry U (TX)
Memorial U of Newfoundland (NL, Canada)
Memphis Coll of Art (TN)
Milwaukee Inst of Art and Design (WI)
Minneapolis Coll of Art and Design (MN)
Minnesota State U Moorhead (MN)
Montserrat Coll of Art (MA)
New World School of the Arts (FL)
Northwest Nazarene U (ID)
Nova Scotia Coll of Art and Design (NS, Canada)
Ohio Northern U (OH)
The Ohio State U (OH)
Ohio U (OH)
Pacific Northwest Coll of Art (OR)
Paier Coll of Art, Inc. (CT)
Pratt Inst (NY)
Rhode Island School of Design (RI)
Rivier Coll (NH)
Rocky Mountain Coll of Art & Design (CO)
Rutgers, The State U of New Jersey, New Brunswick/Piscataway (NJ)
St. Cloud State U (MN)
Sam Houston State U (TX)
San Diego State U (CA)
San Francisco Art Inst (CA)
Sarah Lawrence Coll (NY)
Savannah Coll of Art and Design (GA)
School of the Art Inst of Chicago (IL)
School of the Museum of Fine Arts, Boston (MA)
Seton Hill U (PA)
Shawnee State U (OH)
Simon's Rock Coll of Bard (MA)
State U of NY Coll at Brockport (NY)
State U of NY Coll at Potsdam (NY)
Syracuse U (NY)
Texas Christian U (TX)
Trinity Christian Coll (IL)
The U of Akron (OH)
U of Dallas (TX)
U of Hartford (CT)
U of Houston (TX)
U of Illinois at Urbana–Champaign (IL)
The U of Iowa (IA)
U of Kansas (KS)
U of Massachusetts Dartmouth (MA)
U of Miami (FL)
U of Michigan (MI)
U of Michigan–Flint (MI)
U of Missouri–St. Louis (MO)
U of North Texas (TX)
U of Oregon (OR)
U of Regina (SK, Canada)
U of San Francisco (CA)
The U of the Arts (PA)
U of Washington (WA)
U of Windsor (ON, Canada)
Virginia Commonwealth U (VA)
Washington U in St. Louis (MO)
Western Washington U (WA)
West Virginia Wesleyan Coll (WV)
York U (ON, Canada)
Youngstown State U (OH)

PALEONTOLOGY
Mercyhurst Coll (PA)
North Carolina State U (NC)
San Diego State U (CA)
U of Alberta (AB, Canada)
U of Delaware (DE)
U of Toronto (ON, Canada)

PARKS, RECREATION AND LEISURE
Alabama State U (AL)
Alaska Pacific U (AK)
Alcorn State U (MS)
Alderson-Broaddus Coll (WV)
Arizona State U (AZ)
Arizona State U West (AZ)
Ashland U (OH)
Auburn U (AL)
Belmont U (TN)
Bemidji State U (MN)
Bethany Coll (KS)
Black Hills State U (SD)
Bluffton Coll (OH)
Boston U (MA)
Bowling Green State U (OH)
Brevard Coll (NC)
Bridgewater State Coll (MA)
Brigham Young U (UT)
Brock U (ON, Canada)
California Polytechnic State U, San Luis Obispo (CA)
California State U, Chico (CA)
California State U, Dominguez Hills (CA)
California State U, Fresno (CA)
California State U, Hayward (CA)
California State U, Long Beach (CA)
California State U, Sacramento (CA)
Calvin Coll (MI)
Campbellsville U (KY)
Carson-Newman Coll (TN)
Carthage Coll (WI)
Catawba Coll (NC)
Central Christian Coll of Kansas (KS)
Central Michigan U (MI)
Central Missouri State U (MO)
Central State U (OH)
Central Washington U (WA)
Cheyney U of Pennsylvania (PA)
Chicago State U (IL)
Colorado State U-Pueblo (CO)
Concordia U (QC, Canada)
Cumberland U (TN)
Dalhousie U (NS, Canada)
Davis & Elkins Coll (WV)
Dordt Coll (IA)
Eastern Washington U (WA)
Elon U (NC)
Emporia State U (KS)
Evangel U (MO)
Ferris State U (MI)
Ferrum Coll (VA)
Frostburg State U (MD)
Georgetown Coll (KY)
Georgia Coll & State U (GA)
Georgia Southern U (GA)
Gordon Coll (MA)
Graceland U (IA)
Greenville Coll (IL)
High Point U (NC)
Houghton Coll (NY)
Howard Payne U (TX)
Humboldt State U (CA)
Huntingdon Coll (AL)
Huntington Coll (IN)
Indiana U Bloomington (IN)
Ithaca Coll (NY)
Jacksonville State U (AL)
Johnson State Coll (VT)
Lakehead U (ON, Canada)
Lake Superior State U (MI)
Lock Haven U of Pennsylvania (PA)
Lyndon State Coll (VT)
Mars Hill Coll (NC)
Maryville Coll (TN)
Marywood U (PA)
Memorial U of Newfoundland (NL, Canada)
Messiah Coll (PA)
Metropolitan State Coll of Denver (CO)
Minnesota State U Mankato (MN)
Missouri Valley Coll (MO)
Montclair State U (NJ)
Montreat Coll (NC)
Morgan State U (MD)
Morris Coll (SC)
North Dakota State U (ND)
Northern Arizona U (AZ)
Northern Michigan U (MI)
Northland Coll (WI)
Northwest Nazarene U (ID)
Ohio U (OH)
Oklahoma Baptist U (OK)
Oklahoma Panhandle State U (OK)
Oregon State U (OR)
Pacific Union Coll (CA)
Radford U (VA)
Redeemer U Coll (ON, Canada)
St. Joseph's Coll, Suffolk Campus (NY)
St. Thomas Aquinas Coll (NY)
Salem State Coll (MA)
San Diego State U (CA)
San Francisco State U (CA)
San Jose State U (CA)
Shaw U (NC)
Sheldon Jackson Coll (AK)
Shepherd U (WV)
Shorter Coll (GA)
South Dakota State U (SD)
Southeastern Oklahoma State U (OK)
Southeast Missouri State U (MO)
Southern Connecticut State U (CT)
Southern Illinois U Carbondale (IL)
Southern Wesleyan U (SC)
Southwest Baptist U (MO)
Southwestern Oklahoma State U (OK)
Southwest Missouri State U (MO)
Springfield Coll (MA)
State U of NY Coll at Brockport (NY)
State U of NY Coll at Cortland (NY)
State U of NY Coll of Environ Sci and Forestry (NY)
Sterling Coll (VT)
Taylor U (IN)
Tennessee State U (TN)
Tennessee Wesleyan Coll (TN)
Texas A&M U (TX)
Texas Tech U (TX)
Thomas Edison State Coll (NJ)
Troy State U (AL)
Tyndale U Coll & Sem (ON, Canada)
U of Alberta (AB, Canada)
U of Arkansas (AR)
U of Calgary (AB, Canada)
U of Dubuque (IA)
U of Hawaii at Manoa (HI)
U of Idaho (ID)
U of Illinois at Urbana–Champaign (IL)
The U of Iowa (IA)
The U of Lethbridge (AB, Canada)
U of Maine at Machias (ME)
U of Maine at Presque Isle (ME)
U of Mary Hardin-Baylor (TX)
U of Michigan (MI)
U of Minnesota, Duluth (MN)
U of Mississippi (MS)
U of Missouri–Columbia (MO)
The U of Montana–Missoula (MT)
U of Nebraska at Omaha (NE)
U of Nevada, Las Vegas (NV)
U of Nevada, Reno (NV)
U of New Brunswick Fredericton (NB, Canada)
U of New Hampshire (NH)
U of New Mexico (NM)
The U of North Carolina at Greensboro (NC)
U of Northern Iowa (IA)

U of Ottawa (ON, Canada)
U of Saskatchewan (SK, Canada)
U of South Alabama (AL)
The U of South Dakota (SD)
The U of Tennessee at Chattanooga (TN)
U of the District of Columbia (DC)
U of Toledo (OH)
U of Utah (UT)
U of Vermont (VT)
U of Waterloo (ON, Canada)
U of Windsor (ON, Canada)
U of Wisconsin–Madison (WI)
U of Wisconsin–Milwaukee (WI)
Upper Iowa U (IA)
Utah State U (UT)
Virginia Wesleyan Coll (VA)
Wayne State Coll (NE)
Wayne State U (MI)
Wesley Coll (DE)
Western Michigan U (MI)
Western State Coll of Colorado (CO)
Western Washington U (WA)
Westfield State Coll (MA)
West Virginia State Coll (WV)
West Virginia U (WV)
William Paterson U of New Jersey (NJ)
William Penn U (IA)
Wingate U (NC)
Winona State U (MN)
York Coll of Pennsylvania (PA)

PARKS, RECREATION AND LEISURE FACILITIES MANAGEMENT
Appalachian State U (NC)
Arkansas Tech U (AR)
Asbury Coll (KY)
Ball State U (IN)
California State U, Chico (CA)
California State U, Sacramento (CA)
California U of Pennsylvania (PA)
Central Michigan U (MI)
Clemson U (SC)
Coll of St. Joseph (VT)
Coll of the Ozarks (MO)
Colorado State U (CO)
Concord Coll (WV)
Delaware State U (DE)
East Carolina U (NC)
Eastern Illinois U (IL)
Eastern Kentucky U (KY)
Eastern Michigan U (MI)
Eastern Washington U (WA)
East Stroudsburg U of Pennsylvania (PA)
Florida Ag and Mech U (FL)
Florida Intl U (FL)
Florida State U (FL)
Franklin Pierce Coll (NH)
Georgia Southwestern State U (GA)
Georgia State U (GA)
Grand Valley State U (MI)
Hannibal-LaGrange Coll (MO)
Hastings Coll (NE)
Henderson State U (AR)
High Point U (NC)
Humboldt State U (CA)
Illinois State U (IL)
Indiana Inst of Technology (IN)
Indiana State U (IN)
Indiana U Bloomington (IN)
Indiana U Southeast (IN)
Inter American U of PR, Aguadilla Campus (PR)
John Brown U (AR)
Johnson & Wales U (RI)
Kansas State U (KS)
Kean U (NJ)
Kent State U (OH)
Keystone Coll (PA)
Lake Superior State U (MI)
Lyndon State Coll (VT)
Lynn U (FL)
Marshall U (WV)
Methodist Coll (NC)
Michigan State U (MI)
Middle Tennessee State U (TN)
Minnesota State U Mankato (MN)
Missouri Valley Coll (MO)
Missouri Western State Coll (MO)
Montclair State U (NJ)
Mount Marty Coll (SD)
Murray State U (KY)
New Mexico State U (NM)
North Carolina Central U (NC)
North Carolina State U (NC)
Northland Coll (WI)
Oak Hills Christian Coll (MN)
Ohio U (OH)
Old Dominion U (VA)
Oregon State U (OR)
Penn State U Abington Coll (PA)
Penn State U Altoona Coll (PA)
Penn State U at Erie, The Behrend Coll (PA)
Penn State U Beaver Campus of the Commonwealth Coll (PA)
Penn State U Berks Cmps of Berks-Lehigh Valley Coll (PA)
Penn State U Delaware County Campus of the Commonwealth Coll (PA)
Penn State U DuBois Campus of the Commonwealth Coll (PA)
Penn State U Fayette Campus of the Commonwealth Coll (PA)
Penn State U Hazleton Campus of the Commonwealth Coll (PA)
Penn State U Lehigh Valley Cmps of Berks-Lehigh Valley Coll (PA)
Penn State U McKeesport Campus of the Commonwealth Coll (PA)
Penn State U Mont Alto Campus of the Commonwealth Coll (PA)
Penn State U New Kensington Campus of the Commonwealth Coll (PA)
Penn State U Schuylkill Campus of the Capital Coll (PA)
Penn State U Shenango Campus of the Commonwealth Coll (PA)
Penn State U Univ Park Campus (PA)
Penn State U Wilkes-Barre Campus of the Commonwealth Coll (PA)
Penn State U Worthington Scranton Cmps Commonwealth Coll (PA)
Penn State U York Campus of the Commonwealth Coll (PA)
Slippery Rock U of Pennsylvania (PA)
South Dakota State U (SD)
Southern Virginia U (VA)
Springfield Coll (MA)
State U of NY Coll at Cortland (NY)
State U of West Georgia (GA)
Sterling Coll (VT)
Texas A&M U (TX)
Texas State U-San Marcos (TX)
Thomas U (GA)
Tri-State U (IN)
Union Coll (KY)
Union U (TN)
Unity Coll (ME)
U of Alberta (AB, Canada)
U of Arkansas (AR)
The U of British Columbia (BC, Canada)
U of Connecticut (CT)
U of Delaware (DE)
U of Florida (FL)
U of Houston–Clear Lake (TX)
U of Maine (ME)
U of Maine at Machias (ME)
U of Minnesota, Twin Cities Campus (MN)
The U of North Carolina at Chapel Hill (NC)
The U of North Carolina at Greensboro (NC)
The U of North Carolina at Pembroke (NC)
The U of North Carolina at Wilmington (NC)
U of North Dakota (ND)
U of Northern Colorado (CO)
U of North Texas (TX)
U of St. Francis (IL)
The U of Tennessee (TN)
The U of Tennessee at Martin (TN)
U of Utah (UT)
U of Vermont (VT)
U of Waterloo (ON, Canada)
U of Wisconsin–La Crosse (WI)
U of Wyoming (WY)
Virginia Commonwealth U (VA)
Western Carolina U (NC)
Western Illinois U (IL)
Western Kentucky U (KY)
Western State Coll of Colorado (CO)
West Virginia U (WV)
Winona State U (MN)

PARKS, RECREATION, AND LEISURE RELATED
Brigham Young U (UT)
Chadron State Coll (NE)
Coker Coll (SC)
Culver-Stockton Coll (MO)
Franklin Coll (IN)
Lambuth U (TN)
Madonna U (MI)
Malone Coll (OH)
North Carolina State U (NC)
Plymouth State U (NH)
Providence Coll and Theological Sem (MB, Canada)
Roosevelt U (IL)
St. Edward's U (TX)
Southern Wesleyan U (SC)
State U of NY Coll at Brockport (NY)
U of North Alabama (AL)
U of Toledo (OH)
U of Waterloo (ON, Canada)
Utah State U (UT)
Washington State U (WA)

PASTORAL COUNSELING AND SPECIALIZED MINISTRIES RELATED
Calvary Bible Coll and Theological Sem (MO)
Central Pentecostal Coll (SK, Canada)
Coll of Mount St. Joseph (OH)
Crossroads Bible Coll (IN)
Greenville Coll (IL)
Harding U (AR)
Lancaster Bible Coll (PA)
Malone Coll (OH)
Multnomah Bible Coll and Biblical Sem (OR)
Ouachita Baptist U (AR)
Prairie Bible Coll (AB, Canada)
St. John's U (NY)
Trinity Intl U (IL)
U of Mary (ND)
Vennard Coll (IA)

PASTORAL STUDIES/ COUNSELING
Abilene Christian U (TX)
American Indian Coll of the Assemblies of God, Inc (AZ)
Baptist Bible Coll (MO)
The Baptist Coll of Florida (FL)
Barclay Coll (KS)
Belhaven Coll (MS)
Bellarmine U (KY)
Belmont U (TN)
Bethany Coll (SK, Canada)
Bethel Coll (IN)
Bethesda Christian U (CA)
Biola U (CA)
Briercrest Bible Coll (SK, Canada)
Calvary Bible Coll and Theological Sem (MO)
Campbellsville U (KY)
Campbell U (NC)
Canadian Mennonite U (MB, Canada)
Cedarville U (OH)
Central Christian Coll of Kansas (KS)
Central Pentecostal Coll (SK, Canada)
Charleston Southern U (SC)
Christian Heritage Coll (CA)
Clearwater Christian Coll (FL)
Coll of Santa Fe (NM)
Columbia Intl U (SC)
Concordia U (IL)
Concordia U (NE)
Concordia U Wisconsin (WI)
Cornerstone U (MI)
Crown Coll (MN)
Dallas Baptist U (TX)
Dordt Coll (IA)
East Texas Baptist U (TX)
Emmanuel Coll (GA)
Eugene Bible Coll (OR)
Faith Baptist Bible Coll and Theological Sem (IA)
Faulkner U (AL)
Fresno Pacific U (CA)
Gardner-Webb U (NC)
George Fox U (OR)
Global U of the Assemblies of God (MO)
God's Bible School and Coll (OH)
Grace Bible Coll (MI)
Grace Coll (IN)
Grace U (NE)
Greenville Coll (IL)
Harding U (AR)
Hardin-Simmons U (TX)
Houghton Coll (NY)
John Brown U (AR)
John Wesley Coll (NC)
Kentucky Christian Coll (KY)
Lancaster Bible Coll (PA)
Lenoir-Rhyne Coll (NC)
Liberty U (VA)
Life Pacific Coll (CA)
Lindenwood U (MO)
Madonna U (MI)
Manhattan Christian Coll (KS)
Marylhurst U (OR)
The Master's Coll and Sem (CA)
Messenger Coll (MO)
Milligan Coll (TN)
Multnomah Bible Coll and Biblical Sem (OR)
Newman U (KS)
North Central U (MN)
North Greenville Coll (SC)
Northwest Nazarene U (ID)
Notre Dame Coll (OH)
Nyack Coll (NY)
Oklahoma Baptist U (OK)
Olivet Nazarene U (IL)
Oral Roberts U (OK)
Ouachita Baptist U (AR)
Pacific Union Coll (CA)
Pillsbury Baptist Bible Coll (MN)
Prairie Bible Coll (AB, Canada)
Providence Coll (RI)
Providence Coll and Theological Sem (MB, Canada)
Reformed Bible Coll (MI)
Roberts Wesleyan Coll (NY)
Rochester Coll (MI)
Rocky Mountain Coll (AB, Canada)
Saint Francis U (PA)
St. Gregory's U (OK)
Saint Joseph's Coll (IN)
Saint Mary-of-the-Woods Coll (IN)
St. Thomas U (FL)
Southeastern Bible Coll (AL)
Southeastern Coll of the Assemblies of God (FL)
Southern Christian U (AL)
Southwest Baptist U (MO)
Southwestern Coll (KS)
Tabor Coll (KS)
Taylor U, Fort Wayne Campus (IN)
Trinity Baptist Coll (FL)
Trinity Bible Coll (ND)
Trinity Coll of Florida (FL)
Tyndale U Coll & Sem (ON, Canada)
Union Coll (NE)
Universidad Adventista de las Antillas (PR)
U of Ottawa (ON, Canada)
U of Saint Mary (KS)
U of St. Thomas (TX)
U of Sioux Falls (SD)
Vanguard U of Southern California (CA)
Vennard Coll (IA)
Walsh U (OH)
Warner Pacific Coll (OR)
Western Baptist Coll (OR)
William Jessup U (CA)
Williams Baptist Coll (AR)
William Tyndale Coll (MI)

PATHOLOGIST ASSISTANT
St. John's U (NY)

PATHOLOGY/EXPERIMENTAL PATHOLOGY
U of Calif, Los Angeles (CA)
U of Connecticut (CT)

PEACE STUDIES AND CONFLICT RESOLUTION
American U (DC)
Antioch Coll (OH)
Bethel Coll (KS)
Canadian Mennonite U (MB, Canada)
Chapman U (CA)
Clark U (MA)
Colgate U (NY)
Coll of Saint Benedict (MN)
Coll of the Holy Cross (MA)
Cornell U (NY)
DePauw U (IN)
Earlham Coll (IN)
Eastern Mennonite U (VA)
Elizabethtown Coll (PA)
Fordham U (NY)
Gettysburg Coll (PA)
Goshen Coll (IN)
Guilford Coll (NC)
Hamline U (MN)
Hampshire Coll (MA)
Haverford Coll (PA)
Juniata Coll (PA)
Kent State U (OH)
Le Moyne Coll (NY)
Manchester Coll (IN)
Molloy Coll (NY)
Mount Saint Vincent U (NS, Canada)
Northland Coll (WI)
Ohio Dominican U (OH)
The Ohio State U (OH)
Saint John's U (MN)
Salisbury U (MD)
U of Calif, Berkeley (CA)
U of Calif, Santa Cruz (CA)
U of Missouri–Columbia (MO)
The U of North Carolina at Chapel Hill (NC)
U of St. Thomas (MN)
U of Wisconsin–Milwaukee (WI)
Wayne State U (MI)
Wellesley Coll (MA)
Whitworth Coll (WA)

PEDIATRIC NURSING
British Columbia Inst of Technology (BC, Canada)
U at Buffalo, The State U of New York (NY)

PERFUSION TECHNOLOGY
Medical U of South Carolina (SC)
Rush U (IL)
State U of New York Upstate Medical U (NY)
Thomas Edison State Coll (NJ)

PERIOPERATIVE/OPERATING ROOM AND SURGICAL NURSING
British Columbia Inst of Technology (BC, Canada)
Murray State U (KY)
Texas A&M Intl U (TX)

PERSONAL AND CULINARY SERVICES RELATED
Lexington Coll (IL)

PERSONALITY PSYCHOLOGY
Cornell U (NY)

PETROLEUM ENGINEERING
California State Polytechnic U, Pomona (CA)
Colorado School of Mines (CO)
Louisiana State U and A&M Coll (LA)
Marietta Coll (OH)
Montana Tech of The U of Montana (MT)
New Mexico Inst of Mining and Technology (NM)
Penn State U Abington Coll (PA)
Penn State U Altoona Coll (PA)
Penn State U at Erie, The Behrend Coll (PA)
Penn State U Beaver Campus of the Commonwealth Coll (PA)
Penn State U Berks Cmps of Berks-Lehigh Valley Coll (PA)
Penn State U Delaware County Campus of the Commonwealth Coll (PA)
Penn State U DuBois Campus of the Commonwealth Coll (PA)
Penn State U Fayette Campus of the Commonwealth Coll (PA)
Penn State U Hazleton Campus of the Commonwealth Coll (PA)
Penn State U Lehigh Valley Cmps of Berks-Lehigh Valley Coll (PA)
Penn State U McKeesport Campus of the Commonwealth Coll (PA)
Penn State U Mont Alto Campus of the Commonwealth Coll (PA)
Penn State U New Kensington Campus of the Commonwealth Coll (PA)
Penn State U Schuylkill Campus of the Capital Coll (PA)
Penn State U Shenango Campus of the Commonwealth Coll (PA)
Penn State U Univ Park Campus (PA)
Penn State U Wilkes-Barre Campus of the Commonwealth Coll (PA)
Penn State U Worthington Scranton Cmps Commonwealth Coll (PA)
Penn State U York Campus of the Commonwealth Coll (PA)
Stanford U (CA)
Texas A&M U (TX)
Texas A&M U–Kingsville (TX)
Texas Tech U (TX)
U of Alaska Fairbanks (AK)
U of Alberta (AB, Canada)
U of Kansas (KS)
U of Louisiana at Lafayette (LA)
U of Missouri–Rolla (MO)
U of Oklahoma (OK)
U of Regina (SK, Canada)
U of Southern California (CA)
The U of Texas at Austin (TX)
U of Toronto (ON, Canada)
U of Tulsa (OK)
West Virginia U (WV)

PETROLEUM TECHNOLOGY
Mercyhurst Coll (PA)
Nicholls State U (LA)
Southern Alberta Inst of Technology (AB, Canada)

PHARMACOLOGY
Belmont U (TN)
Campbell U (NC)
Hunter Coll of the City U of NY (NY)
Stony Brook U, State U of New York (NY)
U at Buffalo, The State U of New York (NY)
U of Alberta (AB, Canada)
The U of British Columbia (BC, Canada)
U of Calif, Santa Barbara (CA)
U of Cincinnati (OH)
U of Toronto (ON, Canada)
The U of Western Ontario (ON, Canada)
U of Wisconsin–Madison (WI)

PHARMACOLOGY AND TOXICOLOGY
U of the Sciences in Philadelphia (PA)
Washington State U (WA)
Wright State U (OH)

PHARMACY
Albany Coll of Pharmacy of Union U (NY)
Briar Cliff U (IA)
Butler U (IN)
Campbell U (NC)
Dalhousie U (NS, Canada)
Drake U (IA)
Eastern Nazarene Coll (MA)
Florida Ag and Mech U (FL)
Howard U (DC)
Long Island U, Brooklyn Campus (NY)
Mass Coll of Pharmacy and Allied Health Sciences (MA)
Memorial U of Newfoundland (NL, Canada)
North Dakota State U (ND)
Northeastern U (MA)
Ohio Northern U (OH)
The Ohio State U (OH)
Oregon State U (OR)
Purdue U (IN)
Rutgers, The State U of New Jersey, New Brunswick/Piscataway (NJ)
St. John's U (NY)
St. Louis Coll of Pharmacy (MO)
Saint Vincent Coll (PA)
Simmons Coll (MA)
South Dakota State U (SD)
Southwestern Oklahoma State U (OK)
Texas Southern U (TX)
Université de Montréal (QC, Canada)
Université Laval (QC, Canada)
U of Alberta (AB, Canada)
The U of British Columbia (BC, Canada)
U of Cincinnati (OH)
U of Connecticut (CT)
U of Georgia (GA)
U of Houston (TX)
The U of Iowa (IA)
U of Kansas (KS)
U of Manitoba (MB, Canada)
U of Michigan (MI)
U of Mississippi (MS)
U of Missouri–Kansas City (MO)
The U of Montana–Missoula (MT)
U of New Mexico (NM)
U of Pittsburgh (PA)
U of Rhode Island (RI)
U of Saskatchewan (SK, Canada)
U of the Pacific (CA)
U of Toledo (OH)
U of Toronto (ON, Canada)
U of Utah (UT)
U of Washington (WA)
U of Wisconsin–Madison (WI)
Wayne State U (MI)
West Virginia U (WV)

PHARMACY ADMINISTRATION/ PHARMACEUTICS
DeSales U (PA)
Drake U (IA)
U at Buffalo, The State U of New York (NY)

PHARMACY, PHARMACEUTICAL SCIENCES, AND ADMINISTRATION RELATED
Albany Coll of Pharmacy of Union U (NY)
Campbell U (NC)
Dalhousie U (NS, Canada)
Duquesne U (PA)
Ferris State U (MI)
Long Island U, Brooklyn Campus (NY)
Mass Coll of Pharmacy and Allied Health Sciences (MA)
Ohio Northern U (OH)
St. John's U (NY)
Université Laval (QC, Canada)
U at Buffalo, The State U of New York (NY)
U of Connecticut (CT)
U of the Sciences in Philadelphia (PA)
U of Toledo (OH)
U of Utah (UT)

PHARMACY TECHNICIAN
The U of Montana–Missoula (MT)

PHILOSOPHY
Acadia U (NS, Canada)
Adelphi U (NY)
Agnes Scott Coll (GA)
Albertson Coll of Idaho (ID)
Albertus Magnus Coll (CT)
Albion Coll (MI)
Albright Coll (PA)
Alfred U (NY)
Allegheny Coll (PA)
Alma Coll (MI)
Alvernia Coll (PA)
Alverno Coll (WI)
American Intl Coll (MA)
American U (DC)
The American U in Cairo(Egypt)
Amherst Coll (MA)
Anna Maria Coll (MA)
Antioch Coll (OH)
Aquinas Coll (MI)
Arcadia U (PA)
Arizona State U (AZ)
Arkansas State U (AR)
Asbury Coll (KY)
Ashland U (OH)
Assumption Coll (MA)
Auburn U (AL)
Augsburg Coll (MN)
Augustana Coll (IL)
Augustana Coll (SD)
Aurora U (IL)
Austin Coll (TX)
Austin Peay State U (TN)
Ave Maria Coll (MI)
Ave Maria U (FL)
Azusa Pacific U (CA)
Baker U (KS)
Baldwin-Wallace Coll (OH)
Ball State U (IN)
Bard Coll (NY)
Barnard Coll (NY)
Barry U (FL)
Bates Coll (ME)
Baylor U (TX)
Belhaven Coll (MS)
Bellarmine U (KY)
Belmont Abbey Coll (NC)
Belmont U (TN)
Beloit Coll (WI)
Bemidji State U (MN)
Benedictine Coll (KS)
Benedictine U (IL)
Bennington Coll (VT)
Bentley Coll (MA)
Berea Coll (KY)
Baruch Coll of the City U of NY (NY)
Bethany Coll (KS)
Bethany Coll (WV)
Bethel Coll (IN)
Bethel U (MN)
Biola U (CA)
Birmingham-Southern Coll (AL)
Bishop's U (QC, Canada)
Bloomfield Coll (NJ)
Bloomsburg U of Pennsylvania (PA)
Bluefield Coll (VA)
Boise State U (ID)
Boston Coll (MA)
Boston U (MA)
Bowdoin Coll (ME)
Bowling Green State U (OH)
Bradley U (IL)
Brandeis U (MA)
Briar Cliff U (IA)
Bridgewater State Coll (MA)
Brigham Young U (UT)
Brock U (ON, Canada)
Brooklyn Coll of the City U of NY (NY)
Brown U (RI)
Bryn Mawr Coll (PA)
Bucknell U (PA)
State U of NY Coll at Buffalo (NY)
Butler U (IN)
Cabrini Coll (PA)
California Baptist U (CA)
California Lutheran U (CA)
California Polytechnic State U, San Luis Obispo (CA)
California State Polytechnic U, Pomona (CA)
California State U, Chico (CA)
California State U, Dominguez Hills (CA)
California State U, Fresno (CA)
California State U, Fullerton (CA)
California State U, Hayward (CA)
California State U, Long Beach (CA)
California State U, Los Angeles (CA)
California State U, Sacramento (CA)
California State U, San Bernardino (CA)
California State U, Stanislaus (CA)
California U of Pennsylvania (PA)
Calvin Coll (MI)
Canadian Mennonite U (MB, Canada)
Canisius Coll (NY)
Capital U (OH)
Carleton Coll (MN)
Carleton U (ON, Canada)
Carlow Coll (PA)
Carnegie Mellon U (PA)
Carroll Coll (MT)
Carson-Newman Coll (TN)
Carthage Coll (WI)
Case Western Reserve U (OH)
Catawba Coll (NC)
The Catholic U of America (DC)
Cedarville U (OH)
Centenary Coll of Louisiana (LA)
Central Coll (IA)
Central Connecticut State U (CT)
Central Methodist Coll (MO)
Central Michigan U (MI)
Central Washington U (WA)
Centre Coll (KY)
Chaminade U of Honolulu (HI)
Chapman U (CA)
Christendom Coll (VA)
Christopher Newport U (VA)
City Coll of the City U of NY (NY)
Claremont McKenna Coll (CA)
Clarion U of Pennsylvania (PA)
Clark Atlanta U (GA)
Clarke Coll (IA)
Clark U (MA)
Clemson U (SC)
Cleveland State U (OH)
Coastal Carolina U (SC)
Coe Coll (IA)
Colby Coll (ME)
Colgate U (NY)
Coll Misericordia (PA)
Coll of Charleston (SC)
Coll of Mount Saint Vincent (NY)
The Coll of New Jersey (NJ)
The Coll of New Rochelle (NY)
Coll of Saint Benedict (MN)
Coll of St. Catherine (MN)
Coll of Saint Elizabeth (NJ)
The Coll of Southeastern Europe, The American U of Athens(Greece)
Coll of Staten Island of the City U of NY (NY)
Coll of the Atlantic (ME)
Coll of the Holy Cross (MA)
Coll of the Ozarks (MO)
The Coll of William and Mary (VA)
The Coll of Wooster (OH)
The Colorado Coll (CO)
Colorado State U (CO)
Columbia Coll (NY)
Columbia U, School of General Studies (NY)
Concordia Coll (MN)
Concordia U (IL)
Concordia U (QC, Canada)
Concordia U Coll of Alberta (AB, Canada)
Connecticut Coll (CT)
Cornell Coll (IA)
Cornell U (NY)
Cornerstone U (MI)
Covenant Coll (GA)
Creighton U (NE)
Curry Coll (MA)
Dakota Wesleyan U (SD)
Dalhousie U (NS, Canada)
Dallas Baptist U (TX)
Dartmouth Coll (NH)
Davidson Coll (NC)
Denison U (OH)
DePaul U (IL)
DePauw U (IN)
DeSales U (PA)
Dickinson Coll (PA)
Doane Coll (NE)
Dominican U (IL)
Dordt Coll (IA)
Dowling Coll (NY)
Drake U (IA)
Drew U (NJ)
Drury U (MO)
Duke U (NC)
Duquesne U (PA)
D'Youville Coll (NY)
Earlham Coll (IN)
East Carolina U (NC)
Eastern Illinois U (IL)
Eastern Kentucky U (KY)
Eastern Michigan U (MI)
Eastern U (PA)
Eastern Washington U (WA)
East Stroudsburg U of Pennsylvania (PA)
Eckerd Coll (FL)
Edinboro U of Pennsylvania (PA)
Elizabethtown Coll (PA)
Elmhurst Coll (IL)
Elmira Coll (NY)
Elon U (NC)
Emory & Henry Coll (VA)
Emory U (GA)
Erskine Coll (SC)
Eugene Lang Coll, New School U (NY)
Eureka Coll (IL)
Excelsior Coll (NY)
Fairfield U (CT)
Fairleigh Dickinson U, Florham (NJ)
Fairleigh Dickinson U, Teaneck-Metro Campus (NJ)
Ferrum Coll (VA)
Flagler Coll (FL)
Florida Ag and Mech U (FL)
Florida Atlantic U (FL)
Florida Intl U (FL)
Florida State U (FL)
Fordham U (NY)
Fort Hays State U (KS)
Fort Lewis Coll (CO)
Franciscan U of Steubenville (OH)
Franklin and Marshall Coll (PA)
Franklin Coll (IN)
Freed-Hardeman U (TN)
Frostburg State U (MD)
Furman U (SC)
Gallaudet U (DC)
Gannon U (PA)
Geneva Coll (PA)
George Mason U (VA)
Georgetown Coll (KY)
Georgetown U (DC)
The George Washington U (DC)
Georgia Southern U (GA)
Georgia State U (GA)
Gettysburg Coll (PA)
Gonzaga U (WA)
Gordon Coll (MA)
Goucher Coll (MD)
Grand Valley State U (MI)
Greenville Coll (IL)
Grinnell Coll (IA)
Grove City Coll (PA)
Guilford Coll (NC)
Gustavus Adolphus Coll (MN)
Hamilton Coll (NY)
Hamline U (MN)
Hampden-Sydney Coll (VA)
Hampshire Coll (MA)
Hanover Coll (IN)
Hardin-Simmons U (TX)
Hartwick Coll (NY)
Harvard U (MA)
Hastings Coll (NE)
Haverford Coll (PA)
Heidelberg Coll (OH)
Hendrix Coll (AR)
High Point U (NC)
Hillsdale Coll (MI)
Hiram Coll (OH)
Hobart and William Smith Colls (NY)
Hofstra U (NY)
Hollins U (VA)
Holy Names Coll (CA)
Hood Coll (MD)
Hope Coll (MI)
Houghton Coll (NY)
Howard Payne U (TX)
Howard U (DC)
Humboldt State U (CA)
Hunter Coll of the City U of NY (NY)
Huntington Coll (IN)
Idaho State U (ID)
Illinois Coll (IL)
Illinois State U (IL)
Illinois Wesleyan U (IL)
Indiana State U (IN)
Indiana U Bloomington (IN)
Indiana U Northwest (IN)
Indiana U of Pennsylvania (PA)
Indiana U–Purdue U Fort Wayne (IN)
Indiana U–Purdue U Indianapolis (IN)
Indiana U South Bend (IN)
Indiana U Southeast (IN)
Iona Coll (NY)
Iowa State U of Science and Technology (IA)
Ithaca Coll (NY)
Jacksonville U (FL)
Jamestown Coll (ND)
Jewish Theological Sem of America (NY)
John Carroll U (OH)
The Johns Hopkins U (MD)
Judson Coll (IL)
Juniata Coll (PA)
Kalamazoo Coll (MI)
Kansas State U (KS)
Kent State U (OH)
Kentucky Wesleyan Coll (KY)
Kenyon Coll (OH)
King's Coll (PA)
The King's U Coll (AB, Canada)
Knox Coll (IL)
Kutztown U of Pennsylvania (PA)
Lafayette Coll (PA)
Lake Forest Coll (IL)
Lakehead U (ON, Canada)
La Salle U (PA)
Laurentian U (ON, Canada)
Lawrence U (WI)
Lebanon Valley Coll (PA)
Lehigh U (PA)
Lehman Coll of the City U of NY (NY)
Le Moyne Coll (NY)
Lenoir-Rhyne Coll (NC)
Lewis & Clark Coll (OR)
Lewis U (IL)
Liberty U (VA)
Lincoln U (MO)
Lincoln U (PA)
Linfield Coll (OR)
Lipscomb U (TN)
Lock Haven U of Pennsylvania (PA)
Long Island U, Brooklyn Campus (NY)
Long Island U, C.W. Post Campus (NY)
Loras Coll (IA)
Louisiana Coll (LA)
Louisiana State U and A&M Coll (LA)
Loyola Coll in Maryland (MD)
Loyola Marymount U (CA)
Loyola U Chicago (IL)
Loyola U New Orleans (LA)
Luther Coll (IA)
Lycoming Coll (PA)
Lynchburg Coll (VA)
Macalester Coll (MN)
MacMurray Coll (IL)
Madonna U (MI)
Manchester Coll (IN)
Manhattan Coll (NY)
Manhattanville Coll (NY)
Mansfield U of Pennsylvania (PA)
Marian Coll (IN)
Marietta Coll (OH)
Marlboro Coll (VT)
Marquette U (WI)
Mary Baldwin Coll (VA)
Marymount U (VA)
Mary Washington Coll (VA)
Massachusetts Coll of Liberal Arts (MA)
Massachusetts Inst of Technology (MA)
McDaniel Coll (MD)
McGill U (QC, Canada)
McKendree Coll (IL)
McMurry U (TX)
McPherson Coll (KS)
Memorial U of Newfoundland (NL, Canada)
Mercer U (GA)
Mercyhurst Coll (PA)
Merrimack Coll (MA)
Messiah Coll (PA)
Metropolitan State Coll of Denver (CO)
Metropolitan State U (MN)

Miami U (OH)
Miami U Hamilton (OH)
Michigan State U (MI)
Middlebury Coll (VT)
Middle Tennessee State U (TN)
Millersville U of Pennsylvania (PA)
Millikin U (IL)
Millsaps Coll (MS)
Mills Coll (CA)
Minnesota State U Mankato (MN)
Minnesota State U Moorhead (MN)
Mississippi State U (MS)
Missouri Valley Coll (MO)
Molloy Coll (NY)
Monmouth Coll (IL)
Montana State U–Bozeman (MT)
Montclair State U (NJ)
Moravian Coll (PA)
Morehead State U (KY)
Morehouse Coll (GA)
Morgan State U (MD)
Morningside Coll (IA)
Mount Allison U (NB, Canada)
Mount Holyoke Coll (MA)
Mount Mary Coll (WI)
Mount St. Mary's Coll (CA)
Mount Saint Mary's Coll and Sem (MD)
Mount Saint Vincent U (NS, Canada)
Mount Union Coll (OH)
Mount Vernon Nazarene U (OH)
Muhlenberg Coll (PA)
Murray State U (KY)
Nazareth Coll of Rochester (NY)
Nebraska Wesleyan U (NE)
Newberry Coll (SC)
New Coll of Florida (FL)
New Jersey City U (NJ)
New Mexico State U (NM)
New York U (NY)
Niagara U (NY)
Nipissing U (ON, Canada)
North Carolina State U (NC)
North Carolina Wesleyan Coll (NC)
North Central Coll (IL)
North Dakota State U (ND)
Northeastern Illinois U (IL)
Northeastern U (MA)
Northern Arizona U (AZ)
Northern Illinois U (IL)
Northern Michigan U (MI)
Northland Coll (WI)
North Park U (IL)
Northwestern Coll (IA)
Northwestern U (IL)
Northwest Nazarene U (ID)
Notre Dame de Namur U (CA)
Nyack Coll (NY)
Oakland U (MI)
Oberlin Coll (OH)
Occidental Coll (CA)
Oglethorpe U (GA)
Ohio Dominican U (OH)
Ohio Northern U (OH)
The Ohio State U (OH)
Ohio U (OH)
Ohio Wesleyan U (OH)
Okanagan U Coll (BC, Canada)
Oklahoma Baptist U (OK)
Oklahoma City U (OK)
Oklahoma State U (OK)
Old Dominion U (VA)
Olivet Nazarene U (IL)
Oral Roberts U (OK)
Oregon State U (OR)
Otterbein Coll (OH)
Ouachita Baptist U (AR)
Our Lady of the Lake U of San Antonio (TX)
Pacific Lutheran U (WA)
Pacific U (OR)
Paine Coll (GA)
Palm Beach Atlantic U (FL)
Penn State U Abington Coll (PA)
Penn State U Altoona Coll (PA)
Penn State U at Erie, The Behrend Coll (PA)
Penn State U Beaver Campus of the Commonwealth Coll (PA)
Penn State U Berks Cmps of Berks-Lehigh Valley Coll (PA)
Penn State U Delaware County Campus of the Commonwealth Coll (PA)
Penn State U DuBois Campus of the Commonwealth Coll (PA)
Penn State U Fayette Campus of the Commonwealth Coll (PA)
Penn State U Hazleton Campus of the Commonwealth Coll (PA)
Penn State U Lehigh Valley Cmps of Berks-Lehigh Valley Coll (PA)
Penn State U McKeesport Campus of the Commonwealth Coll (PA)
Penn State U Mont Alto Campus of the Commonwealth Coll (PA)
Penn State U New Kensington Campus of the Commonwealth Coll (PA)
Penn State U Schuylkill Campus of the Capital Coll (PA)
Penn State U Shenango Campus of the Commonwealth Coll (PA)
Penn State U Univ Park Campus (PA)
Penn State U Wilkes-Barre Campus of the Commonwealth Coll (PA)
Penn State U Worthington Scranton Cmps Commonwealth Coll (PA)
Penn State U York Campus of the Commonwealth Coll (PA)
Pepperdine U, Malibu (CA)
Piedmont Coll (GA)
Pitzer Coll (CA)
Plymouth State U (NH)
Point Loma Nazarene U (CA)
Pomona Coll (CA)
Pontifical Catholic U of Puerto Rico (PR)
Pontifical Coll Josephinum (OH)
Portland State U (OR)
Presbyterian Coll (SC)
Princeton U (NJ)
Principia Coll (IL)
Providence Coll (RI)
Purdue U (IN)
Queens Coll of the City U of NY (NY)
Queen's U at Kingston (ON, Canada)
Queens U of Charlotte (NC)
Quincy U (IL)
Randolph-Macon Coll (VA)
Randolph-Macon Woman's Coll (VA)
Redeemer U Coll (ON, Canada)
Reed Coll (OR)
Regis U (CO)
Rensselaer Polytechnic Inst (NY)
Rhode Island Coll (RI)
Rhodes Coll (TN)
Rice U (TX)
The Richard Stockton Coll of New Jersey (NJ)
Rider U (NJ)
Ripon Coll (WI)
Roanoke Coll (VA)
Roberts Wesleyan Coll (NY)
Rockford Coll (IL)
Rockhurst U (MO)
Rocky Mountain Coll (MT)
Roger Williams U (RI)
Rollins Coll (FL)
Roosevelt U (IL)
Rosemont Coll (PA)
Rutgers, The State U of New Jersey, Camden (NJ)
Rutgers, The State U of New Jersey, Newark (NJ)
Rutgers, The State U of New Jersey, New Brunswick/Piscataway (NJ)
Sacred Heart Major Sem (MI)
Sacred Heart U (CT)
St. Ambrose U (IA)
St. Andrews Presbyterian Coll (NC)
Saint Anselm Coll (NH)
St. Bonaventure U (NY)
St. Charles Borromeo Sem, Overbrook (PA)
St. Cloud State U (MN)
St. Edward's U (TX)
St. Francis Coll (NY)
Saint Francis U (PA)
St. Francis Xavier U (NS, Canada)
St. Gregory's U (OK)
St. John Fisher Coll (NY)
St. John's Coll (NM)
Saint John's U (MN)
St. John's U (NY)
Saint Joseph Coll (CT)
Saint Joseph's Coll (IN)
Saint Joseph's Coll of Maine (ME)
Saint Joseph's U (PA)
St. Lawrence U (NY)
Saint Louis U (MO)
Saint Mary's Coll (IN)
Saint Mary's Coll of California (CA)
St. Mary's Coll of Maryland (MD)
Saint Mary's U of Minnesota (MN)
St. Mary's U of San Antonio (TX)
Saint Michael's Coll (VT)
St. Norbert Coll (WI)
St. Olaf Coll (MN)
St. Thomas Aquinas Coll (NY)
St. Thomas U (NB, Canada)
Saint Vincent Coll (PA)
Saint Xavier U (IL)
Salem Coll (NC)
Salisbury U (MD)
Salve Regina U (RI)
Samford U (AL)
Sam Houston State U (TX)
San Diego State U (CA)
San Francisco State U (CA)
San Jose State U (CA)
Santa Clara U (CA)
Sarah Lawrence Coll (NY)
Scripps Coll (CA)
Seattle Pacific U (WA)
Seattle U (WA)
Seton Hall U (NJ)
Shaw U (NC)
Siena Coll (NY)
Siena Heights U (MI)
Simmons Coll (MA)
Simon Fraser U (BC, Canada)
Simon's Rock Coll of Bard (MA)
Simpson Coll (IA)
Skidmore Coll (NY)
Slippery Rock U of Pennsylvania (PA)
Smith Coll (MA)
Sonoma State U (CA)
Southeast Missouri State U (MO)
Southern Connecticut State U (CT)
Southern Illinois U Carbondale (IL)
Southern Illinois U Edwardsville (IL)
Southern Methodist U (TX)
Southern Nazarene U (OK)
Southern Virginia U (VA)
Southwestern U (TX)
Southwest Missouri State U (MO)
Spelman Coll (GA)
Spring Arbor U (MI)
Spring Hill Coll (AL)
Stanford U (CA)
State U of NY at Binghamton (NY)
State U of NY at New Paltz (NY)
State U of NY at Oswego (NY)
Plattsburgh State U of NY (NY)
State U of NY Coll at Brockport (NY)
State U of NY Coll at Cortland (NY)
State U of NY Coll at Fredonia (NY)
State U of NY Coll at Geneseo (NY)
State U of NY Coll at Old Westbury (NY)
State U of NY Coll at Oneonta (NY)
State U of NY Coll at Potsdam (NY)
State U of West Georgia (GA)
Stephens Coll (MO)
Stetson U (FL)
Stevens Inst of Technology (NJ)
Stonehill Coll (MA)
Stony Brook U, State U of New York (NY)
Suffolk U (MA)
Susquehanna U (PA)
Swarthmore Coll (PA)
Sweet Briar Coll (VA)
Syracuse U (NY)
Tabor Coll (KS)
Taylor U (IN)
Texas A&M U (TX)
Texas Christian U (TX)
Texas Lutheran U (TX)
Texas State U-San Marcos (TX)
Texas Tech U (TX)
Thiel Coll (PA)
Thomas Edison State Coll (NJ)
Thomas More Coll (KY)
Thomas More Coll of Liberal Arts (NH)
Toccoa Falls Coll (GA)
Towson U (MD)
Transylvania U (KY)
Trent U (ON, Canada)
Trinity Christian Coll (IL)
Trinity Coll (CT)
Trinity Intl U (IL)
Trinity U (TX)
Trinity Western U (BC, Canada)
Truman State U (MO)
Tufts U (MA)
Tulane U (LA)
Tyndale U Coll & Sem (ON, Canada)
Union Coll (NY)
Union U (TN)
United States Military Acad (NY)
Université de Montréal (QC, Canada)
Université de Sherbrooke (QC, Canada)
Université Laval (QC, Canada)
State U of NY at Albany (NY)
U at Buffalo, The State U of New York (NY)
The U of Akron (OH)
The U of Alabama (AL)
The U of Alabama at Birmingham (AL)
The U of Alabama in Huntsville (AL)
U of Alaska Fairbanks (AK)
U of Alberta (AB, Canada)
The U of Arizona (AZ)
U of Arkansas (AR)
U of Arkansas at Little Rock (AR)
The U of British Columbia (BC, Canada)
U of Calgary (AB, Canada)
U of Calif, Berkeley (CA)
U of Calif, Davis (CA)
U of Calif, Irvine (CA)
U of Calif, Los Angeles (CA)
U of Calif, Riverside (CA)
U of Calif, San Diego (CA)
U of Calif, Santa Barbara (CA)
U of Calif, Santa Cruz (CA)
U of Central Arkansas (AR)
U of Central Florida (FL)
U of Chicago (IL)
U of Cincinnati (OH)
U of Colorado at Boulder (CO)
U of Colorado at Colorado Springs (CO)
U of Colorado at Denver (CO)
U of Connecticut (CT)
U of Dallas (TX)
U of Dayton (OH)
U of Delaware (DE)
U of Denver (CO)
U of Detroit Mercy (MI)
U of Dubuque (IA)
U of Evansville (IN)
The U of Findlay (OH)
U of Florida (FL)
U of Georgia (GA)
U of Guelph (ON, Canada)
U of Hartford (CT)
U of Hawaii at Hilo (HI)
U of Hawaii at Manoa (HI)
U of Houston (TX)
U of Idaho (ID)
U of Illinois at Chicago (IL)
U of Illinois at Urbana–Champaign (IL)
U of Indianapolis (IN)
The U of Iowa (IA)
U of Kansas (KS)
U of Kentucky (KY)
U of King's Coll (NS, Canada)
U of La Verne (CA)
The U of Lethbridge (AB, Canada)
U of Louisiana at Lafayette (LA)
U of Louisville (KY)
U of Maine (ME)
U of Maine at Farmington (ME)
U of Manitoba (MB, Canada)
U of Maryland, Baltimore County (MD)
U of Maryland, Coll Park (MD)
U of Massachusetts Amherst (MA)
U of Massachusetts Boston (MA)
U of Massachusetts Dartmouth (MA)
U of Massachusetts Lowell (MA)
The U of Memphis (TN)
U of Miami (FL)
U of Michigan (MI)
U of Michigan–Dearborn (MI)
U of Michigan–Flint (MI)
U of Minnesota, Duluth (MN)
U of Minnesota, Morris (MN)
U of Minnesota, Twin Cities Campus (MN)
U of Mississippi (MS)
U of Missouri–Columbia (MO)
U of Missouri–Kansas City (MO)
U of Missouri–Rolla (MO)
U of Missouri–St. Louis (MO)
The U of Montana–Missoula (MT)
U of Nebraska at Omaha (NE)
U of Nebraska–Lincoln (NE)
U of Nevada, Las Vegas (NV)
U of Nevada, Reno (NV)
U of New Brunswick Fredericton (NB, Canada)
U of New Hampshire (NH)
U of New Mexico (NM)
U of New Orleans (LA)
The U of North Carolina at Asheville (NC)
The U of North Carolina at Chapel Hill (NC)
The U of North Carolina at Charlotte (NC)
The U of North Carolina at Greensboro (NC)
U of North Dakota (ND)
U of Northern Colorado (CO)
U of Northern Iowa (IA)
U of North Florida (FL)
U of North Texas (TX)
U of Notre Dame (IN)
U of Oklahoma (OK)
U of Oregon (OR)
U of Ottawa (ON, Canada)
U of Pennsylvania (PA)
U of Pittsburgh (PA)
U of Portland (OR)
U of Prince Edward Island (PE, Canada)
U of Puget Sound (WA)
U of Redlands (CA)
U of Regina (SK, Canada)
U of Rhode Island (RI)
U of Richmond (VA)
U of Rochester (NY)
U of St. Thomas (MN)
U of St. Thomas (TX)
U of San Diego (CA)
U of San Francisco (CA)
U of Saskatchewan (SK, Canada)
The U of Scranton (PA)
U of Sioux Falls (SD)
U of South Alabama (AL)
U of South Carolina (SC)
The U of South Dakota (SD)
U of Southern California (CA)
U of Southern Indiana (IN)
U of Southern Maine (ME)
U of South Florida (FL)
The U of Tennessee (TN)
The U of Tennessee at Martin (TN)
The U of Texas at Arlington (TX)
The U of Texas at Austin (TX)
The U of Texas–Pan American (TX)
U of the District of Columbia (DC)
U of the Incarnate Word (TX)
U of the Pacific (CA)
U of the South (TN)
U of the West (CA)
U of Toledo (OH)
U of Toronto (ON, Canada)
U of Tulsa (OK)
U of Utah (UT)
U of Vermont (VT)
U of Victoria (BC, Canada)
U of Virginia (VA)
U of Washington (WA)
U of Waterloo (ON, Canada)
The U of Western Ontario (ON, Canada)
U of West Florida (FL)
U of Windsor (ON, Canada)
U of Wisconsin–Eau Claire (WI)
U of Wisconsin–Green Bay (WI)
U of Wisconsin–La Crosse (WI)
U of Wisconsin–Madison (WI)
U of Wisconsin–Milwaukee (WI)
U of Wisconsin–Oshkosh (WI)
U of Wisconsin–Parkside (WI)
U of Wisconsin–Platteville (WI)
U of Wisconsin–Stevens Point (WI)
U of Wyoming (WY)
Urbana U (OH)
Ursinus Coll (PA)
Ursuline Coll (OH)
Utah State U (UT)
Utica Coll (NY)
Valdosta State U (GA)
Valparaiso U (IN)
Vanderbilt U (TN)
Vassar Coll (NY)
Villanova U (PA)
Virginia Commonwealth U (VA)
Virginia Polytechnic Inst and State U (VA)
Virginia Wesleyan Coll (VA)
Wabash Coll (IN)
Wake Forest U (NC)
Walla Walla Coll (WA)
Walsh U (OH)
Warren Wilson Coll (NC)
Wartburg Coll (IA)
Washburn U (KS)
Washington & Jefferson Coll (PA)
Washington and Lee U (VA)
Washington Coll (MD)
Washington State U (WA)
Washington U in St. Louis (MO)
Wayne State U (MI)
Webster U (MO)
Wellesley Coll (MA)
Wells Coll (NY)
Wesleyan Coll (GA)
Wesleyan U (CT)
West Chester U of Pennsylvania (PA)
Western Carolina U (NC)
Western Illinois U (IL)
Western Kentucky U (KY)
Western Michigan U (MI)
Western Oregon U (OR)
Western Washington U (WA)
Westminster Coll (MO)
Westminster Coll (PA)
Westminster Coll (UT)
Westmont Coll (CA)

West Virginia U (WV)
West Virginia Wesleyan Coll (WV)
Wheaton Coll (IL)
Wheaton Coll (MA)
Wheeling Jesuit U (WV)
Whitman Coll (WA)
Whitworth Coll (WA)
Wichita State U (KS)
Wilkes U (PA)
Willamette U (OR)
William Jewell Coll (MO)
William Paterson U of New Jersey (NJ)
Williams Coll (MA)
Wingate U (NC)
Winthrop U (SC)
Wittenberg U (OH)
Wofford Coll (SC)
Worcester Polytechnic Inst (MA)
Wright State U (OH)
Xavier U (OH)
Xavier U of Louisiana (LA)
Yale U (CT)
York Coll of Pennsylvania (PA)
York Coll of the City U of New York (NY)
York U (ON, Canada)
Youngstown State U (OH)

PHILOSOPHY AND RELIGIOUS STUDIES RELATED

Appalachian State U (NC)
Barton Coll (NC)
Berry Coll (GA)
Bethune-Cookman Coll (FL)
Bridgewater Coll (VA)
Buena Vista U (IA)
California State U, Sacramento (CA)
Capital U (OH)
Claremont McKenna Coll (CA)
Coker Coll (SC)
Coll of the Ozarks (MO)
Columbia Coll (MO)
Cumberland Coll (KY)
Eastern Mennonite U (VA)
Graceland U (IA)
Greenville Coll (IL)
Holy Names Coll (CA)
James Madison U (VA)
Juniata Coll (PA)
Kean U (NJ)
Lambuth U (TN)
Lyon Coll (AR)
McGill U (QC, Canada)
Pace U (NY)
Point Loma Nazarene U (CA)
Radford U (VA)
Roanoke Coll (VA)
Roberts Wesleyan Coll (NY)
St. John's Coll (NM)
St. John's U (NY)
Saint Joseph's Coll (IN)
Samford U (AL)
Sarah Lawrence Coll (NY)
Southwestern Coll (KS)
State U of NY at Oswego (NY)
Sterling Coll (KS)
Syracuse U (NY)
Union U (TN)
The U of North Carolina at Pembroke (NC)
The U of North Carolina at Wilmington (NC)
U of Notre Dame (IN)
The U of Tennessee at Chattanooga (TN)
U of the Ozarks (AR)
Ursinus Coll (PA)
Washington U in St. Louis (MO)
West Virginia Wesleyan Coll (WV)
Wilson Coll (PA)

PHILOSOPHY RELATED

American Public U System (WV)
Claremont McKenna Coll (CA)
Ohio Northern U (OH)
St. John's Coll (NM)
U of Pennsylvania (PA)
U of Southern California (CA)

PHOTOGRAPHIC AND FILM/ VIDEO TECHNOLOGY

Kent State U (OH)
New England School of Communications (ME)
Ohio U (OH)
Rochester Inst of Technology (NY)
Ryerson U (ON, Canada)
St. John's U (NY)

PHOTOGRAPHY

Acad of Art U (CA)
Alberta Coll of Art & Design (AB, Canada)
Albertus Magnus Coll (CT)
American InterContinental U (CA)
American InterContinental U-London(United Kingdom)
Andrews U (MI)
Arcadia U (PA)
Arizona State U (AZ)
Art Acad of Cincinnati (OH)
Art Center Coll of Design (CA)
The Art Inst of Boston at Lesley U (MA)
Atlanta Coll of Art (GA)
Ball State U (IN)
Bard Coll (NY)
Barry U (FL)
Bennington Coll (VT)
Bethel Coll (IN)
Bowling Green State U (OH)
Brigham Young U (UT)
State U of NY Coll at Buffalo (NY)
California Coll of the Arts (CA)
California Inst of the Arts (CA)
California State U, Fullerton (CA)
California State U, Hayward (CA)
California State U, Long Beach (CA)
California State U, Sacramento (CA)
Carroll Coll (WI)
Carson-Newman Coll (TN)
Cazenovia Coll (NY)
Central Missouri State U (MO)
Chester Coll of New England (NH)
The Cleveland Inst of Art (OH)
Coe Coll (IA)
Coker Coll (SC)
Col for Creative Studies (MI)
Coll of Santa Fe (NM)
Coll of Visual Arts (MN)
Colorado State U (CO)
Columbia Coll (MO)
Columbia Coll Chicago (IL)
Columbus Coll of Art & Design (OH)
Concordia U (QC, Canada)
Cornell U (NY)
Dominican U (IL)
Drexel U (PA)
Fordham U (NY)
Gallaudet U (DC)
Governors State U (IL)
Grand Valley State U (MI)
Hampshire Coll (MA)
Hampton U (VA)
Hofstra U (NY)
Indiana U Bloomington (IN)
Indiana U–Purdue U Fort Wayne (IN)
Inter American U of PR, San Germán Campus (PR)
Ithaca Coll (NY)
Kansas City Art Inst (MO)
Long Island U, C.W. Post Campus (NY)
Louisiana Tech U (LA)
Loyola U Chicago (IL)
Maine Coll of Art (ME)
Marlboro Coll (VT)
Maryland Inst Coll of Art (MD)
Marywood U (PA)
Massachusetts Coll of Art (MA)
McNeese State U (LA)
Memorial U of Newfoundland (NL, Canada)
Memphis Coll of Art (TN)
Milwaukee Inst of Art and Design (WI)
Minneapolis Coll of Art and Design (MN)
Montserrat Coll of Art (MA)
Morningside Coll (IA)
Mount Allison U (NB, Canada)
Nazareth Coll of Rochester (NY)
New World School of the Arts (FL)
New York U (NY)
Northern Arizona U (AZ)
Northern Michigan U (MI)
Nova Scotia Coll of Art and Design (NS, Canada)
Ohio U (OH)
Otis Coll of Art and Design (CA)
Pacific Northwest Coll of Art (OR)
Parsons School of Design, New School U (NY)
Point Park U (PA)
Pratt Inst (NY)
Rhode Island School of Design (RI)
Ringling School of Art and Design (FL)
Rivier Coll (NH)
Rochester Inst of Technology (NY)
Rutgers, The State U of New Jersey, New Brunswick/Piscataway (NJ)
Ryerson U (ON, Canada)
St. Edward's U (TX)
St. John's U (NY)
Saint Mary-of-the-Woods Coll (IN)
Salem State Coll (MA)
Sam Houston State U (TX)
San Francisco Art Inst (CA)
Sarah Lawrence Coll (NY)
Savannah Coll of Art and Design (GA)
School of the Art Inst of Chicago (IL)
School of the Museum of Fine Arts, Boston (MA)
Seattle U (WA)
Shawnee State U (OH)
Simon's Rock Coll of Bard (MA)
State U of NY at New Paltz (NY)
State U of NY Coll at Potsdam (NY)
Syracuse U (NY)
Texas A&M U–Commerce (TX)
Texas Christian U (TX)
Texas Southern U (TX)
Thomas Edison State Coll (NJ)
Trinity Christian Coll (IL)
The U of Akron (OH)
U of Calif, Santa Cruz (CA)
U of Central Florida (FL)
U of Dayton (OH)
U of Hartford (CT)
U of Houston (TX)
U of Idaho (ID)
U of Illinois at Chicago (IL)
U of Illinois at Urbana–Champaign (IL)
The U of Iowa (IA)
U of Maryland, Baltimore County (MD)
U of Massachusetts Dartmouth (MA)
U of Miami (FL)
U of Michigan (MI)
U of Michigan–Flint (MI)
U of Missouri–St. Louis (MO)
U of Montevallo (AL)
U of North Texas (TX)
U of Oklahoma (OK)
U of Oregon (OR)
U of Ottawa (ON, Canada)
The U of the Arts (PA)
U of Washington (WA)
Virginia Commonwealth U (VA)
Virginia Intermont Coll (VA)
Washington U in St. Louis (MO)
Watkins Coll of Art and Design (TN)
Weber State U (UT)
Webster U (MO)
Wright State U (OH)
York U (ON, Canada)
Youngstown State U (OH)

PHOTOJOURNALISM

Point Park U (PA)
Rochester Inst of Technology (NY)
St. Gregory's U (OK)
Texas Tech U (TX)
U of Missouri–Columbia (MO)
U of North Texas (TX)

PHYSICAL AND THEORETICAL CHEMISTRY

Cornell U (NY)
Lehigh U (PA)
Michigan State U (MI)
Rice U (TX)

PHYSICAL EDUCATION TEACHING AND COACHING

Abilene Christian U (TX)
Adelphi U (NY)
Adrian Coll (MI)
Alabama Ag and Mech U (AL)
Alabama State U (AL)
Albany State U (GA)
Albertson Coll of Idaho (ID)
Albion Coll (MI)
Alcorn State U (MS)
Alderson-Broaddus Coll (WV)
Alice Lloyd Coll (KY)
Alma Coll (MI)
American U of Puerto Rico (PR)
Anderson Coll (SC)
Appalachian State U (NC)
Aquinas Coll (MI)
Arkansas State U (AR)
Arkansas Tech U (AR)
Armstrong Atlantic State U (GA)
Asbury Coll (KY)
Ashland U (OH)
Athens State U (AL)
Atlantic Union Coll (MA)
Auburn U (AL)
Augsburg Coll (MN)
Augustana Coll (IL)
Augustana Coll (SD)
Augusta State U (GA)
Aurora U (IL)
Austin Coll (TX)
Averett U (VA)
Azusa Pacific U (CA)
Bacone Coll (OK)
Baker U (KS)
Baldwin-Wallace Coll (OH)
Ball State U (IN)
Barry U (FL)
Barton Coll (NC)
Baylor U (TX)
Bellevue U (NE)
Belmont U (TN)
Bemidji State U (MN)
Benedictine Coll (KS)
Berea Coll (KY)
Berry Coll (GA)
Bethany Coll (KS)
Bethany Coll (WV)
Bethel Coll (IN)
Bethel Coll (TN)
Bethel U (MN)
Bethune-Cookman Coll (FL)
Biola U (CA)
Blackburn Coll (IL)
Bluefield Coll (VA)
Blue Mountain Coll (MS)
Boise State U (ID)
Boston U (MA)
Bowling Green State U (OH)
Brewton-Parker Coll (GA)
Briar Cliff U (IA)
Bridgewater State Coll (MA)
Brigham Young U (UT)
Brigham Young U–Hawaii (HI)
Brock U (ON, Canada)
Brooklyn Coll of the City U of NY (NY)
Bryan Coll (TN)
Buena Vista U (IA)
California Lutheran U (CA)
California Polytechnic State U, San Luis Obispo (CA)
California State Polytechnic U, Pomona (CA)
California State U, Chico (CA)
California State U, Dominguez Hills (CA)
California State U, Fresno (CA)
California State U, Fullerton (CA)
California State U, Hayward (CA)
California State U, Long Beach (CA)
California State U, Los Angeles (CA)
California State U, San Bernardino (CA)
California State U, Stanislaus (CA)
Calvin Coll (MI)
Campbellsville U (KY)
Campbell U (NC)
Canisius Coll (NY)
Capital U (OH)
Carroll Coll (MT)
Carroll Coll (WI)
Carson-Newman Coll (TN)
Carthage Coll (WI)
Castleton State Coll (VT)
Catawba Coll (NC)
Cedarville U (OH)
Centenary Coll of Louisiana (LA)
Central Connecticut State U (CT)
Central Methodist Coll (MO)
Central Michigan U (MI)
Central Missouri State U (MO)
Central State U (OH)
Central Washington U (WA)
Chadron State Coll (NE)
Charleston Southern U (SC)
Chicago State U (IL)
Chowan Coll (NC)
Christian Heritage Coll (CA)
Citadel, The Military Coll of South Carolina (SC)
Clark Atlanta U (GA)
Clarke Coll (IA)
Clearwater Christian Coll (FL)
Cleveland State U (OH)
Coastal Carolina U (SC)
Coe Coll (IA)
Coker Coll (SC)
Coll of Charleston (SC)
Coll of Mount St. Joseph (OH)
Coll of Mount Saint Vincent (NY)
The Coll of New Jersey (NJ)
Coll of St. Catherine (MN)
Coll of the Ozarks (MO)
Coll of the Southwest (NM)
The Coll of William and Mary (VA)
Colorado State U-Pueblo (CO)
Columbus State U (GA)
Concord Coll (WV)
Concordia Coll (MN)
Concordia U (IL)
Concordia U (MI)
Concordia U (NE)
Concordia U (OR)
Concordia U, St. Paul (MN)
Concordia U Wisconsin (WI)
Cornell Coll (IA)
Cornerstone U (MI)
Crown Coll (MN)
Culver-Stockton Coll (MO)
Cumberland Coll (KY)
Cumberland U (TN)
Dakota State U (SD)
Dakota Wesleyan U (SD)
Dallas Baptist U (TX)
Dana Coll (NE)
Davis & Elkins Coll (WV)
Defiance Coll (OH)
Delaware State U (DE)
Delta State U (MS)
Denison U (OH)
DePaul U (IL)
DePauw U (IN)
Dickinson State U (ND)
Dillard U (LA)
Doane Coll (NE)
Dordt Coll (IA)
East Carolina U (NC)
East Central U (OK)
Eastern Connecticut State U (CT)
Eastern Illinois U (IL)
Eastern Kentucky U (KY)
Eastern Mennonite U (VA)
Eastern Michigan U (MI)
Eastern Nazarene Coll (MA)
Eastern New Mexico U (NM)
Eastern Oregon U (OR)
Eastern Washington U (WA)
East Stroudsburg U of Pennsylvania (PA)
East Texas Baptist U (TX)
Edinboro U of Pennsylvania (PA)
Elizabeth City State U (NC)
Elmhurst Coll (IL)
Elon U (NC)
Endicott Coll (MA)
Erskine Coll (SC)
Eureka Coll (IL)
Evangel U (MO)
Fairmont State Coll (WV)
Faulkner U (AL)
Fayetteville State U (NC)
Ferrum Coll (VA)
Florida Ag and Mech U (FL)
Florida Intl U (FL)
Florida Southern Coll (FL)
Florida State U (FL)
Fort Hays State U (KS)
Fort Lewis Coll (CO)
Fort Valley State U (GA)
Franklin Coll (IN)
Freed-Hardeman U (TN)
Fresno Pacific U (CA)
Frostburg State U (MD)
Gallaudet U (DC)
Gardner-Webb U (NC)
George Fox U (OR)
George Mason U (VA)
Georgia Coll & State U (GA)
Georgia Southern U (GA)
Georgia Southwestern State U (GA)
Georgia State U (GA)
Gettysburg Coll (PA)
Glenville State Coll (WV)
Gonzaga U (WA)
Goshen Coll (IN)
Grace Coll (IN)
Graceland U (IA)
Grambling State U (LA)
Grand Canyon U (AZ)
Grand Valley State U (MI)
Greensboro Coll (NC)
Greenville Coll (IL)
Gustavus Adolphus Coll (MN)
Hamline U (MN)
Hampton U (VA)
Hannibal-LaGrange Coll (MO)
Hanover Coll (IN)
Harding U (AR)
Hardin-Simmons U (TX)
Hastings Coll (NE)
Heidelberg Coll (OH)
Henderson State U (AR)
Hendrix Coll (AR)
High Point U (NC)
Hillsdale Coll (MI)
Hofstra U (NY)
Hope Coll (MI)
Houghton Coll (NY)
Houston Baptist U (TX)
Howard Payne U (TX)
Howard U (DC)
Humboldt State U (CA)
Hunter Coll of the City U of NY (NY)
Huntingdon Coll (AL)
Huntington Coll (IN)
Husson Coll (ME)

Huston-Tillotson Coll (TX)
Idaho State U (ID)
Illinois Coll (IL)
Illinois State U (IL)
Indiana State U (IN)
Indiana U Bloomington (IN)
Indiana U of Pennsylvania (PA)
Indiana U–Purdue U Indianapolis (IN)
Inter American U of PR, Fajardo Campus (PR)
Inter American U of PR, San Germán Campus (PR)
Iowa Wesleyan Coll (IA)
Ithaca Coll (NY)
Jacksonville State U (AL)
Jacksonville U (FL)
Jamestown Coll (ND)
Jarvis Christian Coll (TX)
John Brown U (AR)
John Carroll U (OH)
Johnson C. Smith U (NC)
Johnson State Coll (VT)
Judson Coll (IL)
Kansas Wesleyan U (KS)
Kean U (NJ)
Keene State Coll (NH)
Kennesaw State U (GA)
Kent State U (OH)
Kentucky State U (KY)
Kentucky Wesleyan Coll (KY)
Lakehead U (ON, Canada)
Lamar U (TX)
Lambuth U (TN)
Lancaster Bible Coll (PA)
Lander U (SC)
Lane Coll (TN)
Laurentian U (ON, Canada)
Lenoir-Rhyne Coll (NC)
LeTourneau U (TX)
Lewis-Clark State Coll (ID)
Lewis U (IL)
Liberty U (VA)
Limestone Coll (SC)
Lincoln Memorial U (TN)
Lincoln U (MO)
Lindenwood U (MO)
Lindsey Wilson Coll (KY)
Lipscomb U (TN)
Livingstone Coll (NC)
Lock Haven U of Pennsylvania (PA)
Long Island U, Brooklyn Campus (NY)
Long Island U, C.W. Post Campus (NY)
Longwood U (VA)
Loras Coll (IA)
Louisiana Coll (LA)
Louisiana State U and A&M Coll (LA)
Louisiana State U in Shreveport (LA)
Louisiana Tech U (LA)
Lubbock Christian U (TX)
Luther Coll (IA)
Lynchburg Coll (VA)
Lyndon State Coll (VT)
MacMurray Coll (IL)
Malone Coll (OH)
Manchester Coll (IN)
Manhattan Coll (NY)
Marian Coll (IN)
Marshall U (WV)
Mars Hill Coll (NC)
Maryville Coll (TN)
The Master's Coll and Sem (CA)
Mayville State U (ND)
McGill U (QC, Canada)
McKendree Coll (IL)
McMurry U (TX)
McNeese State U (LA)
McPherson Coll (KS)
Memorial U of Newfoundland (NL, Canada)
Meredith Coll (NC)
Messiah Coll (PA)
Methodist Coll (NC)
Miami U (OH)
Miami U Hamilton (OH)
Michigan State U (MI)
MidAmerica Nazarene U (KS)
Millikin U (IL)
Minnesota State U Mankato (MN)
Minnesota State U Moorhead (MN)
Minot State U (ND)
Mississippi State U (MS)
Mississippi Valley State U (MS)
Missouri Baptist U (MO)
Missouri Valley Coll (MO)
Monmouth Coll (IL)
Montana State U–Billings (MT)
Montclair State U (NJ)
Morehead State U (KY)
Morehouse Coll (GA)
Morgan State U (MD)
Mount Marty Coll (SD)
Mount Union Coll (OH)
Mount Vernon Nazarene U (OH)
Murray State U (KY)
Nebraska Wesleyan U (NE)
Newberry Coll (SC)
New Mexico Highlands U (NM)
New Mexico State U (NM)
Nicholls State U (LA)
North Carolina Central U (NC)
North Carolina Wesleyan Coll (NC)
North Central Coll (IL)
North Dakota State U (ND)
Northeastern Illinois U (IL)
Northeastern State U (OK)
Northern Arizona U (AZ)
Northern Illinois U (IL)
Northern Michigan U (MI)
Northern State U (SD)
North Georgia Coll & State U (GA)
North Park U (IL)
Northwestern Coll (IA)
Northwestern Coll (MN)
Northwestern Oklahoma State U (OK)
Northwestern State U of Louisiana (LA)
Northwest Nazarene U (ID)
Oakland City U (IN)
Ohio Northern U (OH)
The Ohio State U (OH)
Ohio U (OH)
Ohio Valley Coll (WV)
Ohio Wesleyan U (OH)
Oklahoma Baptist U (OK)
Oklahoma Christian U (OK)
Oklahoma City U (OK)
Oklahoma Panhandle State U (OK)
Oklahoma State U (OK)
Old Dominion U (VA)
Olivet Coll (MI)
Olivet Nazarene U (IL)
Oral Roberts U (OK)
Oregon State U (OR)
Ottawa U (KS)
Otterbein Coll (OH)
Ouachita Baptist U (AR)
Pacific Lutheran U (WA)
Pacific Union Coll (CA)
Palm Beach Atlantic U (FL)
Pepperdine U, Malibu (CA)
Pfeiffer U (NC)
Philadelphia Biblical U (PA)
Pillsbury Baptist Bible Coll (MN)
Pittsburg State U (KS)
Pontifical Catholic U of Puerto Rico (PR)
Purdue U (IN)
Queens Coll of the City U of NY (NY)
Queen's U at Kingston (ON, Canada)
Quincy U (IL)
Radford U (VA)
Reinhardt Coll (GA)
Rhode Island Coll (RI)
Ripon Coll (WI)
Rockford Coll (IL)
Rocky Mountain Coll (MT)
Rowan U (NJ)
Saginaw Valley State U (MI)
St. Ambrose U (IA)
St. Andrews Presbyterian Coll (NC)
Saint Augustine's Coll (NC)
St. Bonaventure U (NY)
St. Cloud State U (MN)
St. Edward's U (TX)
St. Francis Coll (NY)
St. Francis Xavier U (NS, Canada)
Saint Joseph's Coll (IN)
Saint Joseph's Coll of Maine (ME)
Salem State Coll (MA)
Salisbury U (MD)
Samford U (AL)
Sam Houston State U (TX)
San Diego State U (CA)
San Francisco State U (CA)
Schreiner U (TX)
Seattle Pacific U (WA)
Shenandoah U (VA)
Simpson Coll (IA)
Sonoma State U (CA)
South Carolina State U (SC)
South Dakota State U (SD)
Southeastern Louisiana U (LA)
Southeastern Oklahoma State U (OK)
Southeast Missouri State U (MO)
Southern Adventist U (TN)
Southern Arkansas U–Magnolia (AR)
Southern Connecticut State U (CT)
Southern Illinois U Carbondale (IL)
Southern Nazarene U (OK)
Southern Oregon U (OR)
Southern Utah U (UT)
Southern Wesleyan U (SC)
Southwest Baptist U (MO)
Southwestern Oklahoma State U (OK)
Southwestern U (TX)
Southwest Missouri State U (MO)
Spring Arbor U (MI)
Springfield Coll (MA)
State U of NY Coll at Brockport (NY)
State U of NY Coll at Cortland (NY)
State U of NY Coll at Potsdam (NY)
State U of West Georgia (GA)
Sterling Coll (KS)
Syracuse U (NY)
Tabor Coll (KS)
Tarleton State U (TX)
Taylor U (IN)
Tennessee State U (TN)
Tennessee Technological U (TN)
Tennessee Wesleyan Coll (TN)
Texas A&M Intl U (TX)
Texas A&M U–Commerce (TX)
Texas A&M U–Corpus Christi (TX)
Texas A&M U–Kingsville (TX)
Texas Christian U (TX)
Texas Lutheran U (TX)
Texas Southern U (TX)
Texas Wesleyan U (TX)
Towson U (MD)
Transylvania U (KY)
Trevecca Nazarene U (TN)
Trinity Christian Coll (IL)
Trinity Intl U (IL)
Trinity Western U (BC, Canada)
Tri-State U (IN)
Troy State U (AL)
Tusculum Coll (TN)
Union Coll (KY)
Union Coll (NE)
Union U (TN)
Université de Montréal (QC, Canada)
Université de Sherbrooke (QC, Canada)
Université Laval (QC, Canada)
U Coll of the Fraser Valley (BC, Canada)
The U of Akron (OH)
The U of Alabama (AL)
The U of Alabama at Birmingham (AL)
U of Alaska Fairbanks (AK)
U of Alberta (AB, Canada)
The U of Arizona (AZ)
U of Arkansas (AR)
U of Arkansas at Monticello (AR)
U of Calif, Davis (CA)
U of Central Arkansas (AR)
U of Central Florida (FL)
U of Cincinnati (OH)
U of Connecticut (CT)
U of Dayton (OH)
U of Delaware (DE)
U of Dubuque (IA)
U of Evansville (IN)
The U of Findlay (OH)
U of Georgia (GA)
U of Great Falls (MT)
U of Hawaii at Manoa (HI)
U of Idaho (ID)
U of Indianapolis (IN)
U of Kansas (KS)
U of Kentucky (KY)
U of La Verne (CA)
The U of Lethbridge (AB, Canada)
U of Louisiana at Lafayette (LA)
U of Maine (ME)
U of Maine at Presque Isle (ME)
U of Manitoba (MB, Canada)
U of Mary (ND)
U of Mary Hardin-Baylor (TX)
U of Maryland, Coll Park (MD)
U of Maryland Eastern Shore (MD)
U of Massachusetts Boston (MA)
The U of Memphis (TN)
U of Michigan (MI)
U of Minnesota, Duluth (MN)
U of Minnesota, Twin Cities Campus (MN)
U of Missouri–Kansas City (MO)
U of Missouri–St. Louis (MO)
U of Mobile (AL)
The U of Montana–Missoula (MT)
The U of Montana–Western (MT)
U of Nebraska at Omaha (NE)
U of Nebraska–Lincoln (NE)
U of Nevada, Las Vegas (NV)
U of Nevada, Reno (NV)
U of New Brunswick Fredericton (NB, Canada)
U of New Hampshire (NH)
U of New Mexico (NM)
U of New Orleans (LA)
The U of North Carolina at Greensboro (NC)
The U of North Carolina at Pembroke (NC)
The U of North Carolina at Wilmington (NC)
U of North Dakota (ND)
U of Northern Iowa (IA)
U of North Florida (FL)
U of Ottawa (ON, Canada)
U of Pittsburgh (PA)
U of Puerto Rico, Cayey U Coll (PR)
U of Regina (SK, Canada)
U of Rhode Island (RI)
U of Richmond (VA)
U of St. Thomas (MN)
U of San Francisco (CA)
U of Saskatchewan (SK, Canada)
U of Sioux Falls (SD)
U of South Alabama (AL)
U of South Carolina (SC)
U of South Carolina Spartanburg (SC)
The U of South Dakota (SD)
U of Southern Indiana (IN)
U of South Florida (FL)
The U of Tampa (FL)
U of the District of Columbia (DC)
U of the Incarnate Word (TX)
U of the Ozarks (AR)
U of Toledo (OH)
U of Toronto (ON, Canada)
U of Utah (UT)
U of Vermont (VT)
U of Victoria (BC, Canada)
U of Virginia (VA)
The U of West Alabama (AL)
The U of Western Ontario (ON, Canada)
U of Windsor (ON, Canada)
U of Wisconsin–La Crosse (WI)
U of Wisconsin–Madison (WI)
U of Wisconsin–Oshkosh (WI)
U of Wisconsin–River Falls (WI)
U of Wisconsin–Stevens Point (WI)
U of Wisconsin–Superior (WI)
U of Wisconsin–Whitewater (WI)
U of Wyoming (WY)
Upper Iowa U (IA)
Utah State U (UT)
Valdosta State U (GA)
Valley City State U (ND)
Valparaiso U (IN)
Vanguard U of Southern California (CA)
Virginia Intermont Coll (VA)
Virginia State U (VA)
Voorhees Coll (SC)
Waldorf Coll (IA)
Walla Walla Coll (WA)
Walsh U (OH)
Warner Pacific Coll (OR)
Warner Southern Coll (FL)
Wartburg Coll (IA)
Washburn U (KS)
Wayland Baptist U (TX)
Wayne State Coll (NE)
Wayne State U (MI)
Weber State U (UT)
Wesley Coll (DE)
West Chester U of Pennsylvania (PA)
Western Baptist Coll (OR)
Western Carolina U (NC)
Western Illinois U (IL)
Western Kentucky U (KY)
Western Michigan U (MI)
Western State Coll of Colorado (CO)
Western Washington U (WA)
Westfield State Coll (MA)
West Liberty State Coll (WV)
Westminster Coll (MO)
Westmont Coll (CA)
West Virginia State Coll (WV)
West Virginia U (WV)
West Virginia Wesleyan Coll (WV)
Whitworth Coll (WA)
Wichita State U (KS)
William Carey Coll (MS)
William Paterson U of New Jersey (NJ)
William Penn U (IA)
Williams Baptist Coll (AR)
William Woods U (MO)
Wingate U (NC)
Winona State U (MN)
Winston-Salem State U (NC)
Winthrop U (SC)
Wright State U (OH)
Xavier U of Louisiana (LA)
York Coll (NE)
York Coll of the City U of New York (NY)
York U (ON, Canada)
Youngstown State U (OH)

PHYSICAL SCIENCES

Antioch Coll (OH)
Arkansas Tech U (AR)
Asbury Coll (KY)
Auburn U Montgomery (AL)
Augusta State U (GA)
Bard Coll (NY)
Bemidji State U (MN)
Biola U (CA)
Black Hills State U (SD)
Bloomsburg U of Pennsylvania (PA)
Brigham Young U–Hawaii (HI)
Brock U (ON, Canada)
California Inst of Technology (CA)
California Polytechnic State U, San Luis Obispo (CA)
California State U, Hayward (CA)
California State U, Sacramento (CA)
California State U, Stanislaus (CA)
Calvin Coll (MI)
Central Michigan U (MI)
Chowan Coll (NC)
Coe Coll (IA)
Colgate U (NY)
Colorado State U (CO)
Concordia U (IL)
Concordia U (NE)
Concordia U (OR)
Cornell U (NY)
Defiance Coll (OH)
Doane Coll (NE)
Eastern Kentucky U (KY)
Eastern Washington U (WA)
East Stroudsburg U of Pennsylvania (PA)
Emporia State U (KS)
Eureka Coll (IL)
The Evergreen State Coll (WA)
Florida State U (FL)
Fordham U (NY)
Fort Hays State U (KS)
Framingham State Coll (MA)
Freed-Hardeman U (TN)
Georgia Southwestern State U (GA)
Goshen Coll (IN)
Graceland U (IA)
Grand Canyon U (AZ)
Grand Valley State U (MI)
Grand View Coll (IA)
Hampshire Coll (MA)
Hampton U (VA)
Harvard U (MA)
Humboldt State U (CA)
Judson Coll (IL)
Juniata Coll (PA)
Kansas State U (KS)
Kutztown U of Pennsylvania (PA)
Lenoir-Rhyne Coll (NC)
Lincoln U (PA)
Linfield Coll (OR)
Lock Haven U of Pennsylvania (PA)
Long Island U, Brooklyn Campus (NY)
Loras Coll (IA)
Lyndon State Coll (VT)
Mansfield U of Pennsylvania (PA)
The Master's Coll and Sem (CA)
Mayville State U (ND)
McPherson Coll (KS)
Michigan State U (MI)
Michigan Technological U (MI)
Minnesota State U Mankato (MN)
Minot State U (ND)
Muhlenberg Coll (PA)
Northern Arizona U (AZ)
Oakland U (MI)
Oklahoma Baptist U (OK)
Olivet Nazarene U (IL)
Oregon State U (OR)
Otterbein Coll (OH)
Pacific Union Coll (CA)
Penn State U at Erie, The Behrend Coll (PA)
Pittsburg State U (KS)
Radford U (VA)
Rensselaer Polytechnic Inst (NY)
Rhode Island Coll (RI)
Ripon Coll (WI)
Rowan U (NJ)
St. Bonaventure U (NY)
St. Cloud State U (MN)
St. Francis Xavier U (NS, Canada)
St. John's Coll (NM)
St. John's U (NY)
Saint Michael's Coll (VT)
San Diego State U (CA)
San Francisco State U (CA)
Shawnee State U (OH)
Southern Utah U (UT)
Texas A&M Intl U (TX)

Trent U (ON, Canada)
Tri-State U (IN)
Troy State U (AL)
Troy State U Dothan (AL)
United States Naval Acad (MD)
U of Alberta (AB, Canada)
U of Arkansas at Monticello (AR)
U of Calif, Berkeley (CA)
U of Calif, Riverside (CA)
U of Central Arkansas (AR)
U of Dayton (OH)
U of Guelph (ON, Canada)
U of Houston–Clear Lake (TX)
U of Maryland, Coll Park (MD)
U of Michigan–Dearborn (MI)
U of North Alabama (AL)
U of Ottawa (ON, Canada)
U of Pittsburgh (PA)
U of Pittsburgh at Bradford (PA)
U of Southern California (CA)
U of the Pacific (CA)
U of Toledo (OH)
U of Utah (UT)
U of Wisconsin–River Falls (WI)
U of Wisconsin–Superior (WI)
Warner Pacific Coll (OR)
Washington State U (WA)
Washington U in St. Louis (MO)
Wayland Baptist U (TX)
Wayne State Coll (NE)
Wesleyan Coll (GA)
Westfield State Coll (MA)
William Paterson U of New Jersey (NJ)
Winona State U (MN)
Wittenberg U (OH)
York Coll of Pennsylvania (PA)
York U (ON, Canada)

PHYSICAL SCIENCES RELATED

Central Connecticut State U (CT)
Charleston Southern U (SC)
The Coll of St. Scholastica (MN)
Eastern Michigan U (MI)
Florida State U (FL)
Frostburg State U (MD)
Hofstra U (NY)
Ohio U (OH)
Stony Brook U, State U of New York (NY)
The U of North Carolina at Chapel Hill (NC)
U of Toronto (ON, Canada)
U of Utah (UT)
Worcester Polytechnic Inst (MA)

PHYSICAL SCIENCE TECHNOLOGIES RELATED

Southwest Missouri State U (MO)

PHYSICAL THERAPIST ASSISTANT

Mercyhurst Coll (PA)

PHYSICAL THERAPY

Alcorn State U (MS)
American Intl Coll (MA)
Andrews U (MI)
Armstrong Atlantic State U (GA)
Boston U (MA)
Bowling Green State U (OH)
Bradley U (IL)
California State U, Fresno (CA)
Centenary Coll of Louisiana (LA)
Chatham Coll (PA)
Clarke Coll (IA)
Cleveland State U (OH)
Coll of Mount St. Joseph (OH)
Coll of Saint Benedict (MN)
Coll of Staten Island of the City U of NY (NY)
Concordia Coll (MN)
Concordia U Wisconsin (WI)
Daemen Coll (NY)
Dalhousie U (NS, Canada)
Duquesne U (PA)
D'Youville Coll (NY)
Eastern Nazarene Coll (MA)
Eastern Washington U (WA)
Elmhurst Coll (IL)
Florida Ag and Mech U (FL)
Grand Valley State U (MI)
Gustavus Adolphus Coll (MN)
Hamline U (MN)
Hampton U (VA)
Howard U (DC)
Hunter Coll of the City U of NY (NY)
Huntingdon Coll (AL)
Husson Coll (ME)
Indiana U–Purdue U Indianapolis (IN)
Ithaca Coll (NY)
Long Island U, Brooklyn Campus (NY)
Marquette U (WI)
McGill U (QC, Canada)
Merrimack Coll (MA)
Mount Aloysius Coll (PA)
Mount Saint Mary Coll (NY)
Mount Vernon Nazarene U (OH)
Nazareth Coll of Rochester (NY)
New York Inst of Technology (NY)
Northeastern U (MA)
Northern Illinois U (IL)
Northwest Nazarene U (ID)
Oakland U (MI)
The Ohio State U (OH)
Pittsburg State U (KS)
Quinnipiac U (CT)
Russell Sage Coll (NY)
Sacred Heart U (CT)
St. Cloud State U (MN)
Saint Francis U (PA)
Saint John's U (MN)
Saint Louis U (MO)
Saint Mary's U of Minnesota (MN)
Saint Vincent Coll (PA)
Simmons Coll (MA)
Simpson Coll (IA)
Springfield Coll (MA)
State U of NY Health Science Center at Brooklyn (NY)
State U of New York Upstate Medical U (NY)
Tarleton State U (TX)
Tennessee State U (TN)
Texas Southern U (TX)
Thomas Jefferson U (PA)
Université de Montréal (QC, Canada)
Université Laval (QC, Canada)
U of Alberta (AB, Canada)
The U of British Columbia (BC, Canada)
U of Central Arkansas (AR)
U of Connecticut (CT)
U of Evansville (IN)
The U of Findlay (OH)
U of Hartford (CT)
U of Kentucky (KY)
U of Manitoba (MB, Canada)
U of Maryland Eastern Shore (MD)
U of Minnesota, Morris (MN)
U of Minnesota, Twin Cities Campus (MN)
The U of Montana–Missoula (MT)
U of North Dakota (ND)
U of Ottawa (ON, Canada)
U of Saskatchewan (SK, Canada)
The U of Tennessee at Chattanooga (TN)
U of Toledo (OH)
U of Utah (UT)
U of Washington (WA)
The U of Western Ontario (ON, Canada)
U of Wisconsin–Milwaukee (WI)
Utica Coll (NY)
Vanguard U of Southern California (CA)
Villa Julie Coll (MD)
West Virginia U (WV)
Wheeling Jesuit U (WV)
Winona State U (MN)

PHYSICIAN ASSISTANT

Alderson-Broaddus Coll (WV)
Augsburg Coll (MN)
Bethel Coll (TN)
Boise State U (ID)
Butler U (IN)
California State U, Dominguez Hills (CA)
Catawba Coll (NC)
City Coll of the City U of NY (NY)
Coll of Staten Island of the City U of NY (NY)
Daemen Coll (NY)
Duquesne U (PA)
D'Youville Coll (NY)
East Carolina U (NC)
Elmhurst Coll (IL)
Gannon U (PA)
Gardner-Webb U (NC)
The George Washington U (DC)
Grand Valley State U (MI)
High Point U (NC)
Hofstra U (NY)
Howard U (DC)
Le Moyne Coll (NY)
Lenoir-Rhyne Coll (NC)
Long Island U, Brooklyn Campus (NY)
Marquette U (WI)
Mars Hill Coll (NC)
Marywood U (PA)
Medical Coll of Georgia (GA)
Methodist Coll (NC)
Mountain State U (WV)
New York Inst of Technology (NY)
Nova Southeastern U (FL)
Pace U (NY)
Philadelphia U (PA)
Quinnipiac U (CT)
Rochester Inst of Technology (NY)
Rocky Mountain Coll (MT)
St. Francis Coll (NY)
Saint Francis U (PA)
St. John's U (NY)
Saint Louis U (MO)
Saint Vincent Coll (PA)
Salem Coll (NC)
Sam Houston State U (TX)
Seton Hill U (PA)
Southern Illinois U Carbondale (IL)
South U (GA)
Springfield Coll (MA)
State U of NY Health Science Center at Brooklyn (NY)
Stony Brook U, State U of New York (NY)
Union Coll (NE)
The U of Alabama at Birmingham (AL)
The U of Findlay (OH)
U of New Mexico (NM)
U of Saint Francis (IN)
U of Texas Health Science Center at San Antonio (TX)
U of Washington (WA)
U of Wisconsin–La Crosse (WI)
U of Wisconsin–Madison (WI)
Wagner Coll (NY)
Wake Forest U (NC)
Wichita State U (KS)

PHYSICS

Abilene Christian U (TX)
Acadia U (NS, Canada)
Adelphi U (NY)
Adrian Coll (MI)
Agnes Scott Coll (GA)
Alabama Ag and Mech U (AL)
Albertson Coll of Idaho (ID)
Albion Coll (MI)
Albright Coll (PA)
Alfred U (NY)
Allegheny Coll (PA)
Alma Coll (MI)
American U (DC)
The American U in Cairo(Egypt)
Amherst Coll (MA)
Andrews U (MI)
Angelo State U (TX)
Antioch Coll (OH)
Appalachian State U (NC)
Aquinas Coll (MI)
Arizona State U (AZ)
Arkansas State U (AR)
Armstrong Atlantic State U (GA)
Ashland U (OH)
Athens State U (AL)
Auburn U (AL)
Augsburg Coll (MN)
Augustana Coll (IL)
Augustana Coll (SD)
Augusta State U (GA)
Austin Coll (TX)
Austin Peay State U (TN)
Azusa Pacific U (CA)
Baker U (KS)
Baldwin-Wallace Coll (OH)
Ball State U (IN)
Bard Coll (NY)
Barnard Coll (NY)
Bates Coll (ME)
Baylor U (TX)
Belmont U (TN)
Beloit Coll (WI)
Bemidji State U (MN)
Benedictine Coll (KS)
Benedictine U (IL)
Bennington Coll (VT)
Berea Coll (KY)
Berry Coll (GA)
Bethany Coll (WV)
Bethel Coll (IN)
Bethel Coll (KS)
Bethel U (MN)
Bethune-Cookman Coll (FL)
Birmingham-Southern Coll (AL)
Bishop's U (QC, Canada)
Bloomsburg U of Pennsylvania (PA)
Bluffton Coll (OH)
Boise State U (ID)
Boston Coll (MA)
Boston U (MA)
Bowdoin Coll (ME)
Bowling Green State U (OH)
Bradley U (IL)
Brandeis U (MA)
Bridgewater Coll (VA)
Bridgewater State Coll (MA)
Brigham Young U (UT)
Brock U (ON, Canada)
Brooklyn Coll of the City U of NY (NY)
Brown U (RI)
Bryn Mawr Coll (PA)
Bucknell U (PA)
Buena Vista U (IA)
State U of NY Coll at Buffalo (NY)
Butler U (IN)
California Inst of Technology (CA)
California Lutheran U (CA)
California Polytechnic State U, San Luis Obispo (CA)
California State Polytechnic U, Pomona (CA)
California State U, Chico (CA)
California State U, Dominguez Hills (CA)
California State U, Fresno (CA)
California State U, Fullerton (CA)
California State U, Hayward (CA)
California State U, Long Beach (CA)
California State U, Los Angeles (CA)
California State U, Sacramento (CA)
California State U, San Bernardino (CA)
California State U, Stanislaus (CA)
California U of Pennsylvania (PA)
Calvin Coll (MI)
Cameron U (OK)
Canisius Coll (NY)
Carleton Coll (MN)
Carleton U (ON, Canada)
Carnegie Mellon U (PA)
Carthage Coll (WI)
Case Western Reserve U (OH)
The Catholic U of America (DC)
Cedarville U (OH)
Centenary Coll of Louisiana (LA)
Central Coll (IA)
Central Connecticut State U (CT)
Central Methodist Coll (MO)
Central Michigan U (MI)
Central Missouri State U (MO)
Central Washington U (WA)
Centre Coll (KY)
Chadron State Coll (NE)
Chatham Coll (PA)
Christian Brothers U (TN)
Christopher Newport U (VA)
Citadel, The Military Coll of South Carolina (SC)
City Coll of the City U of NY (NY)
Claremont McKenna Coll (CA)
Clarion U of Pennsylvania (PA)
Clark Atlanta U (GA)
Clarkson U (NY)
Clark U (MA)
Clemson U (SC)
Cleveland State U (OH)
Coe Coll (IA)
Colby Coll (ME)
Colgate U (NY)
Coll of Charleston (SC)
Coll of Mount Saint Vincent (NY)
The Coll of New Jersey (NJ)
The Coll of New Rochelle (NY)
Coll of Notre Dame of Maryland (MD)
Coll of Saint Benedict (MN)
Coll of St. Catherine (MN)
The Coll of Southeastern Europe, The American U of Athens(Greece)
Coll of Staten Island of the City U of NY (NY)
Coll of the Holy Cross (MA)
The Coll of William and Mary (VA)
The Coll of Wooster (OH)
The Colorado Coll (CO)
Colorado State U (CO)
Colorado State U-Pueblo (CO)
Columbia Coll (NY)
Columbia U, School of General Studies (NY)
Concordia Coll (MN)
Concordia U (QC, Canada)
Connecticut Coll (CT)
Cornell Coll (IA)
Cornell U (NY)
Covenant Coll (GA)
Creighton U (NE)
Cumberland Coll (KY)
Curry Coll (MA)
Dakota State U (SD)
Dalhousie U (NS, Canada)
Dartmouth Coll (NH)
Davidson Coll (NC)
Delaware State U (DE)
Denison U (OH)
DePaul U (IL)
DePauw U (IN)
Dickinson Coll (PA)
Dillard U (LA)
Doane Coll (NE)
Dordt Coll (IA)
Drake U (IA)
Drew U (NJ)
Drury U (MO)
Duke U (NC)
Duquesne U (PA)
Earlham Coll (IN)
East Carolina U (NC)
East Central U (OK)
Eastern Illinois U (IL)
Eastern Kentucky U (KY)
Eastern Michigan U (MI)
Eastern Nazarene Coll (MA)
Eastern New Mexico U (NM)
Eastern Oregon U (OR)
Eastern Washington U (WA)
East Stroudsburg U of Pennsylvania (PA)
Eckerd Coll (FL)
Edinboro U of Pennsylvania (PA)
Elizabeth City State U (NC)
Elizabethtown Coll (PA)
Elmhurst Coll (IL)
Elon U (NC)
Emory & Henry Coll (VA)
Emory U (GA)
Emporia State U (KS)
Erskine Coll (SC)
Excelsior Coll (NY)
Fairfield U (CT)
Florida Ag and Mech U (FL)
Florida Atlantic U (FL)
Florida Inst of Technology (FL)
Florida Intl U (FL)
Florida State U (FL)
Fordham U (NY)
Fort Hays State U (KS)
Fort Lewis Coll (CO)
Francis Marion U (SC)
Franklin and Marshall Coll (PA)
Frostburg State U (MD)
Furman U (SC)
Gallaudet U (DC)
Geneva Coll (PA)
George Mason U (VA)
Georgetown Coll (KY)
Georgetown U (DC)
The George Washington U (DC)
Georgia Inst of Technology (GA)
Georgian Court U (NJ)
Georgia Southern U (GA)
Georgia State U (GA)
Gettysburg Coll (PA)
Gonzaga U (WA)
Gordon Coll (MA)
Goshen Coll (IN)
Goucher Coll (MD)
Grambling State U (LA)
Grand Valley State U (MI)
Greenville Coll (IL)
Grinnell Coll (IA)
Grove City Coll (PA)
Guilford Coll (NC)
Gustavus Adolphus Coll (MN)
Hamilton Coll (NY)
Hamline U (MN)
Hampden-Sydney Coll (VA)
Hampshire Coll (MA)
Hampton U (VA)
Hanover Coll (IN)
Harding U (AR)
Hartwick Coll (NY)
Harvard U (MA)
Harvey Mudd Coll (CA)
Hastings Coll (NE)
Haverford Coll (PA)
Heidelberg Coll (OH)
Henderson State U (AR)
Hendrix Coll (AR)
Hillsdale Coll (MI)
Hiram Coll (OH)
Hobart and William Smith Colls (NY)
Hofstra U (NY)
Hollins U (VA)
Hope Coll (MI)
Houghton Coll (NY)
Houston Baptist U (TX)
Howard U (DC)
Humboldt State U (CA)
Hunter Coll of the City U of NY (NY)
Idaho State U (ID)
Illinois Coll (IL)
Illinois Inst of Technology (IL)
Illinois State U (IL)
Illinois Wesleyan U (IL)
Immaculata U (PA)
Indiana State U (IN)
Indiana U Bloomington (IN)
Indiana U of Pennsylvania (PA)
Indiana U–Purdue U Fort Wayne (IN)
Indiana U–Purdue U Indianapolis (IN)

Indiana U South Bend (IN)
Iona Coll (NY)
Iowa State U of Science and Technology (IA)
Ithaca Coll (NY)
Jacksonville State U (AL)
Jacksonville U (FL)
James Madison U (VA)
Jarvis Christian Coll (TX)
John Carroll U (OH)
The Johns Hopkins U (MD)
Johnson C. Smith U (NC)
Juniata Coll (PA)
Kalamazoo Coll (MI)
Kansas State U (KS)
Kansas Wesleyan U (KS)
Keene State Coll (NH)
Kent State U (OH)
Kentucky Wesleyan Coll (KY)
Kenyon Coll (OH)
Kettering U (MI)
King Coll (TN)
Knox Coll (IL)
Kutztown U of Pennsylvania (PA)
Lafayette Coll (PA)
Lake Forest Coll (IL)
Lakehead U (ON, Canada)
Lamar U (TX)
Lane Coll (TN)
Laurentian U (ON, Canada)
Lawrence Technological U (MI)
Lawrence U (WI)
Lebanon Valley Coll (PA)
Lehigh U (PA)
Lehman Coll of the City U of NY (NY)
Le Moyne Coll (NY)
Lenoir-Rhyne Coll (NC)
Lewis & Clark Coll (OR)
Lewis U (IL)
Lincoln U (MO)
Lincoln U (PA)
Linfield Coll (OR)
Lipscomb U (TN)
Lock Haven U of Pennsylvania (PA)
Long Island U, Brooklyn Campus (NY)
Long Island U, C.W. Post Campus (NY)
Longwood U (VA)
Loras Coll (IA)
Louisiana Coll (LA)
Louisiana State U and A&M Coll (LA)
Louisiana State U in Shreveport (LA)
Louisiana Tech U (LA)
Loyola Coll in Maryland (MD)
Loyola Marymount U (CA)
Loyola U Chicago (IL)
Loyola U New Orleans (LA)
Luther Coll (IA)
Lycoming Coll (PA)
Lynchburg Coll (VA)
Macalester Coll (MN)
MacMurray Coll (IL)
Manchester Coll (IN)
Manhattan Coll (NY)
Manhattanville Coll (NY)
Mansfield U of Pennsylvania (PA)
Marietta Coll (OH)
Marlboro Coll (VT)
Marquette U (WI)
Marshall U (WV)
Mary Baldwin Coll (VA)
Mary Washington Coll (VA)
Massachusetts Coll of Liberal Arts (MA)
Massachusetts Inst of Technology (MA)
McDaniel Coll (MD)
McGill U (QC, Canada)
McMurry U (TX)
McNeese State U (LA)
Memorial U of Newfoundland (NL, Canada)
Mercer U (GA)
Mercyhurst Coll (PA)
Merrimack Coll (MA)
Messiah Coll (PA)
Metropolitan State Coll of Denver (CO)
Miami U (OH)
Miami U Hamilton (OH)
Michigan State U (MI)
Michigan Technological U (MI)
MidAmerica Nazarene U (KS)
Middlebury Coll (VT)
Middle Tennessee State U (TN)
Midwestern State U (TX)
Miles Coll (AL)
Millersville U of Pennsylvania (PA)
Millikin U (IL)
Millsaps Coll (MS)
Minnesota State U Mankato (MN)
Minnesota State U Moorhead (MN)
Minot State U (ND)
Mississippi Coll (MS)
Mississippi State U (MS)
Missouri Southern State U (MO)
Monmouth Coll (IL)
Montana State U–Bozeman (MT)
Montclair State U (NJ)
Moravian Coll (PA)
Morehead State U (KY)
Morehouse Coll (GA)
Morgan State U (MD)
Morningside Coll (IA)
Mount Allison U (NB, Canada)
Mount Holyoke Coll (MA)
Mount Union Coll (OH)
Muhlenberg Coll (PA)
Murray State U (KY)
Nebraska Wesleyan U (NE)
New Coll of Florida (FL)
New Jersey City U (NJ)
New Mexico Inst of Mining and Technology (NM)
New Mexico State U (NM)
New York Inst of Technology (NY)
New York U (NY)
Norfolk State U (VA)
North Carolina Central U (NC)
North Carolina State U (NC)
North Central Coll (IL)
North Dakota State U (ND)
Northeastern Illinois U (IL)
Northeastern State U (OK)
Northeastern U (MA)
Northern Arizona U (AZ)
Northern Illinois U (IL)
Northern Michigan U (MI)
North Georgia Coll & State U (GA)
North Park U (IL)
Northwestern Oklahoma State U (OK)
Northwestern State U of Louisiana (LA)
Northwestern U (IL)
Northwest Nazarene U (ID)
Oakland U (MI)
Oberlin Coll (OH)
Occidental Coll (CA)
Oglethorpe U (GA)
Ohio Northern U (OH)
The Ohio State U (OH)
Ohio U (OH)
Ohio Wesleyan U (OH)
Okanagan U Coll (BC, Canada)
Oklahoma Baptist U (OK)
Oklahoma City U (OK)
Oklahoma State U (OK)
Old Dominion U (VA)
Oral Roberts U (OK)
Oregon State U (OR)
Otterbein Coll (OH)
Ouachita Baptist U (AR)
Pace U (NY)
Pacific Lutheran U (WA)
Pacific Union Coll (CA)
Pacific U (OR)
Penn State U Abington Coll (PA)
Penn State U Altoona Coll (PA)
Penn State U at Erie, The Behrend Coll (PA)
Penn State U Beaver Campus of the Commonwealth Coll (PA)
Penn State U Berks Cmps of Berks-Lehigh Valley Coll (PA)
Penn State U Delaware County Campus of the Commonwealth Coll (PA)
Penn State U DuBois Campus of the Commonwealth Coll (PA)
Penn State U Fayette Campus of the Commonwealth Coll (PA)
Penn State U Hazleton Campus of the Commonwealth Coll (PA)
Penn State U Lehigh Valley Cmps of Berks-Lehigh Valley Coll (PA)
Penn State U McKeesport Campus of the Commonwealth Coll (PA)
Penn State U Mont Alto Campus of the Commonwealth Coll (PA)
Penn State U New Kensington Campus of the Commonwealth Coll (PA)
Penn State U Schuylkill Campus of the Capital Coll (PA)
Penn State U Shenango Campus of the Commonwealth Coll (PA)
Penn State U Univ Park Campus (PA)
Penn State U Wilkes-Barre Campus of the Commonwealth Coll (PA)
Penn State U Worthington Scranton Cmps Commonwealth Coll (PA)
Penn State U York Campus of the Commonwealth Coll (PA)
Pittsburg State U (KS)
Pitzer Coll (CA)
Point Loma Nazarene U (CA)
Polytechnic U, Brooklyn Campus (NY)
Pomona Coll (CA)
Pontifical Catholic U of Puerto Rico (PR)
Portland State U (OR)
Prairie View A&M U (TX)
Presbyterian Coll (SC)
Princeton U (NJ)
Principia Coll (IL)
Purdue U (IN)
Queens Coll of the City U of NY (NY)
Queen's U at Kingston (ON, Canada)
Ramapo Coll of New Jersey (NJ)
Randolph-Macon Coll (VA)
Randolph-Macon Woman's Coll (VA)
Reed Coll (OR)
Rensselaer Polytechnic Inst (NY)
Rhode Island Coll (RI)
Rhodes Coll (TN)
Rice U (TX)
The Richard Stockton Coll of New Jersey (NJ)
Rider U (NJ)
Roanoke Coll (VA)
Roberts Wesleyan Coll (NY)
Rochester Inst of Technology (NY)
Rockhurst U (MO)
Rollins Coll (FL)
Rose-Hulman Inst of Technology (IN)
Rutgers, The State U of New Jersey, Camden (NJ)
Rutgers, The State U of New Jersey, Newark (NJ)
Rutgers, The State U of New Jersey, New Brunswick/Piscataway (NJ)
Saginaw Valley State U (MI)
St. Ambrose U (IA)
St. Bonaventure U (NY)
St. Cloud State U (MN)
St. Francis Xavier U (NS, Canada)
St. John Fisher Coll (NY)
St. John's Coll (NM)
Saint John's U (MN)
St. John's U (NY)
Saint Joseph's U (PA)
St. Lawrence U (NY)
Saint Louis U (MO)
Saint Mary's Coll of California (CA)
St. Mary's Coll of Maryland (MD)
St. Mary's U of San Antonio (TX)
Saint Michael's Coll (VT)
St. Norbert Coll (WI)
St. Olaf Coll (MN)
Saint Vincent Coll (PA)
Salisbury U (MD)
Samford U (AL)
Sam Houston State U (TX)
San Diego State U (CA)
San Francisco State U (CA)
San Jose State U (CA)
Santa Clara U (CA)
Sarah Lawrence Coll (NY)
Scripps Coll (CA)
Seattle Pacific U (WA)
Seattle U (WA)
Seton Hall U (NJ)
Seton Hill U (PA)
Shaw U (NC)
Shippensburg U of Pennsylvania (PA)
Siena Coll (NY)
Simon Fraser U (BC, Canada)
Simon's Rock Coll of Bard (MA)
Skidmore Coll (NY)
Slippery Rock U of Pennsylvania (PA)
Smith Coll (MA)
Sonoma State U (CA)
South Carolina State U (SC)
South Dakota School of Mines and Technology (SD)
South Dakota State U (SD)
Southeastern Louisiana U (LA)
Southeastern Oklahoma State U (OK)
Southeast Missouri State U (MO)
Southern Adventist U (TN)
Southern Connecticut State U (CT)
Southern Illinois U Carbondale (IL)
Southern Illinois U Edwardsville (IL)
Southern Methodist U (TX)
Southern Nazarene U (OK)
Southern Oregon U (OR)
Southern Polytechnic State U (GA)
Southern U and A&M Coll (LA)
Southwestern Coll (KS)
Southwestern Oklahoma State U (OK)
Southwestern U (TX)
Southwest Missouri State U (MO)
Spelman Coll (GA)
Stanford U (CA)
State U of NY at Binghamton (NY)
State U of NY at New Paltz (NY)
State U of NY at Oswego (NY)
Plattsburgh State U of NY (NY)
State U of NY Coll at Brockport (NY)
State U of NY Coll at Cortland (NY)
State U of NY Coll at Fredonia (NY)
State U of NY Coll at Geneseo (NY)
State U of NY Coll at Oneonta (NY)
State U of NY Coll at Potsdam (NY)
State U of West Georgia (GA)
Stetson U (FL)
Stevens Inst of Technology (NJ)
Stony Brook U, State U of New York (NY)
Suffolk U (MA)
Susquehanna U (PA)
Swarthmore Coll (PA)
Sweet Briar Coll (VA)
Syracuse U (NY)
Talladega Coll (AL)
Tarleton State U (TX)
Taylor U (IN)
Tennessee State U (TN)
Tennessee Technological U (TN)
Texas A&M U (TX)
Texas A&M U–Commerce (TX)
Texas A&M U–Kingsville (TX)
Texas Christian U (TX)
Texas Lutheran U (TX)
Texas Southern U (TX)
Texas State U-San Marcos (TX)
Texas Tech U (TX)
Thiel Coll (PA)
Thomas Edison State Coll (NJ)
Thomas More Coll (KY)
Tougaloo Coll (MS)
Towson U (MD)
Transylvania U (KY)
Trent U (ON, Canada)
Trevecca Nazarene U (TN)
Trinity Coll (CT)
Trinity U (TX)
Truman State U (MO)
Tufts U (MA)
Tulane U (LA)
Tuskegee U (AL)
Union Coll (NE)
Union Coll (NY)
Union U (TN)
United States Air Force Acad (CO)
United States Military Acad (NY)
United States Naval Acad (MD)
Université de Montréal (QC, Canada)
Université de Sherbrooke (QC, Canada)
Université Laval (QC, Canada)
State U of NY at Albany (NY)
U at Buffalo, The State U of New York (NY)
U Coll of the Cariboo (BC, Canada)
U Coll of the Fraser Valley (BC, Canada)
The U of Akron (OH)
The U of Alabama (AL)
The U of Alabama at Birmingham (AL)
The U of Alabama in Huntsville (AL)
U of Alaska Fairbanks (AK)
U of Alberta (AB, Canada)
The U of Arizona (AZ)
U of Arkansas (AR)
U of Arkansas at Little Rock (AR)
The U of British Columbia (BC, Canada)
U of Calgary (AB, Canada)
U of Calif, Berkeley (CA)
U of Calif, Davis (CA)
U of Calif, Irvine (CA)
U of Calif, Los Angeles (CA)
U of Calif, Riverside (CA)
U of Calif, San Diego (CA)
U of Calif, Santa Barbara (CA)
U of Calif, Santa Cruz (CA)
U of Central Arkansas (AR)
U of Central Florida (FL)
U of Chicago (IL)
U of Cincinnati (OH)
U of Colorado at Boulder (CO)
U of Colorado at Colorado Springs (CO)
U of Colorado at Denver (CO)
U of Connecticut (CT)
U of Dallas (TX)
U of Dayton (OH)
U of Delaware (DE)
U of Denver (CO)
U of Evansville (IN)
U of Florida (FL)
U of Guelph (ON, Canada)
U of Hartford (CT)
U of Hawaii at Hilo (HI)
U of Hawaii at Manoa (HI)
U of Houston (TX)
U of Idaho (ID)
U of Illinois at Chicago (IL)
U of Illinois at Urbana–Champaign (IL)
U of Indianapolis (IN)
The U of Iowa (IA)
U of Kansas (KS)
U of Kentucky (KY)
U of King's Coll (NS, Canada)
U of La Verne (CA)
The U of Lethbridge (AB, Canada)
U of Louisiana at Lafayette (LA)
U of Louisville (KY)
U of Maine (ME)
U of Manitoba (MB, Canada)
U of Maryland, Baltimore County (MD)
U of Maryland, Coll Park (MD)
U of Massachusetts Amherst (MA)
U of Massachusetts Boston (MA)
U of Massachusetts Dartmouth (MA)
U of Massachusetts Lowell (MA)
The U of Memphis (TN)
U of Miami (FL)
U of Michigan (MI)
U of Michigan–Dearborn (MI)
U of Michigan–Flint (MI)
U of Minnesota, Duluth (MN)
U of Minnesota, Morris (MN)
U of Minnesota, Twin Cities Campus (MN)
U of Mississippi (MS)
U of Missouri–Columbia (MO)
U of Missouri–Kansas City (MO)
U of Missouri–Rolla (MO)
U of Missouri–St. Louis (MO)
The U of Montana–Missoula (MT)
U of Nebraska at Omaha (NE)
U of Nebraska–Lincoln (NE)
U of Nevada, Las Vegas (NV)
U of Nevada, Reno (NV)
U of New Brunswick Fredericton (NB, Canada)
U of New Hampshire (NH)
U of New Mexico (NM)
U of New Orleans (LA)
U of North Alabama (AL)
The U of North Carolina at Asheville (NC)
The U of North Carolina at Chapel Hill (NC)
The U of North Carolina at Charlotte (NC)
The U of North Carolina at Greensboro (NC)
The U of North Carolina at Pembroke (NC)
The U of North Carolina at Wilmington (NC)
U of North Dakota (ND)
U of Northern Colorado (CO)
U of Northern Iowa (IA)
U of North Florida (FL)
U of North Texas (TX)
U of Notre Dame (IN)
U of Oklahoma (OK)
U of Oregon (OR)
U of Ottawa (ON, Canada)
U of Pennsylvania (PA)
U of Pittsburgh (PA)
U of Portland (OR)
U of Prince Edward Island (PE, Canada)
U of Puget Sound (WA)
U of Redlands (CA)
U of Regina (SK, Canada)
U of Rhode Island (RI)
U of Richmond (VA)
U of Rochester (NY)
U of St. Thomas (MN)
U of San Diego (CA)
U of San Francisco (CA)
U of Saskatchewan (SK, Canada)
U of Science and Arts of Oklahoma (OK)
The U of Scranton (PA)
U of South Alabama (AL)
U of South Carolina (SC)
The U of South Dakota (SD)
U of Southern California (CA)
U of Southern Maine (ME)
U of South Florida (FL)
The U of Tennessee (TN)

The U of Tennessee at Chattanooga (TN)
The U of Texas at Arlington (TX)
The U of Texas at Austin (TX)
The U of Texas at Brownsville (TX)
The U of Texas at Dallas (TX)
The U of Texas–Pan American (TX)
U of the District of Columbia (DC)
U of the Pacific (CA)
U of the South (TN)
U of Toledo (OH)
U of Toronto (ON, Canada)
U of Tulsa (OK)
U of Utah (UT)
U of Vermont (VT)
U of Victoria (BC, Canada)
U of Virginia (VA)
U of Washington (WA)
U of Waterloo (ON, Canada)
The U of Western Ontario (ON, Canada)
U of West Florida (FL)
U of Windsor (ON, Canada)
U of Wisconsin–Eau Claire (WI)
U of Wisconsin–La Crosse (WI)
U of Wisconsin–Madison (WI)
U of Wisconsin–Milwaukee (WI)
U of Wisconsin–Oshkosh (WI)
U of Wisconsin–Parkside (WI)
U of Wisconsin–River Falls (WI)
U of Wisconsin–Stevens Point (WI)
U of Wisconsin–Whitewater (WI)
U of Wyoming (WY)
Ursinus Coll (PA)
Utah State U (UT)
Utica Coll (NY)
Valdosta State U (GA)
Valparaiso U (IN)
Vanderbilt U (TN)
Vassar Coll (NY)
Villanova U (PA)
Virginia Commonwealth U (VA)
Virginia Military Inst (VA)
Virginia Polytechnic Inst and State U (VA)
Virginia State U (VA)
Wabash Coll (IN)
Wagner Coll (NY)
Wake Forest U (NC)
Walla Walla Coll (WA)
Wartburg Coll (IA)
Washburn U (KS)
Washington & Jefferson Coll (PA)
Washington and Lee U (VA)
Washington Coll (MD)
Washington State U (WA)
Washington U in St. Louis (MO)
Wayne State U (MI)
Weber State U (UT)
Wellesley Coll (MA)
Wells Coll (NY)
Wesleyan Coll (GA)
Wesleyan U (CT)
West Chester U of Pennsylvania (PA)
Western Illinois U (IL)
Western Kentucky U (KY)
Western Michigan U (MI)
Western State Coll of Colorado (CO)
Western Washington U (WA)
Westminster Coll (MO)
Westminster Coll (PA)
Westminster Coll (UT)
Westmont Coll (CA)
West Texas A&M U (TX)
West Virginia U (WV)
West Virginia Wesleyan Coll (WV)
Wheaton Coll (IL)
Wheaton Coll (MA)
Wheeling Jesuit U (WV)
Whitman Coll (WA)
Whitworth Coll (WA)
Wichita State U (KS)
Widener U (PA)
Willamette U (OR)
William Jewell Coll (MO)
Williams Coll (MA)
Winona State U (MN)
Wittenberg U (OH)
Wofford Coll (SC)
Worcester Polytechnic Inst (MA)
Wright State U (OH)
Xavier U (OH)
Xavier U of Louisiana (LA)
Yale U (CT)
York Coll of the City U of New York (NY)
York U (ON, Canada)
Youngstown State U (OH)

PHYSICS RELATED

Angelo State U (TX)
Bridgewater Coll (VA)
Bridgewater State Coll (MA)
Brigham Young U (UT)
California State U, Chico (CA)
The Coll of Wooster (OH)
Cornell U (NY)
Drexel U (PA)
Embry-Riddle Aeronautical U (AZ)
Florida Inst of Technology (FL)
Hampden-Sydney Coll (VA)
Lawrence Technological U (MI)
New Jersey Inst of Technology (NJ)
North Carolina State U (NC)
Northern Arizona U (AZ)
Ohio Northern U (OH)
Ohio U (OH)
Oklahoma State U (OK)
Rutgers, The State U of New Jersey, Newark (NJ)
State U of NY Coll at Brockport (NY)
U at Buffalo, The State U of New York (NY)
The U of Akron (OH)
U of Arkansas (AR)
U of Miami (FL)
U of Nevada, Las Vegas (NV)
U of Northern Iowa (IA)
U of North Texas (TX)
U of Notre Dame (IN)
U of Regina (SK, Canada)
U of Rochester (NY)
Wright State U (OH)

PHYSICS TEACHER EDUCATION

Alma Coll (MI)
Appalachian State U (NC)
Arkansas State U (AR)
Auburn U (AL)
Baldwin-Wallace Coll (OH)
Baylor U (TX)
Bethel U (MN)
Bethune-Cookman Coll (FL)
Bishop's U (QC, Canada)
Bridgewater Coll (VA)
Brigham Young U (UT)
Brigham Young U–Hawaii (HI)
Brooklyn Coll of the City U of NY (NY)
Buena Vista U (IA)
Carroll Coll (WI)
Cedarville U (OH)
Centenary Coll of Louisiana (LA)
Central Methodist Coll (MO)
Central Michigan U (MI)
Central Missouri State U (MO)
Chadron State Coll (NE)
Chatham Coll (PA)
Christian Brothers U (TN)
City Coll of the City U of NY (NY)
The Coll of New Jersey (NJ)
Colorado State U (CO)
Concordia Coll (MN)
Concordia U (NE)
Connecticut Coll (CT)
Cornell U (NY)
Delaware State U (DE)
East Central U (OK)
Eastern Michigan U (MI)
Eastern Washington U (WA)
Elmhurst Coll (IL)
Florida Inst of Technology (FL)
Georgia Southern U (GA)
Greenville Coll (IL)
Gustavus Adolphus Coll (MN)
Hardin-Simmons U (TX)
Hastings Coll (NE)
Hofstra U (NY)
Hope Coll (MI)
Illinois Wesleyan U (IL)
Indiana U Bloomington (IN)
Indiana U–Purdue U Fort Wayne (IN)
Indiana U South Bend (IN)
Ithaca Coll (NY)
Juniata Coll (PA)
King Coll (TN)
Lebanon Valley Coll (PA)
Le Moyne Coll (NY)
Louisiana State U in Shreveport (LA)
Louisiana Tech U (LA)
Mansfield U of Pennsylvania (PA)
Maryville Coll (TN)
Mayville State U (ND)
McGill U (QC, Canada)
Miami Dade Coll (FL)
Miami U Hamilton (OH)
Minot State U (ND)
Moravian Coll (PA)
Murray State U (KY)
New York Inst of Technology (NY)
New York U (NY)
North Carolina Central U (NC)
North Carolina State U (NC)
North Dakota State U (ND)
Northern Arizona U (AZ)
Northern Michigan U (MI)
Ohio Dominican U (OH)
Ohio Northern U (OH)
Ohio Wesleyan U (OH)
Pace U (NY)
Pittsburg State U (KS)
Roberts Wesleyan Coll (NY)
St. Ambrose U (IA)
St. Bonaventure U (NY)
St. John's U (NY)
Saint Mary's U of Minnesota (MN)
Saint Vincent Coll (PA)
Shawnee State U (OH)
Southern Arkansas U–Magnolia (AR)
Southwest Missouri State U (MO)
State U of NY Coll at Brockport (NY)
State U of NY Coll at Cortland (NY)
State U of NY Coll at Oneonta (NY)
State U of NY Coll at Potsdam (NY)
State U of West Georgia (GA)
Syracuse U (NY)
Union Coll (NE)
The U of Akron (OH)
The U of Arizona (AZ)
U of Calif, San Diego (CA)
U of Delaware (DE)
U of Illinois at Chicago (IL)
The U of Iowa (IA)
U of Louisiana at Lafayette (LA)
U of Michigan–Flint (MI)
U of Missouri–Columbia (MO)
U of Missouri–St. Louis (MO)
U of Nebraska–Lincoln (NE)
The U of North Carolina at Wilmington (NC)
U of Puerto Rico, Cayey U Coll (PR)
U of Regina (SK, Canada)
U of St. Thomas (MN)
The U of South Dakota (SD)
U of Utah (UT)
U of Waterloo (ON, Canada)
U of Windsor (ON, Canada)
U of Wisconsin–River Falls (WI)
Utah State U (UT)
Utica Coll (NY)
Valparaiso U (IN)
Washington U in St. Louis (MO)
Weber State U (UT)
West Chester U of Pennsylvania (PA)
Western Michigan U (MI)
Wheeling Jesuit U (WV)
Xavier U (OH)
York U (ON, Canada)
Youngstown State U (OH)

PHYSIOLOGICAL PSYCHOLOGY/ PSYCHOBIOLOGY

Albright Coll (PA)
Arcadia U (PA)
Averett U (VA)
Centre Coll (KY)
Claremont McKenna Coll (CA)
Coll of Notre Dame of Maryland (MD)
Florida Atlantic U (FL)
Grand Valley State U (MI)
Hamilton Coll (NY)
Hampshire Coll (MA)
Harvard U (MA)
Hiram Coll (OH)
Holy Names Coll (CA)
The Johns Hopkins U (MD)
Lebanon Valley Coll (PA)
Lincoln U (PA)
Luther Coll (IA)
McGill U (QC, Canada)
Medaille Coll (NY)
Mills Coll (CA)
Mount Allison U (NB, Canada)
Oberlin Coll (OH)
Occidental Coll (CA)
Quinnipiac U (CT)
Ripon Coll (WI)
Saint Mary's Coll of California (CA)
Scripps Coll (CA)
Simmons Coll (MA)
State U of NY at Binghamton (NY)
State U of NY at New Paltz (NY)
Swarthmore Coll (PA)
U of Calif, Los Angeles (CA)
U of Calif, Riverside (CA)
U of Calif, Santa Cruz (CA)
U of Evansville (IN)
U of Miami (FL)
U of New Brunswick Fredericton (NB, Canada)
U of Southern California (CA)
Vassar Coll (NY)
Wagner Coll (NY)
Washington Coll (MD)
Westminster Coll (PA)
Wheaton Coll (MA)
Wilson Coll (PA)
York Coll (NE)

PHYSIOLOGY

Brigham Young U (UT)
California State U, Long Beach (CA)
Cornell U (NY)
Eastern Michigan U (MI)
Michigan State U (MI)
Northern Michigan U (MI)
San Jose State U (CA)
Southern Illinois U Carbondale (IL)
U of Alberta (AB, Canada)
The U of British Columbia (BC, Canada)
U of Calif, Los Angeles (CA)
U of Illinois at Urbana–Champaign (IL)
U of Saskatchewan (SK, Canada)

PIANO AND ORGAN

Abilene Christian U (TX)
Acadia U (NS, Canada)
Andrews U (MI)
Anna Maria Coll (MA)
Augustana Coll (IL)
Baldwin-Wallace Coll (OH)
Ball State U (IN)
Barry U (FL)
Belmont U (TN)
Berklee Coll of Music (MA)
Bethel Coll (IN)
Bethesda Christian U (CA)
Birmingham-Southern Coll (AL)
Blue Mountain Coll (MS)
Boston U (MA)
Bowling Green State U (OH)
Brenau U (GA)
Brigham Young U (UT)
Brigham Young U–Hawaii (HI)
Bryan Coll (TN)
Butler U (IN)
California Inst of the Arts (CA)
California State U, Chico (CA)
California State U, Fullerton (CA)
California State U, Sacramento (CA)
Calvary Bible Coll and Theological Sem (MO)
Calvin Coll (MI)
Campbellsville U (KY)
Campbell U (NC)
Canadian Mennonite U (MB, Canada)
Capital U (OH)
Carson-Newman Coll (TN)
Catawba Coll (NC)
The Catholic U of America (DC)
Cedarville U (OH)
Centenary Coll of Louisiana (LA)
Central Washington U (WA)
Cleveland Inst of Music (OH)
Coker Coll (SC)
The Colburn School of Performing Arts (CA)
Columbia Coll (SC)
Columbus State U (GA)
Concordia Coll (MN)
Concordia U (IL)
Concordia U (NE)
Converse Coll (SC)
Cornish Coll of the Arts (WA)
Dallas Baptist U (TX)
DePaul U (IL)
Dillard U (LA)
Dordt Coll (IA)
Drake U (IA)
East Central U (OK)
Eastern Washington U (WA)
East Texas Baptist U (TX)
Florida State U (FL)
Furman U (SC)
Georgetown Coll (KY)
Grace Coll (IN)
Grace U (NE)
Grand Canyon U (AZ)
Grand Valley State U (MI)
Hannibal-LaGrange Coll (MO)
Hardin-Simmons U (TX)
Hastings Coll (NE)
Heidelberg Coll (OH)
Houghton Coll (NY)
Howard Payne U (TX)
Huntingdon Coll (AL)
Huntington Coll (IN)
Illinois Wesleyan U (IL)
Indiana U Bloomington (IN)
Indiana U–Purdue U Fort Wayne (IN)
Inter American U of PR, San Germán Campus (PR)
Ithaca Coll (NY)
The Juilliard School (NY)
Lamar U (TX)
Lawrence U (WI)
Lipscomb U (TN)
Louisiana Coll (LA)
Loyola U New Orleans (LA)
Manhattan School of Music (NY)
Mannes Coll of Music, New School U (NY)
Mansfield U of Pennsylvania (PA)
Maryville Coll (TN)
The Master's Coll and Sem (CA)
McGill U (QC, Canada)
McMurry U (TX)
Memorial U of Newfoundland (NL, Canada)
Meredith Coll (NC)
Minnesota State U Mankato (MN)
Minnesota State U Moorhead (MN)
Mississippi Coll (MS)
Mount Allison U (NB, Canada)
Newberry Coll (SC)
New England Conservatory of Music (MA)
New World School of the Arts (FL)
New York U (NY)
North Carolina School of the Arts (NC)
Northeastern State U (OK)
Northern Michigan U (MI)
North Greenville Coll (SC)
Northwestern Coll (MN)
Northwestern U (IL)
Notre Dame de Namur U (CA)
Nyack Coll (NY)
Oberlin Coll (OH)
The Ohio State U (OH)
Ohio U (OH)
Oklahoma Baptist U (OK)
Oklahoma City U (OK)
Olivet Nazarene U (IL)
Otterbein Coll (OH)
Ouachita Baptist U (AR)
Pacific Lutheran U (WA)
Pacific Union Coll (CA)
Palm Beach Atlantic U (FL)
Peabody Conserv of Music of Johns Hopkins U (MD)
Pittsburg State U (KS)
Prairie View A&M U (TX)
Queens U of Charlotte (NC)
Rider U (NJ)
Roberts Wesleyan Coll (NY)
Roosevelt U (IL)
St. Cloud State U (MN)
Samford U (AL)
Sarah Lawrence Coll (NY)
Seton Hill U (PA)
Shenandoah U (VA)
Shorter Coll (GA)
Southern Methodist U (TX)
Southern Nazarene U (OK)
Southwestern Oklahoma State U (OK)
Southwestern U (TX)
Spring Arbor U (MI)
State U of NY Coll at Fredonia (NY)
Stetson U (FL)
Susquehanna U (PA)
Syracuse U (NY)
Tabor Coll (KS)
Taylor U (IN)
Texas A&M U–Commerce (TX)
Texas Christian U (TX)
Texas Southern U (TX)
Trinity Christian Coll (IL)
Truman State U (MO)
Union U (TN)
The U of Akron (OH)
U of Alberta (AB, Canada)
The U of British Columbia (BC, Canada)
U of Cincinnati (OH)
U of Delaware (DE)
The U of Iowa (IA)
U of Kansas (KS)
U of Miami (FL)
U of Michigan (MI)
U of Minnesota, Duluth (MN)
U of Missouri–Kansas City (MO)
U of Montevallo (AL)
U of New Hampshire (NH)
The U of North Carolina at Greensboro (NC)
U of North Texas (TX)
U of Oklahoma (OK)
U of Redlands (CA)
U of Sioux Falls (SD)
U of Southern California (CA)
The U of Tennessee at Martin (TN)
U of the Pacific (CA)
U of Tulsa (OK)
U of Victoria (BC, Canada)
U of Washington (WA)
The U of Western Ontario (ON, Canada)
Valparaiso U (IN)
Vanderbilt U (TN)

Walla Walla Coll (WA)
Washburn U (KS)
Weber State U (UT)
Webster U (MO)
West Chester U of Pennsylvania (PA)
Westminster Choir Coll of Rider U (NJ)
Whitworth Coll (WA)
Willamette U (OR)
William Tyndale Coll (MI)
Wingate U (NC)
Xavier U of Louisiana (LA)
York U (ON, Canada)
Youngstown State U (OH)

PLANETARY ASTRONOMY AND SCIENCE
California Inst of Technology (CA)
Cornell U (NY)
U of Waterloo (ON, Canada)
The U of Western Ontario (ON, Canada)

PLANT GENETICS
Brigham Young U (UT)
Cornell U (NY)
Hampshire Coll (MA)

PLANT MOLECULAR BIOLOGY
Pittsburg State U (KS)

PLANT PATHOLOGY/ PHYTOPATHOLOGY
Auburn U (AL)
Clemson U (SC)
Cornell U (NY)
Michigan State U (MI)
New Mexico State U (NM)
The Ohio State U (OH)
State U of NY Coll of Environ Sci and Forestry (NY)
U of Arkansas (AR)
U of Florida (FL)
Washington State U (WA)

PLANT PHYSIOLOGY
Florida State U (FL)
Pittsburg State U (KS)
State U of NY Coll of Environ Sci and Forestry (NY)
Washington State U (WA)

PLANT PROTECTION AND INTEGRATED PEST MANAGEMENT
California State Polytechnic U, Pomona (CA)
Florida Ag and Mech U (FL)
Iowa State U of Science and Technology (IA)
Lubbock Christian U (TX)
Mississippi State U (MS)
North Dakota State U (ND)
State U of NY Coll of Environ Sci and Forestry (NY)
Sterling Coll (VT)
Texas A&M U (TX)
Texas Tech U (TX)
U of Arkansas (AR)
U of Delaware (DE)
U of Georgia (GA)
U of Nebraska–Lincoln (NE)
The U of Tennessee (TN)
West Texas A&M U (TX)

PLANT SCIENCES
Arkansas State U (AR)
Auburn U (AL)
California State U, Fresno (CA)
Colorado State U (CO)
Cornell U (NY)
Lakehead U (ON, Canada)
Louisiana State U and A&M Coll (LA)
Louisiana Tech U (LA)
Lubbock Christian U (TX)
McGill U (QC, Canada)
Middle Tennessee State U (TN)
Montana State U–Bozeman (MT)
Nova Scotia Ag Coll (NS, Canada)
The Ohio State U (OH)
Oklahoma State U (OK)
Rutgers, The State U of New Jersey, New Brunswick/Piscataway (NJ)
Southern Illinois U Carbondale (IL)
State U of NY Coll of A&T at Cobleskill (NY)
State U of NY Coll of Environ Sci and Forestry (NY)
Sterling Coll (VT)
Tuskegee U (AL)
The U of Arizona (AZ)
U of Arkansas (AR)
U of Calif, Los Angeles (CA)
U of Calif, Santa Cruz (CA)
U of Florida (FL)
U of Idaho (ID)
U of Louisiana at Lafayette (LA)
U of Maryland, Coll Park (MD)
U of Massachusetts Amherst (MA)
U of Minnesota, Twin Cities Campus (MN)
U of Missouri–Columbia (MO)
U of Saskatchewan (SK, Canada)
The U of Tennessee (TN)
U of Vermont (VT)
The U of Western Ontario (ON, Canada)
Utah State U (UT)
Washington State U (WA)

PLANT SCIENCES RELATED
Auburn U (AL)
Sterling Coll (VT)
U of Vermont (VT)
Utah State U (UT)
Washington State U (WA)
West Virginia U (WV)

PLASTICS ENGINEERING TECHNOLOGY
Ball State U (IN)
Central Connecticut State U (CT)
Ferris State U (MI)
Pennsylvania Coll of Technology (PA)
Pittsburg State U (KS)
Shawnee State U (OH)
Western Michigan U (MI)
Western Washington U (WA)

PLAYWRITING AND SCREENWRITING
Bard Coll (NY)
Brigham Young U (UT)
Columbia Coll Chicago (IL)
Concordia U (QC, Canada)
DePaul U (IL)
Drexel U (PA)
Emerson Coll (MA)
Fordham U (NY)
Loyola Marymount U (CA)
Metropolitan State U (MN)
New York U (NY)
Ohio U (OH)
Palm Beach Atlantic U (FL)
Sarah Lawrence Coll (NY)
Simon's Rock Coll of Bard (MA)
U of Michigan (MI)
U of Southern California (CA)
York U (ON, Canada)

POLISH
Madonna U (MI)
U of Illinois at Chicago (IL)

POLITICAL COMMUNICATION
Emerson Coll (MA)
Nebraska Wesleyan U (NE)

POLITICAL SCIENCE AND GOVERNMENT
Abilene Christian U (TX)
Acadia U (NS, Canada)
Adams State Coll (CO)
Adelphi U (NY)
Adrian Coll (MI)
Agnes Scott Coll (GA)
Alabama Ag and Mech U (AL)
Alabama State U (AL)
Albany State U (GA)
Albertson Coll of Idaho (ID)
Albertus Magnus Coll (CT)
Albion Coll (MI)
Albright Coll (PA)
Alcorn State U (MS)
Alderson-Broaddus Coll (WV)
Alfred U (NY)
Allegheny Coll (PA)
Alma Coll (MI)
Alvernia Coll (PA)
Alverno Coll (WI)
American Intl Coll (MA)
American U (DC)
American U in Bulgaria(Bulgaria)
The American U in Cairo(Egypt)
Amherst Coll (MA)
Andrews U (MI)
Angelo State U (TX)
Anna Maria Coll (MA)
Antioch Coll (OH)
Appalachian State U (NC)
Aquinas Coll (MI)
Arcadia U (PA)
Arizona State U (AZ)
Arizona State U West (AZ)
Arkansas State U (AR)
Armstrong Atlantic State U (GA)
Ashland U (OH)
Assumption Coll (MA)
Athabasca U (AB, Canada)
Athens State U (AL)
Auburn U (AL)
Auburn U Montgomery (AL)
Augsburg Coll (MN)
Augustana Coll (IL)
Augustana Coll (SD)
Augusta State U (GA)
Aurora U (IL)
Austin Coll (TX)
Austin Peay State U (TN)
Ave Maria Coll (MI)
Averett U (VA)
Avila U (MO)
Azusa Pacific U (CA)
Baker U (KS)
Baldwin-Wallace Coll (OH)
Ball State U (IN)
Barber-Scotia Coll (NC)
Bard Coll (NY)
Barnard Coll (NY)
Barry U (FL)
Barton Coll (NC)
Bates Coll (ME)
Baylor U (TX)
Bellarmine U (KY)
Belmont Abbey Coll (NC)
Belmont U (TN)
Beloit Coll (WI)
Bemidji State U (MN)
Benedictine Coll (KS)
Benedictine U (IL)
Berea Coll (KY)
Baruch Coll of the City U of NY (NY)
Berry Coll (GA)
Bethany Coll (KS)
Bethany Coll (WV)
Bethel U (MN)
Bethune-Cookman Coll (FL)
Birmingham-Southern Coll (AL)
Bishop's U (QC, Canada)
Blackburn Coll (IL)
Black Hills State U (SD)
Bloomfield Coll (NJ)
Bloomsburg U of Pennsylvania (PA)
Boise State U (ID)
Boston Coll (MA)
Boston U (MA)
Bowdoin Coll (ME)
Bowie State U (MD)
Bowling Green State U (OH)
Bradley U (IL)
Brandeis U (MA)
Brenau U (GA)
Brewton-Parker Coll (GA)
Briar Cliff U (IA)
Bridgewater Coll (VA)
Bridgewater State Coll (MA)
Brigham Young U (UT)
Brigham Young U–Hawaii (HI)
Brock U (ON, Canada)
Brooklyn Coll of the City U of NY (NY)
Brown U (RI)
Bryn Mawr Coll (PA)
Bucknell U (PA)
Buena Vista U (IA)
State U of NY Coll at Buffalo (NY)
Butler U (IN)
Cabrini Coll (PA)
Caldwell Coll (NJ)
California Baptist U (CA)
California Lutheran U (CA)
California Polytechnic State U, San Luis Obispo (CA)
California State Polytechnic U, Pomona (CA)
California State U, Chico (CA)
California State U, Dominguez Hills (CA)
California State U, Fresno (CA)
California State U, Fullerton (CA)
California State U, Hayward (CA)
California State U, Long Beach (CA)
California State U, Los Angeles (CA)
California State U, Sacramento (CA)
California State U, San Bernardino (CA)
California State U, San Marcos (CA)
California State U, Stanislaus (CA)
California U of Pennsylvania (PA)
Calumet Coll of Saint Joseph (IN)
Calvin Coll (MI)
Cameron U (OK)
Campbellsville U (KY)
Campbell U (NC)
Canadian Mennonite U (MB, Canada)
Canisius Coll (NY)
Capital U (OH)
Cardinal Stritch U (WI)
Carleton Coll (MN)
Carleton U (ON, Canada)
Carnegie Mellon U (PA)
Carroll Coll (MT)
Carroll Coll (WI)
Carson-Newman Coll (TN)
Carthage Coll (WI)
Case Western Reserve U (OH)
Catawba Coll (NC)
The Catholic U of America (DC)
Cedar Crest Coll (PA)
Cedarville U (OH)
Centenary Coll (NJ)
Centenary Coll of Louisiana (LA)
Central Coll (IA)
Central Connecticut State U (CT)
Central Methodist Coll (MO)
Central Michigan U (MI)
Central Missouri State U (MO)
Central State U (OH)
Central Washington U (WA)
Centre Coll (KY)
Chaminade U of Honolulu (HI)
Chapman U (CA)
Charleston Southern U (SC)
Chatham Coll (PA)
Chestnut Hill Coll (PA)
Cheyney U of Pennsylvania (PA)
Chicago State U (IL)
Christendom Coll (VA)
Christopher Newport U (VA)
Citadel, The Military Coll of South Carolina (SC)
City Coll of the City U of NY (NY)
Claremont McKenna Coll (CA)
Clarion U of Pennsylvania (PA)
Clark Atlanta U (GA)
Clarkson U (NY)
Clark U (MA)
Clemson U (SC)
Cleveland State U (OH)
Coastal Carolina U (SC)
Coe Coll (IA)
Coker Coll (SC)
Colby Coll (ME)
Colgate U (NY)
Coll of Charleston (SC)
The Coll of New Jersey (NJ)
The Coll of New Rochelle (NY)
Coll of Notre Dame of Maryland (MD)
Coll of Saint Benedict (MN)
Coll of St. Catherine (MN)
Coll of St. Joseph (VT)
The Coll of Saint Rose (NY)
Coll of Santa Fe (NM)
The Coll of Southeastern Europe, The American U of Athens(Greece)
Coll of Staten Island of the City U of NY (NY)
Coll of the Holy Cross (MA)
Coll of the Ozarks (MO)
The Coll of William and Mary (VA)
The Coll of Wooster (OH)
Colorado Christian U (CO)
The Colorado Coll (CO)
Colorado State U (CO)
Colorado State U-Pueblo (CO)
Columbia Coll (MO)
Columbia Coll (NY)
Columbia Coll (SC)
Columbia Union Coll (MD)
Columbia U, School of General Studies (NY)
Columbus State U (GA)
Concord Coll (WV)
Concordia Coll (MN)
Concordia U (IL)
Concordia U (QC, Canada)
Concordia U Coll of Alberta (AB, Canada)
Connecticut Coll (CT)
Converse Coll (SC)
Cornell Coll (IA)
Cornell U (NY)
Cornerstone U (MI)
Creighton U (NE)
Cumberland Coll (KY)
Cumberland U (TN)
Curry Coll (MA)
Daemen Coll (NY)
Dalhousie U (NS, Canada)
Dallas Baptist U (TX)
Dartmouth Coll (NH)
Davidson Coll (NC)
Davis & Elkins Coll (WV)
Delaware State U (DE)
Delta State U (MS)
Denison U (OH)
DePaul U (IL)
DePauw U (IN)
DeSales U (PA)
Dickinson Coll (PA)
Dickinson State U (ND)
Dillard U (LA)
Doane Coll (NE)
Dominican U (IL)
Dominican U of California (CA)
Dordt Coll (IA)
Dowling Coll (NY)
Drake U (IA)
Drew U (NJ)
Drury U (MO)
Duke U (NC)
Duquesne U (PA)
Earlham Coll (IN)
East Carolina U (NC)
East Central U (OK)
Eastern Connecticut State U (CT)
Eastern Illinois U (IL)
Eastern Kentucky U (KY)
Eastern Michigan U (MI)
Eastern New Mexico U (NM)
Eastern U (PA)
Eastern Washington U (WA)
East Stroudsburg U of Pennsylvania (PA)
Eckerd Coll (FL)
Edgewood Coll (WI)
Edinboro U of Pennsylvania (PA)
Elizabeth City State U (NC)
Elizabethtown Coll (PA)
Elmhurst Coll (IL)
Elmira Coll (NY)
Elon U (NC)
Emory & Henry Coll (VA)
Emory U (GA)
Emporia State U (KS)
Eugene Lang Coll, New School U (NY)
Eureka Coll (IL)
Evangel U (MO)
The Evergreen State Coll (WA)
Excelsior Coll (NY)
Fairfield U (CT)
Fairleigh Dickinson U, Florham (NJ)
Fairleigh Dickinson U, Teaneck-Metro Campus (NJ)
Fairmont State Coll (WV)
Faulkner U (AL)
Fayetteville State U (NC)
Ferrum Coll (VA)
Flagler Coll (FL)
Florida Ag and Mech U (FL)
Florida Atlantic U (FL)
Florida Gulf Coast U (FL)
Florida Intl U (FL)
Florida Southern Coll (FL)
Florida State U (FL)
Fordham U (NY)
Fort Hays State U (KS)
Fort Lewis Coll (CO)
Fort Valley State U (GA)
Framingham State Coll (MA)
Franciscan U of Steubenville (OH)
Francis Marion U (SC)
Franklin and Marshall Coll (PA)
Franklin Coll (IN)
Franklin Pierce Coll (NH)
Fresno Pacific U (CA)
Frostburg State U (MD)
Furman U (SC)
Gannon U (PA)
Gardner-Webb U (NC)
Geneva Coll (PA)
George Mason U (VA)
Georgetown Coll (KY)
Georgetown U (DC)
The George Washington U (DC)
Georgia Coll & State U (GA)
Georgia Southern U (GA)
Georgia Southwestern State U (GA)
Georgia State U (GA)
Gettysburg Coll (PA)
Gonzaga U (WA)
Gordon Coll (MA)
Goshen Coll (IN)
Goucher Coll (MD)
Grambling State U (LA)
Grand Canyon U (AZ)
Grand Valley State U (MI)
Grand View Coll (IA)
Greensboro Coll (NC)
Grinnell Coll (IA)
Grove City Coll (PA)
Guilford Coll (NC)
Gustavus Adolphus Coll (MN)
Hamilton Coll (NY)
Hamline U (MN)
Hampden-Sydney Coll (VA)
Hampshire Coll (MA)
Hampton U (VA)
Hanover Coll (IN)
Harding U (AR)
Hardin-Simmons U (TX)
Hartwick Coll (NY)

Harvard U (MA)
Hastings Coll (NE)
Haverford Coll (PA)
Hawai'i Pacific U (HI)
Heidelberg Coll (OH)
Henderson State U (AR)
Hendrix Coll (AR)
High Point U (NC)
Hillsdale Coll (MI)
Hiram Coll (OH)
Hobart and William Smith Colls (NY)
Hofstra U (NY)
Hollins U (VA)
Hood Coll (MD)
Hope Coll (MI)
Houghton Coll (NY)
Houston Baptist U (TX)
Howard Payne U (TX)
Howard U (DC)
Humboldt State U (CA)
Hunter Coll of the City U of NY (NY)
Huntingdon Coll (AL)
Huston-Tillotson Coll (TX)
Idaho State U (ID)
Illinois Coll (IL)
Illinois Inst of Technology (IL)
Illinois State U (IL)
Illinois Wesleyan U (IL)
Indiana State U (IN)
Indiana U Bloomington (IN)
Indiana U Northwest (IN)
Indiana U of Pennsylvania (PA)
Indiana U–Purdue U Fort Wayne (IN)
Indiana U–Purdue U Indianapolis (IN)
Indiana U South Bend (IN)
Indiana U Southeast (IN)
Inter American U of PR, San Germán Campus (PR)
Iona Coll (NY)
Iowa State U of Science and Technology (IA)
Ithaca Coll (NY)
Jacksonville State U (AL)
Jacksonville U (FL)
James Madison U (VA)
Jamestown Coll (ND)
John Cabot U(Italy)
John Carroll U (OH)
The Johns Hopkins U (MD)
Johnson C. Smith U (NC)
Johnson State Coll (VT)
Juniata Coll (PA)
Kalamazoo Coll (MI)
Kansas State U (KS)
Kean U (NJ)
Keene State Coll (NH)
Kennesaw State U (GA)
Kent State U (OH)
Kentucky State U (KY)
Kentucky Wesleyan Coll (KY)
Kenyon Coll (OH)
King Coll (TN)
King's Coll (PA)
Knox Coll (IL)
Kutztown U of Pennsylvania (PA)
Lafayette Coll (PA)
LaGrange Coll (GA)
Lake Forest Coll (IL)
Lakehead U (ON, Canada)
Lake Superior State U (MI)
Lamar U (TX)
Lambuth U (TN)
Lander U (SC)
La Salle U (PA)
Laurentian U (ON, Canada)
Lawrence U (WI)
Lebanon Valley Coll (PA)
Lehigh U (PA)
Lehman Coll of the City U of NY (NY)
Le Moyne Coll (NY)
Lenoir-Rhyne Coll (NC)
Lewis & Clark Coll (OR)
Lewis U (IL)
Liberty U (VA)
Lincoln U (MO)
Lincoln U (PA)
Lindenwood U (MO)
Linfield Coll (OR)
Lipscomb U (TN)
Livingstone Coll (NC)
Lock Haven U of Pennsylvania (PA)
Long Island U, Brooklyn Campus (NY)
Long Island U, C.W. Post Campus (NY)
Longwood U (VA)
Loras Coll (IA)
Louisiana State U and A&M Coll (LA)
Louisiana State U in Shreveport (LA)
Louisiana Tech U (LA)
Loyola Coll in Maryland (MD)
Loyola Marymount U (CA)
Loyola U Chicago (IL)
Loyola U New Orleans (LA)
Luther Coll (IA)
Lycoming Coll (PA)
Lynchburg Coll (VA)
Lynn U (FL)
Lyon Coll (AR)
Macalester Coll (MN)
MacMurray Coll (IL)
Malone Coll (OH)
Manchester Coll (IN)
Manhattan Coll (NY)
Manhattanville Coll (NY)
Mansfield U of Pennsylvania (PA)
Marian Coll of Fond du Lac (WI)
Marietta Coll (OH)
Marist Coll (NY)
Marlboro Coll (VT)
Marquette U (WI)
Marshall U (WV)
Mars Hill Coll (NC)
Martin U (IN)
Mary Baldwin Coll (VA)
Marygrove Coll (MI)
Marymount Coll of Fordham U (NY)
Marymount Manhattan Coll (NY)
Marymount U (VA)
Maryville Coll (TN)
Mary Washington Coll (VA)
Massachusetts Inst of Technology (MA)
The Master's Coll and Sem (CA)
McDaniel Coll (MD)
McGill U (QC, Canada)
McKendree Coll (IL)
McMurry U (TX)
McNeese State U (LA)
Memorial U of Newfoundland (NL, Canada)
Mercer U (GA)
Mercy Coll (NY)
Mercyhurst Coll (PA)
Meredith Coll (NC)
Merrimack Coll (MA)
Messiah Coll (PA)
Methodist Coll (NC)
Metropolitan State Coll of Denver (CO)
Miami U (OH)
Miami U Hamilton (OH)
Michigan State U (MI)
Middlebury Coll (VT)
Middle Tennessee State U (TN)
Midwestern State U (TX)
Miles Coll (AL)
Millersville U of Pennsylvania (PA)
Millikin U (IL)
Millsaps Coll (MS)
Mills Coll (CA)
Minnesota State U Mankato (MN)
Minnesota State U Moorhead (MN)
Mississippi Coll (MS)
Mississippi State U (MS)
Mississippi Valley State U (MS)
Missouri Southern State U (MO)
Missouri Valley Coll (MO)
Missouri Western State Coll (MO)
Molloy Coll (NY)
Monmouth Coll (IL)
Monmouth U (NJ)
Montana State U–Bozeman (MT)
Montclair State U (NJ)
Moravian Coll (PA)
Morehead State U (KY)
Morehouse Coll (GA)
Morgan State U (MD)
Morningside Coll (IA)
Morris Coll (SC)
Mount Allison U (NB, Canada)
Mount Aloysius Coll (PA)
Mount Holyoke Coll (MA)
Mount Mercy Coll (IA)
Mount Saint Mary Coll (NY)
Mount St. Mary's Coll (CA)
Mount Saint Mary's Coll and Sem (MD)
Mount Saint Vincent U (NS, Canada)
Mount Union Coll (OH)
Muhlenberg Coll (PA)
Murray State U (KY)
Nazareth Coll of Rochester (NY)
Nebraska Wesleyan U (NE)
Neumann Coll (PA)
Newberry Coll (SC)
New Coll of Florida (FL)
New Jersey City U (NJ)
New Mexico Highlands U (NM)
New Mexico State U (NM)
New York Inst of Technology (NY)
New York U (NY)
Niagara U (NY)
Nicholls State U (LA)
Norfolk State U (VA)
North Carolina Central U (NC)
North Carolina State U (NC)
North Carolina Wesleyan Coll (NC)
North Central Coll (IL)
North Dakota State U (ND)
Northeastern Illinois U (IL)
Northeastern State U (OK)
Northeastern U (MA)
Northern Arizona U (AZ)
Northern Illinois U (IL)
Northern Michigan U (MI)
Northern State U (SD)
North Georgia Coll & State U (GA)
North Park U (IL)
Northwestern Coll (IA)
Northwestern Oklahoma State U (OK)
Northwestern State U of Louisiana (LA)
Northwestern U (IL)
Northwest Nazarene U (ID)
Notre Dame Coll (OH)
Notre Dame de Namur U (CA)
Oakland U (MI)
Oberlin Coll (OH)
Occidental Coll (CA)
Oglethorpe U (GA)
Ohio Dominican U (OH)
Ohio Northern U (OH)
The Ohio State U (OH)
Ohio U (OH)
Ohio Wesleyan U (OH)
Okanagan U Coll (BC, Canada)
Oklahoma Baptist U (OK)
Oklahoma City U (OK)
Oklahoma State U (OK)
Old Dominion U (VA)
Oral Roberts U (OK)
Oregon State U (OR)
Ottawa U (KS)
Otterbein Coll (OH)
Ouachita Baptist U (AR)
Our Lady of the Lake U of San Antonio (TX)
Pace U (NY)
Pacific Lutheran U (WA)
Pacific Union Coll (CA)
Pacific U (OR)
Palm Beach Atlantic U (FL)
Park U (MO)
Penn State U Abington Coll (PA)
Penn State U Altoona Coll (PA)
Penn State U at Erie, The Behrend Coll (PA)
Penn State U Beaver Campus of the Commonwealth Coll (PA)
Penn State U Berks Cmps of Berks-Lehigh Valley Coll (PA)
Penn State U Delaware County Campus of the Commonwealth Coll (PA)
Penn State U DuBois Campus of the Commonwealth Coll (PA)
Penn State U Fayette Campus of the Commonwealth Coll (PA)
Penn State U Hazleton Campus of the Commonwealth Coll (PA)
Penn State U Lehigh Valley Cmps of Berks-Lehigh Valley Coll (PA)
Penn State U McKeesport Campus of the Commonwealth Coll (PA)
Penn State U Mont Alto Campus of the Commonwealth Coll (PA)
Penn State U New Kensington Campus of the Commonwealth Coll (PA)
Penn State U Schuylkill Campus of the Capital Coll (PA)
Penn State U Shenango Campus of the Commonwealth Coll (PA)
Penn State U Univ Park Campus (PA)
Penn State U Wilkes-Barre Campus of the Commonwealth Coll (PA)
Penn State U Worthington Scranton Cmps Commonwealth Coll (PA)
Penn State U York Campus of the Commonwealth Coll (PA)
Pepperdine U, Malibu (CA)
Pfeiffer U (NC)
Piedmont Coll (GA)
Pine Manor Coll (MA)
Pittsburg State U (KS)
Pitzer Coll (CA)
Plymouth State U (NH)
Point Loma Nazarene U (CA)
Point Park U (PA)
Pomona Coll (CA)
Pontifical Catholic U of Puerto Rico (PR)
Portland State U (OR)
Prairie View A&M U (TX)
Presbyterian Coll (SC)
Princeton U (NJ)
Principia Coll (IL)
Providence Coll (RI)
Purdue U (IN)
Queens Coll of the City U of NY (NY)
Queen's U at Kingston (ON, Canada)
Queens U of Charlotte (NC)
Quincy U (IL)
Quinnipiac U (CT)
Radford U (VA)
Ramapo Coll of New Jersey (NJ)
Randolph-Macon Coll (VA)
Randolph-Macon Woman's Coll (VA)
Redeemer U Coll (ON, Canada)
Reed Coll (OR)
Regis Coll (MA)
Regis U (CO)
Rhode Island Coll (RI)
Rhodes Coll (TN)
Rice U (TX)
The Richard Stockton Coll of New Jersey (NJ)
Richmond, The American Intl U in London(United Kingdom)
Rider U (NJ)
Ripon Coll (WI)
Rivier Coll (NH)
Roanoke Coll (VA)
Rockford Coll (IL)
Rockhurst U (MO)
Rocky Mountain Coll (MT)
Roger Williams U (RI)
Rollins Coll (FL)
Roosevelt U (IL)
Rosemont Coll (PA)
Rowan U (NJ)
Russell Sage Coll (NY)
Rutgers, The State U of New Jersey, Camden (NJ)
Rutgers, The State U of New Jersey, Newark (NJ)
Rutgers, The State U of New Jersey, New Brunswick/Piscataway (NJ)
Sacred Heart U (CT)
Saginaw Valley State U (MI)
St. Ambrose U (IA)
St. Andrews Presbyterian Coll (NC)
Saint Anselm Coll (NH)
Saint Augustine's Coll (NC)
St. Bonaventure U (NY)
St. Cloud State U (MN)
St. Edward's U (TX)
St. Francis Coll (NY)
Saint Francis U (PA)
St. Francis Xavier U (NS, Canada)
St. Gregory's U (OK)
St. John Fisher Coll (NY)
Saint John's U (MN)
St. John's U (NY)
Saint Joseph Coll (CT)
Saint Joseph's Coll (IN)
St. Joseph's Coll, Suffolk Campus (NY)
Saint Joseph's U (PA)
St. Lawrence U (NY)
Saint Leo U (FL)
Saint Louis U (MO)
Saint Martin's Coll (WA)
Saint Mary's Coll (IN)
Saint Mary's Coll of California (CA)
St. Mary's Coll of Maryland (MD)
Saint Mary's U of Minnesota (MN)
St. Mary's U of San Antonio (TX)
Saint Michael's Coll (VT)
St. Norbert Coll (WI)
St. Olaf Coll (MN)
St. Thomas U (FL)
St. Thomas U (NB, Canada)
Saint Vincent Coll (PA)
Saint Xavier U (IL)
Salem State Coll (MA)
Salisbury U (MD)
Salve Regina U (RI)
Samford U (AL)
Sam Houston State U (TX)
San Diego State U (CA)
San Francisco State U (CA)
San Jose State U (CA)
Santa Clara U (CA)
Sarah Lawrence Coll (NY)
Schreiner U (TX)
Scripps Coll (CA)
Seattle Pacific U (WA)
Seattle U (WA)
Seton Hall U (NJ)
Seton Hill U (PA)
Shaw U (NC)
Shepherd U (WV)
Shippensburg U of Pennsylvania (PA)
Siena Coll (NY)
Simmons Coll (MA)
Simon Fraser U (BC, Canada)
Simon's Rock Coll of Bard (MA)
Simpson Coll (IA)
Skidmore Coll (NY)
Slippery Rock U of Pennsylvania (PA)
Smith Coll (MA)
Sonoma State U (CA)
South Carolina State U (SC)
South Dakota State U (SD)
Southeastern Louisiana U (LA)
Southeastern Oklahoma State U (OK)
Southeast Missouri State U (MO)
Southern Arkansas U–Magnolia (AR)
Southern Connecticut State U (CT)
Southern Illinois U Carbondale (IL)
Southern Illinois U Edwardsville (IL)
Southern Methodist U (TX)
Southern Nazarene U (OK)
Southern Oregon U (OR)
Southern U and A&M Coll (LA)
Southern Utah U (UT)
Southwest Baptist U (MO)
Southwestern Oklahoma State U (OK)
Southwestern U (TX)
Southwest Missouri State U (MO)
Spelman Coll (GA)
Springfield Coll (MA)
Spring Hill Coll (AL)
Stanford U (CA)
State U of NY at Binghamton (NY)
State U of NY at New Paltz (NY)
State U of NY at Oswego (NY)
Plattsburgh State U of NY (NY)
State U of NY Coll at Brockport (NY)
State U of NY Coll at Cortland (NY)
State U of NY Coll at Fredonia (NY)
State U of NY Coll at Geneseo (NY)
State U of NY Coll at Oneonta (NY)
State U of NY Coll at Potsdam (NY)
State U of West Georgia (GA)
Stephens Coll (MO)
Stetson U (FL)
Stonehill Coll (MA)
Stony Brook U, State U of New York (NY)
Suffolk U (MA)
Susquehanna U (PA)
Swarthmore Coll (PA)
Sweet Briar Coll (VA)
Syracuse U (NY)
Tarleton State U (TX)
Taylor U (IN)
Tennessee State U (TN)
Tennessee Technological U (TN)
Texas A&M Intl U (TX)
Texas A&M U (TX)
Texas A&M U–Commerce (TX)
Texas A&M U–Corpus Christi (TX)
Texas A&M U–Kingsville (TX)
Texas Christian U (TX)
Texas Lutheran U (TX)
Texas Southern U (TX)
Texas State U-San Marcos (TX)
Texas Tech U (TX)
Texas Wesleyan U (TX)
Texas Woman's U (TX)
Thiel Coll (PA)
Thomas Edison State Coll (NJ)
Thomas More Coll of Liberal Arts (NH)
Thomas U (GA)
Tougaloo Coll (MS)
Towson U (MD)
Transylvania U (KY)
Trent U (ON, Canada)
Trinity Coll (CT)
Trinity Coll (DC)
Trinity U (TX)
Trinity Western U (BC, Canada)
Troy State U (AL)
Troy State U Montgomery (AL)
Truman State U (MO)
Tufts U (MA)
Tulane U (LA)
Tuskegee U (AL)
Union Coll (NY)
Union U (TN)
United States Air Force Acad (CO)
United States Coast Guard Acad (CT)
United States Military Acad (NY)
United States Naval Acad (MD)
Université de Montréal (QC, Canada)
Université Laval (QC, Canada)

State U of NY at Albany (NY)
U at Buffalo, The State U of New York (NY)
U Coll of the Cariboo (BC, Canada)
The U of Akron (OH)
The U of Alabama (AL)
The U of Alabama at Birmingham (AL)
The U of Alabama in Huntsville (AL)
U of Alaska Fairbanks (AK)
U of Alaska Southeast (AK)
U of Alberta (AB, Canada)
The U of Arizona (AZ)
U of Arkansas (AR)
U of Arkansas at Little Rock (AR)
U of Arkansas at Monticello (AR)
U of Baltimore (MD)
The U of British Columbia (BC, Canada)
U of Calgary (AB, Canada)
U of Calif, Berkeley (CA)
U of Calif, Davis (CA)
U of Calif, Irvine (CA)
U of Calif, Los Angeles (CA)
U of Calif, Riverside (CA)
U of Calif, San Diego (CA)
U of Calif, Santa Barbara (CA)
U of Calif, Santa Cruz (CA)
U of Central Arkansas (AR)
U of Central Florida (FL)
U of Charleston (WV)
U of Chicago (IL)
U of Cincinnati (OH)
U of Colorado at Boulder (CO)
U of Colorado at Colorado Springs (CO)
U of Colorado at Denver (CO)
U of Connecticut (CT)
U of Dallas (TX)
U of Dayton (OH)
U of Delaware (DE)
U of Denver (CO)
U of Detroit Mercy (MI)
U of Evansville (IN)
The U of Findlay (OH)
U of Florida (FL)
U of Georgia (GA)
U of Great Falls (MT)
U of Guelph (ON, Canada)
U of Hartford (CT)
U of Hawaii at Hilo (HI)
U of Hawaii at Manoa (HI)
U of Houston (TX)
U of Houston–Clear Lake (TX)
U of Idaho (ID)
U of Illinois at Chicago (IL)
U of Illinois at Springfield (IL)
U of Illinois at Urbana–Champaign (IL)
U of Indianapolis (IN)
The U of Iowa (IA)
U of Judaism (CA)
U of Kansas (KS)
U of Kentucky (KY)
U of King's Coll (NS, Canada)
U of La Verne (CA)
The U of Lethbridge (AB, Canada)
U of Louisiana at Lafayette (LA)
U of Louisville (KY)
U of Maine (ME)
U of Maine at Farmington (ME)
U of Maine at Presque Isle (ME)
U of Manitoba (MB, Canada)
U of Mary Hardin-Baylor (TX)
U of Maryland, Baltimore County (MD)
U of Maryland, Coll Park (MD)
U of Massachusetts Amherst (MA)
U of Massachusetts Boston (MA)
U of Massachusetts Dartmouth (MA)
U of Massachusetts Lowell (MA)
The U of Memphis (TN)
U of Miami (FL)
U of Michigan (MI)
U of Michigan–Dearborn (MI)
U of Michigan–Flint (MI)
U of Minnesota, Duluth (MN)
U of Minnesota, Morris (MN)
U of Minnesota, Twin Cities Campus (MN)
U of Mississippi (MS)
U of Missouri–Columbia (MO)
U of Missouri–Kansas City (MO)
U of Missouri–St. Louis (MO)
U of Mobile (AL)
U of Montevallo (AL)
U of Nebraska at Omaha (NE)
U of Nebraska–Lincoln (NE)
U of Nevada, Las Vegas (NV)
U of Nevada, Reno (NV)
U of New Brunswick Fredericton (NB, Canada)
U of New Hampshire (NH)
U of New Haven (CT)
U of New Mexico (NM)
U of New Orleans (LA)
U of North Alabama (AL)
The U of North Carolina at Asheville (NC)
The U of North Carolina at Chapel Hill (NC)
The U of North Carolina at Charlotte (NC)
The U of North Carolina at Greensboro (NC)
The U of North Carolina at Pembroke (NC)
The U of North Carolina at Wilmington (NC)
U of North Dakota (ND)
U of Northern Colorado (CO)
U of Northern Iowa (IA)
U of North Florida (FL)
U of North Texas (TX)
U of Notre Dame (IN)
U of Oklahoma (OK)
U of Oregon (OR)
U of Ottawa (ON, Canada)
U of Pennsylvania (PA)
U of Pittsburgh (PA)
U of Pittsburgh at Bradford (PA)
U of Pittsburgh at Greensburg (PA)
U of Pittsburgh at Johnstown (PA)
U of Portland (OR)
U of Prince Edward Island (PE, Canada)
U of Puget Sound (WA)
U of Redlands (CA)
U of Regina (SK, Canada)
U of Rhode Island (RI)
U of Richmond (VA)
U of Rochester (NY)
U of St. Francis (IL)
U of Saint Mary (KS)
U of St. Thomas (MN)
U of St. Thomas (TX)
U of San Diego (CA)
U of San Francisco (CA)
U of Saskatchewan (SK, Canada)
U of Science and Arts of Oklahoma (OK)
The U of Scranton (PA)
U of Sioux Falls (SD)
U of South Alabama (AL)
U of South Carolina (SC)
U of South Carolina Aiken (SC)
U of South Carolina Spartanburg (SC)
The U of South Dakota (SD)
U of Southern California (CA)
U of Southern Indiana (IN)
U of Southern Maine (ME)
U of South Florida (FL)
The U of Tampa (FL)
The U of Tennessee (TN)
The U of Tennessee at Chattanooga (TN)
The U of Tennessee at Martin (TN)
The U of Texas at Arlington (TX)
The U of Texas at Austin (TX)
The U of Texas at Brownsville (TX)
The U of Texas at Dallas (TX)
The U of Texas at Tyler (TX)
The U of Texas–Pan American (TX)
U of the District of Columbia (DC)
U of the Incarnate Word (TX)
U of the Ozarks (AR)
U of the Pacific (CA)
U of the South (TN)
U of Toledo (OH)
U of Toronto (ON, Canada)
U of Tulsa (OK)
U of Utah (UT)
U of Vermont (VT)
U of Victoria (BC, Canada)
U of Virginia (VA)
The U of Virginia's Coll at Wise (VA)
U of Washington (WA)
U of Waterloo (ON, Canada)
The U of Western Ontario (ON, Canada)
U of West Florida (FL)
U of Windsor (ON, Canada)
U of Wisconsin–Eau Claire (WI)
U of Wisconsin–Green Bay (WI)
U of Wisconsin–La Crosse (WI)
U of Wisconsin–Madison (WI)
U of Wisconsin–Milwaukee (WI)
U of Wisconsin–Oshkosh (WI)
U of Wisconsin–Parkside (WI)
U of Wisconsin–Platteville (WI)
U of Wisconsin–River Falls (WI)
U of Wisconsin–Stevens Point (WI)
U of Wisconsin–Superior (WI)
U of Wisconsin–Whitewater (WI)
U of Wyoming (WY)
Ursinus Coll (PA)
Utah State U (UT)
Utica Coll (NY)
Valdosta State U (GA)
Valparaiso U (IN)
Vanderbilt U (TN)
Vanguard U of Southern California (CA)
Vassar Coll (NY)
Villanova U (PA)
Virginia Commonwealth U (VA)
Virginia Intermont Coll (VA)
Virginia Polytechnic Inst and State U (VA)
Virginia State U (VA)
Virginia Union U (VA)
Virginia Wesleyan Coll (VA)
Voorhees Coll (SC)
Wabash Coll (IN)
Wagner Coll (NY)
Wake Forest U (NC)
Walsh U (OH)
Wartburg Coll (IA)
Washburn U (KS)
Washington & Jefferson Coll (PA)
Washington and Lee U (VA)
Washington Coll (MD)
Washington State U (WA)
Washington U in St. Louis (MO)
Wayland Baptist U (TX)
Waynesburg Coll (PA)
Wayne State Coll (NE)
Wayne State U (MI)
Weber State U (UT)
Webster U (MO)
Wellesley Coll (MA)
Wells Coll (NY)
Wesleyan Coll (GA)
Wesleyan U (CT)
Wesley Coll (DE)
West Chester U of Pennsylvania (PA)
Western Carolina U (NC)
Western Connecticut State U (CT)
Western Illinois U (IL)
Western Kentucky U (KY)
Western Michigan U (MI)
Western New England Coll (MA)
Western Oregon U (OR)
Western State Coll of Colorado (CO)
Western Washington U (WA)
Westfield State Coll (MA)
West Liberty State Coll (WV)
Westminster Coll (MO)
Westminster Coll (PA)
Westminster Coll (UT)
Westmont Coll (CA)
West Texas A&M U (TX)
West Virginia State Coll (WV)
West Virginia U (WV)
West Virginia Wesleyan Coll (WV)
Wheaton Coll (IL)
Wheaton Coll (MA)
Wheeling Jesuit U (WV)
Whitman Coll (WA)
Whitworth Coll (WA)
Wichita State U (KS)
Widener U (PA)
Wilberforce U (OH)
Wilkes U (PA)
Willamette U (OR)
William Jewell Coll (MO)
William Paterson U of New Jersey (NJ)
William Penn U (IA)
Williams Coll (MA)
William Woods U (MO)
Winona State U (MN)
Winston-Salem State U (NC)
Winthrop U (SC)
Wisconsin Lutheran Coll (WI)
Wittenberg U (OH)
Wofford Coll (SC)
Wright State U (OH)
Xavier U (OH)
Xavier U of Louisiana (LA)
Yale U (CT)
York Coll of Pennsylvania (PA)
York Coll of the City U of New York (NY)
York U (ON, Canada)
Youngstown State U (OH)

POLITICAL SCIENCE AND GOVERNMENT RELATED

Buena Vista U (IA)
Capital U (OH)
Claremont McKenna Coll (CA)
Cornell U (NY)
Liberty U (VA)
Monmouth Coll (IL)
North Carolina State U (NC)
Saint Mary's Coll of California (CA)
The U of Akron (OH)
U of Northern Iowa (IA)
Western New England Coll (MA)

POLYMER CHEMISTRY

Carnegie Mellon U (PA)
Clemson U (SC)
Georgia Inst of Technology (GA)
Harvard U (MA)
Rochester Inst of Technology (NY)
State U of NY Coll of Environ Sci and Forestry (NY)
The U of Akron (OH)
U of Wisconsin–Stevens Point (WI)
Winona State U (MN)

POLYMER/PLASTICS ENGINEERING

Ball State U (IN)
Case Western Reserve U (OH)
Eastern Michigan U (MI)
Ferris State U (MI)
Kettering U (MI)
North Dakota State U (ND)
Penn State U at Erie, The Behrend Coll (PA)
The U of Akron (OH)
U of Massachusetts Lowell (MA)
U of Southern California (CA)
Winona State U (MN)

PORTUGUESE

Brigham Young U (UT)
Brooklyn Coll of the City U of NY (NY)
Florida Intl U (FL)
Georgetown U (DC)
Harvard U (MA)
Indiana U Bloomington (IN)
Marlboro Coll (VT)
New York U (NY)
The Ohio State U (OH)
Rutgers, The State U of New Jersey, New Brunswick/Piscataway (NJ)
Smith Coll (MA)
Tulane U (LA)
United States Military Acad (NY)
U of Calif, Los Angeles (CA)
U of Calif, Santa Barbara (CA)
U of Connecticut (CT)
U of Florida (FL)
U of Illinois at Urbana–Champaign (IL)
The U of Iowa (IA)
U of Massachusetts Amherst (MA)
U of Massachusetts Dartmouth (MA)
U of Minnesota, Twin Cities Campus (MN)
U of New Mexico (NM)
U of Southern California (CA)
The U of Texas at Austin (TX)
U of Toronto (ON, Canada)
U of Wisconsin–Madison (WI)
Vanderbilt U (TN)
Yale U (CT)

POULTRY SCIENCE

Auburn U (AL)
Coll of the Ozarks (MO)
Coll of the Ozarks (MO)
Delaware State U (DE)
Mississippi State U (MS)
North Carolina State U (NC)
Sterling Coll (VT)
Texas A&M U (TX)
Tuskegee U (AL)
U of Arkansas (AR)
U of Calif, Davis (CA)
U of Florida (FL)
U of Georgia (GA)
U of Maryland Eastern Shore (MD)
U of Wisconsin–Madison (WI)
Virginia Polytechnic Inst and State U (VA)

PRE-DENTISTRY STUDIES

Abilene Christian U (TX)
Acadia U (NS, Canada)
Adams State Coll (CO)
Albertus Magnus Coll (CT)
Alderson-Broaddus Coll (WV)
Alice Lloyd Coll (KY)
Allegheny Coll (PA)
Alma Coll (MI)
American Intl Coll (MA)
American U (DC)
Aquinas Coll (MI)
Arcadia U (PA)
Ashland U (OH)
Atlantic Union Coll (MA)
Auburn U (AL)
Augsburg Coll (MN)
Augustana Coll (IL)
Augustana Coll (SD)
Baldwin-Wallace Coll (OH)
Ball State U (IN)
Bard Coll (NY)
Barry U (FL)
Baylor U (TX)
Bellarmine U (KY)
Belmont Abbey Coll (NC)
Beloit Coll (WI)
Benedictine U (IL)
Berea Coll (KY)
Bethany Coll (WV)
Bethel Coll (IN)
Bethel Coll (TN)
Birmingham-Southern Coll (AL)
Blackburn Coll (IL)
Bloomfield Coll (NJ)
Blue Mountain Coll (MS)
Boise State U (ID)
Boston U (MA)
Briar Cliff U (IA)
State U of NY Coll at Buffalo (NY)
California State U, Chico (CA)
California State U, Dominguez Hills (CA)
California State U, Hayward (CA)
Calvin Coll (MI)
Campbellsville U (KY)
Campbell U (NC)
Capital U (OH)
Cardinal Stritch U (WI)
Carroll Coll (MT)
Carroll Coll (WI)
Carthage Coll (WI)
Catawba Coll (NC)
Cedar Crest Coll (PA)
Cedarville U (OH)
Centenary Coll of Louisiana (LA)
Central Christian Coll of Kansas (KS)
Central Missouri State U (MO)
Charleston Southern U (SC)
Chicago State U (IL)
Chowan Coll (NC)
Christian Brothers U (TN)
City Coll of the City U of NY (NY)
Claremont McKenna Coll (CA)
Clarkson U (NY)
Clark U (MA)
Coe Coll (IA)
Coll Misericordia (PA)
Coll of Charleston (SC)
Coll of Mount Saint Vincent (NY)
Coll of Saint Benedict (MN)
Coll of St. Catherine (MN)
Coll of Saint Mary (NE)
Coll of the Holy Cross (MA)
Colorado State U (CO)
Colorado State U-Pueblo (CO)
Columbia Coll (MO)
Columbia Union Coll (MD)
Columbus State U (GA)
Concordia Coll (MN)
Concordia U (IL)
Concordia U (NE)
Converse Coll (SC)
Cornerstone U (MI)
Cumberland U (TN)
Dakota State U (SD)
Dalhousie U (NS, Canada)
Davis & Elkins Coll (WV)
Defiance Coll (OH)
DeSales U (PA)
Dickinson Coll (PA)
Dickinson State U (ND)
Dillard U (LA)
Dominican U (IL)
Dordt Coll (IA)
Drake U (IA)
Drury U (MO)
D'Youville Coll (NY)
East Central U (OK)
Eastern Mennonite U (VA)
Eastern Michigan U (MI)
Eastern Oregon U (OR)
Eastern Washington U (WA)
Edgewood Coll (WI)
Elizabethtown Coll (PA)
Elmhurst Coll (IL)
Elmira Coll (NY)
Elms Coll (MA)
Elon U (NC)
Emory & Henry Coll (VA)
Eureka Coll (IL)
Evangel U (MO)
Florida Ag and Mech U (FL)
Florida Southern Coll (FL)
Florida State U (FL)
Fordham U (NY)
Fort Lewis Coll (CO)
Framingham State Coll (MA)
Franklin Pierce Coll (NH)
Furman U (SC)
Gannon U (PA)
Gardner-Webb U (NC)
Georgetown Coll (KY)
The George Washington U (DC)
Georgia Southwestern State U (GA)
Gettysburg Coll (PA)

Goshen Coll (IN)
Graceland U (IA)
Grand Canyon U (AZ)
Grand Valley State U (MI)
Grove City Coll (PA)
Gustavus Adolphus Coll (MN)
Hamline U (MN)
Hampton U (VA)
Harding U (AR)
Hardin-Simmons U (TX)
Harvard U (MA)
Hastings Coll (NE)
Heidelberg Coll (OH)
High Point U (NC)
Hillsdale Coll (MI)
Hiram Coll (OH)
Hobart and William Smith Colls (NY)
Hofstra U (NY)
Houghton Coll (NY)
Humboldt State U (CA)
Huntington Coll (IN)
Illinois Coll (IL)
Immaculata U (PA)
Indiana U Bloomington (IN)
Indiana U–Purdue U Fort Wayne (IN)
Indiana U–Purdue U Indianapolis (IN)
Iowa State U of Science and Technology (IA)
Iowa Wesleyan Coll (IA)
Jacksonville U (FL)
John Carroll U (OH)
Juniata Coll (PA)
Kansas State U (KS)
Kansas Wesleyan U (KS)
Kent State U (OH)
Kentucky Wesleyan Coll (KY)
Kenyon Coll (OH)
Keuka Coll (NY)
King's Coll (PA)
LaGrange Coll (GA)
Lake Erie Coll (OH)
Lake Forest Coll (IL)
Lake Superior State U (MI)
Lamar U (TX)
Lambuth U (TN)
La Salle U (PA)
Lawrence U (WI)
Le Moyne Coll (NY)
Lenoir-Rhyne Coll (NC)
LeTourneau U (TX)
Lewis U (IL)
Limestone Coll (SC)
Lindenwood U (MO)
Lindsey Wilson Coll (KY)
Lipscomb U (TN)
Lock Haven U of Pennsylvania (PA)
Longwood U (VA)
Loyola U Chicago (IL)
Lycoming Coll (PA)
Lynchburg Coll (VA)
MacMurray Coll (IL)
Madonna U (MI)
Manchester Coll (IN)
Marian Coll (IN)
Marian Coll of Fond du Lac (WI)
Marist Coll (NY)
Marquette U (WI)
Mars Hill Coll (NC)
Mary Washington Coll (VA)
Mayville State U (ND)
McKendree Coll (IL)
McPherson Coll (KS)
Mercer U (GA)
Mercy Coll (NY)
Mercyhurst Coll (PA)
Meredith Coll (NC)
Merrimack Coll (MA)
Methodist Coll (NC)
Miami U (OH)
Michigan Technological U (MI)
Millikin U (IL)
Minnesota State U Mankato (MN)
Minnesota State U Moorhead (MN)
Mississippi Coll (MS)
Missouri Southern State U (MO)
Missouri Valley Coll (MO)
Molloy Coll (NY)
Montclair State U (NJ)
Morgan State U (MD)
Morningside Coll (IA)
Mount Allison U (NB, Canada)
Mount Mary Coll (WI)
Mount Mercy Coll (IA)
Mount St. Mary's Coll (CA)
Mount Vernon Nazarene U (OH)
Muhlenberg Coll (PA)
Nazareth Coll of Rochester (NY)
Newberry Coll (SC)
New Mexico Inst of Mining and Technology (NM)
New York U (NY)
Niagara U (NY)
Nicholls State U (LA)
North Central Coll (IL)
Northeastern State U (OK)
Northern Michigan U (MI)
Northern State U (SD)
North Georgia Coll & State U (GA)
Northland Coll (WI)
North Park U (IL)
Northwestern Oklahoma State U (OK)
Notre Dame de Namur U (CA)
Nova Southeastern U (FL)
Oglethorpe U (GA)
Ohio Northern U (OH)
Ohio U (OH)
Ohio Wesleyan U (OH)
Oklahoma Baptist U (OK)
Oklahoma City U (OK)
Oklahoma State U (OK)
Olivet Coll (MI)
Olivet Nazarene U (IL)
Oral Roberts U (OK)
Oregon State U (OR)
Otterbein Coll (OH)
Ouachita Baptist U (AR)
Pacific Union Coll (CA)
Pacific U (OR)
Pepperdine U, Malibu (CA)
Pittsburg State U (KS)
Presbyterian Coll (SC)
Quincy U (IL)
Quinnipiac U (CT)
Redeemer U Coll (ON, Canada)
Regis U (CO)
Rensselaer Polytechnic Inst (NY)
Rhode Island Coll (RI)
Ripon Coll (WI)
Rivier Coll (NH)
Roberts Wesleyan Coll (NY)
Rochester Inst of Technology (NY)
Rockford Coll (IL)
Roger Williams U (RI)
Rollins Coll (FL)
Roosevelt U (IL)
Rutgers, The State U of New Jersey, New Brunswick/Piscataway (NJ)
Sacred Heart U (CT)
Saint Anselm Coll (NH)
St. Bonaventure U (NY)
St. Cloud State U (MN)
Saint Francis U (PA)
St. Francis Xavier U (NS, Canada)
St. Gregory's U (OK)
Saint John's U (MN)
St. Joseph's Coll, Suffolk Campus (NY)
Saint Martin's Coll (WA)
Saint Mary-of-the-Woods Coll (IN)
St. Mary's U of San Antonio (TX)
Saint Michael's Coll (VT)
St. Norbert Coll (WI)
St. Thomas U (FL)
Salem State Coll (MA)
Sam Houston State U (TX)
Sarah Lawrence Coll (NY)
Schreiner U (TX)
Seattle Pacific U (WA)
Seton Hill U (PA)
Siena Coll (NY)
Simmons Coll (MA)
Simpson Coll (IA)
Sonoma State U (CA)
South Carolina State U (SC)
South Dakota State U (SD)
Southern Connecticut State U (CT)
Southern Nazarene U (OK)
Southwestern Oklahoma State U (OK)
Springfield Coll (MA)
Spring Hill Coll (AL)
State U of NY at New Paltz (NY)
State U of NY at Oswego (NY)
State U of NY Coll at Brockport (NY)
State U of NY Coll at Cortland (NY)
State U of NY Coll at Geneseo (NY)
State U of NY Coll at Oneonta (NY)
State U of NY Coll of Environ Sci and Forestry (NY)
Stetson U (FL)
Stevens Inst of Technology (NJ)
Suffolk U (MA)
Susquehanna U (PA)
Syracuse U (NY)
Tabor Coll (KS)
Talladega Coll (AL)
Tarleton State U (TX)
Taylor U (IN)
Tennessee Technological U (TN)
Tennessee Wesleyan Coll (TN)
Texas A&M U–Kingsville (TX)
Texas Lutheran U (TX)
Texas Southern U (TX)
Texas Wesleyan U (TX)
Thiel Coll (PA)
Tougaloo Coll (MS)
Trinity Christian Coll (IL)
Trinity U (TX)
Trinity Western U (BC, Canada)
Troy State U (AL)
Truman State U (MO)
Union U (TN)
Université de Montréal (QC, Canada)
Université Laval (QC, Canada)
U Coll of the Cariboo (BC, Canada)
The U of Akron (OH)
U of Alberta (AB, Canada)
U of Arkansas at Monticello (AR)
U of Bridgeport (CT)
The U of British Columbia (BC, Canada)
U of Colorado at Colorado Springs (CO)
U of Dallas (TX)
U of Dayton (OH)
U of Detroit Mercy (MI)
U of Evansville (IN)
U of Hartford (CT)
U of Houston (TX)
U of Illinois at Chicago (IL)
U of Indianapolis (IN)
The U of Iowa (IA)
U of La Verne (CA)
U of Manitoba (MB, Canada)
U of Mary Hardin-Baylor (TX)
U of Maryland, Baltimore County (MD)
U of Maryland Eastern Shore (MD)
U of Massachusetts Amherst (MA)
U of Minnesota, Duluth (MN)
U of Minnesota, Morris (MN)
U of Minnesota, Twin Cities Campus (MN)
U of Missouri–Rolla (MO)
U of Missouri–St. Louis (MO)
The U of Montana–Western (MT)
U of Montevallo (AL)
U of Nebraska–Lincoln (NE)
U of New Brunswick Fredericton (NB, Canada)
The U of North Carolina at Greensboro (NC)
U of Oregon (OR)
U of Pittsburgh at Johnstown (PA)
U of Portland (OR)
U of Prince Edward Island (PE, Canada)
U of Puget Sound (WA)
U of Regina (SK, Canada)
U of St. Francis (IL)
U of Saint Francis (IN)
U of St. Thomas (TX)
U of San Francisco (CA)
U of Saskatchewan (SK, Canada)
U of Sioux Falls (SD)
The U of Tampa (FL)
The U of Tennessee at Martin (TN)
The U of Texas–Pan American (TX)
U of the Incarnate Word (TX)
U of the Ozarks (AR)
U of Toledo (OH)
U of Victoria (BC, Canada)
U of Windsor (ON, Canada)
U of Wisconsin–Green Bay (WI)
U of Wisconsin–Milwaukee (WI)
U of Wisconsin–Oshkosh (WI)
U of Wisconsin–Parkside (WI)
U of Wisconsin–River Falls (WI)
Upper Iowa U (IA)
Urbana U (OH)
Utah State U (UT)
Utica Coll (NY)
Valley City State U (ND)
Villa Julie Coll (MD)
Virginia Wesleyan Coll (VA)
Wagner Coll (NY)
Walla Walla Coll (WA)
Walsh U (OH)
Washington Coll (MD)
Washington State U (WA)
Washington U in St. Louis (MO)
Waynesburg Coll (PA)
Wells Coll (NY)
Western Connecticut State U (CT)
Western State Coll of Colorado (CO)
West Liberty State Coll (WV)
Westminster Coll (PA)
Westmont Coll (CA)
West Virginia State Coll (WV)
West Virginia Wesleyan Coll (WV)
Wheeling Jesuit U (WV)
Whitworth Coll (WA)
Widener U (PA)
William Jewell Coll (MO)
William Paterson U of New Jersey (NJ)
William Penn U (IA)
Williams Baptist Coll (AR)
Winona State U (MN)
Wittenberg U (OH)
Wofford Coll (SC)
Wright State U (OH)
Xavier U of Louisiana (LA)
York Coll of Pennsylvania (PA)
York U (ON, Canada)
Youngstown State U (OH)

PRE-ENGINEERING

Adams State Coll (CO)
Azusa Pacific U (CA)
Columbia Coll (MO)
Delaware State U (DE)
Lewis & Clark Coll (OR)
McPherson Coll (KS)
Roberts Wesleyan Coll (NY)
The U of Montana–Missoula (MT)
Valley City State U (ND)
Waynesburg Coll (PA)

PRE-LAW STUDIES

Abilene Christian U (TX)
Acadia U (NS, Canada)
Adams State Coll (CO)
Albertus Magnus Coll (CT)
Albion Coll (MI)
Albright Coll (PA)
Alderson-Broaddus Coll (WV)
Alice Lloyd Coll (KY)
Allegheny Coll (PA)
Alma Coll (MI)
Alvernia Coll (PA)
American Intl Coll (MA)
American U (DC)
Andrews U (MI)
Antioch Coll (OH)
Aquinas Coll (MI)
Arcadia U (PA)
Arizona State U (AZ)
Ashland U (OH)
Atlantic Union Coll (MA)
Auburn U (AL)
Augsburg Coll (MN)
Augustana Coll (IL)
Augustana Coll (SD)
Azusa Pacific U (CA)
Babson Coll (MA)
Baldwin-Wallace Coll (OH)
Ball State U (IN)
Barber-Scotia Coll (NC)
Bard Coll (NY)
Barry U (FL)
Baylor U (TX)
Bay Path Coll (MA)
Becker Coll (MA)
Bellarmine U (KY)
Belmont Abbey Coll (NC)
Beloit Coll (WI)
Bemidji State U (MN)
Benedictine U (IL)
Bethany Coll (WV)
Bethel Coll (IN)
Biola U (CA)
Birmingham-Southern Coll (AL)
Blackburn Coll (IL)
Blue Mountain Coll (MS)
Bowling Green State U (OH)
Brenau U (GA)
Brewton-Parker Coll (GA)
Briar Cliff U (IA)
Bridgewater State Coll (MA)
State U of NY Coll at Buffalo (NY)
California State Polytechnic U, Pomona (CA)
California State U, Dominguez Hills (CA)
California State U, Fresno (CA)
Calumet Coll of Saint Joseph (IN)
Calvin Coll (MI)
Campbellsville U (KY)
Campbell U (NC)
Cardinal Stritch U (WI)
Carleton U (ON, Canada)
Carroll Coll (MT)
Carthage Coll (WI)
Catawba Coll (NC)
Cedar Crest Coll (PA)
Cedarville U (OH)
Centenary Coll of Louisiana (LA)
Central Christian Coll of Kansas (KS)
Champlain Coll (VT)
Charleston Southern U (SC)
Chicago State U (IL)
Chowan Coll (NC)
Christian Brothers U (TN)
Christopher Newport U (VA)
City Coll of the City U of NY (NY)
Claremont McKenna Coll (CA)
Clarkson U (NY)
Clark U (MA)
Clearwater Christian Coll (FL)
Coe Coll (IA)
Coll Misericordia (PA)
Coll of Mount Saint Vincent (NY)
The Coll of New Jersey (NJ)
The Coll of New Rochelle (NY)
Coll of Notre Dame of Maryland (MD)
Coll of Saint Benedict (MN)
Coll of St. Catherine (MN)
Coll of St. Joseph (VT)
Coll of Saint Mary (NE)
Coll of the Ozarks (MO)
Colorado State U (CO)
Colorado State U-Pueblo (CO)
Columbia Coll (MO)
Columbia Union Coll (MD)
Columbus State U (GA)
Concordia Coll (MN)
Concordia Coll (NY)
Concordia U (IL)
Concordia U (MI)
Concordia U (NE)
Concordia U Wisconsin (WI)
Converse Coll (SC)
Cornell U (NY)
Cornerstone U (MI)
Covenant Coll (GA)
Creighton U (NE)
Crichton Coll (TN)
Crown Coll (MN)
Cumberland U (TN)
Curry Coll (MA)
Dakota State U (SD)
Dalhousie U (NS, Canada)
Davis & Elkins Coll (WV)
Defiance Coll (OH)
DePaul U (IL)
Dickinson Coll (PA)
Dickinson State U (ND)
Dillard U (LA)
Dominican Coll (NY)
Dominican U (IL)
Dordt Coll (IA)
Drake U (IA)
Drury U (MO)
D'Youville Coll (NY)
Earlham Coll (IN)
East Central U (OK)
Eastern Michigan U (MI)
Eastern Nazarene Coll (MA)
Eastern Oregon U (OR)
Eastern Washington U (WA)
Edgewood Coll (WI)
Elizabethtown Coll (PA)
Elmhurst Coll (IL)
Elmira Coll (NY)
Elms Coll (MA)
Elon U (NC)
Emmanuel Coll (GA)
Emory & Henry Coll (VA)
Eureka Coll (IL)
Evangel U (MO)
Faulkner U (AL)
Florida State U (FL)
Fontbonne U (MO)
Fordham U (NY)
Fort Hays State U (KS)
Fort Lewis Coll (CO)
Framingham State Coll (MA)
The Franciscan U (IA)
Francis Marion U (SC)
Franklin Pierce Coll (NH)
Fresno Pacific U (CA)
Furman U (SC)
Gannon U (PA)
Gardner-Webb U (NC)
Georgetown Coll (KY)
The George Washington U (DC)
Gettysburg Coll (PA)
Goshen Coll (IN)
Graceland U (IA)
Grambling State U (LA)
Grand Canyon U (AZ)
Grand Valley State U (MI)
Grand View Coll (IA)
Grove City Coll (PA)
Gustavus Adolphus Coll (MN)
Gwynedd-Mercy Coll (PA)
Hamline U (MN)
Hampshire Coll (MA)
Hampton U (VA)
Hannibal-LaGrange Coll (MO)
Hardin-Simmons U (TX)
Hartwick Coll (NY)
Harvard U (MA)
Hastings Coll (NE)
Haverford Coll (PA)
Heidelberg Coll (OH)
High Point U (NC)
Hiram Coll (OH)
Hobart and William Smith Colls (NY)
Hofstra U (NY)
Houghton Coll (NY)
Houston Baptist U (TX)
Howard Payne U (TX)
Humboldt State U (CA)
Huntington Coll (IN)

Illinois Coll (IL)
Immaculata U (PA)
Indiana U Bloomington (IN)
Indiana U–Purdue U Indianapolis (IN)
Iowa State U of Science and Technology (IA)
Iowa Wesleyan Coll (IA)
Ithaca Coll (NY)
Jacksonville U (FL)
John Brown U (AR)
John Carroll U (OH)
John Jay Coll of Criminal Justice, the City U of NY (NY)
Judson Coll (IL)
Juniata Coll (PA)
Kansas Wesleyan U (KS)
Kentucky Wesleyan Coll (KY)
Kenyon Coll (OH)
Keuka Coll (NY)
King Coll (TN)
King's Coll (PA)
LaGrange Coll (GA)
Lake Erie Coll (OH)
Lake Forest Coll (IL)
Lake Superior State U (MI)
Lambuth U (TN)
Lasell Coll (MA)
Lawrence U (WI)
Lebanon Valley Coll (PA)
Le Moyne Coll (NY)
Lenoir-Rhyne Coll (NC)
LeTourneau U (TX)
Lewis U (IL)
Limestone Coll (SC)
Lincoln Memorial U (TN)
Lindenwood U (MO)
Lindsey Wilson Coll (KY)
Lipscomb U (TN)
Longwood U (VA)
Louisiana Coll (LA)
Loyola U Chicago (IL)
Lubbock Christian U (TX)
Lycoming Coll (PA)
Lynchburg Coll (VA)
Lynn U (FL)
MacMurray Coll (IL)
Madonna U (MI)
Manchester Coll (IN)
Mansfield U of Pennsylvania (PA)
Marian Coll (IN)
Marian Coll of Fond du Lac (WI)
Marist Coll (NY)
Marlboro Coll (VT)
Marquette U (WI)
Mars Hill Coll (NC)
Marymount Coll of Fordham U (NY)
Mary Washington Coll (VA)
Marywood U (PA)
Massachusetts Coll of Liberal Arts (MA)
The Master's Coll and Sem (CA)
Mayville State U (ND)
McKendree Coll (IL)
Medaille Coll (NY)
Mercy Coll (NY)
Mercyhurst Coll (PA)
Merrimack Coll (MA)
Methodist Coll (NC)
Miami U (OH)
Michigan State U (MI)
Middlebury Coll (VT)
Millikin U (IL)
Minnesota State U Mankato (MN)
Minnesota State U Moorhead (MN)
Mississippi Coll (MS)
Missouri Valley Coll (MO)
Molloy Coll (NY)
Montclair State U (NJ)
Morgan State U (MD)
Morningside Coll (IA)
Mount Allison U (NB, Canada)
Mount Aloysius Coll (PA)
Mount Mary Coll (WI)
Mount Mercy Coll (IA)
Mount Saint Mary Coll (NY)
Mount St. Mary's Coll (CA)
Mount Vernon Nazarene U (OH)
Muhlenberg Coll (PA)
Nazareth Coll of Rochester (NY)
Newberry Coll (SC)
Newbury Coll (MA)
New Mexico Highlands U (NM)
Niagara U (NY)
North Central Coll (IL)
Northeastern State U (OK)
Northern Arizona U (AZ)
Northern Michigan U (MI)
Northern State U (SD)
Northland Coll (WI)
North Park U (IL)
Northwestern Oklahoma State U (OK)
Northwest Nazarene U (ID)
Notre Dame Coll (OH)
Notre Dame de Namur U (CA)
Nova Southeastern U (FL)
Oakland City U (IN)
Oglethorpe U (GA)
Ohio Northern U (OH)
Ohio U (OH)
Ohio Wesleyan U (OH)
Oklahoma Baptist U (OK)
Oklahoma Christian U (OK)
Oklahoma City U (OK)
Oklahoma State U (OK)
Olivet Coll (MI)
Olivet Nazarene U (IL)
Otterbein Coll (OH)
Pacific Union Coll (CA)
Palm Beach Atlantic U (FL)
Peirce Coll (PA)
Pepperdine U, Malibu (CA)
Pfeiffer U (NC)
Pittsburg State U (KS)
Pontifical Catholic U of Puerto Rico (PR)
Presbyterian Coll (SC)
Queens U of Charlotte (NC)
Quinnipiac U (CT)
Redeemer U Coll (ON, Canada)
Regis U (CO)
Rensselaer Polytechnic Inst (NY)
Rhode Island Coll (RI)
Ripon Coll (WI)
Rivier Coll (NH)
Roberts Wesleyan Coll (NY)
Rochester Inst of Technology (NY)
Rockford Coll (IL)
Rollins Coll (FL)
Roosevelt U (IL)
Rutgers, The State U of New Jersey, New Brunswick/Piscataway (NJ)
St. Andrews Presbyterian Coll (NC)
Saint Anselm Coll (NH)
Saint Augustine's Coll (NC)
St. Bonaventure U (NY)
St. Cloud State U (MN)
Saint Francis U (PA)
St. Francis Xavier U (NS, Canada)
St. Gregory's U (OK)
Saint John's U (MN)
Saint Joseph Coll (CT)
St. Joseph's Coll, New York (NY)
St. Joseph's Coll, Suffolk Campus (NY)
Saint Martin's Coll (WA)
Saint Mary-of-the-Woods Coll (IN)
Saint Michael's Coll (VT)
St. Norbert Coll (WI)
St. Thomas U (FL)
Salem State Coll (MA)
Sam Houston State U (TX)
San Diego State U (CA)
Sarah Lawrence Coll (NY)
Schreiner U (TX)
Seattle Pacific U (WA)
Seton Hill U (PA)
Shawnee State U (OH)
Siena Coll (NY)
Siena Heights U (MI)
Simmons Coll (MA)
Simon's Rock Coll of Bard (MA)
Simpson Coll (IA)
Smith Coll (MA)
Sonoma State U (CA)
South Carolina State U (SC)
South Dakota State U (SD)
Southern Connecticut State U (CT)
Southern Nazarene U (OK)
Southern Oregon U (OR)
Southern Vermont Coll (VT)
Southwestern Oklahoma State U (OK)
Springfield Coll (MA)
State U of NY at Binghamton (NY)
State U of NY at New Paltz (NY)
State U of NY at Oswego (NY)
State U of NY Coll at Brockport (NY)
State U of NY Coll at Cortland (NY)
State U of NY Coll at Fredonia (NY)
State U of NY Coll at Geneseo (NY)
State U of NY Coll at Oneonta (NY)
State U of NY Coll of Environ Sci and Forestry (NY)
State U of West Georgia (GA)
Stephens Coll (MO)
Stetson U (FL)
Stevens Inst of Technology (NJ)
Suffolk U (MA)
Susquehanna U (PA)
Syracuse U (NY)
Talladega Coll (AL)
Taylor U (IN)
Taylor U, Fort Wayne Campus (IN)
Tennessee Technological U (TN)
Tennessee Wesleyan Coll (TN)
Texas A&M U–Kingsville (TX)
Texas Lutheran U (TX)
Texas Wesleyan U (TX)
Thiel Coll (PA)
Tiffin U (OH)
Trinity Coll (DC)
Trinity U (TX)
Trinity Western U (BC, Canada)
Tri-State U (IN)
Truman State U (MO)
Tusculum Coll (TN)
Union U (TN)
United States Military Acad (NY)
Université Laval (QC, Canada)
The U of Akron (OH)
U of Alberta (AB, Canada)
U of Arkansas at Monticello (AR)
U of Bridgeport (CT)
The U of British Columbia (BC, Canada)
U of Calif, Riverside (CA)
U of Calif, Santa Barbara (CA)
U of Cincinnati (OH)
U of Colorado at Colorado Springs (CO)
U of Dallas (TX)
U of Dayton (OH)
U of Detroit Mercy (MI)
U of Evansville (IN)
The U of Findlay (OH)
U of Houston (TX)
U of Illinois at Chicago (IL)
U of Indianapolis (IN)
The U of Iowa (IA)
U of La Verne (CA)
U of Louisiana at Lafayette (LA)
U of Manitoba (MB, Canada)
U of Mary Hardin-Baylor (TX)
U of Maryland, Baltimore County (MD)
U of Maryland Eastern Shore (MD)
U of Minnesota, Duluth (MN)
U of Minnesota, Morris (MN)
U of Minnesota, Twin Cities Campus (MN)
U of Missouri–Rolla (MO)
U of Missouri–St. Louis (MO)
The U of Montana–Missoula (MT)
The U of Montana–Western (MT)
U of Montevallo (AL)
U of New Brunswick Fredericton (NB, Canada)
The U of North Carolina at Greensboro (NC)
U of Ottawa (ON, Canada)
U of Pittsburgh at Greensburg (PA)
U of Pittsburgh at Johnstown (PA)
U of Portland (OR)
U of Puget Sound (WA)
U of Regina (SK, Canada)
U of Saint Francis (IN)
U of St. Thomas (TX)
U of Saskatchewan (SK, Canada)
U of Sioux Falls (SD)
The U of Tampa (FL)
U of the Incarnate Word (TX)
U of Toledo (OH)
U of Vermont (VT)
U of Victoria (BC, Canada)
U of West Los Angeles (CA)
U of Windsor (ON, Canada)
U of Wisconsin–Milwaukee (WI)
U of Wisconsin–Oshkosh (WI)
U of Wisconsin–Parkside (WI)
U of Wisconsin–River Falls (WI)
U of Wisconsin–Superior (WI)
Urbana U (OH)
Utah State U (UT)
Utica Coll (NY)
Valley City State U (ND)
Vanguard U of Southern California (CA)
Villa Julie Coll (MD)
Virginia Intermont Coll (VA)
Virginia Wesleyan Coll (VA)
Wabash Coll (IN)
Wagner Coll (NY)
Walla Walla Coll (WA)
Warner Pacific Coll (OR)
Warner Southern Coll (FL)
Washburn U (KS)
Washington Coll (MD)
Washington State U (WA)
Waynesburg Coll (PA)
Webber Intl U (FL)
Wells Coll (NY)
Western Baptist Coll (OR)
Western State Coll of Colorado (CO)
Western Washington U (WA)
Westfield State Coll (MA)
West Liberty State Coll (WV)
Westminster Coll (MO)
Westminster Coll (PA)
Westmont Coll (CA)
West Texas A&M U (TX)
West Virginia Wesleyan Coll (WV)
Wheeling Jesuit U (WV)
Whitworth Coll (WA)
William Jewell Coll (MO)
William Paterson U of New Jersey (NJ)
William Penn U (IA)
Williams Baptist Coll (AR)
William Tyndale Coll (MI)
Wingate U (NC)
Winona State U (MN)
Wittenberg U (OH)
Wofford Coll (SC)
Wright State U (OH)
Xavier U of Louisiana (LA)
York Coll of Pennsylvania (PA)
York U (ON, Canada)
Youngstown State U (OH)

PRE-MEDICAL STUDIES

Abilene Christian U (TX)
Acadia U (NS, Canada)
Adams State Coll (CO)
Adrian Coll (MI)
Alabama State U (AL)
Albertson Coll of Idaho (ID)
Albertus Magnus Coll (CT)
Albion Coll (MI)
Alderson-Broaddus Coll (WV)
Alice Lloyd Coll (KY)
Allegheny Coll (PA)
Alma Coll (MI)
Alvernia Coll (PA)
American Intl Coll (MA)
American U (DC)
Andrews U (MI)
Antioch Coll (OH)
Aquinas Coll (MI)
Arcadia U (PA)
Ashland U (OH)
Atlantic Union Coll (MA)
Auburn U (AL)
Augsburg Coll (MN)
Augustana Coll (IL)
Augustana Coll (SD)
Averett U (VA)
Baldwin-Wallace Coll (OH)
Ball State U (IN)
Bard Coll (NY)
Barry U (FL)
Baylor U (TX)
Bellarmine U (KY)
Belmont Abbey Coll (NC)
Beloit Coll (WI)
Bemidji State U (MN)
Benedictine U (IL)
Bennington Coll (VT)
Berea Coll (KY)
Bethany Coll (WV)
Bethel Coll (IN)
Bethel Coll (TN)
Birmingham-Southern Coll (AL)
Blackburn Coll (IL)
Bloomfield Coll (NJ)
Blue Mountain Coll (MS)
Bluffton Coll (OH)
Boise State U (ID)
Boston Coll (MA)
Bowdoin Coll (ME)
Briar Cliff U (IA)
Bryan Coll (TN)
State U of NY Coll at Buffalo (NY)
California Polytechnic State U, San Luis Obispo (CA)
California State Polytechnic U, Pomona (CA)
California State U, Chico (CA)
California State U, Dominguez Hills (CA)
California State U, Hayward (CA)
Calvin Coll (MI)
Campbellsville U (KY)
Campbell U (NC)
Capital U (OH)
Cardinal Stritch U (WI)
Carroll Coll (MT)
Carroll Coll (WI)
Carthage Coll (WI)
Catawba Coll (NC)
Cedar Crest Coll (PA)
Cedarville U (OH)
Centenary Coll of Louisiana (LA)
Central Christian Coll of Kansas (KS)
Central Missouri State U (MO)
Charleston Southern U (SC)
Chicago State U (IL)
Chowan Coll (NC)
Christian Brothers U (TN)
City Coll of the City U of NY (NY)
Claremont McKenna Coll (CA)
Clarkson U (NY)
Clark U (MA)
Clearwater Christian Coll (FL)
Clemson U (SC)
Coe Coll (IA)
Coll Misericordia (PA)
Coll of Charleston (SC)
Coll of Mount Saint Vincent (NY)
The Coll of New Jersey (NJ)
The Coll of New Rochelle (NY)
Coll of Notre Dame of Maryland (MD)
Coll of Saint Benedict (MN)
Coll of St. Catherine (MN)
Coll of Saint Elizabeth (NJ)
Coll of Saint Mary (NE)
Coll of the Holy Cross (MA)
Coll of the Ozarks (MO)
Colorado State U (CO)
Colorado State U-Pueblo (CO)
Columbia Coll (MO)
Columbia Union Coll (MD)
Columbus State U (GA)
Concord Coll (WV)
Concordia Coll (MN)
Concordia U (IL)
Concordia U (MI)
Concordia U (NE)
Concordia U (OR)
Converse Coll (SC)
Cornell U (NY)
Cornerstone U (MI)
Covenant Coll (GA)
Cumberland U (TN)
Dakota State U (SD)
Dalhousie U (NS, Canada)
Davis & Elkins Coll (WV)
Defiance Coll (OH)
DeSales U (PA)
Dickinson Coll (PA)
Dickinson State U (ND)
Dillard U (LA)
Dominican U (IL)
Dordt Coll (IA)
Drake U (IA)
Drury U (MO)
D'Youville Coll (NY)
Earlham Coll (IN)
East Central U (OK)
Eastern Mennonite U (VA)
Eastern Michigan U (MI)
Eastern Nazarene Coll (MA)
Eastern Oregon U (OR)
Eastern Washington U (WA)
Edgewood Coll (WI)
Elizabethtown Coll (PA)
Elmhurst Coll (IL)
Elmira Coll (NY)
Elms Coll (MA)
Elon U (NC)
Emory & Henry Coll (VA)
Eureka Coll (IL)
Evangel U (MO)
Florida Southern Coll (FL)
Florida State U (FL)
Fontbonne U (MO)
Fordham U (NY)
Fort Lewis Coll (CO)
Framingham State Coll (MA)
The Franciscan U (IA)
Franklin Pierce Coll (NH)
Fresno Pacific U (CA)
Furman U (SC)
Gannon U (PA)
Gardner-Webb U (NC)
Georgetown Coll (KY)
The George Washington U (DC)
Georgia Southwestern State U (GA)
Gettysburg Coll (PA)
Goshen Coll (IN)
Graceland U (IA)
Grand Canyon U (AZ)
Grand Valley State U (MI)
Grinnell Coll (IA)
Grove City Coll (PA)
Gustavus Adolphus Coll (MN)
Hamline U (MN)
Hampshire Coll (MA)
Hampton U (VA)
Harding U (AR)
Hardin-Simmons U (TX)
Hartwick Coll (NY)
Harvard U (MA)
Hastings Coll (NE)
Haverford Coll (PA)
Hawai'i Pacific U (HI)
Heidelberg Coll (OH)
High Point U (NC)
Hillsdale Coll (MI)
Hiram Coll (OH)
Hobart and William Smith Colls (NY)
Hofstra U (NY)
Houghton Coll (NY)
Howard Payne U (TX)
Humboldt State U (CA)
Huntington Coll (IN)
Huston-Tillotson Coll (TX)
Illinois Coll (IL)
Immaculata U (PA)

Indiana U Bloomington (IN)
Indiana U–Purdue U Fort Wayne (IN)
Indiana U–Purdue U Indianapolis (IN)
Inter American U of PR, Bayamón Campus (PR)
Iowa State U of Science and Technology (IA)
Iowa Wesleyan Coll (IA)
Ithaca Coll (NY)
Jacksonville U (FL)
John Brown U (AR)
John Carroll U (OH)
Johnson C. Smith U (NC)
Johnson State Coll (VT)
Judson Coll (IL)
Juniata Coll (PA)
Kansas State U (KS)
Kansas Wesleyan U (KS)
Kentucky Wesleyan Coll (KY)
Kenyon Coll (OH)
Keuka Coll (NY)
Keystone Coll (PA)
King Coll (TN)
King's Coll (PA)
LaGrange Coll (GA)
Lake Erie Coll (OH)
Lake Forest Coll (IL)
Lake Superior State U (MI)
Lambuth U (TN)
La Salle U (PA)
Lawrence U (WI)
Lebanon Valley Coll (PA)
Lehigh U (PA)
Le Moyne Coll (NY)
Lenoir-Rhyne Coll (NC)
LeTourneau U (TX)
Lewis U (IL)
Limestone Coll (SC)
Lincoln Memorial U (TN)
Lindenwood U (MO)
Lindsey Wilson Coll (KY)
Lipscomb U (TN)
Lock Haven U of Pennsylvania (PA)
Long Island U, Brooklyn Campus (NY)
Long Island U, C.W. Post Campus (NY)
Longwood U (VA)
Lourdes Coll (OH)
Loyola U Chicago (IL)
Lycoming Coll (PA)
Lynchburg Coll (VA)
Lynn U (FL)
MacMurray Coll (IL)
Madonna U (MI)
Manchester Coll (IN)
Manhattanville Coll (NY)
Mansfield U of Pennsylvania (PA)
Marian Coll (IN)
Marian Coll of Fond du Lac (WI)
Marist Coll (NY)
Marlboro Coll (VT)
Marquette U (WI)
Mars Hill Coll (NC)
Marymount Coll of Fordham U (NY)
Mary Washington Coll (VA)
Mass Coll of Pharmacy and Allied Health Sciences (MA)
The Master's Coll and Sem (CA)
Mayville State U (ND)
McKendree Coll (IL)
McPherson Coll (KS)
Medgar Evers Coll of the City U of NY (NY)
Memorial U of Newfoundland (NL, Canada)
Mercer U (GA)
Mercy Coll (NY)
Mercyhurst Coll (PA)
Meredith Coll (NC)
Merrimack Coll (MA)
Methodist Coll (NC)
Miami U (OH)
Michigan State U (MI)
Michigan Technological U (MI)
Millikin U (IL)
Minnesota State U Mankato (MN)
Minnesota State U Moorhead (MN)
Mississippi Coll (MS)
Missouri Southern State U (MO)
Missouri Valley Coll (MO)
Molloy Coll (NY)
Montclair State U (NJ)
Morgan State U (MD)
Morningside Coll (IA)
Mount Allison U (NB, Canada)
Mount Mary Coll (WI)
Mount Mercy Coll (IA)
Mount St. Mary's Coll (CA)
Mount Vernon Nazarene U (OH)
Muhlenberg Coll (PA)
Nazareth Coll of Rochester (NY)
Newberry Coll (SC)
New Mexico Highlands U (NM)
New Mexico Inst of Mining and Technology (NM)
New York Inst of Technology (NY)
New York U (NY)
Niagara U (NY)
Nicholls State U (LA)
North Carolina Wesleyan Coll (NC)
North Central Coll (IL)
Northeastern State U (OK)
Northern Arizona U (AZ)
Northern Michigan U (MI)
Northern State U (SD)
North Georgia Coll & State U (GA)
Northland Coll (WI)
North Park U (IL)
Northwestern Oklahoma State U (OK)
Northwestern U (IL)
Northwest Nazarene U (ID)
Notre Dame Coll (OH)
Notre Dame de Namur U (CA)
Nova Southeastern U (FL)
Oakland City U (IN)
Oglethorpe U (GA)
Ohio Northern U (OH)
Ohio U (OH)
Ohio Wesleyan U (OH)
Oklahoma Baptist U (OK)
Oklahoma City U (OK)
Oklahoma State U (OK)
Olivet Coll (MI)
Olivet Nazarene U (IL)
Oral Roberts U (OK)
Oregon Inst of Technology (OR)
Oregon State U (OR)
Otterbein Coll (OH)
Ouachita Baptist U (AR)
Pacific Union Coll (CA)
Pacific U (OR)
Penn State U Abington Coll (PA)
Penn State U Altoona Coll (PA)
Penn State U at Erie, The Behrend Coll (PA)
Penn State U Beaver Campus of the Commonwealth Coll (PA)
Penn State U Berks Cmps of Berks-Lehigh Valley Coll (PA)
Penn State U Delaware County Campus of the Commonwealth Coll (PA)
Penn State U DuBois Campus of the Commonwealth Coll (PA)
Penn State U Fayette Campus of the Commonwealth Coll (PA)
Penn State U Hazleton Campus of the Commonwealth Coll (PA)
Penn State U Lehigh Valley Cmps of Berks-Lehigh Valley Coll (PA)
Penn State U McKeesport Campus of the Commonwealth Coll (PA)
Penn State U Mont Alto Campus of the Commonwealth Coll (PA)
Penn State U New Kensington Campus of the Commonwealth Coll (PA)
Penn State U Schuylkill Campus of the Capital Coll (PA)
Penn State U Shenango Campus of the Commonwealth Coll (PA)
Penn State U Univ Park Campus (PA)
Penn State U Wilkes-Barre Campus of the Commonwealth Coll (PA)
Penn State U Worthington Scranton Cmps Commonwealth Coll (PA)
Penn State U York Campus of the Commonwealth Coll (PA)
Pepperdine U, Malibu (CA)
Pfeiffer U (NC)
Philadelphia U (PA)
Pittsburg State U (KS)
Pitzer Coll (CA)
Pomona Coll (CA)
Pontifical Catholic U of Puerto Rico (PR)
Presbyterian Coll (SC)
Queens U of Charlotte (NC)
Quincy U (IL)
Quinnipiac U (CT)
Redeemer U Coll (ON, Canada)
Regis U (CO)
Rensselaer Polytechnic Inst (NY)
Rhode Island Coll (RI)
Ripon Coll (WI)
Rivier Coll (NH)
Roberts Wesleyan Coll (NY)
Rochester Inst of Technology (NY)
Rockford Coll (IL)
Roger Williams U (RI)
Rollins Coll (FL)
Roosevelt U (IL)
Rutgers, The State U of New Jersey, New Brunswick/Piscataway (NJ)
Sacred Heart U (CT)
St. Andrews Presbyterian Coll (NC)
Saint Anselm Coll (NH)
Saint Augustine's Coll (NC)
St. Bonaventure U (NY)
St. Cloud State U (MN)
Saint Francis U (PA)
St. Francis Xavier U (NS, Canada)
St. Gregory's U (OK)
St. John's Coll (NM)
Saint John's U (MN)
Saint Joseph Coll (CT)
St. Joseph's Coll, Suffolk Campus (NY)
Saint Martin's Coll (WA)
Saint Mary-of-the-Woods Coll (IN)
Saint Michael's Coll (VT)
St. Norbert Coll (WI)
St. Thomas Aquinas Coll (NY)
St. Thomas U (FL)
Salem State Coll (MA)
Samford U (AL)
Sam Houston State U (TX)
Sarah Lawrence Coll (NY)
Schreiner U (TX)
Scripps Coll (CA)
Seattle Pacific U (WA)
Seton Hill U (PA)
Shawnee State U (OH)
Siena Coll (NY)
Simmons Coll (MA)
Simon's Rock Coll of Bard (MA)
Simpson Coll (IA)
Smith Coll (MA)
Sonoma State U (CA)
South Carolina State U (SC)
South Dakota State U (SD)
Southeastern Coll of the Assemblies of God (FL)
Southern Connecticut State U (CT)
Southern Nazarene U (OK)
Southern Oregon U (OR)
Southern Wesleyan U (SC)
Southwestern Oklahoma State U (OK)
Springfield Coll (MA)
Spring Hill Coll (AL)
State U of NY at New Paltz (NY)
State U of NY at Oswego (NY)
State U of NY Coll at Brockport (NY)
State U of NY Coll at Cortland (NY)
State U of NY Coll at Fredonia (NY)
State U of NY Coll at Geneseo (NY)
State U of NY Coll at Oneonta (NY)
State U of NY Coll of Environ Sci and Forestry (NY)
State U of West Georgia (GA)
Stephens Coll (MO)
Stetson U (FL)
Stevens Inst of Technology (NJ)
Suffolk U (MA)
Susquehanna U (PA)
Syracuse U (NY)
Tabor Coll (KS)
Talladega Coll (AL)
Tarleton State U (TX)
Taylor U (IN)
Tennessee Technological U (TN)
Tennessee Wesleyan Coll (TN)
Texas A&M U–Kingsville (TX)
Texas Lutheran U (TX)
Texas Southern U (TX)
Texas Wesleyan U (TX)
Thiel Coll (PA)
Trinity Christian Coll (IL)
Trinity Coll (DC)
Trinity Intl U (IL)
Trinity U (TX)
Trinity Western U (BC, Canada)
Tri-State U (IN)
Troy State U (AL)
Truman State U (MO)
Tusculum Coll (TN)
Union U (TN)
United States Military Acad (NY)
Université de Montréal (QC, Canada)
Université de Sherbrooke (QC, Canada)
Université Laval (QC, Canada)
U Coll of the Cariboo (BC, Canada)
The U of Akron (OH)
U of Alberta (AB, Canada)
U of Arkansas (AR)
U of Arkansas at Monticello (AR)
U of Bridgeport (CT)
The U of British Columbia (BC, Canada)
U of Cincinnati (OH)
U of Colorado at Colorado Springs (CO)
U of Dallas (TX)
U of Dayton (OH)
U of Detroit Mercy (MI)
U of Evansville (IN)
The U of Findlay (OH)
U of Hartford (CT)
U of Houston (TX)
U of Idaho (ID)
U of Indianapolis (IN)
The U of Iowa (IA)
U of Judaism (CA)
U of La Verne (CA)
U of Maine (ME)
U of Maine at Machias (ME)
U of Manitoba (MB, Canada)
U of Mary Hardin-Baylor (TX)
U of Maryland, Baltimore County (MD)
U of Maryland Eastern Shore (MD)
U of Massachusetts Amherst (MA)
U of Minnesota, Duluth (MN)
U of Minnesota, Morris (MN)
U of Minnesota, Twin Cities Campus (MN)
U of Missouri–Rolla (MO)
U of Missouri–St. Louis (MO)
The U of Montana–Missoula (MT)
The U of Montana–Western (MT)
U of Montevallo (AL)
U of Nebraska–Lincoln (NE)
U of Nevada, Reno (NV)
U of New Brunswick Fredericton (NB, Canada)
U of New Hampshire (NH)
The U of North Carolina at Greensboro (NC)
U of Notre Dame (IN)
U of Oregon (OR)
U of Pittsburgh at Johnstown (PA)
U of Portland (OR)
U of Prince Edward Island (PE, Canada)
U of Puget Sound (WA)
U of Regina (SK, Canada)
U of St. Francis (IL)
U of Saint Francis (IN)
U of St. Thomas (TX)
U of San Diego (CA)
U of San Francisco (CA)
U of Saskatchewan (SK, Canada)
U of Sioux Falls (SD)
The U of Tampa (FL)
The U of Tennessee at Martin (TN)
The U of Texas–Pan American (TX)
U of the Incarnate Word (TX)
U of the Ozarks (AR)
U of Toledo (OH)
U of Vermont (VT)
U of Victoria (BC, Canada)
U of Windsor (ON, Canada)
U of Wisconsin–Milwaukee (WI)
U of Wisconsin–Oshkosh (WI)
U of Wisconsin–Parkside (WI)
U of Wisconsin–River Falls (WI)
Upper Iowa U (IA)
Urbana U (OH)
Utah State U (UT)
Utica Coll (NY)
Valley City State U (ND)
Villa Julie Coll (MD)
Virginia Intermont Coll (VA)
Virginia Wesleyan Coll (VA)
Wabash Coll (IN)
Wagner Coll (NY)
Walla Walla Coll (WA)
Walsh U (OH)
Warner Pacific Coll (OR)
Washburn U (KS)
Washington Coll (MD)
Washington State U (WA)
Washington U in St. Louis (MO)
Waynesburg Coll (PA)
Wayne State Coll (NE)
Wells Coll (NY)
West Chester U of Pennsylvania (PA)
Western Connecticut State U (CT)
Western State Coll of Colorado (CO)
Westfield State Coll (MA)
West Liberty State Coll (WV)
Westminster Coll (PA)
Westmont Coll (CA)
West Virginia State Coll (WV)
West Virginia Wesleyan Coll (WV)
Wheaton Coll (MA)
Wheeling Jesuit U (WV)
Whitworth Coll (WA)
Widener U (PA)
William Jewell Coll (MO)
William Paterson U of New Jersey (NJ)
William Penn U (IA)
Williams Baptist Coll (AR)
Wingate U (NC)
Winona State U (MN)
Wittenberg U (OH)
Wofford Coll (SC)
Wright State U (OH)
Xavier U of Louisiana (LA)
York Coll of Pennsylvania (PA)
York U (ON, Canada)
Youngstown State U (OH)

PRE-NURSING STUDIES

Adams State Coll (CO)
Allegheny Coll (PA)
Baylor U (TX)
Brigham Young U (UT)
Canadian Mennonite U (MB, Canada)
Cleveland State U (OH)
Concordia U (NE)
Covenant Coll (GA)
Crichton Coll (TN)
Dordt Coll (IA)
Gettysburg Coll (PA)
Lambuth U (TN)
Limestone Coll (SC)
Lindenwood U (MO)
Marywood U (PA)
Missouri Valley Coll (MO)
Nevada State Coll at Henderson (NV)
Oklahoma City U (OK)
Oklahoma State U (OK)
Ouachita Baptist U (AR)
St. Gregory's U (OK)
Sam Houston State U (TX)
U of La Verne (CA)

PRE-PHARMACY STUDIES

Abilene Christian U (TX)
Adams State Coll (CO)
Allegheny Coll (PA)
American U (DC)
Ashland U (OH)
Auburn U (AL)
Barry U (FL)
Bellarmine U (KY)
Belmont Abbey Coll (NC)
Blue Mountain Coll (MS)
Briar Cliff U (IA)
Campbell U (NC)
Carroll Coll (MT)
Carroll Coll (WI)
Central Christian Coll of Kansas (KS)
Central Missouri State U (MO)
Charleston Southern U (SC)
Christian Brothers U (TN)
Clemson U (SC)
Coll of Saint Benedict (MN)
Coll of the Ozarks (MO)
Colorado State U-Pueblo (CO)
Columbus State U (GA)
Concordia U (NE)
Cumberland U (TN)
Dalhousie U (NS, Canada)
Dordt Coll (IA)
East Central U (OK)
Eastern Michigan U (MI)
Elmhurst Coll (IL)
Florida State U (FL)
Fordham U (NY)
Gardner-Webb U (NC)
Gettysburg Coll (PA)
Iowa Wesleyan Coll (IA)
Juniata Coll (PA)
Keystone Coll (PA)
King Coll (TN)
King's Coll (PA)
Lambuth U (TN)
Le Moyne Coll (NY)
Limestone Coll (SC)
Lindsey Wilson Coll (KY)
Long Island U, C.W. Post Campus (NY)
Longwood U (VA)
Madonna U (MI)
Mayville State U (ND)
McPherson Coll (KS)
Meredith Coll (NC)
Mississippi Coll (MS)
Missouri Southern State U (MO)
Missouri Valley Coll (MO)
Montclair State U (NJ)
Mount Allison U (NB, Canada)
Mount Vernon Nazarene U (OH)
Ohio U (OH)
Oklahoma Baptist U (OK)
Oklahoma City U (OK)
Oklahoma State U (OK)
Ouachita Baptist U (AR)
Roberts Wesleyan Coll (NY)
Roosevelt U (IL)
St. Cloud State U (MN)
St. Gregory's U (OK)
Saint John's U (MN)
Saint Martin's Coll (WA)

Saint Mary-of-the-Woods Coll (IN)
Sam Houston State U (TX)
Southern Nazarene U (OK)
Tarleton State U (TX)
Tennessee Wesleyan Coll (TN)
Texas Southern U (TX)
Truman State U (MO)
Union U (TN)
Université Laval (QC, Canada)
The U of Akron (OH)
U of Connecticut (CT)
The U of Iowa (IA)
U of Mary Hardin-Baylor (TX)
U of Miami (FL)
U of Minnesota, Duluth (MN)
U of Minnesota, Morris (MN)
U of Missouri–St. Louis (MO)
The U of Montana–Missoula (MT)
U of Nebraska–Lincoln (NE)
U of Regina (SK, Canada)
U of Saint Francis (IN)
U of St. Thomas (TX)
U of Saskatchewan (SK, Canada)
The U of Tennessee at Martin (TN)
The U of Texas–Pan American (TX)
U of Utah (UT)
U of Windsor (ON, Canada)
U of Wisconsin–Parkside (WI)
U of Wisconsin–River Falls (WI)
Valley City State U (ND)
Washington U in St. Louis (MO)
Westmont Coll (CA)
West Virginia Wesleyan Coll (WV)
Wright State U (OH)
York U (ON, Canada)
Youngstown State U (OH)

PRE-THEOLOGY/PRE-MINISTERIAL STUDIES
Alma Coll (MI)
Ashland U (OH)
Atlanta Christian Coll (GA)
Ave Maria U (FL)
Blue Mountain Coll (MS)
California Baptist U (CA)
California Christian Coll (CA)
Campbell U (NC)
Central Christian Coll of Kansas (KS)
Christian Brothers U (TN)
Coll of Saint Benedict (MN)
Columbia Intl U (SC)
Concordia Coll (MN)
Concordia U (IL)
Concordia U (MI)
Concordia U (NE)
Concordia U (OR)
Concordia U Coll of Alberta (AB, Canada)
Cornerstone U (MI)
Crossroads Bible Coll (IN)
Florida State U (FL)
Geneva Coll (PA)
Grace U (NE)
Juniata Coll (PA)
Kentucky Mountain Bible Coll (KY)
Lambuth U (TN)
Liberty U (VA)
Loras Coll (IA)
Loyola U Chicago (IL)
Martin Luther Coll (MN)
Minnesota State U Mankato (MN)
Moody Bible Inst (IL)
Mount Allison U (NB, Canada)
Northwestern Coll (MN)
Ohio Northern U (OH)
Ohio Wesleyan U (OH)
Prairie Bible Coll (AB, Canada)
Redeemer U Coll (ON, Canada)
Reformed Bible Coll (MI)
Roberts Wesleyan Coll (NY)
Saint John's U (MN)
Shorter Coll (GA)
Tennessee Wesleyan Coll (TN)
Trinity Christian Coll (IL)
Trinity Intl U (IL)
U of Dallas (TX)
U of Indianapolis (IN)
Viterbo U (WI)
Waynesburg Coll (PA)
Western Baptist Coll (OR)
Westmont Coll (CA)
Williamson Christian Coll (TN)

PRE-VETERINARY STUDIES
Abilene Christian U (TX)
Acadia U (NS, Canada)
Adams State Coll (CO)
Adrian Coll (MI)
Albertus Magnus Coll (CT)
Albion Coll (MI)
Alderson-Broaddus Coll (WV)
Alice Lloyd Coll (KY)
Allegheny Coll (PA)
Alma Coll (MI)
American Intl Coll (MA)
American U (DC)
Andrews U (MI)
Antioch Coll (OH)
Aquinas Coll (MI)
Arcadia U (PA)
Ashland U (OH)
Atlantic Union Coll (MA)
Auburn U (AL)
Augsburg Coll (MN)
Augustana Coll (IL)
Augustana Coll (SD)
Baldwin-Wallace Coll (OH)
Bard Coll (NY)
Barry U (FL)
Bellarmine U (KY)
Belmont Abbey Coll (NC)
Bemidji State U (MN)
Benedictine U (IL)
Bennington Coll (VT)
Berea Coll (KY)
Bethany Coll (WV)
Bethel Coll (IN)
Blackburn Coll (IL)
Bloomfield Coll (NJ)
Blue Mountain Coll (MS)
Boise State U (ID)
Briar Cliff U (IA)
State U of NY Coll at Buffalo (NY)
California State Polytechnic U, Pomona (CA)
California State U, Chico (CA)
California State U, Dominguez Hills (CA)
California State U, Hayward (CA)
Calvin Coll (MI)
Campbellsville U (KY)
Campbell U (NC)
Capital U (OH)
Cardinal Stritch U (WI)
Carroll Coll (MT)
Carroll Coll (WI)
Carthage Coll (WI)
Catawba Coll (NC)
Cedar Crest Coll (PA)
Cedarville U (OH)
Centenary Coll of Louisiana (LA)
Central Christian Coll of Kansas (KS)
Central Missouri State U (MO)
Chicago State U (IL)
Chowan Coll (NC)
City Coll of the City U of NY (NY)
Clarkson U (NY)
Clark U (MA)
Clemson U (SC)
Coe Coll (IA)
Coll Misericordia (PA)
Coll of Notre Dame of Maryland (MD)
Coll of Saint Benedict (MN)
Coll of St. Catherine (MN)
Coll of Saint Elizabeth (NJ)
Coll of Saint Mary (NE)
Coll of the Atlantic (ME)
Coll of the Ozarks (MO)
Colorado State U (CO)
Colorado State U-Pueblo (CO)
Columbia Coll (MO)
Columbia Union Coll (MD)
Columbus State U (GA)
Concord Coll (WV)
Concordia Coll (MN)
Concordia U (NE)
Converse Coll (SC)
Cornell U (NY)
Cornerstone U (MI)
Cumberland U (TN)
Dakota State U (SD)
Dalhousie U (NS, Canada)
Davis & Elkins Coll (WV)
Defiance Coll (OH)
Delaware State U (DE)
DeSales U (PA)
Dickinson State U (ND)
Dillard U (LA)
Dominican U (IL)
Dordt Coll (IA)
Drake U (IA)
Drury U (MO)
D'Youville Coll (NY)
East Central U (OK)
Eastern Mennonite U (VA)
Eastern Michigan U (MI)
Eastern Oregon U (OR)
Eastern Washington U (WA)
Edgewood Coll (WI)
Elizabethtown Coll (PA)
Elmhurst Coll (IL)
Elmira Coll (NY)
Elms Coll (MA)
Elon U (NC)
Emory & Henry Coll (VA)
Eureka Coll (IL)
Evangel U (MO)
Florida Southern Coll (FL)
Florida State U (FL)
Fordham U (NY)
Fort Lewis Coll (CO)
Framingham State Coll (MA)
Franklin Pierce Coll (NH)
Furman U (SC)
Gannon U (PA)
Gardner-Webb U (NC)
Georgia Southwestern State U (GA)
Gettysburg Coll (PA)
Goshen Coll (IN)
Grand Canyon U (AZ)
Grand Valley State U (MI)
Grove City Coll (PA)
Gustavus Adolphus Coll (MN)
Hamline U (MN)
Hampshire Coll (MA)
Hampton U (VA)
Harding U (AR)
Hartwick Coll (NY)
Harvard U (MA)
Hastings Coll (NE)
Haverford Coll (PA)
Heidelberg Coll (OH)
High Point U (NC)
Hillsdale Coll (MI)
Hiram Coll (OH)
Hobart and William Smith Colls (NY)
Hofstra U (NY)
Houghton Coll (NY)
Humboldt State U (CA)
Huntington Coll (IN)
Illinois Coll (IL)
Immaculata U (PA)
Indiana U–Purdue U Indianapolis (IN)
Iowa State U of Science and Technology (IA)
Iowa Wesleyan Coll (IA)
Jacksonville U (FL)
John Brown U (AR)
John Carroll U (OH)
Juniata Coll (PA)
Kansas State U (KS)
Kansas Wesleyan U (KS)
Kentucky Wesleyan Coll (KY)
Kenyon Coll (OH)
Keuka Coll (NY)
Keystone Coll (PA)
King Coll (TN)
King's Coll (PA)
LaGrange Coll (GA)
Lake Erie Coll (OH)
Lake Forest Coll (IL)
Lake Superior State U (MI)
Lambuth U (TN)
La Salle U (PA)
Lawrence U (WI)
Lebanon Valley Coll (PA)
Le Moyne Coll (NY)
Lenoir-Rhyne Coll (NC)
LeTourneau U (TX)
Lewis U (IL)
Limestone Coll (SC)
Lincoln Memorial U (TN)
Lindenwood U (MO)
Lindsey Wilson Coll (KY)
Lipscomb U (TN)
Lock Haven U of Pennsylvania (PA)
Longwood U (VA)
Loyola U Chicago (IL)
Lycoming Coll (PA)
Lynchburg Coll (VA)
MacMurray Coll (IL)
Madonna U (MI)
Manchester Coll (IN)
Marian Coll (IN)
Marian Coll of Fond du Lac (WI)
Marist Coll (NY)
Marlboro Coll (VT)
Mars Hill Coll (NC)
Mary Washington Coll (VA)
Mayville State U (ND)
McKendree Coll (IL)
McPherson Coll (KS)
Mercyhurst Coll (PA)
Meredith Coll (NC)
Methodist Coll (NC)
Miami U (OH)
Michigan State U (MI)
Michigan Technological U (MI)
Millikin U (IL)
Minnesota State U Mankato (MN)
Minnesota State U Moorhead (MN)
Mississippi Coll (MS)
Missouri Southern State U (MO)
Missouri Valley Coll (MO)
Molloy Coll (NY)
Montclair State U (NJ)
Morningside Coll (IA)
Mount Allison U (NB, Canada)
Mount Mary Coll (WI)
Mount Mercy Coll (IA)
Mount Vernon Nazarene U (OH)
Muhlenberg Coll (PA)
Nazareth Coll of Rochester (NY)
Newberry Coll (SC)
New Mexico Inst of Mining and Technology (NM)
Niagara U (NY)
North Central Coll (IL)
Northeastern State U (OK)
Northern Arizona U (AZ)
Northern Michigan U (MI)
North Georgia Coll & State U (GA)
Northland Coll (WI)
North Park U (IL)
Nova Scotia Ag Coll (NS, Canada)
Oakland City U (IN)
Oglethorpe U (GA)
Ohio Northern U (OH)
Ohio U (OH)
Ohio Wesleyan U (OH)
Oklahoma Baptist U (OK)
Oklahoma City U (OK)
Oklahoma State U (OK)
Olivet Coll (MI)
Olivet Nazarene U (IL)
Oregon State U (OR)
Otterbein Coll (OH)
Ouachita Baptist U (AR)
Pacific Union Coll (CA)
Pittsburg State U (KS)
Presbyterian Coll (SC)
Queens U of Charlotte (NC)
Quincy U (IL)
Quinnipiac U (CT)
Redeemer U Coll (ON, Canada)
Regis U (CO)
Rhode Island Coll (RI)
Ripon Coll (WI)
Rivier Coll (NH)
Roberts Wesleyan Coll (NY)
Rochester Inst of Technology (NY)
Rockford Coll (IL)
Roger Williams U (RI)
Sacred Heart U (CT)
St. Andrews Presbyterian Coll (NC)
St. Bonaventure U (NY)
St. Cloud State U (MN)
Saint Francis U (PA)
St. Francis Xavier U (NS, Canada)
Saint John's U (MN)
St. Joseph's Coll, Suffolk Campus (NY)
Saint Martin's Coll (WA)
Saint Mary-of-the-Woods Coll (IN)
Saint Michael's Coll (VT)
St. Norbert Coll (WI)
Salem State Coll (MA)
Sarah Lawrence Coll (NY)
Seton Hill U (PA)
Simpson Coll (IA)
Sonoma State U (CA)
South Carolina State U (SC)
South Dakota State U (SD)
Southern Connecticut State U (CT)
Southwestern Oklahoma State U (OK)
Spring Hill Coll (AL)
State U of NY at Oswego (NY)
State U of NY Coll at Brockport (NY)
State U of NY Coll at Fredonia (NY)
State U of NY Coll at Geneseo (NY)
State U of NY Coll at Oneonta (NY)
State U of NY Coll of Environ Sci and Forestry (NY)
State U of West Georgia (GA)
Stephens Coll (MO)
Stetson U (FL)
Suffolk U (MA)
Susquehanna U (PA)
Syracuse U (NY)
Tarleton State U (TX)
Taylor U (IN)
Tennessee Technological U (TN)
Tennessee Wesleyan Coll (TN)
Texas A&M U (TX)
Texas A&M U–Kingsville (TX)
Texas Lutheran U (TX)
Thiel Coll (PA)
Trinity Christian Coll (IL)
Trinity U (TX)
Trinity Western U (BC, Canada)
Tri-State U (IN)
Troy State U (AL)
Truman State U (MO)
Tusculum Coll (TN)
U Coll of the Cariboo (BC, Canada)
The U of Akron (OH)
U of Alberta (AB, Canada)
The U of Arizona (AZ)
U of Arkansas at Monticello (AR)
U of Bridgeport (CT)
The U of British Columbia (BC, Canada)
U of Cincinnati (OH)
U of Colorado at Colorado Springs (CO)
U of Delaware (DE)
U of Evansville (IN)
The U of Findlay (OH)
U of Hartford (CT)
U of Houston (TX)
U of Illinois at Urbana–Champaign (IL)
U of Indianapolis (IN)
The U of Iowa (IA)
U of Maine (ME)
U of Manitoba (MB, Canada)
U of Mary Hardin-Baylor (TX)
U of Maryland, Baltimore County (MD)
U of Massachusetts Amherst (MA)
U of Minnesota, Duluth (MN)
U of Minnesota, Morris (MN)
U of Minnesota, Twin Cities Campus (MN)
U of Missouri–St. Louis (MO)
The U of Montana–Western (MT)
U of Montevallo (AL)
U of Nebraska–Lincoln (NE)
U of Nevada, Reno (NV)
U of New Brunswick Fredericton (NB, Canada)
U of New Hampshire (NH)
The U of North Carolina at Greensboro (NC)
U of Pittsburgh at Johnstown (PA)
U of Prince Edward Island (PE, Canada)
U of Puget Sound (WA)
U of Regina (SK, Canada)
U of St. Francis (IL)
U of Saint Francis (IN)
U of St. Thomas (TX)
U of San Francisco (CA)
U of Saskatchewan (SK, Canada)
U of Sioux Falls (SD)
The U of Tampa (FL)
The U of Tennessee at Martin (TN)
U of the Ozarks (AR)
U of Toledo (OH)
U of Vermont (VT)
U of Victoria (BC, Canada)
U of Wisconsin–Oshkosh (WI)
U of Wisconsin–Parkside (WI)
U of Wisconsin–River Falls (WI)
Upper Iowa U (IA)
Urbana U (OH)
Utah State U (UT)
Utica Coll (NY)
Valley City State U (ND)
Villa Julie Coll (MD)
Virginia Intermont Coll (VA)
Virginia Wesleyan Coll (VA)
Wabash Coll (IN)
Walla Walla Coll (WA)
Walsh U (OH)
Warner Pacific Coll (OR)
Washington Coll (MD)
Washington U in St. Louis (MO)
Waynesburg Coll (PA)
Wayne State Coll (NE)
Wells Coll (NY)
Western State Coll of Colorado (CO)
Westminster Coll (PA)
Westmont Coll (CA)
West Virginia State Coll (WV)
West Virginia Wesleyan Coll (WV)
Wheeling Jesuit U (WV)
Whitworth Coll (WA)
Widener U (PA)
William Jewell Coll (MO)
Wingate U (NC)
Winona State U (MN)
Wittenberg U (OH)
Wofford Coll (SC)
Wright State U (OH)
Xavier U of Louisiana (LA)
York Coll of Pennsylvania (PA)
York U (ON, Canada)
Youngstown State U (OH)

PRINTING MANAGEMENT
Carroll Coll (WI)
Central Missouri State U (MO)
U of Wisconsin–Stout (WI)

PRINTMAKING
Acad of Art U (CA)
Alberta Coll of Art & Design (AB, Canada)
Arizona State U (AZ)
Art Acad of Cincinnati (OH)
Atlanta Coll of Art (GA)
Ball State U (IN)
Bennington Coll (VT)
Birmingham-Southern Coll (AL)
Brigham Young U (UT)
State U of NY Coll at Buffalo (NY)

California Coll of the Arts (CA)
California State U, Fullerton (CA)
California State U, Hayward (CA)
California State U, Long Beach (CA)
The Cleveland Inst of Art (OH)
Col for Creative Studies (MI)
Coll of Santa Fe (NM)
Coll of Visual Arts (MN)
Colorado State U (CO)
Columbia Coll (MO)
Concordia U (QC, Canada)
Drake U (IA)
Escuela de Artes Plasticas de Puerto Rico (PR)
Framingham State Coll (MA)
Grand Valley State U (MI)
Indiana U–Purdue U Fort Wayne (IN)
Kansas City Art Inst (MO)
Laguna Coll of Art & Design (CA)
Longwood U (VA)
Maine Coll of Art (ME)
Maryland Inst Coll of Art (MD)
Massachusetts Coll of Art (MA)
McNeese State U (LA)
Memorial U of Newfoundland (NL, Canada)
Memphis Coll of Art (TN)
Milwaukee Inst of Art and Design (WI)
Minneapolis Coll of Art and Design (MN)
Minnesota State U Moorhead (MN)
Montserrat Coll of Art (MA)
Mount Allison U (NB, Canada)
New World School of the Arts (FL)
Northern Michigan U (MI)
Nova Scotia Coll of Art and Design (NS, Canada)
Ohio Northern U (OH)
The Ohio State U (OH)
Ohio U (OH)
Pacific Northwest Coll of Art (OR)
Pratt Inst (NY)
Rhode Island School of Design (RI)
Rutgers, The State U of New Jersey, New Brunswick/Piscataway (NJ)
St. Cloud State U (MN)
San Francisco Art Inst (CA)
Sarah Lawrence Coll (NY)
School of the Art Inst of Chicago (IL)
School of the Museum of Fine Arts, Boston (MA)
Seton Hill U (PA)
Simon's Rock Coll of Bard (MA)
Sonoma State U (CA)
State U of NY Coll at Potsdam (NY)
Syracuse U (NY)
Texas Christian U (TX)
Trinity Christian Coll (IL)
The U of Akron (OH)
U of Alberta (AB, Canada)
U of Calif, Santa Cruz (CA)
U of Dallas (TX)
U of Houston (TX)
The U of Iowa (IA)
U of Kansas (KS)
U of Massachusetts Dartmouth (MA)
U of Miami (FL)
U of Michigan (MI)
U of Michigan–Flint (MI)
U of Missouri–St. Louis (MO)
U of Montevallo (AL)
U of North Texas (TX)
U of Oregon (OR)
U of Regina (SK, Canada)
U of San Francisco (CA)
The U of the Arts (PA)
U of Washington (WA)
U of Windsor (ON, Canada)
Washington U in St. Louis (MO)
Western Washington U (WA)
York U (ON, Canada)
Youngstown State U (OH)

PROFESSIONAL STUDIES

Bemidji State U (MN)
Briar Cliff U (IA)
Champlain Coll (VT)
Juniata Coll (PA)
Kent State U (OH)
Missouri Southern State U (MO)
Mount Aloysius Coll (PA)
Saint Mary-of-the-Woods Coll (IN)
Thomas Coll (ME)
U of Dubuque (IA)
The U of Memphis (TN)
U of Oklahoma (OK)
The U of Tennessee at Martin (TN)

PSYCHIATRIC/MENTAL HEALTH NURSING

U at Buffalo, The State U of New York (NY)

PSYCHIATRIC/MENTAL HEALTH SERVICES TECHNOLOGY

Franciscan U of Steubenville (OH)
Pennsylvania Coll of Technology (PA)

PSYCHOLOGY

Abilene Christian U (TX)
Acadia U (NS, Canada)
Adams State Coll (CO)
Adelphi U (NY)
Adrian Coll (MI)
Agnes Scott Coll (GA)
Alabama Ag and Mech U (AL)
Alabama State U (AL)
Alaska Pacific U (AK)
Albany State U (GA)
Albertson Coll of Idaho (ID)
Albertus Magnus Coll (CT)
Albion Coll (MI)
Albright Coll (PA)
Alderson-Broaddus Coll (WV)
Alfred U (NY)
Allegheny Coll (PA)
Alliant Intl U (CA)
Alliant Intl U–México City(Mexico)
Alma Coll (MI)
Alvernia Coll (PA)
Alverno Coll (WI)
American Intl Coll (MA)
American Public U System (WV)
American U (DC)
The American U in Cairo(Egypt)
Amherst Coll (MA)
Anderson Coll (SC)
Andrews U (MI)
Angelo State U (TX)
Anna Maria Coll (MA)
Antioch Coll (OH)
Appalachian State U (NC)
Aquinas Coll (MI)
Arcadia U (PA)
Argosy U/Chicago (IL)
Argosy U/Chicago Northwest (IL)
Argosy U/Dallas (TX)
Argosy U/Phoenix (AZ)
Argosy U/Sarasota (FL)
Argosy U/Seattle (WA)
Argosy U/Tampa (FL)
Argosy U/Twin Cities, Eagan (MN)
Argosy U/Washington D.C. (VA)
Arizona State U (AZ)
Arizona State U West (AZ)
Arkansas State U (AR)
Arkansas Tech U (AR)
Armstrong Atlantic State U (GA)
Asbury Coll (KY)
Ashland U (OH)
Assumption Coll (MA)
Athabasca U (AB, Canada)
Athens State U (AL)
Atlantic Baptist U (NB, Canada)
Atlantic Union Coll (MA)
Auburn U (AL)
Auburn U Montgomery (AL)
Augsburg Coll (MN)
Augustana Coll (IL)
Augustana Coll (SD)
Augusta State U (GA)
Aurora U (IL)
Austin Coll (TX)
Austin Peay State U (TN)
Averett U (VA)
Avila U (MO)
Azusa Pacific U (CA)
Baker U (KS)
Baldwin-Wallace Coll (OH)
Ball State U (IN)
Barclay Coll (KS)
Bard Coll (NY)
Barnard Coll (NY)
Barry U (FL)
Barton Coll (NC)
Bastyr U (WA)
Bates Coll (ME)
Baylor U (TX)
Bay Path Coll (MA)
Beacon Coll and Graduate School (GA)
Becker Coll (MA)
Belhaven Coll (MS)
Bellarmine U (KY)
Belmont Abbey Coll (NC)
Belmont U (TN)
Beloit Coll (WI)
Bemidji State U (MN)
Benedictine Coll (KS)
Benedictine U (IL)
Bennington Coll (VT)
Berea Coll (KY)
Baruch Coll of the City U of NY (NY)
Berry Coll (GA)
Bethany Coll (KS)
Bethany Coll (WV)
Bethany Lutheran Coll (MN)
Bethel Coll (IN)
Bethel Coll (KS)
Bethel Coll (TN)
Bethel U (MN)
Bethune-Cookman Coll (FL)
Biola U (CA)
Birmingham-Southern Coll (AL)
Bishop's U (QC, Canada)
Blackburn Coll (IL)
Black Hills State U (SD)
Bloomfield Coll (NJ)
Bloomsburg U of Pennsylvania (PA)
Bluefield Coll (VA)
Blue Mountain Coll (MS)
Bluffton Coll (OH)
Boise State U (ID)
Boston Coll (MA)
Boston U (MA)
Bowdoin Coll (ME)
Bowie State U (MD)
Bowling Green State U (OH)
Bradley U (IL)
Brandeis U (MA)
Brenau U (GA)
Brescia U (KY)
Brevard Coll (NC)
Brewton-Parker Coll (GA)
Briar Cliff U (IA)
Bridgewater Coll (VA)
Bridgewater State Coll (MA)
Brigham Young U (UT)
Brigham Young U–Hawaii (HI)
Brock U (ON, Canada)
Brooklyn Coll of the City U of NY (NY)
Brown U (RI)
Bryan Coll (TN)
Bryant Coll (RI)
Bryn Mawr Coll (PA)
Bucknell U (PA)
Buena Vista U (IA)
State U of NY Coll at Buffalo (NY)
Burlington Coll (VT)
Butler U (IN)
Cabrini Coll (PA)
Caldwell Coll (NJ)
California Baptist U (CA)
California Lutheran U (CA)
California Polytechnic State U, San Luis Obispo (CA)
California State Polytechnic U, Pomona (CA)
California State U, Chico (CA)
California State U, Dominguez Hills (CA)
California State U, Fresno (CA)
California State U, Fullerton (CA)
California State U, Hayward (CA)
California State U, Long Beach (CA)
California State U, Los Angeles (CA)
California State U, Sacramento (CA)
California State U, San Bernardino (CA)
California State U, San Marcos (CA)
California State U, Stanislaus (CA)
California U of Pennsylvania (PA)
Calumet Coll of Saint Joseph (IN)
Calvin Coll (MI)
Cambridge Coll (MA)
Cameron U (OK)
Campbellsville U (KY)
Campbell U (NC)
Canadian Mennonite U (MB, Canada)
Canisius Coll (NY)
Capital U (OH)
Cardinal Stritch U (WI)
Carleton Coll (MN)
Carleton U (ON, Canada)
Carlos Albizu Univ–Miami (FL)
Carlow Coll (PA)
Carnegie Mellon U (PA)
Carroll Coll (MT)
Carroll Coll (WI)
Carson-Newman Coll (TN)
Carthage Coll (WI)
Cascade Coll (OR)
Case Western Reserve U (OH)
Castleton State Coll (VT)
Catawba Coll (NC)
The Catholic U of America (DC)
Cazenovia Coll (NY)
Cedar Crest Coll (PA)
Cedarville U (OH)
Centenary Coll (NJ)
Centenary Coll of Louisiana (LA)
Central Coll (IA)
Central Connecticut State U (CT)
Central Methodist Coll (MO)
Central Michigan U (MI)
Central Missouri State U (MO)
Central State U (OH)
Central Washington U (WA)
Centre Coll (KY)
Chadron State Coll (NE)
Chaminade U of Honolulu (HI)
Chapman U (CA)
Charleston Southern U (SC)
Chatham Coll (PA)
Chestnut Hill Coll (PA)
Cheyney U of Pennsylvania (PA)
Chicago State U (IL)
Chowan Coll (NC)
Christian Brothers U (TN)
Christian Heritage Coll (CA)
Christopher Newport U (VA)
Citadel, The Military Coll of South Carolina (SC)
City Coll of the City U of NY (NY)
City U (WA)
Claremont McKenna Coll (CA)
Clarion U of Pennsylvania (PA)
Clark Atlanta U (GA)
Clarke Coll (IA)
Clarkson U (NY)
Clark U (MA)
Clayton Coll & State U (GA)
Clearwater Christian Coll (FL)
Clemson U (SC)
Cleveland State U (OH)
Coastal Carolina U (SC)
Coe Coll (IA)
Coker Coll (SC)
Colby Coll (ME)
Colby-Sawyer Coll (NH)
Colgate U (NY)
Coll Misericordia (PA)
Coll of Charleston (SC)
Coll of Mount St. Joseph (OH)
Coll of Mount Saint Vincent (NY)
The Coll of New Jersey (NJ)
The Coll of New Rochelle (NY)
Coll of Notre Dame of Maryland (MD)
Coll of Saint Benedict (MN)
Coll of St. Catherine (MN)
Coll of Saint Elizabeth (NJ)
Coll of St. Joseph (VT)
Coll of Saint Mary (NE)
The Coll of Saint Rose (NY)
The Coll of St. Scholastica (MN)
Coll of Santa Fe (NM)
Coll of Staten Island of the City U of NY (NY)
Coll of the Atlantic (ME)
Coll of the Holy Cross (MA)
Coll of the Ozarks (MO)
Coll of the Southwest (NM)
The Coll of William and Mary (VA)
The Coll of Wooster (OH)
Colorado Christian U (CO)
The Colorado Coll (CO)
Colorado State U (CO)
Colorado State U-Pueblo (CO)
Columbia Coll (MO)
Columbia Coll (NY)
Columbia Coll (SC)
Columbia Intl U (SC)
Columbia Union Coll (MD)
Columbia U, School of General Studies (NY)
Columbus State U (GA)
Concord Coll (WV)
Concordia Coll (MN)
Concordia U (CA)
Concordia U (IL)
Concordia U (MI)
Concordia U (NE)
Concordia U (OR)
Concordia U (QC, Canada)
Concordia U Coll of Alberta (AB, Canada)
Concordia U, St. Paul (MN)
Concordia U Wisconsin (WI)
Connecticut Coll (CT)
Converse Coll (SC)
Cornell Coll (IA)
Cornell U (NY)
Cornerstone U (MI)
Covenant Coll (GA)
Creighton U (NE)
Crichton Coll (TN)
Crown Coll (MN)
Culver-Stockton Coll (MO)
Cumberland Coll (KY)
Cumberland U (TN)
Curry Coll (MA)
Daemen Coll (NY)
Dakota Wesleyan U (SD)
Dalhousie U (NS, Canada)
Dallas Baptist U (TX)
Dana Coll (NE)
Dartmouth Coll (NH)
Davidson Coll (NC)
Davis & Elkins Coll (WV)
Defiance Coll (OH)
Delaware State U (DE)
Delta State U (MS)
Denison U (OH)
DePaul U (IL)
DePauw U (IN)
DeSales U (PA)
Dickinson Coll (PA)
Dickinson State U (ND)
Dillard U (LA)
Doane Coll (NE)
Dominican Coll (NY)
Dominican U (IL)
Dominican U of California (CA)
Dordt Coll (IA)
Dowling Coll (NY)
Drake U (IA)
Drew U (NJ)
Drexel U (PA)
Drury U (MO)
Duke U (NC)
Duquesne U (PA)
D'Youville Coll (NY)
Earlham Coll (IN)
East Carolina U (NC)
East Central U (OK)
Eastern Connecticut State U (CT)
Eastern Illinois U (IL)
Eastern Kentucky U (KY)
Eastern Mennonite U (VA)
Eastern Michigan U (MI)
Eastern Nazarene Coll (MA)
Eastern New Mexico U (NM)
Eastern Oregon U (OR)
Eastern U (PA)
Eastern Washington U (WA)
East Stroudsburg U of Pennsylvania (PA)
East Texas Baptist U (TX)
Eckerd Coll (FL)
Edgewood Coll (WI)
Edinboro U of Pennsylvania (PA)
Elizabeth City State U (NC)
Elizabethtown Coll (PA)
Elmhurst Coll (IL)
Elmira Coll (NY)
Elms Coll (MA)
Elon U (NC)
Emmanuel Coll (GA)
Emory & Henry Coll (VA)
Emory U (GA)
Emporia State U (KS)
Endicott Coll (MA)
Erskine Coll (SC)
Eugene Lang Coll, New School U (NY)
Eureka Coll (IL)
Evangel U (MO)
Excelsior Coll (NY)
Fairfield U (CT)
Fairleigh Dickinson U, Florham (NJ)
Fairleigh Dickinson U, Teaneck-Metro Campus (NJ)
Fairmont State Coll (WV)
Faulkner U (AL)
Fayetteville State U (NC)
Ferrum Coll (VA)
Flagler Coll (FL)
Florida Ag and Mech U (FL)
Florida Atlantic U (FL)
Florida Inst of Technology (FL)
Florida Intl U (FL)
Florida Southern Coll (FL)
Florida State U (FL)
Fontbonne U (MO)
Fordham U (NY)
Fort Hays State U (KS)
Fort Lewis Coll (CO)
Fort Valley State U (GA)
Framingham State Coll (MA)
The Franciscan U (IA)
Franciscan U of Steubenville (OH)
Francis Marion U (SC)
Franklin and Marshall Coll (PA)
Franklin Coll (IN)
Franklin Pierce Coll (NH)
Freed-Hardeman U (TN)
Fresno Pacific U (CA)
Frostburg State U (MD)
Furman U (SC)
Gallaudet U (DC)
Gannon U (PA)
Gardner-Webb U (NC)
Geneva Coll (PA)
George Fox U (OR)
George Mason U (VA)
Georgetown Coll (KY)
Georgetown U (DC)
The George Washington U (DC)
Georgia Coll & State U (GA)
Georgian Court U (NJ)

Georgia Southern U (GA)
Georgia Southwestern State U (GA)
Georgia State U (GA)
Gettysburg Coll (PA)
Gonzaga U (WA)
Gordon Coll (MA)
Goshen Coll (IN)
Goucher Coll (MD)
Governors State U (IL)
Grace Coll (IN)
Graceland U (IA)
Grace U (NE)
Grambling State U (LA)
Grand Canyon U (AZ)
Grand Valley State U (MI)
Grand View Coll (IA)
Greensboro Coll (NC)
Greenville Coll (IL)
Grinnell Coll (IA)
Grove City Coll (PA)
Guilford Coll (NC)
Gustavus Adolphus Coll (MN)
Gwynedd-Mercy Coll (PA)
Hamilton Coll (NY)
Hamline U (MN)
Hampden-Sydney Coll (VA)
Hampshire Coll (MA)
Hampton U (VA)
Hannibal-LaGrange Coll (MO)
Hanover Coll (IN)
Harding U (AR)
Hardin-Simmons U (TX)
Hartwick Coll (NY)
Harvard U (MA)
Hastings Coll (NE)
Haverford Coll (PA)
Hawai'i Pacific U (HI)
Heidelberg Coll (OH)
Henderson State U (AR)
Hendrix Coll (AR)
High Point U (NC)
Hilbert Coll (NY)
Hillsdale Coll (MI)
Hiram Coll (OH)
Hobart and William Smith Colls (NY)
Hofstra U (NY)
Hollins U (VA)
Holy Names Coll (CA)
Hood Coll (MD)
Hope Coll (MI)
Houghton Coll (NY)
Houston Baptist U (TX)
Howard Payne U (TX)
Howard U (DC)
Humboldt State U (CA)
Hunter Coll of the City U of NY (NY)
Huntington Coll (IN)
Huston-Tillotson Coll (TX)
Idaho State U (ID)
Illinois Coll (IL)
Illinois Inst of Technology (IL)
Illinois State U (IL)
Illinois Wesleyan U (IL)
Immaculata U (PA)
Indiana Inst of Technology (IN)
Indiana State U (IN)
Indiana U Bloomington (IN)
Indiana U East (IN)
Indiana U Kokomo (IN)
Indiana U Northwest (IN)
Indiana U of Pennsylvania (PA)
Indiana U–Purdue U Fort Wayne (IN)
Indiana U–Purdue U Indianapolis (IN)
Indiana U South Bend (IN)
Indiana U Southeast (IN)
Inter American U of PR, San Germán Campus (PR)
Iona Coll (NY)
Iowa State U of Science and Technology (IA)
Iowa Wesleyan Coll (IA)
Ithaca Coll (NY)
Jacksonville State U (AL)
Jacksonville U (FL)
James Madison U (VA)
Jamestown Coll (ND)
John Brown U (AR)
John Carroll U (OH)
John F. Kennedy U (CA)
The Johns Hopkins U (MD)
Johnson C. Smith U (NC)
Johnson State Coll (VT)
John Wesley Coll (NC)
Judson Coll (AL)
Judson Coll (IL)
Juniata Coll (PA)
Kalamazoo Coll (MI)
Kansas State U (KS)
Kansas Wesleyan U (KS)
Kean U (NJ)
Keene State Coll (NH)
Kennesaw State U (GA)
Kent State U (OH)
Kentucky Christian Coll (KY)
Kentucky State U (KY)
Kentucky Wesleyan Coll (KY)
Kenyon Coll (OH)
Keuka Coll (NY)
King Coll (TN)
King's Coll (PA)
The King's U Coll (AB, Canada)
Knox Coll (IL)
Kutztown U of Pennsylvania (PA)
Lafayette Coll (PA)
LaGrange Coll (GA)
Lake Erie Coll (OH)
Lake Forest Coll (IL)
Lakehead U (ON, Canada)
Lakeland Coll (WI)
Lake Superior State U (MI)
Lamar U (TX)
Lambuth U (TN)
Lander U (SC)
La Roche Coll (PA)
La Salle U (PA)
Lasell Coll (MA)
Laurentian U (ON, Canada)
Lawrence Technological U (MI)
Lawrence U (WI)
Lebanon Valley Coll (PA)
Lehigh U (PA)
Lehman Coll of the City U of NY (NY)
Le Moyne Coll (NY)
Lenoir-Rhyne Coll (NC)
LeTourneau U (TX)
Lewis & Clark Coll (OR)
Lewis-Clark State Coll (ID)
Lewis U (IL)
Liberty U (VA)
Limestone Coll (SC)
Lincoln Memorial U (TN)
Lincoln U (MO)
Lincoln U (PA)
Lindenwood U (MO)
Lindsey Wilson Coll (KY)
Linfield Coll (OR)
Lipscomb U (TN)
Livingstone Coll (NC)
Lock Haven U of Pennsylvania (PA)
Long Island U, Brooklyn Campus (NY)
Long Island U, C.W. Post Campus (NY)
Long Island U, Southampton Coll (NY)
Longwood U (VA)
Loras Coll (IA)
Louisiana Coll (LA)
Louisiana State U and A&M Coll (LA)
Louisiana State U in Shreveport (LA)
Louisiana Tech U (LA)
Lourdes Coll (OH)
Loyola Coll in Maryland (MD)
Loyola Marymount U (CA)
Loyola U Chicago (IL)
Loyola U New Orleans (LA)
Lubbock Christian U (TX)
Luther Coll (IA)
Lycoming Coll (PA)
Lynchburg Coll (VA)
Lyndon State Coll (VT)
Lynn U (FL)
Lyon Coll (AR)
Macalester Coll (MN)
MacMurray Coll (IL)
Madonna U (MI)
Malaspina U-Coll (BC, Canada)
Malone Coll (OH)
Manchester Coll (IN)
Manhattan Coll (NY)
Manhattanville Coll (NY)
Mansfield U of Pennsylvania (PA)
Marian Coll (IN)
Marian Coll of Fond du Lac (WI)
Marietta Coll (OH)
Marist Coll (NY)
Marlboro Coll (VT)
Marquette U (WI)
Marshall U (WV)
Mars Hill Coll (NC)
Martin U (IN)
Mary Baldwin Coll (VA)
Marygrove Coll (MI)
Marylhurst U (OR)
Marymount Coll of Fordham U (NY)
Marymount Manhattan Coll (NY)
Marymount U (VA)
Maryville Coll (TN)
Maryville U of Saint Louis (MO)
Mary Washington Coll (VA)
Marywood U (PA)
Massachusetts Coll of Liberal Arts (MA)
McDaniel Coll (MD)
McGill U (QC, Canada)
McKendree Coll (IL)
McMurry U (TX)
McNeese State U (LA)
McPherson Coll (KS)
Medaille Coll (NY)
Medgar Evers Coll of the City U of NY (NY)
Memorial U of Newfoundland (NL, Canada)
Mercer U (GA)
Mercy Coll (NY)
Mercyhurst Coll (PA)
Meredith Coll (NC)
Merrimack Coll (MA)
Messiah Coll (PA)
Methodist Coll (NC)
Metropolitan State Coll of Denver (CO)
Metropolitan State U (MN)
Miami U (OH)
Miami U Hamilton (OH)
Michigan State U (MI)
MidAmerica Nazarene U (KS)
Mid-Continent Coll (KY)
Middlebury Coll (VT)
Middle Tennessee State U (TN)
Midway Coll (KY)
Midwestern State U (TX)
Millersville U of Pennsylvania (PA)
Milligan Coll (TN)
Millikin U (IL)
Millsaps Coll (MS)
Mills Coll (CA)
Minnesota State U Mankato (MN)
Minnesota State U Moorhead (MN)
Minot State U (ND)
Mississippi Coll (MS)
Mississippi State U (MS)
Missouri Baptist U (MO)
Missouri Southern State U (MO)
Missouri Valley Coll (MO)
Missouri Western State Coll (MO)
Molloy Coll (NY)
Monmouth Coll (IL)
Monmouth U (NJ)
Montana State U–Billings (MT)
Montana State U–Bozeman (MT)
Montclair State U (NJ)
Moravian Coll (PA)
Morehead State U (KY)
Morehouse Coll (GA)
Morgan State U (MD)
Morningside Coll (IA)
Mount Allison U (NB, Canada)
Mount Aloysius Coll (PA)
Mount Holyoke Coll (MA)
Mount Ida Coll (MA)
Mount Mary Coll (WI)
Mount Mercy Coll (IA)
Mount Saint Mary Coll (NY)
Mount St. Mary's Coll (CA)
Mount Saint Mary's Coll and Sem (MD)
Mount Saint Vincent U (NS, Canada)
Mount Union Coll (OH)
Mount Vernon Nazarene U (OH)
Muhlenberg Coll (PA)
Murray State U (KY)
Naropa U (CO)
National-Louis U (IL)
National U (CA)
Nazareth Coll of Rochester (NY)
Nebraska Wesleyan U (NE)
Neumann Coll (PA)
Nevada State Coll at Henderson (NV)
Newberry Coll (SC)
Newbury Coll (MA)
New Coll of California (CA)
New Coll of Florida (FL)
New Jersey City U (NJ)
Newman U (KS)
New Mexico Highlands U (NM)
New Mexico Inst of Mining and Technology (NM)
New Mexico State U (NM)
New York Inst of Technology (NY)
New York U (NY)
Niagara U (NY)
Nicholls State U (LA)
Nichols Coll (MA)
Nipissing U (ON, Canada)
Norfolk State U (VA)
North Carolina Central U (NC)
North Carolina State U (NC)
North Carolina Wesleyan Coll (NC)
North Central Coll (IL)
Northcentral U (AZ)
North Central U (MN)
North Dakota State U (ND)
Northeastern Illinois U (IL)
Northeastern State U (OK)
Northeastern U (MA)
Northern Arizona U (AZ)
Northern Illinois U (IL)
Northern Michigan U (MI)
Northern State U (SD)
North Georgia Coll & State U (GA)
North Greenville Coll (SC)
Northland Coll (WI)
North Park U (IL)
Northwestern Coll (IA)
Northwestern Coll (MN)
Northwestern Oklahoma State U (OK)
Northwestern State U of Louisiana (LA)
Northwestern U (IL)
Northwest Nazarene U (ID)
Notre Dame Coll (OH)
Notre Dame de Namur U (CA)
Nova Southeastern U (FL)
Nyack Coll (NY)
Oak Hills Christian Coll (MN)
Oakland U (MI)
Oberlin Coll (OH)
Occidental Coll (CA)
Oglethorpe U (GA)
Ohio Dominican U (OH)
Ohio Northern U (OH)
The Ohio State U (OH)
The Ohio State U at Lima (OH)
The Ohio State U at Marion (OH)
The Ohio State U–Mansfield Campus (OH)
The Ohio State U–Newark Campus (OH)
Ohio U (OH)
Ohio Valley Coll (WV)
Ohio Wesleyan U (OH)
Okanagan U Coll (BC, Canada)
Oklahoma Baptist U (OK)
Oklahoma Christian U (OK)
Oklahoma City U (OK)
Oklahoma Panhandle State U (OK)
Oklahoma State U (OK)
Old Dominion U (VA)
Olivet Coll (MI)
Olivet Nazarene U (IL)
Oral Roberts U (OK)
Oregon State U (OR)
Ottawa U (KS)
Otterbein Coll (OH)
Ouachita Baptist U (AR)
Our Lady of the Lake U of San Antonio (TX)
Pace U (NY)
Pacific Lutheran U (WA)
Pacific Union Coll (CA)
Pacific U (OR)
Paine Coll (GA)
Palm Beach Atlantic U (FL)
Park U (MO)
Peace Coll (NC)
Penn State U Abington Coll (PA)
Penn State U Altoona Coll (PA)
Penn State U at Erie, The Behrend Coll (PA)
Penn State U Beaver Campus of the Commonwealth Coll (PA)
Penn State U Berks Cmps of Berks-Lehigh Valley Coll (PA)
Penn State U Delaware County Campus of the Commonwealth Coll (PA)
Penn State U DuBois Campus of the Commonwealth Coll (PA)
Penn State U Fayette Campus of the Commonwealth Coll (PA)
Penn State U Harrisburg Campus of the Capital Coll (PA)
Penn State U Hazleton Campus of the Commonwealth Coll (PA)
Penn State U Lehigh Valley Cmps of Berks-Lehigh Valley Coll (PA)
Penn State U McKeesport Campus of the Commonwealth Coll (PA)
Penn State U Mont Alto Campus of the Commonwealth Coll (PA)
Penn State U New Kensington Campus of the Commonwealth Coll (PA)
Penn State U Schuylkill Campus of the Capital Coll (PA)
Penn State U Shenango Campus of the Commonwealth Coll (PA)
Penn State U Univ Park Campus (PA)
Penn State U Wilkes-Barre Campus of the Commonwealth Coll (PA)
Penn State U Worthington Scranton Cmps Commonwealth Coll (PA)
Penn State U York Campus of the Commonwealth Coll (PA)
Pepperdine U, Malibu (CA)
Pfeiffer U (NC)
Philadelphia U (PA)
Piedmont Coll (GA)
Pikeville Coll (KY)
Pine Manor Coll (MA)
Pittsburg State U (KS)
Pitzer Coll (CA)
Plymouth State U (NH)
Point Loma Nazarene U (CA)
Point Park U (PA)
Pomona Coll (CA)
Pontifical Catholic U of Puerto Rico (PR)
Portland State U (OR)
Prairie View A&M U (TX)
Presbyterian Coll (SC)
Princeton U (NJ)
Providence Coll (RI)
Purdue U (IN)
Queens Coll of the City U of NY (NY)
Queen's U at Kingston (ON, Canada)
Queens U of Charlotte (NC)
Quincy U (IL)
Quinnipiac U (CT)
Radford U (VA)
Ramapo Coll of New Jersey (NJ)
Randolph-Macon Coll (VA)
Randolph-Macon Woman's Coll (VA)
Redeemer U Coll (ON, Canada)
Reed Coll (OR)
Regis Coll (MA)
Regis U (CO)
Reinhardt Coll (GA)
Rensselaer Polytechnic Inst (NY)
Rhode Island Coll (RI)
Rhodes Coll (TN)
Rice U (TX)
The Richard Stockton Coll of New Jersey (NJ)
Richmond, The American Intl U in London(United Kingdom)
Rider U (NJ)
Ripon Coll (WI)
Rivier Coll (NH)
Roanoke Coll (VA)
Roberts Wesleyan Coll (NY)
Rochester Coll (MI)
Rochester Inst of Technology (NY)
Rockford Coll (IL)
Rockhurst U (MO)
Rocky Mountain Coll (MT)
Roger Williams U (RI)
Rollins Coll (FL)
Roosevelt U (IL)
Rosemont Coll (PA)
Rowan U (NJ)
Russell Sage Coll (NY)
Rutgers, The State U of New Jersey, Camden (NJ)
Rutgers, The State U of New Jersey, Newark (NJ)
Rutgers, The State U of New Jersey, New Brunswick/Piscataway (NJ)
Sacred Heart U (CT)
Sage Coll of Albany (NY)
Saginaw Valley State U (MI)
St. Ambrose U (IA)
St. Andrews Presbyterian Coll (NC)
Saint Anselm Coll (NH)
Saint Augustine's Coll (NC)
St. Bonaventure U (NY)
St. Cloud State U (MN)
St. Edward's U (TX)
St. Francis Coll (NY)
Saint Francis U (PA)
St. Francis Xavier U (NS, Canada)
St. Gregory's U (OK)
St. John Fisher Coll (NY)
Saint John's U (MN)
St. John's U (NY)
Saint Joseph Coll (CT)
Saint Joseph's Coll (IN)
St. Joseph's Coll, New York (NY)
Saint Joseph's Coll of Maine (ME)
St. Joseph's Coll, Suffolk Campus (NY)
Saint Joseph's U (PA)
St. Lawrence U (NY)
Saint Leo U (FL)
Saint Louis U (MO)
Saint Martin's Coll (WA)
Saint Mary-of-the-Woods Coll (IN)
Saint Mary's Coll (IN)
Saint Mary's Coll of California (CA)
St. Mary's Coll of Maryland (MD)
Saint Mary's U of Minnesota (MN)
St. Mary's U of San Antonio (TX)
Saint Michael's Coll (VT)
St. Norbert Coll (WI)
St. Olaf Coll (MN)
St. Thomas Aquinas Coll (NY)
St. Thomas U (FL)
St. Thomas U (NB, Canada)
Saint Vincent Coll (PA)

Saint Xavier U (IL)
Salem Coll (NC)
Salem State Coll (MA)
Salisbury U (MD)
Salve Regina U (RI)
Samford U (AL)
Sam Houston State U (TX)
San Diego State U (CA)
San Francisco State U (CA)
San Jose State U (CA)
Santa Clara U (CA)
Sarah Lawrence Coll (NY)
Schiller Intl U(United Kingdom)
Schreiner U (TX)
Scripps Coll (CA)
Seattle Pacific U (WA)
Seattle U (WA)
Seton Hall U (NJ)
Seton Hill U (PA)
Shawnee State U (OH)
Shaw U (NC)
Shenandoah U (VA)
Shepherd U (WV)
Shippensburg U of Pennsylvania (PA)
Shorter Coll (GA)
Siena Coll (NY)
Siena Heights U (MI)
Silver Lake Coll (WI)
Simmons Coll (MA)
Simon Fraser U (BC, Canada)
Simon's Rock Coll of Bard (MA)
Simpson Coll (IA)
Simpson Coll and Graduate School (CA)
Skidmore Coll (NY)
Slippery Rock U of Pennsylvania (PA)
Smith Coll (MA)
Sonoma State U (CA)
South Carolina State U (SC)
South Dakota State U (SD)
Southeastern Coll of the Assemblies of God (FL)
Southeastern Louisiana U (LA)
Southeastern Oklahoma State U (OK)
Southeast Missouri State U (MO)
Southern Adventist U (TN)
Southern Arkansas U–Magnolia (AR)
Southern Connecticut State U (CT)
Southern Illinois U Carbondale (IL)
Southern Illinois U Edwardsville (IL)
Southern Methodist U (TX)
Southern Nazarene U (OK)
Southern Oregon U (OR)
Southern U and A&M Coll (LA)
Southern Utah U (UT)
Southern Vermont Coll (VT)
Southern Wesleyan U (SC)
Southwest Baptist U (MO)
Southwestern Coll (KS)
Southwestern Oklahoma State U (OK)
Southwestern U (TX)
Southwest Missouri State U (MO)
Spelman Coll (GA)
Spring Arbor U (MI)
Springfield Coll (MA)
Spring Hill Coll (AL)
Stanford U (CA)
State U of NY at Binghamton (NY)
State U of NY at New Paltz (NY)
State U of NY at Oswego (NY)
Plattsburgh State U of NY (NY)
State U of NY Coll at Brockport (NY)
State U of NY Coll at Cortland (NY)
State U of NY Coll at Fredonia (NY)
State U of NY Coll at Geneseo (NY)
State U of NY Coll at Old Westbury (NY)
State U of NY Coll at Oneonta (NY)
State U of NY Coll at Potsdam (NY)
State U of NY Inst of Tech at Utica/Rome (NY)
State U of West Georgia (GA)
Stephens Coll (MO)
Stetson U (FL)
Stonehill Coll (MA)
Stony Brook U, State U of New York (NY)
Suffolk U (MA)
Susquehanna U (PA)
Swarthmore Coll (PA)
Sweet Briar Coll (VA)
Syracuse U (NY)
Tabor Coll (KS)
Talladega Coll (AL)
Tarleton State U (TX)
Taylor U (IN)
Taylor U, Fort Wayne Campus (IN)
Teikyo Post U (CT)
Tennessee State U (TN)
Tennessee Technological U (TN)
Tennessee Wesleyan Coll (TN)
Texas A&M Intl U (TX)
Texas A&M U (TX)
Texas A&M U–Commerce (TX)
Texas A&M U–Corpus Christi (TX)
Texas A&M U–Kingsville (TX)
Texas A&M U–Texarkana (TX)
Texas Christian U (TX)
Texas Lutheran U (TX)
Texas Southern U (TX)
Texas State U-San Marcos (TX)
Texas Tech U (TX)
Texas Wesleyan U (TX)
Texas Woman's U (TX)
Thiel Coll (PA)
Thomas Coll (ME)
Thomas Edison State Coll (NJ)
Thomas More Coll (KY)
Thomas U (GA)
Tiffin U (OH)
Tougaloo Coll (MS)
Towson U (MD)
Transylvania U (KY)
Trent U (ON, Canada)
Trevecca Nazarene U (TN)
Trinity Christian Coll (IL)
Trinity Coll (CT)
Trinity Coll (DC)
Trinity Intl U (IL)
Trinity U (TX)
Trinity Western U (BC, Canada)
Tri-State U (IN)
Troy State U (AL)
Troy State U Dothan (AL)
Troy State U Montgomery (AL)
Truman State U (MO)
Tufts U (MA)
Tulane U (LA)
Tusculum Coll (TN)
Tuskegee U (AL)
Tyndale U Coll & Sem (ON, Canada)
Union Coll (KY)
Union Coll (NE)
Union Coll (NY)
Union Inst & U (OH)
Union U (TN)
United States Intl U(Kenya)
United States Military Acad (NY)
Université de Montréal (QC, Canada)
Université de Sherbrooke (QC, Canada)
U du Québec à Hull (QC, Canada)
Université Laval (QC, Canada)
State U of NY at Albany (NY)
U at Buffalo, The State U of New York (NY)
U Coll of the Cariboo (BC, Canada)
U Coll of the Fraser Valley (BC, Canada)
The U of Akron (OH)
The U of Alabama (AL)
The U of Alabama at Birmingham (AL)
The U of Alabama in Huntsville (AL)
U of Alaska Fairbanks (AK)
U of Alberta (AB, Canada)
The U of Arizona (AZ)
U of Arkansas (AR)
U of Arkansas at Little Rock (AR)
U of Arkansas at Monticello (AR)
U of Baltimore (MD)
U of Bridgeport (CT)
The U of British Columbia (BC, Canada)
U of Calgary (AB, Canada)
U of Calif, Berkeley (CA)
U of Calif, Davis (CA)
U of Calif, Irvine (CA)
U of Calif, Los Angeles (CA)
U of Calif, Riverside (CA)
U of Calif, San Diego (CA)
U of Calif, Santa Barbara (CA)
U of Calif, Santa Cruz (CA)
U of Central Arkansas (AR)
U of Central Florida (FL)
U of Charleston (WV)
U of Chicago (IL)
U of Cincinnati (OH)
U of Colorado at Boulder (CO)
U of Colorado at Colorado Springs (CO)
U of Colorado at Denver (CO)
U of Connecticut (CT)
U of Dallas (TX)
U of Dayton (OH)
U of Delaware (DE)
U of Denver (CO)
U of Detroit Mercy (MI)
U of Dubuque (IA)
U of Evansville (IN)
The U of Findlay (OH)
U of Florida (FL)
U of Georgia (GA)
U of Great Falls (MT)
U of Guelph (ON, Canada)
U of Hartford (CT)
U of Hawaii at Hilo (HI)
U of Hawaii at Manoa (HI)
U of Houston (TX)
U of Houston–Clear Lake (TX)
U of Idaho (ID)
U of Illinois at Chicago (IL)
U of Illinois at Springfield (IL)
U of Illinois at Urbana–Champaign (IL)
U of Indianapolis (IN)
The U of Iowa (IA)
U of Judaism (CA)
U of Kansas (KS)
U of Kentucky (KY)
U of King's Coll (NS, Canada)
U of La Verne (CA)
The U of Lethbridge (AB, Canada)
U of Louisiana at Lafayette (LA)
U of Louisville (KY)
U of Maine (ME)
U of Maine at Farmington (ME)
U of Maine at Machias (ME)
U of Manitoba (MB, Canada)
U of Mary (ND)
U of Mary Hardin-Baylor (TX)
U of Maryland, Baltimore County (MD)
U of Maryland, Coll Park (MD)
U of Maryland U Coll (MD)
U of Massachusetts Amherst (MA)
U of Massachusetts Boston (MA)
U of Massachusetts Dartmouth (MA)
U of Massachusetts Lowell (MA)
The U of Memphis (TN)
U of Miami (FL)
U of Michigan (MI)
U of Michigan–Dearborn (MI)
U of Michigan–Flint (MI)
U of Minnesota, Duluth (MN)
U of Minnesota, Morris (MN)
U of Minnesota, Twin Cities Campus (MN)
U of Mississippi (MS)
U of Missouri–Columbia (MO)
U of Missouri–Kansas City (MO)
U of Missouri–Rolla (MO)
U of Missouri–St. Louis (MO)
U of Mobile (AL)
The U of Montana–Missoula (MT)
U of Montevallo (AL)
U of Nebraska at Omaha (NE)
U of Nebraska–Lincoln (NE)
U of Nevada, Las Vegas (NV)
U of Nevada, Reno (NV)
U of New Brunswick Fredericton (NB, Canada)
U of New Hampshire (NH)
U of New Hampshire at Manchester (NH)
U of New Haven (CT)
U of New Mexico (NM)
U of New Orleans (LA)
U of North Alabama (AL)
The U of North Carolina at Asheville (NC)
The U of North Carolina at Chapel Hill (NC)
The U of North Carolina at Charlotte (NC)
The U of North Carolina at Greensboro (NC)
The U of North Carolina at Pembroke (NC)
The U of North Carolina at Wilmington (NC)
U of North Dakota (ND)
U of Northern Colorado (CO)
U of Northern Iowa (IA)
U of North Florida (FL)
U of North Texas (TX)
U of Notre Dame (IN)
U of Oklahoma (OK)
U of Oregon (OR)
U of Ottawa (ON, Canada)
U of Pennsylvania (PA)
U of Pittsburgh (PA)
U of Pittsburgh at Bradford (PA)
U of Pittsburgh at Greensburg (PA)
U of Pittsburgh at Johnstown (PA)
U of Portland (OR)
U of Prince Edward Island (PE, Canada)
U of Puerto Rico, Cayey U Coll (PR)
U of Puget Sound (WA)
U of Redlands (CA)
U of Regina (SK, Canada)
U of Rhode Island (RI)
U of Richmond (VA)
U of Rochester (NY)
U of St. Francis (IL)
U of Saint Francis (IN)
U of Saint Mary (KS)
U of St. Thomas (MN)
U of St. Thomas (TX)
U of San Diego (CA)
U of San Francisco (CA)
U of Saskatchewan (SK, Canada)
U of Science and Arts of Oklahoma (OK)
The U of Scranton (PA)
U of Sioux Falls (SD)
U of South Alabama (AL)
U of South Carolina Aiken (SC)
U of South Carolina Spartanburg (SC)
The U of South Dakota (SD)
U of Southern California (CA)
U of Southern Indiana (IN)
U of Southern Maine (ME)
U of South Florida (FL)
The U of Tampa (FL)
The U of Tennessee (TN)
The U of Tennessee at Chattanooga (TN)
The U of Tennessee at Martin (TN)
The U of Texas at Arlington (TX)
The U of Texas at Austin (TX)
The U of Texas at Brownsville (TX)
The U of Texas at Dallas (TX)
The U of Texas at Tyler (TX)
The U of Texas–Pan American (TX)
U of the District of Columbia (DC)
U of the Incarnate Word (TX)
U of the Ozarks (AR)
U of the Pacific (CA)
U of the Sacred Heart (PR)
U of the Sciences in Philadelphia (PA)
U of the South (TN)
U of the Virgin Islands (VI)
U of the West (CA)
U of Toledo (OH)
U of Toronto (ON, Canada)
U of Tulsa (OK)
U of Utah (UT)
U of Vermont (VT)
U of Victoria (BC, Canada)
U of Virginia (VA)
The U of Virginia's Coll at Wise (VA)
U of Washington (WA)
U of Waterloo (ON, Canada)
The U of West Alabama (AL)
The U of Western Ontario (ON, Canada)
U of West Florida (FL)
U of Windsor (ON, Canada)
U of Wisconsin–Eau Claire (WI)
U of Wisconsin–Green Bay (WI)
U of Wisconsin–La Crosse (WI)
U of Wisconsin–Madison (WI)
U of Wisconsin–Milwaukee (WI)
U of Wisconsin–Oshkosh (WI)
U of Wisconsin–Parkside (WI)
U of Wisconsin–Platteville (WI)
U of Wisconsin–River Falls (WI)
U of Wisconsin–Stevens Point (WI)
U of Wisconsin–Stout (WI)
U of Wisconsin–Superior (WI)
U of Wisconsin–Whitewater (WI)
U of Wyoming (WY)
Upper Iowa U (IA)
Urbana U (OH)
Ursinus Coll (PA)
Ursuline Coll (OH)
Utah State U (UT)
Utica Coll (NY)
Valdosta State U (GA)
Valley City State U (ND)
Valparaiso U (IN)
Vanderbilt U (TN)
Vanguard U of Southern California (CA)
Vassar Coll (NY)
Vennard Coll (IA)
Villa Julie Coll (MD)
Villanova U (PA)
Virginia Commonwealth U (VA)
Virginia Intermont Coll (VA)
Virginia Military Inst (VA)
Virginia Polytechnic Inst and State U (VA)
Virginia State U (VA)
Virginia Union U (VA)
Virginia Wesleyan Coll (VA)
Viterbo U (WI)
Wabash Coll (IN)
Wagner Coll (NY)
Wake Forest U (NC)
Waldorf Coll (IA)
Walla Walla Coll (WA)
Walsh U (OH)
Warner Pacific Coll (OR)
Warner Southern Coll (FL)
Warren Wilson Coll (NC)
Wartburg Coll (IA)
Washburn U (KS)
Washington & Jefferson Coll (PA)
Washington and Lee U (VA)
Washington Coll (MD)
Washington State U (WA)
Washington U in St. Louis (MO)
Wayland Baptist U (TX)
Waynesburg Coll (PA)
Wayne State Coll (NE)
Wayne State U (MI)
Weber State U (UT)
Webster U (MO)
Wellesley Coll (MA)
Wells Coll (NY)
Wesleyan Coll (GA)
Wesleyan U (CT)
Wesley Coll (DE)
West Chester U of Pennsylvania (PA)
Western Baptist Coll (OR)
Western Carolina U (NC)
Western Connecticut State U (CT)
Western Illinois U (IL)
Western Kentucky U (KY)
Western Michigan U (MI)
Western New England Coll (MA)
Western Oregon U (OR)
Western State Coll of Colorado (CO)
Western Washington U (WA)
Westfield State Coll (MA)
West Liberty State Coll (WV)
Westminster Coll (MO)
Westminster Coll (PA)
Westminster Coll (UT)
Westmont Coll (CA)
West Texas A&M U (TX)
West Virginia State Coll (WV)
West Virginia U (WV)
West Virginia Wesleyan Coll (WV)
Wheaton Coll (IL)
Wheaton Coll (MA)
Wheeling Jesuit U (WV)
Whitman Coll (WA)
Whitworth Coll (WA)
Wichita State U (KS)
Widener U (PA)
Wilberforce U (OH)
Wilkes U (PA)
Willamette U (OR)
William Carey Coll (MS)
William Jewell Coll (MO)
William Paterson U of New Jersey (NJ)
William Penn U (IA)
Williams Baptist Coll (AR)
Williams Coll (MA)
William Tyndale Coll (MI)
William Woods U (MO)
Wilmington Coll (DE)
Wingate U (NC)
Winona State U (MN)
Winston-Salem State U (NC)
Winthrop U (SC)
Wisconsin Lutheran Coll (WI)
Wittenberg U (OH)
Wofford Coll (SC)
Worcester State Coll (MA)
Wright State U (OH)
Xavier U (OH)
Xavier U of Louisiana (LA)
Yale U (CT)
York Coll (NE)
York Coll of Pennsylvania (PA)
York Coll of the City U of New York (NY)
York U (ON, Canada)
Youngstown State U (OH)

PSYCHOLOGY RELATED

Arizona State U East (AZ)
Averett U (VA)
Buena Vista U (IA)
Burlington Coll (VT)
Clayton Coll & State U (GA)
Kean U (NJ)
Long Island U, Southampton Coll (NY)
Loyola U Chicago (IL)
Madonna U (MI)
North Carolina State U (NC)
Northwest Christian Coll (OR)
Ohio Northern U (OH)
Saint Mary's Coll of California (CA)
St. Mary's Coll of Maryland (MD)
Skidmore Coll (NY)
State U of NY at Oswego (NY)
Towson U (MD)
U of Michigan–Flint (MI)
U of Puerto Rico, Cayey U Coll (PR)
U of St. Thomas (MN)
U of Toledo (OH)

PSYCHOLOGY TEACHER EDUCATION
Alma Coll (MI)
Brigham Young U (UT)
California Lutheran U (CA)
Campbellsville U (KY)
Carroll Coll (WI)
Cumberland U (TN)
Hardin-Simmons U (TX)
Ohio Wesleyan U (OH)
Pittsburg State U (KS)
St. Ambrose U (IA)
Shawnee State U (OH)
U of Michigan–Flint (MI)
U of Missouri–St. Louis (MO)
Valparaiso U (IN)
Widener U (PA)
York Coll (NE)

PSYCHOMETRICS AND QUANTITATIVE PSYCHOLOGY
North Dakota State U (ND)

PUBLIC ADMINISTRATION
Alfred U (NY)
American Intl Coll (MA)
American Public U System (WV)
Athabasca U (AB, Canada)
Auburn U (AL)
Augustana Coll (IL)
Baylor U (TX)
Baruch Coll of the City U of NY (NY)
Blackburn Coll (IL)
Bloomfield Coll (NJ)
Boise State U (ID)
Bowling Green State U (OH)
Brock U (ON, Canada)
Buena Vista U (IA)
California State Polytechnic U, Pomona (CA)
California State U, Chico (CA)
California State U, Dominguez Hills (CA)
California State U, Fresno (CA)
California State U, Fullerton (CA)
California State U, Hayward (CA)
California State U, San Bernardino (CA)
Calvin Coll (MI)
Campbell U (NC)
Capital U (OH)
Carleton U (ON, Canada)
Carroll Coll (MT)
Cedarville U (OH)
Central Methodist Coll (MO)
Christopher Newport U (VA)
Cleveland State U (OH)
Coll of Santa Fe (NM)
Concordia U (QC, Canada)
Cornell U (NY)
Doane Coll (NE)
Eastern Michigan U (MI)
Eastern Washington U (WA)
Edgewood Coll (WI)
Elon U (NC)
Evangel U (MO)
Ferris State U (MI)
Flagler Coll (FL)
Florida Ag and Mech U (FL)
Florida Atlantic U (FL)
Florida Intl U (FL)
Fordham U (NY)
Framingham State Coll (MA)
George Mason U (VA)
Governors State U (IL)
Grambling State U (LA)
Grand Valley State U (MI)
Hamline U (MN)
Harding U (AR)
Harris-Stowe State Coll (MO)
Hawai'i Pacific U (HI)
Heidelberg Coll (OH)
Henderson State U (AR)
Huntingdon Coll (AL)
Indiana U Bloomington (IN)
Indiana U Northwest (IN)
Indiana U–Purdue U Fort Wayne (IN)
Indiana U–Purdue U Indianapolis (IN)
Indiana U South Bend (IN)
Inter American U of PR, San Germán Campus (PR)
Iowa State U of Science and Technology (IA)
James Madison U (VA)
John Carroll U (OH)
John Jay Coll of Criminal Justice, the City U of NY (NY)
The Johns Hopkins U (MD)
Juniata Coll (PA)
Kean U (NJ)
Kentucky State U (KY)
Kutztown U of Pennsylvania (PA)
La Salle U (PA)
Lewis U (IL)
Lincoln U (MO)
Lincoln U (PA)
Lindenwood U (MO)
Lipscomb U (TN)
Long Island U, C.W. Post Campus (NY)
Louisiana Coll (LA)
Marist Coll (NY)
Marywood U (PA)
Medgar Evers Coll of the City U of NY (NY)
Metropolitan State U (MN)
Miami U (OH)
Miami U Hamilton (OH)
Michigan State U (MI)
Minnesota State U Mankato (MN)
Mississippi Valley State U (MS)
Missouri Valley Coll (MO)
Murray State U (KY)
Nevada State Coll at Henderson (NV)
Northeastern U (MA)
Northern Michigan U (MI)
Northern State U (SD)
North Georgia Coll & State U (GA)
Notre Dame Coll (OH)
Oakland U (MI)
Ohio Wesleyan U (OH)
Park U (MO)
Plymouth State U (NH)
Point Park U (PA)
Pontifical Catholic U of Puerto Rico (PR)
Rhode Island Coll (RI)
Roger Williams U (RI)
Roosevelt U (IL)
Ryerson U (ON, Canada)
Saginaw Valley State U (MI)
St. Ambrose U (IA)
St. Cloud State U (MN)
Saint Francis U (PA)
St. John's U (NY)
Saint Joseph's U (PA)
St. Thomas U (FL)
Samford U (AL)
San Diego State U (CA)
Seattle U (WA)
Shaw U (NC)
Shenandoah U (VA)
Shippensburg U of Pennsylvania (PA)
Siena Heights U (MI)
Southwest Missouri State U (MO)
Stonehill Coll (MA)
Suffolk U (MA)
Syracuse U (NY)
Talladega Coll (AL)
Tennessee State U (TN)
Texas A&M U–Kingsville (TX)
Texas Southern U (TX)
Texas State U-San Marcos (TX)
Thomas Edison State Coll (NJ)
Union Inst & U (OH)
State U of NY at Albany (NY)
The U of Arizona (AZ)
U of Arkansas (AR)
U of Calif, Los Angeles (CA)
U of Calif, Riverside (CA)
U of Central Arkansas (AR)
U of Central Florida (FL)
U of Denver (CO)
U of Houston–Clear Lake (TX)
U of La Verne (CA)
The U of Lethbridge (AB, Canada)
U of Maine (ME)
The U of Maine at Augusta (ME)
U of Maine at Fort Kent (ME)
U of Maine at Machias (ME)
U of Manitoba (MB, Canada)
U of Michigan–Dearborn (MI)
U of Michigan–Flint (MI)
U of Mississippi (MS)
U of Missouri–St. Louis (MO)
The U of North Carolina at Pembroke (NC)
U of Northern Iowa (IA)
U of North Texas (TX)
U of Oklahoma (OK)
U of Oregon (OR)
U of Ottawa (ON, Canada)
U of Pittsburgh (PA)
U of Regina (SK, Canada)
U of St. Thomas (MN)
U of San Francisco (CA)
U of Saskatchewan (SK, Canada)
U of Southern California (CA)
The U of Tennessee (TN)
The U of Tennessee at Martin (TN)
The U of Texas at Dallas (TX)
U of the District of Columbia (DC)
U of Toronto (ON, Canada)
U of Victoria (BC, Canada)
U of Washington (WA)
The U of Western Ontario (ON, Canada)
U of Windsor (ON, Canada)
U of Wisconsin–La Crosse (WI)
U of Wisconsin–Stevens Point (WI)
U of Wisconsin–Whitewater (WI)
Upper Iowa U (IA)
Virginia Intermont Coll (VA)
Virginia State U (VA)
Wagner Coll (NY)
Washburn U (KS)
Washington State U (WA)
Waynesburg Coll (PA)
Wayne State Coll (NE)
Wayne State U (MI)
Western Carolina U (NC)
Western Oregon U (OR)
West Texas A&M U (TX)
Winona State U (MN)
Wright State U (OH)
York Coll of Pennsylvania (PA)
York U (ON, Canada)
Youngstown State U (OH)

PUBLIC ADMINISTRATION AND SOCIAL SERVICE PROFESSIONS RELATED
Coll of Mount St. Joseph (OH)
Columbia Coll (SC)
Cornell U (NY)
Eastern Michigan U (MI)
Kentucky Wesleyan Coll (KY)
Milligan Coll (TN)
Northeastern Illinois U (IL)
Ohio U (OH)
Quincy U (IL)
Roosevelt U (IL)
Southern Christian U (AL)
Texas Woman's U (TX)
U of Phoenix–Colorado Campus (CO)
U of Phoenix–Hawaii Campus (HI)
U of Phoenix–Kansas City Campus (MO)
U of Phoenix–Louisiana Campus (LA)
U of Phoenix–Nevada Campus (NV)
U of Phoenix–New Mexico Campus (NM)
U of Phoenix–Northern California Campus (CA)
U of Phoenix–Oklahoma City Campus (OK)
U of Phoenix–Oregon Campus (OR)
U of Phoenix–Orlando Campus (FL)
U of Phoenix–Phoenix Campus (AZ)
U of Phoenix–Sacramento Campus (CA)
U of Phoenix–St. Louis Campus (MO)
U of Phoenix–San Diego Campus (CA)
U of Phoenix–Southern Arizona Campus (AZ)
U of Phoenix–Southern California Campus (CA)
U of Phoenix–Southern Colorado Campus (CO)
U of Phoenix–Tampa Campus (FL)
U of Phoenix–Utah Campus (UT)
U of Phoenix–Washington Campus (WA)
U of Phoenix–West Michigan Campus (MI)
U of Saint Francis (IN)

PUBLIC/APPLIED HISTORY AND ARCHIVAL ADMINISTRATION
Clayton Coll & State U (GA)
East Carolina U (NC)
Meredith Coll (NC)
U of Calif, Santa Barbara (CA)

PUBLIC HEALTH
Alma Coll (MI)
Boise State U (ID)
Brock U (ON, Canada)
California State U, Dominguez Hills (CA)
California State U, Long Beach (CA)
Central Michigan U (MI)
Dillard U (LA)
Grand Valley State U (MI)
Hampshire Coll (MA)
Hunter Coll of the City U of NY (NY)
Indiana U Bloomington (IN)
Indiana U–Purdue U Indianapolis (IN)
The Johns Hopkins U (MD)
Maryville U of Saint Louis (MO)
Minnesota State U Mankato (MN)
New Mexico State U (NM)
Oregon State U (OR)
The Richard Stockton Coll of New Jersey (NJ)
Rutgers, The State U of New Jersey, New Brunswick/Piscataway (NJ)
Ryerson U (ON, Canada)
St. Joseph's Coll, New York (NY)
Slippery Rock U of Pennsylvania (PA)
Southern Connecticut State U (CT)
Springfield Coll (MA)
Touro U Intl (CA)
Truman State U (MO)
Tufts U (MA)
U of Cincinnati (OH)
U of Minnesota, Twin Cities Campus (MN)
U of Washington (WA)
West Chester U of Pennsylvania (PA)
William Paterson U of New Jersey (NJ)
Winona State U (MN)
York U (ON, Canada)

PUBLIC HEALTH/COMMUNITY NURSING
Capital U (OH)
Northern Illinois U (IL)
Ryerson U (ON, Canada)
U of Washington (WA)
Wright State U (OH)

PUBLIC HEALTH EDUCATION AND PROMOTION
Appalachian State U (NC)
California State U, Long Beach (CA)
Coastal Carolina U (SC)
Dalhousie U (NS, Canada)
Dillard U (LA)
East Carolina U (NC)
Georgia Southern U (GA)
Ithaca Coll (NY)
Laurentian U (ON, Canada)
Louisiana State U in Shreveport (LA)
Malone Coll (OH)
New Mexico State U (NM)
North Carolina Central U (NC)
Plymouth State U (NH)
Southeastern Louisiana U (LA)
U of Michigan–Flint (MI)
The U of North Carolina at Chapel Hill (NC)
The U of North Carolina at Greensboro (NC)
The U of North Carolina at Pembroke (NC)
U of Northern Colorado (CO)
U of North Texas (TX)
U of St. Thomas (MN)
U of Southern California (CA)
U of Toledo (OH)
U of Wisconsin–La Crosse (WI)
Walla Walla Coll (WA)
West Chester U of Pennsylvania (PA)
Western Washington U (WA)

PUBLIC HEALTH RELATED
Concordia U Coll of Alberta (AB, Canada)
Malone Coll (OH)
Maryville U of Saint Louis (MO)
Texas Chiropractic Coll (TX)
U of Calif, Berkeley (CA)
U of Calif, Los Angeles (CA)
U of Illinois at Urbana–Champaign (IL)
Utah State U (UT)
West Chester U of Pennsylvania (PA)

PUBLIC POLICY ANALYSIS
Albion Coll (MI)
Bentley Coll (MA)
Baruch Coll of the City U of NY (NY)
Bloomfield Coll (NJ)
Brigham Young U (UT)
Central Washington U (WA)
Chatham Coll (PA)
Coll of the Atlantic (ME)
The Coll of William and Mary (VA)
Concordia U (QC, Canada)
Cornell U (NY)
DePaul U (IL)
Dickinson Coll (PA)
Duke U (NC)
Eastern Michigan U (MI)
Edgewood Coll (WI)
The George Washington U (DC)
Georgia Inst of Technology (GA)
Grand Valley State U (MI)
Hamilton Coll (NY)
Hampshire Coll (MA)
Harvard U (MA)
Hobart and William Smith Colls (NY)
Indiana U Bloomington (IN)
Indiana U–Purdue U Fort Wayne (IN)
Kenyon Coll (OH)
Mills Coll (CA)
New Coll of Florida (FL)
North Carolina State U (NC)
Northern Arizona U (AZ)
Northwestern U (IL)
Occidental Coll (CA)
Penn State U Harrisburg Campus of the Capital Coll (PA)
Pomona Coll (CA)
Princeton U (NJ)
Rice U (TX)
Rochester Inst of Technology (NY)
St. Cloud State U (MN)
St. Mary's Coll of Maryland (MD)
Saint Vincent Coll (PA)
Sarah Lawrence Coll (NY)
Simmons Coll (MA)
Southern Methodist U (TX)
Stanford U (CA)
Suffolk U (MA)
Trinity Coll (CT)
United States Military Acad (NY)
State U of NY at Albany (NY)
U of Arkansas (AR)
U of Calif, Los Angeles (CA)
U of Chicago (IL)
U of Cincinnati (OH)
U of Massachusetts Boston (MA)
The U of North Carolina at Chapel Hill (NC)
U of Oregon (OR)
U of Ottawa (ON, Canada)
U of Pennsylvania (PA)
U of Rhode Island (RI)
U of Toledo (OH)
U of Wisconsin–Whitewater (WI)
Washington and Lee U (VA)
Wells Coll (NY)
Western State Coll of Colorado (CO)
York U (ON, Canada)

PUBLIC RELATIONS
Delaware State U (DE)

PUBLIC RELATIONS, ADVERTISING, AND APPLIED COMMUNICATION RELATED
Bridgewater State Coll (MA)
Brigham Young U (UT)
Buena Vista U (IA)
California Lutheran U (CA)
Campbell U (NC)
Carroll Coll (WI)
Champlain Coll (VT)
Eastern Kentucky U (KY)
Jones Intl U (CO)
Keystone Coll (PA)
Lambuth U (TN)
Madonna U (MI)
Marietta Coll (OH)
Murray State U (KY)
Notre Dame Coll (OH)
Paine Coll (GA)
Pittsburg State U (KS)
Rochester Inst of Technology (NY)
Shorter Coll (GA)
State U of NY Coll at Brockport (NY)
Texas A&M U (TX)
U Coll of the Cariboo (BC, Canada)
The U of Akron (OH)

PUBLIC RELATIONS/IMAGE MANAGEMENT
Alabama State U (AL)
American U (DC)
Andrews U (MI)
Appalachian State U (NC)
Auburn U (AL)
Ball State U (IN)
Barry U (FL)
Boston U (MA)
Bowie State U (MD)
Bowling Green State U (OH)
Bradley U (IL)
Bridgewater Coll (VA)
State U of NY Coll at Buffalo (NY)
Butler U (IN)
California Lutheran U (CA)
California State Polytechnic U, Pomona (CA)

California State U, Chico (CA)
California State U, Dominguez Hills (CA)
California State U, Fresno (CA)
California State U, Fullerton (CA)
California State U, Hayward (CA)
California State U, Long Beach (CA)
Campbell U (NC)
Capital U (OH)
Cardinal Stritch U (WI)
Carroll Coll (MT)
Castleton State Coll (VT)
Central Michigan U (MI)
Central Missouri State U (MO)
Central Washington U (WA)
Champlain Coll (VT)
Clarke Coll (IA)
Cleveland State U (OH)
Coe Coll (IA)
The Coll of Southeastern Europe, The American U of Athens(Greece)
Coll of the Ozarks (MO)
Colorado State U (CO)
Colorado State U-Pueblo (CO)
Columbia Coll (SC)
Columbia Coll Chicago (IL)
Columbus State U (GA)
Concordia Coll (MN)
Curry Coll (MA)
Defiance Coll (OH)
Doane Coll (NE)
Drake U (IA)
Drury U (MO)
East Central U (OK)
Eastern Kentucky U (KY)
Eastern Michigan U (MI)
Emerson Coll (MA)
Ferris State U (MI)
Florida Ag and Mech U (FL)
Florida Southern Coll (FL)
Florida State U (FL)
Fort Hays State U (KS)
Freed-Hardeman U (TN)
George Fox U (OR)
Georgia Southern U (GA)
Gonzaga U (WA)
Grand Valley State U (MI)
Greenville Coll (IL)
Gwynedd-Mercy Coll (PA)
Hampton U (VA)
Harding U (AR)
Hardin-Simmons U (TX)
Hastings Coll (NE)
Hawai'i Pacific U (HI)
Heidelberg Coll (OH)
Hofstra U (NY)
Howard Payne U (TX)
Huntington Coll (IN)
Illinois State U (IL)
Indiana U Northwest (IN)
Iona Coll (NY)
Ithaca Coll (NY)
John Brown U (AR)
Kent State U (OH)
La Salle U (PA)
Lewis U (IL)
Liberty U (VA)
Lindenwood U (MO)
Lipscomb U (TN)
Long Island U, C.W. Post Campus (NY)
Loras Coll (IA)
Madonna U (MI)
Mansfield U of Pennsylvania (PA)
Marist Coll (NY)
Marquette U (WI)
Marylhurst U (OR)
Marywood U (PA)
The Master's Coll and Sem (CA)
McKendree Coll (IL)
Mercyhurst Coll (PA)
Metropolitan State Coll of Denver (CO)
MidAmerica Nazarene U (KS)
Middle Tennessee State U (TN)
Minnesota State U Mankato (MN)
Minnesota State U Moorhead (MN)
Mississippi Coll (MS)
Monmouth Coll (IL)
Montana State U–Billings (MT)
Montclair State U (NJ)
Mount Mary Coll (WI)
Mount Saint Mary Coll (NY)
Mount Saint Vincent U (NS, Canada)
Murray State U (KY)
New England School of Communications (ME)
North Carolina State U (NC)
Northern Arizona U (AZ)
Northern Michigan U (MI)
Northwestern Coll (MN)
Northwest Nazarene U (ID)
Ohio Dominican U (OH)
Ohio Northern U (OH)
Ohio U (OH)
Ohio U–Zanesville (OH)
Oklahoma Baptist U (OK)
Oklahoma Christian U (OK)
Oklahoma City U (OK)
Oral Roberts U (OK)
Otterbein Coll (OH)
Pacific Union Coll (CA)
Pepperdine U, Malibu (CA)
Pfeiffer U (NC)
Pittsburg State U (KS)
Point Park U (PA)
Pontifical Catholic U of Puerto Rico (PR)
Quincy U (IL)
Quinnipiac U (CT)
Rider U (NJ)
Rochester Inst of Technology (NY)
Rockhurst U (MO)
Roosevelt U (IL)
St. Ambrose U (IA)
St. Cloud State U (MN)
Saint Francis U (PA)
Saint Joseph's Coll of Maine (ME)
Saint Mary-of-the-Woods Coll (IN)
Saint Mary's U of Minnesota (MN)
Salem State Coll (MA)
Sam Houston State U (TX)
San Diego State U (CA)
San Jose State U (CA)
Seattle U (WA)
Simmons Coll (MA)
Southern Adventist U (TN)
Southern Methodist U (TX)
State U of NY at Oswego (NY)
State U of NY Coll at Brockport (NY)
Stephens Coll (MO)
Suffolk U (MA)
Susquehanna U (PA)
Syracuse U (NY)
Tabor Coll (KS)
Taylor U, Fort Wayne Campus (IN)
Texas State U-San Marcos (TX)
Texas Tech U (TX)
Trinity Christian Coll (IL)
Union Coll (NE)
Union U (TN)
The U of Alabama (AL)
U of Dayton (OH)
U of Delaware (DE)
U of Detroit Mercy (MI)
The U of Findlay (OH)
U of Florida (FL)
U of Georgia (GA)
U of Houston (TX)
U of Idaho (ID)
U of Louisiana at Lafayette (LA)
U of Miami (FL)
U of Northern Iowa (IA)
U of North Texas (TX)
U of Oklahoma (OK)
U of Oregon (OR)
U of Pittsburgh at Bradford (PA)
U of Sioux Falls (SD)
U of South Carolina (SC)
U of Southern California (CA)
U of Southern Indiana (IN)
The U of Tennessee at Martin (TN)
The U of Texas at Arlington (TX)
The U of Texas at Austin (TX)
U of Utah (UT)
U of Wisconsin–Madison (WI)
U of Wisconsin–River Falls (WI)
Ursuline Coll (OH)
Utica Coll (NY)
Valparaiso U (IN)
Walla Walla Coll (WA)
Wartburg Coll (IA)
Washington State U (WA)
Wayne State U (MI)
Weber State U (UT)
Webster U (MO)
Western Kentucky U (KY)
Westminster Coll (PA)
West Virginia Wesleyan Coll (WV)
Wheeling Jesuit U (WV)
William Penn U (IA)
William Woods U (MO)
Wingate U (NC)
Winona State U (MN)
Xavier U (OH)
York Coll of Pennsylvania (PA)
Youngstown State U (OH)

PUBLISHING
Benedictine U (IL)
Emerson Coll (MA)
Graceland U (IA)
Pontifical Catholic U of Puerto Rico (PR)
Rochester Inst of Technology (NY)
Saint Mary's U of Minnesota (MN)
U of Missouri–Columbia (MO)

PURCHASING, PROCUREMENT/ ACQUISITIONS AND CONTRACTS MANAGEMENT
American U of Puerto Rico (PR)
Arizona State U (AZ)
Bloomfield Coll (NJ)
California State U, Hayward (CA)
Miami U (OH)
North Georgia Coll & State U (GA)
St. John's U (NY)
Southwestern Coll (KS)
Thomas Edison State Coll (NJ)
U of the District of Columbia (DC)
Wright State U (OH)

QUALITY CONTROL AND SAFETY TECHNOLOGIES RELATED
Madonna U (MI)

QUALITY CONTROL TECHNOLOGY
Bowling Green State U (OH)
California State U, Long Beach (CA)
Eastern Michigan U (MI)
Ferris State U (MI)
San Jose State U (CA)
Winona State U (MN)

RABBINICAL STUDIES
Ohr Somayach/Joseph Tanenbaum Educational Center (NY)
Talmudic Coll of Florida (FL)
Université Laval (QC, Canada)

RADIATION BIOLOGY
Grand Valley State U (MI)
Inter Amer U of PR, Barranquitas Campus (PR)

RADIO AND TELEVISION
Acad of Art U (CA)
Alabama State U (AL)
Appalachian State U (NC)
Arizona State U (AZ)
Arkansas State U (AR)
Ashland U (OH)
Auburn U (AL)
Barry U (FL)
Baylor U (TX)
Belmont U (TN)
Bemidji State U (MN)
Biola U (CA)
Boston U (MA)
Bradley U (IL)
Brooklyn Coll of the City U of NY (NY)
State U of NY Coll at Buffalo (NY)
California State U, Chico (CA)
California State U, Fresno (CA)
California State U, Fullerton (CA)
California State U, Long Beach (CA)
California State U, Los Angeles (CA)
Campbell U (NC)
Castleton State Coll (VT)
Central Michigan U (MI)
Central Missouri State U (MO)
Central State U (OH)
Central Washington U (WA)
Chicago State U (IL)
Colorado State U (CO)
Colorado State U-Pueblo (CO)
Columbia Coll Chicago (IL)
Columbia Coll Hollywood (CA)
Concordia Coll (MN)
Curry Coll (MA)
Delaware State U (DE)
Drake U (IA)
East Central U (OK)
Eastern Kentucky U (KY)
Eastern Nazarene Coll (MA)
Emerson Coll (MA)
Evangel U (MO)
Florida State U (FL)
Fordham U (NY)
Fort Hays State U (KS)
Franklin Pierce Coll (NH)
Freed-Hardeman U (TN)
Gallaudet U (DC)
Gannon U (PA)
Geneva Coll (PA)
George Fox U (OR)
The George Washington U (DC)
Georgia Southern U (GA)
Grand Valley State U (MI)
Grand View Coll (IA)
Hampshire Coll (MA)
Hardin-Simmons U (TX)
Hastings Coll (NE)
Hofstra U (NY)
Howard U (DC)
Indiana State U (IN)
Indiana U Bloomington (IN)
Iona Coll (NY)
Ithaca Coll (NY)
John Brown U (AR)
Kent State U (OH)
Lamar U (TX)
La Salle U (PA)
Lindenwood U (MO)
Lyndon State Coll (VT)
Mansfield U of Pennsylvania (PA)
Marietta Coll (OH)
Marist Coll (NY)
The Master's Coll and Sem (CA)
Mercy Coll (NY)
Mercyhurst Coll (PA)
Messiah Coll (PA)
Michigan State U (MI)
Minot State U (ND)
Murray State U (KY)
New England School of Communications (ME)
New York Inst of Technology (NY)
New York U (NY)
Northeastern U (MA)
Northern Arizona U (AZ)
Northwestern Coll (MN)
Northwestern U (IL)
Ohio Northern U (OH)
Ohio U (OH)
Oklahoma Baptist U (OK)
Oklahoma Christian U (OK)
Oklahoma City U (OK)
Olivet Nazarene U (IL)
Oral Roberts U (OK)
Otterbein Coll (OH)
Pacific Lutheran U (WA)
Pacific U (OR)
Palm Beach Atlantic U (FL)
Pittsburg State U (KS)
Point Park U (PA)
Pontifical Catholic U of Puerto Rico (PR)
Quincy U (IL)
Rider U (NJ)
Roosevelt U (IL)
Ryerson U (ON, Canada)
Sacred Heart U (CT)
St. Ambrose U (IA)
St. Cloud State U (MN)
Sam Houston State U (TX)
San Diego State U (CA)
San Francisco State U (CA)
San Jose State U (CA)
Southern Illinois U Carbondale (IL)
Southern Methodist U (TX)
Spring Arbor U (MI)
Spring Hill Coll (AL)
State U of NY at New Paltz (NY)
State U of NY Coll at Brockport (NY)
State U of NY Coll at Fredonia (NY)
Stephens Coll (MO)
Susquehanna U (PA)
Syracuse U (NY)
Texas A&M U–Commerce (TX)
Texas Christian U (TX)
Texas Southern U (TX)
Texas State U-San Marcos (TX)
Texas Tech U (TX)
Texas Wesleyan U (TX)
Union U (TN)
The U of Alabama (AL)
The U of Arizona (AZ)
U of Arkansas at Little Rock (AR)
U of Central Florida (FL)
U of Cincinnati (OH)
U of Dayton (OH)
U of Detroit Mercy (MI)
U of Florida (FL)
U of Idaho (ID)
U of Kansas (KS)
U of Kentucky (KY)
U of La Verne (CA)
U of Miami (FL)
U of Mississippi (MS)
U of Missouri–Columbia (MO)
The U of Montana–Missoula (MT)
U of Montevallo (AL)
The U of North Carolina at Greensboro (NC)
U of Northern Iowa (IA)
U of North Texas (TX)
U of Oregon (OR)
U of Sioux Falls (SD)
U of Southern California (CA)
U of Southern Indiana (IN)
The U of Tennessee (TN)
The U of Texas at Arlington (TX)
The U of Texas at Austin (TX)
U of Utah (UT)
U of Windsor (ON, Canada)
U of Wisconsin–Madison (WI)
U of Wisconsin–Oshkosh (WI)
U of Wisconsin–River Falls (WI)
U of Wisconsin–Superior (WI)
Valparaiso U (IN)
Vanguard U of Southern California (CA)
Walla Walla Coll (WA)
Washburn U (KS)
Waynesburg Coll (PA)
Wayne State U (MI)
Weber State U (UT)
Webster U (MO)
Western Illinois U (IL)
Western Kentucky U (KY)
Western Michigan U (MI)
Western State Coll of Colorado (CO)
Westfield State Coll (MA)
Westminster Coll (PA)
William Woods U (MO)
Winona State U (MN)
Xavier U (OH)
York Coll of Pennsylvania (PA)
Youngstown State U (OH)

RADIO AND TELEVISION BROADCASTING TECHNOLOGY
Alabama Ag and Mech U (AL)
Asbury Coll (KY)
Eastern Michigan U (MI)
Emerson Coll (MA)
Gardner-Webb U (NC)
Geneva Coll (PA)
Hofstra U (NY)
Iona Coll (NY)
Lewis U (IL)
Liberty U (VA)
New England School of Communications (ME)
Northwest Nazarene U (ID)
Ohio U (OH)
Texas Tech U (TX)
Trevecca Nazarene U (TN)
U of Georgia (GA)

RADIOLOGIC TECHNOLOGY/ SCIENCE
Austin Peay State U (TN)
Baptist Coll of Health Sciences (TN)
Boise State U (ID)
Champlain Coll (VT)
Clarion U of Pennsylvania (PA)
Dalhousie U (NS, Canada)
The George Washington U (DC)
Indiana U Northwest (IN)
Jamestown Coll (ND)
Kent State U (OH)
Manhattan Coll (NY)
Mass Coll of Pharmacy and Allied Health Sciences (MA)
Medical Coll of Georgia (GA)
Midwestern State U (TX)
Mount Aloysius Coll (PA)
North Dakota State U (ND)
The Ohio State U (OH)
Oregon Inst of Technology (OR)
Quinnipiac U (CT)
Saint Joseph's Coll of Maine (ME)
Southwest Missouri State U (MO)
State U of New York Upstate Medical U (NY)
Suffolk U (MA)
U of Charleston (WV)
The U of Findlay (OH)
The U of Iowa (IA)
U of Mary (ND)
U of Michigan (MI)
U of Missouri–Columbia (MO)
U of Nebraska Medical Center (NE)
U of Oklahoma Health Sciences Center (OK)
U of Pittsburgh at Bradford (PA)
U of St. Francis (IL)
U of South Alabama (AL)
Virginia Commonwealth U (VA)

RADIO, TELEVISION, AND DIGITAL COMMUNICATION RELATED
Brigham Young U (UT)
California State Polytechnic U, Pomona (CA)
Campbell U (NC)
Capital U (OH)
Drake U (IA)
Emerson Coll (MA)
Florida State U (FL)
Madonna U (MI)
Sacred Heart U (CT)
State U of NY Coll at Brockport (NY)
Texas Southern U (TX)

RANGE SCIENCE AND MANAGEMENT
Brigham Young U (UT)
California State U, Chico (CA)

Chadron State Coll (NE)
Colorado State U (CO)
Fort Hays State U (KS)
Humboldt State U (CA)
Montana State U–Bozeman (MT)
New Mexico State U (NM)
Oregon State U (OR)
South Dakota State U (SD)
Sterling Coll (VT)
Tarleton State U (TX)
Texas A&M U (TX)
Texas A&M U–Kingsville (TX)
Texas Tech U (TX)
U of Alberta (AB, Canada)
U of Calif, Davis (CA)
U of Idaho (ID)
U of Nebraska–Lincoln (NE)
U of Saskatchewan (SK, Canada)
U of Wyoming (WY)
Utah State U (UT)
Washington State U (WA)

READING TEACHER EDUCATION

Abilene Christian U (TX)
Aquinas Coll (MI)
Baylor U (TX)
Belmont U (TN)
Boise State U (ID)
Catawba Coll (NC)
Central Missouri State U (MO)
Chicago State U (IL)
City Coll of the City U of NY (NY)
Clarion U of Pennsylvania (PA)
Clemson U (SC)
Dordt Coll (IA)
Eastern Michigan U (MI)
Eastern Washington U (WA)
Grand Valley State U (MI)
Harding U (AR)
Jarvis Christian Coll (TX)
Livingstone Coll (NC)
Long Island U, Southampton Coll (NY)
Longwood U (VA)
Lyndon State Coll (VT)
Millersville U of Pennsylvania (PA)
Mount Saint Vincent U (NS, Canada)
Murray State U (KY)
Northeastern State U (OK)
North Georgia Coll & State U (GA)
Oakland U (MI)
Ohio U (OH)
Our Lady of Holy Cross Coll (LA)
Pacific Lutheran U (WA)
St. Cloud State U (MN)
St. John's U (NY)
St. Mary's U of San Antonio (TX)
Sam Houston State U (TX)
State U of NY Coll at Cortland (NY)
State U of NY Coll at Oneonta (NY)
Tennessee State U (TN)
Texas A&M Intl U (TX)
Texas A&M U–Commerce (TX)
Texas Southern U (TX)
Texas Wesleyan U (TX)
Texas Woman's U (TX)
U of Alberta (AB, Canada)
The U of British Columbia (BC, Canada)
U of Central Arkansas (AR)
U of Detroit Mercy (MI)
U of Georgia (GA)
U of Great Falls (MT)
U of Houston–Clear Lake (TX)
U of Mary Hardin-Baylor (TX)
The U of Montana–Missoula (MT)
U of Nebraska–Lincoln (NE)
U of Northern Iowa (IA)
U of the Incarnate Word (TX)
U of Wisconsin–Superior (WI)
Upper Iowa U (IA)
Westfield State Coll (MA)
William Penn U (IA)
Wingate U (NC)
Winona State U (MN)
Wright State U (OH)
York Coll (NE)

REAL ESTATE

Angelo State U (TX)
Arizona State U (AZ)
Ball State U (IN)
Baylor U (TX)
California State Polytechnic U, Pomona (CA)
California State U, Dominguez Hills (CA)
California State U, Fresno (CA)
California State U, Hayward (CA)
California State U, Sacramento (CA)
Clarion U of Pennsylvania (PA)
Colorado State U (CO)
Eastern Kentucky U (KY)
Florida Atlantic U (FL)
Florida Intl U (FL)
Florida State U (FL)
Georgia State U (GA)
Indiana U Bloomington (IN)
Marylhurst U (OR)
Minnesota State U Mankato (MN)
Mississippi State U (MS)
Morehead State U (KY)
New York U (NY)
The Ohio State U (OH)
Peirce Coll (PA)
Saint Augustine's Coll (NC)
St. Cloud State U (MN)
St. John's U (NY)
San Diego State U (CA)
San Francisco State U (CA)
Southern Methodist U (TX)
State U of West Georgia (GA)
Texas A&M U–Kingsville (TX)
Texas Christian U (TX)
Thomas Edison State Coll (NJ)
The U of British Columbia (BC, Canada)
U of Cincinnati (OH)
U of Connecticut (CT)
U of Denver (CO)
U of Florida (FL)
U of Georgia (GA)
U of Guelph (ON, Canada)
U of Hawaii at Manoa (HI)
The U of Memphis (TN)
U of Mississippi (MS)
U of Missouri–Columbia (MO)
U of Nebraska at Omaha (NE)
U of Nevada, Las Vegas (NV)
U of Northern Iowa (IA)
U of North Texas (TX)
U of Pennsylvania (PA)
U of St. Thomas (MN)
U of South Carolina (SC)
The U of Texas at Arlington (TX)
U of Wisconsin–Madison (WI)
U of Wisconsin–Milwaukee (WI)
Washington State U (WA)

RECORDING ARTS TECHNOLOGY

Columbia Coll Chicago (IL)
Lebanon Valley Coll (PA)
New England School of Communications (ME)
Savannah Coll of Art and Design (GA)
Texas State U-San Marcos (TX)

REGIONAL STUDIES

Coll of Santa Fe (NM)
Mercer U (GA)

REHABILITATION AND THERAPEUTIC PROFESSIONS RELATED

Assumption Coll (MA)
Central Michigan U (MI)
East Stroudsburg U of Pennsylvania (PA)
Montana State U–Billings (MT)
Penn State U Abington Coll (PA)
Penn State U Altoona Coll (PA)
Penn State U at Erie, The Behrend Coll (PA)
Penn State U Beaver Campus of the Commonwealth Coll (PA)
Penn State U Berks Cmps of Berks-Lehigh Valley Coll (PA)
Penn State U Delaware County Campus of the Commonwealth Coll (PA)
Penn State U DuBois Campus of the Commonwealth Coll (PA)
Penn State U Fayette Campus of the Commonwealth Coll (PA)
Penn State U Hazleton Campus of the Commonwealth Coll (PA)
Penn State U Lehigh Valley Cmps of Berks-Lehigh Valley Coll (PA)
Penn State U McKeesport Campus of the Commonwealth Coll (PA)
Penn State U Mont Alto Campus of the Commonwealth Coll (PA)
Penn State U New Kensington Campus of the Commonwealth Coll (PA)
Penn State U Schuylkill Campus of the Capital Coll (PA)
Penn State U Shenango Campus of the Commonwealth Coll (PA)
Penn State U Univ Park Campus (PA)
Penn State U Wilkes-Barre Campus of the Commonwealth Coll (PA)
Penn State U Worthington Scranton Cmps Commonwealth Coll (PA)
Penn State U York Campus of the Commonwealth Coll (PA)
Southern Illinois U Carbondale (IL)
Southern U and A&M Coll (LA)
U of North Texas (TX)
U of Pittsburgh (PA)
The U of Texas–Pan American (TX)
U of Texas Southwestern Medical Center at Dallas (TX)
U of Waterloo (ON, Canada)
Wilson Coll (PA)

REHABILITATION THERAPY

Baker Coll of Muskegon (MI)
Boston U (MA)
California State U, Los Angeles (CA)
East Stroudsburg U of Pennsylvania (PA)
Ithaca Coll (NY)
Montana State U–Billings (MT)
Northeastern U (MA)
Southern U and A&M Coll (LA)
Springfield Coll (MA)
Thomas U (GA)
Université de Montréal (QC, Canada)
The U of British Columbia (BC, Canada)
U of Maine at Farmington (ME)
U of Manitoba (MB, Canada)
U of Maryland Eastern Shore (MD)
U of North Texas (TX)
U of Ottawa (ON, Canada)
The U of Texas–Pan American (TX)
Wilberforce U (OH)
York U (ON, Canada)

RELIGIOUS EDUCATION

Andrews U (MI)
Apex School of Theology (NC)
Aquinas Coll (MI)
Asbury Coll (KY)
Ashland U (OH)
Averett U (VA)
Baptist Bible Coll (MO)
The Baptist Coll of Florida (FL)
Barclay Coll (KS)
Bethany Bible Coll (NB, Canada)
Bethesda Christian U (CA)
Biola U (CA)
Bryan Coll (TN)
Calvary Bible Coll and Theological Sem (MO)
Campbellsville U (KY)
Canadian Mennonite U (MB, Canada)
Capital U (OH)
Cardinal Stritch U (WI)
Carroll Coll (MT)
The Catholic U of America (DC)
Cedarville U (OH)
Coll of Mount St. Joseph (OH)
Coll of Saint Benedict (MN)
Columbia Coll (SC)
Columbia Intl U (SC)
Columbia Union Coll (MD)
Concordia U (CA)
Concordia U (IL)
Concordia U (NE)
Concordia U (OR)
Concordia U at Austin (TX)
Concordia U Coll of Alberta (AB, Canada)
Concordia U, St. Paul (MN)
Cornerstone U (MI)
Crossroads Bible Coll (IN)
Crossroads Coll (MN)
Crown Coll (MN)
Cumberland Coll (KY)
Dallas Baptist U (TX)
Davis & Elkins Coll (WV)
Defiance Coll (OH)
Eastern Nazarene Coll (MA)
East Texas Baptist U (TX)
Erskine Coll (SC)
Eugene Bible Coll (OR)
Faith Baptist Bible Coll and Theological Sem (IA)
Faulkner U (AL)
Florida Southern Coll (FL)
Franciscan U of Steubenville (OH)
Gardner-Webb U (NC)
George Fox U (OR)
Global U of the Assemblies of God (MO)
Grace Bible Coll (MI)
Grace U (NE)
Griggs U (MD)
Hannibal-LaGrange Coll (MO)
Harding U (AR)
Hillsdale Free Will Baptist Coll (OK)
Houghton Coll (NY)
Howard Payne U (TX)
Huntingdon Coll (AL)
Jewish Theological Sem of America (NY)
John Brown U (AR)
John Carroll U (OH)
John Wesley Coll (NC)
Kansas Wesleyan U (KS)
Kentucky Christian Coll (KY)
Kentucky Mountain Bible Coll (KY)
LaGrange Coll (GA)
Lancaster Bible Coll (PA)
La Roche Coll (PA)
La Salle U (PA)
Lenoir-Rhyne Coll (NC)
Louisiana Coll (LA)
Loyola U New Orleans (LA)
Malone Coll (OH)
Manhattan Christian Coll (KS)
Marian Coll (IN)
Mars Hill Coll (NC)
Marywood U (PA)
The Master's Coll and Sem (CA)
Master's Coll and Sem (ON, Canada)
McGill U (QC, Canada)
Mercyhurst Coll (PA)
Messenger Coll (MO)
Messiah Coll (PA)
MidAmerica Nazarene U (KS)
Mid-Continent Coll (KY)
Missouri Baptist U (MO)
Moody Bible Inst (IL)
Morris Coll (SC)
Mount Mary Coll (WI)
Mount Vernon Nazarene U (OH)
Multnomah Bible Coll and Biblical Sem (OR)
North Greenville Coll (SC)
Northwestern Coll (IA)
Northwestern Coll (MN)
Northwest Nazarene U (ID)
Nyack Coll (NY)
Oakland City U (IN)
Oklahoma Baptist U (OK)
Oklahoma Christian U (OK)
Oklahoma City U (OK)
Olivet Nazarene U (IL)
Pepperdine U, Malibu (CA)
Pfeiffer U (NC)
Pillsbury Baptist Bible Coll (MN)
Prairie Bible Coll (AB, Canada)
Providence Coll and Theological Sem (MB, Canada)
Reformed Bible Coll (MI)
Rocky Mountain Coll (AB, Canada)
St. Bonaventure U (NY)
St. Edward's U (TX)
Saint John's U (MN)
St. Louis Christian Coll (MO)
Saint Mary's U of Minnesota (MN)
Saint Vincent Coll (PA)
Seattle Pacific U (WA)
Seton Hall U (NJ)
Simpson Coll and Graduate School (CA)
Southeastern Bible Coll (AL)
Southern Adventist U (TN)
Southern Nazarene U (OK)
Sterling Coll (KS)
Talmudic Coll of Florida (FL)
Taylor U (IN)
Taylor U, Fort Wayne Campus (IN)
Texas Wesleyan U (TX)
Thiel Coll (PA)
Toccoa Falls Coll (GA)
Trinity Christian Coll (IL)
Tyndale U Coll & Sem (ON, Canada)
Union Coll (NE)
Universidad Adventista de las Antillas (PR)
U of Dayton (OH)
U of the Ozarks (AR)
Vanguard U of Southern California (CA)
Vennard Coll (IA)
Viterbo U (WI)
Warner Pacific Coll (OR)
Washington Bible Coll (MD)
Wayland Baptist U (TX)
Western Baptist Coll (OR)
Westminster Coll (PA)
West Virginia Wesleyan Coll (WV)
Wheaton Coll (IL)
Williams Baptist Coll (AR)
William Tyndale Coll (MI)
York Coll (NE)

RELIGIOUS/SACRED MUSIC

Alderson-Broaddus Coll (WV)
Aquinas Coll (MI)
Atlantic Union Coll (MA)
Augustana Coll (IL)
Averett U (VA)
The Baptist Coll of Florida (FL)
Barclay Coll (KS)
Baylor U (TX)
Belmont U (TN)
Bethany Lutheran Coll (MN)
Bethel Coll (IN)
Bethel U (MN)
Bethesda Christian U (CA)
Bluefield Coll (VA)
Briercrest Bible Coll (SK, Canada)
Bryan Coll (TN)
Calvary Bible Coll and Theological Sem (MO)
Calvin Coll (MI)
Campbellsville U (KY)
Cedarville U (OH)
Centenary Coll of Louisiana (LA)
Central Baptist Coll (AR)
Central Pentecostal Coll (SK, Canada)
Charleston Southern U (SC)
Christian Heritage Coll (CA)
Clearwater Christian Coll (FL)
Coll of the Ozarks (MO)
Columbia Coll (SC)
Columbia Intl U (SC)
Concordia Coll (NY)
Concordia U (IL)
Concordia U (MI)
Concordia U (NE)
Concordia U at Austin (TX)
Concordia U, St. Paul (MN)
Crossroads Coll (MN)
Dallas Baptist U (TX)
Drake U (IA)
Eastern Nazarene Coll (MA)
East Texas Baptist U (TX)
Emmanuel Coll (GA)
Erskine Coll (SC)
Eugene Bible Coll (OR)
Evangel U (MO)
Faith Baptist Bible Coll and Theological Sem (IA)
Florida Southern Coll (FL)
Fresno Pacific U (CA)
Furman U (SC)
Gardner-Webb U (NC)
God's Bible School and Coll (OH)
Grace U (NE)
Grand Canyon U (AZ)
Greenville Coll (IL)
Gustavus Adolphus Coll (MN)
Hannibal-LaGrange Coll (MO)
Hardin-Simmons U (TX)
Hillsdale Free Will Baptist Coll (OK)
Houston Baptist U (TX)
Howard Payne U (TX)
Johnson Bible Coll (TN)
Lambuth U (TN)
Lancaster Bible Coll (PA)
Lenoir-Rhyne Coll (NC)
Liberty U (VA)
Louisiana Coll (LA)
Loyola U New Orleans (LA)
Malone Coll (OH)
Manhattan Christian Coll (KS)
Mars Hill Coll (NC)
Marywood U (PA)
The Master's Coll and Sem (CA)
McMurry U (TX)
Messenger Coll (MO)
MidAmerica Nazarene U (KS)
Millikin U (IL)
Mississippi Coll (MS)
Missouri Baptist U (MO)
Moody Bible Inst (IL)
Mount Vernon Nazarene U (OH)
Multnomah Bible Coll and Biblical Sem (OR)
Newberry Coll (SC)
North Carolina Central U (NC)
North Central U (MN)
North Greenville Coll (SC)
North Park U (IL)
Northwest Nazarene U (ID)
Nyack Coll (NY)
Oak Hills Christian Coll (MN)
Oklahoma Baptist U (OK)
Oklahoma City U (OK)
Olivet Nazarene U (IL)
Oral Roberts U (OK)
Ouachita Baptist U (AR)
Pacific Lutheran U (WA)
Palm Beach Atlantic U (FL)
Pfeiffer U (NC)
Pillsbury Baptist Bible Coll (MN)
Point Loma Nazarene U (CA)
Rider U (NJ)
Saint Joseph's Coll (IN)
St. Louis Christian Coll (MO)
Samford U (AL)
Seton Hill U (PA)
Shorter Coll (GA)
Southeastern Bible Coll (AL)
Southeastern Coll of the Assemblies of God (FL)
Southern Wesleyan U (SC)

Southwestern Oklahoma State U (OK)
Southwestern U (TX)
Susquehanna U (PA)
Taylor U (IN)
Toccoa Falls Coll (GA)
Trevecca Nazarene U (TN)
Trinity Intl U (IL)
Union U (TN)
U of Mary Hardin-Baylor (TX)
Valparaiso U (IN)
Warner Southern Coll (FL)
Wartburg Coll (IA)
Wayland Baptist U (TX)
Western Baptist Coll (OR)
Westminster Choir Coll of Rider U (NJ)
Westminster Coll (PA)
William Carey Coll (MS)
William Jewell Coll (MO)
Williams Baptist Coll (AR)
William Tyndale Coll (MI)

RELIGIOUS STUDIES

Adrian Coll (MI)
Agnes Scott Coll (GA)
Albertson Coll of Idaho (ID)
Albertus Magnus Coll (CT)
Albion Coll (MI)
Albright Coll (PA)
Alderson-Broaddus Coll (WV)
Allegheny Coll (PA)
Allen U (SC)
Alma Coll (MI)
Alvernia Coll (PA)
Alverno Coll (WI)
Amherst Coll (MA)
Anderson Coll (SC)
Andrews U (MI)
Anna Maria Coll (MA)
Antioch Coll (OH)
Aquinas Coll (MI)
Arizona State U (AZ)
Arkansas Baptist Coll (AR)
Arlington Baptist Coll (TX)
Ashland U (OH)
Athens State U (AL)
Atlantic Baptist U (NB, Canada)
Atlantic Union Coll (MA)
Augsburg Coll (MN)
Augustana Coll (IL)
Augustana Coll (SD)
Austin Coll (TX)
Averett U (VA)
Avila U (MO)
Azusa Pacific U (CA)
Baker U (KS)
Baldwin-Wallace Coll (OH)
Ball State U (IN)
Bard Coll (NY)
Barnard Coll (NY)
Bates Coll (ME)
Baylor U (TX)
Beloit Coll (WI)
Bemidji State U (MN)
Benedictine Coll (KS)
Berea Coll (KY)
Bethany Bible Coll (NB, Canada)
Bethany Coll (KS)
Bethany Coll (WV)
Bethel Coll (KS)
Biola U (CA)
Birmingham-Southern Coll (AL)
Bishop's U (QC, Canada)
Bloomfield Coll (NJ)
Bluefield Coll (VA)
Bluffton Coll (OH)
Boston U (MA)
Bowdoin Coll (ME)
Bradley U (IL)
Brescia U (KY)
Brevard Coll (NC)
Brewton-Parker Coll (GA)
Briercrest Bible Coll (SK, Canada)
Brooklyn Coll of the City U of NY (NY)
Brown U (RI)
Bryn Mawr Coll (PA)
Bucknell U (PA)
Butler U (IN)
Cabrini Coll (PA)
California Lutheran U (CA)
California State U, Chico (CA)
California State U, Dominguez Hills (CA)
California State U, Fresno (CA)
California State U, Fullerton (CA)
California State U, Hayward (CA)
California State U, Long Beach (CA)
Calumet Coll of Saint Joseph (IN)
Calvin Coll (MI)
Campbellsville U (KY)
Campbell U (NC)
Canadian Mennonite U (MB, Canada)
Canisius Coll (NY)
Capital U (OH)
Cardinal Stritch U (WI)
Carleton Coll (MN)
Carleton U (ON, Canada)
Carroll Coll (MT)
Carroll Coll (WI)
Carson-Newman Coll (TN)
Carthage Coll (WI)
Case Western Reserve U (OH)
Catawba Coll (NC)
The Catholic U of America (DC)
Centenary Coll of Louisiana (LA)
Central Christian Coll of Kansas (KS)
Central Coll (IA)
Central Methodist Coll (MO)
Central Michigan U (MI)
Central Washington U (WA)
Centre Coll (KY)
Chaminade U of Honolulu (HI)
Chapman U (CA)
Charleston Southern U (SC)
Chowan Coll (NC)
Christian Brothers U (TN)
Christopher Newport U (VA)
Claremont McKenna Coll (CA)
Clark Atlanta U (GA)
Clarke Coll (IA)
Cleveland State U (OH)
Coe Coll (IA)
Colby Coll (ME)
Colgate U (NY)
Coll of Charleston (SC)
Coll of Mount St. Joseph (OH)
Coll of Mount Saint Vincent (NY)
The Coll of New Rochelle (NY)
Coll of Notre Dame of Maryland (MD)
The Coll of Saint Rose (NY)
The Coll of St. Scholastica (MN)
Coll of Santa Fe (NM)
Coll of the Holy Cross (MA)
Coll of the Ozarks (MO)
The Coll of William and Mary (VA)
The Coll of Wooster (OH)
The Colorado Coll (CO)
Columbia Coll (NY)
Columbia Coll (SC)
Columbia U, School of General Studies (NY)
Concordia Coll (MN)
Concordia Coll (NY)
Concordia U (MI)
Concordia U (OR)
Concordia U (QC, Canada)
Concordia U at Austin (TX)
Concordia U Coll of Alberta (AB, Canada)
Concordia U Wisconsin (WI)
Connecticut Coll (CT)
Converse Coll (SC)
Cornell Coll (IA)
Cornell U (NY)
Cornerstone U (MI)
Culver-Stockton Coll (MO)
Daemen Coll (NY)
Dakota Wesleyan U (SD)
Dalhousie U (NS, Canada)
Dana Coll (NE)
Dartmouth Coll (NH)
Davidson Coll (NC)
Davis & Elkins Coll (WV)
Defiance Coll (OH)
Denison U (OH)
DePaul U (IL)
DePauw U (IN)
Dickinson Coll (PA)
Dillard U (LA)
Doane Coll (NE)
Dominican U (IL)
Dominican U of California (CA)
Dordt Coll (IA)
Drake U (IA)
Drew U (NJ)
Drury U (MO)
Duke U (NC)
Earlham Coll (IN)
Eastern Nazarene Coll (MA)
Eastern New Mexico U (NM)
East Texas Baptist U (TX)
Eckerd Coll (FL)
Edgewood Coll (WI)
Elizabethtown Coll (PA)
Elmira Coll (NY)
Elms Coll (MA)
Elon U (NC)
Emory & Henry Coll (VA)
Emory U (GA)
Erskine Coll (SC)
Eugene Lang Coll, New School U (NY)
Eureka Coll (IL)
Fairfield U (CT)
Faulkner U (AL)
Ferrum Coll (VA)
Flagler Coll (FL)
Florida Ag and Mech U (FL)
Florida Intl U (FL)
Florida Southern Coll (FL)
Florida State U (FL)
Fontbonne U (MO)
Fordham U (NY)
The Franciscan U (IA)
Franklin and Marshall Coll (PA)
Franklin Coll (IN)
Fresno Pacific U (CA)
Furman U (SC)
Gardner-Webb U (NC)
George Fox U (OR)
George Mason U (VA)
Georgetown Coll (KY)
Georgetown U (DC)
The George Washington U (DC)
Georgian Court U (NJ)
Georgia State U (GA)
Gettysburg Coll (PA)
Gonzaga U (WA)
Goshen Coll (IN)
Goucher Coll (MD)
Graceland U (IA)
Grand Canyon U (AZ)
Grand View Coll (IA)
Greensboro Coll (NC)
Greenville Coll (IL)
Griggs U (MD)
Grinnell Coll (IA)
Grove City Coll (PA)
Guilford Coll (NC)
Gustavus Adolphus Coll (MN)
Hamilton Coll (NY)
Hamline U (MN)
Hampden-Sydney Coll (VA)
Hampshire Coll (MA)
Hampton U (VA)
Harding U (AR)
Hartwick Coll (NY)
Harvard U (MA)
Hastings Coll (NE)
Haverford Coll (PA)
Heidelberg Coll (OH)
Hellenic Coll (MA)
Hendrix Coll (AR)
High Point U (NC)
Hillsdale Coll (MI)
Hiram Coll (OH)
Hobart and William Smith Colls (NY)
Hollins U (VA)
Holy Names Coll (CA)
Hood Coll (MD)
Hope Coll (MI)
Houghton Coll (NY)
Houston Baptist U (TX)
Howard Payne U (TX)
Humboldt State U (CA)
Hunter Coll of the City U of NY (NY)
Huntingdon Coll (AL)
Huntington Coll (IN)
Illinois Coll (IL)
Illinois Wesleyan U (IL)
Indiana U Bloomington (IN)
Indiana U of Pennsylvania (PA)
Indiana U–Purdue U Indianapolis (IN)
Iona Coll (NY)
Iowa State U of Science and Technology (IA)
Jamestown Coll (ND)
Jarvis Christian Coll (TX)
Jewish Theological Sem of America (NY)
John Brown U (AR)
John Carroll U (OH)
John Wesley Coll (NC)
Judson Coll (AL)
Judson Coll (IL)
Juniata Coll (PA)
Kalamazoo Coll (MI)
Kansas Wesleyan U (KS)
Kentucky Mountain Bible Coll (KY)
Kenyon Coll (OH)
King Coll (TN)
Lafayette Coll (PA)
LaGrange Coll (GA)
Lakeland Coll (WI)
Lambuth U (TN)
Lane Coll (TN)
La Roche Coll (PA)
La Salle U (PA)
Laura and Alvin Siegal Coll of Judaic Studies (OH)
Laurentian U (ON, Canada)
Lawrence U (WI)
Lebanon Valley Coll (PA)
Lehigh U (PA)
Le Moyne Coll (NY)
Lenoir-Rhyne Coll (NC)
LeTourneau U (TX)
Lewis & Clark Coll (OR)
Lewis U (IL)
Liberty U (VA)
Lincoln U (PA)
Lindenwood U (MO)
Linfield Coll (OR)
Loras Coll (IA)
Louisiana Coll (LA)
Lourdes Coll (OH)
Loyola Coll in Maryland (MD)
Loyola U New Orleans (LA)
Luther Coll (IA)
Lycoming Coll (PA)
Lynchburg Coll (VA)
Macalester Coll (MN)
MacMurray Coll (IL)
Madonna U (MI)
Manchester Coll (IN)
Manhattan Christian Coll (KS)
Manhattan Coll (NY)
Manhattanville Coll (NY)
Marlboro Coll (VT)
Marquette U (WI)
Mars Hill Coll (NC)
Martin U (IN)
Mary Baldwin Coll (VA)
Marygrove Coll (MI)
Marylhurst U (OR)
Marymount U (VA)
Maryville Coll (TN)
Mary Washington Coll (VA)
Marywood U (PA)
The Master's Coll and Sem (CA)
McDaniel Coll (MD)
McGill U (QC, Canada)
McKendree Coll (IL)
McMurry U (TX)
McPherson Coll (KS)
Memorial U of Newfoundland (NL, Canada)
Mercyhurst Coll (PA)
Meredith Coll (NC)
Merrimack Coll (MA)
Messenger Coll (MO)
Messiah Coll (PA)
Methodist Coll (NC)
Miami U (OH)
Michigan State U (MI)
MidAmerica Nazarene U (KS)
Middlebury Coll (VT)
Miles Coll (AL)
Millsaps Coll (MS)
Missouri Baptist U (MO)
Missouri Valley Coll (MO)
Molloy Coll (NY)
Monmouth Coll (IL)
Montclair State U (NJ)
Moravian Coll (PA)
Morehouse Coll (GA)
Morgan State U (MD)
Morningside Coll (IA)
Mount Allison U (NB, Canada)
Mount Holyoke Coll (MA)
Mount Marty Coll (SD)
Mount Mary Coll (WI)
Mount Mercy Coll (IA)
Mount St. Mary's Coll (CA)
Mount Saint Vincent U (NS, Canada)
Mount Union Coll (OH)
Muhlenberg Coll (PA)
Naropa U (CO)
Nazareth Coll of Rochester (NY)
Nebraska Wesleyan U (NE)
Newberry Coll (SC)
New Coll of Florida (FL)
New York U (NY)
Niagara U (NY)
North Carolina State U (NC)
North Carolina Wesleyan Coll (NC)
North Central Coll (IL)
North Central U (MN)
Northern Arizona U (AZ)
North Greenville Coll (SC)
Northland Coll (WI)
North Park U (IL)
Northwestern Coll (IA)
Northwestern U (IL)
Northwest Nazarene U (ID)
Notre Dame de Namur U (CA)
Nyack Coll (NY)
Oakland City U (IN)
Oakland U (MI)
Oberlin Coll (OH)
Occidental Coll (CA)
Ohio Northern U (OH)
The Ohio State U (OH)
Ohio Valley Coll (WV)
Ohio Wesleyan U (OH)
Oklahoma Baptist U (OK)
Oklahoma Christian U (OK)
Oklahoma City U (OK)
Olivet Nazarene U (IL)
Oral Roberts U (OK)
Ottawa U (KS)
Otterbein Coll (OH)
Our Lady of the Lake U of San Antonio (TX)
Pacific Lutheran U (WA)
Pacific Union Coll (CA)
Paine Coll (GA)
Palm Beach Atlantic U (FL)
Penn State U Abington Coll (PA)
Penn State U Altoona Coll (PA)
Penn State U at Erie, The Behrend Coll (PA)
Penn State U Beaver Campus of the Commonwealth Coll (PA)
Penn State U Berks Cmps of Berks-Lehigh Valley Coll (PA)
Penn State U Delaware County Campus of the Commonwealth Coll (PA)
Penn State U DuBois Campus of the Commonwealth Coll (PA)
Penn State U Fayette Campus of the Commonwealth Coll (PA)
Penn State U Hazleton Campus of the Commonwealth Coll (PA)
Penn State U Lehigh Valley Cmps of Berks-Lehigh Valley Coll (PA)
Penn State U McKeesport Campus of the Commonwealth Coll (PA)
Penn State U Mont Alto Campus of the Commonwealth Coll (PA)
Penn State U New Kensington Campus of the Commonwealth Coll (PA)
Penn State U Schuylkill Campus of the Capital Coll (PA)
Penn State U Shenango Campus of the Commonwealth Coll (PA)
Penn State U Univ Park Campus (PA)
Penn State U Wilkes-Barre Campus of the Commonwealth Coll (PA)
Penn State U Worthington Scranton Cmps Commonwealth Coll (PA)
Penn State U York Campus of the Commonwealth Coll (PA)
Pepperdine U, Malibu (CA)
Pfeiffer U (NC)
Philadelphia Biblical U (PA)
Piedmont Coll (GA)
Pikeville Coll (KY)
Pitzer Coll (CA)
Pomona Coll (CA)
Presbyterian Coll (SC)
Princeton U (NJ)
Principia Coll (IL)
Providence Coll and Theological Sem (MB, Canada)
Queens Coll of the City U of NY (NY)
Queen's U at Kingston (ON, Canada)
Queens U of Charlotte (NC)
Randolph-Macon Coll (VA)
Randolph-Macon Woman's Coll (VA)
Redeemer U Coll (ON, Canada)
Reed Coll (OR)
Regis U (CO)
Rhodes Coll (TN)
Rice U (TX)
Ripon Coll (WI)
Roanoke Coll (VA)
Rocky Mountain Coll (MT)
Rollins Coll (FL)
Rosemont Coll (PA)
Rutgers, The State U of New Jersey, New Brunswick/Piscataway (NJ)
Sacred Heart U (CT)
St. Andrews Presbyterian Coll (NC)
St. Francis Coll (NY)
Saint Francis U (PA)
St. Francis Xavier U (NS, Canada)
St. John Fisher Coll (NY)
St. John's Coll (NM)
Saint Joseph Coll (CT)
Saint Joseph's Coll of Maine (ME)
Saint Joseph's U (PA)
St. Lawrence U (NY)
Saint Martin's Coll (WA)
Saint Mary-of-the-Woods Coll (IN)
Saint Mary's Coll (IN)
Saint Mary's Coll of California (CA)
St. Mary's Coll of Maryland (MD)
Saint Michael's Coll (VT)
St. Norbert Coll (WI)
St. Olaf Coll (MN)
St. Thomas Aquinas Coll (NY)
St. Thomas U (FL)
St. Thomas U (NB, Canada)
Saint Xavier U (IL)
Salem Coll (NC)
Salve Regina U (RI)
Samford U (AL)
San Diego State U (CA)
San Francisco State U (CA)
San Jose State U (CA)

Santa Clara U (CA)
Sarah Lawrence Coll (NY)
Schreiner U (TX)
Scripps Coll (CA)
Seattle U (WA)
Seton Hall U (NJ)
Seton Hill U (PA)
Shaw U (NC)
Shenandoah U (VA)
Shorter Coll (GA)
Siena Coll (NY)
Siena Heights U (MI)
Simon's Rock Coll of Bard (MA)
Simpson Coll (IA)
Skidmore Coll (NY)
Smith Coll (MA)
Southeastern Bible Coll (AL)
Southern Adventist U (TN)
Southern Methodist U (TX)
Southern Wesleyan U (SC)
Southwest Baptist U (MO)
Southwestern U (TX)
Southwest Missouri State U (MO)
Spelman Coll (GA)
Spring Arbor U (MI)
Stanford U (CA)
State U of NY Coll at Old Westbury (NY)
Steinbach Bible Coll (MB, Canada)
Stetson U (FL)
Stonehill Coll (MA)
Stony Brook U, State U of New York (NY)
Susquehanna U (PA)
Swarthmore Coll (PA)
Sweet Briar Coll (VA)
Syracuse U (NY)
Tabor Coll (KS)
Taylor U (IN)
Tennessee Wesleyan Coll (TN)
Texas Christian U (TX)
Texas Wesleyan U (TX)
Thiel Coll (PA)
Thomas Edison State Coll (NJ)
Thomas More Coll (KY)
Towson U (MD)
Transylvania U (KY)
Trevecca Nazarene U (TN)
Trinity Christian Coll (IL)
Trinity Coll (CT)
Trinity U (TX)
Trinity Western U (BC, Canada)
Truman State U (MO)
Tulane U (LA)
Union Coll (KY)
Union Coll (NE)
Union U (TN)
Université de Montréal (QC, Canada)
State U of NY at Albany (NY)
The U of Alabama (AL)
U of Alberta (AB, Canada)
The U of Arizona (AZ)
U of Bridgeport (CT)
The U of British Columbia (BC, Canada)
U of Calgary (AB, Canada)
U of Calif, Berkeley (CA)
U of Calif, Davis (CA)
U of Calif, Los Angeles (CA)
U of Calif, Riverside (CA)
U of Calif, San Diego (CA)
U of Calif, Santa Barbara (CA)
U of Calif, Santa Cruz (CA)
U of Central Arkansas (AR)
U of Chicago (IL)
U of Colorado at Boulder (CO)
U of Dayton (OH)
U of Denver (CO)
U of Detroit Mercy (MI)
U of Dubuque (IA)
U of Evansville (IN)
The U of Findlay (OH)
U of Florida (FL)
U of Georgia (GA)
U of Great Falls (MT)
U of Hawaii at Manoa (HI)
U of Illinois at Urbana–Champaign (IL)
U of Indianapolis (IN)
The U of Iowa (IA)
U of Kansas (KS)
U of King's Coll (NS, Canada)
U of La Verne (CA)
The U of Lethbridge (AB, Canada)
U of Maine at Farmington (ME)
U of Manitoba (MB, Canada)
U of Mary (ND)
U of Mary Hardin-Baylor (TX)
U of Miami (FL)
U of Michigan (MI)
U of Minnesota, Twin Cities Campus (MN)
U of Missouri–Columbia (MO)
U of Mobile (AL)
U of Nebraska at Omaha (NE)
U of New Mexico (NM)
The U of North Carolina at Chapel Hill (NC)
The U of North Carolina at Charlotte (NC)
The U of North Carolina at Greensboro (NC)
U of North Dakota (ND)
U of Northern Iowa (IA)
U of Oklahoma (OK)
U of Oregon (OR)
U of Ottawa (ON, Canada)
U of Pennsylvania (PA)
U of Pittsburgh (PA)
U of Prince Edward Island (PE, Canada)
U of Puget Sound (WA)
U of Redlands (CA)
U of Regina (SK, Canada)
U of Richmond (VA)
U of Rochester (NY)
U of Saint Francis (IN)
U of St. Thomas (MN)
U of San Diego (CA)
U of San Francisco (CA)
U of Saskatchewan (SK, Canada)
The U of Scranton (PA)
U of Sioux Falls (SD)
U of South Carolina (SC)
U of Southern California (CA)
U of South Florida (FL)
The U of Tennessee (TN)
The U of Texas at Austin (TX)
U of the Incarnate Word (TX)
U of the Pacific (CA)
U of the South (TN)
U of Toledo (OH)
U of Toronto (ON, Canada)
U of Tulsa (OK)
U of Vermont (VT)
U of Virginia (VA)
U of Washington (WA)
U of Waterloo (ON, Canada)
The U of Western Ontario (ON, Canada)
U of West Florida (FL)
U of Wisconsin–Eau Claire (WI)
U of Wisconsin–Milwaukee (WI)
U of Wisconsin–Oshkosh (WI)
Urbana U (OH)
Vanderbilt U (TN)
Vanguard U of Southern California (CA)
Vassar Coll (NY)
Vennard Coll (IA)
Villanova U (PA)
Virginia Commonwealth U (VA)
Virginia Intermont Coll (VA)
Virginia Wesleyan Coll (VA)
Viterbo U (WI)
Wabash Coll (IN)
Wake Forest U (NC)
Walla Walla Coll (WA)
Walsh U (OH)
Warner Pacific Coll (OR)
Wartburg Coll (IA)
Washburn U (KS)
Washington and Lee U (VA)
Washington Bible Coll (MD)
Washington State U (WA)
Washington U in St. Louis (MO)
Webster U (MO)
Wellesley Coll (MA)
Wells Coll (NY)
Wesleyan Coll (GA)
Wesleyan U (CT)
Western Baptist Coll (OR)
Western Kentucky U (KY)
Western Michigan U (MI)
Westminster Coll (MO)
Westminster Coll (PA)
Westmont Coll (CA)
West Virginia Wesleyan Coll (WV)
Wheaton Coll (IL)
Wheaton Coll (MA)
Wheeling Jesuit U (WV)
Whitman Coll (WA)
Whitworth Coll (WA)
Willamette U (OR)
William Carey Coll (MS)
William Jessup U (CA)
William Jewell Coll (MO)
Williams Baptist Coll (AR)
Williams Coll (MA)
Wingate U (NC)
Winthrop U (SC)
Wittenberg U (OH)
Wofford Coll (SC)
Wright State U (OH)
Yale U (CT)
York Coll (NE)
York U (ON, Canada)
Youngstown State U (OH)

RELIGIOUS STUDIES RELATED

Bryn Athyn Coll of the New Church (PA)
Campbell U (NC)
Claremont McKenna Coll (CA)
Lindsey Wilson Coll (KY)
Ohio Northern U (OH)
Sarah Lawrence Coll (NY)
U of Regina (SK, Canada)
U of the West (CA)
Ursuline Coll (OH)

REPRODUCTIVE BIOLOGY

Goddard Coll (VT)

RESORT MANAGEMENT

Florida Gulf Coast U (FL)
Lakeland Coll (WI)
Rochester Inst of Technology (NY)

RESPIRATORY CARE THERAPY

Armstrong Atlantic State U (GA)
Baptist Coll of Health Sciences (TN)
Bellarmine U (KY)
Boise State U (ID)
Coll of St. Catherine (MN)
Columbia Union Coll (MD)
Dakota State U (SD)
Dalhousie U (NS, Canada)
Florida Ag and Mech U (FL)
Gannon U (PA)
Georgia State U (GA)
Gwynedd-Mercy Coll (PA)
Indiana U of Pennsylvania (PA)
Indiana U–Purdue U Indianapolis (IN)
La Roche Coll (PA)
Loma Linda U (CA)
Long Island U, Brooklyn Campus (NY)
Louisiana State U Health Sciences Center (LA)
Medical Coll of Georgia (GA)
Midwestern State U (TX)
Mountain State U (WV)
National-Louis U (IL)
Nebraska Methodist Coll (NE)
North Dakota State U (ND)
The Ohio State U (OH)
Our Lady of Holy Cross Coll (LA)
Quinnipiac U (CT)
Salisbury U (MD)
Sam Houston State U (TX)
Shenandoah U (VA)
Southwest Missouri State U (MO)
State U of New York Upstate Medical U (NY)
Stony Brook U, State U of New York (NY)
Tennessee State U (TN)
Texas Southern U (TX)
Texas State U-San Marcos (TX)
Thomas Edison State Coll (NJ)
Universidad Adventista de las Antillas (PR)
U Coll of the Cariboo (BC, Canada)
The U of Alabama at Birmingham (AL)
U of Bridgeport (CT)
U of Central Florida (FL)
U of Hartford (CT)
U of Kansas (KS)
U of Mary (ND)
U of Missouri–Columbia (MO)
U of South Alabama (AL)
U of Texas Health Science Center at San Antonio (TX)
U of Texas Medical Branch at Galveston (TX)
U of the Ozarks (AR)
U of Waterloo (ON, Canada)
Washburn U (KS)
Weber State U (UT)
Wheeling Jesuit U (WV)
York Coll of Pennsylvania (PA)
Youngstown State U (OH)

RESPIRATORY THERAPY TECHNICIAN

Dalhousie U (NS, Canada)
Saint Joseph's Coll of Maine (ME)

RESTAURANT, CULINARY, AND CATERING MANAGEMENT

The Art Inst of Atlanta (GA)
The Art Inst of California–San Diego (CA)
Kendall Coll (IL)
Lexington Coll (IL)
Lindenwood U (MO)
U of Illinois at Urbana–Champaign (IL)
Virginia Intermont Coll (VA)
Washington State U (WA)

RESTAURANT/FOOD SERVICES MANAGEMENT

The Art Inst of California–San Diego (CA)
Kendall Coll (IL)
Lexington Coll (IL)
Niagara U (NY)
Oklahoma State U (OK)
Rochester Inst of Technology (NY)
Syracuse U (NY)
U of Missouri–Columbia (MO)
U of San Francisco (CA)
Viterbo U (WI)

RETAILING

Brigham Young U (UT)
Johnson & Wales U (RI)
Syracuse U (NY)
The U of Akron (OH)
Youngstown State U (OH)

ROBOTICS TECHNOLOGY

Indiana State U (IN)
Indiana U–Purdue U Indianapolis (IN)
Lake Superior State U (MI)
Purdue U (IN)

ROMANCE LANGUAGES

Albertus Magnus Coll (CT)
Bard Coll (NY)
Beloit Coll (WI)
Baruch Coll of the City U of NY (NY)
Bowdoin Coll (ME)
Bryn Mawr Coll (PA)
Carleton Coll (MN)
The Catholic U of America (DC)
City Coll of the City U of NY (NY)
Colgate U (NY)
Cornell U (NY)
Dartmouth Coll (NH)
DePauw U (IN)
Dowling Coll (NY)
Eastern Michigan U (MI)
Elmira Coll (NY)
Fordham U (NY)
Franklin Coll Switzerland(Switzerland)
Gettysburg Coll (PA)
Harvard U (MA)
Haverford Coll (PA)
Hunter Coll of the City U of NY (NY)
Judson Coll (AL)
Kenyon Coll (OH)
Manhattanville Coll (NY)
Marlboro Coll (VT)
Mount Allison U (NB, Canada)
Mount Holyoke Coll (MA)
New York U (NY)
Oberlin Coll (OH)
Olivet Nazarene U (IL)
Pitzer Coll (CA)
Point Loma Nazarene U (CA)
Pomona Coll (CA)
Ripon Coll (WI)
St. Thomas Aquinas Coll (NY)
Sarah Lawrence Coll (NY)
Tufts U (MA)
State U of NY at Albany (NY)
U of Alberta (AB, Canada)
The U of British Columbia (BC, Canada)
U of Chicago (IL)
U of Cincinnati (OH)
U of Maine (ME)
U of Michigan (MI)
U of Nevada, Las Vegas (NV)
U of New Brunswick Fredericton (NB, Canada)
U of New Hampshire (NH)
The U of North Carolina at Chapel Hill (NC)
U of Oregon (OR)
U of Toronto (ON, Canada)
U of Victoria (BC, Canada)
U of Washington (WA)
U of Windsor (ON, Canada)
Washington U in St. Louis (MO)
Wesleyan U (CT)
York U (ON, Canada)

ROMANCE LANGUAGES RELATED

The Colorado Coll (CO)
Hood Coll (MD)
Houston Baptist U (TX)
U of Pennsylvania (PA)

RUSSIAN

American U (DC)
Amherst Coll (MA)
Arizona State U (AZ)
Bard Coll (NY)
Barnard Coll (NY)
Bates Coll (ME)
Baylor U (TX)
Beloit Coll (WI)
Boston Coll (MA)
Boston U (MA)
Bowdoin Coll (ME)
Bowling Green State U (OH)
Brandeis U (MA)
Brigham Young U (UT)
Brooklyn Coll of the City U of NY (NY)
Bryn Mawr Coll (PA)
Bucknell U (PA)
Carleton Coll (MN)
Carleton U (ON, Canada)
Carnegie Mellon U (PA)
Claremont McKenna Coll (CA)
Colgate U (NY)
Coll of the Holy Cross (MA)
The Colorado Coll (CO)
Columbia Coll (NY)
Columbia U, School of General Studies (NY)
Connecticut Coll (CT)
Cornell Coll (IA)
Dalhousie U (NS, Canada)
Dartmouth Coll (NH)
Dickinson Coll (PA)
Drew U (NJ)
Duke U (NC)
Eckerd Coll (FL)
Emory U (GA)
Ferrum Coll (VA)
Florida State U (FL)
Fordham U (NY)
Georgetown U (DC)
The George Washington U (DC)
Goucher Coll (MD)
Grinnell Coll (IA)
Gustavus Adolphus Coll (MN)
Harvard U (MA)
Haverford Coll (PA)
Hobart and William Smith Colls (NY)
Hofstra U (NY)
Howard U (DC)
Hunter Coll of the City U of NY (NY)
Indiana U Bloomington (IN)
Indiana U of Pennsylvania (PA)
Juniata Coll (PA)
Kent State U (OH)
Knox Coll (IL)
Kutztown U of Pennsylvania (PA)
La Salle U (PA)
Lawrence U (WI)
Lehigh U (PA)
Lehman Coll of the City U of NY (NY)
Lincoln U (PA)
Loyola U New Orleans (LA)
Macalester Coll (MN)
McGill U (QC, Canada)
Memorial U of Newfoundland (NL, Canada)
Miami U (OH)
Miami U Hamilton (OH)
Michigan State U (MI)
Middlebury Coll (VT)
Mount Holyoke Coll (MA)
New Coll of Florida (FL)
New York U (NY)
Northeastern U (MA)
Northern Illinois U (IL)
Oakland U (MI)
Oberlin Coll (OH)
The Ohio State U (OH)
Ohio U (OH)
Oklahoma State U (OK)
Ouachita Baptist U (AR)
Penn State U Abington Coll (PA)
Penn State U Altoona Coll (PA)
Penn State U at Erie, The Behrend Coll (PA)
Penn State U Beaver Campus of the Commonwealth Coll (PA)
Penn State U Berks Cmps of Berks-Lehigh Valley Coll (PA)
Penn State U Delaware County Campus of the Commonwealth Coll (PA)
Penn State U DuBois Campus of the Commonwealth Coll (PA)
Penn State U Fayette Campus of the Commonwealth Coll (PA)
Penn State U Hazleton Campus of the Commonwealth Coll (PA)
Penn State U Lehigh Valley Cmps of Berks-Lehigh Valley Coll (PA)
Penn State U McKeesport Campus of the Commonwealth Coll (PA)
Penn State U Mont Alto Campus of the Commonwealth Coll (PA)

Penn State U New Kensington Campus of the Commonwealth Coll (PA)
Penn State U Schuylkill Campus of the Capital Coll (PA)
Penn State U Shenango Campus of the Commonwealth Coll (PA)
Penn State U Univ Park Campus (PA)
Penn State U Wilkes-Barre Campus of the Commonwealth Coll (PA)
Penn State U Worthington Scranton Cmps Commonwealth Coll (PA)
Penn State U York Campus of the Commonwealth Coll (PA)
Pitzer Coll (CA)
Pomona Coll (CA)
Portland State U (OR)
Queens Coll of the City U of NY (NY)
Reed Coll (OR)
Rice U (TX)
Rider U (NJ)
Rutgers, The State U of New Jersey, New Brunswick/Piscataway (NJ)
Saint Louis U (MO)
St. Olaf Coll (MN)
St. Thomas U (NB, Canada)
San Diego State U (CA)
San Francisco State U (CA)
Sarah Lawrence Coll (NY)
Scripps Coll (CA)
Seattle Pacific U (WA)
Smith Coll (MA)
Southern Methodist U (TX)
Stony Brook U, State U of New York (NY)
Swarthmore Coll (PA)
Syracuse U (NY)
Texas A&M U (TX)
Trinity Coll (CT)
Trinity U (TX)
Truman State U (MO)
Tufts U (MA)
Tulane U (LA)
United States Military Acad (NY)
State U of NY at Albany (NY)
The U of Alabama (AL)
U of Alberta (AB, Canada)
The U of Arizona (AZ)
The U of British Columbia (BC, Canada)
U of Calgary (AB, Canada)
U of Calif, Davis (CA)
U of Calif, Irvine (CA)
U of Calif, Los Angeles (CA)
U of Calif, Riverside (CA)
U of Calif, San Diego (CA)
U of Chicago (IL)
U of Delaware (DE)
U of Denver (CO)
U of Florida (FL)
U of Georgia (GA)
U of Hawaii at Manoa (HI)
U of Illinois at Chicago (IL)
U of Illinois at Urbana–Champaign (IL)
The U of Iowa (IA)
U of Kentucky (KY)
U of King's Coll (NS, Canada)
U of Manitoba (MB, Canada)
U of Maryland, Baltimore County (MD)
U of Maryland, Coll Park (MD)
U of Michigan (MI)
U of Minnesota, Twin Cities Campus (MN)
U of Missouri–Columbia (MO)
The U of Montana–Missoula (MT)
U of Nebraska–Lincoln (NE)
U of New Brunswick Fredericton (NB, Canada)
U of New Hampshire (NH)
U of New Mexico (NM)
The U of North Carolina at Chapel Hill (NC)
The U of North Carolina at Greensboro (NC)
U of Northern Iowa (IA)
U of Notre Dame (IN)
U of Oklahoma (OK)
U of Oregon (OR)
U of Ottawa (ON, Canada)
U of Pennsylvania (PA)
U of Pittsburgh (PA)
U of Rochester (NY)
U of St. Thomas (MN)
U of Saskatchewan (SK, Canada)
U of Southern California (CA)
U of South Florida (FL)
The U of Tennessee (TN)
The U of Texas at Arlington (TX)
The U of Texas at Austin (TX)
U of the South (TN)
U of Toronto (ON, Canada)
U of Utah (UT)
U of Vermont (VT)
U of Victoria (BC, Canada)
U of Washington (WA)
U of Waterloo (ON, Canada)
The U of Western Ontario (ON, Canada)
U of Windsor (ON, Canada)
U of Wisconsin–Madison (WI)
U of Wisconsin–Milwaukee (WI)
U of Wyoming (WY)
Vanderbilt U (TN)
Vassar Coll (NY)
Wake Forest U (NC)
Washington State U (WA)
Washington U in St. Louis (MO)
Wayne State U (MI)
Wellesley Coll (MA)
Wesleyan U (CT)
West Chester U of Pennsylvania (PA)
Wheaton Coll (MA)
Williams Coll (MA)
Yale U (CT)
York U (ON, Canada)

RUSSIAN STUDIES

American U (DC)
Bard Coll (NY)
Barnard Coll (NY)
Beloit Coll (WI)
Boston Coll (MA)
Boston U (MA)
Brandeis U (MA)
Brock U (ON, Canada)
Brown U (RI)
California State U, Fullerton (CA)
Carleton Coll (MN)
Carleton U (ON, Canada)
Claremont McKenna Coll (CA)
Colby Coll (ME)
Colgate U (NY)
Coll of the Holy Cross (MA)
The Coll of William and Mary (VA)
The Coll of Wooster (OH)
The Colorado Coll (CO)
Columbia Coll (NY)
Concordia Coll (MN)
Cornell U (NY)
Dalhousie U (NS, Canada)
Dartmouth Coll (NH)
DePauw U (IN)
Dickinson Coll (PA)
Florida State U (FL)
Fordham U (NY)
George Mason U (VA)
The George Washington U (DC)
Grand Valley State U (MI)
Gustavus Adolphus Coll (MN)
Hamilton Coll (NY)
Hamline U (MN)
Hampshire Coll (MA)
Harvard U (MA)
Hobart and William Smith Colls (NY)
Indiana U Bloomington (IN)
Iowa State U of Science and Technology (IA)
Kent State U (OH)
Knox Coll (IL)
Lafayette Coll (PA)
La Salle U (PA)
Lawrence U (WI)
Lehigh U (PA)
Louisiana State U and A&M Coll (LA)
Macalester Coll (MN)
Marlboro Coll (VT)
McGill U (QC, Canada)
Middlebury Coll (VT)
Mount Holyoke Coll (MA)
Muhlenberg Coll (PA)
Oberlin Coll (OH)
The Ohio State U (OH)
Randolph-Macon Woman's Coll (VA)
Rhodes Coll (TN)
Rice U (TX)
Rutgers, The State U of New Jersey, New Brunswick/Piscataway (NJ)
St. Olaf Coll (MN)
San Diego State U (CA)
Smith Coll (MA)
Southern Methodist U (TX)
Stetson U (FL)
Syracuse U (NY)
Texas State U-San Marcos (TX)
Texas Tech U (TX)
Tufts U (MA)
Tulane U (LA)
State U of NY at Albany (NY)
U of Alaska Fairbanks (AK)
U of Alberta (AB, Canada)
The U of British Columbia (BC, Canada)
U of Calif, Los Angeles (CA)
U of Calif, Riverside (CA)
U of Calif, San Diego (CA)
U of Calif, Santa Cruz (CA)
U of Chicago (IL)
U of Colorado at Boulder (CO)
U of Connecticut (CT)
U of Houston (TX)
U of Illinois at Urbana–Champaign (IL)
The U of Iowa (IA)
U of Kansas (KS)
U of Manitoba (MB, Canada)
U of Maryland, Coll Park (MD)
U of Massachusetts Amherst (MA)
U of Michigan (MI)
U of Minnesota, Twin Cities Campus (MN)
U of Missouri–Columbia (MO)
The U of Montana–Missoula (MT)
U of New Mexico (NM)
The U of North Carolina at Chapel Hill (NC)
U of Northern Iowa (IA)
U of Rochester (NY)
U of St. Thomas (MN)
U of Southern Maine (ME)
The U of Texas at Austin (TX)
U of the South (TN)
U of Toronto (ON, Canada)
U of Vermont (VT)
U of Victoria (BC, Canada)
U of Washington (WA)
U of Waterloo (ON, Canada)
U of Wisconsin–Milwaukee (WI)
Washington and Lee U (VA)
Washington State U (WA)
Washington U in St. Louis (MO)
Wellesley Coll (MA)
Wesleyan U (CT)
Western Michigan U (MI)
Wheaton Coll (MA)
Wittenberg U (OH)
Yale U (CT)
York U (ON, Canada)

SAFETY/SECURITY TECHNOLOGY

State U of NY at Farmingdale (NY)
John Jay Coll of Criminal Justice, the City U of NY (NY)
Keene State Coll (NH)
Madonna U (MI)
Mercy Coll (NY)
York Coll of Pennsylvania (PA)

SALES AND MARKETING/ MARKETING AND DISTRIBUTION TEACHER EDUCATION

Bowling Green State U (OH)
Central Michigan U (MI)
Colorado State U (CO)
East Carolina U (NC)
Eastern Michigan U (MI)
Eastern New Mexico U (NM)
Fayetteville State U (NC)
Kent State U (OH)
Middle Tennessee State U (TN)
New York Inst of Technology (NY)
North Carolina State U (NC)
San Diego State U (CA)
State U of NY at Oswego (NY)
U of Georgia (GA)
U of Hawaii at Manoa (HI)
U of Nebraska–Lincoln (NE)
U of North Dakota (ND)
U of Wisconsin–Stout (WI)
Utah State U (UT)
Virginia Polytechnic Inst and State U (VA)
Wright State U (OH)

SALES, DISTRIBUTION AND MARKETING

Babson Coll (MA)
Bacone Coll (OK)
Baylor U (TX)
Black Hills State U (SD)
Brock U (ON, Canada)
Central Michigan U (MI)
Champlain Coll (VT)
Colorado Tech U Sioux Falls Campus (SD)
Dalton State Coll (GA)
Dowling Coll (NY)
Fairleigh Dickinson U, Florham (NJ)
Fairleigh Dickinson U, Teaneck-Metro Campus (NJ)
Florida State U (FL)
Hampton U (VA)
Harding U (AR)
HEC Montreal (QC, Canada)
Husson Coll (ME)
Johnson & Wales U (RI)
Long Island U, Brooklyn Campus (NY)
McGill U (QC, Canada)
McKendree Coll (IL)
Metropolitan State U (MN)
Middle Tennessee State U (TN)
Ohio U (OH)
Our Lady of Holy Cross Coll (LA)
Purdue U North Central (IN)
Quinnipiac U (CT)
Ryerson U (ON, Canada)
St. Mary's U of San Antonio (TX)
Seton Hill U (PA)
Sierra Nevada Coll (NV)
Syracuse U (NY)
Texas A&M U (TX)
Thomas Coll (ME)
Thomas Edison State Coll (NJ)
Trinity Christian Coll (IL)
Tuskegee U (AL)
U of Baltimore (MD)
The U of Findlay (OH)
U of Houston (TX)
U of Illinois at Urbana–Champaign (IL)
The U of Memphis (TN)
U of North Texas (TX)
U of Pennsylvania (PA)
U of Wisconsin–Stout (WI)
U of Wisconsin–Superior (WI)
West Chester U of Pennsylvania (PA)
Wichita State U (KS)
York U (ON, Canada)
Youngstown State U (OH)

SANITATION TECHNOLOGY

Grand Valley State U (MI)

SANSKRIT AND CLASSICAL INDIAN LANGUAGES

U of Chicago (IL)

SCANDINAVIAN LANGUAGES

Augsburg Coll (MN)
Augustana Coll (IL)
Concordia Coll (MN)
Gustavus Adolphus Coll (MN)
Harvard U (MA)
North Park U (IL)
Pacific Lutheran U (WA)
St. Olaf Coll (MN)
U of Alberta (AB, Canada)
U of Calif, Berkeley (CA)
U of Calif, Los Angeles (CA)
U of Minnesota, Twin Cities Campus (MN)
U of North Dakota (ND)
The U of Texas at Austin (TX)
U of Washington (WA)
U of Wisconsin–Madison (WI)
Washington State U (WA)

SCANDINAVIAN STUDIES

Gustavus Adolphus Coll (MN)
Luther Coll (IA)
Sterling Coll (VT)
U of Michigan (MI)
U of Washington (WA)

SCHOOL LIBRARIAN/SCHOOL LIBRARY MEDIA

The Coll of St. Scholastica (MN)
Eastern Washington U (WA)
Ohio Dominican U (OH)
U of Great Falls (MT)

SCHOOL PSYCHOLOGY

Crichton Coll (TN)
Fort Hays State U (KS)
St. John's U (NY)
Texas Wesleyan U (TX)
U of Houston–Clear Lake (TX)
Valdosta State U (GA)

SCIENCE TEACHER EDUCATION

Abilene Christian U (TX)
Adrian Coll (MI)
Alabama State U (AL)
Albany State U (GA)
Alderson-Broaddus Coll (WV)
Alfred U (NY)
Alice Lloyd Coll (KY)
Alma Coll (MI)
Alvernia Coll (PA)
Alverno Coll (WI)
Andrews U (MI)
Antioch Coll (OH)
Aquinas Coll (MI)
Arkansas Tech U (AR)
Ashland U (OH)
Athens State U (AL)
Auburn U (AL)
Augustana Coll (IL)
Baldwin-Wallace Coll (OH)
Ball State U (IN)
Baylor U (TX)
Beloit Coll (WI)
Bemidji State U (MN)
Benedictine U (IL)
Bethel Coll (IN)
Bethel U (MN)
Bishop's U (QC, Canada)
Black Hills State U (SD)
Bloomfield Coll (NJ)
Bluefield Coll (VA)
Blue Mountain Coll (MS)
Boise State U (ID)
Boston U (MA)
Bowie State U (MD)
Bowling Green State U (OH)
Brewton-Parker Coll (GA)
Brigham Young U (UT)
Brigham Young U–Hawaii (HI)
Brock U (ON, Canada)
Bryan Coll (TN)
Buena Vista U (IA)
State U of NY Coll at Buffalo (NY)
California Lutheran U (CA)
California State U, Chico (CA)
California State U, San Marcos (CA)
Calumet Coll of Saint Joseph (IN)
Calvin Coll (MI)
Campbellsville U (KY)
Campbell U (NC)
Canisius Coll (NY)
Capital U (OH)
Cardinal Stritch U (WI)
Carroll Coll (WI)
Carthage Coll (WI)
Castleton State Coll (VT)
Cedar Crest Coll (PA)
Cedarville U (OH)
Centenary Coll of Louisiana (LA)
Central Methodist Coll (MO)
Central Michigan U (MI)
Central Missouri State U (MO)
Central State U (OH)
Central Washington U (WA)
Chadron State Coll (NE)
Charleston Southern U (SC)
Chicago State U (IL)
Citadel, The Military Coll of South Carolina (SC)
City Coll of the City U of NY (NY)
Clarion U of Pennsylvania (PA)
Clark Atlanta U (GA)
Clearwater Christian Coll (FL)
Clemson U (SC)
Coe Coll (IA)
Coll of Mount Saint Vincent (NY)
Coll of Saint Mary (NE)
The Coll of St. Scholastica (MN)
Coll of Santa Fe (NM)
Coll of the Atlantic (ME)
Coll of the Ozarks (MO)
Coll of the Southwest (NM)
Colorado State U (CO)
Colorado State U-Pueblo (CO)
Columbus State U (GA)
Concordia Coll (MN)
Concordia Coll (NY)
Concordia U (IL)
Concordia U (MI)
Concordia U (NE)
Concordia U (OR)
Concordia U, St. Paul (MN)
Concordia U Wisconsin (WI)
Cornerstone U (MI)
Culver-Stockton Coll (MO)
Dakota Wesleyan U (SD)
Dallas Baptist U (TX)
Dana Coll (NE)
Defiance Coll (OH)
Delaware State U (DE)
Delta State U (MS)
Dickinson State U (ND)
Dillard U (LA)
Dordt Coll (IA)
Drake U (IA)
Duquesne U (PA)
D'Youville Coll (NY)
East Carolina U (NC)
East Central U (OK)
Eastern Kentucky U (KY)
Eastern Michigan U (MI)
Eastern Washington U (WA)
Elizabethtown Coll (PA)
Elmira Coll (NY)
Elms Coll (MA)
Elon U (NC)
Eureka Coll (IL)
Evangel U (MO)
Fairmont State Coll (WV)
Ferris State U (MI)
Florida Atlantic U (FL)
Florida Inst of Technology (FL)
Florida Intl U (FL)

Florida State U (FL)
Fort Hays State U (KS)
Framingham State Coll (MA)
The Franciscan U (IA)
Freed-Hardeman U (TN)
Fresno Pacific U (CA)
Gettysburg Coll (PA)
Glenville State Coll (WV)
Goshen Coll (IN)
Governors State U (IL)
Grace Coll (IN)
Graceland U (IA)
Grambling State U (LA)
Grand Canyon U (AZ)
Grand Valley State U (MI)
Greensboro Coll (NC)
Grove City Coll (PA)
Gwynedd-Mercy Coll (PA)
Hamline U (MN)
Hannibal-LaGrange Coll (MO)
Harding U (AR)
Hardin-Simmons U (TX)
Hastings Coll (NE)
Heidelberg Coll (OH)
Henderson State U (AR)
Hofstra U (NY)
Hope Coll (MI)
Houston Baptist U (TX)
Howard Payne U (TX)
Hunter Coll of the City U of NY (NY)
Huntington Coll (IN)
Illinois Wesleyan U (IL)
Indiana State U (IN)
Indiana U Bloomington (IN)
Indiana U of Pennsylvania (PA)
Indiana U–Purdue U Fort Wayne (IN)
Indiana U South Bend (IN)
Indiana U Southeast (IN)
Inter American U of PR, San Germán Campus (PR)
Iona Coll (NY)
Ithaca Coll (NY)
Johnson C. Smith U (NC)
Judson Coll (AL)
Judson Coll (IL)
Juniata Coll (PA)
Kent State U (OH)
Lakehead U (ON, Canada)
Lakeland Coll (WI)
La Salle U (PA)
Lebanon Valley Coll (PA)
Le Moyne Coll (NY)
Lenoir-Rhyne Coll (NC)
Lewis-Clark State Coll (ID)
Liberty U (VA)
Lincoln Memorial U (TN)
Lincoln U (MO)
Lindenwood U (MO)
Longwood U (VA)
Louisiana Coll (LA)
Lyndon State Coll (VT)
Madonna U (MI)
Malone Coll (OH)
Manchester Coll (IN)
Mansfield U of Pennsylvania (PA)
Marian Coll of Fond du Lac (WI)
Marquette U (WI)
Mars Hill Coll (NC)
Marymount Coll of Fordham U (NY)
Marywood U (PA)
The Master's Coll and Sem (CA)
McGill U (QC, Canada)
Memorial U of Newfoundland (NL, Canada)
Mercyhurst Coll (PA)
Methodist Coll (NC)
Miami U (OH)
Miami U Hamilton (OH)
Michigan Technological U (MI)
Millersville U of Pennsylvania (PA)
Minnesota State U Mankato (MN)
Minnesota State U Moorhead (MN)
Minot State U (ND)
Mississippi Coll (MS)
Mississippi Valley State U (MS)
Missouri Baptist U (MO)
Missouri Valley Coll (MO)
Montana State U–Billings (MT)
Moravian Coll (PA)
Morningside Coll (IA)
Mount Mercy Coll (IA)
Mount Vernon Nazarene U (OH)
Murray State U (KY)
Nazareth Coll of Rochester (NY)
Nebraska Wesleyan U (NE)
Nevada State Coll at Henderson (NV)
New Mexico Highlands U (NM)
Niagara U (NY)
Nicholls State U (LA)
North Carolina State U (NC)
North Central Coll (IL)
North Dakota State U (ND)
Northern Arizona U (AZ)
Northern Michigan U (MI)
North Georgia Coll & State U (GA)
Northland Coll (WI)
Northwestern Oklahoma State U (OK)
Oakland City U (IN)
Oakland U (MI)
Ohio Dominican U (OH)
Ohio Northern U (OH)
Ohio U (OH)
Ohio Valley Coll (WV)
Oklahoma Baptist U (OK)
Oklahoma Christian U (OK)
Oklahoma City U (OK)
Oklahoma Panhandle State U (OK)
Olivet Nazarene U (IL)
Oral Roberts U (OK)
Otterbein Coll (OH)
Ouachita Baptist U (AR)
Our Lady of Holy Cross Coll (LA)
Pacific Lutheran U (WA)
Pfeiffer U (NC)
Pillsbury Baptist Bible Coll (MN)
Pittsburg State U (KS)
Pontifical Catholic U of Puerto Rico (PR)
Queens Coll of the City U of NY (NY)
Queen's U at Kingston (ON, Canada)
Rhode Island Coll (RI)
Rider U (NJ)
Roberts Wesleyan Coll (NY)
Rockford Coll (IL)
Sacred Heart U (CT)
Saginaw Valley State U (MI)
St. Ambrose U (IA)
St. Cloud State U (MN)
Saint Francis U (PA)
St. John Fisher Coll (NY)
St. John's U (NY)
Saint Joseph's Coll of Maine (ME)
Saint Mary's U of Minnesota (MN)
Samford U (AL)
San Diego State U (CA)
Seattle Pacific U (WA)
Shawnee State U (OH)
Southeastern Coll of the Assemblies of God (FL)
Southeastern Louisiana U (LA)
Southeastern Oklahoma State U (OK)
Southeast Missouri State U (MO)
Southern Arkansas U–Magnolia (AR)
Southern Connecticut State U (CT)
Southern Illinois U Edwardsville (IL)
Southern Nazarene U (OK)
Southern Wesleyan U (SC)
Southwest Baptist U (MO)
Southwestern Oklahoma State U (OK)
Southwest Missouri State U (MO)
Springfield Coll (MA)
State U of NY at New Paltz (NY)
State U of NY at Oswego (NY)
State U of NY Coll at Brockport (NY)
State U of NY Coll at Cortland (NY)
State U of NY Coll at Fredonia (NY)
State U of NY Coll at Old Westbury (NY)
State U of NY Coll at Oneonta (NY)
State U of NY Coll at Potsdam (NY)
State U of NY Coll of Environ Sci and Forestry (NY)
Sterling Coll (VT)
Tabor Coll (KS)
Talladega Coll (AL)
Tarleton State U (TX)
Taylor U (IN)
Texas A&M Intl U (TX)
Texas Christian U (TX)
Texas Wesleyan U (TX)
Texas Woman's U (TX)
Trinity Christian Coll (IL)
Tri-State U (IN)
Troy State U (AL)
Troy State U Dothan (AL)
Union U (TN)
Université Laval (QC, Canada)
State U of NY at Albany (NY)
The U of Akron (OH)
U of Alberta (AB, Canada)
The U of Arizona (AZ)
The U of British Columbia (BC, Canada)
U of Central Arkansas (AR)
U of Central Florida (FL)
U of Charleston (WV)
U of Dayton (OH)
U of Delaware (DE)
U of Detroit Mercy (MI)
U of Evansville (IN)
The U of Findlay (OH)
U of Georgia (GA)
U of Great Falls (MT)
U of Hawaii at Manoa (HI)
U of Illinois at Chicago (IL)
U of Indianapolis (IN)
The U of Iowa (IA)
U of Kentucky (KY)
The U of Lethbridge (AB, Canada)
U of Louisiana at Lafayette (LA)
U of Maine at Farmington (ME)
U of Maine at Machias (ME)
U of Maine at Presque Isle (ME)
U of Manitoba (MB, Canada)
U of Maryland, Coll Park (MD)
U of Michigan–Dearborn (MI)
U of Minnesota, Duluth (MN)
U of Minnesota, Twin Cities Campus (MN)
U of Mississippi (MS)
U of Missouri–Columbia (MO)
The U of Montana–Missoula (MT)
The U of Montana–Western (MT)
U of Nebraska–Lincoln (NE)
U of Nevada, Reno (NV)
U of New Brunswick Fredericton (NB, Canada)
U of New Hampshire (NH)
U of New Orleans (LA)
The U of North Carolina at Pembroke (NC)
U of North Dakota (ND)
U of Northern Iowa (IA)
U of North Florida (FL)
U of Notre Dame (IN)
U of Oklahoma (OK)
U of Pittsburgh at Johnstown (PA)
U of Puerto Rico, Cayey U Coll (PR)
U of Regina (SK, Canada)
U of St. Francis (IL)
U of Saint Francis (IN)
U of St. Thomas (MN)
U of Sioux Falls (SD)
The U of South Dakota (SD)
U of South Florida (FL)
The U of Tennessee at Chattanooga (TN)
The U of Tennessee at Martin (TN)
The U of Texas–Pan American (TX)
U of the Ozarks (AR)
U of Toledo (OH)
U of Utah (UT)
U of Vermont (VT)
U of Washington (WA)
U of West Florida (FL)
U of Windsor (ON, Canada)
U of Wisconsin–Eau Claire (WI)
U of Wisconsin–La Crosse (WI)
U of Wisconsin–Madison (WI)
U of Wisconsin–Platteville (WI)
U of Wisconsin–River Falls (WI)
U of Wisconsin–Superior (WI)
U of Wisconsin–Whitewater (WI)
Upper Iowa U (IA)
Urbana U (OH)
Ursuline Coll (OH)
Utah State U (UT)
Valdosta State U (GA)
Valley City State U (ND)
Valparaiso U (IN)
Villa Julie Coll (MD)
Viterbo U (WI)
Walsh U (OH)
Warner Pacific Coll (OR)
Warner Southern Coll (FL)
Washington U in St. Louis (MO)
Waynesburg Coll (PA)
Wayne State Coll (NE)
Wayne State U (MI)
Weber State U (UT)
West Chester U of Pennsylvania (PA)
Western Carolina U (NC)
Western Kentucky U (KY)
Western Michigan U (MI)
Western State Coll of Colorado (CO)
Western Washington U (WA)
Westfield State Coll (MA)
West Virginia State Coll (WV)
Wheaton Coll (IL)
Wheeling Jesuit U (WV)
Wichita State U (KS)
Widener U (PA)
William Penn U (IA)
William Woods U (MO)
Wilmington Coll (DE)
Wingate U (NC)
Winona State U (MN)
Wright State U (OH)
Xavier U (OH)
Xavier U of Louisiana (LA)
York Coll (NE)
York Coll of Pennsylvania (PA)
York U (ON, Canada)
Youngstown State U (OH)

SCIENCE TECHNOLOGIES RELATED

Arizona State U East (AZ)
Athens State U (AL)
Bridgewater State Coll (MA)
Charleston Southern U (SC)
Clemson U (SC)
Lehigh U (PA)
Madonna U (MI)
Northern Arizona U (AZ)
The U of Arizona (AZ)
U of Wisconsin–Stout (WI)

SCIENCE, TECHNOLOGY AND SOCIETY

Butler U (IN)
California Inst of Technology (CA)
Cleveland State U (OH)
Colby Coll (ME)
Coll of the Ozarks (MO)
Cornell U (NY)
Dalhousie U (NS, Canada)
Eastern Michigan U (MI)
Embry-Riddle Aeronautical U (AZ)
Georgetown U (DC)
Georgia Inst of Technology (GA)
Grinnell Coll (IA)
Hampshire Coll (MA)
James Madison U (VA)
Massachusetts Inst of Technology (MA)
Michigan State U (MI)
New Jersey Inst of Technology (NJ)
North Carolina State U (NC)
Northwestern U (IL)
Pitzer Coll (CA)
Rensselaer Polytechnic Inst (NY)
Rutgers, The State U of New Jersey, Newark (NJ)
Samford U (AL)
Scripps Coll (CA)
Slippery Rock U of Pennsylvania (PA)
Stanford U (CA)
Texas Southern U (TX)
U of King's Coll (NS, Canada)
U of Nevada, Reno (NV)
U of Puget Sound (WA)
U of Windsor (ON, Canada)
Vassar Coll (NY)
Washington U in St. Louis (MO)
Wesleyan U (CT)
Worcester Polytechnic Inst (MA)
York U (ON, Canada)

SCULPTURE

Acad of Art U (CA)
Alberta Coll of Art & Design (AB, Canada)
Antioch Coll (OH)
Aquinas Coll (MI)
Arizona State U (AZ)
Art Acad of Cincinnati (OH)
Atlanta Coll of Art (GA)
Ball State U (IN)
Bard Coll (NY)
Bellarmine U (KY)
Bennington Coll (VT)
Bethany Coll (KS)
Birmingham-Southern Coll (AL)
Boston U (MA)
Bowling Green State U (OH)
Brigham Young U (UT)
State U of NY Coll at Buffalo (NY)
California Coll of the Arts (CA)
California Inst of the Arts (CA)
California State U, Fullerton (CA)
California State U, Hayward (CA)
California State U, Long Beach (CA)
Carnegie Mellon U (PA)
The Catholic U of America (DC)
The Cleveland Inst of Art (OH)
Col for Creative Studies (MI)
Coll of Santa Fe (NM)
Coll of Visual Arts (MN)
Colorado State U (CO)
Concordia U (QC, Canada)
Cornell U (NY)
DePaul U (IL)
Drake U (IA)
Escuela de Artes Plasticas de Puerto Rico (PR)
Framingham State Coll (MA)
Grand Valley State U (MI)
Hampshire Coll (MA)
Hofstra U (NY)
Indiana U Bloomington (IN)
Indiana U–Purdue U Fort Wayne (IN)
Inter American U of PR, San Germán Campus (PR)
Kansas City Art Inst (MO)
Laguna Coll of Art & Design (CA)
Longwood U (VA)
Lyme Acad Coll of Fine Arts (CT)
Maine Coll of Art (ME)
Marlboro Coll (VT)
Maryland Inst Coll of Art (MD)
Massachusetts Coll of Art (MA)
Memorial U of Newfoundland (NL, Canada)
Memphis Coll of Art (TN)
Mercyhurst Coll (PA)
Milwaukee Inst of Art and Design (WI)
Minneapolis Coll of Art and Design (MN)
Minnesota State U Mankato (MN)
Minnesota State U Moorhead (MN)
Montserrat Coll of Art (MA)
Moore Coll of Art & Design (PA)
Mount Allison U (NB, Canada)
New World School of the Arts (FL)
Northern Michigan U (MI)
Northwest Nazarene U (ID)
Nova Scotia Coll of Art and Design (NS, Canada)
Ohio Northern U (OH)
The Ohio State U (OH)
Ohio U (OH)
Otis Coll of Art and Design (CA)
Pacific Northwest Coll of Art (OR)
Parsons School of Design, New School U (NY)
Portland State U (OR)
Pratt Inst (NY)
Rhode Island School of Design (RI)
Rochester Inst of Technology (NY)
Rocky Mountain Coll of Art & Design (CO)
Rutgers, The State U of New Jersey, New Brunswick/Piscataway (NJ)
St. Cloud State U (MN)
San Diego State U (CA)
San Francisco Art Inst (CA)
Sarah Lawrence Coll (NY)
School of the Art Inst of Chicago (IL)
School of the Museum of Fine Arts, Boston (MA)
Seton Hill U (PA)
Simon's Rock Coll of Bard (MA)
Sonoma State U (CA)
State U of NY at New Paltz (NY)
State U of NY Coll at Brockport (NY)
State U of NY Coll at Potsdam (NY)
Syracuse U (NY)
Texas A&M U–Commerce (TX)
Texas Christian U (TX)
Trinity Christian Coll (IL)
The U of Akron (OH)
U of Alberta (AB, Canada)
U of Calif, Santa Cruz (CA)
U of Dallas (TX)
U of Evansville (IN)
U of Hartford (CT)
U of Houston (TX)
U of Illinois at Urbana–Champaign (IL)
The U of Iowa (IA)
U of Kansas (KS)
U of Massachusetts Dartmouth (MA)
U of Miami (FL)
U of Michigan (MI)
U of Michigan–Flint (MI)
U of Montevallo (AL)
The U of North Carolina at Greensboro (NC)
U of North Texas (TX)
U of Oregon (OR)
U of Regina (SK, Canada)
The U of the Arts (PA)
U of Washington (WA)
U of Windsor (ON, Canada)
U of Wisconsin–Milwaukee (WI)
Virginia Commonwealth U (VA)
Washington U in St. Louis (MO)
Western Michigan U (MI)
Western Washington U (WA)
York U (ON, Canada)

SECONDARY EDUCATION

Abilene Christian U (TX)
Acadia U (NS, Canada)
Adams State Coll (CO)
Adrian Coll (MI)
Alabama Ag and Mech U (AL)
Alabama State U (AL)
Albertus Magnus Coll (CT)
Albion Coll (MI)
Albright Coll (PA)
Alcorn State U (MS)
Alderson-Broaddus Coll (WV)
Alfred U (NY)

Alice Lloyd Coll (KY)
Alma Coll (MI)
American Intl Coll (MA)
American U (DC)
Anderson Coll (SC)
Andrews U (MI)
Antioch Coll (OH)
Aquinas Coll (MI)
Arcadia U (PA)
Arizona State U (AZ)
Arizona State U West (AZ)
Arkansas Baptist Coll (AR)
Ashland U (OH)
Assumption Coll (MA)
Athens State U (AL)
Atlantic Union Coll (MA)
Auburn U (AL)
Auburn U Montgomery (AL)
Augsburg Coll (MN)
Augustana Coll (IL)
Augustana Coll (SD)
Baldwin-Wallace Coll (OH)
Ball State U (IN)
Baylor U (TX)
Bellarmine U (KY)
Belmont Abbey Coll (NC)
Beloit Coll (WI)
Bemidji State U (MN)
Benedictine Coll (KS)
Benedictine U (IL)
Berea Coll (KY)
Bethel Coll (IN)
Biola U (CA)
Birmingham-Southern Coll (AL)
Bishop's U (QC, Canada)
Blackburn Coll (IL)
Black Hills State U (SD)
Bluefield Coll (VA)
Boise State U (ID)
Boston Coll (MA)
Bowie State U (MD)
Brescia U (KY)
Brevard Coll (NC)
Brewton-Parker Coll (GA)
Briar Cliff U (IA)
Bridgewater Coll (VA)
Brigham Young U–Hawaii (HI)
Brock U (ON, Canada)
Bryan Coll (TN)
Bucknell U (PA)
Buena Vista U (IA)
State U of NY Coll at Buffalo (NY)
Butler U (IN)
Calumet Coll of Saint Joseph (IN)
Calvary Bible Coll and Theological Sem (MO)
Calvin Coll (MI)
Campbellsville U (KY)
Campbell U (NC)
Canisius Coll (NY)
Capital U (OH)
Cardinal Stritch U (WI)
Carroll Coll (MT)
Carroll Coll (WI)
Carson-Newman Coll (TN)
Carthage Coll (WI)
Catawba Coll (NC)
The Catholic U of America (DC)
Cedar Crest Coll (PA)
Cedarville U (OH)
Centenary Coll (NJ)
Centenary Coll of Louisiana (LA)
Central Coll (IA)
Central Methodist Coll (MO)
Central Missouri State U (MO)
Centre Coll (KY)
Chadron State Coll (NE)
Champlain Coll (VT)
Charleston Southern U (SC)
Cheyney U of Pennsylvania (PA)
Chicago State U (IL)
Christian Heritage Coll (CA)
City Coll of the City U of NY (NY)
Clark Atlanta U (GA)
Clarke Coll (IA)
Clark U (MA)
Clearwater Christian Coll (FL)
Clemson U (SC)
Coastal Carolina U (SC)
Coe Coll (IA)
Coll Misericordia (PA)
Coll of Charleston (SC)
Coll of Mount Saint Vincent (NY)
The Coll of New Jersey (NJ)
Coll of Saint Benedict (MN)
Coll of St. Catherine (MN)
Coll of St. Joseph (VT)
Coll of Saint Mary (NE)
Coll of Santa Fe (NM)
Coll of the Atlantic (ME)
Coll of the Ozarks (MO)
Coll of the Southwest (NM)
Colorado State U-Pueblo (CO)
Columbus State U (GA)
Concord Coll (WV)
Concordia Coll (MN)
Concordia Coll (NY)
Concordia U (IL)
Concordia U (MI)
Concordia U (NE)
Concordia U (OR)
Concordia U at Austin (TX)
Concordia U, St. Paul (MN)
Concordia U Wisconsin (WI)
Connecticut Coll (CT)
Converse Coll (SC)
Cornell Coll (IA)
Cornerstone U (MI)
Crichton Coll (TN)
Cumberland U (TN)
Dakota State U (SD)
Dakota Wesleyan U (SD)
Dallas Baptist U (TX)
Dana Coll (NE)
Davis & Elkins Coll (WV)
Defiance Coll (OH)
Delaware State U (DE)
Delaware Valley Coll (PA)
Delta State U (MS)
DePaul U (IL)
Dickinson State U (ND)
Dillard U (LA)
Doane Coll (NE)
Dominican Coll (NY)
Dordt Coll (IA)
Dowling Coll (NY)
Drake U (IA)
Drury U (MO)
Duquesne U (PA)
D'Youville Coll (NY)
East Central U (OK)
Eastern Connecticut State U (CT)
Eastern Kentucky U (KY)
Eastern Mennonite U (VA)
Eastern Michigan U (MI)
Eastern Nazarene Coll (MA)
Eastern U (PA)
East Stroudsburg U of Pennsylvania (PA)
Elizabeth City State U (NC)
Elizabethtown Coll (PA)
Elmhurst Coll (IL)
Elmira Coll (NY)
Elms Coll (MA)
Elon U (NC)
Emory U (GA)
Emporia State U (KS)
Eureka Coll (IL)
Evangel U (MO)
Fairfield U (CT)
Fairmont State Coll (WV)
Faulkner U (AL)
Ferris State U (MI)
Flagler Coll (FL)
Florida Southern Coll (FL)
Florida State U (FL)
Fontbonne U (MO)
Fordham U (NY)
Fort Lewis Coll (CO)
Framingham State Coll (MA)
The Franciscan U (IA)
Franklin Pierce Coll (NH)
Freed-Hardeman U (TN)
Fresno Pacific U (CA)
Frostburg State U (MD)
Furman U (SC)
Gallaudet U (DC)
Gannon U (PA)
Gardner-Webb U (NC)
Geneva Coll (PA)
Georgetown Coll (KY)
Gettysburg Coll (PA)
Glenville State Coll (WV)
Gonzaga U (WA)
Goshen Coll (IN)
Grace Bible Coll (MI)
Graceland U (IA)
Grace U (NE)
Grambling State U (LA)
Grand Canyon U (AZ)
Grand Valley State U (MI)
Greensboro Coll (NC)
Grinnell Coll (IA)
Grove City Coll (PA)
Guilford Coll (NC)
Gustavus Adolphus Coll (MN)
Gwynedd-Mercy Coll (PA)
Hamline U (MN)
Hampshire Coll (MA)
Hampton U (VA)
Hannibal-LaGrange Coll (MO)
Harding U (AR)
Hardin-Simmons U (TX)
Harris-Stowe State Coll (MO)
Hastings Coll (NE)
Heidelberg Coll (OH)
High Point U (NC)
Hillsdale Coll (MI)
Hiram Coll (OH)
Hofstra U (NY)
Hope Coll (MI)
Houghton Coll (NY)
Houston Baptist U (TX)
Howard Payne U (TX)
Humboldt State U (CA)
Hunter Coll of the City U of NY (NY)
Huntingdon Coll (AL)
Huntington Coll (IN)
Huston-Tillotson Coll (TX)
Idaho State U (ID)
Illinois Coll (IL)
Illinois Wesleyan U (IL)
Immaculata U (PA)
Indiana U Bloomington (IN)
Indiana U East (IN)
Indiana U Northwest (IN)
Indiana U of Pennsylvania (PA)
Indiana U–Purdue U Fort Wayne (IN)
Indiana U–Purdue U Indianapolis (IN)
Indiana U South Bend (IN)
Indiana U Southeast (IN)
Inter Amer U of PR, Barranquitas Campus (PR)
Inter American U of PR, Ponce Campus (PR)
Inter American U of PR, San Germán Campus (PR)
Iona Coll (NY)
Iowa State U of Science and Technology (IA)
Iowa Wesleyan Coll (IA)
Ithaca Coll (NY)
Jacksonville State U (AL)
Jacksonville U (FL)
Jamestown Coll (ND)
Jarvis Christian Coll (TX)
John Brown U (AR)
John Carroll U (OH)
Johnson C. Smith U (NC)
Johnson State Coll (VT)
Judson Coll (AL)
Judson Coll (IL)
Juniata Coll (PA)
Kansas State U (KS)
Keene State Coll (NH)
Kentucky State U (KY)
Kentucky Wesleyan Coll (KY)
Keuka Coll (NY)
King Coll (TN)
King's Coll (PA)
Kutztown U of Pennsylvania (PA)
Lake Forest Coll (IL)
Lakehead U (ON, Canada)
Lakeland Coll (WI)
Lake Superior State U (MI)
Lamar U (TX)
Lambuth U (TN)
Lander U (SC)
La Salle U (PA)
Lawrence U (WI)
Lebanon Valley Coll (PA)
Le Moyne Coll (NY)
Lenoir-Rhyne Coll (NC)
Lesley U (MA)
LeTourneau U (TX)
Lewis U (IL)
Liberty U (VA)
Lincoln Memorial U (TN)
Lincoln U (PA)
Lindenwood U (MO)
Lindsey Wilson Coll (KY)
Lipscomb U (TN)
Lock Haven U of Pennsylvania (PA)
Long Island U, Brooklyn Campus (NY)
Long Island U, C.W. Post Campus (NY)
Longwood U (VA)
Loras Coll (IA)
Louisiana Coll (LA)
Louisiana State U and A&M Coll (LA)
Lubbock Christian U (TX)
Lycoming Coll (PA)
Lynchburg Coll (VA)
Lynn U (FL)
MacMurray Coll (IL)
Madonna U (MI)
Maharishi U of Management (IA)
Manchester Coll (IN)
Manhattanville Coll (NY)
Mansfield U of Pennsylvania (PA)
Marian Coll (IN)
Marian Coll of Fond du Lac (WI)
Marietta Coll (OH)
Marist Coll (NY)
Marquette U (WI)
Marshall U (WV)
Mars Hill Coll (NC)
Martin U (IN)
Marymount Coll of Fordham U (NY)
Maryville U of Saint Louis (MO)
Mary Washington Coll (VA)
Marywood U (PA)
Massachusetts Coll of Liberal Arts (MA)
The Master's Coll and Sem (CA)
McGill U (QC, Canada)
McKendree Coll (IL)
McMurry U (TX)
McNeese State U (LA)
McPherson Coll (KS)
Memorial U of Newfoundland (NL, Canada)
Mercy Coll (NY)
Mercyhurst Coll (PA)
Merrimack Coll (MA)
Methodist Coll (NC)
Miami U (OH)
Michigan Technological U (MI)
MidAmerica Nazarene U (KS)
Midway Coll (KY)
Miles Coll (AL)
Minnesota State U Mankato (MN)
Minnesota State U Moorhead (MN)
Mississippi Coll (MS)
Mississippi State U (MS)
Missouri Southern State U (MO)
Missouri Valley Coll (MO)
Molloy Coll (NY)
Monmouth Coll (IL)
Monmouth U (NJ)
Montana State U–Billings (MT)
Montana State U–Bozeman (MT)
Moravian Coll (PA)
Morehouse Coll (GA)
Morgan State U (MD)
Morningside Coll (IA)
Mount Marty Coll (SD)
Mount Mary Coll (WI)
Mount Mercy Coll (IA)
Mount Saint Mary Coll (NY)
Mount St. Mary's Coll (CA)
Mount Saint Mary's Coll and Sem (MD)
Mount Saint Vincent U (NS, Canada)
Mount Vernon Nazarene U (OH)
Muhlenberg Coll (PA)
Murray State U (KY)
Nazareth Coll of Rochester (NY)
Newberry Coll (SC)
Newman U (KS)
New Mexico Highlands U (NM)
New Mexico State U (NM)
New York U (NY)
Niagara U (NY)
Nicholls State U (LA)
Nichols Coll (MA)
North Carolina State U (NC)
North Carolina Wesleyan Coll (NC)
North Central Coll (IL)
North Central U (MN)
Northeastern State U (OK)
Northern Michigan U (MI)
Northern State U (SD)
North Georgia Coll & State U (GA)
Northland Coll (WI)
North Park U (IL)
Northwestern Coll (IA)
Northwestern Oklahoma State U (OK)
Northwestern State U of Louisiana (LA)
Northwestern U (IL)
Northwest Nazarene U (ID)
Notre Dame de Namur U (CA)
Nyack Coll (NY)
Oakland City U (IN)
Oakland U (MI)
Oglethorpe U (GA)
Ohio Dominican U (OH)
Ohio Northern U (OH)
Ohio U (OH)
Ohio Valley Coll (WV)
Ohio Wesleyan U (OH)
Oklahoma Baptist U (OK)
Oklahoma Christian U (OK)
Oklahoma City U (OK)
Oklahoma Panhandle State U (OK)
Oklahoma State U (OK)
Olivet Coll (MI)
Olivet Nazarene U (IL)
Otterbein Coll (OH)
Ouachita Baptist U (AR)
Our Lady of Holy Cross Coll (LA)
Pacific Lutheran U (WA)
Pacific U (OR)
Palm Beach Atlantic U (FL)
Penn State U Abington Coll (PA)
Penn State U Altoona Coll (PA)
Penn State U at Erie, The Behrend Coll (PA)
Penn State U Beaver Campus of the Commonwealth Coll (PA)
Penn State U Berks Cmps of Berks-Lehigh Valley Coll (PA)
Penn State U Delaware County Campus of the Commonwealth Coll (PA)
Penn State U DuBois Campus of the Commonwealth Coll (PA)
Penn State U Fayette Campus of the Commonwealth Coll (PA)
Penn State U Hazleton Campus of the Commonwealth Coll (PA)
Penn State U Lehigh Valley Cmps of Berks-Lehigh Valley Coll (PA)
Penn State U McKeesport Campus of the Commonwealth Coll (PA)
Penn State U Mont Alto Campus of the Commonwealth Coll (PA)
Penn State U New Kensington Campus of the Commonwealth Coll (PA)
Penn State U Schuylkill Campus of the Capital Coll (PA)
Penn State U Shenango Campus of the Commonwealth Coll (PA)
Penn State U Univ Park Campus (PA)
Penn State U Wilkes-Barre Campus of the Commonwealth Coll (PA)
Penn State U Worthington Scranton Cmps Commonwealth Coll (PA)
Penn State U York Campus of the Commonwealth Coll (PA)
Pepperdine U, Malibu (CA)
Pillsbury Baptist Bible Coll (MN)
Pine Manor Coll (MA)
Pittsburg State U (KS)
Point Park U (PA)
Pontifical Catholic U of Puerto Rico (PR)
Providence Coll (RI)
Queen's U at Kingston (ON, Canada)
Queens U of Charlotte (NC)
Reformed Bible Coll (MI)
Rhode Island Coll (RI)
Rider U (NJ)
Ripon Coll (WI)
Rivier Coll (NH)
Roberts Wesleyan Coll (NY)
Rockhurst U (MO)
Rocky Mountain Coll (MT)
Roger Williams U (RI)
Roosevelt U (IL)
Rowan U (NJ)
Sacred Heart U (CT)
St. Ambrose U (IA)
Saint Anselm Coll (NH)
St. Bonaventure U (NY)
St. Cloud State U (MN)
Saint Francis U (PA)
St. Francis Xavier U (NS, Canada)
Saint John's U (MN)
St. John's U (NY)
Saint Joseph Coll (CT)
Saint Joseph's Coll (IN)
St. Joseph's Coll, Suffolk Campus (NY)
Saint Joseph's U (PA)
Saint Martin's Coll (WA)
Saint Mary-of-the-Woods Coll (IN)
Saint Michael's Coll (VT)
St. Thomas Aquinas Coll (NY)
St. Thomas U (FL)
Salisbury U (MD)
Salve Regina U (RI)
Seton Hall U (NJ)
Shawnee State U (OH)
Sheldon Jackson Coll (AK)
Shepherd U (WV)
Siena Coll (NY)
Siena Heights U (MI)
Simmons Coll (MA)
Simpson Coll (IA)
South Dakota State U (SD)
Southeastern Oklahoma State U (OK)
Southern Connecticut State U (CT)
Southern Nazarene U (OK)
Southern U and A&M Coll (LA)
Southern Utah U (UT)
Southwest Baptist U (MO)
Southwestern Coll (AZ)
Southwestern Oklahoma State U (OK)
Spring Arbor U (MI)
Springfield Coll (MA)
Spring Hill Coll (AL)
State U of NY at New Paltz (NY)
State U of NY at Oswego (NY)
Plattsburgh State U of NY (NY)
State U of NY Coll at Brockport (NY)
State U of NY Coll at Cortland (NY)
State U of NY Coll at Fredonia (NY)
State U of NY Coll at Old Westbury (NY)
State U of NY Coll at Oneonta (NY)

State U of West Georgia (GA)
Stetson U (FL)
Suffolk U (MA)
Susquehanna U (PA)
Tabor Coll (KS)
Tarleton State U (TX)
Taylor U (IN)
Tennessee Technological U (TN)
Tennessee Wesleyan Coll (TN)
Texas A&M U–Commerce (TX)
Texas A&M U–Kingsville (TX)
Texas Christian U (TX)
Texas Southern U (TX)
Thiel Coll (PA)
Thomas U (GA)
Tougaloo Coll (MS)
Trent U (ON, Canada)
Trevecca Nazarene U (TN)
Trinity Baptist Coll (FL)
Trinity Christian Coll (IL)
Trinity Coll (DC)
Trinity Intl U (IL)
Trinity Western U (BC, Canada)
Tri-State U (IN)
Troy State U (AL)
Troy State U Dothan (AL)
Tufts U (MA)
Tusculum Coll (TN)
Union Coll (KY)
Union Coll (NE)
Union U (TN)
Universidad Adventista de las Antillas (PR)
Université de Montréal (QC, Canada)
Université de Sherbrooke (QC, Canada)
U du Québec à Hull (QC, Canada)
Université Laval (QC, Canada)
The U of Akron (OH)
The U of Alabama (AL)
The U of Alabama at Birmingham (AL)
U of Alberta (AB, Canada)
The U of Arizona (AZ)
U of Arkansas (AR)
The U of British Columbia (BC, Canada)
U of Calgary (AB, Canada)
U of Cincinnati (OH)
U of Dallas (TX)
U of Dayton (OH)
U of Delaware (DE)
U of Detroit Mercy (MI)
U of Dubuque (IA)
U of Evansville (IN)
The U of Findlay (OH)
U of Great Falls (MT)
U of Hartford (CT)
U of Hawaii at Hilo (HI)
U of Hawaii at Manoa (HI)
U of Idaho (ID)
U of Illinois at Chicago (IL)
U of Illinois at Springfield (IL)
U of Indianapolis (IN)
The U of Iowa (IA)
U of Kansas (KS)
U of La Verne (CA)
U of Louisiana at Lafayette (LA)
U of Maine (ME)
U of Maine at Farmington (ME)
U of Maine at Presque Isle (ME)
U of Manitoba (MB, Canada)
U of Mary Hardin-Baylor (TX)
U of Maryland, Coll Park (MD)
U of Miami (FL)
U of Michigan (MI)
U of Michigan–Dearborn (MI)
U of Minnesota, Morris (MN)
U of Mississippi (MS)
U of Missouri–Columbia (MO)
U of Missouri–Kansas City (MO)
U of Missouri–Rolla (MO)
U of Missouri–St. Louis (MO)
U of Mobile (AL)
The U of Montana–Missoula (MT)
The U of Montana–Western (MT)
U of Nebraska at Omaha (NE)
U of Nevada, Las Vegas (NV)
U of New Brunswick Fredericton (NB, Canada)
U of New Hampshire (NH)
U of New Mexico (NM)
U of North Alabama (AL)
U of North Florida (FL)
U of Ottawa (ON, Canada)
U of Pittsburgh at Johnstown (PA)
U of Portland (OR)
U of Prince Edward Island (PE, Canada)
U of Puerto Rico, Cayey U Coll (PR)
U of Redlands (CA)
U of Regina (SK, Canada)
U of Rhode Island (RI)
U of Richmond (VA)
U of Saint Francis (IN)
U of St. Thomas (TX)
U of San Francisco (CA)
U of Saskatchewan (SK, Canada)
The U of Scranton (PA)
U of Sioux Falls (SD)
U of South Alabama (AL)
U of South Carolina Aiken (SC)
U of South Carolina Spartanburg (SC)
The U of South Dakota (SD)
The U of Tampa (FL)
The U of Tennessee at Chattanooga (TN)
U of the Incarnate Word (TX)
U of the Ozarks (AR)
U of the Sacred Heart (PR)
U of Toledo (OH)
U of Utah (UT)
U of Vermont (VT)
U of Victoria (BC, Canada)
U of Washington (WA)
The U of Western Ontario (ON, Canada)
U of Windsor (ON, Canada)
U of Wisconsin–La Crosse (WI)
U of Wisconsin–Madison (WI)
U of Wisconsin–Milwaukee (WI)
U of Wisconsin–Oshkosh (WI)
U of Wisconsin–Platteville (WI)
U of Wisconsin–River Falls (WI)
U of Wisconsin–Stevens Point (WI)
U of Wisconsin–Whitewater (WI)
U of Wyoming (WY)
Urbana U (OH)
Utah State U (UT)
Utica Coll (NY)
Valdosta State U (GA)
Valley City State U (ND)
Valparaiso U (IN)
Vanderbilt U (TN)
Vanguard U of Southern California (CA)
Vennard Coll (IA)
Villanova U (PA)
Virginia Intermont Coll (VA)
Virginia Wesleyan Coll (VA)
Wagner Coll (NY)
Walsh U (OH)
Warner Pacific Coll (OR)
Warren Wilson Coll (NC)
Wartburg Coll (IA)
Washington State U (WA)
Washington U in St. Louis (MO)
Waynesburg Coll (PA)
Weber State U (UT)
Webster U (MO)
Wells Coll (NY)
Western Baptist Coll (OR)
Western Connecticut State U (CT)
Western Oregon U (OR)
Western State Coll of Colorado (CO)
Western Washington U (WA)
Westfield State Coll (MA)
West Liberty State Coll (WV)
Westminster Coll (MO)
Westmont Coll (CA)
West Virginia State Coll (WV)
West Virginia U (WV)
West Virginia Wesleyan Coll (WV)
Wheeling Jesuit U (WV)
Whitworth Coll (WA)
Wichita State U (KS)
William Jewell Coll (MO)
William Paterson U of New Jersey (NJ)
William Penn U (IA)
William Woods U (MO)
Wingate U (NC)
Winona State U (MN)
Wright State U (OH)
Xavier U of Louisiana (LA)
York Coll (NE)
York Coll of Pennsylvania (PA)
York U (ON, Canada)
Youngstown State U (OH)

SECONDARY SCHOOL ADMINISTRATION/ PRINCIPALSHIP
Auburn U (AL)
Charleston Southern U (SC)
Eastern Michigan U (MI)
Jones Intl U (CO)

SECURITIES SERVICES ADMINISTRATION
Southwestern Coll (KS)
State U of NY Coll at Brockport (NY)

SECURITY AND LOSS PREVENTION
Eastern Kentucky U (KY)
State U of NY at Farmingdale (NY)
John Jay Coll of Criminal Justice, the City U of NY (NY)
U of New Haven (CT)
York Coll of Pennsylvania (PA)
Youngstown State U (OH)

SECURITY AND PROTECTIVE SERVICES RELATED
Eastern Michigan U (MI)
Franklin U (OH)
Lewis U (IL)
North Dakota State U (ND)
St. Ambrose U (IA)

SELLING SKILLS AND SALES
The U of Akron (OH)
Youngstown State U (OH)

SEMITIC LANGUAGES
Cornell U (NY)
The U of Texas at Austin (TX)

SIGN LANGUAGE INTERPRETATION AND TRANSLATION
Bethel Coll (IN)
Bloomsburg U of Pennsylvania (PA)
Columbia Coll Chicago (IL)
Converse Coll (SC)
Eastern Kentucky U (KY)
Gallaudet U (DC)
Gardner-Webb U (NC)
Goshen Coll (IN)
Idaho State U (ID)
Indiana U–Purdue U Indianapolis (IN)
MacMurray Coll (IL)
Maryville Coll (TN)
Mount Aloysius Coll (PA)
North Central U (MN)
Northeastern U (MA)
Rochester Inst of Technology (NY)
U of Arkansas at Little Rock (AR)
U of Louisville (KY)
U of New Hampshire at Manchester (NH)
U of New Mexico (NM)
The U of North Carolina at Greensboro (NC)
Western Oregon U (OR)
William Woods U (MO)
York U (ON, Canada)

SLAVIC, BALTIC, AND ALBANIAN LANGUAGES RELATED
Rutgers, The State U of New Jersey, Newark (NJ)

SLAVIC LANGUAGES
Boston Coll (MA)
Columbia Coll (NY)
Columbia U, School of General Studies (NY)
Cornell U (NY)
Duke U (NC)
Harvard U (MA)
Indiana U Bloomington (IN)
Northwestern U (IL)
Princeton U (NJ)
Stanford U (CA)
State U of NY at Albany (NY)
U of Alberta (AB, Canada)
The U of British Columbia (BC, Canada)
U of Calif, Berkeley (CA)
U of Calif, Los Angeles (CA)
U of Calif, Santa Barbara (CA)
U of Chicago (IL)
U of Georgia (GA)
U of Illinois at Chicago (IL)
U of Kansas (KS)
U of Manitoba (MB, Canada)
U of Pittsburgh (PA)
U of Saskatchewan (SK, Canada)
U of Southern California (CA)
U of Toronto (ON, Canada)
U of Victoria (BC, Canada)
U of Virginia (VA)
U of Washington (WA)
U of Windsor (ON, Canada)
U of Wisconsin–Madison (WI)
U of Wisconsin–Milwaukee (WI)
Wayne State U (MI)

SLAVIC STUDIES
Barnard Coll (NY)
Baylor U (TX)
Connecticut Coll (CT)
Cornell U (NY)
Lawrence U (WI)
Northwestern U (IL)
U of Ottawa (ON, Canada)
U of Waterloo (ON, Canada)

SMALL BUSINESS ADMINISTRATION
Babson Coll (MA)
Central Christian Coll of Kansas (KS)
Dalhousie U (NS, Canada)
Husson Coll (ME)
Kendall Coll (IL)
Lewis-Clark State Coll (ID)
Northern Michigan U (MI)

SOCIAL AND PHILOSOPHICAL FOUNDATIONS OF EDUCATION
Eastern Michigan U (MI)
Hampshire Coll (MA)
Northwestern U (IL)
Sterling Coll (VT)
Texas Southern U (TX)
Troy State U Dothan (AL)
Washington U in St. Louis (MO)

SOCIAL PSYCHOLOGY
Brigham Young U (UT)
Clarion U of Pennsylvania (PA)
Cornell U (NY)
Florida Atlantic U (FL)
Inter American U of PR, Aguadilla Campus (PR)
Kwantlen U Coll (BC, Canada)
Lawrence U (WI)
Loyola U Chicago (IL)
Marymount U (VA)
Maryville U of Saint Louis (MO)
Paine Coll (GA)
Park U (MO)
Penn State U Abington Coll (PA)
U of Calif, Irvine (CA)
U of Calif, Santa Cruz (CA)
U of Nevada, Reno (NV)
U of Wisconsin–Superior (WI)

SOCIAL SCIENCES
Adams State Coll (CO)
Adelphi U (NY)
Adrian Coll (MI)
Alabama State U (AL)
Albertus Magnus Coll (CT)
Allen U (SC)
Alma Coll (MI)
Alvernia Coll (PA)
Alverno Coll (WI)
American Intl Coll (MA)
Andrews U (MI)
Angelo State U (TX)
Anna Maria Coll (MA)
Antioch Coll (OH)
Aquinas Coll (MI)
Arizona State U West (AZ)
Asbury Coll (KY)
Ashland U (OH)
Augsburg Coll (MN)
Averett U (VA)
Azusa Pacific U (CA)
Ball State U (IN)
Bard Coll (NY)
Bemidji State U (MN)
Benedictine Coll (KS)
Benedictine U (IL)
Bennington Coll (VT)
Berry Coll (GA)
Bethany Lutheran Coll (MN)
Bethel Coll (IN)
Bethel U (MN)
Biola U (CA)
Bishop's U (QC, Canada)
Black Hills State U (SD)
Bloomsburg U of Pennsylvania (PA)
Bluefield Coll (VA)
Bluefield State Coll (WV)
Blue Mountain Coll (MS)
Bluffton Coll (OH)
Boise State U (ID)
Brescia U (KY)
Brewton-Parker Coll (GA)
Brock U (ON, Canada)
Buena Vista U (IA)
Caldwell Coll (NJ)
California Baptist U (CA)
California Inst of Technology (CA)
California Lutheran U (CA)
California Polytechnic State U, San Luis Obispo (CA)
California State Polytechnic U, Pomona (CA)
California State U, Chico (CA)
California State U, Los Angeles (CA)
California State U, Sacramento (CA)
California State U, San Bernardino (CA)
California State U, San Marcos (CA)
California State U, Stanislaus (CA)
California U of Pennsylvania (PA)
Calvin Coll (MI)
Campbellsville U (KY)
Campbell U (NC)
Cardinal Stritch U (WI)
Carnegie Mellon U (PA)
Carroll Coll (MT)
Carthage Coll (WI)
Castleton State Coll (VT)
Cazenovia Coll (NY)
Central Coll (IA)
Central Connecticut State U (CT)
Central Michigan U (MI)
Chaminade U of Honolulu (HI)
Charleston Southern U (SC)
Cheyney U of Pennsylvania (PA)
Christian Heritage Coll (CA)
Clarion U of Pennsylvania (PA)
Clark Atlanta U (GA)
Clarkson U (NY)
Cleveland State U (OH)
Colgate U (NY)
Coll of Mount Saint Vincent (NY)
Coll of Saint Benedict (MN)
Coll of St. Catherine (MN)
Coll of Saint Mary (NE)
The Coll of St. Scholastica (MN)
Coll of the Southwest (NM)
Colorado Christian U (CO)
Colorado State U (CO)
Colorado State U-Pueblo (CO)
Columbia Coll (SC)
Concordia Coll (NY)
Concordia U (MI)
Concordia U (NE)
Concordia U (OR)
Concordia U (QC, Canada)
Concordia U Coll of Alberta (AB, Canada)
Cumberland U (TN)
Dana Coll (NE)
Daniel Webster Coll (NH)
Defiance Coll (OH)
Delta State U (MS)
DePaul U (IL)
Dickinson State U (ND)
Doane Coll (NE)
Dominican Coll (NY)
Dominican U (IL)
Dordt Coll (IA)
Dowling Coll (NY)
Drexel U (PA)
Eastern Mennonite U (VA)
Eastern Michigan U (MI)
Eastern New Mexico U (NM)
East Stroudsburg U of Pennsylvania (PA)
Edgewood Coll (WI)
Edinboro U of Pennsylvania (PA)
Elizabeth City State U (NC)
Elizabethtown Coll (PA)
Elmira Coll (NY)
Emporia State U (KS)
Eugene Lang Coll, New School U (NY)
Eureka Coll (IL)
Evangel U (MO)
The Evergreen State Coll (WA)
Faulkner U (AL)
Ferrum Coll (VA)
Florida Ag and Mech U (FL)
Florida Atlantic U (FL)
Florida Southern Coll (FL)
Florida State U (FL)
Fontbonne U (MO)
Fordham U (NY)
Fort Valley State U (GA)
Framingham State Coll (MA)
The Franciscan U (IA)
Freed-Hardeman U (TN)
Fresno Pacific U (CA)
Frostburg State U (MD)
Gardner-Webb U (NC)
Georgia Southwestern State U (GA)
Gettysburg Coll (PA)
Governors State U (IL)
Graceland U (IA)
Grand Canyon U (AZ)
Grand Valley State U (MI)
Gustavus Adolphus Coll (MN)
Hamline U (MN)
Hampshire Coll (MA)
Hampton U (VA)
Harding U (AR)
Harvard U (MA)
Hawai'i Pacific U (HI)
Hofstra U (NY)
Howard Payne U (TX)

Humboldt State U (CA)
Inter American U of PR, San Germán Campus (PR)
Iona Coll (NY)
Ithaca Coll (NY)
James Madison U (VA)
John Brown U (AR)
The Johns Hopkins U (MD)
Johnson C. Smith U (NC)
Judson Coll (IL)
Juniata Coll (PA)
Kansas State U (KS)
Kansas Wesleyan U (KS)
Keene State Coll (NH)
Kent State U (OH)
Keuka Coll (NY)
The King's U Coll (AB, Canada)
Kutztown U of Pennsylvania (PA)
Lake Erie Coll (OH)
Lake Superior State U (MI)
La Salle U (PA)
Lehigh U (PA)
Lesley U (MA)
Lewis-Clark State Coll (ID)
Liberty U (VA)
Lincoln U (MO)
Lindsey Wilson Coll (KY)
Livingstone Coll (NC)
Lock Haven U of Pennsylvania (PA)
Long Island U, Brooklyn Campus (NY)
Loyola U New Orleans (LA)
Lyndon State Coll (VT)
Lynn U (FL)
Mansfield U of Pennsylvania (PA)
Marian Coll of Fond du Lac (WI)
Marlboro Coll (VT)
Mars Hill Coll (NC)
Marygrove Coll (MI)
Marylhurst U (OR)
Marywood U (PA)
Mayville State U (ND)
McKendree Coll (IL)
McPherson Coll (KS)
Medaille Coll (NY)
Memorial U of Newfoundland (NL, Canada)
Mercyhurst Coll (PA)
Metropolitan State U (MN)
Michigan State U (MI)
Michigan Technological U (MI)
Mid-Continent Coll (KY)
Miles Coll (AL)
Minnesota State U Mankato (MN)
Minot State U (ND)
Mississippi Coll (MS)
Missouri Baptist U (MO)
Moravian Coll (PA)
Morehead State U (KY)
Mount Aloysius Coll (PA)
Mount Holyoke Coll (MA)
Mount Saint Mary Coll (NY)
Mount St. Mary's Coll (CA)
Mount Saint Mary's Coll and Sem (MD)
Mount Saint Vincent U (NS, Canada)
Mount Vernon Nazarene U (OH)
Muhlenberg Coll (PA)
National-Louis U (IL)
Nazareth Coll of Rochester (NY)
New Coll of California (CA)
New Coll of Florida (FL)
New York Inst of Technology (NY)
New York U (NY)
Niagara U (NY)
North Central Coll (IL)
North Dakota State U (ND)
Northern Arizona U (AZ)
Northern Michigan U (MI)
North Georgia Coll & State U (GA)
Northland Coll (WI)
North Park U (IL)
Northwestern Coll (MN)
Northwestern Oklahoma State U (OK)
Northwestern State U of Louisiana (LA)
Northwest Nazarene U (ID)
Notre Dame de Namur U (CA)
Nyack Coll (NY)
Oakland City U (IN)
The Ohio State U (OH)
Ohio U (OH)
Oklahoma Baptist U (OK)
Oklahoma Panhandle State U (OK)
Olivet Coll (MI)
Olivet Nazarene U (IL)
Ouachita Baptist U (AR)
Our Lady of Holy Cross Coll (LA)
Our Lady of the Lake U of San Antonio (TX)
Pace U (NY)
Pacific Union Coll (CA)
Pfeiffer U (NC)
Piedmont Coll (GA)
Pikeville Coll (KY)
Pittsburg State U (KS)
Plymouth State U (NH)
Point Loma Nazarene U (CA)
Point Park U (PA)
Portland State U (OR)
Presbyterian Coll (SC)
Providence Coll (RI)
Providence Coll and Theological Sem (MB, Canada)
Purdue U (IN)
Quinnipiac U (CT)
Radford U (VA)
Ramapo Coll of New Jersey (NJ)
Rensselaer Polytechnic Inst (NY)
Rhode Island Coll (RI)
Richmond, The American Intl U in London(United Kingdom)
Robert Morris U (PA)
Rockford Coll (IL)
Rockhurst U (MO)
Rocky Mountain Coll (AB, Canada)
Roger Williams U (RI)
Roosevelt U (IL)
Rosemont Coll (PA)
St. Bonaventure U (NY)
St. Cloud State U (MN)
St. Gregory's U (OK)
Saint John's U (MN)
St. John's U (NY)
St. Joseph's Coll, New York (NY)
St. Joseph's Coll, Suffolk Campus (NY)
Saint Joseph's U (PA)
Saint Louis U (MO)
Saint Mary-of-the-Woods Coll (IN)
Saint Mary's Coll of California (CA)
Saint Mary's U of Minnesota (MN)
St. Thomas Aquinas Coll (NY)
Saint Xavier U (IL)
Salem State Coll (MA)
Samford U (AL)
San Diego State U (CA)
San Francisco State U (CA)
San Jose State U (CA)
Sarah Lawrence Coll (NY)
Shawnee State U (OH)
Shimer Coll (IL)
Shorter Coll (GA)
Siena Heights U (MI)
Silver Lake Coll (WI)
Simpson Coll (IA)
Southern Connecticut State U (CT)
Southern Illinois U Carbondale (IL)
Southern Methodist U (TX)
Southern Oregon U (OR)
Southern Utah U (UT)
Southern Wesleyan U (SC)
Southwest Baptist U (MO)
Southwestern U (TX)
Spring Arbor U (MI)
State U of NY Coll at Old Westbury (NY)
State U of NY Empire State Coll (NY)
Stetson U (FL)
Stony Brook U, State U of New York (NY)
Suffolk U (MA)
Tabor Coll (KS)
Taylor U (IN)
Texas A&M Intl U (TX)
Texas A&M U–Commerce (TX)
Texas Wesleyan U (TX)
Thomas Edison State Coll (NJ)
Thomas U (GA)
Towson U (MD)
Trent U (ON, Canada)
Trevecca Nazarene U (TN)
Trinity Intl U (IL)
Trinity Western U (BC, Canada)
Tri-State U (IN)
Troy State U (AL)
Troy State U Dothan (AL)
Troy State U Montgomery (AL)
Union Coll (KY)
Union Coll (NE)
Union Coll (NY)
Union Inst & U (OH)
United States Air Force Acad (CO)
Université de Montréal (QC, Canada)
U du Québec à Hull (QC, Canada)
U Coll of the Cariboo (BC, Canada)
The U of Akron (OH)
U of Bridgeport (CT)
The U of British Columbia (BC, Canada)
U of Calif, Irvine (CA)
U of Calif, Riverside (CA)
U of Central Florida (FL)
U of Chicago (IL)
U of Cincinnati (OH)
U of Denver (CO)
The U of Findlay (OH)
U of Great Falls (MT)
U of Houston–Victoria (TX)
U of Kentucky (KY)
U of La Verne (CA)
The U of Lethbridge (AB, Canada)
U of Maine at Fort Kent (ME)
U of Mary (ND)
U of Maryland Eastern Shore (MD)
U of Maryland U Coll (MD)
U of Michigan (MI)
U of Michigan–Dearborn (MI)
U of Michigan–Flint (MI)
U of Minnesota, Morris (MN)
U of Mobile (AL)
The U of Montana–Missoula (MT)
The U of Montana–Western (MT)
U of Montevallo (AL)
U of Nevada, Las Vegas (NV)
U of North Dakota (ND)
U of Northern Colorado (CO)
U of North Texas (TX)
U of Ottawa (ON, Canada)
U of Pittsburgh (PA)
U of Pittsburgh at Bradford (PA)
U of Pittsburgh at Greensburg (PA)
U of Pittsburgh at Johnstown (PA)
U of Puerto Rico, Cayey U Coll (PR)
U of Regina (SK, Canada)
U of St. Thomas (MN)
U of Sioux Falls (SD)
U of Southern Indiana (IN)
U of Southern Maine (ME)
U of South Florida (FL)
The U of Tampa (FL)
The U of Texas–Pan American (TX)
U of the Ozarks (AR)
U of the Pacific (CA)
U of the Sacred Heart (PR)
U of the South (TN)
U of the Virgin Islands (VI)
U of Utah (UT)
U of Washington (WA)
U of West Florida (FL)
U of Windsor (ON, Canada)
U of Wisconsin–Madison (WI)
U of Wisconsin–Platteville (WI)
U of Wisconsin–River Falls (WI)
U of Wisconsin–Stevens Point (WI)
U of Wisconsin–Superior (WI)
U of Wisconsin–Whitewater (WI)
U of Wyoming (WY)
Upper Iowa U (IA)
Utica Coll (NY)
Valley City State U (ND)
Virginia Wesleyan Coll (VA)
Viterbo U (WI)
Warner Pacific Coll (OR)
Warner Southern Coll (FL)
Washington State U (WA)
Washington U in St. Louis (MO)
Wayland Baptist U (TX)
Waynesburg Coll (PA)
Wayne State Coll (NE)
Webster U (MO)
Wesleyan Coll (GA)
Wesleyan U (CT)
Western Baptist Coll (OR)
Western Carolina U (NC)
Western Connecticut State U (CT)
Western Kentucky U (KY)
Western Michigan U (MI)
Western Oregon U (OR)
Western State Coll of Colorado (CO)
Westfield State Coll (MA)
West Liberty State Coll (WV)
Westminster Coll (UT)
Westmont Coll (CA)
West Texas A&M U (TX)
Widener U (PA)
William Carey Coll (MS)
William Paterson U of New Jersey (NJ)
William Tyndale Coll (MI)
Wilson Coll (PA)
Wingate U (NC)
Winona State U (MN)
Winston-Salem State U (NC)
Wisconsin Lutheran Coll (WI)
Wittenberg U (OH)
Worcester Polytechnic Inst (MA)
York U (ON, Canada)
Youngstown State U (OH)

SOCIAL SCIENCES RELATED

Abilene Christian U (TX)
Adelphi U (NY)
Bethel Coll (KS)
Bloomsburg U of Pennsylvania (PA)
Boston U (MA)
Central Michigan U (MI)
Cleveland State U (OH)
Colby-Sawyer Coll (NH)
The Colorado Coll (CO)
Concordia U (CA)
Concordia U at Austin (TX)
Cornell U (NY)
Eastern Michigan U (MI)
Edinboro U of Pennsylvania (PA)
Georgetown U (DC)
Gettysburg Coll (PA)
Greenville Coll (IL)
Lehigh U (PA)
Liberty U (VA)
Long Island U, Southampton Coll (NY)
Marywood U (PA)
Midwestern State U (TX)
Millersville U of Pennsylvania (PA)
Mississippi Coll (MS)
Monmouth U (NJ)
Northwest Christian Coll (OR)
Northwestern U (IL)
Plymouth State U (NH)
Queens Coll of the City U of NY (NY)
Roosevelt U (IL)
Rutgers, The State U of New Jersey, New Brunswick/Piscataway (NJ)
Saint Mary's Coll of California (CA)
Saint Mary's U of Minnesota (MN)
San Diego State U (CA)
Sarah Lawrence Coll (NY)
Simon Fraser U (BC, Canada)
Skidmore Coll (NY)
Swarthmore Coll (PA)
Towson U (MD)
Transylvania U (KY)
The U of Akron (OH)
The U of Alabama at Birmingham (AL)
U of Calif, Berkeley (CA)
U of Denver (CO)
U of Hartford (CT)
U of Massachusetts Amherst (MA)
U of North Texas (TX)
U of Pittsburgh at Bradford (PA)
U of Rochester (NY)
U of Waterloo (ON, Canada)
U of West Florida (FL)
Ursinus Coll (PA)
Washington U in St. Louis (MO)
Wayland Baptist U (TX)

SOCIAL SCIENCE TEACHER EDUCATION

Alma Coll (MI)
Alverno Coll (WI)
Arkansas State U (AR)
Baylor U (TX)
Blue Mountain Coll (MS)
Bridgewater Coll (VA)
Brigham Young U (UT)
Brigham Young U–Hawaii (HI)
Buena Vista U (IA)
California Lutheran U (CA)
California State U, Chico (CA)
Campbellsville U (KY)
Carroll Coll (MT)
Carroll Coll (WI)
Central Methodist Coll (MO)
Central Michigan U (MI)
Central Washington U (WA)
Chadron State Coll (NE)
The Coll of St. Scholastica (MN)
Coll of Santa Fe (NM)
Columbus State U (GA)
Concordia U (IL)
Concordia U (NE)
Cornerstone U (MI)
Dana Coll (NE)
Delta State U (MS)
Dominican Coll (NY)
Dordt Coll (IA)
Eastern Illinois U (IL)
Eastern Mennonite U (VA)
Eastern Michigan U (MI)
East Stroudsburg U of Pennsylvania (PA)
Elmira Coll (NY)
Elon U (NC)
Emmanuel Coll (GA)
Emporia State U (KS)
Fayetteville State U (NC)
Florida Atlantic U (FL)
Florida Intl U (FL)
Florida State U (FL)
Grace U (NE)
Grambling State U (LA)
Hardin-Simmons U (TX)
Hastings Coll (NE)
Howard Payne U (TX)
Johnson State Coll (VT)
Judson Coll (AL)
Kennesaw State U (GA)
Lewis-Clark State Coll (ID)
Liberty U (VA)
Lincoln Memorial U (TN)
Lindenwood U (MO)
Lindsey Wilson Coll (KY)
Lyndon State Coll (VT)
Mansfield U of Pennsylvania (PA)
Marquette U (WI)
Mayville State U (ND)
McGill U (QC, Canada)
McKendree Coll (IL)
Mercyhurst Coll (PA)
Michigan State U (MI)
Millikin U (IL)
Minot State U (ND)
Mississippi Coll (MS)
Mississippi Valley State U (MS)
Montana State U–Billings (MT)
Murray State U (KY)
Nebraska Wesleyan U (NE)
Nevada State Coll at Henderson (NV)
North Dakota State U (ND)
Northern Arizona U (AZ)
Northern Michigan U (MI)
North Georgia Coll & State U (GA)
Northwest Nazarene U (ID)
Oakland City U (IN)
Oklahoma Baptist U (OK)
Point Park U (PA)
Rivier Coll (NH)
Sacred Heart U (CT)
St. Ambrose U (IA)
Saint Mary's U of Minnesota (MN)
Samford U (AL)
San Diego State U (CA)
Seattle Pacific U (WA)
Simpson Coll and Graduate School (CA)
Southern Nazarene U (OK)
Southwest Baptist U (MO)
Southwestern Oklahoma State U (OK)
State U of NY Coll at Oneonta (NY)
Stetson U (FL)
Taylor U (IN)
Union Coll (NE)
State U of NY at Albany (NY)
The U of Akron (OH)
The U of Arizona (AZ)
U of Central Florida (FL)
U of Detroit Mercy (MI)
U of Georgia (GA)
U of Great Falls (MT)
U of Hawaii at Manoa (HI)
U of Illinois at Chicago (IL)
U of Maine at Farmington (ME)
U of Maine at Fort Kent (ME)
U of Maine at Machias (ME)
U of Mary (ND)
U of Minnesota, Twin Cities Campus (MN)
The U of Montana–Missoula (MT)
The U of Montana–Western (MT)
U of Nebraska–Lincoln (NE)
U of Nevada, Reno (NV)
The U of North Carolina at Greensboro (NC)
U of Northern Iowa (IA)
U of Puerto Rico, Cayey U Coll (PR)
The U of South Dakota (SD)
U of South Florida (FL)
U of Utah (UT)
U of Vermont (VT)
U of West Florida (FL)
U of Wisconsin–River Falls (WI)
U of Wisconsin–Superior (WI)
Upper Iowa U (IA)
Utica Coll (NY)
Valley City State U (ND)
Valparaiso U (IN)
Warner Southern Coll (FL)
Wartburg Coll (IA)
Washington U in St. Louis (MO)
Weber State U (UT)
Western Baptist Coll (OR)
Western Michigan U (MI)
Westminster Coll (UT)
Westmont Coll (CA)
William Penn U (IA)
York Coll (NE)
York Coll of Pennsylvania (PA)
York U (ON, Canada)
Youngstown State U (OH)

SOCIAL STUDIES TEACHER EDUCATION

Abilene Christian U (TX)
Alma Coll (MI)
Alverno Coll (WI)
Appalachian State U (NC)
Aquinas Coll (MI)
Arkansas Tech U (AR)
Augustana Coll (SD)
Averett U (VA)
Baylor U (TX)
Bethany Coll (KS)
Bethel Coll (IN)

Bethel U (MN)
Bethune-Cookman Coll (FL)
Bloomfield Coll (NJ)
Bluefield Coll (VA)
Boston U (MA)
Bowling Green State U (OH)
Brescia U (KY)
Brooklyn Coll of the City U of NY (NY)
State U of NY Coll at Buffalo (NY)
Cabrini Coll (PA)
Calumet Coll of Saint Joseph (IN)
Campbellsville U (KY)
Campbell U (NC)
Capital U (OH)
Carlow Coll (PA)
Carroll Coll (WI)
Castleton State Coll (VT)
Cedarville U (OH)
Centenary Coll of Louisiana (LA)
Central Michigan U (MI)
Central Missouri State U (MO)
Central State U (OH)
Charleston Southern U (SC)
Chatham Coll (PA)
Citadel, The Military Coll of South Carolina (SC)
City Coll of the City U of NY (NY)
Clarion U of Pennsylvania (PA)
Clearwater Christian Coll (FL)
Colby-Sawyer Coll (NH)
Coll of St. Catherine (MN)
The Coll of Saint Rose (NY)
Colorado State U (CO)
Colorado State U-Pueblo (CO)
Columbia Coll (SC)
Concordia Coll (MN)
Concordia U (MI)
Concordia U (OR)
Concordia U, St. Paul (MN)
Cornerstone U (MI)
Crown Coll (MN)
Cumberland Coll (KY)
Daemen Coll (NY)
Dakota Wesleyan U (SD)
Dordt Coll (IA)
Dowling Coll (NY)
Duquesne U (PA)
East Carolina U (NC)
Eastern Michigan U (MI)
Eastern Washington U (WA)
East Texas Baptist U (TX)
Edinboro U of Pennsylvania (PA)
Elmira Coll (NY)
Elon U (NC)
Erskine Coll (SC)
Flagler Coll (FL)
Franklin Coll (IN)
George Fox U (OR)
Georgian Court U (NJ)
Glenville State Coll (WV)
Grand Valley State U (MI)
Greensboro Coll (NC)
Greenville Coll (IL)
Gustavus Adolphus Coll (MN)
Harding U (AR)
Hardin-Simmons U (TX)
Hastings Coll (NE)
Hofstra U (NY)
Hope Coll (MI)
Houston Baptist U (TX)
Howard Payne U (TX)
Huston-Tillotson Coll (TX)
Illinois State U (IL)
Indiana State U (IN)
Indiana U Bloomington (IN)
Indiana U Northwest (IN)
Indiana U of Pennsylvania (PA)
Indiana U–Purdue U Fort Wayne (IN)
Indiana U–Purdue U Indianapolis (IN)
Indiana U South Bend (IN)
Indiana U Southeast (IN)
Iona Coll (NY)
Ithaca Coll (NY)
Johnson State Coll (VT)
Juniata Coll (PA)
Kent State U (OH)
Kentucky State U (KY)
Kentucky Wesleyan Coll (KY)
Keuka Coll (NY)
Lebanon Valley Coll (PA)
Le Moyne Coll (NY)
Limestone Coll (SC)
Lincoln U (PA)
Long Island U, Brooklyn Campus (NY)
Long Island U, C.W. Post Campus (NY)
Long Island U, Southampton Coll (NY)
Louisiana State U in Shreveport (LA)
Louisiana Tech U (LA)
Madonna U (MI)
Malone Coll (OH)
Manhattanville Coll (NY)
Mansfield U of Pennsylvania (PA)
Marquette U (WI)
Marymount Coll of Fordham U (NY)
Maryville Coll (TN)
McGill U (QC, Canada)
McNeese State U (LA)
Messiah Coll (PA)
Miami U (OH)
Miami U Hamilton (OH)
MidAmerica Nazarene U (KS)
Millersville U of Pennsylvania (PA)
Minnesota State U Mankato (MN)
Minnesota State U Moorhead (MN)
Mississippi Coll (MS)
Molloy Coll (NY)
Moravian Coll (PA)
Morris Coll (SC)
Mount Vernon Nazarene U (OH)
Murray State U (KY)
Nazareth Coll of Rochester (NY)
New York Inst of Technology (NY)
New York U (NY)
Niagara U (NY)
North Carolina State U (NC)
Northern Michigan U (MI)
Northwestern Coll (MN)
Oakland City U (IN)
Ohio Dominican U (OH)
Ohio Northern U (OH)
Ohio U (OH)
Ohio Valley Coll (WV)
Ohio Wesleyan U (OH)
Oklahoma Baptist U (OK)
Oklahoma Christian U (OK)
Oral Roberts U (OK)
Ouachita Baptist U (AR)
Pace U (NY)
Penn State U Harrisburg Campus of the Capital Coll (PA)
Pfeiffer U (NC)
Philadelphia Biblical U (PA)
Pikeville Coll (KY)
Pillsbury Baptist Bible Coll (MN)
Pittsburg State U (KS)
Pontifical Catholic U of Puerto Rico (PR)
Queens Coll of the City U of NY (NY)
Roberts Wesleyan Coll (NY)
Rocky Mountain Coll (MT)
Saint Augustine's Coll (NC)
St. Bonaventure U (NY)
St. Edward's U (TX)
St. Francis Coll (NY)
Saint Francis U (PA)
St. Gregory's U (OK)
St. John's U (NY)
Saint Joseph's Coll of Maine (ME)
St. Mary's U of San Antonio (TX)
St. Olaf Coll (MN)
Seton Hill U (PA)
Shawnee State U (OH)
Southeastern Coll of the Assemblies of God (FL)
Southeastern Louisiana U (LA)
Southeastern Oklahoma State U (OK)
Southeast Missouri State U (MO)
Southern Arkansas U–Magnolia (AR)
Southern Nazarene U (OK)
Southwest Baptist U (MO)
State U of NY Coll at Brockport (NY)
State U of NY Coll at Cortland (NY)
State U of NY Coll at Old Westbury (NY)
State U of NY Coll at Potsdam (NY)
Syracuse U (NY)
Texas A&M Intl U (TX)
Texas Christian U (TX)
Texas Lutheran U (TX)
Texas Wesleyan U (TX)
Thomas More Coll (KY)
Tri-State U (IN)
Universidad Adventista de las Antillas (PR)
The U of Akron (OH)
The U of Arizona (AZ)
U of Central Arkansas (AR)
U of Charleston (WV)
U of Detroit Mercy (MI)
U of Great Falls (MT)
U of Hawaii at Manoa (HI)
U of Illinois at Urbana–Champaign (IL)
U of Indianapolis (IN)
The U of Iowa (IA)
The U of Lethbridge (AB, Canada)
U of Louisiana at Lafayette (LA)
U of Maryland, Coll Park (MD)
U of Minnesota, Duluth (MN)
U of Mississippi (MS)
U of Missouri–Columbia (MO)
U of Missouri–St. Louis (MO)
U of Nevada, Reno (NV)
U of New Orleans (LA)
The U of North Carolina at Chapel Hill (NC)
The U of North Carolina at Greensboro (NC)
The U of North Carolina at Pembroke (NC)
U of Northern Iowa (IA)
U of Oklahoma (OK)
U of Pittsburgh at Johnstown (PA)
U of Puerto Rico, Cayey U Coll (PR)
U of Regina (SK, Canada)
U of St. Francis (IL)
U of Saint Francis (IN)
U of St. Thomas (MN)
U of the Ozarks (AR)
U of Toledo (OH)
U of Utah (UT)
U of Wisconsin–Eau Claire (WI)
U of Wisconsin–La Crosse (WI)
U of Wisconsin–River Falls (WI)
U of Wisconsin–Superior (WI)
Ursuline Coll (OH)
Utah State U (UT)
Utica Coll (NY)
Valdosta State U (GA)
Virginia Intermont Coll (VA)
Viterbo U (WI)
Waldorf Coll (IA)
Washington U in St. Louis (MO)
Waynesburg Coll (PA)
Wayne State U (MI)
Weber State U (UT)
West Chester U of Pennsylvania (PA)
Western Baptist Coll (OR)
Western Carolina U (NC)
Wheaton Coll (IL)
Wheeling Jesuit U (WV)
Widener U (PA)
William Carey Coll (MS)
Winston-Salem State U (NC)
Wright State U (OH)
Xavier U of Louisiana (LA)
York Coll (NE)
York Coll of Pennsylvania (PA)
York U (ON, Canada)
Youngstown State U (OH)

SOCIAL WORK

Abilene Christian U (TX)
Adelphi U (NY)
Adrian Coll (MI)
Alabama Ag and Mech U (AL)
Alabama State U (AL)
Albany State U (GA)
Albertus Magnus Coll (CT)
Alvernia Coll (PA)
Andrews U (MI)
Anna Maria Coll (MA)
Appalachian State U (NC)
Arizona State U (AZ)
Arizona State U West (AZ)
Arkansas Baptist Coll (AR)
Arkansas State U (AR)
Asbury Coll (KY)
Ashland U (OH)
Atlantic Union Coll (MA)
Auburn U (AL)
Augsburg Coll (MN)
Augustana Coll (SD)
Aurora U (IL)
Austin Peay State U (TN)
Avila U (MO)
Azusa Pacific U (CA)
Ball State U (IN)
Barton Coll (NC)
Baylor U (TX)
Belmont U (TN)
Bemidji State U (MN)
Bethany Coll (KS)
Bethany Coll (WV)
Bethel Coll (KS)
Bethel U (MN)
Bloomsburg U of Pennsylvania (PA)
Bluffton Coll (OH)
Boise State U (ID)
Bowie State U (MD)
Bowling Green State U (OH)
Bradley U (IL)
Brescia U (KY)
Briar Cliff U (IA)
Bridgewater State Coll (MA)
Brigham Young U (UT)
Brigham Young U–Hawaii (HI)
Buena Vista U (IA)
State U of NY Coll at Buffalo (NY)
Cabrini Coll (PA)
California State U, Chico (CA)
California State U, Fresno (CA)
California State U, Hayward (CA)
California State U, Long Beach (CA)
California State U, Los Angeles (CA)
California State U, Sacramento (CA)
California State U, San Bernardino (CA)
California U of Pennsylvania (PA)
Calvin Coll (MI)
Campbellsville U (KY)
Campbell U (NC)
Capital U (OH)
Carleton U (ON, Canada)
Carlow Coll (PA)
Carroll Coll (MT)
Carthage Coll (WI)
Castleton State Coll (VT)
The Catholic U of America (DC)
Cedar Crest Coll (PA)
Cedarville U (OH)
Central Connecticut State U (CT)
Central Michigan U (MI)
Central Missouri State U (MO)
Central State U (OH)
Chadron State Coll (NE)
Champlain Coll (VT)
Chapman U (CA)
Chatham Coll (PA)
Christopher Newport U (VA)
Clark Atlanta U (GA)
Clarke Coll (IA)
Cleveland State U (OH)
Coker Coll (SC)
Coll Misericordia (PA)
Coll of Mount St. Joseph (OH)
The Coll of New Rochelle (NY)
Coll of Saint Benedict (MN)
Coll of St. Catherine (MN)
The Coll of Saint Rose (NY)
The Coll of St. Scholastica (MN)
Coll of Staten Island of the City U of NY (NY)
Coll of the Ozarks (MO)
Colorado State U (CO)
Colorado State U-Pueblo (CO)
Columbia Coll (MO)
Columbia Coll (SC)
Concord Coll (WV)
Concordia Coll (MN)
Concordia Coll (NY)
Concordia U (IL)
Concordia U (OR)
Concordia U Wisconsin (WI)
Cornerstone U (MI)
Creighton U (NE)
Cumberland Coll (KY)
Daemen Coll (NY)
Dalhousie U (NS, Canada)
Dalton State Coll (GA)
Dana Coll (NE)
Defiance Coll (OH)
Delaware State U (DE)
Delta State U (MS)
Dickinson State U (ND)
Dillard U (LA)
Dominican Coll (NY)
Dordt Coll (IA)
East Carolina U (NC)
East Central U (OK)
Eastern Connecticut State U (CT)
Eastern Kentucky U (KY)
Eastern Mennonite U (VA)
Eastern Michigan U (MI)
Eastern Nazarene Coll (MA)
Eastern U (PA)
Eastern Washington U (WA)
Edinboro U of Pennsylvania (PA)
Elizabeth City State U (NC)
Elizabethtown Coll (PA)
Elmira Coll (NY)
Elms Coll (MA)
Evangel U (MO)
Ferris State U (MI)
Ferrum Coll (VA)
Florida Ag and Mech U (FL)
Florida Atlantic U (FL)
Florida Intl U (FL)
Florida State U (FL)
Fordham U (NY)
Fort Hays State U (KS)
Fort Valley State U (GA)
Franciscan U of Steubenville (OH)
Franklin Pierce Coll (NH)
Freed-Hardeman U (TN)
Fresno Pacific U (CA)
Frostburg State U (MD)
Gallaudet U (DC)
Gannon U (PA)
Geneva Coll (PA)
George Fox U (OR)
George Mason U (VA)
Georgian Court U (NJ)
Georgia State U (GA)
Gordon Coll (MA)
Goshen Coll (IN)
Governors State U (IL)
Grace Coll (IN)
Graceland U (IA)
Grambling State U (LA)
Grand Valley State U (MI)
Greenville Coll (IL)
Gwynedd-Mercy Coll (PA)
Hampton U (VA)
Harding U (AR)
Hardin-Simmons U (TX)
Hawai'i Pacific U (HI)
Henderson State U (AR)
Hood Coll (MD)
Hope Coll (MI)
Howard Payne U (TX)
Howard U (DC)
Humboldt State U (CA)
Idaho State U (ID)
Illinois State U (IL)
Immaculata U (PA)
Indiana State U (IN)
Indiana U Bloomington (IN)
Indiana U East (IN)
Indiana U–Purdue U Indianapolis (IN)
Inter American U of PR, Fajardo Campus (PR)
Iona Coll (NY)
Jacksonville State U (AL)
James Madison U (VA)
Johnson C. Smith U (NC)
Juniata Coll (PA)
Kansas State U (KS)
Kean U (NJ)
Kennesaw State U (GA)
Kentucky Christian Coll (KY)
Kentucky State U (KY)
Keuka Coll (NY)
Kutztown U of Pennsylvania (PA)
LaGrange Coll (GA)
Lakehead U (ON, Canada)
Lamar U (TX)
Lancaster Bible Coll (PA)
La Salle U (PA)
Laurentian U (ON, Canada)
Lehman Coll of the City U of NY (NY)
Lewis-Clark State Coll (ID)
Lewis U (IL)
Limestone Coll (SC)
Lincoln Memorial U (TN)
Lindenwood U (MO)
Lipscomb U (TN)
Livingstone Coll (NC)
Lock Haven U of Pennsylvania (PA)
Long Island U, Brooklyn Campus (NY)
Long Island U, C.W. Post Campus (NY)
Longwood U (VA)
Loras Coll (IA)
Louisiana Coll (LA)
Lourdes Coll (OH)
Loyola U Chicago (IL)
Lubbock Christian U (TX)
Luther Coll (IA)
MacMurray Coll (IL)
Madonna U (MI)
Malone Coll (OH)
Manchester Coll (IN)
Mansfield U of Pennsylvania (PA)
Marian Coll of Fond du Lac (WI)
Marist Coll (NY)
Marquette U (WI)
Marshall U (WV)
Mars Hill Coll (NC)
Mary Baldwin Coll (VA)
Marygrove Coll (MI)
Marymount Coll of Fordham U (NY)
Marywood U (PA)
Massachusetts Coll of Liberal Arts (MA)
McDaniel Coll (MD)
McGill U (QC, Canada)
McKendree Coll (IL)
Memorial U of Newfoundland (NL, Canada)
Mercy Coll (NY)
Mercyhurst Coll (PA)
Meredith Coll (NC)
Messiah Coll (PA)
Methodist Coll (NC)
Metropolitan State Coll of Denver (CO)
Metropolitan State U (MN)
Miami U (OH)
Michigan State U (MI)
Middle Tennessee State U (TN)
Midwestern State U (TX)
Miles Coll (AL)
Millersville U of Pennsylvania (PA)
Minnesota State U Mankato (MN)
Minnesota State U Moorhead (MN)
Minot State U (ND)
Mississippi Coll (MS)

Mississippi State U (MS)
Mississippi Valley State U (MS)
Missouri Western State Coll (MO)
Molloy Coll (NY)
Monmouth U (NJ)
Morehead State U (KY)
Morgan State U (MD)
Mountain State U (WV)
Mount Ida Coll (MA)
Mount Mary Coll (WI)
Mount Mercy Coll (IA)
Mount Vernon Nazarene U (OH)
Murray State U (KY)
Nazareth Coll of Rochester (NY)
Nebraska Wesleyan U (NE)
New Mexico Highlands U (NM)
New Mexico State U (NM)
New York U (NY)
Niagara U (NY)
Norfolk State U (VA)
North Carolina Central U (NC)
North Carolina State U (NC)
Northeastern Illinois U (IL)
Northeastern State U (OK)
Northern Arizona U (AZ)
Northern Michigan U (MI)
Northwestern Coll (IA)
Northwestern Oklahoma State U (OK)
Northwestern State U of Louisiana (LA)
Northwest Nazarene U (ID)
Nyack Coll (NY)
Oglethorpe U (GA)
Ohio Dominican U (OH)
The Ohio State U (OH)
Ohio U (OH)
Okanagan U Coll (BC, Canada)
Oklahoma Baptist U (OK)
Oral Roberts U (OK)
Our Lady of the Lake U of San Antonio (TX)
Pacific Lutheran U (WA)
Pacific Union Coll (CA)
Pacific U (OR)
Philadelphia Biblical U (PA)
Pittsburg State U (KS)
Plymouth State U (NH)
Point Loma Nazarene U (CA)
Pontifical Catholic U of Puerto Rico (PR)
Prairie View A&M U (TX)
Presentation Coll (SD)
Providence Coll (RI)
Quincy U (IL)
Radford U (VA)
Ramapo Coll of New Jersey (NJ)
Redeemer U Coll (ON, Canada)
Reformed Bible Coll (MI)
Regis Coll (MA)
Rhode Island Coll (RI)
The Richard Stockton Coll of New Jersey (NJ)
Roberts Wesleyan Coll (NY)
Rochester Inst of Technology (NY)
Rockford Coll (IL)
Rutgers, The State U of New Jersey, Camden (NJ)
Rutgers, The State U of New Jersey, Newark (NJ)
Rutgers, The State U of New Jersey, New Brunswick/Piscataway (NJ)
Ryerson U (ON, Canada)
Sacred Heart U (CT)
Saginaw Valley State U (MI)
St. Augustine Coll (IL)
St. Cloud State U (MN)
St. Edward's U (TX)
Saint Francis U (PA)
Saint John's U (MN)
Saint Joseph Coll (CT)
Saint Joseph's Coll (IN)
Saint Joseph's Coll of Maine (ME)
Saint Leo U (FL)
Saint Louis U (MO)
Saint Mary's Coll (IN)
St. Olaf Coll (MN)
St. Thomas U (NB, Canada)
Salem State Coll (MA)
Salisbury U (MD)
Salve Regina U (RI)
San Diego State U (CA)
San Francisco State U (CA)
San Jose State U (CA)
Seattle U (WA)
Seton Hall U (NJ)
Seton Hill U (PA)
Shaw U (NC)
Shepherd U (WV)
Shippensburg U of Pennsylvania (PA)
Siena Coll (NY)
Siena Heights U (MI)
Skidmore Coll (NY)
Slippery Rock U of Pennsylvania (PA)
South Carolina State U (SC)
Southeastern Coll of the Assemblies of God (FL)
Southeastern Louisiana U (LA)
Southeast Missouri State U (MO)
Southern Adventist U (TN)
Southern Arkansas U–Magnolia (AR)
Southern Connecticut State U (CT)
Southern Illinois U Carbondale (IL)
Southern Illinois U Edwardsville (IL)
Southern Nazarene U (OK)
Southern U and A&M Coll (LA)
Southwestern Oklahoma State U (OK)
Southwest Missouri State U (MO)
Spring Arbor U (MI)
State U of NY at New Paltz (NY)
Plattsburgh State U of NY (NY)
State U of NY Coll at Brockport (NY)
State U of NY Coll at Cortland (NY)
State U of NY Coll at Fredonia (NY)
Stony Brook U, State U of New York (NY)
Suffolk U (MA)
Syracuse U (NY)
Talladega Coll (AL)
Tarleton State U (TX)
Taylor U (IN)
Taylor U, Fort Wayne Campus (IN)
Tennessee State U (TN)
Tennessee Technological U (TN)
Texas A&M U–Commerce (TX)
Texas A&M U–Kingsville (TX)
Texas Christian U (TX)
Texas Southern U (TX)
Texas State U-San Marcos (TX)
Texas Tech U (TX)
Texas Woman's U (TX)
Thomas U (GA)
Trinity Christian Coll (IL)
Troy State U (AL)
Tuskegee U (AL)
Union Coll (NE)
Union Inst & U (OH)
Union U (TN)
Université de Montréal (QC, Canada)
Université de Sherbrooke (QC, Canada)
U du Québec à Hull (QC, Canada)
Université Laval (QC, Canada)
State U of NY at Albany (NY)
U at Buffalo, The State U of New York (NY)
U Coll of the Cariboo (BC, Canada)
U Coll of the Fraser Valley (BC, Canada)
The U of Akron (OH)
The U of Alabama (AL)
The U of Alabama at Birmingham (AL)
U of Alaska Fairbanks (AK)
U of Arkansas (AR)
U of Arkansas at Little Rock (AR)
U of Arkansas at Monticello (AR)
The U of British Columbia (BC, Canada)
U of Calgary (AB, Canada)
U of Calif, Berkeley (CA)
U of Calif, Los Angeles (CA)
U of Central Florida (FL)
U of Cincinnati (OH)
U of Detroit Mercy (MI)
The U of Findlay (OH)
U of Georgia (GA)
U of Hawaii at Manoa (HI)
U of Houston–Clear Lake (TX)
U of Illinois at Chicago (IL)
U of Illinois at Springfield (IL)
U of Indianapolis (IN)
The U of Iowa (IA)
U of Kansas (KS)
U of Kentucky (KY)
U of Maine (ME)
U of Maine at Presque Isle (ME)
U of Manitoba (MB, Canada)
U of Mary (ND)
U of Mary Hardin-Baylor (TX)
U of Maryland, Baltimore County (MD)
U of Maryland Eastern Shore (MD)
The U of Memphis (TN)
U of Michigan–Flint (MI)
U of Mississippi (MS)
U of Missouri–Columbia (MO)
U of Missouri–St. Louis (MO)
The U of Montana–Missoula (MT)
U of Montevallo (AL)
U of Nebraska at Omaha (NE)
U of Nevada, Las Vegas (NV)
U of Nevada, Reno (NV)
U of New Hampshire (NH)
U of North Alabama (AL)
The U of North Carolina at Charlotte (NC)
The U of North Carolina at Greensboro (NC)
The U of North Carolina at Pembroke (NC)
The U of North Carolina at Wilmington (NC)
U of North Dakota (ND)
U of Northern Iowa (IA)
U of North Texas (TX)
U of Oklahoma (OK)
U of Pittsburgh (PA)
U of Portland (OR)
U of Regina (SK, Canada)
U of St. Francis (IL)
U of Saint Francis (IN)
U of St. Thomas (MN)
U of Sioux Falls (SD)
The U of South Dakota (SD)
U of Southern Indiana (IN)
U of Southern Maine (ME)
U of South Florida (FL)
The U of Tennessee (TN)
The U of Tennessee at Chattanooga (TN)
The U of Tennessee at Martin (TN)
The U of Texas at Arlington (TX)
The U of Texas at Austin (TX)
The U of Texas–Pan American (TX)
U of the District of Columbia (DC)
U of the Sacred Heart (PR)
U of the Virgin Islands (VI)
U of Toledo (OH)
U of Utah (UT)
U of Vermont (VT)
U of Victoria (BC, Canada)
U of Washington (WA)
U of Waterloo (ON, Canada)
The U of Western Ontario (ON, Canada)
U of West Florida (FL)
U of Windsor (ON, Canada)
U of Wisconsin–Eau Claire (WI)
U of Wisconsin–Green Bay (WI)
U of Wisconsin–Madison (WI)
U of Wisconsin–Milwaukee (WI)
U of Wisconsin–Oshkosh (WI)
U of Wisconsin–River Falls (WI)
U of Wisconsin–Superior (WI)
U of Wisconsin–Whitewater (WI)
U of Wyoming (WY)
Ursuline Coll (OH)
Utah State U (UT)
Valparaiso U (IN)
Virginia Commonwealth U (VA)
Virginia Intermont Coll (VA)
Virginia State U (VA)
Virginia Union U (VA)
Viterbo U (WI)
Walla Walla Coll (WA)
Warner Pacific Coll (OR)
Warner Southern Coll (FL)
Warren Wilson Coll (NC)
Wartburg Coll (IA)
Washburn U (KS)
Washington State U (WA)
Wayne State U (MI)
Weber State U (UT)
West Chester U of Pennsylvania (PA)
Western Carolina U (NC)
Western Connecticut State U (CT)
Western Illinois U (IL)
Western Kentucky U (KY)
Western Michigan U (MI)
Western New England Coll (MA)
West Texas A&M U (TX)
West Virginia State Coll (WV)
West Virginia U (WV)
Wheelock Coll (MA)
Wichita State U (KS)
Widener U (PA)
William Woods U (MO)
Winona State U (MN)
Winthrop U (SC)
Wright State U (OH)
Xavier U (OH)
York Coll of the City U of New York (NY)
York U (ON, Canada)
Youngstown State U (OH)

SOCIAL WORK RELATED

Miami U Hamilton (OH)

SOCIOBIOLOGY

Beloit Coll (WI)
Cornell U (NY)
Hampshire Coll (MA)
Harvard U (MA)
Tufts U (MA)

SOCIOLOGY

Abilene Christian U (TX)
Acadia U (NS, Canada)
Adams State Coll (CO)
Adelphi U (NY)
Adrian Coll (MI)
Agnes Scott Coll (GA)
Alabama Ag and Mech U (AL)
Alabama State U (AL)
Albany State U (GA)
Albertson Coll of Idaho (ID)
Albertus Magnus Coll (CT)
Albion Coll (MI)
Albright Coll (PA)
Alcorn State U (MS)
Alderson-Broaddus Coll (WV)
Alfred U (NY)
Alma Coll (MI)
American Intl Coll (MA)
American U (DC)
The American U in Cairo(Egypt)
Amherst Coll (MA)
Andrews U (MI)
Angelo State U (TX)
Antioch Coll (OH)
Appalachian State U (NC)
Aquinas Coll (MI)
Arcadia U (PA)
Arizona State U (AZ)
Arizona State U West (AZ)
Arkansas State U (AR)
Arkansas Tech U (AR)
Asbury Coll (KY)
Ashland U (OH)
Assumption Coll (MA)
Athabasca U (AB, Canada)
Athens State U (AL)
Atlantic Baptist U (NB, Canada)
Atlantic Union Coll (MA)
Auburn U (AL)
Auburn U Montgomery (AL)
Augsburg Coll (MN)
Augustana Coll (IL)
Augustana Coll (SD)
Augusta State U (GA)
Aurora U (IL)
Austin Coll (TX)
Austin Peay State U (TN)
Averett U (VA)
Avila U (MO)
Azusa Pacific U (CA)
Baker U (KS)
Baldwin-Wallace Coll (OH)
Ball State U (IN)
Barber-Scotia Coll (NC)
Bard Coll (NY)
Barnard Coll (NY)
Barry U (FL)
Bates Coll (ME)
Baylor U (TX)
Bellarmine U (KY)
Belmont Abbey Coll (NC)
Belmont U (TN)
Beloit Coll (WI)
Bemidji State U (MN)
Benedictine Coll (KS)
Benedictine U (IL)
Bennington Coll (VT)
Berea Coll (KY)
Baruch Coll of the City U of NY (NY)
Berry Coll (GA)
Bethany Coll (KS)
Bethany Lutheran Coll (MN)
Bethel Coll (IN)
Bethune-Cookman Coll (FL)
Biola U (CA)
Birmingham-Southern Coll (AL)
Bishop's U (QC, Canada)
Black Hills State U (SD)
Bloomfield Coll (NJ)
Bloomsburg U of Pennsylvania (PA)
Bluefield Coll (VA)
Bluffton Coll (OH)
Boise State U (ID)
Boston Coll (MA)
Boston U (MA)
Bowdoin Coll (ME)
Bowie State U (MD)
Bowling Green State U (OH)
Bradley U (IL)
Brandeis U (MA)
Brewton-Parker Coll (GA)
Briar Cliff U (IA)
Bridgewater Coll (VA)
Bridgewater State Coll (MA)
Brigham Young U (UT)
Brock U (ON, Canada)
Brooklyn Coll of the City U of NY (NY)
Brown U (RI)
Bryn Mawr Coll (PA)
Bucknell U (PA)
Buena Vista U (IA)
State U of NY Coll at Buffalo (NY)
Butler U (IN)
Cabrini Coll (PA)
Caldwell Coll (NJ)
California Baptist U (CA)
California Lutheran U (CA)
California State Polytechnic U, Pomona (CA)
California State U, Chico (CA)
California State U, Dominguez Hills (CA)
California State U, Fresno (CA)
California State U, Fullerton (CA)
California State U, Hayward (CA)
California State U, Long Beach (CA)
California State U, Los Angeles (CA)
California State U, Sacramento (CA)
California State U, San Bernardino (CA)
California State U, San Marcos (CA)
California State U, Stanislaus (CA)
California U of Pennsylvania (PA)
Calvin Coll (MI)
Cameron U (OK)
Campbellsville U (KY)
Canisius Coll (NY)
Capital U (OH)
Cardinal Stritch U (WI)
Carleton Coll (MN)
Carleton U (ON, Canada)
Carlow Coll (PA)
Carroll Coll (MT)
Carroll Coll (WI)
Carson-Newman Coll (TN)
Carthage Coll (WI)
Case Western Reserve U (OH)
Castleton State Coll (VT)
Catawba Coll (NC)
The Catholic U of America (DC)
Cedarville U (OH)
Centenary Coll (NJ)
Centenary Coll of Louisiana (LA)
Central Coll (IA)
Central Connecticut State U (CT)
Central Methodist Coll (MO)
Central Michigan U (MI)
Central Missouri State U (MO)
Central State U (OH)
Central Washington U (WA)
Centre Coll (KY)
Chadron State Coll (NE)
Chapman U (CA)
Charleston Southern U (SC)
Chestnut Hill Coll (PA)
Cheyney U of Pennsylvania (PA)
Chicago State U (IL)
Christopher Newport U (VA)
City Coll of the City U of NY (NY)
Claremont McKenna Coll (CA)
Clarion U of Pennsylvania (PA)
Clark Atlanta U (GA)
Clarke Coll (IA)
Clarkson U (NY)
Clark U (MA)
Clemson U (SC)
Cleveland State U (OH)
Coastal Carolina U (SC)
Coe Coll (IA)
Coker Coll (SC)
Colby Coll (ME)
Colgate U (NY)
Coll of Charleston (SC)
Coll of Mount St. Joseph (OH)
Coll of Mount Saint Vincent (NY)
The Coll of New Jersey (NJ)
The Coll of New Rochelle (NY)
Coll of Saint Benedict (MN)
Coll of St. Catherine (MN)
Coll of Saint Elizabeth (NJ)
The Coll of Saint Rose (NY)
The Coll of Southeastern Europe, The American U of Athens(Greece)
Coll of the Holy Cross (MA)
Coll of the Ozarks (MO)
The Coll of William and Mary (VA)
The Coll of Wooster (OH)
The Colorado Coll (CO)
Colorado State U (CO)
Colorado State U-Pueblo (CO)
Columbia Coll (MO)
Columbia Coll (NY)
Columbia U, School of General Studies (NY)
Columbus State U (GA)
Concord Coll (WV)
Concordia Coll (MN)
Concordia U (IL)
Concordia U (NE)
Concordia U (QC, Canada)
Concordia U Coll of Alberta (AB, Canada)
Concordia U, St. Paul (MN)

Connecticut Coll (CT)
Converse Coll (SC)
Cornell Coll (IA)
Cornell U (NY)
Cornerstone U (MI)
Covenant Coll (GA)
Creighton U (NE)
Culver-Stockton Coll (MO)
Cumberland U (TN)
Curry Coll (MA)
Dakota Wesleyan U (SD)
Dalhousie U (NS, Canada)
Dallas Baptist U (TX)
Dana Coll (NE)
Dartmouth Coll (NH)
Davidson Coll (NC)
Davis & Elkins Coll (WV)
Delaware State U (DE)
Denison U (OH)
DePaul U (IL)
DePauw U (IN)
Dickinson Coll (PA)
Dillard U (LA)
Doane Coll (NE)
Dominican U (IL)
Dordt Coll (IA)
Dowling Coll (NY)
Drake U (IA)
Drew U (NJ)
Drexel U (PA)
Duke U (NC)
Duquesne U (PA)
D'Youville Coll (NY)
Earlham Coll (IN)
East Carolina U (NC)
East Central U (OK)
Eastern Connecticut State U (CT)
Eastern Illinois U (IL)
Eastern Kentucky U (KY)
Eastern Mennonite U (VA)
Eastern Michigan U (MI)
Eastern Nazarene Coll (MA)
Eastern New Mexico U (NM)
Eastern Oregon U (OR)
Eastern U (PA)
Eastern Washington U (WA)
East Stroudsburg U of Pennsylvania (PA)
East Texas Baptist U (TX)
Eckerd Coll (FL)
Edgewood Coll (WI)
Edinboro U of Pennsylvania (PA)
Elizabeth City State U (NC)
Elizabethtown Coll (PA)
Elmhurst Coll (IL)
Elmira Coll (NY)
Elms Coll (MA)
Elon U (NC)
Emory & Henry Coll (VA)
Emory U (GA)
Emporia State U (KS)
Eugene Lang Coll, New School U (NY)
Eureka Coll (IL)
Evangel U (MO)
Excelsior Coll (NY)
Fairfield U (CT)
Fairleigh Dickinson U, Florham (NJ)
Fairleigh Dickinson U, Teaneck-Metro Campus (NJ)
Fairmont State Coll (WV)
Fayetteville State U (NC)
Flagler Coll (FL)
Florida Ag and Mech U (FL)
Florida Atlantic U (FL)
Florida Intl U (FL)
Florida Southern Coll (FL)
Florida State U (FL)
Fordham U (NY)
Fort Hays State U (KS)
Fort Lewis Coll (CO)
Fort Valley State U (GA)
Framingham State Coll (MA)
Franciscan U of Steubenville (OH)
Francis Marion U (SC)
Franklin and Marshall Coll (PA)
Franklin Coll (IN)
Franklin Pierce Coll (NH)
Frostburg State U (MD)
Furman U (SC)
Gallaudet U (DC)
Gardner-Webb U (NC)
Geneva Coll (PA)
George Fox U (OR)
George Mason U (VA)
Georgetown Coll (KY)
Georgetown U (DC)
The George Washington U (DC)
Georgia Coll & State U (GA)
Georgian Court U (NJ)
Georgia Southern U (GA)
Georgia Southwestern State U (GA)
Georgia State U (GA)
Gettysburg Coll (PA)
Gonzaga U (WA)
Gordon Coll (MA)
Goshen Coll (IN)
Goucher Coll (MD)
Grace Coll (IN)
Graceland U (IA)
Grambling State U (LA)
Grand Canyon U (AZ)
Grand Valley State U (MI)
Greensboro Coll (NC)
Greenville Coll (IL)
Grinnell Coll (IA)
Grove City Coll (PA)
Guilford Coll (NC)
Gustavus Adolphus Coll (MN)
Gwynedd-Mercy Coll (PA)
Hamilton Coll (NY)
Hamline U (MN)
Hampshire Coll (MA)
Hampton U (VA)
Hannibal-LaGrange Coll (MO)
Hanover Coll (IN)
Hardin-Simmons U (TX)
Hartwick Coll (NY)
Harvard U (MA)
Hastings Coll (NE)
Haverford Coll (PA)
Hawai'i Pacific U (HI)
Henderson State U (AR)
Hendrix Coll (AR)
High Point U (NC)
Hillsdale Coll (MI)
Hiram Coll (OH)
Hobart and William Smith Colls (NY)
Hofstra U (NY)
Hollins U (VA)
Holy Names Coll (CA)
Hood Coll (MD)
Hope Coll (MI)
Houghton Coll (NY)
Houston Baptist U (TX)
Howard Payne U (TX)
Howard U (DC)
Humboldt State U (CA)
Hunter Coll of the City U of NY (NY)
Huntington Coll (IN)
Huston-Tillotson Coll (TX)
Idaho State U (ID)
Illinois Coll (IL)
Illinois State U (IL)
Illinois Wesleyan U (IL)
Immaculata U (PA)
Indiana State U (IN)
Indiana U Bloomington (IN)
Indiana U East (IN)
Indiana U Kokomo (IN)
Indiana U Northwest (IN)
Indiana U of Pennsylvania (PA)
Indiana U–Purdue U Fort Wayne (IN)
Indiana U–Purdue U Indianapolis (IN)
Indiana U South Bend (IN)
Indiana U Southeast (IN)
Inter American U of PR, Fajardo Campus (PR)
Inter American U of PR, San Germán Campus (PR)
Iona Coll (NY)
Iowa State U of Science and Technology (IA)
Ithaca Coll (NY)
Jacksonville State U (AL)
Jacksonville U (FL)
James Madison U (VA)
Jarvis Christian Coll (TX)
John Carroll U (OH)
The Johns Hopkins U (MD)
Johnson C. Smith U (NC)
Johnson State Coll (VT)
Judson Coll (IL)
Juniata Coll (PA)
Kalamazoo Coll (MI)
Kansas State U (KS)
Kansas Wesleyan U (KS)
Kean U (NJ)
Keene State Coll (NH)
Kennesaw State U (GA)
Kent State U (OH)
Kentucky State U (KY)
Kentucky Wesleyan Coll (KY)
Kenyon Coll (OH)
Keuka Coll (NY)
King's Coll (PA)
The King's U Coll (AB, Canada)
Knox Coll (IL)
Kutztown U of Pennsylvania (PA)
Lafayette Coll (PA)
Lake Erie Coll (OH)
Lake Forest Coll (IL)
Lakehead U (ON, Canada)
Lakeland Coll (WI)
Lake Superior State U (MI)
Lamar U (TX)
Lambuth U (TN)
Lander U (SC)
Lane Coll (TN)
La Roche Coll (PA)
La Salle U (PA)
Lasell Coll (MA)
Laurentian U (ON, Canada)
Lebanon Valley Coll (PA)
Lehigh U (PA)
Lehman Coll of the City U of NY (NY)
Le Moyne Coll (NY)
Lenoir-Rhyne Coll (NC)
Lewis & Clark Coll (OR)
Lewis U (IL)
Lincoln U (MO)
Lincoln U (PA)
Lindenwood U (MO)
Linfield Coll (OR)
Livingstone Coll (NC)
Lock Haven U of Pennsylvania (PA)
Long Island U, Brooklyn Campus (NY)
Long Island U, C.W. Post Campus (NY)
Long Island U, Southampton Coll (NY)
Longwood U (VA)
Loras Coll (IA)
Louisiana Coll (LA)
Louisiana State U and A&M Coll (LA)
Louisiana State U in Shreveport (LA)
Louisiana Tech U (LA)
Lourdes Coll (OH)
Loyola Coll in Maryland (MD)
Loyola Marymount U (CA)
Loyola U Chicago (IL)
Loyola U New Orleans (LA)
Luther Coll (IA)
Lycoming Coll (PA)
Lynchburg Coll (VA)
Macalester Coll (MN)
Madonna U (MI)
Malaspina U-Coll (BC, Canada)
Manchester Coll (IN)
Manhattan Coll (NY)
Manhattanville Coll (NY)
Mansfield U of Pennsylvania (PA)
Marian Coll (IN)
Marian Coll of Fond du Lac (WI)
Marlboro Coll (VT)
Marquette U (WI)
Marshall U (WV)
Mars Hill Coll (NC)
Martin U (IN)
Mary Baldwin Coll (VA)
Marymount Coll of Fordham U (NY)
Marymount Manhattan Coll (NY)
Marymount U (VA)
Maryville Coll (TN)
Maryville U of Saint Louis (MO)
Mary Washington Coll (VA)
Massachusetts Coll of Liberal Arts (MA)
McDaniel Coll (MD)
McGill U (QC, Canada)
McKendree Coll (IL)
McMurry U (TX)
McNeese State U (LA)
McPherson Coll (KS)
Memorial U of Newfoundland (NL, Canada)
Mercer U (GA)
Mercy Coll (NY)
Mercyhurst Coll (PA)
Meredith Coll (NC)
Merrimack Coll (MA)
Messiah Coll (PA)
Methodist Coll (NC)
Metropolitan State Coll of Denver (CO)
Miami U (OH)
Miami U Hamilton (OH)
Michigan State U (MI)
MidAmerica Nazarene U (KS)
Middlebury Coll (VT)
Middle Tennessee State U (TN)
Midwestern State U (TX)
Millersville U of Pennsylvania (PA)
Milligan Coll (TN)
Millikin U (IL)
Millsaps Coll (MS)
Mills Coll (CA)
Minnesota State U Mankato (MN)
Minnesota State U Moorhead (MN)
Minot State U (ND)
Mississippi Coll (MS)
Mississippi State U (MS)
Mississippi Valley State U (MS)
Missouri Southern State U (MO)
Missouri Valley Coll (MO)
Molloy Coll (NY)
Monmouth Coll (IL)
Montana State U–Billings (MT)
Montana State U–Bozeman (MT)
Montclair State U (NJ)
Moravian Coll (PA)
Morehead State U (KY)
Morehouse Coll (GA)
Morgan State U (MD)
Morris Coll (SC)
Mount Allison U (NB, Canada)
Mount Holyoke Coll (MA)
Mount Mercy Coll (IA)
Mount Saint Mary Coll (NY)
Mount St. Mary's Coll (CA)
Mount Saint Mary's Coll and Sem (MD)
Mount Saint Vincent U (NS, Canada)
Mount Union Coll (OH)
Mount Vernon Nazarene U (OH)
Muhlenberg Coll (PA)
Murray State U (KY)
Nazareth Coll of Rochester (NY)
Nebraska Wesleyan U (NE)
Newberry Coll (SC)
New Coll of Florida (FL)
New Jersey City U (NJ)
Newman U (KS)
New Mexico Highlands U (NM)
New Mexico State U (NM)
New York Inst of Technology (NY)
New York U (NY)
Niagara U (NY)
Nicholls State U (LA)
Nipissing U (ON, Canada)
Norfolk State U (VA)
North Carolina Central U (NC)
North Carolina State U (NC)
North Carolina Wesleyan Coll (NC)
North Central Coll (IL)
North Dakota State U (ND)
Northeastern Illinois U (IL)
Northeastern State U (OK)
Northeastern U (MA)
Northern Arizona U (AZ)
Northern Illinois U (IL)
Northern Michigan U (MI)
Northern State U (SD)
North Georgia Coll & State U (GA)
Northland Coll (WI)
North Park U (IL)
Northwestern Coll (IA)
Northwestern Oklahoma State U (OK)
Northwestern State U of Louisiana (LA)
Northwestern U (IL)
Notre Dame de Namur U (CA)
Oakland U (MI)
Oberlin Coll (OH)
Occidental Coll (CA)
Oglethorpe U (GA)
Ohio Dominican U (OH)
Ohio Northern U (OH)
The Ohio State U (OH)
Ohio U (OH)
Ohio Wesleyan U (OH)
Okanagan U Coll (BC, Canada)
Oklahoma Baptist U (OK)
Oklahoma City U (OK)
Oklahoma State U (OK)
Old Dominion U (VA)
Olivet Coll (MI)
Oregon State U (OR)
Ottawa U (KS)
Otterbein Coll (OH)
Ouachita Baptist U (AR)
Our Lady of the Lake U of San Antonio (TX)
Pacific Lutheran U (WA)
Pacific Union Coll (CA)
Pacific U (OR)
Paine Coll (GA)
Park U (MO)
Penn State U Abington Coll (PA)
Penn State U Altoona Coll (PA)
Penn State U at Erie, The Behrend Coll (PA)
Penn State U Beaver Campus of the Commonwealth Coll (PA)
Penn State U Berks Cmps of Berks-Lehigh Valley Coll (PA)
Penn State U Delaware County Campus of the Commonwealth Coll (PA)
Penn State U DuBois Campus of the Commonwealth Coll (PA)
Penn State U Fayette Campus of the Commonwealth Coll (PA)
Penn State U Harrisburg Campus of the Capital Coll (PA)
Penn State U Hazleton Campus of the Commonwealth Coll (PA)
Penn State U Lehigh Valley Cmps of Berks-Lehigh Valley Coll (PA)
Penn State U McKeesport Campus of the Commonwealth Coll (PA)
Penn State U Mont Alto Campus of the Commonwealth Coll (PA)
Penn State U New Kensington Campus of the Commonwealth Coll (PA)
Penn State U Schuylkill Campus of the Capital Coll (PA)
Penn State U Shenango Campus of the Commonwealth Coll (PA)
Penn State U Univ Park Campus (PA)
Penn State U Wilkes-Barre Campus of the Commonwealth Coll (PA)
Penn State U Worthington Scranton Cmps Commonwealth Coll (PA)
Penn State U York Campus of the Commonwealth Coll (PA)
Pepperdine U, Malibu (CA)
Pfeiffer U (NC)
Piedmont Coll (GA)
Pikeville Coll (KY)
Pittsburg State U (KS)
Pitzer Coll (CA)
Point Loma Nazarene U (CA)
Pomona Coll (CA)
Pontifical Catholic U of Puerto Rico (PR)
Portland State U (OR)
Prairie View A&M U (TX)
Presbyterian Coll (SC)
Princeton U (NJ)
Principia Coll (IL)
Providence Coll (RI)
Purdue U (IN)
Queens Coll of the City U of NY (NY)
Queen's U at Kingston (ON, Canada)
Quinnipiac U (CT)
Radford U (VA)
Ramapo Coll of New Jersey (NJ)
Randolph-Macon Coll (VA)
Randolph-Macon Woman's Coll (VA)
Redeemer U Coll (ON, Canada)
Reed Coll (OR)
Regis Coll (MA)
Regis U (CO)
Reinhardt Coll (GA)
Rhode Island Coll (RI)
Rhodes Coll (TN)
Rice U (TX)
The Richard Stockton Coll of New Jersey (NJ)
Richmond, The American Intl U in London(United Kingdom)
Rider U (NJ)
Ripon Coll (WI)
Rivier Coll (NH)
Roanoke Coll (VA)
Roberts Wesleyan Coll (NY)
Rockford Coll (IL)
Rockhurst U (MO)
Rocky Mountain Coll (MT)
Roger Williams U (RI)
Rollins Coll (FL)
Roosevelt U (IL)
Rosemont Coll (PA)
Rowan U (NJ)
Russell Sage Coll (NY)
Rutgers, The State U of New Jersey, Camden (NJ)
Rutgers, The State U of New Jersey, Newark (NJ)
Rutgers, The State U of New Jersey, New Brunswick/Piscataway (NJ)
Sacred Heart U (CT)
Saginaw Valley State U (MI)
St. Ambrose U (IA)
Saint Anselm Coll (NH)
Saint Augustine's Coll (NC)
St. Bonaventure U (NY)
St. Cloud State U (MN)
St. Edward's U (TX)
St. Francis Coll (NY)
Saint Francis U (PA)
St. Francis Xavier U (NS, Canada)
St. Gregory's U (OK)
St. John Fisher Coll (NY)
Saint John's U (MN)
St. John's U (NY)
Saint Joseph Coll (CT)
Saint Joseph's Coll (IN)
Saint Joseph's Coll of Maine (ME)
St. Joseph's Coll, Suffolk Campus (NY)
Saint Joseph's U (PA)
St. Lawrence U (NY)
Saint Leo U (FL)
Saint Louis U (MO)
Saint Mary's Coll (IN)
Saint Mary's Coll of California (CA)
St. Mary's Coll of Maryland (MD)

Saint Mary's U of Minnesota (MN)
St. Mary's U of San Antonio (TX)
Saint Michael's Coll (VT)
St. Norbert Coll (WI)
St. Olaf Coll (MN)
St. Thomas U (FL)
St. Thomas U (NB, Canada)
Saint Vincent Coll (PA)
Saint Xavier U (IL)
Salem Coll (NC)
Salem State Coll (MA)
Salisbury U (MD)
Salve Regina U (RI)
Samford U (AL)
Sam Houston State U (TX)
San Diego State U (CA)
San Francisco State U (CA)
San Jose State U (CA)
Santa Clara U (CA)
Sarah Lawrence Coll (NY)
Scripps Coll (CA)
Seattle Pacific U (WA)
Seattle U (WA)
Seton Hall U (NJ)
Seton Hill U (PA)
Shawnee State U (OH)
Shaw U (NC)
Shenandoah U (VA)
Shepherd U (WV)
Shippensburg U of Pennsylvania (PA)
Shorter Coll (GA)
Siena Coll (NY)
Simmons Coll (MA)
Simon Fraser U (BC, Canada)
Simon's Rock Coll of Bard (MA)
Simpson Coll (IA)
Skidmore Coll (NY)
Slippery Rock U of Pennsylvania (PA)
Smith Coll (MA)
Sonoma State U (CA)
South Carolina State U (SC)
South Dakota State U (SD)
Southeastern Louisiana U (LA)
Southeastern Oklahoma State U (OK)
Southeast Missouri State U (MO)
Southern Arkansas U–Magnolia (AR)
Southern Connecticut State U (CT)
Southern Illinois U Carbondale (IL)
Southern Illinois U Edwardsville (IL)
Southern Methodist U (TX)
Southern Nazarene U (OK)
Southern Oregon U (OR)
Southern U and A&M Coll (LA)
Southern Utah U (UT)
Southwest Baptist U (MO)
Southwestern U (TX)
Southwest Missouri State U (MO)
Spelman Coll (GA)
Spring Arbor U (MI)
Springfield Coll (MA)
Stanford U (CA)
State U of NY at Binghamton (NY)
State U of NY at New Paltz (NY)
State U of NY at Oswego (NY)
Plattsburgh State U of NY (NY)
State U of NY Coll at Brockport (NY)
State U of NY Coll at Cortland (NY)
State U of NY Coll at Fredonia (NY)
State U of NY Coll at Geneseo (NY)
State U of NY Coll at Old Westbury (NY)
State U of NY Coll at Oneonta (NY)
State U of NY Coll at Potsdam (NY)
State U of NY Inst of Tech at Utica/Rome (NY)
State U of West Georgia (GA)
Stetson U (FL)
Stonehill Coll (MA)
Stony Brook U, State U of New York (NY)
Suffolk U (MA)
Susquehanna U (PA)
Sweet Briar Coll (VA)
Syracuse U (NY)
Tabor Coll (KS)
Talladega Coll (AL)
Tarleton State U (TX)
Taylor U (IN)
Teikyo Post U (CT)
Tennessee State U (TN)
Tennessee Technological U (TN)
Texas A&M Intl U (TX)
Texas A&M U (TX)
Texas A&M U–Commerce (TX)
Texas A&M U–Corpus Christi (TX)
Texas A&M U–Kingsville (TX)
Texas Christian U (TX)
Texas Lutheran U (TX)
Texas Southern U (TX)
Texas State U-San Marcos (TX)
Texas Tech U (TX)
Texas Wesleyan U (TX)
Texas Woman's U (TX)
Thiel Coll (PA)
Thomas Edison State Coll (NJ)
Thomas More Coll (KY)
Thomas U (GA)
Tougaloo Coll (MS)
Transylvania U (KY)
Trent U (ON, Canada)
Trinity Christian Coll (IL)
Trinity Coll (CT)
Trinity U (TX)
Troy State U (AL)
Troy State U Dothan (AL)
Truman State U (MO)
Tufts U (MA)
Tulane U (LA)
Tuskegee U (AL)
Union Coll (NY)
Union U (TN)
Université de Montréal (QC, Canada)
U du Québec à Hull (QC, Canada)
Université Laval (QC, Canada)
State U of NY at Albany (NY)
U at Buffalo, The State U of New York (NY)
U Coll of the Cariboo (BC, Canada)
U Coll of the Fraser Valley (BC, Canada)
The U of Akron (OH)
The U of Alabama (AL)
The U of Alabama at Birmingham (AL)
The U of Alabama in Huntsville (AL)
U of Alaska Fairbanks (AK)
U of Alberta (AB, Canada)
The U of Arizona (AZ)
U of Arkansas (AR)
U of Arkansas at Little Rock (AR)
The U of British Columbia (BC, Canada)
U of Calgary (AB, Canada)
U of Calif, Berkeley (CA)
U of Calif, Davis (CA)
U of Calif, Irvine (CA)
U of Calif, Los Angeles (CA)
U of Calif, Riverside (CA)
U of Calif, San Diego (CA)
U of Calif, Santa Barbara (CA)
U of Calif, Santa Cruz (CA)
U of Central Arkansas (AR)
U of Central Florida (FL)
U of Chicago (IL)
U of Cincinnati (OH)
U of Colorado at Boulder (CO)
U of Colorado at Colorado Springs (CO)
U of Colorado at Denver (CO)
U of Connecticut (CT)
U of Dayton (OH)
U of Delaware (DE)
U of Denver (CO)
U of Detroit Mercy (MI)
U of Dubuque (IA)
U of Evansville (IN)
The U of Findlay (OH)
U of Florida (FL)
U of Georgia (GA)
U of Great Falls (MT)
U of Guelph (ON, Canada)
U of Hartford (CT)
U of Hawaii at Hilo (HI)
U of Hawaii at Manoa (HI)
U of Houston (TX)
U of Houston–Clear Lake (TX)
U of Idaho (ID)
U of Illinois at Chicago (IL)
U of Illinois at Springfield (IL)
U of Illinois at Urbana–Champaign (IL)
U of Indianapolis (IN)
The U of Iowa (IA)
U of Kansas (KS)
U of Kentucky (KY)
U of King's Coll (NS, Canada)
U of La Verne (CA)
The U of Lethbridge (AB, Canada)
U of Louisiana at Lafayette (LA)
U of Louisville (KY)
U of Maine (ME)
U of Maine at Farmington (ME)
U of Maine at Presque Isle (ME)
U of Manitoba (MB, Canada)
U of Mary Hardin-Baylor (TX)
U of Maryland, Baltimore County (MD)
U of Maryland, Coll Park (MD)
U of Maryland Eastern Shore (MD)
U of Massachusetts Amherst (MA)
U of Massachusetts Boston (MA)
U of Massachusetts Dartmouth (MA)
U of Massachusetts Lowell (MA)
The U of Memphis (TN)
U of Miami (FL)
U of Michigan (MI)
U of Michigan–Dearborn (MI)
U of Michigan–Flint (MI)
U of Minnesota, Duluth (MN)
U of Minnesota, Morris (MN)
U of Minnesota, Twin Cities Campus (MN)
U of Mississippi (MS)
U of Missouri–Columbia (MO)
U of Missouri–Kansas City (MO)
U of Missouri–St. Louis (MO)
U of Mobile (AL)
The U of Montana–Missoula (MT)
U of Montevallo (AL)
U of Nebraska at Omaha (NE)
U of Nebraska–Lincoln (NE)
U of Nevada, Las Vegas (NV)
U of Nevada, Reno (NV)
U of New Brunswick Fredericton (NB, Canada)
U of New Hampshire (NH)
U of New Mexico (NM)
U of New Orleans (LA)
U of North Alabama (AL)
The U of North Carolina at Asheville (NC)
The U of North Carolina at Chapel Hill (NC)
The U of North Carolina at Charlotte (NC)
The U of North Carolina at Greensboro (NC)
The U of North Carolina at Pembroke (NC)
The U of North Carolina at Wilmington (NC)
U of North Dakota (ND)
U of Northern Colorado (CO)
U of Northern Iowa (IA)
U of North Florida (FL)
U of North Texas (TX)
U of Notre Dame (IN)
U of Oklahoma (OK)
U of Oregon (OR)
U of Ottawa (ON, Canada)
U of Pennsylvania (PA)
U of Pittsburgh (PA)
U of Pittsburgh at Bradford (PA)
U of Pittsburgh at Johnstown (PA)
U of Portland (OR)
U of Prince Edward Island (PE, Canada)
U of Puerto Rico, Cayey U Coll (PR)
U of Puget Sound (WA)
U of Redlands (CA)
U of Regina (SK, Canada)
U of Rhode Island (RI)
U of Richmond (VA)
U of Saint Mary (KS)
U of St. Thomas (MN)
U of San Diego (CA)
U of San Francisco (CA)
U of Saskatchewan (SK, Canada)
U of Science and Arts of Oklahoma (OK)
The U of Scranton (PA)
U of Sioux Falls (SD)
U of South Alabama (AL)
U of South Carolina (SC)
U of South Carolina Aiken (SC)
U of South Carolina Spartanburg (SC)
The U of South Dakota (SD)
U of Southern California (CA)
U of Southern Indiana (IN)
U of Southern Maine (ME)
U of South Florida (FL)
The U of Tampa (FL)
The U of Tennessee (TN)
The U of Tennessee at Chattanooga (TN)
The U of Tennessee at Martin (TN)
The U of Texas at Arlington (TX)
The U of Texas at Austin (TX)
The U of Texas at Brownsville (TX)
The U of Texas at Dallas (TX)
The U of Texas at Tyler (TX)
The U of Texas–Pan American (TX)
U of the District of Columbia (DC)
U of the Incarnate Word (TX)
U of the Ozarks (AR)
U of the Pacific (CA)
U of Toledo (OH)
U of Toronto (ON, Canada)
U of Tulsa (OK)
U of Utah (UT)
U of Vermont (VT)
U of Victoria (BC, Canada)
U of Virginia (VA)
The U of Virginia's Coll at Wise (VA)
U of Washington (WA)
U of Waterloo (ON, Canada)
The U of West Alabama (AL)
The U of Western Ontario (ON, Canada)
U of West Florida (FL)
U of Windsor (ON, Canada)
U of Wisconsin–Eau Claire (WI)
U of Wisconsin–La Crosse (WI)
U of Wisconsin–Madison (WI)
U of Wisconsin–Milwaukee (WI)
U of Wisconsin–Oshkosh (WI)
U of Wisconsin–Parkside (WI)
U of Wisconsin–River Falls (WI)
U of Wisconsin–Stevens Point (WI)
U of Wisconsin–Superior (WI)
U of Wisconsin–Whitewater (WI)
U of Wyoming (WY)
Upper Iowa U (IA)
Urbana U (OH)
Ursinus Coll (PA)
Ursuline Coll (OH)
Utah State U (UT)
Utica Coll (NY)
Valdosta State U (GA)
Valparaiso U (IN)
Vanderbilt U (TN)
Vanguard U of Southern California (CA)
Vassar Coll (NY)
Villanova U (PA)
Virginia Commonwealth U (VA)
Virginia Polytechnic Inst and State U (VA)
Virginia State U (VA)
Virginia Union U (VA)
Virginia Wesleyan Coll (VA)
Viterbo U (WI)
Voorhees Coll (SC)
Wagner Coll (NY)
Wake Forest U (NC)
Walla Walla Coll (WA)
Walsh U (OH)
Warren Wilson Coll (NC)
Wartburg Coll (IA)
Washburn U (KS)
Washington & Jefferson Coll (PA)
Washington and Lee U (VA)
Washington Coll (MD)
Washington State U (WA)
Waynesburg Coll (PA)
Wayne State Coll (NE)
Wayne State U (MI)
Weber State U (UT)
Webster U (MO)
Wellesley Coll (MA)
Wells Coll (NY)
Wesleyan U (CT)
West Chester U of Pennsylvania (PA)
Western Carolina U (NC)
Western Connecticut State U (CT)
Western Illinois U (IL)
Western Kentucky U (KY)
Western Michigan U (MI)
Western New England Coll (MA)
Western Oregon U (OR)
Western State Coll of Colorado (CO)
Western Washington U (WA)
Westfield State Coll (MA)
West Liberty State Coll (WV)
Westminster Coll (MO)
Westminster Coll (PA)
Westminster Coll (UT)
Westmont Coll (CA)
West Texas A&M U (TX)
West Virginia State Coll (WV)
West Virginia U (WV)
West Virginia Wesleyan Coll (WV)
Wheaton Coll (IL)
Wheaton Coll (MA)
Whitman Coll (WA)
Whitworth Coll (WA)
Wichita State U (KS)
Widener U (PA)
Wilberforce U (OH)
Wilkes U (PA)
Willamette U (OR)
William Paterson U of New Jersey (NJ)
William Penn U (IA)
Williams Coll (MA)
Wingate U (NC)
Winona State U (MN)
Winston-Salem State U (NC)
Winthrop U (SC)
Wittenberg U (OH)
Wofford Coll (SC)
Worcester State Coll (MA)
Wright State U (OH)
Xavier U (OH)
Xavier U of Louisiana (LA)
Yale U (CT)
York Coll of Pennsylvania (PA)
York Coll of the City U of New York (NY)
York U (ON, Canada)
Youngstown State U (OH)

SOIL CHEMISTRY AND PHYSICS

Hampshire Coll (MA)

SOIL CONSERVATION

Ball State U (IN)
California State Polytechnic U, Pomona (CA)
The Ohio State U (OH)
U of Delaware (DE)
U of New Hampshire (NH)
The U of Tennessee at Martin (TN)
U of Wisconsin–Stevens Point (WI)

SOIL MICROBIOLOGY

Hampshire Coll (MA)

SOIL SCIENCE AND AGRONOMY

Colorado State U (CO)
Cornell U (NY)
McGill U (QC, Canada)
Michigan State U (MI)
New Mexico State U (NM)
North Carolina State U (NC)
North Dakota State U (ND)
Penn State U Abington Coll (PA)
Penn State U Altoona Coll (PA)
Penn State U at Erie, The Behrend Coll (PA)
Penn State U Beaver Campus of the Commonwealth Coll (PA)
Penn State U Berks Cmps of Berks-Lehigh Valley Coll (PA)
Penn State U Delaware County Campus of the Commonwealth Coll (PA)
Penn State U DuBois Campus of the Commonwealth Coll (PA)
Penn State U Fayette Campus of the Commonwealth Coll (PA)
Penn State U Hazleton Campus of the Commonwealth Coll (PA)
Penn State U Lehigh Valley Cmps of Berks-Lehigh Valley Coll (PA)
Penn State U McKeesport Campus of the Commonwealth Coll (PA)
Penn State U Mont Alto Campus of the Commonwealth Coll (PA)
Penn State U New Kensington Campus of the Commonwealth Coll (PA)
Penn State U Schuylkill Campus of the Capital Coll (PA)
Penn State U Shenango Campus of the Commonwealth Coll (PA)
Penn State U Univ Park Campus (PA)
Penn State U Wilkes-Barre Campus of the Commonwealth Coll (PA)
Penn State U Worthington Scranton Cmps Commonwealth Coll (PA)
Penn State U York Campus of the Commonwealth Coll (PA)
Sterling Coll (VT)
The U of Arizona (AZ)
The U of British Columbia (BC, Canada)
U of Delaware (DE)
U of Florida (FL)
U of Idaho (ID)
U of Maine (ME)
U of Minnesota, Twin Cities Campus (MN)
U of Nebraska–Lincoln (NE)
U of Saskatchewan (SK, Canada)
U of Vermont (VT)
U of Wisconsin–River Falls (WI)
Utah State U (UT)
Washington State U (WA)

SOIL SCIENCES RELATED

Brigham Young U (UT)
Cornell U (NY)
Sterling Coll (VT)

SOLAR ENERGY TECHNOLOGY

Hampshire Coll (MA)
Sterling Coll (VT)

SOLID STATE AND LOW-TEMPERATURE PHYSICS

George Mason U (VA)

SOUTH ASIAN LANGUAGES

Claremont McKenna Coll (CA)
Northwestern U (IL)
Oakland U (MI)

The U of British Columbia (BC, Canada)
U of Chicago (IL)
Yale U (CT)

SPANISH
Abilene Christian U (TX)
Adams State Coll (CO)
Adelphi U (NY)
Adrian Coll (MI)
Agnes Scott Coll (GA)
Alabama State U (AL)
Albany State U (GA)
Albertson Coll of Idaho (ID)
Albertus Magnus Coll (CT)
Albion Coll (MI)
Albright Coll (PA)
Alfred U (NY)
Allegheny Coll (PA)
Alma Coll (MI)
American Intl Coll (MA)
American U (DC)
Amherst Coll (MA)
Anderson Coll (SC)
Andrews U (MI)
Angelo State U (TX)
Antioch Coll (OH)
Appalachian State U (NC)
Aquinas Coll (MI)
Arcadia U (PA)
Arizona State U (AZ)
Arizona State U West (AZ)
Arkansas State U (AR)
Armstrong Atlantic State U (GA)
Asbury Coll (KY)
Ashland U (OH)
Assumption Coll (MA)
Atlantic Union Coll (MA)
Auburn U (AL)
Augsburg Coll (MN)
Augustana Coll (IL)
Augustana Coll (SD)
Augusta State U (GA)
Austin Coll (TX)
Austin Peay State U (TN)
Azusa Pacific U (CA)
Baker U (KS)
Baldwin-Wallace Coll (OH)
Ball State U (IN)
Bard Coll (NY)
Barnard Coll (NY)
Barry U (FL)
Barton Coll (NC)
Bates Coll (ME)
Baylor U (TX)
Bellarmine U (KY)
Belmont U (TN)
Beloit Coll (WI)
Bemidji State U (MN)
Benedictine Coll (KS)
Benedictine U (IL)
Bennington Coll (VT)
Berea Coll (KY)
Baruch Coll of the City U of NY (NY)
Berry Coll (GA)
Bethany Coll (WV)
Bethel Coll (KS)
Bethel U (MN)
Biola U (CA)
Birmingham-Southern Coll (AL)
Bishop's U (QC, Canada)
Blackburn Coll (IL)
Black Hills State U (SD)
Bloomsburg U of Pennsylvania (PA)
Blue Mountain Coll (MS)
Bluffton Coll (OH)
Boise State U (ID)
Boston U (MA)
Bowdoin Coll (ME)
Bowling Green State U (OH)
Bradley U (IL)
Brandeis U (MA)
Brescia U (KY)
Briar Cliff U (IA)
Bridgewater Coll (VA)
Bridgewater State Coll (MA)
Brigham Young U (UT)
Brock U (ON, Canada)
Brooklyn Coll of the City U of NY (NY)
Brown U (RI)
Bryn Mawr Coll (PA)
Bucknell U (PA)
Buena Vista U (IA)
State U of NY Coll at Buffalo (NY)
Butler U (IN)
Cabrini Coll (PA)
Caldwell Coll (NJ)
California Lutheran U (CA)
California State Polytechnic U, Pomona (CA)
California State U, Chico (CA)
California State U, Dominguez Hills (CA)
California State U, Fresno (CA)
California State U, Fullerton (CA)
California State U, Hayward (CA)
California State U, Long Beach (CA)
California State U, Los Angeles (CA)
California State U, Sacramento (CA)
California State U, San Bernardino (CA)
California State U, San Marcos (CA)
California State U, Stanislaus (CA)
California U of Pennsylvania (PA)
Calvin Coll (MI)
Campbell U (NC)
Canisius Coll (NY)
Capital U (OH)
Cardinal Stritch U (WI)
Carleton Coll (MN)
Carleton U (ON, Canada)
Carnegie Mellon U (PA)
Carroll Coll (MT)
Carroll Coll (WI)
Carson-Newman Coll (TN)
Carthage Coll (WI)
Case Western Reserve U (OH)
Castleton State Coll (VT)
Catawba Coll (NC)
The Catholic U of America (DC)
Cedar Crest Coll (PA)
Cedarville U (OH)
Centenary Coll of Louisiana (LA)
Central Coll (IA)
Central Connecticut State U (CT)
Central Methodist Coll (MO)
Central Michigan U (MI)
Central Missouri State U (MO)
Centre Coll (KY)
Chadron State Coll (NE)
Chapman U (CA)
Charleston Southern U (SC)
Chatham Coll (PA)
Chestnut Hill Coll (PA)
Cheyney U of Pennsylvania (PA)
Chicago State U (IL)
Christopher Newport U (VA)
Citadel, The Military Coll of South Carolina (SC)
City Coll of the City U of NY (NY)
Claremont McKenna Coll (CA)
Clarion U of Pennsylvania (PA)
Clark Atlanta U (GA)
Clarke Coll (IA)
Clark U (MA)
Cleveland State U (OH)
Coastal Carolina U (SC)
Coe Coll (IA)
Coker Coll (SC)
Colby Coll (ME)
Colgate U (NY)
Coll of Charleston (SC)
Coll of Mount Saint Vincent (NY)
The Coll of New Jersey (NJ)
The Coll of New Rochelle (NY)
Coll of Saint Benedict (MN)
Coll of St. Catherine (MN)
Coll of Saint Elizabeth (NJ)
The Coll of Saint Rose (NY)
Coll of Staten Island of the City U of NY (NY)
Coll of the Holy Cross (MA)
Coll of the Ozarks (MO)
The Coll of William and Mary (VA)
The Coll of Wooster (OH)
The Colorado Coll (CO)
Colorado State U (CO)
Colorado State U-Pueblo (CO)
Columbia Coll (NY)
Columbia Coll (SC)
Columbia U, School of General Studies (NY)
Concordia Coll (MN)
Concordia U (MI)
Concordia U (NE)
Concordia U (QC, Canada)
Concordia U Wisconsin (WI)
Connecticut Coll (CT)
Converse Coll (SC)
Cornell Coll (IA)
Cornell U (NY)
Cornerstone U (MI)
Creighton U (NE)
Daemen Coll (NY)
Dakota Wesleyan U (SD)
Dalhousie U (NS, Canada)
Dana Coll (NE)
Dartmouth Coll (NH)
Davidson Coll (NC)
Davis & Elkins Coll (WV)
Delaware State U (DE)
Denison U (OH)
DePaul U (IL)
DePauw U (IN)
DeSales U (PA)
Dickinson Coll (PA)
Dickinson State U (ND)
Dillard U (LA)
Doane Coll (NE)
Dominican Coll (NY)
Dominican U (IL)
Dordt Coll (IA)
Drew U (NJ)
Drury U (MO)
Duke U (NC)
Duquesne U (PA)
Earlham Coll (IN)
East Carolina U (NC)
Eastern Connecticut State U (CT)
Eastern Kentucky U (KY)
Eastern Mennonite U (VA)
Eastern Michigan U (MI)
Eastern New Mexico U (NM)
Eastern U (PA)
Eastern Washington U (WA)
East Stroudsburg U of Pennsylvania (PA)
East Texas Baptist U (TX)
Eckerd Coll (FL)
Edgewood Coll (WI)
Edinboro U of Pennsylvania (PA)
Elizabethtown Coll (PA)
Elmhurst Coll (IL)
Elmira Coll (NY)
Elms Coll (MA)
Elon U (NC)
Emory & Henry Coll (VA)
Emory U (GA)
Erskine Coll (SC)
Evangel U (MO)
Fairfield U (CT)
Fairleigh Dickinson U, Florham (NJ)
Fairleigh Dickinson U, Teaneck-Metro Campus (NJ)
Fayetteville State U (NC)
Ferrum Coll (VA)
Flagler Coll (FL)
Florida Ag and Mech U (FL)
Florida Atlantic U (FL)
Florida Intl U (FL)
Florida Southern Coll (FL)
Florida State U (FL)
Fordham U (NY)
Fort Hays State U (KS)
Fort Lewis Coll (CO)
Framingham State Coll (MA)
Franciscan U of Steubenville (OH)
Francis Marion U (SC)
Franklin and Marshall Coll (PA)
Franklin Coll (IN)
Fresno Pacific U (CA)
Furman U (SC)
Gallaudet U (DC)
Gardner-Webb U (NC)
Geneva Coll (PA)
George Fox U (OR)
Georgetown Coll (KY)
Georgetown U (DC)
The George Washington U (DC)
Georgia Coll & State U (GA)
Georgian Court U (NJ)
Georgia Southern U (GA)
Georgia State U (GA)
Gettysburg Coll (PA)
Gonzaga U (WA)
Gordon Coll (MA)
Goshen Coll (IN)
Goucher Coll (MD)
Grace Coll (IN)
Graceland U (IA)
Grambling State U (LA)
Grand Valley State U (MI)
Greensboro Coll (NC)
Greenville Coll (IL)
Grinnell Coll (IA)
Grove City Coll (PA)
Guilford Coll (NC)
Gustavus Adolphus Coll (MN)
Hamilton Coll (NY)
Hamline U (MN)
Hampden-Sydney Coll (VA)
Hanover Coll (IN)
Harding U (AR)
Hardin-Simmons U (TX)
Hartwick Coll (NY)
Harvard U (MA)
Hastings Coll (NE)
Haverford Coll (PA)
Heidelberg Coll (OH)
Henderson State U (AR)
Hendrix Coll (AR)
High Point U (NC)
Hillsdale Coll (MI)
Hiram Coll (OH)
Hobart and William Smith Colls (NY)
Hofstra U (NY)
Hollins U (VA)
Holy Names Coll (CA)
Hood Coll (MD)
Hope Coll (MI)
Houghton Coll (NY)
Houston Baptist U (TX)
Howard Payne U (TX)
Howard U (DC)
Humboldt State U (CA)
Hunter Coll of the City U of NY (NY)
Huntingdon Coll (AL)
Idaho State U (ID)
Illinois Coll (IL)
Illinois State U (IL)
Illinois Wesleyan U (IL)
Immaculata U (PA)
Indiana State U (IN)
Indiana U Bloomington (IN)
Indiana U Northwest (IN)
Indiana U of Pennsylvania (PA)
Indiana U–Purdue U Fort Wayne (IN)
Indiana U–Purdue U Indianapolis (IN)
Indiana U South Bend (IN)
Indiana U Southeast (IN)
Inter American U of PR, San Germán Campus (PR)
Iona Coll (NY)
Iowa State U of Science and Technology (IA)
Ithaca Coll (NY)
Jacksonville State U (AL)
Jacksonville U (FL)
John Carroll U (OH)
The Johns Hopkins U (MD)
Johnson C. Smith U (NC)
Juniata Coll (PA)
Kalamazoo Coll (MI)
Kansas Wesleyan U (KS)
Kean U (NJ)
Keene State Coll (NH)
Kennesaw State U (GA)
Kent State U (OH)
Kentucky Wesleyan Coll (KY)
Kenyon Coll (OH)
King Coll (TN)
King's Coll (PA)
Knox Coll (IL)
Kutztown U of Pennsylvania (PA)
Lafayette Coll (PA)
LaGrange Coll (GA)
Lake Erie Coll (OH)
Lake Forest Coll (IL)
Lakeland Coll (WI)
Lamar U (TX)
Lambuth U (TN)
Lander U (SC)
La Salle U (PA)
Laurentian U (ON, Canada)
Lawrence U (WI)
Lebanon Valley Coll (PA)
Lehigh U (PA)
Lehman Coll of the City U of NY (NY)
Le Moyne Coll (NY)
Lenoir-Rhyne Coll (NC)
Lewis & Clark Coll (OR)
Liberty U (VA)
Lincoln U (PA)
Lindenwood U (MO)
Linfield Coll (OR)
Lipscomb U (TN)
Lock Haven U of Pennsylvania (PA)
Long Island U, C.W. Post Campus (NY)
Longwood U (VA)
Loras Coll (IA)
Louisiana Coll (LA)
Louisiana State U and A&M Coll (LA)
Louisiana State U in Shreveport (LA)
Louisiana Tech U (LA)
Loyola Coll in Maryland (MD)
Loyola Marymount U (CA)
Loyola U Chicago (IL)
Loyola U New Orleans (LA)
Luther Coll (IA)
Lycoming Coll (PA)
Lynchburg Coll (VA)
Lyon Coll (AR)
Macalester Coll (MN)
MacMurray Coll (IL)
Madonna U (MI)
Malone Coll (OH)
Manchester Coll (IN)
Manhattan Coll (NY)
Manhattanville Coll (NY)
Mansfield U of Pennsylvania (PA)
Marian Coll (IN)
Marian Coll of Fond du Lac (WI)
Marietta Coll (OH)
Marist Coll (NY)
Marlboro Coll (VT)
Marquette U (WI)
Mars Hill Coll (NC)
Mary Baldwin Coll (VA)
Marymount Coll of Fordham U (NY)
Maryville Coll (TN)
Mary Washington Coll (VA)
Marywood U (PA)
McDaniel Coll (MD)
McGill U (QC, Canada)
McMurry U (TX)
McNeese State U (LA)
McPherson Coll (KS)
Memorial U of Newfoundland (NL, Canada)
Mercer U (GA)
Mercy Coll (NY)
Mercyhurst Coll (PA)
Meredith Coll (NC)
Merrimack Coll (MA)
Messiah Coll (PA)
Methodist Coll (NC)
Metropolitan State Coll of Denver (CO)
Miami U (OH)
Miami U Hamilton (OH)
Michigan State U (MI)
MidAmerica Nazarene U (KS)
Middlebury Coll (VT)
Midwestern State U (TX)
Millersville U of Pennsylvania (PA)
Millikin U (IL)
Millsaps Coll (MS)
Mills Coll (CA)
Minnesota State U Mankato (MN)
Minnesota State U Moorhead (MN)
Minot State U (ND)
Mississippi Coll (MS)
Missouri Southern State U (MO)
Missouri Western State Coll (MO)
Molloy Coll (NY)
Monmouth Coll (IL)
Montana State U–Billings (MT)
Montclair State U (NJ)
Moravian Coll (PA)
Morehead State U (KY)
Morehouse Coll (GA)
Morningside Coll (IA)
Mount Allison U (NB, Canada)
Mount Holyoke Coll (MA)
Mount Mary Coll (WI)
Mount St. Mary's Coll (CA)
Mount Saint Mary's Coll and Sem (MD)
Mount Saint Vincent U (NS, Canada)
Mount Union Coll (OH)
Mount Vernon Nazarene U (OH)
Muhlenberg Coll (PA)
Murray State U (KY)
Nazareth Coll of Rochester (NY)
Nebraska Wesleyan U (NE)
Newberry Coll (SC)
New Coll of Florida (FL)
New Jersey City U (NJ)
New Mexico Highlands U (NM)
New York U (NY)
Niagara U (NY)
North Carolina Central U (NC)
North Carolina State U (NC)
North Central Coll (IL)
North Dakota State U (ND)
Northeastern Illinois U (IL)
Northeastern State U (OK)
Northeastern U (MA)
Northern Arizona U (AZ)
Northern Illinois U (IL)
Northern Michigan U (MI)
Northern State U (SD)
North Georgia Coll & State U (GA)
North Park U (IL)
Northwestern Coll (IA)
Northwestern Coll (MN)
Northwestern Oklahoma State U (OK)
Northwestern U (IL)
Northwest Nazarene U (ID)
Oakland U (MI)
Oberlin Coll (OH)
Occidental Coll (CA)
Ohio Northern U (OH)
The Ohio State U (OH)
Ohio U (OH)
Ohio Wesleyan U (OH)
Oklahoma Baptist U (OK)
Oklahoma Christian U (OK)
Oklahoma City U (OK)
Oklahoma State U (OK)
Old Dominion U (VA)
Olivet Nazarene U (IL)
Oral Roberts U (OK)
Oregon State U (OR)
Otterbein Coll (OH)
Ouachita Baptist U (AR)
Our Lady of the Lake U of San Antonio (TX)
Pace U (NY)
Pacific Lutheran U (WA)
Pacific Union Coll (CA)

Pacific U (OR)
Park U (MO)
Peace Coll (NC)
Penn State U Abington Coll (PA)
Penn State U Altoona Coll (PA)
Penn State U at Erie, The Behrend Coll (PA)
Penn State U Beaver Campus of the Commonwealth Coll (PA)
Penn State U Berks Cmps of Berks-Lehigh Valley Coll (PA)
Penn State U Delaware County Campus of the Commonwealth Coll (PA)
Penn State U DuBois Campus of the Commonwealth Coll (PA)
Penn State U Fayette Campus of the Commonwealth Coll (PA)
Penn State U Hazleton Campus of the Commonwealth Coll (PA)
Penn State U Lehigh Valley Cmps of Berks-Lehigh Valley Coll (PA)
Penn State U McKeesport Campus of the Commonwealth Coll (PA)
Penn State U Mont Alto Campus of the Commonwealth Coll (PA)
Penn State U New Kensington Campus of the Commonwealth Coll (PA)
Penn State U Schuylkill Campus of the Capital Coll (PA)
Penn State U Shenango Campus of the Commonwealth Coll (PA)
Penn State U Univ Park Campus (PA)
Penn State U Wilkes-Barre Campus of the Commonwealth Coll (PA)
Penn State U Worthington Scranton Cmps Commonwealth Coll (PA)
Penn State U York Campus of the Commonwealth Coll (PA)
Pepperdine U, Malibu (CA)
Piedmont Coll (GA)
Pittsburg State U (KS)
Pitzer Coll (CA)
Plymouth State U (NH)
Point Loma Nazarene U (CA)
Pomona Coll (CA)
Pontifical Catholic U of Puerto Rico (PR)
Portland State U (OR)
Prairie View A&M U (TX)
Presbyterian Coll (SC)
Princeton U (NJ)
Principia Coll (IL)
Providence Coll (RI)
Queens Coll of the City U of NY (NY)
Queen's U at Kingston (ON, Canada)
Quinnipiac U (CT)
Ramapo Coll of New Jersey (NJ)
Randolph-Macon Coll (VA)
Randolph-Macon Woman's Coll (VA)
Reed Coll (OR)
Regis Coll (MA)
Regis U (CO)
Rhode Island Coll (RI)
Rhodes Coll (TN)
Rice U (TX)
Rider U (NJ)
Ripon Coll (WI)
Rivier Coll (NH)
Roanoke Coll (VA)
Rockford Coll (IL)
Rockhurst U (MO)
Rollins Coll (FL)
Roosevelt U (IL)
Rosemont Coll (PA)
Rowan U (NJ)
Russell Sage Coll (NY)
Rutgers, The State U of New Jersey, Camden (NJ)
Rutgers, The State U of New Jersey, Newark (NJ)
Rutgers, The State U of New Jersey, New Brunswick/Piscataway (NJ)
Sacred Heart U (CT)
Saginaw Valley State U (MI)
St. Ambrose U (IA)
Saint Anselm Coll (NH)
St. Bonaventure U (NY)
St. Cloud State U (MN)
St. Edward's U (TX)
St. Francis Coll (NY)
Saint Francis U (PA)
St. John Fisher Coll (NY)
Saint John's U (MN)
St. John's U (NY)
Saint Joseph Coll (CT)
St. Joseph's Coll, New York (NY)
Saint Joseph's U (PA)
St. Lawrence U (NY)
Saint Louis U (MO)
Saint Mary-of-the-Woods Coll (IN)
Saint Mary's Coll (IN)
Saint Mary's Coll of California (CA)
Saint Mary's U of Minnesota (MN)
St. Mary's U of San Antonio (TX)
Saint Michael's Coll (VT)
St. Norbert Coll (WI)
St. Olaf Coll (MN)
St. Thomas Aquinas Coll (NY)
St. Thomas U (NB, Canada)
Saint Vincent Coll (PA)
Saint Xavier U (IL)
Salem Coll (NC)
Salisbury U (MD)
Salve Regina U (RI)
Samford U (AL)
Sam Houston State U (TX)
San Diego State U (CA)
San Francisco State U (CA)
San Jose State U (CA)
Santa Clara U (CA)
Sarah Lawrence Coll (NY)
Scripps Coll (CA)
Seattle Pacific U (WA)
Seattle U (WA)
Seton Hall U (NJ)
Seton Hill U (PA)
Shenandoah U (VA)
Shippensburg U of Pennsylvania (PA)
Shorter Coll (GA)
Siena Coll (NY)
Siena Heights U (MI)
Simmons Coll (MA)
Simon's Rock Coll of Bard (MA)
Simpson Coll (IA)
Skidmore Coll (NY)
Slippery Rock U of Pennsylvania (PA)
Smith Coll (MA)
Sonoma State U (CA)
South Carolina State U (SC)
South Dakota State U (SD)
Southeastern Louisiana U (LA)
Southeast Missouri State U (MO)
Southern Arkansas U–Magnolia (AR)
Southern Connecticut State U (CT)
Southern Illinois U Carbondale (IL)
Southern Methodist U (TX)
Southern Nazarene U (OK)
Southern Oregon U (OR)
Southern U and A&M Coll (LA)
Southern Utah U (UT)
Southern Virginia U (VA)
Southwest Baptist U (MO)
Southwestern U (TX)
Southwest Missouri State U (MO)
Spelman Coll (GA)
Spring Arbor U (MI)
Spring Hill Coll (AL)
Stanford U (CA)
State U of NY at Binghamton (NY)
State U of NY at New Paltz (NY)
State U of NY at Oswego (NY)
Plattsburgh State U of NY (NY)
State U of NY Coll at Brockport (NY)
State U of NY Coll at Cortland (NY)
State U of NY Coll at Fredonia (NY)
State U of NY Coll at Geneseo (NY)
State U of NY Coll at Old Westbury (NY)
State U of NY Coll at Oneonta (NY)
State U of NY Coll at Potsdam (NY)
State U of West Georgia (GA)
Stetson U (FL)
Stony Brook U, State U of New York (NY)
Suffolk U (MA)
Susquehanna U (PA)
Swarthmore Coll (PA)
Sweet Briar Coll (VA)
Syracuse U (NY)
Talladega Coll (AL)
Tarleton State U (TX)
Taylor U (IN)
Tennessee State U (TN)
Tennessee Technological U (TN)
Texas A&M Intl U (TX)
Texas A&M U (TX)
Texas A&M U–Commerce (TX)
Texas A&M U–Corpus Christi (TX)
Texas A&M U–Kingsville (TX)
Texas Christian U (TX)
Texas Lutheran U (TX)
Texas Southern U (TX)
Texas State U-San Marcos (TX)
Texas Tech U (TX)
Texas Wesleyan U (TX)
Thiel Coll (PA)
Towson U (MD)
Transylvania U (KY)
Trent U (ON, Canada)
Trinity Christian Coll (IL)
Trinity Coll (CT)
Trinity Coll (DC)
Trinity U (TX)
Truman State U (MO)
Tufts U (MA)
Tulane U (LA)
Union Coll (NE)
Union U (TN)
United States Military Acad (NY)
Universidad Adventista de las Antillas (PR)
Université de Montréal (QC, Canada)
Université Laval (QC, Canada)
State U of NY at Albany (NY)
U at Buffalo, The State U of New York (NY)
The U of Akron (OH)
The U of Alabama (AL)
The U of Alabama at Birmingham (AL)
U of Alberta (AB, Canada)
The U of Arizona (AZ)
U of Arkansas (AR)
U of Arkansas at Little Rock (AR)
The U of British Columbia (BC, Canada)
U of Calgary (AB, Canada)
U of Calif, Berkeley (CA)
U of Calif, Davis (CA)
U of Calif, Irvine (CA)
U of Calif, Los Angeles (CA)
U of Calif, Riverside (CA)
U of Calif, San Diego (CA)
U of Calif, Santa Barbara (CA)
U of Calif, Santa Cruz (CA)
U of Central Arkansas (AR)
U of Central Florida (FL)
U of Chicago (IL)
U of Cincinnati (OH)
U of Colorado at Boulder (CO)
U of Colorado at Colorado Springs (CO)
U of Colorado at Denver (CO)
U of Connecticut (CT)
U of Dallas (TX)
U of Dayton (OH)
U of Delaware (DE)
U of Denver (CO)
U of Evansville (IN)
The U of Findlay (OH)
U of Florida (FL)
U of Georgia (GA)
U of Guelph (ON, Canada)
U of Hawaii at Manoa (HI)
U of Houston (TX)
U of Idaho (ID)
U of Illinois at Chicago (IL)
U of Illinois at Urbana–Champaign (IL)
U of Indianapolis (IN)
The U of Iowa (IA)
U of Kansas (KS)
U of Kentucky (KY)
U of King's Coll (NS, Canada)
U of La Verne (CA)
U of Louisiana at Lafayette (LA)
U of Louisville (KY)
U of Maine (ME)
U of Manitoba (MB, Canada)
U of Mary Hardin-Baylor (TX)
U of Maryland, Baltimore County (MD)
U of Maryland, Coll Park (MD)
U of Massachusetts Amherst (MA)
U of Massachusetts Boston (MA)
U of Massachusetts Dartmouth (MA)
U of Miami (FL)
U of Michigan (MI)
U of Michigan–Dearborn (MI)
U of Michigan–Flint (MI)
U of Minnesota, Duluth (MN)
U of Minnesota, Morris (MN)
U of Minnesota, Twin Cities Campus (MN)
U of Mississippi (MS)
U of Missouri–Columbia (MO)
U of Missouri–Kansas City (MO)
U of Missouri–St. Louis (MO)
The U of Montana–Missoula (MT)
U of Montevallo (AL)
U of Nebraska at Omaha (NE)
U of Nebraska–Lincoln (NE)
U of Nevada, Las Vegas (NV)
U of Nevada, Reno (NV)
U of New Brunswick Fredericton (NB, Canada)
U of New Hampshire (NH)
U of New Mexico (NM)
U of New Orleans (LA)
The U of North Carolina at Asheville (NC)
The U of North Carolina at Charlotte (NC)
The U of North Carolina at Greensboro (NC)
The U of North Carolina at Wilmington (NC)
U of North Dakota (ND)
U of Northern Colorado (CO)
U of Northern Iowa (IA)
U of North Florida (FL)
U of North Texas (TX)
U of Notre Dame (IN)
U of Oklahoma (OK)
U of Oregon (OR)
U of Ottawa (ON, Canada)
U of Pennsylvania (PA)
U of Pittsburgh (PA)
U of Portland (OR)
U of Prince Edward Island (PE, Canada)
U of Puerto Rico, Cayey U Coll (PR)
U of Puget Sound (WA)
U of Redlands (CA)
U of Regina (SK, Canada)
U of Rhode Island (RI)
U of Richmond (VA)
U of Rochester (NY)
U of St. Thomas (MN)
U of St. Thomas (TX)
U of San Diego (CA)
U of San Francisco (CA)
U of Saskatchewan (SK, Canada)
The U of Scranton (PA)
U of South Carolina (SC)
U of South Carolina Spartanburg (SC)
The U of South Dakota (SD)
U of Southern California (CA)
U of Southern Indiana (IN)
U of South Florida (FL)
The U of Tampa (FL)
The U of Tennessee (TN)
The U of Tennessee at Chattanooga (TN)
The U of Tennessee at Martin (TN)
The U of Texas at Arlington (TX)
The U of Texas at Austin (TX)
The U of Texas at Brownsville (TX)
The U of Texas at Tyler (TX)
The U of Texas–Pan American (TX)
U of the District of Columbia (DC)
U of the Incarnate Word (TX)
U of the Pacific (CA)
U of the South (TN)
U of Toledo (OH)
U of Toronto (ON, Canada)
U of Tulsa (OK)
U of Utah (UT)
U of Vermont (VT)
U of Victoria (BC, Canada)
U of Virginia (VA)
The U of Virginia's Coll at Wise (VA)
U of Washington (WA)
U of Waterloo (ON, Canada)
The U of Western Ontario (ON, Canada)
U of Windsor (ON, Canada)
U of Wisconsin–Eau Claire (WI)
U of Wisconsin–Green Bay (WI)
U of Wisconsin–La Crosse (WI)
U of Wisconsin–Madison (WI)
U of Wisconsin–Milwaukee (WI)
U of Wisconsin–Oshkosh (WI)
U of Wisconsin–Parkside (WI)
U of Wisconsin–Platteville (WI)
U of Wisconsin–River Falls (WI)
U of Wisconsin–Stevens Point (WI)
U of Wisconsin–Whitewater (WI)
U of Wyoming (WY)
Ursinus Coll (PA)
Utah State U (UT)
Valdosta State U (GA)
Valley City State U (ND)
Valparaiso U (IN)
Vanderbilt U (TN)
Vanguard U of Southern California (CA)
Vassar Coll (NY)
Villanova U (PA)
Virginia Polytechnic Inst and State U (VA)
Virginia Wesleyan Coll (VA)
Viterbo U (WI)
Wabash Coll (IN)
Wagner Coll (NY)
Wake Forest U (NC)
Walla Walla Coll (WA)
Walsh U (OH)
Warren Wilson Coll (NC)
Wartburg Coll (IA)
Washburn U (KS)
Washington & Jefferson Coll (PA)
Washington and Lee U (VA)
Washington Coll (MD)
Washington State U (WA)
Washington U in St. Louis (MO)
Wayland Baptist U (TX)
Wayne State Coll (NE)
Wayne State U (MI)
Weber State U (UT)
Webster U (MO)
Wellesley Coll (MA)
Wells Coll (NY)
Wesleyan Coll (GA)
Wesleyan U (CT)
West Chester U of Pennsylvania (PA)
Western Carolina U (NC)
Western Connecticut State U (CT)
Western Illinois U (IL)
Western Kentucky U (KY)
Western Michigan U (MI)
Western Oregon U (OR)
Western State Coll of Colorado (CO)
Western Washington U (WA)
Westminster Coll (MO)
Westminster Coll (PA)
Westmont Coll (CA)
West Texas A&M U (TX)
Wheaton Coll (IL)
Wheeling Jesuit U (WV)
Whitman Coll (WA)
Whitworth Coll (WA)
Wichita State U (KS)
Widener U (PA)
Wilkes U (PA)
Willamette U (OR)
William Jewell Coll (MO)
William Paterson U of New Jersey (NJ)
Williams Coll (MA)
William Woods U (MO)
Wilson Coll (PA)
Wingate U (NC)
Winona State U (MN)
Winston-Salem State U (NC)
Wisconsin Lutheran Coll (WI)
Wittenberg U (OH)
Wofford Coll (SC)
Worcester State Coll (MA)
Wright State U (OH)
Xavier U (OH)
Xavier U of Louisiana (LA)
Yale U (CT)
York Coll of Pennsylvania (PA)
York Coll of the City U of New York (NY)
York U (ON, Canada)
Youngstown State U (OH)

SPANISH AND IBERIAN STUDIES

Barnard Coll (NY)
Coe Coll (IA)
Fordham U (NY)
Simon's Rock Coll of Bard (MA)
U of Houston (TX)
U of Puerto Rico, Cayey U Coll (PR)
York U (ON, Canada)

SPANISH LANGUAGE TEACHER EDUCATION

Abilene Christian U (TX)
Alma Coll (MI)
Anderson Coll (SC)
Appalachian State U (NC)
Arkansas State U (AR)
Auburn U (AL)
Baylor U (TX)
Berea Coll (KY)
Bethel U (MN)
Bishop's U (QC, Canada)
Blue Mountain Coll (MS)
Bridgewater Coll (VA)
Brigham Young U (UT)
Brooklyn Coll of the City U of NY (NY)
Buena Vista U (IA)
California Lutheran U (CA)
California State U, Chico (CA)
Campbell U (NC)
Carroll Coll (MT)
Carroll Coll (WI)
The Catholic U of America (DC)
Cedarville U (OH)
Centenary Coll of Louisiana (LA)
Central Michigan U (MI)
Central Missouri State U (MO)
Central Washington U (WA)
Chadron State Coll (NE)
Charleston Southern U (SC)
The Coll of New Jersey (NJ)
Coll of St. Catherine (MN)
The Coll of Saint Rose (NY)
Colorado State U (CO)
Colorado State U-Pueblo (CO)
Columbus State U (GA)

Concordia Coll (MN)
Concordia U (NE)
Concordia U Wisconsin (WI)
Daemen Coll (NY)
Delaware State U (DE)
Dordt Coll (IA)
Dowling Coll (NY)
Duquesne U (PA)
East Carolina U (NC)
Eastern Mennonite U (VA)
Eastern Michigan U (MI)
Eastern Washington U (WA)
East Texas Baptist U (TX)
Elmhurst Coll (IL)
Elmira Coll (NY)
Evangel U (MO)
Fayetteville State U (NC)
Flagler Coll (FL)
Framingham State Coll (MA)
Franklin Coll (IN)
Georgian Court U (NJ)
Georgia Southern U (GA)
Grace Coll (IN)
Greensboro Coll (NC)
Greenville Coll (IL)
Hardin-Simmons U (TX)
Hofstra U (NY)
Hope Coll (MI)
Howard Payne U (TX)
Illinois Wesleyan U (IL)
Indiana U Bloomington (IN)
Indiana U Northwest (IN)
Indiana U–Purdue U Fort Wayne (IN)
Indiana U–Purdue U Indianapolis (IN)
Indiana U South Bend (IN)
Inter American U of PR, Aguadilla Campus (PR)
Iona Coll (NY)
Ithaca Coll (NY)
Juniata Coll (PA)
Kennesaw State U (GA)
Kent State U (OH)
Kentucky Wesleyan Coll (KY)
King Coll (TN)
La Roche Coll (PA)
Lebanon Valley Coll (PA)
Le Moyne Coll (NY)
Liberty U (VA)
Lindenwood U (MO)
Long Island U, Brooklyn Campus (NY)
Long Island U, C.W. Post Campus (NY)
Malone Coll (OH)
Manhattanville Coll (NY)
Mansfield U of Pennsylvania (PA)
Marian Coll of Fond du Lac (WI)
Marymount Coll of Fordham U (NY)
Maryville Coll (TN)
Marywood U (PA)
Messiah Coll (PA)
Miami U Hamilton (OH)
MidAmerica Nazarene U (KS)
Minnesota State U Moorhead (MN)
Minot State U (ND)
Missouri Western State Coll (MO)
Molloy Coll (NY)
Montana State U–Billings (MT)
Moravian Coll (PA)
Murray State U (KY)
Niagara U (NY)
North Carolina Central U (NC)
North Carolina State U (NC)
North Dakota State U (ND)
Northern Arizona U (AZ)
Northern Michigan U (MI)
Northwest Nazarene U (ID)
Notre Dame Coll (OH)
Ohio Northern U (OH)
Ohio U (OH)
Ohio Wesleyan U (OH)
Oklahoma Baptist U (OK)
Oral Roberts U (OK)
Pace U (NY)
St. Ambrose U (IA)
St. Bonaventure U (NY)
St. Edward's U (TX)
St. Francis Coll (NY)
St. John's U (NY)
Saint Mary's U of Minnesota (MN)
Saint Xavier U (IL)
Salve Regina U (RI)
San Diego State U (CA)
Seton Hill U (PA)
Southeastern Louisiana U (LA)
Southeastern Oklahoma State U (OK)
Southern Arkansas U–Magnolia (AR)
Southern Nazarene U (OK)
Southwest Baptist U (MO)
Southwest Missouri State U (MO)
State U of NY Coll at Brockport (NY)
State U of NY Coll at Cortland (NY)
State U of NY Coll at Oneonta (NY)
State U of NY Coll at Potsdam (NY)
Taylor U (IN)
Texas A&M Intl U (TX)
Universidad Adventista de las Antillas (PR)
State U of NY at Albany (NY)
The U of Akron (OH)
The U of Arizona (AZ)
U of Illinois at Chicago (IL)
U of Illinois at Urbana–Champaign (IL)
U of Indianapolis (IN)
The U of Iowa (IA)
U of Louisiana at Lafayette (LA)
U of Michigan–Flint (MI)
U of Minnesota, Duluth (MN)
U of Missouri–St. Louis (MO)
U of Nebraska–Lincoln (NE)
The U of North Carolina at Chapel Hill (NC)
The U of North Carolina at Charlotte (NC)
The U of North Carolina at Greensboro (NC)
The U of North Carolina at Wilmington (NC)
U of Puerto Rico, Cayey U Coll (PR)
The U of South Dakota (SD)
The U of Tennessee at Martin (TN)
U of Toledo (OH)
U of Utah (UT)
U of Wisconsin–River Falls (WI)
Valley City State U (ND)
Valparaiso U (IN)
Viterbo U (WI)
Washington U in St. Louis (MO)
Weber State U (UT)
West Chester U of Pennsylvania (PA)
Western Carolina U (NC)
Western Michigan U (MI)
Wheeling Jesuit U (WV)
Widener U (PA)
Winston-Salem State U (NC)
Xavier U of Louisiana (LA)
Youngstown State U (OH)

SPECIAL EDUCATION

Abilene Christian U (TX)
Alabama Ag and Mech U (AL)
Alabama State U (AL)
Albany State U (GA)
Albright Coll (PA)
Alcorn State U (MS)
Alderson-Broaddus Coll (WV)
American Intl Coll (MA)
American U of Puerto Rico (PR)
Anderson Coll (SC)
Arizona State U (AZ)
Arizona State U West (AZ)
Arkansas State U (AR)
Armstrong Atlantic State U (GA)
Ashland U (OH)
Athens State U (AL)
Auburn U (AL)
Augustana Coll (SD)
Augusta State U (GA)
Austin Peay State U (TN)
Avila U (MO)
Ball State U (IN)
Barry U (FL)
Barton Coll (NC)
Baylor U (TX)
Bellarmine U (KY)
Belmont U (TN)
Benedictine Coll (KS)
Benedictine U (IL)
Bethel Coll (TN)
Black Hills State U (SD)
Bloomsburg U of Pennsylvania (PA)
Boise State U (ID)
Boston Coll (MA)
Boston U (MA)
Bowie State U (MD)
Bowling Green State U (OH)
Brenau U (GA)
Brescia U (KY)
Bridgewater Coll (VA)
Bridgewater State Coll (MA)
Brigham Young U (UT)
Brigham Young U–Hawaii (HI)
Buena Vista U (IA)
State U of NY Coll at Buffalo (NY)
Cabrini Coll (PA)
California U of Pennsylvania (PA)
Calvin Coll (MI)
Capital U (OH)
Cardinal Stritch U (WI)
Carlow Coll (PA)
Carson-Newman Coll (TN)
Carthage Coll (WI)
Cedarville U (OH)
Centenary Coll (NJ)
Central Missouri State U (MO)
Central State U (OH)
Central Washington U (WA)
Chadron State Coll (NE)
Chatham Coll (PA)
Cheyney U of Pennsylvania (PA)
Chicago State U (IL)
City U (WA)
Clarion U of Pennsylvania (PA)
Clarke Coll (IA)
Clearwater Christian Coll (FL)
Clemson U (SC)
Cleveland State U (OH)
Coastal Carolina U (SC)
Coker Coll (SC)
Coll Misericordia (PA)
Coll of Charleston (SC)
Coll of Mount St. Joseph (OH)
Coll of Mount Saint Vincent (NY)
The Coll of New Jersey (NJ)
The Coll of New Rochelle (NY)
Coll of Notre Dame of Maryland (MD)
Coll of Saint Elizabeth (NJ)
Coll of St. Joseph (VT)
Coll of Saint Mary (NE)
The Coll of Saint Rose (NY)
Coll of the Southwest (NM)
Columbia Coll (SC)
Columbus State U (GA)
Concord Coll (WV)
Concordia U (NE)
Converse Coll (SC)
Culver-Stockton Coll (MO)
Cumberland Coll (KY)
Cumberland U (TN)
Curry Coll (MA)
Daemen Coll (NY)
Dakota State U (SD)
Dakota Wesleyan U (SD)
Dana Coll (NE)
Defiance Coll (OH)
Delaware State U (DE)
Delta State U (MS)
Dillard U (LA)
Doane Coll (NE)
Dominican Coll (NY)
Dowling Coll (NY)
Duquesne U (PA)
D'Youville Coll (NY)
East Central U (OK)
Eastern Illinois U (IL)
Eastern Kentucky U (KY)
Eastern Michigan U (MI)
Eastern Nazarene Coll (MA)
Eastern New Mexico U (NM)
Eastern Oregon U (OR)
Eastern Washington U (WA)
East Stroudsburg U of Pennsylvania (PA)
Edinboro U of Pennsylvania (PA)
Elizabeth City State U (NC)
Elmhurst Coll (IL)
Elms Coll (MA)
Elon U (NC)
Erskine Coll (SC)
Evangel U (MO)
Fairmont State Coll (WV)
Florida Atlantic U (FL)
Florida Gulf Coast U (FL)
Fontbonne U (MO)
Freed-Hardeman U (TN)
Furman U (SC)
Gannon U (PA)
Geneva Coll (PA)
Georgia Coll & State U (GA)
Georgian Court U (NJ)
Georgia Southern U (GA)
Georgia Southwestern State U (GA)
Glenville State Coll (WV)
Gonzaga U (WA)
Gordon Coll (MA)
Goucher Coll (MD)
Grace Coll (IN)
Grambling State U (LA)
Grand Canyon U (AZ)
Grand Valley State U (MI)
Greensboro Coll (NC)
Greenville Coll (IL)
Gwynedd-Mercy Coll (PA)
Hampton U (VA)
Hastings Coll (NE)
Heidelberg Coll (OH)
High Point U (NC)
Hood Coll (MD)
Houston Baptist U (TX)
Huntington Coll (IN)
Idaho State U (ID)
Illinois State U (IL)
Indiana State U (IN)
Indiana U Bloomington (IN)
Indiana U of Pennsylvania (PA)
Indiana U South Bend (IN)
Indiana U Southeast (IN)
Inter American U of PR, Fajardo Campus (PR)
Inter American U of PR, Ponce Campus (PR)
Jacksonville State U (AL)
Jacksonville U (FL)
Jarvis Christian Coll (TX)
John Brown U (AR)
John Carroll U (OH)
Juniata Coll (PA)
Kansas Wesleyan U (KS)
Kean U (NJ)
Keene State Coll (NH)
Kent State U (OH)
Keuka Coll (NY)
King's Coll (PA)
Kutztown U of Pennsylvania (PA)
Lamar U (TX)
Lambuth U (TN)
Lander U (SC)
La Salle U (PA)
Lesley U (MA)
Lewis U (IL)
Liberty U (VA)
Lincoln U (MO)
Lincoln U (PA)
Lindenwood U (MO)
Lock Haven U of Pennsylvania (PA)
Long Island U, Brooklyn Campus (NY)
Longwood U (VA)
Louisiana Coll (LA)
Louisiana State U in Shreveport (LA)
Louisiana Tech U (LA)
Loyola Coll in Maryland (MD)
Loyola U Chicago (IL)
Lubbock Christian U (TX)
Lynchburg Coll (VA)
Lyndon State Coll (VT)
MacMurray Coll (IL)
Madonna U (MI)
Manchester Coll (IN)
Manhattan Coll (NY)
Mansfield U of Pennsylvania (PA)
Marian Coll (IN)
Marist Coll (NY)
Marymount Coll of Fordham U (NY)
Marymount U (VA)
Marywood U (PA)
McGill U (QC, Canada)
McNeese State U (LA)
McPherson Coll (KS)
Medgar Evers Coll of the City U of NY (NY)
Memorial U of Newfoundland (NL, Canada)
Mercy Coll (NY)
Mercyhurst Coll (PA)
Methodist Coll (NC)
Miami Dade Coll (FL)
Miami U (OH)
Miami U Hamilton (OH)
Michigan State U (MI)
Middle Tennessee State U (TN)
Millersville U of Pennsylvania (PA)
Minnesota State U Moorhead (MN)
Mississippi Coll (MS)
Mississippi State U (MS)
Missouri Southern State U (MO)
Missouri Valley Coll (MO)
Molloy Coll (NY)
Monmouth U (NJ)
Montana State U–Billings (MT)
Morehead State U (KY)
Morningside Coll (IA)
Mount Marty Coll (SD)
Mount Saint Mary Coll (NY)
Mount Vernon Nazarene U (OH)
Murray State U (KY)
Nazareth Coll of Rochester (NY)
Nebraska Wesleyan U (NE)
Newberry Coll (SC)
New Jersey City U (NJ)
New Mexico Highlands U (NM)
New Mexico State U (NM)
New York U (NY)
Niagara U (NY)
Nicholls State U (LA)
Northeastern Illinois U (IL)
Northeastern State U (OK)
Northern Arizona U (AZ)
Northern Illinois U (IL)
Northern Michigan U (MI)
Northern State U (SD)
North Georgia Coll & State U (GA)
Northwestern Oklahoma State U (OK)
Northwestern State U of Louisiana (LA)
Nova Southeastern U (FL)
Oakland U (MI)
Ohio Dominican U (OH)
The Ohio State U (OH)
Ohio U (OH)
Oklahoma Baptist U (OK)
Oral Roberts U (OK)
Our Lady of the Lake U of San Antonio (TX)
Pacific Lutheran U (WA)
Pacific Oaks Coll (CA)
Penn State U Abington Coll (PA)
Penn State U Altoona Coll (PA)
Penn State U at Erie, The Behrend Coll (PA)
Penn State U Beaver Campus of the Commonwealth Coll (PA)
Penn State U Berks Cmps of Berks-Lehigh Valley Coll (PA)
Penn State U Delaware County Campus of the Commonwealth Coll (PA)
Penn State U DuBois Campus of the Commonwealth Coll (PA)
Penn State U Fayette Campus of the Commonwealth Coll (PA)
Penn State U Hazleton Campus of the Commonwealth Coll (PA)
Penn State U Lehigh Valley Cmps of Berks-Lehigh Valley Coll (PA)
Penn State U McKeesport Campus of the Commonwealth Coll (PA)
Penn State U Mont Alto Campus of the Commonwealth Coll (PA)
Penn State U New Kensington Campus of the Commonwealth Coll (PA)
Penn State U Schuylkill Campus of the Capital Coll (PA)
Penn State U Shenango Campus of the Commonwealth Coll (PA)
Penn State U Univ Park Campus (PA)
Penn State U Wilkes-Barre Campus of the Commonwealth Coll (PA)
Penn State U Worthington Scranton Cmps Commonwealth Coll (PA)
Penn State U York Campus of the Commonwealth Coll (PA)
Pfeiffer U (NC)
Piedmont Coll (GA)
Pontifical Catholic U of Puerto Rico (PR)
Presbyterian Coll (SC)
Providence Coll (RI)
Quincy U (IL)
Rhode Island Coll (RI)
Rivier Coll (NH)
Roberts Wesleyan Coll (NY)
Roosevelt U (IL)
Rowan U (NJ)
Saginaw Valley State U (MI)
Saint Augustine's Coll (NC)
St. Bonaventure U (NY)
St. Cloud State U (MN)
Saint Francis U (PA)
St. John Fisher Coll (NY)
St. John's U (NY)
Saint Joseph Coll (CT)
St. Joseph's Coll, Suffolk Campus (NY)
Saint Martin's Coll (WA)
Saint Mary-of-the-Woods Coll (IN)
St. Thomas Aquinas Coll (NY)
Salve Regina U (RI)
Seattle Pacific U (WA)
Seton Hall U (NJ)
Seton Hill U (PA)
Shawnee State U (OH)
Simmons Coll (MA)
Slippery Rock U of Pennsylvania (PA)
South Carolina State U (SC)
Southeastern Louisiana U (LA)
Southeast Missouri State U (MO)
Southern Connecticut State U (CT)
Southern Illinois U Carbondale (IL)
Southern Illinois U Edwardsville (IL)
Southern U and A&M Coll (LA)
Southern Utah U (UT)
Southern Wesleyan U (SC)
Southwestern Oklahoma State U (OK)
Southwest Missouri State U (MO)
Springfield Coll (MA)
State U of NY at New Paltz (NY)
Plattsburgh State U of NY (NY)
State U of NY Coll at Geneseo (NY)
State U of NY Coll at Old Westbury (NY)
Syracuse U (NY)
Tabor Coll (KS)
Tennessee State U (TN)
Tennessee Technological U (TN)
Texas A&M Intl U (TX)
Texas A&M U–Commerce (TX)

Texas Christian U (TX)
Texas Southern U (TX)
Texas Woman's U (TX)
Towson U (MD)
Trinity Christian Coll (IL)
Trinity Coll (DC)
Troy State U (AL)
Tufts U (MA)
Tusculum Coll (TN)
Union Coll (KY)
Union U (TN)
Université de Montréal (QC, Canada)
Université de Sherbrooke (QC, Canada)
U du Québec à Hull (QC, Canada)
The U of Alabama (AL)
The U of Alabama at Birmingham (AL)
U of Alberta (AB, Canada)
The U of Arizona (AZ)
U of Arkansas (AR)
U of Arkansas at Monticello (AR)
The U of British Columbia (BC, Canada)
U of Calif, Los Angeles (CA)
U of Central Arkansas (AR)
U of Central Florida (FL)
U of Cincinnati (OH)
U of Connecticut (CT)
U of Dayton (OH)
U of Delaware (DE)
U of Detroit Mercy (MI)
U of Evansville (IN)
The U of Findlay (OH)
U of Florida (FL)
U of Georgia (GA)
U of Great Falls (MT)
U of Hartford (CT)
U of Hawaii at Manoa (HI)
U of Idaho (ID)
U of Illinois at Urbana–Champaign (IL)
U of Kentucky (KY)
The U of Lethbridge (AB, Canada)
U of Louisiana at Lafayette (LA)
U of Maine at Farmington (ME)
U of Mary Hardin-Baylor (TX)
U of Maryland, Coll Park (MD)
U of Maryland Eastern Shore (MD)
The U of Memphis (TN)
U of Miami (FL)
U of Minnesota, Duluth (MN)
U of Mississippi (MS)
U of Missouri–St. Louis (MO)
U of Nevada, Las Vegas (NV)
U of Nevada, Reno (NV)
U of New Brunswick Fredericton (NB, Canada)
U of New Mexico (NM)
U of North Alabama (AL)
The U of North Carolina at Greensboro (NC)
U of Northern Colorado (CO)
U of Northern Iowa (IA)
U of North Florida (FL)
U of Oklahoma (OK)
U of Ottawa (ON, Canada)
U of St. Francis (IL)
U of Saint Francis (IN)
The U of Scranton (PA)
U of South Alabama (AL)
U of South Carolina Aiken (SC)
The U of South Dakota (SD)
U of South Florida (FL)
The U of Tennessee (TN)
The U of Tennessee at Chattanooga (TN)
The U of Tennessee at Martin (TN)
The U of Texas at Brownsville (TX)
U of the District of Columbia (DC)
U of the Incarnate Word (TX)
U of the Ozarks (AR)
U of the Pacific (CA)
U of Toledo (OH)
U of Utah (UT)
U of Victoria (BC, Canada)
The U of West Alabama (AL)
The U of Western Ontario (ON, Canada)
U of West Florida (FL)
U of Windsor (ON, Canada)
U of Wisconsin–Eau Claire (WI)
U of Wisconsin–Madison (WI)
U of Wisconsin–Milwaukee (WI)
U of Wisconsin–Oshkosh (WI)
U of Wisconsin–Superior (WI)
U of Wisconsin–Whitewater (WI)
U of Wyoming (WY)
Ursuline Coll (OH)
Utah State U (UT)
Valdosta State U (GA)
Vanderbilt U (TN)
Virginia Union U (VA)
Walsh U (OH)
Warner Southern Coll (FL)
Washington State U (WA)
Waynesburg Coll (PA)
Wayne State Coll (NE)
Wayne State U (MI)
Webster U (MO)
West Chester U of Pennsylvania (PA)
Western Carolina U (NC)
Western Illinois U (IL)
Western Kentucky U (KY)
Western State Coll of Colorado (CO)
Western Washington U (WA)
Westfield State Coll (MA)
Westminster Coll (UT)
West Virginia Wesleyan Coll (WV)
Wheelock Coll (MA)
Whitworth Coll (WA)
Widener U (PA)
William Paterson U of New Jersey (NJ)
William Penn U (IA)
William Woods U (MO)
Winona State U (MN)
Winston-Salem State U (NC)
Winthrop U (SC)
Xavier U (OH)
Xavier U of Louisiana (LA)
York Coll (NE)
York U (ON, Canada)
Youngstown State U (OH)

SPECIAL EDUCATION (ADMINISTRATION)
East Central U (OK)
Sterling Coll (VT)
Wright State U (OH)

SPECIAL EDUCATION (EARLY CHILDHOOD)
Canisius Coll (NY)
Cazenovia Coll (NY)
Delaware State U (DE)
Eastern Washington U (WA)
Harding U (AR)
Juniata Coll (PA)
Keuka Coll (NY)
U of Northern Iowa (IA)

SPECIAL EDUCATION (EMOTIONALLY DISTURBED)
Augsburg Coll (MN)
Bradley U (IL)
Central Michigan U (MI)
East Carolina U (NC)
Eastern Mennonite U (VA)
Eastern Michigan U (MI)
Flagler Coll (FL)
Florida Intl U (FL)
Florida State U (FL)
Greensboro Coll (NC)
Hope Coll (MI)
Loras Coll (IA)
Marygrove Coll (MI)
Minnesota State U Moorhead (MN)
Oklahoma Baptist U (OK)
Southern Wesleyan U (SC)
Trinity Christian Coll (IL)
U of Detroit Mercy (MI)
U of Maine at Farmington (ME)
The U of North Carolina at Wilmington (NC)
U of South Florida (FL)
U of Toledo (OH)
Wright State U (OH)

SPECIAL EDUCATION (GIFTED AND TALENTED)
Texas Christian U (TX)
U of Great Falls (MT)
Wright State U (OH)

SPECIAL EDUCATION (HEARING IMPAIRED)
Augustana Coll (SD)
Barton Coll (NC)
Boston U (MA)
Bowling Green State U (OH)
The Coll of New Jersey (NJ)
Eastern Kentucky U (KY)
Eastern Michigan U (MI)
Flagler Coll (FL)
Indiana U of Pennsylvania (PA)
Lambuth U (TN)
MacMurray Coll (IL)
Michigan State U (MI)
Minot State U (ND)
Texas Christian U (TX)
U of Arkansas at Little Rock (AR)
U of Nebraska–Lincoln (NE)
The U of North Carolina at Greensboro (NC)
U of Science and Arts of Oklahoma (OK)
U of Toledo (OH)

SPECIAL EDUCATION (MENTALLY RETARDED)
Augusta State U (GA)
Bowling Green State U (OH)
Bradley U (IL)
Central Michigan U (MI)
East Carolina U (NC)
Eastern Mennonite U (VA)
Eastern Michigan U (MI)
Flagler Coll (FL)
Florida Intl U (FL)
Florida State U (FL)
Greensboro Coll (NC)
Loras Coll (IA)
Minnesota State U Moorhead (MN)
Minot State U (ND)
Northern Michigan U (MI)
Oakland City U (IN)
Oklahoma Baptist U (OK)
Shaw U (NC)
Silver Lake Coll (WI)
Southern Wesleyan U (SC)
State U of West Georgia (GA)
Trinity Christian Coll (IL)
The U of Akron (OH)
U of Maine at Farmington (ME)
U of Mary (ND)
The U of North Carolina at Charlotte (NC)
The U of North Carolina at Pembroke (NC)
The U of North Carolina at Wilmington (NC)
U of Northern Iowa (IA)
U of South Florida (FL)
U of West Florida (FL)
Western Michigan U (MI)
Wright State U (OH)

SPECIAL EDUCATION (MULTIPLY DISABLED)
Bowling Green State U (OH)
Dominican Coll (NY)
Flagler Coll (FL)
Inter Amer U of PR, Barranquitas Campus (PR)
Ohio U (OH)
The U of Akron (OH)
U of Detroit Mercy (MI)
U of Northern Iowa (IA)
U of Toledo (OH)
Wright State U (OH)

SPECIAL EDUCATION (ORTHOPEDIC AND OTHER PHYSICAL HEALTH IMPAIRMENTS)
Eastern Michigan U (MI)
Indiana U of Pennsylvania (PA)
Wright State U (OH)

SPECIAL EDUCATION RELATED
Auburn U (AL)
Harding U (AR)
Juniata Coll (PA)
Lock Haven U of Pennsylvania (PA)
Lycoming Coll (PA)
Minot State U (ND)
Nevada State Coll at Henderson (NV)
Saint Joseph's U (PA)
Southeastern Oklahoma State U (OK)
The U of Akron (OH)
U of Arkansas (AR)
U of Missouri–Columbia (MO)
U of Nebraska–Lincoln (NE)
U of Southern Indiana (IN)
U of Toledo (OH)
U of Wyoming (WY)
Wright State U (OH)
Xavier U of Louisiana (LA)
York Coll of Pennsylvania (PA)

SPECIAL EDUCATION (SPECIFIC LEARNING DISABILITIES)
Appalachian State U (NC)
Aquinas Coll (MI)
Baldwin-Wallace Coll (OH)
Bethune-Cookman Coll (FL)
Bowling Green State U (OH)
Bradley U (IL)
East Carolina U (NC)
Eastern Mennonite U (VA)
Eastern Michigan U (MI)
Elizabeth City State U (NC)
Flagler Coll (FL)
Florida Intl U (FL)
Florida Southern Coll (FL)
Florida State U (FL)
Greensboro Coll (NC)
Harding U (AR)
Hope Coll (MI)
Malone Coll (OH)
Michigan State U (MI)
Minnesota State U Moorhead (MN)
Northwestern U (IL)
Notre Dame Coll (OH)
Oklahoma Baptist U (OK)
Silver Lake Coll (WI)
Southern Wesleyan U (SC)
Trinity Christian Coll (IL)
The U of Akron (OH)
U of Detroit Mercy (MI)
U of Maine at Farmington (ME)
The U of North Carolina at Pembroke (NC)
The U of North Carolina at Wilmington (NC)
U of South Florida (FL)
U of Toledo (OH)
West Virginia Wesleyan Coll (WV)
Wheeling Jesuit U (WV)
Winston-Salem State U (NC)
Wright State U (OH)
Youngstown State U (OH)

SPECIAL EDUCATION (SPEECH OR LANGUAGE IMPAIRED)
Alabama Ag and Mech U (AL)
Baylor U (TX)
Bloomsburg U of Pennsylvania (PA)
Brooklyn Coll of the City U of NY (NY)
State U of NY Coll at Buffalo (NY)
Eastern Kentucky U (KY)
Eastern Michigan U (MI)
Emerson Coll (MA)
Indiana U of Pennsylvania (PA)
Ithaca Coll (NY)
Kutztown U of Pennsylvania (PA)
Long Island U, Brooklyn Campus (NY)
Long Island U, C.W. Post Campus (NY)
Louisiana Tech U (LA)
Minot State U (ND)
New Mexico State U (NM)
New York U (NY)
Northern Arizona U (AZ)
Pace U (NY)
Southeastern Louisiana U (LA)
State U of NY Coll at Cortland (NY)
The U of Akron (OH)
U of Toledo (OH)
Wayne State U (MI)
Western Kentucky U (KY)

SPECIAL EDUCATION (VISION IMPAIRED)
Auburn U (AL)
Eastern Michigan U (MI)
Florida State U (FL)
Kutztown U of Pennsylvania (PA)
St. Francis Coll (NY)
U of Toledo (OH)
Western Michigan U (MI)

SPECIAL PRODUCTS MARKETING
Ball State U (IN)
State U of NY Coll at Buffalo (NY)
Carlow Coll (PA)
Concord Coll (WV)
Dominican U (IL)
Immaculata U (PA)
Iowa State U of Science and Technology (IA)
Johnson & Wales U (RI)
Lindenwood U (MO)
Lipscomb U (TN)
Lynn U (FL)
Madonna U (MI)
Mount Saint Vincent U (NS, Canada)
North Carolina Wesleyan Coll (NC)
Northern Michigan U (MI)
Oregon State U (OR)
Quinnipiac U (CT)
Rochester Inst of Technology (NY)
San Francisco State U (CA)
U of Alberta (AB, Canada)
U of Maryland Eastern Shore (MD)
Wayne State Coll (NE)

SPEECH AND RHETORIC
Abilene Christian U (TX)
Adams State Coll (CO)
Adelphi U (NY)
Alabama State U (AL)
Albany State U (GA)
Alderson-Broaddus Coll (WV)
Anderson Coll (SC)
Appalachian State U (NC)
Arkansas State U (AR)
Arkansas Tech U (AR)
Asbury Coll (KY)
Ashland U (OH)
Auburn U (AL)
Augsburg Coll (MN)
Augustana Coll (IL)
Baker U (KS)
Ball State U (IN)
Bates Coll (ME)
Belmont U (TN)
Bemidji State U (MN)
Bethune-Cookman Coll (FL)
Blackburn Coll (IL)
Black Hills State U (SD)
Bloomsburg U of Pennsylvania (PA)
Blue Mountain Coll (MS)
Bowling Green State U (OH)
Bradley U (IL)
Brigham Young U (UT)
Butler U (IN)
California Polytechnic State U, San Luis Obispo (CA)
California State U, Chico (CA)
California State U, Fresno (CA)
California State U, Fullerton (CA)
California State U, Hayward (CA)
California State U, Long Beach (CA)
California State U, Los Angeles (CA)
Calvin Coll (MI)
Capital U (OH)
Carson-Newman Coll (TN)
Carthage Coll (WI)
Cedarville U (OH)
Central Michigan U (MI)
Central Missouri State U (MO)
Chadron State Coll (NE)
Charleston Southern U (SC)
Clarion U of Pennsylvania (PA)
Clark Atlanta U (GA)
Clemson U (SC)
Coe Coll (IA)
The Coll of New Jersey (NJ)
Coll of Saint Benedict (MN)
Coll of St. Catherine (MN)
Coll of the Ozarks (MO)
Colorado State U (CO)
Concordia Coll (MN)
Concordia U (NE)
Cornell Coll (IA)
Cornerstone U (MI)
Creighton U (NE)
Cumberland Coll (KY)
Defiance Coll (OH)
Denison U (OH)
Dickinson State U (ND)
Dillard U (LA)
Doane Coll (NE)
Dowling Coll (NY)
Drake U (IA)
East Central U (OK)
Eastern Illinois U (IL)
Eastern Kentucky U (KY)
Eastern Michigan U (MI)
East Texas Baptist U (TX)
Emerson Coll (MA)
Evangel U (MO)
Fairmont State Coll (WV)
Florida Atlantic U (FL)
Frostburg State U (MD)
Geneva Coll (PA)
George Mason U (VA)
Georgetown Coll (KY)
The George Washington U (DC)
Georgia Coll & State U (GA)
Georgia Southern U (GA)
Georgia State U (GA)
Gonzaga U (WA)
Governors State U (IL)
Graceland U (IA)
Grand Canyon U (AZ)
Greenville Coll (IL)
Gustavus Adolphus Coll (MN)
Hannibal-LaGrange Coll (MO)
Hardin-Simmons U (TX)
Hastings Coll (NE)
Henderson State U (AR)
Hillsdale Coll (MI)
Hofstra U (NY)
Houston Baptist U (TX)
Howard Payne U (TX)
Humboldt State U (CA)
Huntingdon Coll (AL)
Illinois Coll (IL)
Illinois State U (IL)
Indiana U Bloomington (IN)
Indiana U South Bend (IN)
Iona Coll (NY)
Iowa State U of Science and Technology (IA)
Ithaca Coll (NY)
Judson Coll (IL)
Kansas Wesleyan U (KS)
Kent State U (OH)
Kutztown U of Pennsylvania (PA)
Lehman Coll of the City U of NY (NY)

Lewis U (IL)
Lipscomb U (TN)
Lock Haven U of Pennsylvania (PA)
Long Island U, Brooklyn Campus (NY)
Louisiana Coll (LA)
Louisiana State U and A&M Coll (LA)
Louisiana State U in Shreveport (LA)
Louisiana Tech U (LA)
Lynchburg Coll (VA)
Madonna U (MI)
Manchester Coll (IN)
Mansfield U of Pennsylvania (PA)
Marietta Coll (OH)
Marquette U (WI)
Marshall U (WV)
Marymount Coll of Fordham U (NY)
The Master's Coll and Sem (CA)
McKendree Coll (IL)
McMurry U (TX)
McNeese State U (LA)
Mercy Coll (NY)
Metropolitan State Coll of Denver (CO)
Miami U (OH)
Minnesota State U Mankato (MN)
Minnesota State U Moorhead (MN)
Minot State U (ND)
Mississippi Valley State U (MS)
Missouri Valley Coll (MO)
Monmouth Coll (IL)
Morehead State U (KY)
Morgan State U (MD)
Mount Mercy Coll (IA)
Murray State U (KY)
Nebraska Wesleyan U (NE)
Newberry Coll (SC)
New Mexico State U (NM)
North Central Coll (IL)
North Dakota State U (ND)
Northeastern Illinois U (IL)
Northern Arizona U (AZ)
Northern Michigan U (MI)
Northern State U (SD)
North Park U (IL)
Northwestern Coll (IA)
Northwestern Oklahoma State U (OK)
Northwestern U (IL)
Ohio U (OH)
Oklahoma Baptist U (OK)
Oklahoma Christian U (OK)
Oklahoma City U (OK)
Oklahoma State U (OK)
Old Dominion U (VA)
Olivet Nazarene U (IL)
Oregon State U (OR)
Ouachita Baptist U (AR)
Pace U (NY)
Pepperdine U, Malibu (CA)
Portland State U (OR)
Rhode Island Coll (RI)
Rider U (NJ)
St. Cloud State U (MN)
Saint John's U (MN)
St. John's U (NY)
St. Joseph's Coll, New York (NY)
St. Joseph's Coll, Suffolk Campus (NY)
St. Mary's U of San Antonio (TX)
Samford U (AL)
Sam Houston State U (TX)
San Diego State U (CA)
San Francisco State U (CA)
San Jose State U (CA)
Shippensburg U of Pennsylvania (PA)
Simpson Coll (IA)
South Dakota State U (SD)
Southeast Missouri State U (MO)
Southern Illinois U Carbondale (IL)
Southern Illinois U Edwardsville (IL)
Southern Nazarene U (OK)
Southern U and A&M Coll (LA)
Southern Utah U (UT)
State U of NY at New Paltz (NY)
State U of NY Coll at Brockport (NY)
State U of NY Coll at Cortland (NY)
State U of NY Coll at Oneonta (NY)
State U of NY Coll at Potsdam (NY)
Stonehill Coll (MA)
Suffolk U (MA)
Susquehanna U (PA)
Syracuse U (NY)
Tarleton State U (TX)
Texas A&M U (TX)
Texas A&M U–Kingsville (TX)
Texas Southern U (TX)
Texas State U-San Marcos (TX)
Texas Tech U (TX)
Texas Wesleyan U (TX)
Thomas More Coll (KY)
Trinity U (TX)
Troy State U (AL)
Truman State U (MO)
Union U (TN)
State U of NY at Albany (NY)
The U of Akron (OH)
The U of Alabama (AL)
The U of Alabama in Huntsville (AL)
U of Alaska Fairbanks (AK)
U of Arkansas at Little Rock (AR)
U of Arkansas at Monticello (AR)
U of Calif, Berkeley (CA)
U of Calif, Davis (CA)
U of Central Arkansas (AR)
U of Central Florida (FL)
U of Dubuque (IA)
U of Georgia (GA)
U of Hawaii at Manoa (HI)
U of Houston (TX)
U of Illinois at Chicago (IL)
U of Illinois at Urbana–Champaign (IL)
The U of Iowa (IA)
U of Kansas (KS)
U of Mary Hardin-Baylor (TX)
U of Michigan (MI)
U of Michigan–Dearborn (MI)
U of Minnesota, Morris (MN)
The U of Montana–Missoula (MT)
U of Montevallo (AL)
U of Nebraska at Omaha (NE)
U of New Mexico (NM)
U of North Alabama (AL)
The U of North Carolina at Greensboro (NC)
The U of North Carolina at Wilmington (NC)
U of Northern Iowa (IA)
U of Pittsburgh (PA)
U of Richmond (VA)
U of Sioux Falls (SD)
U of South Florida (FL)
The U of Tennessee (TN)
The U of Texas at Arlington (TX)
The U of Texas at Tyler (TX)
The U of Texas–Pan American (TX)
U of the Incarnate Word (TX)
U of the Virgin Islands (VI)
U of Utah (UT)
U of Washington (WA)
U of Waterloo (ON, Canada)
U of Wisconsin–La Crosse (WI)
U of Wisconsin–Platteville (WI)
U of Wisconsin–River Falls (WI)
U of Wisconsin–Superior (WI)
U of Wisconsin–Whitewater (WI)
Utah State U (UT)
Vanguard U of Southern California (CA)
Wabash Coll (IN)
Walla Walla Coll (WA)
Washburn U (KS)
Wayne State Coll (NE)
West Chester U of Pennsylvania (PA)
Western Kentucky U (KY)
West Texas A&M U (TX)
West Virginia Wesleyan Coll (WV)
Whitworth Coll (WA)
Willamette U (OR)
William Jewell Coll (MO)
Wingate U (NC)
Winona State U (MN)
York Coll of Pennsylvania (PA)
York Coll of the City U of New York (NY)
Youngstown State U (OH)

SPEECH-LANGUAGE PATHOLOGY

Abilene Christian U (TX)
Augustana Coll (IL)
Brooklyn Coll of the City U of NY (NY)
Central Missouri State U (MO)
Columbia Coll (SC)
Duquesne U (PA)
Eastern Michigan U (MI)
Emerson Coll (MA)
Grambling State U (LA)
Harding U (AR)
James Madison U (VA)
Lehman Coll of the City U of NY (NY)
Loyola Coll in Maryland (MD)
Marshall U (WV)
Miami U (OH)
Miami U Hamilton (OH)
Nevada State Coll at Henderson (NV)
Northern Michigan U (MI)
Northwestern U (IL)
Pace U (NY)
Rockhurst U (MO)
St. Cloud State U (MN)
Saint Xavier U (IL)
State U of West Georgia (GA)
Texas Christian U (TX)
Texas Woman's U (TX)
Towson U (MD)
The U of Akron (OH)
U of Maryland, Coll Park (MD)
U of Nebraska–Lincoln (NE)
U of Nevada, Reno (NV)
U of Northern Colorado (CO)
U of Northern Iowa (IA)
U of Oklahoma Health Sciences Center (OK)
U of Science and Arts of Oklahoma (OK)
The U of Tennessee (TN)
U of Toledo (OH)
U of Wisconsin–Whitewater (WI)
Valdosta State U (GA)
Wayne State U (MI)
Xavier U of Louisiana (LA)

SPEECH TEACHER EDUCATION

Arkansas Tech U (AR)
Baylor U (TX)
Brigham Young U (UT)
Brooklyn Coll of the City U of NY (NY)
Buena Vista U (IA)
Capital U (OH)
Central Michigan U (MI)
Central Missouri State U (MO)
Chadron State Coll (NE)
Coll of St. Catherine (MN)
Concordia U (IL)
Concordia U (MI)
Concordia U (NE)
Dana Coll (NE)
Dordt Coll (IA)
East Central U (OK)
East Texas Baptist U (TX)
Elmira Coll (NY)
Evangel U (MO)
Harding U (AR)
Hastings Coll (NE)
Henderson State U (AR)
Howard Payne U (TX)
Indiana U Bloomington (IN)
Indiana U–Purdue U Fort Wayne (IN)
Indiana U–Purdue U Indianapolis (IN)
Kean U (NJ)
Louisiana Tech U (LA)
McNeese State U (LA)
Minnesota State U Moorhead (MN)
Murray State U (KY)
North Dakota State U (ND)
Northwestern Oklahoma State U (OK)
Oklahoma Baptist U (OK)
Pillsbury Baptist Bible Coll (MN)
St. Ambrose U (IA)
Samford U (AL)
Southeastern Louisiana U (LA)
Southeast Missouri State U (MO)
Southern Nazarene U (OK)
Southwest Baptist U (MO)
Taylor U (IN)
Texas Wesleyan U (TX)
The U of Akron (OH)
The U of Arizona (AZ)
U of Indianapolis (IN)
The U of Iowa (IA)
U of Louisiana at Lafayette (LA)
U of Michigan–Flint (MI)
The U of North Carolina at Chapel Hill (NC)
The U of North Carolina at Greensboro (NC)
U of Northern Iowa (IA)
The U of South Dakota (SD)
William Carey Coll (MS)
William Jewell Coll (MO)
York Coll (NE)
Youngstown State U (OH)

SPEECH/THEATER EDUCATION

Augustana Coll (SD)
Bemidji State U (MN)
Boston U (MA)
Briar Cliff U (IA)
Columbus State U (GA)
Culver-Stockton Coll (MO)
Dickinson State U (ND)
Graceland U (IA)
Grambling State U (LA)
Hamline U (MN)
Hastings Coll (NE)
King Coll (TN)
Lewis U (IL)
McKendree Coll (IL)
McPherson Coll (KS)
Missouri Western State Coll (MO)
Northwestern Coll (IA)
Oklahoma City U (OK)
St. Ambrose U (IA)
Southwest Baptist U (MO)
U of Minnesota, Morris (MN)
U of St. Thomas (MN)
U of Windsor (ON, Canada)
Wartburg Coll (IA)
William Woods U (MO)
York Coll (NE)
York U (ON, Canada)

SPEECH THERAPY

Auburn U (AL)
Augustana Coll (IL)
Eastern Kentucky U (KY)
Eastern Washington U (WA)
Elms Coll (MA)
Emerson Coll (MA)
Fontbonne U (MO)
Hampton U (VA)
Indiana U Bloomington (IN)
Iona Coll (NY)
Lamar U (TX)
Murray State U (KY)
Northeastern State U (OK)
Northwestern U (IL)
Ohio U (OH)
Queens Coll of the City U of NY (NY)
St. Cloud State U (MN)
State U of NY at New Paltz (NY)
State U of NY Coll at Fredonia (NY)
State U of NY Coll at Geneseo (NY)
Texas A&M U–Kingsville (TX)
Texas Southern U (TX)
The U of British Columbia (BC, Canada)
U of New Hampshire (NH)
U of Oklahoma Health Sciences Center (OK)
U of Redlands (CA)
The U of Texas–Pan American (TX)
U of Toledo (OH)
U of Wisconsin–Madison (WI)
U of Wisconsin–River Falls (WI)
Xavier U of Louisiana (LA)

SPORT AND FITNESS ADMINISTRATION

Abilene Christian U (TX)
Albertson Coll of Idaho (ID)
Alvernia Coll (PA)
American Public U System (WV)
American U (DC)
Anderson Coll (SC)
Arkansas State U (AR)
Asbury Coll (KY)
Augustana Coll (SD)
Averett U (VA)
Baldwin-Wallace Coll (OH)
Ball State U (IN)
Barber-Scotia Coll (NC)
Barry U (FL)
Barton Coll (NC)
Baylor U (TX)
Becker Coll (MA)
Belhaven Coll (MS)
Bemidji State U (MN)
Bethany Coll (WV)
Bethel Coll (IN)
Black Hills State U (SD)
Bluffton Coll (OH)
Bowling Green State U (OH)
Brock U (ON, Canada)
Buena Vista U (IA)
Campbell U (NC)
Carroll Coll (MT)
Cazenovia Coll (NY)
Cedarville U (OH)
Centenary Coll (NJ)
Central Methodist Coll (MO)
Central Michigan U (MI)
Central Washington U (WA)
Chowan Coll (NC)
Cleveland State U (OH)
Coker Coll (SC)
Colby-Sawyer Coll (NH)
Coll Misericordia (PA)
Columbia Southern U (AL)
Concordia U (NE)
Concordia U (OR)
Concordia U Wisconsin (WI)
Cornerstone U (MI)
Crown Coll (MN)
Daniel Webster Coll (NH)
Davis & Elkins Coll (WV)
Defiance Coll (OH)
Delaware State U (DE)
DeSales U (PA)
Eastern Connecticut State U (CT)
Eastern Mennonite U (VA)
Eastern Michigan U (MI)
Edinboro U of Pennsylvania (PA)
Elmhurst Coll (IL)
Elon U (NC)
Emmanuel Coll (GA)
Endicott Coll (MA)
Erskine Coll (SC)
Faulkner U (AL)
Flagler Coll (FL)
Florida State U (FL)
Franklin Pierce Coll (NH)
Fresno Pacific U (CA)
Frostburg State U (MD)
Gardner-Webb U (NC)
George Fox U (OR)
Georgia Southern U (GA)
Gonzaga U (WA)
Graceland U (IA)
Greensboro Coll (NC)
Greenville Coll (IL)
Guilford Coll (NC)
Hampton U (VA)
Harding U (AR)
Hastings Coll (NE)
Henderson State U (AR)
High Point U (NC)
Howard Payne U (TX)
Huntingdon Coll (AL)
Husson Coll (ME)
Indiana U Bloomington (IN)
Iowa Wesleyan Coll (IA)
Ithaca Coll (NY)
Johnson State Coll (VT)
Judson Coll (IL)
Keene State Coll (NH)
Kennesaw State U (GA)
Kentucky Wesleyan Coll (KY)
Keystone Coll (PA)
Lambuth U (TN)
Laurentian U (ON, Canada)
LeTourneau U (TX)
Liberty U (VA)
Limestone Coll (SC)
Lindenwood U (MO)
Livingstone Coll (NC)
Longwood U (VA)
Loras Coll (IA)
Lubbock Christian U (TX)
Luther Coll (IA)
Lynchburg Coll (VA)
Lyndon State Coll (VT)
Lynn U (FL)
MacMurray Coll (IL)
Malone Coll (OH)
Marian Coll of Fond du Lac (WI)
Mars Hill Coll (NC)
Marymount U (VA)
Medaille Coll (NY)
Mercyhurst Coll (PA)
Meredith Coll (NC)
Methodist Coll (NC)
Miami U (OH)
MidAmerica Nazarene U (KS)
Millikin U (IL)
Minnesota State U Mankato (MN)
Minnesota State U Moorhead (MN)
Minot State U (ND)
Mississippi Coll (MS)
Missouri Baptist U (MO)
Missouri Valley Coll (MO)
Montana State U–Billings (MT)
Montana State U–Bozeman (MT)
Morehead State U (KY)
Morgan State U (MD)
Mount Union Coll (OH)
Mount Vernon Nazarene U (OH)
National American U (SD)
National U (CA)
Nebraska Wesleyan U (NE)
Neumann Coll (PA)
New York U (NY)
Nichols Coll (MA)
North Carolina State U (NC)
North Dakota State U (ND)
Northern Michigan U (MI)
North Greenville Coll (SC)
Northwood U (MI)
Northwood U, Texas Campus (TX)
Notre Dame Coll (OH)
Nova Southeastern U (FL)
Ohio Northern U (OH)
Ohio U (OH)
Old Dominion U (VA)
Olivet Coll (MI)
Olivet Nazarene U (IL)
Otterbein Coll (OH)
Pfeiffer U (NC)
Principia Coll (IL)
Quincy U (IL)
Reinhardt Coll (GA)
Robert Morris U (PA)
Rochester Coll (MI)
Sacred Heart U (CT)
St. Ambrose U (IA)
St. Andrews Presbyterian Coll (NC)
St. John's U (NY)
Saint Joseph's Coll of Maine (ME)
Saint Leo U (FL)

Saint Mary's Coll of California (CA)
St. Thomas U (FL)
Salem State Coll (MA)
Seton Hall U (NJ)
Shawnee State U (OH)
Simpson Coll (IA)
Southeast Missouri State U (MO)
Southern Adventist U (TN)
Southern Nazarene U (OK)
Southern Wesleyan U (SC)
Southwest Baptist U (MO)
Southwestern Coll (KS)
Spring Arbor U (MI)
Springfield Coll (MA)
State U of NY at Oswego (NY)
State U of NY Coll at Brockport (NY)
Stetson U (FL)
Taylor U (IN)
Tennessee Wesleyan Coll (TN)
Texas Lutheran U (TX)
Texas State U-San Marcos (TX)
Texas Wesleyan U (TX)
Thomas Coll (ME)
Towson U (MD)
Tri-State U (IN)
Tulane U (LA)
Tusculum Coll (TN)
Union Coll (KY)
Union Coll (NE)
Union U (TN)
U of Alberta (AB, Canada)
U of Dayton (OH)
U of Georgia (GA)
The U of Iowa (IA)
U of Louisville (KY)
U of Massachusetts Amherst (MA)
The U of Memphis (TN)
U of Michigan (MI)
U of Minnesota, Crookston (MN)
U of Nevada, Las Vegas (NV)
U of New Haven (CT)
U of Pittsburgh at Bradford (PA)
U of Regina (SK, Canada)
U of Saint Mary (KS)
U of Saskatchewan (SK, Canada)
U of South Carolina (SC)
The U of Tennessee (TN)
The U of Tennessee at Martin (TN)
The U of Texas at Austin (TX)
U of the Incarnate Word (TX)
U of Tulsa (OK)
U of Victoria (BC, Canada)
U of Windsor (ON, Canada)
U of Wisconsin–La Crosse (WI)
U of Wisconsin–Parkside (WI)
Valparaiso U (IN)
Virginia Intermont Coll (VA)
Warner Southern Coll (FL)
Wartburg Coll (IA)
Washington State U (WA)
Wayne State Coll (NE)
Webber Intl U (FL)
Western Baptist Coll (OR)
Western Carolina U (NC)
Western New England Coll (MA)
West Virginia U (WV)
West Virginia Wesleyan Coll (WV)
Widener U (PA)
William Penn U (IA)
Wilmington Coll (DE)
Wingate U (NC)
Winona State U (MN)
Winston-Salem State U (NC)
Winthrop U (SC)
Xavier U (OH)
York Coll of Pennsylvania (PA)
York U (ON, Canada)
Youngstown State U (OH)

STATISTICS

American U (DC)
Appalachian State U (NC)
Barnard Coll (NY)
Baruch Coll of the City U of NY (NY)
Bowling Green State U (OH)
Brigham Young U (UT)
Brock U (ON, Canada)
California Polytechnic State U, San Luis Obispo (CA)
California State Polytechnic U, Pomona (CA)
California State U, Chico (CA)
California State U, Fullerton (CA)
California State U, Hayward (CA)
California State U, Long Beach (CA)
Carleton U (ON, Canada)
Carnegie Mellon U (PA)
Case Western Reserve U (OH)
Central Michigan U (MI)
Clarkson U (NY)
The Coll of New Jersey (NJ)
Columbia Coll (NY)
Columbia U, School of General Studies (NY)
Concordia U (QC, Canada)
Cornell U (NY)
Dalhousie U (NS, Canada)
DePaul U (IL)
Eastern Kentucky U (KY)
Eastern Michigan U (MI)
Eastern New Mexico U (NM)
Eastern Washington U (WA)
Florida Intl U (FL)
Florida State U (FL)
Fort Lewis Coll (CO)
The George Washington U (DC)
Grand Valley State U (MI)
Hampshire Coll (MA)
Harvard U (MA)
Hunter Coll of the City U of NY (NY)
Huron U USA in London(United Kingdom)
Indiana U–Purdue U Fort Wayne (IN)
Iowa State U of Science and Technology (IA)
Kansas State U (KS)
Kenyon Coll (OH)
Kettering U (MI)
Lehigh U (PA)
Loyola U Chicago (IL)
Luther Coll (IA)
Marquette U (WI)
McGill U (QC, Canada)
Memorial U of Newfoundland (NL, Canada)
Mercyhurst Coll (PA)
Miami U (OH)
Miami U Hamilton (OH)
Michigan State U (MI)
Michigan Technological U (MI)
Mount Holyoke Coll (MA)
Mount Saint Vincent U (NS, Canada)
New York U (NY)
North Carolina State U (NC)
North Dakota State U (ND)
Northwestern U (IL)
Oakland U (MI)
Ohio Northern U (OH)
Ohio Wesleyan U (OH)
Oklahoma State U (OK)
Penn State U Abington Coll (PA)
Penn State U Altoona Coll (PA)
Penn State U at Erie, The Behrend Coll (PA)
Penn State U Beaver Campus of the Commonwealth Coll (PA)
Penn State U Berks Cmps of Berks-Lehigh Valley Coll (PA)
Penn State U Delaware County Campus of the Commonwealth Coll (PA)
Penn State U DuBois Campus of the Commonwealth Coll (PA)
Penn State U Fayette Campus of the Commonwealth Coll (PA)
Penn State U Hazleton Campus of the Commonwealth Coll (PA)
Penn State U Lehigh Valley Cmps of Berks-Lehigh Valley Coll (PA)
Penn State U McKeesport Campus of the Commonwealth Coll (PA)
Penn State U Mont Alto Campus of the Commonwealth Coll (PA)
Penn State U New Kensington Campus of the Commonwealth Coll (PA)
Penn State U Schuylkill Campus of the Capital Coll (PA)
Penn State U Shenango Campus of the Commonwealth Coll (PA)
Penn State U Univ Park Campus (PA)
Penn State U Wilkes-Barre Campus of the Commonwealth Coll (PA)
Penn State U Worthington Scranton Cmps Commonwealth Coll (PA)
Penn State U York Campus of the Commonwealth Coll (PA)
Purdue U (IN)
Queen's U at Kingston (ON, Canada)
Rice U (TX)
Rochester Inst of Technology (NY)
Roosevelt U (IL)
Rutgers, The State U of New Jersey, New Brunswick/Piscataway (NJ)
St. Cloud State U (MN)
St. Mary's U of San Antonio (TX)
Sam Houston State U (TX)
San Diego State U (CA)
San Francisco State U (CA)
Simon Fraser U (BC, Canada)
Sonoma State U (CA)
Southern Methodist U (TX)
State U of NY Coll at Oneonta (NY)
Stevens Inst of Technology (NJ)
Tulane U (LA)
Université de Montréal (QC, Canada)
Université Laval (QC, Canada)
U Coll of the Fraser Valley (BC, Canada)
The U of Akron (OH)
U of Alberta (AB, Canada)
U of Arkansas (AR)
The U of British Columbia (BC, Canada)
U of Calgary (AB, Canada)
U of Calif, Berkeley (CA)
U of Calif, Davis (CA)
U of Calif, Los Angeles (CA)
U of Calif, Riverside (CA)
U of Calif, Santa Barbara (CA)
U of Central Florida (FL)
U of Chicago (IL)
U of Connecticut (CT)
U of Denver (CO)
U of Florida (FL)
U of Georgia (GA)
U of Guelph (ON, Canada)
U of Houston (TX)
U of Houston–Clear Lake (TX)
U of Illinois at Chicago (IL)
U of Illinois at Urbana–Champaign (IL)
The U of Iowa (IA)
U of King's Coll (NS, Canada)
U of Manitoba (MB, Canada)
U of Maryland, Baltimore County (MD)
U of Michigan (MI)
U of Minnesota, Morris (MN)
U of Missouri–Columbia (MO)
U of Missouri–Kansas City (MO)
The U of Montana–Missoula (MT)
U of Nevada, Las Vegas (NV)
U of New Brunswick Fredericton (NB, Canada)
U of New Hampshire (NH)
The U of North Carolina at Greensboro (NC)
The U of North Carolina at Wilmington (NC)
U of North Florida (FL)
U of Oregon (OR)
U of Ottawa (ON, Canada)
U of Pennsylvania (PA)
U of Pittsburgh (PA)
U of Regina (SK, Canada)
U of Rochester (NY)
U of Saskatchewan (SK, Canada)
U of South Carolina (SC)
The U of Tennessee (TN)
The U of Texas at Dallas (TX)
U of Toronto (ON, Canada)
U of Vermont (VT)
U of Victoria (BC, Canada)
U of Washington (WA)
U of Waterloo (ON, Canada)
The U of Western Ontario (ON, Canada)
U of Windsor (ON, Canada)
U of Wisconsin–Madison (WI)
U of Wisconsin–Milwaukee (WI)
U of Wyoming (WY)
Utah State U (UT)
Virginia Polytechnic Inst and State U (VA)
Washington State U (WA)
Washington U in St. Louis (MO)
Western Michigan U (MI)
Winona State U (MN)
Wright State U (OH)
Xavier U of Louisiana (LA)
York U (ON, Canada)

STATISTICS RELATED

Brigham Young U (UT)
Ohio Northern U (OH)

STRUCTURAL ENGINEERING

Clarkson U (NY)
The Coll of Southeastern Europe, The American U of Athens(Greece)
Cornell U (NY)
Johnson & Wales U (RI)
Penn State U Harrisburg Campus of the Capital Coll (PA)
U at Buffalo, The State U of New York (NY)
U of Calif, San Diego (CA)
U of Southern California (CA)
U of Toledo (OH)
Western Michigan U (MI)

SUBSTANCE ABUSE/ADDICTION COUNSELING

Alvernia Coll (PA)
Calumet Coll of Saint Joseph (IN)
Coll of St. Catherine (MN)
Graceland U (IA)
Indiana U–Purdue U Fort Wayne (IN)
Kansas Wesleyan U (KS)
Martin U (IN)
Metropolitan State U (MN)
Minot State U (ND)
National-Louis U (IL)
Newman U (KS)
St. Cloud State U (MN)
State U of NY Coll at Brockport (NY)
U of Detroit Mercy (MI)
U of Great Falls (MT)
The U of Lethbridge (AB, Canada)
U of Mary (ND)
The U of South Dakota (SD)

SURVEYING ENGINEERING

Cornell U (NY)
U of Maine (ME)

SURVEY TECHNOLOGY

British Columbia Inst of Technology (BC, Canada)
California State Polytechnic U, Pomona (CA)
California State U, Fresno (CA)
Ferris State U (MI)
Idaho State U (ID)
Metropolitan State Coll of Denver (CO)
Michigan Technological U (MI)
New Mexico State U (NM)
Nicholls State U (LA)
The Ohio State U (OH)
Oregon Inst of Technology (OR)
Penn State U Wilkes-Barre Campus of the Commonwealth Coll (PA)
Polytechnic U of Puerto Rico (PR)
Purdue U (IN)
Southern Polytechnic State U (GA)
State U of NY Coll of Technology at Alfred (NY)
Texas A&M U–Corpus Christi (TX)
Thomas Edison State Coll (NJ)
Université Laval (QC, Canada)
The U of Akron (OH)
U of Arkansas at Little Rock (AR)
U of Florida (FL)
U of Maine (ME)
U of New Brunswick Fredericton (NB, Canada)
U of Wisconsin–Madison (WI)

SWEDISH

Augustana Coll (IL)
Brigham Young U (UT)

SYSTEM ADMINISTRATION

American Coll of Computer & Information Sciences (AL)
Bethel Coll (KS)
Champlain Coll (VT)
Coleman Coll, La Mesa (CA)
Dordt Coll (IA)
Huron U USA in London(United Kingdom)
Keystone Coll (PA)
Mt. Sierra Coll (CA)
National American U, Denver (CO)
Rochester Inst of Technology (NY)
State U of NY Coll of Technology at Alfred (NY)
U of Great Falls (MT)
U of Minnesota, Crookston (MN)

SYSTEM, NETWORKING, AND LAN/WAN MANAGEMENT

American InterContinental U Online (IL)
Carroll Coll (WI)
Champlain Coll (VT)
Huron U USA in London(United Kingdom)
Mt. Sierra Coll (CA)
National American U, Denver (CO)
Peirce Coll (PA)
Rochester Inst of Technology (NY)
Southern Nazarene U (OK)
U of Great Falls (MT)
U of Minnesota, Crookston (MN)

SYSTEMS ENGINEERING

Carleton U (ON, Canada)
Case Western Reserve U (OH)
Cornell U (NY)
Delaware State U (DE)
Eastern Nazarene Coll (MA)
Florida Intl U (FL)
George Mason U (VA)
The George Washington U (DC)
Harvard U (MA)
Maine Maritime Acad (ME)
Missouri Tech (MO)
Montana Tech of The U of Montana (MT)
Oakland U (MI)
The Ohio State U (OH)
Ohio U (OH)
Rensselaer Polytechnic Inst (NY)
Richmond, The American Intl U in London(United Kingdom)
Rochester Inst of Technology (NY)
Stevens Inst of Technology (NJ)
United States Military Acad (NY)
United States Naval Acad (MD)
The U of Arizona (AZ)
U of Calif, San Diego (CA)
U of Detroit Mercy (MI)
U of Florida (FL)
U of Houston–Clear Lake (TX)
U of Maine (ME)
The U of Memphis (TN)
U of Missouri–Rolla (MO)
U of Pennsylvania (PA)
U of Regina (SK, Canada)
U of Southern California (CA)
U of Virginia (VA)
U of Waterloo (ON, Canada)
Washington U in St. Louis (MO)
Wright State U (OH)

SYSTEMS SCIENCE AND THEORY

Indiana U Bloomington (IN)
Marshall U (WV)
Miami U (OH)
Providence Coll (RI)
Stanford U (CA)
Sterling Coll (VT)
U of Ottawa (ON, Canada)
Washington U in St. Louis (MO)
Wright State U (OH)
Yale U (CT)

TALMUDIC STUDIES

Jewish Theological Sem of America (NY)
Talmudic Coll of Florida (FL)

TAMIL

U of Chicago (IL)

TAXATION

California State U, Fullerton (CA)
Capital U (OH)
Drexel U (PA)
St. John's U (NY)

TECHNICAL AND BUSINESS WRITING

Alderson-Broaddus Coll (WV)
Allegheny Coll (PA)
Boise State U (ID)
Bowling Green State U (OH)
Carlow Coll (PA)
Carnegie Mellon U (PA)
Carroll Coll (MT)
Cedarville U (OH)
Champlain Coll (VT)
Chicago State U (IL)
Christian Brothers U (TN)
Clarkson U (NY)
Coll of Santa Fe (NM)
Drexel U (PA)
State U of NY at Farmingdale (NY)
Ferris State U (MI)
Florida State U (FL)
Grand Valley State U (MI)
Illinois Inst of Technology (IL)
Iowa State U of Science and Technology (IA)
James Madison U (VA)
La Roche Coll (PA)
Madonna U (MI)
Maryville Coll (TN)
Medaille Coll (NY)
Metropolitan State U (MN)
Miami U (OH)
Miami U Hamilton (OH)
Michigan State U (MI)
Michigan Technological U (MI)
Montana Tech of The U of Montana (MT)
Mount Mary Coll (WI)
New Jersey Inst of Technology (NJ)
New Mexico Inst of Mining and Technology (NM)
New York Inst of Technology (NY)
Northern Michigan U (MI)
Northwestern Coll (MN)
Ohio Northern U (OH)
Oklahoma State U (OK)

Oregon State U (OR)
Pennsylvania Coll of Technology (PA)
Penn State U Berks Cmps of Berks-Lehigh Valley Coll (PA)
Penn State U Lehigh Valley Cmps of Berks-Lehigh Valley Coll (PA)
Pittsburg State U (KS)
San Francisco State U (CA)
Southern Polytechnic State U (GA)
Southwest Missouri State U (MO)
Tarleton State U (TX)
Tennessee Technological U (TN)
U of Arkansas at Little Rock (AR)
U of Baltimore (MD)
U of Delaware (DE)
U of Hartford (CT)
U of Michigan–Flint (MI)
The U of Montana–Missoula (MT)
U of Victoria (BC, Canada)
U of Washington (WA)
U of Wisconsin–Stout (WI)
Weber State U (UT)
Webster U (MO)
Winthrop U (SC)
Worcester Polytechnic Inst (MA)
York Coll of Pennsylvania (PA)
York U (ON, Canada)
Youngstown State U (OH)

TECHNICAL TEACHER EDUCATION

Bowling Green State U (OH)
Eastern Illinois U (IL)
Eastern Kentucky U (KY)
Mississippi State U (MS)
New York Inst of Technology (NY)
The Ohio State U (OH)
San Diego State U (CA)
Texas Christian U (TX)
Université Laval (QC, Canada)
The U of Akron (OH)
U of Idaho (ID)
U of Missouri–Columbia (MO)
U of Saskatchewan (SK, Canada)
The U of Tennessee (TN)
U of Wisconsin–Stout (WI)
Utah State U (UT)
Valley City State U (ND)
Wayne State U (MI)
Wright State U (OH)

TECHNOLOGY/INDUSTRIAL ARTS TEACHER EDUCATION

Alcorn State U (MS)
Appalachian State U (NC)
Brigham Young U (UT)
State U of NY Coll at Buffalo (NY)
California State U, Los Angeles (CA)
Central Connecticut State U (CT)
Central Michigan U (MI)
Central Missouri State U (MO)
Central Washington U (WA)
Chadron State Coll (NE)
Clemson U (SC)
The Coll of New Jersey (NJ)
Coll of the Ozarks (MO)
Concordia U (NE)
Eastern Kentucky U (KY)
Eastern Michigan U (MI)
Elizabeth City State U (NC)
Georgia Southern U (GA)
Grambling State U (LA)
Illinois State U (IL)
Kean U (NJ)
Kent State U (OH)
Lindenwood U (MO)
Middle Tennessee State U (TN)
Mississippi State U (MS)
Missouri Southern State U (MO)
Montana State U–Bozeman (MT)
Murray State U (KY)
New York Inst of Technology (NY)
North Carolina State U (NC)
Northern Arizona U (AZ)
Northern Michigan U (MI)
The Ohio State U (OH)
Oklahoma Panhandle State U (OK)
Pittsburg State U (KS)
Purdue U (IN)
St. Cloud State U (MN)
St. John Fisher Coll (NY)
Sam Houston State U (TX)
Southeast Missouri State U (MO)
Southwestern Oklahoma State U (OK)
State U of NY at Oswego (NY)
Texas Southern U (TX)
Texas Wesleyan U (TX)
U of Arkansas (AR)
U of Georgia (GA)
U of Hawaii at Manoa (HI)
U of Idaho (ID)
The U of Lethbridge (AB, Canada)
The U of Montana–Western (MT)
U of Nebraska–Lincoln (NE)
U of Nevada, Reno (NV)
U of New Mexico (NM)
U of Northern Iowa (IA)
U of Regina (SK, Canada)
U of Wisconsin–Stout (WI)
U of Wyoming (WY)
Utah State U (UT)
Valley City State U (ND)
Virginia Polytechnic Inst and State U (VA)
Viterbo U (WI)
Western Michigan U (MI)

TELECOMMUNICATIONS

Ball State U (IN)
Bowling Green State U (OH)
Butler U (IN)
California State Polytechnic U, Pomona (CA)
California State U, Hayward (CA)
Capitol Coll (MD)
Champlain Coll (VT)
Colorado State U-Pueblo (CO)
Columbia Coll Hollywood (CA)
Golden Gate U (CA)
Grand Valley State U (MI)
Hampshire Coll (MA)
Howard Payne U (TX)
Indiana U Bloomington (IN)
Inter American U of PR, Bayamón Campus (PR)
Ithaca Coll (NY)
Kean U (NJ)
Kutztown U of Pennsylvania (PA)
Michigan State U (MI)
Morgan State U (MD)
Murray State U (KY)
New York Inst of Technology (NY)
Ohio U (OH)
Oklahoma Baptist U (OK)
Pacific U (OR)
Penn State U Univ Park Campus (PA)
Pepperdine U, Malibu (CA)
Rochester Inst of Technology (NY)
Roosevelt U (IL)
St. John's U (NY)
Southern Polytechnic State U (GA)
Syracuse U (NY)
Texas Southern U (TX)
Tusculum Coll (TN)
U of the Sacred Heart (PR)
U of Wisconsin–Platteville (WI)
Western Michigan U (MI)
Westminster Coll (PA)
Wingate U (NC)
Winona State U (MN)
Youngstown State U (OH)

TELECOMMUNICATIONS TECHNOLOGY

Rochester Inst of Technology (NY)
St. John's U (NY)
U of the Sacred Heart (PR)

TEXTILE SCIENCE

Cornell U (NY)
Florida State U (FL)
North Carolina State U (NC)

TEXTILE SCIENCES AND ENGINEERING

Auburn U (AL)
Georgia Inst of Technology (GA)
North Carolina State U (NC)
Philadelphia U (PA)
Texas Tech U (TX)
U of Massachusetts Dartmouth (MA)

THEATRE DESIGN AND TECHNOLOGY

Baylor U (TX)
Boston U (MA)
Brigham Young U (UT)
California Inst of the Arts (CA)
Carroll Coll (MT)
Centenary Coll (NJ)
Chapman U (CA)
Coe Coll (IA)
Coker Coll (SC)
Coll of Santa Fe (NM)
Columbia Coll Chicago (IL)
Concordia U (QC, Canada)
Cornish Coll of the Arts (WA)
DePaul U (IL)
Dickinson Coll (PA)
Elizabethtown Coll (PA)
Emerson Coll (MA)
Five Towns Coll (NY)
Florida State U (FL)
Greensboro Coll (NC)
Hampshire Coll (MA)
Ithaca Coll (NY)
Memorial U of Newfoundland (NL, Canada)
North Carolina School of the Arts (NC)
Ohio U (OH)
Oklahoma City U (OK)
Penn State U Abington Coll (PA)
Penn State U Altoona Coll (PA)
Penn State U at Erie, The Behrend Coll (PA)
Penn State U Beaver Campus of the Commonwealth Coll (PA)
Penn Sta.e U Berks Cmps of Berks-Lehigh Valley Coll (PA)
Penn State U Delaware County Campus of the Commonwealth Coll (PA)
Penn State U DuBois Campus of the Commonwealth Coll (PA)
Penn State U Fayette Campus of the Commonwealth Coll (PA)
Penn State U Hazleton Campus of the Commonwealth Coll (PA)
Penn State U Lehigh Valley Cmps of Berks-Lehigh Valley Coll (PA)
Penn State U McKeesport Campus of the Commonwealth Coll (PA)
Penn State U Mont Alto Campus of the Commonwealth Coll (PA)
Penn State U New Kensington Campus of the Commonwealth Coll (PA)
Penn State U Schuylkill Campus of the Capital Coll (PA)
Penn State U Shenango Campus of the Commonwealth Coll (PA)
Penn State U Univ Park Campus (PA)
Penn State U Wilkes-Barre Campus of the Commonwealth Coll (PA)
Penn State U Worthington Scranton Cmps Commonwealth Coll (PA)
Penn State U York Campus of the Commonwealth Coll (PA)
Rocky Mountain Coll (MT)
Ryerson U (ON, Canada)
Seton Hill U (PA)
Shenandoah U (VA)
Simon's Rock Coll of Bard (MA)
Syracuse U (NY)
Texas Tech U (TX)
Trinity U (TX)
The U of Akron (OH)
U of Alaska Fairbanks (AK)
U of Alberta (AB, Canada)
The U of Arizona (AZ)
U of Calif, Santa Cruz (CA)
U of Connecticut (CT)
U of Delaware (DE)
U of Kansas (KS)
The U of Lethbridge (AB, Canada)
U of Michigan (MI)
U of Northern Iowa (IA)
U of Regina (SK, Canada)
U of Southern California (CA)
The U of the Arts (PA)
Webster U (MO)
Western Michigan U (MI)
William Woods U (MO)
Wright State U (OH)
York U (ON, Canada)
Youngstown State U (OH)

THEATRE LITERATURE, HISTORY AND CRITICISM

Averett U (VA)
Bard Coll (NY)
Boston U (MA)
Buena Vista U (IA)
Cornell U (NY)
Dalhousie U (NS, Canada)
DePaul U (IL)
Hampshire Coll (MA)
Marymount Manhattan Coll (NY)
Memorial U of Newfoundland (NL, Canada)
Moravian Coll (PA)
New York U (NY)
Northwestern U (IL)
Ohio U (OH)
Saint Mary's Coll of California (CA)
Simon's Rock Coll of Bard (MA)
Texas Christian U (TX)
U of Connecticut (CT)
U of Northern Iowa (IA)
Virginia Wesleyan Coll (VA)
Washington U in St. Louis (MO)

THEATRE/THEATRE ARTS MANAGEMENT

Brooklyn Coll of the City U of NY (NY)
California Inst of the Arts (CA)
Campbell U (NC)
Coll of Santa Fe (NM)
East Central U (OK)
Eastern Michigan U (MI)
Elizabethtown Coll (PA)
Hampshire Coll (MA)
Luther Coll (IA)
Miami U Hamilton (OH)
North Greenville Coll (SC)
Ohio Northern U (OH)
Ohio U (OH)
St. Cloud State U (MN)
Seton Hill U (PA)
The U of British Columbia (BC, Canada)
The U of Iowa (IA)
U of Southern California (CA)
Western Michigan U (MI)

THEOLOGICAL AND MINISTERIAL STUDIES RELATED

Brescia U (KY)
California Baptist U (CA)
Central Pentecostal Coll (SK, Canada)
God's Bible School and Coll (OH)
Messenger Coll (MO)
Northwest Christian Coll (OR)
Northwestern Coll (MN)
Palm Beach Atlantic U (FL)
Point Loma Nazarene U (CA)
Prairie Bible Coll (AB, Canada)
Quincy U (IL)
Southeastern Coll of the Assemblies of God (FL)
Southwest Baptist U (MO)
Trinity Coll of Florida (FL)
U of Saint Francis (IN)
Williamson Christian Coll (TN)

THEOLOGY

Alvernia Coll (PA)
American Baptist Coll of American Baptist Theol Sem (TN)
Andrews U (MI)
Apex School of Theology (NC)
Appalachian Bible Coll (WV)
Assumption Coll (MA)
Atlanta Christian Coll (GA)
Atlantic Union Coll (MA)
Augsburg Coll (MN)
Ave Maria Coll (MI)
Ave Maria U (FL)
Azusa Pacific U (CA)
The Baptist Coll of Florida (FL)
Barry U (FL)
Bellarmine U (KY)
Belmont Abbey Coll (NC)
Biola U (CA)
Bluefield Coll (VA)
Boston Coll (MA)
Brewton-Parker Coll (GA)
Briar Cliff U (IA)
Briercrest Bible Coll (SK, Canada)
Caldwell Coll (NJ)
California Baptist U (CA)
Calumet Coll of Saint Joseph (IN)
Calvin Coll (MI)
Canadian Mennonite U (MB, Canada)
Carlow Coll (PA)
Carroll Coll (MT)
Cedarville U (OH)
Central Christian Coll of Kansas (KS)
Central Pentecostal Coll (SK, Canada)
Christendom Coll (VA)
Christian Heritage Coll (CA)
Coll of Emmanuel and St. Chad (SK, Canada)
Coll of Saint Benedict (MN)
Coll of St. Catherine (MN)
Coll of Saint Elizabeth (NJ)
Columbia Union Coll (MD)
Concordia U (CA)
Concordia U (IL)
Concordia U (NE)
Concordia U (OR)
Concordia U (QC, Canada)
Concordia U, St. Paul (MN)
Concordia U Wisconsin (WI)
Creighton U (NE)
Crossroads Coll (MN)
Crown Coll (MN)
Dakota Wesleyan U (SD)
DeSales U (PA)
Dordt Coll (IA)
Duquesne U (PA)
Eastern Mennonite U (VA)
Eastern U (PA)
Elmhurst Coll (IL)
Faulkner U (AL)
Fordham U (NY)
Franciscan U of Steubenville (OH)
Gannon U (PA)
Global U of the Assemblies of God (MO)
Grace Bible Coll (MI)
Grand Canyon U (AZ)
Griggs U (MD)
Hanover Coll (IN)
Harding U (AR)
Hardin-Simmons U (TX)
Hellenic Coll (MA)
Heritage Bible Coll (NC)
Hillsdale Free Will Baptist Coll (OK)
Holy Trinity Orthodox Sem (NY)
Houghton Coll (NY)
Howard Payne U (TX)
Huntington Coll (IN)
Immaculata U (PA)
Intl Coll and Graduate School (HI)
John Brown U (AR)
John Wesley Coll (NC)
King's Coll (PA)
The King's U Coll (AB, Canada)
Laura and Alvin Siegal Coll of Judaic Studies (OH)
Lenoir-Rhyne Coll (NC)
Life Pacific Coll (CA)
Lipscomb U (TN)
Louisiana Coll (LA)
Loyola Marymount U (CA)
Loyola U Chicago (IL)
Manhattan Christian Coll (KS)
Marian Coll (IN)
Martin Luther Coll (MN)
The Master's Coll and Sem (CA)
Master's Coll and Sem (ON, Canada)
Morris Coll (SC)
Mount Saint Mary's Coll and Sem (MD)
Mount Vernon Nazarene U (OH)
Multnomah Bible Coll and Biblical Sem (OR)
Newman U (KS)
North Greenville Coll (SC)
North Park U (IL)
Northwest Nazarene U (ID)
Notre Dame Coll (OH)
Nyack Coll (NY)
Oakland City U (IN)
Ohio Dominican U (OH)
Oklahoma Baptist U (OK)
Olivet Nazarene U (IL)
Oral Roberts U (OK)
Ouachita Baptist U (AR)
Pacific Union Coll (CA)
Pontifical Catholic U of Puerto Rico (PR)
Prairie Bible Coll (AB, Canada)
Providence Coll (RI)
Providence Coll and Theological Sem (MB, Canada)
Quincy U (IL)
Redeemer U Coll (ON, Canada)
Reformed Bible Coll (MI)
Roanoke Coll (VA)
Rockhurst U (MO)
Rocky Mountain Coll (AB, Canada)
St. Ambrose U (IA)
Saint Anselm Coll (NH)
St. Gregory's U (OK)
Saint John's U (MN)
St. John's U (NY)
Saint Joseph's Coll of Maine (ME)
Saint Joseph's U (PA)
Saint Leo U (FL)
St. Louis Christian Coll (MO)
Saint Louis U (MO)
Saint Mary-of-the-Woods Coll (IN)
Saint Mary's Coll of California (CA)
Saint Mary's U of Minnesota (MN)
St. Mary's U of San Antonio (TX)
Saint Vincent Coll (PA)
Seattle Pacific U (WA)
Silver Lake Coll (WI)
Southeastern Bible Coll (AL)
Southern Adventist U (TN)
Southern Nazarene U (OK)
Southern Wesleyan U (SC)
Spring Hill Coll (AL)
Taylor U (IN)
Texas Lutheran U (TX)
Trinity Christian Coll (IL)
Union Coll (NE)
Union U (TN)
Universidad Adventista de las Antillas (PR)
Université de Montréal (QC, Canada)
Université de Sherbrooke (QC, Canada)
Université Laval (QC, Canada)
U of Dallas (TX)
U of Dubuque (IA)
U of Great Falls (MT)
U of Mary (ND)
U of Notre Dame (IN)
U of Ottawa (ON, Canada)

U of Portland (OR)
U of St. Francis (IL)
U of Saint Mary (KS)
U of St. Thomas (TX)
U of San Francisco (CA)
U of Toronto (ON, Canada)
Valparaiso U (IN)
Vennard Coll (IA)
Walla Walla Coll (WA)
Walsh U (OH)
Warner Pacific Coll (OR)
Warner Southern Coll (FL)
Washington Bible Coll (MD)
Western Baptist Coll (OR)
Wheeling Jesuit U (WV)
William Jessup U (CA)
Williams Baptist Coll (AR)
William Tyndale Coll (MI)
Wisconsin Lutheran Coll (WI)
Xavier U (OH)
Xavier U of Louisiana (LA)

THEOLOGY AND RELIGIOUS VOCATIONS RELATED
Abilene Christian U (TX)
Arlington Baptist Coll (TX)
Bethany Coll (SK, Canada)
Bryn Athyn Coll of the New Church (PA)
Central Baptist Coll (AR)
Central Pentecostal Coll (SK, Canada)
Coll of Mount St. Joseph (OH)
Concordia U Coll of Alberta (AB, Canada)
Crossroads Coll (MN)
Lubbock Christian U (TX)
Master's Coll and Sem (ON, Canada)
Missouri Baptist U (MO)
Prairie Bible Coll (AB, Canada)
St. Edward's U (TX)
Simpson Coll and Graduate School (CA)
Union U (TN)
U of St. Thomas (TX)
Wayland Baptist U (TX)
Williamson Christian Coll (TN)

THEORETICAL AND MATHEMATICAL PHYSICS
San Diego State U (CA)
Sweet Briar Coll (VA)
U at Buffalo, The State U of New York (NY)
U of Guelph (ON, Canada)
U of Saskatchewan (SK, Canada)

THERAPEUTIC RECREATION
Alderson-Broaddus Coll (WV)
Ashland U (OH)
Belmont Abbey Coll (NC)
Bridgewater State Coll (MA)
Brigham Young U (UT)
California State U, Chico (CA)
California State U, Hayward (CA)
Catawba Coll (NC)
Central Michigan U (MI)
Coker Coll (SC)
Coll of Mount St. Joseph (OH)
Concordia U (QC, Canada)
Dalhousie U (NS, Canada)
East Carolina U (NC)
Eastern Michigan U (MI)
Eastern Washington U (WA)
Gallaudet U (DC)
Grand Valley State U (MI)
Hampton U (VA)
Indiana Inst of Technology (IN)
Indiana U Bloomington (IN)
Indiana U–Purdue U Fort Wayne (IN)
Ithaca Coll (NY)
Lake Superior State U (MI)
Livingstone Coll (NC)
Longwood U (VA)
Mars Hill Coll (NC)
Messiah Coll (PA)
Minnesota State U Mankato (MN)
Northeastern U (MA)
Northland Coll (WI)
Ohio U (OH)
Pacific Lutheran U (WA)
Pittsburg State U (KS)
St. Cloud State U (MN)
St. Joseph's Coll, Suffolk Campus (NY)
Shaw U (NC)
Shorter Coll (GA)
Southern U and A&M Coll (LA)
Southwestern Oklahoma State U (OK)
Springfield Coll (MA)
State U of NY Coll at Brockport (NY)
State U of NY Coll at Cortland (NY)
The U of Findlay (OH)
The U of Iowa (IA)
U of New Hampshire (NH)
The U of North Carolina at Wilmington (NC)
U of Southern Maine (ME)
U of Waterloo (ON, Canada)
U of Wisconsin–La Crosse (WI)
U of Wisconsin–Milwaukee (WI)
Utica Coll (NY)
Voorhees Coll (SC)
Western Carolina U (NC)
West Virginia State Coll (WV)
Winona State U (MN)
Winston-Salem State U (NC)

TIBETAN
U of Chicago (IL)

TIBETAN STUDIES
Hampshire Coll (MA)

TOOL AND DIE TECHNOLOGY
Utah State U (UT)

TOURISM AND TRAVEL SERVICES MANAGEMENT
Alliant Intl U (CA)
Alliant Intl U–México City(Mexico)
Arkansas State U (AR)
Ball State U (IN)
Becker Coll (MA)
Black Hills State U (SD)
Brigham Young U–Hawaii (HI)
Brock U (ON, Canada)
Champlain Coll (VT)
The Coll of Southeastern Europe, The American U of Athens(Greece)
Concord Coll (WV)
Davis & Elkins Coll (WV)
Delaware State U (DE)
Dowling Coll (NY)
Florida Intl U (FL)
Fort Lewis Coll (CO)
Grand Valley State U (MI)
Hawai'i Pacific U (HI)
Inter American U of PR, Fajardo Campus (PR)
Johnson & Wales U (FL)
Johnson & Wales U (RI)
Johnson State Coll (VT)
Lasell Coll (MA)
Lynn U (FL)
Malaspina U-Coll (BC, Canada)
Mansfield U of Pennsylvania (PA)
Montclair State U (NJ)
Mount Saint Vincent U (NS, Canada)
New Mexico Highlands U (NM)
New York U (NY)
Niagara U (NY)
North Carolina State U (NC)
Northeastern State U (OK)
Our Lady of Holy Cross Coll (LA)
Pontifical Catholic U of Puerto Rico (PR)
Robert Morris U (PA)
Rochester Inst of Technology (NY)
Ryerson U (ON, Canada)
St. Cloud State U (MN)
St. Thomas U (FL)
Salem State Coll (MA)
San Diego State U (CA)
Schiller Intl U (FL)
Schiller Intl U, American Coll of Switzerland(Switzerland)
Sullivan U (KY)
Texas A&M U (TX)
United States Intl U(Kenya)
U of Calgary (AB, Canada)
U of Guelph (ON, Canada)
U of Maine at Machias (ME)
U of Nevada, Las Vegas (NV)
U of New Hampshire (NH)
U of New Haven (CT)
U of the Sacred Heart (PR)
Virginia Polytechnic Inst and State U (VA)
Webber Intl U (FL)
Western Michigan U (MI)
Youngstown State U (OH)

TOURISM AND TRAVEL SERVICES MARKETING
Central Connecticut State U (CT)
Central Missouri State U (MO)
Champlain Coll (VT)
U of Missouri–Columbia (MO)
Western Michigan U (MI)

TOURISM PROMOTION
Bowling Green State U (OH)
Champlain Coll (VT)
New Mexico State U (NM)
Our Lady of Holy Cross Coll (LA)

TOURISM/TRAVEL MARKETING
Eastern Michigan U (MI)
Johnson & Wales U (RI)
Mount Saint Vincent U (NS, Canada)
Rochester Inst of Technology (NY)
U Coll of the Cariboo (BC, Canada)
The U of Montana–Western (MT)
U of the Sacred Heart (PR)

TOXICOLOGY
Ashland U (OH)
Bloomfield Coll (NJ)
Clarkson U (NY)
Coll of Saint Elizabeth (NJ)
Cornell U (NY)
Eastern Michigan U (MI)
Humboldt State U (CA)
Minnesota State U Mankato (MN)
Monmouth U (NJ)
Northeastern U (MA)
St. John's U (NY)
U of Guelph (ON, Canada)
U of Saskatchewan (SK, Canada)
U of Toronto (ON, Canada)
The U of Western Ontario (ON, Canada)
U of Wisconsin–Madison (WI)

TRADE AND INDUSTRIAL TEACHER EDUCATION
Athens State U (AL)
Auburn U (AL)
Ball State U (IN)
Bemidji State U (MN)
State U of NY Coll at Buffalo (NY)
California Polytechnic State U, San Luis Obispo (CA)
California State U, Fresno (CA)
California State U, Long Beach (CA)
California State U, Los Angeles (CA)
California State U, San Bernardino (CA)
Central Washington U (WA)
Clemson U (SC)
The Coll of Saint Rose (NY)
Concordia U (NE)
Dakota State U (SD)
Delaware State U (DE)
Eastern Kentucky U (KY)
Florida Ag and Mech U (FL)
Florida Intl U (FL)
Indiana State U (IN)
Indiana U of Pennsylvania (PA)
Iowa State U of Science and Technology (IA)
Keene State Coll (NH)
Kent State U (OH)
Madonna U (MI)
Memorial U of Newfoundland (NL, Canada)
Murray State U (KY)
New York Inst of Technology (NY)
Norfolk State U (VA)
Northeastern State U (OK)
Oklahoma State U (OK)
Pittsburg State U (KS)
Prairie View A&M U (TX)
San Francisco State U (CA)
South Carolina State U (SC)
Southern Illinois U Carbondale (IL)
State U of NY at Oswego (NY)
Texas A&M U–Commerce (TX)
Texas A&M U–Corpus Christi (TX)
U of Alberta (AB, Canada)
U of Arkansas (AR)
U of Central Florida (FL)
U of Hawaii at Manoa (HI)
U of Idaho (ID)
U of Louisville (KY)
U of Nebraska–Lincoln (NE)
U of Nevada, Reno (NV)
U of New Hampshire (NH)
U of North Florida (FL)
U of Regina (SK, Canada)
U of Saskatchewan (SK, Canada)
U of Southern Maine (ME)
U of South Florida (FL)
U of the District of Columbia (DC)
U of the Virgin Islands (VI)
U of Toledo (OH)
U of West Florida (FL)
U of Wyoming (WY)
Upper Iowa U (IA)
Valdosta State U (GA)
Virginia Polytechnic Inst and State U (VA)
Virginia State U (VA)
Wayland Baptist U (TX)
Western Illinois U (IL)
Western Kentucky U (KY)
Wright State U (OH)

TRANSPORTATION AND HIGHWAY ENGINEERING
Cornell U (NY)
U of Arkansas (AR)

TRANSPORTATION AND MATERIALS MOVING RELATED
Averett U (VA)
Dowling Coll (NY)
St. John's U (NY)
Syracuse U (NY)
United States Merchant Marine Acad (NY)

TRANSPORTATION MANAGEMENT
U of North Florida (FL)
U of Pennsylvania (PA)

TRANSPORTATION TECHNOLOGY
Dowling Coll (NY)
Eastern Kentucky U (KY)
Maine Maritime Acad (ME)
Niagara U (NY)
Pacific Union Coll (CA)
San Francisco State U (CA)
Tennessee State U (TN)
Texas A&M U at Galveston (TX)
The U of British Columbia (BC, Canada)
U of Cincinnati (OH)

TURF AND TURFGRASS MANAGEMENT
Colorado State U (CO)
Delaware Valley Coll (PA)
North Carolina State U (NC)
North Dakota State U (ND)
The Ohio State U (OH)
Penn State U Abington Coll (PA)
Penn State U Altoona Coll (PA)
Penn State U at Erie, The Behrend Coll (PA)
Penn State U Beaver Campus of the Commonwealth Coll (PA)
Penn State U Berks Cmps of Berks-Lehigh Valley Coll (PA)
Penn State U Delaware County Campus of the Commonwealth Coll (PA)
Penn State U DuBois Campus of the Commonwealth Coll (PA)
Penn State U Fayette Campus of the Commonwealth Coll (PA)
Penn State U Hazleton Campus of the Commonwealth Coll (PA)
Penn State U Lehigh Valley Cmps of Berks-Lehigh Valley Coll (PA)
Penn State U McKeesport Campus of the Commonwealth Coll (PA)
Penn State U Mont Alto Campus of the Commonwealth Coll (PA)
Penn State U New Kensington Campus of the Commonwealth Coll (PA)
Penn State U Schuylkill Campus of the Capital Coll (PA)
Penn State U Shenango Campus of the Commonwealth Coll (PA)
Penn State U Univ Park Campus (PA)
Penn State U Wilkes-Barre Campus of the Commonwealth Coll (PA)
Penn State U Worthington Scranton Cmps Commonwealth Coll (PA)
Penn State U York Campus of the Commonwealth Coll (PA)
Rutgers, The State U of New Jersey, New Brunswick/Piscataway (NJ)
State U of NY Coll of A&T at Cobleskill (NY)
Tennessee Technological U (TN)
U of Georgia (GA)
U of Minnesota, Crookston (MN)
U of Rhode Island (RI)

TURKISH
U of Chicago (IL)
The U of Texas at Austin (TX)

UKRAINE STUDIES
Simon's Rock Coll of Bard (MA)

UKRAINIAN
U of Saskatchewan (SK, Canada)

URBAN EDUCATION AND LEADERSHIP
Harris-Stowe State Coll (MO)
U of Missouri–Kansas City (MO)

URBAN FORESTRY
Southern U and A&M Coll (LA)
Texas A&M U (TX)
Université Laval (QC, Canada)

URBAN STUDIES/AFFAIRS
Albertus Magnus Coll (CT)
Aquinas Coll (MI)
Augsburg Coll (MN)
Barnard Coll (NY)
Baylor U (TX)
Boston U (MA)
Brown U (RI)
Bryn Mawr Coll (PA)
State U of NY Coll at Buffalo (NY)
California State Polytechnic U, Pomona (CA)
Calvary Bible Coll and Theological Sem (MO)
Canisius Coll (NY)
Carleton U (ON, Canada)
Cleveland State U (OH)
Coll of Charleston (SC)
Coll of Mount Saint Vincent (NY)
The Coll of Wooster (OH)
Columbia Coll (NY)
Columbia U, School of General Studies (NY)
Concordia U (QC, Canada)
Connecticut Coll (CT)
Cornell U (NY)
Crossroads Bible Coll (IN)
DePaul U (IL)
Dillard U (LA)
Eastern U (PA)
Elmhurst Coll (IL)
Eugene Lang Coll, New School U (NY)
Florida Intl U (FL)
Fordham U (NY)
Furman U (SC)
Georgia State U (GA)
Hamline U (MN)
Hampshire Coll (MA)
Harris-Stowe State Coll (MO)
Harvard U (MA)
Haverford Coll (PA)
Hobart and William Smith Colls (NY)
Hunter Coll of the City U of NY (NY)
Indiana U Bloomington (IN)
Lehigh U (PA)
Lipscomb U (TN)
Loyola Marymount U (CA)
Macalester Coll (MN)
Manhattan Coll (NY)
McGill U (QC, Canada)
Metropolitan State Coll of Denver (CO)
Minnesota State U Mankato (MN)
Montclair State U (NJ)
Morehouse Coll (GA)
Mount Mercy Coll (IA)
New Coll of Florida (FL)
New Jersey City U (NJ)
New York U (NY)
Northeastern Illinois U (IL)
North Park U (IL)
Northwestern U (IL)
Oglethorpe U (GA)
Ohio Wesleyan U (OH)
Portland State U (OR)
Queens Coll of the City U of NY (NY)
Rhodes Coll (TN)
Rockford Coll (IL)
Roosevelt U (IL)
Rutgers, The State U of New Jersey, Camden (NJ)
Rutgers, The State U of New Jersey, New Brunswick/Piscataway (NJ)
Ryerson U (ON, Canada)
St. Cloud State U (MN)
Saint Louis U (MO)
San Diego State U (CA)
San Francisco State U (CA)
Sarah Lawrence Coll (NY)
Southern Nazarene U (OK)
Stanford U (CA)
Taylor U, Fort Wayne Campus (IN)
Trinity U (TX)
Tufts U (MA)
Université de Montréal (QC, Canada)
State U of NY at Albany (NY)
U of Alberta (AB, Canada)
The U of British Columbia (BC, Canada)
U of Calgary (AB, Canada)
U of Calif, Berkeley (CA)
U of Calif, San Diego (CA)
U of Cincinnati (OH)
U of Connecticut (CT)
The U of Lethbridge (AB, Canada)

U of Minnesota, Duluth (MN)
U of Minnesota, Twin Cities Campus (MN)
U of Missouri–Kansas City (MO)
U of New Orleans (LA)
The U of North Carolina at Greensboro (NC)
U of Pennsylvania (PA)
U of Pittsburgh (PA)
U of Richmond (VA)
U of San Diego (CA)
U of Saskatchewan (SK, Canada)
U of Southern California (CA)
The U of Tampa (FL)
The U of Texas at Austin (TX)
U of the District of Columbia (DC)
U of Toledo (OH)
U of Toronto (ON, Canada)
U of Utah (UT)
The U of Western Ontario (ON, Canada)
U of Wisconsin–Green Bay (WI)
U of Wisconsin–Madison (WI)
U of Wisconsin–Milwaukee (WI)
U of Wisconsin–Oshkosh (WI)
Vanderbilt U (TN)
Vassar Coll (NY)
Virginia Commonwealth U (VA)
Virginia Polytechnic Inst and State U (VA)
Washington U in St. Louis (MO)
Wayne State U (MI)
Wittenberg U (OH)
Worcester State Coll (MA)
Wright State U (OH)
York Coll of Pennsylvania (PA)
York U (ON, Canada)

URDU
U of Chicago (IL)

VEHICLE AND VEHICLE PARTS AND ACCESSORIES MARKETING
Northwood U (MI)
Northwood U, Florida Campus (FL)
Northwood U, Texas Campus (TX)

VETERINARY/ANIMAL HEALTH TECHNOLOGY
Becker Coll (MA)
Brigham Young U (UT)
Medaille Coll (NY)
Michigan State U (MI)
Murray State U (KY)
North Dakota State U (ND)
Purdue U (IN)
U of Nebraska–Lincoln (NE)
Wilson Coll (PA)

VETERINARY SCIENCES
Becker Coll (MA)
Lincoln Memorial U (TN)
Mercy Coll (NY)
Northland Coll (WI)
Pontifical Catholic U of Puerto Rico (PR)
Rutgers, The State U of New Jersey, New Brunswick/Piscataway (NJ)
Université de Montréal (QC, Canada)
U of Guelph (ON, Canada)
Wagner Coll (NY)
Washington State U (WA)

VETERINARY TECHNOLOGY
Medaille Coll (NY)
Mercy Coll (NY)
Michigan State U (MI)
Mount Ida Coll (MA)
Newberry Coll (SC)
Quinnipiac U (CT)

VIOLIN, VIOLA, GUITAR AND OTHER STRINGED INSTRUMENTS
Acadia U (NS, Canada)
Augustana Coll (IL)
Ball State U (IN)
Bennington Coll (VT)
Berklee Coll of Music (MA)
Bethesda Christian U (CA)
Brigham Young U (UT)
Butler U (IN)
California Inst of the Arts (CA)
California State U, Fullerton (CA)
Capital U (OH)
Cleveland Inst of Music (OH)
The Colburn School of Performing Arts (CA)
Columbus State U (GA)
Converse Coll (SC)
Cornish Coll of the Arts (WA)
DePaul U (IL)
Five Towns Coll (NY)
Florida State U (FL)
Grand Valley State U (MI)
Hardin-Simmons U (TX)
Hastings Coll (NE)
Heidelberg Coll (OH)
Houghton Coll (NY)
Howard Payne U (TX)
Illinois Wesleyan U (IL)
Inter American U of PR, San Germán Campus (PR)
The Juilliard School (NY)
Lamar U (TX)
Lawrence U (WI)
Lipscomb U (TN)
Manhattan School of Music (NY)
Mannes Coll of Music, New School U (NY)
Mars Hill Coll (NC)
Memorial U of Newfoundland (NL, Canada)
Meredith Coll (NC)
Mount Allison U (NB, Canada)
New England Conservatory of Music (MA)
New World School of the Arts (FL)
Northern Michigan U (MI)
Northwestern U (IL)
Notre Dame de Namur U (CA)
Oberlin Coll (OH)
Oklahoma City U (OK)
Olivet Nazarene U (IL)
Otterbein Coll (OH)
Peabody Conserv of Music of Johns Hopkins U (MD)
Pittsburg State U (KS)
Queen's U at Kingston (ON, Canada)
Roosevelt U (IL)
St. Cloud State U (MN)
Sarah Lawrence Coll (NY)
Seton Hill U (PA)
State U of NY Coll at Fredonia (NY)
Stetson U (FL)
Susquehanna U (PA)
Syracuse U (NY)
The U of Akron (OH)
U of Alberta (AB, Canada)
The U of British Columbia (BC, Canada)
U of Cincinnati (OH)
The U of Iowa (IA)
U of Kansas (KS)
U of Michigan (MI)
U of Missouri–Kansas City (MO)
U of New Hampshire (NH)
U of North Texas (TX)
U of Oklahoma (OK)
U of Southern California (CA)
The U of Tennessee at Martin (TN)
U of Washington (WA)
The U of Western Ontario (ON, Canada)
U of Wisconsin–Milwaukee (WI)
Vanderbilt U (TN)
Washburn U (KS)
Willamette U (OR)
Xavier U of Louisiana (LA)
Youngstown State U (OH)

VISUAL AND PERFORMING ARTS
American Acad of Art (IL)
Angelo State U (TX)
Antioch Coll (OH)
Arizona State U West (AZ)
Armstrong Atlantic State U (GA)
Art Center Coll of Design (CA)
Assumption Coll (MA)
Bard Coll (NY)
Barnard Coll (NY)
Bennington Coll (VT)
Bethel Coll (KS)
Brown U (RI)
California Baptist U (CA)
California State U, San Marcos (CA)
Carroll Coll (MT)
Cazenovia Coll (NY)
Centenary Coll of Louisiana (LA)
Christopher Newport U (VA)
Claremont McKenna Coll (CA)
Columbia Coll (NY)
Concordia U Coll of Alberta (AB, Canada)
Cooper Union for the Advancement of Science & Art (NY)
Cornell U (NY)
Delta State U (MS)
Eastern Connecticut State U (CT)
East Stroudsburg U of Pennsylvania (PA)
Emerson Coll (MA)
The Evergreen State Coll (WA)
Fairleigh Dickinson U, Florham (NJ)
Fairleigh Dickinson U, Teaneck-Metro Campus (NJ)
The Franciscan U (IA)
Frostburg State U (MD)
George Mason U (VA)
Gettysburg Coll (PA)
Iowa State U of Science and Technology (IA)
Ithaca Coll (NY)
Jacksonville U (FL)
Johnson State Coll (VT)
Kutztown U of Pennsylvania (PA)
LaGrange Coll (GA)
Lambuth U (TN)
Lehigh U (PA)
Long Island U, C.W. Post Campus (NY)
Loras Coll (IA)
Loyola U New Orleans (LA)
Maryland Inst Coll of Art (MD)
Marywood U (PA)
Massachusetts Coll of Liberal Arts (MA)
Miami Intl U of Art & Design (FL)
Mississippi State U (MS)
Naropa U (CO)
New Mexico State U (NM)
North Carolina School of the Arts (NC)
Northwestern U (IL)
Oakland U (MI)
Ohio Northern U (OH)
Ohio U (OH)
Penn State U Abington Coll (PA)
Penn State U Altoona Coll (PA)
Penn State U at Erie, The Behrend Coll (PA)
Penn State U Beaver Campus of the Commonwealth Coll (PA)
Penn State U Berks Cmps of Berks-Lehigh Valley Coll (PA)
Penn State U Delaware County Campus of the Commonwealth Coll (PA)
Penn State U DuBois Campus of the Commonwealth Coll (PA)
Penn State U Fayette Campus of the Commonwealth Coll (PA)
Penn State U Hazleton Campus of the Commonwealth Coll (PA)
Penn State U Lehigh Valley Cmps of Berks-Lehigh Valley Coll (PA)
Penn State U McKeesport Campus of the Commonwealth Coll (PA)
Penn State U Mont Alto Campus of the Commonwealth Coll (PA)
Penn State U New Kensington Campus of the Commonwealth Coll (PA)
Penn State U Schuylkill Campus of the Capital Coll (PA)
Penn State U Shenango Campus of the Commonwealth Coll (PA)
Penn State U Univ Park Campus (PA)
Penn State U Wilkes-Barre Campus of the Commonwealth Coll (PA)
Penn State U Worthington Scranton Cmps Commonwealth Coll (PA)
Penn State U York Campus of the Commonwealth Coll (PA)
Providence Coll (RI)
Quincy U (IL)
Ramapo Coll of New Jersey (NJ)
Regis U (CO)
The Richard Stockton Coll of New Jersey (NJ)
Roger Williams U (RI)
Rutgers, The State U of New Jersey, New Brunswick/Piscataway (NJ)
Saint Augustine's Coll (NC)
St. Bonaventure U (NY)
St. Gregory's U (OK)
Saint Joseph's U (PA)
St. Olaf Coll (MN)
San Jose State U (CA)
Sarah Lawrence Coll (NY)
School of the Art Inst of Chicago (IL)
Seton Hall U (NJ)
Shenandoah U (VA)
Simon's Rock Coll of Bard (MA)
South Dakota State U (SD)
Southeast Missouri State U (MO)
Southwest Missouri State U (MO)
State U of NY Coll at Old Westbury (NY)
Texas Southern U (TX)
Texas Wesleyan U (TX)
Trinity Western U (BC, Canada)
U Coll of the Cariboo (BC, Canada)
The U of Alabama at Birmingham (AL)
The U of Arizona (AZ)
The U of British Columbia (BC, Canada)
U of Louisiana at Lafayette (LA)
U of Maine at Machias (ME)
U of Maryland, Baltimore County (MD)
U of Maryland, Coll Park (MD)
U of Miami (FL)
U of Michigan (MI)
U of Michigan–Flint (MI)
U of Pennsylvania (PA)
U of Regina (SK, Canada)
U of St. Francis (IL)
U of Saint Mary (KS)
U of San Francisco (CA)
The U of Tampa (FL)
The U of Tennessee at Martin (TN)
The U of Texas at Austin (TX)
The U of Texas at Dallas (TX)
U of the Sacred Heart (PR)
U of Utah (UT)
U of Windsor (ON, Canada)
Valdosta State U (GA)
Vassar Coll (NY)
Virginia State U (VA)
Viterbo U (WI)
Western Kentucky U (KY)
Western Washington U (WA)
West Virginia U (WV)
Wichita State U (KS)
York U (ON, Canada)

VISUAL AND PERFORMING ARTS RELATED
Adelphi U (NY)
Baldwin-Wallace Coll (OH)
Bridgewater Coll (VA)
Brigham Young U (UT)
Cameron U (OK)
Claremont McKenna Coll (CA)
Clemson U (SC)
Coll of Visual Arts (MN)
Cumberland U (TN)
Dominican U of California (CA)
Fashion Inst of Technology (NY)
Huntingdon Coll (AL)
Illinois State U (IL)
Illinois Wesleyan U (IL)
Kutztown U of Pennsylvania (PA)
Long Island U, C.W. Post Campus (NY)
Maine Coll of Art (ME)
Marywood U (PA)
Meredith Coll (NC)
Ohio Northern U (OH)
Rensselaer Polytechnic Inst (NY)
Rice U (TX)
St. Cloud State U (MN)
Saint Mary's Coll of California (CA)
Samford U (AL)
Sarah Lawrence Coll (NY)
School of the Art Inst of Chicago (IL)
School of the Museum of Fine Arts, Boston (MA)
Scripps Coll (CA)
Simon Fraser U (BC, Canada)
Simon's Rock Coll of Bard (MA)
State U of NY Coll at Geneseo (NY)
Stetson U (FL)
Swarthmore Coll (PA)
U Coll of the Cariboo (BC, Canada)
The U of Akron (OH)
U of Calif, Los Angeles (CA)
U of Oklahoma (OK)
The U of the Arts (PA)
West Virginia U (WV)

VOCATIONAL REHABILITATION COUNSELING
California State U, Los Angeles (CA)
East Carolina U (NC)
Emporia State U (KS)
Florida State U (FL)
U of Arkansas (AR)
U of Northern Colorado (CO)
U of Wisconsin–Stout (WI)
Winston-Salem State U (NC)
Wright State U (OH)

VOICE AND OPERA
Abilene Christian U (TX)
Acadia U (NS, Canada)
Andrews U (MI)
Anna Maria Coll (MA)
Augustana Coll (IL)
Ball State U (IN)
Bard Coll (NY)
Barry U (FL)
Bellarmine U (KY)
Belmont U (TN)
Bennington Coll (VT)
Berklee Coll of Music (MA)
Bethel Coll (IN)
Bethesda Christian U (CA)
Birmingham-Southern Coll (AL)
Black Hills State U (SD)
Blue Mountain Coll (MS)
Boston U (MA)
Bowling Green State U (OH)
Brenau U (GA)
Brigham Young U (UT)
Brigham Young U–Hawaii (HI)
Bryan Coll (TN)
Butler U (IN)
California Inst of the Arts (CA)
California State U, Fullerton (CA)
California State U, Long Beach (CA)
Calvary Bible Coll and Theological Sem (MO)
Calvin Coll (MI)
Campbellsville U (KY)
Canadian Mennonite U (MB, Canada)
Capital U (OH)
Carson-Newman Coll (TN)
Catawba Coll (NC)
The Catholic U of America (DC)
Cedarville U (OH)
Centenary Coll of Louisiana (LA)
Central Washington U (WA)
Chapman U (CA)
Charleston Southern U (SC)
Christian Heritage Coll (CA)
Clarke Coll (IA)
Cleveland Inst of Music (OH)
Coker Coll (SC)
Columbia Coll (SC)
Columbus State U (GA)
Concordia Coll (MN)
Concordia U (IL)
Concordia U (NE)
Converse Coll (SC)
Cornish Coll of the Arts (WA)
Dallas Baptist U (TX)
Delaware State U (DE)
DePaul U (IL)
Dordt Coll (IA)
Drake U (IA)
East Central U (OK)
Eastern Michigan U (MI)
Eastern Washington U (WA)
East Texas Baptist U (TX)
Eureka Coll (IL)
Five Towns Coll (NY)
Florida State U (FL)
Furman U (SC)
Georgetown Coll (KY)
Grace U (NE)
Grand Canyon U (AZ)
Grand Valley State U (MI)
Hannibal-LaGrange Coll (MO)
Hardin-Simmons U (TX)
Hastings Coll (NE)
Heidelberg Coll (OH)
Houghton Coll (NY)
Howard Payne U (TX)
Huntingdon Coll (AL)
Huntington Coll (IN)
Illinois Wesleyan U (IL)
Immaculata U (PA)
Indiana U Bloomington (IN)
Indiana U–Purdue U Fort Wayne (IN)
Inter American U of PR, San Germán Campus (PR)
Ithaca Coll (NY)
Jacksonville U (FL)
John Brown U (AR)
Judson Coll (IL)
The Juilliard School (NY)
Kennesaw State U (GA)
Lamar U (TX)
Lawrence U (WI)
Lindenwood U (MO)
Lipscomb U (TN)
Long Island U, C.W. Post Campus (NY)
Louisiana Coll (LA)
Loyola Marymount U (CA)
Manhattan School of Music (NY)
Mannes Coll of Music, New School U (NY)
Mansfield U of Pennsylvania (PA)
Mars Hill Coll (NC)
Maryville Coll (TN)
The Master's Coll and Sem (CA)
McGill U (QC, Canada)
McMurry U (TX)
Memorial U of Newfoundland (NL, Canada)
Mercyhurst Coll (PA)
Meredith Coll (NC)
MidAmerica Nazarene U (KS)
Millikin U (IL)
Minnesota State U Mankato (MN)
Minnesota State U Moorhead (MN)
Mississippi Coll (MS)

Mount Allison U (NB, Canada)
Mount Mercy Coll (IA)
Mount St. Mary's Coll (CA)
Newberry Coll (SC)
New England Conservatory of Music (MA)
New World School of the Arts (FL)
New York U (NY)
North Carolina School of the Arts (NC)
Northeastern State U (OK)
Northern Michigan U (MI)
Northern State U (SD)
North Greenville Coll (SC)
North Park U (IL)
Northwestern Coll (MN)
Northwestern U (IL)
Notre Dame de Namur U (CA)
Nyack Coll (NY)
Oberlin Coll (OH)
The Ohio State U (OH)
Ohio U (OH)
Oklahoma Baptist U (OK)
Oklahoma Christian U (OK)
Oklahoma City U (OK)
Olivet Nazarene U (IL)
Otterbein Coll (OH)
Ouachita Baptist U (AR)
Pacific Lutheran U (WA)
Palm Beach Atlantic U (FL)
Peabody Conserv of Music of Johns Hopkins U (MD)
Pittsburg State U (KS)
Prairie View A&M U (TX)
Queens U of Charlotte (NC)
Rider U (NJ)
Roberts Wesleyan Coll (NY)
Rochester Coll (MI)
Roosevelt U (IL)
St. Cloud State U (MN)
Samford U (AL)
Sarah Lawrence Coll (NY)
Seton Hill U (PA)
Shorter Coll (GA)
Southern Nazarene U (OK)
Southwestern Oklahoma State U (OK)
State U of NY Coll at Fredonia (NY)
Stetson U (FL)
Susquehanna U (PA)
Syracuse U (NY)
Tabor Coll (KS)
Talladega Coll (AL)
Taylor U (IN)
Texas A&M U–Commerce (TX)
Texas Southern U (TX)
Texas Wesleyan U (TX)
Trinity Christian Coll (IL)
Trinity U (TX)
Truman State U (MO)
Union U (TN)
The U of Akron (OH)
U of Alberta (AB, Canada)
The U of British Columbia (BC, Canada)
U of Charleston (WV)
U of Cincinnati (OH)
U of Delaware (DE)
U of Idaho (ID)
U of Illinois at Urbana–Champaign (IL)
The U of Iowa (IA)
U of Kansas (KS)
U of Miami (FL)
U of Michigan (MI)
U of Missouri–Kansas City (MO)
U of Montevallo (AL)
U of Nebraska at Omaha (NE)
U of New Hampshire (NH)
The U of North Carolina at Greensboro (NC)
U of North Texas (TX)
U of Oklahoma (OK)
U of Oregon (OR)
U of Ottawa (ON, Canada)
U of Redlands (CA)
U of Sioux Falls (SD)
U of Southern California (CA)
The U of Tennessee at Martin (TN)
U of the Pacific (CA)
U of Tulsa (OK)
U of Victoria (BC, Canada)
U of Washington (WA)
The U of Western Ontario (ON, Canada)
U of Wisconsin–Milwaukee (WI)
Valparaiso U (IN)
Vanderbilt U (TN)
Walla Walla Coll (WA)
Washburn U (KS)
Washington U in St. Louis (MO)
Webster U (MO)
West Chester U of Pennsylvania (PA)
Western Baptist Coll (OR)
Westfield State Coll (MA)
Westminster Choir Coll of Rider U (NJ)
Westminster Coll (PA)
Whitworth Coll (WA)
Wilberforce U (OH)
Willamette U (OR)
William Paterson U of New Jersey (NJ)
William Tyndale Coll (MI)
Wingate U (NC)
Winona State U (MN)
York U (ON, Canada)
Youngstown State U (OH)

WALDORF/STEINER TEACHER EDUCATION
Sterling Coll (VT)

WATER QUALITY AND WASTEWATER TREATMENT MANAGEMENT AND RECYCLING TECHNOLOGY
Mississippi Valley State U (MS)
Murray State U (KY)

WATER RESOURCES ENGINEERING
Central State U (OH)
State U of NY Coll of Environ Sci and Forestry (NY)
The U of Arizona (AZ)
U of Guelph (ON, Canada)
U of Nevada, Reno (NV)
U of Southern California (CA)

WATER, WETLANDS, AND MARINE RESOURCES MANAGEMENT
Sterling Coll (VT)
Texas State U-San Marcos (TX)
U of Minnesota, Crookston (MN)

WEB/MULTIMEDIA MANAGEMENT AND WEBMASTER
Acad of Art U (CA)
Baker U (KS)
Champlain Coll (VT)
Dana Coll (NE)
Davenport U, Dearborn (MI)
Davenport U, Grand Rapids (MI)
Davenport U, Holland (MI)
Davenport U, Kalamazoo (MI)
Davenport U, Warren (MI)
Grace U (NE)
Greenville Coll (IL)
Huron U USA in London(United Kingdom)
Lewis-Clark State Coll (ID)
Limestone Coll (SC)
Mt. Sierra Coll (CA)
The New England Inst of Art (MA)
New England School of Communications (ME)
Rochester Inst of Technology (NY)
U of Dubuque (IA)
U of Great Falls (MT)
U of Phoenix–Atlanta Campus (GA)
U of St. Francis (IL)

WEB PAGE, DIGITAL/ MULTIMEDIA AND INFORMATION RESOURCES DESIGN
The Art Inst of Atlanta (GA)
The Art Inst of California–San Francisco (CA)
The Art Inst of Phoenix (AZ)
The Art Inst of Portland (OR)
The Art Inst of Washington (VA)
Atlanta Coll of Art (GA)
Azusa Pacific U (CA)
Bellevue U (NE)
Bloomfield Coll (NJ)
Capella U (MN)
Champlain Coll (VT)
The Cleveland Inst of Art (OH)
Columbia Coll Chicago (IL)
Dakota State U (SD)
Dana Coll (NE)
DePaul U (IL)
Drexel U (PA)
Duquesne U (PA)
Franklin U (OH)
Huron U USA in London(United Kingdom)
The Illinois Inst of Art-Schaumburg (IL)
Medaille Coll (NY)
National American U, Denver (CO)
National American U–Sioux Falls Branch (SD)
Nebraska Wesleyan U (NE)
The New England Inst of Art (MA)
New England School of Communications (ME)
Northface U (UT)
Quinnipiac U (CT)
Rochester Inst of Technology (NY)
Ryerson U (ON, Canada)
San Francisco Art Inst (CA)
School of the Art Inst of Chicago (IL)
Silver Lake Coll (WI)
Southern Virginia U (VA)
Stetson U (FL)
Strayer U (DC)
Tennessee Technological U (TN)
U of Dubuque (IA)
U of Great Falls (MT)
U of Wisconsin–Stevens Point (WI)

WELDING TECHNOLOGY
Excelsior Coll (NY)
Ferris State U (MI)
LeTourneau U (TX)
Lewis-Clark State Coll (ID)
Montana Tech of The U of Montana (MT)

WESTERN CIVILIZATION
Bard Coll (NY)
Belmont U (TN)
Carnegie Mellon U (PA)
The Coll of Southeastern Europe, The American U of Athens(Greece)
Concordia U (QC, Canada)
Gettysburg Coll (PA)
Grand Valley State U (MI)
Harvard U (MA)
St. John's Coll (MD)
St. John's Coll (NM)
Sarah Lawrence Coll (NY)
Thomas Aquinas Coll (CA)
U of King's Coll (NS, Canada)
The U of Western Ontario (ON, Canada)
Western Washington U (WA)

WILDLIFE AND WILDLANDS SCIENCE AND MANAGEMENT
Arkansas State U (AR)
Arkansas Tech U (AR)
Auburn U (AL)
Brigham Young U (UT)
Coll of the Ozarks (MO)
Colorado State U (CO)
Delaware State U (DE)
Delaware Valley Coll (PA)
Eastern Kentucky U (KY)
Eastern New Mexico U (NM)
Fort Hays State U (KS)
Framingham State Coll (MA)
Frostburg State U (MD)
Grand Valley State U (MI)
Humboldt State U (CA)
Lake Superior State U (MI)
Lincoln Memorial U (TN)
Louisiana State U and A&M Coll (LA)
McGill U (QC, Canada)
McNeese State U (LA)
Mississippi State U (MS)
Murray State U (KY)
New Mexico State U (NM)
North Carolina State U (NC)
Northern Arizona U (AZ)
Northland Coll (WI)
The Ohio State U (OH)
Oklahoma State U (OK)
Oregon State U (OR)
Pittsburg State U (KS)
Purdue U (IN)
South Dakota State U (SD)
Southeastern Oklahoma State U (OK)
Southwest Missouri State U (MO)
State U of NY Coll of A&T at Cobleskill (NY)
State U of NY Coll of Environ Sci and Forestry (NY)
Sterling Coll (VT)
Tennessee Technological U (TN)
Texas A&M U (TX)
Texas A&M U–Kingsville (TX)
Texas State U-San Marcos (TX)
Texas Tech U (TX)
U of Alaska Fairbanks (AK)
U of Alberta (AB, Canada)
The U of Arizona (AZ)
U of Arkansas at Monticello (AR)
The U of British Columbia (BC, Canada)
U of Delaware (DE)
U of Georgia (GA)
U of Idaho (ID)
U of Maine (ME)
U of Massachusetts Amherst (MA)
U of Miami (FL)
U of Minnesota, Crookston (MN)
U of Missouri–Columbia (MO)
The U of Montana–Missoula (MT)
U of Nevada, Reno (NV)
U of New Brunswick Fredericton (NB, Canada)
U of New Hampshire (NH)
U of Rhode Island (RI)
The U of Tennessee (TN)
The U of Tennessee at Martin (TN)
U of Washington (WA)
U of Wisconsin–Madison (WI)
U of Wisconsin–Stevens Point (WI)
Utah State U (UT)
Washington State U (WA)
West Texas A&M U (TX)
West Virginia U (WV)
Winona State U (MN)

WILDLIFE BIOLOGY
Baker U (KS)
Ball State U (IN)
Coll of the Atlantic (ME)
Framingham State Coll (MA)
Grand Canyon U (AZ)
Grand Valley State U (MI)
Kansas State U (KS)
McGill U (QC, Canada)
New Mexico State U (NM)
Northeastern State U (OK)
Northern Michigan U (MI)
Northland Coll (WI)
Ohio U (OH)
St. Cloud State U (MN)
State U of NY Coll of Environ Sci and Forestry (NY)
Sterling Coll (VT)
Unity Coll (ME)
U of Guelph (ON, Canada)
U of Michigan (MI)
U of Michigan–Flint (MI)
U of New Brunswick Fredericton (NB, Canada)
U of New Hampshire (NH)
U of Vermont (VT)
Washington State U (WA)
Winona State U (MN)

WIND/PERCUSSION INSTRUMENTS
Acadia U (NS, Canada)
Augustana Coll (IL)
Ball State U (IN)
Berklee Coll of Music (MA)
Bowling Green State U (OH)
Bryan Coll (TN)
Butler U (IN)
California State U, Fullerton (CA)
Capital U (OH)
Chapman U (CA)
Chicago State U (IL)
Cleveland Inst of Music (OH)
Columbus State U (GA)
Concordia U (IL)
DePaul U (IL)
Five Towns Coll (NY)
Florida State U (FL)
Grand Canyon U (AZ)
Grand Valley State U (MI)
Hardin-Simmons U (TX)
Houghton Coll (NY)
Howard Payne U (TX)
Illinois Wesleyan U (IL)
Indiana U Bloomington (IN)
Inter American U of PR, San Germán Campus (PR)
The Juilliard School (NY)
Lawrence U (WI)
Lipscomb U (TN)
Manhattan School of Music (NY)
Mannes Coll of Music, New School U (NY)
Mars Hill Coll (NC)
Maryville Coll (TN)
Memorial U of Newfoundland (NL, Canada)
Mercyhurst Coll (PA)
Meredith Coll (NC)
Minnesota State U Mankato (MN)
Minnesota State U Moorhead (MN)
Mount Allison U (NB, Canada)
New England Conservatory of Music (MA)
New World School of the Arts (FL)
Northern Michigan U (MI)
Northwestern U (IL)
Oberlin Coll (OH)
Oklahoma Baptist U (OK)
Oklahoma Christian U (OK)
Oklahoma City U (OK)
Olivet Nazarene U (IL)
Otterbein Coll (OH)
Palm Beach Atlantic U (FL)
Peabody Conserv of Music of Johns Hopkins U (MD)
Pittsburg State U (KS)
Prairie View A&M U (TX)
Roosevelt U (IL)
Sarah Lawrence Coll (NY)
Seton Hill U (PA)
Southwestern Oklahoma State U (OK)
State U of NY Coll at Fredonia (NY)
Susquehanna U (PA)
Syracuse U (NY)
Texas Southern U (TX)
Texas Wesleyan U (TX)
The U of Akron (OH)
U of Alberta (AB, Canada)
U of Cincinnati (OH)
The U of Iowa (IA)
U of Kansas (KS)
U of Michigan (MI)
U of Missouri–Kansas City (MO)
U of New Hampshire (NH)
U of North Texas (TX)
U of Oklahoma (OK)
U of Sioux Falls (SD)
U of Southern California (CA)
The U of Tennessee at Martin (TN)
The U of Western Ontario (ON, Canada)
U of Wisconsin–Milwaukee (WI)
Vanderbilt U (TN)
Xavier U of Louisiana (LA)

WOMEN'S STUDIES
Agnes Scott Coll (GA)
Albion Coll (MI)
Albright Coll (PA)
Allegheny Coll (PA)
American U (DC)
Amherst Coll (MA)
Antioch Coll (OH)
Arizona State U (AZ)
Arizona State U West (AZ)
Athabasca U (AB, Canada)
Augsburg Coll (MN)
Augustana Coll (IL)
Barnard Coll (NY)
Bates Coll (ME)
Beloit Coll (WI)
Berea Coll (KY)
Bishop's U (QC, Canada)
Bowdoin Coll (ME)
Bowling Green State U (OH)
Brock U (ON, Canada)
Brooklyn Coll of the City U of NY (NY)
Brown U (RI)
Bucknell U (PA)
Burlington Coll (VT)
California State U, Chico (CA)
California State U, Fresno (CA)
California State U, Fullerton (CA)
California State U, Long Beach (CA)
California State U, Sacramento (CA)
California State U, San Marcos (CA)
Carleton Coll (MN)
Carleton U (ON, Canada)
Case Western Reserve U (OH)
Central Michigan U (MI)
Chatham Coll (PA)
City Coll of the City U of NY (NY)
Claremont McKenna Coll (CA)
Colby Coll (ME)
Colgate U (NY)
The Coll of New Jersey (NJ)
The Coll of New Rochelle (NY)
Coll of St. Catherine (MN)
Coll of the Holy Cross (MA)
The Coll of William and Mary (VA)
The Coll of Wooster (OH)
The Colorado Coll (CO)
Columbia Coll (NY)
Columbia U, School of General Studies (NY)
Concordia U (QC, Canada)
Connecticut Coll (CT)
Cornell Coll (IA)
Cornell U (NY)
Curry Coll (MA)
Dalhousie U (NS, Canada)
Dartmouth Coll (NH)
Denison U (OH)
DePaul U (IL)
DePauw U (IN)
Dickinson Coll (PA)
Drew U (NJ)
Duke U (NC)
Earlham Coll (IN)
East Carolina U (NC)
Eastern Michigan U (MI)
Eckerd Coll (FL)
Emory U (GA)
Eugene Lang Coll, New School U (NY)

Florida Intl U (FL)
Florida State U (FL)
Fordham U (NY)
Georgetown U (DC)
Georgia State U (GA)
Gettysburg Coll (PA)
Goucher Coll (MD)
Grand Valley State U (MI)
Grinnell Coll (IA)
Guilford Coll (NC)
Hamilton Coll (NY)
Hamline U (MN)
Hampshire Coll (MA)
Harvard U (MA)
Haverford Coll (PA)
Hobart and William Smith Colls (NY)
Hollins U (VA)
Hunter Coll of the City U of NY (NY)
Illinois Wesleyan U (IL)
Indiana U Bloomington (IN)
Indiana U–Purdue U Fort Wayne (IN)
Indiana U South Bend (IN)
Iowa State U of Science and Technology (IA)
Jewish Theological Sem of America (NY)
Kansas State U (KS)
Kenyon Coll (OH)
Knox Coll (IL)
Lakehead U (ON, Canada)
Laurentian U (ON, Canada)
Louisiana State U and A&M Coll (LA)
Macalester Coll (MN)
Marlboro Coll (VT)
Marquette U (WI)
McGill U (QC, Canada)
Memorial U of Newfoundland (NL, Canada)
Metropolitan State U (MN)
Middlebury Coll (VT)
Mills Coll (CA)
Minnesota State U Mankato (MN)
Mount Holyoke Coll (MA)
Mount Saint Vincent U (NS, Canada)
Nazareth Coll of Rochester (NY)
Nebraska Wesleyan U (NE)
Nipissing U (ON, Canada)
Northeastern Illinois U (IL)
Northeastern U (MA)
Northern Arizona U (AZ)
Northwestern U (IL)
Oakland U (MI)
Oberlin Coll (OH)
Occidental Coll (CA)
The Ohio State U (OH)
Ohio Wesleyan U (OH)
Old Dominion U (VA)
Pacific Lutheran U (WA)
Penn State U Abington Coll (PA)
Penn State U Altoona Coll (PA)
Penn State U at Erie, The Behrend Coll (PA)
Penn State U Beaver Campus of the Commonwealth Coll (PA)
Penn State U Berks Cmps of Berks-Lehigh Valley Coll (PA)
Penn State U Delaware County Campus of the Commonwealth Coll (PA)
Penn State U DuBois Campus of the Commonwealth Coll (PA)
Penn State U Fayette Campus of the Commonwealth Coll (PA)
Penn State U Hazleton Campus of the Commonwealth Coll (PA)
Penn State U Lehigh Valley Cmps of Berks-Lehigh Valley Coll (PA)
Penn State U McKeesport Campus of the Commonwealth Coll (PA)
Penn State U Mont Alto Campus of the Commonwealth Coll (PA)
Penn State U New Kensington Campus of the Commonwealth Coll (PA)
Penn State U Schuylkill Campus of the Capital Coll (PA)
Penn State U Shenango Campus of the Commonwealth Coll (PA)
Penn State U Univ Park Campus (PA)
Penn State U Wilkes-Barre Campus of the Commonwealth Coll (PA)
Penn State U Worthington Scranton Cmps Commonwealth Coll (PA)
Penn State U York Campus of the Commonwealth Coll (PA)
Pitzer Coll (CA)
Pomona Coll (CA)
Portland State U (OR)
Queens Coll of the City U of NY (NY)
Queen's U at Kingston (ON, Canada)
Randolph-Macon Coll (VA)
Rice U (TX)
Roosevelt U (IL)
Rosemont Coll (PA)
Rutgers, The State U of New Jersey, Newark (NJ)
Rutgers, The State U of New Jersey, New Brunswick/Piscataway (NJ)
St. Francis Xavier U (NS, Canada)
Saint Louis U (MO)
Saint Mary's Coll of California (CA)
St. Olaf Coll (MN)
San Diego State U (CA)
San Francisco State U (CA)
Sarah Lawrence Coll (NY)
Scripps Coll (CA)
Simmons Coll (MA)
Simon Fraser U (BC, Canada)
Simon's Rock Coll of Bard (MA)
Skidmore Coll (NY)
Smith Coll (MA)
Sonoma State U (CA)
Southwestern U (TX)
Spelman Coll (GA)
Stanford U (CA)
State U of NY at New Paltz (NY)
State U of NY at Oswego (NY)
State U of NY Coll at Brockport (NY)
State U of NY Coll at Fredonia (NY)
Stony Brook U, State U of New York (NY)
Suffolk U (MA)
Syracuse U (NY)
Towson U (MD)
Trent U (ON, Canada)
Trinity Coll (CT)
Tufts U (MA)
Tulane U (LA)
State U of NY at Albany (NY)
U at Buffalo, The State U of New York (NY)
U of Alberta (AB, Canada)
The U of Arizona (AZ)
The U of British Columbia (BC, Canada)
U of Calgary (AB, Canada)
U of Calif, Berkeley (CA)
U of Calif, Davis (CA)
U of Calif, Irvine (CA)
U of Calif, Los Angeles (CA)
U of Calif, Riverside (CA)
U of Calif, San Diego (CA)
U of Calif, Santa Barbara (CA)
U of Calif, Santa Cruz (CA)
U of Colorado at Boulder (CO)
U of Connecticut (CT)
U of Delaware (DE)
U of Denver (CO)
U of Georgia (GA)
U of Guelph (ON, Canada)
U of Hartford (CT)
The U of Iowa (IA)
U of Kansas (KS)
U of King's Coll (NS, Canada)
U of Louisville (KY)
U of Maine (ME)
U of Maine at Farmington (ME)
U of Manitoba (MB, Canada)
U of Maryland, Coll Park (MD)
U of Massachusetts Amherst (MA)
U of Massachusetts Boston (MA)
U of Miami (FL)
U of Michigan (MI)
U of Michigan–Dearborn (MI)
U of Minnesota, Duluth (MN)
U of Minnesota, Morris (MN)
U of Minnesota, Twin Cities Campus (MN)
The U of Montana–Missoula (MT)
U of Nebraska at Omaha (NE)
U of Nebraska–Lincoln (NE)
U of Nevada, Las Vegas (NV)
U of Nevada, Reno (NV)
U of New Hampshire (NH)
U of New Mexico (NM)
U of New Orleans (LA)
The U of North Carolina at Chapel Hill (NC)
The U of North Carolina at Greensboro (NC)
U of Oklahoma (OK)
U of Oregon (OR)
U of Ottawa (ON, Canada)
U of Pennsylvania (PA)
U of Regina (SK, Canada)
U of Rhode Island (RI)
U of Richmond (VA)
U of Rochester (NY)
U of St. Thomas (MN)
U of Saskatchewan (SK, Canada)
U of South Carolina (SC)
U of Southern California (CA)
U of Southern Maine (ME)
U of South Florida (FL)
U of Toledo (OH)
U of Toronto (ON, Canada)
U of Utah (UT)
U of Vermont (VT)
U of Victoria (BC, Canada)
U of Washington (WA)
U of Waterloo (ON, Canada)
The U of Western Ontario (ON, Canada)
U of Windsor (ON, Canada)
U of Wisconsin–Madison (WI)
U of Wisconsin–Milwaukee (WI)
U of Wisconsin–Whitewater (WI)
U of Wyoming (WY)
Vassar Coll (NY)
Warren Wilson Coll (NC)
Washington State U (WA)
Washington U in St. Louis (MO)
Wayne State U (MI)
Wellesley Coll (MA)
Wells Coll (NY)
Wesleyan U (CT)
West Chester U of Pennsylvania (PA)
Western Illinois U (IL)
Western Michigan U (MI)
Western Washington U (WA)
Wheaton Coll (MA)
Wichita State U (KS)
Wright State U (OH)
Yale U (CT)
York U (ON, Canada)

WOOD SCIENCE AND WOOD PRODUCTS/PULP AND PAPER TECHNOLOGY

Memphis Coll of Art (TN)
Miami U (OH)
Mississippi State U (MS)
North Carolina State U (NC)
Oregon State U (OR)
Pittsburg State U (KS)
State U of NY Coll of Environ Sci and Forestry (NY)
Sterling Coll (VT)
Université Laval (QC, Canada)
The U of British Columbia (BC, Canada)
U of Idaho (ID)
U of Maine (ME)
U of Massachusetts Amherst (MA)
U of Minnesota, Twin Cities Campus (MN)
U of Toronto (ON, Canada)
U of Washington (WA)
U of Wisconsin–Stevens Point (WI)
West Virginia U (WV)

WORD PROCESSING

Huron U USA in London(United Kingdom)

WORK AND FAMILY STUDIES

American Public U System (WV)
Brigham Young U (UT)
Miami U Hamilton (OH)
Texas Tech U (TX)
Ursuline Coll (OH)

YOUTH MINISTRY

Andrews U (MI)
Benedictine Coll (KS)
Bethel Coll (IN)
Bethel Coll (KS)
Bethel U (MN)
Bluffton Coll (OH)
California Baptist U (CA)
Calvary Bible Coll and Theological Sem (MO)
Campbell U (NC)
Canadian Mennonite U (MB, Canada)
Cascade Coll (OR)
Cedarville U (OH)
Central Christian Coll of Kansas (KS)
Central Pentecostal Coll (SK, Canada)
Charleston Southern U (SC)
Colorado Christian U (CO)
Columbia Intl U (SC)
Concordia U Wisconsin (WI)
Crichton Coll (TN)
Crossroads Bible Coll (IN)
Crossroads Coll (MN)
Dordt Coll (IA)
East Texas Baptist U (TX)
Emmanuel Coll (GA)
Eugene Bible Coll (OR)
Gardner-Webb U (NC)
Gordon Coll (MA)
Grace Bible Coll (MI)
Grace U (NE)
Greenville Coll (IL)
Harding U (AR)
Hardin-Simmons U (TX)
Lancaster Bible Coll (PA)
Liberty U (VA)
Lindenwood U (MO)
Lubbock Christian U (TX)
Malone Coll (OH)
Master's Coll and Sem (ON, Canada)
Messenger Coll (MO)
Multnomah Bible Coll and Biblical Sem (OR)
North Central U (MN)
Northwestern Coll (MN)
Ouachita Baptist U (AR)
Pfeiffer U (NC)
Pillsbury Baptist Bible Coll (MN)
Prairie Bible Coll (AB, Canada)
Providence Coll and Theological Sem (MB, Canada)
Rocky Mountain Coll (AB, Canada)
Saint Mary's U of Minnesota (MN)
Southwest Baptist U (MO)
Southwestern Coll (AZ)
Taylor U, Fort Wayne Campus (IN)
Toccoa Falls Coll (GA)
Trinity Coll of Florida (FL)
Trinity Intl U (IL)
Vanguard U of Southern California (CA)
Vennard Coll (IA)
Western Baptist Coll (OR)

YOUTH SERVICES

Cazenovia Coll (NY)
Indiana U–Purdue U Fort Wayne (IN)
Medaille Coll (NY)

ZOOLOGY/ANIMAL BIOLOGY

Andrews U (MI)
Auburn U (AL)
Ball State U (IN)
Brigham Young U (UT)
California State Polytechnic U, Pomona (CA)
California State U, Fresno (CA)
California State U, Long Beach (CA)
Coll of the Atlantic (ME)
Colorado State U (CO)
Connecticut Coll (CT)
Cornell U (NY)
Delaware Valley Coll (PA)
Florida State U (FL)
Fort Valley State U (GA)
Howard U (DC)
Humboldt State U (CA)
Idaho State U (ID)
Iowa State U of Science and Technology (IA)
Juniata Coll (PA)
Kent State U (OH)
Mars Hill Coll (NC)
McGill U (QC, Canada)
Memorial U of Newfoundland (NL, Canada)
Miami U (OH)
Miami U Hamilton (OH)
Michigan State U (MI)
North Carolina State U (NC)
North Dakota State U (ND)
Northeastern State U (OK)
Northern Arizona U (AZ)
Northern Michigan U (MI)
Northland Coll (WI)
The Ohio State U (OH)
Ohio U (OH)
Ohio Wesleyan U (OH)
Oklahoma State U (OK)
Olivet Nazarene U (IL)
Oregon State U (OR)
Quinnipiac U (CT)
Rutgers, The State U of New Jersey, Newark (NJ)
San Diego State U (CA)
San Francisco State U (CA)
Sonoma State U (CA)
Southeastern Oklahoma State U (OK)
Southern Connecticut State U (CT)
Southern Illinois U Carbondale (IL)
Southern Utah U (UT)
State U of NY at Oswego (NY)
State U of NY Coll of Environ Sci and Forestry (NY)
Tarleton State U (TX)
Texas A&M U (TX)
Texas State U-San Marcos (TX)
Texas Tech U (TX)
The U of Akron (OH)
U of Alberta (AB, Canada)
The U of British Columbia (BC, Canada)
U of Calgary (AB, Canada)
U of Calif, Davis (CA)
U of Calif, Santa Barbara (CA)
U of Florida (FL)
U of Guelph (ON, Canada)
U of Hawaii at Manoa (HI)
U of Idaho (ID)
U of Maine (ME)
U of Manitoba (MB, Canada)
U of Michigan (MI)
The U of Montana–Missoula (MT)
U of New Brunswick Fredericton (NB, Canada)
U of New Hampshire (NH)
U of Oklahoma (OK)
U of Rhode Island (RI)
The U of Tennessee (TN)
The U of Texas at Austin (TX)
U of Toronto (ON, Canada)
U of Vermont (VT)
U of Victoria (BC, Canada)
U of Washington (WA)
The U of Western Ontario (ON, Canada)
U of Wisconsin–Madison (WI)
U of Wisconsin–Milwaukee (WI)
U of Wyoming (WY)
Utah State U (UT)
Washington State U (WA)
Weber State U (UT)
Winona State U (MN)

ZOOLOGY/ANIMAL BIOLOGY RELATED

McGill U (QC, Canada)
Oklahoma State U (OK)
U Coll of the Cariboo (BC, Canada)

Geographical Listing of In-Depth Descriptions

U.S. AND U.S. TERRITORIES

Geographical Listing of In-Depth Descriptions

Alphabetical Listing of Colleges and Universities

In this index, the page locations of the profiles are printed in regular type, **Special Messages** in *italics,* and **In-Depth Descriptions** in **bold type.** When there is more than one number in **bold type,** it indicates that the institution has more than one **In-Depth Description;** in most such cases, the first of the series is a general institutional description.

…ersity (NS, Canada) 1089
145
…sity (OH) *759*, **2052**
760
…al Seminary *846*, **2054**
800
390
145
761
303
182, **2056**
182
182
522
554
…15